P9-CJM-189

The New York Times

CROSSWORD PUZZLE DICTIONARY

The New York Times

CROSSWORD PUZZLE DICTIONARY

• Third Edition •

By Tom Pulliam and Clare Grundman

A HUDSON GROUP BOOK

Random House Puzzles & Games

Produced in association with Morningside Editorial Associates, Inc.
Designed by Martin Connell

 Published in the United States by Random House, Inc., New York, and simultaneously in Canada by Random House of Canada Limited, Toronto.

This work was originally published in 1974 as The New York Times Crossword Puzzle Dictionary by Quadrangle Books. An expanded edition of this work was published in 1977 by Quadrangle Books as The New York Times Crossword Puzzle Dictionary—Expanded Edition. A second edition of this work was published in 1984 by Random House, Inc., as The New York Times Crossword Puzzle Dictionary, 2nd Edition.

Library of Congress Cataloging in Publication Data

Pulliam, Tom.
The New York Times crossword puzzle dictionary.

"A Hudson Group book."
1.Crossword puzzles—Glossaries, vocabularies, etc.
I. Grundman, Clare, 1913– II. New York Times.
III. Title
GV1507.C7P83 1984 793.73'2'03 84-40108

Manufactured in the United States of America

9 8 7

Third Edition

PREFACE to the First Edition

THE NEW YORK TIMES CROSSWORD PUZZLE DICTIONARY exceeds in completeness and scope all other puzzle dictionaries. No useful word has been omitted. Not only have puzzles themselves been combed for synonyms that are used over and over, but also a word-for-word reading of major unabridged dictionaries, both current and old, has produced a thoroughly complete and extensive checklist.

Each of us has been solving and compiling puzzles for many years, and our chief purpose has been to design a practical and easy-to-use dictionary, in the belief that your needs and requirements for such a volume closely reflect our own. For example, the synonyms are arranged by the number of letters, and then alphabetized so you can quickly find the very word that fills the spaces in the puzzle. Another feature, one that seems obvious for a crossword puzzle dictionary but is not found in most of them, is that all words are printed in easy-to-read capital letters. The type has been chosen with great care for its legibility, and the three-column format not only provides a short line of type to scan but also enables us to get a very large number of words on each page.

Synonyms of great length have been omitted to give room for the shorter, more useful words. The puzzler can always "fill in" the very long words provided he has a good supply of short common synonyms. We have placed, therefore, an arbitrary ceiling of eight-letter word-lengths, knowing this will satisfy almost all needs. Here and there, however, you will find occasional exceptions to this rule. These are synonyms of such frequent, interesting, and normal usage that their omission might handicap the puzzler.

The "shaded boxes" scattered through the book are a notable and unique feature of THE NEW YORK TIMES CROSSWORD PUZZLE DICTIONARY. They collect under one heading a variety of categories and synonyms that you would have a hard time finding in other dictionaries. For example, when you are confronted by the clue "Brazilian river" merely turn to the shaded area marked BRAZIL, where you will find several excellent possibilities. Similarly, look for a "Philippine native" under PHILIPPINES, or a "Scottish measure" under SCOTLAND.

Another useful feature is the lavish listing of phrases. For instance, instead of being confronted by the simple clue "Sword," you may run up against "Double-edged sword." Under the entry word SWORD in this dictionary you will find ample phrases that qualify the entry word or more sharply specify its meaning. Also, given the definition "Turn aside," simply look under TURN and find that phrase, along with many others.

THE NEW YORK TIMES CROSSWORD PUZZLE DICTIONARY is a versatile reference book that you will want to keep on your desk or next to your chair for help, not only with crossword puzzles, but also for a large variety of other puzzles and contests. In addition, it will be invaluable for writers, speakers, and the like, for (with more than one-half million words) it is one of the largest books of synonyms ever published. Its simple arrangement makes it far easier to use than the standard thesauri.

Our hope is that you will come to use this new word book as we might. Get to know it and be adventuresome! If the first entry you consult does not corner the exact word you are seeking, let any listing at that spot lead you to a cross-reference. Follow this track until you have the right word "treed."

A project of this scope may well have been beyond the ability of only two to accomplish. We have required and welcomed top-flight support during our work. Although many might be named, special note must be given to the efforts of Richard Martz and David House of Dartmouth College, who were responsible for much of the computerization; also, to Gorton Carruth and Robert O'Brien of Morningside Associates. Each made his individual contributions, which we gratefully acknowledge.

Happy word hunting!

Tom Pulliam
Clare Grundman

1974

PREFACE to the Second Edition

This Second Edition of THE NEW YORK TIMES CROSSWORD PUZZLE DICTIONARY greatly augments the First Edition. We have added approximately 100,000 new entry words and synonyms into a new four-column format, which maintains the same easy-to-read features and the large numbers of words per page, including many new longer words. An outstanding innovation of this Second Edition is the inclusion of the titles of major works of literature and music, as well as their authors and composers, and the names of characters in books, plays, operas, etc. Another very important addition is the listing of famous people from various walks of life—painters, physicians, playwrights, botanists, etc.—as well as those men and women who have won Nobel Prizes and who have been inducted into the Hall of Fame. We have also assembled what we believe to be the most comprehensive listing of prefixes, suffixes, and combining forms, which are *listed by meaning,* and the largest list of biblical, mythological, and literary relationships ever to appear in a crossword puzzle dictionary. And, of course, we have retained from the First Edition the unique "shaded boxes" that feature pertinent facts about geographical locations.

We would like to acknowledge once more the excellent assistance of Gorton Carruth and Robert O'Brien of Morningside Editorial Associates and to thank the many puzzlers who have sent us their compliments and suggestions.

Again, we wish you happy word hunting!

T.P.
C.G.

1984

PREFACE to the Third Edition

In the decade since the Second Edition of THE NEW YORK TIMES CROSSWORD PUZZLE DICTIONARY was published, the nature of crossword puzzles has changed in several ways, some obvious and some subtle. These changes, which we determined several years ago would require a Third Edition in order to have an up-to-date dictionary, are reflected in the many alterations and additions you will find in the text. In the last few years writers of crossword puzzles have made the clues less obvious, thus making the puzzles more difficult to solve. We believe that the average solver appreciates this additional challenge. You will discover in this Third Edition, therefore, many alternate and uncommon synonyms of finding words. You will also discover many synonyms consisting of phrases of two or more words unaccompanied by qualifying explanations, such as "two words." For example, under the finding word "succeed" you will find MAKEIT. Consider, AT HOME under "in," SHOOIN under "winner (easy)," the slangy GOAPE under "flip," and the three-word phrase INARUT under "stuck." Please remember that all phrases are listed, just as they are written in puzzles, as one word. This use of phrases makes solving crossword puzzles more interesting, as does the use of "gimmicks" or unifying themes, slang, and words and phrases associated with the space age and the drug culture. You will find a more extensive coverage of these kinds of subjects in this new edition. We have also included a list of "partners," a category that has come into increasing use. For example, the clue asks for the "partner of hither," intending you to fill in YON. These pairings are all listed under the finding word "partners" and written in the dictionary as one word: HITHERYON, KITHKIN, YINYANG, etc. You will find a similar listing under "alternatives," which suggests the use of *or* instead of *and,* as in "alternative of hit" is MISS and is entered as HITMISS. Particularly useful new categories of finding words are those dealing with sports teams and players. For example, under "hockey" or "football" you will find lists of players and teams. Other similar finding words include baseball, golf, and tennis. Finally, we have updated many lists, such as Nobel Prize winners and persons who are well-known for their achievements in their professions, such as "author," "playwright," and "statesman." In short, all these additions confirm that this Third Edition of THE NEW YORK TIMES CROSSWORD PUZZLE DICTIONARY remains the most comprehensive and current puzzle dictionary available.

Once again we would like to acknowledge the excellent and necessary assistance of Gorton Carruth of Morningside Editorial Associates. For this Third Edition we are grateful for the contributions of Edmund Yee, who guided us through the intricacies of the computer, and Bruce Wetterau, who updated the geographical boxes and expanded the categories of occupations. Our thanks also go to Henry Griffin for much of the keyboarding. We are especially grateful to the many puzzlers who have written us over the years with their suggestions and well wishes.

Happy word hunting!

T.P.
C.G.

1995

The New York Times

CROSSWORD PUZZLE DICTIONARY

A AY HA AIR ARY PER ALFA EACH ALPHA
(EVER —) ARROW
AA LAVA
AAL AL MULBERRY
AARDVARK ANTEATER EARTHHOG EDENTATE
AARDWOLF HYAENID
AARON (BROTHER OF —) MOSES
(BURIAL PLACE OF —) HOR
(FATHER OF —) AMRAM
(MOTHER OF —) JOCHEBED
(SISTER OF —) MIRIAM
(SON OF —) ABIHU NADAB ELEAZAR ITHAMAR
(WIFE OF —) ELISHEBA
AARONIC LEVITIC LEVITICAL
AARON'S ROD MULLEIN
AB HATI
ABA ABAYAH
ABACA HEMP FIBER LUPIS LINAGA MANILA
ABACK SHORT
ABACUS SOROBAN SHWANPAN
ABADDON PIT HELL ABYSS SATAN APOLLYON
ABAFT AFT BACK BAFT ABAFF ASTERN BEHIND REARWARD
(— THE BEAM) LARGE
ABALONE EAR PAUA AWABI NACRE ORMER UHLLO ASSEIR MOLLUSK
ABANDON EGO CAST DROP FLEE JUNK QUIT SINK ABAND ALLAY CHUCK DITCH EXPEL LEAVE PLANT REMIT SCRAP WAIVE YIELD ABJURE BANISH BETRAY DESERT DEVEST DISUSE DIVEST EXPOSE FOREGO FORHOO FORLET MAROON RECANT REFUSE REJECT RELENT RESIGN SLOUGH STRAND VACATE DEPLORE DISCARD FORFEIT FORSAKE SCUTTLE ABDICATE FORHOOIE FORSWEAR JETTISON RASHNESS RENOUNCE SURCEASE RELINQUISH
(— EVIL WAYS) REFORM
(WITH —) DESPERATELY
ABANDONED BAD LEFT LORN LOST VACANT WICKED CORRUPT FORLORN PROJECT DEPRAVED DERELICT DESERTED DESOLATE FLAGRANT FORSAKEN
ABANDONING
(PREF.) LIPO
ABANDONMENT BURIAL DUNKIRK APOSTASY ABATEMENT
(— OF RESTRAINT) LETUP
ABANGA ADY
ABAS (FATHER OF —) CELEUS LYNCEUS
(MOTHER OF —) METANIRA HYPERMNESTRA
(SON OF —) PROETUS ACRISIUS
ABASE SINK VAIL AVALE AVILE BLAME DEMIT DIMIT LOWER SHAME ABJECT BEMEAN DEBASE DEFAME DEJECT DEMEAN DEPOSE GROVEL HUMBLE LESSEN MEEKEN REDUCE DEGRADE DEPRESS MORTIFY DIMINISH DISGRACE DISHONOR
ABASED ABAISSE DEJECTED
ABASH AWE COW BASH BAZE DASH AVALE ESBAY SHAME HUMBLE AFFRONT CONFUSE MORTIFY BEWILDER BROWBEAT CONFOUND
ABASHED BLANK CHEAP SHAMED ASHAMED FOOLISH SHEEPISH
ABASHMENT VERGOYNE
ABATE EBB END LOW CALM CURB FAIK FALL MEND OMIT SLOW SOFT VAIL VOID WANE ALLAY ALLOW ANNUL APPAL BREAK CHECK LOWER QUASH RELAX REMIT SLAKE SWAGE ASLAKE DEDUCT LESSEN PACIFY REBATE REDUCE RELENT ABOLISH ASSUAGE CASSARE CHANCER NULLIFY QUALIFY SLACKEN SUBSIDE DECREASE DIMINISH MITIGATE MODERATE OVERBLOW PALLIATE
ABATEMENT DELF FALL ALLAY DELFT DELPH LETUP GUSSET MIOSIS RABATE DECREASE DISCOUNT PROSTRATION
(— OF DISEASE) LYSIS
ABATIS OBSTACLE SLASHING
ABAXIAL DORSAL
ABBA FATHER
ABBAY ABBACY
ABBE MONK CLERIC CURATE PRIEST
ABBESS AMMA VICARESS
ABBEY ABADIA ABBAYE PRIORY CONVENT NUNNERY CLOISTER
ABBOT ABBAS COARB ARCHIMANDRITE
(— OF MISRULE) BISHOP
ABBREVIATE CUT CLIP DOCK PRUNE DIGEST ABRIDGE BOBTAIL CURTAIL SHORTEN CONDENSE CONTRACT TRUNCATE
ABBREVIATED SHORT BOBTAIL CRYPTIC MUTILATE
ABBREVIATION LAPSE SIGLUM SYMBOL
(PL.) SIGLA
ABC ALPHABET
ABDA (FATHER OF —) SHAMMUA
(SON OF) ADONIRAM
ABDEEL (SON OF —) SHELEMIAH
ABDERITE FOOL SCOFFER SIMPLETON
ABDI (SON OF —) KISHI
ABDICATE CEDE QUIT DEMIT EXPEL LEAVE REMIT DEPOSE DISOWN FOREGO RESIGN RETIRE VACATE ABANDON DISCLAIM RENOUNCE
ABDICATION DRIFT
ABDIEL (FATHER OF —) GUNI
(SON OF —) AHI
ABDOMEN BOUK WOMB ALVUS APRON BELLY MELON MIRAC PLEON THARM PAUNCH VENTER STOMACH
(PREF.) CELI COELI VENTR(I)(O)
ABDOMINAL BELLY HEMAL CELIAC COELIAC VENTRAL VISCERAL
ABDON (FATHER OF —) MICAH HILLEL JEHIEL SHASHAK
ABDUCT LURE TAKE STEAL ABDUCE KIDNAP RAVISH SPIRIT CAPTURE
ABDUCTED RAPT
ABDUCTION APAGOGE RAPTURE
ABDUCTION FROM THE SERAGLIO (CHARACTER IN —) OSMIN PASHA BLONDE BELMONTE PEDRILLO CONSTANZE
(COMPOSER OF —) MOZART
ABDUCTOR SPIRIT
ABEAM ABREAST
ABECEDARIAN TYRO NOVICE LEARNER BEGINNER
ABECEDARIUS ABC
ABED SICK RESTING RETIRED SLEEPING
ABEL (BROTHER OF —) CAIN SETH
(FATHER OF —) ADAM
(MOTHER OF —) EVE
(PARENT OF —) ADAM
ABE LINCOLN IN ILLINOIS
(AUTHOR OF —) SHERWOOD
(CHARACTER IN —) ABE ANN GALE MARY SETH TODD GREEN SPEED GRAHAM JIMMIE MENTOR NINIAN BOWLING DOUGLAS EDWARDS HERNDON RUTLEDGE
ABELMOSK MUSK MALLOW
ABENCERAGES (CHARACTER IN —) ALMANSOR
(COMPOSER OF —) CHERUBINI
ABENCERRAJE (AUTHOR OF —) VILLEGAS
(CHARACTER IN —) JARIFA NARVAEZ RODRIGO ABINDARRAEZ
ABERDEEN ANGUS BLACK DODDY DODDIE
ABERRANT WILD CLAMMY DEVIANT ABNORMAL STRAYING VARIABLE
ABERRATION SLIP WARP ERROR FAULT LAPSE MANIA DELIRIUM DELUSION INSANITY
ABESSIVE CARITIVE
ABET AID EGG BACK HELP BOOST COACH ASSIST FOMENT INCITE SECOND SUCCOR UPHOLD COMFORT CONNIVE ESPOUSE FORWARD FURTHER SUPPORT SUSTAIN ADVOCATE BEFRIEND
ABETO ACXOYATL
ABETTING CONFEDERATE
ABETTOR FAUTOR ADVOCATE PROMOTER
ABEYANCE ABEYANCY DORMANCY
(IN —) ONICE
ABEYANT LATENT
ABHIMANYU (FATHER OF —) ARJUNA
(VICTIM OF —) LAKSHMANA
ABHOR UG IRK HATE SHUN AGRISE DETEST LOATHE DESPISE DISLIKE EXECRATE ABOMINATE
ABHORRENCE HATE ODIUM HATRED HORROR DISGUST DISLIKE SCUNNER AVERSION LOATHING
ABHORRENT ODIOUS UGSOME HATEFUL ABSONANT INFAMOUS REPUGNANT
ABI (SON OF —) HEZEKIAH
ABIA (FATHER OF —) BECHER SAMUEL JEROBOAM REHOBOAM
(HUSBAND OF —) HEZRON
ABIATHAR (FATHER OF —) AHIMELECH
ABIDA (FATHER OF —) MIDIAN
ABIDE BE WIN WON BEAR BIDE KEEP LAST LEND LENG LIVE REST STAY WAIT ABEAR AWAIT DELAY EXIST HABIT PAUSE STAND SWELL TARRY ENDURE HARBOR LINGER REMAIN RESIDE SUBMIT INHABIT SOJOURN SUBSIST SUSTAIN CONTINUE TOLERATE
(— BY) HOLD
ABIDING ABY FAST STABLE LASTING
ABIDINGNESS PERMANENCE
ABIEL (SON OF —) KISH
ABIES FIRS CONIFERS
ABIETATE SYLVATE
ABIEZER (FATHER OF —) GILEAD
ABIGAIL MAID
(HUSBAND OF —) DAVID NABAL JETHER
(SON OF —) AMASA DANIEL CHILEAB
ABIGEUS ABACTOR
ABIHAIL (DAUGHTER OF —) ESTHER
(FATHER OF —) HURI ELIAB
(HUSBAND OF —) ABISHUR REHOBOAM
(SON OF —) ZURIEL
ABIHU (BROTHER OF —) NADAB
(FATHER OF —) AARON
(MOTHER OF —) ELISHEBA
ABIHUD (FATHER OF —) BELA
ABIJAH (FATHER OF —) DAVID SAMUEL JEROBOAM REHOBOAM
(SON OF —) ASA HEZEKIAH
ABILITY G CAN MAY CLAY EASE FORM HAND CLASS FLAIR FORCE MIGHT POWER SKILL STUFF VERVE ENERGY ENGINE INGINE MAUGHT

STROKE TALENT CALIBER
CUNNING FACULTY POTENCY
APTITUDE CAPACITY STRENGTH
(— TO ENTER) ACCESS
(— TO THROW) ARM
(BATTING —) STICKWORK
(CREATIVE —) IMAGINATION
(FIELDING —) GLOVE
(INVENTIVE —) CONTRIVANCE
(MENTAL —) INGENY BRAINPOWER
ABIMELECH (BROTHER OF —) JOTHAM
(FATHER OF —) GIDEON ABIATHA
ABINADAB (FATHER OF —) SAUL JESSE
ABINOAM (SON OF —) BARAK
ABIPON CORONADO
ABIRAM (FATHER OF —) HIEL ELIAB
ABISHAI (BROTHER OF —) JOAB ASAHEL
(MOTHER OF —) ZERUIAH
ABISHALOM (DAUGHTER OF —) MAACHAH
ABISHUA (FATHER OF —) BELA PHINEHAS
(SON OF —) BUKKI
ABISHUR (FATHER OF —) SHAMMAI
ABITAL (HUSBAND OF —) DAVID
ABITUB (FATHER OF —) SHAHARAIM
(MOTHER OF —) HUSHIM
ABJECT LOW BASE MEAN POOR SUNK VILE HELOT PRONE SORRY CRAVEN MENIAL PALTRY SORDID SUPINE FAWNING FORLORN IGNOBLE SERVILE SLAVISH BEGGARLY CRINGING DEGRADED DOWNCAST LISTLESS WRETCHED
ABJOINT ABSTRICT
ABJURE DENY NITTE SPURN ESCHEW RECALL RECANT REJECT RESIGN REVOKE ABANDON DISAVOW EJURATE RETRACT ABNEGATE DISCLAIM FORSWEAR RENOUNCE
ABLAUT APOPHONY
ABLAZE ALOW AFIRE ALOWE ABLEEZE BURNING GLOWING RADIANT GLEAMING INFLAMED
ABLE APT BIG CAN FIT FERE ADEPT HABIL SMART THERE CLEVER EXPERT FACILE FITTED HABILE POTENT STRONG BASTANT CAPABLE DOUGHTY DEXTROUS POSSIBLE POWERFUL SKILLFUL SUITABLE TALENTED VIGOROUS
(— TO WALK) FEERIE FEIRIE
(SUFF.) **(— TO)** FUL
ABLE-BODIED YAL YALD YAULD
ABLENESS
(SUFF.) ABILITY IBILITY
ABLUTION BATH WIDU WUDU WUZU LOTION BAPTISM BATHING WASHING
ABNAKI WABANAKI
ABNEGATE DENY ABJURE FOREGO REFUSE REJECT DISAVOW DISCLAIM FORSWEAR IMMOLATE RENOUNCE
ABNER (BROTHER OF —) KISH
(FATHER OF —) NER
(SLAYER OF —) JOAB
(SON OF —) JAASIEL
(WIFE OF —) RIZPAH
ABNORMAL ENORM QUEER UTTER ERRATIC UNUSUAL VICIOUS ABERRANT ATYPICAL FREAKISH TERATOID ANOMALOUS MONSTROUS
(PREF.) ANOM(O) DYS MAL PARA POLY PSEUD(O)
ABNORMALITY ATAXY ATAXIA LETHAL ANOMALY BROWNING DEMENTIA ENORMITY
(CATTLE —) SAWDUST
ABOARD ON ONTO ACROSS ATHWART
ABODE COT DAR HUT INN WON BODE CELL FLAT HALL HOME NEST OMEN REST SEAT TENT WOON BEING BOWER DELAY HAUNT HOUSE MANOR PITCH RESET SIEGE SUITE ABIDAL BIDING ESTATE ADDRESS COTTAGE HABITAT LODGING MANSION SITTING CUNABULA DOMICILE DWELLING RESIANCE TENEMENT
(— OF DEAD) DAR AARU HELL ARALU HADES ORCUS SHEOL HEAVEN SHADES XIBALBA NIFLHEIM
(— OF DELIGHT) ELYSIUM
(— OF EVIL POWERS) ABYSS
(— OF GIANTS) UTGARD
(— OF GODS) MERU ASGARD OLYMPUS
(— OF LOST SOULS) ABADDON
(— OF MEN) MIDGARD
(— OF SOULS) LIMBO
(— OF SPIRITS) HELL
(ANIMAL —) ZOO MENAGERIE
(CELESTIAL —) HEAVEN
(FILTHY —) STY STYE
(MISERABLE —) DOGHOLE
(SHELTERED —) SHADE
ABOLISH END BLOT KILL ABATE ANNUL ERASE FORDO QUASH CANCEL EFFACE FOREDO RECALL REPEAL REVOKE VACATE DESTROY NULLIFY RESCIND REVERSE ABROGATE
ABOLITION EXTINCTION
ABOMA BOA BOM BOMA
ABOMASUM READ REED
ABOMINABLE VILE NASTY RUSTY CURSED ODIOUS ROTTEN BEASTLY HATEFUL HEINOUS MALEDICT NEFANDOUS
ABOMINABLY BEASTLY
ABOMINATE HATE ABHOR DETEST LOATHE EXECRATE
ABOMINATION EVIL CRIME CURSE HORROR PLAGUE DISGUST AVERSION
ABONGO BABONGO
ABORAL DORSAL ABACTINAL
ABORIGINAL ABO YAO FIRST NATAL BINGHI NATIVE SAVAGE NATURAL PRIMARY ORIGINAL
(— WOMAN) GIN
ABORIGINE KA KHA AINU TODA ALFUR BAIGA BLACK BOONG DASYU MAORI MYALL ALFURO ARANDA ARANTA ARUNTA BINGHI INDIAN KIPPER KODAGA NATIVE SAVAGE ADIBASI CHINHWAN WARRAGAL WARRIGAL
(AUSTRALIAN —) ABO
ABORT SLIP
ABORTION ABORT FAILURE CASTLING FETICIDE MISBIRTH
ABORTIVE IDLE VAIN BLIND FUTILE BOOTLESS
ABOUND SNY FLOW SNEE TEEM COVER FLEET SWARM REDOUND OVERFLOW
(SUFF.) ULENT
ABOUNDING RIFE FLUSH ROUTH COPIOUS REPLETE TEEMING UBEROUS ABUNDANT AFFLUENT PROLIFIC
(— IN POSSESSIONS) RICH
(SUFF.) IOUS OSE OUS
ABOUT BY IN OF ON RE SAY ASTO AWAY NEAR SOME UMBE UPON ANENT ASTIR CIRCA ABROAD ACTIVE ALMOST ANENST AROUND CIRCUM TOWARD ENVIRON CIRCITER
(PREF.) AMB(I) AMPH(I)(O) CIRCUM HYPER PERI
ABOUT-FACE FLOP
ABOVE ON UP OER SUP ATOP OVER PAST UPON ABEEN ABOON ABUNE ALOFT SUPRA BEFORE BEYOND HIGHER THEREUP OVERHEAD SUPERIOR
(— GENERAL LEVEL) APART
(PREF.) EP EPH EPI HYPER OVER SUPER SUPRA SUR
ABOVEBOARD HONEST
ABRADE RAW RUB BARK FILE FRET GALL RASP SAND WEAR CHAFE ERASE GRATE GRAZE GRIND SCORE SCUFF TOUCH SCOTCH SCRAPE IRRITATE
ABRADER FILE RASP EMERY SANDER ABRASER GRINDER SCRAPER
ABRAHAM (BIRTHPLACE OF —) UR
(BROTHER OF —) HARAN NAHOR
(CONCUBINE OF —) HAGAR
(FATHER OF —) TERAH
(GRANDFATHER OF —) NAHOR
(GRANDSON OF —) ESAU
(NEPHEW OF —) LOT
(SON OF —) ISAAC MEDAN SHUAH MIDIAN ZIMRAN ISHMAEL JOKSHAN
(WIFE OF —) SARAH KETURAH
ABRASION BURN GALL OUCH SCAR SORE GRAZE BRUISE BLASTING
ABRASIVE SAND EMERY PUMICE QUARTZ SILICA ALUNDUM BORAZON ERODENT ABRADANT CORUNDUM PUMICITE SCRUBBER
ABRAXAS GEM STONE AMULET ABRASAX
ABREAST EVEN AFRONT BESIDE HANGING
ABRET BREAD WAFER
ABRI SHED COVER DUGOUT SHELTER
ABRIDGE CUT DOCK LASK BRIEF ELIDE LIMIT RASEE RAZEE BRIDGE REDUCE SHRINK CURTAIL DEPRIVE REWRITE SHORTEN ABSTRACT BREVIATE COMPRESS CONDENSE CONTRACT DIMINISH RETRENCH SIMPLIFY ABBREVIATE
ABRIDGED TAIL
ABRIDGEMENT BRIEF ABREGE DIGEST PRECIS RESUME SKETCH COMPEND EPITOME PANDECT SUMMARY SUMMULA ABSTRACT BOILDOWN BREVIARY SYNOPSIS ABBREVIATION ABBREVIATURE
ABROAD OFF ASEA AWAY ABOUT ASTIR FORTH ABREED AFIELD ASTRAY WIDELY DISTANT OUTWARD OVERSEA OFFSHORE
ABROGATE ANNUL QUASH REMIT CANCEL REPEAL REVOKE VACATE ABOLISH NULLIFY RESCIND RETRACT DISSOLVE OVERRULE
ABROGATION REPEAL
ABRUPT BOLD CURT DEAD FAST RUDE BLUFF BLUNT BRIEF BRUSK HASTY ICTIC PLUMP QUICK ROUGH SHARP SHEER SHORT STEEP STUNT SURLY TERSE TOTAL CHOPPY CRAGGY CRUSTY PROMPT RUGGED SUDDEN ANGULAR BRUSQUE PRERUPT VIOLENT HEADLONG VERTICAL PRECIPITATE
(NOT —) SOFT
ABRUPTLY BANG SHARP SHORT STEEPLY SUDDENLY
ABSALOM (FATHER OF —) DAVID
(MOTHER OF —) MAACHAH
(SISTER OF —) TAMAR
(SLAYER OF —) JOAB
ABSALOM, ABSALOM (AUTHOR OF —) FAULKNER
(CHARACTER IN —) BON ROSA ELLEN HENRY JUDITH SHREVE SUTPEN THOMAS CHARLES COMPSON GOODHUE QUENTIN MCCANNON COLDFIELD
ABSAROKA CROW
ABSCESS BOIL MORO SORE ULCER FESTER INCOME LESION QUINSY VOMICA EXITURE GUMBOIL PARULIS APOSTEME SQUINACY
ABSCISIC ACID DORMIN
ABSCISSA X COSINE
ABSCISSION APOCOPE
ABSCOND GO FLY RUN BOLT FLEE HIDE QUIT ELOPE SCRAM SMOKE DECAMP DEPART DESERT ELOINE ESCAPE LEVANT WITHDRAW
ABSEILING RAPPEL
ABSENCE CUT LACK VOID WANT BLANK LEAVE DEFECT REMOVE VACUUM DEFAULT FAILURE VACANCY FURLOUGH
(— FROM DUTY) LIBERTY
(— FROM ONE'S COUNTRY) EXILE
(— OF AN ORGAN) AGENESIA AGENESIS
(— OF BIAS) DETACHMENT
(— OF CEREMONY) FAMILIARITY
(— OF FAMILIARITY) DISTANCE
(— OF FEELING) APATHY
(— OF FEVER) APYREXY APYREXIA
(— OF FORM) ENTROPY
(— OF GOVERNMENT) ANARCHY
(— OF INHIBITIONS) ANIMALITY
(— OF LIGHT) BLACK DARKNESS
(— OF MARRIAGE) AGAMY
(— OF MIND) ABSTRACTION
(— OF NAILS) ANONYCHIA
(— OF PAIN) ANODYNIA

(— OF PIGMENTATION) ACHROMA ACHROMIA
(— OF SKULL) ACRANIA
(— OF TAIL) ANURY
(— OF TASTE) AGEUSIA
(— OF TRUMPS) CHICANE
(— OF TRUTH) FALSEHOOD
(PERMITTED —) LEAVE
(PREF.) DYS ECTRO NON
ABSENT CUT OFF OUT AWAY AWOL GONE LOST WANE DESERT MUSING LACKING MISSING NOTHERE WANTING ABSORBED DREAMING
(— IN MIND) ABSTRACT
(PREF.) ECTRO
ABSENTMINDED FLAKY MUSED MUSING DISTRAIT DREAMING ABSTRACTED
ABSENTMINDEDNESS STARGAZING
ABSINTHE AJENJO GENIPI
ABSOLUTE GOD ONE TAO TAT DEAD DOWN FAIR FINE FREE MEAR MEER MERE PLAT PLUM PURE RANK REAL SELF TRUE VERY BLANK CLEAR FIXED PLUMB SHEER STARK STONE TOTAL UTTER WHOLE ENTIRE PROPER SEVERE SIMPLE SQUARE BRAHMAN CERTAIN PERFECT PLENARY ABSTRACT COMPLETE DESPOTIC EVENDOWN EXPLICIT IMPLICIT POSITIVE
(— TEMPERATURE) T
(NOT —) NISI FINITE CONDITIONAL
ABSOLUTELY YEA YES AMEN BONE COLD DEAD FAIR JUST PLAT SLAP PLAIN PLUMB STARK BARELY FAIRLY FLATLY SIMPLY WHOLLY SHEERLY ENTIRELY EVENDOWN
ABSOLUTION EXCUSE PARDON SHRIFT LOOSING SHRIVING
ABSOLUTISM CAESARISM DESPOTISM
ABSOLVE FREE QUIT CLEAR LOOSE REMIT ACQUIT ASSOIL EXCUSE EXEMPT FINISH PARDON SHRIVE UNBIND CLEANSE FORGIVE JUSTIFY RELEASE DISPENSE LIBERATE OVERLOOK
ABSORB EAT FIX SOP SUP BLOT SOAK SUCK TAKE AMUSE DRINK MERGE RIVET UNITE DEVOUR ENGAGE ENGULF ENWRAP IMBIBE INGEST INSORB INWRAP OCCUPY SPONGE STIFLE COMBINE CONSUME ENGROSS IMMERSE INVOLVE OCCLUDE SWALLOW
(— GRADUALLY) OSMOSE
ABSORBED DEEP GONE LOST RAPT SUNK FIXED ABSENT BURIED ENRAPT HIPPED INTENT PLUNGED RIVETED WRAPPED IMMERSED ABSTRACTED
(— BY) ALL
ABSORBENT BASE DOPE FOMES BARYTA SPONGY ANTACID SORBENT ANTIACID BIBULOUS DRINKING
ABSORBER SNUBBER
(— OF MONEY) LICKPENNY
(SHOCK —) BUFFER DAMPER
ABSORPTION AUTISM PREOCCUPATION
(— UNIT) SABIN
ABSORPTIVE SPONGY
ABSQUATULATE DECAMP ABSCOND
ABSTAIN DENY FAST KEEP STAY AVOID CEASE SPARE SPURN WAIVE DESIST DISUSE ESCHEW FOREGO REFUSE REJECT FORBEAR REFRAIN RESTRAIN TEETOTAL WITHHOLD
(— FROM) FAST FORGO LEAVE ABJURE ESCHEW FOREGO REFRAIN
ABSTAINER TOTE RECHABITE
ABSTEMIOUS SOBER ACETIC SLENDER MODERATE
ABSTENTION CELIBACY CHASTITY
ABSTERGE WIPE BATHE CLEAN PURGE RINSE
ABSTINENCE ENCRATY
ABSTINENT SOBER ABSTEMIOUS
ABSTRACT CULL DEED DRAW NOTE PART PURE TAKE BRIEF IDEAL STEAL ABSORB DEDUCT DETACH DIGEST DIVERT DOCKET NOETIC PRECIS REMOVE ABRIDGE COMPEND EPITOME EXCERPT ISOLATE PURLOIN SECRETE SUMMARY VIDIMUS ABSTRUSE ACADEMIC ARGUMENT BREVIATE DISCRETE PRESCIND SEPARATE SYLLABUS SYNOPSIS TABLEITY WITHDRAW METAPHYSICAL
(— SECRETLY) SUBDUCT
(NOT —) CONCRETE
(PL.) PARATITLA PARATITLES
ABSTRACTED REMOTE
ABSTRACTION STUDY ENTITY ABSENCE REVERIE ABSTRACT QUODDITY
(MENTAL —) REVERY REVERIE
ABSTRUSE DARK DEEP HIGH HIDDEN MYSTIC REMOTE SECRET SUBTLE CURIOUS OBSCURE RETIRED ABSTRACT ACROATIC ESOTERIC PROFOUND METAPHYSICAL
ABSTRUSENESS DEPTH
ABSURD HOT RICH WILD DOTTY DROLL FALSE INANE INEPT SILLY SCREWY STUPID ASININE FATUOUS FOOLISH LAPUTAN ABSONANT DOGGEREL FABULOUS COCKAMAMY MONSTROUS RIDICULOUS PREPOSTEROUS
ABSURDITY BETISE FATUITY FOOLERY FOPPERY WALTROT MAGGOTRY NONSENSE UNREASON
ABUNA METRAN
ABUNDANCE WON COPY FLOW MORT SONS WONE CHEAP DEPTH FLUSH FOUTH POWER RIVER ROUTH ROWTH SCADS SONSE STORE WRECK BOUNTY FOISON GALORE LAVISH OODLES PLENTY POWDER RICHES TALENT UBERTY WEALTH FLUENCY LASHINS PLEROMA SATIETY BELLYFUL FULLNESS LASHINGS OPULENCE PLEURISY RIMPTION PLENITUDE REDUNDANCY
(IN —) APLENTY
ABUNDANT FAT OLD FREE LUSH MUCH RANK RICH RIFE AMPLE FLUSH HEFTY LARGE OPIME ROUTH ROWTH STORE DEMOID GALORE HEARTY ROUTHY APLENTY COPIOUS FERTILE FULSOME LIBERAL OPULENT PROFUSE REPLETE TEEMING UBERANT UBEROUS WEALTHY AFFLUENT FRUITFUL GENEROUS NUMEROUS PLENTIFUL
(NOT —) LIGHT SPARE
(PREF.) HADR(O) LARGI
ABUNDANTLY RIFE WELL FREELY PLENTY LARGELY HEARTILY
ABUSE MAR MOB TAX BUSE CALL DRUB FLAY GAFF HARM HURT LACK MAUL RAIL RUIN SLAM TEEN VAIN BASTE BLAST CRIME CURSE FAULT GRIEF SCOLD SLANG SNASH SPOIL BERATE DEFILE INJURE INSULT MALIGN MISSAY MISUSE MUMBLE PUNISH RAVISH REVILE TANCEL TANSEL VILIFY YATTER AFFRONT BACKJAW BEDEVIL DECEIVE DESPITE FALSIFY MISBEDE MISCALL MISNAME OBLOQUY OUTRAGE PERVERT PROFANE SLANDER TRADUCE UPBRAID VIOLATE BALLARAG BUSINESS DISHONOR FRUMPERY LANGUAGE MALTREAT MISAPPLY MISTREAT REPROACH SLAPDASH
(— OF FREEDOM) LICENCE LICENSE
ABUSED DOWNTROD DOWNTRODDEN
ABUSIVE FOUL DIRTY SHREWD CORRUPT SATIRIC CHEATING INSOLENT LIBELOUS
ABUT BUTT JOIN REST TOUCH ADJOIN BORDER BUTTAL PROJECT
ABUTILON MALLOW
ABUTMENT CRIB PIER ALETTE BUTTRESS
ABUTTING FLUSH ADJACENT
ABY ABIDING
ABYSM ABIME BISME DOWNFALL
ABYSMAL DEEP DREARY PROFOUND UNENDING WRETCHED
ABYSS PIT POT DEEP GULF HELL HOLE VOID ABYSM CHAOS CHASM DEPTH GORGE ABRUPT BOTTOM VORAGO ABADDON AVERNUS GEHENNA SWALLOW DOWNFALL INTERVAL
ABYSSAL ABYSMAL BASSALIAN
ABYSSINIA (SEE ETHIOPIA)
ABYSSINIAN SIDI ABASSIN
(— BANANA) ENSETE
ACACALLIS (FATHER OF) MINOS
(MOTHER OF —) PASIPHAE
(SON OF —) GARAMAS AMPHITHEMIS
ACACIA GUM JAM KOA WELD WOLD BABUL GIDYA MULGA MYALL SIRIS THORN TIMBE VEREK WOALD WOULD ARABIC BABLAH BINDER GIDGEA GIDGEE GIDYEA HASHAB LEGUME LOCUST MIMOSA SALLEE WATTLE YARRAN BLUEBUSH BRIGALOW CHAPARRO IRONWOOD ROSEWOOD
ACADEMIC IVY MOOT RIGID FORMAL ACADEME CLASSIC DONNISH ERUDITE LEARNED POMPIER PEDANTIC PLATONIC
(— HEAD) DEAN
ACADEMY LYCEE CRUSCA LYCEUM MANEGE SCHOOL ACADEME COLLEGE SOCIETY YESHIVA SEMINARY
(FRENCH —) FORTY
(RIDING —) MANAGE MANEGE
ACADIAN CAJUN
ACAJOU CAJU CAJOO CAJOU
ACALEPH MEDUSA MEDUSAN
ACAMAS (BROTHER OF —) ARCHELOCHUS
(FATHER OF —) ANTENOR THESEUS EUSSORUS
(MOTHER OF —) THEANO PHAEDRA
(SLAYER OF —) AJAX MERIONES
(SON OF —) MUNITUS
ACANA ALMIQUE
ACANTHA FIN SPINE THORN PRICKLE ACANTHON
ACAPU WALNUT WACAPOU CHAPERNO
ACARID MITE NYMPH NYMPHA OCTOPOD DIBRANCH PROTONYMPH
ACARNAN (BROTHER OF —) AMPHOTERUS
(FATHER OF —) ALCMAEON
(MOTHER OF —) CALLIRRHOE
ACASTUS (FATHER OF —) PELIAS
(SLAYER OF —) PELEUS
(WIFE OF —) HIPPOLYTE
ACAUDAL BOBBED ANUROUS ECAUDATE TAILLESS
ACAULESCENT STEMLESS
ACCEDE LET AGREE ALLOW ENTER GRANT YIELD ACCORD ASSENT ATTAIN COMPLY CONCUR CONCEDE CONFORM CONSENT
ACCELERATE GUN REV RUN HYPO JAZZ RACE SPUR URGE DRIVE FAVOR FORCE HURRY LINAC SPEED HASTEN ADVANCE FORWARD FURTHER QUICKEN ANTEDATE DISPATCH EXPEDITE INCREASE THROTTLE
ACCELERATED (PREF.) TACHY
ACCELERATING (PREF.) AUXO
ACCELERATION PICKUP SPEEDUP
(— OF REACTION) CATALYSIS
(— UNIT) STAPP
ACCELERATOR GAS GUN SPEEDER BETATRON BEVATRON THROTTLE
(LINEAR —) LINAC
ACCENT BEAT BIRR BLAS BURR MARK TONE ACUTE GRAVE ICTUS PITCH PULSE SOUND THROB VERGE BROGUE LENGTH RHYTHM STRESS THESIS EMPHASIS
(DORIC —) PLATEASM
(IRISH —) BROGUE
(MUSICAL —) BEAT
(WITHOUT AN —) ATONIC

ACCENTED FZ SFZ TONIC STRONG MARCATO MARCANDO SFORZATO
ACCENTUATE ACCENT
ACCENTUATION DECLAMATION ENHANCEMENT
ACCEPT BUY EAT BEAR FANG HAVE HOLD JUMP TAKE ADMIT ADOPT AGREE ALLOW HONOR INFER MARRY ASSENT ASSUME AVOUCH POCKET RATIFY AGREEON AGREETO APPROVE BELIEVE CONCEDE EMBRACE ESPOUSE RECEIVE SETTLEFOR
(— AS ONE'S OWN) NOSTRIFICATE
(— AS TRUE) ACCREDIT
(— AT RANDOM) DRAW
(— BETS) BOOK
(— EAGERLY) LEAP
(— INHERITANCE) ADIATE
(— READILY) SWALLOW
(— WITHOUT QUESTION) ABIDE
ACCEPTABLE LIEF VALID SIGHTLY WELCOME GRACIOUS PASSABLE PLEASANT
ACCEPTANCE PASS SNAFF ADITIO TAQLID PASSAGE CREDENCE CURRENCY
(— OF INHERITANCE) CERNITURE
(— OF ORDER) ALLOTMENT
ACCEPTATION MEANING ACCEPTANCE
ACCEPTED GOING VULGAR POPULAR APPROVED CREDITED ORTHODOX STANDARD
(NOT —) OUT
(WIDELY —) INVETERATE
ACCEPTOR BASE
ACCESS FIT WAY ADIT DOOR GATE PATH ROAD ENTRY GOING ROUTE ACCOST AVENUE COMING ENTREE PORTAL STREET ADVANCE APPROACH ENTRANCE PAROXYSM RECOURSE
(— OF DISEASE) ATTACK
ACCESSIBILITY EXPOSURE
ACCESSIBLE NEAR OPEN HANDY PATENT AFFABLE PRESENT FAMILIAR PERVIOUS SOCIABLE GETATABLE
ACCESSION ENTER ACCESS AFFLUX ALLUVIO ILLAPSE ADDITION ALLUVION ENTRANCE INCREASE
ACCESSORY HAT AIDE ALLY DOME TOOL EXTRA SCARF HELPER ABETTOR ADAPTER ADAPTOR ADJUNCT ANCILLA ENCLAVE FITTING FIXTURE ADDITIVE HATSTAND ORNAMENT
(PL.) ADDENDA FIXINGS STAFFAGE
ACCIACCATURA MORDENT
ACCIDENT HAP CASE LUCK EVENT GRIEF PRANG SHUNT CHANCE HAZARD INJURY MISHAP FORTUNE QUALITY CALAMITY CASUALTY DISASTER FORTUITY INCIDENT ROLLOVER
(— IN CAR RACING) SHUNT
(AUTOMOBILE —) FATAL
(EUCHARISTIC —S) SPECIES
(HAVE — WITH) PRANG
ACCIDENTAL ODD CASUAL CHANCE RANDOM EXTERNAL
ACCIPITER ERNE HAWK
ACCLAIM CRY CLAP FAME HAIL LAUD ROOT CHEER CLAIM ECLAT EXTOL SHOUT PRAISE APPLAUD HOSANNA OVATION PLAUDIT RECLAME WELCOME APPLAUSE
(NOISY —) RIOT
ACCLAMATION CRY VOTE CHEER SHOUT ACCLAIM HOSANNA PLAUDIT APPLAUSE
ACCLIMATE ENURE INURE HARDEN SEASON ACCUSTOM
ACCLIMATIZE SALT ADAPT HARDEN ORIENT SEASON
ACCLIVITY BANK BROW HILL RISE GRADE PITCH SLANT SLOPE TALUS ASCENT HEIGHT INCLINE
ACCOLADE EMMY KISS RITE SIGN AWARD HONOR KUDOS MEDAL OSCAR TOKEN EULOGY SYMBOL EMBRACE GARLAND CEREMONY
ACCOMMODATE AID BED BOW FIT CAMP GIVE HELP HOLD LEND SORT SUIT ADAPT BOARD DEFER FAVOR HOUSE LODGE SERVE YIELD ADJUST COMPLY FAVOUR OBLIGE SETTLE CONFORM CONTAIN FASHION ATTEMPER GARRISON
ACCOMMODATING OBLIGING
ACCOMMODATION LOAN BERTH CLASS BERTHAGE GIFFGAFF
(— BILL) KITE
(PL.) PASSAGE
ACCOMPANIED FRAUGHT
ACCOMPANIMENT SON ALBA BACKUP BURDEN ESCORT OOMPAH ADJUNCT DESCANT SUPPORT OBLIGATO
(IMPROVISED —) VAMP
(PLAY JAZZ —) COMP
(PL.) FIXINGS
ACCOMPANIST JONGLEUR
ACCOMPANY SEE BACK FARE FERE JOIN LEAD TEND WAIT BRING PILOT ASSIST ATTEND CONCUR CONVEY CONVOY ESCORT FOLLOW SECOND SQUIRE COEXIST CONDUCT CONSORT SUPPORT CHAPERON
ACCOMPANYING FELLOW ADJUNCT
(PREF.) SYMPHORI
ACCOMPLICE PAL AIDE ALLY CHUM BUDDY CRONY LOUKE SHILL TILER BONNET COHORT FELLOW HELPER ABETTOR FEODARY FEUDARY HUSTLER PARTNER STEERER
ACCOMPLISH DO GO END WIN CHAR FILL WORK ENACT EQUIP FETCH FORTH SWING AFFORD ATTAIN EFFECT FINISH FULFIL MANAGE VIRTUE ABSOLVE ACHIEVE CHEVISE COMPASS EXECUTE EXPLETE FULFILL FURNISH OPERATE PERFECT PERFORM REALIZE SUCCEED COMPLETE CONTRIVE DISPATCH ENGINEER OUTCARRY NEGOTIATE
ACCOMPLISHED APT ABLE ARCH DONE ADEPT ENDED GREAT TERSE BESEEN EXPERT HANDSOME TALENTED
ACCOMPLISHMENT ART END DEED FEAT PASS CRAFT SKILL EFFECT TALENT VIRTUE EARNING QUALITY FRUITION LEARNING
(PRIOR —) ANTICIPATION
ACCORD GIVE JIBE JUMP SUIT UNIT AGREE ALLOW ATONE AWARD BEFIT CHIME CHORD CORDE GRANT LEVEL STAND TALLY UNITY ACCEDE ADJUST ASSENT BESTOW BETEEM COMPLY CONCUR SETTLE UNISON COMPORT COMPOSE CONCEDE CONCERT CONCORD CONGREE CONSENT CONSORT HARMONY RAPPORT RESPOND UNANIME DIAPASON SYMPATHY
(— WITH) SUIT
(IN —) ALONG
ACCORDANCE CONCERT CONSENT
(IN —) ALONG
ACCORDANT EVEN ATTUNED AGREEING COHERENT SUITABLE
ACCORDING (— TO) AD BY AUX SEC EMFORTH ENFORTH PURSUANT SECUNDUM
(— TO ART) SA
(— TO LAW) SL
ACCORDINGLY SO ERGO THEN THUS HENCE IGITUR
ACCORDION LANTUM FLUTINA FLAUTINO
ACCOST BAIL HAIL MASH MEET ABORD ASSAY BOARD GREET SPEAK ACCESS BROACH HALLOO SALUTE ACCOAST ADDRESS SOLICIT APPROACH GREETING
ACCOUCHEUR OBSTETRICIAN
ACCOUCHEUSE MIDWIFE
ACCOUNT TAB BILL BOOK DEEM DRAW ITEM NICK NOTE RATE REDE SAKE TAIL TALE TELL TEXT WORD AUDIT BLAME CHALK COUNT JUDGE SCORE STATE STORY VALUE WORTH BATTEL CREDIT DETAIL ESTEEM HORARY LEGEND NOTICE PROFIT REASON RECKON RECORD REGARD RELATE RENDER REPORT REPUTE TREATY ACCOMPT COMPOST COMPUTE EXPLAIN JOURNAL LEXICON NARRATE PROCESS RECITAL TAILZIE BREVIARY CONSIDER ESTIMATE RELATION TREATISE BORDEREAU MONOGRAPH RECKONING PRESENTATION
(— FOR) SAVE EXPLAIN
(—S FOR PROVISIONS) BATTELS
(ACCURATE —) GRIFF GRIFFIN
(CREDIT —) TICK
(KIND OF —) IRA NOW
(LONG —) ILIAD MEGILLAH
(LONG, INVOLVED —) MEGILLA MEGILLAH
(OFFICIAL —) PROTOCOL
(SAVINGS —) IRA
(SHORT —) KETCH
(TRAVEL —) ITINERARY
(PL.) BATTELS
ACCOUNTABILITY DETAIL LIABILITY
ACCOUNTABLE LIABLE AMENABLE
ACCOUNTANT CLERK SIRCAR SIRKAR AUDITOR PESHKAR PUTWARI KULKARNI MUTSUDDY RECKONER
ACCOUNTANT-GENERAL DAFTARDAR DEFTERDAR
ACCOUNTING TASK REASON COSTING
ACCOUTER ARM RIG GIRD ARRAY DRESS EQUIP ATTIRE CLOTHE OUTFIT BEDIGHT FURNISH HARNESS PROVIDE
ACCOUTERMENTS GEAR TIRE DRESS ATTIRE GRAITH
ACCREDIT ALLOT VOUCH CREDIT DEPUTE APPOINT APPROVE ASCRIBE BELIEVE CERTIFY CONFIRM ENDORSE LICENSE SANCTION
ACCRETION SUM GAIN GROWTH DEPOSIT EXUDATE ADDITION ADHESION INCREASE
(INJURIOUS —) RUST
ACCRUAL ACCRUE DEMERIT
ACCRUE ADD WIN EARN GAIN GROW PILE ARISE ENSUE ENURE INCUR INURE ISSUE MATURE RESULT SPRING ACQUIRE COLLECT REDOUND ACCRESCE CUMULATE INCREASE
ACCUMULATE DRAW FUND GROW HEAP HIVE MASS PILE SAVE AMASS DRIFT HOARD STACK STORE TOTAL ACCRUE GARNER GATHER MUSTER RACKUP SCRAPE COLLECT CONGEST HARVEST INCREASE
ACCUMULATION DRIP DUMP FUND GAIN HEAP MASS PILE LODGE STACK STORE ANLAGE BACKUP BUDGET COLUMN DEBRIS GARNER BACKLOG CUMULUS DEPOSIT DOSSIER MORAINE DIVIDEND INTEREST
(— OF FLUID) EDEMA OEDEMA ASCITES
(— OF FORCE) CHARGE
(— OF SNOW) ALIMENTATION
(— OF TRIFLES) FLOTSAM
(— ON CONCRETE) LAITANCE
ACCURACY NICETY FIDELITY JUSTNESS PRECISION
(— OF ADJUSTMENT) TRAM
(HISTORICAL —) SYNCHRONISM
ACCURATE JUST LEAL NICE TRUE CLOSE EXACT FLUSH RIGHT DEADON NARROW PROPER SEVERE STRICT CAREFUL CORRECT CURIOUS PRECISE FAITHFUL PERQUEER PUNCTUAL RIGOROUS TRUTHFUL
(NOT —) IMPURE
(UNPLEASANTLY —) BRUTAL
ACCURATELY JUST FAIRLY JUSTLY CLOSELY EXACTLY INSOOTH
ACCURSED FEY CURSED DAMNED DOOMED FORBID SACRED WARIED BLASTED MALEDICT
ACCUSATION BEEF WITE BLAME CAUSE CRIME POINT WHITE APPEAL ATTACK CHARGE THREAP THREEP ACCUSAL SCANDAL DELATION
(FALSE —) SUGGESTION
ACCUSATORY WRAYFUL
ACCUSE TAX WRY CALL FILE NOTE SHOW SLUR TASK WITE WRAY

ACOUP ARGUE BLAME PEACH TAINT TOUCH WHITE APPEAL ATTACH ATTACK BECALL BEWRAY CHARGE DEFAME DELATE DETECT INDICT INTENT MURMUR APPEACH ARRAIGN ATTAINT CENSURE IMPEACH IMPLEAD TRADUCE CHASTISE COMPLAIN DENOUNCE QUESTION REDARGUE REPROACH
(— UNJUSTLY) SLANDER
ACCUSER CHARGER DELATOR LIBELANT
ACCUSING CULPATORY DENUNCIATORY
ACCUSTOM URE USE WIN WON HAFT WONT ADAPT BREAK DRILL ENURE FLESH HABIT HAUNT INURE TRAIN ADDICT ADJUST CUSTOM INDUCE ORIENT SEASON CONSORT EDUCATE TOUGHEN ACQUAINT
(— HORSE TO BIT) MOUTH
(— TO PASTURE) HAFT
ACCUSTOMED TAME USED WONE WONT USANT USUAL INURED CHRONIC CURRENT HABITED CONSUETE
ACCUSTOMEDNESS HABIT
ACE AS ALS JOT ONE PIP TIB ATOM CARD HERO MARK TOPS UNIT WHIZ ADEPT BASTO FLYER POINT BULLET EXPERT AVIATOR BRISQUE PARTICLE
(— OF CLUBS) BASTA BASTO
(— OF SPADES) SPADILLE SPADILLO
(— OF TRUMPS) TIB HONOR PUNTO
(THREE —S) GLEEK
ACEDIA SLOTH ACCIDIA ACCIDIE
ACEPHALOUS HEADLESS
ACER NEGUNDO
ACERB ACID HARD SOUR TART ACRID HARSH SHARP BITTER SEVERE
ACERBAS (WIFE OF —) ELISSA
ACERBATE EMBITTER IRRITATE
ACERBITY ACRIMONY ASPERITY CYNICISM SEVERITY TARTNESS
ACESTES (FATHER OF —) CRIMISUS
(MOTHER OF —) EGESTA
(WIFE OF —) ENTELLA
ACETABULUM PAN PYXIS CUPULE ACETABLE HOLDFAST
ACETAL KETAL FORMAL KETATE BUTYRAL
ACETALDEHYDE ETHYL ETHANAL ALDEHYDE
ACETIC SOUR SHARP ZOONIC
ACETOPHENETIDIN PHENACETIN
ACETYLENE TOLAN ALKINE ALKYNE ETHINE ETHYNE TOLANE
ACHAEMENES (BROTHER OF —) XERXES
(FATHER OF —) DARIUS
(SLAYER OF —) INARUS
ACHAEUS (FATHER OF —) XUTHUS
(MOTHER OF —) CREUSA
ACHBOR (FATHER OF —) MICHAIAH
(SON OF —) BAALHANAN
ACHE AKE NAG NIP ECHE GELL HURT LONG PAIN PANG PINE RACK WARK WERK HACHE SMART STANG STOUN THROB THROE WARCH YEARN DESIRE MISERY STITCH STOUND TWINGE TWITCH ANGUISH EARACHE SORENESS
ACHENE CYPSELA UTRICLE
ACHIEVE DO END GET WIN EARN GAIN HACK HAVE MAKE FETCH FORCE NOTCH REACH SCORE AFFORD ARRIVE ATTAIN EFFECT FINISH OBTAIN CHEVISE COMPASS EXPLOIT FULFILL PERFORM PROCURE PRODUCE REALIZE SUCCEED TRIUMPH COMPLETE CONCLUDE CONTRIVE ACCOMPLISH
(— HARMONY) AGREE
(— ORIENTATION) ADJUST
ACHIEVED (SOMETHING EASILY —) GIMME
ACHIEVEMENT ACT JOB DEED FEAT WORK ACTION CAREER RESULT STROKE EXPLOIT HARVEST PROWESS SUCCESS FELICITY
(COMPLETE —) TRIUMPH
ACHILLEA PTARMICA
ACHILLES PELIDES
(COMPANION OF —) PATROCLUS
(FATHER OF —) PELEUS
(FRIEND OF —) PATROCLUS
(GRANDFATHER OF —) AEACUS
(HORSE OF —) XANTHUS
(MOTHER OF —) THETIS
(SLAYER OF —) PARIS
ACHIM (FATHER OF —) SADOC
(SON OF —) ELIUD
ACHING SORE
ACHIOTE OLEANA ACHUETE ANNATTO ARNATTA ARNATTO
ACHRAS SAPOTA
ACHROMACYTE SHADOW
ACHROMATIC GRAY GREY NEUTRAL
ACHSAH (FATHER OF —) CALEB
(HUSBAND OF —) OTHNIEL
ACICULAR SPLINTERY
ACID DRY LSD YAR DIAL DOPA KEEN PABA SOUR TART ACERB ACRID ALGIN AMINO CERIN EAGER HARSH LYSIN MALIC OLEUM RHEIN SHARP ULMIC ABRINE ALLIIN BITING BITTER DORMIN FOLATE GLYCIN LYSINE NIACIN PROLIN SERINE TWEAKY VALINE ACERBIC ACETOSE CERASIN FILICIN GLYCINE PROLINE STEARIN VINEGAR ORNITHINE PENICILLIN
(CRYSTALLINE —) EDTA
(KIND OF —) MALIC ADIPIC KAINIC MURAMIC
(NITRIC —) AQUAFORTIS
(NUCLEIC —) DNA RNA
(SEQUENCE OF NUCLEIC —) INTRON
(PREF.) ACETO OXY
(SUFF.) **(— RADICAL)** OYL
ACID HYDROGEN
(SUFF.) HYDRIC
ACIDITY ACOR VERDURE ACERBITY SOURNESS VERJUICE
ACIDULOUS TART
ACIS (FATHER OF —) FAUNUS
(LOVER OF —) GALATEA
(MOTHER OF —) SYMAETHIS
(SLAYER OF —) POLYPHEMUS
ACIS & GALATEA (CHARACTER IN —) ACIS GALATEA POLYPHEMUS
(COMPOSER OF —) HANDEL
ACKNOWLEDGE NOD OWN AVER AVOW SIGN ADMIT ADOPT ALLOW GRANT KITHE KYTHE THANK YIELD ACCEDE ACCEPT AGNIZE ANSWER ASSENT AVOUCH BEKNOW COUTHE FATHER REWARD CONCEDE CONFESS DECLARE OBSERVE PROFESS DISCLOSE RECOGNIZE
ACKNOWLEDGEMENT GRANT THANK AVOWAL CREDIT SHRIFT APOLOGY AGNITION COGNOVIT COGNISANCE COGNIZANCE RECOGNITION
(— OF MISTAKE) JEOFAIL
(— OF SERVICE) GRAVITY
(— OF SIN) PECCAVI
(WRITTEN —) RECEIPT
ACLE AKLE IRUL JAMBA IRONWOOD PYENGADU
ACLYS HURLBAT
ACME IT ACE CAP TOP APEX CULM HIGH PEAK CREST PITCH POINT STATE APOGEE CLIMAX COMBLE CRISIS CULMEN HEIGHT HEYDAY SUMMIT ZENITH CUMULUS SUBLIME CAPSHEAF CAPSTONE PINNACLE
ACNE WHELK ROSACEA
ACOLYTE BOY HELPER NOVICE SERVER LEARNER PATENER THURIFER
ACOMIA BALDNESS
ACONITE BIKH ACONITUM NAPELLUS
ACORN NUT MAST GLAND OVEST BALANUS BELLOTA BELLOTE
(— CUPS) VALONIA
(PL.) MAST CAMATA PANNAGE CAMATINA
(PREF.) BALAN(I)(O) GLANDI GLANDULI
ACORN-SHAPED BALANOID
ACOUSTICS SONICS PHONICS
ACQUAINT KNOW TELL TEACH VERSE ADVISE INFORM NOTIFY SCHOOL APPRISE APPRIZE POSSESS RESOLVE
ACQUAINTANCE KITH HABIT COUSIN FRIEND GOSSIP PICKUP AFFINITY FAMILIAR INTIMATE
(CLOSE —) HABIT INWARDNESS
(PRACTICAL —) PRACTICE PRACTISE
(PL.) KITH SOCIETY
ACQUAINTED VERSED ACQUENT VERSANT
(CLOSELY —) INTIMATE
ACQUIESCE BOW ABIDE AGREE CHIME YIELD ACCEDE ACCEPT ASSENT COMPLY CONCUR SUBMIT CONCEDE CONFIRM CONFORM CONSENT
ACQUIESCENCE ASSENT
ACQUIRABLE
(PREF.) CTETO
ACQUIRE ADD BAG BUY GET WIN EARN FORM GAIN GRAB HAVE MAKE REAP ADOPT AMASS ANNEX BEGET CHEVY CHIVY GLEAN INCUR LEARN REACH SEIZE STEAL ATTAIN CHIVEY CHIVVY DERIVE EFFECT GARNER OBTAIN SECURE SNATCH COLLECT CONQUER DEVELOP PROCURE RECEIVE CONTRACT
(— DESIRABLE QUALITY) AGE
(— KNOWLEDGE) LERE
ACQUIRED (NOT —) NATURAL
ACQUIREMENT (— OF CONTROL) TAKEOVER
ACQUISITION WIN GAIN LUCRE ACQUEST ACQUIST GETTING CONQUEST ACCESSION
(DISHONEST —) GRAFT
(VALUED —) PRIZE
ACQUISITIVE GRABBY
ACQUIT PAY FREE QUIT CLEAR QUIET ASSOIL BEHAVE BESTOW EXCUSE PARDON ABSOLVE COMPORT CONDUCT RELEASE REQUITE LIBERATE OVERLOOK UNCHARGE ASSOILZIE
ACQUITTAL EXCUSE DISCHARGE ABSOLUTION
ACQUITTANCE QUIETUS RELEASE
ACRE AKER LAND ACKER FIELD STANG ARPENT COLLOP FARMHOLD
(QUARTER —) ROOD
(120 —S) HIDE
(2-3RDS —) COVER
(PL.) ACREAGE
ACREMAN CARUCARIUS
ACRID HOT ACID BASK KEEN SOUR HARSH ROUGH SHARP SURLY BITING BITTER CAUSTIC PUNGENT REEKING UNSAVORY VIRULENT
ACRIMONIOUS MAD ACID KEEN ACRID ANGRY GRUFF HARSH IRATE SHARP SNELL SURLY BITTER CAUSTIC STINGING VIRULENT
ACRIMONY VIRUS ACERBITY ASPERITY PUNGENCY SOURNESS ANIMOSITY
ACRISIUS (BROTHER OF —) PROETUS
(DAUGHTER OF —) DANAE
(FATHER OF —) ABAS
(MOTHER OF —) AGLAIA
(SLAYER OF —) PERSEUS
(WIFE OF —) AGANIPPE EURYDICE
ACROBAT ZANY KINKER GYMNAST TOPPLER TUMBLER BALANCER AERIALIST ROPEWALKER
ACRONYM INITIALISM
ACROPOLIS FORT HILL POLIS CADMEA CITADEL LARISSA
ACROSOME IDIOSOME IDIOZOME
ACROSS OVER SPAN YOND CROSS ABOARD THWART ATHWART OPPOSITE TRAVERSE
(CLEAN —) SHORT
(PREF.) DIA OVER TRANS
ACROSTIC ABC AGLA DORA GAME POEM TANAK PHRASE PUZZLE TANACH
ACRYLIC PROPENOIC
ACT BE DO GO APE LAW LET ACTU AUTO BILL COME DEAL DEED DORA FACT FEAT HOCK JEST MAKE MOVE PART PASS PLAY SKIT SLIM TAKE TURN WORK ACTUS DRAMA EDICT EMOTE ENTRY EXERT FEIGN GRACE KARMA MODEL SCENE

SHIFT SHTIK STUNT ACTION BEHAVE BESTIR DECREE DEMEAN FACTUM MANAGE RAGMAN SHTICK COMPORT EXECUTE EXPLOIT PERFORM PORTRAY PRETEND STATUTE FUNCTION PRETENSE SIMULATE
(— AFFECTEDLY) MIMP POSTURE
(— AGGRESSIVELY) HUSTLE
(— AS WANTON) RIG
(— AWKWARDLY) HOCKER
(— BADLY) HAMFATTER
(— BEFORE) ANTICIPATE
(— BLUNDERINGLY) BULL
(— DECEITFULLY) DOUBLE
(— DISHONESTLY) FUDGE
(— FIRST) LEAD
(— FOOLISHLY) FON FONNE FOLEYE FOOTER FOOTLE
(— FRIVOLOUSLY) FRIVOL FRIBBLE
(— IN A NERVOUS WAY) JITTER
(— INDECISIVELY) DITHER
(— INDEPENDENTLY) SEVER
(— IN THEATER) GAFF
(— OF APPROVAL) EUGE
(— OF BEGGING) CADGE
(— OF CIVILITY) CURTSY DEVOIR CURTSEY
(— OF KINDNESS) CARESS BENEFIT
(— OF LABOR) DILIGENCE
(— OF PRAYER) DEVOTION
(— OF STUPIDITY) BETISE
(— OF TRICKERY) COG
(— OF UNKINDNESS) CUT
(— OUT) ENACT DRAMATIZE
(— PLAYFULLY) DALLY BANTER
(— QUICKLY) GIRD
(— RASHLY) RACKLE
(— SLOWLY) DAWDLE
(— SPORTIVELY) DAFF
(— SUDDENLY) FLASH
(— TIMIDLY) NESH
(— TOGETHER) AGREE COACT CONCUR CONCORD
(— TRIFLINGLY) JANK
(— UPON) TOUCH AFFECT HANDLE
(— UP TO) EVEN
(— VIGOROUSLY) TWIG TURNTO
(— WITHOUT RESTRAINT) FREEWHEEL
(COMICAL —) JIG
(CONVENTIONAL —) AMENITY
(CORRUPT —) DEPRAVITY
(CRIMINAL —) INFAMY
(DARING —) ESCAPADE
(DECEITFUL —) ABUSE
(DECEPTIVE —) FEINT
(ECCENTRIC —) CANTRIP
(EVIL —) MALEFICENCE
(FAULTY —) PARAPRAXIS
(FOOLISH —) DIDO IDIOTISM
(FORBIDDEN —) CRIME
(FORMAL —) CEREMONY
(FRAUDULENT —) SCAM
(HABITUAL—) EXERCISE
(HASTY —) FLING
(HOSTILE —) BLOW
(INJURIOUS —) SPOIL
(KIND OF —) RIOT
(LAUDATORY —) COUP
(LITURGICAL —) LAVABO
(LIVELY —) JIG
(MERITORIOUS —) MITZVAH
(MISCHIEVOUS —) DIDO CANTRAP CANTRIP
(OFFENSIVE —) AFFRONT
(OFFICIAL —S) ACTA
(PLAYFUL —) RALLERY RAILLERY
(PRAISEWORTHY —) DEMERIT
(RUDE —) INCIVILITY
(SUDDEN VIOLENT —) BENSEL BENSIL
(THOUGHTLESS —) FOLLY
(UNMANNERLY —) SOLECISM
(UNUSUAL —) STUNT
(VALOROUS —) WORSHIP
(VARIETY —) SKETCH
(WRONG —) DERELICT DERELICTUM
(PL.) DOINGS
(SUFF.) ADE ATE CY ICE ION ISM TH

ACTAEON **(FATHER OF —)** ARISTAEUS
(MOTHER OF —) AUTONOE

ACTINAL ORAL

ACTING AGENT SERVING HISTRIONIC
(— AGAINST) ADVERSE
(— BY TURN) ALTERN
(— IN RETURN) RECIPROCAL
(— ODDLY) HAYWIRE
(— RAPIDLY) DRASTIC
(UNSKILLFUL —) BUNGLING

ACTINIAN OPELET VESTLET

ACTINOST RADIAL RADIALE

ACTINOZOAN SEAFLOWER

ACTION ACT AIR DAP JOB PAS ACTO CASE DEED FACT FRAY GEST PLAY PLOY PUSH SHOW STEP SUIT WORK ACTIO DOING EDICT FIGHT FLING GESTE ISSUE THING TREAD VENUE AFFAIR AGENCY BATTLE BEFOOT COMBAT PRAXIS CONDUCT FACTION GESTURE MEASURE PROCESS TANQUAM ACTIVITY BEHAVIOR BUSINESS CONFLICT FUNCTION PRACTICE PRACTISE
(— BETWEEN HORSE AND RIDER) APPUI
(— OF DRAMA) EPITASIS
(— OF WIND) EOLATION
(— PAINTING) TACHISM
(— POTENTIAL) SPIKE
(ABSURD —S) BOSH
(ANTAGONISTIC —) ATOMISM
(BLAMEWORTHY —) WITE
(CAPRICIOUS —) FREAK
(CHEMICAL —) ACTINISM
(COARSE —) HARLOTRY
(CONCLUDING —) MOPUP
(CONVULSIVE —) SPASM
(COOPERATIVE —) SYNERGISM
(COURT —) LAW SUIT ASSIZE LAWSUIT QUERELA QUERELE
(CRUEL —) RUTH
(CUSTOMARY —) COURSE
(DIVINE —) THEURGY
(DUE —) ORDER
(EXAGGERATED —) PRODUCTION
(EXTEMPORE —) SCHEDIASM
(FANTASTIC —) ABTIC
(FINAL —) CATASTROPHE
(FOOLISH —) FOPPERY INEPTITUDE
(FRISKY —) FRISKIN
(FRIVOLOUS —) DALLIANCE
(HOSTILE —) OPPOSITION
(IMPULSIVE —) STAMPEDE
(INDIRECT —) WINDLASS
(INITIAL —) LEADOFF INDUCTION
(INTRODUCTORY —) PROLOGUE
(JOINT —) COACTION
(LEGAL —) DEBT SUIT ACCOUNT DETINET DETINUE PROCEEDING
(MEAN —S) DOGGERY
(MILITARY —) SWEEP OPERATION
(ODD —S) JIMJAMS
(PLAYFUL —) FUN FROLIC
(RASH —) HASTE
(REPEATED —) DRUM DOUBLE
(SUDDEN —) FLISK
(SYMBOLIC —) CHARADE
(TACTLESS —) GAUCHERIE
(UNAVOIDABLE —) FORCEPUT
(UNINTERMITTED —) HEAT
(VIOLENT —) AFFRAY
(WHIMSICAL —S) HUMORS HUMOURS
(WILY —) WRINKLE
(PREF.) CIN(O) CINET(O) KIN(O) KINESI KINET(O)
(SUFF.) ADE AL ANCE ANT ARD ATION CY ENCE ESIS ING ISATION IVE IZATION MENT OSIS PRACTIC PRAXIA PRAXIS SIS SOME LE LING

ACTIS **(FATHER OF —)** RHODE
(MOTHER OF —) HELIUS

ACTIVATE SPARK ACTIFY ELICIT
(— BY MIXING WITH WATER) PROOF

ACTIVATION
(SUFF.) KINESIS

ACTIVATOR GOAD

ACTIVE UP YAL YAP YEP BUSY GAIN LISH LIST PERT RASH SPRY TRIG WHAT YALD YARE YEPE YERN ABOUT AGILE ALERT ALIVE ASTIR BRISK DEEDY FRESH LIGHT LINGY LUSTY NIPPY PEART QUICK READY SMART SNELL SPICY SPRIG STOUT SWANK VIVID WIGHT YAULD YERNE ACTUAL BOUNCY CLEVER DIRECT FEERIE FEIRIE FIERCE HEARTY LIVELY LIVING MOVING NIMBLE PROMPT QUIVER SEMMIT SPEEDY SPRACK SPROIL SPRUCE SPRUNT SWANKY WIMBLE DASHING DEEDFUL DELIVER DYNAMIC HOPPING HUMMING KINETIC STHENIC THRODDY YANKING ANIMATED ATHLETIC BRAWLING DILIGENT SPIRITED VIGOROUS
(EXCESSIVELY —) MANIC
(NORMALLY —) ABOUT

ACTIVELY DOWN BUSILY DEEDILY HEARTILY

ACTIVITIES
(PL.) DOINGS

ACTIVITY ACT ADO GOG VIR FIZZ LIFE PLAY PUSH STIR BLAST CAPER EVENT HEART RAJAS RALLY TRADE VIGOR ACTION AGENCY BUSTLE ENERGY HUSTLE SATTVA SPROIL AGILITY CALLING BUSINESS EXERCISE FUNCTION MOVEMENT PARERGON STIRRING OCCUPATION
(— OF INTELLECT) NOESIS
(BUSTLING —) RUSH
(CHOICE OF —) THING
(FRENZIED —) HUSTLE
(FUNCTIONAL —) SHOP
(GAY —) MERRYMAKING
(MENTAL —) CONCEIT BRAINWORK MENTATION
(SHARED —) COMMUNITY
(SPHERE OF —) SCENE
(STORMY —) RAGE
(TEACHING —) REALIA
(TROUBLESOME —) COIL
(PL.) GOINGSON
(SUFF.) OR
(OUTBURST OF —) FEST

ACTON HOGTON HAQUETON

ACTOR HAM DOER HERO LEAD MIME STAR AGENT BUFFO COMIC DROLL EXTRA HEAVY MIMIC PLANT SERIO SUPER ARTIST BUSKER COWBOY DISEUR FEEDER FIDDLE MUMMER PLAYER PUPPET STAGER TOMMER ARTISTE CABOTIN DISEUSE HISTRIO PRIMOMO ROSCIUS STORMER TROUPER AISTEOIR COMEDIAN HISTRION JUVENILE STROLLER THESPIAN
(BROTHER OF —) AUGEAS
(DAUGHTER OF —) POLYMELA
(FATHER OF —) DIOMEDES MYRMIDON
(INDIFFERENT —) JAY
(INEPT —) HAM
(INFERIOR —) SHINE
(MOTHER OF —) DEION PASIDICE
(SON OF —) CTEATUS EURYTUS MENOETIUS
(PREF.) HISTRIO

ACTRESS DIVA STAR INGENUE STARLET FARCEUSE PREMIERE THESPIAN

ACTUAL GOOD HARD REAL TRUE VERY POSIT RIGHT BODILY FACTUAL GENUINE CONCRETE DEFINITE EXISTING MATERIAL POSITIVE TANGIBLE

ACTUALITY ACT FACT BEING VERITY REALITY ENERGEIA REALNESS

ACTUALLY BUT DONE TRULY FAIRLY ITSELF REALLY
(NOT —) NOMINALLY

ACTUATE ACT EGG RUN DRAW MOVE URGE ENACT IMPEL ROUSE START AROUSE COMPEL EXCITE INCITE INDUCE AGITATE ANIMATE ENLIVEN INSPIRE POINTED SHARPEN MOTIVATE PERSUADE

ACUITY FINENESS

ACUMEN WIT INSIGHT CAPACITY KEENNESS SAGACITY

ACUMINATE TAPE

ACUTE ACID FINE HIGH KEEN TART HEAVY QUICK SHARP SMART SNACK SNELL ARGUTE ASTUTE CRYING SHREWD SHRILL SUBTLE TREBLE URGENT CRUCIAL FEELING INTENSE POINTED VIOLENT CRITICAL INCISIVE POIGNANT ACUMINATE PENETRATING PENETRATIVE
(MOST —) DIRE
(NOT —) SLOW GRAVE CHRONIC
(PREF.) OXY

ACUTENESS DEPTH SENSE ACUITY ACUMEN NOSTRIL INCISION SAGACITY SUBTLETY
(— OF SMELL) HYPEROSMIA
ACYCLIC SPIRAL ALIPHATIC
ACYLOIN
(SUFF.) OIN
ADA (BROTHER OF —) PIXODARUS
(HUSBAND & BROTHER OF —) IDRIEUS
ADAD RAMMAN
ADAGE SAW DICT REDE TEXT WORD AXIOM MAXIM MOTTO HOMILY SAYING TRUISM WHEEZE BROMIDE PRECEPT PROVERB APHORISM APOTHEGM PAROEMIA
ADAGIO ADAGE ADAGIETTO
ADAH (HUSBAND OF —) ESAU LAMECH
(SON OF —) JABAL JUBAL ELIPHAZ
ADAIAH (FATHER OF —) SHIMHI JEROHAM
ADALIA (FATHER OF —) HAMAN
ADAM ADE EDIE ADKIN
(GRANDSON OF —) ENOS ENOCH
(SON OF —) ABEL CAIN SETH
(TEACHER OF —) RAISEL
(WIFE OF —) EVE LILITH
ADAM-AND-EVE CRAWFOOT
ADAMANT FIRM GRIM HARD SOLID STONY ADAMAS DIAMOND UNMOVED OBDURATE SOLIDITY STUBBORN
ADAMANTINE FIRM HARD BORON STONE VAJRA ADAMANT
ADAM BEDE (AUTHOR OF —) ELIOT
(CHARACTER IN —) ADAM SETH DINAH HETTY ARTHUR BARTLE IRVINE MARTIN MASSEY MORRIS POYSER SORREL DONNITHORNE
ADAMITE NUDIST PICARD
ADAMS ANSEL
ADAM'S APPLE GUZZLE THROATBOLL
ADAM'S FLANNEL MULLEIN
ADAM'S NEEDLE YUCCA
ADAPT APT FIT PLY PUT EDIT MOLD SORT SUIT AGREE HUMOR INURE SHAPE TALLY ADJUST CHANGE COMPLY DERIVE DOCTOR HUMOUR TEMPER ARRANGE CONFORM CONVERT FASHION PREPARE QUALIFY ATTEMPER CONTRIVE EQUALIZE MODULATE REGULATE ACCOMMODATE
ADAPTABILITY FLUIDITY ELASTICITY
ADAPTABLE LABILE ELASTIC PLASTIC PLIABLE FLEXUOUS
ADAPTATION CONSERTION
(— TO MUSIC) SETTING
ADAPTED FIT FOR FITTED SUITED CONGENIAL
ADAPTER KIT ARRANGER
ADAXIAL SUPERIOR POSTERIOR
ADBEEL (FATHER OF —) ISHMAEL
ADD AD EIK EKE SAY SUM TOT CAST FOOT GAIN JOIN LEND PLUS TOTE AFFIX ANNEX GIVEN PUTON TOTAL UNITE ACCRUE ADJECT APPEND ATTACH CONFER FIGURE RECKON SUPPLY ACCRETE AUGMENT COMBINE COMPILE COMPUTE ENLARGE SUBJOIN SUMMATE INCREASE
(— ALCOHOL) SPIKE
(— AN ENTRY) RUNON
(— FUEL) BEET
(— IN WRITING) ASCRIBE
(— ON) AFFIX ANNEX
(— STRENGTH) HEARTEN
(— TO) ADORN ENRICH AUGMENT ENHANCE
(— UP) SUM TOT COUNT TALLY TOTAL AMOUNT
(— WORT TO BEER) KRAUSEN
ADDA SCINK SKINK LIZARD
ADDAR (FATHER OF —) BELA
ADDAX PYGARG PYGARGUS
ADDED AND EKE PLUS ADJUNCT
(— SOMETHING) TILLY
(RECENTLY —) FRESH
ADDEND SUMMAND
ADDENDUM RIDER
ADDER ATHER KRAIT VIPER ELAPID NADDER NEDDER CRIBBER ELAPOID HAGWORM HOGNOSE HYPNALE
(KIND OF —) MILK
ADDERING (KIND OF —) CRIB
ADDER'S-TONGUE LILY LILIUM COXCOMB ROOSTERS
ADDERWORT BISTORT
ADDI (FATHER OF —) COSAM
(SON OF —) MELCHI
ADDICT FAN BUFF DOPE DOPY HYPE USER WINO COKEY COKIE FIEND HOPPY HOUND JUNKY SLAVE BOTARY DEVOTE JUNKER JUNKIE DELIVER DEVOTEE HABITUE HOPHEAD SNIFTER ACCUSTOM DOPEHEAD SNOWBIRD
ADDICTED GIVEN PRONE HOOKED BIBULOUS
ADDICTION HABIT JONES MONKEY BIBACITY
ADDITION AND EIK EKE ELL TAB TOO ALSO ELSE GAIN PLUS AFFIX ICING RIDER ACCESS ACCRUE AUGEND ENCORE GANSEL INCOME PREFIX ADJUNCT ADVANCE AUCTARY CODICIL JOINING PENDANT UNITING ADDENDUM INCREASE MANTISSA ACCESSION
(— TO ARTICLE) SHIRTTAIL
(— TO BEEHIVE) IMP
(— TO CALENDAR) EPACT
(— TO MASS) FARCE FARSE
(— TO PRICE) ADVANCE
(— TO WORD) PARAGOGE
(EXTRANEOUS —) ACCRETION
(TRIVIAL —) FILIP FILLIP
(PREF.) **IN —)** SUPER
ADDITIONAL NEW ELSE MORE ADDED EXTRA FRESH OTHER TIDDER TOTHER ANOTHER BESIDES FURTHER ACCESSORY PIGGYBACK
ADDITIVE CUMOL CUMENE PRESERVATIVE
(HAND-CREAM —) ALOE
ADDLE EARN HOME IDLE MIRE AMAZE FILTH RIPEN SPOIL CURDLE MUDDLE THRIVE AGITATE CONFUSE BEFUDDLE BEWILDER
ADDLED ASEA EMPTY PUTRID MUDDLED UNSOUND
ADDRA DAMA NANGER
ADDRESS AIM SUE WOO BACK CALL EASE HAIL HOME MINT PRAY TACT TALK TULK TURN ABODE APPLY BOARD COURT DRESS ELOGE GREET POISE SKILL SPEAK TREAT ACCOST ADJUST APPEAL BOUNCE CHARGE DEVOTE DIRECT EULOGY MANNER PARLEY SALUTE SERMON SPEECH BEHIGHT CONDUCT CONSIGN ENTRUST LECTURE ORATION TUTOYER APPROACH DEDICATE DELIVERY DISPATCH FACILITY HARANGUE INSCRIBE PETITION
(— FAMILIARLY) TOM TUTOYER
(— FOR GI) APO
(— SAUCILY) CHYAK CHYACK
(METHOD OF —) TONE
(PART OF —) ZIP
(PULPIT —) KHUTBA KHUTBAH
ADDUCE BEAR CITE GIVE NAME ALLAY ARGUE BRING INFER OFFER QUOTE ALLEGE ASSIGN OBJECT ADVANCE COUNTER MENTION PRESENT
ADE SQUASH
ADELIE PENGUIN
ADEPS FAT LARD
ADEPT ACE APT DON ABLE HANDY ADROIT ARTIST CRAFTY DEACON EXPERT MASTER VERSED ANCIENT ARTISTE CAPABLE DABSTER MAHATMA DEXTROUS SKILLFUL PROFICIENT
ADEQUATE DUE FIT ABLE ENOW FAIR FULL GOOD MEET WELL AMPLE DIGNE EQUAL COMMON DECENT ENOUGH PROPER CONDIGN PASSABLE SUITABLE COMMENSURATE SATISFACTORY
(BARELY —) BRIEF
ADER (FATHER OF —) BERIAH
ADHERE HEW HUG CLAG CLAM CLOG GLUE HOLD JOIN KEEP LINK ABIDE AFFIX APPLY CLEAM CLING STICK UNITE ATTACH CEMENT CLEAVE COHERE FREEZE ACCRETE ANNERRE PERSIST
ADHERENCE CLING ABIDANCE ADHESION ARIANISM FIDELITY
ADHERENT IST ITE AIDE ALLY JAIN SIKH ADEPT BAHAI BLACK BONPA DEIST JAINA SIDER SPIKE STOOP FACTOR KIRKER VOTARY APRISTA BAHAIST CHANIST FASCIST FLACIAN GNOSTIC NICAEAN OWENIAN SECTARY SEQUELA THOMIST AGATHIST BELIEVER BUDDHIST CABALIST DISCIPLE FAITHFUL FATALIST FOLLOWER HUMANIST HYLICIST IMPERIAL PARTISAN RETAINER SERVITOR SOCINIAN UPHOLDER MONTANIST
(PL.) FOLD FOLLOWING
(SUFF.) ITE
ADHERING PERTINACIOUS
ADHESION BLOCKING STICKAGE SYNECHIA
ADHESIVE GUM WAX BOND CLAM GLUE SIZE TAPE DABBY DAUBY PASTE TACKY BINDER CEMENT CLINGY GLUTEN MASTIC PLUCKY SMEARY STICKY HOTMELT MOUNTANT MUCILAGE TENACIOUS
(PREF.) GLUT
ADHESIVENESS STICK
ADHIBIT USE ADMIT AFFIX APPLY ATTACH
ADIANTUM MAIDENHAIR
ADIEL (SON OF —) AZMAVETH
ADIEU ADEW CIAO ADDIO ADIOS LEAVE FAREWELL
AD INFINITUM EVER
ADIPOCERE GRAVEWAX
ADIPOSE FAT HARD SUET FATTY OBESE PURSY SQUAT TALLOW
ADIT DOOK DOOR ENTRY SOUGH STULM ACCESS TUNNEL PASSAGE APPROACH ENTRANCE
ADJACENT NEAR NIGH CLOSE FLUSH HANDY BESIDE NEARBY MEETING VICINAL ABUTTING TOUCHING CONTIGUOUS
(PREF.) **(— TO)** AC AD AF AG AL AP AS AT
ADJECTIVE ADNOUN DIPTOTE EPITHET NOMINAL MODIFIER
ADJOIN ADD ABUT BUTT JOIN LINE TACK COAST MARCH TOUCH UNITE ACCOST APPEND ATTACH BORDER CONTACT NEIGHBOR
ADJOINING VICINAL
ADJOURN END MOVE RISE STAY ARISE CLOSE DEFER DELAY RECESS SUSPEND DISSOLVE POSTPONE PROROGUE
ADJUDGE TRY ARET DEEM FIND GIVE HOLD RATE ALLOT AREAD AREED ARETT AWARD GRANT JUDGE ORDER ADDEEM ADDICT ADDOOM ASSIGN DECERN DECIDE DECREE ORDAIN REGARD BEHIGHT CONDEMN SENTENCE
(— GUILTY) DAMN
(— NOT GUILTY) ABSOLVE
ADJUDICATE ACT TRY HEAR PASS RULE JUDGE DECIDE ESTEEM RECKON REGARD SETTLE ADJUDGE CONSIDER SENTENCE
ADJUNCT AID HELP PART WORD ANNEX DEVICE PHRASE ADJOINT ANCILLA APENAGE EPITHET FITTING GARNISH PERTAIN TEACHER ADDITION ADDITIVE APPANAGE APPENDIX ORNAMENT
ADJURATION OATH APPEAL SWEARING
ADJURE ASK BEG BID BIND ETHE PRAY CRAVE PLEAD SWEAR APPEAL CHARGE OBTEST BESEECH COMMAND CONJURE CONTEST ENTREAT REQUEST UNSWEAR
ADJUST FIT FIX KEY SET CAST EASE FORM FREE GEAR JUST LINE PARE RATE SIZE SORT SUIT TRAM TRIM TRUE TUNE ADAPT ADMIT ALIGN ALINE ALTER ANGLE COAPT EQUAL FRAME PATCH RANGE RIGHT SHAPE ACCORD ATTUNE HAMMER JUSTEN ORIENT SETTLE SQUARE TEMPER WANGLE ADDRESS ARRANGE BALANCE CHANCER

COMPOSE CONCERT CONFORM CORRECT DISPOSE JUSTIFY PREPARE RECTIFY COMPOUND REGULATE CALIBRATE ACCOMMODATE
(— A LOOM) GATE
(— DULY) CONCENT
(— SAIL) FLATTEN
(PREF.) CO
ADJUSTABLE ELASTIC
ADJUSTED KEYED
(ACCURATELY —) TRUE
ADJUSTER FIXER FITTER ASSESSOR
ADJUSTMENT FIT GEAR MISE TRIM FITNESS FITTING CHANCERY
(— OF DISPUTE) MISE
(COST —) COLA
(HARMONIOUS —) TUNE
ADJUTANT AIDE ALLY STORK ARGALA HELPER HURGILA MARABOU OFFICER
ADJUVANT AIDE HELPER ADJUNCT HELPFUL
ADLAI (SON OF —) SHAPHAT
AD-LIB FAKE
ADMAN HUCKSTER
ADMEASURE METE
ADMETUS (FATHER OF —) PHERES
(WIFE OF —) ALCESTIS
ADMINISTER DO RUN DEAL DEEM DOSE GIVE MOVE RULE APPLY SERVE TREAT DIRECT GOVERN MANAGE SETTLE SUPPLY TENDER ADHIBIT CONDUCE CONDUCT CONTROL EXECUTE EXHIBIT FURNISH HUSBAND DISPENSE MINISTER
(— FORCIBLY) HAND
(— SACRAMENT) BISHOP HOUSEL
ADMINISTRATION HELM RULE SWAY POLICY TAHSIL CONDUCT DIOCESE ECONOMY RECTORY REGIMEN CARRIAGE DISPOSAL MINISTRY
(— OF OATH) JURATION
(CORRUPT —) MALVERSATION
(REVENUE —) HACIENDA
ADMINISTRATOR CAID HELM QAID GABBAI ALCAIDE MANAGER TRUSTEE DIRECTOR EXECUTOR MINISTER PROVICAR PROCONSUL
(— OF COMPUTER BOARD) SYSOP
(INCA —) CURACA
(MORMON —) APOSTLE
ADMIRABLE FINE GOOD HIGH NEAT GRAND GREAT LUMMY PROUD DIVINE AMIABLE CAPITAL ELEGANT MIRANDA RIPPING
ADMIRAL (ALSO SEE NAVAL OFFICER) FLAG AMREL AMRELLE CAPITAN FLAGMAN GENERAL NAVARCH
(KIND OF —) RED REAR VICE
ADMIRATION CULT FUROR GLORY ESTEEM LIKING WONDER CONCEIT WORSHIP ADULATION
(— FOR BIGNESS) JUMBOISM
(EXTRAVAGANT —) FUREUR
ADMIRE DIG LIKE LOVE ADORE EXTOL HONOR PRIZE VALUE ESTEEM MARVEL REGARD REVERE WONDER ADULATE APPROVE DELIGHT IDOLIZE RESPECT VENERATE
ADMIRER FAN BEAU LOVER SWAIN AMATEUR DEVOTEE FOLLOWER IDOLATER
(PL.) FOLLOWING
ADMISSION FEE ADIT CALL ENTRY ACCESS CHARGE ENTREE TICKET APOLOGY CONSENT INGRESS ENTRANCE RECEPTION CONCESSION
(— TO BAR) CALL
(— TO MINISTRY) ORDINATION
(CONCLUSIVE —) ESTOPPEL
ADMIT COP KEN LET OWN AVER AVOW BEAR TAKE AGREE ALLOW ENTER GRANT IMMIT INLET ACCEDE ACCEPT ADJUST ASSENT AVOUCH ENROLL INDUCT PERMIT SUFFER ADHIBIT CONCEDE CONFESS INCLUDE PROFESS RECEIVE SUFFICE INITIATE
(— AS MEMBER) INDUCT
(— AS VALID) SUSTAIN
(— OPENLY) OWNUPTO
(— TO HOLY ORDERS) ORDAIN
ADMITTANCE ACCESS ADMITTY ENTRANCE
ADMITTED GIVEN GRANTED
ADMITTING THOUGH
(REGRETFULLY —) AFRAID
ADMIX DALLOP DOLLOP
ADMIXTURE DASH ALLOY BLEND SHADE SPICE TINGE DALLOP DOLLOP FLAVOR LEAVEN STREAK MIXTURE SOUPCON COMPOUND INFUSION
ADMONISH WARN CHIDE SCOLD ADVISE ENJOIN EXHORT NOTIFY REBUKE REMIND SCHOOL CAUTION COUNSEL MONITOR REPROVE
ADMONITION ITEM ADVICE CAVEAT HOMILY CAUTION LECTURE REPROOF WARNING DOCUMENT REMINDER
ADNATE ADHERENT EPIGYNOUS
(— TO CALYX) INFERIOR
ADO DO COIL DEED FLAP FUSS ROUT STIR TODO WORK HOOHA HURRY TOUSE TOWSE BOTHER BUSTLE EFFORT FLURRY HUBBUB POTHER RUCKUS BLATHER BLETHER SPUTTER TROUBLE TURMOIL BUSINESS FOOFARAW
ADOBE MUD CLAY DOBE DOBY SILT BRICK DOBIE TAPIA MUDCAP
ADOLESCENCE TEENS YOUTH NONAGE PUBERTY MINORITY
ADOLESCENT LAD TEEN YOUNG YOUTH TEENER IMMATURE TEENAGER
(DISRUPTIVE —) NED
(PROSPECTIVE —) PRETEEN
ADONIJAH (BROTHER OF —) AMNON ABSALOM CHILEAB
(FATHER OF —) DAVID
(MOTHER OF —) HAGGITH
(SLAYER OF —) BENAIAH
ADONIS ADON
(FATHER OF —) CINYRAS
(MOTHER OF —) MYRRH MYRRHA
ADOPT TAKE STEAL ACCEPT ASSUME ATTACH BORROW CHOOSE FATHER FOLLOW FOSTER MOTHER TAKEON ACQUIRE EMBRACE ESPOUSE RECEIVE WELCOME ADVOCATE ARROGATE MAINTAIN
ADOPTION ESPOUSAL
(— OF DEBTS) ASSUMPTION
ADORABLE LOVELY LOVABLE CHARMING
ADORATION HOMAGE WORSHIP DEVOTION
(— OF GOD) LOVE
ADORE DOTE LAUD LOVE EXALT EXTOL HONOR WURTH ADMIRE ESTEEM PRAISE REVERE GLORIFY IDOLIZE WORSHIP VENERATE
ADORN DUB FIG GEM ORN SET BEAD BUSK DECK DILL DINK FOIL GAUD GILD LACE OUCH PICK PINK POSH STUD SWAG TRIM ADORE ANORN ARRAY BEDUB BEGEM BELAY BESEE BRAVE CROWN DIGHT DRAPE DRESS FRONT GRACE HIGHT INLAY JEWEL MENSK PRANK PRICK PRIDE PRIMP PRINK ROUGE SPLAY SPRIG TRICK AGUISE ATTIRE ATTRAP BECOME BEDECK BETRIM BLAZON BROOCH CLOTHE COLLAR DAMASK DIADEM EMBOSS ENAMEL ENRICH ENROBE FIGURE FINIFY FRIEZE FRINGE GRAITH INSTAL INVEST ORNIFY POUNCE PURFLE QUAINT STATUE SUBORN TASSEL ADONISE APPAREL BEDIGHT BEDIZEN COMMEND CORONET DEPAINT DIGNIFY EMPEARL FEATHER FOLIAGE FURNISH GARNISH GLORIFY GRATIFY IMPLUME SPANGLE VARNISH BEAUTIFY DECORATE EMBLAZON FLOURISH ORNAMENT SPLENDOR
(— WITH MOSAIC) TESSELLATE
ADORNED CLAD BESEEN DAEDAL ORNATE PICKED BRAIDED CLOTHED COLORED DAISIED FIGURED OVERHUNG
(GAUDILY —) TAWDRY
(SHOWILY —) BEPRANKED
ADORNMENT TIRE ADORN DRESS PRIDE BEAUTY DECORE TAHALI TINSEL DECKING OUNDING PRANKING TIREMENT
ADOXY TENET
ADRAMMELECH (BROTHER OF —) SHAREZER
(FATHER OF —) SENNACHERIB
ADRASTUS (BROTHER OF —) MECISTEUS
(DAUGHTER OF —) AEGIA DEIPYLE
(FATHER OF —) TALAUS GORDIUS
(MOTHER OF —) LYSIMACHE
(SISTER OF —) ERIPHYLE
ADRESTUS (BROTHER OF —) AMPHIUS
(FATHER OF —) MENOPS
(SLAYER OF —) DIOMEDES
ADRIANA LECOUVREUR
(CHARACTER IN —) ADRIANA MAURICE BOUILLON MICHONNET
(COMPOSER OF —) CILEA
ADRIEL (FATHER OF —) BARZILLAI
(WIFE OF —) MERAB
ADRIFT ASEA LOST AWAFT LIGAN LOOSE AFLOAT DERELICT FLOATING UNMOORED
ADROIT DEFT EASY FEAT GOOD NEAT SLIM ADEPT HANDY READY SMART SNACK TIGHT TRICK ARTFUL CLEVER EXPERT HABILE NIMBLE CUNNING DEXTROUS HANDSOME SKILLFUL
ADROITNESS ART EASE TACT KNACK SKILL ADDRESS FACILITY
ADSORBENT BASE EARTH SILICA
ADULATE FAWN LAUD GLOSS GLOZE PRAISE REVERE FLATTER
ADULATION GLOSE GLOZE PRAISE INCENSE FLATTERY
ADULT MAN FULL MANLY MATURE EPHEBIC GROWNUP THRIVEN
(SCIENCE OF TEACHING —S) ANDRAGOGY
(YOUNG COLLEGE-EDUCATED —) YUP YUPPIE
ADULTERANT DOPE MULTUM ALMEIDINA
ADULTERATE CUT MIX CARD DASH LOAD ABUSE ALLOY HOCUS TAINT DEACON DEBASE DEFILE DILUTE EXTEND MANAGE WEAKEN BASTARD CORRUPT FALSIFY VITIATE DENATURE IMPURIFY SPURIOUS
(— WINE) LIME
ADULTERATED CUT SHAM IMPURE CORRUPT SPURIOUS
ADULTEROUS ERRING
ADULTERY AVOUTRY CUCKOLDOM CUCKOLDRY MISCONDUCT
ADUMBRATE IMAGE SHADE VAGUE OBSCURE SUGGEST INTIMATE
ADUMBRATION SHADE SHADOW PHANTASM
ADUNCOUS BENT HOOKED
ADUST BURNT FIERY GLOOMY SALLOW PARCHED SCORCHED SUNBURNT
ADVANCE GO AID PAY SOP WAY BULL CITE COME DASH GAIN HELP INCH LAUD LEND LIFT LOAN MARK MOVE NEAR NOSE PASS PUSH RISE SHOW STEP WORM AVANT BOOST BRING CREEP ENTER EXALT EXTOL FAVOR FORGE MARCH OFFER PLACE PREST RAISE SERVE SPEED STAIR STAKE THROW ADDUCE ADMOVE ALLEGE AMOUNT ASSIGN ASSIST AVAUNT BETTER DEGREE EXTEND FAVOUR GROWTH HASTEN INCEDE INROAD PREFER PREPAY SCHOOL STRIDE STRIKE THRIVE TRAVEL VAUNCE BENEFIT DEVELOP ELEVATE ENHANCE FORTHGO FORWARD FURTHER HEADWAY IMPREST IMPROVE PROCEED PROCESS PROMOTE PROMOVE PROPOSE PROSPER PROVECT SUCCEED ADDITION DEVELOPE HEIGHTEN INCREASE PROGRESS PROGRESSION
(— BY CUTTING) DRIVE
(— BY LEAPS) SALTATION

(— IN LIFE) WAY
(— LABORIOUSLY) STRIVE
(— OBLIQUELY) SIDLE
(— OF MONEY) IMPREST
(— ONE'S POINT) TAKE
(— RUDELY) ELBOW
(— SLOWLY) INCH WORM CRAWL CREEP
(— WAVERINGLY) HOBBLE
(— WITH EFFORT) DRAG
(DIFFICULT —) SLOG
(GRADUAL —) ILLAPSE
(STEADY —) SWING
(SUDDEN —) SHOOT
(VIGOROUS —) SWING
(PL.) APPROACHES

ADVANCED FAR DEEP GONE HIGH LATE AHEAD OUTER FORWARD IMPREST LIBERAL VANWARD FOREMOST
(— IN AGE) DEEP ANTIQUATED
(— IN YEARS) SENIOR AGEABLE ELDERLY
(MOST —) EXTREME FARTHEST FOREMOST HEADMOST
(WELL —) AGED

ADVANCEMENT UP GOOD ASCENT INCREASE

ADVANCING RISING
(— BY DEGREES) GRADUAL
(— RAPIDLY) RAKING

ADVANTAGE AD BOT USE VAN BEST BOOT BOTE DRAW DROP EDGE GAIN GOOD HANK JUMP MEND NOTE ODDS PULL SAKE VAIL ASSET AVAIL BULGE BUNCE FAVOR FRAME FRUIT KINCH LAUGH POINT SPEED START STEAD USAGE BEHALF BEHOOF BETTER CARROT EFFECT PROFIT ACCOUNT BENEFIT CAPITAL EXPLOIT FORDEAL FURTHER PROMOTE PURPOSE UTILITY VANTAGE HANDICAP INTEREST LEVERAGE OVERHAND OVERPLUS PERCENTAGE
(ACCIDENTAL —) FLUKE
(UNDUE —) ABUSE
(UNEXPECTED —) WINDFALL

ADVANTAGEOUS GOOD JOLI WELL JOLIE GOLDEN PLUMMY SPEEDY USEFUL ELIGIBLE BEHOVEFUL PROPITIOUS
(PREF.) EU

ADVENT DAWN COMING INCOME ARRIVAL APPROACH PAROUSIA

ADVENTITIOUS CASUAL FOREIGN STRANGE ACQUIRED EPISODIC ACCESSORY

ADVENTURE GEST LARK RISK SEEK WAGE EVENT GESTE PERIL QUEST AUNTER AUNTRE CHANCE DANGER HAZARD EMPRISE EMPRIZE FORTUNE VENTURE ESCAPADE JEOPARDY
(TALE OF —) CONTE

ADVENTURER ROUTIER ARGONAUT PICAROON

ADVENTURESS DEMIREP DEMIMONDAINE

ADVENTUROUS BOLD RASH DARING ERRANT AUNTROUS RECKLESS

ADVERSARY FOE ENEMY RIVAL SATAN FOEMAN OPPONENT
(— OF GOD) DEVIL
(PREF.) ENSTATO

ADVERSE FOE ILL EVIL CROSS LOATH THRAW AVERSE INFEST WITHER AWKWARD COUNTER DIVERSE FROWARD HOSTILE OPPOSED CONTRARY INIMICAL OPPOSING OPPOSITE OVERWART THRAWART
(PREF.) COUNTER

ADVERSITY ILL WOE CROSS DECAY NIGHT MISERY SORROW WITHER ILLNESS TROUBLE CALAMITY DISTRESS MISFORTUNE

ADVERT HEED AVERT RECUR REFER ALLUDE ATTEND RETURN REVERT OBSERVE CONSIDER

ADVERTISE CRY BARK BILL CALL PLUG PUFF STAR WARN BLURB INFORM NOTIFY PARADE DECLARE DISPLAY OBSERVE PLACARD PUBLISH ANNOUNCE PROCLAIM

ADVERTISED AFFICHE

ADVERTISEMENT AD BILL SIGN BLURB CHANT PITCH PROMO ADVERT CACHET DODGER NOTICE POSTER TEASER AFFICHE PLACARD STUFFER CIRCULAR HANDBILL

ADVERTISING BUSH BILLING PUFFERY
(EXTRAVAGANT —) HYPE
(MASS-MEDIA —) ADMASS
(RADIO OR TV —) PLUGOLA

ADVICE AVIS AVYS LORE NEWS REDE AVYSE INPUT STEER ADVISO DEVICE NOTICE CAUTION CONSEIL COUNSEL OPINION TIDINGS GUIDANCE MONITION
(PL.) INFORMATION

ADVICE-BOAT AVISO

ADVISABLE BOOK PROPER PRUDENT

ADVISE SAY READ REDE TELL VISE WARN WISE AREAD AREED COACH GUIDE WEISE WEIZE ADJURE ADVISO BEREDE CONFER DEVISE EXHORT INFORM PONDER REVEAL APPRISE APPRIZE COUNSEL ACQUAINT ADMONISH CONSIDER RECOMMEND
(— AGAINST) DISSUADE
(— STRONGLY) URGE
(— WRONGLY) MISCOUNSEL

ADVISED DELIBERATE

ADVISER AIDE TOUT COACH COMES TUTOR DOCTOR EGERIA LAWYER NESTOR ADVISOR MONITOR STARETS TEACHER ATTORNEY CROUPIER DIRECTOR FIELDMAN PREACHER

ADVISORY URGING PRUDENT

ADVOCACY BOOM FAVOR AVOWRY FAVOUR ARIANISM

ADVOCATE PRO ABET BACK PUSH URGE VOGT ACTOR ADOPT FAVOR PLEAD ASSERT AVOWRY BACKER DEFEND IDEIST LAWYER PATRON SYNDIC ABETTOR APOSTLE DECLAIM ENDORSE ESPOUSE EXPOUND FASCIST GOLDBUG PATRIOT PLEADER PROCTOR PROMOTE SCHOLAR SUPPORT ATTORNEY CHAMPION CLUBBIST DEFENSOR EXPONENT HUMANIST PARTISAN PREACHER PARACLETE PROPONENT
(— FAVORED BY JUDGE) PEAT
(— OF REVOLT) ANARCH
(SUFF.) ARIAN CRAT

ADVOWSON ADVOCACY TENEMENT PATRONAGE

ADZ AX AXE ADZE EDGE ADDIS ADDICE EATCHE THIXLE HATCHET

AEACUS (FATHER OF —) ZEUS JUPITER
(MOTHER OF —) AEGINA
(SON OF —) PELEUS PHOCUS TELAMON
(WIFE OF —) ENDEIS

AECHMAGORAS (FATHER OF —) HERCULES
(MOTHER OF —) PHIALO

AECIUM CAEOMA

AEDON (BROTHER OF —) AMPHION
(FATHER OF —) PANDAREUS
(HUSBAND OF —) ZETHUS POLYTECHNUS
(MOTHER OF —) HARMOTHOE
(SON OF —) ITYLUS

AEETES (DAUGHTER OF —) MEDEA
(FATHER OF —) HELIOS
(MOTHER OF —) PERSA PERSEIS
(SON OF —) APSYRTUS

AEGAEON (BROTHER OF —) GYGES COTTUS
(FATHER OF —) URANUS
(MOTHER OF —) GE GAEA
(WIFE OF —) AEMILIA

AEGEAN SEA (ANCIENT PEOPLE OF —) PSARA PSYRA SAMIAN LELEGES SAMIOTE
(GULF OF —) SAROS
(ISLAND OF —) COS IOS KEOS NIOS RODI SCIO CHIOS LEROS MELOS NAXOS PAROS PATMO SAMOS SIROS TENOS THERA ANDROS IKARIA IMBROS LEMNOS LESBOS RHODES SKYROS
(RIVER INTO —) STRUMA VARDAR MARISTA
(TOWN ON —) CHIOS VATHY MYTILENE

AEGEON (WIFE OF —) AEMILIA

AEGEUS (BROTHER OF —) LYCUS NISUS PALLAS
(FATHER OF —) PANDION
(SON OF —) THESEUS
(WIFE OF —) PYLIA

AEGIA (FATHER OF —) ADRASTUS
(HUSBAND OF —) POLYNICES
(SON OF —) THERSANDER

AEGINA (FATHER OF —) ASOPUS
(MOTHER OF —) METOPE
(SON OF —) AEACUS

AEGIR HLER GYMIR
(WIFE OF —) RAN

AEGIRITE ACMITE

AEGIS EGIS SHIELD AUSPICE DEFENCE DEFENSE

AEGISTHUS (FATHER OF —) THYESTES
(MOTHER OF —) PELOPIA
(SLAYER OF —) ORESTES

AEGLE (BROTHER OF —) PHAETHON
(FATHER OF —) HELIUS
(MOTHER OF —) CLYMENE

AEGYPTUS (BROTHER OF —) DANAUS
(FATHER OF —) BELUS
(MOTHER OF —) ANCHINOE
(SON OF —) LYNCEUS

AENEAS (COMPANION OF —) ACHATES
(FATHER OF —) ANCHISES
(GREAT-GRANDSON OF —) BRUT
(MOTHER OF —) VENUS APHRODITE
(SON OF —) IULUS ASCANIUS
(WIFE OF —) CREUSA LAVINIA

AENEID (AUTHOR OF —) VIRGIL
(CHARACTER IN —) ANNA DIDO JUNO VENUS AENEAS PALLAS TURNUS EVANDER LATINUS LAVINIA ANCHISES ASCANIUS

AENGUS (MOTHER OF —) BOANN

AEOLUS (BROTHER OF —) DORUS XUTHUS
(DAUGHTER OF —) ARNE CANACE ALCYONE HALCYONE
(FATHER OF —) HELLEN HIPPOTES
(MOTHER OF —) ARNE ORSEIS
(SON OF —) ATHAMAS CRETHEUS SISYPHUS SALMONEUS

AEON AGE EON ERA AION AEVUM CYCLE KALPA PERIOD
(PAIR OF —S) SYZYGY

AEPYTUS (FATHER OF —) CRESPHONTES
(MOTHER OF —) MEROPE

AERATE AERIFY CHARGE INFLATE

AERIAL AERY AIRY TWIN AERIE LOFTY DIPOLE UNREAL AEOLIAN ANTENNA ETHEREAL
(ROTATING —) SCANNER
(WIRELESS —) RADIATOR

AERIALIST FLIER FLYER

AERIE AERY AIRE AYRE EYRY NEST AIERY BROOD EYRIE

AERIFORM UNREAL GASEOUS

AEROBE BACTERIUM

AERODROME AIRPORT AIRFIELD

AEROEMBOLISM BENDS

AEROFOIL FOIL SLAT ROTOR CONTROL SURFACE

AEROLITE AEROLITH

AERONAUT PILOT SKYMAN

AERONAUTICS AVIATION

AEROPE (DAUGHTER OF —) ANAXIBIA
(FATHER OF —) CATREUS CERHEUS
(HUSBAND OF —) ATREUS PLISTHENES
(LOVER OF —) THYRESTES
(SISTER OF —) CLYMENE
(SON OF —) MENELAUS AGAMEMNON

AEROPLANE (SEE AIRPLANE) FANJET JALOPY RAIDER PARASOL PROPJET SOCIABLE SPITFIRE

AEROSE BRASSY

AEROSTAT AIRSHIP BALLOON AIRCRAFT

AERUGO RUST PATINA

AESACUS (FATHER OF —) PRIAM
(LOVER OF —) HESPERIA
(MOTHER OF —) ARISBE ALEXIRRHOE

AESEPUS **(BROTHER OF —)** PEDASUS
(FATHER OF —) BUCOLION
(MOTHER OF —) ABARBAREA
(SLAYER OF —) EURYALUS
AESON **(BROTHER OF —)** PELIAS
(FATHER OF —) CRETHEUS
(MOTHER OF —) TYRO
(SON OF —) JASON
(WIFE OF —) ALCIMEDA
AESTHETIC ARTISTIC ESTHETIC TASTEFUL
AETA ITA
AETHALIDES **(FATHER OF —)** HERMES MERCURY
(MOTHER OF —) EUPOLEMIA
AETHRA **(FATHER OF —)** OCEANUS PITTHEUS
(MOTHER OF —) TETHYS
(SON OF —) HYAS THESEUS
AETOLUS **(FATHER OF —)** ENDYMION
(SON OF —) CALYDON PLEURON
(WIFE OF —) PRONOE
AFAR OFF AWAY SAHO FERNE FERREN REMOTE YFERRE DANAKIL DANKALI DISTANT
AFARA LIMBA
AFFABLE FAIR OPEN BLAND CIVIL FRANK SUAVE BENIGN FACILE FORTHY GENIAL SOCIAL URBANE AMIABLE CORDIAL GENERAL LIKABLE CHARMING FAMILIAR FRIENDLY GRACIOUS PLEASANT SOCIABLE TOWARDLY CONVERSABLE
AFFAIR DO JOB PIE BLOW CASE DEAL DUEL GEAR PLOY BRAWL CAUSE EVENT FIGHT LEVEE PARTY THING ACTION BATTLE BEHALF DOMENT EFFEIR MATTER SETOUT SHAURI BLOWOUT CONCERN FUNERAL HOEDOWN JOURNEY LIAISON PALAVER SHEBANG BUSINESS COMETHER ENDEAVOR HYPOTHEC INTRIGUE OCCASION PROCEEDING
(CONFUSED —) SCHEMOZZLE
(CRITICAL —) KANKEDORT
(LOVE —) LOVE AMOUR INTRIGUE
(SOCIAL —) FORMAL JUNKET SUPPER
(STATE —S) ESTATE
(PL.) SQUARES OCCASIONS
AFFECT AIL AIR HIT BEAR MELT MOVE POSE RINE SHAM STIR SWAY ALLOT ALTER ANNOY ASSAY COLOR DRIVE FANCY FEIGN HAUNT IMPEL MINCE SHOCK TOUCH ASPIRE ASSIGN ASSUME CHANGE DESIRE MOLEST SOFTEN STRIKE THRILL ATTAINT ATTINGE BEWITCH CONCERN EMOTION FEELING IMPRESS OPERATE PASSION PRETEND PROFESS ALLOCATE DISPOSED FREQUENT INTEREST SIMULATE
(— BY HANDLING) TOUCH
(— DEEPLY) CUT
(— FAVORABLY) LIKE
(— INJURIOUSLY) INTERESS
(— STRONGLY) HIT HOLD SURPRISE
(— WITH EXCITEMENT) BLOW
(— WITH FEELING) SMITE
AFFECTATION AIR AIRS POSE SHAM FRILL GRACE MINCE CHICHI CONCEIT DISPLAY FOPPERY FROUNCE GRIMACE PIETISM FONDNESS PRETENSE PUPPYISM
(PL.) LUGS
AFFECTED MOY AIRY CAMP FEAT AILED APISH MOVED POSEY CHICHI FALLAL FEISTY FORMAL PRETTY QUAINT SEIZED FEIGNED MINIKIN MISSISH REACHED SMITTEN STILTED TAFFETA TAFFETY TOUCHED INVOLVED PRECIEUX PRECIOUS RECHERCHE
(— BY DECAY) DOTY
(— WITH RABIES) MAD
(EASILY —) SENSIBLE
(SOMETHING —) CAMP
(SUFF.) IC ICAL PATH(IA)(IC)(Y)
AFFECTING AIRIFIED FRAPPANT POIGNANT TOUCHING
AFFECTION LOVE WAFF ALOHA AMOUR BOTCH FLAME HEART CHERTE DOTAGE ESTEEM HYDROA MALADY REGARD THRUSH AILMENT CHARITY EMOTION FEELING PASSION SYMPTOM CHLOASMA DEARNESS DEVOTION FONDNESS KINDNESS MELICERA TENDENCY
(LASTING —) WARMSPOT
(MORBID —) SEQUELA
(PARENTAL —) STORGE
(PROFOUND —) WORSHIP
(PL.) HEART HEARTSTRING
(SUFF.) OMA PATHY
AFFECTIONATE DEAR FOND WARM ARDENT DOTING LOVING TENDER AMOROUS CORDIAL DEVOTED EARNEST ZEALOUS ATTACHED PARENTAL SISTERLY
AFFECTIVE SENSIBLE
AFFERENT BEAR ESODIC SENSORY ADVEHENT INFERENT
AFFIANCE AFFY FAITH TRUST ASSURE ENGAGE ENSURE FIANCE PLEDGE PLIGHT SPOUSE BETROTH PROMISE CONTRACT RELIANCE
AFFIANCED INTENDED
AFFIANT DEPONENT AFFIDAVIT
AFFIDAVIT DAVY OATH AFFIANT AFFIDAVY AFFYDAVY
AFFILIATE ALLY UNIT ADOPT MERGE UNITE ATTACH BRANCH RELATE ASCRIBE CHAPTER CONNECT FILIATE
AFFINITY KIN TELE FAMILY LIKING AVIDITY CHEMISM KINDRED KINSHIP RAPPORT ALLIANCE GOSSIPRY HOMOLOGY RELATION SYMPATHY COGNATION
(PREF.) **(— FOR)** TROP(IDO)(O)
(SUFF.) **(— FOR)** PHIL(A)(AE)(E)(IA)(ISM)(IST)(OUS)(US) TROPE TROPISM
AFFIRM PUT AFFY AVER AVOW TAKE POSIT STATE SWEAR TRUTH VOUCH ADHERE ALLEGE ASSERT ATTEST AVOUCH DEPOSE RATIFY SUBMIT THREAP THREEP VERIFY ASSEVER CONFIRM DECLARE PROFESS PROTEST TESTIFY MAINTAIN PREDICATE
AFFIRMATION SAY VOW YES AMEN OATH WORD DIXIT PONENT THESIS AVERRAL AVERMENT
AFFIRMATIVE AY AYE NOD YAH YEA YEP YES AMEN ATEN YEAH PONENT DOGMATIC POSITIVE
AFFIX ADD FIX PEN PIN SET CASE CLIP FAST JOIN NAIL SEAL SIGN ADDON ANNEX INFIX STAMP UNITE ANCHOR APPEND ATTACH FASTEN SETTLE STAPLE ADHIBIT CONNECT ENTITLE FORMANT IMPRESS PLASTER SUBJOIN
AFFLATUS FURY FUROR FRENZY VISION IMPULSE
AFFLICT AIL RUE TRY VEX COMB FIRE HOLD HURT PAIN PINE RACK TUKE ARRAY ASSAY BESET CURSE GRILL GRIPE HARRY PINCH PRESS SEIZE SMITE TRYST VISIT WOUND WRING BURDEN GRIEVE HARASS HUMBLE INFECT MOLEST PESTER REMORD SCORCH STRAIN STRESS STRIKE CHASTEN INFLICT OPPRESS SCOURGE TORMENT TROUBLE DISTRESS LACERATE STRAITEN
AFFLICTED JOB SAD SORRY AILING WOEFUL GRIEVED HAUNTED SMITTEN IMPAIRED STRICKEN TROUBLED
AFFLICTION WOE EVIL LOSS PAIN SORE TEEN TINE TRAY ASSAY CROSS GRIEF PRESS SMART STOUR BUFFET DURESS MISERY PATHOS PLAGUE SORROW STRESS THRONG AILMENT DISEASE ILLNESS PASSION PURSUIT SCOURGE TORTURE TROUBLE CALAMITY DISTRESS HARDSHIP SEVERITY SICKNESS VEXATION MARTYRDOM
(SECRET —) HAIRSHIRT
(PL.) CUP
(SUFF.) **(— WITH)** ITIS
AFFLICTIVE SAD DIRE SORE SOUR HEAVY SEVERE
AFFLUENCE EASE AFFLUX INFLUX PLENTY RICHES WEALTH FORTUNE OPULENCE
AFFLUENT FAT RICH FLUSH RIVER BRANCH SPRUIT STREAM COPIOUS FLOWING HALCYON OPULENT WEALTHY ABUNDANT INFLUENT
AFFORD GO BEAR GIVE LEND GRANT INCUR OFFER STAND THOLE YIELD CONFER ENDURE MANAGE SUPPLY ACHIEVE FORWARD FURNISH FURTHER PRODUCE PROVIDE MINISTER
AFFRAY FEUD FRAY RIOT ALARM BRAWL BROIL CLASH FIGHT MELEE SCARE SPURN ATTACK BATTLE COMBAT EFFRAY ENFRAI FRIGHT STRIFE TERROR TUMULT ASSAULT CONTEST QUARREL SCUFFLE STARTLE FRIGHTEN STRUGGLE
AFFRIGHT COW FEAR AGAST ALARM DAUNT DOUBT DREAD SCARE AGRISE APPALL DISMAY CONFUSE STARTLE TERRIFY FRIGHTEN
AFFRONT CUT DEFY SLAP ABUSE BEARD PEEVE HARASS INJURE INSULT NETTLE OFFEND SLIGHT STRUNT ASSAULT OFFENCE OFFENSE OUTRAGE PROVOKE CONFRONT DISGRACE ILLTREAT IRRITATE CONTUMELY
AFFUSION POURING INFUSION
AFGHAN RUG GHAN COVER DURANI HASARA HAZARA PATHAN BLANKET PAKHTUN PUKHTUN ACHAKZAI COVERLET
AFGHAN FOX CORSAC CORSAK

AFGHANISTAN

CAPITAL: KABUL
COIN: PUL ABBASI AMANIA AFGHANI
LAKE: HELMAND
LANGUAGE: DARI PASHTO PUSHTU BALOCHI BALUCHI
MEASURE: JERIB KAROH
MOUNTAIN: KOH SAFEO CHAGAI PAMIRS SULAIMAN HIMALAYAS
NATIVE: SISTANI
PARLIAMENT: SHURA
PROVINCE: GHOR FARAH HERAT KABUL KUNAR KUNUZ LOGAR MAZAR ZABUL GHAZNI KAPISA PARWAN WARDAK
RIVER: LORA OXUS CABUL FARAH HARUT INDUS KABUL KHASH KUNAR KOKCHA KUNDUZ HELMAND MURGHAB AMUDARYA
SEA: DARYA
TOWN: RUI JURM NANI WAMA ASMAR BALKH DOSHI HERAT KABUL KUNAR MARUF MATUN MUKUR PAHRA TULAK URGAN CHAMAN GHAZNI KUNDUZ NAUZAD PANJAO RUSTAK SANGAN SAROBI TUKZAR WASHIR BAGHLAN BAMIYAN DILARAM KANDAHAR MAZARESHARIF
TRIBE: SAFI TURK ULUS KAFIR TAJIK UZBEK BALOCH BALUCH HAZARA KIRGIZ PATHAN
WEIGHT: PAU PAW SER SIR KARWAR KHURDS

AFICIONADO FAN AMATEUR DEVOTEE GROUPIE FOLLOWER
AFIELD ABROAD ASTRAY
AFIRE ALOW ALOWE EAGER ABLAZE AFLAME ARDENT BURNING FLAMING
A-FLAT AS AIS
AFLOAT ASEA ASWIM AWAFT AWASH ADRIFT BUOYED NATANT ABROACH FLOODED UNFIXED FLOATING
AFOOT ABOUT AGATE ASTIR ABROAD TOWARD WALKING
AFORE ERE
AFOREMENTIONED SAID SUCH
AFORESAID SAME DITTO NAMED PRIOR PREVIOUS
AFORETIME ERE FORMER FORMERLY
AFRAID RAD REDE ADRAD FRAID PAVID REDDE TIMID AGHAST

CRAVEN FEARED SCARED WROTHE AFEARED ALARMED ANXIOUS ASCARED CHICKEN FEARFUL GASTFUL COWARDLY GHASTFUL TIMOROUS
AFREET JINN AFRIT DEMON GIANT IFRIT JINNI AFRITE EFREET
AFRESH ANEW ANON OVER AGAIN NEWLY DENOVO ENCORE REPEATED

AFRICA
(ALSO SEE SPECIFIC COUNTRIES)
DESERT: NAMIB NEFUD NUBIAN SAHARA ARABIAN KALAHARI
LAKE: CHAD CONGO NYASA VOLTA ALBERT KARIBA MALAWI RUDOLF TURKANA VICTORIA TANGANYIKA
MOUNTAIN: MERU ATLAS ELGON KENYA TEIDE TOUBKAL KARISIMBI RASDASHAN RUWENZORI DRAKENSBERG KILIMANJARO
NATION: CHAD MALI TOGO BENIN CONGO EGYPT GABON GHANA KENYA LIBYA NIGER SUDAN ZAIRE ANGOLA GAMBIA GUINEA MALAWI RWANDA UGANDA ZAMBIA ALGERIA BURUNDI LESOTHO LIBERIA MOROCCO NAMIBIA NIGERIA SENEGAL SOMALIA TUNISIA BOTSWANA CAMEROON DJIBOUTI ETHIOPIA TANZANIA ZIMBABWE SWAZILAND IVORYCOAST MADAGASCAR MAURITANIA MOZAMBIQUE UPPERVOLTA BURKINAFASO SIERRALEONE SOUTHAFRICA GUINEABISSAU
RIVER: NILE ORANGE LIMPOPO SENEGAL ZAMBEZI
WATERFALL: FINCHA TUGELA KALAMBO RUACANA TESSISAT VICTORIA

AFRICAINE, L' (CHARACTER IN —) INEZ DAGAMA SELIKA NELUSKO
(COMPOSER OF —) MEYERBEER
AFRICAN BOER AFRIC
AFRICAN MARIGOLD KHAKIBOS
AFRIKAANS TAAL DUTCH
AFRO NATURAL
AFT BACK REAR ABAFT AFTER ASTERN BEHIND
(FARTHEST —) AFTERMOST
AFTER A AB BY TO AFT EFT FOR SIN ANON NEXT PAST POST SYNE ABAFT APRES ARTER EFTER INFRA LATER SINCE ASTERN BEHIND BEYOND FOLLOW HINDER
(— MEALS) PC
(PREF.) EPH EPI INFRA META POST
AFTERBIRTH HEAM SECUNDINE SOOTERKIN
AFTERBODY TONNEAU
AFTERBURNER AUGMENTER
AFTEREFFECT SEQUEL SEQUELA
(PL.) HANGOVER
AFTERGRASS FOG AFTERFEED
AFTERIMAGE SPECTRUM PHOTOGENE SENSATION
(KIND OF —) PURKINJE
AFTERMATH FOG ETCH LOSS ISSUE ROWEN ROWET TRAIL TRAIN ARRISH EDDISH EDGREW EDGROW EFFECT PROFIT RESULT SEQUEL UPSHOT EAGRASS STUBBLE BACKWASH
AFTERMOST LAST HINDMOST
AFTERNOON AFTER TARDE UNDERN EVENING TEATIME
AFTERPIECE JIG EPODE EXODE EXODIUM POSTLUDE
AFTERSONG EPODE
AFTERSWARM CAST SPEW SPUE CASTLING
AFTERTASTE TWANG FAREWELL
AFTERTHOUGHT FOOTNOTE
AFTERWARD EFT POST SITH THEN APRES LATER INABIT EFTSOON EFTSOONS
AFTERWARDS SYNE
AGA AGHA LORD CHIEF
(WIFE OF —) BEGUM
AGAIN OR TO BIS EFT YET AGIN ANEW ANON AYEN AYIN BACK MORE OVER NEWLY AFRESH DENOVO ENCORE ITERUM EFTSOON FRESHLY FURTHER EFTSOONS MOREOVER
(— AND AGAIN) AND
(PREF.) ANA OVER PALI RE
AGAINST BY IN UP CON GIN NON AGIN ANTI GAIN INTO WITH AGAIN ANENT AYENS UNTIL ANENST AVERSE AYENST CONTRA GAINST UPTILL VERSUS FERNENT FORNENT OPPOSED ADVERSUS CONTRAIR FORENENT FORNENST FORNINST
(— HOPE) AGLEE AGLEY
(PREF.) ANTH ANTI CAT(A) CATH CONTRA ENANTIO GAIN OB
AGAL HEADROPE
AGALLOCH AGGUR ALOES GAROO GARROO GARROW TAMBAC LINALOE AGALWOOD CALAMBAC
AGAMA AGA AGHA GUANA AGAMID IGUANA LIZARD AGAMIAN
AGAMEDE (FATHER OF —) AUGEAS
(HUSBAND OF —) MULIUS
AGAMEMNON (BROTHER OF —) MENELAUS
(DAUGHTER OF —) ELECTRA IPHIGENIA
(FATHER OF —) PLISTHENES
(GRANDFATHER OF —) ATREUS
(MOTHER OF —) AEROPE
(SON OF —) ORESTES
(WIFE OF —) CLYTEMNESTRA
AGAMETE SPORE
AGAMID AGA AGHA BALETE BALITI
AGAPANTHUS TULBAGHIA LOVEFLOWER
AGAPE LOVE OPEN FEAST GAPING YAWNING
AGAR MOSS GELOSE KANTEN GELOSIN GELOSINE
AGARIC BLEWITS BLUSHER FLYBANE LEPIOTA
AGASP EAGER GASPING
AGATE TAW ONYX RUBY SARD ACHATE GAGATE MARBLE PEBBLE QUARTZ
(KIND OF —) MOSS
AGATI SESBANIA
AGAVE ALOE LILY PITA AGAUE AMOLE DATIL SISAL LILIUM MAGUEY MESCAL PULQUE ZAPUPE CANTALA KARATTO KERATTO TEQUILA HENEQUEN HENIQUEN JINIQUEN SOAPWEED
(BROTHER OF —) POLYDORUS
(FATHER OF —) CADMUS
(HUSBAND OF —) ECHION
(MOTHER OF —) HARMONIA
(SISTER OF —) INO SEMELE AUTONOE
(SON OF —) PENTHEUS
AGE ALD BIN DAY ELD EON ERA AEON EDGE GRAY OLAM TIME YUGA AETAT CYCLE EPOCH GETON OLDEN RIPEN SECLE WORLD YEARS MATURE MELLOW PERIOD SIECLE WITHER CENTURY DEVELOP GLACIAL OLDNESS SECULUM SENESCE VORHAND ANCIENTY DURATION ETERNITY LIFETIME MAJORITY MATURITY
(— OF MOON) EPACT
(— OF 100 YEARS) CENTENARY
(ADVANCED —) DOTAGE
(BEING UNDER 13 YEARS OF —) PRETEEN
(EARLY MIDDLE —) SUMMER
(FULL —) MAJORITY
(GREAT —) ANTIQUITY GRANDEVITY
(OLD —) CRUTCH SENIUM VETUSTY SENILITY
(PREF.) **(OLD —)** GERONT(O) PRESBY(O)
(SUFF.) AEVAL EVAL
(HAVING APPROXIMATE — OF) ISH ISTIC
AGED AE AET AGY OLD RIPE ANILE HOARY OLDEN PASSE FEEBLE INFIRM MATURE SENILE WINTRY YEARED ANCIENT ELDERLY OGYGIAN WINTERED
(NOT —) GREEN
(WELL —) STALE
AGEE AJEE AWRY AGLEY ASKEW
(SON OF —) SHAMMAH
AGELESS ETERNAL TIMELESS
AGELONG SECULAR SAECULAR
AGENCY DINT HAND CHECK FORCE LEVER MEANS MOYEN ORGAN PROXY ACTION BUREAU MEDIUM OFFICE ARBITER BENEFIT BROKERY FACULTY LIBRARY MACHINE ACTIVITY COMPTOIR COURTESY MINISTRY
(PUBLIC —) AUTHORITY
(REGULATORY —) QUANGO
(RESTORATIVE —) BALM
(SUPPOSITITIOUS —) ENTELECHY
(THERAPEUTIC —) MODALITY
(WORLD WAR II —) WPA
AGENDA LIST PLAN ROTA OUTLINE
AGENDUM ITEM SLATE DOCKET RECORD RITUAL PROGRAM
AGENOR (BROTHER OF —) BELUS
(DAUGHTER OF —) EUROPA
(FATHER OF —) ANTENOR NEPTUNE
(MOTHER OF —) LIBYA
(SON OF —) CILIX CADMUS PHOENIX
(WIFE OF —) TELEPHASSA
AGENT SPY AMIN DOER ETCH GENE ACTOR AMEEN BUYER CAUSE ENVOY MEANS ORGAN PROXY REEVE RIDER VAKIL WALLA ADUROL ASSIGN ATOPEN BROKER BURSAR COMMIS DEALER DEPUTY ENGINE FACTOR FITTER KEHAYA LEDGER MEDIUM MINION MUKTAR PESKAR SELLER SYNDIC VAKEEL WALLAH BAILIFF BLISTER CHANNEL COUCHER DRASTIC FACIENT FEDERAL HUSBAND LEAGUER MOOKTAR MOUNTAR MUKTEAR MUTAGEN OFFICER PESHKAR PROCTOR SCALPER APPROVER ATTORNEY AUMILDAR CATALYST EMISSARY EXECUTOR GOMASHTA GOMASTAH IMPROVER INCITANT INSTITOR MINISTER MITICIDE MOOKHTAR OPERATOR PROMOTER QUAESTOR RESIDENT SALESMAN VIRUCIDE MIDDLEMAN OPERATIVE SATELLITE SENESCHAL MAINSPRING PROCURATOR PLENIPOTENTIARY
(— AGAINST LEPROSY) DAPSONE
(— INVESTIGATING DRUG VIOLATIONS) NARC NARK
(— OF CROMWELL) AGITATOR
(ANTIKNOCK —) ADDITIVE ALKYLATE
(BINDING —) CHELATOR
(CLEANSING —) SOAP
(CONFIDENTIAL —) AMIN AMEEN
(DESTRUCTIVE —) DEVOURER
(EMPLOYMENT —) PADRONE
(ENFORCEMENT —) LAW
(ENVIRONMENTAL —) ZEITGEBER
(ESPIONAGE —) COURIER
(FISCAL —) STEWARD
(FIXING —) HYPO
(GOVERNMENT —) NARC NARCO
(HEALING —) BALSAM
(LIGHTLY-VALUED —) PAWN
(MEDICINAL —) DRASTIC
(MILK-CURDLING —) RENNET
(NARCOTIC —) NARC NARK GAZER
(OXIDIZING —) NINHYDRIN
(PRESS —) FLACK
(PUBLICITY —) BEATER
(PURCHASING —) CIRCAR SIRCAR SIRKAR
(SECRET —) SBIRRO OPERATIVE
(SPECIAL —) TMAN
(SPIRITUAL —) POWER
(STIMULATING —) FILIP FILLIP
(SUBVERSIVE —) STOOGE
(SWEETENING —) DULCIN
(UNDERCOVER —) SPOOK
(VOLATILE —) SPIRIT
(WETTING —) SPREADER
(SUFF.) ANT FIER STAT(IC)(ICS)
AGE-OLD TIMEWORN
AGESILAUS (BROTHER OF —) AGIS
(FATHER OF —) ARCHIDAMUS
(MOTHER OF —) EUPOLIA
AGGLOMERATE HEAP LUMP MASS PILE SELF SLAG WIND CHAOS GATHER CLUSTER COLLECT
AGGLOMERATION HORDE CONGERY FAVELLA CONGERIE

AGGRANDIZE LIFT BOOST EXALT RAISE ADVANCE AUGMENT DIGNIFY ELEVATE ENLARGE MAGNIFY PROMOTE INCREASE
AGGRAVATE IRK NAG VEX FEED LOAD TWIT ANGER ANNOY TAUNT TEASE BURDEN PESTER WORSEN AGGREGE BEDEVIL ENHANCE ENLARGE MAGNIFY PROVOKE AGGRIEVE HEIGHTEN INCREASE IRRITATE
AGGRAVATED ACUTE
AGGREEABLE ACCEPTABLE
AGGREGATE ADD ALL SET SUM AUGE BAND BULK CLON CLUB COMB DEME FLOC GOUT LATH MASS BLOCK BUNCH CLASS CLONE COVER CROWD FIELD GROSS SHOOT SMEAR TOTAL UNITE WHOLE AMOUNT BALLAS DOMAIN PLUREL VOLUME ASBOLAN COLLECT SCHMEAR SCHMEER ARCULITE ASBOLANE ASBOLITE AXIOLITE COMPOUND COVERAGE CUMULITE ENSEMBLE MANIFOLD MULTEITY TOTALITY
(— OF CELLS) TISSUE
(— OF CRYSTALS) TREE
(— OF MICA) BOOK
(— OF MINERALS) EYE
(— OF ORE) KIDNEY
(— OF POINTS) CELL
(— OF RELATED THINGS) SHMEAR SCHMEAR
(— OF STATEMENTS) AUTHORITY
(— OF TISSUES) BODY
(MATHEMATICAL —) FIELD SEQUENCE
(MOLECULAR —) MICELLE
(SOIL —) PED
(SUFF.) ERY
AGGREGATION HEAD HERD NEST CLUMP CUTIN FLOCK GORGE GROUP LURRY SWARM COLONY FAMILY NATION SYSTEM CLUSTER CONGERY GALLERY SORITES CONGERIE EUMERISM
AGGRESSION WAR RAID ATTACK INJURY ASSAULT OFFENSE INVASION
AGGRESSIVE BUTCH PUSHY PUSHING AGONISTIC TRUCULENT
AGGRESSIVENESS CRUST DEFIANCE BELLICOSITY
AGGRIEVE TRY HARM HURT PAIN HARRY WRONG INJURE AFFLICT OPPRESS TROUBLE DISTRESS
AGGRIEVED SORE OFFENDED
AGHAST AGAST AFRAID
AGHRERATH (FATHER OF —) PESHENG
(SLAYER OF —) AFRASIAB
AGILAWOOD AGALLOCH AGALLOCHUM
AGILE DEFT FAST LISH SPRY WIRY ADEPT ALERT BRISK CATTY ELFIN FLEET LITHE NIFTY NIPPY QUICK WANLE WITHY ACTIVE ADROIT FEERIE FEIRIE LIMBER LISSOM LITHER LIVELY LUTHER NIMBLE QUIVER SUPPLE WANDLE LISSOME SALIENT SPRINGE SPRINGY ATHLETIC
AGILITY LEVITY SPROIL SLEIGHT ACTIVITY LEGERITY SALIENCE
AGING BINNING
(PREMATURE —) GERODERMA GERODERMIA
AGIO BATTA DISAGIO PREMIUM DISCOUNT EXCHANGE
AGIST TAX FEED RATE GRAZE PASTURE
AGITATE FAN IRK JAR VEX WEY FRET FUSS MOVE PLOT RILE ROCK ROIL SEEK STIR TEEM ALARM ALTER BREAK BROIL CHURN DRIVE HARRY IMPEL QUAKE ROUSE SHAKE AROUSE BETOSS BUSKLE DEBATE DEVISE EXCITE FOMENT HARASS INCITE JABBLE JOSTLE JUMBLE JUSTLE LATHER MANAGE RATTLE RUFFLE SEETHE ACTUATE CANVASS COMMOVE CONCUSS DISCUSS DISTURB PERTURB REVOLVE TEMPEST TORMENT TROUBLE ACTIVATE CONTRIVE CONVULSE DISQUIET DISTRACT TRANSACT
(— A LIQUID) SPARGE
AGITATED WILD HECTIC STEWED STORMY YEASTY AGITATO ESTUOUS UNQUIET AESTUOUS FEVERISH FLURRIED SEETHING OVERWROUGHT
AGITATION GOG JAR JOG BOIL FEAR FLAP FRET FURY GUST HEAT ITCH JERK JOLT SNIT STEW ALARM DANCE HURRY QUAKE SHAKE STORM STOUR TWEAK YEAST BREEZE BUSTLE DITHER ENERGY FIZZLE FLIGHT FLURRY FRENZY JABBLE MOTION PUCKER QUIVER RIPPLE SHAKES TAKING TREMOR TUMULT UNREST WELTER EMOTION FERMENT FLUSTER FLUTTER MADNESS RAMPAGE STICKLE SWITHER TEMPEST TURMOIL DISQUIET PAROXYSM UPHEAVAL COMMOTION
(— AND PROPAGANDA) AGITPROP
(— IN LIQUID) JABBLE
(BODILY —) JACTATION
(MENTAL —) STEW
AGITATOR HOG TREATER
AGLAIA (FATHER OF —) JUPITER
(MOTHER OF —) EURYNOME
(SISTER OF —) THALIA EUPHROSYNE
AGLET TAB TAG LACE STUD PLATE AIGLET PENDANT SPANGLE HAWTHORN STAYLACE
AGLEY AWRY AGLEE ASIDE ASKEW WRONG
AGLYCON GENIN NONSUGAR SAPOGENIN
AGNATE AKIN ALLIED COGNATE KINDRED
AGNEL MOUTON
AGNOETE THEMISTIAN
AGNOMEN NAME ALIAS EPITHET SURNAME COGNOMEN NICKNAME
AGNOSTIC ATHEIST DOUBTER SKEPTIC NESCIENT
AGO BY SIN BACK ERST GONE PAST SENS SYNE YGOE YORE ABACK AGONE SINCE YGONE SINSYNE BACKWARD
(LONG —) ANCIENTLY
AGOG AVID KEEN ASTIR EAGER LIVELY EXCITED VIGILANT
AGOING AGATE
AGONIZE BEAR RACK STRAIN WRITHE
AGONIZING GRINDING HARROWING
AGONY ACHE PAIN PANG DOLOR GRIEF GRIPE PANIC STOUR THRAW THROE TRIAL ACHING ANGUISH ANXIETY EMOTION TORMENT TORTURE TRAVAIL DISTRESS PAROXYSM
AGOUTI CAPA CAVY PACA ACUCHI AGOUTY ACOUCHI ACOUCHY
AGRAFFE CLASP
AGRARIAN RURAL PASTORAL PRAEDIAL
AGRAULOS (DAUGHTER OF —) HERSE PANDROSOS
(FATHER OF —) ACTAEUS
(HUSBAND OF —) CECROPS
AGREE FAY FIT GEE HIT PAN YES GIBE GREE JIBE JUMP MEET SIDE SORT SUIT ADMIT ALLOW ATONE BLEND CHECK CLICK CLOSE FADGE GRANT HITCH JUTTY LEVEL MATCH PIECE STAND TALLY UNITE YIELD ACCEDE ACCEPT ACCORD ADHERE ASSENT ASSORT COMPLY CONCUR CONDOG COTTON ENGAGE REWARD SETTLE SQUARE SUBMIT ARRANGE BARGAIN COMPORT CONCEDE CONFORM CONGREE CONGRUE CONSENT CONSIGN DARESAY PACTION PROMISE COINCIDE COMPOUND CONTRACT COVENANT QUADRATE
(— MUTUALLY) STIPULATE
(— TO) ACCEPT
(— TO JOIN) ADHERE
(— UPON) TAILYE TAILZEE TAILZIE
(— WITH) SIT LIKE SIDE TAIL ANSWER
AGREEABLE AMEN EASY FAIR FINE GOOD KIND LIEF NICE SOFT WEME AMENE CANNY DULCE GRATE JOLIE JOLLY LITHE LUSTY QUEME READY SAPID SMIRK SUANT SUAVE SUENT SWEET COMELY COWDIE DAINTY DULCET KINDLY LIKELY MELLOW SAVORY SMOOTH SUITED ADAPTED AMABILE AMIABLE COUTHIE DOUCEUR TUNABLE WELCOME WILLING WINSOME AMENABLE CHARMING DELICATE GRATEFUL LIKESOME LOVESOME OBLIGING PLACABLE PLAUSIVE PLEASANT PLEASING PURSUANT SOCIABLE SUITABLE THANKFUL CONGENIAL PALATABLE
(NOT —) ABHORRENT
(UNPLEASANTLY —) SACCHARINE
AGREED ON DONE CONTENT
AGREEING CONNATE CONTENT ACCORDANT ACCORDING
AGREEMENT GO FIT NOD AXIS BOND DEAL FINE LINE MISE PACT TACK TAIL TRUE WHIZ ATONE COVIN LEASE MATCH TERMS TOUCH TRUTH TRYST UNITY WHIZZ ACCORD ACTION ASSENT CARTEL CAUTIO COMART COMITY COVINE DICKER LEAGUE PACTUM PLEDGE TREATY UNISON ANALOGY BARGAIN CLOSING CLOSURE COMPACT CONCERT CONSENT CONSORT CONSULT ENTENTE HARMONY ONENESS PACTION RAPPORT CONTRACT DIAPASON SANCTION SORTANCE SYMPATHY ACCEPTANCE ACCORDANCE
(— OF SOUND) CHIME
(— TO JOIN) ADHESION
(GRAMMATICAL —) ATTRACTION
(IN —) ASONE
(REPURCHASE —) REPO
(SECRET —) CAHOOT CAHOOTS COLLUSION
AGRICANE (SLAYER OF —) ORLANDO
AGRICULTURAL ARABLE GEOPONIC GEOPONICAL
AGRICULTURE FARMING GAINAGE TILLAGE AGRONOMY
(— SYSTEM) KOLKHOZ
(PREF.) AGRO
AGRICULTURIST THO FARMER GROWER SANTAL PLANTER RANCHER
AMERICAN REID MORTON RUFFIN TAYLOR THOMAS WATSON BORLAUG
CANADIAN MACKAY SAUNDERS
ENGLISH TULL YOUNG
GERMAN NAUMANN
SWISS SAUSSURE
AGRIMONY CLIVE BONESET BORWORT HEMPWEED
AGRIPPINA (SON OF —) NERO
AGRITO AGARITA MAHONIA ALGERITO ASHBERRY
AGRIUS (BROTHER OF —) LATINUS TELEGONUS
(FATHER OF —) ULYSSES ODYSSEUS PORTHAON
(MOTHER OF —) GAEA CIRCE EURYTE
(SON OF —) THERSITES
AGRONOMIST (ALSO SEE AGRICULTURIST)
AGROUND SEWED ASHORE BEACHED STRANDED
AGRYPHA LOGION
AGRYPNIA INSOMNIA SLEEPLESSNESS
AGUACATE AHUACA AVOCADO
AGUAMAS PINGUIN
AGUE CHILL EXIES FEVER MALARIA QUARTAN SHAKING SHIVERS
AGUE TREE SASSAFRAS
AGUEWEED BONESET
AGUR (FATHER OF —) JAKEH
AH AY ACH
AHAB (FATHER OF —) OMRI
(NEIGHBOR OF —) NABOTH
(WIFE OF —) JEZEBEL
AHAR AGEE AJEE
AHARAH (FATHER OF —) BENJAMIN
AHARTALAV YARROW MILFOIL
AHASBAI (SON OF —) ELIPHELET
AHAZ (FATHER OF —) MICAH JOTHAM

AHAZIAH **(FATHER OF —)** AHAB JEHORAM
(MOTHER OF —) JEZEBEL ATHALIAH
AHBAN **(FATHER OF —)** ABISUR
(MOTHER OF —) ABIHAIL
AHEAD ON UP ALEE FORE AFORE ALONG DORMY BEFORE DORMIE ONWARD ALREADY ENDWAYS ENDWISE FORWARD LEADING ADELANTE ADVANCED ANTERIOR
(— OF TIME) FAST
(STRAIGHT —) FORERIGHT
AHEM HUM
AHIAH **(FATHER OF —)** AHITUB JERAHMEEL
(SON OF —) BAASHA
AHIAM **(FATHER OF —)** SHARAR
AHIEZER **(FATHER OF —)** AMMISHADDAI
AHIHUD **(FATHER OF —)** SHELOMI
AHIKAM **(FATHER OF —)** SHAPHAN
(SON OF —) GEDALIAH
AHILUD **(SON OF —)** BAANA JEHOSHAPHAT
AHIMAAZ **(DAUGHTER OF —)** AHINOAM
(FATHER OF —) ZADOK
AHIMELECH **(FATHER OF —)** AHITUB
AHINADAB **(FATHER OF —)** IDDO
AHINOAM **(FATHER OF —)** AHIMAAZ
(HUSBAND OF —) SAUL DAVID
(SON OF —) AMNON
AHIO **(FATHER OF —)** BERIAH JEHIEL ABINADAB
AHIRAM **(FATHER OF —)** BENJAMIN
AHISAMACH **(SON OF —)** AHOLIAB
AHISHAHAR **(FATHER OF —)** BILHAN
AHITUB **(FATHER OF —)** AMARIAH PHINEHAS
(SON OF —) ZADOK AHIJAH AHIMELECH
AHLAI **(FATHER OF —)** SHESHAN
(HUSBAND OF —) JARHA
(SON OF —) ZABAD
AHOAH **(FATHER OF —)** BENJAMIN
AHOLIBAMAH **(FATHER OF —)** ANAH
(HUSBAND OF —) ESAU
AHOY AVAST
AHUEHUETE CEDAR SABINO CYPRESS
AHURA MAZDA ORMAZD
AHUZAM **(FATHER OF —)** ASHUR
(MOTHER OF —) NAARAH
AH WILDERNESS **(AUTHOR OF —)** ONEILL
(CHARACTER IN —) BELLE DAVID MILLER MURIEL RICHARD MCCOMBER
AIAH **(BROTHER OF —)** ANAH
(DAUGHTER OF —) RIZPAH
(FATHER OF —) ZIBEON
AID KEY ABET BACK BEET HAND HELP PONY REDE ALLAY BOOST COACH FAVOR GRANT SERVE SPEED TREAT ASSIST CRUTCH FAVOUR FRIEND PROFIT RELIEF REMEDY RESCUE SECOND SUCCOR SUPPLY UPHOLD ADVANCE AIDANCE ANCILLA BACKING BENEFIT COMFORT ENDORSE FORWARD FURTHER INDORSE RELIEVE SECOURS SERVICE SUBSIDY SUPPORT ADJUVATE AUXILIUM BEFRIEND SUFFRAGE
(— A VESSEL) HOVEL
(— A WAITER) BUS
(— IN MONEY) SUBSIDY
(— SECRETLY) SUBAID
(COMPLEXION —) FUCUS
(FAMILY —) AFDC
(MORMON —) COUNSELOR COUNSELLOR
AIDA **(CHARACTER IN —)** AIDA AMNERIS RADAMES AMONASRO
(COMPOSER OF —) VERDI
AIDAN **(FATHER OF —)** GABRAN
AIDE AID BEAGLE DEPUTY SECOND OFFICER ORDERLY ADJUTANT GALLOPER PARAPROFESSIONAL
(BULLFIGHTER'S —) CAPEADOR
AIDS **(— VIRUS)** HIV
AIGRETTE EGRET HERON PLUME SPRAY AIGRET FEATHERS
AIL ILE AILD EILE EYLE FAIL PAIN PINE AFFECT BOTHER FALTER SUFFER AFFLICT DECLINE TROUBLE COMPLAIN DISTRESS
AILANTHUS SUMAC SUMACH
AILING SICK CRAZY CRONK DONCY DONSY SOBER DONSIE SICKLY UNWELL CRAICHY CREACHY
AILMENT AIL ILL PIP COUGH MALADY DISEASE ILLNESS DISORDER SICKNESS WEAKNESS
(SUDDEN —) WAFF
(WINTER —) STREP
AIM END LAY TRY BEAD BEAM BEND BENT BUTT FINE GLEE GOAL HEAD HOLD LEAD MARK MINT PLAN SAKE SEEK TEMP VIEW VIZY WINK ACIES BLANK DRIVE ESSAY ETTLE GUESS LEVEL POINT PRICK SCOPE SIGHT TRAIN VISIE VIZZY ASPIRE DESIGN DIRECT ESTEEM INTEND INTENT OBJECT SCHEME STRIVE ADDRESS ATTEMPT CHIMERA MEANING PRETEND PURPOSE RESPECT STAGGER CHIMAERA CONSIDER ENDEAVOR ESTIMATE PRETENSE STEERING TENTAMEN
(— A BROADCAST) NARROWCAST
(— A KICK) FLING
(— AT) EYE AFFECT
(— FURTIVELY) STEAL
(— HIGH) LOB
(— INDIRECTLY) GLANCE
AIMED FAST
(— AT) AFFECTED
AIMING LEVEL GUNLAYING
AIMLESS IDLE BLIND CHANCE RANDOM DRIFTING
AIMLESSNESS FLANERIE
AIR AER PEW SKY AERE ARIA AURA AYRE BROW DIRT FEEL LILT LOFT MIEN PORT POSE SONG TELL TUNE VENT WIND AVION ETHER FRILL OZONE UTTER VOICE AERATE AETHER ALLURE ASPECT BROACH CACHET MANNER MELODY OSTENT PIAFFE REGARD REGION STRAIN VANITY WELKIN WITHER BEARING DISPLAY EXHIBIT EXPRESS FANFARE MALARIA NEPHELE PIAFFER ATTITUDE BEHAVIOR CARRIAGE PRESENCE
(— COOLED) WATERLESS
(— EXHALED) BLAST
(— IN MOTION) BREATH
(— OUT) VENT
(— PLANT) LIFELEAF
(AFFECTED —S) FRILLS
(BOASTFUL —) PARADO
(CHEERFUL —) LILT
(CONFIDENT —) BRAVURA
(COOL —) FRESCO
(COQUETTISH —) MINAUDERIE
(FETID —) REEK
(FOUL —) DIRT
(HAUGHTY —S) ALTITUDES
(MUSICAL —) ARIA SOLO TUNE BRAWL MELODY ARIETTA ARIETTE BRAVURA CANZONE MUSETTE CAVATINE
(OPEN —) OUTDOORS OUTOFDOORS
(POISONOUS —) MALARIA
(POMPOUS —) SWELL
(PRETENTIOUS —) SIDE
(PURE —) SERENE
(PUT ON —S) PROSS
(PUT ON THE —) TELEVISE BROADCAST
(STALE —) STEAM
(STIFLING —) SMORE
(THE —) GATE
(WARM —) OAM
(PL.) LUGS FRONT
(PREF.) AER(O) ATM(O) PNEO PNEUM(A)(ATA)(O)(ON)(ONO) PNEUSTA
AIRBORNE ALOFT
AIRCRAFT KITE ABORT BLIMP CRAFT FLYER PLANE GLIDER TRIJET AEROBUS AERONEF AIRSHIP BALLOON AEROBOAT AERODYNE AEROSTAT AIRLINER AIRPLANE AUTOGIRO AUTOGYRO GYRODYNE TILTROTOR GYROCOPTER ROTORCRAFT ORNITHOPTER
(— DESIGN) STEALTH
(— WAITING TO LAND) STACK
(ARMED —) GUNSHIP
(LARGE JET —) WIDEBODY
(SMALL —) STOL
(UNIDENTIFIED —) UFO BOGY BOGEY BOGIE
(UNMANNED —) RPV
AIRCRAFTSMAN ERK
AIRCREWMAN KICKER AIREDALE
AIRFARE **(CLASS OF —)** APEX
AIRFIELD AERODROME SATELLITE
AIRFOIL FIN FLAP SLAT BLADE CANARD SURFACE AEROFOIL ELEVATOR
AIR FORCE **(WOMEN COMPONENTS OF —)** WAF
AIRHEAD SAP
AIRILY JAUNTILY
AIRING OUTING
AIRLESS STUFFY STIFLING
AIRLINE KLM SAS TWA BWIA ELAL ALOHA DELTA USAIR FEEDER IBERIA QANTAS SABENA SKYWAY UNITED NONSKED LUFTHANSA
AIRMAN ACE FLIER FLYER BIRDMAN WARBIRD AERONAUT WASTEMAN
AIRPLANE BUS CUB JET MIG SST BAKA GYRO KILL KITE SHIP ZERO AVION CAMEL CRATE FLIER FLYER FRITZ GOTHA HEINE JENNY LINER PLANE SCOUT SNOOP AIRBUS BOMBER CANARD CESSNA CHASER COPTER FANJET FERRET FESSEL FOKKER GLIDER JENNIE PUSHER SMOKER TANDEM VESSEL VIMANA AERONEF AVIATIK AVIETTE BIPLANE CLIPPER FIGHTER FLIVVER FLYAWAY HOTSHOT PENGUIN SNOOPER SPOTTER STINSON TRACTOR WARBIRD AEROSTAT ALBATROS KAMIKAZE SEAPLANE SKYCOACH SKYCRAFT SOCIABLE STRUTTER TRIPLANE TURBOJET WARPLANE AEROPLANE MONOPLANE
(— ENGINE) RAMJET
(COMMANDEER —) SKYJACK
(JET —) AIRBUS
(JUMPING FROM —) SKYDIVING
(PART OF —) FIN POD TAB FLAP WING BLADE CABIN PYLON RADAR ENGINE RUDDER AILERON COCKPIT COWLING SPOILER ELEVATOR REVERSER STABILIZER SUPPRESSOR
(REMOTE-CONTROLLED —) DRONE
(TYPE OF —) TRIJET
AIR PLANT LIFELEAF LIVELEAF
AIRPORT DROME AIRPARK JETPORT SCUTTLE AIRDROME AIRFIELD
AIRSCREW PUSHER
AIRSHIP (SEE ALSO AIRPLANE AND AIRCRAFT) SHIP BLIMP GASBAG AERONAT AEROSTAT PARSEVAL ZEPPELIN
AIRSTREAM PEW DOWNWASH
AIRSTRIP LILY
AIRTIGHT SEALED AIRPROOF HERMETIC
AIRWAY MONKEY RETURN SKYWAY AIRWAVE WINDWAY WINDROAD
AIRY GAY COOL RARE THIN EMPTY HUFFY LIGHT MERRY WINDY AERIAL BLITHE BREEZY FLUFFY JAUNTY JOCUND LIVELY STARRY AIRLIKE AIRSOME HAUGHTY JOCULAR SFOGATO AFFECTED ANIMATED DEBONAIR DELICATE ETHEREAL FLIPPANT GRACEFUL SPARKISH TRIFLING VOLATILE
AISLE WAY YLE AILE LANE NAVE WALK ALLEE ALLEY FEEDWAY GANGWAY PASSAGE CORRIDOR
AIT OAT EYOT HOLM ILOT ISLE EIGHT ISLET ISLOT
AITCH ACHE
AITCHBONE ICEBONE EDGEBONE
AJA **(FATHER OF —)** RAGHU DILIPA
AJAR OPEN DISCORDANT
AJAX AIAS
(FATHER OF —) OILEUS TELAMON
(MOTHER OF —) ERIBOEA PERIBOEA
AJIGARTA **(SON OF —)** SUNAHSEPA
AJONJOLI SESAME
AJOWAN AJAVA AIWAIN
AKALI SHAHIDI
AKAN **(FATHER OF —)** EZER

AKEAKE AKE HOPBUSH IRONWOOD
AKHA KAW
AKIMBO ANGLED AKEMBOLL AKENBOLD
AKIN SIB LIKE NEAR NIGH ALIKE CLOSE AGNATE ALLIED COUSIN SIBBED TENDER COGNATE CONNATE GERMANE RELATED SIMILAR
(— ON MALE SIDE) AGNATIC
(NOT —) UNSIB
AKKUB (FATHER OF —) ELIOENAI
AKRA ACCRA INKRA
AKU VICTORFISH
AL AAL AWL MULBERRY
ALA AXIL DRUM WING AXILLA RECESS NOSEWING

ALABAMA
CAPITAL: MONTGOMERY
COUNTY: LEE BIBB CLAY DALE PIKE COOSA HENRY LAMAR MACON PERRY BLOUNT BUTLER COFFEE DALLAS ELMORE ETOWAH GENEVA GREENE MARION MONROE MORGAN SHELBY SUMTER WILCOX CHILTON
LAKE: MARTIN
MOUNTAIN: CHEAHA LOOKOUT RACCOON
NATIVE: LIZARD
RIVER: PEA COOSA CAHABA MOBILE SIPSEY TENSAW CONECUH PERDIDO SEPULGA WARRIOR TOMBIGBEE TALLAPOOSA
STATE BIRD: YELLOWHAMMER
STATE FISH: TARPON
STATE FLOWER: CAMELLIA
STATE TREE: PINE LONGLEAF
TOWN: OPP PIPER SELMA ATHENS CORONA HEFLIN JASPER LANETT LINDEN MARION MOBILE SAMSON BREWTON FLORALA GADSDEN ANNISTON SYLACAUGA TUSCALOOSA

ALABASTER GYPSUM TECALI ONYCHITE
ALACK ALAS ALAKE
ALACRITY HASTE SPEED CELERITY RAPIDITY
ALAMEDA MALL WALK
ALAMETH (FATHER OF —) BECHER
ALAN ALAND ALANT ALAUNT
ALANG-ALANG COGON KOGON
ALANS GHUZ OGHUZ
ALANTIN INULIN
ALAR PTERIC WINGED AXILLARY WINGLIKE
ALARBUS (MOTHER OF —) TAMORA
ALARDO (BROTHER OF —) BRADAMANT
ALARM COW DIN BELL FEAR FRAY GAST LARM ALERT BROIL CLOCK DAUNT FEEZE LARUM NOISE PANIC ROUSE SCARE SIREN START STILL UPSET AFFRAY ALARUM APPALL AROUSE ATTACK BUZZER DISMAY EXCITE FRIGHT OUTCRY SIGNAL TERROR TOCSIN DISTURB GLOPNEN GLOPPEN MOUNTEE STARTLE TERRIFY TORPEDO WARNING AFFRIGHT DISQUIET FRIGHTEN SURPRISE CONSTERNATION
(FIRE —) STILL FIREBOX
ALARMED SCARY SCAREY FEARFUL GASTFUL AFFRAYED GHASTFUL SCAREFUL STREAKED
ALARMER HUER
ALARMING SCARY SCAREY FEARFUL SCAREFUL
ALARMIST JITTERBUG
ALAS AY ACH HEU LAS OCH TSK VAE WOE EHEU HECH OIME WALY ALACK HALAS HELAS OIMEE SOSAD HARROW OCHONE OTOTOI WAESUCK ULLAGONE WAESUCKS WELLADAY WELLAWAY

ALASKA
CAPITAL: JUNEAU
GLACIER: MUIR
ISLAND: ADAK ATKA ATTU UMNAK KODIAK UNIMAK AFOGNAK DIOMEDE NUNIVAK
ISLAND GROUP: RAT ALEUTIAN PRIBILOF ANDREANOF
LAKE: NAKNEK ILIAMNA
MOUNTAIN: BONA VETA SPURR KATMAI PAVLOF FORAKER MCKINLEY
MOUNTAIN RANGE: CRAZY BROOKS KAIYUH CHUGACH KILBUCK WRANGELL
NATIVE: ALEUT AHTENA ESKIMO INGALIK KOYUKON TLINGIT
PENINSULA: KENAI SEWARD
PURCHASER: SEWARD
RIVER: CHENA KOBUK YUKON COPPER NOATAK TANANA KOYUKUK SUSITNA CHULITNA COLVILLE KUSKOKWIM PORCUPINE
STATE BIRD: PTARMIGAN
STATE FLOWER: FORGETMENOT
STATE TREE: SPRUCE
TOWN: EEK NOME RUBY KENAI SITKA UMIAT BARROW JUNEAU KODIAK NENANA SKAGWAY KOTZEBUE ANCHORAGE FAIRBANKS KETCHIKAN
VOLCANO: KUKAK SPURR GRIGGS KATMAI MAGEIK MARTIN PAVLOF DOUGLAS ILIAMNA REDOUBT TORBERT TRIDENT WRANGELL

ALASTRIM AMAAS
ALATE WINGY
ALB ALBE AUBE CAMISIA CHRISOM VESTMENT
ALBACORE TUNA TUNNY GERMAN GERMON LONGFIN ALALONGA ALALUNGA MACKEREL SCOMBRID

ALBANIA
ANCIENT PEOPLE: ILLYRIAN
CAPITAL: TIRANA TIRANE
COIN: LEK FRANC QINTAR QINTARKA
KING: ZOG
LAKE: ULZE OHRID PRESPA SCUTARI OHRIDSKO
MOUNTAIN: KORAB SHALA PINDUS KORITNIK
REGION: EPIRUS
RIVER: MAT DRIN OSUM SEMAN BOJANA ERZENI SEMENI VIJOSE SHKUMBI
TOWN: LIN FIER KLOS LESH BERAT CROIA DUKAT KORCE KRUJE PECIN PEQIN QUKES RUBIC SPASH VLONE VLORE AVLONA BERATI BITSAN DARDHE DURRES KORRCE PERMET PRESHE TIRANA VALONA ALESSIO DURAZZO KORITZA SCUTARI SHKODER
TRIBE: GEG CHAM GHEG TOSK

ALBANIAN GEG GHEG GUEG ARNAUT SKIPETAR
ALBATROSS GONY GOON GONEY GOONY NELLY FABRIC GOONEY GOONIE QUAKER SEABIRD ALCATRAS BLUEBIRD STINKPOT
ALBEIT ALL ALBE ALBEE ALLBE THOUGH HOWBEIT
ALBERIC (WIFE OF —) MAROZIA
ALBERTA (CAPITAL OF —) EDMONTON
(LAKE OF —) BANFF JASPER WATERTON
(RIVER OF —) BOW OLDMAN WAPITI ATHABASCA
(TOWN OF —) CALGARY REDDEER LETHBRIDGE MEDICINEHAT
ALBIGENSIANS CATHARI
ALBINISM ALPHOSIS
ALBINO LEUCAETHIOP
ALBITE PERICLINE
ALBIZZIA SIRIS
ALBOIN (FATHER OF —) ALDUIN
(SLAYER OF —) HELMICHIS
(WIFE OF —) ROSAMUNDA
ALBUM ALBE BOOK RECORD VOLUME REGISTER
ALBUMEN WHITE
ALBUMIN ALBUMEN PHASELIN SYNTONIN
ALBUMINOID ELASTIN FIBROIN KERATIN PROTEIN SERICIN COLLAGEN GORGONIN
ALBURNUM SAP BLEA SPLINT SAPWOOD
ALBUS BLANCO
ALCAEUS (DAUGHTER OF —) ANAXO
(FATHER OF —) PERSEUS ANDROGEUS
(MOTHER OF —) ANDROMEDA
(SON OF —) AMPHITRYON
ALCAIDE CADE CAID QAID JUDGE ALCADE
ALCATHOUS (FATHER OF —) PELOPS
(MOTHER OF —) HIPPODAMIA
(SLAYER OF —) OENOMAUS IDOMENEUS
(WIFE OF —) EUACHME
ALCESTIS (AUTHOR OF —) EURIPIDES
(CHARACTER IN —) APOLLO ADMETUS ALCESTIS HERCULES THANATOS
(FATHER OF —) PELIAS
(HUSBAND OF —) ADMETUS
ALCHEMIST ADEPT ARTIST CHEMIC CHEMICK CHEMIST HERMETIC
(AUTHOR OF —) JONSON
(CHARACTER IN —) DOL ABEL FACE SURLY COMMON DAPPER MAMMON PLIANT SUBTLE ANANIAS DRUGGER EPICURE KASTRIL LOVEWIT WHOLESOME TRIBULATION
ALCHEMY ART MAGIC ALCUMY CHYMIA SPAGYRIC
(GOD OF —) HERMES
ALCHFRITH (FATHER OF —) OSWIU
(MOTHER OF —) EANFLAED
(WIFE OF —) CYNEBURH
ALCHORNEA DOVEWOOD
ALCIBIADES (FATHER OF —) CLINIAS
(MOTHER OF —) DINOMACHE
ALCIMEDE (FATHER OF —) PHYLACUS
(HUSBAND OF —) AESON
(MOTHER OF —) CLYMENE
(SON OF —) JASON
ALCIMEDES (BROTHER OF —) ARGUS MEDEUS PHERES MERMERUS TISANDER THESSALUS
(FATHER OF —) JASON
(MOTHER OF —) MEDEA
ALCINA (SISTER OF —) MORGANA LOGISTILLA
(VICTIM OF —) RUGGIERO
ALCINOUS (DAUGHTER OF —) NAUSICAA
(FATHER OF —) NAUSITHOUS
(MOTHER OF —) PERIBOEA
(WIFE OF —) ARETE
ALCIPPE (DAUGHTER OF —) MARPESSA
(HUSBAND OF —) EVENUS METION
(SON OF —) DAEDALUS
ALCIS (FATHER OF —) ANTIPOENUS
(SISTER OF —) ANDROCLEA
ALCITHOE (FATHER OF —) MINYAS
(SISTER OF —) ARSIPPE LEUCIPPE
ALCMAEON (FATHER OF —) AMPHIARAUS
(MOTHER OF —) ERIPHYLE
(WIFE OF —) CALLIRRHOE ALPHESIBOEA
ALCMENE (FATHER OF —) ELECTRYON
(HUSBAND OF —) AMPHITRYON
(SON OF —) HERCULES IPHICLES
ALCOHOL ALKY ETHAL ETHYL IDITE LEDOL NEROL VINYL AMYROL ANDROL CEDROL ELEMOL GLYCOL GUAIOL HYDROL IDITOL LUPEOL LUTEIN METHYL PHYTOL SPIRIT STERIN STERNO STEROL TALITE ACRITOL ADONITE ALDITOL ALKANOL ANISOIN BORNEOL BUTANOL CAROTOL DECANOL ETHANOL FENCHOL HEPTITE HEXITOL INOSITE MANNITE MENTHOL PHORBOL PULEGOL QUINITE SCOPINE SORBITE STETHAL STYRONE TAGETOL TALITOL TROPINE XYLITOL CATECHOL LINALOOL MANNITOL METHANOL GLYCERINE PYRIDOXINE
(ETHYL —) METHS
(NOT USING —) STRAIGHT
ALCOHOLATE SPIRIT ESSENCE

ALCOHOLIC ALKY
(HERBAL — DRINK) SNAPS
(NOT —) SOFT
ALCOHOLOMETER GENOMETER VINOMETER
ALCOVE BAY NOOK BOWER NICHE ORIEL STALL CARREL RECESS CARRELL CUBICLE DINETTE RETREAT SERVERY ALHACENA SNUGGERY TABLINUM
ALCYONARIAN SEAPEN
ALCYONE (BROTHER OF —) EURYSTHEUS
(FATHER OF —) ATLAS AEOLUS
(HUSBAND OF —) CEYX
(MOTHER OF —) ENARETE PLEIONE
(SON OF —) ANTHAS HYRIEUS
ALDABELLA (BROTHER OF —) OLIVIERO BRANDIMARTE
(FATHER OF —) MONODANTES
(HUSBAND OF —) ORLANDO
ALDEHYDE ALDOL CITRAL ALKANAL CHLORAL COGENER DECANAL GLYOXAL HEXANAL RETINAL RETINEL ACROLEIN CONGENER FURFURAL PIPERONAL PYRIDOXINE
ALDER ARN OLER ALNUS ELDER OWLER SAGEROSE
(PREF.) ALNI
ALDERMAN BAILIE SENIOR HEADMAN
ALDFRITH (BROTHER OF —) ECGFRITH
(FATHER OF —) OSWIU
ALE MUM NOG BASS BEER BOCK BREW FLIP MILD NOGG PURL SCUD YELL AUDIT CLINK DARBY JOUGH KVASS LAGER NAPPY STOUT ALEGAR PORTER STINGO SWANKY BITTERS MOROCCO OCTOBER PHARAOH HUGMATEE
(— BREWED WITH BRACKISH WATER) TIPPER
(— MIXED WITH SWEETENER) BRAGGET
(INFERIOR —) SWANKY SWANKEY
(NEW —) SWATS
(SOUR —) ALEGAR
(SPICED —) SWIG
(STRONG —) MUM HUFF BURTON STINGO HUFFCAP
(WEAK —) TWOPENNY
ALEATORY HAZARDOUS
ALEBION (BROTHER OF —) BERGION DERCYNUS
(FATHER OF —) NEPTUNE POSEIDON
(SLAYER OF —) HERCULES
ALECOST COSTMARY
ALECTRYON TITOKI
ALEE AHEAD LEEWARD
ALEHOUSE PUB TAVERN BARROOM MUGHOUSE POTHOUSE
ALEKO (CHARACTER IN —) ALEKO ARENSKY ZEMFIRA
(COMPOSER OF —) RACHMANINOFF
ALEMBIC LIMBEC LIMBECK CUCURBIT
(PART OF —) HEAD LAMP CUCURBIT RECEIVER
ALERT APT GAY HEP HIP YAL YEP FOXY GLEG KEEN LIVE PERT SNAP TRIG WAKE WARN WARY YALD YEPE ACUTE AGILE ALARM ALIVE AWAKE AWARE BREME BRISK EAGER ERECT LEERY MERRY NIPPY PEART PEERT QUICK READY SHACK SHARP SIREN SLICK SWIFT TIGHT WAKER YAULD ACTIVE ALARUM ARRECT BRIGHT DAPPER LIVELY NIMBLE PROMPT SLIPPY SPRACK SUDDEN TIPTOE TOCSIN WACKER CAREFUL KNOWING WAKEFUL WORKING PREPARED THOUGHTY VIGILANT WAKERIFE WATCHFUL
ALERTNESS NOUS SNAP ANTENNA APTNESS APTITUDE
(MENTAL —) WIT
ALETES (FATHER OF —) HIPPOTES AEGISTHUS
(MOTHER OF —) CLYTEMNESTRA
(SLAYER OF —) ORESTES
ALETTE WING ABUTMENT
ALEUT ATKA ORARIAN UNALASKA
ALEUTIANS (ISLANDS AND ISLAND GROUPS OF —) FOX RAT ADAK ATKA ATTU NEAR KISKA UMNAK KODIAK
(TOWN OF —) UNALASKA
(VOLCANO ON —) SHISHALDIN
ALEWIFE BANG ALLICE ALOOFE BUCKIE ALEWHAP HERRING OLDWIFE POMPANO WALLEYE GRAYBACK GREYBACK SAWBELLY SKIPJACK
ALEXANDER ALEX PARIS SAWNY ELLICK SAWNEY SAWNIE ISKANDER
(BIRTHPLACE OF —) PELLA
(FATHER OF —) SIMON
(HORSE OF —) BUCEPHALUS
ALEXIARES (FATHER OF —) HERCULES
(MOTHER OF —) HEBE
ALFA HALFA ESPARTO
ALFALFA HAY MEDIC FODDER LEGUME LUCERN LUCERNE
ALFILARIA ERODIUM FILAREE FILARIA PINWEED PINGRASS
ALFORJA BAG POUCH WALLET ALFARGA ALFORGE
ALGA NORI ALGAL BROWN FUCUS JELLY SLAKE SLOAK SLOKE DESMID DIATOM FUNORI NOSTOC AMANORI GULAMAN HAITSAI OARWEED SEAWEED ANABAENA FERNLEAF GELIDIUM HAIRWEED ROCKWEED SEABEARD SILKWEED SPOROGEN WHIPCORD ZOOGLOEA
ALGAE
(PREF.) PHYC(O)
(SUFF.) PHYCEAE
ALGARROBA CAROB CALDEN
ALGEBRA LOGISTIC
(KIND OF —) LIE LINEAR BOOLEAN
ALGEBRAIC COSSIC
ALGENIB MIRFAK

ALGERIA

BERBER: KABYLE SHAWIA TUAREG
BERBER DIALECT: ZENATA SENHAJA
CAPITAL: ALGIERS
CAVALRYMAN: SPAHI SPAHEE
DEPARTMENT: ORAN ALGER ALGIERS CONSTANTINE
GRASS: ESPARTO
HILL: TELL
HOLY MAN: MARABOUT
MEASURE: PIK REBIS TARRI TERMIN
MONASTERY: RIBAT
MOUNTAIN: AISSA ATLAS AURES DAHRA TAHAT CHELIA AHAGGAR MOUYDIR DJURJURA
NAME: ALGERIE NUMIDIA
NATIVE: BERBER KABYLE
PIRATE: CORSAIR
RIVER: SHELIF CHELIFF MEDJERDA
RULER: BEY DEY BEVLERBEY
SECT: SUNNITE
SETTLER: COLON PIEDNOIR
SHIP: XEBEC
TERRITORY: AINSEFRA GHARDALA TOUGGOURT
TOWN: BONE ORAN AFLOU ARZEW BATNA BLIDA MEDEA SAIDA SETIF TENES ABADLA ANNABA AUMALE BARIKA BECHAR BEJAIA BENOUD BISKRA BOUGIE DELLYS DJANET DJELFA DZIOUA FRENDA GUELMA SKIKDA BOGHARI MASCARA MILIANA NEGRINE NEMOURS OUARGLA TEBESSA TLEMCEN
WEIGHT: ROTL

ALGERINE COOLOOLY KOOLOOLY
ALGID COLD COOL CHILLY CLAMMY
ALGOLOGY VERATRIN PHYCOLOGY
ALGONKIAN CREE EOZOIC
(— ROCKS) UNKAR
ALIAS AKA ELSE OTHER ANONYM AYLESS ASSUMED EPITHET PSEUDONYM
(UNDER AN —) INCOGNITO
ALIBI PLEA EXCUSE APOLOGY PRETEXT
ALIDADE INDEX DIOPTER
ALIEN ET GER DEED FREMD METIC ALAUNT ALLTUD AUBAIN CONVEY EXOTIC INMATE REMOTE ADVERSE DENIZEN FOREIGN FRAMMIT INVADER OUTLAND STRANGE DETAINEE STRANGER TRANSFER
ALIENATE PART WEAN ALIEN AVERT ANNALY CONVEY DEMISE DEVEST FREEZE FORFEIT SUBVERT AMORTIZE DISUNITE ESTRANGE MORTMAIN SEPARATE STRANGER TRANSFER WITHDRAW
ALIENATION GIFT DISTASTE DISUNION DISUNITY DIVISION DONATION INSANITY
ALIENIST PSYCHOPATH PSYCHIATRIST
ALIGHT DROP LAND LEND REST STOP AVALE LATCH LIGHT LODGE PERCH ROOST STOOP SWOOP ARRIVE SETTLE BURNING DESCEND
ALIGN LINE TRAM TRUE ALINE ARRAY DRESS RANGE ADJUST ARRANGE MARSHAL
(— PAPER) JOG
ALIGNED FAIR COLORED COLLINEAR
ALIGNMENT KELTER KILTER GROUPING ORIENTATION
ALII ARIKI
ALIKE AKIN BOTH LIKE SAME EQUAL INLIKE SQUARE YLICHE EQUALLY SIMILAR UNIFORM
(PREF.) HOM(O) ISO
ALIMENT PAP FOOD FUEL BROMA MANNA VIANDS ALIMONY PABULUM RATIONS
ALIMONY ALIMENT
ALINDA (FATHER OF —) ALPHONSO
ALIPHATIC FATTY ACYCLIC
ALIVE VIF BUSY KEEN SPRY VIVE AGILE ALERT ALIFE ASTIR AWARE BEING BRISK FRESH GREEN QUICK VITAL AROUND EXTANT LIVING SLIPPY ANIMATE VIBRANT ANIMATED EXISTENT SENSIBLE SWARMING
(PREF.) VIVI
ALKALI LYE REH BASE BRAK KALI SALT SODA USAR BRACK CAUSTIC
(PREF.) KALI
ALKALINITY (REDUCED —) ACIDOSIS
ALKALOID BASE ERGOT ESERE ARICIN BRUCIN CEVINE CODEIN CONINE CURINE ESERIN QUINIA QUININ ACONINE ARABINE ARICINE ATROPIA BOGAINE BOLDINE BRUCINE CAFFEIN COCAINE CODEINE CONIINE EMETINE HARMINE HYGRINE JERVINE KAIRINE NARCEIN NEOPINE OUABAIN PTOMAIN QUININE SCOPINE SINAPIN SOLANIN SOPHORA VIOLINE CURARINE CYTISINE PIPERINE MESCALINE QUINIDINE YOHIMBINE PAPAVERINE PILOCARPINE VINBLASTINE VINCRISTINE CAMPTOTHECIN
ALKANE BUTANE PARAFFIN
ALKANET BUGLOSS PUCCOON REDROOT
ALKANNIN ORCANET ANCHUSIN ORCHANET
ALKENE OLEFIN
ALKYD GLYPTAL
ALL A AL ANY SUM EACH FULL TOTE AUGHT EVERY GROSS OMNES OUGHT QUITE TOTAL TOTUM TUTTA TUTTO WHOLE ENTIRE SOLELY WHOLLY PLENARY ENTIRELY EVERYONE TOTALITY
(— BUT ABSOLUTELY) ALMOST
(— IN) ALTOGETHER
(— TOGETHER) COLLECTEDLY
(AND —) ANA
(AT —) AVA ANYWISE ANYTHING ANYWHERE
(OF —) AVA
(PREF.) CUNCTI OMN(I) PAM PAN PANT(A)(O) PASI
ALLANITE CERINE CERITE ORTHITE
ALLAY AID LAY CALM CITE COOL EASE HELP HUSH STAY ABATE AGATE ALLOY CHARM CHECK DELAY QUELL QUIET SALVE SLAKE STILL ADDUCE LESSEN PACIFY QUENCH REDUCE SOFTEN SOLACE SOOTHE STANCH SUBDUE TEMPER APPEASE ASSUAGE COMFORT COMPOSE LIGHTEN MOLLIFY RELIEVE REPRESS STAUNCH MITIGATE PALLIATE

ALLAYED DEFERRED
ALL-CREATING OMNIFIC
ALLEGATION PLEA COUNT VOUCH CHARGE ESSOIN AVERRAL FICTION PROFERT SCANDAL SURMISE AVERMENT SCIENTER PRETENSION
ALLEGE LAY SAY AVER AVOW CITE SHOW URGE ALLAY CLAIM FEIGN INFER LEDGE OFFER PLEAD QUOTE STATE SWEAR TRUMP VOUCH ADDUCE AFFIRM ASSERT ASSIGN CHARGE DEPOSE ESSOIN OBTEND RECITE ADVANCE ASCRIBE DECLARE LIGHTEN PRESENT PROFESS PROPOSE MAINTAIN
ALLEGED SUPPOSED SURMISED
ALLEGIANCE FOY TIE DUTY FAITH HONOR FEALTY HOMAGE LYANCE LOYALTY SERVAGE SERVICE TRIBUTE CIVILITY DEVOTION FIDELITY LIGEANCE
ALLEGORICAL PARABOLIC SYMBOLICAL
ALLEGORICALLY SECRETLY
ALLEGORIZE TALMUDIZE
ALLEGORY MYTH TALE FABLE STORY EMBLEM PARABLE APOLOGUE METAPHOR
ALLELE GENE
ALLELOMORPH GENE
ALLELUIA AEVIA LAUDS
ALL-EMBRACING INFINITE SWEEPING
ALLERGEN INHALANT GOLDENROD
ALLERGY ATOPY IDIOBLAPSIS
ALLEVIATE AID BALM CALM CURE EASE HELP ABATE ALLAY QUIET ALIGHT ALLEGE LENIFY LESSEN PACIFY SOFTEN SOLACE SOOTHE SUCCOR SUPPLE TEMPER ASSUAGE COMPOSE CONSOLE CORRECT LENIATE LIGHTEN MOLLIFY RELEASE RELIEVE DIMINISH MITIGATE MODERATE PALLIATE
ALLEVIATION ALAY SOLACE
ALLEY MIG ROW WAY CHAR LANE LEAD MALL MEWS PASS PATH VENT WALK WENT WIND WYND AISLE ALLEE BLIND BYWAY CHARE ENTRY TEWER WEENT ALLEGE PEEWEE SMOOTH TRANCE VENNEL PASSAGE
(BLIND —) LOKE STOP CLOSE POCKET RUELLE IMPASSE
ALL FOR LOVE **(AUTHOR OF —)** DRYDEN
(CHARACTER IN —) ANTONY OCTAVIA OCTAVIUS CLEOPATRA DOLABELLA VENTIDIUS
ALLHALLOWTIDE HOLLANTIDE
ALLHEAL PANACEA VALERIAN WOUNDWORT
ALL-HOLY PANAGIA PANHAGIA
ALLIANCE AXIS PACT UNION ACCORD FUSION LEAGUE LYANCE TREATY COMPACT ENTENTE SOCIETY AFFINITY AGNATION CACTALES COVENANT DREIBUND FEDERACY FUNGALES LILIALES TRIPLICE CONSOCIATION
(— IN WAR) SYMMACHY
ALLICE SHAD ALEWIFE POMPANO
ALLIED SIB AKIN AGNATE COUSIN JOINED LINKED UNITED COGNATE CONNATE FEDERAL GERMANE KINDRED RELATED SIMILAR RELATIVE
ALLIGATOR GATOR NIGER CAIMAN CAYMAN CROTCH JACARE LIZARD TRAVOY YACARE CRAWLER CREEPER LAGARTO TRAVOIS ALAGARTO LORICATE
(— PEAR) ZABOCA AVOCADO AGUACATE
(— TURTLE) LOGGERHEAD
(MALE —) BULL
ALLIGATORING WEBBING
ALLIGATOR PEAR AVOCADO
ALL-INCLUSIVE WIDE GLOBAL
ALLITERATION RHYME LETTER
ALLITERATIVE LITERAL
ALLIUM LILY ONION GARLIC
ALLNESS OMNEITY OMNITUDE
ALLOCATE DEAL DOLE METE RATE ALLOT AWARD SHARE AFFECT ASSIGN DEVOTE OUTPLACE
ALLOCATION DRAW DESIGNATION
ALLODIAL UDAL
ALLODIUM ESTATE
ALLONGE RIDER
ALLOT FIX SET ARET BILL CAST DEAL DOLE GIVE MARK METE PART RATE SORT ALLOW ARETT AWARD CAVEL GRANT SHARE ACCORD AFFECT ASSIGN BESTOW DEPUTE DESIGN DIRECT INTEND ORDAIN RATION ACCOUNT APPOINT DESTINE PRORATE QUARTER SPECIFY TRIBUTE ALLOCATE PROPORTION
(— QUARTERS) CANTON
ALLOTHEIST PAGAN
ALLOTMENT CUT LOT DOLE CAVEL SHARE RATION SIZING LOTMENT LOTTERY PORTION DIVISION PITTANCE
ALL-OUT DEAD
ALLOW LET LOW BEAR GIVE HAVE LEND LOAN ADMIT DEFER GRANT LEAVE STAND THOLE YIELD ACCEPT ACCORD ASSIGN BESTOW BETEEM ENABLE ENDURE PERMIT SUFFER APPROVE CONCEDE CONFESS LICENCE LICENSE SUFFICE SUPPOSE SUSTAIN CONSIDER DISPENSE SANCTION TOLERATE
(— UNWILLINGLY) GRUDGE
ALLOWABLE FREE LICIT LAWFUL PERMISSIBLE
ALLOWANCE BOT FEE ICE AGIO BOTE DOLE EASE EDGE GIFT HIRE ODDS RATE SALT SIZE ARRAS BATTA CLOFF GRANT LEAVE RATIO SHARE STENT STINT BOUCHE BOUNTY CORODY FODDER MARGIN RATING REGAIN SALARY SEQUEL TANTUM ALIMENT ALIMONY CORRODY DIETARY DIOBELY LEAKAGE LOWANCE PENSION PORTION PREBEND SCALAGE STIPEND TEARAGE APPENAGE APPROVAL BREAKAGE DISCOUNT DRAFTAGE ORDINARY QUANTITY SANCTION SOLATIUM VIATICUM
(— FOR EXPENSES) DIET
(— FOR MAINTENANCE) ALIMENT
(— FOR THICKNESS) BOXING
(— FOR WASTE) TARE TRET
(— FOR WEIGHT) BUG TARE DRAFT DRAUGHT
(— OF ARROWS) SHEAF
(— OF FOOD) DIET BOUCHE DIETARY
(— OF TIME OR DISTANCE) LAW
(— TO WORKER'S) MAGS MAGGS
(CLOTHING —) INLAY
(CORRECTIVE —) SALT
(EXTRA —) BUCKSHEE
(NEGATIVE —) INTERFERENCE
(SERVANT'S —) LIVERY
ALLOWED VENIAL LICENTIATE
(NOT —) ILLICIT FORBIDDEN
ALLOWING THOUGH
ALLOY LAY LOY MIX AICH ASEM ALPAX BIDRI BIDRY BRASS CALIN DURAL FLINT INVAR MOKUM MONEL TERNE ALBATA ALNICO ALUMEL BIDREE BILLON BRONZE CERMET GARBLE ILLIUM LATTEN LEAVEN NEOGEN NIELLO OCCAMY OREIDE OROIDE PEWTER SOLDER TAMBAC TOMBAC TOMBAK ACIERAL ALCHEMY AMALGAM BABBITT BIDDERY ELINVAR INCONEL MIXTURE NITINOL PAKTONG PERLITE RHEOTAN RHODITE SEMILOR SIMILOR TAENITE TUTANIA TUTENAG ALFENIDE ARGENTON ARSEDINE AWARUITE CALAMINE CARACOLI CARACOLY DORALIUM ELECTRUM EUTECTIC GUNMETAL HARDENER KAMACITE METALINE NICHROME ORICHALC ROMANIUM STELLITE ZIRCALOY PINCHBECK PORPORINO
ALL-PERVADING UNIVERSAL
ALL-PURPOSE VERSATILE
ALL QUIET ON WESTERN FRONT
(AUTHOR OF —) REMARQUE
(CHARACTER IN —) PAUL KROPP ALBERT BAUMER MULLER TJADENS KEMMERICH STANILAUS KATCYINSKY
ALL RIGHT OK YES OKAY AGREED OKEYDOKE
ALL-ROUND OVERALL OVERHEAD
ALLSEED FLAXSEED BURSTWORT
ALL SOULS' DAY SOULMASS
ALLSPICE BUBBY PIMENTO
ALL'S WELL THAT ENDS WELL
(AUTHOR OF —) SHAKESPEARE
(CHARACTER IN —) DIANA LAFEU HELENA BERTRAM LAVACHE MARIANA PAROLLES VIOLENTA
ALLTHORN JUNCO
ALLUDE HINT IMPLY POINT REFER ADVERT GLANCE RELATE CONNOTE MENTION SUGGEST INDICATE INTIMATE
ALLURE IT AIR COY WIN WOO BAIT DRAW LEAD LURE MOVE SWAY WILE ANGLE BRIBE CHARM COURT DECOY SNARE TEMPT ALLECT ENTICE ENTRAP ILLURE INDUCE INVITE SEDUCE ATTRACT BEGUILE ENSNARE BLANDISH INESCATE INVEIGLE PERSUADE SIRENING
ALLUREMENT BAIT CORD LURE SNARE ALLURE GLAMOR GUDGEON AGACERIE SOLICITATION
ALLURING GREEN TAKING AGACANT SIRENIC SUGARED TAKEFUL CATCHING CHARMING ENTICING FETCHING TEMPTING
ALLUSION HINT TWIT TOUCH GLANCE REFLEX INKLING MENTION INNUENDO INSTANCE REFERENCE
ALLUSIVE CANTING
ALLUVIUM WASH
ALLY PAL AIDE JOIN RANGE UNION UNITE BACKER COHORT COXCOX FRIEND HELPER LEAGUE ALLIANT CONNECT PARTNER ADHERENT CONFEDER FEDERATE
(PL.) FOEDERATI
ALMANAC ORDO PADDY CALENDAR
ALMANDINE GARNET CARBUNCLE
ALMEMAR BEMA BIMA BIMAH
ALMIGHTY GOD GREAT MAKER CREATOR EXTREME JEHOVAH INFINITE POWERFUL PUISSANT OMNIPOTENT
ALMOND DOE PILI BADAM CHUFA JORDAN KAMANI KANARI AMYGDAL BISCUIT TALISAY ALMANDER ALMENDRO AMYGDALA ROSACEAN VALENCIA
(— BROWN) WOOD
(— SHAPED OBJECT) MANDORLA
(PREF.) AMYGDAL(O) MANDEL(O)
ALMONRY AMBRY
ALMOST JUST LIKE MOST MUCH NEAR NIGH ABOUT ANEAR CLOSE AMAIST FECKLY MOSTLY NEARLY NIGHLY MUCHWHAT WELLMOST WELLNEAR WELLNIGH PRACTICALLY
(PREF.) PARA PEN(E)
ALMS DOLE GIFT ALMOIN AUMOUS AWMOUS BOUNTY CORBAN MAUNDY RELIEF ALMOIGN CHARITY HANDOUT PASSADE DEVOTION DONATION GRATUITY OFFERING PITTANCE BENEFACTION
(GIVER OF —) ALMONER
ALMSHOUSE POORHOUSE WORKHOUSE
ALMSMAN BLUECOAT
ALMUCE HOOD AMICE VAGAS TIPPET VAKASS VARKAS
ALODIUM ODAL ODEL ODHAL ESTATE PROPERTY
ALOE PITA AGAVE
(— EXTRACT) ORCIN ORCINAL
ALOEUS **(FATHER OF —)** NEPTUNE POSEIDON
(MOTHER OF —) CANACE
(SON OF —) OTUS EPHIALTES
(WIFE OF —) IPHIMEDIA
ALOFT UP HIGH ABOVE AHIGH UPWARD AHEIGHT SKYWARD OVERHEAD
(PREF.) HYPS(I)(O)
ALONE ALL ONE BARE LANE LORN ONLY SOLE SOLO ALOOF APART

SOLUS SIMPLY SINGLE SOLEIN SOLELY SULLEN UNIQUE ALONELY FORLORN UNAIDED DESOLATE DETACHED ISOLATED SEPARATE SOLITARY
(ALL —) LEELANE LEELONE
(PREF.) MANI MON(O) SOLI
(SUFF.) MONAS
ALONG ON UP VIA AWAY LANG WITH YOND AHEAD LONGS BESIDE FORBYE FOREBY ONWARD ALONGST ENDLONG FORWARD PARALLEL TOGETHER
(— THE MARGIN) DOWN
(— WITH) AND
(WELL —) ENDWAYS ENDWISE
(PREF.) **(— WITH)** SYM
ALONGSIDE AT BY ASIDE CLOSE ABOARD BESIDE ABREAST FORNENT SIDLINS FORNENST PARALLEL
(PREF.) PAR(A)
ALONSOA MASKFLOWER
ALOOF DRY ICY SHY COLD COOL ABACK ALONE APART PROUD ABEIGH FROSTY OTIOSE REMOTE SILENT SKEIGH DISTANT REMOVED STUCKUP RESERVED
ALOPECIA PELADE ATRICHIA BALDNESS
ALOPECIC BALD
ALOPECURUS FOXTAIL
ALOT SLEW
ALOUD OUT
ALPACA PACO
ALPENGLOW AFTERGLOW
ALPENSTOCK STOCK BERGSTOCK
ALPHABET ABC ABCEE ABSEY CUFIC KUFIC LATIN ONMUN ORDER BISAYA BRAHMI CIPHER GLAGOL HANGUL HANKUL KAITHI NAGARI PRIMER ROMAJI SARADA SCRIPT TAGALA VISAYA ALJAMIA FUTHARK KALEKAH LETTERS PESHITO ALJAMIAH CROSSROW GUJARATI GURMUKHI
(— SQUARE) TABLEAU
(ARABIC —) BA FA HA RA TA YA ZA AYN DAD DAL JIM KAF KHA LAM MIM NUN QAF SAD SIN THA WAW ZAY ALIF DHAL SHIN GHAYN
(CELTIC —) OGAM OGHAM
(GREEK —) MU NU PI XI CHI ETA PHI PSI RHO TAU BETA IOTA ZETA ALPHA DELTA GAMMA KAPPA OMEGA SIGMA THETA LAMBDA EPSILON OMICRON UPSILON
(HEBREW —) HE PE MEM NUN SIN TAW VAV WAW AYIN BETH HETH KAPH QOPH RESH SHIN TETH YODH ALEPH GIMEL SADHE ZAYIN DALETH LAMEDH SAMEKH
(OLD IRISH —) OGAM OGHAM
ALPHAEUS (SON OF —) JAMES MATTHEW
ALPHESIBOEA (FATHER OF —) BIAS PHEGEUS
(HUSBAND OF —) ALCMAEON
(SON OF —) ADONIS
ALPS (LAKE IN —) ZUG COMO ISEO THUN GARDA BRIENZ GENEVA ZURICH LUCERNE MAGGIORE CONSTANCE
(PASS IN —) SPLUGA ARLBERG BRENNER SIMPLON SPLUGEN SEMPIONE
(PEAK IN —) ROSA VISO BLANC LEONE TRIGLAV VOLJNAC EISENHUT PARADISO HOCHSTUHL MARMOLADA MONTBLANC KELLERWAND SACCARELLO
(VALLEY IN —) ZERMATT CHAMONIX ENGADINE INTERLAKEN GRINDELWALD LAUTERBRUNNEN
ALREADY EEN NOW DONE EVEN SINCE BEFORE
ALSACE-LORRAINE REICHSLAND
ALSINE ALLBONE
ALSO SO ALS AND EKE TOO YET ERST ITEM MORE PLUS ALONG DITTO BESIDES FURTHER THERETO LIKEWISE MOREOVER
(— KNOWN AS) AKA
ALSO-RAN SLOWPOKE BACKMARKER
ALTAMONT (WIFE OF —) CALISTA
ALTAR ARA BEMA BOMOS TABLE WEVED ACERRA AUTERE HAIKAL SHRINE TRIPOD VEDIKA CHANCEL CHANTRY ESCHARA SCROBIS THYMELE OMPHALOS REPOSOIR REPOSITORY
(— BACK) TABLE
(— TOP) MENSA
ALTARPIECE ANCONA DIPTYCH TRIPTYCH
ALTAZIMUTH ABA
ALTER COOK DRAW EDIT GELD MOVE RASE TURN VARY VEER WEND ADAPT AMEND BREAK ELIDE EMEND FORGE RESET SHAPE SHIFT ADJUST BUSHEL CENSOR CHANGE DEFORM IMMUTE JIGGER MODIFY MUTATE NEUTER REVISE TEMPER UNSAME CHAFFER COMMUTE CONVERT CORRECT CORRUPT DISTORT FASHION QUALIFY RECYCLE STRANGE ACTIVATE EXCHANGE REJIGGER
(— APPEARANCE) WRY
(— BOUNDARIES) DEACON
(— BRANDS) DUFF
(— DIRECTION) BREAK
(— FRAUDULENTLY) FIDDLE
(— STANCE) CLOSE
ALTERATION DOWN CROSS ACTION CHANGE JANGLE DISEASE HEMIOLA MUTATION UPHEAVAL
(— OF BOUNDARY) ERUB ERUV
ALTERATIVE LAPPA FUMARIA
ALTERCATE JANGLE STICKLE WRANGLE
ALTERCATION SPAT TIFF TILT BRAWL BROIL CRASH CROSS FIGHT BARNEY BICKER FRACAS JANGLE STRIFE BRABBLE CONTEST DISPUTE PASSAGE QUARREL WRANGLE SQUABBLE
ALTERED BURNT BROKEN VARIED ANOTHER FEIGNED ADJUSTED
(— BY AGE) STALE
(PREF.) EPH EPI META
ALTERNATE ELSE SWAY VARY OTHER RECUR SHIFT ALTERN CHANGE RINGER ROTATE SECOND SEESAW SPIRAL EXCHANGE INTERMIT TRAVERSE
(— LEAPS AND DIVES) GREYHOUND
(— PLAYERS) PLATOON
(PREF.) CO COUNTER
ALTERNATELY ABOUT RECIPROCALLY
ALTERNATION ADDITION
(— OF GENERATIONS) METAGENESIS
ALTERNATIVE OR FORK HORN BACKUP CHOICE EITHER OPTION DISJUNCT ELECTION
(PREF.) ALLELO
ALTERNATIVES (SEE PARTNERS) DODIE INOUT ONOFF HITMISS WINLOSE FISHFOWL HIDEHAIR ONEOTHER SINKSWIM WHITERYE FACTFANCY HERETHERE WHEREWHEN ALLNOTHING TRICKTREAT
ALTERNATOR MAGNETO
ALTHAEA MALLOW
(FATHER OF —) THESTIUS
(HUSBAND OF —) OENEUS
(SON OF —) MELEAGER
ALTHAEMENES (FATHER OF —) CATREUS
(SISTER OF —) AEROPE CLYMENE APEMOSYNE
ALTHORN SAX ALTO ALTUS SAXHORN
ALTHOUGH ALL EEN SET ALBE ALIF EVEN THAT WHEN WHILE ALBEIT THOUGH WHENAS DESPITE HOWBEIT WHEREAS
ALTITUDE APEX PEAK HIGHT LEVEL PITCH HEIGHT STATURE
(SUN'S GREATEST —) APOGEE
ALTO MEAN ALTUS ALTHORN SAXHORN
ALTOGETHER ALL NUDE QUITE SHEER STICK AGREAT ALGATE BODILY FREELY WHOLLY EXACTLY TOTALLY UTTERLY ALLTHING ENTIRELY
ALTRUISM OTHERISM
ALTRUISTIC HEROIC HEROICAL
ALUDEL POT LUDEL UDELL
ALULA LOBE WING ALULET SQUAMA TEGULA LOBULUS WINGLET CALYPTER
ALULIM ALOROS
ALUM AUM ALME GRAD ALUMEN MIGITE TSCHER STYPTIC HARDENER KALINITE
(FEATHER —) ALUNOGEN
ALUMINA ARGIL ALOXITE
ALUMNUS GRAD PUPIL GRADUATE
ALUMROOT HEUCHERA
ALUR LUR LURI
ALVAN (FATHER OF —) SHOBAL
ALVEARY HIVE BEEHIVE
ALVELOZ SAP
ALVEOLA FAVEOLUS
ALVEOLAR SPUMOID GINGIVAL
ALVEOLATE FAVOSE FAVOUS PITTED
ALWAYS O AY AYE EEN EER EVER SIMLE STILL ALWISE SEMPRE ALGATES FOREVER EVERMORE
ALYSSUM ALISON MADWORT
ALZIRA (CHARACTER IN —) ALZIRA GUSMAN ZAMORO
(COMPOSER OF —) VERDI
AM M AME HAM
(— NOT) NAM AINT AMNT
(I —) CHAM CHYM
AMA CUP AMULA CRUET DIVER VESSEL CHALICE
AMABILE GENTLE TENDER
AMACRATIC AMASTHENIC
AMADAVAT WAXBILL TIGERBIRD
AMADIS (COMPOSER OF —) LULLY
AMADOU PUNK TINDER
AMAH NURSE SERVANT
AMAHL AND THE NIGHT VISITORS (COMPOSER OF —) MENOTTI
AMAIN GREATLY FORCIBLY
AMAL (FATHER OF —) HELEM
AMALA AMLAH
AMALASONTHA (FATHER OF —) THEODORIC
AMALEK (FATHER OF —) ELIPHAZ
(MOTHER OF —) TIMNAH
AMALGAM ALLOY MAGNESIA ARQUERITE
AMALGAMATE MIX FUSE JOIN ALLOY BLEND MARRY MERGE UNITE BLUNGE MINGLE COMBINE COALESCE COMPOUND
AMALGAMATION MERGER ADDITION
AMALGAMATOR PLATEMAN
AMANORI NORI LAVER
AMANUENSIS PENMAN SCRIBE TYPIST RECORDER
AMARANTA (HUSBAND OF —) BARTOLUS
AMARANTH JATACO PIGWEED FLORAMOR
(PL.) LIGHTHOUSES
AMARETTO LIQUEUR MACAROON
AMARIAH (FATHER OF —) BANI MERAIOTH
(SON OF —) AHITUB
AMARILLO FUSTIC
AMARYLLIS LILY AGAVE CRINUM SNOWFLAKE
AMASA (FATHER OF —) ITHRA HADLAI JETHER
(MOTHER OF —) ABIGAIL
AMASAI (SON OF —) MAHATH
AMASHAI (FATHER OF —) AZAREEL
AMASIAH (FATHER OF —) ZICHRI
AMASS HEAP HILL MASS PILE SAVE GROSS HOARD STACK STORE GATHER COLLECT COMPILE CONGEST ENGROSS ASSEMBLE OVERHEAP ACCUMULATE
AMASSMENT HEAP
AMATA (DAUGHTER OF —) LAVINIA
(HUSBAND OF —) LATINUS
AMATEUR HAM LAY TIRO TYRO NOVICE SUNDAY VOTARY ADMIRER DABBLER DEVOTEE FANCIER JACKLEG PATRIOT VARMENT VARMINT BEGINNER
(GOLF —) DUFFER
AMATEURISH BUSH TYRONIC
AMATORY EROTIC LOVING TENDER AMOROUS GALLANT ANACREONTIC

AMAZE AWE WOW MAZE STAM STUN ALARM FERLY FLOOR ASTONY AWHAPE WONDER ASTOUND CONFUSE IMPRESS PERPLEX STAGGER STUPEFY ASTONISH BEWILDER CONFOUND DUMFOUND FRIGHTEN SURPRISE
AMAZED AGAPE INAWE AGAZED BUSHED ASTONIED
AMAZEMENT STAM AMAZE FERLY GHAST FERLIE FRENZY WONDER MADNESS SURPRISE CONSTERNATION
(INTERJECTION TO EXPRESS —) YIKES
AMAZIAH (FATHER OF —) JOASH
AMAZON VIRAGO
AMBARI KANAF KENAF KANAFF
AMBASSADOR AGENT ELCHI ENVOY VAKIL DEPUTY ELCHEE LEDGER LEGATE NUNCIO VAKEEL EMBASSY LEAGUER CAPUCIUS DIPLOMAT MINISTER
AMBASSADORIAL FECIAL FETIAL
AMBASSADORS (AUTHOR OF —) JAMES
(CHARACTER IN —) JIM MAMIE MARIA SARAH JEANNE POCOCK GOSTREY LAMBERT NEWSOME CHADWICK STRETHER WAYMARSH
AMBER GRIS LIME AWMER RESIN FUSTIC LAMMER SUCCIN YELLOW BURMITE AMBEROID ELECTRUM SUNSTONE
(PREF.) ELECTRO SUCCIN(I)(O)
AMBERFISH JUREL CARANX KAHALA RUNNER CARANGID CARANGIN KINGFISH MACKEREL MEDREGAL
AMBERGRIS AMBER AMBRACAN
AMBERINA (KIND OF —) PLATED
AMBERJACK ALMICORE CORONADO
AMBIENCE MILIEU AMBIANCE
AMBIGUITY AMBAGE PARADOX
AMBIGUOUS DARK VAGUE DOUBLE FORKED LOUCHE CRYPTIC DUBIOUS DOUBTFUL SLIPPERY SPURIOUS
(NOT —) EXPRESS
AMBIT LIMIT SCOPE SPACE BOUNDS EXTENT SPHERE CIRCUIT COMPASS BOUNDARY PRECINCT
AMBITION ATE GOAL HOPE WISH GLORY DESIRE PURPOSE PRETENSION
AMBITIONLESS DRIFTING
AMBITIOUS AVID BOLD HIGH KEEN EAGER ETTLE SHOWY EMULOUS ASPIRANT ASPIRING
AMBITUS TENOR
AMBIVALENCE BIPOLARITY
AMBIVALENT EQUIVOCAL
AMBLE FOOL GAIT MOOCH PADNAG MEANDER SAUNTER TRIPPLE
AMBLING TOLUTATION
AMBLYOPIA SNOWBLINDNESS
AMBO DESK PULPIT
AMBOCEPTOR COPULA MEDIATOR
AMBOYNA LINGOA KIABOOCA
AMBROSIA AMRITA AMBROSE HONEYDEW KINGWEED
AMBROSIAL DIVINE FRAGRANT
AMBRY SAFE CHEST NICHE AUMRIE CLOSET PANTRY RECESS ALMONRY ARMOIRE ARMARIUM CUPBOARD
AMBULANCE PANNIER AUXILIUM BRANCARD
(— ATTENDANT) EMT
AMBULATE GAD HIKE MOVE WALK
AMBULATORY ALURE GALLERY PORTICO CLOISTER PERAMBLE
AMBUSCADE WATCH WAYLAY BUSHMENT
AMBUSH NAB LURE LURK TRAP WAIT AWAIT BLIND BUSSE CATCH COVER LURCH SHOMA SNARE STALE TRAIN WATCH INBUSH THREAT WAYLAY FORELAY SCUPPER DISGUISE ENBUSSHE AMBUSCADE
(SUFF.) **(ONE IN —)** DOLOPS
AMCHOOR AMHAR
AMELIA (AUTHOR OF —) FIELDING
(CHARACTER IN —) BOOTH JAMES TRENT AMELIA HARRIS ATKINSON HARRISON MATTHEWS ELIZABETH
AMELIORATE EASE HELP MEND AMEND EMEND BETTER REFORM IMPROVE PROMOTE
AMEN YEA TRULY ASSENT SOBEIT VERILY APPROVAL SANCTION
AMENABLE GAME OPEN LIABLE PLIANT SUBJECT OBEDIENT MALLEABLE
AMEND END BEET HEAL MEND ALTER ATONE BEETE EMEND REDUB BETTER CHANGE DOCTOR REFORM REMEDY REPAIR REPEAL REVISE CONVERT CORRECT ENLARGE IMPROVE RECOVER RECTIFY REDRESS RESTORE CHASTISE
AMENDING COMPENSATION
AMENDMENT RIDER AMENDS REFORM SLEEPER
AMENDS BOOT MEND ASSETH ASSYTH REWARD APOLOGY REDRESS
AMENITY JOY COMITY FEATURE SUAVITY CIVILITY COURTESY MILDNESS
(PL.) AGREMENS FROUFROU NICETIES
AMENT JUL CHAT IDIOT IULUS MORON CATKIN CACHRYS CATTAIL GOSLING IMBECILE NUCAMENT
AMERCE FINE MERCE MULCT TREAT AFFEER PUNISH SCONCE CONDEMN FORFEIT
AMERCEMENT MULCT UNLAW BLOODWIT
AMERICA INDIA
AMERICAN YANK GRINGO YANKEE YANQUI AMERICA WESTERN JONATHAN COLUMBIAN
(— OF EUROPEAN STOCK) WASP
(— OF MEXICAN DESCENT) CHICANA CHICANO
(AUTHOR OF —) JAMES
(CHARACTER IN —) BREAD CINTRE CLAIRE NEWMAN NIOCHE TRISTRAM VALENTIN BELLEGARDE CHRISTOPHER
AMERICAN GRAY JAKO
AMERICANISM HECKERISM
AMERICAN TRAGEDY (AUTHOR OF —) DREISER
(CHARACTER IN —) ALDEN CLYDE SAMUEL SONDRA ROBERTA FINCHLEY GRIFFITHS
AMESTRIS (FATHER OF —) OTANES ONOPHAS
(WIFE OF —) XERXES
AMETHYST ONEGITE CORUNDUM
AMIABILITY DOUCEUR
AMIABLE GOOD KIND WARM SWEET CLEVER GENIAL GENTLE LOVING MELLOW SMOOTH TENDER AFFABLE LOVABLE WINSOME CHARMING ENGAGING FRIENDLY OBLIGING PLEASING
AMICABLE KIND FRIENDLY NEIGHBORLY
AMICE AMIT AMYS CAPE COWL HOOD EPHOD ALMUCE DOMINO TIPPET VAKASS AMICTUS VESTMENT
AMID IN OMEL AMELL AMONG AMIDST DURING IMELLE AMONGST BETWEEN
AMIDAS (BROTHER OF —) BRACIDAS
AMIDE LACTAM SULTAM ANILIDE ARYLIDE PEPTIDE
AMIDST AMONG AMONGST
AMILDAR AUMIL
AMIN IDI
AMINE ANILIN ANILINE PSILOCIN
AMINO ALANINE
AMINO-ACID LYSINE
AMISS ILL MIS AWRY BIAS AGATE AGLEY ASKEW WONKY WRONG ACROSS AGRIEF ASTRAY FAULTY MISTAKE IMPROPER
(PREF.) MIS PAR(A)
AMITRIPTYLINE ELAVIL
AMITTAI (SON OF —) JONAH
AMITY PEACE ACCORD CONCORD HARMONY
AMMA ABBESS MOTHER
AMMIEL (DAUGHTER OF —) BATHSHEBA
(FATHER OF —) OBEDEDOM
(SON OF —) MACHIR
AMMIHUD (SON OF —) TALMAI PEDAHEL SHEMUEL ELISHAMA
AMMINADAB (FATHER OF —) RAM ARAM KOHATH UZZIEL
(SON OF —) NAASSON
AMMISHADDAI (SON OF —) AHIEZER
AMMIZABAD (FATHER OF —) BENAIAH
AMMO BBS
(— FOR TOY GUN) CAP CAPS
AMMONIA HARTSHORN
AMMONIAC OSHAC
AMMONITE POLYPOD AMMONOID BACULITE CACULOID CERATITE SALIGRAM
AMMONIUM CARBONATE HARTSHORN
AMMOPHILA STAR STARR
AMMUNITION AMMO AMMU ARMS SHOT BOMBS FODDER POWDER SHELLS BULLETS BUCKSHOT GRENADES MATERIAL MATERIEL ORDNANCE SHRAPNEL
AMNESIA LAPSE FORGETFULNESS
AMNESTY COWLE PARDON OBLIVION
AMNION SAC CAUL SEROSA INDUSIUM MEMBRANE
AMNON (FATHER OF —) DAVID
(HALF-SISTER OF —) TAMAR
AMOBARBITAL AMYTAL
AMOEBA AMEBA AMEBULA PROTEUS AMOEBULA RHIZOPOD
AMOK MAD AMUCK CRAZY CRAZED VIOLENT FRENZIED
(RUNNING —) ARIOT
AMOLE EMOL AMOULI AMOLILLA MANFREDA
AMON (FATHER OF —) MANASSEH
(SON OF —) JOSIAH
AMONG IN MID AMID INTO MANG MONG OMEL WITH AMANG AMELL MIDST AMIDST BIMONG IMELLE WITHIN BETWEEN
(— OTHER THINGS) IA
(PREF.) EPH EPI INTER
AMOR EROS LOVE CUPID AMOROSO
AMORAL NEUTRAL NONMORAL
AMORET (HUSBAND OF —) SCUDAMORE
(SISTER OF —) BELPHOEBE
AMORINO CUPID
AMORITE CANAANITE
AMOROUS FOND GAMY SOFT WARM CADGY JOLLY MUSHY NUTTY ARDENT COQUET EROTIC LOVELY LOVING SPOONY TENDER WANTON AMATIVE AMATORY AMIABLE FERVENT GALLANT JEALOUS SMICKER LOVESOME VENEREAN
AMOROUSLY SMICKLY
AMORPHOUS VAGUE ATELENE HYALINE DEFORMED FORMLESS INCHOATE RESINOUS
AMORT ALAMORT DEJECTED LIFELESS
AMORTIZE DESTROY MORTISE ALIENATE
AMOUNT GO GOB LOT SUM SUP TOT ANTE BODY COME DOSE DRAW FECK KIND LEVY MESS REAM RISE SOUD SOWD TALE UNIT WARE ADDUP CHUNK COUNT GROSS MOUNT PRICE REACH STACK STORE STUFF TOTAL WHOLE BUDGET DEGREE DOLLOP DOSAGE EFFECT EXTENT FIGURE MATTER NUMBER SUPPLY ADVANCE FOOTING QUANTUM SCRUPLE SIGNIFY SLATHER TODDICK INCREASE QUANTITY SPOONFUL SURMOUNT VALLIDOM
(— BORNE BY BEAST) SEAM
(— CARRIED AT ONE TIME) GANG
(— DUE) BILL SCORE
(— HELD) CAPACITY
(— LEFT IN VESSEL) ULLAGE
(— OF BASS) BOOMINESS
(— OF CONCRETE) LIFT
(— OF DYE) STRIKE
(— OF FLOW) STRENGTH
(— OF FREIGHT) CARLOAD
(— OF GAS) BREATH
(— OF HERRINGS) CRANNAGE

(— OF LEAKAGE) SLIP
(— OF LIQUOR) SLUG
(— OF MEDICINE) DOSAGE
(— OF MONEY) BEAN BOND CASH SCOT
(— OF OIL) ALLOWABLE
(— OF PAYMENT) FOOTAGE
(— OF POWDER) INCREMENT
(— OF SOIL) INTHROW
(— OF WATER) CATCHMENT
(— OF WORK) ASSIGNMENT
(— OWED) LIABILITY OBLIGATION
(— PAID) COST
(— PROVIDED) SUPPLY
(— TURNED BY SPADE) GRAFT
(APPRECIABLE —) BEANS
(COMPLETE —) FULL
(CONSIDERABLE —) MIGHT HANTLE HATFUL
(EXACT —) NICK
(EXTRA —) BONUS
(GREAT —) MICKLE INFINITY MOUNTAIN
(GREATEST —) MAXIMUM
(GROSS —) SLUMP
(INADEQUATE —) DEFICIENCY
(INDEFINITE —) BAIT SNAG SOME
(INFINITESIMAL —) IOTA
(INSIGNIFICANT —) SCRAT PEANUTS PEPPERCORN
(LARGE —) GOB LOB JUNT LUMP MINT RAFT SNAG SWAG SIEGE SLASH SPATE BOODLE SOMDEL BONANZA SOMDIEL CARTLOAD MUCHNESS SOMEDEAL
(LAVISH —) SLATHER
(LEAST —) DIDDLY
(LEAST POSSIBLE —) GRAIN AMBSACE
(LIMITED —) SPRINKLING
(MEDICINAL —) DOSAGE
(MINUTE —) HAIR FLEABITE
(RENT —) GALE
(SIZABLE —) CHUNK SMART
(SLIGHT —) ADDED SNACK TILLY TINGE
(SLIGHTEST —) BEANS
(SMALL —) ACE BIT DAB TAD DITE DOIT DRAB DRAM DRIB FLOW HAET HINT HOOT INCH LICK MITE SNAP SONG SPOT SKOSH SPECK SPURT TRACE DRAPPY PICKLE SMIDGE TICKET CAPSULE DRAPPIE GLIMMER KENNING SMIDGEN SMIDGIN THOUGHT
(SMALLEST —) JOT STIVER MINIMUM STEEVER STUIVER
(SMALLEST —S) MINIMA
(TENFOLD —) DECUPLE
(USUAL —) GRIST
(WHOLE —) ALL SUBSTANCE
(YEARLY —) ANNUITY
(SUFF.) ANCE ANT ENCE
AMOUR DRURY DRUERY AMOURET INTRIGUE PARAMOUR
AMOZ (SON OF —) ISAIAH
AMPERSAND AND ALSO PLUS AMPASSY IPSEAND
AMPHETAMINE SPEED UPPER BENZEDRINE
AMPHIALUS (MOTHER OF —) CECROPIA
AMPHIARAUS (DAUGHTER OF —) EURYDICE DEMONASSA
(FATHER OF —) OICLES
(MOTHER OF —) HYPERMNESTRA
(SON OF —) ALCMAEON AMPHILOCHUS
(WIFE OF —) ERIPHYLE
AMPHIBIA BATRACHIA
AMPHIBIAN EFT OLM FROG HYLA NEWT RANA TOAD ANURA SIREN SNAKE AMPHIB AXOLOTL CAUDATE ERYOPID PROTEUS TADPOLE AISTOPOD SALAMANDER
AMPHIBOLE EDENITE ORALITE URALITE ASBESTOS CROSSITE TREMOLITE SMARAGDITE
AMPHICARPA FALCATA
AMPHICTYON (FATHER OF —) DEUCALION
(MOTHER OF —) PYRRHA
AMPHIGASTRIUM UNDERLEAF
AMPHIGORIC INANE
AMPHILOCHUS (FATHER OF —) AMPHIARAUS
(MOTHER OF —) ERIPHYLE
AMPHION (BROTHER OF —) ZETHUS
(FATHER OF —) ZEUS IASUS JUPITER
(MOTHER OF —) ANTIOPE
(WIFE OF —) NIOBE
AMPHIOXUS LANCELET
AMPHIPOD SHRIMP
AMPHISSA (FATHER OF —) ECHETUS MACAREUS
(MOTHER OF —) CANACHE
AMPHISSUS (FATHER OF —) APOLLO
(MOTHER OF —) DRYOPE
AMPHITHEA (DAUGHTER OF —) ANTICLEA
(HUSBAND OF —) AUTOLYCUS
AMPHITHEATER BOWL OVAL ARENA CAVEA CIRCUS CIRQUE STADIUM THEATER
AMPHITRITE (FATHER OF —) NEREUS OCEANUS
(HUSBAND OF —) NEPTUNE POSEIDON
(MOTHER OF —) TETHYS
(SON OF —) TRITON
AMPHITRYON (AUTHOR OF —) PLAUTUS
(CHARACTER IN —) SOSIA ALCMENA JUPITER MERCURY AMPHITRYON
(DOG OF —) LAELAPS
(FATHER OF —) ALCAEUS
(MOTHER OF —) HIPPONOME
(WIFE OF —) ALCMENE
AMPHORA JUG URN VASE CADUS DIOTA PELIKE
AMPHOTERUS (BROTHER OF —) ACARNAN
(FATHER OF —) ALCMAEON
(MOTHER OF —) CALLIRRHOE
AMPLE BIG FAIR FULL GOOD MUCH RICH SIDE WIDE BROAD GREAT LARGE LUCKY PLUMP ROOMY ROUND SONSY WALLY ENOUGH HEARTY PLENTY PROLIX COPIOUS LIBERAL OPULENT WEALTHY ABUNDANT ADEQUATE BARONIAL GENEROUS HANDSOME SPACIOUS PLENTIFUL
AMPLIFICATION GAIN
AMPLIFIED EXTENDED
AMPLIFIER BOOSTER REPEATER
AMPLIFY PAD FARCE FARSE SWELL WIDEN DILATE EXPAND EXTEND STRESS AUGMENT ENLARGE STRETCH AMPLIATE HEIGHTEN INCREASE LENGTHEN MULTIPLY
AMPLITUDE BULK BREADTH LATITUDE OPULENCE
AMPLY LARGE
AMPUTATE CUT LOP PRUNE SEVER CURTAIL
AMPUTATION APOCOPE ABLATION
AMPYCUS (FATHER OF —) PELIAS
(MOTHER OF —) CHLORIS
(SON OF —) MOPSUS
AMRAM (FATHER OF —) BANI DISHON
(SON OF —) MOSES
AMRITA RASA
AMULA AMA VESSEL
AMULET GEM MET ANKH HAND JUJU MOJO PLUM CHARM IMAGE MENAT SAFFI SAFIE TOKEN FETISH GRIGRI MASCOT SAPHIE SCROLL TABLET ABRAXAS AMALETT ICHTHUS ICHTHYS PERIAPT CHURINGA GREEGREE HAGSTONE LIGATURE ORNAMENT TALISMAN PHYLACTERY
AMULIUS (BROTHER OF —) NUMITOR
(FATHER OF —) PROCAS
(NEPHEW OF —) LAUSUS
AMURRU MARTU
AMUSE GAME LAKE ENJOY MIRTH SHORT SPORT ABSORB DELUDE DIVERT ENGAGE FROLIC PLEASE POPJOY SOLACE TICKLE BEGUILE DISPORT GRATIFY PASTIME BEWILDER DISTRACT RECREATE
(— IMMENSELY) SLAY
(— ONESELF) POPJOY
(— VERY MUCH) SLAY
AMUSEMENT FAD FUN JEU GAME JEST LAKE PLAY MIRTH SPORT LAKING MUSERY PASTIME COTTABUS LAUGHTER PLEASURE (PL.) MIDWAY
AMUSING RICH COMIC DROLL FUNNY MERRY WITTY COMICAL FOOLISH KILLING RISIBLE FARCICAL HUMOROUS PLEASANT SPORTFUL
(SOMEONE —) GIGGLE
(SOMETHING OR SOMEONE —) HOOT
AMYCLAS (FATHER OF —) LACEDAEMON
(MOTHER OF —) SPARTE
(SON OF —) HYACINTHUS
AMYCUS (FATHER OF —) NEPTUNE POSEIDON
(MOTHER OF —) MELIA
(SLAYER OF —) POLLUX
AMYGDALA TONSIL
AMYL AMYDON PENTYL ISOAMYL
AMYLASE PTYALIN DIASTASE
AMYMONE (FATHER OF —) DANAUS
(HUSBAND OF —) ENCELADUS
(SON OF —) NAUPLIUS
AMYNTOR (FATHER OF —) ORMENUS
(SON OF —) PHOENIX
(WIFE OF —) CLEOBULE
AMYTHAON (BROTHER OF —) AESON PHERES
(FATHER OF —) CRETHEUS
(MOTHER OF —) TYRO
(SON OF —) BIAS MELAMPUS
(WIFE OF —) IDOMENE
AN ONE ARTICLE
ANA EVENTS OMNIANA SAYINGS
ANABAPTIST DIPPER ABECEDARIAN
ANABAS MARTINICO
ANABATIC DESCENDING
ANABLEPS FOUREYES
ANABO NABO ANABONG
ANABRANCH BRANCH TALLYWALKA
ANACAONA (BROTHER OF —) BEHECHIO
(HUSBAND OF —) CAONABO
ANACHARSIS (BROTHER OF —) SAULIUS
ANACHRONISM SOLECISM
ANACONDA BOA ABOLLA SUCURI SUCURY CAMOUDIE SUCURUJU
ANACREONTIC TEIAN
ANACRUSIS UPBEAT
ANADEM CROWN DIADEM FILLET WREATH CHAPLET CORONET GARLAND
ANAGNOST LECTOR READER
ANAGOGICAL MYSTICAL
ANAGRAM REBUS PUZZLE METAGRAM LOGOGRIPH (PL.) VERBARIUM
ANAGUA KNACKAWAY KNOCKAWAY
ANAH (DAUGHTER OF —) AHOLIBAMAH
(FATHER OF —) ZIBEON
ANAL PODICAL
ANALABOS CLOAK
ANALGESIC ANODYNE CODEINE QUININE ANTIPYRIN PHENALGIN
ANALOGICAL NORMAL
ANALOGOUS LIKE SIMILAR
ANALOGUE DFDT ANALOG
ANALOGY QIYAS PARALLEL PREDISONE
(CLOSE —) PARITY
ANALYSIS TEST INDEX STUDY ANATOMY AUTOPSY SCANSION SOLUTION
(BLOWPIPE —) PYROLOGY
(CHARACTER —) PSYCHOGRAPH
(ECONOMIC —) DYNAMICS
(LOGICAL —) SYLLOGISM
ANALYST SHRINK
ANALYTIC SUBTLE REGULAR
(NOT —) SYNTHETIC SYNTHETICAL
ANALYTICAL CLINICAL DIVISIVE
ANALYZE RUN PART SIFT ASSAY BREAK PARSE SENSE STUDY WEIGH ASSESS DIVIDE REDUCE DISSECT EXAMINE ITEMIZE RESOLVE TITRATE UNPIECE APPRAISE CONSTRUE DIAGNOSE SEPARATE
(— ACCOUNT) AGE
(— VERSE) SCAN

ANAMITE TWINE
ANANAS ANANA PINGUIN
ANANI (FATHER OF —) ELIOENAI
ANANIAS LIAR SIDRACH
(FATHER OF —) NEDEBAEUS
(WIFE OF —) SAPPHIRA
ANANSI NANCY
ANAPEST ANTIDACTYL
ANARCHIST RED PROVO REBEL ANARCH NIHILIST REDSHIRT SOLECIST
ANARCHY RIOT CHAOS REVOLT LICENSE MISRULE DISORDER
ANASARCA EDEMA DROPSY
ANASAZI PUEBLO PLATEAU
ANASCHISTIC EUMITOTIC
ANASTOMOSIS GLOMUS
ANASTROPHE INVERSION
ANATASE OCTAHEDRITE
ANATH (SON OF —) SHAMGAR
ANATHEMA WO BAN MUD WOE OATH CURSE CENSURE
ANATHEMATIZE BAN CURSE ACCURSE EXECRATE
ANATHOTH (FATHER OF —) BECHER
ANATOMIST AMERICAN TODD ALLEN EVANS SABIN WYMAN DWIGHT KNOWER COGHILL HERRICK STOCKARD
AUSTRIAN HYRTL
BELGIAN VESALIUS
DANISH STENO
DUTCH TULP GRAAF CAMPER COITER DUBOIS
ENGLISH GRAY OWEN JONES QUAIN COWPER HARVEY HAVERS HILTON HUNTER WILLIS
FRENCH ROBIN DUVERNEY DUPUYTREN POISEUILLE CRUVEILHIER
GERMAN HIS FICK ROUX HENLE MEYER BRAUNE EBERTH KRAUSE MECKEL MULLER RATHKE WAGNER FRORIEP SIEBOLD ANDERSCH BISCHOFF HARTMANN MEISSNER SCHULTZE SCHWALBE WRISBERG GEGENBAUR HELMHOLTZ LIEBERKUHN SOEMMERRING WEIDENREICH
GREEK RUFUS HEROPHILUS ERASISTRATUS
ITALIAN CORTI ASELLI PACINI SCARPA VAROLI CALDANI COLOMBO COTUGNO ROLANDO MALPIGHI EUSTACHIO FALLOPIUS PACCHIONI
SCOTTISH BELL MONRO FERRIER GOODSIR PETTIGREW MACALISTER
SWEDISH KEY
SWISS BAUHIN HALLER HARDER BRUNNER
ANATOMIZE ANALYZE DISSECT
ANATOMY TOPOLOGY
(— OF HORSE) HIPPOTOMY
(MICROSCOPIC —) HISTOLOGY
(VEGETABLE —) PHYTOTOMY
ANAX (FATHER OF —) URANUS
(MOTHER OF —) GE GAEA
(SON OF —) ASTERIUS
ANAXARETE (LOVER OF —) IPHIS
ANAXIBIA (DAUGHTER OF —) PELOPEA ALCESTIS PISIDICE
(FATHER OF —) BIAS
(HUSBAND OF —) PELIAS
(SON OF —) ACASTUS
ANAXO (BROTHER OF —) AMPHITRYON
(DAUGHTER OF —) ALCMENE
(FATHER OF —) ALCAEUS
(HUSBAND OF —) ELECTRYON
ANCAEUS (FATHER OF —) ALEUS NEPTUNE LYCURGUS POSEIDON
(MOTHER OF —) ASTYPALAEA
(SON OF —) AGAPENOR
ANCESTOR ION MIL ADAM EBER HETH ROOT SIRE DORUS ELDER STOCK APETUS ATAVUS AUTHOR BELDAM EPONYM FATHER MANNUS MILEDH PARENT STIPES ANCIENT BELDAME BELSIRE EPAPHUS FLEANCE FORBEAR IAPETUS ISHMAEL KACHINA SAKULYA DARDANUS FOREBEAR FOREGOER MILESIUS MYRMIDON RELATIVE PREDECESSOR PRIMOGENITOR
(— CULT) MANISM
(—S OF GOTLANDERS) GEAT
(MAORI —) TIKI TUPUNA
(PL.) OLDERS ANCESTY
ANCESTRAL AVAL AVITAL AVITIC LINEAL FAMILIAL
ANCESTRY KIN RACE SEED ATHEL FAMILY ORIGIN PEOPLE SOURCE STRAIN DESCENT KINDRED LINEAGE BREEDING PEDIGREE
ANCHINOE (FATHER OF —) NILUS
(HUSBAND OF —) BELUS
(SON OF —) DANAUS AEGYPTUS
ANCHISES (FATHER OF —) CAPYS
(MOTHER OF —) THEMIS
(SON OF —) AENEAS
ANCHOR FIX BIND DRAG DRUG HOOK MOOR REST SLUG SPUD STOP AFFIX BERTH BOWER KEDGE RIVET SHEET STOCK ATTACH DROGUE FASTEN HERMIT KEDGER KELLEG SECURE STREAM CHAPLET CONNECT DEADMAN GRAPNEL GROUSER KILLICK MUDHOOK SUPPORT COCKBILL
(— IN PLACE) ACOCKBILL
(— RING) TORUS
(AT —) ASTAY
(BEAM —) WALL
(PART OF —) ARM EYE KEY PEE PIN BALL BILL HEAD HOOP PALM RING CROWN FLUKE STOCK TREND THROAT
ANCHORAGE DOCK STAY HARBOR REFUGE RIDING MOORAGE ABUTMENT BERTHAGE ROOTHOLD
ANCHORITE MONK LONER HERMIT ASCETIC EREMITE RECLUSE STYLITE ANCHORET
ANCHOVY NEHU BOCON SPRAT HERRING SARDINE
(— SAUCE) ALEC
(PL.) ALICI
ANCHUSA OXTONGUE
ANCHUSIN ALKANET
ANCIENT ELD OLD AGED AULD FERN HIGH HOAR IAGO YORE EARLY ELDER HOARY OLDEN BYGONE ENSIGN FORMER NOETIC PISTOL PRIMAL VETUST ANTIENT ANTIQUE ARCHAIC ARCHEAN CLASSIC OGYGEAN OGYGIAN HISTORIC NOACHIAN OBSOLETE PRIMEVAL PRISTINE TIMEWORN
(MOST —) ELDEST
(PREF.) ARCHAE PALAE(O) PALE(O) PALE PALE(O)
ANCIENTLY OLD HIGH
ANCILLA HELPER ADJUNCT SERVANT
ANCON ELBOW CORBEL CONSOLE
AND N U AN ET SO ANT TOO ALSO PLUS BESIDES FURTHER MOREOVER AMPERSAND
(— SO FORTH) ETC USW
(SYMBOL OF —) AMPERSAND
ANDAMAN MINCOPI MINKOPI MINCOPIE
ANDESITE BONINITE TIMAZITE PROPYLITE
ANDHAKA (FATHER OF —) KASYAPA
(MOTHER OF —) DITI
(SLAYER OF —) SHIVA
ANDIRON DOG CHENET COBIRON FIREDOG HESSIAN HANDIRON LANDIRON
ANDORRA (LANGUAGE OF —) CATALAN
(NATIVE OF —) ANDOSIAN
(RIVER OF —) VALIRA
ANDRADITE APLOME GARNET
ANDRAEMON (FATHER OF —) OXYLUS
(MOTHER OF —) GORGE DRYOPE
(SON OF —) THOAS
ANDREA CHENIER (CHARACTER IN —) ANDREA COIGNY GERARD CHENIER MADELEINE
(COMPOSER OF —) GIORDANO
ANDROCLES AND THE LION
(AUTHOR OF —) SHAW
(CHARACTER IN —) LAVINIA MEGAERA ANDROCLES FERROVIUS
ANDROCONIUM STIGMA PLUMULE
ANDROGEUS (FATHER OF —) MINOS
(MOTHER OF —) PASIPHAE
ANDROID ROBOT AUTOMATON
ANDROMACHE (AUTHOR OF —) EURIPIDES
(CHARACTER IN —) PELEUS THETIS ORESTES PYRRHUS HERMIONE MENELAUS MOLOSSUS ANDROMACHE NEOPTOLEMUS
(FATHER OF —) EETION
(HUSBAND OF —) HECTOR HELENUS NEOPTOLEMUS
(SON OF —) PIELUS ASTYANAX MOLOSSUS PERGAMUS
ANDROMEDA (FATHER OF —) CEPHEUS
(MOTHER OF —) CASSIOPEA
(RESCUER OF —) PERSEUS
ANDROMEDE BIELID
ANDRON (FATHER OF —) ANIUS
(SISTER OF —) OENO ELAIS SPERMO
ANECDOTAL LITERARY
ANECDOTE GAG TOY JOKE TALE YARN EVENT STORY SKETCH HAGGADA EXEMPLUM HAGGADAH
(COLLECTION OF —S) ANA
ANECHOIC DEAD
ANEMIA SURRA SURRAH ANAEMIA HYPAEMA HYPHEMA HYPHEMIA ISCHEMIA SPANEMIA CHLOROSIS
ANEMIC LOW PALE WEAK MEALY WATERY LIFELESS
(PREF.) CHLOR(O)
ANEMONE LILY CRASS EMONY POLYP OPELET ACTINIA BOWBELLS SNOWDROP
(KIND OF —) RUE
ANENT ON RE ASTO ABOUT ANENST BESIDE TOWARD AGAINST OPPOSITE
ANESTHESIA BLOCK CORYL SPINAL
ANESTHETIC GAS CRNA ETHER ACOINE EVIPAN OBTUSE OPIATE COCAINE DULLING MENTHOL METOPRYL PARAFORM PROCAINE SEDATIVE PHENOCAIN METHOXYFLURANE
(SUFF.) CAINE
ANESTHETIST CRNA
ANESTHETIZE FREEZE ETHERIZE
ANEW OVER AGAIN NEWLY AFRESH ITERUM NEWLINS NEWLINGS RECENTLY
(PREF.) RE
ANFRACTUOUS SPIRAL BENDING SINUOUS WINDING TORTUOUS
ANGEL MAH DEVA EBUS ANGLE ARDOR ARIEL DAEVA DULIA NAKIR YAKSA ABDIEL ARIOCH BACKER BELIAL CHERUB MONKIR MUNKAR NEKKAR SERAPH SPIRIT THRONE UZZIEL YAKSHA ANGELET EGREGOR ISRAFEL RAPHAEL SPONSOR WATCHER ZADKIEL ZOPHIEL APOLLYON GUARDIAN ITHURIEL SUPERNAL
(— OF DEATH) AZRAEL SAMMAEL
(DESTROYING —) ABADDON
(FALLEN —) SATAN
(FALLEN —S) HELL
(GUARDIAN —) YAKSA YAKSHA YAKSHI
(RECORDING —) SIJIL SIJILL
(PL.) HOST FRAVASHI SERAPHIM
ANGELFISH MONK MUNK ANGEL QUOTT RHINA SQUAT MONACH CICHLID FLATFISH KINGSTON MONKFISH SQUATINA
ANGELIC SAINTLY BEATIFIC CHERUBIC HEAVENLY SERAPHIC
ANGELICA JELLICA ARCHANGEL
(FATHER OF —) GALAPHRON
(LOVER OF —) ORLANDO
ANGELIN PACAY ANGELEEN
ANGELIQUE (CHARACTER IN —) CHARLOT BONIFACE ANGELIQUE
(COMPOSER OF —) IBERT
ANGER ARR IRE IRK MAD VEX BATE BILE BURN CRAB FELL FUME FURY GALL GRIM HUFF MOOD RAGE RILE ROIL RUFF TEEN TIFF ANNOY BIRSE GRAME GRIPE HATEL IRISH PIQUE SPONK SPUNK STURT THRAW WRATH BOTHER CHOLER DANDER ENRAGE EXCITE GRIEVE MADDEN MONKEY NETTLE OFFEND RANCOR SPLEEN TALENT TEMPER WARMTH BURNING DESPITE DUDGEON EMOTION

INCENSE INFLAME PASSION PROVOKE STOMACH ACRIMONY DISTRESS EBENEZER IRRITATE VEXATION
ANGERED SORE AGRAMED PELTISH INCENSED
ANGICO CURUPAY
ANGINA PRUNELLA
ANGIOSPERM HARDWOOD METASPERM
ANGLE IN BOB DIP ELL OUT TEE WRO CANT COIN COOK DRAW FISH FORK HADE KEEN KNEE LEAD NOOK PEAK SITE WICK ANCON ARRIS AXIAL BEVEL BIGHT CHOIL COIGN DRAFT DRIFT ELBOW FLEAM GROIN GUISE INGLE PHASE POINT QUOIN SLANT SLOPE ALLURE ANGULE ASPECT CANTON CORNEL CORNER DIRECT ENGHLE EPAULE HADING LAGGEN LAGGIN OCTANT SCHEME SQUARE TORNUS ANGLIAN ANGULUS ANOMALY AZIMUTH BASTION DRAUGHT GIMMICK KNUCKLE PERIGON RAVELIN SALIENT ARGUMENT DECALAGE DIHEDRAL FISHHOOK INTRIGUE SHOULDER OBLIQUITY
(— OF BEVEL) FLEAM FLEEM
(— OF BOWSPRIT) STEEVE STEEVING
(— OF CLUB HEAD) LIE
(— OF EYELIDS) CANTHUS
(— OFF) JAG
(— OF HAT BRIM) BREAK
(— OF HIPBONE) HOOK
(— OF LEAF) AXIL
(— OF RAFTER) HEEL
(— OF TIMBER KNEE) BREECH
(DRIFT —) LEEWAY
(OBTUSE —) HEEL BULLNOSE
(ROCK —) DIEDRE
(ROOF —) HIP FASTIGIUM
(ROUND —) PERIGON
(SALIENT —) ARIS ARRIS PIEND
(PREF.) ANGULO GON(I)(IO)(Y)(YO)
(SUFF.) GON
ANGLED CANTED NOOKED ANGULATE
(PREF.) ACUTI
ANGLER MONK FRIAR THIEF SLIMER LOPHIID RODSTER SPINNER WIDEGAB WIDEGAP ALLMOUTH FROGFISH MONKFISH PISCATOR TOADFISH WALTONIAN
ANGLESMITH SLABMAN
ANGLEWORM ESS WORM FISHWORM
ANGLICAN EPISCOPAL
ANGLO CAUCASIAN

ANGOLA
CAPITAL: LUANDA
COIN: LWEI KWANZA MACUTA MACUTE
DISTRICT: CABINDA
KINGDOM: BAKONGO
LANGUAGE: BANTU KIMBUNDU
MONEY: KWANZA LWEI
MOUNTAIN: LOVITI
PLATEAU: PLANALTO
PORT: LOBITO LUANDA
RIVER: CONGO CUITO KASAI CUANDO CUANZA CUNENE KUNENE KWANDO KWANZA CUBANGO
TOWN: LOBITO LUANDA LUBANGO BENGUELA MOSSAMEDES NOVALISBOA
TRIBE: BANTU KIKONGO
WATERFALL: RUACANA

ANGORA CAT GOAT ANGOLA RABBIT
ANGRILY ANGERLY IRATELY FUMINGLY
ANGRY MAD ASHY EVIL GRIM GRUM HIGH RILY ROID ROSY SORE WARM WAXY WILD WRAW CROOK CROSS GRAME HUFFY IRATE IROUS MOODY RATTY RILEY SNAKY STUNT VEXED WEMOD WROTH BIRSIT CHAFED CROUSE FRENZY FUMING FUMOUS HEATED IREFUL LOADED SHIRTY SNAKEY STUFFY TICKED ENRAGED FRETFUL FURIOUS HOPPING IRACUND PAINFUL RILEDUP ROPABLE SNAKISH SPLEENY TEEDOFF UPTIGHT CHOLERIC INFLAMED RIGOROUS SEETHING SPITFIRE TEMPERED VEHEMENT WREAKFUL INDIGNANT PASSIONATE
(BE —) STEAM
(MAKE —) FROST
ANGRY-LOOKING THUNDERY
ANGUISH WOE ACHE HARM HURT PAIN PANG RACK TRAY AGONY ANGST ANGUS DOLOR GRIEF THROE MISERY REGRET SORROW ANGOISE ANGWICH REMORSE TORMENT TORTURE TRAVAIL DISTRESS
(CHRIST'S —) AGONY
ANGUISHED GRIEFFUL
ANGULAR BONE BONY EDGY LEAN SLIM THIN GAUNT SHARP ABRUPT POINTED SCRAWNY CORNERED
(NOT —) SOFT
(PREF.) ANG
ANGULARITY EDGINESS
ANGUS FORFAR FORFARSHIRE
ANHYDRIDE LACTAM SULTAM FULGIDE LACTIDE SULTONE GLUCOSAN MANNITAN SORBITAN
ANHYDRITE VULPINITE
ANHYDROUS DRY DESICCATED
ANI WITCH CUCKOO JEWBIRD KEELBILL KEELBIRD TICKBIRD
ANIAM (FATHER OF —) SHEMIDAH
ANIARA (COMPOSER OF —) BLOMDAHL
ANIMADVERSION BLAME REMARK CENSURE COMMENT REPROOF WARNING MONITION REPROACH REFLECTION
ANIMAL (ALSO SEE UNDER SPECIFIC HEADINGS) FAT DEER BEAST BIPED BLACK BRUTE GRADE GROSS LUSTY STORE STRAY BRUTAL CARNAL DAPPLE DESPOT FLESHY KICKER MAMMAL RODENT SILVAN SORREL SPONGE SYLVAN BEASTIE BREEDER CARRION CRITTER EPIZOON FATLING LINSANG SENSUAL BURROWER CREATURE EMIGRANT ORGANISM PREDATOR
(— COLLECTION) LARDER
(— FOR MARKET) STOCKER
(— INHABITED BY SPIRIT) GUACA HUACA
(— LIVING IN CAVES) TROGLOBITE
(— OF LITTLE VALUE) SCALAWAG SKALAWAG
(— RESEMBLING MAN) HOMINOID
(—S AS RENT) CAIN
(— SHOT) KILL
(— VICTIM OF MOTOR VEHICLE) ROADKILL
(— WITH BLACK COAT AND MARKINGS) PARSON
(— WITH DOCKED TAIL) CURTAL
(BEEF —) BONER GRASSER
(BOVINE —) BOSS BRUTE
(BROKEN-DOWN —) CROCK
(CARNIVOROUS —) GENET GENETTE SARCOPHILE
(CASTRATED —) SEG SEGG SPAY SPADO GELDING
(COLD-BLOODED —) ECTOTHERM
(CREATED —) BARAMIN
(DECOY —) COACH
(DOMESTIC —) DOER SCRUB BESTIAL FOLLOWER SCRUBBER
(DRAFT —) AVER AIVER
(EMACIATED —) FRAME SKELETON
(FABULOUS —) KYLIN BUNYIP DRAGON ACEPHAL GRIFFIN GRIFFON GRYPHON UNICORN SEMITAUR TRAGELAPH
(FARM —S) STOCK
(FEMALE —) HEN SHE LADY JENNY SHEDER
(FERAL —) CIMAROON CIMARRON CIMMARON
(FLEA-RIDDEN —) FLEABAG
(FOOTLESS —) APOD APODE
(FOSSIL —) ZOOLITE
(FREAKISH —) FERLY FERLIE
(GRASSHOPPER-EATING —) WHANGAM
(GRAY —) GRIZZLE
(GRAZING —) HERBAGER
(GREEDY —) GORB
(HORNED —) HORN REEM
(HORNLESS —) POLLARD
(HUNTED —) QUARRY
(HYPOTHETICAL —) PROAVIS
(IMAGINARY —) WHANGAM CATAWAMPUS
(LOWER —) BEAST CREATURE
(LUSTY OR PLUMP —) BILCH BILSH
(MALE —) HE TOM BUCK BULL JACK STAG JOHNNY BACHELOR
(MARINE —) LANCELET
(MATURE —) SENIOR
(MEAT —) CHOPPER
(MISCHIEVOUS —) ELF
(MYTHICAL —) HODAG KYLIN MOONACK
(ODD —) SPLACKNUCK
(PACK —) HUNIA SUMPTER
(PARTY —) STAG
(PET —) CADE
(PREMATURE —) SLINK
(PURSUED —S) GAME
(ROASTED —) BARBECUE BARBEQUE
(SADDLE —) LOPER
(SCRAWNY —) SCRAG
(SHORN —) SHEAR
(SKINNY —) SCRAE
(SLUGGISH —) DRUMBLE
(SOLID-HOOFED —) SOLIPED
(SPOTTED —) CALICO
(STOCKY —) BLOCK
(STUNTED —) SHARGAR SHARGER
(THICKSET —) NUGGET
(TOTEM —) EPONYM
(UNBRANDED —) SLICK
(UNCASTRATED —) ENTIRE
(UNDERSIZED —) DURGAN DURGEN SCALAWAG SCALLYWAG
(UNHOUSED —) OUTLER OUTLIER
(UNMANAGEABLE —) OUTLAW
(UNWEANED —) SUCKER
(WANDERING —) STRAY ESTRAY
(WARM-BLOODED —) ENDOTHERM HAEMATHERM
(WATER —) AQUATIC AQUATILE
(WEAK —) DRAG DOWNER
(WILD —) SAVAGE WILDLING
(WING-FOOTED —) ALIPED
(WORNOUT —) KANCKER
(WORTHLESS —) CARRION
(YOUNG —) HOG BIRD HOGG JOEY SHOT TOTO STORE JUNIOR PULLUS FATLING LITTLIN KINDLING LITTLING SUCKLING YOUNGLET
(2-HORNED —) BICORN BICORNE
(4-FOOTED —) TETRAPOD
(PL.) ZOA FAUNA NECTON NEKTON
(PREF.) ZO(E)(IDIO)(IDO)(O) ZOOLOGICO
(RUMINATING —) MERYC(O)
(SUFF.) ACEA AD THERE THERIA THERIUM ZOA ZOIC ZOON
ANIMALCULISM SPERMISM
ANIMALITY HOGGERY
ANIMALS
(SUFF.) ATA IDA IDEA INI
ANIMA MUNDI WELTGEIST
ANIMATE ACT PEP FIRE MOVE PERK STIR URGE ALIVE BRISK CHEER DRIVE FLUSH IMBUE IMPEL LIGHT LIVEN QUICK ROUSE VITAL AROUSE BRIGHT ENSOUL EXCITE INCITE INDUCE INFORM KINDLE LIVING PROMPT SPIRIT VIVIFY ACTUATE COMFORT ENLIVEN INSPIRE QUICKEN ACTIVATE ENERGIZE INSPIRIT VITALIZE
(NOT —) BRUTE
ANIMATED UP GAY VIF GLAD VIVE ALIVE ANIME BRISK QUICK VITAL VIVID ACTIVE ARDENT BLITHE BOUNCY BRISKY LIVELY LIVING SPARKY SPUNKY BUOYANT JOCULAR STHENIC BOUNCING INSTINCT LIFESOME SPIRITED VIGOROUS
ANIMATION BRIO ELAN FIRE HEAT LIFE VERVE SPIRIT SPARKLE
ANIMATOR INFORMER
ANIME COPAL ELEMI RESIN ROSIN ANIMATO
ANIMIKEAN LAWSON
ANIMISM NATURISM
ANIMOSITY HATE PIQUE SPITE ANIMUS ENMITY HATRED MALICE RANCOR DISLIKE ACRIMONY

ANIMUS MIND ONDE WILL EFFORT ENMITY SPIRIT TEMPER ATTITUDE
ANIRUDDHA (FATHER OF —) PRADYUMNA
ANISE ANET DILL CUMEN UMBEL FENNEL SIKIMI SHIKIMI
ANIUS (DAUGHTER OF —) OENO ELAIS SPERMO
(FATHER OF —) APOLLO
(MOTHER OF —) RHOEO CREUSA
(SON OF —) ANDRON
(WIFE OF —) DORIPPE
ANKH TAU
ANKLE COOT CUIT HOCK QUIT ANCLE QUEET TALUS WRIST TARSUS SHACKLE
(COCKED —S) KNUCKLING
(PREF.) TAL(I)(O) TARS(I)(O)
ANKLEBONE TALUS ASTRAGAL
ANKLET SHOE SOCK BANGLE FETTER SHACKLE
ANLAGE INCEPT PROTON INITIAL BLASTEMA
ANNA (FATHER OF —) BELUS
(SISTER OF —) DIDO
ANNA BOLENA (CHARACTER IN —) ANNE JANE HENRY PERCY BOLEYN SEYMOUR
(COMPOSER OF —) DONIZETTI
ANNA KARENINA (AUTHOR OF —) TOLSTOY
(CHARACTER IN —) ANNA KITTY LEVIN ALEXEI STEPAN KARENIN VRONSKY OBLONSKY KONSTANTINE SHTCHERBATSKY
ANNALIST WRITER RECORDER
ANNALS FASTI NIHONGI REGISTER
ANNAM (ALSO SEE VIETNAM) VIETNAM
(BOAT OF —) GAYYOU GAYDIANG
(MEASURE OF —) LY GON NGU QUO SAO TAT PHAN THAT SHITA THUOC TRUONG
(TOWN OF —) HUE VINH TOURANE QUANGTRI
(WEIGHT OF —) CAN BINH DONG
ANNAS (FATHER OF —) SETHI
ANNATTO OTTER URUCU ORLEAN ROUCOU SALMON ACHIOTE ACHUETE ANNOTTO ARNATTO ORLEANS
ANNEAL BAKE FUSE HEAT SMELT TEMPER INFLAME TOUGHEN GRAPHITE
ANNEALER TUBER HEATER
ANNEALING LIGHTING
ANNELID NAID WORM LUGWORM SERPULA ANNULATE SANDWORM SERPULAN OLIGOCHAETE
ANNEX ADD ELL LAY JOIN WING AFFIX SEIZE UNITE ADJECT ANNECT APPEND ATTACH FASTEN ACQUIRE CONNECT FIXTURE POSTFIX SUBJOIN ADDITION ANNEXURE DOCUMENT PENTHOUSE
ANNIE OAKLEY PASS TICKET FREEBEE FREEBIE
ANNIHILATE END OUT KILL RAZE RUIN SLAY ABATE ANNUL ERASE WRECK DELETE DEVOUR NOUGHT QUENCH REDUCE ABOLISH DESTROY EXPUNGE DECIMATE UNCREATE DISCREATE PULVERIZE
ANNIHILATION FANA NEGATION
ANNIVERSARY FETE MASS EMBER FEAST ANNUAL JUBILEE YEARDAY BIRTHDAY FESTIVAL YAHRZEIT
(100TH —) CENTENNIAL
(1000TH —) MILLENIUM
(150TH —) SESQUICENTENNIAL
(200TH —) BIMILLENARY BIMILLENIUM
(25TH —) SEMIJUBILEE
(50TH —) SEMICENTENNIAL
ANNONA ATIS ATTA ATEES
ANNOTATE EDIT NOTE STET GLOSS BENOTE NOTIFY POSTIL REMARK APOSTIL COMMENT EXPLAIN FOOTNOTE
ANNOTATION APOSTIL COMMENT SCHOLION SCHOLIUM
ANNOTATOR NOTIST SCHOLIAST
ANNOUNCE BID CRY BODE CALL DEEM MAKE SCRY SHOW SING TELL BRUIT CLAIM KNELL STATE VOICE ASSERT BLAZON BROACH DENOTE HERALD INFORM PREACH REPORT REVEAL SIGNAL SPRING STEVEN DECLARE DIVULGE FORERUN GAZETTE PUBLISH SIGNIFY DENOUNCE FORETELL INTIMATE PROCLAIM RENOUNCE SENTENCE
ANNOUNCEMENT BID CRY HAT BILL CALL LEAD ALARM BANCO BANNS BLURB EDICT ALARUM DECREE DICTUM NOTICE GAZETTE SENSING BULLETIN CIRCULAR DECISION RESCRIPT PROCLAMATION
(— OF DAWN) AUBADE
(STAGE —) SENNET
ANNOUNCER NEBO PAGE CRIER EMCEE CALLER DEEJAY HERALD NUNCIO VEEJAY GONGMAN GRINDER SPIELER NUNCIATE SPRUIKER
ANNOY ARR BUG DUN EAT EGG GET GIG HOX IRE IRK NAG NOY NYE TRY VEX BAIT BORE BURN FASH FRET FUSS GALL GRIG HALE HARM HAZE HUFF HUMP MIFF NARK PAIN RILE ROIL CHAFE CHASE CHEVY CHIVY DEVIL GRAMY GRATE HARRY PEEVE PIQUE SPITE STURT TEASE THORN UPSET WEARY WORRY BADGER BOTHER CADDLE CHIVEY CHIVVY EARWIG ENRAGE GRAVEL HAGGLE HARASS HATTER HECKLE HECTOR INFEST INJURE MADDEN MOLEST NEEDLE NETTLE OFFEND PESTER POTTER PUTOUT RATTLE REHETE RUFFLE TICKLE BEDEVIL DISTURB HOTFOOT JACKSON TERRIFY TROUBLE ACERBATE CONTRARY DISTRESS IRRITATE PERSECUTE
ANNOYANCE VEX DRAG FASH PEST WEED CROSS GRIEF LOATH SPITE STALL THORN INSECT PESTER DISGUST FASHERY NOYANCE TROUBLE UMBRAGE FASHERIE FLEABITE NOISANCE NUISANCE PINPRICK
ANNOYED SORE TEEDOFF INSULTED
ANNOYING TARE PESKY NOYOUS DISEASY HATEFUL IRKSOME NOISOME PAINFUL TARSOME FASHIOUS FRETSOME NIGGLING SPITEFUL TIRESOME PROVOKING PESTIFEROUS
ANNOYINGLY CONFOUNDED CONFOUNDEDLY
ANNUAL BOOK BUGLE PLANT FLOWER YEARLY ANNUARY BUGSEED BUGWEED ETESIAN GIFTBOOK PERIODIC YEARBOOK
(OLD WORLD —) WELD
ANNUITY CENSO CONSOL INCOME PENSION TONTINE PERPETUITY
ANNUL TOL CASS NULL TOLL UNDO VOID ADNUL AVOID BLANK ELIDE ERASE QUASH REMIT RETEX UNLAW CANCEL FRIVOL NEGATE RECALL REPEAL REVERT REVOKE UNLIVE VACATE ABOLISH CASHIER CASSARE CASSATE DESTROY NULLIFY RESCIND RETRACT REVERSE VACUATE ABROGATE ARROGATE DEROGATE DISANNUL DISSOLVE IMBECILE OVERRIDE OVERRULE
ANNULAR BANDED CYCLIC RINGED ANNULATE CINGULAR CIRCULAR
ANNULARLY RINGWISE
ANNULET RING RIDGE FILLET ANNULUS MOLDING
ANNULLING VACATUR
ANNULMENT UNDOING ABATEMENT
ANNULUS RING ANNULE COLLAR GYROMA INDUSIUM
ANNUNCIATION MARYMASS
ANNUNCIATOR TELLER INDICATOR
ANOA BUFFALO SAPIUTAN
ANODE PLATE ZINCOID
ANODIC ASCENDING
ANODYNE BALM ACOPON BROMAL OPIATE REMEDY EUGENOL SOOTHER NARCOTIC SEDATIVE CHLORODYNE
ANOINT FAT OIL RUB BALM BEAT CERE NARD ANELE ANOIL CREAM CROWN ENOIL LATCH NUNCT PRUNE SALVE SMARM SMEAR SMERL CHRISM GREASE INUNCT SPREAD THRASH MOISTEN UNGUENT
ANOINTMENT CHRISMATORY
ANOMALOUS ODD DIFFORM STRANGE UNUSUAL ABERRANT ABNORMAL ATYPICAL PECULIAR
ANOMALY CREEPER CYCLOPY EPILOIA PARADOX CYCLOPIA
ANON NAN ANEW ONCE SOON AGAIN LATER AFRESH BEDEEN BEDENE THENCE SHORTLY
ANONYMITY NOBODYNESS
ANONYMOUS UNKNOWN NAMELESS UNAVOWED UNSIGNED
ANOPLURA PARASITA PEDICULINA
ANORAK CAGOUL KAGOOL KAGOUL KAGOULE
ANOTHER NEW THAT ALIAS FRESH SECOND TIDDER TOTHER ANITHER FURTHER
(PREF.) ALTERO
(ONE —) ALLELO
ANOXIA ASPHYXIA
ANSHUMANT (FATHER OF —) ASAMANJAS
(GRANDFATHER OF —) SAGARA
ANSWER DO IT SAY SIT ECHO MEET PLEA REIN SUIT ATONE AVAIL COMES COVER JAWAB REACT REPLY SERVE LETTER REJOIN RESULT RETORT RETURN RIPOST ACCOUNT COUNTER DEFENCE DEFENSE FULFILL RESPOND SATISFY ANTIPHON COMEBACK PLEADING REBUTTAL REPARTEE RESPONSE SOLUTION
(— BACK) CHOP
(— FOR) FORM VANG
(— IN FUGUE) COMES
(— OF POPE) RESCRIPT
(— SHARPLY) SNAP
(— THE PURPOSE) DO FIT SUIT AVAIL SERVE
(— TO CHARGE) PLEA
(DECISIVE —) SOCKDOLAGER SOCKDOLOGER
(EXAM —) TRUE FALSE
(GIVE IMPROMPTU —) FIELD
(LEGAL —) DUPLY
ANSWERABLE EQUAL LIABLE FITTING ADEQUATE AMENABLE
ANSWERER USHABTI
ANSWERING
(PREF.) COUNTER
ANT ANAI ANAY ANER ATTA GYNE MIRE AMPTE EMMET KELEP MAXIM MINIM NURSE SAUBA SIAFU SLAVE AMAZON DRIVER ERGATE NASUTE NEUTER WORKER BULLDOG FORAGER FORMICE OUVRIER PISMIRE PISSANT PONERID REPLETE SOLDIER TERMITE ACULEATA DORYLINE FORMICID GYNECOID HONEYPOT MACRANER MICRANER MYRMICID TAPINOMA
(— LION) DOODLEBUG
(— SHRIKE) BATARA
(— STUDY) MYRMECOLOGY
(— THRUSH) PITTA
(— TREE) WORMIGO
(PART OF —) EYE WAIST GASTER ANTENNA MANDIBLE
(WINGED —) ALATE
(WORKER —) ERGATE
(PREF.) FORMI(CI) MYRMECO MYRMO TERMITO
(SUFF.) MYRMEX
ANTA PIER PARASTAS PEDESTAL PILASTER
ANTACID SATURANT
ANTAEUS (FATHER OF —) NEPTUNE POSEIDON
(MOTHER OF —) GE GAEA
ANTAGONISM WAR ANIMUS ENMITY QUARREL AVERSION CONFLICT
(IN —) COUNTER
ANTAGONIST FOE ENEMY PARTY RIVAL FOEMAN BATTLER WARRIOR COPEMATE OPPONENT OPPOSITE WRANGLER

(— OF DRUGS) NALAXONE NALOXONE
ANTAGONISTIC ADVERSE COUNTER HOSTILE ANTERGIC CONTRARY INIMICAL OPPONENT OPPOSITE
(— TO GROWTH) ANTIBLASTIC
(NOT —) SYMPATHETIC
(PREF.) ENANTIO
ANTAGONIZE OPPOSE CONTEST
ANTARCTICA (— CAPE) ADARE
(MOUNTAIN ON —) TYREE GARDNER KIRKPATRICK
(VOLCANO ON —) EREBUS MELBOURNE
ANT BEAR BEAR ERDVARK AARDVARK ANTEATER EDENTATE TAMANOIR
ANTE PAY STAKE
(— UP) KICKIN
ANTEATER TAPIR NUMBAT ECHIDNA TAMANDU AARDVARK AARDWOLF DASYURID EDENTATE PANGOLIN TAMANDUA TAMANOIR
ANTEBRACHIUM CUBIT CUBITAL CUBITUS FOREARM
ANTECEDENT FORE CAUSE PRIOR FORMER REASON WHENCE PREMISE ANTERIOR PREVIOUS PRECEDING PRECEDENCE PREVENIENT
(— OF CANON) GUIDA
ANTECHAMBER LIWAN
ANTEDATE PRECEDE PREDATE FOREDATE PREEXIST
ANTEDATED FORETIMED
ANTELOPE GNU GOA KID KOB RAM SUS ASTE BISA BUCK DODA DUST GUIB IBEX KOBA KUDU ORYX PALA PUKU ROAN SUNI TOPI TORA ADDAX BAIRA BEIRA BEISA BEKRA BOHOR BONGO BOVID BUBAL CHIRU ELAND GORAL GUIBA IPETE LICHI NAGOR NYALA ORIBI PEELE PERON SABLE SAIGA SASIN SEROW TAKIN YAKIN BAGWYN BHOKRA BUBALE CABREE CABRET CABRIE CABRIT CHOUKA DIKDIK DUIKER DUYKER DZEREN DZERIN DZERON GOORAL GRIMME HEROLA IMPALA INYALA KOODOO LECHWE LELWEL NAKONG NILGAI NILGAU PALLAH POOKOO PYGARG RHEBOK ALGAZEL BLAUBOK BLESBOK BUBALIS CHAMOIS CHIKARA DEFASSA GAZELLE GEMSBOK GERENUK GREENUK GRYSBOK MADOQUA REDBUCK RHEEBOK SASSABY STEMBOK AGACELLA BLEEKBOK BLESBUCK BONTEBOK BOSCHBOK BUSHBUCK KORRIGUM LEUCORYX REEDBUCK STEENBOK PRONGHORN HARTEBEEST
(YOUNG —) KID LAMB
ANTEMERIDIEM ACKEMMA
ANTENNA DISH HORN LOOP PALP TIER YAGI AERIAL DIPOLE FEELER TACTOR DOUBLET WHISKER MONOPOLE PARABOLA RADIATOR
(SHORTWAVE —) YAGI
ANTENNATA INSECTA
ANTENOR (FATHER OF —) AESYETES
(MOTHER OF —) CLEOMESTRA
(WIFE OF —) THEANO
ANTERIOR FORNE FRONT PRIOR ATLOID BEFORE FORMER ANTICUS PRORSAL VENTRAL ATLANTAL INFERIOR PREVIOUS PRECEDING
(PREF.) ANTER(O) EPH EPI PRE PRO
ANTEROOM HALL FOYER LOBBY ENTRANCE
ANTEROS (BROTHER OF —) EROS
(FATHER OF —) ARES MARS
(MOTHER OF —) APHRODITE
ANTEWAR PREBELLUM
ANTHAS (FATHER OF —) NEPTUNE POSEIDON
(MOTHER OF —) ALCYONE
ANTHELION HALO NIMBUS ANTISUN AUREOLE
ANTHELMINTIC CUNIC BRAYERA EMBELIN PINKROOT SCAMMONY SANTONICA PIPERAZINE PHENOTHIAZINE
ANTHEM HYMN SONG AGNUS MOTET PAEAN PSALM INTROIT RESPOND ASPERGES ISODICON
(JAPANESE —) KIMIGAYO
ANTHEMIUS (FATHER OF —) PROCOPIUS
ANTHER TIP AGLET CHIVE THECA
ANTHESIS BLOOM BLOSSOM
ANTHILL BANK TUMP
ANTHOCYANIN ENIN OENIN BETANIN PUNICIN VIOLANIN
ANTHOLOGIST RHAPSODE RHAPSODIST
ANTHOLOGY ANA POSY ALBUM SYLVA CORPUS READER GARLAND SYNTAGMA CHRESTOMATHY
ANTHOZOAN CORAL POLYP ANEMONE GULINULA
ANTHRACITE CULM
ANTHRACITIC HARD
ANTHRACONITE STINKSTONE SWINESTONE
ANTHRAX SANG CHARBON BLACKLEG
ANTHROPOLOGIST TOTEMIST CULTURALIST
AMERICAN BIRD BOAS COON MEAD BEALS DIXON HOUGH JENKS LEWIS SAPIR STARR BUTLER DORSEY GEERTE HOLMES HOOTON LAUFER LINTON MERCER POWELL PUTNAM RIPLEY WEAVER BATESON BRINTON FOLKMAR KROEBER LAFARGE MONTAGU SPINDEN WISSLER BENEDICT GWALTNEY HRDLICKA MACCURDY KLUCKHORN MACDONALD HERSKOVITS GOLDENWEISER
AUSTRALIAN DART
AUSTRIAN LUSCHAN
BELGIAN BIEBUYCK
ENGLISH HODGE KEITH PERRY SMITH TYLOR BEDDOE HADDON HOWITT LEAKEY MARETT RIVERS GOODALL TURNBULL MALINOWSKI
FINNISH WESTERMARCK
FRENCH HAMY BROCA DENIKER LAPOUGE TOPINARD DUCHAILLU MORTILLET HOVELACQUE MANOUVRIER
GERMAN WAITZ GUNTHER HARTMANN SCHWALBE BLUMENBACH WEIDENREICH SCHOETENSACK
ITALIAN SERGI MANTEGAZZA
NORWEGIAN HEYERDAHL
SCOTTISH FRAZER MONBODDO
ANTHROPOPHAGITE CANNIBAL
ANTIA (BELOVED OF —) BELLEROPHON
(FATHER OF —) IOBATES
(HUSBAND OF —) PROETUS
ANTIAIRCRAFT ARCHIE
ANTIANEIRA (FATHER OF —) MENETES
(SON OF —) ECHION ERYTUS
ANTIBALLOONER SEPARATOR
ANTIBIOTIC BIOTIC ABIOTIC FILIPIN HUMULON TYLOSIN CIRCULIN CITRININ CLAVACIN CLAVATIN COLISTIN FRADICIN HUMULONE NEOMYCIN NYSTATIN RIFAMPIN SUBTILIN VIOMYCIN POLYMYCIN PUROMYCIN RIFAMICIN GENTAMICIN OLIGOMYCIN PENICILLIN RIFAMPICIN
ANTIBODY LYSIN REAGIN BLOCKER GLUTININ PRECIPITIN
ANTIC TOY DIDO FOOL LARK WILD CAPER CLOWN COMIC DROLL MERRY PRANK STUNT GAMBOL BUFFOON CAPRICE GAMBADE GAMBADO
ANTICHRIST BEAST
ANTICIPATE BALK BEAT HOPE JUMP WISH ALLOT AUGUR AWAIT DREAD PSYCH SENSE STALL DIVINE EXPECT PSYCHE THWART DEVANCE FORERUN FORESEE OBVIATE PORTEND PREPARE PREVENE PREVENT PROPOSE RESPECT SUPPOSE ANTEDATE FORECAST FOREFEEL FORETAKE PROSPECT
ANTICIPATION TYPE ODIUM AUGURY OPINION THOUGHT PROSPECT PROLEPSIS PRESCIENCE PREMONITION
ANTICIPATORY PREVENIENT
ANTICLEA (FATHER OF —) AUTOLYCUS
(HUSBAND OF —) LAERTES
(SON OF —) ULYSSES ODYSSEUS
ANTICLIMAX BATHOS
ANTICLINE ARCH DOME NAPPE ISOCLINE OVERFOLD
ANTICOAGULANT WARFARIN
ANTICYCLONE HIGH
ANTIDEPRESSANT DOXEPIN NIALAMIDE PARGYLINE NORTRIPTYLINE
ANTIDOTE GUACO BEZOAR EMETIC GALENA REMEDY THERIAC DELETERY THERIACA BEZOARDIC MITHRIDATE BLEXIPHARMIC
(— TO POISON) ORVIETAN
ANTIGEN N LYSOGEN BIOLOGIC PRECIPITINOGEN
ANTIGERMANISM VANSITTARTISM
ANTIGONE (AUTHOR OF —) SOPHOCLES
(BROTHER OF —) POLYNICES
(CHARACTER IN —) CREON HAEMON ISMENE ANTIGONE TIRESIAS
(FATHER OF —) OEDIPUS
(MOTHER OF —) JOCASTA
(SISTER OF —) ISMENE
ANTIGORITE SERPENTINE
ANTIGUA & BARBUDA (CAPITAL:) SAINTJOHNS
(COIN:) DOLLAR
(ISLAND:) ANTIGUA BARBUDA REDONDA
(LANGUAGE:) ENGLISH
(TOWN:) CODRINGTON
ANTILOCHUS (FATHER OF —) NESTOR
(MOTHER OF —) ANAXIBIA
(SLAYER OF —) MEMNON
ANTIMALARIAL PENTAQUIN PENTAQUINE
ANTIMASK ANTIC ANTICK
ANTIMONIAL STIBIAL
ANTIMONY SB KOHL REGULUS STIBIUM
(PREF.) STIB(IO)
ANTIMONY SULFIDE SURMA SOORMA
ANTINOMIAN FIDUCIARY
ANTINOMY PARADOX
ANTIOPE (FATHER OF —) NYCTEUS
(HUSBAND OF —) LYCUS THESEUS
(SISTER OF —) HIPPOLYTE
(SON OF —) ZETHUS AMPHION HIPPOLYTUS
ANTIOXIDANT BHA SESAMOL
ANTIPATHY HATE ODIUM ENMITY NAUSEA RANCOR ALLERGY DISGUST DISLIKE AVERSION DISTASTE DYSPATHY LOATHING
ANTIPHON SALVE GRADUAL PLACEBO GRADUALE
ANTIPHONALLY CHOIRWISE ANTHEMWISE
ANTIPHONARY LEDGER
ANTIPHUS (BROTHER OF —) MESTHLES
(FATHER OF —) PRIAM TALAEMENES
(HALF-BROTHER OF —) ISUS
(MOTHER OF —) HECUBA
ANTIPODAL ANTARCTIC
ANTIPYRETIC SALOL MALARIN THALLIN THALLINE
ANTIQUARY ARCHAIST ANTIQUARIAN
ANTIQUATED OLD AGED FUSTY MOSSY PASSE FOGRAM FOSSIL VOIDED ANCIENT ARCHAIC FOGYISH NOACHIAN OBSOLETE OUTDATED OUTMODED TIMEWORN
ANTIQUE ANTIC RELIC SIRUP SYRUP VIRTU ANTICK NOETIC ANCIENT ARCHAIC NOACHIC NOACHIAN OUTMODED ARCHAICAL
(PERSON WHO LOCATES —S) PICKER
ANTIQUITY ELD OLD PAST YORE RELIC OLDNESS ANCIENCE ANCIENCY
(PL.) ARCHEOLOGY ARCHAEOLOGY
ANTIRED WHITE

ANTI-SEMITISM JUDOPHOBIA
ANTISEPTIC CAVA EGOL KAVA SALT AMIDO AMINE EUPAD EUSOL IODOL SALOL AMADOL IATROL IODINE KRELOS PHENOL PICROL ALCOHOL ALUMNOL ARBUTIN ASEPTIC COLYTIC LORETIN STERILE TACHIOL TEUCRIN THALLIN CREOSOTE ICHTHYOL KAVAKAVA METAPHEN TEREBENE THALLINE MERBROMIN ACRIFLAVINE
(SUFF.) IOM
ANTISOCIAL HOSTILE ANARCHIST
ANTISPASMODIC KELLIN SAMBUL SUMBAL SUMBUL KHELLIN PAPAVERINE STRAMONIUM PENTOBARBITAL
ANTISTROPHE REVERT COUNTERTURN
ANTITHESIS AND CONTRAST
ANTITHETICAL OPPOSITE
ANTITOXIN SERUM BIOLOGIC
ANTIVIVISECTIONIST BESTIARIAN
ANTIWAR (— GROUP) DOVES
ANTLER DAG HORN KNOB RIAL TRAY DAGUE RIGHT ROYAL SHOOT SPIKE BOSSET SHOVEL TROCHE SPELLER DEERHORN SURROYAL TROCHING
(— POINT) TROCHING
(BRANCH OF —) TINE PRONG
(PL.) HEAD ATTIRE
ANT LION LACEWING DOODLEBUG NEUROPTERAN
ANTONINA (HUSBAND OF —) BELISARIUS
ANTONY AND CLEOPATRA
(AUTHOR OF —) SHAKESPEARE
(CHARACTER IN —) EROS IRAS MENAS PHILO ALEXAS ANTONY GALLUS SCARUS SEXTUS SILIUS TAURUS AGRIPPA LEPIDUS MARDIAN OCTAVIA THYREUS VARRIUS CANIDIUS CHARMIAN DERCETAS DIOMEDES DOMITIUS MECAENAS OCTAVIUS SELEUCUS CLEOPATRA DEMETRIUS DOLABELLA VENTIDIUS EUPHRONIUS MENECRATES PROCULEIUS
ANTONYM OPP OPPOSITE
ANTOTHIJAH (FATHER OF —) JEROHAM
ANTSHRIKE BATARA
ANTSY EDGY FUSSY TENSE FIDGETY
ANT THRUSH PITTA
ANT TREE HORMIGO
ANUB (FATHER OF —) COZ
ANUS ASS ARSE BUNG VENT SIEGE TEWEL
(PREF.) ANO PROCT(O)
(SUFF.) PROCTA
ANVIL BLOCK INCUS SNARL STAKE STITH TEEST STETHY STITHY ANDVILE ANFEELD BICKERN BEAKIRON
(— SUPPORT) STOCK
(MINIATURE —) STAKE STUMP
(PREF.) INCUD(O)
ANXIETY HOW CARE CARK FEAR FRAY PAIN ALARM ANGOR ANGST DOUBT DREAD PANIC WORRY KIAUGH NERVES PUCKER ANGUISH CAUTION CHAGRIN CONCERN SCRUPLE TENSION THOUGHT TROUBLE DISQUIET SUSPENSE SOLICITUDE
(— ABOUT HEALTH HYPOCHONDRIA
(EXTREME —) RACK
ANXIOUS AGOG BUSY FOND TOEY EAGER FIRST UPSET AFRAID UNEASY ANGUISH CAREFUL CARKING EARNFUL FORWARD TIDIOSE UNQUIET DESIROUS RESTLESS THOUGHTY WATCHFUL CONCERNED
ANY A AN AY AIR ALL ARY ONI ONY AIRY EVER PART SOME WHAT
(— WHATEVER) ALL
(NOT —) NARY
ANYBODY ANY ONE ANYONE SOMEONE
ANYHOW HOW NOHOW NOWAY ALWAYS ANYWAY
ANYONE HE MAN ANYBODY
ANYTHING THAT AUGHT OUGHT
ANYWAY NOHOW ALWAYS
ANYWHERE EIHWER OWHERE UBIQUE ANYPLACE
ANYWISE ANYHOW ANYWAY ANYWAYS
AOUDAD ARUI UDAD AUDAD SHEEP CHAMOIS
APACE FAST QUICK QUICKLY RAPIDLY SPEEDILY
APACHE YUMA PADUCA CIBECUE VAQUERO QUERECHO MESCALERO
APAGOGE ABDUCTION
APAP EPIPHI
APAR APARA BOLITA MATACO
APART BY OFF AWAY BOUT ELSE ALONE ALOOF AROOM ASIDE RIVEN SOLUS SPLIT YTWYN ABREID ATWAIN LONELY SUNDRY ASUNDER ENISLED REMOVED SEVERAL SEVERED SEPARATE PIECEMEAL
(— FROM) BARRING
(TAKE —) UNRIG
(WIDE —) ASPAR
(WIDELY —) ABROAD
(PREF.) CHORI DI DICH
APARTMENT BUT PAD WON DIGS FLAT HALL LOFT ROOM STEW WENE WONE WOON ABODE BOWER OECUS ORIEL ROOMS SALON SOLAR SUITE ANDRON CLOSET DECKER DINGLE DUPLEX GROTTO LYCEUM SALOON SINGLE SOLLAR SPENCE STANZA BUTTERY CHAMBER COCKPIT GALLERY MANSION PRIVACY BUILDING EPHEBEUM SHOWROOM SOLARIUM TENEMENT THALAMUS MAISONETTE
(— FOR IDOL) TING
(— IN CASTLE) BOWER
(— IN CHURCH) SACRISTY
(— OF WARSHIP) COCKPIT
(BACHELOR —) GARCONNIERE
(OUTER —) BUT
(PRIVATE —) MAHAL PARADISE
(RENTED —) LET
(PL.) GYNAECEUM
APATHETIC CALM COLD COOL DEAD DOWF DULL BLASE DOWFF INERT STOIC GLASSY SUPINE TORPID ADENOID PASSIVE UNMOVED LISTLESS SLUGGISH LETHARGIC PERFUNCTORY
APATHY SLOTH ACEDIA CAFARD PHLEGM TORPOR LANGUOR DOLDRUMS DULLNESS LETHARGY OMISSION STOICISM STOLIDITY
(EXTREME —) STUPOR
APATITE IJOLITE MOROXITE PHOSPHORITE
APAYAO ISNEG
APE KRA LAR PAN BOOR COPY DUPE FOOL MAHA MIME MOCK SHAM WILD BEROK CLOWN CRAZY MAGOT MIMIC ORANG PONGO PYGMY APELET BABOON GELADA GIBBON LANGUR MARTEN MARTIN MIRROR MONKEY OURANG PARROT PONGID SIMIAN SIMIID BUFFOON COPYCAT EMULATE GORILLA IMITATE PORTRAY PRIMATE SATYRUS SIAMANG DURUKULI IMITATOR MANTEGAR SIMULATE ORANGUTAN
(— STUDY) PITHECOLOGY
(GO —) FLIP FLIPOUT
(PREF.) PITHEC(O)
(SUFF.) PITHECUS
APEAK VERTICAL
APEIRON MATTER
APELIKE SIMIAN
APER BOAR MIME SNOB CLOWN MOCKER BUFFOON COPYCAT
APERCU DIGEST GLANCE PRECIS SKETCH INSIGHT OUTLINE
APERIENT LAX OPENER CASCARA
APERIODIC DEADBEAT
APERITIF KIR WHET CINZANO DUBONNET
APERTURE F EYE GAP OPE VUE BOLE BORE HOLE LEAK PASS PORE RENT RIMA SLIT SLOT VENT BREAK CHASM CLEFT CRACK LIGHT MOUTH PUPIL STOMA CUTOUT HIATUS KEYWAY LOUVER WINDOW FISSURE KEYHOLE OPENING ORIFICE OSTIOLE PINHOLE PUNCTUM SWALLOW TROMPIL APERTION FENESTRA LOOPHOLE OVERTURE SPIRACLE
(— OF CORROLLA) RICTUS
APEX EPI PIN TIP TOP ACME AUGE CONE CUSP NOON PEAK RUFF CREST HIGHT PITCH POINT SPIRE APOGEE CLIMAX CRISIS CUPULA GENION HEIGHT SUMMIT TITTLE VERTEX ZENITH CACUMEN EVEREST PAPILLA PUNCTUM PINNACLE
(— OF HELMET) CREST
(— OF OBELISK) PYRAMIDION
(PREF.) APIC(O)
(SUFF.) ACE
APHAREUS (BROTHER OF —) LEUCIPPUS
(FATHER OF —) PERIERES
(MOTHER OF —) GORGOPHONE
(SON OF —) IDAS LYNCEUS
(WIFE OF —) ARENE
APHASIA ALALIA ALEXIA JARGON APHEMIA ASYMBOLIA
APHID APHIS LOUSE APTERA BLIGHT COLLIER DIMERAN MIGRANS PUCERON BLACKFLY GREENFLY GYNOPARA HOMOPTER
APHIDAS (DAUGHTER OF —) ANTIA
(FATHER OF —) ARCAS
(MOTHER OF —) ERATO MEGANIRA CHRYSOPELIA
(SON OF —) ALEUS
APHIS ANTCOW GREENFLY
APHORISM SAW ADAGE AXIOM GNOME MAXIM MOTTO SUTRA SUTTA CLICHE DICTUM SAYING WISDOM EPIGRAM PRECEPT PROVERB APOTHEGM PISHOGUE
APHORISTIC GNOMIC
APHRODISIAC DEWTRY DAMIANA VENEREAL VENEREOUS
APHRODITE VENUS CYPRIS URANIA ANTHEIA MYLITTA CYTHEREA PANDEMOS
(FATHER OF —) ZEUS JUPITER
(HUSBAND OF —) VULCAN
(LOVER OF —) ARES
(MOTHER OF —) DIONE
(SON OF —) EROS CUPID AENEAS
APIARIST SKEPPIST
APIARY HIVE SKEP BEEYARD BEEHOUSE
APICULTURE BEEKEEPING
APIECE UP ALL PER APOP EACH SERIATIM
APIKORES BECORESH
APIO ARRACACH ARRACACHA
APIOS SOIA SOJA GLYCINE
APIS HAPI
(FATHER OF —) APOLLO PHORONEUS
(MOTHER OF —) LAODICE
APISH SILLY FOPPISH AFFECTED
APITONG BAGAC HAPITON KERUING
APIUM UMBEL
APLENTY GALORE
APLITE HAPLITE
APLOMB TACT NERVE POISE SURETY COOLNESS
APOCALYPSE DOOM SHOWING REVELATION
APOCRISIARY RESPONSAL
APOCRYPHA (— BOOK) BEL EZRA ABGAR ENOCH TOBIT BARUCH DANIEL ESDRAS JUDITH AERAPHA JUBILEES MANASSES MACCABEES ECCLESIASTICUS
APOCRYPHAL SHAM FALSE UNREAL DOUBTFUL FABULOUS FICTIOUS
APODAL FOOTLESS
APODE EEL
APOGEE ACME APEX AUGE PEAK CLIMAX ZENITH
APOGON AMIA CARDINAL
APOLLO SUN PAEAN DELIUS AGYIEUS APOLLON LYKEIOS PATROUS PHOEBUS PYTHIUS CYNTHIUS PYTHAEUS
(FATHER OF —) ZEUS JUPITER
(MOTHER OF —) LETO LATONA
(SISTER OF —) DIANA ARTEMIS

APOLLYON DEVIL SATAN ABADDON
APOLOGETIC SORRY
APOLOGUE MYTH FABLE STORY APOLOGY PARABLE ALLEGORY
APOLOGY PLEA ALIBI AMENDS EXCUSE PARDON REGRET PRETEXT SCRUPLE APOLOGIA
(INTERJECTION EXPRESSING —) OOPS WOOPS
APOPHONY ABLAUT
APOPHYGE SCAPE ESCAPE
APOPLEXY ESCA SHOCK STROKE POPLESIE
APOSTASY FALL LAPSE
APOSTATE RAT LAPSED CONVERT HERETIC PERVERT SECEDER DEFECTOR DESERTER DISLOYAL RECREANT RENEGADE TURNCOAT
APOSTATIZE DESERT
APOSTLE ESCAPE TEACHER DISCIPLE FOLLOWER PREACHER
(BIBLICAL —) JOHN JUDE LEVI PAUL DENIS JAMES JUDAS PETER SIMON ANDREW PHILIP THOMAS DIDYMUS MATTHEW BARNABAS MATTHIAS
APOSTLE BIRD CATBIRD
APOSTROPHE TUISM TURNWAY TURNTALE
APOTHECARY CHEMIC SPICER CHEMICK DRUGGIST
APOTHECIUM CUP PELTA TRICA SHIELD ARDELLA LIRELLA PATELLA
APOTHEGM SAW DICT ADAGE AXIOM GNOME MAXIM SUTRA DICTUM SAYING SUTTAH PROVERB APHORISM SENTENCE
APOTHEOSIS DEIFICATION CONSECRATION
APOTHEOSIZE DEIFY EXALT ELEVATE GLORIFY CANONIZE
APPAIM (FATHER OF —) NADAB
APPALL STUN APPAL DAUNT SHOCK DISMAY REDUCE REVOLT WEAKEN ASTOUND DEPRESS DISGUST DISMISS HORRIFY PETRIFY TERRIFY AFFRIGHT ASTONISH ENFEEBLE FRIGHTEN OVERCOME
APPALLING AWFUL AWESOME FEARFUL TERRIBLE TERRIFIC
APPANAGE GRANT ADJUNCT APANAGE
APPARATUS AID BOX GUN LOG SET ADON DRAG ETNA FAKE GEAR GRIP HECK HELM LAMP LIFT STOW TIRE TOOL BURET GANCH HOIST HORSE LEECH RELAY SCUBA SHEAR SIREN SONAR SPRAY STILL STOVE SWING BUDDLE BUFFER COILER COOKER DEVICE DINGUS ENGINE FEEDER FILTER FOGGER GADGET GEYSER GRAITH LADDER LIFTER MILKER ORRERY OUTFIT REFLUX RUDDER SEESAW SHEARS SMOKER SMUDGE TACKLE TIPPLE TREMIE TROMPE AERATOR AIRBATH ALEMBIC APPAREL AUTOMAT BAGGAGE BALANCE BASCULE BURETTE DERRICK ECHELON FURNACE GASOGEN GRILLER HOISTER INHALER ISOTRON MACHINE MEGAFOG PINCERS PRESSER SOUNDER SOXHLET SPRAYER STEAMER STIRRER TELEPIX TREMOLO TRIMMER UTENSIL AGITATOR AQUALUNG BLOWDOWN CALUTRON CONVEYER CONVEYOR CRYOSTAT DIALYZER DIAPHOTE DIGESTER DRENCHER DUMBBELL EOLIPILE EQUIPAGE ERGOSTAT GASIFIER GAZOGENE INJECTOR ISOSCOPE JACQUARD OSMOGENE OZONIZER PULMOTOR PURIFIER RECORDER REDUCTOR REHEATER SCRUBBER SOFTENER STRIPPER HANGLIDER ABSORPTIOMETER
(— IN STOMACH OF LOBSTER) LADY
(SEGMENTAL —) BRAINSTEM
(SWIMMING —) SCUBA
(SUFF.) STAT(IC)(ICS)
APPAREL DECK FARE GARB GEAR ROBE SECT TIRE WEAR WEDE ADORN ARRAY BESEE CLOTH DRESS EQUIP HABIT MITER TUNIC ATTIRE CLOTHE GRAITH INFULA OUTFIT PARURE ROBING CLOBBER COSTUME FURNISH GARMENT HARNESS PREPARE RAIMENT VESTURE CLOTHING FOOTWEAR HEADWEAR WARDROBE
(ECCLESIASTIC —) FANON ORALE MANIPLE CHASUBLE CORPORAL
(HEAD —) MILLINERY
(MILITARY —) WARENTMENT
(MOURNING —) WEEDS
(RICH —) ARRAY
APPARENT OPEN BREEM BREME CLEAR OVERT PLAIN FORMAL PARENT PATENT PHANIC CERTAIN EVIDENT GLARING OBVIOUS SEEMING SHALLOW VISIBLE DISTINCT ILLUSORY MANIFEST PALPABLE PROBABLE SEMBLANT SEMBLABLE OSTENSIBLE
APPARENTLY
(PREF.) QUASI
APPARITION HUE HANT SHOW DREAM FANCY FETCH GHOST HAUNT IMAGE LARVA PHASM SHADE SHAPE SPOOK ASPECT DOUBLE IDOLUM SOWLTH SPIRIT SPRITE STOUND SWARTH TAISCH THURSE VISION WRAITH DISPLAY EIDOLON FANTASY FEATURE PHANTOM SPECTER SPECTRE EPIPHANY ILLUSION PHANTASM PRESENCE REVENANT SPECTRUM SEMBLANCE
APPARITOR BEADLE PARURE PARITOR SUMMONER
APPEAL ASK BEG BID CRY CALL CASE PLEA SEEK SUIT APPLY CHARM CLEPE REFER SPEAK ACCUSE ADJURE AVOUCH INVOKE PRAYER SUMMON ADDRESS CONJURE ENTREAT IMPLORE REQUEST SOLICIT APPROACH ENTREATY PETITION ADJURATION
(— FOR CONTRIBUTIONS) WHIP
(— FOR HELP) SOS
(— FOR QUARTER) KAMERAD
(— TO) APPLY AVOUCH INVOKE ARRAIGN
(SEX —) IT OOMPH
(SOLEMN —) OATH
APPEALING CUTE NICE CATCHY CLEVER NELLOW CUNNING SUGARED PLEASANT
(STRIKINGLY —) ZINGY
APPEAR BID CAR EYE GET COME DAWN FARE LOOK LOOM MAKE MEET PEER REAR RISE SEEM WALK ARISE ENTER ISSUE KITHE KYTHE OCCUR SOUND THINK ARRIVE BESEEM EMERGE INFORM REGARD SPRING BLOSSOM COMPEAR DEVELOP OUTCROP RESEMBLE
(— ABOVE GROUND) BREER BRAIRD
(— AND DISAPPEAR) COOK
(— BETTER) GAIN
(— BRIEFLY) GLINT
(— DIRECTLY BEFORE) AFFRONT
(— FAINTLY) GLIMMER
(— SUDDENLY) BURST
(— UNEXPECTEDLY) BLOOM IRRUPT
(PREF.) PHANER(O) PHANTA PHANTO
APPEARANCE AIR CUT HUE CAST FARE FORM GARB IDEA LATE LEEN LOOK MIEN SHOW VIEW BLUSH COLOR EIDOS FAVOR FRONT GUISE HABIT LOOKS PHASE PHASM SHAPE SIGHT SOUND SPICE ASPECT EFFECT FACIES FAVOUR MANNER OBJECT OSTENT REGARD VISAGE ARRIVAL DISPLAY FARRAND FASHION FEATURE GLIMPSE OUTSIDE RESPECT SHOWING SPECIES ARTEFACT ARTIFACT EPIPHANY ILLUSION LIKENESS PRESENCE PRETENSE SEMBLANCE
(— OF LIGHT ON HAIR) HAG
(BRILLANT —) SHINE
(CLOUDED —) HAZE CHILL
(CONSPICUOUS —) FIGURE
(DISTINCTIVE —) AURA
(FIRST —) DAWN DEBUT SPRING
(GENERAL —) RIG
(GUEST —) CAMEO
(IMPOVERISHED —) BEGGARY
(MERE —) INTENTIONAL
(MOCK —) SIMULACRUM
(MOTTLED —) ROE DAPPLE
(MOTTLED SKY —) BLINK
(OF NEAT —) PREPPY PREPPIE
(OUTWARD —) FACE SEEM SHOW FACADE APPAREL BALLOON SEEMING SURFACE
(PERSONAL —) PRESENCE
(SERIES OF —S) ROAD
(STRIPED —) ROE
(SUPERNATURAL —) APPARITION
(SURFACE —) TOUR BLOOM
(UNGAINLY —) ANGULARITY
(VAGUE —) BLUR
(PREF.) SPECTRO
(SUFF.) OPSIA OPSIO OPSIS OPSY PHANE PHANOUS PHANT PHANY
APPEASE LAY PAY CALM EASE HUSH SATE ALLAY ALONE ATONE MEASE PEACE PEASE QUIET SLAKE STILL DEFRAY GENTLE MEEKEN MODIFY PACIFY PLEASE SOFTEN SOOTHE ASSUAGE CONTENT DULCIFY GRATIFY MOLLIFY PLACATE SATISFY STICKLE SUFFICE SWEETEN MITIGATE PROPITIATE
(— APPETITE) STAY
APPEASEMENT MUNICHISM
APPELLATION NAME TERM GODDY STYLE TITLE APPEAL CALLING EPITHET GOODMAN SURNAME COGNOMEN METRONYM NICKNAME
APPEND ADD PIN TAG CLIP HANG JOIN TACK AFFIX ANNEX ADJOIN ATTACH FASTEN AUGMENT POSTFIX SUBJOIN
APPENDAGE ARM AWN FIN LEG TAB TAG ARIL BARB CAUD FLAP HOOK HORN LIMB LOBE SPUR TAIL AFFIX BEARD CAUDA CERAS EXITE RIDER SCALE TROLL WHISK CERCUS CIRRUS CORONA ELATER ENDITE LAGENA LIGULE PALPUS PAPPUS STIPEL STYLET SUFFIX UROPOD ADJUNCT ANTENNA AURICLE CODICIL EARLOBE EMBLAST FIXTURE FURCULA GONOPOD HOUSING MALELLA PENDANT STIPULE SWIMMER THIMBLE TRAILER WINGLET ADDITION ADHERENT ASCIDIUM BRACHIUM EMPODIUM FILAMENT GNATHITE PEDIPALP PENDICLE PHYLLOID PREDELLA RHABDITE SYNTROPE MAXILLIPED
(— ON MOCCASIN) TRAILER
(EAR-SHAPED —) AURICLE
(PL.) ADNEXA ANNEXA FORCEPS
APPENDIX EKE ANNEX LABEL APPEND VERMIX AURICLE CODICIL PENDANT ADDENDUM AURICULA EPILOGUE
APPERCEPTION RECOGNITION
APPERTAIN LIE FALL REFER BELONG EFFEIR RELATE CONCERN PERTAIN
APPETITE MAW YEN LUST PICA TUCK URGE WILL ZEST BELLY BLOOD GORGE GREED GUSTO TASTE TWIST BULIMY DESIRE FAMINE GENIUS GODOWN HUNGER LIKING OREXIS RELISH STROKE TALENT BULIMIA CRAVING EDACITY LONGING PASSION STOMACH SWALLOW WANTING CUPIDITY FONDNESS GULOSITY TENDENCY
(— LOSS) ANOREXIA
(ANIMAL —) BLOOD
(CANINE —) PHAGEDENA
(EXCESSIVE —) LIMOSIS GULOSITY POLYPHAGIA
(PERVERTED —) MALACIA
(RAVENOUS —) LIMOSIS
(SUFF.) OREXIA PHIL(A)(AE)(E)(IA)(ISM)(IST)(OUS)(US)
APPETIZER WET WHET SAUCE CANAPE RAMAKI RELISH RUMAKI SAVORY CEVICHE SASHIMI APERITIF COCKTAIL DUBONNET
(CHICKEN LIVER —) RUMAKI
APPETIZING NICE GUSTY SAVORY GUSTFUL GUSTABLE PALATABLE
APPLAUD HUM CLAP LAUD RISE ROOT RUFF CHEER EXTOL HUZZA

PRAISE ACCLAIM APPROVE COMMENT ENDORSE HOSANNA PLAUDIT
(GROUP HIRED TO —) CLAQUE
APPLAUDER
(PL.) CLAQUE
APPLAUSE CLAP HAND BRAVO CHEER ECLAT HUZZA SALVO HURRAH PRAISE ACCLAIM OVATION CLAPPING
(— WITH THE FEET) RUFF
APPLE MAC PIP CRAB OHIA POME COPEI JAMBO BEEFIN BIFFIN CODLIN DOUCIN ESOPUS GOLDIN KARELA KAVIKA MACUPA MAKOPA PIPPIN PUFFIN RENNET RUSSET BALDWIN BEAUFIN CODLING COSTARD FAMEUSE GOLDING PEELING POMEROY RAMBURE RIBSTON RUDDOCK WAGENER WEALTHY WINESAP AMPALAYA COCCAGEE CORTLAND GREENING JONATHAN MCINTOSH NONESUCH PARADISE PEARMAIN POMANDER POROPORO QUEENING REINETTE ROSACEAN SWEETING WHITSOUR QUARENDEN QUARANTINE
(— OF PERU) JIMSON JIMPSON SHOOFLY
(— OF THE EYE) PUPIL
(BITTER —) COLOCYNTH
(CRAB —) CRAB SCRAB WHARRE POWITCH
(CRUSHED —) POMACE
(EMU —) COLANE
(GOLDEN —) BEL BAEL
(LIKE AN —) POMACEOUS
(PEARLIKE —) SORB
(PEELED —) DUMPLING
(SHRIVELED —) CRUMPLING
(SLICED DRIED —S) SNITS SNITZ SCHNITZ
(SMALL —) CODLIN CODLING
(SMALL —S) GRIGGLES
(STUNTED —) SCRUNT
(THORN —) MAD METEL
(PREF.) POMI POMO
APPLEBERRY DUMPLING
APPLEJOHN DEUSAN DEUZAN
APPLE-POLISH BROWNNOSE
APPLIANCE GEAR GRAB IRON TOOL BRACE CLAMP DEVIL FLIER FLYER GLODE SHADE BONNET BREWER DEVICE ENGINE FABRIC GADGET GAITER JUICER SPLINT WINDLE CHARGER MACHINE SCRAPER STOPPER UTENSIL BALANCER DEVIATOR
(PL.) FURNITURE
APPLICABLE APT FIT MEET PROPER USEFUL FITTING PLIABLE APPOSITE RELATIVE RELEVANT SUITABLE
(STRICTLY —) PROPER
(UNIVERSALLY —) CATHOLIC
(WIDELY —) BROAD
APPLICANT PROSPECT
APPLICATION USE DAUB FORM BLANK TOPIC APPEAL EFFORT ADDRESS EPITHEM REQUEST EPITHEME LENITIVE PETITION PRACTICE SEDULITY
(— OF KNOWLEDGE) PRACTICE PRACTISE
(— OF TESTS) DOCIMASY
(— OF THE MIND) STUDY
(— TO WRONG PURPOSE) ABUSE
(MEDICINAL —) PLASTER DRESSING FRONTING LENITIVE
(MENTAL —) INTENTION
APPLICATOR COLPOSTAT
APPLIED (CLOSELY —) ACCUMBENT
(PREF.) TECHNO
APPLIQUE DAG DAGGE ATTACH DESIGN ORNAMENT
APPLY ASK LAY PLY PUT RUB SET USE BEAR BEND CLAP DAUB GIVE HOLD MOVE SEEK TOIL TURN WORK ADAPT GRIND IMPLY LABOR LIKEN REFER SMEAR ADDICT APPEAL APPOSE BESTOW BETAKE BUCKLE COMPLY DEVOTE DIRECT EMPLOY EXTEND RESORT ADHIBIT COMPARE CONFORM IMPRESS OVERLAY PERTAIN REQUEST SOLICIT UTILIZE DEDICATE DISPENSE MINISTER PETITION
(— BRAKE) BUR
(— COSMETICS) DO POP
(— GRAPHITE) BLACKLEAD
(— GREASE) ARM
(— HOT CLOTHS) FOMENT
(— IMPROPERLY) ABUSE
(— ONESELF) ATTEND INTEND MUCKLE ADDRESS
(— PIGMENT) DRAG
(— TO) CONSULT CONTACT
APPOGGIATURA BACKFALL ACCIACCATURA
(DOUBLE —) FALL
APPOINT ARM FIX SET CALL DECK GIVE MAKE NAME ALLOT ARRAY AWARD COOPT CREST DIGHT ELECT ENACT EQUIP INSET PITCH PLACE POINT SHAPE SLATE ASSIGN ASSIZE ATTACH CREATE DECREE DEPUTE DETAIL DEVISE DIRECT ENTAIL ORDAIN OUTFIT SETTLE STEVEN TAILYE ARRAIGN CONFIRM DESTINE DISPOSE FURNISH GAZETTE RESOLVE TAILZIE DELEGATE DEPUTIZE INDICATE NOMINATE ORDINATE
(— A CLERIC) COLLATE
(— BEFOREHAND) STALL
(— TO BENEFICE) PRESENT
APPOINTED DUE DATIVE
APPOINTEE PLACEMAN
APPOINTMENT SET DATE BERTH ORDER TRYST BILLET OFFICE STEVEN COMMAND STATION CREATION DELEGACY POSITION
(— OF HEIR) INSTITUTION
APPORTION LOT DEAL DOLE MARK METE PART RATE ALLOT AWARD CAVEL GRANT PARAL SHARE SHIFT WEIGH APPLOT ASSESS ASSIGN DIVIDE PARCEL RATION TAVERN ARRANGE BALANCE QUARTER ALLOCATE DESCRIBE ADMEASURE PROPORTION
APPORTIONMENT DIVISION
APPOSITE APT PAT COGENT TIMELY GERMANE INCIDENT RELATIVE RELEVANT SUITABLE
APPRAISAL APPRIZAL
APPRAISE GAGE LOVE METE RATE ASSAY GAUGE JUDGE PRICE PRIZE VALUE ASSESS ESTEEM EVALUE PONDER PRAISE SIZEUP SURVEY ADJUDGE ANALYZE COMMEND ESTIMATE EVALUATE
APPRECIABLE ANY SENSIBLE PERCEPTIBLE
APPRECIATE DIG FEEL LOVE JUDGE PRIZE RAISE SAVOR TASTE VALUE ADMIRE ESTEEM SAVOUR ADVANCE APPRIZE APPROVE CHERISH REALIZE INCREASE TREASURE
APPRECIATION EYE GUSTO SENSE CONCEIT PERCEPTION
APPRECIATIVE AWAKE GRATEFUL
(— OF BEAUTY) ESTHETIC AESTHETIC
APPREHEND COP GET LAG NAB SEE FEAR HEAR KNOW NOTE SCAN TAKE VIEW CATCH DREAD GRASP GRIPE INTUE SEIZE ARREST BEHOLD DETAIN INTEND INTUIT BELIEVE CAPTURE CONCEIT ENDOUTE FORESEE IMAGINE REALIZE RECEIVE SENSATE SUPPOSE CONCEIVE DISCOVER OVERTAKE PERCEIVE
APPREHENDED GRIPPIT
APPREHENSIBLE NOETIC SENSATE SENSIBLE
APPREHENSION CARE FEAR FRAY PAIN PANG SCAN WERE ALARM DOUBT DREAD FANCY WORRY ARREST DISMAY NOESIS ANXIETY CAPTURE CONCERN PRESAGE SUSPECT DISTRUST MISTRUST SUSPENSE COGNITION PREHENSION
APPREHENSIVE APT ANTSY JUMPY FEARED MORBID ANXIOUS FEARFUL JEALOUS NERVOUS STREAKY UPTIGHT DOUBTFUL SOLICITOUS
APPRENTICE CUB BIND BOOT SNOB TYRO CADET DEVIL BURSCH HELPER JOCKEY NOVICE BANKMAN GROMMET LEARNER TRAINEE WAISTER APRENDIZ BEGINNER JACKAROO PRENTICE SERVITOR TURNOVER
(— ON SHIP) BRASSBOUNDER
(LONDON —) FLATCAP
(SHOEMAKER'S —) SNOB
APPRENTICESHIP SERVITUDE
APPRISE WARN LEARN TEACH ADVISE INFORM NOTIFY REVEAL APPRIZE ACQUAINT DISCLOSE INSTRUCT
APPROACH TRY ADIT BUMP BURN CHAT COME COST DRAW NEAR NERE NIGH ROAD ABORD BOARD CLOSE COAST ESSAY STALK VERGE ACCEDE ACCESS ACCOST ADVENT ANIMUS APPEAL BORDER BREAST BROACH COMING GATHER GONEAR IMPEND PROACH TRENCH ADVANCE AGGRESS APPULSE CONTACT PREFACE SEAGATE SUCCEED CONVERGE NEIGHBOR ONCOMING
(— FROM WINDWARD) BEAR
(— GAME) DRAW
(— HOSTILELY) SWAY
(— NEAR) TOUCH
(— OF DEATH) FIT
(— OF NIGHT) FALL
(— TENDENCY) ADIENCE
(GOLF —) SHIPSHOT
(INDIRECT —) FEELER
(INVITING —) PASS
APPROACHABLE COMMON AFFABLE ACCESSIBLE
APPROACHING LIKE COMING TOWARD ONCOMING
APPROBATION TEST FAVOR PROOF TRIAL ASSENT FAVOUR LOANGE PRAISE REGARD REPUTE PLAUDIT APPLAUSE APPROVAL SANCTION
APPROPPRIATELY APROPOS
APPROPRIATE ADD APT DUE FIT LAY PAT AKIN CRIB FEAT GOOD GRAB GRIP HELP JUST MEET SINK SUIT TAKE ALLOT ANNEX FITTY HAPPY RIGHT STEAL USURP ASSELF ASSIGN ASSUME BORROW DECENT DEVOTE DEVOUR DIGEST GATHER GENTIL KINDLY PILFER PIRATE POCKET PROPER TIMELY WORTHY APPROVE APROPOS CABBAGE CONDIGN CONVERT FITTING GERMANE GRABBLE GRADELY IMPOUND PREEMPT PURLOIN RELATED SECRETE SWALLOW ACCROACH APPOSITE ARROGATE BECOMING DESERVED EMBEZZLE GRACEFUL HANDSOME IDONEOUS PECULIAR PROPERTY RELEVANT RIGHTFUL SUITABLE
(— UNLAWFULLY) HEIST STEAL
(MOST —) CHOICE
APPROPRIATED ASSUMED PECULIAR
APPROPRIATENESS APTNESS DECENCY FITNESS APTITUDE
(NICE —) ELEGANCE
APPROPRIATION FUND VOTE DEVOTION
(FRAUDULENT —) CON EMBEZZLEMENT
APPROVAL AMEN ECLAT ASSENT ESTEEM APPROOF CONSENT PLAUDIT SUPPORT APPLAUSE BLESSING SANCTION SUFFRAGE AGREEMENT
(EXPRESSION OF —) VOILA
(FLIGHT —) AOK
APPROVE DO OK BUY DIG TRY AMEN HAVE LIKE OKAY OKEH PASS TEST VOTE ALLOW BLESS CLEAR FAVOR PROVE VALUE ACCEPT ADMIRE BISHOP CONCUR RATIFY AGREEON APPLAUD CERTIFY COMMEND CONFIRM CONSENT ENDORSE EXHIBIT INDORSE SUPPORT ACCREDIT MANIFEST SANCTION
APPROVED TRYE EXPERT PROBAL ACCEPTED ORTHODOX
(NOT —) OUT
APPROVING HEARTY
APPROXIMATE NEAR ABOUT CIRCA CLOSE COAST ROUGH COARSE

GENERAL NOMINAL APPROACH ESTIMATE
APPROXIMATELY SAY AWAY GAIN MUCH NIGH SOME ABOUT CIRCA ALMOST AROUND NEARLY TOWARD CRUDELY ROUGHLY
APPROXIMATING COMPARATIVE
APPROXIMATION CIRCA COUNTERFEIT
APPURTENANCE GEAR ANNEX ASSIGN EFFEIR ADJUNCT COMFORT APPANAGE PENDICLE (PL.) ADDENDA
APRICOT COT UME ANSU MUME ABRICOCK BLENHEIM
(DRIED —S) MEBOS MEEBOS
A PRIORI PURE
APRON BIB CAP BASE BOOT BRAT DICK RAMP SLOP TAYO TIER COVER EPHOD BARVEL BISHOP CANVAS DAIDLE DICKEY NAPRON RUNWAY SHIELD TARMAC TOUSER BRATTLE CANVASS DAIDLIE GREMIAL TABLIER LAMBSKIN PINAFORE PRASKEEN BARMCLOTH
(— OF FURNITURE) PETTICOAT
(— OF SEAT) FALL
(CHILD'S —) TIER BISWOP SLIPPER
(LEATHER —) DICK DICKY BARVEL DICKEY BARMFEL BARVELL BARMSKIN
(MASON'S —) LAMBSKIN
(SILKEN —) GREMIAL
(PL.) ARMITAS
APROPOS APT FIT PAT MEET TIMELY RELEVANT SUITABLE
APSE BEMA APSIS NICHE CHEVET CONCHA EXEDRA RECESS EXHEDRA PROTHESIS
APSIS APSE AUGE
APSYRTUS (FATHER OF —) AEETES
(MOTHER OF —) IDYIA ASTERODIA
(SISTER OF —) MEDEA
APT FIT PAT YAP ABLE DEFT FAIN FEAT GLEG KEEN VAIN WONT ADEPT ALERT HAPPY PRONE QUICK READY ASPERT CLEVER DOCILE KITTLE LIABLE LIKELY PRETTY SUITED TOWARD APROPOS CAPABLE FITTING IDONEAL WILLING APPOSITE DEXTROUS DISPOSED HANDSOME IDONEOUS INCLINED POIGNANT PRACTIVE PREPARED SKILLFUL SUITABLE
(— TO CHANGE) LABILE
(— TO TURN) WALT
APTERYX KIWI RATITE KIVIKIVI KIWIKIWI
APTITUDE ART BENT GIFT HEAD TURN CRAFT FLAIR HABIT KNACK SKILL VERVE GENIUS TALENT ABILITY CONDUCT FACULTY FITNESS LEANING CAPACITY INSTINCT TENDENCY
APTLY PAT
APTNESS GIFT KNACK SKILL APTITUDE FELICITY
APUS CYPSELUS MICROPUS
AQUARIUS SKINKER
AQUATIC (RARE —) MONKSEAL
AQUEDUCT AQUA DUCT CANAL AQUAGE SPECUS CHANNEL CONDUIT PASSAGE
(— OF SILVIUS) ITER
AQUEOUS HYDATOID WATERISH
AQUILA (WIFE OF —) PRISCILLA
AQUILANT (BROTHER OF —) GRYPHON
ARA MACAW
(FATHER OF —) JETHER
ARAB AHL AUS IBAD OMAN SLEB WAIF ARABY GAMIN NOMAD SAUDI TATAR SEMITE SLUBBI URCHIN ARABIAN BEDOUIN SARACEN SOLUBBI AZZAZAME KABABISH LARRIKIN SLOUBBIE YEMENITE
ARABELLA (CHARACTER IN —) MATTEO ZDENKA WALDNER ARABELLA MANDRYKA
(COMPOSER OF —) STRAUSS
ARABESQUE ORNATE MORISCO

ARABIA

COIN: LARI CARAT DINAR KABIK RIYAL
DESERT: NYD ANKAF DEHNA NAFUD NEFUD
DISTRICT: ASIR
GARMENT: ABA HAIK CABAAN BURNOUS
GODDESS: ALLAT
HOLY CITY: MECCA MEDINA
HOLY LAND: HEJAZ
ISLAND: SOCOTRA
JUDGE: CADI
KINGDOM: NEJD
MEASURE: DEN SAA FERK KIST ACHIR BARID CABDA CAFIZ COVID CUDDY MAKUK QASAB TEMAN WOIBE ZUDDA ARTABA ASSBAA COVIDO FEDDAN GARIBA GHALVA CAPHITE FARSAKH FARSANG KILADJA MARHALE NUSFIAH
MOUNTAIN: NEBO HOREB SINAI
PORT: ADEN
RULER: AMIR EMIR AMEER EMEER
STATE: ASIR OMAN YEMEN KUWAIT
TOWN: ABHA ADEN BEDA BERA HAIL RIAD SANA TAIF DUBAI HAUTA HOFUF JIDDA MECCA MOCHA QATIF TAIZZ YENBO ANAIZA MANAMA MATRAH MEDINA RIYADH SALALA SHAQRA BURAIDA HODEIDA MUKALLA ONEIZAH SHARJAH
TRIBE: AUS ASIR IRAD TEMA KEDAR DIENDEL SHUKRIA
WEIGHT: ROTL BAHAR CHEKI KELLA MAUND NASCH NEVAT OCQUE OUKIA RATEL TOMAN VAKIA BOKARD DIRHEM MISKAL FARSALAH

ARABIC CARSHUNI GARSHUNI KARSHUNI THAMUDIC
(— ALPHABET) BA FA HA RA TA YA ZA AYN DAD DAL JIM KAF KHA LAM MIM NUN QAF SAD SIN THA WAW ZAY ALIF DHAL SHIN GHAYN
ARABLE FERTILE PLOWABLE TILLABLE
ARACHNID CRAB MITE TICK TAINT ACARID ACARUS CARTER SPIDER CARTARE OCTOPOD PEDIPALP SCORPION SOLPUGID PSEUDOSCORPION
ARACHNOID KINGCRAB
ARAD (FATHER OF —) BERIAH
ARAGONITE ALABASTER
ARAIN ARRAND
ARAKANESE MAGHI
ARAM (FATHER OF —) ESROM HEZRON KEMUEL SHAMER
ARAMAIC SYRIAC MANDAEAN
(— TRANSLATION) TARGUM
ARAN (BROTHER OF —) UZ
(FATHER OF —) DISHAN
ARANEA EPEIRA
ARAPAIMA PIRARUCU
ARAPONGA BELLBIRD
ARAROBA ZEBRAWOOD
ARAROS (FATHER OF —) ARISTOPHANES
ARAUCANIAN AUCA PAMPA MAPOCHE MOLUCHE PAMPERO PICUNCHE
ARAWA AOTEA MATATUA
ARAWAK ARUA BARE URAN ARAUA BAURE CAMPA CHANE GUANA INERI SIUSI BAINOA BANIVA GUINAU IGNERI GOAJIRO IPURINA CAQUETIO CUSTENAU
ARBALEST BALISTER CROSSBOW
ARBITER REF UMP JUDGE CRITIC ODDMAN UMPIRE ADVISER DAYSMAN ODDSMAN OVERMAN REFEREE DICTATOR STICKLER
ARBITRAGE SHUNTING
ARBITRARY SEVERE THETIC WILLFUL ABSOLUTE DESPOTIC MASTERLY
(NOT —) FREE
ARBITRATE DECIDE MEDIATE
ARBITRATION DAYMENT
ARBITRATOR ARB REF JUDGE UMPIRE ARBITER MUNSIFF REFEREE MEDIATOR
ARBOR BAR AXLE BEAM ABODE BOWER SHAFT STAFF STALK TRAIL ARBOUR BOWERY GARDEN HERBER PANDAL RAMADA VOIDER BERCEAU HARBOUR MANDREL MANDRIL ORCHARD PERGOLA RETREAT SPINDLE TRELLIS FRESCADE TONNELLE
ARBORVITAE AKEKI ALERCE
ARBUTUS IVY MAYFLOWER
ARC BOW ARCH BEND FOIL HALO CURVE HANCE ORBIT SPARK SWING FOGBOW FOLIUM OCTANT RADIAN COMPASS RAINBOW FROSTBOW
(— OF HORIZON) AZIMUTH AMPLITUDE
(ELECTRIC —) SPARK
ARCA BOX CHEST PATEN ARCULA
ARCADE ORB AVENUE LOGGIA STREET GALLERY PORTICO ARCATURE CLOISTER
ARCADIAN CAJUN
ARCANE RUNIC HIDDEN SECRET MYSTERIOUS
ARCAS (FATHER OF —) ZEUS JUPITER
(MOTHER OF —) CALLISTO
ARCESIUS (FATHER OF —) ZEUS JUPITER CEPHALUS
(MOTHER OF —) PROCRIS EURYODIA
(SON OF —) LAERTES
ARCH ARC BOW COY SET SLY BACK BEND COPE COVE DOME HARP HOOP IRIS LEER OGEE PASS PEND PERT SPAN ARCUS CHIEF CURVE FAULD GREAT HANCE HUNCH INBOW JOWEL OGIVE PAUKY PAWKY POKEY PRIME ROACH SAUCY SWEEP VAULT ARCADE BRIDGE CALCAR CAMBER CLEVER DIADEM FOGBOW FORNIX GIRDLE IMPISH INVERT LANCET MANTEL SPRING SUNBOW WICKET ZYGOMA ARCHWAY CONCAVE CUNNING EMINENT GATEWAY ROGUISH SEGMENT SQUINCH SUPPORT TESTUDO TRIUMPH WAGGISH ALVEOLAR ESPIEGLE FOGEATER OVERCAST SCUNCHEON
(— OF FIREPLACE) MANTEL MANTELTREE
(— OF SKY) FIRMAMENT
(— OF WATER) CURL TUBE TUNNEL
(DENTAL —) ARCADE
(LOGGING —) SULKY
(PART OF —) PIER CHORD IMPOST PILLAR ABUTMENT EXTRADOS INTRADOS KEYSTONE SKEWBACK SPANDREL SPRINGER VOUSSOIR
(POINTED —) OGIVE
(PL.) SUBARARCUATION
ARCHAEOCYTE SORITE
ARCHAEOLOGIST POTHUNTER PREHISTORIAN
AMERICAN CLAY LOVE DAVIS EVANS HAWES SHEAR SOREN BARBER BUTLER GLUECK GORDON GORMAN HAYNES HEWETT HOLMES KIDDER MORELY PARKER PORTER SNYDER SQUIER MERRIAM NUTTALL REISNER SAVILLE SPEISER ALBRIGHT BREASTED CUMMINGS HANFMANN ROBINSON STERRETT THOMPSON BANDELIER CARPENTER MOOREHEAD RICHARDSON FROTHINGHAM
AUSTRALIAN CHILDE
AUSTRIAN ARNETH STUDNICZKA
CANADIAN CURRELLY
CZECH HROZNY
DANISH ZOEGA MULLER POULSEN WORSAAE BRONDSTED MATHIASSEN STEENSTRUP
DUTCH GRUYTERE
ENGLISH BELL COOK GANN GELL HALL BIBBY BUDGE EVANS RYMER STEIN CARTER CHILDE LAYARD MURRAY NEWTON PETRIE WARREN BEAZLEY BRAYLEY BURROWS DAWKINS DODWELL FELLOWS GARDNER HERBERT HOGARTH PENROSE WHEELER WOOLLEY GARSTANG HAMILTON LAWRENCE MALLOWAN RIDGEWAY STEPHENS THOMPSON BABINGTON
FRENCH LEBAS MAURY PUGIN VOGUE BORDES BREUIL CAGNAT CHOISY CLARAC COCHET FORBIN GAIDOZ LARTET MORGAN PERROT SAULCY BABELON CHANTRE

CHARNAY DELATRE HOMOLLE LEBLANT PEIRESC POTTIER BERTRAND DIEULAFOY LENORMANT DECHELETTE QUATREMERE WADDINGTON LECHEVALIER
GERMAN MAU ROSS TREU ADLER BRAUN BRUNN CONZE SARRE ANDRAE BECKER HELBIG HILLER MULLER NISSEN SCHOLL CURTIUS GERHARD LASAULX WELCKER WIEGAND BENNDORF BOTTIGER KOLDEWEY KOSSINNA PETERSEN ESSENWEIN LOESCHCKE MICHAELIS SCHLIEMANN FURTWANGLER WINCKELMANN
GREEK TSOUNTAS
ICELANDIC MAGNUSSON
IRISH STOKES ODONOVAN MACALISTER
ISRAELI YADIN SUKENIK
ITALIAN BONI LANZI ROSSI CANINA CESNOLA FIORELLI LANCIANI MARUCCHI VISCONTI
POLISH MICHALOWSKI
RUSSIAN KOPPEN POGODIN CHWOLSON
SCOTTISH RAMSAY BURGESS
SWEDISH BRENNER MONTELIUS
SWISS KELLER
ARCHAIC OLD ANCIENT ANTIQUE HISTORIC OBSOLETE
(PREF.) PALE
ARCHAISM (USE OF —S) GADZOOKERY
ARCHANGEL SATAN URIEL GABRIEL MICHAEL RAPHAEL HIERARCH
ARCHBISHOP HATTO PRELATE PRIMATE ORDINARY
ARCHDEMON BELFAGOR BELFAZOR
ARCHDIOCESE EPARCHY
ARCHDUKE ERZHERZOG
ARCHEAN EOZOIC
ARCHED ARCHY CONVEX ARCUATE EMBOWED VAULTED HOOPLIKE CAMERATED
(— IN) CONCAVE
(PREF.) TOXIC(O) TOX(I)(O)
ARCHEGONIUM CALYPTRA OOANGIUM
ARCHELAUS (BROTHER OF —) PHILIP ANTIPAS
(FATHER OF —) HEROD
(MOTHER OF —) MALTHAKE
ARCHEMORUS (FATHER OF —) LYCURGUS
(MOTHER OF —) EURYDICE
(NURSE OF —) HYPSIPYLE
ARCHER BOW CLIM CLYM BOWER BUTTY CUPID ROVER BOWBOY BOWMAN BOWYER SHOOTER PANDARUS
(EQUIPMENT OF —) TACKLE
ARCHER-FISH DARTER
ARCHERY TOXOLOGY ARTILLERY
(— SPACE) PETTICOAT
(PREF.) TOX(I)(O) TOXIC(O)
ARCHETYPE IDEA MODEL FIGURE SAMPLE ESSENCE EXAMPLE PARAGON PATTERN EXEMPLAR FRAVASHI ORIGINAL PARADIGM PROTOTYPE
ARCHIL CORKE CORCIR CORKER PERSIS CUDBEAR LECANORA ORCHILLA ORSEILLE
ARCHING CAMBER
ARCHITECT MAKER ARTIST ARTISAN BUILDER CREATOR PLANNER BEZALEEL DESIGNER SURVEYOR
AMERICAN DAY ORR PEI COBB COPE CRAM CRET HOOD HOWE HUNT JAHN KAHN MIES PELZ POPE POST SERT TOWN VAUX WANK WARE YEON ADLER ALLEN BACON BAYER BUTTS CASEY CRAMP DAVIS FLAGG GEHRY GOULD HEINS HOBAN MAHER MCKIM MILLS OBATA PELLI PRICE RODIA TANGE WAUGH WHITE BARBER BREUER GEDDES GILMAN GRAHAM HAIGHT HEJDUK HOWARD ITTNER JENNEY KASKEY MIZNER NEUTRA OWINGS ROGERS UPJOHN WALKER WALTER WARREN WRIGHT BRAGDON BRUNNER BURNHAM CARRERE CORBETT EIDLITZ GILBERT GOODHUE GRIFFIN HOWELLS KENDALL KIESLER KIMBALL LAFARGE LATROBE LESCAZE PARSONS PEABODY PEREIRA PLOWMAN RAYMOND STURGIS TUTHILL BENJAMIN BOGARDUS BOSWORTH BULFINCH COOLIDGE DINKELOO HARRISON HASTINGS HOLABIRD MCINTIRE SULLIVAN THOMPSON THORNTON VANBRUNT YAMASAKI MAGONIGLE RICHARDSON STEWARDSON STRICKLAND HARDENBERGH WHEELWRIGHT
AUSTRIAN NULL URBAN GRAVES WAGNER FERSTEL HASENAUER HOLZMEISTER
BELGIAN VELDE POELAERT
BRAZILIAN COSTA NIEMEYER
CZECH ZITEK
DANISH NYROP UTZON HANSEN JACOBSEN
DUTCH OUD KEYSER BERLAGE CUYPERS LOMBARD MOREELSE
EGYPTIAN CALLINICUS
ENGLISH KENT NASH SHAW TITE WEBB WREN ADAMS BAKER BARRY BLORE DANCE GLOAG GOTCH GWILT JONES MOULD SCOTT SOANE STONE WYATT BODLEY CLARKE COOPER HANSOM HUSSEY PAXTON STREET STUART BECKETT BENTLEY GIBBERD JACKSON KNOWLES LUTYENS PEARSON PENROSE RICKMAN ATKINSON CHAMBERS COCKERAM FLETCHER NESFIELD VANBRUGH CHAMPNEYS HAWKSMOOR NICHOLSON WILKINSON CATHERWOOD LANCHESTER WATERHOUSE ABERCROMBIE BUTTERFIELD PENNETHORNE
FINNISH EERO AALTO SAARINEN GESELLIUS
FRENCH DUC ETEX COTTE DUBAN LEVAU MAROT PUGET BENARD BERAIN BROSSE LEDOUX LEFUEL LESCOT NEPVEU ANTOINE BALTARD BLONDEL BULLANT DAVIOUD DELORME FORMIGE GABRIEL GARDNER GARNIER LENOTRE MANSART PERCIER PEVSNER VIOLLET ANDROUET CHALGRIN CUVILLES FELIBIEN FONTAINE HITTORFF LEPAUTRE PERRAULT SOUFFLOT LEMERCIER LECORBUSIER
GERMAN HOLL LENZ ADLER ERWIN GEDON LENNE SPEER KLENZE MESSEL MOLLER SEMPER STULER BEHRENS FRIESEN GROPIUS HOLBEIN NEUMANN OLBRICH POELZIG HEGEMANN LANGHANS SCHINKEL SCHLUTER ALTDORFER ESSENWEIN MENDELSOHN POPPELMANN KNOBELSDORFF
GREEK ICTINUS DOXIADIS MNESICLES SOSTRATUS DINOCRATES HIPPODAMUS POLYCLITUS CALLICRATES
HUNGARIAN STEINDL
IRISH MAGINNIS
ISRAELI SAFDIE
ITALIAN BONI DANTI DOLCI GENGA NERVI PONTI PORTA POZZO VINCI AGNOLO ALESSI BONOMI CIGOLI COSIMO GIOTTO IUVARA PISANO ROMANO SERING SOLARI SUARDI VASARI ALBERTI ALGARDI BELLINI BERNINI BIBIENA CAGNOLA CONTINO CORTONA FONTANA GIORGIO GUARINI LAURANA MADERNA PERUZZI TIBALDI TRIBOLO VIGNOLA AGOSTINO AMMANATI BRAMANTE CIVITALI GIOCONDO LOMBARDO PALLADIO PALLASIO PIRANESI SCAMOZZI BORROMINI PIERMARINI SANMICHELI SERVANDONI VANVITELLI PRIMATICCIO BRUNELLESCHI MICHELANGELO
JAPANESE ISOZAKI
MEXICAN BARRAGAN
POLISH NOWICKI SPYCHALSKI
ROMAN COSMATI COSSUTIUS
RUSSIAN BRYULOV
SCOTTISH ADAM ROSS GIBBS STIRLING MACKINTOSH
SPANISH CANO GAUDI CANDELA HERRERA VILLANUEVA
SWEDISH TESSIN ASPLUND OSTBERG TENGBOM
SWISS FRISCH LECORBUSIER
TURKISH SINAN
ARCHITECTURAL TECTONIC OECODOMIC
ARCHITECTURE DRAVIDA
ARCHITRAVE EPISTYLE PLATBAND
ARCHIVES TABULARY TABULARIUM
ARCHIVOLT RING ARCHBAND HEADBAND
ARCHLUTE THEORBO
ARCHON RULER DIRECTOR OFFICIAL THESMOTHETE
ARCHWAY ARCH PEND ARCUS PAILOO PAILOU
ARC LAMP MONOPHOTE
ARCOGRAPH BOW
ARCO SALTANDO SPICCATO
ARCTIC ICY COLD COOL GELID POLAR BOREAL CHILLY FRIGID GALOSH NORTHERN OVERSHOE
(— VEHICLE) SNOCAT
ARCTIUM LAPPA
ARCTOID URSINE
ARD (FATHER OF —) BELA
ARDENT HOT AVID FOND KEEN LIVE WARM EAGER FIERY GLEDY RETHE SHARP ABLAZE FERVID FIERCE IGNITE STRONG TORRID AMOROUS BURNING CORDIAL DEVOTED EARNEST FEELING FERVENT FLAMING FORWARD GLOWING INTENSE SHINING ZEALOUS DESIROUS EMPRESSE FEVERISH FLAGRANT ROMANTIC SANGUINE SCALDING SPORTIVE VEHEMENT PERFERVID
ARDON (FATHER OF —) CALEB
(MOTHER OF —) AZUBAH
ARDOR DASH EDGE ELAN FIRE GLOW HEAT LOVE ZEAL ZEST ESTRO FLAME GUSTO HEART TAPAS VERVE WRATH DESIRE FERVOR FOUGUE METTLE SPIRIT SPLEEN WARMTH ARDENCY EARNEST ENTRAIN PASSION DEVOTION FEROCITY VIOLENCE VIVACITY
ARDUOUS HARD LOFTY STEEP STIFF SEVERE TRYING ONEROUS EXACTING TIRESOME TOILSOME
ARDYS (FATHER OF —) GYGES
ARE MU RE AIR ARN ARUN HARE
AREA BELT PALE SIZE TREF ZONE BASIN COAST COURT FIELD PLACE RANGE REALM SCENE SCOPE SPACE TRACT ACCENT AREOLA EXTENT GROUND LOCALE MOARIA REGION SECTOR SPHERE SPREAD VOLUME ACREAGE AMENITY AREAWAY CIRCUIT COMPASS CONTENT COUNTRY ENVIRON EXPANSE KINGDOM PURLIEU SURFACE CAPACITY DISTRICT ENCEINTE PLOTTAGE PROVINCE
(— ALONG HIGHWAY) STRIP
(— AROUND MOUTH) DELTA PERISTOME
(— AT INTERSECTION) CIRCUS
(— BETWEEN FILLETS) CANALIS
(— IN BACTERIAL CULTURE) PLAQUE
(— IN CARTOON) BALLOON
(— IN CULTURE) PLAQUE
(— IN FRONT OF HOCKEY GOAL) CREASE
(— IN HOSTILE TERRITORY) AIRHEAD
(— OF ACTIVITY) METIER
(— OF EXPERIENCE) BOOK
(— OF FLAG) CANTON
(— OF INTEREST) SCENE
(— OF OLDER LAND) KIPUKA
(— OF OPEN WATER AMID ICE) POLYNYA
(— OF RIDGES) BILO
(— OF TIMBERLAND) CHENA
(— ON MOON) MARE WANE TERRA
(— OVER GATE) PORTAL
(— RELATE) SPACIAL SPATIAL
(— UNIT) TAN YOKE LABOR VIRGATE PLETHRON PLOWGANG PLOWGATE
(BLANK —) BITE HOLE

(BORDER —) OUTSKIRT OUTSKIRTS
(BORDERED —) PANEL
(COMBAT —) GLACIS
(CONTINENTAL —) MOARIA
(CULTURAL —) HORIZON
(CURLING —) PARISH
(DARK — OF MOON) MARE MARIA
(DENUDED —) BURN
(DIKED —) SLUSHPIT
(DISEASED —) PLAQUE
(ELONGATED —) BELT
(ENCLOSED —) FOLD SEPT
(EXTRAMURAL —) BANLIEUE
(FENCED —) CAGE COMPOUND
(FERTILE —) HAMMOCK
(FLOORING —) SQUARE
(FORTIFIED —) BASTION ENCEINTE
(GATHERING —) MANDAPA
(HOCKEY —) GOALMOUTH
(HOSPITAL —) ICU
(HUNTING —) SURROUND
(IMMOBILE — OF EARTH'S CRUST) CRATON
(INFESTED —) FLYBELT
(ISOLATED —) POCKET
(LARGE —) LANDMASS
(LIMITED —) SPOT
(LOW-LYING —) GLADE SWALE COULEE COULIE GUTTER
(LUMINOUS —) AUREOLA AUREOLE
(MINE —) SQUEEZE
(NUCLEAR —) HEARTH ECUMENE
(OPEN —) COURT LAUND PLAZA CAMPUS SQUARE HAGGARD
(OVERGROWN —) COGONAL
(PASTURE —) SOUM
(PAVED —) CAUSEY
(PLOWED —) BREAK
(RAISED —) TRIBUNE
(RESIDENTIAL —) BANLIEU BANLIEUE
(RURAL —) STICKS BOONIES BOONDOCKS
(SHOPPING —) MALL MART ARCADE EMPORIUM
(SLUM —) STEW
(SMALL —) AREOLA
(SMOKING —) BULLPEN
(STERN —) AFTERPART
(STORAGE —) STACK
(SUBURBAN —) ADDITION FAUBOURG
(SUNKEN —) SAG
(SWAMPY —) SLASH
(TEST —) MILACRE
(TIDAL —) CLAMFLAT
(TRANSITION —) ECOTONE
(TREELESS —) SLICK
(TUMID —) CERE
(UNCLEARED —) BUSH
(UPLAND —) COTEAU
(VOLCANIC —) SOLFATARA
(WASTE —) FOREST
(WOODED —) HAG BOSK BOSQUE
(SUFF.) **(GEOGRAPHIC —)** GAEA GEA
ARECA ARAK ARCHA BETEL
ARELI (FATHER OF —) GAD
ARENA AREA LIST OVAL RING RINK COURT FIELD SCENE SCOPE SPACE STAGE CIRCUS CIRQUE REGION SPHERE COCKPIT STADIUM TERRAIN THEATER BULLRING
(ATLANTA —) OMNI
(JAI ALAI —) FRONTON
ARENACEOUS SANDY GRITTY SABULOUS
AREOLA PIT AREA RING SPOT SPACE CAVITY
ARES MARS ENYALIUS GRADIVUS QUIRINUS
(FATHER OF —) ZEUS JUPITER
(MOTHER OF —) ENYO HERA JUNO
(SON OF —) REMUS CYCNUS ROMULUS
ARETE CREST
(FATHER OF —) DIONYSIUS
(HUSBAND OF —) DION ALCINOUS
(MOTHER OF —) ARISTOMACHE
AREUS (BROTHER OF —) TALAUS LEODOCUS
(FATHER OF —) BIAS
(MOTHER OF —) PERO
ARGALA STORK MARABOU
ARGALI AMMON ARKAR AOUDAD
ARGAN IRONWOOD
ARGANTE (DAUGHTER OF —) OCTAVIA ZERBINETTE
ARGENT LUNA MOON PEARL WHITE BLANCH SILVER CRYSTAL SHINING SILVERY

ARGENTINA
CAPITAL: BUENOSAIRES
COIN: PESO CENTAVO ARGENTINO
DANCE: TANGO CUANDO GAUCHO
FALLS: GRANDE IGUAZU
INDIAN: LULE GUARANI
LAKE: VIEDMA CARDIEL FAGNANO MUSTERS
MEASURE: SINO VARA LEGUA CUADRA FANEGA LASTRE MANZANA
MONEY: AUSTRAL
MOUNTAIN: TORO ANDES CHATO LAUDO MAIPU POTRO CONICO PISSIS RINCON FAMATINA MURALLON OLIVARES TRONADOR ZAPALERI ACONCAGUA INCAHUASI TUPUNGATO MERCEDARIO LLULLAILLACO
PLAIN: PAMPA PAMPAS
PORT: ROSARIO
PROVINCE: CHACO JUJUY SALTA CHUBUT CORDOBA FORMOSA LARIOJA MENDOZA NEUQUEN TUCUMAN MISIONES PATAGONIA
REGION: CHACO PATAGONIA
RIVER: SALI ATUEL CHICO COYLE DULCE LIMAY NEGRO PLATA TEUCO BLANCO CHUBUT CUARTO FLORES GRANDE PARANA QUINTO SALADO BERMEJO DESEADO MENDOZA TERCERO TUNUYAN SENGUERR
TOWN: AZUL GOYA ORAN PUAN BAHIA JUNIN LANUS LUJAN METAN SALTA PARANA RAWSON RUFINO VIEDMA ZARATE BOLIVAR CORDOBA DOLORES FORMOSA LABANDA MENDOZA NEUQUEN POSADAS RAFAELA ROSARIO TUCUMAN USHUAIA GALLEGOS CATAMARCA
VOLCANO: LANIN MAIPU DOMUYO PETEROA TUPUNGATO
WATERFALL: IGUAZU
WEIGHT: LAST GRANO LIBRA QUINTAL TONELADA

ARGES (BROTHER OF —) BRONTES STEROPES
(FATHER OF —) URANUS
(MOTHER OF —) GE GAEA
ARGIA (FATHER OF —) OCEANUS ADRASTUS
(HUSBAND OF —) INACHUS POLYBUS POLYNICES ARISTODEMUS
(MOTHER OF —) TETHYS AMPHITHEA
(SON OF —) ARGUS PROCLES EURYSTHENES
ARGIL CLAY ALUMINA
ARGIOPE (DAUGHTER OF —) EUROPA
(HUSBAND OF —) AGENOR
(SON OF —) CILIX CADMUS THASUS CERCYON PHINEUS PHOENIX
ARGOL TARTAR
ARGOSY SHIP FLEET GALLEON RAGUSYE
ARGOT CALO CANT FLASH LINGO SLANG JARGON PATOIS PATTER DIALECT
ARGUE JAW ARGY CHOP FUSS MEAN MOOT MOVE SPAR TIFF WORD ARGIE CAVIL ORATE PLEAD PROVE TREAT ACCUSE ADDUCE CAFFLE DEBATE EVINCE HASSLE REASON ARRAIGN CONTEND CONTEST COUNTER DISCUSS DISPUTE WRANGLE ERGOTIZE INDICATE MAINTAIN PERSUADE QUESTION TRAVERSE
(— DEDUCTIVELY) SYLLOGIZE
(— SNAPPISHLY) YAFF
(— SUBTLY) DISTINGUISH
ARGUEBUS HAGBUT HACKBUT
ARGUER JAW
ARGUMENT ROW AGON BEEF BLUE CASE FUSS MOOT PLEA SPAR SPAT TEXT TIFF CLASH DEBAT INDEX KNIFE LEMMA PROOF THEME TOPIC BARNEY COMBAT CORKER DEBATE DUSTUP ELENCH HASSLE MATTER TUSSLE APAGOGE CLAMPER DEFENCE DEFENSE DILEMMA DISPUTE ESSENCE FLUBDUB POLEMIC RHUBARB SOPHISM SORITES SUMMARY ABSTRACT CLINCHER COURSING EVIDENCE SPARRING TRILEMMA REASONING PARALOGISM PERSUASION
(— FOR) PRO
(— IN FAVOR) PRO
(ART OF —) POLEMICS
(CONSLUSIVE —) SOCKDOLAGER SOCKDOLOGER
(DECISIVE —) SETTLER
(ILLOGICAL FALLACY
(INVALID —) SOPHISM
(SCHOLASTIC —) QUODLIBET
(THEORETICAL —) ACADEMICS
ARGUMENTATION DEBATE DISPUTE ERGOTISM CHOPLOGIC
ARGUMENTATIVE ERISTIC FRATCHY FORENSIC
ARGUS (FATHER OF —) ZEUS JUPITER PHRIXUS
(MOTHER OF —) ARGIA NIOBE CHALCIOPE
(SLAYER OF —) HERMES MERCURY
ARGUSFISH SCAT
ARHAT MONK LOHAN RAKAN SAINT ARAHANT
ARIA AIR SOLO SONG TUNE MELODY SORTIE ARIETTA ARIETTE SORTITA
ARIADNE (FATHER OF —) MINOS
(HUSBAND OF —) THESEUS
(MOTHER OF —) PASIPHAE
ARIADNE AUF NAXOS
(CHARACTER IN —) ARIADNE BACCHUS ZERBINETTA
(COMPOSER OF —) STRAUSS
ARIAN AGNOETE AGNOITE HOMOEAN ANOMOIAN EUSEBIAN
ARID DRY BALD BARE DULL LEAN BARREN DESERT JEJUNE MEAGER DROUTHY PARCHED STERILE THIRSTY DROUGHTY WITHERED
ARIDAI (FATHER OF —) HAMAN
ARIDATHA (FATHER OF —) HAMAN
ARIDITY DROUTH DROUGHT SICCITY
ARIES RAM
ARIKARA REE
ARIL POD ARILLUS COATING ARILLODE
ARIODANTE (COMPOSER OF —) HANDEL
ARIODANTES (LOVER OF —) GENEURA
ARISAI (FATHER OF —) HAMAN
ARISBE (FATHER OF —) MEROPS
(HUSBAND OF —) PRIAM DARDANUS HYRTACUS
(SON OF —) ASIUS NISUS AESACUS
ARISE WAX COME FLOW FORM GROW LIFT REAR RISE SOAR STEM AWAKE BEGIN BUILD EXIST ISSUE MOUNT RAISE SPRAY STAND START SURGE TOWER WAKEN ACCRUE AMOUNT APPEAR ASCEND ATTAIN DERIVE EMERGE HAPPEN KITTLE SPRING DEVELOP EMANATE EXSURGE PROCEED REDOUND SOURDRE
(— FROM) STEM
ARISING LEVEE EMERGENT
(PREF.) **(— WITHIN)** IDIO
ARISTAEUS (DAUGHTER OF —) MACRIS
(FATHER OF —) APOLLO
(MOTHER OF —) CYRENE
(SON OF —) ACTAEON
(WIFE OF —) AUTONOE
ARISTE (BROTHER OF —) CHRYSALE
ARISTO (BROTHER OF —) SGANARELLE
ARISTOCRACY CLASS ELITE GENTRY ARISTOI SAMURAI NOBILITY OPTIMACY
ARISTOCRAT LORD NOBLE ARISTO JUNKER GRANDEE PARVENU EUPATRID OPTIMATE PATRICIAN
(RUSSIAN —) BOIAR BOYAR BOYARD
(PL.) ARISTOI
ARISTOCRATIC HIGH TONY NOBLE QUALITY CAVALIER BELGRAVIAN

ARISTODEMUS **(BROTHER OF —)** TEMENUS CRESPHONTES
(FATHER OF —) ARISTOMACHUS
(SON OF —) PROCLES EURYSTHENES
(WIFE OF —) ARGEIA
ARISTOTELIAN PERIPATETIC
ARITHMETIC SUM AUGRIM ALGORISM
(— FIGURE) ADDEND
ARITHMOMETER MULTIPLIER

ARIZONA
CAPITAL: PHOENIX
COUNTY: GILA PIMA YUMA PINAL APACHE MOHAVE NAVAJO COCHISE YAVAPAI COCONINO GREENLEE MARICOPA SANTACRUZ
INDIAN: HOPI PIMA YUMA NAVAHO NAVAJO PAPAGO HUALAPAI
MOUNTAIN: BANGS GROOM LEMMON TURRET HUALPAI PASTORA MERIDIAN
MOUNTAIN RANGE: GILA KOFA MOHAWK GALIURO HUALPAI AQUARIUS BUCKSKIN
PEAK: HUMPHREYS
RIVER: GILA SALT ZUNI VERDE PUERCO COLORADO
STATE BIRD: CACTUSWREN
STATE FLOWER: SAGUARO
STATE NICKNAME: OCOTILLO
STATE TREE: PALOVERDE
TOWN: AJO ELOY MESA NACO YUMA GLOBE LEUPP TEMPE BISBEE JEROME MCNARY SALOME TOLTEC TUCSON CLIFTON CORTARO KINGMAN MORENCI NOGALES PHOENIX SAFFORD FREDONIA PRESCOTT FLAGSTAFF TOMBSTONE

ARJUN KUMBUK
ARJUNA **(FATHER OF —)** PANDU
(SON OF —) ABHIMANYU
ARK BIN BOX BOAT SHIP BARGE CHEST HUTCH BASKET COFFER REFUGE WANGAN RETREAT SHELTER WANIGAN FLATBOAT
ARKANSAN ARKANSAWYER

ARKANSAS
CAPITAL: LITTLEROCK
COUNTY: LEE CLAY DREW PIKE POLK POPE YELL BOONE CROSS DESHA IZARD LOGAN SHARP STONE BAXTER CHICOT LONOKE SEARCY CALHOUN PRAIRIE PULASKI OUACHITA
INDIAN: CADDO OSAGE QUAPAW CHOCTAW CHEROKEE
LAKE: CONWAY NIMROD GREESON NORFORK OUACHITA
MOUNTAIN: RICH GAYLOR MAGAZINE
MOUNTAIN RANGE: OZARK OUACHITA
NATIVE: TOOTHPICK
NICKNAME: WONDER
PRESIDENT: CLINTON
RIVER: RED WHITE SALINE BUFFALO CURRENT COSSATOT OUACHITA
STATE BIRD: MOCKINGBIRD
STATE FLOWER: APPLE BLOSSOM
STATE TREE: SHORTLEAFPINE
TOWN: COY CUY KEO OLA ROE ULM ALMA BONO CASA DELL DIAZ MORO ENOLA PERLA RISON RONDO WYNNE ALICIA JASPER PIGGOTT

ARKOSE ARENITE SANDSTONE
ARLECCHINO **(CHARACTER IN —)** LEANDRO BOMBASTO COLUMBINE HARLEQUIN
(COMPOSER OF —) BUSONI
ARLESIANA, L' **(CHARACTER IN —)** ROSA MAMMAI METIFIO VIVETTE FEDERICO
(COMPOSER OF —) CILEA
ARM FIN OAR TOE BOOM HEEL LIMB WING BLADE BOUGH CRANE EQUIP FENCE FIORD FIRTH FJORD FORCE GARDY INLET MIGHT OXTER POWER RIFLE SNORD STOCK BRANCH CRUTCH ENERGY FRETUM GIBBET MEMBER OUTFIT PINION RADIAL SLEEVE TAPPET WEAPON CATCHER DERRICK DRAWARM FLIPPER FOREARM FORTIFY FURNISH GARNISH HARNESS OCKSTER PREPARE PROTECT PROVIDE QUILLON SUPPORT ARMORIAL CROSSARM FOLLOWER FORELIMB PULLDOWN SOUPBONE STRENGTH TRANSEPT
(— FORCES) MIRV
(— HOLDING FLINT) HAMMER
(— OF BARNACLE) CIRRUS CIRRHUS
(— OF CHAIR) ELBOW
(— OF CRANE) JIB GIBBET RAMHEAD
(— OF GIN) START
(— OF PROPELLER) BLADE
(— OF RECORD PLAYER) PICKUP
(— OF SEA) COVE FLOW MEER MERE BRACE CANAL FIRTH FRITH GRAIN FRETUM ESTUARY EURIPUS
(— OF SPINNING MULE) SICKLE
(— OF WINDMILL) VANE WHIP
(— WITH GAFF) HEEL
(INDEX —) DIOPTER
(IRON —) CRANE
(KIND OF —) BOSTON
(LEVER —) SWEEP
(PITCHING —) SOUPBONE
(WINDMILL —) VANE
(PL.) ARMORY ARMAMENT
(PREF.) BRACHI
ARMADA NAVY FLEET FLOTILLA
ARMADILLO APAR PEBA TATU APARA POYOU TATOU BOLITA MATACO MATICO MULITA PELUDO DASYPOD TATOUAY TATUASU EDENTATE KABASSOU LORICATE PANGOLIN
(SMALL —) PICHI PICHICIAGO
ARMAMENT ARMADA BATTERY
ARMATURE ARMING KEEPER LIFTER
ARMBAND BRASSARD
ARMCHAIR CHAIR ELBOW BERGERE FAUTEUIL LOVESEAT
ARMED FLUTE HEELED DAGGERED WEAPONED

ARMENIA
ANCIENT CAPITAL: ANI ARTASHAT ARTAXATA
ANCIENT NAME: MINNI
CAPITAL: EREVAN ERIVAN YEREVAN
COIN: RUBLE
FORTRESS: EREBUNI
HERO: ARA ARAM HAIK ARAME VARTAN
KING: ASHOT GAGIK TRDAT ZAREH DIKRAN ARTAKIAS ARTASHES TIGRANES ZARIADES
KINGDOM: URARTU VANNIC CILICIA SOPHENE ARDSRUNI
LAKE: VAN SEVAN URMIA
LANGUAGE: ARMENIAN
MOUNTAIN: ARA ALAGEZ ARARAT TAURUS ALADAGH ARAGATS KARABAKH
NATIVE: ARMEN GOMER
PLAIN: ARARAT
RIVER: KUR ARAS KURA ARAKS CYRUS DEBET HALYS ZANGA AGSTEV ARAXES RAZDAN TIGRIS HRAZDAN VOROTAN AKHURYAN EUPHRATES
SAINT: SAHAK MESROP
TOWN: VAN SIVAS BITLIS EREVAN KUMAYN SPITAK ERZURUM KUMAIRI TRABZON LENINAKAN

ARMENIAN ERMYN HADJI HAIKH
ARMFUL LOCK YAFFLE
ARMHOLE MAIL SCYE OXTER ARMSCYE ARMSEYE ARMSIZE
ARMIDE **(CHARACTER IN —)** ARMIDA RINALDO
(COMPOSER OF —) GLUCK
ARMINIO **(COMPOSER OF —)** HANDEL
ARMISTICE LULL PEACE TRUCE INDUCIAE
ARMLET BANGLE TABLET TORQUE ARMHOOP
ARMONI **(FATHER OF —)** SAUL
(MOTHER OF —) RIZPAH
ARMOR (AND SPECIFIC PIECES THEREOF) ARMS BACK BOOT EGIS JAMB MAIL TACE WEED ACTON AMURE BARDS BRACE CUISH CULET DORON GUARD GUIGE JAMBE PIECE PLATE PROOF SCALE STEEL TAPUL TASSE TRUSS ARMLET ARMOUR BEAVER BRINIE BRUNIE BYRNIE CAMAIL CORIUM COUTER CRANET CUISSE GORGET GRAITH GREAVE JAMBER POLEYN RONDEL SECRET SHIELD TASSET THORAX TONLET TUILLE VOIDER AILETTE ARMHOOP BESAGNE BROIGNE CORSLET CUIRASS DEFENSE EPAULET HARNESS HAUBERK JAZERAN KNEELET LAMBOYS PALETTE PANOPLY PLACATE POITREL REREDOS ROUNDEL SABATON VENTAIL BRASSARD PAULDRON RAMENTUM VAMBRACE BAINBERGS RONDACHEPALLETTE
(— ON TREE) TROPHY
(— PLATE) TUILLE
(ELBOW —) CUBITIERE
(FOOT —) SABATON SABBATON SOLLERET
(HEAD —) ARMET CASQUE HELMET PALLET SCONCE VENTAIL AVENTAIL
(HORSE —) BARB BARD BARDE CRINET CHAMFRON CRINIERE CHAMFRAIN
(LEATHER —) CORIUM
(LEG —) BOOT JAMB CUISH JAMBE CUISSE GREAVE JAMBER TUILLE JAMBEAU CHAUSSES
(NECK —) COLLAR GORGET
(PADDED —) GAMBESON
(SUIT OF —) CAST STAND
(PREF.) HOPL(O)
ARMOR-BEARER SQUIRE ARMIGER CUSTREL
ARMORED PANZER
ARMORER GUNSMITH ARTIFICER
ARMORICAN BRETON
ARMORY ARSENAL HERALDRY
ARMPIT ALA OXTER AXILLA ARMHOLE
ARMS TACKLE
(PREF.) HOPL(O)
ARMS AND THE MAN **(AUTHOR OF —)** SHAW
(CHARACTER IN —) LOUKA RAINA NICOLA PETKOFF SERGIUS CATHERINE BLUNTSCHLI
ARMY FERD HERE HOST IMPI LEVY MAIN ARRAY CROWD FORCE HERSE HORDE POWER RANKS ZOMBI COHORT HONVED LEGION NUMBER THRONG TROOPS MILITIA BATTALIA CHIVALRY MILITARY
(HOSTILE —) FOE
(MEMBER OF IRISH REPUBLICAN —) PROVO
(VOLUNTEER —) VOLAR
(PL.) SABAOTH
(PREF.) STRATO
ARMY OFFICER (ALSO SEE SOLDIER)
ARMYWORM GRASSWORM
ARNE **(FATHER OF —)** AEOLUS
(HUSBAND OF —) METAPONTUS
(MOTHER OF —) THEA
(SON OF —) AEOLUS BOEOTUS
ARNOTTO ROUCOU
AROAR REBOANT
AROD **(FATHER OF —)** GAD
AROID APII ARAD TARO APIUM KRUBI TANIA KONJAK TANIER YAUTIA PINUELA CALADIUM CUNJEVOI MOCOMOCO CUCKOOPINT
AROMA AURA NOSE ODOR NIDOR SAVOR SCENT SMELL SNUFF SPICE FLAVOR BOUQUET PERFUME REDOLENCE
(— OF WINE) BLOOM
AROMATIC BALMY SPICY SWEET MASTIC ODOROUS PIQUANT PUNGENT FRAGRANT REDOLENT SPICEFUL
AROUND NEAR UMBE ABOUT CIRCA CIRCUM ENVIRON
(PREF.) AMBI AMPHI CIRCUM PERI
AROUSAL INDUCTION
AROUSE SOW CALL CITE FIRE GAIN HEAT MOVE REAR SPUR STIR WAKE WHET ADAWE ALARM

ALERT AWAKE EVOKE FLESH PIQUE RAISE RALLY ROUSE ROUST SHAKE STEER WAKEN ABRAID AWAKEN ELICIT EXCITE FOMENT INCITE INDUCE KINDLE REVIVE STIRUP SUMMON THRILL TURNON ACTUATE AGITATE CONNOTE INCENSE INFLAME INSPIRE PROVOKE STEAMUP SUGGEST WHOMPUP INSPIRIT
(— DISPLEASURE) AGGRAVATE
(— ENMITY) ESTRANGE
(— WRATH) SPLEEN

ARPEGGIATE BREAK

ARPEGGIO SWEEP ROULADE FLOURISH
(— EFFECT) RASGADO

ARPHAXAD (FATHER OF —) SHEM

ARRACACHA APIO ARRA

ARRACK ARAK RACK ARAKI RACKAPEE

ARRAIGN TRY CITE ARGUE PEACH ACCUSE CHARGE IMPUTE INDICT INDITE SUMMON APPOINT IMPEACH DENOUNCE

ARRANGE DO FIX LAY RAY SET CAST COMB EDIT FILE FORM PLAN PLAT RAIL RULE SIDE SIZE SORT TIER TIFT WORK ADAPT AGREE ALIGN ALINE ARRAY BESEE CURRY DRAPE DRESS ETTLE FANCY FRAME GRADE ORDER PITCH RANGE SCORE SHAPE SHIFT SPACE STALL TRICK ADJUST BRANCH CODIFY DAIKER DESIGN DEVISE FETTLE FORMAT INFORM ORDAIN SETTLE SOLUTE TAILYE ADDRESS APPOINT BESPEAK CATALOG COLLATE COMPONE COMPOSE CONCERT DISPOSE ENRANGE GRADATE MARSHAL PERMUTE PREPARE REDRESS SERIATE TAILZEE TAILZIE ALPHABET CLASSIFY CONCLUDE ORGANIZE REGULATE TABULATE COLLOCATE CONJOBBLE NEGOTIATE STIPULATE ORCHESTRATE
(— BEFOREHAND) FORLAY FORELAY
(— FANTASTICALLY) HARLEQUINIZE
(— FASTIDIOUSLY) PREEN
(— HAIR) SET TED COIF TRUSS COIFFE
(— HARMONIOUSLY) GRADATE
(— IN FLOCKS) HIRSEL HIRSLE
(— IN FOLDS) DRAPE
(— IN LAYERS) DESS TIER
(— IN ROW) RACE
(— STRAW) HAULM
(— SYSTEMATICALLY) DIGEST
(— WITH BEST AT TOP) DEACON

ARRANGEMENT FIX FLY LAY RAY DEAL FLOW PLAT RANK TIFF ARRAY BUILD DRAPE INDEX ORDER SETUP BORDER DESIGN HOOKUP LAYOUT SCHEME SETOUT SYNTAX SYSTEM TREATY BLEEDER INTERIM POSTURE TONTINE ATTITUDE CONTRACT DISPOSAL GROUPING POSITURE SEQUENCE ORDONNANCE ORIENTATION BANDSTRATION ORCHESTRATION
(— IN LINE) RANK SERIES
(— IN LOCK) DETECTOR
(— OF BRISTLES) CHAETOTAXY
(— OF CHESS PAWNS) CHAIN
(— OF COMPUTER ELEMENTS) ARRAY
(— OF DRAPERIES) CAST
(— OF FLOWERS) CASCADE CORSAGE IKEBANA PARTERRE
(— OF GRADES) CURVE
(— OF GUNS) ARMADA
(— OF HAIRDO) FORETOP
(— OF HAIRS) SCOPA
(— OF HOOKS) GIG
(— OF LOOM BARS) GRIFF GRIFFE
(— OF PARTS) STRUCTURE
(— OF ROCKS) BEDDING
(— OF TACKLE) BURTON
(— OF TIMBER) ANCHOR
(— OF TROOPS) ECHELON
(BETTING —) PERM
(CIRCULAR —) CYCLE
(DISHONEST —) CROSS
(GEOMETRICAL —) LATTICE
(MUSICAL —) CHART
(ORDERED —) PERMUTATION
(SECRET —) PACK
(TRADITIONAL —) AKOLUTHIA AKOLOUTHIA
(TRAVEL —) CHARTER
(PREF.) TAX(EO)(I)(O)
(LACK OF —) ATAXO
(SUFF.) OSIS TACTIC TAXIS TAXY

ARRANGEMNET (SECRET —) PACKK

ARRANGING ORDONNANT
(JAPANESE ART OF FLOWER —) IKEBANA

ARRANNGEMENT (MUSICAL—) SCORE INSTRUMENTATION

ARRANT BAD THIEF OUTLAW ROBBER VAGRANT OUTRIGHT PRECIOUS RASCALLY

ARRAS ORRIS ARISTE DRAPERY TAPESTRY

ARRASTRA TAHONA

ARRAU JURARA

ARRAY DON DUB FIG ARMY BUSK DECK DOLL FYRD GALA GARB HOST POMP RAIL RANK ROBE VEST ADORN ALIGN ALINE ATOUR DRESS EQUIP HABIT HARKA HEDGE ORDER ADIGHT AGUISE ATTIRE ATTRAP BEDECK CLOTHE DEVISE FETTLE FINERY GRAITH INVEST LAYOUT MUSTER PLIGHT SERIES SETOUT SHROUD ADDRESS AFFAITE AFFLICT APPAREL ARRANGE BATTERY BEDIGHT COMPANY DISPLAY DISPOSE ENVELOP FURNISH FYRDUNG MARSHAL PANOPLY REPAREL ACCOUTER
(— OF CHEMICALS) ARA
(— OF GUNS) BROADSIDE
(— OF TROOPS) PAREL
(— OF WEAPONS) ARMORY
(— TASTELESSLY) DAUB
(BATTLE —) ACIES HERSE BATTALIA
(MATHEMATICAL —) MATRIX

ARRAYED HABITED ABULYEIT

ARREAR DEBT BEHIND UNPAID ARRIERE
(IN —S) BACK BEHIND

ARREST CAP COP FIX FOB LAG NAB NIP VAG BALK BUST CURB FALL GLOM GRAB HALT HOLD JAIL KEEP NAIL NICK PULL REST SHOP SIST STAY STEM STOP ARRET CATCH CHECK DELAY PINCH REEST SEIZE STILL STUNT ATTACH BRIDLE COLLAR DECREE DETAIN ENGAGE FINGER HAULIN HINDER PLEDGE PULLIN RETARD SLOUGH SNEEZE THWART CAPTION CAPTURE CUSTODY SUSPEND IMPRISON OBSTRUCT RESTRAIN
(— DEVELOPMENT) FIXATE
(— OF BLEEDING) HEMOSTASIS
(— OF DEVELOPMENT) ABORTION
(— OF GROWTH) STASIS
(PUT UNDER —) BUST

ARRESTER (SPARK —) BONNET

ARRESTING BOLD SEIZING MAGNETIC PLEASING STRIKING

ARRET EDICT ARREST DECREE DECISION JUDGMENT

ARRHA HANDGELD

ARRIGANTLY HIGH

ARRIS PIEN ANGLE PIEND ARRIDGE

ARRIVAL COMER IKBAL VENUE ADVENT COMING INCOMING REACHING
(— TIME) TOUCHDOWN
(— TIME RECORD) OS
(NEW —) ROOINEK
(UNTIMELY —) LATECOMER

ARRIVE GO SEY COME FALL FLOW GAIN LAND LEND RIVE GETIN LIGHT OCCUR REACH WORTH ACCEDE APPEAR ATTAIN HAPPEN OBTAIN UPCOME CHECKIN COMPASS
(— AT) GET HIT FIND GAIN HENT MAKE BRING EDUCE FETCH GUESS SEIZE ATTAIN DERIVE ESTIMATE
(— AT LAST) ROLLIN

ARRIVED-IN DONE

ARROBA ROVE

ARROGANCE PRIDE SWANK TUMOR BOWWOW HUBRIS BOBANCE CONCEIT DISDAIN EGOTISM HAUTEUR STOMACH BOLDNESS SUCCUDRY SURQUIDY

ARROGANT BOLD COXY HIGH MOOD COBBY COCKY GREAT HUFFY JOLLY LOFTY PROUD STOUT SURLY WLONK ASSUME CHESTY FIERCE LORDLY UPPISH UPPITY WANTON FORWARD FROSTED HAUGHTY HAUTAIN HUFFISH POMPOUS STATELY TOPPING AFFECTED ASSUMING CAVALIER FASTUOUS IMPUDENT SNUFFING SUPERIOR TUMOROUS OVERBEARING OVERWEENING

ARROGATE GRAB TAKE CLAIM SEIZE USURP ASSUME ADROGATE

ARROW FLO PIN ROD SEL BOLT DART REED SELF SELL SHOT VIRE BLUNT DEATH FLANE ROVER SHAFT ARCHER FLIGHT GANYIE GARROT QUARRY SPRITE TACKLE WEAPON BOBTAIL DOGBOLT MISSILE POINTER PROJECT QUARREL SAGITTA SPINNER FISHTAIL FORKHEAD
(— ARUM) TUCKAHOE
(— IN GRASS) GREEN SNAKE
(— IN LEG OF STAND) FOOT
(FIRE —) MALLEOLUS
(PART OF —) TIP BUTT HEAD NOCK PILE POINT SHAFT FEATHER FLETCHING
(POISONED —) DERRID SUMPIT
(WOBBLING —) FISHTAIL
(PREF.) BELO(NO) HASTATO SAGITTI SAGITTO TOX(I)(ICO)(O)

ARROWHEAD BUNT FORK HEAD PILE FLUKE POINT NEOLITH ARTIFACT CROWBILL FORKHEAD SPICULUM

ARROWROOT PIA ARUM MUSA SAGU ARARU CANNA TACCA TIKOR ARARAO CURCUMA

ARROWSMITH (AUTHOR OF —) LEWIS
(CHARACTER IN —) MAX ALMUS JOYCE LEORA SILVA TERRY LANYON MARTIN GUSTAVE WICKETT GOTTLIEB SONDELIUS ARROWSMITH PICKERBAUGH

ARROWWORM SAGITTA CHAETOGNATH

ARROYO DRAW WADI BROOK CREEK GULCH GULLY HONDO ZANJA COULEE RAVINE STREAM CHANNEL BARRANCA BARRANCO

ARRRANGED (— IN BUNDLES) DESMOID

ARSENAL ARMORY SUPPLY MAGAZINE

ARSENOPYRITE MISPICKEL

ARSHIN ARCHIN ALTSCHIN
(ONE-24TH OF —) PARMAK PARMACK

ARSINOE (DAUGHTER OF —) ERIOPIS
(FATHER OF —) PHEGEUS LEUCIPPUS
(HUSBAND OF —) ALCMAEON
(MOTHER OF —) PHILODICE
(SISTER OF —) PHOEBE HILAIRA

ARSIS BEAT ICTUS ACCENT RHYTHM UPBEAT DOWNBEAT

ARSON FIRE CRIME FELONY BURNING

ARSONIST ARSONITE

ARSPHENAMINE SIX SALVARSAN

ART WILE CRAFT KNACK KUNST MAGIC SKILL TRADE MISTER TECHNE ARTWORK CALLING CUNNING DESCANT DISCANT FACULTY FINESSE MYSTERY SCIENCE APTITUDE ARTIFICE BUSINESS LEARNING PRACTICE PRACTISE
(— OF APPLYING TESTS) DOCIMASY
(— OF BLAZONING) ARMORY
(— OF CALCULATING) ALGORISM ALGORITHM
(— OF DEFENSE) SKIRMISH
(— OF FLOWER ARRANGEMENT) IKEBANA
(— OF FLOWER ARRANGING) IKEBANA
(— OF HEALING) LEECHCRAFT
(— OF HORSEMANSHIP) MANEGE
(— OF PREPARING COLORS) GUMPTION

(— OF SELF-DEFENSE) AIKIDO
(— OF SPEECH) RHETORIC
(— OF TYING KNOTS IN PATTERN) MACRAME
(— SUPPLIES) OILS
(DIABOLIC —) DEVILRY DEVILTRY
(DRAMATIC —) STAGE
(IRRATIONAL —) DADA
(JAPANESE — MOVEMENT) YAMATO YAMATOE
(JUNK —) NEODADA
(KIND OF —) OP POP CLIP JUNK MARTIAL OPTICAL
(LEG —) CHEESECAKE
(MAGIC —) WITHERCRAFT
(MYSTERIOUS —) CABALA KABALA CABBALA KABBALA QABBALA CABBALAH KABBALAH QABBALAH
(NOT —) SHLOCK
(OCCULT —) THEURGY
(RUN AN — SHOW) CURATE
(SHODDY —) BONDIEUSERIE
(TYPE OF —) STREETSCAPE
(PREF.) TECHNI TECHNO TYP(I)(O)
(SUFF.) ERY SHIP TECHNICS TECHNY TYPAL TYPE TYPIC TYPY
(RELATING TO —) METRIC

ARTAXERXES (COMPOSER OF —) ARNE

ART DECO DECO MODERNE
(— MASTER) ERTE
(— PAINTER) ERTE

ARTEMIS UPIS DELIA DIANA PHOEBE CYNTHIA AMARYSIA

ARTERY WAY PATH ROAD AORTA PULSE ROUTE COURSE DENTAL FACIAL RADIAL STREET VESSEL ANONYMA CAROTID COELIAC CONDUIT HIGHWAY SCIATIC VAGINAL CEREBRAL CERVICAL CORONARY DORSALIS EMULGENT PROFUNDA
(NECK —) CAROTID

ARTFUL APT FLY SLY FOXY WILY AGILE DOWNY PAWKY SUAVE ADROIT CLEVER CRAFTY FACILE PRETTY QUAINT SCHEMY SHREWD SMOOTH TRICKY CROOKED CUNNING KNOWING PLAITED POLITIC PRACTIC SUBTILE VULPINE DEXTROUS SCHEMING STEALTHY

ARTFULNESS CUNNING ARTIFICE SUBTLETY

ART GRAY QUAKER SEAMIST

ARTHRITIS GOUT CARPITIS

ARTHROPOD GOLACH GOLOCH SPIDER CHILOPOD DIPLOPOD PERIPATUS

ARTHUR (FATHER OF —) UTHER

ARTICHOKE BUR CANADA CYNARA CARDOON CHOROGI CROSNES KNOTROOT

ARTICLE A AN YE LOT ONE THE BOOK ITEM TERM BRIEF CHEAT ESSAY GEANE PAPER PIECE PLANK POINT STORY THEME THING CLAUSE DETAIL LEADER NOTICE OBJECT REPORT FEATURE BROCHURE CAUSERIE DOCTRINE PARTICLE POSTFACE TREATISE
(— OF CLOTHING) DUD DIDO APRON CLOUT DICKY FANCY THING CASUAL DICKEY GARMENT COINTISE CREATION
(— OF FOOD) CATE KNACK
(— OF FURNITURE) STICK
(— OF LITTLE WORTH) DIDO
(— OF SILK) SQUEEZE
(— OF TRADE) PADNAG
(— OF UNUSUAL SIZE) IMPERIAL
(—S OF FAITH) CREDENDA
(—S OF MERCHANDISE) CHAFFER
(CAST-IRON —S) KENTLEDGE
(CHEAP —) CAMELOT
(CHOICE —) VALUABLE
(CONTERFEIT —) DUMMY
(DECORATIVE —) LACKER LACQUER
(FANCY —) CONCEIT
(FIVE —S) HAND
(GENUINE —) GOODS
(HANDICRAFT —) BOONDOGGLE
(INFERIOR —S) SHODDY
(METAL —S) BATTERY
(MISCELLANEOUS —S) SUNDRIES
(NESWPAPER —) STORY LEADER FEATURE
(NONDESCRIPT —) DODAD DOODAB DOODAD WHATNOT
(PALTRY —) GIMCRACK JIMCRACK
(PERSONAL —) CHOSE
(SECONDHAND —) JUNK
(SHOWY —) FRIPPERY
(TRIFLING —) KNICKKNACK
(VALUABLE —S) SWAG
(WORTHLESS —) TRANGAM
(PL.) WARES

ARTICULAATE (INDISTINCTLY —) THICK

ARTICULATE BACK JOIN CLEAR FRAME JOINT SPEAK UNITE UTTER VOCAL ACCENT FLUENT VERBAL EXPRESS JOINTED PHONATE DISTINCT SYLLABLE
(— ASCHILD) LISP
(— CONFUSEDLY) SPUTTER

ARTICULATED BACK BLADE DENTAL DORSAL LABIAL JOINTED ALVEOLAR CEREBRAL VERTEBRATE

ARTICULATION NODE JOINT VOICE SUTURE ARTHRON JUNCTURE SYNTAXIS
(DEFECTIVE —) LALLATION LAMBDACISM

ARTIFACT CELT DISC DISK BATON GUACA HUACA AMGARN BRONZE EOLITH FABRIC GORGET REJECT RONDEL SAGAIE SKEWER ABRADER ARTEFAC DISCOID RACLOIR SCRAPER ARTEFACT DATEMARK RONDELLE TRANCHET
(JAPANESE —S) HANIWA
(PL.) CACHE CERAUNIA

ARTIFICE ART GIN JET GAUD HOAX JOUK PLAN PLOT RUSE TURN WILE BLIND CHEAT COVIN CRAFT CROCK CROOK DODGE DRAFT FEINT FETCH FRAUD GUILE SHIFT SKILL STALL TRAIN TRICK CAUTEL DECEIT DEVICE DOUBLE ENGINE CHICANE COMPASS CUNNING DODGERY DRAUGHT EVASION FINESSE SHUFFLE SLEIGHT COZENAGE DISGUISE DOUBLING INTRIGUE MANAGERY MANEUVER PRACTICE PRACTISE PRETENSE STRATEGY TRICKERY WINDLASS
(PL.) CABAL CRANS

ARTIFICER WRIGHT ARTIFEX WORKMAN DAEDALUS LAPIDARY MECHANIC OPIFICER TVASHTAR TVASHTRI

ARTIFICIAL CUTE SHAM BOGUS DUMMY FAKED FALSE ARTFUL ERSATZ FORCED FORGED STAGEY UNREAL ASSUMED BASTARD FEIGNED PLASTIC AFFECTED FABULOUS FALSETTO POSTICHE POSTIQUE SPURIOUS
(NOT —) REAL NATURAL
(OVERLY —) ALEXANDRIAN
(SOMETHING —) CAMP

ARTIFICIALITY MANNERISM

ARTILLERY (OR PIECE THEREOF) ARMS GUNS DRAKE SAKER CANNON MINION HEAVIES LANTACA LANTAKA CANNONRY ORDNANCE
(— FIRE) STONK RAFALE

ARTILLERYMAN GUN GUNNER LASCAR REDLEG LASHKAR ENGINEER TOPECHEE

ARTISAN FEVER SMITH ARTIST COOPER ARTIFEX TARKHAN WORKMAN KAMMALAN LETTERER MECHANIC OPIFICER OPERATIVE SILVERSMITH

ARTISANSHIP FOLKCRAFT

ARTIST (ALSO SEE PAINTER) DAB NABI POET ACTOR ADEPT BRUSH HILDA RAPIN DANCER ETCHER EXPERT FICTOR MASTER SINGER WIZARD ARTISAN ARTISTE ARTSMAN FAUVIST OPERANT PAINTER PONTIST SCHEMER ANIMATOR COLORIST FUSINIST IDEALIST LADISLAW LETTERER MAGICIAN MUSICIAN SCULPTOR SKETCHER STIPPLER PASTELIST PRIMITIVE MINIMALIST PASTELLIST
(— SCHOOL) LUMINISM
(SIDEWALK —) SCREEVER
(PL.) SCHOOL

ARTISTIC ARTLY DAEDAL EXPERT ESTHETIC PAINTERLY
(— MATERIAL) KITSCH
(— QUALITY) VERTU VIRTU

ARTISTRY FOLKCRAFT

ARTLESS NAIF OPEN FRANK NAIVE PLAIN SEELY CANDID RUSTIC SIMPLE GIRLISH NATURAL INNOCENT

ARTS TRIVIUM
(MARTIAL —) BUDO

ART-SONG LIED

ARTY CHICHI

ARUGULA RUGOLA

ARUM ARAD TARO AROID CALALU DRAGON TAWKEE WAMPEE MANDRAKE TUCKAHOE

ARVIRAGUS CADWAL
(FATHER OF —) CYMBELINE
(WIFE OF —) DORIGEN

ARYAN MEDE SLAV OSSET NORDIC OSSETE
(NOT —) ANARYA

ARZA (SLAYER OF —) ZIMRI

AS S SO ALS FOR HOW QUA ALSO INTO LIKE SOME THAT THUS TILL WHEN EQUAL QUOAD SINCE WHILE BRONZE THEWAY WHENAS BECAUSE EQUALLY SIMILAR QUATENUS
(— FAR AS) TO INTO QUATENUS
(— IT WERE) FAIRLY
(— LONG AS) SOBEIT
(— MUCH) ALSMEKILL
(— SOON) ALSOON ASTITE ALSWITH DIRECTLY
(— TO) QUOAD
(— WELL) EVEN
(— WELL AS) FORBY FORBYE
(— YET) HITHERTO

ASA (FATHER OF —) ABIJAH

ASAFETIDA HING LASER FERULA

ASAHEL (BROTHER OF —) JOAB
(MOTHER OF —) ZERUIAH
(SLAYER OF —) ABNER
(SON OF —) JONATHAN
(UNCLE OF —) DAVID

ASANDER (BROTHER OF —) PARMENION
(FATHER OF —) PHILOTAS

ASAPH (FATHER OF —) BECHERIAH
(SON OF —) JOAH ASARELAH

ASARABACCA HAZEL FOALFOOT

ASAREEL (FATHER OF —) JEHALELEEL

ASARELAH (FATHER OF —) ASAPH

ASBESTOS ABBEST XYLITE AMIANTH ABSISTOS ALBESTON AMIANTUS WOODROCK EARTHFLAX
(BLUE —) CROCIDOLITE

ASCALAPHUS (BROTHER OF —) IALMENUS
(FATHER OF —) ARES MARS ACHERON
(MOTHER OF —) ORPHNE GORGYRA ASTYOCHE
(SLAYER OF —) DEIPHOBUS

ASCEND UP STY RISE SOAR STYE UPGO ARISE CLIMB MOUNT SCALE STAIR TOWER AMOUNT ASPIRE BREAST CLIMAX UPRISE CLAMBER UPCLIMB ESCALATE PROGRESS

ASCENDANCY SWAY POWER CONTROL MASTERY SUCCESS DOMINION OWERANCE PRESTIGE

ASCENDANT ARISING MOUNTANT ASSURGENT

ASCENDING ANODAL ANODIC ORIENT UPHILL UPWARD ANABATIC ASPIRANT SUBERECT
(— WITHOUT A TURN) FLYING

ASCENSION APOTHEOSIS

ASCENT STY HILL RAMP RISE RIST UPGO CLIMB GLORY GRADE MOUNT RAISE SCEND SLOPE STEEP STEPS STILL UPWAY SOURCE STAIRS UPCOME UPGANG UPHILL UPRISE UPWITH INCLINE SCALING UPGRADE UPSWING EMINENCE GRADIENT

ASCERTAIN GET SEE SET TRY FEEL FIND TELL COUNT GLEAN LEARN PITCH PROVE ASSURE ATTAIN FIGURE ANALYSE ANALYZE APPRISE APPRIZE COMPUTE MEASURE UNEARTH DISCOVER

ASCETIC NUN MONK SOFI SUFI YATI YOGI DANDY FAKIR FRIAR SADHU SOFEE STOIC YOGIN CHASTE ESSENE HERMIT SADDHU SEVERE SOOFEE STRICT ADAMITE AUSTERE BHIKSHU DEVOTEE EREMITE RECLUSE SRAMANA STYLITE TAPASVI AVADHUTA MARABOUT NAZARITE SANNYASI
(PL.) THERAPEUTAE
ASCIDIAN POLYP CUNGEBOI CUNGEVOI TETHYDAN TUNICATE
ASCIDIUM PITCHER VASCULUM
ASCOCARP ASCOMA
ASCOGONIUM ARCHICARP
ASCOMA CUPULE
ASCRIBABLE DUE
ASCRIBE LAY ARET EVEN GIVE APPLY BLAME COUNT GUESS IMPLY INFER PLACE REFER TITLE ACCUSE ALLEGE ARETTE ASSIGN ATTACH CHARGE CREDIT IMPUTE PREFER RECKON RELATE ASCRIVE ENTITLE ACCREDIT ARROGATE DEDICATE INSCRIBE INTITULE
ASCRIPTION LAUD CREDIT ADDITION
ASCUS BAG SAC THECA ASCELLUS
ASEA LOST ADDLED ADRIFT PUZZLED SAILING CONFUSED
ASEMIA ASYMBOLIA
ASENATH (FATHER OF —) POTIPHERAH
(HUSBAND OF —) JOSEPH
(SON OF —) EPHRAIM MANASSEH
ASEXUAL AGAMIC NEUTER AGAMOUS
(PREF.) AGAM(O)
ASGARD (GODS OF —) AESIR
ASH AS ALS ASE ASS FIG RON COKE SORB ARTAR ASHEN EMBER FRAIN ROWAN CINDER CORPSE DOTTEL DOTTLE TEPHRA WICKEN CLINKER RESIDUE DOGBERRY FRAXINUS HOOPWOOD WINETREE
(BARILLA —) PULVERINE
(FRUIT OF —) SAMARA
(SILKY —) CEDAR
(PL.) ASE AXAN KELP SOIL ASHEN VAREC WASTE BREEZE CINDERS CREMAINS PULVERIN
ASHAMED MEAN NACE NAIS ABASHED HANGDOG HONTOUS SHAMEFACED
ASHBEL (FATHER OF —) BENJAMIN
ASH-BLOND CENDRE
ASH-COLORED CINEREAL CINEREOUS
ASHEN WAN GRAY GREY PALE WAXEN WHITE PALLID GHASTLY BLANCHED CINEREAL
ASHER (FATHER OF —) JACOB
(MOTHER OF —) ZILPAH
ASHES (— OF CREMATED BODY) CREMAINS
(HUMAN —) CREMAINS
(PREF.) CINE SPODO TEPHRA TEPHRO
ASHKENAZ (FATHER OF —) GOMER
ASHKOKO CONY DAMAN HYRAX
ASHLAR ASELAR RANGEWORK
ASHORE ACOST ALAND AGROUND BEACHED STRANDED
ASHTAVAKRA (FATHER OF —) KAHODA
ASHTRAY SPITKID SPITKIT
ASHUR FEROHER
(FATHER OF —) HEZRON
(MOTHER OF —) ABIAH
(WIFE OF —) HELAH
ASHVATH (FATHER OF —) JAPHLET
ASHY WAN CINEREAL
ASIA (FATHER OF —) OCEANUS
(HUSBAND OF —) IAPETUS
(MOTHER OF —) TETHYS
(SON OF —) ATLAS EPIMETHEUS PROMETHEUS

ASIA

(ALSO SEE SPECIFIC COUNTRIES)
DESERT: GOBI TAKLAMAKAN
LAKE: ARAL URMIA BAYKAL CASPIAN BALKHASH
MOUNTAIN: FUJI DJAJA JANNU KAMET PAMIR ARARAT KUNGUR KUNLUN LHOTSE MAKALU MUZTAG NOSHAQ NUPTSE SEMERU TRIVOR EVEREST RATHONG ANNAPURNA
NATION: IRAN IRAQ LAOS OMAN BURMA CHINA INDIA JAPAN NEPAL QATAR SYRIA TIBET YEMEN BHUTAN ISRAEL JORDAN RUSSIA TAIWAN TURKEY ARMENIA BAHRAIN CROATIA LEBANON VIETNAM CAMBODIA HONGKONG MALAYSIA MONGOLIA PAKISTAN THAILAND INDONESIA KAMPUCHEA SINGAPORE AZERBAIJAN BANGLADESH NORTHKOREA SOUTHKOREA AFGHANISTAN SAUDIARABIA
RANGE: ALTAI KOLYMA HIMALAYA
RIVER: OB SI AMUR LENA URAL INDUS GANGES MEKONG TIGRIS HWANGHO SALWEEN TANGTZE YENISEI EUPHRATES IRRAWADDY
VOLCANO: APO USU FUGI GEDE TAAL AGUNG ALAID DEMPO MAYON RAUNG MARAPI MERAPI SEMERU SINILA SLAMET ULAWUN TAMBORA TJAREME GAMALAMA KERINTJE RINDJANI TOLBACHIK BULOSANSUNDORO
WATERFALL: JOG GOKAK KEGON MEKONG CAUVERY

ASIA MINOR (ANCIENT REGION OF —) IONIA
ASIAN LAO THAI
ASIDE BY BYE OFF AGEE AWAY GONE NEAR PAST AGLEY ALOOF APART ASKEW FORBY ASLANT ASTRAY BESIDE BEYOND BYHAND FORBYE FORTHBY LATERAL PRIVATE WHISPER OVERHAND RESERVED SECRETLY SEPARATE SIDEWISE OVERBOARD TOTHEWIND
ASININE DULL CRASS DENSE INEPT SILLY ABSURD ASSISH OBTUSE SIMPLE STUPID DOLTISH FATUOUS FOOLISH IDIOTIC MORONIC
ASIUS (FATHER OF —) DYMAS HYRTACUS
(SISTER OF —) HECUBA
(SLAYER OF —) AJAX IDOMENUS
ASK BEG SPY SUE FAND PRAY QUIZ CLAIM CRAVE EXACT FRAYN PLEAD QUERY SPEAK SPEER SPEIR SPELL SPERE ADJURE DEMAND DESIRE EXAMIN EXPECT FRAIST FRAYNE INVITE BESEECH BESPEAK CONSULT ENTREAT IMPLORE INQUIRE REQUEST REQUIRE SOLICIT PETITION QUESTION
(— ALMS) CANT THIG
(— FOR) BEG BID CRY DUN LAIT SEEK BESPEAK INQUIRE REQUEST
(— PAYMENT) CHARGE
ASKANCE AWRY ASKEW ASKILE CROOKED SIDEWAYS
ASKEW CAM AGEE ALOP AWRY AZEW AGLEE AGLEY AMISS ATILT CRAZY GLEED TIPSY ASKANT ASLANT ATWIST FLOOEY SKEWED SKIVIE ASQUINT CROOKED OBLIQUE BIASWISE COCKEYED SIDELING
ASKING ROGATION ROGATORY
ASKWARD HAMHANDED
ASLANT ASIDE SLOPE
(PREF.) PLAGI(O)
ASLEEP DEAD FAST IDLE LATENT NUMBED DORMANT NAPPING
ASOCIAL EGREGIOUS
ASOKA (FATHER OF —) BINDUSARA
ASOPUS (DAUGHTER OF —) ORNIA THEBE AEGINA ASOPIS CLEONE PIRENE SINOPE CHALCIS CORCYRA SALAMIS TANAGRA THESPEIA
(SON OF —) ISMENUS PELASGUS
(WIFE OF —) METOPE
ASP ESP ASPIC COBRA SNAKE VIPER ASPIDE URAEUS CERASTES
ASPAR (FATHER OF —) ARDABURIUS
ASPARAGUS LILY GRASS SPRUE ASPERGE SPARAGE SPERAGE
(— GARNISH) PRINCESS
(— UNIT) SPEAR
(INFERIOR —) SPRUE
ASPATHA (FATHER OF —) HAMAN
ASPECT AIR HUE WAY AURA BROW FACE HAND KIND LEER LOOK MIEN SIDE VIEW VULT ANGLE COLOR DECIL FACET GUISE IMAGE NORMA PHASE SIGHT STAGE TRINE VISOR VIZOR DECILE FACIES FIGURE GLANCE MANNER PHASIS REGARD VISAGE APPAREL BEARING ESSENCE FEATURE MALEFIC OUTLOOK RESPECT RETRAIT SEXTILE SHOWING SPECIES CARRIAGE CONSPECT FOREHEAD OUTSIGHT PROSPECT QUINTILE CHARACTER SEMBLANCE
(— OF CURVE) INSIDE
(— OF EMOTION) AFFECT
(— OF MOON) CRESCENT
(— OF MUSICAL NUANCES) AGOGICS
(BALEFUL —) DISASTER
(CULTURAL —) EMANATION
(DETERMINING —) HEART
(DORSAL —) NOTUM
(EXTERNAL —) PHYSIOGNOMY
(FACIAL —) EXPRESSION
(LANGUAGE —) DURATIVE
(OF PLANETS) QUARTILE
(OF STARS) QUINCUNX
(PRIMARY —) HIGHWAY
(QUARTILE —) SQUARE
(SECONDARY —) BYWAY
ASPEN APS ASP ALAMO NITHER POPLAR POPPLE QUAKER QUAKING TREMBLE
ASPER AKCHA AKCHEH OTHMANY
ASPERGILLUM HYSSOP SPRINKLE STRINKLE
ASPERITY IRE RIGOR ACERBITY ACRIMONY TARTNESS ANIMOSITY
ASPERSE SKIT SLUR SPOT ABUSE DECRY LIBEL SPRAY DEFAME DEFILE MALIGN REVILE SHOWER VILIFY APPEACH BLACKEN DETRACT LAMPOON SLANDER TARNISH TRADUCE BESMIRCH FORSPEAK SPRINKLE
ASPERSION SLUR BAPTISM CALUMNY INNUENDO
ASPHALT BREA PITCH SLIME FILLER MANJAK BITUMEN CUTBACK MANJACK BYERLITE UINTAITE GILSONITE
ASPHALTUM CONGO
ASPHODEL KNAVERY AFFODILL
ASPHYXIA APNEA APNOEA ACROTISM SUFFOCATION
ASPIC JELLY GELATIN GELATINE LAVENDER
ASPIRANT (— TO KNIGHTHOOD) DONZEL SQUIRE
ASPIRATE ROUGH SPIRITUS
ASPIRATION GOAL IDEAL DESIRE RECOIL SIGHTS AMBITION PRETENSION
ASPIRE AIM STY HOPE LONG MINT RISE SEEK SOAR WISH ETTLE MOUNT TOWER YEARN ASCEND ATTAIN DESIRE PRETEND
ASPIRIN FEBRIFUGE
ASPIRING ASPIRANT
ASRIEL (FATHER OF —) GILEAD
ASS DOLT FOOL JADE KHUR MOKE BURRO CHUMP CUDDY DICKY DUNCE EQUID GUDDA HINNY NINNY CUDDIE DAPPLE DICKEY DONKEY ONAGER ASINEGO ASSHEAD JACKASS LONGEAR MALTESE SOLIPED IMBECILE
(FEMALE —) JENNY JENNET
(MALE —S) JACKSTOCK
(WILD —) KIANG KULAN KYANG KIYANG KOULAN ONAGER HEMIPPE CHIGETAI GHORKHAR HEMIONUS
(PL.) JACKSTOCK
(PREF.) ONISCI ONO
ASSAI MANICOLE
ASSAIL WOO BASH BEAT FRAY HOOT JUMP PELT SAIL ASSAY BESET FLYAT PRESS SETAT SHOCK STONE WHACK WHANG ACCUSE ATTACK BATTER BICKER BULLET HURTLE IMPUGN INFEST INSULT INVADE MALIGN MOLEST OFFEND OPPUGN RAGEAT RATTLE SAILYE SCATHE STRIKE ASSAULT ATTEMPT BELABOR BESEIGE BOMBARD CATCALL ENFORCE ASSEMBLE BLUDGEON TOMAHAWK
(— WITH DIN) PEAL

(— WITH LANGUAGE) REVILE BULLYRAG BALLLYRAG
(— WITH RAILLERY) BANTER
(— WITH WORDS) TONGUE
ASSAILANT ONSETTER
ASSAM (MOUNTAIN OF —) JAPVO
(STATE OF —) KHASI MANIPUR
(TOWN OF —) IMPHAL SADIYA GAUHATI SHILLONG
(TRIBE OF —) AO AKA AOR AHOM GARO NAGA
ASSARACUS (BROTHER OF —) ILUS GANYMEDE
(FATHER OF —) TROS
(MOTHER OF —) CALLIRRHOE
(SISTER OF —) CLEOPATRA
(SON OF —) CAPYS
ASSART SART THWAITE
ASSASSIN THAG THUG BRAVE BRAVO FEDAI FIDAI NINJA CUTTLE FIDAWI HITMAN KILLER SLAYER RUFFIAN STABBER TORPEDO HACKSTER MURDERER SICARIUS
ASSASSINATE KILL SLAY MURDER REMOVE
ASSASSINATION THUGGEE
ASSAULT MUG BEAT BLOW COSH FRAY RAID SLUG ABUSE ALARM ASSAY BRUNT HARRY ONSET POISE POUND SHOCK SMITE STORM STOUR VENUE AFFRAY ALARUM ASSAIL ATTACK BREACH BUFFET CHARGE ENGINE EXTENT HOLDUP INSULT INVADE NAPALM ONFALL STOUND STOUSH THRUST YOKING ATTEMPT BOMBARD DESCENT LAMBAST PURSUIT RUNNING VIOLATE INVASION OUTBURST BUSHWHACK
ASSAY RUN SAY TRY TEST ESSAY PROOF PROVE TOUCH TRIAL ASSAIL ATTACK EFFORT ANALYZE ATTEMPT EXAMINE TASTING ANALYSIS APPRAISE ENDEAVOR ESTIMATE HARDSHIP
ASSAYER POTDAR TESTER
(CONTAINER OF —) CUPEL
ASSAYING DOCIMASY
ASSEMBLAGE ARMY BODY CAMP CLOT COMA CREW HERD HOST MASS PACK RUCK BUNCH CHOIR COURT CROWD DRIFT DROVE FLOCK GROUP LEVEE POSSE QUIRE SALON SHOCK SWARM TRIBE CONVOY GALAXY HOOKUP RESORT SPREAD SYSTEM THRONG CIRCUIT CLUSTER COLLEGE COMPANY COMPLEX CONVENT CULTURE SOCIETY STATION STATUTE TABAGIE ASSEMBLY AUDITORY CONGRESS MULTIPLE PARLIAMENT
(— OF FOSSILS) COLONY
(— OF INTEGERS) IDEAL
(CONFUSED —) FARRAGO
ASSEMBLE FIT LAY POD SAM BULK CALL HERD HOST KNOT MASS MEET ROUT SAMM AMASS ASAME FLOCK GROUP PIECE RALLY TROOP UNITE COUPLE GATHER HUDDLE MUSTER SUMMON COLLATE COLLECT COMPILE CONDUCE CONVENE CONVOKE RECRUIT CONGRESS CONGREGATE
(— CARDS) BUNCH
ASSEMBLED ACCOYLD
ASSEMBLER BONDER
ASSEMBLING MUSTER PARADE ROUNDUP
ASSEMBLY HUI SUM BAUD BEVY BOGY DIET DRUM DUMA FEIS HOEY MALL MOOT RAAD ROUT SEJM SEYM TING AGORA BOGEY BOULE COURT COVEN CURIA DOUMA FORUM GROUP JUNTA LEVEE PARTY PRESS SABHA SETUP SOBOR SYNOD THING TROOP AENACH AONACH ASSIZE BOBBIN BUSING CHAPEL COETUS COVINE GEMOTE MAJLIS PARADE PLENUM POWWOW SEIMAS SENATE STEVEN CHAMBER CHAPTER COLLEGE COMITIA COMMAND COMPANY CONCION CONSORT CONVENT COUNCIL DIETINE EOTATES FOLKMOT HUSTING LANDTAG MEETING PENSION SERVICE SESSION SOCIETY SYNAGOG SYNAXIS TEMPEST TYNWALD ZEMSTVO AUDIENCE CONCLAVE CONGRESS ECCLESIA FOLKMOOT PLACITUM PORTMOTE PRESENCE SEDERUNT SOBRANJE TINEWALD TRIBUNAL VOLKSTAG WARDMOTE CONCOURSE
(— HOUSE) KASHIM
(— OF BLESSED) HEAVEN
(— OF CONDUCTORS) BUS
(— OF DEPUTIES) AMPHICTYONA
(— OF ELDERS) KGOTLA
(— OF WITCHES) COVEN SABBAT SABBATH
(AFTERNOON —) LEVEE
(BOY SCOUT —) JAMBOREE
(CLOSED —) CONCLAVE
(CROWDED —) SQUEEZE
(EVENING —) ROUT
(FASTENER —) SEMS
(FULL —) PLENUM
(GRENADE —) BOUCHON
(IRELAND —) DAIL SEANAD
(IRISH —) DAIL
(RIOTOUS —) MOB DONNYBROOK
(PL.) PLENA COMITIA
ASSENT AYE BOW NOD YEA YES AMEN SEAL SENT ADMIT AGREE GRANT YIELD ACCEDE ACCEPT ACCORD BELIEF CHORUS COMPLY CONCUR SUBMIT UNISON APPROVE CONCEDE CONFESS CONFORM CONSENT ADHESION CONSTATE OKEYDOKE SANCTION SUFFRAGE ACCESSION OKEYDOKEY
(— TO) GOWITH
ASSERT LAY BRAG SHOW POSIT VOICE AFFIRM ALLEGE ASSURE AVOUCH DEFEND DEPONE DEPOSE INTEND INTENT THREAP UPHOLD ADVANCE BETOKEN CONFIRM CONTEND DECLARE PROTEST SUPPORT ADVOCATE CHAMPION CONSTATE MAINTAIN OUTSTAND POSITIVE PREDICATE
ASSERTING (POSITIVELY —) THETIC
ASSERTION VOW FACT HOTI CLAIM VOUCH AVERMENT
(— OF MASCULINITY) MACHISMO
(BOASTFUL —) JACTATION
(DUBIOUS —) PLINYISM
ASSERTIVE BRASH DOGMATIC POSITIVE
ASSESS LAY TAX CESS DOOM LEVY MISE RATE SCOT TOLL AGIST CENSE PRICE STENT SUMUP TEIND VALUE AFFEER ASSIZE CHARGE EXTEND IMPOSE SAMPLE MEASURE APPRAISE ESTIMATE
ASSESSMENT FEE LUG TAX CESS DUTY LEVY SCOT TOLL CULET JUMMA PRICE RATAL STENT TITHE WORTH EXTENT IMPOST PURVEY SURTAX TARIFF SCUTAGE BRIGBOTE TAXATION
ASSESSOR JUDGE MUFTI RATER TAXER CESSOR LISTER TASKER AUDITOR STENTOR TAXATOR
(PL.) FINTADORES
ASSET PLUS HONOR GETPENNY PROPERTY RESOURCE STRENGTH
ASSETS GOODS MEANS MONEY STOCK CREDIT WEALTH CAPITAL EFFECTS ACCOUNTS PROPERTY RESOURCE
ASSEVERATE SAY VOW AVER AVOW STATE SWEAR AFFIRM ALLEGE ASSERT ASSURE DECLARE PROTEST
ASSEVERATION VOW OATH STATING
ASSHUR (FATHER OF —) SHEM
ASSIDUOUS BUSY GREAT ACTIVE DEVOTED PENIBLE STUDIED DILIGENT FREQUENT SEDULOUS STUDIOUS
ASSIGN FIX LET PUT SET ARET CAST CEDE DEAL DOLE DRAW GIVE METE RATE SEAL SHOW SIGN ALLOT ALLOW APPLY ARETT AWARD DIGHT ENDOW REFER SHIFT TITLE ADDUCE AFFECT ALLEGE ATTACH CHARGE CONVEY DESIGN DIRECT ENTAIL ORDAIN ACCOUNT ADJUDGE APPOINT ASCRIBE CONSIGN DISPOSE ENTITLE SPECIFY STATION TRIBUTE ALLOCATE ANTEDATE ARROGATE DELEGATE INSCRIBE TRANSFER
(— QUARTERS) BILLET
(— TASK) STINT
ASSIGNATION DATE MEET TRYST MEETING
ASSIGNMENT DECK DUTY TASK CHORE GRIND STENT STINT TUNCA CESSIO LESSON CESSION BUSINESS HOMEWORK PLACEMENT
(FOREIGN —) POST
ASSIGNOR CEDOR CEDENS CEDENT
ASSIMILATE MIX ONE FUSE ADAPT ALTER BLEND LEARN MERGE ABSORB DIGEST IMBIBE COMPARE CONCOCT RESEMBLE
ASSIMILATION ECHOISM HOMEOSIS RECOGNITION
(— OF FOOD) CONCOCTION
ASSINIBOIN HOHE
ASSIR (FATHER OF —) KORAH EBIASAPH JECONIAH
ASSIST AID ABET BACK HELP JOIN AVAIL BOOST COACH FAVOR NURSE SERVE SPEED STEAD ATTEND ESCORT PROMPT SECOND SQUIRE SUCCOR BENEFIT COMFORT FURTHER RELIEVE SUPPORT SUSTAIN ADJUVATE BEFRIEND
(— A READER) FESCUE
(— AT) STAY
ASSISTANCE AID ALMS CAST GIFT HAND HELP LIFT BOOST FAVOR HEEZE RELIEF REMEDY SUCCOR SUPPLY ADJUTOR COMFORT SECOURS SUBSIDY SUPPORT AUXILIUM EASEMENT GIFFGAFF LARGESSE
ASSISTANT CAD AIDE ALLY HAND HELP MAID MATE PUNK SOUS ZANY CLERK GROOM USHER VALET AIDANT BUMPER COMMIS CURATE DEPUTY FLUNKY HELPER LEGATE NIPPER SECOND TULTUL YEOMAN ABETTOR ACOLYTE ADJOINT ADJUNCT DOORMAN DRESSER HOGGLER PADRINO PARTNER PROVOST RUBBLER SHIFTER STRIKER SWAMPER ADJUTANT ADJUVANT FELDSHER GOMASHTA LECTURER MINISTER OFFSIDER PARASITE SERVITOR SIDESMAN SUBPRIOR
(— TO ANIMAL SHOW JUDGE) STEWARD
(AUCTIONEER'S —) SPOTTER
(BOY —) NIPPER
(DOCTOR'S —) FELDSHER
(DYEING —) CARRIER
(GUNNER'S —) MATROSS
(MASON'S —) GOUJAT
(MATADOR'S —) CHULO
(POLICE —) CORPORAL
(SURVEYOR'S —) CHAINMAN
(WAITER'S —) BUSBOY OMNIBUS
ASSOCIATE MIX PAL AIDE ALLY BAND CHUM HERD JOIN LINK MATE MOOP MOUP PEER WALK WIFE YOKE BLEND BUDDY CRONY HABER MATCH TRAIN TROOP ASSORT ATTACH ATTEND CHABER COHORT COUSIN FASTEN FELLOW FRIEND HELPER HOBNOB MARROW MEDDLE MEMBER MINGLE PUISNE PUISNY RELATE SOCIUS SPOUSE TRAVEL ADJUNCT ASSOCIE BRACKET COALITE COMMUNE COMPANY COMPEER COMRADE CONNECT CONSORT HUSBAND PARTNER PEWMATE SOCIATE COMPLICE CONFRERE CONJOINT CONVERSE COPEMATE FAMILIAR FEDERATE FOLLOWER FREQUENT GADSHILL IDENTIFY INTIMATE PARTAKER ACCOMPANY ACCOMPLICE
(— WITH) FRAT MOOP MOUP
(DEMON —) FLY
(PL.) ENTOURAGE
ASSOCIATED
(PREF.) SYM
(SUFF.) (— WITH) IC(AL)

ASSOCIATION HUI BODY BOND BUND CLUB GILD HONG HUNT TONG ARTEL BOARD GUILD HANSA HANSE SANGH TRUCK UNION CARTEL CERCLE CHAPEL COMITY CONGER GRANGE LEAGUE LEGION LYCEUM PLEDGE SANGHA SCHOLA VEREIN CIRCUIT COMBINE COMPANY CONSORT CONTACT CONVENT COUNCIL SOCIETY SOROSIS SYNOECY AFFINITY ALLIANCE ASSEMBLY ATHENEUM CONVERSE HABITUDE INTIMACY SODALITY SYNOMOSY TAALBOND ORGANIZATION
(— OF FOSSILS) FAUNULA FAUNULE
(ANTAGONISTIC —) ANTIBIOSIS
(BANK —) SANDL
(BOOK-SELLERS' —) CONGER
(CLOSE —) HARNESS INTIMACY
(EMPLOYERS' —) GREMIO
(FARMERS' —) GRANGE
(IN —) ALONG
(LABOR —) ARTEL UNION
(RELIGIOUS —) SAMAJ
(SECRET —) CABAL
(STUDENTS' —) CORPS
(SYMBIOTIC —) ACAROPHILY
ASSOIL RID SOIL ATONE CLEAR SOLVE ACQUIT PARDON REFUTE ABSOLVE DELIVER EXPIATE FORGIVE RELEASE RESOLVE
ASSONANCE PUN RHYME PARAGRAM
ASSORT BOLT CULL SUIT WINNOW
(— COINS) SHROFF
ASSORTED CHOW CHOWCHOW
ASSORTER FEEDER LOOKER
ASSORTMENT BAG LOT SET OLIO BATCH BUNCH GROUP SUITE RAGBAG MIXTURE
(— OF COLORS) PALETTE
(— OF TYPE) BILL FONT
(COMPLETE —) STANDARD
ASSUAGE BEET CALM EASE LIOS LISS ABATE ALLAY CHARM DELAY LISSE MEASE SALVE SLAKE STILL SWAGE LENIFY LESSEN MODIFY PACIFY QUENCH REDUCE SOFTEN SOLACE SOOTHE TEMPER APPEASE COMFORT MOLLIFY QUALIFY RELIEVE SATISFY DIMINISH MITIGATE MODERATE
ASSUASIVE MILD LENIENT LENITIVE SOOTHING
ASSUME DON PUT SAY SET BEAR DARE FANG GIVE MASK PULL SHAM SHIP TAKE ADOPT ANNEX CLOAK ELECT ENDUE FEIGN GUESS INDUE INFER RAISE USURP ACCEPT AFFECT BETAKE CLOTHE FIGURE ASSUMPT BELIEVE PREMISE PRESUME PRETEND RECEIVE SUBSUME SUPPOSE SURMISE ACCROACH ARROGATE SIMULATE PERSONATE POSTULATE UNDERTAKE
(— CHARACTER) ACT AFFECT
(— FORM) ENGENDER
(— OFFICE) ACCEDE
(— PAINTING STANCE) BACK
ASSUMED ALIAS FALSE GIVEN FEIGNED AFFECTED BORROWED
ASSUMING LOFTY UPPISH UPPITY AFFECTED ARROGANT SUPERIOR
ASSUMPTION ALSOB DONNEE THESIS BALLOON FICTION SURMISE HOMEOSIS MARYMASS PRETENCE PRETENSE PRESUMPTION
(BASIC —) BEGINNING
(EMPTY —) IMAGINATION
ASSURANCE FACE GALL SEAL BRASS CHEEK FAITH NERVE POISE TRUST APLOMB AVOUCH BELIEF CAUTIO CREDIT PLEVIN PLIGHT SAFETY COURAGE PROMISE WARRANT AUDACITY BOLDNESS COOLNESS FIRMANCE FOREHEAD SECURITY SUREMENT
ASSURE AFFY AVER SURE TELL CINCH HIGHT SEWUP VOUCH AFFEER ASSERT AVOUCH ENSURE INSURE PLEDGE SECURE SEKERE SICCAR SICKER WITTER BETROTH CERTIFY CONFIRM DECLARE HEARTEN PROMISE PROTEST RESOLVE WARRANT AFFIANCE CONVINCE EMBOLDEN PERSUADE
ASSURED BOLD CALM COLD FIRM PERT SURE BOUND SIKER SLUSH FACILE PROBAL SECURE SICCAR SICKER CERTAIN POSITIVE
(— OF SUCCESS) MADE
(BLUNTLY —) KNOCKDOWN
ASSUREDLY AMEN SOON INDEED PERDIE REDELY SICCAR SICKER SURELY VERILY HARDILY WITTERLY
ASSYRIA ASHUR ASSUR ASSHUR
(CAPITAL OF —) CALAH NINEVEH
ASSYRIAN NESTORIAN
(— PLUM) SEBESTEN
ASTER ARNICA COCASH AMELLUS BEEWEED BONESET EUASTER ASTROFEL COMPOSIT CYTASTER MONASTER STARWORT STOKESIA
ASTERIA (DAUGHTER OF —) HECATE
(FATHER OF —) COEUS
(HUSBAND OF —) PERSES
(MOTHER OF —) PHOEBE
(SISTER OF —) LETO LATONA
ASTERISK MARK STAR ASTER ASTERISM WINDMILL
(THREE —S) ASTERISM
ASTERIUS (BROTHER OF —) AMPHION
(FATHER OF —) ANAX HYPERASIUS
(SLAYER OF —) MILETUS
ASTERN AFT BAFT HIND REAR ABAFT APOOP BEHIND OCCIPUT BACKWARD
ASTEROID EROS HEBE IRIS JUNO CERES DIONE FLORA IRENE METIS VESTA ASTREA EGERIA EUROPA HYGEIA PALLAS PLANET PSYCHE THALIA THEMIS THETIS ELECTRA EUNOMIA FORTUNA LUTETIA CALLIOPE MASSALIA PLANTOID STARFISH STARLIKE VICTORIA
ASTHMA PHTHISIC
ASTHMATIC POUCY PURSY POUCEY WHEEZY PANTING PUFFING
ASTIR UP AGOG ABOUT AFOOT AGATE ALERT GOING ACTIVE AROUND ASTEER MOVING ROUSED ABROACH EXCITED STIRRING VIGILANT
ASTONISH AWE DAZE STAM AMAZE KNOCK SHOCK DAMMER MARVEL STOUND ASTOUND GLOPPEN IMPRESS STARTLE AMERVEIL BEWILDER CONFOUND SURPRISE
ASTONISHING AMAZING FABULOUS MARVELOUS MARVELLOUS MINDBOGGLING
ASTONISHMENT MUSE FERLY DISMAY FARLEY MARVEL STOUND WONDER SURPRISE
ASTOUND BEAT STUN ABASH AMAZE APPAL SHOCK STOUN APPALL STOUND STAGGER STUPEFY STUPEND TERRIFY ASTONISH CONFOUND SURPRISE
ASTOUNDED STUPENT
ASTOUNDING STUNNING
ASTRAEA (FATHER OF —) ZEUS JUPITER
(MOTHER OF —) THEMIS
(SISTER OF —) PUDICITIA
ASTRAEUS (BROTHER OF —) PALLAS PERSES
(FATHER OF —) CRIUS
(MOTHER OF —) EURYBIA
ASTRAGAL TALUS CHAPLET CORNICE BAGUETTE
ASTRAGALAR (PREF.) TALO
ASTRAGALUS TALUS VETCH HUCKLEBONE
ASTRAKHAN BOKHARA
ASTRAL REMOTE STARRY STELLAR ASTRAEAN SIDEREAL STARLIKE
ASTRAY AWRY LOST WILL ABORD AGATE AGLEE AGLEY AMISS ASIDE GLEED WRONG ABROAD AFIELD ERRANT ERRING FAULTY DEPAYSE DEVIOUS FORLORN SINNING WILSOME MISTAKEN STRAYING
ASTRIDE ATOP ABOARD ACHEVAL SPANNING
ASTRINGENCY ACERBITY ACRIMONY
ASTRINGENT ACID ALUM COTO SOUR TART ACERB HARSH ROUGH SAPAN STERN TONER CORNUS MASTIC PONTIC SEVERE TANNIN ALUMNOL AUSTERE BINDING CATECHU PUCKERY RHATANY STYPTIC GERANIUM TRILLIUM
(NOT —) SOFT
ASTROLOGER JOTI JOSHI ARTIST JOTISI MERLIN ZADKIEL SCHEMIST
ASTROLOGY STARCRAFT MATHEMATICALS
ASTRONAUT (— ACTIVITY) SPACEWALK
ASTRONOMER JOTI JOSHI JOTISI
AMERICAN BOK SEE BOND BOSS HALE HALL HILL POOR REES TODD VERY ABELL ADAMS BAADE BAUER BOWEN CHASE ELKIN FROST HOUGH HYNEK MAURY PEASE SAGAN SWIFT YOUNG AITKEN BAILEY CANNON DRAPER HOLDEN HUBBLE HUSSEY JACOBY KEELER KUIPER LOOMIS LOWELL PEIRCE PETERS PORTER RENIZE ROGERS SEARES STRUVE WALKER WATSON WILSON BARNARD BURNHAM EASTMAN FLEMING GILLIES JASTROW LANGLEY LITTELL MERRILL MITCHEL MOULTON NEWCOMB PERRINE RITCHEY RUSSELL SAFFORD SHAPLEY SLIPHER WHITNEY ASHBROOK BOWDITCH CAMPBELL CHANDLER COMSTOCK DOUGLASS HARKNESS STEBBINS TOMBAUGH WINTHROP WOODWARD ALEXANDER DOOLITTLE LEUSCHNER MOREHOUSE PICKERING PRITCHETT HARRINGTON RUTHERFURD SCHAEBERLE RITTENHOUSE SCHLESINGER EICHELBERGER
AUSTRIAN FALB HAGEN LITTROW PURBACH
BELGIAN QUETELET
CANADIAN KLOTZ PLASKETT
CZECH KOHOUTEK
DANISH BRAHE DREYER HANSEN ROEMER SCHUMACHER LONGOMONTANUS
DUTCH BLAEU SITTER HUYGENS KAPTEYN
EGYPTIAN PTOLEMY
ENGLISH AIRY HIND POND RYLE TODD WARD ADAMS BAILY DIXON DYSON INNES JEANS JONES MASON MILNE MURIS WALES CLERKE DARWIN HALLEY LOVELL BRADLEY CHALLIS CLAXTON DELARUE GREGORY HUGGINS LOCKYER LUBBOCK MICHELL PARSONS PENROSE PROCTOR BRISBANE COPELAND EDDINTON GLAISHER GOMPERTZ HERSCHEL HORROCKS EDDINGTON FLAMSTEED MASKELYNE PRITCHARD CARRINGTON GELLIBRAND GROOMBRIDGE SHEEPSHANKS
FINNISH STONE
FRENCH BIOT FAYE LYOT PONS WOLF HENRY LOEWY RAYET BAILLY FERNEL MOREUX PICARD VALLOT BORELLY BOUVARD CASSINI DELISLE JANSSEN LALANDE LAPLACE MARALDI MESSIER MOUCHEZ PUISEUX DELAMBRE DELAUNAY LACAILLE LAGRANGE BIGOURDAN CHACORNAC LEMONNIER LEVERRIER TISSERAND BURCKHARDT FLAMMARION MAUPERTUIS
GERMAN BEER BODE WOLF ZACH BAYER BIELA ENCKE GALLE GAUSS GRAFF KEMPF KNOPF MAYER ARNOLD ARREST AUWERS BESSEL BRUHNS HANSEN HARZER IDELER KEPLER LAMONT MADLER MARIUS MOBIUS MULLER OLBERS PETERS RUMKER SPORER STRUYE TEMPEL AMBRONN APIANUS BRENDEL BRUNNOW LAMBERT SCHONER SCHWABE FOERSTER GUTHNICK HARTMANN HERSCHEL HEVELIUS LINDENAU MERCATOR RHATICUS SCHEINER WINNECKE FABRICIUS PALITZSCH SCHONFELD
GREEK CONON METON PTOLEMY AUTOLYCUS CALLIPPUS

CLEOMEDES OENOPIDES SOSIGENES HIPPARCHUS THEODOSIUS ANAXIMANDER ARISTARCHUS CLEOSTRATUS ERATOSTHENES
INDIAN ARYABHATA BRAHMAGUPTA
IRISH BALL PARSONS HAMILTON MOLYNEUX
ITALIAN AMICI FRISI DONATI ORIANI PIAZZI SECCHI BORELLI GALILEI GALILEO RICCIOLI TACCHINI BIANCHINI BOSCOVICH FRACASTORO SCHIAPARELLI
NORWEGIAN HANSTEEN
POLISH COPERNICUS
RUSSIAN BREDICHIN SHKLOVSKY
SCOTTISH GILL NICHOL WILSON GREGORY ANDERSON FERGUSON HENDERSON
SWEDISH DUNER BOHLIN GYLDEN CELSIUS ANGSTROM BACKLUND BRANTING STROMGREN
SWISS ZWICKY

ASTRONOMICAL FAR HUGE GREAT URANIC DISTANT IMMENSE URANIAN COLOSSAL INFINITE
(— INSTRUMENT) ARMILL

ASTRONOMY WAGON WAGONER WAGGONER

ASTROPHEL PENTHIA STARLIGHT

ASTUTE SLY FOXY KEEN WILY ACUTE CANNY QUICK SHARP SMART CLEVER CRAFTY NASUTE SHREWD CUNNING KNOWING SKILLED

ASTYAGES (FATHER OF —) CYAXARES

ASTYANAX (FATHER OF —) HECTOR
(MOTHER OF —) ANDROMACHE

ASTYDAMIA (FATHER OF —) PELOPS
(MOTHER OF —) HIPPODAMIA
(SON OF —) AMPHITRYON

ASTYOCHE (DAUGHTER OF —) PHYLEUS
(LOVER OF —) HERCULES
(SON OF —) TLEPOLEMUS

ASUNDER ATWO APART SPLIT ATWAIN SUNDER SUNDRY DIVIDED DIVORCED YSOWNDIR
(PREF.) AP(H) DI DICH(O)

ASURA VARUNA

ASVATTHAMAN (FATHER OF —) DRONA
(MOTHER OF —) KRIPA

ASYLUM ARK HOME JAIL ALTAR COVER GRITH HAVEN BEDLAM HARBOR REFUGE ALSATIA COLLEGE HOSPICE RETREAT SHELTER BUGHOUSE MADHOUSE NUTHOUSE

ASYMMETRIC PEDIAL

AS YOU LIKE IT (AUTHOR OF —) SHAKESPEARE
CHARACTER IN — ADAM CELIA CORIN PHEBE AMIENS AUDREY DENNIS JAQUES LEBEAU OLIVER CHARLES MARTEXT ORLANDO SILVIUS WILLIAM ROSALIND FREDERICK TOUCHSTONE

AT A AL AU BY IN TO ALS TIL TILL UNTO ATTEN THERE HEREAT
(— ALL) ANY AVA EER EVER HALF OUGHT SOEVER HOWEVER

ATABAL DRUM TABOR ATTABAL

ATALANTA (CHARACTER IN —) MERCURY ATALANTA MELEAGER
(COMPOSER OF —) HANDEL
(FATHER OF —) IASUS
(HUSBAND OF —) MELANION HIPPOMENES
(MOTHER OF —) CLYMENE

ATAMAN CHIEF JUDGE HETMAN HEADMAN

ATARAH (HUSBAND OF —) JERAHMEEL
(SON OF —) ONAM

ATAVISM REVERSION

ATELIER SHOP STUDIO BOTTEGA WORKSHOP

ATEO WAKEA

ATES SWEETSOP

ATHALARIC (FATHER OF —) EUTHELRIC
(MOTHER OF —) AMALASUINTHA

ATHALIAH (FATHER OF —) AHAB
(HUSBAND OF —) JEHORAM
(MOTHER OF —) JEZEBEL

ATHAMAS (DAUGHTER OF —) HELLE
(FATHER OF —) AEOLUS
(MOTHER OF —) ENARETE
(SON OF —) PHRIXUS LEARCHUS PALAEMON
(WIFE OF —) INO NEPHELE

ATHANAGILD (DAUGHTER OF —) BRUNEHILDE GALESWINTHA

ATHANOR OVEN ATHENOR FURNACE

ATHAPASKAN HAW HARE HUPA KATO KASKA AHTENA BEAVER CHETCO GILENO LASSIK SARCEE SEKANI CARRIER CHILULA KOYUKON KUTCHIN

ATHEIST ZENDIK DOUBTER INFIDEL NASTIKA AGNOSTIC APIKOROS NETHEIST

ATHENA ALEA AUGE NIKE ALERA AREIA ERGANE HIPPIA HYGEIA ITONIA PALLAS POLIAS AIANTIS MINERVA APATURIA

ATHENIAN ATTIC CHORAGUS CHOREGUS

ATHLAI (FATHER OF —) BEBAI

ATHLETE PRO BLUE JOCK KEMP STAR BOXER COLOR CRACK CUTEY CUTIE TURNER ACROBAT AMATEUR GYMNAST STICKER TUMBLER VARMINT GAMESTER REPEATER WRESTLER PENTATHLETE
(COLLEGE —) REDSHIRT

ATHLETIC AGILE BURLY LUSTY VITAL BRAWNY GYMNIC ROBUST SINEWY STRONG BOARDLY BOORDLY MUSCULAR POWERFUL VIGOROUS

ATHLETICS GAMES SPORT EXERCISE

AT-HOME ASSEMBLY

ATHWART CROSS ABOARD ACROSS ASLANT OBLIQUE SIDEWISE TRAVERSE

ATLANTIC CROAKER HARDHEAD

ATLANTIC OCEAN POND MILLPOND

ATLAS BOOK LIST MAPS TOME TITAN TELAMON MAINSTAY
(DAUGHTERS OF —) ATLANTIDES
(FATHER OF —) IAPETUS
(MOTHER OF —) CLYMENE
(WIFE OF —) PLEIONE

ATLE ETHEL

ATMAN ATMA ATTA SELF

ATMOSPHERE AIR SKY AURA FEEL LIFT MOOD TONE AROMA CLIME DECOR ETHER PLACE SMELL FROWST MIASMA NIMBUS SPHERE WELKIN FEELING HYALINE QUALIFY AMBIANCE AMBIENCE
(— OF DISCOURAGEMENT) CHILL
(CHARACTERISTIC —) VIBE
(EMOTIONAL —) VIBE VIBES
(NOXIOUS —) MIASMA
(OUTERMOST PART OF —) GEOCORONA
(SECTION OF —) SOLENOID
(SENSED —) KARMA
(STALE —) FROUST FROWST
(STUFFY —) FUG
(SUFFOCATING —) STIFLE

ATMOSPHERIC AERIAL METEORIC

ATMOSPHERICS STATIC STRAYS SFERICS SPHERICS

ATOLL LAGOON

ATOM ACE BIT ION JOT DIAD DYAD HAET HATE IOTA MITE MOTE WHIT ATOMY HENAD LABEL MONAD SHADE SPECK TINGE ADATOM BRIDGE CARBYL HEPTAD ISOBAR TETRAD ATOMIZE BODIKIN IONOGEN ISOTOPE NUCLIDE RADICAL SPECIES FUNCTION ISOSTERE MOLECULE PARTICLE PERISSAD QUANTITY CORPUSCLE SCINTILLA
(— TOTALITY) MATTER
(COMBINING —) ACCEPTOR
(TAGGED —) TRACER
(PL.) SMITHERS SMITHEREENS

ATOMIC TINY MINUTE NUCLEAR
(— PARTICLE) MUON

ATOMIZE PULVERIZE

ATOMIZER SPRAY SPARGE SCENTER SPRAYER AIRBRUSH ODORATOR PERFUMER
(CONTENTS OF —) SCENTS

ATOMS
(PREF.) **(CONTAINING 20 —)** EICOS
(CONTAINING 4 CARBON —) BUT
(HAVING ARRANGEMENT OF —) GALA GALACTO
(PRESENCE OF 2 NITROGEN —) DIAZ

ATONE AGREE AMEND ACCORD ANSWER ASSOIL RANSOM REDEEM REPENT APPEASE EXPIATE RESTORE SATISFY
(— FOR) ABY BYE ABYE MEND ABIDE ABEGGE

ATONEMENT MEND RANSOM MICHTAM PENANCE SATISFACTION ACCEPTILATION

ATOP ACOR OVER UPON

ATORAI DAURI

ATOSSA (FATHER OF —) CYRUS
(HUSBAND OF —) DARIUS SMERDIS CAMBYSES

ATRABILIOUS SAD GLUM ADUST GLOOMY MOROSE SULLEN

ATRAMENTOUS INKY

ATRAX (DAUGHTER OF —) CAENIS HIPPODAMIA
(FATHER OF —) PENEUS
(MOTHER OF —) BURA

ATREUS (BROTHER OF —) THYESTES
(FATHER OF —) PELOPS
(HALF-BROTHER OF —) THYESTES
(MOTHER OF —) HIPPODAMIA
(SON OF —) MENELAUS
(WIFE OF —) AEROPE

ATRIP AWEIGH

ATRIUM HALL ATRIO COURT CAVITY AURICLE CHAMBER PASSAGE

ATROCIOUS BAD DARK RANK VILE AWFUL BLACK CRUEL GROSS ATROCE BRUTAL ODIOUS SAVAGE WICKED HEINOUS UNGODLY VIOLENT FLAGRANT GRIEVOUS HORRIBLE TERRIBLE MONSTROUS

ATROPHIC AUANTIC

ATROPHY RUST STUNT TABES MACIES MOLDER SHRINK STARVE SWEENY WITHER SWINNEY WASTING STULTIFY
(PREF.) NECR(O)

ATROPINE DATURINE

ATTACH ADD FIX PUT SET SEW TAG TIE BIND BOLT GLUE HANG JOIN LINK NAIL SPAN TAKE VEST WELD ADOPT AFFIX ANNEX BEWED CLING FOUND HINGE HITCH LATCH PASTE SCREW SEIZE SPEND STICK TACHE TATCH UNITE ACCUSE ADDICT ADHERE ADJOIN APPEND ARREST CEMENT DEVOTE ENGAGE ENTAIL ENTIRE FASTEN FATHER INDICT SPLINE ADHIBIT APPOINT ASCRIBE CONNECT ESPOUSE SUBJOIN
(— TEMPORARILY) SECOND

ATTACHED FAST FOND ADNATE DOTING ADJUNCT BIGOTED SESSILE ADSCRIPT INSERTED

ATTACHING INCIDENT ALLIGATION

ATTACHMENT ARM GAG BAIL BALE DRUM FLAY HEAD HECK LOVE MOTE SHIM SHOE AMOUR CHUCK CRUSH DOBBY DODAD FENCE GUARD STRIG AFFAIR BEATER BINDER BUMPER DAMSEL DOBBIE DOCTOR DOODAD DREDGE FELLER FETICH FETISH HEMMER HILLER LAPPET LAYBOY MARKER PACKER PICKUP SECTOR SHIELD SIDING ADAPTOR AFFAIRE BIGOTRY BRAIDER CREASER DROPPER FAGOTER FITTING GIGBACK HEADSET HOLDING JOINTER KNOCKUP LEVELER SPANNER SPRAYER DEVOTION DINGDONG FASTNESS FIXATION FONDNESS GOVERNOR HEADREST

ATTACK FIT HIT HOP MUG SIC BAIT BOMB BOUT CLAW COSH DINT FAKE FANG FORK FRAY GANG GIVE HOOK JUMP MACE PAIL PANG RAID RISE RUSH SAIL SICK SLOW

TACK TURN WADE YOKE ABUSE ALARM ASSAY BEGIN BESET BLAST BLITZ BOARD BRASH BRUNT CATCH CHECK DRIVE FIGHT FLUSH FORAY FORCE GLIDE HARRY HOUND ICTUS ONSET POISE PULSE SALLY SCUFF SETON SMITE SOUSE SPASM SPELL STORM ACCESS ACCUSE ACTION AFFRAY AFFRET ASSAIL ATTAME BATTLE BICKER BODRAG CHARGE CRISIS DOUBLE ENVAYE EXPUGN EXTENT GRUDGE INDICT INFEST INSULT INVADE OFFEND ONFALL ONRUSH POUNCE RUFFLE SAVAGE SHOWER SORTIE STOUND STRIKE STROKE TACKLE TAKING THRUST AGGRESS ASPERSE ASSAULT ATTEMPT BARRAGE BELABOR BELIBEL BESEIGE BOMBARD CENSURE CRUSADE DESCENT OFFENSE PICKOUT POTSHOT RUNNING SCALING SEIZURE STACKER CAMISADE CAMISADO ENDEAVOR ESCALADE PAROXYSM SKIRMISH SURPRISE TOMAHAWK OFFENSIVE ONSLAUGHT PENETRATION
(— FEEDBAG) TIEIN
(— IN COCKFIGHT) SHUFFLE
(— OF ILLNESS) GO
(— OFILLNESS) FIT
(— OF ILLNESS) DWAM DWALM ACCESS
(— OFILLNESS) ONFALL SEIZURE
(— OF SICKNESS) WHIP SEIZURE
(— TO ROB) THUG
(— WITH SHOUTS) HUE
(— WITH WORDS) STOUSH
(— ZEALOUSLY) CRUSADE
(BOMBING —) PRANG
(CHESS —) FORK
(CRITICAL —) SLATING
(FENCING —) GLIDE
(LIGHT —) TOUCH
(NIGHT —) CAMISADO
(PROLONGED —) SIEGE
(SLIGHT —) WAFF
(SUDDEN —) ICTUS RAPTUS SURPRISE
(SUICIDAL —) KAMIKAZE
(SURPRISE —) ALARM ALARUM
(VERBAL —) FIRE SALVO BLUDGEON
(SUFF.) LEPSIA LEPSIS LEPSY LEPT(IC)

ATTACKER AGGRESSOR OFFENDANT
(SUFF.) MASTIX

ATTACK ON THE MILL
(CHARACTER IN —) MERLIER DOMINIQUE FRANCOISE MARCELLINE
(COMPOSER OF —) BRUNEAU

ATTAI (FATHER OF —) REHOBOAM
(MOTHER OF —) AHLAI MAACHAH

ATTAIN GO GET HIT WIN BUMP COME EARN GAIN RISE SORT ARISE CATCH COVER CROSS FETCH PROVE REACH TOUCH ACCEDE AMOUNT ARRIVE ASPIRE EFFECT OBTAIN SECURE STRIKE ACHIEVE ACQUIRE COMPASS PROCURE SUCCEED OVERTAKE
(— TO ACCOMPLISH) FIND FORCE

ATTAINMENT ARRIVAL ADEPTION ENERGEIA PURCHASE
(— OF NIRVANA) MOKSHA
(SCHOLARLY —) LETTERS

ATTAR ITR OIL ATAR OTTO ATHAK OTTAR ESSENCE PERFUME

ATTEMPT GO PUT SAY SHY TRY BASH BOUT BURL DARE DASH FAND FIST FOND HACK JUMP MIND MINT MIRD OSSE SEEK SHOT SLAP STAB WAGE WORK ASSAY BEGIN ESSAY ETTLE FLING FRAME OFFER ONSET PRESS PROOF PROVE START TEMPT TRIAL WHACK ASSAIL ATTACK EFFORT FRAIST STRIVE ENFORCE IMITATE PRETEND PROFFER STAGGER VENTURE CONATION ENDEAVOR EXERTION PURCHASE TENTAMEN
(— TO AROUSE) AGITATE
(— TO BRIBE) APPROACH
(— TO INFLUENCE) AGITATION
(— TO THROW RIDER) ESTRAPADE
(ABORTIVE —) FUTILITY
(FIRST —) DEBUT
(PREF.) PEIRA

ATTEND GO HO HOA HOO SEE BEAT FAND HARK HEAR HEED LIST MIND OYES OYEZ STAY TEND WAIT WALK APPLY AUDIT AWAIT GUARD NURSE SERVE TREAT VISIT WATCH ASSIST CONVEY ESCORT FOLLOW HARKEN INTEND LACKEY LISTEN SECOND SHADOW SQUIRE CONDUCT CONSORT ESQUIRE HEARKEN LACQUEY PERPEND RETINUE ACCOMPANY
(— A LADY) WAIT
(— FUNERAL) FOLLOW
(— REGULARLY) KEEP
(— TO) MIND TREAT FETTLE INTEND
(— UPON) TENT CHASE CHAPERON

ATTENDANCE GATE SUIT CHAPEL NUMBER OFFICE REGARD SERVICE PRESENCE

ATTENDANT BOY FLY LAD JACK MAID MUTE PAGE PEON SYCE ZANY CADDY COMES GILLY GROOM GUIDE JAGER USHER VALET ALEXAS CADDIE DACTYL DAMSEL EMILIA ESCORT FRIEND GESITH GILLIE HAIDUK HOGMAN JAEGER KAVASS MINION PORTER SQUIRE STOCAH TUBMAN VARLET VERGER WAITER YEOMAN ALIPTES ARMORER BULLDOG CHOBDAR COURIER CROSSER DAMOSEL FAMULUS FENELLA FOOTBOY GHILLIE HALLMAN HOSTESS JACKMAN LINKMAN ORDERLY PAGEBOY PIQUEUR PRESSER SEQUENT SERVANT SHIPBOY SPOUTER TRABANT TRESSEL ATTENDEE BEACHBOY CHASSEUR CORYBANT CRUTCHER FEWTERER FOLLOWER GATHERER HANDMAID HENCHBOY HENCHMAN HOUSEMAN MINISTER MYRMIDON OBSERVER OUTRIDER ROSALINE SERGEANT SERJEANT STAFFIER TIPSTAFF WATERMAN OBSERVANT PURSUIVANT CHAMBERLAIN
(— OF CYBELE) CORYBANT
(ARMED —) CAVASS KAVASS
(CROSSING —) GATEMAN
(FLIGHT —) STEW STEWARD STEWARDESS
(FUNERAL —) MUTE
(KNIGHT'S —) SWAIN CUSTREL ESQUIRE
(PALACE —S) BOSTANGI
(PROCTOR'S —) BULLDOG
(SHIP'S —) STEWARD
(YOUNG —) BOY LAD JACK PAGE KNIGHT
(PL.) MEINY STAFF CORTEGE RETINUE

ATTENDED FRAUGHT

ATTENDER (HABITUAL —) PATRON

ATTENTION EAR CARE GAUM HEED HIST MARK MIND NOTE RUSH SHUN TENT COURT FLOOR GUARD STUDY TASTE DETAIL FAVORS NOTICE REGARD ACCOUNT ACHTUNG ADDRESS EARNEST HEARING RESPECT THOUGHT AUDIENCE
(— FROM SUPERIOR) TASHRIF TASHREEF
(— TO PETTY ITEMS) MICROLOGY
(AMOROUS —) GALLANTRY
(FIXED —) DHARANA
(FLATTERING —) HOMAGE
(INTERJECTION TO ATTRACT —) YOOHOO
(PLEASING —) INCENSE
(SPECIAL —) ACCENT
(PL.) FUSS

ATTENTIVE WARY ALERT AWAKE CIVIL CLOSE SHARP TENTY ARRECT INTENT POLITE ALLEARS CAREFUL GALLANT HEEDFUL LISTFUL MINDFUL PRESENT DILIGENT OBEDIENT STUDIOUS THOUGHTY VIGILANT WATCHFUL
(— TO) IMMINENT

ATTENUATE SAP DRAW FINE THIN WATER DILUTE LESSEN RAREFY REDUCE WEAKEN SLENDER AVIANIZE DECREASE DIMINISH EMACIATE ENFEEBLE TAPERING

ATTENUATED RARE THIN GAUNT AERIAL DILUTED SPINDLY FINESPUN SMORZATO

ATTENUATION LOSS

ATTENUATOR PAD

ATTEST CHOP SEAL SIGN PROVE STATE SWEAR VOUCH ADJURE AFFIRM INVOKE RECORD WITTEN CERTIFY CONFESS CONFIRM CONSIGN TESTIFY WARRANT WITNESS EVIDENCE INDICATE MANIFEST

ATTESTATION VOUCH DOCKET RECORD

ATTESTED SWORN CERTIFIED

ATTIC LOFT CELER SOLAR SOLER GARRET TALLET GRENIER COCKLOFT
(— SIDE) SKEELING

ATTILA (BROTHER OF —) BLEDA
(CHARACTER IN —) LEO EZIO ATTILA FORESTO ODABELLA
(COMPOSER OF —) VERDI
(FATHER OF —) MUNDZUK
(WIFE OF —) HILDA ILDICO

ATTIRE (ALSO SEE DRESS) BEGO BUSK GARB SUIT TIRE ADORN ARRAY BIGAN DRESS GETUP HABIT AGUISE ENROBE PLIGHT REVEST TOILET ADDRESS APPAREL DUBBING PANOPLY ACCOUTER CLEADING EQUIPAGE FEATHERS
(EPISCOPAL —) PONTIFICAL
(FORMAL —) BALLDRESS
(SHINING —) SHEEN

ATTIRED TRICKSY
(— IN FINERY) BRAW

ATTITUDE AIR CUE SET BIAS MIEN MOOD POSE SIDE ANGLE FRAME HEART PHASE SHAPE SHELL SIGHT SLANT STAND ACTION ANIMUS ASPECT MANNER SPIRIT STANCE BEARING FEELING GESTURE POSTURE STATION STOMACH BEHAVIOR CARAPACE CROTCHET HABITUDE POSITION PREPOSSESSION
(— OF HUNTING DOG) POINT
(HABITUAL —) SONG
(MENTAL —) SENSE
(PREVAILING —) STREAM

ATTITUDINIZE POSE POSTURE

ATTORNEY DOER AGENT AVOUE PROXY VAKIL DEPUTY FACTOR FISCAL LAWYER LEGIST MUKTAR SYNDIC VAKEEL PROCTOR ADVOCATE PROSECUTOR

ATTRACT BAIT CALL DRAW LURE PULL TILL WIND BRING CATCH CHARM COURT FETCH TEMPT ALLURE ATTACH ENGAGE ENLIST ENTICE GATHER INVITE SEDUCE STRIKE BEWITCH PROCURE INTEREST MAGNETIZE
(— FISH) CHUM

ATTRACTANT (MOTH SEX —) GYPLURE

ATTRACTION TUG BAIT CALL CARD CLOU DRAW PULL CHARM DRAFT FAVOR SPELL TRACT APPEAL DESIRE FAVOUR MAGNET BLOWOFF COITION DRAUGHT GRAVITY INDRAFT ADHESION AFFINITY COHESION CONTRACT PENCHANT SIDESHOW WITCHERY
(KIND OF —) ADDED
(SEX —) GYPLURE

ATTRACTIVE FLY BRAW CHIC CUTE FAIR FOXY GOOD NICE BONNY DISHY FATAL JOLLY NIFTY QUEME SONSY SWEET COMELY FLASHY FRUITY HEPPEN LOVELY LURING PRETTY SAVORY SEEMLY SNAZZY TAKING TRICKY AMIABLE CIRCEAN CUNNING EYEABLE EYESOME GRADELY LIKABLE WINNING WINSOME ALLURING CHARMING ENGAGING ENTICING FEATURED FETCHING GRACEFUL GRACIOUS HANDSOME INVITING SPECIOUS TEMPTING VENEREAN PERSONABLE PREPOSSESSING
(— TO OPPOSITE SEX) EPIGAMIC
(FALSELY —) MERETRICIOUS
(NOT —) FOUL INCURIOUS
(STRIKINGLY —) ZINGY

ATTRACTIVENESS CHARM GRACE LOOKS BEAUTY GLAMOR AMENITY GLITTER AFFINITY HARLOTRY
ATTRIBUTABLE DUE
ATTRIBUTE FOX OWE PUT GIVE MARK SIGN TYPE ALLOT BADGE BLAME CHARM PLACE POWER REFER TRAIT ALLEGE ALLUDE ARRECT ASSERT ASSIGN BESTOW CHARGE CREDIT IMPUTE PREFER REPUTE SYMBOL ADJUNCT APANAGE ASCRIBE COUNTER ESSENCE PERTAIN QUALITY ACCREDIT APPANAGE ARROGATE GRANDITY INTITULE PROPERTY PROPRIUM STRENGTH
(—S OF ROCKS) GEOLOGY
(— WRONGFULLY) FOIST
(PL.) SARIRA SHARIRA
ATTRIBUTION ACCENT THEORY ANIMISM ETIOLOGY
ATTRITION WEAR GRIEF REGRET SORROW ANGUISH ABRASION BLASTING FRICTION
ATTUNE KEY TUNE ADAPT AGREE ACCORD ADJUST TEMPER PREPARE
ATUA AKUA DEMON SPIRIT
ATYPICAL RARE BIZARRE ABERRANT GROTESQUE
AUBADE ALBA
AUBERGE INN ALBERGO
AUBERGINE EGGPLANT
AUBURN ABRAM BLOND CACHA CUTCH BLONDE CACHOU CATECHU GOREVAN TULIPWOOD
AU COURANT CONTEMPORARY
AUCTION CANT ROUP SALE SELL VEND COKER TRADE BARTER BRIDGE HAMMER OUTCRY TROVER VENDUE OUTROOP UNCTION DISPOSAL KNOCKOUT PORTSALE
AUCTIONEER CRIER CRYER OUTCRIER
AUDACIOUS BOLD BRASH BRAVE FRACK HARDY SAUCY AUDACE BRAZEN CHEEKY DARING FORWARD ARROGANT FEARLESS IMPUDENT INSOLENT INTREPID SPIRITED BAREFACED DEVILMAYCARE
(NOT —) CIVIL
(PIQUANTLY —) SASSY SAUCY
AUDACITY CHEEK NERVE COURAGE BOLDNESS TEMERITY HARDIHOOD PRESUMPTION
AUDIBLE RIFE ALOUD CLEAR HEARD AUTOMATIC
AUDIBLY ALOUD
AUDIENCE EAR PIT FANS AUDIT COURT FLOOR HOUSE PUBLIC GALLERY HEARING ASSEMBLY AUDITORY TRIBUNAL
AUDIT SCAN CHECK PROBE APPOSE RECKON VERIFY ACCOUNT EXAMINE INQUIRE INSPECT ESTIMATE
AUDITION READ HEARING
AUDITOR CENSOR HEARER APPOSER AUDIENT PITTITE COUNTOUR DISCIPLE LISTENER
AUDITORIUM HALL ROOM CAVEA FRONT ODEUM THEATER AUDITORY
AUDITORY ORAL OTIC AURAL AUDILE ACOUSTIC AUDITIVE
AUGE (FATHER OF —) ALEUS
(HUSBAND OF —) TEUTHRAS
(MOTHER OF —) NAERA
(SON OF —) TELEPHUS
AUGER BIT POD BORE BORAL BORER GRILL BORING GIMLET NAUGER WIMBLE PIERCER TEREBRA
(PREF.) TRYPAN(O)
AUGHT ACHT EAWT AUCHT OWNED CIPHER NAUGHT WORTHY NOTHING VALIANT ANYTHING
AUGMENT ADD EKE FEED GROW HELP URGE BOOST EXALT SWELL APPEND DILATE EXPAND EXTEND AMPLIFY BALLOON ENHANCE ENLARGE IMPROVE INFLAME MAGNIFY COMPOUND HEIGHTEN INCREASE MAJORATE MULTIPLY
(— IN STRENGTH) INGROSS
AUGMENTATION RISE EKING SWELL GROWTH AUCTARY ADDITION
AUGMENTED SHARP EXTREME
AUGUR BODE OMEN SEER SPEAK AUSPEX DIVINE BETOKEN CONJECT FORESEE OMINATE PORTEND PREDICT PRESAGE PROMISE PROPHET SIGNIFY DENOUNCE FOREBODE FORESHOW FORETELL FOREWARN INDICATE PROPHESY
AUGURY ORE OMEN RITE SIGN SOOTH TOKEN HANSEL RITUAL AUSPICE HANDSEL PRESAGE CEREMONY
AUGUST AWFUL GRAND NOBLE KINGLY SERENE SOLEMN EXALTED STATELY IMPOSING MAJESTIC
(FIRST DAY OF —) LAMMAS LUGNAS LUGHNAS LUGNASAD
(PREF.) SEBASTO
AUGUSTINIAN AUSTIN ASSUMPTIONIST
AUHUHU HOLA
AUK FALK LOOM ARRIE DIVER LEMOT MURRE NODDY SCOOT SCOUT SKOUT MARROT PUFFIN ROTCHE STARIK TINKER DOVEKEY DOVEKIE PENGUIN PYGOPOD SEAFOWL WILLOCK GAIRFOWL GAREFOWL ROCKBIRD RAZORBILL
AULA HALL COURT EMBLIC
AUNT TIA BAWD AUNTY NAUNT TANTA TANTE AUNTIE GOSSIP
(— SALLY) STICKS
AURA AIR HALO ODOR PUFF AROMA NUMEN SAVOR SMELL BREEZE NIMBUS BUZZARD ESSENCE FEELING
(CHARACTERISTIC —) VIBE
(SENSED —) KARMA
(VITALIZING —) VIBE VIBES
AURAL OTIC AUDIAL
AUREATE GOLDEN ORNATE ROCOCO YELLOW
AUREOLE HALO CROWN GLORY LIGHT AREOLA CORONA GLORIA NIMBUS VESICA GLORIOLE MANDORLA
AUREUS (HALF —) SEMIS
AURICLE EAR PINNA ATRIUM EARLET TRUMPET PAVILION
AURICULAR OTIC
AURICULATE EARED
AURIGA WAGONER WAGGONER
AURIST OTOLOGIST
AUROCHS TUR UROX URUS BISON WISENT BONASUS
AURORA EOS DAWN DRAPERY MORNING
AURORA BOREALIS DANCERS STREAMERS
AUSPICE CARE OMEN SIGN AUGURY PORTENT GUIDANCE
(PL.) EGIS AEGIS
AUSPICIOUS FAIR GOOD TWINE WHITE BRIGHT CHANCY DEXTER CHANCEY FAVORING PROPITIOUS PROSPEROUS
AUSTERE BARE COLD HARD SOUR BLEAK BUDGE GRAVE GRUFF HARSH RIGID ROUGH SHARP STERN STIFF STOUR BITTER CHASTE FORMAL RUGGED SEVERE SIMPLE SOMBER STRICT SULLEN TETRIC ASCETIC CRABBED DANTEAN EARNEST SERIOUS GRANITIC RIGOROUS TETRICAL ASTRINGENT PURITANICAL
AUSTERITY RIGOR CATOISM RIGORISM SIMPLICITY
AUSTRAL SOUTHERN

AUSTRALIA

ABORIGINE: MYALL
CAPE: HOWE
CAPITAL: CANBERRA
COIN: DUMP POUND SHILLING
DESERT: STURT GIBSON TANAMI SIMPSON
HARBOR: DARWIN BRISBANE FREMANTLE MELBOURNE NEWCASTLE
ISLAND: CATO COCOS FRASER KOOLAN CORINGA KANGAROO LACEPEDE MELVILLE ROTTNEST TASMANIA
LAKE: EYRE COWAN FROME BARLEE BULLOO LEFROY AMADEUS BLANCHE EVERARD GREGORY TORRENS GAIRDNER NABBEROO DISAPPOINTMENT
LANGUAGE: YABBER
MEASURE: SAUM
MOUNTAIN: OLGA BRUCE LEGGE CRADLE GARNET GAWLER MAGNET STUART BONGONG GREGORY WILHELM CUTHBERT JUSGRAVE MULLIGAN KOSCIUSKO
MOUNTAIN RANGE: DARLING FLINDERS
NATIVE: ABO MARA BINGE ARANDA ARUNTA AUSSIE DIGGER BILLIJIM KANGAROO WARRAGAL WARRIGAL JINDYWOROBAK
PENINSULA: EYRE
RIVER: DALY SWAN BULLO COMET FINKE ISAAC PAROO ROPER SNOWY YARRA BARCOO BARWON CULGOA DAWSON DEGREY DARLING FITZROY LACHLAN STAATEN WARREGO BURDEKIN FLINDERS GEORGINA VICTORIA
SEA: CORAL TIMOR TASMAN ARAFURA
SOLDIER: DIGGER SWADDY BILLIJIM
STATE: TASMANIA VICTORIA QUEENSLAND
STRAIT: TORRES
TOWN: AYR YASS DUBBO PERTH WAGGA ALBURY AUBURN CAIRNS CASINO COBURG DARWIN HOBART MACKAY SYDNEY BENDIGO GEELONG KOGARAH MILDURA MITCHAM ADELAIDE BRISBANE ESSENDON RANDWICK RINGWOOD MELBOURNE TOOWOOMBA
VALLEY: GROSE JAMIESON MEGALONG
WATERFALL: TULLY COOMERA WALLAMAN WENTWORTH WOLLOMOMBI
WATER HOLE BILLABONG
WOMAN: LUBRA

AUSTRALIAN ANZAC AUSSIE DIGGER AUSTRAL CURRENCY KANGAROO WARRAGAL WARRIGAL
(— GIRL) LUBRA

AUSTRIA

ANCIENT PEOPLE: HUNS AVARS RAETIANS SLOVENES BAVARIANS
CAPITAL: WIEN VIENNA
CELTIC KINGDOM: NORICUM
COIN: DUCAT KRONE FLORIN HELLER ZEHNER GROSCHEN SCHILLING
DUCHY: STYRIA CARNIOLA CARINTHIA
EMPEROR: CHARLES FRANCIS FERDINAND
LAKE: ALMSEE FERTOTO MONDSEE BODENSEE TRAUNSEE CONSTANCE NEUSIEDLER
MEASURE: FASS FUSS JOCH MASS MUTH YOKE HALBE LINIE MEILE METZE PFIFF PUNKT ACHTEL BECHER SEIDEL DLAFTER VIERTEL DREILING
MOUNTAIN: STUBAI EISENERZ RHATIKON KITZBUHEL
NATIVE: STYRIAN TYROLEAN
NOBILITY: RITTER
PASS: LOIBL ARLBERG BRENNER PLOCKEN
PROVINCE: TIROL TYROL STYRIA VIENNA SALZBURG CARINTHIA VORARLBERG
RIVER: INN MUR DRAU ENNS KAMP LECH MURZ RAAB DONAU MARCH SALZA THAYA TRAUN DANUBE SALZACH
RIVER PORT: LINZ KREMS VIENNA
ROMAN PROVINCE: RAETIA NORICUM PANNONIA
TOWN: ENNS GRAZ LECH LINZ RIED WELS WIEN GMUND LIENZ STEYR

TRAUN LEOBEN VIENNA BREGENZ MODLING SPITTAL VILLACH DORNBIRN SALZBURG INNSBRUCK
WATERFALL: KRIMML GASTEIN GOLLING
WEIGHT: MARC SAUM UNZE DENAT KARCH PFUND STEIN CENTNER PFENNIG VIERLING

AUTACOID HORMONE INCRETION
AUTARCHIC FREE
AUTHENTIC ECHT PURE REAL SURE TRUE EXACT PUCCA PUCKA PUKKA RIGHT VALID ACTUAL DINKUM PROPER CORRECT CURRENT GENUINE SINCERE CREDIBLE OFFICIAL ORIGINAL RELIABLE
AUTHENTICATE SEAL PROVE VOUCH ATTEST SIGNET VERIFY APPROVE CONFIRM LEGALIZE
AUTHOR DOER JUDE SIRE JUDAS MAKER RULER AUCTOR FACTOR FORGER LOKMAN PARENT PENMAN SCRIBE SOURCE WRITER ANCIENT CLASSIC CREATOR ELOHIST FOUNDER LOLLIUS ANCESTOR BEGETTER COMPILER COMPOSER IDEALIST IMMORTAL INVENTOR JEHOVIST ORIGINAL PAYYETAN PRODUCER
(BAD —) BLOTTER
(PL.) SS
AMERICAN ADE BOK GAY ILG LEA LEE NIN NYE POE ZIM AGAR AGEE AUEL BABB BATE BAUM BEER BELL BODE BOVA BOYD BUCK BURT CAIN CARO CARR COIT COOK DANA DAHL DYER EDDY EDEL ERTE EWEN FARB GALE GANN GASS GRAU GREY HALL HAHN HUIE HUME HUNT JONG KEMP KREY KYNE LANE LASH LONG LOOS LUCE MACY MAYO NASH PAUL POST POHL PUZO RAND ROTH SHAW SUHL URIS WARD WATT WEBB WEST WOOD WOUK AARON ADAMS ADLER AIKEN ALBEE ALGER ALSOP AMORY ANSON ANTIN ARNOW BACON BARTH BASSO BATES BAUGH BEACH BEEBZ BENET BINNS BOLES BOYLE BRITT BROWN BRUSH CABLE CAHAN CANBY CHILD CLAPP COOKE CORLE CRANE CREWS CUPPY DAVIS DEISS DIETZ DOBIE DODGE DRURY DUNNE EARLE EATON ELLIS EVANS FAUST FOESS FOOTE GATES GOYEN GRAFF GREEN HARTE HECHT HOBAN HORAN HULME HURST HYAMS IRWIN JAFFE JAKES KELLY KESEY KEYES KIELY KOVEL LAPPE LEECH LEWIS LILLY LODGE LORTZ LYNES LYTLE MABEE MAJOR MARCH MASON MASUR MCFEE MERTZ NIZER OATES ODELL OGDEN OHARA PAINE PANEK POOLE POTOK PUSEY QUEEN RAINE RECHY REESE REEVE RIVES ROARK SELBY SEUSS SIMAK SIMMS SMITH STEIN STONE STONG STOUT STOWE TEALE TEVIS THANE THARP TRINE TRYON TUDOR TULLY TWAIN UHNAK VANCE VIDAL VORSE WALSH WATTS WELTY WEEMS WELLS WHITE WHYTE WILEY WOLFE WYLIE YERBY ADAMIC ALCOTT ALGREN ANGELL ARTHUR ASIMOV AUSTIN BAILEY BARNES BECKER BELLOW BESSIE BISHOP BOWLES BRALEY BRINIG BROWNE BURMAN BURNET CABELL CAPOTE CARMER CARSON CATHER CATLIN CATTON CHIANG CLARKE COLTON COOPER CORBIN CORLEY CROUSE DANNAY DARGAN DAVIES DELAND DEVOTO DIDION DILLON DOWNEY ELLROY EVARTS FARSON FERBER FIELDS FINLEY FISHER FLAVIN FLEBBE FORBES FULLER GADDIS GILMAN GINOTT GORMAN GUNTER HALPER HARRIS HAWKES HERBST HOBART HOLMES HOLZER HOOKER HORGAN HOSMER HOWARD HUGHES IRVING JAHODA JEWETT KELLER KESTER KUMMER LAIKEN LARCOM LEGUIN LIBBEY LONDON LOVETT LUDLUM LUMMIS MAILER MANNES MARCUM MARTIN MCEVOY MILLAY MILLER MORLEY MORROW MUNSON NATHAN NORRIS PARKER PITKIN POLITI PORTER POWELL PROUTY RHODES RIFKIN RIPLEY ROURKE RUNYON SALTUS SENDAK SEVERN SHEEHY SONTAG STEELE STREET STRONG STYRON SUCKOW SWADOS TALESE TAYLOR TERKEL THAYER THOMAS TOLAND TOOMER TRUMAN TUTTLE UPDIKE VEBLEN WALLOP WARNER WATKIN WERNER WILDER WILLIS WILSON WINTER WINWAR WISTER WRIGHT YERKES ALDRICH ANDREWS BABBITT BANNING BELLAMY BENNETT BIGELOW BIGGERS BOYESEN BOYNTON BURGESS BURNETT CALKINS CARROLL CHEEVER CHILTON CLEMENS COMFORT COURNOS COZZENS CUMMINS CURWOOD DERLETH DREISER EDMONDS ELLIOTT ELLISON ERSKINE FARRELL FAWCETT FERNALD FINEMAN FOLLETT FRANKEN FREEMAN GALLICO GARLAND GIFFORD GLASGOW GRATTAN GUNTHER HAMMETT HEYWARD HOLDING HOPKINS JANIFER JOHNSON KAILLOR KELLAND KEROUAC KILVERT KOMROFF LAFARGE LARDNER LINCOLN LINDSAY LOSSING MASTERS MULFORD MUMFORD MURFREE NABOKOV OSTENSO OURSLER PARRISH PARROTT PEATTIE PRESTON PRUETTE ROBERTS ROLVAAG SAMPSON SAROYAN SEIFERT SKINNER TARBELL TERHUNE THEROUX THOREAU THURBER TRAUBEL VANDINE VANDYKE VANLOON VOELKER VOLLMER WAKEMAN WEBSTER WESCOTT WHARTON WHITNEY WINSLOW WOOLSEY WOOLSON YOUMANS ATHERTON ATKINSON AYSCOUGH BAKELESS BARRETTO BENCHLEY BILLINGS BRADFORD BURDETTE CALDWELL CANTWELL CHAMBERS CLEGHORN COLLISON CONNOLLY CONVERSE CRAWFORD DONNELLY FAULKNER FERGUSON FREDERIC GELLHORN GLASPELL GOODRICH HAGEDORN HARRISON HEINLEIN JOHNSTON KEMELMAN KIRKLAND KOSINSKI KRUMGOLD LATHBURY MACAULAY MACGRATH MARQUAND MELVILLE MICHENER MITCHELL NORDHOFF PERELMAN PETERKIN PHILLIPS PROKOSCH RAWLINGS REPPLIER RICHARDS RINEHART SALINGER SANDBURG SEDGWICK SINCLAIR SPILLANE SPINGARN SPOFFORD STANFORD STARRETT STEPHENS STOCKTON STODDARD TIETJENS TOLEDANO TORRENCE TURNBULL VANDOREN VONNEGUT WESTCOTT WIDDEMER WILLIAMS ALTSHELER BACHELLER BERCOVICI BODENHEIM BROMFIELD BURROUGHS CARPENTER CHURCHILL DOSPASSOS EGGLESTON GRANBERRY HAWTHORNE HEMINGWAY ISHERWOOD KORZYBSKI LANCASTER LOCKRIDGE MCCULLERS NICHOLSON OSULLIVAN SANTAYANA SCHULBERG SIGOURNEY STALLINGS STEINBECK STEVENSON STRIBLING WOOLLCOTT CLENDENING FITZGERALD MCCUTCHEON SOUTHWORTH TARKINGTON TROWBRIDGE UNTERMEYER VANVECHTEN CANTACUZENE CHAMBERLAIN GERSTENBERG MINNIGERODE SCHLESINGER STRATEMEYER HERGESHEIMER
ARGENTINIAN PUIG BORGES GALVEZ MARMOL SABATO CANDIOTI TIMERMAN CAPDEVILA
AUSTRALIAN STOW WEST BECKE COWAN GREER WHITE BROWNE CLARKE LAWSON PORTER POWELL CALVERT COLLINS DAVISON EGERTON TRAVERS PRICHARD SOUTHALL VILLIERS BRINSMEAD CAMBRIDGE MOOREHEAD RICHARDSON
AUSTRIAN LIND ADLER BAYER KAFKA PRAED ZWEIG WERFEL BARTSCH COLERUS NEUMANN PICHLER ROSEGGER SCHREKER ALTENBERG BURCKHARD SCHREIBER SCHNITZLER VONDODERER
BELGIAN COSTER HYMANS PICARD EEKHOUD SIMENON DECOSTER LEMONNIER
BRAZILIAN AMADO CUNHA MORAES TAUNAY GUIMARAES LISPECTOR VERISSIMO
BULGARIAN VAZOV CANETTI
CANADIAN COX ROY CARR GROVE MOWAT SETON SULTE ATWOOD BIRNEY BRIAND ERDMAN HAILEY LEVINE MILLAR MOODIE PARKER CAMERON GLASSCO LEACOCK MCLUHAN NEUHAUS RICHLER SERVICE TRUDEAU CHAMBERS LAURENCE MCDOWELL STRINGER SULLIVAN CALLAGHAN DELAROCHE MACDONALD MACLENNAN PICKTHALL VANPAASEN
CHILEAN CORTES ALLENDE
COLOMBIAN CARO REYES CUERVO CARRASQUILLA
CZECH HASEK MUCHA LANGER HOLECEK JIRASEK KUNDERA COMENIUS VANCURRA
DANISH BANG NEXO HERTZ KIDDE SKRAM BLIXEN LARSEN RORDAM BAUDITZ CLAUSEN DINESEN PALUDAN TANDRUP ANDERSEN FREUCHEN INGEMANN JACOBSEN BUCHHOLTZ COUPERIUS DRACHMANN GJELLERUP JORGENSEN MICHAELIS BREGENDAHL KIERKEGAAD
DUTCH LOOY EEDEN BEKKER CREMER DEJONG EMANTS JENSEN LENNEP DEVRIES ERAMUS DEHARTOG MAARTENS
ENGLISH DAY LEE PYM AMIS AYER BECK BEHN BELL BRAY COLE DANE ERTZ FENN FORD GLYN HONE HULL HUME KOPS LAMB LEEK LEON LEVY LONG LYLY MORE MUIR PAUL PAYN REED REID PHYS RICE SAKI SHAW SNOW WAIN WARD WEBB WEST WOOD WREN ADAMS AMORY AYRES BARRY BATES BAYLY BERRY BLOOM BRETT BRYCE BURKE CAINE COMBE CORVO CRABB CRAIK CRISP CROWE DAVIE DEFOE DIGBY DIXON DOYLE ELIOT ELLIS EWING FRAYN GIBBS HARDY HEARD HEVER HINDE HOLME INNES JAMES JEANS KEOWN LEVER LEWIS LOCKE LOFTS LOWRY LUCAS MASON MAYNE MCFEE MILNE MOORE MUNRO MURRY ORCZY OUIDA POWYS RAMEE READE ROPES SCOTT SHARP SHIEL SHUTE SMITH STEEL STERN SWIFT WAUGH WELLS WOOLF WYLIE YONGE YOUNG ALDISS ALLSOP AMBLER ANGELL ASCHAM ASHTON ASTELL AUBREY AUSTEN AUSTIN BARING BARRIE BAWDEN BELLOC BENSON BESANT BLOUNT BLYTON BORROW BRAINE BRIDGE BRONTE BROPHY BULLEN BUNYAN BURGIN BURTON CALDER CANNAN CASTLE CHURCH CONRAD CRONIN ESSLIN FARNOL FELKIN FOSTER GODWIN GOUDGE GRAHAM GRAVES GREENE HILTON HOBBES HOLTBY HORLER HOWELL HOWITT HUDSON HUGHES HUXLEY JEROME LANDON LANDOR LYTTON MACHEN MORGAN MORTON MOSLEY MURRAY NESBIT NORTON ONIONS ORMSBY ORWELL PALMER PORTER POWELL PUDNEY REEVES RUSKIN SANDYS SANSOM SAYERS SEWELL SHANKS SOUTAR SPRING STERNE SYMONS TAYLOR WALTON WARNER WARREN WARTON WATSON WEYMAN WRIGHT AGUILAR ASHFORD BAGNOLD BALCHIN BALDWIN BARCLAY BENNETT BENTLEY BERNERS BIRRELL BOLITHO BOTTOME BULLETT BUNBURY CHAMIER CHATWIN CLELAND COCKTON COLLINS

CORELLI CRISPIN DAICHES DEEPING DICKENS DODGSON DOUGLAS DUDENEY EDWARDS FARJEON FIRBANK FORSTER FORSYTH FREEMAN GARNETT GASKELL GIBBONS GISSING GOLDING GUTHRIE HAGGARD HASSALL HAWKINS HAZLITT HEWLETT HICHENS HORNUNG HOUSMAN JACKSON JOHNSON KENNEDY KIPLING LAMBURN LECARRE LEHMANN LESSING LOVESEY LOWNDES MARRYAT MAUGHAM MAXWELL MCKENNA MITFORD MONTAGU MORISON NICHOLS OXENHAM PEACOCK PERTWEE RANSOME RITCHIE ROBERTS SASSOON SHELLEY SITWELL SMEDLEY SOWERBY SPENDER SURTEES TOLKIEN TOYNBEE VACHELL WADDELL WALLACE WALPOLE ZIMMERN BARBAULD BARTLETT BEERBOHM BRITTAIN CHRISTIE DASHWOOD DEIGHTON FIELDING FLETCHER FORESTER HAMILTON HARRADEN KERNAHAN KINGSLEY KNOBLOCK KOESTLER LAWRENCE LEIGHTON MACAULAY MARRIOTT MEREDITH MORDAUNT OLIPHANT OLLIVANT PATTISON SINCLAIR SMOLLETT STANNARD STOPPARD STRETTON THIRKELL TROLLOPE WALMSLEY ZANGWILL AINSWORTH ALDINGTON BERESFORD BLACKMORE BLACKWOOD BROUGHTON CARPENTER CHURCHILL DEQUINCEY DUMAURIER GERHARDIE GOLDSMITH GREENWELL GREENWOOD HENRIQUES KINGSMILL LINKLATER LITVINOFF LLEWELLYN MANSFIELD MITCHISON MONKHOUSE OPPENHEIM PEMBERTON PHILLPOTS PICKTHALL PRIESTLEY PRITCHETT RADCLIFFE ROBERTSON SCHREINER SOUTHWOLD STACPOOLE STAPLEDON THACKERAY TREVELYAN WHITEHEAD WILKINSON WILLCOCKS WODEHOUSE FOTHERGILL GALSWORTHY HUTCHINSON MEYERSTEIN MUGGERIDGE RICHARDSON SHORTHOUSE SWINNERTON WILLIAMSON DANGERFIELD YOUNGHUSBAND
ESTONIAN TAMMSAARE
FINNISH AHO KIVI CANTH KALLAS CYGNAUS SALMINEN SILLANPAA TAVASTSTJERNA
FRENCH FOA GAY NAU SUE AIDE ARON AYME BLOY GIDE HUGO KARR MAEL SADE SAND UZES ZOLA ABOUT BAZIN BEDEL BLOCH BOVET BUTOR CAMUS CARCO CEARD COLET DUMAS DURAS FABRE GENET GIONO HEMON LOUYS OHNET PEYRE ROSNY SAGAN VERNE ACHARD AGOULT ARAGON ARGENS ARLAND AULNOY AVENEL BALZAC BEDIER BENOIT BERAUD BISSON BIYIDI BLOUET BODARD BOULLE BRUEYS BUFFON CASSOU CLADEL CRAVEN DAUDET DONIOL EPINAY ELUARD FAYARD FRANCE HALEVY HUZARD IMBERT JAMMES LACLOS LEROUX LESAGE MOULIE PROUST REBOUX SARTRE SCHURE TROYAT VERCEL VOLNEY ANCELOT ARNAULT BAUMANN BEHAINE BERNARD BERQUIN BONNARD BOSSUET BOURGET BOUVIER CAZOTTE COCTEAU COLETTE DEBERLY DELTEIL DURTAIN FEYDEAU FONTANE GAUTIER HERMANT HERVIEU HOFFMAN IONESCU LAVEDAN LEBLANC LERMINA MALRAUX MAURIAC MAUROIS MERIMEE MONNIER PREVOST REGNIER ROLLAND ROMAINS SANDEAU SARASIN SIMENON TENDRON ASSOLANT BANVILLE BARBUSSE BEAUVOIR BENJAMIN BERENGER BERNANOS BERTRAND BONVALOT BORDEAUX BOYLESVE BRUNHOFF CENDRARS CHARTIER CLARETIE DORGELES DUFRESNY ESTAUNIE FEUILLET FLAUBERT FOUCAULT GENEVOIX GONCOURT GREVILLE HOUSSAYE HUYSMANS KOCKLOTI LATAILLE MALHERBE MARIETON MARIVAUX MONTEPIN MONTFORT PERRAULT RABELAIS ROUSSEAU SAVIGNON SCHOPFER SOUPAULT STENDHAL VALLETTE VOLTAIRE BEAUCHAMP BOUHELIER CHERVILLE COULEVAIN DESCHANEL FONTAINAS MARMONTEL MIOMANDRE POURTALES SENANCOUR BAZANCOURT CHARLEVOIX DESJARDINS FAUCONNIER MAUPASSANT APOLLINAIRE MARGUERITTE
GERMAN APEL BALL BAUM BOLL BURG HEYM HOLZ HUCH KURZ MANN ARNDT BULOW BUSSE EBERS ERNST GRASS GROTH HAGEN HALBE HAUFF HESSE HEYSE HUBER KUHNE LANGE LAUBE MAREK MUGGE MUNDT RAABE UNRUH ZESEN ZWEIG BECKER BEREND BINZER BLUNCK BUICKE CONRAD DAUMER DEWOHL DREYER HAUSER HEYDEN JENSEN JOHNST KLEIST KNIGGE LEWALD LUDWIG MILLER MORIKE MUSAUS REUTER SCHMID VIEBIG WERNER BERTUCH BRONNEN CONRADI DAUBLER FALLADA FREYTAG GLAESER GUTZKOW HEIBERG KASTNER KRETZER LAROCHE NEUMANN OSTWALD REDWITZ RICHTER SEGHERS VULPIUS AUERBACH BORKENAU BRENTANO ECKSTEIN FRAENKEL HAUSMANN HOCHHUTH HOFFMANN KOTZEBUE LIENHARD MEISSNER REMARQUE ROQUETTE WOLZOGEN ZSCHOKKE BEYERLEIN GANGHOFER IMMERMANN SCHUCKING SIODMAKK SUDERMANN UECHTRITZ WILBRANDT WITZLEBEN ZERKAULEN ZOBELTITZ FLAISCHLEN GERSTACKER KELLERMANN SPIELHAGEN WASSERMANN WILDERMUTH HASENCLEVER FEUCHTWANGER SCHOPENHAUER
GREEK AESOP HOMER BARDIS IOPHON LONGUS LUCIAN BABRIUS PLUTARCH ARISTOTLE ONOSANDER KAZANTZAKIS
GUATEMALAN ASTRUIAS
HUNGARIAN FAY BIRO JOKAI DOBOZY FARAGO FOLDES JOSIKA KARMAN SALTEN HEGEDUS VAMBERY HARSANYI KOESTLER KORMENDI
ICELANDIC KAMBAN ARNASON LAXNESS SAEMUND GUNNARSSON THORODDSEN GUDMUNDSSON
INDIAN ALI ABBAS ANAND GHOSE MEHTA RUSHDIE SORABJI CHATTERJI SHRIDHARANI KRISHNAMURTI
IRISH DALY WEST BEHAN BOWEN COYLE CROLY DOYLE GWYNN JOYCE KEANE LECKY LETTS LOVER MOORE MOYES STERN TYNAN WILDE BARLOW BROOKE CROFTS ERVINE GRAVES LEFANU LESLIE MARTIN OBRIEN OGRADY OKELLY PEARSE STOKER TREVOR BECKETT CCOGARTY ORKERY DUNSANY LARDNER LAWLESS MACGILL MATURIN MAXWELL MURDOCH OCONNER STARKIE CARELTON CHILDERS KAVANAGH ODONNELL OFAOLAIN ORIORDAN STEPHENS OFLAHERTY TODHUNTER WARBURTON WIBBERLEY BARRINGTON MCALLISTER SOMERVILLE
ISRAELI OZ BROD AGNON BUBER
ITALIAN VARE BRUNO PULCI SERAO TASSO AMICIS FARINA MAFFEI PAPINI PAVESE SILONE ALBERTI BARRILI BARZINI BONATTI CARCANO DELEDDA GALIANI GIACOMO MANZONI MOHAVIA PELLICO ALBRIZZI BERSEZIO SABATINI BOCCACCIO CHIARELLI CORRADINI DANNUNZIO FOGAZZARO GUERRAZZI BELGIOIOSO BERTINELLI PREZZOLINI CASTELNUOVO PIRANDELLO
JAPANESE ENDO BAKIN NAGAI OZAKI TAMAI MISHIMA FUKUZAWA KAWABATA MURASAKI
LATVIAN RAINIS
MEXICAN AZUELA GAMBOA TRAVEN FUENTES
NEW ZEALAND EDEN ADAMS MARSH DUGGAN BOLITHO LYTTLETON MANSFIELD RUSSELL
NIGERIAN ALUKO ACHEBE DELANO SOYINKA TUTUOLA
NORWEGIAN LIE BULL BOJER FONHUS HAMSUN UNDSET COLLETT GARBORG INGSTAD ELVESTAD KIELLAND ASBJORNSEN
PERUVIAN PALMA URETA ALEGRIA CACERES
POLISH REJ ASCH PRUS STRUG ANCZYC BERENT CONRAD GOETEL BALUCKI REYMONT WITTLIN ZAPOLSKA ZELENSKI ZEROMSKI ZULAWSKI MILKOWSKI NALKOWSKA DANILOWSKI KONOPNICKA KRASZEWSKI CHMIELOWSKI OSSENDOWSKI SIENKIEWICZ KORZENIOWSKI ANDREZEJEWSKI
PORTUGUESE LOBO BRAGA SOUSA DANTAS MORAES
ROMAN LUCAN APULEIUS PHAEDRUS VELLEIUS PETRONIUS
RUMANIAN BEIN GOGA NEGRUZZI CARAGIALE RADULESCU
RUSSIAN BLOK BABEL BUNIN FEDIN GOGOL GORKI FADEEV GLINKA HERZEN KRYLOV KUPRIN LEONOV LESKOV AKSAKOV ALDANOV AMALRIK ANDREEV CHEKHOV GARSHIN GLADKOV KATAYEV PILNYAK PUSHKIN ROMANOV TOLSTOI BULGAKOV KARAMZIN POTEKHIN SHALAMOV SHUKSHIN TURGENEV USPENSKI VERESAEY BESTUZHEV EHRENBURG GONCHAROV KOROLENKO LERMONTOV PASTERNAK SHOLOKHOV SUMAROKOV USPENSKII DOSTOEVSKI YUSHKEVICH ZOSHCHENKO AMFITEATROV ARTSYBASHEV GRIGOROVICH LAZHECHNIKOV SOLZHENITSYN
SCOTTISH TEY DENT GALT GUNN HOGG LANG BEITH BROWN COMBE JACOB MUNRO SCOTT SHARP SPARK YOUNG AYTOUN BARRIE BROGAN BUCHAN GIBBON SHAIRP WATSON BALFOUR CHESNEY FERRIER HERRIOT MACLEAN MACLEOD BUCHANAN CRAUFURD CROCKETT LOCKHART MAITLAND MARSHALL OLIPHANT URQUHART FINDLATER MACDONALD MACKENZIE MITCHISON MOLESWORTH
SOUTH AFRICA HEAD SEED PATON CLOETE MILLIN PLOMER
SOUTH AFRICAN BLOOM COETZEE GORDIMER BALLINGER
SPANISH ALAS BAREA PEREZ RIVAS ROJAS TRIGO ALEMAN BAROJA ESPRIU PEREDA SENDER AGUILAR ALARCON ESPINEL MACHADO CABALLERO CERVANTES
SWEDISH AURELL CARLEN EDGREN MOBERG MWRDAL WAHLOO AHLGREN LIDGREN SJOWALL ALMQVIST LAGERLOF SCHWARTZ BACKSTROM LUNDEGARD LAGERKVIST STRINDBERG STREINDBERG WETTERBERGH
SWISS ROD FREY HEER KING HESSE WYSS SPYRI FRISCH FUSELI KAISER BITZIUS FEDERER KERLLER OLIVIER DURRENMATT
WELSH MAP EVANS PRYCE WYNNE DAVIES THOMAS ARUNDEL POLLETT LLEWELLYN
YUGOSLAVIAN ANDRIC DJILAS DEDIJER

AUTHORITATIVE GRAVE CLASSIC OFFICIAL ORACULAR POSITIVE TEXTUARY MAGISTERIAL (PREF.) CURIO

AUTHORITY LAW ROD SEE BALL RULE SWAY ADEPT BOARD FAITH

POWER RICHE RIGHT SAYSO STAMP SWING TITLE ARTIST AUTHOR CREDIT DANGER EMPERY EXPERT FASCES PUNDIT REGENT REGIME SWINGE WEIGHT AMITATE COMMAND CONTROL DYNASTY FACULTY LEADING LICENCE LICENSE POTENCY SCEPTER WARRANT DISPOSAL DOMINION DOMINIUM HEGEMONY LORDSHIP PRESTIGE SANCTION STRENGTH PROCURATION
(— OF SWITZERLAND) BUNDESRAT
(ARBITRARY —) ABOVE
(CHALLENGE —) REBEL
(COLLEGE —) DON
(MORAL —) MANA
(ONE HIGHEST IN —) SUPREMO
(PAPAL —) VATICAN
(ROYAL —) SCEPTRE SOVRANTY
(SPIRITUAL —) KEYS KHILAFAT
(SUPREME —) SAY SIRCAR SIRKAR
(TEACHING —) MAGISTERIUM
(UNLIMITED —) AUTOCRACY
(PL.) ISNAD SIRCAR
(SUFF.) CRACY CRAT(IC)

AUTHORIZATION FIAT BARAT BERAT PASSPORT SANCTION WARRANTY PERMISSION

AUTHORIZE LET LEAL VEST ALLOW CLEAR CLOTHE PERMIT RATIFY APPROVE EMPOWER ENDORSE ENTITLE INDORSE JUSTIFY LICENSE WARRANT ACCREDIT DELEGATE LEGALIZE SANCTION

AUTHORIZED LEGAL OFFICIAL

AUTHORSHIP PENCRAFT PATERNITY

AUTO (ALSO SEE AUTOMOBILE) CRATE CHUMMY LIZZIE
(— RACING MANEUVER) SLINGSHOT
(— RACING PROBLEM) SPINOUT
(CONVERTIBLE —) RAGTOP
(UNSATISFACTORY —) LEMON

AUTOBIOGRAPHY VITA MEMOIR

AUTOCHTHONOUS NATIVE EDAPHIC ENDEMIC

AUTOCLAVE DIGESTER DIGESTOR

AUTOCRACY MONARCHY

AUTOCRAT CHAM CZAR TSAR TZAR MOGUL CAESAR DESPOT AUTARCH MONARCH DICTATOR MONOCRAT

AUTOCRATIC ABSOLUTE

AUTO-DA-FE AUTO SERMO

AUTOGRAPH NAME SIGN MANUAL INSCRIBE

AUTOLYCUS (DAUGHTER OF —) ANTICLEA
(FATHER OF —) HERMES MERCURY
(HALF-BROTHER OF —) PHILAMMON
(MOTHER OF —) CHIONE

AUTOMATIC REFLEX MACHINE MECHANICAL
(PREF.) SELF

AUTOMATON GOLEM ROBOT AUTOMA ANDROID MACHINE

AUTOMOBILE BUG BUS CAR SIX AUTO FOUR HEAP JEEP PONY TRAP BUGGY COACH COUPE CRATE EDSEL EIGHT MOTOR PONEY RACER SEDAN BUCKET CHUMMY CUSTOM JALOPY JUNKER SALOON WHEELS AUTOCAR COMPACT FLIVVER HACKNEY HARDTOP MACHINE MINICAR MINIVAN PHAETON STEAMER TORPEDO VOITURE CARRYALL DRAGSTER ELECTRIC FASTBACK ROADSTER SQUADROL SUBURBAN VICTORIA HATCHBACK NOTCHBACK
(CONVERTIBLE —) RAGTOP DROPHEAD
(DEMONSTRATOR —) DEMO
(KIND OF —) RENTACAR
(MIDGET —) DOODLEBUG
(NOISY —) BANGER
(SMALL —) MINI

AUTONOE (FATHER OF —) CADMUS
(HUSBAND OF —) ARISTAEUS
(MOTHER OF —) HARMONIA
(SISTER OF —) AGAVE
(SON OF —) ACTAEON

AUTONOMOUS FREE SEPARATE

AUTONOMY SOVEREIGNTY SEPARATENESS
(— OF GOD) ASEITY ASEITAS

AUTOPSY NECROPSY

AUTUMN FALL KHARIF AUTOMPNE FALLTIME MATURITY

AUXILIARY AID SUB AIDE ALLY ANSAR AIDING BRANCH DONKEY HELPER ABETTER ABETTOR ADJUNCT HELPING PARTNER ADJUTANT ANCILLARY PERIPHERAL
(PL.) FOEDERATI

AVAIL DO AID DOW USE BOOT HELP FADGE SERVE SKILL STEAD VALUE MOMENT PROFIT BENEFIT BESTEAD PREVAIL SERVICE SUCCEED SUFFICE UTILIZE SUBSERVE
(— ONESELF) EMBRACE IMPROVE SUBSERVE

AVAILABLE FIT FREE OPEN FLUSH HANDY LOOSE ONTAP READY PATENT USABLE PRESENT VISIBLE ATSTORES

AVALANCHE SLIDE LAWINE VOLLENGE

AVANT-COURIER HERALD SCURRIER

AVANT-GARDE LITERATI

AVARICE GREED MAMMON MISERY AVIDITY CUPIDITY RAPACITY

AVARICIOUS CLOSE SLOAN GREEDY HAVING HUNGRY SORDID STINGY GRIPING GRIPPLE ITCHING MISERLY COVETOUS GRASPING

AVATAR BALARAMA EPIPHANY

AVELLANEOUS HAZEL

AVENGE REPAY RIGHT VISIT WRACK WREAK AWREAK PUNISH BEWREAK REQUITE REVENGE SATISFY CHASTISE

AVENGER KANAIMA NEMESIS WREAKER

AVENS GEUM BENNET BAREFOOT

AVENTURINE SUNSTONE GOLDSTONE

AVENUE RUE WAY GATE MALL PIKE ROAD ALLEE ALLEY DRIVE ENTRY ACCESS ARCADE ARTERY DROMOS RIDING STREET AVENIDA OPENING PASSAGE

AVER SAY AIVER CLAIM PROVE STATE SWEAR AFFIRM ALLEGE ASSERT ASSURE AVOUCH DEPOSE VERIFY DECLARE JUSTIFY PROFESS PROTEST

AVERAGE PAR SUM DUTY FAIR MEAN NORM RULE SOSO RATIO USUAL VALUE CHARGE MEDIAL MEDIAN MEDIUM MIDDLE NORMAL TARIFF ARRIAGE ESTIMATE MEDIOCRE MIDDLING MODERATE ORDINARY OVERHEAD QUANTITY STANDARD
(DOW-JONES —) DOW
(NOT —) BORDERLINE

AVERNAL HELLISH INFERNAL

AVERSE LOTH BALKY LOATH AFRAID ADVERSE AGAINST OPPOSED BACKWARD INIMICAL OPPOSITE PERVERSE RELUCTANT
(— TO) ABOVE

AVERSION TOY HATE DERRY ODIUM ENMITY HATRED HORROR PHOBIA REGRET DESPITE DISDAIN DISGUST DISLIKE MISLIKE DISTASTE ABOMINATION
(— TO FOOD) APOSITIA
(— TO WORK) ERGOPHOBIA

AVERT WRY BEND FEND MOVE SHUN TURN WARD AVOID DETER DODGE EVADE PARRY SHEER TWIST DEFRAY DIVERT RETARD SHIELD DECLINE DEFLECT EXPIATE PREVENT ALIENATE ESTRANGE FOREFEND WITHTURN

AVESTA ZEND

AVIARY CAGE HOUSE VOLARY ORNITHON

AVIATOR ACE FLIER FLYER PILOT AIRMAN FLYING ICARUS BIRDMAN LOOPIST LUFBERY MANBIRD SOLOIST

AVID LSD AGOG KEEN WARM EAGER ARDENT GREEDY HUNGRY JEJUNE ANXIOUS ATHIRST CRAVING LONGING THIRSTY DESIROUS GRASPING

AVIDITY AVARICE CUPIDITY

AVIFAUNA BIRDS ORNIS BIRDLIFE

AVIKOM JACKS

AVOCADO COYO PEAR PALTA AHUACA CHININ MARROW PERSEA ZABOCA ABACATE ABBOGADA AGUACATE ALLIGATO

AVOCET BARKER TILTER YELPER SCOOPER

AVOID FLY SHY BALK FLEE HELP MISS PASS QUIT SAVE SHUN VOID WARE ABHOR ANNUL AVERT BURKE DITCH DODGE ELUDE EVADE EVITE FEIGN HEDGE PARRY SHIFT SHIRK SKIRT SKULK SLACK SPAIR SPARE START WANDE WONDE ABJURE BLENCH BYPASS DETOUR ESCAPE ESCHEW REFUTE REMOVE VACATE ABSTAIN DECLINE EVITATE FORBEAR FORSAKE REFRAIN
(— A PUNCH) SLIP
(— COMMITMENT) FUDGE
(— EXPENSE) HELP MISS SKIVE
(— OVERWORKING) FAVOR
(— RESPONSIBILITY) BLUDGE
(— SUPERHIGHWAY) SHUNPIKE
(PREF.) PHYGO

AVOIDANCE DODGE OUTLET EVASION ESCHEWAL
(— OF RISK) CAUTION
(PREF.) PHOB(O)

AVOIDING (— BATTLE) FABIAN

AVOIRDUPOIS HEFT

AVOUCH AVER ASSERT

AVOW OWN BIND WARE ADMIT STATE AFFIRM ASSERT AVOUCH DEPONE DEPOSE DEVOTE CONFESS DECLARE JUSTIFY PROFESS MAINTAIN

AVOWAL OATH WORD AVOURE PROTEST

AVOWED FRANK SWORN STATED DECLARED

AWAIT BIDE HEED KEEP PEND STAY TEND WAIT ABIDE TARRY WATCH ATTEND EXPECT IMPEND REMAIN WAYLAY
(— PAYMENT) CARRY

AWAITING BEFORE BIDING

AWAKE DAW STIR WAKE ADAWE ALERT ALIVE AWARE ROUSE ABRADE ABRAID ACTIVE AROUSE AWAKEN EXCITE CAREFUL HEEDFUL STARTLE VIGILANT

AWAKEN DAW STIR ALERT AROUSE BESTIR EXCITE KINDLE

AWAKENER (ARMY —) BUGLE

AWAKENING REVIVAL WAKEFUL

AWARD LAW ARET CLIO GIVE HUGO KUDO MARK MEED METE OBIE TONY WARD ALLOT ARETT EDGAR GRANT MEDAL PRICE PRIZE ACCORD ACTION ADDEEM ADDOOM ADWARD ASSIGN BESTOW BOUNTY CONFER DECIDE GRAMMY MODIFY ADJUDGE APPOINT CONSIGN CUSTODY KEEPING ACCOLADE SENTENCE
(ATHLETIC —) LETTER
(DETECTIVE FICTION —) EDGAR
(MOVIE —) OSCAR
(MYSTERY-NOVEL WRITING —) EDGAR
(RADIO OR TELEVISION —) CLIO
(RECORDING —) GRAMMIE
(STATUETTE —) GRAMMY REUBEN
(TELEVISION —) EMMY
(THEATER —) OBIE
(THEATRICAL —) TONY
(WRITING —) HUGO
(PL.) DESERTS

AWARE HEP HIP RECK SURE WARE WARY WISE ALERT ALIVE AWAKE JERRY BEWARE KNOWING MINDFUL APPRISED INFORMED SENSIBLE SENTIENT VIGILANT WATCHFUL
(— OF) ONTO
(KEENLY —) HIP

AWARENESS EAR FEEL SENSE FEELING INSIGHT COGNITION SENSATION PERCEPTION

(— OF SUPERNATURAL) VISION
(— OF WORTH) APPRECIATION
AWASH ASEA ADRIFT AFLOAT FLOODED SWAMPED FLOATING
AWAY BY TO AWA FRO OFF OUT VIA WAY AFAR GONE PAST SCAT YOND ALONG APART ASIDE FORTH HENCE ABROAD ABSENT BEGONE ONWARD THENCE DISTANT FROWARD FAREWELL TOTHEWIND
(— FROM) DOWN WITH ALONE ALOOF APART BESIDE
(— FROM HOME) AFIELD OUTLAND
(— FROM MOUTH) ABORAL
(— FROM PORT) AFLOAT
(FARTHER —) BEYOND
(PREF.) DE E
(— FROM) APH APO
AWE COW WOW FEAR AMAZE DAUNT DREAD SCARE FRIGHT HORROR REGARD TERROR WONDER BUFFALO RESPECT ASTONISH BEWILDER OVERCOME RELIGION
AWED SOLEMN
AWEIGH ATRIP
AWE-INSPIRING GODFUL SOLEMN AWESOME RELIGIO FEARSOME OLYMPIAN
AWESOME EERY FELL HOLY AWFUL EERIE WEIRD SOLEMN DREADED GHOSTLY
AWESTRUCK SILENT
AWETO WERI
AWFUL DIRE FINE UGLY DREAD GHAST AUGUST HORRID AWESOME FEARFUL HIDEOUS SATANIC DREADFUL SHOCKING TERRIBLE
AWFULLY AWFUL FIERCE
AWHILE FORABIT
AWKWARD AWK CAR GAUM UNCO BLATE CRANK DODGY FALSE FUDGY GAUMY GAWKY GOATY INAPT INEPT SPLAY STIFF UNCOW UNKED UNKID CLUMSY GAUCHE RUSTIC STICKY THUMBY UNEASY WOODEN ADVERSE BOORISH CUBBISH FROWARD HALTING LOUTISH LUMPISH STILTED UNCANNY UNCOUTH UNHANDY UNREADY BUNGLING CLOWNISH FECKLESS LUBBERLY PERVERSE UNGAINLY UNTOWARD UNWIELDY CLOUTERLY GRACELESS MALADROIT
(— LOOKING) HORSY
(— PERSON) CLOUT KLUTZ TAWPY TUMFIE
(NOT —) FACILE
AWKWARD PERSON GALOOT
AWL BROD BROG NAIL NALL PROD PROG ALENE BRODE ELSEN NALLE BROACH DRIVER ELSHIN FIBULA GIMLET BRADAWL SCRIBER STABBER
AWN AIL EAR JAG BARB BEAK JAGG PILE ARISTA BRISTLE
(— OF BARLEY) HORN
(— OF OATS) JAG JAGG
(PL.) BEARD
AWNED BARBATE
AWNING TILT BLIND SHADE VELUM CANOPY SEMIAN SHADER TIENDA TENTORY SEMIANNA SUNBLIND SUNSHADE VELARIUM
AWNLESS NOT NOTT HUMBLE HUMMEL POLLARD MUTICOUS
AWRY CAM WRY AGEE BIAS SKEW AGLEY AMISS ASKEW GLEED GLEYD SNAFU WONKY WRONG ACROSS ASIDEN BLOOEY BLOOIE CAMMED FLOOEY SKIVIE THRAWN ASKANCE ASQUINT ATHWART CROOKED OBLIQUE PERVERSE
AX ADZ AXE CAN ADZE EAWT FIRE HACHE MATAX BIFACE CANCEL CUTOUT PICKEL PIOLET POLEAX THIXLE TWIBIL BESAGUE BOUCHER BROADAX CHOPPER CLEAVER HATCHET JEDDING PULASKI TWIBILL FRANCISC PALSTAVE SUNDERER TOMAHAWK
(DOUBLE —) LABRYS
(HEADSMAN'S —) MANNAIA
(MASON'S —) CAVEL
(PART OF —) EAR EYE BUTT FACE HAFT HEAD POLL BLADE HELVE HANDLE
(WOODEN —) MACANA
(PREF.) SECURI
AXENIC GERMFREE
AXHAMMER CAVEL CAVIL KEVEL KNAPPER
AXIAL VENTRAL
AXIL ALA
AXILLA AXIS ARMPIT SHOULDER
AXILLARY ALAR
AXIOM SAW ADAGE MAXIM MOTTO BYWORD DICTUM SAYING TRUISM DIGNITY PRECEPT PROVERB APHORISM APOTHEGM DIGNITAS PETITION SENTENCE POSTULATE
AXIOMATIC PRIMITIVE
AXIS AXE NUT AXLE STEM ARBOR HINGE STALK ARBOUR CAUDEX CENTER CHITRA RACHIS CAULOME CORNCOB DENTATA POLAXIS SPINDLE SUCCULA SYMPODE TENDRIL AXLETREE MONOPODE
(— OF A FLOWER) CYME SPIKE UMBEL CORYMB RACEME PANICLE
(— OF COCHLEA) MODIOLUS
(PREF.) AX(I)(IO)(O)(ONO)
AXLE EX BAR COD PIN AXIS BOGY ARBOR BOGEY BOGIE EXTRE SHAFT AXTREE SLEEVE MANDREL SPINDLE SUCCULA
AXOLOTL SIREDON
AXON PROCESS
AYAH IYA CHAY EYAH MAID NURSE
AYE I AY EY EYE PRO YEA YES EVER ALWAYS ASSENT FOREVER
AYESHA (HUSBAND OF —) MOHAMMED
AYU AI SWEETFISH
AZALEA ERICA MINERVA CARDINAL
AZALIAH (SON OF —) SHAPHAN
AZANIAH (SON OF —) JESHUA
AZAREEL (FATHER OF —) BANI JEROHAM
(SON OF —) AMASHAI MAASIAI
AZARIAH (FATHER OF —) JEHU ODED ETHAN NATHAN AHIMAAZ JEROHAM JOHANAN MAASEIAH JEHALELEL ZEPHANIAH JEHOSHAPHAT
(SON OF —) JOEL
AZAZ (SON OF —) BELA
AZAZEL EBLIS
AZAZIAH (SON OF —) HOSHEA
AZERBAIJAN (ALSO SEE RUSSIA)
(CAPITAL OF —) BAKU
(CAPITOL OF —) BAKU
AUTONOMOUS REGION: NAGORNOKARABAKH
AUTONOMOUS REPUBLIC: NAKHICHEVAN
CANAL: SHIRVAN KARABAKH
CAPITAL: BAKU BAKY
COIN: MANAT
LAKE: GEYGYOL
LANGUAGE: AZERI
MOUNTAIN: TUFAN SHAKHDAG BAZARDYUZYU KYUMYURKYOY
MOUNTAIN RANGE: TALISH TALYSH CAUCASUS MUROVDAG SHAKHDAG ZANGEZUR
PLAIN: MUGAN SHIRVAN LENKORAN MILSKAYA
RIVER: ARAS KURA ARAKS
TOWN: GANJA SUMGAIT KIROVABAD
AZIMUTH ZN ARC BEARING
AZMAVETH (SON OF —) PELET JEZIEL
AZOLE PYRROLE
AZOR (FATHER OF —) ELIAKIM
AZRIEL (SON OF —) SERAIAH
AZRIKAM (FATHER OF —) AZEL NEARIAH
(SLAYER OF —) ZICHRI
AZTEC AZTECA MEXICA MEXICAN TENOCHCA
AZUBAH (HUSBAND OF —) CALEB
(SON OF —) JEHOSHAPHAT
AZUR (SON OF —) HANANIAH JAAZANIAH
AZURE BICE BLUE HURT JOVE COBALT JOVIAL JUPITER CERULEAN SAPPHIRE
AZZAN (SON OF —) PALTIEL

B

B SI BEE BAKER BRAVO
(— FLAT) ZA BEMOL
BA TRIPOS
BAA MAA MAE BLEAT
BAAL BEEZEBUB
BAANA (FATHER OF —) AHILUD
(SON OF —) ZADOK
BAANAH (BROTHER OF —) RECHAB
(FATHER OF —) HUSHAI RIMMON
(SLAYER OF —) DAVID
(SON OF —) HELEB HELED
BAARA (HUSBAND OF —) SHAHARAIM
BAASHA (FATHER OF —) AHIJAH
BABBAR UTU UTUO
BABBITT PHILISTINE
(AUTHOR OF —) LEWIS
(CHARACTER IN —) TED MYRA PAUL TANIS ZILLA GEORGE VERONA BABBITT JUDIQUE REISLING
BABBLE CHAT GASH KNAP PURL TOVE BABIL BLATE CLACK CLYDE GLOCK HAVER PRATE TAVER WLAFF CACKLE DITHER GABBLE GAGGLE GLAVER GOSSIP JANGLE MURMUR PALTER PIFFLE RABBLE TAIVER TUMULT BLABBER BLATHER BLETHER BLUSTER BRABBLE CHATTER CHIPPER CLATTER PRATTLE SMATTER TWADDLE TWATTLE GLAISTER
BABBLER CACKLER BLATEROON STIPITURE
BABBLING LALLATION
(PREF.) LALO
BABE NAIF INFANT
BABEL DIN MEDLEY TUMULT CHARIVARI CONFUSION
BABESIA APIOSOMA NUTTALIA PIROPLASMA
BABOON APE PAP PAPA DRILL ADONIS BAVIAN CHACMA GIRRIT PAPION SPHINX BABUINA MANDRILL HAMADRYAD
BABUL SANT SUNT ACACIA BABOOT GARRAT GONAKE NEBNEB ATTALEH GONAKIE
BABUSHKA SCARF KERCHIEF
BABY MOP BABA BABE CHAP DOLL JOEY NENE TOTO WEAN BAIRN CHILD HUMOR SPOIL WAYNE CHRISM CODDLE FONDLE INFANT MOPPET PAMPER POUPEE PUPPET SQUALL WEANIE BAMBINO CHRISOM INDULGE PAPOOSE PREEMIE WADDLER PAPPOOSE
(— FOOD) PAP
BABY CARRIAGE PRAM BUGGY WAGON GOCART STROLLER PERAMBULATOR
BABYISH TIDDY PULING SIMPLE PUERILE CHILDISH
BABYLONIA CHALDEA
BABYLONIAN (— CYCLE) SAROS
BABY'S BREATH GYP GYPSOPHILA
BACALAO MURRE SCAMP ABADEJO CODFISH GROUPER GUILLEMOT
BACCATE BERRIED
BACCHANAL DEVOTEE REVELER CAROUSER
BACCHANTE FROW MAENAD
BACCHUS LIBER LYAEUS BROMIUS DIONYSUS
(AUNT OF —) INO
(FATHER OF —) ZEUS JUPITER
(MOTHER OF —) SEMELE
BACHELOR BACH SEAL BATCH GARCON WANTER BACULERE BENEDICT CELIBATE
BACILLUS GERM VIRUS MICROBE
BACK AID FRO TUB VAT ABET BAKE BECK FULL HIND HINT NAPE NATA REAR TAIL ABACK AGAIN ANGEL BOOST BROAD CHINE DORSE FAVOR NOTUM SPINE SPLAT STERN VOUCH ASSIST DORSUM HINDER RETRAL SECOND SOOTHE TERGUM TROUGH UPHOLD VERIFY CISTERN ENDORSE FINANCE POSTERN RIGGING SPONSOR SUPPORT SUSTAIN BACKWARD FULLBACK HALFBACK MAINTAIN
(— A ROWBOAT) STERN
(— OF ANIMAL) RIG TERGUM
(— OF ARCHERY TARGET) BOSS
(— OF AWNING) RIDGEROPE
(— OF BOOK) DORSE SPINE
(— OF BULL) ROOF
(— OF HAND) OPISTHENAR
(— OF HEAD) INION NODDLE NIDDICK OCCIPUT
(— OF INSECT) NOTUM
(— OF NECK) NAPE NUQUE SCRUFF
(— OF PAGE) FV
(— OUT) BEG JIB DUCK FLUNK CRAWFISH
(— TO BACK) ADDORSED
(— UP) ABET PROVE VERIFY
(— WATER) STERN SHEAVE
(ANIMALS' —S) DORSA
(BROUGHT —) REDUX
(SHOWING —) TERGANT
(PREF.) ANA DORSI DORSO NOT(O) OPISTH(O) POST RE RETRO TERGI TERGO
(AT THE — OF) OPISTH(O) POSTERO
(BENT —) POSTERO RECURVI RECURVO
(SUFF.) NOTUS
BACKACHE NOTALGIA
BACKBAND RIGWIDDIE RIGWOODIE
BACKBITING CATTY DETRACTION
BACKBOARD BANK MONITOR
BACKBONE BACK GRIT GUTS CHINE NERVE PLUCK RIDGE SPINA SPINE LADDER METTLE SPIRIT GRISTLE RIGBANE SPINULE STAMINA VERTEBRA
(— OF FISH) GRATE
BACKCHAT MOUTH CROSSTALK
BACK-COMB TEASE
BACKCOUNTRY BUSH STICKS BOONIES BACKLAND BACKVELD BOONDOCKS
BACKDROP OLEO SCENERY SETTING
BACKER ANGEL
BACKFIELD SECONDARY
BACKFIRE BOOMERANG
BACKFLASH GUTTER
BACKGAMMON IRISH LURCH TABLE FAYLES GAMMON TABLES BACKGAME TICKTACK VERQUERE
(— MAN) BLOT TABLEMAN
BACKGROUND FOND REAR GROUND OFFING LINEAGE SETTING BACKDROP DISTANCE EXTERIOR OFFSCAPE TRAINING EDUCATION
(— OF FLOWERS) BOCAGE
(MUSICAL —) SUPPORT
BACKHANDED AWKWARD
BACKHOE PULLSHOVEL
BACKHOUSE PRIVY OUTHOUSE
BACKING AID EGIS AEGIS BACKUP BEHIND LINING MUSLIN REFUSE SUPPORT HEARTING FINANCING
(LEGAL —) STRENGTH
BACKLASH LASH SHAKE SLACK
BACKLOG RESERVE SURPLUS BACKBRAND
BACKPACK GEAR LOAD
BACKPIECE DOSSIERE
BACKPLATE REREDOS
BACKREST LAZYBACK
BACKROPE GOBLINE
BACKSEY SEY SIRLOIN
BACKSLIDE FALL LAPSE DESERT REVERT RELAPSE
BACKSPIN DRAG UNDERCUT UNDERSPIN
BACKSTITCH PURL PEARL
BACKSTOP BUTT
BACK TALK LIP SASS
BACKWARD FRO JAY LAX YON BACK CRAB DARK DULL LOTH ABACK AREAR BLATE INAPT LOATH THRAW UNAPT ARREAR ASTERN AVERSE BYGONE POSTIC RETRAD RETRAL STUPID ARRIERE BASHFUL LAGGARD LAGGING REVERSE UPSTAGE DILATORY IGNORANT LATEWARD PERVERSE REARWARD RINKYDINK TAILFIRST
(PREF.) OPISTH(O) RE RETRO
BACKWARDNESS DARKNESS BARBARISM
BACKWARDS YON ABACK AROUND
(PREF.) OPISO PALI(M)(N)
BACKWASH SLIPSTREAM
BACKWATER EBB COVE SLEW SLUE SNYE BAYOU BOGAN SHEAVE SLOUGH RETRACT RETREAT BACKWASH BILLABONG
BACKWOODS BRUSH
BACKWOODSMAN HICK WOODSY BUCKSKIN HILLBILLY
BACKWORT COMFREY
BACON PIG BARD MEAT PORK BARDE JAMON PRIZE SPECK FLITCH GAMMON RUSTIC SAWNEY GAMBONE SOWBELLY
(UNSMOKED —) PANCETTA
BACOPA BRAMIA
BACTERIOLOGIST AMERICAN GAY KAHN NOVY PARK BURKE CRAIG ERNST MOORE PLOTZ BERGEY ENDERS JORDAN FRANCIS KENDALL NOGUCHI THEILER ZINSSER
BELGIAN BORDET
BRAZILIAN CHAGAS
CANADIAN WESBROOK
CUBAN AGRAMONTE
ENGLISH TWORT FLEMING
FRENCH ROUX RAMON MARTIN LAVERAN NICOLLE CHAMBERLAND
GERMAN KOCH FLUGGE GAFFKY GRUBER HUEPPE BEHRING EHRLICH GARTNER LOFFLER FRAENKEL PFEIFFER UHLENHUTH WASSERMANN
JAPANESE HATA SHIGA KITAZATO
RUMANIAN BABES
RUSSIAN METCHNIKOFF
SPANISH FERRAN
SWISS YERSIN
BACTERIUM ROD COLI GERM AEROBE COCCUS CYTODE ANTHRAX CHOLERA LYSOGEN MICROBE PROTEUS SARCINA VIBRION BACILLUS LISTERIA PATHOGEN SHIGELLA BOTULINUS CYTOPHAGA HEMOPHILE INFECTANT INFECTION SPIRILLUM MICROCOCCUS PNEUMOCOCCUS SCHIZOMYCETE PNEUMOBACILLUS
BAD BIG DUD ILL SAD EVIL FULL HARD LEWD POOR PUNK QUED SICK SOUR VILE WICK ADDLE GAMMY LOUSY NASTY SORRY WEARY WORST WRONG ARRANT FAULTY LITHER LUTHER NOUGHT ROTTEN SEVERE SHREWD SINFUL UNGOOD UNKIND WICKED BALEFUL BANEFUL CHRONIC CORRUPT FEARFUL HARMFUL HEINOUS HURTFUL IMMORAL INUTILE NAUGHTY SPOILED TAINTED UNLUCKY UNMORAL UNSOUND VICIOUS ANNOYING CRIMINAL DEPRAVED DOGGEREL FIENDISH FLAGRANT INFERIOR PRECIOUS SINISTER UNSUITED

(— MANNERS) TROLLOPE
(ASTROCIOUSLY —) PIACULAR
(OUTRAGEOUSLY —) GRIEVOUS
(OUTSTANDINGLY —) ARRANT PIACULAR
(RATHER —) INDIFFERENT
(VERY —) FEARFUL ALMIGHTY GODAWFUL EXECRABLE
(PREF.) CAC(O) CACH DYS KAK(O) MAL(E) MIS
(SUFF.) CACE
BADDERLOCKS MURLIN PURSES HENWARE SEAWEED HONEYWARE
BADEBEC (HUSBAND OF —) GARGANTUA
(SON OF —) PANTAGRUEL
BADGE PIN BLUE MARK SIGN STAR COLOR CREST CROSS FAVOR HONOR ORDER PATCH TOKEN WINGS BUTTON BUZZER COLLAR EMBLEM ENSIGN FASCES GARTER GIGLIO PLAQUE SHIELD SYMBOL TIPONI WEEPER CHEVRON EPAULET FEATHER BRASSARD EPISEMON INSIGNIA SCAPULAR VERNICLE EPAULETTE COGNISANCE
(— OF VIRGINITY) SNOOD
(JAPANESE —) MON KIRIMON
(PILGRIM —) SCALLOP
(RUSSIAN —) ZNAK
(PL.) INSIGNIA
BADGER NAG PAT BAIT GRAY GREY GRIS MELE PATE ANNOY BRACE BROCK BRUSH CHEVY CHIVY HURON MELES PAHMI RATED RATEL TAXEL TAXUS TEASE WORRY BAUSON BAWSON BOTHER BRAROW CHIVVY HAGGLE HARASS HAWKER HECKLE KIDDER MELINE PESTER TELEDU WOMBAT BAUSOND GRISARD TORMENT BRAIREAU BULLYRAG CARCAJOU HUCKSTER IRRITATE STINKARD MISTONUSK
(— STATE) WISCONSIN
(AUSTRALIAN —) WOMBAT
(BURROW OF —) SET SETT
(COMPANY OF —S) CETE
(LIKE A —) MELINE
BADGER-DOG DACHSHUND
BADINAGE FOOL CHAFF JOKER BANTER RAILLERY TRIFLING
BADLANDS MALPAIS
BADLY BAD ILL EVIL HARD ILLY SICK SADLY EVILLY HARDLY POORLY UNWELL FAULTILY WICKEDLY VICIOUSLY
(PREF.) MAL
BADMINTON POONA
BADNESS MALICE PRAVITY UNVALUE EVILNESS
(SUFF.) CACE
BADROULBOUDOUR (HUSBAND OF —) ALADDIN
BAD-TEMPERED CRANKY STROPPY CROTCHETY FOUL ANGRY STINGY CRABBED GROUCHY
BAFF LOFT
BAFFLE FOX GET BALK BEAT FOIL LICK MATE POSE STOP UNDO CHEAT CHECK ELUDE EVADE FLING STICK STUMP BLENCH BOGGLE DEFEAT DELUDE FICKLE INFAMY OUTWIT PUZZLE RESIST THWART BUFFALO CONFUSE DECEIVE QUIBBLE STONKER BEWILDER CONFOUND DISGRACE JUGGLING
BAFFLED FOXED BEATEN
BAFFLING SHREWD ELUSIVE
BAG COD KIT LOT MAT NET PAD POD POT SAC CELL DRAG GRIP HOBO KILL LAND LOBE MAIL POCK POKE SACK TOOT TOTE TRAP WOMB BELLY BOUGE BULSE CATCH DILLI DILLY EMERY FLOAT HUSSY PETER POUCH PURSE SCRIP SEIZE SHOOT SNARE STEAL BLOUSE BUDGET CAVITY ENTRAP FOLLIS GASBAG MATAPI PAGGLE POCKET POUNCE SACHET SEABAG VALISE WALLET ALFORJA BALLOON BEANBAG BLISTER BUCKRAM CANTINA CAPCASE CAPTURE CUSHION DESTROY GAMEBAG GOMUKHI HANDBAG HOLDALL RETICLE SANDBAG SARPLER SATCHEL TRAVOIS BALLONET CARRYALL CORNSACK ENTRAILS ENVELOPE FOLLICLE KNAPSACK MONEYBAG OVERSLIP POCHETTE RETICULE RUCKSACK SUITCASE WINESKIN MULTIWALL WEEKENDER PORTMANTEAU
(— BULGING) SWAG
(— FOR DIAMONDS) BULSE
(— FOR LETTERS) MAIL POUCH KAREETA MAILBAG POSTBAG
(— FOR TOOLS) WALLET
(— OF ANISEED) DRAG
(— OF PERFUME) SACHET
(— OF WOOL) POCKET
(— WITH POCKETS) TIDE TIDY
(ANATOMICAL —) CECUM CAECUM STOMACH
(AUSTRALIAN —) SWAG DILLI SHIRT SHAMMY
(GAS —) CELL
(GRAB —) FISHPOND
(HAWSE —) JACKASS
(KIND OF —) DOGGY DOUGLAS
(LEATHER —) JAG JAGG ASKOS BUDGE BOUGET MUSSUK
(NET —) SNOOD GARLAND
(SEWING —) HUSSY
(SLEEPING —) FUMBA FLEABAG SLEEPER
(WATER —) CHAGAL CHAGEN CHAGUL
(PREF.) UTRI
(SUFF.) SACCATE SACCI SACCO
BAGASSE BEGASS LINAGA MEGASS
BAGATELLE CANON TRUNK VERSE CANNON TRIFLE NOTHING
BAGEL ROLL BIALY
(PARTNER OF —) LOX
BAGGAGE ARMS GEAR MINX SWAG CUTTY HUZZY NASTY SAMAN STUFF TENTS TRASH WENCH HARLOT REFUSE TRASHY TRUNKS CLOTHES DUNNAGE EFFECTS FARDAGE PLUNDER RUBBISH SALMARY SUMPTER VALISES CARRIAGE HARLOTRY RUBBISHY UTENSILS
BAGGAGE CAR WAGON FOURGON
BAGGER SACKER BATCHER
BAGGING SOUTAGE
BAGGY LOOSE POCKY PURSY FLABBY PUFFED PURSIVE SACCATE
BAGNIO BAIN BATH BAGNE PRISON BROTHEL HOTHOUSE
BAGPIPE MUSE PIPE PIVA DRONE TITTY BIGNOU BINIOU CHORUS GEWGAW MUSETTE PIFFERO SAMBUKE DULCIMER SYMPHONY ZAMPOGNA CORNAMUTE CORNEMUSE SYMPHONIA
(PART OF —) BAG CORD PIPE DRONE MOUNT STOCK TASSEL CHANTER WINDBAG BLOWPIPE
BAGUETTE CHAPLET
BAH PO FIE FOH PAH POH ROT RATS FAUGH PSHAW NONSENSE
BAHAMAS (CAPITAL OF —) NASSAU
(ISLAND OF —) ABACO EXUMA ANDROS BIMINI
(TOWN IN —) FREEPORT
BAHIA (CAPITAL OF —) SALVADOR
BAHRAIN (CAPITAL OF —) MANAMA
(MONEY OF —) FILS DINAR
(TOWN OF —) RIFAA JIDHAFS
BAIL BOW DIP ANDI BALE BOND HOOP LADE LAVE RING RYND YOKE LADLE SCOOP THROW VOUCH BUCKET HANDLE PLEDGE SECURE SURETY VADIUM CAUTION CUSTODY DELIVER RELEASE REPLEVY BAILSMAN BULWARKS SECURITY GUARANTEE
(— OUT) ABANDON
BAILEE LESSEE POSITOR CONDUCTOR
BAILER SPOUCHER
BAILIFF FOUD GRAB HIND AGENT REEVE SAFFO SCULT STAFF BAILIE BAILLI BEADLE BEAGLE DEPUTY FACTOR GRIEVE LOOKER OFFICE PORTER PREVOT SCHOUT VARLET BUMTRAP GRIPPER PROVOST PUTTOCK SHERIFF STEWARD APPROVER HUISSIER OVERSEER TIPSTAFF CATCHPOLE CATCHPOLL CONSTABLE HUNDREDER PORTREEVE SENESCHAL WAPENTAKE
BAILIWICK AREA FIELD DOMAIN OFFICE SPHERE PROVINCE
BAILMENT MUTUUM
BAILOR LESSOR
BAIN NEAR LITHE READY SHORT DIRECT LIMBER SUPPLE FORWARD WILLING
BAIRN WEAN
BAIT BAD BOB COG DAP LUG BITE CAST CHUM FEED HALT HANK LURE PLUG TAIL DECOY HOUND LEGER SHACK SLATE SQUID STALE TEMPT TRAIN WORRY ALLURE APPAST ATTACK BADGER BERLEY ENTICE HARASS HECKLE HECTOR KILLER LEDGER REPAST SHRAPE SLIVER FULCRUM GUDGEON PROVOKE TAGTAIL TOLLING TORMENT BRANLING CUNGEBOI BRANDLING
(— FOR BIRDS) SHRAP SHRAPE
(— FOR COD) CAPELIN
(— WITH DOGS) SLATE
(GREASY —) ROGUE
(GROUND —) BERLEY
(MAGGOT —) GENTLE
(SCENTED —) DRAG
(SPINNING —) PROPELLER
BAITING HANK
BAIZE BAY BAYES BAYETA DOMETT BOCKING
BAKE DRY BURN COCT COOK FIRE BATCH BROIL GRILL PARCH ROAST ANNEAL HARDEN BISCUIT PISTATE SCALLOP CLAMBAKE ESCALLOP
(— EGGS) SHIRR
(— THOROUGHLY) SOAK
BAKED CASINO COCTILE
(— IN EARTH OVEN) KALUA
(— PRODUCT) KICHEL
BAKER OVEN FIRER BAXTER BURNER FURNER PISTOR FURNACE OVENMAN ROASTER
BAKER BIRD HORNERO
BAKERY PIZZERIA
BAKING CUIT BATCH COCTION FURNAGE ASSATION
BAKONGO FIOT
BALAAM (FATHER OF —) BEOR
BALACHONG NGAPI
BALAK (FATHER OF —) ZIPPOR
BALANCE BEAM EVEN PEIS REST SWAY TRIM COVER ERASE PEISE POISE SCALE TRONE WEIGH WEIHE ADJUST AUNCEL CANCEL EMBLEM EQUATE KELTER KELVIN KILTER LAUNCE OFFSET SANITY SQUARE STRIKE DESEMER LIBRATE OVERRUN RESIDUE TRABUCH TRUTINE EQUALITY EQUALIZE EQUATION SERENITY WESTPHAL TREBUCHET PROPORTION
(— DUE) ARREAR
(— IN ACCOUNT) CREDIT
(— OF SAILS) ATRY
(MAKE —) EQUATE
(MENTAL —) HEAD
(PREF.) STATO
BALANCED EVEN EQUAL LEVEL TRUED APOISE KITTLE WEIGHED COMPLETE QUADRATE TOGETHER
(PREF.) SYM
BALANCER HALTER ACROBAT GYMNAST HALTERE
BALATA ICICA BULLACE BEEFWOOD BORRACHA
BALCONY POY ORIEL PORCH STOOP CIRCLE GAZEBO PIAZZA PODIUM SOLLAR BALAGAN GALLERY MIRADOR PERGOLA TERRACE BRATTICE CANTORIA VERANDAH MEZZANINE
BALD RAW BARE BASE BOLD CRUDE DODDY NAKED PLAIN CALLOW PALTRY PEELED PILLED SIMPLE CALVOUS EPILOSE LITERAL POLLARD GLABROUS HAIRLESS TONSURED
(— HEAD) PILGARLIC
(— SPOT) TONSURE
(PREF.) PHALACRO
BALDACHIN CANOPY CIBORIUM
BALDER BALDR BALDUR BAELDAEG
(CHILD OF —) FORSETE FORSETI
(FATHER OF —) ODIN

(SLAYER OF —) HOTH LOKE LOKI HOTHR
(WIFE OF —) NANNA
BALDERDASH ROT GUFF PUNK GOOEY TRASH TRIPE DRIVEL JARGON FLUBDUB NONSENSE BALDUCTUM RIGMAROLE
BALDMONEY MEU SPIGNEL SPICKNEL
BALDNESS ACOMIA CALVITY ALOPECIA ATRICHIA OPHIASIS CALVITIES
BALDPATE ZUISIN POACHER
BALDRIC BELT LACE GIRDLE ZODIAC BALTEUS SUPPORT NECKLACE
BALE NO GIB NOT WOE EVIL FIRE HARM LAVE PACK PYRE BLOCK CRATE DEATH FARDO SERON BALLOT BUNDLE EMBALE SEROON SORROW PACKAGE SARPLER
BALEARIC ISLANDS (ISLAND OF —) IBIZA CABRERA MAJORCA MINORCA CONEJERA
(MEASURE OF —) PALMO MISURA QUARTA QUARTIN BARCELLA
(TOWN OF —) IBIZA MAHON PALMA
(WEIGHT OF —) CARGO CORTA QUARTANO
BALEEN WHALEBONE
BALEFUL BAD EVIL DEADLY MALIGN SACRED SULLEN MALEFIC NOXIOUS RUINOUS SIDERAL SINISTER WRETCHED MALEFICENT
BALI (CAPITAL OF —) DENPASAR
(DANCE OF —) ARDJA BARIS KRISS BARONG KETJAK MONKEY DJANGER
(MOUNTAIN OF —) AGOENG
(MUSICAL INSTRUMENT OF —) GAMELAN
(RICE FIELD OF —) SAWAII
(STRAIT OF —) LOMBOK
(TOWN OF —) SINGARADJA
BALIN (BROTHER OF —) SUGRIVA
(SLAYER OF —) RAMA
BALINGHASAY ANAM ANAN
BALK GAG HEN HUE JIB JUB SHY BEAM BILK BUCK BULL COND FOIL GORM HADE HEAP LICK LOFT MISS OMIT PROP SHUN SKIP SLIP STAY STOP AVOID BAULK BLOCK CHECK CLAMP DEMUR HUNCH MOUND REBEL REEST RIDGE STAKE STICK WAVER BAFFLE DEFEAT FALTER HINDER IMPEDE OUTWIT RAFTER REFUSE STRAIN THWART BLUNDER CODLING GALLOWS ISTHMUS MISTAKE
(— IN FISHING) HUE COND
(HALF —) FLITCH
(PL.) MIDDLES
BALKAN (— COIN) NOVCIC
(— COUNTRY) GREECE SERBIA ALBANIA RUMANIA BULGARIA
(— INSTRUMENT) GUSLA
(— RIVER) JIU OLT IBAR JIUL SAVA TISA OLTUL DANUBE MORAVA
(— SEA) BLACK AEGEAN IONIAN ADRIATIC
BALKER HUER CONNER
BALKY NAPPY STICK MULISH REESTY RESTIVE CONTRARY STUBBORN OBSTINATE
BALL IN BAL BOB FLY HOP NOB ORB PEA TOY BEAD BOWL CLEW CLUE KNOB KNOP KNUR PICK PILL POME PROM TRAP DANCE EDGER FAULT FLOAT GLOBE GLOME HURLY ORBIT PEARL PUPPY SHAPE SNACK SPORT TRUCK BULLET BUTTON HOOKER HURLEY MOONIE MUDDLE PEELEE PELLET PELOTA POMMEL POMPON RONDEL RUNDLE SPHERE SQUASH BALLOON CONFUSE FLOATER GLOBULE INCURVE INSHOOT KNAPPAN LEATHER MANDREL PELOTON RIDOTTO SLITTER ASSEMBLY BASEBALL BISCAYEN FANDANGO FOOTBALL GROUNDER HANDBALL QUENELLE SOFTBALL SPHEROID TRAPBALL
(— AS SHIP'S SIGNAL) SHAPE
(— FOR MUSKET) GOLI SLUG
(— OF CLAY) KNICKER
(— OF FIRE) DYNAMO
(— OF RICE OR MEAT) PINDA
(— OF THREAD) COP CLEW CLUE GOME BOTTOM COPPIN WHARROW
(— OF THUMB) THENAR CUSHION
(— OF WASTE IRON) COBBLE
(—S OF MEDICI FAMILY) PALLE
(— USED IN SHINTY) PEG
(BILLIARD —) SPOT IVORY SNOOKER
(BOWLED —) TICE CURVE SKYER BAILER BUMPER FIZZER GOOGLY KICKER POODLE SEAMER YORKER CREEPER SNORTER SPINNER BREAKBACK CROSSOVER INSWINGER
(BOWLING —) DODO JACK
(CORK —) PLUMBER
(CRICKET —) SNICK SHOOTER
(CROQUET —) ROVER
(DECORATIVE —) DRAGEE
(FIVES —) SNACK
(FORCEMEAT —) QUENELLE
(FRIED —) RISSOLE
(GOLF —) PUTTY
(HARD —) SNUG
(HOCKEY —) NUN NUR ORR
(INK —) PUMPET
(JAI ALAI —) PELOTA
(KIND OF —) MINIE
(MEAT —S) CECILS
(PLASTIC —) WIFFLE
(SKITTLE —) CHEESE
(SPONGE —) NERF
(TENNIS —) PALM
(WOODEN —) KNUR
(PREF.) GLOBI GLOBO SPHAER(O) SPHER(O)
(SUFF.) SPHAERA SPHERE SPHERIC(AL)
BALLAD JIG LAI LAY LILT MELE POEM SONG CAROL DERRY FANCY BALLET BYLINA CARVAL SONNET BALLANT CANZONE CORRIDO GWERZIOU SINGSONG
BALLAST BED CRIB LOAD TRIM METAL POISE STONE BOTTOM BURDEN GRAVEL WEIGHT BALANCE LASTAGE SANDBAG DRAGROPE KENTLEDGE SABURRATE
BALLERINA DANCER DANSEUSE
BALLET BALLAD MASQUE BOURREE PANTOMIME
(— COACH) REPETITEUR
(— LEAP) CABRIOLE ENTRECHAT
(— MOVEMENT) VOLE FERME TEMPS APLOMB CHASSE OUVERT POINTE RELEVE RETIRE ALLONGE ARRONDI ASSEMBLE ATTITUDE ARABESQUE
(— POSE) ARABESQUE
(— PROP) BARRE
(— SPIN) PIROUETTE
BALLHOOTER BRUTTER
BALLISTA SWEEP MANGONEL
BALLOON BAG BALL BLIMP EXPAND GASBAG AIRSHIP DISTEND DRACHEN INFLATE SAUSAGE SKYHOOK AEROSTAT ENVELOPE DIRIGIBLE
(TRIAL —) KITE
BALLOONING BOSOMY
BALLOONIST AERONAUT AEROSTAT
BALLOON VINE FAROLITO HEARTPEA HEARTSEED
BALLOT BALE POLL PROX VOTE ELECT PROXY VOICE BILLET CHOICE POLICY TICKET SUFFRAGE
BALLROOM SALOON
BALLYHOO BALLY HOOPLA
BALM OIL BEEB BITO DAUB ODOR SALVE ANOINT BALSAM EMBALM LOTION RELIEF SOLACE SOOTHE ANODYNE BESMEAR COMFORT PERFUME UNGUENT OINTMENT
(— OF GILEAD) CANADA OPOBALSAM
(BURN —) ALOE
BALMORAL CAP BOOT SHOE
BALMY DAFT MILD SOFT BLAND DAFFY MOONY SPICY SUNNY SWEET GENTLE INSANE SERENE HEALING LENIENT AROMATIC BALSAMIC DRESSING FRAGRANT SOOTHING
BALONEY BULL BUNK CROCK HOOEY BUNKUM BUSHWA BUSHWAH
BALSA RAFT FLOAT GUANO POLAK POLACK BOBWOOD CORKWOOD
BALSAM BALM RIGA TOLU UMIRI COPALM GURJAN GURJUN STORAX AMPALEA COPAIBA CREEPER AMPALAYA BDELLIUM BENJAMIN OINTMENT
BALSAM APPLE KARELA AMARGOSA AMPALAYA BALSAMINE
BALSAM FIR SAPIN BAUMIER
BALSAM POPLAR TACAMAHAC
BALSAMROOT SUNFLOWER
BALSAMWEED MOONSHINE FEATHERWEED
BALT YOD ESTH LETT ESTONIAN
BALTIC (— GULF) RIGA DANZIG BOTHNIA FINLAND
(— ISLAND) AERO DAGO FARO OSEL ALAND ALSEN OESEL OLAND GOTLAND HIIUMAA BORNHOLM
(— PORT) KIEL RIGA MEMEL REVAL DANZIG GDANSK TALINN LEIPAJA
(— RIVER) ODER ODRA DVINA VIADUA
(— TOWN) MEMEL DANZIG GDANSK LEIPAJA
BALUCHISTAN (— CULTURE) QUETTA
BALUSTER SPOKE COLUMEL BANISTER COLUMELLA
BALUSTRADE BARRER PARAPET RAILING BALCONET BANISTER
BAMBI (AUNT OF —) ENA
BAMBOO DHA CANE REED BATAK GLUMAL GUADUA TONKIN BATAKAN WANGHEE WHANGEE
(SACRED —) NANDIN
(WOVEN —) SAWALI
BAMBOOZLE DUPE HAVE CHEAT COZEN GRILL CAJOLE HUMBUG BUFFALO BUMBAZE DECEIVE DEFRAUD MYSTIFY PERPLEX
BAN BAR WOE TABU VETO BANAL BANUS BLOCK CURSE EDICT ORDER TABOO BANISH CENSOR ENJOIN FORBID HINDER INVOKE NOTICE OUTLAW CONDEMN EXCLUDE ANATHEMA DENOUNCE EXECRATE PROHIBIT
(— ON NEWS) BLACKOUT
(LEGAL —) ESTOP
BANA (DAUGHTER OF —) USHA
BANAK UCUUBA
BANAL FLAT CORNY INANE SILLY STALE TRITE VAPID JEJUNE INSIPID MUNDANE TRIVIAL
BANANA FEI FIG MUSA SABA BERRY ENSETE FINGER SAGING LACATAN PLATANO SAGUING SUNBEAM PLANTAIN
(KIND OF —) TOP
BANANAS BALMY BATTY DAFFY
BAND BAR GAD HUB TIE TUB ZON BEAD BELT BEND BOND CAME CASH CORD CREW CUFF FALL FERD FESS GANG GATE GIRT HOOD HOOP KNOT LACE LIST RING SASH SHOE TAPE WISP ZONA ZONE AMPYX BANDY BRAID CHOIR CLAMP CORSE COVEY COVIN CRAPE CROWN FEMUR FLOCK FRAME GIRTH GORGE GUARD JATHA LABEL MEINY NOISE PANEL PATTE PRIDE QUIRE SABOT SNOOD STRAP STRIP STROP TAPIS TORSE TRACK TRIBE UNITE WERED WITHE ARMLET BENDEL BINDER BORDER BOYANG BRIDGE BUNDLE CIMBIA CLAVUS COHORT COLLAR COLLET COPULA COVINE CRANCE CRAVAT DECKLE FASCIA FETTER FILLET FRIEZE FRINGE FUNNEL GAMMON GARTER GASKET GIRDLE HYPHEN LEGLET MATRIX NIPPER NORSEL PLEDGE RADULA REGULA ROLLER SCREED STRAKE STRING STRIPE SWATHE TAENIA TETHER TISSUE WEEPER BINDING BLANKET CHAMBUL CIRCLET COMPANY ENOMOTY FERRULE FRONTAL GARLAND HATBAND HEADING NECKTIE ORPHREY PALLIUM PIGTAIL PROMISE SEQUELA SHACKLE SHOEING SWADDLE VINCULUM
(— ACROSS SUNSPOT) BRIDGE
(— AROUND MAST) PARREL

(— AT BOTTOM OF WALL) PLINTH
(— FOR HEAD) VITTA
(— IN BRAIN) LIGULA FRENULUM FUNICULUS
(— IN ROCKS) FAHLBAND
(— OF CLAY) COTTLE
(— OF COLOR) SOCK SLASH STRIA LACING FASCIOLE SPECTRUM
(— OF CRAPE) WEED SCARF
(— OF FUR) TIPPET
(— OF INDIANS) SHIVWITS
(— OF LIGHT) STREAMER
(— OF PILLAGERS) SKINNERS
(— OF PIPERS) POVERTY
(— OF PLASTER) SCREED
(— OF PURPLE) CLAVUS
(— OF STARS) GALAXY
(— OF STRAW) GAD SIMMON
(— OF TISSUE) TENDON TISSUE
(— OF 13 WITCHES) COVEN
(— ON HORSE'S HOOF) FROG
(— ON SHIELD) ENDORSE
(— TO COMPRESS CHEEKS) CAPISTRUM
(— TOGETHER) BANDY
(— UNDER TONGUE) LYTTA
(ARMED —) JATHA POSSE
(ARMOR —) TONLET
(CIRCULAR —) HOOP RING ANNULE WREATH
(DANCE —) CHORO COMBO
(DECORATIVE —) PATTE LEGLET CORNICE ARCHIVOLT
(DIVIDING —) CLOISON
(EUCHARISTIC —) MANIPLE
(FOREHEAD —) INFULA
(HEAD —) BANDEAU
(IRON —) FRET GATE TRUSS FUNNEL STRAKE
(LACE —) SCALLOP
(MUSICIANS —) CONCERT
(NOISY —) CALLITHUMP
(RADIO —) CHANNEL
(RAISED —) RIB
(RESONANCE —) FORMANT
(STREET —) MARIACHI
(TRIBAL —) AIMAK
(PL.) GRIPES INTERLACERY
(PREF.) TAENI(A)(O) ZON(I)(O)
(SUFF.) **(CILIATED —)** TROCH(A)(AL)(OUS)(US)
BANDAGE BAND BELT BIND TAPE BLIND BRACE CLOUT DRESS GALEA LINEN SLING SPICA SWARF SWATH TRUSS BINDER COLLAR CRAVAT FASCIA FETTLE FILLET LIGATE NIPPER ROLLER SWARTH SWATHE SWEATH REVERSE ROLLING SWADDLE TRUSSER ACCIPTER CAPELINE CINCTURE GAUNTLET LIGAMENT LIGATURE SCAPULAR STOCKING CAPISTRUM
(— FOR NOSE) ACCIPITER
(EYE —) MUFFLER
(FINGER —) HOVEL
(JAW —) FUNDA
(PL.) SWADDLING
BANDALORE QUIZ
BANDANNA WEB TURBAN BANDANA PULICAT PULICATE PULLICAT
BANDAR RHESUS
BANDEAU BRA BAND STRIP FILLET BRASSIERE
BANDICOOT RAT MARL BILBI BILBY BADGER BIELBY PINKIE QUENDA
BANDIT CACA TORY BRAVO THIEF BANISH HAIDUK HEYDUK OUTLAW ROBBER BANDIDO BRIGAND LADRONE TULISAN BUSHWACK MARAUDER MIQUELET PICAROON RAPPAREE BANDOLERO
(PL.) MANZAS
BANDLEADER MASTER MAESTRO CHORAGUS CONDUCTOR
BANDORE PANDORA PANDURA
(PREF.) PANDURI
BANDSMAN WINDJAMMER
BANDSTAND KIOSK STAND
BANDY VIE BAND CART CHOP SWAP TRADE LEAGUE RACKET STRIVE CHAFFER CONTEND DISCUSS CARRIAGE EXCHANGE SHUTTLECOCK
(— WORDS) REVIE GIFFGAFF
BANE BAN WOE BONE EVIL HARM KILL PEST RUIN CURSE DEATH VENOM INJURY MURDER POISON SLAYER NEMESIS SCOURGE MISCHIEF MURDERER NUISANCE
BANEBERRY COHOSH REDBERRY TOADROOT GRAPEWORT
BANEFUL BAD ILL EVIL VILE SWART HARMFUL HURTFUL NOXIOUS RUINOUS VENOMOUS SINISTRAL PERNICIOUS
BANG POM RAP BAFF BEAT BLOW BOOT DASH DOCK DRUB POUF RUSH SCAT SLAM SWAP SWOP TANK BLAFF CLASH CRACK DRIVE EXCEL FORCE IMPEL POUND SLAKE SLUMP SOUND SPANG STRAM THUMP WHACK WHANG WHUMP BOUNCE CUDGEL ENERGY FRINGE STRIKE THRASH THUNGE THWACK SARDINE SURPASS THUNDER FORELOCK
(— ON HEAD) BRAIN
BANGLADESH (CAPITAL OF —) DACCA
(MONEY OF —) TAKA
(NATIVE OF —) BENGALI
(PAISA OF —) POISHA
(RIVER OF —) GANGES
(TOWN IN —) KHULNA CHITTAGONG
COIN: TAKA
BANGLE ORNAMENT
BANGTAIL NAG
BANG-UP SLAP CRACK TIPTOP
BANISH BAN FREE ABAND EJECT EXILE EXPEL FLEME WAIVE WREAK BANDIT DEPORT DISPEL DISTER FORSAY OUTLAW ABANDON CONDEMN CONFINE DISMISS DIVORCE EXCLUDE DISPLACE RELEGATE EXPATRIATE
BANISHED FUGITIVE
BANISHMENT EXILE BANNIMUS OUTLAWRY XENELASY OSTRACISM XENELASIA
BANISTER RAILING BALUSTER
BANJO BOX BANJORE BANJORINE
(— SITE) KNEE
BANK BAR BAY COP JUG RIM ROW BINK BRAE BREW BUTT CAJA DIKE DUNE DYKE EDGE HEAD HILL LINK MASS PILE RAKE RAMP RELY RIPA RIVE SAND SCAR SEAT SIDE TIER WEIR BANCO BENCH BLUFF BRINK COAST DITCH EARTH FENCE HOVER HURST LEVEE MARGE MOUND MOUNT RIDGE SAVER SHARE SHELF SHOAL SHORE SLOPE STACK STAGE TRUST BANQUE BORROW CAISSE CAUSEY CRADGE DEGREE DEPEND DOUBLE MARGIN RANDOM RECKON RIVAGE STRAND ANTHILL BANKING CUSHION DEPOSIT LOMBARD POTTERY SANDBAG SHALLOW WINDROW BARRANCA PLATFORM TRAVERSE
(— A FIRE) REST
(— ASSOCIATION) SANDL
(— FOR DRYING BRICKS) HACK
(— OF CANAL) BERM BERME HEELPATH
(— OF EARTH) COP DAM DITCH
(— OF RIVER) RIPA WHARF STRAND
(— OF SAND OR MUD) BAR SCALP
(— OF SNOW) WREATH SNOWDRIFT
(— OF TURF) SUNK
(KIND OF —) STILL
(OVERHANGING —) BREW HOVER
(RUSSIAN —) CRAPETTE
(SAVINGS —) THRIFT
(STEEP —) HEUCH HEUGH WOUGH BARRANCA BARRANCO
(PREF.) RIPI
BANKER BOOK SETH SETT FACTOR FINDER SAHKAR SHROFF SOUCAR SOWCAR LOMBARD MARWARI MONEYER SPONSOR TAILLEUR BANQUETER FINANCIER
BANKNOTE CRISP FLIMSY SCREEN
(FORGED —) STUMER
(PL.) CABBAGE
BANKRUPT SAP BONG BUNG BUST DUCK RUMP BREAK BROKE DRAIN SMASH STRIP BROKEN BUSTED DYVOUR QUISBY CRACKED DEPLETE
BANKRUPTCY SMASH FAILURE SMASHUP
BANKSMAN LANDER HILLMAN
BANLIEUE LOWY ENVIRONS
BANNER FANE FLAG JACK SIGN COLOR BUMPER ENSIGN FANNON PENNON LABARUM LEADING PENNANT SALIENT BANDEROL BRATTACH FOREMOST GONFALON ORIFLAMB STANDARD STREAMER VEXILLUM BEAUSEANT ORIFLAMME
(— ON TRUMPET) TABARD
(FUNERAL —) BANNEROL GUMPHEON GUMPHION
(PL.) ENSIGNRY
BANNOCK PANAK DIGGER JANNOCK
BANNS CRY BANS CRIES NOTICE SIBRET SIBRIT SIBREDE SPURRINGS
BANQUET FETE MEAL DIFFA FEAST DINNER JUNKET MANGER REGALE REGALO REPAST SEUDAH SPREAD AHAAINA CONVITO CONVIVE NAMGERY REGALIO CAROUSAL FESTIVAL SYMPOSIUM SYSSITION
BANQUETER CONVIVE SYMPOSIAST
BANQUETING EPULATION TRENCHERING
BANQUETTE FIRESTEP
BANSHEE BOW SIDHE TROLL
BANTAM COCK GRIG BANTY DANDY SAUCY CHICKEN SEBRIGHT COMBATIVE
BANTENG OX TSINE BANTIN TEMADAU
BANTER COD KID RAG ROT CHIP FOOL JEST JOKE JOSH MOCK QUIZ RAIL RAZZ BORAK CHAFF DRAPE JOLLY QUEER RALLY ROAST TAUNT TRICK DELUDE DERIDE HAGGLE SATIRE BADINER STASHIE BADINAGE CHAFFING GIFFGAFF RAILLERY RIDICULE
BANTING DIET DUGOUT
BANTU ILA BULU GOGO GUHA HEHE YAKA ZULU DUALA KAFIR KAMBA KIOKO KONDE KONGO LAMBA SHONA SWAZI BANYAI BASUTO DAMARA HERERO KAFFIR NATIVE THONGA WAGUHA YAKALA CABINDA MASHONA SWAHILI WACHAGA
(— LANGUAGE) ILA RONGA NYANJA THONGA KIRUNDI NYAMWEZI
BANTUSTAN HOMELAND
BANYAN BUR BURR BANIYA BUNNIA JAGUEY
BAOBAB MOWANA IMBONDO TEBELDI CALABASH ADANSONIA
BAPTISM CLEANSING IMMERSION PALINGENY PERFUSION
BAPTISMAL FONTAL
BAPTIST DIPPER DOPPER DIDAPPER SEPARATE TRASKITE
BAPTIZE DIP DEPE FULL NAME HEAVE VOLOW PLUNGE PURIFY ASPERSE CLEANSE IMMERSE CHRISTEN SPRINKLE
BAPTIZED ILLUMINATE
BAR BAN DAM FID FOX GAD INN LAW LEG RIB ROD TAP AXLE BALK BAND BANK BAUR BEAM BOLT BOOM BULL CAKE CHAR CORE CROW DRAG FLAT GATE HIDE JOKE LOCK MAKE OUST POLE RACK RAIL REEF SAVE SETT SHUT SKID SLAB SLAT SLIP SLOT SNIB STOP TREE YARD ARBOR BAULK BENCH BETTY BILBO BLOCK BLOOM BRACE CATCH CLASP CLOSE COURT CRAMP CREEL DEBAR DETER DOLLY EASER EMBAR ESTOP FENCE FORCE GEMEL HEDGE HORSE HUMET LEVER PERCH PILOT PINCH PITCH RANCE RATCH SHADE SHAFT SHAPE SIGHT SLOTE SNEEK SPELL SPOON SPRAG STAFF STANG STAVE STEEK STRAP STRIP STRUT SWIPE TRACE YAIRD ANCONY BARRET BATTEN BILLET BISTRO BODEGA BROOCH BUMPER CRUTCH DOFFER DOLLEY DOLLIE EVENER EXCEPT EYEBAR FASTEN FORBAR FORBID FORCER FORSET GRILLE HEAVER HINDER LADDER

MEAGRE NORMAN PEELER RABBLE RADIAL RETURN RIFFLE SALOON SHADES SHANTY STOWER STRIPE TABLET TANGLE TILLER TOGGLE BARRACE BARRAGE BARRIER BOBSTAY BOLSTER BUVETTE CHANNEL CHARIOT CONFINE COUNTER DRAWBAR EXCLUDE GALLOWS MANDREL MANDRIL OVERARM PREVENT SCRATCH SIDEBAR SNIBBLE SPINDLE STEMMER TOMBOLO TOPRAIL TRUNDLE WIREBAR ASTRAGAL KNIFEWAY MURDERER PESSULUS
(— FOR TAPPING FURNACE) LANCET
(— IN CHIMNEY) SWEE
(— IN FABRIC) BARRE
(— IN RIVER) CHAR SANDBAR
(— IN SEA) SWASH
(— OF CULTIVATOR) ARCH
(— OF DOOR) SLOT STANG
(— OF ELECTRIC SWITCH) BLADE
(— OF GATE) SPAR LEDGE
(— OF HARROW) BULL
(— OF LOOM) EASER SWORD BATTEN BACKSTAY
(— OF METAL) ZED
(— OF RAYS) SHOOT
(— OF SAND) TOMBOLO
(— OF STEEL) BLOOM BILLET STIRRUP
(— OF WAGON) SHETH
(— OF WHEEL) SPOKE
(— ON BOWSPRIT) WHISKER
(— ON SIDE OF BOWSPRIT) WHISKER
(— ON WINDMILL) UPLONG
(— SUPPORTING MILLSTONE) MOLINE
(— WITH SHACKLES) BILBOES
(— WITH SPIKES) HERISSON
(CAST IRON —) SOW
(CONNECTING —) ZYGON
(HERALDIC —) FESS FESSE HUMET LABEL
(JOINTED —) CHILL
(KIND OF —) RAW WET CASH FERN NERF OPEN SWAY SALAD DATING OYSTER SINGLES
(MINING —) MOIL
(NOTCHED —) RISP SKEY
(PAIR OF —S) GEMEL GEMMEL
(REFRESHMENT —) BUFFET CANTEEN
(SOAP FRAME —) SESS
(STIRRING —) CRUTCH
(TAMPING —) STEMMER
(TYPEWRITER —) BAIL BALE SPACER SHUTTLE
(UNSAVORY —) DIVE
(WEAVING —) TEMPLE
(WHEEL —) AXLE SPOKE
BARABARA HUT
BARACHEL (SON OF —) ELIHU
BARAK (FATHER OF —) ABINOAM
BARANI BRANDY
BARB AWN BUR JAG MOW BURR CLIP FILE FLUE HAIR HERL HOOK JAGG BEARD HORSE POINT RIDGE SHAFT SPEAR PIGEON STRAIN TIPPET WITTER BARBARY BARBULE BRISTLE FILAMENT KINGFISH
(— OF ANCHOR) FLUKE
(— OF ARROW) HOOK WING BEARD WITTER
(— OF FEATHER) HARL HERL RAMUS PINNULA FILAMENT
(— OF HARPOON) FLUE FLUKE
(THROW —S AT) ZING
(PREF.) ONC(O)
BARBADOS (CAPITAL OF —) BRIDGETOWN
(MOUNTAIN OF —) HILLABY
(NATIVE OF —) BIM BAJAN
BARBADOS CHERRY ACEROLA
BARBADOS PRIDE SANDALWOOD
BARBAREA CAMPE
BARBARIAN HUN BOOR GOTH RUDE WILD ALIEN BRUTE SAVAGE VANDAL RUFFIAN FOREIGNER HOTTENTOT UNTUTORED TRAMONTANE
BARBARIC GROSS ATROCIOUS
BARBARISM CANT DATISM SAVAGISM SOLECISM
BARBARITY FERITY CRUELTY FELLNESS FEROCITY RUDENESS SAVAGERY BRUTALITY
BARBAROUS FELL RUDE WILD CRUEL BRUTAL FIERCE GOTHIC BESTIAL FOREIGN HUNNISH INHUMAN SLAVISH UNCIVIL IGNORANT CUTTHROAT FEROCIOUS PRIMITIVE
BARBARY MAGOT MAGHRIB MOGHRIB
(— STATE) TUNIS ALGIERS MOROCCO TRIPOLI
BARBASCO CUBE JOEWOOD
BARBECUE ASADO BOCAN BUCCAN
(— ITEM) KABOB
BARBEL BEARD CIRRUS WATTLE BARBLET CYPRINID
BARBER NAI FIGARO POLLER SHAVER TONSOR SCRAPER TONSURE
(— FISH) TANG
BARBER OF BAGDAD (CHARACTER IN —) ABUL BEKAR CALIPH MARGIANA NUREDDIN
(COMPOSER OF —) CORNELIUS
BARBER OF SEVILLE (CHARACTER IN —) BERTHA FIGARO ROSINA BARTOLO LINDORO ALMAVIVA
(COMPOSER OF —) ROSSINI
BARBERRY MAHONIA
BARBET BARBION BARMKIN DREAMER BARBICAN PUFFBIRD WATERRUG IRONSMITH PEARLBIRD THICKHEAD TIGERBIRD
BARBITAL VERONAL
BARBITURATE DOWNER SECONAL GOOFBALL SECOBARBITAL PENTOBARBITAL PHENOBARBITAL
BARBULE RADIUS RADIOLUS
BARCHESTER TOWERS (AUTHOR OF —) TROLLOPE
(CHARACTER IN —) BOLD SLOPE ARABIN BERTIE NERONI ELEANOR GRANTLY HARDING OBADIAH PROUDIE SEPTIMUS STANHOPE CHARLOTTE ETHELBERT QUIVERFUL
BARD BHAT MUSE POET SCOP SWAN DRUID OVATE RUNER SCALD SKALD OSSIAN SHAPER SINGER BARDING PENBARD MINSTREL MUSICIAN TALIESEN DEMODOCUS SEANNACHIE
BARE DRY BALD LEAN MERE NUDE POOR THIN ALONE BLEAK CRUDE EMPTY NAKED PLAIN PLUME SCANT STARK STRIP WASTE BARISH BARREN CALLOW DENUDE DIVERT DIVEST EXPOSE HISTIE MARGIN MEAGER MEAGRE PALTRY PILLED REVEAL SCARRY SIMPLE DIVULGE EXPOSED UNARMED UNCOVER DENUDATE DESOLATE DISCLOSE STRIPPED DESTITUTE
(— SKIN) BUFF
(— TEETH) TUCK
(NOT —) COOL
(PREF.) GYMN NUDI PSIL(O)
BAREFACED GLARING IMPUDENT AUDACIOUS SHAMELESS
BAREFOOT UNSHOD
BARELY JIMP JUST ONLY FANIT HARDLY MERELY POORLY SIMPLY UNEATH UNNETH NAKEDLY UNNETHE EDGEWAYS SCANTILY SCARCELY SLIGHTLY
BARER NAVVY DELVER FEIGHER MUCKMAN CALLOWER
BARFISH DORAB
BARFLY SOT TOSSPOT
BARGAIN GO BUY RUG WOD COPE DEAL HUCK KOOP MART MISE PACT PICK RUGG SALE SELL SNIP SONG TROG WHIZ CHEAP FIGHT PRICE STEAL TROKE TRUCK WHACK WHIZZ BARTER DICKER HAGGLE HIGGLE INDENT NIFFER PALTER CHAFFER CHEAPEN COMPACT CONTEND CONTEST DISPOSE PACTION TRAFFIC CONTRACT COVENANT PENNORTH PURCHASE STRUGGLE WANWORTH PENNYWORTH
(— HARD) PRIG
(— IN MINING) STURT
BARGAINER NIP KITE COPER COWPER CHAFFERER
(SHARP —) SCREW
BARGAINING MART ACHATE CHAFFER CHEAPING HUCKSTERY
(KIND OF —) PLEA
BARGE ARK BOX BOY HOY TOW TUB BARK BOAT FUST LUMP PRAM RAFT SCOW TROW BARCA CASCO DUMMY FOIST LUNGE LURCH PRAAM SCOLD SHREW VIXEN BARQUE BERATE BUGERO DREDGE GALLEY GYASSA PRAHAM REBUKE STUMPY TENDER THRUST WHERRY BALLOON BIRLING BIRLINN CHALANA DROGHER GABBARD GABBART GONDOLA LIGHTER OMNIBUS TOWBOAT TUMBLER TUMBRIL BILLYBOY BUDGEROW CARRIAGE BUCENTAUR MOORPUNKY
(COAL —) KEEL
(FRENCH —) TOUE
(TOWED —) BUTTY
BARGEMAN PUG BARGEE BARGER HOYMAN HUFFLER
BARGHEST PADFOOT
BARITE CAUK CAWK TIFF CAULK BARYTES BARYTINE HEPATITE
BARITONE DEEP
BARK AGO BAG BAY OUF RUB TAN WAP YAP YIP BAFF BOAT BOOF COAT COTO DITA HOWL HUSK OPEN PEEL PELT PILL REND RIND ROSS SKIN SNAP TAPA WAFF YAFF YAWP YELP YIPE AABEC BALAT BARCA BARGE COUGH MOCHA NIEPA SHELL SHOUT SPEAK STRIP TIMBE YAMPH YOUFF ABRADE AGAMID AVARAM BARKEY BOWWOW CASSIA CORNUS CORTEX GIRDLE MASSOY SINTOC TRANKY WAFFLE YAFFLE CASCARA MALAMBO MESENNA PEREIRA PHLOEUM SOLICIT TANBARK DOUNDAKE EUONYMUS FRANGULA GRANATUM MEZEREUM WOODSKIN RHYTIDOME QUERCITEON
(AROMATIC —) CANELLA CULILAWAN
(EXTERIOR OF —) ROSS
(INNER —) BAST
(LAVER OF —) HAT
(PREF.) CORTICI CORTICO PHELLO PHLO(E)(EO) QUIN(O)
BARKER BUFFER DOORMAN GRINDER SPIELER SPUDDER SPRUIKER CHARLATAN
BARKING BAY SPUD QUEST LATRANT LATRATION
BARLEY BIG BEAR BENT BERE BIGG GRAIN SPRAT LICORN HORDEUM WHITECORN
(AWN OF —) HORN
(GROUND —) TSAMBA
(HULLED —) PTISAN
(REFUSE —) SHAG FLINTS
(PREF.) ALPHITO CRITHO
BARLEY CAKE
(PREF.) MAZO
BARN BYRE AMBAR LATHE STALL GRANGE STABLE SKIPPER COWHOUSE
(— OWL) LULU MADGE
(COW —) SAUR SHIPPON
(PART OF —) BAY HIP DOOR EAVE APRON GABLE RIDGE VERGE AWNING CUPOLA DORMER PENTHOUSE VENTILATOR WEATHERVANE
BARNACLE BRAY BREY ACORN LEPAS CYPRIS ANATIFA BALANID LEPADID CIRRIPED GNATHOPOD SACCULINA
BARNBURNER SOFT
BARNSTORM TOUR
BARNYARD PIGHTLE BACKSIDE FARMYARD STRAWYARD
BAROMETER GLASS ANEROID OROMETER STATOSCOPE
BARON THANE DAIMIO BARONET FREEMAN FREIHERR
(COURT —) HALLMOOT
BARONET SIR
BARONY HAN DOMAIN

BAROQUE GOTHIC ORNATE ROCOCO GROTESQUE IRREGULAR
BAROTO VINTA
BARRACK CAMP BOTHY CASERN CANNABA CUARTEL
BARRACKS HOOCH HOOTCH
(DETENTION —) GLASSHOUSE
BARRACUDA CUDA KAKU SPET BARRY PELON SNAKE SNOEK SNOOK BECUNA PICUDA SCOOTS SENNET VICUDA KATONKEL SCOOTERS
BARRAGE BAR SALVO ATTACK VOLLEY BARRIER DRUMBEAT DRUMFIRE UMBRELLA CANNONADE FUSILLADE
BARRAMUNDA SALMON CYCLOID DIPNOAN FLATHEAD CERATODUS
BARRED CUCKOO RIBBED STRIPED
BARREL FAT HUB KEG TUN VAT BUTT CADE CASK DRUM KANG TREE WOOD BOWIE QUILL SHELL STAND UNION FESSEL GIRNAL GIRNEL HOGGET RUMBLE RUNLET TIERCE TUMBLE VESSEL CALAMUS CISTERN PACKAGE RATTLER RUNDLET TUMBLER CYLINDER HOGSHEAD KILDERKIN
(— OF FEATHER) CALAMUS
(— OF REVOLVER) CHAMBER
(— ROW) LONGER
(— WITH CRANKS) VANGEE
(CAPSTAN —) SPOOL
(CORE —) LANTERN
(HERRING —) CADE CRAN
(PART OF —) HEAD HOOP CHIME STAVE BOTTOM
(SMALL —) KEG KIT CADE KNAG RUNLET BARRICO RUNDLET
(TAR —) CLAVIE
(PL.) ALOT
BARRELHOUSE GUTBUCKET
BARREN DRY ARID BARE BOWY DEAD DEAF DOUR DULL EILD GAST GELD LEAN NUDE POOR SALT SECK YELD YELL ADDLE BLEAK BLUNT BOWEY DRAPE DUSTY EMPTY GAUNT GHAST GUESS NAKED STARK STERN WASTE YEILD DESERT EFFETE FALLOW HISTIE HUNGRY JEJUNE MEAGER STUPID SAPLESS STERILE DESOLATE IMPOTENT TEEMLESS TREELESS
(NOT —) FACILE FECUND
(PL.) LANDES
(PREF.) STEIRO
BARREN GROUND (AUTHOR OF —) GLASGOW
(CHARACTER IN —) JASON RUFUS GENEVA JOSIAH NATHAN OAKLEY PEDLAR DORINDA ELLGOOD GREYLOCK
BARRENNESS DEARTH VACANCY EMPTINESS
BARRICADE BAR STOP BLOCK CLOSE FENCE ABATIS PRISON BARRAGE BARRIER DEFENSE FORTIFY OBSTRUCT RAMFORCE REVETMENT ROADBLOCK
(— OF TREES) ABATIS
BARRIER ALP BAR DAM BALK BOMA BOOM CRIB CROY DIKE DOOR DYKE FOSS GATE LINE LOCK PALE STOP WALL WEIR BAULK BOUND CHAIN FENCE FOSSE GRILL HEDGE LIMIT STILE STUMP CORDON GLACIS GRILLE HURDLE SCREEN TREBLE BARRAGE CEILING CHICANE CURTAIN GALLERY PARAPET RAILING RAMPART BOUNDARY FORTRESS FRONTIER STOCKADE STRENGTH TRAVERSE
(— ACROSS RIVER) STILL KIDDLE
(— IN TRUCK) HEADER
(— OF STAKES) STOCKKADE
(— OF TREES) SHELTERBELT
(ARTIFICIAL —) FOSS FOSSE
(OIL SPILL —) BOOM
(PROTECTIVE —) REDOUBT
(RACECOURSE —) RAILS
(SPIKED —) TURNPIKE
(TRAFFIC —) SEPARATOR
(PL.) BAIL
(PREF.) HERCO
BARRING BUT SAVE CLOSED
BARRISTER COLT BARMAN JUNIOR LAWYER TUBMAN COUNSEL POSTMAN TEMPLAR ADVOCATE ATTORNEY SERJEANT
(PL.) BAR
BARROOM PUB CAFE HOUSE BISTRO SALOON CANTINA DOGGERY GROCERY TAPROOM DRAMSHOP DRINKERY EXCHANGE GROGGERY GROGSHOP
BARROW HOD HOG BANK BIER DUNE GALT HILL MOTE TUMP CARRY GRAVE GURRY HURLY MOUND SEDAN TRUCK BURROW GALGAL KURGAN NAVETA HILLOCK TROLLEY TUMULUS MOUNTAIN PUSHCART
BARRULET VIVRE
BARTENDER MIXER BARMAN BARMAID SKINKER TAPSTER
BARTER CHAP CHOP COPE COUP HAWK MANG MONG SELL SWAP TROG VEND CORSE TRADE TROKE TRUCK DICKER NIFFER SCORSE BARGAIN CAMBIUM CHAFFER PERMUTE TRAFFIC TRUCKLE COMMERCE EXCHANGE TRUCKAGE
BARTERED BRIDE (CHARACTER IN —) JASEK JENIK KECAL MICHA TOBIAS MARENKA ESMERALDA
(COMPOSER OF —) SMETANA
BARTERER COPER COWPER TRUCKER
BARUCH (FATHER OF —) NERIAH ZABBAI COLHOZEH
BARYTES CAUK CAWK HEPATITE
BARZILLAI (SON OF —) ADRIEL
BASAL BASIC BASILAR RADICAL
BASALT MARBLE NAVITE DIABASE GHIZITE KULAITE POTTERY AUGANITE BANDAITE BASANITE DOLERITE ANAMESITE ARAPAHITE MELAPHYRE SUDBURITE VARIOLITE
(DECOMPOSED —) WACKE
BASE BED DEN HUB LOW TUT ANIL CLAM EVIL FOOT FOUL HUBB HUNK LEWD MEAN POOR RELY REST ROOT SACK STAY STEM STEP VILE BASIS BLOCK CHEAP DIRTY FIRST FLOOR FOUND LACHE MUDDY PETTY SNIDE SOCLE STAND STOOL WORSE ABJECT BOTTOM BRASSY COARSE COMMON DEMISS GROUND GRUBBY HARLOT HUMBLE MENIAL NOUGHT PALTRY PATAND PATTEN PERRON PODIUM RASCAL SECOND SHABBY SORDID VULGAR BASTARD CAITIFF COMICAL CURRISH DEBASED FOOTING HANGDOG HILDING HOUSING IGNOBLE OUTPOST PEASANT ROINISH SERVILE SLAVISH STADDLE STANDER SUBBASE SUPPORT CHURLISH COISTREL COISTRIL DEGRADED DRAWHEAD HARLOTRY HOLDFAST INFAMOUS INFERIOR MECHANIC MESCHANT PEDESTAL PEDIMENT RASCALLY SCULLION SHAMEFUL STANDARD STEPPING SUBSTRAT UNWORTHY WRETCHED NIDDERING
(— IN GAME) HOME
(— IN QUALITY) LEADEN
(— OF BRANCK) KNOT
(— OF CANNON) SOUL
(— OF OPERATIONS) BOOK HOME
(— OF OVULE) CHALAZA
(— OF PETAL) CLAW
(— OF PILLAR) PATTEN
(— OF PLANT) CAUDEX
(— OF POLLINIUM) DISC DISK
(— OF ROCK) MAGMA MAGMO
(— OF TUBER) HEEL
(— OF WORD) STEM
(CHEMICAL —) ALKALI ACRIDAN ADENINE ANSERIN CHOLINE GUANINE ACRIDANE ACTININE AGMATINE ALDIMINE ALKALOID ANSERINE CONYRINE GALEGINE KETIMINE LEPIDINE SEMIDINE
(HIDDEN —) LAIR
(HOME —) DEN
(LEAF —) FOVEA
(LOGARITHM —) E RADIX
(OFF —) AWOL
(PROJECTING —) PLINTH
(SECOND —) KEYSTONE
(STALKLIKE —) CNIDOPOD
(PREF.) BASI TAPIN(O)
(SUFF.) HEDRAL
BASEBALL PILL APPLE DUSTER FLOATER INSHOOT LEATHER BEANBALL HARDBALL HORSEHIDE STICKBALL
(— DOUBLEHEADER) TWINIGHT
(— FLY) POPUP
(— PLAYER) OTT COBB DEAN FORD MAYS ROSE RUTH RYAN AARON BANKS BENCH BERRA BROCK CAREW EVERS LYONS PAIGE REESE SPAHN YOUNG FELLER GEHRIG GOSLIN KEELER KOUFAX MANTLE MUSIAL SEAVER CARLTON DYKSTRA HORNSBY JACKSON JOHNSON CLEMENTE DIMAGGIO DRYSDALE ROBINSON STARGELL WILLIAMS YANNIGAN BOTTOMLEY KILLEBREW CAMPANELLA STRAWBERRY YASTRZEMSKI
(— PRACTICE) FUNGO
(— TEAM) CUBS METS REDS EXPOS TWINS ANGELS ASTROS BRAVES GIANTS PADRES REDSOX ROYALS TIGERS BREWERS DODGERS INDIANS MARLINS ORIOLES PIRATES RANGERS ROCKIES YANKEES BLUEJAYS MARINERS PHILLIES WHITESOX ATHLETICS CARDINALS
(— THROW) PEG TOSS
(HIGH-BOUNCING —) CHOPPER
(MODIFIED —) TBALL
BASEBOARD GRIN SKIRT PLINTH EASEMENT MOPBOARD SKIRTING WASHBOARD
BASE-DEALING BROKING
BASELESS IDLE UNFOUNDED
BASEMAN SACKER
BASEMENT BASE CELLAR TAHKHANA
BASENESS FELONY VILITY BEGGARY SQUALOR TURPITUDE
BASH BAT LAM TRY BEAT BLOW DENT GALA MASH SWAT WHAM WHOP ABASH BEANO PARTY SLOSH SMASH ASSAIL BRUISE STRIKE ATTEMPT BLOWOUT JAMBOREE
BASHEMATH (FATHER OF —) ISHMAEL
(HUSBAND OF —) ESAU
BASHFUL COY SHY HELO SHAN BLATE HELOE TIMID MODEST PUDENT ASHAMED DAUNTED BACKWARD BLUSHING DAPHNEAN DISMAYED LOATHFUL PUDIBUND RETIRING SACKLESS SHAMEFUL SHEEPISH SKITTISH VERECUND SHAMEFACED
BASHFULNESS PUDOR SHYNESS
BASIC NET BASE BASAL VITAL BOTTOM BEDROCK CANONIC CENTRAL CLASSIC PRIMARY ZINCOUS CARDINAL ULTIMATE ELEMENTAL ESSENTIAL SUBSTRATE
BASIL TULASI
BASILICA (PART OF —) APSE BEMA NAVE AISLE ALTAR NARTHEX TRANSEPT
BASIN DOP PAN BOWL COMB COVE DISH DOCK EWER FLOW FONT GULF LAKE PARK SINK SLAD TALA TANK COMBE LAVER SLAKE STOUP BASSON BULLAN CHAFER CIRQUE HOLLOW LAVABO LEKANE LOUTER MARINA VALLEY VESSEL CUVETTE PISCINA RECEIPT URCEOLE BIRDBATH CESSPOOL LAVATORY RECEPTOR VANITORY WASHBOWL GEMELLION
(— FOR RAINWATER) IMPLUVIUM
(DESERT —) PLAYA
(GEOLOGICAL —) BOLSON
(MOUNTAIN —) HOYA PUNA
(OYSTER —) PISCINA
(ROCK —) KEEVE KIEVE
(SEA —) FLOW
(PREF.) LECAN(O)
BASIS BASE FOND FOOT FORM FUND ROOT SILL AXIOM RADIX STOCK ANLAGE BOTTOM GROUND ACCOUNT BEDROCK FOOTING PREMISE SUPPORT GRAVAMEN STRENGTH AUTHORITY CRITERION

FUNDAMENT GROUNDSEL SUBSTANCE
BASK SUN BEEK LAZE WARM ACRID BATHE ENJOY REVEL BITTER REJOICE APRICATE
BASKET IE ARK COB FAN HOT KIT LUG PAD PED PEG POT RIP TAP TOP BUCK CAUL COBB COOP CORB CORF CRIB FLAT GOAL HOTT IEIE KIPE KISH KIST KITT LEAP MAND MAUN SKEP TAPE TILL TOUR TRUG WEEL CABAS CASSY CESTA CHEST CRAIL CRASH CRATE CREEL DEVIL DILLI DILLY FRAIL GRATE MAUND MOLLY NATTE RUSKY SCULL SWILL WILLY BEACON BOKARK CASSIE CLEAVE COFFIN COURGE CRADLE DORSEL DORSER DOSSER FANNER FASCET GABION HAMPER HOBBET HOBBIT HOPPET JICARA JUNKET KIBSEY KIPSEY MOCOCK MOLLIE MURLIN PEGALL PETARA POTTLE PUNNET SEQUIN SERPET TAPPET TEANAL TOPNET VOIDER WINDEL WINDLE WISKET ZEQUIN CANASTA CORBEIL CRESSET FLASKET HANAPER MURLAIN PANNIER PATTARA PITARAH PRICKLE SCUTTLE SEEDLIP SHALLOW SKEOUGH SKIPPET WATTAPE WHISKET CALATHUS CANISTER CHEQUEEN ZECCHINO
(— BOTTOM) SLATH
(— FOR CRUMBS) VOIDER
(— FOR EELS) BUCK COURGE
(— FOR FIGS) TAP CABAS FRAIL TAPNET
(— FOR FISH) CREEL
(— FOR FRUIT) CALA MOLLY CALATHOS
(FISH —) CRAN HASK
(JAI ALAI —) CESTA
(PART OF —) RIB RIM FOOT JOIN RAND SLEW WALE FITCH STAKE UPSET BORDER HANDLE
(REFUSE —) SIEVE
(WICKER —) RIP
BASKETBALL HOOP
(— ATTEMPT) SETSHOT
(— FOUL) HACK
(— GOAL) TIPIN
(— PLAYER) BIRD REED WEST EWING ONEAL PIVOT BAYLOR ERVING JABBAR JORDAN MALONE MCHALE PARISH PETTIT THOMAS UNSELD WALTON WORTHY BARKLEY FRAZIER GRUENIG JOHNSON RUSSELL ALCINDOR HAVLICEK OLAJUWON PIVOTMAN SWINGMAN ROBERTSON STEINMETZ DEBUSSCHERE
(— SHOT) JAM DUNKSHOT SLAMDUNK
(— TEAM) BING HEAT JAZZ NETS SUNS BARRY BUCKS BULLS COUSY HAWKS KINGS MAGIC SPURS LAKERS PACERS BRADLEY BULLETS CELTICS HORNETS NUGGETS PISTONS ROCKETS CLIPPERS WARRIORS CAVALIERS MAVERICKS CHAMBERLAIN SUPERSONICS TIMBERWOLVES TRAILBLAZERS SEVENTYSIXERS KNICKERBOCKERS
(DUNK SHOT) JAM
(FREE-THROW LANE IN —) PAINT
(KIND OF — PASS) SPOT OUTLET
BASKET MAKER ANASAZI
BASKETRY UPSET
BASKETWORK TEE SLEW WALE SLATH STAKE SLATHE STROKE SLEWING
BASMATH (FATHER OF —) SOLOMON
(HUSBAND OF —) AHIMAAZ
BASQUE VASCON EUSCARA EUSCARO IBERIAN BISCAYAN
(— DIALECT) LABOURDIN
(PL.) VASCONA VASCONES
BAS-RELIEF PLAQUETTE
BASS LOW PES CHUB DEEP DRUM FOOT ROCK BASSO DRONE HURON ROCHE SWEGO VOICE BORDUN BRASSE BURDEN CHERNA GROUND JUMPER REDEYE SINGER STRIPE ACHIGAN BARFISH BOURDON BROWNIE GROWLER JEWFISH STRIPER BACHELOR BIGMOUTH BLUEFISH CABRILLA CONTINUO ROCKFISH SPOTTAIL STREAKER TALLYWAG WELSHMAN LINESIDES
(— DRUM) TAMBURONE
(— PART) ALBERTI
(DRONE —) BOURDON
(GROUND —) OSTINATO
(LEADING —) SUCCENTOR
(THOROUGH —) BC
BASSOON REED CURTAL FAGOTT BOMBARD FAGOTTE FAGOTTO WOODWIND
(PART OF —) BELL BOOT BUTT WING CROOK JOINT
BASSWOOD LIN BASS WAHOO LINDEN WICOPY DADDYNUT WHITEWOOD
BAST LIBER RAMIE PHLOEM NOSEBURN
BASTARD GET SOB BASE FALSE CANNON COWSON GALLEY HYBRID IMPURE MAMZER BYSPELL GETLING LOWBRED MONGREL WOSBIRD BANTLING BASEBORN MISBEGET NAMELESS SPURIOUS WHORESON
(PREF.) NOTH(O)
BASTE SEW BEAT CANE COOK DRUB LARD TACK FLAMB SAUCE CUDGEL JIPPER PUNISH STITCH THRASH
BASTION JETTY BULWARK LUNETTE MOINEAU
(PART OF —) FACE RAMP ANGLE FLANK GORGE CURTAIN BANQUETTE
BAT CAT HIT WAD BACK BAKE BATE BEAT CLUB FOWL GAIT JACK LUMP MASS SWAT TRAP WINK BANDY BATON BRICK CHUCK FUNGO HARPY PIECE SPREE STICK ALIPED BACKIE BASTON BEETLE CUDGEL DRIVER KALONG PADDLE POMMEL RACKET STRIKE STROKE WILLOW BAUCKIE FLUTTER JAVELIN MORMOPS NOCTULE VAMPIRE BLUDGEON ROUSETTE SEROTINE BARBASTEL REARMOUSE REREMOUSE CHEIROPTER
(GO TO — FOR) AID
(PART OF —) KNOB MEAT LABEL BARREL HANDLE SIGNATURE
(PREF.) NYCTERI
(SUFF.) NYCTERIS
BATAK (— DIALECT) TOBA
BATCH LOT BAKE BREW CAST CROP FINE MASS MESS RAFT SORT BUNCH FLOOR GROUP BAKING CHEESE MAKING BOILING BREWING FORMULA MIXTURE RAISING QUANTITY
(— OF EGGS) SETTING
(— OF GRAIN) GRIST
(— OF MAIL) SEPARATION
BATCHER BAGGER
BATE BAIT BEET PARE PUER PURE GRAIN
BATELEUR BERGHAAN
BATEMAN DRENCHER
BATFISH ANGLER DIABLO MALTHE DEVILFISH
BATH DIP TUB BAIN BATE LOSS PERT TOSH BATHE LAVER STEEP THERM BAGNIO DOUCHE LIQUOR MIKVAH PICKLE PLUNGE SHOWER SPONGE BALNEUM LAVACRE ABLUTION BALNEARY
(FOOT —) PEDILUVIUM
(HOT —) STEW SCALD STUFE THERM STUPHE THERME
(HOT-AIR —) STOVE
(MUD —) ILLUTATION
(PHOTOGRAPHIC —) FIXER
(SITZ —) BIDET SITZBAD SEMICUPE INSESSION
(SPINNING —) DOPE
(STEAM —) SAUNA
(TANNING —) BATE SOAK
(TURKISH —) HAMMAM HUMMUM HOTHOUSE
(WHIRLPOOL —) JACUZZI
(PREF.) BALNE(O)
BATHE BAY TUB BAIN BASK DOOK LAVE STEW WASH CLEAN DOUSE DOWSE EMBAY SOUSE STEEP ENWRAP FOMENT SHOWER SPLASH EMBATHE IMMERSE PERVADE SUFFUSE PERMEATE
BATHHOUSE SEW STEW SAUNA STUFE BAGNIO CABANA HAMMAM STUPHE BALNEARY
BATHING LAVACRE LAVEMENT
(— SUIT) SLIP TOGS MAILLOT
(SAND —) SABURRATION
BATHROBE PEIGNOIR
BATHROOM BIFFY BALNEARY
BATHSHEBA (FATHER OF —) ELIAM AMMIEL
(HUSBAND OF —) DAVID URIAH
(SON OF —) NATHAN SHIMEA SHOBAB SOLOMON
BATHTUB TUB TOSH LAVACRE
BATIA (FATHER OF —) TEUCER
(HUSBAND OF —) DARDANUS
(SON OF —) HIPPOCOON ERICHTHONIUS
BATON ROD BEND BURN WAND STAFF STICK BAGUET BASTON CUDGEL BOURDON SCEPTER SCEPTRE BAGUETTE CROSSBAR TRUNCHEON
BATSMAN BAT BATTER HITTER SLOGGER SLUGGER STRIKER
BATTALION WARD CONREY
BATTEN END LAY RIB SLAT SLEY CLEAT LEDGE BATTON BEATER ENRICH FATTEN REEPER THRIVE FERTILIZE
(PL.) SPARRING
BATTER RAM BEAT DENT MAIM MAUL PELT CLOUR DINGE FRUSH PASTE POUND SMASH BALLER BRUISE BUFFET HAMMER HATTER HITTER PUMMEL THRING TUMBLE BATSMAN BOMBARD CRIPPLE DESTROY FRITTER SHATTER SLUGGER STRIKER DEMOLISH
BATTERCAKE WAFFLE CRUMPET
BATTERING BLAST LACING
BATTERY PILE SINK TIRE TROOP RADEAU EXCITER SINKBOX SINKBOAT ACCUMULATOR
(GUN —) SWINGER
BATTLE WAR CAMP DUEL FEUD FRAY MART MEET TILT TOIL UNDO BRUSH FIELD FIGHT JOUST STOUR ACTION AFFAIR AFFRAY CAMLAN COMBAT SHOWER STRIVE CONTEND CONTEST HOSTING JOURNAL JOURNEY WARFARE CONFLICT SKIRMISH STRUGGLE ENCOUNTER NAUMACHIA THEOMACHY
(PREF.) MACHO
(SUFF.) MACHIA MACHY
BATTLE-AX WIFLE POLEAX SPARTH TWIBIL BROADAX HALBERD TWIBILL WHIFFLE FAUCHARD FRANCISC
BATTLE CRY CRY BANZAI ENSIGN GERONIMO SLUGHORN BEAUSEANT
BATTLEFIELD ARENA BLAIR CHAMP TAHUA CHAMPAIGN
BATTLEGROUND COCKPIT TERRAIN
BATTLEMENT KERNEL MERION PINION BARMKIN CORNELLE MURDRESS
(PART OF —) CRENEL MERLON MACHIOLATION
BATTLE OF LEGNANO
(CHARACTER IN —) LIDA ARRIGO ROLANDO FREDERICK BARBAROSSA
(COMPOSER OF —) VERDI
BATTLESHIP MAINE CARRIER
BATTOLOGIZE ITERATE
BATTUS (FATHER OF —) POLYMNESTUS
(MOTHER OF —) PHRONIMA
BATTY BATS BUGGY CRAZY SILLY BANANAS BATLIKE FOOLISH
BAUBLE BOW TOY BEAD GAUD BUTTON GEWGAW TRIFLE MAROTTE TRINKET GIMCRACK PLAYTHING
BAWD AUNT HARE DIRTY MADAM DEFILE MADAME PANDER COMMODE MACKEREL PROCURER PURVEYOR
BAWDINESS RAUNCH
BAWDRY SCULDUDDERY

BAWDY LEWD DIRTY SCARLET SKULDUGGERY
BAWL CRY HOWL ROAR ROUT YAUP YAWP BLORE GOLLY SHOUT BELLOW BOOHOO GOLLAR OUTCRY GLAISTER
(— OUT) JUMP CRACK SCOLD
BAY ARM COD DAM RIA VOE BANK BARK CHOP COVE GULF HOLE HOPE HOWL LOCH ROAN TREE WICK YAUP YAWP BAHIA BASIN BAYOU BERRY BIGHT COLOR CREEK FIORD FJORD FLEET HAVEN HORSE INLET LOUGH MOUTH ORIEL QUEST SINUS SPEAK TRAVE BABBLE HARBOR LAUREL RECESS SEVERY TONGUE WINDOW BADIOUS BAYGALL ENCLOSE ESTUARY MALABAR SILANGA ULULATE BREWSTER CHESTNUT
(— OF BARN) GOAF SKEELING SKILLING SKILLION
(— OF LIBRARY) CLASSIS
(— STATE) MASSACHUSETTS
(SWEET —) BREWSTER BEAVERWOOD
BAYBERRY AUSU PIMIENTA WAXBERRY
BAYOU SLEW SLOO SLUE BROOK CREEK INLET RIVER OUTLET SLOUGH STREAM RIVULET BACKWATER
BAY WINDOW ORIEL MIRADOR
BAZAAR FAIR FETE SALE AGORA BURSE CHAWK CHOWK MARKET ALCAZAR CANTEEN BOOKFAIR EMPORIUM BEZESTEEN
BDELLIUM GUGAL GUGUL GOOGUL
BE ABE ARE BES BEEN BETH BIST LIVE ABIDE EXIST OCCUR WORTH REMAIN BREATHE CONSIST SUBSIST CONTINUE
(TO —) SER ETRE SEIN
BEACH AIR BANK CHIP MOOR NARD RIPA SAND SLIP COAST PLAGE PLAYA PRAYA SHORE GROUND SHILLA STRAND HARDWAY SEASIDE SHINGLE LAKESHORE
(— PROTECTOR) SEAWALL
(— RIDGE) FULL
(PROJECTING —) CUSP
(SANDY —) MACHAIR
(PREF.) THIN(O)
BEACH APPLE CANAJONG
BEACHCOMBER SEASONER STRANDLOOPER
BEACHED AGROUND
BEACH FLEA SCUD SCREW SANDBOY
BEACH GRASS STAR SPIRE MARRAM BENTSTAR
BEACON MARK PIKE SIGN BAKEN FANAL GUIDE PHARE RACON ENSIGN PHAROS RAMARK SIGNAL CRESSET SEAMARK WARNING BALEFIRE NEEDFIRE SIGNPOST STANDARD
(RADAR —) RACON NAVAID
BEAD NIB POT DROP FOAM GAUD AGGRI AGGRY BUGLE FILET GRAIN KNURL PEARL QUIRK SIGHT STAFF ARANGO BAGUET BAUBLE BICONE BUBBLE CORNET FILLET HEISHE HEISHI PELLET PIPPER POPPET PRAYER RONDEL WAMPUM CABLING DEWDROP GLOBULE MOLDING SPARKLE TRINKET AVEMARIA CABOCHON
(PREHISTORIC —) ADDERSTONE
(ROSARY —) GAUD PATERNOSTER
(SHELL —S) SEWAN
BEADING VEINING
(PL.) TASBIH
BEADLE CRIER MACER POKER USHER BEDRAL BUMBLE HARMAN HERALD BAILIFF NUTHOOK OFFICER SERVITOR SUMMONER APPARITOR MESSENGER
BEADSMAN BEGGAR HERMIT BLUEGOWN GOWNSMAN
BEAK NEB NIB BECK BILL CLAP NOSE PIKE PROW LORUM SNOUT SWORD TUTEL MASTER NOZZLE SPERON WEAPON EMBOLON EMBOLUM FOREBOW MOLDING ROSTRUM BEAKHEAD MANDIBLE CAPITULUM
(— OF SHELL) UMBO
(— OF SHIP) SPERON
(— OF SWORDFISH) SWORD
(PREF.) RHAMPH(O) RHYNCH(O) ROSTR(I)(O)
(SUFF.) RHYNCHUS RHYNCUS ROSTRAL
BEAKED NASUTE
BEAKER CUP HORN TASS BIKER BOCAL BOUSE GLASS BARECA
BEAM BAR LEG RAY TIE BALK BEAK BOOM EMIT GLOW GRIN PLAT SILE SILL SKID SPAR STUD ARBOR BAULK CABER FLASH GLEAM GLEED JOIST LIGHT RAYON SHAFT SHAPE SHINE SHOOT SMILE SPEAR STANG STOCK TRAVE BINDER BULKER CAMBER CHEESE COLLAR FLITCH GIRDER GLANCE HEADER MANTEL NEEDLE RAFTER SUMMER TIMBER TRABES TREVIS WALKER BALANCE BUMPKIN CATHEAD CHANNEL CHEVRON DORMANT DRAWBAR FRIJOLE MADRIER PINRAIL RADIATE SLEEPER SUPPORT TRANSOM TRIMMER TYNDALL AXLETREE BROWPOST HERISSON PADSTONE PLOWHEAD ROOFTREE STENTREL TEMPLATE BRESSUMMER
(— OF LIGHT) CHINK GLEED RAYON SHAFT PENCIL SIGNAL STREAM SUNBEAM STRICTURE
(HIGH —) BRIGHTS
(LARGE —) BALK LACE BAULK SUMMER
(LOW —) DIM
(POWERFUL —) LASER
(SANIO'S —) CRASSULA
(WEAVER'S —) TRAM TAVIL
(PL.) CRANEWAY
(PREF.) DOCO
BEAMER SMILER SCUDDER
BEAMING GAY ROSY BRIGHT LUCENT MASSIVE RADIANT SHINING
BEAMY BROAD BRIGHT JOYOUS LUCENT MASSIVE RADIANT MIRTHFUL
BEAN BON NIB URD CHAP FABA FAVA GRAM HABA HEAD LIMA POLE SNAP TEKE TICK BRAIN CARAT PULSE SIEVA SKULL TONKA CACOON CASTER COLLAR FELLOW KIDNEY LABLAB LENTIL NIPPLE NOGGIN RUNNER RUTTEE SEEWEE STRIKE TEPARY THRASH TRIFLE CALABAR FRIJOLE MAZAGAN PHASEMY SNAPPER WINDSOR BONAVIST BONNYVIS RAMBUTAN TICKBEAN TORNILLO
(— CURD) TOFU
(— OF CHINA AND JAPAN) ADZUKI
(BROKEN COFFEE —S) TRIAGE
(KIND OF —) GOA MOTH MUNG PINTO TONKA TEPARY WINGED
(LOCUST —) CAROB
(MESCAL —) SOPHORA
(PL.) NIBS FASELS FESELS PODDER PODWARE
(PREF.) FABI
BEANFEAST BEANO
BEANIE DINK
BEAN-SHAPED FABIFORM
BEANSHOOTER TRUNK PEASHOOTER
BEAN TREE BOGUM
BEAN TREFOIL LABURNUM
BEAR GO CUB LUG BALU BERN BORN CAST DREE DUBB FURE GEST GIVE HAVE HOLD LIFT TEEM TOTE URSA WEAR YEAN ABEAR ABIDE ALLOW BALOO BEGET BHALU BREED BRING BROOK BROWN BRUIN CARRY DREIE DRIVE GESTE ISSUE KOALA POLAR PRESS SPARE STAND STICK THOLE THROW WEIGH WIELD YIELD AFFORD BEHAVE BRUANG CONVEY ENDURE IMPORT INFANT KADIAK KINDLE KODIAK PIERCE RENDER SUFFER THRUST UPHOLD URSULA WOMBAT WOOBUT ABROOKE ARCTOID BROWNIE COMPORT CONDUCT EPHRAIM FORBEAR GRIZZLY MUSQUAW PRODUCE STOMACH SUPPORT SUSTAIN UNDERGO FISSIPED SILVERTIP
(— A PART) CONTRIBUTE
(— DOWN) BROWBEAT OVERSWAY
(— EVIDENCE) ASSERT
(— EXPENSES) DEFRAY
(— FLOWERS) FLOURISH
(— FRUIT) FRUCTIFY
(— IN MIND) REMEMBER
(— INVESTIGATION) WASH
(— ON) CONCERN
(— OUT) PROPORT
(— PATIENTLY) DIGEST
(— UP) CAPE ENDURE SUSTAIN
(— WITH CREDIT) BROOK
(— WITNESS) TEEM SPEAK ATTEST DEPOSE
(— YOUNG) FIND YEAN CALVE CHILD
(MALE —) BOAR
(NYMPH CHANGED TO —) CALLISTO
(SLOTH —) ASWAIL
(STUFFED —) TEDDY
(PREF.) ARCT(O) URSI
(SUFF.) FER(ENCE)(ENT)(OUS) GEN(E)(ESIA)(ESIS)(ETIC)(IC)(IN)(OUS)(Y) GER(ENCE)(ENT)(OUS)
BEARBERRY LARB WHORTLE BILBERRY DOGBERRY FOXBERRY CREASHAKS
BEARCAT PANDA
BEARD ANE AWN AVEL BARB DEFY FACE FUZZ NECK NOSE PEAK TUFT ZIFFS ARISTA BEAVER GOATEE TASSEL AFFRONT BARBULE CHARLEY CHARLIE VANDYKE IMPERIAL STILETTO WHISKERS BILLYGOAT
(— OF GRAIN) AIL AWN
(— TREATISE) POGONOLOGY
(KIND OF —) GYPSUM
(SMALL —) BARBET
(PREF.) ATHERO POGON(O)
(SUFF.) POGON
BEARDED AWNIE HAIRY BARBED BARBATE HIRSUTE POGONIATE WHISKERED
BEARDLESS NOT NOTT IMBERBE POLLARD
BEARDTONGUE PENSTEMON
BEARER NEWS HAMAL MACER BEADLE HAMMAL HOLDER PACKER PORTER ANCIENT CARRIER JAMPANI PINCERN CHAPRASI ESCUDERO PORTATOR STANDARD MESSENGER SUPPORTER
(— OF GREAT BURDEN) ATLAS
(ARMOR —) ESQUIRE
(BURDEN —) HAMAL HAMMAL
(CROZIER —) CROCIARY
(CUP —) SAKI COPPER
(PALANQUIN —) BOY SIRDAR MUSAHAR
(SHIELD —) SQUIRE ESCUDERO
(STANDARD —) ANCIENT
(STRETCHER —) BRANCARDIER
(SWORD —) PORTGLAVE PORTGLAIVE
(PREF.) PORTE
BEARING AIM AIR COD BALL DUCT GEST MIEN ORLE PORT RUBY BIRTH FRONT GESTE HABIT JEWEL POISE SETUP TENUE TREND ALLURE APPORT ASPECT BILLET CHARGE COURSE DEPORT GERENT GIGLIO MANNER ORIENT SADDLE STANCE THRUST VOIDER ADDRESS AZIMUTH CONDUCT FASHION GESTURE MEANING POSTURE PURPORT RHODING SUPPORT AMENANCE ATTITUDE BEHAVIOR BIRTHING CARRIAGE DELIVERY DEMEANOR FOOTSTEP PEDESTAL PRESENCE PRESSURE RELATION STANDARD TENDENCY TOURNURE YIELDING REFERENCE
(— AWAY) DEFERENT
(— FRUIT) FRUCTED
(— OUTWARD) EFFERENT
(— UPON) RELEVANT
(ARROGANT —) HUFF
(CONSEQUENTIAL —) POMP
(HERALDIC —) GAD DELF ENTE GORE MARK ORLE PALL WEEL CROWN DELFT DELPH FUSIL LAVER PHEON BILLET DEVICE ENSIGN

GOUTTE CHAPLET CLARION DEMIVOL PLASQUE QUARTER ORDINARY QUENTISE TRESSURE
(PERSONAL —) GARB
(PREF.) PHOR(O)
(SUFF.) GEROUS IGEROUS PARA PAROUS PHORA PHORE(SIS) PHORIA PHOROUS PHORUS
BEARLIKE URSINE
BEAR'S-EAR AURICULA
BEAR'S-FOOT OXHEAL PEGROOTS
BEARSKIN BUSBY
BEAR STATE ARKANSAS
BEAST BETE HOOF BRUTE VACHE ANIMAL JUMENT CRITTER MONSTER MUSIMON VENISON BEHEMOTH BLIGHTER OPINICUS
(— OF BURDEN) JUMENT SUMPTER
(CASTRATED —) SPADO
(DEAD —) MORKIN
(FABULOUS —) YALE THRIS BAGWYN BICORN TRICORN UNICORN DINGMAUL EPIMACUS OPINICUS GYASCUTUS
(HORNED —) RETHER ROTHER
(STURDY —) NUGGET
(WILD —) FERIN FERINE OUTLAW UNBEAST
(WILD —S) ZIIM
(3-HORNED —) TRICORN
(PREF.) THER(A)(IO)(O)
(SUFF.) THERE THERIA THERIUM
BEASTLIKE THEROID
BEASTLY GROSS PRONE ANIMAL BRUTAL WICKED BESTIAL BRUTISH INHUMAN SWINISH OFFENSIVE
BEAT BAT BUM COB DAD FAN FIB LAM PIP PLY PUG PUN RUN TAN TAP TAW TEW TIE WAX BAFF BAIT BANG BASH BATE BELT BEST BLOW BOLT BRAY BUFF BURN CANE CAST CHAP CLAP CLUB COIL COLT COMB CRAB DAUD DING DINT DRUB DUMP DUNT FELL FIRK FLAP FLAX FLOG FRAM FRAP FRAT GROW HAZE JOWL KILL LACE LAMP LASH LICK LOUK LUMP LUSH MAUL MELL MEND MILL PAIK PALE PANT PELT POLT POSS PRAT ROUT SCAT SLAM SLAT SLOG SOCK SOLE SOWL STUB SWAP SWOP TACK TAKD TICK TRIM TUCK TUND TWIG WALK WARP WELT WHIP WHOP WIPE BANDY BASTE BATON BEPAT BERRY BIRCH BLESS CHURN CLINK CREAM CURRY DOUSE DRASH DRESS DRIVE FEEZE FIGHT FILCH FLAIL FLANK FORGE ICTUS INLAY KNOCK LABOR NEVEL NOINT PASTE PATCH POUND PULSE PUNCH ROUGH ROUND SCATT SCOOP SCOUR SKELP STAMP STRAP SWACK SWING TARGE THREP THROB THUMP TREAD TRUMP UPEND WADDY WHACK WHANG WORST ACCENT ANOINT BAMBOO BATTER BENSEL BETTLE BOUNCE BUFFET COTTON CUDGEL DEFEAT DOWSEL FEAGUE FETTLE HAMMER HAMPER JACKET KNEVEL LARRUP LATHER NEAVIL NODDLE OUTRUN PUMMEL RADDLE REBUKE REESLE RHYTHM SCUTCH SQUASH STOUND STOUSH STRIKE STRIPE STROKE SUGGIL SWINGE SWITCH TANSEL TEWTAW TEWTER THRASH THREAP THREIP THREPE THRESH TICKLE WAGGLE WALLOP WATTLE WUTHER ASSAULT BATTUTA BELABOR BLATTER BLISTER CADENCE CANVASS CONQUER CONTUSE EXHAUST FATIGUE FLYFLAP KNUCKLE LAMBACK LAMBAST LOBTAIL LOUNDER PULSATE REESHIE SHELLAC SURPASS SWABBLE SWADDLE TROLLOP TROUNCE VIBRATE MALLEATE PALPITATE SPIFLICATE
(— ABOUT) BUSK BANGLE
(— AGAINST) BLAD
(— AGAINST THE WIND) LAVEER
(— BACK) REBUFF
(— BARLEY) PAIL WARM
(— CLOTHES) BATTLE
(— COVERT) TUFT
(— DOWN) LAY FELL FULL ABATE FLASH
(— EGGS) CAST
(— FIBERS) BRUSH
(— FLAX) SCUTCH
(— HIGH) LEAP
(— IT) LAM
(— OF DRUM) RUFF RAPPEL RATTAN
(— OF HEART) DUNT STROKE
(— ON BUTTOCKS) COB
(— OUT) THRESH
(— SEVERELY) DRUB LUMP SOAK BASTE SOUSE LATHER
(— SMALL) CHAP
(— TO AND FRO) BANDY
(— TO WINDWARD) LAVEER
(— UP) WHISK SWITCH WORKOVER
(— VIOLENTLY) WETHER
(— WINGS) BATE FLAP
(— WITH HAMMER) DOLLY
(— WITH WHIP) SJAMBOK
(— WOODS) TUSK
(MUSICAL —) SALSA BOUNCE BATTUTA
(WEAK —) ARSIS
(PREF.) TYPTO
BEATEN BEAT BETE BATTU PARTY TRITE TRADED
BEATER RAB MAUL SEAL CANER LACER STOCK DASHER DRIVER MALLET TRIMMER SCUTCHER THRESHER
BEATIFIC DEIFIC ELYSIAN
BEATIFIED BLEST BLESSED
BEATIFY SAINT HALLOW HEAVEN ENCHANT GLORIFY SANCTIFY
BEATING COB COBB LICK TUND BEANS DOUSE JESSE PULSE STICK HAZING HIDING HOSING ROPAND TATTOO BASHING BATTERY BELTING CLANKER DASHING DUSTING LICKING SKELPIN WELTING WHALING BIRCHING DRESSING DRUBBING RIBROAST SLOSHING WHIPPING JACKETING STRAPPADO PERCUSSION
BEATITUDE JOY BLISS BENISON MACARISM HAPPINESS
BEATRICE DI TENDA (CHARACTER IN —) AGNESE FILIPPO BEATRICE VISCONTI OROMBELLO
(COMPOSER OF —) BELLINI
BEATRICE ET BENEDICT
(CHARACTER IN —) HERO CLAUDIO BEATRICE BENEDICT SOMARONE
(COMPOSER OF —) BERLIOZ
BEAU BEW BOY CHAP BLADE DANDY FLAME LOVER SPARK SWELL ADONIS ESCORT FELLOW GARCON STEADY SUITOR TATTLE ADMIRER AIMWELL BRAVERY COURTER COXCOMB CUPIDON GALLANT SPARKER FOLLOWER
BEAU GREGORY COCKEYE
BEAUISH DOGGY
BEAUT PIP DILLY
BEAUTIFUL FAIR FINE GLAD GOOD MEAR MEER MERE WALY BELLE BONNY KALON LUSTY SHEEN WLITY WLONK BLITHE BONNIE COMELY DECORE FREELY LOVELY POETIC PRETTY VENUST ANGELIC ELEGANT FORMOSE FORMOUS TEMPEAN TOKALON CHARMING DELICATE ESTHETIC FAIRSOME GORGEOUS GRACEFUL HANDSOME LUCULENT SPECIOUS MAGNIFICENT
(PREF.) CALI CALLI CALLO CALO PULCHRI
BEAUTIFY FAIR GILD ADORN GRACE HIGHT PREEN PRIMP PRUNE BEAUTY BEDECK DECORE ENAMEL QUAINT ADONIZE ENHANCE GARNISH GLORIFY DECORATE FAIRHEAD EMBELLISH PULCHRIFY
BEAUTY GEM FACE FAIR FORM GLEE BEAUT BELLE CHARM FAVOR GLORY GRACE PRIDE WLITE FINERY LOOKER LOVELY POLISH DECORUM FEATURE TOKALON SPLENDOR FORMOSITY
(— OF FORM) SYMMETRY
(— OF STYLE) ELEGANCE
(PREF.) CALI CALLI CALLO CALO PULCHRI
BEAVER BOOMER CASTOR RODENT PRALINE MUSHROOM SEWELLEL STARLING
(— SKIN) PLEW
(— STATE) OREGON
(DARK —) NUTMEG
BEBAI (SON OF —) ZECHARIAH
BEBEERINE CURINE
BEBEERU SWEETWOOD GREENHEART
BECAUSE AS SO FOR THAT BEING CAUSE SINCE THERE FORWHY THROUGH INASMUCH
BECCAFICO FIGEATER FIGPECKER
BECHE-DE-MER PIDGIN TREPANG
BECHER (FATHER OF —) EPHRAIM BENJAMIN
BECHORATH (FATHER OF —) APHIAH
BECK RUN VAT BECON BROOK CREEK
(— AND CALL) DEVOTION
BECKEN CYMBALS
BECKET SQUILGEE SQUILLGEE
BECKON BOW NOD WAG BECK WAFT WAVE CURTSY SUMMON BIDDING COMMAND CURTSEY GESTURE
BECKONING WAFTURE
BECLOUD HIDE MASK BEDIM DARKEN MUDDLE MYSTIFY OBSCURE OBNUBILATE
BECLOUDED FOGGY
BECOME GO FIT GET RAX SET SIT WAX COME FALL GROW LIKE PASS SUIT TAKE TILL WEAR ADORN BEFIT GRACE PROVE WORTH ACCORD BEFALL BESEEM BETIDE CHANGE IWORTH BEHOOVE FLATTER PROCEED
(— A PARTY) ACCEDE
(— AUDIBLE) ARISE
(— BETTER) GAIN
(— BIGGER) SPREAD
(— DAMP) EVE
(— DAZED) DWAM DWALM
(— DIM) DASWEN
(— DROWSY) DOW
(— EVENTUALLY) ENDUP
(— FAT) GRAZE
(— FLUID) FLOW FLUX LEACH
(— KNOWN) GO KITHE KYTHE SPUNK
(— MEMBER) JOIN
(— MOLDY) FUST MOUL FINEW
(— MOROSE) SOUR
(— ROUND) GLOBE
(— SOUR) FOX BLINK CARVE
(SUFF.) IZE
BECOMING FIT FEAT GOOD BHAVA FITTY RIGHT COMELY DUEFUL GAINLY PROPER DECORUM FARRAND FARRANT DECOROUS HANDSOME SUITABLE WISELIKE
(SUFF.) ESCENT ESCENCE ESCENCE
BECOMINGLY TALLY
BED COT HAY KIP LIT PAD PAN TYE BAND BASE BODY BUNK DOSS DOWN FLOP FORM LAIR PLOT SACK VEIN WADI WADY BERTH BOIST COUCH FLASK FLOCK GRATE GROVE LAYER ROOST THORE BORDER BOTTOM COUCHE CRADLE GIRDLE HOTBED LIBKEN LIBKIN LITTER MATRIX OSIERY PALLET STRATA CHANNEL CHARPOY FLEABAG HAMMOCK LODGING QUARTER REPOSAL SEEDBED SETTING STRATUM SUBSOIL TRUCKLE TRUNDLE BASSINET CAPSTONE LENTICLE PLANCHER SHAKEDOWN
(— DOWN) DOSS
(— IN WAGON) KATEL
(— OF ANIMAL) LAIR KENNEL
(— OF CLAY) CLOD
(— OF COAL) BRAT DELF SEAM
(— OF EMBERS) GRIESHOCH
(— OF FIRE CLAY) THILL
(— OF FURNACE) HEARTH
(— OF GUN-CARRIAGE) FLASK
(— OF HAND PRESS) COFFIN
(— OF OYSTERS) PLANT
(— OF REFUSE) NITRIARY
(— OF ROCK) CAP PLUM
(— OF ROSES) ROSARY

(— OF SEDIMENT) WARP
(— OF SHELLFISH) BANK
(— OF STONES) SHINGLE
(— OF STREAM) DRAW WASH NULLAH BILLABONG STREAMWAY
(— SIZE) KING TWIN QUEEN DOUBLE SINGLE
(CREEK —) COULEE COULIE
(DRIED LAKE —) CHOTT SEBKA SHOTT
(FEATHER —) TIE TYE
(FOLDING —) SLAWBANK
(GO TO —) SACKOUT
(LOW —) LOWBOY
(OYSTER —) STEW LAYER SCALP CLAIRE LAYING OYSTERAGE
(RUBBLE —) CALLOW
(SEED —) SEMINARY
(WATER-BEARING —) AQUAFER AQUIFER
(WOODEN —) RUSTBANK
(PREF.) CLIN(O) STRATI STROMATI STROMATO
(SUFF.) STROMA
BEDAD (SON OF —) HADAD
BEDAN (FATHER OF —) GILEAD
BEDAUB CLAG CLAT DAUB MOIL SOIL SLAKE SMEAR PARGET SLUBBER SLAISTER BEPLASTER
BEDBUG BUG CHINK CIMEX CHINCH CHINTZ COREID PUNESE VERMIN CIMICID PUNAISE REDCOAT CONENOSE HEMIPTER HOUSEBUG
BEDCHAMBER RUELLE BEDROOM CUBICLE
BEDCLOTHES COVER BEDDING CLOTHES
BEDCOVER COMFORTER PALAMPORE
BEDDING BEDROLL DOMESTICS
BEDECK GEM BEDO LARD TRAP ADORN ARRAY DIGHT GRACE PRINK ORNAMENT EMBELLISH
BEDECKED PRINKY
BEDEGUAR SPONGE
BEDEIAH (FATHER OF —) BANI
BEDEVIL ABUSE ANNOY BESET WORRY HARASS MUDDLE PESTER BEWITCH CONFUSE TORMENT
BEDEW DEW DAMPEN SHOWER EMBATHE IRRORATE
BEDIZEN DAUB ADORN ARRAY DIZEN BEDAUB
BEDLAM ZOO RIOT NOISE RUDAS ASYLUM TUMULT UPROAR MADNESS MADHOUSE BETHLEHEM
BEDLAMITE MADMAN
BEDOUIN ABSI ARAB BEDU MOOR NOMAD BADAWI BEDAWEE SHAMMAR HOWEITAT
BEDQUILT POURPOINT
BEDRAGGLE DAG DRABBLE TRACHLE
BEDRAGGLED FORLORN SHOPWORN
BEDRAIL RAVE RATHE
BEDRIDDEN ILL AILING BEDFAST
(NOT —) AFOOT
BEDROCK LEDGE NADIR SHELF BOTTOM HARDPAN STONEHEAD
BEDROLL BINDLE
BEDROOM FLAT BERTH CABIN BEDDER DORMER BOUDOIR CHAMBER CUBICULO WARDROBE GARDEROBE
BEDSORE ANACLISIS DECUBITUS
BEDSPREAD ALEZE STRAIL BEDCOVER COVERLET COVERLID
BEDSTAFF SLAT
BEDSTEAD BED COT CRIB HATCH STEAD STAPLE ANGAREP CHARPOY
BEDSTRAW CRUDWORT CURDWORT FLEAWEED BEDFLOWER CROSSWORT SCRAMBLER
BED TESTER SPARVER
BEDWARMER CURATE
BEDWEAR PJS
BEE DOR FLY APIS BEVY KING RING KARBI MASON NOMIA NURSE PARTY DINGAR DRONEL DRONER FROLIC INSECT NOTION TORQUE TSETSE WORKER ANDRENA DEBORAH KOOTCHA MELISSA RAISING SERPENT STINGER SWERVER TRIGONA ANDRENID ANGELITO HONEYBEE QUILTING SCOPIPED SHUCKING WAXMAKER GATHERING
(KIND OF —) KILLER
(PERTAINING TO —S) APIAN
(QUEEN —) KING
(PL.) BEEN BONE HIVE SPEW SOCIALES
(PREF.) API
BEEBREAD CERAGO AMBROSIA
BEECH BUCK BIRCH MYRTLE FLINDOSA FLINDOSY
(PREF.) FAGI FAGO
BEECHNUT SPLITNUT
(PL.) BUCK MAST PANNAGE
BEEF JERK BEEVE BULLY GRIPE JERKY VIFDA VIVDA CASSON CUTTER CHARQUI TOPSIDE COMPLAIN COMPOUND PASTRAMI PIPIKAULA
(— FOR SLAUGHTER) MART
(BOILED —) BOUILLI
(BROILED —) CHURRASCO
(CORN —) BULLY
(CUT OF —) SEY LOIN RUMP SIDE BARON CHINE CHUCK FLANK ROAST ROUND SHANK STEAK ALOYAU CUTLET SADDLE BRISKET KNUCKLE QUARTER SIRLOIN EDGEBONE SHOULDER AITCHBONE NINEHOLES RATTLERAN
(GROUND —) HAMBURGER
(INFERIOR —) COMPOUND
(JERKED —) TASAJO BILTONG CHARQUE CHARQUI
(LEAN —) LIRE
(PIECE OF —) PAILLARD
(SALTED —) JUNK VIFDA
(STRIPS OF —) FAJITA
BEEF BREAD SWEETBREAD
BEEFEATER OXBIRD BUPHAGA OXBITER OXPECKER TICKBIRD
BEEFWOOD TOA BELAH BELAR FILAO
BEEFY HEAVY HEFTY SOLID BRAWNY FLESHY
BEE GLUE PROPOLIS
BEEHIVE GUM BUTT GUME HIVE SKEP PYCHE STAND STATE STOCK SWARM APIARY HAIRDO HOPPET ALVEARY SWARMER BEEHOUSE PRAESEPE
(— STATE) UTAH
(— TOMB) TREASURY
BEEKEEPER HIVER BEEMAN BEEHERD APIARIST SKEPPIST
BEELIADA (FATHER OF —) DAVID
BEELZEBUB DEVIL
BEEN BE BON SEE BONE
BEEPER PAGER
BEE PLANT GUACO STINKWEED
BEER ALE MUM BIER BOCK BREW FARO GAIL GROG GYLE HOPS KVAS MALT MILD QUAS SCUD SUDS BELCH CHANG CHICA GROUT KVASS LAGER POMBE QUASS SCUDS STOUT WEISS CHICHA DOUBLE GATTER LIQUOR PORTER SPRUCE STINGO SWANKY SWIPES WALLOP ZYTHUM CERVEZA PANGASI PHARAOH PILSNER TANKARD TAPLASH TAPWORT CERVISIA PILSENER
(ADD TO —) KRAUSEN
(BAD —) TACK TAPLASH
(HOT — AND GIN) PURL
(INFERIOR —) BELCH SWANKY
(KIND OF —) NEAR
(SMALL —) TIFF GROUT
(SOUR —) BEEREGAR
(STRONG —) HUFF NAPPY DOUBLE STINGO
(THIN —) PRITCH SWIPES
(TIBETAN —) CHANG
(WARM — AND OATMEAL) STORRY
(WEAK —) BEVERAGE
BEERA (FATHER OF —) ZOPHAH
BEER-GARDEN BRASSERIE
BEERHOUSE KNEIPE TIDDLYWINK
BEERI (DAUGHTER OF —) JUDITH
(SON OF —) HOSEA
BEESWAX CAPPING
BEET CHARD MANGEL MANGOLD STECHLING
(SUGAR —) BOLTER
BEETLE BAT BOB BUG DOR JUT RAM BEAT BUZZ FLEA FOWL GOGA GOGO IPID MAUL MELL STAG TROX TURK UANG AMARA ATLAS BORER BULGE CAROB CHUCK CLOCK DRIVE FIDIA GOGGA HISPA LYCID MELOE SAGRA TIGER BATLET CHAFER CLERID COCUYO CUCUYO ELATER GOLACH GOLOCH HISTER JUTOUT KHAPRA LICTUS MALLET MELOID PESTLE PRUNER PTINID SAWYER SCARAB WEAVER WEEVIL ADELOPS BRUCHID BUZZARD CADELLE CARABID CARABUS CLOCKER CUCUJID FIDDLER FIREFLY GIRDLER GOLDBUG HORNBUG LADYBUG LUCANID PAUSSID PRIONID PROJECT SILPHID SKIPPER SNAPPER SOLDIER TANBARK TICKLER ATEUCHUS CALOSOMA CETONIAN COCKTAIL CURCULIO DYTISCID ENGRAVER EROTYLID FIGEATER GLOWWORM HARDBACK LADYBIRD LAMPYRID LOWERING OVERHANG RUTELIAN SCOLYTID SEARCHER SHARNBUD SHARNBUG SKIPJACK SPHINDID SQUASHER SQUEAKER SYMPHILE TOKTOKJE WHIRLWIG DEDEMERID LONGICORN OSTOMATID TUMBLEBUG TWIRLIGIG WHIRLIGIG SCAPHIDIUM RHYNCHOPHORAN
(KIND OF —) OIL
(RHINOCEROS —) UANG SCARABAEID
(PL.) XYLOPHAGA
BEEWEED ASTER TONGUE
BEFALL HAP COME LIMP SORT TIDE TIME CHEFE CHIVE OCCUR SHAPE ASTART BECOME BETIDE HAPPEN PERTAIN
BEFIT DOW SIT COME LONG SEEM SORT SUIT BESET SERVE BECOME BEHOVE BESEEM BETIDE BEHOOVE
BEFITTING FIT AFTER DECENT PROPER WORTHY SEEMING THRIFTY BECOMING DECOROUS SORTABLE
(PROFESSIONALLY —) ETHICAL
(SUFF.) LY
BEFOG GAUM CLOUD OBSANE CONFUSE MYSTIFY
BEFOOL BOB FON SOT BURN COLT CRAP DOLT DUPE FODE JADE POOP ASSOT ELUDE FONNE BEFLUM DIDDLE TRIFLE FOOLIFY
BEFOOLING BITE
BEFORE OR TO AIR BUT ERE FOR GIN TIL ANTE FORE SAID TILL YORE AFORE AHEAD ANENT AVANT CORAM FIRST FORBY FORNE FRONT PRIOR SOPRA UNTIL ERENOW FORBYE FORMER RATHER SOONER TOFORE WITHIN AGAINST ALREADY EARLIER FORTHBY FORWARD
(— LONG) SOON ERELONG
(JUST —) TOWARD FORMERLY
(PREF.) FORE OB PRAE PRE PRO PROTER(O)
BEFOREHAND AFORE
BEFORE-MENTIONED SAID SUCH
BEFOUL FILE SLUT SOIL BERAY DIRTY GRUFT BEMIRE DAGGLE DARKEN DEFILE DRABBLE FEWMAND POLLUTE SLUTTER BESQUIRT ENTANGLE
BEFOULED SHARNY
BEFRIEND AID ABET HELP FAVOR ASSIST FOSTER FRIEND SUCCOR BENEFIT SUPPORT SUSTAIN
BEFUDDLE BOX GAS ADDLE BESOT MUDDLE BECLOUD CONFUSE FLUSTER MYSTIFY STUPEFY
BEFUDDLED REE MUSED
BEG ASK BID CRY SUE WOO CANT COAX KICK MOVE MUMP PRAY PRIG SEEK SORN SUIT THIG TRAM CADGE CRAVE MAUND MOOCH PLEAD SCAFF SHOOL TEASE YEARN ADJURE FLEECH BESEECH ENTREAT IMPLORE MAUNDER REQUEST SKELDER SOLICIT PETITION OBSECRATE PANHANDLE

BEGET GET WIN BEAR HAVE KIND SIRE BREED YIELD BIGATE CREATE FATHER ACQUIRE ENGRAFF CONCEIVE ENGENDER GENERATE PROCREATE
(PREF.) GONIDIO GONIMO GONIO GON(O)
BEGETTER SIRE AUTHOR FATHER MOTHER PARENT
BEGETTING
(SUFF.) GON(E)(IDIUM)(IMO)(IUM)(Y)
BEGGAR BLOB PROG RUIN ASKER HALFY LAZAR RANDY ROGUE THRUM TRAMP ARMINE BACACH BIDDER CADGER CANTER DYVOUR MUMPER PARIAH PAUPER SORNER WRETCH ABRAHAM ALMSMAN BAIRAGI BEGSTER JARKMAN LAZARUS MAUNDER PARDHAN PROCTOR RUFFLER SCAFFER SORNARI STEMMER THIGGER ABRAMMAN BADGEMAN BEADSMAN BESOGNIO BEZONIAN BLUEGOWN DUMMERER GLASSMAN PALLIARD STROLLER WHIPJACK MENDICANT SCHNORRER
(— DESCRIPTION) PASS
(SWINDLING —) JARKMAN
(VIOLENT —) RANDY RANDIE
(PL.) GUEUX
BEGGARED PEELED
BEGGARLY MEAN POOR CHEAP PETTY SORRY ABJECT PALTRY PILLED PEGRALL BANKRUPT INDIGENT HUNGARIAN
BEGGAR'S-LICE STICKWEED
BEGGARS' OPERA (AUTHOR OF —) GAY
(CHARACTER IN —) LUCY POLLY LOCKIT PEACHUM MACHEATH
BEGGAR-TICK CUCKOLD
(PL.) BOOTJACKS
BEGGARY THIG WANT INDIGENCE PAUPERISM
BEGGING MAUND CRAVING OPENERS MENDICANT THOMASING
(— FOR FOOD) SCRANNING
(FRAUDULENT —) TRUANDISE
BEGHARD PICARD
BEGIN GIN GYN HIT FALL FANG HEAD JUMP LEAD OPEN RISE TAME YOKE ARISE ENTER FRONT START ATTACK ATTAME INCEPT SPRING STREAK TEEOFF INSTATE COMMENCE GETGOING INCHOATE INITIATE
(— AGAIN) RENEW REOPEN RESUME
(— IN EARNEST) SETTO
(— TO APPEAR) PEEP
(— TO MELT) GIVE
(— TO WORK) GEL
BEGINNER BOOT PUNK TIRO TYRO ROOKY SOFTA GINNER NOVICE ROOKIE SOPHTA AMATEUR ENTRANT RECRUIT RUBBLER STUDENT TRAINEE FRESHMAN INCEPTOR NEOPHYTE NEWCOMER NOVELIST ABECEDARIAN
BEGINNING EGG ORD DAWN EDGE GERM HEAD RISE ROOT SEED ALPHA BIRTH DEBUT ENTRY FIRST FRONT ONSET START VAUNT AURORA INCOME INSTIL ONCOME ORIGIN OUTSET SETOUT SOURCE SPRING CALENDS DAWNING GENESIS HANDSEL INCIPIT INFANCY INITIAL INITION KALENDS NASCENT OPENING SUNRISE ENTRANCE EXORDIUM INCHOATE OUTSTART RUDIMENT
(— OF A TRILL) RIBATTUTA
(FROM THE —) ABOVO
(NEW —) EPOCH
(PL.) INCUNABULA
(PREF.) ACR(O)
(SUFF.) ARCH ARCHIC ARCHY ESCENT
BEGONE OFF OUT VIA AWAY SCAT SHOO SCOOT SCRAM AROINT AVAUNT DEPART SKIDOO SKIDDOO VAMOOSE
BEGONIA GAIETY GAYETY
BEGRIME COOM SOIL COLLY DITCH GRIME BECOOM SMIRCH SMUDGE BRUCKLE
BEGRIMED DIRTY GRIMY SMUDGY CINDERY SMIRCHY
BEGRUDGE ENVY GRUDGE MALIGN JALOUSE
BEGTI NAIR COCKUP
BEGUILE FOX COAX FODE FOIL FOND GULL LURE VAMP WILE WISE AMUSE CHARM CHEAT COZEN ELUDE EVADE GUILE TEMPT TRICK TROLL TRYST WEIZE BRIGUE BUTTER DELUDE DIVERT ENTRAP JUGGLE VAMPEY DECEIVE ENSNARE FLATTER FLUMMER MISLEAD MOUNTEBANK
BEHALF HALF PART SAKE SIDE FAVOR SCORE STEAD AFFAIR MATTER PROFIT BENEFIT DEFENCE SUPPORT INTEREST
BEHAVE DO ACT LET BEAR FARE HAVE KEEP MAKE PLAY WALK WORK ABEAR CARRY REACT TREAT ACQUIT DEMEAN DEPORT HANDLE COMPORT CONDUCT CONTAIN DISPORT GESTURE MANAGER FUNCTION REGULATE RESTRAIN
(— AFFECTEDLY) MOP
(— AWKWARDLY) GAUM HOCKER
(— BOLDLY) GAUSTER
(— BRASHLY) HOOK
(— CHURLISHLY) CARL
(— EVASIVELY) DODGE
(— FOOLISHLY) DOLT
(— IRRATIONALLY) FREAK
(— MEANLY) SNEAK
(— MISCHIEVOUSLY) LARK
(— NOISILY) HELL REHAYTE
(— OSTENTATIOUSLY) SWANK
(— RIOTOUSLY) ROLLICK GALRAVAGE GILRAVAGE
(— VULGARLY) RAMP
BEHAVING
(SUFF.) ANT ENT
BEHAVIOR AIR MIEN PORT RULE THEW WALK FRONT GUISE HABIT LATES USAGE ACTION COURSE GOINGS MANNER ACTIONS BEARING BIGOTRY COMPORT CONDUCT DECORUM ERGASIA FACTION FASHION HAVANCE HAVINGS AMENANCE ATTITUDE BLINDISM BREEDING BYRONICS CARRIAGE FUNCTION MAINTAIN PERFORMANCE
(AMOROUS —) SPORT
(ARROGANT —) SIDE SWAGGER
(COURTEOUS —) COMITY COURTESY
(DECENT —) CIVILITY
(EXCITED —) RAMPAGE RAMPAUGE
(FOOLISH —) SIMPLES SOTTISE
(GOAL-DIRECTED —) HORME
(GOOD —) STRAIGHT
(IMPROPER —) MISCONDUCT
(LIVELY —) TITTUP
(LOUTISH —) BUFFOONERY
(RIOTOUS —) RAMPAGE
(SILLY —) SPOONISM
(SLEAZY —) SMARM
(STUDIED —) ART
(SUSPICIOUS —) SUS
(UNDERHANDED —) SKULLDUGGERY
(VIOLENT —) THUGGERY
BEHEAD NECK
BEHEST BID LAW HEST RULE ORDER DEMAND BIDDING COMMAND MANDATE
BEHIND AFT HINT PAST RUMP ABACK ABAFF ABAFT AFTER AHIND AREAR LATER PASSE TARDY ARREAR ASTERN DERERE BACKWARD DILATORY
(— TIME) OVERDUE
(PREF.) META POST POSTERO RETRO
BEHINDHAND TARDY LAGGARD DILATORY HINDERLY
BEHOLD LA LO EYE SEE SPY ECCE ESPY GAZE HOLD KEEP LOOK SCAN STOP TOOT VIEW VISE WAIT HOLDE OCULE SIGHT VOILA WATCH ASPECT DESCRY MIRROR REGARD RETAIN DISCERN OBSERVE SURVISE WITNESS
BEHOLDEN OWING AFFINED BOUNDEN OBLIGED INDEBTED
BEHOOVE DOW FIT NEED SUIT THAR BEFIT OUGHT THARF BELONG PROPER REQUIRE
BEIGE HOP TAN ECRU HOPI GREGE DORADO GREIGE STRING SUNBURN
BEING ENS ESSE FEAL SELF ENTIA GNOME HUMAN SHAPE TROLL ANIMAL ENTITY EXTANT LIVING MORTAL PERSON SYSTEM ESSENCE PRESENT REALITY VIVENCY CREATURE EXISTENT ONTOLOGY PRESENCE STANDING
(ANIMATE —) LIFE JAGAT
(BIONIC HUMAN —) CYBORG
(CELESTIAL —) ANGEL CHERUB SERAPH WATCHER DIVINITY
(DIMINUTIVE —) ELF GNOME
(DIVINE —) DEV DEVA DEMIGOD
(ESSENCE OF —) SAT
(ETERNAL —) EON AEON
(EVIL —) DEVIL GHOUL
(FABULOUS —) TENGU TORNIT
(HAVING REAL —) ONTIC
(HUMAN —) BODY BUCK JACK SOUL BLADE HUMAN SLIME ANIMAL ADAMITE CREATURE RATIONAL CHRISTIAN
(IDEAL —) IMMORTAL
(ILL-FAVORED —) BLASTIE
(IMAGINARY —) SYLPH TERMAGANT
(INNER —) INWARD SPRITE INBEING
(INNERMOST —) HEART
(INTRINSIC —) ESSENCE
(LEGENDARY —) GIANT
(LIVING —) BLOOD WIGHT
(MATERIAL —) HYLIC
(PERFECT —) GOD
(PHYSICAL —) FLESH
(SEMIDIVINE —) SHEDU LAMASSU
(SMALL —) INCHLING
(SO —) SAEBEINS
(SUPERNATURAL —) DEV MAN AKUA ATUA DEVA JANN ZEMI ADARO BALAM DAEVA DEMON FAIRY TROLL WIGHT DAEMON GARUDA GODKIN SPIRIT GODLING FOLLETTO HAMINGJA
(SUPREME —) DEITY MONAD NYAMBE NZAMBI CREATOR
(TRUE —) OUSIA
(PREF.) ONT(O) ZO(E)(IDIO)(IDO)(O) ZOOLOGICO
(HUMAN —) ANTHROP(O)
(SUFF.) IC(AL) ZOA ZOIC ZOON
BELA (FATHER OF —) AZAZ BEOR BENJAMIN
BELABOR PLY BEAT DRUB LASH WORK ASSAIL BOUNCE CUDGEL HAMMER HAMPER THRASH THWACK
BELARUS (ALSO SEE RUSSIA)
CANAL: DNIEPERBUG
CAPITAL: MINSK
COIN: RUBLE
LAKE: NARACH NAROCH DRISVYATY DRYSVYATY ASVEYSKAYE OSVEYSKOYE
MARSH: PRIPET PALESSE POLESYE
MOUNTAIN: DZERZHINSKAYA DZYARZHINSKAYA
NAME: BYELARUS BELORUSSIA BYELORUSSIA
PEOPLE: BELARUS RUSSIAN BELORUSSIAN WHITERUSSIAN
PLAIN: BEREZINA
RIVER: BUG DRUT SOZH DISNA DNEPR DVINA DYSNA NEMAN SLUCH DNEPRO PRIPET PTITCH DAUGAVA DNIEPER NEMUNAS PRIPYAT SHCHARA YASELDA BEREZINA PRYPYATS SVISLOCH BYAREZINA MUKHAVETS
TOWN: BREST GOMEL HOMEL PINSK GRODNO HRODNA BORISOV MOGILEV VITEBSK ZHODINO BOBRUISK BOBRUYSK MOGILYOV MOLODECHNO BRESTLITOVSK
BELAY BESET BELAGE INVEST WAYLAY BESEIGE
BELCH YEX BOCK BOKE BOLK BURP GALP RASP RIFT ERUCT FRUCT REBOKE ERUCTATE
BELCHING BRASH
BELDAM HAG FURY TROT CRONE RUDAS ALECTO ERINYS RUDOUS

VIRAGO BELDAME JEZEBEL TISIPHONE
BELEAGUER BELAY BESET INVEST ASSAULT BESEIGE LEAGUER BLOCKADE SURROUND
BELEAGUERING SIEGE
BELEM PARA
BELEMNITE ARTIFACT KERAUNION
BELFRY SHED TOWER BEFFROY CLOCHER CLOGHEAD BELLHOUSE
BELGIAN FLEMING
BELGIAN CONGO (CAPITAL OF —) LEOPOLDVILLE
(LAKE IN —) KIVU MWERU ALBERT
(PROVINCE OF —) KIVA KASAI EQUATOR KATANGA ORIENTAL
(RIVER IN —) RUKI KASAI LINDI LOMAMI LUKUGA UBANGI ARUWIMI LULONGA
(TOWN IN —) BOMA LULUABOURG

BELGIUM
CANAL: YSER UNION ALBERT CAMPINE
CAPITAL: BRUSSELS BRUXELLES
GAUL TRIBE: REMI BELGAE NERVII
MEASURE: VAT AUNE LAST PIED CARAT PERCHE BOISSEAU
MOUNTAIN: BOTRANGE
NAME: BELGIE BELGIQUE
PLATEAU: ARDENNES HOHEVENN
PORT: OSTEND ANTWERP
PROVINCE: LIEGE NAMUR ANTWERP BRABANT HAINAUT LIMBURG FLANDERS HAINAULT
RIVER: LYS DYLE LEIE MAAS MARK YSER BOUCQ DEMER LESSE MEUSE NETHE RUPEL SENNE DENDER ESCAUT MANJEL OURTHE SAMBRE SEMOIS VESDRE WARCHE AMBLEVE SCHELDT
TOWN: AS AAT ANS ATH HAL HUY MOL SPA AATH AMAY ASSE BOOM BREE DOEL GAND GEEL GENK GENT HOEI LIER LOOZ MONS VISE WAHA ZELE AALST ALOST ARLON CINEY EEKLO ESSEN EUPEN EVERE GENCK GHENT HEIST IEPER JETTE JUMET LIEGE NAMUR RONSE TIELT UCCLE VORST WEZET YNOIR YPRES AARLEN ANVERS BERGEN BILZEN BRUGES DEURNE ELSENE IZEGEM LEUVEN LIERRE MERXEM OPWIJK OSTEND ANTWERP ARDOOIE BERCHEM DOORWIK HERSTAL HOBOKEN IXELLES LOUVAIN MECHLIN ROULERS SERAING TONGRES TOURNAI BRUSSELS COURTRAI KORTRIJK MECHELEN MOUSCRON TONGEREN TURNHOUT VERVIERS WATERLOO
WEIGHT: LAST CARAT LIVRE POUND CHARGE CHARIOT ESTERLIN

BELIE BELONG DEFAME BESEIGE FALSIFY PERTAIN SLANDER TRADUCE DISGUISE STRUMPET SURROUND MISREPRESENT
BELIEF CRY FAY ISM LEVE MIND SECT TAKE TROW VIEW VOTE WEEN CAUSE CREDO CREED DOGMA FAITH OBEAH TENET TROTH TRUST CREDIT GROUND CRIANCE FEELING HOLDING OPINION TROWING ARYANISM BITHEISM CREDENCE DOCTRINE FINALISM HUMANISM RELIANCE THANATISM PREPOSSESSION
(— HANDED DOWN) TRADITION
(— IN DEVILS) DIABOLISM
(— IN GHOSTS) EIDOLISM
(— IN GOD) DEISM THEISM
(— IN MAGIC) OBEAH
(CONVENTIONAL —) PIETY
(FALSE —) DELUSION
(GROUNDLESS —) CANARD
(MORTAL —) HALL
(READY —) ACCEPTATION
(SHALLOW —) BALLOON
(SUPERSTITIOUS —) FREET
(TRADITIONAL —) ICON IKON EIKON
(UNFOUNDED —) FICTON
(UNIMPORTANT —) FAD
BELIEVABLE PLAUSIBLE
BELIEVE BUY WIS DEEM FEEL HOLD TAKE TREW TROW WEEN CREED FAITH FANCY GUESS JUDGE SEPAD THINK TRUST ACCEPT CREDIT ESTEEM EXPECT DARESAY SUPPOSE ACCREDIT CONSIDER CREDENCE
(— ERRONEOUSLY) FEIGN
(— NAIVELY) SWALLOW
(— UNCRITICALLY) EAT
(HARD TO —) TALL
BELIEVER IST LEVER BOTARY KITABI CREDENS ADHERENT ARMINIAN (SUFF.) ARIAN
BELIEVING CREDENT FAITHFUL
BELISARIO (CHARACTER IN —) ANTONIA EUTRIPIO BELISARIUS
(COMPOSER OF —) DONIZETTI
BELISE (BROTHER OF —) PHILAMINTE
BELITTLE DIS DUMP DECRY DWARF SNEER BEMEAN DEMEAN MINISH SLIGHT DETRACT DIMINUE LIGHTLY MINIMIZE VILIPEND DENIGRATE DISCREDIT DISPARAGE
BELITTLER ZOILUS
BELIZE (CAPITAL OF —) BELMOPAN
BELL HUB TOM CALL FAIR GONG HUBB RING ROAR CHIME CLOAK CLOCK CODON FLARE KNELL SWELL TENOR BASKET BELLOW BUBBLE CLOCHE CROTAL CURFEW PHONIC SOCKET TAPPER TOCSIN TOLLER TREBLE TRIPLE VESPER ANGELUS BLOSSOM CAMPANA CAMPANE COROLLA COWBELL JANGLER JINGLER LOWBELL SKELLAT SKILLET TAMBOUR TANTONY TINKLER CASCABEL COCKBELL DINGDONG DOORBELL HANDBELL HAWKBELL MORTBELL PAVILLON STARTLER TINGTANG
(ALARM —) TOCSIN
(CLOSED —) CROTAL
(EVENING —) CURFEW
(FUNERAL —) TELLER
(HAND —) CLAG
(LARGE —) SIGNUM
(LOWEST —) BORDON BOURDON
(PART OF —) BOW LIP HEAD CROWN MOUTH WAIST CLAPPER SHOULDER
(PASSING —) KNELL
(SACRING —) SQUILLA
(SLEIGH —) GRELOT CROTALUM
(PREF.) CAMPANI CAMPANO
BELLABELLA HAELTZUK HEILTSUK
BELLADONNA DWALE MANICON BANEWORT DAFTBERRY DWAYBERRY MYDRIATIC NIGHTSHADE
BELLARIA (HUSBAND OF —) PANDOSTO
BELLARMINE GRAYBEARD GREYBEARD LONGBEARD
BELLBIRD MAKO SHRIKE COTINGA ARAPUNGA KORIMAKO MAKOMAKO CAMPANERO
BELLBOY BUTTONS
BELLE SPARK TOAST
(SPANISH —) MAJA
BELLEEK POTTERY CHAMPAGNE
BELLE HELENE, LE (COMPOSER OF —) OFFENBACH
BELLEROPHON (FATHER OF —) GLAUCUS
(MOTHER OF —) EURYMEDE
BELLFLOWER LOBELIA RAMPION BELLWORT HASKWORT IVYBELLS MILKWORT
BELLHOP PAGE BELLBOY HALLBOY CHASSEUR
BELLICOSE MAD IRATE WARFUL HOSTILE WARLIKE MILITANT
BELLIGERENT BRISTLY HOSTILE SCRAPPY STROPPY WARLIKE CHOLERIC FIGHTING JINGOIST COMBATIVE IRASCIBLE LITIGIOUS WRANGLING PUGNACIOUS
BELLISANT (HUSBAND OF —) ALEXANDER
(SON OF —) ORSON VALENTINE
BELLOW CRY LOW MOO YAP BAWL BEAL BELL GAPE ROAR ROME ROUT YAUP YAWP BELVE BLART BLORE CROON ROUST SHOUT TROAT BULLER CLAMOR RUMMES BLUSTER RUMMISH THUNDER ULULATE
BELLOWING ROUT ROUST BELLING BLATANT BOATION MUGIENT
BELLOWS BELY LUNGS BULIES FEEDER SANDER WINKER SYLPHON WINDBAG EXPELLER
(SMALL —) PLUFF
(STORAGE —) RESERVOIR
(PREF.) PHYSA PHYSALLO PHYSO
BELLOWS FISH BUGLER SNIPEFISH
BELL RINGER TOLL YOUTH TOLLER CLINKUM
BELL-TOWER BELFRY CAMPANILE
BELLWETHER MASTER
BELLY BAG COD GIE GUT MAW POD BOUK BUNT FILL KYTE MARY WAME WEAM WOMB BINGY BOSOM BULGE FRONT GORGE PLEON TABLE THARM THERM TRIPE BAGGIE BINGEE HUNGER PAUNCH VENTER ABDOMEN BALLOON STOMACH TUMBREL APPETITE
(PREF.) CELI COELI(O) GASTER(O) GASTR(I)(O) VENTRI VENTRO
(SUFF.) GASTER GASTRIA
BELLYACHE CARP YAMMER COMPLAIN COLLYWOBBLES
BELLYBAND WANTY
BELLYING BUNTING PREGNANT
BELLY-UP BANKRUPT
BELONE SEAPIKE
BELONG BE GO FIT LIE BEAR FALL RELY APPLY BELIE GROUP AFFEIR INHERE RELATE RETAIN BEHOOVE PERTAIN APPERTAIN SUBSCRIBE
BELONGING
(SUFF.) EAE
(— TO) AR ARY EAN INE ISE ORIUM
BELONGINGS ALLS DUDS FARE GEAR GOODS TRAPS ASSETS DUFFEL DUFFLE ESTATE USINGS BAGGAGE EFFECTS CHATTELS PROPERTY PURPRISE FURNITURE HOUSEHOLD PARAPHERNALIA
BELOVED DEAR IDOL LIEF AIMEE BOSOM CHERI SWEET ADORED CHERIE MINION DARLING PRECIOUS INAMORATA INAMORATO
(MOST —) ALDERLIEFEST
BELOW ALOW BAJO DOWN ABLOW AFTER INFRA NEATH SOTTO UNDER BEHIND BENEATH
(PREF.) INFERO INFRA SUB
BELT LAS AREA BAND BEAT BLOW CEST FELT GIRD LACE LIST MARK RING SASH SLUG ZONE GIRTH MITER MITRE PATTE STRAP STRIP SWATH TRACT WAIST WHACK ZONAR ZONIC BODICE CENTER CESTUS CINGLE FETTLE GIRDLE INVEST LUNGER REGION STRAIT STRIPE SWATHE ZONNAR ZONULE BALDRIC BALTEUS CIRCUIT PASSAGE BALTHEUS CEINTURE CINCTURE CINGULUM ELEVATOR ENCIRCLE MECHANIC SURROUND CUMBERBUND CUMMERBUND
(— OF FOG) BLANKET
(AMMUNITION —) BANDOLEER BANDOLIER
(ASTROLOGICAL —) CLIMATE
(CONVEYOR —) HAUL
(ENDLESS —) APRON CREEPER
(GREEK —) ZOSTER
(HINDU SWAMP —) TERAI
(KIND OF —) VANALLEN
(MACHINE —) SWIFTER
(MINERAL —) RANGE
(PACKHORSE'S —) WANTY
(PART OF —) TIP HOLE FRAME PANEL PRONG BUCKLE FILLER KEEPER LINING PIPING TONGUE STITCHING
(TREE —) BERM BERME
(PL.) BALTEI
(PREF.) ZON(O)
BELTED ZONATE GIRDLED CINCTURED
(— WITH WHITE) SHEETED
BELUGA HUSE HUSO HAUSEN MARSOON WHITEFISH
BELUS (BROTHER OF —) AGENOR
(FATHER OF —) NEPTUNE POSEIDON
(MOTHER OF —) LIBYA EURYNOME

(SON OF —) DANAUS CEPHEUS AEGYPTUS
BELVEDERE GAZEBO LOOKOUT
BELVIDERA (FATHER OF —) PRIULI
(HUSBAND OF —) JAFFIER
BELVIDERE MIRADOR
BEMIRE DAG SOIL JARBLE
BEMOAN RUE MEAN MOAN SIGH WEEP MOURN PLAIN BEWAIL LAMENT DEPLORE
BEMUSE SOT BULL DAZE AMUSE
BEMUSED DOPY DOPEY PIXILATED MOONSTRUCK
BENAIAH (FATHER OF —) JEHOIADA
(SON OF —) PELATIAH
BENCH PEW BANC BANK BENK BERM BINK DAIS DEAS FORM MESA SEAT SILL STEP TRAM BASIN BASON BERME BREAK CABIN CHAIR FORME JUDGE PLANK STALL STOOL BANCUS BANKER SCONCE SEDILE SETTEE SETTLE SITTER COUNTER DRESSER REPOSAL SHAMBLE SITTING TRESTLE TRIBUNE ALEBENCH
(— FOR DAIRY TUBS) TRAM
(— FOR KNEADING DOUGH) BREAK
(CHURCH —) PEW
(KNEELING —) PRIEDIEU
(OUTDOOR —) EXEDRA EXHEDRA
(PLAYER'S —) WOOD
(ROWER'S —) BANK THOFT ZYGON THWART
(SHOEMAKER'S —) FORME
(TAILOR'S —) SHOPBOARD
(WORKMAN'S —) SIEGE
BEND BOW ESS NID NIP PLY SAG SET SNY WIN WRY ABOW ARCH BENT BOOL BUCK COPE CURB DOME FAUD FLEX FOLD GENU HOOK KINK LEAN LOUT PLOY RUMP TURN VERT WEEP ANGLE BATON BIGHT BREAK COUCH COUDE COURB CRANK CRIMP CRINK CROOK CULGE CURVE DROOP FLECT FRESE HINGE HUNCH INBOW KNEEL PLASH PLICA QUIRL ROUND SCRAG SKELP SLANT STOOP TREND TWINE TWIST BOUGHT BUCKLE CAMBER CONVEX COTICE CROUCH SPRING COMPASS FLEXURE RECLINE GENUFLECT
(— IN) INFLECT
(— IN HANDRAIL) RAMP
(— IN PIPE) TRAP DIPTRAP
(— IN REVERENCE) PROSTRATE
(— IN SHIP'S TIMBER) SNY
(— KNEE) KNUCKLE
(RIVER —) OXBOW
(SUFF.) FLECT(ION) FLEX(ION)
BENDER BUM JAG LEG BUST KNEE TEAR DRUNK SPREE BRIDGE WHOPPER GUZZLING SIXPENCE BRANNIGAN INFLECTOR
BENDING BOW SAG KNEE KNOT PLIE CROOK CURVE LITHE TWIST PLIANT SUPPLE TWISTY ANFRACT FLEXION HOGGING SINUOUS BUCKLING FLECTION
(— DOWNWARD) RECLINATE
(— OF ROCK) DRAG
(BALLET —) PLIE
(PREF.) SPHINGO
BENDLETS FRET
BENDY TREE MIRO MAHOE
BENEATH ALOW ANETH BELOW LOWER UNDER ANEATH
(PREF.) HYPO INFRA SUB
BENEDICITE BENISON CANTICLE
BENEDICT NEOGAMIST
BENEDICTINE CLUNIAC CAMALDOLESE TIRONENSIAN
BENEDICTION ABOT AMEN ABOTH NANDI AMIDAH BROCHO PRAYER BENISON BERAKAH BLESSING
BENEFACTION ALMS BOON GIFT PRESENT DONATION GRATUITY
BENEFACTOR AGENT ANGEL DONOR FRIEND HELPER PATRON SAVIOR MAECENAS PROMOTER
BENEFICE FEE FEU FEUD FIEF FAVOR SCARF CURACY LIVING BENEFIT CANONRY PRELACY RECTORY TOTQUOT DONATIVE KINDNESS SINECURE VICARAGE PLURALITY
BENEFICENCE BOON GIFT GRACE BOUNTY CHARITY GOODNESS KINDNESS
BENEFICENT KINDLY AMIABLE BENEFIC GRACIOUS
BENEFICIAL GOOD USEFUL HEALTHY HELPFUL BONITARY SALUTARY SANATIVE SINGULAR AVAILABLE BENIGNANT DESIRABLE ENJOYABLE HEALTHFUL LUCRATIVE REWARDING WHOLESOME PROFITABLE
BENEFICIARY HEIR USER DONEE CESTUI CESTUY USUARY VASSAL LEGATEE FEUDATORY
(SUFF.) EE
BENEFIT AID USE BOON BOOT GAIN GIFT GOOD HELP PERK PROW SAKE AVAIL BOOST FRUIT SELTH STEAD VISIT ASSIST BEHALF BEHOOF BETTER FRINGE PROFIT SALUTE USANCE ADVANCE BESPEAK CONCERT DESERVE IMPROVE SERVICE UTILITY BEFRIEND INTEREST
(— SUCCESSFULLY) FLY
BENEVOLENCE JEN BOUNTY GOODNESS GOODWILL HUMANITY
BENEVOLENT GOOD KIND BENIGN KINDLY LOVING AMIABLE LIBERAL GENEROUS AVUNCULAR BENIGNANT ALTRUISTIC PROPITIOUS HUMANITARIAN PHILANTHROPIC
(WEAKLY —) GOODYGOODY
BENHANAN (FATHER OF —) SHIMON
BEN HUR (AUTHOR OF —) WALLACE
(CHARACTER IN —) HUR IRAS JUDAH ESTHER TIRZAH MESSALA BALTHASAR SIMONIDES
BENIGN BOON GOOD KIND MILD BLAND SWEET TRINE GENIAL GENTLE AFFABLE BENEFIC BENEDICT GRACIOUS INNOCENT SALUTARY FAVORABLE WHOLESOME
BENIGNANT KIND BLAND GENIAL LIBERAL GRACIOUS MERCIFUL
BENIN (CAPITAL OF —) PORTONOVO
(TOWN IN —) COTONOU
BENISON BOON BENEDICTION
BENJAMIN BENZOIN
(FATHER OF —) HARIM JACOB BILHAN
(MOTHER OF —) RACHEL
(SON OF —) ARD EHI BELA GERA ROSH ASHBEL BECHER HUPPIM MUPPIM NAAMAN
BENNET CLOVEWORT
BENNISEED SESAME
BENO TUBA
BENT AIM BOW SET BIAS CAST CURB GIFT TURN BANDY BOUND BOWED BOWLY COUDE COURB CRANK CRUMP FLAIR HUMOR KNACK LURCH PRONE SQUAT SWING TASTE TREND AKIMBO ANLAGE BENNET BIASED BRACED COURBE COURSE CURVED DOGLEG ENERGH GENIUS HOOKED INTENT LIKING NECKED SQUINT SWAYED TALENT ADUNCAL ARCUATE BUCKLED CROOKED CURVANT EMBOWED FLEXION FLEXURE IMPETUS INTENSE LEANING LEVELED PRONATE PURPOSE STOOPED TENSION ADUNCOUS APTITUDE ARCUATED CRUMPLED DECLINED FLECTION IMMINENT INFLEXED PENCHANT REFLEXED TENDENCY
(— AT THE END) HAMATE HOGGED GRYPANIAN
(— DOWNWARD) BOWED DECURVED INCUMBENT RECLINATE
(— IN) INCAVATE
(— INWARD) ADUNC
(— OF MIND) GEME AFFECTION
(EASILY —) LITHY
(NATURAL —) SWING
(SPECIAL —) VERVE
(PREF.) ANKYL(O) CAMPTO CURVI CYPH(O) CYRT(O) SCOLIO
BEN-TEAK NANDI NANAWOOD
BENT-GRASS FIBRIN REDTOP
BENUMB NIP DAZE DUNT NUMB STUN CHILL DAVER DOZEN SCRAM SHRAM CUMBER DEADEN PERISH STOUND BINOMEN FRETISH FRETIZE STIFFEN STUPEFY TORPEDO TORPEFY
BENUMBED CHILL SCRAM ASLEEP CLUMSE CLUMSY FROZEN TORPID CLUMPST SHRAMMED
BENUMBING LEADEN
BENVENUTO CELLINI (CHARACTER IN —) POMPEO TERESA ASCANIO CELLINI BALDUCCI SALVIATA BENVENUTO FIERAMOSCA
(COMPOSER OF —) BERLIOZ
BENZAYDA (LOVER OF —) OZWY
BENZENE PHENE BENZIN BENZOL PHENENE
(SUFF.) PHEN(E)
BENZINE
(PREF.) PHEN(O)
BENZOIN BENJOIN LINDERA BENJAMIN FIXATIVE
(SUFF.) OIN
BEOR (SON OF —) BELA BALAAM
BEOWULF (AUTHOR OF —) UNKNOWN
(CHARACTER IN —) WIGLAF BEOWULF GRENDEL HIGELAC UNFERTH AESCHERE HONDSCIO HROTHGAR
BEQUEATH GIVE WILL ENDOW LEAVE OFFER BESTOW COMMIT DEMISE DEVISE LEGATE QUETHE BEQUEST COMMEND TRANSMIT
BEQUEST GIFT WILL LEGACY BEQUEATH HERITAGE PITTANCE ENDOWMENT BENEFACTION
BERACHIAH (SON OF —) ASAPH
BERAIAH (FATHER OF —) SHIMHI
BERATE JAW NAG DRUB LASH RAIL ABUSE BASTE CHIDE SCOLD SCORE SLATE REVILE CENSURE REPROVE UPBRAID CHASTISE
BERBER RIF RIFF KABYL SHLUH KABYLE SHILHA HARATIN MZABITE SHILLUH HARRATIN MOZABITE
(— CHIEF) CAID
BERCEUSE CRADLESONG WIEGENLIED
BEREAVE ROB STRIP WIDOW DIVEST SADDEN DEPRIVE DESPOIL
BEREAVED ORB BEREFT VIDUOUS WIDOWED DESOLATE
BEREAVEMENT ORBITY ORBITUDE VIDUATION
BERECHIAH (SON OF —) ASAPH MESHULLAM ZECHARIAH
BEREFT ORB LORN LOST POOR QUIT WIDOW ORBATE FORLORN FORFAIRN DESTITUTE
BERG FLOE BARROW ICEBERG FLOEBERG
BERGAMOT BOSE BERGAMA BURGAMOT
BERGERE SEAT
BERGYLT ROSEFISH
BERI (FATHER OF —) ZOPHAH
BERIAH (FATHER OF —) ASHER EPHRAIM
BERIBERI KAKKE
BERITH BRIS BRISS BRITH
BERM BERME LISIERE HEELPATH
BERMUDA PETREL CAHOW
BERNICE (FATHER OF —) HEROD
BERRY BAY DEW HAW ALEY BEAT CRAN POHA RASP BACCA BLACK CUBEB FRUIT GRAIN GRAPE LANSA MOUND SALAL SAVIN BURROW LANSAT LANSEH SABINE THRESH CURRANT ETAERIO HILLOCK ACROSARC ALLSPICE COWBERRY DEWBERRY HAWEBAKE PERSIMMON POKEBERRY SASKATOON PEPPERCORN SHEEPBERRY POMEGRANATE
(ACID —) CURRANT
(COFFEE —) CHERRY
(DRIED —) PASA
(JUMPER —) ABHAL
(LAUREL —) BAY
(POISONOUS —) BANEBERRY
(PREF.) BACCI COCC(I)(O)
BERRY-LIKE BACCATE ACINIFORM
BERTH BED JOB BUNK DOCK SLIP SOPT CABIN PLACE UPPER BILLET OFFICE SECURE LODGING

MOORING SLIPWAY POSITION ANCHORAGE
BERTHA **(FATHER OF —)** CARIBERT
(HUSBAND OF —) PEPIN HEREWARD
(SON OF —) CHARLES
BERYL EMERALD AEROIDES HELIODOR GOSHENITE MORGANITE AQUAMARINE
BERYLLIA GLUCINA GLUCINE
BERYLLIUM GLUCINUM
BESEECH ASK BEG BID CRY SUE WOO PRAY CRAVE HALSE PLEAD PRESS ADJURE APPEAL OBTEST CONJURE ENTREAT IMPLORE SOLICIT IMPETRATE OBSECRATE
BESET PLY SET SIT BEGO SAIL STUD ALLOT BELAY BIGAN HARRY PRESS SIEGE SPEND STEAD ASSAIL ATTACK HARASS INFEST OBSESS WAYLAY ARRANGE BESIEGE OVERSET PERPLEX BLOCKADE ENCUMBER ENTHRONG OBSTRUCT SURROUND BELEAGUER
(— WITH DIFFICULTIES) SCABROUS
BESHOW SKIL CUDDY CUDDEN CUDDIE BADDOCK COALFISH SKILFISH
BESIDE BY HEAR INBY NEXT ALONG ANENT ASIDE FORBY ABREAST AGAINST FORNENT ADJACENT FORNENST
(— ONE ANOTHER) ABREAST
(— ONESELF) FEY
(PREF.) EPH EPI PAR(A)
BESIDES BY TO AND BUT TOO YET ALSO ELSE MORE OVER PLUS THEN UNTO WITH ABOVE AGAIN FORBY SUPRA BESIDE BEYOND EXCEPT FORBYE WITHAL THERETO WITHOUT LIKEWISE MOREOVER
(PREF.) EPH EPI PROS
BESIEGE GIRD GIRT BELAY BELIE BESET SIEGE STORM ATTACK OBSESS OBSIDE PESTER PLAGUE COMPASS SOLICIT SURROUND BELEAGUER
BESMEAR RAY BALM DAUB SOIL APPLY COVER GRIME GRUFT MUDDY SLAKE SMEAR SULLY TAINT BEDAUB PLATCH BESLIME SMOTHER BESMIRCH BESLUBBER
BESMIRCH TAR DASH SLUR SOIL SMEAR SULLY TAINT SLURRY SMIRCH ASPERSE BLACKEN DRAGGLE TURPIFY DISCOLOR
BESMIRCHED MACULATE MACULATED
BESMUT CROCK
BESOM COW MAP DRAB BISME BROOM SWEEP SLOVEN HEATHER
BESOT DULL ASOTE ASSOT MUDDLE STUPID STUPEFY BEFUDDLE
BESOTTED BEDAZED DRUNKEN INFATUATED
BESPANGLE DOT STAR STUD ADORN JEWEL INVENT SPRINKLE
BESPATTER BLOT DASH JAUP SOIL SPOT MUDDY PLASH STAIN SULLY BEGARY SPARGE ASPERSE SCATTER SMOTTER REPROACH SPRINKLE
BESPEAK CITE HINT SHOW ARGUE IMPLY ORDER SPEAK TRYST ACCOST ATTEST ENGAGE STEVEN ADDRESS ARRANGE BENEFIT BETOKEN DISCUSS EXCLAIM RESERVE FORETELL INDICATE
BESPECKLE DASH
BESPECTACLED SPECCY
BESPRINKLE DROP SHED POWDER ASPERSE BESTREW BESPRING SPRINKLE BEQUIRTLE
BEST O ACE BEAT GOOD LACE MOST PICK TOPS WALE CREAM ELITE EXCEL PRIZE WORST CHOICE DEFEAT FINEST FLOWER OUTWIT SUNDAY TIPTOP UTMOST ARISTOS CONQUER GARLAND LARGEST OPTIMUM PALMARY DAMNDEST GREATEST KOHINOOR OUTMATCH OUTSTRIP POSSIBLE TOPNOTCH VANQUISH
(SUNDAY —) BRAWS
(PREF.) ARIST(O)
BESTIAL LOW VILE WILD BRUTE FERAL PRONE BRUTAL FILTHY BEASTLY BRUTISH INHUMAN SENSUAL BARBARIC BELLUINE DEPRAVED
BESTIR STIR AWAKE SHIFT STEER AROUSE HUSTLE
(— ONESELF) LEG
BEST MAN PARANYMPH
BESTOW ADD PUT USE CAST DEAL DOTE GIVE SEND STOW TAKE WARE ALLOT ALLOW APPLY AWARD BESET GRANT INFER LODGE PLACE SPEND THOLE WREAK ACCORD BETEEM CONFER DEMISE DEVOTE DIVIDE DONATE DOTATE EMPLOY ENTAIL ESTATE EXTEND IMPART IMPOSE RENDER SHOWER COLLATE COMMEND DISPOSE ENLARGE EROGATE INDULGE INSTATE PARTAKE PRESENT QUARTER TRIBUTE BEQUEATH
(— LAVISHLY) HEAP
(— UPON) GIFT
BESTOWAL DOLE DISPOSAL COLLATION LARGITION
(— OF PRAISE) ACCOLADE
BESTOWED GIVEN
BESTRIDE HORSE STRIDE STRADDLE OVERSTRIDE
BET GO UP BAS BOX LAY PUT SET VIE WAD ANTE BACK BRAG CHIP GAGE HOLD JACK NOIR PAIR PLAY PLOT PUNT RISK WAGE BOUND CARRE HEDGE ROUGE SAVER SPORT STAKE WAGER GAMBLE HAZARD IMPAIR MANQUE MILIEU PLEDGE DERNIER PREMIER ACCUMULATOR
(— AGAINST) MILK COPPER
(— AT LONG ODDS) SKINNER
(— BOLDLY) BLUFF
(— CHIP) CHECK
(FARO —) SLEEPER
(HEDGING —) SAVER
(MULTIPLE —) PARLAY
(POKER —) BLIND
(RACE —) WIN SHOW PLACE DOUBLE EXACTA PARLAY TRIPLE TRIFECTA
(RACING —) WIN SHOW PLACE DOUBLE EXACTA PARLAY TRIPLE PERFECTA QUINELLA TRIFECTA
(UP THE —) RAISE
BETA AND GAMMA GUARDS
BETA-BLOCKER TIMOLOL
BETAKE GO GET HIE MOVE TAKE APPLY CATCH GRANT ASSUME COMMIT REMOVE REPAIR RESORT COMMEND JOURNEY WITHDRAW
(— ONESELF) BUN HIT BOUN MARK PIKE TEEM AVOID FOUND HAUNT REFER TRUSS YIELD
(— ONESELF TO MILL) SUE
BETEL PAN IKMO ITMO SERI SIRI SIRIH PINANG PUPULO
BETEL LEAF PAN BUYO PAUN PAWNE
BETEL NUT BONGA BONYA BUNGA SUPARI
BETHABARA NOIBWOOD GREENHEART
BETHEL BETHESDA
BETHINK TAKE THINK ADVISE DEVISE RECALL REFLECT CONSIDER REMEMBER RECOLLECT
(— ONE'S SELF) MIN MINE UMBETHINK
BETHLEHEM BEDLAM
BETHROOT TRILLIUM
BETHUEL **(DAUGHTER OF —)** REBEKAH
(FATHER OF —) NAHOR
(MOTHER OF —) MILCAH
(UNCLE OF —) ABRAHAM
BETHUMP POUND PUMMEL LOUNDER
BETIDE HAP TIDE BEFIT OCCUR TRITE WORTH BECOME BEFALL CHANCE HAPPEN BETOKEN PRESAGE
BETIMES ANON RATH SOON EARLY RATHE TIMEOUS SPEEDILY FORTHWITH
BETOKEN MARK NOTE SHOW SIGN AUGUR TOKEN ASSERT BETIDE DENOTE EVINCE IMPORT SHADOW BESPEAK EXPRESS OBLIQUE PORTEND PRESAGE SIGNIFY FOREBODE FORESHOW INDICATE
BETONY BROOMWORT
BETRAY BLAB BLOW BOIL GULL SELL SHOP SILE SING SPOT TELL TRAY UNDO WRAY ABUSE CROSS FALSE PEACH ROUND SPILL SPLIT SWICK SWIKE ACCUSE BEWRAY DELUDE DESCRY DESERT QUATCH REVEAL SEDUCE SNITCH SQUEAL BEGUILE DECEIVE FALSIFY MISLEAD PROMOTE TRAITOR DISCLOSE DISCOVER
(— CONFIDENCES) SPILL
BETRAYAL RAP ABUSE ACCUSE TREASON GIVEAWAY PRODITION
BETRAYER RAT JUDAS SKUNK SEDUCER TRAITOR DERELICT RECREANT SQUEALER
BETRAYING TELLTALE
BETROTH AFFY EARL TOKEN TROTH TRUTH ASSURE ENGAGE ENSURE PLEDGE PLIGHT ESPOUSE PROMISE AFFIANCE CONTRACT DESPOUSE HANDFAST
BETROTHAL ESPOUSAL HANDFAST
BETROTHED SURE VOWED ASSURED ENGAGED HANDFAST INTENDED COMBINATE
(AUTHOR OF —) MANZONI
(CHARACTER IN —) LUCIA RENZO RODRIGO ABBONDIO BORROMEO CRISTOFORO
BETTA PLAKAT
BETTER AID TOP BEET MEND AMEND EMEND EXCEL SAFER WISER BIGGER EXCEED REFORM ADVANCE CHOICER CORRECT GREATER IMPROVE PROMOTE RECTIFY RELIEVE SUPPORT SURPASS EMINENCE INCREASE SUPERIOR
(— A SCORE) BREAK
(— THAN ORDINARY) EXTRA
BETTING ACTION GAMBLING
(— ARRANGEMENT) PERM
(— SYSTEM) PAROLI ALEMBERT
BETTOR ORALER
BETTY JENNY COTBETTY JOCRISSE MOLLYCOT WIFECARL
BETWEEN AMID EMEL AMELL AMONG ENTRE TWEEN YTWYN ATWEEN ATWIXT TWEESH AVERAGE BETWIXT
(PREF.) DI INTER INTRA
BEUDANITE CORKITE
BEVEL BLOW CANT CONE EDGE PUSH REAM ANGLE BEARD BEZEL MITER MITRE SLANT SLOPE SNAPE SPLAY ASLANT CIPHER RHYMER CHAMFER INCLINE OBLIQUE
(— EDGES) BEARD
(WITHOUT —) FLAT
BEVERAGE ADE ALE AVA CUP NOG POP RUM SAP TEA BEER BREW CHIA GROG MABI MATE MEAD MILK NIPA SODA WHIG WINE CHOCA CIDER CLARY COCOA DRAFT DRINK JULEP LAGER LEBAN MORAT MULSE NEGUS PUNCH SHRUB SMASH TREAT TWIST WATER BISHOP COFFEE EGGNOG LIQUID LIQUOR NECTAR PORTER SPRUCE TISWIN BUNNELL CASSINA CORDIAL LIMEADE OENOMEL POTABLE STEPONY TULAPAI ALEBERRY COCKTAIL LEMONADE LIBATION PIQUETTE POTATION SANGAREE SWITCHEL BADMINTON CALIBOGUS CHOCOLATE GINGERADE ORANGEADE POMPERKIN SOMETHING
(— FROM COW'S MILK) KEFIR KEPHIR
(— FROM PEPPERS) KAVA KAVAKAVA
(— FROM SAP) TUBA
(— OF BUTTERMILK AND WATER) BLAND
(— OF CHAMPAGNE) POPE
(— OF GODS) NECTAR
(— OF HONEY AND WATER) HYDROMEL METHEGLIN
(— OF HOT MILK) POSSET
(— OF PORT WINE) BISHOP

(— OF VINEGAR AND WATER) POSCA
(— OF WINE AND WATER) SPRITZER
(ALCOHOLIC —) DEW ARAK SAKE SAKI ARRAK BASIG SHRUB SNAPS STUFF ARRACK FIREWATER STIMULANT
(COLA —) DOPE
(EFFERVESCENT —) FIZZ
(FERMENTED —) BASI KAVA KUMYS KUMISS
(FRUIT —) BEVERAGE
(INSIPID —) WASH
(JAPANESE —) SAKE SAKI
(MEXICAN —) TEPACHE
(POLYNESIAN —) AVA KAVA
(WEAK —) LAP
(PL.) WAIPIRO

BEVY HERD PACK COVEY DROVE FLOCK GROUP SWARM FLIGHT SCHOOL COMPANY

BEWAIL CRY RUE WEY KEEN MOAN RAME SIGH WAIL WEEP MOURN PLAIN BEMOAN GRIEVE LAMENT PLAINT SORROW THROPE DEPLORE COMPLAIN

BEWARE WAR CAVE GARE HEED SHUN TENT WARD AVOID SPEND ESCHEW WARNING

BEWILDER FOG FOX MAR BEAT DAZE FOIL GAUM MAZE STUN ABASH ADDLE AMAZE AMUSE DEAVE DIZZY BAFFLE BEMIST BEMUSE BOTHER DAZZLE DUDDER MOIDER MOMBLE MUDDLE PUZZLE WANDER WILDER BUFFALO BUMBAZE CONFUSE FLASKER MYSTIFY NONPLUS PERPLEX STAGGER STUPEFY ASTONISH CONFOUND DISTRACT ENTANGLE OVERMUSE SQUATTER SURPRISE
(PREF.) PLAZO

BEWILDERED MAR ASEA LOST MANG WILL AGAPE ATSEA DAZED MAZED MUZZY BUSHED MAPPED BEMAZED STUPENT WILSOME CONFUSED HELPLESS WILLYARD PERPLEXED

BEWILDERMENT AWE FOG DAZE MISMAZE STICKLE AMAZEMENT CONFUSION PERPLEXITY

BEWITCH HEX WISH BLINK CHARM MAGIC OBEAH SPELL WITCH ENAMOR ENTICE GLAMOR GRIGRI HOODOO STRIKE THRILL ATTRACT BEDEVIL DELIGHT ENCHANT GLAMOUR ENSORCEL FORSPEAK GREEGREE OVERLOOK

BEWITCHED RAPT ENRAPT HAGGED

BEWITCHING SIREN

BEYOND BY FREE OVER YOND ABOVE ASIDE AYOND FORBY ULTRA BEHIND BEYANT YONDER BENEATH BESIDES FORTHBY FURTHER OUTGATE PASSING WITHOUT OVERMORE SUPERIOR HEREAFTER
(— CONTROL) MASTERLESS
(— DOUBT) ASSURED
(— HOPE) DESPERATE
(— ORDINARY METHODS) AFIELD
(— THE MARK) GONE
(— THE MOUNTAINS) TRAMONTANE
(— THE SEA) ULTRAMARINE
(— THIS) STILL
(GO —) OVERSHOOT
(PREF.) EXTRA HYPER META OVER PARA PERI PRETER SUPER TRANS ULTRA

BEYOND HUMAN POWER
(AUTHOR OF —) BJORNSON
(CHARACTER IN —) SANG CLARA ELIAS HANNA ADOLPH RACHAEL ROBERTS

BEZALEEL (FATHER OF —) URI

BEZANT SOLIDUS

BEZEL RIM TOP EDGE OUCH SEAL BEVIL BEZIL CROWN FACET CHATON FLANGE MARQUISE TEMPLATE

BEZER (FATHER OF —) ZOPHAH

BEZIQUE PENCHANT

BEZOAR GOATSTONE HIPPOLITH

B-GIRL SITTER

BHAKTA BHAGAVATA

BHANG BANG BENG BENJ HEMP HASHISH

BHARAL TUR HALL NAHOOR BURRHEL

BHARTRIHARI (BROTHER OF —) VIKRAMADITYA

BHIKSHU GELONG

BHIMA (FATHER OF —) VAYU PANDU
(MOTHER OF —) KUNTI PRITHA

BHUTAN (ASSEMBLY OF —) TSONGDU
(CAPITAL OF —) THIMPHU
(COIN OF —) CHETRUM
(CURRENCY OF —) PAISA RUPEE CHETRUM NGULTRUM
(LANGUAGE OF —) DZONGKHA
(MONEY OF —) NGULTRUM
(RIVER OF —) MACHU MANAS AMOCHU

BHUTAN PINE KAIL

BIANCA (HUSBAND OF —) FAZIO LEONTIO
(SISTER OF —) KATHERINE

BIANNUAL BIYEARLY

BIANOR (FATHER OF —) TIBERIS
(MOTHER OF —) MANTO

BIAS PLY WRY AWRY BENT CANT SWAY WARP AMISS COLOR FAVOR POISE SLANT SLOPE SWING TWIST BIGOTRY INCLINE OBLIQUE SUGGEST CLINAMEN COLORING DIAGONAL TENDENCY PREJUDICE PROCEDURE SPECTACLE
(— IN NEWS REPORTING) PLUGOLA
(BROTHER OF —) MELAMPUS
(FATHER OF —) AMYTHAON
(MOTHER OF —) IDOMENE
(WIFE OF —) PERO IPHIANASSA

BIASED SLANT ANGLED COLORED OBLIQUE PARTIAL SLANTED
(— ONE) BIGOT

BIB SIP BRAT POUT APRON BLAIN DRINK BRASSY FEEDER TIPPLE TUCKER BAVETTE
(CHILD'S —) BISHOP
(LEATHER —) DICK

BIBLE BOOK ITALA VULGATE SCRIPTURE
(— TEXT) MIKRA MIQRA
(BOOK OF —) EX CHR COL COR DAN EPH GAL GEN HAB HAG HEB HOS JER JOB KIN LAM LEV MAL MIC NAH NEH NUM PET REV ROM SAM TIM ACTS AMOS CANT DEUT EZEK EZRA JOEL JOHN JUDE JUDG LUKE MARK MATT OBAD PHIL PROV RUTH SONG ZECH ZEPH HOSEA JAMES JONAH KINGS MICAH NAHUM PETER THESS TITUS DANIEL ECCLES ESTHER EXODUS HAGGAI ISAIAH JOSHUA JUDGES PHILEM PSALMS ROMANS SAMUEL EZEKIEL GENESIS HEBREWS MALACHI MATTHEW NUMBERS OBADIAH TIMOTHY JEREMIAH NEHEMIAH PHILEMON PROVERBS CANTICLES EPHESIANS GALATIANS LEVITICUS ZECHARIAH ZEPHANIAH CHRONICLES COLOSSIANS REVELATION CORINTHIANS DEUTERONOMY PHILIPPIANS ECCLESIASTES LAMENTATIONS THESSALONIANS
(SYRIAC VERSION OF —) PESHITO

BIBLE LEAF COSTMARY

BIBULOUS DRINKING BIBACIOUS

BICEPS HAMSTRING

BICKER JAR WAR BOWL SPAR TIFF ARGUE BRAWL CAVIL FIGHT SCRAP ASSAIL ATTACK BATTLE CONTEND DISPUTE PICKEER QUARREL QUIBBLE WRANGLE PETTIFOG SKIRMISH SQUABBLE

BICKERN ANVIL BEAKIRON

BICUSPID PREMOLAR

BICYCLE BIKE QUAD CORGI CORGY CYCLE HOBBY MOUNT STEED WHEEL JIGGER ORNARY SAFETY TANDEM ORDINAR TRIPLET ORDINARY ROADSTER TENSPEED
(— FOR TWO) TANDEM
(— MANEUVER) WHEELIE
(PART OF —) ARM LUG RIM CLIP FORK POST RACK RING SEAT STAY STEM TIRE CHAIN GUARD PEDAL SHIFT SPOKE FENDER HANGER SADDLE DOWNTUBE SPROCKET CHAINWHEEL DERAILLEUR
(PLACE WHERE —S ARE SERVICED) CYCLERY
(STATIONARY —) EXERCYCLE

BID GO BEG NAP BEDE BODE CALL GIVE HEST HIST PRAY TELL WISH CHEAP CLEPE FRAGE OFFER ORDER ADJURE CHARGE DIRECT ENJOIN INVITE REVEAL SIMPLE SUMMON TENDER BALANCE CHEAPEN COMMAND DECLARE DROPVIE ENTREAT PROFFER ANNOUNCE PROCLAIM PROPOSAL
(— ADIEU) TEACH
(— AT AUCTION) CRY
(— IN CARDS) CUE FROG JUMP PASS SKIP SOLO FRAGE GRAND NULLO SHIFT BOSTON DEFEND DEMAND DENIAL DOUBLE SMUDGE BLUCHER COMMAND SHUTOUT SUPPORT CONTRACT REDOUBLE SCHMEISS
(FIRST —) OPENER OPENERS
(MAKE FIRST —) OPEN
(SEALED —) TICKET

BIDDING BEHEST AUCTION BIDDANCE DIRECTIVE

BIDE FACE STAY WAIT ABIDE AWAIT DWELL TARRY WATCH ENDURE REMAIN SUFFER SOJOURN CONTINUE TOLERATE

BIDENS CUCKOLD MANZANILLA

BIDET SITZBAD INSESSION

BIDRI VIDRY BIDDERY TUTENAG

BIENNIAL TRIETERIC

BIER BEAR PYRE FRAME GRAVE HANDY HORSE TABUT COFFIN HEARSE LITTER SUPPORT FERETORY FERETRUM

BIFURCATION WYE FORK SPLIT BRANCH CROTCH CRUTCH FORKING DIVISION DICHOTOMY

BIG FAT BARO BOLD HUGE MUCH VAST BULKY CHIEF GAUCY GRAND GREAT GROSS HUSKY LARGE GAUCIE MIGHTY BIGGISH BUMPING EMINENT HUMMING LEADING MASSIVE POMPOUS UPRIGHT VIOLENT BOASTFUL BOUNCING ENORMOUS GENEROUS GIGANTIC IMPOSING PLUMPING PREGNANT SLAPPING SWANKING SWAPPING THUMPING
(— C) CANCER
(— WITH YOUNG) FULL GRAVID
(FAIRLY —) TIDY
(MARVELOUSLY —) TREMENDOUS
(VERY-) SKELPING SLASHING
(PREF.) MAGNI

BIGFOOT SASQUATCH

BIGHORN ARGAL AOUDAD ARGALI CIMARRON

BIGHT BAY BEND BITE COIL GULF LOOP ROVE ANGLE CURVE INLET NOOSE BOUGHT CORNER HOLLOW POCKET

BIGMOUTH BLAB

BIGNESS BULK

BIGOT CAFARD ZEALOT FANATIC MUMPSIMUS

BIGOTED BIASED NARROW HIDEBOUND ILLIBERAL SECTARIAN

BIGOTRY INTOLERANCE

BIGROOT MANROOT BITTERROOT

BIG SHOT HEAVY MUCKAMUCK

BIG SKY COUNTRY MONTANA

BIGWIG SWELL

BIKE (KIND OF —) MOTOR TRAIL

BIKINI TANGA
(TOPLESS —) MONOKINI

BILE BOIL GALL HUMP VENOM CHOLER GROWTH RANCOR ATRABILE MELANCHOLY
(PREF.) BILI CHOL(E)(O)
(SUFF.) CHOLIA CHOLY

BILGE PUMP SCUM BOUGE BULGE BILLAGE THURROCK

BILHAH (SON OF —) DAN NAPHTALI

BILHAN (FATHER OF —) JEDIAEL

BILIMBI CAMIAS KAMIAS CUCUMBER

BILINGUAL DIGLOT

BILIOUS GALLISH LIVERISH

BILIOUSNESS LIVER CHOLER

BILK DO GYP BALK DUPE HOAX CHEAT COZEN TRICK DELUDE FLEECE SWEDGE DECEIVE DEFRAUD SWINDLE

BILL ACT DUN GET LAW NEB NIB TAB BEAK CHIT CLAP GETT KITE NOTE PECK SHOT CHECK ENTRY LIBEL SCORE VISOR CARESS CHARGE DOCKET INDICT LAWING PECKER PICKAX POSTER STRIKE DERTRUM INVOICE LAMPOON MATTOCK PLACARD PROGRAM REMANET STATUTE BILLHOOK DOCUMENT HEADLAND INNOCENT PETITION TREASURY RECKONING ACCEPTANCE
(— OF ANCHOR) PEE PEAK
(— OF COMPLAINT) QUERELA
(— OF CREDIT) ANGEL
(— OF DIVORCE) GET GETT
(— OF EXCHANGE) SOLA HUNDI DEVISE
(— OF FARE) MENU CARTE
(— OF PARCELS) FACTURE
(ACCOMMODATION —) KITE
(COUNTERFEIT —S) STIFF
(DOLLAR —) BUCK SPOT SINGLE FROGSKIN
(POSTPONED —) REMANET
(REVOLUTIONARY —) ASSIGNAT
(TAVERN —) RECKONING
(10-DOLLAR —) TEN TENNER SAWBUCK
(100-DOLLAR —) CENTURY
(2-DOLLAR —) DEUCE
(5-DOLLAR —) FIN VEE FIVE FIVER
BILLET BAR GAD HUT LAY LOG LOOP NOTE PASS POST SPOT BERTH ENROL HOUSE LODGE ORDER SHIDE SPRAG STICK STRAP BALLOT BULLET COUPON ENROLL HARBOR LETTER LIBBET NOTICE TICKET BEARING EPISTLE MISSIVE POLLACK COALFISH DOCUMENT FIREWOOD ORNAMENT POSITION QUARTERS
(— SOLDIERS) CESS
BILLET-DOUX CAPON
BILLETING LIVERY
BILLFISH GAR LONGJAWS SAILFISH SPEARFISH
BILLFOLD WALLET NOTECASE
BILLHOOK BILL DHAW HOOK PAWPAW SLASHER SNAGGER SCIMITAR
BILLIARD (— STROKE) LAG
(KIND OF — SHOT) BANK CAROM
BILLIARD BALL IVORY
BILLIARD CUE MACE MAST
(TIP OF —) LEATHER
BILLIARDS PILLS TRUCKS
(— SHOT) CAROM
(LAWN —) TROCO
BILLIKEN MASCOT
BILLINGSGATE ABUSE SLAPDASH
BILLION MILLIARD
(PREF.) GIGA
BILLIONTH
(PREF.) BICRO NANO
BILL OF MARRIAGE (CHARACTER IN —) MILL FANNY SLOOK TOBIAS EDOARDO
(COMPOSER OF —) ROSSINI
BILLON BAIOC VELLON BAJOCCO
BILLOW SEA BLOW WAVE BULGE CLOUD FLOAT SURGE SWELL RESACA RIPPLE ROLLER WALLOW BREAKER UNDULATE
BILLY CAW CHAP CLUB GOAT MACE MATE BATON FANNY NEDDY CUDGEL FANNIE FELLOW BROTHER COMRADE BILLIKIN BILLYCAN BLUDGEON JACKSHAY BLACKJACK TRUNCHEON
BILLY BUDD (CHARACTER IN —) BUDD VERE BILLY CLAGGART
(COMPOSER OF —) BRITTEN
BILLYCOCK DERBY
BILSHAN (COMPANION OF —) ZERUBBABEL
BIMAH ALMEMAR ALMEMOR
BIMHAL (FATHER OF —) JAPHLET
BIN ARK BOX CUB GUM BING BONE CART CRIB VINA FRAME HUTCH KENCH PUNGI STALL STORE WAGON BASKET BUNKER GARNER HAMPER MANGER POCKET TROUGH WITHIN BLEACHER
(— FOR CEMENT) SILO
(— FOR FISH) KENCH
(— FOR GRAIN) ARK
BINARY HYDRIDE
BINATE DUAL DOUBLE PAIRED COUPLED TWOFOLD GEMINATE
BINAURAL DIOTIC
BIND JAM LAP TIE WAP EARL FAST FRAP GIRD GYVE HOLD HOOP JOIN KNIT KNOT LASH MAIL NAIL TAPE YERK BRACE CADGE CHAIN CINCH EDDER GIRTH SNAKE STICK STRAP TRUSS ATTACH BUNDLE COMMIT EMBIND ENGAGE FETTER FREEZE GARTER GIRDLE LIGATE OBLIGE PICKLE STRAIN SWATHE TETHER WRITHE ARTICLE ASTRAIN BANDAGE CONFINE EMBOUND ENCHAIN GRAPPLE SHACKLE SWADDLE ASTRINGE CONCLUDE FLIGHTER HANDFAST INNODATE LIGATURE OBLIGATE RESTRAIN
(— A FALCON) MAIL
(— BY LEASE) THIRL
(— BY OATH) SACRAMENT
(— BY PLEDGE) GAGE SWEAR
(— IN BUNDLE) KID BAVIN
(— INTO SHEAVES) GAVEL THRAVE
(— ONESELF) ADHERE
(— ROUND) WHIP
(— TOGETHER) LIME FAGOT SEIZE CEMENT FAGGOT ASTRINGE RELIGATE COLLIGATE
(— TO SECRECY) TILE
(— UP) KILT BAVIN TRUSS UPBAND ASTRICT REVOLVE
(— WINGS) PINION
(— WITH THREAD) OOP
(PREF.) SPHINGO
(SUFF.) SPHINX
BINDER BAND BEAM BOND CORD ROPE BALER COVER FRAME LEVER FILLET FOLDER GIRDER HEADER LIGNIN STAPLE TARMAC HAYBAND BONDSTONE BOOKMAKER
(— OF SAND-DUNES) MARRAM MARRUM
BINDING TAG BAND CORD GARD HARD LEAR ROPE TAPE YAPP COVER VALID CADDIS EDGING RIBBON BOUNDEN CADDICE GALLOON LAPPING MOUSING WEBBING FAITHFUL LIGATIVE LIGATORY STRINGENT OBLIGATORY
(— FAST) IRON
(— OF BOOK) BOCK FACE YAPP
(— OF GOLD) BISSET
(— ON DRESS) FENT
(SUFF.) DESIS
BINDLESTIFF BUM
BINDLE STIFF HOBO
BINDWEED BINE WIRE CREEPER TIEVINE BEARBIND BEARBINE BELLBINE BINEWEED CORNBIND HELLWEED MILKMAID WOODBINE WITHYWIND
BINE WIRE
BINGE BAT BOW HIT BLOW BUST SOAK TEAR TOOT TOPE BEANO PARTY SOUSE SPRAY SPREE CRINGE BLOWOFF CAROUSAL
(ON A —) ONATEAR
BINGO KENO BEANO LOTTO BRANDY SCREENO TOMBOLA
BINNACLE PYX BITTACLE
BINNUI (FATHER OF —) HENADAD
(SON OF —) NOADIAH
BINOCULARS GLASS
BINOMIAL DIONYM BINOMEN
BIOCHEMIST AMERICAN LI BERG CORI LOEB BLOCH BOYER DOISY KAMEN MOORE OCHOA SHEAR TATUM ASIMOV BEADLE CORDES SLOTTA WATSON ALSBERG AXELROD LIPMANN OSBORNE SCHALLY SHAFFER KORNBERG NORTHRUP NIRENBERG
ARGENTINIAN LELOIR
CANADIAN COLLIP
DANISH DAM
ENGLISH CHAIN KREBS PERUTZ PORTER SANGER HOPKINS MITCHELL
FRENCH MONOD DUCLAUX
GERMAN LYNEN LIPMANN
SWISS THEORELL
BIODEGRADABLE SOFT
BIOGEOGRAPHY CHOROLOGY
BIOGRAPHER PLUTARCH
AMERICAN DAY BEER COFFIN HENDRICK VANDOREN
ENGLISH CECIL ROWSE FORSTER DRINKWATER
ROMAN SUETONIUS
SCOTTISH BOSWELL LOCKHART
BIOGRAPHY BIO LIFE VITA MEMOIR ACCOUNT HISTORY RECOUNT PSYCHOGRAPH
(— OF A SORT) OBIT
(— OF SAINTS) HAGIOGRAPHA HAGIOGRAPHY
(KIND OF —) TELLALL
BIOLOGIST NATURALIST
AMERICAN EAST JUST LUTZ MAYR WALD BRONK CHILD CLARK LURIA MINOT PEARL SABIN SAGAN SHULL TYLER WOODS BAILEY BEADLE BUMPUS CARREL COTTAM FISHER JORDAN LITTLE OSBORN PALADE SPERRY WELLER CONKLIN EHRLICH HERRICK HERSHEY WETMORE CHAMBERS DELBRUCK DISABATO HARRISON SEDGWICK STOCKARD VISHNIAC
AUSTRALIAN BURNET
AUSTRIAN STEINACH
BELGIAN CLAUDE
CUBAN FINLAY
ENGLISH CRICK GEDDES HUXLEY MIVART SANGER BATESON COBBOLD KENDREW MEDAWAR ROMANES CUMMINGS MILSTEIN NICHOLSON ABERCROMBIE
FRENCH GIARD CARREL NOCARD BOUCHARD LEDANTEC
GERMAN WOLFF DRIESCH EHRLICH HAECKEL SPEMANN UEXKULL WEISMANN MUCKERMANN
IRISH ALLMAN
NORWEGIAN MJOEN
RUSSIAN BAER GURVICH LYSENKO MEDVEDEV METCHNIKOFF
SCOTTISH GEDDES THOMSON
SWISS ARBER
BIONIC (— HUMAN BEING) CYBORG
BIOPHORE BIOGEN PLASOME
BIOPLAST MICELLA MICELLE
BIOTITE MICA ANOMITE MEROXENE RUBELLAN
BIOTOPE STATION
BIPARTITE
(PREF.) DIPHY
BIPED DIPODE HINDQUARTERS
BIRCH COW BIRK CANE FLOG WHIP ALDER ALNUS CANOE SWISH BETULA BIRKEN TAWHAI HICKORY
BIRCHBARK CANOE
BIRD ANI DAW DOG JAY NUN PIE TIT TUI CHAT COOT CROW DOVE FOWL HERN IBIS JACK KAGU KITE KNOT LARK QUIT RUFF TERN TODY WING WREN BAKER BRANT CHUCK CLEAR COVEY EGRET FINCH FLIER FLYER GOOSE HOBBY JUNCO LARID LIVER PEWEE PEWIT RAVEN ROBIN SNIPE STILT SWIFT TEREK TURCO TWITE VIREO BULBUL DICKEY DIPPER DRIVER DRONGO DUCKER DUNLIN FALCON FINGER GROUSE GUINEA HOOPOE HOOTER JACANA JAEGER LINNET MARTEN MOCKER NESTER ORIOLE OSCINE PHOEBE PLOVER SHRIKE SILVAN SINGER SITTER SYLVAN THRUSH TROGON TURNIX VERDIN YAWPER ANTBIRD BABBLER BLUEJAY BUNTING BUSTARD BUZZARD CATBIRD CHIRPER COTINGA COURLAN FEATHER FLAPPER FLICKER FLIGGER FLOPPER GRACKLE HALCYON HORNERO HURGILA INCOMER IRRISOR JACAMAR JACKDAW KINGLET MINIVET MOULTER ORTOLAN PEACOCK PERCHER QUILLER REDWING SCRAPER SKINNER SKYLARK SPARROW SUNBIRD SWALLOW TANAGER TINAMOU TITLARK TOMFOOL WARBLER WAXWING WAYBUNG ACCENTOR AIRPLANE AMADAVAT ANNOTINE BLACKCAP BLACKNEB BLUEBIRD BOATBILL BOBOLINK BOBWHITE BUBBLING CAGELING CARINATE COCKBIRD COCORICO

DREPANID FERNBIRD FIREBIRD FIRETAIL GROSBEAK GRUIFORM IBISBILL JUVENILE KILLDEER KINGBIRD LOBEFOOT LONGSPUR OXPECKER PALMIPED PHEASANT PLUMIPED POORWILL PREACHER REDSTART SALTATOR SONGBIRD STARLING SURFBIRD SWAMPHEN TAPACOLO THRASHER THROSTLE TITMOUSE TREMBLER UMBRETTE WHINCHAT WOODCHAT WOODCOCK YEARBIRD COCKYOLLY CROSSBILL ROADRUNNER MOCKINGBIRD
(— CHASED BY HAWK) QUARRY
(— OF BRILLIANT PLUMAGE) TODY JALAP BARBET ORIOLE TROGON JACAMAR KIROMBO MINIVET TANAGER
(— OF INDIA) BAYA KALA SHAMA
(— OF OMEN) WAYBIRD
(— OF PREY) OWL HAWK KITE EAGLE ELANT GLEAD GLEDE STOOP EAGLET ELANET BUZZARD GOSHAWK STOOPER VULTURE ACCIPITER
(AFRICAN —) TAHA QUELEA TOURACO UMBRETTE NAPECREST
(AUSTRALIAN —) EMU ROA LORY ARARA LEIPOA BOOBOOK BUSTARD FIGBIRD WAYBUNG BELLBIRD LORIKEET LYREBIRD MANUCODE
(BIG-BEAKED —) BECARD HORNBILL
(CRESTED —) KAGU COPPY HOATZIN TOPKNOT
(CROCODILE —) TROCHIL
(DECOY —) CALL STOOL
(DIVING —) AUK LOON GREBE DARTER DOPPER DUCKER GRAYLING PLUNGEON
(EUROPEAN —) ANI DAW MEW QUA CIRL DARR KITE MALL MORO QUIS ROOK STAG WHIM YITE AMSEL BOONK GLEDE MAVIS MERLE OUSEL OUZEL SACER SAKER SERIN TARIN TEREK TERIN WHAUP AVOCET CUCKOO CUSHAT GAYLAG GODWIT MARTEN MERLIN MISSEL REDCAP WHEWER WINDLE WINNEL WRANNY BITTERN BUSTARD HAYBIRD KESTREL MOTACIL ORTOLAN SAKERET STARNEL WHISKEY WINNARD WITWALL BARGOOSE CHEPSTER DOTTEREL GARGANEY REDSTART WHEATEAR WHEYBIRD WHIMBREL WRANNOCK YOLDRING
(EXTINCT —) MOA DODO JIBI KIWI MAMO RUKH OFFBIRD
(FABULOUS —) FUM ROC FUNG HALCYON OOFBIRD WHISTLER
(FEMALE —) HEN JENNY
(FICTITIOUS —) JAYHAWK PHOENIX
(FISH-CATCHING —) OSPREY CRABIER
(FLEDGLING —) SQUAB
(FLIGHTLESS —) EMU GOR MOA DODO EYAS GORB GULL KAGU KIWI CALLOW GORLIN APTERYX GORLING NESTLER OSTRICH PENGUIN BUBBLING NESTLING
(FRIGATE —) IOA IWA
(FRUIT-EATING —) COLY
(GALLOWS —) HEMPY HEMPIE
(GAME —) QUAIL SNIPE COLIMA GROUSE INCOME FLAPPER INCOMER PHEASANT PARTRIDGE
(GREEN —) SIRGANG
(HAWAIIAN —) IO OO AVA IOA IWA OOA IIWI JIBI KOAE MAMO MOHO OMAO OOAA KAMAO PALILA
(HORN-HEADED —) KAMICHI
(INJURED —) CRIPPLE
(LARGEST —) LAMMERGEIER
(LIMICOLINE —) PRATINCOLE
(LONG-TOED —) JACANA
(MADAGASCAR —) KIROMBO
(MECHANICAL —) ORTHOPTER
(MYTHICAL —) FUM ROC GANZA SIMURG SIMURGH
(NEW ZEALAND —) KEA MOA OII ROA HUIA KAKA KIWI KOKO KUKU KULU PEHO RURU TITI WEKA POAKA KAKAPO KOKAKO KUKUPA APTERYX KORIMAKO MOREPORK NOTORNIS
(NIGHT —) OWL OWLET
(NOISY —) PIE MAGPIE
(PASSERINE —) QUIT FINCH SPARROW STARNEL SWALLOW SYLVIID DREPANID FALCONET FERNBIRD GRALLINA JACKBIRD OVENBIRD
(PERTAINING TO —S) OSCINE
(PISCATORY —) ERNE TERN
(RAPACIOUS —) SKUA JAEGER
(RASORIAL —) SCRATCHER
(RUNNING —) COURSER
(SAMOAN —) IAO
(SEA —) AUK ERN ERNE GONY GULL PINK SKUA SMEW TERN EIDER MURRE SOLAN FULMAR GANNET HAGDON OSPREY PETREL PUFFIN PELICAN SEAFOWL MURRELET MALLEMUCK
(SHORE —) REE RAIL SORA SNIPE STILT WADER AVOCET CURLEW PLOVER WILLET WRYBILL SHEATHBILL
(SHORT-TAILED —) BREVE
(SINGING —) LARK WREN PIPIT ROBIN VEERY VIREO CANARY LINNET MOCKER ORIOLE OSCINE SINGER THRUSH WARBLER FAUVETTE REDSTART NIGHTINGALE
(SMALL —) TIT TODY WREN DICKY PEGGY PIPIT TYDIE VIREO DICKEY LINNET SISKIN TOMTIT CREEPER SPARROW TITLARK COCORICO GNATSNAP PERCOLIN STARLING WHEATEAR
(SOUTH AMERICAN —) GUAN MINA MITU MYNA RARA TOCA BAKER CHAJA JOPIM TURCO BARBET BECARD CHUNGA TOUCAN CARIAMA OILBIRD BELLBIRD BOATBILL CARACARA GUACHARO HOACTZIN PUFFBIRD SCREAMER TAPACOLO TAPACULO TERUTERO
(STYLIZED —) DISTELFINK
(TROPICAL —) ANI GUAN KOAE TODY BOS'N BOSUN JALAP BARBET BECARD MOTMOT TROGON JACAMAR MANAKIN WIGTAIL LONGTAIL SALTATOR
(WADING —) HERN IBIS RAIL SORA CRANE HERON SNIPE STILT STORK ARGALA AVOCET GODWIT JACANA LIMPKIN BOATBILL FLAMINGO SHOEBILL SHOEBIRD SANDERLING
(WILD —S) GALLINAE
(WITCH —) ANI
(YEAR-OLD —) ANNOTINE
(YOUNG —) EYA GULL PIPER CHEEPER FLAPPER NESTLER BIRDIKIN NESTLING
(PL.) AVIFAUNA POLYMYODI PRAECOCES
(PREF.) AVI ORNIS ORNITH(I)(O)
(SUFF.) ORNIS ORNITHES

BIRD BOLT BURBOLT QUARREL
BIRDBRAIN SIMP
BIRD CAGE AVIARY PINJRA VOLARY VOLERY PADDOCK
BIRDCATCHER FOWLER
BIRD CHERRY DOGWOOD EGGBERRY HACKWOOD HAGBERRY
BIRDLIFE ORNIS
BIRD-LIKE ORNITHOID
BIRDLIME GLUE LIME BELIME VISCUM BIRDGLUE
BIRD OF PARADISE APUS MANUCODE RIFLEBIRD
BIRD-REARING AVINCULTURE
BIRDS (AUTHOR OF —) ARISTOPHANES
(CHARACTER IN —) EPOPS TEREUS BASILEIA EUELPIDES PISTHETAERUS
BIRD'S-FOOT FOWLFOOT SERRADELLA
BIRD'S KNEE SUFFRAGO
BIRD'S MANTLE STRAGULUM
BIRDY AVIAN
BIRENO (WIFE OF —) OLIMPIA
BIRETTA SARRET
BIRI BIDI
BIRL ROTATE
BIRTH KIN BEAR FALL YEAN BLOOD BURDEN GENTRY ORIGIN BEARING BORNING DESCENT GENESIS LINEAGE DELIVERY GENITURE NASCENCY NATALITY NATIVITY
(FALSE —) SOOTERKIN
(GENTLE —) GENTILITY
(GENTLE —)0 GENTRICE
(GIVE —) CALVE
(HIGH —) PARAGE
(HONORABLE —) BLOOD
(OF LOW —) CRESTLESS
(OF NOBLE —) CORONETED
(PREF.) NATI
(SUFF.) **(GIVING —)** PARA PAROUS
BIRTHMARK MOLE IMAGE NAEVE NEVUS BLEMISH SPILOMA SIGNATURE
BIRTHPLACE INCUNABULA
BIRTHRATE NATALITY FERTILITY
BIRTHRIGHT KIND BIRTHDOM HERITAGE
BIRTHROOT BATHROOT BATHWORT DEATHROOT DISHCLOTH SQUAWROOT
BIRTHSTONE (APRIL —) DIAMOND
(AUGUST —) SARDONYX
(DECEMBER —) TURQUOISE
(FEBRUARY —) AMETHYST
(JANUARY —) GARNET
(JULY —) RUBY
(JUNE —) PEARL
(MARCH —) BLOODSTONE
(MAY —) EMERALD
(NOVEMBER —) TOPAZ
(OCTOBER —) OPAL
(SEPTEMBER —) SAPPHIRE
BIRTHWORT GUACO ASARUM BATHROOT
BISAYAN AKLAN CEBUAN AKLANON CEBUANO
BISCUIT BUN NUT BAKE ROLL RUSK SNAP WOOD BREAD COOKY SCONE WAFER BISQUE COOKIE DODGER MALLOW MUFFIN PARKIN PERKIN SIMNEL CRACKER GALETTE PENTILE PRETZEL RATAFIA RATIFIA CRACKNEL HARDTACK ZWIEBACK GINGERSNAP
(ALMOND —) RARAFIA
(BROKEN —S) DUNDERFUNK
(COLOR —) DOE PAWNEE
(SHIP —) HARDTACK DANDYFUNK DUNDERFUNK
BISECT FORK CROSS HALVE SPLIT CLEAVE DIVIDE MIDDLE SEPARATE
BISECTION MEDIATION
BISEXUAL ACDC
BISHOP EP ABBA EPUS LAWN PAPA POPE ANGEL COARB DENIS ARCHER BUSTLE DESPOT EPARCH EXARCH MAGPIE PRESUL PRIEST PRIMUS ROCHET ROCKAT PONTIFF PRELATE PRIMATE TULCHAN ANTISTES DIOCESAN DIRECTOR ORDINARY OVERSEER PONTIFEX PATRIARCH METROPOLITAN
(— AND MARTYR) EM
(ANGLICAN —) MAGPIE
(CHESS —) ALFIN ALPHYN ARCHER
(NEIGHBOR OF —) KING QUEEN KNIGHT
(PL.) PURPLE
BISHOPRIC SEE
BISHOP'S-WEED AMMI AMMEOS KHELLA WILLIAM BOLEWORT BULLWORT GOUTWEED TOOTHPICK
BISHOPWEED GOUTWEED GOUTWORT
BISKOP BRUSHER STEENBRAS
BISMARK KRAPFE KRAPFEN
BISMUTH WISMUTH TINGLASS
BISON BUGLE BOVINE MITHAN WISENT AUROCHS BONASUS BUFFALO
BISTORT PATIENCE ADDERWORT ASTROLOGE SNAKEWEED SNAKEWORT
BISTRO BAR CAFE TAVERN WINESHOP ESTAMINET NIGHTCLUB
BIT ACE FID FIP GAG JOT NIP ORT PIP TAD WEE ATOM BITE BITT CHIP CROP CURB DITE DOIT DRIB FLAW FOOD GRUE HAET HATE HOOT IOTA ITEM LEVY MITE MOTE PART RIFF SLUT SNAP SNIP SPOT TOOL WHIT AUGER BLADE CHECK CRUMB DRILL GROAT PATCH PEZZO PIECE POINT SCRAP SHRED SHTIK SKOSH SMACK SNACK SPECK STEEK TASTE THRUM WIGHT BITTIE BRIDLE CANNON EATING MORSEL PELHAM PICKLE

SCATCH SHTICK SIPPET SMIDGE SPLICE STITCH STIVER TITTLE TRIFLE BRADOON BRIDOON CHILENO GLIMMER MODICUM MORCEAU PALLION PORTION SCHTICK SMIDGEN SMIDGIN SNAFFLE THOUGHT TRANEEN FISHTAIL FRACTION FRAGMENT QUANTITY SMIDGEON SMITCHIN TWOPENNY
(— OF GOSSIP) HEARING
(— OF INFORMATION) GRIFF GRIFFIN WRINKLE
(— OF KEY) WEB
(— OF LAND) CROOK
(— OF METAL) FLITTER
(— OF TOAST) SNIPPET
(—S AND PIECES) GUBBINS GUBBINGS
(—S OF COKE) BREEZE
(—S OF WRITING) EXCERPTA
(— TO EAT) MUNGEY
(A —) SOME
(COMIC —) SIGHTGAG
(CUTTING —) CHASER
(DRILL —) CROWN
(FANCIFUL —) FLAM
(FIPPENY —) SIXPENCE
(FLORID —) FLOURISH
(HORSE'S —) KEVEL SNODE CANNON PELHAM SCATCH SNAFFLE BASTONET
(LEAST —) FIG JOT RAP DAMN HANG LICK GHOST GROAT RIZZOM STITCH
(LITTLE —) PICK TOUCH BITTOCK REMNANT SOUPCON
(ONE — PER SECOND) BAUD
(ONE-QUARTER —) GILL
(ONE BILLION —S) GIGABIT
(SEQUENCE OF —S) BYTE
(SMALL —) BLEB GLIM SPUNK
(SMALL —S) SMATTER
(THEATRICAL —) SHTICK SCHTICK
(TINY —) TAD SPECK DRIBBLE SCRINCH TODDICK
(PL.) SMITHERS SMITHEREENS
BITCH DO GYP BICK LAMP SLUT BRACH BROOD CHEAT GROUSE COMPLAIN
BITE BIT CUT EAT JAW NIP BAIT CHAM CHEW ETCH FOOD GASH GNAP GNAW HOLD KNAP MEAL RIVE SNAP TAKE CHACK CHAMM CHAMP CHEAT GNASH PINCH SEIZE SMART SNACK STING TOOTH TRICK CRUNCH MORSEL NIBBLE PIERCE SAVAGE BUGBITE CHEATER CORRODE FORBITE IMPRESS MORSURE MUNCHET PARTAKE SHARPER SLANDER
(— AT) HIT
(— GREEDILY) HANCH
(— REPEATEDLY) CHAMP
BITER
(SUFF.) DECTES
BITHIAH (HUSBAND OF —) MERED
BITING BIT HOT ACID HOAR KEEN ACRID NIPPY QUICK SHARP SNELL BITTER RODENT SEVERE SHREWD STINGY TEETHY TWEAKY CAUSTIC CUTTING MORDANT MORSURE NIPPING PUNGENT SUBACID DRILLING INCISIVE PIERCING POIGNANT SCALDING SCATHING STINGING ACIDULOUS MORDACIOUS
BITIS ECHIDNA
BITO BALM HAJILIJ
BITON (BROTHER OF —) CLEOBIS
(MOTHER OF —) CYDIPPE
BITT BLOCK KNIGHT BOLLARD
(PL.) RANGEHEADS
BITTER AWA GAL ACID ACRE ASIM BASK KEEN MARA RUDE SALT SORE SOUR TART ACERB ACRID AMARA ASPER BLEAK EAGER HARSH IRATE SHARP SNELL BITING PICRIC SEVERE AUSTERE CAUSTIC CRABBED CUTTING FERVENT GALLING GALLISH PAINFUL PUNGENT SATIRIC POIGNANT SARDONIC STINGING SUBAMARE VIRULENT ASTRINGENT ACRIMONIOUS
(NOT —) MILD
(PREF.) PICR(O)
(SUFF.) PICRIN
BITTER APPLE COLOCYNTH
BITTER BIT SMALLPOX
BITTERBUSH SNAKEROOT
BITTER CLOVER YELLOWTOP
BITTERLY SOUR FELLY BITTER ROUNDLY CURSEDLY
BITTERN BUMP SOCO BOONK BUTOR EGRET HERON BITORE BUMBLE BUMMLE BUTTAL KAKKAK BLITTER BUMMLER ERICIUS DUNKADOO GRUIFORM LONGNECK
(FLOCK OF —) SEDGE SIEGE
BITTERNESS RUE ACOR BILE FELL GALL ATTER MARAH ENMITY MALICE RANCOR AMARITY ACERBITY ACRIDITY ACRIMONY ASPERITY FERVENCY SEVERITY WORMWOOD
(EXTREME —) VIRULENCE
(WITH —) AMAREVOLE
BITTER PIT STIPPEN
BITTERROOT LEWISIA TOBACCOROOT
BITTERS AMER
BITTER SPAR DOLOMITE
BITTERSWEET FELLEN DOGWOOD LOBSTER SOLANUM WAXWORK DULCAMARA FELONWOOD FELONWORT FEVERTWIG WITHYWIND WOLFBERRY
BITTER VETCH ERS
BITTERWEED RAGWEED HORSEWEED
BITTERWORT FELWORT DANDELION
BITUMEN TAR CONGO PITCH SLIME MALTHA ASPHALT CARBENE ALKITRAN ALCHITRAN ELATERITE
BIVALENT DIATOMIC
BIVALVE HEN CLAM SPAT PINNA COCKLE DIATOM MUSSEL OYSTER MOLLUSK NUCULID PANDORA SCALLOP TOHEROA
BIVOUAC CAMP ETAPE WATCH ENCAMP SHELTER
BIZARRE ODD ANTIC DEDAL GONZO OUTRE QUEER QUAINT ANTICAL BAROQUE CURIOUS FANCIFUL ECCENTRIC FANTASTIC GROTESQUE OUTLANDISH
BLAB LAB CHAT BLART BLATE CHEEP CLACK PEACH PRATE BABBLE BETRAY GOSSIP REVEAL SQUEAL TATTLE BLABBER CHATTER CLATTER
BLABBERMOUTH YENTA
BLACK DHU JET WAN CALO CROW DARK EBON FOUL INKY NOIR PIKY SOOT BUGLE COLLY DUSKY DWALE MURKY NEGRO NOIRE RAVEN SABLE SOOTY TARRY THICK ATROUS BRUNET DISMAL ETHIOP GLOOMY MURREY PITCHY SULLEN ABAISER AFRICAN BLACKEN DIAMOND MELANIC NEGRITO NIGRINE NIGROUS PICEOUS SCHWARZ SWARTHY UNCLEAN MOURNFUL
(— AND BLUE) LIVID
(— OUT) CONK
(BONE —) SPODIUM
(BROWNISH —) LAVA
(GREENISH —) CORBEAU
(IVORY —) ABAISER
(LIGHT-SKINNED —) BROWN
(RATHER —) DUSKISH
(VIOLET —) CROW
(PREF.) ATRO MAVRO MEL(A) MELAN(O) NIGRI
(SUFF.) MELANE
BLACKAMOOR BLECK NEGRO MORIAN NEGRESS ETHIOPIAN
BLACK ARROW (AUTHOR OF —) STEVENSON
(CHARACTER IN —) DICK ELLIS OATES DANIEL JOANNA OLIVER SEDLEY LAWLESS RICHARD SHELTON BRACKLEY DUCKWORTH
BLACK ASH HOOPWOOD
BLACKBALL PIP PILL BALLOT EXCLUDE HEEBALL OSTRACIZE
BLACK BASS HURON TROUT ACHIGAN GROWLER OCHIGAN
BLACKBERRY AGAWAM LAWTON BRAMBLE DEWBERRY MULBERRY ROSACEAN
(— BUSH) MORE
BLACKBIRD ANI DAW PIE CROW MERL AMSEL COLLY MERLE OUSEL OUZEL RAVEN BLACKY COLLEY MAIZER BLACKIE COWBIRD GRACKLE JACKDAW REDWING WOOFELL TROOPIAL
BLACKBOARD SLATE CHALKBOARD GREENBOARD
BLACKBREAM TARWHINE
BLACK-BROWED GLOOMY
BLACK BRYONY LILY LILIUM OXBERRY BINDWEED MANDRAKE
BLACK BUCK SASIN
BLACKCAP GULL JACK PEGGY HAYBIRD WARBLER MOCKBIRD TITMOUSE JACKSTRAW RASPBERRY
BLACKCOCK GROUSE
BLACKDAMP STYTH STYTHE CHOKEDAMP
BLACKDRINK YAPON YAUPON
BLACKEN INK TAR CHAR CORK SMUT SOIL SOOT BLECK CLOUD COLLY JAPAN SMOKE SULLY BEFOUL BLATCH DARKEN DEFAME MALIGN SMEETH SMIRCH SMUTCH VILIFY ASPERSE BENEGRO NIGRIFY SLANDER SMOLDER TRADUCE BESMIRCH
BLACKENED REECHY
BLACKENING SWART SWARTH
BLACKEYE COWPEA
BLACKFELLOW BLACKBOY YAMMADJI
BLACKFIN CISCO SESIS
BLACKFISH GRIND TAUTOG BORLASE DOGFISH GRAMPUS POTHEAD HARDHEAD
BLACKFLY GNAT SIMULIID
BLACKFOOT BLOOD KAINAH PIEGAN SIKSIKA SIHASAPA
BLACK GROUPER MERO AGUAJI WARSAW GARRUPA
BLACKGUARD CUR SHAG BLECK CATSO GAMIN GUARD SNUFF SWEEP ROTTER LADRONE SKELLUM VAGRANT BLAGGARD CRIMINAL LARRIKIN VAGABOND SCOUNDREL
BLACK GUILLEMOT CUTTY TYSTE SCRABE DOVEKEY DOVEKIE SCRABER PUFFINET
BLACK GUM TUPELO HORNPIPE STINKWOOD
BLACK HAW SLOE BOOTS ALISIER STAGBUSH VIBURNUM
BLACKHEAD COMEDO
BLACK HOLE COLLAPSAR
BLACK HOREHOUND HENBIT ARCHANGEL
BLACK HORSE SUCKER SUCKEREL
BLACKING LINK BLECK BLATCH BLEACH ATRAMENT
BLACK IRONWOOD AXMASTER AXEMASTER
BLACKISH DUSKY MOREL SWART BLACKY
BLACKJACK OAK SAP CLUB COSH DUCK FLAG JACK BILLY BEETLE BLENDE JERKIN BOMBARD NATURAL BLUDGEON
BLACKLEG LEG FIRE SCAB SNOB ANTHRAX GAMBLER JACKLEG APOSTATE BLACKNEB BLACKNOB SWINDLER KNOBSTICK
BLACK LETTER GOTHIC
BLACKLY SABLY
BLACK MAGIC VODUN VODOUN DIABLERIE
BLACKMAIL BLEED BRIBE CHOUT COERCE EXTORT RANSOM TRIBUTE CHANTAGE
BLACKMAILER GHOUL BRIBER LEECHER
BLACK MANGROVE COURIDA
BLACK MEDIC HOP TREFOIL NONESUCH SHAMROCK
BLACKNESS GRIME DARKNESS NIGRITUDE
BLACK NIGHTSHADE MOREL DUSCLE SOLANUM BLUEBERRY MOONSHADE TROMPILLO
BLACK OLIVE OXHORN
BLACKOUT SKIT
BLACK PEPPER PIMENTA
BLACK PINE MATAI
BLACK POISON WALNUT

BLACK RHINOCEROS BORELE KEITLOA UPEYGAN
BLACK SALLY SALLEE MUZZLEWOOD
BLACK SANICLE LUNGWORT MASTERWORT
BLACK SHANK LANAS
BLACK SKIMMER CUTWATER SHEARBILL
BLACKSMITH GOW SMUG LOHAR SHOER SMITH PLOVER SMITHY VULCAN BROOKIE FARRIER STRIKER BURNEWIN IRONSMITH
BLACKSNAKE WHIP QUIRT RACER ELAPID RUNNER COLUBRID
BLACK SPECK DARTROSE
BLACK SPURGE FLUXWEED
BLACKTAIL DASSY DASSIE
BLACK TERN DARR STARN
BLACKTHORN HAW SLOE SNAG SCROG GRIBBLE SLOEBUSH SLOETREE SNAGBUSH
BLACKTOP PAVE
BLACK-VARNISH TREE THEETSEE
BLACK VULTURE URUBU CORBIE ZOPILOTE
BLACK WALNUT NOGAL
BLACKWATER STATE NEBRASKA
BLACK WIDOW POKOMOO
BLACK WOLF KARAKURT
BLACKWOOD BITI LIGHTWOOD
BLACKWORT COMFREY
BLADDER SAC VES ASCO VESICA AMPULLA BLATHER BLISTER INFLATE UROCYST UTRICLE VESICLE
(AIR —) POKE SWIM SOUND SINGALLY
(PL.) ASCI
(PREF.) ASC(I)(IDI)(IDIO)(O) CYST(I)(O) PHYSO VESICO
(SUFF.) CYST(IS)
BLADDER-AND-STRING BUMBASS
BLADDER CAMPION BEHN BEHEN SILENE COWBELL SNAPPER RATTLEBOX
BLADDER KETMIE MODESTY
BLADDERNUT BAGNUT
BLADDER-WORM CESTODE
BLADDERWORT POPWEED
BLADDER WRACK CUTWEED KELPWARE
BLADE BIT FIN FOP OAR SAW WEB BLOW BONE BOWL EDGE EPEE FLAG HEAD LEAF LIMB TANG WEAK BLOOD BRAND DANDY FLUKE GRAIN GUIDE HEALD KNIFE LANCE SHEAR SPARK SPEAR SPIRE SWORD BLUNGE BUCKET BUSTER CUTTER DOCTOR FOIBLE HEDDLE LAMINA PAGINA RIPPER ROARER SCYTHE SICKLE TOLEDO BAYONET CHIPPER GALLANT POLESAW SCALPEL SCAPULA SCRAPER SPINNER MOLDBOARD PROPELLER
(— OF FAN) VANE
(— OF GRASS) PILE CHIRE SPEAR SPIRE STRAP TRANEEN
(— OF KNIFE) TANG GRAIN
(— OF LEAF) LIMB LAMINA
(— OF MORION) COMB
(— OF OAR) PALM PEEL PELL WASH
(— OF PROPELLER) FAN
(— OF SCISSORS) BILL
(— OF YOUNG GRAIN) SORAGE
(BROAD —) SPATULA
(CULTIVATOR —) SWEEP DUCKFOOT
(MIXER —) BEATER
(NARROW —) DISC
(SKATE —) RUNNER
(SURGICAL —) LEUCOTOME
(SUFF.) SPATH
BLAES CAM CAN CALM CAUM
BLAFFERT PLAPPERT
BLAGGERMOUTH YENTA GOSSIP
BLAH DRAB DULL MEDIOCRE
BLAIN RUBY SORE BULLA BLISTER INFLAME PUSTULE
BLAKE MCKAY
BLAMABLE FAULTY CULPABLE
BLAME RAP CALL CHOP HURT LACK ONUS SAKE SPOT TWIT WITE CHIDE FAULT GUILT ODIUM PINCH PINON SHEND SNAPE SWICK SWIKE THANK TOUCH WHITE ACCUSE ATTASK BUMBLE BURDEN CHARGE DIRDUM PLIGHT REBUKE REVILE SCANCE APPOINT ASCRIBE CENSURE CONDEMN CULPATE OBLOQUY REPROOF REPROVE SLANDER UPBRAID WITHNIM REPROACH
BLAMED BLINDING BLISTERING
BLAMELESS PURE ENTIRE PERFECT INNOCENT SACKLESS SPOTLESS WITELESS RIGHTEOUS
BLAMEWORTHY GUILTY CRIMINAL CULPABLE REPROBATE
BLANCH FADE PALE BLENK CHALK SCALD WHITE APPALL ARGENT BIANCA BLEACH BLENCH FALLOW WHITEN ETIOLATE
BLANCHED ASHEN MEALY ETIOLATE BLOODLESS COLORLESS
BLANCMANGE FLUMMERY
BLAND COLD KIND MILD OILY OPEN SOFT SLEEK SUAVE BENIGN BREEZY GENIAL GENTLE SMOOTH URBANE AFFABLE AMIABLE LENIENT VANILLA FAVONIAN GRACIOUS UNCTUOUS
BLANDISH COAX CHARM ALLURE BLANCH CAJOLE FONDLE SMOOTH FLATTER WHEEDLE HONEYFUGLE
BLANDISHMENT SOOTH LISALVE
(PL.) TREACLE
BLANDLY CREAMILY
BLANK BARE BURR FLAN FORM SHOT VOID ANNUL BLIND BREAK CHASM CLEAN EMPTY FALSE RANGE SPACE WASTE WHITE COUPON VACANT ANTIQUE BRINDLE NONPLUS UNMIXED VACUOUS UNFILLED
(MAY BE —) STARE
BLANKED BLIND
BLANKET RUG BROT MAUD WRAP BLUEY COTTA COVER CUMLY LAYER MANTA PATTU QUILT SHEET SUGAN THROW AFGHAN COOLER CUMBLY GLOBAL KAMBAL MANTLE PALLET PONCHO PUTTOO SERAPE SOOGAN SPREAD STIFLE STROUD TILPAH CHIRIPA DOUBLER SMOTHER WHITTLE COVERLET MACKINAW
(— A VESSEL) WRONG
(— OF SKINS) KAROSS
(— WITH BOMBS) SATURATE
(BUSHMAN'S —) BLUEY
(HORSE —) MANTA
(QUILTED —) BROT
(SADDLE —) CORONA
(PREF.) REGO
BLANKETING DUFFEL DUFFLE
BLANKNESS VACUITY NEGATION
BLARE PEAL BLART BLAST BLEAR NOISE BLAZON SCREAM FANFARE TANTARA TRUMPET
BLARNEY CON TAFFY BUTTER CAJOLE SAWDER FLATTER WHEEDLE
BLAS GIL RUY
BLASPHEME ABUSE CURSE DEFAME REVILE PROFANE
BLASPHEMOUS BAD RIBALD IMPIOUS PROFANE
BLASPHEMY CALUMNY CURSING IMPIETY ANATHEMA SWEARING
BLAST BUB NIP WAP BANG BLOW FRAP GALE GUST RUIN RUST SHOT TOOT WAFF WIND BLAME BLIST BLORE SPLIT STUNT TRUMP ATTACK BLIGHT BUGGER FORBID NIDDER NITHER REBUFF VOLLEY WITHER BLUSTER DESPOIL EXPLODE SHATTER SHRIVEL DYNAMITE OUTBURST PROCLAIM WHIRLPUFF
(— OFF) START
(— OF WIND) GUST RISE PERRY PIRRIE VENTOSITY
(— ON HORN) TOOT PRYSE
(— WITH COLD) SNEAP
(FURIOUS —) SNIFTER
(MILITARY —) SALVO
(RAINY —) BLATTER
BLASTED BLAME BLAMED BLIGHTED BLINDING BLINKING
BLASTER FROSTER SHOOTER SHOTMAN
BLASTING SCATHING SHOOTING STELLATION
(— METHOD) MUDCAP
BLASTOMERE MESOMERE MACROMERE MICROMERE
BLASTULA PLACULA PLANULA PLANULAN
BLATANT GLIB LOUD BRASH GROSS NOISY SILLY VOCAL COARSE GARISH TONANT VULGAR BRAWLING STRIDENT
BLATHER ADO RAVE STIR BLEAT BABBLE WAFFLE BLITHER PRATTLE NONSENSE
BLAUBOK ETAAC BLUEBUCK
BLAZE LOW BURN FIRE GLOW HACK LEAM LOWE LUNT MARK SHOT SPOT FLAME FLARE FLASH GLARE GLEAM GLORY INGLE RATCH SHINE STARE STEAM TORCH BLAZON BLEEZE BONFIRE PIONEER SPLENDOR
(— OUT) FLAP
(HEAVENLY —) NOVA
BLAZING AFIRE FIERY FLAMY LIGHT TORRID FLAMING FLARING
BLAZING STAR LIATRIS GRUBROOT SNAKEROOT
BLAZON DECK SHOW ADORN BLARE BLAZE BOAST DEPICT SHIELD DECLARE DISPLAY EXHIBIT PUBLISH EMBLAZON INSCRIBE
BLAZONED ARMED BANNERED
BLEACH SUN WASH BLEAK CHALK CROFT POACH BLANCH BLENCH CHLORE PURIFY WHITEN DECOLOR LIGHTEN BLONDINE ETIOLATE PEROXIDE
(— PULP) POTCH
BLEACHER WHITSTER
BLEACHERS SCAFFOLD
BLEAK DIM RAW BLAE BLAY COLD DOUR GRAY PALE ABLET OURIE SPRAT STARK SWALE ALBURN BITTER BLEACH DISMAL DREARY FRIGID PALLID CUTTING DESOLATE CHEERLESS
BLEAK HOUSE (AUTHOR OF —) DICKENS
(CHARACTER IN —) JO ADA JOHN ALLAN CLARE FLITE GUPPY KROOK BUCKET ESTHER RAWDON DEDLOCK JELLYBY RICHARD WILLIAM CARSTONE CHADBAND JARNDYCE SKIMPOLE LEICESTER SUMMERSON WOODCOURT TULKINGHORN
BLEAT BAA MAA BLAT BLEA YARM BLART BLATE BLATHER BLUSTER WHICKER
BLEATING BALANT
BLEB BLOB BULLA BUBBLE BLISTER PUSTULE VESICLE SWELLING
BLEED RUN FLUX MILK WEEP BLOOD LEECH MULCT SWEAT SWINDLE TEICHER PHLEBOTOMIZE
BLEEDER STICKER
BLEEDING BLOODY SANGLANT
BLEEDING HEART EARDROP DICENTRA
BLEMISH MAR BLOT BLUR DENT FLAW GALL LACK MAIM MARK MOIL MOLE RIFT SAKE SCAR SLUR SPOT TASH VICE WANT AMPER BLAME BOTCH BRECK CLOUD CRACK FAULT FLECK MULCT NAEVE SPECK STAIN SULLY TACHE TAINT TOUCH BLOTCH BREACH DEFAME DEFECT IMPAIR INJURE MACULA MACULE MAYHEM SMIRCH STIGMA BUBUKLE CATFACE DEFAULT FAILING FISSURE SUNSPOT MACULATION
(— IN CLOTH) AMPER SULLY
(— IN PAPER) FISHEYE
(PRINTING —) MACKLE
BLEMISHED BAD WEMMY
BLENCH FOIL SHUN WILE AVOID ELUDE EVADE QUAIL SHAKE SHIRK TRICK BAFFLE BLANCH BLEACH FLINCH RECOIL SHRINK DECEIVE
BLEND MIX RUN BLOT FADE FUSE JOIN MELD MELT MENG MOLD ADMIX BLIND CREAM GRADE MERGE MOULD PUREE SHADE SMEAR SPOIL STAIN TINGE UNITE BLUNGE COMMIX CRASIS DAZZLE MINGLE TEMPER COMBINE CONFUSE CORRUPT DECEIVE

GRADATE MIXTURE POLLUTE COALESCE CONCRETE IMMINGLE TINCTURE CONTEMPER
(— OF NOISES) CHARM
(— OF SHERRY) SOLERA
(— OF WINES) CUVEE
BLENDE JACK SPHALERITE
BLENDED FONDU FUSED MIXED MERGED MINGLED CONFLATE CONFLUENT
BLENDING FUSION HOTCHPOT
BLENNY GUNNEL SHANNY EELPOUT JUGULAR KELPFISH SENORITA WOLFFISH WRYMOUTH QUILLFISH ROCKSKIPPER
BLESBOK NUNNI BLESBUCK
BLESS KEEP SAIN WAVE ADORE ANELE BENSH CROSS EXTOL FAVOR GUARD THANK VISIT WOUND CROUCH FAVOUR HALLOW PRAISE THRASH APPROVE BEATIFY EMBLISS GLORIFY PROTECT MACARIZE PRESERVE SANCTIFY
BLESSED HOLY BLEST HAPPY SEELY DIVINE JOYFUL SACRED SEELFUL BENEDICT BHAGAVAT BLISSFUL BLOOMING HALLOWED HEAVENLY CELESTIAL
(— MAN) BEATI
(— WOMAN) BEATA
BLESSEDNESS BLISS FELICITY BEATITUDE HAPPINESS
BLESSING BOON GIFT SAIN BLISS DUKAN GRACE SORRA BARAKA DUCHAN PRAISE BENISON DARSHAN WORSHIP BERACHAH FELICITY MACARISM BEATITUDE
(PL.) CUP
BLEU DE ROI SEVRES
BLIGHT NIP FIRE RUIN RUST SMUT SOKA BLAST BRANT EDEMA FROST SNEAP MILDEW NITHER TAKING WITHER DESTROY
(— OF HOPS) FIREBLAST
(PREF.) UREDO
BLIGHTER GUY SOD FELLOW
BLIND BET POT ANTE BOMA DARK DEAD DULL HIDE HOOD SEEL BISME BLANK BLEND CHICK CLOAK DUNCH SHADE STAKE STALL WAGER AMBUSH BISSON BLENDE DARKEN DAZZLE SCREEN SECRET AIMLESS ANTIQUE BANDAGE BATTERY BENIGHT ECLIPSE EYELESS OBSCURE PRETEXT RAYLESS SHUTTER ABORTIVE ARTIFICE BAYARDLY BLINDING EXCECATE HOODWINK IGNORANT INVOLVED JALOUSIE OUTSHINE PURBLIND UMBRELLA VENETIAN
(— IN ONE EYE) PEED GLEED GLEYD
(— MAN) MOLE
(HALF —) STARBLIND
(PART OF —) SLAT
(PL.) PERSIENNES
(PREF.) CECO TYPHL(O)
BLIND ALLEY LOKE STOP POCKET IMPASSE
BLINDER FLAP HOOD BLIND BLUFF LUNET WINKER BLINKER EYEFLAP LUNETTE HOODWINK BLINDFOLD
BLINDFOLD MOP DARK BLINK BLUFF SCARF MUFFLE BANDAGE BLINDER OBSCURE ENCLOSER HEEDLESS HOODWINK RECKLESS CONCEALED
BLINDING BISME BISSON
BLINDMAN'S BLUFF POST HOODWINK
BLINDNESS BISSON CECITY MYOPSY ABLEPSY ANOPSIA MEROPIA ABLEPSIA DARKNESS IGNORANCE
(— TO TRUTH) AVIDYA AVIJJA
(COLOR —) ACHROBIA MONOCHROMATISM
(DAY —) HEMERALOPIA
(NIGHT —) NYCTALOPIA
(PARTIAL —) MEROPIA HEMIOPSIA
(RED-GREEN —) DALTONISM
(SNOW —) CHIONABLEPSIA
(STUDY OF —) TYPHLOLOGY
(TEMPORARY —) MOONBLINK
BLINDSTITCH FELL
BLINDWORM SLOW ORVET ANGUID HAGWORM SLOWWORM
BLIND-YOUR-EYES GANGWA ALIPATA
BLINK BAT PINK SHUN WINK BLUSH CHEAT FLASH GLEAM SHINE TRICK GLANCE IGNORE OBTUSE WAPPER BLINTER CONDONE GLIMMER GLIMPSE NEGLECT NICTATE SPARKLE TWINKLE
BLINKER EYE BLINK BLUFF LIGHT EYELID SIGNAL WAPPER WINKER BLINDER FLASHER GOGGLES COQUETTE HOODWINK MACKEREL
BLINKING PINK OWLISH
BLINTZE BLIN BLINTZ PANCAKE
BLIP PIP ECHO
(SONAR —) ECHO
BLISS JOY EDEN KAIF SEEL SEIL BLESS GLORY ANANDA HEAVEN DELIGHT ECSTASY GLADDEN NIRVANA RAPTURE FELICITY GLADNESS PARADISE PLEASURE
BLISSFUL HOLY SEELY BLITHE EDENIC BLESSED ELYSIAN UTOPIAN BEATIFIED GLORIFIED
BLISTER BEAT BLAB BLEB BLOB BLOW BOIL BURN LASH QUAT APTHA BLAIN BLIBE BULGE BULLA TOPIC VESIC APHTHA BUBBLE CUPOLA SCORCH SOTTER TETTER BLADDER BLUSTER SCALDER SKELLER VESICLE VESICATE
(PREF.) PUSTULI VESICUL(O)
BLISTERED BULLATE
BLISTERING VESICANT
BLITHE GAY GLAD BONNY BUXOM HAPPY JOLLY MERRY BONNIE JOVIAL JOYOUS LIVELY GAYSOME JOCULAR WINSOME CHEERFUL GLADSOME SPRIGHTLY
BLITZ REDDOG
BLIZZARD BLOW GALE WIND BURAN PURGA RETORT SNIFTER SQUELCHER
(— STATE) SD SDAK
BLOAT BLOW BLAST BLOWN FLOAT HOOVE HOVEN PUFFY SWELL BOWDEN EXPAND TUMEFY DISTEND FERMENT INFLATE
BLOATED FOZY BLOAT BROSY CURED FOGGY HOVEN PUFFY TUMID GOTCHY SODDEN TURGID POMPOUS REPLETE
BLOATER MOONEYE
BLOB LIP WEN BEAD BLEB BLOT BOIL CLOT DAUB DROP GLOB GOUT LUMP MARK MASS BUBBLE DALLOP DOLLOP PIMPLE SPLASH BLEMISH BLISTER BLOSSOM GLOBULE PUSTULE SPLOTCH
BLOC RING BLOCK CABAL PARTY UNION CLIQUE BENELUX FACTION
BLOCK AME BAR COB COG DAM DIE DIT DOG FID HOB HUB JAM KEY NOG ROW TOP VOL BALK BASE BEAR BILK BLOC BUCK BUNT CAKE CLOG CUBE DRUM FOIL FOUL FROG GLUT HEAD JAMB LEAD MASK MASS MOCK QUAR STAY STEP STOP TRIG BAULK BRICK CHAIR CHECK CHEEK CHUMP CLAMP CLEAT CLOSE COVER DETER DOLLY DUMMY EMBAR FLOAT HEART HORST JUMBO NUDGE PARRY PATCH SHAPE SLUMP SPIKE SPOKE STOCK STUFF STUMP ASSIZE DENTIL DOLLEY DOMINO FIPPLE FORMER HAMPER HINDER IMPEDE KIBOSH MONKEY MUFFLE MUTULE OPPOSE OUTWIT QUERRE RIPPER SADDLE SCOTCH SNATCH SQUARE STREET STYMIE TAPLET THWART TROLLY WAYLAY BOLLOCK BOLSTER BUCKLER CONDEMN DEADEYE ERRATIC INHIBIT OUTLINE PREVENT QUADREL RAMHEAD STONKER TRIGGER TROLLEY BLOCKADE DEADHEAD ELECTRET FOLLOWER KEYSTONE MONOLITH OBSTACLE OBSTRUCT STOPPAGE WITHSPAR BRIQUETTE
(— AT SPAR END) STEEVE
(— A WHEEL) SCOTE
(— FOR SKIDDING LOGS) BICYCLE
(— FOR SLAVE SALES) CATASTA
(— IN SPEAKING) STAMMER
(— OF BUILDINGS) INSULA
(— OF COAL) JUD JUDD
(— OF EARTH'S CRUST) HORST
(— OF GRANITE) SET
(— OF ICE) SERAC
(— OF LAND) FORTY
(— OF SEATS) CUNEUS
(— OF SHARES) TRANCHE
(— OF TIMBER) BOLT JUGGLE
(—S OF STONE) DIMENSION
(— SUPPORTING MAST) STEP
(— THE WAY) SCOAT
(— UP) BAR DAM CLOY QUIRT CONDEMN OPPILATE FORECLOSE
(— WITH HOLE IN IT) WAPP EUPHROE
(— WITH PROJECTING CORE) SETTLE
(ARCHITECTURAL —) DRUM STONE DENTIL IMPOST MUTULE PLINTH DOSSERET
(BUILDING —) MEGALITH
(CHOPPING —) HACKLOG
(CLAY —) DRAWBAR
(FAULT —) MASSIF
(FELTED —) DAMPER
(FOOTBALL —) CRACKBACK
(FULCRUM —) GLUT
(FUSE —) CUTOUT
(HOSPITAL —) PAVILION
(IRON —) USE VOL BITT ANVIL CHAIR
(LOGGING —) LEAD JUMBO
(NAUTICAL —) CHOCK HEART STOCK SADDLE DEADEYE FAIRLEAD
(ORNAMENTAL —) BOSS MODILLION
(PAVING —) SET CUBE SETT STONE WHEELER
(PLASTER —) BATTER
(POLISHING —) BUFF FLOAT RABOT
(PRINTING —) CUT QUAD RISER QUADRAT
(PULLEY —) CRAWL
(SANDSTONE —) SARSEN
(SQUARED —) MITCHEL
(STUMBLING —) HURTING
(TACKLE —) CALO TONGUE
(VAULTING —) BUCK HORSE
BLOCKADE DAM FERM BESET BLOCK EMBAR SIEGE WHISKY BESIEGE EMBARGO BLOCKAGE OBSTRUCT BARRICADE BELEAGUER
BLOCKAGE LOGJAM
BLOCKER CASER BRACER
(CHANNEL —) NIFEDEPINE
BLOCKHEAD ASS LUG OAF SAP BUST CLOT COOF COOT DAFF DOLT FOOL MOME NOWT STUB BLOCK BOOBY CHUMP CUDDY GOLEM GOOSY IDIOT NINNY SNIPE SUMPH CUDDIE DIMWIT DISARD NITWIT NOODLE TUMPHY TURNIP ASSHEAD BUZZARD DIZZARD DULBERT JACKASS LACKWIT MUDHEAD NOGHEAD TOMFOOL BEEFHEAD BONEHEAD CLODPATE CLODPOLL CODSHEAD DULLHEAD DULLPATE DUMBHEAD DUMMKOPF GAMPHREL HARDHEAD JOLTHEAD LUNKHEAD
BLOCKHOUSE SPUR PUNTAL GARRISON
BLOCKING JAM JAMB DUNNAGE BLOCKADE CROSSING
BLOCKISH STOLID
BLOKE EGG GUY MAN CHAP COVE TOFF BLOAK JOKER FELLOW
BLOLLY BEEFWOOD CORKWOOD PORKWOOD
BLOND BAN FAIR LIGHT BLONDE FLAXEN GOLDEN YELLOW LEUCOUS BLONDINE
(AUTUMN —) FAWN
BLOOD KIN SAP GORE LIFE MASS MOOD RACE SANG SANK BLADE BLUDE BLUID CRUOR FLESH FLUID SERUM STOCK CLARET INDRED KAINAH SLUDGE GALLANT KINSHIP KINSMAN LINEAGE RELATION TROPHEMA
(— CONDITION) SICKLEMIA
(— OF GREEK GODS) ICHOR
(— RELATED) HEMAL
(CORRUPT —) YOUSTIR
(HALF —) DEMISANG
(PREF.) HAEM(A)(O) HAEMAT(O)

HEM(A)(O) HEMAT(O) SANGUI SANGUINO SANO
(SUFF.) AEMIA EMIA HAEMIA HEMIA
BLOOD CLOT
(PREF.) THROMB(O)
BLOODCURDLING GORY HORROR
BLOODFLOWER HIPPO REDHEAD BLOODWEED
BLOODHOUND LYM LYAM LYME HOUND LIMER SLOTH BANDOG LEAMER SLEUTH TIEDOG LYAMHOUND SLEUTHHOUND
BLOODIED BEBLED
BLOODLESS DEAD ANEMIC ANAEMIC INHUMAN TURNIPY LIFELESS UNFEELING
BLOODLETTER BLEEDER
BLOOD-LETTING PHLEBOTOMY
BLOODLIKE HEMATOID HAEMATOID
BLOOD PHEASANT ITHAGINE
BLOOD PUDDING BLUTWURST
BLOOD-RED SANGUINE
BLOODROOT PUCCOON REDROOT BOLOROOT COONROOT CORNROOT TURMERIC SANGUINARIA
BLOODSHED DEATH CARNAGE VIOLENCE SLAUGHTER
BLOODSHOT RED INFLAMED
BLOODSTAINED GORY
BLOODSTONE SANGUINE HEMACHATE
BLOODSUCKER LEECH SPONGER VAMPIRE
BLOODTHIRSTINESS ACHARNEMENT
BLOODTHIRSTY BLOODY CARNAL SANGUINE TIGERISH FEROCIOUS MURDEROUS SANGUINARY
BLOOD VESSEL VEIN COMES HEMAD ARTERY CAPILLARY
(PREF.) ANGIO
BLOODWOOD AJHAR JAROOL
BLOODY GORY RUDE BALLY BLODE CRUEL RUDDY BLUGGY CRUENT GRISLY PLUCKY CRIMSON BLEEDING DEATHFUL HEMATOSE INFAMOUS SANGLANT BUTCHERLY CRUENTOUS FEROCIOUS MERCILESS MURDEROUS SANGUINARY
BLOODY BARK LANCEPOD
BLOOM DEW BLOW CAST HAZE KNOT BLURT BLUSH CHILL BLOOTH BLOWTH BLOSSOM BLOWING ANTHESIS BLOOMING FLOREATE FLOURISH
(— OF WILLOW) GULL
(— ON INSECT) POLLEN
(— ON SHELL) CUTICLE
(— ON TREE) GOSLING
(FULL —) HEYDAY
(METAL —S) HEAT
(POWDERY —) PRUINA
BLOOMER ERROR BLOWER BLUNDER FAILURE
BLOOMERS KNICKERS PANTALETS
BLOOMERY FORGE HEARTH FURNACE
BLOOMING PERT ROSY FLUSH FRESH GREEN PRIME ABLOOM FLORID BLOWING FLAMING ROSEATE BLINKING
BLOOPER BLOOMER
BLOSSOM BUD BELL BLOB BLOW CHIP SILK BLOOM LEHUA FLOWER BLOWING BURGEON PROSPER BOURGEON FLOURISH
(BLIGHTED —) BLAST
(HERALDIC —) FRASE FRAISE
(PL.) SET BLOSSOMRY
BLOSSOMING BLOWTH FLORAISON FLORULENT
(— AFTER NOON) POMERIDIAN
BLOT MAR BLOB BLUR DAUB SOIL SPOT BLACK BLANK BLEND BLOTE ERASE SMEAR SPECK STAIN SULLY BLOTCH CANCEL DAMAGE EFFACE IMPAIR MACULA SHADOW SMIRCH SMOUCH SMUDGE SMUTCH STIGMA BLEMISH ECLIPSE EXPUNGE INKBLOT OBSCURE SPLOTCH TARNISH DISGRACE REPROACH
(— OUT) OUT BURY ANNUL ERASE CANCEL DELETE EXPUNGE
BLOTCH DAB BLOT DASH GOUT MONK SPOT AMPER PATCH SMEAR SPLAT STAIN MACULA MOTTLE PLOTCH PURPLE SMIRCH SPLASH STIGMA BLEMISH PUSTULE SPLOTCH ERUPTION MACULATE
(PL.) BLIBE
(PREF.) MACUL(I)(O)
BLOTCHED SCABBY PIEBALD MACULATE SCABROUS SPLASHED MACULATED
(SUFF.) MACULATE
BLOTCHY SCOVY
BLOTTER BLAD
BLOTTO LIT
BLOUSE CHOLI MIDDY SHIRT SMOCK TUNIC WAIST CAMISA GUIMPE JUMPER CASAQUE VAREUSE CAMISOLE CASAQUIN JIRKINET
(ABBREVIATED —) HALTER
(BUSHMAN'S —) BLUEY
(KIND OF —) PEASANT
BLOW BOB COB COP CUT DAB DAD DUB FAN FIB HIT JAB JAR NAP ONE PAT PEG POP RAP TAP TIP TIT WAP ANDE BAFF BANG BASH BEAT BELT BIFF BIRR BLAD BLAW BRAG BUFF BULL BUMP BUTT CHAP CHOP CONK COUP CRIG CUFF DASH DAUD DENT DING DINT DIRD DOLE DRAW DRUB DUNT DUSH FLAP FLEG FLIG FUFF FUNK GALE GOWF GUST HACK HUFF HURT JOLT KNAP KNEE LASH LEAD LEFT LICK LOUK LUSH MINT ONER PAIK PALT PANT PASS PICK PIRR PLUG POLT PUCK PUFF PUSH SCAT SCUD SHOT SLAM SLAP SLAT SLUG SOCK SPAT STOP SWAP SWAT SWOP SWOT THUD WELT WHAP WHOP WIND WIPE YANK BINGE BLADE BLAST BLIZZ BLOOM BOAST BRUNT BURST CLAUT CLINK CLOUR CLOUT CLUMP CLUNK CRUMP CRUNT CURSE DEVEL DOUSE DOWSE DUNCH FACER FILIP FLACK FLICK FLIRT GOWFF ICTUS IMPEL KNOCK OUTER PALMY PANDY PASTE PEISE PLUMP PLUNK PUNCH RIGHT SHAKE SHOCK SKELP SKIRL SKITE SLASH SLIPE SLOSH SMACK SMASH SMITE SNICK SOUND SOUSE SPANK SPEND STORM STRIP SURGE SWACK SWEEP SWIPE THROW THUMP TOUCH TRICE WHACK WHANG WHIFF WHOOF WHUFF BELTER BENSEL BENSIL BETRAY BOUNCE BUFFET CONKER DEPART DIRDUM DUNDER EXPAND FILLIP FISTER FLOWER FROLIC HANDER HUFFLE LARRUP REBUKE SIFFLE STOUSH STRIPE STROKE SWITCH THUNGE THWACK WALLOP WINDER AFFLATE ASSAULT ATTAINT BELLOWS BENSAIL BLOSSOM BLOWOUT BLUSTER BOASTER COUNTER CRUSHER DESTROY INFLATE KNOCKER LAMBACK LOUNDER MOUTHER PUBLISH SHATTER SMACKER SPANKER SQUELCH WHAMPLE WHIFFLE WHIRRET WHITHER CALAMITY DISASTER KNOCKOUT PASHWAFF SASARARA SICKENER SIDEWINDER
(— ABRASIVES) BLAST
(— CEMENT) KIBOSH
(— GUSTILY) FLAW TUCK WINNOW
(— IN PUFFS) FAFF
(— NOSE) SNITE
(— OFF STEAM) SNIFT
(— OF WHALE) SPOUT
(— ON CHEEK) ALAPA
(— ON HEAD) NOB CONK CLOUR CONKER NOBBER TOPPER NOBBLER
(— ON NOSE) NOSER CANKER NOZZLER SMELLER
(— SMOKE) NOSE
(— SOFTLY) BREATHE
(— UP) BOMB BLAST DYNAMITE SUFFLATE
(— UPON) WINNOW
(— VIOLENTLY) STORM
(— WITH CUDGEL) DUB DRUB CRUNT
(— WITH FIST) BOP BOX PEG BELT HOOK CLOUT BUFFET ROUNDHOUSE
(— WITH FOOT) BOOT KICK SPURN
(BOXING —) BLAST FACER
(DECISIVE —) SOCKDOLAGER SOCKDOLOGER
(FENCING —) MONTANT
(GENTLE —) CHUCK
(GLANCING —) SCUFF
(HARD —) SLOG STOT YANK BEVEL SWACK TWITCHER
(HEAVY —) DAD DONG DRUB DUNT ONER SLAM SLUG CLOUT KNOCK POISE SOUSE SQUAT STAVE SWASH STOUND PLUMPER REEMISH
(LIGHT —) WAFF
(MOCK —) FEINT
(NOISY —) DUNDER DUNNER
(RESOUNDING —) CLAP CRACK
(SHARP —) BAT NAP CLIP KNAP SLAP SPAT CLICK FLICK FLEWIT STINGER
(SLIGHT —) SCLAFF
(SMART —) CLIP FLIP SKELP SKITE YANKER
(SUDDEN —) ZAP
BLOWCASE EGG
BLOWER PAN DRIER DRYER WHALE FANNER PUFFER BELLOWS BLOOMER BOOSTER MUMBLER BRAGGART OUTBURST
(GLASS —) GAFFER
BLOWGUN SUMPIT SUMPITAN SARBACANE PEASHOOTER
BLOWHOLE BLOW GLOUP SPOUT SPIRACLE
(— IN STEEL) ROAK
BLOWING ABLOW BLAST BLORE GUSTY BLUSTER BLUSTERY
(— AT LOW SPEED) SLACK
(— AT RIGHT ANGLES) SIDE
(— OF WHALE) SPOUT
BLOWN STALE TIRED OPENED WINDED BLOSSOM SWOLLEN TAINTED BETRAYED FLYBLOWN INFLATED
BLOWOUT BASH BLOW FEED MEAL BURST VALLEY FLAMEOUT WINGDING WHINGDING
BLOWPIPE HOD SUMPIT SUMPITAN SARBACANE
(PEWTERER'S —) HOD
BLOWSY DOWDY BLOUSY BLOWZY FROWZY
BLOWY DUSTY
BLUBBER CRY FAT SOB BLUB FOAM WAIL WEEP BIBLE MELON PIECE SPECK SPICK SWELL THICK WHINE BUBBLE FLITCH LIPPER LUBBER MEDUSA NETTLE SEETHE BLABBER BLUSTER SLOBBER SWOLLEN WHIMPER
(— AT WHALE'S NECK) CANT
(CUT WHALE —) FLENSE
(REFUSE —) FENKS FOOTING FRITTERS
BLUDGEON BAT HIT SAP CLUB COSH MACE BILLY STICK TOWEL COERCE COURSE BLACKJACK TRUNCHEON
BLUE (ALSO SEE COLOR) HAW LOW SAD SKY AQUA BICE BLAE BLEU CYAN GLUM SAXE TEAL WOAD AZURE BERYL LIVID NIKKO PERSE SMALL WAGET COBALT GLOOMY INDIGO LUPINE ORIENT PEWTER RISQUE SEVERE TRYPAN CELESTE CYANINE GENTIAN GOBELIN HYPPISH LEARNED LIBERTY LOBELIA MATELOT MISTBLU MURILLO NATTIER PEACOCK QUIMPER REGATTA WATCHET CERULEAN DEJECTED LABRADOR LARKSPUR LITERARY MAZARINE MIDNIGHT NATIONAL SAPPHIRE WEDGWOOD POMPADOUR
(— DYE) METHYL
(BLACKISH —) BLO BLOO
(DEEP —) SMALT
(DULL —) HAW
(ROYAL —) HATHOR
(SHADE OF —) INDE COPEN
(PREF.) CYAN(O) INDICO IND(I)(O)
(SUFF.) **(— PIGMENT)** CYAN(IC)
BLUEBELL CROWBELL HAREBELL

BLUEBERRY OHELO STONER PALBERRY RABBITEYE VACCINIUM
BLUEBIRD (— GUIDE) LEADER
BLUE-BLACK BLO
BLUEBLOSSOM LILAC
BLUEBONNET CAP SCOT BLUECAP
BLUEBOTTLE BLUET BLAVER BARBEAU BLAWORT BLOWFLY BLUECAP BLUECUP BRUSHES HARDOCK BLUEBLAW HYACINTH CORNBINKS
BLUE CREEPER LOVE
BLUE CURLS FLEASEED FLEAWEED
BLUE-EYED GRASS PIGROOT SATINFLOWER
BLUEFIN TUNNY
BLUEFISH ELF BASS ELFT SHAD TUNA HORSE SAURY DARZEE TAILER TAILOR FATBACK SKIPJACK WEAKFISH
(YOUNG OF —) SNAPPER WHITEFISH
BLUEGILL BREAM SUNFISH PONDFISH PUMPKINSEED
BLUE GOOSE BALDHEAD
BLUEGRASS STATE KENTUCKY
BLUE GREEN VENICE
BLUE GUM FEVERGUM EUCALYPTUS
BLUE HEN STATE DELAWARE
BLUE HERON CRANE NAILROD
BLUEJACKET SAILOR DRAGMAN
BLUEJOINT REDTOP BLUETOPS
BLUENESS CYANOSIS
(— OF SKIN) CYANOSIS
BLUENOSE PRUDE
BLUE-PENCIL EDIT EMEND
BLUE PETER ASK
BLUE PINE LIM
BLUE POINTER MAKO
BLUEPRINT MAP PLAN PLOT DRAFT TRACE SKETCH DIAGRAM PROJECT CYANOTYPE
BLUE RUNNER JUREL
BLUES MARE DUMPS CAFARD DISMAL GLOOMS DISMALS HORRORS HUMDRUM MEGRIMS SADNESS DOLDRUMS DOLEFULS MULLIGRUBS
BLUE SHEEP BURHEL
BLUE SLATE SKAILLIE
BLUESTOCKING BLUE PEDANT BASBLEU
BLUE SUCCORY CATNACHE CUPIDONE
BLUET PISSABED EYEBRIGHT INNOCENCE
BLUE TIT NUN STONECHAT
BLUE TITMOUSE YAUP TYDIE TIDIFE BLUECAP
BLUETONGUE THICKHEAD
BLUE VERVAIN IRONWEED
BLUE VINNY DORSET
BLUEWEED ECHIUM IRONWEED ADDERWORT
BLUFF ALTO BANK BRAG CURT FOOL RUDE BLUNT BRAVE BURLY CLIFF FRANK GRUFF SHORT SURLY SWANK WINDY ABRUPT BOUNCE CRUSTY BLINDER BLINKER BLUFTER BRUSQUE DECEIVE UNCIVIL BARRANCA BARRANCO CHURLISH HOODWINK IMPOLITE
BLUISH BLEUATRE
BLUISH-GRAY MERLE
BLUISH-GREEN AQUAMARINE
BLUMEA PLACUS
BLUNDER ERR MIX BALK BONE BOOB BUBU BULL DOLT FLUB GAFF ROIL SKEW SLIP STIR TRIP BEVUE BLOOP BONER BOTCH BREAK ERROR FAULT FLUFF GAFFE LAPSE MISDO BOGGLE BOOBOO BUMBLE BUMMLE BUNGLE ESCAPE FUMBLE GAZEBO HOWLER MAFFLE MINGLE MUDDLE SLIPUP BLOOMER BLOOPER CLANGER CONFUSE DERANGE FAILURE FLOATER MISSTEP MISTAKE OVERSEE SOTTISE STUMBLE PRATFALL SOLECISM
((AMUSING —) HOWLER
(— IN LANGUAGE) BULL
(— IN SPEECH) SOLECISM
(HUMILIATING —) PRATFALL
(VERBAL —) SLIPSLAP SLIPSLOP
BLUNDERBUSS TRABU TRABUCO TRABUCHO TROMBONE ESPINGOLE
BLUNDERER BUMBLER BUMMLER KNOTHEAD LUMBERER
BLUNDERING AWKWARD BUMBLING
BLUNT BALD BATE BULL CURT DAMP DULL FLAT MULL SNUB ABATE BLATE BLUFF BRUSK DUBBY FRANK INERT MORNE PLAIN PLUMP STUNT TERSE CANDID CLUMSY DEADEN DIRECT OBTUND OBTUSE REBATE RETUND SHEATH STUBBY STUPID BRUSQUE DISEDGE HACKNEY SHEATHE SNUBBED SPADISH STUBBED STUPEFY HEBETATE
BLUNTED MORNED (PREF.) OBTUSI
BLUNTLY PLAT PLUMP FLATLY CRUDELY FRANKLY
BLUR DIM FOG HUM BLOB BLOT FADE FUZZ MIST SLUR SOIL SPOT BLEAR CLOUD FUDGE SHAKE SMEAR STAIN SULLY MACKLE MACULE SMUDGE STIGMA BLEMISH CONFUSE FEATHER OBSCURE TAILING
BLURB AD BOLT PUFF RAVE BRIEF PROMO NOTICE
(PROMOTIONAL —) PROMO
BLURRED FAINT FUZZY MUZZY VAGUE WOOZY BLEARY BLURRY CLOUDY SMEARY SMUDGY SWIMMY WOOLLY CLOUDED COMATIC EDGELESS FLANNELLY
BLURRING HALATION
BLURT BLAT BOLT PLUMP BLUNDER EXCLAIM
BLUSH BLUE GLOW BLINK COLOR FLUSH GLEAM PAINT ROUGE TINGE CHANGE GLANCE MANTLE REDDEN CRIMSON FLICKER SCARLET LIKENESS JOSEPHINE
BLUSHING RED ROSY ABLUSH ROSEATE FLUSHING ROSACEOUS
BLUSTER GAS BEEF BLOW DING HUFF RAGE RAIL RANT RAVE BLAST BLEAT BLORE BOAST BRACE BULLY NOISE STORM SWANK BABBLE BELLOW BOUNCE FRAPLE HECTOR HUFFLE TUMULT WUTHER BLUBBER BRAVADO FLUSTER GAUSTER ROISTER SWAGGER WHITHER BOASTING BULLYING THREATEN RODOMONTADE
BLUSTERER SWAG FLASH HECTOR HUFFER FRAPLER HUFFCAP TEARCAT CACAFOGO FANFARON
BLUSTERING BOG LOUD BLUFF BRASH BULLY VAPORS HUFFCAP VAPOURS ARROGANT BULLYING
BLUSTERY RAW
BOA BOM BOID BOMA ABOMA JIBOA SCARF THROW ABOLLA ADJIGA GIBOIA JOBOYA PYTHON ADJIGER CAMOODI EMPEROR PEROPOD ANACONDA CORALLUS
BOADICEA (HUSBAND OF —) PRASUTAGUS
BOAR HOG APER SUID BRAWN SWINE BARROW HOGGET TUSKER BRAWNER SOUNDER SUIDIAN VENISON WILRONE BRISTLER SANGLIER HOGGASTER
(— CRY) FREAM
(— HEAD) HURE
(— IN 2ND YEAR) HOGGET
(— IN 3RD YEAR) HOGSTEER HOGGASTER
(— STY) FRANK
(YOUNG —) GRISE SOUNDER (PREF.) SUI
BOARD EAT LAG PAX TOE DAIL DEAL DECK DIET EATS FARE FLIP HACK JOIN KEEP LATH MEAT SHIP SIGN SLAT TRAY TRIP ASTEL BUIRD CHESE CLEAR COARD COUCH COURT ENTER FOUND GETIN GETON HOUSE LODGE MEALS PANEL PLANK RATCH SHIDE STAGE STALL SWALE TABLE THEAL ABACUS ACCOST ASTYLL COMMON PALLET PLANCH RANDOM RIBBON SHIELD SIDING TUCKER CABINET CHAMBER COUNCIL CRIMPER DUOVIRI ENPLANE ENTRAIN KNEELER PALETTE PENSION PLANCHE SCRAPER TABLING TRANSOM WHATMAN APPROACH ASSEMBLY BOXBOARD CUPBOARD EXCLUDER FETIALES KEYBOARD LAPBOARD PEGBOARD TRIBUNAL PRESSBOARD MORTARBOARD
(— FOR FALCON'S MEAT) HACK
(— OF BRIDGE) CHESS
(— OF LOOM) CARD
(— OF MILL WHEEL) AWE
(— ON CALF'S NOSE) BLAB
(— OVER) BERTH
(— WITH GROOVE) COULISSE
(— WITH HANDLE) CLAPPER
(— WITH NUMBER) SLATE
(— WITH PINS) RIDDLE
(— WITH TEETH) HACKLE RUFFER
(BLOCKHEAD —) DOLL
(CHANNEL —) PAN
(CHESS —) TABLER
(DRAWING —) COQUILLE
(EXHIBITION —) FRAME
(FLOOR —) KEY
(GAME —) HALMA
(HEART-SHAPED —) PLANCHET
(KIND OF —) OUIJA MALIBU
(MORTAR —) HAWK
(NOTCHED —) HORSE
(OTTER —) DOOR
(POLING —) RUNNER
(PRESSED —S) FELT
(PULP-PRESSING —) COUCH
(RABBETED —S) SHIPLAP
(SHEATHING —S) SARKING
(STRIKE —) SCREED
(TANNING —) BEAM
(THIN —) SHIDE SARKING
(THIN —S) SLITWORK
(WARPING —) BARTREE
BOARDED PLANCHED
BOARDER MEALER TABLER GRAINER PENSIONER SOJOURNER TRANSIENT
BOARDING LIVERY
BOARDINGHOUSE FONDA HOUSE PENSION
BOARDWALK MARINA DUCKBOARD
BOARWOOD CHEWSTICK
BOAST BOG GAB JET BEEF BLAW BLOW BRAG CROW POMP PUFF RAVE VANT WIND WOST YELP BLAST BRAVE CRACK CRAKE EXTOL EXULT GLORY PRATE QUACK ROOSE SCOLD SKITE VAPOR VAUNT VOUST YOLPE AVAUNT BLAZON BLEEZE BOUNCE CLAMOR FLAUNT INSULT MENACE OUTCRY SPLORE BLUSTER BRAVING CLAMOUR DEVAUNT DISPLAY GLORIFY SWAGGER FLOURISH THREATEN VANTERIE VAUNTERY
BOASTER BLOW HUFF GALAH SKITE BLOWER CROWER GASCON PEDANT PRATER SHAKER BLOWOFF BOUNCER BRAGGER BRAVADO CRACKER RUFFLER BLOWHARD BRAGGART CACAFUGO FANFARON GLORIOSO JINGOIST RODOMONT TARTARIN WOUSTOUR
BOASTFUL BIG BRAG HIGH COCKY LARGE BRAGGY PARADO BOBADIL JACTANT VAUNTIE FANFARON GLORIOUS GASCONADE THRASONIC
BOASTFULLY SIDE LARGE
BOASTFULNESS GLORY EGOTISM WINDINESS
BOASTING BLOW HUFF YELP BOAST CRACK PRATE ROOSE QUACKY BOBANCE GASSING JACTANCE JACTANCY QUACKISH VAPORING VAUNTAGE VENTOSITY RODOMONTADE
(EMPTY —) GAS
BOAT ARK BUM BUN CAT COG COT DOW GIG MON TUB ACON BAIT BARK BOOT BRIG CARV CHOP COCK DHOW DINK DORY DUMP FLAT FOUZ JUNK PAIR PLAT PRAM PUNT RAFT SCOW SHIP SKAG TACK TODE TOPO TROW WAKA YAWL

YOLE ACCON AVISO BANCA BARCA BARGE BARIS BATEL BIDAR BOLIA BOYER BULLY BUYER CANOE COBLE CRAFT DHONI DINGY FERRY FOIST FORTY FUNNY JOLLY KETCH LAKER LINER NADIR OOLAK PIECE PILOT PRAAM RACER SHELL SHOUT SIKAR SKIFF SKIFT SMACK TOPPO UMIAK WAAPA WHIFF XEBEC ZEBEC BAIDAK BANGKA BATEAU BAWLEY BELLUM BILALO BORLEY BOTTOM BOUTRE CAIQUE CARVEL CAYUCO CHEBEC COCKLE CRUISE CUTTER DINGHY DREDGE DRIVER DROVER DUGOUT FLATTY GALLEY GARVEY GAYYOU GLIDER HOOKER JAGGER JIGGER KEELER KICKER KUPHAR LATEEN LERRET MAILER NAGGAR NUGGAR PACKET PEAPOD PEDULE PICARD PINKIE PLAYTE PULWAR RANDAN ROCKER SANDAL SCAPHE SCHOUW SCHUYT SETTEE SINGLE SKERRY STRUSE TANKER TENDER TIMBER TOGGER TORPID TRANKY TROUGH VESSEL WAFTER WHERRY ZEBECK AIRBOAT ALMADIA ANGEYOK BALLOEN BALLOON BAULEAH BUMBOAT CAISSON CARRIER CATCHER CORACLE COROLAN CRUISER CURRACH DOGBODY DRIFTER DROGHER FLATTIE FLEETER FLYBOAT FOYBOAT FRIGATE GAIASSA GASBOAT GEORDIE GONDOLA HOVELER HUFFLER KELLECK LIGHTER MACHINE MASOOLA NACELLE PEARLER PEDIWAK PINNACE PIRAGUA POOKAWN PUTELEE SCOOTER SCULLER SHALLOP SHARPIE SHIKARA SIKHARA SKAFFIE SKIPPET SPONGER SPYBOAT STEAMER TRAWLER TUCKNER TUMBREL TUMBRIL VEDETTE WHIRREY BALANGAY BARANGAY BILLYBOY BOOMBOAT BULLBOAT BUMBARGE CANALLER CHALOUPE CHEBACCO CHELINGA CHELINGO COCKBOAT COROCORE DAHABEAH DUCKBOAT FIREBOAT FLAGBOAT KEELBOAT LIFEBOAT MACKINAW MONOXYLE NEWSBOAT OYSTERER PALANDER PANCHWAY PESSONER PESSULUS PULLBOAT SAILBOAT SCHOKKER SCHOONER SURFBOAT TONGKANG TRANSFER OUTRIGGER
(— OF MALTA) DGHAISA
(— WITH SAILS AND OARS) LYMPHIAD
(ABANDONED —) DERELICT
(CANAL — OF VENICE) VAPORETTO
(CHEMICAL —) CAPSULE
(CHINESE —) JUNK SAMPAN
(CLUMSY —) HOOKER DROGHER
(COLLEGE —) TORPID
(DISPATCH —) AVISO PACKET
(ESKIMO —) KAMIK UMIAK OOMIAC UMIACK
(FERRY —) BAC CUTT
(FISHING —) COG BOVO BUSS DONI CANOA COBLE DHONI NOBBY PYKAR SMACK VINTA BALDIE BAWLEY BORLEY DOGGER DROVER FISHER KUPHAR NICKEY SANDAL SCAFFY SEINER SEXERN TOSHER VOLYER WHALER CARAVEL CRABBER DRAGGER FOLLYER POOKAUN SHARPIE SKAFFIE TRAWLER DRAGBOAT GAROOKUH SHRIMPER
(FLAT-BOTTOM —) ARK BAC BUN DORY FLAT PLAT PRAM PUNT SCOW BARGE COBLE DOREY FLOAT MOSES PRAAM SHOUT BATEAU BUGEYE GAYYOU PUTELI GONDOLA LIGHTER FLATBOAT GUNDELOW JOHNBOAT
(FLY —) BUSS FLUTE FLIGHT
(GANGES —) PUTELI
(HIGHLAND —) BIRLINN
(INCENSE —) NEF SHIP NAVICULA
(MALAY —) COROCORE GALLIVAT
(MORTAR —) PALANDER
(OPEN —) WHIFF LERRET SHALLOP
(PATROL —) SPITKID SPITKIT
(PLEASURE —) FUNNY PEDALO
(RACING —) SIX FOUR EIGHT SCULL SHELL SINGLE TORPID SCULLER
(SHIP'S —) GIG MOSES DINGEY DINGHY LAUNCH TENDER PINNACE
(SKIN —) BIDAR BAIDAR ANGEYOK BIDARKA BULLBOAT
(SMALL —) CARTOPPER
(WICKER —) KUFA GOOFA GOOFAH CORACLE
(3-OAR —) RANDAN
(6-OAR —) SEXERN
(8-OAR —) SHIP
(PL.) LIGHTERAGE
(PREF.) CYMBI CYMBO
(SUFF.) SCAPH
BOATBUILDING SETWORK
BOATHOOK STOWER HITCHER
BOATMAN DANDI DANDY PHAON BARGER BOWMAN CHARON YAWLER HOBBLER HOVELER HUFFLER COBLEMAN VOYAGEUR WATERMAN GONDOLIER
BOAT SEAT TAFT
BOAT-SHAPED NAVICULAR
(PREF.) SCAPH(O)
BOAT SHELL YET SWEETMEAT
BOATSWAIN BOSN BOSUN SERANG TINDAL
BOAZ (FATHER OF —) SALMA SALMON
(SON OF —) OBED
(WIFE OF —) RUTH
BOB BAB BOW CUT DAB DIP HOD JOG POP RAP TAP BALL BLOW BUFF CALF CLIP CLOD COIN CORK DUCK GRUB JEER JERK JEST KNOB MOCK WORM BUNCH CHEAT DANCE FILCH FLOAT FLOUT SHAKE TAUNT TRICK BINGLE BOBBER BOBBLE BUFFET CURTSY DELUDE HOBBLE POMMEL POPPLE STRIKE WEIGHT BOBSLED BOBTAIL CLUSTER HAIRCUT PAGEBOY PENDANT PLUMMET REFRAIN SHINGLE SHILLING
(— UP) LOLLOP
BOBAC PAHMI TARBAGAN
BOBBER CORK DUCK FLOAT BOBFLY
BOBBIN PIN CONE CORD PIRN REEL BRAID QUILL SPOOL BROCHE HANGER SKREEL TAVELL WORKER RATCHET SPINDLE TARELLE TORCHON
(PL.) BONES
BOBBINET ILLUSION
BOBBING DOOK
BOBBLE ERROR
BOBOLINK DEER REED SUCKER BUNTING MAYBIRD ORTOLAN REEDBIRD RICEBIRD
BOBSLED BOB DRAY BOBLET RIPPER TRAVERSE
BOBWHITE COLIN QUAIL PARTRIDGE
BOBWIG DALMAHOY
BOCACCIO JACK TOMCOD
BOCCACCIO TRECENTIST
BOCCARELLA NOSEHOLE
BOCCARO YIHSING
BOCE BOGUE OXEYE
BOCHERU (FATHER OF —) AZEL
BODE OMEN SIGN STOP AUGUR OFFER HERALD MESSAGE PORTEND PRESAGE FOREBODE FORECAST FORESHOW FORETELL INDICATE
BODHISATTVA KWANNON MAITREYA AVALOKITA PADMAPANI
BODICE JUPE CHOLI GILET JUMPS WAIST BASQUE BOLERO CORSET JELICK LYFKIE CORSAGE OVERBODY SLIPBODY
BODIERON BOREGAT
BODILESS MOONSHINE
BODILY SOLID SOMAL ACTUAL CARNAL FLESHLY SOMATIC CORPORAL ENTIRELY EXTERNAL MATERIAL PERSONAL PHYSICAL SARKICAL VISCERAL CORPOREAL
(NOT —) INTERIOR
BODKIN AWL PIN POINT BROACH DAGGER NEEDLE POPPER HAIRPIN PONIARD STILETTO EYELETEER
BODLE TURNER
BODO CACHARI
BODY BOD BAND BELL BOLE BOOK BOUK BUCK BULK CREW DEHA FORM HEAD LICH MASS MOLD NAVE RIND RUPA SOMA STEM ATOMY FLESH FRAME HABIT MOULD SHANK STIFF TORSO TRUNK CORMUS CORPSE CORPUS CUERPO EXTENT FUSEAU LICHAM PERSON SARIRA AIRFOIL ANATOMY CADAVER CARCASS COMPANY ECONOMY QUANTUM SKINFUL SUPTION TEXTURE CORSAINT DEMARCHY EXTENSUM MAJORITY PHYSIQUE QUARROME TENEMENT PERSONNEL
(— OF ARROW) SHAFT STELE
(— OF BASILICA) NAVE
(— OF BEES) SWARM
(— OF BELIEVERS) FAITH
(— OF CANONS) CHAPTER
(— OF CARDINALS) CONCLAVE
(— OF CEREMONIES) RITUAL
(— OF CHILDREN) INFANTRY
(— OF CHRISTIANS) KOINONIA COMMUNION
(— OF CONSTABLES) POSSE
(— OF CORINTHIAN CAPITAL) VASE
(— OF DOCTRINES) DOGMA
(— OF ECHINODERM) DISC DISK
(— OF EVIDENCE) CASE CORPUS
(— OF FIBERS) FORNIX
(— OF FOLLOWERS) SECT
(— OF GUARDS) WARD
(— OF HELMET) BELL
(— OF ISLAMIC CUSTOM) SUNNA SUNNAH
(— OF JUDGES) JUDICIARY
(— OF KNOWLEDGE) STUFF
(— OF LAW) CODE SHAR HALAKA SHARIA PANDECT SHARIAT HALACHAH
(— OF LEGEND) SAGA
(— OF MANKIND) HERD
(— OF MUSCLE) BELLY
(— OF NOTIONS) FOLKLORE
(— OF OFFICERS) BUREAU
(— OF ORE) BUNCH MANTO
(— OF PIGMENT) EYESPOT IMPASTO
(— OF POETRY) EPOS
(— OF PRINCIPLES) ORGANON
(— OF ROCK) DIKE DYKE HORSE STOCK BIOHERM MUDFLOW INTRUSION
(— OF SINGERS) CHORUS
(— OF STATUTE) PURVIEW
(— OF STUDENTS) CLASS
(— OF TEN) DECURY
(— OF TENANTS) GAVEL HOMAGE
(— OF THIEVES) SCHOOL
(— OF TRADITIONS) HADIT HADITH
(— OF TROOPS) FORCE TAXIS AMBUSH BATTLE CONREY SCREEN SQUARE BRIGADE LASHKAR SUPPORT BATTALIA GARRISON
(— OF TYPE) SHANK
(— OF VASSALS) BAN MANRED
(— OF WARRIORS) IMPI
(— OF WATER) BAY RIP SEA BAHR FORD HEAD LAKE LAVE POND POOL WAVE ABYSS BAYOU DRINK FLOOD OCEAN SHARD SHERD SWASH LAGOON NYANZA STREAM FLOWAGE SWALLOW
(— OF WELLBORN MEN) COMITATUS
(— OF WRITINGS) SMRTI SMRITI
(— OF 12 MEN) DOUZAINE
(— POLITIC) ESTATE
(— RIDDLED BY BULLETS) SIEVE
(CAROTID —) GLOMUS
(CART —) SIRPEA
(CELESTIAL —) SUN BALL COMET PLANET SPHERE ELEMENT ASTEROID PLANETOID SATELLITE PLANETESIMAL
(CIRCULAR —) DISC DISK
(COMPACT —) GLOBE
(CONDUCTING —) GROUND
(CORPORATE —) SOCIETY
(DEAD —) LICH MORT GHOST CADAVER CARCASS CARRION SUBJECT
(DEFEATED —) ROUT
(ECCLESIASTICAL —) CLASSIS
(ELASTIC —) CUSHION
(EXTENDED) LENGTH
(FAT —) EPIPLOON
(FRUITING —) CONK CLAVA ASCOCARP MAZAEDIUM

(**GALACTIC —**) SPINAR
(**GLOBULAR —**) NOB KNOB
(**GOVERNING —**) KAHAL SYNOD DURBAR SENATE DECARCHY DIRECTORY
(**HAT —**) HOOD
(**HEAVENLY —**) SUN LAMP STAR COMET LIGHT CANDLE
(**HOLLOW —**) TUBE
(**HUMAN —**) EARTH
(**HYALINE —**) DRUSE
(**IMMUNE —**) DESMON
(**JUDICIAL —**) FORUM
(**KIND OF —**) LIFTING
(**LEGISLATIVE —**) CHAMBER ASSEMBLY CONGRESS LAGTHING PARLIAMENT
(**MAIN — OF ARMY**) BATTLE
(**MATHEMATICAL —**) FILAMENT
(**MORMON —**) BISHOPRIC
(**MORTAL —**) KHET
(**POROUS —**) MADREPORITE
(**PRESBYTERIAN —**) SESSION JUDICATORY
(**RELIGIOUS —**) SECT CONVENT
(**REPRODUCTIVE —**) EGG GEMMA SPORE GEMMULA
(**ROUND —**) GLOBE
(**SONOROUS —**) PHONIC
(**SPIRITUAL —**) SAHU
(**SWELLING —**) BOSS
(**UNICELLUAR —**) SPORE
(**WAGON —**) BED BUCK PUNT
(PREF.) CORPORI SOMAT(O) SOMATICO SOMO
(SUFF.) CY DEMA SOMA(TO)(TOUS) SOME SOMIA SOMIC SOMOUS SOMUS
(**— OF A KIND**) ID

BODYGUARD THANE ESCORT INWARD HUSCARL RETINUE TRABANT THINGMAN WARDCORS
(**CRIMINAL'S —**) MINDER

BOER TAKHAAR AFRIKANER

BOG BUG CAR DUB FEN GOG HAG BOLD CARR CESS FLOW MIRE MOOR MOSS OOZE QUAG SINK SLEW SLUE SPEW STOG SUDS SYRT WASH LETCH MARSH MIZZY SAUCY SLADE SLOCK SWAMP MORASS MUSKEG POLDER SLOUGH CRIPPLE FORWARD PEATERY TURBARY QUAGMIRE
(**MARSH —**) QUAG
(**PEAT —**) CESS MOSS PETARY YARPHA
(PREF.) HELO

BOG ASPHODEL KNAVERY

BOGEY BUG COW HAG BOGIE BOGLE DEVIL GNOME TRUCK BOGGLE BOOGER GOBLIN BOGGARD BOGGART BUGABOO BUGBEAR SPECTER SPECTRE

BOGGED SLOUGHED

BOGGLE JIB SHY BALK FOIL STOP ALARM BOTCH DEMUR SCARE START STICK BAFFLE BUNGLE GOBLIN SHRINK BAUCHLE BLUNDER PERPLEX SCRUPLE STUMBLE FRIGHTEN HESITATE

BOGGY WET DEEP MIRY SOFT FENNY FOGGY GOUTY HAGGY MOSSY SNAPY SPEWY MARISH MARSHY QUAGGY SLOBBY SWAMPY WAUGHY BOGGISH QUEACHY SQUASHY

BOGIER RIDER GEARMAN

BOGLAND SLADE

BOGLE GOBLIN

BOG MANGANESE WAD LAMPADITE

BOGO ABILO ABILAO

BOGOMILE PATARIN PATARINE

BOGUS FAKE SHAM FALSE PHONY SPURIOUS

BOGY GOBLIN

BOHEME, LA (**CHARACTER IN —**) MIMI COLLINE MUSETTA RODOLFO MARCELLO SCHAUNARD
(**COMPOSER OF —**) PUCCINI

BOHEMIAN ARTY PICARA PICARD PICARO ARTISTIC
(**— RIVER**) ELBE VLTAVA LUZNICE BEROUNKA
(**— TOWN**) PISEK PLZEN PRAHA TABOR PILSEN PRAGUE

BOHEMIAN GIRL (**COMPOSER OF —**) BALFE

BOHOR REEDBUCK

BOIL FRY PET STY BILE BLOB BOLL BRAN BREW BUCK BUMP COCT COOK COWL LEEP PLAY PUSH QUAT RAGE SEED SORE STEW STYE TEEM WALL WALM WELL BLAIN BOTCH BREDE STEAM BETRAY BUBBLE BULDER BULLER BURBLE DECOCT GALLOP PIMPLE RISING SEETHE SIMMER TOTTLE WABBLE WOBBLE ANTHRAX BEALING BREEDER CATHAIR ELIXATE ESTUATE INFLAME AESTUATE EBULLATE FURUNCLE PHLEGMON CARBUNCLE
(**— IN LYE**) BUCK
(**— SYRUP**) PEARL
(**SAND —**) BLOWOUT
(PREF.) COCTO DOTHI(EN)(O) ZEO

BOILED SOD SODDEN
(**— WITHOUT SAUCE**) ANGLAISE

BOILER YET REEF STILL COPPER KETTLE RETORT TEACHE ALEMBIC CALDRON FURNACE
(**SALT —**) WELLER

BOILERMAKER (**PART OF —**) BEER

BOILING WALM ABOIL FERVID COCTION FERVENT SCALDING SEETHING ELIXATION

BOILING POINT
(PREF.) COCTO

BOISTERER (**MASTER OF —**) FORTUNIO

BOISTEROUS GURL HIGH LOUD RUDE WILD BURLY GURLY NOISY RANDY ROARY ROUGH WINDY COARSE RUGGED SHANDY STOCKY STORMY STRONG UNRULY FURIOUS MASSIVE ROARING VIOLENT BIGMOUTH CUMBROUS LARRIKIN STRIDENT VEHEMENT ROBUSTIOUS

BOLD BIG BOG MOD YEP DERF HARD KEEN PERT RASH RUDE TALL WHAT YEPE APERT BARDY BIELD BRASH BRAVE BRENT FRACK FREAK FRECK GALLY HARDY JOLLY LARGE MANLY NERVY PAWKY PEART POKEY RUDAS SAUCY STEEP STOUT WLONK ABRUPT AUDACE BRASSY BRAZEN CROUSE DARING FIERCE HEROIC PLUCKY PRETTY STRONG ASSURED DASHING DEFIANT FORWARD GRIVOIS HAUGHTY MASSIVE VALIANT ARROGANT FAMILIAR FEARLESS IMMODEST IMPUDENT INTREPID MALAPERT POWERFUL RESOLUTE TEMEROUS
(**NOT —**) GENTEEL

BOLDFACE BOLD BLACK FULLFACE

BOLDLY CRANK BARELY CROUSE HARDLY HARDILY ROUNDLY STRONGLY

BOLDNESS BROW DARE FACE GALL BIELD CHEEK NERVE PLUCK VIGOR DARING BRAVERY COURAGE FREEDOM AUDACITY TEMERITY HARDIHOOD
(**— OF SPEECH**) PARRHESIA

BOLDO NUTMEG

BOLE CLAY DOSE STEM BOLUS CRYPT TRUNK RUDDLE TIMBER

BOLETUS CEPE

BOLIDE METEOR FIREBALL

BOLIVIA PILE

BOLIVIA

CAPITAL: LAPAZ SUCRE
COIN: TOMIN CENTAVO
DEPARTMENT: LAPAZ ORURO PANDO ELBENI POTOSI TARIJA
FORMER CAPITAL: ORURO
INDIAN: URO INCA ITEN MOXO URAN ARAWAK AYMARA CHARCA CHICHA IXIAMA TACANA PUQUINA QUECHUA SIRIONE TUMUPASA
LAKE: POOPO COIPASA ROGAGUA AULLAGAS TITICACA
MEASURE: LEAGUE CELEMIN
MOUNTAIN: JARA CUSCO CUZCO PUPUYA SAJAMA SORATA ILLAMPU ANCOHUMA ILLIMANI ZAPALERI
MOUNTAINS: ANDES SUNSAS SANSIMON SANTIAGO
PANPIPE: SICU SIKU
PLATEAU: ALTIPLANO
RIVER: BENI YATA ABUNA APERE BOOPI LAUCA ORTON BAURES GRANDE ICHILO ITENEZ MADIDI MAMORE MIZQUE TARIJA YACUMA GUAPORE ITONAMA MACHUPO BENECITO INAMBARI PARAGUAY PARAPETI
SALT DEPOSIT: UYUNI EMPEXA
SWAMP: IZOZOG
TOWN: IVO ICLA ITAU MOJO POJO SAYA YACO YATA YURA CLIZA LAPAZ LLICA ORURO QUIME SUCRE UNCIA UYUNI ZONGO GUAQUI POTOSI TARIJA
VOLCANO: OLLAGUE
WEIGHT: LIBRA MARCO

BOLL BOW POD BULB KNOB SNAP ONION BUBBLE CAPSULE
(**FOURTH —**) FIRLOT

BOLLARD BITT KEVEL DOLPHIN DEADHEAD
(**—S AND BITTS**) APOSTLES

BOLLER STRIPPER

BOLL WEEVIL PICUDO

BOLO MACHETE SUNDANG

BOLSHEVIK RED MAXIMALIST

BOLSHEVISM COMMUNISM SOVIETISM

BOLSHEVIST BOLO

BOLSTER AID PAD JACK PILLOW CUSHION HEADING STIFFEN SUPPORT BACKSTOP BALUSTER COMPRESS MAINTAIN

BOLT BAR JAG KEY LUE PEN PIN ROD RUN BEAT BURR CRAM DART DUMP FLEE GULP LOCK PAWL SHUT SIFT SLOT SNIB SPAR STUD ARROW BILBO CLOSE ELOPE FLASH FLOUR GORGE LATCH RIVET SETUP SHAFT STOCK ASSORT DECAMP DESERT FASTEN FLIGHT GANYIE GARBLE MOOTER PINTLE PURIFY QUARRY REFINE SAFETY SEARCE SECURE SNIBEL STREAK STRONG TOGGLE WINNOW ABSCOND BAYBOLT DOGBOLT EYEBOLT MISSILE QUARREL SETBOLT SHACKLE SLABBER THUNDER DRAWBOLT FASTENER FISHBOLT FLATHEAD KINGBOLT RINGBOLT SEPARATE SLUMMOCK STAMPEDE
(**— FOOD**) SKOFF
(**DOOR —**) DRAWBOLT
(**FIERY —**) RESHEPH
(**LIGHTNING —**) SHAFT
(**THUNDER —**) FULMEN
(PREF.) GOMPHO

BOLTER BOLT SIEVE DRESSER MUGWUMP

BOLTHEAD MATRASS

BOLUS BALL PILL

BOMB DUD EGG ROC AZON BOOM FRAG BLARE CRUMP PRANG RAZON SHELL SQUIB ASHCAN SALUTE AEROSOL BALLOON BOMBARD GRENADE MARMITE TORPEDO AEROBOMB FIREBALL WHIZBANG PINEAPPLE INCENDIARY
(**— RELEASE**) TOGGLE
(**FLYING —**) DOODLEBUG
(**KIND OF —**) SKIP
(**TRENCH —**) MINNIE
(**UNEXPLODED —**) DUD
(PL.) STICK

BOMBARD BOMB PELT CRUMP SHELL ATTACK BATTER BOTTLE STRAFE

BOMBARDMENT BLITZ SIEGE ATTACK RAFALE STRAFE BATTERY SHELLING

BOMBARDON TUBA NICOLO POMMER BRUMMER

BOMBAST GAS PAD PUFF RAGE RANT RAVE STUFF TUMOR BLUSTER FUSTIAN TYMPANY BALLYHOO BOASTING RHAPSODY TURGIDITY

BOMBASTIC PUFFY TUMID VOCAL WINDY FLUENT HEROIC MOUTHY TURGID BLOATED BOMBAST

FLOWERY FUSTIAN OROTUND POMPOUS RANTING STILTED SWOLLEN INFLATED SWELLING
(— STYLE) TYMPANY
BOMBAY DUCK BUMALO BUMMALO
BOMBER (TYPE OF —) STEALTH
BOMBINATE HUM BUZZ
BONACE TREE NOSEBURN
BONACI AGUAJI
BONA FIDE LEVEL GENUINE AUTHENTIC
BONANZA BUNCH
BONANZA STATE MONTANA
BONBON CANDY CREAM GOODY DAINTY CARAMEL COSAQUE SNAPPER CONFETTO
(PL.) CONFETTI
BOND BON DOG TIE VOW ANDI BAIL BAND DUTY FIVE FOUR GILT GLUE GYVE HOLD KNOT LINK NOTE YOKE BOUND CHAIN NEXUS SWATH BINDER CEDULA CEMENT CONNEX COPULA COUPLE ENGAGE ESCROW FETTER LEAGUE PLEDGE SOLDER SWATHE FOREIGN HUSBAND LIAISON LIBERTY LINKAGE MANACLE SHACKLE STATUTE ADHESIVE CONTRACT COVENANT LIGAMENT LIGATION LIGATURE MORTGAGE SECURITY VADIMONY VINCULUM
(EMOTIONAL —) RAPPORT
(KIND OF —) JUNK
(PL.) IRON KHAKIS SHORTS
(PREF.) DESM(A)(IDI)(IDIO)(O) ETHMO OSSE(O) OSSI OST(E)(EO)
(SUFF.) **(CONTAINING TRIPLE —)** OLIC
BONDAGE YOKE THRALL HELOTRY SERFDOM SLAVERY BONDSHIP THIRLING CAPTIVITY SERVITUDE
BONDED CATTED ENGAGED
BONDMAN CARL ESNE PEON SERF CHURL HELOT SLAVE STOOGE SURETY THRALL VASSAL CHATTEL PEASANT SERVANT VILLEIN BONDSMAN
BONDSTONE BINDER BONDER KEYSTONE
BONE OS DIB HIP LUZ RIB TOT BANE ULNA BLADE FEMUR HYOID ILIUM INCUS JUGAL MALAR SLATE STONE TALUS TIBIA UNION VOMER CANNON COCCYX CONCHA COPULA CUBOID EPURAL FIBULA FILLET HAMATE NUCHAL PECTEN RADIAL SPLINT STAPES TRIPOD UNGUIS ZYGOMA DENTARY PALATAL PROOTIC CORACOID PALATINE PARIETAL PERIOTIC PISIFORM QUADRATE TEMPORAL NAVICULAR OPERCULAR METACARPAL
(— OF ARM) RADIU
(— OF DIGIT) PHALANX
(— OF NOSE) VOMER TURBINAL
(ANKLE —) TALUS
(EAR —) INCUS HAMMER STAPES MALLEUS TYMPANIC
(HEEL —) CALCANEUM
(HIP —) HUGGIN
(HORSE'S —) RACK
(PELVIC —) PUBIS
(PUBIC —) PECTEN
(SHIN —) CNEMIS
(SKULL —) SQUAMOSAL
(SMALL —) OSSICLE
(THIGH —) FEMUR
(WRIST —) RADIALE SCAPHOID TRAPEZOID
(PL.) DICE CLAPPERS ETHMO KNACKERS SKELETON
(PREF.) ETHMO OSSE(O) OSSI OST(E)(EO)
(SUFF.) OST(EON)(EUS)(OSIS)
BONE-BLACK SPODE SPODIUM
BONED
(SUFF.) OSTEUS
BONEFISH OIO MACABI GRUBBER BONYFISH LADYFISH
BONEHEAD SAP BOOB STUPE
BONER BUBU FLUB ROCK ERROR BRODIE STAYER STUMER BLOOMER BLOOPER BLUNDER MISTAKE STEELER STUMOUR
BONES
(PREF.) **(— OF HAND OR FOOT)** PHALANGI(A)
BONESET COMFREY AGUEWEED EUPATORY HEMPWEEK
BONEYARD STOCK
BONFIRE BLAZE TANDLE TAWNIE BALEFIRE BURNFIRE NEEDFIRE
BONGO DOR BUNGO CANOE
BONI MUNI
BONIFACE HOST
BONING SAP
BONITO AKU ATU NICE COBIA SARDA BONITA ROBALO ALBACORE KATONKEL MACKEREL SCOMBRID SKIPJACK
BONNET CAP HAT COWL HOOD POKE POXY SCON COVER DECOY SCONE SHAPE TOQUE CAPOTE MOBCAP SLOUCH CHAPEAU COMMODE CORONET LEGHORN SOWBACK VOLUPER BALMORAL BONGRACE HEADGEAR
BONNET MONKEY ZATI MUNGA TOQUE MACACO RILAWA MACAQUE
BONNY GAY FINE MERRY PLUMP BLITHE BONNIE PRETTY STRONG HEALTHY BUDGEREE HANDSOME BEAUTIFUL
BONTOK IGOROT
BONUS GIN TIP GIFT MEED PLUM PLUS AWARD BRIBE BUNCE BUNTS PILON PRIZE SPIFF REGALO REWARD CUMSHAW DOUCEUR PREMIUM SUBSIDY BOUNTITH DIVIDEND TANTIEME LAGNIAPPE
BON VIVANT SPORT EPICURE GOURMET
BON VIVEUR FLANEUR
BONY HARD LANK THIN LANKY STIFF TOUGH OSTEAL SKINNY ANGULAR OSSEOUS SCRAGGY SKELETAL
BONYFISH MENHADEN
BOO FIE HUMBUG
BOOB ASS OAF FOOL GOON GOOP DUNCE GOONY NEDDY NITWIT
BOOBOOK OWL PEHO RURU CUCKOO MOPOKE MOPEHAWK MOREPORK
BOOB TUBE BOX
BOOBY GAWK GONY SULA DUNCE IDIOT LOSER PATCH PRIZE SILLY SLEIGH STUPID CAMANAY PIQUERO GOOSECAP
BOOBYALLA DOGWOOD WATERBUSH
BOODLE LOOT SWAG CROWD GRAFT BUDDLE NOODLE PAYOFF PLUNDER CABOODLE
BOOGEYMAN PADFOOT TANKERABOGUS
BOOJUM SNARK
BOOK MO LIL LOG CHAP CODE FORM HEFT OPUS PAGE TEXT TOME ALBUM ALDUS BIBLE CANON CANTO CODEX DETUR DIARY DIVAN ENTER FLETA FOLIO FROST GUIDE KITAB LIBEL LIBER QUAIR QUIRE RAZEE ZOHAR ALDINE ANONYM BODONI CURSUS DOCKET ENGAGE HERBAL LEDGER MAHZOR MANUAL MISSAL NUMBER REBIND RECORD RITUAL SCHOOL TICKET TROPER VOLUME BLOTTER CATALOG COUCHER DIETARY DISCARD FEODARY GARLAND GRAMMAR JOURNAL LAWBOOK LEXICON MANDALA OCTAPLA OMNIBUS ORDINAL OUTBOOK PEERAGE RECITER SAMHITA SERVICE SLEEPER SPEAKER SPELLER SYNAXAR TERRIER TICKLER TRAVAIL TRIGLOT TYPICON TYPICUM WRITING BANKBOOK BROCHURE CALCULUS CASEBOOK CASHBOOK CHAPBOOK COOKBOOK COPYBOOK DECRETAL DOCUMENT FESTIVAL GIFTBOOK GOSPELER HANDBOOK HARDBACK HERDBOOK JESTBOOK JUVENILE LIBRETTO PASTORAL POMANDER POSTBOOK REGISTER SONGBOOK STUDBOOK SYNAXARY TALEBOOK TRIODION TWENTYMO VESPERAL PAPERBACK PONTIFICAL NOMENCLATOR PROCESSIONAL PHARMACOPOEIA
(— BACK) DORSE
(— FOR HARVARD GRADUATE) DETUR
(— OF CHARTS) WAGONER PORTOLAN
(— OF DEVOTIONS) ORARIUM
(— OF HERALDRY) ARMORY ARMORIAL
(— OF HOMILIES) POSTIL
(— OF MAPS) ATLAS
(— OF PSALMS) PSALTER TEHILLIM
(— OF RULES) HOYLE
(— OF SERVICES) PIE
(— OF SOLUTIONS) KEY
(— OF THE MASS) ORDO
(— SECTION) OCTAVO QUARTO
(—S KEPT IN PRINT) BACKLIST
(— THAT DOESN'T SELL) PLUG
(CHEAP —) BLOOD
(CHINESE —) CHING
(COMIC —) COMIX
(COMMONPLACE —) ADVERSARIA
(ELEMENTARY —) PRIMER
(FIRST READING —) ABC ABCEE ABSEY
(FOLDED —) ORIHON
(HOLY —) VEDA
(IMPROPER —S) FACETIAE
(INSTRUCTION —) METHOD
(JOKE —) JOE JESTBOOK
(LOST HEBREW —) JASHAR JASHER
(MEMORANDUM —) AGENDA JOTTER TICKLER
(MINIATURE —) BIBELOT
(PART OF —) CASE FLAP COVER HINGE JOINT SPINE TITLE JACKET LINING ENDLEAF BACKBONE ENDPAPER HEADBAND BACKSTRIP SHELFBACK
(PRAYER —) PORTAS SIDDUR PORTASS PORTHORS
(READING —) ABC ABCEE ABSEY
(RECORD —) LIBER TICKLER
(RELIGIOUS —) KITAB KORAN QURAN GOSPEL HORARY KYRIAL PROSAR GRADUAL KYRIALE BREVIARY MEGILLAH ORDINARY SYNAXARY
(SACRED —) KORAN QURAN PURANA
(SERVICE —) COMES GRAIL TEXTUS
(SLOW-SELLING —) PLUG
(STRANGE —S) CURIOSA
(UNBOUND —) CAHIER
(PL.) LIBRI SHELF STUDY EROTICA SCRIPTURE
(PREF.) BIBLIO LIBRI
BOOKBINDING STUB YAPP STRING
BOOKBINDINNG LAWCALF
BOOKCASE DESK STAGE STALL SCRINE PLUTEUS CREDENZA
BOOK COVER LID SIDE FOREL RECTO VERSO FORREL REVERSE REVERSO
BOOKISH BOOKY ERUDITE INKHORN PEDANTIC STUDIOUS
BOOKLET FOLDER NOVELET BROCHURE
BOOK LOUSE PSOCID
BOOKMAKER LAYER BOOKER BOOKIE
BOOKMARK MARKER TASSEL REGISTER
BOOK PALM TARA TALIERA
BOOKSELLER STATIONER BIBLIOPOLE
BOOKSHELF DESK PLUTEUS
(PL.) CLASSIS
BOOKWORM GOME GRUB NERD TOOL WONK CEREB GNURD GRIND SQUID SPIDER WEENIE
BOOM JIB BEAM BOMB BUMP CRIB POLE ROAR SPAR BRAIL CHAIN CRANE CROON PROBE BUMPKIN CATHEAD CURTAIN RESOUND SUPPORT BOWSPRIT FLOURISH
(CRANE —) ARM GIB JIB
BOOMBOX (SOUND FROM —) BLARE
BOOMER TNT
BOOMERANG KALIE KILEY KYLIE WANGO ATLATL BOUNCE RECOIL LEEWILL REBOUND WOMERAH WOOMERA BACKFIRE HORNERAH LEEANGLE RICOCHET TROMBASH
BOOMING HUMMING ROARING
BOOM IRON WITHE CRANCE

BOON GAY BENE GIFT GOOD KIND BOUND FAVOR GRANT MERRY ORDER BENIGN BOUNTY GOODLY JOVIAL PRAYER BENEFIT COMMAND PRESENT BLESSING INTIMATE PETITION BENEFACTION
BOONDOCKS STICKS BOONIES
BOOR CAD OAF BOER BORE CARL HICK JACK KERN LOUT PILL RUNT SLOB CARLE CHUFF CHURL CLOWN KERNE SLAVE BUMKIN CARLOT CLUNCH HOBLOB JOBSON JOSKIN LUBBER LUMMOX RUSTIC BUMPKIN CAUBOGE GROBIAN PEASANT VILLAIN BOEOTIAN BOSTHOON CLODHOPPER
BOORISH ILL RUDE CRASS GAWKY ROUGH RUNTY SURLY CLUMSY RUSTIC SAVAGE SULLEN VULGAR WOOLEN AWKWARD CRABBED HIRSUTE HOBLIKE KERNISH LOUTISH PEAKISH ROISTER UNCOUTH VILLAIN WOOLLEN BOEOTIAN CARTERLY CHURLISH CLODDISH CLOWNISH LUBBERLY SWAINISH TACTLESS UNGAINLY
BOORISHNESS VILLAINY GROBIANISM
BOOST AID LEG ABET BACK BOOM HELP LIFT PLUG PUSH COACH EXALT HOIST HOOSH RAISE ASSIST ADVANCE COMMEND ELEVATE ENDORSE PROMOTE INCREASE
BOOT PAC PAD USE CURE GAIN HALF HELP HOOF KICK PUNT SHOE SOCK AVAIL BOOTY DERBY EJECT EVICT JEMMY KAMIK PEWEE SPOIL BOOTEE BUDGET BUSKIN CASING CHUKKA CRAKOW ENRICH FUMBLE GAITER GALOSH INSHOE JEMIMA JOCKEY MUKLUK PEDULE SHEATH BENEFIT BOTTINE COTHURN COWHIDE CRUISER HESSIAN HIGHLOW SEABOOT SHOEPAC VANTAGE BALMORAL BOTTEKIN CHASSURE COVERING FINNESKO JACKBOOT LARRIGAN NAPOLEON COTHURNUS WAFFLESTOMPER
(— OF CARRIAGE) FOREBOOT
(— ON SADDLE) GAMBADE GAMBADO
(CAR —) BUSTLE
(CLIMBING —) SCARPETTO
(HALF —) PAC BUSKIN COCKER SKILTY BRODEKIN
(HIKING —) WAFFLESTOMPER
(HOB-NAILED —) BAT
(HORSE'S —) SCALPER
(KIND OF —) DENVER
(LUMBERMAN'S —) CRUISER
(MARINE —) SKINHEAD
(RIDING —) JEMMY JIMMY JODHPUR
(SEALSKIN —) KAMIK
(STOUT —) STOGA STOGY
(TO —) ALSO
(TORTURE —) SQUEEZER
(WATERPROOF —) WADER
(PL.) OVERS WADER FINNESKO HESSIANS
BOOTBLACK SHINER BLACKER SHOEBOY
BOOTED OCREATE
BOOTES WAINMAN HERDSMAN
BOOTH BOX BULK COOP DESK LOGE SHED SHOP SOOK BOTHY CABIN CRAME HOUSE KIOSK LIWAN LODGE PITCH SLANG STALL STAND BOTHAN PAGODA PANDAL PAYBOX SUCCAH SUKKAH TIENDA BALAGAN COCKSHY TABERNA
BOOTLACE LACET THONG
BOOTLEG SHY SLY ILLEGAL ILLICIT
BOOTY BOOT FANG GAIN LOOT PELF PREY SACK SWAG BUTIN CHEAT FORAY GRAFT PRIZE CREAGH FLEECE SPOILS DESPOIL PILLAGE PLUNDER SPREAGH SPREATH STEALTH PURCHASE SPUILZIE STEALAGE
BOOZE BOLL BOUT BUDGE DRINK HOOCH SPREE FUDDLE LIQUOR
BOOZY TIPPLE LIQUORY
BOP POP JIVE DANCE SHUFFLE
BOPHUTHATSWANA (CAPITAL OF —) MMABATHO
(TOWN OF —) TEMBA MABOPANE GARANKUWA
BORAGE ANCHUSA
BORAX FLUX TINCAL
(— SOURCE) KERNITE
BORDER CUT HEM RIM TAB ABUT BABK BRIM CURB DADO EAVE EDGE LIMB LINE LIST LOVE MARK NARK ORLE RAND ROON RUND SIDE TRIM WELL WELT BOARD BOUND BRAID BRINK CHEEK COAST COSTA DRAFT FILET FLANK FOREL FRAME FRILL GUARD LIMIT MARCH MARGE MARLI PLAIT SHORE SKIRT STRIP SWAGE TOUCH VERGE ACCOST ADJOIN COTISE EDGING FILLET FORREL FRINGE IMPALE LACING LIMBUS LISERE MARGIN ORFRAY PURFLE QUADRA SCREED STRIPE TANIKO WEEPER CONFINE DRAUGHT FIMBRIA FLOROON MARGENT SELVAGE VALANCE BOUNDARY DOUBLING FRONTIER MARCHESE NEIGHBOR OUTSKIRT PLATBAND SKIRTING SURROUND TERMINUS TRESSOUR TRESSURE
(— OF EXTERNAL EAR) HELIX
(— OF LACE) PICOT
(— OF ROCK) SALBAND
(— OF SAIL) DOUBLING
(— OF SHIELD) BORDURE
(— OF STREAM) ROND
(— ON) ABUT ACCOST AFFRONT NEIGHBOR
(FLOWERED —) FLOROON
(ORNAMENTAL —) PURL WAGE FRAME FRINGE MATTING DENTELLE TRESSURE
(RIBBON —) FRILAL
(PL.) CONFIN PURLIEU CONFINS
(PREF.) CRASPEDO LIMBI
BORDERED ORLE LIMBATE
BORDERER MARCHMAN
BORDERING MARGENT FRONTIER
BORDERLAND BOUNDS
(— OF HELL) LIMBO
BORE BIT CUT EAT IRK JET TAP DRAG FLAT HOLE JUMP PALL PILL POKE REAM RUSH SINK SIZE TIDE TIRE TOOL ANNOY AUGER CHINK DRILL EAGRE ENNUI GAUGE GOUGE OUGHT PLONK PRICK PUNCH SUGUR TEWEL THIRL TRICK VAPOR WEARY BEFOOL CANNON GIMLET PIERCE THRILL THRUST TUNNEL WIMBLE YAWNER BROMIDE CALIBER CALIBRE CONCAVE CREVICE HUMDRUM NUDNICK OPENING AIGUILLE CAPILLUS DIAMETER DRAWBORE GRATIANO POROROCA
(— OF CANNON) SOUL CHASE
(PREF.) FORAMINI
BOREAL NORTHERN
BOREAS AQUILO AQUILON
(BROTHER OF —) NOTUS HESPERUS ZEPHYRUS
(DAUGHTER OF —) CLEOPATRA
(FATHER OF —) ASTRAEUS
(MOTHER OF —) EOS AURORA
(SON OF —) ZETES CALAIS
BORED BLASE HOHUM WEARY ENNUYEE TEDIOUS SATIATED
BOREDOM YAWN BLAHS ENNUI ACEDIA TEDIUM
(FEELING OF —) BLAHS
BORELE KEITLOA UPEYGAN
BORER MOLE BARDEE WIMBLE HAGFISH TANBARK TERMITE TERRIER FLATHEAD SHIPWORM WOODWORM
(PREF.) TRYPAN(O)
BORING DIM DRY FLAT SLOW HOHUM BROACH STODGY STUPID TIRING LUMPISH TEDIOUS PIERCING TIRESOME TEREBRANT
(— TOOL) AUGER GIMLET WIMBLE AIGUILLE
(SOMETHING —) DRAG
BORIS GODUNOV (CHARACTER IN —) BORIS PIMEN DMITRY GRIGORY MISSAIL RANGONI SHUISKY VARLAAM
(COMPOSER OF —) MUSSORGSKY
BORN N NEE NATE INNATE NASCENT NATURAL UTERINE ORIGINAL
(— OUT OF WEDLOCK) BASTARD
(NEWLY —) NEONATE
(NOBLY —) GENEROUS
(PREMATURELY —) SLINK ABORTIVE
(WELL —) FREE EUGENIC
(SUFF.) GEN(E)(ESIA)(ESIS)(ETIC)(IC)(IN)(OUS)(Y)
BORNE RODE NARROW CARRIED ENDURED
(— AFFRONTEE) CABOCHED
(— LOWER THAN USUAL) ABASED
(— ON WATER) AFLOAT
(WIND —) EOLIAN

BORNEO
BAY: ADANG KUMAI SAMPIT
CAPE: ARU DATU LOJAR PUTING SAMBAR SELATAN
MOUNTAIN: RAJA SARAN NIJAAN TEBANG
MOUNTAINS: IRAN MULLER SCHWANER
NAME: KALIMANTAN
NATIVE: DYAK DAJAK
RIVER: ARUT IWAN BAHAU BERAU KAJAN PADAS PAWAN BARITO KAPUAS SEBUKU KAHAJAN MAHAKAM MENDAWI PEMBUANG
TOWN: KUMAI SAMBAS SAMPIT MALINAU PAGATAN SANGGAU SINTANG TARAKAN KETAPANG
TREE: KAPOR KAPUR
WEIGHT: PARA CHAPAH

BORO MARIANA
BORON BORAX ULEXITE
BORORO COROADO
BOROUGH BURG CITY PORT TOWN WICK BORGO BRUSH BURGH CASTLE COUNTY CITADEL FORTESS VILLAGE TOWNSHIP
(SUFF.) BURG
BORROW BOT BITE COPY HIRE KICK LOAN SHIN TAKE THIG ADOPT STEAL TOUCH DESUME DUPLEX PLEDGE STRIKE SURETY CHEVISE HOSTAGE MUTUATE TITHING
BORROWED SECONDHAND
BORROWER BOT CRIB MUTUARY
BORROWING ECLECTIC
BORS (BROTHER OF —) BAN
(UNCLE OF —) LANCELOT
BORSCHT (— INGREDIENT) BEETS
BOS OX NEAT TAURUS
BOSH END ROT JOKE SHOW TALK TOSH FUDGE TRASH BUSHWA FIGURE FLAUNT HUMBUG TRIVIA HOGWASH TOSHERY GALBANUM NONSENSE POPPYCOCK
BOSKY BUSHY TIPSY WOODY FUDDLED
BOSNIA & HERZEGOVINA (ALSO SEE YUGOSLAVIA)
CAPITAL: SARAJEVO
COIN: DINAR
LANGUAGE: BOSNIAN SERBOCROATIAN
MOUNTAIN: MAGLIC
MOUNTAIN RANGE: GRMEC CINCAR RADUSA VITOROG KLEKOVACA PLJESIVICA
PEOPLE: SERB SLAV CROAT
RIVER: UNA SAVA BOSNA DRINA VRBAS NERETVA
SEA: ADRIATIC
TOWN: MOSTAR RAGUSA BANJALUKA DUBROVNIK
BOSNIA-HERZEGOVINA (RIVER OF —) BOSNA DRINA NERETVA
(TOWN OF —) TUZLA MAGLAJ MOSTAR VISOKO SARAJEVO
BOSOM LAP BARM BUST CLOSE DICKY HEART SINUS BREAST CAVITY DESIRE DICKEY RECESS BELOVED EMBRACE GREMIAL INCLOSE INTIMATE POITRINE
(— OF DRESS) SQUARE
(FALSE —) PLUMPER
BOSS BUR HUB MOP NOB ORB PAD POP BAAS BEAD BOCE BUHR BURR CAPO COCK CZAR KNOB KNOP KNOT NAIL NAVE NULL STUD TSAR BULLA BULLY BWANA CHIEF EMPTY JEWEL KNOSP ORDER OWNER PEARL ANCHOR BROOCH BUCKRA BUTTON CHEESE DIRECT HOLLOW HONCHO MANAGE MASTER OCULUS PATERA PELLET

SHIELD BULLION CACIQUE CAPATAZ CAPTAIN CUSHION FOREMAN HASSOCK HEADMAN HOBNAIL MANAGER PADRONE PHALERA SPANGLE SPONSON DIRECTOR DOMINATE DOMINEER MISERERE OMPHALOS OVERSEER UMBILICUS
(— OF LOGGING CAMP) BULLY
(— OF SHIELD) UMBO
(FIRE —) GASMAN
(LEATHER —) BUTTON
(MINE —) SHIFTER SHIFTMAN
(POLITICAL —) CACIQUE CAUDILLO
(STRAW —) BULL LEADER
(PREF.) UMBO
BOSSY PUSHY
BOSTONIAN HUBBITE
BOT OESTRUM OESTRUS
BOTANIST HERBALIST HERBARIAN
AMERICAN AMES BEAL COOK GRAY HOWE ROSE BROWN CLUTE GAGER HEALD JAMES JONES LOGAN MOORE PURSH SEARS SHULL SMALL VASEY BAILEY BESSEY CANNON CARVER CUTLER DUDLEY DUGGAR FARLOW HARRIS HOWELL JEPSON LEMMON PEIRCE SHANTZ TAYLOR TORREY WATSON BARTRAM BIGELOW BRITTON COULTER CROCKER ELLIOTT FERNALD GOODALE HOLLICK JOHNSON MERRILL PEATTIE POLLARD RYDBERG SWINGLE THURBER CALDWELL CAMPBELL COPELAND KNOWLTON MARSHALL TRELEASE BLAKESLEE FAIRCHILD LONGWORTH NIEUWLAND OSTERHOUT SULLIVANT UNDERWOOD CHAMBERLAIN
AUSTRIAN UNGER KERNER MENDEL JACQUIN HABERLANDT
BELGIAN LINDEN
CANADIAN SAUNDERS
DANISH HANSEN WARMING JOHANNSEN RAUNKIAER
DUTCH TREUB DODOENS
ENGLISH WARD BOWER BUDDLE CLARKE DARWIN GERARD HOOKER HUDSON MARTYN PAXTON TURNER BENNETT FORSYTH HAWORTH HENSLOW JACKSON LINDLEY DRYANDER SIBTHORP BABINGTON
FRENCH BORNET MAGNOL MIRBEL THURET TRECUL BONNIER JUSSIEU LECLUSE MICHAUX TULASNE DECAISNE MILLARDET JACQUEMONT TOURNEFORT VANTIEGHEM DESFONTAINES
GERMAN BOCK COHN KOCH LINK MOHL ZINN BLUME DRUDE FUCHS KUNTH SACHS ENGLER GLOXIN GMELIN GOEBEL HEDWIG KUNTZE MIGULA REINKE CORRENS EICHLER FITTING GARTNER JUNGIUS KARSTEN KUTZING MOLISCH PFEFFER RIVINUS WARBURG BRUNFELS LEDEBOUR LONITZER SPRENGEL DILLENIUS GRISEBACH KOLREUTER CAMERARIUS HOFMEISTER PRINGSHEIM REICHENBACH STRASBURGER
HUNGARIAN ENDLICHER
IRISH HARVEY
ITALIAN TONI CORTI ALPINI BECCARI CESALPINO
JAPANESE IKENO
NORWEGIAN GUNNERUS
RUSSIAN BUNGE FAMINTSYN
SCOTTISH AITON BROWN DOUGLAS FORTUNE MORISON FALCONER
SPANISH CAVANILLES
SWEDISH DAHL KALM FRIES RETZIUS ACHARIUS AFZELIUS LINNAEUS THUNBERG ANDERSSON BROMELIUS
SWISS BAUHIN VAUCHER CANDOLLE
BOTANY HERBARISM PHYTOLOGY
BOTCH MAR MUX BOIL BOSS FLUB MEND MESS MULL SORE BITCH BODGE BUTCH FLUFF FUDGE SPOIL STICK BOGGLE BOLLIX BUMBLE BUNGLE COBBLE JUMBLE MUCKER REPAIR TINKER BLUNDER BUTCHER CLAMPER SCAMBLE SCLATCH SLUBBER SWELLING
BOTCHER GRILSE SALMON TINKER BUNGLER BUTCHER CLOUTER COBBLER
BOTCHERY PATCHERY
BOTE KINBOT MAGBOTE CARTBOTE FRITHBOT PLOWBOTE WAINBOTE
BOTFLY BOTT BREEZE GADBEE GADFLY NITTER CANOPID OESTRID TORSALO DIPTERAN OESTRIAN
BOTH BO ALL TWO BAITH EQUALLY
(PREF.) AMBI AMBO AMPH(I)(O) BIS
(— SIDES) AMPHI
BOTHER ADO AIL BUG IRK NAG VEX FASH FAZE FUSS JADE WORK ANNOY DEAVE HARRY KNOCK PHASE TEASE TRADE WORRY BADGER BUSTLE CUMBER DITHER FLURRY GRAVEL HARASS HASSLE MEDDLE MITHER MOIDER MOLEST MUCKLE PESTER PLAGUE POTHER POTTER PUTTER PUZZLE TAMPER CONFUSE DISTURB FASHERY GRIZZLE PERPLEX TERRIFY TRACHLE TROUBLE BEWILDER DISTRESS IRRITATE NUISANCE
BOTOCUDO BORUN AIMORE AYMORO
BOTONEE TREFLEE FLEURONE
BO TREE PIPAL

BOTSWANA
CAPITAL: GABORONE GABERONES
COIN: PULA RAND THEBE
DESERT: KALAHARI
LAKE: DOW NGAMI
LANGUAGE: BANTU CLICK KHOISAN SETSWANA
MONEY: PULA THEBE
MOUNTAIN: TSODILO
NATIVE: BANTU TSWANA BUSHMAN
RIVER: NATA OKWA CHOBE NOSOB CUANDO MOLOPO SHASHI CUBANGO LIMPOPO OKAVANGO
TOWN: KANYE ORAPA TSANE SEROWE LOBOTSI MOCHUDI PALAPYE THAMAGA GABERONES

BOTTLE JUG BOSS SKIN VIAL VIOL AMPUL ASKOS BETTY BOCAL BUIRE BURET CADUS COOJA CROFT CRUET CRUSE FIFTH FLASK GIRBA GLASS GOURD HOUSE PHIAL SPLIT VERRE ALUDEL BACBUC BUNDLE CARAFE CARBOY CASTER CASTOR CHAGUL CHATTY CREWET DORUCK DUBBER FESSEL FIASCO FLACON FLAGON GOGLET GUTTUS JORDAN LAGENA MAGNUM MARINE MATARA NURSER PACKER SIPHON VESSEL WOULFF BALLOON BIBERON BOMBARD BOMBOLA BURETTE CANTEEN CARAFON COSTREL DEADMAN FLACKET FLOATER GRENADE INKHORN BOMBONNE BORACHIO BUILDING CALABASH DECANTER DEMIJOHN GARDEVIN JEROBOAM MARIOTTE PRESERVE REHOBOAM PEPPERBOX
(— IN WICKER) CARBOY DEMIJOHN
(EGYPTIAN —) DORUCK
(EMPTY —) MARINE
(HOT-WATER —) PIG
(LARGE —) KIT JEROBOAM
(LEATHER —) BOOT JACK DUBBA BUDGET DUBBER DUPPER MATARA BOMBARD BORACHIO WHINNOCK WINESKIN
(MEDICINE —) VIAL PHIAL
(OVERSIZED —) BALTHAZAR
(PAIR OF —S) GEMEL GEMMEL
(PART OF —) LIP CORK KICK NECK PUNT MOUTH MUZZLE CAPSULE SHOULDER
(PILGRIM'S —) AMPULLA
(SMALL —) VIAL AMPUL CRUET PHIAL SPLIT FLACON AMPOULE TICKLER CRUISKEN CRUISKEEN
(18 —S OF WINE) RIDDLE
(40 —S) KEMPLE
(PREF.) UTRI
BOTTLE CAP CAPSULE
BOTTLE CARRIER FASCET
BOTTLE CASE CELLAR
BOTTLEHEAD DOEGLING
BOTTLER COOPER
BOTTOM ASS BED ARSE BASE DALE DOUP FLAT FOND FOOT FUND HOLM LEES REAR ROOT ABYSS BASIS DREGS FLOOR LAIGH NADIR BATHOS FOUNCE FUNDUS GROUND GUTTER LAAGTE LEEGTE BEDROCK LOWLAND SUPPORT SURFACE BUTTOCKS INTERVAL SEDIMENT TETRAPOD
(— LINE) NET
(— OF BENCH) TOE
(— OF CUPOLA) HEARTH
(— OF FURROW) SOLE
(— OF GRATE) NIGGARD
(— OF PAGE) TAIL
(— OF PISTOL GRIP) BUTT
(— OF POT) POTSTONE
(— OF PRINTER'S GALLEY) SLICE
(— OF PULLEY BLOCK) BREECH
(— OF SEA) GROUND BENTHOS
(— OF SOLE) NAUMK NAUMKEAG
(— OF STACK) STADDLE
(MARSHY —) SIKE
(ROCK —) HARDPAN
(PL.) HOLM HOLME
BOTTOM-DWELLING DEMERSAL
BOTTOMER FOOTMAN STATIONMAN
BOTTOMLAND STRATH
BOTTOMLESS ABYSMAL
BOTTOM LINE CRUX UPSHOT OUTCOME SUMMARY CONCLUSION
BOTULISM LAMSIEKTE LAMZIEKTE
BOUDOIR ROOM BOWER CABIN BEDROOM CABINET
BOUGH ARM LEG LIMB TWIG CHUCK SHOOT SPRAY SPRIG BRANCH RAMAGE SHROUD GALLOWS PHYLLIS OFFSHOOT SHOULDER
(— ON TAVERN) BUSH
(— USED AS TORCH) ROUGHIE
(DRY —) ROUGHY ROUGHIE
(PL.) RAMAGE DUNNAGE RAMMAGE
BOUGHT KEFT STORE ZEBINA
BOUGIE CANDLE COLLYRIE FILIFORM
BOUILLABAISSE POTPOURRI
BOULDER NOB KELK KNOB ROCK STONE GIBBER BOOTHER DORNICK ERRATIC GRAYBACK HARDHEAD MEGALITH POTSTONE
BOULE BIRNE
BOULEVARD DRIVE PRADO AVENUE STREET ALAMEDA HIGHWAY TERRACE CORNICHE
BOULTER TRAWL SPILLER SPILLET
BOUNCE DAP HOP BANG BLOW BRAG BUMP DING DIRD FIRE GATE JUMP LEAP OUST SACK STOT BOAST BOUND BULLY CAROM CHUCK EJECT KNOCK SCOLD THUMP VERVE BLAGUE MORGAY SPIRIT SPRING STRIKE ADDRESS BLUSTER CHOUNCE DISMISS REBOUND SWAGGER PINGPONG PROCLAIM RICOCHET
(— A BABY) DANDLE
(— BACK) RECOVER
BOUNCER BUMPER CHUCKER SCROUGER
BOUNCING BIG BUXOM LUSTY STOUT BOUNCY HEALTHY WALLOPING
(— OF TONGUE) FLAP
BOUNCING BET SOAPWORT
BOUND DAP END HOP LOP BENT BIND BOND BONE BROW BUTT DART GIRT JUMP LEAP LIST MERE RAMP RISE SCUD SKIP STEM STOT SURE TERM WALL AMBIT BORNE BOURN FIXED GOING LIMIT READY SALLY SCOUP SKELP START STEND STING TILED VAULT VERGE BORDER BOUNCE BOURNE BUTTAL CAVORT CURVET DEFINE DOMAIN FINISH GAMBOL GIRDED HURDLE JETTED LIABLE LOLLOP OBLIGE PRANCE SPRING AFFINED BARRIER CERTAIN CHAINED CLOSURE CONFINE CONTAIN COSTIVE DELIMIT DRESSED GAMBADO INCLUDE REBOUND SALTATE SECURED SUBSULT TERMINE TRUSSED BOUNDARY CONFINED DESTINED ENCLOSED FASCIATE FRONTIER HANDFAST

LANDMARK LIMITATE OBLIGATE PINIONED PRECINCT PREPARED RESTRICT SHACKLED
(— ALONG) SLING
(— BY OATH) SWORN
(— BY OBLIGATION) AFFINED
(— CLUMSILY) LOLLOP
(NOT —) SOLUTE
(RIGIDLY —) STATIC STATICAL
(PL.) PALE AMBIT MOUND CLOSURE COMPASS CONFINE PURLIEUS PERIPHERY

BOUNDARY AHU END RIM DOLE DOOL EDGE FINE FORM LINE LIST MARK MEAR MEER MERE META METE PALE SURF TERM TRIG WALL AMBIT BOURN CLOSE FENCE FRAME FRONT HEDGE LIMES LIMIT MARCH MEITH MOUND SHORE VERGE BORDER COLLET DEFINE OCTROI OCTROY TROPIC BARRIER BOUNDER BUTTING COMPASS FURLONG OUTLINE CURBLINE FRONTIER LANDLINE LIMITARY PRECINCT TERMINUS UMSTROKE PERIMETER PERIPHERY MAGNETOPAUSE
(— OF EARTH'S CRUST-MANTLE) MOHO
(PL.) ABUTTALS ENVIRONS
(PREF.) HORO LIMI ORI TERMINO
(— OF AIR MASS) FRONTO TERMINO

BOUNDER CAD HARE RAKE ROUE ROTTER

BOUNDING (— LINE) RUBICON

BOUNDLESS VAST UNTOLD ENDLESS ETERNAL INFINITE UNLIMITED

BOUNDLESSNESS INFINITY

BOUNTEOUS BOON CROWNED LIBERAL PLENTEOUS

BOUNTIFUL GOOD LUSH RICH AMPLE FREELY LAVISH LIBERAL PROFUSE ABUNDANT GENEROUS

BOUNTY BOON GIFT MEED AWARD BONUS GRANT LARGE VALOR WORTH BONTEE REWARD VIRTUE LARGESS PREMIUM PRESENT PROWESS SUBSIDY DONATIVE GOODNESS GRATUITY KINDNESS

BOUQUET BOB AURA ODOR POSY AROMA BLOOM CIGAR POSEY SHEAF SPRAY BOWPOT BUSKET SHOWER CORSAGE NOSEGAY BOUGHPOT
(— GARNI) FAGOT FAGGOT
(DEVELOP —) BREATHE

BOURDON BURDEN

BOURGEOIS ORGON COMMON POOTER STUPID BOORISH BURGHER
(KIND OF —) PETIT

BOURGEOIS GENTILHOMME
(AUTHOR OF —) MOLIERE
(CHARACTER IN —) CLEANTE LUCILLE COVIELLE JOURDAIN

BOURSE SALE BOLSA BORSE CAMBIO

BOURTREE ELDER

BOUT GO JOB BOOT FALL PULL TURN BOOZE BRASH CRASH ESSAY FIGHT MATCH PLUCK ROUND SCRAP SIEGE TRIAL VENNY VENUE ATTACK COURSE FRACAS YOKING ASSAULT ATTEMPT CAROUSE CIRCUIT CONTEST DEBAUCH OUTSIDE WITHOUT CONFLICT
(— OF INDULGENCE) JAG
(DRINKING —) BAT BEND BUST TIRL BOOZE SPRAY SPREE RANDAN SCREED SPLORE CAROUSE GAEDOWN WASSAIL POTATION

BOUTONNIERE BOUQUET BUTTONHOLE

BOUW BAHU BAHOE

BOVAARISM EGO

BOVATE OSKEN OXGANG OXGATE OXLAND
(TWO —S) HUSBANDLAND

BOVINE OX BOS COW BOSS BULL CALF DULL NEAT SLOW ZEBU BEAST BISON STEER ANIMAL COWISH HUMLIE HUMMEL OXLIKE ROTHER BULLOCK TAURINE BANGTAIL LEPTOBOS

BOW ARC LEG LUG NOD SAW TIE YEW ARCH BAIL BEAK BECK BEND BENT CURB DUCK FOLD FORE GORA JOUK KNEE KNOT LATH LOUT MOVE PROW SELF STEM SWIM TRUE TURN WEND BINGE CLINE CONGE COQUE COUCH CROOK CRUSH CURVE DEFER GOURA HONOR KNEEL NOEUD SHIKO STICK STOOP VENIE YIELD ARCHER ASSENT BAUBLE BUCKLE CONGEE CRINGE CROUCH CURTSY FIDDLE FOGBOW RIBBON SALAAM SALUTE SCRAPE SUBMIT SWERVE TOURTE WEAPON DEPRESS FOREBOW FORMBOW HANDBOW INCLINE INFLECT LONGBOW NECKTIE RAINBOW ARBALEST COURTESY CRESCENT ENTRANCE FOGEATER GREETING STONEBOW TRUELOVE OBEISANCE
(— DOWN) ALOUT HUMBLE
(— IN ONE PIECE) SELF
(— LOW) BINGE
(— OF PLOW) DRAIL
(— OF VESSEL) HEAD PROW STEM HAWSE ENTRANCE
(— ON SCRAPER) BAIL BALE
(— ON SEA) ATRY
(— OUTWARD) CONVEX
(— SLIGHTLY) ADDRESS
(OVERHANGING —) SWIM
(PART OF —) DIP TIP BACK FACE GRIP LIMB LOOP NOCK BELLY BRIDGE HANDLE RECURVE SERVING BOWSTRING
(PART OF VIOLIN —) NUT TIP FROG HAIR HEAD POINT SCREW STICK
(WITH THE —) ARCO
(PREF.) ARCI ARCO TOX(I)(ICO)(O)

BOWDLERIZE EDIT

BOWED ARCO BENT BANDY KNEED ARCATE ARCATO CURVED BULGING CURVANT SHAMBLE DOWNBENT
(PREF.) TOX(I)(O)

BOWELS GUT GUTS WOMB BELLY COLON ROPES VISCERA ENTRAILS
(PREF.) VISCER(I)(O)

BOWER RUN BOOR JACK NOOK SALE ABODE ARBOR JOKER KNAVE ANCHOR BOWERY LEFSEL PANDAL BERCEAU CABINET CHAMBER COTTAGE EMBOWER ENCLOSE LEVESEL PERGOLA RETREAT SHELTER TRELLIS THALAMUS
(— FOR SNAKES) KISI
(GARDEN —) ALCOVE

BOWERBIRD CATBIRD COLLARBIRD

BOWFIN AMIA GANOID LAWYER MORGAY SAWYER CHOUPIC DOGFISH GRINDAL GRINDLE GRINNEL MUDFISH

BOWIE STATE ARKANSAS

BOWING CERNUOUS FEATHERING

BOWL CAP CUP PAN TUN COUP ROLL TASS TRAY WOOD ARENA BASIN BOWIE DEPAS GUARD JORUM KITTY LAVER MAZER PHIAL PITCH ROGAN SCALE TANOA TAZZA TREEN TROLL BEAKER BICKER CHAWAN CLOSET COOTIE CRATER FESSEL JICARA KETTLE LEKANE MAZARD MORTAR PIGGIN TROUGH TUREEN VESSEL BRIMMER DITCHER DOUBLER DUGGLER SCYPHUS SKYPHOS SPILLER STADIUM TOUCHER TRINDLE TRUNDLE WHISKIN AQUARIUM BRIDECUP FISHBOWL JEROBOAM LAVATORY MONTEITH REHOBOAM PORRINGER
(— ILLEGALLY) JERK
(— OF PIPE) CHILLUM STUMMEL
(— ON PEDESTAL) TAZZA SALVER
(— OUT) YORK
(— THAT TOUCHED JACK) TOUCHER
(— WITH TWO HANDLES) CAP DEPAS
(DRINKING —) TUN TASS
(MARBLE CUTTER'S —) SEBILLA
(OBLONG —) PITCHI
(PUNCH —) SNEAKER
(SHALLOW —) CAP COUPE WHISKIN
(SMALL —) JACK
(SOUP —) ECUELLE
(SUGAR —) SUGAR SUCRIER
(TOILET —) HOPPER
(WOODEN —) CAP BOWIE COGIE KITTY ROGAN BASSIE BICKER COGGIE COOTIE

BOWLEG OUTKNEE

BOWLEGGED BANDY VALGUS

BOWLER HAT POT DERBY KEGLER PINMAN SPINNER TRUNDLER
(CRICKET —S) ATTACK

BOWLINE BOWLIN FARGOOD

BOWLING BOWLS ATTACK KEGLING TENPINS
(— GAME) BOCCI

BOWLS RINK BOCCE BOCCIE

BOWMAN ARCHER

BOW-SHAPED ARCATE

BOWSPRIT SPAR

BOWSTRING SERVING

BOWYER BOWER ARTILLER

BOX BED BIN CAR EAR FUR GIG KIT LOB LUG PIX PYX TYE ARCA BARK BODY BOOT CAGE CAJA CASE CIST CRIB CUFF CYST DRAB FLAT HEAD LOGE MILL PACK PUNG SCOB SEAT SLAP SLUG SPAR STOW TILL TRAY ARBOR BARGE BIJOU BOIST BUIST BUXUS CADDY CAPSA CHEST CLOUT CRATE FIGHT FRAME HUTCH LADLE POUCH PUNCH SHRUB STALL TRUNK ASCHAM BRUISE BUFFET BUNKER CARTON CASKET COFFER COFFIN DRAWER GRILLE HAMPER HATBOX HAYBOX HOPPER ICEBOX MAROON MOCUCK PATRON PETARA PILLAR SAGGER SHRINE STRIKE TARBOX VANITY ARCANUM BANDBOX BATTERY BOXTREE BOXWOOD CABINET CAISSON CARRIER CASHBOX CASQUET CASSONE COFFRET CONFINE COREBOX DICEBOX DREDGER DUSTBOX ENCLOSE EXHAUST FOSTELL FREEZER HANAPER JACKBOX PACKAGE PILLBOX PITARAH PRINTER SANDBOX SCATULA SHELTER TRUMMEL WHERRET BOXTHORN DOVECOTE DRAGEOIR JUNCTION LAVARIUM MATCHBOX POMANDER SHOWCASE SLIPCASE SOLANDER SWEATBOX PEPPERBOX PHYLACTERY
(— FOR CARRYING COAL) DAN
(— FOR CARRYING ICE) YAKHDAN
(— FOR CLOTHES) PETARA PITARA PITARAH
(— FOR COSMETICS) PUFFBOX
(— FOR CUTLERY) CANTEEN
(— FOR FIRE) CHAUFFER
(— FOR FISH) CAR NID
(— FOR MONEY OFFERING) ARCA LADLE
(— FOR SALT) DRAB
(— FOR SEAL) SKIPPET
(— FOR SEED) LEAP
(— FOR TOBACCO) BUTT DOSS CADDY SARATOGA
(— FOR TROUSSEAU) GLORYBOX
(— IN TIMEPIECE) BARREL
(— IN WHEEL HUB) FUR
(— OF BIRCHBARK) MOCUCK
(— OF CYLINDER) BUSH
(— OF FIRE CLAY) SAGGAR SAGGER
(— OF ORGAN) BOOT SWELL
(— SHAPED LIKE BOOK) SOLANDER
(— TO SHELTER BELL) SCONCE
(— USED AS DARKROOM) TENT
(BALLOT —) URN
(BERRY —) HALLOCK
(BREAD —) BARGE
(CANDLE —) BARK
(CIRCULAR —) THIMBLE
(COLLECTION —) BROD
(COMPASS —) KETTLE BINNACLE
(DICE —) RATTLE
(FANCY —) ETUI ETWEE
(FLOATING —) CAISSON
(FOUNDRY —) FRAME
(IRON —) HANGER
(JAPANESE —) INRO
(JUGGLER'S —) TRANKA
(KIND OF —) FUZZ READY
(MONEY —) CASH SAFE PIRLIE
(ORE —) SKIP
(PERFUME —) CASSOLETTE
(PIVOTING —) TOUR
(PRESENTATION —) COFFRET

(PRINTING —) TURTLE
(REFRIGERATOR —) COOLER
(SHADOW —) SPAR
(SHALLOW —) FLAT BACKET HARBOR
(SNUFF —) MILL MULL
(TEA —) CADDY
(TELEPHONE —) KIOSK
(TIN —) TRUMMEL VASCULUM
(WITNESS —) PETER STAND
(PREF.) CAPSULI CAPSULO CISTO PYXID(O)
BOX BRIER INDIGO INKBERRY
BOXCAR LOWRY STOCKCAR
BOX ELDER MAPLE NEGUNDO
BOXER PUG CHAMP DARES BANTAM MILLER NOBBER TANKER WELTER BRUISER CRUISER FIGHTER SLUGGER SPARRER BUFFETER PUGILIST SOUTHPAW
BOXFISH CHAPIN COWFISH SHELLFISH TRUNKFISH
BOXING PLUG RING FANCY SAVATE PARINGS SCIENCE SPARRING
(— GLOVE) MUFFLE
(— JAB) LEFT RIGHT
BOXING-GLOVE CESTUS MUFFLE
BOX TORTOISE COOTER
BOXWOOD KNYSNA DUDGEON
BOXY BLOCKY
BOY BO BUB FAG GUY HIM LAD PUR TAD BOYO CHAP LOON NINO PAGE PUER BILLY BUBBY BUDDY CHABO CHILD CRACK GAMIN GILPY GROOM KNAVE PUTTO ROGUE SWAIN VALET YOUTH BIRKIE BUTTON CALLAN CHOKRA GAFFER GARCON MANNIE MASTER NIPPER RASCAL SHAVER STIRRA UMFAAN URCHIN BOUCHAL CALLANT DRAWBOY GLEANER GOSSOON GRUMMET JACKBOY RUBBLER SERVANT SPADGER TRAPPER CLERGION HENCHBOY MUCHACHO SPALPEEN
(— DRESSED AS WOMAN) MALINCHE
(— IN LIVERY) TIGER
(— NOT YET 13) PRETEEN
(— OF FREE BIRTH) CAMILLUS
(ALTAR —) ACOLYTE THURIFER
(AWKWARD —) CUB CALF GRUMMET
(BABY —) NENE
(BLESSED —) BEATUS
(BOISTEROUS —) GILPY GILPEY
(BOLD —) SPALPEEN
(CHIMNEY SWEEPER'S —) CHUMMY
(CHOIR —) CHILD
(CLEANING —) BUSBOY
(COLLIER'S —) HODDER
(EFFEMINATE —) SISSY MOLLYCODDLE
(ERRAND —) GALOPIN
(FIRST-YEAR —) GYTE
(FIRST YEAR —) GYTE
(GOOD OLD —) BUBBA
(HEAD —) SENIOR CAPTAIN
(HOMELESS —) ARAB
(ILL-MANNERED —) CUB
(LOVER —) ROMEO
(MESSENGER —) PAGE
(MISCHIEVOUS —) NICKUM
(MY —) AVICK
(NATIVE —) MOWGLI
(NON-JEWISH —) SHEGETZ
(OFFICE —) DUFTRY DUFTERY
(PERT —) CRACK
(POOR —) HERO
(ROGUISH —) CRACK GAMIN URCHIN
(SAUCY —) NACKET
(SERVING —) KNAVE PEDEE CHOKRA MOUSSE FOOTBOY GOSSOON
(SILLY —) CALF
(SMALL —) BO BUDDY UMFAAN SPADGER
(SPRIGHTLY —) CRACK
(STABLE —) MAFU MAFOO MEHTAR
(TEDDY —) DUCKTAIL
(TOWN —) CAD
(WINGED —) PUTTO
(YOUNG —) LAD SONNY YOUTH NIPPER
(PL.) BOYHOOD
(PREF.) PAED(O) PAID(O) PED(O)
BOYCOTT MITE SHUN AVOID DEBAR BLACKBALL
BOYFRIEND BEAU STEADY
BOYISH GAMIN GAMINE
BRA BANDEAU
BRABANTIO (DAUGHTER OF —) DESDEMONA
BRACE DUO LEG MAN TIE TWO BEND BIND CASE FRAP GIRD JACK KNEE LACE MARK PAIR PROP SPUR STAY STEM STUD CLAMP CRANK DWANG GIRTH HOUND NERVE POISE RIDER SHORE STEEL STOCK STRUT ANKLET BINDER BRACHE CLENCH COLLAR COUPLE CRUTCH FASTEN FATHOM HURTER SPLINT STRING WIMBLE BOTTINE BRACKET EMBRACE REFRESH SPANNER STIFFEN SUPPORT ACCOLADE BITBRACE BITSTALK BITSTOCK BUTTRESS CROSSBAR ENCIRCLE ORTHOTIC
(— ACROSS CABLE) STUD
(— AND HALF) LEASH
(— A YARD) TRAVERSE
(— BETWEEN FRAMES) TOM
(— FOR POST) SPUR
(— UP) ACCINGE SHARPEN
(PART OF —) BOW HEAD JAWS PAWL RING CHUCK CRANK QUILL SHELL HANDLE RATCHET
(PL.) BRIDGING
BRACED BENT
(— ABACK) ABOX
BRACELET BAND RING ARMIL CHAIN ARMLET BANGLE GRIVNA ARMILLA CIRCLET MANACLE POIGNET RACETTE WRISTER BARRULET HANDCUFF MUFFETEE WRISTLET
(— USED AS MONEY) MANILLA
(SHELL —) SANKHA
BRACER TONIC SHORER BLOCKER ARMGUARD STIFFENER STIMULANT
BRACHIAL HUMERAL
BRACHIOPOD ATREMATE ATRYPOID SPIRIFER
BRACHIUM ARM
BRACHYCEPHALIC ROUNDHEADED
BRACING CRISP QUICK TONIC DUNNAGE
BRACKEN FERN TARA BRAKE PLAID
BRACKET BIBB COCK CONK FORK GATE PUNK ANCON BELOW BRACE CLASS CONCH COUCH CRANE CRANK CROOK LEVEL SHELF STRUT TRUSS ANCONE BECKET BRIDGE CORBEL COUPLE GUSSET HANGER LADDER MUTULE SADDLE SCONCE BECKETT CONSOLE DERRICK FEATHER FIXTURE GATELEG LOOKOUT POTENCE SPONSON SPOTTED BRAGWORT CATEGORY CROTCHET MISERERE SPECKLED STRADDLE MODILLION CANTILEVER
(PL.) HOOKS CROOKS
BRACKISH YAR FOIST SALTY BRACKY SALINE BREACHY SALTISH NAUSEOUS
BRACT HUSK LEAF GLUME LEMMA PALEA PALET SCALE SPADIX SPATHE BRACTLET PHYLLARY
BRACTEOLE PROPHYLL
BRAD PIN NAIL PRIG RIVET SPRIG
BRADAMANT (BROTHER OF —) RINALDO
(HUSBAND OF —) ROGERO
BRAE BANK BRAY BROW HILL CLEVE SLOPE WOUGH CLEEVE VALLEY
BRAG GAB JET BLAH BLAW BLOW CROW DEFY FACE HUFF PUFF WIND WOST YELP BLUFF BOAST CRACK FLIRD PREEN SKITE STRUT VAUNT BLEEZE BOUNCE INSULT SPLORE SPROSE SQUIRT DISPLAY GAUSTER ROISTER SWAGGER BRAGGART FLOURISH PRETENSE THREATEN
BRAGGART BRAG PUFF BOAST FACER BLOWER CROWER GASBAG GASCON HECTOR POTGUN SKITER THRASO BLOWOFF BOASTER BOBADIL BOUNCER CRACKER RUFFLER SHALLOW VAPORER BANGSTER BLOWHARD CACAFUGO FANFARON PAROLLES PUCKFIST RENOWNER RODOMONT SKIPJACK
BRAGGARTISM COCKALORUM
BRAGGING ROOSE JACTANCE RODOMONT THRASONIC
BRAHMA KA SELF BRAMAH
BRAHMAN ARYAN HINDU PUNDIT SMARTA BRAHMIN
BRAID CUE BRAY GIMP JERK LACE PLAT TAIL TRIM BREDE FANCY FREAK JIFFY LACET MILAN ONSET ORRIS PLAIT PLEAT QUEUE START TAGAL TRACE TRADE TRESS TRICK TWINE VOMIT WEAVE BOBBIN BORDER CORDON EDGING GALLON LACING MOMENT PLIGHT RIBBON RICRAC SENNET SNATCH STRING BANDING BULLION CAPRICE ENTWINE UPBRAID BRANDISH ORNAMENT REPROACH RICKRACK SOUTACHE TRIMMING
(— FOR HATS) SENNET SINNET
(— OF WIG) SNAKE
(LINEN —) INKLE
BRAIDER RATCHER
BRAIDING FROG BREDE
BRAIDWORK LACET
BRAIN MAD BEAN HARN MIND PATE UTAC WITS AXION HAIRN HAURN SKULL GENIUS NODDLE PSYCHE FURIOUS SENSORY THINKER CEREBRUM HEADPIECE
(— WAVE PATTERN) THETA
(IN THE —) UPSTAIRS
(KIND OF —) PEA
(MUDDLED —) SMOKEJACK
(PART OF —) PONS CORTEX FORNIX THALAMUS VENTRICLE
(PL.) HARN PATE SCONCE HEADPIECE
(PREF.) CEREBELLI CEREBELLO CEREBR(I)(O) ENCEPHAL(O)
(SUFF.) ENCEPHALIA ENCEPHALUS ENCEPHALY
BRAINCHILD IDEA
BRAINLESS SILLY STUPID FOOLISH WITLESS
BRAINPAN PAN HARNPAN PANNICLE
BRAIN SAND SABULUM
BRAIZE BECKER
BRAKE COW BULL BURR CAGE CLOG CURB DRAG FERN LOCK RACK SKID SLOW STAY TARA TRAP TRIG BLOCK CHECK COPSE DELAY DETER GRIPE SNARE SPOKE SPRAG VOMIT BRIDLE CONVOY HARROW HINDER REMORA RETARD STAYER WARABI BRACKEN DEADMAN DILEMMA SLIPPER STOPPER THICKET TRIGGER DRAGROPE RETARDER
(— PART) DISC SHOE
BRAKEMAN GUARD SHACK SHAKE BRAKIE NIPPER DILLIER SNAPPER SWAMPER DILLYMAN INCLINER TRAINMAN
BRAKES ANCHORS
BRAMBLE WHIN BRIER RHAMN THIEF THORN BUMBLE JAGGER LAWYER STICKER DEWBERRY MAYBERRY NESSBERRY
(PREF.) BATO
BRAMBLE BUSH TUTU GRANJENO
BRAMBLING KATE SNOWHAMMER
BRAMBLY DUMAL SPINY THORNY PRICKLY
BRAN GRIT SEED DARAK TREAT CEREAL CHESIL CHISEL POLLARD TOPPING BEESWING
(— AND MEAL) SHORTS
(CORNMEAL —) HUSK
(FINE —) POLLEN
(UNSORTED —) RUBBLES
(PREF.) PITYRO
BRANCH ARM BOW COW KOW LAP LEG LOP RAY RUN BARB BROG BUSH CHAT FANG FORK LIMB PALM PART RAME RICE RISE SNAG SNUG SPUR STEM STUD TANG TWIG YARD AXITE BAYOU BOUGH BREAK BRIAR BRIER CREEK DRUPA GRAIN LAYER LULOV PLASH PRONG RAMUS REISE SCROG SHOOT SHRAG SPRAY SPRIG STICK TWIST VIMEN WITHE BUREAU CLADUS DIVIDE DRUKPA EXOPOD

GERMEN GREAVE GROWTH LEADER MEMBER OFFSET OUTLET PHYLUM PORTIO RADDLE RAMAGE RAMIFY RUNNER SHROUD SPRANG STOLON STREAM TAPOUN CHAPTER CLADODE DIALECT DIVERGE ENDOPOD FURCATE LATERAL PHYLLIS RAMULUS TENDRIL TORRENT ANAPHYTE BRONCHUS DISTRICT EFFLUENT OFFSHOOT PEASTICK SCAFFOLD SPRANGLE TRAILING PHYLLOCLADE RAMIFICATION
(— OF ANTLER) SPELLER ADVANCER
(— OF COLONY) STIPE
(— OF CRAFT) INDUSTRY
(— OF FAMILY) SEPT
(— OF FEATHER) BARB
(— OF HORN) RIAL ANTLER
(— OF IVY) BUSH
(— OF LEARNING) ART STUDY FACULTY KNOWLEDGE
(— OF MATHEMATICS) ALGEBRA CALCULUS
(— OF THALLUS) STICHID
(— OF TREASURY) FISCUS
(DEAD —) FLAG
(EVERGREEN —S) GREENS
(LANGUAGE —) INDIC
(LOCAL —) COURT
(MINE —) LEADER
(PALM —) LULAB
(RAILWAY —) LYE
(SHORT THICK —) STUMP
(SLENDER —) WHIP
(SMALL —) RICE
(YOUNGER —) CADET
(PL.) LOFT RAMI SKIRT SPRAY RAMAGE CYPRESS DEADWOOD
(PREF.) CLON(O) FRONDI RAMI RAMOSO RAMULI
(SUFF.) RAMOSE

BRANCHED FORKY FORKED RAMATE RAMOSE CLADOSE TROCHED RAMIFORM
(SUFF.) CLADOUS

BRANCHES
(SUFF.) **(HAVING —)** CLEMA

BRANCHIA GILL

BRANCHING ARMY RAMOSE FURCATE DICHOTOMY

BRANCHIOPOD SHRIMP

BRANCHLET RAMULUS SPILLER

BRAND BIRN BLOT BURN CHOP FLAW KIND MARK NOTE SEAR SMIT SMOT SORT VENT WIPE BUIST INURE LABEL SCEAR STAIN STAMP SWORD TAINT TORCH BARREL MARQUE STIGMA FLAMBEAU NAMEPLATE STIGMATIZE

BRANDED INFAMOUS

BRANDIMART (SLAYER OF —) GRADASSO
(WIFE OF —) FLORDELIS

BRANDING IRON BRAND CAUTER SEARER CAUTERY

BRANDISH WAG DART STIR WAVE WIND BLESS BRAID SHAKE SWING WIELD FLAUNT HURTLE QUAVER RUFFLE STRAIN WINNOW FLUTTER GLITTER SWAGGER VIBRATE WAMPISH FLOURISH VAMBRASH

BRANDY DOP VSO BOOF FINE JACK MARC VSOP BINGO MOBBY NANTS NANTZ PEACH RAKIA VVSOP CINDER COGNAC GRAPPA KIRSCH PUPELO RAKIJA VISNEY ANISADO AQUAVIT QUETSCH ARMAGNAC CALVADOS SLIVOVIC SLIVOVITZ AGUARDIENTE
(— AND WATER) MAHOGANY
(PLUM —) SLIVOVITZ SLIVOWITZ
(SOUTH AFRICAN —) SMOKE

BRANDYWINE (VICTOR AT —) HOWE

BRANK MUMPS BRIDLE PILLORY

BRANLE BRAWL

BRAN-LIKE PITYROID

BRANT ROUT ERECT PROUD QUINK SHEER STEEP ROUGHT

BRASH GAY BOLD FACY RASH HASTY NERVY SAUCY STORM ATTACK RUBBLE BRITTLE FORWARD IMPUDENT TACTLESS BALDFACED

BRASQUE STEEP

BRASS CASH ALLOY CHEEK MONEY NERVE BRAZEN BRONZE MASLIN ORMOLU OFFICER ORICHALC
(— PLAYER) WINDJAMMER
(PREF.) CHALC(O) CHALK(O)

BRASSARD ARMBAND

BRASSEY BIB

BRASSICA CABBAGE

BRASSIERE BANDEAU

BRASSWARE DINANDERIE

BRASSY LOUD RUDE BRAZEN COARSE SHRILL IMPUDENT STRIDENT OVERBLOWN

BRAT BIB GET IMP BROT FILM SCUM APRON BAIRN BILSH BROLL CHILD CLOAK GAITT SCAMP INFANT MANTLE TERROR URCHIN GARMENT BANTLING

BRATTICER AIRMAN CANVASMAN

BRAVADO POMP BRAVE PRIDE STORM SWASH HECTOR BLUSTER BOMBAST BRAVERY SWAGGER VAUNTERY GASCONISM

BRAVE BOLD BRAW DARE DEFY FACE FINE GAME GOOD PROW TALL WILD ADORN BOAST BRAVO BULLY FELON HARDY JOLLY MANLY MOODY ORPED ROMAN STIFF STOUT VAUNT WIGHT BRAWLY BREAST DARING HEROIC MANFUL PLUCKY SANNUP STURDY BRAVADO DOUGHTY GALLANT HAUTAIN SOLDIER SWAGGER VALIANT VENTURE WARRIOR CAVALIER DEFIANCE EMBOLDEN FEARLESS INTREPID LIONLIKE STALWART SUPERIOR VALOROUS VIRTUOUS

BRAVELY BIG FINELY

BRAVE NEW WORLD (AUTHOR OF —) HUXLEY
(CHARACTER IN —) JOHN MARX MOND CROWNE LENINA WATSON BERNARD MUSTAPHA HELMHOLTZ

BRAVERY GRIT VALOR SPIRIT VIRTUE BRAVADO BRAVURA COURAGE HEROISM JOLLITY MANHEAD MANHOOD PROWESS BOLDNESS CHIVALRY

BRAVO OLE RAH EUGE THUG BRAVE BULLY BANDIT CUTTER BRAVADO SHABASH VILLAIN APPLAUSE ASSASSIN

BRAWL DIN ROW BEEF CLEM DUST FRAY RIOT BLIND BROIL CHIDE CLASH FIGHT FLYTE MELEE REVEL RISSA SCOLD SCRAP AFFRAY BICKER FRACAS FRATCH HABBLE REVILE RUFFLE RUMPUS SHINDY STOUSH STRIFE TUMULT UPROAR YATTER BAGARRE BOBBERY BRABBLE BRANGLE DISCORD DISPUTE QUARREL SCUFFLE TUILYIE WRANGLE COMPLAIN RIXATION SQUABBLE STRAMASH

BRAWLER FRATCH NICKER SQUARER FRAMPLER NIGHTCAP OUTCRIER

BRAWLING NOISY BLATANT FLITING SCAMBLING SHEMOZZLE

BRAWN BEEF BOAR LIRE PORK FLESH SINEW FATTEN MUSCLE MANPOWER STRENGTH
(MOCK —) HEADCHEESE

BRAWNY BEEFY FLESHY ROBUST SINEWY SQUARE STRONG STURDY CALLOUS MUSCULAR POWERFUL STALWART

BRAXY BRADSOT

BRAY CRY MIX RUB BEAT ROUT TOOL CRUSH GRIND NOISE POUND STAMP BRUISE HEEHAW OUTCRY PESTLE THRASH WHINNY

BRAYERA KOSO CUSSO KOSSO

BRAZEN BOLD CALM HARD PERT BRASS HARDY HARSH SASSY AENEAN BRASSY BLATANT CALLOUS FORWARD IMMODEST IMPUDENT INSOLENT METALLIC

BRAZENFACED CHEEKY

BRAZIER HEARTH MANGAL BRASERO HIBACHI REREDOS SCALDINO

BRAZIL ROSET
BAY: MARAJO IGRANDE SEPETIBA GUANABARA
BIRD: MITU MITUA
CAPE: FRIO BLANCO BUZIOS GURUPY ORANGE SAOTOME SAOROQUE
CAPITAL: BRASILIA
COIN: JOE REIS CONTO DOBRA CENTAVO HALFJOE MILREIS CRUZEIRO
DAM: FURNAS ITAIPU PEIXOTO
DANCE: SAMBA MAXIXE
ESTUARY: PARA
FALLS: IGUACU IGUASSU
INDIAN: ANTA ACROA ARARA ARAUA BRAVO CARIB GUANA ARAWAK CARAJA CARAYAN JAVAHAI TARIANA BOTOCUDO CHAMBIOA
ISLAND: MARACA MARAJO BANANAL CARDOSO CAVIANA MEXIANA COMPRIDA
LAKE: AIMA FEIA MIRIM
MEASURE: PE MOIO PIPA SACK VARA BRACA FANGA LEGOA MILHA PALMO PASSO TONEL CANADA COVADO CUARTA LEAGUE QUARTO TAREFA ALQUIER GARRAFA ALQUEIRE
MONETARY UNIT: CRUZADO
MOUNTAIN: URUCUM BANDEIRA ITATIAIA
MOUNTAINS: MAR GERAL ORGAN PIAUI ACARAI GURUPI ORGAOS PARIMA AMAMBAI CARAJAS GRADAUS RONCADOR TOMBADOR
NATIVE: CABOCLO CURIBOCA MAMELUCO PAULISTA
PORT: RIO PARA BAHIA BELEM CEARA NATAL SANTOS PELOTAS SALVADOR
PRESIDENT: BRAS DUTRA FILHO VARGAS
RIVER: APA ICA DOCE GEIO IVAI JARI PARA PARU SONO TEFE ABUNA ANAUA APORE CAPIM CLARO CORUA ICANA IRIRI ITAPI JURUA JUTAI MANSO NEGRO PARDO PIAUI PRETO TIETE TURVO URUBU VERDE XINGU AJUANA AMAZON ARINOS BALSAS BRANCO CANUMA CONTAS CUIABA DEMINI GRAJAU GRANDE GURUPI IBICUI IGUACU JAPURA JAVARI MEARIM MORTES MUCURI PARANA PURPUS RONURO SANGUE TACUTU TIBAGI UATUMA UAUPES VELHAS CORUMBA IGUASSU MADEIRA PARAIBA SUCURIU TAPAJOS TAQUARI TEODORO URUGUAI ARAGUAIA PADAUIRI PARACATU PARAGUAI PARNAIBA SOLIMOES TARAUACA
STATE: ACRE PARA AMAPA BAHIA CEARA GOIAS GOYAZ PIAUI PARANA PIAUHY ALAGOAS GUAPORE PARAIBA RORAIMA SERGIPE AMAZONAS MARANHAO PARAHIBA PARAHYBA RONDONIA SAOPAULO
TOWN: ACU EXU ICO IPU ITU JAU LUZ RIO UBA BAGE FARO IBIA IJUI ITAI LAPA LINS PARA PIUI TUPA UNAI BAHIA BAIAO BAURU BELEM CEARA NATAL NEVES CAMPOS CUIABA ILHEUS MACEIO MANAOS MANAUS OLINDA RECIFE SANTOS ARACAJU CARUARU CITORIA GOIANIA ITABUNA JUNDIAI NITEROI PELOTAS TAUBATE UBERABA ANAPOLIS BRASILIA CAMPINAS CURITIBA LONDRINA SALVADOR SOROCABA TERESINA
TREE: APA ICICA UCUUBA ARARIBA WALLABA
WATERFALL: GLASS IGUAZU
WEIGHT: BAG ONCA LIBRA ARROBA OITAVA ARRATEL QUILATE QUINTAL TONELADA

BRAZIL NUT JUVIA CASTANA

BRAZILWOOD SAPPAN VERZINO HYPERNIC PEACHWOOD SAPPANWOOD

BREACH GAP CHAP FLAW GOOL RENT RIFT SLAP BRACK BRECK BURST CHASM CLEFT CRACK PAUSE SPLIT WOUND BRUISE HARBOR HERNIA HIATUS INROAD

SCHISM SCREED SLUICE ASSAULT BLEMISH DISPUTE FISSURE OPENING QUARREL RUPTURE BREAKING CREVASSE FRACTION FRACTURE INTERVAL OUTBREAK SOLUTION TRESPASS
(— IN DIKE) GOOL
(— IN SEAWAY) GOOL
(— OF CHASTITY) SCULDUDDRY SKULDUDDERY
(— OF CONTINUITY) SALTUS
(— OF DUTY) BARRATRY
(— OF ETIQUETTE) SOLECISM
(— OF FAITH) TREASON
(— OF GRAMMAR) SOLECISM
(— OF MORALITY) SCAPE VAGARY
(— OF PEACE) AFFRAY DISORDER FRACTION
(— OF RULES) FOUL
(— OF SYNTAX) SOLECISM
(— OF UNITY) SOHISM
BREAD BAP BUN NAN PAN BODY BRAD DIET FARE FOOD LOAF NAAN PAIN PITA PONE RIMA ROLL ROTI RUSH RUSK TOKE AZYME BABKA BATCH BATON BOXTY CAPER CHEAT KISRA LIMPA MICHE POORI ROOTY TOMMY CHALLA CHAPON COCKET DAMPER DODGER ENZYME HALLAH KANKIE MASLIN MATZOS PANNAM SIMNEL TAMMIE WASTEL YANNAM ALIMENT ANADAMA BANNOCK CHALLAH EULOGIA MANCHET POPOVER STOLLEN TOASTER CORNCAKE FOCACCIA HARDTACK SOFTTACK TORTILLA ZWIEBACK PUMPERNICKEL
(— AND MILK) POBS PANADA POBBIES
(— BOX) PANETIERE
(— QUALITY) PANEITY
(BATCH OF —) CAST
(BUTTERED —) CAPER
(DRY —) TOKE
(EUCHARISTIC —) BODY HOST AZYME
(FANCY —) BRAID
(INDIAN —) NAN
(ITALIAN —) FOCACCIA
(KIND OF —) FRY PITA POCKET
(MAIZE —) PIKI
(OATMEAL —) ANACK JANNOCK
(POTATO —) FADGE
(QUICK —) SCONE
(S. AFRICAN —) DIKA
(SLICE OF —) TARTINE TRENCHER
(SMALL LOAF OF —) COB
(SMALL PIECE OF —) SIPPET MEALOCK
(SOPPED —) MISER BREWIS BROWIS
(SWEET —) BUN BROWNIE STOLLEN
(TOASTED —) SIPPET
(TWICE-BAKED —) ZWIEBACK
(UNLEAVENED —) AZYM AZYME BANNOCK CHAPATTI
(WHEAT —) CHEAT HOVIS COCKET MANCHET PARATHA
(YEAST-LEAVENED —) SALLYLUNN
(PREF.) ARTO PANI
BREADBOARD PANEL
BREADED ANGLAISE
BREADFRUIT MASI RIMA RIMAS DUGDUG NANGCA CAMANSI CASTANA ANTIPOLO BREADNUT CHESTNUT
BREADNUT RAM
BREADROOT PSORALEA
BREADTH BEAM WIDTH LATITUDE
(— OF PLANK) STRAIK STRAKE
(FINGER'S —) DIGIT
BREADWINNING GAP BOON BUST DASH HINT KNAP PICK PLOW REND RENT RIFT RIVE
BREAK GO CUT JAR LOP TEN ABRA BUST CHIP DRAG FALL FLAW KNAP PART RUIN RUSH SLIP SNAP STEP STOP TEAR TURN UNDO WASH WORK ALTER BLANK BRACK BURST CHECK CHINK CLEFT COMMA CRACK CRAZE DAUNT FALSE FRACT FRUSH LAPSE PAUSE PLUCK ROUGH SEVER SMASH SOLVE SPAWN SPELT STAVE SWING WOUND BRUISE CABBLE CHANGE CLEAVE CRANNY CUTOUT DEFEAT HIATUS IMPAIR LACUNA PIERCE SALTUS SHREND SPRING TEWTAW TEWTER BLUNDER CAESURA CRACKLE CRANKLE CREVICE CRUMBLE DESTROY DISABLE DISPART DISRUPT EXHAUST FISSURE GRITTLE INFRACT INTERIM OPENING RESPITE RUPTURE SHATTER TAILING VARIATE BREATHER CREVASSE DIERESIS DIFFRACT FRACTION FRACTURE FRAGMENT INFRINGE INTERVAL SEPARATE SOLUTION STRAMASH
(— APART) SUNDER DISRUPT SHATTER
(— AWAY) BOLT PEEL ESCAPE
(— BOULDERS) BULLDOZE
(— DOWN) CONK FAIL GIVE CRAZE CROCK PLASH TRAIK UNMAN BRUISE TUMBLE ANALYZE FOUNDER REFRACT COLLAPSE INFRINGE
(— FORCE) BAFFLE
(— FORTH) BOIL ERUPT EVENT FLASH EXPLODE
(— FROM ICE MASS) CALVE
(— GLASS) SHREND DRAGADE
(— IN) ENTER
(— IN PIECES) CHAP DICE KNAP CRASH CRAZE SMASH SMOKE SHIVER CRUMBLE FRITTER SMATTER DEMOLISH DIFFRACT DISJOINT SPLINTER STRAMASH
(— INTO) BROACH IRRUPT
(— INTO FOAM) COMB
(— INWARD) STAVE
(— IN WAVES) JABBLE
(— IN YARN) SMASH
(— LANCE) TAINT
(— OF CONTINUITY) SALTUS
(— OFF) NUB DROP SNAP CEASE LEAVE ABRUPT DIREMPT INTERMIT PRETERMIT
(— OFF END) SNUB
(— OPEN) BUST CHOP FORCE
(— ORE) COB SPALL SPAWL
(— OUT) ERUPT START ASSURD STRIKE
(— RANKS) DISMISS
(— SHARPLY) KNACK
(— SILENCE) QUATCH QUETCH
(— SKIN) GALL
(— SLATE) SCULP
(— STONE) CAVIL KEVEL
(— THE BACK) CHINE
(— THROUGH) BEAT FORCE BREACH
(— THROUGH SHELL) PIP
(— UP) BUCK FALL MELT FLOUR SEVER SPALE SPLIT STASH INCIDE DEGRADE DIFFUSE DISBAND DISSECT DISTURB REFRACT SCARIFY SCATTER CROSSCUT DISJOINT DISPERSE DISSOLVE DISUNIFY FRAGMENT
(— UP EARTH) HACK FALLOW
(— UP SIEGE) LEVY
(— WATER) FIN
(— WINDOWS) NICK
(INDUSTRY —) SHAKEOUT
(STEM —) BROWNING
(SUFF.) CLASE CLASIA CLAST(IC)
BREAKABLE BRITTLE BRUCKLE FRIABLE DELICATE FRANGIBLE
BREAKAGE GRIEF
BREAKAX IRONWOOD
BREAKDOWN JUBA EDGER BURNOUT DEBACLE HOEDOWN ANALYSIS COLLAPSE DILUTION
(— OF RIND) ADUSTIOSIS
(ELECTRIC —) AVALANCHE
BREAKER JUMP SURF WAVE BARECA BEAKER BILLOW COMBER ROLLER CRACKER SLEDGER LEDGEMAN SCRAPPER
(— OF WORD) WARLOCK
(CIRCUIT —) CUTOUT
(ROCK —) ALLIGATOR
(PL.) BREACH
(SUFF.) CLASTIC
BREAKFAST BRUNCH DEJEUNE DISJUNE DEJEUNER DISJEUNE
(— FOOD) GRANOLA
BREAKING BREACH BREAKUP FRACTION FRACTURE SOLUTION
(— COVER) GETAWAY
(— DOWN) LYSIS
(— FORTH) ERUPTIVE
(— OFF) CHIPPING ABRUPTION
(— OF OATH) PERJURY
(— UP) DEBACLE ANALYSIS DISUNION
(SUFF.) CLASE CLASIA CLAST(IC)
(— INTO SMALL PIECES) THRIPSIS
BREAKSTONE SAXIFRAGE
BREAK-UP DEBACLE
BREAKWATER COB DAM COBB CROY DIKE MOLE PIER PILE QUAY JETTY GROYNE REFUGE BULWARK STOCKADE
BREAM TAI BRIM CARP CHAD SCUP SHAD ZOPE BROOM ROMAN BALEEN BARWIN BRAISE SARGUS OLDWIFE SUNFISH WAREHOU CYPRINID FLATFISH TARWHINE STEENTJIE
BREAST DUG BOOB BUMP CROP FACE BOOBY BOSOM BRAVE BUBBY CHEST HEART MAMMA PETTO STALL BAZOOM PECTUS POMMEL THORAX BRISKET COUNTER KNOCKER FOREBOWS
(— OF HORSE) COUNTER
(PHOTOGRAPH OF —S) MAMMOGRAM
(PL.) BUST
(PREF.) MAMM(I)(ILLI) MAST(O) MAZ(O) PECTORI STERN(O) STETH(O)
BREASTBAND HORSE
BREASTBONE BREAST STERNUM XIPHOID
BREASTHOOK CRUTCH FOREHOOK
BREASTPIECE RABAT RABBI
BREASTPLATE EGIS URIM AEGIS BREAST BYRNIE GORGET LORICA ORACLE SHIELD THORAX CUIRASS PALETTE POITREL PECTORAL PLASTRON RATIONAL
(HIGH PRIEST'S —) RATIONAL
BREASTS
(SUFF.) MASTIA
BREASTWORK FORT REDAN SANGAR SCHANZ SCHERM SCONCE SUNGAR BRATTLE PARAPET PLUTEUS RAMPART BARBETTE BRATTICE
BREATH AIR ANDE GASP HUFF LIFE ONDE PANT PECH PUFF SIGH WAFT WIND BLAST PAUSE SCENT SMELL VAPOR WHIFF WHIFT BREEZE FLATUS PNEUMA HALITUS INSTANT RESPITE SUSPIRE SPIRACLE
(— OF WIND) SPIRIT
(BAD —) OZOSTOMIA
(DIVINE —) NEPHESH
(LIFE —) PRANA SPIRIT
(STINKING —) FUMOSITY
(PREF.) PNEO PNEUM(A)(O) PNEUMATO PNEUMON(O) RESPIRO SPIRACULI SPIRO
(SUFF.) PNEA PNEUSTA PNOEA
BREATHE ANDE LIVE ONDE PANT PECH PUFF SIGH VENT EXIST EXUDE SPEAK SPIRE UTTER ASPIRE EXHALE INHALE WHEEZE AFFLATE EMANATE RESPIRE SUSPIRE
(— HEAVILY) FOB PECH FNESE SOUGH THROTTLE
(— LABORIOUSLY) GASP
(— NOISILY) SOUGH SNOTTER
(— OUT) EXPIRE
(— UPON) FAN
BREATHER PAUSE
BREATHING AIR ALIVE PNEUMA SPIRIT GASPING AFFLATUS SPIRITUS SPIRATION
(— HEAVILY) SUSPIRIOUS
(LABORED —) ASTHMA
(ROUGH —) ASPER
(SMOOTH —) LENE LENIS
BREATHING-SPACE BARLEY RESPIRATION
BREATHLESSNESS TIFT
BREATHY HOLLOW ADENOID
BRECCIA BROCKRAM
BRED (WELL —) FREE
BREECH BORE BUTT DOUP BLOCK BRICK CULOTTE DRODDUM BUTTOCKS CYLINDER DERRIERE
(— OF SECURITY) LEAK
BREECHBLOCK BLOCK VENTPIECE
BREECHCLOTH HIPPEN HIPPING

BREECHES HOSE CHAPS JEANS LEVIS SLOPS STOCK TREWS BRACAE BRAGAS BREEKS GASKIN SMALLS TIGHTS TROUSE TRUSSES BOMBARDS BREEKUMS JODHPURS KICKSIES KNICKERS LEATHERS TROUSERS PANTALOON SMALLCLOTHES
(KNEE —) SMALLS
BREED GET ILK BEAR KIND RACE REAR SORT BEGET BROOD CASTE CAUSE CLASS FANCY HATCH ISSUE RAISE STOCK STORE TRAIN CREATE GENDER STRAIN EDUCATE NOURISH PRODUCE PROGENY SPECIES VARIETY ENGENDER GENERATE INSTRUCT MULTIPLY PULLULATE
(— OF BEEF CATTLE) BEEFALO
(— OF CATS) RAGDOLL
(— OF SWINE) LACOMBE
(DWARF —) TOY
(DWARF—) TOY
BREEDER RANCHER AURELIAN HERDSMAN HORSEMAN
(FISH —) MILTER
BREEDING ORIGIN DESCENT NURTURE TUPPING BEHAVIOR CIVILITY PREGNANT TRAINING
(— PLACE) NIDUS
(GOOD —) GENTRY
BREEZE AIR AURA BLOW FLAW GALE GUST PIRR SNAP STIR WIND BLAST RUMOR SLANT WALTZ BREATH DOCTOR REPORT SLATCH SPIRIT ZEPHYR FRESHEN MUZZLER QUARREL VIRASON WHISPER
(COOL —) DOCTOR
(GENTLE —) AIR AURA ZEPHYR
(LAND —) TERRAL
(SHOOT THE —) GAB JAW
(STIFF —) STOUR TIFTER
BREEZE FLY WHAME
BREEZY AIRY BRISK FRESH WINDY AIRISH
BRETHREN IKHWAN
BRETON ARMORICAN
BREVE NOTE WRIT BRIEF MINIM ORDER SHORT PRECEPT
BREVIARY ORDO CURSUS DIGEST LEDGER PORTAS COUCHER EPITOME SUMMARY ABSTRACT PORTESSE PORTHORS
(— CONTENTS) PRAYERS
BREVITY SYNTOMY LACONISM UNLENGTH BRIEFNESS SHORTNESS TERSENESS BRACHYLOGY
BREW ALE MIX BEER BOIL MAKE PLOT POUR DRINK HATCH STEEP STOUT BROWST DEVISE DILUTE FOMENT GATHER LIQUOR SEETHE CONCOCT INCLINE PREPARE CONTRIVE
(HOME —) SAMOGON
BREWER TUNNER
BREWERY BRASSERIE
BREWING GAIL GYLE BROWST BUMMOCK
BRIBE BUD BUY FEE FIX OIL ROB SOP TIP BAIT DASH GIFT HAVE HIRE MEED MOIL PALM VAIL WAGE BONUS CUDDY GRAFT OFFER STEAL SUGAR TEMPT TOUCH BOODLE EXTORT GREASE HAMPER NOBBLE PAYOLA SQUARE SUBORN CORRUPT DOUCEUR SWEETEN TICKLER GRATUITY VENALIZE
(— TO A POLICEMAN) NUT
(— TO POLICEMAN) NUT
BRIBERY MEED
(OPEN TO —) VENAL
BRIC-A-BRAC CURIO VERTU VIRTU BIBELOT TROCKERY TRUMPERY
BRICK BAT BUR BURR GLUT MARL PAVE TILE BLOCK GAULT QUARL SLOPE SPLIT STOCK STONE TOOTH CUTTER FELLOW HEADER PAMENT PAVIOR BACKING CLINKER FLETTON GRIZZLE PERPEND SOLDIER BURNOVER
(— WALL) NECK
(CRACKED —) CHUFF SHUFF
(FINAL HALF —) JACK
(IMPERFECT —) SHIPPER BURNOVER
(PILE OF —S) HACK CLAMP
(PULVERIZED —) SOORKY SOORKEE
(SECOND-RATE —) GRIZZLE
(SECOND QUALITY —S) BRINDLES
(SOFT —) CUTTER RUBBER PICKING
(SQUARE —) QUADREL
(STACK OF —) LIFT
(SUN-DRIED —) BAT ADOBE
(UNBURNT —) ADOBE
(WOODEN —) DOOK
(PL.) CLAYWARE
(PREF.) PLINTHI
BRICKBAT GIBE
BRICKLAYER BRICKY MASONER
BRICKMAKER MOLDER
BRICKWORK HOB BRICKING
BRIDAL NUPTIAL BRIDALTY
BRIDE KALLAH SPOUSE SHULAMITE SWEETENER
BRIDE OF LAMMERMOOR
(AUTHOR OF —) SCOTT
(CHARACTER IN —) LUCY CALEB EDGAR FRANK ASHTON HAYSTON WILLIAM RAVENSWOOD BALDERSTONE
BRIDE-PRICE LOBOLD LOBOLO
BRIDESHEAD REVISITED (AUTHOR OF —) WAUGH
(CHARACTER IN —) BOY REX CARA KURT BERYL CELIA JULIA RYDER BRIDEY ANTHONY BLANCHE CHARLES MOTTRAM CORDELIA MUSPRATT SAMGRASS MARCHMAIN MULCASTER SEBASTIAN BRIDESHEAD
BRIDESMAID PARANYMPH
BRIDEWELL JAIL MILLDOLL
BRIDGE WAY BRIG LINK NOSE PONS PONT REST SPAN WIEN CROSS SIRAT TOWIE GANTRY ISLAND JIGGER RIALTO RUNWAY SANGAR AUCTION BASCULE BIFROST CHANNEL CONNECT CULVERT EXOSTRA PASSAGE PASSING PINNOCK PONCEAU PONTOON PROPONS TRAJECT TRESTLE VIADUCT CONTRACT TRAVERSE DUPLICATE
(— BID) SPLINTER
(— BUILDER) PONTIFEX
(— HAND) YARBOROUGH
(— HOLDING) HONORS TENACE YARBOROUGH
(— MARKER) PYLON
(— OF MUSICAL INSTRUMENT) MAGAS CHEVALET CHEVILLE
(— PLAY) RUFF UPPERCUT
(— SEAT) EAST WEST DUMMY NORTH SOUTH
(— TO PARADISE) ALSIRAT
(ARCADED —) RIALTO
(BILLIARDS —) JIGGER
(CONTRACT —) CHICAGO GHOULIE PLAFOND
(FLUE —) ALTAR
(GATEWAY —) GOUT
(HOSE —) JUMPER
(IMPEDANCE —) DIPLEXER
(NATURAL —) ARCH
(PLANK —) LIGGER
(RAISE — BID) JUMP
(ROPE SUSPENSION —) JOOLA
(RUDE —) CLAPPER
(PREF.) GEPHYR(O) PONTI PONTO
BRIDGEMAKER PONTIFEX
BRIDGEMAN EBBMAN
BRIDGE OF SAN LUIS REY
(AUTHOR OF —) WILDER
(CHARACTER IN —) PIO JAIME PILAR MANUEL PEPITA ESTEBAN JUNIPER PERICHOLE MONTEMAYOR
BRIDGING ASTRIDE STRUTTING
BRIDLE BIT CURB REIN RULE BRAKE BRANK BRIDE CHECK GUARD GUIDE STRUT DIRECT GOVERN HALTER MASTER SIMPER SUBDUE BLINDER CONTROL LORMERY REPRESS SNAFFLE SWAGGER CAVESSON RESTRAIN SUPPRESS
BRIDLE PATH SPURWAY
BRIEF FEW CURT LIST RIFE WRIT BLURB BREVE CHARM PITHY QUICK SHORT TERSE ABRUPT COMMON CURTAL FLYING HOURLY LETTER LITTLE SNIPPY SUDDEN ABRIDGE CAPSULE COMPACT COMPOSE CONCISE CRYPTIC INVOICE LACONIC MANDATE OUTLINE PRECEPT SUMMARY BREVIATE CONDENSE FLEETING FLITTING SNATCHED SNIPPETY SUCCINCT SYLLABUS
(PL.) BIKINI
(PREF.) BREVI
BRIEF CASE FOLIO TASHIE
BRIEFED (WELL —) UPON
BRIEFLY BRIEF ENFIN SHORTLY
BRIEFS JOCKEY
BRIER BARB PIPE BRIAR ERICA THORN SMILAX BRUYERE PRICKER INKBERRY
BRIER TREE PIPER
BRIG RIG JAIL PRISON GEORDIE
BRIGADE TERZO CAMPOO
BRIGAND THIEF USKOK BANDIT KLEPHT LATRON PIRATE ROBBER CATERAN KETTRIN LADRONE ROUTIER SOLDIER PICAROON BANDOLERO
(PL.) TCHETNITSI
BRIGANDAGE DACOITY
BRIGANDINE PLACCATE
BRIGHT APT GAY NET FINE GILD GLAD GLEG HIGH LIVE ROSY ACUTE AGLOW ALERT ANIME BEAMY BRAVE CLEAR CRISP EAGLE FLARY FRESH GEMMY JOLLY LIGHT LUCID NITID PRINT QUICK RIANT SHARP SHEEN SHEER SHINY SMART SMOLT STEEP SUNNY TINNY VIVID WHITE WITTY BERTHA CHEERY CLEVER FLASHY FLORID GARISH LIMPID LIVELY LUCENT ORIENT SERENE SHRILL SILVER BEAMISH DIAMOND DILUCID FORWARD FULGENT LAMBENT RADIANT RINGING SHINING ANIMATED CHEERFUL FLASHING GLEAMING LIGHTFUL LUMINOUS LUSTROUS SPLENDID SPLENDOR STARLIKE SUNSHINY
(— IN COLOR) NEON
(BLINDINGLY —) GLARING
(NOT —) SOFT
(OFFENSIVELY —) GARISH
(SOFTLY —) LAMBENT
(TOO —) ROARY ROARIE
(VULGARLY —) GAUDY
(PREF.) AETHIO AGLAO LAMPR(O)
BRIGHTEN GILD LAMP BLOOM CHEER CLEAR FLAME GLOZE LIGHT LIVEN SHINE SNUFF CANTLE ENGILD POLISH ANIMATE BURNISH EMBRAVE ENLIVEN FURBISH LIGHTEN REFRESH SMARTEN ILLUMINE
BRIGHTENED LITUP
BRIGHTENER FLUOROL
BRIGHTLY GAY CLEAR LIGHT SHEEN BRIGHT FRESHLY SHEENLY
BRIGHTNESS SUN BLAZE BLOOM ECLAT FLAME GLARE GLEAM GLINT GLORY GLOSS LIGHT NITOR SHEEN SHINE ACUMEN BRIGHT CANDOR FULGOR LUSTER CLARITY GLISTEN GLITTER LAMBERT NITENCY SPARKLE RADIANCE SPLENDOR BRILLIANCE
(— OF TOBACCO) FLASH
(— UNIT) STILB
(UNIT OF —) NIT
(PREF.) GANO
BRIGUE BLAT
BRILLIANCE FAME BLARE BLAZE ECLAT FLAME GLARE GLORY SHINE VALUE KEENNESS RADIANCE SPLENDOR VIVACITY REFULGENCE
BRILLIANCY FIRE BLARE ECLAT GLORY REFLET CLARITY GLITTER ORIENCY RADIANCE SPLENDOR
BRILLIANT GAY GOOD KEEN SAGE WISE BREME QUICK VIVID BRIGHT CLEVER GIFTED LIVELY PURPLE SIGNAL BRAVURA BRITTLE EMINENT FLAMING GLARING LAMBENT LAMPING LOZENGE PRISMAL RADIANT SHINING BLINDING DAZZLING DIZZYING GLORIOUS INSPIRED LUCULENT LUMINOUS SLASHING SPLENDID PRISMATIC
(TRANSIENTLY —) METEORIC
BRIM LIP RIM RUT SEA EDGE TURF BLUFF BRINK MARGE OCEAN

VERGE WATER BORDER MARGIN TURNUP COPULATE STRUMPET
(— OF HAT) FLAP LEAF POKE BRINK TARFE SLOUCH
BRIMFUL TIPFUL TOPFUL CROWNED
BRIMMING BIG FULL ABRIM
BRIMSTONE SULFUR VIRAGO SULPHUR BRINSTON SPITFIRE
(PREF.) THI(O)
BRIMSTONY LURID
BRINDLED TABBY TAWNY BRANDED FLECKED STREAKED
BRINE SEA MAIN SALT BRACK LEACH OCEAN TEARS PICKLE MARINADE
BRINER COBBERER
BRING DO LAY TEE WIN BEAR BUCK CALL FIRK LEAD STOP TAKE TEEM CARRY DRIVE ENDUE FETCH INCUR APPORT ARRIVE CONVEY DEDUCE CONDUCE CONDUCT EXHIBIT PROCURE PRODUCE
(— ABOUT) DO SEE BREW MAKE STAY TEEM CAUSE DIGHT FRAME INFER MOYEN SETUP SHAPE SWING CREATE EFFECT INVOKE SECURE SPIRIT COMPASS CONDUCE INSPIRE OPERATE PROCURE PRODUCE CATALYZE OCCASION TRANSACT PERPETRATE
(— ABOUT CAPTURE) ACCOUNT
(— BACK) REFER EFFECT RECALL REDUCE REDUCT RELATE RETURN REVIVE REVOKE PRODUCE RESTORE OCCASION RETRIEVE TRANSACT
(— BEFORE) HAUL
(— CHARGE) APPEACH
(— DOWN) LAY DROP FALL FELL STOP ABATE COUCH EMBASE SOFTEN DECLINE DESCEND DISMOUNT OVERTHROW
(— DOWN STEER) HOOLIHAN
(— FORTH) CAST FOAL GIVE MAKE TEEM YEAN EDUCE HATCH ISSUE SPAWN THROW PROFER DELIVER TRADUCE ENGENDER PROCREATE
(— FORTH YOUNG) EAN KID YEAN
(— FORWARD) CITE LEAD INFER ADDUCE ALLEGE ADJOUST ADVANCE PROPOSE
(— IN) EARN INFER USHER IMPORT INDUCE INVECT REPORT RETURN ADHIBIT
(— INTO BATTLE) COMMIT
(— INTO COURT) SIST
(— INTO DISGRACE) FOUL
(— LOW) AVALE DEGRADE SUPPLANT
(— ON) INFER INDUCE
(— ONESELF) GET
(— OUT) DRAW ACCENT ELICIT DISINTER HEIGHTEN
(— OVER) CONVERT
(— SHIP INTO POSITION) EASE
(— TO A HALT) STICK
(— TO AN END) DO END FIT DOCK DRAW REDD CEASE FORDO DECIDE EXPIRE FINISH FOREDO FULFIL DISJOIN INCLUDE COMPLETE CONCLUDE DISSOLVE SURCEASE
(— TO BAY) CORNER
(— TO BEAR) EXERT
(— TOGETHER) JOIN AMASS RAISE UNITE ADDUCT CONFER CORRAL ENGAGE ENLINK GATHER SUMMON COLLATE COLLECT COMPILE COMPORT ASSEMBLE CONFLATE ENSEMBLE
(— TO HEEL) FACE
(— TO LIFE) EVOKE ANIMATE
(— TO LIGHT) GRUB REAP DREDGE ELICIT EXPOSE REVEAL UNEARTH DISCLOSE DISCOVER
(— TO NAUGHT) DASH FOIL UNDO NEGATE CONFUTE DESTROY
(— TO PERFECTION) RIPEN
(— TO STOP) CURB HALT ARREST
(— TO THE GROUND) GRASS
(— UP) REAR BREED NURSE RAISE TRAIN NURSLE NUZZLE UPREAR EDUCATE NOURISH
(SUFF.) FER(ENCE)(ENT)(OUS)
(— ABOUT) FIC(AL)(ATE)(ATION)(ATIVE)(ATOR)(ATORY)(E)(ENCE)(ENT)(IAL)(IARY)(IENT) FIQUE
BRING-DOWN LETDOWN COMEDOWN
BRINGER (— OF BABIES) STORK
(— OF BAD LUCK) JINX JONAH
(— OF BAD NEWS) SCREECHOWL
(— OF DREAMS) MAB
(— OF GOOD LUCK) MASCOT
BRINGING-UP BREEDING EDUCATION
BRINJAL EGGPLANT
BRINK END EVE LIP RIM SEA BANK BRIM EDGE FOSS MARGE SHORE VERGE BORDER MARGIN MARGENT PRECIPICE THRESHOLD
BRINY BRACK SALTY SALINE BRACKISH MURIATED
BRIOCHE ROLL STICH SAVARIN
BRISE-SOLEIL BLIND SUNBREAK SUNSHADE
BRISK GAY BRAG BUSY CANT FAST KEEN PERK PERT RACY RASH SPRY TRIG VIVE YARE YERN AGILE ALERT ALIVE BUDGE BUXOM CANTY COBBY CRANK CRISP FRESH FRISK KEDGE NIPPY PEART PEPPY PERKY QUICK ROUND ZIPPY ACTIVE BREEZY COCKET CROUSE DAPPER FLICKY LIVELY NIMBLE SNAPPY SPRACK SPRUNT TROTTY VIVACE ALLEGRO CHIPPER HUMMING ROUSING ANIMATED BRUSHING FRISKFUL GALLIARD RATTLING SMACKING SPANKING SPIRITED
(SOMEWHAT —) ALLEGRETTO
BRISKLY YERN SHARP YERNE BUSILY CROUSE ALLEGRO ROUNDLY
BRISKNESS ALACRITY VIRITOOT
BRISTLE AWN JAG RIB BARB HAIR JAGG SETA TELA BIRSE BRUSH PARCH PREEN STARE STRUT STYLE TOAST AVISTA CHAETA PALPUS RUFFLE SETULA STIVER STRIGA STYLET GLOCHIS SMELLER STUBBLE WHISKER ACICULUM FRENULUM SPICULUM VIBRISSA VIBRACULUM
(PREF.) CHAET(I)(O) CHETO HIRSUTO HORRI SETI SETULI
(SUFF.) CHAETA CHAETES CHAETUS
BRISTLED HERISSE HORRENT
BRISTLE-SHAPED STYLOID
BRISTLING ROUGH HISPID HORRID SETOSE THORNY HORRENT SCRUBBY SPINOUS
BRISTLY BIRSY PENNY SETOSE STUBBY SCRUBBY STICKLE
BRITAIN
(PREF.) BRITO
BRITISH ENGLISH BRITANNIC WHITEHALL
BRITISH COLUMBIA (CAPITAL OF —) VICTORIA
(MOUNTAINS OF —) COAST CARIBOO CASCADE PURCELL SELKIRK MONASHEE
(RIVER OF —) NASS LIARD PEACE FRASER SKEENA STIKINE
(TOWN OF —) KELOWNA KAMLOOPS VANCOUVER
BRITISH GUM DEXTRIN DEXTRINE
BRITISH HONDURAS (BAY OF —) CHETUMAL
(CAPITAL OF —) BELMOPAN
(FORMER CAPITAL OF —) BELIZE
(MOUNTAIN RANGE OF —) MAYA
(TOWN OF —) CAYO STANN COROZAL
BRITOMARTIS (FATHER OF —) ZEUS JUPITER
(MOTHER OF —) CARME
BRITON BRIT CELT SCOT BRYTHON
BRITTANY ARMORICA
(NATIVE OF —) BRETON
BRITTLE DRY FROW WEAK BRASH CANDY CRIMP CRISP CRUMP EAGER FRAIL FROWY FRUSH SHORT SPALT CRISPY CRUMPY FEEBLE FICKLE FROUGH GINGER INFIRM SLIGHT BRICKLE BRUCKLE CRACKLY FRAGILE FRIABLE REDSEAR SHIVERY SMOPPLE BRITCHEL DELICATE SNAPPISH
(— AT HIGH HEAT) REDSHORT
BRITTLEBUSH ENCELIA
BRITTLE STAR OPHIUROID
BROACH AIR AWL CUT PIN ROD TAP OPEN OUCH SHED SPIT SPUR STAB TAME VEER VENT BEGIN DRESS DRIFT PRICK RIMER SPOOL START VOICE ATTAME BORING BROOCH DRIVER FIBULA LAUNCH PIERCE REAMER RHYMER STRIKE ENLARGE EXPRESS PUBLISH SPINDLE SQUARER VIOLATE WIDENER APPROACH DEFLOWER DRIFTPIN INCISION PORPOISE
BROAD DEEP FREE VAST WIDE AMPLE BEAMY BRAID DORIC GROSS LARGE LARGO PLAIN ROOMY SPLAY SQUAB STOUT THICK WOMAN COARSE GLOBAL BELCHER EVIDENT GENERAL GRIVOIS LIBERAL OBVIOUS PLATOID BARNYARD SPACIOUS TOLERANT
(— AND FLAT) PLATOID
(NOT —) STRAIT
(PREF.) EURY LATI PLAT(Y)
BROADBILL GAYA RAYA GAPER SCAUP BOATBILL SHOVELER SWORDFISH
BROADCAST AIR SOW SEED SEND CARRY RADIO STREW AIRING SPREAD DECLARE DIFFUSE PUBLISH SCATTER ANNOUNCE TELEVISE TRANSMIT
BROADCLOTH CASTOR SUCLAT TAUNTON
BROADEN BREDE WIDEN DILATE EXPAND EXTEND SPREAD ENNOBLE
BROADHORN ARK
BROADLOOM CARPET
BROAD-MINDED LIBERAL
BROADNESS BIGNESS LIBERALITY
BROADSIDE RAM TIRE BROAD GARLAND
BROADSWORD BILL KRIS GLAIVE HANGER SPATHA CUTLASS FERRARA CLAYMORE MONTANTO SCIMITAR
BROBDINGNAGIAN HUGE
BROCADE ACCA BROCHE KINCOB KINKHAB NISHIKI BAUDEKIN DAMASSIN
BROCADED BROCHE
BROCCOLI ASPARAGUS
BROCCOLI BROWN GOAT LOAM PLOVER RABBIT
BROCCOLI RABE RAPINI RAPPINI
BROCHURE TRACT BOOKLET PAMPHLET TREATISE
BROCKET PITA STAG BROCK SPITTER
BRODIAEA GRASSNUT
BROGAN STOGA STOGY BROGUE STOGIE
BROGUE STOGY STOGIE
BROIL ROW BURN CHAR FEUD FRAY GRID HEAT TOIL ALARM BRAWL GRILL MELEE SCRAP SWELT AFFRAY BIRSLE BRAISE GRILLY SPLORE SQUEAL TUMULT BRANDER BRULYIE CARBONE CONTEST DISCORD DISPUTE EMBROIL FRIZZLE GARBOIL QUARREL SIMULTY BARBECUE BLOODWIT CONFLICT GRILLADE STRAMASH
BROILED CASINO
BROILER GRILL SEARER CHICKEN POUSSIN
BROKE HOG LOW BUST SKINT STONY STONEY CHICANE UPTIGHT BANKRUPT
BROKEN DOWN DUFF RENT RUDE TORN BLOWN BROKE BURST FRACT GAPPY HAIRY KAPUT ROMPU ROUGH TAMED BRASHY HACKLY RUINED SHAKEN CRACKED CRUSHED FRACTED REDUCED SUBDUED VICIOUS WHIPPED BANKRUPT CONTRITE OUTLAWED RUPTURED TATTERED WEAKENED
(— BUT NOT TRAINED) GREEN
(— IN) STOVEN
(— IN HEALTH) CRAZY
(— OFF) ABRUPT
(EASILY —) GINGER
(PREF.) FRACTO
BROKEN-DOWN HAYWIRE DISJASKED DISJASKIT
BROKER AGENT CRIMP BANIAN BANYAN CORSER DEALER FACTOR

JOBBER BROGGER CHANGER COURSER MONEYER PEDDLER REALTOR SCALPER HUCKSTER INSTITOR MERCHANT
BROKERAGE AGIOTAGE
BROMATIUM KOHLRABI
BROME CHEAT
BROMEGRASS CHESS
BROMIA (HUSBAND OF —) SOSIA
BROMO ACID EOSIN EOSINE
BROMUS DRAWK
BRONCHITIS HUSK HOOSE HOOZE
BRONCO PONY PONEY CAYUSE BRONCHO MUSTANG
BRONCOBUSTER BUSTER GINETE BUCKAROO
BRONZE AES TAN BUST ALLOY BROWN COWBOY ORMOLU STATUE ASIATIC GUNMETAL
(— AGE CULTURE) UBAID
(ANTIQUE —) CACAO
(GILDED —) VERMEIL
(MEDAL —) CALABASH
(PREF.) CHALC(O) CHALK(O)
BRONZEWING SQUATTER
BROOCH BAR PIN BOSS LACE OUCH PRIN PROP CAMEO CLASP MORSE PREEN SLIDE SPRAY SPRIG FIBULA NOUCHE PLAQUE SHIELD FERMAIL PETALON CROTCHET ORNAMENT SUNBURST
BROOD EYE FRY NYE SET SIT MOPE NEST NIDE RACE STEW TEAM TRIP WEEP AERIE BREED CLOCK COVER COVEY FLOCK GLOOM GROUP HATCH HOVER ISSUE SEDGE STOCK WORRY YOUNG CLETCH CLUTCH FAMILY KINDLE LITTER PONDER PROGENY SPECIES CLECKING COGITATE INCUBATE KINDLING MEDITATE
(— OF BIRDS) AERY AERIE COVEY EYRIE SEDGE SIEGE
(— OF PHEASANTS) EYE NID NYE NIDE
BROODER HOVER MOTHER NURSERY
BROOK RUN BEAR BECK BURN GHYL GILL LAKE RILL RUSH SIKE ABIDE BAYOU BOURN CREEK FLEET GLIDE STAND STELL TCHAI ARROYO BRANCH CANADA DIGEST ENDURE GUTTER RINDLE RIVOSE RUNLET RUNNEL SICKET STREAM SUFFER ABROOKE COMPORT CONCOCT STOMACH QUEBRADA TOLERATE
(RIPPLING —) PURL
(SALT —) LICK
BROOKLET BECK DOKE RILL RILLET RUNNEL RILLOCK RIVULET
BROOM COW MOP FRAY SWAB WISP BESOM BISME BREAM BRUSH SCRUB SPART SWEEP UALIS WHISK GENISTA HAGWEED WHISKER HACKWEED SPLINTER
(DYER'S —) GENET DYEWOOD
(NATIVE —) DOGWOOD
(TOPS OF —) SCOPARIUS
(PREF.) SCOPI SCOPULI
BROOMCORN HURL
BROOMCORN MILLET HIRSE PANIC PANICLE KADIKANE
BROOMRAPE HELLROOT HERBBANE
BROOMROOT SACATON ZACATON
BROSE ATHOLE CROWDIE
BROTH SEW BREE BROO FOND KAIL KALE SOUP DASHI GLAZE STOCK BREWIS CULLIS JUSSAL JUSSEL LIQUOR SKILLY CALDERA POTTAGE SOUCHIE SUPPING BOUILLON CONSOMME PISHPASH POSSODIE POWSOWDY
(FISH —) DASHI
BROTHEL KIP CRIB STEW BAGNE HOUSE BAGNIO BORDEL CORINTH LUPANAR SHEBANG BORDELLO CATHOUSE HOOKSHOP HOTHOUSE JOYHOUSE SERAGLIO
BROTHER FR BUB FRA KIN PAL SIB BHAI BRER EGIL FRAY MATE MONK PEER BILLY BUBBY BUDDY CADET FRERE FRIAR FELLOW FRAILE FRATER GERMAN COMRADE SIBLING FOSTERER
(HUSBAND'S —) LEVIR
(LAY —) SCOLOG
(WIFE'S —) AFFINE
(YOUNGER —) CADET
(PL.) FF ADELPHI BRETHREN CURIATII HARLUNGEN
(PREF.) ADELPHO FRATRI
(SUFF.) ADELPHIA ADELPHOUS
BROTHERHOOD GILD GUILD LODGE ORDER PAPEY FRIARY BRATSVO CHISHTI THIASOS THIASUS BRODHULL SODALITY
(— OF FREEMASONS) CRAFT
(LITERARY —) FELIBRIGE
BROTHER-IN-LAW MAUGH
BROTHERS KARAMAZOV
(AUTHOR OF —) DOSTOEVSKI
(CHARACTER IN —) IVAN ALEXEY DMITRI FYODOR ALYOSHA KATRINA ZOSSIMA GRUSHENKA SMERDYAKOV
BROUGHAM PILLBOX CARRIAGE
BROUGHT BROCHT
(— FROM ELSEWHERE) DERIVED
(— TO BAY) CORNERED
(— TOGETHER) CONFLATE
(— UP BY HAND) CADE
BROUHAHA SCRAP
BROW TOP BRAE EDGE MIEN SNAB BOUND BRINK CREST EAVES FRONT RIDGE SLOPE BOLDNESS FOREHEAD
BROWBEAT BOSS CARP FACE ABASH BULLY BOUNCE HECTOR DEPRESS DUMBCOW OUTFACE SWAGGER
BROWBEATEN HACKED
BROWN (ALSO SEE COLOR) ART DUN LES TAN ARAB COIN COOK DARK GOAT LION SEAR ABRAM ACORN ARGUS BRUNO DUSKY HAZEL KAFFA MOSUL PABLO PENNY QUAIL SEDGE SEPIA TAWNY TENNE TOAST UMBER APACHE BEAVER BRUNET BURNET GLOOMY MALAGA MANILA MASTIC MOHAWK PALOMA PLOVER PONGEE RABBIT RUSSET SENNET TANNED TURTLE WIGWAM ASPHALT FUSCOUS HARVEST LIBERIA MUSCADE OAKWOOD OXBLOOD POMPEII PRAIRIE REDWOOD TANBARK TOBACCO VESUVIN BRUNETTE MOCCASIN MUSHROOM PHEASANT PERSIMMON PYGMALION
(CONDOR —) TIFFIN
(DARK —) BURNET
(GRAYISH —) DUN
(HAIR —) ARGALI
(LIGHT —) BRAN ALOMA ALESAN STRING
(OLIVE —) BARK AUTUMN
(REDDISH —) BAY ROAN SORE SEPIA AUBURN CROTAL GINGER RUSSET SORREL AMBROSIA
(YELLOWISH —) AZTEC ALMOND BAMBOO BLONDE BEESWAX ALDERNEY
(PREF.) AITHO
BROWNBACK DOWITCH DOWITCHER
BROWNED ADUST
BROWN HEART RAAN
BROWNIE ELF NIS COOKY DOBBY NISSE URISK DOBBIE GOBLIN URUISG
BROWNING SCALD SCORCH SUNTAN
BROWNISH UMBER BURNET
(— BLACK) LAVA
BROWN LUNG DISEASE BYSSINOSIS
BROWNSTONE CHESTNUT
BROWSE BRUT CROP FEED GRAZE FORAGE NIBBLE PASTURE
BRUCITE NEMALITE
BRUISE JAM BASH BRAY BUBU DENT DUNT HURT JAMB MAIM MAUL SORE STUN TUND BLACK BREAK BRIZZ CRUSH CURRY DELVE DINGE FRUSH POUND PUNCH SQUAT BATTER BREACH HATTER INJURY INTUSE MANGLE POUNCE SHINER STOUND SUGGIL BATTERY CONTUND CROWNER DAMMISH DISABLE
(— FLAX) BRAKE
BRUISED HURT LIVID FROISSE
BRUIT DIN FAME RALE ROAR TELL NOISE RUMOR SOUND BLAZON CLAMOR REPORT DECLARE HEARSAY
BRUNEI (— WEIGHT) PARA CHAPAH
(COIN OF —) SEN
(TOWN OF —) SERIA
BRUNET DARK BLACK BROWN GIPSY GYPSY MORENA SWARTHY BRUNETTE MORENITA
BRUNHILD (HUSBAND OF —) GUNTHER
BRUNT JAR BLOW JOLT CLASH FORCE ONSET SHOCK ATTACK EFFORT IMPACT STRAIN STRESS ASSAULT OUTBURST VIOLENCE
BRUSH DIP DUB PIG TIP BOSH CARD COMB DUST FLAP FLAT FRAY KIYI SKIM SWAB BROOM CHAPE CLEAN COPSE FIGHT FITCH GRAZE LINER SABLE SCOPA SCRUB SCUFF SWEEP SWOOP WHISK BADGER BATTLE BRIGHT BROSSE DABBER DAUBER DUSTER MOGOTE PALLET PENCIL PICKUP PUTOIS RIGGER RUBBER SPONGE STROKE TEASEL CLEANSE FOXTAIL GRAINER GROOMER MOTTLER STIPPLE STRIPER THICKET SCRUBBER SKIRMISH SOFTENER STIPPLER TARBRUSH NAILBRUSH PAINTBRUSH
(— ASIDE) SCUFF
(— IN DANCING) SCUFFLE
(— OF HIR) PENCIL
(— OF TWIGS) COW
(— TO CLEAN SHIP BOTTOM) HOG
(BLUNT —) BLENDER
(DENSE —) BUNDOCKS BOONDOCKS
(ELECTRIC —) DOCTOR
(EMPHASIZED —) SLAP
(FLESH —) SCRAPER STRIGIL
(GROWTH OF —) SYLVAGE
(POLLEN —) SCOPA SAROTHRUM
(SMALL —) TOOL FITCH FITCHEW
(PREF.) MUSCARI SCOPI
BRUSHER LIMBER LIPPER
BRUSH MAKER FLIRTY FLICKER
BRUSH SHUNT PIGTAIL
BRUSHWOOD HAG RICE RONE RUSH BAVIN BRAKE BRUSH COPSE FRITH REISE SCROG SCRUB SPRAY COPPET GARSIL MALLEE RAMMEL SCRAWL SCRUNT SHROGS TINNET TINSEL COPPICE ROUGHIE TEENAGE THICKET WOODRIS BUSHWOOD OVENWOOD
BRUSQUE CURT RUDE BLUFF BLUNT GRUFF HASTY ROUGH SHORT ABRUPT VIOLENT CAVALIER IMPOLITE
BRUT DRY
BRUTAL CRUEL FERAL GROSS CARNAL COARSE FERINE SAVAGE BEASTLY BESTIAL BRUTISH CADDISH DOGGISH INHUMAN BELLUINE INHUMANE INSOLENT RUTHLESS
BRUTALITY SADISM
BRUTE BETE BEAST GROSS YAHOO ANIMAL BRUTAL SAVAGE BEASTLY BESTIAL BRUTISH GORILLA RUFFIAN
BRUTISH FELL CRUEL BRUTAL CARNAL FIERCE SAVAGE STUPID BESTIAL INHUMAN SENSUAL GADARENE
BRYONY HOP NEP ALRAUN COWBIND MANDRAKE
(— FRUIT) OXBERRY
BRYOPHYTE MOSS ANOPHYTE LIVERWORT
BRYOPHYTIC MOSSY MOSSED
BRYOZOAN POLYZOAN
BRYTHONIC CYMRIC KYMRIC BRITTONIC
BUBBLE AIR BUB BEAD BELL BLEB BLOB BOIL BOLL DUPE FOAM GLOB SCUM SEED CAPER CHEAT EMPTY VAPOR BURBLE DELUDE HOTTER POPPLE SEETHE SOTTER TRIFLE BLISTER BLUBBER DECEIVE GLOBULE DELUSIVE
(— IN GLASS) BOIL REAM SEED BLISTER

(FORMATION OF —S) EBULLISM
(PL.) SUDS
(PREF.) BULLI
BUBBLING GAY BULLER BURBLY BOILING GASSING EFFUSIVE
BUBINGA KEVAZINGO
BUBO EMEROD
BUCCANEER PIRATE RIFLER ROBBER VIKING CORSAIR MARINER SPOILER MAROONER PICAROON
BUCHMANITE GROUPER
BUCHU BUKA DIOSMA
BUCK FOB RAM BOIL BUTT DEER DUDE MALE PRIG REAR SOAK STAG TOFF WASH BLOOD DANDY MONEY PITCH SASIN STEEP BASKET DOLLAR OPPOSE RESIST STRIVE SAWBUCK BUCKJUMP BUCKWASH
(— IN 1ST YEAR) FAWN
(— IN 2ND YEAR) PRICKET
(— IN 3RD YEAR) SORREL
(— IN 4TH YEAR) SORE
(— STEADILY) SUNFISH
(— UP) BRACE
BUCKBEAN BOGBEAN THREEFOLD
BUCKER DOLLYMAN
BUCKET SAY TUB BAIL BOOT BOWK CAGE GRAB MEAL PAIL SKIP BOWIE CHEAT SCOOP SKEEL STOOP STOUP BAILER DIPPER DRENCH HOPPET KIBBLE SITULA SUCKER VESSEL FERMAIL GRAPPLE SNAPPER SWINDLE CANNIKIN HEDGEHOG PAINTPOT
(— ON MILL WHEEL) AW AWE EIE
(— ON WHEELS) SKIP
(GLASS-MAKING —) CUVETTE
(GRAVEL —) GRAB
(HOISTING —) HUDGE
(PART OF —) EAR RIM BAIL BODY CURL HANDLE
(TWO —S OF WATER) GAIT
BUCKEYE CANOE
BUCKEYE STATE OHIO
BUCKLAW HAYSTON
BUCKLE BOW BEND CURL KINK OUCH TACH TACK WARP BRACE CLASP MARRY STRAP TACHE TWIST FIBULA CONTEND FERMAIL GRAPPLE FASTENER STRUGGLE
BUCKLER CRAB BLOCK PELTA SCUTE TARGE SHIELD TAIRGE TARGET BUCKLUM BUCKRAM ROTELLA ROUNDEL SHUTTER RONDACHE
BUCKLING KINK UPSET
BUCK RAKE SWEEP
BUCKRAM STIFFENER
BUCKS BREAD DOUGH MONEY MOOLA DINERO
BUCKTHORN COMA RHAMN SCROG WAHOO ALATERN CASCARA BEARWOOD FRANGULA LOTEBUSH WAYTHORN STINKWOOD
BUCKTHORN BROWN SUMAC SUMACH
BUCKWHEAT BUCK CRAP BRANK WRIGHT KNOTWEED SARRAZIN POLYGONUM
(PL.) FAGOPYRUM
BUCOLIC IDYL LOCAL NAIVE RURAL FARMER RUSTIC SIMPLE COWHERD ECLOGUE AGRESTIC HERDSMAN PASTORAL
BUCOLION (FATHER OF —) LAOMEDON
(SON OF —) AESEPUS PEDASUS
(WIFE OF —) ABARBAREA
BUD BUR EYE GEM IMP PIP BULB BURR CION FORM GERM GIRL GROW KNOP KNOT WORK CAPOT CHILD CLOVE GEMMA GRAFT SCION SHOOT SPRIT SPURT YOUTH BUDLET BULBIL BUTTON FLOWER GERMIN OCULUS OILLET SPROUT BLOSSOM BROTHER CABBAGE GEMMULE PLUMULE ROSEBUD TENDRON BOURGEON BULBILLA
(BLIGHTED —) BLAST
(BROOD —) SOREDIUM
(UNDERGROUND —) TURION
(UNDEVELOPED —) EYE
(UNOPENED —) KNOSP
(PL.) CAPERS
(PREF.) BLAST(O) GEMMI GEMMO
BUDDENBROOKS (AUTHOR OF —) MANN
(CHARACTER IN —) TOM JEAN TONI ERICA GERDA HANNO JOHANN THOMAS ANTONIE GRUNLICH CHRISTIAN PERMANEDER
BUDDHA FO FOH BUTSU JATAKA GAUTAMA SRAMANA DAIBUTSU
(— STORY) JATAKA
(FATHER OF —) SUDDHODANA
(SON OF —) KAHULA
BUDDHISM DAIJO FOISM KEGON CHANISM LAMAISM HINAYANA
(— CODE) VINAYA
(BRANCH OF —) MAHAYANA
BUDDHIST (— DOCTRINE) ANATTA TRIKAYA
(— FESTIVAL) WESAK
(— MOUNTAIN) OMEI
(— PATH) VEHICLE
(— SCHOOL) RITSU
(— SECT) SHIN TENDAI
(— TEACHER) GURU
(— WHO ATTAINED NIRVANA) ARHAT ARAHAT
BUDDLE TYE FRAME BODDLE SLIMER STRIPE TROUGH
BUDDY BO BOY BUD DOC PAL JACK MATE COBBER DIGGER BROTHER COMRADE COMPADRE TENTMATE
BUDGE FUR JEE BOGY MOVE STIR BOOZE BRISK MUDGE STIFF THIEF JOCUND LIQUOR SOLEMN AUSTERE POMPOUS MOVEMENT
BUDGET BAG BOGY BOOT PACK PLAN ROLL BATCH BOGEY BOGIE BUNCH STOCK STORE BOTTLE BUNDLE PARCEL SOCKET WALLET PROGRAM
BUFF ASH BOB FAN TAN BLOW COAT CURT FIRM SHINE SNUFF SPARK BUFFET POLISH STURDY DEVOTEE STAMMER STUTTER NAUMKEAG
(TILLEUL —) ALABASTER
BUFFALO OX ANOA ARNA ARNI BUFF STAG ARNEE BISON BUGLE BUFFLE HAMPER KERBAU MURRAH WUNTEE CARABAO CARIBOU GAZELLE OVERAWE TIMARAU ZAMOUSE BEWILDER SAPIUTAN SELADANG
(WATER —) ARNEE
BUFFALO CHIPS BODEWASH
BUFFALO FISH SUCKER BUFFALO BIGMOUTH GOURDHEAD
BUFFER DOG PAD FROG RACK BUMPER FENDER HURTER PISTOL CUSHION
BUFFET BAR BOB BOX BEAT BLAD BLOW BUFF CUFF GOWF PLAT SCAT SLAP TOSS YANK FILIP KNOCK SCUFF SCUFT SMITE STOOL ABACUS BATTER FILLIP FLEWIT SERVER SETOUT STRIKE STRIVE THRASH COLPHEG CONTEND COUNTER HASSOCK SMACKER SQUELCH CREDENCE CREDENZA CUPBOARD SPANGHEW
BUFFETING DIRD SKITE DUSTING
BUFFLEHEAD DUCK FOOL CLOWN BUFFLE DIPPER DOPPER MARIONET WOOLHEAD MERRYWING
BUFFOON DOR WAG WIT APER FOOL JAPE MIME MOME VICE ZANY ACTOR ANTIC BUFFO CLOWN COMIC DROLE DROLL HARLOT JESTER MUMMER STOOGE ANTIQUE BOUFFON FARCEUR JUGGLER PIERROT PLAYBOY SCOGGIN TOMFOOL BALATRON GRACIOSO HUMORIST MACAROON MERRYMAN OWLGLASS PLEASANT RIDICULE PANTALOON SCARAMOUCH PUNCHINELLO
BUFFOONERY JAPERY ZANYISM CLOWNERY TOMFOOLERY
BUFO TOAD
BUG (ALSO SEE INSECT) DOR FLU FLAW GERM IDEA MITE BOGEY BULGE FIEND LYGUS ROACH ARADID BEDBUG BEETLE BUGGER CAPSID CHINCH COREID CORUCO ELATER GLITCH INSECT SALDID SCHEME TINGID BELLIED BOATMAN BUGBEAR CIMICID CORSAIR FORWARD POMPOUS STRIDER ASSASSIN BARBEIRO CONENOSE HEMIPTER HOBBYIST NAUCORID VINCHUCA
(— OFF) LEAVE
(KIND OF —) LYGUS DAMSEL
(RED —) CHIGGA CHIGGER
(SOW —) SLATER
(PREF.) CIMI(CI)
(SUFF.) CORIS
BUGABOO BOGY FEAR GOGA GOGO OGRE TURK ALARM BOGEY BOGIE GOGGA BODACH GOBLIN BUGBEAR SPECTER SPECTRE WORRICOW
BUGANDA (— KING) KABAKA
BUGBANE COHOSH BUGWORT RICHWEED HELLEBORE
BUGBEAR BUG COW BOGY OGRE BOGEY BOGIE CADDY MORMO POKER BOGGLE BOGGART BUGABOO FEARBABE SCAREBUG
BUGGER SOD CHAP BOOGER FELLOW PERSON RASCAL HERETIC
BUGGY CART NUTS PRAM SHAY TRAP NUTTY CALESA CABOOSE CALESIN FOOLISH VEHICLE DEMENTED INFESTED ROADSTER STANHOPE
BUGLE BEAD HORN AJUGA BLACK BUFFALO BULLOCK CLARION HUTCHET TRUMPET KEYBUGLE
(— CALL) WARISON
(PART OF —) CUP RIM BELL BITE EDGE
(YELLOW —) IVA
BUGLER WINDJAMMER
BUGLEWEED IVA AJUGA
BUGLOSS ALKANET ANCHUSA BLUEWEED OXTONGUE
BUILD BIG SET FORM LEVY MAKE REAR TELD DRIVE EDIFY ERECT FOUND FRAME HOUSE PUTUP RAISE SHAPE THROW CREATE FABRIC GRAITH TAILLE TIMBER COMPILE EXTRUCT FASHION ASSEMBLE PHYSIQUE
(— FIRE) CHUNK
(— HASTILY) CLAP
(— NEST) AERIE NIDIFY
(— UP) AGGRADE
(BODY —) HABITUS STATURE
BUILDER EPEUS MAKER BIGGAR EPEIUS HANGER ERECTOR ENGINEER TECTONIC
(DAM —) DAMMER
(PREF.) TECTO
(SUFF.) TECT
BUILDING GIN CASA CRIB DOME FLAT HALL IGLU JAIL LAND PILE SHED SHOP SLAB SPOT TELD ABBEY AEDES ARENA BLOCK COURT FOLLY FRAME HOTEL HOUSE IGLOO JAWAB STORE STUDY ARMORY BIGGIN BOTTLE CASING CHAPEL FABRIC GARAGE HAMMAM INSULA LYCEUM PALACE SCHOOL SUCCOR BREWERY BROODER CARBARN COLLEGE DIORAMA EDIFICE FACTORY FLATTOP FOUNDRY KURHAUS MANSION PALAZZO SALTERN STATION SYNAGOG ATHENEUM BAGHOUSE BASILICA BROLETTO CHANCERY DIPTEROS DRYHOUSE DWELLING DYEHOUSE ELEVATOR EPHEBEUM FIRETRAP FOURPLEX GASHOUSE GINHOUSE HOTHOUSE ICEHOUSE MAGAZINE NYMPHEUM PANORAMA SERAPEUM STEMMERY TAXPAYER TENEMENT VELODROME OBSERVATORY OUTBUILDING PLANETARIUM MEETINGHOUSE
(— BLOCK) MEGALITH
(— FOR AIRCRAFT) DOCK
(— GROUPS) HAM
(— OF STONE) KAABA CASHEL TRUDDO TRULLO
(— ON POSTS) PATAKA
(— WITH TRIANGULAR FRONT) AFRAME
(BUDDHIST —) TOPE
(CIRCULAR —) THOLE THOLOS ROTUNDA
(CRUDE —) SHANTY

(DILAPIDATED —) FLEAPIT ROOKERY FIRETRAP
(EXHIBITION —) MUSEUM
(FARM —) BARN STABLE HACIENDA
(FORTIFIED —) CASTLE
(GLOOMY —) MAUSOLEUM
(GRAIN —) GARNER
(GROUP OF —S) CLUSTER
(JAI ALAI —) FRONTON
(MOVABLE —) TURRET
(ORNAMENTAL —) ALCOVE
(PUBLIC —) CASINO THEATER THEATRE COLISEUM
(QUADRANGULAR —) TETRAGON
(QUARANTINE —) LAZARET
(ROUND —) THOLUS
(SACRED —) CHURCH MOSQUE TEMPLE SACRARY PANTHEON SARAPEUM
(SERIES OF —S) SWEEP
(SLIGHT —) SHED
(SMALL —) HUT COOP HOCK EDICULE
(SPORTS —) CAGE
(STATELY —) DOME
(STORAGE —) BARN HORREUM
(SUBSIDIARY —) ANNEX
(TALL —) SKYSCRAPER
(TRADE —) HALL
(UNCOMFORTABLE —) ARK
(PL.) FUNDUS

BUILD-UP GROWTH

BUILT SET BOUKIT STACKED TIMBERED
(COMPACTLY —) CORKY
(HEAVILY —) BLOCKY
(LOOSELY —) GANGLING
(STRONGLY —) BURLY GROSS QUARRY
(WELL —) BUIRDLY

BUKIDNON MONTES BINOKID

BUKKI (FATHER OF —) JOGLI ABISHUA
(SON OF —) UZZI

BULB BUD SET BLUB CORM IXIA KNOB LAMP ROOT SEED SEGO CAMAS CHIVE CLOVE FLOAT GLOBE ONION SWELL TUBER BULBIL BULBUS CAMASS CROCUS GARLIC OFFSET SCILLA BABIANA GALTONIA SPARAXIS TRITONIA PHOTOFLASH
(— OF PERCUSSION) CONCHOID
(CUBICAL —) FLASHCUBE
(LIGHT —) HELION
(ONION —) BUTTON
(PL.) SQUILL
(PREF.) BULBI BULBO

BULBIL CHIVE BULBLET
(PL.) SPAWN

BULBLET CHIVE CORMEL BULBULE NUCLEUS PROPAGO

BULBUL KALA BUHLBUHL GREENBUL LEAFBIRD

BULGARIA

ASSEMBLY: SOBRANJE SOBRANYE
CAPE: EMINE SABLA KURATAN
CAPITAL: SOFIA
COIN: LEV LEW STOTINKA
COMMUNE: SLIVEN SLIVNO SISTOVA
GULF: BURGAS
MEASURE: OKA OKE KRINE LEKHE
MOUNTAIN: BOTEV SAPKA MUSALA VIKHREN
MOUNTAINS: PIRIN BALKAN RHODOPE
PEOPLE: SLAV TATAR BULGAR SLAVIC
RIVER: LOM VIT ARDA OSMA ISKER MESTA DANUBE MARICA OGOSTA STRUMA YANTRA MARITSA STRYAMA TUNDZHA
TOWN: RILA RUSE AYTOS BUTAN BYCLU ELENA ISKRA STARA VARNA BLEVEN BURGAS DULOVO LEVSKY PLEVNA SHUMEN SHUMLA SLIVEN SLIVNO WIDDIN YAMBOL ZAGORA GABROVO KARLOVO PLOVDIV SISTOVA TIRNOVO RUSTCHUK
WEIGHT: OKA OKE TOVAR

BULGARIAN POMAK

BULGE BAG BUG JUT SAG BIAS BULB BUMP CASK HUMP KNOB LUMP PANT BILGE BLOAT BOUGE FLASK POUCH START STRUT SWELL BEETLE BILLOW COCKLE EXTEND PUCKER WALLET BLISTER PROJECT OVERHANG PROTRUDE SWELLING PROJECTION
(— OUT) TUT BELLY BOWDEN STRUNT
(OFFENSIVE —) SALIENT

BULGING FULL BOMBE BOWED BUGGY GOUTY PUDGY TUMID BAGGED BUNCHY CONVEX GOOGLY TOROSE GAMPISH GIBBOUS GOUTISH SWOLLEN BOUFFANT PROPTOSIS

BULK BODY BOUK FECK HEAP HEFT HOLD HULK HULL LUMP MASS MOLE PILE SIZE BURLY CARGO GROSS MIGHT POWER SLUMP STALL SWELL CORPSE EXPAND EXTENT FIGURE VOLUME BIGNESS MAJORITY QUANTITY
(PREF.) ONCO

BULKHEAD CHECK BATTERY PARTITION

BULKY BIG MAIN BURLY GROSS LARGE LUSTY PUDGY STOUT CLUMSY STODGY HULKING LUMPING MASSIVE VOLUMED WEIGHTY CUMBROUS UNWIELDY
(PREF.) PYCN(O)

BULL COP SEG APIS BEEF BILL JEST MALE ROAN SEAL SEGG SLIP STOT TORO ZEBU BACIS BEEVE BOBBY BONER BOVID BRUTE CROCK DRINK EDICT ERROR ANIMAL BOVINE BUSHWA LETTER PEELER TAURUS BULLOCK BUSHWAH CRITTER CRUSADE NOVILLO TAURINE CAJOLERY DOCUMENT FLATTERY IRISHISM
(— AREA) QUERENCIA
(— KILLING) VOLAPIE
(HORNLESS —) DODDY DODDIE
(HUMAN-HEADED —) SHEDU CAMASSU
(YOUNG —) STOT BUGLE MICKY STIRK STOTT BULLOCK
(PL.) BATTERY
(PREF.) TAUR(I)(O)

BULLA BLEB BULL SEAL BLAIN BLISTER VESICLE

BULL CELL TORIL

BULLDOG BULL BULLER BULLDOZE

BULLDOZE COW RAM BULLY FORCE SCOOP COERCE BROWBEAT BULLYRAG RESTRAIN

BULLDOZER (PART OF —) ARM EYE SHOE TANK BLADE FRAME IDLER LEVER LIGHT STRUT TRACK CANOPY FENDER GRILLE ROLLER CLEANER HOUSING MUFFLER CYLINDER

BULLET ACE GUN BALL LEAD PILL SHOT SLUG TOWEL CONOID DUMDUM PELLET PICKET SINKER TRACER DINGBAT MISSILE PELLOCK PROJECT SPITZER BISCAYAN MUSHROOM WADCUTTER
(— SIZE) CALIBER
(KIND OF —) MAGIC
(PL.) BALL LEAD STUFF

BULLETIN ITEM MEMO NOTICE POSTER REPORT SERIAL PROGRAM NEWSBILL

BULLETIN BOARD (OPERATOR OF —) SYSOP

BULLFIGHT CORRIDA NOVILLADA

BULLFIGHTER TORERO MATADOR PICADOR CAPEADOR TOREADOR NOVILLERO

BULLFIGHTING REJONEO TAUROMACHY
(— MOVEMENT) PASE
(PASE IN —) VERONICA

BULLFINCH ALP OLP HOOP MAWP MONK NOPE OLPH POPE HEDGE TANNY TAWNY MONACH REDBIRD REDHOOP SHIRLEY BLOODALP TONYHOOP

BULLHEAD CUR POUT POGGE COTTOID

BULLHEADED SET

BULLHORN HAILER LOUDHAILER

BULLIMONG FARRAGE

BULLION BILLOT

BULLISH STIFF

BULLOCK HOG HOGG NEAT NOWT STOT BUGLE COACH KNOUT STEER STIRK BOVINE
(AUSTRALIAN —) SNAIL
(BAD-TEMPERED —) RAGER
(DECOY —) COACH

BULL-ROARER BUZZ BUMMER BUZZER ROARER TUNDUN HUMBUZZ TURNDUN WHIZZER

BULL'S-EYE EYE BULL DUMP GOLD BLANK OXEYE WHITE TARGET ROUNDEL

BULL SNAKE GOPHER

BULL TROUT TRUFF

BULLY COW NUT BOAT BOSS FACE FINE GOOD HAZE HUFF MATE BRAVE BRAVO GREAT JOLLY SNOOL TIGER VAPOR BOUNCE CUTTER CUTTLE HARASS HECTOR HUFFER JOVIAL RUFFLE TYRANT BLUSTER BOUNCER BULLOCK DARLING DASHING GALLANT GAUSTER HUFFCAP ROISTER RUFFIAN RUFFLER SLASHER SOLDIER SWAGGER BANGSTER BARRATER BLUDGEON BROWBEAT BULLDOZE DOMINEER FRAMPLER NIGHTCAP RABIATOR
(MASTIC —) ACOMA

BULLY TREE BALATA BULLACE GAUSTER BEEFWOOD

BULRUSH REED RISP RUSH TULE SEDGE BUMBLE GLUMAL AKAAKAI CATTAIL PAPYRUS SCIRPUS TUSSOCK

BULWARK BAIL FORT WALL FENCE JETTY MANTA MOUND TOWER SCONCE WARDER BASTION DEFENCE DEFENSE PARAPET PROTECT RAMPART WEREWALL

BUM BEG DIN BOMB BOOM HOBO DRINK DRONE IDLER MOOCH SHACK STIFF TRAMP FROLIC GUZZLE ROTTER SPONGE SQUEEF GUZZLER LAYABOUT VAGABOND BINDLESTIFF

BUMBERSHOOT GAMP

BUMBLE ERR

BUMBLEBEE DOR CLOCK BUMBEE BUMBLE CARDER BUMBLER

BUMBLER OAF IDIOT KLUTZ

BUMMER FLOP FAILURE SKIDDER STINKER

BUMP CRY HIP HIT NOB BANG BLOW BOOM BUNK DIRD JOLT JOWL KNOB LUMP NERF WHAP WHOP BARGE BULGE CLASH CLOUR CLOUT DUNCH KNOCK ORGAN THUMP BOUNCE CANNON IMPACT JOUNCE NODULE STRIKE BITTERN COLLIDE CONFLICT SWELLING
(— IMPOLITELY) KNEE
(— IN SKI RUN) MOGUL
(— OFF) KILL SCRAG MURDER
(— ON SKI RUN) MOGUL
(— ON WHALE'S HEAD) HOVEL

BUMPER BOWL FINE GOOD FACER GLASS ROUSE BUFFER CASABE FENDER GOBLET HURTER KELTIE BOUNCER BRIMMER DINGMAN CARANGID
(— GUARD) OVERRIDER

BUMPER CAR DODGEM

BUMPKIN JAY YAP BEAM BOOM BOOR CHAW CLOD GAWK HICK LOUT PUTT RUBE SWAB SWAD TIKE TYKE CHURL CLOWN ROBIN YAHOO YOKEL FARMER JOSKIN LUMMOX RUSTIC BUCOLIC CAUBOGE HAWBUCK CHAWBACON

BUMPTIOUS COXY BRASH COCKSY

BUN PUG CHOU BRICK COOKIE CRESCENT
(PL.) BUTTOCKS

BUNAH (FATHER OF —) JERAHMEEL

BUNCH BOB SET WAD BALE BOSS CHOU CLEW CLOT CLUB CLUE COMA KICK KNOB KNOT PACK SWAD TUFT WISP BREAK CLUMP FAGOT FLOCK KNOLL PAHIL THUMP CLUTCH GAGGLE HUDDLE CLUSTER
(— OF BANANAS) HAND STEM
(— OF FEATHERS) LURE PLUME

(— OF FLAX) HEAD STRICK
(— OF FLOWERS) POSY BOWPOT BOUGUET BOUQUET NOSEGAY BOUGHPOT
(— OF FOLIAGE) FINIAL
(— OF FRUIT) HOG STRAP
(— OF GRAIN) RIP
(— OF GRAPES) RAISIN
(— OF GRASS) WHISK
(— OF HAIR) COB
(— OF HERBS) BOUQUET
(— OF IVY) BUSH
(— OF RAGS) MOP
(— OF TOBACCO LEAVES) HAND BREAK
(— OF TWIGS) COW KOW ROD
(— UP) SHRUG
(LONG —) STRING
(SMALL —) WISP
BUNCHER BINDER
BUNCHY TRUSS
BUNCO SCAM CHEAT
BUNCOMBE HOOEY BUNKUM
BUND BAND QUAY PRAYA LEAGUE SOCIETY
BUNDLE KID LOT PAD TOD WAD WAP BALE BAND BEAT BOLT BOOK BUNG DRUG DRUM GARB HANK HAUL HEAD KNOT LOCK PACK ROLL SWAG BLUEY BULTO BUNCH FADGE FAGOT GAVEL GLEAN GROUP LITCH NICKY PETER SHEAF SKEIN TARRY TRACE TRUSS TURSE WADGE BARSOM BATTEN BINDLE BOTTLE BUDGET DRIVER DUFTER FAGGOT FARDEL FASCES FUMBLE GATHER KNITCH LOGGIN NUMBER PACKET PARCEL SCROLL THRAVE DORLACH FASCINE GARBAGE MATILDA PACKAGE FASCICLE TROUSSEAU
(— BARLEY) SHEAVE
(— OF BOARDS) BOLT
(— OF CELLULOSE) MICROFIBRIL
(— OF FASCINES) ROULEAU
(— OF FIBRILS) AXONEME
(— OF FILAMENTS) BYSSUS
(— OF FLAX) BEET HEAD
(— OF HAIR) LEECH
(— OF HAY, STRAW, ETC.) WAP WASE WISP GAVEL SHEAF BATTEN BOLTIN BOTTLE TIPPLE WINDLING
(— OF HEATH) KID
(— OF HIDES) KIP
(— OF NERVE FIBERS) TRACT COLUMN
(— OF PAPERS) SPUR DUFTER
(— OF RODS) FASCES
(— OF SACKS) BADGER
(— OF SACRED TWIGS) BARSOM
(— OF THONGS) KNOUT
(— OF TOBACCO) CARROT
(— OF TWIGS) BIRCH BROOM FAGGOT
(— OF WOOD) PIMP BAVIN FAGOT
(— OF YARN) HAUL SLIP
(— OF 60 SKINS) TURN
(— UP) EMBALE
(BUSHMAN'S —) DRUM BLUEY
BUNG CORK DOOK PLUG SHIVE SPILE STOPPER
BUNGEY KIT
BUNGI-BUNGI STAVEWOOD
BUNGLE ERR BOOB DUFF FLUB GOOF MESS MUCK MUFF MULL BLUNK BOTCH FAULT FLUFF FUDGE MISDO SPOIL STICK BOGGLE BOLLIX BUMBLE FOOZLE FUMBLE MANGLE MOMBLE MUCKER MUDDLE TAILOR TOGGLE BAUCHLE BLUNDER BUTCHERY SHAMMOCK
BUNGLER MUFF LUMMOX PUDDLE TINKER BLUNKER BUMBLER BUMMLER FOOZLER DAUBSTER SCHLEMIEL
BUNGLING FLUFF FUDGY INERT CLUMSY AWKWARD TINKERLY MUDDLEHEADED
BUNGO BONGO CANOE
BUNG START FLOGGER
BUNION ONION WYROCK CARBUNCLE
BUNJI-BUNJI CUDGERIE
BUNK BED CAR BLAA BLAH CASE JUNK SACK ABIDE BERTH BUNKO FRAME HOKUM HOOEY LEAVE LODGE SLEEP TRUCK BUNKUM TIMBER BALONEY BOLSTER CHICORY HEMLOCK TWADDLE BUNCOMBE COBBLERS MALARKEY NONSENSE
BUNKHOUSE BULLPEN
BUNKUM BLAH BULL BUNK CROCK FUDGE HOKUM HOOPLA BALONEY BUNCOMBE MALARKEY
BUNTAL BURI BANGKOK
BUNTING EBB POP CIRL FLAG PAPE POPE CHINK DUMPY FINCH PLUMP COTTON STOCKY TOWHEE UNTIDY COWBIRD ETAMINE GARMENT OATFOWL ORTOLAN ROUNDED BELLYING BOBOLINK PRUSIANO RICEBIRD RINGBIRD SLOVENLY NONPAREIL
BUNTON DIVIDER
BUNUS (FATHER OF —) HERMES
(MOTHER OF —) ALCIDAMEA
BUOY DAN NUN WAFT BAKEN ELATE FLOAT LAGAN RAISE BEACON MARKER DOLPHIN SUSTAIN DEADHEAD LEVITATE MAKEFAST SONOBUOY
(KIND OF —) SONOBUOY
BUOYANCY BALON BALLON LEVITY SPRING ELATION
BUOYANT GAY CORKY HAPPY LIGHT BLITHE BOUNCY FLOATY LIVELY ELASTIC HOPEFUL JOCULAR LILTING SPRINGY ANIMATED CHEERFUL SANGUINE SPIRITED VOLATILE
BUPHAGUS (FATHER OF —) IAPETUS
(MOTHER OF —) THORNAX
(SLAYER OF —) ARTEMIS
BUR BUZZ TEAZEL STICKER
BURBARK AKONGE BOXBUSH BURRBARK
BURBOT COD CONY CUSK LING LOTA CONEY LOCHE LAWYER MORGAY DOGFISH EELPOUT GUDGEON BIRDBOLT
BURBUNG BORA
BURDEN TAX VEX BIRN CARE CARK CLAG CLOG DRAG DUTY FARE FOOT GANG LADE LOAD MUCK ONUS PORT SEAM TACK TASK BIRTH CARGO CROWD CRUSH DRONE HEAVY LABOR MIDST CHARGE CUMBER ENTAIL FARDEL HAMPER IMPOSE LADING SADDLE THRACK WEIGHT BALLAST BURTHEN CONVETH FRAUGHT FREIGHT HAGRIDE ONERATE OPPRESS REFRAIN REPRISE SUMPTER TROUBLE CAPACITY CARRIAGE ENCUMBER ENGREGGE HANDICAP OVERCOME PRESSURE QUANTITY RUMBELOW MILLSTONE RESPONSIBILITY
(— OF SONG) WHEEL FADING HOLDING OVERTURN OVERWORD
(FINANCIAL —) EXPENSE
BURDENED HEAVY LADEN GRAVID FRAUGHT HARASSED
BURDENER INCUBUS
BURDENSOME HEAVY IRKSOME ONEROUS WEIGHTY CUMBROUS GRIEVOUS GRINDING LOADSOME
BURDOCK DOCK GOBO CLITE CLOTE CLOTS DRAIN LAPPA BARDANE BURWEED BUZZIES CADILLO CLOTBUR HARDOCK HAREBUR CLEAVERS HAULBACK
BUREAU DESK CHEST AGENCY EXCISE OFFICE CENTRAL DRESSER AGITPROP
BUREAUCRAT MANDARIN
BURFISH ATINGA
BURGEON BUD GROW ERUPT SHOOT SPROUT
BURGESS CITIZEN FREEMAN PORTMAN COMMONER GORGIBUS (PL.) BURGWARE
BURG GRASS SANDBUR COCKSPUR SANDSPUR
BURGH ROYALTY
BURGLAR YEGG CRACK THIEF GOPHER ROBBER RAFFLES YEGGMAN PETERMAN PICKLOCK
(— TOOL) LOID
BURGLARY BREAK CRACK THEFT LARCENY ROBBERY STEALAGE
BURGLE ROB SCREW
BURGUNDY MACON POMMARD VOUGEOT TONNERRE
BURIAL FUNERARY INTERMENT
(— MOUND) TOLA HUACA
BURIAL PLACE AHU TOMB GRAVE BURIAL GIGUNU LAYSTOW PYRAMID CATACOMB CEMETERY GOLGOTHA LAYSTALL
BURIED HIDDEN HUMATE SEPULT ABSORBED IMBEDDED
(NOT —) UNRESTED
(RECENTLY —) GREEN
BURIN GRAVER PLASTIC
BURKINA FASO (CAPITAL OF —) OUAGADOUGOU
(LANGUAGE OF —) BOBO LOBI SAMO MANDE MOSSI
(MOUNTAIN IN —) TEMA
(NATIVE OF —) BOBO LOBI SAMO BISSA HAUSA MANDE MARKA MOSSI PUEHL TUAREG SENOUFO VOLTAIC YATENGA MANDINGO
(RIVER IN —) VOLTA SOUROU
(TOWN OF —) PO LEO DORI PAMA YAKO DJIBO GAOUA LAWRA HOUNDE TOUGAN BANFORA
BURL BURR KNAR KNOT LUMP KNAUR PIMPLE PUSTULE
BURLAP GUNNY CROCUS BAGGING HESSIAN SACKING WRAPPING
BURLER LECKER SPILER
BURLESQUE APE ODD COPY JEST MIME SKIT BURLY DROLL FARCE REVUE COMEDY OVERDO PARODY BUFFOON JOCULAR MIMICRY MOCKERY OVERACT DOGGEREL RIDICULE TRAVESTY
BURLY BIG FAT BLUFF BULKY GROSS HEAVY HUSKY LARGE LUSTY NOBLE OBESE STOUT THICK TRAMP BOWERLY BUIRDLY MASTIFF STATELY IMPOSING
BUR MARIGOLD BACLIN CUCKOLD
BURMESE KADU BIRMAN ARAKANESE
BURN GYP BREN BREW CHAR FIRE GLOW PLOT RAZE RILL SEAR SERE TEND TIND ADUST BLAZE BROIL BROOK CENSE CHARK CLAMP FLAME FLARE OUTDO PARCH PLOUT QUICK ROAST SCALD SCAUM SINGE SWEAL WASTE WATER CLOZLE IGNIFY SCORCH SIZZLE STREAM CHARPIT COMBURE COMBUST CONSUME CREMATE CROZZLE FLICKER FRIZZLE INCENSE OXIDIZE RIVULET SCOWDER SMOLDER SWINDLE FLAGRATE SQUANDER AMBUSTION
(— FEEBLY) GUTTER
(— FITFULLY) FLICKER
(— IN) INURE
(— MIDNIGHT OIL) LUCUBRATE
(— OUT) GUT
(— THOROUGHLY) ASH
(— UP) ADUST EXUST
(— WITH LITTLE FLAME) SMUDGE
(LET —) BISHOP
(PREF.) COMBURI
BURNED ADUST COMBUST
(PREF.) AITHO
BURNER BEAK ETNA KORO BAKER PILOT ARGAND BUNSEN CENSER BATSWING CALCINER GASLIGHT THURIBLE WELSBACH
BURNET SELFHEAL BLOODWORT
BURNING HOT FIRE LIVE ADUST AFIRE ANGRY BLAZE CALID EAGER FIERY FLAME GLEDY QUICK SCALD URENT ABLAZE ARDENT FERVID FIRING LIVING TORRID USTION ADURENT CAUSTIC CAUTERY FERVENT FLAMING GLARING GLOWING INTENSE MORDANT SCOWDER SHINING ARDUROUS EXCITING FLAGRANT INUSTION MUIRBURN PARCHING SCOUTHER
(— BRIGHTLY) LIGHT
(— OF FORESTS IN INDIA) JHOOM
(MALICIOUS —) ARSON
(NO LONGER —) EXTINCT
(PREF.) IGNI

BURNING BUSH WAHOO
BURNISH RUB GLAZE GLOSS INLAY POLISH FURBISH
BURNISHED BROWN WHITE
BURNISHER AGATE BUFFER GLAZER FROTTON POLISHER
BURNT ADUST BRULE COMBUST
BURP BOKE BELCH BUBBLE
BURR NUT PAD RIB BARB BIRR BOSS BUZZ HALO KNOB PILE RING ROVE SLUG WHIR BRIAR BURGH CROUP WHARL WHIRR BANYAN CIRCLE CORONA TEASEL TUNNEL WASHER CORONET STICKER PARASITE
(— IN WOOD) GNAR KNAR
(— OF ANTLER) CORONET
(— ON TYPE) RAG
BURRO ASS DONKEY
BURROW BED DEN DIG SET BURY HEAP HOLE HOWK MINE MOLE PIPE ROOT TUBE BERRY COUCH EARTH MOUND FURROW ROOTLE TUNNEL CLAPPER GALLERY PASSAGE SHELTER EXCAVATE WORMHOLE
(— AS EEL) MUD
(— IN) MOIL
(— OF BADGER) SET
(— OF OTTER) COUCH
(FOSSIL —) SCOLITE
BURROWS TOWN
BURSA SAC SACK POUCH CAVITY BURSULA
BURSAR BOWSER PURSER TERRAR BOUCHER CASHIER
BURSE CASE SHOP FOREL BAZAAR BOURSE POCKET
BURST FIT FLY POP BLOW BUST DASH GUSH GUST LOSS LOUP REND SCAT TILT BLAST BLOUT BREAK CRACK ERUPT FLAFF FLASH GRAZE REAVE SALVO SCATT SHOUT SPASM SPLIT START STAVE BROKEN DAMAGE INJURY SPROUT EXPLODE IMPLODE RUPTURE SHATTER AIRBURST OUTBREAK SUNDERED
(— ASUNDER) OUTRIVE
(— FORTH) ERUPT SALLY EXPIRE BALLOON
(— IN) IRRUPT IMPLODE
(— INTO FRAGMENTS) FLITTER
(— INTO LAUGHTER) BUFF
(— OF ACTIVITY) BRASH SPURT SPRINT SPLURGE
(— OF ARTILLERY) GRAZE RAFALE
(— OF CHEERS) SALVO
(— OF ENERGY) BANG
(— OF FIRING) COUGH
(— OF HARMONIOUS SOUND) DIAPASON
(— OF LIGHT) FLASH GLORY
(— OF SPEED) KICK FLUTTER
(— OF TEARS) BLURT
(— OF TEMPER) FUFF BOUTADE
(— OF WIND) FLAW
(— OPEN) DEHISCE UPBRAST
(— OUT) BUFF PRORUMP
(— THE HEART) RIVE
(SUFF.) RRHAGE RRHAGIA RRHAGY
BURSTER GALE LUGGER CRACKER
BURSTING TUMID ABURST BLOWOUT RUPTION ERUPTING

BURUNDI
CAPITAL: BUJUMBURA
COIN: FRANC
LAKE: RUGWERO TSHOHOHA
NATIVE: TWA HUTU BANTU PYGMY TUTSI WATUSI
PEOPLE: WATUSI
RIVER: KAGERA RUVUBU RUZIZI AKANYARU MALAGARAZI
TOWN: NGOZI BURURI KITEGA MUYINGA BUJUMBURA

BURY URN CAMP HIDE MOOL RAKE TURF VEIL CLOAK COVER EARTH GRAVE INTER INURN PLANT VAULT WHELM ENTOMB ENWOMB HEARSE INHUME SEPULT SHROUD BEDELVE CONCEAL ENGROSS IMMERSE PITHOLE REPRESS SECRETE FUNERATE INHEARSE SUBMERGE SEPULCHER
BUS CLEAR CAMION JITNEY JEEPNEY MINIBUS DOUBLEDECKER
(PRIVATE —) PIRATE
BUSBOY OMNIBUS PICCOLO
BUSH TOD BUTT BOSCH BURSE CLUMP GROVE PLASH SCRAY SHRUB BOUCHE BRANCH BUSKET MAQUIS TAVERN BOSCAGE BOUCHON CLUSTER OUTBACK THICKET BUSHLAND
(— OF HAIR) GLIB
(— SICKNESS) TAURANGA
(BLACKBERRY —) BRAMBLE
(PRICKLY —) GORSE
(ROSE —) ROSIER ROSIERE
(STUNTED —) SCROG
(WILD ROSE —) BRIAR BRIER
(PL.) RUFFMANS
(PREF.) THAMN(O)
BUSHBUCK BONGO
BUSH CLOVER HAGI
BUSH COW ZAMOUSE
BUSHEL FOO FOU GOB LOT MET EPHA EPHI EPHAH BUCKET MODIUS STRICK
(1.6 —) FANEGA
(1-HALF —) TOVET
(1-HALF TO 3-4THS —) CABOT
(1-4TH —) PECK
(3-4THS —) SKIPPLE
(3 TO 5 —S) SACK
(4 —S) COMB COOMB
(41.28 —) WEY
(8 —S) SEAM
BUSHER SWAMPER
BUSHGRASS WOODREED
BUSHING BUSH COAK DRILL LINER BOUCHE COLLET LINING SLEEVE BOUCHON FERRULE GROMMET PADDING
(HALF —) STEP
BUSHMAN GUNG BUSHY KHUAI ABATOA ABATWA WHALER BUSHBOY SWAGMAN NEGRILLO
(PL.) SAN SAAN
BUSHMASTER CURUCUCU SURUCUCU
BUSHWHACKER PAPAW PAWPAW
BUSHY BOSKY SHOCK DUMOSE DUMOUS BUSHMAN QUEACHY
BUSIED VERSANT
BUSILY THRANG
BUSINESS ADO ART BIZ FAT JOB PIE CARE FEAT FIRM FUSS GAME GEAR LINE NOTE TASK WORK CAUSE CRAFT ERGON TRADE TRUCK AFFAIR CUSTOM EMPLOY ERRAND MATTER METIER NEGOCE OFFICE PIDGIN PIGEON RACKET TURKEY ACCOUNT BEESWAX CALLING CONCERN JOURNEY PALAVER TRADING TRAFFIC ACTIVITY AGIOTAGE BESOIGNE COMMERCE FOLLOWER INDUSTRY INTEREST VOCATION OCCASIONS OCCUPATION
(— WITHOUT ASSETS) SHELL
(COMIC —) LAZZO
(MONKEY —) JOUKERY PAWKERY
(STAGE —) BYPLAY
BUSINESSMAN TYCOON POACHER BOURGEOIS CONVERTER
BUSKIN BOOT SHOE CALIGA BOTTINE COTHURN BRODEKIN COTHURNUS
BUSS SMOUCH
BUSSU UBUSSU TROOLIE
BUST BUMP FAIL RUIN TAME BOSOM BREAK BURST BUSTO CHEST EDGAR FLUNK SPREE BRONZE DEMOTE REDUCE STATUE TURKEY DEGRADE DISMISS FAILURE PROTOME PORTRAIT
(— SHAPE) TAILLE
BUSTARD KORI OTIS WATO PAAUW TURKEY BEBILYA HOUBARA KORHAAN FLORICAN GOMPAAUW
(PREF.) OTIDI
BUSTIC AUSUBO CASSADA
BUSTLE ADO TEW BUZZ FIKE FRAY FUSS JUMP STIR WHEW WHIR FRISK HASTE HYPER KNOCK PAVIE STEER WHIRL WHIRR BISHOP BUMBLE ENERGY FISSLE FISTLE FLURRY FUSTLE HUDDLE HUSTLE POTHER PUDDER RACKET ROMAGE RUFFLE TATTER THRONG TUMULT UNREST UPROAR CLATTER CLUTTER CONTEND LOUSTER SCOWDER SCUFFLE SCUFTER SPUFFLE ACTIVITY IMPROVER SPLUTTER STRUGGLE TOURNURE CRINOLETTE
(—ABOUT) TROT
BUSTLING ADO BUSY FUSSY SPOFFISH STIRRING
BUST-UP SCUFFLE
BUSY FAST FELL APPLY BRISK QUICK ACTIVE ATWORK EIDENT EMPLOY INTENT LIVELY OCCUPY ORNATE STEERY THRONG UNIDLE ENGAGED HOPPING HUMMING OPEROSE TROUBLE WORKING DILIGENT EMPLOYED EXERCISE OCCUPIED SEDULOUS TIRELESS UNTIRING PRAGMATIC PRAGMATICAL
(— ONESELF) STRAP
(— WITH TRIFLES) FIDDLE FIDDLING
(NOT —) SLACK
BUSYBODY BUSY SNOOP YENTA EARWIG SPOFFY ARDELIO MARPLOT MEDDLER SNOOPER FACTOTUM QUIDNUNC PRAGMATIC
BUT AC LO MA BIT SED YEA YET MERE ONLY SAVE ARRAH STILL ALWAYS EXCEPT UNLESS BESIDES HOWBEIT HOWEVER
BUTCHER KILL SLAY BUTCH SPOIL BUNGLE KIDDER LEGGER LEMMER MURDER VENDOR BOTCHER BRAINER BRITTEN FLESHER MEATMAN PORKMAN KILLCALF PIGSTICK SLAUGHTER
BUTCHERBIRD SHRIKE MATAGASSE
BUTCHER'S-BROOM RUSCUS BRUSCUS
BUTCHERY MURDER CARNAGE MASSACRE SHAMBLES SLAUGHTER
BUTEA DHAK
BUTEO BUZZARD
BUTES (BROTHER OF —) ERECHTHEUS
(FATHER OF —) NEPTUNE PANDION POSEIDON
(SISTER OF —) PROCNE PHILOMELA
(WIFE OF —) CHTHONIA
BUTLER SOMLER YEOMAN BOTELER SERVANT SPENCER STEWARD CELLARER CONSUMAH KHANSAMA STEPHANO MAJORDOMO
BUTT JUR JUT MOT PIT PUT RAM RUN TOY TUP BUCK BUNT BURT BUSH CART CASK DISH DOSS FOOL GOAD GOAL GOAT HORN JOLT JURR PIPE POLL PUCK PUSH STUB TANG TOPE TURR BOUND DUNCH HINGE JOINT MOUND ROACH SCOPE STOCK STUMP BREECH TARGET THRUST BEEHIVE BUTTOCK PARAPET PROJECT REVERSE STUMMEL ARIETATE FLATFISH FLOUNDER RIDICULE SACKBUTT
(— FOR RIDICULE) GAME SPORT STALE COCKSHY
(— OF CIGAR) DOCK SNIPE
(— OF HORSEHIDE) SHELL
(— OF JOKE) JEST SCOGGIN JESTWORD
(CIGARETTE —) BUMPER
(HALF —) BEND
BUTTE HILL PICACHO
BUTTER RAM GOAT SHEA CLART COCUM BAMBUK BEURRE CAJOLE LEKVAR SPREAD BLARNEY FLATTER
(— MEASURE) SPAN
(— SUBSTITUTE) VANASPATI
(ARTIFICIAL —) BOSH OLEO BOSCH MARGARINE
(ASTRONOMICAL —) ARIES
(BROWNED IN —) NOISETTE
(PRUNE —) LEKVAR
(SEMIFLUID —) GHI GHEE
BUTTER-AND-EGGS RANSTEAD TOADFLAX
BUTTERBUR CLEAT CLOTE ELDIN GALON GALLON OXWORT GILTCUP FLEADOCK
BUTTERCUP BOLT CYME CRAZY ANEMONE CRAISEY CROWTOE GILTCUP GOLDCUP KINGCOB

KINGCUP CRAWFOOT CROWFOOT FROGWORT PASQUEFLOWER
BUTTERFISH GUNNEL POMPANO WHITING PALOMETA SKIPJACK
BUTTERFLY IO BLUE ARGUS COMMA ELFIN GHOST NYMPH QUEEN SATYR SWIFT WHITE ZEBRA ADONIS ALPINE APOLLO CALIGO COPPER DANAID HOPPER IDALIA JUGATE MORPHO PIERID PROGNE PSYCHE SULFUR THECLA URSULA VIOLET YELLOW ADMIRAL BUCKEYE DIURNAL DOLPHIN EMPEROR FRENATE MONARCH PIERINE SATYRID SKIPPER SULPHUR TROILUS TUSSOCK VANESSA VICEROY ARTHEMIS CECROPIA CRESCENT GRAYLING HESPERID ITHOMIID WANDERER METALMARK
(— BREEDER) AURELIAN
BUTTERFLY FISH MOJARRA FLATFISH
BUTTERFLY WEED FLUXROOT MILKWEED WINDROOT
BUTTERMILK WHIG JOCOQUE SOURDOOK
(— AND WATER) BLAND
BUTTERSCOTCH TOFFY
BUTTERTREE MAHWA
BUTTERWORT BEANWEED ROTGRASS SHEEPWEED
BUTTERY BOTRY LARDER SPENCE BUTLERY SPICERY
BUTTOCK CHEEK
BUTTOCKS ASS BUM BUN CAN FUD HAM ARSE BUNS BUTT CULE DOCK DOUP DUFF LEND MOON POOP PRAT SEAT TAIL TOBY TUSH CROUP FANNY NATES SLATS STERN TOUTE TUSHY BEHIND BOTTOM BREECH CHEEKS CURPIN HEINIE HINDER TUSHIE CROUPON CRUPPER DRODDUM HURDIES KEISTER BACKSIDE DERRIERE NATIFORM POSTERIOR
(PRACTICE OF EXPOSING —) MOONING
(PREF.) NATI PYG(O)
(SUFF.) PROCTA PYGAL PYGE PYGIA(N) PYGOUS PYGUS
BUTTON BUD ZIP BOSS CHIN DOME HOOK KNOB KNOP SPUR TUFT BADGE CATCH GLIDE OLIVE PEARL PRILL BARREL BAUBLE BOUTON BUCKLE GLIDER SHINER TOGGLE TROCHE DEWDROP HORNTIP KNICKER NETSUKE PRESSEL REGULUS DOORBELL FASTENER OLIVETTE
(— MAN) SOLDIER
(KIND OF —) PANIC
BUTTONBUSH BUCKBRUSH SWAMPWOOD
BUTTONHOLE EYE LOOP SLIT
BUTTON SNAKEROOT LIATRIS SAWWORT
BUTTONWOOD COTONIER
BUTTRESS NOSE PIER PILE PROP SPUR STAY BRACE BRICK ALLETTE OUTCAST OUTSHOT SUPPORT TAMBOUR ABUTMENT
(— MEMBER) TIRE
BUTYL TETRYL
BUXOM MILD AMPLE JOLLY PLUMP PRONE SONSY BLITHE CRUMBY CRUMMY FLORID FODGEL HUMBLE PLIANT SONSIE BOWERLY BOUNCING FLEXIBLE OBEDIENT OBLIGING YIELDING JUNOESQUE
BUY CHAP COFF COUP GAIN HAVE SHOP SNIP TAKE BRIBE CLAIM TRADE ABEGGE MARKET RANSOM REDEEM SECURE ACQUIRE CHAFFER PURCHASE
(— BACK) REPRISE
(— OFF) BRIBE APPEASE
(— UP STOCKS) COVER
(GOOD —) DEAL
BUYER CHAP AGENT CATER BEGGER EMPTOR PATRON VENDEE CHAPMAN SHOPPER ACHATOUR CUSTOMER PROSPECT
(— OF CLOTH) REDUBBER
BUYING ACATE ACHATE EMPTION
(— MANIA) ONIOMANIA
BUZ (FATHER OF —) NAHOR
(MOTHER OF —) MILCAH
BUZI (SON OF —) EZEKIEL
BUZZ HUM BURR CALL DASH HISS HUSS HUZZ RING WHIR FANCY FLING PHONE RUMOR BUMBLE NOTION WHOOSH WHISPER
BUZZARD AURA FOOL HAWK PERN BUTEO GLADE GLEDE HARPY STOOP BEETLE CURLEW PREYER STUPID PUDDOCK PUTTOCK VULTURE BROMVOEL
BUZZER BEE BELL ALARM HOWLER SIGNAL WHIZZER
BY A P X AB AT OF TO AGO BYE GIN PAR PER TIL ABUT ANON INTO NEAR PAST TILL APART ASIDE CLOSE FORBY BESIDE TOWARD BESIDES THROUGH
(— AND —) ANON
(— AND BY) BELIVE BIMEBY
(— FAR) EASILY
(— HEART) PERQUEIR
(— HOOK OR CROOK) HABNAB
(— MEANS OF) PER MOYENANT
(— NO MEANS) NA
(— REASON OF THIS) HEREAT
(— STEALTH) STOWLINS
(— SURPRISE) ABACK
(— THE DAY) PD
(— THE ORDER OF) O
(— THE WAY) APROPOS
(— THIS TIME) ALREADY
(— WAY OF) VIA
(GONE —) AGO PAST
(NEAR —) GIN
(PREF.) PRETER
BY-BIDDER FUNK CAPPER PUFFER
BYBLIS (BROTHER OF —) CAUNUS
(FATHER OF —) MILETUS
(MOTHER OF —) IDOTHEA
BY-CHANNEL BAYOU BRANCH
BYCOKET ABACOT ABOCOCKET
BYGONE PAST YORE OLDEN BYPAST FORMER ANCIENT ANTIQUE ELAPSED BACKWARD DEPARTED FOREPAST PRETERIT
BYPASS JUMP SHUN AVOID BURKE EVADE SHUNT CUTOFF DETOUR CIRCUIT OUTFLANK
BYPATH LANE BYWAY UNDERWALK
BY-PRODUCT SPINOFF SCRAP SHORTS EFFLUVIUM MIDDLINGS OUTGROWTH
BYRE SHIPPEN COWHOUSE
BYRNIE ARMOR
BYROAD BOREEN
BYWAY LANE PATH ALLEY BYPATH BYWALK OUTWAY SIDEWAY
BYWORD ADAGE AXIOM MOTTO BYNAME DIVERB PHRASE SAYING NAYWORD PROVERB NICKNAME REPROACH
BY-WORK PARERGON

C

C DO CEE DOH COCA CHARLIE HUNDRED
CAAMA FOX ASSE SILVER
CAB FLY KAB HACK TAXI ARABA ARANA CABIN NODDY GHARRI CRAWLER HACKNEY SHOWFUL TAXICAB VETTURA COUPELET MOTORCAB
(HINDU —) JUDKA
(KIND OF —) GYPSY
(LOW-HUNG —) HERDIC
(2-PONY —) KOSONG
(4-WHEELED —) BOUNDE BOUNDER DROSHKY GROWLER
CABAL PLOT RING JUNTA JUNTO PARTY BRIGUE CLIQUE SCHEME SECRET CHATTER CONSULT COUNCIL DISPUTE FACTION TALKING INTRIGUE CAMARILLA
CABALASSOU ARMADILLO
CABALISTIC MYSTIC
CABARET CAFE TAVERN
CABASSOU XENURUS
CABBAGE CAB CHOU CRIB KALE WORT CROUT FILCH SAVOY STEAL STOCK PECHAY PILFER TAILOR BOWKAIL OXHEART PAKCHOI PALMITO PURLOIN BORECOLE COLEWORT CRUCIFER CULTIGEN DRUMHEAD KOHLRABI KERGUELEN
(CHINESE —) BOKCHOY PAKCHOI
(KIND OF —) NAPA
(STUFFED —) HOLISHKES
(PL.) WORTS
CABBAGE BARK ANGELIM ANGELIN
CABBAGE SOUP SHCHI STCHI SHTCHEE
CABBAGE STALK CASTOCK
CABBIE HACK
CABDRIVER HACK MUSH CABBY CABMAN COCHER MUSHER COCHERO HACKMAN
CABIN BOX CAB COT DEN HUT CAVE CELL CREW CRIB SHED TILT BOOTH CHOZA COACH CUDDY FELZE HOVEL LODGE SHACK BOHAWN CABANA CASITA LITTER REFUGE SALOON SHANTY SHELTY WIGWAM BEDROOM BOUDOIR COTTAGE HUDDOCK MUDSILL
(— ON SHIP'S DECK) TEXAS ROUNDHOUSE
(DOUBLE —) SADDLEBAG
(PASSENGER —) VAN
(RUSSIAN LOG —) IZBA
CABIN-BOY GRUMMET
CABINET ARK BOX BUHL CASE FILE SINK AMBRY BAHUT BOARD CABIN CHEST BAFFLE BUREAU CLOSET ICEBOX ALMIRAH BOUDOIR COMMODE CONSOLE COUNCIL ETAGERE FREEZER JUKEBOX WHATNOT CELLARET CUPBOARD MINISTRY SHOWCASE VARGUENO MONOCLEID
(FILING —) MORGUE
CABINET-MAKER EBENISTE
CABINETMAKER EBENISTE
CABLE GUY TOW BOOM COAX CORD FAST JUNK LINK ROPE STAY WIRE CABLET GANGER STRAND TETHER COAXIAL GUNLINE SKYLINE CATENARY HIGHLINE TELEGRAM UMBILICAL
(— WITH EYE AT EACH END) STRAP
(— WOUND) KECKLING
(CHAIN —) BOOM
(DERRICK —) BACKSTAY
(SPLICED —) SHOT
(SUSPENDED —) ROPEWAY
CABLE CAR TELFER TELPHER
CABLED RUDENTED
CABMAN IZVOZCHIK
CABOCHON CAB SHELL CARBUNCLE
CABOODLE KIT LOT CALABASH
CABOOSE CAB CAR VAN CRIB HACK BUGGY CRUMMY GALLEY PALACE BOUNCER COOKROOM DOGHOUSE
CABRILLA CONY GAPER GROUPER
CABRIOLE LEG
CABSTAND HASARD HAZARD
CABUYA PITEIRA
CACAO BROMA COCOA ARRIBA COCKER CRIOLLO FORASTERO
CACHARI BODA
CACHE BURY HIDE DEPOT STASH STORE MEMORY SCREEN CONCEAL DEPOSIT TREASURE
CACHELOT WHALE
CACHET SEAL STAMP WAFER ESSENCE KONSEAL
CACIQUE BUNYAH CASSICAN HANGNEST
CACKEREL MENDOLE
CACK-HANDED CLUMSY AWKWARD
CACKLE CANK CONK CLACK LAUGH BABBLE GABBLE GAGGLE GIGGLE GOSSIP KECKLE TITTER CHACKLE CHATTER SNICKER TWADDLE LAUGHTER
CACKLING GAGGLING
CACKLING GOOSE GREASER
CACOMISTLE CIVET ARCTOID RINGTAIL BASSARISK
CACOON SEGRA SEQUA
CACOPHONOUS HARSH RAUCOUS JANGLING STRIDENT
CACTUS BLEO DILDO NOPAL BAVOSO CARDON CEREUS CHAUTE CHENDE CHINOA CHOLLA COCHAL MESCAL PEYOTE PEYOTL TASAJO AIRAMPO BISAGRE BISNAGA SAGUARO ALICOCHE CHICHIPE PITAHAYA XEROPHIL
(— FRUIT) MUYUSA
(KIND OF —) RATTAIL
CAD CUR BOOR CHUM HEEL CHURL LOUSE SWEEP BRAKJE MUCKER RASCAL ROTTER BOUNDER BUDMASH DASTARD BLIGHTER ASSISTANT
CADASTRAL UNIT YOKE
CADAVER BODY STIFF CORPSE CARCASS SUBJECT SKELETON
CADAVEROUS PALE GAUNT LIVID PALLID GHASTLY HAGGARD
CADDIE NACKET
CADDIS FLY DUN CADEW SEDGE CADBIT
CADDISWORM PIPER
CADDO ADAI TEXAS EYEISH HAINAI KICHAI HASINAI
CADE LAMB SOCK
CADENAS NEF
CADENCE BEAT FALL IAMB LILT PACE TONE CLOSE METER METRE PULSE SOUND SWING THROB DACTYL IAMBUS JINGLE RHYTHM BACCHIC ANAPAEST CLAUSULA MOVEMENT MEDIATION
(GREGORIAN —) TROPE
CADENZA MELISMA BARIOLAGE
CADET SON DODO GOAT PLEBE YOUTH EMBRYO JUNIOR SERGEANT
CADGE BEG BOT BUM TIE BIND HAWK CARRY MOOCH PEDDLE SPONGE SCROUNGE
CADGER BOT BUM DEALER HAWKER CARRIER PACKMAN SPONGER HUCKSTER SCAMBLER
CADGY KEDGY MERRY WANTON AMOROUS LUSTFUL CHEERFUL MIRTHFUL
CADMUS (DAUGHTER OF —) INO AGAVE SEMELE AUTONOE
(FATHER OF —) AGENOR
(MOTHER OF —) TELEPHASSA
(SISTER OF —) EUROPA
(SON OF —) POLYDORUS
(WIFE OF —) HARMONIA
CADRE CORE FRAME
CADUCEUS WAND STAFF SCEPTER SCEPTRE KERYKEION
CAECUM TYPHLON
(PREF.) ILEO TYPHL(O)
CAESAR (WORDS FROM —) ETTU
CAESURA REST STOP BREAK PAUSE INTERVAL DIAERESIS
CAFE BAR PUB CAFF AGOGO TAVERN BARROOM CABARET TAVERNA ESTAMINET
(— AU LAIT) ALESAN
(ROADSIDE —) BUVETTE
CAFE CREME SUEDE
CAFETERIA AUTOMAT
CAFFEINE THEIN THEINE
CAGAYAN IBANAG
CAGE BOX CAR GIG MEW PEN COOP CORF CRIB GOAL BRAKE CAVEA GRATE HUTCH AVIARY BASKET BUCKET CHAPEL ENCAGE FLIGHT PRISON CHANTRY CONFINE ENCLOSE LANTERN SHELTER TUMBREL TUMBRIL CARRIAGE ELEVATOR IMPRISON LAVARIUM RETAINER SCAFFOLD STRAINER
(— FOR HAWKS) MEW
(— FOR HENS) CAVEY CAVIE
(— FOR MOUTH) MUZZLE
(— OF MINE SHAFT) GIG
(— OF TRAM) CABIN
(BIRD —) AVIARY PINJRA VOLARY BIRDCAGE
(FIRE —) CRESSET
(KIND OF —) RIB
(LOBSTER —) CORF CREEL
(REVOLVING —) TUMBLER
CAGED PENT CAPTIVE
CAGER ONSETTER
CAGEY CAGY WARY COONY
CAGMAG KEGMEG
CAGOT AGOTE
CAHITA YAQUI
CAHOT PITCHHOLE
CAIMAN CAYMAN JACARE ALLIGATOR
CAIN (BROTHER OF —) ABEL SETH
(FATHER OF —) ADAM
(MOTHER OF —) EVE
(SON OF —) ENOCH
CAINAN (FATHER OF —) ENOS ARPHAXAD
(SON OF —) SALA MAHALALEEL
CAINGANG COROADO AWEIKOMA CORONADO
CAIRN MAN PIKE MOUND RAISE GALGAL CATSTONE STONEMAN
CAIRNGORM MORION SMOKESTONE
CAISSON BOX PONT CAMEL CHEST WAGON COFFER PONTON SAUCER CAMAILE CHAMBER LACUNAR PONTOON
(— DISEASE) BENDS
CAITIFF BASE MEAN VILE COWARD WICKED CAPTIVE COWARDLY PRISONER WRETCHED
CAJOLE COG CON JIG COAX FLAM FLUM PALP WORD CARNY CHEAT CURRY DECOY FRAIK INGLE JOLLY TEASE BEFLUM CARNEY DELUDE DIDDLE ENTICE FRAISE HUMBUG WHILLY BEGUILE BEHONEY CUITTLE FLATTER PALAVER SOOTHER TWEEDLE WHEEDLE BLANDISH

CAJOLERY FRAIK SOOTH TAFFY WILES BUTTER FRAISE WHILLY BLARNEY DAUBERY FLATTERY
CAKE BAR BUN NUT WIG BAKE BALL FLAE FOOL LUMP MASS MOLE PUFF TART ARVAL BATTY BLOCK BOXTY COOKY CRUST CUPID FADGE KYAAK PATTY SCONE SHIVE TORTE WAFER WEDGE BARKLE CIMBAL COOKIE DAMPER ECLAIR GATEAU HALLAH HARDEN KICHEL KUCHEN NACKET PARKIN PASTRY POPLIN SIMNEL TABLET WASTEL ASHCAKE BANBURY BANNOCK BRIOCHE BROWNIE CAKETTE CARAWAY CASSATA CROZZLE CRUMPET CUPCAKE FAIRING GALETTE GENOISE HOECAKE MANCHET NUTCAKE OATCAKE PANCAKE PLASTER POPADAM CHRIMSEL CLAPCAKE KUGELHOF MADELINE MARZIPAN SEEDCAKE SOLIDIFY SOULCAKE TORTILLA TURNPIKE
(— OF CLAY) PLATTEN
(— OF COCONUT PULP) POONAC
(— OF MEAL) DODGER
(— OF RUBBER) BISCUIT
(ALMOND —) RATAFIA
(CORN —) PONE
(CREOLE RICE —) CALA
(EASTER —) TANSY
(FANCY —) SUNKET
(FLAT —) PLATE BUNUELO GALETTE PLACENT CHRIMSEL
(FOURTH PART OF —) FARL FARLE
(FRIED —) WONDER CRULLER DOUGHNUT
(GINGER —) BOLIVAR
(GRIDDLE —) LATKE FLIPPER FRITTER FLAPJACK
(HOLIDAY —) SIMNEL
(HONEY —) LEKACH
(INDIAN —) PARATHA
(KIND OF —) LANE FUNNEL
(LAMB AND WHEAT —) KIBBE KIBBEH
(LEAVENED —) BAP
(NEW YEAR'S —) HAGMENA HOGMANAY
(OATEN —) BANNOCK
(OIL —) GRIT POONAC
(PIECE OF —) CINCH BREEZE
(PLUM —) SIMNEL
(POTATO —) FADGE
(PRESS —) CACHAZA
(RAISIN —) BABA
(RUM —) BABA
(SEED —) WIG SEEDCAKE
(TEA —) LUNN SCONE PIKELET
(THIN —) WAFER JUMBLE BANNOCK TORTILLA
(UNLEAVENED —) CHAPATI CHAPATTI
(YEAST —) KOJI SAVARIN
(PL.) AMSATH COLYBA
CAKED CLIT
CAKE PULLER KNOCKER
CAKES AND ALE (AUTHOR OF —) MAUGHAM
(CHARACTER IN —) AMY KEAR KEMP ALROY ROSIE EDWARD GEORGE ASHENDEN TRAFFORD DRIFFIELD
CALABA BIRMA GALBA
CALABASH GOURD CURUBA JICARA
CALABASH TREE HIGUERO
CALABOOSE JUG BRIG JAIL STIR POKEY COOLER PRISON CABOOSE BASTILLE HOOSEGOW
CALABUR TREE CAPULI CAPULIN SILKWOOD
CALAIS (BROTHER OF —) ZETES
(FATHER OF —) BOREAS
(MOTHER OF —) ORITHYIA
CALAMANCO MANKIE
CALAMINE CADMIA
CALAMINT BASIL
CALAMITOUS BAD SAD DIRE EVIL BLACK FATAL BITTER DISMAL TRAGIC WOEFUL ADVERSE BALEFUL DIREFUL HAPLESS RUINOUS UNHAPPY UNLUCKY GRIEVOUS TRAGICAL WRETCHED
CALAMITY ILL WOE BLOW DOOM EVIL RUIN RUTH SLAP HYDRA STORM WRACK MISERY ONCOME PLAGUE SORROW EXTREME SCOURGE ACCIDENT DISASTER DISTRESS FATALITY JUDGMENT MISCHIEF
CALAMONDIN ORANGE CALAMANSI
CALAMUS PEN CANE REED QUILL ACORUS RATTAN ROTANG
CALANGAY ABACAY COCKATOO
CALANTHA (FATHER OF —) AMYCLAS
CALASH CALESA GALECHE
CALCANEUM FIBULARE HYPOTARSUS
CALCAR OVEN SPUR FURNACE CALCARIUM PREHALLUX
CALCEOLARIA FAGELIA IONIDIUM
CALCIFY CRETIFY
CALCINING BURNING
CALCINO MUSCADINE
CALCITE APHRITE CALCSPAR ALABASTER ARAGONITE ARGENTINE HISLOPITE
CALCIUM LIME
CALCIUM CARBONATE WHITING DRIPSTONE
CALCIUM HYDROXIDE LIME
CALCIUM SULPHATE PLASTER
CALCULATE AIM SUM CALK CAST PLAN RATE TELL COUNT FRAME THINK CIPHER DESIGN EXPECT FIGURE NUMBER RECKON ACCOUNT AVERAGE CALLATE COMPUTE PREPARE CONSIDER ESTIMATE FORECAST
(— BY ASTROLOGY) ERECT
CALCULATED COLD MEASURED
CALCULATING COLD WISE BRITTLE CAUTIOUS
CALCULATION CARE SHARE CALCUL ACCOUNT CAUTION WORKING CALCULUS FORECAST HINDCAST PRUDENCE
(PL.) FIGURES
CALCULATOR TABLE ABACUS ABACIST SOROBAN CALCULER COMPUTER ISOGRAPH
CALCULUS STONE UROLITH ANALYSIS
(PREF.) LITH(O)
(SUFF.) LITE LITH(IC) LITIC
CALDRON POT RED VAT LEAD ALFET BOILER KELDER KETTLE TRIPOD VESSEL CALDERA CAULDRON
CALEB (DAUGHTER OF —) ACHSAH
(FATHER OF —) HEZRON JEPHUNNEH
(SON OF —) HUR
CALENDAR ORDO DIARY FASTI ALMANAC CALENDS JOURNAL KALENDS REGISTER SCHEDULE
(— ADDITION) EPACT
(— OF MARTYRS) MENOLOGY
(— SIGN) ZODIAC
(ADDITION TO —) EPACT
(PL.) FASTI
CALENDER TABBY SCHREINER
CALENDERER CANROYER SMOOTHER
CALENDS K KAL
CALF CA BOB BOX BOY LEG BOSS BUSS DOLT VEAL VEAU BOBBY BOSSY BUNCH DOGIE MOGGY PODDY RANNY SOOKY YOUTH MUSCLE VEALER WEANER BULCHIN FATLING SLEEPER CALFLING
(LIKE A —) VITULINE
(OF LEG —) SURAL
(PREMATURE —) SLINK
(STRAY —) MAVERICK
(UNBRANDED —) LONGEAR SLEEPER
(YEARLING —) BUD DAIRT
(YOUNG —) DEACON
(PL.) CAURE
CALF'S-FOOT JELLY SULZE FISNOGA
CALFSKIN OOZE COROVA VELLUM GRASSER TULCHAN VEALSKIN
CALIBER BORE RANK DEGREE TALENT ABILITY BREADTH COMPASS QUALITY CAPACITY DIAMETER MAGNITUDE
(HIGH —) STATURE
CALIBRATED BRIX BEAUME BALLING
CALICHE CALCRETE TEPETATE NITRATINE
CALICO BLAY PINTO SALLO CHINTZ SALLOO CROYDON SPOTTED DUNGAREE GOLDFISH
CALICO ASTER WISEWEED
CALICOBACK STINKBUG
CALICO BASS CRAPPIE BACHELOR
CALICO-BUSH KALMIA
CALICUT KOZHIKODE

CALIFORNIA
CAPITAL: SACRAMENTO
COLLEGE: MILLS POMONA WHITTIER
COUNTY: INYO KERN MONO NAPA YOLO YUBA MARIN MODOC COLUSA LASSEN MERCED PLACER PLUMAS SHASTA SOLANO SONOMA SUTTER TEHAMA TULARE ALAMEDA VENTURA SISKIYOU CALAVERAS
DESERT: MOJAVE COLORADO
INDIAN: HUPA POMO YANA YUKI KAROK MAIDU MIWOK WAPPO WIYOT YUROK PATWIN SHASTA TOLOWA YOKUTS CHUMASH LUISENO SALINAN SERRANO DIEGUENO
LAKE: MONO SODA EAGLE OWENS TAHOE SALTON TULARE ALMANOR BERRYESSA
MOUNTAIN: MUIR LASSEN SHASTA WHITNEY
NAME: ELDORADO
PARK: LASSEN SEQUOIA YOSEMITE
PRESIDENT: NIXON
PRISON: ALCATRAZ
RESORT: OJAI
RIVER: EEL MAD PIT KERN OWENS PUTAH STONY FEATHER KLAMATH RUBICON TRINITY SACRAMENTO
STATE BIRD: QUAIL
STATE FLOWER: POPPY
STATE NICKNAME: GOLDEN
STATE TREE: REDWOOD
TOWN: LODI AZUSA CHICO CHINO INDIO BLYTHE CARMEL COVINA EUREKA FRESNO LOMPOC MERCED OXNARD POMONA SONOMA TULARE ALAMEDA BURBANK GARDENA NEEDLES SALINAS VALLEJO VISALIA ALTADENA BERKELEY PASADENA REDLANDS CUCAMONGA
UNIVERSITY: USC UCLA CALTECH STANFORD

CALIPER JENNY ODDLEGS CALIPERS
CALIPH ABU ALI BEKR IMAM OMAR CALIF OTHMAN ABBASID UMAYYAD
CALISTA (HUSBAND OF —) ALTAMONT CLEANDER
(LOVER OF —) LOTHARIO LYSANDER
CALISTO, LA (CHARACTER IN —) PAN JOVE JUNO DIANA LYCAON CALISTO MERCURY ENDYMION
(COMPOSER OF —) CAVALLI
CALIXTINE UTRAQUIST
CALK (ALSO SEE CAULK) JAG NAP PAY COPY CORK FILL STOP CAULK CLOSE HORSE ROUGH CAREEN CALTROP CHINTZE OCCLUDE SILENCE
CALKING OAKUM
CALL HO KA BAN BID CRY CUP DUB HOY SAY SEE CITE COOP DIAL HAIL JERK NAME NOTE PAGE PIST ROUP STOP TERM TOOT YELL BEDUB CHUCK CLAIM CLEPE CLOCK ELECT HALLO HIGHT HOLLA PHONE ROUSE SHOUT SPEAK STYLE UTTER VISIT VOUCH WAKEN YODEL ACCUSE APPEAL AROUSE BECALL CHANGE DEMAND HALLOA HALLOO INVITE INVOKE MUSTER QUETHE SUMMON TEKIAH TERUAH YELPER ACCLAIM ADDRESS APPOINT BEHIGHT BETITLE COLLECT COMMAND CONVENE CONVOKE DECLARE ENTITLE IMPEACH INQUIRE INSTYLE MOUNTEE WHISTLE ANNOUNCE

APPELATE ASSEMBLE NOMINATE PROCLAIM TRANSFER VOCATION
(— A BET) STAY
(— ALOUD) COUNT
(— BACK) RSVP RECALL REVOKE
(— COARSELY) ROOP ROUP
(— DOWN) BRAWL DEVOCATE IMPRECATE
(— FOR) CRY TAKE CLAIM EXACT DEMAND DESIRE COLLECT SOLICIT
(— FOR HELP) SOS
(— FOR HOGS) SOOK SOOEY
(— FOR PARLEY) CHAMADE
(— FORTH) STIR EVOKE BECKON ELICIT INDUCE INVOKE ATTRACT PROVOKE SUGGEST
(— HOUNDS) LIFT
(— IN ANGER) GREET
(— IN CHILDRENS' GAMES) FAN FEN FIN VENTS
(— IN MARBLES) DUBS
(— INTO QUESTION) IMPUGN OPPUGN
(— IN WHIST) ABUNDANCE
(— LOUDLY) CRY HAIL ACCLAIM
(— MAN BY MAN) ARRAY
(— ON TELEPHONE) BUZZ
(— OUT) HAIL LURE ASCRY EVOKE HALLO GOLLAR GOLLER HOLLER HULLOO
(— THE GAME) UMP
(— TO ACCOUNT) AREASON CONTROL
(— TO ARMS) ALARM ALARUM RAPPEL
(— TO BELLBOY) FRONT
(— TO CAT) CHEET
(— TO COURT) ARRAIGN
(— TO COWS) PROO SOOK COBOSS SOOKIE
(— TO DUTY) TURNOUT
(— TO FOOD) SOSS
(— TO HORSE) HIE HUP WAY PROO
(— TO MIND) CITE MING RECORD BETHINK RECOLLECT
(— TO PRAYER) ADAN AZAN
(— TO READINESS) ALERT
(— TO SPARROW) PHIP PHIPPE
(— TO WITNESS) APPEAL
(— UPON) ASK SEE CITE GREDE HALSE BECALL DEPOSE ENGAGE SUMMON ADDRESS BESEECH IMPLORE
(BIRD'S —) WEET
(BOATSWAIN'S —) WINDING
(BRIDGE —) DOUBLE
(BUGLE —) POST HALLALI STABLES
(CLOSE —) TOUCH
(DUCK —) SQUAWKER
(FRIENDLY —) CEILIDH
(HUNTING —) MOT RECHATE RECHEAT
(KIND OF —) ROLL COLLECT
(MORNING —) MATIN
(NAUTICAL —) AHOY
(SHEPHERD'S —) OVEY
(SOCIAL —) VISIT
(SPORTSMAN'S —) HOICKS YOICKS HALLALI
(SQUARE DANCE —) GEE HAW
(STAGE TRUMPET —) SENNET SINNET
(TRUMPET —) BERLOQUE

CALLA ARUM LILY DRAGON MAYFLOWER
CALLBOY FRONT CALLER HALLBOY
CALLED NEMPT
CALLER FLOORMAN
CALLIGRAPHER PENMAN WRITER COPYIST ENGROSSER
CALLIGRAPHY LETTERING CHIROGRAPHY
CALLING ART JOB WAY CALL HAIL RANK TRADE CAREER METIER NAMING OUTCRY MISSION MYSTERY PURSUIT STATION SUMMONS WARNING BUSINESS FUNCTION POSITION SHOUTING VOCATION
(— TO ACCOUNT) AUDIT
(— TOGETHER) MUSTER
CALLIOPE (FATHER OF —) ZEUS JUPITER
(MOTHER OF —) MNEMOSYNE
(SON OF —) ORPHEUS
CALLIRRHOE (FATHER OF —) OCEANUS
(HUSBAND OF —) TROS ALCMAEON
(SON OF —) ILUS GANYMEDE ASSARACUS
CALLISTO (FATHER OF —) LYCAON
(SON OF —) ARCAS
CALLITHRIX HAPALE JACCHUS
CALLOP YELLOWBELLY
CALLOSAL TRABAL
CALLOSITY SEG CALLUS SITFAST TYLOSIS CHESTNUT
CALLOUS HARD HORNY TOUGH BRAWNY OBTUSE SEARED TORPID WAUKIT DEDOLENT OBDURATE HEARTLESS
CALLOUSED BRAWNY
CALLOW BALD BARE CRUDE GREEN SQUAB JEJUNE MARSHY IMMATURE UNFORMED YOUTHFUL
CALLUS SEG POROMA TYLOMA CALLOUS
(— ON HORSE) RINGBONE
(PREF.) PORA PORO
CALM LAY LEE COOL DILL EASY EVEN FAIR FLAT HUSH LOWN LULL MEES MILD REST SOFT STAY ABATE ALLAY CHARM LEVEL LITHE LOUND MEASE PEACE QUELL QUIET SLEEK SMOLT SOBER STILL STOIC STREW APLOMB DEFUSE DOCILE GENTLE GLASSY IRENIC PACIFY PLACID SEDATE SERENE SETTLE SILENT SLATCH SLIGHT SMOOTH SOOTHE STEADY APPEASE ASSUAGE CALMATO COMPOSE GLACIAL HALCYON MOLLIFY PACIFIC PATIENT PLACATE QUALIFY QUIETEN RESTFUL UNMOVED CALMNESS COMPOSED DECOROUS MODERATE PEACEFUL PLACABLE RESTRAIN SERENITY TRANQUIL UNRUFFLE POSSESSED PHILOSOPHIC
(INTERNAL —) HARMONY
(NOT —) BOISTEROUS
CALMING SEDATIVE
CALMLY COOLY COOLLY STILLY
CALMNESS CALM LULL POISE PHLEGM REPOSE SERENE TEMPER ATARAXY COOLNESS SERENITY SOBRIETY STILLNESS
CALNO KULLANI
CALOMEL TURPETH
CALORIC THERMOGEN
CALORIE THERM THERME
CALQUE LOANSHIFT
CALTROP CROWTOE GALTRAP BULLHEAD CROWFOOT
CALUMET PIPE PEACEPIPE
CALUMNIATE BLOT SLUR TEEN BELIE LIBEL ACCUSE ATTACK BEFOUL DEFAME MALIGN REVILE VILIFY ASPERSE BLACKEN SLANDER TRADUCE
CALUMNIATION SATIRE ASPERSION
CALUMNY SLUR ATTACK DEPRAVE OBLOQUY SLANDER ASPERSION
CALVA CALOTTE SINCIPUT
CALVARIA SKULLCAP
CALVARY GOLGOTHA
CALVE FRESHEN
CALVINIST GENEVAN GOMARIAN
CALYCE (FATHER OF —) AEOLUS
(MOTHER OF —) ENARETE
(SON OF —) ENDYMION
CALYCULUS CELL CALYX
CALYPTER ALULA SQUAMA
CALYPTRA CAP VEIL EPIGONIUM
CALYX CUP POP HULL HUSK LEAF CULOT SEPAL SHUCK
(PREF.) CALYC(I)(O)
CAM COG AWRY LOBE TRIG ASKEW CATCH SNAIL WIPER LIFTER TAPPET CROOKED TRIPPET KNOCKOFF PERVERSE ROLLBACK
CAMACHILE INGA HUAMUCHIL
CAMAGON MABOLO
CAMAS LOBELIA
CAMBER SET ARCH BEND SWEEP ROUNDUP CROSSFALL

CAMBODIA

CAPE: SAMIT
CAPITAL: PNOMPENH PHNOMPENH
COIN: SEN RIEL PUTTAN PIASTER
GULF: SIAM
LAKE: TONLESAP
MOUNTAIN: PAN AURAL
MOUNTAINS: DANGREK CARDAMOM ELEPHANT
NAME: CAMBOJA CAMBODGE KAMPUCHEA
NATIVE: CHAM KHMER
RIVER: SAN SEN BASSAC MEKONG PORONG SREPOK SEKHONG TONLESAP
RUINS: ANGKORWAT
TOWN: REAM TAKEO KAMPOT KRATIE PURSAT KOHNIEH KRACHEH ROVIENG SAMRONG PNOMPENH SISOPHON
WEIGHT: MACE TAEL

CAMBODIAN KHMER
CAMBRIC LAWN BATISTE PERCALE
CAMBUSCAN (SON OF —) CANACE CAMBALLO ALGARSIFE
CAME BAND CALM
CAMEL COLT OONT DELOUL DROMED FENDER HAGEEN MEHARI CAISSON TYLOPOD BACTRIAN RUMINANT DROMEDARY
CAMEL GRASS SCHOENANTH
CAMELLIA JAPONICA
CAMEL LIP CHILOMA
CAMELOPARD GIRAFFE
CAMEO GEM GAMAHE CAMAIEU CARVING PHALERA RELIEVO ANAGLYPH
(— MATERIAL) ONYX
CAMERA KINO KODAK CHAMBER MINICAM PANORAM ENLARGER MINIATURE VERASCOPE CAMCVORDER
(— AND RECORDER) PORTAFAX PORTAPACK
(— SHOT) PAN
(— TUBE) VIDICON
(KIND OF —) REFLEX
(PART OF —) LUG BODY DOOR KNOB LENS LOCK CRANK DRIVE FOCUS LATCH SCALE STRAP TIMER BUTTON SENSOR SOCKET WINDOW ADVANCE BELLOWS LANYARD RELEASE SHUTTER PHOTOCELL TRANSDUCER VIEWFINDER
(SHIELD FOR —) GOBO
(VIDEO —) CAMCORDER
CAMERAMAN LENSMAN
CAMEROON (CAPITAL OF —) YAOUNDE
(RIVER OF —) DJA NYONG SANAGA
(TOWN OF —) EDEA POLI YOKO BAFIA KRIBI DOUALA
CAMILLA (FATHER OF —) METABUS
(SLAYER OF —) ARUNS
CAMILLE (AUTHOR OF —) DUMAS
(CHARACTER IN —) DUVAL ARMAND NANINE CAMILLE GAUTIER PRUDENCE VARVILLE
CAMIRUS (FATHER OF —) CERCAPHUS
(MOTHER OF —) CYDIPPE
CAMISOLE WAISTCOAT
CAMLET MOHAIR PARAGON BARRACAN
CAMOMILE OXEYE MORGAN MAYWEED
CAMOUFLAGE FAKE HIDE DAZZLE MUFFLE SCREEN CONCEAL DISGUISE
CAMOUFLET STIFLER
CAMP TAN PEST TENT DOUAR ETAPE HORDE SIEGE TABOR CASTLE LAAGER SUGARY BIVOUAC HUTMENT LASHKAR LODGING MAHALLA PALANKA ZAREEBA QUARTERS
(— OF INDIAN SOLDIERS) LASHKAR
(— OUT) MAROON OUTLIE
(HOBO —) JUNGLE
(LABOR —) GULAG
(LUMBER —) CHANTIER
(PRISONER —) OFLAG STALAG
(PREF.) CASTRA
(SUFF.) CASTER CESTER CHESTER
CAMPA ANDA ANDI ANTI
CAMPAIGN BLITZ DRIVE PLAIN WHOOP CANVASS CRUSADE JOURNEY SERVICE SOLICIT WARFARE
(STUNT —) JIHAD

CAMPANA GUTTA
CAMPANERO COTINGA ARAPUNGA BELLBIRD COTINGID
CAMPANILE TOWER BELFRY CLOCHER STEEPLE CARILLON
CAMPANULA BELLWORT
CAMPESTRAL AGRARIAN
CAMP-FOLLOWER BOY BUMMER LASCAR
CAMPHOL BORNEOL
CAMPHOR ASARONE BORNEOL MENTHOL
(ANISE —) ANETHOLE
CAMPHOR TREE KADUR KAPOR
CAMPING BIVOUAC
CAMPION ROBIN COWBELL
CAMPUS GATE QUAD YARD FIELD
CAN CUP JUG MAY MOW POT TIN ABLE FIRE JAIL SACK BILLY CADDY COULD ESHIN OILER PUTUP SHALL SKILL BOTTLE VESSEL ABILITY BOMBARD CANIKIN CAPABLE CREAMER DISMISS GROWLER PIPETTE BILLYCAN CONSERVE PRESERVE
(— FOR LIQUOR) JACK
(— ON WHEELS) DANDY
(BULGED —) SWELL FLIPPER
(DEFECTIVE —) SPRINGER
(LEAKY —) LEAKER
(MILK —) CHURN
(SPRAY —) AEROSOL
(TIN —) DESTROYER
(TRASH —) DUSTBIN
(PREF.) SCYPH(I)(O)
CANAAN (FATHER OF —) HAM
CANAANITE ARKITE HIVITE AMORITE HIVVITE JEBUSITE
CANACE (BROTHER OF —) MACAREUS
(FATHER OF —) AEOLUS
(MOTHER OF —) ENARETE
(SON OF —) TRIOPAS

CANADA

(ALSO SEE SPECIFIC PROVINCES)
BAY: JAMES HUDSON UNGAVA GEORGIAN
CAPITAL: OTTAWA
INDIAN: CREE COMOX HAIDA NISKA SARSI STALO MICMAC NAHANE NOOTKA SARCEE SEKANE CARRIER NANAIMO SHUSWAP SONGISH TAHLTAN ALGONKIN COWICHAN LILLOOET MALECITE SQUAMISH TSATTINE
ISLAND: READ BANKS BYLOT COATS DEVON SABLE BAFFIN MANSEL VICTORIA ANTICOSTI VANCOUVER
ISLANDS: PARRY BELCHER BATHURST MAGDALEN
LAKE: BEAR CREE GARRY RAINY SLAVE LOUISE SIMCOE ABITIBI DUBAWNT NIPIGON KOOTENAY OKANAGAN NIPISSING
MEASURE: MINOT PERCH ARPENT CHAINON
MOUNTAIN: LOGAN ROYAL ROBSON TREMBLANT
MOUNTAIN RANGE: SKEENA CARIBOO PEMBINA STELIAS COLUMBIA LAURENTIAN
NATIVE: CANUCK
PARK: YOHO BANFF ACADIA JASPER
PENINSULA: GASPE BOOTHIA MELVILLE
PROVINCE: BC NB NS MAN ONT PEI QUE ALTA SASK QUEBEC ALBERTA ONTARIO MANITOBA NOVASCOTIA NEWBRUNSWICK NEWFOUNDLAND SASKATCHEWAN
PROVINCIAL CAPITAL: QUEBEC REGINA STJOHN HALIFAX TORONTO EDMONTON VICTORIA WINNIPEG CHARLOTTETOWN
RIVER: HAY RED BACK PEEL PEACE SLAVE YUKON FRASER NELSON OTTAWA SKEENA THELON KOKOSAK PEMBINA PETAWAWA SAGUENAY MACKENZIE RICHELIEU
STRAIT: CABOT DEASE HECATE HUDSON GEORGIA
SYMBOL: MAPLELEAF
TERRITORY: YUKON
TOWN: HULL BANFF LAVAL GUELPH OSHAWA REGINA SARNIA CALGARY HALIFAX LACHINE MONCTON NANAIMO SUDBURY TORONTO WELLAND WINDSOR KINGSTON MONTREAL VICTORIA WINNIPEG SASKATOON VANCOUVER
UNIVERSITY: MCGILL DALHOUSIE
WATERFALL: DELLA PANTHER TAKAKKAW

CANADA BLUEBERRY SOURTOP
CANADA GOOSE HONKER BUSTARD OUTARDE
CANADA JAY MEATBIRD MOOSEBIRD
CANADA LYNX PISHU LUCIVEE
CANADA PLUM CHENEY
CANADA VIOLET JUNEFLOWER
CANADIAN CANUCK
CANAILLE MOB FLOUR RABBLE DOGGERY RIFFRAFF
CANAL CUT CANO DUCT LODE PIPE SHAT TUBE BAYOU DITCH DRAIN FOSSA GRAFF KLONG SCALA ZANJA ESTERO GROOVE KENNEL STRAIT TRENCH VAGINA ACEQUIA APHODUS CHANNEL CONDUIT FOREBAY RACEWAY SHIPWAY TOWPATH AQUEDUCT EMISSARY IRRIGANT MILLRACE PROSODUS VOLKMANN
(— LABORER) NAVIGATOR
(ALIMENTARY —) GUT ENTERON INTESTINE
(ANATOMICAL —) SCALA MEATUS
(CARINAL —) LACUNA
(PREF.) MEATO
CANARD DUCK HOAX RUMOR GRAPEVINE
CANARY DICKY FRILL SERIN LIZARD ROLLER CAYENNE CHOPPER JONQUIL SQUEALER
(— HYBRID) MULE

CANARY ISLAND

CAPITAL: SANTACRUZ
ISLAND: ROCA CLARA FERRO LOBOS PALMA ROCCA GOMERA HIERRO INFERNO GRACIOSA TENERIFE LANZAROTE
MEASURE: FANEGADA
MOUNTAIN: TEYDE LACRUZ ELCUMBRE TENERIFE
PROVINCE: LASPALMAS
TOWN: LAGUNA ARRECIFE VALVERDE
VOLCANO: TENEGUIA

CANARY MOSS CORKIR
CANASTA SAMBA BOLIVIA
(— PLAY) MELD
CANCEL AX BLOT DASH DELE OMIT UNDO VENT WIPE ABORT ADEEM ANNUL BELAY CROSS ERASE QUASH REMIT SCORE SCRUB DELETE EFFACE KILLER RECALL REMOVE REVOKE STROKE ABOLISH DESTROY EXPUNGE NULLIFY RESCIND RETRACT SCRATCH SUBLATE UNWRITE ABROGATE OVERRIDE WRITEOFF OBLITERATE
CANCELED OFF NOGO
CANCELER BUMPER STAMPER
CANCELLATION GRID CANCEL REVOKE RECISION SURRENDER
CANCER BIGC WOLF KASHYAPA SCIRRHUS
(PREF.) CARCIN(O)
CANCERWORT FLUELLIN
CANDAREEN FAN FEN
CANDELABRUM PHAROS MENORAH GIRANDOLE
CANDID FAIR JUST OPEN PURE BLUNT CLEAR FRANK NAIVE PLAIN HONEST ARTLESS JANNOCK SINCERE EVENDOWN INNOCENT SPLENDID STRAIGHT PLAINSPOKEN
CANDIDA (AUTHOR OF —) SHAW
(CHARACTER IN —) MORELL CANDIDA MARCHBANKS
CANDIDATE AGREGE LEGACY ESQUIRE NOMINEE ASPIRANT GRADUAND ORDINAND PROSPECT
(DOCTORAL) ABD
(DOCTORAL —) ABD
(LIST OF —S) SLATE
(TEACHING —) AGREGE
CANDIDE (AUTHOR OF —) VOLTAIRE
(CHARACTER IN —) CACAMBO CANDIDE PANGLOSS PAQUETTE CUNEGONDE
CANDIDIASIS MONILIASIS
CANDIED GLACE
CANDLE DIP WAX GLIM SIZE SLUT LIGHT SPERM TAPER TOLLY TORCH BOUGIE CIERGE MORTAR PLANET SHAMUS SLUSHY TALLOW TORTIS CANDELA PERCHER PRICKET SHAMMES AMANDINE
(IMITATION —) JUDAS
(SQUARE —) QUARRIER
CANDLEFISH SKIL EULACHON HOOLAKIN OOLACHAN SKILFISH SABLEFISH
CANDLEHOLDER SPIDER
CANDLEMAKER CHANDLER TALLOWER
CANDLEMAS TERM MARYMASS
CANDLENUT AMA LAMA BIABO KUKUI IGUAPE KEMIRI LUMBANG ABURAGIRI
CANDLESNUFFER DOUTER
CANDLESTAND TORCHERE
CANDLESTICK BUGIA DYKER JESSE STICK CRUSIE LAMPAD MORTAR SCONCE PASCHAL PRICKET CHANDLER DICERION FLAMBEAU STANDARD TORCHERE TRIKERION
(TALL ORNAMENTAL —) TORCHERE
CANDLEWICK MATCH SNAST SHROUD
(CHARRED PART OF —) SNOT SNUFF SNUFFING
CANDLEWOOD CIRIO OCOTILLO TABANUCO
CANDOR PURITY FAIRNESS KINDNESS INTEGRITY SIMPLICITY
CANDY DROP DUMP KISS PIPE ROCK CREAM CRISP DULCE FUDGE GLACE GUNDY LOLLY NABIT SPICE SQUIB SWEET TAFFY BONBON COMFIT DRAGEE HUMBUG NOGADA NOUGAT PATTIE PENIDE BRITTLE CANDIEL CARAMEL CONGEAL FLATTER FONDATE GUMDROP SWEETEN SWEETIE TORRONE ALPHENIC LOLLIPOP STICKJAW PEPPERMINT
(DECORATIVE —) DRAGEE
(PL.) CUTS CONFETTI
CANDYTUFT CRUCIFER
(PL.) IBERIS
CANE ROD BEAT CRAB DART FLOG PIPE REED STEM TUBE WAND WHIP BIRCH GIBBY GUNDY LANCE STAFF STICK SWISH TOLLY WADDY BAMBOO JAMBEE KEBBIE PUNISH RATTAN CALAMUS HICKORY KIPPEEN MALACCA SCOURGE STADDLE TICKLER WHANGEE GIBSTAFF
(BLACK —) JAPAN
(END OF —) FRAZE
(SPLIT —) CANEWORK
(TIP OF —) FERRULE
CANELLA CINNAMON WHITEWOOD
CANELO CIXO
CANESCENT HOARY
CANE TREE BEJUCO
CANFIELD KLONDIKE
CANICULA SIRIUS
CANINE CUR DOG FOX PUP FISC TUSH WOLF DOGLY DOGLIKE LANIARY EYETOOTH
CANING RATTAN BIRCHING
CANISTEL TIES EGGFRUIT
CANNA ACHIRA GOLDBIRD
CANNABIS BHANG GANJA GUAZA GUNJA HEMPWORT
(— TOPS) TAKROURI
CANNEL BONE FURCULE
CANNEL COAL AMPELITE
CANNER CANMAN TINNER
CANNIBAL WINDIGO LESTRIGON THYESTEAN
CANNON BIT EAR GUN BASE SHOT TUBE ASPIC CAROM CRACK MOYEN PIECE SACRE SACRI SAKER SHANK SLING THIEF BARKER BICORN CURTAL FALCON FOWLER JINGAL LICORN MORTAR POTGUN

BASTARD BOMBARD BULLDOG CHAMBER HANDGUN LOMBARD MOYENNE ROBINET SERPENT STINGER UNICORN BASILISK CULVERIN HOWITZER MURDERER OERLIKON ORDNANCE SPITFIRE CARAMBOLE CARRONADE ZUMBOORUK
(— OF BELL) EAR
(CARRIAGE OF —) NADRIER
(DISCHARGE OF —) TIRE
(DUMMY —) QUAKER
(PART OF —) BASE BORE FACE KNOB NECK OGEE RING VENT CHASE FILET SWELL BREECH BUTTON FILLET MUZZLE CHAMBER DOLPHIN GUNLOCK RIMBASE ASTRAGAL CASCABEL TRUNNION REINFORCE
CANNONBALL GUN PILL TEAR BULLET GUNSTONE
CANNON BOSS TRUNNION
CANNON PLUG TAMPION
CANNOT CANT CANNA DONNA DOWNA UNABLE
CANNULA TROCAR
CANNY SLY COZY SNUG WARY WILY WISE COONY LUCKY PAWKY QUIET SAVVY CLEVER FRUGAL GENTLE SHREWD STEADY CAREFUL CUNNING KNOWING PRUDENT QUIETLY THRIFTY CAUTIOUS SKILLFUL WATCHFUL
CANOE AMA KIAK LISI PAHI PROA WAKA AOTEA ARAWA BANCA BIRCH BONGO BUNGO CANKA KAYAK KOLEK PRAHU SKIFF TONEE UMIAK VINTA WAAPA BAIDAR BALLAM BAROTO CORIAL CUNNER DUGOUT OOMIAK PAOPAO PITPAN PUNGEY TAINUI TROUGH WHERRY ALMADIA BIDARKA BUCKEYE CANADER CASCARA CORACLE CURIARA CURRANE HOROUTA LAKATOI PIRAGUA PIROGUE BALANGAY BARANGAY FALTBOAT FOLDBOAT MONOXYLE MONTARIA TAKITUMU THAMAKAU TSUKUPIN WOODSKIN
CANON FEN LAW CODE FUGA HYMN LAUD LIST ROTA RULE SONG AXIOM GORGE GULCH MODEL NODUS ROUND TABLE TENET ACTION DECREE GNOMON BROCARD LIBRARY PRECEPT STATUTE DECISION MATHURIN STAGIARY STANDARD SACRISTAN PREBENDARY PREMONSTRATENSIAN
(BODY OF —S) CHAPTER
CANONICAL CANONIC ACCEPTED ORTHODOX
(NOT —) APOCHRYPHAL
CANOODLE PET CARESS FONDLE
CAN OPENER CHURCHKEY
CANOPY SKY CEIL COPE DAIS HOOD TILT CHUPA CROWN HOVEL SHADE STATE VAULT AWNING BUBBLE CELURE ESTATE FINIAL GABLET HUPPAH PELMET SHADOW TESTER CEILING HEAVENS MARQUEE SHELTER SPARVER BASILICA CIBORIUM COVERING OVERWOOD PAVILION SEMIANNA SHAMIANA TABERNACLE
(— ABOVE THRONE) STATE
(— FOR LIVESTOCK) HOVEL
(— OF ALTAR) DAIS CIBORIUM
(— OF HEAVEN) VAULT
(— OVER BROODER) HOVER
(BED —) TESTER SPARVER
(HEARSE —) MAJESTY
CANT TIP COAX HEEL LEAN LIST NOOK SING TILT TURN ARGOT BEVEL CHANT DRIFT FLASH HIELD LINGO LUSTY MERRY NICHE PITCH SHARE SLANG SLANT SLOPE WHINE CAREEN CASTER CORNER INTONE JARGON LIVELY PATOIS PATTER SNIVEL AUCTION DIALECT INCLINE PORTION SINGING WHEEDLE CHEERFUL PRETENSE VIGOROUS
CANTABRIGIAN CANTAB CAMBRIDGE
CANTALA MAGUEY
CANTALOUPE MELON MUSKMELON
CANTANKEROUS ILL CURSED CUSSED ORNERY KICKISH PIGGISH CANKERED CONTRARY PERVERSE
CANTATA MOTET SERENATA PASTORALE VILLANCICO
(CHILDREN'S —) KINDERSPIEL
CANTEEN BAR FLASK BAZAAR CANTINA
CANTER JOG RUN GAIT LOPE PACE RACK AUBIN ROGUE BEGGAR WHINER TRIPPLE SNUFFLER VAGABOND
CANTERBURY BELL MILKWORT CAMPANULA
CANTERBURY TALES (AUTHOR OF —) CHAUCER
(CHARACTER IN —) NUN COOK DYER HOST MONK WIFE CLERK FRIAR REEVE DOCTOR KNIGHT MILLER PARSON PRIEST SQUIRE WEAVER YEOMAN CHAUCER PLOWMAN SHIPMAN FRANKLIN MANCIPLE MERCHANT PARDONER PRIORESS SERGEANT SUMMONER CARPENTER HABERDASHER
CANTICLE ODE HYMN LAUD SONG CANTO ANTHEM CANTIC HIRMOS BRAVURA MAGNIFICAT
CANTILEVER LOOKOUT SEMIBEAM CARTOUCHE
CANTING CANT PIOUS SNUFFLING
CANTO AIR FIT BOOK DUAN PACE RUNE SONG VERSE MELODY PASSUS CANTICLE
CANTON ANGLE UNION CORNER VOLOST PORTION QUARTER SECTION DISTRICT DIVISION
(HALF —) ESQUIRE
CANTOR HAZAN HAZZAN SINGER CHANTER CHAZZAN SOLOIST PSALMIST
CANVAS FLY PAT DUCK GLUT PATA SAIL TARP TENT TEWK CLOTH COAST SCRIM TOILE VITRY BALINE BURLAP CATGUT LINING MUSLIN PICTURE POLDAVY SACKING SCUTAGE DRABBLER PAINTING VANDELAS SAILCLOTH
(— COVER) TARP
(— FOR CONVEYING GRAIN) APRON
(OLD CONDEMNED —) RUMBOWLINE
(RUBBERIZED —) TOSH
(STUFFED —) BOLSTER
(TARRED —) COAT
CANVASBACK CAN DIVER CHEVAL DUCKER POCHARD BULLNECK
CANVASS BEAT CASE DRUM HAWK POLL SIFT RANDY STUDY DEBATE PEDDLE SEARCH AGITATE DISCUSS EXAMINE SOLICIT TROUNCE CAMPAIGN CONSIDER
CANVASSER AGENT POLLER ROADMAN
CANYON CAJON CHASM COULE GORGE GULCH ARROYO CANADA RAVINE
CANZONE ODE
CAOUTCHOUC RUBBER ELATERITE
CAP CUP FEZ HAT LID PAD POT TAJ TAM TIP TOP ACME CALL COIF CORK COWL DINK DOME DOWD ETON GAGE HOOD HURE JOAN KEEP KEPI MATE SHOE SHOW TOPI BERET BOINA BUSBY CHIEF COVER CROWN EXCEL FANON GALEA HOUVE KULAH MATCH MUTCH OUTDO PHANO PUNCH SEIZE SHAKO TOPEE TRUMP ARREST BARRAD BARRET BEANIE BIGGIN BIRRUS BONNET CALPAC CLIMAX COCKUP CORNET GALERA HELMET HUBCAP JINNAH MOBCAP PILEUS PINNER PRIMER PUZZLE SUMMIT TABARD TURBAN ALOPEKE BIRETTA CALOTTE CAMAURO CAPITAL CEREVIS CHAPEAU CHECHIA CLOSURE COMMODE FERRULE FLATCAP FORAGER HEADCAP OVERLIE OVERTOP PERPLEX PETASOS PILLBOX PILLION SOWBACK SURPASS THIMBLE TURNCAP ACROSOME BALMORAL BEARSKIN BYCOCKET CAPELINE CHAPERON COONSKIN ELECTRIC FOLLOWER HEADGEAR PHRYGIUM SKEWBACK SKULLCAP SURPRISE TARBOOSH
(— FOR PILEDRIVER) PUNCH
(— OF FLAGSTAFF) TRUCK
(— OF FOAM) HOOD
(— OF MUSHROOM) PILEUS
(— OF PIER) CUSHION
(— OF PYXIDIUM) LID
(— OF WATCH) DOME CROWN
(— ON MAST) TRUCK
(ACADEMIC —) MORTARBOARD
(BISHOP'S —) HURA HURE
(CANADIAN —) TUQUE
(CHIMNEY —) GRANNY
(HORSEMAN'S —) MONTERO
(HUNTER'S —) MONTERA MONTERO
(ICE —) BRAE CALOTTE
(JESTER'S —) COXCOMB FOOLSCAP
(MILITARY —) KEPI BUSBY SHAKO CHAPKA CZAPKA
(MOUNTAIN —) SCALP
(OLD WOMAN'S —) TOY
(PERCUSSION —) AMORCE CAPSULE
(PERUVIAN —) CHULLO
(POPE'S —) CAMAURO
(ROMAN —) PILEUS
(ROOT —) CALYPTRA
(TRIANGULAR —) CALPAC KALPAK CALPACK
(WOMAN'S —) TOY CAUL DOWD JOAN KELL MUTCH COMMODE VOLUPER BIGGONET
(WOOLEN —) BOINA TOQUE TUQUE
(PREF.) PILEI PILEO PILO
CAPABILITY POWER STROIL ABILITY CONDUCT FACULTY POTENCY CAPACITY
CAPABLE APT CAN FIT ABLE GOOD ADEPT CAPAX FENDY TIGHT EXPERT SKILLED POWERFUL
(— OF BEING DEFENDED) TENABLE
(— OF BEING DRAWN OUT) DUCTILE
(— OF BEING SEVERED) SEVTILE
(— OF BEING THROWN) MISSILE
(— OF BEING UTTERED) EFFABLE
(— OF FLYING) VOLANT
(— OF SUBMISSION) AMENABLE
(NORMALLY —) ABOUT
(SUFF.) ABLE IBLE
(— OF) ILE
CAPACIOUS FULL SIDE WIDE AMPLE BROAD LARGE ROOMY WOMBY GOODLY ROOMFUL CAPTIOUS ROOMSOME SPACIOUS
CAPACITOR CONDENSER
CAPACITY BACK BENT BIND DISH GIFT GIVE SIZE TURN BLAST FLAIR FORCE KNACK MODEL POWER SKILL SPACE AGENCY BOTTOM BURDEN ENERGY ENGINE EXTENT GENIUS MODULE SPREAD TALENT VOLUME ABILITY CALIBER CALIBRE CONTENT FACULTY FITNESS QUALITY APTITUDE INSTINCT STRENGTH INFLUENCE
(— FOR EATING) STROKE
(— FOR ENDURANCE) STAY
(— FOR HIGHER KNOWLEDGE) INTELLECT
(— OF LATHE) SWING
(— OF SHIP) BURDEN
(— TO UNDERSTAND LANGUAGE) ORACY
(CIVIL —) CAPUT
(INNATE —S) STAMINA
(INTELLECTUAL —) BROW
(LOAD-PULLING —) DRAFT DRAUGHT
(MENTAL —S) BELFRY
(SPECIAL —) KNACK
(UNIT OF —) MUD MUID LAGEN KISHEN MEDIMNUS KILDERKIN
(UNLIMITED —) INFINITY
CAPANEUS (FATHER OF —) HIPPONOUS BELLEROPHON
(SLAYER OF —) JUPITER
(SON OF —) STHENELUS
(WIFE OF —) EVADNE
CAPARISON DECK TRAP HOUSE COVERING TRAPPING
CAPARISONED BARDED
CAPE RAS COPE GAPE HEAD HOOK LOOK NAZE NECK NESS SKAW TANG WRIT AMICE CAPPA CLOAK FICHU ORALE POINT SAGUM

STARE STOLE TALMA BERTHA BYRRUS CABAAN CHAPEL DOLMAN MANTLE SONTAG TABARD TIPPET CHLAMYS LEATHER MANTEEL MOZETTA SALIENT TANJONG VANDYKE CIRCULAR COLLARET HEADLAND LAMBSKIN MANTILLA MOZZETTA PALATINE PELERINE SEALSKIN INVERNESS RAINPROOF
(— OF SKINS) KAROSS
(— OF STRAW) MINO
(BULLFIGHTER'S —) CAPA
(CLERGICAL —) ALMUCE
(DRESSING —) TOILET
(FEATHER —) AHUULA
(HOODED —) HUKE DOMINO
(LACE OR SILK —) VISITE
(LOW —) TANG
(PAPAL —) FANO FANON FANUM ORALE PHANO
(RAIN —) CAPOTE
CAPE ANTEATER AARDVARK
CAPE ARMADILLO PANGOLIN
CAPE DUTCH TAAL
CAPE GOOSEBERRY POHA
CAPE HARTEBEEST CAAMA
CAPE HEN STINKER STINKPOT
CAPEK (— DRAMA) RUR
CAPELIN SMELT ICEFISH
CAPE PIGEON PINTADO
CAPE POLECAT ZORIL MUISHOND
CAPER HOP JET DIDO HOIT JUMP LEAP ROMP SKIP SKIT ANTIC BRANK DANCE FLING FLISK FRISK PRANK SAUCE SCOUP SHRUB CAVORT CURVET FRISCO FROLIC GAMBOL GAMOND PRANCE SPRING TITTUP VAGARY CORSAIR COURANT FRISCAL GAMBADO PRANKLE CAPRIOLE MARIGOLD
(— ABOUT) FLING CAVORT
(SILLY —) SHINE
CAPER SPURGE CATEPUCE
CAPE TOWN BOVENLAND
CAPE VERDE ISLANDS (CAPITAL OF —) PRAIA
(TOWN OF —) MINDELO
(VOLCANO ON —) FOGO
CAPHITE KIST
CAPITAL CAP CASH CITY FUND GOOD LIMA MAIN RARE SEAT BASIC CHIEF FATAL GREAT MAJOR MONEY MUANG STOCK VITAL DEADLY HEADLY IMPOST LETTER LISBON MORTAL PRIMAL UNCIAL WEALTH CENTRAL CHATTEL DRESDEN LEADING RADICAL SERIOUS WEIGHTY CABECERA CATALLUM CHAPITER CHAPTREL DOSSERET SWINGING
(— OF HEAVEN) AMARAVATI
(— OF HELL) PANDEMONIUM
(DIVISION OF —) ABACUS
(GAMBLER'S —) STAKE
(INADEQUATE —) SHOESTRING
CAPITALIST MONEYER
CAPITATUM MAGNUM
CAPITELLUM KNOP
CAPITOL STATEHOUSE
CAPITOLINE SATURNIAN
CAPITULATE DEFER
CAPITULATION MUNICH TREATY
CAPITULUM HEAD KNOP ANTHODIUM
CAPO DON BOSS HEAD
CAPOTE HOOD CAPPO CLOAK BONNET MANTLE TOPPER
CAPPED PILEATE PILEATED
CAPPER CORKER SEALER STEERER
CAPPY TALLOWY
CAPRICCIO (CHARACTER IN —) FLAMAND OLIVIER MADELEINE
(COMPOSER OF —) STRAUSS
CAPRICE FAD TOY KINK MOOD WHIM ANTIC BRAID CRANK FANCY FREAK HUMOR QUIRK CHANGE MAGGOT NOTION SPLEEN TEMPER VAGARY WHIMSY BOUTADE CONCEIT CROCHET IMPULSE TANTRUM WHIMSEY
CAPRICIOUS DIZZY DODDY FLUKY MOODY CHANCY FICKLE FITFUL KITTLE PLATTY WANTON COMICAL ERRATIC FLIGHTY MAGGOTY MOONISH PEEVISH VAGRANT WAYWARD EPISODAL FANCIFUL FREAKISH HUMOROUS PERVERSE SKITTISH UNSTEADY VARIABLE VOLATILE CROTCHETY FANTASTIC VAGARIOUS
CAPRICIOUSNESS FREAK
CAPRICORN GOAT
CAPRIPEDE SATYR
CAPRYL RUTYL DECANOYL
CAPSHEAF CAP HOOD
CAPSICUM AJI PEPPER PAPRIKA
(— SAUCE) TABASCO
CAPSID MIRID
CAPSIZE COUP KEEL PURL UPEND UPSET WRONG WHEMMLE OVERTURN
CAPSTAN CRAB DRUM DANDY HOIST LEVER CYLINDER WINDLASS
CAPSTONE ACME LECH TOPSTONE
CAPSULE CAP POD URN BOLL CASE CYST PILL SEED PEARL PERLE SHELL THECA WAFER AMPULE BARROW CACHET COCOON OOCYST SHEATH AMPOULE EYEBALL OTOCYST SEEDBOX SILIQUE VANILLA PERICARP PYXIDIUM
(— OF LSD) MICRODOT
(DRUG —S) RED REDS
(PERSON WHO TAKES —S) PILLHEAD
(SPACE —) TERRELLA
(PREF.) THEC(A)(I)(O)
CAPTAIN BO BOH CID BAAS HEAD JOAB RAIS REIS BARAK CHIEF LEADER MASTER NAAMAN SOTNIK CAPITAN FOREMAN HEADMAN MANAGER PATROON SKIPPER FLUELLEN GOVERNOR SUBAHDAR
(— OF ARAB VESSEL) NACODAR
(— OF CAVALRY) RESSALDAR RITMASTER
(— OF CRICKET TEAM) SKIPPER
(— OF CURLING TEAM) SKIP
(— OF PRIVATEER) CAPER
(— OF SHIP) WAFTER
(STRICT —) SUNDOWNER
CAPTAINS COURAGEOUS (AUTHOR OF —) KIPLING
(CHARACTER IN —) DAN JACK DISKO TROOP CHEYNE HARVEY MANUEL SALTERS
CAPTAIN'S DAUGHTER (AUTHOR OF —) PUSHKIN
(CHARACTER IN —) MARIA PETER ALEXEI ZOURIN EMELYAN GRINEFF GRINYEV EGOROVNA IVANOVNA MIRONOFF PUGACHEV SHVABRIN VASILISA SAVELITCH POUGATCHEFF
CAPTION TITLE LEADER LEGEND CUTLINE HEADING SUBHEAD CITATION HEADLINE SUBTITLE
CAPTIOUS CRAFY TESTY CRAFTY SEVERE CARPING CYNICAL FRETFUL PEEVISH TETTISH ALLURING CATCHING CAVILING CONTRARY CRITICAL
CAPTIOUSLY TUTLY
CAPTIVATE WIN TAKE CATCH CHARM RIVET ALLURE ENAMOR PLEASE RAVISH SUBDUE ATTRACT BEWITCH CAPTIVE CAPTURE ENCHANT ENTHRALL INTEREST OVERTAKE SURPRISE
CAPTIVATED EPRIS EPRISE CAPTIVE
CAPTIVATING TAKING KILLING WINNING WINSOME CATCHING
CAPTIVE SLAVE DANIEL ENAMOR THRALL BRISEIS CAITIFF CAITIVE PRISONER
(— OF HERCULES) IOLE
CAPTIVITY BOND IRON BONDS CHAINS DURESS BONDAGE SERFDOM SLAVERY
(— OF THE JEWS) EXILE
CAPTOR TAKER VICTOR CATCHER
CAPTURE BAG COP FIX GET NAB NET WIN FALL FANG GRAB HOOK LAND PREY SNIB TAKE TRAP TREE CARRY CATCH FORCE PINCH PRIZE PURSE RAVEN SEIZE SWOOP ARREST COLLAR CORRAL ENTRAP GOBBLE OBTAIN PIRACY REDUCE TAKING CAPTIVE LOWBELL SEIZURE WINNING EXCHANGE SURPRISE UNDERNIM
(— BACKGAMMON PIECE) HIT
(— BIRDS) TOODLE
(— GAME) SATCHEL
(— OF ALL PRIZES) SWEEP
(— TROUT) TICKLE
CAPTURED COLLARED
CAPUCHIN MONKEY CAY SAI CEPID SAJOU WEEPER SAPAJOU RINGTAIL
CAPULIN CEREZA
CAPYBARA CAVY CARPINCHO
CAPYS (FATHER OF —) ASSARACUS
(SON OF —) ANCHISES
(WIFE OF —) THEMISTE
CAR BOX BUS PIG AUTO BOGY BUNK DOLL DRAG DUMP GRIP JEEP RATH TRAM ZULU BOGEY COACH CRATE DINER DUMMY GURRY HUTCH JIMMY RATHA SEDAN STOCK TRAIN TRUCK WRONG BASKET BOXCAR BUFFET CHIPPY DINGEY DINGHY DUPLEX HOPPER JIGGER JINGLE SALOON SETOFF SMOKER TOURER AWKWARD CARROCH CHARIOT COMBINE FLATCAR FREEZER GIRAFFE GONDOLA HANDCAR MINIVAN SIDECAR TELPHER TRAILER TROLLEY VEHICLE VETTURA AMPHICAR DRAGSTER HORSECAR OUTSIDER QUADRIGA ROADSTER SINISTER
(— FOR TRAIN CREW) CABOOSE
(— ON RAIL) TROLLEY
(BAGGAGE —) BLIND
(BRAND OF —) FORD SAAB CHEVY DODGE MAZDA VOLVO PLYMOUTH
(CABLE —) GONDOLA
(COAL —) HUTCH JIMMY WAGON WAGGON
(CONVERTIBLE —) RAGTOP
(DEALER'S —) DEMO
(ELECTRIC —) TELFER TELPHER
(ELEVATOR —) CAB CAGE
(EMPTY —) EMPTY IDLER
(ENCLOSED CABLE —) GONDOLA
(FUNNY —) DRAGSTER
(GO BY —) AUTO MOTOR
(JAUNTING —) SIDECAR
(KIND OF —) PACE PROWL SQUAD HEARSE MUSCLE
(KIND OF POLICE —) PANDA
(LOG —) BUNK
(LOW-WHEELED —) HUTCH TRUCKLE
(MINE —) SKIP LARRY BARNEY GIRAFFE GUNBOAT
(MONORAIL —) GYROCAR
(OBSERVATION —) BUGGY
(OLD —) HEAP CRATE JUNKER
(OLD-TIME —) REO NASH EDSEL ESSEX STUTZ DESOTO HUDSON MAXWELL
(POLICE —) CRUISER
(POLICE PATROL —) PANDA
(SMALL —) MINICAB ECONOBOX
(STYLE OF —) COUPE SEDAN
(TOURING —) PHAETON
(TOY RACING —) SLOTCAR
(TROLLEY —) SHORT
(USED —) DOG
CARABAO BUFF BUFFALO
CARACAL GORKUN SYAGUSH
CARACARA HAWK CARANCHA CHIMANGO
CARACOLE FRISK CAREER
CARADOC BALA CRADOCK
CARAFE CROFT BOTTLE
CARAGUATA CHAGUAR
CARAJURA CHICA
CARAMBOLA BLIMBING BALIMBING
CARAMEL BLACKJACK
CARAPA CRAB CRAPPO CRABWOOD
CARAPACE CRUST SHELL LORICA SHIELD CALAPASH
(SUFF.) STEGE STEGITE
CARAT (HUNDREDTH OF —) POINT
CARATE PINTA
CARATHIS (SON OF —) VATHEK
CARAVAN VAN TREK TRIP FLEET TRAIN CAFILA COFFLE CONVOY SAFARI TRAVEL JOURNEY VEHICLE CONDUCTA
CARAVANSARY INN CHAN KHAN HOTEL SERAI ZAYAT HOSTEL IMARET CHOULTRY HOSTELRY SERAGLIO
CARAVEL NINA
CARAWAY CARVY UMBEL
CARBAMATE MEPROBAMATE
CARBAMIDE UREA

CARBINE STEN DRAGON MUSKET DRAGOON ESCOPET
(BRITISH —) STEN
CARBOHYDRATE SUGAR AMYLAN GELOSE INULIN STARCH FUCOSAN GLUCIDE CELLULIN DEXTRINE DEXTROSE GLYCOGEN GRAMININ PENTOSAN TRITICIN CELLULOSE PARAMYLUM POLYSACCHARIDE
CARBON COAL COKE COPY SOOT NORIT CRAYON DIAMOND REPLICA CHARCOAL GRAPHITE SCHUNGITE
(PREF.) ANTHRAC(O)
(SUFF.) ANE
CARBONADO BORT BOART BOORT CARBON
CARBONATE BURN CHAR FIZZ AERATE ALKALI ENLIVEN ENERGIZER
CARBONATOR GASMAN
CARBON DIOXIDE CHOKEDAMP
(SUFF.) CAPNIA
CARBONIZE CHAR
CARBONIZER PICKLER
CARBORUNDUM EMERY ABRASIVE SILUNDUM
CARBOXYL
(SUFF.) **(CONTAINING —)** OIC ONIC
CARBUNCLE RUBY PYROPE ANTHRAX CHARBOCLE
(PREF.) ANTHRAC(O)
CARBURETOR CARB DIFFUSER VAPORIZER
CARCASS BEEF BODY BOUK CASE CULL BLOCK MUMMY CORPSE CARRION
(— OF WHALE) CRANG KRANG KRENG
CARCERULE SARCOBASIS
CARD ACE MAP PAM WAG CLUB COMB DRAW FACE FIVE FOUR JACK KING MENU PLAN ROVE STOP BALOP BLANK CARTE CHART CHECK DEUCE DUMMY EIGHT ENTRY EQUAL FICHE FLATS GREEN HEART HONOR JOKER LOSER PIECE QUEEN SPADE STAMP STIFF TAROT TEASE BENDER CARTEL CONVEX FILLER KICKER KNIGHT PIGEON READER SECOND TICKET TOWSER BRAGGER BRISQUE DIAMOND PROGRAM RELEASE STARTER STOPPER TAROCCO TRIUMPH BOOKMARK COMOQUER DECKHEAD DRAWCARD SCHEDULE SCRIBBLE SQUEEZER STRIPPER TIMECARD
(— GAME) WAR
(— IN OMBRE) MANILLE
(— LAST IN BOX) HOCK HOCKELTY
(— WOOL) TUM ROVE
(ACE OF CLUBS —) BASTA BASTO MATADOR PUPPYFOOT
(ACE OF SPADES —) MATADOR SPADILLE
(ACE OF TRUMPS —) TIB
(AVIATOR'S —) CARNET
(CLUB —) OAK
(COMPASS —) FLY ROSE
(CREDIT —) PLASTIC
(CRIBBAGE —S) CRIB
(DEAD —) SLEEPER
(DIAMOND —) PICK CARREAU
(DISCARDED —S) CRIB
(DRAWING —) BLOWOFF
(FARO —) SODA
(FOUR —) CATER QUATRE
(FOURTH —) CASE
(HIGHEST UNPLAYED —) COMMAND
(IN THE —S) PROBABLE
(JOKER —) BRAGGER MISTIGRIS
(KIND OF —) PUNCH REPORT HOLLERITH
(KING, QUEEN OR KNAVE —) COST FACE
(KNAVE —) PAM TOM JACK BOWER EQUES MAKER NODDY COQUIN KNIGHT PICARO VARLET WENZEL CUSTREL PEASANT VILLAIN VARLETTO
(LAYOUT OF —S) TABLEAU
(LOW —) GUARD
(MARKED —) STAMP
(POSTAL —) COVER
(PULLING —S) TIRE
(QUEEN AND KNAVE —S) INTRIGO INTRIGUE
(RUN OF —S) SEQUENCE
(SPADE —) PICK DIGGER
(STOCK —) TALON
(THIRD HIGHEST TRUMP —) BASTA
(THREE —) TREY THREE
(WILD —) FREAK
(3 —S IN SEQUENCE) TIERCE FOURCHETTE
(3 —S OF KIND) TRIO TRICON PAIRIAL TRIPLET
(3 ACE —S) CORONA
(3 FACE —S) GLEEK
(4 OF TRUMPS —) TIDDY
(5 FACE —S) BLAZE
(7, 8 AND 9 —S) VOIDS
CARDAMOM KNOBWOOD
CARDBOARD CARD PALL BLANK BOGUS CARTON BRISTOL TAGBOARD PAPERBOARD
(SMALL PIECES OF —) CHAD
(TWO —S) SPHEROGRAPH
CARDER TOZER TEASER TUMMER
CARDIALGIA HEARTBURN
CARDIGAN CORGI WAMUS FABRIC JACKET WAMPUS SWEATER
CARDINAL RED MAIN BASIC CHIEF CLOAK VITAL ALEPHA CLERIC DATARY PRINCE RADICAL ALEFNULL ALEFZERO CAMPEIUS PENITENTIARY
CARDINALATE PURPLE
CARDINAL BIRD CARNAL REDBIRD REDLEGS GROSBEAK REDSHANK
CARDINAL FISH FUCINITA ALFONCINO
CARDSHARP TRAMPOSO
CARDSHARPER GREEK SHARPER SPIELER
CARE DO DOW HOW CARK CURE DUTY FASH FRET HEED KEEP KEPE MIND PASS RECK SOIN TEND TENT WISH YEME COUNT GRIEF GUARD NURSE PAINS SORGE TRUST WORRY BURDEN CARIEN CHARGE CUMBER DESIRE GRIEVE KIAUGH LAMENT REGARD SORROW ANXIETY AUSPICE CAUTION CHERISH CONCERN CULTURE CUSTODY KEEPING RESPECT RUNNING SCRUPLE THOUGHT TUITION BUSINESS PERIERGY TENDMENT NURTURANCE PRECAUTION SOLICITUDE
(— FOR) KNOW MIND RECK TEND WARD FORCE NURSE SAVOR FATHER MATTER REGARD CHERISH PROCURE
(— FOR ONESELF) BACH
(— OF HOUSEHOLD) HUSBANDRY
(— OF LIVESTOCK) CHORE
(— OF THE OLD) GERIATRY
(GIVE EXCESSIVE — TO) WETNURSE
(JUDICIOUS —) LEISURE
(WATCHFUL —) TENDANCE OVERSIGHT
CAREEN GIP CANT HEEL KEEL LIST TILT VEER LURCH SLOPE SWIFT INCLINE
CAREENING ALIST AREEL
CAREER RUN WAY LIFE ROAD RUSH SPEED TRADE CHARGE COURSE GALLOP CALLING CARIERE PURSUIT
(— SUMMARY) BIO VITA
(MILITARY —) ARMS SERVICE
(SELECT A —) GOINTO
CAREFREE EASY FRANK HAPPY BREEZY DEGAGE HOLIDAY DEBONAIR
CAREFUL BUSY WARY CANNY CHARY CLOSE EXACT HOOLY TENTY CHOICE DAINTY EIDENT EYEFUL FRUGAL NARROW TENDER ANXIOUS CURIOUS ENVIOUS GUARDED HEEDFUL PAINFUL PRUDENT THRIFTY ACCURATE CAUTIOUS CRITICAL DILIGENT DISCREET DREADFUL GINGERLY MOURNFUL PUNCTUAL TROUBLED VIGILANT WATCHFUL OBSERVANT METICULOUS SOLICITOUS PUNCTILIOUS
CAREFULLY HOOLY NARROW CANNILY CHARILY TENTILY CHOICELY GINGERLY
CAREFULNESS CAUTION
CARELESS LAX COOL EASY LASH RASH MESSY SLACK CASUAL OVERLY RAKISH REMISS SECURE SLOPPY SUPINE UNTIDY UNWARY CURSORY LANGUID SLIGHTY UNCANNY HEEDLESS LISTLESS MINDLESS RECKLESS SLATTERN SLIPSHOD SLOVENLY YEMELESS NEGLECTFUL SLATTERNLY
CARELESSLY SLACK OVERLY SLACKLY SLIGHTLY
CARELESSNESS LACHES LAXITY INCAUTION
CARESS COY HUG PAT PET BILL CLAP DAUT DAWT KISS MUCH NECK INGLE NURSE CODDLE COSSET CUDDLE FONDLE PAMPER STROKE CHERISH EMBRACE FLATTER BLANDISH CANOODLE LALLYGAG
CARETAKER KEEPER WARDER JANITOR
CAREWORN HAGGARD
CARGO BULK LAST LOAD BURDEN LADING FREIGHT PACKAGE PORTAGE CARGASON PROPERTY SHIPLOAD SHIPMENT TRAFFICS
CARIAMA CHUNGA SERIEMA
CARIB GALIBI CALINAGO
CARIBBEAN (— GULF) DARIEN HONDURAS
(— ISLAND) CUBA SABA ARUBA HAITI NEVIS BEQUIA NASSAU TOBAGO ANTIGUA BARBUDA BONAIRE CURACAO GRENADA JAMAICA TORTOLA ANGUILLA BARBADOS DOMINICA TRINIDAD GUADELOUPE MONTSERRAT
(— ISLAND GROUP) TURKS CAICOS CAYMAN LEEWARD ANTILLES WINDWARD
CARIBE PIRAI PIRANHA CHARACINE
CARIBOU STAG RANGIFER REINDEER
CARICATURE APE COPY MOCK SKIT FARCE LIBEL MIMIC SQUIB OVERDO PARODY SATIRE CARTOON TRAVESTY BURLESQUE
CARILLON PEAL
CARILLONNEUR CAMPANIST BELLMASTER
CARINA KEEL
CARIOUS ROTTEN
CARMELITE EXTERN TERESIAN
CARMEN (CHARACTER IN —) JOSE CARMEN ZUNIGA MICAELA ESCAMILLO
(COMPOSER OF —) BIZET
CARMI (FATHER OF —) REUBEN
(SON OF —) ACHAN
CARMINATIVE GINGER CALAMUS CAMPHOR ANETHOLE VALERIAN
CARMINE RED LAKE CRIMSON SCARLET
CARNAGE WAL MURDER POGROM STRAGE BUTCHERY MASSACRE BLOODSHED SLAUGHTER
CARNAL CROW LEWD GROSS ANIMAL BODILY SEXUAL BESTIAL BRUTISH EARTHLY FLESHLY SECULAR SENSUAL WORLDLY MATERIAL PANDEMIC PHYSICAL TEMPORAL
CARNATION JACK PINK FLAKE BIZARRE PICOTEE DAYBREAK DIANTHUS GRENADINE MALMAISON
CARNELIAN SARD COPPER
(BEAD OF —) ARANGO
CARNIVAL FETE SHOW CARNY CANVAS APOKREA CANVASS REVELRY FASCHING FESTIVAL
CARNIVORE CAT DOG FOX BEAR COON LION LYNX MINK PUMA SEAL WOLF CIVET GENET HYENA OTTER PANDA PEKAN RATEL SABLE STOAT TIGER BADGER COUGAR ERMINE FELINE FERRET FISHER FOUSSA JACKAL JAGUAR MARTEN OCELOT POSSUM SERVAL WEASEL DASYURE GLUTTON LEOPARD MEERKAT POLECAT RACCOON TIGRESS AARDWOLF MONGOOSE OPPOSSUM PREDACEAN ZOOPHAGAN
(FOSSIL —) CREODONT

CARNIVOROUS SARCOPHAGOUS
CAROB HUSK LOCUST ALGAROBA
CAROL LAY NOEL SING SONG DITTY YODEL WARBLE WASSAIL MADRIGAL AGUINALDO
CAROLINA ALLSPICE SHRUB
CAROLINE ISLANDS (— ISLAND GROUP) PALAU
(ISLAND OF —) YAP HALL PALU TRUK PELEW PULAP OROLUK PONAPE WOLEAI PELELIU
(TOWN OF —) LOT NIF RUNU KOROR MUTOK TOMIL PONAPE MALAKAL GARUSUUN
CAROLINGIAN KARLING
CAROM SHOT BOUNCE CANNON GLANCE STRIKE REBOUND BILLIARD CARAMBOLE
CAROUSAL BAT GELL LARK ORGY RIOT ROMP TOOT BINGE FEAST RANDY REVEL ROUSE SPRAY SPREE FROLIC SHINDY SPLORE BANQUET CAROUSE REVELRY WASSAIL DRINKING FESTIVAL JAMBOREE
CAROUSE JET BOUT HELL RANT TEAR TOOT BINGE BIRLE BOUSE DRINK QUAFF RANDY REVEL ROUSE SPREE TOAST COURANT JOLLIFY WASSAIL CAROUSAL
CAROUSER BACCHANT BACCHANAL
CAROUSING REVEL RAFFING
(— OF ICEBOUND SEAMEN MALLE MOLLIE
CARP KOI NAG BITE DRUM SING SNAG TALK YERK CAVIL PINCH PRATE SCOLD SPEAK CENSOR GROUSE NIBBLE RECITE TWITCH CENSURE CHATTER CRUCIAN QUIBBLE COMPLAIN CYPRINID GOLDFISH
(CRUCIAN —) GIBEL
(LAKE —) DRUM LAKER
(PREF.) CYPRIN(O)
CARPAL ACTINOST
CARPEL ACHENE CARPID COCCUS MERICARP CARPOPHYL
(PL.) CORE
CARPENTER ANT LOHAR FITTER FRAMER HOUSER JOINER PINNER WRIGHT BUILDER HOWSOUR WOODMAN INDENTER TECTONIC TIMBERER PITWRIGHT SHIPWRIGHT
(SHIP'S —) CHIPS
(PREF.) TECTO
CARPENTRY WOODWORK WRIGHTRY
CARPER MOME CRITIC KNOCKER
CARPET MAT RUG AGRA KALI KUBA HERAT KILIM SARUK SCOLD SUMAK TAPET TAPIS TEKKE USHAK AFGHAN FLOSSA FRIEZE KASHAN KIDDER KIRMAN LAVEHR NAMMAD RUNNER SAROUK SAXONY SELJUK SMYRNA TABRIZ VELVET WILTON DHURRIE GIORDES HAMADAN INGRAIN ISFAHAN ISPAHAN SHEMAKA TEHERAN AKHISSAR AMRITSAR BRUSSELS COVERING FOOTPACE KARABAGH MOQUETTE TAPESTRY TURCOMAN VENETIAN AXMINSTER SITRINGEE
(HOLY —) KISWA
(PILELESS —) KILIM GELEEM
CARPETING FILLING
CARPET SHARK WOBBEGONG
CARPET SHELL EEROCK PULLET
CARPETWEED FICOID FICOIDAL MESEMBRYANTHEMUM
CARPING CRAB CAPTIOUS CAVILING CRITICAL
CARPSUCKER QUILLBACK
CARPUS WRIST CARPOPODITE
CARRAGEEN KILLEEN
CARREL STALL CUBICLE
CARRIAGE AIR CAB CAR FLY GIG RIG RUT SET VIS ARBA BIGA CART CHAR DRAG DUKE EKKA GAIT GARB HACK LOAD MIEN PORT RUTH SHAY TEAM TRAP WYNN ARABA BANDY BRAKE BREAK BRETT BUGGY CHAIR COACH COUPE ESSED FRONT JUTKA MIDGE NODDY PANEL POISE SADOO SETUP SULKY TENUE TONGA TRUCK WAGON BURDEN CALASH CHAISE CHARET CISIUM CONVOY DENNET DROSKY FIACRE GHARRY GOCART HANSOM HERDIC KOSONG LANDAU MANNER MOTION PORTER REMISE SADDLE SPIDER STANCE SURREY TANDEM TELEGA TROIKA BAGGAGE BEARING BERLINE BOUNDER BRITSKA CALECHE CALESIN CARAVAN CARIOLE CAROCHE CHARIOT COACHEE CONDUCT CROYDON DOGCART DOSADOS DROSHKY FORECAR GESTURE HACKMAN HACKNEY MINIBUS PHAETON POSCHAY SHANDRY SKYHOOK TALLYHO TARTANA TILBURY TRANSIT TROLLEY UNICORN VECTURE VEHICLE VETTURA VOITURE VOLANTE WAFTAGE BAROUCHE BEHAVIOR BROUGHAM CARRIOLE CARRYALL CLARENCE CURRICLE DEARBORN DEMEANOR DORMEUSE EQUIPAGE PORTANCE PRESENCE ROCKAWAY SOCIABLE STANHOPE TARANTAS TOURNURE VICTORIA
(— IN PHILIPPINES) CALESA
(— OF HANDPRESS) COFFIN
(— OF HORSE) AIR
(AMMUNITION —) CAISSON
(CEREMONIAL —) RATH
(ELEVATED —) LIFT
(GUN —) CHASSIS
(INDIAN —) RUT EKKA BANDY GHARRI GHARRY
(JAVANESE —) SADO SADOO
(LIVERY —) REMISE
(LOG —) DRAG
(PUBLIC —) FLY OMNIBUS
CARRIAGE HOUSE REMISE
CARRIAGEWAY SWEE
CARRIED (— AWAY) RAPT ENLEVE
CARRIER HOD BASE JEEP SHIP TRAM BUGGY HAMAL KAHAR MACER PLANE SABOT TAMEN TIGER BARKIS BEARER CADGER COOLIE HAMMAL HODMAN JAGGER PACKER PORTER RUNNER TAILER WEASEL DRAYMAN DROGHER FLATTOP POSTMAN REMOVER TACULLI TROTTER VEHICLE CARGADOR CARRYALL PORTATOR RAILROAD TEAMSTER SUBSTRATE
(— OF DISEASE) VECTOR
(COAL —) FLATIRON
(COLOR —) LURRIER
(CRANE —) GANTRY
(ENDLESS —) TAILER
(FIRE —) PORTFIRE
(MAIL —) COURIER POSTMAN
(ORE —) BARGE BOXCAR
(WATER —) BHISTI BHEESTY
(PREF.) PORTE
CARRION KET VILE OFFAL CORPSE HOODIE REFUSE ROTTEN CARCASS CORRUPT DOGMEAT CROWBAIT
CARRION BIRD SCAVENGER
CARRION CROW DOWP HOODY URUBU CORBIE HOODIE GERCROW
CARROT UMBEL CONIUM DAUCUS CACHRYS SECRETE BUPLEVER HILLTROT
(DEADLY —) DRIAS
(PERUVIAN —) ARRACACH
(PREPARED WITH —S) CRECY
CARROTING SECRETAGE
CARROUSEL RIDE WHIRLGIG QUADRILLE
CARRY CAR HUG JAG LUG BEAR BUCK CART DRAY FARE GEST HAUL HAVE HOLD HUMP LEAD PACK PORT SHOW TAKE TOTE TUMP BRING BROOK CADGE CROSS FERRY GESTE GUIDE POISE WALTZ WEIGH BEHAVE CONVEY CONVOY DELATE DEPORT DERIVE EXTEND COMPORT CONDUCT CONTAIN ENTRAIN PORTAGE PRODUCE SUPPORT SUSTAIN UNDERGO BAJULATE CONTINUE TRANSFER TRANSMIT
(— AWAY) FIRK DRAIN REAVE SWEEP TRUSS ABLATE ASPORT
(— CLUBS) CADDY CADDIE
(— EFFIGY) GUY
(— FORWARD) EXTEND
(— IN OXCART) KURVEY
(— INTO EFFECT) FULFIL FULFILL
(— IN TRIUMPH) CHAIR
(— LIQUOR) BOOTLEG
(— OFF) RAP HENT LIFE SACK FETCH HEAVE RIFLE SCOUR SWOOP ABDUCT ASPORT BRAZEN KIDNAP SPIRIT
(— ON) DO RUN WAR HAVE LEAD LEVY WAGE APPLY DRIVE ENSUE FIGHT TRAIN CREATE DEMEAN FOLLOW MANAGE OCCUPY CONDUCT EXERCISE MAINTAIN TRANSACT
(— ONESELF) HOLD
(— ONWARD) CONTINUE
(— OUT) DO ACT END GIVE LAST HONOR AFFORD EFFECT ACHIEVE EXECUTE FULFILL PERFORM SATISFY PERPETRATE
(— TOO FAR) OVERDO
(— UPWARD) RAP ESCALATE
(SUFF.) GER(ENCE)(ENT)(OUS) PHER PHORA PHORE(SIS) PHORIA PHOROUS PHORUS
(— ON) IZE
CARRYALL BUS CASE WAGON CARRIAGE
CARRY-ALONG TOTE
CARRYING BURDEN GERENT FRAUGHT
(— AWAY) REVEHENT
(— ON) GESTION
(— WEIGHT) EFFECTIVE
(PREF.) **(— ON)** PHORO
CART CAR JAG POT RUT BUTT CHAR COOP COUP DRAY HAUL JANG LEAD LOAD PLOW PUTT RUTH TOTE WAIN ARABA BANDY BOGEY BOGIE CADDY CARRY DANDY DILLY DOLLY SULKY TONGA TRUCK WAGON BARROW CADDIE CHAISE CHARET CISIUM CONVEY DOLLIE DUMPER GHARRI GHARRY JIGGER JINKER KURUMA LIMBER PLOUGH SPIDER CARIOLE CARRETA CHARIOT DOGCART GUJERAT HACKERY MORFREY SHALLOW SHANDRY TROLLEY TRUNDLE TUMBLER TUMBREL TUMBRIL VEHICLE BUCKCART DUMPCART HANDCART PUSHCART
(— WITH TANK) TUMBLER
(BULLOCK —) BANDY HACKERY
(COSTER'S —) TROLL
(COVERED —) JINGLE CARIOLE
(FARMER'S —) PUTT GAMBO MORPHREY
(FREIGHT —) CARRETON
(LOG —) TUG BUNK
(LUMBER —) GILL BUMMER
(MILKMAN'S —) PRAM
(OX —) RECKLA
(PARCELS —) FLY
(TIMBER —) CUTS
(TIP —) COOP COUP COUPE
(UNDERSLUNG —) FLOAT
(2-PONY —) KOSONG
(2-WHEELED —) BANDY BUGGY SULKY CARRETA TUMBREL
(3-WHEELED —) PORTER
CARTE MAP CARD LIST MENU CHART CHARTER DIAGRAM
CARTE BLANCHE BLANK
CARTEL CARD DEFY PACT POOL SHIP PAPER TRUST CORNER LETTER TREATY CONTRACT SYNDICATE
CARTER CARMAN JAGGER LEADER DRAYMAN LADEMAN TRUCKER HORSEMAN TEAMSTER
CART-HORSE AVER
CARTILAGE COPULA TISSUE CRICOID EPIURAL GRISTLE RADIALE STERNUM TARSALE THYROID CHONDRUS EPIPUBIS HYPOHYAL SESAMOID TURBINAL
(— UNDER DOG'S TONGUE) LYTTA
(PREF.) CHONDR(I)(IO)(O) CRICO
(SUFF.) CHONDRIA CHONDRY CRINUS
CARTILAGINOUS CHONDRIC
CARTLOAD SEAM FOTHER
CARTOGRAPH MAP PLAT CHART

CARTOGRAPHER CHARTIST MAPMAKER
AMERICAN GANNETT HUTCHINS SOUTHACK STEVENSON
ENGLISH SPEED
GERMAN KIEPERT STIELER PETERMANN WALDSEEMULLER
RUSSIAN KAULBARS
SWISS SIEGFRIED
CARTON BOX CASE SHELL
CARTOON EPURE ANIMATION
CARTOONING (— AWARD) REUBEN
CARTOONIST AMERICAN DAY FOX KEY REA ARNO BAER BALD BODE CADY CAPP DODD DUNN HELD HESS LUKS NAST BARKS BLOCK BURCK CRUMB DARCY DIRKS DUFFY EDSON ERNST GOULD HATLO KIRBY LANTE MCCAY NEHER OPPER PLUMB SAXON SEGAR STEIG TERRY YATES YOUNG ADDAMS BERNDT BRIGGS CANIFF DEITCH DISNEY DORGAN FISHER KEMBLE KOTSKY MUSIAL NEWELL NOWLAN POWERS RIPLEY SCHULZ SOGLOW DARLING GRUELLE KEPPLER MAULDIN MCMANUS TRUDEAU WEBSTER GOLDBERG HERBLOCK OUTCAULT SCHULTZE WESTOVER WILLIAMS NANKIVELL STEINBERG HERSHFIELD FITZPATRICK
AUSTRALIAN LINDSAY
BELGIAN CULLIFORD
DUTCH RAEMAEKERS
ENGLISH LOW SPY DYSON LEECH SMYTHE FURNISS GILLRAY HAMPSON TENNIEL ROBINSON LANCASTER BAIRNSFATHER
FRENCH GOSCINNY
GERMAN MEGGENDORFER
MEXICAN ARRIOLA COVARRUBIAS
WELSH BATEMAN ILLINGWORTH
CARTOUCHE MESA OVAL DURANGO CARTRIDGE
CARTRIDGE BAG CASE HULL BLANK SHELL SHORT BULLET MAGNUM PATRON CAPSULE TORPEDO HANDLOAD SHOTSHELL
(PART OF —) RIM CASE HEAD NOSE SLUG CRIMP BULLET JACKET PRIMER
(TAPE —) CASSETTE
(TYPE OF —) POPIN
CARTULARY COUCHER
CARTWHEEL CLOGWHEEL
CARUCATE CARVE PLOWLAND
(ONE EIGHTH —) OXGANG OXGATE OXLAND
CARUNCLE ARIL COMB STROPHIOLE
CARVE CUT ALAY SIDE BEHEW BREAK GRAVE KIRVE MINCE SHEAR SPLAY SPOIL THIGH INCISE QUINSE SCULPT THWITE TRENCH UNLACE ENCHASE ENGRAIL ENGRAVE DISJOINT MALAHACK SCULLION
(— A BIRD) WING
(— AN EEL) TRUNCHEON
(— CHICKEN) FRUSH
(— GOOSE) REAR
(— HEN) SPOIL
(— PEACOCK) DISFIGURE
(— PLOVER) MINCE
(— SWAN) LIFT
(PREF.) GLYPHO GLYPT(O) SCULPTO
(SUFF.) GLYPH
CARVED CARVEN GLYPHIC INCISED
(PREF.) GLYPT(O)
CARVER BODGER KIRVER CROPPER FROSTER IVORIST CISELEUR TRENCHER
CARVING CAMEO GLYPH IVORY ENTAIL SCRIVE GLYPTIC MASKOID NICKING APLUSTRE INTAGLIO TRIPTYCH PETROGLYPH
(— ON MOLDING) GADROON
(— ON TREE) DENDROGLYPH
(CIRCULAR —) TONDO
CARYA HICORIA
CARYATID TELAMON CANEPHORA
(PART OF —) GAINE
CARYOCAR SOUARI
CARYOPHYLLUS JAMBOSA
CARYOPSIS SEED
CASABLANCA (CHARACTER IN —) ILSA
CASANOVA AMORIST
CASCABEL POMMEL POMMELION
CASCADE LIN FALL LINN FORCE SPOUT CATARACT
CASCARA BUCKTHORN WAHOO SHITTIM
CASCARILLA CROTON GOATWEED SWEETWOOD
CASE BAG BOX CUP HAP LEG POD POT PYX BIND BOOT BUNK BURR CASK COPE DEED DESK DOCK DOME FILE PACK PAIR ROLL SUIT TICK BRACE BRIEF BULLA BURSE CADDY CASUS CAUSE CHAPE COVER CRATE EVENT FOLIO FOREL HUSSY HUTCH PRESS PYXIS SHELL STATE THECA THING TRIAL ACTION AFFAIR APPEAL BARREL BINDER BOXING CARTON CASING CELLAR CHANCE CHRISM COFFIN COUPLE LOCKET LORICA MATTER PATRON PENNER PETARD POPPET QUIVER RIDDLE SHEATH SHRINE STATOR SURVEY TASHIE TWEEZE VALISE VANITY CABINET CAMISIA CAPCASE CAPSULE COUNTER CUSHION DIECASE ENCLOSE ENVELOP EXAMPLE GEARBOX HOLDALL HOLSTER HOUSING HUMIDOR INCLOSE LAWSUIT LUNETTE PACKAGE REMANET SATCHEL SHIPPER WARDIAN ACCIDENT ARGUMENT BOOKCASE CARRYALL CUPBOARD ENVELOPE EQUIPAGE EXEMPLAR GARDEVIN INSTANCE KNAPSACK PACKSACK PORTFIRE SHOWCASE SITUATED SOLANDER TANTALUS CARTRIDGE PORTFOLIO
(— CONTAINING ELEVATOR BELT) LEG
(— ENCLOSING CLOCK DIAL) HOOD
(— FOR BOTTLES) CELLARET
(— FOR CARDS) SHOE
(— FOR COMPASS) BINNACLE
(— FOR DECANTERS) TANTALUS
(— FOR EXPLOSIVES) TRUNK
(— FOR JEWELS) TYE
(— FOR MAINSPRING) BARILLET
(— FOR MOLD) COPE CHAPE
(— FOR MONEY WALLET
(— FOR MUMMY) SLEDGE
(— FOR PISTOL) HOLSTER
(— FOR PULLEY) BLOCK
(— FOR RIFLE) BOOT
(— FOR SEWING ITEMS) HUSSY
(— FOR TOOLS) TROUSSE
(— FOR TWEEZERS) BUBBLEBOW
(— FOR WRITING MATERIALS) STANDISH
(— IN WATCH) DOME BARREL
(— OF) A
(— OF FLOUR BOLTER) HUTCH
(— OF VENETIAN BLIND) HEADBOX
(— WITH COMPARTMENTS) RIDDLE
(BONY —) CARAPACE
(CARTRIDGE —) DOP CARTOUCHE
(COSMETIC —) COMPACT
(COURT —) LAWSUIT
(EGG —) OVISAC OOTHECA
(EMPTY —) SHELL
(FIREWORKS —) LANCE
(GRAMMATICAL —) DATIVE ESSIVE LATIVE ELATIVE FACTIVE ABLATIVE EQUATIVE ERGATIVE GENITIVE ILLATIVE LOCATIVE VOCATIVE ACCUSATIVE
(HOPELESS —) GONER
(LARVA —) INDUSIUM
(LUGGAGE —) IMPERIAL
(ORNAMENTAL —) ETUI
(PAPER —) COFFIN
(PILLOW —) SLIP
(SMALL —) MINAUDIERE
(SPORE —) ASCUS
(WICKER —) HASK BARROW HANAPER
(WING —) SHARD
(WRITING —) KALAMDAN
(PREF.) THEC(A)(I)(O)
(EGG —) OOTHEC(O)
(SUFF.) THECA THECIUM
CASED BOUND
CASEMENT SASH LUKET WINDOW
CASE OF SERGEANT GRISCHA
(AUTHOR OF —) ZWEIG
(CHARACTER IN —) BABKA LYCHOW GRISCHA WILHELMI WINFRIED BJUSCHEFF PAPROTKIN PONSANSKI SCHIEFFENZAHN
CASH (SHORT OF —) STRAPPED
CASHEW ACAJOU ANACARD
CASHEW TREE ACAJOU
CASHIER CASS CAST BREAK DEALER POTDAR PURSER TELLER CHECKER DISMISS
CASHIERED BROKEN DEGOMME
CASHMERE KASHMIR PRUNELL
CASH REGISTER DAMPER REGEST GREFFIER RECORDER REGISTER
CASING BODY BOOT BUNG CASE CURB HULL SHOE SKIN TIRE APRON BELLY DERMA EPHOD GAINE LINER ROUND STOCK TRUNK BOXING COFFIN COLLET JACKET KISHKE LINING SCROLL SHEATH VOLUTE COWLING FEEDBOX HOUSING MANHEAD OUTCASE STAVING THIMBLE CACHEPOT COVERING PLOWSHOE SHIRTING WHEELBOX
(— FOR BRAIN) HARNPAN
(— FOR SHAFT) TUB
(BOILER —) JACKET
CASINO BAKED BROILED
(— CALL) HITME
(— EMPLOYEE) DEALER
CASK KEG PIN TUB TUN VAT BOSS BUTT CADE COWL DRUM KNAG PIPE RAPE RIER SLIP TREE WOOD ANKER BOWIE BULGE FOIST STAND UNION BARECA BARREL CARDEL CASQUE DOLIUM FIRKIN FOODER LONGER OCTAVE TIERCE WINGER BARRICO BREAKER FOSTELL LEAGUER RUNDLET SACKBUT CASSETTE HOGSHEAD PUNCHEON QUARDEEL ROUNDLET KILDERKIN
(BREWING —) UNION
(LOCKED —) TANTALUS
(PERFORATED —) POT
(SMALL —) KEG TUB KNAG STOOP STOUP
(WINE —) FAT TUN BOSS BUTT PIPE TIERCE HOGSHEAD
(PL.) COOPERAGE
CASKET BOX PIX TYE CASE CASK CIST TILL TOMB BUIST CHEST ACERRA CHASSE COFFER COFFIN SHRINE CADENAS FOSTELL CASSETTE
CASK-STAND STILLAGE STILLION
CASPIAN (— FEEDER) YSER
CASQUE CASK HORN GALEA HELMET BRASSET
CASSABANANA CURUBA
CASSANDRA SEER
(BROTHER OF —) HELENUS
(FATHER OF —) PRIAM
(HUSBAND OF —) AGAMEMNON
(MOTHER OF —) HECUBA
(SLAYER OF —) CLYTEMNESTRA
CASSAREEP CAXIRI
CASSAVA AIPI YUCA AIPIM YUCCA CASIRI CAZIBI MANIOC TAPIOCA
(— DISH) TAPIOCA
CASSEROLE TUREEN COCOTTE MARMITE TERRINE TZIMMES
CASSETTE TAPE MAGAZINE CARTRIDGE
CASSIA KEZIA SENNA SICKLEPOD
CASSIA FISTULA AMALTAS
CASSIMERE ZEPHYR
CASSINI OLEG
CASSITERITE TINSTONE
CASSITES KUSHSHU
CASSOCK GOWN SLOP VEST APRON GIPPO SIMAR SYMAR PRIEST PELISSE SIMARRE SOUTANE ZIMARRA
CASSOWARY EMU MURUP MOORUP RATITE
CAST MEW PUT SET AURA BILL DART HURL MOLD MOLT PICK SHED SLAT SLIP SPEW SWAK TINT TOSS TREE TURN WHAP WHOP WURP BLOCK BRAID CHUCK COOST DEUCE DRIVE EJECT ERECT FLING FLIRT FOUND FUSIL HEAVE IMAGE KEIST PITCH SHADE SHAPE SHOOT SLING STAMP THROW TINGE COLLAR INJECT NOSING

STRIKE STRIND THRILL AGARWAL CASHIER DEPOSIT DISCARD MOULAGE VIBRATE CASTLING CONSPECT OUTSLING POLYTYPE TINCTURE
(— ASIDE) DICE FLING
(— A SPELL) TAKE HOODOO BESPELL BEWITCH FORSPEAK
(— ASPERSIONS) SLUR SKLENT APPEACH
(— AWAY) DUMP SHOVE DEJECT REJECT
(— DICE) WHIRL
(— DISCREDIT) GLANCE
(— DOWN) DASH DUMP HURL SINK ABASE AMATE AMORT AWARP STREW ABATTU ABJECT DECAST DEJECT DEMISS THRING ECLIPSE RUINATE DEJECTED
(— FORTH) SPEW SPUE WARP BELCH BRAID LAUNCH
(— GLOOM) DUSK CLOUD DARKEN DEPRESS
(— IN A MOLD) STRIKE
(— LOTS) CAVEL
(— METAL) YET
(— OF DICE) COUP DEUCE
(— OFF) DAFF JILT MOLT SHED DITCH LOSSE SHAKE SLIRT SLUFF WAIVE CASTEN DEVEST REFUSE REJECT SLOUGH ABDICATE RENOUNCE
(— OF HERRINGS) WARP
(— OF LANGUAGE) IDIOM
(— OF NET) SHOT SHOOT
(— ON GROUND) TERRE
(— OUT) EGEST EJECT EXPEL BANISH ABANDON EXTRUDE OSTRACIZE
(— SHADOW) ADUMBRATE
(— UP) SUM LEVY UPBRAID
(FRESHLY —) GREEN
(PLASTER —) CUIRASS
(SUFF.) JECT

CASTANET CLICKER KNACKER KNOCKER SNAPPER TCHAPAN CROTALUM

CASTAWAY WAIF WEFT TRAMP CRUSOE REJECT OUTCAST DERELICT STRANDED

CASTE (OR CASTE MEMBER) DOM MEO AHIR BHAR BHAT GOLA JATI KOLI KORI MALI MINA PASI TELI BAGDI BANIA DHOBY GOALA IRAVA KAHAR KUMNI KUNBI KURMI LADHA LOHAR MAHAR PALLI PUGGI SAMAR SANSI SINGH SONAR SUDRA TANTI VARNA ARORAS BAIDYA BALIJA BANIAN BHANGI CHAMAR CHETTY CHUHRA DHANUK DHOBIE DOSADH DURZEE HOLEYA HOLIYA ILAVAN JAJMAN KALWAR KAMBOH KHATRI KUMHAR KURUBA LOHANA MADIGA NATION PALLAR PRABHU PULAYA PULIAN PURVOE RAJPUT VAISYA AGARWAL BRAHMAN BRAHMIN DHANGAR GADARIA HARIJAN KAYASTH KOMATRI KURUMBA NISHADA VELLALA KAMMALAN KHANDAIT PARAIYAN POVINDAH RAJBANSI VAKKALIGA
(LOWER —S) PANCHAMA

CASTER VIAL CRUET CRUSE PHIAL CASTOR HORRAL HURLER MASTER ROLLER FOUNDER PITCHER TRUCKLE TRUNDLE
(SURF —) SQUIDDER

CASTIGATE LASH EMEND SCARE SCORE BERATE PUNISH REVISE STRAFE SUBDUE CANVASS CENSURE CHASTEN CORRECT LEATHER REPROVE CHASTISE KEELHAUL LAMBASTE FUSTIGATE OBJURGATE

CASTIGATION HELL LASHING DRESSING

CASTILIAN BROWN TANAGRA

CASTING DIE PIG CAST FONT KEEP MOLD TYMP BLOCK CHOCK CHUCK FOUND MOULD BILLET BUMPER MATRIX MISRUN SPIDER COULAGE DARTING SEGMENT SEPARATOR SORTILEGE
(— LOTS) SORTITION
(— OF HOROSCOPE) APOTELESM
(— OF NET) SHOT
(— OVERBOARD) JETTISON
(PL.) SPRAY FOUNDRY

CAST IRON YETLING

CASTLE BURY FORT HALL KEEP ROCK ROOK ABODE BROCH COURT MORRO PIECE CASBAH BASTILE BOROUGH CHATEAU CITADEL SCHLOSS UDOLPHO BASTILLE CASTELET CASTILLO FASTNESS FORTRESS STAROSTY TINTAGEL
(— IN CHESS) JUEZ ROOK TOUR JUDGE TOWER
(PART OF —) KEEP MOAT WARD MOUNT TOWER WHARF BAILEY BRIDGE DONJON TURRET BASTION BULWARK DUNGEON OUTWORK RAMPART BARBICAN CASEMATE GATEHOUSE BATTLEMENT DRAWBRIDGE PORTCULLIS
(SMALL —) PEEL TOWER CASTLET CHATELET

CASTLE OF OTRANTO (AUTHOR OF —) WALPOLE
(CHARACTER IN —) CONRAD JEROME MANFRED MATILDA ISABELLA THEODORE

CAST-OFF DISCARD

CASTOR BEAVER LEATHER TRUCKLE TRUNDLE BARKSTONE
(— AND POLLUX) TWINS GEMINI DIOSCURI
(MOTHER OF —) LEDA

CASTOR AND POLLUX
(CHARACTER IN —) CASTOR PHOEBE POLLUX JUPITER MERCURY TELAIRA
(COMPOSER OF —) RAMEAU

CASTOR-OIL
(PREF.) RICIN(I)

CASTOR-OIL PLANT KIKI MAMONA PALMCRIST

CASTRATE CUT FIX GIB LIB GELD GLIB SPAY SWIG TRIM ALTER CAPON DESEX PRUNE STEER CHANGE DOCTOR EUNUCH NEUTER EVIRATE CAPONIZE MUTILATE SATURNIZE

CASTRATED CUT GIBBED NEUTER UNPAVED
(NOT —) STONE ENTIRE

CASTRATO EUNUCH EVIRATO TENORINO

CASUAL GLIB ORRA STRAY BLITHE BYHAND CHANCE FOLKSY RANDOM CASALTY CURSORY LEISURE NATURAL OFFHAND RUNNING GLANCING INFORMAL PROMISCUOUS

CASUALTY LOSS DEATH CADUAC CHANCE HAZARD INJURY MISHAP ACCIDENT DISASTER

CASUARINA BEEFWOOD

CASUIST JESUIT

CAT GIB RAT REX SOW TAB CHAT EYRA FLOG GATO LION LYNX MANX MISS PARD PUMA PUSS CHAUS CIVET FELID GATOL KITTY KORAT MANUL MEWER MOGGY OUNCE PUSSY SMOKE TABBY TIGER TILER WHITE ZIBET ANGORA BIRMAN BOMBAY COUGAR FELINE JAGUAR KITTEN KODKOD MALKIN MARGAY MAWKIN MIAUER MOGGIE MOUSER MUSION NEUTER OCELOT PAJERO PURRER SERVAL SOMALI TIBERT TORTIE BURMESE CARACAL CATHEAD CATLING CHEETAH KITLING KUICHUA LEOPARD LINSANG PANTHER PERSIAN SIAMESE TIGRESS WILDCAT WRAWLER BAUDRONS DASYURID FISSIPED PUSSYCAT RINGTAIL TONKINESE
(— CRY) WAW MEOW MIAOW
(— GROUP) CLOWDER
(BREED OF —) CYMRIC CHARTREUX
(BREED OF —S) RAGDOLL
(FAMOUS —) MORRIS GARFIELD MEHITABEL HEATHCLIFF
(FEMALE —) QUEEN WHEENCAT
(MALE —) GIB TOM TOMCAT
(PART OF —) EAR EYE PAW TOE HEEL KNEE LIPS LOIN NAPE NECK RUMP TAIL BELLY BREAK ELBOW FLANK SHANK THIGH WRIST FEELER DEWCLAW LEATHER WHISKER FOREHEAD SHOULDER VIBRISSA METATARSUS
(ROOF-PROWLING —) TILER
(TAILLESS —) RUMPY
(PREF.) AELUR(O) AILUR(O) FELIN(O)

CATACHRESIS ABUSION

CATACHRESTICAL ABUSIVE

CATACLYSM FLOOD DELUGE DEBACLE DISASTER UPHEAVAL

CATACOMB TOMB CRYPT VAULT CEMETERY HYPOGEUM
(PL.) ARENARIAE

CATADROMOUS SEAGOING

CATAFALQUE BIER COFFIN

CATALECTIC HEMIAMB TRUNCATED

CATALEPSY TRANCE SEIZURE CATATONY

CATALOG PIE PYE BILL BOOK LIST ROLL ROTA BRIEF CANON FLIER FLYER INDEX PINAX AUTHOR RAGGER RAGMAN RECORD ROSTER ARRANGE BEADROW DIPTYCH NOTITIA BEADROLL BULLETIN CALENDAR CLASSIFY REGISTER SCHEDULE SYLLABUS CATALOGUE DIDASCALY INVENTORY

CATALUFA SCAD TORO BIGEYE

CATALYST CARRIER SAUSAGE ZIEGLER CATALYTE HOPCALITE
(NEGATIVE —) INHIBITER

CATAMARAN NAG RAFT TROW BALSA FLOAT NAGGER GUNBOAT JANGADA MONITOR AUNTSARY

CATAMITE INGLE GUNSEL NINGLE PATHIC BARDASH GANYMEDE

CATAMOUNT LION LYNX PUMA COUGAR

CATAPLASM PELOID POULTICE

CATAPULT GUN BIBLE SLING SWEEP THROW HURTLE LAUNCH ONAGER TREPAN ALACRAN BRICOLE PEDRERO TORMENT TRABUCH WARWOLF BALLISTA CROSSBOW DONDAINE LAUNCHER MANGONEL MARTINET SCORPION SPRINGAL STONEBOW

CATARACT LIN FALL LINN FALLS FLOOD PEARL DELUGE CASCADE NIAGARA CATADUPE OVERFALL VICTORIA

CATARRH MUR COLD MURR POSE RHEUM CORYZA NASITIS

CATASTROPHE ACCIDENT CALAMITY DISASTER CATACLYSM

CATCALL HOOT

CATCH BAG COB COG COP GET GIN KEP NAB NET NIP DRAW FANG GLOM HASP HAUL HAWK HENT HOLD HOOK LAND MAKE MEET MESS NAIL NICK PAWL SAVE SEAR SNAG SNAP SNIB STOP TAKE TRAP TREE VANG BENET CHAPE CLASP CLEEK CREEL FETCH GLOVE GRASP HITCH KETCH KNACK LASSO LATCH PLANT SEIZE SNARE SNICK SWOOP TRICK TROLL ARREST ATTAIN BUTTON CLUTCH CORNER CORRAL DETECT DETENT ENGAGE ENMESH ENTRAP IMMESH LOCKET NOBBLE NOODLE SNATCH SPRENT TAIGLE TAKING TURNEL ATTRACT CAPTURE ENSNARE GIMMICK GRAPNEL RELEASE SNIGGLE SPRINGE TRIGGER CONTRACT CRANNAGE ENTANGLE FASTNESS HOLDBACK HOLDFAST OVERTAKE SNAPHAAN SURPRISE
(— A FLYBALL) SHAG
(— AT PROPER TIME) NICK
(— ATTENTION) FLAG
(— BIRDS) BATFOWL BIRDLIME
(— EELS) SNIGGLE
(— FIRE) SPUNK IGNITE KINDLE
(— FISH) JAB JIG GILL HANG GILLNET
(— FISH WITH HANDS) GUDDLE GRABBLE HANDFAST
(— HOLD OF) GRIP GRASP
(— IN THE ACT) NAB
(— IN VOICE) FETCH
(— OF DOOR) LATCH SNECK SNICK
(— OF FISH) FARE HAUL SHOT TACK TRIP SHACK
(— ON) GET GETIT

(**— ONE'S BREATH**) GASP CHINK
(**— SIGHT OF**) SPY ESPY SPOT DESCRY
(**CRICKET —**) DOLLY
(**EASY —**) POPUP
(**RATCHET —**) CLICK
(**SAFETY —**) CLEVIS
CATCHALL RAGBAG
CATCHER TAKER BIRDER FANGER LARKER RECEIVER
CATCHFLY SILENE FLYBANE
CATCHING CATCHY TAKING ALLURING ARRESTING
CATCH-PHRASE SLOGAN WHEEZE
CATCHPOLE BAILIFF PUTTOCK
CATCHWEED CLEAVERS
CATCHWORD CUE TAG MOTTO BYWORD PHRASE SLOGAN STARTER CATCHCRY SHIBBOLETH
CATCHY CATCHING APPEALING
CATCH-22 DILEMMA
CATECHISE QUIZ
CATECHISM QUIZ GUIDE MANUAL CARRITCH QUESTIONS
CATECHU COTCH CUTCH KHAIR GAMBIER
CATECHUMEN PUPIL AUDIENT AUDITOR CONVERT BEGINNER NEOPHYTE COMPETENT
CATEGORICAL DIRECT ABSOLUTE EXPLICIT KNOCKDOWN
CATEGORIZE ZAG CODE HAVE SORT
CATEGORY WAY KING RANK TALE CLASS FIELD GENRE GENUS ORDER STYLE FAMILY LEAGUE NUMBER RUBRIC SERIES SPECIES DIVISION PIGEONHOLE PREDICAMENT
(**— OF TENSES**) INFECTUM
(**BIOLOGICAL —**) TAXON
(**HIGHEST —**) IDEA
(**PRIMARY —**) SUBSTANCE
(**TAXONOMIC —**) FORM FORMA GENUS TAXON COHORT LEGION SUBCLASS SUBGENUS SUBFAMILY
CATENARY ARC
CATER CUT FEED HUMOR SERVE TREAT PANDER PURVEY SUPPLY PROVIDE
(PREF.) OPSONI OPSONO
CATERCOUSIN PAL FRIEND
CATERER ACATER MANCIPLE
CATERINA CORNARO (**CHARACTER IN —**) ANDREAS GERARDO CATERINA MOCENIGO LUSIGNANO
(**COMPOSER OF —**) DONIZETTI
CATERPILLAR CAT MUGA AWETO ERUCA CANKER LOOPER PALMER PORINA RISPER TAILOR WOUBIT CUTWORM TRACTOR WEBWORM HANGWORM HORNWORM SILKWORM SKINWORM WORTWORM PALMERWORM
(PREF.) CAMPO ERUCI
(SUFF.) CAMPA
CATERWAUL CRY HOWL WAIL MIAUL WRAWL
CATFACE ARR SCAR
CATFISH MUD CUSK ELOD POUT RAAD SHAL WOOF BAGRE DORAD RAASH BARBER DOCMAC GLANIS GOONCH GOUJON HASSAR MADTOM MUDCAT BARBUDO CANDIRU COBBLER FIDDLER PYGIDID SILURID WALLAGO BULLHEAD BULLPOUT CORYDORA FLATHEAD MATHEMEG PLOTOSID SQUEAKER STONECAT
CATGUT THARM THAIRM CATLING WHIPCORD
CATHARI BULGARI PATARINE
CATHARTIC ALOIN BRYONY PHYSIC CALOMEL RHUBARB SCOURER EUONYMUS EVACUANT HYDRAGOG KALADANA LAPACTIC LAXATIVE SCAMMONY SOLUTIVE SOLUTORY PURGATIVE PODOPHYLLIN
CATHAYAN KITAN
CATHEDRA SEE
CATHEDRAL DOM SEE DUOMO SOBOR MARTYRY MEMORIA MINSTER BASILICA
(**PART OF —**) ARCH ROOF CROSS GABLE IMAGE LABEL SPIRE TOWER BELFRY FINIAL LINTEL LOUVER PORTAL WINDOW CROCKET GALLERY LOZENGE MOLDING MULLION TRACERY TREFOIL PINNACLE TYMPANUM DRIPSTONE THROATING TRIFORIUM CINQUEFOIL CLERESTORY QUATREFOIL
CATHEXIS CHARGE
CATHODE K KA FILAMENT ELECTRODE HYDROGODE
CATHOLIC BROAD GENERAL LIBERAL TOLERANT
(**— ORDER**) MARIST DOMINICAN FRANCISCAN
CATHOLICISM PAPISM POPERY
CATHOLICON PANACEA
CATKIN RAG TAG CHAT GULL AGLET AMENT IULUS PUSSY CACHRYS CATTAIL GOSLING
(PREF.) AMENTI
CATMINT NEP NIP
CATNAP NAP DOZE
CATNIP NEP CATARIA CATMINT CATWORT
CATREUS (**DAUGHTER OF —**) AEROPE CLYMENE APEMOSYNE
(**FATHER OF —**) MINOS
(**MOTHER OF —**) PASIPHAE
(**SON OF —**) ALTHAEMENES
CAT'S-CLAW LONGPOD ESCAMBRON
CAT'S CRADLE HEI
CAT'S-EAR GOSMORE CAPEWEED FLATWEED
CAT'S EYE CHATOYANT
CAT'S-FOOT PUSSYTOE
CAT'S-PAW TOOL PROPERTY
CAT'S-TAIL BULRUSH
CATTAIL DOD DODD FLAG MUSK RUSH TULE AMENT BAYON BLECK CLOUD RAUPO REREE WONGA CATKIN GLADEN TOTORA BULRUSH GLADDON MATREED BLACKCAP CARBUNGI FLAXTAIL
CAT THYME HULWORT
CATTLE ZO BOW FEE GIR AVER DHAN GAUR KINE NEAT NOWT OXEN ZEBU ZOBO DEVON STOCK ANKOLI DURHAM GALYAK ONGOLE ROTHER SINDHI SUSSEX BESTIAL NELLORE REDPOLL COMPOUND OUTSIGHT TUBICORN
(**— CARRIED OFF**) SPREATH
(**ASIAN DAIRY —**) REDSINDHI
(**BREED OF —**) ANGUS BORAN DEVON FJALL KERRY KYLOE SANGA SANGU ANGONI ANKOLE ANKOLI DEXTER DURHAM FULANI JERSEY SUSSEX BAROTSE BRAFORD BRAHMAN BRANGUS COASTER CRIOLLA GUZERAT HARIANA SAHIWAL ALDERNEY AYRSHIRE CHARBRAY FRIBOURG FRIESIAN GALLOWAY GUERNSEY HEREFORD HOLSTEIN KANGAYAM LIMOUSIN LONGHORN
(**DWARF —**) NATA NIATA
(**WILD YOUNG —**) KANGAROO
(PREF.) BOVI
CATTLE-BREEDER AHIR ALUR
CATTLE DEALER DROVER
CATTLEHIDE BUFF CROUPON
CATTLEMAN FAZENDEIRO
CATTLE MARKET SALEYARD
CATTLE PEN KRAAL
CATTLE RAID SPRAITH SPREAGH
CATTLE RUN STATION
CATTLE STEALER ABACTOR ABIGEUS
CATTLE YARD CANCHA
CATTY KIN KATI SNIDE
CAUCASIAN OSSET WHITE OSSETE IRANIAN EUROPEAN JAPHETIC PALEFACE
(**— LANGUAGE**) UDI UDIC UDIN
(PL.) MELANOI
CAUCHO ULE RUBBER
CAUCUS BLOC PRIMARY
CAUDAL POSTERIOR
(PREF.) UR(O)
CAUDATA URODELA
CAUDEX STEM STIPE
CAUGHT GRIPPIT ENTANGLED
(**— AT FAULT**) TARDY
CAUL HOW WEB KEEL KELL TRUG VEIL GALEA HOUVE DORLOT CREPINE KERCHER NETWORK OMENTUM MEMBRANE SILLYHOW TRESSOUR TRESSURE
(PREF.) AMNIO OMENT(O)
CAULDRON KOHUA CALDRON
CAULICLE SCAPEL ROSTELLUM
CAULIFLOWER BROCCOLI SNOWBALL CHOUFLEUR
CAULK CALK CORK FILL FLAG CHINSE
CAUNUS (**FATHER OF —**) MILETUS
(**MOTHER OF —**) CYANEE
(**SISTER OF —**) BYBLIS
CAUSAL GENETIC
CAUSE DO AIM GAR ISM KEY LET WAY CASE CHAT FATE HOTI LEAD MAKE MOVE ROOT SAKE SPUR SUIT AGENT ARCHE BASIS BREED CAUSA FRAME PARTY SETUP SKILL SLAKE WREAK YIELD ADDICT CREATE EFFECT ELICIT GOSSIP GROUND INDUCE INVOKE MALADY MANNER MATTER MOTIVE OBJECT ORIGIN PARENT REASON RESORT SOURCE SPEECH SPRING CHESOUN CONCERN DISEASE LAWSUIT PROCURE PRODUCE PROVOKE QUARREL SUBJECT BUSINESS ENGENDER GENERATE INSTANCE MOVEMENT OCCASION WHEREFORE MAINSPRING
(**— A SORE**) RANKLE
(**— DAMAGE**) DAMNIFY
(**— FOR COMPLAINT**) COMEBACK
(**— OF ANXIETY**) BUGABOO
(**— OF IRRITATION**) GALL
(**— OF PAIN**) DISEASE
(**— OF QUARREL**) GRUDGE
(**— OF RUIN**) BANE
(**— OF SORROW**) GRIEF
(**— OF TERROR**) AFFRIGHT
(**— OF TROUBLE**) TRACHLE
(**— PAIN**) URN
(**— TO ARCH**) ROACH
(**— TO CONTRACT**) PUCKER
(**— TO CROUCH**) COUCH
(**— TO DESERT**) DEFECT
(**— TO END**) ACHIEVE
(**— TO GO**) HAVE
(**— TO MOVE RAPIDLY**) GIG
(**— TO PROJECT**) JET
(**— TO RESULT**) ISSUE
(**— TO STICK**) MIRE
(**— TO SWELL**) BINGE EMBOSS
(**— TO THICKEN**) CURD
(**COMMITTED TO A —**) ENGAGE
(**FINAL —**) END
(**FORM-GIVING —**) IDEA
(**IMMEDIATE —**) SIGNAL
(**PRIMAL —**) URGRUND
(PREF.) AETIO AITIO CAUSI ETIO
(SUFF.) FIC(AL)(ATE)(ATION)(ATIVE)(ATOR)(ATORY)(E)(ENCE)(ENT)(IAL)(IARY)(IENT) FIQUE
CAUSED
(SUFF.) (**— BY**) IC(AL)
CAUSER (**— OF TROUBLE**) BOLSHEVIK
CAUSERIE CHAT
CAUSEWAY WAY DIKE ROAD HIGHWAY CHAUSSEE
CAUSING
(SUFF.) ABLE FACIENT FACT(ION)(IVE)(ORY) FIC IBLE
CAUSTIC LYE ACID TART ACRID QUICK SALTY SHARP SNELL ACIDIC BITING BITTER SEVERE BURNING CAUTERY CUTTING ERODENT MORDANT NIPPING PUNGENT PYROTIC SATIRIC ALKALINE DIERETIC SCATHING SNAPPISH STINGING ACIDULOUS SARCASTIC MORDACIOUS
CAUSTICITY ACRIMONY
CAUTERIZATION USTION INUSTION
CAUTERIZE BURN CHAR FIRE SEAR BRAND INUST SINGE
CAUTERY MOXA
CAUTION CARE FEAR HEED WARN GUARD ADVICE CAUTEL CAVEAT EXHORT ANXIETY COUNSEL PRECEPT PROVISO WARNING ADMONISH FORECAST FOREWARN MONITION PRUDENCE WARINESS
CAUTIOUS SHY CAGY SAFE WARE WARY ALERT CANNY CHARY SIKER FABIAN HOOLIE SICKER TENDER TIPTOE CAREFUL CURIOUS ENVIOUS FEARFUL FERDFUL

GUARDED PRUDENT DISCREET SUSPENSE VIGILANT CAUTELOUS
CAUTIOUSLY CANNY CANNILY CHARILY EASYLIKE GINGERLY TENDERLY
CAVAL
(PREF.) VEN(I)(O)
CAVALCADE RAID RIDE MARCH TRAIN PARADE SAFARI COMPANY JOURNEY PAGEANT
CAVALIER GAY CAVY CURT EASY FINE BOSSY BRAVE FRANK MOUNT RIDER ESCORT KNIGHT BRUSQUE GALLANT HAUGHTY OFFHAND SOLDIER CAVALERO ROYALIST CHAMBERER CHEVALIER COMMANDER
CAVALLA CERO JACK TORO ULUA JUREL CARANX CARANGID CREVALLE SCOMBRID
CAVALLERIA RUSTICANA
(CHARACTER IN —) LOLA ALFIO TURIDDU SANTUZZA
(COMPOSER OF —) MASCAGNI
CAVALRY HORSE HEAVIES CHIVALRY HORSEMEN YEOMANRY
CAVALRYMAN SOWAR SPAHI SUWAR HUSSAR JINETE LANCER REITER ARGOLET COURIER DRAGOON PLUNGER SABREUR TROOPER GENDARME HORSEMAN SILLADAR STRADIOT
(PRUSSIAN —) UHLAN
(PL.) FORAGERS
CAVATINA SOLO
CAVE DEN TIP COVE HOLE LAIR MINE REAR SINK TOSS WEEM ANTAR ANTRE CABIN CACHE CALVE CAVEA CRYPT DELVE FOGOU SLADE SPEOS STORE UPSET BEWARE CAVERN CAVITY CELLAR DUGOUT GROTTO HOLLOW LARDER LUSTER PANTRY PLUNGE SHROUD MANSION RESERVE SPELUNK CASTILLO COLLAPSE OVERTURN MITHRAEUM
(— IN) COLT
(ANIMAL LIVING IN —) TROGLODYTE
(ONE WHO EXPLORES —S) SPELUNKER
(PREF.) SPELEO
CAVEAT BEWARE NOTICE CAUTION WARNING
CAVE-DWELLER HORITE TROGLODYTE
CAVE-DWELLING NATUFIAN
(PREF.) TROGLO
CAVEMAN NEANDERTHAL
CAVER SPELUNKER
CAVERN DEN CAVE COVE GROT HOLE LAIR WEEM CROFT VAULT ANTRUM CAVITY GROTTO HOLLOW SPELUNK
(PREF.) ANTR(O)
CAVERNOUS ERECTILE
CAVESSON CHAIN
CAVETTO GULA GORGE
CAVIAR OVA ROE IKRA GARUM IKARY BELUGA OSETRA OSSETRA SEVRUGA
CAVIL CARK CARP HAFT QUIP HAGGLE CAPTION CHICANE QUARREL QUIBBLE PETTIFOG QUIDDITY FORMALIZE
CAVILER CRITIC GIRDER HAFTER ZOILUS
CAVILING CAPTIOUS CRITICAL PICAYUNE
CAVITIED
(SUFF.) COELOUS COELUS
CAVITY BAG CUP PIT SAC ABRI AXIL CASE CAVE CELL DALK DENT DUCT HOLE MIND MINE VEIN VOID WELL WOMB ABYSS BOSOM BURSA CRYPT DRUSE FOSSA GEODE GOUGE LUMEN MOUTH ORBIT SCOOP SINUS ANTRUM AREOLA AREOLE ATRIUM AXILLA BORING CAECUM CAMERA CAVERN COELIA COELOM COTYLE CRATER DEBLAI GROTTO HOLLOW LACUNA POCKET RECESS SCAPHA SOCKET VACUUM VOMICA ABDOMEN CHAMBER CISTERN CYATHUS DIOCOEL KYATHOS LOCULUS MORTISE VACUITY VACUOLE VESICLE ALVEOLUS BROODSAC EPICOELE FOLLICLE WELLHOLE VESTIBULE
(— IN BONE) LACUNA
(— IN CASTING) PIPE
(— IN FRUIT) VITTA
(— IN GLASS) TEAR
(— IN HEAD OF WHALE) CASE
(— IN HEART) AURICLE
(— IN HILLSIDE) ABRI
(— IN LAVA) AMYGDALE AMYGDULE
(— IN MINE) BAG
(— IN ROCK) KETTLE
(— MADE BY SEALS) IGLOO
(— OF SEA-SHELL) FLUE
(ALTAR —) TOMB
(ANATOMICAL —) LUMEN
(BAKING —) OVEN
(BODY —) GUT BELLY CLOACA THORAX ABDOMEN STOMACH PSEUDOCOEL PERICARDIUM
(CHEST —) THORAX
(CRYSTAL-LINED —) VUGG DRUSE GEODE
(DEEP —) WOMB
(EAR —) CONCHA COCHLEA
(GUN —) BORE
(NASAL —) CAVUM
(SUBTERRANEAN —) SLUGGA
(UNFILLED — IN ROCK) VUG
(PREF.) ALVEOL(I)(O) ANTR(O) CAEC(I)(O) CEC(I)(O) CEL(I)(O) COEL(I)(O)
(SUFF.) CELE COELE COELUS
CAVORT PLAY BOUND CAPER CURVET GAMBOL PRANCE
CAVY PACA PONY AGOUTI APEREA CAYUSE CAPYBARA
(FEMALE —) SOW
CAW KA CRY CALL CROAK QUARK QUAWK
CAY ILOT
CAYMAN JACARE
CAYSTER (DAUGHTER OF —) SEMIRAMIS
(FATHER OF —) ACHILLES
(MOTHER OF —) PENTHESILEA
CAYUSE CAVY PONY BRONCO MUSTANG
CEASE HO BOW CUT DIE END LIN BALK BLIN DROP FINE HALT HOLD LIFT LISS QUIT REST SACE SHUT STAY STOP STOW AVAST CLOSE DOWSE LEAVE PAUSE PETER STINT SWICK WAIVE DESIST DEVALL EXPIRE FINISH FORGET ABSTAIN OUTGIVE REFRAIN SUSPEND INTERMIT OVERGIVE SURCEASE
(— FIGHTING) YIELD
(— MILKING COW) SINE
(— TEMPORARILY) LIFT
(— TO ASSERT) ABANDON
(— TO EXIST) VANISH
(— TO FLOW) STANCH STAUNCH
CEASELESS EVER ENDLESS ETERNAL IMMORTAL UNENDING
CEASING CESSER CESSATION
CEBUS SAI
CECILIA SIS SISSU
CECROPS (DAUGHTER OF —) HERSE AGLAUROS PANDROSOS
(WIFE OF —) AGLAURUS
CECUM
(PREF.) TYPHL(O)
CEDAR SUGI TOON SAVIN AROLLA DEODAR SABINA TUMION CYPRESS JUNIPER WAXWING CALANTAS PAHAUTEA
CEDAR SWAMP GREENING
CEDAR WAXWING RECOLLET
CEDE CESS GIVE AWARD GRANT LEAVE WAIVE YIELD ASSIGN RESIGN SUBMIT CONCEDE RENOUNCE TRANSFER
CEDILLA TITTLE
CEIBA KAPOK BENTANG POCHOTE
CEIL LINE SYLE OVERLAY WAINSCOT
CEILING CAP TOP DOME LACE LOFT CHUTT CUPOLA LINING SCREEN SOFFIT SYLING CURTAIN LACUNAR PLAFOND TESTUDO COVERING DECKHAND OVERHEAD PANELING PLANCHER SEMIDOME
CELAENO (FATHER OF —) ATLAS
(MOTHER OF —) PLEIONE
(SON OF —) LYCUS NYCTEUS
CELANDINE FICARY KILLWORT PILEWORT WARTWEED WARTWORT FELONWORT JEWELWEED
CELEBES (GULF OF —) BONE TOLO TOMINI
(ISLAND OF —) MUNA BUTUNG PELENG SULAWESI
(PEOPLE OF —) TORAJA
(TOWN OF —) BUOL LUWUK MANADO MAKASAR
CELEBRANT REVELER
CELEBRATE FETE KEEP SING CHANT DITTY EXTOL HONOR REVEL SACRE SOUND SPEAK BESING CHAUNT EXTOLL PRAISE RECORD RENOWN REPEAT ELEGIZE EXECUTE GLORIFY MAFFICK OBSERVE TRUMPET EMBLAZON EULOGIZE PROCLAIM
(— VICTORY) TRIUMPH
(— 2 MASSES) BINATE DUPLICATE
CELEBRATED KEPT FAMED NOTED FAMOUS EMINENT FEASTED RENOMME STORIED FABULOUS GLORIOUS NOTIFIED OBSERVED RENOWNED
CELEBRATION EED FETE GALA POPE RITE FESTA REVEL COOLIN CUSTOM DOMENT EASTER FIESTA HOOPLA POWWOW RENOWN SIMHAH BLOWOUT HAGMENA HOLIDAY JUBILEE PASCHAL SHINDIG SIMCHAH BINATION BIRTHDAY HOGMANAY MAKAHIKI OCCASION OLYMPIAD POTLATCH SHIVAREE FESTIVITY HOOLAULEA JUNKETING MERRIMENT MILLENIUM
(LIVELY —) RAVEUP
(STUDENT —) GAUDEAMUS
(UNRESTRAINED —) ORGY
(WILD —) ORGY SATURNALIA
CELEBRATOR JUBILIST
CELEBRITY FAME LION NAME STAR CELEB ECLAT RENOWN REPUTE
(PL.) GLITTERATI
CELERITY HASTE HURRY SPEED DISPATCH RAPIDITY VELOCITY SWIFTNESS
CELERY SIT ACHE STICK UMBEL KARPAS SALARY CELERIAC SMALLAGE
CELESTIAL HOLY ASTRAL DIVINE HEAVEN URANIC ANGELIC CHINESE ETHERED EMPYREAL ETHEREAL HEAVENLY OLYMPIAN
(— OBJECT) QUASAR
CELESTITE APOTOME
CELEUS (SON OF —) DEMOPHON TRIPTOLEMUS
(WIFE OF —) METANIRA
CELIBACY CHASTITY VIRGINITY
CELIBATE CLERK CHASTE SINGLE BACHELOR SPINSTER
CELL BOX EGG BAND BOOT CAGE CYTE DISC DISK GERM GONE HOLE JAIL KILL ASCUS CABIN CAROL CLINK CRYPT CYTON FIBER FIBRE GHOST GLAND GROUP OOTID TMEMA TORIL VAULT ZOOID ANAXON CEPTOR COCCUS COOLER CYTODE GAMETE GONIUM INAXON NEURON PRISON SHIELD SIPHON SYPHON WESTON ZYGOTE AGAMETE AMEBULA APOCYTE CELLULE CHAMBER CLOCHAN CLOSTER COCCOID CUBICLE DIPLOID DUNGEON ELEMENT EPICYTE EUPLOID HAPLOID HEMATID INITIAL LOCULUS MYOCYTE NEURONE OOBLAST PAPILLA PLASTID RENETTE SEGMENT SPORONT STEREID TRISOME UTRICLE VESICLE AMACRINE BASOCYTE BASOPHIL BIFORINE BIOPLAST CLOGHAUN DIKARYON FAVEOLUS GLIOCYTE GONIDIUM GONOCYTE HEMOCYTE HOLDOVER IDIOSOME LOCELLUS MYOBLAST ORGANULE PROSORUS RECEPTOR SCLEREID SPERMULE SYNERGID TRACHEID TRIPLOID ZOOBLAST MACROCYTE MICROCYTE MYELOCYTE

OSTEOCYTE PHAGOCYTE PROGAMETE MELANOCYTE MOTONEURON NEUTROPHIL OSTEOCLAST MELANOBLAST MELANOPHORE ODONTOBLAST
(— CONTAINING LATEX) LATICIFER
(— OF LEADERS) CADRE
(— OF TEMPLE) NAOS
(BEE —) PIPE
(CLUSTER OF —S) MORULA
(DETENTION —) BULLPEN
(DRY —) NICAD
(EGG —) OVUM
(KIND OF —) LIP HELA KILLER MOTHER
(NERVE —) NEURON NEURONE
(PART OF —) SAP NUCLEUS PLASTID VACUOLE MEMBRANE CENTRIOLE ECTOPLASM ENDOPLASM NUCLEOLUS RETICULUM CENTROSOME CHONDRIOSOME
(PHOTOELECTRIC —) EYE PEC PHOTOCELL
(PLANT —) LATICIFER
(PRISON —) BING HOLE CABIN CLINK COOLER JIGGER
(RECLUSE'S —)) ANCHORAGE
(STAB —) BAND
(THIN-WALLED —S) STOMIUM
(VOLTAIC —) BATTERY
(PL.) SPOR LAURA POTLINE SWEATBOX
(PREF.) CYT(IO)(O) GAMET(O) GONIDI ONT(O) THYRE(O) THYRO
(SUFF.) BLAST(IC)(Y) CYTE PHAG(A) (E)(O)(OUS)(US)(Y) PLASIA PLASIS PLASM(A)(IA)(IC) PLAST PLATI(IC)(Y) SPONGIA(E)(N) SPONGIUM THYRIS

CELLA NAOS
CELLAR CAVE VAULT BODEGA PALACE FAVISSA HYPOGEE BASEMENT HYPOGEUM MATAMORO VAULTAGE
(WINE —) BODEGA
CELLARET TANTALUS
CELLARMAN SOMMELIER
CELL-DIVISION MEIOSIS
CELLULAR
(SUFF.) ENCHYMA ENCHYMATA
CELLULOID XYLONITE
CELLULOSE CRUMB AMYLOID LIGNOSE TAMIDINE
CELT GAEL GAUL KELT MANX IRISH WELSH BRETON BRITON EOLITH GADHEL GOIDEL BRYTHON CORNISH PALSTAFF PALSTAVE
(PL.) CYMRY KYMRY
CELTIC ERSE GAEL SCOTCH
CEMBALO DULCIMER ZIMBALON
CEMENT FIX KIT TIE GLUE HEAL JOIN KNIT LIME LUTE SLIP BETON GROUT IMBED PASTE PUTTY SIMON STICK TABBY UNITE BINDER CHUNAM COHERE FASTEN FILLER GULGUL KIBOSH MALTHA MASTIC MORTAR OOGLEA SOLDER ASPHALT MIXTION ADHESIVE ALBOLITE ALBOLITH CEMENTUM HADIGEON SOLIDIFY SOLUTION
(BEES' —) PROPOLIS
(SUFF.) LITE LITH(IC) LITIC
CEMENTER GLUER GLUEMAN SMEARER
CEMENT MIXER TEMPERER
CEMETERY HOWF KILL LAIR LITTEN CHARNEL BONEYARD CATACOMB GOLGOTHA URNFIELD NECROPOLIS
CENCHRIAS (FATHER OF —) POSEIDON
(MOTHER OF —) PIRENE
(SLAYER OF —) ARTEMIS
CENCI (AUTHOR OF —) SHELLEY
(CHARACTER IN —) CENCI MARZIO ORSINO CAMILLO GIACOMO OLIMPIO SAVELLA BEATRICE BERNARDO LUCRETIA
CENERENTOLA, LA (CHARACTER IN —) TISBE RAMIRO ALIDORO DANDINI ANGELINA CLORINDA MAGNIFICO CINDERELLA
(COMPOSER OF —) ROSSINI
CENOBITE NUN MONK FRIAR ESSENE RECLUSE MONASTIC SYNODITE
CENOTAPH TOMB
CENSE THURIFY
CENSER INCENSER THURIBLE CASSOLETTE
CENSOR CRITIC SCREEN SYNDIC LAUNDER RESTRICT SUPPRESS
CENSORIOUS SEVERE BLAMING CARPING BLAMEFUL CAPTIOUS CRITICAL CULPABLE SLASHING
CENSORSHIP WRAPS ASSIZE CENSURE
CENSURABLE TAXABLE BLAMABLE CULPABLE
CENSURE BAN HIT NIP RAP TAP TAX WIG CALL CARP DEEM DRUB FLAY HELL LASH RATE SLAP TASK WITE BEANS BLAME CHIDE CURSE DECRY FAULT HOKER JUDGE PINCH SCOLD SLANG SLASH SLATE TAUNT TOUCH WHITE ACCUSE ATTACK BERATE CHARGE REBUFF REBUKE REFORM REMORD STRAFE TARGUE TIRADE APPEACH BLISTER CHASTEN CONDEMN CONTROL DECRIAL DYSLOGY IMPEACH IMPROVE INVEIGH REPROOF REPROVE SCARIFY TRADUCE TROUNCE UPBRAID BACKBITE CHASTISE DISALLOW JUDGMENT LANGUAGE REPROACH SATIRIZE SENTENCE STRICTURE ADMONITION
(GOD OF —) MOMUS
CENSUS LIST POLL CENSE COUNT LUSTER LUSTRUM CAPITATION
CENT RED DUIT SANT BROWNIE CENTAVO STUIVER
(FIVE —S) JITNEY NICKEL
(ODD —S) BREAKAGE
(ONE —) PENNY
(TEN —S) DIME
(TWENTY-FIVE —S) QUARTER
(12 1-2 —S) LEVY
CENTAUR CHIRON NESSUS HORSEMAN BUCENTAUR SAGITTARY
CENTAURUS (FATHER OF —) IXION
(MOTHER OF —) NEPHELE
CENTAURY BEHN BEHEN SABBATIA EARTHGALL
CENTENNIAL STATE COLORADO
CENTER COR EYE GIG HUB MID AXIS CORE NAVE SEAT SNAP YOLK FOCUS FOYER GLOME HEART MIDST NEXUS PIVOT SPINE BOTTOM CENTRE MIDDLE PIPPER STAPLE TEMPLE CENTRUM ESSENCE LINEMAN NUCLEUS UMBILIC INCENTER OMPHALOS SNAPBACK
(— FOR SPINDLE) GIG
(— FOR TARGET) EYE PIN PINHOLE
(— OF ACTIVITY) HUB HIVE
(— OF ARCH) COOM
(— OF ASSURANCE) FORTRESS
(— OF ATTRACTION) FOCUS STAGE CYNOSURE POLESTAR
(— OF BASKET) SLATHER
(— OF CITY) DOWNTOWN
(— OF CULTIVATION) HOME
(— OF CULTURE) ATHENS
(— OF DIAMOND) WELL
(— OF ESCUTCHEON) NOMBRIL
(— OF FIGURE) CENTROID
(— OF FISHING NET) BUNT
(— OF FLOWER) EYE
(— OF HURRICANE) EYE
(— OF OPERATIONS) SHOP
(— OF POPULATION) CITY
(— OF POWER) SEE SIEGE
(— OF STAGE) LIMELIGHT
(— OF STRENGTH) GANGLION
(— PIECE) HUB
(BASKETBALL —) PIVOTMAN
(COLLECTION —) ENTREPOT
(COMMERCIAL —) MALL MART MACHI EMPORIUM
(HARD —) KNOT
(INTIMATE —) BOSOM
(KIND OF —) NERVE
(LATHE —) PIKE
(NERVOUS —) BRAIN NIDUS
(NEURAL —) APPESTAT
(OFF —) ALOP
(PROPAGANDA —) AGITPUNKT
(RECREATION —) ARCADE
(REHABILITATION —) HOSTEL
(SHOPPING —) MALL
(TOWARD —) ENTAD
(TRADING —) BEACH EXCHANGE
(VITAL —) HEARTH HEARTBEAT
(PREF.) CENTR(I)(O)
(SUFF.) CENTRIC
CENTERING COOM COOMB CENTRY FANTAIL
CENTERPIECE ROSACE DORMANT EPERGNE DUCHESSE
CENTETES TENREC
CENTIARE LI
CENTIGRADE CELSIUS
CENTIME RAPPEN
CENTIMETER GAL
CENTIPEDE VEI VERI EARWIG GOLACH GOLOCH POLYPOD CHILOPOD MULTIPED MYRIAPOD SANTAPEE SCUTIGER SCOLOPENDRA
CENTRAL MID AXIAL BASIC CHIEF FOCAL MIXED POLAR PRIME MEDIAN MIDDLE CAPITAL CENTRIC LEADING NUCLEAR PIVOTAL PRIMARY CARDINAL DOMINANT
(PREF.) CENTR(I)(O)

CENTRAL AFRICAN REPUBLIC
CAPITAL: BANGUI
COIN: FRANC
NATIVE: BAYA SARA BANDA BWAKA SANGO YAKOMA BANZIRI MANDJIA
RIVER: BOMU NANA CHARI KOTTO MBARI MPOKO OUAKA OUHAM CHINKO LOBAYE SANGHA UBANGI
TOWN: OBO IPPY BIRAO BOUAR KEMBE NDELE NGOTO PAOUA RAFAI ZEMIO BABOUA BAKALA BANGUI BOZOUM BAMBARI GRIMARI ZEMONGO BERBERATI BOSSANGOA

CENTRAL AMERICAN LADINO
(— NATION) BELIZE PANAMA HONDURAS COSTARICA
(— TREE) TUNO TUNU
CENTRANTH SPURFLOWER
CENTRIFUGAL EFFERENT RADIATING
CENTRIFUGE CYCLONE SEPARATOR
CENTRIPETAL AFFERENT
CENTROSOME CENTRUM CENTRIOLE
CENTRUM CORE
CENTURIED SECULAR
CENTURY AGE TON SECLE SIECLE
(14TH —) TRECENTO
(17TH —) SEICENTO
CENTURY PLANT ALOE PITA AGAVE MAGUEY CANTALA TEQUILA MONOCARP
CENWALH (FATHER OF —) CYNEGILS
CEPHALALGIA SODA HEADACHE
CEPHALIC CRANIAL ATLANTAL CEREBRAL
CEPHALOPOD SQUID CUTTLE INKFISH OCTOPUS SPIRULA DIBRANCH SCAPHITE
CEPHALOTHORAX PROSOMA
CEPHALUS (FATHER OF —) DEION
(MOTHER OF —) DIOMEDE
(WIFE OF —) PROCRIS
CEPHEUS (BROTHER OF —) DANAUS AEGYPTUS AMPHIDAMAS
(DAUGHTER OF —) ANDROMEDA
(FATHER OF —) ALEUS BELUS
(MOTHER OF —) ANCHINOE
(WIFE OF —) CASSIOPEA
CERAMIC (— WARE) WEDGWOOD
CERAMICS TILES POTTERY
CERAMUS (FATHER OF —) BACCHUS DIONYSUS
(MOTHER OF —) ARIADNE
CERASTES ASP VIPER
CERATE WAX LARD SALVE UNGUENT OINTMENT
CERCYON (DAUGHTER OF —) ALOPE
(FATHER OF —) NEPTUNE POSEIDON HEPHAESTUS
(SLAYER OF —) THESEUS
CEREAL RYE BEAN BRAN CORN MUSH OATS RICE SAMP TEFF ARZUN GRAIN MAIZE SPELT WHEAT BARLEY BINDER FARINA HOMINY PABLUM OATMEAL SOYBEAN PORRIDGE
CEREAL LEAF FLAG

CEREBRAL CEPHALIC INVERTED (PREF.) PSYCH(O)
CEREBRATION THOUGHT
CEREBROSIDE KERASIN
CEREMENT SHROUD
CEREMONIAL FORM PRIM RITE STIFF FORMAL RIALTY RITUAL SOLEMN PRECISE STUDIED TRIUMPH UPANAYA AVERSION SPLENDOR
(FOOLISH —) MUMMERY
CEREMONIOUS GRAND LOFTY STIFF FORMAL PROPER SOLEMN PRECISE STATELY STUDIED
CEREMONY BRIS FETE FORM GAUD HAKO ORGY POMP RITE SEAL SHOW SIGN SING BERIT DANCE DOSEH STATE ACTION AUGURY BERITH BRIDAL BURIAL EXEQUY GOMBAY HOMAGE KERIAH MALKAH MAUNDY NIPTER OFFICE PARADE POWWOW REVIEW RITUAL SALUTE BAPTISM DISPLAY KIDDUSH MELAVEH OVATION PAGEANT PANAGIA PORTENT PRODIGY TAHARAH ACCOLADE APOLUSIS ASPERGES COEMPTIO CRIOBOLY ENCAENIA EXERCISE FUNCTION HABDALAH HAKAFOTH HERALDRY MARRIAGE OCCASION SKEYTING INAUGURAL INDUCTION ORDINANCE CORONATION OBSERVANCE
(GRADUATION —) CAPPING
(HAZING —) CREELING
(MARRIAGE —) ESPOUSAL
(TEA —) CHANOYU
(PL.) DEGREE HOLIES AGENDUM FERALIA JUSTMENTS
CERES DEMETER
(DAUGHTER OF —) PROSERPINE PHERREPHATTA
(FATHER OF —) SATURN
(MOTHER OF —) VESTA
CERINTHE HONEYWORT
CERO SEARER SIERRA CAVALLA PINTADO KINGFISH
CERTAIN COLD COOL DEAD FAST FIRM FREE REAL SEAL SURE TRUE BOUND CLEAR EXACT FIXED PLAIN SIKER ACTUAL MEMORY SECURE SICKER STATED WITTER ASSURED PERFECT PRECISE SETTLED SRADDHA ABSOLUTE APPARENT CONSTANT DEFINITE OFFICIAL PALPABLE POSITIVE RELIABLE RESOLVED UNERRING CONFIDENT
CERTAINLY AY AYE WIS AMEN IWIS SOON SURE WHAT YWIS TRULY CERTES INDEED PERDIE SICCAR SICKER SURELY VERILY HARDILY EVERMORE FORSOOTH SECURELY NATURALLY
(MOST —) SO
CERTAINTY YEA CERT PIPE SNIP CINCH POLICY SURETY SURENESS CONSTANCY
(LACK OF —) SCRUPLE
CERTIFICATE BOND CHIT CHECK DEMIT JURAT LIBEL SCRIP TALON TITLE AMPARO ATTEST CEDULA COUPON INDENT PATENT POTTAH RETURN TICKET VERIFY CERTIFY CONSTAT DIPLOMA VOUCHER WARRANT WAYBILL AEGROTAT JUDGMENT KABBALAH NAVICERT REGISTER REGISTRY SECURITY TESCARIA TESTAMUR TEZKIRAH NOTARIZATION
(CUSTOMHOUSE —) COCKET
(MARRIAGE —) LINES
(MINER'S —) LICENCE LICENSE
(PILOT'S —) BRANCH
(SERVANT'S —) CHIT
CERTIFICATION PASS STAMP APPROVAL HECHSHER CLEARANCE DISCHARGE
CERTIFIED SWORN
CERTIFY AVOW VISE AUDIT SWEAR AFFIRM ASSURE ATTEST DEPOSE EVINCE VERIFY WITTER APPROVE ENDORSE LICENSE TESTIFY ACCREDIT
CERTITUDE CERTAIN CONFIDENCE
CERULEAN BLUE AZURE COELIN CYANEAN CYANEOUS
CERUMEN WAX EARWAX
CERVIX NECK
CESS BOG TAX CEDE DUTY LEVY LUCK RATE ABWAB SLOPE YIELD IMPOST MEASURE SURRENDER
(BAD —) SORRA
CESSATION HO END HOO BLIN HALT HUSH LISS LULL REST STAY STOP BREAK CEASE CLOSE DEVAL LETUP LISSE PAUSE SLACK STINT TRUCE CUTOFF DEMISE DISUSE OFFSET PERIOD RECESS CEASING CLOSURE RESPITE ABEYANCE BLACKOUT DESITION INTERVAL SHUTDOWN STOPPAGE SURCEASE SUSPENSE
(— OF HOSTILITIES) TRUCE INDUCIAE ARMISTICE
(— OF LIFE) DEATH
(— OF RESPIRATION) APNEA APNOEA
(— OF WAR) PEACE
(— OF WORK) HARTAL
(DECREED —) MORATORIUM
(TEMPORARY —) RESPITE
CESSPOOL SINK SUMP SINKER CISTERN JAWHOLE SINKHOLE SUSPIRAL
CESTODE POLYZOAN TAPEWORM
CESTRUM POISONBERRY
CESTUS CEST CESTON HURLBAT GAUNTLET WHIRLBAT
CETACEAN ORC CETE ORCA SUSU WHALE BELUGA COWFISH DOLPHIN GRAMPUS NARWHAL MUTILATE PORPOISE
CETO (BROTHER OF —) PHORCYS
(DAUGHTERS OF —) GRAEAE GORGONS HESPERIDES
(FATHER OF —) PONTUS
(MOTHER OF —) GAEA
CEYLON (SEE SRI LANKA) SERENDIP TAPROBANE
CEYLONESE CEYLON BURGHER
CEYLON MOSS GULAMAN
CGS UNIT STILB STOKE
CHA TSIA CHAIS
CHACMA BAVIAN BOBBEJAAN

CHAD
CAPITAL: NDJAMENA
COIN: FRANC FRANCCFA
LAKE: CHAD
NATIVE: ARAB SARA KREDA MASSA TOUBOU KAMADJA MOUNDAN
PLATEAU: ENNEDI
RIVER: CHARI SHARI LOGONE BAHRAOUK
TOWN: ATI BOL LAI MAO FADA FAYA MONGO ABECHE BOKORO BONGOR LARGEAU MOUNDOU FORTLAMY MOUSSORO

CHADOR PHULKARI
CHAETA UNCINUS
CHAETOCHLOA SETARIA
CHAETOPOD SCALEBACK
CHAETURA DRAB BEAR
CHAFE IRK RUB VEX FRET FRIG FROT FUME GALD GALL HEAT JOSH RAGE STEW WARM WEAR ANGER ANNOY CHAFF GRIND SCOLD SNUFF WORRY WRING ABRADE BANTER EXCITE FRIDGE HARASS INJURY NETTLE RANKLE INCENSE INFLAME SNUFFLE FRICTION IRRITATE RAILLERY
CHAFER CRESSET
CHAFF GUY HAY PUG RAG ROT BRAN CAFF CHIP GRIT GUFF JOSH MOCK PULU QUIZ RAZZ BORAK CHIAK CHYAK DROSS GLUME HULLS HUSKS JOLLY RALLY SLACK STOUR STRAW TEASE TRASH BANTER BHOOSA REFUSE CAVINGS TAILING RAILLERY RIDICULE SHELLING
CHAFFER BANDY SIEVE WARES BUYING DICKER HAGGLE HIGGLE MARKET PALTER BARGAIN CHATTER SELLING TRAFFIC EXCHANGE
CHAFFINCH PINK CHINK SPINK TWINK ROBERD SCOBBY SHILFA SKELLY ROBINET SNABBIE WETBIRD
CHAFFY SCALY ACEROSE ACEROUS PALEATE
CHAFING GALLING IMPATIENCE
CHAFING-DISH HEARTH
CHAGRIN ENVY SPITE VEXATION
CHAGRINED SICK ASHAMED
CHAIN FOB GUY NET ROW SET TEW TIE TOE TOW TUG TYE BIND BOND CURB FALL FAST FILE GYVE JOIN LINE LINK SEAL SOAM TEAM BRAIL CABLE GROUP GUARD LEASH SHANK SHEET SLANG SLING SUITE TRACE TRAIN WRASE CARCAN CATENA COLLAR CORDON FASTEN FETTER GANGER HANGER HOBBLE JACKER JIGGER LINKER RACKAN SECURE SERIES STRING TETHER TOGGLE BOBSTAY CATFALL CHIGNON CONNECT EMBRACE ENSLAVE LASHING MANACLE NETWORK PAINTER PENDANT SAUTOIR SHACKLE TACKLER BACKROPE BRACELET CARCANET GLEIPNIR LINKWORK NECKLACE RECEPTOR RESTRAIN RIGWIDDY STROBILA WOOLDING
(— FOR ANCHOR) CATFALL PAINTER
(— FOR BINDING) JACKER TACKLER
(— FOR WRAPPING MAST) WOOLDING
(— OF AUTHORITIES) ISNAD
(— OF DUNES) SAIF SEIF
(— OF MOUNTAINS) RANGE
(— OF ROCKS) REEF
(— ON CONVICT'S LEG) SLANG
(— TO BIND CATTLE) SEAL
(DECORATIVE —) FESTOON
(ENDLESS —) CREEPER
(KIND OF —) MARKOV
(MAGIC —) GLEIPNIR
(SHORT —) SHANK
(SUSPENDED —) CATENARY
(WATCH —) FOB ALBERT
(PL.) IRONS CONVEYOR
(PREF.) HORMO STREPHO STREPSI STREPT(O)
CHAIN LINK SHUT COPULA SWIVEL
CHAINMAN CLASHY CLASHEE LINEMAN TAPEMAN
CHAIN-SHAPED CATENOID
CHAIR KEEP SEAT SHOP HORSE SEDAN STOOL ESTATE OFFICE PULPIT ROCKER SADDLE SITTER TONJON CACOLET COMMODE FANBACK GONDOLA SITTING VOYEUSE WINDSOR ARMCHAIR CARRIAGE CATHEDRA FAUTEUIL KANGAROO SGABELLO VOLTAIRE
(— FOR PRAYING) PRIEDIEU
(— OF SANCTUARY) FRITHSTOOL
(— OF STATE) THRONE
(— SLUNG FROM POLE) KAGO TALABON
(— WITH CANOPY) STATE
(BISHOP'S —) CATHEDRA FALDSTOOL
(EASY —) COGSWELL
(GREEK —) KLISMOS
(KIND OF —) EAMES
(LEAVE THE —) ARISE
(MINING —) DOG
(PART OF —) ARM EAR LEG BACK POST RUNG SEAT SLAT CREST SPLAT STILE STUMP ROCKER ARMREST SPINDLE BACKRAIL HEADPIECE
(PORTABLE —) SEDAN
(SEDAN —) NORIMONO
(SPRING —) PERCH
(THRONE —) SHINZA
CHAIRMAN HEAD CHAIR EMCEE PRESES SPEAKER CONVENER DIRECTOR MODERATOR PROLOCUTOR
(PREF.) SYMPOSI
CHAISE GIG SHAY CHAIR CALESIN CARRIAGE CURRICLE SHANDRYDAN
CHAISE LONGUE DAYBED DUCHESSE
CHALAZA TREAD TREADLE GALLATURE
CHALAZION STYE
CHALCEDONY ONYX OPAL SARD AGATE CHERT PRASE CATEYE JASPER PLASMA QUARTZ

CARNEOL OPALINE SARDINE SARDIUS ENHYDROS CORNELIAN
(RED —) CARNELIAN
CHALCIOPE (FATHER OF —) AEETES
(HUSBAND OF —) PHRIXUS
(MOTHER OF —) ASTERODIA
(SISTER OF —) MEDEA
(SON OF —) ARGUS MELAS PHRONTIS CYTISSORUS
CHALCIS (CHILDREN OF —) CURETES CORYBANTES
(FATHER OF —) ASOPUS
(MOTHER OF —) METOPE
CHALCOPYRITE RUN
CHALDEAN SEER KALDANI BABYLONIAN
(— MEASURE) CANE FOOT MAKUK QASAB ARTABA GARIBA GHALVA MANSION
(— RIVER) TIGRIS EUPHRATES
(— TOWN) UR
CHALICE AMA CUP BOWL CALIX GRAIL REGAL GOBLET KRASIS
CHALK CAUK CORK PALE SCAR TALC TICK CRETA FLOUR SCORE BLANCH BLEACH CRAYON CREDIT RUBBLE WHITEN ACCOUNT WHITING
(GREEN —) PRASINE
(HARD —) HURLOCK
(RED —) RUBRIC
(SURVEYOR'S —) KEEL
(PREF.) CALCAREO CALC(I)(IO)(O)
CHALKBOARD GREENBOARD
CHALKSTONE TOPHUS
CHALKY CRETACIC CRETACEOUS
CHALLENGE HEN VIE BRAG CALL DARE DEFY FACE GAGE ASSAY BANCO BLAME BRAVE CLAIM QUERY STUMP ACCUSE APPEAL BANTER CARTEL CHARGE DACKER DAIKER DEMAND DESCRY FORBID IMPUGN INFIRM INVITE RECUSE SERDAB ARRAIGN CENSURE IMPEACH PROVOKE REPROVE SOLICIT SUMMONS CHAMPION DARRAIGN DEFIANCE GAUNTLET QUESTION REPROACH
(— A BULL) CITE
CHALLENGING PIQUANT BLOODSHOT
CHALONE AUTACOID
CHALYBEATE MARTIAL
CHALYBITE SIDERITE
CHAMBER ODA AGER CELL CIST DOME FLAT FOLD HALL IWAN KIVA ROOM SALE TOMB BOWER CAVUM COURT GOMER HOUSE SENAT SHAFT SOLAR SOLER STOVE ATRIUM CAMARA CAMERA COFFER HEADER HOLLOW MIHRAB SENADO SENATE SOLLAR SPRING STANZA WILSON BEDROOM CAISSON CHALMER CHANNEL CHAUMER CONCAVE CUBICLE FAVISSA FIREBOX GALLERY GEHENNA MANSION RECEIPT CASEMATE CYLINDER DIFFUSER FOUNTAIN GROSSRAT SMOKEBOX SNEMOVNA THALAMUS
(— FOR MOLTEN GLASS) FONT
(— IN FURNACE) SHAFT DOGHOUSE
(— OF EAR) SACCULE UTRICLE
(— POT) JORDAN JEROBOAM
(AIR —) SPONSON
(AUDIENCE —) DURBAR
(BOMBPROOF —) CASEMATE
(CLIMATE CONTROL —) BIOTRON
(FIRE —) ARCH STOVE COCKLE FIREBOX
(FORTIFICATION —) BUNKER
(JUDGE'S —) CAMERA
(OPEN —) LANTERN
(ORGAN —) SWELL
(PERTAINING TO —) CAMERAL
(PISTON —) BARREL
(PRIVATE —) CLOSET CONCLAVE
(PUEBLO —) KIVA ESTUFA
(SLEEPING —) BEDROOM WARDROBE
(SMALL —) LOCULUS
(SUPPLY —) MAGAZINE
(UNDERGROUND —) CAVE CRYPT CAVERN SERDAB HYPOGEE
(WATERTIGHT —) CAISSON
(PREF.) THALAM(I)(O)
(SUFF.) CELE COELE COELUS
CHAMBERLAIN EUNUCH FACTOR SERVANT STEWARD PALATINE POLONIUS
CHAMBERPOT POT JERRY POTTY JORDAN
CHAMELEON ANOLE ANOLI LACERT SAURIAN
CHAMFER BEVEL CHIMB CHIME CHINE FLUTE CIPHER FURROW GROOVE
CHAMOIS GEMS IZARD AOUDAD SHAMMY ANTELOPE
CHAMOMILE MAYWEED MARGUERITE
CHAMONT (SISTER OF —) MONIMIA
CHAMP BITE CHAW FIRM HARD MASH CHANK CHOMP FIELD GNASH TRAMPLE
CHAMPAGNE AY BUBBLY SIMKIN BELLEEK SILLERY CHAMPERS
(IMITATION —) GOOSEBERRY
CHAMPAIGN PLAIN
CHAMPION ACE AID FAN ABET BACK BOSS DEFY HERO KEMP GHAZI ASSERT ATTEND DEFEND KEMPER KNIGHT PATRON SQUIRE VICTOR APOSTLE ESPOUSE FIGHTER PALADIN PROTECT ADVOCATE DEFENDER PALMERIN PROTAGONIST
CHAMPIONING
(PREF.) PRO
CHAMPIONSHIP TITLE LAURELS ADVOCACY
CHAMPLEVE ENAMEL INLAID
CHANCE DIE HAP LOT CASE CAST DINT DRAW FATE LINE LUCK ODDS RISK SHOT SHOW TIDE BREAK ETTLE STAKE WHACK BETIDE CASUAL GAMBLE HAPPEN HAZARD MISHAP RANDOM SQUEAK STRIKE TUMBLE AIMLESS FORTUNE OPENING STUMBLE VANTAGE VENTURE ACCIDENT CASUALTY EVENTUAL FORTUITY QUESTION ALEATORIC OPPORTUNITY PERADVENTURE
(— OF LOSS) RISK
(— OF SUCCESS) PROSPECT
(ADVERSE —) HAZARD
(EVEN —) TOSSUP
(HAPPY-) MERCY
(ILL —) MISHAP
(SLIGHT —) PRAYER
(SLIM —) PRAYER
(UNFORTUNATE —) PITY
(PL.) PROSPECTS
(PREF.) TYCH(O)
CHANCEL BEMA CHOIR ADYTUM
CHANCELLOR LOGOTHETE
CHANCY DODGY ALEATORY
CHANDELIER CORONA LUSTER PHAROS PENDANT CHANDLER GASELIER GIRANDOLE
CHANDLER TALLOWER
CHANE OREJON
CHANGE MEW CHOP FLOP MOLT MOVE ODDS PEAL TURN VARY VEER WARP WEND ADAPT ALTER AMEND BREAK COINS EMEND MOULT SHIFT THROW ADJUST BECOME DIFFER DIGEST IMMUTE MODIFY MUANCE MUTATE REMOVE REVAMP REVISE SWITCH WISSEL WRIXLE COMMUTE CONVERT CUTOVER DEVIATE FLUXION MORTIFY BECOMING DENATURE EXCHANGE INNOVATE LENITION MUTATION REVISION TRANSFER TRANSUME VARIANCE PERMUTATION METAMORPHISM MODIFICATION METAMORPHOSIS
(— APPEARANCE) DISGUISE
(— BACK) REVERT
(— COLOR) TURN
(— COURSE) GYBE JIBE
(— DIRECTION) CUT CANT CHOP HAUL KNEE VEER ANGLE BREAK SHIFT
(— FOR BETTER) HELP
(— FORM) DEVELOP
(— FOR WORSE) BEDEVIL
(— GAIT) BREAK
(— GRADUALLY) PASS GRADUATE
(— IN COURSE) SHEER
(— IN DIRECTION) JOG KNEE STEP
(— IN ELEVATION) FORK
(— IN LAKE LEVEL) SEICHE
(— IN SIZE) ASTOGENY
(— INTO VAPOR) FLASH
(— MONEY) WISSEL
(— OF FORM) SET
(— OF FORTUNE) PERIPETY
(— OF GEAR) KICKDOWN
(— OF HABITAT) MIGRATE
(— OF KEY) TRANSITION
(— OF LIFE) MENOPAUSE
(— OF MIND) CAPRICE
(— OF MOOD) VARY
(— OF PITCH) MOTION INFLECT
(— OF POLICY) TACK
(— OF POSITION KINESIS
(— OF SEA LEVEL) EUSTACY
(— OF SOUND) BREAKING
(— OF WORD) ANAGRAM
(— ONE'S HEART) REPENT
(— PACE) BREAK
(— POSITION) STIR FLEET HOTCH
(— QUICKLY) FLY
(— RESIDENCE) FLIT
(— SHAPE) DRAW CREEP DEFORM
(— SIDES) RAT
(ABNORMAL —) LESION
(ABRUPT —) DOGLEG SALTATION
(GEAR —) KICKDOWN
(GRADUAL —) DRIFT
(MAKE NO —) STANDPAT
(ONE WHO OPPOSES —) AGINNER
(PRESSURE —) ALLOBAR
(SHORT —) FLUFF
(SMALL —) GROCERY
(UNEXPECTED —) SWITCH
(PL.) DOUBLES PLASTIQUE
(PREF.) ALLAGO ALLASSO AMOEBI AMOEBO MUTA MUTO
(SUFF.) MUTE
CHANGEABLE EEMIS GIDDY IMMIS LIGHT WINDY CHOPPY FICKLE FITFUL GERFUL KETCHY LABILE MOBILE MOTLEY MUABLE SHIFTY WANKLE BRUCKLE ERRATIC MUTABLE PROTEAN UNSTAID VARIANT VARIOUS VOLUBLE AMENABLE CATCHING GLIBBERY MOVEABLE SKITTISH TICKLISH UNSTABLE VARIABLE VEERABLE VOLATILE WEATHERY CHAMELEON VERSATILE
CHANGEABLENESS LEVITY CAPRICE VIBRATION
CHANGED VARIED ANOTHER
(PREF.) META
CHANGEFUL FICKLE SHIFTY MUTABLE RESTLESS
CHANGELESS CONSISTENT
CHANGELING AUF AWF OAF DOLT FOOL CHILD DUNCE IDIOT WAVERER IMBECILE KILLCROP RENEGADE TURNCOAT
CHANGEOVER SWITCH
CHANGING FLUXIBLE ALTERNATE
(— MONEY) AGIO
(CONTINUALLY —) FLOATING
CHANK SANK CONCH
CHANNEL CUT GAT POD REE RUT SOW CANO CAVA DEEP DIKE DUCT DYKE FLUE GATE GOOL GOTE GOUT GURT KILL KYLE LAKE LANE PACE PIPE RACE SLEW SLOO VALE VEIN WADI WADY WASH BAYOU CANAL CARRY CHASE COWAL DITCH DRAIN DRILL FLUME FLUTE GLYPH GUIDE INSET LATCH QUIRK RIVER SINUS SLIDE SOUND STOOL STOVE STRIA SWASH AIRWAY ALVEUS ARROYO ARTERY BRANCH COURSE CUTOFF ESTERO FURROW GROOVE GULLET GUTTER HOLLOW KENNEL KEYWAY LAGOON MEDIUM OFFLET OILWAY RABBET RESACA RIVOSE RUNWAY SLOUGH SLUICE SPECUS STRAIT STRAND STREAM THROAT TROUGH CHAMFER CONDUCT CONDUIT CULVERT CUNETTE EURIPUS OFFTAKE PASSAGE RACEWAY RIVULET SHIPWAY SILANGA STRIGIL THALWEG TIDEWAY WASHOUT AQUEDUCT FLOODWAY GUIDEWAY GUNKHOLE RACELINE SCOURWAY SPILLWAY CANNELURE

(— FOR MOLTEN METAL) SOW GATE RUNNER
(— IN CLOTH) FLUTE
(— IN ICE FIELD) LEAD
(— IN MOLD) SPRAY
(— OF AQUEDUCT) SPECUS
(— OF BRAIN) ITER
(— ON A DECK) CHIMB CHIME
(— ON WHALE) SCARF
(ARTIFICIAL —) GAT GOUT
(DRAINAGE —) GAW
(ENGLISH —) SLEEVE
(INCLINED —) SHOOT
(INFORMATION —) PIPELINE
(IRRIGATION —) AUWAI DROVE
(LYMPH —) CISTERNA
(SECONDARY —) BINNACLE
(SLOPING —) CHUTE SHUTE
(PREF.) CANALI RHYN(O) SOLEN(O) VAS(I)(O)
CHANNELBILL RAINFOWL
CHANNELED FLUTED
CHANT CANT MELE SING SONG TONE CAROL PSALM SOUGH ANTHEM CANTUS INTONE LITANY MANTRA WARBLE CHORTLE INTROIT PROSODE REQUIEM WORSHIP ALLELUIA ANTIPHON CANTICLE INTONATE SINGSONG PLAINSONG CANTILLATE
CHANTER STICK CANTOR SINGER BAGPIPE SONGSTER CHALUMEAU
(— OF BAGPIPE) OBOE
CHANTERELLE CANTINO
CHANTING RAP CHARM HAZANUT ANTIPHONY CHAZZANUT
CHANTLATE SPROCKET
CHANTRY CAGE
CHAOS NU NUN PIE APSU GULF HYLE MESS VOID ABYSS BABEL CHASM BEDLAM JUMBLE MATTER TOPHET ANARCHY MIXTURE DISORDER SHAMBLES TAILSPIN TOHUBOHU
CHAOTIC MUDDLED CONFUSED FORMLESS TUMULTUARY
CHAP BOY BUY DOG LAD MAN RAP WAG BEAN BEAT BIRD BLOW CHIP CHOP COVE DICK DUCK HIND JOHN KIBE MASH MATE NABS SNAP BILLY BLOKE BUCKO BULLY BUYER CHAFT CHINK CLEFT CRACK FRUIT KNOCK LOVER RUMMY SCOUT SPLIT SPORT SPRAY SWIPE TRADE YOUTH BARTER BOHUNK BREACH BUGGER CALLAN CHOOSE CODGER CUFFIN FELLOW FOUTER FOUTRA GAFFER GEEZER JOSSER KIPPER SHAVER STRIKE STROKE TURNIP BASTARD BROTHER CALLANT FISSURE HUSBAND ROUGHEN BLIGHTER CUSTOMER DIVISION MERCHANT
(— HANDS) RACK SPRAY
(— IN SKIN) KIN KIBE
(FINE —) BULLY
(OLD —) BO GEEZER
(PLUCKY —) COCK
(QUEER —) GALOOT
(S.AFRICAN —) KEREL
(YOUNG —) GAFFER
(PL.) CHOPS
CHAPARRAL MONTE CHAMISAL BUCKTHORN
CHAPARRO YAYA
CHAPBOOK CHAP GARLAND
CHAPE CRAMPET MORDANT
CHAPEL CAGE CAPE COPE COWL HOOD CLOAK CRYPT PORCH SALEM BETHEL BEULAH CHARRE CHURCH HAIKAL MORADA SHRINE CAPELLA CHANTRY CHAPLET CHARNEL CHHATRI GALILEE MARTYRY MEETING MEMORIA ORATORY SACRARY SERVICE BETHESDA DEACONRY DIACONIA FERETORY FERETRUM PARABEMA SACELLUM SODALITY
(UNDERGROUND —) SHROUDS
CHAPERON HOOD ATTEND DUENNA ESCORT MATRON GRIFFIN PROTECT GUARDIAN SHEEPDOG TRAPPING
CHAPLAIN PADRE LEVITE ALMONER CONDUCT ALTARIST ORDINARY
CHAPLAINCY SCARF
CHAPLET BEAD ORLE STUD CROWN ANADEM ANCHOR CIRCLE FILLET JAMBER JAMMER ROSARY STAPLE TROPHY WREATH CORONAL CORONET GARLAND MOULDING NECKLACE ORNAMENT
(PREF.) STEMMATI
CHAPLIN (WIFE OF —) OONA
CHAPMAN CHAP BUYER DEALER HAWKER TRADER COPEMAN PEDDLER CUSTOMER MERCHANT
CHAPPIE JOCKEY
CHAPS FLEWS BREECHES LEGGINGS OVERALLS
CHAPTER BODY CELL PACE POST CAPUT COURT LODGE BRANCH CABILDO CAPITAL CORRECT COUNCIL MEETING SECTION ASSEMBLY
(— OF BOOK) CAPITAL
(— OF KORAN) SURA SURAH
(— OF SOCIETY) CAMP CIRCLE
CHAPTER-HOUSE FRATRY
CHAR BURN CART COAL SEAR BROIL CHARK CHORE SHARD SINGE TROUT SCORCH BLACKEN CHARIOT TORGOCH REDBELLY SAIBLING SALMONID SANDBANK
(PL.) SALVELINI
CHARA MUSKGRASS
CHARACIN DORADO DOURADE BLOODFIN
CHARACTER AURA BALL BENT CARD CASE CLAY CLEF DASH ECAD FLAT FOND FORM HAIR KIND MAKE MARK MOLD NOTE PART ROLE RUNE SIGN SORT TONE TRIM TYPE BRAND COLOR ETHIC ETHOS FIBER HABIT HEART HUMOR INDEX SAVOR STAMP TENOR TOKEN TRAIT WRITE CARACT CIPHER COCKUP DAGGER DIRECT EMBLEM FIGURE GENIUS HANGER LETTER MANNER METTLE NATURE REPUTE SIGLUM SPIRIT STRIPE SYMBOL CALIBER CLOTHES EDITION ENGRAVE ESSENCE IMPRESS QUALITY CAPACITY FRACTION IDENTITY IDEOGRAM INFERIOR INSCRIBE LIGATURE SELFHOOD SYLLABIC DESCENDER PARAGRAPH PERSONAGE
(— IN DRAMA) CHORUS
(— IN PLAY) DAME BESSY
(— OF SOIL) LAIR
(ASSUMED —) ROLE FIGURE INCOGNITO
(BAD —) DROLE BUDMASH
(BASIC —) BOTTOM
(CELTIC —) OGAM OGHAM
(CHIEF —) AGONIST
(CHINESE —) SHOU RADICAL
(COMIC —) PIERROT
(COMMON —) COMMUNITY
(ESSENTIAL —) ALLOY
(FICTIONAL —) PERSONA
(FIRM —) BACKBONE
(GIVE — TO) TONE
(GREEK —) SAMPI
(JAPANESE —S) HIBUNCI
(MENDELIAN —) ALLEL ALLELE
(PHYSICAL —) ARMENOID
(PRIME —) ESSENCE
(SHIFTLESS —) BEAT
(STOCK —) BESSY MACCUS
(TESTED —) ASSAY
(TRIED —) TOUCH
(VULGAR —S) ONMUN
(PL.) MANA
(SUFF.) ERY
(HAVING — OF) IC(AL)
CHARACTERISTIC CAST COST MARK MIEN ANGLE AROMA GRACE POINT TACHE TOKEN TRAIT TRICK ACCENT BEAUTY NATURE STIGMA STROKE ADJUNCT AMENITY FEATURE IMPRESS QUALITY SPECIES TYPICAL ACTIVITY HEADMARK PECULIAR PROPERTY SYMBOLIC PARAMETER PROPRIETY PECULIARITY PARTICULARITY QUALIFICATION
(— OF ANTIBODIES) AVIDITY
(— OF PARTICLES) CHARM
(ADVENTITIOUS —) ACCIDENT
(DISTINGUISHING —) SPECIES HALLMARK BIRTHMARK
(PECULIAR —) IDIOPATHY
(PL.) CORNERS FACULTY
(SUFF.) IC(AL)
(— OF) ISH ISTIC LY
CHARACTERIZATION ELOGY ELOGIUM
CHARACTERIZE MARK STYLE DEFINE DEPICT TITULE ENGRAVE ENTITLE IMPRINT PORTRAY DESCRIBE INDICATE INSCRIBE
CHARACTERIZED
(SUFF.) **(— BY)** AL FUL IAL IC(AL) LEW
CHARACTERLESS INANE
CHARADES GAME
CHARCOAL COAL CARBO CHARK CARBON FUSAIN PENCIL BLACKEN SPODIUM SCRIBBET
CHARD BEET
CHARGE FEE LAP LAY RAP TAX BEEF BILL BUCK CALL CARE CARK CAST COST CURE DUES DUTY FILL GIBE KEEP LADE LIEN LOAD NICK NOTE ONUS RACK RATE REST RUSH SHOT SIZE SOAK SPAR TASK TOLL WARD WIKE AGIST BLAME CAUSE CHALK COUNT CRIME DEBIT EXTRA GYRON ONSET ORDER PRICE REFER SCORE SHOCK STICK STING THING TRUST ACCUSE ADJURE ALLEGE APPEAL ASSESS ATTACK BEHEST BURDEN CAREER CENSUS COURSE CREDIT DAMAGE DEFAME DEMAND DITTAY ENJOIN ENURNY EXCESS IMPOSE IMPUTE METAGE OBJECT OFFICE PIPAGE REATUS SURMIT SURTAX TARIFF TOWAGE WEIGHT ACIDIZE ANNULET ARRAIGN ARTICLE ASCRIBE ASSAULT AVERAGE BOATAGE CARTAGE CENSURE CHEVRON CLAMPER COMMAND CONCERN CONJURE CORKAGE CORNAGE CUSTODY DOCKAGE DRAYAGE EMBASSY EXPENSE FLOTAGE HAULAGE IGNITER IMPEACH KEEPING MANDATE MILEAGE MISSION MIXTURE MOORAGE PANNAGE QUAYAGE REPRISE SIDEAGE SLANDER SLIDAGE SURMISE WARPAGE BILLBACK BRASSAGE CASUALTY CHASTISE CRESCENT DELAYAGE DENOUNCE LEGATION ORDINARY OVERLOAD PLANKAGE POUNDAGE PROVINCE QUESTION SLINGING SPENDING STANDAGE TUTORAGE VIGORISH COMPLAINT ACCUSATION ACCUSEMENT
(— AGAINST) TILT
(— BATTERY) SOAK BOOST
(— EXCESSIVELY) FLEECE
(— FALSELY) SURMISE
(— FOR GRAZING) AGIST
(— OF FIREARM) LOAD AMORCE
(— OF MENTAL ENERGY) CATHEXIS
(— OF METAL) HEAT
(— OF ORE) POST
(— TO BE PAID) LAW
(— UPON PROPERTY) LIEN
(— WITH CRIME) ACCUSE DELATE INDICT ARTICLE ATTAINT IMPEACH
(— WITH GAS) AERATE
(AGGREGATE —S) BOOK
(CANNON —) GRAPE
(COVER —) COUVERT
(DEPTH —) CAN ASHCAN
(EXPLOSIVE —) CAP BLAST SNAKE SQUIB TULIP BOOSTER BURSTER IGNITER
(FALSE —) CALUMNY
(HERALDIC —) DELF DROP GIRON GYRON LABEL BEZANT BILLET DRAGON GURGES BEARING ESQUIRE
(MAILING —) FRANKAGE
(POWDER —) GRAIN
(SHAPED —) BEEHIVE
(SPIRITUAL —) CURE
(TEMPORARY —) CARE
(WINE —) CORKAGE
CHARGEABLE GUILTY
CHARGED UP HOT LADEN BELAST BILLETY BILLETTE ELECTRIC INSTINCT
(— WITH EMOTION) SWOLLEN

CHARGEHAND CLICKER
CHARGEMAN BLASTER
CHARGER DISH HORSE MOUNT STEED ACCUSER COURSER PLATTER TROOPER
CHARILY FRUGALLY GINGERLY
CHARIOT CAR BIGA CART CHAR RATH WAIN BUGGY CHAIR ESSED RATHA TRIGA WAGON CHARET QUADRIGA
CHARIOTEER AURIGA CARTER DRIVER IOLAUS LEADER CARTARE WAGONER MYRTILUS AUTOMEDON
CHARITABLE KIND BENIGN HUMANE LENIENT LIBERAL GENEROUS
CHARITY ALMS DOLE GIFT LOVE PITY RUTH MERCY BASKET BOUNTY CARITAS HANDOUT LARGESS LENIENCE TZEDAKAH
(SYMBOL OF —) PELICAN
CHARIVARI BABEL SHALLAL SERENADE SHIVAREE
CHARLATAN FAKE CHEAT FAKER FRAUD QUACK CABOTIN EMPIRIC IMPOSTER MAGICIAN SYCOPHANT MOUNTEBANK QUACKSALVER
CHARLES II DAVID
CHARLIE MCCARTHY STOOGE
CHARLOCK KRAUT RUNCH HARLOCK KEDLOCK KERLOCK MUSTARD SINAPIS YELLOWS CHARDOCK CHEDLOCK SKEDLOCK SKELLOCH
CHARM IT GBO KEY OBI CALM CHIC HAND JINX JUJU JYNX LUCK MOJO PLAY RUNE SNOW SONG TAKE TILL ZOGO ALLAY AROMA BRIEF CATCH FAVOR FREET FREIT GRACE LAMIN MAGIC OBEAH OOMPH SAFFI SAFIE SPELL VENUS WANGA WEIRD ALLURE AMULET BEAUTY CARACT DEASIL DISARM ENAMOR ENGAGE ENTICE FETISH GLAMOR GRIGRI INCANT MANTRA MELODY PLEASE SAPHIE SCARAB SOOTHE SUBDUE SUMMON VOODOO ABRAXAS ASSUAGE ATTRACT BEGUILE BEWITCH CANTION CANTRIP CONJURE CONTROL DELIGHT ENCHANT ENTHRAL FLATTER HEITIKI PERIAPT PHILTER PHILTRE SINGING SORCERY BLESSING BRELOQUE COMETHER COQUETRY ENTHRALL ENTRANCE GLAUMRIE GREEGREE PISHOGUE PRACTICE TALISMAN CAPTIVATE MAGNETIZE PATERNOSTER
(MAGNETIC —) CHARISMA
CHARMED CAPTIVE
CHARMER HOURI SIREN EXORCIST MAGICIAN SORCERER ENCHANTER
CHARMING LEPID SWEET GOLDEN WIZARD AMIABLE DARLING EYESOME TEMPEAN WINNING WINSOME ADORABLE DELICATE GRACEFUL LOVESOME PICTURESQUE
CHARNEL GHASTLY CEMETERY GOLGOTHA
CHARNEL-HOUSE OSSUARY GOLGOTHA
CHARON (FATHER OF —) EREBUS
(MOTHER OF —) NOX
CHARPOY BED COT
CHARQUI JERKY XARQUE
CHART MAP BILL CARD MARK PLAN PLAT PLOT ROSE CARTE GRAPH SCORE STILL RECORD SCHEME DIAGRAM EMAGRAM EXPLORE ISOTYPE OUTLINE PROJECT DOCUMENT DOPEBOOK MERCATOR PLATFORM
(— BOOK) WAGONER
(— FROM AIR) AEROVIEW
(— MARK) VIGIA
(— OF A COURSE) RUTTER
(MARINER'S —) ROSE RUTTER
(WEATHER —) ANALOGUE NEPHANALYSIS
CHARTER FIX LET BOND BOOK DEED HIRE RENT CARTE CHART FUERO GRANT LEASE SANAD CHARTA PERMIT SUNNUD DIPLOMA CONTRACT GRUNDLOV HEIRLOOM LANDBOOK MONOPOLY PANCHART
CHARTERHOUSE OF PARMA
(AUTHOR OF —) STENDHAL
(CHARACTER IN —) GINA CONTI DONGO MOSCA CLELIA FAUSTA GILETTI FABRIZIO FERRANTE MARIETTA PIETRANERA
CHARWOMAN CHARER CHARLADY PORTRESS JANITRESS
CHARY SHY DEAR WARY CHERE SCANT SPARE DAINTY FRUGAL PRIZED SKIMPY CAREFUL CURIOUS SPARING CAUTIOUS HESITANT PRECIOUS RESERVED SPAREFUL VIGILANT
CHASE FOG SIC SUE FALL HUNT JERL SHAG SHOO SICK ANNOY CATCH CHEVY CHIVY DRIVE HARRY HOUND SCORE SHACK CACCIA CHIVVY CHOUSE EMBOSS FOLLOW FRIEZE FURROW GALLOP GROOVE HALLOO HARASS HOLLOW INDENT PURSUE QUARRY SCORSE TRENCH CHANNEL ENGRAVE HUNTING PURSUIT ORNAMENT PURCHASE
(— GAME) COURSE
(— HARD) RATTLE
CHASER RAM DRINK HOUND FROGGER
(WOMAN —) SHEEPBITER
CHASING CISELURE
(— OF GAME) DRIVE
CHASM GAP KIN PIT GULF RIFT YAWN ABYSS BLANK CANON CHAOS CLEFT GORGE BREACH CANYON HIATUS FISSURE MEGARON SWALLOW VACANCY APERTURE CREVASSE INTERVAL VACATION
CHASSE SLIP GLIDE SASHAY
CHASSEUR HUNTER BELLBOY DOORMAN FOOTMAN HUNTSMAN
CHASSIS SASH FRAME FIGURE
CHASTE CAST PURE ATTIC CLEAN ZONED DECENT HONEST MODEST PROPER SEVERE VESTAL VIRGIN CLEANLY PUDICAL REFINED CELIBATE INNOCENT VIRGINLY VIRTUOUS CONTINENT
CHASTEN RATE ABASE SMITE SMOTE SNEAP SOBER HUMBLE PUNISH REBUKE REFINE SUBDUE TEMPER AFFLICT CENSURE CORRECT NURTURE CHASTISE MODERATE RESTRAIN
CHASTISE BEAT FIRK FLOG LASH SLAP TRIM WHIP AMEND BLAME FEEZE SCOLD SPANK SPILL STRAP TAUNT ACCUSE ANOINT BERATE CHARGE DISPLE PUNISH PURIFY REBUKE REFINE STRAFE SWINGE TEMPER THRASH TICKLE CHASTEN CORRECT REPROVE SCOURGE SHINGLE SUSPECT CASTIGATE
CHASTISEMENT ROD HELL TOCO TOKO CENSURE PAYMENT FLOGGING
(DIVINE —) WRATH
CHASTITY HONOR PURITY VIRTUE HONESTY MODESTY PUDENCY CELIBACY GOODNESS PUDICITY INNOCENCE
CHASUBLE CASULA DEACON INFULA PLANET PAENULA PIANETA VESTMENT
CHAT GAS JAW MAG RAP BIRD CHIN CONE COZE DISH GIST TALK TELL TOVE TWIG YARN AMENT CAUSE COOSE CRACK DALLY PITCH POINT PRATE PROSE PROSS SPEAK SPIKE VISIT BABBLE BRANCH CATKIN CONFAB COURSE DEVICE GABBLE GIBBER GOSSIP GOSTER HOBNOB JABBER NATTER POTATO POTTER SAMARA CHAFFER CHATTER SHMOOZE CAUSERIE CHATTERY CONVERSE SCHMOOZE SPIKELET STROBILE
CHATEAU HOUSE TOWER CASTLE MANSION SCHLOSS CHATELET FORTRESS
CHATON BASIL BEZEL BEZIL STONE COATING SETTING
CHATTEL CATTLE PLEDGE DEODAND FIXTURE CATALLUM PERSONAL
(DISTRAINT OF —S) NAAM
(PL.) STUFF FARLEU FARLEY COMODATO HOUSEHOLD
CHATTER GAB JAW MAG RAP YAK YAP BLAB CARP CHAT CHIN CLAP CLAT DISH GASH HACK KNAP RICK TALK TEAR YIRR CABAL CLACK CLASH GARRE HAVER PRATE SHAKE BABBLE BRUDGE CACKLE CLAVER GABBLE GIBBER GOSSIP JABBER JANGLE JARGON PALTER RATTLE SHIVER TATTER TATTLE TINKLE YAMMER YATTER BLABBER BRABBLE CHACKLE CHAFFER CHIPPER CHITTER CLACKET CLATTER CLITTER GABNASH NASHGOB PALAVER PRABBLE PRATING PRATTLE SHATTER SMATTER TRATTLE TWATTLE TWITTER TWITTLE WHITTER BABBLING LOLLYGAG SCHMOOSE SCHMOOZE VERBIAGE
(SUFF.) LALIA
CHATTERBOX JAY MAG PIET BUCCO CLACK CRYSTE GOSSIP MAGPIE
CHATTERER JAY MAG PIE BLAB CHUET CHEWET GABBER MAGPIE RATTLE HAVERER
CHATTERING PIET BABBLY CHAVISH POPPING TWITTER BABBLING
CHATTY CHIRRUPY GARRULOUS
CHAUFFEUR DRIVER SHOVER TESTER
CHAUVINISM JINGOISM
CHAUVINIST JINGO JINGOIST
CHAW JAW VEX CHEW ENVY MULL GRIND PONDER
CHAYOTE CHOCHO TALLOTE HUISQUIL MIRLITON
CHEAP LOW BASE GAIN POOR VILE BORAX CLOSE FLASH GAUDY GROSS KITCH LIGHT MUCKY NASTY PRICE SNIDE TATTY TIGHT TINNY VALUE ABJECT BRUMMY CHEESY COMMON CRUMBY CRUMMY JITNEY LEADEN PLENTY SHODDY SLEAZY SORDID STINGY TAWDRY TRASHY UNDEAR BARGAIN CHINTZY POPULAR TINHORN INFERIOR PENNORTH SIXPENNY TWOPENNY BRUMMAGEM PINCHBECK
(— ITEM) TWOFER
(PREF.) VILI
CHEAPEN DOCK STALE VILIFY SMALLEN
CHEAPSKATE PIKER STIFF
CHEAT DO BAM BOB COG CON FOB FOP FUB GIP GUM GYP JIG NIP TOP BEAT BILK BITE BULL BURN CLIP COLT CRIB DISH DUFF DUPE FAKE FIRK FLAM FLUM GECK GULL HAVE HOAX HOSE JILT JINK JOUK KNAP LIAR MACE MUMP NAIL NICK NOSE POOP PULL REAM ROOK SCAM SELL SHAM SILE SKIN SLUR SNAP SWAP SWOP TRIM WEED WIPE BITCH BLINK BOOTY BUNCO BUNKO COZEN CROOK CULLY DODGE FAKER FLING FOIST FOURB FRAUD FUDGE GLEEK GOUGE GREEK GUILE HOCUS KNAVE LURCH MULCT PINCH PLOAT RATON ROGUE SCAMP SCREW SHARP SHORT SLANG SPOIL STICK STIFF STING SWICK SWIKE TOUCH TRICK VERSE WRINK BAFFLE BLANCH BUBBLE BUCKET CHIAUS CHISEL CHOUSE CLOYNE COGGER DADDLE DECEIT DELUDE DERIDE DIDDLE DOODLE DUFFER EMUNGE EUCHRE FIDDLE FLEECE GAZUMP GREASE HUMBUG HUMMER HUSTLE ILLUDE INTAKE JOCKEY NIGGLE NOBBLE NUZZLE OUTWIT RADDLE RENEGE RIPOFF SHAVER SHICER SNUDGE SUCKER TWICER ABUSION BEGUILE BUBBLER CHICANE COZENER CULLION DECEIVE DEFRAUD ESCHEAT FAITOUR FINAGLE FINESSE FOISTER GUDGEON JUGGLER MISLEAD PLUNDER QUIBBLE SHARPER SHIFTER SKELDER SLICKER SWINDLE VERNEUK ARTIFICE BEJUGGLE CHALDESE CHISELER DELUSION HOODWINK

IMPOSTOR INTRIGUE OUTREACH OVERTAKE PICAROON SHAMMOCK SWINDLER BAMBOOZLE CIRCUMVENT SHORTCHANGE
CHEATED SOLD
CHEATER BITE GULL SPEC KNAVE BILKER INTAKE TOPPER SHARPER FINAGLER TREACHER
CHEATING HOCUS BARRAT ODLING ABUSIVE FUBBERY MICHERY ROGUERY CHEATERY JUGGLING TRICKERY
CHECH DUD BOUNCER
CHECK BIT DAM HAP LID NAB NIP SAY SET TAB BAIL BALK BEAT BILK BILL CHIP CHIT COOK CRIB CURB DAMP FACE FOIL GAGE HURT ITEM KITE PAWL REIN SKID SNEB SNIB SNIP SNUB STAY STEM STOP STUB TAKE TEST TICK TRIG TURN TWIT WERE ABORT ALLAY ANNUL BAULK BLOCK BRAKE CATCH CHIDE CHILL CHING CHOKE CRACK CROOK DAUNT DELAY DETER DRAFT EMBAR FACER FAULT GAUGE LIMIT MODER PAUSE QUELL REPEL SNAPE SPOKE STALL STILL STUNT TALLY TAUNT THROW TOKEN TRASH WAVER ARAYNE ARREST ATTACK BAFFLE BOTTLE BRIDLE CHEQUE COUPON DAMPEN DEFEAT DETAIN DETENT DURESS GRAVEL HAFFET HAFFIT HINDER IMPEDE OPPOSE OUTWIT PULLUP QUENCH RABBET REBATE REBUFF REBUKE RETURN SCOTCH STANCH STAYER STIFLE STYMIE TICKET VERIFY ANSTOSS AWEBAND BACKSET BECLOUD COMMAND CONTAIN CONTROL COUNTER CURTAIN DRAUGHT INHIBIT MONITOR REFRAIN REPRESS REPROOF REPROVE REPULSE REVERSE SETBACK SNAFFLE STAUNCH STOPPER TRAMMEL TROUBLE BULKHEAD ENCUMBER HOLDBACK OBSTRUCT PULLBACK RESTRAIN WITHHOLD
(— ENTHUSIASM) DISMAY
(— GRADUALLY) CUSHION
(— GROWTH) BLAST STINT STUNT
(— IN) ARRIVE
(— IN GLASS) SPLIT
(— IN TIMBER) STARSHAKE
(— MOTION) SPRAG
(— OF HORSE) SACCADE
(— PASSER) PAPERHANGER
(— PROGRESS) DEFEAT
(FORGED —) STIFF STUMER
(HOLD IN —) COMPESCE
(ILLEGAL — IN HOCKEY) SPEARING
(RESTAURANT —) LAWING
(WORTHLESS —) DUD STUMER
(WRITE A BAD —) BOUNCE
(PREF.) ISCH(O)
CHECKED CHECK BEATEN CLOSED CAPTIVE STOPPED
CHECKER DAM DICE FRET KING CHECK FREAK FRECK PIECE WHITE DAMPER DRAUGHT
CHECKERBERRY JINKS DRUNKARD TEABERRY
CHECKERBOARD TABLE DAMBROD DAMBOARD
CHECKERED PIED VAIR DICED PLAID CHECKY MOTLEY
CHECKERS DRAFTS CHEQUERS DRAUGHTS
CHECKERWORK TESSEL CHECKER TESSERA
CHECKING REST BLOCK SETBACK EBRILLADE
(— OF HEMORRHAGE) TORSION
(SUFF.) SCHESIS SCHETIC
CHECKMATE LICK MATE STOP UNDO BAFFLE CORNER DEFEAT OUTWIT STYMIE THWART SUIMATE
CHECKSTONE CHUCK
CHEDDAR CHEESE
CHEEK CHAP CHOP GALL GENA JAMB JOLE JOWL LEER SASS WANG WANK BUCCA CHOKE CHYAK CRUST NERVE SAUCE SHICK CHYACK HAFFET HAFFIT OXCHEEK AUDACITY TEMERITY
(— OF SPUR) SHANK
(— OF VISE) CHAP
(PREF.) BUCCO MEL PAREI(A)
CHEEKBONE MALAR ZYGOMA
CHEEK-POUCH (— OF BABOON) ALFORJA
CHEEKY BOLD FRESH
CHEEP PIP YAP YIP CHIP HINT PEEP PULE CHIRP CREAK TWEET SQUEAK TATTLE
CHEER OLE RAH FARE FOOD MIND ROOT VIVA YELL BRAVO BRISK CHIRK ELATE ERECT FEAST HEART HUZZA JOLLY MIRTH SHOUT SPORT TIGER WHOOP CANTLE CHERRY GAIETY HOORAY HURRAH HUZZAH REHETE SOLACE VIANDS ACCLAIM ANIMATE APPLAUD CHERISH COMFORT CONSOLE ENCHEER GLADDEN HEARTEN JOLLITY LIGHTEN REFRESH REJOICE SUPPORT UPRAISE APPLAUSE BRIGHTEN HILARITY INSPIRIT RECREATE VIVACITY
(BURST OF —S) SALVO
(GOOD —) WELFARE
(JAPANESE —) BANZAI
(SORRY —) PENANCE
CHEERFUL GAY CANT GLAD GLEG GOOD HIGH ROSY BONNY CADGY CANTY CHIRK DOUCE HAPPY JOLLY LIGHT MERRY PEART READY RIANT SAPPY SUNNY VAUDY BLITHE BRIGHT CHEERY CHIRPY CROUSE GAWSIE GENIAL HEARTY HILARY JOCUND LIVELY RIDENT BUOYANT CHEERLY CHIPPER HOLIDAY JOCULAR SMILING WINSOME CHEERING CHIRRUPY EUPEPTIC FRIENDLY GLADSOME HOMELIKE SANGUINE SUNBEAMY SUNSHINE
(PREF.) HILARO
CHEERFULLY GLADLY CANTILY CHEERLY JOLLILY LIGHTLY CHEERILY GENIALLY
CHEERFULNESS JOY GLEE TAIT CHEER CHERTE GAIETY GAYETY LEVITY SPIRIT JOLLITY BUOYANCY FESTIVAL GLADNESS HILARITY
(MORE THAN —) GLEE
CHEERING GLAD CORDIAL CHEERFUL CHIRPING
CHEERIO BYE CIAO TATA LATER HOORAY HOOROO
CHEERLESS SAD BLAE COLD DIRE DRAB GLUM GRAY BLEAK DREAR ELYNG WASTE DISMAL DREARY GLOOMY WINTRY DOLEFUL FORLORN JOYLESS SUNLESS DEJECTED DESOLATE LITHLESS
CHEER PINE CHIL
CHEERY BUXOM BRIGHT BOBBISH GAYSOME
CHEESE OKA BLUE BRIE EDAM FETA HAND JACK TOME TRIP APPLE BRICK COLBY CREAM DAISY DERBY GOUDA GRANA KENNO MAHON QUESO SWISS TOMME WHEEL ZIEGA ZIGER ASIAGO BARRIE BONDON BRYNZA BURGOS CANTAL CASSAN DUNLOP GLARUS JUNKET MYSOST ROMANO RONCAL SAANEN SBRINZ TILSIT ZAMORA ZIEGER ANGELOT CHEDDAR CHEVRET COTTAGE CROWDIE FONTINA FROMAGE GJEDOST GRUYERE HAVARTI KASSERI KEBBUCK LASELVA PRIMOST PROVOLA RICOTTA SAPSAGO SERRANO STILTON TETILLA TRUCKLE AMERICAN CABRALES CHESHIRE EMMENTAL LONGHORN MUENSTER PARMESAN PECORINO RACLETTE SANSIMON SLIPCOAT TRONCHON LEICESTER MOUSETRAP PROVOLONE ROQUEFORT WILTSHIRE MOZZARELLA NEUFCHATEL SERVILLETA
(— COATING) MOLD
(— DISH) RACLETTE
(— FANCIER) TUROPHILE
(— IN OATMEAL) CABOC
(— ROLLED IN OATMEAL) CABOC
(COTTAGE —) CROWDIE
(CREAM —) JUNKET
(DANISH —) HAVARTI
(GOAT —) CHEVRE
(HUNGARIAN —) LIPTAUER
(INCIPIENT —) CURD
(INFERIOR —) DICK
(KIND OF —) RAT RATTRAP
(LARGE —) KEBBOC
(MELTED —) FONDUTA
(MILD FRENCH —) REBLOCHON
(SAY —) SMILE
(SOFT —) STRACCHINO
(STORE —) CHEDDAR
(WELSH —) CAERPHILLY
(PREF.) CASE(O) TURO TYR(O)
CHEESELIKE CASEOUS
CHEESEPARING STINGY
CHEESE VAT CHESSEL CHESSART
CHEESEWOOD BONEWOOD WHITEWOOD
CHEETAH CAT OUNCE YOUSE YOUZE GUEPARD
CHEF COOK COMMIS SAUCIER CUISINIER
(PASTRY —) PATISSIER
CHEFOO YENTAI
CHELA HAND MANUS NIPPER PINCER
CHELATE COMPLEX
CHELICERA FALX FANG FALCER MANDIBLE
CHELLIAN ABBEVILLIAN
CHELONIAN TURTLE TURTOISE
CHELUBAI (FATHER OF —) HEZRON
CHEMICAL (ALSO SEE SPECIFIC HEADINGS) ACID BASE SALT ALKALI BLEACH CHEMIC DODGER SAFENER ADDITIVE ALGICIDE CATALYST DEHORNER
(— FROM HEMP RESIN) THC
(— IN MARIJUANA) THC
(— WARFARE AGENT) SARIN
(PREF.) ACETO ALCO ALDO AMIDO AMYL(I)(O) AZ(O) BENZ(O) BOR(O) BROM(O) BUT(YR)(YRO) CADM(I)(O) CAPRO CARB(O) CHAVI(O) CUMO DIAZO DIOL DUPLO EKA ESTERI FORM(O) GLY(O) IDO IMIDO IMINO KER(O) KET(O) LAUR LIP LYSO LYXO MAL(O) MENTH(O) MERCUR(O) METH MOLYBD MURIO NAPHTH NITRATO NITRILO NITROSO NOR OLEO ORTHO OSMIO OX OXAL(O) OXIDI OXIDO OXIMIDO OXO OXY OZO PENT(A) PERI PHLOR(O) PHTHAL(O) PIPTO PLUMB(I)(O) POLY PROP PROS PROTE(O) PYRROL(O) SYN TOL(U)
(SUFF.) AMIN(E)(O) ANE ASE ATE ENE ID(E) ILE INE INOL INONE ION ITE ITOL IUM OIC OIN OL OLE OLIC OLID(E) ON(E) ONIC ONIUM OSAN OSE OSIDE OUS OYL PHORE RETIN THIN(E) YL YNE ZYME
CHEMIN-DE-FER SHIMMY
CHEMISE SARK SHIFT SHIRT SIMAR SMOCK CAMISA SHIMMY LINGERIE
CHEMISETTE SHAM GUIMPE TUCKER PARTLET
CHEMIST ANALYST ASSAYER CHEMICK BENCHMAN COLORIST DRUGGIST
AMERICAN DOW ABEL CADY CRAM DANA HALE HALL HARE HART HASS HUNT KING LAMB LIND LOEB LONG MARK REID UREY WATT CLARK COOKE CROSS DEBYE DROWN DUMEZ FLORY GIBBS GOOCH HAMOR HERTY KRAUS LEWIS LIBBY MOORE NOYES POWER SEMON SMITH SNELL STINE WILEY BROWNE BUCHER BURTON CALVIN CARVER CLARKE CRAFTS DARKEN DEDUVE DORSET DUDLEY EGLOFF HOLMES HOOVER JULIAN LANDIS LEVENE MENDEL MORGAN MUNROE PALMER REMSEN ROBLIN ROGERS SHIMER SUMNER TORREY WARREN WESSON ALDRICH ANDREWS ATWATER CASSIDY CASTNER CUSHMAN DUSHMAN EDELMAN GIAUQUE GODLOVE GOMBERG GUTHRIE HARKINS KHORANA MIDGLEY ONSAGER PAULING SEABORG SHERMAN SLOSSON WHITNEY BANCROFT BENEDICT CHANDLER COOLIDGE COTTRELL DJERASSI FRANKLIN HORSFORD LANGMUIR LIPSCOMB MCCOLLUM MCMILLAN MIDGELEY MULLIKEN RICHARDS SILLIMAN SPRINGER

STODDARD WILLIAMS WOODWARD ALEXANDER CAROTHERS HENDERSON NIEUWLAND PATTERSON CHITTENDEN HILLEBRAND
ARGENTINE LELOIR
AUSTRIAN KUHN EMICH PREGL PRECHTL WELSBACH ZSIGMONDY
BELGIAN STAS SOLVAY HELMONT BAEKELAND PRIGOGINE
CANADIAN HERZBERG MCLAUGHLIN
CZECH BRAUNER HEYROVSKY
DANISH OERSTED THOMSEN BRONSTED KJELDAHL SORENSEN
DUTCH COHEN MULDER HOMBERG
ENGLISH ABEL BELL DAVY POPE SWAN TODD ABNEY BOYLE CROSS DAKIN DEWAR HENRY MARSH PROUT SODDY SYNGE YOUNG BARTON BRANDE DALTON DONNAN GREGOR HARDEN INGOLD MARTIN MILLER PERKIN PORTER RAMSAY THORPE TILDEN WATSON ANDREWS CROOKES DANIELL FARADAY HAWORTH HODGKIN NORRISH TENNANT TRAVERS HATCHETT MITCHELL PLAYFAIR ROBINSON WILLIAMS ARMSTRONG CAVENDISH CORNFORTH FRANKLAND GLADSTONE PRIESTLEY WILKINSON HINSHELWOOD
FINNISH VIRTANEN
FRENCH LEHN BAUME BEHAL CONTE CURIE DUFAY DUMAS FREMY LEBEL LEBON WURTZ BALARD CLAUDE DARCET DULONG GERNEZ GUIMET LEMERY NAQUET ORFILA PERRIN PROUST RAOULT WERNER CHAPTAL DAUBENY FRIEDEL GLENARD LAURENT LEBLANC LUMIERE MACQUER MOISSAN PASTEUR PELOUZE THENARD BERTRAND CAVENTOU CHEVREUL COURTOIS DEBIERNE DEMARCAY FOURCROY FOURNEAU GERHARDT GRIGNARD KUHLMANN REGNAULT SABATIER BERTHELOT LAVOISIER LECLANCHE LENORMAND PELLETIER VAUQUELIN BERTHOLLET CHARDONNET DUBRUNFAUT LECHATELIER BOUSSINGAULT SCHUTZENBERGER
GERMAN CARO HAHN KOPP KUHN MOND ADLER ALDER BOSCH DIELS EIGEN FRANK HABER KNORR KOLBE LUNGE MEYER STAHL ACHARD BAEYER BECHER BREDIG BUNSEN DOMAGK FITTIG GIESEL GRAEBE KOSSEL LIEBIG MAGNUS NERNST TRAUBE WOHLER BERGIUS BISCHOF BORRGER BUCHNER CASSIUS CURTIUS ERDMANN FEHLING FISCHER GLAUBER HOFMANN OSTWALD TIEMANN WALLACH WIELAND WINDAUS ZIEGLER KLAPROTH MARGGRAF SPRENGEL BEILSTEIN BUTENANDT FRESENIUS LADENBURG LAMPADIUS SCHEIBLER SCHONBEIN STRASSMAN WIEDEMANN ZSIGMONDY BODENSTEIN DOBEREINER ERLENMEYER LIEBERMANN STAUDINGER STROHMEYER WILLSTATER GOLDSCHMIDT UNVERDORBEN WILLSTATTER MITSCHERLICH
HUNGARIAN HEVESY
IRISH KIRWAN STEWART
ITALIAN LEVI NATTA SOVET COVELLI FABRONI SOBRERO AVOGADRO CIAMICIAN CANNIZZARO BRUGNATELLI
JAPANESE FUKUI TAKAMINE
NORWEGIAN WAAGE HASSEL GULDBERG
POLISH CURIE MOSCICKI
RUSSIAN BACH WALDEN SEMENOV BUTLEROV MENDELEV ZELINSKI PRIGOGINE
SCOTTISH URE BELL HALL BLACK BROWN DEWAR YOUNG BEILBY GRAHAM THOMSON MACINTOSH
SPANISH RODRIGUEZ
SWEDISH GAHN CLEVE BERGMAN SCHEELE MOSANDER SEFSTROM SVEDBERG TISELIUS ARRHENIUS BERZELIUS CRONSTEDT BLOMSTRAND ABDERHALDEN
SWISS NEF GLASER KARRER MULLER PICTET PRELOG WERNER RUZICKA MARIGNAC SAUSSURE REICHSTEIN

CHEMOSTERILANT METEPA
CHENAANAH (FATHER OF —) BILHAN
CHENDE CHINOA
CHENFISH KINGFISH
CHENILLE SNAIL
CHEQUEEN BASKET SEQUIN ZEQUIN CECCHINE ZECCHINO
CHEQUER DICE
CHERAN (FATHER OF —) DISHON
CHERAW SARA
CHEREMIS MARI
CHERISH AID HUG PET BEAR DOTE HAVE HOPE LIKE LOVE SAVE ADORE BOSOM BROOD CHEER CLING COWER ENJOY NURSE PRIZE VALUE CARESS ESTEEM FADDLE FONDLE FOSTER GRUDGE HARBOR MOTHER NESTLE NUZZLE PAMPER PETTLE REVERE COMFORT EMBOSOM EMBRACE INDULGE NOURISH NURTURE PROTECT SUPPORT SUSTAIN ENSHRINE INSPIRIT PRESERVE TREASURE
CHERISHED PET DEAR BOSOM DANDILY AFFECTED PRECIOUS
CHEROOT MANILA TRICHI TRICHY
CHERRY BING CHOP DUKE FUJI GEAN MERRY MOREL CORNEL MAZARD BURBANK CAPULIN CHAPMAN LAMBERT MAHALEB MARASCA MAYDUKE MORELLO OXHEART PITANGA WINDSOR AMARELLE DURACINE EGGBERRY LUKEWARD NAPOLEON ROSACEAN BIGARREAU MARASCHINO MONTMORENCY
CHERRY BLOSSOM HEBE
CHERRY-COLORED CERISE
CHERRY ORCHARD (AUTHOR OF —) CHEKHOV
(CHARACTER IN —) ANYA GAYEV VARYA YASHA DUNYASHA LOPAKHIN RANEVSKY TROFIMOV CHARLOTTE
CHERRY PLUM MYROBALAN
CHERRY STONE PAIP
CHERT BOONE WHINSTONE
CHERUB AMOR EROS ANGEL CUPID SERAPH SPIRIT AMORINO AMORETTO CHERUBIM
CHERVIL BUN KECK ARFOIL CERFOIL COWWEED HONEWORT MILKWEED RATSBANE
CHESED (FATHER OF —) NAHOR
CHESS CHEAT SHOGI CHECKER SKITTLES
(— CHAMPION) TAL
(— EXPERT) TAL
(— MOVE) ZUGZWANG
(INEPT — PLAYER) PATZER POTZER
CHESSBOARD CHESS TABLE CHECKER
CHESSMAN PIN KING PIECE CHECKER CHEQUER
(— SET) MEINY MEINIE
(ANY — BUT PAWN) OFFICER
(BISHOP —) ALFIN ALPHIN ARCHER
(CASTLE —) JUEZ ROOK TOUR UDGE JUDGE LEDGE TOWER
(KNIGHT —) HORSE CHEVALIER
(PAWN —) PON POUNE
(QUEEN —) FERS FIERS PHEARSE
CHEST ARK BOX CUB FIX KIT PIX PYX ARCA BUST CAJA CASH CIST CYST FUND KIST SAFE SCOB AMBRY BAHUT BUIST CADDY FRONT HOARD HUTCH RAZEE SISTA TRUNK ALMOIN BASKET BREAST BUNKER BUREAU CAISSE CAJETA CASKET COFFER COFFIN FORCER GIRNAL GIRNEL HAMPER JORDAN LARNAX LOCKER LOWBOY SCRINE SHRINE SPRUCE STRIPE THORAX WANGAN BRAZIER BRISKET CAISSON CAPCASE CASSONE COMMODE DEPOSIT DRAWERS DRESSER ENCLOSE HIGHBOY TOOLBOX WANIGAN WINDBAG CISTVAEN CUPBOARD FORCELET MANIFOLD STANDARD TREASURE TREASURY
(— FOR CUTLERY) CANTEEN
(— FOR FISH) CAUF
(— OF ORES) CAXON
(— PROTECTOR) BIB
(FRONT OF —) BREAST
(MEDICINE —) INRO
(SMALL —) COFFRET
(PREF.) STERN(O) STETH(O) THORAC(I)(O)
CHESTERFIELD COAT SOFA
CHESTNUT GAG JOKE LING RATA BROWN HORSE STORY CASTOR MARRON SATIVA CRENATA DENTATA
(HORSE —) CONKER
(POLYNESIAN —) RATA
(WATER —) LING
(PREF.) CASTANO
CHESTNUT-COLORED BAY ROAN BADIOUS
CHEST PROTECTOR PECTORAL
CHEVAL-DE-FRISE TURNPIKE
CHEVAL GLASS PSYCHE
CHEVALIER CADET NOBLE KNIGHT GALLANT CAVALIER HORSEMAN
CHEVET APSE
CHEVILLE PEG
CHEVIN CHUB CHEVESNE
CHEVRON BEAM MARK WOUND RAFTER STRIPE ZIGZAG
CHEVROTAIN MUSK NAPU DEERLET KANCHIL MEMINNA PLANDOK TRAGULE BOOMORAH PEESOREH RUMINANT
CHEVY TEASE
CHEW CUD EAT GUM TAW BITE CHAM CHAW GNAW NOSH QUID CHAMP CHONK GRIND MUNCH RUMEN CRUNCH MUMBLE CHUMBLE MEDITATE RUMINATE MANDUCATE
(— OUT) SCOLD
(— THE CUD) RUMINATE
(— THE FAT) GAB JAW YAK
(— UP NOISILY) CHANK GROUZE
CHEWING GUM GUM CHICCLE
CHEWINK FINCH JOREE TOWHEE GRASSET
CHEYENNE DOG
CHIAN SCIAN
CHIANTI FLORENCE
CHIASTOLITE MACLE ANDALUSITE
CHIBCHA MUISCA
CHIC GOGO PERT POSH TRIG TRIM KIPPY NATTY NIFTY SMART CHICHI DAPPER GIGOLO JAUNTY MODISH TRENDY ELEGANT STYLISH
(KIND OF —) RADICAL
(NO LONGER —) OUT
CHICAGO PORKOPOLIS
CHICANE DECEPTION
CHICANERY DIRT RUSE WILE FEINT TRICK ARTIFICE INTRIGUE TRICKERY DECEPTION PETTIFOGGERY
CHICHI ARTY TONY
CHICK BIRD GIRL PEEP TICK CHILD NATTY POULET SCREEN SEQUIN SPROUT CHICKEN CHUCKIE
CHICKADEE TOMTIT BLACKCAP TITMOUSE
CHICKAREE BOOMER
CHICKEN HEN KIP COCK FOWL BIDDY CAPON CHICK CHILD CHOOK CHUCK DEEDY FRYER LAYER MANOC POULT SILKY TIMID AFRAID CHICKY PULLET SULTAN SUSSEX TURKEN ANCOBAR BOARDER BROILER DIBBLER LEGHORN POUSSIN ROASTER ROOSTER SCRATCH ARAUCANA COCKEREL PHASANID SPRINGER
(— OUT) WIMPOUT
(— PIECES ON SKEWER) YAKITORI
(— SHELTER) MOTHER
(FRIED —) ESCABECHE
(STRIPS OF —) FAJITA
CHICKEN COOP CAVY CAVIE
CHICKEN-FEED PEANUTS
CHICKEN POX SOREHEAD VARICELLA
CHICK-PEA CHIT GRAM CHICH CICER COWGRAM SOWGRAM GARBANZO GARVANCE
(PL.) FASELS

CHICKWEED BLINK BLINKS SPURRY ALLBONE STARWORT
CHICO SAPODILLA
CHICORY BUNK CREPIS ENDIVE SUCCORY WITLOOF BLUEWEED COMPOSIT RADICCHIO
CHIDE BAN FUSS RAIL RATE BLAME CHECK FLITE FLYTE SCOLD SNEAP BERATE REBUFF REBUKE SCHOOL THREAP THREAT THREEP TONGUE CENSURE REPROVE UPBRAID WRANGLE ADMONISH BETONGUE LAMBASTE REPROACH
CHIDING ROW
CHIEF (ALSO SEE CHIEFTAIN) BO AGA BIG BOH CAP CID COB DUX MIR MOI TOP AGHA ALII AMIR ARCH ARII BOSS CAID CHEF COCK DATO DEAN DOEG DUCE DUKE EMIR HEAD HIER HIGH INCA JARL JEFE KAID KHAN KING MAIN MICO MOST NAIK ONLY QAID RAIS RAJA REIS TYEE ALDER ALPHA ARIKI DATTO ELDER FIRST GREAT MAJOR MATAI NAYAK PRIMA PRIME PRIMO RAJAH RULER THANE TITAN VITAL ZAQUE ZIPPA ADALID CABEZA DEPUTY FLAITH HEADLY INKOSI KEHAYA KUBERA KUVERA LEADER LULUAI MASTER MIRDHA NAIQUE PENLOP PRABHU PRIMAL RECTOR SACHEM SAYYID SHAYKH SHEIKH SHERIF STAPLE SUDDER TOPMAN TURNUS CAPITAL CAPTAIN CENTRAL EMINENT FOREMAN GENERAL HEADMAN INGOMAR LEADING LEMPIRA MUGWUMP OVERMAN PADRONE PALMARY POLYGAR PRELATE PREMIER PRIMARY SHEREEF STELLAR SUPREME TOPSMAN TRIBUNE CABOCEER CAPITANO CARDINAL DECURION DIRECTOR DOMINANT ELDORADO ESPECIAL FOREMOST GOVERNOR HEADSMAN HIERARCH INTIMATE MOKADDAM PREMIERE SAGAMORE STAROSTA SUBCHIEF PENDRAGON
(— IN INDIA) PRABHU SIRDAR
(— OF ADVOCATES) BATONNIER
(— OF RELIGIOUS ORDER) GENERAL
(— OF TITHING) BORSHOLDING
(— OF 10 MEN) DEAN
(CHINOOK —) TYEE
(CLAN —) TOISECH
(INDIAN —) SUNCK SACHEM SUNCKE CACIQUE MOCUDDUM SAGAMORE
(MALAY —) RAJA RAJAH
(MOHAMMEDAN —) DATO DATTO SAYID SAYYID
(SCHOOL —) DUX
(SCOTTISH —) MAORMOR
(TIBETAN —) POMBO
(TURKISH —) AGA AGHA
(VIKING —) SEAKING
(PREF.) ARCH(I) PROT(O)
CHIEFLY MAINLY LARGELY
CHIEFTAIN BEG AMIR CHAM EMIR HEAD JARL KHAN ASTUR CHIEF EMEER LEADER SIRDAR CAUDILLO HIAWATHA
CHIEFTAINCY STOOL CHIEFRY
CHIEFTAINESS QUEEN
CHIFFCHAFF PEGGY CHIPCHAP CHIPCHOP
CHIFFON SHEER
CHIFFONIER BUREAU CABINET COMMODE
CHIGGER BICHO PIQUE CHIGGA CHIGOE GIGGER JIGGER LEPTUS REDBUG WHEELWORM
CHIGNON COB KNOT COBBE TWIST
CHIGOE FLEA SIKA BICHO NIGUA PIQUE SCREW CHIGGA ENIGUA JIGGER SANDBOY SANDWORM
CHIH FU PREFECT
CHILBLAIN KIBE MULE BLAIN MOOLS MOULS PERNIO
CHILD BEN BOY BUD ELF GET IMP KID LAD SON SOT TAD TOT WAY BABA BABE BABY BATA BIRD BRAT CHAP CHIT CION FOOD GIRL GYTE PAGE PUSS TIKE TINY TOTO TROT TYKE WEAN BAIRN BIRTH BROLL BROWL CHICK CHIEL COOKY ELFIN GAMIN ISSUE KEIKI OLIVE POULT SCION TIDDY TRICK WAYNE WENCH WHELP CHERUB COLLOP COOKIE ENFANT FILIUS FOSTER INFANT MOPPET NIPPER PLEDGE PROLES SHAVER STUMPY TACKER TODDLE URCHIN BAMBINO CHOOKIE CHOPPER CHRISOM COCKNEY DICKENS GANGREL GYTLING KINCHIN KITLING LAMBKIN PAPOOSE PRETEEN PROGENY STICHEL SUBTEEN TIDDLER TODDLER TROTTIE WRAWLER YOUNKER BANTLING CHISELER DAUGHTER EPIGONUS JUVENILE LITTLING NURSLING PRATTLER RUNABOUT WEANLING WHIMLING PRESCHOOLER
(— AT BAPTISM) CHRISOM CHRISTOM
(— IN THE WOMB) BURDEN
(— OF THE WORLD) WELTKIND
(— UNDER 7 YEARS) INFANS
(ANNOYING —) BRAT
(BAD-MANNERED —) GOOP
(BAPTISMAL —) CHRISOM
(CHUBBY —) CHUNK
(CODDLED —) COCKNEY
(ELF'S —) AUF OAF CHANGELING
(FAVORITE —) BENJAMIN
(FAVORITE —) BENJAMIN
(FORWARD —) JACKANAPES
(FOSTER —) DAULT NORRY NURRY FOSTER REARLING
(ILLEGITIMATE —) MISHAP BASTARD
(INNOCENT —) CHRISOM
(LAST-BORN —) DILLING
(LOVED —) JOY
(MERRY —) SUNBEAM
(MEXICAN —) NINO
(MISCHIEVOUS —) IMP LIMB TIKE DICKENS
(NAKED —) SCUDDY
(NEGLECTED —) WAIF WASTREL
(NEWBORN —) NEONATE STRANGER
(NURSERY —) PREEMIE
(PAUPER —) MINDER
(PLAYFUL —) ELF WANTON
(PLUMP —) FOB FUB
(PRECOCIOUS —) PRODIGY
(PURE —) DOVE
(ROWDY —) HOODLUM
(SMALL —) TAD TOT MITE SPUD GAITT KIDDY TIDDY TOTUM KIDLET PEEWEE TACKER BAIRNIE
(SPOILED —) CADE COSSET WANTON COCKNEY
(STUNTED —) URF
(SWEET —) CHERUB
(TROUBLESOME —) PICKLE STICHEL
(UNMANNERLY —) SMATCHET
(UNWEANED —) SUCKLING
(YOUNG —) BABY JOEY INFANT SQUIRT GANGREL NESTLER TODDLER BANTLING INNOCENT LITTLING SUCKLING
(YOUNGEST —) WRIG DILLING
(PREF.) INFANTI PAED(O) PAID(O) PED(O) TECHNO TECNO TEKNO
CHILDBED JIZZEN
CHILDBIRTH LABOR CRYING INLYING TRAVAIL OXYTOCIA
(— WOMAN) PUERPERA
(OF A METHOD OF —) LAMAZE
(PREF.) LOCHIO LOCHO TOCO TOKO
(SUFF.) TOCIA TOCO(US) TOKIA TOKO(US)
CHILDHOOD INFANCY CHILDAGE
(2ND —) DOTAGE TWICHILD
CHILDISH TID WEAK DANSY NAIVE PETTY SILLY YOUNG CHITTY PULING SIMPLE WEANLY ASININE BABYISH CHILDLY FOOLISH KIDDISH PEEVISH PROGENY PUERILE UNMANLY BAIRNISH BRATTISH IMMATURE TOOTLING
CHILDISHNESS DOTAGE
CHILDLESS ORBATE
CHILDREN ISSUE PROLES STRAIN PROGENY OFFSPRING
(NUMBER OF —) PARITY
(SUFF.) PAEDES
CHILE SOCOMPA
(— INDIAN) FUEGIAN

CHILE

BAY: COOK EYRE NENA TARN LOMAS OTWAY SARCO DARWIN INUTIL MORENO STOKES TONGOY DYNELEY INGLESA SKYRING DESOLATE
CAPE: DYER HORN CHOROS HORNOS QUILAN TABLAS DESEADO BASCUNAN CARRANZA
CAPITAL: SANTIAGO
CHANNEL: ANCHO CHEAP BEAGLE COCKBURN MORALEDA
COIN: PESO LIBRA CONDOR ESCUDO CENTAVO CONDORS CONDORES
DESERT: ATACAMA
GULF: ANCUD GUAFO PEÑAS ARAUCO
INDIAN: ONA AUCA INCA ONAN ARAUCA CHANGO YAHGAN FUEGIAN MAPUCHE MOLUCHE PAMPEAN PATAGON RANQUEL ALIKULUF PICUNCHE TSONECAN
ISLAND: LUZ PRAT BYRON GUAFO HOSTE MOCHA NUEVA NUNEZ VIDAL CHILOE DAWSON EASTER LENNOX PIAZZI PICTON QUILAN RIESCO STOSCH TALCAN ANGAMOS CAMPANA HANOVER REFUGIO TRANQUI CLARENCE HUAMBLIN NALCAYEC NAVARINO TRAIGUEN
ISLANDS: CHONOS HERMITE PAJAROS CHAUQUES
ISTHMUS: OFQUI
LAKE: TORO RANCO YELCHO PUYEHUE RUPANCO
MEASURE: VARA LEGUA LINEA CUADRA FANEGA
MOUNTAIN: MACA TORO CHATO MAIPO PAINE POTRO PULAR TORRE YOGAN APIWAN BURNEY CONICO JERVIS POQUIS RINCON CHALTEL COPIAPO FITZROY PALPANA VELLUDA COCHRANE TRONADOR YANTELES
MOUNTAINS: ANDES DARWIN ALMEIDA DOMEYKO
NATIVE: PATAGONIAN
PENINSULA: HARDY LACUY TAITAO TUMBES
POINT: TORO GALLO LILES LOBOS LOROS MORRO TALCA TETAS VIEJA CACHOS GALERA MOLLES ANGAMOS LAVAPIE
PORT: LOTA TOME ARICA COQUIMBO
PROVINCE: AISEN ARICA AYSEN MAULE NUBLE TALCA ARAUCO BIOBIO CAUTIN CHILOE CURICO OSORNO ATACAMA LINARES MALLECO COQUIMBO OHIGGINS SANTIAGO TARAPACA VALDIVIA
RIVER: LOA LAJA YALI ALHUE AZAPA BRAVO BUENO ELQUI ITATA LAUCA LLUTA MAIPO MAULE PUELO RAHUE RAPEL VITOR BIOBIO CAMINA CHOAPA CHOROS CISNES COLINA HUASCO LIMARI MORADO PALENA POSCUA TOLTEN COPIAPO VALDIVIA
SHRUB: LITRE
STRAIT: NELSON MAGELLAN
TOWN: BOCO CUYA LEBU LOTA OCOA TOCO TOME ARICA TALCA ARAUCO CURICO GATICO OSORNO SERENA TEMUCO VICUNA YUMBEL YUNGAY CALDERA CHILLAN COPIAPO COQUIMBO RANCAGUA SANTIAGO VALDIVIA
TREE: RAULI
VOLCANO: LANIN MAIPO ANTUCO LASCAR LLAIMA OSORNO OYAHUE TACORA LAUTARO PETEROA SOCOMAP VILLARICA GUALLATIRI
WEIGHT: GRANO LIBRA QUINTAL
WIND: SURES

CHILEAB (FATHER OF —) DAVID
(MOTHER OF —) ABIGAIL
CHILE-BELLS COPIHUE LAPAGERIA
CHI-LIN KYLIN UNICORN
CHILION (DAUGHTER OF —) ORPAH
(MOTHER OF —) NAOMI

CHILL ICE RAW AGUE COLD COOL DAZY ALGID ALGOR DAVER GELID OURIE RIGOR SCHEL SHAKE FRAPPE FREEZE FRIGID FROSTY SHIVER SNELLY DEPRESS FRETISH FRISSON MALARIA COLDNESS
(— OUT) RELAX
CHILLED ICED ACOLD CHILL FROZEN STARVEN
CHILLING ICY COLD EERY BLEAK EERIE NIPPY CHILLY WINTRY GLACIAL NIPPING SHIVERY
CHILLNESS COLD
CHILLY ICY RAW COLD COOL LASH ALGID BLEAK HUNCH NIPPY PARKY AGUISH AIRISH ARCTIC CRIMMY FROSTY FROZEN LEEPIT CAULDRIFE
CHIMAERA BELUE DRAGON CATFISH PLACOID RATFISH RATTAIL DOODSKOP
CHIME DIN RIM BELL EDGE PEAL RING SUIT TING TINK AGREE CHIMB CHINE PRATE ACCORD CLOCHE CYMBAL JINGLE MELODY CONCORD HARMONY SINGSONG
(PL.) BELL
CHIMER CYMAR SIMAR CHIMAR TABARD
CHIMERA FANCY MIRAGE MOSAIC POMATO ILLUSION
CHIMERE ROBE
CHIMERICAL VAIN WILD INSANE UTOPIAN DELUSIVE FANCIFUL ROMANTIC IMAGINARY
CHIMNEY BAG LUM TUN FLUE LUMM PIPE TUBE VENT GULLY STACK STALK TEWEL CHIMLA FUNNEL LOUVER SMOKER TUNNEL FISSURE OPENING ORIFICE FUMIDUCT SMOKESTACK
CHIMNEY CAP TURNCAP
CHIMNEY CORNER FIRESIDE INGLENOOK
CHIMNEY COWL COW
CHIMNEY HOOD JACK
CHIMNEY PIECE PAREL
CHIMNEY PIPE TALLBOY
CHIMNEY POST SPEER
CHIMNEY-POT TOPHAT
CHIMNEY SEAT SCONCE
CHIMNEY SWEEP SWEEP CHUMMY FLUEMAN RAMONEUR
CHIMP (SPACE —) ENOS
CHIMPANZEE APE CHIMP JACKO JOCKO PIGMY PYGMY NCHEGA PIGMEW PYGMEAN
CHIN JAW RAP CHAT TSIN MENTUM CHOLLER
(— POINT) MENTON POGONION
(DOUBLE —) BUCCULA CHOLLER
(PREF.) GENIO MENTI MENTO
CHINA WARE JAPAN LENOX SPODE CATHAY PARIAN SEVRES TEASET CERAMIC CHEENEY DRESDEN LIMOGES MEISSEN POTTERY CINCHONA CROCKERY EGGSHELL
(BONE —) WEDGWOOD
(KIND OF —) HOTEL

CHINA

ABORIGINE: YAO MANS MIAO MANTZU YAOMIN MIAOTSE
AREA UNIT: MU MOU MOW
BASIN: TARIM
BAY: LAICHOW HANGCHOW
BUDDHA: FO
CAPE: OLWANPI
CAPITAL: PEKING TAIPEI PEIPING
CHANNEL: BASHI
COIN: PU CASH CENT MACE TAEL TIAO YUAN CHIAO SYCEE DOLLAR
CURRENCY: RENMINBI
DEPRESSION: TURFAN
DESERT: GOBI ORDOS SHAMO ALASHAN TAKLAMAKAN
DIALECT: WU MIN AMOY HAKKA CANTON HSIANG SWATOW FOOCHOW WENCHOW KANHAKKA MANDARIN
DRY LAKE: LOPNOR
DYNASTY: WU HAN SHU SUI WEI YIN CHIN CHOU HSIA HSIN MING SUNG TANG YUAN CHING SHANG
GULF: POHAI CHIHLI TONKIN PECHILI LIAOTUNG
ISLAND: AMOY FLAT MACAO MATSU NAMKI CHUSAN HAINAN PRATAS QUEMOY TAIWAN YUHWAN FORMOSA HUNGTOW TUNGSHA CHOUCHAN KULANGSU STAUNTON
ISLANDS: PENGHU TACHEN CHUSHAN MIAOTAO
LAKE: TAI CHAO KAOYU OLING TELLI BAMTSO BORNOR EBINOR ERHHAI KHANKA LOPNOR NAMTSO POYANG CHALING HUNGTSE KARANOR KOKONOR HULUNNOR MONTCALM TAROKTSO TELLINOR TIENCHIH TSINGHAI TUNGTING
MEASURE: HO HU KO LI MU PU TO TU FAN FEN PAU TOU TUN YIN CHIH FANG KISH PARA QUEI SHIH TSUN CHANG CHING SHENG SHING CHUPAK KUNGHO KUNGLI KUNGMU KUNGFEN KUNGYIN KUNGCHIH
MOUNTAIN: OMI OMEI SUNG KAILAS POBEDA EVEREST MUZTABH SUNGSHAN
MOUNTAINS: ALTAY KUNLUN ALASHAN KUENLUN MEILING MINSHAN NANLING NANSHAN TANGLHA BOGDOULA HIMALAYA TAPASHAN TAYULING TIENSHAN WUYLISHAN
NAME: CATHAY
NATIVE: PAT
PENINSULA: LEICHU LUICHOW LIAOTUNG
PORT: AMOY WUHU AIGUN SHASI ANTUNG CANTON CHEFOO DAIREN ICHANG NINGPO PAKHOI SWATOW SZEMAO WUCHOW YOCHOW FOOCHOW HUNCHUN MENGTSZ NANKING SAMSHUI SANTUAO SOOCHOW WENCHOW CHANGSHA HANGCHOW KIUKIANG KONGMOON LUNGCHOW SHANGHAI TENGYUEH TIENTSIN TSINGTAO WANHSIEN
PROVINCE: HONAN HOPEH HOPEI HUNAN HUPEI HUPEN JEHOL KANSU KIRIN TIBET ANHWEI FUKIEN SHANSI SHENSI TAIWAN YUNNAN KIANGSI KWANGSI NGANHUI CHEKIANG KWEICHOW LIAONING MONGOLIA SHANTUNG SZECHWAN TSINGHAI MANCHURIA
RELIGION: JU SHINTO TAOISM BUDDHISM
RESERVOIR: SUNGARI
RIVER: SI HAN ILI MIN NEN PEI WEI AMUR HUAI LIAO LOHO TUNG YALU YUAN YUEN ARGUN FENHO MACHU PEIHO TARIM TUMEN WEIHO CHUMAR DRECHU DZACHU KHOTAN KUMARA LIAOHO MANASS MEKONG OCHINA URUNGU YELLOW HOANGHO HWANGHO KERULEN KIALING SALWEEN SIKIANG SUNGARI TSANGPO WUKIANG YANGTZE YARKAND YUKIANG CHERCHEN HANKIANG HUNGSHUI MINKIANG
RULER: WANG
SEA: ECHINA SCHINA YELLOW
STRAIT: HAINAN TAIWAN FORMOSA
TOWN: BAI NOH AHPA AMOY ANSI ANTA AQSU FUYU GUMA HAMI HUMA IPIN KIAN KISI LINI LOHO LUTA MOHO MOYU MULI NIYA NOHO NURA OMIN OWPU RIMA SAKA SIAN TALI TAYU WUHU WUSU WUTU YAAN CHIAI FUSIN HOFEI ICHUN JEHOL KIRIN KOKLU LHASA MACAO PENKI SHASI TAIAN TALAI TUTZE TUYUN TZEPO WUHAN WUSIH YENKI YULIN YUMEN ANSHAN ANTUNG CANTON CHENDU DAIREN FUCHAU FUSHUN HANKOW HANTAN HARBIN HOIHOW KALGAN LOYANG LUSHUN MUKDEN NINGPO PAOTOW PEKING PENGPU SUCHOW SWATOW TAINAN TAIPEI TALIEN TSINAN YUNNAN CHUNGTU FATSHAN FOOCHOW HANYANG HUHEHOT KAIFENG KUNMING KWEISUI LANCHOW NANKING PAOTING PEIPING SOOCHOW TAIYUAN TIANJIN TZEKUNG URUMCHI WUCHANG YENPING CHANGSHA CHAOCHOW CHENGTEH CHINCHOW HANGCHOW KIAOCHOW KWEIYANG NANCHANG QARAQASH SHANGHAI SHENYANG SIANGTAN TANGSHAN TENGCHOW TIENTSIN TSINGTAO TUNGCHOW CHUNGKING
WEIGHT: LI TA FAN FEN HAO KIN SSU TAN YIN CHEE CHIN DONG MACE SHIH TAEL CATTY CHIEN LIANG PICUL TCHIN HAIKWAN KUNGFEN KUNGSSU KUNGCHIN

CHINABERRY LILAC AZEDARACH CHINABALL SOAPBERRY
CHINA BLUE NIKKO
CHINA-GRASS RAMI RAMEE RAMIE
CHINA HAT HAELTZUK HEILTSUK
CHINAMAN CHOW JOHN JOHNNY CELESTIAL
(PL.) TANKA
CHINA ROSE MANETTI HIBISCUS
CHINA STONE PETUNSE
CHINA TREE LILAC HAGBUSH
CHINAWARE CRACKLE
CHINCHILLA ABROCOME VIZCACHA
CHINE BACK IKAT CHINK CRACK CREST GORGE RIDGE SPINE CLEAVE RAVINE SPROUT CREVICE
CHINESE PAT BABA CHOW CERAI CHINK SERES SERIC SINIC MANZAS MONGOL ASIATIC CATAIAN CHINOIS PIGTAIL SANGLEY
(COMMUNIST —) CHICOM
(PREF.) CHINO SINICO SINO
CHINESE ARTICHOKE CROSNE CHOROGI CROSNES STACHYS KNOTROOT
CHINESE CABBAGE PECHAY PAKCHOI
CHINESE DATE BER JUJUBE
CHINESE GELATIN AGAR
CHINESE PARSLEY CILANTRO
CHING TSING
CHINGPAW KACHIN SINGPHO YAWYINS
CHINIOFON YATREN
CHINK GAP BORE CASH CHAP COIN JINK KINK RENT RIFT RIME SCAR BOORE CHECK CHINE CHUNK CLEFT CRACK GRIKE KNACK MONEY CRANNY RICTUS SPRAIN CHINKLE CREVICE FISSURE APERTURE
CHINPIECE BARBEL
CHINQUAPIN OAK BONNET NUTLET BONNETS CANDOCK CHESTNUT WANKAPIN YOCKERNUT
CHINTZ PINTADO SALAMPORE
CHIONE (FATHER OF —) BOREAS DAEDALION
(HUSBAND OF —) NEPTUNE
(MOTHER OF —) ORITHYIA DAEDALION
(SLAYER OF —) DIANA
(SON OF —) EUMOLPUS AUTOLYCUS PHILAMMON
CHIOT SCIOT
CHIP BIT CPU CUT DIB GAG HEW NIG BONE CHAP CLIP HACK KNAP KNOP NICK PARE SAND SKIN SNIP SNUB BEACH CHECK CRACK FLAKE PIECE SCRAP SKELF SLICE SPALE SPALL SPALT SPAWL SPELL SPOON WASTE BORING CHISEL GALLET MARKER NOODLE COUNTER SHAVING CHIPPING COSSETTE FRAGMENT SPLINTER WHITLING
(— IN) ANTE
(— OF SOLDER) LINK
(— OF WOOD) SPOON
(— OUT) DESEAM
(BUFFALO —S) BODEWASH
(COMPUTER MEMORY —) DRAM
(CORN —S) FRITOS
(MEMORY —) DRAM
(POTATO —) CRISP
(SUPPLY OF —S) STACK
(TORTILLA —) NACHO
CHIP BASKET PUNNET
CHIPMAN SCRAPMAN

CHIPMUNK CHIPPY GOPHER GRINNY HACKEE GRINNIE SQUIRREL
CHIPOLATA SAUSAGE
CHIPPENDALE AFGHAN
CHIPPER GAY SPRY CHIRP PERKY BABBLE COCKEY FIERCE HACKER KIPPER LIVELY CHATTER CHIRRUP TWITTER CHEERFUL
CHIPPINGS SWARF
CHIRO BONYFISH FRANCESCA
CHIROGRAPHY WRITING
CHIRON (— AS CONSTELLATION) SAGITTARIUS
(FATHER OF —) SATURN
(MOTHER OF —) PHILYRA
CHIROPODIST PEDICURE CORNCUTTER
CHIROPTEROUS BATTY
CHIRP PEW PIP PEEK PEEP PIPE PULE TWIT WEAK CHEEP CHELP CHIRK CHIRL CHIRM CHIRT TWEET TWINK CHIPPER CHIRRUP CHITTER REJOICE SHATTER TWEEDLE TWITTER WHEETLE WHITTER
CHIRPPING TWITTER
CHIRR PITTER
CHIRU SUS
CHISEL BUR CUT GAD CHIP ETCH FORM MOIL PARE SEAT SETT TANG TOOL BRUZZ BURIN CARVE CHEAT DROVE GOUGE HARDY POINT SCOOP SLICK STIFF BROACH CHESIL FIRMER FORMER GRAVEL HAGGLE POMMEL QUARRY REAMER TOOLER BARGAIN BOASTER BOLSTER CHIPPER ENGRAVE GRADINE GRUBBER POINTER QUARREL SCOOPER SCORPER SHINGLE CROSSCUT SPLITTER
(BLACKSMITH'S —) HARDY HARDIE
(FLINT —) TRANCHET
(ICE —) SPUD
(JEWELER'S —) SCAUPER SCORPER
(PREHISTORIC —) CELT
(STONEMASON'S —) TOOL DROVE POMMEL TOOLER SPLITTER
(TOOTHED —) GRADINE
(TRIANGULAR —) BUR BURR
(WHEELWRIGHT'S —) BRUZZ
(PREF.) CELTI
CHISELER CHEAT CROOK COYOTE GOUGER
CHISLON (SON OF —) ELIDAD
CHIT DAB IOU TAB BILL NOTE DRAFT LETTER VOUCHER
CHITARRONE ARCHLUTE
CHITCHAT GAB GASH GUFF TALK BANTER GOSSIP GOSSIPRY BAVARDAGE
CHITINOUS SHELLY
CHITON EXOMIS DIPLOIS EXOMION
CHITTAMWOOD IRONWOOD
CHITTERLINGS SOULFOOD
CHIVALROUS BRAVE CIVIL NOBLE PREUX GENTLE POLITE GALLANT GENTEEL VALIANT WARLIKE KNIGHTLY
CHIVE CIVE SIVE CIVET SITHE ALLIUM
CHIVY RUN VEX BAIT HUNT RACE CHASE CHEVY TEASE BADGER CHIVVY FLIGHT HARASS PURSUE PURSUIT SCAMPER TORMENT MANEUVER
CHLAMYDIA BEDSONIA
CHLOASMA MOTH
CHLOR LEMON
CHLORDIAZEPOXIDE LIBRIUM
CHLORIDE BUTTER CALOMEL MURIATE VIOLOGEN ALEMBROTH
CHLORINE OXYGEN
CHLORION SPHEX
CHLORIS (BROTHER OF —) AMYCLAS
(FATHER OF —) AMPHION
(HUSBAND OF —) NELEUS ZEPHYRUS
(MOTHER OF —) NIOBE
(SON OF —) NESTOR
CHLORITE AMESITE
CHOANA COLLAR
CHOBDAR USHER CHOPDAR
CHOCK COG PAD BLOCK BRACE CHUCK CLEAT SPOKE SPRAG WEDGE SCOTCH
(PL.) STOWWOOD
CHOCKABLOCK SOLID
CHOCOLATE BUD CANDY COCOA NORFOLK JACOLATT
(— MIXTURE) GANACHE
(— SNACK) OREO
CHOGAK SHOQ
CHOICE BET ODD TRY BEST FINE FORE GOOD MIND PICK RARE WALE WEAL WILL CREAM ELITE PRIME VOICE CHOSEN DAINTY DESIRE FLOWER OPTION PICKED PLUMMY SELECT DILEMMA ELEGANT EXCERPT PERMISS DELICATE ELECTION EXIMIOUS UNCOMMON VOLITION RECHERCHE PREFERENCE
(FAVORITE —) STANDBY
(FREE —) SWING DRUTHERS
(PARTICULARLY —) RECHERCHE
CHOICEST PICK PRIMROSE
CHOIR KERE QUIRE CHAPEL CHORUS CHORALE CONCERT KAPELLE PSALMODY
CHOIRBOY CLERGEON CHORISTER
CHOIR LEADER CANTOR CHORAGUS CHORISTER PRECENTOR
CHOIRMASTER CHORAGUS
CHOKE DAM GAG GOB CLOG DAMP PLUG QUAR STOP WARP CHECK CHOCK CLOSE GRAIN GRANE SCRAG WORRY ACCLOY HINDER IMPEDE STIFLE SWARVE CONGEST QUACKLE QUEAZEN QUERKEN REPRESS SILENCE SMOLDER SMOTHER OBSTRUCT QUEASOME SCUMFISH STOPPAGE STRANGLE SUPPRESS THROTTLE
(— OFF) BESET
(— UP) CLOY GORGE STUFF
CHOKEBERRY DOGBERRY SOAPBERRY
CHOKED FOUL WOOLY WOOLLY CLOTTED
CHOKEDAMP STYTHE BLACKDAMP
CHOKERMAN CHAINER CHAINMAN
CHOKWE KIOKO
CHOLER IRE BILE FURY RAGE ANGER WRATH SPLEEN TEMPER DISTEMPER
CHOLERIC MAD ANGRY CROSS FIERY HUFFY TESTY FUMISH IREFUL TOUCHY BILIOUS ENRAGED IRACUND PEEVISH PEPPERY WASPISH WRATHFUL IMPATIENT
CHOLIAMB SCAZON
CHONDRIOME CYTOME
CHOOSE OPT TRY CHAP CULL LIKE LIST LOVE LUST PICK TAKE VOTE WALE WEAL ADOPT ELECT PRICK ANOINT DECIDE GOWITH PLEASE PREFER SELECT EMBRACE ESPOUSE EXTRACT SEPARATE
(— ABRUPTLY) PLUMP
(— A CAREER) GOINTO
(— EASIEST COURSE OF ACTION) WIMPOUT
(— TO WEAR) FAVOR
CHOOSING OPTION ECLECTIC
CHOOSY PICKY CHOICY FINICAL
CHOP AX AXE CUT HAG HEW JAW LOP CHAP CHIP DICE GASH HACK HASH HOWL RIVE SLIT CARVE CLEFT CRACK KNOCK MINCE NOTCH SLASH STAMP TRADE TRUCK WHANG BARTER CHANGE CLEAVE INCISE EXCHANGE
(— OFF) SNIG
(— SMALL) DEVIL MINCE
(— UP) HACKLE
(— WITH DULL AX) BUTTE
(DOG'S —) FLEW
(PORK —) GRISKIN
CHOPINE CIOPPINO PANTOFLE
CHOPPED CUT CHAPPED
CHOPPER SAX MINCER CLEAVER SLASHER TRANCHET
CHOPPINESS CHOP JABBLE
CHOPPING BLOCK HACKLOG
CHOPPING TOOL (— CULTURE) SOAN SOHAN
CHOPPY BUMPY LOPPY LUMPY PECKY ROUGH SHORT POPPLY
CHORAL (— SOCIETY) ORPHEON
CHORD CORD DYAD ROLL TONE CORDE NERVE TRIAD TRINE ACCORD STRING TENDON TETRAD CADENCE CONCORD HARMONY ARPEGGIO DIAMETER FILAMENT SFORZANDO
(STRIKE A —) RESONATE
(TOUCH A —) RESONATE
CHORDATA VERTEBRA
CHORE JOB JOT CHAR DUTY TASK CHARE KNACK STINT ERRAND BUSINESS
CHOREA JUMP JERKS
CHOREOGRAPHY TERPSICHORE
CHORION SEROSA
CHORISTER SINGER CHANTER CHOIRBOY
CHORTLE TITTER
CHORUS SONG CHOIR DRONE QUIRE ACCORD ASSENT BURDEN UNISON CHORALE HOLDING REFRAIN RESPONSE THYMELICI
(— IN PLAY) GREX
CHOSEN ELECT ELITE SORTED ELECTED FANCIED AFFECTED SELECTED
(CAREFULLY —) RECHERCHE
(PREF.) LECTO
CHOUGH COW CHANK CHEWET CORBIE CHOCARD
CHOWDER BOUILLABAISSE
CHOWRY COWTAIL
CHRISM CREAM CREME MURON MYRON
CHRIST X KING LORD TRUE JUDGE RANSOM VERITY MESSIAH SAVIOUR DRIGHTEN PARAMOUR
(INFANT —) BAMBINO
CHRISTEN DUB NAME KIRSEN BAPTIZE
CHRISTENING GOSSIPING
CHRISTIAN XN XT XTIAN UNIATE GENTILE THOMEAN CHRISTEN EBIONITE GALILEAN MELCHITE NAZARENE ORIENTAL STONEITE TRADITOR COLOSSIAN
(— MONOGRAM) IHS
(— VISITOR TO JERUSALEM) HAJI HADJI HAJJI
(EARLY —) COPT
(EASTERN —) UNIAT
(JEWISH —) JUDAIZER
(PL.) FLOCK LAPSED ACEPHALI FAITHFUL
CHRISTIANIA CRISTY
CHRISTIANITY WAY XTY XNTY
CHRISTMAS NOEL YULE HOLIDAY NATIVITY YULETIDE MIDWINTER
CHRISTMAS ROSE BEARFOOT LUNGWORT MELAMPOD PEDELION
CHRISTOPHE COLOMB
(COMPOSER OF —) MILHAUD
CHRIST'S-THORN NABK JUJUBE ZIZYPHUS
CHROMA COLOR QUALITY
CHROMATIC HUEFUL FLAMING SEMITONAL
CHROMATOPHORE ALLOPHORE LIPOPHORE UNIVALENT RHODOPLAST
CHROMOLITHOGRAPH OLEOGRAPH
CHROMOSOME DIAD DYAD IDANT HOMOLOG ALLOSOME AUTOSOME IDIOSOME MONOSOME KARYOMERE LEPTONEMA PLANOSOME
(ENLARGED REGION OF —) PUFF
(PL.) GEMINI
(SUFF.) **(HAVING — NUMBER)** PLOID
CHROMOSPHERE SIERRA
CHROMOTROPE DYE
CHRONIC FIXED SEVERE INTENSE CONSTANT STUBBORN
CHRONICLE BRUT ANNAL DIARY ENACT RECORD ACCOUNT HISTORY RECITAL CORNICLE REGISTER
(PL.) ANNALS ARCHIVE PARALIPOMENON
CHRONICLER WRITER CHRONIST COMPILER RECORDER HISTORIAN SEANNACHIE
CHRONOLOGICAL TEMPORAL
CHRONOMETER DIAL HACK CLOCK TIMER WATCH
CHRYSAL FRET
CHRYSALIS KELL PUPA AURELIA

CHRYSANTHEMUM MUM KIKU OXEYE SPOON BRUTUS POMPON KIKUMON KIRIMON AZALEAMUM PYRETHRUM MARGUERITE
CHRYSEIS (FATHER OF —) CHRYSES
CHRYSIN FLAVONE
CHRYSIPPUS (FATHER OF —) PELOPS
(MOTHER OF —) ASTYOCHE
(SLAYER OF —) HIPPODAMIA
CHRYSOBERYL CATEYE CHRYSOPAL CYMOPHANE
CHRYSOLITE OLIVINE PERIDOT CHRYSOPAL
CHRYSOTILE ASBESTOS
CHTHONIAN INFERNAL
CHUB DACE DOLT FOOL KIYI LOUT POLL CHOPA CHEVIN SHINER CYPRINID FALLFISH MACKEREL CHAVENDER HORNYHEAD
CHUBBY FAT CHUFF FUBSY PLUMP PUDGY CHOATY CHUFFY PLUMPY ROTUND ROLYPOLY
CHUB MACKEREL TINK TINKER HARDHEAD SCOMBRID
CHUCK HEN LOG PIG CHUG GRUB HURL JERK LUMP TOSS CHOCK CLUCK HEAVE PITCH THROW BOUNCE CHUCKY COLLET CHUCKLE DISCARD
CHUCK-A-LUCK SWEAT HAZARD BIRDCAGE
CHUCKER CROZER
CHUCK-FARTHING CHUCK KNICKER
CHUCKHOLE CAHOT CHUGHOLE
CHUCKIE-STANES DIBS
CHUCKLE CHUCK CLUCK EXULT LAUGH GIGGLE GIZZEN KECKLE SMUDGE TITTER CHORTLE
CHUCKLEHEAD DIMWIT
CHUD VEPS VEPSE
CHUDDAR PHULKARI
CHUFA SEDGE GLUMAL CYPRESS EARTHNUT GALANGAL TIGERNUT GROUNDNUT
CHUM CAD PAL BAIT MATE PARD TOLE TOLL BUDDY BUTTY CRONY SPROG AIKANE CHUMMY COBBER COPAIN FRIEND PARDNER ROOMMATE
(— AROUND) HOBNOB
CHUMMY GREAT MATEY PALLY FAMILIAR
CHUMP ASS DOLT HEAD BLOCK PUMPKIN ENDPIECE SCHLEMIEL
CHUNCHO CHAMA
CHUNK DAB DAD FID GOB PAT WAD JUNK JUNT SLUG CHOCK CHUCK CLAUT PIECE THROW WHANG WHANK GOBBET DORNICK KNUCKLE LUNCHEON
CHUNKY LUMPY PLUMP SQUAT STOUT THICK TRUSS BLOCKY CHUBBY STOCKY CHUNKED
CHURCH DOM SEE DOME FANE FOLD HIGH KILL KIRK KURK TERA ABBEY AUTEM FAITH FLOCK KOVIL SAMAJ TITLE BETHEL CHAPEL CHARGE HIERON SPOUSE TEMPLE EDIFICE FANACLE IGLESIA LATERAN MEMORIA MINSTER ORATORY RECTORY STATION TEMPLET BASILICA EBENEZER ECCLESIA PECULIAR PROCATHEDRAL
(— BOOK) TRIODION
(AREA OF —) APSE BEMA
(CHRISTIAN —) BODY ISRAEL HERITAGE
(EASTERN —) UNIATE
(KIND OF —) STAVE
(MEMBER OF UNIFICATION —) MOONIE
(PREF.) ECCLESIASTICO ECCLESI(O)
CHURCHMAN ALDER ELDER DEACON KIRKMAN PRELATE
(HIGH —) PUSEYITE PRELATIST
(LOW —) SIM LOWBOY SIMEONITE
CHURCH-OFFICER BEADLE BEDRAL BEDERAL
CHURCH SERVICE HEARING TENEBRAE
CHURCHWARDEN PIPE STRAW WARDEN WARNER
CHURCHYARD HAW LITTEN CEMETERY KIRKYARD LYNCHGATE
CHURL CAD MAN OAF BOOR CARL GNOF HIND LOUT SERF CARLE CEORL CHUFF GNOFF KNAVE MISER BODACH CARLOT HARLOT LUBBER RUSTIC VASSAL YEOMAN BONDMAN FREEMAN HASKARD HUSBAND NIGGARD PEASANT VILLAIN VILLEIN CURMUDGEON
CHURLISH MEAN BLUFF GRUFF ROUGH RUNTY SURLY URSAL CRABBY RUSTIC SORDID SULLEN VULGAR BOORISH CARLAGE CARLISH CRABBED CURRISH DOGGISH INCIVIL PEEVISH VIOLENT
CHURN BEAT BOIL KIRN MOIL STIR DRILL SHAKE BUBBLE SEETHE AGITATE BARATTE TRUNDLE
CHUTE RUSH SLIP TUBE FLUME HURRY RAPID SHOOT SLIDE HOPPER TROUGH DECLINE DESCENT DOWNFALL STAMPEDE TELEGRAPH
(MINING —) PASS TELEGRAPH
CHUTZPAH CRUST
CHUZA (WIFE OF —) JOANNA
CIBOL SYBO ONION SYBOW SHALLOT
CIBORIUM PIX PYX CANOPY CIVORY COFFER CIMBORIO
CICADA CAD CIGALE JARFLY LOCUST TETTIX LYREMAN HOMOPTER
(SOUND OF —) CHIRR
CICATRICE FESTER
CICATRICLE TREAD GALLATURE
CICATRIX EYE MARK SCAB SCAR SEAM
CICATRIZE FESTER SCARIFY
CICELY MYRRH
CICERO TULLY
CICERONE GUIDE PILOT MENTOR ORATOR COURIER SIGHTSMAN
CICERONIAN TULLIAN
CICHLID JEWELFISH
CID HERO CAMPEADOR
(AUTHOR OF —) CORNEILLE
(CHARACTER IN —) GOMES DIEGUE SANCHE CHIMENE FERNAND URRAQUE RODRIGUE
CID, EL (COMPOSER OF —) MASSENET
CIDER PERRY PERKIN SWANKY SYDDIR POMMAGE SCRUMPY BEVERAGE COCCAGEE
(HARD —) APPLEJACK
(INFERIOR —) SWANKY
CIGAR PURO TOBY WEED BREVA CLARO SEGAR SHUCK SMOKE CONCHA CORONA HAVANA MADURA MADURO MANILA STOGIE TWOFER BOUQUET CHEROOT CULEBRA LONDRES REGALIA TRABUCO COLORADO LOCOFOCO PANATELA PERFECTO PICKWICK PURITANO
(PART OF —) BAND FOOT HEAD TUCK FILLER WRAPPER
CIGARETTE CIG FAG BIRI BUTT KING PILL SKAG CIGGY CUBEB JOINT SHUCK SMOKE WHIFF CIGGIE GASPER REEFER CIGARITO
(— BUTT) ROACH
(— SUBSTANCE) TAR
(MARIHUANA —) JOINT STICK
(MARIJUANA —) JAY JOINT SPLIFF
(PART OF —) BAND FOOT PAPER FILTER
CIGARFISH SCAD QUIAQUIA
CILIATION
(SUFF.) TRICHA TRICHI(A) TRICHOUS TRICHY
CILIUM HAIR LASH EYELASH UNCINUS BARBICEL CILIOLUM
(PREF.) BLEPHAR(O)
CILIX (BROTHER OF —) CADMUS THANUS PHINEUS PHOENIX
(FATHER OF —) AGENOR
(MOTHER OF —) TELEPHASSA
(SISTER OF —) EUROPA
CILLOSIS LIFEBLOOD
CIMBALOM CEMBALON DULCIMER
CIMEX BEDBUG ACANTHIA
CIMON (FATHER OF —) MILTIADES
(MOTHER OF —) HEGESIPYLE
CINCH BELT GIRD GRIP PIPE SNAP GIMME GIRTH GRAVY BREEZE CINCHA FASTEN WRAPUP PIANOLA SINECURE
CINCHONA CHINA QUINA
CINCHONA BARK
(PREF.) QUIN(O)
CINCINNATI PORKOPOLIS
CINCTURE BAND BELT GIRD HALO LIST RING ZONE GIRTH CENTER CESTUS COLLAR FILLET GIRDLE BALDRIC COMPASS ENCIRCLE SURCINGLE
CINDER ASH TAP COAL GRAY SCAR SLAG CHARK DROSS EMBER DANDER SCORIA CLINKER FOXTAIL RESIDUE
(REFUSE —) BREEZE
(VOLCANIC —) LAPILLUS
(PL.) GLEEDS
CINEMA FILMS DRIVEIN THEATER
CINEMATIZE FILMIZE
CINEMATOGRAPH KINO VERISCOPE VITAGRAPH
CINEPHILE CINEAST
CINERARIA URNS SENECIO
CINGULUM BAND RIDGE GIRDLE
CINNABAR MINIUM
CINNAMON CANEL SPICE CASSIA SANELA STACTE CANELLA BARBASCO
(WILD —) BAYBERRY
CINNAMONROOT FLYBANE FLEAWORT
CINNAMON STONE GARNET ESSONITE
CINQUEFOIL FRASIER COWBERRY HARDHACK ROSACEAN QUINTFOIL SILVERWEED
CINYRAS (DAUGHTER OF —) MYRRHA
(FATHER OF —) APOLLO
(SON OF —) ADONIS
CION BUD IMP SECT SLIP GRAFT SCION SHOOT UVULA SARMENT GRAFTING
CIPHER KEY NIL CODE NULL ZERO ALBAM AUGHT OUGHT DECODE DEVICE FIGURE LETTER NAUGHT NOUGHT NUMBER SYMBOL ATHBASH NULLITY MONOGRAM VIGENERE NOTHINGLY
CIRCASSIAN ADIGHE KABARD CHERKESS KABARDIN
CIRCE SIREN TEMPTER
(BROTHER OF —) AEETES
(FATHER OF —) SOL
(LOVER OF —) ULYSSES ODYSSEUS
(MOTHER OF —) PERSE
(NIECE OF —) MEDEA
(SON OF —) TELEGONUS
CIRCINATE SCORPIOID
CIRCLE DOT LAP ORB RED SET CLUE CULT DISK GYRE HALO HOOP IRIS LOOP MARU ORBE RING RINK ROLL TOUR TURN ZONE BLACK CAROL CLASS CROWN CYCLE FETCH FRAME GROUP KREIS MONDE ORBIT PEARL REALM RHOMB RIGOL ROUND ROWEL SKIRT SWIRL TWIRL BEZANT BROUGH CIRCUS CIRQUE CLIQUE COLLET COLURE CORDON CORONA DIADEM EQUANT GIRDLE RONDEL ROTATE RUNDLE SPIRAL SYSTEM TROPIC AZIMUTH CHUKKAR CHUKKER CIRCLET CIRCUIT COMPANY COMPASS CORONET COTERIE ENCLOSE HORIZON MONTHON REVOLVE RINGLET DEFERENT ECLIPTIC FROSTBOW ROUNDURE SURROUND
(— AROUND ORGAN) ANNULET
(— IN BULL'S-EYE) CARTON
(— OF FRIED DOUGH) POPADUM
(— OF HELL) MALEBOLGE
(— OF MONOLITHS) CROMLECH
(— TRACED BY HORSE) VOLT
(ASTRONOMICAL —) EQUANT EPICYCLE
(DANCE —) GALLEY
(EIGHTH PART OF —) OCTANT
(FAIRY —) RINGLET
(FULL —) AMBIT
(GREAT —) EQUATOR ECLIPTIC MERIDIAN
(IMAGINARY —) CYCLE DEFERENT
(INNER —) BOSOM
(MYSTIC —) MANDALA
(PARHELIC —) FROSTBOW

(QUARTER —) ARC
(STONE —) CAROL HURLER GORSEDD CROMLECH
(TRAVERSE —) RACER
(TWO —S) CACHET
(PREF.) CYCL(O) GYRO
CIRCLET BAND HALO HOOP RING CROWN RIGOL VERGE BANGLE CIRQUE CORONA WREATH CIRCUIT CORONET VALLARY BRACELET HEADBAND
(PREF.) STEPHAN(O)
CIRCUIT LAP AREA BOUT EYRE ITER LOOP TOUR WEND ZONE AMBIT CHAIN CYCLE ORBIT ROUND ROUTE VIRON AMBAGE BUFFER CIRCLE DETOUR DOUBLE HOOKUP SPHERE UMGANG ZODIAC ADAPTER ADDRESS COMARCA COMPASS COUNTER DIOCESE ACCEPTER DIPLEXER DISTRICT PERIPLUS PROGRESS
(BRANCH —) LEG
(COMPUTER —) NOR NAND
(ELECTRIC —) LEG LOOP DOUBLER SQUELCH SECONDARY
(ELECTRONIC —) GATE
(INTEGRATED —) CHIP MICROCHIP
(JUNCTION —) TRUNK
CIRCUITOUS MAZY CURVED CROOKED DEVIOUS OBLIQUE SINUOUS TWISTED VAGRANT WINDING FLEXUOUS INDIRECT RAMBLING TORTUOUS AMBAGIOUS DECEITFUL DEVIATING WANDERING ROUNDABOUT
(— METHOD) WINDLASS
CIRCUITOUSLY ROUND
CIRCULAR O BILL FLIER FLYER LIBEL ORBAL ORBED ROUND DODGER FOLDER RINGED WHEELY ANNULAR COMPASS CYCLOID DISCOID DISLIKE HANDOUT PERFECT RUNDLED COMPLETE DOPEBOOK ENCYCLIC GLOBULAR INFINITE NUMMULAR PAMPHLET DOPESHEET ORBICULAR
CIRCULAR-KNIT SEAMLESS
CIRCULATE GO AIR MIX MOVE PASS RISE TURN WALK WIND BANDY TROLL CANARD PURVEY ROTATE SCURRY SPHERE SPREAD WANDER CANVASS CONVECT DIFFUSE PUBLISH CONVOLVE
CIRCULATING WAIF AFLOAT AMBIENT CURRENT
CIRCULATION ISSUE COURSE COVERAGE CURRENCY
CIRCUMCISER MOHEL
CIRCUMCISION BRITH PERITOMY
CIRCUMFERENCE ARC AUGE AMBIT APSIS GIRTH VERGE BORDER BOUNDS CIRCLE LIMITS COMPASS BOUNDARY SURROUND
(— OF SHELL) LIMBUS
CIRCUMFERENTOR PLANCHETTE
CIRCUMFLEX DOGHOUSE
(INVERTED —) HACEK
CIRCUMLOCUTION AMBAGE CIRCUIT WINDING VERBIAGE
CIRCUMLOCUTORY WORDY
CIRCUMNAVIGATION PERIPLUS
CIRCUMSCRIBE BOUND FENCE LIMIT DEFINE CAPTURE CONFINE ENCLOSE ENVIRON ENCIRCLE RESTRAIN RESTRICT SURROUND CONSCRIBE
CIRCUMSCRIBED NARROW INSULAR LIMITED
(PREF.) CIRCUM
CIRCUMSPECT SHY WARY WISE ALERT CHARY CAREFUL GUARDED PRUDENT CAUTIOUS DISCREET VIGILANT WATCHFUL
CIRCUMSPECTION RESPECT PRUDENCE WARINESS
CIRCUMSTANCE GO FIX CASE FACT ITEM NOTE EVENT PHASE POINT START STATE THING AFFAIR DETAIL FACTOR PICKLE CALLING ELEMENT EPISODE INCIDENT INSTANCE POSITION OCCURRENCE PARTICULAR
(BAFFLING —) WARK
(CRITICAL —S) EXTREMES
(DIFFICULT —) WANTS
(EXECRABLE —) ATROCITY
(LUDICROUS —) JEST
(PL.) CIRCS STATE TERMS ESTATE FORTUNE
CIRCUMSTANCED OFF
CIRCUMSTANTIAL EXACT FORMAL MINUTE PRECISE DETAILED ITEMIZED PARTICULAR
CIRCUMSTANTIATE SUPPORT EVIDENCE
CIRCUMVENT BALK BEAT DISH DUPE FOIL CHEAT CHECK COZEN EVADE OUTGO TRICK BAFFLE DELUDE ENTRAP NOBBLE OUTWIT THWART CAPTURE DECEIVE DEFRAUD ENSNARE PREVENT OUTFLANK SURROUND UNDERFONG
CIRCUS RING SHOW ARENA CANVAS CIRCLE CIRQUE CARNIVAL
(— LOT) TOBER
(— RING) TAN
CIRQUE CWM CIRC BASIN CIRCLE CIRCUS CORRIE RECESS CIRCLET EROSION
CIS SYN NERAL NORMAL
CISCO KIYI BLOAT BLOATER BLUEFIN LONGJAW MOONEYE BLACKFIN GRAYBACK TULLIBEE WHITEFIN
CISKEI (CAPITAL OF —) BISHO
(TOWN OF —) ALICE ZWELITSHA
CISSA SIRGANG
CISSEUS (BROTHER OF —) GYAS
(COMPANION OF —) HERCULES
(FATHER OF —) MELAMPUS
(SLAYER OF —) AENEAS
CISSUS TREEBINE
CIST BOX KIST TOMB CHEST CISTA QUOIT CASKET CHAMBER KISTVAEN
CISTERCIAN TRAPPIST
CISTERN BAC FAT SAC TUB URN VAT BACK PANT SUMP TANK URNA WELL LAVER CAVITY CAISSON CHULTUN CUVETTE STEEPER FEEDHEAD
CITADEL ARX FORT HALL ALAMO BURSA BYRSA TOWER CASTLE BOROUGH CHESTER KREMLIN ALHAMBRA FASTNESS FORTRESS TOOTHILL ACROPOLIS
CITATION CITAL NOTICE MENTION SUMMONS EPIGRAPH MONITION AUTHORITY EVOCATION
CITE CALL NAME SIST TELL ALLAY EVOKE QUOTE REFER ACCITE ACCUSE ADDUCE ALLEGE AROUSE AVOUCH EXCITE INVOKE NOTIFY RECITE REPEAT SUMMON ADVANCE ARRAIGN BESPEAK CONVENT EXCERPT EXTRACT IMPEACH MENTION INDICATE INSTANCE REHEARSE
CITHARA CITHER CITOLE PHORMINX
CITHERN ZITTERN LANGSPEL
CITIZEN CIT ALLY VOTER NATIVE BURGESS BURGHER CITOYEN CLERUCH DENIZEN ELECTOR FLATCAP FREEMAN OPPIDAN SUBJECT TOWNMAN AMERICAN CIVILIAN COMMONER CONSCIVE DOMESTIC NATIONAL OCCUPANT RESIDENT
(— OF SECOND CLASS) KNIGHT HIPPEUS
(—S OF MEDINA) ANSAR
(FOREIGN-BORN —) ALIEN
(LATIN — OF U.S.) YANQUI
(PL.) SUBJECT PERIOECI CITIZENRY
(SUFF.) ITE
CITIZENRY COUNTRY SUBJECT
CITRAL GERANIAL
CITRON LIME CEDRA LEMON CEDRAT ETHROG YELLOW BERGAMOT
CITTERN LAUD CITHERN PENORCON
CITY FU WON BURG DORP TOWN URBS WOON ZION BURGH CALNO EKRON JEBUS LILLE MANOA PIECE PLACE POLIS SETTE STEAD VILLE CALNEH CENTER CIUDAD CUTHAH GILEAD JAMNIA JEBUSI LAGADO NAGARA PITHOM STAPLE BABYLON CAMBALU CHESTER ELLASAR FREEDOM JABNEEL MECHLIN CABECERA ELDORADO MAGAZINE PALENQUE
(— LIFE) ASHCAN
(— OF GOD) SION ZION
(ANCIENT —) PERGAMUM
(CAPITAL —) SEAT
(CATHEDRAL —) SEE
(CHIEF —) CAPITAL CABECERA MEGAPOLIS
(RICH —) MAGAZINE
(TREASURE —) RAAMSES
(WICKED —) BABYLON
(PREF.) URBI
(SUFF.) GRAD POLE POLIS POLITAN POLITE
CITY-STATE POLIS CIVITAS
CIVET CAT CIT GENET RASSE ZIBET BONDAR FOUSSA MUSANG PAGUMA ZIBETH CIVETTA FOSSANE LINSANG NANDINE POLECAT ZIBETUM ZINSANG FANALOKA MONGOOSE TANGALUNG
CIVIC LAY CIVIL SUAVE URBAN POLITE URBANE CIVICAL SECULAR
CIVIL FAIR HEND HENDE SUAVE POLITE URBANE AFFABLE AMIABLE COURTLY ELEGANT GALLANT POLITIC REFINED SECULAR DISCREET GRACIOUS OBLIGING POLISHED WELLBRED
CIVILIAN CIT CIVIE CIVIL CIVVY PEKIN MOHAIR CITIZEN TEACHER CIVILIST GOWNSMAN OUTSIDER NONCOMBATANT
(— ENTERTAINING SOLDIER) PYKE
CIVILITY BONTE COURT COMITY NOTICE AMENITY COURTESY URBANITY GENTILITY
(PL.) HONORS HONOURS
CIVILIZATION ISLAM KULTUR POLICE CULTURE ECUMENE CIVILITY
(GREEK —) HELLENISM
CIVILIZE TAME TEACH TRAIN POLISH REFINE EDUCATE HUMANIZE URBANIZE
CIVILIZED CHRISTIAN
CIVVIES MUFTI
CLABBER LOP MUD MIRE CURDLE LOPPER CLAUBER
CLACKDISH CLICKET
CLAD DREST ROBED BESEEN CLEDDE DECKED ADORNED ARRAYED ATTIRED CLOTHED COVERED DRESSED SHEATHED
(— IN PURPLE) PORPORATE
(SCANTILY —) SINGLY
CLADOSE RAMOSE CLADINE BRANCHED
CLAIM ASK DUE AVER AVOW CALL CASE DIBS LIEN MINE NAME PLEA COLOR DRAFT EXACT PLEAD RIGHT SHOUT TITLE ALLEGE ASSERT DEMAND DESIRE ELICIT EQUITY INTEND RECKON ACCLAIM COLLECT DERECHO DRAUGHT PRETEND PRETEXT PROFESS RECLAIM REQUIRE SOLICIT ARROGATE DARRAIGN INTEREST MAINTAIN PRETENCE PRETENSE PROCLAIM SUBCLAIM CHALLENGE POSTULATE PRETENSION PRESCRIPTION
(— IN BUSINESS) CAPITAL
(— IN LEASE) REDDENDO REDDENDUM
(— TO BE BELIEVED) AUTHORITY
(FALSE —) JACTATION
(FORESTER'S —) PUTURE
(INDIAN LEGAL —) HAK HAKH
(JUST —) RIGHT
(MINING —) SHICER
CLAIMANT CLAIMER USURPER PRETENDER
CLAIRE PARK
CLAIRVOYANCE ESP INSIGHT VOYANCE LUCIDITY SAGACITY TELOPSIS PRECOGNITION
CLAIRVOYANT FEY SEER OMENER PROPHET SEERESS
CLAM MYA BASE CLOG DAUB GLAM HUSH MEAN BLUNT CLAMP CRASH GAPER GLAUM GRASP GROPE PAHUA RAZOR SHELL SMEAR SOLEN SPOUT STICK VENUS ADHERE CLUTCH GWEDUC QUAHOG STICKY BIVALVE CLANGOR COQUINA MOLLUSK

STEAMER ADHESIVE ARROGATE BULLNOSE SHIPWORM NANNINOSE
(KIND OF —) RAZOR
(PART OF —) BEAK FOOT SHELL VALVE MANTLE SIPHON UMBONE ORIFICE
CLAMBAKE BAKE RALLY CLAMAROO SQUANTUM
CLAMBER CLIMB SCALE CLAVER SCRAWM SPRAWL RAMMACK SCRABBLE SCRAMBLE SPRACHLE STRUGGLE
CLAMMY DAMP DANK SOFT WACK MOIST SAMMY STICKY WAUGHY FLACCID SQUIDGY CLAMMISH
CLAMOR CRY DIN HUE BARK BERE BUNK GAFF RANE RERD ROAR ROUP ROUT SONG UTAS WAIL BLARE BOAST BRUIT CHIDE CHIRM NOISE OUTAS RERDE RUMOR SHOUT BELLOW BOWWOW HUBBUB OUTCRY QUETHE RACKET TUMULT UPROAR YATTER CLAMOUR EXCLAIM ORATION STASHIE NORATION PILILLOO PULLALUE SHOUTING
(— AGAINST) DECRY
CLAMOROUS NIP LOUD AROAR NOISY VOCAL BLATANT CLAMANT DINSOME YELLING BRAWLING DECRYING OPENMOUTHED OBSTREPEROUS
CLAMP DOG HOG LUG NIP PIN SET BAIL BALE BEND BOLT BURY CLAM GLAM GRIP JACK MUTE NAIL VISE YOKE BLOCK BRACE CLASP CRAMP GLAND GLAUM HORSE CLINCH FASTEN MOPHEAD STIRRUP FASTENER HOLDFAST
(— FOR BASS DRUM) SPUR
(— FOR CORK) AGRAFE AGRAFFE
(— FOR FLASK) GLAND
(— ON TUBE) PINCHCOCK
(STORAGE —) GRAVE
CLAMSHELL CLAM GRAB SHUCK
CLAN ATI HAN KIN SET SIB CULT GENS HAPU NAME RACE SECT SEPT SIOL UNIT AIMAK AYLLU CLASS GENOS GROUP HORDE PARTY TRIBE ABUSUA CLIQUE FAMILY SENAAH ABIEZER KINDRED PHRATRY SATSUMA SOCIETY ZADRUGA CALPULLI DIVISION
(— SUBDIVISION) OBE
CLANDESTINE BYE SLY FOXY HEDGE PRIVY QUIET SNEAK COVERT HIDDEN SECRET BOOTLEG FURTIVE ILLICIT BACKDOOR HIDLINGS STEALTHY
CLANG DIN DING PEAL RING TONK CLANK CLASH NOISE JANGLE TIMBRE
CLANGER STUMER
CLANGING JANGLE
CLANGOR DIN CLAM ROAR CLANG HUBBUB UPROAR
CLANGOROUS BRAZEN PLANGENT
CLANGULA HARELDA
CLANK RING RACKLE
CLAP BANG CHOP FLAP PEAL SLAP SPAT TACK CHEER CLINK CRACK SMITE POSTER STRIKE STROKE APPLAUD CHATTER CLAPPER PLAUDIT HANDCLAP
(— OF THUNDER) DINT
(— ON) CRACK
CLAPBOARD KNAPPLE CLAPHOLT
CLAPNET DAYNET
CLAPPER CLAP CLACK RATTLE TONGUE JINGLET KNACKER KNOCKER CROTALUM
(— OF BELL) TONGUE
(PL.) BONES
CLAPPING APPLAUSE
CLAPTRAP HOKUM TRASH TRIPE BLAGUE BUNKUM DEVICE EYEWASH FUSTIAN BUNCOMBE NONSENSE TRICKERY
CLARE MINORESS
CLARENCE GROWLER
CLARET TERSE PONTAC LAFITTE BORDEAUX BADMINTON
CLARIAS HARMOOT KARMOUTH
CLARIBEL (HUSBAND OF —) PHAON
CLARICE (BROTHER OF —) HUON
(HUSBAND OF —) RINALDO
CLARIFIED PURED LAUTER
CLARIFY CLAY FINE CLEAN CLEAR PURGE SNUFF PURIFY REFINE RENDER SERENE SETTLE CLEANSE DESPUME EXPLAIN GLORIFY DEFECATE DEPURATE ELIQUATE SIMPLIFY
CLARIN ACOCOTL
CLARINET BEN BIN BON BEEN BONE REED AULOS CLARY PUNGI CLARONE LAUNEDDAS
(PART OF —) KEY PAD BELL CORK REED CLAMP COVER BARREL LIGATURE MOUTHPIECE FINGERPLATE
CLARION REST CLARE CLARY CLEAR CLARINO SUFFLUE TRUMPET
CLARISSA HARLOWE (AUTHOR OF —) RICHARDSON
(CHARACTER IN —) HOWE JOHN JAMES MORDEN ROBERT SOLMES BELFORD HARLOWE WILLIAM ARABELLA CLARISSA LOVELACE SINCLAIR
CLARITY GLORY SPLENDOR STRENGTH CLEARNESS SIMPLICITY
CLARY ORVAL CLARRE SALVIA
CLASH JAR BANG BOLT BUMP DASH FRAY NEWS SLAM BRAWL BRUNT CHECK CRASH CROSS FIGHT FRUSH KNOCK OCCUR PRATE SHOCK AFFRAY DIFFER GOSSIP HURTLE IMPACT JOSTLE STRIFE STRIKE TATTLE THRUST THWART COLLIDE DISCORD SCANDAL ARGUMENT CONFLICT
(— OF WORDS) BARGE
CLASHING HARSH CONFLICT FRICTION COLLISION
CLASP HUG PIN CLIP DOME FOLD GRAB GRIP HASP HOLD HOOK HOOP KEEP OUCH STAY TACH BRACE CATCH CLING GRASP MORSE PREEN SEIZE SLIDE SPANG TACHE ACCOLL AGRAFE AMPLEX BECLIP BROOCH BUCKLE CLENCH CLUTCH ENFOLD ENWRAP FASTEN FIBULA GIMMER GIMMOR INCLIP INFOLD JIMMER STRAIN TASSEL AGRAFFE AMPLECT EMBRACE ENTWINE FERMAIL HOLDING MOUSING TENDRIL BARRETTE CORSELET FASTENER SURROUND
(— HANDS) SHAKE WRING
CLASPING AMPLECTANT
CLASS ILK BRAN CHOP FORM KIND RACE RANK RATE SECT SORT SUIT TYPE YEAR BREED CASTE GENRE GENUS GRADE GROUP ORDER RANGE TRIBE VARNA VERGE ASSORT CIRCLE CLINIC DECURY FAMILY GENDER LEAGUE MISTER NATION PHYLUM RATING RECKON REMOVE RUBRIC STRAIN STRIPE CATALOG FACTION LECTURE REGIMEN SEMINAR SPECIES VARIETY CATEGORY DESCRIBE DIVISION GENOTYPE GEOMOROI
(— OF BARDS) THULIR
(— OF GOODS) BRAND
(— OF OUTCASTS) ETA
(— OF PEOPLE) FOLK SALARIAT
(— OF SECURITIES) LEGAL
(— OF SHASTRAS) SRUTI SHRUTI
(— OF SLAVES) HELOTRY
(— OF SOUNDS) ENDING
(— OF TEASELS) KINGS
(ARISTOCRATIC —) ARISTOI
(CHOICEST —) ROBUR
(DEPRESSED —) PANCHAMA
(FIRST —) GAY
(HEREDITARY —) CASTE
(INTERMEDIATE —) SHELL REMOVE
(JAPANESE —) HEIMIN KWAZOKU
(LABORING —) PARAIYAN PROLETARIAT
(LEARNED —) VATES CLERISY
(LOWER —) BELOW GENTE
(LOWER —S) MASSES
(LOWEST —) LAG SCUM
(MIDDLE —) BOURGERIS BOURGEOISIE
(PEASANT —) JACQUERIE
(PRIVILEGED —) ARISTOCRACY
(SLAVEHOLDING —) CHIVALRY
(SOCIAL —) ESTATE SHIZOKU
(WAGE EARNINNG —) PROLETARIAT
(WEALTHY —) PLUTOCRACY
(WITH —) INTASTE
(WORKING —) TOIL
(PREF.) CRATO
(SUFF.) CY OIDA OIDEA OIDEI
CLASSIC VINTAGE AUGUSTAN TEXTBOOK
CLASSICAL PURE ATTIC GREEK LATIN ROMAN CHASTE CLASSIC ACADEMIC HELLENIC MASTERLY
(NOT —) BASE
CLASSICALLY IDEALLY
CLASSIFICATION FILE RANK RATE SORT CODEN GENRE GENUS GRADE ORDER TAXIS RATING SYSTEM ANALYSIS CATEGORY DIVISION TAXONOMY BREAKDOWN
CLASSIFIED SECRET
CLASSIFIER COUNTER SEPARATOR
CLASSIFY CODE LIST RANK RATE SIZE SORT SUIT TAPE TYPE BREAK CLASS DRAFT GRADE GROUP LABEL RANGE TRIBE ASSORT CODIFY DIGEST DIVIDE IMPOST TICKET ACCOUNT ARRANGE BRACKET BRIGADE CATALOG DISPOSE DRAUGHT GRAMMAR MARSHAL SUBSUME REGISTER PIGEONHOLE
(— TOGETHER) SLUMP
CLASSIS CONFERENCE
CLASSY TONY SMOOTH
CLATHRATE LATTICED
CLATTER DIN JAR CLACK NOISE RUMOR BABBLE GABBLE GOSSIP HOTTER HURTLE RACKLE RATTLE TATTLE BLATTER CHATTER CLUNTER CLUTTER PRATTLE REESHLE SHATTER SLAMBANG
CLATTERING CLATTERY SLITHERING
CLAUSE ITEM PART CLOSE COMMA JOKER PLANK RIDER SALVO TROPE MEMBER PHRASE ADJUNCT ARTICLE COMMATA PASSAGE PROVISO SLEEPER APODOSIS CLAUSULA PARTICLE PETITION REDDENDO SENTENCE TENENDAS TENENDUM NOVODAMUS
(— IN CREED) FILIOQUE
(— IN WRIT) TESTE
(— OF DEED) TESTATUM
(— OF WILL) DEVISE
(ADDED —) RIDER
(ADDITIONAL —) RIDER
(CONDITIONAL —) PROTASIS
(SAAVING —) SALVO
(SUBORDINATE —) PROTASIS
CLAVACIN PATULIN
CLAVER PRATE CLOVER GOSSIP CHATTER CLABBER CLAIVER CLAMBER
CLAVICHORD CLAVIER MANICORD UNICHORD CLARIGOLD MONOCHORD
CLAVICLE FURCULE COLLARBONE
CLAVICOR HORN
CLAVIER MANUAL KLAVIER
CLAVUS CORN BUNION HELOMA
CLAW DIG PEG CLEE CRAB FANG FAWN HAND HOOK NAIL PULL SERE TEAR UNCE CHELA CLAUT CLOOF CLUFE COURT GRASP GRIFF ONGLE SCLAW SEIZE TALON UNCUS CLUNCH CLUTCH CRATCH NIPPER POUNCE SCRAPE SINGLE UNGUAL UNGUIS UNGULA WEAPON CRUBEEN FALCULA FLATTER SCRATCH SHUTTLE WHEEDLE SCRABBLE
(HAWK'S —) POUNCE
(LOBSTER —) CHELA
(PL.) CLUTCH
(PREF.) CHEL(I)(O) ONYCH(O) UNGUI
(SUFF.) ONYCHA ONYCHES ONYCHIA ONYCHUS ONYX
CLAY BAT COB PUG WAD WAX BASS BEND BODY BOLE BOTT GALT GLEY LOAM LUTE MARL MIRE PAPA SMIT TILL ARGIL BRICK CLOAM EARTH GAULT LOESS OCHRE PASTE RABAT TASCO BINDER CLEDGE CLUNCH KAOLIN PUDDLE SAGGER DAUBING MOULDER RASHING CAMSTANE CAMSTONE CIMOLITE FIRECLAY

GUMBOTIL LATERITE LIFELESS SINOPITE SMECTITE
(— FOR MELTING POTS) TASCO
(— IN GLASS) TEAR
(— IRON) BULL
(— LAYER) VARVE
(— USED MEDICALLY) FANGO
(COVERED WITH —) LUTOSE
(HARD —) BEND
(HARDENED —) METAL
(INDURATED —) BASS CLUNCH
(PIECE OF FIRED —) TILE
(PIPE —) CAMSTANE CAMSTONE
(POTTER'S —) SLIP ARGIL PETUNTSE
(REMOVE —) UNLUTE
(SURPLUS —) SPARE
(TOUGH —) LECK
(3-ARMED, HARD-FIRED —) STILT
(PREF.) ARGILL(O) ARGILLACEO PEL(O)
CLAYEY BOLAR HEAVY MALMY MARLY CLEDGY LUTOSE ARGILLIC
CLAYMORE FERRARA MORGLAY
CLAY PIGEON BIRD CLAY
CLAYSTONE LECK
CLAYWARE GLOST
CLEADING CLOTHING
CLEAN DO FAY FEY HOE MOP NET DRUM DUST FAIR NEAT PURE REDD RIPE SIDE SMUG SWAB TRIM WASH WIPE CLEAR CURRY EMPTY FEIGH GRAVE SCOUR SCRUB SMART SWEEP TERSE TOSHY BARREL CHASTE CLEVER KOSHER PURIFY SPANDY APINOID BANDBOX CHAMOIS CLEANLY CLEANSE CLEARLY FURBISH PERFECT SWINGLE ABSTERGE BACKWASH BRIGHTLY DEXTROUS ENTIRELY RENOVATE SCAVENGE SPOTLESS UNSOILED
(— A FUR) DRUM
(— A PIPE) REAM
(— A QUILL) DUTCH
(— BOAT) CAREEN
(— BY SCRAPING) GRAVE
(— BY SMOKE) SMEEK
(— CANNON) SCALE
(— FEATHERS) PREEN
(— FIREARM) WORM
(— FLAX) SWINGLE
(— IN ACID) BLANCH
(— OUT) USH SPEAR
(— SHIP'S BOTTOM) HOG BREAM GRAVE
(— UP) DISPATCH
(— WITH VACUUM) HOOVER
(COME —) FESSUP
(RITUALLY —) KOSHER
CLEAN-CUT CRISP
CLEANED BRIGHT
CLEANER SOAP BORAX PURER FOLDER GUMMER RAMROD FLUEMAN SPOTTER CLEANSER
(AIR —) CAN
(GRAIN —) KICKER
(STREET —) ORDERLY
CLEAN-LIMBED CLEVER
CLEAN-LINED SPRUCE
CLEANLY PURE CLEAN ADROIT ARTFUL CHASTE FAIRLY SPANDY CORRECT ELEGANT INNOCENT SKILLFUL
CLEANNESS PURITY
CLEANSE FAY BRAN CARD COMB FARM HEAL PICK SOAP WASH BROOM BRUSH CLEAN CLEAR DIGHT DRESS FEIGH FLAME FLUSH PURGE RINSE SCOUR SCRUB SNUFF BOTTOM CAREEN EMUNGE PICKLE PURIFY REFINE SPONGE WILLOW BAPTIZE CLARIFY DEBRIDE DETERGE EXPIATE LAUNDER MUNDIFY SWEETEN ABSTERGE DEPURATE OFFSCOUR RENOVATE SCAVENGE SPRINKLE
CLEANSER LYE SOAP CLEANER PURIFIER DETERGENT DETERSIVE
CLEANSING BATH FLUSH ABLUENT CLYSMIC WASHING ABLUTION CLEANING LAVATION DETERGENT MENDATORY PURGATORY ABSTERGENT
(CEREMONIAL —) LAVABO PURGATION
CLEANTE (FATHER OF —) HARPAGON
(LOVER OF —) ANGELIQUE
(SISTER OF —) ELMIRE
CLEANTHE (BROTHER OF —) SIPHAX
CLEANTHIS (HUSBAND OF —) SOSIA
CLEANUP KILLING SWEEPUP
CLEAR HOT JAM NET PEN RID WAY CAST EASY FAIR FINE FLAT FREE GAIN GRUB JAIL JUMP NEAT OPEN OVER PURE PUTE QUIT REDD RIFE SHUT SLAM VOID ACUTE ATRIP AZURE BREAK BREME BRENT BROAD CHUCK CLEAN CRISP DRIVE LIGHT LUCID NAKED PLAIN PRINT PRUNE SCOUR SHARP SMOLT SUNNY SUTEL SWEEP UNTIE VIVID ACQUIT AERIAL ASSOIL BRIGHT CANDID CLEVER EXCUSE EXEMPT FLUTED LAUTER LIMPID LIQUID LUCENT PATENT PURIFY REMBLE SERENE SETTLE SHRILL SMOOTH UNSTOP ABSOLVE CAPITAL CLARIFY CLARION CRYSTAL DELIVER DILUCID EVIDENT EXPLAIN EXPRESS GLARING GRAPHIC LIGHTEN OBVIOUS PERVIAL RELEASE SILVERY THROUGH ACCREDIT APPARENT BRIGHTEN BULLDOZE DEFINITE DISTINCT EXPLICIT LUCULENT LUMINOUS MANIFEST PELLUCID REVELANT PERSPICUOUS
(— AWAY) FAY FEY FEIGH BANISH DISPEL DISCUSS
(— FROM) ALOOF
(— FROM CRITICISM) VINDICATE
(— IN TONE) SILVER
(— LAND) CURE BRUSH SLASH DEADEN BUSHHOG
(— OF BLAME) QUIT
(— OFF) QUIT
(— OF FINE HAIR) SLATE
(— OF GROUND) ATRIP AWEIGH
(— OF GUILT) PURGE
(— OF MUD) SLUTCH
(— OF SCUM) SKIM
(— OF SEEDS) GIN RIPPLE
(— OF TUFTS) HOB
(— OUT) BLOW HOOK SWAMP SKIDDOO HIGHTAIL DISCHARGE
(— PATH) FRAY HACK BUSHWACK
(— TABLE) DISSERVE
(— TABLES) BUS
(— THROAT) HOICK HOUGH HARRUMPH
(— UP) SOLVE ASSOIL RESOLVE DISSOLVE UNSHADOW
(ALL —) COPACETIC COPESETTIC
(NOT —) DULL DUSKY FOGGY INEVIDENT
CLEARANCE CHOP ROOM RUNBY BACKLASH ALLOWANCE
(— FOR SHIP) PRATIQUE
CLEAR-CUT LUCID SHARP DIRECT CONCISE DECIDED CHISELED DEFINITE DISTINCT INCISIVE TRENCHANT
CLEARED (— FOR ACTION) PREDY
CLEARHEADED LUCID
CLEARING SART FIELD FRITH GLADE SHADE TRACT ALCOVE ASSART RIDING RIDDING SLASHING
(FOREST —) SLASH SLASHING
CLEARLY FAIR CLEAR LIGHT REDLY FAIRLY FRANKLY PATENTLY WITTERLY
CLEAR-MINDEDNESS LUCIDITY
CLEARNESS CLARITY FINESSE EVIDENCE FINENESS
CLEAR-SIGHTED SEEING
CLEARWEED RICHWEED
CLEAT BITT STUD BLOCK CHOCK KEVEL LEDGE RANGE WEDGE BATTEN RIFFLE BOLLARD COXCOMB GROUSER SIRMARK SUPPORT SURMARK
CLEAVAGE RIFT CLEFT WASSIE FISSION FISSURE WEDGING DIVISION SCISSION
(PREF.) SCHISTO SCHIZ(O)
(SUFF.) CLASE SCHISIS SCHIST
CLEAVE CUT RIP CHOP HANG HOLD JOIN LINK PART RELY REND RIFT RIVE SLIT TEAR BREAK CARVE CHAWN CHINE CLAVE CLEFT CLING CLOVE CRACK KNIFE SEVER SHALE SHARE SHEAR SLIVE SPLAT STICK ADHERE BISECT COHERE DIVIDE FURROW PIERCE SLEAVE SUNDER DISPART FISSURE SEPARATE
(— OFF) AXE SCIND
CLEAVER CLIVE CLEAVE FROWER PARANG CHOPPER HATCHET PARANGI
CLEAVERS GRIP CLOTE CLOTS CLITHE HAIRIF HAIRUP BURHEAD LOVEMAN PIGTAIL BIRDLIME
CLEAVING DYSTOME FISSION DYSTOMIC
(— READILY) EUTOMOUS
CLECHE URDE URDY URDEE
CLEF KEY CLIVE CHIAVETTA
CLEFT CUT GAP JAG CHAP CHOP FENT FLAW GASH NOCK REFT RIFT RILL RIMA RIVE SLIT BIFID BREAK CHASM CHAWN CHINK CLOFF CLOVE CRACK CREEK CRENA GULCH KLOOF RILLE RIVEN SINUS SPLIT BREACH CHAPPY CLEAVE CLOUGH CLOVEN CRANNY CROTCH DIVIDE LISSOM PARTED RECESS RICTUS STIGMA BLASTED CHIMNEY CREVICE DIVIDED FISSURE OPENING SLIFTER APERTURE CREVASSE FRACTURE INCISION INCISURA MULTIFID SCISSURA SCISSURE PALMATIFID
(— BETWEEN HILLS) SLACK RAVINE
(— IN HOOF) SEAM
(— IN ROCK) RIVA
(— IN THE POSTERIORS) NOCK
(— OF BUTTOCKS) CREASE
(PREF.) FISSI SCHISTO SCHIZ(O)
(SUFF.) FID FIDATE
CLEMATIS PIPESTEM CURLYHEAD
CLEMENCY ORE PITY GRACE MERCY LENITY QUARTER KINDNESS LENIENCY MILDNESS
CLEMENT MILD SOFT WARM GENTLE LENIENT MERCIFUL
CLEMENZA DI TITO (CHARACTER IN —) TITUS ANNIUS SEXTUS BERENICE SERVILIA VITELLIA
(COMPOSER OF —) MOZART
CLENCH FIST GRIP GRIT HOLD NAIL BRACE CLASP CLENK CLINT CLOSE GRASP CLINCH CLUTCH DOUBLE
(— FIST) GRIPE
CLEONTE (LOVER OF —) LUCILLE
CLEOPATRA (BROTHER OF —) ILUS ZETES CALAIS GANYMEDE ASSARACUS
(FATHER OF —) IDAS TROS BOREAS PTOLEMY
(HUSBAND OF —) PHILIP PHINEUS PTOLEMY MELEAGER
(MOTHER OF —) MARPESSA ORITHYIA CALLIRRHOE
CLEPE CLUPIEN
CLEPSYDRA GURRY GHURRY
CLERGY CLOTH CRAPE CHURCH CLERISY MINISTRY
(BODY OF —) PULPIT
CLERGYMAN ABBA ABBE DEAN PAPA CANON CLERK FROCK PADRE PILOT PRIOR RABBI VICAR BISHOP CLERIC CURATE DEACON DIVINE DOMINE PAROCH PARSON PASTOR PRIEST RECTOR SUPPLY CASSOCK PRELATE CARDINAL CHAPLAIN CLERICAL DIOCESAN EMERITUS LECTURER MINISTER ORDINARY PREACHER REVEREND SQUARSON PRESBYTER PREBENDARY REVIVALIST
CLERIC ABBE CURE CLERK FROCK DEACON GALLAH LEVITE PRIEST ACOLYTE GOLIARD ANAGNOST
(DISREPUTABLE —) GOLIARD
CLERICAL BLACK CLERIC CLERKISH PARSONIC PARSONLY
(NOT —) LAIC
CLERIMOND (BROTHER OF —) FERRAGUS
(HUSBAND OF —) VALENTINE
CLERIMONT (LOVER OF —) CLARINDA
CLERK NUN BABU MONK AGENT AWARD BABOO CLARK FILER RALPH WRITE BILLER CHASER CLERIC COMMIS GRADER HERMIT KITMAN LAYMAN MAPPER MASTER MUNSHI PANDIT PENMAN PRIEST PUNDIT RALPHO SCRIBE SIRCAR TELLER WRITER YEOMAN ACOLYTE ACTUARY BOOKMAN CARCOON

COMPOSE DOPSTER GOMASTA PIARIST SCHOLAR SHIPPER SHOPMAN STUFFER CLERGEON CLERGION CLERKESS CURSITOR EMPLOYEE GREFFIER MUTSUDDY PENCLERK RECORDER SALESMAN
(— OF ST PAUL) BARNABITE
(CHIEF —) PROTHONOTARY
(HOTEL —) DESKMAN
CLERKLY LEARNED SCRIBAL CLERGIAL SCHOLARLY
CLEVE BRAE CLIFF CLEEVE HILLSIDE
CLEVER APT SLY ABLE CUTE DEFT FEAT FELL FINE FOXY GLEG GNIB GOOD HEND KEEN NEAT SLIM SPRY AGILE ALERT CANNY CLEAN CLEAR CUNNY FALSE FEATY FENDY HANDY HEADY HENDE LITHE QUICK SHARP SLICK SMART SNACK WITTY ACTIVE ADROIT ARTFUL ASTUTE BRIGHT CRAFTY EXPERT HABILE HEPPEN KITTLE KNACKY NEATLY NIMBLE PRETTY SHREWD SPIFFY STALKY SUBTLE AMIABLE CUNNING GNOSTIC PARLISH PARLOUS VARMENT VARMINT DEXTROUS HANDSOME OBLIGING SKILLFUL TALENTED
CLEVERLY SLICK FEATLY TIDELY SMARTLY ASTUTELY
CLEVERNESS CAN CHIC NOUS TACT KNACK SKILL ESPRIT INDUSTRY DEXTERITY
CLEVIS COP DEE HAKE CLEVY COPSE BRIDGE BRIDLE MUZZLE SHACKLE PLOWHEAD
CLEW BALL CLUE HINT GLOBE GLOME SKEIN BOTTOM HURDLE THREAD
CLICHE COMMONPLACE
CLICK DOG DOT DASH MESH PAWL SLAP TICK AGREE CATCH FORGE SNECK SNICK DETENT PALLET RATCHET
(— HORSE'S SHOES) FORGE
(HEEL —S) BELLS
(TELEGRAPH —) DASH
CLICK BEETLE DOR ELATER
CLICKER CASTANET
CLIENT CEILE JAJMAN PATRON PATIENT CUSTOMER HENCHMAN RETAINER
CLIENTELE TRADE PUBLIC CLIENTRY
CLIFF HOE NIP CRAG HILL KLIP ROCK SCAR BLUFF CLEVE CLINT HEUCH HEUGH KRANS SCARP SHORE SLOPE STEEP CLEEVE HEIGHT KRANTZ PISKUN CLOGWYN HILLSIDE PALISADE TRAVERSE
(BROKEN —) CRAG
(ICE —) ICEBLINK
(LINE OF —S) PALISADE
(PREF.) CREMNO
CLIFFY SCARRY
CLIMATE SKY SUN MOOD CLIME HEAVEN REGION TEMPER ATTITUDE
(SCIENCE OF —) PHENOLOGY
(PREF.) METEOR(O)
CLIMAX CAP TOP ACME APEX HEAD NEAR PEAK SHUT CREST CROWN MOUNT SCALE TIGHT APOGEE ASCEND FINISH HEIGHT PAYOFF SHINNY SUMMIT ZENITH BLOWOFF EVEREST CAPSHEAF CAPSTONE EPIPLOCE CULMINATION
CLIMB GAD STY COON RAMP RISE SHIN SKIN SOAR STYE CREEP GRIMP MOUNT SCALE SKLIM SPEED SPEEL SWARM TWINE ASCEND ASCENT BREAST SCLIMB SCRAWM SHINNY SWARVE SWERVE CLAMBER SCRAMBLE TRAVERSE
(— ABOARD) HOP
(— DOWN) LIGHT UNSCALE
(— IN MOUNTAINEERING) CHIMNEY
(— OVER) SURMOUNT
CLIMBER CUBE AKALA AKELA KAIWI TIMBO RIGGER SCALER COWHAGE CRAMPON CREEPER
(MOUNTAIN —) ALPINIST
CLIMBING RAMPANT SCANDENT
(MOUNTAIN —) ALPINISM
CLIMBING FERN NITO AGSAM
CLIMBING IRON SPUR PRICK CRAMPET CRAMPIT CRAMPON CREEPER PRICKER CRAMPBIT
CLIMBING PALM RATTAN
CLIMBING PEPPER BETEL
CLIMBING ROSE SCRAMBLE
CLINCH FIX GET HUG ICE TOE BIND GRIP LOCK NAIL SEAL CLAMP CLING CLINK CLINT GRASP RIVET SEIZE CLENCH CLUTCH FASTEN SECURE SNATCH CONFIRM EMBRACE GRAPPLE SCUFFLE COMPLETE CONCLUDE HOLDFAST
CLING HUG BANK HANG HOLD RELY CLASP HITCH STICK TRUST ADHERE CLEAVE CLINCH COHERE DEPEND FASTEN SHRINK WITHER CHERISH EMBRACE SHRIVEL CONTRACT
CLINGER LIMPET
CLINGFISH SUCKER TESTAR TETARD SUCKFISH
CLINGING CLUNG HUGGING ADHAMANT ADHERENT OSCULANT
CLINK ALE JUG PUT RAP BEAT BLOW BRIG CASH CLAP COIN JAIL MOVE RING SLAP CHINK KLINK LATCH MONEY RHYME SEIZE CLINCH JINGLE LOCKUP MOMENT PRISON STRIKE TINKLE INSTANT JINGLING
CLINKER BUR DUD BUHR BURR SCAR SLAG WASTE HOLLANDER
(PL.) BREEZE
CLINKER-BUILT SHINGLED LAPSTRAKE
CLINKSTONE PHONOLITE
CLINOMETER TRIMMER
CLINTONIA BLUEBEAD DOGBERRY COWTONGUE
CLIP BAT BOB CUT DOD HUG LIP LOP MOW NIG NIP BARB BEAK CHIP COLL CROP DOCK DODD FLAG HOLD PACE PARE POLL SNIP TRIM BRUSH CLASP DRESS FORCE LUNET MINCE PRUNE SHAVE SHEAR SHRIP SNICK STEEK CLUPPE CLUTCH CRUTCH FASTEN GADGET HINDER HOLDER LACING CALIPER CURTAIL CURTAIN EMBRACE HICKORY LUNETTE SCISSOR SHORTEN DIMINISH ENCIRCLE RETAINER
(— A COIN) SHORTEN
(— OF LEAD) TINGLE
(— WOOL) CRUTCH
(CARTRIDGE —) CHARGER
(HAIR —) BARRETTE
(SPRING —) JACK
CLIP-FASTENER DOME
CLIPPED SHORN TONSURED
CLIPPER BOAT SHIP DOCKER SLICER CHAINER CLAMMER CLEANER GRABMAN GRIPPER SHEARER SNAPPER
CLIPPING BOB SCROW CUTTING SNIPPING
(—S OF METAL) SCISSEL
(PL.) BRASH SHORTS EXCERPTA
CLIQUE COT MOB SET BLOC CLAN CLUB GANG KNOT PUSH RING CABAL CROWD GROUP JUNTO MAFIA WRITE CIRCLE CLETCH SCHISM COTERIE FACTION CONCLAVE SODALITY CAMARILLA
CLISTHENES (FATHER OF —) MEGACLES
(MOTHER OF —) AGARISTA
CLITANDRE (LOVER OF —) LUCINDE CELIMENE ANGELIQUE
CLITELLUM GIRDLE SADDLE CINGULUM
CLOAK ABA HAP BRAT CAPA CAPE COPE HIDE HUKE IZAR MANT MASK PALL RAIL ROBE VEIL WRAP AMICE BURKA CAPOT CHOGA COVER GREGO GUISE JELAB MANTA MANTO PILCH SAGUM SHUBA TALAR TALMA TILMA ABOLLA AHUULA ASSUME BAUTTA CAMAIL CAPOTE CASTER CHAMMA CHAPEL CHIMER DOLMAN JOSEPH MANTLE MANTUA PHAROS PONCHO RHASON SCREEN SERAPE SHIELD SHROUD TABARD VISITE ALICULA BAVAROY CASSOCK CHLAMYS CHUDDAR CONCEAL COURTBY GARMENT MANTEAU PAENULA PALLIUM PELISSE PELLARD PRETEXT ROKELAY SHELTER SURCOAT ZIMARRA ALBORNOZ BURNOOSE CAPUCHIN CARDINAL DISGUISE INTRIGUE MANTILLA PALLIATE ROQUELAURE
(— OF FEATHERS) MAMO AHUULA
(— WITH CROSSES) ANALABOS
(ARAB —) GALABIA GALLABIA GALABIYAH
(BULLFIGHTER'S —) CAPA
(CORONATION —) SACCOS
(FUR —) PILCH
(HOODED —) HUKE CAPOT BAUTTA BIRRUS BAVAROY CARDINAL DJELLABA
(INQUISITION —) SANBENITO
(RED —) CAPE
(RUSSIAN —) SARAFAN
(SHORT —) MANTELET
(SOLDIER'S —) SAGUM MANTEEL
(WATERPROOF —) GOSSAMER
(PREF.) PALLIO
CLOAKED PALLIATE
CLOAKROOM VESTRY VESTIARY
CLOAM DAUB CLOMB CROCKERY
CLOCHE BELL
CLOCK NEF BELL CALL DIAL GOER GONG TIME WRAP BUNDY CLUCK GURRY HATCH HURRY KNOCK METER QUIRK STYLE VERGE WATCH BEETLE CROUCH GHURRY ORLAGE TICKER SKELPER STRIKER TATTLER HOROLOGE INCUBATE ORNAMENT RECORDER SOLARIUM TELLTALE
(— IN FORM OF SHIP) NEF
(— ON STOCKING) QUIRK GUSHET GUSSET
(— WITH PENDULUM) PENDULE
(KIND OF —) CESIUM
(PART OF —) BOB ROD BASE DIAL DOOR FACE FOOT HAND HOOD RING ROPE CHAIN CREST PLATE TRUCK FINIAL PLINTH WEIGHT CHAPTER NUMERAL PENDULUM SPANDREL
(TIME —) BUNDY
(WATER —) GURRY GHURRY SOLARIUM CLEPSYDRA
CLOCKER SIZER TIMER RAILBIRD
CLOCKWISE DEASIL DESSIL SUNWISE POSITIVE
CLOD SOD CLAT CLOT DOLT DULL LOUT LUMP SLOB TURF CLOUT CLOWN DIVOT EARTH GLEBE GROSS KNOLL YOKEL CLATCH GROUND STUPID BUMPKIN
CLODDISH GROSS STUPID BOORISH
CLODDY GLEBY GLEBOUS
CLODHOPPER BOOR CLOD SHOE RUSTIC HOBNAIL PLOWMAN
CLODIA LESBIA
CLODPATE CLOT DOLT FOOL RAMHEAD CLODPOLE CLODPOLL IMBECILE
CLODPOLE BOOR BUMPKIN
CLOG FUR GUM JAM LOG BALL CLAG CLAM CLOY CURB DRAG GAUM GLUB LEAD LOAD LUMP SHOE SKID STOP BLIND BLOCK CHECK CHOKE DANCE SABOT SPOKE TRASH ACCLOY ADHERE BURDEN CHOPIN COBCAB DAGGLE ENCLOG FETTER FREEZE GALOSH HAMPER HOBBLE IMPEDE PATINE PATTEN REMORA SANDAL SECQUE WEIGHT CONGEST CREEPER ENGLEIM FETLOCK PERPLEX SHACKLE SPANCEL TRAMMEL TRIGGER BEDAGGLE COALESCE ENCUMBER OBSTRUCT OVERSHOE RESTRAIN
(— A FILE) PIN
(WOODEN —S) GETA GETAS
CLOG ALMANAC STAFF
CLOGGED FOUL FURRY PINNY FROZEN CLOTTED BEGUMMED
CLOGGING CLOGGY FOULING CUMBROUS
CLOGGY DULL HEAVY LUMPY STICKY
CLOISONNE SHIPPO
CLOISTER HALL STOA ABBEY AISLE ARCADE FRIARY IMMURE PIAZZA PRIORY CLOSTER CONVENT NUNNERY MONASTERY

CLOISTER AND THE HEARTH
(AUTHOR OF —) READE
(CHARACTER IN —) KATE DENYS ELIAS GILES MARIE PETER BRANDT GERARD MARTIN PIETRO ELIASON MARGARET GHYSBRECHT
CLOISTERED RECLUSE
CLONE DESMA REPLICA SPICULE
CLORINDA (SLAYER OF —) TANCRED
CLOSE BY IN CAP END GUM HAW HOT TYE ZOP AKIN BUNG CHOP CLAP CLIT DAUB FAST FILL FINE FIRM GRIP HARD HIDE LOUK MEET NEAR NIGH QUIT SEAL SHUT SLAM SNUG SPAR STOP TINE WINK WYND ZERO ANEAR BLOCK BOSOM BREAK CEASE CHEAP CHIEF COAPT DENSE FENCE FINIS FLIRT GARTH GROSS ISSUE MUGGY SNECK SOLID STEEK STICK STIVY THICK TIGHT BUCKLE BUTTON CLAUSE CLENCH CLUTCH DOUBLE EFFECT EXPIRY FINALE FINISH INSTOP INWARD NARROW NEARBY PERIOD SECRET SETTLE SILENT STANCH STINGY STITCH STRAIT STRICT STUFFY THRONG ADJOURN BOROUGH CLOSING CLOSISH COMPACT CONDEMN CONTEXT COSTIVE EXTREME GRAPPLE MISERLY OCCLUDE POCKETY PUTHERY RAMPIRE RECLUDE SHUTTER SIMILAR STAUNCH STOPPER ACCURATE ADJACENT BLOCKADE CLAUSULA COMPLETE COMPRESS CONCLUDE ENCEINTE ESPECIAL FAMILIAR FINALIZE HAIRLINE IMMINENT INTIMATE OBTURATE PARCLOSE PRECLUDE STIFLING PROXIMATE
(— BY) FORBY AROUND BESIDE FOREBY HEREBY FORTHBY SISTERING
(— EYES OF HAWK) SEEL
(— IN) BESET ENCLOSE INCLOSE
(— IN ON) TAKE
(— THE MOUTH) STOPPLE
(— TIGHTLY) SEALOFF
(— TO) BY INBY NEAR NIGH ANEAR INBYE ALMOST AGAINST
(— TO BATSMAN) SILLY
(— TO COMMUNICATION) CORDON
(— TOGETHER) COLLAPSE
(— TO QUARRY) HOT
(— TO THE HEART) DEAR
(— TO THE WIND) SHARP
(— UP) DIT CORK DITT FILL FOLD STOP SERRY UPCLOSE
(— WITH) BIND
(— WITH A CLICK) SNECK
(AS — AS POSSIBLE) CHOCK
(NOT —) UNNEAR
(PARTIALLY —) HOOD
(VERY —) CHIEF STINGY
(PREF.) PLESI(O) PYCN(O) STEN(O)
(SUFF.) STENOSIS
CLOSE-COUPLED COMPACT
CLOSE-CUT SHAVEN
CLOSED DARK DOWN SHUT CLOSE LUCKEN UNOPEN BLOCKED COVERED
(— AT ONE END) BLIND
(PREF.) CLEIST CLIST OCCLUSO
CLOSEFISTED MEAN NEAR FISTY TIGHT SNIPPY STINGY MISERLY HANDFAST
CLOSE-FITTING FIT HARD MEET SNUG THEAT THEET TIGHT THIGHT PRINCESS SUCCINCT PRINCESSE
CLOSE-IN SILLY
CLOSE-KNIT TRUSSED
CLOSE-LIPPED SILENT
CLOSELY FAST JUST NEAR WELL SADLY ALMOST BARELY HARDLY NARROW NEARLY JUNCTLY STRICTLY
CLOSEMOUTHED SECRET SILENT TACITURN
(NOT —) LEAKY
CLOSENESS DENSITY SECRECY FIDELITY INTIMACY NEARNESS PARSIMONY
CLOSER VAMPER CLOSURE
CLOSE-SET THICK SERRIED
CLOSE-SMELLING FROWSTY
CLOSEST NEXT NEAREST
CLOSESTOOL STOLE
CLOSET ARK LOO EWRY ROOM SAFE ZETA AMBRY CUBBY CUDDY PRESS LOCKER PANTRY SECRET CABINET CONCEAL PRIVATE STORAGE CONCLAVE CUPBOARD GARDEVIN WARDROBE
CLOSING FLY SLAM SNAP CLINCH CLOSURE CLOTURE CLAUDENT PHASEOUT BUTTONING
(— DOWN OF OPERATIONS) PHASEOUT
(MUSICAL —) CODA
(TEMPORARY —) SHUTDOWN
CLOSURE END GAG BOLT SEAL BOUND LIMIT POPTOP ATRESIA CLOTURE FERRULE TENSION CLAUSURE FINALITY KANGAROO
(FABRIC —) VELCRO
(SUFF.) CLEISIS CLISIS
CLOT DOT GEL CLAG CLAT GOUT JELL LUMP MASS MOLE SHED CLART CLUMP GRUME BALTER COTTER LAPPER LOPPER CLODDER CONGEAL EMBOLUS THICKEN CLODPATE COAGULUM CONCRETE SOLIDIFY THROMBUS
(— OF BLOOD) THRUMBUS
(— OF DIRT) SPLATCH
(PREF.) THROMB(O)
CLOTH DAB RAG BLUE COAT DRAB DRAP ECRU FELT FILE PALL SEAM WARE WOOF BEIGE BLUET CABAN CLOUT DITTO FOULE GOODS GREEN KENTE LODEN LUNGI MOORY PRINT STUPE TAMMY TAWNY TIBET TOILE TWEED TWILL WIGAN ALPACA AWNING BENGAL BYSSUS CANAMO CANVAS CHADOR CLAITH CLERGY COVERT DOMETT DORSEL DOSSAL DOSSER DRAPET DUSTER FABRIC LIVERY LONGYI LOWELL MELLAY MULETA NAPKIN RENGUE REXINE SARONG SURNAP TILLOT WITNEY ACETATE BAGGING BOULTEL CHADDAR CHRISOM COATING CRIMSON DRAPERY DUSTRAG FALDING GARMENT JACONET ORLEANS PANUELO RAIMENT SACKING SURNAPE TEXTILE WATCHET WORSTED BATSWING CHRISMAL COMPRESS CORPORAL CRAMOISY DWELLING FROCKING HOMESPUN LAMBSKIN MATERIAL PHULKARI RADEVORE SHAATNEZ SHEETING THICKSET TOILINET
(— FOR BELT) SHROUD
(— FOR SWEAT) SUDARY SUDARIUM
(— FOR WIPING TABLE) FILE
(— FOR WRAPPING CHILD) PILCH
(— FOR WRAPPING FABRICS) TILLET
(— FOR WRAPPING THE DEAD) CEREMENT
(— HANGING FROM WAISTBAND) LANGOOTY
(— OF GOLD) LAME
(— OF GOLD) SONERI
(— OF GOLD) SONERIE CICLATON CHECKLATON
(— OF SINGLE WIDTH) STRAITS
(— REMAINING AFTER CUTTING) CABBAGE
(— TEXTURE) WALE
(— WORN LIKE KILT) LAVALAVA
(ALTAR —) TOWEL PENDLE PALLIUM VESPERAL CATASARKA
(ARABIAN —) HAIK CABAN CABAAN
(BAPTISMAL —) CHRISOM
(BARK —) TAPA TAPPA
(BED —) COVER SPREAD
(BLACK —) KISWA KISWAH
(BLUE —) PERSE
(COARSE —) KELT DOZEN DUROY RUDGE BURREL CANGAN DOWLAS DOZENS FORFAR FRIEZE HODDEN KERSEY KHARVA KHARWA STAMIN STROUD TAPALO WADMAL CAMBAYE COTONIA DRUGGET FORFARS RAPLOCH RUGGING SARPLER SOUTAGE FLUSHING RADEVORE SARCILIS
(COMMUNION —) FANON SINDON ANIMETTA CORPORAL PURIFICATOR
(CORDED —) REP REPP
(COTTON —) BAFT JEAN TOBE ADATI BLUET CAFFA CRASH DURRY JEANS KHADI KHAKI SURAT BEAVER CALICO CANGAN DOWLAS DURRIE GANZIE HUMHUM KALMUK NANKIN PENANG CAMBAYE FUSTIAN GALATEA GINGHAM JACONET KHADDAR LASTING NANKEEN REGATTA BOGOTANA CRETONNE DOMESTIC MUSLINET
(CRIMSON —) CRAMASIE CRAMOISY
(DECORATIVE —) SCARF
(DRAB —) KHAKI
(DRIVING —) TOWEL
(EMBROIDERED —) SAMPLER BAUDEKIN
(FINE —) SINDON SCARLET
(FIORE —) PINA
(GLASS —) DORON
(GOAT-WOOL —) ABA ABBA ABAYA SLING
(GREEN —) KENDAL
(GUNNY —) TAT
(HAIR —) ABA ABBA CILICE
(HEMP —) PINAYUSA
(HOMESPUN —) KELT KHADI PATTU PUTTOO HEADING KHADDAR
(INFERIOR —) MOCKADO
(KIND OF —) LOIN PINA
(LAP —) GREMIAL
(LINEN —) BRIN LINE GULIX DOWLAS FORFAR BRABANT LOCKRAM SILESIA BLANCARD CORPORAL DRILLING GAMBROON GHENTING LINCLOTH
(LONG —) LUNGI WHITE LUNGEE
(ORNAMENTAL —) TRAP DOSSAL DOSSEL
(PACK —) MANTA
(PACKING —) SOUTAGE
(PIECE OF —) APRON CLOUT GODET LANGOOTY
(PURLOINED —) CABBAGE
(RICH —) SCARLET
(ROUGH —) PETERSHAM
(ROYAL —) PURPLE
(SADDLE —) PANEL NUMNAH SHABRACK
(SILK —) CAFFA BENGAL PATOLA LUSTRINE LUSTRING
(SOAKED —) BUCK
(SOFT —) RUGINE
(STAGE —) BACKDROP
(STARCHED —) GUIMPE
(STRIPED —) RAY
(STRONG —) CANVAS DURANCE BARRACAN
(TARTAN —) PLAID
(TURBAN —) SASH
(TWILLED —) JANE JEAN BARATHEA GAMBROON
(UNDYED —) HODDEN
(VARI-COLORED —) MEDLEY MOTLEY
(WASHING —) SHAMMY CHAMOIS
(WATERPROOF —) MAC MACK
(WAX —) MUMJUMA
(WET —) DAB
(WOOL —) SAY DRAB PUKE BEIGE BUREL DOZEN DUROY LAINE STARA TAMIS TAMMY BURNET DOZENS DUFFEL HODDEN KENDAL KERSEY MEDLEY MELTON MUSTER SATARA SAXONY STAMIN TAMINY TARTAN BASTARD BLANKET DUNSTER FLANNEL RAPLOCH ROPLOCH RUGGING BEARSKIN BOMBAZET BUCKSKIN FLORENCE SARCILIS VENETIAN PETERSHAM BOMBAZETTE
(WORSTED —) RASH SHAG BOTANY BOMBAZET
(PREF.) HISTI(O)
CLOTHE DON DUB HAP LAP RIG TOG BUSK COAT DECK GARB GIRD GOWN ROBE VEST ADORN ARRAY CLEAD CLEED DRESS ENDOW ENDUE FLESH FROCK HABIT INDUE ATTIRE BEWRAP SHRIDE SHROUD SWATHE ADDRESS APPAREL FEATHER RAIMENT VESTURE ACCOUTER ACCOUTRE
(PLAIN —) MUFTI
CLOTHED CLAD BECLAD HABITED
CLOTHES CASE DUDS GARB GEAR GORE KAPA SUIT TACK TOGS WEAR BRAWS CLAES DUCKS HABIT ATTIRE FARDEL SHROUD

THREAD TROGGS APPAREL BAGGAGE COSTUME IRONING RAIMENT REGALIA THREADS TOGGERY VESTURE WEARING CLOTHING FEATHERS FRIPPERY GARMENTS INDUMENT
(CASTOFF —) FRIPPERY
(CIVILIAN —) MUFTI CIVVIES
(COLORFUL —) TRAPPINGS
(DAINTY —) PRETTIES
(DRESS —) WAMPUM
(FINE —) BRAWS
(HANDSOME —) BRAVERY
(MOURNING —) DOLE
(READY-TO-WEAR —) PRETAPORTER
(SHOWY —) LUGS
(SOAKED —) BUCK
(TRACK —) SILKS
CLOTHES DRYER AIRER TUMBLER
CLOTHES-HORSE MAIDEN SCREEN
CLOTHESPIN PEG
CLOTHESPRESS ARMOIRE TALLBOY WARDROBE
CLOTH FOLDER CUTTLER
CLOTHING (ALSO SEE CLOTHES) BACK BLUE BRAT COAT GARB GEAR SEAM WEAR ARRAY BUREL CLOTH DRESS GREEN HABIT JABOT STUFF ATTIRE FARDEL ROBING VESTRY APPAREL CLOBBER CLOTHES CRIMSON DRAPERY FISHNET OUTWALL RAIMENT THREADS VESTURE WEEDERY INDUMENT KNITWEAR MENSWEAR ORNAMENT SLOPWORK VESTIARY VESTMENT BEACHWEAR
(ARTICLE OF —) VINE
(BLACK —) SABLE
(COARSE —) BUREL
(INFORMAL —) PLAYWEAR
(LOWER —) LAP
(MUSLIM —) IHRAM
(NAUTICAL —) SLOPS
(OF CLASSIC —) PREPPY PREPPIE
(SHEER —) FLIMSIES
(SHOWY —) SHEEN FINERY
(WOMEN'S —) FRILLIES
(WORK —) FATIGUES
(SUFF.) ESTHES
CLOTHING DEALER HOSIER
CLOTHWORKER FULLER
CLOTILDA (FATHER OF —) CHILPERIC
(HUSBAND OF —) CLOVIS AMALARIC
(UNCLE OF —) GUNDEBALD
CLOTTED GORY CLOTTY CLOUTED GARGETY GRUMOUS LIVERED
CLOTURE GAG CLOSURE
CLOUD DOG FOG NUE SKY BLUR DAMP DARK DUST FOOL HAZE HELM HIDE MIST PUFF REEK SMUR ARCUS BEDIM BEFOG BLOOM DRIFT GLOOM MUDDY NUBIA OXEYE SHADE STAIN SULLY SWARM TAINT VAPOR CIRRUS DAMAGE DARKEN DEEPEN DEFAME FUNNEL MUDDLE NEBULA NIMBUS PILEUS POTHER SCREEN SHADOW STIGMA BLACKEN CONFUSE CUMULUS ECLIPSE FUMULUS GRANULE OBSCURE POOTHER STRATUS SUNSPOT TARNISH CLOUDCAP CLOUDLET COCKTAIL NIGHTCAP NUBILATE OVERCAST WOOLPACK
(— BEFORE STORM) MESSENGER
(— OF DROPS) SPRAY
(— OF DUST OR VAPOR) STEW SMOTHER
(— OF MIST) SOP
(— OVER MOUNTAIN) HELM
(CIRRUS —S) GOATSHAIR
(DRIVINNG —) SCUD
(FLYING —) RACK
(FUNNEL —) TORNADO
(HIGH —) CIRRUS
(HORIZONTAL —) STRATUS
(KIND OF —) OORT
(LAYER OF —S) DECK
(MASS OF HIGH —S) RACK
(MASSY —) CUMULUS
(NUCLEAR —) FIREBALL
(RAIN —) NIMBUS
(PL.) SCUD SOUP CARRY GASHES
(PREF.) CIRR(I)(O) CIRRH(I)(O) NEBULI NEPHEL(I)(O) NEPHO NIMBI NUBI
CLOUDBERRY AKPEK MOLKA AVERIN
(FRUIT OF —) NOOP
CLOUDED HAZY DIRTY DUSTY FILMY JASPE MUCKY SHADY ACLOUD GLOOMY TURBID INFUMATE NEBULOUS
CLOUDINESS FAIR HAZE GLOOM MUDDLE NUBECULA
CLOUDING DAPPLE
(— OF EYE) CATARACT
CLOUDLESS AZURE CLEAR BRIGHT
CLOUDLIKE NEBULOUS NUBIFORM
CLOUDY DIM DARK DULL HAZY BLEAR FILMY FOGGY MISTY MUDDY MURKY SHADY GLOOMY LOWERY OPAQUE SMURRY VEILED BLURRED CLOUDED NEBULAR OBSCURE CONFUSED NEBULOSE NUBILOUS OVERCAST VAPOROUS
CLOUGH CLUF CLEFT CLOES CLEUCH CLEUGH RAVINE VALLEY
CLOUT BAT BOX DAB HIT LAP BEAT BLOW BUMP CLOD CLUB CUFF JOIN MEND NAIL PULL SLAP SLUG SWAT JUICE PATCH SMITE WHACK KLOWET STRIKE TACKET TARGET THRASH WASHER BANDAGE BOSTHOON INFLUENCE
CLOVE GAP NAIL CHIVE CLEFT GILLY BUTTON CLEAVE RAVINE SHERRY GILLIVER
CLOVE BROWN EAGLE
CLOVEN CLEFT SPLIT DIVIDED BISULCATE
CLOVEN-FOOTED SLIT FISSIPED
CLOVE PINK GELOFER GRENADIN
CLOVER RED HAGI SEED HUBAM LOTUS MEDIC NARDU PUSSY ALSIKE BERSIM LADINO LEGUME LUXURY NARDOO ALFALFA BERSEEM BERSINE CLAIVER COMFORT LUCERNE MELILOT SAPLING TREFOIL TRIFOLY COWGRASS HAREFOOT NAPOLEON PUSSYCAT SHAMROCK SUCKLING YELLOWTOP
(KIND OF —) LADINO
CLOVER DODDER AILWEED EPITHYME HAILWEED HAIRWEED HALEWEED
CLOWN HOB OAF PUT APER BOOR FOOL GAUM GOFF JOEY LOUT MIME MOME SWAD ZANY ANTIC BUFFO CHUFF CHURL COMIC FESTE IDIOT MIMER PATCH PUNCH WAMBA ZANNI AUGUST BODACH CHOUGH HOBBIL JESTER JOSKIN LUBBER RUSTIC STOOGE AUGUSTE BODDAGH BUFFOON BUMPKIN CHARLEY COSTARD KOSHARE LAVACHE LOBSTER MUDHEAD PEASANT PIERROT PLAYBOY SCOFFER TOMFOOL COVIELLO KOYEMSHI MERRYMAN WHITEFACE PUNCHINELLO
CLOWNISH RAW RUDE ZANY GAWKY ROUGH BORREL CLUMSY COARSE RUSTIC AWKWARD BOORISH BORRELL HOBLIKE KERNISH LOBBISH LOUTISH UNCIVIL VILLAIN BOEOTIAN CLUBBISH SWADDISH UNGAINLY
CLOY CLOG GLUT NAIL PALL SATE GORGE PRICK ACCLOY PIERCE SATIATE SATISFY SURFEIT SATURATE
(— WITH ADORATION) BESOT
CLOYED BLASE
CLOYER SNAP
CLOYING GOOEY SWEET VANILLA CLOYSOME LUSCIOUS SACCHARINE
CLUB BAT DOG HIT HUI SET BEAT CANE JOIN MACE MALL MAUL MERE POLT TEAM BAFFY BANDY BATON BILLY BUNCH CLOUT HURLY KEBBY LODGE MASHY ORDER STAFF STICK TOWEL UNITE YOKEL ZONTA BULGER CERCLE CIRCLE CLIQUE CUDGEL HURLEY KEBBIE LIBBET MACANA MASHIE MENAGE MUCKLE NULLAH PRIEST STRIKE TAIAHA VEREIN WEAPON WHITES BOURDON CAMBUCA COLLEGE COUNCIL HETAERY HETAIRY SOROSIS ATHENEUM BLUDGEON CATSTICK SODALITY SORORITY SPONTOON TERTULIA KNOBKERRY
(— IN PLAYING CARDS) OAK
(— OF ANTENNA) CLAVUS
(BASEBALL —) FARM
(GOLF —) IRON WOOD BAFFY CLEEK MASHY SPOON STICK WEDGE BRASSY BULGER DRIVER JIGGER LOFTER MASHIE PUTTER BLASTER MIDIRON NIBLICK PITCHER
(INTERNATIONAL SERVICE —) GYRO
(MAORI —) MERE MERAI MARREE
(MEMBER OF SERVICE —) SERTOMAN
(POLICEMAN'S —) SAP BILLY PANTOON SPONTON SPONTOON NIGHTSTICK LATHI
(POLITICAL —) ROTA FASCIO HETAERY HETAIRY
(SINGERS' —) GLEE
(SPIKED —) ALLIDE
(SPORTS —) BAT
(WAR —) WADDY
(WOMEN'S —) SOROSIS SORORITY CIRCLE
(PREF.) CLAVI CORDYL(O) RHOPAL(O)
(SUFF.) CORYNUS
CLUB CARRIER CLAVIGER
CLUBFOOT TALUS VARUS VALGUS TALIPES CYLLOSIS POLTFOOT
CLUB, GOLF (PART OF —) TOE FACE GRIP HEAD HEEL NECK NOSE SOLE HOSEL SHAFT
CLUB MOSS MOSS FOFEET LYCOPOD PILIGAN CROWFOOT FERNWORT
CLUBROOT CLUB ANBURY ANBERRY HANBURY CLUBBING CLUBFOOT
CLUB RUSH RUSH SEDGE GLUMAL DEERHAIR
CLUB-SHAPED CLAVATE
CLUCK HEN FUSS CHUCK CLACK CLICK CLOCK CLOOK
CLUE KEY TIP BALL CLEW HINT IDEA LEAD GUIDE TWINE BOTTOM CLAVIS THREAD INNUENDO
CLUMP SOP TOD BLOW BUSH CLOT HEAP KNOT LUMP MASS MOSS MOTT TOPE TUFT TUMP TURB BLUFF BUNCH CLAMP GROUP GROVE HOUSE PATCH PLUMP STUMP TREAD WUDGE CLUNCH DOLLOP LUMPER BOSCAGE CLUMPER CLUSTER THICKET
(— OF BRIERS OR ROSES) ROAN RONE
(— OF CELLS) SLUDGE
(— OF SHRUBS) BUSH
(— OF SPORANGIA) SORUS
(— OF TREES) BLUFF HOUSE HURST HYRST BOSQUE
CLUMSILY SOUSE GREENLY GAUCHELY
CLUMSINESS GAUCHERIE
CLUMSY AWK FLOB LEWD NUMB RUDE BLUNT BULKY GAUMY GAWKY HOGGY HULKY INAPT INEPT SCRAM SPLAY STIFF STOGY CLUMPY CLUNKY GAUCHE LUBBER NOGGEN THUMBY WOODEN AWKWARD BOORISH CHUCKLE LOUTISH LUMPISH UNHANDY UNREADY BENUMBED BUNGLING CLOWNISH FOOTLESS GAUMLESS HANDLESS LUMBERLY TACTLESS UNGAINLY UNWIELDY CLOUTERLY PONDEROUS HIPPOPOTAMIC
(— PERSON) KLUTZ
(NOT —) FINE
CLUPEID HERRING
CLUSTER BOB BOG BUSH CLOT COMA CONE CYME KNOT LUMP TUFT BUNCH CLUMP DRUSE GROUP PLUMP SHEAF SORUS CENTER COLONY GATHER MORULA PLEIAD REGIME BOUROCK CLUTHER DOLPHIN ENVIRON FOLIAGE FASCICLE NUCLEATE SURROUND

(— AS BEES) BALL KNIT
(— OF BANANAS) HAND
(— OF BRANCHES) SPRAY
(— OF CELLS) ROSETTE
(— OF CRYSTALS) DRUSE
(— OF FEATHERS) MUFF
(— OF FIBERS) NEP
(— OF FLOWERS) CYME TRUSS CORYMB ANTHEMY PANICLE
(— OF HAIRS) MYSTAX
(— OF METAL BALLS) GRAPE
(— OF NODULES) GRAPES
(— OF PILES) DOLPHIN
(— OF PLANTS) BED
(— OF RAYS) AIGRETTE
(— OF SPORES) SORUS
(— OF STARS) PRAESEPE
(— OF TINES) TROCHE
(— OF WOOL) NEP
(CONFUSED —) SPLATTER
(GERM CELL —) MORULA
(SUSPENDED —) SWAG
(PREF.) CORYMBI CYM(I)(O) KYM(I)(O) RACEMI RACEMO

CLUSTER BEAN GUAR

CLUSTERED TUFTED RACEMOSE AGGREGATE CONGLOMERATE

CLUTCH HUG NAB SET CLAM CLAW CLEM CLIP FIST GLAM GRAB GRIP NEST BROOD CATCH CLASP CLAUT CLEEK CLICK GLAUM GRASP GRIPE GRISP HATCH LEVER POWER SEIZE TALON CLEACH CLENCH CLETCH CLINCH CUTOUT FASTEN RETAIN SNATCH CLAUGHT CONTROL CRAMPON COUPLING
(— OF EGGS) SET LAWTER LAYING SETTING SITTING LAUGHTER

CLUTCHING GRIP GRIPING

CLUTTER MESS STUFF BUSTLE CUMBER LITTER CLATTER DISORDER CONFUSION

CLUTTERED CLATTY CLOTTED

CLYMENE (DAUGHTER OF —) ALCIMEDE
(FATHER OF —) MINYAS CATREUS OCEANUS
(HUSBAND OF —) IAPETUS NAUPLIUS PHYLACUS
(MOTHER OF —) TETHYS
(SON OF —) OEAX ATLAS IPHICLUS PHAETHON MENOETIUS PALAMEDES

CLYPEUS NASUS EPISTOME PRELABRUM

CLYSTER LAVEMENT INJECTION

CLYTEMNESTRA (BROTHER OF —) CASTOR POLLUX POLYDEUCES
(DAUGHTER OF —) ELECTRA LAODICE IPHIGENIA IPHINASSA CHRYSOTHEMIS
(FATHER OF —) TYNDAREUS
(HUSBAND OF —) TANTALUS AGAMEMNON
(LOVER OF —) AEGISTHUS
(MOTHER OF —) LEDA
(SISTER OF —) HELENA
(SON OF —) ORESTES

CLYTIUS (BROTHER OF —) PRIAM
(FATHER OF —) EURYTUS LAOMEDON
(MOTHER OF —) GAEA
(SLAYER OF —) HERCULES
(SON OF —) CALETOR

COACH BUS CAR FLY DRAG HACK HELP ARABA BOGEY BOGIE BRIEF CABIN FLIER FLYER PILOT PRIME STAGE TEACH TRAIN TUTOR ADVISE DIRECT FIACRE JARVEY MENTOR SALOON ADVISER CHARIOT COACHER CONCORD GONDOLA PREPARE RATTLER TALLYHO TRAINER CARRIAGE DORMEUSE PUPILIZE
(BALLET —) REPETITEUR
(FAST —) FLIER FLYER
(HACKNEY —) FIACRE JARVEY
(HEAVY —) DRAG
(SLOW —) SLOWPOKE
(3-WHEELED —) TRICYCLE

COACHDOG DALMATIAN

COACH-HOUSE REMISE

COACHMAN FLY FISH JEHU WHIP PILOT COACHY DRIVER COACHEE COACHER YAMSHIK YEMSCHIK

COACTION EXPLOITATION

COADJUTOR PRIOR

COAGULANT CURD RENNET STYPTIC COAGULUM GELATINE

COAGULATE GEL SET CAKE CLOD CLOT CURD JELL QUAIL YEARN COTTER CURDLE LAPPER LOBBER LOPPER POSSET CLABBER CLOTTER CONGEAL PECTIZE THICKEN COAGULUM CONCRETE SOLIDIFY

COAGULATED CRUDY CURDY LIVERED

COAGULATION GOUT CLOTTER

COAGULUM CLOT THROMBUS

COAK-LIKE PHELLOID

COAL RIB BASS DUFF FUEL SWAD BLOCK CHARK EMBER GHOST GLEED STOKE BARING BRAZIL BURGEE CANNEL CARBON CINDER FIRING SPLINT BACKING BOGHEAD BRIGHTS BYERITE COBBLES LIGNITE RATTLER VITRAIN AMPELITE LANDSALE
(— IN PLACE) SOLID
(— MINE) COLLIERY
(— MINER) COLLIER
(— PILLAR) STOOK
(— SLAB) SKIP
(BAD —) SMUT
(BED OF —) SEAM
(BROWN-) LIGNITE
(DIRTY —) RASH
(FINE —) DUFF SCREENINGS
(IMPURE —) SWAD
(INFERIOR —) CROW
(LARGE BLOCK OF —) JUD JUDD
(LIVE OR GLOWING —) GLEED GLEYD
(REFUSE —) BREEZE
(SIZE OF —) EGG NUT PEA LUMP RICE SLACK STOVE BARLEY BROKEN CHESTNUT WALLSEND BUCKWHEAT
(SLATY —) BASS BONE BONY
(SMALL LUMP OF —) NUBBLING
(SMALL PORTION OF UNCUT —) PANEL
(PREF.) ANTHRAC(O) CARBONI

COAL BED SEAM

COALBIN BUNKER

COAL BROKER CRIMP

COAL CAR JIMMY

COAL CHUTE DOCK

COAL DUST COOM CULM SMUT COOMB

COALESCE MIX CLOG FUSE JOIN BLEND MERGE UNITE COHERE EMBODY MINGLE SINTER COMBINE

COALESCENCE UNION FUSION LEAGUE CAPTURE SYNANTHY

COAL-FACE BANK

COALFISH SEY PARR COLEY CUDDY SEITH BESHOW BILLET CUDDEN PODLER SAITHE SILLOC BADDOCK GLASHAN GLASSIN PILTOCK POLLACK
(YOUNG —) PODLER PODLEY COMAMIE POODLER SILLOCK GRAYFISH

COALITION FRONT TRUST UNION FUSION LEAGUE MERGER ENTENTE ALLIANCE

COAL OIL KEROSENE

COALRAKE HOE FREGGIN FRUGGAN SCRAPPLE

COAL WORKER GEORDIE HURRIER

COAL YARD REE

COAMING CURB LEDGE COMBING

COARSE FAT LOW RAW BASE BULL DANK FOUL HARD HASK LEWD LOUD RANK RUDE SOUR VILE BAWDY BRASH BROAD CRASS CRUDE DIRTY GREAT GROFF GROSS HARSH HASKY HEAVY LARGE LOOSE PLAIN RANDY ROUGH ROUTH ROWTY RUDAS STOGY STOUR THICK UNORN BLOWSY BRAZEN BRUTAL CALLOW CHUFFY COMMON DUDGEN EARTHY IMPURE INCULT RANDIE RIBALD ROUDAS RUDOUS RUGGED RUSSET RUSTIC SORDID SULTRY UNFELE VULGAR BLATANT CARLAGE CARLISH CRIBBLE FULSOME GOATISH LOUTISH LOWBRED OBSCENE PROFANE RAPLOCH RAUCOUS ROINISH SENSUAL BARBARIC CLOWNISH HOMESPUN IMMODEST INDECENT PLEBEIAN STUBBORN UNCHASTE

COARSE-FIBERED STRONG

COARSE-GRAINED DRY GRUFF

COARSELY BROADLY HARSHLY

COARSEN HACKNEY

COARSENESS RAUNCH HOGGERY

COAST BANK LAND RIPA BEACH BOARD CLIFF SHORE SLIDE WARTH ADJOIN BORDER RIVAGE STRAND BOBSLED SEASIDE APPROACH SEABOARD SEASHORE ROLLALONG

COASTAL ORARIAN

COASTER MAT SLED TILE DOLLY TROUT BARCON CRADLE CREEPER MISTICO TOBOGGAN

COAST GUARD (U.S. — WOMAN) SPAR

COASTLAND MAREMMA

COAT FUR LAY PEE SAC TOG BARK BLUE BUFF CONY DAUB FOIL FOLD HIDE HUSK JACK JAMA JUPE MIDI PINK RIND SACK SCAB SEAL TOGE ZINC BENNY CLOTH CONEY COVER CRUST FLASH FROCK GLACE GLAZE HABIT JAMAH JEMMY LAYER OILER PAINT PLATE QUYTE SAQUE SHELL TERVE ALPACA BYRNIE COATEE DUSTER ENAMEL ENROBE EXTIMA GROUND HACKLE INTIMA INVEST JACKET JOSEPH KIRTLE LACKER MANTLE MELOTE PARGET PELAGE RABBIT REEFER SEALER SILVER SLOUGH STUCCO TABARD VENEER BEESWAX BOBTAIL CASSOCK COATING COURTBY CRISPIN CUTAWAY GARMENT GROGRAM INCRUST KARAKUL LACQUER OILCOAT OVERLAY PALETOT PELISSE PLASTER SHELLAC SHOOTER SPENCER STRATUM SUBCOAT SURCOAT SURTOUT SWAGGER TOGEMAN TOPCOAT VESTURE BENJAMIN COURTEPY GRAPHITE INTONACO MACKINAW MEMBRANE OVERCOAT ROCKELAY SEALSKIN SHERWANI SILICATE TEGUMENT TRENCHER OUTERCOAT PETERSHAM REDINGOTE CHESTERFIELD
(— FOOD) DREDGE
(— LENS) BLOOM
(— OF ARMS) CREST BLAZON BEARINGS
(— OF BIRD SKINS) TEMIAK
(— OF BLOOD VESSEL) MEDIA
(— OF CARIBOU SKINS) KOOLETAH
(— OF DEFENSE) JACK
(— OF EYE) CHOROID
(— OF EYEBALL) SCLERA
(— OF GRAVEL) BLOTTER
(— OF INDIA) ACHKAN
(— OF MAIL) FROCK BRINIE BYRNIE SECRET HAUBERK HABERGEON CATAPHRACT
(— OF ORGAN) INTIMA
(— OF OVULE) PRIMINE
(— OF PLASTER) SET ARRICCIO BROWNING INTONACO
(— OF SEED) ARIL BRAN EPISPERM
(— OF WOOL) FLEECE
(— WITH ALLOY) TERNE
(— WITH PITCH) PAY
(— WORN UNDER ARMOR) GAMBESON
(CLOSE-FITTING —) TRUSS
(DEER'S WINTER —) BLUE
(FIRST — OF TIN) LIST
(FUR —) ANARAK ANORAK
(HAIR —) MELOTE
(HERALD'S —) TABARD
(HOODED —) GREGO CAPOTE
(KIND OF —) TRENCH
(LONG —) MAXI JIBBA JIBBAH KAPOTE DJIBBAH MAXICOAT NEWMARKET
(LOOSE —) CASSOCK PALETOT INVERNESS
(MILITARY —) TUNIC BLOUSE BUFFCOAT
(OLD —) MUMMOCK
(RIDING —) JOSEPH
(SACKCLOTH —) SANBENITO
(SEALSKIN —) NETCHA
(SEED —) ARIL

(SHEEPSKIN —) ZAMARRA ZAMARRO
(SHORT —) PEA JUMP MIDI SACK TERNE JERKIN REEFER PEACOAT
(THREE-QUARTER LENGTH —) ACHKAN
(WATERPROOF —) BURSATI SLICKER
(WOMAN'S —) CARACO DOLMAN
(WOOLLY —) LANUGO
COATED GLACE BACKED FURRED LOADED PLATED CANDIED
(— WITH FLOUR AND CRUMBS) MILANESE
COAT HANGER SHOULDER
COATI NASUA TEJON NARICA PISOTE ARCTOID
COATING (ALSO SEE COAT) FUR GUM ARIL DOPE DRAB FILM FLOR HAIR HOAR SKIN BLOOM FLASH GLACE GLAZE ICING SCALE BEAVER CHATON COVERT CRUSTA FINISH JACKET PATINA VENEER BACKING DIPCOAT FURRING GILDING LACQUER OVERLAY PLATING TINNING ACIERAGE CAMBOUIS CLADDING EMULSION FLOODING MUCILAGE OVERCOAT PERIDIUM PLASTERING
(— FOR METAL) SLUSH
(— OF BACTERIA) SLIME
(— OF GLASS) MOILES FOLIATION
(— OF GLUE) ENAMEL
(— OF ICE) GLAZE
(— OF SEED) TESTA
(— OF TONGUE) ATTER
(CHEESE —) MOLD
(CORROSION —) RUST
(METAL —) CLAD CLADDING
(MIRROR —) FOIL
(OUTSIDE —) CRUST
(POWDERY —) DOWN
(PROTECTIVE —) RESIST
(PRUINOUS —) FARINA
(SEED —) TESTA
(WALL —) GROUT
COATLICUE **(HUSBAND OF —)** MIXCOATL
(SON OF —) HUITZILOPOCHTLI
COATTAIL LABIE LAPPET
COAX BEG COY PET CANT DUPE FAGE FAWN LURE URGE WILE JOLLY TEASE BANTER CAJOLE CUITLE CUTTER ENTICE FLEECH SEDUCE BEGUILE CROODLE CROWDLE CRUDDLE FLATTER IMPLORE SOOTHER WHEEDLE BLANDISH COLLOGUE INVEIGLE PERSUADE
COAXIAL CONCENTRIC
COB EAR LOB MEW COBB
COBALT **(— EXPORTER)** ZAIRE
COBBERER ROARER ROUSER
COBBLE DARN MEND PAVE SOLE BOTCH PATCH STONE BUNGLE COGGLE REPAIR RESOLE
COBBLER PIE SNOB SHEEP SOLER SUTOR ARTIST COZIER SOUTER BOTCHER CATFISH CRISPIN POMPANO SADDLER CHUCKLER SCORPION SNOBSCAT
COBBLERFISH COBBLER SUNFISH SHOEMAKER
COBBLESTONE COGGLE
COBBY STOUT HEARTY LIVELY STOCKY COMPACT
COBIA SNOEK SNOOK
COBLE MULE KOBIL
COBNUT COB OUABE HOGNUT PIGNUT
COBRA ASP NAG HAJE NAGA NAJA KRAIT VIPER ELAPID URAEUS
COBWEB NET TRAP SNARE WEVET GOSSAMER
COCA CUCA KHOKA TRUXILLO
COCAINE BLOW COKE SNOW TOOT CRACK FLAKE FREEBASE
(— MIXED WITH HEROIN) SPEEDBALL
(— USER) COKEHEAD
(— WITH HEROIN) SPEEDBALL
(TAKE —) SPEEDBALL
COCASH ASTER SWANWEED
COCCOID BERRYLIKE
COCCULUS CEBATHA FISHBERRY
COCCUS COFFEEBUG
COCCYX RUMPBONE
(PREF.) COCCYGEO COCCYG(O)
COCHE MOCOA
COCHINEAL GRAIN BLANCO COCCUS GRANILLA
COCHINEAL FIG NOPAL
COCHINEAL INSECT VERMIL VERMEIL VERMILION
COCK COX TAP BANK BOOT COIL FOWL HEAP KORA PILE RICK SPAN COCKY COQUE FIGHT FUGIE GALLO SHOCK STACK STRUT VALVE YOWLE CRAVEN FAUCET HAMMER HEELER LEADER CONTEND GORCOCK PETCOCK ROOSTER SWAGGER ASTROLOG COCKBIRD COCKEREL COXBONES GAMECOCK JERMONAL STOPCOCK
(— GUNLOCK) NAB
(— OF HAY) HIPPLE
(— OF THE WALK) KINGFISH
(— WITHOUT COURAGE) CRAVEN
(— WITHOUT SPURS) MUCKNA
(FIGHTING —) FUGIE HEELER TURNPOKE
(TURKEY —) STAG
(WATER —) KORA
(WEATHER —) FANE VANE
(PREF.) ALECTORO ALECTRYO GALLI
COCKADE KNOT BADGE COCKARD ROSETTE TRICOLOR
COCKATIEL QUARRION
COCKATOO ARA ARARA COCKY GALAH MACAW ABACAY COCKIE PARROT CORELLA JACATOO CALANGAY GANGGANG
COCKATOO BUSH BLUEBERRY
COCKBOAT COG COCK SCULL COGBOAT
COCKCHAFER MAYBUG OAKWEB BUZZARD HUMBUZZ MAYBEETLE
COCKCROW DAWN
COCKED HAT SCRAPER RAMILLIE
COCKER CODDLE COGGER CUITER QUIVER SPANIEL
COCKEREL COCK SLIP BANTAM
COCKFIGHT MAIN SPAR
COCKINESS BRAVADO SWAGGER
COCKLE COCK GALL GITH KILN OAST BULGE KAKEL SHELL STOVE DARNEL NUCULA PALOUR PUCKER RIPPLE WABBLE ZIZANY CUCKOLD WRINKLE HARDHEAD
(PREF.) CONCH(O)
COCKLEBUR COTS CLOTE COCKLE BURDOCK BURWEED CADILLO CLOTBUR CUCKOLD CLOTWEED DITCHBUR
COCKNEY ARRY ORTHERIS LONDONESE
COCKPIT PIT RING RINK WELL ARENA CABIN FIELD GALLERA
COCKROACH BUG DRUM ROACH BEETLE BLATTID DRUMMER KNOCKER
COCKSCOMB CREST COXCOMB
COCKSFOOT HARDGRASS
COCKSPUR FINGRIGO GARABATO
COCKTAIL SOUR ZOOM BRONX CRUSTA GIBSON GIMLET MAITAI COBBLER MARTINI NEGRONI SAZERAC SIDECAR STINGER SWIZZLE APERITIF DAIQUIRI MARGARITA GRASSHOPPER TEQUILASUNRISE
(— INGREDIENT) SAZERAC
(KIND OF —) MOLOTOV
COCK-UP MESS
COCKY PERK PERT CRANK PERKY CROUSE FARMER JAUNTY COCKING ARROGANT
COCO KOKO BROMA COCOA COKER YUNTIA
COCOA MAHAL TURTLE PATASHTE
COCOA BROWN PUEBLO
COCONUT COCO COCKER NARGIL COCOANUT
COCONUT FIBER COIR KAIR KYAR CAYAR
COCONUT MEAT COPRA
COCONUT PALM KOKO NIOG
COCOON POD CLEW CLUE KELL SCAB SHED SHELL BOTTOM DOUPION FOLLICLE
COCO PLUM ICACO HICACO
COCOWOOD KOKRA
COCOYAM TARO YAUTIA
COCUSWOOD KOKRA
COD BAG BIB COR KID POD AXLE BANK CUSK FOOL GADE HOAX HUSK POOR ROCK BELLY DORSE DROUD GADID POUCH SCROD SHALE SHAUP TORSK BURBOT CODGER CULTUS ESCROD FELLOW MULVEL PILLOW POCKET TOMCOD WACHNA BACALAO CODFISH CODLING CUSHION KEELING KILLING MILWELL MORRHUA SCROTUM CABELIAU DOLEFISH KABBELOW KLIPFISH ROCKLING
(BUFFALO —) LING
(CURED —) DUNFISH
(DRIED —) STOCK
(PILE OF DRIED —) YAFFLE
(SALTED —) COR KLIPFISH HABERDINE
(YOUNG —) SPRAG
CODA END CAUDA RONDO EPILOG FINALE CODETTA EPILOGUE POSTLUDE
CODDLE PET BABY CADE COOK MUCH HUMOR NURSE SMALM SPOIL CARESS COCKER COSSET COTTON FONDLE PAMPER PTISAN QUADLE PARBOIL
CODE BCD LAW FLAG ASCII CANON CODEX DOGMA FUERO CIPHER DIGEST SECRET SIGNAL MULTEKA PRECEPT DOOMBOOK MICROCODE
(— OF CEREMONIES) RITUAL
(— OF CHIVALRY) BUSHIDO
(— OF LAWS) ADA ADAT PANDECT SHERIAT DOOMBOOK
(— OF REGULATIONS) RULE
(— OF RULES) VINAYA
(— OF WHAT IS FITTING) DECORUM PROTOCOL
(— WORD) ALFA XRAY ZULU ROGER ROMEO TANGO SIERRA VICTOR YANKEE WHISKEY
(COMPUTER —) BCD ASCII
(INFORMATION —) EBCDIC
(KIND OF —) ZIP AREA MORSE PENAL
(PUNCHCARD —) HOLLERITH
(PUNCH CARD —) HOLLERITH
(READ BAR —S) SCAN
CODETTA CONDUIT
CODE WORD EUPHEMISM
CODEX ALEF CODE ALEPH ANNAL
CODFISH POOR SPRAG TORSK KEELING
CODGER COD CUFF CHURL CRANK MISER FELLOW NIGGARD
CODICIL ANNEX LABEL SCRIPT
CODIFY INDEX DIGEST CLASSIFY
CODLING HAKE
CODOL RETINOL
CODON TRIPLET
CODSWALLOP TRIPE
COEFFICIENT CUMULANT AUSTAUSCH
COELENTERATE POLYP MEDUSA ACALEPH RADIATE ACALEPHE
COENOBIUM COLONY
COENOCYTE SYMPLASM SYMPLAST SYNCYTIUM
COENZYME NAD NADH NADP NADPH COFACTOR
COERCE COW CURB MAKE BULLY CHECK DRIVE FORCE ORDER COHERT COMPEL HIJACK CONCUSS ENFORCE REPRESS SANDBAG BLUDGEON BULLDOZE DISTRAIN RESTRAIN RESTRICT BLACKJACK
COERCION HEAT FORCE DURESS COMMAND
COEUR D'ALENE SKITSWISH
COEUS **(BROTHER OF —)** ENCELADUS
(DAUGHTER OF —) LETO LATONA ASTERIA
(FATHER OF —) URANUS
(MOTHER OF —) GAEA
(SISTER OF —) FAMA RUMOR
(WIFE OF —) PHOEBE
COFFEE JO JOE RIO CAFE COHO COHU JAVA MILD DECAF MOCHA BOGOTA BRAZIL CAUFLE CHAOUA JAMOKE SANTOS TRIAGE ARABICA BOURBON MELANGE SUMATRA

ESPRESSO MAZAGRAN MEDELLIN TRILLADO CAPUCCINO CAPPUCCINO
(— DISPENSER) URN
(DECAFFEINATED —) DECAF
(KIND OF —) DECAF
(MORNING —) ELEVENS
COFFEE BEAN QUAKER
COFFEEBERRY JOJOBA CASCARA SOYBEAN PEABERRY
COFFEE CAKE KUCHEN
COFFEECAKE (ROUND —) TEARING
COFFEE-CUP FINGAN FINJAN
COFFEEHOUSE INN CAFE CAFENEH CAFENER CAFENET
COFFEEMAKER SILEX
COFFEEPOT PERCOLATOR
COFFEE TREE BONDUC CHICOT VIRGILIA
COFFER ARK BOX DAM PYX CHEST HUTCH TRUNK CASKET FORCER FORCET SPRUCE TRENCH CAISSON CASHBOX CASSOON COFFRET LACUNAR LAQUEAR CIBORIUM STANDARD
COFFIN BIER CASE CIST KIST MOLD PALL SHELL BASKET CASING CASKET COFFER HEARSE TROUGH THROUGH
(LEADEN —) COPE
COG CAM LIE NOG CAUK COCK GEAR JEST CATCH CHEAT CHOCK CHUCK COGUE COZEN TENON TOOTH TRICK WEDGE WHEEL CAJOLE COGGING DECEIVE PRODUCE QUIBBLE WHEEDLE
COGENT GOOD PITHY VALID POTENT STRONG TELLING FORCIBLE POWERFUL PREGNANT
COGITATE MULL MUSE PLAN THINK PONDER CONNATE MEDIATE REFLECT CONSIDER
COGNATE KIN AKIN ALIKE ALLIED COGENER KINDRED RELATED SIMILAR BANDHAVA RELATIVE APOPHONIC
COGNITION GNOSIS NOESIS KENNING KNOWLEDGE PERCEPTION
(SUFF.) GNOSIA GNOSIS GNOSTIC GNOSY
COGNITIVE KNOWING EPISTEMIC
COGNIZANCE KEN WIT HEED MARK BADGE CREST EMBLEM NOTICE BEARING COCKADE KNOWING PRIVITY WITTING
COGNIZANT WARE WISE AWAKE AWARE GUILTY KNOWING WITTING ACKNOWNE SENSIBLE
(BE —) DEEM
COGNIZE KNOW
COGNOMEN NAME BYNAME AGNOMEN SURNAME NICKNAME PATRONYM
COGON ILLUK KUNAI LALANG
COGWOOD CERILLO
COHABIT BED LIVE DWELL ADHERE OCCUPY COMPANY ACCUSTOM
CO-HEIR PARCENER
COHERE FIT BOND GLUE SUIT AGREE CLING SEIZE STICK UNITE ADHERE CEMENT CLEAVE CONNECT COINCIDE
COHERENCE UNION CONSENT CONTEXT COHESION STRENGTH
COHERENT SERRIED
COHESION BOND ADHESION HARDNESS STRENGTH
COHESIVE FATTY GLUEY TENACIOUS
COHESIVENESS TENACITY
COHOBA PARICA
COHORT PAL ALLY BUDDY FRIEND PARTNER
COHOSH SQUAWROOT PAPOOSEROOT
COHUNE COROJO COROZO
COIF CAP HOW HOOD HOUVE BEGGIN BIGGIN BURLET HAIRDO QUAIFE ARRANGE CALOTTE BIGGONET COIFFURE SKULLCAP
COIFFURE COIF HEAD HAIRDO TUTULUS TRESSURE
(KIND OF —) BOB BUN AFRO PAGEBOY
COIL ADO WIN WIP ANSA CLEW CURL FAKE FANK FURL FUSS HANK LINK LOOP ROLL TUFT WIND ENROL FLAKE HELIX QUERL QUILE ROUND SPIRE TENSE TESLA TWINE TWIRL TWIST WHORL WRING BOBBIN BOTTOM BOUGHT DIMMER ENROLL GLOMUS HEATER RENDER RUNDLE SPIRAL TEASER TOROID TUMULT UPWIND VOLUME WINDUP WREATH ENTRAIL HAYCOCK INVOLVE PRIMARY RINGLET ROULEAU SNAKING TICKLER TROUBLE WREATHE COFUSION CONVOLVE ENCIRCLE INDUCTOR OVERCOIL
(— IN STILL) SCROLL
(— INTO BALL) WIRE
(— OF CAPILLARIES) TUFT
(— OF HAIR) BUN PUG
(— OF SNAKE) FOLD
(— OF WIRE) BOBBIN SOLENOID
(— OF YARN) SKEIN
(INDUCTION —) JIGGER
(PREF.) SPIRILLO SPIR(I)(O)
COILED GYRATE TORTILE WRITHEN TURBINAL
COILER FLARER
COILING SPIRY
COIN AS BU PU AVO BAN BIT BOO COB DAM DIE DUB ECU FIL JOE KIP LAT LEK LEU LEV LEY ORI PUL SEN SOL TRA WEN WON ZUZ ABAS ANNA ATTE BAHT BATZ BESA CASH CENT CHIP CHON DEMY DIME DOIT DONG DOTT DUMP DURO FELS FILS GILL GROS GROT HARP HOON HWAN JACK JANE KRAN KYAT LEVY LION MAIL MAKE MERK MILL MINT MITE MULE OBAN ONZA OORD PARA PAUL PESA PESO PICE POND POUL QUAN RAND RIAL ROCK RYAL SCAD SENT SINK SIZE SLUG TAEL TARA TARE TARI TARO TIAO TREY TYPE UNIT ACKEY AGNEL AGORA AKCHA ALBUS ALTIN ALTUN AMANI ANGEL ANGLE ASPER BAIOC BAIZA BATTE BEKAR BELGA BETSO BEZZO BISTI BLANC BLANK BODLE BROAD BROWN CHINK CLINK COIGN CONTO COROA CROSS CROWN CUNYE DARIC DINAR DISME DOBLA DUCAT EAGLE EYRIR FANAM FANON FODDA FRANC GAZET GRANO GROAT GROSZ HALER HECTE JACOB JULIO JUSTO KOBAN KRONA KRONE KROON LIARD LIBRA LITRA LIVRE LOUIS MEDAL MEDIN MEDIO MILAN MOHUR MOPUS NOBLE NOMOS OBANG ORKEY ORKYN PAISA PAOLO PARDO PENNY PERAU PESSA PIECE PLACK PLATE POALI POALO PROOF PRUTA QUART QUINE RAPPE REBIA RIDER RIYAL ROYAL RUBLE RUPIA SAIGA SAPEK SCEAT SCUDO SCUTE SEMIS SHAHI SICCA SMASH SOLDO STAMP STYCA SUCRE TALER TANGA TANKA TEMPO THRIP TICAL TRIME UNCIA UNITE WHITE ABASSI ABBASI AFGHAN AHMADI ARGENT ASSARY AUREUS AZTECA BALBOA BAUBEE BAWBEE BEAVER BEZANT BIANCO BLANCO BOGACH BRONZE CARLIN CENTAS CHAISE COBANG CONDOR COPPER CORONA CUARTO CUNZIE DECIME DENARY DENIER DERHAM DINDER DIOBOL DIRHAM DIXAIN DIZAIN DOBLON DODKIN DOLLAR DOPPIA DOUBLE ESCUDO FILLER FLORIN FOLLIS FORINT GEORGE GIULIO GOURDE GRIVNA GROSSO GUINEA GULDEN HARPER HELLER ICHIBU ITZEBU JUSLIK KLIPPE KOPECK KORONA KORUNA LAUREL LEPTON MACUTA MAHBUB MAIDEN MANCUS MEDINO MISKAL NICKEL NORKYN OCHAVO OCTAVE ONGARO PADUAN PAGODA PARDAO PATACA PATART PHILIP PRUTAH QUEZAL ROSARY SALUNG SALUTE SATANG SEQUIN SESKIN SHEKEL SHIELD SIGLOS SINKER SIXAIN SOMALO SOVRAN STATER STELLA STIVER TALENT TARGET TESTAO TESTER TESTON THALER THOMAN TOSTON TRIENS TUMAIN TUNGAH TURNER TURNEY TURTLE UNGARO VINTEM XERIFF YUZLIK ZECHIN ZEHNER ZEQUIN ALFONSO ALTILIK ANGELET ANGELOT ANGOLAR ANGSTER BAIOCCO BAJOCCO BARBONE BOLIVAR CARDECU CARLINE CARLINO CAROLIN CAROLUS CENTAVO CHALCUS CHALKOS CORDOBA COUNTER CRUSADO DAMPANG DRACHMA DUCATON DUPLONE ESCALAN FANTASY JACOBUS JOANNES KASBEKE KREUZER LEMPIRA LEONINE LEOPARD LUIGINO MANGOUR MARENGO MOIDORE MONARCH MUZOONA NOUMMOS ONCETTA PAHLAVI PARISIS PATACAO PATAGON PATAQUE PENNING PFENNIG PISTOLE QUADRIN QUARTER QUATTIE QUETZAL QUINYIE REDDOCK RUDDOCK RUSPONE SANTIMS SCRUPLE SEXTANS SILIQUA SIZEINE SOLIDUS SPECIES STAMPEE STOOTER STUIVER SULTANE TALLERO TEECALL THRYMSA TORNESE TRIOBOL UNICORN XERAFIN ALBERTIN AMBROSIN AQUILINO AUGUSTAL AUKSINAS BAETZNER BAGATINE BECHTLER BLAFFERT BLANKEEL BLANKILO BROCKAGE CAVALIER CHINKERS CHUCKRAM COLONIAL COURONNE CROCKARD CRUZEIRO DECUSSIS DENARIUS DIDRACHM DIOBOLON DOUBLOON EQUIPAGA FARTHING FILIPPIC FREDERIK GAZZETTA GENOVINO GIGLIATO GIUSTINA GROSCHEN HARDHEAD HYPERPER IMPERIAL ISABELLA JOHANNES KREUTZER LUSHBURG MACARONI MAJIDIEH MARAVEDI MARCELLO METALLIK MILESIMA PATACOON PAVILION PICAYUNE PIEDFORT PISTOLET PLAPPERT PORTAGUE QUADRANS QUADRINE QUARTINE QUINCUNX RESTRIKE RIGMAREE RISDALER RIXDALER SCUDDICK SEMUNCIA SESTERCE SHILLING SIXPENCE SKILLING SLEEPING SOLIDARE STERLING STOTINKA SULTANIN TENPENNY TETROBOL THIRTEEN TWOPENCE ZECCHINO BRACTEATE
(— AROUND NECK) TALI
(— FLIP CALL) HEADS TAILS
(— HAVING MINTING ERROR) FIDO
(— IMPERFECTLY MINTED) BROCKAGE
(— OF TRIFLING VALUE) RAP
(BASE —) SHAND SHEEN SINKER
(CLAD —) SANDWICH
(COUNTERFEIT —) RAP GRAY GREY SLIP SHEEN SHOFUL STUMER STUMOR
(ISRAEL —) AGORA
(ISRAEL —S) AGOROT
(PLUGGED —) PLUG
(SMALL THICK —) DUMP
(PL.) AGOROT CHANGE CHINKS SERIES COINAGE
(PREF.) NUMISMATO NUMMI
COINAGE FICTION GALUMPH MINTAGE
COINCIDE FIT GEE JIBE JUMP AGREE TALLY CONCUR
COINCIDENCE SYNCHRONY
COINCIDENT EVEN TOGETHER
COINCIDING CONGRUENT CONSILIENT
COINER MONIER MONEYER SMASHER
COINS CHANGE
COITION SOIL VENERY MEETING CONGRESS
COKE ASK COAL COLK CORE DOPE CHARK COCAINE
(BROKEN —) BREEZE
COL GAP NEK HALS JOCH PASS HALSE SWIRE SADDLE
COLANDER SIEVE STRAINER
COLAXAIS (BROTHER OF —) ARPOXAIS LIPOXAIS
(FATHER OF —) TARGITAUS
COLCOTHAR SAFFRON TUSCANY
COLD FLU ICY MUR NIP COOL DEAD DULL FRIO HARD HASK HOAR

MURR ROUP SOUR ACALE ACOLD AGUED ALGID BLEAK CHILL CRISP FISHY FROID FRORE GELID GLACE GLARE OORIE OURIE PARKY POOSE RHEUM SHARP SNELL STONY VIRUS ARCTIC BITTER BOREAL CHILLY CLAMMY CRIMMY FREDDO FRIGID FRIGOR FROSTY GLASSY MARBLY STECKY WAIRCH WINTRY BRITTLE CATARRH CHILLED COLDISH COSTIVE DISTANT FROSTED GLACIAL INHUMAN MORFOND SHIVERY STRANGE FREEZING MORFOUND PIERCING RESERVED RHIGOSIS STANDOFF UNHEATED REPULSIVE
(— IN HEAD) POSE POOSE CORYZA CATARRH GRAVEDO SNIVELS SNIFFLES SNIFTERS
(BITTER —) ARCTIC
(VERY —) ICY GELID FRIGID PEEVISH
(PREF.) CRY(O) FRIGO FRIGORI KRY(O) PSYCHRO
COLD-BLOODED BRUTAL LEEPIT
COLD CUTS ASSIETTE
COLD-HEARTED COLD FROZEN BLOODLESS
COLDLY DRILY DRYLY
COLDNESS COLD FROST STEEL PHLEGM ALGIDITY ASPERITY DISTANCE FROIDEUR
COLDONG FRIARBIRD
COLE CALE KAIL KALE COLZA FRIGOR COLEWORT
COLE-SEED COLZA NAVEW
COLESEED NAVEW
COLEUS KOORKA
COLEWORT COLE KALE RIBE STOCK CABBAGE
(SPROUT OF —) STOVEN
COLIC BATS FRET BATTS GUTTIE BELLYACHE
COLICROOT UNICORN ALOEROOT HUSKROOT HUSKWORT STARWORT
COLIMA TAPA IRONWOOD
COLISEUM HALL STADIUM THEATER COLOSSEUM
COLL HUG CLIP CULL POLL PRUNE EMBRACE
COLLABORATE AID ASSIST COOPERATE
COLLAGEN OSSEIN
COLLAPSE CAVE FALL FLOP FOLD GIVE SINK WILT CRASH SLUMP WRECK BUCKLE SHRINK TUMBLE CAPSIZE CROPPER CRUMBLE CRUMPLE DEBACLE DEFLATE FAILURE FLUMMOX FOUNDER SMASHUP CONTRACT DOWNFALL MELTDOWN TAILSPIN PROSTRATION
(— OF NUCLEUS) SYSTOLE
COLLAPSED QUAT CLUNG
COLLAPSIBLE FOLDING
COLLAPSING FAILURE COLLABENT
COLLAR CAP FUR NAB BAND BOSS ETON FALL FANO GILL GRAB POKE RING RUFF CHAIN DICKY FANON FANUM FICHU PHANO RUCHE SEIZE STOCK TRASH WHISK BERTHA CARCAN CHOKER COLLET COLLUM DICKEY GORGET PARRAL PARREL RABATO REBATO SADDLE SLEEVE TACKLE TORQUE TUCKER TURNUP BOBACHE BOBECHE CAPTURE CHIGNON CIRCLET PANUELO PARTLET POTHOOK REBATER SHACKLE STICKUP VANDYKE CARCANET CINCTURE NECKBAND NECKLACE RABATINE STARCHER TURNDOWN
(— FOR HORSE) BARGHAM BRECHAM
(HIGH —) GILLS JAMPOT
(HORSE —) BRECHAM
(IRON —) JOUG JOUGS CARCAN POTHOOKS
(LACE —) SCALLOP
(MAGISTRATE'S —) GOLILLA
(ROMAN —) RABAT
(WHEEL-SHAPED —) RUFF
(WOODEN —) CANG CANGUE
COLLAR BEAM SPANNER SPANPIECE
COLLARBONE CLAVICLE
COLL'ARCO ARCATO
COLLARED ACCOLLE ACCOLLEE TORQUATE
COLLAR PAD AFTERWALE
COLLATE BESTOW CONFER VERIFY COMPARE
COLLATERAL SIDE ASSETS MARGIN OBLIQUE INDIRECT PARALLEL SECURITY
COLLATION TEA MEAL BEVER LUNCH REPAST SERMON ADDRESS READING DEJEUNER HOTCHPOT TREATISE
COLLEAGUE AIDE ALLY UNITE DEPUTY SOCIUS ADJUNCT COLLEGE COMPEER CONSORT PARTNER CONFRERE CONSPIRE
COLLECT JUG SAM TAX CALL CARD CULL DRAW HEAP LEVY LIFT PICK PILE POOL REAR SAMM SAVE AMASS CROWD GLEAN GROUP HOARD RAISE STORE SWEEP ACCOIL ACCRUE CENTER CONFER GARNER GATHER MUSTER PRAYER SEMBLE SHEAVE UPTAKE ARCHIVE CLUSTER COMPILE CONGEST ENGROSS IMPOUND RAMMASS RECUEIL SCAMBLE SYNAPTE ASSEMBLE CONFLATE CONTRACT CUPBOARD INGATHER RESEMBLE SCRAMBLE SCROUNGE
(— AND DRIVE INTO ENCLOSURE) WEAR
(— FOOD) FORAGE
(— GRAIN) GAVEL
(— INTO COVEY) JUG
(— MONEY) NOB
(— WAGES) UPLIFT
COLLECTED CALM COOL SOBER SERENE PRESENT COMPOSED
(PREF.) ATHRO
COLLECTION ANA BAG KIT SET BAND BEVY BOOK CLAN CROP FILE HEAD HEAP KNOT LEVY OLIO RAFT SORT ALBUM ANNEX ARRAY BATCH BUDGE BUNCH DEPOT FLOCK GLEAN GROUP HOARD KITTY SHEAF STORE SUITE SWATH TROVE AFFLUX BUDGET BUNDLE CONGER CORPUS FARDEL MISHNA PARCEL RAGBAG RECULE SORITE SPRING SWATHE TUMBLE ACCOUNT BOILING BULLARY CLUSTER COLLECT CONGERY EXHIBIT FERNERY FISTFUL FLUTTER GALLERY QUOTITY RECUEIL SAMHITA SMATTER SMYTRIE SYLLOGE TERRIER ASSEMBLY CABOODLE CONGERIE CUSTOMAL FASCICLE GATHERUM GLOSSARY JINGBANG ROMESCOT ROMESHOT SYNTAGMA
(— AT FOX HUNT) CAP
(— OF ALMS) QUEST
(— OF ANIMALS) ZOO HEAD
(— OF BOOKCASES) STACK
(— OF BOOKS) SET BIBLE CANON LIBRARY
(— OF CONIFERS) PINETUM
(— OF DATA) GROUND
(— OF FORMULAS) CODEX
(— OF FOUR) TETRAD
(— OF HUTS) BUSTEE
(— OF JOKES) SOTTISIER
(— OF LAWS) CODE
(— OF MAPS) ATLAS
(— OF OBJECTS) AFFAIR
(— OF OPINIONS) SYMPOSIUM
(— OF PERSONS) BOODLE
(— OF PLANTS) SERTULE
(— OF POEMS) DIVAN DIWAN SYLVA ANTHOLOGY
(— OF PUS) ABSCESS HYPOPYON
(— OF REVENUES) TAHSIL TEHSIL
(— OF ROCKS) SUITE
(— OF RULES) SUTRA SUTTA
(— OF SAMPLES) SWATCH
(— OF SAYINGS) ANA SUTRA SUTTA
(— OF SMALL THINGS) SMYTRIE
(— OF SPECIMENS) CABINET
(— OF STAFFS) SYSTEM
(— OF STORIES) LEGEND
(— OF TIPS) TRONC
(— OF TOOLS) LAYOUT
(— OF TREES) SERINGAL
(— OF UNWANTED ANIMALS) LARDER
(— OF VIEWS) SYMPOSIUM
(— OF WIVES) SERAGLIO
(— OF WRITINGS) CORPUS
(— OF 24 SHEETS) QUIRE
(CHURCH —) PLATE
(CONFUSED —) CLUTTER
(MISCELLANEOUS —) OLIO FARDEL SMYTRIE
(VALUABLE —) TROVE
(VAST —) CLOUD
(SUFF.) ERY
COLLECTION-BOX LADLE
COLLECTIVE ARTEL GROUP AGGREGATE
COLLECTIVELY ASONE
COLLECTIVIST COMMUNIST SOCIALIST
COLLECTOR COMB CAMEIST CURIOSO DUSTMAN FURIOSO UPTAKER ANTIQUER COUNTOUR GATHERER OOLOGIST STAMPMAN VIRTUOSO ZAMINDAR
(— ITEMS) RARIORA
(— OF BUTTERFLIES) AURELIAN
(— OF HERBS) SIMPLER
(— OF REVENUE) AUMIL AUMILDAR TALUKDAR ZAMINDAR
(— OF UNNEEDED ITEMS) PACKRAT
(BILL —) DUNNER
(CUSTOMS —) HOPPO CUSTOMER
(INDISCRIMINATE —) MAGPIE
(ITEMS OF —) VIRTU
(TAX —) CAID QAID GABBAI PUBLICAN TAHSILDAR
COLLECTORATE TALUK
COLLEEN GIRL LASS MISS BELLE CAILIN DAMSEL
COLLEGE TOL HALL AGGIE HOUSE LYCEE CAMPUS COLAGE SCHOOL SIWASH ACADEMY MADRASA SEMINARY SORBONNE
(KIND OF —) CLUSTER
(MUSLIM —) MADRASA MADRASSAH
COLLEGER TUG
COLLET BAND NECK RING CHUCK CULET CASING CIRCLE COLLAR COLLUM FLANGE BUSHING
COLLIDE HIT RAM BUMP DASH FRAY HURT BARGE CLASH CRASH KNOCK SHOCK SMITE WRECK CANNON HURTLE STRIKE THRUST
(— HEAD-ON) RAM
(— WITH) PRANG
(— WITH) IMPINGE
COLLIE KELPIE BEARDIE
COLLIER MINER PLOVER GEORDIE COILYEAR FLATIRON SCUTCHER
COLLIERY MINE
COLLIMATE ALIGN
COLLINATE ALIGN
COLLIQUATION SYNTEXIS
COLLISION HIT FOUL CLASH CRASH PRANG SHOCK SHUNT HURTLE IMPACT JOSTLE PILEUP SMASHUP CLASHING CONFLICT
COLLOCATE SET PLACE ARRANGE
COLLOID GEL
COLLOP PIECE
COLLOQUIAL FAMILIAR INFORMAL
COLLOQUIUM INDUCEMENT
COLLOQUY CHAT TALK PARLEY DIALOGUE
COLLOTYPE ARTOTYPE HELIOTYPE
COLLUDE PLOT SCHEME CONNIVE COLLOGUE CONSPIRE
COLLUM NECK
COLLUSION DECEIT CAHOOTS SECRECY PRACTICE PRACTISE
COLLUSIVE COVINOUS COLLUSORY

COLOMBIA

CAPE: VELA AGUJA MARZO AUGUSTA
CAPITAL: BOGOTA
CAY: VELA VIGIA RONCADOR
COIN: PESO REAL CONDOR PESETA CENTAVO
FORMER NAME: DARIEN NEWGRANADA
GULF: URABA CUPICA DARIEN TIBUGA TORTUGAS
INDIAN: BORO CUNA HOKA MACU MUZO PAEZ CARIB CATIO CHOCO COFAN COGUI CUBEO GUANE PIJAO SEONA ARAWAK BETOYA CALIMA INGANO SALIVA TAHAMI

TUCANO TUNEBO YAHUNA ACHAGUA ANDAQUI CHIBCHA CHIMILA GUAHIBO GUAJIRO PANCHES PUINAVE PUITOTO QUECHUA TAIRONA GUARAUNO MOTILONE
INLET: TUMACO
ISLAND: BARU NAIPO FUERTE GORGONA CUSACHON
MEASURE: VARA AZUMBRE CELEMIN
MOUNTAIN: CHITA HUILA PURACE TOLIMA
MOUNTAINS: ABIBE ANDES BAUDO COCUY AYAPEL PERIJA TUNAHI CHAMUSA ORIENGAL
PLAINS: LLANOS
POINT: CRUCES LACRUZ SOLANO CARIBANA GALLINAS
PORT: LORICA CARTAGENA
PROVINCE: META CAUCA CHOCO HUILA VALLE ARAUCA BOYACA CALDAS NARINO TOLIMA VAUPES BOLIVAR CAQUETA GUAJIRE VICHADA AMAZONAS PUTUMAYO
RIVER: UVA BITA META MUCO SINU TOMO UPIA YARI BAUDO CAUCA CESAR ISANA MESAI NECHI PATIA PAUTO SUCIO AMAZON ARAUCA ARIARI ATRATO CAGUAN VAUPES YAPURA CAQUETA GUAINIA INIRIDA TRUANDO VICHADA APAPORIS CASANARE GUAVIARE PUTUMAYO MAGDALENA
TOWN: TEN ANZA BUGA CALI MITU MUZO PAEZ SIPI TADO TOLU YARI BELLO CHINU GUAPI NEIVA PASTO TUNJA BOGOTA CUCUTA IBAGUE QUIBDO SANGIL CARTAGO LETICIA PALMIRA PEREIRA POPAYAN GIRARDOT MEDELLIN MONTERIA CARTAGENA
TREE: ARBOLOCO
VOLCANO: PURACE
WEIGHT: BAG SACO CARGA LIBRA QUILATE QUINTAL

COLON CROWN POINT HEMISTICH MESYMNION
COLONEL (— OF LIFEGUARDS) GOLDSTICK
COLONIAL OVERSEA OVERSEAS
COLONIST BOOR COLON FATHER CUTHEAN PIONEER PLANTER SETTLER EMIGRANT
(— IN AFRICA) BOER
(— IN SICILY) SIKELIOT
(AUSTRALIAN —) STERLING
(PL.) DEHAITES DEHAVITES
COLONIZE ECIZE FOUND PLANT GATHER SETTLE MIGRATE
COLONIZER OECIST OEKIST
COLONNADE ROW STOA PORCH PARVIS PIAZZA XYSTUS EUSTYLE GALLERY PARVISE PERGOLA PORTICO TERRACE CHOULTRY DIASTYLE PERISTYLE
COLONNETTE COLUMELLA
COLONUS SERF TENANT
COLONY STATE STOCK SWARM CENOBE CORMUS APOIKIA COLONIA CENOBIUM GANNETRY PLANTATION POLYZOARIUM
(— OF BEES) HIVE SKEP SWARM
(BRYOZOAN —) ESCHARA
COLOPHONY ROSIN
COLOR (ALSO SEE SPECIFIC COLOR) DIP DYE HUE BLEE CAST FAKE FLAG PUKE SUIT TINT TONE BADGE BLUSH GLAZE GLOSS GRAIN PAINT SHADE STAIN TAINT TASTE TENNE TINCT TINGE TOUCH BANNER BLEACH BOTTOM BRIDGE CHROMA ENSIGN INFECT LOCKET MANTLE RADDLE REDDEN STREAK TEMPER COULEUR DEPAINT DISTORT ENGRAIN PENNANT PIGMENT SPECKLE COLORING STANDARD TERTIARY TINCTURE
(— IMPARTED TO HERRINGS) GILDING
(— LOSS) POLIOSIS
(— OF BIRD) SMUT
(— OF BODY) HEAT
(— OF EYES OF FOWLS) DAW
(— OF HONEY) AMBER
(— OF HUMAN FLESH) CARNATION
(— OF REFLECTED LIGHT) OVERTONE
(— OF ROCK) STONE
(AUTUMN —) OCHER
(BLUE —) FOG JAY SKY WAD AQUA BICE CIEL CYAN DELF DUSK IRIS NAVY PAON SAXE WADE WOAD ZINC AZURE BERYL BLUET CADET CAPRI CHING COPEN DELFT DELPH DIANA DRAKE EMAIL GRAPE METAL NIKKO ORION PEARL ROYAL SLATE SMALT SMOKE VANDA CANTON CENDRE COELIN ENSIGN GROTTO HATHOR INDIGO LUPINE MARINE MASCOT MIGNON ORIENT PENSEE ROMANY SEVRES VENICE ZENITH CELESTE CERAMIC CHICORY DUSTBLU GOBELIN HORIZON LIBERTY LOBELIA LOGWOOD MATELOT PEACOCK PETUNIA RAMESES SISTINE SIXTINE ABSINTHE BLUEBIRD BLUEWOOD BRITTANY CAESIOUS CATTLEYA CERULEAN CERULEUM DUCKLING ELECTRIC GENDARME HYACINTH INFANTRY LABRADOR LARKSPUR MASCOTTE MAZARINE MIDNIGHT MOONBEAM NATIONAL SAPPHIRE TWILIGHT WEDGWOOD
(BROWN —) BAY ELK FOX OAK TAN ARAB BARK BOLE BRAN BURE CAIN CLAY CORK CUBA DATE DEER DRAB DUST ECRU FAON FAWN GOAT GOLD HOPI IRON LAMA LION MAST MESA MUSK PUCE SEAL SIAM TEAK ACORN ADUST ALOMA AZTEC BEIGE BISON BLOND BLUSH BOLUS BRIAR BRICK BRIER BROWN BUNNY CACAO CAMEL CANNA CLOVE COCOA CONGO EAGLE FRIAR FUDGE GIPSY GRAIN GYPSY HAZEL HENNA KAFFA KHAKI LIVER MAHAL MALAY MECCA MINIM MUMMY NEGRO OTTER PABLO QUAIL SABEL SEDGE SEPIA SIENA SIRUP SNUFF SUDAN SUEDE SUMAC SYRUP TABAC TAFFY TENNE TOAST TOPAZ AFGHAN ALESAN ALMOND APACHE ARGALI AUBURN BAMBOO BEAVER BISQUE BISTER BISTRE BLONDE BRONCO BRONZE BURNET COCHIN COFFEE CONDOR COOKIE COWBOY CROTAL DORADO ESKIMO FALLOW GINGER GRAVEL GROUSE HAVANA ISABEL LOUTRE MAROON MERIDA MOHAWK MUFFIN NUTMEG ORIOLE PAWNEE PLOVER PUEBLO RABBIT RACKET RUDDLE RUSSET SAHARA SANTOS SHERRY SORREL SPHINX SPONGE STRING STUCCO SUMACH SUNTAN THRUSH TIFFIN TURTLE ASPHALT BADIOUS BEESWAX BITUMEN BRACKEN BRONCHO CALDRON CATTAIL CIGARET COCONUT COTRINE CRACKER DOGWOOD DURANGO FEUILLE FILBERT GAZELLE GOREVAN HARVEST LEATHER LIBERIA MALABAR MIRADOR MORDORE MOROCCO MUSCADE MUSTANG NORFOLK OAKWOOD PERIQUE PRALINE RACQUET ROSARIO SABELLA SUNBURN SUNDOWN TALLYHO TANBARK TOBACCO TUSCANY ALDERNEY ALGERIAN AMBROSIA BISMARCK BOBOLINK CALABASH CARTOUCH CAULDRON CINNAMON CLAYBANK CORDOVAN DOUBLOON ETRUSCAN EUCHROME HAZELNUT ISABELLA KOLINSKY LEAFMOLD MANDALAY MOCCASIN MOLESKIN MOROCCAN MUSHROOM NOISETTE PHEASANT SAUTERNE SHAGBARK STARLING TAMARACK TEAKWOOD TERRAPIN TORTOISE WOODBARK
(DEAD-LEAF —) FILEMOT
(DEEP —) DARK
(FAST —) GRAIN
(FAWN —) WHEATEN
(GREEN —) BOA FIR IVY ALOE BICE FERN JADE LEEK MOSS NILE SAGE ALOES CEDRE CHLOR DRAKE FAIRY HOLLY KELLY LOVAT OLIVE SPRAY CANNON EMPIRE HUNTER JASPER LAUREL LIERRE LIZARD MEADOW MOUSSE MYRTLE SPRUCE VERDET CELADON CITRINE CORBEAU CRESSON CYPRESS EMERALD INGENUE JADEITE JUNIPER MESANGE NEPTUNE OLIVINE PERIDOT SEAFOAM SERPENT TILLEUL VERDURE BAYBERRY CHASSEUR COPPERAS EMERAUDE GLAUCOUS GLOWWORM PARAKEET PERRUCHE PISTACHE POPINJAY SHAMROCK TARRAGON VIRIDIAN WOODLAND
(GRIZZLED —) AGOUTI AGOUTY
(LACK OF —) PALLOR
(LOSE —) FADE
(OF A DARKISH —) SUBFUSE
(OTHER —S) OR ASH BAT DOE DUN JET TEA CHIP CORN CROW DAWN DOVE GRAY GREY GULL HEMP LAVA LEAD MODE MOLE NICE NUDE PLUM PORT PUKE ROAN RUST SAND SOOT WOOD AMBER BEACH BLACK CAMEO CERES CHILE CHILI COPRA CRANE CRASH CREAM DWALE EBONY FLESH GRAPE GREBE GREGE MAUVE MOUSE PANSY PHLOX PLOMB PRAWN PRUNE PUTTY RIFLE SABLE SPICE STEEL THYME TWINE ANATTO AURORA AUTUMN CASTOR CINDER COLLIE CORCIR DAHLIA DAMSON DENVER EVEQUE FIESTA FUSTIC GAMBIA GRIEGE KASPER MALLOW MODENA NAVAHO NAVAJO NIMBUS NUTRIA ONDINE ORCHID OXFORD OYSTER PEANUT PEBBLE PIGEON QUAKER RAISIN RESEDA ROUCOU SEASAN SILVER TUSCAN VANITY VESTAL VIOLET WALNUT ADMIRAL ANNATTO ARBUTUS ARDOISE ARNATTA BEGONIA BERMUDA BLOSSOM BRINDLE CARAIBE CARAMEL CORBEAU COTRINE COWSLIP CRACKER CRUISER MORELLO MURILLO NATURAL OPHELIA PELICAN PONTIFF POPCORN PRELATE PUMPKIN QUIMPER REGATTA ROSEBUD SAKKARA SANDUST SPARROW SUNBEAM THISTLE TUSSORE VERVAIN VIOLINE WEIGELA WHEATEN ALUMINUM AMARANTH AMETHYST BLONDINE CARMETTA CHARCOAL CLEMATIS COCOBOLO COQUETTE CREVETTE CYCLAMEN EGGPLANT EMINENCE FELDGRAU FLAMINGO GILLIVER GRAPHITE GUNMETAL HONEYDEW IMPERIAL JACINTHE LAVENDER MARATHON MORILLON MULBERRY PALMETTO ROSEWOOD SAUTERNE SQUIRREL SUNBURST WIRELESS WISTARIA WISTERIA CARNELIAN
(RED —) DAWN FLEA GOLF GOYA HEBE LAKE MIST PUCE RUBY TULY WINE AGATE BRASS BRICK CANNA CANON CEDAR CORAL CUTCH EMBER FLAME FLASH GULES LILAC MELON NYMPH PEACH PEONY POPPY ROSET SIENA SPARK TOTEM ACAJOU ARCHIL AURORE AUTUMN AZALEA BRAZIL CANYON CARROT CATSUP CERISE CHERRY CHERUB CLARET COGNAC DAMASK FRAISE GAIETY GARNET GAYETY GRANET JOCKEY KERMES MADDER MALAGA MIKADO MURREY NECTAR ORCHIL PATISE SALMON SANDIX SHRIMP SIERRA SULTAN TITIAN TOMATO AFRICAN ANAMITE ANEMONE BEGONIA BISCUIT BOKHARA CARMINE CASTORY CATAWBA CATCHUP CATECHU CRIMSON CURRANT FIREFLY FUCHSIA FUCHSIN GRANATE GRANITE HEATHER INDIANA KETCHUP LACQUER LOBSTER MAGENTA MASCARA NACARAT OXBLOOD PAPRIKA POMPEII PONCEAU REDWOOD ROSETAN ROSETTE RUBELLE SAFFLOR SARAVAN SCARLET SINOPLE STAMMEL SULTANA VERMEIL ALKERMES AMARANTH ARCHILLA BISMARCK BORDEAUX BURGUNDY CAMELLIA CARDINAL CHAUDRON CHEROKEE CHERUBIM CHESTNUT COCOANUT CONFETTI DAMONICO DIANTHUS DUBONNET EVENGLOW GERANIUM GRENADIN GRIDELIN MAHOGANY

MANDARIN MAROCAIN NACARINE TOREADOR
(SOLID —) SOLID
(TONE —) TIMBRE
(YELLOW —) HAY RAT WAX BEAR BUFF CLAY CORN CUIR ECRU FLAX GOLD LARK LIME MOTH WELD WOLD ACIER ALOMA AZTEC BEIGE BLAKE BRASS CRASH CREAM GRAIN HONEY IVORY LEMON MAIZE MAPLE SHELL STRAW TAUPE WOULD ACACIA ALMOND BANANA CANARY CATHAY CHROME CITRON CITRUS CROCUS DORADO FALLOW MANILA MASTIC MIMOSA NANKIN NUGGET OXGALL SULFUR SUNRAY SUNSET ANTIQUE APRICOT BISCUIT CAVALRY CHAMOIS GAMBOGE JASMINE JONQUIL LEGHORN MEXICAN NANKEEN PRAIRIE RHUBARB SAFFRON SULPHUR SUNGLOW ANTELOPE CALABASH CAPUCINE COCKATOO DAFFODIL EGGSHELL GENERALL GOLDMIST MARIGOLD ORPIMENT PRIMROSE SNOWSHOE
(PL.) FLAG
(PREF.) CHROM(AT)(ATO)(I)(IDIO)(O)
(HAVING DARK —) FUSCO
(SUFF.) CHROIA CHROIC CHROID CHROMASIA CHROME CHROMIA CHROMY CHROOUS
COLORABLE SPECIOUS PLAUSIBLE

COLORADO
CAPITAL: DENVER
COLLEGE: REGIS
COUNTY: BACA MESA YUMA OTERO OURAY ROUTT GILPIN CHAFFEE
MOUNTAIN: OSO LONGS PIKES ELBERT
MOUNTAIN RANGE: ROCKY
NATIVE: ROVER
PARK: ESTES
RIVER: YAMPA DOLORES APISHAPA ARIKAREE GUNNISON PURGATOIRE
STATE FLOWER: COLUMBINE
STATE NICKNAME: CENTENNIAL
STATE TREE: SPRUCE
TOWN: ASPEN DELTA LAMAR GOLDEN PUEBLO SALIDA ALAMOSA BOULDER DURANGO GREELEY GUNNISON LOVELAND TRINIDAD

COLORANT STAIN
COLORATION BLEE PILE FLASH CLOUDING COLORISM SCHILLER PIGMENTATION
COLORATURA GORGIA SOPRANO
COLOR-BLIND MONOCHROMATIC
(— TO RED) PROTANOPIC
COLOR-BLINDNESS DALTONISM
COLORED FAW HUED MALE TINCT BIASED DEPAINT STAINED
(— IN RED) RUBRIC
(— LIKE PIPE BOWL) TROUSERED
(BRILLIANTLY —) SUPERB FLAMING PSYCHEDELIC
(GORGEOUSLY —) FLAMBOYANT
(HIGHLY —) CHROMATIC PRISMATIC
(PARTI —) PIED PIEBALD
(UNIFORMLY —) HARD
(PREF.) CHROM(AT)(ATO)(I)(IDIO)(O)
(SUFF.) CHROME CHROOUS
COLORFUL GAY BRAVE JUICY VIVID COLORY GOLDEN FREAKED GORGEOUS
COLORING DYE BLEE TINT PAINT TINGE TINGENT BRONZING PAINTING TINCTURE
(— FOR EYELASHES) MASCARA
(— MATTER) TINCTION
(GARISH —) JAZZ
(SUFF.) CHROMY
COLORING MATTER
(SUFF.) PHYLL(A)(OUS)(UM)(Y)
COLORLESS WAN DRAB DULL PALE ASHEN BLAKE BLANK PLAIN ANEMIC MOUSEY PALLID HUELESS NEUTRAL ACHROMIC ACHROOUS BLANCHED ETIOLATE LIFELESS
(PREF.) LEUC(O)
COLOSSAL BIG HUGE VAST GREAT JUMBO LARGE IMMENSE TITANIC ENORMOUS GIGANTIC MONSTROUS
COLOSSUS GIANT TITAN STATUE COLOSSO MONOLITH
COLOSTRUM FOREMILK AFTERINGS
COLT FOAL STAG FILLY POTRO STAIG HOGGET POLEYN STAGGIE EQUULEUS
COLTER LAVER COOTER COULTER FOREIRON
COLTSFOOT DOCK CLOTE HOOFS CLEATS FARFARA LAGWORT SOWFOOT BULLFOOT CLAYWEED FOALFOOT
COLUGO COBEGO
COLUMBATE NIOBATE
COLUMBIA SINKIUSE
COLUMBINE AQUILEGE BLUEBELL CHUCKIES ROCKBELL
COLUMBITE DIANITE NIOBITE
COLUMBUS (BIRTHPLACE OF —) GENOA
COLUMELLA STALACE
COLUMN COG LAT ROW ANTA FILE FUST GOAL LINE POLE POST PROP STUB BAGUE LALLY SHAFT STELA STELE TORSO TRUNK WURTZ ASOKAN CORNER GNOMON PILLAR SCAPUS STAPLE STRING TSWETT COLUMEL SUPPORT VIGREUX CYLINDER PILASTER
(— IN EAR) MODIOLUS
(— OF FIGURES) SUM
(— OF FILAMENTS) SYNEMA
(— OF MOLTEN ROCK) PLUME
(BUDDHIST —) LAT
(FIGURE USED AS —) ATLAS TELAMON
(PART OF —) BASE DADO NECK OVOLO SHAFT TORUS ABACUS PLINTH REGLET SCOTIA CAPITAL ECHINUS FLUTING ASTRAGAL CINCTURE COLARENO PEDESTAL
(PART OF A —) SOCLE
(ROCK —) HOODOO
(ROULETTE —) DERNIER
(SPINAL —) HORN SPINE BACKBONE
(STRUCTURAL —) LALLY
(TWISTED —) TORSO
COLUMNAR TERETE STELENE COLUMNAL VERTICAL
COLUMNIST WRITER ANALYST
COLY MOUSEBIRD
COLZA SARSON
COMA TUFT BUNCH CARUS SLEEP SOPOR STUPOR SUBETH TORPOR TRANCE SEMICOMA CHEVELURE
COMATOSE OUT DROWSY LETHARGIC
COMB CARD GILL KAME LASH PICK RACK RAKE REDD REED SEEK TOZE BREAK BRUSH CAMBE CLEAN CREST CTENE CURRY FLISK RAVEL TEASE HACKLE SMOOTH CUSHION HATCHEL WRAITHE BEATILLE CARUNCLE TORTOISE
(KIND OF —) HOT
(WEAVING —) RADDLE
(PREF.) CTEN(O) LOPH(I)(IO)(O) PECTINATO
COMBAT WAR BLOW BOUT COPE DUEL FRAY MEEK MEET RUSH TILT CLASH FIGHT JOUST REPEL STOUR ACTION AFFRAY BATTLE MEDLEY OPPOSE RESIST SHOWER STRIFE CONTEND CONTEST COUNTER DERAIGN DISPUTE EXPLOIT SCUFFLE SERVICE ARGUMENT CONFLICT STRUGGLE
(— BETWEEN KNIGHTS) JOUST
(FUTILE —) SCIAMACHY
(SHAM —) SCIOMACHY
(SINGLE —) DUOMACHY
COMBATANT DUELER BATTLER FIGHTER CHAMPION GLADIATOR
COMBATIVE BANTAM MILITANT AGONISTIC BELLICOSE DEPENDENT PUGNACIOUS AGONISTICAL
COMBE HOPE
COMBED CRESTED
COMBER WAVE HANDER BREAKER KEMPSTER
COMBINATION KEY BLOC CLUB GANG PACT POOL RING CABAL COMBO GROUP JUNTO PARTY TRUST UNION CARTEL CLIQUE CORNER CRASIS FUSION LEAGUE MEDLEY MERGER AMALGAM BATTERY COMBINE CONSORT COTERIE FACTION HARMONY JOINING MIXTURE ADDITION ALLIANCE ENSEMBLE MONOPOLY GOODLIBET
(— OF CARDS) SET BUILD FLUSH SPREAD STRAIGHT
(— OF CIRCUMSTANCES) ACTION
(— OF COLORS) HARLEQUIN
(— OF FACES) FORM
(— OF FIRMS) TRUST
(— OF INTAGLIO FORMS) GRYLLI
(— OF NUMBERS) GIG SADDLE
(— OF TACKLES) JEERS
(— OF TONES) CHORD
(— OF 10) DECUPLET
(DANCE —) SEQUENCE
(HARMONIOUS —) CONCORD
(NOSE-JAW —) LAYBACK
(SCORING —) IMPERIAL
(PREF.) HAPT(O)
COMBINE ADD FIX MIX WED BIND BLOC CLUB JOIN NICK POOL BLEND GROUP JOINT MARRY MERGE TOTAL UNITE ABSORB CONCUR LEAGUE MEDDLE MERGER MINGLE SPLICE ACCRETE AMALGAM COMPACT CONJOIN CONJURE MACHINE COALESCE COMPOUND CONCRETE CONDENSE CONFLATE CONSTRUE CONTRACT CUMULATE FEDERATE ORCHESTRATE
(— AGAINST) BOYCOTT
(— WITH GAS) AERATE
(— WITH WATER) AQUATE
COMBINED GUM BOUND FIXED JOINT UNITED CONJOINT
COMB-LIKE PECTINAL
COMBO (SMALL —) TRIO
COMBUST START
COMBUSTIBLE FUEL FIERY ARDENT CINDER PICEOUS BURNABLE
COMBUSTION FIRE HEAT FLAME THERM TUMULT BURNING BACKFIRE
COME BE GET LAY COOP DRAW FALL GROW HAUL PASS WHEN ARISE CHIVE FETCH ISSUE LIGHT OCCUR REACH ACCRUE ADVENE APPEAR ARRIVE BECOME BEFALL EMERGE HAPPEN OBTAIN SPRING ADVANCE DEVELOP EMANATE PROCEED APPROACH PRACTICE
(— ABOUT) ARISE OCCUR CHANCE
(— AFTER) SUE FOLLOW
(— APART) FRAY SHED BREAK STAVE
(— BACK) REVERSE
(— BACK TO LIFE) REVIVE
(— BEFORE) FORERUN PREVENE ANTECEDE ANTEDATE
(— BETWEEN) INTERPOSE INTERVENE
(— DOWN) AVALE SWOOP ALIGHT DESCEND SUCCEED DISMOUNT
(— FORTH) EMIT BREAK ISSUE ACCEDE FORTHGO FURNACE
(— FORWARD) ACCEDE
(— IN CONTACT) ATTINGE
(— IN SECOND) PLACE
(— IN THIRD) SHOW
(— INTO BLOOM) BURST BLOSSOM
(— INTO COLLISION) MEET CLASH COLLIDE
(— INTO EXISTENCE) FORM BEGIN ACCRUE HAPPEN SPRING
(— INTO POSSESSION) ACQUIRE INHERIT
(— OF AGE) MAJORIZE
(— OFF) HARL PEEL
(— OUT) ISSUE APPEAR EMERGE EMANATE
(— SUDDENLY) CLAP PLUMP
(— THROUGH) DELIVER
(— TO) TOUCH ADVENE STRIKE RECOVER REVERSE
(— TO AN END) PASS
(— TO BELIEVE IN) ADOPT
(— TO CONCLUSION) DECIDE
(— TO DIE) DO DIE SET DROP EXPIRE FINISH SURCEASE
(— TOGETHER) ADD HERD JOIN MEET AMASS CONCUR COUPLE GATHER COLLECT COMBINE CONVENE ASSEMBLE

(— TO GRIEF) FOUNDER
(— TO HAND) OFFER
(— TO LIGHT) SPUNK DEVELOP
(— TO MIND) OCCUR STRIKE
(— TO NOTHING) ABORT
(— TO PASS) SORT BREAK LIGHT BEFALL BETIDE HAPPEN
(— TO PERFECTION) RIPEN
(— TO REST) LODGE SETTLE
(— TO STAND STILL) STOP
(— TO TERMS) AGREE TRYST ACCORD BARGAIN COMPOSE COMPOUND ACCOMMODATE
(— TO THE SURFACE) RISE
(— UNDER) SUBVENE
(— UPON) FIND CROSS INVENT STRIKE OVERTAKE
(FULLY —) EXPIATE

COMEBACK RALLY ANSWER RETORT RETURN REBOUND RIPOSTE HAULBACK RECOVERY REPARTEE

COMECRUDO CARRIZO

COMEDIAN WAG WIT CARD ACTOR ANTIC CLOWN COMIC GAGMAN JESTER BUFFOON FUNSTER COMOEDUS FUNMAKER FUNNYMAN PATTERER

COMEDO BLACKHEAD

COMEDOWN BATHOS DESCENT LETDOWN

COMEDY SOCK DRAMA FARCE LAZZO REVUE SITCOM COMEDIA TEMACHA COMOEDIA TRAVESTY BACCHIDES SLAPSTICK
(HEROIC —) NATAKA
(KIND OF —) STANDUP
(SITUATION —) SITCOM
(PREF.) COMICO

COMEDY OF ERRORS (AUTHOR OF —) SHAKESPEARE
(CHARACTER IN —) LUCE PINCH AEGEON ANGELO DROMIO ADRIANA AEMILIA EPHESUS LUCIANA SOLINUS BALTHAZAR ANTIPHOLUS

COMELINESS GRACE DECORUM FEATURE VENUSTY PULCHRITUDE

COMELY FAIR GOOD HEND PERT TALL TIDY WEME BONNY BUXOM HENDE QUEME SONCY SONSY TIGHT DECENT FORMAL GOODLY LIKELY LIKING LOVELY PRETTY PROPER SEEMLY SONSIE VENUST FARRANT FORMFUL SIGHTLY BECOMING DECOROUS FEATURED GRACEFUL HANDSOME PLEASING SUITABLE

COME-ON TEASER

COMET STAR METEOR XIPHIAS SUNGRAZER
(— HEAD) COMA

COMEUPPANCE REBUKE DESERTS BUSINESS

COMFIT CANDY SUCKLE CONFECT PRALINE CONSERVE PRESERVE
(PL) CONFETTI

COMFORT AID EASE REST STAY BIELD CHEER LIGHT SOOTH VISIT ENDURE RELIEF REPOSE SOLACE SOOTHE SUCCOR ANIMATE ASSUAGE CHERISH CONFIRM CONSOLE ENLIVEN GLADDEN REFRESH RELIEVE SUPPORT SUSTAIN INSPIRIT NEPENTHE PLEASURE REASSURE GEMUTLICH

COMFORTABLE RUG BEIN BIEN COSH COSY COZY EASY FEEL FEIL LIKE SNUG TOSH TRIG CANNY COMFY COUTH CUSHY LITHE QUEME QUILT SCARF SONCY COUTHY HEPPEN PENTIT SONSIE RELAXED RESTFUL CHEERFUL DELICATE EUPHORIC HOMELIKE WRISTLET GEMUTLICH

COMFORTABLE-LOOKING SONSY SONSIE

COMFORTABLY SWEETLY

COMFORTED CONSOLATE

COMFORTER PUFF COVER DUVET EIDER NAHUM QUILT SCARF TIPPET CHEERER PACIFIER

COMFORTING TOSY TOSIE FRIENDLY

COMFORTLESS DREARY FORLORN UNCOUTH DESOLATE EITHLESS

COMFREY DAISY BONESET BACKWORT KNITBACK BRUISEWORT

COMIC WAG CLOWN DROLL FUNNY STRIP BUFFONE COMIQUE THALIAN COMEDIAN FARCICAL

COMICAL LOW BASE BUFFO DROLL FUNNY MERRY QUEER STRIP WITTY BOUFFE AMUSING CARTOON JOCULAR RISIBLE STRANGE TRIVIAL HUMOROUS TICKLISH BURLESQUE SPLITTING

COMING DUE ANON COME NEXT VENUE ADVENT FUTURE TOWARD ARRIVAL FOOTING FORWARD BECOMING DESERVED NAISSANT PAROUSIA
(— AFTER) LATTER
(— AND GOING) FITFUL
(— FORTH) NAISSANT
(— INTO BEING) BIRTH GENESIS
(— NEAR) ACCESSION
(— NEXT) FOLLOWING
(— OUT) DEBUT ISSUE EGRESS
(— TO) ADIT
(— TOGETHER) SEANCE CONGRESS COUPLING GATHERING
(— TO OFFICE) ACCESS ACCESSION
(SECOND —) PAROUSIA
(SECOND — OF CHRIST) PAROUSIA

COMMA POINT VIRGULE
(SCRATCH —) DIAGONAL

COMMAND DO BID SAW SOH BECK BODE BOON CALL COME EASY FIAT HEST HETE MAND RATE RULE SWAY WARN WILL WISH WORD BEKEN CHECK COVER EDICT EXACT FORCE HIGHT ORDER POWER SWEEP UKASE ADJURE BEHEST CHARGE COMPEL DECREE DEMAND DEVICE DIRECT ENJOIN GOVERN HOOKUM IMPOSE MASTER ORACLE ORDAIN STEVEN SUMMON APPOINT BEHIGHT BIDDING CONCERN CONTROL DICTATE JUSSION JUSSIVE LEADING MANDATE OFFICER PRECEPT REQUIRE SKIPPER WARRANT BIDDANCE DOMINEER IMPERATE INSTRUCT MANDAMUS RESTRAIN
(— EMOTIONS) GRIP
(— OF ARMY) CONDUCT
(— TO COMPUTER TO STORE DATA) SAVE
(— TO DOGS) MUSH
(— TO HORSE) GEE HAW HUP HUPP WHOA GIDDAP HUDDUP
(— TO TURN LEFT) HAW
(— TO TURN RIGHT) GEE HUP HUPP
(EXCLUSIVE —) MONOPOLY
(MAGICIAN'S —) PRESTO
(NAUTICAL —) AVAST
(ORGANIC —) PERACID

COMMANDANT GOVERNOR KILLADAR

COMMANDED IMPERATE

COMMANDEER PRESS HIJACK
(— AIRCRAFT) SKYJACK
(— AN AIRPLANE) SKYJACK

COMMANDER CID CIO DUX DUKE EMIR HEAD JEFE BLOKE CHIEF EMEER ADALID LEADER MASTER RAMMER TARTAN ALCALDE CAPTAIN CROWNER DECARCH DEKARCH DRUNGAR EMPEROR GENERAL KHALIFA MARSHAL NAVARCH OFFICER VAIVODE HERETOGA HIPPARCH LOCHAGER LOCHAGUS MYRIARCH PHYLARCH RISALDAR SERASKER TAXIARCH TETRARCH VINTENER PROCONSUL
(— IN CHIEF) SIRDAR TARTAN TURTAN ADMIRAL GENERAL
(ANGLO-ASIAN) SIRDAR
(CAVALRY —) RISALDAR

COMMANDERY PRECEPTORY

COMMANDING DOMINANT IMPERANT IMPERIAL IMPOSING

COMMANDMENT LAW RULE ORDER COMMAND MITZVAH PRECEPT BODEWORD
(DIVINE —) LAW
(TEN —S) DECALOG DECALOGUE

COMMANDO RAIDER RANGER CHINDIT FEDAYEE STORMER
(MEMBER OF — GROUP) FEDAYEE

COMMELINA DEWFLOWER

COMMEMORATE FETE KEEP FEAST REMENE EPITAPH MEMORATE MONUMENT REMEMBER MEMORIALIZE

COMMEMORATION AWARD MEDAL COMMEM PLAQUE JUBILEE MEMORIA MENTION SERVICE EBENEZER ENCAENIA MEMORIAL REMEMBRANCE

COMMEMORATIVE HONORARY MEMORIAL

COMMENCE FALL FANG FILE MOVE OPEN ARISE BEGIN FOUND START ARRAME EMBARK INCEPT LAUNCH SPRING STREAK STREEK INITIATE

COMMENCEMENT ONSET ORIGIN OUTSET KICKOFF OPENING ENTRANCE

COMMENCING INITIAL NASCENT INCIPIENT

COMMEND KEN PAT GIVE LAUD ADORN ALOSE BEKEN BOOST EXTOL GRACE OFFER BESTOW BETAKE COMMIT PRAISE RESIGN APPLAUD APPROVE BESPEAK BETEACH DELIVER ENTRUST INTRUST BEQUEATH

COMMENDABLE GOOD WORTHY LOVABLE LOWABLE LAUDABLE

COMMENDATION LAUD PRAISE CITATION
(EFFUSIVE —) SLAVER
(MARKED —) APPLAUSE

COMMENSAL EPIZOON MESSMATE

COMMENSALISM SYNOECY SYMPHILY COMMUNISM

COMMENSURATE EVEN EQUAL ENOUGH ADEQUATE RELEVANT

COMMENT BARB BRAG GIBE JIBE NOTE TALK WORD ASIDE BREAK DUNCE GLOSS GLOZE INPUT CUTTER DILATE GAMBIT NOTATE POSTIL REMARK SCANCE CAPTION DESCANT DISCUSS EXPLAIN EXPOUND ADDENDUM SCHOLION SCHOLIUM DISPRAISE
(— DISAPPROVINGLY) HARRUMPH
(BITING —) BARB
(CAUSTIC —) SATIRE
(ILL-TIMED —) CLANGER
(MARGINAL —) APOSTIL
(WITTY —) RIFF

COMMENTARY GLOSS GEMARA MEMOIR SATIRE ACCOUNT COMMENT MEKILTA POSTILS FOOTNOTE GLOSSARY TREATISE
(RABBINICAL —) HAKAM AGADAH HAGGADA HAGGADAH
(PL.) MIDRASHIM

COMMENTATOR HAKAM CRITIC GLOZER ANALYST GLOSSIST SCHOLIAST

COMMERCE TRADE BARTER CHANGE TRAFFIC BUSINESS EXCHANGE MERCATURE NAVIGATION

COMMERCIAL STORE TRADY TRADAL MERCHANT TRADEFUL
(— ESTABLISHMENT) HONG

COMMERCIALISM HUCKSTERISM MERCANTILISM

COMMINGLE MIX FUSE JOIN BLEND IMMIX MERGE UNITE MINGLE COMBINE COMINGE EMBROIL COMEDDLE

COMMINUTE MILL CRUSH GRIND POUND POUNCE POWDER

COMMINUTED FINE

COMMISERATE PITY

COMMISERATION EMPATHY SYMPATHY

COMMISSION PLAT SEND TASK BOARD PRESS TRUST BRANCH BREVET CHARGE DEMAND DEPUTE ERRAND LEGACY OFFICE ORDAIN PERMIT COMMAND CONSIGN DUOVIRI EMPOWER FITTAGE GOSPLAN MANDATE MISSION SQUEEZE WARRANT CORNETCY DELEGATE ENCHARGE INTERPOL OVERRIDE POUNDAGE
(— AS CAPTAIN) POST
(CHARGING NO —) NOLOAD

COMMISSIONAIRE CADDY CADDIE DUBASH

COMMISSIONER ENVOY TRIER LEDGER ARRAYER OFFICER PRISTAW DELEGATE

COMMISSURE VINCULUM
COMMIT DO GIVE PULL STOW TAKE ALLOT ARRET HIGHT LEAVE REFER TEACH ARETTE ASSIGN BETAKE ENGAGE PERMIT REMAND BEHIGHT BETEACH COMMAND COMMEND COMMISE CONFIDE CONSIGN DELIVER DEPOSIT ENTRUST INTRUSE INTRUST BEQUEATH DEDICATE DELEGATE IMPRISON RELEGATE RECOMMEND PERPETRATE
(— ERROR) SNAPPER
(— MONEY) INVEST
(— TO BATTLE) LAUNCH
(— TO JAIL) JUG
(— TO MEMORY) CON LEARN MEMORIZE
(— VIOLENCE) TOUCH
(— WASTE) ESTREPE
COMMITMENT OBLIGATION
COMMITTAL COMPROMISE
COMMITTED ENGAGED
(— TO) ENGAGE
COMMITTEE BODY JURY RUMP BOARD GROUP JUNTA TABLE BUREAU SOVIET COUNCIL DELEGACY POLITBURO PRESIDIUM SYNDICATE
COMMIXTURE MIXTURE HOTCHPOT CONFUSION IMMISSION
COMMODE CAP CHEST STOOL TOPKNOT CUPBOARD FONTANGE
COMMODIOUS FIT AMPLE ROOMY PROPER USEFUL SPACIOUS SUITABLE CAVERNOUS
COMMODITY ITEM WARE GOODS STUFF EXPORT FUTURE STAPLE ARTICLE SHIPMENT
(— SOLD SHORT) BEAR
(UNSALABLE —) DRUG
(PL.) KIND SPOTS CHANDLERY
COMMON LAY LOW NOA TYE BASE MEAN RIFE TOWN VILE BANAL BRIEF CHEAP EJIDO EXIDO GREEN GRIMY GROSS JOINT LEASE OFTEN SLACK STALE TACKY TRITE USUAL COARSE DEMOID FAMOUS MODERN MUTUAL ORNERY PROPIO PUBLIC SIMPLE VULGAR AVERAGE CURRENT DEMOTIC GENERAL GENERIC IGNOBLE NATURAL POPULAR PROFANE RAFFISH REGULAR TRIVIAL UNNOBLE VILLAIN BANAUSIC EPIDEMIC FAMILIAR FREQUENT HABITUAL MECHANIC MEDIOCRE ORDINARY PANDEMIC PLEBEIAN TRIFLING TRITICAL RECIPROCAL
(— OF ESTOVERS) BOT BOTE
(IN —) ALIKE
(NOT —) UNTRADED
(PL.) COMMUNE
(PREF.) CAEN(O) CEN(O) COEN(O) HOM(O)
COMMONER SNOB CEORL PLEBE SIMPLE BURGESS CITIZEN STUDENT ROTURIER
COMMONLY OFTEN VULGO FAMILIARLY
COMMONNESS IDIOTISM COMMUNITY VULGARITY
COMMON PEOPLE VULGUS
COMMONPLACE DULL FADE WORN BANAL DAILY PLAIN PROSE PROSY STALE TOPIC TRIPY TRITE USUAL COMMON DEJAVU GARDEN HOMELY MODERN TRUISM VULGAR FADAISE HUMDRUM INSIPID PROSAIC TEDIOUS TRIVIAL BANALITY BROMIDIC COPYBOOK EVERYDAY ORDINARY RUMTYTOO PLATITUDE PEDESTRIAN
COMMONPLACENESS BATHOS HUMDRUM
COMMON SENSE WIT NOUS SALT GUMPTION
COMMONWEAL WEAL REPUBLIC
COMMONWEALTH POLIS STATE ESTATE PUBLIC WEALTH COMONTE COUNTRY COMMONTY
(IDEAL —) UTOPIA
COMMONWEALTH OF INDEPENDENT STATES (SEE RUSSIA)
COMMOTION DO ADO DIN BREE DUST FLAP FRAY FUSS HEAT HELL RIOT STIR TODO TOSS WHIR ALARM FLARE FUROR HURLY HURRY STORM STOUR WHIRL BUSTLE CATHRO FISSLE FISTLE FLURRY FRACAS FRAISE FURORE GARRAY HOOPLA HOTTER MOTION MUTINY PHRASE POTHER RUFFLE SHINDY SPLORE SQUALL STEERY TUMULT UNREST UPSTIR WELTER BLATHER BLUSTER CATOUSE CLATTER KIPPAGE SHINDIG TAMASHA TEMPEST TURMOIL DISORDER ERUPTION REMOTION STIRRAGE STRAMASH TIRRIVEE UPHEAVAL UPRISING
COMMUNAL EJIDAL
COMMUNE MIR AREA DEME TALK ARGUE REALM SHARE TREAT ADVISE CONFER DEBATE IMPORT PARLEY REVEAL CONSULT DISCUSS DIVULGE COMMERCE CONVERSE DISTRICT STANITZA TOWNSHIP
(DUTCH —) EDE
COMMUNICABLE OPEN FRANK CATCHING SOCIABLE
COMMUNICATE SAY GIVE SHOW SIGN TELL BREAK DRILL SPEAK TELEX YIELD BESTOW COMMON CONVEY IMPART INFECT INFORM REVEAL SIGNAL ADDRESS BREATHE DECLARE DICTATE DIVULGE CONVERSE DESCRIBE INTIMATE
(— BY ALLUSION) IMPLY
COMMUNICATION CALL NOTE WORD CABLE FAVOR LETTER SPEECH ADDRESS DIVULGE GALLERY MESSAGE COMETHER LANGUAGE TELEGRAM MEMORANDUM
(— SERVICE) TELEX
(— SYSTEM) VOICEMAIL
(ESTABLISH —) LOGIN LOGON
COMMUNICATIVE FREE SOCIABLE EXPANSIVE
COMMUNION CULT HOST MASS SECT TALK CREED FAITH SHARE UNITY CHURCH HOMILY COMMUNE CONCORD NAGMAAL SYNAGOG ANTIPHON COMMERCE CONVERSE KOINONIA VIATICUM
(— SERVICE) ACTION
COMMUNISM LENINISM SOVIETISM
COMMUNIST RED COMMIE SOVIET COMRADE
COMMUNITY MIR BODY BURG CITY CLAN DESA MARK MURA DESSA FIRCA STATE THORP CENOBY CLIMAX COLONY FAMILY HAMLET MILLET NATION POLITY PUBLIC SOCIES ANTHILL BOHEMIA COMMUNE COMONTE CONVENT HERONRY KINGDOM PHALANX SOCIETY VILLAGE ZADRUGA AUTONOMY COMMONTY DISTRICT LIKENESS PRIORATE PROVINCE SODALITY SWEEPDOM TOWNSHIP
(— OF ANCHORITES) LAURA
(— OF INTERESTS) KINSHIP
(— OF KNIGHTS TEMPLARS) PRECEPTORY
(— OF NATURE) RACE
(— OF ORGANISMS) GAMODEME
(— OF TURKS) KIZILBASH
(ANCIENT GREEK —) DEME
(CHURCH —) BODY FOLD FLOCK SYNOD PARISH
(COOPERATIVE —) PHALANSTERY
(ECOLOGICAL —) SERE PROCLIMAX
(JEWISH —) JEWRY KOLEL ALJAMA SHTETL JUDAISM SHTETEL SYNAGOG KEHILLAH
(MAORI —) KAIK KAIKA
(PERUVIAN —) AYLLU COMUNIDAD
(PLANT —) HEATH FOREST ALTERNE ENCLAVE
(RELIGIOUS —) CENOBY SAMGHA SANGHA CONVENT CENOBIUM
(RUSSIAN —) MIR
(UTOPIAN —) PANTISOCRACY
(VILLAGE —) IKHWAN
COMMUTATE COMMUTE UNDIRECT
COMMUTATIVE ABELIAN
COMMUTATOR BREAK BREAKER RHEOTROPE
COMMUTE ALTER CHANGE TRAVEL CONVERT EXCHANGE
COMMUTER (GROUP OF —S) VANPOOL
COMOROS (CAPITAL OF —) MORONI
(ISLAND OF —) MWALI MOHELI NZWANI ANJOUAN NJAZIDJA
(VOLCANO OF —) KARTHALA
COMPACT SAD BALL BOND CASE FAST FIRM HARD KNIT PACK PACT PLOT SNUG TRIM TRUE BRIEF CLOSE COVIN CROWD DENSE GROSS HARDY HORNY MATCH PITHY SOLID SPISS TERSE THICK TIGHT BEETLE COMART HARDEN LEAGUE SHRINK SPISSY STOCKY TREATY VANITY BARGAIN CONCISE CONCORD CROWDED NUGGETY PACTION SERRIED TABLOID ALLIANCE CONDENSE CONTRACT COVENANT FLAPJACK HEAVYSET SOLIDIFY SUCCINCT PELLETIZE
(PREF.) GLOMERO GLOMERULO PYCN(O) PYKN(O)
COMPACTED SAD CROWDED
(PREF.) PECTO
COMPACTNESS BODY DENSITY FASTNESS SOLIDITY INTENSITY
COMPANION PAL SOC CHUM FERE MAKE MATE PEER TWIN WIFE BILLY BUDDY BULLY BUTTY CHINA COMES CRONY CULLY DARES GREEK MATCH MATEY MAUGH RIVAL SPORT ATTEND BELAMY BILLIE BROLGA COBBER COHORT COMATE CUMMER CUPMAN DUENNA EGERIA ESCORT FELLOW FRIEND GESITH GOSSIP KIMMER MARROW PANION SHADOW SPOUSE STEADY TROJAN ACHATES COMPANY COMPEER COMRADE CONSORT ELPENOR FRANION HUSBAND PARTNER SOCIATE SOCIETY SPECIAL BARNACLE BEAUPERE COMPADRE CORRIVAL EPHESIAN EPHESINE FAITHFUL FAMILIAR HELPMATE PARALLEL PLAYFERE SYNODITE
(ARCHER'S —) BUTTY
(DRINKING —) CUPMATE
(POT —) ALEKNIGHT
(READING —) LECTRICE
(TABLE —) CONVICTOR
(PL.) SOCIETY
(PREF.) HETAERO
COMPANIONABLE FERE MATEY SOCIAL CORDIAL FELLOWLY GRACIOUS SOCIABLE
COMPANION-AT-LARGE BILLY BILLIE
COMPANIONS (SEE PARTNERS)
COMPANIONSHIP FERE SHIP HAUNT COMPANY SOCIETY AFFINITY
COMPANY CIE CRY MOB SET BAND BEVY BODY CORE CREW CRUE FARE FERE FIRM GANG GEST GING HERD HOST MANY PUSH ROUT SORT TEAM TURM AERIE COVEN COVEY CROWD FLOCK FLOTE GESTE GROUP GUEST HORDE JATHA MEINY PARTY SQUAD SUITE TROOP TURMA CIRCLE CLIQUE COHORT COVINE CURNEY DECURY LOCHUS OUTFIT RESORT THRAVE THRONG TROUPE TWENTY VOLLEY BATTERY COLLEGE CONDUCT CONSORT HOLDING JIMBANG MANIPLE SOCIETE SOCIETY THIASOS THIASUS VISITOR ASSEMBLY FAISCEAU FOLKMOOT JINGBANG PRESENCE
(— OF BADGERS) CETE
(— OF BIRDS) BANK
(— OF BOOKSELLERS) CONGER CONGENER
(— OF DANCERS) COMPARSA
(— OF HERDSMEN) BOOLY BOOLEY
(— OF HERONS) SEDGE SIEGE
(— OF HORSEMEN) TROOP
(— OF LIONS) PRIDE
(— OF MARTENS) RICHESSE
(— OF MUSICIANS) ORCHESTRA
(— OF PEACOCKS) MUSTER
(— OF PERFORMERS) TROUPE

(— OF PLOVERS) STAND
(— OF SINGERS) CHOIR QUIRE CHORUS
(— OF SWANS) BANK
(— OF TEN) DECURY DECURIA
(— OF THE FAITHFUL) FOLD
(— OF TRAVELERS) CAFILA CAVALCADE
(— OF WOMEN) GAGGLE
(— OF WORSHIPERS) THIASUS
(— OF WORSHIPPERS) THIASUS
(EXCLUSIVE —) CROWD
(FINANCIAL —) FACTOR
(FIRE —) SQUAD
(MILITARY —) WATCH DECURY VENLIN PELOTON VEXILLUM
(RECORDING —) LABEL
(SUITABLE —) BESORT
COMPARABLE LIKE SAME SIMILAR
COMPARATIVE
(SUFF.) ER IOR
COMPARE VIE EVEN LIKE SIZE APPLY EQUAL LIKEN MATCH SCALE TALLY ALLUDE CONFER PARIFY RELATE SEMBLE BALANCE BRACKET COLLATE EXAMINE SENIBLE SIGNIFY STACKUP ASSEMBLE CONFRONT CONTRAST ESTIMATE PARALLEL RESEMBLE SIMILIZE
(— WITH) TO
COMPARISON SIMILE ANALOGY BALANCE COMPARE PARABLE PARAGON DISIMILE LIKENESS LIKENING METAPHOR PARALLEL
(— OF HOROSCOPES) SYNASTRY
COMPARTMENT BAY BIN BOX CAB POD CELL DECK FLUE PANE PART SLOT WELL ABODE CABIN HATCH HUTCH PANEL STALL VOLET ABACUS ALCOVE BUNKER GARAGE HOPPER MUFFLE REGION SEVERY SMOKER ALVEOLE CABINET CAPSULE CELLULE CHAMBER FIREBOX HOUSING KITCHEN LOCULUS MANSION ROTONDE SECTION ALVEOLUS COALHOLE DIVISION FOREPEAK GRINTERN LOCELLUS STEERAGE TRAVERSE PIGEONHOLE
(— FOR COAL) BUNKER
(— FOR TREATING ORE) KITCHEN
(— IN BAR) SNUG SNUGGERY
(— IN BARN) BAY
(— IN CAR) BOOT
(— IN STOVE) BROILER
(— OF COACH) IMPERIAL
(— OF ROOF) SEVERY
(— OF VAULTING) SEVERY
(— OF WINDOW) LIGHT
(— ON GAMEBOARD) STORE
(— ON ROULETTE WHEEL) EAGLE
(— ON TRAIN) COUCHETTE
(CARGO —) HOLD
(DECOMPRESSION —) POD
(DETACHABLE —) POD
(GAS-TIGHT —) BALLONET
(GUNNER'S —) BLISTER
(REFRIGERATOR —) CHILLER
(SCREENED —) TRAVERSE
(SLEEPING —) CUBICLE
(STAGECOACH —) COUPE
(STORAGE—) BOOT
COMPASS BOW AREA DIAL GAIN ROOM ROSE SIZE TOUR AMBIT FIELD GAMUT RANGE REACH SCOPE SWEEP TENOR WHEEL ARRIVE ATTAIN BOUNDS CIRCLE DEGREE DEVICE DIACLE EFFECT EXTENT MERIST MODULE SPHERE SPREAD VOLUME ACHIEVE AZIMUTH CALIBER CIRCUIT CONFINE DIVIDER EMBRACE ENCLOSE ENVIRON HORIZON IMAGINE PELORUS PURVIEW TRAMMEL BOUNDARY CINCTURE CIRCUITY DIAPASON PRACTICE PRACTISE SURROUND
(— IN SHIP'S CABIN) TELLTALE
(— NEEDLE END) LILY
(— OF MELODY) AMBITUS
(— OF TONES) DIAPASON
(— OF VOICE) GAMUT SCALE
(— POINT) RHUMB
(BELL-MAKING —) CROOK
(PART OF —) PIN CARD DOME HOOD PIVOT HOUSING BINNACLE
COMPASS BOX KETTLE
COMPASS CARD ROSE PEDRERO PERRIER
COMPASSION RUE PITY RUTH GRACE HEART MERCY PIETY SORRY KARUNA LENITY REMORSE STOMACH CLEMENCY HUMANITY KINDNESS SYMPATHY
COMPASSIONATE MEEK RUTH SOFT HUMAN GENTLE TENDER CLEMENT PIETOSO PITEOUS PITIFUL GRACIOUS MERCIFUL
COMPASS PLANT PILOTWEED ROSINWEED
COMPASS QUARTER PLAGE
COMPASS SIGHT VANE
COMPATIBILITY MATCH
COMPATIBLE AKIN CIVIL ARTISTIC SUITABLE
COMPATRIOT NATIVE PATRIOT SYNETHNIC
COMPEL GAR MAKE MOVE URGE BRING CAUSE COACT DRIVE EXACT FORCE IMPEL PRESS SHOVE COERCE ENJOIN EXTORT INCITE OBLIGE THREAT ACTUATE AFFORCE ATTRACT COMMAND DRAGOON ENFORCE NECESSE REQUIRE VIOLENCE NECESSITATE
(— TO GO) HALE
(— TO PAY) STICK
COMPELLED HAS FAIN MUST BOUND FORCED ENFORCED
COMPELLING COGENT STRONG TELLING BRUISING FORCEFUL
COMPELLINGLY BADLY
COMPENDIOUS BRIEF SHORT TERSE DIRECT COMPACT CONCISE SUMMARY SUCCINCT
COMPENDIUM LIST BRIEF APERCU DIGEST PRECIS SKETCH SURVEY CATALOG COMPEND EPITOME LEXICON MEDULLA OUTLINE PANDECT SUMMARY SYLLOGE ABSTRACT BREVIARY BREVIATE LANDSKIP SYLLABUS SYNOPSIS ABRIDGEMENT
(— OF DOCTRINE) SYMBOL
COMPENSATE PAY JIBE AGREE ATONE COVER REPAY TALLY OFFSET RECOUP REDEEM REWARD SQUARE COMMUTE CORRECT PLASTER REDRESS REPRISE REQUITE RESTORE SATISFY COMPENSE DISPENSE EQUALIZE
COMPENSATION BOT FEE PAY UTU BOOT BOTE HIRE MEND TOLL BONUS LOWER WAGES AMENDS ANGILD GERSUM OFFSET REWARD SALARY SETOFF DAMAGES FREIGHT PAYMENT REDRESS SALVAGE STIPEND BREAKAGE DONATIVE EARNINGS INTEREST OCTOGILD PILOTAGE PITTANCE REQUITAL SOLATIUM
(— FOR INJURY) SATISFACTION
(— FOR KILLING MAN) MANBOT MANBOTE
(MEAGER —) PITTANCE
(WORKER'S —) COMPO
COMPENSATORILY EVEN
COMPETE PIT VIE COPE KEMP TEND CLASH MATCH RIVAL STRIVE CONTEND CONTEST EMULATE CORRIVAL
(— WITH) BUCK
COMPETENCE SKILL ABILITY FACULTY CAPACITY
COMPETENCY MAY CAPACITY
COMPETENT UP APT CAN FIT ABLE GOOD HOME MEET SANE ADEPT CAPAX SMART SWEET TIGHT INTACT LAWFUL WORTHY CAPABLE ENDOWED SKILLED ADEQUATE SUITABLE QUALIFIED
COMPETITION VIE DRAW GAME HEAT JUMP RACE MATCH PRIZE TRIAL WAGER CONTEST PARAGON RIVALRY BIATHLON CONCOURS CONFLICT
(— AMONG REAPERS) KEMP
(ATHLETIC —) MEET
(DRIVING —) RALLY RALLYE
(VERSE —) TENSON
COMPETITOR FOE ENEMY MATCH RIVAL WAGER COUSIN PLAYER AGONIST ENTRANT CORRIVAL FAVORITE GAMESTER OPPONENT
(FORMIDABLE —) TIGER
COMPILATION ANA BOOK CODE CENTO DIGEST CASEBOOK DIRECTORY GATHERING
COMPILE ADD EDIT AMASS GATHER SELECT ARRANGE COLLECT COMPOSE PREPARE
COMPILER AUTHOR EDITOR COLLATOR GATHERER GLOSSIST SCISSORER
COMPLACENT CALM SMUG PLACID FATUOUS PRIGGISH
COMPLACENTLY FATLY
COMPLAIN AIL NAG YAP YIP BEEF CARP CRIB FRET FUSS GREX KEEN KICK KREX MEAN MOAN MOOT MUTE RAIL RULE WAIL YELP YIRN BITCH BLEAT BRAWL CRAKE CROAK CROON GRIPE GROWL GRUMP GRUNT PINGE PLAIN WHINE BEWAIL CHARGE COTTER CREATE GRIEVE GROUSE GRUTCH HOLLER KVETCH MURMUR PEENGE REPINE SQUAWK THREAP THROPE WHINGE YAMMER CHUNNER DEPLORE GRIZZLE GRUMBLE INVEIGH NITPICK PROTEST BELLYACHE
COMPLAINANT ACTOR ASKER ORATOR ACCUSER PLAINER QUERENT RELATOR
COMPLAINER CRAB WHINER CRYBABY KVETCHER
COMPLAINING BRAY PULY WHINY LATRANT QUERENT DOLEANCE QUERULOUS
COMPLAINT RAP BEEF CARP FUSS HOWL MEAN MOAN WAIL BITCH GRIPE GROWL WHINE CHESON GROUCH GROUSE GRUDGE GRUTCH HOLLER KVETCH LAMENT MALADY NIGGLE PLAINT REPINE SQUAWK AILMENT DISEASE GRUMBLE ILLNESS PROTEST QUARREL QUERELE RECLAMA TRAGEDY COMPLAIN DISORDER DOLEANCE GRAVAMEN JEREMIAD
(SUBDUED —) MURMUR
COMPLAISANCE AMENITY SUAVITY FACILITY URBANITY
COMPLAISANT BON ABLE EASY KIND BUXOM CIVIL SUAVE BONAIR POLITE SMOOTH SUPPLE URBANE AFFABLE AMIABLE BOWABLE LENIENT GRACIOUS OBLIGING PLEASING
COMPLEMENT CREW GANG FORCE TALLY ALEXIN AMOUNT COUSIN ADJUNCT OBVERSE PENDANT
(MILITARY —) STRENGTH
COMPLEMENTARY OPPOSITE
(PREF.) COUNTER
COMPLETE DO ALL CAP END BLUE DASH DEAD DEEP DONE FAIR FILL FINE FULL JUST PASS PURE RANK VERY CLEAN CLOSE CROWN EVERY GROSS LARGE PLAIN PLUMB POINT PUCCA PUKKA QUITE RIPEN ROUND SOLID SOUND STARK STONE TOTAL UTTER WHOLE CHOATE DAMPEN DEADLY EFFECT ENTIRE FINISH GLOBAL HOLLOW INTACT MATURE PROPER SINGLE STRICT VESTED ACHIEVE CONFIRM EXECUTE EXPLETE FULFILL GERMANE OUTWORK PERFECT PLENARY REALIZE REPLETE SPHERAL ABSOLUTE BLINKING CIRCULAR CONCLUDE FINALIZE IMPLICIT INTEGRAL OUTRIGHT OVERCOME PRECIOUS PROFOUND THOROUGH BODACIOUS NEGOTIATE ACCOMPLISH
(— CARELESSLY) HUDDLE
(— IN SYLLABLES) ACATHLECTIC
(REMARKABLY —) SPLENDID
(PREF.) HOL(O) TEL(E)(EO)
COMPLETED PAU OVER CLOSED SUMMED COMPLETE FINISHED
(NOT —) DURATIVE
COMPLETELY ALL JAM BARE BUCK FAIR FLAT GOOD SLAM SLAP SPAN BLACK CLEAN CLOSE FULLY PLUMB QUITE SHEER SMACK

SPANG STARK STICK STOCK UTTER BODILY ENTIRE GAINLY HOLLOW PURELY SPANDY WHOLLY ALGATES BLANKLY THROUGH CLEVERLY DIRECTLY ENTIRELY HEARTILY OUTRIGHT WHOLEHOG (PREF.) DE DIS OB PAN

COMPLETENESS DEPTH ALLNESS FULLNESS RIPENESS INTEGRITY PLENITUDE

COMPLETION END CROWN FINISH (PREF.) TELEUT(O)

COMPLEX HARD MAZY BEING ETHOS FIELD HYOID MIXED ADDUCT DESERT KNOTTY SYSTEM CULTURE NETWORK SAMKARA SINUOUS TANGLED TWISTED ABSTRUSE COMPOUND EQUATION EXCHANGE INVOLVED MANIFOLD SAMSKARA SYNDROME CISPLATIN MACROCOSM
(— OF CHARACTERISTICS) PERSONALITY
(— OF DIALECTS) HINDI
(— OF HORMONES) CALINE
(— OF IDEAS) EGO SYSTEM
(— OF SHOPS) MALL
(BASEMENT —) FLOOR
(NOT —) SIMPLE

COMPLEXION HUE RUD BLEE CAST LEER LOOK RUDD TINT COLOR HUMOR STATE TENOR TINGE ASPECT TEMPER COLORING
(BAD —) DYSCHROA

COMPLEXITY NODUS SCHEME TANGLE INTRIGUE

COMPLIANCE TRUE ASSENT MUNICH CESSION CONSENT HARMONY OBSEQUY ABIDANCE CIVILITY FACILITY FORMALITY

COMPLIANT EASY MEEK OILY SOFT BUXOM FACILE PLIANT SUPPLE COMMODE DUCTILE DUTIFUL WILLING AMENABLE OBEDIENT TOWARDLY YIELDING TRACTABLE

COMPLICATE INTORT PUZZLE TANGLE EMBROIL INVOLVE PERPLEX BEWILDER INTRIGUE INTRICATE

COMPLICATED HARD KNOTTY PROLIX COMPLEX GORDIAN SNARLED TANGLED INVOLVED PLEXIFORM

COMPLICATION KNOT NODE PLOT NODUS SNARL TANGLE INTRIGUE
(— IN STORY) NODE

COMPLIMENT GIFT KUDO LAUD EXTOL EULOGY PRAISE SALAAM SALUTE ADULATE APPLAUD BOUQUET COMMEND DOUCEUR FLATTER TRIBUTE ENCOMIUM FLUMMERY GRATUITY GREETING
(EMPTY —) FLUMMERY

COMPLY PLY CEDE OBEY ABIDE ADAPT AGREE APPLY YIELD ACCEDE ACCORD ASSENT ENFOLD SUBMIT CONFORM EMBRACE OBSERVE
(— WITH) OBEY SERVE OBSERVE SATISFY

COMPONE GOBONE GOBONY

COMPONENT KEY DRAG FORM ITEM PART UNIT GIVEN FACTOR MEMBER SIMPLE ELEMENT FORMANT PARTIAL CONJUNCT INTEGRAL
(— OF ARMY) CAVALRY
(— OF CELL WALLS) CALLOSE
(ELECTRIC —S) CIRCUITRY
(PHYSICAL —S) HARDWARE
(PRINCIPAL —) BASIS

COMPORT ACT BEAR HAVE HOLD JIBE KEEP SUIT ABEAR AGREE BROOK CARRY TALLY ACCORD ACQUIT BEHAVE DEMEAN ENDURE SQUARE CONDUCT

COMPORTMENT DEALING BEHAVIOR DEMEANOR

COMPOSE BAT PEN SET CALM COMP DITE FORM LULL MAKE ALLAY BREVE BRIEF CLERK CLINK COUCH DIGHT DRAFT FRAME ORDER PATCH PIECE SPELL STICK WRITE ACCORD ADJUST CREATE DESIGN GRAITH INDITE NOTATE RECITE REDACT SETTLE SOOTHE STEADY ARRANGE COMPACT COMPILE COMPONE CONCOCT CONFORM DICTATE DISPOSE DRAUGHT FASHION PATIENT PRODUCE TYPESET COMPOUND COMPRISE REGULATE
(— POETRY) MAKE SING

COMPOSED SET CALM COOL QUIET SOBER WROTE DEMURE DIGEST PLACID SEDATE SERENE COMPACT WRITTEN COMPOUND DECOROUS TOGETHER TRANQUIL
(— IN METER) FOOTED
(ILL —) LAME

COMPOSEDNESS SOSSIEGO

COMPOSER BARD POET LYRIC ODIST AUTHOR LYRIST PENMAN WRITER CONTEUR ELEGIST FANTAST MAESTRO COLORIST ELEGIAST IDYLLIST ILIADIST MELODIST MONODIST MUSICIAN PHANTAST TUNESMITH
AMERICAN FRY BIRD BOND CAGE COLE IVES KERN ROOT BEACH BLOCH DANKS FOOTE HANDY HAYDN HOMER LEHAR NEVIN OHARA PRATT ROREM SCOTT SOUSA WEILL BARBER CADMAN HARRIS KRENEK LOOMIS PALMER PARKER PISTON PORTER SEEGER SPEAKS SUESSE TAYLOR WINNER ANTHEIL BRISTOW CHASINS COPLAND DEKOVEN GILBERT GOLDMAN HAESCHE HERBERT MENOTTI PARROTT RODGERS SCHUMAN THOMSON YOUMANS BARTLETT BROCKWAY BURLEIGH CHADWICK CONVERSE GERSHWIN GOODRICH GRAINGER KREISLER SESSIONS THOMPSON ARMSTRONG BERNSTEIN CARPENTER ELLINGTON MACDOWELL
ARGENTINIAN CASTRO
AUSTRIAN FUX GAL BERG WOLF BRULL DRDLA MOTTL ZAYTZ BLEYLE CZERNY EYBLER LANNER MOZART BITTNER NEUKOMM STRAUSS BRUCKNER DIABELLI GYROWETZ KORNGOLD REZNICEK SCHUBERT HEUBERGER MILLOCKER SCHONBERG GANSBACHER ALBRECHTSBERGER
BELGIAN FETIS LEKEU BENOIT BERIOT BLOCKX BRASIN DUMONT FRANCK GRISAR JONGEN GEVAERT HUBERTI LEMMENS MATHIEU CAMPENHOUT
BRAZILIAN GOMES VILLALOBOS
CANADIAN BRANSCOMB
CZECH BENDL NOVAK DVORAK FIBICH FORSTER JANACEK KUBELIK SMETANA DESPAUER NESWADBA KALLIWODA KOVAROVIC MYSLIVECEK
DANISH ENNA GADE HAMERIK NIELSEN HARTMANN
DUTCH FODOR OBRECHT ARCADELT WAGENAAR SWEELINCK
ENGLISH BAX TYE ARNE BLOW BYRD CARR CLAY HOOK MONK BACHE BLISS BOYCE CAREY COOKE COWEN CROFT ELGAR ELVEY FIELD HOLST LAWES LOCKE PARRY SCOTT TOVEY ARNOLD ASHTON AUSTIN AVISON BARNBY BISHOP BRIDGE COATES COWARD CRAMER CROTCH CROUCH CUSINS DAVIES DELIUS DIBDIN GERMAN GLOVER GREENE HANDEL LAMOND LINLEY MCEWEN ONEILL PARKER TALLIS THOMAS WALTON WILSON ATTWOOD BANTOCK BARNETT BENNETT CELLIER COLEMAN DUNHILL FARRANT GIBBONS HORSLEY IRELAND JACKSON LATROBE NOVELLO PURCELL STAINER STORACE BENJAMIN BOUGHTON SULLIVAN TYRWHITT ARMSTRONG CALDICOTT HESELTINE MACFARRNE MACKENZIE SOMERVELL GOLDSCHMIDT RAVENSCROFT
FINNISH PACIUS KAJANUS MADETOJA MELARTIN PALMGREN SIBELIUS WEGELIUS JARNEFELT MERIKANTO
FRENCH ERB HUE ADAM INDY LALO ALARD ALKAN AUBER AURIC BAZIN BIZET COHEN DAVID DUKAS FAURE GOUVY HERVE IBERT LULLY MASSE MEHUL RAVEL REBER REYER SATIE WIDOR AUBERT AUDRAN CAMPRA CHOPIN DANCLA DAQUIN DUBOIS DUPARC GODARD GOSSEC GOUNOD HALEVY HEROLD LECOCQ LEROUX PIERNE STRAUS THOMAS BERLIOZ BERTINI BOESSET BRUNEAU CAMBERT CHELARD COQUARD DEBUSSY DELIBES DUCASSE GUIRAUD LACOMBE LAPARRA LECLAIR LESUEUR MARTINI MILHAUD POULENC SCHMITT CHABRIER CHAUSSON COUPERIN DALAYRAC ERLANGER GOUDIMEL GUILMANT HONEGGER LEFEBVRE MAILLART MASSENET MESSAGER MONSIGNY BOELLMANN BOIELDIEU CHAMINADE OFFENBACH WECKERLIN BURGMULLER DESAUGIERS DESTOUCHES PLANQUETTE WALDTEUFEL CHARPENTIER
GERMAN ABT ETT AHLE BACH BOHM BOTT DORN GOTZ HAAS KAUN LOBE ORFF RAFF ABERT BIBER BLECH BOEHE BRUCH DANZI EBERS FASCH FESCA FINCK FRANK GENEE GLUCK GRAUN GRELL KLEIN LOEWE NEEFE WEBER ALBERT AMBROS BECKER BERGER BOHNER BRAHMS COMMER CRUGER ECKERT EITNER FLOTOW HILLER JENSEN KOHLER KUCKEN KUHLAU KUHNAU LINCKE MAHLER WAGNER WINTER BARGIEL CONRADI EBERLIN HASSLER JARNACH MOLIQUE NAUMANN RICHTER SILCHER STRAUSS WULLNER ZOLLNER AGRICOLA BENEDICT BRAMBACH DIETRICH DRAESEKE EBERWEIN HOFFMANN HOLSTEIN KAMINSKI KEUSSLER KIRCHNER KREUTZER PFITZNER REINECKE SCHUMANN VOLKMANN AIBLINGER AMBROSIUS BEETHOVEN BRAUNFELS BUXTEHUDE CANNABICH DELLINGER HINDEMITH KLUGHARDT MARSCHNER MATTHESON MEYERBEER NEITHARDT REICHARDT BELLERMANN BLUMENTHAL DESTOUCHES PRAETORIUS SCHARWENKA HUMPERDINCK MENDELSSOHN FRANCKENSTEIN LEICHTENTRITT
HUNGARIAN ERKEL HUBAY LEHAR LISZT BARTOK KODALY KUSSER JOACHIM ROMBERG DOHNANYI GOLDMARK
IRISH BALFE OSBORNE WALLACE
ITALIAN LOTI PAER PERI ARAIA BAINI BOITO BRAGA CESTI CLARI COSTA VERDI ALFANO ANERIO ARDITI ARTUSI BUSONI CIAMPI COCCIA MERULO NANINI PACINI PEROSI VECCHI ALBERTI ALLEGRI ANFOSSI ARIOSTI BASSANI BAZZINI BELLINI BERTONI BIANCHI CACCINI CALDARA CAMBINI CASELLA CAVALLI COLONNA CONCONE CORELLI DURANTE FERRARI FLORIMO PICCINI PORPORA PUCCINI ROSSINI SALIERI TARTINI TOSELLI VIADANA VIVALDI ZACCONI ZARLINO AGOSTINI ALBINONI BERNABEI CLEMENTI FIORILLO GABRIELI GAGLIANO GIORDANI GIORDANO JOMMELLI LEGRENZI MARCELLO MASCAGNI PRATELLA RAIMONDI RESPIGHI SPONTINI ANIMUCCIA BANCHIERI BONONCINI BOTTESINI BRAMBILLA CARISSIMI CAVALIERI CHERUBINI DONIZETTI GUGLIELMI LOCATELLI MALIPIERO MARCHETTI MORLACCHI PAISIELLO PERGOLESI SCARLATTI TOMMASINI VICENTINO BOCCHERINI CAMPAGNOLI MERCADANTE MONTEVERDI PALESTRINA PONCHIELLI ZINGARELLI LEONCAVALLO
MEXICAN CHAVEZ CARRILLO
NORWEGIAN GRIEG KJERULF NORDRAAK SVENDSEN SCHJELDERUP

POLISH KOLBERG FITELBERG KAMIENSKI KARLOWICZ MONIUSZKO NOSKOWSKI SZYMANOWSKI
PORTUGUESE ARNEIRO MACHADO BOMTEMPO PORTOGALLO
RUMANIAN ENESCO OTESCUA
RUSSIAN LVOV SEROV GLINKA LIADOV ONEGIN TANEEV ARENSKI BORODIN REBIKOV GODOWSKY LIPAUNOV SCRIABIN BALAKIREY CHEREPNIN GLAZOUNOV KASHPEROV KASTALSKI MUSORGSKI PROKOFIEV KALINNIKOV MOUSORGSKY STRAVINSKY AZANCHEVSKI BORTNYANSKI TCHAIKOVSKY KHACHATURIAN RACHMANINOFF SHOSTAKOVICH
SCOTTISH GOW SPOTTISWOODE
SPANISH ARBOS FALLA CASALS ALBENIZ MARTINI PEDRELL BARBIERI GUERRERO VICTORIA
SWEDISH ALFVEN HALLEN ATTERBERG HALLSTROM WENNERBERG
SWISS EGLI HEGAR HUBER
VENEZUELAN CARRENO
WELSH EVANS PARRY

COMPOSITE HYBRID ITALIC MOTLEY COMPLEX COMPOSED CONCRETE INTEGRAL

COMPOSITION ANA DITE MASS OPUS WORK CENTO DITTY DRAMA FUGUE GETUP MURKY PIECE POESY STUCK THEME ACCORD EULOGY FILLER HAIKAI LESSON MAGGOT MONODY THESIS THREAD VULGUS ARTICLE COMPOST CONSIST DISPLAY EBURINE EPISTLE MIXTURE PICTURE STOPPER WRITING ACROSTIC CAUSERIE COMPOUND DIALOGUE DIAPENTE EXERCISE FANTASIA FROTTAGE HEELBALL
(— FOR BILLIARD BALLS) COMPO
(— TO BE ACTED) PLAY DRAMA
(— TO FILL LEATHER) STUFF
(AMOROUS —) EROTIC
(ARTISTIC —) COLLAGE
(BAGPIPE —) PORT
(BANKRUPT'S —) COMPO
(BUILDING —) STAFF
(CHORAL —) MOTET CANTATA ORATORIO
(GUMMY —) GROUND
(HAND —) CASEWORK
(HUMOROUS —) BURLA
(IMPERFECT —) SOOTERKIN
(INSTRUMENTAL —) AIR GATO FANCY RONDO GROUND SKETCH SONATA TIENTO BOURREE CANZONE BERCEUSE CONCERTO FANTASIA RHAPSODY SYMPHONY PASSACAGLIA
(LITERARY —) BOOK CENTO DEBAT ESSAY PIECE COMEDY SATIRE SKETCH THESIS TREATISE
(MAGIC —) HELLBROTH
(MUSICAL —) DUET GLEE IDYL OPUS SOLO SONG TRIO BURLA CANON DANCE ELEGY ETUDE FUGUE GAZEL IDYLL MESTO MOTET NONET SCORE STUDY ADAGIO ARIOSO AZIONE ENTREE GHAZEL HOCKET HOQUET SEPTET SEXTET BALLADE BOURREE BOUTADE BRAVURA ORGANUM QUARTET SCHERZO TOCCATA CAVATINA CHACONNE CLAUSULA CONCERTO INNOMINE SERENADE SINFONIA STANDARD SYMPHONY ANTIPHONY OFFERTORY PROCESSIONAL
(NARRATIVE —) BALLAD
(PLASTIC —) CEMENT
(POETIC —) GLOSS KAVYA
(RAMBLING —) SATIRE RHAPSODY
(RELIGIOUS —) MOTET ANTHEM HYMNIC CANTATA ORATORIO
(RUBBER —) GUM
(VEDIC —) GAYATRI
(VITREOUS —) ENAMEL
(VOCAL —) ARIA SOLO SONG CANON ANTHEM ELEVATIO CONDUCTUS
(WORDLESS —) VOCALISE
(PL.) JUVENILIA LITERATURE

COMPOSITOR COMP TYPO ADMAN SETTER BANKMAN CASEMAN CLICKER PRINTER STONEMAN

COMPOST PELF SOIL MINGLE COMPOTE MIXTURE COMPOUND DRESSING

COMPOSURE BOND MIEN POISE QUIET UNION REPOSE TEMPER BALANCE POSTURE CALMNESS SERENITY
(LOSE —) CHOKE

COMPOTATION SYMPOSIUM

COMPOTE BOWL COMPORT COMPOST

COMPOUND LSD MIX NTA BASE DIOL ENOL FILL JOIN MIXT SOUR TEPA ALKYL ALLOY AMIDE AMINE BLEND DIENE ESTER FURIL IMIDE OXIDE UNION ACETAL ADJUST ALKIDE BORANE COMMIX COPULA IODIDE JUMBLE KETONE MEDLEY PHENOL POLYOL PTERIN PYRONE SETTLE TEMPER URACIL URAMIL AGATHIN ALCOHOL ALLICIN ALLOXAN AMALGAM AMIDATE AMIDINE AMINATE AMMONIA ARGYROL CARBENE COMBINE COMPLEX COMPONE COMPOSE COMPOST DVANDVA KAMPONG KHELLIN PHORBIN PREPARE SPIRANE STEROID AGLUCONE AGLYCONE ALIZARIN ALKOXIDE AMMONATE ANTIPODE APIGENIN BRAZILIN CEROMIDE COMPOSED FUCHSONE GARDENIN GENTISIN GOSSYPOL IODOFORM ISOLOGUE STYRACIN CARBORANE YELLOWCAKE
(ADHESIVE —) SALVE
(CHEMICAL —) PCB
(COLORLESS —) FURAN FURANE
(COMBINING —) ACCEPTOR
(CRYSTALLINE —) TEPA
(EXPLOSIVE —) TNT
(HALOCARBON —) DBCP
(OF A CHEMICAL —) ORGANO
(ORGANIC —) ENOL
(POISONOUS —) KETENE CACODYL GLYCINE HELENIN STIBINE
(SYNTHETIC —) ANDROGEN SORBITAN
(PREF.) **(PARENT —)** NOR
(SUFF.) GENIN
(CARBON —) ENE

COMPOUNDED CONCRETE COMPOSITE

COMPOUNDER TANKER

COMPOUNDING INTIMACY

COMPREHEND GET SEE KNOW TAKE TWIG COVER GRASP IMPLY LATCH REACH SAVVY SEIZE SENSE SKILL SMOKE SPELL ATTAIN BOTTOM DIGEST EMBODY FATHOM FOLLOW PIERCE UPTAKE COMPASS CONTAIN DISCERN EMBRACE ENCLOSE IMAGINE INCLUDE INVOLVE REALIZE RECEIVE SWALLOW COMPRISE CONCEIVE CONCLUDE PERCEIVE

COMPREHENSIBLE EXOTERIC INCLUDED SENSABLE SCRUTABLE

COMPREHENSION HOLD SABE GRASP SAVVY SENSE ESPRIT FATHOM NOESIS UPTAKE EPITOME INSIGHT KNOWING SUMMARY BEARINGS PREHENSION
(OF READING —) CLOZE

COMPREHENSIVE BIG FULL WIDE BROAD GRAND LARGE GLOBAL SCOPIC CAPABLE CONCISE GENERAL GENERIC CATHOLIC ENCYCLIC SPACIOUS

COMPREHENSIVENESS POWER SCOPE EXTENT BREADTH WIDENESS LARGENESS

COMPRESS NIP TIE BALE BIND FIRM LACE WRAP CLING CRAMP CROWD CRUSH PINCH PRESS SMASH BUNDLE DEFORM DIGEST GATHER SHRINK STRAIN THRONG ABRIDGE ASTRICT BOLSTER CABBAGE COMPACT CURTAIL DEFLATE EMBRACE FLATTEN PLEDGET REPRESS SQUEEZE SQUINCH ASTRINGE CONDENSE CONTRACT LAMINATE PEMMICAN RESTRAIN SUPPRESS
(— WOOL) DUMP
(HOT —) STUPE
(MEDICAL —) BOLSTER PLEDGET

COMPRESSED STRICT CROWDED SUCCINCT ANGUSTATE COARCTATE

COMPRESSION CRUSH SQUEEZE PRESSURE THLIPSIS
(PREF.) SYMPIESO SYMPIEZO

COMPRESSOR PUMP ROTARY CONDENSER

COMPRISE HOLD COVER IMPLY SEIZE ATTACH CONFER EMBODY EMPLOY MUSTER COMPOSE CONTAIN EMBRACE ENCLOSE INCLUDE INVOLVE CONCEIVE PERCEIVE

COMPROMISE FINE TRIM COMMIT INTERIM COMPOUND ENDANGER PALLIATE TEMPORIZE

COMPROMISED BRULE

COMPROMISING FALSE

COMPULSION NEED URGE FORCE PRESS DURESS STRESS IMPULSE COACTION COERCION DISTRESS EXACTION PERFORCE NECESSITY

COMPULSORY COERCIVE FORCIBLE NECESSARY
(NOT —) OPTIONAL

COMPUNCTION QUALM REGRET SORROW REMORSE SCRUPLE PENITENCE

COMPURGATOR COJUROR COSWEARER

COMPUTATION COMPOT ACCOUNT COMPUTE CALCULUS COMPUTUS ESTIMATE RECKONING

COMPUTE ADD SUM CAST ITEM RATE COUNT TALLY VALUE ASSESS CIPHER FIGURE NUMBER RECKON ACCOUNT BALANCE SUPPUTE ESTIMATE CALCULATE

COMPUTER HOST MINI ADDER ENIAC LAPTOP MANIAC DESKTOP MAINFRAME PROCESSOR MINICOMPUTER
(— ADD-ON) ESE
(— ALL-PURPOSE CODE) BASIC
(— BINARY DIGIT) BIT
(— CAPACITY) RAM ROM
(— CHIP) CPU
(— CIRCUIT) NOR NAND
(— CIRCUIT BOARD) SIMM
(— CODE) BCD ASCII
(— COLLECTION OF DATA) DATABASE
(— COMPANY) AST IBM NEC ACER DELL APPLE COMPAQ GATEWAY MACINTOSH PACKARDBELL HEWLETTPACKARD
(— COMPONENT) CHIP
(— CORRECTION) PATCH
(— CURSOR MOVER) MOUSE TRACKBALL
(— DATA) FILE PUSHDOWN
(— DEVICE) WAND MOUSE
(— DISK) FLOPPY MINIFLOPPY
(— DISK OPERATING SYSTEM) MSDOS PCDOS
(— FAILURE) CRASH
(— GATE) AND
(— GATEWAY) PORT
(— HARDWARE PC CPU DRIVE MONITOR PRINTER KEYBOARD
(— INDEX) KWIC
(— INFORMATION) DATA DATABASE
(— INFORMATION UNIT) BYTE MEGABYTE
(— INSERT) DISK
(— INSTRUCTION) MACRO
(— INTERFACE) PORT
(— KEY) ALT END ESC TAB CTRL HOME ENTER
(— LANGUAGE) ADA APL BCD RPG LISP LOGO ALGOL BASIC COBOL PASCAL PROLOG FORTRAN
(— LIST) MENU
(— MEMORY) RAM ROM PAGE CACHE EPROM STACK SCRATCHPAD
(— MEMORY CHIP) DRAM
(— MEMORY MODULE) CHIP SIMM
(— MONITOR) VGA SVGA
(— MOVIE) HAL
(— NERD) WEENIE
(— NETWORK) LAN
(— PRINTED TEXT) HARDCOPY PRINTOUT

(— PROGRAM) WORM VIRUS EDITOR LOADER FORTRAN SPREADSHEET BULLETINBOARD
(— PROGRAMMABLE MEMORY) EPROM
(— PROGRAMS) SOFTWARE
(— SEQUENCE OF BITS) BYTE
(— SOCKET) BANK PORT
(— SOFTWARE) DRIVER MONITOR
(— SOFTWARE NAME) LOTUS
(— SOUND) BEEP
(— STORAGE) FIELD
(— SYMBOL) ICON
(— SYSTEM) KLUGE KLUDGE TRSDOS
(— SYSTEMS COMMUNICATION) GATEWAY
(— UNIT) BIT BYTE ONEK
(— VIDEO DEVICE) MONITOR
(— VIDEO DISPLAY OF TASKS) MENU
(— WHIZ) HACKER
(ADMINISTRATOR OF — BOARD) SYSOP
(COMMAND TO — TO STORE DATA) SAVE
(COPY OF — FILE) BACKUP
(ENTER — DATA INTO MEMORY) WRITE
(ENTER A — PROGRAM) LOAD
(FLASHING — CUE) CURSOR
(FUNCTIONING PERIOD OF —) UPTIME
(HEART OF —) CPU
(HINT ON — TO CONTINUE) PROMPT
(INDICATOR ON — SCREEN) CURSOR
(INTEGRATED — CIRCUIT) CHIP
(KIND OF) ANALOG HYBRID DIGITAL
(KIND OF —) DESKTOP
(LINK FOR TWO —S BY PHONE) MODEM
(MAGNETIC — RECORD) DISK
(MOVE — DISPLAY UP OR DOWN) SCROLL
(NETWORK —) HOST
(OPERATOR OF — PROGRAM) SYSOP
(PARTS OF — SYSTEM) HARDWARE
(PHYSICAL PARTS OF — SYSTEM) HARDWARE
(PRODUCER OF — SYSTEMS) OEM
(READY A —) BOOT
(RELATING TO — DISK) WINCHESTER
(STORED — MEMORY) FIRMWARE
(STORE OF — DATA) PUSHDOWN
(PL.) CYBER

COMRADE PAL ALLY CHUM MATE PEER BILLY BUDDY BUTTY CRONY HABER HAVER TOWNY BURSCH CHABER CHAVER COPAIN COUSIN DIGGER ENGIDU FELLOW FRATER FRIEND GOSSIP HEARTY BROTHER COMPEER CONVIVE BEAUPERE CAMARADA CAMARADE COMORADO CONFRERE COPEMATE TOVARICH SKAINSMATE
(— AT TABLE) CONVIVE
(PL.) SOCE

COMRADESHIP CAMARADERIE

CON DO RAP ANTI KNOW LEAD LOOK PORE QUIN READ SCAN CHEAT CUNNE GUIDE KNOCK LEARN STEER STUDY DIRECT PERUSE REGARD VERSUS AGAINST DECEIVE EXAMINE INSPECT OPPOSED SWINDLE

CONCAVE CAVE VOID CAMUS MINUS ARCHED DISHED HOLLOW SIMOUS VAULTY VAULTED CRESCENT INCURVED
(SUFF.) COELOUS COELUS

CONCAVITY COVE DISH CONCHA HOLLOW VENTER KNEEPAN

CONCEAL MEW WRY BURY DERN FEAL HIDE KEEP LENE MASK SCUG SILE VEIL VEST WRAP BLIND BOSOM CACHE CLOAK COUCH COVER FEIGN LAYNE PLANT SHADE BURROW CLOSET DOCTOR ELOIGN EMBOSS HUDDLE HUGGER IMBOSK OCCULT POCKET SCREEN SHADOW SHIELD SHROUD STIFLE VIZARD ABSCOND ENVELOP OPPRESS PLASTER SECRETE SMOTHER BESCREEN DISGUISE ENSCONCE PALLIATE PRETENCE PRETENSE WITHHOLD
(— A FUGITIVE) HARBOR
(— A TRAIL) TRASH
(— INFORMATION) LAYNE
(— PROFITS) SKIM
(— TO AVOID TAX) SKIM

CONCEALED DERN SCUG SNUG BLIND PERDU PRIVY BURROW COVERT HIDDEN LATENT OCCULT PERDUE SECRET VEILED COVERED LARVATE WRAPPED ABSTRUSE CRYPTOUS HIDEAWAY RECONDITE
(— BY) BENEATH
(PREF.) ADEL(O)

CONCEALING DESIGNING OBVELATION

CONCEALMENT MEW LAIN COVER FRAUD NIGHT STALE SECRECY CELATION VELATION SECRETION
(— OF TREASURE) MISPRISION
(IN —) DOGGO

CONCEDE OWN CEDE GIVE ADMIT AGREE ALLOW GRANT WAIVE YETTE YIELD ACCORD ASSENT BETEEM CONFESS OTTROYE BEGRUDGE ACKNOWLEDGE
(— AS ADVANTAGE) SPOT

CONCEIT EGO TOY IDEA SIDE WIND CRANK FANCY KNACK POESY PRIDE QUIRK BABERY DEVICE NOTION VAGARY VANITY BIGHEAD CAPRICE EGOTISM OUTRAGE TYMPANY CONCETTO FLIMFLAM
(VIVID —) VISION

CONCEITED BUG BRAG COXY FESS VAIN CHUFF COCKY FLORY HUFFY PENSY PROUD SAUCY CLEVER BIGGETY BIGGITY ARROGANT DOGMATIC NOSEWISE PENSEFUL PRIGGISH SNOBBISH

CONCEIVABLE EARTHLY POSSIBLE

CONCEIVE FORM HOLD MAKE PLAN TEEM WEEN BEGIN BRAIN CATCH DREAM FANCY FRAME GUESS IMAGE THINK DESIGN DEVISE IDEATE INTEND PONDER SETTLE GESTATE IMAGINE REALIZE SUPPOSE SUSPECT COMPRISE CONTRIVE ENVISAGE

CONCENTRATE AIM FIX MASS PILE BUNCH COACT EXALT FOCUS PURSE UNIFY ARREST ATTEND CENTER CITRIN DECOCT DISTIL FIXATE GATHER SINGLE COMPACT CONGEST DISTILL ENGROSS ESSENCE EXTRACT THICKEN ABSOLUTE APPROACH ASSEMBLE CONDENSE CONTRACT FOCALIZE GRADUATE
(— ORE) STRAKE

CONCENTRATED HARD DENSE FIXED INTENT STRONG EXALTED INTENSE
(NOT —) DIFFUSE

CONCENTRATION BRIX TITER CENTER BALLING SAMADHI ACTIVITY FIXATION PELMANISM
(— OF ARTILLERY FIRE) STONK
(— OF ENERGY) EXCITON
(— OF GRAPE JUICE) BESHMET
(— OF PLANTS) BED
(— OF SOLUTION) MOLARITY
(EXCESS —) MONOMANIA

CONCEPT GUT GUTS IDEA PLAN FANCY IMAGE BEGRIFF CONCEIT OPINION THOUGHT ABSOLUTE CATEGORY PLURALISM PERCEPTION

CONCEPTION ENS IDEA VIEW EIDOS FANCY FETUS IMAGE BELIEF DESIGN EMBRYO ENTITY NOTION CONCEIT CONCEPT PROJECT PURPOSE CATEGORY ESTHETIC NOTATION RATIONAL
(— OF IDEA) HENT
(— OF ONESELF) BOVARISM BOVARYSM
(ABSTRACT —) ARCHETYPE
(FALSE —) IDOL DELUSION
(QUICKNESS OF —) PREGNANCY

CONCEPTUAL IDEAL NOTIONAL

CONCEPTUALISM SERMONISM

CONCERN BUG BEAR CARE FEAR FIRM GEAR HAND PART RECK SAKE APPLY CAUSE CERNE DRIVE EVENT GRIEF HEART SORGE STAND TOUCH WORRY AFFAIR AFFECT BEHOLD CHARGE DIRECT EMPLOY FINGER IMPORT MATTER REGARD THRUST ANXIETY ARTICLE BOTTLER COMPANY DISTURB FUNERAL INVOLVE PERTAIN RESPECT SHEBANG SOLICIT TROUBLE BUSINESS HYPOTHEC INTEREST JEALOUSY
(— ONESELF) DEAL PASS TOUCH INTERMIT
(INDUSTRIAL —) COLOSSUS
(PRUDISH —) COMSTOCKERY
(SOMETHING CAUSING —) ALBATROSS
(SPECIAL —) ACCENT
(WORLDLY —S) EARTH
(SUFF.) **(— FOR)** ITIS

CONCERNED INTENT ANXIOUS VERSANT WORRIED ATWITTER BOTHERED

CONCERNING BY OF ON RE TO FOR TIL TILL ABOUT ANENT ANENST APROPOS TOUCHING

CONCERT POP PLAN RECK UNITE ACCORD DEVISE SMOKER ARRANGE BENEFIT CONCENT CONCORD CONSORT CONSULT HARMONY POPULAR RECITAL NEGOTIATE

CONCERT-HALL ODEON ODEUM

CONCERTINA ORGAN LANTUM SQUIFFER BANDONION MELOPHONE

CONCESSION BOON FAVOR GRANT LEASE STOOP ASSENT GAMBIT OCTROY CESSION EPITROPE MYNPACHT ADMISSION ALLOWANCE PRIVILEGE

CONCESSIONAIRE GRIFTER

CONCH CONK PUNK SHELL COCKLE MUSSEL STROMB STROMBUS SCUNGILLI

CONCIERGE SUPER PORTER SUISSE WARDEN DVORNIK JANITOR

CONCILIATE GET CALM EASE GAIN ATONE HONEY THING ADJUST PACIFY SOFTEN ACQUIRE APPEASE CONCILE MOLLIFY PLACATE SATISFY PROPITIATE

CONCILIATOR ARBITRATOR

CONCILIATORY MILD SOFT GENTLE GIVING IRENIC LENIENT PACIFIC WINNING IRENICAL LENITIVE TREATABLE

CONCISE CURT NEAT TRIG BRIEF CRISP PITHY SHORT TERSE COGENT CUTTED COMPACT LACONIC POINTED PRECISE SERRIED SUMMARY TABLOID MUTILATE PREGNANT SUCCINCT

CONCISELY PRESSLY ELLIPTICALLY

CONCISENESS BREVITY ECONOMY SYNTOMY FASTNESS SYNTOMIA BRACHYOLOGY

CONCLAMATION SHOUT

CONCLAVE SOBOR CLOSET CHAMBER MEETING AREOPAGY ASSEMBLY

CONCLUDE BAR END AMEN FINE REST TAKE CLOSE DRIVE ESTOP INFER JUDGE LIMIT CLINCH DECIDE DEDUCE EXPIRE FIGURE FINISH GATHER INDUCE PERIOD REASON RECKON SETTLE ACHIEVE ARRANGE COLLECT CONFINE EMBRACE ENCLOSE RESOLVE SUPPOSE COMPLETE DISPATCH ESTIMATE GRADUATE PARCLOSE RESTRAIN

CONCLUDED OVER COMPLETE

CONCLUDING LAST DESITIVE

CONCLUSION END AMEN CODA ERGO FINE LAST TERM CLOSE ENVOY EVENT FINIS ISSUE LOOSE OMEGA POINT ENDING FINALE FINISH PERIOD RESULT SEQUEL THIRTY UPSHOT CLOSURE CURTAIN FINDING OUTCOME SEQUELA VERDICT APODOSIS DECISION EPILOGUE FINALITY FRUITION GODSPEED ILLATION ILLATIVE JUDGMENT PARCLOSE SENTENCE

(— OF ARIA) CABALETTA
(FINAL —) ISSUE
(RANDOM —) SURMISE
(PL.) COLLATION
CONCLUSIVE LAST FINAL VALID COGENT CERTAIN EVIDENT EXTREME TELLING DECISIVE DEFINITE ULTIMATE
CONCOCT MIX BREW COOK FAKE PLAN PLOT VAMP FRAME HATCH THINK DECOCT DEVISE DIGEST INVENT MINGLE REFINE SCHEME COMPOSE CONFECT DREAMUP PERFECT PREPARE COMPOUND INTRIGUE
CONCOCTION PLAN PLOT MUMMY DEVICE MUMMIA BREWING MIXTURE SNEEZER BUSINESS COMPOUND
CONCOMITANT SEQUELA INCIDENT ACCESSORY ASSOCIATE ATTENDANT ATTENDING COMPANION CONJOINED COOPERANT SATELLITE
CONCORD PART AGREE AMITY PEACE TERMS UNION UNITY TREATY UNISON COMPACT CONCENT CONCERT HARMONY ONENESS QUARTER COVENANT SYMPATHY COMMUNITY
(— OF SOUNDS) SYMPHONIA
CONCORDANT UNISON TUNABLE TUNEFUL HARMONIC UNISONAL UNISONOUS
CONCORDE SST
CONCOURSE CROWD HAUNT PLACE POINT REPAIR RESORT THRONG COMPANY ASSEMBLY FREQUENCE
(INFERNAL —) HELL
CONCRESCENCE ADHESION
CONCRETE CLOT FIRM HARD REAL BETON GROUT SOLID UNITE ACTUAL CEMENT GUNITE COMBINE CONGEAL SPECIAL COALESCE COMPOUND POSITIVE TANGIBLE AEROCRETE
CONCRETION CLOT KNOT MESS FLINT FUSIL PEARL STONE BEZOAR DOGGER NODULE TOPHUS LITHITE OTOLITH CALCULUS HAIRBALL POTSTONE SEBOLITH GALLSTONE
(— IN BAMBOO) TABASHIR TABASHEER
CONCUBINAGE KARAO KAREWA HETAERISM
CONCUBINE DASI MOLL HAGAR RIZPAH BEDMATE HETAIRA ODALISK MISTRESS ODALISQUE
CONCUPISCENCE DESIRE
CONCUPISCENT ANTSY
CONCUR HAND JIBE JOIN AGREE CHECK CHIME UNITE ACCEDE ACCORD ASSENT CONDOG APPROVE COMBINE CONSENT CONVENT COINCIDE CONSPIRE CONVERGE
(— IN) SUBSCRIBE
CONCURRENCE UNION ASSENT BESTOW CONSENT CONSORT MEETING ADHESION SYNDROME ADMISSION
CONCURRENT COEVAL UNITED MEETING COPUNCTAL
CONCUSSION BUMP SHOCK IMPACT ICEQUAKE COMMOTION
CONDEMN BAN CAST DAMN DEEM DOOM FILE FINE HISS BLAME BLESS DECRY JUDGE AMERCE ATTAIN AWREAK BANISH DETEST ADJUDGE CENSURE CONVICT DENOUNCE FORJUDGE REPROACH SENTENCE PROSCRIBE
(— AS SPURIOUS) OBELIZE
CONDEMNATION BAN DOOM BLAME CENSURE DECRIAL BRICKBAT
CONDEMNATORY SEVERE ADVERSE
CONDEMNED FATAL DAMNED
CONDENSATION BAN STORY DIGEST CAPSULE BOILDOWN
CONDENSE CUT JIG BRIEF UNITE DECOCT DIGEST HARDEN LESSEN NARROW REDUCE SHRINK ABRIDGE CAPSULE COMBINE COMPACT DEFLATE DENSATE DISTILL SHORTEN SQUEEZE THICKEN COMPRESS CONTRACT DIMINISH PEMMICAN SOLIDIFY
CONDENSED CURT BRIEF CAPSULE COMPACT CONCISE SUMMARY TABLOID ABSORBED
CONDENSER ALUDEL REFLUX BALANCER CAPACITOR
CONDER HUER
CONDESCEND DEIGN FAVOR GRANT SNOOT STOOP ASSENT OBLIGE SUBMIT CONCEDE DESCEND
CONDESCENDING AVUNCULAR
CONDESCENSION STOOP DISDAIN COURTESY DIGNATION
CONDIGN DUE FIT FAIR JUST SEVERE WORTHY ADEQUATE SUITABLE
CONDIMENT SOY HERB KARI MACE SAGE SALT CAPER CURRY DULCE DULSE SAUCE SPICE THYME AIWAIN AJOWAN CATSUP CLOVES GARLIC PEPPER RELISH SAMBAL TAMARA BADIANE CANELLA CHUTNEY KETCHUP MUSTARD OREGANO PAPRIKA VINEGAR ALLSPICE BALACHAN BLATJANG DRESSING SEASONER TURMERIC
CONDITION IF AND FIG PLY WAY CASE FORM HOOD MODE NICK PASS RANK ROTE TERM TIFF TRIM ANGLE BIRTH CAUSE CENSE CLASS COLOR COVIN ESTRE FACET JOKER PLACE POINT SHAPE STAGE STATE THEAT WHACK AGENCY DEGREE DONNEE ESTATE FETTLE GENTRY MORALE MUSCLE PLIGHT STATUS STRING ARTICLE CALLING FEATHER FOOTING PLISKIE PREMISE PREPARE PROVISO STATION SUSPEND COVENANT OCCASION POSITION PROTASIS STANDING PREDICAMENT REQUIREMENT
(— IN LIFE) NICHE SPHERE
(— OF ANXIETY) CARK
(— OF BODY) HEAT AFFECTION
(— OF FATIGUE) FRAZZLE
(— OF FLUCTUATION) EURIPUS
(— STATED BEFOREHAND) PREMISE
(BEING IN DIRTY —) GRUNGY
(CHANCE —) ACCIDENT
(CRUSHED —) MASH
(DEBASED —) CACHEXY CACHEXIA
(DEPRESSED —) DOWNBEAT
(DETERMINING —) GROUND
(DIRTY —) CLAT
(DISEASED —) DIEBACK
(DISGRACEFUL —) IGNOMINY
(DRUNKEN —) BUN
(DUE —) ORDER
(FAULTY —) MALADY
(FLOURISHING —) HEALTH
(GENERAL —) VOGUE
(HABITUAL —) TENOR
(LOW —) NOTHING
(MEAN —) DUST
(MISERABLE —) SQUALOR
(MORBID —) HOLDOVER
(MOST APPROPRIATE —) CHECKER
(NECESSARY —) MEAN
(NEUROTIC —) LATAH
(ORDERLY —) DECENCY
(PAINFUL —) CRICK
(PERMANENT —) HEXIS
(PROPER —) KILTER
(PROTECTIVE —) CALLUS CALLOUS
(SCURFY —) BUCKSKIN
(STATIONARY —) JIB
(SUBLIME —) HEAVEN
(SURROUNDING —) AIR
(TRUE —) SIZE
(UNEQUAL —) ODDS
(UNPROSPEROUS —) ILLTH
(UNWHOLESOME —) MALADY
(WEATHER —S) ELEMENTS
(PL.) HAND TERMS STRINGS
(SUFF.) ACITY ATION DOM ERY ICE ICITY ILITY ION ISM MENT NESS OR OSIS SHIP TH TY
(MORBID —) IASIS
CONDITIONAL EVENTUAL CONNEXIVE PROVISORY QUALIFIED
CONDITIONED FINITE LIMITED
CONDITIONER DEGGER
CONDITIONING EDUCATION HYPOTHESIS
CONDOLE MOAN
CONDOLENCE PITY RUTH EMPATHY SYMPATHY
CONDOM JOHNNY RUBBER JOHNNIE PROPHYLACTIC
CONDONE BLINK REMIT ACQUIT EXCUSE FORGET IGNORE PARDON ABSOLVE FORGIVE OVERLOOK
CONDOR TIFFIN BUZZARD VULTURE
CONDUCE GO AID HELP HIRE LEAD TEND BRING GUIDE CONFER EFFECT ENGAGE ADVANCE CONDUCT FURTHER REDOUND
CONDUCT ACT CON RUN USE WIN BEAR CALL COND CONN DEED FACT FARE FIRK FORM GARB GEST HAND KEEP LEAD MIEN PLAY QUIT RULE SHOW TAKE WAGE WALK BATON CARRY CHAIR DRESS DRIVE FETCH GESTE GUARD GUIDE HABIT MAYNE SITHE TRADE TRAIN USAGE USHER ACTION ATTEND BEHAVE COLORS CONVEY CONVOY COURSE DEDUCE DEMEAN DEPORT DIRECT ESCORT GOVERN INDUCT MANAGE MANNER SQUIRE ACTIONS BEARING CHANNEL COMPERE COMPORT CONDITE CONDUCE CONDUIT CONTAIN CONTROL EXECUTE GALLANT GESTION OFFICER OPERATE WIREWAY ARRIVISM BEHAVIOR CARRIAGE CHAPLAIN COURTESY DEMEANOR GUIDANCE REGULATE SHEPHERD TRANSACT
(— AROUND) TROT
(— ONESELF) DO ACT ACQUIT BEHAVE BESTOW DEMEAN DEPORT COMPORT CONTAIN DISPORT ENTREAT MAINTAIN
(APPROPRIATE —) DHARMA
(BRASH —) FACE
(CONVENTIONAL —) PRAXIS
(DISORDERLY —) RANDAN
(DORMANT —) LATENCY
(DUTIFUL —) PIETY
(ETHICAL —) HONOR
(MORAL —) LIFE
(NORMAL —) WAY
(PROPER —) CRICKET
(RECKLESS —) DEVILRY DEVILTRY
(RIGHT —) TE TAO
(RIOTOUS —) RANDAN
(SAFE —) KOWL COWLE
(SEDITIOUS —) MISPRISION
(SHOWY —) BRAVADO
(SLOPPY —) SWASH
(SOCIAL —) MANNERS
(VAINGLORIOUS —) HEROICS
(WANTON —) RUFF
(WEAK —) FOLLY
CONDUCTANCE G
(UNIT OF —) MHO SIEMENS
CONDUCTION COURSING
CONDUCTOR CON BOND CADE LEAD MAIN BRUSH GUARD SHUNT SPOUT TRUNK BRIDGE BUSMAN CARMAN CONVOY COPPER ESCORT FEEDER LEADER OFFSET RETURN CAPTAIN CATHODE MAESTRO MANAGER AQUEDUCT BATONIST CICERONE CONVEYOR DIRECTOR EMPLOYEE FILAMENT STICKMAN ANELECTRIC
(— OF FESTIVAL) SKUDLER
(ELECTRIC —) FILAMENT
(LIGHTNING —) ROD
(OMNIBUS —) CAD
(WOMAN —) CLIPPIE
(PL.) SERVICE
(SUFF.) EER
CONDUIT BOSS DUCT GOUT MAIN PIPE SINK TUBE WIRE CABLE CANAL CUNDY SEWER STACK HEADER SLUICE TROUGH CARRIER CHANNEL CHIMNEY CONDITE CONDUCT CULVERT CUNDITE EXHAUST FOGGARA LATERAL LAUNDER PASSAGE WIREWAY AQUEDUCT OLEODUCT PENSTOCK UTILIDOR WASTEWAY
(PL.) LIMBERS
CONDYLOMA SYCOMA
CONE CAP YOW CHAT KING MOXA PINA TOOT CONUS CRACK SCREW SHAPE SPIRE YOWIE BOBBIN

CONOID MONTRE PASTIL CLUSTER CONELET CONIOLE FISSURE FRUSTUM PROLONG PYRAMID STROBIL THIMBLE CANNELON DUMPLING GALBULUS PASTILLE PINECONE STROBILE STROBILUS
(— OF CLOTH) VANE
(— OF FIR) YOW YOWIE STROBIL STROBILE STROBILUS
(— OF GUNPOWDER) PEEOY
(— OF HOP PLANT) BUR BURR
(— OF SILVER AMALGAM) PINA
(— ON LOG END) CAP
(— ON SHOE) CLEAT
(— STRUCTURE) NURAGHE
(HALF —) FORME NAPPE
(ICE CREAM —) ICE CORNET
(INVERTED —) HOPPER
(KIND OF —) NOSE
(PAPER —) SPILL COFFIN
(ROPE-MAKING —) TOP
(TOP CUT FROM —) UNGULA
(TRAFFIC —) PYLON
(VOLCANIC —) PUY MONTICULE
(PL.) HOPS
(PREF.) CON(I)(ICO)(O) STROBILI
CONENOSE BEDBUG BARBEIRO
CONE-SHELL ADMIRAL
CONESTOGA WAGON CARAVAN
CONEY CONY HYRAX HYRACID GUATIBERO
CONFAB CHAT TALK POWWOW CONFLAB PRATTLE
CONFABULATE TALK
CONFECTION CHOW MOSS CANDY DULCE FUDGE MEBOS SWEET BONBON COCKLE COMFIT DAINTY DRAGEE HALVAH JUNKET MAJOON NOUGAT SWEETY TABLET CARAMEL CONFECT FONDANT MIXTURE POMFRET PRALINE SEATRON SUCCADE ANGELICA CHOWCHOW CODINIAC COMPOUND CONSERVE DELICACY MARZIPAN PRESERVE QUIDDANY SUBTLETY MARSHMALLOW
(TURKISH —) HALVAH
CONFECTIONERY CIMBAL TUCKSHOP CONFISERIE
CONFEDERACY BUND COVIN CREEK JUNTA KEDAR UNION COVINE LEAGUE COMPLOT ALLIANCE COVENANT FEDERACY ILLINOIS BLACKFOOT
CONFEDERATE AID PAL REB ALLY BAND PUFF COVER REBEL STALL UNITE LEAGUE SANTAR ABETTER ABETTOR CONJURE FEDARIE FEDERAL FEODARY PARTNER STEERER CONSPIRE FEDERARY FEDERATE
(— SOLDIER) CONFED JOHNNY GRAYBACK GRAYCOAT GREYBACK
(PICKPOCKET'S —) STALL
CONFEDERATION BODY BUND ZUPA GUEUX UNION LEAGUE COMPACT HASINAI SOCIETY ALLIANCE COVENANT
(— OF VILLAGES) ZUPA
CONFER DUB GIVE MEET TALK AWARD ENDOW FEOFF GRANT INFER PARLE SPEND TREAT ADVISE BESTOW COMMON CONFAB DONATE ENTAIL HUDDLE IMPARL IMPART INVEST PARLEY POWWOW COLLATE COMMUNE COMPARE CONDUCE CONSULT CONTACT COUNSEL DISCUSS INSTATE PRESENT COLLOGUE COMPRISE CONVERGE NEGOTIATE
(— DEGREE UPON) CAP
(— KNIGHTHOOD UPON) DUB
CONFERENCE DIET TALK SYNOD TREAT TRUST CAUCUS CONFAB HUDDLE INDABA KORERO PARLEY PARVIS POWWOW SUMMIT CIRCUIT COUNCIL MEETING PALAVER PARLING SEMINAR COLLOQUE COLLOQUY CONCLAVE CONGRESS PRACTICE PRACTISE TUTORIAL PARLIAMENT
(SCIENCE —) PUGWASH
CONFERRING GRANT DATION
CONFESS OWN AVOW FESS KNOW SING ADMIT GRANT KITHE ACKNOW AGNISE ATTEST AVOUCH BEKNOW COUTHE RENDER REVEAL SHRIFT SHRIVE SQUEAK CONCEDE DIVULGE PROFESS WHITTLE DISBOSOM DISCLOSE DISCOVER MANIFEST ACKNOWLEDGE
CONFESSION ALHET CREDO CREED GRANT AVOWAL SHRIFT SHRIVE VIDDUI ASHAMNU FORMULA PECCAVI COGNOVIT
(MUTUAL —) SHARING
CONFESSIONAL SHRIFT MALCHUS
CONFESSOR FATHER SHRIFT SHRIVER
CONFIDANT PRIVY FRIEND INWARD INSIDER PRIVADO INTIMATE
CONFIDE AFFY RELY TELL TRUST COMMIT DEPEND LIPPEN BELIEVE CONSIGN ENTRUST INTRUST
(— IN) VENTURE
CONFIDENCE FACE HARK HOPE BIELD CHEEK FAITH STOCK TRUST APLOMB BELIEF CREDIT FIANCE FIDUCE METTLE MORALE SECRET SPIRIT SURETY COUNSEL COURAGE PRIVITY AFFIANCE BOLDNESS CREDENCE RELIANCE SECURITY SURENESS
(—GAME) SCAM STING
CONFIDENT BOLD SMUG SURE COCKY CRANK HARDY SIKER CROUSE SECURE SICKER TRAIST ASSURED CERTAIN HOPEFUL RELIANT CONSTANT FEARLESS FIDUCIAL IMPUDENT POSITIVE SANGUINE TRUSTFUL
CONFIDENTIAL PACK BOSOM PRIVY CLOSET COVERT HUSHED INWARD SECRET PRIVATE ESOTERIC FAMILIAR INTIMATE
CONFIDING TRUSTY CREDENT RELIANT TRUSTFUL CONFIDENT
CONFIGURATION FORM SHAPE FIGURE BANDING CONTOUR DIAMOND GESTALT OUTLINE GEOMETRY POSITURE OPPOSITION PERSPECTIVE
(CELESTIAL —) SYZYGY
CONFINE BAR BOX CUB DAM HEM MEW NUN PEN PIN STY TIE BAIL BIND BOOM CAGE COOP CRIB FOLD HASP JAIL KEEP LACE LOCK PEND SEAL SHUT SPAN STEW STOP STOW BOUND CABIN CHAIN COART CRAMP CROWD DELAY FENCE HOUSE LIMIT MARCH PINCH POUND STICK STINT THIRL BORDER BOTTLE COARCT CORRAL EMBANK FETTER FORBAR HAMPER HURDLE IMMURE IMPALE IMPARK INTERN KENNEL PINION POCKET PRISON SHUTIN STRAIN TETHER ASTRICT CHAMBER COMPASS CONTAIN IMPOUND INCLUDE MANACLE PINFOLD POISTER RECLOSE SECLUDE SHACKLE TRAMMEL BASTILLE BOUNDARY CLOISTER CONCLUDE DISTRAIN FOCALIZE IMPRISON RESTRAIN STRAITEN WAREHOUSE
(— IN HANDKERCHIEF) MAIL
(PL.) AMBIT PURLIEU PERIPHERY
CONFINED ILL FAST PENT BOUND CAGED CLOSE CRAMP BEDRID IMPALE IMPENT PENTIT SEALED CAPTIVE CRAMPED CRIBBED LIMITED SQUEEZY IMPENDED IMPLICIT INTERNED PAROCHIAL
(— TO CERTAIN AREA) ENDEMIC
(—TO ONE) PROPER
(— TO SELECT GROUP) ESOTERIC
CONFINEMENT MEW BOND HOLD JAIL WARD CRYING GATING DURANCE INLYING JANKERS WARDING CLAUSURE FIRMANCE GROANING LOCKDOWN SOLITARY
CONFINES AMBIT
CONFINING NARROW
CONFIRM FIX SET FIRM SEAL PROVE VOUCH AFFEER AFFIRM ASSENT ASSURE ATTEST AVOUCH BISHOP CLINCH FASTEN HARDEN RATIFY REABLE SECOND SETTLE STABLE VERIFY APPROVE COMFORT COMPACT CONSIGN ENDORSE FORTIFY JUSTIFY PROPORT SUPPORT SUSTAIN THICKEN ACCREDIT CONVINCE CORROBER ENTRENCH INSTRUCT SANCTION STRENGTH VALIDATE CORROBORATE REDETERMINE
CONFIRMATION PROOF CHRISM SANCTION
CONFIRMED SET FIXED SWORN ARRANT STABLE CERTAIN CHRONIC AFFEERED HABITUAL HARDENED RATIFIED
CONFISCATE GRAB SEIZE USURP CONDEMN CONFISK ESCHEAT PUBLISH DISTRAIN
CONFISCATION ESCHEAT INCENSION
CONFLAGRATION WAR FIRE BLAZE FEVER BURNING INFERNO
CONFLICT JAR WAR AGON BATE BOUT BUMP CAMP DUEL FRAY MEET MUSS RIFT AGONY BROIL BRUSH CLASH FIGHT GRIPS MIXUP STOUR ACTION BATTLE COMBAT MUTINY OPPOSE SCRAPE SHOWER STRIFE CONTEND CONTEST DISCORD SCUFFLE WARFARE ANTIMONY CLASHING DISAGREE MILITATE SKIRMISH STRIVING STRUGGLE COLLISION COLLUCTATION
(DRAMATIC —) AGON
(FINAL —) ARMAGEDDON
CONFLICTING ADVERSE ABHORRENT
CONFLUENCE FORK CROWD INFALL CONFLUX MEETING JUNCTION
CONFLUENT FORK
CONFORM DO GO FIT HEW BEND LEAN OBEY SORT SUIT ABIDE ADAPT AGREE APPLY SHAPE YIELD ACCEDE ADJUST ASSENT COMPLY CONFER SETTLE SQUARE SUBMIT COMPOSE CONFIRM
(— TO) KEEP MEET ANSWER BEHAVE SATISFY
CONFORMABLE DONE SUING SUITED CONFORM PURSUANT QUADRANT
CONFORMATION FORM BUILD
(MENTAL —) SAMSKARA
CONFORMING FAIR SAME COMELY DECENT CORRECT CONGRUOUS
CONFORMIST BOY COMPLIER
CONFORMITY FIT ACCORD DHARMA EQUITY REASON HARMONY JUSTICE KEEPING ACCURACY AFFINITY JUSTNESS LIKENESS SYMMETRY CONGRUITY FORMALITY ACCORDANCE CONSERTION
(— TO LAW) DECENCY LEGALITY
(— WITH GOOD MANNERS) PROPRIETY
CONFOUND MIX BLOW DASH MATE MAZE ROUT STAM STUN WHIP ABASH ADDLE AMAZE APPAL BLAST FOUND SHEND SPOIL STUMP WASTE AWHAPE BAFFLE BUNKER COMMIT DISMAY DUDDER MINGLE MUDDLE RABBIT RATTLE ASTOUND BUMBAZE CONFUSE CONFUTE CORRUPT DESTROY FLUMMOX FORLESE MISTAKE NONPLUS PERPLEX PETRIFY STUMBLE STUPEFY ASTONISH BABELIZE BEWILDER DISTRACT DUMFOUND SURPRISE SPIFLICATE
CONFOUNDED MATE BALLY BLAME RUDDY BLAMED DEUCED POCKED BLASTED BLESSED MURRAIN PEEVISH DUMMERED JIGGERED SWITCHED CONSARNED
(BE —) ABAVE ABAWE
CONFRATERNITY BODY UNION SOCIETY CONFRAIRY
CONFRONT DARE DEFY FACE MEET NOSE BEARD BRACE BRAVE CROSS FRONT STAND ACCOST ASSAIL BREAST OPPOSE RESIST VISAGE AFFRONT COMPARE OUTFACE PROPOSE ENVISAGE THREATEN
CONFRONTATION FACEOFF
CONFRONTING BEFORE ADVERSE ABUTTING CONFRONT
CONFUSE BOX FOX MIX BALL DASH DAZE DOIT DOZE DUST GAUM HARL MAZE MUSS ROIL ROUT ABASH ADDLE AMAZE BEFOG BITCH BLEND CLOUD DEAVE DIZZY

MUDDY SHEND SHENT SNARL STEER TWIST UPSET BAFFLE BEDAZE BEMUSE BOTHER BURBLE CADDLE COMMIT CORPSE DUDDER DUDDLE FLURRY FUDDLE GRAVEL JUMBLE MADDLE MAFFLE MAMMER MASKER MIZZLE MOIDER MOMBLE MUDDLE PUZZLE RAFFLE RATTLE TWITCH WIMPLE BECLOUD BEDEVIL BLUNDER BUMBAZE DERANGE DIFFUSE EMBROIL FLUSTER GARBOIL GIDDIFY MISTAKE MYSTIFY NONPLUS PERPLEX PERTURB SCATTER SHUFFLE STUPEFY UNRAVEL BEFUDDLE BEWILDER CONFLATE CONFOUND DISORDER DISTRACT DUMFOUND ENTANGLE MISORDER SQUATTER OBFUSCATE
(— AN ACTOR) CORPSE
(— BY NOISE) DUDDER
CONFUSED ASEA LOST ADDLE DIZZY FOGGY FUZZY HEAVY MISTY MUDDY MUZZY VAGUE WESTY WOOLY BLOTTO CLOUDY DOILED DOITED DRUMLY JUMBLY MEDLEY MOPISH MUSHED SHAGGY TAVERT WOOLLY BEMUSED BLURRED CHAOTIC CLOUDED CONFUSE DIFFUSE MIFFLED OBSCURE RATTLED STUPENT COCKEYED DERANGED FLURRIED INVOLVED STREAKED FLUSTERED INDISTINCT SCRAMBLING MUDDLEHEADED
(— IN LANGUAGE) BABYLONIAN
(EASILY —) BASHFUL
CONFUSEDLY PELLMELL
CONFUSING DIZZY MAZEFUL BAFFLING BLINDING DIZZYING
CONFUSION PI DIN PIE COIL DUST FLAP FUSS HARL MESS MOIL RIOT AMAZE ATAXY BABEL CHAOS CHEVY CHIVY DERAY FRASE HAVOC HURLY LARRY LURRY SNAFU SNARL STROW ATAXIA BABBLE BAFFLE BALLUP BEDLAM BUMBLE CHIVVY DUDDER FRAISE HABBLE HOBBLE HUBBUB HUDDLE JABBLE JUMBLE MASTIC MUCKER MUDDLE POTHER PUCKER RABBLE RUFFLE RUMPUS THRONG TOPHET TUMULT UPROAR WELTER ANARCHY BLUNDER BLUSTER CLUTTER COBWEBS FARRAGE FLUTTER GARBOIL HURLING KIPPAGE LOUSTER MISMAZE MISRULE ROOKERY RUMMAGE SCADDLE SCOWDER TOPHETH TURMOIL WHEMMEL WIDDRIM BABELISM DISARRAY DISORDER EQUIVOKE HOOROOSH SCOUTHER SHAMBLES SPLUTTER STRAMASH TOHUBOHU
CONFUTATION DISPROOF
CONFUTE DENY EVICT REBUT EVINCE EXPOSE REFUTE FALSIFY IMPROVE SILENCE SUBVERT CONCLUDE CONFOUND CONVINCE DISPROVE INFRINGE OVERCOME REDARGUE
CONGEAL GEL ICE SET GEAL JELL CANDY COTTER CURDLE FREEZE HARDEN STIFFEN STORKEN THICKEN CONCRETE SOLIDIFY
(— INTO HOARFROST) RIME
CONGEALED FROZEN
CONGELATION FROST
CONGENER BEAVER DOTTREL DOTTEREL
CONGENIAL SIB BOON HAPPY NATAL NATIVE AMIABLE CONNATE KINDRED
CONGENITAL INNATE CONNATE CONNATAL GENETOUS
CONGER SEAEEL
CONGERIES CALCULARY COLLECTION
CONGEST STUFF IMPACT
CONGESTED INJECTED
CONGESTION JAM HEAP LAMPAS LAMPERS CROWDING STOPPAGE
CONGLOMERATE HEAP MASS PILE ROCK STACK BANKET PSEPHITE NAGELFLUH
(—S OF JAPAN) ZAIBATSU
(JAPANESE —) ZAIBATSU
CONGLOMERATION HUDDLE GLOMMOX IMBROGLIO
CONGO MUMMY ASPHALTUM

CONGO
CAPITAL: BRAZZAVILLE
COIN: FRANC FRANCCFA
LAKE: MWERU TUMBA UPEMBA LEOPOLD
NATIVE: SUSA VILI MANTU PYGMY BATEKE MBOCHI WABUMA BAKONGO BANGALA
PLATEAU: BATEKE
RIVER: UELE CONGO KWILU LULUA NGOKO NIARI SANGA WAMBA KWENGE LOANGE SANGHA UBANGI KOUILOU LUBILASH
TOWN: EWO EPENA HOLLE JACOB OKOYO SEMBE MAKOUA OUESSO ZANAGA DOLISIE ENYELLE LOUBOMO SOUANKE DJAMBALA BRAZZAVILLE
TRIBUTARY: LOMAMI UBANGI ARUWIMA LUALABA LUAPULA ITIMBIRI

CONGOU KEEMUN
CONGRATULATE HUG JOY LAUD GREET SALUTE FLATTER MACARIZE
(— ONESELF) PREEN
CONGRATULATION PARABIEN (PL.) GRATTERS
CONGREGATE HERD MASS MEET PACK TEEM GROUP SWARM TROOP GATHER MUSTER COLLECT CONVENE ASSEMBLE
CONGREGATION PEW BODY FOLD HERD HOST MASS FLOCK SAMAJ SWARM CHURCH PARISH COMPANY MEETING ORATORY SYNAXIS ASSEMBLY BRETHREN CHAPELRY
(— OF WITCHES) COVEN
(JEWISH —) KOLEL ALJAMA SYNAGOG
(PL.) CHARGE
CONGRESS MOD DAIL DIET SYNOD UYEZD OBLAST OUYEZD POWWOW COUNCIL GORSEDD MEETING ASSEMBLY CONCLAVE
(— OF BARDS) EISTEDDFOD
CONGRESSMAN SENATOR DOUGHFACE
CONGRUITY ACCORD CONCORD FITNESS HARMONY KEEPING SYMMETRY COHERENCE
CONGRUOUS CONGRUE HARMONIC SUITABLE ACCORDING
CONICAL CONIC TAPER COPPED MITRAL COPPLED TAPERING (PREF.) TURBINATO TURBIN(I)(O)
CONICALLY (PREF.) TURBINATO
CONIDIUM CIDIUM ARTHROSPORE
CONIFER FIR YEW PINE CEDAR LARCH SPRUCE SOFTWOOD EVERGREEN
CONIFERAE PINALES
CONIUM HEMLOCK
CONJECTURE AIM CAST PLOT ROVE SHOT VIEW AUGUR ETTLE FANCY GUESS OPINE THINK BELIEF DIVINE THEORY CONJECT IMAGINE OPINION PRESUME SUPPOSE SURMISE SUSPECT HINDCAST SUPPOSAL
CONJOIN JOIN KNIT ATTEND EMPALE IMPALE ALLIGATE
CONJOINED JOINED JUGATE LINKED JUGATED CONJUNCT TOUCHING
CONJOINTLY JUNCTLY TOGETHER
CONJUGAL SPOUSAL CONNUBIAL
CONJUGATE YOKED JOINED UNITED COUPLED INFLECT PARONYMOUS
CONJUGATION SYNGAMY ZYGOSIS CYTOGAMY ENDOGAMY SYNOPSIS
CONJUNCTION AS ET IF OR AND BUT NOR TIE THAN JOINT SINCE SYNOD UNION UNITY THOUGH COITION CONSORT JOINDER CONJUNCT RATIONAL
(PREF.) **(IN —)** CO
CONJUNCTIVITIS PINKEYE
CONJUNCTURE SEASON
CONJURATION ART CHARM MAGIC SPELL VOODOO EXORCISM
CONJURE PRAY WISH CHARM HALSE ADJURE ENJOIN INVENT INVOKE SUMMON BESEECH COMBINE ENTREAT IMAGINE CONSPIRE CONTRIVE EXORCIZE
(— UP) RAISE
CONJURE MAN CUNJAH CUNJER GOOFER GUFFER
CONJURER MAGE PELLAR POWWOW SHAMAN WIZARD JUGGLER WARLOCK WIELARE ANGEKKOK JONGLEUR MAGICIAN PYTHONIC SORCERER
CONJURING JADU JADOO CONJURY VOODOOISM
CONK FAIL HEAD KONK NOSE FAINT KNOCK STALL BRACKET
CONNECT COG PUT TIE ALLY BIND BOND GEAR GLUE JOIN KNIT KNOT LINK AFFIX CHAIN MARRY NITCH UNITE ATTACH BRIDGE CEMENT COHERE COMMIT CONNEX COUPLE ENLINK FASTEN PLUGIN RELATE SPLICE COMBINE ENCHAIN INVOLVE APPARENT CATENATE CONTINUE DOVETAIL INTERTIE
(— TREADLE) CORD
CONNECTED ALLIED CONNEX AFFINED COUPLED HANGING
(— WITH) ABOUT
(ELECTRICALLY —) ALIVE
(NOT —) FOREIGN ASYNARTETE
(SYNTACTICALLY —) ABSOLUTE
(SUFF.) **(— WITH)** ARIA ARIUM AST ORIAL

CONNECTICUT
CAPITAL: HARTFORD
COLLEGE: TRINITY
COUNTY: TOLLAND WINDHAM
INDIAN: PEQUOT MOHEGAN NIANTIC
STATE BIRD: ROBIN
STATE FLOWER: LAUREL
STATE NICKNAME: NUTMEG
STATE TREE: OAK
TOWN: AVON BETHEL CANAAN COSCOB DARIEN MYSTIC SHARON STORRS WILTON DANBURY MERIDEN NIANTIC NORWALK NORWICH TOLLAND WINDSOR NEWHAVEN SIMSBURY WESTPORT GREENWICH RIDGEFIELD
UNIVERSITY: YALE WESLEYAN

CONNECTING BETWEEN SYNDETIC
CONNECTION Y HUB TAP TIE BOND LINK HITCH NEXUS UNION BUCKLE CLEVIS FAMILY GROUND REPORT SUTURE SWIVEL BEARING BOLSTER CONTACT DESCENT FERRULE HOLDING KINSHIP LIAISON LINKAGE RAPPORT SIAMESE SIBNESS SOCIETY AFFINITY ALLIANCE COMMERCE CONNEXUS INTIMACY JUNCTION LIGATION RELATIVE SYNDETIC RELATIONSHIP
(— BETWEEN UNIVERSES) WORMHOLE
(ELECTRICAL —) GROUND
(FISH-LINE —) LEADER
(FORKED —) BRANCH
(MECHANICAL —S) LEADOUT
(WORKING —) GEAR
CONNECTIVE IZAFAT SUTURAL JUNCTION LIGATIVE SYNDETIC VINCULAR
CONNECTOR AND
CONNING TOWER SAIL
CONNIVANCE CAHOOT CAHOOTS
CONNIVE ABET PLOT WINK BLINK CABAL ASSENT FOMENT INCITE COLLUDE
(— AT MEDICAL TREATMENT) COVER
CONNIVING FOXY
CONNOISSEUR JUDGE CRITIC EXPERT CAMEIST EPICURE GOURMET CIDERIST DILETANT LAPIDARY COGNOSCENTE MEDIEVALIST
(— OF WINES) OENOPHILE
CONNOTATION DEPTH INTENT MEANING

CONNOTE MEAN
CONNUBIAL MARITAL CONJUGAL DOMESTIC
CONQUER GET WIN BEAT BEST DOWN FIRK GAIN LICK ROUT TAME WHIP CRUSH DAUNT DEBEL EVICT DEBELL DEFEAT EVINCE HUMBLE IMPORT MASTER REDUCE SUBDUE VICTOR ACQUIRE PREVAIL SUBJECT SURPASS TRIUMPH OVERCOME OVERGANG SURMOUNT VANQUISH
CONQUEROR HERO MASTER VICTOR WINNER TRIUMPHER
CONQUEST MASTERY SCALING TRIUMPH VICTORY WINNING
CONSANGUINEOUS AKIN CARNAL KINDRED NATURAL RELATED
CONSANGUINITY BLOOD NASAB KINSHIP AFFINITY
CONSCIENCE WORD DAENA HEART INWIT SENSE SCRUPLE THOUGHT
CONSCIENTIOUS FAIR JUST EXACT RIGID EIDENT HONEST STRICT DUTIFUL UPRIGHT FAITHFUL
CONSCIENTIOUSNESS RELIGION
CONSCIOUS KEEN WARE ALIVE AWAKE AWARE JERRY GUILTY FEELING KNOWING WITTING RATIONAL SENSIBLE SENTIENT CONSCIENT
(— OF) ONTO
CONSCIOUSNESS EGO HEART SENSE SPIRIT ANOESIS FEELING THOUGHT SENTIENT AWARENESS PERCEPTION
(HALF —) DOVER
(REGAIN —) COMETO
CONSCRIPT LEVY CHOCO DRAFT ENROL ENLIST MUSTER DRAFTEE DRAUGHT RECRUIT JEANJEAN
CONSCRIPTION LEVY
CONSECRATE VOW FAIN HOLY SAIN SEAL BLESS DEIFY HEAVE SACRE ANOINT DEVOTE HALLOW ORDAIN SACRATE CONSACRE DEDICATE SANCTIFY
CONSECRATED BLEST OBLATE SACRED VOTARY VOTIVE BLESSED SACRATE HALLOWED HIERATIC
CONSECRATION IHRAM SACRE SACRY SACRING DEVOTION HOLINESS
CONSECUTIVELY TOGETHER
CONSECUTIVENESS SEQUENCE
CONSENT HEAR AGREE ALLOW GRANT YIELD ACCEDE ACCORD AFFORD ASSENT BETEEM COMPLY CONCUR PERMIT APPROVE GOODWILL PERMISSION
CONSENTIENT UNANIMOUS
CONSEQUENCE AND END BORE EVENT FORCE FRUIT ISSUE SUITE WORTH BROWST CHARGE EFFECT ENTAIL FIGURE GROWTH IMPORT MOMENT REPUTE RESULT SEQUEL WEIGHT CONCERN OUTCOME PRODUCE PURPOSE SEQUELA SEQUENT BACKLASH INTEREST MISCHIEF OCCASION SEQUITUR COROLLARY OUTGROWTH CONSECTARY RAMIFICATION
(DONE IN —) PURSUANT
(HARMFUL —) EVIL
(ILL —) MISCHIEF
(PERSON OF —) HEAVY
(PL.) AFTERINGS
CONSEQUENT COMES THESIS ADJUNCT
CONSEQUENTIAL HEAVY POMPOUS COROLLARY MOMENTOUS
CONSEQUENTLY SO ERGO THEN THUS HENCE LATER PURSUANT PRESENTLY
CONSERTAL SUTURAL
CONSERVATION HUSBANDRY
CONSERVATISM BOURBONISM
CONSERVATIVE SAFE TORY FUSTY QUIET STAID FABIAN HUNKER STABLE BOURBON DIEHARD HARDHAT MODERATE UNIONIST
CONSERVATORY STOVE SCHOOL ACADEMY
CONSERVE CAN JAM SAVE GUARD GUMBO JELLY DEFEND SECURE SHIELD UPHOLD HUSBAND PROTECT SEATRON SUSTAIN MAINTAIN PRESERVE
(GRAPE —) UVATE
CONSIDER AIM BAT LET SEE CALL CAST DEEM GAUM GIVE HASH HEAR HEED HOLD MULL MUSE RATE SEEM TAKE TALE VIEW VISE WISE ALLOW BESEE COUNT ENTER ETTLE JUDGE PANSE POISE SPELL STUDY THINK VERSE VOLVE WEIGH ADVERT ADVISE BEHOLD DEBATE DEVISE DIGEST ESTEEM EXPEND FIGURE IMPUTE PONDER REASON RECKON REGARD REWARD SURVEY ACCOUNT BELIEVE BETHINK CANVASS CONSULT EXAMINE INSPECT PERPEND PREPEND REFLECT RESPECT REVOLVE SUPPOSE COGITATE ESTIMATE MEDITATE PERPENSE RUMINATE
(— FAVORABLY) CREDIT
(— PROS AND CONS) ARGUE
(— SEPARATELY) SPECIALIZE
CONSIDERABLE GAY GEY FAIR GOOD TIDY BONNY CANNY GEYAN GREAT LARGE SMART STARK GOODLY PRETTY GOODISH HEALTHY INTENSE NOTABLE SEVERAL HANDSOME POWERFUL SENSIBLE UNLITTLE
CONSIDERABLY FAR GAY GEY WELL GEYAN PRETTY SMARTLY
CONSIDERATE KIND MILD NICE GENTLE TENDER CAREFUL HEEDFUL PRUDENT SERIOUS TACTFUL DELICATE GRACIOUS ATTENTIVE
CONSIDERATENESS GRACE
(MUTUAL —) SHU
CONSIDERATION GUT GUTS SAKE COUNT PRICE STUDY TOPIC ADVICE ASPECT COMITY DEBATE ESTEEM MOMENT MOTIVE NOTICE REASON REFLEX REGARD SURVEY ACCOUNT INSIGHT PREMIUM RESPECT THOUGHT ALTRUISM COURTESY DELICACY EMINENCE EMPHASIS GRATUITY PROSPECT SANCTION
(BASIC —) BEDROCK
(ETHICAL —) SCRUPLE
(THOUGHTFUL —) THEORIA
(UNDER —) ONTHETAPIS
CONSIDERED ADVISED DELIBERATE
CONSIDERING IF FOR SINCE SEEING
CONSIGN DOOM GIVE MAIL SEND SHIP ALLOT AWARD CHECK DIGHT REMIT SHIFT YIELD ASSIGN COMMIT DESIGN DEVOTE REMAND RESIGN ADDRESS BETEACH CONFIDE DELIVER DEPOSIT ENTRUST INTRUST BEQUEATH DELEGATE RELEGATE TRANSFER
(— FOR DESTRUCTION) ACCURSE
(— TO OBLIVION) BURY EXPUNGE
(— TO PERDITION) DAMN CONDEMN
CONSIGNEE AGENT FACTOR SHIPPER RECEIVER
CONSIGNMENT INVOICE FOREDOOM SHIPMENT
(— OF TEA) BREAK
CONSIST LIE HOLD RELY REST DWELL EXIST STAND INHERE RESIDE CONTAIN EMBRACE COMPRISE
CONSISTENCY BODY UNION DEGREE CONCENT CONCORD HARMONY KEEPING COMPAGES EVENNESS FIRMNESS SOLIDITY SYMMETRY
CONSISTENT EVEN FIRM STEADY DURABLE LOGICAL REGULAR UNIFORM COHERENT ENDURING SUITABLE COMPATIBLE SEQUACIOUS
(— WITH NATURE) KIND KINDLY
(BE —) ACCORD
(MAKE —) CLEAR
CONSISTING
(PREF.) **(— OF)** DIA
(SUFF.) **(— OF)** IC(AL)
CONSOCIES
(SUFF.) ETUM
CONSOLATION SOP FINE RELIEF SOLACE COMFORT SPIRITING
CONSOLE CALM ALLAY ANCON CHEER ORGAN TABLE SOLACE SOOTHE BRACKET CABINET COMFORT RELIEVE SUPPORT SUSTAIN CARTOUCH
CONSOLER PARACLETE
CONSOLIDATE COG MIX KNIT MASS POOL WELD BLEND CLOSE MERGE UNIFY UNITE HARDEN MINGLE SETTLE COMBINE COMPACT ANKYLOSE COALESCE COMPRESS CONDENSE ORGANIZE SOLIDIFY
CONSOLIDATED CONFLATE
CONSOLS GOSCHENS
CONSOMME MADRILENE
CONSONANCE ACCORD UNISON HARMONY DIAPASON DIAPENTE SYMPATHY SYMPHONY
CONSONANT WAW MUTE STOP DENTAL FORTIS LABIAL LETTER LIQUID SONANT UNISON LATERAL MUTABLE PALATAL PLOSIVE SPIRANT UNIFIED ALVEOLAR ASPIRATA ASPIRATE BILABIAL EJECTIVE GEMINATE HARMONIC SUITABLE
(CONSECUTIVE —S) CLUSTER
(SMOOTH —) LENE LENIS
(TENSE AND STRONG —) FORTIS
(VOICELESS —) SURD SPIRATE
CONSORT COT AIDE ALLY JOIN MATE MOUP WIFE YOKE GROUP TROOP UNITE ACCORD ATTEND ESCORT MINGLE SPOUSE COMPANY COMRADE CONCERT DAMKINA EMPRESS HUSBAND PARTNER ACCUSTOM ASSEMBLY PRINCESS
(VISHNU'S —) LAKSHMI
CONSPECTUS LIST APERCU SURVEY OUTLINE THEATER THEORIC SPECTRUM SYNOPSIS
CONSPICUOUS BIG BOLD RANK CLEAR FAMED NOISY PLAIN STARY EXTANT FAMOUS MARKED PATENT SIGNAL BLATANT EMINENT GLARING NOTABLE OBVIOUS POINTED SALIENT SIGHTLY STARING VISIBLE APPARENT EMPHATIC FLAGRANT KENSPECK MANIFEST STRIKING PROMINENT NOTICEABLE OUTSTANDING
(— ONE) STANDOUT
CONSPIRACY COUP PLAN PLOT RING CABAL COVIN JUNTO PARTY COVINE SCHEME COMPACT COMPLOT INTRIGUE CATILINISM
CONSPIRATOR PACKER PLOTTER SCHEMER
CONSPIRE ABET PACK PLOT CABAL UNITE LEAGUE SCHEME COLLUDE COMPLOT CONJURE CONNIVE COLLOGUE CONTRIVE
CONSTABLE COP BULL PEON SLOP BEADLE BEAGLE HARMAN KAVASS KEEPER KOTWAL WARDEN BAILIFF CORONER DOZENER NUTHOOK OFFICER STALLER SUBASHI ALGUAZIL DOGBERRY TIPSTAFF CASTELLAN CATCHPOLE CATCHPOLL BORSHOLDER
CONSTANCE (FATHER OF —) FONDLOVE NONESUCH
(HUSBAND OF —) ALLA
(SON OF —) ARTHUR
CONSTANCY ZEAL ARDOR FAITH TRUTH FEALTY HONESTY LOYALTY ONENESS PURPOSE DEVOTION FIDELITY
CONSTANT K SET EVEN FIRM JUST LEAL TRUE FIXED LOYAL SOLID STILL TIGHT TRIED ITHAND STABLE STEADY CERTAIN CHRONIC DURABLE FOREVER LASTING REGULAR STAUNCH UNIFORM DEFINITE ENDURING FAITHFUL POSITIVE RESOLUTE SEDULOUS STANDING PERENNIAL
(KIND OF —) HUBBLE
CONSTANTLY AWAY EVER ALWAYS THRONG
CONSTANT NYMPH (AUTHOR OF —) KENNEDY
(CHARACTER IN —) DODD KATE CARYL LEWIS SUSAN TESSA ALBERT

SANGER TERESA ANTONIA PAULINA FLORENCE CHURCHILL SEBASTIAN
CONSTELLATION ARA CUP FLY FOX LEO APUS ARGO COLT CROW CRUX DOVE GOAT GRUS HARE HARP LION LYNX LYRA MAST PAVO PLOW SIGN SWAN TAUR URSA VELA WAIN WOLF ALTAR ARIES CAMEL CETUS CLOCK CRANE DRACO EAGLE GROUP HYDRA INDUS LEPUS LIBRA LUPUS MALUS MENSA MUSCA NORMA ORION PYXIS RAVEN TABLE VIRGO WAGON WHALE ANTLIA AQUILA AURIGA BOOTES CAELUM CANCER CARINA CORVUS CRATER CYGNUS DIPPER DORADO FORNAX GEMINI HYDRUS INDIAN LIZARD OBELUS OCTANS OKNARI PICTOR PISCES PISCIS PLOUGH PUPPIS SCALES SCUTUM TAURUS TIGRIS TOUCAN TUCANA VOLANS ALGEBAR CEPHEUS CLUSTER COLUMBA COMPASS DOLPHIN FURNACE GIRAFFE LACERTA MONARCH OETAEUS PATTERN PEACOCK PEGASUS PERSEUS PHOENIX RHOMBUS SAGITTA SCORPIO SERPENS SERPENT SEXTANS SEXTANT XIPHIAS AQUARIUS ASTERISM CHAMPION CIRCINUS CYNOSURE EQUULEUS ERIDANUS HERCULES HERDSMAN KASHYAPA QUADRANS REINDEER RETICULE SCORPION SCORPIUS SCULPTOR TRIANGLE
(— OF VEGA) LYRA
CONSTERNATION FEAR ALARM PANIC DISMAY FRIGHT HORROR TERROR TREPIDITY
CONSTIPATE BIND ASTRICT
CONSTIPATED BOUND COSTIVE STENOTIC
CONSTIPATION STENOSIS
CONSTITUENCY BOROUGH
CONSTITUENT ATOM ITEM PART PIECE VOTER DETAIL FACTOR FUSAIN MATTER MEMBER SIMPLE ELECTOR ELEMENT FEATURE TAGMEME INTEGRAL
(— OF BLOOD SERUM) OPSONIN
(— OF CLINKER) ALITE CELITE
(— OF COAL) DURAIN FUSAIN
(— OF DURAIN) ATTRITUS
(— OF MUSCLE) CREATINE
(— OF STEEL) PEARLITE
(—S OF BEER) EXTRACT
(NECESSARY —) ESSENCE
(PL.) MATTER BIOSESTON
CONSTITUTE BE FIX SET FORM MAKE ENACT ERECT FORGE FOUND SHAPE SPELL CREATE DEPUTE GRAITH ORDAIN APPOINT COMPOSE FASHION STATION COMPOUND COMPRISE
CONSTITUTION LAW SET CODE SETT BEING CANON FRAME FUERO HUMOR SETUP STATE CHARTE CRASIS CUSTOM DESIGN ESTATE HEALTH NATURE TEMPER CHARTER HABITUS SYNODAL GRONDWET GRUNDLOV HABITUDE PHYSIQUE POLITEIA
(— STATE) CONNECTICUT
(BODILY —) HABIT SPIRITS
(GERMINAL —) HEREDITY
CONSTITUTIONAL WALK HECTIC INNATE RIKKEN EXERCISE
CONSTITUTIVE FORMAL
CONSTRAIN ART PUT TIE ARCT BEND BIND CURB DOOM FAIN HALE HOLD LEAD URGE CHAIN CHECK CLASP COART CRAMP DETER DRIVE FORCE IMPEL LIMIT PRESS COERCE COMPEL EVINCE OBLIGE RAVISH SECURE STRAIN THRAST ASTRICT CONFINE CONJURE ENFORCE MANACLE OPPRESS REPRESS VIOLATE COMPRESS CONCLUDE DISTRESS OBLIGATE PERFORCE POUNDAGE RELIGATE RESTRAIN
CONSTRAINED FAIN TIED VAIN BOUND FORCED FORMAL UNEASY COACTED
CONSTRAINING UNEASY COMPELLENT
CONSTRAINT BOND CRAMP FORCE BRIDLE DURESS STRESS RESERVE STRAINT COERCION DISTRESS PRESSURE
CONSTRICT TIE BIND CURB GRIP CHOKE CRAMP LIMIT STRAP HAMPER SHRINK STRAIN STRAIT ASTRICT DEFLATE SQUEEZE STIFFEN TIGHTEN ASTRINGE COMPRESS CONDENSE CONTRACT DISTRAIN RESTRICT
CONSTRICTED STRAIT STRICT ADENOID
(— AT INTERVALS) MONILIFORM
CONSTRICTION KNOT CHOKE ISTHMUS STENOSIS THLIPSIS
CONSTRICTOR BOA ABOMA NOOSE GUAVINA
CONSTRUCT UP BIG ATOM FORM IDEA LEVY MAKE REAR BUILD CRAFT DIGHT EDIFY ERECT FRAME MODEL WEAVE BURROW DEDUCE DESIGN DEVISE FABRIC ARRANGE CARPENT COMBINE COMPILE COMPOSE CONCEPT CONFECT CONTOUR EXTRUCT FASHION CONSTRUE ENGINEER PRACTISE SLIPFORM
(— ARCH) TURN
CONSTRUCTED BUILT EDIFICATE
(CAREFULLY —) CLEVER
(HASTILY —) GIMCRACK JIMCRACK
CONSTRUCTION BOOM ALTAR FRAME FABRIC MONSTER SYNESIS APPROACH BUILDING DWELLING ERECTION
(— OF NAME) ABSTRACTION
(— SET) ERECTOR
(ABSTRACT —) STABILE
(GRAMMATICAL —) SYNESIS APPOSITION
(POINTED —) BEAK
CONSTRUCTIVE PONENT FACTIVE HELPFUL VIRTUAL CREATIVE IMPLICIT INFERRED
CONSTRUCTOR ENGINEER
CONSTRUE INFER PARSE STRUE INTEND RENDER ANALYZE CONSTER DISSECT EXPLAIN EXPOUND RESOLVE
CONSUL SUFFECT
CONSULT LOOK SEEK TALK ADVISE CONFER EMPARL IMPARL COUNSEL RESOLVE
CONSULTANT EXPERT ADVISER COUNSEL
CONSULTATION ADVICE COUNCIL COUNSEL
CONSUL, THE (CHARACTER IN —) JOHN MAGDA SOREL
(COMPOSER OF —) MENOTTI
CONSUME EAT SUP USE BOLT BURN CHEW FANG FARE FEED FRET GULP IDLE KILL RUST TAKE TUCK WEAR DALLY DRINK FLAME LURCH RAVEN SHIFT SPEND TOOTH WASTE ABSORB BEZZLE BROWSE CANKER DEVOUR ENGAGE EXPEND FINISH IMBIBE INHALE PERISH PUNISH VANISH CORRODE DESTROY DWINDLE ENGROSS EXHAUST SWALLOW CONTRIVE SQUANDER
(— IN LARGE QUANTITY) PUNISH
(— TOTALLY) KILL
(— VORACIOUSLY) HOG
CONSUMED ALL PAU DOWN BURNT SPENT COMBUST OUTWORN
CONSUMER MOUTH
(UNPRODUCTIVE —) CATERPILLAR
CONSUMING EATING SACRED BURNING FLAMING
CONSUMMATE END FINE FULL RIPE CLOSE IDEAL SHEER ARRANT EFFECT FINISH FULFIL RATIFY ACHIEVE CONSUME CROWNED FULFILL PERFECT PERFORM ABSOLUTE COMPLETE MERIDIAN THOROUGH
CONSUMMATION CROWN PERIOD UPSHOT
CONSUMPTION USE DECAY WASTE EXPENSE WASTING PHTHISIS SPENDING
(PREF.) PHTHISIO
CONSUMPTIVE LUNGY HECTIC PREDATORY
CONTACT ABUT JOIN KISS MEET SLED CROSS TOUCH TRUCK UNION ARRIVE IMPACT SYZYGY EPHAPSE HOLDING MEETING TACTION JUNCTION TANGENCY TOUCHING
(— BY RADIO) RAISE
(— OF TELEGRAPH KEY) ANVIL
(ELECTRICAL —) HUB HUBB POINT
(EVIL —) CONTAGION
(FLEETING —) BRUSH
(FORCIBLE —) IMPACT
(3-POINT —) OSCNODE
(PREF.) HAPT(O) THIGMO
CONTAGION POX TAINT VIRUS MIASMA POISON
CONTAGIOUS TAKING NOXIOUS SMITTLE CATCHING EPIDEMIC
CONTAIN RUN HAVE HOLD KEEP STEM STOW TAKE CARRY CHECK CLOSE COVER HOUSE EMBODY ENFOLD ENSEAM HARBOR RETAIN COMPILE EMBRACE ENCLOSE INCLUDE INVOLVE RECEIVE SUBSUME SUSTAIN COMPRISE RESTRAIN
(PREF.) CHADA
CONTAINED IN
CONTAINER BAG BOX CAN CUP HAT JAR JUG KEG LUG NIN PAN POD POT TIN TUB URN VAT BAIL BOMB CAGE CASE CASK CRIB DISH DRUM EWER FILE FLAT JACK SACK SALT SILO SINK SKIP TANK TUBE VASE VIAL ALBUM BASIN BILLY CADDY CHEST CRATE CRUET CRUSE DEWAR EMPTY FLASK GLASS GOURD POUCH SCOOP SCRAY STAND STOOP STOUP BARREL BASKET BOTTLE BUCKET BUSHEL CARBOY CARTON CASTER CASTOR COOLER CRADLE DUSTER HAMPER HATBOX HOLDER INKPOT MAILER PICNIC RABBIT RIDDLE SHAKER WITJAR AEROSOL AMPULLA BANDBOX BLADDER CAPSULE COASTER COSTREL CRISPER FEEDBOX HANAPER HOLDALL INKWELL OILDRUM PACKAGE SEEDLIP SHIPPER SNIFTER SPOONER STEEPER CANISTER DECANTER DEMIJOHN ENVELOPE HOGSHEAD HONEYPOT INHOLDER KNAPSACK PENTAGON PUNCHEON SLIPCASE RELIQUARY POCKETBOOK
(— FOR BEER) GROWLER
(— FOR BOBBINS) BUFFALO
(— FOR BRANDY) SNIFTER
(— FOR COINS) BANK
(— FOR EXPLOSIVE CHARGE) CAP
(— FOR FISH) BASS
(— FOR GOLD DUST) SHAMMY
(— FOR HOLY OIL) STOCK
(— FOR LEFTOVER FOOD) DOGGYBAG DOGGIEBAG
(— FOR PLANTS) BAND
(— HUNG FROM OBI) INRO
(— IN WHICH TO HEAT DRUGS) COOKER
(— MADE OF HOLLOW LOG) GUM
(— OF ASSAYER) CUPEL
(COFFEE —) INSET
(DESSERT —) COUPE
(DRINK —) DOP
(EARTHENWARE —) STEAN
(FIRECLAY —) SETTER
(KITCHEN —) CANISTER
(RAILROAD —S) BUNKER
(SHELVED —) CABIN
(SHIPPING —) KIT
(SNUFF —) WEASAND
(TOBACCO —) SARATOGA
(VENTILATED —) CHIP
(5-GALLON —) JERICAN JERRICAN
(PL.) CONVEYER CONVEYOR
CONTAINING
(SUFF.) IC(AL)
CONTAMINATE FOUL HARM SLUR SMIT SOIL STAIN SULLY TAINT BEFOUL DEBASE DEFILE INFECT INJURE POISON ATTAINT CORRUPT DEBAUCH FLYBLOW POLLUTE TARNISH VITIATE DISHONOR
CONTAMINATED DIRTY DEGRADED INFECTED

CONTAMINATION INFECTION TAINTMENT
(— IN GLASS) STONE
CONTE TALE CRAYON
CONTEMN HATE FLOUT SCORN SPURN REJECT SLIGHT DESPISE DISDAIN CONTEMPT INDIGNIFY
CONTEMPLATE FACE MUSE PLAN SCAN VIEW DEIGN STUDY THINK WEIGH BEHOLD DESIGN PONDER REGARD SURVEY CHERISH PROPOSE REFLECT CONSIDER ENVISAGE ENVISION MEDITATE
CONTEMPLATION MUSE STUDY DHYANA MUSING PRAYER REGARD THEORY INSIGHT MOONING REQUEST THEORIA PETITION RECOLLECTION
(— OF PAST) RETROSPECT RETROSPECTION
CONTEMPLATIVE BROODY PENSIVE THEORIC STUDIOUS
CONTEMPORANEOUS COEVAL LIVING MODERN CURRENT EXISTING
CONTEMPORARY EQUAL COEVAL FELLOW CURRENT PRESENT YEALING EXISTENT SIMULTANEOUS
CONTEMPT PRUT SCORN SHAME SNEER SLIGHT CONTEMN DESPECT DESPITE DISDAIN HETHING MOCKERY DEFIANCE DERISION DESPISAL DISGRACE MISPRIZE MISPRISION OPPROBRIUM
(— FOR DANGER) TEMERITY
(— OF OPPOSITION) DEFIANCE
(ONE HELD IN —) FINK
CONTEMPTIBLE LOW BASE MEAN POOR VILE BALLY CHEAP DIRTY DUSTY LOUSY MANGY MUCKY PETTY POCKY RUDDY SCALD SORRY ABJECT BLOODY CRUDDY GRUBBY MEASLY PALTRY SCABBY SCUMMY SCURVY SHABBY SNOTTY SORDID YELLOW BROKING LIGHTLY PEEVISH PELTING PITIFUL SCALLED SCORNED SHITTEN SLAVISH SQUALID BAUBLING BEGGARLY FRIPPERY INFAMOUS INFERIOR PICAYUNE PITIABLE PRECIOUS SNEAKING UNWORTHY WRETCHED MISBEGOTTEN
(— PERSON) CRUD
(SUFF.) **(— ONE)** EEN EER
CONTEMPTIBLENESS BEGGARY
CONTEMPTUOUS SLIGHT SNEERY SNOOTY HAUGHTY LIGHTLY SLIGHTY SPITOUS ARROGANT FLOUTING INSOLENT SCOFFING SCORNFUL
CONTEND TUG VIE WAR WIN CAMP COCK COPE DEAL FRAB KEMP PLEA RACE WAGE ARGUE BANDY BRAWL CHIDE CLAIM FIGHT FLITE PRESS ASSERT BATTLE BICKER BREAST BUCKLE BUFFET BUSTLE COMBAT DEBATE DIFFER JOSTLE JUSTLE MEDDLE OPPOSE PINGLE REASON STRIVE BARGAIN COMPETE CONTEST COUNTER DISPUTE PROPUGN QUARREL SCUFFLE STICKLE SUSTAIN WRESTLE CONFLICT CONTRAST CONTRIVE MAINTAIN MILITATE SQUABBLE STRUGGLE
(— FOR) SUPPORT
CONTENDER ATHLETE STICKLER
CONTENT PAY CALM EASE GIST GLAD PAID RATH SATE APPAY HAPPY HUMOR RATHE SERVE AMOUNT CUBAGE PLEASE APPEASE CONTENU GRATIFY PERFECT REPLETE SATIATE SATISFY SUFFICE WILLING BLISSFUL CAPACITY CONTINEU WILCWEME
(—S OF SACK) BUDGET
(—S OF STOMACH) COOKIES
(CUBICAL —) VOLUME
(ENERGY —) STRENGTH
(HEAT —) ENTHALPY
(SUPERFICIAL —S) AREA
(PL.) LINING
CONTENTED COZY FAIN VAIN QUIET SATED CONTENT PLEASED CHEERFUL
CONTENTION WAR BAIT BATE CASE FEUD PLEA RIOT TIFF TOIL BROIL CHEST CLAIM STRUT BICKER COMBAT DEBATE ESTRIF JANGLE STRIFE CHIDING CONTEKE CONTEST DISCORD DISPUTE OPINION QUARREL RIVALRY WRANGLE ARGUMENT CONFLICT SQUABBLE STRUGGLE VARIANCE COLLUCTATION
(VERBAL —) WORDS
CONTENTIOUS CROSS BATEFUL PEEVISH PERVERSE BELLICOSE
CONTENTMENT EASE BLISS HEAVEN PLEASURE SATISFACTION
CONTERMINOUS NEXT ADJACENT FRONTIER PROXIMAL
CONTEST GO IT BEE FIX RUN SUE TRY VIE AGON BOUT CAMP COPE DUEL FEUD FRAY GAME HOLD KEMP LAKE MART PULL RACE SHOW SPAR TIFF TILT TURN YOKE AGONY ARGUE BROIL CLASH DERBY EVENT FIGHT MATCH PLATE PRIZE RODEO ROLEO SCRUB SPORT TRIAL WAGER ACTION ADJURE AFFRAY BATTLE BISLEY COMBAT DEBATE DEFEND FLIGHT OPPOSE RESIST RUBBER SEESAW STRIFE STRIVE TUSSLE YOKING BARGAIN BRABBLE CLASSIC COMPETE CONTECK CONTEND DERAIGN DISPUTE GRAPPLE PROTEST SHUTOUT TOURNEY WARFARE ARGUMENT CONCOURS CONFLICT DOGFIGHT HANDICAP LITIGATE SKIRMISH SLUGFEST STRIVING STRUGGLE WALKAWAY WALKOVER PANCRATIUM PENTATHLON
(— EASILY WON) LAUGHER
(— IN WORDS) SPAR
(— NARROWLY WON) SQUEAKER
(ATHLETIC —) AGON BIATHLON
(AUTOMOBILE — ON FROZEN LAKE) ICEKHANA
(BEAUTY —) PAGEANT
(CLOSE —) DICE
(DRAWN —) TIE DRAW STALEMATE
(MOCK —) SCIAMACHY
(MOST IMPORTANT —) SUPERBOWL
(RACING —) DRAG
(REAPING —) KEMP
(PREF.) MACHO
(SUFF.) AGONIST(IC) MACHIA MACHY
CONTESTANT VIER RIVAL WAGER PLAYER AGONIST ENTRANT SCRATCH FINALIST PROSPECT
CONTIGUITY ADJACENCY CONFINITY IMMEDIACY
CONTIGUOUS NEAR NEXT NIGH NEARBY TANGENT ABUTTING ADJACENT TOUCHING
CONTINENT ASIA MASS PORE SOBER AFRICA CHASTE EUROPE CONTENT CAPACITY MAINLAND MODERATE ABSTINENT
(VANISHED —) LEMURIA
CONTINGENCY BOOK CASE EVENT CHANCE ADJUNCT CONTACT VENTURE ACCIDENT CASUALTY FORTUITY INCIDENT JUNCTURE PROSPECT
CONTINGENT TROOP CASUAL CHANCE DOUBTFUL EVENTUAL INCHOATE POSSIBLE TOUCHING ACCIDENTAL DELEGATION
CONTINUAL STILL HOURLY ABIDING ENDLESS ETERNAL LASTING REGULAR UNDYING UNIFORM CONSTANT ENDURING UNBROKEN
CONTINUALLY AY AYE EVER STILL ALWAYS EVERLY HOURLY STEADY ENDLESS ETERNAL FOREVER MINUTELY
CONTINUANCE STAY WHEN DELAY LEASE SEQUEL ABIDING DURANCE LASTING ABIDANCE DURATION STANDING SURVIVAL
CONTINUANT OPEN LIQUID DURATIVE
CONTINUATION SEQUEL CONTANGO DURATION PROLONGATION PERSEVERATION
(— OF DOUBLET) BASQUE
CONTINUE BE DO ABY SUE ABYE BIDE DURE HOLD JUMP KEEP LAST LIVE STAY TIDE ABIDE CARRY EXIST PERGE STICK UNITE ABEGGE BELEVE ENDURE EXTEND PURSUE REMAIN RESUME BELEAVE CONNECT CONTUNE PERSIST PROCEED PROLONG SUBSIST SURVIVE SUSTAIN PROTRACT
(— UNALTERED) TARRY
CONTINUED STILL SERIAL CHRONIC CONSTANT
CONTINUING ABIDING DURABLE LASTING DURATIVE PERPETUAL PERSISTENT OUTSTANDING
(— FOR LONG TIME) CHRONIC
(— TO BE) YET
CONTINUITY TRACT SCRIPT COHESION SCENARIO CONTINUUM
(PREF.) SYNECHIO
CONTINUOUS RUN EVEN ANEND EIDENT ENTIRE EYDENT STEADY CHRONIC ENDLESS RUNNING UNBROKEN PERENNIAL PERPETUAL
CONTINUOUSLY AWAY EVER FAST ANEND OUTRIGHT
CONTORT WRY BEND COIL CURL TURN WARP GNARL SCREW TWIST WREST CRINGE DEFORM WRITHE DISTORT PERVERT SQUINCH WREATHE OBVOLUTE
CONTORTED WRY WRIED KNOTTY CRISPED KNOTTED SCREWED WRITHEN OBVOLUTE
CONTORTION SCREW STITCH WRITHE MURGEON WORKING
CONTOUR FORM LINE CURVE GRAPH SHAPE SWEEP AMOEBA FIGURE OUTLINE PROFILE CARTOUCH CONTORNO MANDORLA PLANFORM TOURNURE
(— ON SHIP) HANCE
CONTRA CONTRE AGAINST COUNTER OPPOSED
CONTRABAND HOT GOODS ILLEGAL ILLICIT SMUGGLED UNLAWFUL
CONTRABASS BASS OCTOBASS
CONTRACEPTIVE SHEATH MINIPILL
(ORAL —) PILL
CONTRACT GET BOND DRAW FARM FORM HALE KNIT PACT SALE TACK CATCH CLOSE COACT COUCH CRAMP FEVER INCUR LEASE LIMIT NEXUM PINCH SHRUG SNURP CARTEL COCKLE COMMIT CRINGE ENGAGE FUTURE GATHER HIRING INDENT LESSEN MUTUUM NARROW PIGNUS PLEDGE POLICY PROMPT PUCKER REDUCE SHRIMP SHRINK SUBLET TREATY ABRIDGE APPALTO BARGAIN BUMMERY CHARTER COMPACT CRIMPLE CRUMPLE CURTAIL DEFLATE FIDUCIA MANDATE PROMISE SCRUNCH SHORTEN SHRIVEL SOCIETY WRINKLE ASSIENTO BOTTOMRY CONDENSE COVENANT HANDFAST HARDNESS LOCATION RESTRICT STEELBOW STRAITEN SYNGRAPH ABBREVIATE OBLIGATION
(— BROW) FROWN
(— INTO WRINKLES) KNIT
(BRIDGE —) SOLO AUCTION
(MARRIAGE —) KETUBA AFFIANCE HANDFAST BETROTHAL SPONSALIA
CONTRACTED BOXY CRAMP BOOKED ASTRICT INGROWN INSULAR SCREWED CONTRACT
CONTRACTILITY MOTILITY
CONTRACTION HM ANT NIP TIC TIS AINT CANT ISNT KNIT MAAM WONT CRAMP HADNT HASNT NISUS SPASM CRASIS GATHER INTAKE MUSTNT SHRINK TWITCH ELISION EPITOME WOULDNT APNEUSIS TRACTION ABRIDGMENT ABRIDGEMENT
(— OF HEART) SYSTOLE
(— OF SYLLABLES) SYNIZESIS
(PL.) TREPPE
CONTRACTOR KHOT BUTTY BUILDER REMOVER SUPPLIER

CONTRADICT DENY BELIE CROSS REBUT FORBID IMPUGN NEGATE OPPOSE RECANT REFUTE THREAP COUNTER GAINSAY REVERSE WITHSAY CONTRARY DISPROVE DOWNFACE NEGATIVE OUTSTAND
CONTRADICTION CLASH DENIAL DEMENTI PARADOX WITHSAW ANTILOGY ANTIMONY ANTILOQUY
(LUDICROUS —) BULL
CONTRADICTORY OPPOSE ANTINOME OPPOSITE THWARTING
CONTRAPTION RIG TOOL DEVICE DOODAD GADGET JIGGER CONCERN MACHINE DOOHICKEY HOOTNANNY
CONTRARIETY DISCORD
CONTRARILY BACKWARD CRISSCROSS
CONTRARIWISE CONTRA CONTRARY
CONTRARY BALKY CROSS KICKY SNIVY AVERSE CONTRA CUSSED ORNERY SNIVEY THRAWN ADVERSE COUNTER CRABBED FROWARD HOSTILE INVERSE OPPOSED PEEVISH RESTIVE REVERSE STROPPY WAYWARD ABSONANT ANTIPODE CAPTIOUS CONTRAIR INIMICAL OPPOSITE PERVERSE PETULANT SINGULAR ABHORRENT
(— EXPRESSION) OXYMORON
(— TO) BESIDE AGAINST ATHWART
(— TO HAPPINESS) ILL
(— TO REASON) SILLY ABSONANT
(PREF.) CONTRA COUNTER DIS RETRO
CONTRAST CLASH STRIFE COMPARE CONTEND DISCORD ANTIMONY DIVISION DYNAMICS OPPOSITE
CONTRASTING
(PREF.) CONTRA
CONTRAVENE DEFY DENY HINDER OPPOSE THWART DISPUTE VIOLATE INFRINGE OBSTRUCT
CONTRAVENTION SIN VICE CRIME BREACH OFFENSE
CONTRETEMPS SLIP BONER HITCH MISHAP SCRAPE ACCIDENT INCIDENT
CONTRIBUTE AID ANTE FORK GIVE HELP MAKE TEND CAUSE ENTER GROUT PUTUP SERVE ASSIST BESTOW CONCUR CONFER DONATE PUNGLE RENDER SUPPLY TENDER ANIMATE CONDUCE FURNISH FURTHER PROVIDE THROWIN
CONTRIBUTING ACCESSORY
CONTRIBUTION BIT SUM TAX ALMS BOON GIFT SCOT SHOT ESSAY INPUT SHARE IMPOST SYMBOL ARTICLE LARGESS PAYMENT PRESENT RENEWAL WRITING DONATION EXACTION OFFERING ROMESHOT
(CHURCH —) TITHE
(LITERARY —) PAPER
(SMALL —) MITE
CONTRITE WORN SORRY HUMBLE RUEFUL PENITENT SORROWFUL
CONTRITION SORE SORROW PENANCE PENITENCE
CONTRIVANCE (ALSO SEE DEVICE) ART BOW FLY GIN JET JIG LEG DROP GEAR HARP JACK KITE LURE PAGE PLAN PLOT RASP REED TOOL ALARM BRAKE CARRY CHECK DOLLY DRAFT FLOAT FRAME GUIDE HICKY KNACK MIXER QUIPU SHIFT SNARE STOCK ANCHOR DAMPER DECEIT DESIGN DEVICE DOCTOR DOLLIE ENGINE FABRIC FANGLE GABION GADGET GIMBAL HANGER HARROW HEATER HICKEY HOLDER JIGGER JINKER MARKER MORTAR MUZZLE POLICY RATTLE SCHEME SLUICE SPIDER TEASEL WEIGHT WHEEZE WINDAS WRENCH BOLSTER CLEANER CLEARER CONCERN COUPLER CUNNING DINGBAT DRAUGHT FICTION FISHWAY HUMIDOR KNOCKER MACHINE PAGEANT PROJECT REDUCER ROASTER SCRAPER SHEBANG SPANNER STOPPER TOASTER TRIPPER VOLVELL ADAPTION ARTIFICE CROTCHET DUTCHMAN EUPYRION FAKEMENT FORECAST GOVERNOR INDUSTRY MOLITION OXIDATOR REGISTER RESOURCE SCISSORS SQUEEZER SUBTLETY WITCRAFT
CONTRIVE GET LAY BREW CAST DRAW FIND FIRK MAKE PLAN PLOT WORK FRAME FUDGE HATCH SHAPE STAGE WEAVE AFFORD DESIGN DEVISE DIVINE ENGINE FIGURE INVENT MANAGE SCHEME WANGLE ACHIEVE AGITATE COMMENT COMPASS CONCOCT CONJURE CONSULT CONTEND FASHION IMAGINE MACHINE PROCURE PROJECT REPAREL CONSPIRE ENGINEER FORECAST INTRIGUE PURCHASE
CONTRIVED PAT SLICK STAGED TIMBERED
CONTRIVER DAEDAL DAEDALUS ENGINEER
CONTRIVING FASHION SCHEMERY
CONTROL BIT LAP LAW MAN POT RUN CONN CURB EGIS GRIP HAND HANK HAVE HOLD REDE REIN RULE STAY SWAY WIND AEGIS BOOST CHARM CHECK COACT DAUNT DUMMY GRASP GUIDE LEASH ORDER POWER STEER SWING THEAT TREAT TUTOR VERGE WIELD BANDON BRIDLE CHARGE CLUTCH COERCE CORNER DANGER DIRECT EMPERY GOVERN HANDLE MANAGE POCKET TEMPER AMENAGE COMMAND CONDUCT CONTAIN CUSTODY FORBEAR MASTERY MONITOR QUALIFY STRINGS COACTION DOMINATE DOMINIUM IMPERIUM MODERATE REGULATE SERVOTAB POSSESSION
(— A BULL) MANDAR
(— OF RESOURCES) HUSBANDRY
(— OVER WIFE) MANUS
(ABSOLUTE —) BECK
(FIRE —) BLANKET
(GET EXCLUSIVE — OF) SEWUP
(GOVERNMENT —) DIRIGISM SQUADRISM
(MANUAL —) JOYSTICK
(NONCLERICAL —) LAICISM LAICITY
(OUT OF —) RUNAWAY
(VOLUME —) GAIN
CONTROLLED STEADY SERVILE CONTAINED
CONTROLLER FENCER GERENT MASTER STARTER
(SPEED —) GOVERNOR RHEOCRAT
CONTROLLING MASTER LEADING DOMINANT HEGEMONIC
CONTROVERSIAL ERISTIC POLEMIC
CONTROVERSIALIST ERISTIC POLEMIC DISPUTANT GLADIATOR
CONTROVERSY FLAP PLEA SPAT SUIT CHEST FUROR BATTLE COMBAT DEBATE FURORE HASSEL HASSLE HOORAH HURRAH STRIFE TUSSLE DISPUTE POLEMIC QUARREL WRANGLE ARGUMENT TRAVERSE CONTENTION
(ART OF —) POLEMICS
CONTROVERT DENY FACE MOOT ARGUE DEBATE DEFEND OPPOSE OPPUGN REFUTE CONTEST DISPUTE GAINSAY DISPROVE
CONTUMACIOUS UNRULY RIOTOUS CONTUMAX INSOLENT MUTINOUS PERVERSE STUBBORN
CONTUMELY ABUSE SCORN INSULT CONTECK DISDAIN REPROOF UPBRAID CONTEMPT RUDENESS
CONTUSE BEAT POUND THUMP BRUISE INJURE SQUEEZE
CONTUSION POUND BRUISE
CONUNDRUM PUN WHIM GUESS ENIGMA PUZZLE RIDDLE CONCEIT CROTCHET
CONURE ARATINGA
CONVALESCE MEND GUARISH RECOVER
CONVENANCE FORM
CONVENE SIT CALL HOLD MEET UNITE GATHER MUSTER SUMMON CONVENT CONVOKE ASSEMBLE CONVERGE
CONVENIENCE GAIN BEHOOF URINAL LEISURE COMMODITY
CONVENIENT FIT GAIN HEND NIGH HANDY HENDE READY ATHAND CLEVER FITTED PROPER SUITED USEFUL ADAPTED AVENANT COMMODE HELPFUL BECOMING EXPEDITE SUITABLE OPPORTUNE COMMODIOUS
CONVENIENTLY WELL HANDILY CLEVERLY
CONVENT ABBEY HOUSE TEKKE TEKYA CENOBY COVENT FRIARY PRIORY MEETING RECLUSE CLOISTER LAMASERY MOTHERHOUSE
CONVENTION DIET FEIS FORM MISE RULE TABU SYNOD TABOO USAGE CARTEL CAUCUS CUSTOM TREATY DECORUM MEETING ASSEMBLY ASSIENTO CONCLAVE CONGRESS CONTRACT COVENANT PRACTICE PRECEDENT
(LONG-ESTABLISHED —) TRADITION
(SET OF —S) PROTOCOL
(STAGE —) ASIDE
(PL.) DECENCIES
CONVENTIONAL MORE NOMIC RIGHT TRITE USUAL DECENT FORMAL MODISH PROPER CORRECT POMPIER REGULAR ACADEMIC ACCEPTED COPYBOOK ORTHODOX CUSTOMARY
(RIGIDLY —) UPTIGHT
CONVENTIONALITY FORM ACADEMISM FORMALITY GRUNDYISM
CONVENTIONALIZE STYLIZE
CONVERGE JOIN MEET FOCUS CONCUR CORNER CONNIVE DESCEND APPROACH FOCALIZE
CONVERSANT ADEPT BUSIED EXPERT VERSED SKILLED FAMILIAR OCCUPIED
CONVERSATION RAP SAY CALL CHAT CHIN RUNE TALE TALK BOARD CRACK PROSE CACKLE CONFAB DEVICE GOSSIP PARLEY POWWOW SPEECH YABBER CEILIDH COMMUNE CONDUCT PALAVER PURPOSE BACKCHAT BEHAVIOR CAUSERIE CHITCHAT COLLOGUE COLLOQUY DIALOGUE GIFFGAFF HARANGUE PARLANCE QUESTION COLLOCUTION
(— BETWEEN WHALERS) GAM
(LIGHT —) SMALLTALK
CONVERSATIONALIST TALKER CAUSEUR
CONVERSE CHAT CHIN LIVE MOVE TALK DWELL SPEAK CACKLE COMMON CONFER DEVISE HOMILY PARLEY REASON COMMUNE CONVERT DISCUSS OBVERSE PROPOSE REVERSE COLLOQUE EXCHANGE OPPOSITE QUESTION
CONVERSION CHANGE EXCHANGE METRICATION PROSELYTISM
(— INTO VAPOR) FLASH
(— OF IRON) FINING
CONVERT TAW TURN WEND ALTER AMEND APPLY MAULA RENEW CHANGE DECODE DETECT DIRECT MAWALI NOVICE SHAIKH SOUPER COMMUTE CONCOCT RESOLVE RESTORE REVERSE ACTIVATE CONVERSE DISCIPLE NEOPHYTE PERSUADE PROSELYTE
(— COTTON) LAP
(— INTO CASH) NEGOTIATE
(— INTO LEATHER) TAN TAW
(— INTO LIQUID) BREW
(— INTO MONEY) REALIZE
(— INTO PELLETS) PRILL
(— INTO SOAP) SAPONIFY
(— INTO STEEL) ACIERATE
(— INTO STONE) LAPIDIFY
(— INTO VAPOR) EVAPORATE
(— SOAP) CLOSE
(— TO CARBON) CHAR
(— TO ISLAM) SHEIK
CONVERTER ROTARY SELECTOR
CONVERTIBLE AUTO DROPHEAD
(— CAR) RAGTOP

CONVERTIPLANE STOL
CONVEX BOWED ARCHED CAMBER CURVED BULGING EMBOWED GIBBOUS ROUNDED
CONVEXITY CAMBER ARCUATION
CONVEY JAG BEAR BOOK CART CEDE DEED DUCT HAVE LEAD MEAN PASS SEND SIGN TAKE TOTE WAIN WILL BRING CARRY DRIVE FETCH GRANT GUIDE HURRY STEAL ARRIVE ASSIGN CONVOY DEDUCE DELATE DEMISE DEVISE ELOIGN GIGGIT IMPART IMPORT REMOVE YMMOTE AUCTION CHANNEL CHARIOT CHARTER CONDUCT DELIVER DERRICK DISPONE DISPOSE LIGHTER RESTORE ALIENATE BEQUEATH DESCRIBE TRANSFER TRANSMIT
(— AN ESTATE) DEMISE
(— BY ALLUSION) IMPLY
(— FORCIBLY) HUSTLE
(— HORIZONTALLY) ADVECT
(— LEGALLY) DEED GRANT LEASE DEMISE ELOIGN DISPONE
(— NEARER) BRING
(— SECRETLY) CRIM
CONVEYANCE BUS CAR AUTO CART DEED DRAG GIFT LOAD SLED TAXI TRAM GRANT SEDAN STAGE TAUGA THEFT TRAIN WAGON DEMISE JINGLE CHARTER CONDUCT COURIER MACHINE RATTLER TRAILER TRAJECT TRANSIT TROLLEY VECTURE VEHICLE WAFTAGE CARRIAGE CARRYING CONVEYAL DELATION FERRIAGE STEALING TRANSFER
CONVEYOR LIFT WORM DRAPER LADDER SHAKER CARRIER CREEPER HURRIER SCRAPER CAROUSEL CONVEYER ELEVATOR
CONVICT LAG CAST FIND STAR ARGUE EXILE FELON LIFER PROVE TAINT ATTAIN FORCAT LAGGER TERMER TRUSTY APPROVE ATTAINT CAPTIVE CONDEMN CULPRIT EXPIREE IMPEACH REPROVE CRIMINAL JAILBIRD PRISONER REDARGUE SENTENCE
CONVICT FISH MANINI HINALEA
CONVICTION CREDO CREED DOGMA FAITH HEART SENSE TAINT TENET BELIEF CREDIT CONCERN OPINION SENTENCE
CONVINCE SELL EVICT FETCH ASSURE EVINCE REPROVE RESOLVE SATISFY CONCLUDE
(— OF ERROR) CONVICT
CONVINCED FIRM SOLD SURE CERTAIN ABSOLUTE POSITIVE
CONVINCING SOUND VALID COGENT POTENT EVIDENT TELLING FORCIBLE LUCULENT POWERFUL PREGNANT
CONVIVIAL GAY BOON FESTAL GENIAL JOVIAL SOCIAL FESTIVE HOLIDAY JOCULAR REVELING ANACREONTIC
CONVIVIALITY REVEL FESTIVAL MERRYMAKING
CONVOCATION DIET SYNOD CALLING COUNCIL MEETING SUMMONS ASSEMBLY CONGRESS VOCATION
CONVOKE CALL HOLD GATHER SUMMON CONVENE ASSEMBLE
CONVOLUTE COIL ROLL WIND TWIST TANGLE WRITHE CONTORT INVOLUTE OBVOLUTE
CONVOLUTED GYRATE
CONVOLUTION COIL CURL FOLD TURN WRAP GYRUS SWIRL TWINE TWIRL TWIST WHORL CUNEUS GYROMA VOLUME VOLUTION
CONVOLUTIONAL SNAKY
CONVOLVE TURN WIND TWIST ENFOLD ENWRAP INFOLD WRITHE
CONVOLVULUS BINDWEED SCAMMONY
CONVOY LEAD WAFT CARRY GUARD GUIDE PILOT TRADE WATCH ATTEND CONVEY ESCORT MANAGE CONDUCT WAFTAGE SAFEGUARD
CONVULSE ROCK STIR SHAKE EXCITE AGITATE DISTURB
CONVULSION FIT SHRUG SPASM THROE ATTACK TUMULT UPROAR CONVULSE LAUGHTER PAROXYSM COMMOTION
CONVULSIVE FITFUL EPILEPTIC
CONY DAS HARE PIKA CONEY CUNNY DAMAN DASSY GANAM HUTIA HYRAX BURBOT CONEEN DASSIE GAZABO GAZEBO RABBIT WABBER ASHKOKO BOOMDAS HYRACID KLIPDAS HYRACOID KLIPDACH
COO CROO CURR WOOT CHIRR CHIZZ CROOD MURMUR CROODLE CRUDDLE
COOEE BIRD KOEL
COOK DO FIX FRY BAKE BOIL CHEF COCT FAKE MAKE SEAR STEW BROIL CUIRE CUSIE FRIZZ GRILL POACH ROAST SCALD SHIRR STEAM SWING BRAISE CODDLE COOKIE COOPER DECOCT DIGEST PORTER SAUTEE SEETHE SIMMER ARTISTE BROILER FRIZZLE GRIDDLE PASTLER PERCOCT POTAGER PREPARE PROCESS SERVANT SMOTHER SWAMPER BAWARCHI BOBACHEE COCINERO CUSINERO GRILLADE MAGIRIST PASTERER MICROWAVE
(— IN BOILING LIQUID) POACH
(— IN MICROWAVE) ZAP NUKE
(— TOO LONG) OVERDO
(— UP) BUILD
(BULL —) FLUNKY FLUNKEY GREASER
(SHIP'S —) DOCTOR SLUSHY SKILLET SLUSHER
(PREF.) MAGIRO
COOKED DONE FRIED BOILED
(— BY BOILING) AUBLEU
(— IN CLAY OVEN) TANDOORI
(— IN EARTHENWARE OVEN) TANDOORI
(— IN EARTHEWARE OVEN) TANDOORI
(— WITH SUGAR) CANDIED
(PREF.) COCTO
COOKEE FLUNKY HASHER FLUNKEY
COOKER CANNER HAYBOX DIGESTER
COOKERY CURY CUISINE KITCHEN MAGIRICS
COOKHOUSE GALLEY
COOKIE CAKE OREO ROCK SNAP COOKY HERMIT KIPFEL SPRITZ BISCUIT BROWNIE OATCAKE PLACENT BISCOTTO CRESCENT SEEDCAKE
(KIND OF —) FORTUNE
COOKING COCTION
(— UTENSIL) WOK
(INDIAN —) TANDOORI
(STYLE OF —) HUNAN
COOKING KIND OF —) TEXMEX
COOKROOM CUDDY
COOKWARE (KIND OF —) TEFLON
COOL AIR FAN HEP HIP ICE RAD CALM COLD DOWN KEEL AKELE ALGID ALLAY ALOOF CHILL EVENT FRESH GELID NERVY QUEEL SOBER STAID WHOLE AIRISH CALLER CHILLY PLACID QUENCH SEDATE SERENE TEMPER UNWARM COOLISH DISTANT RADICAL REFROID UNMOVED CARELESS CAUTIOUS COMPOSED MITIGATE MODERATE TRANQUIL NERVELESS POSSESSED NONCHALANT UNFLAPPABLE
(— IN WATER) SLACK SLACKEN
(— OF EVENING) SERENE
(— OFF) FAN
(BLOW ONE'S —) LOSEIT
COOLED COLD FRAPPE
COOLER PEN COLA ICER JAIL KEEL OLLA SINK POKEY ICEBOX LOCKUP PRISON SINKER KEELFAT ALCOGENE
(WINE —) GLACIER
COOLIE CHANGAR MADRASI MAZDOOR
COOLING REFRESHING
COOLNESS COOL FROST NERVE SWALE APLOMB PHLEGM SERENITY SANGFROID
COOM CULM GAUM SMUT SOOT COOMB GRIME SLACK
COONTIE SAGO ZAMIA COMPTIE
COOP COT CUB CUP MEW PEN POT RIP CAGE COOB COTE JAIL CRAMP HUTCH BASKET CORRAL CONFINE
(— UP) PEN IMMEW INCOUP
(HEN —) CAVEY CAVIE BARTON
COOPER BUNGS COPER COWPER HEADER HOOPER TUBBER TUBBIE TUBMAN
COOPERATE HAND TEND AGREE COACT UNITE CONCUR COMBINE CONDUCE CONNIVE COADJUTE CONSPIRE
COOPERATION SOCIETY COURTESY TEAMWORK
COOPERATIVE COOP ARTEL SOCIAL SYNERGIC
(RUSSIAN —) ARTEL
(SOVIET—) ARTEL
(SOVIET —) ARTEL
CO-OPT ABSORB
COORDINATE MESH SINE ADAPT EQUAL ADJUST ARRANGE SYNTONY ABSCISSA CLASSIFY ENSEMBLE
COORDINATION BOND SKILL HARMONY LIAISON
COORG KADAGA
COOT CUIT DUCK RAIL QUEET SMYTH BELTIE GORHEN PELICK SCOTER HENBILL LOBIPED PULLDOO LOBEFOOT RAILBIRD SWAMPHEN
COP BAG NAB ROB BANK BLOW BULL HEAD HEAP JOHN LIFT PILE TRAP TUBE ADMIT CATCH CREST FILCH MOUNT QUILL SHOCK SNARE STEAL STOCK SWIPE BOBBIN COPPIN PEELER SPIDER STRIKE CAPTURE
(— OUT) EVADE
COPA YAYA COPITA
COPAL BOEA LOBA ANIME CONGO KAURI KAURY RESIN COWRIE DAMMAR CHAKAZI
COPE VIE WAR CAPE DUTY FACE LIFT MEET CAPPA CLOAK COVER DRESS EQUAL FIGHT MATCH NOTCH RIVAL VAULT WIELD BARTER CANOPY CHAPEL COMBAT MANTEL MUZZLE OPPOSE SEMBLE STRIKE STRIVE ANABATA CHLAMYS CONTEND CONTEST GRAPPLE MANDYAS PLUVIAL COMPLETE EXCHANGE FACTABLE SEMICOPE STRUGGLE VESTMENT
COPEHAN WINTUN
COPEPOD CALANID CAYENNE DIAPTOMID
COPIAPITE MISY MISSY IHLEITE
COPIER COPIST SCRIBE JOHNSONIAN
COPING CAP COPE FLUE SKEW CORDON CAPSTONE FACTABLE
COPING STONE TABLET TABLING
COPIOUS FREE FULL GOOD LUSH RANK RICH AMPLE LARGE FLUENT LAVISH DIFFUSE FLOWING FULSOME LENGTHY PROFUSE REPLETE TEEMING UBEROUS ABUNDANT AFFLUENT FRUITFUL GENEROUS NUMEROUS PLENTIFUL
COPIOUSNESS COPY PLENTY
COPPER AES COP BULL CENT BOBBY METAL PENNY VENUS CUPRUM PEELER VELLON BLISTER CARNELIAN
(GILDED —) VERMEIL
(OF —) AEN
(PREF.) CHALC(O) CHALK(O) CUPR(I)(O)
(SUFF.) CHALCITE
COPPERAS COPEROSE INKSTONE COQUIMBITE
COPPERHEAD REDEYE MOCCASIN
COPPERSMITH TINKERBIRD
COPPER SULFATE BLUESTONE
COPPER SULFIDE FERRETTO COVELLINE COVELLITE
COPPERY CUPREOUS
COPPICE COP BROW WOOD COPPY COPSE FIRTH FRITH GROVE COVERT FOREST GROWTH SPROUT THICKET ARBUSTUM
(SUFF.) DRYMIUM

COPREUS (FATHER OF —) PELOPS
(HORSE OF —) ARION
(MOTHER OF —) HIPPODAMIA
COPSE CUT HAG HASP HEWT HOLT MOTT SHAW TRIM DROKE HURST CLEVIS SPINNY COPPICE LOWWOOD SHACKLE SPINNEY ARBUSTUM COPEWOOD
COPULA BAND LINK UNION
COPULATE RUT BULL LINE RIDE COVER MOUNT SERVE TREAD GENDER
COPY APE CALK CAST ECHO EDIT LOAD MIME MOCK NICK TEXT DITTO DUMMY GROSS IMAGE MIMIC MODEL PRINT REVIE STICK STUFF TRACE XEROX CALQUE DOUBLE ECTYPE EFFIGY FILLER FLIMSY FOLLOW MATTER RECORD REFLEX SAMPLE SHADOW EDITION EMULATE ENGROSS ESTREAT EXTRACT IMITATE PATTERN REDRAFT REPLICA REPRINT RUBBING TRACING VIDIMUS APOGRAPH AUTOTYPE EXEMPLAR EXSCRIBE EXSCRIPT KNOCKOFF LIKENESS MANIFOLD POROTYPE PORTRAIT RESEMBLE SPECIMEN MICROCOPY MINIATURE PHOTOSTAT
(— EDITOR) SLOT
(— ILLEGALLY) PIRATE
(— IN COMPUTER) DUMP
(— OF DOCUMENT) EXTRACT PROTOCOL
(— OF DRESS) FORD
(DUPLICATE — OF PROGRAM) BACKUP
(ENLARGED —) MACROCOPY
(EXACT —) TENOR
(FIRST —) DRAFT
(LITERARY —) STUFF
(MAKE A — OF) CLONE
(PRINTING —) KILL BOGUS
(SMALL —) MINATURE
(UNREMUNERATIVE —) LEAN
(WORTHLESS —) BALAAM
(XEROX —) REPRO
COPYING MIMICRY INSINUATION
COPYIST COPIER PENMAN SCRIBE COPYCAT SCRIVENER
COPYREAD EDIT SUBEDIT
COQUET TOY VAMP COPPY DALLY FLIRT TRIFLE BLINKER CELIMENE
COQUETRY AGACERIE
COQUETTE TOYER
COQUILLE SHELL
COQUINA DONAX
CORA NAYARIT
(HUSBAND OF —) ALONZO
CORACIIFORM NONPASSERINE
CORACLE SCOW CURAGH CURRACH CURRANE
CORAL RED PINK AKORI BLOOD POLYP ALCYON PALULE PORITE FUNGIAN OCULINA ACROPORE ASTRAEAN CORALLUM FAVOSITE POLYPITE STAGHORN TUBIPORE ZOOPHYTE MADREPORE MILLEPORE
CORAL BEAN SOPHORA FRIJOLILLO
CORAL-BELLS HEUCHERA
CORALBERRY BUCKBUSH
CORALFISH DOLLFISH
CORALROOT ORCHID CRAWLEY
CORAL SNAKE ELAPID ROLLER ELAPOID SCYTALE
CORAL TREE GABGAB ERYTHRINA
CORBEIL PANNIER
CORBEL KNOT ANCON CORBET TIMBER BRAGGER RESPOND CARTOUCH SPRINGER
CORBELING SQUINCH
CORBIESTEP CATSTEP CROWSTEP
CORCIR CORKE ARCHIL CORKER ORCHIL ARCHILLA
CORD AEA RIB AGAL BAND BIND BOND FILE LACE LASH LINE ROPE WELT BRAID CHORD FUNIS GUARD LEASH LIGNE MATCH NERVE OLONA TWINE TWIST BINDER BOBBIN BRIDLE BUNGEE CATGUT CHORDA CORDON FIADOR GIRDLE LASHER LISERE RACHIS SENNET STRING TENDON TOGGLE AMENTUM BOWYANG BULLION CORDING FUNICLE LANIARD LANYARD MACRAME SEAMING SEIZING SKIRREH TIEBACK URACHUS BELLPULL CHENILLE DRAWCORD HAIRLINE SHOELACE WHIPCORD
(— AROUND BOWSTRING) SERVING
(— FOR PIPING) BOBBIN
(— OF CANDLENUT BARK) AEA
(CROCHETING —) CORDE
(ELASTIC —) BUNGEE
(ELECTRIC —) FLEX
(EMBROIDERY —) ARRASENE
(FACE —) RANK
(FRINGED —) LLAUTU
(HAMMOCK —S) CLEW
(HAWK'S —) CREANCE
(KIND OF —) RIP
(MASON'S —) SKIRREH
(ORNAMENTED —) AGLET AIGLET
(PARACHUTE —) SHROUD
(SACRED —) KUSTI
(SPINAL —) EON AEON NUKE
(TWISTED —) TORSADE
(PL.) PANTS
(PREF.) CHORD(O)
CORDAGE DA COIR ERUC FERU HEMP IMBE JUTE KYAR ROPE HAMBER SENNIT RIGGING
(LENGTH OF —) CATENARY
CORDATE HEARTED
CORDED TIED JETTED REPPED RIBBED WELTED TWILLED
CORDELIA (SISTER OF —) REGAN
COR-DE-NUIT PASTORITA
CORDER RUFFER
CORDIAL REAL WARM CREAM ARDENT CASSIS CLOVES DEVOUT ELIXIR GENIAL HEARTY PASTIS CORDATE DIAMBER LIQUEUR PERSICO RATAFIA ROSOLIO SINCERE ZEALOUS ANISETTE FRIENDLY GRACIOUS PERSICOT VIGOROUS BENEDICTINE
(NOT —) DISTANT STANDOFF
(PL.) SWEETS
CORDIERITE IOLITE FAHLUNITE
CORDITE (INVENTOR OF —) ABEL
CORDON BLEU BENGALEE
CORDONNET CRESCENT
CORDUROOY DUROY
CORDWOOD BODYWOOD
CORE AME COB HUB NUT BONE COKE COLK GIST KNOT NAVE PITH BLOCK FOCUS HEART NOWSE RUMPF SPOOL BARREL CENTER CENTRE HEATER KERNEL MATRIX MIDDLE NODULE POCKET STAPLE CENTRUM CHEMISE COMPANY CORNCOB ESSENCE NUCLEUS FILAMENT HEARTING
(— OF COAL) STOCK
(— OF COLUMN) BELL HEART
(— OF CRICKET BALL) QUILT
(— OF LOG) PITH
(— OF MOLD) NOWEL
(EARTH'S HYPOTHETICAL —) NIFE
(WATER —) GLASSINESS
CORE ARBOR STALK
COREE CORANINE
CORELIGIONIST BROTHER
COREMIUM SYNEMA SYNNEMA
COREOPSIS TICKSEED TICKWEED LEPTOSYNE
CORF TUB CAGE CAWF COFF CORB SKIP CREEL BASKET DOSSER
CORFU CORCYRA KERKYRA SCHERIA
CORGI CARDIGAN PEMBROKE
CORIANDER (— LEAVES) CILANTRO
CORIOLANUS (AUTHOR OF —) SHAKESPEARE
(CHARACTER IN —) CAIUS TITUS BRUTUS JUNIUS TULLUS LARTIUS MARCIUS VALERIA AUFIDIUS COMINIUS MENENIUS SICINIUS VIRGILIA VOLUMNIA
CORIUM CUTIS DERMA LAYER DERMIS
CORK BUNG PLUG FLOAT SHIVE SUBER BOBBER BOUCHON CRINKLE PHELLEM SOBERIN STOPPER STOPPLE
(PREF.) PHELL(O) SUBERI
CORKED BOUCHE
CORKER LULU ONER WHIZ BEAUT DILLY RAKER WHIZZ CUTTER DOOZER HUMDINGER
CORKSCREW WORMER
CORKWING CONNER GOLDFINNY
CORKWOOD BALSA GUANO HAREFOOT
CORM SET BULB SEED CORMEL CORMUS FREESIA UINTJIE
CORMEL BULBLET
(PL.) SPAWN
CORMORANT SHAG CRANE GORMA NORIE SCARF SCART DUIKER DUYKER GORMAW GUANAY SCARFE SCARTH GLUTTON SHAGLET
CORN ZEA DANA DENT MAIS SALT SAMP GRAIN MAIZE SPIKE WYROK AGNAIL CALLUS CLAVUS HELOMA INDIAN KERNEL MEALIE NOCAKE NUBBIN POWDER WYROCK FORMITY FRUMENT FRUMENTY PRESERVE SAUTERNE
(— SALAD) MACHE
(— SPURREY) YARR
(CROW —) COLICROOT
(CRUSHED —) STAMP
(DECORATED EAR OF —) TIPONI
(EAR OF —) ICKER
(GUINEA —) DURRA DHURRA
(INDIAN —) MAIZE INDIAN NOCAKE
(PARCHED —) ROKEE NOCAKE PINOLE YOKAGE GRADDAN ROKEAGE YOKEAGE
(STRING OF —) TRACE
(UNRIPE EAR OF —) TUCKET
CORNAGE HORNGELD
CORN BREAD PONE KANKIE BANNOCK
CORNCOB COB
CORN COCKLE GITH COCKLE POPPLE COCKWEED HARDHEAD MELANTHY
CORNCRACKER STATE KENTUCKY
CORNCRAKE RAIL CORNBIRD
CORN CROWFOOT JOY GOLDWEED HELLWEED JACKWEED
CORNEL DOGWOOD REDBRUSH KILLIKINICK KINNIKINICK
CORNEOUS HORNLIKE KERASINE
CORNER IN GET OUT WRO BEND CANT COIN HALK HERN JAMB NOOK POOL TRAP TREE WICK ANCON ANGLE BIGHT CATCH COIGN ELBOW HERNE INGLE JAMBE NICHE QUOIN TRUST BOTTLE CANTLE CANTON COLLAR CORNEL CRANNY RECESS SQUARE OUTSIDE QUINYIE TURNING MONOPOLY
(— IN A DRIFT) ARRAGE
(— OF EYE) CANTHUS
(— OF GUNSTOCK) TOE
(— OF MOLDBOARD) SHIN
(— OF SAIL) CLEW CLUE TACK GOOSEWING
(CHIMNEY —) LUG
(LOWER —) CLEW CLUE
(RE-ENTRANT —) DIEDRE
(ROUNDED —) FILET FILLET
(SECRET —) CREEK
(TIGHT —) BOX
(PREF.) KERAT(O)
(— OF EYE) CANTH(O)
CORNERPIECE BUMPER CANTLE
CORNERSTONE COIN BASIS COIGN QUOIN HEADSTONE
CORNET CONE HORN ZINK TWIST ZINKE ZINCKE CORONET CORNETTO CORNOPEAN
CORNETFISH FLUTEMOUTH HEMIBRANCH
CORN-FED RUSTIC
CORNFIELD MOW
CORN FLAG LEVERS
CORNFLOWER BLUET BLAVER BARBEAU BLUECAP BLUECUP BLAEWORT
CORN GROMWELL SALFERN
CORNHUSK CAP
CORNHUSKER STATE NEBRASKA
CORNHUSKING SHUCKING
CORNICE CAP BAND DRIP EAVE JOPY ANCON CROWN JOWPY DETAIL GEISON PELMET ANTEFIX MOLDING SURBASE ASTRAGAL SWANNECK
(UNDER SIDE OF —) PLANCIER
(PREF.) GEISSO
CORNICHON GHERKIN

CORNICLE SIPHON SYPHON
CORNISHMAN CELT KELT
CORN MARIGOLD GOLD GOOLS BODDLE BOODLE BUDDLE GOWLAN GOLDING GOLLAND
CORN MEAL MASA SAMP ATOLE HOECAKE
CORN PARSLEY UMBEL
CORN POPPY BLAVER CANKER COCKLE COPROSE EARACHE PONCEAU REDWEED SOLDIER
CORN SALAD MACHE FETTICUS MILKGRASS
CORN SPURREY YARR
CORN STACK HOVEL
CORNSTALKS KARBI
CORNSTARCH BINDER
CORNU HORN THYROHYAL
CORNUCOPIA HORN CORNU COFFIN
CORNUS CORNIN REDBRUSH
CORN VIOLET SPECULARIA
CORN WOUNDWORT STACHYS
CORNY BANAL STALE TRITE MICKEY BUCKEYE
COROADO BORORO
CORODY CONRED
COROEBUS (FATHER OF —) MYGDON
(SLAYER OF —) DIOMEDES
COROLLA CUP BELL COROL CUPULE LIGULE PERIANTH
COROLLARY DOGMA PORISM RESULT TRUISM ADJUNCT THEOREM CONSECTARY
COROMANDEL COLCOTHAR
CORONA BUR BURR CIGAR CROWN GLORY AURORA FILLET ROSARY WREATH AUREOLE CIRCLET CORONET GARLAND LARMIER SCYPHUS
CORONAL CRONET CORONEL CROWNAL
CORONATION ABHISEKA CROWNMENT
CORONATION OF POPPAEA
(CHARACTER IN —) NERONE OTTONE SENECA OTTAVIA POPPAEA DRUSILLA
(COMPOSER OF —) MONTEVERDI
CORONER ELISOR CROWNER EXAMINER SEARCHER
CORONET BAND BURR CROWN TIARA ANADEM CIRCLE CRONET DIADEM TIMBRE WREATH CHAPLET CORONAL CROWNAL CROWNET GARLAND CROWNLET
CORONIS (FATHER OF —) PHLEGYAS PHORONEUS
(HUSBAND OF —) BUTES
(LOVER OF —) APOLLO ISCHYS
(SON OF —) ASCLEPIUS
CORONOPUS CARARA
CORPORAL NYM FANO NAIG NAIK PALL FANON FANUM NAYAK PHANO BODILY EXEMPT GUNNER NAIGUE NAIQUE SINDON TINDAL
CORPORATE UNITED COMBINED
CORPORATION BODY CITY FIRM POUCH TRUST SCHOLA BOROUGH COLLEGE COMMUNE FREEDOM GUILDRY SOCIETY SPONSOR
CORPOREAL REAL HYLIC SOMAL ACTUAL BODILY CARNAL FLESHLY SOMATIC MATERIAL PHYSICAL TANGIBLE
CORPOSANT HERMO
CORPS CORE ORDU VELITES SERAGLIO
(— DE BALLET) ENSEMBLE
(MEMBER OF WOMEN'S ARMY —) WAC
CORPSE BIER BODY CLAY DUST LICH MORT GHOST MUMMY RELIC STIFF TRUCK ZOMBI CORPUS DEADER ZOMBIE ANATOMY CADAVER CARCASS CARRION CROAKER DEADMAN FLOATER
(— WASHING) TAHARAH
(PREF.) NECR(O)
CORPSELIKE CADAVEROUS
CORPSMAN MEDIC BEARER
CORPULENCE FAT FATNESS STOUTNESS
CORPULENT FAT BEEFY BULKY BURLY FATTY GROSS HUSKY OBESE PLUMP PURSY STOUT TUBBY FLESHY GREASY PORTLY ROTUND ADIPOSE BELLIED WEIGHTY
CORPUSCLE CELL GHOST GLOBULE HEMATID HAEMATID HEMOCYTE
CORRAL PEN STY COOP ATAJO POUND TAMBO CONFINE ENCLOSE STOCKAGE SURROUND
(ELEPHANT —) KRAAL KEDDAH
CORRECT DUE FIT FIX TIC BEET BOOK EDIT JAKE JUST LEAL LEAN MARK MEND NICE OKAY SMUG TRUE AMEND CHECK CLEAN EMEND EXACT ORDER RIGHT SOUND SPILL ADJUST BETTER CHANGE DEADON INFORM PROPER PUNISH REBUKE REFORM REMEDY REPAIR REVAMP REVISE SEEMLY STRICT ADDRESS CHAPTER CHASTEN CORRIGE ELEGANT IMPROVE PERFECT PRECISE RECLAIM RECTIFY REDRESS REGULAR REPROVE RIGHTON SINCERE ACCURATE CHASTISE DEFINITE EMENDATE EQUALIZE REGULATE RIGOROUS STRAIGHT TRUTHFUL CASTIGATE
(APPROXIMATELY —) BALLPARK
(GRAMMATICALLY —) CONGRUE
(MATHEMATICALLY —) PURE
(NOT —) INEXACT
(PREF.) ORTH(O)
CORRECTABLE CORRIGIBLE
CORRECTED TRUE
(NOT —) RAW
CORRECTION YARD REFORM CENSURE FLEXURE IMPRINT REDRESS SCOURGE FUGACITY
(— IN COMPUTER PROGRAM) PATCH
CORRECTIVE SALT REMEDY
CORRECTLY JUST RIGHT ARIGHT MEETLY RIGHTLY SOUNDLY PROPERLY
CORRECTNESS TRUTH DECORUM FITNESS JUSTICE ACCURACY JUSTNESS VERACITY
CORREGIDOR, DER (CHARACTER IN —) TIO LUCAS MERCEDES FRASQUITA CORREGIDOR
(COMPOSER OF —) WOLF
CORRELATE PARALLEL HARMONIZE
CORRELATIVE OR NOR THEN EQUAL STILL EITHER MUTUAL NEITHER ANALOGUE CONJOINT REDDITIVE
CORRESPOND FIT GEE JIBE SUIT AGREE MATCH TALLY WRITE ACCORD ANSWER CONCUR SQUARE COMPORT RESPOND COINCIDE PARALLEL QUADRATE
(— IN SOUND) ASSONATE
(— TO) ENSUE
CORRESPONDENCE MAIL TALLY ANALOGY CONSENT HARMONY KEEPING LETTERS TRAFFIC FUNCTION HOMOGENY HOMOLOGY SYMMETRY SYMPATHY SIMILARITY SIMILITUDE PARALLELISM RESEMBLANCE
(— IN SOUND) RIME RHYME
(INCOMPLETE —) ASSONANCE
(OFFICIAL —) BUMF
CORRESPONDENT NEWSMAN QUADRATE RELEVANT STRINGER SUITABLE STRINGMAN
CORRESPONDING LIKE SIMILAR PARALLEL ACCORDANT CONGRUENT
(PREF.) COUNTER
CORRESPONDINGLY SORTLY SIMILARLY
CORRIDA BULLFIGHT
CORRIDOR HALL AISLE ORIEL VISTA ARCADE COULOIR GALLERY PASSAGE COULISSE HALLCIST TRESANCE
CORRIE CIRQUE
CORRIGENDUM ERROR ERRATUM
CORROBORATE PROVE SECOND APPROVE COMFORT CONFIRM SUPPORT SUSTAIN ROBORATE
CORRODE EAT BITE BURN ETCH FRET GNAW RUST DECAY ERODE EXEDE TOUCH WASTE BEGNAW CANKER IMPAIR CONSUME GRAPHITE
CORRODING BITE RODENT ESURINE
CORROSION EROSION EMBAYMENT
CORROSIVE ACID ACRID ARDENT BITING CORSIE EATING CAUSTIC EROSIVE ESURINE FRETFUL MORDANT DIERETIC
CORRUGATE GIMP CRIMP CRISP FURROW RUMPLE CRINKLE CRUMPLE WRINKLE
CORRUGATED PLAITED WRINKLY FURROWED WRINKLED
CORRUGATION BAT FOLD GILL REED RUGA CREASE PUCKER CRINKLE WRINKLE
CORRUPT BAD ILL LOW ROT WEM BENT EVIL RANK SICK SOIL VILE ADDLE BLEND BRIBE FALSE SPOIL STAIN SULLY TAINT VENAL VENOM WEMMY AUGEAN CANKER DEBASE DEFILE FESTER IMPURE INFECT PALTER POISON PUTRID RAVISH ROTTEN SEPTIC ABUSIVE ATTAINT BEDEVIL BEGRIME BESHREW CARRION CORRUMP CROOKED DEBAUCH DEFINED DEGRADE DEPRAVE ENVENOM FALSIFY IMMORAL PECCANT PERVERT POLLUTE PUTREFY SUBVERT TRADING VIOLATE VITIATE CONFOUND DECADENT DEPRAVED EMPOISON PERVERSE POLLUTED PRACTICE PRACTISE SINISTER VITIATED PERVERTED ADULTERATE CONTAMINATE PECKSNIFFIAN
CORRUPTED SICK
CORRUPTION DIRT SOIL VICE DECAY SPOIL TAINT JOBBERY PRAVITY SQUALOR ADULTERY BARRATRY INFECTION MALVERSATION PUTREFACTION
CORSAC ADIVE KARAGAN
CORSAGE WAIST BODICE BOUQUET CANEZOU
CORSAIR BUG CAPER PIRATE ROBBER CURSARO PICAROON ROCKFISH
CORSAIR, THE (CHARACTER IN —) SEID MEDORA CORRADO GULNARA
(COMPOSER OF —) VERDI
CORSELET LORICA THORAX ALLECRET HALECRET
CORSET BELT BUSK STAY STAYS GIRDLE LORICA SUPPORT
CORSICA (CAPITAL OF —) AJACCIO
(HARBOR OF —) BASTIA
(MOUNTAIN OF —) CINTO ROTONDO
(RIVER OF —) GOLO TARAVO GRAVONE
(TOWERLIKE STRUCTURES OF —) TORRI
(TOWN OF —) CALVI CORTE ALERIA BASTIA AJACCIO SARTENE
(VEGETATION OF —) MAQUIS
CORSICAN PINE LARCH
CORTEGE POMP SUITE TRAIN PARADE RETINUE
CORTEX BARK PEEL RIND MANTLE PALLIUM PERIBLEM PERIDIUM
CORUNDUM RUBY SAND EMERY ADAMAS ALUMINA ABRASIVE AMETHYST CORINDON SAPPHIRE BARKLYITE
(SYNTHETIC —) EMERALD
CORUSCATE BLAZE FLASH GLEAM SHINE GLANCE GLISTEN GLITTER RADIATE SPARKLE BRANDISH
CORVEE POLO
CORVINO (WIFE OF —) CELIA
CORYPHENE DORADO
CORYTHUS (FATHER OF —) ZEUS PARIS JUPITER
(SON OF —) DARDANUS
(WIFE OF —) ELECTRA
CORYZA COLD
COSAM (FATHER OF —) ELMODAM
COSA RARA, UNA (CHARACTER IN —) TITA LILLA CORRADO LISARGO GIOVANNI
(COMPOSER OF —) SOLER
COSCET COTTAR COTARIUS COTSETLE
COSETTE (MOTHER OF —) FANTINE
COSH SANDBAG
COSI FAN TUTTE (CHARACTER IN —) ALFONSO DESPINA FERRANDO DORABELLA GUGLIELMO FIORDILIGI
(COMPOSER OF —) MOZART

COSMETIC KOHL WASH CREAM FUCUS HENNA LINER PAINT PETER ROUGE BLANCH CERUSE CRAYON ENAMEL POMADE POWDER BLUSHER BRONZER GLEAMER MASCARA PANCAKE STIBIUM AMANDINE LIPSTICK STIBNITE
(— PREPARATION) TONER
COSMIC VAST MUNDANE ORDERLY CATHOLIC INFINITE
COSMOLABE PANTACOSM
COSMOPOLITAN URBAN ECUMENIC PANDEMIC AMPHIGEAN
COSMOS EARTH GLOBE ORDER REALM WORLD FLOWER HEAVEN HARMONY UNIVERSE
COSSACK TURK TATAR ATAMAN HETMAN TARTAR ZAPOROGUE
COSSET MUD PET LAMB CARESS CODDLE CUDDLE FONDLE PAMPER TIDDLE
COSSETTE CHIP SLICE STRIP SCHNITZEL
COST SIT GAFF LOSS PAIN SOAK BASIS PRICE SPEND STAND VALUE CHARGE DAMAGE OUTLAY SCATHE EXPENSE FREIGHT REPRISE ESTIMATE SPENDING
(LOW —) LOWBALL

COSTA RICA

CAPE: ELENA VELAS BLANCO
CAPITAL: SANJOSE
COIN: COLON CENTIMO
DANCE: PUNTO TORITO
GULF: DULCE NICOYA PAPAGAYO
INDIAN: BORUCA GUAYMI
ISLAND: COCO
LAKE: ARENAL
MEASURE: VARA CAFIZ CAHIZ FANEGA TERCIA CAJUELA CANTARO MANZANA
MOUNTAIN: BLANCO CHIRRIPO
PENINSULA: OSA NICOYA
POINT: QUEPOS CAHUITA GALONOS LLERENA
PORT: LIMON PUNTARENAS
RIVER: POAS IRAZU MATINA SIXAOLA TENORIA TARCOLES
TOWN: CANAS LIMON VESTA BORUCA NICOYA BAGACES CARTAGO GOLFITO HEREDIA LIBERIA NEGRITA ALAJUELA COLORADO GUAPILES
VOLCANO: POAS IRAZU
WEIGHT: BAG CAJA LIBRA

COSTERMONGER COSTER HAWKER NIPPER PEARLY PEDDLER BARROWMAN
COSTIVE BOUND EMPLASTIC
COSTLINESS DEARTH DEARNESS
COSTLY DEAR FINE HIGH RICH SALT PRICY DAINTY LAVISH PRICEY SILVER COSTFUL COSTLEW GORGEOUS PLATINUM PRECIOUS PRODIGAL SPLENDID PRICELESS
COSTMARY TANSY ALECOST MAUDLIN ROSEMARY
COSTREL KEG HEAD FLASK BOTTLE COYSTREL
COSTUME RIG DRAG GARB ROBE SARI SUIT BURKA DRESS GETUP HABIT SHAPE TRUSS ATTIRE DOMINO FORMAL SETOUT TOILET APPAREL BLOOMER CLOTHES POLLERA RAIMENT SCARLET UNIFORM CHARSHAF CLOTHING ENSEMBLE TOILETTE VENETIAN
(ACADEMIC —) GUISE
(JUDO —) JUDOGI
(KARATE —) GI GIE
COSTUSROOT PACHAK PUTCHOCK
COSY FEEL FEIL SNUG INTIME
COT BED HUT MAT PEN BOAT COOP COTE FOLD ABODE BOTHY CABIN COUCH COVER HOUSE STALL COTEEN CRADLE GURNEY PALLET SHEATH TANGLE CHARPAI CHARPOY COTTAGE SHELTER BEDSTEAD COTHOUSE DWELLING STRETCHER
COTERIE SET RING CABAL JUNTO MONDE CIRCLE CLIQUE GALAXY SETOUT CENACLE CIRCUIT COLLEGE PLATOON SOCIETY
COTHURNUS BOOT BUSKIN COTHURN
COTILLION GERMAN
COTINGA CHATTERER
COTO OREJON
COTTA KATHA STOLE MANTLE BLANKET SURPLICE VESTMENT
COTTAGE BOX COT HUT BACH BARI COSH CRIB SHED WALK BOTHY BOWER CABIN HOUSE HOVEL LODGE SHACK BOHAWN BOTHIE CABANA CHALET SHELTER BUNGALOW COTHOUSE SHEELING SHIELING THALTHAN
(RUSSIAN —) DACCA
COTTAGE CHEESE SKYR SMEARCASE SMIERCASE
COTTAGER MAILER
COTTER KEY MAT PIN VEX CLOT BOWPIN COTMAN FASTEN MAILER POTTER PUCKER SHRINK TOGGLE WITHER CONGEAL COTTIER PEASANT SHRIVEL VILLEIN COTARIUS COTTAGER COTTEREL ENTANGLE FORELOCK LINCHPIN
COTTON SAK BEAT DRAB FLOG MALO PIMA AGREE BAYAL BOLLY DERRY MATTA SAKEL SURAT BROACH CODDLE COMBER DHURRY FABRIC MAARAD MALLOW NANKIN PEELER STAPLE ALGODON BENDERS BOMBACE CANTOON DHURRIE GARMENT GINNING SILESIA SUCCEED
(— SQUARE) TZUT TZUTE
(BOLL OF —) SNAP
(NAPPED —) LAMBSKIN
(PAINTED —) INDIENNE
(PIECE OF —) SPONGE
(PRINTED —) CHINTZ SARONG
(RAW —) LINT BAYAL
(SILK —) FLOSS
(STOUT —) THICKSET
(STRIPED —) BENGAL
(TREE —) MACO
(TWILLED —) JEAN SALLO SALLOO
(WAD OF —) TAMPON
(WASTE —) GRABBOTS
(PREF.) BYSSI BYSSO
COTTON GRASS CANNA CANNACH DRAWLING
COTTON PLANT LAMB
(— FLOWER) SQUARE
COTTON TREEE SIMAL
COTTONWOOD ALAMO POPLAR
COTTON-WOOL BOMBAST WADDING
COTYLEDON BUTTON PICHURIM SARCOLOBE
COUCAL PHEASANT
COUCH BED COT KIP LAY LIE HIDE LAIR LURK SOFA SUNK DIVAN INLAY LODGE PRESS SKULK SLINK SNEAK SNOOP SQUAB SQUAT UTTER BURROW CLOTHE DAYBED LITTER PALLET PLINTH SETTEE CONCEAL EXPRESS HAMMOCK OTTOMAN OVERLAY RECLINE TRANSOM RECAMIER
(NUPTIAL —) THORE
(WOODEN —) RUSTBANK
(PREF.) CLIN(O) STROMATI STROMATO
(SUFF.) STROMA
COUCH GRASS CUTCH KUTCH QUACK QUICK TWICH QUITCH SCOTCH SCUTCH STROIL QUICKEN WITHVINE
COUGAR CAT PUMA PAINTER PANTHER CARCAJOU
COUGH YEX YOX BAFF BARK HACK HOST KINK CHINK CROUP HOAST HOOSE HOOZE TISICK TUSSIS
COUGH DROP PASTIL TROCHE LOZENGE PASTILLE
COUGH SYRUP LINCTUS
COULEE DRAW GORGE GULCH COOLEY RAVINE
COULOMB WEBER
COUMA SORVA HYAHYA
COUNCIL BODY BULE DAEL DIET DUMA FONO RAAD REDE YUAN BOARD BOULE BUNGA CABAL CAPUT DIVAN DIWAN DOUMA JIRGA JUNTA JUNTO SABHA SOBOR STATE SYNOD THING JIRGAH LUKIKO MAJLIS POWWOW QUORUM SENATE SOVIET TARYBA CABILDO CABINET CHAMBER CONSULT GERUSIA HUSTING MEETING PENSION WHITLEY ASSEMBLY CONCLAVE CONGRESS FOLKMOOT FOLKMOTE HEEMRAAD HEEMRAAT MINISTRY PLACITUM RIGSRAAD CAMARILLA PARLIAMENT AMPHICTYONS
(— CHAMBER) DIVAN
(MORMON —) PRESIDENCY
COUNCILLOR RAT VIZIR ENDUNA INDUNA VIZIER FAIPULE SENATOR WISEMAN DECURION
(PL.) ANZIANI
COUNSEL RAD LORE REDE RULE RUNE SILK WARD WARN AREED CHIDE DEVIL GUIDE ADVICE ADVISE CONFER LEADER ABOGADO CAUTION COUNCIL LECTURE ADMONISH ADVOCATE PRUDENCE
(JUNIOR LEGAL —) DEVIL
(KING'S —) SILK
(SACRED —) TORAH
COUNSELOR RAT SAGE WITE CONSUL LAWYER MENTOR NESTOR ADVISER ADVISOR COUNSEL ECHEVIN GONZALO PROCTOR STARETS ADVOCATE ATTORNEY REDESMAN UCALEGON
COUNT ADD GAN SUM TOT BANK CAST EARL FOOT GANO GRAF NAME RELY RIME SIZE TALE TELL TOTE COMES COMPT COMTE GRAVE JUDGE RHYME SCORE TALLY WEIGH CENSUS CONSUL COUNTY DEPEND ESTEEM FIGURE IMPUTE MATTER NUMBER RECKON TOTTLE ACCOUNT ARTICLE ASCRIBE COMPUTE GANELON ADNUMBER NUMERATE SANCTION CALCULATE PALSGRAVE
(— IN BILLIARDS) DOUBLE
(— OF A FIBER) GRIST
(— OF SHEEP OR CATTLE) BREAK
(— ON) LITE RELY
(— UNIT) WARP
COUNTABLE DISCRETE
COUNTE COMTE
COUNTENANCE AID MUG OWN RUD ABET BROW FACE GIZZ LEER MIEN PUSS SHOW VULT CHEER FAVOR FRONT GRACE ASPECT ENDURE UPHOLD VISAGE APPROVE BEARING CONDUCT ENDORSE FEATURE PROFFER SUPPORT BEFRIEND DEMEANOR FOREHEAD SANCTION SEMBLANCE
(PREF.) PROSOP(O)
COUNTER BAR DIB LOT BANK BUCK CENT CHIP DESK DUMP EDDY FISH JACK KIST PAWN STOP CAROM CHECK FORCE HATCH JETON MERIL PIECE SHELF STALL STAND TABLE TOTER BUFFET COMBAT GEIGER ISLAND JETTON MARKER OPPOSE SQUAIL ADVERSE BUTTOCK CONTEND CURRENT FANTAIL SHAMBLE CONTRARY MAHOGANY OPPOSITE TELLTALE
(— TO) AGAINST
(LEADEN —) DUMP
(LUNCH —) PLACE
(PREF.) ANTI GAIN
COUNTERACT CHECK CANCEL OPPOSE RESIST THWART BALANCE CORRECT DESTROY NULLIFY ANTIDOTE NEGATIVE
COUNTERACTION DEADLOCK
COUNTERACTIVE REMEDY ADVERSE
COUNTERBALANCE COVER WEIGH CANCEL SETOFF BALANCE
COUNTERCLOCKWISE DIRECT DIRECTLY
COUNTERCURRENT BACKSET
COUNTEREARTH ANTICHTHON
COUNTERFEIT ACT BASE COIN COPY DAUB DUFF FAKE IDOL MOCK SHAM BELIE BOGUS DUMMY FALSE FEIGN FLASH FORGE FUDGE GAMMY MIMIC PHONY QUEER SNIDE AFFECT ASSUME CHEMIC ERSATZ FORGED PSEUDO TINSEL BASTARD CHEMICK DUFFING FALSIFY FASHION FEIGNED FORGERY

IMITANT IMITATE SIMULAR BORROWED DEFORMED PHANTASM POSTICHE POSTIQUE RESEMBLE SIMILIZE SIMULATE SPURIOUS SUPPOSED BRUMMAGEM
(PREF.) PSEUD(O)
COUNTERFEITER COINER JACKMAN JARKMAN SCRATCHER
COUNTERFEITERS (AUTHOR OF —) GIDE
(CHARACTER IN —) LAURA VEDEL ARMAND GEORGE ROBERT BERNARD EDOUARD LILLIAN OLIVIER VINCENT DOUVIERS GRIFFITH MOLINIER PASSAVANT GHERIDANISOL PROFITENDIEU
COUNTERFEITING COINING FICTION POSTICHE POSTIQUE
COUNTERFOIL FOIL STUB CHECK
COUNTERFORT SCONCE BUTTRESS
COUNTERION GEGENION
COUNTERIRRITANT MOXA GINGER IODINE PEPPER MUSTARD CANTHARIS
COUNTERMAND STOP ANNUL CANCEL FORBID RECALL REVOKE ABOLISH RESCIND REVERSE UNORDER ABROGATE PROHIBIT
COUNTERMOVE DEMARCHE
COUNTERMOVEMENT BACKFIRE
COUNTERPANE PANE QUILT LIGGER BEDSPREAD
COUNTERPART COPY LIKE MATE SPIT TWIN FETCH IMAGE MATCH MORAL SHELL TALLY COUSIN DOUBLE SHADOW BALANCE COUNTER OBVERSE PENDANT SIMILAR ANTIPART PARALLEL RESCRIPT SIMILITUDE
(SPEECH —) A
COUNTERPOINT FOIL DESCANT CONTRAST FABURDEN
COUNTERPOISE POISE OFFSET BALANCE EQUALIZE MAKEWEIGHT
COUNTERPOISON ORVIETAN
COUNTERSIGN BACK MARK SEAL SIGN SIGNAL CONFIRM ENDORSE PASSWORD SANCTION
COUNTERSINK DISH REAM BEVEL CHAMFER
COUNTERSTATEMENT ANSWER
COUNTERSUN ANTHELION
COUNTER-TENOR ALTO
COUNTERTENOR ALTO
COUNTERWEIGHT TARE MAKEWEIGHT
COUNTERWORD ANIMAL COUNTER
COUNTESS OLIVIA COMTESSE CONTESSA
COUNTING ACCOUNT
COUNTLESS INFINITE NUMBERLESS
(PREF.) MYRI(A)(O)
COUNT OF MONTE CRISTO
(AUTHOR OF —) DUMAS
(CHARACTER IN —) FARIA ALBERT DANTES EDMOND HAIDEE MONDEGO MORRELL DANGLARS MERCEDES FERDINAND VALENTINE VILLEFORT CADEROUSSE MAXIMILIAN
COUNTRIFIED JAY RURAL BUCOLIC LOBBISH AGRESTIC CORNPONE HOBNAILED
COUNTRY SOD DESH EARD HICK HOME KITH LAND PAIS SOIL ADDLE CLIME EARTH FAIRY FRITH MARCH PLAGE REALM STATE TRACT WEALD GROUND KINTRA KINTRY NATION PEOPLE REGION STICKS UPLAND IMAMATE KWINTRA MONKERY MUFASAL BACKVELD DISTRICT DOMINION ELDORADO LANDWARD MAGAZINE MOFUSSIL REGALITY PRINCIPALITY
(— DANCE) CLOG
(— OF ETHIOPIA) SEBA
(— OF ORIGIN) HOMELAND
(— OF PERFECTION) EUTOPIA
(— ON SEA) SEABOARD
(— STYLE) PAYSANNE
(ANCIENT —) ARAM
(BIBLICAL —) SHEBA
(CABIN —) LOBBY
(FRONTIER —) BORDER
(HOME —) BLIGHTY
(IMAGINARY —) EREWHON LILLIPUT RURITANIA
(LIMESTONE —) KARST
(MARITIME —) MAREMMA
(MYTHICAL —) UTOPIA LEONNOYS SVITHIOD SWITHIOD TEUTONIA
(OPEN —) BLED VELD FIELD VELDT WEALD CAMPAIGN
(PETTY —) TOPARCHY
(ROUGH —) STICKS BOONIES BOONDOCK BUNDOCKS BOONDOCKS
(RURAL —) OUTBACK
(PREF.) RURI
(SUFF.) STAN
COUNTRYMAN HOB BOOR HIND KERN TIKE CHURL CLOWN HODGE KERNE SWAIN YOKEL GAFFER GIBARO JIBARO GRANGER HAYSEED LANDMAN PAESANO PAISANO PEASANT PLOWMAN LANDSMAN
(PL.) KITH
COUNTRY-ROCK METAL
COUNTRY-SEAT CHATEAU
COUNTRYSIDE BLED BOCAGE MOFUSSIL
COUNTRY WIFE (AUTHOR OF —) WYCHERLEY
(CHARACTER IN —) HORNER ALITHEA HARCOURT SPARKISH PINCHWIFE
COUNTY AMT LAN SEAT FYLKE SHIRE DOMAIN PARISH BOROUGH COMITAT NORFOLK DISTRICT
COUP BUY BLOW DEAL PLAN PLAY COUPE FAULT SCOOP UPSET ATTACK BARTER PUTSCH REFAIT STRIKE STROKE CAPSIZE TRAFFIC OVERTURN
COUP DE POING BOUCHER HANDSTONE
COUPE CUT CABRIOLET LANDAULET
COUPED HUMETTY HUMETTEE
COUPLE DUO TIE TWO BOND CASE DYAD JOIN LINK MATE PAIR SPAN TEAM TWIN YOKE BRACE LEASH MARRY TWAIN UNITE GEMINI SPLINE SWINGE BRACKET CONNECT COUPLER COUPLET DOUBLET SHACKLE TWOSOME VOLTAIC ACCOUPLE ASSEMBLE COPULATE ACCOMPANY
(— OF HAWKS) CAST
(ROMANTIC —) ITEM
COUPLED GEMEL YOKED JOINED WEDDED GEMELED COPULATE GEMINATE
COUPLER LINK RING BOBBER COPULA JANNEY LINKER SUTURE UNITER DRAGBAR DRAWBAR REDUCER SHACKLE SNAPPER TIRASSE DRAGBOLT DRAWBOLT DRAWGEAR SHACKLER
COUPLET BAIT COPLA ELEGIAC
COUPLING HUB HICKY UNION CLUTCH HICKEY NIPPLE SHACKLE SHACKLER
COUPON TWOFER VOUCHER
COURAGE BIEL FIRE GRIT GUTS MIND MOOD PROW SAND SOUL BIELD CREST HEART HONOR MOXIE NERVE PLUCK SPUNK VALOR DARING DAUBER METTLE PECKER SPIRIT VIRTUE VIRTUS BRAVERY COJONES CORAGIO HEROISM MANHEAD MANHOOD MANSHIP PROWESS STOMACH VENTURE AUDACITY BOLDNESS CORRAGIO FIRMNESS TENACITY
(— OF CONVICTION) STAMINA
(MORAL —) STRENGTH
(PREF.) THYM(O)
(SUFF.) THYMIA
COURAGEOUS BOLD GAME GOOD TALL BRAVE GUTSY HARDY LUSTY MANLY STOUT WIGHT DARING GRITTY HEROIC MANFUL PLUCKY SPUNKY CORIAUS GALLANT SPARTAN STAUNCH VALIANT FEARLESS GENEROUS INTREPID VALOROUS
COURAGEOUSLY BIG BRAVELY
COURANT ROMP CAPER DANCE LETTER CORANTO CURRENT GAZETTE RUNNING
COURBARIL JATOBA LOCUST GUAPINOL CUAPINOLE
COURGETTE ZUCCHINI
COURIER NEWS POST GUIDE SCOUT KAVASS NEWING POSTER ESTAFET ORDERLY PATAMAR POSTBOY POSTMAN SOILAGE CICERONE CURSITOR DRAGOMAN HORSEMAN ORDINARY PATTAMAR
COURLAN LIMPKIN
COURONNE CROWN
COURSE FLY LAP RUN WAY BEAT BENT FLOW GAGE GAME GANG GATE HEAT HUNT LANE LINE LODE MESS MODE PACE PATH RACE RACK RAIK RAND RILL RING RINK ROAD ROTA ROTE WENT CLASS COURS CRUST CURRY CURVE CYCLE DRAFT DRIFT DRIVE EMBER GAUGE GREAT LAPSE LAYER LEDGE MARCH MOYEN ORBIT PLATE POINT ROUTE SENSE SITHE SPACE STEPS SWELT SWING TENOR TRACK TRACT TRADE TRAIL TREND WEENT ARTERY CAREER COPING CURSUS DROMOS FURROW GALLOP GIRDER GUTTER HONORS MANNER METHOD MOTION RESACA SCHOOL SERIES SPHERE STREAM STREET SYSTEM TRIPOS ZODIAC AZIMUTH BEELINE CHANNEL CIRCUIT CONDUCT DIAULOS DRAUGHT HIGHWAY LECTURE PASSADE PASSAGE PATHWAY PROCESS ROUTINE RUNNING SEMINAR SERVICE STRETCH SUBJECT SUCCESS TIDEWAY TRAJECT TRUNDLE CURRENCY CURRICLE DIADROME DISTANCE ELECTIVE PROGRESS RECOURSE SEQUENCE STEERAGE TENDENCY MOTORDROME
(— OF ACTION) LARK TACK TROD VEIN DANCE CUSTOM ROUTINE DEMARCHE
(— OF ACTIVITY) SIDELINE
(— OF A ROPE) LEAD
(— OF BOAT) LEG
(— OF BRICK) BED ROWLOCK SCINTLE CREASING
(— OF FEEDING) DIET
(— OF KNITTING) BOUT
(— OF LIFE) GOINGS PILGRIMAGE
(— OF LIGHTNING) STREAK
(— OF LUCK) FORTUNE
(— OF MASONRY) BAHUT STILT COPING HEADING SKEWBACK
(— OF NATURE) TAO
(— OF PROCEDURE) RULE
(— OF PROCEEDING) FORE
(— OF PURSUIT) SCENT
(— OF ROADBED) SUBCRUST
(— OF STONES) BED PLINTH
(— OF STUDY) DEBATE COLLEGE LECTURE SEMINAR ELECTIVE
(— OF SUN) JOURNEY
(— OF TREATMENT) CURE
(— OF WALL) CORNICE
(— WITH GREYHOUNDS) GREW
(BELL-RINGING —) HUNT
(CIRCULAR —) SWEEP CHUKKAR CHUKKER COMPASS
(COLLEGE —) PRECEPTORIAL
(CURVING —) SWING
(CUSTOMARY —) GUISE
(DOWNWARD —) DIP DECLINE TOBOGGAN
(DUE —) TRAIN
(EASY —) PIPE
(EASY COLLEGE —) GUT
(EXACT —) BEAM
(FIRST —) ANTEPAST
(FIXED —) RUT
(FREE —) FORTH
(HONEST —) UPANDUP
(IRREGULAR —) ERROR
(LAST —) VOID
(MIDDLE —) MIDS TEMPER
(NATURAL —) RITA
(NORMAL —) WAY
(OBLIQUE —) SKEW
(OFF —) ASTRAY
(OVERHANGING —) JET
(PREDETERMINED —) DESTINY
(RACING —) RINK
(REGULAR —) ORBIT ROUTINE
(ROUNDABOUT —) DETOUR WINDLASS

(SETTLED —) BIAS GROOVE
(SKIING —) SCHUSS
(ZIGZAG —) TACK
(PREF.) DROM(O)
COURSER HORSE RACER STEED CUSSER CHARGER
COURSING CURSIVE
COURT BAR BID HOF SEE SUE WOO AREA BAIL BODY CLAW FUSS GATE GIRL LEET QUAD ROTA SEAT SEEK SUIT TOWN WALE WARD WYND YARD ARENA BENCH BUREO CURIA CURRY DAIRI DIVAN FAVOR FORUM FUERO GARTH JUDGE PATIO SHIRE SPACE SPARK SPOON SWEET TEMPT THING THINK TOURN TRAIN YAMEN ADALAT ALLURE ATRIUM BAILEY COUNTY DARGAH DURBAR DURGAH GEMOTE HOMAGE INVITE PALACE PARVIS PURSUE SPLUNT SUITOR TOLSEY ADAWLUT ADDRESS ASSIZES ATTRACT BARMOTE DUOVIRI EPHETAE FOREIGN HELIAEA HUSTING JUSTICE PARVISE RETINUE SOLICIT TEMENOS TOURNEL AUDIENCE BURHMOOT CHANCERY FOUJDARY LAWCOURT MARKMOOT MARKMOTE QUARANTY SERENADE SESSIONS SWANMOTE TRIBUNAL WOODMOTE PERIBOLOS PARLIAMENT
(— FAVOR) FAWN
(— OF A HUNDRED) MALL MALLUM MALLUS
(— OF CIRCUIT JUDGES) EYRE
(— OF FORTRESS) PEEL
(— OF MIKADO) DAIRI
(— ORDER) VACATUR
(— THE GREAT) LEVEE
(ECCLESIASTICAL —) ROTA CURIA SYNOD COLLOQUY AUDIENCIA
(EXERCISE —) EPHEBEUM
(FORTIFIED —) BAWN
(GERMAN —) FEHM VEHM
(INNER —) PATIO
(MUSLIM —) DIVAN DIWAN
(REFORMED —) CLASIS
(SMALL —) WIND WYND CORTILE
(SUPREME —) SUDDER
(TAKE TO —) SUE
(TURKISH —) GATE
COURTEOUS FAIR HEND BUXOM CIVIL GENTY SUAVE BONAIR GENTLE POLITE SMOOTH URBANE AFFABLE CORDIAL GALLANT GENTEEL GENTILE REFINED DEBONAIR FAMILIAR GRACIOUS OBLIGING
COURTEOUSLY FAIR FAIRLY GENTLY KINDLY AFFABLY
COURTEOUSNESS COMITY
COURTESAN MADAM QUAIL THAIS WHORE COURTY GEISHA LALAGE MADAME PLOVER AMOROSA ASPASIA CANIDIA DELILAH LORETTE PUCELLE DEVADASI
(PL.) DEMIMONDE
COURTESY MENSK COMITY EXTENT GENTRY MANSHIP TASHRIF BREEDING CALIDORE CORTEISE ELEGANCE GENTRICE GRATUITY URBANITY
(PL.) HONORS
COURTHOUSE CUTCHERY KACHAHRI
COURTIER CURAN OSRIC WOOER OSRICK COURTER IACHIMO COURTMAN DAMOCLES POLONIUS
COURTING SUING SPLUNT
COURTLY HEND AULIC CIVIL HENDE POLITE AULICAL ELEGANT REFINED STATELY POLISHED DIGNIFIED
COURT-NOUE RONCET
COURTSHIP SUIT AMOUR DRURY SPARKING
COURTYARD AREA WYND CLOSE CURIA PATIO ATRIUM TRANCE BALLIUM CORTILE TETRAGON CURTILAGE
COUSIN COZ KIN AKIN HERO ALLIED NEPHEW
COUSIN BETTE (AUTHOR OF —) BALZAC
(CHARACTER IN —) HULOT AGATHE CREVEL MONTES ADELINE LISBETH HORTENSE MARNEFFE VICTORIN CELESTINE STEINBOCK
COUSINRY KITH
COVE CO BAY DEN CAVE CHAP FILE GILL HOLE NOOK PASS SUMP BASIN BAYOU BIGHT CREEK INLET ARMLET COVING FELLOW HOLLOW RECESS VALLEY MOLDING CALANQUE GUNKHOLE
COVENANT BIND BOND BRIS MISE PACT TRUE AGREE BERIT BRITH TOUCH ACCORD BERITH CARTEL COMART CONAND ENGAGE INDENT LEAGUE PATISE PLEDGE TREATY BARGAIN COMPACT CONCORD PROMISE ALLIANCE CONTRACT DOCUMENT HANDFAST TREATISE
COVENANTER HILLMAN TRUEBLUE
COVER DO CAP COT HAP LAP LAY LID NAP TOP TUP WRY BIND CEIL CLAD COAT COOM CURE DAUB DECK FACE FADE FALL FURL GARB GATE HEAD HEAL HEEL HIDE HILL HOOD LATH LEAD LEAP LINE MASK PAVE ROOF SILE SPAN TELD TICK TIDE TILT VEIL WRAP APRON BATHE BOARD CLOAK CLOUT COPSE CROWN DRAPE DRESS FENCE FLESH FLOOD GUISE HATCH KIVER MOUNT RECTO SCARF SERVE SHADE STREW STUDY THEAK THEEK TOWEL TREAD VERSO WELME WHALM AWNING BATTER BINDER BLAZON CANOPY CHALON CLOTHE DOUBLE EARLAP ENAMEL ENCASE ENFOLD ENROBE ENTIRE ENVEIL FOLDER HACKLE IMMASK INVEST JACKET KIRTLE MANTLE OVERGO POTLID RUNNER SCONCE SCREEN SHADOW SHEATH SHIELD SLEEVE SPREAD SPRING SWATHE TOILET TOPPER WHAUVE APPAREL ASPHALT BANDAGE BESTREW BLANKET CAPSULE CONCEAL CONTECT COUVERT ELYTRON EMBRACE ENCRUST FASCINE HEADCAP HOUSING INCRUST KNEECAP MANHEAD OBSCURE OMNIBUS OVERLAY PRETEXT SHEATHE SHELTER SHUTTER TAMPION THIMBLE BEDCOVER COMPRISE COVERCLE DEBRUISE ENCLOTHE ENSCONCE HOODWINK IMMANTLE OVERHAIL OVERSILE OVERWEND PALLIATE PRETENCE PRETENSE SLIPOVER SURPOOSE
(— A FIRE) BANK DAMP
(— AROUND FLOWER) CYMBA
(— BRICKS) SCOVE
(— BY EXCUSES) ALIBI PALLIATE
(— DISPERSEDLY) STREW
(— FOR ALEMBIC) HEAD
(— FOR CHAIR BACK) TIDY
(— FOR CHALICE) PALL
(— FOR DIAPER) SOAKER
(— FOR ENGINE) COWLING
(— FOR FOOD) BELL
(— FOR GUN) TAMPION
(— FOR MILITARY CAP) HAVELOCK
(— FOR PISTON) FOLLOWER
(— FOR POWDER PAN) HAMMER
(— FOR REAL PURPOSE) STALE
(— FOR WIRES) BOOTLEG
(— GROUND) HEAT
(— HEARTH) FETTLE
(— OF BALL) CARCASS
(— OF BOILER) VOMIT
(— OF COFFIN) COOM
(— OF HAWSEHOLE) BUCKLER
(— OF MATTRESS) TICK TICKING
(— OF MINE CAGE) BONNET
(— OF RIFLE MAGAZINE) GATE
(— OF SPORANGIUM) EPIGONE
(— OF VEGETATION) GROWTH
(— OPPRESSIVELY) SMOTHER
(— OVER) RAKE WELME WHELM QUELME SHEUGH BECLOUD OVERDECK WITHHELE OVERWHELM
(— PLANTS) BAG
(— PROTECTIVELY) SHROUD SHEATHE
(— ROAD) BLIND
(— SOIL WITH CLAY) GAULT
(— UP) HAP BELY FOLD BELIE SALVE SLEEK HUDDLE
(— WITH ASHES) SOIL
(— WITH BACON) BARD
(— WITH BOMBS) SATURATE
(— WITH CLAY) CLOAM
(— WITH COWL) MOB
(— WITH CRUMBS) BREAD
(— WITH DOTS) CRIBBLE
(— WITH DROPS) DAG
(— WITH EARTH) BURY HEAL INTER
(— WITH FILM) SKIM
(— WITH FLESH) INCARN
(— WITH FOAM) EMBOSS
(— WITH GOLD) GILD
(— WITH MEAL) MELVIE
(— WITH MUD) BEMUD BELUTE
(— WITH OAKUM) FOTHER
(— WITH PITCH) PAY
(— WITH PLASTER) PARGET
(— WITH SHEATH) GLOVE
(— WITH SOLDER) SPLASH
(— WITH STONE) ASHLAR
(— WITH STRAW) THATCH
(— WITH TIN) BLANCH
(— WITH TOPSOIL) KELLY
(— WITH WATER) DOUSE DOWSE FLOOD WHELM OVERFLOW
(— WITH WAX) CERE
(— WITH WEAVING) GRAFT
(— WITH WINGS) BROOD
(BED —S) HEALING
(BEEHIVE —) QUILT
(BOOK —) CASE SIDE
(CANVAS —) TARP TARPAULIN
(GLASS —) STRIKE
(KIND OF —) MAIL
(PACK —) MANTA
(PILLOW —) CASE SHAM
(POSTAL —) ENTIRE
(POT —) BRED
(RAIN —) TARP
(SADDLE —) PILCH HOUSING
(SEED —) TESTA
(SLIDING —) BRIDGE
(TABLE —) BAIZE DUCHESSE
(WING — OF BEETLE) SHARD
(PREF.) OPERCULI
COVERAGE PROTECTION
COVERALL GOWN JUMPER
COVERED CLAD FULL SHOD TECT BLIND MOSSY CLOSED COVERT HIDDEN ENCASED OBTECTED SCREENED
(— WITH CRYSTALS) DRUSY
(— WITH FEATHERS) HIRSUTE
(— WITH FOREST) HYLEAN
(— WITH HAIRS) COMATE VILLOUS
(— WITH PROTUBERANCES) HUMPY
(— WITH SCALES) SCUTATE
(— WITH SEAWEED) TANGLY
(— WITH WHITE DUST) PRUINOSE
(THINLY —) BARISH
(PREF.) CALYPT(O) CRYPT(O) KRYPT(O)
COVERED WAGON WHITETOP BUCKWAGON
COVERER DECKER
COVERING (ALSO SEE COVER) BOX COT FUR HAP KEX LAG ARIL BARB BARK BOOT CASE CAUL COAT CUFF DECK FILM HAME HEAD HOOD HULL HUSK KELL MASK OVER PALL PUFF ROBE ROOF SLIP SPAT TARP TILE TILT TRAP VEIL APRON ARMOR BRAID BURSE CRUST DRESS GLOBE GLOVE HATCH QUILT SCALE SHELL SKIRT STALL SWARD TESTA TUNIC TWEEL WREIL ARMING ATTIRE AWNING BANCAL BANKER CANOPY CANVAS COVERT DRAPET EMBRYO ENAMEL FACING FENDER GAITER GANOIN HACKLE HATCAP HELMET JACKET MUZZLE PELAGE SADDLE SCREEN SHEATH SHROUD SINDON TEGMEN VERNIX BLANKET BUFFONT CAMISIA CAPPING CAPSULE CEILING COATING COWLING EARFLAP ENVELOP EXCIPLE GRATING HAPPING HEALING HEELCAP HOUSING MUFFLER OVERLAY PURPORT SARPLER SHADING SHELTER SHOEING SLIPPER TECTURE TEGMENT VESTURE WRAPPER ARMGUARD BLAZONRY BOARDING CASEMENT CLEADING CLOTHING COMPRESS COVERLET EGGSHELL

EPISPORE INDUMENT INDUSIUM MANTELET MANTLING OVERCAST PAVILION PERICARP SETATION UMBRELLA TECTORIAL PILLOWCASE
(— FOR ANTENNA) RADOME
(— FOR BENCH) BANKER
(— FOR BOXERS' HANDS) CESTUS
(— FOR CHEST) STOMACHER
(— FOR EGG) COSY
(— FOR FOREHEAD) BONGRACE
(— FOR NECK) TUCKER PARTLET
(— FOR ROOF APEX) EPI
(— FOR SHOULDERS) STOLE
(— FOR SKI) SKIN
(— FOR STIRRUP) HOOD
(— FOR TEAPOT) COSY COZY
(— OF BED) TIKE
(— OF BELL ROPE) GRIP
(— OF BIRD) INDUMENT
(— OF BOW HANDLE) ARMING
(— OF CASH SHORTAGE) LAPPING
(— OF EYEBALL) CORNEA
(— OF FEATHERS) DOWN
(— OF GILLS) OPERCULUM
(— OF MUMMY) CARTONAGE CARTONNAGE
(— OF NUTMEG) MACE
(— OF PIE) CRUST
(— OF ROOT) CALYPTRA
(— OF ROPE) SERVICE
(— OF VEGETATION) FLEECE
(— OVER DRESS) PINAFORE
(—S FOR NIPPLES) PASTIES
(— WITH IRON) ACIERAGE
(CAST —S) EXUVIAE
(CHIMNEY —) COWL
(CLOTH —) TOILET
(COARSE —) CADDOW TILLET
(DEFENSIVE —) ARMOR KICKER
(EAR —) EARLAP EARFLAP EARMUFF OREILET
(EYE —S) GOGGLES
(FLOOR —) RUG TILE CRASH CARPET LINOLEUM OILCLOTH
(FOUL —) SCUM
(HEAD —) CAP HAT WIG HAIR HIVE HOOD CURCH BONNET HELMET BIRETTA CHAPEAU CHAPERON HAVELOCK HEADRAIL TROTCOZY
(LEATHER —) GAMBADO
(LEG —) BOOT HOSE STOCK GAITER LEGGIN PEDULE KNEELET LEGGING STOCKING
(LIGHT —) GRIMING
(LINEN —) BARB
(OUTER —) BARK HIDE HULL HUSK CRUST TESTA JACKET CARAPACE
(PLANT —) PERIDERM
(PROTECTIVE —) APRON ARMOR SHELL COCOON
(SADDLE —) MOCHILA
(SEED —) PERIGONE
(SHELF —) OILCLOTH
(SLIGHT —) CYMAR
(SOFT —) DOWN
(STAGE —) HEAVENS
(STERILE —) DRAPE
(STICKY DAMP —) GLET
(THIN —) FILM SCRUFF WASHING
(PREF.) CALYPT(O) COLE STEG(O) STRATI STRATO
(SUFF.) DERM(A)(ATOUS)(IA)(IS)(Y)
(— OF PLATE) STEGE

COVERLET PANE HELER HOUSE QUILT REZAI THROW AFGHAN CADDOW CHALON COLCHA LIGGER SPREAD BLANKET BUFFALO COVERLID DAGSWAIN
COVER-SHAME SAVIN SAVINE
COVERT DEN LAY LIE SLY LAIR VERT EARTH NICHE PRIVY ASYLUM HARBOR HIDDEN LATENT MASKED MYSTIC REFUGE SECRET COVERED DEFENSE PRIVATE SHELTER TECTRIX THICKET DISGUISE INVOLVED
(PL.) CRISSUM
COVERTLY CLOSE CLOSELY
COVET ACHE ENVY PANT WANT WISH CRAVE YEARN YISSE DESIRE GRUDGE HANKER
COVETOUS AVID GAIR GARE EAGER FRUGAL GREEDY SORDID STINGY ENVIOUS GRIPPLE MISERLY DESIROUS GRASPING
COVETOUSNESS GREED MISERY AVARICE YISSING COVETISE CUPIDITY PLEONEXIA
COVEY BEVY FALL BROOD FLOCK HATCH COVERT COMPANY
COVIN BAND CREW FRAUD COVINE COMPANY CONVENE ASSEMBLY TRICKERY
COW AWE KEY NOT BEEF BOGY BOSS COWL CUSH FAZE MOIL MULL NOTT ROAN RUNT VACA ABASH ALARM BEEVE BOSSY BROCK BULLY CUSHA DAUNT DOMPT DRAPE MOGGY QUAIL SCARE SNOOL VACHA BOVINE BULLER COLLOP CRUMMY GOBLIN HAWKEY HAWKIE HEIFER MAILIE MILKER MULLEY ROTHER SUBDUE BOARDER BUGBEAR BULLOCK CRITTER CRUMMIE DEPRESS MESTENO MILCHER OVERTOP SQUELCH TERRIFY ALDERNEY AUDHUMLA BROWBEAT COWBRUTE DISPIRIT FRIGHTEN STRIPPER THREATEN
(— ABOUT 3 FEET HIGH) GYNEE
(— BEFORE CALVING) SPRINGER
(BAD-TEMPERED —) RAGER
(BARREN —) DRAPE BARRENER
(DRY —) KEY SEW
(HORNLESS —) NOT MOIL NOTT DODDY MULEY DODDIE HUMLIE MAILIE HUMBLIE POLLARD MOULLEEN
(NOTED —) ELSIE
(PART OF —) HIP JAW RIB CROP HOCK HOOF HORN KNEE LOIN NECK POLL RUMP TAIL TEAT CHEST CHINE FLANK GIRTH PLATE THIGH THURL UDDER BARREL BRIDGE DEWLAP MUZZLE SWITCH THROAT BRISKET DEWCLAW PASTERN PINBONE WITHERS FOREHEAD
(PREGNANT —) CALVER INCALVER
(WHITE-FACED —) HAWKEY HAWKIE
(YOUNG —) QUEY STIRK HEIFER
(PL.) KYE KINE DAIRY
(PREF.) VACCI(NI)(NO)

COWARD COW CUR COOF DAFF FUNK FUGIE LACHE PIKER CRAVEN FUNKER PIGEON BUZZARD CAITIFF CHICKEN COUCHER DASTARD MEACOCK NITHING PANURGE QUITTER NIDERING POLTROON RECREANT TURNBACK TURNTAIL VILLIAGO
COWARDICE DASTARDY LASHNESS POLTROONERY
COWARDLINESS PUSILLANIMITY
COWARDLY SHY ARGH FAINT LACHE TIMID AFRAID COWARD COWISH CRAVEN TURPID YELLOW CAITIFF CHICKEN GUTLESS HILDING MEACOCK FACELESS NIDERING POLTROON RECREANT SNEAKING POLTROONISH PIGEONHEARTED
COW BARN BYRE SAUR BARTH SHIPPON VACCARY
COWBIRD BECCO BUNTING CUCKOLD OXBITER COKEWOLD LAZYBIRD
COWBOY HAZER RIDER ROPER SCREW WADDY CHARRO GAUCHO GINETE HERDER JINETE WADDIE COWHAND COWHERD COWPOKE GRAZIER HERDBOY LLANERO PANIOLO PUNCHER REFUGEE VAQUERO BUCKAROO DALLYMAN JACKAROO NEATHERD NOWTHERD OUTRIDER PASTORAL RANCHERO SWINGMAN WRANGLER
COWCATCHER GUARD LASSO PILOT FENDER
COWED HANGDOG DOWNCAST
COWER HUG COUR FAWN RUCK HOVER QUAIL SHRUG SNOOL SQUAT STOOP TOADY WINCE COORIE CRINGE CROUCH HURKLE SHRINK CROODLE CRUDDLE
COWFISH TORO BECCO CUCKOLD MANATEE SIRENIA
COWHAGE KIWACH
COWHAND PEELER FLANKER STOCKMAN
COWHERB COCKLE SOAPWORT
COWHERD HERDSMAN NEATHERD
COWHOUSE BYRE SHIPPEN SHIPPON
COWL CAP COW LID SOE TUB COUL HOOD MONK MITER BONNET CUCULE CAPUCHE SCUTTLE CAPUCHIN
COW PARSNIP MADNEP CADWEED HOGWEED PIGWEED BEARWORT BUNDWEED
COWPEA SITAO FRIJOL FRIJOLE TOWCOCK BLACKEYE BLACKPEA
COWPEN CUPPEN CUPPIN
COW PILOT PINTANO
COWPOX PAPPOX KINEPOX VACCINA VACCINIA
COWRIE COWRY VENUS ZIMBI CYPRAEID
COWSHED STALL
COWSLIP PAIGLE PRIMULA SHOOTER AURICULA CYCLAMEN MARIGOLD PRIMROSE
COXA HIP HAUNCH
COXCOMB FOP NOB BUCK DUDE FOOL PRIG TOFF CLEAT DANDY HINGE PRINCOX POPINJAY PRINCOCK
COXCOMBRY FOPPERY
COXSWAIN PATROON
COY PAL SHY ARCH COAX NICE ALOOF CHARY DECOY QUIET SQUAB STILL ALLURE CARESS DEMURE MODEST PROPER SKEIGH BASHFUL DISTANT PEEVISH STRANGE RESERVED SKITTISH VERECUND KITTENISH
COYNESS SHYNESS
COYO CHININ
COYOL COROJO COROZO
COYOTE VARMINT
(— STATE) SOUTHDAKOTA
COYPU DEGU NUTRIA
COZBI (FATHER OF —) ZUR
COZEN COG CON BILK FOOL GULL POOP CHEAT TRICK CHISEL GREASE BEGUILE DECEIVE DEFRAUD SWINDLE HOODWINK
COZENER SNAP SNECKDRAW
COZENING SIMILATE
COZIER CADGER CODGER COSIER
COZY RUG BEIN BIEN COSY EASY HOMY SAFE SNUG BIELD CANNY COMFY CUSHY HOMEY CHATTY PENTIT SECURE TOASTY COVERING FAMILIAR HOMELIKE SOCIABLE
CPU CHIP
CRAB GIN UCA BOCO JUEY MAJA ZOEA ANGER ARROW AYUYU BLUEY MAIAN MAIID MAJID RACER SANDY THIEF WINCH BUSTER CANCER GROUCH GROUSE HARPER HERMIT KABURI NIPPER PARTAN PEELER PUNGAR PUNGER RACING SCRAWL SPRITE BUCKLER BUCKLUM BURSTER CABOUCA CANCRID DECAPOD FIDDLER GRUMBLE INACHID OCYPODE PANFISH POLYPOD SHEDDER SOLDIER SPECTER SPECTRE SURIQUE ARACHNID CRABFISH DORIPPID GRAPSOID HORSEMAN IRRITATE LIMULOID LITHODID OCHIDORE OXYSTOME PAGURIAN PORTUNID RANINIAN TRAVELER WINDLASS BRACHYURA
(KIND OF —) SNOW PURSE
(MATING —) DOUBLER
(PREF.) CANCERI CANCERO CANCRI CARCIN(I)(O)
CRAB APPLE CRAB SCRAB SCROG COLING
CRABBED SOUR UGLY CABBY CRANK CROSS SURLY TESTY BITTER COPPED CROOSE CROUSE CRUSTY MOROSE RUGGED SULLEN TEETHY TRYING BOORISH CANKERY CRABBIT CRAMPED CRONISH CROOKED FRABBIT GNARLED KNOTTED OBSCURE PEEVISH CANKERED CHURLISH CONTRARY CRABBISH LIVERISH PETULANT VINEGARY
CRABBEDNESS ACRIMONY ASPERITY
CRABCATCHER CRABIER
CRABER VOLE AGOUARA
CRABGRASS DRAWK FONIO PANIC

DARNEL PANICLE CRABWEED ELEUSINE
CRAB LOUSE CRAB MORPION MOREPEON
CRAB PLOVER DROME
CRAB'S-EYE JEQUIRITY
CRAB TREE GRIBBLE
CRABWOOD ANDIROBA POISONWOOD
CRACK GAG KIN POP BANG BLOW CHAP CHIP CHOP CLAP CONE DOKE FENT FLAW GAIG JEST JIBE JOKE KIBE LEAK LICK QUIP REND RIFT RIME RIVE SCAR SLAT SNAP YERK BRACK BREAK CHARK CHECK CHICK CHINE CHINK CLACK CLEFT CRAKE CRAZE FLAKE FLANK FLASH GRIKE KNACK KNICK SCORE SHAKE SLASH SOLVE SPANG SPLIT CLEAVE CRANNY SLITER SPIDER SPRING BLEMISH CRACKLE CREVICE FISSURE SLIFTER SLITHER FRACTURE HAIRLINE STRAMASH
(— A WHIP) YERK FLANK
(— IN FLESH) KIN CHAP KIBE
(— IN FLOOR) STRAKE
(— IN INGOT) SPILL
(— IN MAST) SPRING
(— IN ROCK) GRIKE JOINT
(— IN SEA ICE) RIFTER
(— IN STEEL) CHECK SPILL
(— OPEN) SEAM
(— PETROLEUM) BURN
(— WHILE FIRING) DUNT
(FILLER FOR —S) SPACKLE
(PL.) CRAZE
(PREF.) RIMI
CRACKAJACK NAILER NAILING
CRACKBRAINED BATS CRAZY NUTTY CRACKY ERRATIC
CRACKED BATS FLED NECKED CHAPPED COMICAL TOUCHED CRACKERS
CRACKER BAKE LIAR WAFER BONBON POPPER BISCUIT BOASTER BREAKER BURSTER COSAQUE REDNECK SALTINE SNAPPER
(— STATE) GEORGIA
(BOILED —S) CUSH
(BROKEN —S) DUNDERFUNK
CRACKERJACK ACE TRUMP
CRACKING CRAZE SHIVERING
(PL.) SCRAP
CRACKLE SNAP BREAK CRACK CRISP BRUSTLE CRINKLE SPARKLE SPUTTER CREPITATE
CRACKLING CRISP GREAVE SNAPPY CRACKEL CRACKLE CREMANT GREAVES CRACKNEL CRITLING CREPITANT
(— OF PAPER) RATTLE
(PL.) SCRAPS GRIEBEN
CRACKNEL SIMNEL CRACKLING
CRACKPOT NUT CRACK ERRATIC LUNATIC CRANKISH
CRACKSMAN YEGG BURGLAR PETEMAN
CRADLE BED COT CRIB REST ROCK WOMB CRATE FRAME CRECHE MATRIX ROCKER SADDLE TROUGH BERCEAU SHELTER BASSINET CUNABULA
(— FOR SHIP) BED SLEE
(— FOR VATS) STILLING STILLION
(— IN ARCHERY) PURSE
(CERAMICS —) CHUM
(GRAIN —) CADAR CADER
(PL.) CHOCKS
CRADLESONG BERCEUSE
CRADLING BRACK
CRAFT ART BARK BOAT SAIL FRAUD GUILE SKILL TRADE BARQUE BATEAU CAUTEL DECEIT DROGER METIER MISTER POLICE ROADER STRUSE TALENT VESSEL ABILITY CUNNING DROGHER MYSTERY PANURGY SLEIGHT APTITUDE ARTIFICE BASKETRY VOCATION
(ANTIQUATED OR CLUMSY —) HOOKER
(CLUMSY —) ARK
(LANDING —) DUCK
(PREF.) TECHNI TECHNO
(SUFF.) TECT
CRAFTILY FOXILY
CRAFTINESS DESIGN SLEIGHT SLYNESS
CRAFTSMAN CARL HAND CARLE CRAFT NAVVY ARTIST WRITER ARTISAN TOHUNGA WORKMAN LETTERER MECHANIC ARTIFICER MACHINIST
CRAFTY SLY ARCH DEEP DERN FINE FOXY NOUP SLIM WILY WISE ADEPT COONY PAWKY SLAPE SLEEK ADROIT ARTFUL ASTUTE CALLID QUAINT SHREWD SOLERT SUBTLE TRICKY CUNNING POLITIC SLEEKIT SLEIGHT SUBTILE VAFROUS VERSUTE VULPINE CAPTIOUS DEXTROUS ENGINOUS FETCHING JESUITIC SLEIGHTY CAUTELOUS
CRAG TOR CRAW KNEE NECK ROCK SCAR SPUR ARETE BRACK CLIFF CLINT CRAIG HEUCH HEUGH THROAT
(PREF.) CREMNO
CRAGGY ROUGH ABRUPT CLIFFY CLIFTY KNOTTY PAMPER RUGGED CRAGGED KNAGGED
CRAKE CROW RAIL ROOK RAVEN CORNBIRD RAILBIRD
CRAKOW BEAKER CRACOWE POULAINE
CRAM BAG MUG RAM WAD BONE CRAP FILL GLUT LADE PACK PANG PORR PURR STOW TRIG TUCK URGE CROWD CRUSH DRIVE FARCE FORCE FRANK GORGE GRIND LEARN PRESS SCRAM STECH STUDY STUFF TEACH AGROTE BONEUP CROMME PESTER STEEVE STODGE THRACK
(— WITH RICH FOOD) PAMPER
CRAMMED PANG STODGY CHOCKFUL JAMPACKED
CRAMMER CRAM FEEDER
CRAMMING GAVAGE
CRAMP ART ARCT COOP CRIB KINK PAIN TUCK CRICK CRIMP CROWD DOWEL PINCH STUNT TRAMP AGRAFE DOGTIE HAMPER HINDER KNOTTY PESTER CONFINE CRAMPER CRAMPET COMPRESS CONTRACT RESTRAIN RESTRICT
CRAMPED POKY CRIMP POKEY NIGGLY BOUNDED CRIMPED SQUEEZY NIGGLING
CRAMPFISH TORPEDO
CRAMPING UNEASY
CRAMPON CRAMP CRAMPET CRAMPOON
CRANBERRY BERRY CRANE ERICAD BOGWORT PEMBINA ACROSARC BILBERRY BOGBERRY COWBERRY FENBERRY FOXBERRY CROWBERRY
(— BUSH) PIMBINA
CRANBERRY TREE PEMBINA SNOWBALL VIBURNUM
CRANE JOB GRUS HOOK SWAY CYRUS DAVIT HERON HOIST JENNY RAISE SARUS TITAN WADER BROLGA COOLEN JIGGER KULANG SAHRAS COOLUNG CRAWLER DERRICK GOLIATH KAIKARA WHOOPER ADJUTANT GRUIFORM TRAVELER
(— FOR FIREPLACE) COTTREL COTTEREL
CRANE ARM GIB JIB GIBBET RAMHEAD COTTEREL
CRANE-FLY LONG-LEGS
CRANESBILL ALUMROOT DOVEFOOT FLUXWEED
CRANIUM PAN HEAD CRANE CRANY SKULL BRAINPAN
(PART OF —) INION
CRANK NUT WIT BENT SICK WALT WEAK WHIM WIND BRACE GRUMP LOOSE ROGUE SHAKY THROW WALTY WINCH AILING BOLDLY CRANKY EVENER GROUCH HANDLE INFIRM AWKWARD BRACKET FANATIC LUSTILY
(SOMEWHAT —) TENDER
CRANKCASE SUMP
CRANKINESS ANGULARITY
CRANKY UGLY CRAZY CRONK CROSS LUSTY SHAKY TESTY AILING CRANNY FIFISH INFIRM SICKLY CROOKED GROUCHY PERVERSE TORTUOUS
CRANNY HOLE NOOK CHINK CLEFT CRACK CORNER CRANNEL CREVICE FISSURE
CRANTARA TARIE
CRANTS WREATH CORANCE GARLAND
CRAPE BAND CURL FRIZ CREPE CRIMP DRAPE GAUZE SHROUD MOURNING
CRAPE MYRTLE JAPONICA ASTROMEDA
CRAPPIE BACH SHAD BATCH CALICO CROPPIE BACHELOR BACULERE NEWLIGHT SACALAIT TINMOUTH CHINKAPIN
CRAPS CRAP HAZARD
CRASH BASH FAIL FALL RACK BLAST BURST CLOTH CRUSH FRUSH PRANG SHOCK SMASH SOUND FIASCO FRAGOR HURTLE FAILURE SHATTER STENTER COLLAPSE ICEQUAKE SPLINTER STRAMASH
(— OF THUNDER) CLAP
CRASHING ROPAND SMASHING
CRASH-LAND DITCH
CRASS RAW DULL LOUD RUDE CRUDE DENSE GROSS ROUGH THICK COARSE OBTUSE STUPID
CRASSNESS SQUALOR
CRATCH CRIB RACK CRITCH MANGER GRATING
CRATE BOX CAR CASE CRIB FLAT PLANE SERON BASKET CRADLE ENCASE HAMPER HURDLE CACAXTE CANASTA CARRIER PACKAGE VEHICLE
(EMPTY —) EMPTY
CRATER CUP PIT CONE HOLE DINOS FOVEA NICHE CELEBE HOLLOW CALDERA
(— FORMED BY STEAM) MAAR
(LUNAR —) LINNE
(VOLCANIC —) MAAR
CRATUS (FATHER OF —) PALLAS URANUS
(MOTHER OF —) GAEA STYX
CRAUNCH CRANCH SCRANCH
CRAVAT TIE TECK ASCOT FRONT SCARF STOCK CHOKER GRAVAT BANDAGE NECKTIE OVERLAY SOUBISE CRUMPLER
CRAVE ASK BEG GAPE ITCH LONG NEED PINE PRAY SEEK WISH COVET GREED YEARN DESIRE HANKER HUNGER LINGER THIRST YAMMER BESEECH ENTREAT IMPLORE REQUEST REQUIRE SOLICIT APPETITE
CRAVEN AFRAID COWARD SCARED DASTARD COWARDLY DEFEATED OVERCOME POLTROON RECREANT SNEAKING
CRAVING AVID ITCH WANT LETCH DESIRE HUNGER THIRST LONGING APPETITE LIKEROUS TICKLING APPETENCE
(— FOR LIQUOR) DRY
(— FOR UNNATURAL FOOD) PICA
(ABNORMAL —) BULIMY BULIMIA BOULIMIA
CRAW MAW CRAG CROP STOMACH
CRAWFISH KREEF
CRAWL LAG COON DRAG FAWN INCH LOOP RAMP SHUG SWIM CREEP KRAAL SLIDE SLIME SNAKE TRAIL BUSTLE CRINGE GROVEL SCRAWL SCRIDE CLAMBER SLITHER SNIGGLE TRUDGEN INCHWORM SCRABBLE
CRAWLING
(SUFF.) **(— CREATURE)** ERPETON
CRAWLY CREEPY
CRAYFISH DAD CRAB YABBY YABBIE CAMARON CRAWDAD LOBSTER CAMBARUS CRABFISH CRAWFISH
CRAYON KEEL PLAN CHALK CONTE SAUCE PASTEL PENCIL SKETCH SANGUINE
CRAZE BUG FAD FLAW MAZE MODE RAGE BREAK CRACK CRUSH FEVER FUROR MANIA VOGUE DEFECT IMPAIR MADDEN MADDLE WEAKEN WHIMSY DERANGE DESTROY FASHION SHATTER WHIMSEY DISTRACT

(NEWSPAPER —) STUNT
(PREF.) MANIC
CRAZED MAD REE AMOK LOCO WILD WOOD WOWF ZANY BALMY BATTY DAFFY DOTTY GIDDY MANIC NUTTY POTTY WACKY COOCOO DOTTLE INSANE LOONEY BERSERK FANATIC LUNATIC DATELESS DELEERIT DEMENTED DERANGED POSSESSED
CRAZINESS CRAZE LUNACY DEMENTIA
CRAZY (ALSO SEE CRAZED) APE OFF REE WET BATS BUGS GAGA GYTE HITE LOCO NUTS WILD ZANY BATTY BEANY BUGGY DAFFY DIPPY DOILT DOTTY FLAKY GOOFY KOOKY LOOLY LOONY POTTY WACKO WACKY WIGGY CRANKY CUCKOO DOTTLE FLAKEY FRUITY INSANE KOOKIE LOCKET MENTAL SCATTY SCREWY WHACKO WHACKY BANANAS BONKERS CRACKED LUNATIC PEEVISH SCRANNY BUGHOUSE COCKEYED CRACKERS DERANGED HALLICET HALUCKET MESHUGGA
CREAK CRY GIG GEIG GIRG JARG RASP YIRR CHARK CHEEP CHIRK CRAIK CRANK CROAK GRIND GROAN FRATCH SCREAK SCRIKE SCROOP SKRAIK SQUEAK COMPLAIN
(— OF TIN) CRY
CREAKING JARG SCREAK SCRIKE
CREAKY ARTHRITIC
CREAM DIP BEAT BEST FOOL HEAD REAM CREME ELITE FROTH REAME SAUCE WHOMP BONBON CHOICE TRIFLE COLOGNE FATNESS EMULSION OINTMENT
(ICE —) GELATA
CREAMING MANTLING
CREAM PUFF PUFF DUCHESSE
CREAMY RICH REAMY ACREAM SMOOTH LUSCIOUS
CREASE GAW CLAM FOLD LINE LIRK RUCK RUGA SEAM BLOCK CRESS CRIMP PLAIT PLEAT PRESS SCARF SCORE FURROW SCARPA SUTURE WREATH CRUMPLE CRUNKLE WRIMPLE WRINKLE
(SERIES OF —S) BREAK
(PL.) RASCETA
CREASED CRUMPLED ACCORDION
CREASELESS (HAVING — LEGS) STOVEPIPE
CREATE COIN CREE FORM MAKE PLAN BUILD CAUSE ERECT FORGE IMPEL RAISE SETUP SHAPE WRITE AUTHOR DESIGN IMPOSE INVENT COMPACT COMPOSE CONJURE FASHION IMAGINE PRODUCE COMPOUND GENERATE CONSTRUCT
(— A DISTURBANCE) RIOT
(— CONFUSION) GARBOIL
(NEWLY -D) SUNRISE
CREATING CREANT
CREATION WORLD COSMOS EFFECT NATURE POETRY EDITION FACTURE FASHION POIESIS PRODUCT SHAPING BERESHIT BUSINESS CREATURE UNIVERSE
(MENTAL —) FANTASY PHANTASY
(VISIONARY —) DREAM
CREATIVE FERTILE FORMFUL PLASTIC POIETIC FORGEFUL GERMINAL NATURING POMATIVE PROMETHEAN ORIGINATIVE
CREATOR MAKER AUTHOR FATHER FORMER VARUNA WORKER KHEPERA TAGALOA DESIGNER INVENTOR OPERATOR PRODUCER TANGALOA
CREATURE MAN FOOD TOOL BEAST BEING DABBA JOKER SLAVE THING TRICK WIGHT ANIMAL FELLOW MINION PERSON WRETCH CRITTER GANGREL MINIKIN MINIMUS SHAPING CRAYTHUR CREATION HELLICAT
(— OF LITTLE VALUE) SHOT
(CANNIBALISTIC —) WENDIGO WINDIGO
(CHARMING —) FAIRY
(DEFORMED —) MOONCALF
(DISORDERLY —) ROIT ROYT
(DWARF —) FAIRY GNOME
(ELFLIKE —) PERI
(EVIL —) HELLICAT
(FABLED —) LUNG SIREN MERMAN WIVERN ALBORAK MERMAID
(FRIVOLOUS —) MOTH
(LITTLE —) MITING
(MANGY —) RONION RONYON
(MANLIKE —) HOMINID HOMONID HOMINIAN
(MEAN —) LEFT
(MECHANICAL —) GOLEM
(MISERABLE —) SNAKE
(NONSENSE —) SNARK
(POOR —) EARTHWORM
(SILLY —) GOOSE
(SMALL —) ATOM GRIG BEASTIE
(SPRY —) WHIPPET
(STUNTED —) WIRL URLING WIRLING
(SUPERNATURAL —) MAN DRAGON
(TINY —) ELF ATOMY
(UNDERDEVELOPED —) SLINK
(UNDERSIZED —) DURGAN
(USELESS —) HUSHION
(VICIOUS —) DEVIL
(WICKED —) HELLICAT
(WORTHLESS —) SCULPIN SNIPJACK
(WRETCHED —) ARMINE
(3 —S OF A KIND) LEASH
(PL.) CREATION
CRECHE CRIB PUTZ MANGER NURSERY
(— FIGURES) MAGI
CREDENCE FAITH TRUST BELIEF BUFFET CREDIT CREANCE CREDENZA
CREDENTIAL VOUCHER CREDENCE
CREDENZA NICHE SHELF TABLE BUFFET SERVER CREDENCE CUPBOARD
CREDIBILITY FAITH CREDIT
CREDIBLE LIKELY CREDENT FAITHFUL PROBABLE TROWABLE PLAUSIBLE
CREDIT LOAN TICK ASSET CHALK ENDOW FAITH HONOR IZZAT MENSK MERIT STRAP TENET TRUST BELIEF CHARGE ESTEEM IMPUTE RENOWN REPUTE TICKET WEIGHT ACCOUNT ASCRIBE BELIEVE CREANCE JAWBONE OPINION WORSHIP ACCREDIT CREDENCE HEADMARK PRESTIGE
(HOCKEY —) ASSIST
CREDITABLE HONEST CREDIBLE REPUTABLE
CREDITOR DEBTEE SHYLOCK TRUSTER ADJUDGER APPRIZER CRANSIER CREANCER
(TROUBLESOME —) DUN
CREDO FAITH
CREDULITY EASINESS
CREDULOUS FOND SIMPLE SPOONY SPOONEY BOOBYISH CREDIBLE GULLIBLE
CREED ISM LAY CULT SECT CREDO DOGMA FAITH TENET BELIEF KELIMA SYMBOL CREANCE KALIMAH TROWING DOCTRINE SYMBOLUM
(KIND OF —) NICENE
CREEK BAY CUT GEO GIO GUT POW RIA RIO RUN VLY VOE BECK BURN COVE HOPE KILL PILL RILL SLEW SLUE VLEI VLEY WASH WICK BACHE BAYOU BIGHT BOGUE BROOK CRICK DRAFT FLEET INLET ZANJA ARROYO BRANCH BREACH CANADA ESTERO SLOUGH STREAM DRAUGHT ESTUARY RIVULET ZANJONA MUSKOGEE
(AUSTRALIAN —) COWAL
(TIDE —) SLAKE
CREEK SEDGE THATCH
CREEL RIP CAUL CAWL HASK JACK KELL RACK TRAP HARSK BASKET JUNKET
(— FOR BOBBINS) BANK SKEWER
CREELER TUBER LIGGER
CREEP COON FAWN GEEK INCH NERD RAMP CRAWL CROPE DRIFT GLIDE PROWL SKULK SLINK SMOOT STEAL TRAIL CRINGE GROVEL SCRIDE SPRAWL TIPTOE WEIRDO CRAMBLE CRAMMEL SNIGGLE WEIRDIE TAURANGA
(— AS IVY) RIZZLE
(PL.) WILLIES
(PREF.) HERPETI HERPETO
CREEPER IVY JITI SHOE VINE WORM CREEP CROPE SNAKE COWAGE CRADLE IPECAC REPENT ROMPER TECOMA CLAMPER CLIMBER COWHAGE COWITCH CRAWLER REPTANT REPTILE RUNNING TRAILER FOXGLOVE GUITGUIT PICUCULE WOODBINE PERIWINKLE
CREEPING SLOW REPTANT REPTILE SERVILE SARMENTOUS SERPIGINOUS
(— OF FLESH) GREW GRUE
(PREF.) HERPET(I)(O)
(SUFF.) **(— CREATURE)** ERPETON
CREEPING CROWFOOT SITFAST CRAWFOOT
CREEPING JENNY MONEYWORT
CREEPING SNOWBERRY MOXA TEABERRY
CREESE KRIS STAB CRESS CRISE SWORD DAGGER
CREMATE BURN
CREMATION SUTTEE
(PLACE OF —) GHAT GHAUT
CRENEL LOOP CORNEL KERNEL CRENELET
CREOLE KRIO PATOIS CRIOLLO DIALECT HAITIAN MESTIZO
(— STATE) LOUISIANA
(ENGLISH-BASED —) SRANAN
CREON (DAUGHTER OF —) GLAUCE
(FATHER OF —) MENOECEUS
(SISTER OF —) JOCASTA HIPPONOME
CREOSOTE BUSH LARREA
CREPE CRAPE FRIZZED NACARAT PANCAKE CHIRIMEN CRINKLED WRINKLED
CREPITATE SNAP GRATE RATTLE CRACKLE
CRESCENT HORN LUNE MOON ROOL CURVE LUNAR LUNOID LUNULE MOONED SICKLE WAXAND LUNETTE DEMILUNE MENISCUS
(END OF —) CUSP HORN
(PREF.) MENISCI MENISCO
CRESCENTLIKE BICORN
CRESCENT-SHAPED MOONY LUNATE LUNATED
(PREF.) SELEN(O)
CRESCIVE WAXING GROWING INCREASING
CRESOL FROTHER
CRESPHONTES (BROTHER OF —) TEMENUS ARISTODEMUS
(FATHER OF —) ARISTOMACHUS
(SON OF —) AEPYTUS
CRESS EKER KERSE CUCKOO MADWORT CRUCIFER WHITETOP PEPPERGRASS
CRESSET TORCH BASKET BEACON SIGNAL CRISSET FLAMBEAU
CREST COP TIP TOP ACME APEX COMB EDGE HOOD KNAP PEAK RUFF SEAL TUFT CHINE CROWN PLUME RIDGE COPPLE CREASE CRISTA CUMBRE FINIAL HEIGHT HELMET SUMMIT TIMBER TIMBRE BEARING FEATHER TOPKNOT CENTROID CRESTING ECTOLOPH METALOPH PINNACLE WHITECAP
(— OF BREAKER) SEEGE
(— OF HELMET) COMB CIMIER
(— OF HILL) KNAP
(— OF MINERAL VEIN) APEX
(— OF MOUNTAIN RANGE) ARETE SAWBACK
(— OF PEACOCK) CHAPLET
(— OF RIDGE) EDGE
(— OF SNOW) CORNICE
(— ON BIRD) CROWN ECKLE COPPLE
(IMPERIAL —) KIKUMON
(WAVE —) FEATHER WHITECAP
(PREF.) CRISTI LOPH(I)(IO)(O)
(SUFF.) LOPH(US)
CRESTED COMBED MUFFED TAPPET TAPPIT COPPLED CRISATE CROWNED CRISTATE PILEATED CRISTATED
CRESTED GREBE CARGOOSE
CRESTED QUAIL COPPY

CRESTFALLEN COWED DEJECTED
CRESTING CHENEAU
CRETACEOUS CHALKY
CRETAN KEFTI MINOAN CANDIOT
CRETAN SPIKENARD PHU

CRETE
BAY: SUDA KANCA KISAMO MESARA
CAPE: BUZA LIANO SALOME SIDERO SPATHA STAVROS LITHINON SIDHEROS
CAPITAL: CANEA
GULF: KHANIA MERABELLO
MOUNTAIN: IDA DIKTE JUKTAS LASITHI THEODORE
NAME: CRETA KRETE CANDIA
TOWN: HAG LATO CANEA KHORA SITIA ZAKRO ANOYIA CANDIA KHANIA KISAMO RETIMO KISAMOS KASTELLI HERAKLION

CRETHEUS **(FATHER OF —)** AEOLUS **(MOTHER OF —)** ENARETE **(SLAYER OF —)** TURNUS **(SON OF —)** AESON PHERES AMYTHAON **(WIFE OF —)** TYRO
CRETIN IDIOT
CREUSA GLAUCE GLAUKE **(FATHER OF —)** CREON PRIAM ERECHTHEUS **(HUSBAND OF —)** AENEAS XUTHUS **(MOTHER OF —)** HECUBA PRAXITHEA **(SLAYER OF —)** MEDEA **(SON OF —)** ION DORUS ACHAEUS ASCANIUS
CREVALLE JACK JUREL
CREVASSE CHASM SPLIT MOULIN SCHRUND CLEAVAGE BERGSCHRUND
CREVICE KIN BORE LEAK NOOK PEEP SEAM VEIN BREAK CHINE CHINK CLEFT CRACK CREEK CUNNE GRIKE CRANNY STRAKE CRANNEL FISSURE GUNNIES KRAVERS OPENING SLIFTER CREVASSE PEEPHOLE **(VOLCANIC —)** SOLFATARA
CREW LOT MEN MOB SET BAND GANG GING HERD OARS SHIP TEAM UNIT COVIN EIGHT HANDS MEINY PARTY SQUAD STAFF COVINE MEINIE SEAMEN THRONG AIRCREW COMPANY FACULTY MANNING MEMBERS RETINUE EQUIPAGE **(— OF SHEARERS)** BOARD
CREWEL CRUEL CADDIS CADDICE
CRIB BED BIN BOX CAB COT CUB HUT KEY BOOM CRUB CURB DIVE JACK PONY RACK RAFT SKIN TROT BOOSE BOOSY CHEAT CRATE FRAME HOVEL STALL STEAL BUNKER CRATCH CRECHE CRITCH MANGER PIGSTY PILFER CABBAGE ENGLISH PURLOIN BASSINET CORNCRIB CRIBBAGE CRIBBING CRIBWORK
CRIBBER SHORER STUMPSUCKER
CRICK KINK CREEK HITCH SPASM TWIST
CRICKET GRIG MOLE SNOB CHANGA SADDLE GRYLLID TWIDDLER ORTHOPTERAN **(— HIT)** SLOG **(— SCORE OF 100 RUNS)** TON **(KIND OF —)** MORMON (PREF.) GRYLLO
CRICKETER CUT COLT PLAYER RABBIT GENTLEMAN
CRICKET ON THE HEARTH **(AUTHOR OF —)** DICKENS **(CHARACTER IN —)** DOT MAY JOHN CALEB BERTHA EDWARD PLUMMER FIELDING TACKLETON PERRYBINGLE
CRIER HUER CRYER BEADLE HERALD WAILER BELLMAN MUEZZIN WRAWLER OUTCRIER
CRIME ACT SIN EVIL FACT LACK ABUSE ARSON BLAME CAPER FOLLY LIBEL WRONG FALSUM FELONY INCEST MURDER PIACLE FORFEIT FORGERY MISDEED OFFENCE OFFENSE INIQUITY SABOTAGE VILLAINY MALEFACTION MISDEMEANOR **(— PHRASE)** DOESNTPAY **(ORGANIZED —)** GANGLAND
CRIME AND PUNISHMENT **(AUTHOR OF —)** DOSTOEVSKI **(CHARACTER IN —)** SONIA DOUNIA LUZHIN PORFIRY PETROVICH RAZUMIHIN MARMELADOV RASKOLNIKOV SVIDRIGAILOV
CRIMINAL BAD SORE YEGG CROOK FELON TOUGH APACHE BASHER DACOIT GUILTY GUNMAN INMATE KILLER NOCENT SLAYER WARGUS WICKED CONVICT CULPRIT HEINOUS HOODLUM ILLEGAL ILLICIT MOBSTER NOXIOUS SEVENER VAUTRIN CRIMEFUL CULPABLE GANGSTER GAOLBIRD HABITUAL HARDCASE JAILBIRD PIACULAR SCELERAT **(HABITUAL —)** RECIDIVIST **(PETTY —)** ROUNDER **(VIOLENT —)** DESPERADO (PL.) AMALAITA
CRIMINATE IMPEACH
CRIMP BEND CURL FOLD FRIZ POKE POTE WAVE WEAK CLAMP CRISP FLUTE FRILL FRIZZ PINCH PLAIT BUCKLE GOFFER RUFFLE CRIMPER CRIMPLE CRINKLE FRIABLE GAUFFER WRINKLE OBSTACLE
CRIMSON LAC RED PINK GRAIN BLOODY JOCKEY MAROON MODENA CARMINE SCARLET CRAMOISY CREMOSIN **(— TIDE)** BAMA
CRIMSON CLOVER NAPOLEON
CRIMSON LAKE SULTAN
CRINE HAIR
CRINED MANED
CRINGE BOW BEND CURB CURR DUCK FAWN JOUK BINGE COWER CRAWL CREEP QUAIL SNEAK SNOOL STOOP WINCE YIELD BUCKLE CROUCH GROVEL SHRINK SUBMIT ADULATE CRINKLE DISTORT SCRINGE TRUCKLE
CRINGER FLUNKEY
CRINGING ABJECT HANGDOG SERVILE SPANIEL
CRINKLE BEND CURL KINK TURN WIND CREPE CRISP PUCKER RIPPLE RUMPLE RUSTLE CRACKLE CRANKLE FRIZZLE WRINKLE
CRINKLED CRIMP CURLY BUCKLED ENCOMIC CRISPATE
CRINKLY CREPY CREPEY
CRINOID POLYP CRINITE CAMERATE COMATULA **(BODY OF —)** CROWN
CRINOLINE CRIN HOOP
CRIPPLE MAR CRIP GIMP HARM HURT LAME MAIM BACACH HOBBLE IMPAIR INJURE SCOTCH WEAKEN CRAPPLE CRUMPET DISABLE LAMETER LAMIGER LAMITER HANDICAP LAMESTER MUTILATE PARALYZE (PL.) LAMZIEKTE
CRIPPLED GIMPY LAMED COUPLED DISABLED
CRIPPLING MAIM MAYHEM
CRISIS FIT ACME CRUX FLAP HEAD JUMP PASS TURN BRUNT CARDO CRISE PANIC PERIL PINCH POINT STATE STORM TRIAL STRAIT DUNKIRK DECISION JUNCTURE MOUNTAIN **(AUTHOR OF —)** CHURCHILL **(CHARACTER IN —)** BRICE GRANT CARVEL COLFAX ABRAHAM LINCOLN STEPHEN WHIPPLE CLARENCE VIRGINIA
CRISP NEW COLD CURL FRIZ FROW HARD BRISK CLEAR CRIPS CRUMP CURLY FRESH FRIZZ NIPPY PITHY SHARP SHORT SPALT STIFF TERSE BITING BRIGHT CRISPY LIVELY SNAPPY BRACING BRITTLE CONCISE CRACKLY CRUNCHY CUTTING FRIABLE FRIZZLE SMOPPLE INCISIVE POTATOCHIP
CRISPED FUZZY FRIZZLY CRISPATE
CRISPINELLA **(SISTER OF —)** BEATRICE
CRISPNESS SNAP
CRISSCROSS AWRY CROSS NETWORK CONFUSED
CRITERION LAW NORM RULE TEST TYPE AXIOM CANON CHECK GAUGE MODEL PROOF TOUCH CRISIS METRIC INDICIA MEASURE PLUMMET STANDARD SHIBBOLETH
CRITIC MOME BOOER JUDGE MOMUS RATER CARPER CENSOR CORNER EXPERT PUNDIT SLATER SYNDIC ZOILUS STYLIST ZOILIST COLLATOR CRITIQUE DEBUNKER OVERSEER REVIEWER THONGMAN ARISTARCH **AMERICAN** CARY GILL KAEL KERR LAHR MORE SOBY TATE AIKEN BANGS BOGAN BREEN BROWN CANBY CRIST CUPPY EBERT ELSON FINCK FISKE GIBBS HEWES KALEM KAZIN KOBBE LEVIN MABIE POUND SIMON WHITE ALLSOP BECKER BROOKS CHENEY DOWNES FULLER GILMAN HUTTON KRASNA KRUTCH LEDOUX LOWELL MANTLE MILLER MUNSON NATHAN PARKER PHELPS SHALIT SISKEL SONTAG TAYLOR WILSON ALDRICH ANDREWS AVAKIAN FIEDLER GRANICK HUNEKER POIRIER SMAROFF VENDLER WHIPPLE WIMSATT ATKINSON BOOKSPAN CROWTHER HAGEDORN SAARINEN ROSENFELD WOOLLCOTT CHOTZINOFF **AUSTRALIAN** HUGHES TURNER **AUSTRIAN** KUH KRAUS **CANADIAN** FRYE SMITH BIRNEY **CZECH** HANSLICK **DANISH** LANGE BRANDES GERSTENBERG **DUTCH** BRINK BILDERDIJK JONCKBLOET VALCKENAER **ENGLISH** BAX FRY BELL LAMB READ SHAW WAIN WEST AGATE BOWRA DILKE ELIOT ELWIN GAUNT GOULD GREIN LAVES LEVIN MERES PAGET PATER PATES RYMER SCOTT TYNAN WAUGH ARNOLD BINYON COLLES COLVIN DENNIS EMPSON HUXLEY LEAVIS MORGAN PALMER RUSKIN SYMONS THOMAS WALKER WARTON AINSLIE BENTLEY BRADLEY COLLIER COLLINS FREEMAN GIFFORD GISSING JOHNSON KERMODE LUBBOCK RALEIGH SHORTER SITWELL STEPHEN TOYNBEE WALKLEY WHIBLEY BEERBOHM MARRIOTT SECCOMBE STEPHENS MACCARTHY PARTRIDGE SAINTSBURY SWINNERTON **FINNISH** WALTARI **FRENCH** GIDE BAYLE BAZIN BIDOU BLAZE DENIS GILLE TAINE CASSOU FAGUET FRANCE LANSON MENDES OZANAM SARCEY VALERY BARTHES BATTEUX BOURGET BREMOND GAUTIER MERIMEE REGNIER AUBIGNAC MEZIERES MONTEGUT VALLETTE BRUNETIERE APOLLINAIRE **GERMAN** BAB EYE KERR MERCK MUNDT OPITZ MENZEL SCHOLL WAAGEN LESSING NICOLAI RIBBECK ZARNCKE ACIDALIUS **GREEK** ELYTIS ZOILUS ARISTARCHUS CALLIMACHUS **HUNGARIAN** KOLCSEY **ICELANDIC** BLONDAL **INDIAN** ANAND **IRISH** BOYD DEVERE MARTYN **ITALIAN** PRAZ CECCHI OJETTI OVIDIO BARETTI CAPUANA MONTALE ZANELLA CARDUCCI CHIARINI ALGAROTTI DESANCTUS CASTELVETRO CAVALCASELLE **MEXICAN** PAZ **NORWEGIAN** WELHAVEN **POLISH** LANGE **PORTUGUESE** VASCONCELLOS **RUSSIAN** PYPIN STASOV BELINSKI **SCOTTISH** DENT MUIR ARCHER WILSON JEFFREY **SPANISH** CANETE **SWEDISH** SIREN LEOPOLD KELLGREN LEVERTIN **SWISS** BODMER **WELSH** SYMONS
CRITICAL EDGY HIGH NICE ACERB ACUTE VITAL CHILLY CRITIC

NASUTE SEVERE URGENT ACERBIC ADVERSE CARPING EXIGENT NERVOUS PARLOUS CAPTIOUS CARDINAL CAVILING DECISIVE EXACTING JUDICIAL PRESSING SLASHING TICKLISH CLIMACTERIC
CRITICISM DIG RAP FIRE FLAK GAFF SLAM BLAME KNOCK SLATE ATTACK CRITIC REVIEW STATIC CENSURE COMMENT DESCANT LITCRIT PANNING QUIBBLE SLASHER SLATING ZOILISM BLUDGEON CRITIQUE DIATRIBE JUDGMENT STRICTURE
(PETTY —) NITPICKING
(POINTED —) JAB
(UNJUSTIFIED —) NITPICKING
CRITICIZE HIT PAN RAP RIP CARP CRAB FLAY FLOG RIDE SKIN SLAM SLUR TIDE YELP BLAME BLAST CAVIL DECRY GRIPE JUDGE KNOCK ROAST SCORE SLASH SLATE TRASH BERATE CRITIC REBUKE REVIEW CENSURE COMMENT CONDEMN CRITIZE EXAMINE NITPICK SCARIFY BADMOUTH CRITIQUE DENOUNCE TOMAHAWK
(— MINUTELY) NITPICK
(— SEVERELY) FLAY JUMP
(— SLASHINGLY) SLASH SLATE
CRITIQUE CRITIC REVIEW CRITICISM
CRIUS (FATHER OF —) URANUS
(MOTHER OF —) GAEA
(SON OF —) PALLAS PERSES ASTRAEUS
CRO CROY PAYMENT
CROAK CAW DIE GASP KILL PORK ROUP CRAKE CREAK CRONK PLUNK QUALM QUARK SPEAK CROAPE GRUMBLE COMPLAIN FOREBODE
CROAKER SPOT RONCO CROCUS RONCHO TOMCOD BUBBLER CABEZON CORBINA CORVINA CABEZONE HARDHEAD KINGFISH SCIAENID
CROAKING CROAKY HOARSE RANARIAN COAXATION
CROAT CHORWAT CHROBAT SYRMIAN
(PL.) HRVATI HERVATI
CROATIA (ALSO SEE YUGOSLAVIA)
CAPITAL: ZAGREB
COIN: DINAR
GULF: KOTOR
LANGUAGE: CROATIAN SERBOCROATIAN
MOUNTAIN: TROGLAV
MOUNTAIN RANGE: DINARIC ZAGORJE
PENINSULA: ISTRIAN
PLAIN: PANNONIAN PARAPANNONIAN
REGION: ISTRIA DALMATIA
RIVER: UNA KRKA KUPA SAVA DRAVA CETINA
SEA: ADRIATIC
TOWN: SPLIT OSIJEK RIJEKA
WIND: BORA BURA JUGO MISTRAL
CROCARD BRABANT SCALDING SLEEPING
CROCHET HOOK KNIT BRAID PLAIT WEAVE CROTCHET
CROCK JAR PIG POT SMUT SOIL SOOT STEAN STEEN STOOL CHATTY CRITCH GOOLAH PANMUG SMUDGE CRAGGAN TERRINE POTSHERD
CROCKERY CHINA CLOAM DISHES PIGGERY POTWARE CLAYWARE
CROCODILE GOA CROC GATOR MAGAR CAYMAN GAVIAL JACARE LIZARD MUGGER YACARE CRAWLER CREEPER DIAPSID REPTILE SAURIAN SERPENT LORICATE
CROCODILE BIRD SICSAC TROCHIL MESSMATE
CROCUS IRID LILY SAFFRON COLCHICUM
CROFT FARM TORP CRAFT CRYPT FIELD GARTH VAULT BLEACH CAVERN PARROCK PIGHTLE
CROMLECH QUOIT CIRCLE DOLMEN CROMMEL GORSEDD
CROMORNA CREMONA KRUMHORN
CRONE HAG AUNT TROT CRONY WITCH BELDAM RIBIBE BELDAME
CRONOS (DAUGHTER OF —) HERA
CRONY PAL CHUM BILLY GOSSY NETOP GIMMER GOSSIP
CROOK BEND HOOK TURN WARP CHEAT CHINK CLEEK CRANK CROMB CROOM CRUMP CURVE GANEF HUNCH NIBBY PEDUM STAFF THIEF TRICK CRUMMY INDENT TWICER CAMBUCA CROSIER CROZIER CRUMMIE INCURVE POTHOOK SLICKER ARTIFICE CHISELER CRUMMOCK SWINDLER
(— A FINGER AT) BECKON
(— IN BRANCH) KNEE
(— OF HEAD) HEEL
(SHEPHERD'S —) CROTCH KEBBIE
CROOKBACKED CROUCHIE
CROOKED CAM WRY AGEE ALOP AWRY BENT GAME WOGH AGLEY ASKEW BANDY BOWLY CRANK CRUMP FALSE GLEED KINKY SNIDE THRAW TIPSY WRONG ACROOK AKIMBO ARTFUL ASLANT CAMMED CAMSHO CRABBY CRAFTY CRANKY CURVED DOGLEG HURLED THRAWN TRICKY WEEWAW WEEWOW ZIGZAG ASKANCE ASQUINT CORRUPT CRABBED CURVOUS OBLIQUE TURNING TWISTED WINDING CAMSHACH THRAWART TORTUOUS
(PREF.) ANKYL(O) CROM
CROOKEDNESS PRAVITY RHEBOSIS
CROOKNECK CASHAW CUSHAW
CROON HUM LOW BOOM LULL SING WAIL CHIRM CRONY WHINE LAMENT MURMUR TEEDLE COMPLAIN
CROP BOB COW CUT LOP MAW SET TOP CLIP CRAP CRAW KNAP MINE REAP SETT SNIP STOW TRAP TRIM WHIP FRUIT GRAZE PLANT QUIRT SHAVE SHEAR SHIFT SWATH TILTH TRASH BROWSE BURDEN DECERP GATHER GEBBIE SILAGE BEARING BURTHEN CRAPPIN CURTAIL CUTTING HARVEST MAMMONI MASHLUM TILLAGE GLEANING PROFICHI TRASHIFY INGLUVIES
(— CANDLEWICK) SNUFF
(— OF A HAWK) GORGE
(— OF BIRDS) INGLUVIES
(— OF FRUIT) HANG
(— OF GRASS) LEA LEY SWATH SWARTH SWATHE
(— OF OYSTERS) SET
(— OF POTATOES) GARDEN
(— OUT) BASSET
(— UP) EMERGE
(GREEN —S) SOILAGE
(INDIAN —) RABI KHARIF
(LARGE —) HIT
(RIDING —) ROP
(SECOND-GROWTH —) ROWEN AFTERMATH
(PL.) FEED TILLAGE
CROPPED GOTCH SHAVED GOTCHED
CROPPER CARVER MUCKER PURLER GRINDER PLUMPER
CROPPING EARMARK
CROQUET ROQUE BOMBARD
CROQUETTE CECIL OYSTER KROMESKI KROMESKY
CROSIER BAGLE CROCE CROOK PEDUM STAFF POTENT BACULUS CAMBUCA CROZIER PASTORAL
CROSS GO CAM CUT MIX TAU ANKH CRUX FORD FUNK MARK PASS ROOD SIGN SOUR SPAN TREE WOOD ANGRY CANGY CHUFF CORSE GAMMY GURLY IRATE SURLY TEATY TESTY THRAW TRAVE TRIAL YAPPY BISECT CHUFFY CRABBY CRANKY CROUCH DENIAL EMBLEM FRANZY GIBBET GROUTY GRUMPY HIPPED OUTWIT PATCHY SIGNUM SNAGGY SNASTY SNUFFY SULLEN SYMBOL TEETHY THWART TOUCHY WICKED WOOLLY ATHWART BECROSS CALVARY CRABBED CROSIER CROZIER CRUSADE CRUSADO FRABOUS FRETFUL FROWARD OBLIQUE PASSAGE PATIBLE PEEVISH PETTISH POTENCE SALTIER SALTIRE CAMSHACH CRANTARA CROCIATE CROISADE CROSSLET CROTCHED CRUCIFIX DEBRUISE DEMISANG FRAMPOLD FRATCHED FRUMPISH OVERPASS PECTORAL PETULANT PHRAMPEL SNAPPISH SWASTIKA THUNDERY TRAVERSE VEXILLUM WINDMILL
(— BETWEEN GRAPEFRUIT AND TANGERINE) UGLI
(— BY PLANE) HOP
(— ONESELF) SAIN
(— OVER) SPAN TRAJECT
(DOUBLE —) BUSINESS
(KIND OF —) TAU
(MALTESE —) FIREBALL
(PREF.) CRUCI STAUR(O)
CROSSARM WISHBONE
CROSSBAR RUNG CROWN JUGUM DRIVER TRANSOM
(— IN GATE) SWORD
(— IN SHAFT) STEMPEL STEMPLE
(— OF BALANCE) BEAM
(— OF DOOR) SLOAT
(— OF WINDOW) LOCKET
CROSSBEAM BAR BUNK SPUR TRAVE GIRDER BOLSTER DORMANT TRANSOM TRAVERSE
CROSSBEARER CRUCIFER SPREADER
CROSSBILL FINCH
CROSSBOW PROD RODD BRAKE LATCH PIECE PRODD TILLER SLURBOW ARBALEST BALISTER BALLISTA STEELBOW STOCKBOW STONEBOW
(PART OF —) NUT IRON LOCK GUARD SIGHT STOCK WEDGE GROOVE STIRRUP TRIGGER BOWSTRING
CROSSBREED CUR HUSKY METIS SANGA SANGU HYBRID
CROSS CARRIER CRUCIFER
CROSSCURRENT EDDY SURGING
CROSSCUT DRIFT OFFSET TUNNEL COUPURE
CROSSCUT SAW BRIAR
CROSSCUTTER BUCKER
CROSSE STICK
CROSSED ACROSS SQUINT WOOFED CRUCIAL THWARTING
(PREF.) CHIASTO
CROSSER STICKER
CROSSETTE EAR ANCON ELBOW ANCONE CROSET
CROSS-EXAMINE GRILL TARGE
CROSSEXAMINE TARGE
CROSS-EYE ESOTROPIA
CROSS-EYED SQUINT
CROSS-FERTILIZATION ALLOGAMY PHYTOGAMY
CROSS FORM URDE URDY
CROSS-GRAINED THWART UGLY NURLY GNARLED HICKORY CONTRARY FRAMPOLD
CROSSHEAD YOKE
CROSSING XG PASS CROSS LACED MIXTURE PASSAGE TRAJECT CRUCIATE OPPOSING OVERPASS TRAVERSE CROSSOVER
(KIND OF —) ZEBRA
(NAVE —) TRANSEPT
CROSSLIKE CRUCIAL
CROSS-LINE (— OF LETTER) SERIF
CROSSPATCH BEAR CRAB CRANK GROUCH
CROSSPIECE BAR BAIL SPAR STEP YOKE BEARD GLAND GRILL ROUND STOCK PUTLOG THWART TOGGEL TOGGLE BOLSTER TRANSOM CROSSARM CROWFOOT FOOTRAIL HEADRAIL TRAVERSE CHOPSTICK
(PL.) CROSSTREE
CROSS-QUESTION GRILL TARGE TAIRGE
CROSSROAD LEET VENT WENT WEENT CAREFOX CARFOUR COMPITUM CROSSWAY
(PL.) TRIVIA
CROSSRUFF SAW SEESAW
CROSS-SHAPED CRUCIAL CRUCIATE
CROSS-STAFF CROSS RADIUS CROSIER CROZIER ARBALEST
CROSS STROKE BIND
CROSS-TEMPERED FRUMPISH

CROSSWALK ZEBRA
CROSSWISE CROSS ACROSS ATHWART ACROSTIC DIAGONAL OVERWART TRAVERSE WEFTWISE CROSSWAYS
CROSSWORD (— PUZZLER) CRUCIVERBALIST
CROSSWORT MAYWORT MUGWEED MUGWORT
CROTALUM CROTAL CYMBAL
CROTCH FORK POLE POST CLEFT NOTCH STAKE CRATCH CRUTCH GRAINS CROTCHET
CROTCHET FAD TOY HOOK KINK WHIM CRANK FANCY FREAK FIZGIG MAGGOT VAGARY CORCHAT CRANKUM
(HALF —) QUAVER
CROTCHETY KINKY CRANKY SNARKY
CROUCH HUG BEND CLAP COOK CURB DARE DROP FAWN FORM ROOK RUCK COWER HOVER SQUAT STOOP COORIE CRINGE CROOCH HUDDLE HUNKER HURKLE HURTLE SCOOCH SCOUCH CROODLE CROWDLE SCROOCH SCRUNCH SQUATTER
CROUCHING SQUAT CROUCHANT
CROUD SCROUGE
CROUP CRUP HIVES CRUPPER
CROUPIER DEALER TOURNEUR
CROUTON DIABLOTIN
CROW AGA CAW CRY DAW BRAG BRAN CRAW DOWP ROOK AYLET BOAST CRAKE CROWD EXULT GLOAT HOODY KELLY RAVEN VAUNT CARNAL CHOUGH CORBIE CORVUS HOODIE KOKAKO GORCROW GRAPNEL JACKDAW SWAGGER ABSAROKA BALDHEAD BLACKNEB GAVELOCK GRAYBACK GREYBACK
(PREF.) CORACO CORVI
(SUFF.) CORAX
CROWBAR PRY SET CROW BETTY JEMMY JIMMY LEVER SETUP SWAPE FORCER GABLOCK PITCHER GAVELOCK HANDSPEC
CROWBERRY HEATH HEATHER
CROWD FRY HUG JAM MOB SET TAG TIP BIKE CRAM CRUT FARE GANG HEAP HERD HOST JOSS MONG PACK PAVE PILE PUSH RAFT ROCK ROTE ROUT RUCK SERR SKIT SLUE SORT STOW SWAD TURB WOOD BUNCH CLOUD COHUE COVEY CRAMP CRUSH CRWTH DROVE FLOCK GROUP HORDE HURRY PLUMP POSSE PRESS ROTTA SERRY SHACK SHOAL STECH STIVE STUFF SWARM THREE VOLGE WEDGE BOODLE CHORUS CLIQUE HUBBLE HUDDLE HUSTLE IMPACT JOSTLE MITHER MOIDER OUTFIT PESTER RABBLE RESORT SCRUZE THRAVE THREAD THRIMP THRONG THRUST TOURBE TYMPAN VOLLEY BOUROCK CHROTTA CLUSTER COMPANY CONGEST IMPRESS JIMBANG SCROOGE SCROUGE SQUEEZE THICKEN THRUTCH CABOODLE ENTHRONG FREQUENT JINGBANG SANDWICH SATURATE VARLETRY CONCOURSE GATHERING MULTITUDE CLAMJAMFRY
(— ABOUT) FLOCK
(— AROUND) MOB BESIEGE
(— OUT) DISPLACE
(— TOGETHER) HUG HOTTER HOWDER HUDDLE CLUTTER CONTRUDE
(CONFUSED —) HURRY
(MOVING —) DROVE
(NOISY —) ROUT
(PREF.) OCHLO
CROWDED PANG CLOSE DENSE SPISS STIFF THICK FILLED SPISSY THRONG BUNCHED COMPACT OPPLETE POPULAR SERRIED STIPATE STUFFED TEEMING NUMEROUS POPULOUS JAMPACKED
CROWFOOT JOY PAGLE CREATE EXOGEN PAIGLE EELWARE GOLDCUP GOLLAND GOWLAND BANEWORT CRAWFOOT GOLDWEED HELLWEED
CROWING COCK
CROWN CAP TAJ TIP TOP BULL COIN GULL HELM PALE PATE PEAK POLL RIGO TIAR ADORN BASIL BEZEL BEZIL CREST MITER MITRE MURAL POLOS REGAL ROUND ROYAL TIARA ANADEM CANTLE CIRCLE CLIMAX CORONA DIADEM DOLLAR FILLET INVEST LAUREL POTONG REWARD SUMMIT TIMBER TROPHY UPWARD VALLAR VERTEX WREATH AUREOLE CHAPLET CORNICE CORONAL CORONET FORETOP GARLAND INSTALL PSCHENT STEPHEN TONSURE CORONATE CORONULE ENTHRONE PINNACLE SURMOUNT TURNPIKE
(— OF CHICORY) ENDIVE
(— OF EGYPT) ATEF PSCHENT
(— OF HEAD) NOLL PATE SKULL CANTLE POMMEL FORETOP
(— OF HILL) KNAP
(— OF LAUREL) BAY
(— OF ROCK) KRANTZ
(HALF —) GEORGE ALDERMAN
(PIECE OF —) BULL
(PLANT —) STOOL
(PREF.) CORONI CORONO STEPHAN(O)
CROWNED CORONATE LAURELED
(— WITH ROSES) ROSATED
CROW SHRIKE MAGPIE SQUEAKER
CROW'S NEST LOOKOUT
CROZER CHUCKER
CRUCIAL KEY ACUTE PIVOT NEEDLE SEVERE TRYING PIVOTAL SUPREME TELLING CRITICAL DECISIVE
CRUCIAN CARP GIBEL
CRUCIBLE POT DISH ETNA SHOE TEST CRUCE FOYER TRIAL CRUSET HEARTH MONKEY RETORT FURNACE CROSSLET
CRUCIFIX PAX ROOD CROSS
CRUCIFIXION RANSOM
CRUCIFY VEX HANG KILL HARRY MORTIFY TORMENT TORTURE CRUCIATE
CRUDE ILL RAW BALD BARE RUDE BRUTE CRASS GREEN GROSS HAIRY HARSH ROUGH TACKY CALLOW COARSE DOUGHY INCULT KUTCHA SAVAGE UNRIPE VULGAR ARTLESS GLARING SQUALID UNCOUTH AGRESTIC IGNORANT IMMATURE IMPOLITE INDIGEST PRIMITIVE
(NOT —) DELICATE
CRUDELY HARSHLY GAUCHELY
CRUDITY RUDENESS BARBARITY CRASSNESS GAUCHERIE ROUGHNESS
CRUEL ILL FELL GRIL GRIM HARD BLACK BREEM BREME BRUTE FELON HARSH RETHE SADIC STERN WROTH BITTER BLOODY BRUTAL DIVERS DREARY FIERCE IMMANE SAVAGE SEVERE UNJUST UNKIND UNMEEK UNMILD UNRIDE WANTON WICKED BESTIAL BOARISH BRUTISH GRIMFUL INHUMAN NERONIC SCADDLE SPITOUS WILROUN BARBARIC DIABOLIC FELONOUS FIENDISH INHUMANE PITILESS RUTHLESS SADISTIC TYRANNIC TRUCULENT
(THOUGHTLESSLY —) WANTON
CRUELLY FELL HARD CRUEL FELLY HARSHLY
CRUELTY RIGOR DURESS SADISM DEVILRY DEVILTRY FELLNESS SEVERITY
CRUET AMA JAR JUG VIAL BURET CRUSE BOTTLE CASTER CREVET CREWET GUTTUS AMPULLA BURETTE URCEOLE
CRUISE SAIL TRIP JUNKET STOOGE
(— AS A PIRATE) BUSK
CRUISER SHIP VALUER VESSEL WARSHIP ESTIMATOR
CRUISING ASEA
CRULLER WONDER OLYCOOK OLYKOEK TWISTER DOUGHNUT
CRUMB BIT ORT MURL NIRL PIECE LITTLE MORSEL CRIMBLE CRUMBLE MEALOCK MURLACK REMNANT FRAGMENT
(PL.) PANADA PANURE MOOLINGS
CRUMBLE ROT CRIM MULL MURL MUSH BREAK BROCK CRUSH DECAY RAVEL SLAKE SPALL SPOIL BUCKLE MOLDER MYRTLE PERISH SLOUGH CORRADE CRIMBLE MOULDER COLLAPSE
(— DOWN) GRUSH
(— UNDER OVERWEIGHT) FLUSH
CRUMBLED UNDURE
(EASILY —) CRIMP BRUCKLE CRUMBLY
CRUMBLING SAMEL SAMMEL POWDERY
CRUMBLY NESH MURLY CRUMBY CRUMMY FRIABLE PULVERULENT
CRUMPET CAKE MUFFIN PIKELET
CRUMPLE FOLD MOOL MUSS ROOL WISP CRUSH SCREW BUCKLE CREASE FURROW RAFFLE RUCKLE RUMPLE CRIZZLE CRUNKLE FRUMPLE SCRUNCH WRINKLE COLLAPSE CONTRACT SCRUMPLE
CRUNCH BITE CHEW MUCH CHOMP CRASH CRUMP CRUSH GNASH GRIND PRESS RUNCH CRANCH CRINCH GRANCH GROWSE CRAUNCH SCRANCH SCRUNCH
CRUPPER CROUP CURPEL CURPIN TAILBAND
CRUSADE WAR JEHAD JIHAD CROISEE CAMPAIGN CROCIATE
CRUSADER PILGRIM TEMPLAR EQUITIST REFORMER
(PL.) CROISES
CRUSADER IN EGYPT (CHARACTER IN —) ADRIANO ALADINO ARMANDO PALMIDE DORVILLE ELMIRENO
(COMPOSER OF —) MEYERBEER
CRUSH BOW HUG JAM BEND BORE BRAY CASE CHEW CRAM DASH MASH MILL MULL PASH RAVE STUB BRAKE BREAK BRIZZ CHAMP CHECK CRASH CRAZE CREEM CROWD FORCE FRUSH GRIND GRUSH PRESS QUASH QUELL SMASH SMUSH SQUAB SQUAT STAMP TREAD UNMAN BRUISE BURDEN CRUNCH DEFOIL DEFOUL KNATCH KNETCH SCOTCH SCRUSH SCRUZE SQUASH SQUISS SUBDUE THRING THRONG THWACK ACCABLE BECRUSH CONQUER CONTUSE CRACKLE CRUMPLE DEPRESS DESTROY OPPRESS OVERRUN REPRESS SCRUNCH SCRUNGE SHATTER SQUEEZE SQUELCH SUCCUMB TRAMPLE COMPRESS FORBREAK OVERCOME SQUABASH SUPPRESS OVERWHELM
(— BEANS) NIB
(— HAT) BONNET
(— IN) STAVE
(— ROCK) DOLLY DOLLEY DOLLIE
(— SPIRIT) BREAK
CRUSHABLE QUASHY
CRUSHED TAME BROKEN ECRASE MUSHED CONTRITE CRUMPLED
CRUSHER NIBBER
CRUSHING FIERCE BRUISING SMASHING SQUABASH
(SUFF.) TRIPSY
CRUST FUR PIP CAKE HULL RIND SCAB SHELL SKULL COFFIN CRUSTA ESCHAR GRATIN HARDEN RONDLE SCRUFF ABAISSE CALICHE COATING ENCRUST INCRUST CARAPACE PELLICLE SCUTULUM WINEBALL DURICRUST
(— IN BOILER) FUR
(— OF DIKE) SALBAND
(— OF DYKE) SALBAND
(— OF EARTH) SIAL SIMA
(— ON WINE) ARGAL ARGOL
(PIE —) HUFF COFFIN
(PL.) SORDES
CRUSTA PES
CRUSTACEAN BUG APUS CRAB FLEA SCUD ZOEA ALIMA CARID KRILL LOUSE PRAWN SCREW SCROW CYPRID ENDITE ISOPOD SHRIMP SLATER SQUILL ARTEMIA COPEPOD CRAYLET DAPHNID DECAPOD GRIBBLE HAYSEED LOBSTER SQUAGGA SQUILLA AMPHIPOD BARNACLE CIRRIPED

CRAYFISH GAMMARID LERNAEAN MONOCULE OSTRACOD PAGURIAN SQUILLID BRACHYURA PHYLLOPOD SCHIZOPOD SHELLFISH MALACOSTRACAN RHIZOCEPHALAN
(FEMALE —) HEN
CRUSTADE DARIOLE
CRUSTY CURT BLUFF BLUNT RUSTY TESTY MOROSE SULLEN CRABBED PEEVISH PETTISH STARCHY SNAPPISH
CRUTCH FORK STILT CLUTCH CRATCH CROTCH POTENT SADDLE SCATCH STADDLE
CRUX NUB GIST HALF PITH CROSS POINT PUZZLE RIDDLE PROBLEM
CRUX ANSATA ANKH
CRWTH ROTA ROTE CROWD CRUTH ROTTA ROTTE CROUTH CHROTTA
CRY HO AHA BOO CAW CRI FAD HOA HUE OLE PIP SOB YIP BAWL BELL BUMP CALL COWL CROW EVOE FALL GLAM GOWL HAIL HAWK HOOT HOWL KEEN MEWL NOTE OYES OYEZ PULE RAGE RAME RANE REEM RERD ROOP SCRY SIKE TOOT WAIL WEEP YELL YELP YOWL BARLA BLART BLORE CHEVY CLEPE CRAKE CROUP CRUNK GREDE GREET GROAN QUEAK RUMOR SHOUT SOUND TROAT UTTER VOGUE WHEWL WHINE WHULE WRAWL BARLEY BELLOW BOOHOO CHIVVY CLAMOR DEMAND ENSIGN LAMENT OUTCRY QUETHE SCREAM SHRIEK SLOGAN SNIVEL SQUALL SQUAWL SQUEAL TONGUE WIMICK YAMMER EXCLAIM FASHION HOSHANA SCREECH SPRAICH GARDYLOO PROCLAIM SCRONACH
(— ALOUD) BLART GREDE
(— AT SIGHT OF WHALE) FALL
(— DOWN) DOWNCRY BERATTLE
(— FOR TRUCE) BARLA BARLY BARLEY
(— HOARSELY) CROUP
(— LIKE ELEPHANT) BARR TRUMPET
(— LIKE PIG) WRINE
(— MOURNFULLY) YOWL
(— OF A BAT) CHIP
(— OF ABORIGINES) COOEE
(— OF BACCHANALS) EVOE
(— OF BIRD) CAW COO PEW BOOM CAWK CLANG BIRDCALL
(— OF BITTERN) BILL
(— OF CAT) MEW MEWL MIAOU MIAOW MIAUL MIAUW CALLING
(— OF CONTEMPT) BOO
(— OF DEER) BELL
(— OF DELIGHT) WHEE YIPES
(— OF DISCOVERY) EUREKA
(— OF DISGUST) PAH
(— OF ENTHUSIASM) BANZAI
(— OF GOOSE) HONK YANG
(— OF GUINEA HEN) POTRACK
(— OF HORROR) ACK
(— OF HOUND) MUTE MUSIC
(— OF JACKAL) PHEAL PHEALE PHEEAL
(— OF MOURNING) KEEN TANGI
(— OF NEWBORN CHILD) VAGITUS
(— OF RAVEN) QUALM
(— OF SHEEP) BAA BLAT BLEAT
(— OF SNIPE) SCAPE
(— OF SORROW) ULLAGONE
(— OF SURPRISE) ACK
(— OF SURRENDER) KAMERAD
(— OF WATCHMAN) WATCH
(— OUT) BAY BAWL BRAY GALE GAPE HOOT HOWL JERK SCRY BLORE CHIRM CLAIM ESCRY SHOUT HALLOO HOLLER SCREAM SHRIEK THREAP THROPE BREATHE EXCLAIM RECLAIM DISCLAIM PROCLAIM
(— TO CLEAR PASSAGE) HALL
(— TO COMBATANTS) BAILE
(— UP) CRACK
(BATTLE —) CRY ENSIGN MONTJOY GERONIMO MONTJOYE
(DERISIVE —) BOO FIE POOF POOH HUMBUG
(DISMAL —) HOWL WAIL YOWL
(DRINKING —) RIVO
(HOARSE —) CROAK
(HUNTING —) TIVY CHEVY CHIVY CHEVVY STABOY YOICKS TALLYHO TANTARA TANTIVY PILILLOO
(KIND OF —) FAR
(MAGICIAN'S —) PRESTO
(PROLONGED —) RANE
(RALLYING —) SLOGAN
(RAUCOUS —) CATCALL
(SHRILL) SKIRL SQUEAK SQUEAL SCREECH YALLOCK
(WAR —) DIN ALALA HAVOC BANZAI SLOGAN
(WORDLESS —) KEEN ULULU
CRY-BABY MARDY
CRYING PIPING URGING CLAMANT HEINOUS VAGIENT PRESSING RECREANT
(— OF HOUND) BELLING
CRYPT PIT CRAFT CROFT CROWD VAULT CAVERN GROTTO RECESS SHROUD CHAMBER FOLLICLE
CRYPTIC DARK VAGUE HIDDEN OCCULT SECRET OBSCURE ELLIPTIC MYSTICAL SIBYLLIC
CRYPTOGAM ACROGEN
CRYPTOGAMOUS AGAMIC AGAMOUS
CRYPTOGRAM CODE CRYPT CIPHER
CRYPTOGRAPH GEMATRIA
CRYPTOGRAPHER VIGENERE
CRYPTORCHID RIDGLING
CRYSTAL XL ICE DIAL DOME HARD IRIS SEED XTAL CLEAR CRANK GLASS GRAIN LUCID LUNET NICOL TABLE GLASSY LIMPID MIRROR NEEDLE PEBBLE QUARTZ TABLET ACICULA DIAMOND DIPLOID GLASSIE LUNETTE ORTHITE SPICULE TWOLING ULEXITE YAJEINE ZOISITE FIVELING FOURLING PELLUCID TRICHITE TRILLING PERIMORPH PHENOCRYST
(— FOREIGN TO ROCK) XENOCYST
(— OF GREAT STRENGTH) WHISKER
(FINE —) BERYL
(ICE —S IN WATER) FRAZIL
(NEEDLE-SHAPED —S) RAPHIDES
(ROCK —) BRISTOL CITRINE
(TWIN —) TWIN MACLE TWINDLE TWOLING FOURLING
(PL.) DRUSE GRAIN
(PREF.) CHRYSTO
(SUFF.) BLAST(IC)(Y) HEDRON
CRYSTAL GAZE SCRY
CRYSTAL GAZER SEER SCRYER SKRYER
CRYSTALLINE PURE CRYSTAL PELLUCID
CRYSTALLITE BELONITE TRICHITE BACILLITE SCOPULITE
CRYSTALLIZE FIX FIRM JELL CANDY SUGAR NEEDLE CONGEAL SOLIDIFY
CRYSTALLOGRAPHY LEPTOLOGY
C-SHAPED SIGMATE
CTENIDIUM COMB
CTENOPHORE RIB NUDA CESTOID CYDIPPID JELLYFISH
CUADRA MANZANA
CUB FRY PEN BEAR CHIT COOP SHED TOTO STALL WHELP LIONET NOVICE CODLING REPORTER
(— SCOUT) WEBELOS

CUBA

BAY: NIPE PIGS
CAPE: CRUZ MAISI LUCRECIA
CAPITAL: HAVANA
CIGAR: HAVANA
COIN: PESO CENTAVO CUARENTA
DANCE: CONGA RUMBA DANZON RHUMBA GUARACHA PACHANGA
FALLS: TOA AGABAMA CABURNI
GULF: MEXICO ANAMARIA BATABANO
INDIAN: CARIB TAINO ARAWAK
ISLAND: PINES
ISLANDS: SABANA CAMAGUEY
MEASURE: VARA BOCOY TAREA CORDEL FANEGA
MOUNTAIN: TURQUINO
MOUNTAINS: CRISTAL MAESTRA ORGANOS TRINIDAD
PROVINCE: HAVANA ORIENTE CAMAGUEY MATANZAS
RIVER: ZAZA CAUTO
SWAMP: ZAPATA
TOWN: COLON MANES ALAMAR BAYAMO GUINES HAVANA BARACOA HOLGUIN PALMIRA ARTEMISA CAMAGUEY GUAYABAL MATANZAS SANTIAGO
TREE: JIQUE JIQUI
WEIGHT: LIBRA TERCIO

CUBAN LILY SCILLA
CUBBYHOLE CELL NOOK CUBBY
CUBE CUT DIE NOB KNOB BLOCK EIGHT SOLID TIMBO BABASCO CUBELET TESSERA BARBASCO QUADRATE TESSELLA
(— OF BREAD) CROUTON
(— OF COLORED GLASS) SMALTO
(— WITH 21 SPOTS) DIE
(MEAT —S) CABOB KABOB KEBOB
(PUZZLE —) RUBIC
(PL.) DICE
CUBIC SOLID CUBOID CUBICAL
CUBICALLY DIEWISE
CUBIC CENTIMETER FLUIGRAM
CUBICLE BAY CELL ROOM BOOTH CABIN NICHE STALL ALCOVE CARREL CARRELL
CUBIC METER STERE
CUBIT ELL CODO HATH COVID HASTA COUDEE
CUBITUS ULNA
CUB SHARK LAMIA GALEID REQUIEM
CUCKING STOOL THEW TUMBLER TUMBREL TUMBRIL
CUCKOLD TUP HORN BECCO VULCAN WITTOL ACTAEON CORNUTE CORNUTO HORNIFY RAMHEAD COKEWOLD
CUCKOLDED FORKED UNICORN
CUCKOLDISE GRAFT
CUCKOLD-MAKING HORNING
CUCKOLDRY HORNWORK
CUCKOO ANI GAG COWK CUCK FOOL GOUK GOWK KOEL KOIL CLOCK CRAZY KOKIL SILLY COUCAL DIDRIC HUNTER KOBIRD BOOBOOK CHATAKA DIEDRIC KOWBIRD SIRKEER CHOWCHOW PICARIAN RAINBIRD RAINFOWL
(PREF.) CUCULI
CUCKOOFLOWER HEAD PAGLE SPINK CUCKOO PAIGLE HEADACHE MILKMAID
CUCKOOPINT ARUM RAMP AARON AROID BOBBIN DRAGON BUCKRAM OXBERRY MANDRAKE
CUCKOO SPIT WOODSERE
CUCULLATE COWLED HOODED COVERED
CUCUMBER CUKE PEPO GOURD CONGER CUCURB PEPINO PICKLE GHERKIN PICKLER CUCURBIT PEPONIDA PEPONIUM
(BITTER —) COLOCYNTH
(SHRIVELED —) CRUMPLING
(WILD —) SICYOS CREEPER
(PREF.) CUCUMI
CUCURBIT BODY FLASK GOURD CUCURB ALEMBIC MATRASS
CUD CHEW QUID BOLUS QUEED RUMEN CUDGEL
CUDBEAR CORK PERSIO PERSIS CUDWEED
CUD-CHEWING RUMINANT
CUDDLE HUG LAP PET CARESS COSSET FONDLE HUGGLE KIDDLE KIUTLE NESTLE PETTLE CROODLE CRUDDLE EMBRACE SMUGGLE SNOOZLE SNUGGLE CANOODLE
CUDDLESOME HUGGABLE
CUDDY ASS LOUT BRIBE CABIN DONKEY GALLEY PANTRY CUDEIGH
(BELOVED OF —) BUXOMA
CUDGEL BAT CUD BEAT CANE CLUB CRAB DRUB KENT MACE RACK RUNG TREE BASTE BATON BILLY DRIVE KEBBY KEVEL LINCH LINGE SHRUB STAFF STAVE STICK THUMP TOWEL ALPEEN BALLOW BASTON BILLET GIBBET KEBBIE LIBBET THRASH WASTER BELABOR BOURDON DRUBBER SWADDLE SWINGLE TROUNCE BLUDGEON SHILLALA THWACKER SHILLALAGH
CUDWEED ENAENA CATFOOT
CUE QU NOD TAG TIP HINT MAST TAIL WINK BRAID CLUFF PLAIT

QUEUE TWIST PROMPT SIGNAL PIGTAIL
(BILLIARD —) MACE MAST STICK
(MUSICAL —) PRESA
(PART OF —) TIP BUTT HILT JOINT POINT SHAFT BUMPER FERRULE
(SHUFFLEBOARD —) SHOVEL
(TIP OF —) LEATHER
CUFF BOX BANK BLOW GOWF SLAM SLAP SLUG SWAT TURF CLOUT FIGHT GOWFF MISER SCUFF SCUFT SMITE SOUSE BUFFET CODGER FENDER MITTEN STRIKE TURNUP COLPHEG SCUFFLE WHERRET GAUNTLET HANDBLOW HANDCUFF TURNBACK
CUIR DORADO
CUIRASS CURACE CURATE CURIET LORICA THORAX
CUIRASSIER LOBSTER
CUISINE FOOD MENU TABLE COOKERY KITCHEN
(KIND OF —) HAUTE
(SOUTHERN —) CAJUN CREOLE
CUITLATEC TECO
CUL-DE-SAC POCKET STRAIT IMPASSE
CULL OPT CAST COIL DUPE GULL PICK PIKE SIFT SORT ELECT GLEAN PLUCK ASSORT CHOOSE GARBLE GATHER REMOVE SELECT CULLING SEPARATE
CULLET SCRAP
CULLODEN MOOR
CULM COOM HAULM SLACK COOMBE REFUSE DEPOSIT
(PL.) SIRKI SIRKY
CULMINATE CLIMAX
CULMINATION END ACME APEX AUGE CULM NOON ROOF BLOOM CREST CROWN HIGHT POINT APOGEE CLIMAX CULMEN CUMBLE HEIGHT PAYOFF PERIOD SUMMIT VERTEX ZENITH BLOWOFF
CULOTTE PANTDRESS
CULOTTES GAUCHOS
CULPABILITY BLAME FAULT GUILT DEMERIT
CULPABLE FAULTY GUILTY LACHES SINFUL IMMORAL TOBLAME BLAMABLE CRIMINAL
CULPRIT FELON CONVICT CRIMINAL OFFENDER
CULT CLAN DADA SECT CREED KUKSU CHURCH CULTUS DOMNEI MANISM NUDISM RITUAL SCHOOL SHINTO AMIDISM DADAISM ICONISM MYALISM MYSTERY WORSHIP DEVILISM HUMANISM SATANISM
(— OF MALE VIRILITY) MACHISMO
(ADHERENT OF RELIGIOUS —) RASTA RASTAMAN
(SUFF.) ISM
CULTCH CUTCH STOOL SCULCH
CULTIVATE EAR HOE CROP DISC DISK FARM GROW PLOW REAR TEND TILL WORK DRESS EARTH LABOR NURSE RAISE STUDY TRAIN AFFECT FOSTER FURROW HARROW MANAGE MANURE PLOUGH RATOON SARCLE SCHOOL ACQUIRE CHERISH CONTOUR CULTURE EDUCATE EMBRACE EXPLOIT HUSBAND IMPROVE NOURISH PREPARE SCRATCH CIVILIZE
(— FAVOR) BOOTLICK
CULTIVATED ABAD TAME CIVIL GROWN POLITE SATIVE TOILED POLITIC REFINED CULTURED ARTIFICIAL
(ARTIFICIALLY —) HOTHOUSE
CULTIVATION CROP TILTH FINISH GROWTH CULTURE TILLAGE TILTURE LABORAGE MANURAGE REFINEMENT
(— IN MANNERS) FINISH
(MENTAL —) HUMANITY
CULTIVATOR JAT KMET RYOT ILAVA SULKY FARMER GADABA HARROW ILAVAN MAMOTY MILLER RIDGER TILLER FLORIST GRUBBER HUSBAND MEADOWER ROSARIAN SCUFFLER
(— GANG) RIG
(PL.) LAETI
CULTURAL HUMANIST
CULTURE ART AGAR STAB KULLI NASCA NAZCA SHAKE SLANT SLOPE TAJIN TASTE TILTH JHUKAR KULTUR POLISH STREAK WILTON ABASHEV ANANINO AZILIAN IRANISM JHANGAR KAYENTA SOCIETY STARTER TILLAGE HUMANISM LEARNING
(ESKIMO —) DORSET
(MEXICAN —) MAZAPAN
(MIDDLEBROW —) MIDCULT
(PREF.) ETHEO
CULTURED CIVIL POLITE LETTERED
CULVERIN SLING CULVER LANTACA PELICAN SPIROLE
CULVERT FOX GOUT DRAIN SLUIT BRIDGE CONDUIT CULBERT PINNOCK PONCEAU OVERPASS
CUMBER BURDEN CUMMER SHACKLE
CUMBERSOME GOURD HEAVY CLUMSY UNRIDE AWKWARD LUGSOME ONEROUS WEIGHTY CUMBROUS UNWIELDY
CUMMER GIRL LASS WOMAN KIMMER
CUMMERBUND BAND BELT SASH
CUMMUTATIVE ABELIAN
CUMULATE HEAP GATHER COMBINE
CUMULATIVE CHAIN SUMMATIVE
CUNA CUEVA DARIEN
CUNEIFORM ULNARE WEDGED
CUNNER CANOE NIPPER WRASSE BURGALL CHOGSET GOLDNEY NIBBLER BERGGYLT BLUEFISH CORKWING GILTHEAD
CUNNING ART OLD SHY SLY WIT ARCH CUTE DEEP FAST FINE FOXY KEEN SLIM SNOD TRAP WILY WISE CANNY CRAFT DOWNY FAVEL GUILE LOOPY PAUKY PAWKY POKEY SHARP SMART ADROIT ARTFUL ASTUTE CALLID CLEVER CRAFTY DAEDAL DECEIT ENGINE FOXERY PRETTY QUAINT SHREWD SUBTLE SUPPLE TRICKY WISDOM COMPASS CRAFTLY CURIOUS FINESSE KNOWING PARLISH PARLOUS POLITIC PRACTIC SLEIGHT SUBTILE VARMINT VULPINE CONTOISE DEXTROUS MANAGERY QUENTISE SKILLFUL SLEIGHTY STEALTHY YEPELEIC
CUNNING LITTLE VIXEN
(CHARACTER IN —) LAPAK PRIEST HARASTA TERYNKA FORESTER SHARPEARS GOLDENMANE SCHOOLMASTER
(COMPOSER OF —) JANACEK
CUNNINGLY YEPLY YEPELY
CUP AMA BOX CAN DOP MUG NOG POT TOT TUN TYG CELL DOPP HORN LOTA PECE SHOE SKEW TASS TOSS BOUSE CALIX CHARK COGUE COPPE CRUSE CYLIX DEPAS GLASS GODET GRAIL KITTY PHIAL SCALE STEIN STOOP STOUP TASSE TAZZA THECA BEAKER BICKER BUCKET BUMPER CAPPIE CHOANA COTYLA CRATER CUPULA DOBBIN EGGCUP EYECUP FALSIE FESSEL FINJAN GOBLET JICARA KOTYLE MAZARD NAGGIN NOGGIN OXHORN POTION RUMKIN TASSIE VESSEL BRIMMER CAPSULE CHALICE CHEERER CYATHUS GODDARD KYATHOS QUONIAM SCYPHUS SHERBET STIRRUP THIMBLE TRINKET VENTOSE BRIDECUP GRADUATE PANNIKIN STANDARD TJANTING
(— FOR HOLDING DIAMOND) DOP DOPP
(— FOR PERFUMES) CONCH
(— FOR YEAST) SKEP
(— IN SAUCER OF ALCOHOL) ETNA
(— OF FLOWER) BELL
(— OF TEA) DISH CUPPA SPEED OYSTER
(— ON BULLET) GASCHECK
(— WITH COVER) HANAP
(ASSAYING —) CUPEL
(CAFE —) TASSE
(DRINKING —) CAN MUG NUT TIG TUN TYG CANN HORN TASS TOSS GODET BEAKER GOBLET HOLMOS QUAICH RUMMER CHALICE GODDARD TRINKET
(FAIRY —) COOLWORT
(FILLED —) BUMPER
(IRISH —) MADDER METHER
(IRON —) CULOT MUSHROOM
(LARGE —) FACER BLACKJACK
(LEATHER —) WELL GISPIN
(LONG-HANDLED —) CYATH DIPPER CYATHUS KYATHOS
(MAPLE —) MAZER
(NAUTICAL —) THIEF
(ORNAMENTAL —) TAZZA
(PAPER —) DIXIE
(PASTRY —) DARIOLE
(PRIZE —) PEWTER
(SACRED —) GRAIL
(SHALLOW —) CYLIX TAZZA TASTER CAPSULE
(SMALL —) DOP NOG TOT DOPP TASS DOBBIN NAGGIN NOGGIN TASSIE
(SQUARE —) MADDER METHER
(STIRRUP —) BONAILIE
(WINE-TASTING —) TASTEVIN
(WOODEN —) COG COGUE CAPPER CAPPIE METHER QUAICH
(PL.) VALONIA
(PREF.) CALATHI CALICI COTYL(I)(O) CUPULI CYATH(I)(O) POCILLI SCYPH(I)(O)
(SUFF.) COTYL(LY)(OUS)
CUPBEARER HEBE SAKI CUPPER GANYMEDE
CUPBOARD CUB KAS BOLE CASE COIN SAFE AMBRY CHEST CUBBY CUDDY HUTCH PRESS ABACUS AUMBRY AWMRIE BUFFET CLOSET LARDER LOCKER PANTRY SPENCE ALMIRAH ARMOIRE CABINET DRESSER PIESAFE SKIBBET ALHACENA CREDENCE CREDENZA TROSTERA
(ARCHERY —) ASCHAM
CUPEL TEST
CUPFUL CUP CAROUSE
CUP HOLDER ZARF
CUPID DAN AMOR EROS LOVE PUTTO CHERUB AMORINO AMOURET AMORETTO
(PL.) PUTTI
CUPIDITY LUST GREED DESIRE AVARICE AVIDITY LONGING APPETITE RAPACITY
CUPOLA DOME KILN TYPE VAULT BELFRY TURRET CALOTTE FURNACE LANTERN LOOKOUT CIMBORIO COCKLOFT
(ROUND —) THOLUS
CUPOLAMAN HEATER
CUPPED GLENOID
CUPPING GLASS VENTOSE
CUPSEED NUTSEED
CUP-SHAPED PEZIZOID SCYPHATE
CUPULE CUP BOLSTER CYATHUS THUMBMARK
CUR DOG YAP FICE FIST FYCE MUTT TIKE TYKE FEIST KEOUT BRAKJE MESSAN MESSIN BOBTAIL MONGREL WHAPPET
CURABLE SANABLE
CURARE URARE URARI OORALI WOORALI
CURASSOW MITU COPPY HOCCO MITUA PAUXI
CURATE ABBE CURA AGENT VICAIRE MINISTER
CURATIVE HEALING IATRICAL PHYSICAL REMEDIAL SALUTARY SANATIVE
CURATOR KEEPER STEWARD GUARDIAN OVERSEER
CURB BIT LID CRUB FOIL KERB REIN SKID SNIP SNUB BRAKE CHECK CRIMP CURVE GUARD LEASH LIMIT MOUND ARREST BOTTLE BRIDLE COERCE COLLAR DECKLE GOVERN HAMPER STIFLE STRAIN SUBDUE THWART CONTROL CURBING INHIBIT REFRAIN REPRESS SHACKLE ATTEMPER COMPESCE MODERATE RESTRAIN RESTRICT WITHHOLD
(OFFICIAL —) LID
(WELL —) PUTEAL
CURCULIO TURK WEEVIL
CURCUMA ZEDOARY

CURD CRUD DAHI CHEESE CURDLE CASEINE CLABBER CONGEAL COAGULUM
(— IN MILK) ZIEGA
(—S AND WHEY) SLIP PINJANE
(BEAN —) TOFU
(PL.) SKYR FLEETINGS
(PREF.) THROMB(O)
CURDLE CAP LOP RUN SAM SET CRIM CURD EARN LEEP QUAR SAMM SOUR TURN WHIG YERN CARVE QUAIL QUARL SPOIL YEARN CAILLE LAPPER LOBBER LOPPER POSSET QUARLE CLABBER CONGEAL CRIDDLE CRUDDLE THICKEN CONDENSE
CURDLED CURDLY QUARRED SHOTTEN
(NOT —) UNCRUDDED
CURE DIP DRY DUN FIX BEEF BOOT CARE CORN HEAL HEED HELP JERK MEND SALT SANE SAVE AMEND BLOAT BOTEN LEECH REEST SMEEK SMOKE CHARGE CURATE KIPPER PHYSIC PRIEST RECURE REMEDY SEASON SUCCOR TEMPER WARISH BESMOKE RECOVER RESTORE THERAPY TREACLE ANTIDOTE BARBECUE CURATION GUERISON PRESERVE REVOCERY
(— A HABIT) BREAK
(— BY SMOKING) GAMMON SMUDGE
(— FISH) DUN ROUSE
(— GRASS) HAY
(— HAY) WIN
(— HERRINGS) BLOAT
(— IN SUN) RIZZAR
(— SKINS) DRESS
(COUGH —) SAPA SAPE
CURE-ALL BALM AVENS ELIXIR REMEDY PANACEA THERIAC
CURED SALT BLOATED
CURIO DOODAD
CURIOSITY CURIO ODDITY INTEREST
(— OF SMALL VALUE) GABION
(—S OF THE CITY) LIONS
(PL.) CURIOSA
CURIOUS ODD NOSY RARE SELI QUEER SELLE SELLY PRYING QUAINT SNOOPY CUNNING STRANGE UNUSUAL FREAKISH MEDDLING PECULIAR SINGULAR
(— ONE) PANDORA
CURL BOB BEND COIL FEAK FURL KINK LOCK PURL ROLL TUBE WAVE WIND ACKER CANON CRIMP CRISP DILDO FRILL FRIZZ QUIRL SPIRE TRESS TWIRE TWIST BERGER BUCKLE CANNON CRUCHE CURDLE FROWSE MULLET RIPPLE SPIRAL TUNNEL WRITHE CRIDDLE CRIMPLE CRINKLE CROCKET CRUDDLE EARLOCK FLEXURE FRIZZLE FROUNCE RINGLET SERPENT TENDRIL WHISKER FAVORITE LOVELOCK SQUIGGLE
(— HAIR) CROOK
(— OF SMOKE) WREATH
(— OF WIG) SNAKE
(— ON FOREHEAD) CRUCHE CROUCHE
(— OVER) BREAK
(— UP) CRUMP HUNCH SNIRL HUDDLE SHRINK SNUGGLE
(FRINGE OF —S) FRISETTE FRIZETTE
(METAL —) CHIP
(SMALL —) CROCK
(PREF.) CIRR(I)(O) CIRRH(I)(O)
CURLED CRISP FUZZY KINKY SPIRY CIRRATE COCKLED CRISPED FRIZZLY SAVOYED WREATHY CRISPATE CRUMPLED GAUFFRED GOFFERED HELICINE SCROLLED
CURLER GOFFER TEASER CRIMPER FRIZZER MULLETS
CURLEW FUTE JACK SPOW KIOEA SNIPE SPOWE WHAAP WHAUP DIKKOP MARLIN SMOKER BANKERA BUSTARD DOEBIRD BLUELEGS WHIMBREL SICKLEBILL
CURLICUE ESS CAPER CURVE CASSIS PARAPH SQUIRL FLOURISH PURLICUE SCRIGGLE SQUIGGLE
CURLING CRISP
CURLING MARK TEE
CURLING MATCH SPIEL
CURLING STONE IRON STONE LOOFIE GRANITE
(— SPIN) RAISE
CURL-PAPER CRACKER PAPILLOTE
CURLY WAVY CRISP CRULL OUNDY CRIMPY RIPPLED CRINKLED
(— HAIR) VEDDOID
CURMUDGEON CRAB CHURL HUNKS MISER GLEYDE GROUCH NIGGARD
(LIKE A —) CRUSTY
CURMUDGEONLY STINGY
CURRANT PASA BERRY CASSIS RAISIN RIZZAR RIZZLE CORINTH
(PL.) RIBES SPICE
CURRANT BUN WIG WIGG
CURRAWONG SQUEAKER STREPERA
CURRENCY CASH COIN PASS BILLS CATER MONEY SCRIP SERIES SPECIE PASSAGE WILDCAT
(FRACTIONAL —) SPONDULIX
(SHELL —) UHLLO
CURRENT NOW WAY EDDY FLOW FLUX FORD RACE RIFE TIDE VEIN WAFT ALIVE DRIFT GOING RAPID ROUST SCOUR SWIFT TENOR TESLA TREND USUAL ABROAD ACTUAL COEVAL COMMON COURSE DOUCHE DURANT FLUENT LATEST LIVING MOTION MOVING OFFSET OUTSET RECENT RIZZER RULING SLUICE STRAND STREAM TONGUE VOLANT COUNTER DRAUGHT FLOWING FRESHET GENERAL INDRAFT INSTANT PASSANT PRESENT RUNNING STICKLE THERMAL TORRENT BACKWASH CURRANCE DOWNCAST FREQUENT MILLRACE OCCURENT PASSABLE TIDERACE TODAYISH UNDERTOW
(— IN SPEECH) WAIF
(— INSTRUMENT) AMMETER
(AIR —) DRAFT SHEET SPLIT BREEZE DRAUGHT DOWNCAST DOWNFLOW
(ELECTRIC —) STRAY
(HOT —) BACK
(JAPAN —) KUROSHIO KUROSIWO
(KIND OF —) RIP
(PREVAILING —) MAINSTREAM
(RAPID —) SWIFT TONGUE
(SOUND —) DISTORTION
(STRONG —) GALE ROOST ROUST
(PREF.) RHEO
CURRENTLY ANYMORE
CURRICULUM STREAM PROGRAM PROGRAMME
CURRISH BASE CYNICAL DOGGISH IGNOBLE SNARLING
CURRY COMB DRUB KARI CLEAN DRESS GROOM BRUISE CAJOLE CARREE POWDER PREPARE TARKEEAN
(— FAVOR) HUG NUT QUILL COTTON SMOOGE CUITTLE SMOODGE
CURSE BAN HEX POX BANE BLOW CUSS DAMN JINX OATH PIZE WARY BLAST BLESS CORSE SHREW SPELL SWEAR WEARY WINZE DETEST DEVOTE GOOFER GUFFER MAKUTU MALIGN MAUGER MAUGRE ACCURSE BESHREW MALISON SWEARAT ANATHEMA EXECRATE FORSPEAK MALEDICTION
CURSED DASH CUSSED DAMNED DASHED ACCURSED
CURSER WARIER
CURSING BLESSING BLASPHEMY
CURSIVE RUNNING
CURSORILY OBITER
CURSORY FAST BRIEF HASTY QUICK SHORT FITFUL ROVING SPEEDY PASSANT PASSING SHALLOW CARELESS RAMBLING
CURT BUFF RUDE TART BLUFF BLUNT BRIEF BRUSK NIPPY SHORT SQUAB TERSE ABRUPT CURTAL CUTTED SNIPPY BRUSQUE CONCISE CRYPTIC LACONIC CAVALIER SNAPPISH SNIPPETY SUCCINCT
CURTAIL CUT LOP CLIP CROP DOCK PARE STOP ABATE ELIDE SHORT SLASH STUNT TRUNK DECURT LESSEN REDUCE ABRIDGE BOBTAIL CRACKLE SHORTEN DIMINISH MINORATE RETRENCH
CURTAILED TAIL CUTTY SHORT STUNT CURTAL BOBTAIL CONCISE ABRIDGED
CURTAIN END BOOM DROP IRIS MASK VEIL WALL BLIND DRAPE SCENE SHADE SHEET VELUM COSTER HANGER PURDAH SCREEN SHROUD CEILING CONCEAL CORTINE DRAPERY HANGING VITRAGE ASBESTOS PORTIERE TRAVERSE
(CHURCH —) CLOTH RIDDEL ENDOTYS ENDOTHYS
(THEATER —) IRON SCRIM TEASER TRAVELER TORMENTER
(PL.) END DEATH
CURTAIN ROD TRINGLE
CURTAIN STRETCHER SCRAY STRAINER
CURTAL CRAPE COURTAL CURTLAX
CURTSY BOB BOW DIP DOP BECK DROP JOUK KNEE CONGE HONOR CURCHY
CURUBA CASSA BANANA
CURVATED STUNT HOOKED
CURVATURE ARC PLY ARCH BENT BOOL CURL CURVE SHEER SINUS CAMBER CURVITY ADUNCITY APOPHYGE CYRTOSIS GRYPOSIS KYPHOSIS LORDOSIS
(— OF BONE) ARCUATION
(— OF DECK) SHEER
(— OF LEGS) RHEBOSIS
(— OF SHOE SOLE) SWING
(— OF SPINE) KYPHOSIS SCOLIOSIS
(— OF STOMACH) FUNDUS
(— OF STRAKE) SPILING
CURVE ARC BOW CUP ESS SAG ARCH BEND BOUT COME CURB FADE HOOK KNEE LINE OGEE TURN VEER WIND AMBIT BIGHT BREAK CONIC CROOK CRUMP CUBIC HELIX NONIC OGIVE PEDAL POLAR QUIRK SLICE SWEEP SWIRL TARVE TREND TWIST WITCH BOUGHT CAMBER CIRCLE DEFLEX JORDAN LITUUS SOLVUS SPIRAL SPRING TOROID WIMPLE ADIABAT BRACKET CAUSTIC CIRCUIT CISSOID COMPASS CONCAVE CONTOUR COSEISM CURVITY CYCLOID ELLIPSE ENVELOP FESTOON FLEXURE INCURVE INFLECT LIMACON PHUGOID PROFILE QUARTIC SCALLOP SINUATE SOLIDUS CARDIOID CATENARY CONCHOID DYGOGRAM ELASTICA EXTRADOS FADEAWAY INTRADOS INVOLUTE LIGATURE LIQUIDUS OPHIURID PARABOLA SINUSOID TONOGRAM TRACTRIX TROCHOID STROPHOID CATACAUSTIC
(— DESCRIBED BY GRAPH) GRAM
(— IN HANDRAIL) KNEE
(— IN PLANKING) HANG
(— IN SAIL) ROACH
(— OF ARCH) INTRADOS
(— OF BALL) DROP
(— OF BIT) LIBERTY
(— OF COLUMN) APOPHYGE
(— OF FINGERNAIL) GRYPOSIS
(— OF HORSE'S NECK) CREST
(— OF PLANK) SNY
(— OF SHIP'S BOW) FLAIR FLARE
(— OF TIMBER) CUP
(— SATISFYING EQUATION) BRANCH
(— SPACE) KNOT
(— WHEN DRAWN) COME
(BASEBALL —) SNAKE
(CRICKET —) SWERVE
(DOUBLE —) CIMA CYMA
(KIND OF —) LAFFER LEARNING PRACTICE
(PLANE —) ROSE STROPHOID
(PLANE CUBIC —) WITCH
(VERTICAL —) RAMP
CURVED BENT SOFT ADUNC CORBE CURVE CURVY ROUND WOUND CONVEX CURVEY GYRATE HAMATE TURNED ARCUATE ARRONDI

CONCAVE CROOKED CURVANT EMBOWED FALCATE SIGMOID ADUNCOUS ANCHORAL AQUILINE ARCIFORM CRUMPLED CYGNEOUS DECURVED EXCURVED SCROLLED ARCHIFORM
(PREF.) ANCYLO ANKYLO CAMPTO CAMPYL(O) CURVI CURVO CYRT(O)
(SUFF.) CLASTIC
CURVET HOP LEAP LOPE SKIP TURN BOUND CAPER FRISK PRANK VAULT CAVORT CROUPE FROLIC GAMBOL PRANCE PANNADE CORVETTO CROUPADE
CURVING SPIRY SIMOUS TWISTY AQUILINE DRAWDOWN
(— IN) CONCAVE
(— OUTWARD) BOMBE
(DOWN —) EPINASTY
(SMOOTHLY —) FAIR
CUSH (FATHER OF —) HAM
CUSH-CUSH CARA YAMPEE
CUSHION BAG COD MAT PAD PIG BALL BANK BOSS PUFF SEAT SUNK TRIM GADDI GADHI PANEL SQUAB TRUSH BUFFER INSOLE JOCKEY MUSNUD PILLOW SACHET BOLSTER BRIOCHE COSSHEN HASSOCK KNEELER MUFFLER PILLION REPOSAL ROOTCAP CUTIDURE OREILLER PULVINAR PINCUSHION
(KIND OF —) WHOOPEE
(LACE-MAKERS —) BOTT
(PIN —) PRINCOD
(SEAT —) BANKER
(TAILOR'S —) HAM
(PREF.) PULVILLI PULVINI
CUSHIONING DUNNAGE
CUSHIONLIKE PULVINAR
CUSHION PLANT POLSTER
CUSHIONY PADDY
CUSHITIC NUBIAN
CUSHY PLUM
CUSK COD TUSK TORSK BURBOT CATFISH
CUSP APEX CONE HORN PEAK ANGLE POINT STYLE TOOTH CORNER SPINODE ENTOCONE HYPOCONE METACONE PARACONE
CUSPID CANINE
CUSPIDOR GABOON CRACHOIR SPITTOON
CUSSO KOSO KOUSSO BRAYERA BRAZERA
CUSTARD FLAN FOOL CREME FLAWN DOUCET DOWCET CHARLET PARFAIT FLUMMERY DIABLOTIN ZABAGLIONE
(— PIE) QUICHE
CUSTARD APPLE ANONA ANNONA PAWPAW CORAZON SWEETSOP
CUSTODIAN HACK GUARD BAILEE CUSTOS KEEPER SEXTON WARDEN WARDER CURATOR JANITOR CERBERUS CLAVIGER GUARDIAN CONCIERGE
CUSTODY LAP BAIL CARE HOLD KEEP WARD TRUST ARREST CHARGE SAFETY YEMSEL CONTROL DURANCE KEEPING TUITION COMMENDA CUSTODIA HANDFAST SECURITY WARDSHIP
CUSTOM FAD LAW MOS PAD TAX URE USE WON ASAL DUTY FORM GARB MODE MORE RITE ROTE RULE THEW TOLL WONE WONT FUERO GUISE HABIT HAUNT RITUS STYLE SUNNA TRADE TREAD TRICK USAGE VOGUE BYRLAW DASTUR DHARMA GROOVE IMPOST MANNER MINHAG MONTEM PRAXIS SUNNAH USANCE COSTUME DUSTOOR DUSTOUR FASHION FORMULA HALAKAH TRIBUTE USAUNCE WARNOTH BUSINESS ENDOGAMY HABITUDE PRACTICE ASSUETUDE CONSUETUDE PRESCRIPTION
(BINDING —) LAW
(BUSINESS —) TRADE GOODWILL
(CHILDBIRTH —) COUVADE
(CHURCH —) COMITY
(CORRUPT —) ABUSE
(FESTIVAL —) HOCKING
(OUTMODED —) ARCHAISM
(PRIMITIVE —) COUVADE
(RURAL —) HEAVING
(SECRET —) SANDE
(TEMPORARY —) FAD VOGUE
(PL.) MORES MOEUR HAIKWAN FOLKLORE PROPRIETIES
CUSTOMARILY USUALLY CUSTOMLY
CUSTOMARY PER RIFE TAME USED NOMIC USUAL BEATEN COMMON SOLEMN VULGAR WONTED CLASSIC GENERAL REGULAR USITATE EVERYDAY FAMILIAR HABITUAL ORTHODOX
(NOT —) INSOLENT
CUSTOMER CHAP COVE BUYER CLIENT PATRON SUCKER ACCOUNT CALLANT CHAPMAN PATIENT SHOPPER MERCHANT PROSPECT
(PRINTER'S —) AUTHOR
(PROBABLE —) PROSPECT
(TOUGH —) HARDCASE
(PL.) CUSTOM CLIENTELE
CUSTOMHOUSE ADUANA DOGANA DOUANE
CUSTOM-MADE BESPOKE BESPOKEN
CUSTOMS OFFICER SHARK WAITER
CUT AX ADZ AXE BOB DAG DAP DIE HAG HEW KIT LOP MOW NIP RIT SAW SNY TAP ADZE BANG BITE BOLO BOLT BUZZ CHIP CHOP CLIP CROP DADO DOCK FACE FELL FILE GASH GIRD HACK HASH HEWN JERK KNAP LIMB MAKE MODE MUSH NICK OCHE PARE RACE RASH RAZE REAP SIDE SKIN SLIT SLOT SMIT SNEE SNEG SNIP SNUB STOW SUMP SWAP SWOP TAME TRIM VELL VIDE BEVEL BLOCK BREAK CANAL CANCH CARVE CHIVE CHYND CLEFT COPSE COUPE CRIMP DRESS FLICK FRAZE FRITH GOUGE GRAVE GRIDE GROOP HOWEL KITTE KNIFE LANCE LATHE MINCE NOTCH PLATE PRUNE RAZEE SABER SABRE SCALP SCARP SCIND SCORE SEVER SHAPE SHARE SHEAR SHIVE SHRED SKICE SKISE SLASH SLICE SLICK SLISH SLIVE SNICK SPLIT STAMP SWEEP SWIPE SWISH TOUCH TWITE VOGUE WHITE ABLATE AJOURE BARBER BISECT BROACH CAMBER CHISEL CLEAVE CORNER CUTTED DIVIDE EXCISE FIGURE FLETCH FLITCH FRENCH GROOVE GULLET HACKLE HAGGLE IGNORE INCIDE INCISE INDENT LESSEN MANGLE OUTPUT RASURE REDUCE RIPPLE SCORCH SCOTCH SCRIBE SCYTHE SLIGHT SLIVER SNATHE STRAIT STREAK SULLET SWINGE TAILYE THWITE TRENCH AFFRONT CONVERT CURTAIL CUTTING DIACOPE DISCIDE DISSECT DRAWCUT ENGRAVE FASHION FRITTER HATCHET RAKEOFF SCALPEL SCISSOR SCUTTLE SECTILE TAILZEE WHITTLE DISSEVER FRACTION INCISION INCISURE INTAGLIO LACERATE MALAHACK RETRENCH THWITTLE
(— AN OPENING) BREACH
(— ASLANT) RAKE
(— AT ANGLE) CANT BEVEL
(— A THREAD) CHASE
(— AT RANDOM) SLASH
(— AWAY) COPE SLIT UNDO ABATE CONCISE
(— BACK) HEAD SPUR
(— BARK) CHIP
(— BEAM) KERF
(— CARS) LIFT
(— CHEESE) HARP
(— CLAY) SLING
(— CORNERS) SKIRT CHAMFER CHAMPHER
(— CRUST) CHIP
(— DEEPER) REENTER
(— DEEPLY) DIG SHANK
(— DIAGONALLY) CATER SLANT
(— DOWN) HEW MOW FELL STAG STUB RAZEE SCANT SCARP ABRIDGE SHORTEN RETRENCH
(— FANCY FIGURE) DASH
(— FINELY) DICE
(— FISH) SOLAY STEAK
(— FOR FODDER) CHAFF
(— GEAR TEETH) RATCH
(— GLASS) SPLIT
(— GRAIN) BAG FAG CRADLE SWINGE
(— HAIR) DOD
(— IN) INSECT INCISED
(— IN A TREE) FACE
(— IN BARK) RING
(— IN BARREL STAVE) HOWEL
(— IN CURVES) SCALLOP
(— IN EXCAVATIONS) GULLET
(— IN LARGE SLICES) WHANG
(— IN RELIEF) ENCHASE
(— IN SOFT ROCK) CAVATE
(— IN SQUARES) CHECK
(— INTO LARGE SLICES) WHANG
(— INTO SLIPS) ZEST
(— INTO STRIPS) JERK FLETCH FLITCH JULIENNE
(— INTO TREE) BOX
(— IN WHALE'S CARCASS) SCARF
(— JAGGEDLY) HACK SNAG
(— LEDGES) BENCH
(— LOGS) LUMBER
(— OFF) BOB LOP CLIP CROP DOCK KILL PARE SHUT SLIT STAG BELEE CROSS ELIDE PRUNE SCIND SEVER SHAVE SHEAR SKIVE SLIPE SPIKE COUPED DECIDE EXEMPT FORCUT RESECT SHIELD STIFLE SWATCH ABJOINT ABSCIND ABSCISE ABSCISS CURTAIL EXSCIND ISOLATE PRECIDE RESCIND AMPUTATE CLEIDOIC DESECATE RESECATE RETRENCH TRUNCATE LANDLOCKED
(— OFF BY BITS) DRIB
(— OFF END) BUTT
(— OF FISH) JOWL
(— OFF WOOL) DOD DODD
(— OF GEM) STAR BAGUET BAGUETTE
(— OF GRAIN) MELL
(— OF MEAT) ARM SEY CROP HOCK SHIN SIDE CHUCK SHANK STEAK BRISKET FORESEY ICEBONE SIRLOIN EDGEBONE FORERIBS
(— OF RIFLING) GROOVE
(— OPEN) SPLAY
(— OUT) AX DESS DINK CLICK BROACH EXCIDE EXCISE EXSECT
(— PATH) FRAY
(— SALMON) CHINE
(— SHEEP) TOMAHAWK
(— SHORT) BOB COW HOG LOP BANG CROP DOCK JIMP SNIB BOBBED CURTAL HOGGED BOBTAIL CHAPPED CONCISE SCANTLE PRESCIND
(— TENDONS) ENERVATE
(— THE THROAT) JUGULATE
(— THE WAVES) SNORE
(— THINLY) CURL
(— TO PIECES) CHOP DICE MINCE BRITTLE FRITTER
(— TO SIZE) TAIL
(— TURF) VELL
(— UNDER) KIRVE
(— UNEVENLY) CHATTER
(— UP) TUSK CARVE CHINE JOINT PRANK SPOIL TRAIN GOBBET COLLOPED
(— UP SWAN) LIFT
(— WHALE BLUBBER) LEAN FLENSE
(— WITH BACKWARD SLOPE) COOT
(— WITH DIE) DINK BLANK
(— WITH SHEARS) SHIRL
(— WITH SICKLE) BAG REAP
(COLD —S) ASSIETTE
(CREW —) BUTCH FLATTOP
(DEEP NARROW —) JAD
(FENCING —) STRAMAZON
(LARGE — OF FOOD) DODGE
(NOT —) UNCORVEN
(SHORT —) ATAJO
(SLIGHT —) SNICK SCOTCH
(THIN —) TARGET
(PREF.) SEC(O) TEMNO TOMC
(SUFF.) COPATE COPE SECT SECTED TOMA TOME TOMIC TOMOUS TOMY
CUT-AND-DRIED CANNED
CUTANEOUS DERMAL
CUTCH GAMBIR CATECHU GAMBIER

CUTE COY KEEN TWEE COONY DINKY DUCKY SHARP CLEVER PRETTY SHREWD CUNNING DARLING
CUTICLE DERM HIDE SKIN SHUCK THECA MEMBRANE PELLICLE
(— OF EGGSHELL) BLOOM
CUTLASS SWORD CURTAL DUSACK HANGER TESACK CURTAXE MACHETE SHABBLE CAMPILAN
CUTLASS FISH HIKU SAVOLA KALKVIS MACHETE HAIRTAIL
CUTLERY SILVER FLATWARE
CUTLET SCHNITZEL
(KIND OF —) PORK VEAL
CUTOVER COUPE
CUTPURSE NIP BUNG THIEF HORNTHUMB
CUTTER DIE BEEF BOAT IRON MILL PONE SLED BRAVO FACER FRAZE SLOOP SMACK BAYMAN CHERRY COLTER COTTER DOCKER EDITOR FRAZER MINCER SLEIGH SLICER CLIPPER COULTER DROMOND INCISOR RUFFIAN KNIFEMAN REVENUER SCHOKKER SHEPSTER
(— OF STONES) LAPIDARY
(BRICK —) RUBBER
(PEAT —) PINER
(WIRE —) SECATEUR
CUTTERHEAD WABBLER WOBBLER
CUTTHROAT THUG BRAVO CUTTER RUFFIAN SWORDER
CUTTHROAT TROUT MYKISS
CUTTING CUT HAG RAW SET ACID CARF CURT KEEN KERF SECT SETT SLIP TART TWIG ACUTE BLEAK CHECK CRISP EAGER EDGED GRIDE SCION SCRAP SCROW SHARP SMART BITING BITTER BORING ENTAIL GODOWN GORING JAGGED PHYTON PIPING SECANT SEVERE SNITHE BURNING CAUSTIC GRIBBLE INCISAL MORDANT NICKING OVERCUT PAINFUL PIQUANT POLLING SARMENT SATIRIC SECTION SLICING CHILLING CLEARING INCISIVE PIERCING POIGNANT QUICKSET SCATHING SCISSION SNAPPISH WOUNDING TRENCHANT
(— FOR DIRT-CAR TRACK) GULLET
(— FOR WATER) TAJO
(— FROM PLANT) SLIP SHROUD SARMENT PROPAGULE TRUNCHEON
(— OF DEER) SAY
(— OFF) AVULSION
(— OF TREES) HAG
(— SHORT) ABORTIVE
(— TOOL) HOB
(DRILL —S) MUD
(OBLIQUE —) BARBING
(SECOND —) ROWEN
(WASTE —) SELVAGE SELVEDGE
(SUFF.) THEMA THESIS TOMA TOME TOMIC TOMOUS TOMY
(— OUT) ECTOMY
CUTTLEBONE SEPIA SEPION SEPIUM GLADIUS SEPIARY
CUTTLEFISH SEPIA SHELL SQUID CUDDLE CUTTLE SCRIBE CATFISH DECAPOD INKFISH MOLLUSK OCTOPUS SCUTTLE
(PREF.) TEUTHIS
CUVETTE POT TUB TANK BASIN BUCKET TRENCH CISTERN
CYANEE (DAUGHTER OF —) BYBLIS
(FATHER OF —) MAEANDER
(HUSBAND OF —) MILETUS
(SON OF —) CAUNUS
CYANIDE NITRILE CYANURET PRUSSIATE
CYANIPPUS (FATHER OF —) PHARAX
(WIFE OF —) LEUCONE
CYANITE SAPPARE DISTHENE
CYANOGEN PRUSSIN PRUSSINE
CYANOTYPE BLUEPRINT
CYBELE RHEA KYBELE AGDISTIS
(DAUGHTER OF —) JUNO
(FATHER OF —) URANUS
(HUSBAND OF —) SATURN
(MOTHER OF —) GAEA
(SON OF —) JUPITER NEPTUNE
CYCAD BANGA CICAD ZAMIA COONTIE CYCADITE
CYCHREUS (DAUGHTER OF —) GLAUCE
(FATHER OF —) NEPTUNE POSEIDON
(MOTHER OF —) SALAMIS
CYCLADES (ISLAND OF —) IOS KEOS DELOS MELOS NAXOS PAROS SYROS TENOS ANDROS AMORGOS KYTHNOS SANTORIN SERIPHOS
CYCLAMEN BACCHAR PRIMWORT SOWBREAD
CYCLE AGE EON ERA AEON BIKE EPOCH KALPA PEDAL PRIME ROUND SAROS SECLE WHEEL BAKTUN CIRCLE COURSE CYCLUS PERIOD BICYCLE CIRCUIT DICYCLE TRICYCLE
(— FURIOUSLY) SCORCH
(— OF TIME) ORB
(— OF WORK) ROTA JOURNEY
(— OF 3600 YEARS) SAROS
(—S CAUSED BY KARMA) SAMSARA SANSARA
(BUSINESS —) JUGLAR KITCHIN
(GO THROUGH —S) ROTATE
(KIND 0F —) CALVIN
(LUNAR —) SAROS
(ONE — PER SECOND) HERTZ
(SECONDARY —) EPICYCLE
CYCLIC CYCLAR ANNULAR CYCLICAL PERIODIC
CYCLING (— TRACK) VELODROME
CYCLIST CYCLER WHEELER WHEELMAN
CYCLOLITH CROMLECH
CYCLOMETER ODOGRAPH VIAMETER
CYCLONE GALE GUST WIND BLAST STORM BAGUIO TORNADO TWISTER TYPHOON SECONDARY NEUTERCANE
CYCLOPARAFFIN NAPHTHENE
CYCLOPEAN HUGE VAST STRONG MASSIVE COLOSSAL GIGANTIC
CYCLOPS ARGES BRONTES COPEPOD STEROPES
CYCLORAMA CYKE PANORAMA
CYCLOSIS STREAMING
CYCLOSTOME HAGFISH
CYCNUS (DAUGHTER OF —) HEMITHEA
(FATHER OF —) ARES MARS NEPTUNE POSEIDON
(MOTHER OF —) CALYCE PYRENE PELOPIA
(SON OF —) TENES
(WIFE OF —) PROCLEA PHYLONOME
CYLINDER CAN EKE GIG TIN BEAM BOMB BURR CAGE CANE DRUM LEAD MUFF PIPE PRIM ROLL SLUG TUBE WELL BLOCK CORER DRAIN FIBER FIBRE FUDGE SCREW SHELL SPOOL STELA STELE SWIFT BARREL BOBBIN BUTTON COLUMN COPPER DECKER DOFFER DUSTER FILTER GABION PISTON PLATEN ROLLER SCREEN TIPITI TUMBLE URCHIN WORKER CUTCHER SLEEVER SLUDGER SUCCULA FOLLOWER GRADUATE NEURAXIS SPARKLET
(— AROUND MOLD) COTTLE
(— FOR DANCE RHYTHM) CLAVE
(— OF STEAM WHISTLE) BELL
(— OF TISSUE) CORTEX
(— OF YARN) CAKE
(— ON LOOM) BEAM
(—S PULLED THROUGH DUCT) MANDREL
(— WITH PERFORATIONS) FLUSHER
(ARMORED —) BARBETTE
(GLASS —) MUFF
(HOLLOW —) PIPE TUBE
(MARKING —) LEAD
(NAPPING —) GIG
(RELAY —) BATON
(REVOLVING —) BEATER ROLLER
(TOOTHED —) SPROCKET
(WATERMARK —) DANDY
CYLINDRICAL ROUND TERETE TOROSE CENTRIC TUBULAR TERETIAL
(PREF.) TERETI
CYMA GOLA GULA OGEE DOUCINE MOLDING CYMATIUM
CYMA REVERSA HEEL
CYMBA YET
CYMBAL ZEL ZILL CHIME TARGET CROTALUM KYMBALON
(PAIR OF —S) HIGHHAT
(PL.) TAL BECKEN PIATTI
CYMBELINE (AUTHOR OF —) SHAKESPEARE
(CHARACTER IN —) CAIUS HELEN CLOTEN IMOGEN LUCIUS MORGAN IACHIMO PISANIO BELARIUS LEONATUS PHILARIO ARVIRAGUS CORNELIUS CYMBELINE GUIDERIUS POSTHUMUS
(SON OF —) ARVIRAGUS GUIDERIUS
CYMBIUM MELO
CYME AXIS CYMULE BOSTRYX
CYMLING SIMNEL CYMBLIN SCALLOP PATTYPAN
CYMOSE DEFINITE SYMPODIAL
CYMRY KYMRI WELSH
CYNIC SATYR TIMON DOUBTER SNEERER APEMANTUS
CYNICAL CYNIC SULLEN CURRISH DOGGISH DOGLIKE CAPTIOUS SARDONIC SNARLING JAQUESIAN MISOGYNIC PESSIMISTIC MISANTHROPIC
CYNOCEPHALUS AANI
CYNORTES (BROTHER OF —) HYACINTHUS
(FATHER OF —) AMYCLAS
(MOTHER OF —) DIOMEDE
(SON OF —) PERIERES
CYNOSURE SHOW LODESTAR
CYPRESS CULL SABINO SIPERS FIREBALL AHUEHUETE BELVEDERE
CYPRESS SPURGE BALSAM NAPOLEON
CYPRIPEDIUM CYP DUCK NERVINE

CYPRUS

CAPE: GATA GRECO ANDREAS ARNAUTI ZEVGARI
CAPITAL: NICOSIA
COIN: PARA
MEASURE: OKA OKE PIK CASS DONUM KOUZA GOMARI KARTOS MEDIMNO
MOUNTAIN: TROODOS
RIVER: PEDIAS PEDIEOS
TOWN: POLIS CITIUM PAPHOS KYRENIA LARNACA MORPHOU NICOSIA LIMASSOL FAMAGUSTA
WEIGHT: OKA OKE MOOSA KANTAR

CYRANO DE BERGERAC (AUTHOR OF —) ROSTAND
(CHARACTER IN —) CYRANO ROXANE VALVERT DEGUICHE CHRISTIAN
CYRENE (FATHER OF) HYPSEUS
(MOTHER OF —) CHLIDANOPE
(SON OF —) IDMON DIOMEDES ARISTAEUS
CYRILLA TITI
CYRUS KORESH
CYST BAG SAC WEN POUCH CYSTUS RANULA DERMOID HYDATID HYGROMA SACCULE VESICLE ATHEROMA DACRYOPS MUCOCELE STEATOMA
CYSTOPTERIS FILIX
CYTOKININ ZEATIN
CYTOLYSIN AMBOCEPTOR
CYTOME SPHEROME
CYTOPLASM MASSULA OOPLASM PLASMON DIASTEMA
(PREF.) PLASTO
CZAR CSAR IVAN TSAR TZAR PETER AUTOCRAT NICHOLAS
CZARDAS CSARDAS
(SECTION OF —) FRISS LASSU FRISZKA
CZECH CECH TSECH TSCEKH BOHEMIAN

CZECH REPUBLIC

CAPITAL: PRAHA PRAGUE
COIN: CROWN DUCAT HALER HELLER KORUNA
DANCE: POLKA REDOWA FURIANT
FOREST: BOHEMIAN
FORMER NAME: CZECHOSLAVAKIA
MEASURE: LAN SAH MIRA KOREC LATRO STOPA MERICE STRYCH
MOUNTAIN: SNEZKA
MOUNTAIN RANGE: ORE GIANT

SUMAVA SUDETEN KRKONOSE JAVORNIKY CARPATHIAN KRUSNEHORY BILEKARPATY
PEOPLE: ROMA CZECH GYPSY MORAVIAN
PLATEAU: BOHEMIAN
REGION: BOHEMIA MORAVIA
RIVER: MZE DYJE EGER ELBE ISER LABE NISA ODER ODRA OHRE OLSE OLZA OPPA BECVA OPAVA JIZERA MOLDAU MORAVA SAZAVA VLTAVA LUZNICE BEROUNKA
TOWN: AS ASCH BRNO CHEB EGER MOST ZLIN BRUNN OPAVA PLZEN PRAHA TABOR AUSSIG BILINA KLADNO OSTROV PILSEN VSETIN BUDWEIS HAVIROV JIHLAVA OLOMOAC OSTRAVA TEPLICE TEPLITZ KARLOVYVARY

D

D DE DEE DOG DELTA
DA DUCKTAIL
DAB DAP DOB DOT DUB HIT PAT BLOW CHIT DAUB LICK LUMP PECK SPOT CLOUT DHABB DIGHT LEMON SMEAR BLOTCH EXPERT STRIKE DABSTER PORTION SPLOTCH FLATFISH FLOUNDER MARYSOLE SANDLING
DABBER BALL PROD TAMPON
DABBING PICKING
DABBLE DAB DIB MESS DALLY DIBBLE MEDDLE MUDDLE PADDLE POTTER SOSSLE SPLASH TAMPER TRIFLE DRABBLE MOISTEN PLOUTER PLUTTER SMATTER SPATTER DELIBATE SPRINKLE
(— WITH BLOOD) ENGORE
DABBLER AMATEUR DABSTER
DABBLING PLOUTER PLOWTER
DABCHICK GREBE DIPPER DOBBER DOPPER PUFFER HENBILL DIDAPPER DOPCHICK
DACE CHUB DARE DART CYPRINID GRAYLING
DACHSHUND DACHS TECKEL BADGERER
DACOIT DAKU DAKOO ROBBER CRIMINAL
DACTYL TOE FOOT FINGER
(— AND IAMB) FEET
DACTYLOPODITE POLLEX
DACTYLOZOOID PALPON
DACTYLUS DACTYL DIGITUS
DAD BEAT BLOW DAUD HUNK LUMP PAPA KNOCK THUMP FATHER STRIKE
DADA (FOUNDER OF —) ARP
DADAIST (— PAINTER) ARP
(— POET) TZARA
DADDY BABBO DEDDY
DADDY LONGLEGS SPINNER LONGLEGS PHALANGID
DADO DIE GROOVE SOLIDUM
DAEDALUS (ANCESTOR OF —) ERECHTHEUS
(NEPHEW OF —) TALUS
(SON OF —) ICARUS
DAEMON (ALSO SEE DEMON) GHOST DAIMON PYTHON EUDAEMON MISTRESS
(PL.) CURETES
DAFFODIL GLEN LILY DAFFY DILLY JONQUIL ASPHODEL BELLWORT CROWBELL
DAFT GAY MAD LOCO WILD ZANY BALMY BATTY CRAZY DAFFY GIDDY LOONY POTTY SILLY INSANE FOOLISH IDIOTIC IMBECILE
DAG JAG DAGG STAB SLASH DAGGLE PIERCE DAGGING DAGLOCK PRICKET
DAGAME SALAMO MADRONA LEMONWOOD
DAGGER DAG SAX DIRK ITAC KRIS SAEX SNEE SPUD STAB TANG CRISE DAGUE KATAR KREES POINT PRICK SKEAN STEEL ANLACE BODKIN COUTEL CREESE DIESIS HANGER KIRPAN KUTTAR PANADE PINKER POPPER SKHIAN STYLET BALARAO BAYONET COUTEAU DUDGEON HANDJAR KANDJAR KHANJAR OBELISK PONIARD SLASHER STABBER BASELARD PUNCHEON PUNTILLA STILETTO
(— AS CERAMICS COVER) HILLER
(— REFERENCE MARK) SPIT
(— WITH WAVY BLADE) KRIS CREESE KREESE
(DOUBLE —) DIESIS
(PART OF —) HAFT BLADE
(SACRED —) KIRPAN
(PREF.) MACHAIRO
DAGOMBA DAGBANE DAGBANI
DAH DAO DOW DHAO
DAHLIA JICAMA POMPON
DAHOMEY (CAPITAL OF —) PORTONOVO
(PEOPLE OF —) FON FONG BARIBA
(RIVER OF —) NIGER OUEME
(TOWN IN —) KANDI NIKKI ABOMEY OUIDAH COTONOU
DAIL ASSEMBLY
DAILY ADAY ADAYS DIARY DIURNAL QUOTIDIAN
DAINCHA NARDOO
DAINTIES EST ESTE SOCK CATES DIABLOTIN
DAINTILY CHOICELY GINGERLY MINIONLY
DAINTINESS FLUTTER DELICACY
DAINTY CATE FINE NICE RARE TEAR TWEE ACATE DAINT DENTY FRILL GENTY NAISH TREAT BONBON CHOICE COSTLY FRIAND MIGNON MINION PICKED REGALO SCARCE SPICED SUNKET CURIOUS ELEGANT FINICAL FINICKY MINIKIN REGALIA TAFFETA TAFFETY DAINTITH DAINTREL DELICACY DELICATE ETHEREAL LIKEROUS MIGNIARD TRYPHOSA
(PREF.) ABRO HABRO
DAIRY TAMBO LACTARY VACCARY CREAMERY DEYHOUSE
(— PRODUCTS) MILCHIGS
DAIRYMAID DEE DEY DEYWOMAN MILKMAID
DAIRYMAN AHIR MILKMAN
DAIS PACE SEAT BENCH LEWAN STAGE TABLE CANOPY ESTATE LISSOM PODIUM PULPIT SETTLE ESTRADE TERRACE TRIBUNE CHABUTRA FOOTPACE HALFPACE HATHPACE HUSTINGS PLATFORM
DAISY BULL GOLD DANDY GOWAN OXEYE BENNET MORGAN SHASTA BONESET BOWWORT COMFREY DOGBLOW BACKWORT BONEWORT COMPOSIT HEXAFOIL KNITBACK PISSABED MOONPENNY BRUISEWORT MARGUERITE
DAISY CUTTER GRUB
DAISY FLEABANE ERIGERON SCABIOUS
DAKOTA SIOUX LAKOTA
DALE HAW DELL DENE GLEN VALE SPOUT BOTTOM DINGLE TROUGH VALLEY
DALEA PAROSELA
DALIBOR (CHARACTER IN —) BENES ZDENEK DALIBOR MAILADA
(COMPOSER OF —) SMETANA
DALLES DELLS RAPIDS
DALLIANCE TOY CHAT PLAY TALK SPORT GOSSIP TOUSEL TOUSLE TRIFLE COLLING
DALLIER PINGLER
DALLY TOY CHAT DAFF FOOL IDLE JAKE JAUK PLAY SWAN WAIT DELAY FLIRT SPORT TARRY COQUET DABBLE DAWDLE LINGER LOITER PINGLE TRIFLE WANTON DRINGLE SLIDDER PHILANDER
DALLYING COQUETRY SISSETON
DALMATIAN COACHDOG
DALMATIC TUNICLE
DALPHON (FATHER OF —) HAMAN
DAM BAR BAY PEN REE BUND DAME HEAD POND SADD SPUR STAY STEM STOP SUDD WEIR BLOCK CAULD CHECK CHOKE GARTH MOUND POUND STANK ANICUT CAUSEY HINDER MOTHER PARENT ANNICUT BARRAGE BARRIER BURROCK MILLDAM PENHEAD RAMPIRE TAPPOON ABOIDEAU BLOCKADE GRANDDAM OBSTACLE OBSTRUCT RESTRAIN
(PART OF —) GATE PIER POOL SILL WALL BASIN CREST OUTLET SLUICE ROADWAY TAINTOR OVERFLOW SPILLWAY POWERHOUSE
DAMAGE MAR BLOT BURN COST HARM HURT JEEL LOSS RUIN SKIN TEEN BLITZ BURST CLOUD CRACK HAVOC PRANG SPOIL WOUND WRONG BANJAX BATTER CHARGE DANGER DEFACE DEFECT HINDER IMPAIR INJURE INJURY INSULT LESION SCATHE SORROW AFFLICT DAMNIFY DEGRADE DISTURB EXPENSE FOUNDER OFFENCE OFFENSE PAYMENT SCRATCH SCUTTLE SHATTER ACCIDENT BUSINESS DISSERVE FRACTURE FRETTING MISCHIEF SABOTAGE
(MINOR SURFACE —) DING
(PREF.) DAMNI
DAMAGED HURT CRAZY LESED BROKEN CRACKED INJURED
DAMAGES INTEREST HAMESUCKEN
(EXCESSIVE —) SMART SMARTMONEY
DAMAGING HARMFUL HURTFUL SCATHING
DAMAN DAS CONY CONEY CUNNY DASSY GANAM HYRAX DASSIE WABBER ASHKOKO CHEROGRIL
DAMA PADEMELON TAMMAR WALLABY
DAMASCENED WATERED
DAMASCENE WORK KOFTGARI
DAMASK LINEN DARNEX DORNIC DORNICK VALANCE DAMASSIN DRAWLOOM
DAMAYANTI (HUSBAND OF —) NALA
DAME DINT LADY DAMIE WOMAN MATRON
DAME BLANCHE, LA (CHARACTER IN —) ANNA BROWN JENNY GEORGE DICKSON GAVESTON
(COMPOSER OF —) BOIELDIEU
DAME'S VIOLET EVEWEED
DAMKINA (HUSBAND OF —) EA
DAMMARA AGATHIS
DAMN DEE DEM DOG RAT BLOW BURN DANG DARN DASH DING DRAT DUMB DURN BLAME BLANK BLAST BLESS CURSE FETCH TARAL WHOOP BEDAMN BUGGER DEMPNE DEVOTE GODDAM CONDEMN CONSARN DOGGONE GODDAMN GOLDARN GOLDURN CONFOUND EXECRATE
DAMNABLE RUDDY DAMNED ODIOUS ACCURSED INFERNAL
DAMNABLY DEUCED CURSEDLY DEUCEDLY
DAMNATION NATION PERDITION
DAMNATION DE FAUST (CHARACTER IN —) FAUST MARGUERITE MEPHISTOPHELES
(COMPOSER OF —) BERLIOZ
DAMNED DEE DAMN DARN DEED DURN LOST BALLY DOOMS BLAMED BLOODY DARNED DASHED DURNED GODDAM GORMED TARNAL BLASTED BLESSED CONSARN DOGGONE ETERNAL GOLDARN GOLDURN MUCKING ACCURSED BLANKETY BLINKING DASHEDLY FREAKING INFERNAL JIGGERED
DAMO (FATHER OF —) PYTHAGORAS
(MOTHER OF —) THEANO
DAMP DEG FOG RAW WAK WET

CLAM DANK DEWY DULL MIST ROKY SOFT WACK BLUNT DABBY HUMID JUICY MALMY MOCHY MOIST MOOTH MUGGY MUNGY MUSTY RAFTY RAINY RAWKY SAPPY SEEPY SOBBY SOGGY THONE WAUGH WEAKY BLIGHT CLAMMY DAMPEN DEADEN MUFFLE QUENCH RHEUMY STUPOR BEDEWED DAMPISH DEPRESS MOISTEN SQUIDGY DEJECTED DISPIRIT HUMIDIFY HUMIDITY MOISTURE
(— OF EVENING) SERENE
(CHOKE —) STYTHE
(PREF.) HUMI(DI)
DAMPED SORDO
DAMPEN DEG DAMP MOIL CHILL CRAMP FREEZE SPONGE MOISTURE
DAMPENER MULLER
DAMPER DAMP MUTE BREAD CHECK CHECKER SORDINE REGISTER
DAMPNESS CLAM DAMP HUMIDITY
DAMSEL GIRL MISS WENCH MAIDEN MOPPET DAMOSEL DAMOZEL PUCELLE DONZELLA PRINCESS
DAMSELFISH PINTANO
DAMSELFLY NAIAD ODONATE
DAN GI DEN
(MOTHER OF —) BILHAH
DANAKIL AFAR
DANAUS ANOSIA
(BROTHER OF —) AEGYPTUS
(DAUGHTER OF —) AMYMONE
(FATHER OF —) BELUS
(MOTHER OF —) ANCHINOE
DANCE BAL BOB HOP JIG MAI SON BALL DRAG DUET DUMP FISH FOOT FRUG HEEL HOOF HORA JAZZ JIVE JUBA JUKE KOLO LEAP LOPE LOUP MASK MILL MOVE PROM REEL SAIL SHAG SKIT STEP BAILE BAMBA BONGO BOOGY BRAWL CANON CAPER CAROL CONGA DANZA DISCO ENTRY FLING FLISK FRIKE FRISK GOPAK HORAH LASYA LIMBO LINDY MAMBO PAVAN POLKA RINKA RUMBA SALLY SAMBA STOMP SWING TANGO TRACE TREAD TWIST VOLTA WALTZ ALTHEA AREITO BALLET BALTER BOLERO BOOGIE BOSTON BRANLE CANARY CANCAN CEBELL CHACHA CORDAX DANZON DIDDLE DREHER FADING FORMAL FROLIC GERMAN HORMOS MASQUE MINUET MOBBLE MONKEY MORRIS NRITTA PASSAY RACKET RHUMBA SHIMMY TODDLE TRESCA TUMBLE VALETA VELETA ANTHEMA BEGUINE CALINDA CANTICO COURANT CZARDAS DANSANT FADDING FARRUCA FOOTING FOXTROT FURLANA GAVOTTE MEASURE MORISCO PATTERN SALTATE SARDANA SHUFFLE TEMPETE TRESCHE TRIPPLE VOLTIZE ZIGANKA ANGLAISE AURRESCU BAMBOULA BUNNYHUG CACHUCHA CAKEWALK CHACONNE COMPARSA COONJINE COTILLON ENTRACTE ESTAMPIE FANDANGO FANTASIA FLAMENCO GALLIARD GALOPADE GUARACHA HABANERA HEYDEGUY HORNPIPE KOLATTAM MATELOTE MERENGUE SALTATION SHAKEDOWN CARMAGNOLE SCHOTTISCHE
(— ART) NATYA ORCHESIS
(— ATTENDANCE) LACKEY LACQUEY
(— CLUMSILY) BALTER
(— DRAMA) NO NOH
(— FACE TO FACE) SET
(— FORM) PIVA
(— IN CIRCLE) JIGGER
(— METHOD) LABAN
(— NIMBLY) CANARY
(— RESEMBLING THE POLKA) BERLIN
(— STEP) RIFF PICKUP
(— STYLE) ABHINAYA
(— SUGGESTIVELY) BUMP GRIND
(— TYPE) TANDAVA
(ACROBATIC —) ADAGIO
(AFRICAN —) SHOUT
(ARGENTINE —) CUANDO
(AUSTRIAN —) LANDLER
(BALINESE —) KEBYAR LEGONG
(BALLROOM —) SON CONGO TWOSTEP COTILLON
(BOHEMIAN —) REDOWA FURIANT
(BRAZILIAN —) SAMBA
(CARNIVAL —) COOCH FOLIA COOTCH
(CEREMONIAL —) AREITO CANTICO DUTUBURI
(COQUETTISH —) PURPOSE
(COUNTRY —) HAY CLOG RANT CONFESS LANDLER MUSETTE ZIGANKA ANGLAISE SARABAND
(COURTSHIP —) CUECA BATUQUE LEZGINKA
(DANISH —) SEXTUR
(FIESTA —S) AKRIEROS
(FLAMENCO —) ALEGRIAS
(FRENCH —) BAL BOREE BRAWL GAVOT BRANLE BOURREE BOUTADE BRANSLE GAVOTTE LAVOLTA ALLEMANDE
(GAY —) RANT GAILLARD GALLIARD
(GESTURE —) SIVA
(GREEK —) CORDAX KORDAX ROMAIKA SIRTAKI SIKINNIS
(GYPSY —) FARRUCA
(HAITIAN —) JUBA
(HAWAIIAN —) HULA
(HOBBYHORSE —) CALUSAR
(HOLIDAY —) PATTERN
(HUNGARIAN —) KOS
(IMPROMPTU —) BOUTADE
(INDIAN —) IRUSKA KATHAK KANTIKOY
(IRISH —) FADING PLANXTY
(ITALIAN —) FORLANA FURLANA BERGAMASK SALTARELLO
(JAPANESE —) BUGAKU KAGURA
(JAVANESE —) SERIMPI
(KIND OF —) TAP
(LIVELY —) JIG REEL GALOP GIGUE POLKA RUMBA BOLERO CANARY RHUMBA SPRING BOURREE CORANTO FURLANA HOEDOWN GALLIARD GALOPADE HORNPIPE
(MAORI —) HAKA
(MARTIAL —) PYRRHIC
(MEXICAN —) JARABE HUAPANGO SANDUNGA
(MOURNFUL —) DUMP
(NORWEGIAN —) HALLING
(OLD-FASHIONED —) LOURE PASSACAGLIA
(OLD ENGLISH —) CEBELL MORRIS ARGEERS ANGLAISE
(PEASANT —) JOTA DANZON BALITAO
(PERUVIAN —) CUECA KASWA CACHUA
(POLISH —) POLACCA KUJAWIAK POLONAISE VARSOVIENNE
(POLYNESIAN —) HULA
(PORTUGUESE —) FADO
(ROMAN —) TRIPUDIUM
(ROUND —) RAY BRAUL CAROL WALTZ CAROLE MAXIXE
(RUSSIAN —) ZIGANKA
(RUSTIC —) HAY HEY HAYMAKER
(SPANISH —) JOTA POLO JALEO BOLERO JARABE CHACONNE FLAMENCO GUARACHA MALAGUENA ZAPATEADO SEGUIDILLA
(SPEAR —) BARIS
(SQUARE —) SQUARE ARGEERS HOEDOWN LANCERS QUADRILLE
(STATELY —) PAVAN PAVANE EMMELEIA SARABAND POLONAISE
(SWORD —) BACUBERT MATACHIN
(VENEZUELAN —) JOROPO
(WEDDING —) CANACUAS
(WEST INDIAN —) LIMBO
(WHIRLING —) TARANTELLA
(PREF.) CHORE(I)(O) CHORO ORCHESO
DANCE-DRAMA NOH
(JAPANESE —) NO
DANCER PONY CLOWN PONEY ARTIST CORNER EXOTIC HOOFER HOPPER MAENAD APSARAS CLOGGER DANSEUR PASCOLA PRANCER PRANKER SAILOUR STEPPER TODDLER BALADINE BAYADERE DANSEUSE DEVADASI FIGURANT MORRICER
(BALLET —) ETOILE SOLISTE CORYPHEE
(EGYPTIAN —S) GHAWAZI GHAWAZEE
(JAVANESE —) SERIMPI
(JAVANESE —S) BEDOYO
(MASKED —S) GAHE
(SQUARE —S) FLOOR
(SWORD —) MATACHIN
(ZUNI —) SHALAKO
DANCE-TUNE BRAWL BRANTLE
DANCING SWING ADANCE BALLET CHANGE FROLIC MORRIS SALTANT SURGING STEPPING TRIPSOME
(— MANIA) TARANTISM
DANCING-GIRL ALMA ALME ALMEH ALAMAH BAYADERE
DANDELION BLOW BLOWER CANKER DINDLE CHICORY HAWKBIT BLOWBALL COMPOSIT PISSABED
(RUSSIAN —) KOKSAGYZ
DANDELION HEAD PUFF CLOCK BUFFBALL BULLFICE BULLFIST PUFFBALL
DANDER ANGER DUTCH SCURF STROLL TEMPER WANDER HACKLES PASSION SAUNTER DANDRUFF
DANDIFIED SPRUCE BUCKISH ADONIZED
DANDIFY ADONIZE DANDYIZE
DANDLE DANCE DIDDLE DOODLE FADDLE FONDLE PAMPER
DANDRUFF SCURF DANDER FURFUR PORRIGO
DANDY FOP JAY ADON BEAU BUCK DAND DUDE FINE JAKE MAJO PRIG TOFF TRIG YAWL BLOOD DILDO JEMMY SWELL ADONIS MIZZEN BUCKEEN CAPSTAN COXCOMB ELEGANT FOPPISH JESSAMY MACARONI MUSCADIN SAILBOAT
DANDY HORSE HOBBY DRAISINE
DANDYISHNESS SPIFF
DANDYISM BUCKISM
DANE DANSKER LOCHLIN DUBHGALL
DANEWORT EBULUS LOCHLIN DANEBALL DANEWEED DEADWORT WALLWORT
DANGER FEAR RISK DOUBT PERIL WATHE HAZARD PLIGHT EXTREME PITFALL VENTURE DISTRESS JEOPARDY
(— SIGNAL) RED
(MORAL —) SNARE
DANGEROUS BAD HOT ILL RUM DEAR FOUL GRAVE NASTY RISKY FICKLE KITTLE SCATHY SHREWD UNSURE AWKWARD FEARFUL PARLOUS UNCANNY DOUBTFUL INSECURE PERILOUS UNCHANCY BREAKNECK WANCHANCY PRECARIOUS PESTIFEROUS
(MAKE LESS —) DEFUSE
(NOT —) CUSHY
(VERY —) TOXIC
DANGLE BOB LOP HANG LOLL DROOP SWING DANDLE SHOGGLE SHOOGLE SUSPEND SWINGLE TROLLOP
DANGLER (— AFTER WOMEN) PHILANDER
DANGLIN DANLI
DANGLING PENDANT VERSATILE
DANIEL (FATHER OF —) DAVID
(MOTHER OF —) ABIGAIL
DANK WET DAMP DONK HUMID MADID MOIST CLAMMY COARSE DAMPEN DANKISH DRIZZLE WETNESS MOISTURE
DANSEUSE DANCER BALLERINA
DANUBE (— FEEDER) INN
DANZIG GDANSK
(— LIQUEUR) RATAFIA
DAPHNE (CHARACTER IN —) GAEA APOLLO DAPHNE PENEIOS LEUKIPPOS
(COMPOSER OF —) STRAUSS
DAPPER CHIC COOL NEAT TRIM

NATTY SNAZZY SPRUCE FINICAL FOPPISH SPARKISH
DAPPLE COVER FLECK FRECK
DAPPLED BLOCKY DOTTED POMELY FLECKED MOTTLED SPOTTED FRECKLED
DAPPLE-GREY LIARD
DARBHA KUSA KUSHA
DARDA (FATHER OF —) MAHOL
DARDANUS (CHARACTER IN —) VENUS IPHISE TEUCER ANTENOR ISMENOR DARDANUS
(COMPOSER OF —) RAMEAU
(DAUGHTER OF —) IDAEA
(FATHER OF —) ZEUS JUPITER
(MOTHER OF —) ELECTRA
(SON OF —) ILUS DEIMAS IDAEUS ERICHTHONIUS
DARE OSS DAST DEFY FACE OSER OSSE RISK BRAVE STUMP ASSUME BANTER DACKER ATTEMPT BRAVADE FASHION PRESUME VENTURE
(— NOT) DASSNT DAURNA DASSENT
DAREDEVIL MADCAP HARDYDARDY
DARING BOLD DARE DERF PERT RACY RASH WILD BRAVE HARDY MANLY NERVE PREST FELONY HEROIC COURAGE DAIROUS DAREFUL BOLDNESS DEVILISH FEARLESS STALWART
DARIOLE MADELINE
DARK DIM DUN MUM SAD WAN BASE BLAE DEEP DERK DERN DUSK EBON HARD MALE MIRK MURK BLACK BLIND BROWN CLOUD DINGY DUSKY FAINT MIRKY MURKY ROOKY SHADY SOOTY SWART UMBER UNLIT VAGUE CLOSED CLOUDY CYPRUS DIMPSY DISMAL DRUMLY GLOOMY OPAQUE SOMBER SOMBRE SWARTH WICKED APHOTIC DARKISH DUSKISH MELANIC OBSCURE PITMIRK RAYLESS STYGIAN SUNLESS SWARTHY THESTER UNCLEAR ABSTRUSE DARKLING DARKSOME GLOOMFUL GLOOMING IGNORANT LOWERING SINISTER CIMMERIAN CALIGINOUS
(PREF.) AITHO MAVRO MEL(A) MELAN(O)
(SUFF.) MELANE
DARK BEAVER PRALINE
DARK-COLORED SAD SWART SOMBER SOMBRE SWARTH SWARTHY
(PREF.) FUSCO
DARK-COMPLEXIONED BROWN MELANOUS
DARKEN DIM DUN BLUR DULL DUSK BEDIM BLIND CLOUD GLOAM GLOOM POCHE SHADE SULLY SWART UMBER DEEPEN ENDARK SHADOW BECLOUD BENIGHT BLACKEN ECLIPSE EMBROWN OBSCURE OPACATE PERPLEX SLUBBER TARNISH OVERCAST OBFUSCATE OVERSHADOW
(— HAIR) BLEND
DARKENED SABLE CLOUDY BLINDED LAMPLESS
DARKENING SCURF
DARK HORSE MOREL
DARKISH DIM
DARKLY DARK CLOSE SABLY MISTILY
DARKNESS DARK DERN DUSK MIRK MURK BLACK GLOOM NIGHT SHADE TAMAS SHADOW DIMNESS PITMIRK PRIVACY SECRECY TENEBRA GLOAMING INIQUITY MIDNIGHT TENEBRES TWILIGHT NIGRITUDE
(PLACE OF —) EREBUS
(PREF.) SCOTO TENEBRI
DARKNESS AT NOON (AUTHOR OF —) KOESTLER
(CHARACTER IN —) ARLOVA BOGRAV IVANOV GLETKIN HARELIP KIEFFER MICHAEL NICHOLAS RUBASHOV
DARLING JO JOE PET CHOU CONY DEAR DUCK LIFE LOVE NOBS PEAT ROON AROON ARUIN BULLY CHERI DEARY DUCKS LIEVE SWEET WHITE CHERIE DAUTIE DAWTIE MINION MOPPET OCHREE POPPET ACUSHLA ASTHORE BUNTING CUSHLAM DILLING MINIKIN PIGSNEY PINKENY QUERIDA STOREEN DEARLING DUMPLING FAVORITE LIEBCHEN LOVELING MACUSHLA PRECIOUS SWEETING MAVOURNIN MAVOURNEEN
DARLING PEA INDICO INDIGO
DARN DOG BLOW DERN DURN MEND PATCH BUGGER RENTER REPAIR DOGGONE
DARNED BLAME BLAMED DAGNAB DAGNAG DANGED DEUCED DURNED BLESSED BLINDING DOWNGONE
DARNEL RAY CRAP TARE WEED CHEAT CHESS DRANK DRAWK DRUNK EAVER GRASS IVRAY NEELE COCKLE EGILOPS AEGILOPS
DART JET POP BOLT BUZZ CANE CHOP COLP FLIT JOUK LEAP LICK PILE PLAN PLAY ROUT ARROW BOUND FLAME FLING FLIRT GLEAM GLINT LANCE SCAMP SCOOT SHAFT SHOOT SKITE SKIVE SPEAR SPEED SPRIT START ANCHOR BULTEN DARTLE ELANCE GLANCE LANCET LAUNCH METHOD SCHEME SPRING SQUIRT STRIKE SUMPIT THRUST JAVELIN MISSILE STRALET VERUTUM BRANDISH GAVELOCK JACULATE SPICULUM BANDERILLA
(— ABOUT) SPRINKLE
(— OF LIGHTNING) STREAK
(— OF MOLDING) ANCHOR
(— REPEATEDLY) DARTLE
(PART OF —) POINT SHAFT BARREL FLIGHT
(PREF.) JACULI TELI
DARTER SPECK
DARTING SALLY ARROWY
DARTLIKE SPICULAR
DASH DAD DAH PEP ZIP BANG BOLT CAST DING DIVE ELAN GIFT HINT HURL LASH LINE LUSH PASH PELT POSS RACE RASH RUIN RULE RUSH SHOW SLAM SOSH TICK VEIN WHAP WHOP ABASH ARDOR BLANK BREAK CHAFE CLASH CRASH CRUSH DRIVE ECLAT FLASH FLING FRUSH KNOCK PLASH PLOUT SKITE SLASH SLOSH SMASH SPEED SPEND SPICE SPURN START STYLE SWASH SWELL TASTE THROW TOUCH TRICK BEDASH DALLOP DASHEE DOLLOP ENERGY HURTLE HYPHEN JABBLE RELISH SHIVER SPIRIT SPLASH SPRINT STRAIN STROKE THRUST ABANDON BRAVURA BREENGE COLLIDE DEPRESS DISPLAY HUNDRED IMPINGE PANACHE SHATTER SPATTER SPLOTCH TANTIVY VIRETOT CONFOUND GRATUITY SPLINTER
(— ABOUT WILDLY) GAD REEL
(— AGAINST) BEAT
(— DOWN) QUELL STRAM STRAMASH
(— IN PIECES) CRASH
(— OF LIQUID) JAW
(— OF SPIRITS) LACE LACING
(— OUT) QUELL
(— TOGETHER) COLLIDE
(— UP) FLURR
(— WITH WATER) JAW BLASH SLASH
DASHARATHA (FATHER OF —) AJA
(SON OF —) RAMA BHARATA LAKSHMANA SHATRUGHNA
(WIFE OF —) KAIKEYI SUMITRA KAUSHALYA
DASHBOARD DASH FACIA DASHER FASCIA
DASHED SWITCHED
DASHEEN TARO
DASHER DASH BEATER PLUNGER
DASHING BOLD BULLY DASHY DOGGY SHOWY SMART SPICY SWASH JABBLE SPANKY SWANKY VELOCE DOGGISH GALLANT GALLOWS LARKING STYLISH SWAGGER VARMINT SLASHING SPANKING SPIRITED
DASSIE HYRAX
DASTARD CAD SOT DAFF SNEAK COWARD CRAVEN DULLARD HILDING VILLAIN WITHING POLTROON
DASTARDLY BASE FOUL VILLAIN COWARDLY POLTROON SNEAKING
DASYLIRION SOTOL
DASYPUS TATU
DASYURE TIGER YABBI DAPPLE
DATA DOPE FILE FACTS IMPUT INPUT MATERIAL
(— RETRIEVAL SYSTEM) VIDEOTEX
(— STRUCTURE) ARRAY
(COMPUTER —) FILE PUSHDOWN
(ENTER —) READIN
(INACCURATE —) GARBAGE
(SHORT SECTION OF —) PACKET
(STORE OF —) PUSHDOWN
(USELESS —) GARBAGE
DATE DAY ERA SEE DRAG FARD FUSS DATUM EPOCH FARDH FRUIT SAIDI TRYST CUTOFF FRIEND HALAWI JUJUBE RECKON GALLANT ANTEDATE ASHARASI DEADLINE
(— BACK) TRACE RELATE
(— FIXED UPON) TERM
(— OF DEATH) OBIT
(— RIPENING) KIMRI RUTAB KHALAL
(CHINESE —) BER
(REGULAR —) STEADY
DATED GIVEN PASSE STALE OUTMODED
DATELESS STAG
DATE PLUM LOTUS SAPOTE ZAPOTE
DATHAN (FATHER OF —) ELIAB
DATING (KIND OF —) OPEN
DATOLITE BAKERITE HUMBOLDTITE
DATUM FACT ITEM GIVEN DONNEE
DATURA DUTRA STRAMONY TOGUACHA
DAUB DAB DOB MUD BALM BLOB BLOT CLAG CLAM CLAT CLAY COAT GAUM MOIL SOIL TEER CLAIK CLART CLEAM COVER DITCH FLICK PAINT SLAKE SLAUM SMEAR BEDAUB CLATCH GREASE LABBER SMUDGE SPLASH BESMEAR DRIBBLE PLASTER SCLATCH SLUBBER SPLATCH SPLOTCH SLAISTER
DAUBE LARD
DAUBED GAUMY
DAUBING DUBBING MOILING
DAUBY BLOTTY
DAUGHTER ANAC BINT DAME GIRL CHILD FILLE FILLY KIBEI REGAN ALUMNA CADETTE DOCHTER GONERIL CORDELIA
(NISEI —) SANSEI
(PANTALOON'S —) COLUMBINE
(PRIEST'S —) NIECE
(PREF.) FILI
DAUGHTER OF THE REGIMENT
(CHARACTER IN —) MARIE TONZIO SULPICE COUNTESS
(COMPOSER OF —) DONIZETTI
DAUNT AWE COW DAW ADAW DARE DAZE FAZE MATE PALL STUN TAME ABASH ACCOY AMATE BREAK CHECK DETER DOMPT QUAIL APPALL DANTON DISMAY SUBDUE CONQUER CONTROL OVERAWE REPRESS STUPEFY TERRIFY DISPIRIT OVERCOME
DAUNTED MATE
DAUNTLESS BOLD GOOD BRAVE AWELESS SPARTAN FEARLESS INTREPID
DAUNUS (DAUGHTER OF —) EUIPPE
(FATHER OF —) PILUMNUS
(MOTHER OF —) DANAE
(SON OF —) TURNUS
(WIFE OF —) VENILIA
DAVENPORT DESK SOFA COUCH DIVAN
DAVID TAFFY DAWKIN
(COMPANION OF —) JONATHAN
(DAUGHTER OF —) TAMAR
(FATHER OF —) JESSE
(SON OF —) AMNON ABSALOM
(WIFE OF —) ABIGAIL AHINOAM
DAVID COPPERFIELD (AUTHOR OF —) DICKENS
(CHARACTER IN —) HAM DICK DORA HEEP JANE MICK ROSA AGNES BETSY CLARA DAVID EMILY

JAMES MEALY TOMMY URIAH BARKIS DARTLE GRINBY STRONG WALKER CREAKLE SPENLOW WILKINS MICAWBER PEGGOTTY TRADDLES TROTWOOD MURDSTONE WICKFIELD STEERFORTH
DAVIDIST JORIST
DAVIT CRANE
DAW DA DAWN DRAB DAUNT MAGPIE DAWPATE JACKDAW SLATTERN SLUGGARD
DAWDLE LAG IDLE JAUK LOAF MOON MUCK MULL POKE TOIT DALLY DELAY DRILL KNOCK DADDLE DAIDLE DIDDLE DOODLE DRETCH FADDLE LINGER LOITER MUCKER PICKLE PIDDLE PINGLE POTTER PUTTER TANTLE TRIFLE DRIDDLE FINNICK QUIDDLE SAUNTER LALLYGAG LOLLYGAG SHAMMOCK SLUMMOCK
DAWDLER DAWDLE MUSARD LOUTHER
DAWN DAW ROW EOAN MORN BREAK CREEK LIGHT PRIME SHINE SUNUP AURORA MORROW ORIENT SPRING UPRISE DAWNING GREKING MORNING SUNRISE COCKCROW DAYBREAK (PREF.) EO EOSINO
DAWN-HORSE EOHIPPUS
DAY DA DEI ERA SUN YOM DATE DIEM DIES DIET JOUR TIME EPOCH LIGHT FRIDAY MONDAY PERIOD SUNDAY JOURNEY TUESDAY LIFETIME SATURDAY THURSDAY WEDNESDAY
(— AND NIGHT) KALPA
(— BEFORE) EVE
(— OF BRAHMA) CALPA KALPA
(— OF JOY)) FEAST
(— OF JUDGMENT) INQUEST DOOMSDAY
(— OF ORIGIN) BIRTHDAY
(— OF REST) SABBATH
(— OF ROMAN MONTH) IDES NONES CALENDS KALENDS
(DOG —S) CANICULE
(EVERY —) ALDAY
(EVIL —S) DISMAL
(FAST —) ASHURA FASTEN
(FIRST — OF AUGUST) LAMMAS
(FIRST — OF MAY) BELTANE BEALTINE
(HOLY —) FEAST HOLIDAY
(HOT —) BROILER ROASTER SCORCHER
(LAST — OF FESTIVAL) APODOSIS
(LAST — OF YEAR) HOGMANAY
(MARKET —) NUNDINE TIANGUE
(NO FLESH —) MAIGRE
(PATRON SAINT'S —) PATTERN
(QUARTER —) TERM
(SAINT'S —) FESTA FIESTA
(TWELFTH —) EPIPHANY
(UNLUCKY —S) DISMAL
(WEEK —) FERIA
(WORK —) WARDAY
(40 —S) QUARANTINE
(5 NAMELESS —S) UAYEB
(60TH OF —) GHURRY
(8TH — AFTER FEAST) UTAS
(PREF.) HEMER(O)
(LASTING BUT —) EPHEMERO
DAYAK DYAK IBAN BAHAU DUSUN KAYAN KENYA KENYAH KELABIT
DAYBOOK BOOK DIURNAL JOURNAL
DAYBREAK DAWN MORN SUNUP DAWNING DAYDAWN DAYLIGHT (PREF.) EO EOSINO
DAYDREAM DWAM MUSE DREAM DWALM FANCY VISION FANTASY REVERIE PHANTASY
DAYDREAMER MITTY REVEUR
DAYFLOWER COHITRE
DAYLIGHT DAY LIGHT DAYSHINE
(BROAD —) FUIRDAYS
DAYWORKER DILKER
DAZE FOG DAMP DARE MAZE ROCK STUN DAUNT DAVER DIZZY DOZEN GALLY SWOON ASTONY BEDAZE BEMUSE BENUMB DAZZLE DEAFEN MUDDLE STUPOR TRANCE CONFUSE PETRIFY STUPEFY TORPIFY ASTONISH BEWILDER DUMFOUND PARALYZE
DAZED MAD ASEA DAMP ASSOT DIZZY DOYLT MUZZY SILLY TOTTY WOOZY CUCKOO DOILED GROGGY ROTTEN BEMUSED DONNERT SPOILED WITLESS ASTONIED BESOTTED DITHERED DONNERED WITHERED
DAZEDLY GROGGILY
DAZZLE DARE DAZE BLEND BLIND DROWN GLAIK SHINE FULGOR ECLIPSE BEWILDER OUTSHINE SURPRISE
DAZZLED BLINDED
DAZZLING FLARE FLASH GLAIK FLASHY GARISH ADAZZLE FLARING FULGENT GLARING RADIANT DIZZYING GORGEOUS
DDT TDE DICOPHANE
DEACON ADEPT CLERIC DOCTOR LAYMAN LEVITE MASTER PHILIP MINISTER
DEACONESS WIDOW
DEACTIVATE MOTHBALL
DEAD FEY LOW AWAY BONG BUNG COLD DEAF DOWD DULL FLAT GONE MORT NUMB POKY SURE TAME ADEAD AMORT BLIND DEEDS INERT NAPOO POKEY QUIET SLAIN STARK VAPID ASLEEP BYGONE FALLEN LAPSED NAPOOH PARTED REFUSE DEADISH DEFUNCT EXACTLY EXPIRED EXTINCT INSIPID SAINTED STERILE TEDIOUS ABSOLUTE COMPLETE DECEASED DEPARTED INACTIVE LIFELESS OBSOLETE SCUPPERED
(— AT TOP) RAMPICK
(BLESSED —) SAINT
(PREF.) NECR(O)
DEAD-ARM NECROSIS
DEAD-DRUNK BLIND
DEADEN DAMP DRUG DULL DUMB KILL MULL MUTE NUMB SEAR STUN BLUNT SLAKE BENUMB DAMPEN MUFFLE OBTUND OPIATE RETARD STIFLE WEAKEN MORTIFY PETRIFY REPRESS SLUMBER SMOTHER AMORTIZE ASTONISH ENFEEBLE
(— A SCENT) FOIL
DEAD END PLACE
(AUTHOR OF —) KINGSLEY
(CHARACTER IN —) KAY JACK DRINA TOMMY GIMPTY HILTON MARTIN BABYFACE
DEADENED DEAD DEAF SEAR SERE
DEADENING PUGGING
DEADFALL SNARE
DEADHEAD SINK BOBBER SINKER
DEADHOUSE MORGUE MORTUARY
DEAD LETTER NIX
DEADLINE DATELINE
DEADLINESS LETHALITY
DEADLOCK TIE DRAW LOGJAM IMPASSE STANDOFF STOPPAGE
DEADLY WAN DIRE FELL MORT FATAL FERAL TUANT DEATHY FUNEST LETHAL MORTAL CAPITAL DEATHLY FATEFUL RUINOUS MORTIFIC VENOMOUS VIRULENT PESTILENT THANATOID PERNICIOUS
DEADLY CARROT DRIAS THAPSIA
DEADLY-NIGHTSHADE DWALE
DEAD NETTLE HENBIT
DEADS MULLOCK
DEAD SOULS (AUTHOR OF —) GOGOL
(CHARACTER IN —) PAVEL ALEXEI PLATON KLOBUEFF KOPEYKIN MANILOFF NOZDREFF LYENITZEN PLATONOFF PLIUSHKIN SOBAKEVITCH KOSTANZHOGLO TCHITCHIKOFF TENTETNIKOFF BETRISHTCHEFF
DEAF SURD DUNCH DUNNY SORDA SORDO (PREF.) SURDI SURDO
DEAFEN DIN DORR DEAVE DEADEN
DEAFENING DEEVEY
DEAF-MUTE FENELLA SURDOMUTE
DEAFNESS ASONIA SURDITY ANACUSIA ANACUSIS COPHOSIS
DEAL GO END JOB DAIL DOLE LEND PART SALE TALE WHIZ ALLOT BOARD BROKE FETCH PLANK SERVE SEVER SHAKE SHARE SHIFT TRADE TREAT TROKE TRUCK WIELD YIELD BATTEN BESTOW DIVIDE HANDLE MEDDLE NUMBER PARCEL BARGAIN DELIVER INFLICT PIANOLA PORTION SCATTER TRUCKLE WRESTLE DISPENSE SEPARATE
(— CARDS) DRAW TALLY
(— CLANDESTINELY) TRINKET
(— DISHONESTLY) SHORTCHANGE
(— IN) SELL VEND
(— IN A TRIFLING WAY) PIDDLE
(— IN BRIDGE) BOARD
(— IN GRAIN) SWALE
(— OF CARDS) COUP SPOIL GOULASH
(— OUT) HELP METE
(— SHREWDLY) JOCKEY
(— SPARINGLY) TAPE
(— WITH) HAND COVER DIGHT TOUCH TREAT BUCKET CUSTOM DEMEAN HANDLE ENTREAT NEGOTIATE
(GOOD —) HANTLE
(GREAT —) MORT LOADS MIGHT SIGHT JUGFUL OODLES SKINFUL
(POLITICAL —) DICKER
DEALER BANK CHAP AGENT COPER BADGER BANKER BROKER CADGER EGGLER GROCER JOBBER JUNIOR MONGER SELLER TRADER BUTCHER CHAPMAN KEELMAN YOUNGER CHANDLER MERCHANT OCCUPIER OPERATOR STICKMAN TAILLEUR
(— IN CATTLE) COUPER COWPER DROVER
(— IN CHEMICALS) SALTER DRYSALTER
(— IN DRY GOODS) DRAPER
(— IN GRAIN) SWALER
(— IN OLD CLOTHES) FRIPPER
(— IN PAINTS) COLORMAN
(— IN TEXTILES) MERCER
(CARDS —) FARMER
(COAL —) COLLIER
(EXTORTIONATE —) SHAVER
(HORSE —) COPER COUPER COWPER CHANTER SCORSER
(SCRAP —) TOTTER DIDAKAI
(SLAVE —) MANGO
(STOCK —) STAG JOBBER OUTSIDER
DEALFISH VAAGMAR VAAGMAER RIBBONFISH
DEALING DOLE PRICE TRUCK TAFFIC TRADING EXCHANGE
(BUSINESS —S) TROKE
(JUST —) DOOM
(TRICKY —) BROKING
(PL.) DEAL TRAFFIC BUSINESS COMMERCE PRACTICE PRACTISE
(SUFF.) **(— WITH)** IC(AL)
DEAN DECAN DOYEN DEANER SENIOR VERGER PREFECT PROVOST SUBDEAN ARCHDEAN PRAEFECT
DEAR JO GRA HON JOE PET AGRA CARA CHER CHOU CONY FAIR FOND GOOD HIGH LAMB LIEF LOVE NEAR NOBS SALT ANGEL BOSOM CHARY CHERE CHERI CHUCK DEARY HONEY LOVED PRICY SWEET TIGHT CHERIE COSTLY DAUTIE DAWTIE DEARIE DEARLY POPPET PRICEY SCARCE SEVERE SQUALL TENDER WORTHY BELOVED DARLING LOVABLE PIGSNEY QUERIDA SPECIAL TOOTSIE ESPECIAL ESTEEMED GLORIOUS PRECIOUS VALUABLE
(SUFF.) **(— ONE)** EEN
DEARLY DEAR ALIFE DEEPLY KEENLY RICHLY HEARTILY
DEARNESS CHERTE DEARTH
DEARTH LACK WANT CHERTE FAMINE PAUCITY POVERTY DEARNESS SCARCITY SOLITUDE (SUFF.) PENIA
DEASPIRATION PSILOSIS
DEATH DEE END BALE BANE DEAD DOOM EXIT FAIL FATE KILL MORS MORT OBIT PASS REST WINK ANKOU DECAY GRAVE GRUEL LETHE NIGHT SLEEP CHAROS CHARUS DEMISE DEPART ENDING EXITUS EXPIRY MURDER PERIOD

REAPER WAGANG ACHERON CURTAIN DECEASE FUNERAL PARTING PASSAGE QUIETUS SILENCE BIOLYSIS CASUALTY CURTAINS FATALITY NECROSIS RAWBONES THANATOS MORTALITY NOTHINGNESS
(— ANGEL) AZRAEL
(— BY BURNING) STAKE
(— BY HANGING) HALTER
(— OF TISSUE) GANGRENE
(PREF.) LETHI THANAT(O)
(SUFF.) THANASIA
DEATH ADDER ELAPID ELAPOID
DEATH-AGONY (— OF WHALE) FLURRY
DEATH CAMASS LOBELIA
DEATH INSTINCT THANATOS
DEATH IN VENICE (CHARACTER IN —) TADZIO ASCHENBACH
(COMPOSER OF —) BRITTEN
DEATHLESS ETERNAL UNDYING IMMORTAL
DEATHLESSNESS ATHANASY
DEATHLIKE CHARNEL DEATHLY GHASTLY MACABRE GHASTFUL MORIBUND MORTUOUS
DEATHLY DEAD FATAL DEADLY MORTAL GHASTLY STYGIAN DEATHFUL MORTALLY
DEATH OF A SALESMAN (AUTHOR OF —) MILLER
(CHARACTER IN —) BIFF HAPPY LINDA LOMAN WILLY
DEATH'S-HEAD SKULL
DEBACLE ROUT COLLAPSE STAMPEDE
DEBAR DENY TABU CROSS ESTOP REPEL TABOO DISBAR FORBID HINDER REFUSE BOYCOTT DEPRIVE EXCLUDE OUTSHUT PREVENT SECLUDE SUSPEND PRECLUDE PROHIBIT
DEBARK LAND GOASHORE
DEBARRED FROZEN OUTSHUT
DEBASE SINK ABASE ALLAY ALLOY AVILE DIRTY LOWER STOOP BEMEAN DEFILE DEMEAN DILUTE EMBASE IMPAIR NIDDER NITHER REDUCE REVILE VILIFY CORRUPT DEBAUCH DECLINE DEGRADE DEPRAVE PERVERT PROFANE TRADUCE VILLAIN VITIATE DEROGATE PROSTITUTE
DEBASED BASE VILE HEDGE BASTARD CORRUPT SQUALID CANKERED DEGRADED DEROGATE
DEBASEMENT TARNISH PROSTITUTION
DEBASING DOWNWARD
DEBATABLE MOOT DISPUTABLE
DEBATE AGON BEAT FRAY MOOT ARGUE FIGHT PLEAD STUDY ARGUFY COMBAT HASSEL HASSLE REASON STRIFE AGITATE CANVASS CONTEND CONTEST DISCEPT DISCUSS DISPUTE EXAMINE MOOTING PALAVER QUARREL WRANGLE ARGUMENT COLLOQUY CONSIDER CONTRARY MILITATE PARLANCE QUESTION CONTENTION
(VIGOROUS —) SETTO
DEBATER PICADOR
DEBAUCH BUM BOUT FILE SPREE TAINT WHORE DEBASE DEBOSH DEFILE GUZZLE MISUSE SEDUCE SPLORE VILIFY CORRUPT DEBOISE DEPRAVE MISLEAD POLLUTE VIOLATE DISHONOR SQUANDER STRUMPET STUPRATE
DEBAUCHED LEWD RAKELY RAKISH DEBOIST DEBOSHED RAKEHELL
DEBAUCHEE RIP RAKE ROUE HOLOUR LECHER RAKEHELL
DEBAUCHERY RIOT RAKERY DEBAUCH PRIAPISM
DEBENTURE BOND SECURITY
DEBENZOLIZE STRIP
DEBILITATE SINK
DEBILITATED WEAK SEEDY FEEBLE INFIRM SAPPED ASTHENIC
DEBILITY ATONY ADYNAMY ASTHENY LANGUOR MALAISE ADYNAMIA ASTHENIA WEAKNESS MYASTHENIA
(PREF.) ASTHEN(O)
(SUFF.) ASTHENIA
DEBIR (SLAYER OF —) JOSHUA
DEBIT DEBT LOSS CHARGE
DEBONAIR AIRY JAUNTY POLITE CAVALIER GRACEFUL GRACIOUS
DEBORA E JAELE (CHARACTER IN —) JAELE DEBORA SISERA
(COMPOSER OF —) PIZZETTI
DEBOUCH FALL MOUTH
DEBOUCHMENT EXIT INFLUX INFLUXION
DEBRIS GUCK SLAG DECAY FRUSH TRADE TRASH WASTE RAFFLE REFUSE RUBBLE RUDERA CRUMBLE ELUVIUM RUBBISH SLIDDER DETRITUS
(— AT BASE OF CLIFF) SCREE
(— IN WOOL) BUR BURR
(— OF INSECTS) FRASS
(— OF ROCKS) HEAD DRIFT SCREE TALUS ELUVIUM
(FLOATING —) LAGAM JETSAM FLOTSAM
(FLUFFY —) FLUE
(FOREST —) SLASH
DEBT DUE SIN CHIT POST DEBIT FAULT STOCK ARREARS DEBITUM JUDGMENT TRESPASS
(PL.) OBLATA WANIGAN ARREARAGE
DEBTOR OWER PEON SKIP DYVOUR DEBITOR YIELDER
DEBUT OPENING ENTRANCE
DEBUTANTE BUD DEB BELLE DEBBY INGENUE ROSEBUD
DECADENT EFFETE DECAYED HOTHOUSE OVERRIPE
DECAHYDRATE SODA
DECALOGUE WITNESS
DECAMP GUY PUT BOLT HIKE KITE ELOPE MOSEY SCOOT SCOUR SLOPE VAMOS DEPART ESCAPE LEVANT MIZZLE MORRIS POWDER VAMOSE ABSCOND DISCAMP VAMOOSE ABSQUATULATE
DECAMPING GUY
DECAN DECURION
DECANT EMIT POUR RACK UNLOAD TRANSFER
DECANTER CARAFE CARAFON URCEOLE GARDEVIN INGESTER
DECAPITATE BEHEAD DECOLLATE
DECAPITATION DECOLL HEADING
DECAPOD CRAB BUSTER
DECARBONIZE DECOKE
DECATING SPONGING
DECAY EBB ROT ROX BLET CONK DOAT DOTE DOZE FADE FAIL RUIN SEED WANE WEAR CROCK DEATH SHANK SLOOM SLOUM SPOIL WASTE BLIGHT CANKER CARIES FADING MARCOR MILDEW MOLDER MOSKER SICKEN WITHER CRUMBLE DECLINE FAILURE FORFAIR MORTIFY PUTREFY DECREASE FORDWINE
(— IN WOOD) CONK DOZE
(— OF FRUIT) BLETTING
(INCIPIENT —) BLET
(TOOTH —) CARIES
(PREF.) SAPR(O)
(TOOTH —) CARIO
DECAYED BAD DEAF DOZY ROXY FRUSH SEEDY DAISED MARCID PUTRID ROTTEN SPAKED CARIOUS RUINOUS SNAGGLED
DECAYING COLD DOTY SHABBY CARIOUS
DECEASE DIE FAIL OBIT PASS DEATH DEMISE PASSAGE
DECEASED DEAD LATE PARTED DEFUNCT EXTINCT UMWHILE DEPARTED UMQUHILE
DECEIT GAB DOLE FLUM GAFF GULL RUSE SHAM TRAP TRAY WILE ABUSE COVIN CRAFT DOLUS FRAUD GUILE SARAB SWICK SWIKE CAUTEL FELONY WOIDRE CUNNING DISSAIT FAITERY FICTION ARTIFICE COZENAGE FALSEDAD INTRIGUE SPOOFERY SUBTLETY TRICKERY TRUMPERY WILINESS
(— IN LOVE) COQUETRY
DECEITFUL JIVE RUSE BLIND BRAID FALSE GAUDY JANUS LOOPY PUNIC SLAPE SNAKY ARTFUL COVERT CRAFTY DOUBLE FICKLE HOLLOW ROTTEN TRICKY CUNNING EVASIVE FICTIVE SIRENIC SLEEKIT SLIDDER UNWREST WINDING COVINOUS GUILEFUL ILLUSIVE INDIRECT SHAMMISH TORTUOUS MENDACIOUS
DECEITFULLY DOUBLE FALSELY
DECEITFULNESS SHAM DECEIT FALSITY
DECEIVE BOB COG CON DOR FOB FUB GAB GAS GUM KID LIE BILK BRAG BUNK CRAP DUPE FAKE FLAM FOOL GAFF GULL HAVE HOAX HYPE JILT JOUK MOCK SCAM SELL SHAM SILE SNOW TURN WILE ABUSE AMUSE BLEAR BLEND BLENK BLIND BLINK BLUFF CATCH CHEAT COZEN CROSS CULLY DODGE DORRE FEINT GLEEK GLOZE HOCUS LIETO LURCH PATCH SHUCK SPOOF SWICK SWIKE TRICK TROIL TRUFF TRUMP TRYST BAFFLE BARRAT BEDOTE BEFLUM BEFOOL BETRAY BLANCH BUBBLE CAJOLE CLOINE CLOYNE DELUDE DIVERT EUCHRE GAMMON HUMBUG ILLUDE JUGGLE MISUSE NIGGLE SUCKER TAKEIN WIMPLE BEGUILE DEFRAUD MISLEAD OVERSEE TRAITOR BEJUGGLE FLIMFLAM HOODWINK OUTREACH
DECEIVER ANGLE CHEAT HOCUS COGGER FAITOR FALSER GUILER MOCKER TRAPAN TREPAN FALSARY ILLUSOR JUGGLER SHARPER SPOOFER TRUMPER WARLOCK WERNARD IMPOSTOR LOSENGER LOTHARIO MAGICIAN TREGETOUR
DECEIVING FALSE ILLUSIVE
DECELERATE SLOW
DECENCY GRACE DECORUM HONESTY MODESTY CHASTITY
DECENNIUM DECADE
DECENT FAIR CHASTE COMELY HONEST MODEST PRETTY PROPER SEEMLY FITTING GRADELY JANNOCK SHAPELY SIGHTLY DECOROUS GRAITHLY WISELIKE
DECENTLY WHITE
DECEPTION BAM COG DOR GAG LIE DOLE FLAM FLUM GAFF GULL HOAX HYPE MAZE RIDE RUSE SELL SHAM WILE ABUSE BLIND BLUFF CHEAT COVIN CRAFT CURVE DOLUS DORRE FAVEL FRAUD GLAIK GLEEK GUILE MAGIC SHUCK SNARE SPOOF TRICK BARRAT CAUTEL DECEIT DUPERY HUMBUG JUGGLE ABUSION BLAFLUM CHICANE CUNNING EVASION FALLACY FALSERY FICTION GULLAGE GULLERY KNAVERY PRETEXT SLYNESS ARTIFICE DISGUISE FALSEDAD FLIMFLAM ILLUSION INTRIGUE PHANTASM PRESTIGE SUBTLETY TRICKERY TRUMPERY WILINESS
DECEPTIVE FLAM FALSE ARTFUL BUBBLE SIRENIC TRICKSY DELUSIVE DELUSORY FLIMFLAM ILLUSORY IMPOSING SHAMMISH UNSICKER
DECEPTIVENESS FANTASTRY
DECIBEL (10 —S) BEL
DECIDE FIX CAST DEEM HOLD RULE TELL WILL AWARD JUDGE PATCH PITCH DECERN DECISE DECREE FIGURE REWARD SETTLE ADJUDGE DERAIGN RESOLVE CONCLUDE SENTENCE
(— UPON) SET ELECT CHOOSE TERMINE
(RIGHT TO —) SAY
DECIDED FIRM FLAT MAIN FORMED SETTLED DECISIVE RESOLUTE
DECIDEDLY DIRECTLY DISTINCTLY
DECIDUA CADUCA
DECIGRAM LI
DECIMA TENTH TITHE
DECIMAL DENARY REPEATER
(— PART) MANTISSA
DECIMATE TENTH DESTROY
DECIPHER READ SOLVE CIPHER DECODE DETECT REVEAL DECRYPT DISCOVER INDICATE UNPUZZLE
DECIPHERING EPIGRAPHY

DECISION ACT END CALL DOOM FIAT GRIT ARRET AWARD CANON FAITH ISSUE PARTY PLUCK POINT ACTION CHOICE CRISIS DECREE DIKTAT RULING ACUERDO CONSULT INTERIM PRACTIC VERDICT FINALITY JUDGMENT PLACITUM SENTENCE SUFFRAGE UMPIRAGE
(— BY MAJORITY) VOTE
(— OF COURT) HOLDING ABSOLVITOR
(— OF REFEREE) TKO
(— OF UMPIRE) OUT FOUL SAFE
(EXISTENTIAL —) LEAP
(FINAL —) ISSUE
(LEGAL —) FETWA
(MUSLIM LEGAL —) FETWA
DECISIVE FATAL FINAL CRISIC PAYOFF VIRILE CRUCIAL DECIDED CRITICAL CRUSHING DECRETAL POSITIVE
DECISIVELY FINALLY
DECK FIG TOG BANK BUSK BUSS DAUB DINK FLAT HEAP PINK POOP PROW TIER TRIG ADORN ARRAY COVER DIZEN DRESS EQUIP FLOOR HATCH PRANK PRINK STORE AWNING BEDECK BETRIM BLAZON CLOTHE ENRICH FETTLE FOCSLE LAUREL APPAREL BEDIGHT BEDIZEN FEATHER FLOUNCE GEMMATE TERRACE BEAUTIFY DECORATE EMBLAZON PLATFORM FLYBRIDGE
(— OF CARDS) BOOK
(— OUT) BARB TIFF ARRAY DIZEN SPICK BEDECK DAIKER FANGLE FINIFY BEDIGHT
(HIGH —) POOP
(LOWEST —) ORLOP
DECKED CLAD BESEEN ARMORIED LAURELED
(— OUT) CLAD SPIFFED
DECKHAND BOATMAN TRIMMER BARGEMAN ROUSTABOUT
DECKHOUSE CABOOSE CAMBOOSE PILOTHOUSE
DECKLE DECKEL FEATHEREDGE
DECKMAN TRIPPER LEVERMAN
DECLAIM GALE RANT RAVE ROLL MOUTH ORATE SPEAK SPOUT BLEEZE RECITE ELOCUTE INVEIGH DENOUNCE DISCLAIM HARANGUE PERORATE SINGSONG
DECLAIMER BARD SPEECHIFIER
DECLAMATION FROTHING HARANGUE RHETORIC SPOUTING PHILIPPIC
DECLARATION BILL CALL DICK NARR TALE WORD COUNT FUERO LIBEL PAROL AVOWAL DECEIT MISERE ORACLE PAROLE PLACET SAYING EXPRESS PROMISE RESOLVE MANIFEST PLATFORM
(— IN BRIDGE) MAKE AUCTION
(— OF HOSTILITIES) DEFIANCE
(OFFICIAL —) AUTHORITY
(PUBLIC —) MANIFESTO
DECLARE BID KEN LAY SAY VOW AVER AVOW DENY MAKE READ SHOW SNUM SWAN TROW VOTE AREAD AREED BRUIT KEETH KITHE KYTHE POSIT SNORE SOUND SPEAK STATE TRUTH VOUCH AFFIRM ALLEGE ASSERT ASSURE AUTHOR AVOUCH BLAZON COUTHE DEPONE DESCRY EXPONE HERALD INDICT NOTIFY PATEFY RELATE SPRING UPGIVE ACCLAIM BEHIGHT DISCUSS EXPRESS OUTTELL PROFESS PROTEST PUBLISH SIGNIFY TERMINE TESTIFY ANNOUNCE DENOUNCE DESCRIBE INDICATE INTIMATE MAINTAIN MANIFEST NUNCIATE PROCLAIM RENOUNCE PREDICATE
(— ARBITRARILY) GAVEL
(— A SAINT) CANONIZE
(— INVALID) ANNUL
(— PUBLICLY) CRY
(— TRUE) SOOTHE
(— UNTRUE) DENY
(— WAR) DEFY
(SOLEMNLY —) AFFY SWEAR
DECLARED AVOWED STATED
DECLARER LAWMAN VIVANT
DECLINATION BIAS DECAY SLOPE REGRET DECLINE DESCENT REFUSAL SOUTHING SWERVING
DECLINE BEG DIP EBB SAG SET BALK BEND BUST DENY DIVE DOWN DROP FADE FAIL FALL FLAG FLOP HELD SINK SLIP TURN VAIL WANE WELK BAULK CHUTE DECAY DROLL DROOP DWINE FAINT HEALD HIELD LAPSE LOWER QUAIL REPEL SLACK SLOPE SLUMP SPURN STOOP STRAY TABES WAIVE DEBASE DEVALL FALTER REFUSE REJECT RENEGE SICKEN WEAKEN ATROPHY DESCEND DESCENT DETRECT DEVIATE DISAVOW DWINDLE ECLIPSE FAILURE FALLOFF FORBEAR INFLECT LETDOWN SINKAGE DECREASE DOWNBEAT DOWNTURN FOREBEAR LANGUISH MELTDOWN TOBOGGAN WITHDRAW REPUDIATE
(— IN MARKET PRICE) SPILL
(— IN POPULATION) CRASH
(ECONOMIC —) SLUMPFLATION
(INTO A STATE OF —) SOUTH
(PREF.) CLIN
DECLINING DOWN AWANE BEARISH FALLING WESTERN DECADENT
DECLIVITY BENT BREW FALL HANG SIDE SKUG CLIFF COAST DEVEX PITCH SCARP SLENT SLOPE CALADE HANGER DECLINE DESCENT HANGING DOWNHILL
DECLIVOUS PRONE SLOPING
DECOCT BOIL COOK SMELT EXCITE KINDLE REFINE EXTRACT
DECOCTION BANG OOZE SAVE BHANG APOZEM CREMOR PTISAN TISANE APOZEMA DECOCTUM
DECODE CLEAR DECRYPT
DECOHERER TAPPER
DECOLLETE LOW
DECOMPOSE ROT FOUL FRIT DECAY ATTACK DIGEST DEGRADE DISSOLVE
DECOMPOSED BAD PUTRID
DECOMPOSITION DECAY BREAKUP BIOLYSIS EXCHANGE
(DOUBLE —) METATHESIS
(SUFF.) LYSE LYSIS LYST LYTE LYTIC LYZE
DECORATE DO BIND BUSK CHIP CITE DECK EDGE FRET GAUD PINK RAIL RULE TIFF TIRE TRIM ADORN DRESS FLOCK FRILL GRAIN INLAY MENSE PANEL POKER TRAIL TRICK BEDECK BUTTON DAIKER DAMASK DECORE EMBOSS FLOWER FRESCO PARGET POUNCE PURFLE SPONGE SUBORN BECROSS CORONET ENCHASE FESTOON FURNISH GADROON GARNISH HISTORY IMPASTE INWEAVE MINIATE PERFORM BELETTER FLOURISH ORNAMENT OVERWORK TITIVATE
DECORATED GIDDY LACED AJOURE FLAMBE ORNATE ADORNED DAMASSE FROGGED INCISED WROUGHT COCKADED DISTINCT FLORETED
(— WITH PENDANTS) SCARFED
(ELABORATELY —) RICH
DECORATING LIMNERY
DECORATION KEY BUHL FALL FUSS IKAT BOULE DECOR DODAD HONOR MEDAL PRIDE BOULLE DECKER DECORE DESIGN DOODAB DOODAD FINERY FLORET FRIEZE GOTHIC NIELLO PLAQUE SETOFF TINSEL ARTWORK BARBOLA DECKING EPERGNE FLUTING GARNISH TRACERY BAYADERE DENTELLE DIAMANTE ESCALLOP FILIGREE FLOURISH FOOFARAW FRETTING FRETWORK FRIPPERY FURBELOW INTARSIA ORNAMENT
(— IN GUEST CHAMBER) XENIUM
(— OF LEAVES) VIGNETTE
(— OF MONKEYS) SINGERIE
(— TECHNIQUE) PLANGI
(BOOK-COVER —) DENTELLE
(CURVED —) OGEE
(CUTOUT —) APPLIQUE
(ENAMEL —) WUTSAI
(FESTIVE —) GALA
(INESSENTIAL —) SPINACH
(INLAID —) BUHL BOULE BOULLE
(MURAL —) TOPIA
(MUSICAL —) GRACE
(PAINTED —) ROSEMALING
(PORCELAIN —) KAKIEMON
(POTTERY —) BRODERIE
(RICH —) PARAMENT
(SCANDINAVIAN —) ROSEMALING
(TABLE —) DOILY
(WALL —) ARRAS
(WALL —S) TENTURE
(PL.) COLORS BUNTING GREENERY
DECORATIVE FANCY FIKIE
(OVERLY —) DITSY DITZY
DECORATOR PAINTER
DECOROUS CALM DONE GOOD NICE PRIM DOUCE GRAVE QUIET SOBER STAID CHASTE DECENT DEMURE MODEST POLITE PROPER SEDATE SEEMLY SERENE STEADY BECOMED FITTING ORDERLY REGULAR SETTLED BECOMING COMPOSED MANNERLY
DECOROUSLY FITLY
DECOROUSNESS CHASTITY POLITESSE
DECORTICATE FLAY HULL HUSK PARE PEEL PILL SKIN STRIP DENUDE
DECORUM DECENCY DIGNITY FITNESS HONESTY MODESTY PROPRIETY
DECOY COY BAIT CALL GOAD LURE TOLE TOLL COACH CRIMP DRILL PLANT ROPER SHILL STALE STALL STOOL TEMPT TRAIN ALLURE BUTTON CALLER CAPPER ENTICE ENTRAP PIGEON SEDUCE TOLLER TREPAN BARNARD BERNARD DECOYER INVEIGLE SQUAWKER
(— FOR GAMBLERS) CAPPER
(— FOR SWINDLERS) BARNARD BERNARD
(AUCTIONEER'S —) BONNET BUTTON
DECREASE EBB BATE DROP FALL LOSS SINK WANE WELK WILK ABATE CROCK DECAY LAPSE SWAGE TAPER WANZE WASTE CHANGE DECESS DECREW IMPAIR LESSEN NARROW REDUCE SHRINK ATROPHY CUTDOWN DECLINE DWINDLE SHORTEN SLACKEN SUBSIDE ABLATION DECIMATE DIMINISH DOWNTURN MODERATE RETRENCH
(— IN FORCE) LAY
(— IN VOLUME) ABLATION
(— IN WIDTH) INTAKE
(— OF EFFICIENCY) FATIGUE
(— STITCHES) FASHION
DECREE ACT DIT LAW SAW SET DOOM FIAT REDE RULE WILL WITE AREAD AREED ARRET CANON EDICT ENACT FIANT GRACE HATTI IRADE JUDGE ORDER POINT SHAPE TENET UKASE WRITE ARREST ASSIZE DECERN DICTUM DIKTAT FIRMAN INDICT MODIFY ORDAIN PLACIT RECESS ADJUDGE APPOINT BESLUIT COMMAND CONSULT DECREET DICTATE DIVORCE ESCRIPT GEZERAH MANDATE SETNESS STATUTE WORKING DECISION DECRETUM JUDGMENT PLACITUM PSEPHISM RESCRIPT ROGATION SANCTION SENTENCE ORDINANCE ABSOLVITOR
(— BEFOREHAND) DESTINE
(ECCLESIASTICAL —) CANON SYNODICAL
(JUDICIAL —) AUTO
(MOHAMMEDAN —) IRADE
(OFFICIAL —) RESCRIPT
(PAPAL —) BULL DECRETAL
DECREPIT LAME WEAK UNORN BEDRID CREAKY FEEBLE INFIRM SENILE FAILING INVALID FORFAIRN
DECRY BOO CRAB SLUR LOWER ROGUE DESCRY LESSEN ASPERSE BARRACK CENSURE CONDEMN DEBAUCH DEGRADE DETRACT BELITTLE DEROGATE MINIMIZE
DECRYPT BREAK DECODE

DECURRENT DEFLUENT
DECUSSATION CHIASM CHIASMA
DEDAN (FATHER OF —) RAAMAH JOKSHAN
(MOTHER OF —) KETURAH
DEDANS HAZARD
DEDICATE VOW VOTE DEVOW SACRE SACRI DEVOTE DEVOVE DIRECT HALLOW OBLATE ASCRIBE ENTITLE CHRISTEN INSCRIBE INTITULE SEPARATE NUNCUPATE
(— TO CHURCH) IMMOLATE
DEDICATED HOLY OBLATE SACRED VOTIVE
DEDICATION CULT WAKF DEVOTION
DEDUCE PUT DRAW LEAD TAKE BRING DRIVE FETCH GUESS INFER TRACE DEDUCT DERIVE ELICIT EVOLVE GATHER COLLECT EXPLAIN EXTRACT SUBSUME CONCLUDE
DEDUCT BATE DOCK TAKE ABATE ALLOW SHAVE DEFALK REBATE RECOUP REDUCT REMOVE CURTAIL SUBDUCT TAKEOUT TRADUCE ABSTRACT DISCOUNT SEPARATE SUBTRACT
DEDUCTION AGIO SALT CREDIT DEDUCT REBATE BEAMAGE DOCKAGE IMPRESS OFFTAKE REPRISE DISCOUNT ERGOTISM ILLATION STOPPAGE ABATEMENT COROLLARY
(YEARLY —) REPRISE
DEDUCTIVE DOGMATIC
DEE DUANT
DEED DO ACT BILL BOOK CASE FACT FAIT FEAT FIAT GEST HARD JEST TURN WORK ACTUM ACTUS BROAD CHART DOING GESTE ISSUE SANAD THING TITLE ACTION CONVEY ESCROW FACTUM POTTAH REMISE SASINE SUNNUD TAILYE CHARTER EXPLOIT FACTION TAILZIE CHIVALRY HEIRLOOM PARERGON PRACTICE PRACTISE TRANSFER HARDIMENT PERFORMANCE
(BRUTAL —) ATROCITY
(CHARITABLE —S) ALMS
(DARING —) GESTE
(EVIL —) PRANK MALEFACTION
(GOOD —) BENEFIT MITZVAH
(HEBREW —) STARR
(KIND —) FAVOR
(PART OF —) HABENDUM
(VALIANT —) VALIANCE
(WICKED —) ILL
(PL.) DOINGS SERVICE MUNIMENTS
DEEM LET SAY SEE GIVE HOPE RECK SEEM TELL JUDGE OPINE THINK ESTEEM EXPECT ORDAIN RECKON REGARD ACCOUNT ADJUDGE BELIEVE RECOUNT RESPECT SURMISE ANNOUNCE CONSIDER JUDGMENT PROCLAIM
DE-EMPHASIZE DOWNPLAY
DEEMSTER DOOMSMAN
DE-ENERGIZE KILL CLEAR
DEEP LOW SAD SEA BASS BOLD DUAT HOLL HOWE NEAL RAPT ABYSS BROAD DEWAT GRAVE GREAT GRUFF HEAVY OCEAN SOUND STIFF STOOR STOUR HOLLOW INTENT STRONG SULLEN ABYSMAL INTENSE SERIOUS UNMIXED ABSORBED ABSTRUSE COMPLETE POWERFUL PROFOUND THOROUGH RECONDITE
(— IN COLOR) RICH
(— IN THE THROAT) GRUM
(PREF.) **(— SEA)** BATH(O)(Y)
DEEP-DYED ENGRAINED
DEEPEN CLOUD DARKEN DREDGE ENHANCE THICKEN HEIGHTEN
DEEPEST INMOST DEEPMOST
DEEPLY DEEP INLY ADEEP DEARLY SOUNDLY DEVOUTLY GROUNDLY INWARDLY
DEEP-SEA DIPSY BATHYL DIPSEY BATHYAL
DEEP-SEATED CHRONIC DEEP INTIMATE PROFOUND INGRAINED
DEEP-TONED STOUR
DEER ELK RED REH ROE AXIS BUCK DAIM HART HIND MILU MUSK OLEN PARA PUDU RUSA SHOU SIKA STAG WILD BROCK GEMUL MARAL MOOSE SABIR SPADE STAIG CERVID CHITAL CHITRA FALLOW GUEMAL HANGUL HEARST HUEMUL PARRAH RASCAL SAMBAR SAMBUR THAMIN VENADA BROCKET BROWZER CARIBOU CERVINE CERVOID CHEETAL DEERLET FANTAIL GUAZUTI KASTURA MUNTJAC PLANDOK SAMBHAR THAMENG VENISON BOBOLINK CARIACOU CARJACOU ELAPHURE RUMINANT
(— IN 3RD YEAR) SPAY SOREL SPAYAD SPAYARD
(— UNDER 1 YEAR) KID
(CASTRATED —) HAVIER
(FEMALE —) DOE ROE HIND
(FEMALE — IN 2ND YEAR) TEG HEARST
(HINDQUARTERS OF —) FOUCH FOURCHE
(MALE — IN 2ND YEAR) PRICKET
(MALE — IN 4TH YEAR) SORE STAGGARD STAGGART
(MALE — OVER 5 YEARS) HART STAG
(RED —) OLEN SPAY MARAL BROCKET
(RUSINE —) AXIS
(YOUNG —) KID FAWN SPITTER
(2-YEAR OLD —) KNOBBER
(PREF.) CERVI
DEER BUSH SOAPBUSH
DEER FERN HARDFERN
DEERFLY TABANID
DEERHAIR SEDGE BULRUSH
DEERHOUND DEERDOG BUCKHOUND
DEERSKIN BUCK DEER
DEERSLAYER (AUTHOR OF —) COOPER
(CHARACTER IN —) HARRY HETTY NATTY UNCAS BUMPPO HUTTER JUDITH THOMAS CHINGACHGOOK
DEFACE MAR FOUL RUIN SCAR ERASE SHAME SPOIL CANCEL DAMAGE DAMASK DEFAME DEFOIL DEFORM DEFOUL EFFACE INJURE INJURY DESTROY DETRACT DISTORT SLANDER DISGRACE DISHONOR MALAHACK MUTILATE OUTSHINE
DEFACED FOUL
DEFACING DIMINUTION
DEFALCATE DRIB DEFALK
DEFAMATION LIBEL SMEAR DEFAME DEFAMY DEPRAVE SCANDAL SLANDER ASPERSION
DEFAMATORY SCANDALOUS
DEFAME FOUL ABASE BELIE CLOUD LIBEL NOISE SMEAR ACCUSE CHARGE DEFACE DEFOIL DEFOUL FORGAB INFAME INJURE MALIGN REVILE SUGGIL VILIFY ASPERSE BLACKEN BLEMISH DEBAUCH DETRACT DIFFAME PUBLISH SCANDAL SLANDER SPATTER TRADUCE DISHONOR INFAMIZE VILIPEND
DEFAMER SYCOPHANT
DEFAULT FAIL FLAW LOSS MORA ERROR FAULT OFFEND BLEMISH FAILURE MISTAKE NEGLECT OFFENSE OMISSION
(— ON DEBT) LEVANT
DEFAULTER DUCK
(PL.) JANKERS
DEFEASANCE DEFEAT UNDOING
DEFEASIBLE IMPERFECT
DEFEAT ACE EAT PIP WIN BALK BEAT BEST BOWL CAST DING DOWN DRUB FOIL HAVE JINK KILL LACE LICK LOSS ROUT RUIN RUSH SINK SKIN STOP TOLL TOSS TRAP TRIM UNDO WHAP WHIP WHOP AVOID BREAK CHECK FACER FALSE FLING FLOOR OUTDO PASTE SHEND SKUNK SMITE SWAMP THROW UPEND WASTE WHACK WORSE WORST WRACK BAFFLE CUMBER DEROUT EUCHRE HOSING LARRUP MASTER MURDER OUTGUN REBUFF STOUSH THWACK THWART WAGGLE WEAKEN CLOBBER CONQUER DEPRIVE DESTROY LICKING OVERSET PEREMPT REVERSE SCOMFIT SETBACK SHELLAC SNOOKER SUBVERT TROUNCE INFRINGE IRRITATE OUTFIGHT OVERCOME SLOSHING VANQUISH WATERLOO OVERPOWER OVERTHROW
(— BY INGENUITY) OUTWIT
(— COMPLETELY) SKUNK
(— DECISIVELY) EAT DRUB SACK BLAST CLEAN FLATTEN SHELLAC
(— IN BRIDGE) SET
(— IN LAWSUIT) CAST
(DECISIVE —) CLEANUP CLEANING PLASTERING
(INTO —) DOWN
(UTTER —) MATE ROUT DEROUT
DEFEATED DOWN LOST KAPUT BEATEN CRAVEN WHIPPED
DEFEATIST BOLO FATALIST
DEFECT BUG FLAW LACK MAIM MOTE TWIT VICE WANE WANT WART BOTCH CLOUD CRAZE ERROR FAULT MINUS MULCT TOUCH DAMAGE DESERT HIATUS INJURY LACUNA MALADY MAYHEM PLIGHT VICETY VITIUM ABSENCE BLEMISH DEMERIT FAILING MISPICK PEELING PINHOLE COLOBOMA CRESCENT DRAWBACK WEAKNESS SHORTCOMING
(— IN ARTICULATION) PSELLISM
(— IN CRYSTAL) HOLE
(— IN ENAMEL) SCAB SAGGING SCUMMING
(— IN FABRIC) GOUT SCOB BARRE BRACK SMASH
(— IN GLASS) KNOT TEAR STONE WREATH THREADS
(— IN IRON) SEAM
(— IN MARBLE) TERRAS TERRACE TERRASSE
(— IN METAL) SNAKE BLOWHOLE
(— IN PRINTING PLATE) HICKY HICKEY
(— IN STEEL) LAP
(— IN TIMBER) LAG SHAN COLLAPSE
(— IN YARN) SINGLING CORKSCREW
(— OF CHARACTER) HOLE SHADE HAMARTIA
(LINT —) SPOT
(SPEECH —) BALBUTIES CLUTTERING
(TELEVISION —) FLOPOVER
DEFECTION LETDOWN APOSTASY DESERTION
DEFECTIVE BAD ILL EVIL FOXY LACK LAME MANK POOR SICK BAUCH BAUGH BLIND FALSE FLAWY PASUL COMMON FAULTY FLAWED MANGUE MEAGER MEAGRE RAGGED HALTING TOMFOOL VICIOUS DISGENIC DYSGENIC MUTILOUS VITIATED
(— PRODUCT) LEMON
(MENTALLY —) WANTING
(PREF.) ATEL(O)
DEFECTOR APOSTATE DESERTER FUGITIVE
DEFEND FEND HOLD KEEP SAVE WARD WARN WEAR COVER GUARD SHEND WATCH ASSERT FORBID SCREEN SECURE SHIELD UPHOLD WARISH BUCKLER BULWARK CONTEST DERAIGN ESPOUSE EXPOUND FLANKER JUSTIFY PREVENT PROPUGN PROTECT SHELTER SUPPORT WARRANT ADVOCATE CHAMPION CONSERVE GARRISON MAINTAIN PRESERVE PROHIBIT SAFEGUARD
(— WITH SUCCESS) VINDICATE
DEFENDANT REA REUS ACCUSED AVOWANT APPELLEE
DEFENDER FENDER PATRON ADVOCATE ASSERTER ASSERTOR CHAMPION GUARDIAN UPHOLDER
DEFENSE EGIS FORT PALE ROCK WALL WARD WEAR AEGIS ALIBI FENCE GRITH GUARD TOWER ABATIS ANSWER BEHALF COVERT FRAISE SCONCE BARRACE BARRIER BASTION BULWARK CONTEST COUNTER DEFENCE

DILATOR OUTWORK PARADOS RAMPART SHELTER WARDING WARRANT ADVOCACY APOLOGIA BOUNDARY FRONTIER GALAPAGO GARRISON MUNITION SECURITY SEPIMENT
DEFENSELESS BARE COLD NAKED SILLY UNARMED HELPLESS
DEFENSIBLE TENABLE JUSTIFIABLE
DEFER BOW RISE STAY WAIT DELAY DRIVE HONOR REFER REMIT STAVE TARRY TRACK WAIVE YIELD ESTEEM HUMBLE RETARD REVERE SUBMIT ADJOURN SUSPEND CONSIDER INTERMIT POSTPONE PROROGUE PROTRACT SUSPENSE
DEFERENCE VAIL COURT HONOR CRINGE ESTEEM HOMAGE REGARD RESPECT WORSHIP CIVILITY OBEISANCE
DEFERENT ECCENTRIC
DEFERENTIAL DUTIFUL OBEISANT
DEFERMENT STAY
DEFERVESCENCE LYSIS DECLINE
DEFIANCE DARE DEFI DEFY GAGE BRAVE DEFIAL CHALLENGE
DEFIANT BOLD BARDY BRAVE STOUT DARING STOCKY INSOLENT STUBBORN OBSTREPEROUS
DEFIANTLY ACOCK
DEFICIENCY FAIL LACK WANT ANOIA ERROR FAULT MINUS DEARTH DEFECT INLAIK ULLAGE ABSENCE ANOESIA BLEMISH DEFICIT FAILING FAILURE POVERTY DELETION SCARCITY SHORTAGE SHORTFALL SHORTCOMING
(— OF BLOOD) ISCHEMIA
(— OF NERVOUS ENERGY) ANEURIA
(— OF OXYGEN) ASPHYXIA
(CARBON DIOXIDE —) ACAPNIA
(MENTAL —) IDIOCY AMENTIA
(PL.) SHORTS
(PREF.) ISCH
(SUFF.) PENIA
DEFICIENT BAD LEAN WANE BLUNT MINUS SCANT BARREN FEEBLE MEAGER MEAGRE SCARCE SCRIMP SKIMPY BOBTAIL DISGENIC DYSGENIC INDIGENT
(— IN BEAUTY) PLAIN
(— IN HEALTH) INVALID
(— IN TURGOR) FLACCID
(MENTALLY —) SOFT
(SUFF.) PRIVIC
DEFICIT SHORTAGE UNDERAGE
DEFILE GUT RAY ABRA BAWD BEDO FILE FOIL FOUL GATE GOWL HALS LIME MOIL MUCK PACE PASS SLIP SLOT SLUT SMUT SOIL ABUSE BERAY CLEFT CROCK DIRTY FILTH GLACK GORGE HALSE NOTCH SLACK SMEAR STAIN SULLY TAINT BEWRAY DEBASE GULLET IMBRUE INFECT RAVISH SMOUCH SMUTCH CORRUPT DEBAUCH DEPRAVE DISTAIN PASSAGE POLLUTE PROFANE SLOTTER SMATTER TARNISH VIOLATE DISHONOR MACULATE
DEFILED DIRTY IMPURE SPOTTY UNCLEAN MACULATE
DEFILEMENT MOIL SOIL SULLAGE TAINTURE
(PREF.) MEASMATO MIASMO MYS(O)
DEFILING PIKY PITCHY
DEFINE END FIX SET MERE TERM BOUND LIMIT DECIDE CLARIFY DELIMIT EXPLAIN EXPOUND DESCRIBE DISCOVER
DEFINED FORMED STRICT
(SHARPLY —) HARD
DEFINITE SET FIRM HARD SURE CLEAR FINAL FIXED SHARP FINITE FORMED LIQUID STRAIT CERTAIN EXPRESS LIMITED POINTED PRECISE DISTINCT EMPHATIC EXPLICIT LIMITING POSITIVE PUNCTUAL SPECIFIC
DEFINITELY BUT WELL FAIRLY EVERMORE
DEFINITION GLOSS CLARITY DIORISM
(— OF FORM) SFUMATO
(PREF.) ORISMO
DEFINITIVE LAST FINAL GRAND ORISTIC DEFINITE
DEFLATE EMPALE IMPALE CONTRACT
DEFLATED FLAT
DEFLATING SETDOWN
DEFLATION HANGOVER
DEFLECT CUT WRY BEND COCK SWAY WARP PARRY WREST WRING BAFFLE DETOUR DIVERT SWERVE DEVIATE DIVERGE INFLECT REFLECT REFRACT
DEFLECTION DROOP SWEEP WINDAGE
(— ON METER) KICK
(PREF.) SPHINGO
DEFLECTOR (AIR —) SPOILER
DEFLOWER FRAY DEFOIL DEFOUL FORLIE RAVAGE RAVISH DEFLORE DESPOIL VIOLATE UNMAIDEN UNVIRGIN
DEFORM MAR FLOW WARP GNARL DEFACE BLEMISH CONTORT DISFORM DISTORT DIFFORME DISGUISE DISHONOR MISSHAPE SHAUCHLE
DEFORMATION CREEP SPRING STRAIN FLEXURE FLOWAGE
DEFORMED GAMMY WRONG INFORM PAULIE CROOKED HIDEOUS MISBORN FORMLESS UNMACKLY MISCREATE MISCREATED
(PREF.) CACH CAC(O)
(SUFF.) CACE
DEFORMITY GALL VICE BLEMISH HARELIP PRAVITY CLUBFOOT CLUBHAND FLATFOOT WANSHAPE
DEFRAUD ROB BEAT BILK FAKE GULL NICK ROOK SCAM TRIM WIPE CHEAT COZEN GOUGE LURCH MULCT SLICK STICK TRICK WRONG BOODLE CHOUSE CHOWSE RIPOFF DECEIVE SKELDER SWINDLE
DEFRAY PAY BEAR AVERT COVER ABSORB EXPEND PREPAY APPEASE REQUITE SATISFY DISBURSE
DEFT FEAT GAIN NEAT TALL TRIM AGILE HANDY NATTY QUICK SLICK ADROIT EXPERT HEPPEN NIMBLE SPRACK SPRUCE DELIVER DEXTROUS SKILLFUL
DEFTEST EFTEST
DEFTLY LIGHTLY SLICKLY DELIVERLY
DEFTNESS SLEIGHT
DEFUNCT DEAD EXTINCT DECEASED DEPARTED FINISHED
DEFY BRAG DARE DEFI FACE MOCK BEARD BRAVE FLOUT STUMP TEMPT CARTEL FORBID MAUGER MAUGRE REJECT AFFRONT BRAVADE DESPISE DISDAIN OUTDARE OUTFACE CHAMPION DEFIANCE OUTSCOUT RENOUNCE CHALLENGE
DEGENERATE ROT SINK DEBADE EFFETE UNKIND DEGENER DEGRADE DEPRAVE DESCEND DEGENDER DEROGATE
(— IN IDLENESS) RUST
(— TOWARD BARBARISM) WILDER
DEGENERATION WALLER ATROPHY ADIPOSIS PEJORATION
DEGRADATION FALL WOHL SHAME DEMISS DECLINE DESCENT ADULTERY COMEDOWN DEPOSURE IGNOMINY ABJECTION
DEGRADE BUST SINK ABASE BREAK DECRY LOWER SHAME SHEND STOOP STRIP UNMAN DEBASE DEMEAN DEMOTE DEPOSE EMBASE HUMBLE LESSEN REDUCE VILIFY CORRUPT DECLINE DEPRESS IMBRUTE REGRADE VILLAIN DIMINISH DISGRACE DISHONOR DISMOUNT DISPLUME SUPPLANT
DEGRADED BASE BROKE SEAMY ABJECT DEMISS FALLEN SORDID DEBASED DEGREED GRIECED OUTCAST
DEGRADING BASE VILE MENIAL SHAMEFUL
(PREF.) LY(O)
DEGRAS MOELLON
DEGREE PEG PIP POL BANK CAST DEAL FORM GREE HEAT PEEP POLL RANK RATE RUNG STEP TERM TIER CLASS GRADE GRADO GRECE GRICE HONOR LEVEL NOTCH ORDER PITCH PLACE POINT PRICK SHADE STAGE STAIR EXTENT GRIECE LENGTH MEDIUM SOEVER DESCENT DIGNITY MEASURE SAENGER STATION ACCURACY AEGROTAT QUANTITY STANDING STRENGTH
(— OF CLOSENESS) FIT
(— OF COLOR) SHADE
(— OF COMBINING POWER) VALENCE
(— OF CONTRAST) GAMMA
(— OF DEVIATION) LEEWAY
(— OF DISTINCTION) PHD
(— OF ELEVATION) ASCENT
(— OF ENGAGEMENT) DEPTH
(— OF EXCELLENCE) DIGNITY
(— OF FLAWLESSNESS) CLARITY
(— OF FORCE) KICK
(— OF HEIGHT) GRADE
(— OF IMPORTANCE) CALIBER CALIBRE
(— OF INFESTATION) BURDEN
(— OF INTOXICATION) EDGE
(— OF KNOWLEDGE) SCIENTER
(— OF LIGHTNESS) VALUE
(— OF MIXTURE) ALLOY
(— OF OPACITY) DENSITY
(— OF PLENTIFULNESS) ABUNDANCE
(— OF PRESTIGE) PLACE
(— OF QUALITY) VALUE
(— OF SLOPE) PITCH SPLAY
(— OF STREAMLINING) FAIRNESS
(— OF THE SOUL) RUACH
(— OF WATER HARDNESS) GRAIN
(— OF WHITENESS) BLEACH
(CONFUSING —) WHIRL
(EXCESSIVE —) EXTREME
(GREATEST —) UTMOST OPTIMUM
(HIGHEST —) PINK SUMMIT SUPREME SUBLIMITY
(INDEFINITE —) SEEM
(LEAST —) MINIMUM
(MINUTE —) DROP SHADE
(MUSICAL —) SPACE SUBTONIC
(RABBINICAL —) SEMICHA SEMIKAH SEMICHAH
(SMALL —) ACE TAD HAIR INCH IOTA SHADOW GLIMMER
(SOME —) BIT
(TO A GREAT —) INSPADES
(TO A MODERATE —) RATHER SORTOF
(UTMOST —) MAX NTH SUM ACME HEIGHT EXTREME EXTREMITY
(10 —S OF LONGITUDE) FACE
(15 —S) HOUR
(PREF.) **(OF THE THIRD ALGEBRAIC —)** CUB(I)(O)
(SUFF.) ANCE ANT ENCE ITY NESS TY
DEGU OCTODONT
DEGUM STRIP
(— SILK) SOUPLE
DEHGAN SWAT SWATI
DEHORN SNUB DISBUD
DEHWAR DEHKAN
DEHYDRATE DRY DESICCATE
DEIANIRA (BROTHER OF —) TYDEUS MELEAGER
(FATHER OF —) OENEUS
(HUSBAND OF —) HERCULES
(MOTHER OF —) ALTHAEA
DEIDAMIA HIPPODAMIA
(FATHER OF —) LYCOMEDES
(LOVER OF —) ACHILLES
(SON OF —) PYRRHUS NEOPTOLEMUS
DEIFICATION APOTHEOSIS
DEIFY GOD BEGOD DIVINE GODDIZE DIVINIFY DIVINIZE
DEIGN STOOP VOUCHSAFE
DEILEON (BROTHER OF —) PHLOGIUS AUTOLYCUS
(FATHER OF —) DEIMACHUS
DEION (DAUGHTER OF —) ASTERODIA
(FATHER OF —) AEOLUS
(MOTHER OF —) ENARETE
(SON OF —) ACTOR AENETUS CEPHALUS PHYLACUS
(WIFE OF —) DIOMEDE

DEIPHOBUS (BROTHER OF —) PARIS HECTOR
(FATHER OF —) PRIAM
(MOTHER OF —) HECUBA
(WIFE OF —) HELEN
DEIPYLE (FATHER OF —) ADRASTUS
(HUSBAND OF —) TYDEUS
(SISTER OF —) AEGIA ARGIA
(SON OF —) DIOMEDES
DEIPYLUS (FATHER OF —) POLYMNESTOR
(MOTHER OF —) ILIONE
DEITY (ALSO SEE GOD AND GODDESS) EA EL KA RA RE SU ABU BEL GAD GOD RAN SHU SOL AKAL AMEN AMON BAAL CAGN DEVA FAUN FURY GWYN MIND MORS RANA SIVA SOBK ALALA ALALU AMIDA AMITA AMMON DAGAN DAGON HAOMA HOBAL HORUS HUBAL INUUS JANUS MIDER MITRA MONAD SATYR SEBEK SHIVA SIRIS SURYA ZOMBI ASHIMA ATHTAR BATALA BUNENE CAISSA FATHER FAUNUS IASION MARDUK MOLOCH NIBHAZ OANNES ORISHA ORMAZD ORMUZD RIMMON SOMNUS SUCHOS SYLVAN VARUNA ZOMBIE ALASTOR FORSETE FORSETI GODDESS GODHEAD GODLING GODSHIP HERSHEF IAPETUS KHEPERA MANITOU NINURTA NISROCH PHORCUS PHORKYS RESHEPH SETEBOS SILENUS TAGALOA TARANIS VIRBIUS BAALPEOR BEELPEOR BELFAGOR DEVARAJA DIVINITY ELAGABAL GOVERNOR HACHIMAN MELKARTH MERODACH PICUMNUS PILUMNUS SEILENOS SILVANUS TANGALOA TUTELARY ZEPHYRUS ZOOMORPH
(AVENGING —) ALASTOR
(BIBLE —) ELI ABBA ELOI
(HEATHEN —) IDOL
(INFERIOR —) GODKIN GODLING DEMIURGE PETTYGOD
(PRESIDING —) NUMEN
(SHINTO —) KAMI
(SUPREME —) HANSA
(TUTELARY —) LAR NUMEN GENIUS
(ZOROASTRIAN —) HAOMA
(PL.) CABIRI PENATES
DEJECT ABASE LOWER HUMBLE LESSEN FLATTEN DISPIRIT DOWNCAST
DEJECTA EGESTA
DEJECTED BAD LOW SAD DAMP DOWN GLUM POOR SUNK AMORT MUDDY WAPED ABASED ABATTU DEJECT DEMISS DROOPY GLOOMY PINING SOMBER SOMBRE ALAMORT DUMPISH HANGDOG HANGING HUMBLED LUMPISH UNHAPPY DOWNCAST DOWNWARD REPINING WOBEGONE WRETCHED MELANCHOLY
DEJECTEDLY HEAVILY
DEJECTION CRAB DAMP GLOOM SLOTH DISMAY DISMALS HUMDRUM SADNESS MELANCHOLY
DEJEUNER LUNCH BREAKFAST COLAZIONE COLLATION
DEKASTERE (ABBR.) DAS
DEL NABLA
DELAIAH (FATHER OF —) MEHETABEEL
(SON OF —) SHEMAIAH

DELAWARE
CAPITAL: DOVER
COUNTY: KENT SUSSEX NEWCASTLE
INDIAN: LENAPE
STATE BIRD: BLUEHEN
STATE FLOWER: PEACH
STATE NICKNAME: FIRST BLUEHEN DIAMOND
STATE TREE: HOLLY
TOWN: LEWES NEWARK SMYRNA ELSMERE CLAYMONT WILMINGTON

DELAY LAG LET BLIN BODE HOLD HONE LENG LING LITE MORA SIST SLOW SLUG STAY STOP WAIT ABIDE ABODE ALLAY BLINE CHECK DALLY DEFER DEMUR DETER DRIFT DWELL FRIST PAUSE REPRY SLOTH STALL STENT STICK STINT TARDY TARRY TRACT ARREST ATTEND BACKEN BELATE DAWDLE DETAIN DILATE DILUTE DRETCH ESSOIN FUTURE HINDER HOLDUP IMPEDE LINGER LOITER QUENCH REMORE RETARD TAIGLE TARROW TEMPER WEAKEN ADJOURN ASSUAGE BARRACE CONFINE DRUTTLE FORSLOW PROLONG RESPECT RESPITE SLACKEN SOJOURN DEMURRAL DILATION FORESLOW FOURCHER HANGFIRE HESITATE MACERATE MITIGATE MORATION OBSTRUCT POSTPONE PROTRACT REPRIEVE STOPPAGE DEMURRAGE CUNCTATION OBSTRUCTION
(— IN COUNTDOWN) HOLD
(— IN EXECUTION) REPRIEVE
(— IN EXPLOSION) HANGFIRE
(— TRIAL) TRAVERSE
(LEGAL —) DILATOR INDUCIAE
(UNDUE —) LACHES
(WITHOUT —) PRONTO
(PL.) AMBAGES
DELAYED LATE TARDY LAGGED BELATED OVERDUE
DELAYING TRAIN DILATORY
DELECTABLE TASTY DESIROUS PLEASING BEAUTIFUL EXQUISITE
DELECTATE PLEASE
DELEGATE NAME SEND ASSIGN COMMIT DELATE DEPUTE DEPUTY LEGATE NUNCIO APPOINT CONSIGN EMPOWER ENTRUST EMISSARY RELEGATE TRANSFER
DELEGATION MISSION DELEGACY
(ATHENIAN —) DELIA
DELETE DELE EDIT OMIT BLACK ERASE PURGE SLASH CANCEL CENSOR DELATE REMOVE STRIKE DESTROY EXPUNGE STONKER CASTRATE
DELETERIOUS BAD PRAVE HARMFUL HURTFUL NOXIOUS PRAVOUS DAMAGING DELETERY PERNICIOUS
DELI (— ORDER) BLT
DELIBERATE COOL PORE RUNE SLOW STUDY THINK VOULU ADVISE CONFER DEBATE PONDER REGARD ADVISED BALANCE BETHINK CONSULT COUNCIL COUNSEL DELIBER DELIVER REFLECT RESOLVE STUDIED WILLING WITTING CONSIDER DESIGNED MEASURED MEDITATE PERPENSE PREPENSE PROPENSE STUDIOUS
DELIBERATELY COOLY COOLLY APURPOSE ADVISEDLY
DELIBERATENESS MATURITY
DELIBERATION ADVICE COUNCIL COUNSEL LEISURE THOUGHT VISEMENT
DELICACY BIT ROE CATE EASE NORI TACT ACATE FRILL KNACK TASTE CAVIAR DAINTY DELICE JUNKET LUXURY NICETY REGALO TIDBIT FINESSE RAREBIT REGALIA TENUITY TRINKET AIRINESS DAINTITH DAINTREL DELICATE KICKSHAW LEGERETE NICENESS PLEASURE SUBTLETY
(STUFFED —) DERMA
(PL.) CATES ACATES
DELICATE SLY AIRY FINE LACY NESH NICE SOFT TEAR TWEE ZART DELIE DORTY ELFIN FAIRY FRAIL LIGHT SILKY TEWLY CASHIE CHOICE DAINTY FLIMSY GENTLE GINGER INCONY KITTLE MINION PASTEL PETITE PULING QUEASY SILKEN SLIGHT SUBTLE TENDER TICKLE TWIGGY ELEGANT EPICENE FINICAL FRAGILE MINIKIN REFINED SLIMMER SUBTILE SUMMERY TAFFETA TAFFETY TENUOUS TIFFANY WILLOWY ARANEOUS CHARMING ETHEREAL FEATHERY GOSSAMER GRACEFUL HOTHOUSE LUSCIOUS MIGNIARD PINDLING PLEASANT SENSIBLE SUMMERLY TICKLISH UNLUSTIE
(— IN APPEARANCE) HUNGRY
(AFFECTEDLY —) ROSEWATER
(PREF.) ABRO HABRO
DELICATELY FINE SMALLY FAIRILY MELTINGLY
DELICATESSEN DELI DELLY GASTRONOME CHARCUTERIE
DELICIOUS TASTY YUMMY DAINTY FRIAND DELICATE SCRUMPTIOUS
DELIGHT JOY GLEE GUST LITE LOVE SEND TAKE BLESS BLISS CHARM EXULT FEAST GRACE GUSTO MIRTH REVEL SAVOR SMACK ADMIRE ARRIDE DELICE DIVERT LIKING PLEASE RAVISH REGALE RELISH TICKLE DISPORT ECSTASY ENCHANT GLADDEN GRATIFY JOYANCE JOYANCY LECHERY RAPTURE REJOICE DELICATE ENTRANCE GLADNESS PLEASURE SAVORING
(— IN) LOVE SAVOR
(PL.) DELICIAE
DELIGHTED GLAD
DELIGHTFUL NICE GREAT JAMMY JOLLY MERRY SOOTH DREAMY SAVORY ELYSIAN LEESOME ADORABLE CHARMING DELICATE DELITOUS GLORIOUS GORGEOUS HEAVENLY LUSCIOUS SCRUMPTIOUS
DELIMER DRENCHER
DELIMIT FIX DEFINE SUBTEND
DELIMITATION
(PREF.) HORISMO
DELIMITED MERED MEERED
DELINEATE MAP DRAW ETCH LIMN LINE CHALK CHART FENCE IMAGE PAINT STELL TABLE TOUCH TRACE TRICK BLAZON CIPHER DELINE DEPICT DESIGN DEVISE SKETCH SURVEY DEPAINT EXPRESS LINEATE OUTLINE PICTURE PORTRAY DECIPHER DEFIGURE DESCRIBE TRAVERSE
DELINEATION DRAFT DESIGN SKETCH SURVEY DRAUGHT
(CARELESS —) PERIGRAPH
DELINQUENCY FAULT GUILT FAILURE MISDEED OFFENSE OMISSION
DELINQUENT CRIMINAL
(JUVENILE —) HALBSTARKER
(PL.) KALANG
DELIQUESCE MELT LIQUEFY DISSOLVE
DELIRIOUS FEY MAD OFF REE GYTE LIGHT MANIC INSANE RAVING FLIGHTY FRANTIC LUNATIC MADDING BRAINISH DELEERIT DELIERET DERANGED FRENETIC FRENZIED
DELIRIUM FURY MAZE MANIA FRENZY LUNACY RAVERY RAVING MADNESS DELIRACY IDLENESS INSANITY
DELIRIUM TREMENS JUMP HORRORS JIMJAMS JIMMIES POTOMANIA
DELITESCENT LATENT
DELIVER DO HIT LAY LET RID BAIL BORN DEAL FREE GIVE LEND REDD SAVE SELL SEND TAKE BEKEN BRING COUGH LIVER SERVE SPEAK UTTER ADDICT ASSIZE ASSOIL BETRAY COMMIT CONVEY EXEMPT PREACH RANSOM REDEEM RENDER RESCUE RESIGN SUCCOR UNBIND BETEACH BITECHE COMMEND CONSIGN DECLAIM DICTATE OUTTAKE PRESENT RECOVER RELEASE RELIEVE DISPATCH EXORCISE EXORCIZE LIBERATE
(— BALL) BOWL
(— BLOW) LEND POKE SEND
(— BLOWS ON HEAD) NOB
(— CHILD) LIGHT
(— FORCEFULLY) FASTEN
(— FORMALLY) SERVE
(— FROM EVIL SPIRIT) EXORCIZE
(— FROM SIN) SAVE
(— LECTURES) READ
(— LOGS) STOCK
(— MERCHANDISE) UTTER
(— OVER) BETAKE CONSIGN

(— RHETORICALLY) DECLAIM
(— SERMON) PREACH
(— SPEECH) ADDRESS
DELIVERANCE BOOT ESCAPE RANSOM RESCUE SAVING DELIVERY RIDDANCE SOLUTION VOIDANCE SALVATION
(FESTIVAL OF —) PURIM
DELIVERED LANDED
(— FREE) FRANCO
(PRECISELY —) FLUSH
DELIVERER SOTER SAVIOR DRAYMAN SAOSHYANT
DELIVERY FLY BAIL FLIER FLYER ISSUE LIVERY RESCUE ADDRESS AIRDROP BAILMENT SHIPMENT ACCOUCHEMENT
(— IN SPEAKING) DICTION
(— OF BALL) BOWL
(— WAGON) FLY
(MAIL —) TAPPALL TAPPAUL
(PREF.) TOCO TOKO
(SUFF.) TOCIA TOCO(US) TOKIA TOKO(US) TOKY
DELL DEN HOW DALE DEAN DENE DILL DRAB GLEN VALE SLACK SLADE TRULL WENCH DARGLE DIMBLE DINGLE RAVINE VALLEY
(PL.) DALLES
DELPHINIUM DAUPHIN DOLPHIN LARKSPUR
DELPHUS (FATHER OF —) APOLLO NEPTUNE POSEIDON
(MOTHER OF —) CELAENO MELANTHO
DELUDE BOB JIG BILK DUPE FOOL HOAX MOCK AMUSE CHEAT COZEN ELUDE EVADE GLAIK SPOOF TRICK BAFFLE BANTER BEFOOL BUBBLE CAJOLE DIDDLE ILLUDE BEGUILE DECEIVE ENCHANT MISLEAD OVERSEE BEJUGGLE HOODWINK INVEIGLE OVERSILE
DELUGE SEA FLOW FLOOD SWAMP DILUVY CATARACT INUNDATE OVERFLOW SATURATE SUBMERGE CATACLYSM
DELUNDUNG LINSANG ZINSANG VIVERRINE
DELUSION MAZE MOHA ABUSE DWALE FRAUD TRICK MIRAGE VISION CHIMERA FALLACY FANTASM PHANTOM WANHOPE ILLUSION NIHILISM PHANTASM
DELUSTER DULL
DELUXE PALACE ELEGANT ELABORATE SUMPTUOUS
DELVE DEN DIG DIP PIT CAVE DINT MINE DITCH PLUMB BRUISE BURROW EXHUME FATHOM INDENT IMPRESS EXCAVATE INSCRIBE
DEMAGNETIZE DEPERM DEPOLARIZE
DEMAGOGUE CLEON LEADER ORATOR ROUSER DEMAGOG JACOBIN SPEAKER TRIBUNE JAWSMITH OCHLOCRAT
DEMAND ASK CRY TAX USE CALL NEED RAME SALE CLAIM CRAVE DRAFT EXACT GAVEL ORDER QUERY SIGHT BEHEST CHARGE DESIRE ELICIT EXPECT SNATCH SUMMON ARRAIGN COMMAND CONSIST DRAUGHT INQUIRE MANDATE REQUEST REQUIRE SOLICIT INSTANCE QUESTION POSTULATE SCISCITATION
(— HIGHER PRICE) GAZUMP
(— PAYMENT) DUN CALL
(— RECOGNITION) CLAIM ASSERT
(STRONG —) PRESSURE
(PL.) EXIGENCE EXIGENCY
DEMANDABLE DUE EXIGIBLE
DEMANDED COMPULSORY
DEMANDING HEFTY EXIGENT
(— ATTENTION) ACUTE
DEMANTOID EMERALD OLIVINE
DEMARCATE DELIMIT SEPARATE
DEMARCATION CELL
DEMEAN ABASE CARRY LOWER BEHAVE DEBASE DEPORT CONTAIN DEGRADE DESCEND DEROGATE MALTREAT
DEMEANOR AIR GARB MIEN PORT FRONT HABIT ACTION HAVIOR BEARING CONDUCT DISPOSE FASHION CARRIAGE PORTANCE
(COLD —) MORGUE
DEMENTED MAD NUTS BUGGY CRAZY LOONY NUTTY INSANE SKEWED FATUOUS
DEMENTIA FATUITY INSANITY
DEMERIT MARK FAULT DESERT BROWNIE
(PL.) GIG
DEMESNE MANOR PLACE REALM DOMAIN ESTATE REGION DISTRICT
DEMETER CERES MISTRESS
DEMETRIUS (BELOVED OF —) CELIA HERMIA
(MOTHER OF —) TAMORA
DEMIGOD AITU HERO KAMI YIMA ADAPA SATYR GARUDA PAGODA TRITON GODLING
(PL.) NEPHILIM
DEMIGODDESS URD NORN HEROINE
DEMILUNE RAVELIN
DEMISE WILL DEATH CONVEY DECEASE BEQUEATH
DEMISED LETTEN
DEMIT LOWER HUMBLE RESIGN ABDICATE
DEMOCRACY POPULACY COMMONALTY
DEMOCRAT DEMO DANITE HUNKER SNAPPER DEMOCRAW LOCOFOCO POPOCRAT
(CONSERVATIVE —) HARD
DEMOCRATIC LEFT POPULAR
DEMODULATE DETECT
DEMOISELLE KULM CRANE COOLEN KAIKARA
DEMOLISH RASE RAZE RUIN ABATE BREAK ELIDE LEVEL TOTAL WASTE WRECK BATTER SLIGHT DESTROY RUINATE SHATTER SUBVERT UNBUILD DOWNCAST STRAMASH PULVERIZE
DEMOLITION END FALL
DEMON ALP DEV HAG IMP NAT OKI AITU ATUA BADB BALI BHUT DEVA DOOK OGRE OKEE PUCK RAHU SURT WADE ASURA DEVIL DHOUL FIEND GENIE GHOST JUMBY LAMIA LESHY LESIY OTKON SATAN SATYR SHEDU SURTR TAIPO WITCH ABIGOR AFREET ARIOCH BILWIS DAEMON DAIMON DAITYA GENIUS JUMBIE MAMMON PILWIZ PISACA THURSE VRITRA YAKSHA YAKSHI ASMADAI ASMODAY DEMONIO HARPIER INCUBUS PISACHA VILLAIN WARLOCK ALICHINO ASHMODAI ASMODEUS BAALPEOR BEELPEOR CURUPIRA EUDAEMON OBIDICUT SUCCUBUS WATERMAN
(— OF WOODS) LESHY LESIY LESHEY
(ARABIC —) AFRIT AFREET AFRITE EFREET
(DESERT —) SATYR
(EVIL —) SHEDU
(FEMALE —) HAG LAMIA PISACHI SUCCUBUS
(NATURE —) GENIUS
(PETTY —) IMP
(WATER —) NICKER
(PL.) DASYUS
DEMONASSA (FATHER OF —) AMPHIARAUS
(HUSBAND OF —) THERSANDER
(MOTHER OF —) ERIPHYLE
(SON OF —) TISAMENUS
DEMONIAC DEMONIC LUNATIC SATANIC DEVILISH DIABOLIC FIENDISH INFERNAL
DEMONIACAL DEMONIAC INFERNAL
DEMONICE (FATHER OF —) AGENOR
(MOTHER OF —) EPICASTE
(SON OF —) MOLUS EVENUS PHYLUS THESTIUS
DEMONSTRABLE ACTUAL
DEMONSTRATE GIVE SHOW CLEAR PROVE SPEAK EVINCE CONVICT DISPLAY PORTRAY CONVINCE INSTANCE MANIFEST
DEMONSTRATION SHOW SIGN TIME PROOF OVATION APODIXIS BALLYHOO DARSHANA MANIFEST
(— OF POWER) MANIFESTATION
(OSTENTATIOUS —) SPLURGE
DEMONSTRATIVE THAT THIS THESE THOSE EFFUSIVE EVINCIVE
DEMOPHON (FATHER OF —) CELEUS THESEUS
(MOTHER OF —) PHAEDRA METANIRA
(NURSE OF —) DEMETER
DEMORALIZE UNMAN WEAKEN CONFUSE CORRUPT DEPRAVE PERVERT
DEMORALIZING INFECTIOUS SHATTERING
DEMOTE BUMP BUST REDUCE UNRANK DEGRADE DISRATE
DEMOTIC POPULAR ENCHORIAL
DEMOTION BUMP
DEMULCENT MANNA SALEB SALEP BORAGE GINSENG EMULSION SOOTHING
DEMUR COY GIB JIB SHY BALK STAY DELAY DOUBT PAUSE QUALM STICK BOGGLE LINGER OBJECT STRAIN DEMEORE SCRUPLE STICKLE STUMBLE SUSPEND DEMURRER HESITATE SUSPENSE
DEMURE COY MIM SHY MURE PRIM GRAVE SPAKE STAID SUANT SUENT MODEST SEDATE PRENZIE PRIMSIE COMPOSED DECOROUS
DEN MEW CAVE COVE DEAN DELL DIVE GLEN HELL HOLE HOLT HUNK LAIR LAKE NEST ROOM SHED SINK BIELD CABIN CAVEA COUCH DELVE HAUNT LODGE SLADE STUDY BURROW CAVERN COVERT GROTTO HOLLOW KENNEL RAVINE SHROUD LIBRARY RETREAT SPELUNK HIDEAWAY SNUGGERY WORKROOM
(— OF BEAR) WASH
(— OF INIQUITY) DOMDANIEL
(DRINKING —) BOTHAN
(FOUL —) SPITAL
(GAMBLING —) DEADFALL
DENARIUS DENAR PENNY DINDER
DENATURANT PYRIDINE
DENDRITE PROCESS
DENIAL NO NAY WARN DENAY DENIER NAYSAY DEFENSE DEMENTI REFUSAL REPULSE CONTRARY NEGATION TRAVERSE
(— OF AUTHORITY) ANARCHY
(— OF REALITY) NIHILISM
(— OF TRUTH) HERESY
DENIED LOST
DENIER DINERO NEGATOR DENARIUS DINHEIRO
(HALF —) MAIL MAILLE
DENIGRATE BEFOUL CRUCIFY DEROGATE
DENIM DUNGAREE
DENIZEN CITIZEN RESIDENT
(— BY BIRTH) NATIVE
(— OF HELL) HELLION

DENMARK
CAPITAL: COPENHAGEN
CHEESE: SAMSO
COIN: ORA ORE KRONE
COUNTY: AMT FYN RIBE SORO VEJLE AARHUS MARIBO ODENSE TONDER VIBORG AALBORG RANDERS AABENRAA BORNHOLM
INLET: ISE LIM FJORD VEJLE NISSUM ODENSE HORSENS LOGSTOR MARIAGER
ISLAND: OE ALS FYN MON AARO AERO FANO FOHR MORS ROMO BAAGO FAROE LAESO SAMSO SANDO AMAGER FAEROE SEJERO SUDERO FALSTER SEELAND ZEALAND
MEASURE: ELL FOD MIL POT ALEN FAVN RODE ALBUM KANDE LINJE PAEGL TOMME ACHTEL PAEGEL SKEPPE LANDMIL OLTONDE SKIEPPE VIERTEL FJERDING
PARLIAMENT: RIGSRAAD FOLKETING LANDSTING
PENINSULA: JUTLAND
POSSESSION: FAROE ICELAND GREENLAND
RIVER: ASA HOLM OMME STOR GUDEN SKIVE SUSAA VARDE GELSAA STORAA VORGOD GUDENAA LILLEAA LONBORG
SETTLERS: OSTMEN
STRAIT: KATTEGAT SKAGERRAK

TOWN: ARS HOV HALS KOGE NIBE SORO VRAA FARUM HOBRO SKIVE AARHUS DRAGOR KORSOR NYBORG ODENSE SKAGEN STRUER VIBORG AALBORG HERNING HORSENS KOLDING RANDERS ALSINORE BALLERUP GENTOFTE GLOSTRUP ROSKILDE HELSINGOR COPENHAGEN
TRIBE: DANES JUTES ANGLES CIMBRI TEUTONS
TRIBUNAL: RIGSRAD RIGSRET
WEIGHT: ES LOD ORT VOG LAST MARK PUND UNZE CARAT KVINT POUND QUINT TONDE CENTNER LISPUND QUINTIN LISPOUND SKIPPUND

DENOMINATE CALL NAME STYLE TITLE DENOTE CHRISTEN INDICATE NOMINATE
DENOMINATION CULT NAME SECT CLASS FAITH TITLE VALUE CHURCH SCHOOL SOCIETY CATEGORY
DENOMINATIONAL SECTARIAN CONFESSIONAL
DENOTATION SIGN TOKEN EXTENT NOTION SPHERE AMBITUS BREADTH REFERENCE
DENOTE GIVE MARK MEAN NAME NOTE SHOW SOUND IMPORT NOTIFY BETOKEN CONNOTE EXPRESS SIGNIFY DENOTATE DESCRIBE INDICATE
DENOUEMENT END ENVOY ISSUE PAYOFF OUTCOME SOLUTION ANAGNOSIS
DENOUNCE BAN DAMN WRAY ASCRY BASTE BLAST DECRY TAUNT ACCUSE DELATE DESCRY DETEST MENACE SCATHE ARRAIGN CONDEMN DECLAIM DECLARE UPBRAID EXECRATE PROCLAIM THREATEN OBJURGATE
DENOUNCEMENT DELATION
DENSE SAD FAST FIRM CLOSE CRASS DUNCH FOGGY GROSS HEAVY MASSY MURKY SILLY SOLID SOUND SPISS STIFF THEET THICK TIGHT WOOFY OBTUSE OPAQUE SPISSY STUPID THICKY THIGHT COMPACT CROWDED INTENSE SERRIED CONDENSE
(NOT —) TENUOUS
(PREF.) PACHY PYCN(O) PYKN(O)
DENSELY CLOSE
DENSITY FOG CANDY FASTNESS GAUSSAGE SOLIDITY
(UNIT OF —) TESLA
(PREF.) DASY
DENT BASH BURT DING DINT DOKE DUNT FAZE NICK CLOUR DELVE DINGE NOTCH STOVE TOOTH BATTER DUNTLE HALLOW INDENT BLEMISH DEPRESS
(— OF REED) SPLIT
(PL.) BEER
DENTAL POINT
DENTATE TOOTHED
DENTICLE RASP
DENTICULATE SERRATE SERRATED
DENTICULATION JAG JAGG
DENTIFRICE WASH
DENTIL DENTEL DENTELLO DENTICLE
DENTINE IVORY DENTIN
DENTIST ODONTIST OPERATOR
DENTISTRY PROSTHODONTICS
DENTURE PLATE BRIDGE
(PL.) WALLIES
DENUDE BARE SCALP SHAVE STRIP DIVEST NUDATE DESPOIL DENUDATE
DENUNCIATION BAN THREAT THUNDER ANATHEMA DIATRIBE
DENY NAY NAIT NICK NITE WARN BELIE DEBAR NITTE RENAY REPEL WERNE ABJURE DISOWN FORBID IMPUGN NAYSAY NEGATE OPPOSE REFUSE REFUTE REJECT RENEGE CONFUTE DEPRIVE DISAVOW DISPUTE FORSAKE GAINSAY PROTEST SUBLATE WITHSAY ABNEGATE DENEGATE DISALLOW DISCLAIM FORSWEAR NEGATIVE RENOUNCE TRAVERSE WITHHOLD REPUDIATE
(— ACCESS) CLOSE
(— RECOGNITION) BLINK
DEODORANT ROLLON
DEOXIDIZE REDUCE
DEOXIDIZED
(PREF.) DESOXY
DEPART GO DIE MOG OFF WAG BLOW EXIT FLIT HOOK MOVE PACK PART PASS PIKE QUIT SHED STEP VADE VARY VOID WALK WEND WITE AVOID BREAK FOUND LEAVE MOSEY SEVER SHAKE SHIFT START TRUSS AVAUNT BEGONE DECAMP DECEDE DEMISE DESIST DIVIDE PERISH RECEDE REMOVE RETIRE SKIDOO SUNDER SWERVE WANDER ABSCOND DEVIATE DISCEDE FORSAKE RETREAT SKIDDOO TAKEOFF VAMOOSE DISCOAST FAREWELL SEPARATE TRESPASS WITHDRAW
(— FROM HARBOR) SORTIE
(— FROM LIFE) DECEASE
(— IN HASTE) BREEZE
(— IN HURRY) SKIVE LAMMAS
(— SECRETLY) ABSCOND ABSQUATULATE
(— SUDDENLY) FLEE DECAMP MIZZLE
(— WITH SPEED) VAMOOSE
DEPARTED DEAD BYGONE DEFUNCT DECEASED DECEDENT
DEPARTMENT END PART OKRUG REALM AGENCY BRANCH BUREAU EXCISE MEMBER OKROOG SPHERE FOUNDRY HANAPER PORTION REVENUE SPICERY AGITPROP CHANCERY DIVISION INDUSTRY NOMARCHY PROVINCE SCULLERY
(— IN CHINA) FU
(— OF CHANCERY) HAMPER HANAPER
(— OF KNOWLEDGE) STUDY
(ACADEMIC —) FACULTY
(NEWSPAPER —) COLUMN FEATURE
(TREASURY —) CAMERA
DEPARTURE BUNK EXIT BREAK DEATH EXODE GOING LEAVE LUCKY OUTGO CHANGE CONGEE DEPART EGRESS EXODUS HEGIRA SETOFF WAGANG WAYING DECEASE EASTING OUTGANG PARTING PARTURE RETREAT SAILING TRUNDLE WAYGATE DEPARTER FAREWELL OFFGOING REMOTION
(— FROM CORRECTNESS) ATROCITY
(— FROM SUBJECT) ASIDE
(— FROM THEME) CADENZA
(— OF SHIP) SORTIE
(CHARACTER IN —) LUISE TROTT GILFEN
(COMPOSER OF —) D'ALBERT
(EMERGENCY —) BAILOUT
(GEOLOGICAL —) ANOMALY
(SECRET —) GUY SLIP
DEPEND BANK HANG LEAN PEND RELY REST RIDE STAY TURN BUILD COUNT FOUND HINGE TRUST LIPPEN CONFIDE
DEPENDABILITY SECURITY
DEPENDABLE GOOD SURE TRIG SIKER SOLID SOUND THERE SECURE SICCAR SICKER STANCH STEADY CERTAIN STAUNCH RELIABLE SILVENDY SUREFIRE
DEPENDENCE MAINSTAY RELIANCE SERVILITY
DEPENDENCY TALUK COLONY APANAGE APPANAGE
DEPENDENT CHILD CLIENT HANGBY MINION SPONGE VASSAL FEODARY FEUDARY PRONEUR RELIANT SERVILE SPONGER SUBJECT WRAPPED BEHOLDEN CLINGING CREATURE ENCLITIC EVENTUAL FOLLOWER RETAINER
(— ON) ILLATIVE
(— ON DRUGS) HOOKED
(— PERSON) JUNKIE
(NOT —) ABSOLUTE
DEPENDING ATTENDANT
(— ON UNCERTAIN EVENTS) ALEATORY
DEPICT HUE DRAW ETCH LIMN PICT UNDO ENTER IMAGE PAINT SPEAK WRITE BLAZON SHADOW DEPAINT DISPLAY EXPRESS IMPAINT PICTURE PORTRAY DESCRIBE EMBLAZON RESEMBLE
(— IN MOSAIC) IMPAVE
(— WITH EXAGGERATION) OVERPAINT
DEPICTED DEPAINT
(— AS BROKEN) ROMPU
DEPICTION SCAN SCHEMA
(PHOTOGRAPHIC —) RENOGRAM
DEPILATION PSILOSIS
DEPILATORY RUSMA EPILATOR PELADORE PSILATRO
DEPILOUS BALD
DEPLETE DRAIN EMPTY PUNISH REDUCE UNLOAD EXHAUST BANKRUPT DIMINISH
DEPLETED WASTE BANKRUPT
DEPLETION DRAIN EROSION
DEPLORABLE SAD WOFUL WOEFUL DOLOROUS GRIEVOUS WAILSOME WRETCHED
DEPLORABLY SADLY
DEPLORE RUE MOAN SIGH WAIL MOURN BEMOAN BEWAIL GRIEVE LAMENT REGRET COMPLAIN
DEPLOY UNFOLD DISPLAY
DEPLOYMENT FORMATION
DEPOLYMERIZE DEGRADE
DEPONE SWEAR DEPOSE TESTIFY
DEPONENT AFFIANT DEPONER EXAMINATE
DEPOPULATE RAVAGE DESOLATE DISPEOPLE
DEPORT BEAR EXILE EXPEL BANISH BEHAVE DEMEAN BEARING CONDUCT DISPORT RELEGATE
DEPORTMENT AIR GEST MIEN PORT GESTE HABIT TENUE ACTION DEPORT HAVING MANNER ADDRESS BEARING COMPORT CONDUCT GESTURE HAVANCE BREEDING CARRIAGE DEMEANOR MAINTAIN PORTANCE
DEPOSE AVER ABASE PRIVE SWEAR AFFIRM ASSERT BANISH DEPONE DIVEST REDUCE REMOVE DEGRADE DEPOSIT DESTOOL TESTIFY DETHRONE DISCROWN DISPLACE
DEPOSIT FUR LAY PUT SET ADHI BANK CAKE CAST CRUD DROP DUMP FUND HIDE HOCK PAWN BLOOM CHEST COUCH COVER DEPOT LODGE PLACE SCURF STORE TOSCA BESTOW DEPONE DEPOSE ENTOMB ESCROW FLYSCH GARNER IMPOSE INHUME PLEDGE REPOSE SALINE SCORIA SCROLL SETTLE SINTER TOPHUS ASHFALL CONSIGN HORIZON DILUVIUM FOULNESS SANDBANK PRECIPITATION
(— BALLOT) CAST
(— DRIFT-SAND) SUD
(— EGGS) BLOW SPAWN
(— FOR COPYRIGHT) ENTER
(— FROM HOT SPRINGS) SINTER
(— IN CHAMPAGNE) GRIFFE
(— IN EARTH) INTER INHUME
(— IN GUN BORE) FOULING
(— IN WINE CASK) CRUST TARTAR
(— OF DEBRIS) BRECCIA
(— OF LOAM) LOESS
(— OF ORE) BANK FLAT
(— OF PEBBLES AND SAND) BEACH CASCALHO
(— OF SALT WATER) SOAK
(— ON LEATHER) BLOOM
(— ON LEAVES) HONEYDEW
(— STOLEN ARTICLES) FENCE
(— USED AS FERTILIZER) FALUN
(ALLUVIAL —) APRON DELTA
(ARCHAEOLOGICAL —) LENS LENSE
(BANK —S) CASH
(BLACK —) STUPP
(BROKER'S —) MARGIN
(CORNEA —) ARCUS
(DEEP-SEA —) OOZE
(EARTHY —) GUHR MARL
(GEOLOGIC —) BLANKET HORIZON
(GLACIAL —) TILL DRIFT ESKAR ESKER SHEET PLACER MORAINE
(GOUTY —) TOPHUS
(GRANULAR —) SABURRA
(GRAVEL —) LEAD
(KIDNEY —) GRAVEL

(MASS OF SEDIMENTARY —S) GOBI
(MINERAL —) FLAT LODE CARBONA
(MUDDY —) SLUDGE SLUMGULLION
(POWDERY —) BERGMEHL
(SEDIMENTARY —) SILT VARVE TURBIDITE
(SHELLY —) CRAG
(SHOAL-WATER —) CULM
(SKELETAL —) CORAL
(STOMACH —) SABURRA
(TARRY —) GUM
(VALUABLE —) VEIN
(WELDING —) TACK
(PREF.) THESO

DEPOSITARY POSITOR SEQUESTER

DEPOSITION PAD BURIAL DEPOSIT OPINION SILTING DEPOSURE SEDIMENT

DEPOSITORY BANK DROP SAFE AMBRY ATTIC VAULT DEPOSIT OSSUARY SENTINE DEPOSITO ESCROWEE OSSARIUM

DEPOT BANK BASE GARE AURANG AURUNG STAPLE STATION MAGAZINE TERMINAL TERMINUS
(MISSILE —) SILO

DEPRAVE TAINT DEBASE DEFILE INFECT MALIGN REVILE BESHREW CORRUPT PERVERT VITIATE

DEPRAVED BAD EVIL UGLY VILE PRAVE ROTTEN SHREWD WICKED BESTIAL CORRUPT IMMORAL PRAVOUS VICIOUS MISCREANT

DEPRAVITY VICE ABYSS ILLNESS PRAVITY VILLAINY TURPITUDE

DEPRECATE PRAY INVOKE BESEECH

DEPRECATORY PEJORATIVE

DEPRECIATE FALL LACK SLUR ABASE AVILE DECRY SLUMP DEBASE EMBASE LESSEN MINISH REDUCE SHRINK CHEAPEN DEBAUCH DEGRADE DEPRAVE DEPRESS DETRACT DISABLE SLANDER SMALLEN BELITTLE DEROGATE DISCOUNT DISPRIZE DISVALUE MINIMIZE PEJORATE VILIPEND WRITEOFF

DEPRECIATION AGIO DECRIAL DISCOUNT

DEPREDATION PREY RAPINE PILLAGE

DEPRESS BOW COW HIP LOW BATE BEAR BORE DAMP DASH DENT FALL FLAT SINK SUMP ABASE APPAL BREAK CHILL COUCH CRUSH FAINT LOWER SLUMP VAPOR WEIGH APPALL DAMPEN DEBOSS DISMAY HUMBLE INDENT LESSEN MURDER SADDEN SETTLE SICKEN SLOUCH STRIKE WEAKEN DECLINE DEGRADE DESTROY FLATTEN OPPRESS REPRESS BROWBEAT DIMINISH DISPIRIT DOWNBEAR ENFEEBLE
(— STRINGS OF INSTRUMENT) FRET

DEPRESSANT HELLEBORE

DEPRESSED LOW SAD BLUE DAMP DULL FLAT SICK SUNK COWED WROTH BROODY BUMMED DISHED GLOOMY HIPPED HOLLOW LONELY OBLATE SOMBER TRISTE ACCABLE LETDOWN DEJECTED DOWNCAST DOWNSOME
(— AT THE POLES) OBLATE
(ECONOMICALLY —) HARD

DEPRESSING SAD BLUE COLD BLEAK CHILL DREAR DUSKY MUZZY OURIE DISMAL DREARY GLOOMY SOMBER SOMBRE TRISTE OPPRESSIVE

DEPRESSION COL DIP EYE GAT PAN PIT BUST CROP DAMP DELK DENT DOKE DOWN FALL FOSS FUNK GASH GLEN HOLL HOWE SLEW SLOT SLUE WELL ATRIO BASIN BLAHS BLUES BOSOM CANON COWAL CRYPT DELVE DINGE FOSSA FOSSE FOVEA GLOOM GROIN NADIR NAVEL ORBIT POLJE SALAR SCOOP SELLA SINUS SLUMP SWALE AMPHID BLIGHT BUCKLE CAFARD CANYON CAVITY CRATER CUPULE DIMPLE DISMAY FURROW GROOVE GULLEY GUTTER INDENT LACUNA RAVINE SAUCER SLOUGH SPLEEN VALLEY WALLOW ALVEOLA BLOWOUT BOGHOLE CHAGRIN CLAYPAN CONCAVE COUNTER FOSSULA FOSSULE FOVEOLA JIMMIES SADNESS SALTPAN SINKAGE SINKING VARIOLE BOTHRIUM DOLDRUMS DOWNBEND FAINTING FOLLICLE FOREDEEP FOSSETTE FOSSULET PUNCTURE SINKHOLE SOAKAWAY EPHIPPIUM MELANCHOLY OPPRESSION
(— BEHIND COW'S SHOULDERS) CROP
(— BETWEEN BREASTS) CLEAVAGE
(— BETWEEN HILLS) SWIRE
(— IN BOARD) SKIP
(— IN BOTTLE BOTTOM) KICK
(— IN DECK) COCKPIT
(— IN DOG'S FACE) STOP
(— IN FRUITS) EYE
(— IN GROUND) DALK DELK SOAK SWAG WELL SWALE CHARCO
(— IN MILLSTONE) BOSOM
(— IN NILE VALLEY) KORE
(— IN RANGE) PASS
(— IN RIDGE) COL
(— IN SNOW) SITZMARK
(— IN VELD) COMITJE KOMMETJE
(— OF EAR) SCAPHA
(— OF SPIRITS) JAWFALL
(— PRONE) VAPORISH
(ARTICULAR —) GLENE
(OBLONG —) CIRCUS
(SMALL —) DENT DIMPLE LACUNA FOLLICLE

DEPRIVATION COST LOSS MAIM WANT MAYHEM AMOTION MISTURE DEPRIVAL
(— OF SIGHT) DARKNESS
(SUFF.) STERESIS

DEPRIVE BAR ROB BATE DENY DOCK EASE GELD TWIN ABATE BENIM BREAK DEBAR EMPTY EXUTE PREVE SPOIL STRIP WRONG AMERCE DEFEAT DENUDE DEPOSE DEVEST DISMAY DIVEST FAMISH FORBAR HINDER HUSTLE REMOVE ABRIDGE BEGUILE BEREAVE CASHIER CURTAIL DECEIVE DEFORCE DEPRAVE DESPOIL DESTROY DISABLE EXHAUST FOREBAR GUDGEON PRIVATE UNDRESS BANKRUPT DENATURE DESOLATE DISANNUL EVACUATE
(— BY TRICKERY) NOSE MULCT
(— FRAUDULENTLY) GUDGEON
(— OF BRILLIANCE) DEADEN
(— OF COLOR) STAIN
(— OF COURAGE) UNNERVE
(— OF FOOD) STARVE
(— OF FREEDOM) FETTER
(— OF INDIVIDUALITY) FORDIZE
(— OF LIFE) DEADEN
(— OF OFFICE) DEPOSE
(— OF PAY) DOCK
(— OF POSSESSIONS) FLAY
(— OF REASON) DEMENT
(— OF SENSATION) BENUMB
(— OF SENSE) INEBRIATE
(— OF SIGHT) SEEL
(— OF STRENGTH) ENERVATE
(— OF VIRGINITY) DEFLOWER
(— WRONGFULLY) ROB
(PREF.) **(— OF)** DE DIS

DEPRIVED REFT SANS BANKRUPT DESOLATE

DEPTH DIP BURY DEEP DROP MOHO ABYSS MIDST SIDTH FATHOM HEIGHT ALTITUDE DEEPNESS PROFOUND SOUNDING STRENGTH PENETRATION
(— CHARGE) ASHCAN
(— OF NIGHT OR WINTER) HOLL HOWE
(— OF SAIL) HOIST
(— OF SHIP) GAGE GAUGE
(— OF SIN) SLOUGH
(— OF SPADE) SPIT GRAFT
(— OF WATER) DRAFT DRAUGHT
(—S OF SEA) PROFOUND
(LOWEST —) GROUND
(MORAL —) ABYSS
(PL.) MUD ABYSS HEART
(PREF.) BATH(O)(Y)

DEPUTATION MISSION THEORIA LEGATION

DEPUTE SEND ALLOT ASSIGN DEVOTE APPOINT DELEGATE

DEPUTY AIDE VICE AGENT ENVOY NABOB PROXY VICAR ANGELO COMMIS CURATE DEPUTE EXARCH FACTOR KEHAYA LEGATE MINION ADJOINT BAILIFF ESCALUS SUBDEAN CAIMACAM DELEGATE ORDINARY PYLAGORE QAIMAQAM TENIENTE VICARIAN
(— OF BISHOP) VICAR VIDAME
(BISHOP'S —) VIDAME
(PREF.) CO

DERACINATE UPROOT

DERAIL TOAD DERAILER THROWOFF FRUSTRATE

DERANGE TURN CRAZE UNWIT UPSET HAMPER RUFFLE CONFUSE DERAIGN DISEASE DISTURB PERTURB UNSHAPE DISORDER DISPLACE UNSETTLE

DERANGED OUT GYTE CRAZY CRAZED SKIVIE FRANTIC FURIOUS BUGHOUSE DEMENTED DETRAQUE INFORMAL

DERANGEMENT MANIA UPSET FRENZY LUNACY DISEASE MADNESS PHRENSY RUMMAGE DELIRIUM DISORDER INSANITY

DERBY POT CADY KATY RACE BOXER CADDY DICER KELLY SHIRE BOWLER POTHAT BILLYCOCK

DERBY BLUE ELDERBERRY

DERELICT REMISS STREET FAILURE BETRAYER CASTAWAY

DERELICTION FAILURE RELICTION

DERIDE BOO GECK GIBE HOOT JAPE JEER JIBE LOUT MOCK RAZZ TWIT DRAPE FLEER FLOUT KNACK LAUGH RALLY SCOFF SCORN SCOUT TAUNT EXPOSE ILLUDE IRRIDE CATCALL LOWBELL RIDICULE

DERIDER IRRISOR

DERISION GECK JEER MOCK HOKER SCORN SPORT MOWING ASTEISM MOCKERY CONTEMPT IRRISION RIDICULE
(EXPRESS —) SNEER SNORT

DERISIVE JEERY SNIDE MOWING SNEERY SNOOTY SATANIC DERISORY IRRISORY SARDONIC SCOFFING

DERIVATION ORIGIN DESCENT PEDIGREE PARENTAGE

DERIVATIVE FURAN LININ SLOPE ACOINE ACYLAL BORANE FURANE INDOLE PHENOL RETENE ALKYLOL ANALGEN DERIVED ENOLATE FLAVONE FLUXION FULGIDE FULVENE GERMANE SUCRATE ALBUMOSE ANALGENE FLAVONOL FORMAZAN HEMATINE INDAZOLE STANNANE SECONDHAND ADSCITITIOUS

DERIVE GET DRAW STEM TAKE BRING CARRY DRIVE FETCH INFER TRACE BORROW CONVEY DEDUCE DESUME ELICIT EVOLVE GATHER OBTAIN SPRING DESCEND EXTRACT PROCEED RECEIVE TRADUCE
(IMPROPERLY —) WREST

DERIVED
(SUFF.) **(— FROM)** IC(AL)

DERMA LAYER CORIUM DERMIS KISHKE

DERMATITIS ICH ICK CASCADO CUTITIS

DERMATOGEN PROTODERM

DERMIS CUTIS DERMA CORIUM

DERNIER LAST FINAL DARREIN

DERNIER CRI CRY KICK LATEST NEWEST FASHION

DEROGATE ANNUL DECRY LESSEN REPEAL DETRACT SLANDER RESTRICT WITHDRAW

DEROGATORY BAD

DERRICK JIB RIG LIFT SPAR CRANE DAVIT HOIST STEEVE TACKLE ERECTER ERECTOR GALLOWS HANGING HANGMAN STIFFLEG JINNYWINK

DERRIS TUBA DEGUELIA

DERVISH AGIB FAKIR FAKEER SADITE SANTON DARWESH WHIRLER CALENDER

DESALT DEIONIZE

DESATURATE SADDEN

DESCANT SING SONG COPULA MELODY REMARK WARBLE COMMENT QUINIBLE
DESCEND DIP SYE DIVE DROP DUCK FALL SHED SINK SKIN VAIL AVALE LIGHT LOWER SQUAT STOOP SWOOP ALIGHT DERIVE DEVALL DEVAUL SETTLE DECLINE DELAPSE DEVOLVE SUBSIDE SUCCEED DISMOUNT PREPONDERATE
(— BY ROPE) RAPPEL
(— INTO HELL) HARROW
DESCENDANT SON CION GHUZ HEIR SEED SLIP CHILD GHUZZ SCION BRANCH LINEAL DESCENT AARONITE ASHERITE DAUGHTER EPIGONUS
(— OF IMMIGRANTS) BRAVA
(— OF JEW) CHUETA
(— OF MOHAMMED) EMIR
(— OF NOAH) AD
(—S OF MOHAMMED) ASHRAF
(INSIGNIFICANT —) TAG
(PL.) SEED DONMEH DUNMEH STRAIN PROGENY OFFSPRING POSTERITY
(SUFF.) ITE
DESCENDING FALL CADENT DOWNWARD
(— FROM COMMON ANCESTOR) AKIN
DESCENT JET KIN SET DIVE DOWN DROP FALL KIND VAIL BIRTH BLOOD CANCH CHUTE ISSUE PITCH SCARP SHUTE SLOPE STOCK CLEUCH CLEUGH ESCARP RAPPEL STRAIN ASSAULT DECLINE DISSENT EXTRACT FALLOUT INCLINE KINDRED LINEAGE PROGENY ANCESTRY BREEDING COMEDOWN DOWNCOME DOWNFALL DOWNGATE DOWNHILL GLISSADE INVASION PEDIGREE PARENTAGE
(— IN MOUNTAINEERING) ABSEIL
(— OF AIRPLANE) LETDOWN APPROACH
(— OF BIRD) STOOP
(— OF DEITY) AVATAR AVATARA
(— OF LIQUID) DRIBBLE
(— OF MASS) SLIDE
(— OF RIVER) LEAP
(FAMILIAR —) HAVAGE
(OVERWHELMING —) AVALANCHE
(PARACHUTE —) JUMP BAILOUT
(PLUNGING —) SPIN
DESCHAMPSIA AIRA
DESCRIBE DRAW GIVE LIMN READ TELL BLAZE IMAGE LABEL PAINT POINT STYLE WRITE DEFINE DENOTE DEPICT DEVISE DILATE RELATE REPORT SKETCH TITULE DECLARE DEPAINT DISPLAY EXPLAIN EXPRESS NARRATE OUTLINE PICTURE PORTRAY PRESENT RECOUNT STORIFY DESCRIVE INSCRIBE REHEARSE
(— A LINE) CUT
(— AS) CALL
(— BRIEFLY) KODAK
(— GRAMMATICALLY) PARSE
(— VIVIDLY) PICTURE
DESCRIBER (VIVID —) PAINTER
DESCRIBING GRAPHIC
DESCRIPTION KIN IMAGE BLAZON SKETCH SURVEY ACCOUNT DICTION DISPLAY PICTURE LANDSKIP RELATION TREATISE
(— OF A COUNTRY) FACE
(— OF VISION) AISLING
(BRIEF —) LEGEND
(RUSTIC —) IDYL IDYLL
(VIVID —) PICTURE PAINTING
DESCRY SEE SPY ESPY MAKE SCRY ASCRY SIGHT BEHOLD BETRAY DETECT REVEAL DISCERN DISPLAY DENOUNCE DESCRIBE DISCLOSE DISCOVER PERCEIVE
DESDEMONA (FATHER OF —) BRABANTIO
(HUSBAND OF —) OTHELLO
DESECRATE ABUSE DEFILE POLLUTE PROFANE VIOLATE TEMERATE UNHALLOW
DESECRATION PROFANATION
DESENSITIZE DRUG DEADEN
DESERT DUE ERG RAT RUN AREG ARID BOLT FAIL FLEE MEED SAND SERT TURN VAST DITCH GUILT LEAVE LURCH MERIT PLANT SERIR START WAIVE WASTE WORTH BARREN BETRAY DEFECT EXPOSE LONELY RENEGE REWARD SHRINK THIRST WESTEN ABANDON ABSCOND CHICKEN DEMERIT FORSAKE HORNADA OVERRUN WASTERN WASTINE DESOLATE RENOUNCE SOLITARY SOLITUDE WASTABLE
(PL.) GUILT
(PREF.) EREM(O)
DESERTED DEAD LONE WYSTY LONELY FORLORN DESOLATE FORSAKEN SOLITARY
(— WOMAN) AGUNAH
DESERTER RAT BOLTER BUGOUT APOSTATE BUSHWACK FUGITIVE RECREANT RENEGADE RUNAGATE TURNTAIL
DESERTION BUGOUT RATTERY APOSTASY
DESERT LEMON KUMQUAT
DESERVE EARN MEED RATE MERIT REPAY SERVE ASSERVE BENEFIT DEMERIT DISSERVE PROMERIT
DESERVED JUST COMING WORTHY CONDIGN
DESERVING WORTHY CONDIGN WORTHFUL ADMIRABLE MERITORIOUS
DESICCATE DRY ARID SEAR SERE DRAIN DEHYDRATE
DESICCATION XERANSIS
DESIDERATUM NEED DESIRE
DESIGN AIM END MAP CAST DRAW GOAL IDEA MARK MEAN PLAN PLAT PLOT TOOL TREE WORK ALLOT CHECK DECAL DECOR DODAD DRAFT DRIFT ETTLE FANCY MODEL MOTIF NOTAN QUILT SHAPE STAMP STUDY STYLE BOWPOT CACHET CORNER CREATE DEVICE DEVISE DOODAD DOODLE EMBLEM FIGURE FLORAL FLOWER INCUSE INTEND INTENT INVENT LAYOUT MODULE OBJECT OBTENT PROJET SCHEME SKETCH SYSTEM VERVER ALLOVER BOSCAGE CARTOON CARVING CHASING COMPOSE CONCERT COUNSEL CROQUIS DESTINE DIAGRAM DRAUGHT ETCHING FANTASY FASHION OUTLINE PATTERN PRETEND PROJECT PROPOSE PURPORT PURPOSE REVERSE SCALLOP SLEIGHT THOUGHT APPLIQUE BAYADERE BOUGHPOT CONTRIVE CYMATION CYMATIUM ENGINEER FILIGREE FLOCKING FORECAST GRAFFITO GROOVING INTAGLIO PHANTASY PLATFORM REMARQUE SINGERIE STRIPING SUNBURST GOFFERING SCHEMATISM
(— AS TITLE PAGE) VIGNETTE
(— ON BOOK) TOOL
(— ON CARPET) MEDALLION
(— ON COIN) BEADING
(— ON FABRIC) BATIK BATTIK
(AIRCRAFT —) STEALTH
(ARTFUL —) MACHINATION
(BOOK —) FILET FILLET
(COMPUTER —) CAD
(CUP-SHAPED —) HUSK
(EMBLEMATIC —) IMPRESS
(ESSENTIAL —) BONES
(FASHION —) FORD
(OPENWORK —) POINTELLE
(OUTLINE —) KEYSTONE
(PERFORATED —) POUNCE
(SPOTTED —) SEME
(STRIPED —) STRIA STRIE
(TESSELLATED —) MOSAIC
(TEXTILE —) STRIPE HAIRLINE
DESIGNATE SET HAIL MARK MEAN NAME SHOW ELECT LABEL SPEAK STYLE TITLE ANOINT ASSIGN DENOTE DESIGN FINGER INTEND SETTLE TARGET APPOINT EARMARK ENTITLE EXPRESS SPECIFY SURNAME ALLOCATE DESCRIBE IDENTIFY INDICATE NOMINATE PRESCRIBE
DESIGNATION NAME TERM TYPE LABEL STYLE TITLE CAPTION HOMONYM ADDITION
(— OF PLACE) ADDRESS
DESIGNED PREPENSE SUPPOSED
(— FOR MALE AND FEMALE) UNISEX
DESIGNER ERTE STYLER FANCIER PLANNER PLOTTER SCHEMER STYLIST COLORIST ENGINEER MEDALIST MOSAICIST
(FASHION —) DIOR FENLI RENTA CASSINI
(PL.) COUTURE
DESIGNING ARTFUL CUNNING JESUITIC PLANNING PLOTTING SCHEMING
DESIRABLE FAIR GOOD KEEN WORTH PLUMMY AMIABLE GRADELY HEALTHY OPTABLE WELCOME WISHFUL DESIROUS ELIGIBLE ENVIABLE PLEASING SALUTARY
DESIRE HOT YEN ACHE CARE ENVY EROS FAIN HAVE HOPE HOTS ITCH KAMA KEEP LEST LIST LOAD LUST MIND NEED PANT URGE WANT WILL WISH WIST ARDOR BOSOM BRAME COVET CRAVE FANCY GIMME GREED GROAN HEART MANGE MANIA NISUS QUEST STUDY TANHA TASTE WILNE YEARN YISSE AFFECT APPETE ASPIRE BEHEST BESOLN DEMAND DEVICE HANKER HUNGER OREXIS POTHOS PREFER TALENT THIRST UTINAM YAMMER AVARICE AVIDITY CONATUS COURAGE CRAVING EROTISM FANTASY HIMEROS HOPEFOR INKLING LONGING PASSION STOMACH VOLUNTY WILLING AMBITION APPETITE COVETISE CUPIDITY PLEASING NECESSITY
(— FOR LIFE) TANHA
(— WITH EAGERNESS) ASPIRE
(ARDENT —) THIRST
(IRRITATING —) ITCH
(SEXUAL —) HOTS PRIDE
(STRONG —) CUPIDITY SLAVERING
(UNCONTROLLABLE —) CACOETHES
(PREF.) **(SEXUAL —)** ERO EROTO
(SUFF.) OREXIA
DESIRE UNDER THE ELMS
(AUTHOR OF —) ONEILL
(CHARACTER IN —) EBEN ABBIE CABOT PUTNAM EPHRAIM
DESIROUS AVID FAIN FOND LIEF VAIN EAGER FRACK FRECK LUSTY ARDENT WILFUL ANXIOUS THIRSTY WILLFUL WILLING WISHING APPETENT COVETOUS LIKEROUS PRURIENT SPIRITED
DESIST HO LIN EASE HALT QUIT REST SIST STOP WHOA CEASE LEAVE SPARE STINT SWICK SWIKE WONDE DEPART ABANDON FORBEAR FORFEIT RESPITE SUBSIST SURCEASE
(— FROM) CUT LEAVE REMIT FORBEAR
DESK PEW AMBO SCOB BOARD DESSE TABLE BUREAU CAISSE PULPIT CONSOLE LECTERN PLUTEUS COPYDESK STANDISH VARGUENO
(KIND OF —) ROLLTOP
DESMA CLON CLONE
DESMAN MOLE SQUASH MUSKRAT ONDATRA
DESMANTHUS ACUAN
DESOLATE SAD BARE LORN RUIN SACK SOLE VAST WILD ALONE BLEAK DREAR GAUNT GUBAT OURIE STARK UNKED UNKET UNKID WASTE WASTY WYSTY BARREN DESERT DISMAL DREARY GLOOMY GOUSTY LONELY RAVAGE DESTROY FORLORN GOUSTIE HOWLING LACKING UNCOUTH WIDOWED WILSOME DEPRIVED DESERTED FORSAKEN SOLITARY WASTEFUL WOBEGONE
DESOLATION WOE RUIN GLOOM GRIEF HAVOC WASTE RAVAGE SADNESS
DESPAIR GLOOM UNHOPE WANHOPE

DESPAIRING HOPELESS
DESPERADO BRAVO BADMAN BANDIT RUFFIAN CRIMINAL RESOLUTE
DESPERATE MAD DIRE RASH ACHARNE DESPERT EXTREME FORLORN FRANTIC HEADLONG HOPELESS PERILOUS RECKLESS
DESPERATELY BONE
DESPICABLE BUM BASE MEAN ORRA VILE CHEAP DIRTY FOUTY SCALY ABJECT PALTRY ROTTEN SHABBY SORDID CAITIFF IGNOBLE PITIFUL REPTILE PITIABLE UNWORTHY WRETCHED
DESPICABLY DIRTILY
DESPISE DEFY HATE SCORN SCOUT SPISE SPURN DETEST FORHOO LOATHE SLIGHT VILIFY CONTEMN DESPITE DISDAIN DISPRIZE MISPRIZE VILIPEND
DESPITE BY VEX SPITE MALGRE DESPISE
DESPOIL ROB PELF PILL POLL RAID RAPE RUIN SKIN BOOTY HARRY PLUME RAVEN REAVE RIFLE SPOIL STRIP STRUB TRICE BEZZLE DIVEST FLEECE HESPEL HUSPEL RAVAGE RAVISH REMOVE BEREAVE DEPRIVE DISROBE PILLAGE PLUNDER UNSPOIL DEFLOWER DISARRAY SPOLIATE SPUILZIE UNCLOTHE
DESPOINA KORE PERSEPHONE
DESPONDENCY DUMP HUMP BLUES DUMPS GLOOM ATHYMY MISERY ATHUMIA ATHYMIA DESPAIR DESPOND
DESPONDENT SAD BLUE GLOOMY FORLORN DEJECTED DOWNCAST HOPELESS
DESPOT CZAR TSAR TZAR ANARCH SATRAP TYRANT AUTARCH MONARCH AUTOCRAT
DESPOTIC LORDLY ABSOLUTE DOMINANT
DESPOTISM TYRANNY AUTARCHY SULTANISM
DESQUAMATE PEEL
DESSERT EIS ICE PIE BABA CAKE FOOL SKYR SNOW VOID BETTY BOMBE COUPE DOLCE FRUIT GLACE GRUNT JELLY LACTO SLUMP AFTERS ECLAIR JUNKET MOUSSE PASTRY POSTRE SPONGE SWEETS TRIFLE BAKLAVA BANQUET PARFAIT PAVLOVA PUDDING SHERBET SOUFFLE SPUMONE STRUDEL SUPREME DUMPLING FLUMMERY FRUMENTY NAPOLEON PANDOWDY SILLABUB DACQUOISE ENTREMETS SOPAPILLA SOPAIPILLA
(BAKED —) CRISP
(CARAMEL) FLAN
DESTINATION END GOAL PORT BOURN BILLET BOURNE
DESTINE DOOM EURE FATE MARK ALLOT SHAPE SLATE WEIRD DEPUTE DESIGN DEVOTE INTEND ORDAIN APPOINT PURPOSE SENTENCE
DESTINY LOT DOLE DOOM EURE FATE SORT KARMA MOIRA STARS WEIRD KHARMA KISMET DESTINE FORTUNE PORTION FOREDOOM
DESTITUTE BARE NACE POOR SANS VOID CLEAN EMPTY NAKED NEEDY WASTE BEREFT DEVOID VACANT WASTED FORLORN LACKING NAUGHTY VIDUATE WANTING BANKRUPT BEGGARED DEFEATED DEPRIVED DESOLATE FORSAKEN HELPLESS INDIGENT INNOCENT VIDUATED PENNILESS
(— OF) BUT
(— OF FEATHERS) DEPLUMATE
(— OF LEAVES) APHYLLOUS
(— OF LIGHT) DARK
(— OF TEETH) EDENTATE
(— OF WATER) ANHYDROUS
(SUFF.) **(— OF)** LESS
DESTITUTION NEED WANT FAMINE PENURY BEGGARY DEFAULT POVERTY
DESTROY BAG EAT END GUT MOW RID ZAP BLOW CHEW FRAP FULL KILL NUKE NULL RASE RAZE RUIN RUSH SINK SLAY SMIT STRY TINE UNDO VOID BREAK CRACK CRAZE DECAY ELIDE ERASE ERODE FORDO HAVOC MISDO PRANG QUADE QUAIL QUELL SHEND SHOOT SMASH SMITE SPEED SPEND SPILL SPLIT SPOIL STROY SWAMP TOTAL TRASH WASTY WRACK WRECK BLIGHT CANCEL CUMBER DEFACE DEFEAT DELETE DEVOID DEVOUR EFFACE FAMISH FOREDO MURDER PERISH QUENCH RANKLE RAVAGE STARVE STIFLE UNMAKE UNPILE UNWORK UPROOT UPTEAR ABOLISH CONSUME CORRODE DEPRIVE DISTURB ENECATE EXPUNGE FLATTEN FORFARE FORLESE MORTIFY NULLIFY OVERRUN PEREMPT RUINATE SHAMASH SHATTER SMOTHER SUBVERT TERRIFY UNBUILD WHITTLE AMORTIZE CONFOUND DECIMATE DEMOLISH DESOLATE DESTRUCT DISANNUL DISPLANT DISSOLVE FRACTURE FRAGMENT IMMOLATE INFRINGE MUTILATE OVERTURN PARALYZE SABOTAGE STRAMASH OBLITERATE
(— BARK) GIRDLE
(— BY FIRE) CONSUME
(— COMPLETELY) RUBOUT
(— FERTILITY) EXHAUST
(— FOR FUN) TRASH
(— SELF-POSSESSION) ABASH
(— TOTALLY) SMASH SWEEP CUMBER SCUTTLE
(SUFF.) CLASE CLASIA CLAST(IC)
DESTROYED FLAT BLOWN KAPUT KAPUTT
DESTROYER CAN HUN DEATH TINCAN UNDOER VANDAL VICTOR FLIVVER STROYER UNMAKER WARSHIP APOLLYON DEVOURER SABOTEUR
(— OF MACHINERY) LUDDITE
(SUFF.) CIDAL CIDE PHTHORA
DESTROYING FELL (PREF.) ANTI (SUFF.) CLASTIC
DESTRUCTIBLE FRAIL
DESTRUCTION BAR END HEW BANE DOGS DOOM FIRE LOSS RACK RUIN STRY TALA CRUSH DEATH DECAY GRAVE HAVOC SMASH STRIP STROY WASTE WRACK DEFEAT DISMAY ENDING EXPIRY WONDER ABADDON CARNAGE EROSION UNDOING COLLAPSE DELETION DISPOSAL DOWNFALL EVERSION EXCISION SHAMBLES SMASHERY RUINATION
(— OF BONES) CARIES
(— OF ENVIRONMENT) ECOCIDE
(— OF SHIP'S PAPERS) SPOLIATION
(CELL —) LYSIS
(GOD OF —) SIVA
(GRADUAL —) CORROSION
(MALICIOUS —) SABOTAGE
(UTTER —) PERDITION
(SUFF.) LYSE LYSIS LYST LYTE LYTIC LYZE
DESTRUCTIVE FELL FATAL DEADLY MORTAL BALEFUL BANEFUL DEATHLY EXITIAL FATEFUL HARMFUL HUMLIKE HURTFUL NOISOME NOXIOUS RUINOUS ANERETIC DEATHFUL EXITIOUS WASTEFUL WRACKFUL WREAKFUL ANAERETIC PESTILENT
(— TO LIFE) BIOCIDAL
DESUETUDE BREACH DISUSE
DESULTORY IDLE HASTY LOOSE ROVING AIMLESS CURSORY RAMBLING UNSTEADY WAVERING IRREGULAR
DETACH CUT DRAFT LOOSE SEVER AVULSE LOOSEN UNBIND UNGLUE UNWORK CRACKLE DISJOIN DRAUGHT ISOLATE UNHINGE UNRIVET UNSEIZE ABSTRACT DISSOLVE DISUNITE PRESCIND SEPARATE UNFASTEN WITHDRAW
DETACHABLE SLIP
DETACHED CUT COLD FREE ALONE ALOOF LOOSE DEADPAN INSULAR PORTATO SCIOLTO ABSTRACT CLINICAL DISCRETE ISOLATED OUTLYING SEPARATE SPICCATO UNBIASED IMPERSONAL
(PREF.) APH APO
DETACHMENT POINT POSSE ATARAXY OUTPOST ATARAXIA AVULSION OUTGUARD
(SUFF.) LYSE LYSIS LYST LYTE LYTIC LYZE
DETAIL CREW ITEM DODAD POINT ACCENT ASSIGN DOODAB DOODAD NICETY PARCEL RELATE RETAIL ACCOUNT APPOINT ARTICLE ITEMIZE MINUTIA NARRATE NULLING RESPECT SEVERAL SPECIFY INSTANCE REHEARSE SALIENCE PARTICULAR PARTICULARITY
(—S OF MAP) CULTURE
(CLIMACTIC —) BEAUTY
(PETTY —) CHICKEN
(SPECIFIC —S) NITTYGRITTY
(UNIMPORTANT —S) TRIVIA
(PL.) DOPE FROUFROU FURNITURE
DETAILED NARROW PROLIX CLOSEUP SPECIAL PUNCTUAL TIRESOME
DETAIN BAIL HOLD KEEP STAY STOP CHECK DELAY TARRY ARREST ATHOLD COLLAR HINDER RETARD TAIGLE IMPRISON RESTRAIN WITHHOLD
DETECT SEE SPY ESPY FIND NOSE SPOT CATCH SCENT SENSE SMOKE SNIFF TRACE DESCRY DIVINE EXPOSE REVEAL DEVELOP DISCERN UNCOVER DECIPHER DISCOVER OVERTAKE
DETECTIVE EYE TEC BULL BUSY DICK JACK TRAP PLANT SNOOP SPADE BEAGLE MOUSER RUNNER SHADOW SHAMUS SLEUTH TAILER TRACER GUMSHOE MAIGRET SCENTER SNOOPER SPOTTER TEMPLAR TRAILER BEAUMONT DETECTOR FLATFOOT HAWKSHAW HOUSEMAN OPERATOR SHERLOCK OPERATIVE PINKERTON PLAINCLOTHESMAN
(— FICTION AWARD) EDGAR
(— OF FICTION) LUPIN
(— STORY) WHODUNIT
(FICTIONAL —) CHAN LUPIN QUEEN TRACY VANCE CARTER HOLMES MARPLE POIROT CHARLES
DETECTOR ASDIC COHERER REAGENT SFERICS SPHERICS
(ELECTRONIC —) SOLION
(KIND OF —) METAL
(LIE —) POLYGRAPH
DETENT DOG PALL PAWL CATCH CLICK RATCH PALLET RATCHET
DETENTION DELAY ARREST CAPTURE DETINUE JANKERS DETAINER STOPPAGE
DETER BAR FEAR BLOCK BLUFF CHECK DELAY DEHORT HINDER RETARD PREVENT TERRIFY DISSUADE PRECLUDE RESTRAIN
DETERGE PURGE CLEANSE MUNDIFY
DETERGENT SOAP SYNDET ABLUENT PURGING RHYPTIC SMECTIC SOLVENT CLEANSER GARDINOL
DETERIORATE GO FAIL GIVE SLIP SOUR WEAR DECAY ERODE SPILL WORST APPAIR APPERE DEBASE IMPAIR SICKEN WORSEN DECLINE PERVERT FIREFANG
DETERIORATED MUSTY
DETERIORATING DECADENT
DETERIORATION DECAY IMPAIR MALADY DECLINE EROSION FAILURE DOLDRUMS PEJORATION
DETERMINABLE FIXED DEFINITE DEFINABLE GAUGEABLE
DETERMINANT CYTOGENE JACOBIAN CIRCULANT WRONSKIAN PLASTOGENE
DETERMINATE CERTAIN ORISTIC DEFINITE RESOLUTE RESOLVED SPECIFIC
DETERMINATION ACT HEST WILL ASSAY BLANK CAUSE ADVICE BEARING CONSULT PURPOSE

RESOLVE ANALYSIS BACKBONE BIOASSAY DECISION DIVISION FIRMNESS FORECAST JUDGMENT JUDICIAL SENTENCE VOLITION
DETERMINATIVE FINAL FORMANT SHAPING LIMITING
(MOST —) DOMINANT
DETERMINE END FIT FIX GET RUN TEST WILL ASSAY AWARD JUDGE PITCH WIELD ADJUST ASSESS ASSIGN ASSOIL CHOOSE DECERN DECIDE DECREE DEFINE DESCRY DETECT DETERM DEVISE FIGURE GOVERN PERFIX SETTLE ACCOUNT ADJUDGE ANALYZE APPOINT ARRANGE COMPUTE DELIMIT DERAIGN DISPOSE RESOLVE TERMINE COGNOSCE CONCLUDE DISCOVER PINPOINT INFLUENCE
(— FINENESS) SET SETT
(— PATERNITY) AFFILIATE
(— RATE) ASSESS
(— ROOT) EXTRACT
DETERMINED SET BENT DERN FIRM GRIM BOUND GIVEN STOUT UPSET BITTER DOGGED GRITTY INTENT MULISH STURDY DECIDED SETTLED DECISIVE FOREGONE PERVERSE RESOLUTE RESOLVED STUBBORN
DETERMINER GENE CHANCE PLASMAGENE
DETERMINING CRUCIAL
DETERMINIST JABARITE
DETEST DAMN HATE ABHOR CURSE LOATHE CONDEMN DESPISE DISLIKE DENOUNCE EXECRATE ABOMINATE
DETESTABLE FOUL HORRID ODIOUS BLASTED HATABLE HATEFUL HELLISH HIDEOUS ACCURSED DAMNABLE HATEABLE INFAMOUS INFERNAL MALEDICT ABHORRENT ABOMINABLE
DETESTATION ODIUM HATRED HORROR LOATHING ANTIPATHY
DETHRONE DEPOSE DIVEST UNCROWN
DETONATE FIRE BELCH BLAST SHOOT EXPLODE DETONIZE
DETONATION BLAST KNOCK AMBITUS PINGING PINKING
DETONATOR CAP FUSE FUZE FUSEE FUZEE SQUIB TORPEDO INITIATOR
DETOUR BYPASS CIRCUIT REROUTE DIVERSION ROUNDABOUT
DETRACT TAKE DECRY DEDUCT DEFAME DETRAY DIVERT VILIFY ASPERSE TRADUCE BELITTLE DEROGATE DIMINISH DISTRACT MINIMIZE PROTRACT SUBTRACT WITHDRAW
(— FROM) IMPEDE
DETRACTION CALUMNY SCANDAL SLANDER ZOILISM
DETRIMENT COST HARM HURT LOSS SORE WOUND DAMAGE DAMNUM DENIAL INJURY BEATING EXPENSE JACTURE DISFAVOR MISCHIEF
DETRIMENTAL ADVERSE CAPITAL HARMFUL HURTFUL LOSSFUL DAMAGING INVIDIOUS PERNICIOUS PREJUDICIAL
(— TO HEALTH) HARD
DETRITUS OUTWASH SHINGLE SHEETWASH
DEUCALION (FATHER OF —) PROMETHEUS
(MOTHER OF —) CLYMENE
(SON OF —) HELLEN ORESTHEUS AMPHICTYON
(WIFE OF —) PYRRHA
DEUCE TWO DIANTRE DICKENS
(WILD —) FREAK
DEUCEDLY BLAME BLAMED
DEUEL (SON OF —) ELIASAPH
DEUTERIUM DIPLOGEN
DEUTEROGAMY DIGAMY
DEUTOMALA LABIUM
DEUX JOURNEES, LES
(CHARACTER IN —) ARMAND MIKELI MAZARIN
(COMPOSER OF —) CHERUBINI
DEVA DEV DEWA SURA ANGEL DEITY
DEVASTATE NUKE EXILE HARRY HAVOC WASTE DEVAST RAVAGE ATOMIZE DESTROY PILLAGE PLUNDER SCOURGE DEMOLISH
DEVASTATED WASTE
DEVASTATING DEADLY LETHAL SAVAGE CRUSHING FEROCIOUS MURDEROUS
DEVASTATION RUIN SACK EXILE HAVOC WASTE WRACK HARASS RAVAGE SACCAGE SACKAGE SACCADGE
DEVASTATOR LOCUST
DEVELOP BUD RUN BOOM COOK FORM GROW STEM TILL ARISE BREAK BREED BUILD ERECT RIPEN SHOOT APPEAR BRANCH DETECT EVOLVE EXPAND FLOWER FULFIL MATURE REVEAL UNFOLD UNFURL BLOSSOM BURGEON BURNISH EDUCATE ENLARGE EVOLUTE EXPOUND FULFILL UNCOVER DEVELOPE DISCLOSE DISCOVER DISVELOP ENGENDER GENERATE INCUBATE MANIFEST
(— A HEAD) HEART
(— BULB) BOTTOM
(— COLOR) AGE
(— CRACKS) ALLIGATOR
(— FLAVOR) BREATHE
(— WELL) COTTON
DEVELOPABLE TORSE
DEVELOPED DEEP FORWARD
(— AFTER BIRTH) ACQUIRED
(FULLY —) BOLD ADULT FLORID FORMED SUMMED
(GREATLY —) ADVANCED
(IMPERFECTLY —) ABORTIVE
(INCOMPLETELY —) SEED
DEVELOPER ELON SOUP METOL ORTOL AMIDOL GLYCIN KACHIN QUINOL BUILDER GLYCINE RODINAL
DEVELOPING
(SUFF.) PLASTIC
DEVELOPMENT WAX DRIFT EVENT HATCH ESTATE GROWTH DESCENT GENESIS PROCESS STATURE BREEDING INCREASE ONTOGENY PEDIGREE UPGROWTH UPSPRING
(— OF SEX) DIOECISM
(FULL —) BLOW MATURITY
(HIGHEST —) BLOOM
(NORMAL —) APHANISIA
(SUBSEQUENT —) SEQUEL
(THEMATIC —) CONTINUITY
(UNEXPECTED —) ACCIDENT
(PREF.) PLASTO
(SUFF.) PLASIA PLASIS PLASM(A) (IA)(IC) PLAST(IC)(Y) PLASY
DEVI UMA KALI DURGA GAURI CHANDI SHAKTI BHAVANI BHOWANI HIMAVAT MAHADEVI HAIMAVATI
(FATHER OF —) HIMAVAT
(HUSBAND OF —) SHIVA
DEVIANT KINKY ABERRANT DIVERGENT
DEVIATE ERR RUN WRY YAW LEAN MISS VARY VEER BEVEL BREAK DRIFT LAPSE SHEER SPORT START STRAY WAIVE CHANGE DEPART DETOUR DIVERT RECEDE SQUINT SWERVE WANDER DECLINE DEFLECT DIGRESS DIVERGE INCLINE REFLECT ABERRANT ABERRATE DEROGATE
(— FROM VERTICAL) HADE
DEVIATING SKEW DEVIANT DEVIOUS ERRATIC SINUOUS ABERRANT INDIRECT
DEVIATION BOW YAW HELM JUMP SKEW TURN DRIFT LAPSE QUIRK SHEER TWIST ABRASH BATTER CHANGE DETOUR FIGURE SPREAD ANOMALY BRISURE LICENCE LICENSE ACCURACY DRIFTAGE LATITUDE SOLECISM VARIANCE ABERRATION
(— OF COLOR) ABRASH
(STANDARD —) SIGMA
DEVICE (ALSO SEE INSTRUMENT) ARM ART DIE DOG DOP EYE FAN FLY FOB GAG GIN GUN HOG JIG KEY MOP MOT PEN SET TIP TUP WAY WIT ARCH BELL BOND BOOM BUFF COIN COMB COUP DARE DOPP DRAG DRIP FAKE FIRE FLAG FORK FROG FUSE FUZE GAGE GATE GOBO GRAB GRIP GYRO HASP HAUL HEAD HECK HORN IRIS IRON JACK KEEP KITE LAMP LENS LOCK MOVE MULE MUTE NAIL PACE PAGE PAWK PLAN PLOW POKE PUMP REEL SEAL SHOE SHUT SIGN SLAY SLEY SLUR SNAP SPUD STOP STUD SUMP TOOL TRAP TRIP VICE WEIR WHIM WHIP WIND WING WOLF ALARM APRON BADGE BALUN BITCH BLOCK BREAK BRUSH CHECK CLAMP CODER COVIN CRAMP CROSS DODGE DRIER DRIFT DRIVE DRYER DUMMY FADER FANCY FLAIL FLARE FLASH FLIRT FLOAT GAUGE GLAND GORGE GRIPE GUARD GUIDE GUILE HICKY HINGE HOKUM IMAGE KAZOO KEYER LADLE LASER LATCH LEVEL LIDAR LINAC MATCH MODEM OTTER PARER PLATE PROBE PUNKA SCREW SHADE SHANK SHIFT SIEVE SIGHT SIGIL SIREN SIZER SKATE SLAVE SLICK SLIDE SLING SONDE SPOOL SPOUT SQUIB STAMP STILL STOOL STOVE SWEEP SWELL TABLE TABUT TAMER THIEF TIMER TORCH TRUER TUNER UNION VERGE AGRAFE AIRWAY ALARUM ALINER ANCHOR ARREST BAILER BASTER BEACON BEATER BECKET BEDDER BEEPER BINDER BLOWER BOBBIN BOOMER BRIDLE BROOCH BUCKLE BUFFER BULLEN BUMPER BUNGEE BUNTER BURNER BUTTON CHARGE CIPHER COOKER DASHER DECEIT DERAIL DESIGN DIMMER DOFFER DOTTER DRIVER DROGUE DUMPER EMBLEM ENGINE EVENER FABRIC FALLER FEEDER FENDER FILLER FILTER FINDAL FINDER FORMER GADGET GLAZER GOFFER GOGGLE GRADER GRATER GRISLY GUIDER HANGER HEATER HICKEY HOLDER HOOTER INVENT JIGGER JOGGER KEEPER KICKER LAYBOY LETOFF LIFTER LOOPER MARKER MIRROR MODULE MORTAR MOTHER NAVAID NIPPLE NONIUS NOTION PACKER PEELER PICKUP PLAYER PLOUGH PORTER POTEYE PULLER PUNKAH REROLL RINGER ROCKET ROLLER ROOTER ROTULA ROUTER SACKER SADDLE SAFETY SANDER SCALER SCHEME SCREEN SEALER SEEKER SENSOR SETTER SHAKER SHIELD SIFTER SIGNAL SINKER SIPPER SLEIGH SLICER SLIDER SLIMER SLOPER SLUICE SOCKET SOLION SORTER SPACER SPRING STONER STYLUS SUCKER SWITCH TACTIC TAGGER TAPPER TELLER TEMPLE TESTER TILLER TRACER TUCKER TUNNEL TURNER WARMER WASHER WEANER WEEDER WHEEZE WINDER WINNOW WORKER ADAPTER ADJUNCT AERATOR AGRAFFE ALIGNER AUTOCUE BALANCE BECKETT BIMETAL BIMORPH BINDING BLEEDER BLEEPER BLENDER BLINKER BLOCKER BLOWOFF BLOWOUT BOOKEND BOOSTER BREAKER CALTROP CHIPPER CLAPPER COMPASS DASHPOT DISHMOP DIVISOR DRAWOFF DRESSER DRINKER EARPICK EDUCTOR EJECTOR EMPRESA EXCITER FACEBOW FASHION FETLOCK FICELLE FICTION FITMENT FIXTURE FLASHER FLIPPER FLUSHER FLYFLAP FRISKET GAUFFER GIMMICK GLASSES GRAINER GRENADE GRIDDLE GRILLER GRINDER GRIPPER GRIZZLY GROMMET GROOVER GROWLER GUDGEON GUZZLER HATCHER HELIDON IGNITER IMAGINE IMPRESA IMPRESS INFUSER INHALER IRONMAN KICKOFF KNOTTER LIGHTER MACHINE MUFFLER OOGRAPH PIGTAIL PLOTTER POINTER PRESSER RATCHET RATTLER RECEDER

REDUCER RELEASE ROASTER ROSETTE SAMPLER SCALPER SCANNER SCOGGAN SCRAPER SCUPPER SERVANT SETBACK SETOVER SETWORK SHACKLE SHEDDER SHIFTER SHIPPER SHOOFLY SHUTTER SHUTTLE SINKBOX SKIMMER SLAPPER SLEEVER SLINGER SLITTER SLUDGER SLUSHER SNAPPER SNIFFER SNIGGLE SNORKEL SNUBBER SNUFFER SNUGGER SONOVOX SOUNDER SPARGER SPEEDER SPLICER SPOTTER SPRAYER SQUEEZE STACKER STAPLER STARTER STEMMER STENTER STIRRER STOPPER STRIKER STRIPER SUCTION SWATTER SWEEPER SYRINGE TAMBOUR TENDRIL TENSION THEORIC THINNER TICKLER TOKAMAK TREADLE TRINDLE TRIPPER TRIPPET TUMBLER TURNOUT TWISTER WASHOUT WRINGER ABSORBER ADJUSTER AQUASTAT BACKSTAY BAROSTAT BIOMETER BLOCKING BOOTJACK BRAILLER BREATHER BRONTEUM BUSINESS BUSYBODY CATAPULT CATHETER COLOPHON CONTOISE COUPLING CROTCHET CRYOTRON DAMPENER DEHORNER DERAILER DIFFUSER DIRECTOR DISPOSER DOORSTOP DROPHEAD DUPLEXER EARPHONE EPISEMON ESPRESSO EXPLODER FAIRLEAD FAKEMENT FASTENER FLASHGUN FLYBRUSH FUELIZER GASCHECK GATHERER GIMCRACK GUNSTICK GYROSTAT HALLMARK HANDTRAP HEADGEAR HOLDBACK IMPROVER INKSTAND IRENICON IRISCOPE ISOLATOR KNOCKOUT LAUNCHER LEEBOARD LOXOCOSM LUNARIUM MNEMONIC MOLITION NEOSTYLE ODOGRAPH OVERLIFT OVERRIDE PACIFIER PARAVANE PENWIPER PINWHEEL PULSATOR PYROSTAT QUADRANT QUENTISE REFILTER REHEATER REPEATER RETARDER REVERSER SCORCHER SCOTCHER SCRAWLER SCUTCHER SELECTOR SHRINKER SILENCER SILVERER SINKBOAT SMOOTHER SNOWPLOW SNOWSHOE SPLITTER SPREADER SPROUTER SQUEEGEE SQUEEZER STOPWORK STRAINER STRINGER STRIPPER STROPPER SURFACER SWEATBOX TELETYPE TELLTALE TERMINAL THROWOFF THROWOUT TRAVELER TRAVERSE TRIANGLE NEURISTOR PINSETTER PROJECTOR STRATAGEM MARTINGALE PERIPHERAL PINSPOTTER ACCELERATOR
(— FOR BENDING PIPE) HICKEY
(— FOR BORING WELLS) TIGER
(— FOR CONCENTRATING ORE) JIGGER
(— FOR PUTTING IN GEAR) STRIKER
(— IN LOOM) FEELER TEMPLE
(— ON FLAG) UNION
(— PLACED OVER CHIMNEY) JACK
(— PROTECTING DENTIST'S HAND) THIMBLE
(— THAT CONVERTS SIGNALS) MODEM
(— TO LOCATE AN OBJECT) LIDAR
(— TO RETAIN COFFEE GROUNDS) GRECQUE
(ARTIFICIAL —) PROSTHESIS
(AUTOMATIC —) BRAIN
(BRAKE —) CALIPER
(CENTRIFUGAL —) CYCLONE
(CLEVER —) COUP KNACK
(COMPUTER —) WAND MOUSE TERMINAL ACCUMULATOR
(COMPUTER CONTROL —) PADDLE
(CONVERTING —) MODEM
(CUBICAL BULB —) FLASHCUBE
(DISTINGUISHING —) SPOT
(ELECTORNIC —) MASER
(ELECTRICAL —) OVONIC
(ELECTRONIC —) DME NEURISTOR
(FILM —) MOVIOLA
(FILM EDITING —) MOVIOLA
(GAMBLING —) HOLDOUT
(GLASSBLOWER'S —) DUMMY
(HAMPERING —) HOBBLES
(HEATING —) ETNA
(HERALDIC —S) ARMS
(LISTENING —) BUG
(LITERARY —) FRAME
(MAGICIAN'S —) FAKE FEKE CRAFT
(MIXING —) CRUTCHER
(MUSIC —) HOOK
(NAVIGATIONAL —) LORAN
(OPTICAL —) NIGHTSCOPE
(PAGING —) BEEPER
(POLISHING —) WAGWAG
(PYROTECHNIC —) FOUNTAIN
(RHETORICAL —) ANAPHORA
(ROTATION —) TACH
(SHIELDING —) GOBO
(SIGHTING —) ALIDADE
(SIGNALLING —) CRICKET
(SKILLFUL —) ART
(SOUND —) PINGER
(SPEECH —) ITALICS
(SWIMMING —) SNORKEL
(THEATRICAL —) SLOAT SLOTE
(TIMEKEEPING —) HOROLOGE
(TOROIDAL —) TOKAMAK
(WATER-RAISING —) JANTU SWEEP CHURRUS
(WEAVING —) BOAT ENGINERY
(SUFF.) STAT(IC)(ICS)
(MUSICAL —) INA INE

DEVIL DEL IMP BENG BHUT BOGY DEIL HAZE MAHU NICK PUCK QUED WOLF WOND ANNOY BOBBY BOGEY BOGIE CHORT CLOOT DEMON DEUCE EBLIS FIEND HARRY SATAN SCRAT SHEDU TAIPO TEASE AMAMON BELIAL DAEMON DIABLE DIABLO HORNIE NICKIE PESTER RAGMAN SORROW THURSE AMAIMON ANHANGA CLOOTIE DIANTRE DICKENS GREMLIN LUCIFER MAHOUND RUFFIAN SERPENT SHAITAN TORMENT WARLOCK WENDIGO WINDIGO APOLLYON BAALPEOR BEELPEOR BELFAGOR CAGNAZZO CURUPIRA DEVILING DEVILKIN DIABOLUS MEPHISTO MISCHIEF OBIDICUT PLOTCOCK WIRRICOW WORRICOW WORRYCOW BEELZEBUB
(BLUE —S) MARE
(PREF.) DIABOL(O)

DEVILFISH RAY MANTA
DEVIL-IN-A-BUSH NIGELLA
DEVILISH DARING DEUCED DEVILY RAKISH WICKED DEMONIC EXTREME FIENDLY HELLISH INHUMAN SATANIC DEMONIAC DIABOLIC FIENDISH INFERNAL SATURNINE
DEVILISHLY DEUCED DEUCEDLY
DEVILKIN IMP
DEVIL'S CLUB FATSIA
DEVIL'S COACHHORSE DARDAOL
DEVIL'S DISCIPLE (AUTHOR OF —) SHAW
(CHARACTER IN —) DICK ESSIE JUDITH DUDGEON ANDERSON BURGOYNE
DEVIL'S-MILK WARTWEED WARTWORT
DEVIL'S-TREE DITA
DEVIOUS DEEP ERRING LOUCHE ROVING SHIFTY SUBTLE TRICKY OBLIQUE PLAITED VAGRANT WINDING HAVERING INDIRECT RAMBLING SCHEMING TORTUOUS AMBAGIOUS MEALYMOUTHED
DEVISE AIM CAST COOK FIND GIVE PLAN PLOT WARP WILL ARRAY FANCY FRAME FUDGE IMAGE LEAVE SHAPE WEAVE ADVISE CONVEY DECOCT DESIGN DEVICE DIVIDE DIVINE INVENT SCHEME AGITATE APPOINT ARRANGE BETHINK COMMENT COMPASS CONCERT CONCOCT CONSULT IMAGINE PREPARE PROJECT BEQUEATH CONTRIVE
DEVISED INVENIT
DEVISER FINDER ARTIFICER
DEVISING DEVICE DEVISAL FORGERY
DEVITALIZE DULL DEADEN
DEVITALIZED DEGENERATE
DEVITRIFIED AMBITTY
DEVOID FREE VAIN VOID EMPTY BARREN EXPERT VACANT SINCERE WANTING DESOLATE
(— OF) BOUT EMPTY
(— OF HELP) AIDLESS
(— OF KINDNESS) CRUEL
(— OF MERCY) BRUTAL
(— OF MIND) AMENTAL
(— OF VALUE) HOLLOW
DEVOLUTION DESCENT
DEVOLVE FALL PASS VEST RESULT BLOSSOM SUCCEED OVERTURN TRANSFER TRANSMIT
DEVOTE VOW ALLY AVOW DOOM GIVE LEND TAKE TURN APPLY DEVOW ADDICT ATTACH BESTOW DEPUTE DESIGN DEVOVE DIRECT EMPLOY INTEND RESIGN ADDRESS APPOINT CONSIGN DESTINE DEDICATE VENERATE
(— TIME) BOTHER
(— TO MISERY) ACCURSE
DEVOTED MAD HIGH TRUE LIEGE LOYAL PIOUS ARDENT DEVOUT DOOMED ENTIRE FERVID LOVING OBLATE VOTARY VOTIVE ADORING ARDUOUS JEALOUS SERIOUS ZEALOUS ADDICTED ATTACHED CONSTANT FAITHFUL
(— TO COUNTRY) PATRIOTIC
(— TO ENJOYMENT) APOLAUSTIC
(OVERLY —) SUPERSTITIOUS
DEVOTEE CAT FAN NUN BUFF MONK YATI ADEPT JNANI ADDICT BHAGAT BHAKTA DEVOTO DEVOUT HEPCAT VOTARY VOTEEN ZEALOT ADMIRER AMATEUR BOPPIST BOPSTER CINEAST FANATIC HEPSTER HIPSTER SHAVIAN TARTUFE AMOURIST BURNSIAN CABALIST DEVOTARY FOLLOWER IBSENITE PARTISAN PRIAPIAN SAVOYARD SIMPLIST TARTUFFE VOTARESS VOTARIST ALLIGATOR AFICIONADO
DEVOTION CULT ZEAL ARDOR PIETY BHAKTI NOVENA ANGELUS ARABISM CULTISM LOYALTY PIETISM FIDELITY IDOLATRY JEALOUSY KAVVANAH KAWWANAH RELIGION NATIONALISM
(— OF ONESELF) VOW NARCISSISM
(— TO HUMAN WELFARE) HUMANISM
(— TO LADIES) GALLANTRY
(FERVENT —) ADORATION
(PARENTAL —) PROGENITY
(PL.) HOLIES
(SUFF.) LATER LATRIA LATROUS LATRY
DEVOTIONAL PIOUS SOLEMN
DEVOUR EAT JAW FRET GULP SWAP SWOP VOUR GORGE RAVEN SCOFF WASTE AFRETE ENGULF CONSUME ENGORGE FRAUNCH SWALLOW
(— GREEDILY) SWILL
(RAVENOUSLY —) WOLF
(SUFF.) VORA VORE VOROUS
DEVOURER LOCUST
DEVOURING PREY EATING GREEDY VORANT EDACIOUS
DEVOUT GOOD HOLY WARM FROOM GODLY GRACY PIOUS HEARTY INWARD SOLEMN CORDIAL DEVOTED GODLIKE PITEOUS SAINTLY SINCERE REVERENT PIETISTIC PRAYERFUL RELIGIOUS PIETISTICAL SANCTIMONIOUS
(NOT —) LINK
DEVOUTNESS PIETY DEVOTION
DEW DAG RIME BLOOM FROST TEARS MOISTEN REFRESH MOISTURE
(— METER) PAGOSCOPE
(NIGHT —) SERENE
(PREF.) DROSO RORI
DEWBERRY MAYES
DEWDROP PEARL
DEWLAP JOWL GULLET JOLLOP CHOLLER WATTLES
(— OF MALE MOOSE) BELL
DEWY DAMP RORY MOIST RORAL RORIC RORID GENTLE ROSCID
DEXTERITY ART CHIC CRAFT KNACK SKILL STROIL ABILITY ADDRESS AGILITY APTNESS CUNNING

FINESSE SLEIGHT APTITUDE DEFTNESS FACILITY
(— IN ARMS) CHIVALRY
DEXTEROUS APT FLY DEFT FEAT HEND NEAT WISE ADEPT CANNY CLEAN FEATY HANDY HAPPY HENDE JIMMY QUICK READY SMART TIGHT ADROIT ARTFUL CLEVER DRAFTY CUNNING SLEIGHT DEXTROUS HANDSOME SKILLFUL SLEIGHTY
DEXTEROUSLY YARELY HANDILY
DEXTRAN GLUCOSAN
DEXTROROTATORY POSITIVE
DEXTRORSE EUTROPIC
DEXTROSE AME CERELOSE
DHAK DAK PALAS PULAS
DHAVA BAKLI
DHOLE KOLSUN
DHOW BUGALA LATEEN SAMBUK SAMBOUK LATEENER
DHRITARASHTRA (BROTHER OF —) PANDU
(FATHER OF —) VYASA VICHITRAVIRYA
(SON OF —) DURYODHANA
(WIFE OF —) GANDHARI
DHYANA JHANA
DIABASE OPHITE DOLERITE THOLEITE
DIABOLICAL CRUEL WICKED DEMONIC HELLISH INHUMAN SATANIC VIOLENT DEMONIAC DEVILISH DIABOLIC FIENDISH INFERNAL
DIABOLISM SATANISM
DIACETATE ACETIN
DIACONATE DEACONRY
DIACONICON PARABEMA
DIACRITIC HACEK TILDE UMLAUT MODIFIER
DIAD DIGONAL TWOFOLD
DIADEM TAJ MIND CROWN TIARA ANADEM CIRCLE EMBLEM FILLET CIRCUIT CORONET HEADBAND
DIAERESIS TREMA CESURA CAESURA DIALYSIS
DIAGNOSE ANALYZE IDENTIFY KNOWLEDGE
DIAGONAL BIAS SLANT SLASH COUNTER SOLIDUS VIRGULE BENDWISE DIAGONIC
DIAGONALLY BIAS ASLOPE BENDWAYS BENDWISE
DIAGRAM MAP PLAN PLOT TREE CARTE CHART EPURE GRAPH PARSE DESIGN FIGURE SCHEMA SCHEME SYMBOL YANTRA ISOGRAM ISOTYPE SECTION VIAGRAM PICTOGRAM PICTOGRAPH
(KIND OF —) FEYNMAN
DIAGRAMMATIC GRAPHIC
DIAGRAPH OE
DIAL NOB CALL FACE KNOB WATCH DIACLE JIGGER AZIMUTH CRYSTAL DECLINER HOROLOGE INCLINER RECLINER
DIAL BIRD DAYAL DHYAL
DIALECT (ALSO SEE LANGUAGE) HO KA WU GEG GIZ KHA LAI SAC TWI AMOY CANI CANT DRAA EFIK EGBA EPIC GEEZ GHEG GONA GUEG IOWA ITZA KORA MANX NAMA NORN OGAM PALI SAUK SHOR SOGA TALK TCHI TOSK TUBA ALTAI ARGOT ASURI ATTIC CONOY DORIC FANTI GHEEZ GHESE HAKKA IDIOM IONIC IOWAY IRAQI KANSA KAREL KOINE LADIN LINGO MAZUR MOPAN MUKRI NGOKO OGHAM PARSI PUNIC SABIR SAXON SCOTS SLANG TIGRE TSCHI VALVE VOGUL ZMUDZ AEOLIC AGNEAN ASANTE ATSINA AWADHI BADAGA BRETON BROGUE CANTON CREOLE DEBATE DUNGAN FAEROE FANTEE FURLAN GASCON GULLAH GUTNIC HARARI HARAYA IBANAG ISINAI ITAVES JARGON KABYLE KANSAS KHAMIR KORANA KVITSH LADAKI LADINO LAHULI LALLAN LEDDEN LIBYAN PARSEE PATOIS PATTER PICARD SANTEE SCOTCH SCOUSE SHARRA SKAGIT SPEECH SUDANI SWATOW SYRIAC SZEKEL TAVAST TONGUE TUSCAN YANKEE ZENAGA ACADIAN AEOLIAN AMOYESE ANGLIAN ASHANTI BHOTANI BHUTANI BUNDELI CATALAN CHILULA CHUVASH CLATSOP COCKNEY CORNISH CUZCENO CYPRIOT FAYUMIC FOOCHOW GEECHEE GHEGISH GUTNISH JAIPURI KARAITE KENTISH KITKSAN KONKANI LADAKHI LALLAND LEONESE LESBIAN MALTESE MARSIAN MARWARI MERCIAN MIDLAND MULTANI MUNDARI OLONETS PANAYAN PRAKRIT SAHIDIC SANPOIL SHORTZY SOKOTRI SPOKANE SQUAXON SWABIAN SZEKLER TIGRINA VAUDOIS WALLOON ABANEEME ACHMIMIC AKHMIMIC ALGERINE ARCADIAN ASSYRIAN BASILECT BAVARIAN BHOJPURI BISCAYAN BOEOTIAN BOHAIRIC CLAKAMAS COLVILLE CORSICAN CYPRIOTE FALERIAN FALISCAN FAROEISH FRANCIEN FRIULIAN GARHWALI HARARESE IZCATECO KANESIAN KARELIAN KERMANJI KICKAPOO KINGWANA LACANDON LANGUAGE LAWLANTS MAGHREBI MAGHRIBI MAITHILI MANDAEAN MANDARIN MANISIAN MAZATECO MAZURIAN MEMPHITE NABATEAN NEENGATU PANAYANO PEKINESE RABBINIC SALTEAUX SOULETIN SOUTHERN TAUNGTHU TIGRINYA TIRHUTIA TUNISIAN VENERIAN VIENNESE NORTHUMBRIAN
(ENGLISH — IN LIVERPOOL) SCOUSE
(ESKIMO —) INUIT INUKTITUT
(STRANGE —) GIBBERISH
(PL.) WU ANGLIAN
DIALECTIC PILPUL
DIALOGUE ION CRITO DIALOG EPILOG PATTER PHAEDO TIMAEUS COLLOQUY DUOLOGUE EPILOGUE EXCHANGE PHAEDRUS COLLOCUTION
(—S OF BUDDHA) SUTRA SUTTA
(COMIC —) LAZZO
DIAMETER BORE GAGE GEAR MOOT GAUGE WIDTH MODULE
(— OF BULLET) CALIBER CALIBRE
(— OF PELVIS) CONJUGATA
(— OF PUPIL) APERTURE
(— OF WIRE) GAGE GAUGE
DIAMOND GEM ICE BORT LASK PICK ROCK ROSE BAHIA BOORT BORTZ DORJE FANCY FIELD JAGER JEWEL LOZEN MACLE MELEE POINT RHOMB RIVER SANCY SPARK STONE TABLE VAJRA ADAMAS BOARTS CANARY CARBON JAEGER LASQUE ORLOFF PENCIL REGENT RONDEL SHINER TABLET ADAMANT BRIOLET CARREAU CRYSTAL FISHEYE INFIELD LOZENGE PREMIER RHOMBUS SPARKLE CORUNDUM KOHINOOR RONDELLE SPARKLER BRIOLETTE
(— CUT TOO THIN) FISHEYE
(— MOLDER) DOP
(— STATE) DELAWARE
(— UNIT) INNING
(— USED FOR ENGRAVING) SHARP
(BLACK —) CARBONADO
(FLAT —) LASQUE
(GLAZIER'S —) QUARREL
(IMITATION —) SCHLENTER
(INFERIOR GRADE OF —) FLAT
(PASTE —) RHINESTONE
(PERFECT —) PARAGON
(PURE WHITE —) RIVER
(ROUGH —) BRAIT
(SINGLE —) SOLITAIRE
(TRANSPARENT —) CRYSTAL
(YELLOW —) CANARY
(PL.) MELANGE
DIAMOND BIRD PARDALOTE
DIAMORPHINE HEROIN
DIANA LUCINA TRIVIA ARTEMIS
(BROTHER OF —) APOLLO
(FATHER OF —) JUPITER
(MOTHER OF —) LATONA
DIANA MONKEY ROLOWAY
DIAPASON MONTRE DIAPASE
DIAPAUSE BLOCK
DIAPER FUR DIDY CLOUT DIDIE NAPPY HIPPEN HIPPIN NAPKIN NAPPIE DIAPERY
DIAPHANOUS CLEAR SHEER FRAGILE DIAPHANE VAPOROUS
DIAPHONY ORGANUM TRIPHONY
DIAPHORETIC BUCCO BUCHU BUCKU BORAGE DIAPNOIC HIDROTIC SUDATORY SASSAFRAS PILOCARPINE
DIAPHRAGM IRIS RIFF SLIT APRON PHREN SKIRT WAFER DECKER PLATEN MIDRIFF PHRAGMA SKIRTING TRAVERSE TYMPANUM
(KIND OF —) IRIS
(PREF.) PHREN(O)
DIAPHRAGMATIC PHRENIC
DIARIST ENTERER
DIARRHEA LAX FLUX LASK GURRY RELAX SCOUR SPRUE PURGING SQUIRTS LIENTERY
DIARY LOG RECORD DAYBOOK DIURNAL JOURNAL REGISTER EPHEMERIS
DIASKEUAST EDITOR REVISER
DIASPORA GALUT GOLAH GALUTH
DIASPORE MIGRULE
DIASTASE MALT ENZYME AMYLASE
DIATOM BRITTLEWORT ASTERIONELLA
DIATOMITE TRIPOLI
DIATONIC ACHROMATIC
DIATRIBE SATIRE SCREED HARANGUE INVECTIVE
DIAZAPAM VALIUM
DIB DAP DIP DIBBLE DIBSTONE
DIBBLE DAP DIB DABBLE DIBBER KIPPIN TRIFLE DIBBLER KIPPEEN
DIBRI (SON OF —) SHELOMITH
DIBS COCKAL
DICAST HELIAST JURYMAN
DICE CHOP CUBE DEES BONES CRAPS FLATS LOWMEN REJECT CHECKER IVORIES
(— GAME) SET RAPHE MUMCHANCE
(— HAVING FOUR SPOTS) QUATRE
(FALSE —) GOAD TATS GOURD GRAVIERS SQUARIER STOPDICE
(HIGHEST THROW AT —) APHRODITE
(LOADED —) TOPS DOCTOR
(LOWEST THROW AT —) AMBSACE
(PAIRED NUMBERS AT —) DUPLET DOUBLETS
(2, 3, OR 12 ON 1ST —) MISSOUT
(PREF.) ASTRAGAL(O)
DICE-BOX RATTLE
DICE PLAYER THROWSTER
DICER HAT DERBY GAMBLER GRAINER
DICERION DYKER
DICHASIAL BIPAROUS
DICHLORVOS DDVP
DICHONDRA LAWNLEAF
DICHOTOMY DUALITY
DICHROITE IOLITE
DICK TEC
DICKENS HECK DEUCE
(LITTLE —) IMP
DICKER ICRE SWAP DAKER BARTER HAGGLE BARGAIN CHAFFER EXCHANGE
DICKEY POOP WEAK DICKY FRONT GILET SHAKY DONKEY RUMBLE VESTEE HADDOCK PLASTRON
DICKIE SHAM DICKY FRONT SQUARE TUCKER STARCHER
DICLINOUS IMPERFECT
DICTATE SAW SAY DITE TELL UTTER WRITE DECREE DICTUM ENJOIN IMPOSE INDITE OCTROY ORDAIN SCHOOL COMMAND DELIVER REQUIRE SUGGEST WARRANT DICTAMEN PRESCRIBE
DICTATION DICTAMEN
DICTATOR CHAM CZAR DUCE TSAR CAESAR PENDRAGON
DICTATORIAL BOSSY LORDLY CZARIST POMPOUS TSARIST ARROGANT DOGMATIC ORACULAR POSITIVE ARBITRARY MAGISTERIAL
DICTION STYLE TERMS PHRASE IMAGERY LANGUAGE PARLANCE VERBIAGE
(BAD —) CACOLOGY
(SUFF.) ESE
DICTIONARY GRADUS ALVEARY CALEPIN LEXICON GLOSSARY WORDBOOK THESAURUS

(BRITISH —) OED
(PREF.) LEXICO
DICTUM SAY ADAGE AXIOM EDICT DECREE SAYING DICTATE EFFATUM OPINION APOTHEGM PRINCIPLE STATEMENT
DID D CAN DED DEDE DYDE
(— NOT) DIDNA DIDNT
DIDACTIC DRY PREACHY SERMONIC
DIDO ANTIC CAPER PRANK TRICK
(BROTHER OF —) PYGMALION
(FATHER OF —) BELUS
(HUSBAND OF —) SICHAEUS
(LOVER OF —) AENEAS
DIDO AND AENEAS (CHARACTER IN —) DIDO AENEAS BELINDA MERCURY
(COMPOSER OF —) PURCELL
DIE GO BED DEE DOD END HOB HUB PIP ROT SIX TAT BOSS COIN CONK CUBE DADO DEAD DICE DROP EXIT FADE FAIL FALL FINE FIVE FLIT KICK MARK MOLD PART PASS PIKE PILE SEAL TATT TINE WANE CROAK FORCE FUDGE GHOST IVORY NAPOO PATAY PRINT PUNCH QUAIL SHAPE SNUFF SOUGH SPILL STALL STAMP STOCK SWELT CHANCE DEMISE DEPART DOCTOR EXPIRE FAMISH FINISH FORCER FORMER FULLAM MATRIX MULLAR PATRIX PERISH ROLLER STARVE STRIKE TORFEL TORFLE TRANCE VANISH WITHER BLOCKER DECEASE STEPOUT SUCCUMB TESSERA INTAGLIO LANGUISH MISCARRY PUNCHEON TRESPASS TRUSSELL
(— AWAY) FAIL SWOON
(— BEFORE) PREDECEASE
(— BY HANGING) SWING
(— DOWN) FLIT SINK ABATE
(— FOR DRAWING WIRE) WHIRTLE WHORTLE
(— FOR MAKING DRAINPIPE) DOD
(— FOR MOLDING BRICK) KICK
(— FROM HUNGER) AFFAMISH
(— OF COLD) STARVE
(— OF HUNGER) STARVE
(— OF PEDESTAL) SOLIDUM
(— WITH 4 SPOTS) QUATRE
(— WITH 6 SPOTS) CISE SICE SISE SIZE
(COINING —) SICCA
(FRAUDULENT —) FULHAM FULLAM FULLOM
(HOLLOW —) GOURD
(IMPROPER —) FLAT
(LOADED —) TAT DOCTOR FULHAM HIGHMAN LANGRET
(LOWER —) BED
(REVOLVING —) DREIDEL
DIEBACK STAGHEAD EXANTHEMA
DIED DYDE OBIIT WRATE
DIEHARD TORY BLIMP
DIESIS FEINT
DIET BANT FARE FAST FOOD SEIM SEYM BOARD HOFTAG REDUCE SEIMAS VIANDS VICTUS BANTING DIETINE LANDTAG REGIMEN RIKSDAG CONGRESS KREISTAG VOLKSTAG
DIETARY LOCAL
(— LAWS) KASHRUTH
DIETER SLIMMER
DIETETICS SITOLOGY
DIETHER APIOL APIOLE DIOXANE
DIETING BANTING
DIFFER VARY RECEDE SQUARE COMPARE DISCORD DISSENT DIVERGE DISAGREE
DIFFERENCE SHED CHASM CLASH FAVOR BREACH CHANGE DIFFER ANOMALY BRISURE DISCORD DISPUTE QUALITY VARIETY DISTANCE DIVISION IMPARITY VARIANCE
(— IN ELEVATION) HEAD
(— IN EXCHANGE) AGIO
(— IN LATITUDE) SOUTHING
(— IN LONGITUDE) EASTING
(— IN PITCH) COMMA INTERVAL
(— IN PRESSURE) DRAFT DRAUGHT
(— IN WIDTH) BILGE
(— OF OPINION) DISSENT ARGUMENT
(— OF VESSEL'S DRAFT) DRAG
(ANGULAR —) EXPLEMENT
(GRADED —) GRADIENT
(MAKE A —) MATTER
(MINUTE —) SHADE
(POTENTIAL —) EMF
(PRICE —) BASIS
(SMALL —) NUANCE HAIRLINE
DIFFERENT FAR MANY SERE FRESH OTHER PARTY DIVERS SCREWY SUNDRY UNLIKE ANOTHER DISTANT DIVERSE SEVERAL STRANGE UNALIKE UNUSUAL VARIANT VARIOUS CONTRARY DISTINCT MANIFOLD SEPARATE OTHERWISE OTHERGUESS NONIDENTICAL
(NOT —) IDENTIC INDENTICAL
(VERY —) WISE
(PREF.) DIVERSI HETER(O)
DIFFERENTIA MARK LIMIT
DIFFERENTIAL FLUXION
DIFFERENTIATE APLITE DIFFER DISCERN HAPLITE CONTRAST SPECIATE
DIFFERENTIATION ANABOLY DEVIATION DICHOTOMY
(PREF.) ALL(O)
DIFFERING DIVERSE SINGULAR DIVERGENT
DIFFICULT ILL HARD WICK CRAMP CRANK GREAT HEAVY SPINY STEEP STIFF AUGEAN CRABBY CRANKY KNOTTY SEVERE STICKY STRAIT STRONG TICKLE TRAPPY UNEASY UNEATH UPHILL WENETH WICKED ARDUOUS AWKWARD BRITTLE COMPLEX CRABBED DIFFUSE LABORED NERVOUS OBSCURE PAINFUL PERPLEX PRACTIC SERIOUS STICKLE UNNETHE ABSTRACT CUMBROUS FIENDISH PUZZLING SCABROUS STRUGGLE STUBBORN TICKLISH
(— TO BEAR) BITTER
(— TO COMPREHEND) STRANGE
(— TO FOLLOW) DIRTY
(— TO GRASP) FUGITIVE
(— TO HANDLE) SPINOUS
(— TO MANAGE) SURLY STURDY
(— TO OBTAIN) CLOSE
(— TO OVERCOME) STRONG
(— TO PLEASE) CURIOUS
(— TO PRONOUNCE) BREAKJAW
(— TO RAISE) DORTY
(— TO SATISFY) CHOOSY CHOOSEY
(— TO UNDERSTAND) DEEP HIGH SUBTLE CRABBED ABSTRACT ABSTRUSE ESOTERIC
(PREF.) DYS MOGI
DIFFICULTY ADO BAR BOX ILL JAM RUB BUMP CLOG COIL HEAT JAMB KNOT LOCK NODE PAIN PINE SNAG SORE WERE CHECK DOUBT GRIEF NODUS PRESS RIGOR STAND STOUR TRADE APORIA BOGGLE BUNKER HABBLE HOBBLE PLIGHT PLUNGE RUBBER SCRAPE STRAIT TIFTER BARRIER DICKENS GORDIAN PITFALL PROBLEM SQUEEZE ASPERITY DISTRESS HARDNESS HARDSHIP OBSTACLE SEVERITY STRUGGLE
(TEMPORARY —) HICCUP
(UNEXPECTED —) SNAG
(WITH —) SCARCELY
(PREF.) (WITH —) DYS MOGI
DIFFIDENCE DOUBT MODESTY RESERVE SHYNESS DISTRUST HUMILITY TIMIDITY
DIFFIDENT SHY BLATE CHARY MODEST BASHFUL BACKWARD RESERVED RETIRING SHEEPISH
DIFFUSE FULL SHED BLEED EXUDE LARGE STREW WORDY DEFUSE DERIVE DILATE DIVIDE EXPAND EXTEND OSMOSE PROLIX SPREAD SPRING COPIOUS DIALYSE DIALYZE DIFFUND PERFUSE PERPLEX PERVADE PUBLISH RADIATE SCATTER SPARKLE SPRAWLY SPRENGE SUFFUSE VERBOSE CONFUSED DIFFUSED DIOSMOSE DISPERSE PATULENT PATULOUS SPRANGLE
(NOT —) STRICT COMPACT
DIFFUSION SPREAD OSMOSIS BLEEDING DEFUSION
DIG GET HOE JOB NIP CLAW DIKE DYKE GIRD GORE GRUB HOWK LIKE MINE MOOT PICK PION POKE PROD ROOT SINK SLAM SMUG SPIT SPUD SUMP SWOT DELVE DITCH DWELL GAULT GRAFT GRAVE LODGE POACH PROBE SNOUT SPADE START STOCK BURROW DREDGE EXHUME GRAVEL HOLLOW PLUNGE SHOVEL THRUST TUNNEL BEDELVE COSTEAN SPUDDLE UNEARTH EXCAVATE UNDERSTAND
(— IN) EAT ENTRENCH
(— OUT) SCOOP STUMP EXHUME
(— OUT CREVICES) FOSSICK
(— PEAT) SHEUGH
(— POTATOES) LIFT
(— TRENCHES) GRIP LABOR COSTEAN COSTEEN
(— UP) CAST GRUB STUB SPADE STOCK EXHUME UPGRAVE DISINTER
(— WITH NAILS) SCRAPE
(— WITH SNOUT) GROUT
(— WITH STICK) CROW
DIGAMMA VAU
DIGEST COCT CODE DEFY ENDEW ENDUE INDUE RIPEN CODIFY DECOCT DOCKET MATURE SEETHE CONCOCT EPITOME PANDECT SUMMARY CONDENSE SYLLABUS
(— OF ROMAN LAWS) PANDECTS
DIGESTION PEPSIS COCTION EUPEPSY EUPEPSIA
(SUFF.) PEPSIA PEPTIC
DIGESTIVE PEPSIN PEPTIC DIGERENT
DIGGER DIG PAL PLOW MINER BANKER BILDAR DRUDGE PLOUGH COMRADE PEATMAN PIONEER PLODDER TRENCHER
(POST HOLE —) LOY
DIGGING DIG DIKAGE DYKAGE STRIPPING
DIGHT DAB RUB DECK DINK DITE WIPE ADORN DICHT DRESS EQUIP ORDER RAISE TREAT MANAGE REPAIR WINNOW APPOINT CONSIGN PERFORM PREPARE
DIGIT TOE BYTE ONEK UNIT DOIGT POINT THUMB DACTYL FIGURE FINGER HALLUX MEDIUS NUMBER DEWCLAW DIGITAL INTEGER
(BINARY —) BIT BINIT
(EXTRA —) PREPOLLEX
(GROUP OF EIGHT BINARY —S) BYTE
(PREF.) DACTYLIO DACTYL(O)
(SUFF.) DACTYLIA DACTYLOUS
DIGITAL KEY MANUAL
DIGITATE DIGITAL FINGERED
DIGNIFIED GRAND LOFTY MANLY NOBLE REGAL STAID AUGUST LORDLY SEDATE SOLEMN COURTLY EXALTED STATELY TOGATED ELEVATED ENNOBLED MAJESTIC
DIGNIFY DUB ADORN CROWN EXALT GRACE HONOR RAISE ELEVATE ENNOBLE PROMOTE
DIGNITARY DON WIG BABA RAJA CANON RAJAH PRIEST SHERIF DIGNITY HUTUKTU PRELATE PROVOST SHEREEF ALDERMAN HUTUKHTU VESTIARY
DIGNITY DOG CHIC FACE RANK BENCH DINES HONOR IZZAT PRIDE STATE AFFAIR BARONY LAUREL REPOSE BARONRY BEARING DECORUM DUKEDOM EARLDOM FITNESS GRAVITY MAJESTY SHAHDOM STATION WORSHIP CHIVALRY EARLSHIP GRANDEUR NOBILITY
(— OF BISHOP) LAWN
(— OF CARDINAL) HAT
(— OF KING) PURPLE
(ACCIDENTAL —) JOY HAYZ
(EPISCOPAL —) MITER MITRE CATHEDRA
(PAPAL —) TIARA
(SUFF.) DOM SHIP
DIGRAPH CH OE PH RH TH RRH BIGRAM LIGATURE DIPHTHONG
DIGRESS VEER EXCUR DIVERT SWERVE WANDER DEVIATE

DIVERGE EXCURSE DISGRESS DIVAGATE
DIGRESSION ASIDE VAGARY DIGRESS ECBASIS EPISODE EXCURSE PASSAGE TANGENT DISGRESS EXCURSUS SIDESLIP PARENTHESIS
(RHETORICAL —) ECBOLE
DIKE BAR RIB BANK BUND DICE DICK DYKE GALL POND POOL DIGUE DITCH GROIN LEVEE CAUSEY CRADGE CHANNEL DIKELET POWDIKE ABOIDEAU CAUSEWAY ESTACADE SPREADER
DIKER COWAN COWEN
DIKETONE BENZIL BIACETYL DIMEDONE
DIKLAH (FATHER OF —) JOKTAN
DILACTONE LACTIDE ANEMONIN
DILAPIDATE DESTROY
DILAPIDATED BAD BEATEN CREAKY RAGGED RUINED SHABBY WRECKY CRAICHY CREACHY RUINOUS DESOLATE TATTERED WOBEGONE
DILAPIDATION RUIN DECAY DECREPITY DISREPAIR
DILATATION BULB SINUS VARIX JARBOT SPREAD AMPULLA ECTASIA ECTASIS ANEURISM DILATION MYDRIASIS
(— OF ARTERY) ANEURYSM
(— OF TRACHEA) AIRSAC
(SUFF.) ECTASIA ECTASIS
DILATE TENT DELAY PLUMP SWELL WIDEN DELATE EXPAND EXTEND SPREAD AMPLIFY BROADEN DESCANT DIFFUSE DISTEND ENLARGE INFLATE PROLONG STRETCH DISPERSE INCREASE LENGTHEN PROTRACT DISCOURSE
DILATED TURGID VARICOSE
DILATING
(SUFF.) EURYSIS
DILATOR DIOPTER DIOPTRA DIOPTRY DIVULSOR SPECULUM
DILATORY LATE SLOW SLACK SPARE TARDY FABIAN REMISS DILATOR LAGGARD LATREDE TEDIOUS BACKWARD DELAYING INACTIVE SLUGGISH
DILEMMA FIX FORK LOCK NODE BRIKE POSER CHOICE PICKLE PLUNGE CORNUTE SNIFTER JEOPARDY QUANDARY
DILETTANTE LOVER SUNDAY ADMIRER AMATEUR DABBLER DABSTER ESTHETE AESTHETE
DILIGENCE HIE CARE HEED DILLY EFFORT CAUTION HORNING BUSINESS INDUSTRY SEDULITY ASSIDUITY
DILIGENT BUSY HARD TIDY ACTIVE EIDENT ITHAND STEADY CAREFUL EARNEST HEEDFUL OPEROSE PAINFUL PATIENT WORKFUL CAUTIOUS CONSTANT LABOROUS SEDULOUS STUDIOUS
DILL ANET CALM SOYA ANISE UMBEL PICKLE SOOTHE DILLWEED
DILLIDALLY TARRY
DILLY ONER
DILLYDALLY LAG TOY LOAF DELAY DILLY STALL LOITER TRIFLE
DILOGY ECHO
DILUENT CARRIER VEHICLE
DILUTE CUT BREW FUSE LEAN THIN WEAK ALLAY BLUNT DELAY WATER RAREFY REDUCE WEAKEN WHITISH DIMINISH LENGTHEN WATERISH
(— LIQUOR) BREW SPLIT
(— WINE) GALLIZE
(VERY —) SMALL
DILUTED WASHY DILUTE REMISS
DILUTING ATTENUANT
DILUTION (— OF A SERUM) TITER
DIM DIP WAN BLUR DARK DULL FADE GRAY HAZY MIST PALE PALL VEIL BEDIM BLEAK BLEAR BLIND DUSKY DUSTY FAINT FOGGY MISTY STAIN UNLIT BEMIST BLEARY CLOUDY DARKEN DASWEN DIMPSY GLOOMY OBTUSE SHADOW TWILIT BECLOUD DARKISH DISLIMN ECLIPSE OBSCURE OPACATE SHADOWY TARNISH DARKLING OVERCAST CALIGINOUS CREPUSCULAR
(NOT —) FRESH
DIME HOG HOGG DISME TENPENCE TENPENNY
(HALF —) PICAYUNE
DIMEDON METHONE
DIMENHYDRINATE DRAMAMINE
DIMENSION BODY BULK SIZE SCOPE WIDTH ASSIZE DEGREE EXTENT HEIGHT LENGTH MOISON BREADTH PROPORTION MEASUREMENT
(COLOR —) CHROMA
(TYPE —) EM EN
(PL.) GAGE SIZE GAUGE GIRTH EXTENT SIDING MEASURE
DIMENSIONS
(PREF.) **(THREE —)** STERE(O)
DIMER (— IN EXCITED STATE) EXCIMER
DIMERCAPROL BAL
DIMIDIATE HALVED
DIMINISH GO CUT EBB SAP BATE BURN CHOP DAMP DROP EASE FADE FAIL FINE FRET MELT PARE PINK SINK WANE WEAR ABATE ALLAY BREAK CLOSE DRAFT DWARF ELIDE ERODE LOWER MINCE PETER SLACK SMALL TAPER DAMPEN DEBATE DECOCT DEDUCT DILUTE IMPAIR LESSEN MINISH REBATE REDUCE SLOUGH VANISH WITHER ABRIDGE ASSUAGE CORRODE CURTAIL DEGRADE DEPLETE DEPRESS DETRACT DIMINUE DRAUGHT DWINDLE FRITTER INHIBIT QUALIFY REFRACT RELIEVE TARNISH ADMINISH AMOINDER CONDENSE DECREASE DIMINUTE DISCOUNT MINORATE MITIGATE MODERATE RETRENCH
(— FRONT) PLOY
DIMINISHED SLACK ABATED GRAYED DIMINUTE
DIMINISHING TAPER CRITICAL FLAGGING
(— IN LOUDNESS) CALANDO
DIMINUTION FALL WASTE RABATE DECREASE PERDITION
DIMINUTIVE TOY WEE BABY TINY BANTY DWARF PETTY RUNTY SMALL YOUNG BANTAM LITTLE MIDGET PETITE POCKET MANIKIN MIDGETY MINIKIN SHRIMPY EXIGUOUS
(— OF BAR) SCARP CLOSET SCARPE
(SUFF.) CLE CULE CULUS EL ET ETTE KIN OCK SY ULA ULE
DIMLY DULLY DARKLY FEEBLY SHADOWY
DIMMED BLEARY CLOUDY GRAYED BLEARED
DIMMING GRAYOUT
DIMNESS DIM HAZE MIST SLUR GLOOM CALIGO DARKNESS
DIMPLE DOKE AHMADI AHMEDI RIPPLE GELASIN FOSSETTE
DIM-SIGHTED PURBLIND
DIMWIT DODO DOLT DUMMY AIRHEAD DINGDONG
DIN BUM DUN REEL RERD RIOT UTIS ALARM BABEL BRUIT CHIME CHIRM CLANG DEAVE DEEVE FRUSH NOISE RERDE ALARUM BELDER CLAMOR FRAGOR HUBBUB RACKET RANDAN RATTLE STEVEN TUMULT UPROAR CLANGOR CLATTER DISCORD TURMOIL DINGDONG TINTAMAR
DINAH (BROTHER OF —) LEVI SIMEON
(FATHER OF —) JACOB
(MOTHER OF —) LEAH
DINAR DENARE MARAVEDI
DINARZADE (SISTER OF —) SCHEHERAZADE
DINDLE RING QUIVER THRILL TINGLE TINKLE TREMOR STAGGER VIBRATE
DINE EAT SUP FARE FEAST REGALE
DINER EPICURE GOURMAND
DING DIN BEAT DANG DASH KICK PUSH RING WHIP CLANG DRIVE EXCEL FLING KNOCK PITCH POUND PUNCH THUMP STROKE THRASH THRUST
DINGE DENT DINT BATTER BRUISE TARNISH
DINGHY PRAM SKIFF DINGEY ROWBOAT SHALLOP SNOWBIRD
DINGLE DEN DALE DELL GLEN VALE DIMBLE DUMBLE HOLLOW VALLEY
DINGMAN BUMPER
DINGO WARRAGAL WARRIGAL
DINGUS GADGET DOOHICKEY
DINGY DUN DARK BLACK DIRTY DUSKY GRIMY OURIE SMOKY DINGHY FUSCOUS SUBFUSC SMIRCHED
DINING CENATION
(— HALL) MESS
(PREF.) DEIPNO
DINING ROOM TRICLINIUM
DINKA JANGHEY
DINNER DINE HALL KALE MEAL MEAT NOON BEANO FEAST DINING REPAST BANQUET PUCHERO FUNCTION
(— AT HOME) EATIN
(CEREMONIAL —) SEDER
(PERTAINING TO —) PRANDIAL
(PREF.) DEIPNO
DINOSAUR DIAPSID SAURIAN DUCKBILL NODOSAUR SAUROPOD TROODONT ORNITHISCHIAN
DINT BEAT BLOW DENT DUNT NICK CLOUR DELVE DINGE FORCE NOTCH ONSET POWER PRESS SHOCK ATTACK CHANCE EFFORT STRIKE STROKE IMPRINT EFFICACY STRIKING
DIOCESAN EPISCOPAL
DIOCESE SEE EPARCHY DISTRICT BISHOPRIC
DIODE LED KENOTRON
(— THAT EMITS LIGHT) LED
(KIND OF —) ZENER
(LIGHT-EMITTING —) LED
(TYPE OF —) ZENER
DIOLEFIN DIENE ALLENE HEXADIENE
DIOMEDES (FATHER OF —) MARS TYDEUS
(MOTHER OF —) CYRENE DEIPYLE
(WIFE OF —) AEGIALE
DION (DAUGHTER OF —) EUPHRASIA
(FATHER OF —) HIPPARINUS
(SISTER OF —) ARISTOMACHE
(SLAYER OF —) CALLIPPUS
(TEACHER OF —) PLATO
(WIFE OF —) ARETE
DIONYSUS BACCHUS BROMIOS BROMIUS LENAEUS LIKNITES
DIONYZA (HUSBAND OF —) CLEON
DIOPSIDE VIOLAN ALALITE PYROXENE
DIORITE CORSITE DIABASE ORNOITE APPINITE TONALITE
DIOSCURI ALCIS ANACES ANAKES CASTORES
DIOXIDE SILICA BINOXIDE
DIOXIN TCDD AGENTORANGE
DIP DAP DIB DOP SOP BAIL DROP DUCK DUNK LADE LAVE SINK SOAK BATHE DELVE LADLE LOWER MERSE PITCH SCOOP SLOPE SOUSE SWOOP TAINT CANDLE HOLLOW PLUNGE BAPTIZE DECLINE IMMERGE IMMERSE INCLINE MOISTEN DIPSTICK SUBMERGE GUACAMOLE
(— AND THROW) BAIL BALE
(— IN DANCING) CORTE
(— IN HOT WATER) PLOT
(— INTO) SAMPLE
(— OUT) KEACH
DIPENTENE CINENE CAJUPUTENE
DIPHOSPHATE UDP
DIPHTHONG BIVOCAL
DIPHTHONGIZED BROKEN
DIPLOIDIZE SPERMATIZE
DIPLOMA SANAD DEGREE SUNNUD CHARTER CODICIL PARCHMENT SHEEPSKIN
DIPLOMACY TACT POLICE TREATY
(KIND OF —) GUNBOAT SHUTTLE
DIPLOMAT DEAN ENVOY CONSUL ATTACHE MINISTER
(ISRAELI —) EBAN
DIPLOMATIC SUAVE FECIAL FETIAL
DIPLOPIA POLYOBA AMBIOPIA
DIPNOAN DIPNOID MUDFISH
DIPODY METER METRE DIIAMB SYZYGY
DIPPER BAIL GAWN PIET PLOW GOURD HANDY LADLE SCOOP

SPOON BUCKET DUNKER PIGGIN PLOUGH TUNKER DUNKARD PICKLER CALABASH
(ASTRONOMICAL —) WAGON WAGGON
DIPPING DOOK MERSION
(SUFF.) CLINIC CLINOUS
DIPSOMANIA ENOMANIA POTOMANIA
DIPTERAN SYRPHID
DIPTEROCARP GURJUN
DIPTERON DIPTER
DIPTEROUS BIALATE
DIRDUM BLOW BLAME DURDUM OUTCRY REBUKE TUMULT UPROAR SCOLDING
DIRE DERN EVIL FELL AWFUL FATAL DEADLY DISMAL DREARY FUNEST TRAGIC WOEFUL DIREFUL DOLEFUL DRASTIC FEARFUL DREADFUL FUNESTAL HORRIBLE TERRIBLE ULTIMATE
DIRECT AIM BID CON KEN SAY SET WIS AGYE AIRT BAIN BEAM BEND BOSS CAST DEAD EDIT EVEN FLAT FULL GAIN HEAD HELM HOLD LEAD NEAR NIGH OPEN REIN SEND SOON SWAY TELL TURN WAFT WEND WILL WISE AIRTH APPLY AREAD AREED BLANK BOUND BURLY COACH DRESS ETTLE FLUSH FRAME FRANK GUIDA GUIDE HIGHT INDEX LEVEL ORDER PLUMP POINT REFER RIGHT SPEED STEER TEACH TRAIN UTTER WEISE WRITE ADVERT ARRECT CUSTOS DEVOTE ENJOIN ENSIGN FASTEN GOVERN GRAITH HANDLE HOMELY HONEST IMPART INDITE INFORM INTEND LINEAL MANAGE MASTER MOSTRA REFORM SQUARE STEADY STRECK TEMPER WITTER ADDRESS APPOINT COMMAND CONDUCT CONTROL CONVERT DEICTIC DESTINE EXECUTE EXPRESS FRONTAL GENERAL INSTANT MARSHAL OFFICER PRESIDE SPADISH ABSOLUTE ADMONISH CONVERSE DEDICATE DIRECTOR HOMESPUN IMMEDIAL INSTRUCT INTIMATE MANUDUCE MANUDUCT MINISTER OUTRIGHT REGULATE STRAIGHT
(— AGAINST) LAUNCH
(— ATTENTION) ATTEND
(— BLOW) MARK
(— DOGS) BLOW
(— FALL OF TREE) GUN
(— HELMSMAN) CON CONN
(— HORSE) HUP
(— ITSELF) TENT
(— ONE'S COURSE) HIT
(— PROCEEDINGS) PRESIDE
(— SECRETLY) STEAL
(— SIDEWAYS) SKLENT
(— TO GO) ADDRESS
(— UPWARD) MOUNT
DIRECTED FAST COMPULSORY
(— BACKWARD) RETROGRADE
(— FORWARD) ANTRORSE
(— TOWARD GOAL) HORMIC
(— UPWARD) ERECT
DIRECTING AIM LEADING PRINCIPAL
DIRECTION (ALSO SEE MUSICAL DIRECTION) AIM RUN WAY AIRT BENT CARE DUCT EAST EGIS GATE HAND LEFT PART ROAD RULE WEST WORD YARD AEGIS ANGLE COAST DRIFT EAVER KIBLA NORTH ORDER PARTY POINT QIBLA RANGE ROUTE SENSE SOUTH TENOR TREND ASPECT COURSE DESIGN ADDRESS BEARING BIDDING CHANNEL COMMAND CONDUCT CONTROL COUNSEL DICTATE HEADING HELMAGE MANDATE PRECEPT STRETCH BEARINGS CALENDAR DELEATUR DIAGONAL GUIDANCE STEERAGE STEERING TENDENCY ORDINANCE ORIENTATION PRESCRIPTION
(— IN WOOD) GRAIN
(— OF CURRENT) AXIS
(— OF FLOW) SET
(— OF ROCK CLEAVAGE) GRAIN
(— OF WIND) EYE CORNER
(— OUTWARD) BEAM
(—S FOR DELIVERY) ADDRESS
(DANCE —) CALL
(GENERAL —) RUN
(HORIZONTAL —) COURSE AZIMUTH
(MUSICAL —) SEGUE
(NEW —) TURN
(OBLIQUE —) SKEW
(OPPOSITE —) EYE COUNTER
(SINGING —) GIMEL GYMEL
(PREF.) PHORO
(SUFF.) ERLY ERN
(— TO) WARD
DIRECTIVE MEMO GUIDE DICTATE CIRCULAR
DIRECTLY DUE BANG BOLT DEAD FLAT GAIN JUST MEAN PLAT PLUM SLAP SOON PLAIN PLUMB PLUNK POINT ROUND SHEER SMACK SOUSE SPANG STANG ARIGHT CLEVER SIMPLY SQUARE RIGHTLY SHEERLY OUTRIGHT PROMPTLY SLAPDASH STRAIGHT PRESENTLY
DIRECTNESS CLARITY IMMEDIACY
DIRECTOR BOSS HEAD COACH GUIDE PILOT STAFF ARCHON AUTEUR BISHOP LEADER MASTER RECTOR WARDEN CURATOR DESKMAN MANAGER PREFECT STARETS STERNER TRAINER ACCENTOR DISPOSER GOVERNOR PRAEFECT PRODUCER TETRARCH
(BALLET —) REGISSEUR
(FILM —) AUTEUR
DIRECTORY PIE BOOK
DIRGE KEEN SONG ELEGY KINAH LINOS LINUS QINAH TANGI HEARSE LAMENT MONODY THRENE EPICEDE REQUIEM CORONACH THRENODY ULLAGONE
(PREF.) THREN(O)
DIRIGIBLE BLIMP AIRSHIP
DIRK SNEE SKEAN SWORD DAGGER SKHIAN SKIVER WHINGER WHINIARD
DIRT FEN MUD PAY CRUD DUST GORE GUCK MOOL MUCK NAST SOIL SUMP CROCK EARTH FILTH GRIME GROUT SEUCH SEUGH TRASH FULYIE FULZIE GRAVEL GROUND GRUNGE REFUSE MULLOCK SLOTTER MUCKMENT
(— ON PRINTING TYPE) PICK
DIRT-COLORED SORDID
DIRTINESS GRIME JAKES
DIRTY LOW RAY BASE CLAT DIRT FOUL MOIL MUSS SOIL WORY BAWDY BLACK CABBY DINGY FOGGY GRIMY GUSTY HORRY MUDDY NASTY POUSY SOILY SULLY BEMIRE CLARTY CLATTY DEFILE DIRTEN FILTHY FULYIE FULZIE GREASY GRUBBY GRUNGY IMPURE MUSSED POUCEY REECHY SCRIMY SLASHY SLURRY SMIRCH SMUTTY SOILED SORDID STORMY BEGRIME BROOKED BROOKIE BRUCKLE CLOUDED GRUFTED IMBROIN MUDDIED PIGGISH RAUNCHY ROYNOUS SCRUFFY SLOTTER SMUTCHY SQUALID SULLIED TARNISH UNCLEAN AMURCOUS SLOBBERY SLOTTERY SOAPLESS
DIS BELITTLE
DISABLE OUT HOCK LAME MAIM BREAK CHINK CROCK GRUEL UNFIT WRECK BRUISE DISMAY UNABLE WEAKEN CRIPPLE
(— CANNON) SPIKE
(— HORSE) NOBBLE
(— TANK) BELLY
DISABLED LAME INVALID
DISABLING BUM
DISACCHARIDE BIOSE LACTOSE MALTOSE SUCROSE
DISACCUSTOM DISUSE
DISACKNOWLEDGE DISCLAIM
DISADVANTAGE HURT MISS RISK LURCH WORRY DAMAGE DENIAL INJURY STRIKE DICKENS PENALTY UNSELTH UNSPEED DISAVAIL DISFAVOR DRAWBACK HANDICAP
DISADVANTAGEOUS HURTFUL INCONVENIENT
DISAFFECT DEBAUCH ALIENATE ESTRANGE
DISAFFECTED FALSE UNTRUE DISEASED DISLOYAL FORSWORN PERJURED RECREANT
DISAFFECTION DECEIT MUTINY DISEASE DISGUST DISLIKE DISORDER HOSTILITY
DISAFFIRM DENY ANNUL REVERSE DISCLAIM
DISAGREE VARY ARGUE CLASH DIFFER DISCEPT DISCORD DISSENT QUARREL CONFLICT
DISAGREEABLE BAD ILL ACID EVIL FOUL PERT SOUR UGLY VILE AWFUL CROSS HARSH NASTY STIFF GREASY PUTRID ROTTEN SNUFFY STICKY UNEASY UNGAIN BEASTLY CHRONIC COMICAL GHASTLY HATEFUL INGRATE IRKSOME NAUGHTY UNLUSTY CHISELLY KINDLESS TERRIBLE UNGENIAL UNLIKELY UNLOVELY UNSAVORY
DISAGREEABLENESS ILLNESS ASPERITY
DISAGREEABLY HARSHLY
DISAGREEING ODD DISSENTIVE
DISAGREEMENT BREE CLASH CROSS FIGHT BREACH FRATCH DISCORD DISGUST DISPUTE DISSENT FISSURE MISLIKE QUARREL WRANGLE ARGUMENT CLASHING DISTANCY DIVISION FRICTION SQUABBLE VARIANCE MISUNDERSTANDING
(IN —) APART
DISALLOW FORBID REJECT CENSURE DISCLAIM DISPROVE PROHIBIT
DISAPPEAR DIE FLY DROP FADE FALL FLEE LIFT PASS SINK WEND WHOP BREAK CLEAR FAINT LAPSE SLIDE SLOPE SNUFF REMOVE RETIRE VANISH EVANISH IMMERGE DISSOLVE EVANESCE
(— GRADUALLY) ELY FADE DRAIN EVANESCE
(— SUDDENLY) COOK DUCK BURST MIZZLE
(— UNEXPECTEDLY) LEVANT
DISAPPEARANCE ECLIPSE FADEAWAY
DISAPPOINT BALK BILK FAIL FALL MOCK SOUR UNDO CHEAT SNAPE BAFFLE DEFEAT DELUDE OUTWIT THWART BEGUILE DECEIVE DESTROY FALSIFY NULLIFY DISPOINT
DISAPPOINTED OUTED BUMMED THROWN SOREHEAD
DISAPPOINTING FIERCE FALLACIOUS
DISAPPOINTMENT RUE BALK DRAG SUCK BAULK LURCH DENIAL DOWNER LETDOWN COMEDOWN
DISAPPROBATION ODIUM DISLIKE
DISAPPROVAL BAN BOOH HISS VETO CATCALL CENSURE DISFAVOR DISGRACE
(EXPRESSION OF —) TUT TUTTUT
(SHOW —) HISS
DISAPPROVE NIX GROAN REJECT RESENT CENSURE CONDEMN DISLIKE MISTAKE PROTEST DISALLOW DISPROVE HARRUMPH
DISAPPROVED DISTASTED
DISAPPROVER WOWSER
DISARM SUBDUE UNSTEEL
DISARRANGE MESS MUSS DEFORM GARBLE RUFFLE TIFFLE UNTIDY UNTUNE CLUTTER CONFUSE DERANGE DISTURB RUMMAGE SLATTER TROUBLE COCKBILL DISHEVEL DISORDER UNSETTLE
(— TYPE) SQUABBLE
DISARRANGEMENT DISARRAY
DISARRAY MESS TASH RIFLE STRIP CADDLE DISRAY FUFFLE HUDDLE DESPOIL UNDIGHT DISHEVEL DISORDER
DISARRAYED UNKEMPT
DISASSEMBLE UNDO STRIP DEMOUNT DISMOUNT
(— CASK) SHAKE
DISASSEMBLY TAKEDOWN TEARDOWN
DISASSOCIATE SEVER SEPARATE
DISASTER ILL WOE BALE BLOW EVIL FATE RUIN GRIEF MISHAP

STROKE REVERSE ACCIDENT CALAMITY CASUALTY EXIGENCY FATALITY
(ONE WHO PREDICTS —) CASSANDRA
DISASTROUS BAD ILL FATAL WEARY SINISTER
DISAVOW DENY DEVOW ABJURE DISOWN RECANT REFUSE DECLINE RETRACT ABNEGATE DISCLAIM DISVOUCH RENOUNCE
DISAVOWAL DENIAL
DISBAND BREAK REDUCE REFORM ADJOURN CASHIER DISMISS RELEASE SCATTER DISSOLVE
DISBAR EXCLUDE
DISBELIEF ATHEISM SCRUPLE ACOSMISM
(EXPRESSION OF —) TUT TUTTUT
DISBELIEVE DOUBT REJECT SUSPECT DISCOUNT DISCREDIT
DISBELIEVER ATHEIST HERETIC INFIDEL
DISBURDEN RID EASE CLEAR UNLOAD DELIVER DISLOAD RELIEVE
(— BY CONFESSION) SHRIVE
DISBURSE SPEND DEFRAY EXPEND OUTLAY DEBURSE
DISC (ALSO SEE DISK) DIAL DISK GONG BLANK MEDAL PATEN PLATE QUOIT COLTER RECORD RONDEL SQUAIL COULTER DISCOID FRISBEE PLATTER ROUNDEL TROCHUS
(— FOR PRESSING HERRINGS) DAUNT
(— ON BIT) ROWEL
(— ON SPINDLE) WHORL
(— ON TAMBOURINE) JINGLE
(— ON TARGET) GONG FRISBEE ROUNDEL
(CILIATED —) VELUM
(COPPER —) ROSETTE
(FLESHY —) SARCOMA
(FLOPPY —) DISKETTE
(HOCKEY —) PUCK
(JELLYFISH —) UMBRELLA
(KIND OF —) LASER SECCHI
(POLISHING —) LAP
(TELEVISION —) SCANNER
DISCANT HOCKET
DISCARD CAST DECK DEFY JILT JUNK MOLT OMIT OUST SHED CHUCK DITCH FLING SCRAP SHUCK SLUFF THROW TRASH CHANGE DECARD DISUSE DIVEST EXCUSS REJECT SLOUGH ABANDON CASHIER DISMISS EXPUNGE FORSAKE ABDICATE JETTISON
(— IN BRIDGE) ECHO
DISCARDED DORMANT OFFCAST
DISCARDING DISPOSAL
DISCERN KEN SEE SPY WIT DEEM ESPY KNOW READ SCAN JUDGE SIGHT BEHOLD DESCRY DETECT DEVISE NOTICE PIERCE SCERNE DIGNOSCE DISCOVER PERCEIVE
(— BY SMELL) SCENT
DISCERNIBLE EVIDENT VISIBLE APPARENT MANIFEST OBSERVABLE
DISCERNING SAGE WISE NASUTE SHREWD SUBTLE SAPIENT SAGACIOUS PERCEPTIVE PERCIPIENT PENETRATING
DISCERNMENT EYE DOOM GOUT TACT FLAIR SENSE SKILL TASTE ACUMEN INSIGHT ELECTION JUDGMENT SAGACITY SAPIENCE PERCEPTION PENETRATION
DISCHARGE AX DO AXE CAN GUN LET RUN BOLT BOOT CASS DUMP EMIT FIRE FLOW FLUX FREE GIVE KICK PASS POUR QUIT RIFF SACK SEND SHOT VENT VOID BLAST BLEED BRUSH CLEAR DRAIN EGEST EJECT EMPTY EXPEL EXUDE FRUSH GLEET GRASS ICHOR ISSUE LOOSE OZENA PURGE RHEUM SHOOT SPEED START VOMIT WHIFF YIELD ACQUIT ASSOIL BOUNCE DEFRAY EFFECT EXCERN EXEMPT EXHALE FEEDER LOCHIA OZAENA TICKET UNLADE UNLOAD ABSOLVE CASHIER DEBOUCH DEFEASE DEHISCE DELIVER DERAIGN DISBAND DISMISS EXCRETE EXHAUST MISSION PAYMENT PERFORM QUIETUS RELEASE RELIEVE SATISFY SKITTER SOLUTIO CATAPULT COMPOUND DEFECATE DESPATCH DISGORGE DISPATCH DISPLACE DISPLODE EMISSION EVACUATE MITTIMUS OUTSHOOT PERSOLVE SEPARATE SOLUTION STREAMER
(— ARROW) TWANG
(— AT RANDOM) ROVE
(— BULLET) DRIVE
(— CARGO) STRIKE
(— DEBT) MEET CLEAR ACQUIT LOOSING
(— DUTY) SERVE
(— FROM HORSE'S FOOT) FRUSH
(— FROM NOSE) RHEUM OZAENA
(— FROM RESERVOIR) HUSHING
(— FROM WOUND) SANIES
(— MATTER) WEEP
(— OF DEBT) SETOFF
(— OF GAS) FEEDER
(— OF STREAM) FALL SPOUT
(— SUDDENLY) HIKE
(BLOODY —) SHOW SANIES
(CANNON —) TIRE CANNON
(CONCENTRATED —) BARRAGE
(CONTINUOUS — OF FIREARMS) FUSILLADE
(DISHONORABLE —) BOBTAIL
(ELECTRIC —) ARC SPARK LEADER EFFLUVE STREAMER LIGHTNING
(ELECTRIC —S) STATIC
(HEAVY —) STORM
(MENSTRUAL —) PERIOD
(SIMULTANEOUS —) SALVO BROADSIDE FUSILLADE
(SUFF.) CENOSIS RRHAGIA RRHEA RRHOEA
DISCHARGED SPED SATISFIED
DISCHARGER EXCITATOR
DISCHARGING LABILE
DISCIPLE SON JOHN MARK CHELA JUDAS MURID PETER PUPIL TEACH TRAIN ANANDA DISPLE DORCAS HEARER PUNISH APOSTLE AUDITOR MATTHEW OVIDIAN SCHOLAR SECTARY SRAVAKA STUDENT ADHERENT FOLLOWER GALENIST SECTATOR
DISCIPLINARIAN RAMROD TRAINER MARTINET
DISCIPLINARY STRICT
DISCIPLINE THEW WHIP BREAK DRILL INURE TEACH TRAIN TUTOR CHURCH ETHICS FERULA FERULE GOVERN INFORM PUNISH SEASON TAIRGE VIRTUE CHASTEN CORRECT CULTURE EDUCATE FURNACE NURTURE SCOURGE DISCIPLE DOCTRINE EXERCISE INSTRUCT LEARNING MATHESIS PEDAGOGY REGULATE RESTRAIN TEACHING TRAINING TUTORING PHILOSOPHY CASTIGATION
(CHINESE —) TAICHICHUAN
(MENTAL —) YOGA
(RELIGIOUS —) CHURCH PENANCE SADHANA
DISCIPLINED INURED STEADY
DISCLAIM DENY DEVOW WAIVE ABJURE DISOWN REFUSE DISAVOW ABDICATE ABNEGATE DISALLOW RENOUNCE
DISCLOSE OPE RIP BARE BLOW CALL KNOW OPEN TELL BREAK COUGH UNRIP UNWRY UTTER BETRAY BEWRAY DESCRY DIVINE EVOLVE EXPOSE IMPART REVEAL SHRIVE UNBURY UNCASE UNHASP UNHIDE UNLOCK UNROLL UNSEAL UNSHUT UNVEIL UNWRAP CONFESS DEVELOP DISCUSS DISPLAY DIVULGE EXHIBIT EXPLAIN PROPALE UNCLOSE UNCOVER DISCOVER INDICATE MANIFEST UNBUNDLE UNKENNEL UNSECRET UNTHATCH
(— PARTIALLY) ADUMBRATE
DISCLOSED OUT
DISCLOSURE REVEAL SHRIFT COLORING DESCRIAL DISCLOSE OVERTURE APOCALYPSE
DISCOLOR FOX BURN FADE SPOT BLACK SMOKE STAIN TINGE SMIRCH STREAK DISTAIN TARNISH BESMIRCH
DISCOLORATION CORN BLEED SCALD SPECK STAIN TINGE FOXING LIVEDO MILDEW ARGYRIA BURNING MELASMA BRONZING BROWNING CHLOASMA CYANOSIS DYSCHROA SCALDING
(— IN FISH) PINKEYE
(— OF FRUIT) SUNBURN
(— OF TURKEYS) BLUEBACK
(— ON CHOCOLATE) BLOOM
(— ON CURED FISH) RUST
(SMALL —) FRECKLE
(SUFF.) CHROIA
DISCOLORED HAW FOUL DINGY FOXED RUSTY STAINED SCORCHED USTULATE
(— BY DECAY) DOTY FOXED
DISCOMFIT MATE ROIT ABASH ABAVE AFLEY SHEND SHENT UPSET WORST BAFFLE DEFEAT FEAGUE SQUASH CONFUSE CONQUER DISTURB
DISCOMFITURE LURCH
DISCOMFORT HELL PAIN UNEASE MALAISE PURGATORY
(FEELING OF —) BLAHS
DISCOMPOSE FEEZE PERTURB
DISCONCERT BASH BOWL FAZE FUSS HACK ABASH BLANK DAUNT FEEZE PHASE UPSET WORRY BAFFLE BLENCH MISPUT PUZZLE RATTLE SQUASH CONFUSE DISTURB FLUMMOX NONPLUS PERTURB SQUELCH BROWBEAT DISORDER
DISCONCERTED BLANK ASHAMED RATTLED CONFUSED
DISCONCERTING BAFFLING
DISCONNECT UNDO SEVER DIVIDE UNDOCK UNYOKE DISJOIN DISSOLVE DISUNITE SEPARATE UNCOUPLE
DISCONNECTED LOOSE ABRUPT BROKEN CHOPPY CURSORY DECOUSU SNATCHY RAMBLING STACCATO ASYNARTETE
DISCONSOLATE SAD GLOOMY WOEFUL DOLEFUL FORLORN UNCOUTH DEJECTED DESOLATE DOWNCAST HOPELESS
DISCONTENT ENVY ENNUI DISQUIET SOURNESS
DISCONTENTED DUMPY RESTLESS MALCONTENT
DISCONTINUANCE BREAK LAPSE DEMISE CUTBACK DISUNION SHUTDOWN CESSATION
DISCONTINUE END DROP HALT QUIT STOP BREAK CEASE CLOSE LETUP DESIST DISUSE SUNDER DISRUPT SUSPEND INTERMIT SURCEASE
DISCONTINUITY JAR BREAK COMMA BREACH HIATUS
DISCONTINUOUS BROKEN DISJUNCT SALTATORY
DISCORD DIN JAR BROIL JANGLE SCHISM STRIFE DISLIKE FACTION FISSURE JARRING MISTONE CONFLICT DISTANCE DIVISION FRACTION MISCHIEF UNSAUGHT VARIANCE CACOPHONY
DISCORDANT AJAR RUDE CRONK HARSH FROWZY HOARSE JANGLY HIDEOUS JARRING SQUAWKY ABSONANT CONTRARY JANGLING SCORDATO
DISCOTHEQUE AGOGO DISCO
DISCOUNT AGIO BATTA SHAVE REBATE REDUCE DISCOMPT
DISCOURAGE CARP DAMP CHILL DAUNT DETER FROST DAMPEN DEJECT DISMAY FREEZE STIFLE DEPRESS FLATTEN INHIBIT DISPIRIT DISSUADE
DISCOURAGEMENT COLD DAMP CHILL DAUNT REBUFF LETDOWN PUTBACK
DISCOURAGING CHILL DREARY
DISCOURSE SAW CARP RANT READ TALE TALK TELL WORD DROOL FABLE ORATE PAPER SPEAK SPELL THEME TRACT TREAT COMMON DILATE EULOGY HOMILY PARLEY PREACH REASON SCREED SERMON THESIS TONGUE TREATY

ACCOUNT ADDRESS COMMENT CONTEXT DECLAIM DELIVER DESCANT DIETARY DISCANT DISCUSS DISSERT ENTREAT EXPOUND GRAMMAR LECTURE NARRATE ORATION PARABLE PRATING PRELECT PURPOSE RECITAL TALKING ARGUMENT COLLOQUY CONVERSE EXERCISE LOCUTION LOQUENCE PARLANCE SPEAKING SPELLING TRACTATE TREATISE PHILIPPIC PROLUSION
(— OF LITTLE VALUE) STUFF
(— POLICY) GLASNOST
(LAUDATORY —) PANEGYRIC
(LONG —) SCREED
(OBSCENE —) SMUT
(PROLONGED —) DIATRIBE
(RAMBLING —) RHAPSODY RIGMAROLE
(SERIOUS —) HOMILY
(SIMPLE —) PAP
(UNIMAGINATIVE —) PROSE
(PL.) EXOTERICS
(PREF.) LOG(O)
(SUFF.) LOG(ER)(IA)(IAN)(IC)(ICAL)(IST)(UE)(Y)

DISCOURTEOUS RUDE SCURVY UNCIVIL UNHENDE CAVALIER IMPOLITE UNGENTLE
DISCOURTESY CUT SLIGHT
DISCOVER RIP SEE SPY WIT ESPY FEEL FIND PICK TWIG CATCH LEARN SPELL DEFINE DESCRY DETECT DIVINE EXPOSE IMPART INVENT LOCATE OVERGO REVEAL STRIKE UNHIDE CONFESS DESCURE DEVELOP DISCERN DISCURE DISPLAY DIVULGE EXHIBIT EXPLORE UNCOVER UNEARTH CONTRIVE DECIPHER DESCRIBE DISCUREN MANIFEST UNKENNEL
DISCOVERABLE VISIBLE
DISCOVERER SPY SCOUT COLUMBUS EXPLORER INVENTOR
DISCOVERY FIND TROVE DESCRY ESPIAL STRIKE DESCRIAL
DISCREDIT FOUL SLUT DECRY DOUBT REFEL DEFACE DEFECT ASPERSE BLEMISH DESTROY IMPEACH SCANDAL SUSPECT BELITTLE DISGRACE DISHONOR DISTRUST REPROACH UNCREDIT
(SUFF.) ARD ART
DISCREDITABLE BLACK UNHONEST
DISCREET SAGE WARY WISE CIVIL WITTY HUSHED POLITE SILENT CAREFUL GUARDED POLITIC PRUDENT CAUTIOUS RESERVED RETICENT
DISCREETLY SENSIBLY
DISCREPANCY VARIANCE
DISCREPANT VARIANT CONTRARY DISSONANT
DISCRETE ETERNAL DISTINCT
DISCRETION TACT OPTION WISDOM CONDUCT RETENUE COURTESY JUDGMENT PRUDENCE
DISCRETIONARY ARBITRARY
DISCRIMINATE PART SEVER SECERN DISCERN PERCEIVE SEPARATE
DISCRIMINATED DISTINCT
DISCRIMINATING GOOD NICE ACUTE SHARP ASTUTE CHOICE NASUTE SELECT CHOOSEY CRITICAL EXPLICIT
DISCRIMINATINGLY CHOICE FINELY
DISCRIMINATION EYE BIAS DOOM TACT TASTE ACUMEN AGEISM CHOICE SEXISM FINESSE RESPECT DELICACY SAPIENCE
(— AGAINST ANIMALS) SPECIESISM
(SYMBOL OF —) HANSA
DISCRIMINATIVE RESPECTIVE
DISCURSIVE ROVING CURSORY RAMBLING DESULTORY
DISCURSIVELY WIDE
DISCUS DISC DISK QUOIT DISKOS DISCOID
DISCUSS AIR MOOT RUNE TALK ARGUE BANDY COVER DANDY TRACT TREAT COMMON CONFER DEBATE DICKER EMPARL EXCUSS IMPARL PARLEY AGITATE BESPEAK CANVASS COMMENT CONSULT DESCANT DISCANT DISCEPT DISCUTE DISPUTE DISSERT EXAMINE NARRATE TRAVERSE CONJOBBLE
(— AT LENGTH) BAT
(— CASUALLY) MENTION
(— EXCITEDLY) AGITATE
(— LIGHTLY) BANDY
(— QUICKLY) SKIP
(— SECRETLY) ROUN
(— TERMS) CHAFFER
(— THOROUGHLY) EXHAUST
(— TO EXCESS) VEX
DISCUSSION MOOT DEBAT FORUM COMMON CONFAB DEBATE HASSEL HOMILY HUDDLE PARLEY TREATY BARGAIN CANVASS COMMENT COUNSEL DISCUSS DISPUTE MOOTING PALAVER PRIBBLE ARGUMENT CAUSERIE CHINFEST COLLOQUY DIATRIBE ENTREATY EXCURSUS QUESTION
(CONTROVERSIAL —) DISPUTE
(DIDACTIC —) HARANGUE
(HEATED —) FLAK
DISDAIN COY TUT DAIN DEFY PRIDE SCORN SDAIN SPURN SDEIGN SLIGHT CONTEMN DESPISE CONTEMPT
DISDAINFUL COY DIGNE PROUD SAUCY TOSSY SCORNY SLIGHT SNIFFY SNUFFY DAINFUL HAUGHTY ARROGANT DEIGNOUS PROUDFUL SCORNFUL SNIFFISH TOPLOFTY
DISDAINFULLY SMALL SNIFFILY
DISEASE BUG FLU MAL ROT AIDS BATS COTH CRUD EVIL FLAW GOUT GRIP KURU NOMA PEST PHOS SORE AGROM BATTS BEJEL BENDS CAUSE COTHE CROUP DECAY DOLOR FEVER GRIEF LUPUS PHOSS PINTA PINTO SCALL SHAKE SPRUE SURRA AINHUM ANGINA CANCER CARATE CORYZA COURAP DENGUE GRAVEL GRIPPE HERPES MALADY MORBUS PALMUS PIEDRA POPEYE SCURVY SICKEN SURRAH THRUSH UROSIS ZOOSIS AILMENT CHOLERA COXALGY DECLINE ENDEMIC ENTASIA LANGUOR LEPROSY MALEASE MISLIKE MYCOSIS MYIASIS PATHEMA RAPHANY SCOURGE SEQUELA SERPIGO SIBBENS SORANCE SYCOSIS TETANUS XERASIA ZYMOTIC ADENOSIS ALASTRIM ATHEROMA BERIBERI COXALGIA CRIPPLER CYNANCHE DIAMONDS ENZOOTIC JAUNDICE LEUKEMIA PALUDISM PANDEMIC PELLAGRA RAPHANIA SCABBADO SHINGLES SICKNESS SMALLPOX SORRANCE STAGGERS SYPHILIS UNHEALTH XANTHOMA ZOONOSIS
(— OF ANIMALS) SURRA
(— OF ANIMALS, GENERAL) ROT CLAP CORE FIRE GOUT HUSK LICK WEED APTHA CLEFT CLING CLOSH COTHE CROOK DRUSE FARCY FLAPS NENTA NGANA PAINS SPEED SWEAT TAINT APHTHA AVIVES BROSOT CANKER CARNEY CREEPS FARCIN GARGET GRAPES LAMPAS NAGANA ROUGET SPAVIN SURRAH WOBBLE ANTHRAX BIGHEAD CALCINO CALORIS CARCEAG DOURING EARWORM EQUINIA FASHION FISTULA FOUNDER FROUNCE KETOSIS LAMPERS MURRAIN MURRINA QUITTER QUITTOR SLOBBER SOLDIER TAKOSIS BULLNOSE CRATCHES CRIPPLES FERNSICK FOOTHALT HORSEPOX HYSTERIA MAWBOUND SLOBBERS SNUFFLES THWARTER VACCINIA EPIZOOTIC
(— OF APPLES) CORK BLOTCH
(— OF BANANAS) SIGATOKA SQUIRTER
(— OF BARLEY) STRIPE
(— OF BEES) SACBROOD
(— OF BEETS) HEARTROT
(— OF BIRDS) GOUT
(— OF BLUEBERRY) BLUESTEM
(— OF CABBAGE) ANBURY CLUBROOT
(— OF CATERPILLARS) WILT FLACHERY
(— OF CATS) PANLEUCOPENIA
(— OF CATTLE) PUCK TURN BARBS BLAIN CLOSH FARCY HOOVE HOOZE SLOWS COWPOX GARGET GRAPES HAMMER HEAVES ANTHRAX BLACKLEG BLOATING
(— OF CEREALS) BRAND ERGOT
(— OF CHICKEN) PIP CORYZA
(— OF CHILDREN) PROGERIA
(— OF COTTON) HYBOSIS CYRTOSIS STENOSIS
(— OF DUCKLING) KEEL
(— OF EYES) WALL GLAUCOMA SYNECHIA TRACHOMA
(— OF FIGS) SMUT
(— OF FINGERNAILS) FLAW
(— OF FLAX) BROWNING
(— OF FOWLS) PIP CRAY ROUP GAPES SOREHEAD
(— OF GRAIN) ILIAU ICTERUS
(— OF GRAPES) COLEUR ERINOSE ROUGEAU ROUGEOT SHELLING
(— OF HAWKS) RYE CRAY CROAK CROAKS FROUNCE FILANDER
(— OF HORSES) HAW CLAP CURB MOSE MULE WEED FARCY LEUMA VIVES APHTHA SCALMA THRUSH BARBELS DOURINE QUITTOR SARCOID AZOTURIA GLANDERS HORSEPOX SCRATCHES STRANGLES
(— OF INSECTS) POLYHEDROSIS
(— OF LAMB) SWAYBACK
(— OF LETTUCE) STUNT
(— OF NARCISSUS) SMOLDER SMOULDER
(— OF ONION) SMUDGE
(— OF ORANGE) LEPROSIS
(— OF PALMS) KOLEROGA
(— OF PLANTS) SCAB NECROSIS
(— OF PLANTS, GENERAL) POX ROT BUNT CORK DROP FIRE GOUT KNOT PULP SMUT BLAST DWARF EDEMA ERGOT FLECK FLOCK GRUBS SCALD SCALE SCURF SEREH SPIKE STUNT TUKRA TWIST AUCUBA BLIGHT BLOTCH BLUING BRAUNE CALICO CANKER COLEUR GIRDLE OEDEMA OIDIUM PETECA SMUDGE STREAK STRIPE VIROSE BLISTER BLUEING BRINDLE CRINKLE DIEBACK ERINOSE EYESPOT FROGEYE HYBOSIS MEASLES PRURIGO ROSETTE SHATTER SMOLDER STIPPEN TIPBURN TOMOSIS VIRUELA WALLOON BLUESTEM BREAKING BROWNING BUCKSKIN CLUBROOT CYRTOSIS DARTROSE EXANTHEM FLYSPECK GUMMOSIS KOLEROGA LEPROSIS MELANOSE MELAXUMA POLEBURN PSOROSIS RAPHANIA SMOULDER STENOSIS VIROSITY WHIPTAIL WILDFIRE CHLOROSIS
(— OF POTATO) CURL HAYWIRE
(— OF RABBITS) SNUFFLES
(— OF RICE) BLAST SPECK
(— OF RODENTS) TULAREMIA
(— OF SHEEP) CAW COE GID MAD RAY ROT BANE BELT CORE HALT SHAB WIND BLAST BLOOD BRAXY GILLAR OVINIA PINING STURDY ANTHRAX BRADSOT DAISING RUBBERS SCRAPIE THWARTER WILDFIRE BREAKSHARE
(— OF SILKWORM) UJI CALCINO GATTINE PEBRINE FLACHERY
(— OF SUGARCANE) ILIAU SEREH EYESPOT
(— OF SWINE) GARGET
(— OF TOBACCO) ETCH CALICO BRINDLE FROGEYE
(— OF TOMATO) FERNLEAF GRAYWALL
(— OF TONGUE) AGROM
(— OF TREES) KNOT CANKER
(— OF TULIPS) SHANKING
(— OF UNKNOWN ORIGIN) AINHUM ACRODYNIA
(AGENT OF PLANT —) VIROID
(CAISSON —) CHOKES
(FATAL — OF NERVOUS SYSTEM) KURU
(FOOT-AND-MOUTH —) AFTOSA
(FUNGUS —) PECK MYCOSIS
(KIDNEY —) RIPPLE

(KIND OF —) LYME KISSING MINAMATA
(LUNG —) CON
(MUSHROOM —) FLOCK
(PINK —) ACRODYNIA
(PLANT —) ESCA YAWS
(SKIN —) ACNE SCAB FAVUS HIVES LEPRA MANGE PSORA RUPIA SCALL TINEA ECZEMA LICHEN TETTER EXORMIA PORRIGO PRURIGO PURPURA SERPIGO VERRUGA CHLOASMA IMPETIGO MILIARIA MYCETOMA SHINGLES VERRUGAS VITILIGO PEMPHIGUS
(SWELLING —) EDEMA
(VENEREAL —) BURNING SYPHILIS
(WINE —) GRAISSE
(WOOLSORTER'S —) ANTHRAX
(PREF.) MORBI NOS(O) PATH(O)
(SUFF.) IASIS ITIS NOSUS OMATOSIS OSIS SIS
(FUNGUS —) OSIS

DISEASED BAD EVIL SICKLY MORBOSE PECCANT VICIOUS MORBIFIC
(PREF.) CACH CAC(O) DYS
(SUFF.) CACE

DISEMBARK LAND ALIGHT ARRIVE DEBARK UNBARK UNBOAT DISBOARD

DISEMBARKATION LANDING

DISEMBARRASS EXTRICATE

DISEMBODIED SEPARATE DISBODIED FLESHLESS

DISEMBODIMENT SOUL SPIRIT

DISEMBOGUE MOUTH

DISEMBOWEL GUT HULK PAUNCH DEBOWEL EMBOWEL GARBAGE UNTRIPE GRALLOCH

DISEMIC DIMORIC DICHRONOUS

DISENCHANT DISMAY

DISENCHANTED SOUR

DISENCUMBER RID FREE REDD UNCUMBER

DISENCUMBERMENT RIDDANCE

DISENGAGE FREE CLEAR EDUCE UNTIE DETACH EVOLVE LOOSEN CUTOVER DISGAGE RELEASE UNRAVEL LIBERATE UNCLUTCH

DISENGAGED OFF CLEAR

DISENTANGLE CARD COMB FREE REED TOSE TOZE CLEAR LOOSE RAVEL TEASE EVOLVE SCUTCH SLEAVE UNMAZE UNMESH RESOLVE UNRAVEL UNREAVE UNTWINE UNTWIST OUTTWINE UNTANGLE

DISENTANGLEMENT SOLUTION

DISESTEEM UMBRAGE DISVALUE

DISFAVOR DUTCH ODIUM DISLIKE OFFENCE OFFENSE UMBRAGE MALGRACE

DISFIGURE MAR BLUR FOUL MAIM SCAR TASH AGRISE DEFACE DEFEAT DEFORM INJURE MANGLE BLEMISH DISGRACE DISGUISE MUTILATE

DISFIGURED FOUL DEFET DEFEIT DEFORMED

DISFIGUREMENT SCAR BLEMISH CATFACE DEFORMITY

DISGORGE SPEW VENT EGEST EJECT EMPTY VOMIT

DISGRACE BLOT FOIL FOUL HISS LACK SLUR SMIT SOIL SPOT TASH ABASE CRIME ODIUM SCORN SHAME SHEND SPITE STAIN TAINT BAFFLE BEFOUL BISMER HUMBLE INFAMY REBUKE STIGMA VILIFY AFFRONT ATTAINT DEGRADE OBLOQUY OFFENCE OFFENSE REPROOF SCANDAL SLANDER UMBRAGE CONTEMPT DISHONOR IGNOMINY REPROACH SHENDING UNWORTHY VILLAINY OPPROBRIUM
(PUBLIC —) ATIMY

DISGRACEFUL MEAN SOUR FILTHY INDIGN IGNOBLE CRIMINAL DEFAMOUS INHONEST SHAMEFUL

DISGRUNTLED SORE PEEVISH

DISGUISE DAUB FACE HIDE LAIN LEAN MASK VEIL BELIE CLOAK COLOR COUCH COVER FEIGN GLOZE GUISE SHADE VISOR VIZOR COVERT DEFORM IMMASK MANTLE MASQUE VIZARD CONCEAL OBSCURE PRETEND PURPORT COLORING DISLIKEN MISGUISE PALLIATE PRETENCE PRETENSE TRAVESTY UMBRELLA SMOKEANDMIRRORS
(— INFORMATION) LAYNE

DISGUISED COVERT FUCATE GILDED LATENT MYSTIC FEIGNED PALLIATE TRAVESTY INCOGNITA INCOGNITO

DISGUST IRK UGH CLOY PALL BLECH LOATH REPEL SHOCK STALL DEGOUT HORROR NAUSEA OFFEND REVOLT SICKEN SCUNNER STOMACH SURFEIT AVERSION DISTASTE KREISTLE LOATHING NAUSEATE SCOMFISH SICKNESS
(EXPRESSION OF —) BAH ICK ROT RATS YECH YUCK PSHAW YECCH PHOOEY
(INTERJECTION TO EXPRESS —) YUK TUCK YECH YECCH
(SOUND OF —) RAZZ RASPBERRY
(WORD OF —) ICK

DISGUSTED IRK SICK IRKSOME

DISGUSTING FOUL PERT VILE LOUSY MUCKY NASTY FILTHY SCRIMY SICKLY BEASTLY CLOYING FULSOME HATEFUL LOATHLY MAWKISH NOISOME OBSCENE SHITTEN FOULSOME LOATHFUL NAUSEOUS SHOCKING VOMITOUS

DISH CAP CAUP CUSH DISC DISK FOOL MEAT MOLD PLAT SOLE BASIN BATEA COMAL DEVIL MOULD NAPPY PATEN PINAX PLATE SHAPE BASQUE BASSIE BICKER BLAZER BUTTER CHAFER CRITCH CUSCUS ENTREE FONDUE GOSSIP LUGGIE NAPPIE OLIVES PADDLE PANADA PATERA PATINA PHIALE RECIPE SAUCER SUNDAE TAMALE TUREEN BALANCE BOBOTEE BOBOTIE CAPSULE CEVICHE CHARGER COCOTTE COMPORT COMPOTE CRESSET DORMANT DOUBLER EPERGNE PAPBOAT PATELLA PLATEAU PLATTER RAMEKIN SCUTTLE STIRFRY SUPREME TERRINE TIMBALE AMATORIO CIOPPINO CLAPDISH COQUILLE COUSCOUS GALATINE KEDGEREE MAZARINE POWSODDY STANDARD ENTREMETS
(— IN PYRAMID STYLE) BUISSON
(— OF FISH) SUSHI
(— OF MEAT AND EGGPLANT) MOUSSAKA
(— OF RAW FISH) SEVICHE
(— OF SLOPPY FOOD) SOSS
(— WITH TOAST) RAREBIT
(BAKING —) SCALLOP SCOLLOP
(BRAISED —) HASLET
(CASSEROLE —) POTAUFEU
(CHAFING —) CHAFER CHOFFER SCALDINO
(CHEESE —) RACLETTE
(CHINESE —) LOMEIN SUBGUM
(CHOICE —) REGALE
(CONE-SHAPED —) BOMBE
(CURRIED MEAT —) VINDALOO
(EXQUISITE —) AMBROSIA
(FANCY —) SURPRISE
(FIRST —) STARTER
(FISH —) CIOPPINO
(FLAT —) ASHET COMAL CHARGER
(FRIED —) SKIRL
(HIGH-FLAVORED —) HOGO
(INDIAN —) BIRYANI BURIANI
(INDIAN — OF LEGUMES) DAL DAHL DHAL
(IRISH —) COLCANNON
(JAPANESE —) SUSHI TEMPURA TERIYAKI YAKITORI
(JEWISH —) CHOLENT
(LIGHT —) SOUFFLE
(MEAT —) SPIEDINO
(PASTA —) CARBONARA
(PHILIPPINE —) BURO
(PHILIPPINE FISH —) DOBO
(PIE —) COFFIN
(PILE OF —S) BUNG
(RICE —) PILAU
(ROMAN —) LANX PATERA PATINA
(SAILOR'S —) BURGOO SCOUSE
(SAUSAGE —) CHIPOLATA
(SCOTTISH —) BROSE
(SIDE —) OUTWORK
(SPANISH —) ADOBO
(SPANISH MEAT —) ADOBO
(SWEET —) JUNKET FLUMMERY
(TASTY —) MORSEL
(WARMED-UP —) RECHAUFFE
(WOODEN —) CUP CAUP BOWIE GOGGAN LUGGIE KICKSHAW
(PL.) GARNISH BAKEWARE FLATWARE ENTREMETS
(PREF.) LECO

DISHABILLE MOB DISARRAY DISORDER NEGLIGEE

DISHAN (FATHER OF —) SEIR

DISHARMONY SCHISM ADHARMA FRACTION

DISHCLOTH DISHRAG TORCHON

DISHCLOTH GOURD LOOFAH PATOLA DISHRAG

DISHEARTEN AMATE DAUNT FAINT DEJECT DEPRESS FLATTEN UNHEART UNNERVE DISHEART DISPIRIT

DISHEARTENED DULL GLUM GLOOMY DOWNCAST DEPRESSED

DISHEARTENING GLOOMY DESOLATE

DISHEVEL MUSS TOWSE RUFFLE TOUSEL TOUSLE TUMBLE TRACHLE DISARRAY DISORDER

DISHEVELED ROOKY BLOUSY BLOWZY FROWZY TUMBLED UNKEMPT FROWZLED SHEVELED SLIPSHOD TATTERED

DISHON (FATHER OF —) ANAH

DISHONEST BENT FOUL LEWD CRONK CROSS FALSE LYING QUEER SNIDE TWISTY UNFAIR UNJUST CORRUPT CROOKED JACKLEG KNAVISH INDECENT INDIRECT SHAMEFUL SINISTER UNCHASTE UNHONEST MENDACIOUS

DISHONESTLY DOUBLY FALSELY

DISHONESTY IMPROBITY

DISHONOR FILE FOUL ABASE ABUSE ATIMY ODIUM SHAME SPITE STAIN WRONG DEFAME DEFILE DEFORM INFAMY VILIFY DEGRADE DISTAIN OBLOQUY SLANDER VIOLATE DISGLORY DISGRACE DISPLUME IGNOMINY REPROACH VILLAINY ATTAINDER

DISHONORABLE BASE FOUL MEAN BLACK NASTY SHABBY YELLOW DISLEAL IGNOBLE SHAMEFUL UNHONEST UNWORTHY

DISHONORED DEFAMED

DISHPAN KEELER

DISH RACK FIDDLE

DISHWASHER SWILLER

DISILLUSION SOUR DISMAY

DISINCLINATION NILL UNLUST UNWILL DISLIKE QUARREL AVERSION DISTASTE

DISINCLINED LOTH LOATH AFRAID AVERSE HESITANT
(— TO) ABOVE

DISINFECT SCRUB SEASON CLEANSE SWEETEN

DISINFECTANT LYSOL IODINE PHENOL CREOLIN EUGENOL TACHIOL FUMIGANT HALAZONE PARAFORM ANTISEPTIC

DISINFECTION ANTISEPSIS

DISINGENUOUS FALSE UNFAIR OBLIQUE

DISINHERIT DEPRIVE DISHEIR ABDICATE DISHERIT

DISINTEGRATE BEAT DUST MELT BREAK DECAY ERODE GRUSH SLAKE SPLIT MOLDER CRUMBLE DISBAND RESOLVE SHATTER COLLAPSE DISSOLVE SEPARATE

DISINTEGRATING ROTTEN SCHIZOID
(SUFF.) CLASTIC

DISINTEGRATION DECAY BREAKUP EROSION BIOLYSIS COLLAPSE HEARTROT SOLUTION
(SUFF.) LYSE LYSIS LYST LYTE LYTIC LYZE

DISINTER EXHUME UNBURY UNTOMB UNGRAVE

DISINTERESTED FAIR CANDID APATHETIC IMPARTIAL

DISJOIN PART UNDO SEVER DETACH SUNDER UNTACK UNYOKE DISSOLVE DISUNITE SEPARATE
DISJOINED BITTY SEJOINED DIAZEUTIC
DISJOINTED BITTY
DISK (ALSO SEE DISC) EYE NOB ORB PAN SAW WAX WEB BURR CHAD DIAL DISC FLAN FLAT KNOB PALM PUCK STAR TUFT CAKRA DAUNT LAMIN MEDAL PATEN PLATE ROUND SABLE SABOT SPILL TOKEN TRUCK WAFER WHEEL WHORL BEZANT BOTTOM BUCKET BUMPER BUTTON CACHET CARTON CHAKRA CONCHA CONCHO CORONA DISCUS FLOPPY GHURRY HARROW PALLET PELLET RECORD RIFFLE RONDEL SEQUIN SHEAVE SQUAIL WASHER WEIGHT ZEQUIN ACETATE BLOTTER BOBECHE CHECKER CHIPPER CLIPEUS DIOPTER DISCOID FREEBEE FRISBEE GOGGLES KNICKER MEDALET PHALERA ROSETTE SLITTER SPINNER SPOTTER TONDINO DIFFUSER EYEPIECE HOLDFAST PLANCHET RONDELLE ROUNDLET ZECCHINO
(— FOR BARRELING HERRING) DAUNT
(— FOR CHEESE) FOLLOWER
(— FOR STRIKING HOURS) GHURRY
(— OF JELLYFISH) BELL
(— OF LAMELLAE) THYLAKOID
(— OF WAX) AGNUS
(— ON WOODEN ROD) SPILL
(— OPERATING SYSTEM) DOS
(BULL'S-EYE —) CARTON
(COIN-MAKING —) FLAN PLANCHET
(COMPUTER —) FLOPPY MINIFLOPPY
(CONTENTS OF —) DATA
(DOUBLE —) YOYO
(ECCENTRIC —) SHEAVE
(FLESHY —) SARCOMA
(FLOPPY —) DISKETTE
(HANDLED —) RIFFLE
(HOCKEY —) PUCK
(KIND OF —) FLOPPY
(MEDICATED —) LAMELLA
(METAL —) SLUG MEDAL
(ORNAMENTAL —) BANGLE SPANGLE
(PADDED IRON —) SPINNER
(PAPER —S) CONFETTI
(PLASTIC —) FRISBEE
(POTTER'S —) BAT
(REVOLVING —) WAFTER
(ROTATING —) SCANNER
(SOLAR —) ATEN ATON
(SUN —) ATEN CAKRA CHAKRA
(TROCHAL —) CORONA
(WINGED —) FEROHER
(PREF.) DISC(I)(O)
DISLIKE DEFY DOWN HATE LOTH LUMP MIND DERRY LOATH SPITE DETEST PHOBIA REGRET RESENT SPLEEN UNLIKE DESPISE MISLIKE QUARREL SCUNDER SCUNNER STOMACH AVERSION DESPISAL DISFAVOR DISTASTE DYSPATHY
(— OF CHILDREN) MISOPEDIA
(FOOLISH —) TOY
DISLOCATE LUX SLIP BREAK SPLAY UNSET LUXATE DISLOCK UNWREST DISJOINT DISPLACE SEPARATE
DISLOCATED SHOTTEN DISLOCATE
DISLOCATION BREAK SHIFT SLIDE THROW
(PL.) SETTLEMENTS
DISLODGE BEAT BOLT BUCK BUMP EXPEL SHAKE SHIFT SWOOP REMOVE DISROOT UNHORSE UNHOUSE UNLODGE DISHABIT
(— BY BLASTING) BRUSH
(— FROM SADDLE) THROW
DISLODGING BULLING
DISLOYAL FALSE FELON UNTRUE DISLEAL
DISLOYALTY SWICK SWIKE UNLEWTY UNTRUTH
DISMAL SAD WAN BLUE DARK DIRE DOWF DREE DULL EERY GASH GLUM GRAY GREY BLACK BLEAK DOWFF DREAR EERIE LURID MORNE OORIE OURIE SABLE SORRY SURLY SWART WASTE WISHT DREARY DREICH DREIGH GLOOMY GOUSTY LENTEN SULLEN TRISTE DIREFUL DOLEFUL FUNERAL GASHFUL GHASTLY GOUSTIE JOYLESS OMINOUS POCOSIN STYGIAN UNCOUTH UNHAPPY DESOLATE DOLESOME DOLOROUS FUNEREAL GROANFUL LONESOME NOVEMBRY SOLITARY WEARIFUL MELANCHOLY
DISMAL-LOOKING GASH WOBEGONE
DISMALLY DERNLY DIRELY
DISMANTLE RASE RAZE STRIP DIVEST STRIKE DEPRIVE DESTROY UNCLOAK DISMOUNT
DISMAY BOWL FEAR RUIN ALARM AMATE APPAL DAUNT DREAD FLUNK APPALL ASTONY CHASSE FRIGHT SUBDUE TERROR DEPRESS DEPRIVE FOUNDER HORRIFY TERRIFY AFFRIGHT CONFOUND CONSTERNATION
(INTERJECTION EXPRESSING —) OOPS WOOPS
DISMAYED ASTONIED
DISMAYING HIDEOUS
DISMEMBER LIMB MAIM PART REND SEVER MANGLE UNLIMB DISCERP DISLIMB DISSECT QUARTER DISJOINT MUTILATE
DISMISS AX AXE CAN PUT BOOT BUMP BUST CASH CAST DAFF DROP DRUM FIRE KICK OUST QUIT SACK SEND SHAB SWAP SWOP TURN VAIK VOID AMAND AMOVE BREAK BRUSH CHUCK DEMIT DIMIT DITCH EJECT EXPEL FLIRT FLUNK LOOSE SCOUT BANISH BOUNCE CHASSE CONGEE DEHIRE DISMIT DISOWN REJECT REMOVE SHELVE CASHIER DISBAND DISCARD LICENCE LICENSE TURNOFF DESELECT DISGRACE DISPATCH DISPOINT RELEGATE SETASIDE WITHDRAW
(— LIGHTLY) SNEEZEAT
DISMISSAL AX BOOT SACK BRUSH CHUCK CONGE SHAKE AVAUNT BOUNCE OUSTER KICKAXE REMOVAL DISPATCH MITTIMUS REDUNDANCY
(LARGE-SCALE —) PURGE
(UNCEREMONIOUS —) CONGE CONGEE
DISMISSED DEGOMME
(ONE WHO IS —) PUSHOUT
DISMOUNT AVALE AVOID LIGHT ALIGHT DEVOID DESCEND FLYAWAY UNHORSE UNMOUNT DISHORSE UNSTRIDE
DISOBEDIENCE CONTEMPT
DISOBEDIENT BAD FORWARD FROWARD NAUGHTY UNBUXOM UNGODLY WAYWARD MUTINOUS
DISOBEY SIT REJECT
DISOBLIGE OFFEND REFUSE AFFRONT NEGLECT
DISOBLIGING MEAN UNBAIN UNBANE
DISORDER ILL MUX PIE CRUD FLAW MESS MUSS RIOT RUFF STIR TOUT CHAOS CRACK DERAY GRIME HAVOC REVEL SNAFU SPLIT TOUSE TUKRA UPSET BURBLE CHOREA DEFUSE DESRAY HUDDLE JUMBLE LITTER MALADY MASTIC MUCKER MUDDLE RUFFLE TOUSLE TROPPO TUMULT UNTIDY WALTER AILMENT CLUTTER COBWEBS CONFUSE DERANGE DISEASE DISTURB EMBROIL FERMENT FLUTTER GARBOIL ILLNESS MISDEED MISRULE OUTRAGE PERTURB SHATTER TROUBLE UNRAVEL UNSHAPE DISARRAY DISHEVEL EPILEPSY MILIARIA MISORDER NEUROSIS ROWDYISM SICKNESS UNSETTLE COMMOTION CONFUSION POLLINOSIS
(— OF BIRDS) PIP
(— OF EYES) HIPPUS
(— OF VISION) DIPLOPIA
(— OF WINES) CASSE
(COMPLETE —) CHAOS ANARCHY
(EATING —) BULIMIA
(MENTAL —) INSANITY PARANOIA
(NERVOUS —) VAPORS
(SPEECH —) LALOPATHY
(SUFF.) **(SPEECH —)** PHASIA PHEMIA PHRASIA
DISORDERED ILL SICK WILD CRAZY GAUMY LIGHT MESSY UNRID BLOTTO FROUZY FROWSY FROWZY INCULT INSANE MUSSED TURBID CHAOTIC CLOUDED FORLORN TUMBLED UNGLUED UNSIDED CONFUSED DERANGED DISEASED FEVERISH FLURRIED INCHOATE SHAMBOLIC
DISORDERING CRIMP
DISORDERLY RAND RANDY ROWDY RABBLE UNRULY BUNTING LAWLESS ROARING CONFUSED FAROUCHE LARRIKIN SLIPSHOD SLOVENLY SLUTTISH SLATTERNLY
DISORGANIZE SHOCK UPSET CONFUSE CONTUSE DERANGE DISBAND DISRUPT DISORDER DISSOLVE
DISOWN DENY RENAY UNOWN REJECT DISAVOW RETRACT ABDICATE DISALLOW DISCLAIM RENOUNCE REPUDIATE
DISPARAGE LACK SLUR ABUSE DECRY LOWER TRASH DEBASE LESSEN SLIGHT BACKCAP DEBAUCH DEGRADE DEMERIT DEPRESS DETRACT DISABLE DOWNCRY IMPEACH RUBBISH RUNDOWN BELITTLE DEROGATE DIMINISH DISCOUNT DISHONOR DISPRIZE MINIMIZE MISLIKEN VILIPEND
DISPARAGEMENT DIASYRM SNIDERY WASHWAY
DISPARAGING SNIDE SLIGHTING PEJORATIVE
DISPARATE UNEQUAL SEPARATE
DISPARITY DISSENT DISTANCE IMPARITY
DISPASSIONATE CALM COOL FAIR STOIC SEDATE SERENE CLINICAL COMPOSED MODERATE
DISPATCH RID FREE KILL MAIL NOTE POST SEND SLAY WING BRIEF ENVOY FLASH HASTE HURRY SHOOT SPEED DIRECT EMPLOY HASTEN ADDRESS COMMAND DELIVER DISPEED EXPRESS HATCHET BREVIATE CELERITY CONCLUDE DESPATCH EXPEDITE TELEGRAM
DISPATCH BOAT AVISO PACKET
DISPATCHER STARTER
DISPEL FRAY SHOO CHASE ASSOIL BANISH DISCUSS SATISFY SCATTER DISPERSE
DISPENSATION LAW LILA GRACE LIVERY ECONOMY FACULTY QUIENAL TOTQUOT COVENANT DISPOSAL
DISPENSE DEAL DOLE HELP SHED WEIGH EFFUSE EXCUSE EXEMPT FOREGO MANAGE SPREAD ABSOLVE ARRANGE DISPEND DRIBBLE MINISTER
(— WITH) MISS WANT SPARE SUSPENSE
DISPENSER BOMB MANAGER STEWARD
DISPERSE DOT SOW FRAY MELT PART ROUT SHED LOOSE SCALE SEVER SKAIL STREW BAFFLE DEFEAT DILATE DISPEL FANOUT SKIVER SPARSE SPERSE SPREAD UNKNIT VANISH WINNOW DIFFUSE DISBAND DISJECT DISMISS DRIBBLE FRITTER SCATTER SHATTER SPARKLE SPARPLE SPERPLE DISSOLVE DISTRACT SEPARATE SQUANDER STAMPEDE
DISPERSEDLY PASSIM
DISPERSING SCALE
(— SHADOWS) SCIALYTIC
DISPERSION CUT FOAM STAIN SPREAD DEBACLE SCATTER DIASPORA EMULSOID SOLUTION STAMPEDE
(PREF.) LYO
DISPIRIT COW DAMP MATE MULL CHILL DAUNT DEJECT DEPRESS FLATTEN OPPRESS

DISPIRITED SAD BLUE DOWN DOWY DOWIE ABATTU ABATTUE LETDOWN SHOTTEN DOWNCAST DOWNSOME SACKLESS UNHEARTY WOBEGONE
DISPIRITING COLD BLEAK CHILL DISMAL
DISPLACE BUMP EDGE MOVE STIR BANISH DEPOSE LUXATE MISLAY REMOVE WINKLE DERANGE SWALLOW UNHINGE UNPLACE ANTEVERT DISLODGE DISPLANT MISPLACE SUPPLACE SUPPLANT UNSETTLE
(— LATERALLY) HEAVE
DISPLACED ATOPIC DEPAYSE
DISPLACEMENT JEE BUMP SLIP HEAVE SCEND SHIFT START CUBAGE OFFSET UPSLIP FALLING EVECTION
(— OF FAULT) THROW
(— OF STAR) ABERRATION
(DOWNWARD —) PTOSIS
(OPTICAL —) PARALLAX
(ROCK —) HITCH
DISPLAY ACT AIR BRAG DASH GAUD OOZE ORGY POMP SHOW SIGN STAR WEAR AGONY ARRAY BINGE BLAZE BOAST DERAY ECLAT EMOTE FLASH PRIDE SCENE SHINE SIGHT SPLAY SPORT STAGE VAUNT BLAZON DEPLOY DESCRY ESTATE EVINCE EXPOSE EXTEND FLAUNT MUSTER OSTENT OUTLAY PARADE REVEAL RUFFLE SETOUT SPLASH SPRANK SPREAD UNCASE APPROVE BALLOON BRAVERY ETALAGE EXHIBIT EXPRESS FANFARE FLUTTER GAUDERY PAGEANT PRESENT SHOWING SPLURGE TRADUCE UNCOVER BEEFCAKE BLAZONRY BOOKFAIR CEREMONY DISCLOSE DISCOVER EMBLAZON EQUIPAGE EVIDENCE EXERCISE EXPOSURE FLOURISH INDICATE MANIFEST PARAFFLE SPLENDOR TINSELRY
(— EXCITEMENT) FAUNCH
(— GLARINGLY) FLARE
(— OF COMPUTER TASKS) MENU
(— OF EMOTION) GUSH
(— OF GOODS) ETALAGE
(— OF SKILL) APPERTISE
(— OF STRONG COLORS) RIOT
(BOASTFUL —) JACTATION
(BOISTEROUS —) SPLURGE
(COMPUTER VIDEO — OF TASKS) MENU
(DARING —) BRAVURA
(EMPTY —) GAUD EYEWASH
(EXCESSIVE —) OSTENTATION
(FLASHY —) CLAPTRAP
(FLORAL —) BLOW BLANKET
(IMPRESSIVE —) SWELL
(LAVISH —) PROFUSION
(LIGHT —) LED
(MOVE COMPUTER — UP OR DOWN) SCROLL
(OSTENTATIOUS —) DOG GAUDERY SWAGGER
(PRETENTIOUS —) PARAFLE PARAFFLE
(RADAR —) SCAN
(SHOWY —) PYROTECHNICS
DISPLAYED SPLAY EXPANDED
DISPLEASE VEX MIFF ANGER ANNOY PIQUE MISPAY MISSET OFFEND DISLIKE DISSUIT MISLIKE PROVOKE IRRITATE
DISPLEASED MAD GLUM UNEASY UNFAIN
DISPLEASING BAD DRY PUTRID IRKSOME TEDIOUS UNLOVELY
DISPLEASURE IRE ANGER MUMPS PIQUE INJURY STRUNT UNLUST UNWILL DISLIKE OFFENSE TROUBLE UMBRAGE UNTHANK DISFAVOR DISGRACE DISTASTE
DISPORT PLAY AMUSE FRISK SPORT DIVERT FROLIC GAMBOL DISPLAY
DISPOSAL SALE BANDON CLEANUP PROPINE BESTOWAL DEVOTION DISPATCH
(— OF DEAD) FUNERAL
(ARBITRARY —) WILL
(QUICK —) WASHWAY
DISPOSE APT SET BEND CAST DUMP GIVE MIND TRIM YARK ARRAY BRUSH DIGHT ORDER PLACE POSIT ADJUST ATTIRE BESTOW DIGEST SETTLE TEMPER APPOINT ARRANGE DISPONE GESTURE INCLINE PREPARE RESOLVE DISPATCH REGULATE
(— OF) JOB SELL SCRAP FINISH HANDLE WORKOFF
(— VARIOUSLY) STAGGER
DISPOSED APT FIT SET SIB LIEF DIGHT GIVEN PRONE READY WRAST MINDED MINDFUL SUBJECT WILLING ADDICTED AFFECTED PREGNANT PROCLIVE PROPENSE PROTENSE TALENTED
(— AT INTERVALS) ALTERNATE
(— TO ACTION) ACTIVE
(— TO ASSOCIATE WITH ONE GROUP) CLANNISH
(— TOWARD) AFFECTED
(FAIRLY —) CANDID
(FAVORABLY —) PROPITIOUS
(KINDLY —) FOND
(OPENLY —) LOOSE
(WELL —) FAIN INCLINED
DISPOSITION BENT BIAS MAKE MIND MOOD RACE SORT TRIM TURN DRIVE ETHOS FRAME GRAIN HABIT HEART HUMOR SHAPE SPITE TACHE AFFECT ANIMUS DESIGN GENIUS HEALTH KIDNEY NATURE PTYXIS SPIRIT SPRITE STRIND TALENT TEMPER CONCEPT COURAGE DISPOSE FACULTY STOMACH APTITUDE ATTITUDE DISPOSAL POSITURE PERSONALITY
(— OF DRAPERIES) CAST
(— OF PARTS) SYMMETRY
(— OF PAWNS) SKELETON
(— OF STRATA) OVERLAP
(— TO ANGER) CHOLER
(— TO RESIST) DEFIANCE
(BRIGHT —) OPTIMISM
(DEVILISH —) SATANISM
(GENEROUS —) HEART
(GENIAL —) BONHOMIE
(INHERITED —) RACE
(KINDLY —) CHARITY HUMANITY
(NATURAL —) KIND GRAIN TARAGE INDOLES
(ORNAMENTAL —) DECOR
(ULTIMATE —) FATE
DISPOSITIONN (FORGIVING —) MERCY
DISPOSSESS OUST EJECT EVICT EXPEL STRIP WRONG DEPOSE DIVEST BEREAVE CASHIER DEPRIVE DISSEIZE SEPARATE
DISPOSSESSED LUMPEN
DISPOSSESSION OUSTER
DISPRAISE BLAME CENSURE
DISPROOF ELENCH REFUTE IMPROOF REPROOF
DISPROPORTIONATE UNEQUAL
DISPROVE BREAK REBUT REFEL NEGATE REFUTE CONFUTE EXPLODE IMPROVE REPROVE DISALLOW NEGATIVE REDARGUE
DISPUTABLE MOOT VAGUE UNSURE DUBIOUS FALLIBLE
DISPUTANT FENCER POLEMIC WRANGLER
DISPUTATION PARVIS PILPUL POLEMIC PROBLEM WRANGLE ARGUMENT COURSING DEBATING EXERCISE QUODLIBET
DISPUTATIOUS POLEMIC LITIGIOUS POLEMICAL
DISPUTE JAR ROW TAX CALL CHOP DENY FEUD FRAY FUSS HOLD MOOT ODDS RIOT SAKE SPAR SPAT TILT ARGUE BRAWL BROIL CABAL CHEST FLITE FLYTE HURRY PLEAD SPUTE SQUIB ARGUFY BARNEY BICKER CAMPLE CANGLE DABBER DACKER DAIKER DEBATE DIFFER FITTER FRATCH HAGGLE HASSLE IMPUGN MATTER NAGGLE SHARRY SQUALL SQUEAL THREAP BRABBLE CONTEND CONTEST DERAIGN DISCEPT DISCUSS DISSERT FACTION GAINSAY PRIBBLE QUARREL WRANGLE ARGUMENT CATFIGHT CONTRARY POLEMIZE QUESTION SKIRMISH SPARRING SPLUTTER SQUABBLE
(POETICAL —) FLYTING PARTIMEN
DISQUALIFY DEBAR UNFIT OUTLAW DISABLE
DISQUIET VEX FEAR FRET PAIN TOSS UNRO EXCITE UNCALM UNEASE UNREST AGITATE ANXIETY DISREST DISTURB INQUIET PERTURB SOLICIT TROUBLE TURMOIL UNPEACE UNQUIET
DISQUIETED UNEASY
DISQUIETING UGLY
DISQUIETINGLY UGLY
DISQUIETUDE CHAGRIN WANREST WANRUFE
DISRAELI DIZZY
DISREGARD BY SIT BLOW MOCK OMIT PASS WANE BELAY FLING WAIVE FORGET HUBRIS IGNORE SLIGHT UNHEED CASHIER DESPISE FORHEED LICENCE LICENSE NEGLECT OVERSEE DISCOUNT DISFAVOR DISPENSE DISVALUE EASINESS OVERHALE OVERLOOK OVERPASS UNREGARD
DISRELISH DISLIKE DISTASTE
DISREPUTABLE LOW BASE GAMY HARD WAFF GAMEY SEAMY SEEDY SHADY TOUGH LOUCHE SHODDY RAFFISH SHAMEFUL UNHONEST
DISREPUTABLENESS BEGGARY
DISREPUTE DISFAME DISFAVOR DISHONOR REPROACH
DISRESPECT AFFRONT CONTEMPT RUDENESS
DISRESPECTFUL HARM SAUCY UNCIVIL IMPOLITE IMPUDENT INSOLENT
DISROBE STRIP CHANGE DIVEST DESPOIL UNDRESS
DISRUPT GASH REND TEAR BREAK CROSS HAMPER DISRUMP DISTRACT SONICATE
(— WITH SOUND TREATMENT) SONICATE
DISRUPTED BROKEN DISRUPT
DISRUPTION BREACH BREAKUP DEBACLE RUPTURE SOLUTION
DISSATISFACTION PAIN DISTASTE VEXATION
(FEELING OF —) BLAHS
DISSATISFIED UNEASY MALCONTENT
DISSATISFY MISPAY
DISSECT BAR ANALYZE DISJOIN SCALPEL UNPIECE
DISSECTED MATURE
DISSECTION ANATOMY ANALYSIS
DISSEMBLE ACT FOX LIE HIDE MASK CLOAK FEIGN BOGGLE SEMBLE CONCEAL DISGUISE SIMULATE SIMULIZE
DISSEMBLER SIMULAR
DISSEMBLING SLY BRAIDE IRONIC FICTION AESOPIAN IRONICAL
DISSEMINATE SOW BEAR BLAZE STREW EFFUSE SPREAD DIFFUSE PUBLISH SCATTER SPARPLE DISPERSE SEMINATE
DISSEMINATION PROPAGATION
DISSENSION JAR ODDS DEBATE STRIFE DISCORD DISLIKE DISSENT FACTION MISLIKE BROILERY DISPEACE DISTANCE DISUNION DISUNITY DIVISION FRACTION FRICTION SEDITION
DISSENT VARY DIFFER HERESY CONTEND PROTEST DISAGREE
DISSENTER HERETIC SECTARY RECUSANT SEPARATE RASKOLNIK (PL.) SEPARATION
DISSENTING PANTILE
DISSEPIMENT REPLUM SEPTUM PHRAGMA
DISSERTATION ESSAY THEME TRACT DEBATE MEMOIR SCREED THESIS DESCANT LECTURE MEMOIRS EXCURSUS EXERCISE TRACTATE TREATISE
(— ON TEA) TSIOLOGY
DISSERVE HARM
DISSERVICE HARM DAMAGE INJURY MISCHIEF
DISSIDENT FRONDEUR
DISSIMILAR UNLIKE DIFFORM DIVERSE UNLIKEN
DISSIMILATE UNLIKEN
DISSIMULATION IRONY DECEIT

DISSIPATE BURN FRAY SPEND WASTE BANISH DISPEL EXPEND CONSUME DIFFUSE DISCUSS FRITTER RESOLVE SCAMBLE SCATTER SHATTER SWATTLE TARNISH DISPERSE DISSOLVE EMBEZZLE EVANESCE SQUANDER
DISSIPATED FAST HIGH LOST SPORTY OUTWARD RACKETY
DISSIPATION RAKERY
DISSOLUTE LAX LEWD WILD LOOSE SLACK RAKELY RAKISH SUBURB UNTIED WANTON IMMORAL LAWLESS VICIOUS DESOLATE RAKEHELL RECKLESS RESOLUTE SUBURBAN UNCURBED
DISSOLUTION END RUIN DECAY BREAKUP DECEASE DIVORCE DIALYSIS
(PREF.) LYS(I)
DISSOLVE CUT END DEFY FADE FUSE MELT SOLV THAW BREAK FLEET LOOSE SOLVE UNFIX DIGEST DISTIL RELENT SOLUTE UNBIND UNGLUE UNKNIT ADJOURN DESTROY DISBAND DISJOIN DISTILL DIVORCE LIQUEFY RESOLVE DISCANDY DISUNITE SEPARATE
(— MEAT PARTICLES) DEGLAZE
(— OUT) LEACH
(PREF.) LY(O)
DISSOLVED SOLUT REMISS SOLUTE RESOLUTE
DISSOLVING
(SUFF.) LYSE LYSIS LYST LYTE LYTIC LYZE
DISSONANCE WOLF DISCORD DIAPHONY
DISSONANT AJAR HARSH RAGGED GRATING JARRING JANGLING
DISSUADE BLUFF DETER DEHORT DIVERT RETIRE
DISTAFF ROCK FEMALE
DISTAFFINA (LOVER OF —) BOMBASTES
DISTANCE DX HOP WAY BLUE GAIT GATE LOOK PIPE SPAN STEP DEPTH DRAFT RANGE SPACE GROUND HEIGHT LENGTH SPREAD STANCE STITCH BOWSHOT BREADTH DRAUGHT FARNESS JOURNEY MILEAGE MILEWAY RESERVE STRETCH YARDAGE COLDNESS COSECANT DIAMETER FOOTSTEP HANDSPAN INTERVAL LATITUDE OFFSCAPE OUTSTRIP
(— ALONG TRACK) LEAD
(— BETWEEN BATTENS) GAG
(— BETWEEN GEAR TEETH) PITCH
(— BETWEEN MASTS) INTERVAL
(— BETWEEN RAILS) GAGE GAUGE
(— BETWEEN RIVET-HEADS) GRIP
(— BETWEEN TACKS) REACH
(— FOR PUTTING COAL) RENK
(— FROM BELLY TO BACK) BODY
(— FROM CENTER) RADIUS
(— FROM EQUATOR) HEIGHT
(— FROM LOCK FACE) BACKSET
(— FROM THE EYE) DEPTH
(— IN ADVANCE) START
(— OF ARCHERY RANGE) BUTT
(— OF BOW SHOT) CAST
(— OF GOLF BALL) CARRY
(— OF HAUL) LEAD LEADAGE
(— OF TURNING SHIP) ADVANCE
(— OF VISION) KEN
(— ON FISHHOOK) BITE
(— ON GEAR WHEEL) ADDENDUM
(— OVER WHICH WIND BLOWS) FETCH
(— UPWARDS) HEIGHT
(ANGULAR —) ANOMALY
(AT A —) LARGE
(GREAT —) INFINITY
(INTERVENING —) GAP
(PERPENDICULAR —) DROP CAMBER ALTITUDE
(REMOVE TO A —) ELOIN
(SAFE —) BERTH
(SEA —) OUTING STEAMING
(SHOOTING —) SHOOT
(SHORT —) HAIR INCH SPIT STEP SPELL BITTIE FOOTSTEP
(SHORT — AWAY) OUTBYE
(SMALL —) HAIR STEP
(UNIT OF —) LI YOJAN PARASANG
DISTANT DX COY FAR OFF AFAR AWAY BACK COLD SIDE YOND ALOOF CHILL FERNE HENCE FERREN REMOTE YONDER FARAWAY FOREIGN FROSTED REMOVED STRANGE RESERVED
(— FROM COAST) MIDLAND
(— IN TIME) EARLY
(— PART) OFFSCAPE
(MORE —) YOND YONDER ULTERIOR
(MOST —) OUTMOST OUTERMOST
(PREF.) TEL(E)(EO)
DISTASTE HATE DEGOUT UNLUST DISGUST DISLIKE MISLIKE AVERSION MISTASTE
(— FOR FOOD) APOSITIA
DISTASTEFUL ICKY SOUR YUCKY AUGEAN BITTER BEASTLY HATEFUL BRACKISH NAUSEOUS SHOCKING UNSAVORY REPUGNANT
DISTEMPER SOAK STEEP CHOLER DILUTE GARGET GARGIL GARGLE MALADY PANTAS AILMENT DISEASE ILLNESS DISORDER DYSCRASE SICKNESS UNSETTLE
(— OF COLT) STRANGLES
DISTEND BAG BLOW FILL GROW HEFT BLOAT PLUMP STRUT SWELL WIDEN DILATE EXPAND EXTEND INTEND SPREAD BALLOON ENLARGE INFLATE STRETCH
DISTENDED BIG FULL PENT TAUT TRIG WIDE BLOWN POOCH TUMID ASTRUT GRAVID BLOATED DISTENT SWOLLEN INFLATED PATULENT PATULOUS
DISTENDEDLY ASTRUT
DISTENTION BLOAT DISTENT TYMPANY
DISTHENE CYANITE KYANITE
DISTICH SLOKA PROODE COUPLET
DISTILL DROP ELIX EMIT RATE STILL DISTIL EXTILL INFUSE ALEMBIC LIMBECK TRICKLE
DISTILLATE GUNDY ROSIN BENZIN ALCOHOL BENZINE
DISTILLATION RUN DESCENT
DISTILLER ABKAR STILLER
DISTILLERY STILL JIGGER STILLERY
DISTINCT HOT FAIR FREE VIVE BREME BRISK CLEAR PLAIN SHARP VIVID PLUCKY PROPER SECRET SUNDRY ANOTHER ASUNDER DIVERSE EVIDENT LEGIBLE OBVIOUS PRECISE SCIOLTO SEVERAL SPECIAL APPARENT DISCRETE DIVIDUAL PALPABLE PECULIAR SEPARATE TRENCHANT
(— FROM) BESIDE
(NOT —) DIM OBSCURE
(PREF.) CHORI CHORIST(O) IDIO
DISTINCTION MARK NOTE RANK SHED TEST CLASS GLORY HONOR FIGURE LAUREL LUSTER LUSTRE RENOWN DIORISM QUALITY QUILLET ACCESSIT DIVISION GRANDEZA SUBTLETY REFINEMENT
(ACADEMIC —) HONORS HONOURS
(LACKING —) VANILLA
(WITHOUT —) COMMON
DISTINCTIVE RARE JUICY DIRECT PROPER SIGNAL PECULIAR PHONEMIC SEPARATE SPANKING TALENTED
DISTINCTIVENESS EMPHASIS
DISTINCTLY CLEAR REDLY FAIRLY CLEARLY
DISTINCTNESS PLUCK CLARITY SEVERALTY
(LACKING —) SMUDGY
DISTINGUISH DEEM KNOW MARK SORT BADGE JUDGE LABEL SEVER SKILL STAMP DECERN DEFINE DESCRY DEVISE DIVIDE ENSIGN SECERN SINGLE CONCERN DISCERN DESCRIBE PERCEIVE SEPARATE
DISTINGUISHED CLEAR GREAT NOTED SWELL BANNER FAMOUS GENTLE MARKED SOLEMN EMINENT INSIGNE NOTABLE SIGNATE SPECIAL TOPPING DISTINCT ESPECIAL LAUREATE RENOWNED SPLENDID CONSPICUOUS
DISTINGUISHING BETWEEN
DISTORT WRY SKEW WARP CLOUD COLOR FUDGE SCREW TWIST WREST WRING CRINGE DEFACE DEFORM DETORT GARBLE MANGLE SHEVEL WRENCH WRITHE BLUBBER CONTORT FALSIFY GRIMACE PERVERT SHACHLE SHACKLE SLANDER OUTIMAGE WIREDRAW
DISTORTED WRY AWRY BENT SKEW ASKEW CRANK SKEWED WARPED CROOKED DISTORT GNARLED LOXOTIC WRITHEN CAMSHACH DEFORMED DEGRADED STRAINED TORTIOUS PERVERTED
DISTORTING CONVULSION
DISTORTION FIB HOG SAG WOW WREST STRAIN FLUTTER GRIMACE GARBLING SKEWNESS
(— IN WOOD) WARP DIAMONDING
(FACIAL —) GRIMACE
DISTRACT MAD AMUSE CRAZE STROY BEMUSE DETRAY DIVERT HARASS INSANE MADDEN MITHER MOIDER PUZZLE TWITCH AGITATE CONFUSE DETRACT DISTURB EMBROIL PERPLEX SCATTER BEWILDER CONFOUND FORHAILE
DISTRACTED GYTE WILD CRAZY EPERDU STRACT FRANTIC MADDING SCRANNY FRENETIC SCATTERED
DISTRACTION ALARM BLIND ALARUM ESCAPE FRENZY TUMULT ECSTASY
DISTRAIN NAM NAAM DRIVE POIND STRAIN STRESS DISTRESS POUNDAGE
DISTRAINT NAM NAAM POIND
DISTRAUGHT MAD CRAZED FRANTIC DERANGED DISTRACT DISTRAIT STRAUGHT
DISTRESS AIL ILL MAR VEX BITE CARK GNAW HURT MOAN NEED PAIN PORT PUSH TEAR TEEN AGONY ANGER ANNOY DOLOR GRATE GRIEF GRILL GRIPE LABOR PINCH PRESS SMART TRYST TWEAK WORRY WOUND WRING BARRAT DANGER DURESS GRIEVE GRUDGE HARASS HARROW LAMENT MISERY SORROW STRESS TAKING THRONG WORRIT AFFLICT ANGUISH ANXIETY CHAGRIN DAYMARE DESTROY DISEASE EXTREME HERSHIP MISEASE OPPRESS PASSION PENANCE PERPLEX STURBLE TORMENT TORTURE TRAVAIL TROUBLE UNQUERT AGGRIEVE CALAMITY DARKNESS DISTASTE DISTRAIN EXIGENCE FORHAILE PRESSURE SORENESS STRAITEN WANDRETH GRIEVANCE
DISTRESSED WRUNG DOWNGONE
DISTRESSFUL STRAIT
DISTRESSING BAD HOT SAD GRIM HARD SORE BLEAK CHARY CRUEL DIRTY SHARP BITTER SEVERE SHREWD THORNY CARKING FEARFUL GRIPING PAINFUL GRIEVOUS
DISTRIBUTE DOT SOW CAST DEAL DOLE GRID METE SEED SORT TAME ALLOT CLASS DIVVY ISSUE PLACE SHARE SHIFT SPEND ASSIGN ASSORT DEPART DEVISE DIGEST DIVIDE EXPEND IMPART PARCEL REPART SPARSE SPREAD ARRANGE DISPEND DISPOSE EROGATE PRORATE SCATTER ALLOCATE CLASSIFY DESCRIBE DISBURSE DISPENSE DISPERSE SEPARATE SPRINKLE
(— GUNFIRE) SEARCH
(— SEED) SOW SEED DRILL
(— TYPE) DISH THROW
DISTRIBUTED BALANCED DISPERSE
DISTRIBUTION DOLE SALE ARRAY DIVVY DETAIL DIVIDE PARTING DISPOSAL DIVIDEND
DISTRIBUTIVELY EACH APIECE
DISTRIBUTOR SOWER SHARER CARRIER ZANJERO
DISTRICT DO AMT GAU LAN SOC WAY WON AREA COIL FARM HUNT LEET LIWA PALE PART SIDE SLUM SOKE TEMA WARD WENE WICK

WOON AIMAK ANNEX COILA EXURB HARSH JAGIR JEWRY MAHAL OKRUG PAGUS PARTY SHIRE SOKEN TALUK TEMAN TRACT VICUS AGENCY BARRIO BOWERY CANTON CERCLE CIRCLE COUNTY FOREST JAGHIR MARKAZ MEMBER MERINA OKROOG PARAMO PARISH POLLAM REGARD REGION SIRCAR STAPLE STREET SYSSEL VINTRY ZILLAH CALABAR CIRCUIT CLASSIS COMARCA COMMUNE COUNTRY CURRAGH DEMESNE DIOCESE ENCLAVE FREEDOM LIBERTY MAHALLA MALACCA MAYFAIR MELIZKI MISSION PIMLICO PURLIEU QUARTER SEASIDE SLUMDOM THANAGE THEBAID UPRIVER CHAPELRY CIMARRON DISTRITO DIVISION FAUBOURG GILDABLE LEGATION MACASSAR MAGAZINE MONTANAS PRECINCT PROVINCE REGIMENT MAGISTRACY PREFECTURE
(— BORDERING RIVER) WATER
(— FOR GAME HUNTING) SHOOTING
(— OF COURT) LEET
(— OF JAPAN) DO KEN
(ADMINISTRATIVE —) ZILA ZILLAH TOWNSHIP
(BROTHEL —) STEW
(BURNED —) QUEMADO
(CHINESE —) HIEN
(COASTAL —) RIVIERA
(ECCLESIASTICAL —) SYNOD CLASSIS DIOCESE
(HUNTING —) WALK
(ICELANDIC —) SYSSEL
(ISLE OF MAN —) SHEADING
(JUDICIAL —) CIRCUIT
(MARKED-OFF —) PALE
(MOUNTAINOUS —) HIGHLAND
(OUTER —) END
(OUTWARD —) END
(OVERCROWDED —) WARREN
(POOR —) SLUM SLUMS
(POSTAL —) RAYON
(RURAL —) WAYBACK
(RURAL —S) STICKS
(RUSSIAN —) OBLAST STANITSA STANITZA
(TENANT —) THIRL
(THEATER —) RIALTO
(TRIBAL —) GAU
(TURKISH —) ORDU SANJAK
(PL.) GAELTACHT

DISTRUST FEAR DOUBT DREAD STRIFE DIFFIDE SUSPECT UNFAITH UNTRUST DEFIANCE DISFAITH MISFAITH MISTRUST QUESTION WANTRUST

DISTRUSTFUL SHY LEERY JEALOUS

DISTURB JEE VEX BUSY FAZE FRET FUSS JOLT RILE ROCK ROIL STIR TOSS ALARM ANNOY BRASH DROVE FEEZE KNOCK PHASE ROUSE SHAKE STEER UPSET AFFRAY BOTHER HARASS JOSTLE MOLEST RUFFLE SQUEAK UNCALM UNEASE AGITATE COMMOTE COMMOVE CONCUSS DERANGE DISREST DRUMBLE FRAZZLE GARBOIL INQUIET MISMAKE PERTURB SCUFFLE SOLICIT STURBLE TEMPEST TROUBLE CONVULSE DISJOINT DISORDER DISQUIET DISTRACT DISTRESS FRIGHTEN
(— BY HANDLING) TOUCH
(— SUDDENLY) START
(— THE PEACE) RIOT INQUIET

DISTURBANCE VEX BOIL BREE CAIN COIL DUST RIOT ROUT STIR WIND WORK ALARM BEANO BRAWL BROIL DERAY FUGUE FUROR HURRY SHINE SHOCK STEER STORM STROW STURT TOUSE AFFRAY BOTHER BREEZE CATHRO DESRAY FRACAS FRAISE FURORE HUBBUB KICKUP POTHER RUCKUS RUMBLE RUMPUS SHINDY SQUALL STATIC TUMULT TURNUP UPROAR BLUNDER BOBBERY BRULYIE BRULZIE CHAGRIN CLATTER CLUTTER DISTURB EMOTION FERMENT GRINDER MADNESS ROOKERY RUCTION TROUBLE TURMOIL BROILERY BUSINESS DISORDER FOOFARAW INCIDENT REELRALL STRAMASH TRAVALLY RABBLEMENT PERTURBATION
(— OF OCEAN) SEA
(ATMOSPHERIC —) STORM GRINDER
(DIGESTIVE —) BLOAT
(MENTAL —) FRENZY PHRENSY DELIRIUM
(SEISMIC —) SEAQUAKE

DISTURBED CRACKED INQUIET MAKADOO TROUBLE AGITATED FLURRIED STREAKED

DISTURBING BREAK NASTY HAUNTING

DISUNION DIVORCE

DISUNITE RIP PART SEVER UNTIE DETACH DIVIDE SUNDER UNKNIT UNLIME DISBAND DISJOIN DISLINK DISSENT DIVORCE UNRAVEL ALIENATE DISSEVER DISSOLVE ESTRANGE SEPARATE UNSOLDER

DISUNITY DISCORD DISUNION DIVISION

DISUSE MISUSE OUTAGE ABANDON DISCARD DISUSAGE MISAPPLY

DISUSED DEAD WASTE DESUETE EXOLETE OBSOLETE

DITCH GAW RUT SAP SOW DELF DICK DIKE DYKE FOSS GOOL GOUT GRIP GURT HOLL LEET LODE MOAT SEEK SICK SIKE SINK TRIG CANAL CLAUD DELFT DELVE FENCE FLEAM FOSSA FOSSE GRAFF GRAFT GRAVE GRIPE GROOP GULLY PUDGE RHEEN RHINE RIGOL SEWER SHORE SLONK SLUIT SOUGH STANK STELL ZANJA GUTTER GUZZLE HOLLOW RELAIS SHEUCH SHEUGH TRENCH ZANJON ABANDON ACEQUIA CHANNEL GRINDLE GRIPPLE LATERAL VANFOSS ZANJONA WATERING
(— AROUND ARENA) EURIPUS
(MUDDY —) LETCH
(NARROW —) RELAIS
(OPEN —) STELL
(WIDE —) SLOT
(PREF.) FOSSI

DITCH GRASS ENALID

DITCH MILLET HUREEK PASPALUM

DITCH REED SPIRE BENNEL

DITHER FLAP STEW SHAKE TIZZY BOTHER LATHER SHIVER TROUBLE

DITI (FATHER OF —) DAKSHA
(HUSBAND OF —) KASHYAPA

DITROCHEE DIPODY

DITSY CRAZY DIZZY GIDDY INANE SILLY SPACY WIFTY SPACEY

DITTO SAME REPEAT LIKEWISE

DITTY DIT LAY DITE DYTE POEM SING SONG THEME VERSE SAYING DICTATE VINETTA

DIURETIC ZEA CAVA KAVA BUCCO BUCHU CUBEB LAPPA PICHI SABAL NASROL DROSERA EMICTORY FUROSOMIDE PIPSISSEWA

DIVAGATE ROVE

DIVAN SOFA OTTOMAN SOCIABLE

DIVE BAR DEN DASH DUCK DUMP JOINT SOUSE GAINER HEADER PLUNGE SALOON BROTHEL RATTRAP JACKNIFE SUBMERGE JACKKNIFE
(— DEEP) SOUND
(KIND OF —) SWAN TWIST GAINER JACKKNIFE
(MAKE A NOSE —) PEARL

DIVER AMA LOON DUCKER PEARLER PLUNGER PLUNGEON
(SCUBA —) AQUANAUT
(SUFF.) DYTA DYTES

DIVERGE LEAVE BRANCH DIFFER DIVIDE RAMIFY SPREAD SQUARE SWERVE DEVIATE DIGRESS DIVERSE DISAGREE DIVAGATE

DIVERGENCE DIP ERROR CHANGE SPREAD SWERVE VAGARY CONTRAST OBLIQUITY
(UNDUE —) OUTRAGE

DIVERGENT OFF APART REMOTE TANGENT VARIANT
(MORE —) FARTHER

DIVERS EVIL MANY CRUEL SUNDRY SEVERAL VARIOUS PERVERSE DIFFERING
(PREF.) PARTI PARTY

DIVERSE EVIL SERE MOTLEY SUNDRY UNLIKE VARIED ADVERSE SEVERAL VARIOUS DISTINCT PERVERSE SEPARATE VARIETAL
(PREF.) PARTI PARTY POLY VARI(O)

DIVERSIFIED MOTLEY EXTENDED

DIVERSIFY DOT FRET VARY CHECK FRECK BEGARIE CHECKER VARIATE SPRINKLE

DIVERSION JEU GAME MASK PLAY ALARM FEINT FRISK HOBBY SPORT ATTACK DEDUIT DIVERT LAUGHS SCHEME SOLACE DISPORT PASTIME ESCAPISM PLEASURE SIDESHOW VARIORUM
(— OF STREAM) CAPTURE

DIVERSITY CHANGE DISCORD DISSENT VARIETY CONTRAST
(PREF.) POLY

DIVERT SWAY AMUSE BLANK RELAX SHUNT SPORT WRING DERAIL DERIVE DETURN SIPHON SWITCH SYPHON TICKLE BEGUILE CELIGHT DECEIVE DEFLECT DETRACT DISPORT PASTIME PERVERT REFLECT ABSTRACT DISSUADE DISTRACT ESTRANGE RECREATE
(— ATTENTION) COVER
(— HEADWATERS) BEHEAD
(— STREAM) CAPTURE
(— WATER) FLUME

DIVERTED MERRY AMUSED DISTRACT

DIVERTICULUM UTERUS OLEOCYST

DIVERTING DROLL AMUSING FOOLISH PLEASANT SPORTFUL LAUGHABLE

DIVEST BARE DOFF REFT TIRL EMPTY EXUTE REAVE SHEAR SPOIL STRIP DELAWN DENUDE DEPOSE DEVEST DISMIT UNVEST BEREAVE DEPRIVE DESPOIL DISROBE UNCOVER UNDRESS DENATURE DETHRONE UNCLOTHE
(— OF) ABDICATE
(— OF ARMOR) DEMAIL
(— OF VALUE) DEVALUE

DIVIDE CUT LOT CAST DEAL FORK MERE PART RIFT SHED SLIP TEAR ZONE BREAK CARVE CLASS CLEFT DIVVY GAVEL JOINT SCALE SCIND SEVER SHARE SHIFT SLICE SNACK SPACE SPLIT SPRIT WHACK BEPART BISECT BRANCH CANTLE CANTON CLEAVE COTEAU DEPART DEVISE DIFFER DOMIFY INDENT PARCEL RAMIFY SECTOR SEJOIN SLEAVE SUNDER ALIQUOT ANALYZE ATOMIZE AVERAGE BRITTEN COMPART DIFFUSE DIREMPT DISCIDE DISPART DISSECT DIVERGE FISSURE FRITTER PARTAKE PRORATE ALLOCATE CLASSIFY CROSSCUT DISCRETE DISSEVER DISTRACT DISUNITE FRACTION FRAGMENT GRADUATE HEMISECT MEDISECT SEPARATE STRATIFY UNSEEDER
(— BEEF) BLOCK
(— FILAMENTS) SLEAVE
(— INTO DISTRICTS) CANTON
(— INTO MEASURES) BAR
(— INTO PIECES) GOBBET
(— INTO 2 PARTS) HALVE BISECT
(— INTO 4 PARTS) QUARTER
(— LAND) STINT
(— NATURALLY) FALL
(— SMALL) SCANTLE

DIVIDED ENTE REFT SIDE CLEFT FORKY SPLIT ATOMIC CLOVEN PRONGY FISSATE FOURCHE GYRONNY PARTITE SEPTATE AEROLATE CAMERATE DIVIDUAL FOURCHEE
(— BY VERTICAL LINES) PALY
(— INTO 4 PARTS) PALY QUARTERED
(— IN TWO) FOURCHE DIMIDIATE
(— TWICE) RETAILLE
(NOT —) GLOBAL
(PREF.) CHORI(ST)(STO) FISSI PARTI PARTY SCHIZ(O)
(SUFF.) FID FIDATE SECT SECTED TOMOUS

DIVIDEND BONUS SHARE

DIVIDER BUNTON MERIST SEPTUM SHARER BUNTING COMPASS MULLION SEVERER DIVIDANT
DIVI-DIVI LIBIDIBI
DIVINATION OMEN SORS SORT AUGURY MANTIC SORTES AUSPICE SCRYING SORCERY GEOMANCY TAGHAIRM
(— SCIENCE) MANTIC
(PREF.) MANTO
(SUFF.) MANCER MANCY MANTIC
DIVINE HOLY SORT SPAE TWIG AREAD AREED ATMAN AUGUR DIVUS GODLY GUESS PIOUS DEIFIC DETECT DEVISE GODFUL HALSEN PRIEST SACRED BLESSED FORESEE GODLIKE PORTEND PREDICT PRESAGE ARIOLATE CONTRIVE FOREBODE FOREKNOW FORETELL HEAVENLY IMMORTAL MINISTER PERCEIVE UBIQUIST SPIRITUAL
DIVINER SEER AUGUR SIBYL ARUSPEX AUGURER PROPHET HARUSPEX
DIVING BELL NAUTILUS
DIVING BOARD RISE
DIVING SUIT GANGAVA
DIVINING ROD TWIG DOWSER
DIVINITY (ALSO SEE GOD AND GODDESS) JOSS LLEU LLEW TIEN AHURA DEITY HYBLA NUADA NUADU NYMPH POWER ATHTAR VEDUIS GLAUCUS GODDESS GODHEAD GODSHIP HYBLAEA TARANIS VIRBIUS TEUTATES VEDIOVIS
(— CIRCUIT BINDING) YAPP
(PL.) CABIRI ELOHIM
DIVISIBLE SECABLE DIVIDUAL PARTIBLE
(— BY 2) AIM
DIVISION BAY BOX CUT DAG FIT JAG LEG CHAP CLAN DOLE FARM FAUN FORK GELD GELT GORE HOLD LITH NEAT PACE PANE PART RANK RAPE RIFT CAPUT CHASM CLASS CLEFT CURIA DIGOR DIVVY DULAN DULAT FIELD FIGHT GENOS GRANT GROUP IJORE MURUT PERES REALM SHARD SHARE SUBAH TAXIS THEME TOMAN WHEEN BARONY CANTON COHORT DECADE DECURY DEGREE DIVIDE EOGAEA HAWIYA IMAHAL JHURIA PORTIO SCHISM SEASON SECTOR SUNDER VOLOST ZILLAH BREAKUP COMARCA CUSTODY DIOCESE DUALISM ENOMOTY FISSURE FURLONG HASHIYA KINGDOM KITKSAN NATUARY PARTAGE PARTING ROULADE SECTION SEGMENT SUBRACE ARPEGGIO CATEGORY CLEAVAGE DECANATE DIERESIS DISTRICT FASCICLE MEROTOMY PARGANNA PRECINCT SCISSION SCISSURE SHEDDING SQUADRON SUBCLASS
(— BETWEEN PIERS) BAY
(— BETWEEN STALLS) BAIL
(— FOR TAXATION) GELD
(— IN DENMARK) AMT
(— IN HUNGARY) COMITAT
(— IN MINING BED) CLEAVE
(— OF ANGELS) CHOIR
(— OF ARMY) BATTLE LOCHUS
(— OF BEJA) BISHARIN
(— OF BOOK) CHAPTER FASCICLE
(— OF BUDDHIST CANON) PITAKA
(— OF BUILDING) STORY STOREY
(— OF CHAPTER) VERSE
(— OF CHARIOTEERS) FACTION
(— OF CHURCH) AISLE
(— OF COMPASS) POINT
(— OF CONTEST) HEAT INNING
(— OF COUNTY) RAPE BARONY HUNDRED
(— OF CROPLAND) FLAT
(— OF DISCOURSE) HEADING
(— OF DRAMA) ACT SCENE
(— OF FAMILY) BRANCH
(— OF FIELD) RIG
(— OF FOOT) SEMEION
(— OF FOREST) WARD
(— OF GEOLOGICAL TIME) ERA EPOCH PERIOD
(— OF GRASS) SPRIG
(— OF GREAT HORDE) DULAN DULAT KANGLA KANGLI
(— OF HEADLINE) BANK DECK
(— OF HERALDIC SHIELD) POINT
(— OF ISLE OF MAN) SHEADING
(— OF KENT) LATHE
(— OF LAND) LAINE KONOHIKI
(— OF LEAF) LOBE
(— OF LEGION) COHORT HASTATI MANIPLE TRIARII
(— OF LOG LINE) KNOT
(— OF MANCHU ARMY) BANNER
(— OF MANKIND) RACE
(— OF MEAL) COURSE
(— OF MUSICAL COMPOSITION) MOVEMENT
(— OF NIGHT) WATCH
(— OF ORANGE) LITH
(— OF PARTED HAIR) LIST
(— OF PEOPLE) STREAM
(— OF PLAY) ACT SCENE
(— OF POEM) FIT DUAN CANTO STANZA STROPHE
(— OF PROCESS) STAGING
(— OF ROAD) LANE
(— OF ROCKS) SYSTEM
(— OF ROSARY) DECADE CHAPLET
(— OF SCHOOL YEAR) TERM SESSION
(— OF SOCIETY) CASTE ATOMISM
(— OF SONG) FIT
(— OF STOPE) FLOOR
(— OF STRUCTURE) STAGE
(— OF SUSSEX) RAPE
(— OF TREF) RANDIR
(— OF TRIBE) CURIA
(— OF UTTERANCE) COLON
(— OF WINDOW) DAY
(— OF YEAR) SEASON
(— OF YORKSHIRE) RIDING
(— OF ZILLAH) PARGANA PERGUNNAH
(— OF ZODIAC) SIGN DECAN
(— OVER ISSUE) BREACH
(— SIGN) OBELUS
(ADMINISTRATIVE —) FU LATHE CHARGE CIRCLE COUNTY EYALET CUSTODY DIOCESE TOWNSHIP
(ANTHROPOLOGICAL —) STOCK
(ARMY —) MORA
(ASTROLOGICAL —) FACE
(CELL —) MITOSIS AMITOSIS
(ECCLESIASTICAL —) SCHISM SOCIETY PRECINCT
(GEOLOGICAL —) ERA LIAS MALM BUNTER KEUPER LUDIAN SERIES LARAMIE ARNUSIAN RICHMOND
(HINGED —) LEAF
(ISLE OF MAN —) SHEADING
(MUSICAL —) ALLEGRO
(NUCLEAR —) FISSION
(PHILIPPINE —) ATO
(POLICE —) TANA THANA
(POLITICAL —) ATO CITY LATHE STATE COUNTY PARISH BOROUGH HUNDRED SURPLUS DISTRICT PURCHASE WAPENTAKE
(POPULATION —) STRATUM
(SOCIAL —) HORDE
(TRIBAL —) CLAN
(SUFF.) KINESIS
DIVITIACUS (BROTHER OF —) DUMNORIX
DIVORCE GET GETT AHSAN HASAN KHULA SEVER TALAK SUNDER ASUNDER DISBAND DISMISS MUBARAT UNMARRY DISSOLVE DISUNION DISUNITE SEPARATE
DIVOT CLOD TURF
DIVULGATION (UNAUTHORIZED —) LEAK
DIVULGE BARE CALL SHOW TELL BLURT BREAK SPILL UTTER VOICE BABBLE BEWRAY EVULGE EXPOSE IMPART REVEAL SPREAD UNFOLD PROPALE PUBLISH UNCOVER DISCLOSE DISCOVER EVULGATE PROCLAIM
DIZZINESS HILO SWIM DINUS TIEGO MEGRIM VANITY MERLIGO SCOTOMY VERTIGO SWIMMING WILLNESS
DIZZY DUNT AREEL CRAZY DITSY DITZY FAINT GIDDY LIGHT TOTTY WESTY WOOZY FICKLE STUPID FOOLISH SWIMMING UNSTEADY
DJIBOUTI (GULF OF —) TADJOURA
DNA (— SEGMENT) CISTRON
(— SEQUENCE) HOMEOBOX
DO D ACT DIV FAY TRY BILK BURN CHAR COME DEAL DOST MAKE PASS SUIT AVAIL BITCH CHEAT EXERT GUISE SERVE SHIFT TRICK ANSWER COMMIT NOBBLE RENDER ACHIEVE EXECUTE PERFORM PRODUCE SATISFY SUFFICE TRANSACT
(— AWAY WITH) BURK ABATE BURKE FORDO BANISH FOREDO ABOLISH AMOLISH CASHIER CONSUME ABROGATE DEMOLISH DISSOLVE IMBOLISH RETRENCH
(— BUSINESS) CHAFFER
(— CARELESSLY) SLIM
(— CASUAL WORK) GRASS
(— FOR) FIX GET JACK POOP SINK FETCH NAPOO DIDDLE SCUPPER
(— IMPERFECTLY) HUDDLE
(— INJURY) BANE
(— IN SLOVENLY WAY) SLUBBER
(— NOT) DONT DINNA
(— OVER) REVAMP REMODEL
(— PENANCE) SATISFY
(— PIECEWORK) DACKER
(— SMARTLY) LINK
(— THOROUGHLY) FLOOR
(— WITHOUT) LACK SPARE FORBEAR DISPENSE
(— WRONG) ERR SIN MISCARRY
(— YE) DEE
DOABLE AGIBLE
DOBLON ISABELLA
DOBRA JO JOE OCTAVE
DOCENT TUTOR TEACHER LECTURER
DOCILE CALM MEEK TALL TAME TAWIE FACILE GENTLE DOCIOUS DUCTILE DUTIFUL BIDDABLE OBEDIENT TOWARDLY
DOCK BOB CUT PEN BANG CLIP MOOR PIER QUAY RUMP SCUT BASIN SHORE WHARF CAMBER COFFER DOCKEN FIDDLE HAMBLE MARINA SORREL STRUNT BOBTAIL CURTAIL PARELLA PARELLE SHORTEN CANAIGRE PATIENCE SHIPSIDE
(SPACE BETWEEN —S) SLIPWAY
DOCKAGE BERTHAGE
DOCKET LIST AGENDA
DOCKMACKIE VIBURNUM
DOCKWORKER (—S GROUP) ILA
DOCKYARD ARSENAL
(— WORKMAN) MATEY
DOCTOR (ALSO SEE PHYSICIAN) DOC COOK DOPE DOSE FAKE PILL BRUJO HAKIM LEECH SUGAR TREAT CROCUS DEACON EXTERN HAIKUN HEALER INTERN MAULVI POWWOW CROAKER KORADJI TEACHER MEDICATE PHYSICIAN MANIPULATE
(— OF CANON LAW) JCD
(— OF LAWS) JD
(— UP) COOK FAKE EYEWASH
(— WINE) STUM
(IRISH —) OLLAV OLLAMH
(KIND OF —) SPIN
(PLAY —) FIXER
(QUACK —) CROCUS
(WITCH —) BOCOR BOKOR GOOFER GUFFER WIZARD WITCHMAN
DOCTOR'S DILEMMA (AUTHOR OF —) SHAW
(CHARACTER IN —) LOUIS RALPH CULLEN COLENSO DUBEDAT PATRICK RIDGEON WALPOLE JENNIFER BONINGTON BLENKINSOP
DOCTRINAIRE ISMY
DOCTRINAL CREEDAL
DOCTRINE ISM DOXY LEAR LORE RULE CREDO CREED DOGMA LIGHT MAXIM TABLE TENET ZOISM AHIMSA BABISM BELIEF DHARMA EGOISM EROTIC GOSPEL HOLISM MALISM MONISM NOETIC THEORY ACROAMA AMIDISM ANIMISM ARTICLE ATAVISM ATHEISM ATOMISM BAHAISM DUALISM EGOTISM EVANGEL KARAISM KRYPSIS MISHNAH NEOLOGY NOETICS OPINION PEELISM PRECEPT PROGRAM REALISM SENSISM TRIKAYA ACTIVISM AGATHISM ANALYTIC ARIANISM ARYANISM BAJANISM CHILIASM

CYNICISM DARBYISM DEVILISM DOCETISM DYNAMISM ENERGISM FATALISM FINALISM GOBINISM HEDONISM HYLOLOGY IDENTISM IDEOLOGY ISLAMISM MOLINISM NIHILISM PAJONISM PAMNESIA PEJORISM POSITION POSOLOGY PSYCHISM REGALISM RHEMATIC SIDERISM SOLIDISM SPHERICS TYPOLOGY UBIQUITY VITALISM DITHESISM MECHANISM MUTUALISM PANTHEISM PESSIMISM PLURALISM NATURALISM
(BAD —) CACODOXY
(BUDDHIST —) ANATTA ANATMAN
(CONTRARY —) HERESY
(ESOTERIC —) CABALA QABBALA CABALISM
(EVIL —) MOLOCH
(MUSLIM —) TAUHID TAWHID
(PL.) ESOTERY SCOTISM CREDENDA DONATISM LABADISM SCRIBISM
(SUFF.) ISM LOGER LOGIA(N) LOGIC(AL) LOGIST LOGUE LOGY OLOGY

DOCUMENT DOC GET BILL BOND BOOK CALL CHOP DEED FORM GETT OLLA SEAL WRIT CHART DEMIT DIMIT GRIEF LEASE PAPER PROOF SCRIP SCRIT STIFF TARGE TEACH TITLE BILLET BREVET CADJAN CAJANG CEDULA COCKET DOCKET PATENT RAGMAN SCHOOL SCRIPT SOURCE SURVEY TICKET VOLUME ARCHIVE CONDUCT DIPLOMA ELOHIST ESCRIPT EXHIBIT INQUEST LICENSE MISSIVE PLACARD PRECEPT WARRANT WAYBILL WHEREAS WRITING CITATION CONTRACT COVENANT FURLOUGH INSTRUCT MORTGAGE SCHEDULE SECURITY TRANSIRE BORDEREAU
(CONDITIONAL —) SCRIP
(COPY OF —) VIDIMUS
(COURT —) WRIT PRODUCTION
(REGISTRATION —S) LOGBOOK
(PL.) BUMF ARCHIVE ARCHIVE PALAPALA

DODAVAH (SON OF —) ELIEZER

DODDER SCAD SCALD SHAKE DODDLE DOTHER FIDEOS TOTTER TREMBLE FLAXDROP HAIRWEED HALEWEED HELLWEED MULBERRY

DODDERING OLD ANILE INANE INFIRM SENILE FOOLISH

DODDER LAUREL WOEVINE MISTLETOE

DODDIE HUMLIE

DODECANESE (— ISLAND) KOS SYME KASOS LEROS TELOS KHALKE LIPSOS PATMOS NISYROS KALYMNOS

DODGE RIG SHY BILK DUCK GAME JINK JOUK LURK RUSE AVOID CHEAT ELUDE EVADE FENCE FUDGE GLOSS LURCH PARRY PLANT SHIFT SHIRK SHUNT STALL TRICK ESCAPE FIDDLE PALTER RACKET WHEEZE DECEIVE EVASION PROFFER ARTIFICE CROTCHET GILENYIE MALINGER SIDESTEP

DODGER FLIER FLYER SOGER HAGGLER HANDBILL
(DRAFT —) BUSHWACK

DODGING JINK

DODO (SON OF —) ELEAZAR ELHANAN

DOE DA ROE TEG FAUN HIND NANNY ALMOND BISCUIT
(— IN 1ST YEAR) FAWN
(BLUE —) FLIER FLYER

DOER ACTOR AGENT MAKER AUTHOR FACTOR FEASOR WORKER FACIENT MANAGER ATTORNEY EXECUTOR
(— OF ODD JOBS) JACK
(SUFF.) AST ATOR IST OR STER STRESS

DOES S DOTH DUSE
(— NOT) DONT DISNA DOESNT

DOFF OFF DAFF VAIL AVALE DOUSE DOWSE STRIP DIVEST REMOVE UNDRESS

DOFFER DRUM DUFFER

DOFFING CAP

DOG CUR LAB MUT PUG PUP YAP ALAN ALCO CHOW DANE FAUS GOER HUND KIYI MONG MUTT PAWL STAG TIKE TRAY TYKE ALAND ALANT ARGOS BAWTY BEDOG BESET BOUCH BOXER CALEB CANID CHIEN CORGI DERBY DODGE HOUND HUSKY LIMER PELON POOCH PUPPY RACHE RAKER RATCH SILKY SLING SPITZ STALK WHELP AFGHAN BANDOG BARBET BARKER BASSET BAWTIE BEAGLE BELTON BORZOI BOSTON BOWWOW BRIARD BUFFER CANINE COCKER COLLIE COONER DANCER DETENT DRIVER ESKIMO FINDER GUNDOG HEADER HEELER HUNTER JOWLER KELPIE KENNET MISSET POODLE RANGER RATTER SALUKI SEIZER SETTER SHADOW SHOUGH SIRIUS SUSSEX TALBOT TANUKI TOLLER TOWSER VIZSLA YAPPER YAUPER YELPER BASENJI BOARDER BULLDOG CARRIER COURSER CRAMPON CREEPER DOGGESS DROPPER GRIFFON HARRIER LURCHER MALTESE MASTIFF MONGREL OWTCHAH POINTER SCOTTIE SHARPAI SKIRTER SLEUGHI SPANIEL SPORTER STARTER TERRIER TUMBLER WHIPPET YAPSTER ABERDEEN AIREDALE ALEUTANT ALSATIAN CERBERUS COACHDOG COCKAPOO CYNHYENA DEMIWOLF DOBERMAN ELKHOUND FISSIPED FOXHOUND KEESHOND LABRADOR LANDSEER LONGTAIL MALEMUTE MALINOIS PAPILLON PEKINESE SAMOYEDE SEALYHAM SHEPHERD SIBERIAN SPRINGER TURNSPIT VERMINER WATCHDOG WATERRUG PEKINGESE POMERANIAN AFFENPINSCHER
(— OF BUSTER BROWN) TIGE
(— OF INDIA) PARIAH
(— OF LATHE) DRIVER
(— OF ORPHAN ANNIE) SANDY
(— TRAINED AS DECOY) TOLLER
(BELGIAN —) SCHIPPERKE
(BIRD —) BOLTER
(CHAINED —) BANDOG
(CHINESE —) SHARPEI SHIHTZU
(COMICS —) OTTO
(COMMON NAME FOR —) ZEKE
(CORN —) FRANKFURTER
(DECOY —) PIPER
(ESKIMO —) HUSKY SIWASH
(FAMOUS —) ASTA FALA TIGE TOTO
(FARM —) KOMONDOR
(FEMALE —) GYP SLUT BITCH DOGGESS
(FICTIONAL —) LAD TOBY SANDY
(FOXLIKE —) COLPEO
(GERMAN —) ROTTWEILER
(GUIDE —) SEEINGEYE
(HOUSE —) WAP WAPP
(HUNGARIAN —) PULI KUVASZ
(HUNTING —) ALAN BRACH RACHE RATCH ALAUND BASSET HUNTER KENNET LUCERN RACCHE SALUKI SEIZER SETTER SLOUGH COURSER DROPPER HARRIER POINTER STRIKER
(JAPANESE —) AKITA
(KIND OF —) FOO
(LAP —) MESSAN SHOUGH
(LARGE —) DANE TOWSER MASTIFF KOMONDOR
(LIKE A —) CYNIC
(LONG-EARED —) BEAGLE
(LONG-HAIRED —) ALCO SHOCK
(MONGREL —) CUR BRAKJE DEMIWOLF
(MOVIE —) ASTA LADY TOTO BENJI TRAMP CHANCE LASSIE OLDYELLER RINTINTIN
(NON-BARKING —) BASENJI
(PARTI-COLORED —) PIE PYE
(PART OF —) PAD PAW TOE ARCH BACK DOME HOCK KNEE LOIN RUMP STOP CHEEK CHEST CREST CROUP ELBOW FLEWS THIGH CARPUS DEWLAP MUZZLE STIFLE BRISKET CUSHION KNUCKLE LEATHER OCCIPUT PASTERN WITHERS FOREHEAD HEELKNOB
(PET —) MINX LAPDOG MOPPET
(POPULAR — NAME) FIDO LADY SHEP SPOT ROVER
(PRESIDENT'S —) FALA MINNIE CHECKERS
(PUG —) MOPS
(PUNCH'S —) TOBY
(RACCOON —) TANUKI
(RUNNING —) LACKEY
(SHAGGY —) RUG OWTCHAH
(SHEEP —) CUR COLLIE KELPIE BEARDIE MALINOIS SHEPHERD
(SHORT-BODIED —) PUG
(SMALL —) TOY FICE FIST DOGGY FEIST LAIKA PIPER DOGGIE AMERTOY SPANIEL PAPILLON PEKINESE
(VICIOUS —) TAEPO
(WATCH —) CUR GARM GARMR
(WELSH —) CORGI
(WILD —) ADJAG DHOLE DINGO GUARA JACKAL AGOUARA CIMARRON
(YELPING —) WAPPET
(PL.) DOGGERY
(PREF.) CYN(O)

DOGBANE KENDIR KENDYR ECHITES FLYTRAP ALSTONIA MILKWEED OLEANDER PERIWINKLE

DOGBOAT PIG

DOGCART GADDER TUMTUM BOUNDER GADABOUT

DOG COLLAR TRASH

DOG DAYS CANICULE

DOG EAR LEATHER

DOG FENNEL HOGWEED

DOGFIGHT SCRAMBLE

DOGFISH DOG HOE HUSS TOPE FLAKE HOUND HURSE MANGO TOPER BOUNCE DAGGAR GALEID MORGAY BONEDOG GABBACK SPURDOG TRIAKID GRAYFISH SEAHOUND
(PREF.) SCYLLIO SQUALI SQUALO

DOGGED DOUR SULLEN DOGGISH DOGLIKE STUBBORN OBSTINATE

DOGGEREL NOMINY TRIVIA DOGGREL SINGSONG

DOGGONE BLESSED DOWNGONE

DOGIE CALF LEPPY STRAY

DOG KEEPER FEWTERER

DOGLIKE CYNIC CYNOID DOGGED

DOGMA CREED TENET DICTUM DOCTRINE DOCUMENT

DOGMATIC THETIC PONTIFIC POSITIVE ARBITRARY CONFIDENT PONTIFICAL

DOGMATISM BOWWOW

DOGMATIST BIGOT PHILODOX

DOG POUND GREENYARD

DOG ROSE BUCKY CANKER BEDEGUAR DOGBERRY

DOG SALMON CHUM KETA MORGAY DOGFISH

DOGSBODY DRUDGE

DOGSHORE DOG DAGGER

DOG'S MERCURY SAPWORT

DOG SNAPPER JOCU

DOGSTAIL BENT

DOGSTAR SIRIUS

DOGWOOD OSIER SUMAC CORNEL CORNUS GAITER WIDBIN BARBASCO FISHWOOD

DOILY MAT TIDE TIDY NAPKIN

DOING ACT DEED FACT STIR EVENT ACTION FUNCTION PRACTIVE
(PL.) FARE GEAR
(SUFF.) ANT ENT PRACTIC PRAXIA PRAXIS

DOIT DODKIN

DO-IT-YOURSELF DIY

DOLE LOT ALMS DEAL DOOL GIFT GOAL METE PART VAIL ALLOT FRAUD GRIEF GUILE MOURN POGEY SHARE DECEIT GRIEVE RELIEF SORROW CHARITY DEALING DESTINY HANDOUT PAYMENT PORTION BOUNDARY DIMENSUM DISPENSE DIVISION GRATUITY LANDMARK PITTANCE

DOLEFUL SAD DOWY DOWIE DREAR HEAVY DISMAL DOOLFU DREARY FUNEST RUEFUL FLEBILE DOLESOME DOLOROUS FUNESTAL MOURNFUL TRAGICAL

DOLERITE DIABASE
DOLICHOTIS MARA
DOLL GAL TOY BABE BABY MOLL ARRAY DOLLY DOLLIE KEWPIE MAIDEN MAUMET MOPPET MUNECA POPPET POUPEE PUPPET KACHINA KATCINA KATCHINA MISTRESS
(— UP) PRIMP SWANK
(PASTEBOARD —) PANTINE
(PREF.) PUPI
DOLLAR BALL BEAN BONE BUCK CASE CLAM DURO FISH ROCK SCAD SKIN SPOT ADOBE BERRY DALER EAGLE PLONK PLUNK WHEEL GOURDE PATACA DAALDER RINGGIT SMACKER FROGSKIN PATACOON SIMOLEON
(FIVE —S) NICKEL
(ONE MILLION —S) MEGABUCK
(SILVER —) SINKER
(SPANISH —) COB DURO COBBE
(TEN —S) DIME
(THOUSAND —S) GEE THOU GRAND
DOLLARFISH SHINER MOONFISH STARFISH
DOLLOP GLOB
DOLL'S HOUSE (AUTHOR OF —) IBSEN
(CHARACTER IN —) NORA RANK HELMER LINDEN TORVALD KROGSTAD CHRISTINA
DOLLY DRAB HOBBY PEGGY PUNCH SWAGE MAIDEN FOLLOWER MISTRESS SLATTERN
DOLLYMAN BUCKER
DOLLYWAY DOCK
DOLMEN SENAM TOLMEN CROMMEL CROMLECH MEGALITH
DOLOMITE ANKERITE PEARLSPAR
DOLOR CALOR GRIEF SORROW ANGUISH SADNESS DISTRESS MOURNING
DOLOROUS SAD DISMAL DOLEFUL GRIEVOUS PATHETIC
DOLPHIN INIA SUSU BOUTO WHALE DORADO KILLER PALACH TURSIO BOLLARD COWFISH PELLOCK PULLOCK SNUFFER CETACEAN MAHIMAHI MUTILATE PORPOISE
(PREF.) DELPHIN DELPHO
(SUFF.) DELPHIS
DOLPHIN STRIKER MARTINGALE
DOLT ASS OAF PUT ASSE BOZO CALF CHUB CLOD COOF DULT FOOL GOFF MOKE PEAK POOP STUB BOOBY CHUMP CLUNK DOBBY DUMMY DUNCE FUNGE GOLEM IDIOT NUMPS PATCH THICK BEFOOL CUDDEN DIMWIT DOODLE DULTIE HOBBIL NITWIT OXHEAD AIRHEAD BLUNTIE DAWCOCK DULLARD JACKASS SAPHEAD SCHNOOK BONEHEAD BOSTHOON CLODPATE CLODPOLL DUMBBELL IMBECILE LUNKHEAD MACAROON MOONCALF NUMSKULL LAMEBRAIN
DOLTISH DULL STUPID FOOLISH PEAKISH SOTTISH TOMFOOL BESOTTED BLOCKISH DOLTLIKE
DOMAIN LAND BOUND BOURN REALM SCOPE STATE WORLD BARONY BOURNE COUNTY DEMAIN EMPERY EMPIRE ESTATE SPHERE DEMESNE EARLDOM BIRTHDOM DOMINION LORDSHIP PROVINCE SEIGNORY STAROSTY
(— OF SULTAN) SOLDAN
(— OF THE UNCONSCIOUS) SHADOWLAND
(MATHEMATICAL —) FIELD
(NETHER —) HELL
(TRANSCENDENT —) HEAVEN
(WOMAN'S —) DISTAFF
DOMBEYA ASSONIA
DOMBEY AND SON (AUTHOR OF —) DICKENS
(CHARACTER IN —) GAY PAUL EDITH CARKER CUTTLE DOMBEY WALTER GRANGER FLORENCE
DOME CAP CIMA TYPE CROWN VAULT COCKLE CUPOLA THOLOS CALOTTE EDIFICE CIMBORIO HEMIDOME
(— OVER TOMB) WELI
(BUDDHIST —) TOPE
(KIND OF —) ONION
(OBSERVATION —) BLISTER
(POINTED —) IMPERIAL
(ROUND —) THOLUS
(SNOW-CAPPED —) CALOTTE
DOMER CLASPER
DOME-SHAPED BEEHIVE
DOMESTIC HIND HOME MAID MOZO DOMAL TABBY FAMILY HAMEIL HAMELT HEYDUC HOMELY HOMISH HOUSAL INLAND INMATE INWARD MENIAL NATIVE FAMELIC HEYDUCK ONSHORE SCALDER SERVANT FAMILIAR HOMEBRED HOMEMADE INTIMATE
(PL.) FOLK
DOMESTICALLY ONSHORE
DOMESTICATE TAME ENTAME AMENAGE RECLAIM CIVILIZE
DOMESTICATED CADE TAME GENTLE INWARD DOMESTIC FAMILIAR
DOMICILE CRIB HOME SHED ABODE HOUSE MENAGE DWELLING RESIDENCE
DOMINANCE SWAY INFLUENCE
DOMINANT BOSSY CHIEF FIFTH TENOR MASTER RULING SOVRAN CENTRAL REGNANT SUPREME DOMINULE SUPERIOR PARAMOUNT OVERBEARING PREPONDERANT
DOMINATE TOP BOSS HAVE RULE CHARM REIGN COERCE DIRECT GOVERN VASSAL BEWITCH COMMAND CONTROL ENVELOP POSSESS BESTRIDE DOMINEER OVERRIDE OVERSWAY OVERTONE
(— THE MIND) POSSESS
(— THE WILL) MESMERIZE
DOMINATING SUPERIOR BREATHLESS
DOMINATION EMPIRE CONTROL STRINGS BOVARISM BOVARYSM DOMINION POSSESSION
DOMINEER BOSS BRAG LORD RULE BULLY FEAST REVEL TOWER COMPEL COMMAND SWAGGER DOMINATE OVERBEAR OVERLEAD OVERLORD
(— OVER) RIDE HECTOR
DOMINEERING SURLY LORDLY HAUGHTY ARROGANT DESPOTIC MASTERLY MASTERFUL
DOMINICA (CAPITAL OF —) ROSEAU
(MOUNTAIN PEAK IN —) MORNEDIABLOTIN
DOMINICAN JACOBIN JACOBITE PREACHER PREDICANT

DOMINICAN REPUBLIC
BAY: OCOA YUMA NEIBA RINCON SAMANA ISABELA CALDERAS ESCOCESA
CAPE: BEATA FALSO CABRON ENGANO CAUCEDO ISABELA MACORIS
CAPITAL: SANTODOMINGO
COIN: ORO PESO
INDIAN: TAINO
ISLAND: BEATA SAONA ALTOVELO CATALINA HISPANIOLA
LOWLAND: CIBAO
MEASURE: ONA TAREA FANEGA
MOUNTAIN: TINA GALLO DUARTE
MOUNTAINS: NEIBA BAHORUCO ORIENTAL
RIVER: YUNA OZAMA
TOWN: AZUA BANI MOCA PENA POLO BONAO COTUI NAGUA NEIBA NIZAO SOSUA HIGUEY OVIEDO SANCHEZ BARAHONA SANTIAGO
VALLEY: REAL NEYBA

DOMINIE MASTER PASTOR
DOMINION RULE SWAY CROWN REALM REIGN DITION DOMAIN EMPERY EMPIRE REGNUM CONTROL DIOCESE DYNASTY KHANATE MASTERY POUSTIE REGENCY CALIFATE IMPERIUM LORDSHIP SEIGNORY SIGNORIA SOVRANTY OBEDIENCE
(PL.) DUCHY
DOMINO DIE BONE CARD FIVE MASK TILE BLANK JETON STONE DOUBLE JETTON MATADOR VENETIAN
(FIRST — PLAYED) SET
(PL.) MATATADOR MUGGINS BONEYARD
DOMINO NOIR, LE (COMPOSER OF —) AUBER
DOMITILLA (DAUGHTER OF —) DOMITILLA
(HUSBAND OF —) VESPASIAN
(SON OF —) TITUS DOMITIAN
DOM PEDRO SNOOZER
DON CAPO WEAR ARRAY DRESS ENDUE INDUE PUTON THROW ASSUME CLOTHE INVEST ADDRESS NOBLEMAN
DONALBAIN (FATHER OF —) DUNCAN
DONATE GIE GIFT GIVE BESTOW PRESENT
DONATION GIFT GRANT DONATIO PRESENT DONATIVE BENEFACTION
(—S RECEIVED BY SINGERS) CARL
DON CARLOS (CHARACTER IN —) EBOLI CARLOS PHILIP VALOIS CHARLES RODRIGO ELISABETH
(COMPOSER OF —) VERDI
DONE GAR DEEN OVER BAKED ENDED GIVEN COOKED THROUGH FINISHED
(— AS DUTY) PERFUNCTORY
(— BY HAND) MANUAL
(— BY WORD OF MOUTH) PAROL PAROLE
(— CARELESSLY) SCAMBLING
(— FOR) GONE SUNK KAPUT KAPUTT FINISHED
(— IN FAITH) AF
(— IN PLAIN SIGHT) BRAZEN
(— POORLY) BOTCHY
(— THOROUGHLY) PERFECT
(— TOGETHER) CONCERTED
(— WITH) BY
(— WITHOUT DELIBERATION) SNAP
(— WRONG WAY) AWK
(TO BE —) PASS
DONEE DONATOR HERITOR RECEIVER
DON GIOVANNI (CHARACTER IN —) ANNA ELVIRA MASETTO OTTAVIO ZERLINA GIOVANNI LEPORELLO
(COMPOSER OF —) MOZART
DONJON KEEP ROCCA DUNGEON
DON JUAN (MOTHER OF —) INEZ
DONKEY ASS BUSS DONK FUSS MOKE BURRO CHUMP CUDDY DICKY EQUID GENET GUDDA HINNY HORSE JENNY NEDDY BRAYER CUDDLE DICKEY JENNET ONAGER ASINEGO BUSSOCK FUSSOCK JACKASS LONGEAR CARDOPHAGUS
(MILNE —) EEYORE
DONKEY ENGINE DOCTOR DONKEY ROADER YARDER DOLLBEER
DONNA DEL LAGO (CHARACTER IN —) ELENA DOUGLAS GIACOMO MALCOLM RODERICK
(COMPOSER OF —) ROSSINI
DONNA DIANA (COMPOSER OF —) REZNICEK
DONNYBROOK MELEE
DONOR GIVER DONATOR
DO-NOTHING DONNOT DONOUGHT FAINEANT
DON PASQUALE (CHARACTER IN —) NORINA ERNESTO PASQUALE SOFRONIA MALATESTA
(COMPOSER OF —) DONIZETTI
DON QUIXOTE (AUTHOR OF —) CERVANTES
(CHARACTER IN —) PANZA PEDRO PEREZ ALONZO DAPPLE SAMSON SANCHO TOBOSO GUINART QUIXOTE CARRASCO DULCINEA NICHOLAS ROSINANTE
DONUM GIVER DEUNAM
DOODAD DODAD DOODAB DOFUNNY TRINKET GIMCRACK JIMCRACK
DOOHICKEY GISMO
DOOM KER LAW LOT DAMN FATE RUIN CURSE DEATH JUDGE ADDEEM DECREE DEVOTE STEVEN CONDEMN DESTINE DESTINY FORTUNE STATUTE DECISION FOREDOOM SENTENCE

DOOMED FEY DEAD DONE LORN FATAL DAMNED FORLORN ACCURSED FINISHED
DOOM PALM DOUM
DOOMSAYER DOOMSTER DOOMSDAYER
DOOMSMAN LAWMAN
DOOMSTER JUDGE
DOOR LID DROP EXIT FOLD GATE HECK SHUT TRAP ENTRY HATCH JANUA VALVE DAMPER JIGGER PORTAL RADDLE WICKET BARRIER DOORWAY INGRESS OPENING OUTDOOR PASSAGE POSTERN ANTEPORT ENTRANCE FOREDOOR POSTICUM SERVIDOR STOPPING TRAVERSE VOMITORY
(— IN MINE) STOPPING
(— OF ASH PIT) ARCH
(— OF MASONIC LODGE) TILE
(ADIT —) STULM
(AIRPLANE —) CLAMSHELL
(HALF —) HECK HATCH
(PART OF —) RAIL SILL STILE LINTEL MULLION
(ROMAN —S) FORES
(SLIDING —) SHUT SHOJI FUSUMA TRAVERSE
(STORM —) DINGLE
(STRONG —) OAK
(TRAP —) SLOT SCRUTO VAMPIRE VAMPYRE
(PREF.) THYRE(O) THYRO
(SUFF.) THYRIS
DOORFRAME BUCK
DOORHEAD DERNER
DOORKEEPER TILER TILIA USHER DURWAN PORTER WARDEN DOORMAN JANITOR OSTIARY DOORWARD HUISSIER JANITRIX PORTRESS WISKINKY
DOOR KNOCKER HAMMER RAPPER
DOOR LATCH SNECK HAGGADAY
DOORMAN FOOTMAN HALLMAN DOORWARD
DOORMAT COCOMAT
DOORPOST DURN JAMB PIER POST ALETTE POSTEL
DOORSILL SOIL
DOORSTOP BUMPER HOLDBACK
DOORWAY DOOR EXIT PORTAL OPENING
DOOZER PIP DARB LULU BEAUT DILLY CORKER SNORTER HUMDINGER
DOOZY LULU HUMDINGER
DOPATTA UPARNA DOOPUTTY
DOPE HOP LUG BOOB DRUG GOFF GOON GOOP INFO BOOBY OPIUM PASTE STUPE HEROIN INSIDE OPIATE SKINNY LOWDOWN PREDICT STUPEFY NARCOTIC
(— SMUGGLER) MULE
DOPED CRONK
DOPER GREASER
DOR BEE DORR JOKE MOCK BONGO CLOCK DORRE JOKER SCOFF TRICK BEETLE DRONER BUFFOON DECEIVE MOCKERY
DORADO CUIR XIPHIAS GOLDFISH
DORALICE (HUSBAND OF —) PHODOPHIL MANDRICARDO
(LOVER OF —) RODOMONT
DORBEETLE DOR CLOCK DRONER BUZZARD BUMCLOCK
DORIGEN (HUSBAND OF —) ARVIRAGUS
(LOVER OF —) AURELIUS
DORIMENE (HUSBAND OF —) SGANARELLE
(LOVER OF —) DORANTE
DORINDA (HUSBAND OF —) AIMWELL
(SISTER OF —) MIRANDA
DORIS (BROTHER AND HUSBAND OF —) NEREUS
(FATHER OF —) OCEANUS
(MOTHER OF —) TETHYS
DORK JERK NERD DWEEB
DORMANCY TORPOR ABEYANCE
DORMANT FIXED INERT ASLEEP LATENT TORPID RESTING SLEEPER INACTIVE LATITANT SLEEPING CONNIVENT
DORMER WINDOW LUCOMB MEMBER DORMANT EYEBROW LUCARNE LUTHERN
DORMITORY DORM HALL HOUSE DORMER DORTER HOSTEL BULLPEN COLLEGE DORTOUR CUBATORY QUARTERS
DORMOUSE LOIR DRYAD LEROT GLIRID SLEEPER
(PREF.) GLIRI
DORNICK DONEY LINEN DARNEX DONACK DONNICK
DORPER DORSIAN
DORSAL NOTAL DORSER DOSSER NEURAL TERGAL ABAXIAL HANGING SUPERIOR POSTERIOR
(PREF.) OPISTH(O)
DORSUM BACK
DORUS (BROTHER OF —) LAODOCUS POLYPOETES
(FATHER OF —) APOLLO HELLEN XUTHUS
(MOTHER OF —) CREUSA ORSEIS PHTHIA
(SLAYER OF —) AETOLUS
DOSAGE (RADIATION —) REM REP REPP
(SCIENCE OF —) POSOLOGY
DOSE BOLE DOST SHOT BROMO DATIO DOSIS DRAFT STORE TREAT DATION DOCTOR DOSAGE DRENCH POTION BOOSTER BROMIDE CAPSULE DRAUGHT QUANTITY
(— OF SUBSTANCE) PULSE
(DRUG —) HIT
(NARCOTIC —) LOCUS BINDLE LOCUST
DOSS BOW DOS KNOT TUFT BUNCH
DOSSERET PULVINO
DOT SET CLOT DOTE LUMP MOTE PECK SPOT STAR TICK COVER DOWER DOWRY POINT PRICK PUNTO SPECK BULLET CENTER CENTRE DOTLET PERIOD STIGME TITTLE TOCHER PUNCTUM PUNCTUS SPECKLE SPOTTLE STIPPLE FLYSPECK PARTICLE SPRINKLE
(— IN CODE) DIT
(— ON DICE) PIP
(— ON FOREHEAD) BOTTU
(— ON PATCH OF DIFFERENT COLOR) ISLET
(BLACK —) DARTROSE
(PL.) LEADERS
DOTAGE DOTE FOLLY DRIVEL SENILITY TWICHILD
DOTARD DOBBY DOTER SILLY DOBBIE DOTANT SENILE DOTTREL DOTTEREL IMBECILE LIRIPIPE LIRIPOOP
DOTCHIN STEELYARD
DOTE ROT DOVE DOZE FOND LIKE LOVE TIRE ADORE DECAY ENDOW BESTOW DOTAGE DOTARD DRIVEL STUPOR IMBECILE
DOTING FON FOND GAGA DOTAGE PAWING UXORIOUS
DOTTED SEME CRIBLE SEMEED TICKED TOUCHY SPOTTED PUNCTATE SPECKLED STIPPLED STELLATED
(— SWISS) LAPPET
DOTTER SPOTTER
DOTTEREL DUPE GULL WIND PLOVER DOTTREL MORINEL
DOTTY TOTY CRAZY TOTTY FEEBLE SPOTTY
DOUBLE KA BOW PLY DUAL FOLD SORE TWIN CRACK DUPLE FETCH ROUND SOSIE BIFOLD BINARY BINATE DOPPIO DUPLEX MIDDLE DIPLOID DOUBLET TWOFOLD BIVALENT GEMINATE BIFARIOUS SIMILITUDE
(— IMPRESSION) MACKLE
(— IN POKER) STRADDLE
(— MUSICAL NOTES) AUGMENT
(— UP) BUCK JACKKNIFE
(PHANTOM —) FETCH
(PREF.) BI BIN(I)(O) DI(S) DIPHY DIPL(O) DISS(O) DITTO GEMINI
DOUBLE BASSOON FAGOTTONE
DOUBLE CHIN CHOLLER
DOUBLECROSS BITCH CHEAT BETRAY DECEIVE SWINDLE BUSINESS
DOUBLE-CROSSER RAT HEEL
DOUBLED GEMEL GEMINOUS
(PREF.) BIS
DOUBLE DAGGER DIESIS
DOUBLE-DEALING DECEIT DUPLICITY
DOUBLE FLUTE DIAULOS
DOUBLEHEADER (BASEBALL —) TWINIGHT
DOUBLENESS DUALITY PLENITUDE
(— OF ASPECT) POLARITY
DOUBLE-RIPPER BOBSLED BOBSLEIGH
DOUBLE-RUNNER SKATE
DOUBLET SNIFF DOUBLE DUPLET PALTOCK PLACCATE POURPOINT
DOUBLE-TALK NEWSPEAK RAZZMATAZZ
DOUBLETREE EVENER SPREADER
DOUBLING LAP FOLD HEAD LOOP
(— OF THE BLIND) STRADDLE
DOUBLOON ONZA
DOUBLY
(PREF.) BI
DOUBT FEAR WEIR DEMUR DREAD DWERE QUERY WAVER NIGGLE BALANCE DIFFIDE DUBIETY SCRUPLE SKEPSIS SUSPECT SWITHER UMBRAGE DISTRUST DUBITATE HESITATE MISTRUST QUESTION STAGGERS MISLIPPEN
(EXTREME —) RACK
(PROFESSED —) APORIA
DOUBTER CYNIC SKEPTIC DUBITANTE
DOUBTFUL JUBUS DOUBTY UNSURE DUBIOUS FEARFUL JEALOUS PERHAPS WILSOME BOGGLISH DREADFUL JUBEROUS PERILOUS WAVERING QUESTIONABLE PROBLEMATICAL
DOUBTING DUBIOUS DUBITANT
DOUBTLESS WITTERLY
DOUCEUR TIP BONUS POURBOIRE
DOUCHE RINSE EYEWASH
DOUGH CASH DUFF FILO MASA CRUST DAIGH MONEY MOOLA PASTE PUPPY CHANGE DINERO HALLAH NOODLE PHYLLO SPONGE WAMPUM BRIOCHE CABBAGE MANDLEN TEIGLACH
(BISCUIT —) CAKE
(BREAD —) SPONGE
(CASE OF —) PIROGI PIEROGI
(FERMENTING —) LEAVEN
(FRIED —) SPUD
(NOODLE —) FARFEL FERFEL
(PASTRY —) PHYLLO
(SWEET SQUARE OF —) SOPAPILLA SOPAPAILLA
DOUGHBOY YANK
DOUGHNUT NUT SINK DONUT TORUS CYMBAL SINKER BEIGNET CRULLER FATCAKE NUTCAKE OLYCOOK OLYKOEK SIMBALL TWISTER ZEPPOLE BISMARCK FASNACHT
(SHAPED LIKE —) TOROIDAL
DOUGHTY FELL PREU TALL BRAVE VALIANT INTREPID
DOUGHY SAD DUNCH SODDEN
DOUR DERN GLUM GRIM HARD SOUR ROUGH STERN GLOOMY MOROSE SEVERE STRONG SULLEN OMINOUS TACITURN
DOUSE BEAT BLOW DOFF DUCK QUIT STOW CEASE DOWSE RINSE SOUSE DRENCH PLUNGE SLUICE STRIKE STROKE IMMERSE DOWNPOUR
(— WITH LIQUOR AND IGNITE) FLAMBE
DOUZEPER ANSEIS PALADIN
DOVE DOO DOW DOZE KUKU JONAH CULVER CUSHAT JEMIMA PIGEON COLUMBA DOVELET LAUGHER NAMAQUA SLUMBER DOVELING RINGDOVE
(— SOUND) CURR
(GROUND —) ROLA
(RING —) TOOZOO
(ROCK —) SOD
(SCALE —) INCA
DOVECOTE DOOCOT LOUVER DOVECOT DOWCOTE PIGEONRY COLUMBARY
DOVEKIE AUK ALLE BULL ROTCH ROTGE DOVEKEY BULLBIRD DOVELIKE

DOVETAIL COG JAG JAGG MESH MERGE TENON
DOWDINESS FRUMPERY
DOWDY POKY FRUMP MOPSY POKEY TACKY BLOWZY SHABBY STODGY UNTIDY FRUMPISH SLOVENLY
DOWEL NOG PEG PIN COAK STUD SPRIG JOGGLE PINTLE DULEDGE
DOWER DOS DOWRY ENDOW TOCHER DOARIUM PORTION HERITAGE MARITAGE
DOWITCHER SNIPE DRIVER SLEEPER GRAYBACK GREYBACK LONGBEAK
DOWN BAS EAT HUP OFF BETE CAST COOL DOON DOWL FELL FLIX FLUE FUZZ HILL LINT MOXA PILE SOUR ADOWN BELOW DOWLE EIDER FLOOR FLUFF SOUTH BEDOWN FRIEZE LANUGO PAPPUS CONSUME HANDOUT HILLOCK PLUMAGE DOWNLAND
(— AND OUT) QUISBY
(— AT THE HEEL) SLIPSHOD
(— THAT WAY) DOWNBY DOWNBYE
(— THE LINE) ALONG
(BE — WITH) HAVE
(BEAVER —) FLIX
(FAR —) DEEP DEEPLY
(FARTHEST —) BOTTOMMOST
(GO —) SET
(STRAIGHT —) DOWNRIGHT
(PREF.) CAT(A)(O) CATH DE HYPO KAT(A) LACHN(O) OB PTIL(O) SUB
DOWN-AND-OUT DERELICT
DOWNBEAT THESIS
DOWNCAST BAD LOW SAD DOWN ABJECT GLOOMY HANGING DEJECTED HOPELESS
DOWNER DRAG
DOWNFALL PIT FALL FATE RUIN TRAP ABYSS DECAY FINISH DESCENT ECLIPSE UNDOING COLLAPSE DOWNCOME FLAMEOUT TAILSPIN
(AUTHOR OF —) ZOLA
(CHARACTER IN —) JEAN WEISS HONORE GOLIATH GUNTHER MAURICE SILVINE FOUCHARD MACQUART HENRIETTE LEVASSEUR DELAHERCHE GARTLAUBEN
DOWNFEED OVERHEAD
DOWNFLOW VAIL DEFLUX
DOWNFOLD SADDLE DOWNWARP
DOWNGRADE DERATE
DOWNHILL DOWNDALE
(SKI —) WEDEL
DOWN-HOME CORNPONE
DOWNPOUR POUR RAIN BRASH DOUSE DOWSE FLOOD PLASH SPILL SPOUT DELUGE TORRENT CATARACT AVALANCHE
DOWNRIGHT FAIR FLAT PURE RANK BLANK BLUNT PLAIN PLUMB PLUMP ROUND SHEER STARK ARRANT DIRECT FAIRLY STURDY REGULAR ABSOLUTE EVENDOWN POSITIVE THOROUGH
DOWNSPOUT SPOUT DOWNPIPE DOWNTAKE
DOWNSTAIRS BELOW
DOWNSTROKE DOWNBEAT
DOWNSWING DOLDRUMS
DOWNWARD ADOWN BELOW LOWER PRONE DEORSUM DOWNWITH
(— ON ONE SIDE) SIDEWAYS
(PREF.) BATH(O)(Y) CAT(A)(O) CATH
DOWNWIND LEEWARD
DOWNY SOFT FLUEY MOSSY NAPPY PILAR PLUMY QUIET CALLOW FLEDGY FLOSSY FLUFFY PILARY PLACID COTTONY CUNNING KNOWING SOOTHING
(PREF.) HEBE
DOWRY DOS DOT GIFT DOWER SULKA DOWAGE LOBOLA LOBOLO TALENT PORTION
DOWSE WITCH
DOXOLOGIZE LAUD
DOXOLOGY GLORIA KADDISH
DOXY WENCH HARLOT
DOYEN DEAN DOYENNE
DOZE NAP NOD ROT DARE DORM DOTE DOVE DECAY DOVER SLEEP SLOOM CATNAP DROWSE MUDDLE SNOOZE DROPOFF MEMENTO PERPLEX SLUMBER SNOOZLE STUPEFY
DOZEN DIZZEN DOSAIN
(FIVE —) TALLY
(TWO —) THRAVE
DOZING DOGSSLEEP
DRAB BOX DAW FOX SAD BLAH DELL DRUG DULL BESOM BLEAK DINGY DOLLY DREAR GRAVE GRAZE HEAVY MOUSY TRULL WENCH WHORE DREARY FRUMPY ISABEL MALKIN POISON PUSSEL STODGY PROSAIC PUCELLE SUBFUSC DOLLYMOP EVERYDAY POMPLESS
(CHAETURA —) BEAR
DRABBLE DRAGGLE
DRACHM DRAM
DRACO ANGUIS DRAGON
DRAFT NIP SIP CHIT DOSE DRAG DRAM DRAW GLUT GULF GUST ITEM LEVY PLAN PLOT SUCK SWIG TOOT WORK BLAST CHECK DRINK EPURE SLOCK SWILL SWIPE TAPER WRITE DESIGN DRENCH GODOWN MINUTE POTION PROJET REDACT RETURN SCHEME SCROLL SKETCH WAUCHT WAUGHT ABBOZZO DRAUGHT DRAWING OUTLINE PATTERN PHILTER PROJECT BEVERAGE POTATION PROTOCOL
(— OF AIR) COOKE
(— OF A VESSEL) GAGE GAUGE
(— OF COMPOSITION) SCORE
(— OFF) SHED
(— OF LAW) BILL
(— OF PATTERN) STRIP
(HEAVY —) WHITTER
(LARGE —) SCOUR CAROUSE
(MIDDAY —) NOONING
(ORIGINAL —) PROTOCOL
(ROUGH —) EBAUCHE BROUILLON SCANTLING
(SECOND —) REDO REWRITE
(SLEEPING —) DORTER
(SMALL —) NIP SIP SUCK TIFF TIFT
DRAFTER HORSER
DRAFTSMAN DRAWER TRACER TIPPLER
DRAG DOG LAG TOW DRUG HALE HONE HOOK KITE RASH SHOE SKID SLUR TOLE TOLL TUMP CREEP DEVIL DRAWL DRIFT FLOAT GETUP LURRY NOWEL PLUCK RALLY SLIDE SNAKE SWEEP TEASE TRAIL TRAIN TRAWL TRICE DAGGLE DOWNER DROGUE LINGER OUTFIT REMORA SCHOOL TAIGLE TRAYNE DRAGBAR DRAGGLE GRAPNEL GRAPPLE SCHLEPP SKIDPAN ARRASTRA DRAGSHOE
(— ALONG) LUG CRAWL SHOOL TRAYNE TRACHLE TRAUCHLE
(— CARELESSLY) HIKE
(— DOWN) DEGRADE
(— FEET) SLODGE
(— FORCIBLY) SNAKE
(— HOME CARCASS OF GAME) TUMP
(— IN DEEP WATER) CREEP
(— JERKILY) SNIG
(— LOGS) SKID
(— OFF) HARRY
(— OUT) DRAWL
(PLANK —) RUBBER
DRAGGING LEADEN
(— DEAD BULL FROM RING) ARRASTRE
DRAGGLE LAG DRAIL DAGGLE DRABBLE TRACHLE
DRAGNET FLUE TRAIN TRAWL DRAWNET TRAINEL
DRAGON AHI LUNG WORM DRAKE RAHAB NIDHOG VRITRA WYVERN BASILISK DRAGONET NIDHOGGR NITHHOGG
(— WITH 7 HEADS) HYDRA
(SEA —) QUAVIVER
(WINGLESS —) LINDWORM
(PREF.) DRACO(NT)(NTO)
DRAGONET FOX ILLECK FOXFISH GOWDNIE GURNARD JUGULAR SCULPIN LORICATE QUAVIVER
DRAGONFLY NAIAD ODONATE SKIMMER LIBELLULA
DRAGON TREE DRACAENA
DRAGROPE DRAG GUSS
DRAGSTER FUELER SLINGSHOT
DRAIN DRY FRY GAN GAW SAP SEW TOP BUZZ COUP DAIL DALE DELF DIKE DRAG DRAW GOUT GRIP GURT LADE LODE MILK SIKE SINK SOAK SUFF SUMP TEEM TILE BLEED BUNNY CANAL DELFT DRAFT DREEN DRILL DROVE EMPTY FLEET GROOP GULLY LEECH RHINE SEUCH SEUGH SEWER SHORE SIVER STANK STELL EMULGE FILTER FURROW GUZZLE RIGGOT SHEUCH SHEUGH SIPHON SPONGE SWOUGH SYPHON TRENCH TROGUE TROUGH ZANJON ACEQUIA ALBERCA CAROUSE CARRIER CHANNEL CULVERT DEPLETE DRAUGHT EXHAUST GRINDLE GRIPPLE SCUPPER ZANJONA CANALIZE CARRIAGE SINKHOLE SUBDRAIN THURROCK
(— DRY) JIB
(— IN CHURCH) PISCINA
(— IN FEN) LEAM
(— IN MINE) SOUGH
(— IN STABLE) GROOP
(— SUGAR) POT
(COVERED —) THURROCK
(OPEN —) SIVER STELL KENNEL
(SMALL —) TRONE
DRAINAGE ADIT SAUR SOCK SULLAGE SUMPAGE
DRAINAGEWAY DRAW
DRAINER COLANDER
DRAINING SEEPAGE DRAINAGE EMULGENT
DRAINPIPE SINK SHELL WHELM LEADER QUELME
DRAKE STAG STAIG DRAKELET
DRAM GO NIP MITE SLUG TIFF TIFT DRAFT DRINK SOPIE CALKER CHASSE DRACHM JIGGER CAULKER SNIFTER MERIDIAN POTATION QUANTITY
(— OF LIQUOR) TOT SLUG SNIFTER
(— OF SPIRITS) NOBBLER
DRAMA RAS AUTO MIME PLAY LEGIT OPERA COMEDY NATAKA SCENES SOAPER TRAGIC ATELLAN COMEDIA HISTORY PROVERB THEATRE TRAGEDY DUODRAMA MONODRAM OPERETTA PASTORAL
(DANCE —) KATHAKALI
(JAPANESE —) NO NOH KABUKI
(MUSICAL —) OPERA SAYNETE OPERETTA
DRAMATIC WILD VIVID SCENIC THESPIAN
(— REPRESENTATION) WAYANG
(— WORK) PREQUEL
(HAVING LYRIC AND — QUALITIES) SPINTO
DRAMATIST (ALSO SEE PLAYWRIGHT) OG ACTOR IBSENITE
DRAMSHOP GROGSHOP
DRAPE HANG PALL VEST ADORN COVER CRAPE WEAVE CURTAIN FESTOON HANGING VALANCE
DRAPED BEHUNG
DRAPER TAILOR LINENMAN
DRAPERY SWAG BAIZE DRAPE SCENE CURTAIN REREDOS VALANCE MOURNING
(— ON BEDSTEAD) PAND
(PIECE OF —) HANGING
DRAPING BLOUSE DRAPERY
DRASTIC DIRE HARSH EXTREME RADICAL RIGOROUS
(NOT —) BLAND
DRAT DARN NUTS RATS PSHAW PHOOEY RABBIT SHUCKS DOGGONE
DRATTED BLESSED
DRAUGHT (ALSO SEE DRAFT) SLUG WAUGHT OENOMEL
DRAUPADI (FATHER OF —) DRUPADA
DRAVIDIAN GOND KOTA TODA TULU ARAVA COORG GONDI KHOND KLING MALTO ORAON TAMIL ANDHRA BADAGA BIRHOR BRAHUI KODAGU KURUKH TELEGU TELUGU COLLERY DRAVIDA TAMILIC KANARESE TAMILIAN
DRAW LUG TEE TIE TOW TUG DRAG DUCT HALE HAUL LADE LIMN LINE

LURE PUFF PULL RAKE SPAN TILL TIRE TOLL TREK VENT CATCH DRAFT DRILL EDUCE ENDUE EXACT HEAVE PAINT SKINK TRACE TRAIN TRECK ALLURE BUCKET DEDUCE DEPICT DERIVE DESIGN DEVISE ELICIT ENGAGE ENTICE INDUCE INHALE SELECT SKETCH STRIKE ATTRACT BEGUILE CONTOUR DETRACT DOGFALL DRAUGHT EXTRACT INSPIRE PORTRAY SCREEVE SCUMBLE INSCRIBE INVEIGLE OUTBRAID STANDOFF
(— A CARD) CUT
(— AIR) BREATHE
(— ALONG) TRACK TRAIN
(— APART) REAM DIVEL DIDUCE DIVERGE
(— ASIDE) SEDUCE
(— ASUNDER) TEAR
(— AT A PIPE) SHOOH SHAUGH
(— AWAY) ARACE DRAFT ABDUCT ARACHE DRAUGHT ENTRAIN ABSTRACT DISTRACT
(— AWKWARDLY) SCRAWL
(— BACK) FADE REVEL START WINCE ARREAR RETIRE REVOKE SHRINK CRINKLE RECLAIM RETRACT RETREAT WITHTEE
(— BACK FROM) BLENCH FLINCH RESILE TORFEL TORFLE DETRECT
(— BACK LIPS) GRIN
(— BOLT) SLOT
(— BY SUCTION) ASPIRATE
(— DEEP BREATH) SUSPIRE
(— DRINK) BIRL
(— EARTH AROUND) HILL
(— FIRST FURROW) FEER
(— FORTH) EDUCE EVOKE FETCH ELICIT DEPROME EXHAUST
(— IN) PINK TRAP ENTRAP
(— IN DOTS) STIPPLLE
(— OFF) BROACH
(— ON) INDUE INDUCE SOLICIT
(— ON PAVEMENT) SCREEVE
(— ON UNCOLLECTED FUNDS) KITE
(— OUT) MILK SLUB EDUCE EVOKE EXACT SKINK TRACT ELICIT EXHALE EXTEND EXTORT EXTRACT
(— STITCHES TIGHT) YERK
(— TIGHT) FRAP THRAP STRAIN
(— TOGETHER) COWL LACE COART GATHER CRIMPLE
(— UP) FORM MAKE HUCKLE INKNIT UPWALE
(— WITH FORCE) STRAIN
DRAWBACK OUT LETDOWN TAKEOFF DISCOUNT PULLBACK
DRAWBAR DRAGBAR BULLNOSE DRAWLINK SLIPRAIL
DRAWBRIDGE PONTLEVIS
DRAWEE ACCEPTER
DRAWER TILL LIMNER LOCKER TILLER ENTERER INTAKER SHUTTLE
(— OF WATER) GIBEONITE
(BOTTOM —) GLORYBOX
(CASH —) TILL
(COAL —) PUTTER
(TYPEWRITER —) BED
DRAWER-DOWN KNOBBLER
DRAWER-IN ENTERER HEALDER HEDDLER
DRAWER-OFF RACKER
DRAWERS PANTS SHORTS LININGS PANTIES SHALWAR CALSOUNS CALZOONS SHINTYAN PANTALETS PANTELETS SHULWAURS PANTALETTES
DRAWGATE SLACKER
DRAWING DRAW CHALK DRAFT ENVOI EPURE SEPIA TUSHE CRAYON DESIGN DETAIL FIGURE FUSAIN SKETCH CAMAIEU CARTOON CROQUIS DIAGRAM DRAUGHT HAULING ISOTYPE PULLING RETRAIT TOUSCHE ADDUCENT CHARCOAL CROSSING DOODLING FREEHAND FROTTAGE HATCHING LINEWORK SANGUINE SLUBBING SPECULUM STICKMAN TRACTION TRANSFER TRICKING
(— ASUNDER) DIVELLENT
(— BACK) ABDUCENT
(— IN) INDRAFT
(— IN RED CHALK) SANGUINE
(— LIQUOR) BIRLING
(— OFF) DERIVATION
(— OF LOTS) BALLOT
(— OUT) BATTUE
(— TOGETHER) STYPTIC
(CHARCOAL —) FUSAIN
(COMIC —) CARTOON DROLLERY
(MARGINAL —) REMARK
(PREHISTORIC —) PICTOGRAM PICTOGRAPH
(PREPARATORY —) SINOPIA
(SIDEWALK —) SCREEVE
(PL.) GRAFFITI
(PREF.) GRAMO
(SUFF.) GRAM
DRAWING-IN DRAW ENTERING
DRAWING-ROOM SALON
DRAWING ROOM SALON PARLOR
DRAWKNIFE SHAVE JIGGER
DRAWL DRANT DRATE DRUNT TRAIN LOITER PROLATE
DRAWN DRAFT STREIT DRAUGHT GRAPHIC HAGGARD
(— APART) DISTRACT
(— AWAY) ABSTRACT
(— CLOSE) STRICT
(— OFF) DRAINED
(— OUT) DREE DREICH DREIGH EXTENDED
DRAWPLATE AGATE FLATTER
DRAWSHEET TYMPAN
DRAWSTRING LATCH STRING
DRAY CART LORRY SCOOT SLOOP WAGON CAMION JIGGER ROLLEY RULLEY SLOVEN WHEERY
DREAD AWE DREE FEAR FRAY FUNK WARD WERE ANGST AWFUL DOUBT GRISE TIMOR ADREAD AGRISE DISMAY ESCHEW HORROR TERROR ANXIETY DISMISS DRIDDER REDOUBT AFFRIGHT DREDDOUR GASTNESS MISDREAD TERRIBLE
(SUFF.) PHOBE PHOBIA(C) PHOBIC PHOBOUS
DREADED AWESOME BEDREAD
DREADFUL DERN DIRE AWFUL CRUEL DISMAL GRISLY HORRID AWESOME CAREFUL DIREFUL DRIDDER FEARFUL GHASTLY GRIMFUL HIDEOUS UNCOUTH DOUBTFUL DOUBTOUS GHASTFUL HORRIBLE HORRIFIC PERILOUS SCAREFUL SHOCKING TERRIBLE TERRIFIC
DREADFULLY DIRELY GRISLY ABYSMALLY
DREADNOUGHT TANK DAREALL WARSHIP FEARLESS
DREAM METE MOON MUSE REVE FANCY SWEVEN VISION AISLING AVISION CHIMERA FANTASY IMAGINE NIRVANA REVERIE ROMANCE CHIMAERA DAYDREAM PHANTASM SOMNIATE
(— UP) ENVISION
(FRIGHTENING —) NIGHTMARE
(PREF.) ONEIR(O) ONIR(O)
DREAMER POET METER MUSARD FANTAST IDEALIST PHANTAST
DREAMINESS LANGUOR
DREAMING ADREAM TRAUMEREI
DREAMTIME ALCHERA
DREAMY KEF SOFT MOONY VAGUE POETIC FARAWAY LANGUID MUSEFUL ONEIRIC PENSIVE DREAMFUL FANCIFUL SOOTHING
DREAR DERN BLEAK DISMAL GLOOMY DOLEFUL
DREARY SAD DIRE DOWY DREE DULL FLAT GLUM BLEAK CRUEL DOWIE DRURY OURIE WASTE WISHT DISMAL DREICH ELENGE GLOOMY GOUSTY LONELY DOLEFUL GOUSTIE HOWLING WILSOME GRIEVOUS WEARIFUL
DREDGE MOP DRAG DREG SIFT SCOOP TRAIN DEEPEN DRUDGE SCRAPE SPONGE TANGLE GANGAVA SCALLOP EXCAVATE SPRINKLE
(KIND OF —) EKMAN
(NATURALIST'S —) TANGLE
DREDGER DUSTER HEDGEHOG
DREDGING JILLING
DREGS LAG MUD CRAP FAEX LAGS LEES SCUT SILT SUDS TAIL DRAFF DREST DROSS DRUGS FECES FOOTS GROUT JAUPS MAGMA BOTTOM DRAINS DUNDER FECULA MOTHER REFUSE SORDES SORDOR ULLAGE DRIBBLE GROUNDS GRUMMEL HEELTAP OUTWALE RESIDUE RINSING GRUMMELS REMNANTS SEDIMENT SETTLING
(— OF LIQUOR) TAPLASH
(— OF MOLTEN GLASS) DRIBBLE
(— OF SOCIETY) WASH LEGGE CANAILLE
(— OF TALLOW) GREAVES
DREIBUND TRIPLICE
DREIDEL TRENDEL
DREI PINTOS, DIE (CHARACTER IN —) GOMEZ PINTO GASTON AMBROSIO CLARISSA PANTALEONE
(COMPOSER OF —) MAHLER
DRENCH SOP DOSE HOSE SIND SINK SOAK TOSH BLASH DOUSE DOWSE DRAFT DRINK DROKE DROUK DROWN SLOCK SLUSH SOUSE STEEP SWILL BUCKET DELUGE DOUCHE IMBRUE INFUSE POTION SLUICE DRUNKEN EMBATHE IMMERSE INDRENCH PERMEATE SATURATE SUBMERGE
DRENCHED DRUNKEN
DRENCHER INFUSER
DRENCHING DOUSE DOWSE DOWNPOUR
DRESS AX AXE BED DON DUB FIG FIT HOE KIT RAG RAY RIG TOG BARB BEGO BOWN BUSK BUSS CLAY COAT COMB DESK DILL DINK GALA GARB GEAR GORE GOWN HONE HUKE KNAP MIDI MILL MINI RAIL ROBE SUIT TIFF TIRE TRIM TUBE TUCK VEST WEAR ADORN ARRAY BIGAN BRAWS CLEAN CLOTH CRUMB CRUSH CURRY DIGHT DIZEN EQUIP FLOAT FROCK GUISE HABIT IHRAM MAGMA PREEN PRICK PRIMP PRINK PRUNE SHAPE SHIFT TENUE THING TRICK AGUISE ATTIRE ATTRAP BARBER BETRIM BROACH CLOTHE ENROBE FANGLE FETTLE FRAISE GRAITH INVEST JELICK JUMPER KIRTLE MAGPIE MULLET MUUMUU OUTFIT PLIGHT REVEST SARONG SHEATH SHROUD TOILET ADDRESS AFFAITE APPAREL BANDAGE BEDIZEN CHEMISE CLOTHES COSTUME DALLACK DUBBING GARMENT GARNISH HARNESS HATCHEL RAIMENT TOGGERY VESTURE ACCOUTER ACCOUTRE CLEADING CLOTHING DECORATE FEATHERS HANDMADE ORNAMENT SUNDRESS TAILLEUR VESTMENT EMBELLISH
(— A SKIN) WHEEL
(— DOWN) BRACE BERATE
(— ELEGANTLY) DINK
(— FISH) CALVER
(— FLAX) TED
(— FLINT) NAP KNAP
(— FOOD) SAUCE
(— FOR FELTING) CARROT
(— HAIR) TIRE TRUSS BARBER
(— HIDES) BEAM
(— HURRIEDLY) HUDDLE
(— IN FINE CLOTHES) DIKE BRANK
(— MEAT) LARD SHROUD
(— NEGLIGENTLY) MOB
(— OF OFFICE) ROBE
(— ORE) VAN
(— OVER) STOP
(— SHEEPSKINS) TAW
(— SHOWILY) PRANK
(— SMARTLY) DALLACK
(— STONE) DAB NIG DAUB DRAG FACE GAGE HACK GAUGE NIDGE POINT SCABBLE SCAPPLE
(— TAWDRILY) BEDIZEN
(— UNTIDILY) MAB
(— UP) BUSK DILL ADORN ARRAY PRANK PRIMP PRINK SPICK WATER FETTLE TOGGLE BECLOUT BEDRESS TITIVATE
(— VULGARLY) DAUB
(— WITH CHISEL) DROVE
(— WITH SLIT SKIRT) CHEONGSAM
(— WITH TROWEL) STRIKE
(— WORN BY MAN) DRAG
(— WOUND) PANSE BANDAGE
(CIVILIAN —) MUFTI

(COAT —) SIMAR SYMAR SIMARRE
(EVENING —) FORMAL
(FESTIVE —) GALA
(HAWAIIAN —) MUUMUU
(HIGHLANDER —) FILABEG
(HOMESPUN —) RUSSET
(INCOMPLETE —) DISARRAY
(LONG —) MAXI
(LOOSE —) SACK SACQUE
(MORNING —) PEIGNOIR
(ONE-PIECE —) CAGE
(ORIENTAL —) CHEONGSAM
(PECULIAR —) LIVERY
(POPLIN —) TABINET TABBINET
(RUSSIAN NATIONAL —) SARAFAN
(SHOWY —) BRAVERY
(SLEEVELESS —) SKIMMER
(STYLE OF —) GETUP
(SUFF.) ESTHES

DRESSED CLAD DONE BOUND BECLAD COATED COMBED HABITED GOFFERED
(— GAILY) FRESH SPARKISH
(— IN WHITE) CANDIDATE
(LOOSELY —) DISCINCT
(NOT —) UNDIGHT
(RICHLY —) BROCADED
(ROUGHLY —) HEWN
(SHOWILY —) BEPRANKED
(STYLISHLY —) SMART
(WELL —) BRAW GASH

DRESSER AMBRY AWMRY ROBER TAWER BUREAU FRAMER ENROBER MODISTE CUPBOARD
(LEATHER —) LEVANTER
(WELSH —) TRIDARN

DRESSING CAST MAYO GRAVY BANDAGE BEATING BLANKET IODOFORM RAVIGOTE REMOLADE SCOLDING STUFFING MAYONNAISE
(— FOR WOUNDS) LINT SPONGE
(— OF STONE) SKIFFLING
(HAIR —) LACKER LACQUER
(KIND OF —) RANCH

DRESSING-GOWN KIMONO PEIGNOIR

DRESSING ROOM SHIFT VESTRY CAMARIN VESTUARY

DRESSING-TABLE LOWBOY

DRESSMAKER SEWER SEAMER MODISTE STITCHER COUTURIER TIREWOMAN

DRESSMAKING COUTURE

DRESS RACK FRIPPERY

DRESSY SHARP

DRIBBLE DRIB DRIP DROP CARRY DRIVEL DRIBLET DRIPPLE DRIZZLE SLABBER

DRIBLET CLOT PIECE
(PL.) SMALLS

DRIED SEAR SERE ADUST GIZZEN TORRID WIZENED GIZZENED

DRIFT FAN JET SAG DENE DUNE FORD HERD PLOT RACK SILT TIDE TILL DRIVE DROVE FLEET FLOAT FLOCK IOWAN SENSE SLIDE SLOOM SLOUM TENOR TREND BROACH COURSE DESIGN DEVICE DRIVER OFFSET PODGER SCHEME STREAM TUNNEL WINDLE CURRENT DIPHEAD DRIBBLE GALLERY HEADING IMPETUS IMPULSE LATERAL OUTWASH PASTURE PROCESS PURPORT SETBOLT DILUVIUM DRIFTPIN TENDENCY
(— LANGUIDLY) SWOON
(— OF CLOUDS) CARRY
(— OF SAND OR SNOW) WREATH
(— SIDEWISE) CRAB
(— WITH ANCHOR DOWN) CLUB
(DOWNWARD —) DROOP
(GLACIAL —) CARY TILL IOWAN
(RUBBLE —) HEAD

DRIFTER HOBO TRAMP DROVER SWAGMAN VAGRANT

DRIFTING ADRIFT DRIFTAGE

DRIFT PLUG DUMMY

DRIFTWAY DROVE

DRIFTWOOD WAFTURE

DRILL GAD JAR JIG RIG SOW TAP BORE CORE SPUD AUGER BORER CHARK CHURN DECOY DREEL PADDY THIRL TRAIN TUTOR TWIRL WHIRL ALLURE BROACH ENTICE FURROW JUMPER PIERCE SCHOOL SEEDER SINKER STOPER THRILL CHANNEL DRIFTER JANKERS PLUGGER STARTER EXERCISE INSTRUCT PRACTICE
(— SYSTEM) MARTINET
(MASONRY —) AIGUILLE
(WEAPONS —) MANUAL

DRILLMAN STOPER

DRINK GO ADE ALE BIB BUM FIX GIN HUM KIR LAP MOP NOG PEG POT RUM RYE SIP SUP TEA TOT WET BALL BEER BEND BENO BOLL BOSA BOZA BREW BULL BUMP CHIA CHUG COKE COLA DRAG DRAM FIZZ FLIP GROG HAVE HORN JAKE LUSH MEAD MIST NIPA NOGG PULL PURL SHOT SIND SLUG SOAK SOMA SOPE SPOT SWIG TIFF TOOT TOPE WHET AIRAH ASSAI BEVER BINGE BLAND BOMBO BOOZE BOUSE BOZAH BUBUD BUMBO CIDER CRUSH DAISY DRAFT FLOAT GLOGG HAOMA JULEP LAGER MORAT NEGUS PAINT POSCA PUNCH QUAFF ROUSE SETUP SKINK SLING SLOCK SMACH SMASH SMILE SMOKE SNIFF SNORT SOPIE SOUSE SWATS SWILL THING TOAST TODDY VODKA WHIFF ZOMBI ABSORB BEZZLE BRACER BRANDY BUMPER BURTON CALKER CASIRI CATLAP CAUDLE CHASER COFFEE COOPER DIBBLE DRENCH EGGHOT EGGNOG FUDDLE GIMLET GODOWN GUGGLE GUZZLE HOOKER IMBIBE MESCAL POSSET POTION PTISAN RICKEY ROBROY SCREED SHANDY SIPPLE SIRPLE SWANKY SWINGE TACKLE TAMPOY TASTER TIPPLE VELVET WAUCHT WAUGHT ZOMBIE BRAGGET BRIMMER CAROUSE CHEERER CHIRPER COBBLER COLLINS CONSUME CORDIAL DILUENT DRAUGHT EXHAUST FLANNEL GUARANA GUARAPO INHAUST MORNING NOONING PROPOMA SHERBET SIDECAR SNEEZER SNIFTER SUCTION SUPPAGE SWALLOW TANKARD TRILLIL AMARETTO APERITIF BEVERAGE BRIDECUP BULLSHOT CHUGALUG COCKTAIL HIGHBALL LIBATION MAHOGANY NIGHTCAP POTATION QUENCHER REFRESCO RUMBARGE SANGAREE SPRITZER SYLLABUB TEQUILLA PHOSPHATE SUNDOWNER
(— AFTER A MEAL) DIGESTIF
(— AT DRAFT) TOP
(— EXCESSIVELY) TOPE BIBLE SOUSE BEZZLE BIBBLE TIPPLE SWIZZLE
(— FROM FERMENTED MILK) AIRAN KEFIR
(— GREEDILY) SLOP SWACK SWILL GUTTLE GUZZLE
(— HEAVILY) TOOT SWINK
(— INTOXICATING LIQUOR) IRRIGATE
(— LIQUOR) TIP DRAM SOAK BOOZE PAINT
(— NOISILY) SLURP
(— OF BEER) BUTCHER
(— OF BEER AND BUTTERMILK) BONNY CLABBER
(— OF BEER AND GINGERALE) SHANDYGAFF
(— OFF) COUP
(— OF HONEY AND MULBERRY JUICE) MORAT
(— OF IMMORTALITY) SOMA
(— OF INDIA) SHRAB
(— OF LIQUEUR) FRAPPE
(— OF LIQUOR) WET DRAM JOLT SHOT SPOT TASS WHET SETUP WHIFF CALKER JIGGER TASTER WETTING HIGHBALL NIGHTCAP
(— OF MOLASSES) SWITCHEL
(— OF THE GODS) AMRITA NECTAR
(— OF VINEGAR AND WATER) POSCA
(— SOCIALLY) BIRL HOBNOB
(— SPARINGLY) BLEB
(— TOAST) PLEDGE
(— TO EXCESS) SOAK
(— TO EXCITE LOVE) PHILTER
(— TO LAST DROP) BUZZ
(— UP) CRUSH EPOTE CAROUSE EXHAUST
(— WITHOUT PAUSE) CHUGALUG
(ACID —) SOUR
(ADDITIONAL —) EIK EKE
(ALCOHOLIC —) BENO BINO MIST NIPA BOMBO BUDGE BUMBO DRAIN JOUGH SHRAB SLING SNORT SNIFTER
(AUSTRALIAN —) BEAL
(BRAZILIAN —) ASSAI ASSAHY
(BUTTERMILK AND WATER —) BLAND
(CURRANT —) CASSIS
(DIETETIC —) POSSET
(DRUGGED —) HOCUS
(FARINACEOUS —) PTISAN
(FERMENTED —) BOSA MEAD BALCHE MUSHLA PULQUE CASSIRI GUARAPO
(FREE —) SHOUT
(FRUIT —) SQUASH
(GREAT —) JORUM
(HALF-SIZED —) CHOTAPEG
(HEADY —) HUFFCAP
(HERBAL —) SNAPS
(HOT —) COPUS NEGUS SALOP TODDY BISHOP EGGHOT PLOTTY SALOOP CARDINAL
(INCLINED TO —) OUTWARD
(INSIPID —) SLUM
(INTOXICATING —) AVA GROG SUCK BOOZE KUMISS SCOTCH DRAPPIE PAIWARI SWIZZLE SKOKIAAN
(INTOXICATING —S) SAUCE BOTTLE
(LONG —) SWIPE HIGHBALL
(MAKE A — LAST) NURSE
(MEAN —) LAP
(MEDICINAL —) TISANE ADVOCAAT
(MIDDAY —) NOONING MERIDIAN
(MIXED —) TWIST
(NARCOTIC —) KAVA
(NON-ALCOHOLIC —) GAZOZ COOLER
(PALM —) ASSAI
(PARTING —) BONAILIE
(POISONOUS —) DRENCH
(RUSSIAN —) OBARNE OBARNI
(SACRED —) HOMA AMRIT HAOMA AMRITA
(SACRIFICIAL —) HOMA SOMA
(SMALL —) PEG DRAM SOPIE DALLOP WETTING
(SOFT —) SLUSH
(SOUR —) ALEGAR
(SPANISH —) SANGRIA
(STRONG —) BUB HUM BENO SICER FUDDLE SHICKER
(TASTELESS —) SLOP
(THIN —) SLOSH
(WEAK —) LAP BOOL BULL CATLAP
(WEST INDIES —) SANGAREE

DRINKER SOT LUSH TANK POTER TOAST TOPER BARFLY BENDER CUPMAN LUSHER SOAKER SPONGE IMBIBER INTAKER QUAFFER DRUNKARD
(EXCESSIVE — OF TEA) THEIC
(HEAVY —) JUICEHEAD
(WATER —) HYDROPOT

DRINKING BEVER DRAFT DRINKY GUZZLE DRAUGHT POTTING CAROUSAL POTATION
(CONTINUOUS —) BOUT

DRINKING-BOUT CAROUSE

DRIP LIP SIE SYE DROP LEAK SEGE SILE WEEP CANAL DRILL EAVES LABEL STILL DRIBBLE DRIPPLE LARMIER TRICKLE TRINKLE TRINTLE
(— WITH TINKLING SOUND) PINK
(PREF.) STALACTI(TI) STALAGMO

DRIPPING ADRIP ALEAK STAXIS WEEPING

DRIPSTONE BAT DING LABEL HOODMOLD

DRIVE CA CAW COT FOG HOY JOG AUTO BANG BEAR BEAT BUTT CALL CRAM DING DRUB DRUM FIRE FIRK FLOG GOAD HACK HERD HUNT HURL JASM JEHU KICK LASH MOVE PICK PILE POSS PUSH RACK RIDE SEND SERR SINK SLOG SPUR STAB STUB TOOL TOUR TURN URGE BRAWL CHASE CHECK COACT CROWD DRIFT DROVE FEEZE FLAIL FORCE HORSE HURRY IMPEL INFER LODGE MOTOR PEDAL POACH

PRESS PULSE PUNCH REPEL ROUST SHOVE SLASH SMITE SPANK SWEEP TEASE ATTACK BATTER BEETLE BENSEL CHARGE COMPEL CUDGEL DEDUCE DERIVE FERRET HAMMER HASTEN IMPACT JARVEY JOSTLE PLUNGE PROPEL BLUSTER ENFORCE IMPULSE OVERTAX SETDOWN TRAVAIL CATAPULT CONATION SHEPHERD TENDENCY MOTIVATION
(— A BALL) LACE SEND
(— A HORSE ONWARD) WHIG
(— AIR) BLOW
(— ANIMALS) HAZE
(— AT TOP SPEED) BARREL CAREER
(— AWAY) RID FIRK HUSH SHOO BANDY EXILE FEEZE FLEME HOOSH REPEL SMOKE SWEEP AROINT BANISH DEFEND DISPEL ENCHASE DISPLACE EXORCISE
(— BACK) RUSH REBUT REPEL CULBUT DEFEND REBATE REBUFF RETUND REPULSE REFRINGE
(— BACK AND FORTH) TENNIS
(— BEFORE STRONG WIND) SPOON
(— BRISKLY) JUNE
(— CLOSE BEHIND WHILE RACING) DRAFT
(— CRAZY) BUG
(— DISTRACTED) BEDEVIL
(— FORTH) ISH
(— FURIOUSLY) SCORCH
(— HARD) RAM SWEAT HACKNEY
(— HOME) CLINCH
(— HURRIEDLY) BUM BUCKET
(— IN) CRAM DINT PILE TAMP INJECT
(— IN A PARK) TOUR
(— INTO THE GROUND) STUB
(— INTO WATER) ENEW
(— LEISURELY) TOOTLE
(— LOGS) SPLASH
(— OFF) KEEP LIFT EXCOCT
(— OFF STAGE) EXPLODE
(— ON BACK ROADS) SHUNPIKE
(— OUT) BOLT FIRE DEPEL DROWN EJECT EXPEL KNOCK WREAK AROINT EXTURB ABANDON DISLODGE EXORCISE PROPULSE
(— RECKLESSLY) COWBOY
(— ROUGHLY) CHOUSE
(— RUDELY IN TRAFFIC) CUTIN
(— SLANTINGLY) TOE
(— SLOWLY) TAXI
(— TO BAY) EMBOSS
(— TO MADNESS) FRENZY
(— VIOLENTLY) THUD SMASH HURTLE
(— WITH BLOWS) SKELP COURSE
(— WITH SHOUTS) HOY HUE
(FREE GOLF —) MULLIGAN
(RECREATIONAL —) SPIN

DRIVEL GOO BLAH DOTE DRIP MUSH DROOL SLUSH DOTAGE DRUDGE FOOTLE HUMBUG MENIAL SLAVER DRIBBLE EYEWASH MAUNDER SLABBER TWADDLE NONSENSE SALIVATE CODSWALLOP

DRIVELING INANE SLAVERY FOOTLING IMBECILE SLOBBERY BLITHERING

DRIVEPIPE POINT

DRIVER MUG HACK JEHU MUSH WHIP DRABI URGER CABMAN CALLER COWBOY DROVER FLYMAN HAULER JARVEY JOCKEY MALLET MIZZEN MUSHER PONIER STAGER VANMAN WAINER CATCHER COCHERO FLANKER HACKMAN HOODLUM HURRIER JITNEUR PHAETON SPANKER SPEEDER SUMPTER TOPSMAN TRUCKER WHIPMAN BANDYMAN BULLOCKY CALESERO CAMELEER COACHMAN DRAGSMAN ENGINEER GALLOWAY GOADSMAN IMPULSOR JITNEUSE MOTORMAN OVERSEER REINSMAN TEAMSTER WHIPSTER
(— OF ANIMALS) DROVER SKINNER
(— OF ELEPHANT) MAHOUT
(— OF OMNIBUS) PIRATE
(CAMEL —) SARWAN CAMELEER
(FAST —) JEHU SPEEDER
(FIELD —) HAYWARD
(PACK-HORSE —) SUMPTER
(SKILLFUL —) REINSMAN
(TOWPATH —) HOGGY HOGGEE
(PREF.) ELATRO

DRIVEWAY DRIVE SWEEP AVENUE DRIFTWAY

DRIVING PELTING COACHING SLASHING
(— ALONG) SCUD
(— OF GAME) BATTUE
(— OF WIND) GUST
(— TOGETHER) DRIFT
(— TOWARD) APPULSE

DRIZZLE DEG MUG DANK DRIP DROW HAZE LING RAIN SMUR STEW DRISK MISLE SMURR MIZZLE DRISSEL SCOUTHER SPRINKLE
(— OF RAIN) SKEW

DRIZZLY SOFT DRIPPY MIZZLY

DROGUE DRAG DRUG SLEEVE

DROLL ODD RUM WRY COMIC DROLE FUNNY MERRY QUEER WITTY JESTER JOCOSE AMUSING BUFFOON COMICAL JOCULAR STRANGE WAGGISH FARCICAL HUMOROUS

DROLLERY WIT JEST FARCE HUMOR DROLERIE

DROMEDARY OONT CAMEL DELUL DELOUL HAGEEN HAGEIN HYGEEN MEHARI CAMAILE CAMELUS DROMOND

DRONE BEE BUM HUM DRUM SLUG SPIV DRANT DROLL IDLER SNAIL THRUM BUMBLE BURDEN CHORUS DRAUNT DRONEL DRONET LUBBER BAGPIPE BUMBARD BUMBASS HUMMING SHIRKER SLEEPER SOLDIER SPEAKER LOITERER SLUGGARD

DRONE BASS FOOT

DRONGO FORKTAIL

DRONING BOURDON HUMDRUM HUMMING SINGSONG

DRONISH SLOW INDOLENT SLUGGISH

DROOL FLAT DRIVEL SLAVER DRIBBLE SLABBER SLOBBER SALIVATE

DROOP FAG LOB LOP SAG BEND DROP FADE FLAG HANG LAVE LOLL PEAK PINE SINK SWAG WEEP WILT DAVER DREEP DROWK FLACK HEALD HIELD MOURN BANGLE BLOUSE DANGLE DEPEND NUTATE SLOUCH CURTAIN DECLINE FLITTER LANGUISH PENDENCY

DROOPING LOP DRAG FLAG LANK LAZY LIMP GOTCH OURIE ADROOP DROOPY FLAGGY NUTANT SLOUCH SOPITE GOTCHED HANGING LANGUID NODDING POPPIED CERNUOUS TRAILING
(— OF EARS) LAVE
(— OF EYELID) PTOSIS

DROOPY DREEPY SLIMPSY

DROP DAP DIP SIE SYE BEAD BEDE BLOB CAST DRIB DRIP DUMP FALL GLOB GOUT OMIT SEGE SHED SILE SINK SPOT STOP TEAR BREAK CLOTH DROOP FLUMP GUTTA LAPSE LOWER MINIM PEARL PLUMP PLUNK SLUMP STILL SWOOP CANCEL DISTIL DRAPPY EXTILL FUMBLE GOBBET GOUTTE PLUNGE SINKER SLOUGH SPRINK TUMBLE ABANDON CURTAIN DESCENT DEWDROP DISCARD DISMISS DISTILL DRAPPIE DRIBBLE DRIBLET DROPLET EXPUNGE FORSAKE GLOBULE GUTTULA GUTTULE INCURVE LETDOWN MELDROP PLUMMET RELEASE SPATTER DECREASE DROPLING
(— ANCHOR) SLIP
(— ARGENT) LARME
(— AS SEEDS FROM A POD) ROSE
(— AWAY) DESERT
(— BAIT IN WATER) DAP
(— BY DROP) DROPWISE GUTTATIM
(— DOWN) VAIL
(— IN) STOP HAPPEN INSTIL INSTILL
(— INTO LIQUID) PLUMP
(— OFF) NAP NOD DOZE SNOOZE
(— OF GIN) DAFFY
(— OF SEALING-WAX) KISS
(— OUT) FLOUNCE
(ARCHITECTURAL —) GUTTA
(CHOCOLATE —) DRAGEE
(THEATRICAL —) TAB SCRIM
(UNEXPECTED —) DOYST
(PL.) GTT GUTT
(PREF.) GUTTI STAGMO STAGONO STILLI

DROP-CURTAIN GREENY

DROP ELBOW PIERDROP

DROPLET GLOBULE
(PL.) DEW

DROPLIGHT PENDANT

DROPPER SINK BOBBER SINKER PIPETTE

DROPPING FALL SCAT SKAT SHARD COWSHARD
(— ABRUPTLY) BOLD
(— SHARPLY) ABRUPT
(PL.) SOIL SPOOR FLYINGS

DROPSICAL PUFFY EDEMIC DROPSIED HYDROPIC

DROPSY EDEMA OEDEMA ASCITES ANASARCA

DROPWORT HORSEBANE DEADTONGUE

DROSS KISH LEES SCUM SLAG CHAFF DREGS DRUSH SCOBS SLACK SPRUE WASTE GARBLE REFUSE SCORIA SCRUFF SHRUFF SINTER CINDERS LEAVING OFFSCUM

DROSSEL SLUT HUSSY DRAZEL DRAZIL

DROUGHT DRYTH DROUTH THIRST ARIDITY DRYNESS ARIDNESS

DROVE MOB SENT ATAJO CROWD DRIFT FLOCK MANADA BOASTER DISTURB TROUBLE DRIFTWAY

DROVER DEALER DRIVER TOPMAN TOPSMAN WHACKER HERDSMAN

DROWN DEAFEN DRENCH STIFLE ADRENCH DRUNKEN INDRENCH INUNDATE OVERTONE

DROWNED ADRENT

DROWNING NOYADE

DROWSE NOD SOG DOZE DOVER DRONE SLEEP SNOOZE SLUMBER

DROWSINESS COMA DULLNESS LETHARGY NARCOSIS

DROWSING DORMANT

DROWSY DOZY DULL LOGY HEAVY NODDY SLEEPY SNOOZY SOPITE STUPID SUPINE SWOONY DORMANT LULLING NODDING POPPIED COMATOSE COMATOUS OSCITANT SLUGGISH LETHARGIC

DRUB TAP WAP BANG BEAT BLOW DRUM PAIK ARRAY CREAM CURRY PASTE STAMP THUMP WHALE ANOINT CUDGEL SCUTCH THRASH BELABOR DRYBEAT SHELLAC

DRUBBING PAIK LICKING SACKING

DRUDGE DIG FAG TUG DROY DRUG GRUB HACK MOIL PEON PLOD SERF TOIL DROIL DRONE GRIND SCRAT SCRUB SLAVE SWEAT DIGGER DRIVEL ENDURE JACKAL MOILER SCODGY SCOGIE SLAVEY SLUDGE SUFFER GRUBBER HACKNEY PLODDER SLAVERY SWEATER TRACHLE DOGSBODY

DRUDGERY FAG MOIL SLOG TOIL WORK GRIND LABOR SWEAT SWINK FAGGERY SLAVERY TRACHLE TURMOIL DRUDGISM
(ROUTINE —) TREADMILL

DRUG (ALSO SEE NARCOTIC) DEX DOM HOP STP ACID ALOE ALUM BUKU CURE DOPE DRAB DULL HEMP LOAD MDMA NUMB SCAG SINA BUCHU HOCUS JALAP LDOPA LOCUS MECON NSAID OPIUM RUTIN SALOL SENNA SPECE SPEED SULFA TONGA TRUCK COOLER DEWTRY DOWNER ELAVIL FINGER HEROIN IPECAC JAMBUL LOCUST MYOTIC NOBBLE OPIATE PEYOTE PEYOTL PITURI POTION SIDDHI SIMPLE SULPHA ANODYNE ASPIRIN ATEBRIN BOTANIC CUSHION DAMIANA DAPSONE DILATER ECBOLIC ECSTASY ETHICAL HASHISH JAMBOOL LIBRIUM METOPON PHILTER PHILTRE QUASSIA STUPEFY STYPTIC SURAMIN ZEDOARY ADJUVANT AROMATIC ASPIDIUM ATARAXIC BANTHINE HYPNOTIC KOROMIKO

LAETRILE LAXATIVE MEDICATE MEDICINE MERSALYL NARCOTIC NEPENTHE PEMOLINE QUAALUDE SALIVANT SEDATIVE SPECIFIC THIAZIDE TOXICANT ZERUMBET ATARACTIC BARBITONE BEMEGRIDE BRETYLIUM CAPTOPRIL CLONIDINE COLCHICUM IBUPROFEN MELPHALAN NIALAMIDE SALURETIC AMANTADINE CLOFIBRATE CLOMIPHENE PAINKILLER
(— CAPSULE) QUAALUDE
(— CAPSULES) RED REDS
(— DOSE) HIT
(— IN TABLET OF VARIOUS COLORS) RAINBOW
(— SMUGGLER) MULE
(— USER) DOPER FREAK DRUGGY DRUGGIE ACIDHEAD JOYPOPPER
(BITUMINOUS —) MUMMY
(DEPRESSANT —) DOWNER
(FIVE DOLLAR — PACKET) NICKEL
(FREE FROM — ADDICTION) CLEAN
(INHALE A —) SNORT
(INJECT —) SKINPOP
(INJECT —S) SHOOT
(KIND OF —) SULFA ORPHAN DESIGNER
(NONUSER OF —S) STRAIGHT
(NOT USING —S) STRAIGHT
(ONE WHO USES —S) DRUGGY DRUGGIE
(ONE WHO USES A —) HEAD
(ONE WHO USES ILLICIT —S) FREAK
(ORAL DIURETIC —) THIAZIDE
(RENDER FREE FROM —S) DETOX
(STIMULANT —) UPPER
(STRENGTHENING —) ROBORANT
(TAKE —S ORALLY) POP
(TAKE —S THROUGH THE MOUTH) DROP SWALLOW
(TAKE A — THROUGH THE MOUTH) DROP
(TO INJECT —) SHOOT
(VEGETABLE —) FINGER
(PL.) DRUGGERY
(PREF.) PHARMACO

DRUGGED POPPIED
DRUGGET BAUGE BOCKING
DRUGGIST CHEMIST DRUGGER GALLIPOT APOTHECARY
DRUGSTORE APOTHEC PHARMACY
DRUID SARONIDE
DRUM BAZ GIN GON GOO GYO BOWL CAGE CHIH DRUB LALI MUYU POPO QASA ROUT SKIN SPOT TOPH TRAP ZUZU ADAPU BONGO CONGA CRAWL DAVUL DRONE DUGGI ENNEN EWTIE FOUCT FURIN GUMBE GUMBY JAIRA KENON MBIRA NAKER QABIB REBAB SARON SHAPE SNARE SWASH TABOR THRUM TOMBE TUPAN ZURLA AFUCHE AMBIRA ATABAL BAMBUS BARREL CROCUS GAMAKA GRELOT KANOON KEMPUL KHANSI KURTAR LIVIKA RIGGER TABRET TAMBOR TIMBRE TUMBLE TUMMER TYMPAN UDAKKI ANACARA BODHRAN BUBBLER CROAKER DAULBAZ ENCLUME FRUSTUM GHIRBAL GRUNTER RATTLER REDFISH SLENTEM SNUBBER TABORIN TAMBOUR TEMPEST TIMBREL TUMBLER VOSHAGA ZAMBONA BAMBOULA BARBUKKA CANISTER CYLINDER DERBUKKA DRUMFISH HUEHUETI HUEHUETL MAQQAREH MOULINET MRIDANGA TYMPANUM ABURUKUWA BRONTERON DUMTAKTAK MRIDANGAM PUTTIPUTI ROMMELPOT TSANATSEL CACCAVELLA
(— AS SHIP'S SIGNAL) SHAPE
(— FOR WINDING ROPE) CAGE
(— IN WINCH) GIPSY GYPSY
(— MADE FROM HOLLOW TREE) GUMBE GUMBY
(— OF CAPSTAN) RUNDLE MOULINE
(— OF INDIA) MRIDANGA MRIDANGAM
(— ON WINDLASS) WILDCAT
(— UP BUSINESS) HUSTLE
(— UP INTEREST) BALLYHOO
(HEATED —) DRIER DRYER
(IGOROT —) GANGSA
(KIND OF —) STEEL
(NARROW —) RIGGER
(PAIR OF —S) TABLA
(PAIR OF HINDU —S) TABLA
(REVOLVING —) GURDY BARREL RATTLER
(SUMERIAN —) ALA ALAL

DRUMBEAT DUB FLAM RUFF TUCK MARCH RUFFLE SHUFFLE ASSEMBLY BERLOQUE BRELOQUE
(— SOUND) TUCK

DRUM-BELLY HOOVE
DRUMFISH SPOT CROCUS BUBBLER CROAKER DRUMMER DRUMSLER SCIAENID
DRUMLIN DRUM SOWBACK
DRUMMER DRUM TABOR STICKS TABRET ROADMAN SWASHER TAMBOUR TUMBLER DRUMSLER SALESMAN
DRUMMING TATTOO
DRUM ROLL DIAN DIANA
DRUMS ALONG THE MOHAWK
(AUTHOR OF —) EDMONDS
(CHARACTER IN —) HON JOHN LANA MARK YOST BRANT JURRY NANCY WOLFF ARNOLD GAHOTA JOSEPH MARTIN DEMOOTH GILBERT MCLONIS SCHUYLER MAGDELANA MCKLENNAR

DRUMSTICK LEG STICK BAGUET TAMPON BAGUETTE
DRUNK CUT FAP FOU REE WET GONE HIGH LUSH NASE PAID RIPE SOSH BLIND BOOZE BOSKY CLEAR DRINK GONZO LITUP LUMPY LUSHY MALTY MOPPY OILED QUEER SHICK STIFF TIGHT TIPSY BAGGED BLOTTO BOILED BOMBED BUZZED CANNED FLUFFY GROGGY JAGGED LOADED LOOPED MORTAL POTTED RIPPED SLOPPY SODDEN SOSHED SOUSED SOZZLY SPONGY SPRUNG STEWED STINKO STONED TIDDLY UPPISH UPPITY ZONKED BLOTTER BONKERS BOTTLED CROCKED DRUNKEN JINGLED MAUDLIN PICKLED SCREWED SHICKER SLOPPED SLOSHED SMASHED SOZZLED SQUIFFY SWACKED UNSOBER WRECKED COCKEYED GLORIOUS MUCKIBUS PLEASANT SQUIFFED STINKING WIPEDOUT BLITHERED PIXILATED
DRUNKARD SOT LUSH SOAK WINO BLOAT DIPSO DRUNK GULCH RUMMY SOUSE TOPER BARFLY LUSHER SOAKER SPONGE DRUNKER FUDDLER POTSHOT SHICKER STEWBUM TIPPLER TOSSPOT BORACHIO HABITUAL SWILLTUB
DRUNKEN REE WAT GONE WINY BLIND BOUSY DROWN DRUNK BLOTTO FLUFFY SODDEN BACCHIC DRUCKEN PICKLED SOTTISH WHIPCAT DRENCHED SATURATE SQUIFFED VINOLENT WOODSERE
DRUNKENNESS BUN IVRESSE POTSHOT METHYSIS
DRUPE TRYMA DRUPEL DRUPELET DRUPEOLE
DRUPELET GRAIN ACINUS
DRUPE STONE NUTLET
DRUSE GEODE
DRUSILLA (BROTHER OF —) CALIGULA
(FATHER OF —) HEROD CALIGULA GERMANICUS
(HUSBAND OF —) FELIX AZIZUS AUGUSTUS
(MOTHER OF —) CYPROS CAESONIA AGRIPPINA
(SON OF —) AGRIPPA TIBERIUS

DRY EBB KEX SEC TED WIN ADRY ARID BAKE BLOT BRUT DULL EILD GELD HASK KEXY KILN PINE SAVE SERE SOUR WELT WIPE AREFY CORKY DRAIN FROST GUESS HASKY JUSKY MEALY PARCH PROSY SANDY SECCO SMEEK SWEAT VAPID WIZEN BARKEN BARREN BIRSLE BORING CHIPPY ENSEAR GIZZEN HISTIE JEJUNE SCORCH STARKY AREFACT BRUSTLE INSIPID SAHARAN SAPLESS SICCATE SQUALID STERILE THIRSTY TORREFY XEROTIC BARBECUE DROUGHTY INFUMATE TIRESOME WOODSERE
(— HERRINGS) DEESE
(— IN SUN) RIZZAR
(— OFF) TOWEL
(— OF MILK) SEW EILD
(— PARTLY) SAMMY
(— UP) SERE WELK WITHER AREFACT FORWELK SKELLER
(— WITH SMOKE) REAST REEST
(— WOOD) BEATH SWEAT SEASON
(KIND OF —) DRIP
(NOT —) SWEET
(PREF.) DEHYDR(O) JEJUN(O) SCLER(O) SICCI TORRE XER(O) XER(O)

DRYAD DRYAS NYMPH CAISSA YAKSHA YAKSHI WOODMAID
DRYER DRIER STOVE SIROCCO
DRY GOODS DRAPERY
DRYING SICCANT
DRYING RACK CRIB
DRYNESS DROUTH ARIDITY DROUGHT SICCITY XEROSIS XEROTES HASKNESS AREFACTION
(— OF THE HAIR) XERASIA

DRYOPE (FATHER OF —) EURYTUS
(HUSBAND OF —) ANDRAEMON
(SISTER OF —) IOLE
(SON OF —) AMPHISSUS

DUAL TWIN BINARY DOUBLE DUALIST TWOFOLD
DUALISM DVAITA
DUALITY DUAD TWINE TWONESS
DUANT DE DEE
DUB DIB RUB ADUB BLOW CALL NAME POOL ADORN ARRAY DRESS STYLE THUMP CLOTHE KNIGHT PUDDLE SMOOTH STRIKE ENTITLE BEGINNER DRUMBEAT ORNAMENT
DUBBIN DAUBING
DUBIOUS DICKY FISHY JUBUS DOUBTY BEARISH DOUBTFUL DOUBTING JUBEROUS PRECARIOUS QUESTIONABLE
(NOT —) EXPRESS

DUCA D'ALBA, IL (CHARACTER IN —) AMELIA EGMONT MARCELLO
(COMPOSER OF —) DONIZETTI

DUCHY SAVOY DUCATUS DUCHERY DUKEDOM PARMESAN
DUCK AIX BOB BOW CAN DIG DIP DOP MIG PET WIO CHAP COLK COOT DIVE DOGS DOGY DOKE DUKW JOUK LADY LORD PATO ROOK SMEE SMEW TEAL TEUK BOOBY BUNTY CRICK DILLY DODGE DOUSE DOWSE DUCKY EIDER EVADE HOUND MOMMY NODDY PADDY POKER RODGE ROUEN SCAUP SHIRK SOUSE SPIKE SPRIG STOOL BOBBER CALLOO CALLOW CANARD CANNET DUCKIE FELLOW GARROT HARELD PEKING PERSON PLUNGE QUANDY RUNNER SCOTER SMETHE ANATINE BARWING BLACKIE BOWSSEN BUMMALO CANETTE CRACKER DABBLER DARLING DRABBET DUCKING DUCKLET DUNBIRD FIDDLER FLAPPER GADWALL GEELBEC GREASER MALLARD OLDWIFE PENTAIL PINKEYE PINTAIL POCHARD REDHEAD REDLEGS REDWING SCOOTER SLEEPER SPATTER WADDLER WIDGEON YAGUAZA BALDPATE BLUEBILL BLUEWING BOATBILL BULLNECK DUCKLING DUCKWING GARGANEY GRAYBACK GREYBACK HARDHEAD IRONHEAD MOONBILL MORILLON PIKETAIL REDSHANK RINGBILL RINGNECK SHOVELER SHUFFLER SQUEALER WIRETAIL BERGANDER
(— AT CRICKET) BLOB
(— EGGS) PIDAN
(DEAD —) GONER
(KIND OF —) PEKING SITTING
(MALE —) DRAKE
(PART OF —) EAR EYE WEB BEAN BILL CAPE HEAD NECK RUMP TAIL WING FLUFF SHANK BREAST SADDLE COVERTS NOSTRIL

SHOULDER PRIMARIES SECONDARIES
(STUFFED —) DUMPOKE
(YOUNG —) CANETON FLAPPER FLOPPER
DUCKBILL OOTOCOID PLATYPUS TAMBREET MONOTREME
DUCKING SOUSE
DUCKTAIL DA HAIRSTYLE
DUCKWEED GLIT GRAIN LEMNAD LENTIL DIGMEAT DUCKMEAT FROGFOOT
DUCT VAS MAIN PIPE TUBE VEIN CANAL ALVEUS BUSWAY DUCTUS MEATUS URETER CHANNEL CONDUIT DUCTULE DUCTURE LACTEAL LEADING PASSAGE TRACHEA AQUEDUCT CALIDUCT DOWNTAKE EFFERENT EMISSARY EXHALANT GONADUCT GUIDANCE OLEODUCT
(PREF.) RHYN(O) VAS(I)(O)
DUCTILE SOFT DOCILE FACILE PLIANT PLASTIC PLIABLE TENSILE FLEXIBLE TRACTILE
(PREF.) ELAST(O)
DUD TOG FLOP LEMON STUMER STUMOR FAILURE
DUDE FOP DANDY DUDINE JOHNNY COXCOMB JACKEEN
DUDEGON PIQUE
DUDGEON IRE RAGE ANGER PIQUE OFFENSE
(HIGH —) IRE
DUE HAK LOT OWE BACK CENS DEBT FAIR FARM FLAT HAKH JUST MEED OWED TOLL DROIT ENDOW ENDUE FATED MERIT OWING COMING CUSTOM DESERT EXTENT LAWFUL MATURE PROPER UNPAID CONDIGN EXACTLY FALDFEE FITTING JETTAGE TALLAGE ADEQUATE DIRECTLY HEREGELD HEREZELD RIGHTFUL SUITABLE TRUNCAGE
DUEL TILT FENCE FIGHT AFFAIR COMBAT DUELLO MENSUR CONTEST MEETING CONFLICT DUELLIZE HOLMGANG
DUELIST FIGHTER SPADASSIN
DUENNA DRAGON GRIFFIN GRIFFON CHAPERON
DUES TOLLS DROITS CHIEFRY INWARDS JETTAGE PAYMENT PENSION QUAYAGE ALTARAGE HAVENAGE SOUNDAGE THIRLAGE WHARFAGE
DUET DUO TWO DUETTO TWOSOME
(BALLET —) ADAGIO
DUFF ALTER BRAND CHEAT FLOOR PUDDING
DUFFER DUB MUFF SHAM CHEAT BUFFER GEEZER HAWKER RABBIT SHICER PEDDLER
DUG TEAT
(— UP) HOWKIT
(PREF.) ORYCTO
DUGONG SEACOW YUNGAN COWFISH MANATEE HALICORE MUTILATE SIRENIAN
DUGOUT ABRI BOAT BURY CAVE BANCA BONGO BUNGO CANOE DONGA DUNGA SHELL BAROTO BUNKER CAYUCA CAYUCO CORIAL TROUGH BANTING PIRAGUA PIROGUE SHELTER BLINDAGE LIPALIPA
DUHSHASANA (FATHER OF —) DHRITARASHTRA
DUIKER IPITI DUYKER BLAUBOK
DUKE DUC DUX KNEZ PEER AYMON CHIEF KNIAZ HERZOG LEADER ORSINO AUMERLE GORLOIS SOLINUS STEENIE HERETOGA PROSPERO
DUKEDOM DUCHY ALBANY DUCATUS
DULCET SWEET DULCID SIRUPY SYRUPY SOOTHING
DULCIAN CURTAL
DULCIMER ROTA CANUN CITOLE SANTIR CEMBALO MAGADIS SANTOUR CYMBALOM PANTALON SAUTERIE ZIMBALON
DULIA ADORATION
DULL DIM DOW DRY FAT LAX MAT SAD ARID BLAH CLOD COLD DAMP DEAD DILL DOWD DOWF DOWY DRAB DREE DRUG DUMB FLAT GRAY GREY LOGY MOPE MULL POKY SLOW TAME THIN TURN BESOT BLACK BLAND BLATE BLEAR BLIND BLUNT BRUTE CRASS DENSE DINGY DOWFF DOWIE DOWLY DREAR DUBBY DUNCH DUNNY DUSTY FISHY FOGGY GLAZY GRAVE GROSS HEAVY HOHUM INERT LOURD MATTE MORON MOSSY MUDDY MUSTY MUZZY NOOSE PLUMP POKEY PROSE PROSY SHADE SLACK SOGGY STARY STILL SULKY TERNE THICK UNAPT VAPID WASTE BARREN BLEARY BOVINE CLOUDY DAMPEN DARKEN DEADEN DISMAL DRAGGY DREARY DRIECH DRIEGH DROWSY EARTHY FRIGID FRUMPY GLASSY HEBETE JEJUNE LEADEN LOURDY MUFFLE OBTUND OBTUSE OPAQUE PALLID REBATE RETUND SLEEPY SLOOMY SODDEN SOMBER SOMBRE STODGY STOLID STUFFY STUPID SULLEN TIMBER TORPID TRISTE TURBID URLUCH WOODEN ADENOID BLUNTED CONFUSE DEADISH DISEDGE DOLTISH DOWFART DRAINED DULLISH DUMPISH HUMDRUM INSIPID IRKSOME LANGUID LUMPISH MUMPISH PEAKISH PINHEAD PROSAIC SHEATHE SOTTISH STUPEFY TEDIOUS UNLUSTY VACUOUS BACKWARD BANAUSIC BEFUDDLE BLOCKISH BOEOTIAN BROMIDIC COMATOSE COMATOUS DIDACTIC DISCOLOR DULLSOME EDGELESS FRUMPISH GAUMLESS HEBETATE INFICETE LIFELESS LISTLESS LOURDISH OVERCAST PLODDING SLOTTERY SLUGGISH SOULLESS STAGNANT TIRESOME PINHEADED PONDEROUS SATURNINE
(— EDGE OF) ABATE
(— IN MOTION) LOGY
(— IN SPEECH) PROSY
(— SCENT) FOIL
(— WITH LIQUOR) SEETHE
(BECOME —) PALL RUST
(MENTALLY —) DOPY DOPEY BARREN
(PREF.) AMBLY(O) BRADY
DULLARD DOLT BOOBY DUNCE IDIOT MORON DODUNK STUPID BROMIDE DASTARD DOLDRUM DULBERT POTHEAD BLINKARD DULLHEAD
DULLED EMPTY HEAVY JADED BROKEN CLOUDY GRAYED SODDEN STUPID BLEARED
DULLISH DIRTY
DULL-LOOKING OWLISH
DULLNESS DRAB HAZE YAWN CLOUD TAMAS FADEUR PHLEGM TORPOR DIMNESS DOLDRUM DULLITY DUNCERY FATUITY LANGUOR OPACITY DUMBNESS HEBETUDE SLOWNESS SOPITION VAPIDITY SEGNITUDE STOLIDITY
(— OF SIGHT) AMBLYOPIA
DULL-SPIRITED MUZZY
DULL-WITTED FOZY WITLESS BESOTTED DONNERED
(— PERSON) MOREPORK
DULLY FLATLY HEAVILY
DULSE DILLESK DILLISK SEAWEED
DULY DUE FITLY RIGHT RITELY PROPERLY
DUMAH (FATHER OF —) ISHMAEL
DUMB DULL MUTE STONY SILENT STONEY STUPID IDIOTIC
(— OX) BOZO
DUMBBELL DODO DUMMY DUNCE IDIOT HALTER AIRHEAD KNOTHEAD
DUMBFOUND DAZE STUN AMAZE CONFUSE CONFOUND SURPRISE
DUMBFOUNDED AWED STUPENT
DUMBNESS SILENCE APHRASIA
DUMBWAITER LIFT DUMMY
DUM-DUM AIRHEAD KNUCKLEHEAD
DUMMY COPY DOLT MUTE SHAM DUMBY FAGOT EFFIGY FAGGOT PONTIC SHADOW SILENT PHANTOM DUMBBELL
(SWORDSMAN'S —) PEL
DUMNORIX (BROTHER OF —) DIVITIACUS
DUMP SUM TIP BEAT CASH COIN COUP FALL HOLE JAIL MUSE NAIL TOOM EMPTY HOUSE SHOOT GRIEVE PLUNGE TIPPLE UNLOAD BOGHOLE COUNTER DEPOSIT REVERIE SADNESS STORAGE
(MINE —) BURROW
(PL.) SUDS MOPES SADNESS
DUMPCART DUMPER TUMBREL TUMBRIL
DUMPER TIPMAN
DUMPLING COB CRUST KNODEL PIROGI KNAIDEL NOCKERL PIEROGI SPATZLE DOUGHBOY QUENELLE SPAETZLE AGNOLOTTI
(POLISH —) PIEROGI
(RUSSIAN MEAT —S) PELMENI PELMENY
(PL.) KLOSSE GNOCCHI
DUMPY DUNCH GROSS PUDGY SQUAB SQUAT DUMPTY STOCKY SQUATTY
DUN BUM TAN FORT KICK URGE ANNOY BROWN CRAVE CROWD DINGY FAVEL MOUND PRESS SEPIA DUNNER LEADEN PESTER PLAGUE DUNNISH SWARTHY
DUNCE ASS CLOD DODO DOLT DULT GABY GONY BOBBY BOOBY DOBBY IDIOT NINNY DULTIE HOBBIL PEDANT DULLARD SOPHIST NUMSKULL STUNPOLL TOMNODDY WISEACRE
DUN-COLORED
(PREF.) PHAEO PHEO
(SUFF.) PHAEIN PHEIN
DUNDERHEAD OAF CLOD DOLT SAPE DUNCE TURNIP GOMERIL
DUNE BAR DENE MEAL MOUND TOWAN TWINE BARKAN BARCHAN BARKHAN
(SAND —) DRAB SAIF SEIF
DUNG MIS CACK CHIP DOLL FIME GORE MERD MUCK MUTE SOIL TATH ARGAL ARGOL FECES FILTH FUMET MIXEN SCARN SHARN BILLET CASSON FIANTS LESSES MANURE ORDURE SCUMBER SCUMMER TREDDLE COWSHARD DROPPING STALLAGE
(— AS FUEL) ARGOL CASSON CASSONS
(— OF BEAST OF PREY) LESSES
(— OF DEER) FUMET FEWMET
(COW —) MIST UPLA COWSHARD COWSHARN
(OTTER'S —) SPRAINTS
(SHEEP —) BUTTONS TREDDLE TROTTERS
(PREF.) COPR(O) FIMI GUANI GUANO MERDI SCAT(O) SCORI SPATILO STERCO STERCOR(I)
DUNG BEETLE SCARAB
DUNGEON PIT CELL HELL HOLE LAKE VAULT CACHOT DONJON PRISON CONFINE OUBLIET REVOLVER OUBLIETTE
DUNGHILL MIXEN MIDDEN MIXHILL
DUNGON DONGON SUNDARI
DUNK DIP SOP SOAK STEEP IMMERSE MOISTEN
(— SHOT) JAM
DUNKER DIPPER TAUFER TUNKER DUMPLER DUNKARD TUMBLER
DUNLIN STIB OXEYE PURRE STINT DORBIE OXBIRD REDBACK LEADBACK
DUNNAGE FARDAGE
DUODECIMO TWELVEMO
DUPE APE BAM FOB FOP MUG BOOB COAX CONY CULL DUST FOOL GECK GULL HOAX LAMB ROOK SCAM TOOL CHEAT CHUMP COKES CONEY CULLY HEALD MOOTH MOUTH PROOF REPRO SLANG STALE TRICK BEFOOL BUBBLE CHOOSE CHOUSE COUSIN DELUDE DERIDE MONKEY PIGEON PLOVER SQUARE SUCKER TAKEIN VICTIM BECASSE CATSPAW CHICANE CULLION DECEIVE GUDGEON MISLEAD SAPHEAD SWINDLE YOUNKER DOTTEREL HOODWINK RODERIGO DUPLICATE
DUPERY RAMP

DUPLE BINARY DOUBLE TWOFOLD
DUPLEX DOUBLE TWOFOLD
DUPLEXITY EQUIVOKE
DUPLICATE BIS COPY DUPE ALIKE DITTO SPARE TALLY DOUBLE FLIMSY REPEAT COUNTER ESTREAT MISLEAD REPLICA TWOFOLD LIKENESS (PREF.) COUNTER
DUPLICATION DISOMATY
DUPLICATOR MIMEOGRAPH
DUPLICITY ART GUILE DECEIT TRICKERY
DUPONDIUS BRONZE
DURABILITY WEAR FIBER FIBRE STEEL DURANCE STAMINA
DURABLE FIRM HARD LASTY PAKKA PUKKA STOUT STABLE STAPLE LASTING SERVICE CONSTANT ENDURING LIVELONG
DURABLENESS DURATION
DURAMEN HEARTWOOD
DURANCE DURANT DURESS CUSTODY
DURANGO CARTOUCH
DURATION AGE DATE LAST LIFE SPAN TERM TIME WHEN DUREE KALPA SPACE LENGTH PERIOD DURANCE LASTING INFINITE LIFETIME STANDING
(— BREEZE) SLATCH
(— OF DWELLING) RESIDENCE
(BOUNDLESS —) INFINITE
(INFINITE —) ETERNITY
(RELATIVE —) VALUE
DURAZZO (WARD OF —) CALDORO
DURESS FORCE DANGER CRUELTY DURANCE COERCION HARDNESS PRESSURE
DURGA KALI CHAMUNDA
(HUSBAND OF —) SHIVA
DURIAN JAK JACK JAKFRUIT
DURING IN ON BIN AMID OVER TIME AMONG INTRA WHILE AMIDST WHILST WITHIN AMONGST DURANTE PENDING ENDURING (PREF.) DIA INTRA
DURRA DARI DURA MILO JOWAR CHOLUM DHURRA JONDLA SORGHUM FETERITA
DURUM WHEAT
DURYODHANA (BROTHER OF —) PANDU
(FATHER OF —) DHRITARASHTRA
(SON OF —) LAKSHMANA
(WIFE OF —) DRAUPADI
DUSACK TESACK
DUSHYANTA (SON OF —) BHARATA
(WIFE OF —) SHAKUNTALA
DUSK DIM EVE DARK DIMPS GLOAM GLOOM DIMMET DIMPSY DIMNESS DUCKISH DARKNESS GLOAMING OWLLIGHT TWILIGHT NIGHTFALL
DUSKINESS PHAEISM
DUSKY DIM DUN SAD WAN DARK DUSK ADUSK BLACK BROWN DINGY GRIMY MOORY TAWNY GLOOMY PHAEIC SMUTTY SOMBER SOMBRE SWARTH DARKISH DARLING OBSCURE SUBFUSC SUBFUSK SWARTHY BLACKISH (PREF.) PERCNO PHAEO
DUST ROW COOM DIRT FOGO MUCK MULL PILM SMUT BRISS CLEAN COOMB FLOUR POUCE STIVE STOUR DREDGE FILLER KITTEN POLLEN POWDER SMEECH BEFLOUR EBURINE REMAINS SAWDUST SMEDDUM TURMOIL ANTELOPE BULLDUST PUMICITE
(— IN FLOUR MILLS) STIVE
(— IN QUARTZ MILL) SLICKENS
(BLOOD —) HEMOCONIA
(CHOKING —) POTHER
(COAL —) COOM CULM DUFF COOMB
(COKE —) BREEZE
(COSMIC —) STARDUST
(DIAMOND —) SEASONING
(FIBER —) FLOCK
(FLAX —) POUCE POUSE
(THICK —) SMOTHER
(PREF.) CON(I)(ICO)(IDIO)(O)
(SUFF.) CONITE
DUST CLOUD STEW
DUST COVER WRAPPER
DUSTER COAT DEVIL WILLOW ZEPHYR TORCHON DUSTCOAT
DUSTMAN GARBO
DUST-STORM DEVIL
DUST-UP TODO
DUSTY ADUST MOTTY MOTTLE POUCEY STOURY POWDERY UNDUSTED
DUTCH (SEE NETHERLANDS) HOGEN HOLLAND
DUTCH FOIL ORSEDE ORSEDUE
DUTCH GOLD CLINQUANT
DUTCHMAN HANS HOGEN BLANDA DUTCHY BELANDA DUTCHER MYNHEER BATAVIAN
DUTCHMAN'S-BREECHES DICENTRA
DUTCHWOMAN FROW
DUTIFUL PIOUS DOCILE LAWFUL DEBTFUL DUTEOUS OBEDIENT OFFICIAL REVERENT OFFICIOUS
DUTIFULNESS PIETY
DUTY DO END JOB LOT TAX CALL CARE FYRD MUST ONUS PART PROW ROLE TAIL TASK TOLL WIKE CHORE DEVER ERMIN LADLE LIKIN OUGHT PREST RIGHT STINT WIKEN BLANCH BURDEN CHARGE COCKET DEVOIR DHARMA EXCISE EXITUS HERIOT IMPOSE IMPOST INGATE OFFICE RIVAGE TARIFF AVERAGE BAILAGE BOOMAGE FOSSAGE FURDUNG GRANAGE INDULTO KEELAGE LASTAGE PONTAGE PRIMAGE ROYALTY SCAVAGE SERVICE STATION TONNAGE TRIBUTE TRONAGE TUNNAGE BALLIAGE BUSINESS FUNCTION MALIKANA MALTOLTE REDDENDO WEIGHAGE OBLIGATION
(— FOR LEAD ORE) COPE
(— OF SPARING LIFE) AHIMSA
(CHINESE TRANSIT —) LIKIN
(CUSTOMS —) OCTROI
(FEUDAL —) HERIOT
(IMPORT —) ERMIN INDULTO
(MILITARY —) STABLES
(TIRING —) FATIGUE
(PL.) CUSTOMS INGATES ACTIVITY
DUX CHIEF LEADER SUBJECT HERETOGA
DWALE BELLADONNA
DWARF ELF PUG URF AETA CRUT GRIG GRUB NANA RUNT CRILE CROWL GALAR GNOME KNURL MIDGE PIGMY PYGMY SCRUB STUNT TROLL ABLACH ALVISS CONJON DROICH DURGAN DURGEN MIDGET SHRIMP ANDVARI ANDWARI BLASTIE CONGEON MANIKIN OVERTOP PACOLET WRATACK ALBERICH BELITTLE HOMUNCIO HOMUNCLE HUCKMUCK KNURLING MENEHUNE NANANDER (PL.) CERCOPES NIBLUNGS NIBELUNGS (PREF.) NAN(O) NANN(O)
DWARF DANDELION KRIGIA
DWARFED STUNTY STUNTED
DWARF ELDER WALLWORT
DWARFING BRACHYSM
DWARFISH ELFIN PIGMY PYGMY GRUBBY KNURLY NANOID RUNTISH STUNTED
DWARFISHNESS NANISM
DWARFISM NANISM ATELIOSIS
DWARF MALLOW CHEESE PELLAS
DWARF RASPBERRY PLUMBOG
DWEEB NERD
DWELL BIG COT DIG SIT WIN WON BIDE BIGG HAFT HARP LIVE STAY TELD WINE WONT ABIDE BIELD BOWER BROOD BUILD DELAY HOUSE LODGE PAUSE SHACK STALL TARRY LINGER REMAIN RESIDE TENANT CLIMATE COHABIT INHABIT CONVERSE
(— IN) BIG BIGG BEDWELL INHABIT
(— IRRITATINGLY) GRATE
(— ON) HARP BROOD GLOAT
DWELLER TENANT WONNER DENIZEN PALEMAN DOWNSMAN HABITANT OCCUPANT RESIDENT
(— BY SEA) PARALIAN
(BUSH —) HATTER
(CAVE —) CAVEMAN TROGLODYTE
(CITY —) SLICKER
(COAST —) BUFFALO ORARIAN
(LAKE —) LACUSTRIAN
(PL.) HUTHOLD
(SUFF.) ITE
DWELLING DAR HUT INN SEE WON CASA FARM FLAT FORT HAFT HALL HOME NEST ROOF SLUM TENT WIKE WONE ABODE BOWER CABIN DOMUS HOGAN HOOCH HOTEL HOUSE HOVEL JOINT MANSE MOTEL PLACE CASTLE DUGOUT DUPLEX HOMING HOOTCH MALOCA SHANTY TEEPEE WIGWAM WONING COTTAGE LODGING MANSION SALTBOX TRAILER TRIPLEX WONNING BUILDING BUNGALOW DOMICILE TENEMENT PENTHOUSE RESIDENCE
(— IN UNDERWORLD) CHTHONIC
(— PLACE) HOWF HOWFF
(— WITH ANOTHER) INMATE
(ATTRACTIVE —) BOWER
(CRUDE —) SHED SHEBANG
(ESKIMO —) IGLOO
(HERMIT'S —) CELL
(LAKE —) CRANNOG PALAFITTE
(MEAN —) SHANTY
(MISERABLE —) BURROW DOGHOLE
(NAVAJO —) HOGAN
(NEOLITHIC —) TERRAMARA
(ONE-ROOM —) CELL
(OVERCROWDED —) WARREN
(PORTABLE —) CAMPER
(RAMSHACKLE —) HUMPY
(RUDE —) BOTHY BOTHIE
(SMALL —) CRIB
(SUBTERRANEAN —) WEEM
(SWISS —) CHALET
(TEMPORARY —) BOTHY BOTHIE
(WRETCHED —) HOVEL
(PL.) HOUSING
DWINDLE FADE FAIL FINE MELT PINE WANE DECAY DRAIN PETER TAPER TRAIL WASTE MOLDER SHRINK CONSUME DECLINE FRITTER MOULDER DECREASE DIMINISH FORDWINE
DWINDLING DOWN FLAGGING
DYAD PAIR
DYBBUK GILGUL
DYE (ALSO SEE DYESTUFF) AAL AZO DIP LIT ANIL BLUE COLOR EMBUE FUCUS IMBUE LOKAO STAIN SUDAN TINCT VENOM ARCHIL IMBRUE INFECT MADDER TINGER ENGRAIN INTINCT LACMOID LOGWOOD PUCCOON ZAMBESI AMARANTH COLORANT DYESTUFF FUGITIVE INDIGOID TINCTURE
(— FUR) FEATHER
(— NOT FAST) FUGITIVE
(BLACK —) GUAKO
(BLUE —) RUM ANIL ROOM SAXE WOAD INDIGO METHYL ANILINE CYANINE DICYANINE
(BROWN —) CACHOU
(GENERAL —S) NIL NILL AZINE BROWN EOSIN GREEN DIANIL EOSINE ISAMIN ORANGE PURPLE VIOLET CYANINE FUCHSIN METANIL PONCEAU PRIMULA ALIZARIN AURANTIA CIBACRON DICYANIN EURHODOL FUCHSINE HYPERNIC INDULINE NIGROSIN TURNSOLE VIRIDINE NIGROSINE SAFRANINE
(HAIR —) RASTIK
(KIND OF —) AZO SRA
(ORANGE —) KAMALA ROUCOU
(PURPLE —) CASSIUS GALLEIN TURNSOLE
(RED —) AAL ANATO AURIN EOSIN GRAIN HENNA RUBIN ANATTO AURINE CERISE EOSINE RELBUN RUBINE ALKANET ANNATTO CORINTH CRIMSON MAGENTA PONCEAU SAFFLOR ALIZARIN AMARANTH BORDEAUX CORALLIN CROCEINE
(SCARLET —) TULY GRAIN
(VIOLET —) MAUVE ARCHIL ORCHIL LACMOID ARCHILLA
(VIOLET — SOURCE) MUREX
(YELLOW —) ARUSA FLAVIN

CHRYSIN FISETIN FLAVINE LAWSONE WONGSHY AURAMINE
DYED INGRAIN
(PERMANENTLY —) FAST
DYED-IN-THE-WOOL INVETERATE
DYEING TINCTION
DYEPOT JIG VAT LEAD DYEBECK
DYER LISTER TINGER TINTER DYESTER FIELDER SKEINER TAINTOR TINTIST
DYERMA ZARMA ZAREMA
DYERS' MULBERRY FUSTIC
DYERS'-WEED SOLIDAGO
DYESTUFF (ALSO SEE DYE) DYE LIT WELD WOAD CHICA LOKAO WOULD ANATTO BRAZIL KAMALA LITMUS ORCEIN RELBUN ALKANET ARNATTO CUDBEAR DYEWARE SAFFRON INDULINE LUTEOLIN PITTACAL PURPURIN
DYEWEED WOODWAX
DYEWOOD FUSTET FUSTIC BARWOOD CAMWOOD HYPERNIC
DYING FEY DEATH MORENDO PARTING MORIBUND
(— AWAY) CALANDO DILUENDO MANCANDO PERDENDO SMORZATO
DYNAMIC POTENT DRIVING KINETIC FORCEFUL
DYNAMITE BLAST DUALIN SAWDUST RENDROCK GELIGNITE
DYNAMO EXCITER TORNADO
(PART OF —) BRUSH FIELD FRAME RIGGING ARMATURE COUPLING COMMUTATOR
DYNASTY (OR MEMBER THEREOF) HAN KIN SUI WEI YIN CHIN CHOU HSIA RACE SUNG TANG YUAN BUYID CHING PIAST REALM RULER SHANG HAFSID PRINCE SAFAVI SELJUK ABBASID ALMOHAD ARSACID ATTALID AYUBITE AYYUBID BOUIDES FATIMID HAFSITE IDRISID JAGELLO LAKHMID MONARCH OMAYYAD ROMANOV SAADIAN SAFAWID SAMANID TULUNID ABBASIDE AGHLABID AGLABITE ASMONEAN BUWAIHID CAPETIAN CHALUKYA DOMINION EDRISITE GOVERNOR IDRISITE JAGIELLO LORDSHIP SAFFARID SARGONID SASANIAN SELEUCID SOFFARID SASSANIDE
DYSENTERY FLUX SCOUR MENISON TOXEMIA DIARRHEA
DYSPEPTIC CACOGASTRIC
DYSPHORIA FIDGET
DYSSODIA BOEBERA
DZIGGETAI HEMIONUS

E

E EASY ECHO
EA HEA ENKI
EACH A EA UP ALL ILK THE UCH ILKA UCHE EVERY APIECE EITHER EVERYONE
(OF —) ANA
EAGER HOT RAD YAN ACID AGOG AVID EDGY FAIN FELL FOND FREE GAIR HIGH KEEN RATH SOUR TARE THRO VAIN WARM WAVE YARE YERN AFIRE AGASP ANTSY BRIEF FIRST FRACK FRECK HASTY HIGRE ITCHY PRIME READY SHARP SNELL YIVER ARDENT FIERCE GREEDY HETTER INTENT STRONG TIPTOE ANXIOUS ATHIRST BRITTLE BURNING EMULOUS EXCITED FERVENT FORWARD ITCHING PROVOKE DESIROUS IRRITATE SPIRITED VIGOROUS YEARNING SOLICITOUS
(— IN PURSUIT) SHARP
(— TO KNOW) INQUISTITIVE
(VERY —) WILD
(WILDLY —) CRAZY
EAGERLY FAST FELL YERN HOTLY BELIVE TIPTOE YARELY YEPELY PRESTLY HUNGRILY INTENTLY
EAGERNESS GOG ELAN GARE ZEAL ARDOR DESIRE FERVOR ARDENCY AVIDITY ALACRITY CUPIDITY DEVOTION FAINNESS FERVENCY
EAGLE AAR ERN CROW ERNE GIER TERN HARPY AQUILA BERGUT EAGLET FALCON FORMAL FORMEL RAPTOR ALLERION BATALEUR BATELEUR BEARCOOT BERGHAAN RINGTAIL
(KIND OF —) LEGAL
(SEA —) ERN ERNE PYGARG PYGARGUS
(PREF.) AET(O)
(SUFF.) AETUS
EAGLE OWL KATOGLE
EAGLESTONE AETITES
EAGLET BIRD LAIGLON
EAGLEWOOD AGAR ALOE AGILA ALOES AGALLOCH AQUILARI
EAGRE BORE WAVE AEGIR HYGRE
EANFLED (FATHER OF —) EADWINE
(HUSBAND OF —) OSWIU
EAR LUG NEB CLIP HEAR HEED HOOK LIST OBEY PLOW TILL AURIS BRACE PINNA SENSE SOUSE SOWSE SPIKE CANNON CONCHA CROSET EARLET LISTEN AURICLE HEARING SENSORY AUDIENCE PAVILION RECEPTOR
(— OF BELL) CANON CANNON
(— OF CORN) COB ICKER MEALIE NUBBIN CORNCOB
(— OF GRAIN) RISOM SPIKE RIZZOM
(— OF WHEAT) SPICA WHEATEAR
(—S OF GRAIN) CAPES EARHEAD
(KIND OF —) TREE
(KIND OF —S) RABBIT
(OF THE —) AURICULAR
(PART OF —) LOBE TUBE CANAL HELIX INCUS PINNA CONCHA MEATUS SCAPHA STAPES TRAGUS COCHLEA MALLEUS MEMBRANE TYMPANUM ANTIHELIX ANTITRAGUS
(UNRIPE — OF CORN) TUCKET
(PREF.) AUR(I) AURICULO OT(ICO) (IO)(O) SPICI SPICULI SPICULO
(— OF CORN) ATHERO STACHY(O)
(SUFF.) OTIC
EARACHE OTALGY OTALGIA
EAR-BONE OTOLITH
EARCOCKLE PURPLES
EARDRUM TABOR TABOUR TYMPAN MYRINGA DRUMHEAD TYMPANUM
(PREF.) TRYPAN(O) TYMPAN(O)
EARED SEAL SEALION
EARFLAP LUG EARLAP EARTAB EARMUFF
EARINE (LOVER OF —) AEGLAMOUR
EARL EORL GRAF JARL LORD PEER COMES NOBLE CONSUL SIWARD
(— OF COVENTRY) SNIPSNAPSNORUM
EARLDOM DERBY COUNTY
EARLIER ERE OLD ERST FORE ELDER SUPRA UPPER BEFORE FORMER HITHER RATHER SOONER FIRSTER FURTHER PIONEER PREMIER PREVIOUS
(PREF.) FORE PROTER(O)
(— THAN) PRE PRO
EARLIEST ERST FIRST ELDEST MAIDEN PIONEER PREMIER RATHEST FURTHEST PRIMROSE ABORIGINAL
(PREF.) EO
EAR LOBE LUG EARLAP
(— PEOPLE) OREJON
EARLY AIR ERE OLD GOOD HIGH RARE RATH SOON FORME PRIMY RATHE VERTY REARLY SUDDEN TIMELY ANCIENT BETIMES ERLICHE FORWARD YOUTHFUL MATUTINAL
(UNDULY —) PREMATURE
(PREF.) EO PALAE(O) PALE(O)
EARMARK BIT CROP SIGN SPLIT LUGMARK OVERBIT SLEEPER ALLOCATE OVERCROP UNDERBIT
EAR MUFF OREILET
EARN GET WIN FANG GAIN MAKE TILL VANG ADDLE ETTLE GLEAR MERIT GARNER HUSTLE OBTAIN ACHIEVE ACQUIRE CHEVISE DEMERIT DESERVE
(— BY LABOR) ADDLE SWINK BESWINK
EARNEST ARRA DEAR DERN HARD PAWN ARLES EAGER GRAVE SMART SOBER STAID ARDENT ENTIRE HANSEL HEARTY INTENT SEDATE SOLEMN EMULOUS ENGAGED FERVENT FORWARD HANDSEL INTENSE SERIOUS SINCERE ZEALOUS DILIGENT EMPHATIC STUDIOUS
(IN —) AGOOD
EARNESTLY HARD DEARLY WISHLY WISTLY EARNEST DEVOUTLY DINGDONG ENTIRELY HEARTILY INTENTLY INWARDLY
EARNESTNESS GLOW FERVOR WARMTH GRAVITY DEVOTION DILIGENCE
EARNINGS GET MAKING ADDLINS PICKING ADDLINGS
EARPIECE BUTTON
EARPLUG STOPPLE TEMBETA EARSPOOL
EARRING DROP GRIP EARBOB EARLET PENDLE EARCLIP EARDROP PENDANT EARSCREW
(— LOCALE) LOBE
EARS (KIND OF —) RABBIT
EAR SHELL ORMER ABALONE
EARSHOT SOUND HEARING EARREACH
EARTH ERD ORB SET BALL BANK BURY BYON CLAY CLOD DIRT DUST FLAG FOLD GRIT LAND LOAM MARL MASS MEAL MOLD MOOL MUCK ROCK SOIL SORY STAR VALE YIRD ADOBE CRUMB FLOSS GLEBE GLOBE GROOT INTER LOESS MOULD REGUR TERRA TRASS UMBER WORLD CENTER CENTRE COARSE GROUND YACATA KOKOWAI MIDGARD TERRENE TIERRAS TOPSOIL TRIPOLI MAGNESIA MIDGARTH
(— FOR RAMPART) REMBLAI
(— INHABITANT) TERRAN
(— PROVIDING OCHER) KOKOWAI
(— SUITABLE FOR CULTIVATION) LAYER
(BLACK —) MUCK SORY KILLOW AMPELITE CHERNOZEM
(BLUE —) KIMBERLITE
(BROWN —) UMBER
(CLAYEY —) LAME LOAM
(DRY —) MOOL GROOT
(FULLER'S —) CRETA CIMOLITE SMECTITE
(GEM-BEARING —) BYON
(HEAVY —) BARYTA
(LOOSE —) CRUMB GEEST
(MOIST —) SLAB SLIME
(POOR —) RAMMEL
(RAMMED —) PISE
(RED —) RUDDLE
(REFUSE —) MURGEON
(RIVER-BANK —) GREWT
(SMALL —) TERRELLA
(SOAP —) SOAPROCK
(STRAW-YELLOW —) BISMITE
(SUN-DRIED —) SWISH
(VITRIFIED —) FLOSS
(VOLCANIC —) TRASS TARRASS
(PREF.) AGRO GE(O) TELLUR(I) TERR(A)(E)(I)
(SUFF.) GAEA GEA
EARTHEN FICT DIRTEN EARTHLY YARTHEN
EARTHENWARE PIG POT DELF CHINA CLOAM CROCK DELFT CLAYEN JASPER ASTBURY BISCUIT FAIENCE POTTERY TICKNEY BUFFWARE CROCKERY MAJOLICA TALAVERA
(BROKEN PIECE OF —) CROCK
EARTHINESS SALT TERREITY
EARTHKIN TERRELLA
EARTHLY LAIRY CARNAL EARTHY MORTAL EARTHEN GLEBOUS MUNDANE SECULAR TERRAIN TERRENE WORLDLY SUBLUNAR TELLURIC TEMPORAL
EARTHMAN TERRAN
EARTHNUT ARNOT ARNUT CHUFA HOGNUT JARNUT PEANUT PIGNUT HARENUT HAWKNUT TRUFFLE
EARTH PIG ERDVARK AARDVARK
EARTHQUAKE QUAKE SEISM SHAKE SHOCK TEMBLOR SEAQUAKE
(PREF.) SEISMO SISMO
(SUFF.) SEISM SEISMAL SEISMIC
EARTHSTAR GEASTER
EARTH STATION DISH
EARTHWALL TRINCHERA
EARTH WOLF AARDWOLF
EARTHWORK BANK RATH RING AGGER CASTLE SCONCE PARADOS RAMPART TERRACE
(PL.) PARADOS
EARTHWORM ESS MAD WORM ANNELID DEWWORM IPOMOEA MADDOCK ANGLEDOG BRANDLIN EACEWORM FISHWORM RAINWORM TWATCHEL BRANDLING LUMBRICID OLIGOCHATE
EARTHY GROSS SALTY WORMY CLODDY VULGAR EARTHLY TERRENE BARNYARD TERREOUS VISCERAL
EAR TICK PINOLIA
EAR TRUMPET CORNET AEROPHONE
EARWAX CERUMEN
(PREF.) CERUMINI
EARWIG GOLACH GOLOCH TOUCHBELL
EARWORM BOLLWORM
EASE CALM COSY COZY EASY REST

ABATE ALLAY KNACK LETUP PEACE QUIET RELAX SLAKE LOOSEN PACIFY REDUCE RELIEF REPOSE SAUGHT SMOOTH SOFTEN SOOTHE APPEASE ASSUAGE COMFORT CONTENT FACULTY FLUENCY FREEDOM LEISURE LIBERTY LIGHTEN RELIEVE SLACKEN SUBSIDE DIMINISH FACILITY MITIGATE MODERATE PALLIATE PLEASURE SECURITY UNBURDEN
(— GENTLY) SLIDE
(— OF A BURDEN) LIGHT
(— OFF) FLOW CHECK START SLOUGH
(APATHETIC —) INDOLENCE
(AT —) OTIOSE
(CAREFREE —) ABANDON
EASEL FRAME SUPPORT SCAFFOLD
EASEMENT EASE EASING RELIEF HERBAGE TURBARY SERVITUS WAYLEAVE
EASE-TAKING PICKTOOTH
EASIEST EFTEST
EASILY EASY EATH WELL LIGHT EATHLY GENTLY GLIBLY HANDILY LIGHTLY READILY SLIGHTLY SMOOTHLY
(PREF.) EU
EASINESS GRACE FACILITY
EASING DETENTE
EAST OST ASIA MORN LEVANT ORIENT SUNRISE EASTWARD
(— OF) FOLLOWING
EAST AFRICA (— TREE) PODO
EASTER PT PACE PASCH EOSTRE PASCHA PASQUE
EASTERN LEVANT ORTIVE AURORAL ORIENTAL
EASTERNER DUDE
EAST INDIAN (— TREE) SAL AMLA DHAK TEAK KOKAN LANSA MAHUA MOHWA NIEPA PALAS PULAS ROHAN ROHUN SALAI SIMAL
EASTLAND ESTRICHE
EASTWARD EAST EASEL EASSEL
EASY CALM COZY CRIP EATH EITH GAIN GLIB MILD RIFE SNAP SOFT CUSHY JAMMY LARGE LIGHT PLAIN PRONE ROYAL SUAVE YEZZY CASUAL COMODO FACILE FLUENT FRUITY GENTLE GENTLY SECURE SIMPLE SMOOTH UNHARD ARTLESS GRADUAL LENIENT NATURAL CAREFREE CARELESS CAVALIER EXPEDITE FAMILIAR FRIENDLY GRACEFUL HOMELIKE MODERATE TRANQUIL UNFORCED
(— IN MIND) SECURE
(— TO HANDLE) HANDSOME
(— TO SPEAK TO) AFFABLE
(— TO UNDERSTAND) PELLUCID
(— TO USE) CLEVER
(TAKE IT —) SIT LAZE
EASYGOING LAX QUIET DEGAGE
EAT FOG KAI SUP BITE CHOP CHOW DINE FARE FEED FRET GNAW GRUB HAVE HEYT MAKE PECK RUST TUCK DIGIN ERODE FEAST GRAZE MANGE MUNCH SCOFF STOKE TASTE WASTE ABSORB BEGNAW DEVOUR INGEST NIBBLE RAVAGE CONSUME CORRODE DESTROY SWALLOW VICTUAL
(— A MEAL) GRUB
(— AS HOGS) SLUICE
(— A SNACK) NOSH
(— AWAY) GNAW ERODE RANKLE CORRODE
(— BETWEEN MEALS) NOSH
(— BIG MEAL) STOKE
(— CRUNCHINGLY) GROUZE
(— GLUTTONOUSLY) GUDGE STUFF
(— GREEDILY) GAMP GAWP SLAB SLOP TUCK CHAUM MOOCH SCARF SCOFF GOBBLE GOFFLE GUTTLE GUZZLE PIGOUT RAUNGE GLUTTON GOURMAND
(— HEARTILY) THORN
(— IN GULPS) LAB
(— MINCINGLY) PICK PICKLE PIDDLE
(— NOISILY) SLOP GULCH SLURP GUTTLE SLOTTER
(— OUT) EXEDE
(— RUDELY) TROUGH
(— SLOVENLY) SLUP MUMMICK
(— SPARINGLY) DIET NIBBLE
(— TO EXCESS) COLF BEZZLE
(— UP) DEMOLISH
(— VORACIOUSLY) CRAM WORRY
(— WITH GUSTO) SMOUSE
(— WITHOUT CHEWING) BOLT
(SUFF.) ESTES PHAG(A)(E)(IA)(ISM)(IST)(O)(OUS)(US)(Y) VORA VORE VOROUS
EATABLE FOODY COOKER EDIBLE ESCULENT
EATEN CANKERED
(HALF —) SEMESE
(PREF.) BROTO
EATER PECKER DEVOURER
(GREEDY —) GOURMAND
EATING BIT FOOD ESURINE
(— BETWEEN MEALS) TIFFIN
(— COARSE FOOD) FOUL
(— DISORDER) BULIMIA
(— INTO) CANKEROUS
(— OUT) EXESION
(PREF.) PHAG(O)
EAVES EASE EASING
EAVESDROP DARK HARKEN LISTEN HEARKEN
EAVESDROPPER COWAN EARWIG SNOOPER DRAWLATCH
EAVES TROUGH CHENEAU
EBAL (FATHER OF —) SHOBAL
EBB FAIL FALL FLAG SINK WANE ABATE DECAY RECEDE REFLOW REFLUX RETIRE TIDING DECLINE REFLOAT SUBSIDE DECREASE DIMINISH
(— AND FLOW) ESTUS AESTUS FLUIDITY
EBBING AWANE REFLUENT REFLUOUS
(— AND FLOWING) TIDAL
EBED (FATHER OF —) JONATHAN
(SON OF —) GAAL
EBER (FATHER OF —) SALAH ELPAAL
EBLIS JANN IBLIS
EBONY EBON BLACK GABON GABOON WAMARA HEBENON IRONWOOD
EBULLIENCE OVERFLOW ELEVATION
EBULLIENT BRASH FERVID YEASTY BOILING
EBULLIOSCOPE ZEOSCOPE
EBULLITION SEETHE FERMENT OUTBURST
ECAD ECOPHENE
ECCENTRIC FEY NUT ODD OFF CARD DOER NUTS CRANK DOTTY KINKY OUTRE QUEER WEIRD WIPER CRANKY LOCOED OUTISH PSYCHO SCREWY SHAGGY WEIRDO WEIRDY BIZARRE CURIOUS DEVIOUS DINGBAT ERRATIC ODDBALL STRANGE TOUCHED ABNORMAL CRACKPOT FITIFIED PECULIAR SINGULAR
(— PERSON) KOOK
ECCENTRICITY KINK FERLY ODDITY ANOMALY CROTCHET QUIDDITY
(— OF CURVE) E
ECCLESIASTES KOHELETH QOHELETH
ECCLESIASTIC ABBE ABBOT CLERK VICAR ARCHON FATHER LECTOR LEGATE PRIEST KIRKMAN PRELATE SECULAR EPISTLER SUBDEACON
ECCLESIASTICAL CHURCH CANONIC CHURCHLY CHRISTIAN SPIRITUAL
ECHELES (FATHER OF —) ACTOR
(FOSTER SON OF —) EUDORUS
(WIFE OF —) POLYMELA
ECHEVIN SCABINE SCABINUS
ECHIDNA NODIAK ANTEATER EDENTATE MONOTREME PORCUPINE
(CHILD OF —) HYDRA LADON ORTHUS SPHINX CERBERUS CHIMAERA
(FATHER OF —) PHORCYS CHRYSAOR
(MOTHER OF —) CETO CALLIRRHOE
(SLAYER OF —) ARGUS
ECHINODERM CYSTID CRINOID BLASTOID STARFISH
ECHINOPANAX FATSIA
ECHINO-SOREX GYMNURA
ECHION (FATHER OF —) MERCURY
(MOTHER OF —) ANTIANIRA
(SON OF —) PENTHEUS
(WIFE OF —) AGAVE
ECHO APE ECO BLIP RING SING CHORUS REPEAT REVERB SECOND IMITATE ITERATE RESOUND RESPEAK RESPOND REVOICE REDOUBLE RESPONSE
(— EFFECT) REVERB
(RADAR —) ANGEL
(RADIO —) ANGEL
ECLAT FAME GLORY RENOWN ACCLAIM SCANDAL APPLAUSE FACILITY PRESTIGE SPLENDOR
ECLECTIC BROAD LIBERAL
ECLIPSE DIM BIND BLOT HIDE BLIND CLOUD SHADE STAIN SULLY DARKEN DAZZLE DEFECT EXCEED OCCULT DEFAULT OBSCURE PRODIGY TRAVAIL OUTRIVAL OCCULTATION
ECLOGUE IDYL IDYLL BUCOLIC
ECOLOGIST BIONOMIST
ECOLOGY BIOLOGY BIONOMY MESOLOGY
ECONOMIC
(PREF.) EC(O) OEC(O) OIKO
ECONOMICAL WARY CHARY FENDY FRUGAL SAVING CAREFUL PRUDENT SPARING THRIFTY SCREWING
ECONOMICS PLUTONOMY
ECONOMIST HUSBAND MANAGER PHYSIOCRAT
AMERICAN DAY ELY GRAY OKUN POOR ADAMS ARROW ARROW BALCH BURNS CAREY CLARK DEWEY GRAMM HANEY HAUGE HICKS LUBIN MEYER SOLOW TOBIN WELLS WITTE YOUNG CARVER DEBREU DUNBAR DURAND ECCLES FISHER FOSTER GEORGE HADLEY HARVEY KATONA MILLIS RAGUET RIPLEY RIVLIN SPLAWN SUMNER TUCKER TURNER VEBLEN WALKER WEAVER WILLIS BULLOCK COMMONS CROWELL GARRETT JOHNSON KUZNETS TAUSSIG TUGWELL ANDERSON FRIEDMAN KEMMERER KOOPMANS LAUGHLIN LEONTIEF MITCHELL ROSOVSKY GALBRAITH HENDERSON HOLLANDER SAMUELSON MODIGLIANI WILLOUGHBY JANEWAY
AUSTRALIAN DONALD
AUSTRIAN BOHM HAYEK MISES SPANN MENGER
BELGIAN ZEELAND LEVELEYE MOLINARI
CANADIAN HOWE MAVOR ERDMAN LALONDE LEACOCK
DUTCH TINBERGEN
ENGLISH JAY COLE MILL WARD WEBB WEST HAYEK HICKS HIRST JAMES MEADE PAISH PETTY PRICE STAMP ASHLEY BARBON BAXTER COBDEN FARRER GIFFEN HOBSON JEVONS KEYNES KIRKUP LAYTON LESLIE REEVES ROGERS SALTER SENIOR SHANKS TUCKER WILSON BAGEHOT CHAPMAN CLAPHAM FAWCETT GRESHAM MALTHUS MALYNES RICARDO TOYNBEE BELLERBY MARSHALL BEVERIDGE EDGEWORTH HOLLOWOOD MACMILLAN MARTINEAU NICHOLSON OVERSTONE CUNNINGHAM
FINNISH PROCOPE
FRENCH SAY LEVY RIST BODIN GUYOT CAMBON HAUSER MONNET ALPHAND BASTIAT BLANQUI BLONDEL COURNOT FAUCHER GARNIER GOURNAY MONTYON QUESNAY SCHUMAN MIRABEAU PECQUEUR ROEDERER WOLOWSKI CHEVALIER LEVASSEUR SIEGFRIED
GERMAN RAU BONN HAHN ENGEL FUCHS HARMS JUSTI KNIES LANGE BRIEFS BUCHER CONRAD ECKERT ERHARD GESELL GOSSEN HIRSCH SERING ANDREAE DUHRING EHEBERG GERLOFF HEIMANN JASTROW LEDERER MICHELS ROSCHER HUFELAND SCHAFFLE BAMBERGER RODBERTUS SCHMOLLER FLURSCHEIM

HAXTHAUSEN HELFFERICH KESSELRING RAIFFEISEN SCHUMPETER OPPENHEIMER
GREEK ANDREADES
IRISH SMIDDY CAIRNES BASTABLE CANTILLON
ITALIAN BODIO CARLI GIOJA LORIA NITTI PELLA ROSSI BOTERO PARETO GALIANI BECCARIA GENOVESI LUZZATTI SCIALOIA CERNUSCHI PANTALEONI
NORWEGIAN FRISCH
POLISH GRABSKI WOJCIECHOWSKI
RUSSIAN BUNGE KANTOROVICH VOZNESENSKI
SCOTTISH MILL SMITH MACLEOD ANDERSON MCCULLOCH
SWEDISH OHLIN CASSEL MYRDAL
SWISS SISMONDI CHERBULIEZ
URUGUAYAN COSIO

ECONOMIZE HAIN SAVE SKIMP STINT SCRAPE SCRIMP HUSBAND UTILIZE RETRENCH
ECONOMY SPARE SAVING SYSTEM THRIFT MANAGERY PARSIMONY
ECOTONE EDGE
ECSTASY JOY BLISS POWER SWOON TRANCE DELIGHT EMOTION MADNESS RAPTURE RHAPSODY
ECSTATIC HOT RAPT PYTHIAN GLORIOUS
ECTENE IRENICON
ECTODERM EXODERM EPIBLAST
ECTOMORPHIC LINEAR ASTHENIC LEPTOSOME
ECTROPION EVERSION
ECU CROWN SCUTE SHIELD

ECUADOR

ANCIENT NAME: QUITO
CAPE: ROSA PASADO PUNTILLA
CAPITAL: QUITO
COIN: SUCRE CONDOR CENTAVO
INDIAN: CARA INCA PALTA CANELO JIVARO
ISLAND: PUNA WOLF MOCHA PINTA BALTRA CHAVES DARWIN PINZON WENMAN ISABELA
ISLANDS: COLON GALAPAGOS
LANGUAGE: JIBARO QUECHUA SPANISH
MEASURE: CUADRA FANEGA
MOUNTAIN: ANDES SANGAY CAYAMBE ANTISANA COTOPAXI
NATIVE: MONTUVIO
PROVINCE: LOJA AZUAY CANAR COLON ELORO CARCHI GUAYAS MANABI BOLIVAR LOSRIOS COTOPAXI IMBABURA
RIVER: COCA MIRA NAPO DAULE PINDO TIGRE GUAYAS TUMBES ZAMORA CURARAY PASTAZA AGUARICO BOBONAZA CONONACO NARANJAL PUTUMAYO
TOWN: JAMA LOJA MERA NAPO PUYO TENA CANAR GUANO MANTA PAJAN PINAS PIURA QUITO YAUPI AMBATO CUENCA IBARRA PUJILI TULCAN ZARUMA AZOGUES CAYAMBE GUAMOTE MACHALA PELILEO PILLARO SALINAS BABAHOYO GUARANDA RIOBAMBA
WATERFALL: AGOYAN
WEIGHT: LIBRA

ECUMENE HEARTH
ECUMENICAL LIBERAL CATHOLIC
ECZEMA TETTER EARWORM MALANDERS
EDACITY GREED APPETITE VORACITY
EDDA SAGA
EDDISH ETCH ARRISH EEGRASS
EDDO TARO COCOYAM
EDDY CURL GULF PURL WASH WEEL WELL ACKER GURGE SHIFT SWIRL TWIRL WHIRL SWOOSH VORTEX WIRBLE BACKSET WREATHE (PREF.) DINO
EDDYING WALE
EDEMA BRAXY TUMOR DROPSY BIGHEAD HYDROPS ANASARCA SWELLING
EDEMATOUS BLOATED HYDROPIC
EDEN ADEN HEAVEN UTOPIA ARCADIA ELYSIUM PARADISE **(FATHER OF —)** JOAH
EDENTATA BRUTA
EDENTATE SLOTH AARDVARK ANTEATER
EDGE AGE BIT HEM JAG LIP RIM BANK BERM BRIM BROW CURB DRAW FACE KANT LIMB LIST RAND SIDE TRIM WELL WHET ARRIS BERME BEVEL BLADE BOARD BRINK CHIMB CHIME CREST EAVES FRILL KNIFE LABEL LEDGE MARGE PEARL RULER SHARP SIDLE SPLAY VERGE BORDER CANTLE DECKLE FLANGE FORAGE IMPALE LABRUM MARGIN NOSING PLANGE MARGENT NOSEOUT SELVAGE SHARPEN VANDYKE BOUNDARY EMBORDER KEENNESS MAJORITY OUTSKIRT SELVEDGE STICKING UMSTROKE
(— FORWARD) CREEP
(— IN MINING DRIFT) ARRAGE
(— OF BASKET) FOOT
(— OF BED) STOCK
(— OF BIRD'S BILL) TOMIUM
(— OF BOOK) FERRULE BACKBONE
(— OF BOOK COVER) FLAP
(— OF BRILLIANT) GIRDLE
(— OF CASK) CHIME CHINE
(— OF COAL PILE) RUN
(— OF DAM) CREST
(— OF DUMP) TOE
(— OF FABRIC) SELVAGE SELVEDGE
(— OF FLAG) HOIST
(— OF MESA) CEJA
(— OF MINERAL VEIN) APEX
(— OF ROADWAY) SHOULDER
(— OF RUDDER) BEARDING
(— OF RUFFLE) HEADING
(— OF SAIL) FOOT HEAD LEACH LEECH
(— OF SAW) SAFE
(— OF SHELL) HINGE
(— OF STRATUM) BASSET
(— OF STREAM) HAG
(— OF TOOL) BEZEL BEZIL
(— OF TOOTH) SCALPRUM
(— OF TROUSERS) CREASE
(— OF VAULT) GROIN
(— OF WOOD) WOODRIME
(—S OF COAT) LAP
(BEVELED —) CHAMFER
(CUTTING —) SHOE FRONTIER VANGUARD
(DOUBLE —) FLAT
(EMBROIDERED —) SURFLE SURPHUL
(EXTERIOR —) AMBITUS
(FRONT — OF BOOK) FACE
(HAVING IRREGULAR —) EROSE
(ORNAMENTAL —) FRILL
(RAGGED —) RAG
(ROCKY —) ARETE
(ROUGH —S) FASH
(SHARP —) ARRIS BEARD
(UNPLOWED — OF FIELD) RAND
(UNTRIMMED —) DECKLE
(PREF.) AMBO
EDGED EDGY EROSE SHARP CRENATE CUTTING **(— BY ARCS)** INVECTED
EDGER WHETTER STRANDER
EDGEWISE (NOT —) FLATLONG
EDGING HEM CURB EDGE LACE LIST FILET FRILL LEDGE PICOT BORDER FILLET FRINGE LIMBUS BEADING BINDING GIMPING HAMBURG COQUILLE FRILLING PUNTILLA RICKRACK SKIRTING SURROUND PASSEMENTERIE **(— TO COLLAR)** PIKADELL PICCADILL PICCADILLO PICCADILLY **(GRASS —)** VERGE
EDGY ANTSY EAGER FUSSY SHARP TENSE ANGULAR NERVOUS CRITICAL SNAPPISH
EDIBLE EDULE ALIBLE EATABLE ESCULENT
EDICT ACT BAN LAW BULL FIAT TYPE ARRET BANDO BULLA IRADE ORDER SANAD UKASE ASSIZE DECREE DICTUM NOTICE COMMAND EMBARGO PLACARD PROCESS PROGRAM STATUTE ECTHESIS RESCRIPT
EDIFICE DOME CHURCH TURBEH BUILDING ERECTION TETRAGON
EDIFY GROW BUILD FAVOR TEACH BENEFIT IMPROVE PROSPER CONVINCE INSTRUCT ORGANIZE
EDIFYING HIGH SAVORY ELEVATED
EDIT CUT EMEND DIRECT REDACT REVIEW REVISE ARRANGE COMPILE CORRECT PREPARE PUBLISH REWRITE COPYREAD
EDITION KIND EXTRA FINAL FIRST ISSUE PRINT STAMP ALDINE DIGLOT SOURCE AUSGABE BULLDOG HEXAPLA OCTAPLA VERSION PRINCEPS VARIORUM **(FIRST —)** PRINCEPS
EDITOR AUTHOR OVERSEER REDACTOR
AMERICAN BOK DAY BOVA BOYD BURR BYRD CARY DANA DELL DUNN FARB FOSS FUNK HILL HOWE LUCE REID ROSS SHAW WARE YUST ALLEN BACON BYERS CANBY CLARK COLBY DEBOW DUBAY ELSON FENNO FODOR FOLEY GOULD GRADY KNOTT LASCH LOCKE LYNES MABIE MOORE NILES PAINE PRATT PUSEY RENSE RIDER RUDER SHAWN SWOPE WHITE ABBOTT AIKENS ANGELL ANGOFF BALLOU BARRON BIRNIE BOWKER BOWLES CAPPER CATTON CHURCH CLARKE COWLEY DABNEY DANIEL DENNIE DUBOIS FINLEY FLOWER FORBES GILDER GIROUX HANSEN HEARST HOOPER LARSEN LAWSON LUMMIS MALONE MANTLE MARKEL MARTIN MERWIN MONROE MUNSON NATHAN PALLEN RASCOE WILLIS ALDRICH BROWLES BURNETT COUSINS DREISER EASTMAN FADIMAN FERNALD FREEMAN GANNETT HAPGOOD HAZLITT HOFFMAN HOLLAND HUBBARD JOHNSON LINCOLN LITTELL LOVEJOY LOWNDES MENCKEN NAVASKY ONASSIS STEDMAN TAGGARD VIERECK WALLACE ALLIBONE ANDERSON BARSOTTI BENJAMIN CRAWFORD DOCTOROW GINGRICH GRINNELL GRUENING HUZTABLE LIPPMANN PETERSON RUKEYSER SEDGWICK STRUNSKY TAISHOFF THOMPSON VANDOREN WHEELOCK ALTSHELER BARTHOLDT BLACKWELL DUYCKINCK KAEMPFFERT UNTERMEYER CHAMBERLAIN CROWNINSHIELD
CANADIAN MCGEE NEWMAN
ENGLISH LEE MEE FELL FENN OPIE PEEL READ RHYS RYLE TODD CRAIG GIBBS HICKS WAUGH ALLOTT BARNES BOOSEY DELANE GARVIN HAWKES HUTTON HUXLEY KELTIE SEAMAN BOWDLER BURNAND CHAPMAN DUGDALE HYAMSON KNOWLES VERRALL CHISHOLM GOLDRING MUIRHEAD PROTHERO QUENNELL RICKWORD SPEDDING BOTTOMLEY CUSHENDUN HOLINSHED HOLLOWOOD PEMBERTON RAPPOPORT MONTGOMERY
FINNISH WALTARI
FRENCH MIGNE MORTIER YRIARTE CHAUMEIX HACHETTE
GERMAN BARTH HUBER MULLER
HUNGARIAN HARSANYI
IRISH RUSSELL ALLINGHAM
ITALIAN ASCOLI
MALTESE BUTTIGIEG
PANAMANIAN ARIAS
RUSSIAN CAHAN ARBATOV BLEEKER
SCOTTISH DYCE LAING CURRIE DAVIES HERVEY SPENCE ANDERSON HASTINGS LOCKHART FINDLATER MOTHERWELL
EDITORIAL LEADER
EDO BENI BINI
EDRED (BROTHER OF —) EDMUND **(FATHER OF —)** EDWARD **(MOTHER OF —)** EADGIFU
EDUCATE REAR BREED TEACH TRADE TRAIN EXPAND INFORM SCHOOL DEVELOP NURTURE INSTRUCT

EDUCATED BRED CIVIL TAUGHT TRAINED INFORMED LETTERED LITERATE
EDUCATION CLERGY NURTURE BREEDING LEARNING NORTELRY PEDAGOGY TRAINING
(— GROUP) NEA
(LIBERAL —) HUMANITY
(PHYSICAL —) GYM
EDUCATOR TEACHER
AMERICAN BOK DAY FEW GAY HAM ILG AMES BATE BLOW BODE CASE CHEW COLN CONE FORD FRYE HALL HART HESS HILL HOLT HOPE HULL HYDE KOHL LEVI LIDZ LYND LYON MANN MAYR MOON ODUM PAGE RAND ROOS ROOT RUGG TARR TRUE WARD WARE WEST AARON ADAMS ADLER AIKEN AVERY AYRES BAKER BATES BAUGH BEARD BEERS BEGLE BERRY BOLEY BROWN BRYAN BYRNE CANBY CAPEN CAPPS CHASE CLAPP CLARK COONS CROSS CURRY DAMON DENNY DEWEY DOBIE ELIOT EWING FLORY FRANK FUESS GATES GAUSS GOULD HEDGE HUBEL JAMES JENKS JONES KNOTT KOZOL KRAPP KRAUS KUSCH LANGE LOCKE LOWES MANLY MEYER MEZES MINOT ORTON PATRI PERRY POUND PUSEY RILES ROLFE ROSSI SCOTT SHERA SMITH SMYTH SZASZ TAUBE TEMIN TYLER UNGER UPHAM WHITE WOLFF YOUNG ANGELL BAGLEY BAILEY BARNES BARZUN BASCOM BAXTER BOVARD BOWKER BOWMAN BRIGGS BUMPUS BUTLER CARMER CARTER CARVER CHIANG CONANT COOPER CORSON COUNTS CRONIN DABNEY DAVIES DOMAGK DONHAM DRAPER DUBOIS DURANT EURICH FERRIS FINLEY FINNEY FOWLER GAYLEY GEDDES GILMAN GOEBEL GRAVES GRIMKE HADLEY HARPER HARRIS HAWKES HAZARD HIBBEN HIGHET HOWARD JESSUP JEWETT JUDSON KELLER KEPPEL LANDIS LERNER LOVETT LOWELL MARTIN MATHER MCAFEE MEARNS MILLIS MONROE NORTON PALMER PARKER PEFFER PEIRCE PHELPS PORTER SARETT SCOPES SLOANE SPARKS SPROUL STRONG STROUP STUART THOMAS THWING WIGGIN WILDER WRIGHT AGASSIZ ANAGNOS ANDREWS BABBITT BARBOUR BARNARD BARROWS BENEZET BETHUNE BRADLEY BRAWLEY CALKINS CARDOZO CLAXTON COFFMAN COLBURN COMFORT CONNELY DENNETT DOHERTY DYKSTRA ERSKINE FARRAND GARNETT GARRATY GARRETT GILMORE GOODNOW GOODWIN GOUCHER GUMMERE HASKINS HERRICK HOPKINS HOUSTON HUEBNER HULBERT HULBURT JACKSON JARDINE JOHNSON KHORANA KIMBALL KIMPTON LEONARD LINCOLN LINDSAY MATHEWS MCMURRY PADOVER PATRICK PEABODY RAYMOND RICKERT ROLLINS SCUDDER SHUSTER TATLOCK TAUSSIG THACHER VANDYKE VANHISE VIERECK VOELKER WALLACE WHEELER WILLARD WIMSATT WOOLSEY ZEITLIN ALDERMAN BANCROFT BASHFORD BLANDING BREWSTER BRITTAIN CALLAHAN CHANDLER COMMAGER COMSTOCK COPELAND DJERASSI FLETCHER FOERSTER GRISWOLD HARNWELL HARRISON HOLLOWAY HUTCHINS LANGSTON LAWRENCE MARQUAND MATTHEWS MCGUFFEY MCKNIGHT PENNIMAN PHILLIPS ROBINSON SCHURMAN SEASHORE SILLIMAN STODDARD SUZZALLO TUTWILER WHEELOCK WILLIAMS WOODBURN WOODWARD ARMSTRONG AYDELOTTE CARPENTER CHAUVENET FAIRBANKS FAIRCHILD GOODSPEED GRANDGENT GREENOUGH HENDERSON KITTREDGE LOUNSBURY PARTRIDGE PATTERSON PENDLETON SCHELLING SHARPLESS SPAULDING THORNDIKE WENTWORTH BLOOMFIELD CHADBOURNE KILPATRICK LONGSTREET PARRINGTON STURTEVANT WASHINGTON GILDERSLEEVE
ARGENTINIAN HOUSSAY SAAVDEDRA AVELLANEDA
AUSTRALIAN GREER HOLME CALDWELL
AUSTRIAN NEURATH
BELGIAN HEYMANS LAFONTAINE
CANADIAN ABEL GRANT OSLER PRATT WIGLE CAPPON HUTTON MACKAY MURRAY LEACOCK MACLEAN MCLUHAN
CZECH KELSEN COMENIUS
DANISH LUND KROGH
DUTCH ASSER DEVRIES EIJKMAN LORENTZ ZERNIKE COUPERIUS
ECUADORIAN ROCAFUERTE
EGYPTIAN HUSSEIN
ENGLISH DENT KING KLUG ALLEN BEALE BOWRA CECIL CHAIN DYSON ELTON FITCH GRANT KEBLE LUCAS OGDEN PETTY ROUSE SMITH SWANN ARNOLD BARNES CATLIN COTTON FARMER HADDON HOGBEN INGOLD KEYNES MORANT RAIKES RIPMAN SADLER BAINTON BALFOUR BALLARD COGHILL KENDREW STARKIE WESTRUP CHAMBERS CUNLIFFE SIDGWICK SPURGEON MANSBRIDGE ABERCROMBIE
FRENCH EPEE ANDLER BOUTMY CAMPAN DORIOT FONCIN WAILLY ABELARD BELJAME BIDAULT BUISSON CHINARD RENAULT BOUTROUX COMPAYRE
GERMAN AHN ALER BAUR KERN LAUE REIN CAMPE GRAFE LANGE STURM CARNAP GEDIKE JENSEN LIEBIG NATORP WITTIG ZIMMER BECKMAN FISCHER FROEBEL JASPERS SPEMANN DORPFELD FOERSTER DIESTERWEG TROTZENDORF
HUNGARIAN BEOTHY MANNHEIM
INDIAN HUSAIN GOKHALE
IRISH HUNTER WALTON STARKIE
ISRAELI SCHOLEM
ITALIAN PEI NATTA FEDELE DAPONTE VILLARI BELTRAMI GALLENGA LOMBROSO MALPIGHI MONTESSORI
JAPANESE NAGAI SUZUKI YUKAWA ASAKAWA NEESIMA FUKUZAWA
MEXICAN CAMPOS
NORWEGIAN HASSEL ONSAGER
PORTUGUESE EGAS
RUSSIAN BAER RUBIN
SCOTTISH BELL BLAIR NEILL AYTOUN DALGARNO
SWEDISH SIREN SIEGBAHN
SWISS HESS BLOCH PAULI GIRARD KARRAR TOPFFER DUCOMMUN FELLENBERG
EDUCE DRAW EVOKE ELICIT EVOLVE EXTORT EXTRACT
EEL ELE APOD GRIG LING OPAH SNIG TUNA APODE ELVER MORAY SIREN APODAN CARAPO CONGER FAUSEN MOREIA MURENE CONGRIO KWATUMA LAMPREY MURAENA SNIGGLE WRIGGLE CONGEREE GYMNOTID KINGKLIP
(KIND OF —) MORAY
(YOUNG —) GRIG ELVER OLIVER YELVER
(25 —S) STICK SWARM
EELGRASS DREW WRACK ENALID
EELPOUT BARD LING POUT QUAB BURBOT CONGER GUFFER YOWLER LYCODOID
EELSKIN (10 —S) TIMBER
EELSPEAR PILGER
EELWORM EEL NEMA
EERIE EERY SCARY TIMID WEIRD WISHT CREEPY DISMAL GLOOMY GOUSTY SPOOKY AWESOME GHOSTLY GOUSTIE MACABRE STRANGE UNCANNY ELDRITCH GHOULISH POKERISH
EFFACE BLOT DASH DELE RASE RAZE WEAR ERASE CANCEL DEFACE SPONGE STRIKE DESTROY DISLIMN EXPUNGE NULLIFY UNPAINT WEAROUT
EFFECT DO SEE DENT DOES FECK HAVE PRAY PREY TEEM WORK CAUSE CLOSE ECLAT ENACT ETTLE EVENT FORCE FRUIT ISSUE STAMP ACTION ENERGY GROWTH INDUCE INTENT OBTAIN RESULT SECURE SEQUEL STEREO UPSHOT ACHIEVE ACQUIRE ARRANGE COMPASS CONDUCE EMOTION EXECUTE FULFILL IMPRESS IMPRINT OPERATE OUTCOME PERFORM PROCURE PRODUCE PURPORT REALIZE CAUSATUM COMPLETE CONCLUDE CONTRIVE FRUITAGE CONSEQUENT
(— OF PAST EXPERIENCE) MNEME
(BLURRED —) FUZZ
(COUNTERBALANCING —) STANDOFF
(DAZZLING —) ECLAT
(DECORATIVE —) CHIPPING
(ELECTRICAL —) STRAY
(ESTHETIC —) ATMOSPHERE
(FALSE —) FACADE
(FINAL —) AMOUNT
(GRANULAR —) SPECKLE
(ILL —) EVIL
(INTENSE —) STRESS
(KIND OF —) BOHR GUNN COANDA DOMINO RIPPLE DOPPLER PLACEBO HAWTHORNE MOSSBAUER
(MOTTLED —) SPRINKLE
(MUSICAL —) BEND SHADING
(OPTICAL —) PHANTASMAGORIA
(PAINFUL —) JAR
(PAINTING —) STIPPLE
(PENETRATING —) SEARCH
(PERNICIOUS —) BLAST
(PERSONAL —S) DUNNAGE
(SECONDARY —) OVERTONE
(SHATTERING —) BRISANCE
(THEATRICAL —) CURTAIN
(TO HAVE —) MILITATE
(TOTAL —) ENSEMBLE
(TOXIC —S) THEISM
(TREMOLO —) BEBUNG
(VISIBLE —) TOUCH
(SUFF.) ERGATE ERGY
EFFECTIVE ABLE HOME MEAN REAL ALIVE GREAT HAPPY PITHY SIKER SOUND VALID ACTIVE ACTUAL CAUSAL COGENT DEADLY DIRECT FRUITY POTENT SEVERE SICKER SOVRAN CAPABLE FECKFUL OPERANT TELLING VIRTUAL ADEQUATE FORCEFUL POWERFUL SMASHING STRIKING VIGOROUS TRENCHANT
EFFECTIVELY NAITLY
EFFECTIVENESS AIM BANG CHIC EDGE TEETH VOLTAGE EFFICACY LEVERAGE
EFFECTUAL ACTUAL TOOTHY ADEQUATE POWERFUL MAGISTRAL
EFFECTUATE FULFIL FULFILL COMPLETE
EFFEMINATE NICE SOFT MILKY MISSY NELLY SAPPY SISSY BITCHY EFFETE FEMALE LYDIAN NELLIE NIMINY PRISSY SILKEN TENDER WANTON WEAKLY CITIZEN EPICENE MEACOCK WOMANLY FEMINATE FEMININE LADYLIKE OVERSOFT WOMANISH
EFFERENT EXODIC
EFFERVESCE FIZZ HUFF KNIT BUBBLE SPARKLE CARBONATE
EFFERVESCENCE FRET CRACKLE SPARKLE
EFFERVESCENT UP BRISK FIZZY QUICK BUBBLY ABUBBLE ELASTIC BUBBLING
EFFERVESCING BRISK
EFFETE SERE WEAK JADED PASSE SPENT BARREN DECADENT ETIOLATE MORIBUND OUTMODED
EFFICACIOUS VALID MIGHTY POTENT FORCIBLE POWERFUL SINGULAR VIGOROUS VIRTUOUS OPERATIVE
EFFICACY DINT FECK DEVIL FORCE GRACE MIGHT POWER DEGREE VIRTUE POTENCY VALIDITY OPERATION

EFFICIENCY POWER SKILL AGENCY ABILITY FACULTY DISPATCH EFFICACY PERFORMANCE
EFFICIENT ABLE GOOD SMART VALID POTENT CAPABLE FECKFUL POWERFUL SPEEDFUL
EFFIGY GUY IDOL POPE SIGN DUMMY IMAGE LIKENESS MONUMENT
EFFLORESCE GERMINATE
EFFLORESCENCE RASH BLOOM BLOSSOM ROSEOLA ANTHESIS ERUPTION WHITEWASH
EFFLUENCE ISSUE EFFLUX ELAPSE EMANATE
EFFLUVIA SCENT
EFFLUVIUM AURA ODOR MIASMA FLUXION SPECIES APORRHEA EMISSION OUTGOING EMANATION
EFFLUX OUTGO OUTFLOW EFFUSION
EFFORT JOB TRY TUG DINT FIST HUMP JUMP MINT PASS SHOT TOIL ASSAY BRUNT BURST CRACK DRIVE ESSAY FLING LABOR NISUS PAINS POWER REACH STUDY THROE TRIAL ANIMUS DEVOIR FAVORS FIZZLE FUFFLE PINGLE STRAIN STROKE THRIFT ATTEMPT CONATUS MOLIMEN NITENCY SPLURGE STRETCH TENSURE TROUBLE WORKING ENDEAVOR EXERTION GOODWILL INDUSTRY MOLITION REACHING STRIVING STRUGGLE
(— FOR ONESELF) FEND
(ABORTIVE —) FIZZLE
(AGONIZED —) THROE
(ARTICULATIVE —) ACCENT
(EARNEST —) STUDY
(EFFECTIVE —) LICK
(FINAL —) CHARETTE
(INITIAL —) ASSAY
(MAXIMUM —) BEST
(SALVATIONIST —) ATTACK
(SINGLE —) HEAT TRICE
(STRENUOUS —) HASSEL HASSLE
(UNSUCCESSFUL —) ATTEMPT CLUNKER
(UTMOST —) DEVOIR BUSINESS
(VIOLENT —) BURST STRAIN OUTRAGE STRUGGLE
EFFORTLESS EASY
EFFORTLESSNESS EASE
EFFRONTERY BROW FACE GALL BRASS FRONT BRONZE AUDACITY BOLDNESS CHUTZPAH FOREHEAD TEMERITY
EFFULGENCE BLAZE GLORY RADIANT RADIANCE SPLENDOR
EFFULGENT BRIGHT FULGENT RADIANT SHINING
EFFUSE GUSH SHED FLING EFFUND EMANATE DISPENSE
EFFUSION EFFLUX FOISON SCREED SPILTH STREAM
EFFUSIVE GOOEY GUSHY LAVISH SLOPPY GUSHING BUBBLING
EFFUSIVENESS SLOP
EFT ASK EVET NEWT LIZARD TRITON
EGAD ADAD ECOD IGAD SGAD
EGEST VOID EXCRETE ELIMINATE
EGEUS (DAUGHTER OF —) HERMIA

EGG AI ABET GOAD GOOG OEUF OVUM PROD SEED SPUR URGE CHECK HUEVO OVULE SPORE DARNER INCITE OOCYTE PEEWEE ZYGOTE ACTUATE COCKNEY COKENEY OOPLAST OOSPERM PROTOVUM
(— CASE) POD
(— CLUTCH) LAUGHTER
(— OF FISH OR LOBSTER) BERRY
(— ON) HAG ABET EDGE GOAD URGE
(— ON ONE'S FACE) EMBARRASSMENT
(— PRODUCT) ZOON
(—S OF BEES) BROOD
(—S OF SILKWORM) GRAINE
(— WITH BACON) COLLOP
(ACID —) SLOWCASE
(CRACKED —) CHECK CRACK LEAKER
(DRIED —S) AHUATLE
(DUCK —S) PIDAN
(FLY'S —) BLOW FLYBLOW
(FOSSIL —) OVULITE
(GOLDEN —S) SUNCUP
(GOOSE —) BLOB
(HAVE AN —) LAY
(HUNT BIRDS' —S) OOLOGIZE
(INFERTILE —) CLEAR
(INSECT —) NIT BLOW
(PART OF —) YOLK SHELL WHITE ALBUMEN CHALAZA MEMBRANE BLASTODISC
(SHAPED LIKE AN —) OVOID
(SHAPE LIKE AN —) OVOID
(SMALL —) OVULE OVULUM
(PL.) OVA ROE SEED EYREN SPAWN CLUTCH ETTING AHUATLE
(PREF.) OARI(O) OIDIO OO OV(I)(O)
(— CASE) OOTHEC(O)
EGG AND DART ECHINUS
EGG CAPSULE OVISAC
EGG-CELL GAMETE
EGGFRUIT LUCUMA CANISTEL
EGGHEAD EINSTEIN HIGHBROW INTELLECTUAL
EGGNOG NOG CAUDLE ADVOCAAT
EGGPLANT BRINJAL SOLANUM BRINGELA EGGFRUIT
EGG-SHAPED OOID OVAL OVATE OVOID OOIDAL OBOVOID OVALOID OVIFORM
EGGSHELL SHARD CASCARON
EGG WHITE GLAIR ALBUMEN
EGG YOLK YELLOW VITELLUS
EGLAH (HUSBAND OF —) DAVID
EGLANTINE (FATHER OF —) PEPIN
(HUSBAND OF —) VALENTINE
EGO I ATTA SELF ATMAN EGOITY FYLGJA CONCEIT SUBJECT
EGOCENTRIC INSEEING
EGOISM PRIDE ONEISM VANITY CONCEIT EGOTISM OWNHOOD SELFNESS NARCISSISM
EGOIST (AUTHOR OF —) MEREDITH
(CHARACTER IN —) DALE LUCY CLARA HARRY OXFORD VERNON DECRAYE CROSSJAY DARLETON LAETITIA PATTERNE WHITFORD MIDDLETON CONSTANTIA WILLOUGHBY

EGOTISM EGO PRIDE EGOISM VANITY CONCEIT EGOMANIA SELFLOVE
EGREGIOUS FINE GROSS CAPITAL EMINENT FLAGRANT PRECIOUS SHOCKING
EGREGIOUSLY BEASTLY
EGRESS EXIT ISSUE OUTGO OUTLET EXITURE OUTCOME OUTGATE PASSAGE REGRESS OUTGOING
EGRET HERON PLUME GAULIN KOTUKU AIGRETTE GAULDING
EGYPT MIZRAIM

EGYPT

BAY: FOUL
CALENDAR: AHET APAP TYBI PAYNI SHEMU THOTH CHOIAK HATHOR MECHIR MESORE PAOPHI PACHONS
CANAL: SUEZ
CAPE: BANAS RASBANAS
CAPITAL: CAIRO ELQAHIRA
CHRISTIAN: COPT COPTIC
COIN: FILS DINAR GIRSH POUND DIRHAM GUINEA JUNAYH PIASTER MILLIEME
DAM: ASWAN
DESERT: LIBYAN
GOVERNORATE: SUEZ CAIRO CANAL SINAI BAHARIYA BAHRIYAH ALEXANDRIA
GULF: AQABA
ISTHMUS: SUEZ
KING: AY IB KA ITI ITY TUT DJER DJET HUNY PAMI PEPI SETI TEOS TETI UNIS ARSES BEBTI FOUAD ITETI KEBEH KHUFU KNIAN MENES NEBKA NECHO NEFER UDIMU ZEMTI ZOSER CHEOPS DARIUS FAROUK KHAFRE NARMER RANSES SENEDJ XERXES MENKURE PHARAOH PTOLEMY RAMESES SALADIN CHEPHREN THUTMOSE
LAKE: EDKU IDKU MARYUT MOERIS MANZALA BURULLUS MAREOTIS
LAKES: BITTER
MEASURE: APT DRA HEN PIK ROB DRAA KHET ROUB THEB ABDAT ARDAB CUBIT FARDE KELEH KILAH SAHME ARTABA AURURE FEDDAN KEDDAH ROBHAH SCHENE CHORYOS DARIBAH MALOUAH ROUBOUH TOUMNAH KASSABAH KHAROUBA
MOUNTAIN: SINAI GHARIB KATHERINA
NAME: UAR
NATIVE: ARAB COPT NILOT BERBER MUSLIM NUBIAN
OASIS: SIWA DAKHLA KHARGA FARAFRA BAHARIYA
OLD CAPITAL: SAITE
PENINSULA: SINAI
PORT: TOR SUEZ ATTUR DUMYAT QUSEIR RASHID SAFAGA SALLUM ROSETTA DAMIETTA HURGHADA PORTSAID ALEXANDRIA
PROVINCE: GIZA QENA QINA ASWAN ASYUT MINYA SOHAG DUMYAT FAIYUM SAWHAJ TAHRIR ALJIZAH BEHEIRA BENISUEF DAMIETTA GHARBIYA MINUFIYA SHARQIYA
RESERVOIR: ASWAN
RIVER: NILE
RUINS: ABYDOS THEBES MEMPHIS PYRAMIDS
SUN GOD: RA RE ATUM
TOWN: NO MUT DUSH GIZA IDFU ISNA QENA SAIS SIWA SUEZ ZOAN ASWAN ASYUT BENHA BULAQ CAIRO ELTUR FAYID GIRGA GIZEH LUXOR NAKHL SALUM SOHAG TAHTA TANIS TANTA ABYDOW AKHMIN DUMYAT ELQASR HELWAN RASHID THEBES BURSAID ROSETTA ZAGAZIG BENISUEF DAMIETTA ISMAILIA
WEIGHT: KAT KET OKA OKE HEML KHAR OKIA ROTL ARTAL ARTEL DEBEN KERAT MINAE MINAS OKIEH POUND RATEL UCKIA HAMLAH KANTAR DRACHMA QUINTAL
WELL: BIRTABA
WIND: KAMSIN SIROCCO KHAMSEEN

EGYPTIAN ARAB COPT GIPPY GYPPY TASIAN PHARIAN BADARIAN MEMPHIAN
EHUD (FATHER OF —) GERA BILHAN
EIDER COLK WAMP DIVER EDDER DUCKER SHOREYER
EIDOLON ICON GHOST IMAGE IDOLUM PHANTOM LIKENESS
EIGHT ETA ECHT AUGHT CHETH OCTAD OCTET OCTAVE OGDOAD OCTONARY
(PREF.) OCT(A)(O)(U)
EIGHTEENMO OCTODECIMO
EIGHTEEN-WHEELER RIG
EIGHTFOLD OCTUPLE
EIGHTH AUGHT
(— PART OF CIRCLE) OCTANT
EIGHTH NOTE UNCA CROMA CHROMA QUAVER
EIGHTY FOURSCORE
EIGHTY-SIX EJECT
EINSTEIN BRAIN
EIRE (SEE IRELAND)
EITHER ANY EDDER ITHER OTHER WHETHER
EJACULATE BELCH BLURT EJECT FLING EXCLAIM EMISSION
EJACULATION HOW COADS ZOWIE BEGORRA CRIMINE UTTERING
(MYSTIC —) OM
EJACULATORY SPUTTERY
EJECT OUT BLOW BOOT CAST EMIT FIRE HOOF OUST SHED SPAT SPEW SPIT VOID WARP AVOID BELCH CHUCK ERUCT ERUPT EVICT EXPEL SHAKE SHOOT SPOUT SPURT VOMIT BANISH BOUNCE REJECT SQUIRT DEFORCE DISMISS EXCLUDE EXTRUDE OBTRUDE DISGORGE OUTBRAID
(— DROPS) SPUTTER
EJECTION BLOW OUSTER OUTING EVICTION
EJECTOR LIFTER EDUCTOR
EKE IMP ALSO YEKE AUGMENT ENLARGE HUSBAND STRETCH

APPENDIX INCREASE LENGTHEN LIKEWISE UNDERLAY
ELABORATE LUSH FIKIE GREAT LABOR DELUXE DRESSY ELABOR ORNATE QUAINT REFINE CURIOUS DEVELOP ENLARGE LABORED PERFECT
(OVERLY —) NIGGLING
ELABORATED WROUGHT
ELABORATELY FANCILY
ELABORATENESS FINENESS CURIOSITY
ELABORATION FINISH
(PETTY —) NIGGLING
ELAH (FATHER OF —) UZZI CALEB BAASHA
(SLAYER OF —) ZIMRI
(SON OF —) HOSHEA
ELAINE (FATHER OF —) PELLES BRANDEGORIS
(SON OF —) GALAHAD
ELAIS (FATHER OF —) ANIUS
(MOTHER OF —) DORIPPE
(SISTER OF —) OENE SPERMO
ELAMITE SUSIAN ANZANITE
ELAN DASH ZEST ARDOR DRIVE FLAIR GUSTO VERVE SPIRIT WARMTH PANACHE POTENCY
ELAND ORYX IMPOFO
ELAN VITAL ZOISM
ELAPS MICRURUS
ELAPSE GO RUN PASS ROLL SLIP GLIDE SPEND EXPIRE RUNOUT
ELAPSED PAST
ELAPSING CURRENT
ELASAH (FATHER OF —) SHAPHAN
ELASMOBRANCH PLACOID
ELASTIC QUICK GARTER RUBATO SPONGY BUOYANT SPRINGY STRETCH CHEVEREL CHEVERIL FLEXIBLE STRETCHY VOLATILE
ELASTICITY GIVE LIFE ELATER SPRING STRETCH
ELATE BYOU PUFF CHEER EXALT EXULT FLUSH LOFTY RAISE SETUP ELATED EXCITE PLEASE THRILL ELEVATE GLADDEN INFLATE SUBLIME SUCCESS ELEVATED HEIGHTEN INSPIRIT JUBILATE
ELATED RAD HIGH RADE CHUFF ELATE GIDDY HAPPY PROUD VAUDY VOGIE WLONK CHUFFY JOVIAL UPPISH UPPITY EXCITED EXULTED JOCULAR SUBLIME EUPHORIC EXULTANT GLORIOUS INFLATED JUBILANT PRIDEFUL UPLIFTED
ELATER BEETLE CRINULA SKIPJACK
ELATION JOY GLEE RUFF RUFFE BUOYANCY
ELATUS (FATHER OF —) ARCAS
(MOTHER OF —) ERATO CHRYSOPELIA
(SON OF —) CYLLEN ISCHYS PEREUS AEPYTUS STYMPHALUS
(WIFE OF —) LAODICE
ELBOW ELL BEND ANCON JOINT NUDGE SHOVE CROSET ELBUCK JOSTLE JUSTLE SPRING PIERDROP
(OUT AT THE —S) SEEDY
(PREF.) CUBITO ULNO
ELCAJA MAFURA
ELDER AIN IVA AINE WITE ELLER OLDER PRIOR MAHANT PRIMUS SENIOR ANCIENT NEGUNDO STAROST TRAMMON ANCESTOR BOUNTREE BOURTREE CARELESS DANEWORT ELDERMAN PRESBYTER
ELDERLY AGED GRAY ALDER ANILE ELDERN SENILE BADGERLY GERIATRIC
ELDEST AYNE EIGNE OLDEST PRIMUS
ELDRICH EERIE
ELEASAH (FATHER OF —) HELEZ RAPHA
ELEAZAR (BROTHER OF —) ABIHU NADAB ITHAMAR
(FATHER OF —) AARON ELIUD MAHLI PAROSH ABINADAB PHINEHAS
(GRANDFATHER OF —) MERARI
ELECAMPANE INULA CANADA ELFWORT SCABWORT
ELECT CALL PICK VOICE ASSUME CHOOSE CHOSEN DECIDE ISRAEL PREFER SELECT
ELECTION PROXY CHOICE LECTION PRIMARY
ELECTIONEERING HUSTINGS
ELECTIVE OPTION OPTIONAL
ELECTOR VOTER ELISOR CHOOSER ELIGENT INTRANT ELECTANT
ELECTORATE PEOPLE COUNTRY
ELECTRA LAODICE
(BROTHER OF —) ORESTES
(DAUGHTER OF —) IRIS AELLO OCYPETE
(FATHER OF —) ATLAS OCEANUS AGAMEMNON
(HUSBAND OF —) PYLADES THAUMAS
(MOTHER OF —) ERATO TETHYS PLEIONE CLYTEMNESTRA
(SON OF —) IASION DARDANUS
(UNCLE OF —) MENELAUS
ELECTRIC
(PREF.) POTAM(O)
(— RAY) NARC(O)
ELECTRICIAN WIRER GAFFER JUICER BOARDMAN
ELECTRICITY JUICE POWER PYROGEN ELECTRIC GALVANISM
(GENIUS OF —) TESLA
ELECTRIFY EXCITE THRILL STARTLE
ELECTROCARDIOGRAPHIC (— EXAMINATION) STRESSTEST
ELECTROCUTE BURN EXECUTE
ELECTROCUTION CHAIR
ELECTRODE DE DEE GATE GRID ANODE PLATE DYNODE CATHODE IGNITER CROWFOOT REOPHORE
(PL.) ELEMENT
ELECTRODEPOSIT STRIKE REGULINE
ELECTROLYTE STRIKE IONOGEN
ELECTROMAGNETIC (— UNIT) OERSTED ABAMPERE
ELECTRON ION NEGATON POLARON NEGATRON POSITRON CORPUSCLE
ELECTRONIC RADIONIC
(— DEVICE) WAWAPEDAL
ELECTRONICS (— WHIZ) TECHIE
(BRANCH OF —) OVONICS
ELECTRONOGRAPHY ONSET
ELECTRON TUBE TRIODE
ELECTROPHONE MARTENOT
ELECTROPLATE SILVER
ELECTROTYPE PATCH CLICHE WORKER ELECTRO
ELECTRUM AMBER ELECTRE ORICHALC
ELECTRYON (DAUGHTER OF —) ALCMENE
(FATHER OF —) PERSEUS
(MOTHER OF —) ANDROMEDA
ELECTUARY DIASCORD LECTUARY THERIACA MITHRIDATE
ELEGANCE CHIC GARB LUXE TONE CLASP GRACE STYLE SWANK TASTE FINERY GAIETY GAYETY LUXURY NICETY POLISH COURTESY EUPHUISM FINENESS FRIPPERY GRANDEUR SPLENDOR
ELEGANT CHIC DINK FAIR FEAT FINE FIXY GENT JIMP POSH CIVIL COMPT FANCY GRAND NOBBY RITZY SHARP SLEEK SWANK SWISH CHOICE CLASSY DAINTY DELUXE DRESSY FACETE MINION POLITE PRETTY QUAINT SUPERB SWANKY URBANE VENUST CAPITAL CLEANLY COURTLY FEATISH FEATOUS GENTEEL MINIKIN REFINED SMICKER DEBONAIR DELICATE GINGERLY GRACEFUL GRAZIOSO HANDSOME POLISHED TASTEFUL CONCINNOUS
ELEGANTLY FINE TALLY FAIRLY GENTLY GINGERLY
ELEGIAC MOURNFUL EPICEDIAL
ELEGY POEM SONG DIRGE KINAH QINAH LAMENT MONODY EPICEDE
ELEKTRA (CHARACTER IN —) OREST AEGISTH ELEKTRA CHRYSOTHEMIS KLYTEMNESTRA
(COMPOSER OF —) STRAUSS
ELEMENT AIR ATOM DIAD DYAD RECT WOOF BEARD ETHER FIBER FIBRE IODIN METAL MONAD PUNCT STUFF AETHER ARTIAD COSTAL FACTOR HEPTAD LOSSER MATTER MOMENT SIMPLE ACTINON ADAPTER BUNCHER CARRIER CATCHER ESSENCE FEATURE ACTINIDE BACKBONE CEREBRAL EQUATION PERISSAD RUDIMENT SELECTOR THERBLIG
(— IN GRAPH) SPIKE
(— IN WAVE) DART
(— IN WORD GROUP) KOINON
(— OF ALCHEMIST) AIR FIRE EARTH WATER
(— OF EXISTENCE) DHARMA
(— OF MACHINE) HORN SPIDER
(— OF WEALTH) COMMODITY
(— ON TV SCREEN) PIXEL
(ALIEN —) ALLOY
(ARCHITECTURAL —) SLAB
(BINDING —) CEMENT
(CHARACTER —) STRAIN
(CHARACTERISTIC —) PARAMETER
(CHEMICAL —) TIN GOLD IRON LEAD NEON ZINC ARGON BORON RADON XENON BARIUM CARBON CERIUM CESIUM COBALT COPPER CURIUM ERBIUM HELIUM INDIUM IODINE MURIUM NICKEL OSMIUM OXYGEN RADIUM SILVER SODIUM SULFUR ARSENIC BISMUTH BROMINE CADMIUM CALCIUM FERMIUM GALLIUM HAFNIUM HOLMIUM IRIDIUM KRYPTON LITHIUM MERCURY NIOBIUM RHENIUM RHODIUM SILICON TERBIUM THORIUM THULIUM URANIUM WOLFRAM YTTRIUM ACTINIDE ACTINIUM ANTIMONY ASTATINE CHLORINE CHROMIUM EUROPIUM FLUORINE FRANCIUM HYDROGEN LUTETIUM MASURIUM NITROGEN NOBELIUM NONMETAL PLATINUM POLONIUM RUBIDIUM SAMARIUM SCANDIUM SELENIUM TANTALUM THALLIUM TITANIUM TUNGSTEN VANADIUM METALLOID PALLADIUM PLUTONIUM
(COMMUNION —) GIFT
(CRIMINAL —) GANGLAND
(DECORATIVE —S) ART
(DOMINANT —) CAPSHEAF
(ELECTRIC —) IMPEDOR
(ESSENTIAL —) CORPUS
(EUCHARISTIC —S) HAGIA SPECIES
(FATAL —) BANE
(FIRST —) PRIMORDIAL
(FUNDAMENTAL —) STAMEN KEYSTONE
(GLOOMY —) PALL
(HEATING —) CALANDRIA
(HYPOTHETICAL —) CORONIUM
(IMAGE —) PIXEL
(INTERFERING —) CRIMP
(LAMP —) GLOWER
(LEADING —) HEAD
(LINGUISTIC—) SERVILE INTENSIVE
(MILITARY —) SUPPORT
(MODIFYING —) LEAVENING
(MORAL —) DAENA
(MOST IMPORTANT —) CAPSTONE
(PRIMAL —) GUNA SALT ARCHE
(PRINCIPAL —) STAPLE
(SKELETAL —) SCLERE
(STRUCTURAL —) ARCUALE
(SUPPOSED —) PROTYLE WELSIUM VICTORIUM
(SUSTAINING —) BREAD STAPLE
(TRACE —) MICRONUTRIENT
(TRANSITORY —S) SKANDHAS
(UNITING —) BOND
(UNSOUND —) ULCER
(PL.) DETAIL ALPHABET
(PREF.) **(FIRST —TH)** STOICHIO
(SUFF.) AD IUM
(CHEMICAL —) ID IDE INE IUM
ELEMENTAL PURE BASIC PRIMAL SIMPLE PRIMARY ULTIMATE PRIMITIVE
ELEMENTARY PRIMAL SIMPLE INITIAL PRIMARY INCHOATE ULTIMATE RUDIMENTARY
ELEMI ANEMI ANIME MATTI RESIN CONIMA
ELEPHANT COW BULL CALF HINE PUNK BABAR HATHI HATTY JUMBO ROGUE MUCKNA TUSKER KOOMKIE AIRAVATA LOXODONT MASTODON OLIPHANT PACHYDERM PROBOSCIDEAN
(— BOY) SABU
ELEPHANT BIRD AEPYORNIS

ELEPHANT FISH JOSEF JOSUP JOSEPH
ELEPHANTIASIS TYRIASIS
ELEPHANTINE HUGE ENORMOUS
ELEPHANT'S-EAR TARO
ELEPHANT'S -EARS BEGONIA
ELEPHANT SHREW JUMPER
ELEUT KALMUK KALMYK KALMUCK
ELEVATE HAIN JUMP LIFT REAR RISE EDIFY ELATE ENSKY ERECT EXALT EXTOL GRIMP HEAVE HOIST MOUNT RAISE TOWER REFINE UPLIFT ADVANCE DIGNIFY ENHANCE ENNOBLE GLORIFY PROMOTE SUBLIME UPRAISE HEIGHTEN INSPIRIT
ELEVATED EL FINE HIGH GREAT LOFTY NOBLE RISEN STEEP AERIAL AMOTUS ELATED RAISED RISING WINGED BULLATE ELEVATO EXALTED MOUNTED STILTED SUBLIME MAJESTIC UPLIFTED
(— IN CHARACTER) HIGH
(NOT —) COMICAL
ELEVATION UP ARM BAND BANK DOME DRUM GLEE HIGH HILL HUMP LIFT RISE SPUR TOFT TOOT UMBO AGGER BULLA GRADE KNOLL MOUND PITCH RAISE RIDGE SHOAL SWELL TOWER WHEAL CONULE CRISTA HEIGHT PAPULE UPLIFT DIGNITY FURCULA MAJESTY UPRIGHT ALTITUDE EMINENCE EVECTION HIGHNESS LEVATION MOUNTAIN SWELLING MONTICULE
(— OF CARTILAGE) ANTHELIX
(— OF CUTICLE) BLEB
(— OF SKIN) BLISTER
(— OF VOICE) ARSIS
(— ON TOOTH) STYLE
(— SEPARATING CREEKS) BUGOR
(ANGULAR —) STEEVE
(GUN —) RANDOM
(TURRET —) HOOD
(PREF.) ORO
ELEVATOR BIN CAGE LIFT SILO HOIST BRIDGE LIFTER TEAGLE HOISTER STACKER UPTAKER UPLIFTER UPRAISER
(TAKE THE —) RIDEUP
ELEVEN
(PREF.) HENDEC(A) UNDEC(A)
ELEVENTH ELFT
ELF FAY HAG HOB IMP OAF PUG DROW FANE OUPH PERI PIXY PUCK DWARF ELFIN FAIRY GNOME OUPHE PIGMY PIXIE ELFKIN GOBLIN SPIRIT SPRITE URCHIN BLASTIE BROWNIE INCUBUS SUCCUBUS
ELFIN ELF FEY CHILD ELFIC ELFISH URCHIN
ELFISH ELFIN ELVAN ELVISH IMPISH URCHIN ELFLIKE TRICKSY
ELFRIDA (HUSBAND OF —) EDGAR
(SON OF —) AETHELRED
ELIA LAMB
ELIAB (BROTHER OF —) DAVID
(DAUGHTER OF —) ABIHAIL
(FATHER OF —) HELON NAHATH
(SON OF —) ABIRAM DATHAN
ELIADA (FATHER OF —) DAVID
ELIADAH (SON OF —) REZON
ELIAKIM (FATHER OF —) ABIUD MELEA HILKIAH
(SON OF —) AZOR JONAN
ELIAM (DAUGHTER OF —) BATHSHEBA
ELIASAPH (FATHER OF —) LAEL
ELIASHIB (FATHER OF —) BANI ZATTU
ELICIT CALL DRAW MILK PUMP CLAIM EDUCE EVOKE EXACT FETCH WREST WRING DEDUCE DEMAND ENTICE EXTORT INDUCE EXTRACT PROVOKE SOLICIT
ELIDE OMIT SKIP ANNUL IGNORE CURTAIL DESTROY NULLIFY DEMOLISH SUPPRESS
ELIEZER (FATHER OF —) JORIM MOSES BECHER ZICHRI DODAVAH
ELIGIBILITY FITNESS
ELIGIBLE FIT ACTIVE WORTHY SUITABLE
(— IN POKER) ACTIVE
ELIMELECH (SON OF —) MAHLON CHILION
(WIFE OF —) NAOMI
ELIMINATE FAN COMB EDIT KILL EDUCE EXPEL PURGE SCRUB DELETE EFFACE EXCEPT IGNORE REMOVE SCREEN WINNOW ABOLISH BLANKET BRACKET DIVULGE EXCLUDE EXCRETE RELEASE RULEOUT SCISSOR SILENCE SUBLATE TAKEOUT SEPARATE
ELIMINATION STRIP
ELIOENAI (FATHER OF —) NEARIAH
ELIPHAL (FATHER OF —) UR
ELIPHALET (FATHER OF —) DAVID
ELIPHAZ (FATHER OF —) ESAU
(MOTHER OF —) ADAH
(SON OF —) TEMAN
ELIPHELET (FATHER OF —) DAVID ESHEK
ELISABETH (HUSBAND OF —) ZACHARIAS
(SON OF —) JOHN
ELISHA (FATHER OF —) SHAPHAT
ELISHAH (FATHER OF —) JAVAN
ELISHAMA (FATHER OF —) DAVID
(SON OF —) NETHANIAH
ELISHAPHAT (FATHER OF —) ZICHRI
ELISHEBA (BROTHER OF —) NAHSHON
(FATHER OF —) AMMINADAB
(HUSBAND OF —) AARON
ELISHUA (FATHER OF —) DAVID
ELISION SYNCOPE
ELISIR D'AMORE (CHARACTER IN —) ADINA BELCORE NEMORINO DULCAMARA
(COMPOSER OF —) DONIZETTI
ELISSA (BROTHER OF —) PYGMALION
(FATHER OF —) BELUS METGEN
(HUSBAND OF —) ACERBAS SYCHAEUS SICHARBAAL
(SISTER OF —) ANNA
ELITE BEST LITE PINK CREAM CHOICE CIRCLE FLOWER GENTRY SELECT PERFECTI
ELIUD (FATHER OF —) ACHIM
ELIXIR DAFFY AMRITA SPIRIT AMREETA ARCANUM CORDIAL CUREALL ESSENCE PANACEA MEDICINE
(ALCHEMIST'S —) TINCT
ELIZAPHAN (FATHER OF —) UZZIEL
ELK ALCE DEER LAMA LOSH ALAND ALCES ELAND LOSHE MOOSE CERVID SAMBAR WAPITI SAMBHUR WAMPOOSE
(— HIDE) LOSH
(YOUNG —) DEACON
ELKANAH (FATHER OF —) KORAH
(SLAYER OF —) ZICHRI
(SON OF —) SAMUEL
ELK BARK BIGBLOOM
ELL ULNA WING ELBOW ALNAGE ADDITION
ELLIPSE OVAL
ELLIPSIS BRING ELLIPSE
ELLIPSOGRAPH TRAMMEL
ELLIPSOID CONOID ELLIPTIC SPHEROID
ELLIPSOIDAL OVAL
ELLIPTICAL OVAL OVATE OVOID OBLONG
ELLOBIUM AURICULA
ELM ULME ELVEN ULMUS WAHOO MEZCAL CHEWBARK ORHAMWOOD
(FRUIT OF —) SAMARA
ELMODAM (FATHER OF —) ER
ELMSEED
(PREF.) SAMARI
ELNAAM (SON OF —) JERIBAI JOSHAVIAH
ELOCUTION SPEECH DICTION ORATORY
ELOCUTIONIST READER RECITER
ELOIGN CONVEY REMOVE ABSCOND CONCEAL
ELON (FATHER OF —) ZEBULUN
ELONGATE EXTEND REMOVE STRETCH LENGTHEN PROTRACT
(— RAPIDLY) SHOOT
ELONGATED LANK LONG LINEAR OBLONG PROLATE SLENDER HAIRLIKE PRODUCED
ELOPE DECAMP ESCAPE ABSCOND
ELOQUENCE FACUND FLUENCY ORATORY
ELOQUENT VOCAL DISERT FACUND FERVID FLUENT SILVER RENABLE SPEAKING ORATORICAL
ELPAAL (BROTHER OF —) ABITUB
(FATHER OF —) SHAHARAIM
(MOTHER OF —) HUSHIM
ELPALET (FATHER OF —) DAVID

EL SALVADOR
CAPITAL: SANSALVADOR
COIN: PESO COLON CENTAVO
DANCE: PASILLO
DEPARTMENT: LAPAZ CABANAS MORAZAN SONSONATE
GULF: FONSECA
INDIAN: PIPIL
LAKE: GUIJA ILOPANGO
MEASURE: VARA CAFIZ CAHIZ FANEGA TERCIA BOTELLA CAJUELA CANTARO MANZANA
POINT: REMEDIOS
PORT: CUTUCO ACAJUTLA
RIVER: JIBOA LAPAZ LEMPA
RUINS: TAZUMAL
TOWN: CUTUCO IZALCO CORINTO METAPAN ACAJUTLA USULUTAN SONSONATE AHUACHAPAN
VOLCANO: IZALCO
WEIGHT: BAG CAJA LIBRA

ELSE OR ENS ENSE OTHER BESIDES INSTEAD
ELSEWHERE ALIBI EXCEPT THENCE
(FROM —) ALIUNDE
ELUCIDATE CLEAR LUCID EXPLAIN SIMPLIFY
ELUDE BEAT FLEE FOIL JINK MISS MOCK SLIP AVOID DODGE EVADE BAFFLE BEFOOL DELUDE DOUBLE ESCAPE BEGUILE DECEIVE HEDGEHOP
ELUSIVE EELY LUBRIC SHIFTY SUBTLE TRICKY TWISTY EVASIVE BAFFLING FUGITIVE SLIPPERY
ELYSIUM EDEN ANNWFN PARADISE
ELYTRON HUSK SCUTE SHARD SHERD SHEATH
ELYTRUM SHARD TEGMEN
ELZAPHAN (FATHER OF —) UZZIEL
EM EMMA
(HALF —) EN
EMACIATED LEAN POOR EMPTY GAUNT MEAGER PEAKED SKINNY WASTED TABETIC WASTREL MARASMIC SKELETAL WANTHRIVEN
EMACIATING MARCID
EMACIATION NITON TABES MACIES ATROPHY POVERTY ASTHENIA MARASMUS
EMANATE FLOW ARISE EMANE EXUDE ISSUE DERIVE EFFUSE EXHALE OUTRAY SPRING BREATHE OUTCOME PROCEED RADIATE
EMANATING EFFLUENT
EMANATION FUG AURA BEAM BLAS AROMA GLORY NITON AZILUT BREATH EFFLUX ELAPSE EIDOLON MOFETTE OUTCOME PROCESS SEPHIRA EMISSION PROCESSION
(— FROM A MEDIUM) ECTOPLASM
(SENSED —) KARMA
(PL.) SCENT
EMANCIPATE FREE MANUMIT RELEASE LIBERATE UNFETTER
EMANCIPATION FREEDOM RELEASE
(FINAL —) NIRVANA
EMASCULATE GELD SOFTEN EVIRATE CASTRATE ENERVATE
EMATHION (BROTHER OF —) MEMNON
(FATHER OF —) TITHONUS
(MOTHER OF —) EOS
(SLAYER OF —) HERCULES
EMBALM BALM CERE MUMMY SPICE BALSAM SEASON CONDITE MUMMIFY
EMBANK BUND
EMBANKMENT BAY BAND BANK BUND DIKE DYKE FILL QUAY ARGIN DIGUE LEVEE MOUND REVET SCARP BUNKER ESCARP STAITH BACKING BANKING PARADOS PILAPIL RAMPART RAMPIRE

SEAWALL APPROACH STRENGTH REVETMENT
EMBARGO EDICT ORDER IMBARGE BLOCKADE STOPPAGE
EMBARK BANK SAIL SHIP ENGAGE ENLIST INSHIP INVEST LAUNCH IMBARGE
EMBARRASS SET CHAW CLOG FAZE HACK LAND POSE ABASH ANNOY SHAME UPSET BOGGLE CUMBER GRAVEL HAMPER HINDER HOBBLE IMPEDE PLUNGE PUZZLE RATTLE CONFUSE ENTRIKE FLUMMOX INVOLVE NONPLUS BEWILDER CONFOUND DUMFOUND ENCUMBER ENTANGLE HANDICAP IMPESTER OBSTRUCT STRAITEN
EMBARRASSED AWKWARD FLURRIED SHEEPISH
EMBARRASSING STICKY AWKWARD HIDEOUS
EMBARRASSINGLY AWKWARDLY
EMBARRASSMENT FIX GENE LURCH SHAME STAND CADDLE CUMBER HOBBLE PUZZLE CHAGRIN NONPLUS CONFUSION
EMBASSY SAND ERRAND AMBASSY MESSAGE MISSION INBASSAT LEGATION
EMBATTLED BATTLED CRENELE BRETESSE CRENELEE
EMBAY BATHE DETAIN ENCLOSE SHELTER SUFFUSE ENCIRCLE SURROUND
EMBAYMENT FIORD FJORD
EMBDEN GOOSE
EMBED BED SET BOND IMBED LAYIN STAMP CHARGE ENGAGE EMBOWEL IMMERSE
(— IN SAND) DOCK
EMBEDDED INNATE ENGAGED IMMERSED
EMBELLISH GEM DECK GILD LARD TRIM ADORN DRESS FUDGE GRACE BEDECK BETRIM BLAZON EMBOSS ENRICH FIGURE FLOWER APPAREL BEDRAPE EMBLAZE GARNISH MYSTIFY VARNISH BEAUTIFY DECORATE FLOURISH ORNAMENT
EMBELLISHED FLORID GESTED ORNATE COLORED FUCUSED BROCADED SPLENDID
EMBELLISHMENT FILIP GRACE FILLIP RELISH AGREMEN GARNISH GILDING WINDING AGREMENT FLOURISH MOUNTING ORNAMENT PARERGON TRAPPING TRICKING PASSAGGIO
(MUSICAL —) SERIF MELISMA ROULADE ARABESQUE
(PL.) FIXINGS
EMBER ASH COAL AIZLE GLEED IMBER CINDER
(RED-HOT —S) BAGA
EMBEZZLE STEAL PECULATE SQUANDER
EMBEZZLEMENT THEFT PLUNDERAGE
EMBITTER SOUR BITTER CURDLE ACIDIFY ENVENOM ACERBATE EMPOISON VERJUICE
EMBITTERED SOURED ACERBATE ENFESTED
EMBLAZON LAUD ADORN EXTOL BLAZON DISPLAY EMBLAZE EXHIBIT GLORIFY
EMBLAZONED CLOUE CLOUEE CRINED CRESTED BRISTLED
(— WITH ANTLERS) ATTIRED
(— WITH BEARD) BARBED
EMBLAZONMENT HERALDRY
EMBLEM BAR ANKH ATEN LOGO MACE ORLE SEAL SIGN STAR TYPE AWARD BADGE CREST CROSS EAGLE FAVOR IMAGE TIARA TOKEN DEVICE DIADEM ENSIGN FIGURE KAHILI SABCAT SHIELD SIGNAL SYMBOL TRISUL CHARACT IMPRESA IMPRESE SCEPTER SCEPTRE ALLEGORY CADUCEUS COLOPHON INSIGNIA
(— OF AUTHORITY) ROD SCEPTER
(— OF CUCKOLD) HORN
(— OF ENGLAND) ROSE
(— OF IMMORTALITY) AMARANTH
(— OF IRELAND) SHAMROCK
(— OF PIRACY) CROSSBONES
(— OF SCOTLAND) THISTLE
(— OF SOVEREIGNTY) GLOBE
(— OF VENGEANCE) SWORD
(— OF WALES) LEEK
(AUTOMOBILE —) MARQUE
(FLYER'S —) WINGS
(PRINTING —) COLOPHON
(SACRED —) HIEROGRAM
EMBLEMATIC TYPAL FIGURAL TYPICAL SYMBOLIC
EMBLIC AMLA AULA MYROBALAN
EMBODIMENT MAP SON SELF AVATAR GENIUS EPITOME IMAGERY BODIMENT
(— OF JUSTICE) ARISTIDES
(— OF PERFECTION) FLOWER
(VISIBLE —) PICTURE
EMBODY BODY UNITE INBODY CONTAIN EXPRESS COALESCE ORGANIZE
(— IN FLESH) INCARNATE
EMBOLDEN BOLD BIELD BRAVE ERECT NERVE ASSURE BOWDEN ENHARDY HEARTEN STOMACH
EMBOLUS CLOT STYLE
EMBOSOM BOSOM FOSTER CHERISH ENCLOSE IMBOSOM SHELTER SURROUND
EMBOSS BOSS HIDE KNOB KNOT ADORN BLOCK CHASE GOFFER INDENT POUNCE ANTIQUE CONCEAL ENCLOSE EXHAUST GAUFFER INFLATE ORNAMENT
EMBOSSED BOSSED RAISED ANTIQUE CHAMPED MATELASSE
EMBOSSING CELATURE
EMBOUCHURE LIP CHOPS LIPPING
EMBOWER BOWER
EMBOWERED ARBORED
EMBRACE ARM HUG CLIP COLL FOLD LOVE NECK PLAT SIDE ZONE ADOPT BOSOM BRACE CHAIN CLASP CLING CRUSH ENARM GRASP HALCH HALSE INARM OXTER PRESS TWINE ABRAZO ACCEPT ACCOLL AMPLEX BECLIP CARESS CLINCH COMPLY CUDDLE ENFOLD FATHOM HUDDLE INCLIP INFOLD PLIGHT SHRINE AMPLECT CHERISH CONTAIN ENCLOSE ESPOUSE INCLUDE INVOLVE ACCOLADE AMPLEXUS CANOODLE COMPLECT COMPRESS COMPRISE CONCLUDE ENCIRCLE
EMBRACING COLLING OSCULANT AMPLECTANT
EMBRASURE LOOP PORT VENT CRENEL CRENELLE PORTHOLE
EMBROCATION ARNICA EMBROCHE LINIMENT
EMBROIDER RUN TAT DARN FRET LACE BROUD COUCH FAGOT PANEL SMOCK BEWORK EMBOSS FAGGOT FRIEZE NEEDLE PURFLE STITCH SURFLE TISSUE BROIDER TAMBOUR ORNAMENT
EMBROIDERED BRODE BRODEE BROWDEN BROCADED
EMBROIDERER SPRIGGER
EMBROIDERY KANT LACE OPUS WORK BREDE ASSISI BONNAZ CREWEL EDGING HEDEBO APPAREL CHICKEN CUTWORK ORPHREY SETWORK TAMBOUR ARRASENE BRODERIE BROIDERY COUCHING FAGOTING LISTWORK PHULKARI SMOCKING TAPESTRY CREWELLERY NEEDLEPOINT
EMBROIL BROIL JUMBLE INVOLVE PERPLEX TROUBLE DISORDER DISTRACT ENTANGLE
EMBRYO GERM CADET FETUS OVULE FOETUS EMBRYON NEURULA PLANULA ACANTHOR BLASTULA GASTRULA PRINCIPE
(PREF.) BLAST(O)
EMBRYONIC GERMINAL
EMCEE HOST
EME AUNT YEME UNCLE FRIEND NEIGHBOR
EMEND (ALSO SEE AMEND) EDIT MEND ALTER AMEND BETTER REFORM REPEAL REVISE CORRECT IMPROVE RECTIFY REDRESS EMENDATE
EMERALD BERYL GREEN EMRAUD EMERANT PRASINE SMARAGD
EMERALD FISH ESMERALDA
EMERGE BOB DIP BOLT LOOM PEER RISE BREAK ERUPT EXUDE ISSUE START APPEAR BECOME PLUNGE SPRING DEBOUCH EXTRUDE
(— FROM EGGSHELL) HATCH ECLOSE
(— FROM SLEEP) AWAKE
(— SLOWLY) PEEK
EMERGENCE NEED BIRTH PINCH EGRESS GROWTH PRICKLE BECOMING DEBOUCHE ECLOSION EMERSION ERUPTION EXIGENCE TENTACLE
(— FROM DARKNESS) BREAK
(SUDDEN —) OUTCROP
EMERGENCY NEED PEND PUSH PINCH CRISIS STRAIT SUDDEN EMERGENT EXIGENCY JUNCTURE
EMERGENT RISING ONCOMING
EMERGING EMANANT EMERGENT
EMERITA HIPPA
EMERY EMERIL SMIRIS ABRASIVE CORUNDUM
EMETIC ALUM PICK PUKE PUKER VOMIT IPECAC EVACUANT VOMITIVE VOMITORY
EMIGRANT EMIGRE EXODIST PATARIN SETTLER COLONIST PATERINE STRANGER
(— FROM MECCA) COMPANION
EMIGRATE MOVE REMOVE MIGRATE
EMIGRATION EXODUS HEGIRA HEJIRA SWARMING
EMILIA (HUSBAND OF —) IAGO PALAMON
EMINENCE DUN NAB BALL BERG CRAG KNOT MONS MOTE NOTE POLE RANK RISE SCAR TOOT CHIEF HOYLE KNOLL PERCH STATE WHEAL WORTH ASCENT HEIGHT KRANTZ RENOWN RIDEAU STATURE ALTITUDE GRANDEUR TUBERCLE
(— OF HAND) SUBVOLA
EMINENT BIG ARCH HIGH CHIEF GRAND GREAT LOFTY NOBLE NOTED FAMOUS MARKED SIGNAL EXCELSE SUBLIME TOPPING GLORIOUS RENOWNED SINGULAR TOWERING PROMINENT CONSPICUOUS
EMIR AMIR AMEER NOBLE RULER LEADER PRINCE ADMIRAL GOVERNOR
EMISSARY SPY AGENT SCOUT LEGATE DELEGATE
EMISSION FUME GUST PUFF VENT ESCAPE
EMISSIVE EMITTENT EXHALANT
EMIT RUN BARK BEAM CAST DRIP GIVE GUSH HURL LASH MOVE OOZE PASS POUR REEK SEND SHED SPIT VENT VOID WARP AVOID BELCH EJECT ERUCT EXERT EXUDE FLASH FLING ISSUE UTTER YIELD DECANT DONATE EVOLVE EXHALE EXPIRE SPREAD BREATHE DISTILL EMANATE EXHAUST OUTSEND RADIATE REFLAIR ERUCTATE TRANSMIT
(— COHERENT LIGHT) LASE
(— FOAM) SPURGE
(— FORCEFULLY) FIRE
(— IN PUFFS) PLUFF
(— LIGHT) GLOW
(— ODOR) REEK STEAM
(— OUTCRIES) CHUNNER CHUNTER
(— PLAY OF COLORS) OPALESCE
(— RAYS) RADIATE IRRADIATE
(— SMOKE) SMEECH
(— SOUND) BUFF MOVE
(— SPARKS) SNAP
(— SPITTLE) SPAWL
EMITTING EMISSIVE SOUNDING
(SUFF.) **(— LIGHT)** ESCENT
EMMA (AUTHOR OF —) AUSTEN
(CHARACTER IN —) EMMA JANE BATES ELTON FRANK SMITH GEORGE MARTIN ROBERT WESTON FAIRFAX HARRIET CHURCHILL KNIGHTLEY WOODHOUSE
EMMENAGOGUE ALOE SAFFRON GROUNDSEL

EMMER SPELTZ AMELCORN
EMMET ANT ENEMY PISMIRE FORMICID
EMMOR (SON OF —) SHECHEM
EMOLLIATE SOFTEN
EMOLLIENT BALM LOTION LENIENT ICHTHYOL LENITIVE MALACTIC MOLLIENT SUPPLING
EMOLUMENT FEES WAGES INCOME PROFIT SALARY BENEFIT STIPEND
(PL.) PERK
EMOTE HAM OVERACT
EMOTION IRE LOVE ONDE PANG STIR AGONY ANGER CHORD GRIEF HEART SHAME AFFECT EFFECT MOTION RAPTUS SNIVEL SPLEEN ECSTASY FEELING PASSION VULTURE GRAMERCY MOVEMENT SURPRISE SENTIMENT
(CONTROLLING —) LEITMOTIF LEITMOTIV
(CONVULSIVE —) SPASM
(EVIL —) DEMON DAEMON
(PAINFUL —) PANG
(PERIOD OF —) CRISIS
(PREF.) THYM(O)
(SUFF.) THYMIA
EMOTIONAL MUSHY DRIPPY EMOTIVE AFFECTIVE
(OPENLY —) TOUCHYFEELY
(UNDULY —) SPOONY SPOONEY RHAPSODIC
EMOTIONLESS COLD
EMPATHY SYMPATHY
EMPEROR I IMP CZAR INCA KING TSAR AKBAR RULER TENNO CAESAR DESPOT KABAKA KAISER SULTAN BAGINDA MONARCH VIKRAMA AUGUSTUS IMPERIAL PADISHAH
(ROMAN —) GETA NERO OTHO OTTO CARUS GALBA NEPOS NERVA TITUS ADRIAN CAESAR JULIAN HADRIAN CALIGULA
EMPERY DOMAIN EMPIRE EMPIRY DOMINION
EMPHASIS ANGLE ACCENT STRESS WEIGHT EMPIRISM SALIENCE
EMPHASIZE HIT CLICK PINCH PRESS RUBIN ACCENT BETONE CHARGE HARPON PLAYUP STRESS FOREGROUND
EMPHATIC LOUD STRONG EARNEST MARCATO SERIOUS ENFATICO FORCIBLE MARCANDO POSITIVE RESOUNDING
EMPHATICALLY FLATLY STRONGLY POINTEDLY
EMPHYSEMA HEAVES
EMPIRE RULE SWAY POWER REALM REIGN STATE DIADEM DOMAIN EMPERY CONTROL KINGDOM IMPERIUM
(— STATE) NEWYORK
(— STATE OF SOUTH) GEORGIA
(SELJUK —) RUM ROUM
EMPIRIC QUACK IMPOSTOR
EMPIRICAL POSITIVE
EMPIRICIST VIRTUOSO
EMPLACEMENT BATTERY GALLERY PLATFORM
EMPLOY FEE PAY USE BUSK BUSY HIRE PLOY TAKE WAGE WISE ADOPT APPLY BESET IMPLY SPEND BESTOW ENGAGE ENLIST INFOLD INVOKE OCCUPY SUPPLY CONCERN CONDUCT ENCLOSE IMPROVE INVOLVE SERVICE UTILIZE PRACTICE
(— FLATTERY) COLLOGUE
(— ONESELF ABOUT) TOSS
(— SHIFTS) CHICANE
EMPLOYED APPLIED ENGAGED
EMPLOYEE HAND HELP BOOTS CLERK FACTOR LEADER BELLBOY BOOTBOY CALLBOY CARRIER SERVANT CHASSEUR CIVILIAN FLOORMAN IMPROVER
(— PROGRAM) ESOP
(— WHO RUNS ERRANDS) GOFER GOPHER
EMPLOYER BOSS JOSS BLOKE GAFFER ENGAGER MANAGER PADRONE GOVERNOR
(SMALL —) CORK
EMPLOYMENT FEE JOB USE CALL HIRE NOTE TASK TOIL USER WORK CRAFT TRADE TREAD USAGE MISTER THRIFT CALLING PURPOSE PURSUIT SERVICE USAUNCE BUSINESS EXERCISE POSITION RETAINER VOCATION
(CASUAL —) GRASS
EMPORIUM MART SHOP BAZAR STORE BAZAAR EMPORY MARKET STAPLE MONOPOLE
EMPOWER POWER ENABLE ENTITLE DELEGATE DEPUTIZE
EMPRESS IMPX EMPERESS IMPERIAL KAISERIN
EMPTIED DRAINED
EMPTILY TOOMLY
EMPTINESS VAIN VOID INANE ANEMIA VACUUM VANITY ANAEMIA INANITY VACANCY VACUITY LEERNESS
(— OF SPIRIT) ENNUI
EMPTY DRY FAT RID TIM AIRY BARE BOSS BUZZ CANT DEAF DUMP EMPT FALL FARM FREE GLIB HOWE IDLE LEER NEAR POUR ROOM TEEM TOOM VAIN VIDE VOID ADDLE AVOID BLANK BLEED CLEAN CLEAR DRAIN EQUAL EXPEL HUSKY INANE LEERY MOUTH SCOOP SHOOT SKAIL STARK START STRIP SWAMP TINNY WINDY BARREN BUBBLE CHAFFY DEVOID GOUSTY HOLLOW JEJUNE STRIKE SWASTY UNEMPT UNLOAD VACANT VACATE DELIVER DEPLETE EXHAUST EXPRESS UNTAKEN VACUATE VACUOUS VIDUOUS DISGORGE EVACUATE EVANESCE NEGATION UNFILLED
(— AN EGG) BLOW
(PREF.) CEN(O) JEJUN(O) KEN(O)
EMPTY-HEADED VAIN DOLLISH
EMPTYING EVACUANT
(ACT OF —) KENOSIS
EMPTY-SOUNDING TOOM
EMPUSA MONSTER SPECTER SPECTRE
EMPYREAN ETHER AETHER HEAVENS EMPYREUM
EMU EMEU RHEA RATITE
EMU APPLE COLANE
EMU BUSH BERRIGAN
EMULATE APE VIE COPY EMULE EQUAL EXCEL RIVAL COMPETE IMITATE
EMULATION STRIFE CONTEST PARAGON RIVALRY
EMULATOR RIVAL
EMULOUS EMULATE ENVIOUS CORRIVAL
EMULOUSLY AVIE
EMULSIFIABLE SOLUBLE
EMULSION PAP FLUID LATEX
(SENSITIVE —) PHOTOGENE
EMU WREN STIPITURE
EN NUT
ENABLE ABLE EMPOWER ENTITLE QUALIFY INHABILE
ENACT LIVE MAKE PASS ADOPT STAGE DECREE EFFECT ORDAIN ACTUATE APPOINT PERFORM PORTRAY
ENACTMENT LAW DOOM ENACT NOVEL ASSIZE DECREE MEASURE PASSAGE STATUTE ENACTION ENACTURE
ENAMEL AMEL FLUX SLIP EMAIL GLAZE GLOSS PAINT SLUSH AUMAIL SHIPPO SMALTO DENTINE LIMOGES SCHMELZ
(KIND OF —) CANTON
ENAMOR LOVE CHARM SMITE CAPTIVE
ENAMORED FOND EPRIS EPRISE MASHED AMOROUS CHARMED SMITTEN
(VAINLY —) FOOLISH
ENARCHUS (NEPHEW OF —) MUSIDORUS
(SON OF —) PYROCLES
ENCAMP TELD TENT LODGE PITCH INCAMP LAAGER BIVOUAC LEAGUER
ENCAMPMENT CAMP DOUAR ETAPE SIEGE LAAGER BIVOUAC CASTRUM HUTMENT TOLDERIA
ENCASE CASE WRAP HOUSE SHELL INCASE ENCHASE INCLOSE SURROUND ENCAPSULE
ENCELIA INCIENSO
ENCEPHALON CEREBRUM
ENCHAIN FETTER INCHAIN
ENCHANT CHARM DELUDE GLAMOR INCANT ATTRACT BECHARM BESPELL BEWITCH DELIGHT GLAMOUR BEDAZZLE ENSORCEL CAPTIVATE
ENCHANTED RAPT HAGGED CAPTIVE
ENCHANTER MAUGIS CHARMER MAGICIAN MALAGIGI ARCHIMAGE
ENCHANTING ORPHIC WIZARD HEAVENLY SPELLFUL
ENCHANTMENT HEX TAKE CHARM FAIRY MAGIC SPELL SPOKE CARACT CHANTRY DEVILRY GRAMARY SORCERY SORTIARY WITCHERY
ENCHANTRESS CIRCE FAIRY MEDEA ACRASIA URGANDA
ENCHARGE ENJOIN ENTRUST
ENCHASE INFIX ENRICH ENGRAVE
ENCHIRIDION MANUAL HANDBOOK TREATISE
ENCHORIAL NATIVE DEMOTIC DOMESTIC
ENCIPHER CODE CIPHER ENCRYPT
ENCIRCLE ORB BAND BELT BIND CLIP COIL GIRD GIRT HALO HOOP PALE RING RINK STEM WIRE ZONE BELAY BESET BRACE CLASP CROWN EMBAY EMBOW GIRTH HEDGE INORB ROUND TWINE TWIST BECLIP BEGIRD CIRCLE EMBALL ENGIRT ENLACE ENRING ENWIND FATHOM GIRDLE IMPALE SWATHE WRITHE BETREND COMPASS EMBRACE ENCLAVE ENCLOSE ENTWINE ENVIRON ENWHEEL SERPENT WREATHE CINCTURE CORSELET ENSPHERE IMMANTLE SURROUND
ENCIRCLED GIRT CINCT BELTED SUCCINCT
ENCIRCLEMENT EMBRACE
ENCIRCLING AROUND AMBIENT EMBRACE CORONARY ENCYCLIC
(PREF.) AMPLEXI
ENCLAVE INLIER
(— IN SOUTH AFRICA) BANTUSTAN
ENCLOAK MANTLE
ENCLOSE IN BAY BOX CAN HEM LAP MEW ORB PAR PEN PIN RIM BANK BUNG CAGE CASE COOP FORT GIRD HAIN HOOP PALE SPAR TINE WALL WARD WOMB YARD BOSOM BOUND BOWER BRICK CHEST CLOSE DITCH EMBAR EMBED EMBOX FENCE FRAME GARTH GRIPE HEDGE HOUSE IMBED INURN BOUGHT CARTON CASTLE CAVERN CIRCLE CORDON CORRAL EMBANK EMBOSS EMPALE EMPARK EMPLOY ENCASE ENCYST ENFOLD ENGULF ENLOCK FASTEN IMMURE IMPALE IMPARK INCASE INCLIP INHOOP INSACK INWALL JACKET PICKET POCKET SHUTIN TACKLE APPROVE CAPSULE COMPASS CONFIDE CONTAIN CURTAIN EMBOSOM EMBOWEL EMBOWER EMBRACE ENCHASE ENCLAVE ENGLOBE ENHEDGE ENVELOP HARNESS IMBOSOM IMMERSE IMPOUND INBOUND INCLUDE INFIELD PARROCK PINFOLD SHEATHE BULKHEAD COMPRISE COMPRIZE CONCLUDE CONVOLVE EMBORDER ENCIRCLE ENSHRINE ENSPHERE IMPRISON LANDLOCK PALISADE PARCLOSE SURROUND
(— IN ARMOR) EMPANOPLY
(— LOGS) CRIB
ENCLOSED BOUND CLOSED INDOOR OBTECT SHUTIN INGROWN INTERNAL
ENCLOSING LIMITARY
(PREF.) PERI
ENCLOSURE HAG HAW HOK MEW PAR PEN REE STY TYE BAWN BOMA BYTH CAGE CAVE CELL COOP DOCK FOLD HAIN HOCK HOPE KILN LIST PALE PEEL SEPT SKIT SLOT TIGH TOWN WALL WEIR

YARD ALTIS ATAJO BASIN BLIND BOOLY BOOTH BOSOM CAROL CLOSE COURT CRAWL CREEP CUBBY FENCE FRANK GARTH GOTRA HOARD KENCH KRAAL LOBBY MARAI PLECK POUND REEVE STALL STELL AVIARY BOOLEY BOXING CANCHA CARREL CORRAL COWPEN CRUIVE DRYLOT GARDEN HURDLE INTAKE KENNEL OUTSET PALING PRISON SERAIL TAMBOR TEOPAN TINING VIVARY WARREN BELLOWS BOROUGH BULLPEN CLOSURE COCKPIT EMBRACE GALLERY GONDOLA HAINING HENNERY HOUSING HUMIDOR LANTERN PADDOCK PIGHTLE PUDDOCK SEVERAL STUFFER TAMBOUR AEDICULA CASEMATE CHIPYARD CINCTURE CLAPNEST CLAUSURE CLOISTER COMPOUND DELUBRUM ENCEINTE ENCHASER PARADISE POUNDAGE PRECINCT PURPRISE SEPIMENT SERAGLIO SKIRTING STOCKADE VIVARIUM
(— ABOUT ALTAR) BEMA
(— FOR BOWLING) ALLEY
(— FOR COCKPIT) CANOPY
(— FOR FISH) CROY YAIR YARE KENCH SPILLER SPILLET
(— FOR JURY) BOX
(— FOR KNIGHTLY ENCOUNTERS) BARRACE
(— FOR LIGHT) LANTERN
(— FOR ROASTING ORE) STALL
(— OF HOUSE) BAWN
(— ON AIRPLANE) NACELLE
(— SURROUNDED BY DITCH) COP
(ELEPHANT —) KEDDAH
(OBLONG —) CIRCUS
(PORTABLE —) PLAYPEN
(POULTRY —) HENNERY
(PRIVATE SEAT —) SKYBOX
(ROOFED —) SKYBOX
(SACRED —) SECOS SEKOS
(PREF.) CLAUSTRO SEPTATO
(SUFF.) SEPTATE

ENCOLPION PANAGIA
ENCOLURE MANE
ENCOMIAST EULOGIST
ENCOMIUM ELOGE ENCOMY EULOGY PRAISE PLAUDIT TRIBUTE PANEGYRIC
ENCOMPASS BEGO BELT CLIP GIRD PALE RING SPAN WALL WRAP BELIE BERUN BESET BIGAN BRACE CLOSE CROWN ROUND BEGIRD BEGIRT CIRCLE ENGIRD BESEIGE COMPASS EMBOWEL EMBRACE ENCLOSE ENVIRON INCLUDE SUBSUME UMBESET CINCTURE ENCIRCLE ENGIRDLE PURPRISE SURROUND
(— WITH ARMS) FATHOM
ENCOMPASSED AMID BAYED AMIDST BEGIRT
ENCOMPASSING ROUND AMBIENT CINCTURE PROFOUND INCLUSIVE
ENCORE BIS AGAIN RERUN ANCORA RECALL REPEAT
ENCOUNTER BIDE BUMP COIL COPE FACE FIND KEEP MEET MOOT RINK BRUSH CLOSE FIGHT FORCE GREET INCUR OCCUR ONSET SHOCK STOUR VENUE ACCOST AFFRAY ANSWER ASSAIL ATTACK BATTLE BREAST CAREER COMBAT JOSTLE JUSTLE OPPOSE RUFFLE ADDRESS AFFRONT CONTEST COUNTER DISPUTE HOSTING JOINING PASSAGE CONFLICT CONFRONT CONGRESS REANSWER RECONTER SKIRMISH COLLISION
(— HOSTILELY) CROSS
(HOSTILE —) CLOSE
(MILITARY —) ACTION
(PUGILISTIC —) MILL

ENCOURAGE DAW EGG ABET BACK FIRM URGE BOOST CHEER ERECT FAVOR FLUSH HEART IMPEL NERVE SERVE STEEL ADVISE ASSURE EXHORT FOMENT FOSTER HALLOO HARDEN INCITE INDUCE INVITE NUZZLE REHETE SECOND SPIRIT UPHOLD ADVANCE ANIMATE CHERISH COMFORT CONFIRM CONSOLE ENFORCE ENLIVEN FLATTER FORTIFY FORWARD HEARTEN INSPIRE PROMOTE STOMACH UPCHEER UPRAISE EMBOLDEN INSPIRIT REASSURE
ENCOURAGED BUCKED CONFIRMED
ENCOURAGEMENT BOOST FLUSH HURRAH COMFORT FOMENTO IMPETUS BLESSING SANCTION
ENCOURAGING HELPFUL FAVORING
ENCRATITE TATIAN AQUARIAN
ENCROACH JET PINCH POACH IMPOSE INVADE TRENCH IMPINGE INTRUDE SHINGLE ENTRENCH INFRINGE INTRENCH TRESPASS
ENCROACHING INVASIVE
ENCROACHMENT BREACH INROAD ENCROACH INVASION
ENCRUST CAKE CANDY BARKEN BARKLE INCRUST
ENCRUSTATION SCALE
ENCRUSTED CAKED SCABROUS
ENCUMBER CLOG LOAD PACK BESET CHECK CRAMP CROWD TRASH ACCLOY BEMOIL BURDEN FELTER HAMPER HINDER IMPEDE LUMBER MITHER MOIDER RETARD SADDLE WEIGHT BEPAPER INVOLVE OPPRESS ACCUMBER ENTANGLE HANDICAP OBSTRUCT OVERCOME OVERLOAD
ENCUMBERED HEAVY CONGESTED
ENCUMBRANCE CLOG LIEN LOAD CLAIM BURDEN CHARGE CUMBER TROUBLE MORTGAGE ALBATROSS
ENCYCLICAL PASCENDI
ENCYCLOPEDIA TOME
(GAME —) HOYLE
ENCYSTED CYSTIC SACCATE SACCATED
END EN AIM DAG EAR FAG TIP BUTT CUSP DATE DOUP FACE FATE FINE FOOT GOAL HALT HEEL LAST MAIN MARK SAKE STOP TAIL TERM VIEW AMEND ANNUL ARTHA BLOCK BREAK CAUSE CEASE CLOSE DEATH ENSUE EVENT FINIS ISSUE LIMIT LOOSE NAPOO OMEGA POINT PRICK RAISE SCOPE SCRAP SHANK START STASH THULE DECIDE DEFINE DESIGN DOMINO EFFECT EFFLUX ENDING EXITUS EXPIRE EXPIRY FINALE FINISH INTENT NAPOOH OBJECT PERIOD RESULT THIRTY UPSHOT UTMOST WINDUP ABOLISH ACHIEVE CLOSURE CURTAIN DESTROY FANTAIL FINANCE LINEMAN MEANING OUTGIVE PURPOSE REMNANT BOUNDARY COMPLETE CONCLUDE DESITION DISSOLVE FINALITY SURCEASE TERMINAL TERMINUS ULTIMATE
(— DEBATE) CLOTURE
(— OF ANTENNA) CLAVA
(— OF ANVIL) BICKIRON
(— OF ARCHERY PILE) STOPPING
(— OF ARROW) NOCK
(— OF BEEF LOIN) BUTT
(— OF BLANKET) DAGON
(— OF BONE) EPIPHYSIS
(— OF BOOM) JAW
(— OF BOW) EAR
(— OF BRICK) HEADING
(— OF BRISTLE) FLAG
(— OF BUILDING) GABLE
(— OF CAN) BREAST
(— OF CANE) FRAZE
(— OF CART) TIB
(— OF CRESCENT) HORN
(— OF EAR CANAL) AMPULLA
(— OF EGG) DOUP
(— OF EXISTENCE) DEMISE
(— OF FABRIC) FENT
(— OF FISHHOOK) SPEAR
(— OF FLAG) FLY
(— OF FROG) TOE
(— OF HALTER) CAPITULUM
(— OF HAMMER) CLAW POLL
(— OF HAMMERHEAD) PEEN
(— OF HORSE-COLLAR) GULLET
(— OF INGOT) CROP
(— OF KEEL) GRIPE
(— OF LEVER) FORK
(— OF LOAF) HEEL
(— OF MINERAL LODE) SLOVAN
(— OF MINE TUNNEL) FACE
(— OF MINING LEVEL) DEAN
(— OF MUZZLE) MUFFLE
(— OF NAIL) CLENCH
(— OF ONE'S LIFE) DOOM
(— OF PIER) CUTWATER
(— OF PIPE) TAFT SPIGOT
(— OF POCKETKNIFE HANDLE) BOLSTER
(— OF RAILROAD CAR) BEND
(— OF ROAD) ROADHEAD
(— OF ROD) FORKHEAD
(— OF SHEEP SHEARING) CUTOUT
(— OF SHIP) STERN
(— OF SPINE) ACRUMION
(— OF TENON) HAUNCH
(— OF TOOL) BUTT
(— OF UTERUS) FUNDUS
(— OF WEAVER'S THREAD) THRUM
(— OF WORLD) PRALAYA
(— OF YARD) ARM YARDARM
(— ON) ABUT
(— ON POND) FOREBAY
(—S OF RIBBONS) FATTRELS
(—S OF SATURN'S RINGS) ANSA
(— UP WITH) NET
(CANDLE —) DOUP SNUFF
(DOMINO —) ACE
(FAG —) RUMP
(HANGING —) DAG DAGGE
(JAGGED —) SHRAG
(KIND OF —) TIGHT
(LOOSE —) TAG
(NARROWED —) NEB
(NORTH — OF COMPASS NEEDLE) LILY
(POINTED —) APEX
(POSTERIOR —) BOTTOM
(REEF —S) DEADMAN
(ROPE'S —) COLT FEAZE PIGTAIL FEAZINGS
(SPECIAL —) SAKE
(TAPERING —) POINT
(TATTERED —) FRAZZLE
(ULTIMATE —) SUM TELOS
(UNPLEASANT —) GRIEF
(UPPER —) HEAD
(WARP —S) ACCIDENTAL
(PREF.) ACR(O) FINI TEL(IO)

ENDANGER DANGER HAZARD IMPERIL SCUPPER
ENDANGERED BESTED BESTEAD FRAUGHT
ENDANGERER MARPLOT
ENDEARMENT LOVE CARESS
ENDEAVOR DO AIM PUT TRY WIN BEST MINT SEEK WORK ASSAY ESSAY ETTLE EXERT OFFER STUDY TEMPT TRIAL AFFAIR ASSAIL DEVOIR EFFORT INTEND STRIFE STRIVE AFFORCE ATTEMPT CONATUS CONTEND CULTURE EMPRISE EMULATE IMITATE MOLIMEN NITENCY WORKING EXERTION PURCHASE STRUGGLE
(— TO CONCLUSION) STUDY
(BEST —) DEVOIR
(EARNESTLY —) FEND
ENDED DONE OVER PAST FINISHED
(— BY CONSONANT) CHECKED
ENDEMIC LOCAL ENDEMIAL
ENDING END CLOSE DEATH GRAVE FINALE BREAKUP FINANCE DESITION
(KIND OF —) NERVE
(MUSICAL —) CODA
(NERVE —) SPINDLE
(ROMAN —) CODA
ENDIVE CHICORY WITLOOF ESCAROLE SCARIOLE
ENDLESS ANANTA ETERNE ETERNAL FOREVER UNDYING UNENDED UNENDLY DATELESS FINELESS IMMORTAL INFINITE UNENDING
ENDMOST TIPMOST FARTHEST REMOTEST
ENDOCARP STONE PYRENA PUTAMEN
ENDOGENOUS INNATE AUTOGENIC
ENDOMORPHIC PYCNIC PYKNIC
ENDOPITE PETASMA
ENDOPLEURA TEGMEN
ENDORSE BACK SIGN ADOPT BOOST DOCKET ENDOSS SECOND APPROVE CERTIFY INDORSE

SPONSOR SUPPORT ADVOCATE SANCTION RECOMMEND
ENDORSEE HOLDER
ENDORSEMENT FIAT FORM VISA RIDER BACKING APPROVAL HECHSHER SANCTION
ENDOSPERM FARINA ALBUMEN
ENDOSPORIUM INTINE
ENDOW DOW DUE DOTE GIFT RENT VEST BLESS CROWN DOWER ENDUE EQUIP FOUND INDUE SEIZE STATE STUFF ASSIGN CLOTHE DOTATE ENABLE ENRICH ENSOUL ESTATE IMPART INVEST CHARTER ENLARGE FURNISH INSTATE APPANAGE BENEFICE BEQUEATH ENTALENT
(— WITH FORCE) DYNAMIZE
ENDOWED ABLE GIFTED FAVORED
ENDOWMENT CLAY FINE GIFT WAKF WAQF DOWER DOWRY GRACE GRANT CORPSE GENIUS TALENT APANAGE CHANTRY CHARISM FACULTY APPANAGE DOTATION PATRIMONY BENEFACTION
(NATURAL —S) BUMP DOTES TALENT
(PL.) ALTARAGE
ENDPAPER FLYLEAF
ENDPIECE BRACE CHUMP
(— OF STETHOSCOPE) BELL
ENDUE DUE ENDOW INDUE TEACH CLOTHE INVEST INSTRUCT
ENDURABLE LIVABLE BEARABLE LIVEABLE PORTABLE
ENDURANCE GAME LAST TACK PLUCK BOTTOM BEARING COMFORT DURANCE GRANITE LASTING STAMINA BEARANCE DURATION GAMENESS HARDSHIP PATIENCE STRENGTH
ENDURE GO ABY SIT VIE ABYE BEAR BIDE DREE DURE HOLD KEEP LAST TAKE TIDE WEAR ABEAR ABIDE ALLOW BROOK CARRY DRIVE POUCH SPARE STAND STICK STOUT THOLE TOUGH WIELD ABROOK ACCEPT DRUDGE HARDEN REMAIN SUFFER ABROOKE COMFORT FORBEAR PERSIST STOMACH SUPPORT SUSTAIN SWALLOW TOUGHEN UNDERGO WEARING CONTINUE FOREBEAR TOLERATE
(— LONGER) OUTLAST
ENDURING FAST SURE STOUT BIDING DURING STABLE STURDY ABIDING DURABLE ETERNAL LASTING PATIENT IMMORTAL REMANENT STUBBORN PERENNIAL
ENDWAYS ANEND ENDWISE
ENDYMION (DAUGHTER OF —) EURYDICE
(FATHER OF —) ZEUS JUPITER AETHELIUS
(MOTHER OF —) CALYCE
(SON OF —) EPEUS PAEON AETOLUS
(WIFE OF —) CROMIA ASTERODIA HYPARIPPE
ENEMA CLYSMA CLYSTER COLONIC LAVEMENT
ENEMY FOE AXIS BOYG FEID DEVIL FIEND SATAN FOEMAN HOSTILE CONTRARY OPPONENT
(— OF MANKIND) DEVIL FIEND SATAN
(PERSONAL —) HATER
ENEMY OF THE PEOPLE (AUTHOR OF —) IBSEN
(CHARACTER IN —) KIIL PETER MORTEN HORSTER HOVSTAD ASLAKSEN STOCKMANN
ENERGETIC BUSY FAST FELL HARD LIVE RASH SPRY BRISK DASHY LUSTY PITHY STOUT TIGHT VITAL YAULD ZIPPY ACTIVE HEARTY HUSTLE LIVELY SPROIL ACTIOUS ANIMOSO ARDUOUS DASHING DRIVING DYNAMIC ENERGIC FURIOUS NERVOUS PUSHFUL PUSHING VIBRANT EMPHATIC ENERGICO FORCEFUL FORCIBLE HUSTLING VIGOROUS
(— PERSON) TOWSER
ENERGETICALLY MANLY FURIOUSLY
ENERGID PROTOPLAST
ENERGIZE LIVEN EXCITE ANIMATE
ENERGIZING KINETIC VIRTUAL
ENERGY U W GO GAS PEP VIM ZIP BANG BENT BIRR DASH EDGE JASM LIFE SAKT SNAP TUCK ZING ARDOR ECLAT FORCE INPUT MOXIE NERVE OOMPH POWER STEAM VIGOR EFFORT FOISON INTAKE ORGONE OUTPUT SPIRIT SPRAWL SPRING SPROIL STARCH VIRTUE POTENCY SPIRITS ACTIVITY AMBITION DYNAMISM ENERGEIA MOTIVITY PRAKRITI STRENGTH VIVACITY
(— PEAK) NUCLEUS
(EMOTIONAL —) LIBIDO
(LIBINAL —) CATHEXIS
(LIFE —) JIVA SAKTI SHAKTI
(LIGHT —) RAD
(LOW IN —) COLD
(MENTAL —) DOCITY PSYCHURGY
(POINT OF PHYSICAL —) CHAKRA
(POTENTIAL —) ERGAL
(QUANTUM OF —) PLASMON
(RADIANT —) SOUND ACTINISM EINSTEIN
(VITAL —) HORME PANZOISM
(PREF.) **(RADIANT —)** PENETRO
(SOLAR —) HELI(O)
ENERVATE SAP COOK FLAG MELT SOFTEN WEAKEN MOLLIFY UNNERVE UNSINEW ENFEEBLE
ENERVATED LIMP BEDRID EFFETE LANGUID LIFELESS BEDRIDDEN
ENERVATING MUGGY DREARY
ENERVATION COLLAPSE
ENFEEBLE SAP NUMB FAINT SHAKE APPALL DEADEN FEEBLE IMPAIR SOFTEN WEAKEN DEPRESS UNSINEW AFFEEBLE ENERVATE IMBECILE UNSTRONG
ENFEEBLED FEY NUMB
ENFILADE RAKE
ENFOLD (ALSO SEE INFOLD) LAP FURL ROLL WRAP CLASP COVER DRAPE ENROL IMPLY COMPLY ENLACE ENROLL ENWIND ENWRAP INCLIP INFOLD INWIND SHADOW SWATHE WATTLE EMBRACE ENCLOSE ENVELOP ENVIRON INCLUDE INVOLVE UMBELAP CONVOLVE
ENFORCE BULL LEVY EXACT FORCE PRESS COERCE COMPEL EFFECT FOLLOW INVOKE EXECUTE IMPLANT
ENFORCED COMPULSORY
ENFORCER EXECUTOR MUSCLEMAN
ENFRAMEMENT CARTOUCH
ENG AGMA
ENGAGE DIP WED BOOK BUSY GAGE HAVE HIRE JOIN LIST MESH RENT SIGN TAKE WAGE AGREE AMUSE CATCH ENTER LEASE PITCH TRADE TRYST ABSORB ARREST EMBARK EMPLOY ENLIST INDUCE OBLIGE OCCUPY PLEDGE PLIGHT TAKEON BESPEAK BETROTH CONCERN CONDUCE CONSUME ENGROSS IMMERSE INVOLVE PROMISE THROWIN AFFIANCE CONTRACT COVENANT ENTANGLE INTEREST INTRIGUE PERSUADE PREOCCUPY
(— ATTENTION) INTEREST
(— DEEPLY) DROWN
(— IN) GO CUT SUE HAVE JOIN LEAD PROSECUTE
(— IN ARGUMENT) BALK BAULK
(— IN COMBAT) DEBATE STRIKE
(— IN DEBATE) STONEWALL
(— IN DISCUSSION) CONTEND
(— IN PRANKS) LARK
(— IN TILT) JUST JOUST
(— OVERMUCH) TROUBLE
(— WHOLLY) ABSORB CONSUME IMMERSE
(SUFF.) **(— IN)** IZE
ENGAGED BENT BUSY FAST GONE HIRED ACTIVE BONDED BOOKED MESHED ASSURED BESPOKE EARNEST ENTERED PLEDGED TOKENED VERSANT ABSORBED ATTACHED EMBEDDED EMPLOYED INSERTED INTEREST INVOLVED OCCUPIED PROMISED
(— IN) ABOUT
(— IN CONTROVERSY) DISPUTANT
(MENTALLY —) VERSANT
(WARMLY —) ZEALOUS
ENGAGEMENT AVAL DATE COWLE SPURN ACTION AFFAIR BATTLE COMBAT ESCROW PLIGHT STANZA SURETY BARGAIN BOOKING DUSTING SERVICE CONFLICT RETAINER SKIRMISH WARRANTY
(— OF GEARS) MESH
(— TO MARRY) TRYST
(MILITARY —) DO SHOW
(SHORT —) RUN SNAP
(SINGLE —) GIG
(THEATRICAL —) SHOP
(WRITTEN —) COWLE
ENGAGING SOFT SAPID SWEET TAKING
ENGENDER BEGET BREED CAUSE EXCITE GENDER DEVELOP PRODUCE GENERATE INGENDER OCCASION
ENGIDU EABANI
ENGINE GAS JET SIX FOUR GOAT TANK EIGHT JINNY MOTOR OILER STEAM BANKER DIESEL DOCTOR DUDLER DUDLEY INGENE JORDAN KICKER PUFFER RADIAL RAMJET ROADER YARDER MACHINE POACHER POTCHER SKIDDER STEAMER TRACTOR TURBINE BULLGINE COMPOUND DOLLBEER EXPANDER GASOLINE IMPULSOR SCRAMJET
(— FOR HAULING LOGS) DUDLER DUDLEY
(— FOR THROWING MISSILES) GIN PETRARY SPRINGAL
(— OF TORTURE) GIN RACK
(— OF WAR) RAM SWEEP HELEPOLE
(— PART) STATOR
(AIRPLANE —) SCRAMJET
(DONKEY —) DOCTOR
(FIRE —) TUB
(JET —) ATHODYD
(KIND OF —) PLASMA WANKEL
(MILITARY —) BOAR TOWER BRICOL FABRIC TREPAN BRICOLE DONDINE PERRIER PETRARY TORMENT WARWOLF BALLISTA DONDAINE MANGONEL MARTINET SCORPION
(RAILROAD —) HOG GOAT YARDER SWITCHER
(REACTION —) THRUSTER THRUSTOR
(ROCKET —) ARCJET VERNIER
(SMOOTH RUNNING —) HUMDINGER
(TYPE OF ROTARY —) WANKEL
ENGINEER PLAN GUIDE DRIVER FANNER HOGGER MANAGE SAPPER HOGHEAD PLANNER PLOTTER CONTRIVE DESIGNER INGENIER INVENTOR MANEUVER
AMERICAN AMY BURR BUSH DORR DUNN EADS HERR HILL KRUG LAKE LEAR PECK RICE ROUS WANG ALLEN CARTY ELLET GANTT HAUPT HENCH LAMME MILLS MOORE OWENS PRATT STOUT TESLA AMDAHL ARNOLD BEATTY BOGART COFFIN CONRAD COOPER COWLES CRAVEN FERRIS GARAND GREENE HAMMER HOLLEY HOLLIS HOUDRY HUTTON JACOBY JENNEY LAMONT LITTLE MORGAN NEWELL PARKER PENDER PINCUS PORTER RUMSEY STUMPF WILSON WRIGHT BALDWIN BARRELL BEHREND CLEMSON CROCKER DEJONGH DRINKER EHRICKE FANNING FREEMAN GODFREY GRAYDON HASWELL KINEALY KINTNER KNOWLES LATROBE LEONARD PACKARD PARSONS PATRICK SERRELL STRAUSS WHIPPLE AMSTRUTZ DINKELOO EDGERTON ELLSBERG ERICSSON GOETHALS HARRISON HARTNESS HUNSAKER KENNELLY MCALPINE MODJESKI OVINGTON REYNOLDS RICHARDS ROEBLING ZWORYKIN ARMSTRONG CARPENTER GILLESPIE KETTERING STEINMETZ TRAUTWINE ZACHARIAS FARNSWORTH LETOURNEAU

LINDENTHAL RIESENBERG STRICKLAND WORTHINGTON ALEXANDERSON BRECKENRIDGE
AUSTRALIAN CLAPP
AUSTRIAN BIRAGO ENGERTH MANNLICHER
CANADIAN DUMAS KLOTZ MARKLE
CHINESE KWOH
CUBAN MENOCAL
CZECH SKODA
DANISH POULSEN
DUTCH NORDEN STEVIN MUSSERT
ENGLISH FOX AIRD PAUL BAKER BOYLE CLARK COOKE GABOR GOOCH GROVE KEMPE MANCE ROYCE AYRTON BRAMAH BRUNEL CAYLEY CLARKE CUBITT DONKIN FLOREY FOWLER HARRIS HEDGES HINTON MCADAM WALLIS BERKLEY BOULTON CAUTLEY CRAPPER DUDDELL FLEMING HARTLEY MURDOCK SIEMENS SMEATON ANDERSON BRINDLEY BUCHANAN CRAMPTON FERRANTI HAWKSHAW REDMAYNE SYDENHAM GREATHEAD GRIFFITHS HOPKINSON ISSIGONIS WILLCOCKS WIMSHURST HORNBLOWER TREVITHICK BRAITHWAITE FITZMAURICE
FRENCH LAME ARCON MALUS PRONY BERTIN CHAPPE COANDA CUGNOT DEPREZ EIFFEL LEPLAY MARTIN RATEAU RIQUET ALPHAND BELIDOR BERLIER BERNARD BIERIOT BLERIOT CLERGET GIFFARD LEBLANC LENFANT LESSEPS TELLIER BELGRAND PONCELET FOURNEYRON HENNEBIQUE
GERMAN BACH BENZ KOCH OTTO BOSCH KNORR AMMANN CRELLE DIESEL GERBER LANGEN WANKEL CARNALL CULMANN DAIMLER SIEMENS FLETTNER EYTELWEIN BAUERSFELD LILIENTHAL BAUERNFEIND GOLDSCHMIDT HASELWANDER
ITALIAN NERVI VINCI BUGATTI CODAZZI FABRONI MARCONI
LATVIAN MOISSEIFF
POLISH NARUTOWICZ
RUSSIAN THEREMIN FEOKTISOV
SCOTTISH BARR BELL WATT BAIRD CLERK ELDER EWING MCADAM MURRAY NAPIER RANKINE TELFORD BRUNLEES FAIRBAIRN STEVENSON SYMINGTON
SPANISH CIERVA CANDELA
SWEDISH DALEN LAVAL POLHEM BRINELL DAHLBERG
SWISS ILG FAVRE

ENGINEMAN HOISTER HOISTMAN
ENGINERY TIRE
ENGIRDLED CINCT
ENGLAND HOME ALBION LOGRIA BLIGHTY BRITAIN LOEGRIA HOMELAND

ENGLAND

AIRFORCE: RAF
BAY: TOR LYME WASH START MOUNTS BIGBURY BIDEFORD CARDIGAN FALMOUTH TREMADOC WEYMOUTH
CAPITAL: LONDON
CHANNEL: SOLENT BRISTOL ENGLISH SPITHEAD
CHANNEL ISLAND: HERM SARK JERSEY ALDERNEY GUERNSEY
COIN: ORA RIAL RYAL ACKEY ANGEL CROWN GROAT NOBLE PENCE PENNY POUND SPRAT UNITE BAWBEE FLORIN GUINEA SESKIN TESTON ANGELET CAROLUS HAPENNY TUPPENY FARTHING SHILLING SIXPENCE TUPPENCE
CONSERVATIVE: TORY
COUNTY: KENT DEVON ESSEX HANTS NOTTS SALOP WIGHT DORSET DURHAM LONDON SURREY SUSSEX NORFOLK RUTLAND SUFFOLK CHESHIRE CORNWALL SOMERSET
DANCE: MORRIS
FIRTH: SOLWAY
FOREST: ARDEN EPPING EXMOOR DARTMOOR SHERWOOD
HEAD: SPURN BEACHY FORMBY LIZARD CEMMAES TREVOSE
HILLS: MENDIP BRENDON CHEVIOT MALVERN CHILTERN COTSWOLD
INVADER: DANE PICT ROMAN SAXON NORMAN
ISLAND: HOLY LUNDY WIGHT COQUET MERSEA THANET TRESCO WALNEY BARDSEY HAYLING IRELAND SHEPPEY ANGLESEA ANGLESEY FOULNESS HOLYHEAD
ISLANDS: FARNE SCILLY CHANNEL
KING: HAL LUD BRAN BRUT CNUT COLE KNUT LEAR HENRY JAMES SWEYN ALFRED BLADUD BRUTUS CANUTE EDWARD EGBERT GEORGE ARTEGAL ELIDURE RICHARD WILLIAM GORBODUC
LAKE: CONISTON
LIBERAL: WHIG
MEASURE: CUT ELL LEA MIL PIN ROD RUN TON TUN VAT ACRE BIND BOLL BUTT CADE COMB COOM CRAN FOOT GILL GOAD HAND HANK HEER HIDE INCH LAST LINE MILE NAIL PACE PALM PECK PINT PIPE POLE POOL ROOD ROPE SACK SEAM SPAN TRUG TYPP WIST YARD YOKE BODGE CABOT CHAIN COOMB CUBIT DIGIT FLOAT FLOOR FLUID HUTCH JUGUM MINIM OUNCE PERCH POINT PRIME QUART SKEIN STACK TRUSS BARREL BOVATE BUSHEL CRANNE FATHOM FIRKIN GALLON HOBBET HOBBIT LEAGUE MANENT OXGANG POTTLE RUNLET SECOND SQUARE STRIKE SULUNG THREAD TIERCE AUCHLET FURLONG KENNING QUARTER RUNDLET SEAMILE SPINDLE TERTIAN VIRGATE CARUCATE CHALDRON HOGSHEAD LANDYARD PUNCHEON QUADRANT QUARTERN STANDARD
MOUNTAIN: PEAK SCAFELL SKIDDAW SNOWDON
MOUNTAINS: BLACK PENNINE SNOWDON CAMBRIAN CUMBRIAN
NAME: ALBION BRITAIN BRITANNIA
PENINSULA: PORTLAND
POINT: NAZE LYNAS MORTE SALES DODMAN LIZARD PRAWLE HARTLAND LANDSEND GIBRALTAR
POLICEMAN: BOBBY COPPER PEELER
RACE TRACK: ASCOT
RESORT: BATH BRIGHTON BLACKPOOL
RIVER: CAM DEE DON ESK EXE LEA NEN URE WYE AIRE AVON EDEN LUNE NENE NIDD OUSE PENK TAME TEES TILL TYNE WEAR YARE ANKER COLNE DEBEN STOUR SWALE TAMAR TAWAR TRENT TWEED HUMBER KENNET MERSEY RIBBLE ROTHER SEVERN THAMES WENSUM WHARFE WITHAM DERWENT PARRETT WAVENEY WELLAND TORRIDGE
ROCKS: MANACLES
ROYAL HOUSE: YORK TUDOR STUART HANOVER WINDSOR LANCASTER PLANTAGENET
SCHOOL: ETON RUGBY HARROW
SEA: IRISH NORTH
SEAPORT: POOLE
SETTLER: JUTE PICT ANGLE SAXON NORMAN
SOLDIER: TOMMY REDCOAT FUSILEER
STRAIT: DOVER
TOWN: ELY BATH DEAL ETON HULL RYDE WARE YORK BLYTH BRENT DERBY DOVER ERITH FLINT LEEDS RIPON TRURO WIGAN BARNET BOLTON BOOTLE CAMDEN DURHAM EALING EXETER HANLEY JARROW LEYTON LONDON OLDHAM OXFORD YEOVIL BRISTOL BROMLEY BURNLEY CHELSEA CROYDON ENFIELD GRIMSBY HALIFAX HORNSEY IPSWICH LAMBETH NEWPORT NORWICH PRESTON SALFORD SEAFORD WESTHAM BRADFORD BRIGHTON CORNWALL COVENTRY DEWSBURY HASTINGS PLYMOUTH ROCHDALE WALLASEY WALLSALL GREENWICH LIVERPOOL SHEFFIELD BIRMINGHAM MANCHESTER
TRIBE: ICENI
UNIVERSITY: LONDON OXFORD CAMBRIDGE
VALLEY: COOM EDEN TEES TYNE COMBE COOMB COQUET
WEIGHT: BAG KIP TOD TON KEEL LAST MAST MAUN BARGE FAGOT GRAIN MAUND POUND SCORE STAND STONE TRUSS BUSHEL CENTAL FANGOT FIRKIN FOTHER FOTMAL POCKET QUARTER QUINTAL SARPLER

ENGLISH SPIN SAXON AUSTRAL BRITISH ENGLAND SAXONISH SOUTHRON STANDARD
(— DIALECT IN LIVERPOOL) SCOUSE
(— MIXED WITH SPANISH) SPANGLISH
(IN —) ANGLICE
(TEACHING —) TEFL TESL TESOL
(PREF.) ANGLO
ENGLISHMAN PONGO SAXON BRITON BRONCO GODDAM GRINGO JOHNNY ROOINEK MACARONI SOUTHRON ENGLISHER
(— IN INDIA) QUIHIQUIHYE
(— IN SOUTH AFRICA) ROOTNEK
(RICH —) MILOR MILORD
ENGLISHWOMAN INGLESA
ENGORGE GLUT GORGE DEVOUR SWALLOW
ENGRAFT INSET
ENGRAM TRACE
(— PATTERN) MEANING
ENGRAVE CUT ETCH RIST CARVE CHASE GRAVE HATCH PRINT SCULP CHISEL INCISE SCULPT CRIBBLE ENCHASE EXARATE IMPRESS IMPRINT INSCULP STIPPLE INSCRIBE ORNAMENT
ENGRAVED GRAVEN GRAPHIC INCISED
(PREF.) GRAPTO
ENGRAVER POINT CHASER ETCHER GRAVER ARTISAN INSCULP BURINIST MEDALIST SCULLION WRIGGLER
(— OF STONES) LAPIDARY
ENGRAVING CUT PRINT SCULP STAMP GRAVERY GRAVING GRAVURE WOODCUT AQUATINT DRYPOINT HATCHING INTAGLIO LINEWORK MEZZOTINT
(PREF.) GLYPHO GLYPT(O)
ENGROSS BURY SINK SOAK AMASS GROSS ABSORB ENGAGE ENROLL ENWRAP OCCUPY SCROLL COLLECT CONSUME IMMERSE INVOLVE PREOCCUPY
ENGROSSED DEEP FULL RAPT INTENT BEMUSED WRAPPED ABSORBED IMMERSED PREOCCUPIED
ENGULF GULF ABYSM ABYSS SOUSE SWAMP WHELM ABSORB DEVOUR INVADE QUELME SLOUGH ENGORGE SWALLOW SUBMERGE
ENHANCE FOIL LIFT BUILD ENARM ENDOW EXALT RAISE DEEPEN AUGMENT ELEVATE ENLARGE EXHANCE GREATEN IMPROVE SHARPEN HEIGHTEN INCREASE
ENHANCEMENT SAKE
ENHYDRA LATAX
ENID (HUSBAND OF —) GERAINT
ENIGMA WHY EGMA GRIPH REBUS PUZZLE RIDDLE SPHINX GRIPHUS MYSTERY PROBLEM PROVERB
ENIGMATIC HUMAN MYSTIC CRYPTIC OBSCURE ELLIPTIC MYSTICAL ORACULAR PUZZLING RIDDLING MYSTIFYING PERPLEXING
ENISLE MAROON
ENJAMBMENT OVERFLOW
ENJOIN BID JOIN WILL ENIUN ORDER CHARGE DECREE DIRECT

FORBID COMMAND DICTATE REQUIRE ADMONISH PROHIBIT
ENJOY GO JOY FAIN HAVE LIKE BROOK FANCY PROVE SAVOR TASTE WIELD ADMIRE DEVOUR GROOVE RELISH DELIGHT
(— AT LEISURE) SIP
(— ONESELF) FEAST LAUGH
ENJOYABLE GOOD FRUITY AMIABLE BLESSED CAPITAL GLORIOUS SAVOROUS SPLENDID
ENJOYING FRUITIVE
ENJOYMENT FUN JOY USE BANG BASK BOOT EASE GUST KAMA PLAY ZEST FEAST GUSTO LIKING RELISH COMFORT DELIGHT JOLLITY JOYANCE JOYANCY FELICITY FRUITION PLEASURE SKITTLES
(— FROM OTHERS' TROUBLES) SCHADENFREUDE
ENKINDLE WARM STIRUP INCENSE INFLAME
ENLARGE ADD EKE BORE GROW HONE HUFF OPEN REAM ROOM BUILD FARCE LARGE SWELL WIDEN BIGGEN BRANCH BROACH DIDUCE DILATE EXPAND EXTEND FRAISE GATHER LARGEN OMNIFY SPREAD AMPLIFY AUGMENT DISTEND ENHANCE GREATEN IMPROVE INGREAT MAGNIFY STRETCH AMPLIATE CUMULATE FLOURISH INCREASE
(— COAL MINE) SNUB
ENLARGED TUMID BLOATED CLUBBED SWELLED SWOLLEN AMPLIATE CAPITATE EXPANDED EXTENDED VARICOSE ACCRESCENT
ENLARGEMENT BULB DISC DISK KNOP NODE CLAVA SWELL BLOWUP BUNION GIBBER GROWTH SCYPHA ENLARGE FOOTING SCYPHUS STATION ANEURYSM INCREASE SWELLING PROPAGATION
(— IN MINE SHAFT) STATION
(— IN MUSCLE) KNOT
(— OF BONE) EXOSTOSIS
(— OF GLAND) GOITER GOITRE
(— OF GULLET) CROP
(— OF MOLD) RAPPAGE
(— OF NERVE FIBER) BOUTON
(— OF ORGAN) STRUMA
(— ON HORSE'S LEG) SPLINT
(ABNORMAL —) ANEURYSM
(BONY —) SPAVIN SPAVINE
(MORBID —) TUMOR
(PREF.) MACR(O) MEG(A) MEGAL(O) PLETHYSMO
(SUFF.) AUXE MEGALY
ENLARGING EVASE SWELLING
(PREF.) MICR(O)
ENLIGHTEN OPEN CLEAR EDIFY TEACH ILLUME INFORM UNSEEL EDUCATE LIGHTEN CIVILIZE ENKINDLE INSTRUCT
ENLIGHTENED WISE LUMINOUS
ENLIGHTENMENT BODHI LIGHT SATORI WISDOM CULTURE INSIGHT SAMADHI AUFKLARUNG
ENLIST DRUM JOIN LEVY SOUD ENROL ENTER HITCH PREST ENGAGE ENROLL INDUCT JOINUP SIGNUP IMPRESS RECRUIT REGISTER
(— AGAIN) REUP
ENLISTMENT LEVY HITCH PREST LISTING
ENLIVEN DASH JAZZ WARM BRACE BRISK CHEER PEPUP QUICK RAISE ROUSE KITTLE REVIVE ANIMATE COMFORT INSPIRE REFRESH SMARTEN BRIGHTEN INSPIRIT RECREATE
ENLIVENED MERRY
ENLIVENING GENIAL LIVELY VIVIFIC CHIRPING
ENMESH TRAP CATCH SNARL IMMESH ENSNARE ENTANGLE
ENMITY WAR FEUD SPITE WRAKE ANIMUS HATRED MALICE RANCOR STRIFE FOEHOOD AVERSION
ENNEAGON NONAGON
ENNOBLE LORD EXALT HONOR NOBLE RAISE GENTLE UPLIFT DIGNIFY ELEVATE GLORIFY GREATEN NOBLIFY SUBLIME
ENNUI BORE TEDIUM ACCIDIE BOREDOM DOLDRUM
ENOCH (FATHER OF —) CAIN JARED
(SON OF —) METHUSALEH
ENOCH ARDEN (AUTHOR OF —) TENNYSON
(CHARACTER IN —) LEE RAY LANE ANNIE ARDEN ENOCH MIRIAM PHILIP
ENORMITY GRAVITY
ENORMOUS BIG GOB HUGE REAM VAST ENORM GREAT HEROIC MIGHTY UNRIDE IMMENSE ABNORMAL COLOSSAL FLAGRANT GIGANTIC WHAPPING WHOPPING
ENOS (FATHER OF —) SETH
(GRANDFATHER OF —) ADAM
(SON OF —) CAINAN
ENOUGH BAS ENOW WELL WHEN AMPLE ASSAI BASTA BELAY ANEUCH PLENTY APLENTY SUFFICE ADEQUATE
(— SAID) VERBUMSAP
(HARDLY —) SKIMP
(MORE THAN —) PLENTY APLENTY
ENOUNCE STATE UTTER AFFIRM DECLARE PROCLAIM
ENRAGE RAGE ANGER GRIEVE MADDEN INCENSE INFLAME STOMACH
ENRAGED MAD ASHY WODE WOOD ANGRY IRATE LIVID SAVAGE AGRAMED BERSERK CHOLERIC INCENSED MADDENED
ENRAPTURE RAVISH TRANCE ECSTASY ENCHANT ENRAVISH ENTRANCE
ENRAPTURED RAPT ENRAPT TRANCED ECSTATIC
ENRICH FAT BOOT FEED FRET LARD RICH ADORN CROWN ENDOW GUANO BATTEN FATTEN INVEST FEATHER FORTIFY FURNISH GUANIZE INCREASE ORNAMENT TREASURE
(— A GAS) CARBURET
(— A MINE) SALT
(— FUEL MIXTURE) CHOKE
ENRICHED FLORID
ENRICHMENT DITATION
ENROLL BEAR JOIN LIST POLL ENROL ENTER WRITE ATTEST BILLET ENFOLD ENLIST INDUCT MUSTER RECORD ASCRIBE IMPANEL INITIATE INSCRIBE REGISTER
ENROLLMENT LISTING REGISTRY
ENROOT ENRACE IMPLANT
ENSCONCE HIDE COVER SETTLE CONCEAL SHELTER
ENSEMBLE CORPS DECOR WHOLE COSTUME PANTSUIT
(— OF ARMS) ARMORY
(WOMAN'S —) PANTSUIT
ENSHEATHE EMBOSS
ENSHRINE SAINT SHRINE ENCHASE ENTEMPLE
ENSHROUD WRAP
ENSIFORM ENSATE XIPHOID GLADIATE
ENSIGN FLAG IAGO SIGN BADGE COLOR SENYE AQUILA BANNER BEACON PENNON PISTOL SIGNAL SYMBOL ALFEREZ ANCIENT INSIGNE DANEBROG GONFALON ORIFLAMB PAVILION STANDARD
(—S ARMORIAL) ARMS
(IMPERIAL —) TUT
(JAPANESE —) SUNBURST
(PL.) ENSIGNRY HERALDRY
ENSILE SILO SILAGE
ENSLAVE THEW CHAIN SLAVE THIRL ENTHRAL NESLAVE SLAVISH ENTHRALL
ENSLAVED SLAVE THRALL
ENSLAVEMENT DULOSIS SLAVERY
ENSNARE NET WEB GIRN LACE LIME MESH TOIL TRAP WRAP BENET CATCH NOOSE SNARE SNARL ALLURE ATTRAP ENGINE ENMESH ENTOIL ENTRAP TANGLE TREPAN BEGUILE DECEIVE ENGLEIM SNIGGLE SPRINGE BIRDLIME INVEIGLE OVERTAKE SURPRISE
ENSNARL ENTANGLE
ENSPHERE INORB SPHERE
ENSTATITE BRONZITE
ENSUE FOLLOW RESULT SUCCEED
(— UPON) SUE
ENSUING NEXT SUING SEQUENT
ENSURE ASSURE INSURE SECURE BETROTH ESPOUSE WARRANT AFFIANCE
ENTABLATURE (PART OF —) CORONA FRIEZE TAENIA CORNICE CYMATIUM ARCHITRAVE
ENTADA LENS
ENTAIL TAIL INCUR IMPOSE CONTAIN INVOLVE REQUIRE TAILZIE
ENTAILED AYNE TAIL EIGNE
ENTAMOEBA LOSCHIA
ENTANGLE ELF LAP MAT TAT WEB BALL CAST COLL FOUL HARL KNIT KNOT LIME MESH MIRE TOIL WRAP BROIL CATCH HALCH RAVEL SNAFU SNARE SNARL TWIST BEFOUL COMMIT COTTER ENGAGE ENLACE ENMESH ENTRAP ENWRAP FANKLE FELTER HAMPER HANKLE HATTER INMAZE INMESH PESTER PUZZLE RAFFLE RANGLE TACKLE TAIGLE TANGLE WRAPLE CONFUSE EMBRAKE EMBROIL ENSNARL ENTRIKE IMBRIER INVOLVE PERPLEX TRAMMEL BEWILDER ENCUMBER IMPESTER INTRIGUE STRAPPLE
ENTANGLED DEEP FOUL COTTY TANGLY COMPLEX KNOTTED IMPLICIT
ENTANGLEMENT WEB FOUL KNOT TWIT HITCH BUNKER COBWEB ENTRAIL HEDGEHOG OBSTACLE PERPLEXITY
ENTASIS SWELL
ENTELLUS HANUMAN
ENTENTE TREATY ALLIANCE
ENTER BOX DIP SET BEAR BOOK JOIN POST ADMIT BEGIN BOARD BREVE ENROL GETIN INCUR PROBE SHARE START ACCEDE APPEAR BILLET ENGAGE ENLIST ENROLL ENTRER INCEPT INVADE PIERCE RECORD SPREAD INGRESS INTRUDE COMMENCE ENCROACH INITIATE INSCRIBE NOMINATE REGISTER PENETRATE
(— A COMPUTER PROGRAM) LOAD
(— BY FORCE) BREAK IRRUPT INTRUDE
(— COMPUTER PROGRAM) BOOT
(— DATA) INPUT
(— HASTILY) BULGE
(— IN ATTACK) FORCE
(— IN BOOK) ACCESS
(— IN BOOKS) ACCRUE
(— INFORMATION INTO COMPUTER) WRITE
(— INTO) JOIN INTERN
(— NOISILY) STOMPIN TROMPIN
(— PROGRAM INTO COMPUTER) LOAD
(— SLOWLY) SEEP
(— UNNOTICED) CREEP
(— UPON CAREER) INCEPT
(— UPON DUTIES) ASSUME
(— WITHOUT RIGHT) ABATE
ENTERING ENTRY INGOING INGRESS INTRANT INCOMING
ENTEROTOXEMIA STRUCK
ENTERPRISE FIRM IRON PUSH TOGT DRIVE ESSAY ACTION EMPIRE SPIRIT VOYAGE ATTEMPT EMPRISE HOLDING PROJECT VENTURE BUSINESS CARNIVAL GUMPTION VIRITOOT
(CRIMINAL —) JOB
(HARD —) DIFFICULTY
(REMEDIAL —) CRUSADE
(SPECULATIVE —) ADVENTURE
(UNPROFITABLE —) SINKHOLE
ENTERPRISING BOLD FORTHY PUSHFUL PUSHING
ENTERTAIN INN BEAR BUSK EASE FETE HAVE HOLD HOST AMUSE ENJOY FEAST GUEST SPORT TREAT DIVERT FROLIC GESTEN HARBOR JUNKET RECULE REGALE RETAIN

SOLACE TICKLE ACCOURT BEGUILE CHERISH DISPORT KITCHEN CONSIDER INTEREST RECREATE
(— IN THE MIND) HAVE
(— WITHOUT CHARGE) DEFRAY
ENTERTAINED OUGHT
ENTERTAINER BHAT HOST ACTOR AMUSER ARTIST BUSKER DANCER FIDDLE HARLOT SINGER ACTRESS ARTISTE DISEUSE GLEEMAN HETAERA HOSTESS REGALER SPEAKER BEACHBOY COMEDIAN HOSTELER MAGICIAN MINSTREL
(WEST AFRICA —) GRIOT
ENTERTAINING GOOD RICH TREAT PRETTY AMUSING BEDSIDE GUESTING SPORTFUL
ENTERTAINMENT BASH BILL FARE FETE GALA GLEE PLAY SHOW BOARD CHEER FEAST GAUDY OPERA REVUE SPORT CIRCUS DIVERT DOMENT GAIETY GAYETY HOSTEL INFARE KERMIS NAUTCH SETOUT SHIVOO WATTLE BANQUET BENEFIT BUMMACK BUMMOCK BURLESK CEILIDH CONCERT COSHERY FESTINE FESTINO JOLLITY KERMESS PASTIME RIDOTTO TAMASHA CAKEWALK CARNIVAL COMMORTH DROLLERY EASEMENT ENTREATY ENTREMES FUNCTION GESTNING GESTONIE GUESTING HOGMANAY JONGLERY MUSICALE WAYZGOOSE
(BLUE —) NUDIE
(FAREWELL —) FOY
(OF INDIA —) TAMASHA
(TRIVIAL —) PAP
(VARIETY —) VODVIL VAUDEVILLE
ENTERTAINMNET (CHEAP —) HONKYTONK
ENTHALPY H
ENTHRALL SEND CHARM THIRL THRALL ENSLAVE ENTHRAL CAPTIVATE
ENTHRALLED AGOG RAPT HOOKED
ENTHRONE CROWN EXALT STALL ENSEAT THRONE THRONIZE
ENTHUSIASM BUG ELAN FIRE FURY ZEAL ZEST ZING ARDOR ESTRO FEVER FLAME FUROR HEART MANIA OOMPH VERVE FERVOR HURRAH SPIRIT WARMTH ABANDON ARDENCY AVIDITY MADNESS MUSTARD DEVOTION LYRICISM
(— IN BATTLE) EARNEST
(CONTAGIOUS —) FUROR FURORE
(EXCESSIVE —) MANIA
(LOSE —) COOL SOUR
(WILD —) DELIRIUM
ENTHUSIAST BUG FAN NUT BUFF BIGOT DEMON FREAK ROOTER VOTARY ZEALOT BOOSTER DEVOTEE EUCHITE FANATIC FANCIER GROUPIE FOLLOWER VOTARESS VOTARIST
(PHOTOGRAPHY —) SHUTTERBUG
(PL.) ARDITI
ENTHUSIASTIC GAGA KEEN NUTS WARM HAPPY NUTTY RABID ARDENT GUNGHO HEARTY STOKED CRACKED FERVENT GLOWING CRACKERS PASSIONATE
(BECOME —) FLIP
(EXCESSIVELY —) FANATIC
(VAINLY —) FOOLISH
ENTICE COG COY PUT WIN BAIT COAX DRAW DRIB LEAD LOCK LURE TICE TOLE TOLL WILE CHARM DECOY DRILL LATHE SIREN SLOCK STEAL TEMPT TRAIN TROLL TULLE ALLECT ALLURE ATTICE CAJOLE ENLURE INCITE INDUCE INVITE SEDUCE ATTRACT BEWITCH SOLICIT SUGGEST INVEIGLE PERSUADE
ENTICEMENT BAIT CORD LURE TICE
ENTICING SIREN ALLURING
ENTIRE ALL DEAD EVEN FULL HALE MEAR MERE SOLE CLEAN EVERY GROSS PLAIN QUITE ROUND SOUND STARK TOTAL TUTTO UTTER WHOLE VERSAL PERFECT PLENARY ABSOLUTE COMPLETE ENDURING GLOBULAR INTEGRAL LIVELONG OUTRIGHT TEETOTAL UNBROKEN
(NOT —) PARTIAL
(PREF.) HOL(O) INTEGRI
ENTIRELY DEAD DEIN FAIR FULL PURE CLEAN CLEAR FULLY PLAIN QUITE STARK WHOLE BODILY WHOLLY EXACTLY QUITELY THROUGH CLEVERLY ABSOLUTELY
ENTIRETY WHOLE ENTIRE TOTALITY
(PREF.) PAM PAN
ENTITLE DUB CALL NAME TERM AFFIX STYLE ENABLE CAPTION EMPOWER QUALIFY INTITULE NOMINATE
ENTITLED APPARENT ELIGIBLE
ENTITY ENS BODY FORM UNIT BEING HABIT OUSIA SPACE THING ENERGY ESSENCE INTEGER TOTALITY
ENTOMB BURY TOMB INTER INURN ENCAVE HEARSE IMMURE INHUME SHRINE
ENTOMBMENT BURIAL
ENTOMOLOGIST BUGHUNTER
AMERICAN SAY DYAR HORN BANKS BRUES RILEY FORBES HARRIS HOWARD MORGAN BURGESS PACKARD POLLARD SCHWARZ COMSTOCK COQUILLETT
DANISH FABRICIUS
DUTCH LYONNET
ENGLISH SCOTT LEFROY HAWORTH ORMEROD WESTWOOD
FRENCH FABRE AUDOUIN LATREILLE LACORDAIRE
GERMAN BRAUER
SWISS FOREL SAUSSURE
ENTOMOLOGY BUGOLOGY
ENTOMOPHTHORA EMPUSA
ENTOTROPHI DIPLURA
ENTOURAGE TRAIN COMITES RETINUE
ENTRACTE INTERACT INTERVAL INTERMEZZO
ENTRAIL BOWEL TRAIL INTRAIL
(PREF.) SPLANCHN(O)
ENTRAILS GUT GUTS DRAFT TRIPE FIBERS GIBLET HALLOW HASLET INWARD JAUDIE MUGGET PAUNCH QUARRY QUERRE UMBLES INSIDES NUMBLES CHAWDRON GRALLOCH PUDDINGS PURTENANCE
(DEER'S —) QUARRY
ENTRANCE ADIT BOCA CUSP DOOR GATE HALL PEND BOCCA CHARM DEBUT ENTER ENTRY FOYER GORGE INLET MOUTH PORCH STULM THIRL TORAN ACCESS ATRIUM ENTREE INFAIR INGANG INGATE INROAD PORTAL RAVISH TORANA TRANCE ZAGUAN DELIGHT GATEWAY HALLWAY INGOING INGRESS INITIAL INTRADO INTROIT PASSAGE POSTERN ENTRESSE FOREGATE VOMITORY PROPYLAEUM
(— TO SEWER) JAWHOLE
(— TO VALLEY) CHOPS
(ASTROLOGICAL —) CUSP
(CELLAR —) ROLLWAY
(FORCIBLE —) INROAD
(FORMAL —) DEBUT
(HARBOR —) BOCA
(HOSTILE —) INVASION
(HURRIED —) BOUT
(MINE —) EYE ADIT
(PRIVATE —) POSTERN
ENTRANCED RAPT CHARMED TRANCED ECSTATIC
ENTRANCEMENT SPELL
ENTRANCING ORPHIC
ENTRANT INTRANT STARTER BEGINNER
ENTRAP BAG EBB NET HOOK SNIB TOIL TRAP CATCH CRIMP DECOY NOOSE SNARE ALLURE AMBUSH ATTRAP CAJOLE ENGAGE ENTOIL TAIGLE TANGLE TREPAN BEGUILE ENSNARE PITFALL ENTANGLE INVEIGLE
ENTRAPMENT SETUP
ENTRAPPED (— IN SEDIMENT) CONNATE
ENTREAT ASK BEG BID SUE WOO PRAY PRIG SEEK URGE CRAVE HALSE PLEAD PRESS TREAT ADJURE APPEAL DESIRE INVOKE BESEECH CONJURE EXORATE IMPLORE PREVAIL PROCURE REQUEST SOLICIT PERSUADE PETITION
ENTREATING TREAT CRAVING
ENTREATY DO CRY PLEA SUIT APPEAL DEESIS PRAYER TREATY BESEECH BIDDING ENTREAT PURSUIT REQUEST URGENCY PETITION PLEADING
ENTRECHAT (PERFORM —S) LEAP
ENTREE ENTRY ACCESS BOUDIN OSTIUM ENTRADA INTRADA SOUFFLE ENTRANCE FRICANDO MAZARINE
ENTREMES SAINETE SAYNETE
ENTRENCH DIGIN INVADE SCONCE TRENCH ENCROACH TRESPASS
ENTRENCHED (BECOME —) DIGIN
ENTRENCHMENT CLOSURE COUPURE LODGMENT
ENTROPY S
ENTRUST ARET FIDE GIVE STOW BEKEN TRUST CHARGE COMMIT CREDIT LIPPEN ADDRESS BEHIGHT COMMEND CONFIDE CONSIGN DEPOSIT INTRUST BEQUEATH DELEGATE ENCHARGE RECOMMEND
(— TO DEPUTY) DEVIL
ENTRY ADIT HALL ITEM STET BREAK CLOSE DEBIT AUTHOR CREDIT DOCKET ENTREE PORTAL POSTEA RECORD RINGER TRANCE ENTRADA INGRESS INTRADO PASSAGE ENTRANCE ENTRESSE ENTRYWAY NOTANDUM REGISTER VOCATION
(— IN CHRONICLE) ANNAL
(— WORD) HEADWORD
(LEDGER —) POSTING
ENTWINE FOLD LACE WIND BRAID CLASP IMPLY PLASH TWINE TWIST WEAVE ENLACE INWIND ENTWIST INVOLVE SERPENT WREATHE
ENTWINED ACCOLLE BRAIDED INWOVEN ACCOLLEE
ENUMERATE POLL TELL COUNT SCORE DETAIL NUMBER RECITE RECKON RELATE COMPILE COMPUTE ITEMIZE RECOUNT ESTIMATE REHEARSE
ENUMERATION LIST TALE COUNT SCORE CENSUS ACCOUNT CATALOG RECITAL CITATION
ENUNCIATE SAY UTTER DECLARE DELIVER ENOUNCE ANNOUNCE PROCLAIM
ENUNCIATION DICTION DELIVERY
(IMPERFECT —) LALLATION
ENVELOP BUR FOG LAP LOT POD WEB BURR CASE COMA FOLD HUSK MAIL ROLL BRACE CLOUD COVER KNIFE ROUND BEGIRD BEGIRT BEMIST BINDLE CLOTHE COCOON CORONA CUPULE ENFOLD ENGIRT ENTIRE ENWRAP FARDEL FOLDER INFOLD INVEST JACKET MANTLE MUFFLE POCKET SHEATH SHROUD STIFLE SWATHE WRIXLE CALYMMA CAPSULE CHORION ENCLOSE ENVIRON INVOLVE SWADDLE SWALLOW VESTURE WRAPPER ENSPHERE ENVELOPE MANTLING PERIANTH PERIDIUM POCHETTE SURROUND WRAPPAGE
(— CLOSELY) SMOTHER
(— IN SMOKE) ENFUME
(GLASS —) BULB
(LUMINOUS —) CORONA
(NEBULOUS —) CHEVELURE
(OPEN —) JACKET
(PAY —) PACKET
(STAMPED —) ENTIRE
(VEGETABLE —) COD
ENVELOPE (— ENCLOSURE) SASE
(FRUIT —) CUPULE
(SUN'S —) CORONA
(PREF.) **(OUTER —)** PERIDI
(SUFF.) LEMMA
ENVELOPED WOMPLIT
ENVELOPING AMBIENT
ENVENOM VENOM CORRUPT VITIATE EMBITTER EMPOISON
ENVIOUS YELLOW EMULOUS JEALOUS ENVIABLE

ENVIRON HEM BEGO GIRD BIGAN LIMIT VIRON ENVIRE GIRDLE SUBURB COMPASS ENVELOP INCLOSE INVOLVE PURLIEU DISTRICT ENCIRCLE SURROUND
(PL.) SKIRT UMLAND BANLIEU SUBURBS PRECINCT
ENVIRONMENT HOTBED MEDIUM MILIEU AMBIENT CONTEXT ELEMENT HABITAT SETTING TERRAIN AMBIANCE CINCTURE PRECINCT
(— OF NURTURE) LAP
(ACADEMIC —) ACADEME
(DOMESTIC —) INTERIEUR
(NORMAL —) HOME
(PREF.) EC(O) OEC(O) OIK(O)
ENVISAGE FACE CONFRONT ENVISION
ENVISION PICTURE
ENVOY AGENT ELCHI ENVOI DEPUTY ELCHEE LEGATE LENVOY NUNCIO EMBASSY TORNADA ABLEGATE LEGATION METATRON
ENVY CHAW ONDE COVET GRUDGE EMULATE BEGRUDGE GRUDGERY JEALOUSY
ENWRAP FOLD ROLL CLASP IMPLY ENFOLD INFOLD KIRTLE ENGROSS ENVELOP OBVOLVE CONVOLVE ENVELOPE INSWATHE
ENZOOTIC RABIES
ENZU SIN
ENZYME ASE ZYM ZYMO LYASE RENIN CYTASE KINASE LIGASE LIPASE LOTASE MUTASE OLEASE PAPAIN PEPSIN RENNIN UREASE ZYMASE ACYLASE ADENASE AMIDASE AMINASE AMYLASE APYRASE CASEASE CYCLASE EMULSIN ENOLASE EREPSIN FERMENT GUANASE HYDRASE INULASE LACCASE LACTASE MALTASE MYROSIN OXIDASE PECTASE PEPSINE PHYTASE PLASMIN PRUNASE TANNASE TRYPSIN ALDOLASE ARGINASE BROMELIN CATALASE CATALYST CYTOLIST DIASTASE ELASTASE EREPTASE ESTERASE FUMARASE INVERTIN LYSOZYME NUCLEASE PERMEASE PROTEASE RACEMASE SEMINASE SYNTHASE THROMBIN TRYPTASE UROKINASE
(PREF.) ZYM(O)
(SUFF.) ASE EIN EINE IN INE
EOANTHROPUS DAWNMAN
EOS MORNING
(SISTER OF —) SELENE
EPAPHUS (DAUGHTER OF —) LIBYA
(FATHER OF —) ZEUS JUPITER
(MOTHER OF —) IO
(WIFE OF —) MEMPHIS
EPAULET KNOT SWAB SWOB WING SCALE SHELL
EPENDYTES HAPLOMA
EPENTHESIS ANAPTYXIS
EPEUS (BROTHER OF —) AETOLUS
(DAUGHTER OF —) HYRMINA
(FATHER OF —) ENDYMION PANOPEUS
(WIFE OF —) ANAXIROE
EPHAH BATH
(FATHER OF —) JAHDAI MIDIAN
EPHELIS FRECKLE
EPHEMERAL BRIEF VAGUE HORARY DIURNAL FUNGOUS PASSANT PASSING EPISODAL EPISODIC FUGITIVE MUSHROOM STAYLESS MOMENTARY
EPHEMERIS DIARY TABLE RECORD ALMANAC JOURNAL CALENDAR
EPHER (FATHER OF —) EZRA MIDIAN
EPHIPPIUM SADDLE
EPHOD VAKASS
(SON OF —) HANNIEL
EPHRAIM (FATHER OF —) JOSEPH
(MOTHER OF —) ASENATH
EPHRATAH (HUSBAND OF —) CALEB
(SON OF —) HUR
EPHRON (FATHER OF —) ZOAR
EPHTHALITE HAITHAL
EPI PEAK SPIRE FINIAL PINNACLE
EPIBLAST ECTODERM
EPIC EDDA EPOS SAGA GRAND ILIAD NOBLE BYLINA EPOPEE HEROIC LUSIAD BEOWULF EPYLLION KALEVALA RAMAYANA MAHABHARATA
(SUFF.) AD
EPICALYX CALYCLE
EPICARP HUSK RIND EXOCARP
EPICENE SEXLESS
EPICURE FRIAND FEASTER GLUTTON GOURMET GOURMAND PALATIST GASTRONOME GASTRONOMER
EPICUREAN APICIAN SENSUOUS
EPIDEMIC FLU PLAGUE POPULAR PANDEMIA PANDEMIC
EPIDERMIS SKIN CUTICLE ECDERON VELAMEN
EPIDOTE SCORZA
EPIGLOTTIS FLAP WEEZLE
EPIGRAM POEM ENGLYN EPITAPH
EPIGRAMMATIC LACONIC POINTED
EPIGRAPH EPIGRAM IMPRINT
EPILEPTIC FITIFIED
EPILOGUE CLOSE FINALE APPENDIX
EPIMANIKION CUFF
EPIMETHEUS (WIFE OF —) PANDORA
EPINAOS POSTICUM
EPINEPHRINE ADRENINE
EPINICION ODE
EPIPACTIS SERAPIAS
EPIPHANY TWELFTH
EPIPHARYNX PALATE EPIGLOTTIS
EPIPHRAGM TYMPANUM
EPIPHYTE KARO EPIPHYLL
EPIPHYTOTIC EPIDEMIC
EPIRUS (KING OF —) PYRRHUS
EPISCOPACY BISHOPRIC PRELATISM
EPISCOPAL PRELATIC
EPISODE GAG EPOCH EVENT SCENE STORY AFFAIR INCIDENT SEQUENCE OCCURRENCE
(COMIC —) BURLA SIGHTGAG
(MUSICAL —) COUPLET
EPISPASTIC VESICANT
EPISPERM TESTA
EPISTAXIS NOSEBLEED
EPISTERNUM MANUBRIUM
EPISTLE CANON JAMES LETTER PISTLE MISSIVE WRITING DECRETAL
EPISTLER SUBDEACON
EPISTOLOGRAPHIC DEMOTIC
EPISTROPHE EPODE ABGESANG
EPISTYLE PLATBAND
EPITHELIUM ENDODERM
EPITHET AKAL GOOD NAME TERM LABEL SMEAR TITLE BYWORD MONETA PHRASE AGNOMEN JAPHETIC MULCIBER
(PL.) LANGUAGE
EPITOME MAP SUM FLETA DIGEST PRECIS SCHEME COMPEND PITOMIE SUMMARY SUMMULA ABSTRACT BREVIARY LANDSKIP SYLLABUS SYNOPSIS ABRIDGMENT CONSPECTUS
EPITOMIZE RESUME ABRIDGE CURTAIL ABSTRACT COMPRESS CONDENSE CONTRACT DIMINISH
EPITONIUM SCALA
EPIZOA PARASITA
EPOCH AGE ERA DATE ECCA TIME DWYKA EVENT EOCENE PERIOD CLINTON OLIGOCENE
EPONYM LIMMU ANCIENT
EPOPEUS (BROTHERS OF —) ALOIDAE
(FATHER OF —) ALOEUS POSEIDON
(MOTHER OF —) CANACE IPHIMEDIA
(WIFE OF —) ANTIOPE
EQUABLE EVEN JUST EQUAL SUANT SMOOTH STEADY UNIFORM TRANQUIL
EQUAL AEQ PAR TIE COPE EGAL EVEN FERE JUST LIKE MAKE MATE MEET PEEL PEER SAME ALIKE LEVEL MATCH PARTY RIVAL TOUCH DOUBLE EQUATE EVENLY FELLOW MARROW PAREIL ABREAST BALANCE COMPEER EMULATE EQUABLE IDENTIC PARAGON PAREGAL UNIFORM ADEQUATE EQUALIZE EVENHAND PATCHING TRANQUIL
(— A BET) SEE
(— IN MEANING) BE
(— QUANTITY) ANA
(— TO) ANOTHER
(NOT —) UNMEET UNMETE
(PREF.) AEQUI EQUI IS(O) PARI
EQUALING TO
EQUALITY PAR TIE EQUITY OWELTY PARAGE PAREIL PARITY BALANCE EGALITE EGALITY ISOTELY EQUATION EVENHAND EVENNESS FAIRNESS
(— BEFORE THE LAW) ISONOMY
(— OF ELEVATION) ISOMETRY
(—OF MEASURE) ISOMETRY
(— OF POWER) ISOCRACY
(— OF RATIOS) ANALOGY
(— STATE) WYOMING
EQUALIZATION EQUATION DISCHARGE
EQUALIZE EVEN KNOT EQUAL LEVEL EQUATE SQUARE BALANCE ADEQUATE
EQUALIZER EVENER
EQUALLY AS BOTH LIKE ONCE SAME ALIKE EGALLY EVENLY JUSTLY EMFORTH
EQUANIMITY POISE PHLEGM TEMPER BALANCE EGALITY CALMNESS EVENNESS SERENITY SANGFROID
EQUATE EQUAL BALANCE EQUALIZE
EQUATING COMPARISON
EQUATION CUBIC IDENTITY
EQUATOR LINE GIRDLE EQUINOX
(— CROSSER) POLLIWOG
EQUATORIAL GUINEA (CAPITAL OF —) MALABO
(COIN OF —) EKUELE EKPWELE
(MONEY OF —) EKUELE EKPWELE
(MONEY 0F —) CENTIME
(RIVER 0F —) MUNI CAMPO BENITO
(TOWN OF —) BATA NSOK SANTAISABEL
EQUES KNIGHT
EQUIDISTANT CENTRAL HALFWAY
EQUILIBRIUM POISE APLOMB BALANCE STATION EQUATION EVENHAND ISOSTASY
(— OF FLUID) LEVEL
(PREF.) STATO
EQUINE COLT FOAL MARE FILLY HORSE ZEBRA EQUOID EQUINAL HORSELY
EQUINIA MALLEUS
EQUIP ARM FIT IMP KIT RAY RIG ABLE BEAM DECK FEAT FIND GEAR GIRD GIRT HEEL REEK TRIM ARRAY DIGHT DRESS ENARM ENDOW POINT SPEED STUFF AGUISE ATTIRE BUCKLE ORDAIN OUTFIT SUBORN APPAREL APPOINT BEDIGHT FORTIFY FRAUGHT FURNISH GARNISH HARNESS PLENISH PREPARE QUALIFY ACCOUTER ACCOUTRE ACCOMPLISH
(— FOR ACTION) ARM
EQUIPAGE RIG CREW SAMAN SUITE TRAIN SUPPLY RETINUE TURNOUT UNICORN CARRIAGE
EQUIPMENT KIT FARE GEAR TIRE STOCK STUFF ATTIRE CONREY DUFFEL DUFFLE FITOUT GRAITH OUTFIT SETOUT TACKLE APPAREL BAGGAGE FITMENT HARNESS PANOPLY ARMAMENT EQUIPAGE MATERIAL MATERIEL MOUNTING SUPELLEX
(— FOR CATCHING FISH) CRAFT
(— FOR JOURNEY) FARE
(CLASSROOM —) REGALIA
EQUIPOISE POISE BALANCE
EQUIPOTENTIAL LEVEL
EQUIPPED SEEN ARMED BODEN THERE EQUIPT ARMORED INSTRUCT WEAPONED
(FULLY —) SUMMED
(INADEQUATELY —) HAYWIRE
(LIGHTLY —) EXPEDITE
EQUISETUM CANDOCK
EQUITABLE EVEN FAIR JUST EQUAL RIGHT EVENLY HONEST EQUABLE UPRIGHT BONITARY RATIONAL RIGHTFUL
EQUITY LAW EPIKY MARGIN EPIKEIA HONESTY JUSTICE EQUALITY EVENHAND FAIRNESS
EQUIVALENCE AMOUNT PARITY

EQUIVALENT KIND SAME EQUAL NODEL COUSIN UNISON ANALOGUE EVENHAND
(— IN MONEY) CHANGE
(— OF TWO BUSHELS) HUTCH
(FAIR —) VALUE
EQUIVOCAL FISHY SHADY DOUBLE FORKED DUBIOUS EVASIVE HALFWAY OBSCURE DOUBTFUL HAVERING PUZZLING SIBYLLIC
EQUIVOCATE HAW HEM LIE DODGE EVADE SHIFT BOGGLE ESCAPE PALTER TRIFLE WAFFLE WEASEL QUIBBLE SHUFFLE SCRAFFLE PUSSYFOOT PREVARICATE
EQUIVOCATION QUIP QUIRK EVASION QUIBBLE SHUFFLE EQUIVOKE
EQUIVOQUE PUN
EQUULEUS FOAL
ER (FATHER OF —) JOSE
(SON OF —) ELMODAM
ERA AGE AEON DATE TIME EPOCH STAGE PERIOD CENOZOIC PALEOZOIC PROTEROZOIC
(EMPEROR'S —) KIMIGAYO
(GEOLOGICAL —) QUATENARY
(HINDU —) SAMVAT
(MUSLIM —) HEGIRA HEJIRA
ERADICATE DELE ROOT SLAY WEED CROSS ERASE STAMP DELETE EFFACE REMOVE UNROOT UPROOT ABOLISH DESTROY EXPUNGE OUTROOT SUPPLANT
(— HAIR) EPILATE
ERADICATOR ERASER
ERAL MOINE
ERAN (GRANDFATHER OF —) EPHRAIM
ERASE BLOT DASH DELE RACE RASE RASH RAZE ANNUL PLANE CANCEL DEFACE DELETE EFFACE EXCISE REMOVE SCRAPE SPONGE DESTROY EXPUNGE OUTRAZE SCRATCH UNWRITE WEAROUT OBLITERATE
ERASER RASER RUBBER
ERASTE (LOVER OF —) JULIE LUCILLE ORPHISE
ERASURE RASURE ERASION DELETION EXCISION
ERD SHREW RANNY
ERE OR AIR SOON EARLY PRIOR BEFORE EREWHILE FORMERLY
EREBUS (FATHER OF —) CHAOS
(SISTER OF —) NOX
(SON OF —) CHARON
ERECHTHEUS (DAUGHTER OF —) CREUSA PROCRIS CHTHONIA ORITHYIA
(FATHER OF —) PANDION
(SLAYER OF —) JUPITER
(SON OF —) MERION CECROPS PANDORUS
(WIFE OF —) PRAXITHEA
ERECT BIG SET BIGG LEVY REAR RECT STEP STEY SWAY TELD AREAR BRANT BUILD DRESS EXALT FRAME MOUNT ONEND PUTUP RAISE SETUP STAND ARRECT UPLIFT UPREAR ADDRESS ATROPAL BRISTLE ELEVATE STATELY UPRAISE UPRIGHT UPSTART STANDING STRAIGHT VERTICAL
(— HASTILY) RUNUP
(— TENT) PITCH
(NOT —) LAZY COUCHED
ERECTED UPSET
ERECTION DOME HARD FABRIC CHORDEE MACHINE
(— FOR SPECTATORS) STAND
(TEMPORARY —) SCAFFOLD
ERELONG ANON SOON
EREMITE LONER HERMIT ASCETIC RECLUSE ANCHORET
EREWHILE ERE WHILOM
EREWHON (AUTHOR OF —) BUTLER
(CHARACTER IN —) HIGGS GEORGE STRONG ZULORA CHOWBOK AROWHENA NOSNIBOR
ERG REG EROGON
(PL.) AREG
ERGINUS (FATHER OF —) CLYMENUS POSEIDON
(SON OF —) AGAMEDES TROPHONIUS
ERGO SO ARGO ARGAL HENCE
ERGOT SPUR CLAVUS ECBOLIC
(STAGE OF —) SPHACELIA
ERI (FATHER OF —) GAD
ERICHTHONIUS (FATHER OF —) VULCAN DARDANUS
(MOTHER OF —) ATTHIS
(SON OF —) PANDION
ERIDANUS (FATHER OF —) OCEANUS
(MOTHER OF —) TETHYS
ERIE WENRO
ERIGONE (FATHER OF —) ICARIUS AEGISTHUS
(MOTHER OF —) CLYTEMNESTRA
ERINYS FURY ALECTO MEGAERA
(PL.) DIRAE FURIAE SEMNAE EUMENIDES
ERIOPHORUM DRAWLING
ERIPHYLE (FATHER OF —) TALAUS
(HUSBAND OF —) AMPHIARAUS
(SON & SLAYER OF —) ALCMAEON
ERISTIC DIALECTIC
ERITREA (CAPITAL OF —) ASMARA
ERMINE VAIR VARE STOAT WEASEL ERMELIN FUTERET FUTTRAT MINIVER CLUBSTER WHITRACK WHITTRET
ERNANI (CHARACTER IN —) CARLO GOMEZ SILVA ELVIRA ERNANI
(COMPOSER OF —) VERDI
ERODE EAT ROT COMB ETCH GNAW GULL WEAR CLIFF GULLY SCOUR ABRADE DENUDE CORRODE DESTROY
ERODIUM HERONBILL
EROS AMOR KAMA CUPID AENGUS POTHOS
EROSE ERODED UNEVEN
EROSION PIPING CHIMNEY NIVATION SCOURING
(MECHANICAL —) PLANATION
ERO THE JOKER (COMPOSER OF —) GOTOVAC
EROTIC SEXY LOVING STEAMY AMATORY AMOROUS CURIOUS LESBIAN THERMAL
EROTICA CURIOSA FACETIAE
ERR MAR SIN BOOT FAIL MISS SLIP ABERR LAPSE MISGO STRAY BUNGLE FORVAY SLIPUP WANDER BLUNDER DEVIATE MISPLAY MISTAKE SCRITHE STUMBLE MISCARRY MISJUDGE
(— AT BRIDGE) RENEGE
ERRAND CHORE ENVOY JOURNEY MISSION LEGATION
(— BOY) LOBBYGOW
(RUNNER OF —S) GOFER GOPHER
ERRANT STRAY ASTRAY ERRING DEVIOUS PRICKANT
ERRATIC WILD CRAZY HUMAN LOONY QUEER WACKY CRANKY WHACKY STRANGE TANGENT VAGRANT ACROSTIC ERRABUND FITIFIED PLANETAL PLANETIC TRAVELED VAGABOND PLANETARY
ERRATUM ERROR
ERRING ASTRAY ERRANT DEVIOUS
ERRINGLY FALSE
ERRONEOUS AMISS FALSE WRONG UNTRUE ERRATIC MISTAKEN STRAYING WRONGFUL
(PREF.) PSEUD(O)
ERRONEOUSLY AWRY
ERRONEOUSNESS FALLACY
ERROR X HOB SIN BALK BUBU BULL FLUB HELL MUFF SLIP TRIP TYPO BEARD BEVUE BONER DEVIL FAULT FLUFF LAPSE SCAPE BOBBLE BOOBOO FUMBLE GARBLE HOWLER LAPSUS MISCUE NAUGHT SPHALM BLOOMER BLUNDER DEFAULT ERRATUM FALLACY FALSITY LITERAL MISPLAY MISSTEP MISTAKE OFFENSE RHUBARB SNAPPER STUMBLE DELUSION HAMARTIA MISPRINT MISSMENT SOLECISM OVERSIGHT MISPRISION
(— IN PLEADINGS) JEOFAIL
ERS VETCH KERSANNE
ERSATZ FAUX
ERSE ERSCH IRISH CELTIC GAELIC SCOTTISH
ERST ONCE FORMERLY RECENTLY
ERSTWHILE ONCE FORMER FORMERLY
ERUCT RASP BELCH
ERUCTATION BRASH
ERUDITE LEARNED CLERGIAL DIDACTIC
ERUDITION WIT LORE WISDOM LETTERS LEARNING
ERUPT BOIL SPEW BELCH BURST EJECT IRRUPT
ERUPTING ACTIVE
ERUPTION ITCH RASH REEF RUSH AGRIA BLAIN BRASH BURST RUPIA SALLY SALVO STORM BLOTCH HYDROA NIRLES ACTERID BLOWOUT ECTHYMA MORPHEA MORPHEW PUSTULE SAWFLOM SUDAMEN SYCOSIS EMPYESIS ENANTHEM EXANTHEM MALANDER OUTBREAK OUTBURST
(— ON CHIN) MENTAGRA
(CUTANEOUS —) HUMOR
(SKIN —) SPOT REDGUM TETTER
(SUFF.) ANTHEMA PHLYSIS
ERVUM LENS LENTILLA
ERYSICHTHON (FATHER OF —) CECROPS TRIOPAS
(MOTHER OF —) AGRAULOS
(SISTER OF —) IPHIMEDIA
ERYSIPELAS POX ROSE BLAST WILDFIRE
ERYTHROBLASTOSIS HYDROPSY
ERYX (FATHER OF —) BUTES
(MOTHER OF —) VENUS
(SLAYER OF —) HERCULES
ESAU EDOM
(BROTHER OF —) JACOB
(FATHER OF —) ISAAC
(LIKE —) HAIRY
(MOTHER OF —) REBEKAH
(SON OF —) JEUSH KORAH REUEL JAALAM ELIPHAZ
(WIFE OF —) ADAH BASHEMATH
ESCALADE SCALE SCALADE SCALADO ESCALADO
ESCAPADE LARK CAPER FLING PRANK SALLY SCHEME SCRAPE SPLORE RUNAWAY FREDAINE
ESCAPE FLY GUY LAM RUN BAIL BALE BEAT BLOW BOLT FLEE GATE HISS JINK JUMP LEAK MISS SHUN SKEW SLIP VENT AVOID BREAK CHAPE DODGE ELOPE ELUDE EVADE FLANK ISSUE SCAPE SHIFT SKIRT SMOKE SPILL ASTERT DECAMP ESCHEW OUTLET POWDER SQUEAK ABSCOND AVOLATE BLOWOUT ELUSION EXHAUST GETAWAY LEAKAGE MISTAKE OUTFLOW SCRITHE SQUEEZE WILDING BLOWBACK BREAKOUT ESCAPADE ESCAPAGE EXSHEATH OUTSCAPE OVERSLIP RIDDANCE WITHSLIP
(— FROM) FLY SHUN ILLUDE
(— FROM WORK) SNIB
(— LEGAL PROCESS) ABSCOND
(— NOTICE) ELUDE
(— OF FLUID) EFFUSION
(CUT OFF FROM —) HEMIN
(NARROW —) SHAVE
ESCAPEMENT SCAPE CRUTCH ESCAPE FOLIOT VIRGULE KARRUSEL
ESCARGOT SNAIL
ESCAROLE ENDIVE SCAROLA
ESCARPMENT EDGE
ESCHAR SCAB CRUST ASCHER
ESCHAROTIC CAUSTIC
ESCHEAT FALL LAPSE REVERT EXCHEAT FORFEIT
ESCHEW SHUN ABHOR AVOID FORGO ESCAPE FOREGO ABSTAIN
ESCOLAR PALU ROVET OILFISH ROVETTO MACKEREL
ESCORT MAN SEE SET TRY BEAR BEAU COND LEAD SHOW TEND WAIT BRING CARRY GUARD USHER ATTEND CONVEY CONVOY FOLLOW SQUIRE COLLECT CONDUCT CONSORT ESQUIRE GALLANT CAVALIER CHAPERON SHEPHERD SAFEGUARD
(PAID —) GIGOLO
ESCRITOIRE DESK BUREAU LECTERN
ESCULENT EDIBLE EATABLE

ESCUTCHEON CREST SHIELD
(CENTER OF —) NOMBRIL
ESHBAN **(FATHER OF —)** DISHON
ESHCOL **(BROTHER OF —)** ANER MAMRE
(COMPANION OF —) ABRAHAM
ESKER AS OS OSE KAME ESKAR HOGBACK
ESKIMO ITA HUSKY INUIT INNUIT AGOMIUT AMERIND ANGAKOK KUNMIUT OKOMIUT ORARIAN AGLEMIUT ESQUIMAU IKOGMIUT KIDNELIK KINIPETU MAGEMIUT MALEMIUT NUGUMIUT SINIMIUT
(— ASSEMBLY HOUSE) KASHIM
(— CULTURE) PUNUK
(— ISLAND) ALEUT
(— TENT) TUPEK TUPIK
ESLI **(FATHER OF —)** NAGGE
ESOPHAGUS GULLET SWALLOW WEASAND
(PREF.) LAEMO LEMO
ESOTERIC DEEP INNER ARCANE MYSTIC ORPHIC SECRET PRIVATE ABSTRUSE RAREFIED RARIFIED
ESPADON ESPADA SPADON SPADROON
ESPALIER CORDON LATTICE RAILING TRELLIS PALISADE
ESPARTO ALFA HALFA SPART STIPA ATOCHA
ESPAVE CARACOLI
ESPECIAL VERY CHIEF SPECIAL PECULIAR UNCOMMON
ESPECIALLY SUCH EXTRA RATHER CHIEFLY OVERALL SPECIAL
ESPIAL SPY ESPY EYING SCOUT NOTICE
ESPINAL MONTE
ESPIONAGE SPYING
ESPLANADE BUND WALK DRIVE MAIDAN MARINA
ESPOUSAL CEREMONY SPOUSAGE BETROTHAL
ESPOUSE WED AFFY MATE ADOPT MARRY DEFEND ENSURE SPOUSE BETROTH EMBRACE HUSBAND SUPPORT ADVOCATE MAINTAIN
ESPOUSED HANDFAST
ESPRESSO COFFEE
ESPUNDIA UTA
ESPY SEE ASPY SPOT ASCRY SIGHT WATCH BEHOLD DESCRY DETECT LOCATE NOTICE DISCERN OBSERVE DESCRIBE DISCOVER
ESQUIRE RADMAN ARMIGER ESCUDERO SERGEANT
ESSAY TRY SEEK ASSAY CHRIA OFFER PAPER PROVE TASTE THEME TRACT TRAIL CASUAL EFFORT MEMOIR SAILYE SATIRE SCREED THESIS ARTICLE ATTEMPT PROFFER VENTURE WRITING CAUSERIE ENDEAVOR EXERCISE EXERTION TRACTATE TREATISE TURNOVER
(PRELIMINARY —) STUDY
ESSAYIST **AMERICAN** DAY MORE VERY ADAMS GRANT WHITE YOUNG BROOKS COFFIN FISHER GUINEY HOLMES HUTTON KILMER KRUTCH LOWELL EMERSON LAZARUS SISSMAN WHIPPLE WHITMAN WHITTER KOSINSKI REPPLIER STRUNSKY TUCKERMAN SCHAUFFLER
AUSTRIAN BLEI
BELGIAN MAETERLINCK
CANADIAN MACMECHAN
CZECH CAPEK
ENGLISH HUNT LAMB BACON DRAKE MUNRO MYERS PAGET PATER POWYS SMITH GARROD MACHEN MARTIN SEELEY STEELE TEMPLE ADDISON BUDGELL CHAPONE HAYWARD HAZLITT HEWLETT MEYNELL RALEIGH SYMONDS CHAMBERS CONGREVE DISRAELI NEVINSON STERLING THOMPSON DICKINSON STEVENSON CHESTERTON DOBSONLEGALLIENNE
FRENCH ALAIN CAMUS ARAGON MOUREY CHAMSON STAPFER CHARTIER SCHOPFER MONTAIGNE
GERMAN ZWEIG FONTANE
GREEK XENOPHON
IRISH BOYD LECKY MAGEE
ITALIAN BRACCO CECCHI
MEXICAN REYES
POLISH BELCIKOWSKI MAKUSZYNSKI
SCOTTISH SMITH WILSON CARLYLE THOMSON STEVENSON
SWEDISH EKELUND
ESSE BEING
ESSENCE ENS NET ALMA ATAR BASE BONE CORE CRUX DRAW ESSE GIST GUTS KIND ODOR OTTO PITH QUID RASA SOUL YOLK ATTAR BASIC BASIS BEING EIDOS FIBER FIBRE FUMET HEART JUICE OTTAR OUSIA STUFF BOTTOM EFFECT ENTITY FLOWER INWARD MARROW NATURE SPRITE ALCOHOL ELEMENT EXTRACT FUMETTE GODHEAD INBEING MEDULLA PERFUME RATAFIA BERGAMOT CONCRETE ESSENTIA
(— OF BEING) SAT
(— OF FLOWERS) CONCRETE
(— OF GOD) SPIRIT DIVINITY
(— OF MEAT) BLOND
(— OF TEA) DRAW
(— OF VITAL MATTER) GLAME
(INNERMOST —) ATMAN
(UNIVERSAL —) FORM
(VITAL —) STAMINA
ESSENE ESSEE ASCETIC
ESSENTIAL KEY MUST REAL BASAL BASIC VITAL ENTIRE FORMAL INWARD CENTRAL CRUCIAL NEEDFUL CARDINAL CRITICAL INHERENT MATERIAL OBLIGATE NECESSARY
(— TO LIFE) BIOGENOUS
(NOT —) ACCIDENTAL
(PL.) ABCS
ESSENTIALLY AUFOND
ESSONITE GARNET HYACINTH
ESTABLISH BED FIX PUT SET BASE FAST FIRM FOOT MAKE REAR REST ROOT SEAT BUILD DEFIX EDIFY ENACT ERECT EVICT FOUND PLANT PROVE RAISE SEIZE SETUP START STATE STELL ATTEST AVOUCH BOTTOM CEMENT CLINCH CREATE ENROOT FASTEN FICCHE GROUND INVENT INVEST LOCATE ORDAIN RATIFY SETTLE STABLE VERIFY ACCOUNT APPOINT APPROVE CONFIRM ENSTATE INSTALL INSTATE INSTORE POSSESS PREEMPT SUSTAIN COLONIZE CONSTATE CONTRACT ENSCONCE ENTRENCH IDENTIFY INITIATE INSTRUCT RADICATE REGULATE STABLISH VALIDATE ASCERTAIN
(— FACT) APPROVE
(— FIRMLY) HAFT INDURATE
(— MORALS) ETHIZE
(— TRUMP) PITCH
ESTABLISHED SAD FAST FIRM SURE LEGAL ROOTED SEATED SICCAR STABLE STAPLE STATED STRONG CERTAIN SETTLED STANDING
ESTABLISHMENT HONG MILL SHOP STAB DAIRY FORGE JOINT PLANT POWER SALON STORE AGENCY CAISSE CENOBY ECESIS LAYOUT MENAGE SALOON SCHOOL ARSENAL ATELIER BROTHEL COENOBY CONCERN DOWNSET FACTORY FISHERY FOUNDRY FUNDUCK SHEBANG AQUARIUM AVERMENT BUSINESS CHEESERY CREAMERY ERECTION HACIENDA
(— IN NEW HABITAT) ECESIS
(— OF COLONY) DEDUCTION
(BATHING —) THERM HAMMAM HOTHOUSE
(DOMESTIC —) MENAGE
(DRINKING —) STUBE SALOON BARROOM SHEBEEN
(GAMBLING —) HOUSE TRIPOT
(HORSE-BREEDING —) HARAS
(MONASTIC —) CLOISTER
(NAVAL —) DOCKYARD
(WHITE —) MAN
ESTAFETTE COURIER STAFETTE
ESTAMINET CAFE
ESTATE FEE ALOD COPY FEOD FIEF HOME LAND POMP RANK UDAL ACRES ALLOD DAIRA DOWER DOWRY ESTER ESTRE ETHEL FINCA FUNDO HABIT HOUSE MANOR STATE TALUK VILLA ABBACY BARONY DEMISE DOMAIN ENTAIL GROUND LIVING MISTER QUINTA TALUKA ALODIUM CHATEAU COMMONS DEMESNE DIGNITY DISPLAY FORTUNE HAVINGS MAJORAT ALLODIUM BENEFICE COPYHOLD DOMINION EXECUTRY FREEHOLD HACIENDA JOINTURE LIFEHOLD LONGACRE MESNALTY POSITION PROPERTY SENATORY STANDING STAROSTY PATRIMONY PERPETUITY
(— OF REBEL) FISC FISK
(— WITH SERFS) HAM
(CATTLE —) ESTANCIA
(HINDU —) CHAK
(PORTION OF —) LEGITIM
(REAL —) FUNDUS
(PL.) AMANI
ESTEEM AIM LET USE DEEM HOLD RATE TALE ADORE COUNT FAVOR HONOR PRICE PRIDE STEEM THINK VALUE WEIGH WORTH ADMIRE CREDIT EXTIME REGARD REPUTE REVERE TENDER WONDER ACCOUNT CONCEIT OPINION RESPECT SUSPECT APPRAISE CONSIDER ESTIMATE VENERATE
ESTEEMED DEAR PRECIOUS
ESTER ADP FMN BIXIN ETHER OLEIN SARIN TABUN BORATE CAPRIN ERUCIN FOLATE HUMATE LAURIN MALATE OLEATE ACETATE ADIPATE ANISATE AZELATE CINERIN ELAIDIN FORMATE FUROATE GALLATE HEPARIN INDICAN LACTATE LACTONE LAURATE MALEATE MELLATE NITRATE OCTOATE OXALATE OXAMATE PECTATE PEPSIDE PICRATE SORBATE STEARIN SULTONE ABIETATE ACRYLATE ARSENATE ARSENITE ARSONATE BEHENATE BENZOATE CAFFEATE CONGENER DIPHENAN ESTOLIDE FLUORIDE FUCOIDIN KETIPATE LINOLATE LINOLEIN MALONATE MARGARIN MYRISTIN NUCLEATE PALMITIN PIMELATE PIPERATE RACEMATE SEBACATE SELENATE SILICATE SINAPATE STEARATE SUBERATE TARTRATE TOSYLATE PYRETHRIN
(SUFF.) OATE
ESTHER **(COUSIN OF —)** MORDECAI
(FATHER OF —) ABIHAIL
(HUSBAND OF —) AHASUERUS
ESTHER WATERS **(AUTHOR OF —)** MOORE
(CHARACTER IN —) FRED RICE LATCH SARAH ESTHER JACKIE PEGGIE TUCKER WATERS PARSONS WILLIAM BARFIELD
ESTIMABLE GOOD SOLID WORTH GENTLE HONEST WORTHY THRIFTY VALUABLE
ESTIMATE AIM SET CALL CAST GAGE RANK RATE READ RECK ASSAY AUDIT CARAT CENSE COUNT GAUGE GUESS JUDGE MOUNT PLACE PRIZE SCALE STOCK TALLY VALUE WEIGH ASSESS BUDGET ESTEEM RECKON REGARD SURVEY ACCOUNT AVERAGE BALANCE CENSURE COMPUTE CONCEIT MEASURE APPRAISE CONSIDER CRITIQUE CALCULATE
(— OF ONE'S SELF) OPINION
(— TOO HIGHLY) OVERRATE
(KIND OF —) POINT
(LOW COST —) LOWBALL
ESTIMATION AIM EYE CESS FAME NAME ODOR PASS RATE COUNT HONOR PRICE SIEGE VALUE CHOICE ESTEEM REGARD REPUTE ACCOUNT OPINION JUDGMENT PRESTIGE
(— OF STRAIGHTNESS) BONING
(HIGH —) CONCEIT
(LOW —) DISREPUTE
ESTIMATOR RATER CRUISER

ESTOC STOCK SWORD
ESTOILE STAR ETOILE

ESTONIA
CAPITAL: TALLINN
COIN: SENT KROON ESTMARK
DIALECT: TARTU
ISLAND: DAGO MUHU OESEL SAARE VORMSI HIIUMAA SAAREMAA
LAKE: PEIPUS
MEASURE: TUN ELLE LIIN PANG SUND TOLL TOOP FADEN VERST SAGENE VERSTA KULIMET VERCHOC TONNLAND
NATIVE: ESTH AESTI
PROVINCE: SAARE
RIVER: EMA NARVA PARNU KASARI
TOWN: NARVA PARNU REVAL TARTU TALLINN
WEIGHT: LOOD NAEL PUUD

ESTONIAN ESTH
ESTOP BAR FILL PLUG STOP DEBAR PREVENT
ESTRANGE PART WEAN ALIEN AVERT DIVERT ALIENATE DISUNITE STRANGER
ESTRANGED ALIEN FRAIM FREMIT
ESTRANGEMENT STANCE DISTASTE
ESTRAY STRAY WANDER
ESTREAT COPY FINE EXACT RECORD STREET EXTRACT EXTREAT
ESTREPEMENT STRIP
E STRING QUINT
ESTRIOL THEELOL
ESTROGEN MESTRANOL TAMOXIFEN
ESTRONE THEELIN
ESTRUS HEAT SEASON
ESTUARY ARM RIA PARA WASH CREEK FIRTH FLEET FRITH INLET LIMAN ESTERO
ESURIENCE GREED HUNGER
ETCETERA ETC KTL
ETCH BITE FROST ENGRAVE AQUATINT INSCRIBE
ETCHED FROSTED
ETCHER POINT
ETCHING ETCH AQUATINT
ETEOCLES (BROTHER OF —) POLYNICES
(FATHER OF —) OEDIPUS
(MOTHER OF —) JOCASTA
ETERNAL ETERNE TARNAL AGELESS ENDLESS LASTING UNAGING ENDURING IMMORTAL TIMELESS UNCAUSED
ETERNALLY AKE EER EVER ALWAYS ETERNE FOREVER
ETERNITY AGE EON AEON OLAM GLORY ETERNE ETERNAL EWIGKEIT INFINITY PERPETUITY
ETESIAN ANNUAL PERIODIC
ETHAN (FATHER OF —) KISHI MAHOL
ETHANE DIMETHYL
ETHAN FROME (AUTHOR OF —) WHARTON
(CHARACTER IN —) ETHAN FROME ZEENA MATTIE PIERCE SILVER ZENOBIA
ETHANOL ISOMER
ETHBAAL (DAUGHTER OF —) JEZEBEL
ETHER AIR SKY APIOL ESTER PINOLE ANISOLE ASARONE EPOXIDE ETHYLIN HARMINE SAFROLE SESAMIN SESAMOL SOLVENT ACACETIN ELEMICIN EMPYREAN GUAIACOL PHENETOLE
ETHEREAL AERY AIRY SKYEY AERIAL SKYISH AIRLIKE ETHERIC FRAGILE SLENDER DELICATE HEAVENLY SUPERNAL VAPOROUS
ETHICAL ETHIC MORAL HONORABLE
ETHICS HEDONICS PHILOSOPHY

ETHIOPIA
ANCIENT CAPITAL: AXUM AKSUM
CAPITAL: ADDISABABA
COIN: BESA BIRR AMOLE GIRSH DOLLAR TALARI ASHRAFI PIASTER
DEPRESSION: DANAKIL
FALLS: TISISAT BLUENILE
ISLANDS: DAHLAK
LAKE: ABE TANA ABAYA SHOLA ZEWAY RUDOLF STEFANIE
LANGUAGE: GEEZ TIGRE SOMALI AMHARIC GALLINYA TIGRINYA
MARRIAGE: DAMOZ QURBAN SEMANYA
MEASURE: TAT KUBA SINJER SINZER FARSAKH FARSANG
MOUNTAIN: BATU GUGE GUNA TALO
MOUNTAINS: AHMAR CHOKE
NAME: ABYSSINIA
NATIVE: AFAR GALLA ABIGAR AMHARA ANNUAK HAMITE SEMITE SOMALI TIGRAI CUSHITE DANAKIL FALASHA
PORT: ASSAB MASSAWA
PRINCE: RAS
PROVINCE: BALE KEFA WELO ARUSI GOJAM HARER SHEWA TIGRE SIDAMO ERITREA
RIVER: OMO WEB BARO DAWA GILA ABBAI AKOBO AWASH FAFAN TAKKAZE
TOWN: EDD DESE GOBA GORE JIMA THIO ADOLA ADUWA AKSUM ASSAB AWASH DIMTU HARAR HARER JIMMA MOJJO ASMARA DESSYE DUNKUR GONDAR MAKALE MEKELE GARDULA MASSAWA NAKAMTI NEKEMTE DIREDAWA LALIBALA MUSTAHIL
VALLEY: RIFT
WATERFALL: FINCHA DALVERME TESISSAT
WEIGHT: KASM NATR OKET ALADA NETER WAKEA WOGIET FARASULA

ETHIOPIAN SIDI HAMITE HARARI AETHIOP AFRICAN CUSHITE FALASHA
ETHIOPIC GIZ GEEZ GHEEZ
ETHNAN (FATHER OF —) ASHUR
(MOTHER OF —) HELAH
ETHNIC RACIAL
(— GROUP) ACHANG
ETHNOLOGIST AMERICAN GIBBS HODGE LOWIE MASON SMITH FEWKES MOONEY MORGAN THOMAS BARROWS GODDARD HENSHAW PILLING FLETCHER GATSCHET GRINNELL CHURCHILL SCHOOLCRAFT
AUSTRIAN MULLER LUSCHAN WINTERNITZ
DANISH RASMUSSEN
DUTCH STEINMETZ NIEUWENHUIS
ENGLISH HADDON LATHAM PRICHARD
FINNISH CASTREN
GERMAN BOEHM FINSCH GROSSE KRAUSE BASTIAN GERLAND STEINEN FROBENIUS FRIEDERICI
RUSSIAN KOPPEN
ETHOS MANNER
ETHYLENE ELAYL ETHENE ETHERIN
ETIOLATED DRAWN
ETIQUETTE FORM DECORUM MANNERS
(— OF DRINKING TEA) CHANOYU
ETRUSCAN TUSCAN RASENNA ETRURIAN TYRRHENE
(PL.) TURSENOI TYRRHENI
ETUDE STUDY
ETUI CASE ETWEE TWEEZE TWEEZER EQUIPAGE RETICULE
ETYMOLOGY ORIGIN DERIVATION
ETYMON RADIX
EUAECHME (DAUGHTER OF —) PERIBOEA
(FATHER OF —) MEGAREUS
(HUSBAND OF —) ALCATHOUS
EUBOEANS ABANTES
EUCALYPT GUM YATE APPLE BIMBIL CARBUN JARRAH MALLEE MYRTAL CARBEEN CUTTAIL MESSMAN COOLABAH IRONBARK MESSMATE WHITETOP YERTCHUK
EUCALYPTOLE CINEOL CINEOLE
EUCALYPTUS TUART MALLEE TEWART BLUEGUM EUCALYPT IRONBARK SUGARGUM WHIPSTICK
EUCHARIST HOUSEL MAUNDY SUPPER MYSTERY VIATICUM
EUCHARISTIC (— ELEMENTS) HAGIA
EUCHITE SATANIST ADELPHIAN MESSALIAN
EUCHRE LOVE
(— HAND) JAMBONE JAMBOREE
EUDAEMONIA HAPPINESS
EUDOCIMUS GUARA
EUDOXIA (FATHER OF —) BAUTO
(HUSBAND OF —) ARCADIUS
(SON OF —) THEODOSIUS
EUGENE ONEGIN (CHARACTER IN —) OLGA GREMIN LARINA ONEGIN OLENSKY TATYANA TRIQUET
(COMPOSER OF —) TCHAIKOVSKY
EUGENIE GRANDET (AUTHOR OF —) BALZAC
(CHARACTER IN —) NANON CHARLES CRUCHOT EUGENIE GRANDET DEGRASSINS
EULALIA NETI
EULENSPIEGEL OWLGLASS
EULOGIST PRAISER LAUREATE PANEGYRIST
EULOGISTIC EULOGIC EPENETIC MAGNIFIC LAUDATORY
EULOGY PRAISE TONGUE ADDRESS ELOGIUM ORATION ENCOMIUM PANEGYRE
EUMOLPUS (FATHER OF —) NEPTUNE
(MOTHER OF —) CHIONE
(SON OF —) ISMARUS
EUNEUS (BROTHER OF —) THOAS
(FATHER OF —) JASON
(MOTHER OF —) HYPSIPYLE
EUNICE (SON OF —) TIMOTHEUS
EUNUCH CAPON SPORUS WETHER GELDING HALFMAN CASTRATE
EUPHAUSID SHRIMP
EUPHEMISM DEE FIB GEE GOR DASH GOSH GOLES GOLLY LAWKS DIANTRE DICKENS CODEWORD GRACIOUS
(— FOR DAMN) HANG
(— FOR MURDER) REMOVAL
EUPHEMUS (FATHER OF —) NEPTUNE POSEIDON
(MOTHER OF —) EUROPA
(SON OF —) BATTUS
EUPHONIOUS TUNEFUL
EUPHORIA BLISS ELATION
EUPHORIC GIDDY
EUPHROSYNE JOY
EUPHUISM GONGORISM
EURASIAN BURGHER FERINGI
EUREKA RED PUCE
EURIPIDES (TRAGEDY OF —) ELECTRA
EURO WALLAROO
EUROPA (BROTHER OF —) CILIX CADMUS THASUS PHINEUS PHOENIX
(FATHER OF —) AGENOR
(HUSBAND OF —) ASTERIUS
(MOTHER OF —) TELEPHASSA
(SON OF —) MINOS SARPEDON RHADAMANTHYS

EUROPE
(ALSO SEE SPECIFIC COUNTRIES)
LAKE: COMO GARDA ONEGA VANEM GENEVA LADOGA LUGANO PEIPUS VANERN ZURICH BALATON MALAREN SCUTARI VATTERN MAGGIORE CONSTANCE NEUCHATEL
MOUNTAIN: DOM ETNA ELBRUS KAZBEK LYSKAMM SHKHARA JUNGFRAU NADELHORN WEISSHORN ZUGSPITZE MATTERHORN
NATION: ITALY SPAIN FRANCE GREECE LATVIA MONACO NORWAY POLAND RUSSIA SWEDEN ALBANIA ANDORRA AUSTRIA BELGIUM DENMARK ENGLAND ESTONIA FINLAND GERMANY HOLLAND HUNGARY ICELAND IRELAND ROMANIA BULGARIA PORTUGAL SCOTLAND SLOVAKIA SLOVENIA SANMARINO LUXEMBOURG YUGOSLAVIA NETHERLANDS SOVIETUNION SWITZERLAND VATICANCITY LIECHTENSTEIN CZECHOSLOVAKIA
RANGE: ALPS URAL BALKAN KJOLEN RHODOPE SUDETEN

CAUCASUS PYRENEES APENNINES CARPATHIAN
RIVER: PO AAR DON AARE EBRO ELBE ODER DOURO DVINA LOIRE RHINE RHONE SEINE TAGUS TIBER VOLGA DANUBE THAMES DNIEPER VISTULA DNIESTER

EUROPEAN FRANK SAHIB BOHUNK EUROPE FRINGE INDIAN FERINGI TOPIWALA
(— IN INDIES) BLIJVER
(WESTERN —) FRANK
EUROPEAN BARRACUDA SPET
EUROPEAN BASS BRASSE
EUROPEAN BISON AUROCHS
EUROPEAN CLOVER ALSIKE
EUROPEAN GULL MEW
EUROPEAN HERRING SPRAT
EUROPEAN JUNIPER CADE
EUROPEAN KITE GLEDE
EUROPEAN LAVENDER ASPIC
EUROPEAN LINDEN TEIL
EUROPEAN MINT HYSSOP
EUROPEAN OAK DURMAST
EUROPEAN PERCH RUFF RUFFE
EUROPEAN POLECAT FITCHEW
EUROPEAN PORGY BESUGO
EUROPEAN RABBIT CONY
EUROPEAN SHARK TOPE
EUROPEAN SPARROW WHITECAP
EUROPEAN STARLING STARNEL
EUROPEAN SWALLOW MARTIN
EUROPEAN THRUSH MAVIS OUZEL
EUROPEAN WIDGEON WHIM WHEWER
EUROPEAN WREN STAG
EURYANTHE (CHARACTER IN —) ADOLAR LYSIART EGLANTINE EURYANTHE
(COMPOSER OF —) WEBER
EURYBIA (FATHER OF —) PONTUS
(MOTHER OF —) GAEA
(SON OF —) PALLAS PERSES ASTRAEUS
EURYNOME (DAUGHTERS OF —) GRACES CHARITES
(FATHER OF —) CHAOS OCEANUS
EURYPTERID SERAPHIM
EURYPYLUS (FATHER OF —) NEPTUNE TELEPHUS
(MOTHER OF —) ASTYOCHE
(SLAYER OF —) PYRRHUS HERCULES
EURYSACES (FATHER OF —) AJAX
(MOTHER OF —) TECMESSA
EURYSTHEUS (FATHER OF —) STHENELUS
(MOTHER OF —) NICIPPE
(SLAYER OF —) HYLLUS
EURYTUS (DAUGHTER OF —) IOLE
(FATHER OF —) ACTOR AUGEAS MELANEUS
(MOTHER OF —) GAEA
(SLAYER OF —) HERCULES
EUTECTIC STEADITE
EUTERPE (FATHER OF —) JUPITER
(MOTHER OF —) MNEMOSYNE
EUXANTHONE PURRONE
EUXOA AGROTIS
EVACUATE PASS VENT VOID AVOID EMPTY EXPEL STOOL VACATE DEPRIVE EXCRETE EXHAUST NULLIFY VACUATE PERSPIRE
EVACUATION OFFICE DUNKIRK MEDEVAC
EVADE BEG GEE BILK DUCK FLEE FOIL JOUK JUMP SHUN SLIP VOID AVERT AVOID BLINK DALLY DODGE ELUDE FENCE FLANK PARRY SHIRK SKIRT SKIVE BAFFLE BLENCH BYPASS COPOUT DELUDE ESCAPE ILLUDE BEGUILE FINESSE OUTSLIP QUIBBLE TURNOFF HEDGEHOP LEAPFROG SIDESTEP
(— LEGAL PROCESS) ABSCOND
(— PAYMENT) BILK
(— QUESTIONS) QUIBBLE SHUFFLE
(— WORK) JOUK BLUDGE
EVADNE (FATHER OF —) PELIAS NEPTUNE POSEIDON
(HUSBAND OF —) CAPANEUS
(MOTHER OF —) IPHIS PITANA
(SON OF —) IAMUS
EVALUATE RATE ASSESS PONDER RECKON DISSECT APPRAISE ESTIMATE
EVALUATION STOCK ESTIMATE
EVANDER (FATHER OF —) HERMES
(MOTHER OF —) CARMENTA
EVANESCE FADE VANISH
EVANESCENCE ANICCA
EVANESCENT FLEET EVANID BRITTLE CURSORY EVASIVE FRAGILE DELICATE FLEETING FLITTING FUGITIVE STAYLESS
EVANGELICAL GOSPEL SIMEONITE
(— ACTIVITY) WARFARE
EVANGELIST LUKE MARK EVANGEL GOSPELER SALVATIONIST
EVAPORATE DRY EXHALE AVOLATE CONDENSE VAPORIZE
EVAPORATING (— QUICKLY) VOLATILE
EVAPORATOR BOILER EFFECT
EVASION JINK SLIP DODGE QUIRK SALVE SHIFT AMBAGE ESCAPE SNATCH ELUSION OFFCOME SHUFFLE TWISTER ARTIFICE ESCAPISM VOIDANCE
(— OF DUTY) COMEOFF
(ARTFUL —) QUIRK
EVASIVE SLY EELY DODGY SHIFTY SUBTLE TWISTY ELUSIVE ELUSORY TRICKSY SLIPPERY SLIPSKIN
(TO BE —) STONEWALL
EVE DUSK EREB EREV EVEN VIGIL SUNSET SUNDOWN
(NEW YEAR'S —) HAGMENA HOGMANAY
EVELINA (AUTHOR OF —) BURNEY
(CHARACTER IN —) JOHN DUVAL ARTHUR HOWARD ANVILLE BELMONT CLEMENT EVELINA ORVILLE VILLARS WILLOUGHBY
EVEN ALL DEN EEN TIE YET FAIR HUNK JUST PAIR TIED TILL ALINE CLEAN EQUAL EVERY EXACT FLUSH GRADE HUNKY LEVEL MATCH PLAIN RIVAL STILL SUANT SUENT SWEET DIRECT ITSELF PLACID SILKEN SMOOTH SQUARE STEADY ABREAST BALANCE EQUABLE FLATTEN REGULAR UNIFORM UPSIDES EQUALIZE MODERATE PARALLEL SOMUCHAS
(— NUMBERS) PAIR
(— OFF) LEVEL
(— THOUGH) IF ALTHO ALBEIT ALTHOUGH
(MAKE —) WEIGH STEADY
(PREF.) ARTIO HOMAL(O) LEUR(O)
EVENING DEN EVE EREB EVEN SOIR ABEND TARDE SUNSET VESPER EVENTIDE VESPERAL
(— BEFORE PASSOVER) PARASCEVE
(— OF SONG) CEILIDH
(AT —) TEEN
(EARLY —) UNDERN
(YESTERDAY —) STREEN
EVENING PRIMROSE SUNCUP SCABIOUS
EVENING STAR VENUS HESPER VESPER EVESTAR HESPERUS
EVENLY FAIR PLAIN FLATLY EQUALLY
EVENNESS EQUALITY
EVENSONG VESPERS
EVENT HAP CASE FACT FATE FEAT TILT CASUS DOING EPOCH FRAME ISSUE THING ACTION EFFECT FACTUM RESULT TIDING TIMING EPISODE FIXTURE MIRACLE PORTENT TRAGEDY INCIDENT OCCASION OCCURRENCE PHENOMENON
(AMUSING —) COMEDY
(CHANCE —) ACCIDENT FORTUITY
(EXTRAORDINARY —) MIRACLE
(FORTUITOUS —) HAZARD
(GRAVE —) CALAMITY
(HAPPY —) GODSEND
(IMPORTANT —) ACE ERA
(INTRODUCTORY —) PROLOGUE
(KIND OF —) MEDIA
(PAST —S) HISTORY
(SEISMIC —) STARQUAKE
(SET OF —S) EPISODE
(SIGNIFICANT —) CRISIS
(SKI —) DOWNHILL
(SOCIAL —) BENEFIT
(SPORTING —) STAKE
(STAGED —) FRAMEUP
(SUPERNATURAL —) MIRACLE
(THEATRICAL —) DRAW
(TURNING-POINT —) LANDMARK
(UNEXPECTED —) STUNNER ACCIDENT AFTERCLAP
(UNPLEASANT —) BUMMER
(YEARLY —) ANNUAL
EVENTFUL LIVELY NOTABLE
EVENTIDE VESPER EVENING
EVENTUAL LAST FINAL ULTIMATE
EVENTUALITY EVENT
EVENTUALLY YET FINALLY
EVENTUATE GO LEAD ISSUE RESULT SUCCEED ULTIMATE
EVENUS (DAUGHTER OF —) MARPESSA
(FATHER OF —) ARES MARS
EVER O AY SO AYE EER ONCE STILL ALWAYS ETERNE FOREVER
EVERGLADE STATE FLORIDA
EVERGREEN BOX FIR IVY YEW ASIS ATLE BAGO ILEX PINE TAWA ATLEE BOLDO CAROB CEDAR HEATH HOLLY LARCH SAVIN THUYA TOYON BAUERA COIGUE DAHOON LAUREL MASTIC SPRUCE BANKSIA BARETTA BEBEERU BILIMBI GOWIDDE HEMLOCK JASMINE TARATAH BOXTHORN CALFKILL CARAUNDA IRONWOOD TAMARISK TILESEED
(— SHRUB) GORSE
(PL.) CHRISTMAS
EVER-INCREASING ACCRESCENT
EVERLASTING ETERNE AEONIAL AEONIAN AGELESS AGELONG DURABLE ENDLESS ETERNAL FOREVER LASTING TEDIOUS ENDURING IMMORTAL INFINITE TIMELESS PERPETUAL
EVERLASTINGLY ALWAYS FOREVER
EVERSION BLOWOUT BEARINGS
EVERT UPSET EVERSE SUBVERT OVERTURN
EVERY ALL ANY ILK PER THE EACH EVER ILKA ENTIRE EVERICH COMPLETE
(— DAY) QD QUOTID
(— HOUR) QH
(— NIGHT) QN
(PREF.) PAM PAN
EVERYBODY ALL EACH EVERYMAN EVERYONE
EVERYDAY USUAL HOMELY PROSAIC ORDINARY WORKADAY
EVERY MAN IN HIS HUMOUR
(AUTHOR OF —) JONSON
(CHARACTER IN —) EDWARD KITELY BOBADIL BRIDGET CLEMENT KNOWELL MATTHEW WELLBRED BRAINWORM
EVERYTHING ALL ATHING
(— TAKEN INTO ACCOUNT) ALLINALL
(COUNTING —) INALL
EVERYWHERE PASSIM UBIQUE ALGATES AYWHERE OVERALL ALLWHERE
EVICT OUST EJECT EXPEL
EVICTION OUSTER
EVIDENCE CLUE MARK SHOW SIGN TEST PROOF SCRIP SMOKE TOKEN TRACE TRIAL ATTEST AVOUCH BETOKE RECORD REVEAL CHARTER EXHIBIT HEARSAY SHOWING SUPPORT ARGUMENT DISPROOF DOCUMENT EVICTION INDICATE MANIFEST MONUMENT MUNIMENT WARRANTY ADMINICLE
(— OF DISEASE) SYMPTOM
(— OF FRESHNESS) BLOOM
(— OF RIGHT) TITLE
(— OF WRONGDOING) GOODS
(POSITIVE —) CONSTAT
(VERBAL —) PAROL
EVIDENT LOUD OPEN PERT APERT BROAD CLEAR FRANK GROSS NAKED PLAIN EXTANT LIQUID PATENT WITTER EMINENT GLARING OBVIOUS PROBATE VISIBLE APPARENT DISTINCT FLAGRANT LUCULENT MANIFEST PALPABLE
(PREF.) DELO
EVIL BAD DER ILL SIN BALE BASE DIRE HARM LEWD PAPA POOR SORE VICE VILE WICK YELL CRIME

CURSE DEVIL FELON FOLLY HYDRA MALUM QUEDE SORRY WATHE WRONG CANCEL DIVERS INJURY MALIGN MENACE NAUGHT PLAGUE ROTTEN SHREWD SINFUL UNFEEL UNFELE UNGOOD UNWELL WICKED WONDER ADVERSE BALEFUL CORRUPT DISEASE DIVERSE HEINOUS HURTFUL IMMORAL MISDEED NOXIOUS SATANIC UNHAPPY UNSOUND VICIOUS CALAMITY DEPRAVED DEVILISH DISASTER GANGRENE IMPROPER INIQUITY MISCHIEF QUEDSHIP SINISTER NEFARIOUS
(— BEING) MARE
(— OF MANY PHASES) HYDRA
(— SPIRIT) JUMBIE
(IMAGINARY —) WINDMILL
(IMPENDING —) MENACE IMMINENCE
(SOCIAL —) SCOURGE
(SPIRITUAL —) SCAB
(PREF.) MAL(E) PONERO
EVIL-DOER VILLAIN
EVILDOER BADMASH BUDMASH SLASHER
EVIL EYE DROCHUIL MALOCCHIO
EVINCE SHOW ARGUE PROVE SUBDUE BREATHE CONQUER DISPLAY EXHIBIT EVIDENCE INDICATE MANIFEST
EVISCERATE GUT DRAW BOWEL PAUNCH GARBAGE
EVOCATION SADHANA
EVOCATIVE REDOLENT
EVOKE FIT MOVE STIR EDUCE AROUSE ELICIT SUMMON EVOCATE PROVOKE SUGGEST
EVOLUTION DRIFT GROWTH BIOGENY DIOECISM HOROTELY MANEUVER BRADYTELY
(PL.) AEROBATICS
EVOLUTIONISM DARWINISM
EVOLVE COOK EMIT EDUCE DERIVE UNFOLD UNROLL BLOSSOM DEVELOP EVOLUTE CONCEIVE UNPLIGHT
EWE KEB TEG CROCK CRONE DRAPE SHEEP GIMMER LAMBER RACHEL THEAVE CHILVER
(— AND LAMB) COUPLE
(OLD —) BIDDY CROCK CRONE BIDDIE
(YOUNG —) THEAVE
EWER JUG CREW LAIR BASIN UDDER PITCHER URCEOLE
EXACERBATE SOUR ENRAGE FERMENT EMBITTER IRRITATE
EXACERBATION PAROXYSM
EXACT ASK DUE DEAD EVEN FINE FLAT HAVE JUMP JUST LEVY NEAT NICE TRUE VERY PRESS SCREW WREAK WREST COMPEL DEMAND ELICIT EVINCE EXTORT FORMAL GRAITH MINUTE NARROW PROPER SEVERE SQUARE STRAIT STRICT CAREFUL CERTAIN COLLECT COMMAND CORRECT ENFORCE ESTREAT EXPRESS EXTRACT LITERAL PARTILE PERFECT POINTED PRECISE PRECISO REFINED REGULAR REQUIRE ACCURATE CRITICAL EXPLICIT FAITHFUL RIGOROUS SPECIFIC
(— BY FINE) ESTREAT
(— SATISFACTION) AVENGE
(NOT —) PLATIC
(VERY —) RELIGIOUS
(PREF.) ORTH(O)
EXACTING NICE HARSH PICKY STERN STIFF TIGHT SCREWY SEVERE STRAIT STRICT ARDUOUS EXIGENT FINICKY ONEROUS CRITICAL IMPOSING IRONCLAD PRESSING SCREWING PARTICULAR PERSNICKETY
(— EXCLUSIVE DEVOTION) JEALOUS
EXACTION FEE TAX MART GOUGE GRIPE
(— OF PROVISIONS) CESS COYNE COIGNY
(ANCIENT IRISH —) SOREHON
(UNDUE —) EXTORTION
EXACTITUDE RIGOR
EXACTLY DUE AMEN BANG DEAD EVEN FLAT FLOP FULL JUMP JUST VERY PLUMB PLUNK QUITE RIGHT SHARP SPANG TRULY ARIGHT EVENLY ITSELF JUSTLY NICELY PERFECT SLAPDAB DIRECTLY MINUTELY SMACKDAB
EXACTNESS RIGOR TRUTH NICETY ACCURACY DELICACY DISPATCH FIDELITY IDENTITY JUSTNESS SAPIENCE SEVERITY PRECISION PARTICULARITY
(FUSSY —) FIKE
EXAGGERATE GAB MORE COLOR BOUNCE CHARGE COLOÜR EXTEND OVERDO AMPLIFY ENHANCE ENLARGE MAGNIFY OUTLASH ROMANCE STRETCH INCREASE OVERDRAW OVERLASH OVERPLAY OVERTELL OVERSTATE OVERCHARGE
(— OPENING OF MOUTH) CHINK
EXAGGERATED CAMP SLAB TALL COLORED FUSTIAN FABULOUS INFLATED OVERDONE OVERSHOT OVERWEENING
EXAGGERATING ARROGANT
EXAGGERATION BLAH REACHER HYPERBOLE
EXALT HAUT LAUD REAR AREAR BUILD DEIFY ELATE ENSKY ERECT EXTOL HEAVE HEEZE HONOR MOUNT RAISE TOWER ALTIFY ASCEND EXHALE PREFER REFINE THRONE UPREAR WORTHY ADVANCE AUGMENT DIGNIFY ELEVATE ENHANCE ENNOBLE FEATHER GLORIFY GREATEN INSPIRE MAGNIFY PROMOTE SUBLIME DIVINIZE ENTHRONE GRADUATE HEIGHTEN INHEAVEN PEDESTAL
EXALTATION LAUD AVATAR ANAGOGE ANAGOGY ELATION RAPTURE ERECTION
EXALTED HAUT HIGH ELATE GRAND LOFTY NOBLE SHEEN SKYEY SOARY ASTRAL TIPTOE TOPFUL HAUGHTY SUBLIME ELEVATED EXALTATE MAGNIFIC
EXALTING HUMAN
EXAM MUG
(— ANSWER) TRUE FALSE
(— TAKER) TESTEE
(HIGH SCHOOL —) PSAT
EXAMINATION EX MAY EXAM FACE QUIZ TEST ASSAY AUDIT BOARD CHECK FINAL GREAT POINT PROBE STUDY TRIAL BIOPSY EXAMEN NOTICE REVIEW SCHOOL SEARCH SURVEY TRIPOS AUTOPSY BEARING CANVASS CHECKUP DIVVERS EXAMINE HEARING INQUEST INQUIRY MIDYEAR OPPOSAL TUGGERY ANALYSIS CRITIQUE DOCIMASY EXERCISE NECROPSY PHYSICAL RESEARCH SCANNING SCRUTINY PRACTICAL PRELIMINARY
(BRITISH —) SLEVEL
(ELECTROCARDIOGRAPHIC —) STRESSTEST
(PL.) HOURS
(SUFF.) SCOPE SCOPIC SCOPUS SCOPY
EXAMINE ASK CON FAN SEE SPY TRY BOLT CASE COMB FEEL LAIT LINE LOOK OGLE QUIZ RIPE SCAN SEEK SIFT TEST VIEW ASSAY AUDIT CHECK ENTER GROPE PROBE QUEST QUOTE SAMEN SENSE SOUND STUDY VISIT APPOSE BEHOLD CANDLE DEBATE PERUSE PONDER REVIEW SCREEN SEARCH SURVEY ANALYZE CANVASS COLLATE DISCUSS EXPLORE INQUIRE INSPECT OVERSEE PALPATE RUMMAGE COGNOSCE CONSIDER OVERHAUL TRAVERSE
(— BY TOUCH) PALPATE
(— CAREFULLY) SCAN SIFT PONDER
(— LAND) SOUM
EXAMINER POSER TRIER CENSOR CONNER SABORA ANALYST APPOSER AUDITOR CORONER PROBATOR SEARCHER
EXAMPLE A CASE CAST COPY LEAD NORM TYPE BEAUT BYSEN ESSAY LIGHT MODEL PIECE EMBLEM PRAXIS SAMPLE BOUNCER LEADING LECTURE PATTERN PURPOSE SAMPLER THEATER CALENDAR ENSAMPLE EXEMPLAR EXEMPLUM FORBYSEN FOREGOER INSTANCE PARADIGM SPECIMEN
(CHOICE —) PEACH
(DISGRACEFUL —) BIZEN BYSEN BYZEN MONSTROSITY
(EXTREME —) CAUTION
(FINEST —) PEARL
(INFERIOR —) EXCUSE
(INSTRUCTIVE —) LESSON
(NOTABLE —) MONUMENT
(OLDEST —) DOYEN
(PERFECT —) APOTHEOSIS
(STANDARD —) PROTOTYPE
(SUPERLATIVE —) BLINGER
EXANTHEMA DIEBACK ERUPTION
EXASPERATE IRE IRK MAD BAIT GALL HEAT URGE ANNOY BLOOD ENRAGE EXCITE NETTLE EXASPER INFLAME PROVOKE ROUGHEN ACERBATE IRRITATE
EXASPERATED SNAKY WROTH SNAKEY SNAKISH ACERBATE
EXASPERATION AGRO GALL HEAT AGGRO WRATH
EXCAVATE CUT DIG PIT HOLE HOWK MINE MOLE MUCK PION SINK DELVE DRILL DRIVE GRAVE NAVVY SCOOP STOPE BURROW DREDGE EXCAVE GULLET HOLLOW QUARRY
EXCAVATION CUT DIG PIT HOLE MINE REDD SINK SUMP BERRY DELFT DELPH DITCH GRAFT GRAVE HEUGH PILOT STOPE BURROW CAVITY DUGOUT GROOVE TRENCH BREAKUP CUTTING PADDOCK TUTWORK WORKING DENEHOLE SLUSHPIT
(TRIAL —) SONDAGE
EXCAVATOR DIG BILDAR CLEOID DIGGER DIPPER DRIFTER HATCHET PIONEER
EXCEED COW TOP BEST PASS EXCEL OUTDO OUTGO BETTER OUTRUN OUTVIE OVERDO OVERGO ECLIPSE OUTPASS OVERRUN OVERTAX PRECEDE SURPASS OUTRANGE OUTREACH OUTSTRIP OVERCOME OVERGANG OVERSTEP OVERWEND SURMOUNT PREPONDERATE
(— IN IMPORTANCE) OVERSHADOW
(— THE RESOURCES) BEGGAR
EXCEEDING VILE
EXCEEDINGLY ALL DONE PURE TRES VERY AMAIN BLAME BLAMED MASTER PROPER PURELY AWFULLY LICKING PARLOUS PASSING HEARTILY HEAVENLY HORRIBLE PROPERLY
(PREF.) PRE ULTRA
EXCEL CAP COB TOP BANG BEAT BEST DING FLOG MEND PASS STAR BLECK OUTDO OUTGO SHINE TRUMP BETTER EXCEED MASTER OUTRAY OVERDO OVERGO PRECEL ECLIPSE EMULATE OUTPEER SURPASS OUTCLASS OUTRANGE OUTRIVAL OUTSHINE OUTSTRIP OVERPEER SUPERATE SURMOUNT
EXCELLENCE ARETE MERIT PRICE VIRTU WORTH BEAUTY DESERT HEIGHT VIRTUE DIGNITY PROWESS GOODNESS SPLENDOR BRILLIANCE PREROGATIVE
(— OF QUALITY) STRIKE
(MORAL —) GRACE
(PL.) SANCTITIES
EXCELLENT FAB GAY RUM BEST BOSS BRAW COOL FINE GOOD HEND HIGH PURE RARE RIAL SLAP TALL TRIM ATHEL BEAUT BONNY BONZA BRAVE BULLY BURLY CRACK GREAT JAMMY JOLLY LUMMY PIOUS PRIME PRIMO SOLID SUPER SWELL TOUGH TRIED WALLY BONNIE BONZER BOSKER BUMPER CHEESY CHOICE CLASSY FAMOUS FREELY GENTLE GOODLY MELLOW PRETTY PROPER SELECT SPIFFY TIPTOP WICKED WIZARD WORTHY YANKEE BLIGHTY BOSHTER CAPITAL CORKING

CURIOUS ELEGANT GALLANT IMMENSE QUALITY SNIFTER STAVING TOPPING CLIPPING COLOSSAL EXIMIOUS GENEROUS KNOCKOUT SPIFFING STUNNING SUPERIOR VALUABLE VIRTUOUS WAUREGAN YNGOODLY GANGBUSTERS
(— IN QUALITY) FRANK
(MOST —) BEST
EXCELLENTLY BRAWLY CLEVER FINELY FREELY PROUDLY DIVINELY FAMOUSLY
EXCELLING BEST PASSANT
EXCEPT BAR BUT CEP NOR NOT BATE BOUT OMIT ONLY SAVE ABATE FORBY SEVER EXEMPT FORBYE NOBBUT SAVING SCUSIN UNLESS BARRING BESIDES EXCLUDE OUTCEPT OUTSIDE OUTTAKE OUTWITH RESERVE WITHOUT FORPRISE OUTTAKEN RESERVED
(PREF.) PRETER
EXCEPTING BATING EXCEPT SAVING UNLESS BARRING
EXCEPTION DEMUR SALVO SAVING DISSENT OFFENSE DEMURRER FALLENCY FORPRISE INSTANCE
(— TO JUROR) CHALLENGE
(WITHOUT —) BARNONE
EXCEPTIONAL RARE EXEMPT ROUSING STRANGE UNUSUAL ABERRANT ABNORMAL ESPECIAL SINGULAR UNCOMMON
EXCEPTIONALLY AMAZING SPANKING
EXCERPT CITE PATCH QUOTE SCRAP EXTRACT OFFPRINT
(— FROM SONG) SNATCH
EXCESS OVER PLUS RIOT FLOOD INORD LUXUS PRIDE ACRASY SPILTH ACRASIA BALANCE DEBAUCH EXTREME MISRULE NIMIETY OUTRAGE OVERAGE OVERSET PROFUSE RIOTISE SURFEIT SURPLUS EXCEDENT GLUTTONY INTEREST OVERLASH OVERMUCH OVERPLUS PLEONASM PLETHORA PLEURISY SATURNALIA OVERABUNDANCE
(— OF ACTION) OVERKILL
(— OF LOGS) BANK
(— OF METAL) FEEDHEAD
(— OF SOLAR MONTH) EPACT
(— OF VOTES) PLURALITY
(SUFF.) ARD ART
EXCESSIVE TOO OVER RANK ENORM FANCY STEEP STIFF THICK UNDUE DEADLY DEUCED WOUNDY BURNING EXTREME FURIOUS NIMIOUS OVERDUE SURFEIT ABNORMAL CRIMINAL DEVILISH ENORMOUS HORRIBLE INSOLENT OVERMUCH TERRIBLE TERRIFIC PLETHORIC
(PREF.) POLY SUR
EXCESSIVELY TOO SUPER DEADLY OVERLY STRONG UNDULY PARLISH PARLOUS PASSING PLAGUEY WOUNDLY DEVILISH PLAGUILY
(PREF.) HYPER
EXCHANGE RAP SET CASH CAUP CHOP CODE COPE COUP KULA MART SELL SWAP SWOP BANDY BOARD BOLSA CORSE SHIFT STORE TRADE TROKE TRUCK BARTER BOURSE CAMBIO CHANGE DICKER EXCAMB MARKET NIFFER RESALE RIALTO SCORSE SHOPPE TOLSEL TOLZEY VALUTA WISSEL WRIXLE BARROOM CAMBIUM CHAFFER COMMUTE CONVERT DEALING PERMUTE TRAFFIC COMMERCE TRADEOFF TRUCKAGE
(— COURTESIES) GAM
(— IN CHECKERS) CUT SHOT
(— OF BLOWS) HANDPLAY
(— OF PRISONERS) CARTEL
(— OF SYLLABLES) ANACLASIS
(— PREMIUM) AGIO
(— SMALL TALK) CHAFFER
(— THOUGHTS) CONVERSE
(— VISITS) GAM
(DANCE —) CROSSOVER
(FAIR —) GIFFGAFF
(FOREIGN —) DEVISE
(POETICAL —) FLYTING
(POST —) CANTEEN
(TELEPHONE —) CENTRAL
(PREF.) CAMBI(O)
EXCHEQUER FISC PURSE COFFER KHALSA CHECKER FINANCE TREASURY
EXCIPIENT OXYMEL
EXCISE CUT TAX CROP DUTY GELD TOLL SLASH EXCIDE EXSECT IMPOST RESECT EXSCIND ALCABALA RETRENCH
EXCISEMAN GAGER GAUGER EXCISOR
EXCISION CUT ERASURE ABLATION
EXCITABLE HYPER NAPPY NERVY NERVOUS RACKETY
EXCITATION LASH
(CONVULSIVE —) SHOCK
EXCITE HOT CITE FIRE HEAT HYPO SEND SPUR STIR URGE WAKE WHET WORK YERK ALARM AMOVE ANGER CHAFE ELATE ERECT FLAME FLUSH IMPEL PIQUE RAISE ROUSE SCALD SPOOK AROUSE AWAKEN BOTHER DAZZLE DECOCT FLURRY FOMENT GROOVE IGNITE INCEND INCITE INVOKE JANGLE KINDLE LATHER PROMPT SALUTE TICKLE TURNON UPREAR WECCHE AGITATE ANIMATE COMMOVE ENCHAFE FERMENT INCENSE INFLAME PHILTER PROVOKE QUICKEN STARTLE WHITTLE DISQUIET ENGENDER EXCITATE IRRITATE
(— MIRTH) DIVERT
EXCITED UP APE GAY HOT AGOG GAGA GYTE PINK ABOIL AGLOW CADGY EAGER MANIC PROUD RANTY SKEER WIRED BLEEZY ELATED HEATED STEAMY ATHRILL FEVERED HAYWIRE SKEERED WAKENED AGITATED ATWITTER ELEVATED FEVERISH FLURRIED FRENETIC STARTLED OVERWROUGHT
(EASILY —) KITTLE
(INTENSELY —) MAD AMOK
EXCITEMENT ADO GOG BUZZ FUME FUSS GLOW HEAT HWYL KICK RUFF STIR TOSS UNCO FEEZE FEVER FUROR KICKS LARRY MANIA SETUP SPARK STOUR UNCOW FRENZY SPLASH WARMTH FERMENT FRISSON NERVISM TAMASHA WIDDRIM BROUHAHA DELIRIUM INTEREST RACKETRY
(FILLED WITH —) HECTIC
(GREAT —) FEVER
(MENTAL —) WIDDRIM
(PLEASANT —) SUSPENSE
(SHOW —) ENTHUSE
(VIOLENT —) GARE
EXCITING HOT HIGH KICKY ZINGY HECTIC AGACANT BURNING PARLOUS RACKETY ROUSING EXCITANT EXCITIVE PATHETIC STIRRING TERRIFIC FASHIONABLE
(— HORROR) DIRE DIREFUL
(ENJOYABLY —) ZINGY
EXCLAIM CRY HOWL BLURT ESCRY SNORT CLAMOR OUTCRY BESPEAK
(— IN AMAZEMENT) OOH
(— IN PROTEST) RECLAIM
EXCLAMATION (ALSO SEE INTERJECTION) O AH AI AY BO EH EY HA HI HO LA LO MY OH OW SO ST YO AHA AIE BAH BAM BOO FEN FIE FOH GEE GIP GRR GUP HAI HAW HAY HEM HEP HEY HIC HOY HUH NOW OCH OFF OHO OUF OUT PAH PEW POH POX ROT SEE SUZ TCH TCK TUT UGH VOW WEE WOW YAH YOW AHEM ALAS AVOY BUFF DEAR DRAT EGAD EVOE FAST GARN GOOD HAIL HECH HECK HIST HOLA HUFF HUNH HUSH HYKE OONS OUGH PHEW PHOO PHUT PIFF PISH POOH PRUT PUGH RATS RIVO SCAT SIRS SOFT SOHO TCHU TUSH WALY WEEK WEET WELL WHAM WHAT WHEE WHEW WHIR WHIT WUGG YOOP YULE ALACK BRAVO EWHOW FAINS FANCY FAUGH FEIGH GLORY GOODY HEIGH HELLO HOLLA HUFFA HULLO HUMPH HUZZA JOSSA OHONE PSHAW RIGHT SALVE SHISH SKOAL SORRY SUGAR TEREU WAUGH WELOO WHING WHISK WHIST WHOOP WIRRA WOONS CARAJO CLAMOR ENCORE HALLOO HEYDAY HOOTAY HURRAH INDEED OUTCRY PERFAY QUOTHA RATHER RIGHTO SHUCKS STEADY WALKER WHOOSH ZOUNDS CARAMBA DOGGONE GODSAKE HOSANNA JEEPERS JIGGERS KERCHOO KERWHAM NICHEVO PRITHEE RUBBISH SALAMAT TANTIVY THUNDER WELCOME WHOOPEE FAREWELL WAESUCKS WELLAWAY
(— OF DISGUST) AUH FIE FOH PAH UGH AUGH AVOY PHEW PISH POOT PSHA PUGH FAUGH FEICH FEIGH PSHAW WELOO
(— OF DISTRESS) AI AIE HARO HARROW
(— OF DOUBT) HUM HUMPH
(— OF IMPATIENCE) GIP PHEW
(— OF INCREDULITY) AHEM INDEED WALKER
(— OF REPUGNANCE) UGH
(— OF SURPRISE) HA OW GIP LAW HEIN HUNH LACK LAND LAWK LORD ODSO BABAI HEUGH LAWKS MARRY CRIMINE CRIMINY HEAVENS JUCKIES GORBLIMY GRAMERCY
(— OF TRIUMPH) AH IO GRIG HEUCH HOOCH HURRAH
(BIBLICAL —) SELAH
(IRISH —) ARRA
(PROFANE —) BAN
EXCLAMATION POINT BANG SHOUT SCREAMER
EXCLUDE BAR SHUT SINK CLOSE DEBAR EJECT EXPEL FENCE BANISH DISBAR EXCEPT EXEMPT FORBAR FORBID REJECT BLANKET DEFAULT EXPUNGE FOREBAR FOREIGN OUTTAKE OUTWALL REPULSE RULEOUT SECLUDE SHUTOUT SUSPEND OSTRACIZE
(PREF.) DIS
EXCLUDED EXEMPT FOREIGN
EXCLUDING BAR BUT LESS BARRING
EXCLUSION TABU TABOO OSTRACISM
EXCLUSIVE ALL ONLY RARE SOLE VERY ALONE ELECT WHOLE NARROW SELECT CLANNISH CLIQUISH ENTIRELY RECHERCHE
(— OF) BEFORE
EXCLUSIVELY ALL ONLY ALONE SINGLY ENTIRELY
EXCOGITATE CONSIDER
EXCOMMUNICATE CURSE UNCHURCH
EXCOMMUNICATION BAN CURSE HEREM EXCISION
EX-CONVICT LAG LAGGER
EXCORIATE FLAY GALL SCORE STRIP ABRADE SCATHE SCORCH BLISTER LAMBASTE
EXCREMENT LEE CRAP DIRT DREG DUNG FRASS JAKES SIEGE HOCKEY ORDURE REFUSE VOIDING CROTTELS COLLUVIES
(— OF EARTHWORM) CAST
(— OF FOXES) SCUMBER
(— OF HARES) CROTTELS
(— OF INSECTS) FRASS
(PL.) DEJECTA
(PREF.) COPR(O) MERDI
EXCRESCENCE NOB PIN WEN BURL BURR GALL HORN KNOB KNOT KNUR LUMP SCAB WART FUSEE FUZEE KNURL THORN EXCESS HURTLE MORULA NUBBLE PIMPLE BOLSTER PUSTULE RATTAIL SPINACH CARUNCLE EPITHEMA TUBERCLE
(— ON BIRD'S THROAT) WATTLE
(— ON HORSE'S FOOT) FIG TWITTER
(— ON WHALE'S HEAD) BONNET
(FLESHY —) SARCOMA
(TUBERCULOUS —) WOLF
(PREF.) GANGLI GANGLO
EXCRETA EGESTA
EXCRETE EGEST SWEAT EXCERN SECERN DEFECATE PERSPIRE

EXCRETION SORDES ECRISIS PERISARC
EXCRUCIATE RACK GRIND AGONIZE TORMENT TORTURE
EXCRUCIATING GRINDING
EXCULPATE FREE CLEAR REMIT ACQUIT EXCUSE PARDON ABSOLVE FORGIVE JUSTIFY RELEASE PALLIATE
EXCULPATION EXCUSE
EXCURSION DIP HOP ROW DIET RIDE SAIL SPIN TOUR TRIP ESSAY JAUNT RANGE SALLY START TRAMP AIRING CANTER CRUISE FLIGHT JUNKET OUTING PASEAR RAMBLE SASHAY VAGARY VOYAGE JOURNEY OUTLOPE OUTRIDE OUTROAD CAMPAIGN ESCAPADE
EXCURSIONIST TRIPPER
EXCUSABLE VENIAL
EXCUSE OUT FAIK PLEA ALIBI COLOR GLOSS PLANE REMIT SALVO SCUSE STORY ACQUIT ESSOIN EXEMPT PARDON REASON REFUGE SCONCE SECURE SUNYIE ABSOLVE APARDON APOLOGY CONDONE ESSOIGN EVASION EXCUSAL FORGIVE OFFCOME PRETEXT DISPENSE OCCASION OVERLOOK PALLIATE PRETENCE
(CONSCIENTIOUSLY —) SCRUPLE
EXCUSS SHAKE DISCARD DISCUSS
EXECRABLE BAD CURST CURSED DAMNED HEINOUS ACCURSED DAMNABLE WRETCHED
EXECRATE BAN DAMN ABHOR CURSE DETEST DEVOTE
EXECRATION CURSE ANATHEMA MALEDICTION
EXECUTE DO ACT CUT TOP BURN DASH FILL GIVE HANG HAVE KILL OBEY PASS PLAY SLAY FRAME GANCH LYNCH SCRAG YIELD DESIGN DIRECT EFFECT FINISH FULFIL GARROT GIBBET MANAGE ACHIEVE CONDUCT ENFORCE FULFILL GAROTTE PERFORM STRETCH COMPLETE DISPATCH EXPEDITE PRACTICE PRACTISE
(— BOW) WREATHE
(— POORLY) DUB
(— SUCCESSFULLY) COMPLETE
EXECUTED GIVEN
(— EXQUISITELY) CURIOUS
(— WITH CARE) ACCURATE
(CRUDELY —) DAUBY
EXECUTION GANCH TOUCH EFFECT FACTURE GARROTE HANGING TECHNIC CARRIAGE GARROTTE PRACTICE PERFORMANCE
(— BY BURNING) STAKE
(— BY DROWNING) NOYADE
(— OF WILL) FACTUM
EXECUTIONER BURRIO HEADER TORTOR BUTCHER HANGMAN HEADMAN LOCKMAN CARNIFEX EXECUTOR HEADSMAN CRUCIFIER
EXECUTIVE BOSS DEAN EXEC MAYOR WARDEN CASHIER MANAGER PODESTA PREMIER GOVERNOR OFFICIAL
(— OFFICER) CEO
EXECUTOR DOER AGENT ALBACEA SECUTOR ENFORCER MINISTER
EXEGESIS ANAGOGE ANAGOGY MIDRASH HAGGADAH
EXEMPLAR COPY TYPE MODEL FATHER MIRROR MODULE EIDOLON EXAMPLE PARABLE PATTERN PARADIGM
EXEMPLARY LAUDABLE
EXEMPLIFICATION SOUL SAMPLE CONSTAT EXAMPLE
EXEMPLIFY SAMPLE SATISFY ENSAMPLE MODELIZE
EXEMPT EXON FREE EXEEM EXEME FRANK SEVER SPARE EXPERT FIDATE IMMUNE EXCLUDE RELEASE DISPENSE EXCEPTED PRIVILEGE
(— FROM DEATH) IMMORTAL
(PREF.) IMMUNO
EXEMPTION GRACE CHARTER FREEDOM LIBERTY SWEATER BLOODWIT IMMUNITY IMPUNITY
EXEQUATUR PLACET
EXERCISE ACT AIR DIP PLY URE USE BEAR HAVE DRILL ETUDE EXERT HALMA LATIN LONGE SWEAT AIRING BREATH CAREER EMPLOY EXERCE LESSON MANUAL PARADE PRAXIS PUSHUP SCHOOL AUFGABE BREATHE DISPLAY ENHAUNT JOGGING PROBLEM ACTIVITY EXERTION FORENSIC PALESTRA PRACTICE PRACTISE
(— AUTHORITY) COMMAND
(— CONTROL) BOSS PRESIDE
(— HORSE) BREEZE
(— POWER) RULE
(—S TO REDUCE WEIGHT) SLIMNASTICS
(ACADEMIC —) PRACTICUM
(BRIEF —) THEME
(CAVALRY —) MELEE
(DEVOTIONAL —) ANGELUS
(GYMNASTIC —) PRESSUP
(MARTIAL —) BARRIERS
(MUSICAL —) ETUDE SOLFEGE VOCALISE
(PRACTICE —) DRYRUN
(PRELIMINARY —) WARMUP PROLUSION
(PUNISHMENT —) PENSUM
(REDUCING —S) SLIMNASTICS
(RHYTHMICAL —) MEDAU
(STRONG —) INTENSION
(SYSTEM OF —) AEROBICS
(UNWARRANTED —) STRETCH
(PL.) ALLEGRO ATHLETICS
EXERT DO PLY PUT DRAW EMIT HUMP STIR DRIVE SPEND SWING BESTIR EXTEND PUTOUT REVEAL STRAIN AFFORCE ENFORCE IMPRESS CHARETTE ENDEAVOR EXERCISE
(— A SPELL) TAKE
(— POWER) ACT BEAR
(— PRESSURE) PRESS SQUEEZE
(— TRACTION) HAUL
EXERTING (— POWER) AGENT
EXERTION DINT HEFT BURST ESSAY LABOR NISUS TRIAL WHILE ACTION EFFORT MOTION PINGLE STRESS STRIFE ATTEMPT TROUBLE ENDEAVOR EXERCISE STRUGGLE
(EXCESSIVE —) STRAIN
(STRENUOUS —) HUMP
EXFOLIATE SCALE SPALL SPAWL
EXFOLIATION FURFUR
EXHALATION AURA FUME REEK STEAM BREATH EXPIRY MIASMA HALITUS MALARIA FUMOSITY MEPHITIS
EXHALE CAST EMIT REEK EXUDE STEAM WHIFF EXPIRE BREATHE FURNACE REFLAIR RESPIRE EXHALATE PERSPIRE
EXHALED SFOGATO
EXHAUST DO FAG SAP BEAT BURN COOK COWL EMIT FAIL FLAG FLOG JADE KILL MATE SOAK TIRE TUCK BLAST BREAK CLEAN DRAFT DRAIN EMPTY FORDO GRUEL LEECH PETER SHOOT SPEND SWINK WASTE WEARY ABRADE BETOIL BOTTOM BUGGER EMBOSS FINISH FOREDO HARASS HATTER OVERDO TAIGLE TUCKER BREATHE CONSUME DEPLETE DEPRIVE DRAUGHT EXTRACT FATIGUE OUTWEAR SCOURGE SURREIN TRACHLE WEAROUT DISTRESS EDUCTION EVACUATE FORSPEND FORSWINK FORWEARY OVERWEAR OVERSPEND
EXHAUSTED TAM BEAT DEAD DONE DUNG GONE WEAK WORN BLOWN EMPTY JADED SPENT STANK TIRED BARREN BEATEN BUSHED EFFETE GROGGY MARCID PLAYED TOILED TRAIKY ATTAINT DRAINED EMPTIED FORDONE FORSUNG FORWORN TEDIOUS WHACKED WORNOUT BANKRUPT CONSUMED FOREDONE FOREWORN FORFAIRN FORSPENT FOUGHTEN HARASSED OUTSPENT OVERWORN
(— OF AIR) HIGH
EXHAUSTING ARDUOUS IRKSOME PREYING
EXHAUSTION EXHAUST FATIGUE SELLOUT SOOREYN DISTRESS GONENESS HEATSTROKE PROSTRATION
EXHAUSTIVE FULL MINUTE THOROUGH
EXHIBIT AIR PEN FAIR HAVE SHEW SHOW TURN WEAR CARRY SPORT STAGE BLAZON DEMEAN EVINCE EXPOSE OPPOSE OSTEND PARADE REVEAL APPROVE CONCENE DIORAMA DISPLAY EXPRESS MONSTER PERFORM PRESENT PRODUCE PROJECT PROPOSE TRADUCE BOOKFAIR BRANDISH CONCEIVE DISCLOSE DISCOVER EMBLAZON EVIDENCE FORTHSET MANIFEST SHOWCASE
(— ALARM) GLOFF
(— DOGS) BENCH
(— IN SNARLING) GRIN
EXHIBITION EXPO FAIR SALE SHOW DROLL ENTRY SALON SIGHT ANNUAL PARADE SALARY ACADEMY DISPLAY EXHIBIT PAGEANT PENSION PRESENT SHOWING STAGERY EXERCISE PERFORMANCE
(— OF DOGS) BENCH
(— ON STAGE) STAGERY
(ART —) SALON
(POETICAL —) FLYTE
(PUBLIC —) SPECIES
(RIDING —) CAROUSEL
EXHIBITIONER SERVITOR
EXHIBITIONIST HAM FLASHER HAMFATTER
EXHIBITOR SHOWER
EXHILARANT GOOFBALL
EXHILARATE AMUSE CHEER ELATE ANIMATE ELEVATE ENLIVEN GLADDEN
EXHILARATED RAD GLAD HAPPY HEADY STOKED ELEVATED SPIRITED
EXHILARATING RACY SAPID BREEZY LIVELY
EXHILARATION GAIETY JOLLITY GLADNESS HILARITY
EXHORT URGE WARN CHARM ADHORT ADVISE CHARGE DEHORT ENGAGE INCITE PREACH CAUTION ADMONISH DISSUADE
EXHORTATION ADVICE EXHORT HOMILY COUNSEL PROPHECY PREACHMENT
EXHORTER HORTATOR PREACHER
EXHUME DIG DELVE UNBURY UNTOMB UNEARTH DISINTER EXHUMATE
EXIGENCY NEED PUSH WANT EXIGENT URGENCY JUNCTURE OCCASION PRESSURE
EXIGENT DIRE VITAL URGENT CRITICAL EXACTING PRESSING
EXIGUITY PAUCITY
EXIGUOUS MEAGER MEAGRE
EXILE EXUL POOR RUIN THIN EXPEL GALUT WREAK BANISH DEPORT GALUTH OUTLAW SCANTY WRETCH EXULATE GERSHOM OUTCAST PILGRIM REFUGEE SLENDER DIASPORA FUGITIVE OUTLAWRY RELEGATE OSTRACIZE
(PLACE OF —) ELBA
EXILED FOREIGN FUGITIVE
EXIST AM BE IS ARE LIE COME GROW LIVE MOVE PASS DWELL CONSIST SUBSIST
(— IN FULL SUPPLY) FLOW
EXISTENCE ENS ESSE LIFE SEIN BEING DASEIN ENTITY IDEATE INESSE ESSENCE IDEATUM REALITY ENERGEIA IDENTITY STANDING SURVIVAL PERSONALITY
(— AFTER DEATH) AFTERLIFE
(DULL —) DEATH
(ETERNAL —) SAT
(EVER-CHANGING —) SAMSARA SANSARA
(FIRST —) ORIGIN
(IN —) GOING AROUND EXTANT
(INDEPENDENT —) ASEITY PERSEITY
(PERMANENT —) INHERENCE
(WAKING —) JAGRATA
(PREF.) ONTO
EXISTENT HARD REAL ALIVE BEING ACTUAL EXTANT EXISTING

(— IN DIFFERENT FORMS) ALLOTROPIC
(CONTINUALLY —) STUBBORN
EXISTING GOING ACTUAL EXTANT PRESENT EXISTENT
(— IN NAME ONLY) DUMMY
(SUFF.) ANT ENT
EXIT ISH DOOR GATE VENT GOING ISSUE LEAVE EGRESS EXITUS OUTLET OUTWAY EXITION OUTGATE OUTPORT PASSAGE DEBOUCHE
(HURRIED —) BOUT
EXITE BRACT
EX LIBRIS BOOKPLATE
EXOCYCLIC IRREGULAR
EXODUS EXODY EXITUS FLIGHT HEGIRA HEJIRA EXODIUM
EXON EXEMPT
EXONERATE FREE ALIBI CLEAR ACQUIT EXCUSE EXONER UNLOAD ABSOLVE RELIEVE EXCULPATE
EXOPODITE EXOPOD SQUAMA
EXORABLE PRAYABLE
EXORBITANT STEEP UNDUE ABNORMAL
EXORCISE LAY
EXORCIST BENET
EXORDIUM PREFACE PRELUDE
EXOSKELETON CORSLET CORSELET
EXOSPORIUM EXINE EXTINE EXOSPERM
EXOSTOSIS POROMA SPLINT OSSELET RINGBONE
EXOTIC ALIEN FOREIGN STRANGE ADVENTIVE RECHERCHE
EXOTOSPORE BLAST
EXOTROPIA WALLEYE
EXPAND OPE WAX BLOW BULK FLAN FLUE FOAM GROW HUFF OPEN FARCE FLASH RETCH SPLAY SWELL WIDEN DIDUCE DILATE EXTEND INTEND SPREAD SPROUT UNFOLD UNFURL AMPLIFY BALLOON BLOSSOM BOLSTER BROADEN BURGEON DEVELOP DIFFUSE DISPAND DISPLAY DISTEND EDUCATE ENLARGE EXPANSE EXPLAIN INFLATE STRETCH DISPREAD INCREASE LENGTHEN OUTREACH
(— AS A VESSEL) FLAN
(— FEATHERS) PRIDE
(— INTO PODS) KID
EXPANDED NOWY OPEN OVERT DILATE PATENT SPREAD DILATED SWOLLEN INFLATED PATULENT PATULOUS
EXPANDER EXTENDER
EXPANDING BOSOMY
EXPANSE AREA ROOM BOSOM BURST FIELD REACH TRACT EXTENT LENGTH SPREAD COUNTRY STRETCH DISTANCE EXPANSUM SEPARATE
(— OF ICE) SHEET
(— OF SEA ICE) FIELD
(— OF SPACE) VOID
(— OF WATER) OCEAN
(BROAD —) ACRE MAIN
(FLAT —) LEVEL
(GREAT —) MAIN
(IMMEASURABLE — OF TIME) ETERNITY
(IMMENSE —) OCEAN
(INDEFINITE —) VAGUE
(UNBROKEN —) MASS
(VAST —) SEA
(WIDE —) BREADTH
EXPANSIBILITY ELATER
EXPANSION ALA BULB WING FLUSH SPLAY GROWTH SPREAD ECTASIA ECTASIS EXPANSE HASTULA ACROCYST COQUILLE DIASTOLE DILATION INCREASE SWELLING
(— IN SEEDS) ALA WING
(— OF COBRA'S NECK) HOOD
(— OF DECK) SPONSON
(— OF LEAF-BASE) SPUR
(— OF RIVER) BROAD
(— OF ROADWAY) LAYBY
(FOLIOSE —) LAMINA
(LITURGICAL —) EMBOLISM
EXPANSIVE FREE WIDE BROAD GENIAL ELASTIC LIBERAL GENEROUS SPACIOUS SWELLING
EXPATIATE DWELL DILATE EXPAND SPREAD AMPLIFY BROADEN DESCANT DIFFUSE ENLARGE SATISFY
EXPATRIATE EXILE EXPAT EXPEL BANISH OUTLAW OUTCAST
EXPATRIATION EXILE
EXPECT ASK DEEM HOPE LITE LOOK STAY TEND TROW WAIT WEEN ABIDE AWAIT THINK ATTEND DEMAND INTEND LIPPEN RECKON PRESUME REQUIRE SUPPOSE SUSPECT CALCULATE
(— CONFIDENTLY) TRUST
(— TOO MUCH) OVERWEEN
EXPECTANT ATIP ATIPTOE CHARGED HOPEFUL INCHOATE
EXPECTANTLY AGOG TIPTOE
EXPECTATION HOPE VIEW WAIT WEEN TRUST EXPECT FUTURE ESPEIRE OPINION SUPPOSE THOUGHT WEENING PROSPECT
(CONFIDENT —) TRUST
EXPECTED DUE NATURAL SUPPOSED
EXPECTORANT CINEOL STORAX CINEOLE EMETINE AMMONIAC CREOSOTE GUAIACOL TEREBENE
EXPECTORATE SPIT
EXPECTORATION EMPTYSIS
EXPEDIENCE ARTIFICE
EXPEDIENT FIT WISE ATAJO CRAFT DODGE JOKER KNACK SALVO SHIFT DEVICE RESORT STRING DODGERY POLITIC STOPGAP ARTIFICE RESOURCE DESIRABLE MAKESHIFT
EXPEDITATE LAW
EXPEDITATION LAWING
EXPEDITE HIE EASY FREE HURRY SPEED EXPEDE GREASE HASTEN QUICKEN DISPATCH
EXPEDITION CAMP FARE PLOY ROAD TREK DRAVE HASTE HURRY RANGE SCOUT TRADE SAFARI VOYAGE CARAVAN CRUSADE ENTRADA JOURNEY OUTLOPE SERVICE WARFARE WARPATH COMMANDO HEADHUNT PROGRESS
(FISHING —) DRAVE
(HUNTING —) SAFARI
(MILITARY —) HARKA CRUSADE HOSTING JOURNEY WARPATH
EXPEDITIOUS FAST HASTY QUICK RAPID READY SHORT PROMPT SPEEDY
EXPEL CAN OUT USH BLOW BOLT DRUM DUMP FIRE OUST VOID WARP AVOID CHASE CHECK DEPEL EJECT ERUPT EVICT EXILE KNOCK SPURT BANISH BOUNCE DEBOUT DEPORT DEVOID DISBAR DISOWN OUTPUT OUTRAY REFUSE ABANDON EXCLUDE EXPULSE EXTRUDE OBTRUDE SCRATCH SECLUDE SUSPEND DISLODGE DISPLACE EVACUATE FORJUDGE
(— AIR) COUGH
(— FROM MEMBERSHIP) HAMMER
(— GAS) BELCH
(— SUDDENLY) SLIRT
(PREF.) DIS
EXPEND USE LEND SPEND SPORT WASTE WREAK DEFRAY IMPEND OCCUPY OUTLAY PONDER CONSUME DISPEND EROGATE EXHAUST OVERUSE DISBURSE SQUANDER
EXPENDITURE COST MISE OUTGO PENSE CHARGE OUTLAY EXPENSE OUTFLOW PENSION SPENDING
(— OF ENERGY) EFFORT
EXPENSE EX COST GAFF LOSS BATTA PRICE SUMPT CHARGE DAMAGE GERSUM ONCOST OUTLAY OUTSET AVERAGE OVERHEAD SUMPTURE
(— OF CARRYING) CARRIAGE
(— OF TREAT) SAM
(PL.) BATTA COSTS MISES
EXPENSIVE DEAR HIGH SALT PRICY STEEP STIFF COSTLY LAVISH PRICEY APICIAN LIBERAL THRIFTY
(— IN DIET) APICIAN
EXPERIENCE SEE TRY FEEL FIND GUST HAVE HENT HOLD KNOW LIVE TEST ASSAY EVENT PROOF PROVE SKILL TASTE TRIAL USAGE BEHOLD EXPERT FRAIST ORDEAL SAMPLE SUFFER APPROVE CALVARY CONTACT FEELING FURNACE KNOWING REALIZE SUSTAIN UNDERGO ESCAPADE
(— GOOD OR ILL FORTUNE) SPEED
(— OF INTENSE SUFFERING) CALVARY
(— WITH BITTERNESS) BEAR
(CALAMITOUS —) ADVERSITY
(DRUG —) TRIP
(ENJOYABLE —) GROOVE
(EXCITING —) TRIP
(FIRST —) TIROCINIUM
(HALLUCINATORY —) TRIP FREAKOUT
(HORRIFYING —) NIGHTMARE
(HUMILIATING) PRATFALL
(IRRITATING —) RUB
(ORDINARY —) USE
(PAINFUL —) FIT
(PARTIAL —) GUST
(TASTE —) GUST
(TEDIOUS —) DRAG
(TRYING —) ORDEAL
(UNPLEASANT —) BUMMER MISERY
(VISIONARY —) PHANTOM
(WARNING —) LESSON
EXPERIENCED HAD MET OLD SEEN USED SALTY EXPERT SALTED TRADED ANCIENT PRACTIC THRIVEN VETERAN WEIGHED SEASONED
(— INTENSIVELY) ACUTE
(ACTUALLY —) SPECIOUS
EXPERIENTIAL EMPIRIC
EXPERIMENT SHY TRY TEST ASSAY ESSAY TRIAL ATTEMPT CONTROL
(PREF.) EMPIRICO EMPIRIO
EXPERIMENTAL SAMPLE
(NOT —) STANDARD
EXPERT ACE DAB PRO DEFT FULL GOOD GURU PERT ADEPT CRACK FLASH MAVEN MAVIN READY SHARP SWELL ADROIT ARTIST CLEVER FACILE HABILE KAHUNA MASTER MAYVIN PANDIT PERTLY QUAINT SUBTLE WIZARD ARTISTE ATTACHE CAPABLE DABSTER MEISTER PERFECT PERITUS SKILLED DEXTROUS GAINSOME SKILLFUL SPEEDFUL VIRTUOSO PROFESSED PROFICIENT
(— IN JEWISH LAW) DAYAN
(— LEVEL IN JUDO) DAN
(— ON DRIVING LOGS) LAKER
(BANK —) SHROFF
(GREAT —) ONER
(SCIENTIFIC —) BOFFIN
(PL.) PERITI
(SUFF.) ICIAN
EXPERTISE MOXIE
EXPERTNESS SAVVY SKILL FACILITY HABILITY
EXPIATE ABY SKUG ATONE AVERT ASSOIL RANSOM
EXPIATORY PIACULAR
EXPIRATION END DEATH BREATH EFFLUX ELAPSE EXPIRE EXPIRY
(SPASMODIC —) SNEEZE
EXPIRE DIE END EMIT FALL EXPEL GHOST LAPSE ELAPSE EXHALE INLAIK OUTRUN PERISH RUNOUT
EXPIRED UP DEAD EXPIATE
EXPIRING DYING
EXPIRY ISH CLOSE DEATH EFFLUX
EXPLAIN OPEN REDE SAVE SCAN UNDO WISE AREAD AREED CLEAR GLOSS GLOZE PLANE RECHE SOLVE SPEED TOUCH DEFINE EXPAND EXPLAT EXPONE REMENE RIDDLE UNFOLD ABSOLVE ACCOUNT AMPLIFY CLARIFY COMMENT CONTRUE DECLARE DEVELOP DISCUSS EXHIBIT EXPOUND JUSTIFY RESOLVE CONSTRUE DESCRIBE MANIFEST SIMPLIFY UNPLIGHT UNWONDER
(— BY HYPOTHESIS) SALVE
EXPLAINER EXPONENT
EXPLAINING EXPONENT
EXPLANATION KEY NOTE FARSE GLOSS SALVE SALVO ANSWER CAVEAT ACCOUNT APOLOGY

ADDENDUM EXEGESIS INNUENDO NOTATION SOLUTION
(PRELIMINARY —) PREFACE
EXPLETIVE ACH AND GEE BOSH EGAD GOSH OATH BEGAD MODAL BEHEAR SDEATH TUNKET DAMMISH MORBLEU GOODYEAR GRACIOUS
EXPLICATE OPEN CLEAR EXPAND UNFOLD ACCOUNT EXPLAIN
EXPLICATION CRIB ANALYSIS
EXPLICIT OPEN CLEAR EXACT FIXED PLAIN EXPRESS PRECISE ABSOLUTE DEFINITE IMPLICIT POSITIVE PUNCTUAL SPECIFIC
EXPLICITLY BARELY DIRECT FORMALLY
EXPLODE POP BLOW FIRE BELCH BLAST BURST CRUMP ERUPT GOOFF PLUFF SHOOT SQUIB SPRING BACKFIRE DETONATE DISPLODE
EXPLOIT ACT USE DEED FEAT GEST JEST MILK WORK GESTE GOUGE STUNT PERFORM SUCCESS CHIVALRY PARERGON PROPERTY
(— FINANCIALLY) RIPOFF
(— SUCCESSFULLY) PARLAY
EXPLOITATION RIPOFF
EXPLOITER KULAK
EXPLORATION SPY PROBE SEARCH EXPLORE
(— OF CAVES) SPELEOLOGY
EXPLORATORY FRONTIER PROBATIVE PROBATORY
EXPLORE DO DIP MAP SPY DIVE DRAG FEEL VIEW CHART COAST DELVE RANGE SCOUT SOUND SEARCH EXAMINE PALPATE BOTANIZE DISCOVER
(— CAVES) SPELUNK
(— FOR MINERALS) PROSPECT
EXPLORER CAVEMAN PIONEER COLUMBUS
AMERICAN BOYD BYRD COOK GRAY HALL KANE LONG PIKE BEEBE CLARK FIALA GOULD HAYES JAMES LEWIS MUSIL NILES PEARY RONNE AKELEY ASHLEY BRYANT CARVER CATLIN COLTER DELONG EKLUND GIMBEL GREELY HENSON HERVEY LUMMIS RAINEY WILKES AGASSIZ ANDREWS BALCHEN BALDWIN BURNHAM FREMONT POULTER STANLEY VERRILL WELLMAN WORKMAN BRAINARD BRIDGMAN LOCKWOOD MELVILLE SCHWATKA ELLSWORTH MACMILLAN DANENHOWER HUNTINGTON HALLIBURTON
AUSTRALIAN WILLS MAWSON STUART FORREST KENNEDY LINDSAY WILKINS BERNACCHI
AUSTRIAN HUGEL PAYER GLASER BAUMANN PAULITSCHKE
BELGIAN GERLACHE
CANADIAN MACKAY JOLLIET SIMPSON BARTLETT PALLISER IBERVILLE VINCENNES STEFANSSON
COLOMBIAN REYES
DANISH BOCK HOLM KOCH FREUCHEN MIKKELSEN RASMUSSEN
DUTCH TASMAN NIEUWENHUIS
ENGLISH BACK BASS BENT BYNG COOK EYRE BAKER BATES BRUCE DAVYS EVANS FUCHS GRANT OATES PARRY SCOTT SPEKE STURT YOUNG BAILEY BURTON CONDER GROGAN HEARNE HOWITT LANDER MAWSON OSBORN PHILBY SABINE WILSON CAMERON CHESNEY DAMPIER DEWINDT GREGORY HOLDICH JACKSON WEDDELL WHYMPER WICKHAM FLINDERS FRANKLIN GRENFELL JOHNSTON SCORESBY ALEXANDER VANCOUVER WARBURTON INGLEFIELD MCCLINTOCK SCHOMBURGK SHACKLETON LIVINGSTONE YOUNGHUSBAND
FRENCH BONIN MONTS BINGER BRAZZA CALLIE DULUTH GENTIL HAARDT ABBADIE CARTIER CRAMPEL CREVAUX FOUREAU GARNIER LASALLE NICOLET BONVALOT COUDREAU HENNEPIN MARCHAND RADISSON CAILLIAUD CHAMPLAIN IBERVILLE MARQUETTE VINCENNES
GERMAN EMIN LENZ BARTH PFEIL POGGE REISS VOGEL DECKEN FLEGEL JUNKER PETERS ROHLFS FISCHER NEUWIED NIEBUHR OVERWEG WEGENER DENHARDT FILCHNER FRANCOIS HUMBOLDT KOLDEWEY KOTZEBUE WISSMANN FEDERMANN GUSSFELDT WEYPRECHT LEICHHARDT SCHLAGINTWEIT
ICELANDIC ERICSON
IRISH BURKE SHACKLETON
ITALIAN ZENO CABOT CAGNI GESSI CASATI NOBILE ABRUZZI BELZONI CODAZZI FILIPPI PIAGGIA ALBERTIS ANTINORI BECCARIA COLUMBUS CADAMOSTO VERRAZANO SCHIAPARELLI
NEW ZEALAND HAAST HILLARY
NORWEGIAN ASTRUP NANSEN WISTING AMUNDSEN JOHANSEN SVERDRUP HEYERDAHL JOHANNESEN BORCHGREVINK
PORTUGUESE CABRAL DAGAMA CABRILLO COVILHAO MAGELLAN FERNANDES
RUSSIAN TOLL PAPANIN POTANIN WRANGEL PRZHEVALSKI BELLINGSHAUSEN
SCOTTISH RAE PARK ROSS BRUCE LAING LAIRD BAIKIE CADELL FORBES THOMSON MITCHELL MACKENZIE CLAPPERTON LIVINGSTONE
SPANISH ANZA OJEDA AYLLON BALBOA CABEZA CORTES DESOTO AGUIRRE ALARCON CORDOBA MENDOZA PIZARRO BASTIDAS CARDENAS CORONADO GRIJALVA ORELLANA VIZCAINO ESCALANTE ESTAVANICO
SWEDISH HEDIN ANDREE NATHORST PALANDER ANDERSSON NORDENSKJOLD
SWISS BODMER PICCARD MUNZINGER
EXPLOSION POP BANG BLOW BLAST BURST CRUMP SALVO BLOWUP BOUNCE REPORT PLOSION INCIDENT OUTBURST
(FUEL —) BACKFIRE
(SLIGHT —) PLUFF
EXPLOSIVE EGG TNT MINE AMVIS AMATOL JOVITE LIMPET POWDER TETRYL TONITE TORPEX TOUCHY TRITON ABELITE AMMONAL AZOTINE DUNNITE LIGNOSE LYDDITE PLOSIVE PRIMING PUDDING SHIMOSE THORITE AMMONITE CHEDDITE DYNAMITE ECRASITE ERUPTIVE GELATINE MAXIMITE MELINITE PYROLITE ROBURITE SABULITE SAXONITE SECURITE VOLATILE RACKAROCK SAMSONITE
(— COMPOUND) TNT
(CHARGE OF —) TULIP RESPONDER
(NOT —) SOFT
EXPONENT INDEX POWER
(SUFF.) ICIAN
EXPORT OUTCARRY
(— HERRING) KLONDIKE
EXPORTATION EXPORT OUTPORT
EXPOSE AIR BARE GIVE OPEN RISK SHOW STRIP BEWRAY DEBUNK DETECT EXPONE GIBBET OBJECT OPPOSE REVEAL UNHUSK UNMASK DISPLAY EXHIBIT EXPOUND PILLORY PROPINE PUBLISH SUBJECT UNCOVER UNEARTH UNTRUSS BRANDISH DISCLOSE DISCOVER MUCKRAKE RIDICULE SATIRIZE UNCLOTHE UNSHROUD
(— FOR BLEACHING) CROFT
(— INDECENTLY) FLASH
(— ORE) HUSH
(— PLAYING CARD) BURN
(— SELF TO) WAGE
(— SUDDENLY) FLASH
(— TO AIR) AERATE
(— TO ATTENTION) PARADE
(— TO DANGER) JUMP COMMIT SUBMIT
(— TO FUMES) FUMIGATE
(— TO HAZARD) RISK
(— TO HEAT) AIR
(— TO INFAMY) GIBBET
(— TO MOISTURE) RET
(— TO RADIATION) PUMP
(— TO SCORN) PILLORY
(— TO SULFUR DIOXIDE) STOVE
(— TO SUN) INSOLATE SOLARIZE
(— TO SUN AND AIR) FIELD
EXPOSED AIRY BARE OPEN BLEAK LIABLE PUBLIC UNSAFE SUBJECT VEILLESS
(— TO) AGAINST
(— TO DANGER) INSECURE
EXPOSITION EXPO FAIR GECK SHOW ZEND TRACT APERCU EXPOSE METHOD SURVEY ACCOUNT EXPOSAL MIDRASH ANALYSIS EXEGESIS EXPOSURE EXTHESIS HAGGADAH TREATISE
(— OF FEAST) SYNAXARY
EXPOSITORY EXEGETIC
EXPOSTULATE ARGUE OBJECT DISCUSS EXAMINE PROTEST
EXPOSTULATION PROTEST
EXPOSURE ASPECT EXPOSE EXPOSAL FLASHING FRONTAGE PROSPECT
(— OF CARDS) SPREAD
(— OF KING) CHECK
(— TO AIR) AERATE AIRING
(BODY —) FLASH
(PHOTOGRAPHIC —) SHOT
(PUBLIC —) NOTORIETY
EXPOUND OPEN REDE UNDO GLOZE SENSE TREAT DEFINE EXPONE EXPOSE COMMENT DEVELOP DISCUSS EXPLAIN EXPOSIT EXPRESS CONSTRUE SIMPLIFY PHILOSOPHIZE
(— SCRIPTURES) PROPHESY
EXPOUNDER MUFTI MULLAH SCRIBE EXPRESS EXPONENT HERMETIC
(— OF THEORY) ALFAQUI PHILOSOPHER
EXPRESS AIR BID PUT SAY CAST EMIT FAST PASS POST VENT COUCH EMOTE FRAME OPINE SPEAK STATE UTTER VOICE WIELD BROACH DEMEAN DENOTE DIRECT EVINCE IMPORT PHRASE ABREACT BREATHE DECLARE DICTATE EXPOUND EXPREME TESTIFY DEFINITE DESCRIBE DISPATCH EXPLICIT INTIMATE MANIFEST
(— APPROVAL) AGREE ACCEDE APPLAUD
(— AS LANGUAGE) LAY
(— AT LENGTH) EXPAND
(— A VIEW) OPINE
(— BY GESTURE) BECK
(— BY LAUGHTER) LAUGH
(— CONCERN) CLUCK
(— DISAPPROVAL) BOO CHIDE DECRY GROAN CATCALL
(— DISDAIN) TUT
(— EFFERVESCENTLY) CHORTLE
(— FOLLY) EXPAND
(— GRATITUDE) THANK AGGRATE
(— GRIEF) DEPLORE
(— INDIRECTLY) IMPLY
(— IN OTHER WORDS) REDUCE PARAPHRASE
(— IN WORDS) SAY DRAW SPEAK PHRASE
(— NUMERICALLY) EVALUATE
(— ONE'S FEELINGS) FLOW
(— SORROW) LAMENT COMPLAIN
(— WILLINGNESS) CONSENT
(NOT AN —) LOCAL
EXPRESSION DIT HIT SAY CAST EUGE FACE FORM MIEN POSE SHOW SIGN TERM VULT WORD ADIEU GLIFF IDIOM SNEER TOKEN VOICE BYWORD DILOGY DIVERB EFFECT FACIES ORACLE PHRASE SPEECH SYMBOL COMMENT DESCANT EPITHET EXPRESS GRIMACE ALLEGORY AUSDRUCK DANICISM FELICITY LACONISM MONOMIAL
(— IN FEW WORDS) BREVITY
(— OF ANNOYANCE) SOH
(— OF APPROVAL) EUGE PLACET
(— OF ASSENT) CONTENT
(— OF BEAUTY) ART
(— OF CHOICE) VOTE
(— OF CONTEMPT) COBLOAF

(— OF DELIGHT) WHEE
(— OF DISPLEASURE) FROWN
(— OF DISTASTE) FACE
(— OF HOMAGE) OVATION
(— OF JOY) GREETING
(— OF OPINION) EDITORIAL
(— OF RESPECT) DUTY
(— OF SADNESS) SHADE
(— OF SCORN) GECK
(— OF SINGLE IDEA) RHEME
(APT —) FELICITY
(CHEMICAL —) EQUATION
(COMMONPLACE —) BROMIDE
(CORRECT —) SUMPSIMUS
(CURT —) LACONIC
(FACIAL —) GRIN CHEER SCOWL SMILE
(HACKNEYED —) CLICHE
(HIGH-FLOWN —) EUPHUISM
(INCONGRUOUS —) BULL
(LOUD —) CLAMOR
(MATHEMATICAL —) INDEX SERIES BINOMIAL EQUATION FUNCTION INTEGRAL
(MOCKING —) SCOFF
(MOMENTARY —) SHADE
(PECULIAR —) IDIOM
(PET —) CANT
(PUERILE —) BOYISM
(SARCASTIC —) GIBE JIBE
(SERIOUS —) EARNEST
(SINCERE —) CANDOR
(SYMBOLIC —) FORMULA
(TENDER —) LANGUISH
(TRITE —) CLICHE
(UNRESTRAINED —) EFFUSION
(VERBAL —) LETTER
(VOCAL —) TONE
(VULGAR —) SOLECISM
(WISE —) ORACLE
(SUFF.) LOG(ER)(IA)(IAN)(IC)(ICAL)(IST)(UE)(Y)

EXPRESSIONLESS BLANK STONY GLASSY LEADEN SODDEN VACANT WOODEN TONELESS
EXPRESSIVE POETIC TONGUED ELOQUENT EMPHATIC SPEAKING
EXPRESSIVENESS DICTION DELICACY TOURNURE ELOQUENCE
EXPRESSLY NAMELY EXPRESS PRESSLY FORMALLY
EXPRESSWAY FREEWAY SPEEDWAY
EXPROBATE CENSURE UPBRAID
EXPULSION EXILE BOUNCE OUSTER BANNIMUS EJECTION EXCISION
(— OF SPORES) ABJECTION
EXPUNGE BLOT DELE ERASE SLASH CANCEL DELETE EFFACE EXCISE SCRAPE DESTROY SCRATCH DISPUNGE
EXPURGATE GELD PURGE CASTRATE
EXPURGATION BOWDLERISM
EXQUISITE FOP DUDE FINE NICE PERT PINK RARE DANDY EXACT CHOICE DAINTY CAREFUL ELEGANT GEMLIKE PERFECT REFINED AFFECTED DELICATE ETHEREAL MACARONI RECHERCHE
EXQUISITELY CHOICELY
EXSCIND CUT SEVER EXCISE
EXTANT ALIVE BEING LIVING VISIBLE EXISTING MANIFEST
(PREF.) NEO
EXTEMPORE SUDDEN OFFHAND IMPROVISO
EXTEMPORIZE ADLIB
EXTEND GO EKE LIE RUN BEAR BUSH COME DATE DRAW GROW LAST OPEN PASS PUSH RISE ROLL SPAN SPIN BREDE BULGE CARRY COVER FARCE REACH RENEW RETCH SEIZE SHOOT STENT VERGE WIDEN AMOUNT DEEPEN DEPLOY DILATE EXPAND INTEND OUTLIE SPREAD SPRING STRAIN STREAK THRUST TRENCH AMPLIFY BROADEN DIFFUSE DISPLAY DISTEND ENLARGE OVERLAP OVERRUN PORRECT PORTEND PRODUCE PROFFER PROJECT PROLONG PROMOTE PROTEND RADIATE STRETCH CONTINUE ELONGATE INCREASE LENGTHEN OUTREACH PROROGUE PROTRACT PROTRUDE OUTSPREAD PROPAGATE OUTSTRETCH
(— ACTIVITIES) BRANCH
(— AROUND) GIRTH
(— HAND) RAX
(— IN SPACE) DURE
(— IRREGULARLY) TRAIL
(— OVER) SPAN COVER CROSS CONTAIN OVERLAP OVERRIDE
(— SAIL) SHEET
(— THE FRONT) DEPLOY
(— TO) LINE REACH
EXTENDED FAT LONG OPEN BROAD EXTENT SPREAD EXTENSE LENGTHY PROLATE SPLAYED EXPANDED INTENDED
(PREF.) MEG(A) MEGAL(O)
EXTENDER INERT FILLER LIGNIN
EXTENDING BROAD
(— OVER) ASTRIDE
EXTENSION ARM EKE ELL AREA CAPE LIMB SCOPE POCKET SATTVA SPHERE SPREAD BREADTH STRETCH ADDENDUM ADDITION DURATION INCREASE PROTENSE
(— OF BUILDING MATERIAL) APRON
(— OF CREDIT) DATING
(— OF MINERAL VEIN) FLAT
(— OF RACE TRACK) CHUTE SHUTE
(— OF SHELL) LAPPET
(— OF TIME) RESPITE
(— OF WAGON FRAME) THRIPPLE
(BALLET —) BATTEMENT
EXTENSIVE HUGE VAST WIDE AMPLE BROAD LARGE EXTENSE IMMENSE EXPANDED FARFLUNG INFINITE SPACIOUS SWEEPING
EXTENT DUE RUN TAX AREA BODY BULK DEAL GAGE LEVY PASS SIZE WRIT AMBIT DEPTH FIELD GAUGE LIMIT RANGE REACH SCOPE SPACE STENT SWEEP TRACK AMOUNT ASSIZE ATTACK DEGREE LENGTH SPREAD STREEK ACREAGE ASSAULT BREADTH COMPASS CONTENT EXPANSE PURVIEW SEIZURE STRETCH VARIETY DISTANCE INCREASE LATITUDE OUTREACH QUANTITY STRAIGHT
(— OF FRONT) FRONTAGE
(— OF JURISDICTION) VERGE
(— OF LAND) HEIGHT CONTINENT
(— OF SPACE) ROOM
(— OF TIME) SPACE
(BROAD —) SWEEP MAGNITUDE
(GREATEST —) MAX MAXIMUM
(RELATIVE —) SCALE
(SOME —) BIT
(UNLIMITED —) INFINITY
(UTMOST —) FULL
(VAST —) DEEP
(VERTICAL —) ALTITUDE
EXTENTION (— OF LETTER) TAIL
EXTENUATE THIN GLOZE MINCE EXCUSE LESSEN SOOTHE WEAKEN DIMINISH PALLIATE
EXTERIOR CRUST ECTAD ECTAL OUTER SHELL EXTERN OUTSIDE OUTWARD SURFACE EXOTERIC EXTERNAL OUTLYING
(PREF.) OUT
EXTERMINATE WIPE EXPEL UPROOT ABOLISH DESTROY
EXTERMINATION (RACIAL —) GENOCIDE
EXTERNAL OUT OUTER EXTERN OUTSIDE OUTWARD STRANGE EXOTERIC EXTERIOR INCIDENT PHYSICAL PERIPHERAL
(PREF.) ECT(O) OUT
EXTERNALITY OUTNESS
EXTERNALIZE OBJECTIFY
EXTERNALLY OUTWARD WITHOUT
EXTINCT DEAD BYGONE DEFUNCT QUENCHED
(— MAN) KANJERA
(PREF.) NECR(O)
EXTINCTION DOOM FINE DEATH EXPIRY DELETION
EXTINGUISH OUT DAMP DOUT REDD STUB ANNUL CHOKE CRUSH DINCH DOUSE DOWSE DROWN QUELL REPEL SLAKE SNUFF STAMP ASLAKE QUENCH STANCH STIFLE ABOLISH BLANKET DESTROY ECLIPSE EXPIATE EXTINCT OBSCURE OPPRESS SLOCKEN STAUNCH SUPPRESS
(— BY CRUSHING) DINCH
(— CIGARETTE) SNUB
EXTINGUISHED OUT DEAD EXTINCT
EXTINGUISHER DOUTER STAUNCH BACKPACK QUENCHER STANCHER
EXTIRPATE DELE ROOT STUB ERASE EXPEL STAMP STOCK EXCISE EXTIRP UPROOT DESTROY EXSCIND OUTROOT SUPPLANT
EXTIRPATION ROOTAGE EXCISION
EXTOL CRY FETE HYMN LAUD BLESS CRACK EXALT KUDOS ROOSE SPEAK EXTOLL PRAISE ADVANCE APPLAUD COLLAUD COMMEND ELEVATE ENHANCE GLORIFY MAGNIFY RESOUND UPRAISE EMBLAZON EULOGIZE PROCLAIM
EXTOLMENT PRECONY
EXTORT MILK PEEL PILL RAMP BLEED BRIBE EDUCE EXACT FORCE PINCH WREST WRING COMPEL ELICIT SPONGE STRAIN WRENCH WRITHE EXTRACT OUTWREST
EXTORTION CHOUT GOUGE EXTORT HOLDUP SCOTAL BRIBERY PILLAGE CHANTAGE EXACTION RAPACITY SHAKEDOWN
EXTORTIONATE HARD CRIMINAL GRINDING
EXTORTIONER BRIBER POLLER SHAVER BLEEDER VAMPIRE
EXTORTIONIST POLLER
EXTRA ODD GASH MORE ORRA OVER PLUS ADDED SPARE SPECIAL SURPLUS SUPERIOR LAGNIAPPE
(PREF.) HYPER SUPER
EXTRACT DIG PRY CITE COPY DRAW KINO KOLA MILK PULL SOAK ANIMA BLEED CUTCH DRAFT EDUCE ELUTE EXACT KUTCH KYPOO QUOTE RENES RUSOT SCRAP STEEP WRING CORTIN CURARE DECOCT DEDUCE DERIVE DEWTRY DISTIL ELICIT ELIXIR EVULSE EXTORT GOBBET GUACIN MULIUM OVARIN REMOVE RENDER RUSWUT TRIPOS UZARON ABORTIN AMALTAS ARCANUM CATECHU DESCENT DISTILL DRAUGHT ERGOTIN ESSENCE ESTREAT EXCERPT EXHAUST FUMARIA INTRAIT LIMBECK MONESIA PASSEWA SUMMARY VANILLA ACETRACT AMBRETTE GINGERIN HYPERNIC INFUSION LICORICE PERICOPE SEPARATE TIKITIKI TINCTURE WITHDRAW
(— BY BOILING) DECOCT ELIXATE
(— BY DIGGING) GRUB
(— DATA FROM COMPUTER) READ
(— FORCIBLY) MULCT EVULSE
(— FROM ACACIA) KATH CASHOO CATECHU
(— FROM BERBERIS) RUSOT RUSWUT
(— OF BARK) EUONYMIN
(— OF GINGER) JAKE JAKEY
(— ORE) STOPE
(— WITH LIQUID) LEACH
(ALOE —) ORCIN ORCINOL
(TANNING —) AMALTAS
EXTRACTION KIN BIRTH BROOD STOCK ORIGIN DESCENT EDITION ESSENCE EXTRACT EXTREAT BREEDING TINCTURE
(— OF ROOTS) EVOLUTION
(— OF STEAM) BLEEDING
EXTRACTIVE AGAR BANG BHANG AMAROID CARAGEEN
EXTRACTOR JUICER
EXTRADITE BANISH
EXTRANEOUS ALIEN OUTER EXOTIC FOREIGN OUTLYING SPURIOUS
EXTRAORDINARILY BYOUS
EXTRAORDINARY ODD FREM ONCO RARE BYOUS ENORM SMASH DAMNED EXEMPT MIGHTY RAGING SIGNAL AWESOME CORKING CURIOUS HUMMING NOTABLE SPECIAL STRANGE UNUSUAL ABNORMAL ESPECIAL EXIMIOUS FORINSEC FRABJOUS SINGULAR SMASHING UNCOMMON PHENOMINAL PRODIGIOUS
EXTRARETINAL PAROPTIC
EXTRATERRESTRIAL ALIEN

EXTRAVAGANCE CAMP FRILL PRIDE WASTE LUXURY EXPENSE RAMPANCY SQUANDER UNTHRIFT WILDNESS PROFUSION SATURNALIA
(MENTAL —) MADNESS
EXTRAVAGANT MAD HIGH LUSH WILD FANCY FISHY FOLLE LARGE OUTRE COSTLY GOTHIC HEROIC LAVISH SHRILL WANTON BAROQUE BIZARRE COSTLEW FANATIC FLAMING FURIOUS NIMIOUS PROFUSE RAMPANT VAGRANT INSOLENT PRODIGAL RECKLESS ROMANTIC UNTHRIFT WANDERER WASTEFUL BOMBASTIC PROFLIGATE
EXTRAVAGANTLY LARGE
EXTRAVAGANZA FEERIE
EXTRAVAGATION VIBEX
EXTRAVASATION EFFUSION
EXTREME NTH BLUE DEEP DIRE HIGH LAST RANK SORE VILE ACUTE BLACK CLOSE CRUEL DENSE DIZZY FINAL GREAT LIMIT PITCH STEEP ULTRA UNDUE UTTER ARDENT ARRANT BRAZEN DEADLY FAROUT FIERCE HEROIC LENGTH MORTAL SAVAGE SEVERE STRONG UTMOST WOUNDY ABYSMAL DRASTIC FEARFUL FORWARD FRANTIC HOWLING INTENSE OUTWARD PROFUSE RADICAL SURFEIT VICIOUS VIOLENT ALMIGHTY DEVILISH DREADFUL EGYPTIAN ENORMOUS FABULOUS FARTHEST GREATEST MERCIFUL SPENDFUL TERRIBLE TERRIFIC ULTIMATE EXQUISITE
(NOT —) SWEET
(TO THE —) INSPADES
(PL.) PASO
(PREF.) ACR(O) ARCH
EXTREMELY SO BIG DOG TOO WAY BONE DEAD EVER FULL MAIN RANK SELI THAT UNCO VERY AWFUL BLACK BULLY BYOUS CRAZY CRUEL EXTRA HEAPS RIGHT SELLE SOWAN SUPER BITTER DAMNED DEADLY DEUCED HIGHLY MIGHTY NATION POISON SORELY SURELY UNCOLY APLENTY AWFULLY BOILING CRUELLY EXTREME GALLOWS HOPPING INNERLY SOPPING STAVING ALMIGHTY ENORMOUS MORTALLY PRECIOUS PROPERLY
EXTREMISM JACOBINISM
EXTREMIST CRAZY ULTRA JACOBIN RADICAL SANSCULOTTE
EXTREMITY END TIP HEAD NEED PUSH TAIL CLOSE LIMIT SHIFT START VERGE BORDER FINGER EXIGENT EXTREME ACROSTIC ALTITUDE DISASTER JUNCTURE OUTRANCE TERMINAL
(— OF MOON) HORN
(— OF TENDRIL) HOLDFAST
(— OF TOOTH ROOT) APEX
(HORSE'S —) POINT
(REMOTEST —) CORNER
(PREF.) ACR(O)
EXTRICATE FREE HELP WIND CLEAR LOOSE RESCUE SQUIRM OUTWIND EXPEDITE LIBERATE UNTANGLE
(— ONESELF) WANGLE
EXTRINSIC ALIEN EVERY FOREIGN OUTWARD EXTERNAL OUTLYING
EXTROVERT SYNTONIC
EXTRUDE BEAR SPEW EJECT EXPEL SHOOT PROJECT PROTRUDE
EXUBERANCE BEANS PRICE EXCESS LUXURY PLENTY ABANDON LAUGHTER OVERFLOW RAMPANCY
EXUBERANT RANK BOUNCY FEISTY LAVISH COPIOUS FERTILE GLOWING PROFUSE RAMPANT EFFUSIVE
EXUDATE GUM SPEW SPUE MANNA DIKAMALI GUAIACUM HONEYDEW SARCOCOL
EXUDATION DIP GUM LAC SAP TAR BALM KINO COPAL PITCH RESIN ROSIN SUDOR ULMIN CHARAS MASTIC SANIES CHURRUS GALIPOT MOCHRAS SPEWING BLEEDING EXUDENCE LAITANCE MOISTURE
EXUDE GUM DRIP EMIT OOZE REEK SPEW BLEED STILL SWEAT EXTILL STRAIN STREAM EXUDATE GUTTATE SCREEVE SECRETE SWELTER PERSPIRE
EXULT JOY CROW LEAP BOAST GLOAT GLORY INSULT SPRING MAFFICK REJOICE TRIUMPH
EXULTANT PROUD ELATED PRIDEFUL
EXULTATION JOY GLEE PAEAN OVATION RAPTURE
EXULTING EXULTANT JUBILANT
EXUVIATE MOLT
EYALET VILLAYET
EYAS NESTLING
EYE O EE HE ORB SPY DISC GAZE GLIM LAMP LOOP MIEN OEIL OGLE SCAN UVEA VIEW GLARE GLASS GLENE NAVEL OPTIC SENSE SHANK SIGHT TOISE WATCH BEHOLD COLLAR EUCONE EYELET GOGGLE OCULAR OCULUS OILLET PEEPER POPEYE REGARD ROLLER SHINER STEMMA VISION WINDOW WINKER BLINKER EUCONIC EXOCONE EYEBALL EYEHOLE OBSERVE OCELLUS PIERCER PIGSNEY PINKANY PINKENY SENSORY WITNESS LATCHING NOISETTE OMMATEUM RECEPTOR
(— AMOROUSLY) OGLE
(— DISEASE) STYE PINKEYE
(— FORMED BY ROPE) TONGUE
(— IN BIGHT) COLLAR
(— IN EGYPTIAN SYMBOLISM) UTA
(— MAKEUP) KOHL MASCARA
(— MOVEMENT) REM
(— OF BEAN) HILUM
(— OF CAMERA) LENS
(— OF FRUIT) NOSE
(— OF HINGE) GUDGEON
(— OF INSECT) STEMMA
(— OF POTATO) BUD
(— OF RA) SEKHET
(— SORENESS) LIPPITUDE
(BLACK —) KEEK MOUSE SHINER
(EVIL —) DROCHUIL MALOCCHIO
(JERKY — MOVEMENT) SACCADE
(KIND OF —) RIB LAZY
(METAL —) HONDA
(PART OF —) IRIS LENS FOVEA PUPIL CORNEA MACULA SCLERA CHAMBER CHOROID LIGAMENT CONJUNCTIVA
(PRIVATE —) GUMSHOE
(PL.) EEN EES NIE YEN YES EYNE LAMPS LIGHTS SEEING GOGGLES KEEKERS GLAZIERS GLIMMERS
(PREF.) OCELLI OCUL(I)(O) OMMA(TO) OPHTHALM(O) OPTI(CO) OPTO
(SUFF.) OMMA OPHTHALMA OPHTHALMUS OPIS OPS
(DEFECT OR CONDITION OF —) OPE OPIA OPIC OPIS OPS OPY
EYEBALL EYE BALL GLASS GLOBE
(— MOVEMENT) VERGENCE
(PREF.) OPHTHALM(O)
EYEBOLT SPRIG RINGBOLT
(INTERLOCKING —S) SNIBEL
EYEBRIGHT EYEWORT EUPHRASY
EYEBROW BREE BROW EEBREE WINBROW WRIGGLE
EYE-CATCHING BOLD
EYE-CORNER
(PREF.) CANTH(O)
EYECUP EYEGLASS
EYED
(SUFF.) OPIS OPS
EYEGLASS QUIZ NIPPER MONOCLE
EYEGLASSES GLIMS SPECS LENSES GLASSES LORGNON NIPPERS BIFOCALS
EYEHOLE EYELET EYEPIT
EYELASH BREE LASH CILIUM WINKER EYEBREE
(LOSS OF —S) MADAROSIS
(PL.) CILIA EAVES
(PREF.) CILI(I)(O)
EYELET MAIL PINK OELET AGRAFE OILLET POUNCE AGRAFFE CRINGLE GROMMET PEEPHOLE
EYELID HAW LID BREE WINDOW EYEBREE PALPEBRA
(PL.) EAVES
(PREF.) BLEPHAR(O) CILI(I)(O)
(SUFF.) BLEPHARON CIL
EYEPIECE OCULAR EYEGLASS
(— OF TELESCOPE) POWER
EYESHADE VISOR OPAQUE
EYESHOT RANGE REACH EYESIGHT
EYESIGHT VIEW LIGHT SIGHT
EYE SOCKET ORBIT
EYESORE DESIGHT
EYESPOT EYEDOT STIGMA EYEHOLE OCELLUS EYEPOINT
EYESTALK STIPES
EYETOOTH CUSPID DOGTOOTH
EYEWASH COLLYRIE EYEWATER COLLYRIUM
EYING ESPIAL
EYOT AIT EIGHT ISLET
EYRE AIR ITER
EZBAI (SON OF —) NAARAI
EZBON (FATHER OF —) GAD BELA
EZEKIEL (FATHER OF —) BUZI
EZER (FATHER OF —) EPHRAIM
(SON OF —) HUSHAH
EZRA (SON OF —) EPHER
EZRI (FATHER OF —) CHELUB

F

F EF FF EFF FOX DIGAMMA FOXTROT
FABA VICIA
FABLE MYTH TALE FEIGN STORY LEGEND TRIFLE FICTION PARABLE POETIZE UNTRUTH ALLEGORY APOLOGUE FABULATE FABULIZE
(— OF GOLD COAST) NANCY
(MORAL —) EMBLEM
(PREF.) MYTHO
FABRIC ABA BAN ACCA CORD DUCK GOLD GROS HAIR HUCK IKAT SILK SUSI TAPA TARS TUKE BATIK CHECK CREPE DHOTI DOBBY DYNEL FANCY GAZAR MOIRE NINON PRINT RUMAL SCRIM SPLIT STUFF SUPER SURAH SURAT TABBY TAMMY TARSE TERRY TEWKE TULLE TWEED TWILL UNION VICHY VOILE WEAVE WIGAN WOVEN AGARIC ALACHA BENGAL BROCHE BYSSUS CAFFOY CARPET COTTON CREPON CYPRUS DACRON DAMASK DIAPER DOBBIE EPONGE ESTRON FLEECE HARDEN LAPPET LUSTER LUSTRE MARBLE MASHRU MURREY PLISSE POODLE SENNIT STRIPE TAMINY TANJIB TARTAN TRICOT TUSSAH VELURE VELVET WADMAL WINCEY ZENANA ACETATE ALEPINE ALLOVER BANDALA BANDING BELTING BEWPERS BINDING BUCKRAM CANILLE CHALLIS CHEKMAK CHIFFON CYPRESS DAMASSE DOESKIN DRABBET EDIFICE ELASTIC EPINGLE FACONNE FISHNET FUSTIAN MIXTURE MORELLA ORGANZA PAISLEY PLUMBET RASCHEL SAYETTE SEGATHY SILESIA SUITING TABARET TABINET TAFFETA TEXTILE TIFFANY VESSETS AGABANEE BARRACAN BOCASINE BOURETTE BROCATEL CAMELINE CANNELLE CASEMENT CHAMBRAY CRETONNE DIAMANTE DUCHESSE FIBRANNE HAIRLINE HANDMADE HARATEEN JACQUARD KNITTING LUSTRINE MATERIAL METALLIC MOLESKIN OSNABURG SHANTUNG SHIRTING SICILIAN SKIRTING SWANSKIN TAPESTRY TARLATAN VALENCIA POINTELLE VELVETEEN
(— CLOSURE) VELCRO
(— CONTAINING GOLD OR SILVER THREAD) ACCA TASH TASS KINCOB
(— FOR STIFFENING) WIGAN
(— OF TWO OR MORE MATERIALS) UNION
(— RESEMBLING TOWELING) AGARIC
(— WITH INWOVEN SCENES) ARRAS
(ABSORBENT —) HUCK
(BROCADED —) LAME LAMPAS
(CARPET —) DURRIE
(COARSE —) TAT BAFT CRASH HAIRE DUFFEL RATINE STAMIN BAGGING BOCKING DRABBET SACKING STAMMEL DAGSWAIN FIBRANNE
(CORDED —) REP PIQUE DUCAPE POPLIN OTTOMAN BENGALINE
(COTTON —) CREA DUCK JEAN LENO LINO SUSI BAIZE BASIN DENIM DRILL RUMAL SUPER SWISS VICHY WIGAN BURRAH CALICO CANVAS CATGUT CHILLO CHINTZ COUTIL COVERT DIMITY MADRAS MUSLIN PENANG SATEEN BLANKET BUSTIAN CANTOON DAMASSE ETAMINE FLANNEL GALATEA GINGHAM HICKORY HOLLAND JACONET ORGANDY ORLEANS PERCALE TICKING BOCASINE BUCKSKIN COTELINE COUTILLE CRETONNE DRILLING DUNGAREE INDIENNE SHEETING SILKALINE MARSEILLES
(CURTAIN —) NINON
(DECORATED —) DIAMANTE
(DELICATE —) HUSI JUSI
(DURABLE —) SCRIM SERGE
(ELASTIC —) GORING ELASTIC
(EMBOSSED —) CLOKY CLOQUE
(EMBROIDERED —) BALDAQUIN
(FIGURED —) BROCADE BROCATEL
(FINE —) PIMA SILK SUSI LINEN DIMITY MERINO MOHAIR BATISTE PERCALE
(GAUZELIKE —) BAREGE GOSSAMER
(GLAZED —) CIRE
(GLOSSY —) SATIN GLORIA SATEEN PERCALINE
(GOAT'S-HAIR —) ABA TIBET
(HEAVY —) GROS CRASH DENIM DRILL BURLAP CATGUT FRIEZE LINENE TOBINE WHITNEY
(JUTE —) BALINE BURLAP
(KNITTED —) SUEDE BOUCLE JERSEY TRICOT CHIFFON
(LIGHTWEIGHT —) GLORIA BUNTING DELAINE FORTISAN PARAMATTA SEERSUCKER
(LINEN —) HARN SINDON BEWPERS BUCKRAM CAMBRIC DRABBET HOLLAND NACARAT CRETONNE
(METALLIC —) LAME
(MOTTLED —) CHINE
(MOURNING —) ALMA
(MUSLIN —) TANJIB
(NYLON —) VELCRO
(OPEN-WEAVE —) LENO
(OPENWORK —) LACE SKIPDENT
(ORNAMENTAL —) GIMP LACE LAMPAS GALLOON
(PEBBLY-SURFACED —) ARMURE
(PILED —) TERRY BOLIVIA KRIMMER CHENILLE
(PRINTED —) BATIK CALICO ALLOVER PERCALE TOURNAY
(RAFFIA —) RABANNA
(RIBBED —) CORD GROS PIQUE COTELE FAILLE SOLEIL DROGUET CORDUROY MAROCAIN MOGADORE WHIPCORD
(RICH —) SAMITE SATEEN
(ROUGH —) TERRY HOPSACK HOMESPUN
(SATIN —) CAMLET ETOILE CHARMEUSE
(SHEER —) LAWN NINON SHEER SWISS BAREGE DIMITY BATISTE SOUFFLE VALENCE GOSSAMER MOUSSELINE MARQUISETTE
(SHORT-NAPPED —) RAS
(SILK —) ACCA ALMA FUGI FUJI GROS IKAT MOFF RASH ATLAS CARDE NINON PEKIN RAJAH RUMAL SATIN SHIKH SURAH TIRAZ ARMURE BROCHE CAMACA CHAPPE CREPON DIAPER DUCAPE FAILLE KHAIKI MANTUA PONGEE SAMITE SENDAL ALACHAH ALAMODE BROCADE EPINGLE GROGRAM SARSNET SCHAPPE YESTING BARATHEA DUPPIONI EOLIENNE IMPERIAL ORMUZINE SARCENET SARSENET SHAGREEN SIAMOISE MARCELINE MESSALINE BROCATELLE
(SOFT-NAPPED —) PANNE DUVETYN
(SOFT SILK —) KASHA BARATHEA
(STRIPED —) ABA STRIPE BAYADERE MERALINE
(THIN —) CRISP GAUZE VOILE PONGEE TAMISE HERNANI MARABOU ORGANZA PERSIAN
(TWILLED —) REP SAY DENIM KASHA SERGE SURAH COUTIL RUSSEL BOLIVIA ESTAMIN FLANNEL ZANELLA CAMELINE CASHMERE CORDUROY DIAGONAL MARCELLA SHALLOON VENETIAN
(UNBLEACHED —) DRABBET
(UNGLAZED —) CRETONNE
(UPHOLSTERY —) FRISE FRIEZE BROCATEL MOQUETTE
(VELVETY —) TRIPE DUVETYN
(VINYL —) NAUGAHYDE
(VINYL-COATED —) NAUGAHYDE
(WATERPROOF —) MACINTOSH MACKINTOSH
(WOOLEN —) REPP BAIZE DOILY OSSET SERGE TAMIS TWEED BUFFIN BURNET COTTON DJERSA DUFFEL FRISCA MANTLE MOREEN MOTLEY PERPET SAXONY SHAYAK SHODDY STAMIN TAMISE VICUNA WADMAL WITNEY BATISTE BOCKING BOLIVIA CHEVIOT CHEYNEY CRYSTAL DELAINE DRUGGET FRISADO HEATHER RATTEEN STAMMEL ALGERINE BATSWING BURBERRY CASHMERE CATALOON CHIVERET HARATEEN LAMBSKIN PRUNELLA RATTINET SHALLOON SHETLAND WOOLENET ZIBELINE
(WORSTED —) TABBY COBURG ESTAMIN ETAMINE SAGATHY BARATHEA
(WOVEN —) LENO TWEED TWILL SOLBIL TISSUE GROGRAM TEXTURE VALENCIA
FABRICATE COIN COOK FAKE FORM MAKE MINT VAMP WARP BUILD FORGE FRAME FRUMP WEAVE DEVISE FANGLE INVENT CONCOCT FASHION IMAGINE PRODUCE CONTRIVE
(— CLOTH) DRAPE
(— PAPER) CONVERT
FABRICATION LIE WEB TRIFLE CHIMERA FICTION FINGURE FORGERY UNTRUTH BASKETRY PRETENSE
(PL.) INVENTARY
FABRICATOR LIAR COINER FORGER
FABULIST LIAR AESOP FABLER
FABULOUS FAB FEIGNED MYTHICAL ROMANTIC
FACADE FACE FRONT FUCUS FRONTAL FRONTLET
(— FEATURE) CEDILLA
FACE JIB MAP MUG NEB PAN BIDE CHIV CLAD COPE DARE DEFY DIAL GIZZ HEAD LEER LINE MASK MEET MOUE MUNS PHIZ PUSS SIDE ABIDE BEARD BRAVE BRICK BRUNT CASTE CHECK CHEER COVER FACET FAVOR FRONT GUARD INDEX REVET STAND STONE VISOR VIZOR ASPECT BRAZEN FACADE FACIES KISSER MAZARD MUZZLE OPPOSE PHIZOG VENEER VISAGE AFFRONT BAZOOKA COMMAND DIGLYPH FASHION FEATURE GRIMACE GRUNTLE PROPOSE RESPECT REVERSE SURFACE UPRIGHT CONFRONT ENVISAGE EXTRADOS FEATURES FROGFACE FRONTAGE FRONTIER PROSPECT SEMBLANT PERPENDICULAR
(— DOWN) DEFACE
(— IN DEFIANCE) AFFRONT
(— OF ANIMAL) MASK
(— OF CUBE) SQUARE
(— OF CUTTING TOOL) BEZEL BEZIL
(— OF GLACIER) SNOUT
(— OF PEDIMENT) TYMPANUM
(— OF STEAM HAMMER) TUP

(— OF STUMP) SCARF SCARPH
(— ON DOOR KNOCKER) MASCARON
(— ONE'S DANCING PARTNER) SET
(— THE EAST) ORIENTATE
(— TO FACE) AFRONT BEFORE FACIAL DIRECTLY
(— WITH MARBLE) PIN
(— WITH MASONRY) REVET
(— WITH PLASTER) STUCCO
(— WITH STONE) BATCH
(CLOCK —) DIAL TABLE WATCH
(CRYSTAL —) PINAKOU
(CURVED —) EXTRADOS INTRADOS
(DIE —) ACE
(FANTASTIC —) ANTIC
(HALF DOMINO —) END
(HAVING SHORT BROAD —) LATERAL
(INNER —) CONCAVE
(MADE-UP —) MOP
(MINING —) BANK BREAST FOREHEAD LONGWALL
(MOCKING —) MOE MOWE
(QUARRY —) HEUGH
(ROCK —) CLIFF
(UPPER —) BROW
(WRY —) MOUTH GRIMACE
(PREF.) FACIO PROSOP(O)
FACE-ARBOR KNIFE
FACED
(SUFF.) PROSOPOUS
FACE GUARD FRONTAL
FACEMAN HAGGER WINNER
FACEPLATE FRONT DOGPLATE
FACER BUMPER DRIFTER TANKARD
FACET PANE STAR BEZEL CULET PHASE COLLET STEMMA FACETTE LOZENGE TEMPLET
FACETIAE CURIOSA
FACETIOUS FUNNY MERRY SMART WITTY FACETE JOCOSE JOCULAR HUMOROUS POLISHED
FACIAL
(PREF.) FACIO
FACIENT DOER
FACILE PAT ABLE EASY GLIB QUICK READY EXPERT FLUENT GENTLE AFFABLE DUCTILE LENIENT
FACILITATE AID EASE HELP FAVOR SPEED ASSIST GREASE EXPEDITE
FACILITY ART EASE FEEL HELP ECLAT KNACK SKILL ADDRESS COMMAND FREEDOM PROWESS EASINESS
(PL.) ADDITIONS
FACING DADO HARL FRONT HARLE LAPEL LINER PANEL SKIRT BEFORE TOWARD VENEER AGAINST FORNENT SURFACE BLACKING CAMPSHOT CONFRONT COVERING FACEWORK FORNENST OPPOSITE PITCHING
(— AGAINST GLACIER) STOSS
(— AHEAD) FULL
(— APEX) ACROSCOPIC
(— AUDIENCE OBLIQUELY) EFFACE
(— EACH OTHER) AFFRONTE AFFRONTY
(— FOR WALLS) CASE
(— FROM GLACIER) STOSS
(— INWARD) INTRORSE
(— OF BODICE) VEST
(— OUTWARDS) EXTRORSE
(PREF.) OB
FACSIMILE FAX COPY IMAGE MODEL REPLICA AUTOTYPE
FACT CASE DEED FAIT DATUM EVENT SOOTH TRUTH DONNEE EFFECT FACTUM VERITY COMPERT FORMULA GENERAL INDICIA KEYNOTE LOWDOWN REALITY PARTICULAR
(CONCLUSIVE —) CRUSHER
(DECISIVE —) CLINCHER
(FUNDAMENTAL —) KEYNOTE
(OBVIOUS —) TRUISM
(TRUE —S) STRENGTH
(PL.) DATA FEAT
FACTION BLOC NERI PART SECT SIDE WING CABAL JUNTO PARTY BRIGUE CLIQUE SCHISM BIANCHI DISPUTE PINFOLD QUARREL INTRIGUE SPLINTER
(— OF SECEDERS) CAVE
(PARTY —) STASIS
FACTITIOUS SHAM WHIPPED KRITRIMA
FACTOR GEN DOER GENE ITEM AGENT ALLEL CAUSE MAKER ALLELE AUTHOR CENTER DETAIL BAILIFF CONTROL COUCHER CUSHION ELEMENT ENTROPY FACTRIX ISOLATE STEWARD ADHERENT AUMILDAR COFACTOR DOMINANT EQUATION GOMASHTA INCIDENT INCITANT PARAMETER
(—S IN EVOLUTION) ANTICHANCE
(CYTOPLASMIC —) KAPPA
(DECISIVE —) CAPSTONE
(ECOLOGICAL —) INFLUENT
(ENVIRONMENTAL —) GEOGEN
(HEREDITY —) GENE INSTINCT
(HINDERING —) CRIMP
(INTELLIGENCE —) G
(MATHEMATICAL —) ROOT
(PERSONALITY —) SURGENCY
(RESTRICTIVE —) BARRIER
(UNFORSEEN —) JOKER
FACTORY HONG MILL SHOP PLANT USINE AURANG AURUNG FABRIC SUGARY CANNERY HATTERY HOSIERY OFICINA SOAPERY BUILDING COMPTOIR FABRIQUE FILATURE HACIENDA OFFICINA STAMPERY WORKSHOP MANUFACTORY
FACTOTUM SIRCAR FAMULUS COMPRADOR
(INDIAN —) SIRCAR SIRKAR
FACTUAL HARD REAL TRUE ACTUAL BEDROCK EARTHLY EMPIRIC LITERAL PROSAIC
(INSUFFICIENTLY —) ABSTRACT
FACTUALLY INSOOTH
FACULTY ART WIT BOOM BUMP EASE GIFT WILL FANCY POWER SENSE TASTE BREATH BUDDHI GIFTIE SEEING TALENT ABILITY COLLEGE COUNSEL HABITUS APTITUDE CAPACITY FELICITY
(— FOR DETECTING) NOSE
(— OF EXPRESSION) LANGUAGE
(CRITICAL —) JUDGMENT
(MENTAL —) HEADPIECE
(POETIC OR CREATIVE —) IDEALITY PRINCIPLE
(REASONING —) DISCOURSE
(PL.) INDULTS
FAD BUG CULT FIKE RAGE WHIM CRAZE FANCU HOBBY FOIBLE MAGGOT CROCHET FASHION WRINKLE
FADDISH TRENDY
FADDIST CRANK
FADE DIE DIM DOW FLY WAN BRIT CAST FATE FLAT GIVE PALE PEAK PINE PINK VADE WELK WILK WILT BLANK DAVER DECAY FLEET PASSE PETER QUAIL SWING SWOON DARKLE PERISH VANISH WITHER DECLINE INSIPID LIGHTEN DIMINISH DISCOLOR DISSOLVE EVANESCE LANGUISH
(— AWAY) DOW BREAK FLEET WALLOW
FADED PASSE SHABBY EXOLETE SHOPWORN
FADELESS AMARANTIN
FADGE FAY FIT SUIT
FADING FUGITIVE MANCANDO SWINGING
FAERIE QUEENE (AUTHOR OF —) SPENSER
(CHARACTER IN —) UNA GUYON IRENE TALUS ACRASY AMORET ARTHUR DUESSA TIMIAS ASTRAEA MALEGER ARTEGALL CALIDORE GLORIANA ORGOGLIO RADIGUND ARCHIMAGO BELPHOEBE BRITOMART FLORIMELL GRANTORTO SCUDAMOUR
FAFNIR (FATHER OF —) HREIDMAR
(SLAYER OF —) SIGURD
FAG FLAG JADE TIRE TOIL DROOP WEARY DRUDGE HARASS MENIAL EXHAUST FATIGUE FRAZZLE
FAG-END LAG BUTT
FAGGED TASKIT
FAGGOT BROSNA CHUMPA FAGALD
FAGOT KID BUNT PILE PIMP BAVIN FADGE NICKY NITCH FAGGOT KNITCH GARBAGE
FAIL GO CUT EBB ERR PIP BANK BOMB BUST CONK FALL FLAG FLOP FOLD LACK LOSE MISS SINK SKEW SPIN WANE APPAL BREAK BURST CRACK FAULT FLUFF FLUKE FLUNK PETER QUAIL SLAKE SMASH SPILL VAILE APPALL BETRAY COPOUT DEFAIL DEFECT DESERT FALTER FIZZLE REPINE WINDER BACKOUT DECLINE DEFAULT EXHAUST FALSIFY FINKOUT FLICKER FLUMMOX FOUNDER MISFARE MISGIVE SCANTLE LANGUISH
(— AT) FLUB
(— IN DUTY) LAPSE
(— IN EARLY STAGES) ABORT
(— IN HEALTH) SINK BREAK
(— IN SPIRIT) QUAIL
(— IN STUDIES) BILGE
(— ON RIFLE RANGE) BOLO
(— TO ADVANCE) STICK
(— TO FOLLOW SUIT) RENIG RENEGE
(— TO GAIN ALTITUDE) MUSH
(— TO GROW) MISS
(— TO NOTICE) OVERLOOK
(— TO PERFORM) CHOKE
FAILING BAD ILL BLOT FAULT FOIBLE SENILE BLEMISH FAILURE FRAILTY ABORTIVE WEAKNESS
(NEVER —) PERENNIAL
FAILURE DUD BALK BOMB BUST FAIL FLOP FLUB FOIL LACK LOSS MISS MUFF TRIP BAULK BILGE CRASH DECAY ERROR FAULT FLUKE FLUNK FROST GRIEF GUILT LAPSE LEMON PLUCK SMASH BRODIE BUMMER FIASCO FIZZLE OUTAGE STUMER STUMOR TURKEY BLOOMER CROPPER DEBACLE DECLINE DEFAULT FLIVVER FLUMMOX NEGLECT STUMBLE ABORTION COLLAPSE DISASTER FAILANCE FLOPEROO OMISSION
(— OF DAM) BLOW
(— OF FIREARM) STOPPAGE
(— OF MILK SECRETION) AGALAXY AGALAXIA
(— OF MUSCLE) ACHALASIA
(— OF PAVEMENT) BLOWUP
(— OF PRIMER) HANGFIRE
(— OF VITALITY) DELIQUIUM
(— TO MEET) GAPE
(— TO NOTICE) OVERSIGHT
(— TO PLAY) GO
(— TO RAISE OAR) CRAB
(COMPUTER —) CRASH
(FLAT —) DUD
(POWER —) OUTAGE
(RIDICULOUS —) FIASCO
FAIN FOND GLAD LIEF EAGER PLEASED WILLING DESIROUS INCLINED
FAINEANT IDLE LAZY LOAFER
FAINT GO DIM LOW WAN WAW COLD CONK COOL DARK PALE PALL SOFT THIN WEAK LIGHT QUEAL QUEER SHADY SWELT SWOON TIMID WAUFF WAUGH WERSH EVANID FEEBLE REMISS REMOTE SICKLY WAMBLY FEIGNED FORGONE LANGUID OBSCURE SWITHER SYNCOPE WEARISH COWARDLY DELICATE LANGUISH LISTLESS SLUGGISH TIMOROUS
(— FROM HEAT) SWELTER
(— FROM HUNGER) LEERY
(— OF SCENT) COLD WAUGH
FAINTHEARTED TIMID COWARD CRAVEN COWARDLY UNHEARTY
FAINTHEARTEDNESS QUALM
FAINTING AFAINT SYNCOPE DELIQUIUM
(— SPELL) DROW DWAM DWALM
FAINTLY DIMLY FAINT SMALL
FAINTNESS TENUITY GONENESS WEAKNESS
FAINT-VOICED INWARD
FAIR GAY GEY MOP BEAU BELL CALM EVEN FINE GAFF GALA GOOD HEND JUST MART PLAY TIDE TIDY BAZAR BLOND CLEAN CLEAR EQUAL FERIA HENDE LARGE RIGHT ROUND SHEER TRYST WHITE AONACH BAZAAR

BLONDE CANDID COMELY DECENT DINKUM HONEST KERMIS PRETTY SERENE SQUARE EXHIBIT JANNOCK KERMESS STATUTE BOOKFAIR DISTINCT FESTIVAL HORNFAIR MIDDLING RATIONAL STRAIGHT UNBIASED EQUITABLE OBJECTIVE REASONABLE
(— AND CALM) SETTLED
(— AND SQUARE) DINKUM
(HINDU —) MELA
(VILLAGE —) WALK
FAIR-DEALING HONEST
FAIRER SHIPWRIGHT
FAIRING SPAT SPINNER FAIRLING
FAIR-LEAD WAPP
FAIRLY WELL GAILY GAYLY GEYAN EVENLY JUSTLY MEANLY HANDILY PLAINLY RIGHTLY MIDDLING PROPERLY SUITABLY
FAIRNESS FAIR CANDOR EQUITY HONESTY JUSTICE EQUALITY EVENNESS FAIRHEAD FAIRHOOD
FAIRWAY HOLE WATERWAY
(ANGLED —) DOGLEG
FAIR-WEATHER SUNSHINE
FAIRY ELF FAY FEE HOB IMP FAIN PERI PIXY PUCK SHEE VILA OUPHE PECHT PIXIE SIDHE WIGHT COURIL FAERIE HATHOR KEWPIE SPIRIT SPRITE YAKSHA YAKSHI ARGANTE BANSHEE ORIANDA SHEOGUE SYLPHID URGANDA FOLLETTO MELUSINA
(— QUEEN) MAB
(IRISH —) SHEE SIDHE
(TRICKSY —) PUCK
(PL.) GENTRY
FAIRY BELL FOXGLOVE
FAIRYFOLK SHEE SIDHE
FAIRYLAND ANNWN ANNWFN FEERIE ELFLAND
FAITH DIN FAY FOY LAW LAY VAY FACK FAIX FEGS SLAM TROW CERTY CREED HAITH STOCK TOUCH TROTH TRUST TRUTH BELIEF CERTIE CREDIT GOSPEL CREANCE FACKINS AFFIANCE RELIANCE RELIGION
(BAD —) DUPLICITY
(MUSLIM —) CRESCENT
(RELIGIOUS —) SRADH SRADDHA SHRADDHA
(SHOW OF GOOD —) GESTURE
(PREF.) FIDE(I) PISTIO PISTO
FAITHFUL FAST FEAL FIRM GOOD JUST LEAL LIKE REAL TRIG TRUE FALSE HEMAN LIEGE LOYAL PIOUS SOOTH SWEER TIGHT TREST TRIED AEFALD ARDENT ENTIRE FIDELE HONEST LAWFUL PISTIC STANCH STEADY TRUSTY DEVOTED SINCERE STAUNCH ACCURATE CONSTANT RESOLUTE SPEAKING RELIGIOUS
FAITHFULNESS HSIN FEALTY VERITY LOYALTY FIDELITY TRUENESS
FAITHFUL SHEPHERDESS
(AUTHOR OF —) FLETCHER
(CHARACTER IN —) CHLOE ALEXIS AMORET CLORIN THENOT DAPHNIS PERIGOT AMARILLIS
FAITHLESS FALSE PUNIC FICKLE HOLLOW ROTTEN UNJUST UNTRUE ATHEIST APOSTATE DELUSIVE DISLOYAL SHIFTING UNSTABLE NIDDERING PERFIDIOUS
FAITHLESSNESS FALSITY PERFIDY UNTRUTH
FAKE DUD DUFF DUPE FEKE HOAX HOKE SHAM BOGUS CHEAT FALSE FEIGN FLAKE FRAUD FUDGE PHONY WANGLE DUFFING FALSIFY FURBISH GUNDECK PRETEND SWINDLE SIMULATE SPURIOUS ADULTERINE
(— OF STOWED ROPE) FLEET
(— OUT OF POSITION) JUKE
(FOOTBALL —) JUKE
(PREF.) PSEUD(O)
FAKER FAKIR QUACK HUMBUG CAMELOT PEDDLER
(— OF ART) TRUQUEUR
FAKIR FAKIH FAQUIR DERVISH
FALCHION FALX
FALCON EYAS HAWK SORE BESRA HOBBY SAKER STOOP GENTLE JAGGER JUGGER LANNER LUGGAR LUGGER MERLIN MUSKET PREYER RAPTOR SHAHIN TERCEL KESTREL SAKERET BERIGORA BOCKEREL FALCONET PEREGRIN SOREHAWK
(— BOARD) HACK
(— IN FIRST YEAR) SORE SOREHAWK
(FEMALE —) FORMAL FORMEL LANNER
(MALE —) TASSEL TERCEL SAKERET
(SMALL —) HOBBY MERLIN KESTREL
(WHITE —) ICELANDER
FALCONER HAWKER OSTREGER
FALCONRY HAWKING
FALDSTOOL ORATORY
FALL GO EBB SAG SYE TIP BACK BAND COME COUP DIVE DRIP DROP DUNT FLOP HANG PICK PLOP RASH RUIN RUSE SHED SILE SINK SLIP SWAK SWAP SWAY SWOP TILT WHAP WHOP ABATE CHUTE CLOIT CRASH DROOP HANCE INCUR JABOT LAPSE LIGHT LODGE PITCH PLUMB PLUMP RAPID SAULT SHAKE SHOOT SKITE SLIPE SLUMP SPILL SQUAB SQUAT THROW TRACE TWINE ALIGHT AUTUMN BRODIE DEVALL DOUNCE DRYSNE FOOTER HAPPEN HEADER JOUNCE PERISH PLUNGE RECEDE SEASON SLOUGH STREEK STRIKE TOPPLE TUMBLE CASCADE CROPPER CROWNER DECLINE DEGRADE DEPRESS DESCEND DEVOLVE DRIBBLE ESCHEAT ILLAPSE PLUMMET RELAPSE RETREAT SQUELCH STUMBLE SUBSIDE CATARACT COLLAPSE COMMENCE DECREASE DOWNCOME PRECIPITATE
(— ABRUPTLY) DUMP
(— APART) BREAK SHIVER COLLAPSE DISUNITE
(— AWAY) DEFECT
(— BACK) RECEDE RESORT
(— BEHIND) LAG
(— DIZZILY) SPIN
(— DOWN) CAVE FLOP SWAP SLUMP REVERSE SWITHER
(— DUE) ACCRUE BEFALL
(— FAST) HOP
(— FLAT) PLAT FLIVVER
(— FOR) BITE
(— FORWARD) PECK PITCH PROLAPSE
(— FROM A HORSE) PURL VOLUNTARY
(— FROM SURFBOARD) WIPEOUT
(— FROM UNDERMINING) CALVE
(— FROM VIRTUE) LAPSE
(— GRADUALLY) EBB SAG
(— GUY) GOAT CHUMP SCAPEGOAT
(— HEAVILY) DING LUMP SOSS CLOIT CLYTE GULCH PLOUT PLUMP SOUSE SWACK THROW
(— ILL) TRAIK
(— IN) CAVE FOUNDER
(— IN DROPS) DRIP STILL DRIBBLE
(— IN FLURRIES) SPIT
(— IN FOLDS) BLOUSE
(— IN RIVER) SAULT
(— INTO) STRIKE
(— INTO ERROR) SLIP STUMBLE
(— INTO FAINT) DWAM DWALM
(— INTO RUIN) DECAY
(— INTO SLUMBER) DROWSE
(— INTO TRAP) DECOY
(— INTO WATER) DOP
(— IN WITH) INCUR
(— OF DEW) SEREIN SERENE
(— OFF) BATE SLIP SLACK
(— OF RAIN) SKIFF SKIFT ONDING SHOWER
(— OF SNOW) SKIFF SKIFT ONCOME SCOUTHER SNOWFALL
(— OF WICKETS) ROT
(— ON BACK) BACKER
(— ON SUCCESSIVE DAYS) CONCUR
(— ON THE NOSE) NOSER
(— OUT) BREAK LIGHT FORTUNE QUARREL
(— PRONE) GRABBLE
(— RAPIDLY) SKID
(— SHORT) DROP FAIL FAULT
(— SLOWLY) SETTLE
(— SUDDENLY) BOLT PLOP SLUMP
(— THROWING HORSE AND RIDER) CRUMPLER
(— TO NOTHING) DISSOLVE
(— TO PIECES) BUCKLE CRUMBLE
(— UPON) WARP
(— VIOLENTLY) BEAT
(BAD —) BUSTER
(HEAVY —) PASH POUR SWAG BLASH CLOIT GULCH SKELP SOUSE SQUAT MUCKER
(INCOMPLETE WRESTLING —) FOIL
(SOFT —) SCLAFF
(SUDDEN —) HANCE SQUAT SQUASH TAILSPIN
FALLACIOUS SLY WILY ABSURD CRAFTY UNTRUE DELUSIVE GUILEFUL ILLUSORY
FALLACY IDOL ERROR FALLAX IDOLUM SOPHISM EQUIVOKE ILLUSION
(PL.) IDOLA
FALLEN DOWN FAUN FLAT SHED LAPSED DECLASSE
(— IN) SUNKEN
FALLER GILL FLATHEAD
FALLFISH CHUB DACE CORPORAL
FALLGUY PATSY
FALL HERRING TAILOR
FALLIBLE HUMAN ERRANT ERRABLE
FALLING SIT CADENT CAVING PROLAPSE WINDFALL
(— BACK) ESCHEAT
(— BEHIND) LAG
(— DOWN) RUIN
(— IN FOLDS) FLOWING
(— IN RUINS) DERELICT
(— INTO) INFALL
(— OFF) CADUCE LEEWAY CADUCOUS
(— OF MINE ROOF) SIT
(— OF RAIN) SPIT
(— ON SOMETHING) INCIDENT
(— OUT) DIFFICULTY
(— SHORT) DEFICIT
(PREF.) CADUCI
(SUFF.) PTOMA PTOSIS
FALLOPIAN TUBE TUBAL
(PREF.) FALL(O)
FALLOVER OSTREGER
FALLOW LEA PALE HOBBY BARREN VALEWE
(PREF.) POLI(O)
FALLOW DEER DAMINE DAPPLE
FALLOWING ARDER
FALSE DEAD FAKE FLAM SHAM BOGUS FAUSE LYING PASTE PHONY WRONG FICKLE HOLLOW LUTHER PSEUDO UNTRUE ASSUMED BASTARD CROOKED FEIGNED APOSTATE DISLOYAL ILLUSIVE RECREANT RENEGADE SPECTRAL SPURIOUS MENDACIOUS
(PREF.) PSEUD(O)
FALSE BEACHDROPS PINESAP
FALSE CRAWLEY PINEDROPS
FALSE FOXGLOVE FEVERWEED
FALSE HELLEBORE EARTHGALL
FALSEHOOD COG FIB LIE BUNG CRAM FLAM TALE CRACK ERROR FABLE STORY FALSET UNFACT YANKER CRAMMER CRETISM FALSAGE FALSERY FALSITY FIBBERY FICTION LEASING PERFIDY PHANTOM ROMANCE UNTRUTH FALSHEDE ROORBACK STRAPPER
FALSE MERMAID FLOERKEA LIMNANTH
FALSENESS SHAM DECEIT
FALSE WINTERGREEN PYROLA
FALSEWORK CENTERING
FALSIES CHEATERS
FALSIFIER LIAR FALSER FORGER FALSARY
FALSIFY LIE COOK FAKE WARP ABUSE BELIE FEINT FORGE BETRAY DOCTOR FIDDLE WANGLE GUNDECK VIOLATE EMBEZZLE MISREPRESENT
FALSITY LIE ERROR VANITY UNTRUTH INVERITY
FALSTAFF (CHARACTER IN —) MEG FORD JOHN PAGE ALICE BROOK

CAIUS FENTON QUICKLY FALSTAFF NANNETTA
(COMPOSER OF —) VERDI
FALTER FAIL HALT LIMP PAUSE WAVER BOGGLE FLINCH TOTTER FRIBBLE STAMMER STUMBLE TREMBLE HESITATE
FALTERING HINK HALTING
FALX FALCULA
FAME BAY CRY LOSE NAME STAR WORD BRUIT ECLAT GLORY HONOR KUDOS PRICE RUMOR VOICE ESTEEM LAUREL RENOWN REPORT REPUTE TONGUE HEARSAY STARDOM WORSHIP
(HALL OF —) OF (SEE HALL FAME)
(ILL —) OPPROBRIUM
FAMED RIFE KNOWN NOTED EMINENT RENOMEE RENOWNED
FAMEUSE APPLE
FAMILIAR FLY BAKA BOKO BOLD COZY EASY FREE FULL HOMY TAME TOSH CLOSE CONNU GREAT HOMEY KNOWN PRIVY THICK USUAL ATHOME BEATEN CHUMMY COMMON ENTIRE FOLKSY GERMAN HOMELY INWARD KENNED STRAIT THRONG VERSED AFFABLE FAMULAR FOLKSEY POPULAR FREQUENT HABITUAL INTIMATE SOCIABLE STANDARD
(— FEELING) DEJAVU
(— WITH) KNOWING
(MAKE —) POST
(PRESUMPTUOUSLY —) INSOLENT
FAMILIARITY HABIT FREEDOM LIBERTY PRIVACY PRIVITY TRAFFIC HABITUDE INTIMACY CONSUETUDE
FAMILIARIZE HAFT VERSE ACCUSTOM ACQUAINT FREQUENT
FAMILIARLY HOMELY
FAMILY ILK KIN AIGA CLAN GING KIND LINE NAME RACE TEAM TRIP CINEL CLASS FLESH GOTRA GROUP HOUSE MEINY STIRP STOCK CLETCH FAIMLY PARAGE STEMMA STIRPS STRAIN ZEGRIS DYNASTY KINDRED LINEAGE ORLEANS PROGENY CATEGORY FIRESIDE
(COSMOPOLITAN —) FELIDAE FABACEAE
(FIRST —) FF
(LANGUAGE —) CHON BANTU CLICK COCHE CUNAN KADAI STOCK AIMARA ATALAN AYMARA CHOLON GILIAK HUARPE LENCAN SERIAN URALIC BOTOYAN CADDOAN CARIBAN CATIBAN CHINOOK CHOLONA CHUMASH COPEHAN ESSELEN KARTHLI KARTVEL KERESAN SHASTAN ATAKAPAN CHANGOAN
(LARGE —) QUIVERFUL
(ONE-PARAMETER —) PENCIL
(RAISE A —) PARENT
(SUPER —) APINA APOIDEA
FAMINE LACK PINE WOLF DEARTH HUNGER SCARCITY
FAMISH KILL STARVE DESTROY ENFAMISH
FAMOUS MERE BREME FAMED GRAND NOBLE NOTED FAMOSE NAMELY EMINENT NAMABLE NOTABLE RENOWNED
FAMULUS WAGNER SERVANT
FAN ONE RUN VAN BEAT BLOW BUFF COOL WASH DELTA PUNKA WHIFF BASKET BLOWER CHAMAR COLMAR FANNER FLABEL FLIGHT PUNKAH ROOTER SHOVEL SPREAD VENTOY WINNOW ADMIRER DEVOTEE FLABRUM FLYFLAP MPANGWE PAHOUIN WHISKER EVENTAIL FOLLOWER RHIPIDION
(— FOR BLOWER) WAFTER
(— OF ROCK GROUP) GROUPIE
(ALLUVIAL —) CONE APRON DELTA
(FEMALE — OF ROCK MUSICIAN) GROUPIE
(FOOTBALL —) GRIDDER
(JAZZ —) CAT
(WINNOWING —) SAIL LIKNON
(PL.) FOLLOWING
(PREF.) FLABELLI RHIPI(D)(DO)
FANALOKA FOSSA FOUSSA
FANATIC MAD NUT BIGOT CRAZY FIEND RABID ULTRA ZEALOT DEVOTEE FURIOSO PHANTIC PULAHAN PULIJAN BABAYLAN FRENETIC
(TYPE OF —) PURIST
FANATICAL RABID ULTRA EXTREME FURIOUS
FANCIED UNREAL DREAMED AFFECTED
FANCIFUL ODD ANTIC FAIRY IDEAL QUEER VIEWY DREAMY QUAINT UNREAL BIZARRE CURIOUS FANCIED LAPUTAN STRANGE WHIMSIC CHIMERIC FANCICAL FILIGREE NOTIONAL ROMANTIC VAPAROUS WHIMSICAL
FANCY BEE FAD GIG IDEA ITEM LIKE LOVE MAZE TROW WEEN WHIM BRAID BRAIN DREAM FREAK GUESS HUMOR SHINE AFFECT BEGUIN FANGLE FIGURE FLOSSY IDEATE LIKING MAGGOT MEGRIM NOTION ORNATE SHINDY VAGARY VISION WHIMSY CAPRICE CHIMERA CONCEIT CONCEPT CROCHET FANCIED FANCIFY FANTASY PROPOSE ROMANCE SUSPECT THOUGHT WRINKLE CHIMAERA CONCEIVE CROTCHET DAYDREAM ILLUSION PHANTASM PHANTASY
(FOOLISH —) CHIMERA CHIMAERA
(PASSING —) FIKE
(PERVERSE —) CROTCHET
(WILD —) TOY MAZE
(PL.) DREAMERY
FANDANGO MURCIANA
FANE FLAG BANNER FANACLE
FANFARE TUSCH HOOPLA HOORAY HURRAH TUCKET TANTARA FANFARON FLOURISH
FANFARONADE BLUSTER FANFARE SWAGGER BOASTING
FANFLOWER TACCADA
FANG FAN EARN FALX TAKE TANG TUSK VANG BEGIN PRONG SEIZE SNARE TOOTH ASSUME OBTAIN PANGWE CAPTURE PAHOUIN PROCURE
FANON CAPE ORALE PHANO FANNEL MANIPLE
FAN PALM YARAY ERYTHEA FANTREE TALIPOT
FAN-SHAPED FLABELLATE ALARY RHIPIDATE
FANTAIL COMET SHAKER WAGTAIL
FAN-TAN PARLIAMENT
FANTASIA FANTASY QUODLIBET
FANTASTIC ODD WILD ANTIC LUCIO OUTRE QUEER ABSURD GOTHIC ROCOCO TOYISH UNREAL ANTICAL BAROQUE BIZARRE WHIMSIC FANCIFUL FREAKISH ROMANTIC SINGULAR
(— PERSON) KICKSHAW
FANTASY IDEA MYTH DREAM FANCY DESIRE VISION CAPRICE CHIMERA PHANTOM ROMANCE CHIMAERA PHANTASM PHANTASY
(FUTURISTIC —) SPACEOPERA
FANTINE (DAUGHTER OF —) COSETTE
FAR AWAY LONG MUCH ROOM SIDE WELL WIDE CLEAN SIZES WIDEN REMOTE DISTANT FARAWAY ROOMWARD
(— AND AWAY) STREETS
(— OFF) OUTBYE
(— ON) ADVANCED
(— OUT) RAD WOW RADICAL
(— UP) HIGH
(SO —) ASYET UPTONOW
(PREF.) TEL(E) TELOTERO
FARAMONDO (COMPOSER OF —) HANDEL
FARCE MIME DROLL EXODE FORCE STUFF COMEDY GARLIC SOTTIE EXODIUM MOCKERY TEMACHA BURLETTA DROLLERY FARCETTA
(RELATING TO —) ATELLAN
FARCEUR WAG JOKER FORCER
FARCICAL BUFFO COMIC DROLL ATELLAN
FARCTATE STUFFED
FARCY FARCIN EQUINIA FASHION
FARE DO GO EAT TRY COME DIET FEND FOOD PATH RATE TIME TOLL WEND CHEER CHEFE CHIVE FRAME GOING LIGHT PRICE SPEED TABLE TOKEN TRACK VIAND COMMON FARING FETTLE HAPPEN TRAVEL CARFARE JOURNEY MAKEOUT PASSAGE PROCEED PROSPER WAFTAGE WAYFARE FERRYAGE PROGRESS
(— FOR FERRY) NAULUM FERRYAGE
(— WELL) SPEED
(COARSE —) HAWEBAKE
(USUAL —) ORDINARY
FAREWELL AVE BYE CIAO TATA VALE ADIEU ADIOS ALOHA CONGE FINAL LEAVE BYEBYE CHEERO SOLONG BONALLY CHEERIO GOODBYE LEAVING LULLABY PARTING
FAREWELL TO ARMS (AUTHOR OF —) HEMINGWAY
(CHARACTER IN —) HENRY BARKLEY RINALDI FREDERIC CATHERINE
FARFETCHED FARFET FORCED DEVIOUS STRAINED EXQUISITE
FAR-FETCHED (NOT —) NATURAL
FAR-FLUNG EXTENDED
FAR FROM THE MADDING CROWD (AUTHOR OF —) HARDY
(CHARACTER IN —) OAK TROY FANNY ROBIN GABRIEL BOLDWOOD EVERDENE BATHSHEBA
FARIDUN (FATHER OF —) ABTIN
(MOTHER OF —) FIRANAK
(SON OF —) TUR IRAJ SALM
FARINA MEAL FLOUR FARINE POLLEN STARCH
FARKLEBERRY BLUET
FARL PARLY FARREL
FARM FEU PEN CROP TACK TILL TORP TOWN WALK CROFT DAIRY EMPTY FIRMA HARAS MAINS MILPA PLACE RANCH RANGE STEAD BARTON BOWERY CHACRA ESTATE FURROW GRANGE RANCHO TYDDEN TYDDYN CLEANSE HENNERY KOLKHOZ MAILING POTRERO POULTRY SOVKHOS VACCARY ESTANCIA HACIENDA HATCHERY LABORING LOCATION STEADING TOWNSHIP
(— OUT) DIMIT ARRENT
(AUSTRALIAN —) STATION
(COLLECTIVE —) ARTEL KIBBUTZ KOLKHOZ
(COMMUNAL —) KVUTZA KVUTZAH
(DAIRY —) WICK
(KIND OF — AS ASYLUM) FUNNY
(LARGE —) RANCH BARTON
(RENTED —) MAILING
(SMALL —) CHACRA
(STOCK —) ESTANCIA
(STUD —) STUD HARAS
(WEST INDIAN —) PEN
FARMER HOB MEO CARL FARM HOBB KHOT KYLE RUBE RYOT TATE AILLT AUMIL BOWER CARLE CEILE CLOWN COLON HODGE KISAN COCKIE GROWER HOGMAN JIBARO TILLER YEOMAN BUCOLIC BUSHMAN BYWONER COTTIER CROFTER GRANGER HAYSEED HUSBAND LANDMAN METAYER PLANTER PLOWMAN RANCHER SCULLOG TILLMAN TRUCKER AGRONOME COCKATOO PRODUCER PUBLICAN RURALIST SELECTOR AGRONOMIST
(AUSTRALIAN —) SELECTOR
(NORWEGIAN —) BONDER
(POOR —) PIKE
(PROSPEROUS —) KULAK
(SMALL —) BOOR COCKIE
(TENANT —) AILLT GEBUR SIRDAR COLONUS SHAREMAN SHARECROPPER
FARMHAND HAND HELP
FARMHOLD CROFT
FARMHOUSE FARM TOWN ONSET GRANGE QUINTA CASERIO ONSTEAD STEADING
FARMING SOIL FARMERY HUSBANDRY
(— SYSTEM) NOTILL METAYAGE
FARMLAND ACREAGE
FARMSTEAD TOWN WICK STEAD FARMERY ONSTEAD

FARMYARD WERF CLOSE BARTON RICKYARD
FARO MONTE STUSS TIGER PHARAOH
(— CARD) SODA
FARO BANK TIGER
FAR-OFF DISTANT
FAR-OUT RAD GONZO KINKY
FARRAGO OLIO
FAR-REACHING GREAT FARGOING
FARRIER SHOER SMITH MARSHAL
FARROW PIG ROW RAKE DRAPE LITTER
FARSEEING ORACULAR
FARSIGHTED SHREWD SIGHTY
FARTHER YOND AHEAD STILL LONGER FURTHER REMOTER THITHER
FARTHEST ULTIMA ENDMOST EXTREME FARMOST LONGEST OUTMOST DOWNMOST FURTHEST REMOTEST ULTIMATE
FARTHING RAG GRIG JACK QUAD FADGE FERLING QUARTER QUADRANS QUADRANT
(HALF —) CUE
(THREE —S) GILL
FARTHINGALE FERDEGEW VERTUGAL
FASCIA BAND SASH FACIA FILLET BANDAGE MOLDING LIGATURE PLATBAND
FASCICLE BUNDLE PHALANGE
FASCICULUS HEFT BUNDLE COLUMN TRACTUS
FASCINATE DARE CHARM RIVET SEIZE WITCH ALLURE ENAMOR ATTRACT BEWITCH ENCHANT ENGROSS GLAMOUR PHILTER PHILTRE ENSORCEL ENTRANCE INTEREST INTRIGUE SIRENIZE CAPTIVATE
FASCINATED HOOKED BESOTTED
FASCINATING NUTTY ORPHIC TAKING SIRENIC CHARMING FETCHING MESMERIC
FASCINATION CHARM SPELL WITCHERY
FASCINE FAGOT FAGGOT SAUCISSE
FASCIOLA DISTOMA DISTOMUM
FASCIOLE SEMITA
FASCIST BLACK FASCISTA
FASHION GO CRY CUT FAD LAT TON WAY CHIC FEAT FORM GARB GATE KICK MAKE MODE MOLD RAGE RATE SORT TURN TWIG WEAR WISE BUILD CRAZE FEIGN FORGE FRAME GUISE MODEL MOULD SHAPE STYLE TASTE VOGUE WEAVE AGUISE ASSIZE BUSTLE CAMBER CREATE CUSTOM DESIGN FANGLE INVENT MANNER METHOD TAILOR ALAMODE COMPOSE IMAGERY PORTRAY QUALITY CONTRIVE
(LATEST —) KICK
(OF PAST —) RETRO
(PREVAILING —) CRY
(SPECIAL —) TOUCH
FASHIONABLE HIP CHIC GOGO LATE PINK POSH TONY DASHY DOGGY DOSSY NOBBY RITZY SMART SWELL SWISH VOGUE GIGOLO JAUNTY MODISH TIMISH TONISH TRENDY DASHING GALLANT GENTEEL STYLISH SWAGGER BELGRAVIAN
(NOT —) DEMODE
FASHIONABLY SMARTLY
FASHIONED HUED CARVED SHAPED WROUGHT FEATURED
FASHIONING FINGENT
FASHION PLATE SWELL
FASSAITE PYRGOM
FAST HOT HUT COLD FIRM HARD LENT SOON SURE WIDE AGILE APACE BRISK CHEAP FIXED FLASH FLEET HASTY QUICK RAPID ROUND SADLY STUCK SWIFT TIGHT TOSTO CARENE ESTHER FASTLY LIVELY SECURE SPEEDY SPORTY STABLE STARVE ABIDING EXPRESS HOTSHOT HURRIED PROVISO RASPING SETTLED SIKERLY STATION TAANITH ENDURING FAITHFUL SPINNING SPORTING WIKIWIKI
(— DAY) ASHURA
(DANGEROUSLY —) BREAKNECK
(MUSLIM —) MOHARRAM
(SUFF.) **(MAKING —)** PEXIA PEXIS PEXY
FAST-DYED INGRAIN
FASTEN BAR DOG FAY FIX GAD GIB KEY LAG PEN PIN SEW TAG TIE YOT BELT BEND BIND BITT BOLT BRAD CLIP FRET GIRD GIRT GLUE GRIP HANG HANK HASP HOOK HOOP HORN KILT KNIT KNOT LACE LASH LINK LOCK MOOR NAIL ROPE SEAL SNIB SOUD SPAN SPAR STAY WELD WIRE AFFIX ANNEX BELAY BIGHT BRACE CABLE CATCH CHAIN CHOCK CINCH CLAMP CLASP CLING COPSE CRAMP DEFIX GIRTH HALSH HITCH INFIX LATCH PASTE RIVET SCREW SEIZE SLOUR SNECK STEEK STICK STRAP TRUSS WITHE ANCHOR ATTACH BATTEN BUCKLE BUTTON CEMENT CLINCH COTTER COUPLE ENGAGE ENTAIL FATHER GARTER HAMPER HANKLE INKNOT PICKET SECURE SKEWER SOLDER STAPLE STITCH STRAIN TETHER BRACKET CONFINE CONNECT EMBRACE GRAPPLE GROMMET PADLOCK BARNACLE FORELOCK INTERTIE OBLIGATE TRANSFIX
(— ABOUT) THRAP
(— ANCHOR) SCOW
(— A SAIL) CROSS
(— AS SPURS) SPEND
(— IN) EMBAR
(— PROMPTLY) CLAP
(— THE LEGS) HOBBLE
(— TO) TAG
(— TOGETHER) COAPT SEIZE SPLICE CONNECT
(— WINGS ON) IMP
(— WITH A GIRTH) WARRICK
(— WITH NOTCHES) GAIN
(PREF.) HAPT(O)
FASTENED FAST SHUT BOUND FIXED BOUNDEN
(PREF.) **(— TOGETHER)** SYNAPTO
FASTENER BAR GIB GIN NUT PIN AGAL BOLT DOME FAST FROG HASP LOCK NAIL SNAP STUD TACK CATCH CLAMP CLASP LATCH RIVET SCREW SPIKE STRAP TATCH THONG BUCKLE BUTTON HATPIN STAPLE ZIPPER FIXATOR LATCHET PADLOCK SNAPPER TENDRIL FASTNESS STAYLACE
FASTENING TEE TIE FROG HASP SEAL SNAP SNIB STAY TACK TACHE BUCKLE CLINCH LACING MUZZLE STRIKE TINGLE BINDING CLOSURE LATCHET MOUSING PINNING SEIZING FORELOCK KNITTING
(— FOR HAWK'S WING) BRAIL
(— OF COPE) MORSE
(— ON HARPOON IRON) HITCH
(HOOK AND LOOP —) AGRAFE AGRAFFE
(PL.) GRIPES
(PREF.) DESM(A)(IDI)(IDIO)(O)
(SUFF.) PEXIA PEXIS PEXY
FAST-GOING CLIPPING
FASTIDIOUS FINE NEAT NICE CHARY DONCY FEEST FUSSY NAISH NATTY PAWKY PICKY CHOICE CHOICY CHOOSY DAINTY DONSIE MOROSE PICKED QUAINT QUEASY SPRUCE CHOOSEY CURIOUS ELEGANT FINICAL FINICKY HAUGHTY PICKING REFINED TAFFETA TAFFETY CRITICAL DELICATE EXACTING GINGERLY OVERNICE PICKSOME PRECIOUS SCORNFUL SQUEAMISH PARTICULAR PERSNICKETY SCRUMPTIOUS
(NOT —) GROSS
(OVERLY —) SAUCY
FASTIDIOUSNESS DAINTY NICETY DELICACY
FASTIGIATE CONIC
FASTING RAMADAN
(PREF.) NEST(I)
FAST-MOVING SUDDEN
FASTNESS FORT CASTLE CITADEL RETREAT FORTRESS
FAST-WORKING HOTSHOT
FAT GHI OIL TUB FOZY GHEE GRAS LARD LIPA MORT RICH SAIM SUET ADEPS BEEFY BROSY CETIN CHUFF COCUM ESTER FLECK FLICK FOGGY GROSS JUICY KEDGE KOKUM LARDY LIPID LIPIN LUSTY OBESE PLUMP PODGY PORKY PUDDY PUDGY PURSY SAAME SPICK SQUAB STOUT SUMEN THICK WASTY AXUNGE BLOWSY CHOATY CHUBBY CHUFFY DEGRAS FATTED FINISH FLESHY GREASE LIPIDE LIPOID PLUFFY PORTLY PUBBLE PUNCHY PYKNIC ROTUND STOCKY STUFFY TALLOW UCUUBA ADIPOSE BLOATED BLUBBER CEROTIN FATNESS FERTILE FLESHLY FULSOME LANOLIN OPULENT PINGUID PURSIVE REPLETE STEARIN EXTENDED FRUITFUL MARROWED MURUMURU PALMITIN UNCTUOUS
(— AROUND WHALE'S NECK) KENT
(— MEAT) SPECK
(— OF HIPPOPOTAMUS) SPECK
(— PERSON) SQUAB
(ANIMAL —) GLOR SAIM SUET ADEPS GLORE GREASE TALLOW
(CHEW THE —) GAB JAW YAK
(FLOATING —) FLOT
(LARD —) FLARE FLECK FLICK
(LOW IN —S) SPA
(LUMP OF —) KEECH
(LUMPY —) CELLULITE
(NATURAL —) ESTER
(POULTRY —) SCHMALZ SCHMALTZ
(SOLID —) LARD KIKUEL STEARIN
(PREF.) ADIP(O) LIP(O) LIPAR(O) PI(O) PIA(R)(RO) PINGUE PINGUI SEBI STEAR(O) STEAT(O)
FATAL FEY DIRE MORT FERAL VITAL DEADLY DISMAL DOOMED FUNEST LETHAL MORTAL TRAGIC CAPITAL DEATHLY EXITIAL FATEFUL KILLING OMINOUS RUINOUS UNSONSY BASILISK DESTINED EXITIOUS FUNESTAL MORTIFIC
FATALITY DOOM ACCIDENT CALAMITY DISASTER
FATA MORGANA MIRAGE
FAT-BELLIED GUTTY
FATE DIE END KER LOT CAST DOLE DOOM EURE NORN RUIN SORT STAR CAVEL EVENT GRACE KARMA MOIRA MORTA WEIRD WHATE WRITE ANANKE CHANCE KISMET DESTINY FORTUNE OUTCOME PORTION DOWNFALL FATALITY
(INEXORABLE —) HEAVEN
(PREF.) FATI
FATED DUE FEY FATAL DOOMED DECREED DESTINED
FATEFUL FATAL FATED DEADLY DOOMFUL OMINOUS DOOMLIKE
FATES CLOTHO MOERAE PARCAE ATROPOS LACHESIS
(ONE OF —) URD NONA PARCA SKULD CLOTHO DECUMA ATROPOS LACHESIS VERDANDE
FATHEAD REDFISH
FATHEADED FOZY
FATHEADEDNESS FOZINESS
FATHER BU DA PA ABU AMA DAD POP TAT ABBA ABOU AMBA ANBA ATEF BABA BAPU DADA PAPA PERE SIRE ADOPT BABBO BEGET DADDY FRIAR PADRE PATER VADER PARENT PRIEST SUBORN ELKANAH GENITOR TATINEK BEAUPERE GENERATE GOVERNOR PATRIARCH PATERFAMILIAS
(CHURCH —) APOLOGIST
(SEMIDIVINE —) PITRI
(SIDE OF —) AGNATE
(PL.) PP
(PREF.) PARRI PATR(I)(IO)(O)
FATHER GORIOT (AUTHOR OF —) BALZAC
(CHARACTER IN —) EUGENE GORIOT VAUTRIN DELPHINE ANASTASIE DERESTAUD TAILLEFER VICTORINE DENUCINGEN DEBEAUSEANT DERASTIGNAC
FATHERLAND KITH HOMELAND
FATHER-LASHER GUNDIE COTTOID SCULPIN BULLHEAD LORICATE
FATHERLESS ORBATE SIRELESS

FATHERS AND SONS (AUTHOR OF —) TURGENEV
(CHARACTER IN —) KATYA PAVEL ARKADY VASILY NIKOLAI BAZAROFF FENICHKA KIRSANOFF ODINTZOFF SITNIKOFF
FATHOM BRACE BRASS DELVE FADME PLUMB SOLVE SOUND TOUCH BOTTOM MEASURE PLUMMET
FATIGUE FAG HAG TEU BEAT BORE COOK JADE TASH TIRE TRAY SPEND STALL TARRY THRIE TRAIK TRASH WEARY HARASS OVERDO TAIGLE TUCKER EXHAUST LANGUOR TRACHLE FATIGATE VEXATION
(FLIGHT —) AERONEUROSIS
FATIGUED BEAT GONE JADED TIRED WEARY TASKIT OUTWORN WEARIED FATIGATE HARASSED OVERDONE TUCKERED
FATIGUING HARD IRKSOME
FATLIKE LIPOID
FATNESS BLOOM GREASE
FATTEN FAT BEEF LARD SOIL BRAWN FARCE FLESH FRANK PROVE SMEAR STALL BATTEN BATTLE ENRICH FINISH TALLOW THRIVE PINGUEFY SAGINATE
FATTENING FRANK BATTEL BATTABLE
FATTY SUETY BACONY GREASY ADIPOSE ADIPOUS FATLIKE PINGUID SEBIFIC STEARIC LIPAROID LIPAROUS UNCTUOUS ALIPHATIC
(PREF.) LIPAR(O)
FATUITY INANITY
FATUOUS DOPY GAGA DOPEY INANE SILLY SIMPLE STUPID UNREAL FATUATE FOOLISH IDIOTIC WITLESS DEMENTED ILLUSORY IMBECILE
FAUCES JAWS
FAUCET BIB TAP BIBB COCK QUILL SPOUT VALVE CUTOFF DOSSIL DOZZLE OFFLET SPIGOT BIBCOCK HYDRANT PETCOCK TURNCOCK
(WOODEN —) HORSE
FAUGH BAH FOH VAH
FAUJDAR PHOUSDAR
FAULT BUG RUB SIN BEAM CLAG COUP DEBT FAIL FLAW FLUB GALL HOLE LACK LAST MOLE SAKE SLIP SPOT VICE WANT WITE ABUSE AMISS BLAME BREAK CULPA ERROR FLUFF GUILT LAPSE SCAPE SHIFT SLIDE SWICK TACHE BLOTCH DEFECT FOIBLE RUNNER THRUST VICETY VITIUM BLEMISH BLISTER BLUNDER DEFAULT DEMERIT EYELAST FAILING FAILURE FRAILTY MISTAKE NEGLECT OFFENSE FAULTING PECCANCY WEAKNESS
(— IN BADMINTON) SLING
(AT —) CULPABLE
(MINING —) COUP LEAP CHECK HITCH
(TRIFLING —) PECCADILLO
(PL.) FAULTAGE
FAULTFINDER MOMUS CARPER CHIDER CRITIC MOMIST CAPTION KNOCKER NAGSTER
FAULTFINDING CARPING CAPTIOUS CRITICAL
FAULTILY BADLY
FAULTLESS PURE CLEAN RIGHT CORRECT PERFECT PRECISE FLAWLESS
FAULTY BAD ILL SICK AMISS UNFIT WRONG FLAWED FAULTED PECCANT VICIOUS BLAMABLE CULPABLE SPURIOUS
(PREF.) DYS PARA
FAUN SATYR WOODMAN WOODWOSE
FAUNA ANIMALS FAUNULA FAUNULE ZOOLOGY
(FOSSIL —) BIOCHRON
FAUSSEBRAIE VAMURE VAUMURE
FAUST (AUTHOR OF —) GOETHE
(CHARACTER IN —) FAUST HELEN SIEBEL WAGNER GRETCHEN VALENTINE HOMUNCULUS MARGUERITE MEPHISTOPHELES
(COMPOSER OF —) GOUNOD
FAUX PAS GAFF SLIP BONER ERROR GAFFE BLOOMER FLOATER MISSTEP MISTAKE SNAPPER
FAVOLA D'ORFEO (CHARACTER IN —) PLUTO APOLLO CHARON ORPHEUS MESSENGER PROSERPINA
(COMPOSER OF —) MONTEVERDI
FAVOR AID FOR ORE PRO BOON ESTE FACE GREE HEAR HELP LIKE MAKE BLESS BRIBE GRACE LEAVE MENSK SERVE SPARE SPEED THANK TREAT ASSIST ERRAND ESTEEM FAVOUR LETTER NOTICE PENCEL UPHOLD ADVANCE AGGRACE BENEFIT ENFAVOR FEATURE FORWARD GRATIFY INDULGE RESPECT SUPPORT ADVOCACY BEFRIEND COURTESY FAVORIZE GOODWILL KINDNESS RESEMBLE SYMPATHY ACCEPTANCE
FAVORABLE HOT BOON FAIR FREE GOOD HIGH KIND ROSY TIDY CIVIL CLEAR HAPPY LARGE MERRY TRINE WHITE WILLY BENIGN DEXTER GENIAL GOLDEN KINDLY TOWARD BENEFIC EXALTED OPTIMAL POPULAR PRESENT FAVONIAN FRIENDLY GRACIOUS PLEASING PROPENSE SPEEDFUL TOWARDLY BENIGNANT PROPITIOUS PROSPEROUS
(— TO PURCHASER) KEEN
(NOT —) INFAUST
FAVORABLY FAIR WELL HIGHLY
FAVORED WELL FAURD HAPPY FAURED GIFTED BLESSED FAVOURED
FAVORER FAUTOR FRIEND FAVORITE
FAVORING FAVONIAN
(PREF.) PRO
(SUFF.) ABLE IBLE
FAVORITE BOY PET POT DEAR PEAT CHALK GREAT INGLE WHITE MINION DARLING FANCIED MINIKIN POPULAR SPECIAL GRACIOSO WHITEBOY
FAVORITE, LA (CHARACTER IN —) GUSMAN ALFONSO LEONORA FERNANDO
(COMPOSER OF —) DONIZETTI
FAVORITISM BIAS FAVOR NEPOTISM
FAVUS TILE WHITECOMB
FAWN COG BUCK CLAW DEER FAON JOUK ROOT COWER CRAWL CREEP GLOZE HONEY SMARM TOADY WHELP CRINGE CROUCH GROVEL KOWTOW SHRINK SLAVER ADULATE CROODLE CRUDDLE FLATTER FLETHER HANGDOG SERVILE SPANIEL TOADEAT TRUCKLE WHEATEN BOOTLICK
(— UPON) SUCK SMOOGE ADULATE
FAWN-COLORED CERVINE
FAWNIA (LOVER OF —) DORASTUS
FAWNING SLEEK CRINGE GREASE MENIAL SLEEKY SMARMY SUPPLE FLETHER GLOZING HANGDOG SERVILE SPANIEL FLATTERY
FAWNSKIN NEBRIS
FAY ELF FEY FAIRY FEIGH
FAZE DAUNT FEEZE PHASE WORRY
FEALTY FEE FEWTE HOMAGE LOYALTY SERVICE TREWAGE FIDELITY
FEAR UG AWE DREE FLAY FUNK WARD ALARM DOUBT DREAD JELLY PANIC AFFRAY ALARUM DANGER DISMAY FRIGHT HORROR PHOBIA TERROR ANXIETY SUSPECT AFFRIGHT DISQUIET DISTRUST EERINESS MISDOUBT VENERATE
(— OF CROSSING STREETS) DROMOPHOBIA
(— OF DRAFTS) AEROPHOBIA
(— OF FALLING) BATHOPHOBIA HYPSOPHOBIA
(— OF HOME SURROUNDINGS) ECOPHOBIA
(— OF OPEN PLACES) AGORAPHOBIA
(— OF THUNDER) ASTRAPHOBIA
(INTERJECTION TO EXPRESS —) YIKES
(IRRATIONAL —) PARANOIA
(PREF.) PHOB(O)
(SUFF.) PHOBE PHOBIA(C) PHOBIC PHOBOUS
FEARFUL ARGH DIRE AWFUL FERLY PAVID TIMID WINDY WROTH AFRAID COWISH FRIGHTY GHASTLY NERVOUS PANICKY WORRIED CAUTIOUS DOUBTFUL DREADFUL GREWSOME GRUESOME HORRIBLE HORRIFIC PARANOID SHOCKING SKITTISH TERRIBLE TERRIFIC TIMOROUS
(PREF.) DEIN(O) DIN(O)
FEARLESS BOLD BRAVE DARING HEROIC AWELESS IMPAVID INTREPID
FEASIBLE FIT LIKELY POSSIBLE PROBABLE SUITABLE
FEAST (ALSO SEE FESTIVAL) EAT FOY PIG SUP DINE FARM FETE LUAU MEAL TUCK UTAS AZYME CHEER CHOES CITUA DIRGY FESTA FESTY GAUDY REVEL TREAT ARTHEL AVERIL BRIDAL DEVOUR DINNER DOUBLE INFARE ISODIA JUNKET MAUNDY REGALE REPAST SIMPLE SMOUSE SPREAD AHAAINA BANQUET BRIDALE DELIGHT FESTINO GRATIFY GREGORY LAMBALE LEMURIA SHEVUOS SYNAXIS ANALEPSY CAROUSAL DOMINEER EPIPHANY FESTIVAL GESTNING GESTONIE HANUKKAH KOIMESIS PASSOVER POTLATCH SHABUOTH VESTALIA
(— BEFORE JOURNEY) FOY
(— OF BOOTHS) SUCCOS SUKKOTH
(— OF LANTERNS) HON
(— OF LOTS) PURIM
(— OF WEEKS) SHEVUOS SHABUOTH
(— PLACE) IDGAH
(DRINKING —) BANQUET
(FUNERAL —) ARVAL ARVEL DIRGY DIRGIE DREDGIE
(HARVEST —) BUSK
(JEWISH —) SENDAH
(LOVE —) AGAPE
(RELIGIOUS —) CANAO KANYAW PENTECOST
(VILLAGE —) TANSY
(PREF.) DAPI FESTI FESTO HEORTO
(SUFF.) **(— DAY)** MAS
FEASTER CONVIVE
FEASTING FEAST CARNIVAL
FEAT ACT KIP DEED FATE GEST WORK GESTE SPLIT STUNT TRICK CRADDY CUTOFF EXPLOIT MASTERY MIRACLE WORSHIP DEXTROUS PERFORMANCE
(— IN SURFING) SPINNER QUASIMODO
(ACROBATIC —) SPLITS
(CRICKETER'S —) DOUBLE
(EASY —) PICNIC
(EFFECTIVE —) STROKE
(TUMBLING —) SCISSORS
(PL.) DAGS
FEATHER BOO PEN TAB DECK DOWN FLAG HERL SETA STUB VANE ADORN AXIAL PENNA PINNA PLUMA PLUME QUILL REMEX CLOTHE COVERT CRINET FLEDGE FLETCH FLIGHT HACKLE MANUAL PINION SARCEL SICKLE SQUAMA TIPPET TONGUE AXILLAR BRISTLE FLEMISH IMPLUME PRIMARY RECTRIX REMICLE STIPULE TECTRIX TERTIAL TOPPING AXILLARY SCAPULAR STREAMER TERTIARY
(BRISTLELIKE —) VIBRISSA
(HAWK'S —S) BRAIL BRAILS
(HORSE —) SPEAR
(NECK —) HACKLE
(NEW —) STIPULE
(OSTRICH TAIL —) BOO
(PINION —) SARCEL
(PRIMARY —) MANUAL
(TAIL —) SICKLE RECTRIX
(YELLOW —S) HULU
(PL.) GIG BOOT CAPE DOWN FLUE MAIL BRAIL CRISSUM CUSHION FLIGHTS PLUMAGE REMIGES SPURIAE

(PREF.) PENNAT(I)(O) PENNI PENNO PINN(I)(O) PINNAT(I)(O) PLUMI PTER(O) PTIL(O)
(SUFF.) PENNATE PENNINE PTILE PTILUS
FEATHER BED TYE
FEATHER CLOAK AHUULA TEMIAK
FEATHERED FLEDGE FLEDGY PLUMED PENNATE PINNATE FLIGHTED
(PREF.) PTENO
(SUFF.) PINNATE
FEATHERHEAD FOOL
FEATHERING STOCKING
FEATHER KEY FIN STOP SPLINE FEATHER
FEATHER-LEGGED COOTY COOTIE
FEATHERLIKE PINNATE
FEATHERY LIGHT PLUMY FLEDGY FLUFFY PLUMOSE PLUMEOUS
FEATLY NEATLY FOOTINGLY
FEATURE WAY FACE ITEM NOTE STAR BREAK FAVOR GRACE MOTIF TOKEN TRACT TRAIT TREAT ASPECT CACHET FAVOUR SPLASH AMENITY OUTLINE HALLMARK SALIENCE
(— OF WORD FORM) ASPECT
(ATTRACTIVE —) AMENITY
(DETERMINING —) LIMIT
(DISTINGUISHING —) TRAIT STROKE HALLMARK
(ESSENTIAL —) CHARACTER
(FATAL —) BANE
(LINGUISTIC —) ISOGLOSS SURVIVAL
(MAIN —) CRUX
(MOST COGENT —) BEAUTY
(OBJECTIONABLE —) DISCOUNT DRAWBACK
(SALIENT —) MOTIF
(TOPOGRAPHIC —) ARC
(TOPOGRAPHIC —S) LIE
(PL.) LAY FACE CONTOUR FASHION GEOLOGY RETRAIT
FEAZE FRAY FAIZE ROUGHEN
FEBRIFUGE PEREIRA ANGOSTURA
FEBRILE PYRETIC FEVERISH
FECES DRAST HOCKEY ORDURE
(PREF.) COPR(O)
FECKLESS WEAK FEEBLE
FECULENCE DREG
FECULENT DREGGY
FECUND FERTILE FRUITFUL PROLIFIC
FED FAT MEATED
FEDERATION BUND CROM UNION LEAGUE NATION COUNCIL ALLIANCE FEDERACY TRIALISM
FEDORA (CHARACTER IN —) LORIS FEDORA IPANOV ROMANOV
(COMPOSER OF —) GIORDANO
FEE FEU DUES DUTY FEAL FEUL FIEF FIER HIRE RATE WAGE CAULP EXTRA HANSE PRICE RIGHT ALNAGE AMOBER BARONY CHARGE DASTUR EMPLOY EXCISE REWARD SALARY SHEKEL BUOYAGE DASTURI DUMPAGE DUSTOOR FALDAGE FIRNAGE FURNAGE GAOLAGE GARNISH GRATIFY GUIDAGE HALLAGE HOUSAGE JAILAGE MULTURE PAYMENT PINLOCK PREFINE STIPEND STORAGE TALLAGE TRIBUTE VANTAGE BOOTHAGE BOUNTITH CHUMMAGE EXACTION FAREWELL GRATUITY MALIKANA POUNDAGE REREFIEF RETAINER SHIPPAGE WHARFAGE
(— TO LANDOWNER) TERRAGE
(— TO TEACHER) MINERVAL
(CUSTOMARY —) DASTUR
(CUSTOMS —) LOT
(ENTRANCE —) HANSA HANSE INCOME
(GRINDING —) THIRLAGE
(INITIATION —) FOOTING
(INSTALLATION —) FOOTING
(PHYSICIAN'S —) SOSTRUM
(ROAD —) PIKE
(UNAUTHORIZED —) GARNISH
(PL.) EXHIBITS
FEEBLE LOW WAN FLUE LAME MEAN PALE POOR PUNY SOFT WEAK DONCY DOTTY FAINT SEELY SILLY SOBER UNORN WANKY WASHY WERSH WONKY CADUKE DEBILE DONSIE DOTAGE FAINTY FLABBY FLIMSY FOIBLE INFIRM PAULIE PUISNE SCANTY SEMMIT SICKLY SIMPLE TANGLE UNFIRM WANKLE WEANLY DWAIBLY DWEEBLE FRAGILE INVALID LANGUID QUEECHY RICKETY SAPLESS SHILPIT SLENDER SLIMPSY THREADY UNWIELD UNWREST WEARISH DECREPIT DROGHLIN FEATLESS IMBECILE IMPOTENT INFERIOR LUSTLESS MALADIVE RESOLUTE SACKLESS THEWLESS THOWLESS UNSTRONG UNWIELDY WATERISH YIELDING NERVELESS
FEEBLE-MINDED ANILE DOTTY DOTTLE FOOLISH MORONIC WANTING IMBECILE
FEEBLENESS DOTAGE FEEBLE POVERTY CADUCITY DEBILITY WEAKNESS
FEED EAT HAY BAIT BEET BRAN CROP DIET DINE FILL FOOD GLUT GRUB MEAL MEAT OATS SATE AGIST FLESH FLUSH GORGE GRASS GRAZE NURSE SERVE STOKE TABLE BATTLE BROWSE FODDER FOSTER INFEED NOODLE REFETE REPAST SUCKLE SUPPLY BLOWOUT FURNISH GRATIFY HERBAGE INDULGE KEEPING NOURISH NURTURE PASTURE PROVENT SATIATE SATISFY SUBSIST SURFEIT SUSTAIN VICTUAL PROVENDER
(— ABUNDANTLY) STOKE
(— ANIMAL) SORT SERVE
(— AT NIGHT) SUP
(— CATTLE) SOIL
(— FOR CATTLE) FODDER STOVER TACKLE
(— FORCIBLY) CRAM
(— GLUTTONOUSLY) BATTEN
(— GREEN FOOD TO CATTLE) SOIL
(— HIGH) FRANK
(— IN STUBBLE) SHACK
(— ON FLIES) SMUT
(— RAVENOUSLY) FRAUNCH
(— STOCK) FOG SOIL SOILING
(— TO REPLETION) ENGORGE
(— TO THE FULL) SATIATE
(— WELL) BATTLE
(GROUND —) CHOP
(HORSE'S —) OATS
(POULTRY —) SCRATCH
(RED —) HAYSEED
(STOCK —) BRAN
(WHALE —) GRIT
(PREF.) THREP(SO)
FEEDBOARD DECK
FEEDER HOGGER HOPPER PECKER STOCKER
(YARN —) CARRIER
FEEDHEAD RISER FEEDER SINKHEAD
FEEDING RELIEF FOLDAGE PANNAGE
(— GROUND FOR FISH) MEADOW
(— THROUGH TUBE) GAVAGE
(FREE-CHOICE —) CAFETERIA
(IMPROPER —) MISDIET
(PREF.) PHAG(O)
FEEL FIND PALP GROPE SENSE THINK TOUCH FIMBLE FINGER HANDLE RESENT EXAMINE EXPLORE FEELING SENSATE PERCEIVE
(— ACUTELY) SUFFER
(— AVERSION FOR) HATE LOATHE
(— CHILLY) CREEM
(— COMPASSION) PITY YEARN
(— DEJECTION) REPINE
(— FEAR) UG GRUE UGGE TREMBLE
(— GRIEF) GRIEVE DEPLORE
(— HAPPY OR BETTER) LIGHT
(— NAUSEA) WAMBLE
(— OF CLOTH) HAND
(— ONE'S WAY) GROPE FUMBLE GRAMMEL
(— OUT) SOUND
(— PAIN) URN
(— REPUGNANCE) ABHOR
(— SHAME) BLUSH
(— WANT OF) MISS
FEELER DRAW KITE PALP SNIFF PALPUS TACTOR ANTENNA SMELLER PROPOSAL TENTACLE
(PREF.) ANTENNI
FEELING AURA FEEL PITY TACT VIBE VIEW CHEER HEART HUMOR SENSE SORGE TOUCH VIBES AFFECT CEMENT MORALE CONSENT EMOTION OPINION PASSION VELUNGE ATTITUDE SENTIENT SENSATION PRESENTIMENT
(— ILL) HOWISH
(— MIRTH) JOCUND
(— OF ACCORD) SYMPATHY
(— OF AMUSEMENT) CHARGE
(— OF ANTIPATHY) ALLERGY
(— OF ANXIETY) ANGST
(— OF CONTEMPT) DISDAIN
(— OF DISGUST) UG
(— OF DOUBT) SCRUPLE
(— OF HAVING SEEN BEFORE) DEJAVU
(— OF HORROR) CREEP CREEPS
(— OF HOSTILITY) ANIMUS
(— OF JOY) GLOAT
(— OF LOSS) REGRET
(— OF NAUSEA) WAMBLE
(— OF OPPOSITION) KICK
(— OF PLEASURE) THRILL
(— OF RESENTMENT) GRUDGE
(— OF ROMANCE) STARDUST
(— OF UNEASINESS) MALAISE
(— OF WARMTH) GLOW
(— OF WEARINESS) ENNUI
(— OF WELL-BEING) EUPHORIA
(— PRODUCED BY DRUG) RUSH
(ACTIVE —) SWANKY
(ANGERED —) DUDGEON
(AWKWARD —) LUBBER
(BODILY —) TABET
(BRISTLING —) GOOSEFLESH
(COMPASSIONATE —) REMORSE
(CONCEITED —) SWELLING
(EXALTED —) ECSTASY
(FAMILIAR —) DEJAVU
(HUMILIATING —) SHAME
(ILL —) HARDNESS
(INMOST —S) HEART
(INTUITIVE —) HUNCH
(KINDLY —) GOODWILL
(LOW-BORN —) LOON
(MISCHIEVOUS —) SPALPEEN
(OFFENDED —) PET
(PALTRY —) SQUIB
(PLEASANT —) BUZZ
(RAGGED —) SNUDGE
(RAKISH —) RAFF
(REPRESSION OF —) STOICISM
(SCURVY —) SCALD
(SHOCKED —) SCANDAL
(SICKLY —) QUALM
(STRONG —) STAB
(STRONG, POSITIVE —) SOUL
(TENDEREST —S) QUICK
(TRIFLING —) TOMFOOL
(UNKIND —) ILLWILL
(PL.) HEART WITHERS
(PREF.) SENSI
(SUFF.) PATH(IA)(IC)(Y)
FEEN, DIE (CHARACTER IN —) ADA GROMA ARINDAL
(COMPOSER OF —) WAGNER
FEET DOGS TONGS STAMPS WALKERS GUNBOATS TRILBIES PETTITOES
(— WASHING) MAUNDY
(BOARD —) FOOTAGE
(LARGE —) GUFFINS
(PREF.) PED(I)
(SUFF.) PEDE
(MEASURE OF —) METER
FEIGN ACT FAKE MINT MOCK SEEM SHAM VEYN AVOID FABLE FALSE FORGE PAINT PUTON SHAPE SHIRK AFFECT ASSUME GAMMON INVENT POSSUM CONCEAL FALSIFY FASHION IMAGINE POETIZE PRETEND ROMANCE DISGUISE SIMULATE
(— ASSENT) COLLOGUE
(— IGNORANCE) CONNIVE
(— ILLNESS) MALINGER
FEIGNED SHAM FALSE FEINT POETIC PSEUDO SHADOW ASSUMED COLORED FICTIVE PAINTED FABULOUS FICTIOUS SIMULATE SUPPOSED
(PREF.) PSEUD(O)

FEIGNING FICTION FORGERY SIMULATION
FEIJOA ANDRE
FEINT FAKE MINT RUSE APPEL FAINT SHIFT SPOOF TRICK FALSIFY FEIGNED FEINTER FINCTURE PRETENSE REVIRADO
FELDSPAR ALBITE AMBITE GNEISS CELSIAN SYENITE ADULARIA ANDESINE FELSPATH PERTHITE PETUNTZE SANIDINE SUNSTONE MOONSTONE
FELICIA AGATHAEA
FELICITATE HUG BLESS MACARIZE
FELICITOUS FIT HAPPY
FELICITOUSLY HAPPILY
FELICITY JOY BLISS SONSE HEAVEN
FELINE CATTISH
FELL CUR FEN HEW COSH DOWN DROP FALL HIDE HILL MOOR PELT RUIN SKIN VERY CRUEL EAGER FIELD GRASS GREAT SHARP DEADLY FIERCE FLEECE INTENT MIGHTY SAVAGE SHREWD TUMBLE BRUTISH CRASHED DOUGHTY HIDEOUS INHUMAN STRETCH TUMBLED MOUNTAIN SPIRITED VIGOROUS
(— A TREE) HEW LODGE
FELLER GIDEON
FELLING FALL CUTTING
FELLOE BOD FELF FALLY
FELLOW S BO BOY BUB COD DON EGG FOX GUY JOE LAD MAC MAN MUN NUT WAG WAT YOB BALL BEAN BEAU BIRD BOZO BUFF CARL CHAL CHAP COOT COVE CUSS DEAN DICK DUCK DUDE DULL GENT GILL GINK HIND HUSK JACK JAKE JOHN LOON MATE NABS PEER PRIG SNAP BILLY BIMBO BLOKE BROCK BUDDY BULLY CARLE CHIEL COVEY CULLY FRUIT GROOM GUEST JOKER MATCH PARTY SCOUT SKATE SLAVE SPORT SPRIG SWIPE BEGGAR BILLIE BIRKIE BOHUNK BOOGER BUDDIE BUFFER BUGGER BUSTER CALLAN CHIELD CODGER CUFFIN CUTTER FELLER FOOTER FOUTER FOUTRA GALOOT GAZABO GEEZER HOMBRE JASPER JOCKEY JOHNNY JOSSER KIPPER PERSON SHAVER SINNER SIRRAH SISTER SOCIUS TURNIP BASTARD BROTHER CALLANT CHAPPIE COMRADE CULLIES CULLION CUSTRON KNOCKER PARTNER SCROYLE SNOOZER BLIGHTER CONFRERE DOTTEREL MERCHANT NEIGHBOR SYNODITE
(AWKWARD —) JAY OAF CLUB GAWK CLOWN LOOBY GALOOT SLOUCH
(BASE —) CARL CARLE CULLION
(BASHFUL —) SHEEP
(BOLD —) HEARTY
(BRUTAL —) CLUBFIST
(CLOWNISH —) COOF BAYARD LOBLOLLY
(CLUMSY —) BOOB FILE CAMEL FARMER LUBBER PALOOKA
(COMMON —) JACK LOUT
(CONCEITED —) JEMMY DALTEEN PRINCOX
(CONTEMPTIBLE —) DOG SCUT SMAIL SNAKE RABBIT SMATCH PEASANT
(CONTENTIOUS —) SQUARER
(CORPULENT —) POMPION
(COUNTRY —) JAKE JASPER
(CRUDE —) STIFF
(DASHING —) BUCK BLADE
(DASTARDLY —) HOUND
(DECEITFUL —) KNAVE
(DESPICABLE —) FOUTER FOUTRA HANGDOG SMATCHET
(DIRTY —) SCAB BROCK
(DISAGREEABLE —) GLEYDE
(DISSOLUTE —) RAKE ROUE RAKEHELL
(DROLL —) CARD
(DROWSY —) LUNGIS
(DRUNKEN —) BORACHIO
(DULL —) BUFF DRIP FOGY CHUFF SUMPH LUNGIS HUMDRUM
(ENERGETIC —) HUSTLER
(FAT —) HIND GULCH GLUTTON
(FIERCE-LOOKING —) KILLBUCK
(FINE —) BAWCOCK
(FOOLISH —) SOP GABY GOFF ZANY GANDER JACKSON WIDGEON
(GAY —) GALLIARD
(GOOD —) BRICK BULLY TRUMP HEARTY TROJAN
(GOOD-FOR-NOTHING —) JACKEEN
(GREEDY —) SLOTE
(IDLE —) FANION FOOTER STOCAH LOLLARD SKULKER
(IGNORANT —) GOBBIN
(ILLBRED —) LARRIKIN
(IMPERTINENT —) JACK WHISK
(INSIGNIFICANT —) SQUIB
(JOLLY —) VAVASOR VAVASOUR
(LAZY —) BUM LUSK TOOL LENTO
(LOW —) RAG WAFF SWEEP LIMMER VARLET MECHANIC WHORESON
(LUBBERLY —) HULK
(MEAN —) CAD DOG BOOR BOUCH BUCKO CAVEL CHURL SCURF RASCAL CULLION BEZONIAN COISTREL COISTRIL SNEAKSBY SPALPEEN STINKARD
(NIGGARDLY —) SNUDGE
(NOISY —) MOUTH
(OLD —) GLYDE GAFFER GEEZER
(OLD-FASHIONED —) FOGY
(OVERBEARING —) GRIMSIR
(PROSAIC —) PRUNE
(PUNY —) SMAIK
(QUARRELSOME —) HECTOR
(QUEER OLD —) CODGER GEEZER
(RESIDENTIAL —) DON
(ROGUISH —) DOG
(RUDE —) BOOR JACK ROUGH
(SHABBY —) SHAB SQUEEF
(SHEEPISH —) SUMPH
(SHIFTLESS —) PROG SHACK PROGGER
(SHREWD —) COLT
(SILLY —) TOT GUMP ZANY SHEEP SMAIK BUFFER DOTTEREL MUSHHEAD
(SIMPLE —) DOODLE
(SLOVENLY —) SLUTE
(SLY —) FOX COON
(SNEAKING —) SNUDGE
(SORDID —) HUNKS
(SOUTH AFRICAN —) KEREL
(SPIRITED —) BRICK
(SPORTY —) PLAYBOY
(STRANGE —) CODGER
(STRAPPING —) SWANKY SWANKIE
(STUPID —) ASS BOOB CLOD COOF DAFF DOLT GUMP HASH MUFF SIMP BOOBY CUDDY DUNCE MORON STIRK BAYARD BUFFER FARMER FOOZLE GANDER ASINOCO DOWFART HUMDRUM CLODPATE CLODPOLE CLODPOLL CODSHEAD SOCKHEAD
(STURDY —) HUSKY
(SULLEN —) GLUMP
(SURLY —) CHUFF CHOUGH
(TEDIOUS —) FOOZLE
(TRICKISH —) HUMBUG
(TRICKY —) ROOK GREEK KNAVE SCAMP DODGER RASCAL
(UNCIVIL —) RUDESBY
(UNCOUTH —) JAKE KEMP TIKE
(VILE —) RAT SKUNK
(VULGAR —) TIGER
(WORTHLESS —) BUM CUR DOG HASH PROG RAFF WAFF JAVEL ROGUE SCAMP SHOAT SNAKE STUMER BROTHEL BUDMASH PROGGER VAURIEN TARTARET
(WRETCHED —) DEVIL DOGBOLT
(YOUNG —) BILLY BUCKO CADIE CADDIE
(PREF.) CO
(SUFF.) ENGRO
FELLOWMAN BROTHER NEIGHBOR
FELLOWSHIP GUILD HAUNT UNION FAMILY COMPANY ALLIANCE SODALITY
(CHRISTIAN —) KOINONIA
FELLY RIM FELF FELLOE KEENLY CRUELLY BITTERLY FIERCELY SAVAGELY TERRIBLY
FELO-DE-SE SUICIDE
FELON WILD CRUEL FETLOW FIERCE WICKED CONVICT CULPRIT PANARIS VILLAIN WHITLOW PHLEGMON RUNROUND MALEFACTOR
FELONY ARSON CRIME OFFENSE
FELT JIG PLAIT FILTER NUMNAH SENSED SOLEIL VELOUR DOUBLER FELTING PANNOSE
(— INTENSIVELY) ACUTE
(— THROUGH SENSES) SENSATE
(DEEPLY —) CORDIAL INTENSE
(PERSONALLY —) CONSCIOUS
(PL.) CLOTHING
(PREF.) PIL(O)
FELTWORK NEUROPIL
FEMALE DOE EWE HEN HER SHE SOW DAME GIRL GYNE LADY MORT ADULT JENNY SMOCK SQUAW WOMAN WAHINE WEAKLY DISTAFF FEMINAL WOMANLY DAUGHTER FEMININE GYNAECIC LADYLIKE WOMANISH PETTICOAT
(— ANCESTOR) TAPROOT
(IMPERFECT —) FREEMARTIN
(PARTHOGENETIC —) AMAZON
(PREF.) FEMINO GYN(AE)(AECO)(AEO)(ANDRO)(E)(ECO)(EO)(O) THELY
(SUFF.) ESS ETTE GYN(E)(IST)(OUS) INE TRIX
FEMININE FAIR SOFT WEAK WOMAN FEMALE TENDER WAHINE FEMINAL WOMANLY WOMANISH PETTICOAT
(SUFF.) ENNE INA INE
FEMININE WILES (CHARACTER IN —) BELLINA LEONORA FILANDRO GIAMPOLO ROMUALDO
(COMPOSER OF —) CIMAROSA
FEMININITY MUSLIN FEMINITY MULIEBRITY
FEMME FATALE VAMP SIREN
FEMORAL CRURAL
(PREF.) CRURO
FEMUR THIGH
FEN BOG CARR FAIN FELL FOWL MERE MOOR WASH BROAD FAINS MARSH SNIPE SWAMP VENTS MORASS MUSKEG QUAGMIRE
FENCE BAR HAW HAY BANK DIKE DUEL DYKE HAHA HAIN PALE PLAY RAIL STUB WALL WEIR WIRE BEARD DODGE FRITH GUARD HEDGE MOUND PALIS STICK STUMP DETENT FENDER FRAISE GLANCE HURDLE LEADER PALING PICKET RADDLE RASPER SCHERM SCRIME TIMBER BARRIER BULWARK CYCLONE DEFENSE ENCLOSE FENCING FENSURE IMPALER PASSAGE RAILING SWAGMAN BACKSTOP ENCHASER ENCLOSER GRAFFAGE HOARDING PALISADE PALISADO SEPIMENT SKIRMISH BRANDRETH BRANDRITH
(— AROUND BULLRING) BARRERA
(— AROUND MACHINERY) BRATTICE
(— CLOSING DITCH) WOLF
(— OF LOCK) STUB
(— OF LOGS) GLANCE
(CATTLE —) OXER WIPE SKERM SCHERM
(FISH —) WEIR KIDDLE LEADER
(METAL —) RAIL RAILING
(PREF.) HERCO PHRAGMO SEPTATO
(SUFF.) SEPTATE
FENCER DUELIST IMPALER PARRIER PROVOST SCRIMER SWORDER FOILSMAN BACKSWORD
FENCE RAIL DRAWBAR
FENCE SECTION PANE
FENCE-SITTER MUGWUMP
FENCING WIRE FENCE PALING ESCRIME PASSAGE SCIENCE SWORDING
(— THRUST) PASSADO
(JAPANESE —) KENDO
FEND WARD PARRY SHIRK DEFEND FORBID RESIST SUPPORT
FENDER SKID WING CAMEL GUARD SKATE BUFFER BUMPER SHIELD DOLPHIN PUDDING BOWGRACE MUDGUARD SPLASHER
(— FOR FIREPLACE) CURB KERB
(— NEAR HOLE) TELLTALE

(ROPE —) PUDDENING
(SHIP'S —) SKID
FENDER SKID GLANCER
FENESTRA FORAMEN
FENGHUANG FUM PHOENIX
FENKS FRITTERS
FENMAN WEBFOOT
FENNEC ZERDA
FENNEL ANIS DILL HEMP SOYA FERULE FINKEL COWBANE HOGWEED SPINGEL FINOCHIO FLORENCE CAROSELLA
FENNER ZERDA
FENRIS (FATHER OF —) LOKI
(MOTHER OF —) ANGURBODA
(SISTER OF —) HEL
(SLAYER OF —) VIDAR
FENSTER WINDOW
FENUGREEK BAUMIER MELLILOT
(SEEDS OF —) HELBEH
FERAL WILD BRUTAL DEADLY FERINE SAVAGE BESTIAL UNTAMED FUNEREAL UNBROKEN
FER-DE-LANCE BONETAIL JARARACA
FERMATA HOLD PAUSE TENOR CORONA
FERMENT FRY LOB ZYM BARM BREW FRET HEAT SOUR TURN WORK ZYME FEVER SWEAT YEAST DANDER ENZYME FLOWER FOMENT SEETHE SIMMER TUMULT UPROAR AGITATE QUICKEN TURMOIL DISORDER
(— IN SALIVA) PTYALIN
(DIGESTIVE —) TRYPSIN
(PREF.) ZYM(O)
(SUFF.) ZYME
FERMENTATION SWEAT CUVAGE FERMENT MOWBURN WORKING ZYMOSIS
FERMENTED SOD HARD
(IMPROPERLY —) FOXY
FERMENTING BARMY WORKING
FERN HEII NITO PULU TARA WEKI BRAKE DUGAL EKAHA FROND NARDO PITAU PONGA ULUHI WHEKI AMAMAU DOODIA NARDOO OSMUND PTERIS ACROGEN ATERACH BOGFERN BRACKEN OSMUNDA SYNANGE WOODSIA ADIANTUM ASPIDIUM BAROMETZ BUCKHORN BUNGWALL CETERACH DAVALLIA DENDRITE FERNWORT FILICITE GOLDBACK HARDFERN KOLOKOLO MOONWORT MULEWORT PARAREKA PILLWORT POLYPODY SPOROGEN STAGHORN MAIDENHAIR
(KIND OF —) MALE
(PART OF —) AXIS CASE LEAF STEM BLADE FROND PINNA STIPE TOOTH MIDRIB RACHIS LEAFLET PETIOLE PINNULE SUBLEAFLET
(PL.) FILICES
(PREF.) PTERID(O)
(SUFF.) PTERIS
FERN LEAF FROND CROSIER
FERNLIKE FERNY PTEROID
FEROCIOUS ILL FELL GRIM RUDE WILD BRUTE CRUEL FERAL BLOODY BRUTAL FEROCE FIERCE GOTHIC RAGING SAVAGE ACHARNE INHUMAN OMINOUS VIOLENT WOLFISH PITILESS RAVENOUS RUTHLESS TARTARLY
FEROCITY FERITY SAVAGERY VIOLENCE ACHARNEMENT
FERRARA ANDREW
FERRET HOB MONK TAPE PADOU MONACH WEASEL POLECAT
(— OUT) FOSSICK
(FEMALE —) GIL GILL JILL BITCH
(MALE —) HOB HOBB
FERRIAGE WAFTAGE
FERRIC OXIDE CROCUS
FERROCYANIDE PRUSSIATE
FERROTYPE GLAZE TINTYPE
FERROUS SIDEROUS
FERRULE CAP TIP CUFF RING SHOE VIRL COLLET PULLEY RUNNER VERREL VIROLE ARMGARN BUSHING CRAMPET
FERRY FORD PASS PONT SCOW PASSAGE TRAJECT TRANECT TRANSFER
FERRYBOAT BAC PONT SCOW FERRY
FERRYMAN CHARON FERRIER WATERMAN
FERTILE FAT GOOD RANK RICH GLEBY ARABLE BATFUL BATTLE FECUND HEARTY STRONG TEEMING ABUNDANT BATTABLE FRUITFUL GENEROUS PREGNANT PROLIFIC SPAWNING
FERTILITY HEART FATNESS
(PATRON OF —) YAKSHA
FERTILIZATION ENDOGAMY POROGAMY
FERTILIZE FAT DUNG FISH LIME MARL CHALK BATTEN ENRICH FRUCTIFY
FERTILIZER FAT MARL GUANO HUMUS ALINIT FLOATS MANURE POLLEN POTASH CARRIER COMPOTE HUMOGEN KAINITE NITRATE TANKAGE AMMONITE CINEREAL NITROGEN
FERULA NARTHEX
FERULE ROD RULER COLLET FENNEL FERULA PALMER
FERVENCY WARMTH CANDENCY
FERVENT HOT KEEN WARM EAGER FIERY ARDENT BITTER FERVID FIERCE INWARD RAGING SAVAGE BOILING BURNING GLOWING INTENSE PECTORAL ROMANTIC VEHEMENT RELIGIOUS
FERVID HOT ARDENT TROPIC BOILING BURNING FERVENT GLOWING ZEALOUS UNCTUOUS VEHEMENT
FERVOR FIRE HEAT HWYL RAGE SOUL ZEAL ARDOR SPIRIT WARMTH PASSION CANDENCY DEVOTION STRENGTH VIOLENCE
(— IN PRAYER) KAVVANAH KAWWANAH
FESCUE VESTER
FESS BAR BAND PERT DANCE HUMET
(DIMINUTIVE —) TRANGLE
FEST GALA
FESTAL GAY GALA GAUDY FESTIVE FESTUAL FEASTFUL
FESTER ROT BEAL RANK SCAR RANKLE PUSTULE PUTREFY
FESTERING RANK FRETTY
FESTIVAL (ALSO SEE FEAST) ALE BON PWE BUSK FAIR FEIS FETE GALA HOLI MELA PUJA TIDE UTAS WAKE DELIA FEAST FERIA FESTA GAUDY HALOA PURIM REVEL ROUSE SEDAR ADONIA BAIRAM BRIDAL CARNEA DEWALI DIASIA DIPALA FIESTA HOHLEE HUFFLE KERMIS KWANZA LAMMAS LENAEA OPALIA PONGOL POOJAH POSADA SUCCOS AGONIUM AGRANIA BANQUET BELTANE DASAHRA EQUIRIA FESTIAL HILARIA KERMESS KWANZAN MATSURI PALILIA SUKKOTH THIASOS TOXCATL UPHELYA VINALIA AGRIONIA AIANTEIA APATURIA ATHENAEA BEALTINE BRUMALIA CARNIVAL COTYTTIA DASAHARA DIIPOLIA DIONYSIA DUSSERAH ENCAENIA FASNACHT FLORALIA HANUKKAH HIGHTIDE KALENDAE LUPERCAL MARYMASS MATRALIA MITHRIAC MUHARRAM MUNYCHIA NATIVITY NEOMENIA POTLATCH STAMPEDE TAARGELIA SATURNALIA
(FALL —) OCTOBERFEST
(HIGHLAND —) MOD
(MUSICAL —) EISTEDDFOD
(PL.) MOED VOTA
(SUFF.) MAS
FESTIVE GAY GALA JOLLY FESTAL GENIAL JOYOUS FEASTLY HOLIDAY JOCULAR CONVIVAL FEASTFUL MIRTHFUL SPORTIVE CONVIVIAL
(— TIME) TET
FESTIVITY GALA GAUD UTAS UTIS BEANO FEAST MIRTH RANDY REVEL GAIETY GAYETY SPLORE HOLIDAY JOLLITY JOYANCE PATTERN FESTIVAL FUNCTION MERRIMENT MERRYMAKING
(RIOTOUS —) RAG
FESTOON SWAG TRIM WREATH GARLAND DECORATE
(PL.) ENCARPUS
FETCH FET FESH GASP GIVE SHAG TACK TAKE TEEM WAIN BRING SWEEP TRICK DOUBLE STROKE WRAITH ACHIEVE ATTRACT ARTIFICE FETCHING INTEREST
FETCHED FOSH
FETCHING SWEET CRAFTY CUNNING ALLURING PLEASING SCHEMING
FETE FAIR GALA FEAST HONOR ROAST BAZAAR FIESTA HOLIDAY
FETID OLID RANK MUSTY PUTID ROTTEN VIROSE NOISOME SANIOUS MALODOROUS
FETIDLY FOULLY
FETISH OBI IDOL JUJU OBIA ZEME ZEMI ZOGO ANITO ASCON CHARM GUACA HUACA OBEAH OBIAH TOTEM AMULET FETICH GRIGRI NAGUAL VOODOO SHINTAI SORCERY FETISHRY GREEGREE TALISMAN
FETLOCK COOT FOOTLOCK
FETTER BAND BEND BOLT BOND FIND GYVE IRON SPAN BASIL BEWET BILBO CHAIN SLANG SWATH ANKLET GARTER HALTER HAMPER HOBBLE HOPPLE IMPEDE LANGEL RACKAN SWATHE CLINKER CONFINE ENCHAIN ENSLAVE FETLOCK GARNISH MANACLE SHACKLE SPANCEL TRAMMEL RESTRAIN
(PL.) IRONS LINKS DARBIES GARNISH GARTERS
FETTERBUSH PIPESTEM PIPEWOOD
FETTLE BEAT DECK FUSS MULL TIDY TWIG VEIN DRESS GROOM WHACK YARAK GIRDLE REPAIR SETTLE STRIKE ARRANGE BANDAGE FEATHER HARNESS
FETTLER BILLYER NOBBLER
FETTLING FIX FETTLE FIXING
FETUS BIRTH CHILD YOUNG AMELUS BREECH EMBRYO FOETUS ABORTUS CYCLOPS FEATURE AMORPHUS
(PREF.) EMBRY(O) FETI FETO FOETI FOETO
FEUD FIEF FRAY BROIL AFFRAY ENMITY FEODUM FEUDUM STRIFE CONTEST DISPUTE QUARREL VENDETTA
FEUDATORY FIEF VASSAL ZAMINDAR ZEMINDAR
FEUILLE MORTE PHILAMOT
FEVER AGUE FIRE ARDOR CAUMA DANDY LEUMA OCTAN CAUSUS DENGUE FEBRIS HECTIC SEPTAN SEXTAN SODOKU TYPHIA TYPHUS VOMITO AMAKEBE FERMENT FEVERET HELODES HOTNESS MALARIA PINKEYE PYREXIA QUARTAN TERTIAN TYPHOID SYNOCHUS TERTIANA TYPHINIA CALENTURE
(— OF HORSE) WEED SCALMA
(— OF PERU) VERRUGA
(— OF SHEEP) BRAXY
(BRAIN —) PHRENITIS
(HAY —) RHINITIS
(KIND OF —) LASSA
(MALARIAL —) TAP
(MARSH —) HELODES
(SPLENIC —) ANTHRAX
(TEXAS —) TRISTEZA
(WITHOUT —) APYRETIC
(YELLOW —) VOMITO
(PREF.) FEBRI PYR(ET)(ETO)
(SUFF.) PYRA
FEVERED DISEASED
FEVERFEW MAYWEED MUGWORT PELLITORY
FEVERISH HOT FIERY FEVERY HECTIC EXCITED FEBRILE FRANTIC RESTLESS
FEVERLESS APYREXIA
FEVERROOT GENSON
FEVER TREE BITTERBARK
FEVERWEED FITWEED
FEVERWORT BONESET
FEW LIT CURN LESS SOME SCANT THREE WHEEN WHONE CURRAN PICKLE SPOTTY LIMITED SEVERAL EXIGUOUS
(PREF.) OLIG(O) PAUCI

FEWER LESS
(PREF.) MI(O)
FEWNESS PAUCITY
FEY DEAD CRAZY DYING ELFIN FATAL DOOMED TOUCHED UNLUCKY PIXILATED
FEZ TARBOOSH
FIADOR THEODORE
FIANCE TRUST SPOUSE FIANCEE PROMISE AFFIANCE INTENDED
FIASCO CRASH FLASK FROST FIZZLE FAILURE DISASTER
FIAT EDICT ORDER UKASE DECREE COMMAND DECISION SANCTION
FIB LIE YED FLAW WHID SLANT STORY FITTEN PUMMEL SKLENT TARADIDDLE
FIBBER LIAR
FIBER TAL ADAD BASS BAST COIR ERUC FERU FLAX HARL HEMP IMBE JUTE LINE PITA SILK SUNN TULA ABACA AGUST AZLON CAJUN CAROA CHOEL ERIZO FIBRE GRAIN HARLE ISOTE ISTLE IXTLE IZOTE KAPOK KENAF KITUL LYCRA MESTA MURVA OAKUM RAMIE RAPHE SIMAL SISAL STRAW TERAP TOSSA TUCUM VIVER AMIRAY ARAMID ARGHAN BINDER BUNTAL BURITI CABUYA CATENA DACRON EMBIRA FIBRIL FIMBLE HINOKI KANAFF KENDIR KOHEMP MUCUNA NYTRIL RAFFIA SALAGO STAPLE STRAND STRING SUTURE THREAD TUCUMA TURURI VINYON YACHAN ZAPUPE ACETATE ACRYLIC ANONANG ARAMINA BASSINE CANTALA CASCARA CHANDUL CHINGMA COQUITA ESPARTO FILASSE FUNICLE GEBANGA GRAVATA GUAXIMA GUMIHAN HUARIZO KERATTO KITTOOL MOCMAIN PALMITE PANGANE PAUKPAN POCHOTE SABUTAN CANAPINA CURRATOW FILAMENT HARAKEKE HENEQUEN PIASSAVA TOQUILLA TRONADOR
(— FROM PEACOCK FEATHERS) MARL
(— OF PALM) DOH LIF ERUC COYOL COROZO GOMUTI KITTUL COQUITA GEBANGA
(—S OF FLAX) HARE
(CLUSTER OF —S) NEP
(COARSE —) KEMP
(COCONUT —) COIR KYAR
(COTTON —) LINT STAPLE
(FLAX —) TOW
(KNOT OF —) NOIL
(MANUFACTURED —) DYNEL ORLON ESTRON ACRILAN SPANDEX
(MATTED —) SHAG
(MINERAL —) ASBESTOS
(MUSCLE —) RHABDIUM
(NERVE —) EFFERENT DEPRESSOR
(PULVERIZED —) FLOCK
(SILKY —) PULU KAPOK KUMBI YACHAN CASTULI
(TEXTILE —) SPANDEX
(TWISTED —S) STRAND
(WASTE —) FLY GOUT
(WASTE —S) FLOSS
(WOODY —) BAST GRAIN SCUTCH
(PL.) FUZZ KERATTO
(PREF.) FIBRO IN(O)
FIBRIL AXONEME DESMOSE MYONEME MYOPHAN
FIBRILS
(SUFF.)
(NETWORK —) SPONGIA(E)(N) SPONGIUM
FIBRIN GLUTEN MYOSIN
FIBROCARTILAGE FABELLA MENISCUS
FIBROID DESMOID
FIBROMA INOMA FIBROID
FIBROUS FIBROSE STRINGY NEMALINE
FIBULA LACE CLASP BROOCH BUCKLE PERONE SPLINT
(PREF.) PERONEO PERONO
FICHE FILMCARD
FICKLE GERY DIZZY FALSE GIDDY LIGHT UNSAD HARLOT KITTLE MOBILE PUZZLE SHIFTY VOLAGE WANKLE WANKLY CASALTY CASELTY FLATTER MOONISH MOVABLE MUTABLE VAINFUL VARIANT VOLUBLE GOSSAMER MOVEABLE SKITTISH STIRRING UNSTABLE UNSTEADY VARIABLE VOLATILE WAVERING
FICKLENESS CHANGE LEVITY EASINESS FICKLETY VARIANCE
FICO FIG FIGO TANTI
FICTILE FIGULINE
FICTION BAM TALE FABLE FALSE NOVEL ROMAN STORY DECEIT DEVICE FABULA FITTEN LEGEND COINAGE FANTASY FIGMENT FORGERY MARCHEN NOVELRY ROMANCE ROMANZA KAILYARD PHANTASY PRETENCE PRETENSE
(CRIME —) NOIR
FICTITIOUS MADE BOGUS DUMMY FALSE PHONY FABLED POETIC ASSUMED FEIGNED PHANTOM FABULOUS FICTIOUS MYTHICAL ROMANTIC SIMULATE SPURIOUS LEGENDARY
(PREF.) PSEUD(O)
FICUS PYRULA
FID PRICK NORMAN PRICKER SPLICER
FIDDLE BOW BOX GIG SAW VIOL CHEAT CROWD GEIGE GIGUE GUDOK CHORUS DIDDLE FITHEL POTTER TRIFLE URHEEN VIOLIN CHROTTA SARANGI SWINDLE HUMSTRUM
(— STRING) THAIRM
(— WITH) TWIDDLE
(BASS —) GUTBUCKET
(OLD —) REBEC
FIDDLER CRAB VIOLER VIOLIN CROWDER SCRAPER SIXPENCE
FIDDLER CRAB RACER FIDDLER OCYPODE SOLDIER
FIDDLESTICKS POOH PSHAW FIDDLE
FIDELIO (CHARACTER IN —) ROCCO FIDELIO LEONORE PIZARRO JACQUINO FLORESTAN MARZELLINE
(COMPOSER OF —) BEETHOVEN
FIDELITY TRUE ARDOR FAITH PIETY TROTH TRUTH FEALTY HONESTY LOYALTY ADHESION DEVOTION RELIGION VERACITY CONSTANCY
FIDGET MOP FIKE FIRK FUSS ROIL FIDGE FITCH HOTCH SHRUB SHRUG WORRY BREVIT FIGGLE FISSLE FISTLE FRIDGE FUSSER HIRSEL JIFFLE JIGGET NESTLE NIBBLE NIGGLE TIDDLE TRIFLE VIGGLE WORRIT NERVOUS RESTLESS TWITCHET
(— ABOUT TRIFLES) SPOFFLE
(STATE OF —) FANTAD FANTOD
(PL.) JUMPS
FIDGETY ANTSY FIKIE FUSSY ITEMY FEISTY FIGENT FLISKY KITTLE UNEASY RESTIVE TWITCHY RESTLESS
FIDUCIARY TRUSTEE TRUSTFUL
FIE SISS FAUGH
FIEF FEE HAN FEUD FEOFF TIMAR ZIAMET SATSUMA SUBFIEF BENEFICE
(— HOLDER) TIMARIOT
FIELD LEA LOT ACRE AGER AREA BENT CAMP FELL FLAT HADE INAM LAND LIST MEAD PALE PARK PLAY RAND TOWN WONG BRECK CAMPO CHAMP CLOUR CROFT EARTH GLEBE INNAM LAYER MILPA NILPA PADDY RANGE ROWEN SAWAH TILTH VELDE ARRISH CAMPUS CAREER CHAMPE DOMAIN FURROW GARDEN GROUND MACHAR MATTER MEADOW PADANG PINGLE SHIELD SPHERE CHARMEL COMPASS CULTURE DIAMOND FERRING GARSTON INFIELD MOWLAND NEWTAKE PADDOCK PARROCK PIGHTLE PURVIEW QUILLET TERRAIN THWAITE TILLAGE CLEARING PROVINCE
(— ADJOINING HOUSE) CROFT
(— AT CRICKET) SCOUT
(— OF ACTIVITY) GAME ARENA BARONY SPHERE TERRAIN
(— OF BATTLE) PLAIN
(— OF BLOODSHED) ACELDAMA AKELDAMA
(— OF CONTROL) DOMAIN
(— OF ENDEAVOR) BUSINESS
(— OF SNOW) NEVE SNOWPACK
(— OF STUDY) MAJOR GROUND
(— ON WHICH GRASS IS GROWN) MEAD MEADOW
(— SOWN FOR TWO SUCCESSIVE YEARS) HOOK
(ENCLOSED —) AGER TOWN CLOSE CROFT
(FOOTBALL —) GRIDIRON
(FRUITFUL —) CHARMEL
(GRASSY —) LEA PEN GARSTON
(HOP —) HOPYARD
(KIND OF —) SKEW
(LAVA —) PEDREGAL
(LITTLE-KNOWN —) BYWAY
(NEW GOLD —) RUSH
(PLOWED —) FURROW
(RICE —) SAWAH
(SMALL —) HAW CLOSE CROFT PADDOCK
(SPORTS —) ARENA PITCH
(STUBBLE —) HIRSH ROWEN ARRISH GRATTEN GRATTON
(TILTING —) LISTS
(TOBACCO —) VEGA
(UNEXPLOITED —) FRONTIER
(UNPLOWED EDGE OF —) RAND
(PL.) FIELDEN
(PREF.) AGRI AGRO ARVI CAMPI
FIELD BALM SHEEPMINT
FIELD CAMOMILE OXEYE
FIELDER GLOVEMAN
(CRICKET —) SLIP COVER FIELD GULLY POINT SCOUT GULLEY INFIELDER
FIELDFARE FELT JACK REDLEG FELLFARE HILLBIRD JACKBIRD REDSHANK SNOWBIRD VELTFARE
FIELDING (— ABILITY) GLOVE
FIELD MADDER SPURWORT
FIELD MOUSE VOLE MIGALE
FIELDPIECE GUN AMUSETTE GALLOPER
FIELD SCABIOUS BLUECAP
FIELDWORK LUNET REDAN LUNETTE REDOUBT
FIEND FEN FOE PUG FEND FYND DEMON DEVIL ENEMY SATAN TRULL WIZARD SHAITAN SUCCUBA TITIVIL BARBASON SUCCUBUS
FIENDISH CRUEL WICKED DEMONIC FIENDLY SATANIC DEMONIAC DEVILISH DIABOLIC INFERNAL
FIERCE ILL BOLD FELL GRIM KEEN RUDE THRO WILD WOOD ASPER BREME CRUEL EAGER FELON HATEL ORPED RETHE SHARP SMART STARK STERN STOUR STOUT WROTH ARDENT FEROCE GOTHIC HETTER IMMANE LUPINE RAGING RUGGED SAVAGE STURDY UNMEEK UNMILD WICKED BRUTISH FERVENT FURIOSO FURIOUS GRIMFUL INHUMAN MANKIND RABIOUS RAMPANT SCADDLE VICIOUS VIOLENT STERNFUL TIGERISH
(PREF.) LABRO
FIERCE-EYED WALLEYED
FIERCELY FELL HARD FELLY FIERCE
FIERCENESS FURY FEROCITY
FIERY HOT RED ADUST FIRED QUICK SHARP ARDENT FLASHY IGNITE BURNING FERVENT FLAMING FURIOUS GLOWING HOTHEAD IGNEOUS PARCHED PEPPERY VIOLENT ADUSTIVE CHOLERIC FEVERISH FRAMPOLD INFLAMED PHRAMPEL SPIRITED SPITFIRE VEHEMENT
FIERY ANGEL (CHARACTER IN —) RENATA AGRIPPA HEINRICH RUPPRECHT MEPHISTOPHELES
(COMPOSER OF —) PROKOFIEV
FIERY RED SANDIX
FIERY-TEMPERED SPUNKY
FIESTA FETE FERIA PARTY HOLIDAY
(— COSTUME) POLLERA
FIFE STICK PIFERO PIFFERO
FIFTEEN FIVE
(PREF.) PENTADEC(A)
FIFTEENTH DOUBLETTE
FIFTH QUINT QUINTIN HEMIOLIA
(— ABOVE TONIC) DOMINANT

(PERFECT —) HEMIOLA HEMIOLIA
(PREF.) QUINT(I)
FIFTY (— YEAR ANNIVERSARY) JUBILEE
FIFTY-FIFTY EVEN
FIG RIG FICO ARRAY BREBA DRESS ELEME ELEMI PIPAL SABRA TANTI BALETE BALITI FOUTER FOUTRA GINGER LOBFIG PEEPUL TRIFLE FURBISH GONDANG SICONUS SYCONUS WARINGIN
(— CROP) MAMME
(PREF.) FICI SYCO
FIG BASKET CABAS
FIGHT BOX MIX WAP WAR WIN BEAT BEEF BLUE BOUT CAMP CLEM COCK COPE COWP CRAB CUFF DUEL DUKE FLOG FRAY LAKE MEET MELL MILL SHOW SLUG SPAR TILT WAGE YOKE BANDY BRAWL CLASH FIELD FLOLT HURRY JOUST MATCH MELEE MIXUP RAMMY SCRAP SETTO SHINE SPURN STOUR TOUSE AFFAIR AFFRAY BARNEY BATTLE BICKER BLOWUP COMBAT DEBATE FEUCHT FRACAS FRAISE HASSLE IMPUGN MEDDLE OPPOSE RELUCT REPUGN RESIST RIPPIT RUFFLE SHOWER STOUSH STRIFE STRIKE STRIVE TOUSEL TURNUP BARGAIN BRABBLE CONTEND CONTEST COUNTER JOURNEY QUARREL RUCTION SIMULTY TUILYIE WARFARE CONFLICT DOGFIGHT DUOMACHY FINISHER GUNFIGHT MILITATE SKIRMISH SLUGFEST SQUABBLE STRUGGLE TIRRIVEE TIRRWIRR TRAVERSE
(— AGAINST) BUCK OPPUGN
(— BETWEEN TWO) DUEL DUOMACHY
(— FOR) SERVE CHAMPION
(— WITH CLUB) TIMBER
(FIST —) RIPPIT TURNUP
(GANG —) RUMBLE
(SEA —) NAUMACHY
(STREET —) HABBLE RUMBLE
(SUFF.) MACHIA MACHY
FIGHTER PUG VAMP BOXER COCKER BATTLER DUELIST SLUGGER SOLDIER WARRIOR ANDABATA BARRATER BARRATOR CHAMPION GUERILLA PUGILIST SCRAPPER
(FIRE —) EXEMPT HOTSHOT
(GUERILLA —) MAQUIS BUSHWHACKER
(GUERILLA —S) MUJAMIDEEN
FIGHTING BLOW ACTION AFFRAY DEBATE WARLIKE CONFLICT MILITANT
(— WITH SHADOW) SCIAMACHY
FIGHTING FISH PLAKAT
FIGLIA DI JORIO, LA (CHARACTER IN —) MILA ALIGI LAZARO
(COMPOSER OF —) PIZZETTI
FIG MARIGOLD SAMH MESEM FICOID FOXCHOP FICOIDAL ICEPLANT
FIGMENT IDEA FICTION
FIGPECKER BECCAFICO
FIGURATE FLORID FIGURAL FIGURED FIGURATO
FIGURATION FORM SHAPE DESIGN OUTLINE
FIGURATIVE FLORID FIGURAL FIGURED FLOWERY TYPICAL ALLUSIVE TROPICAL
FIGURE FIG HUE VOL BOSH DOLL FORM IDEA SIGN STAR ANGLE ANTIC DATUM DIGIT FLIRT FRAME IMAGE MAGOT MOTIF SHAPE SPADE SPRIG AUMAIL BABOON CHANGE CIPHER COCKUP CUTOUT DEVICE EFFIGY EMBLEM ENTAIL FIGGER GOOGOL INCUSE NUMBER PERSON SCHEME SYMBOL TAILLE TATTOO CHASSIS CHEVRON CHIFFER CHIFFRE COMPUTE CONTOUR DRAWING GESTALT IMPRESS NUMERAL OUTLINE STATURE DIHEDRAL FIGURATE GRAFFITO HEXAGRAM LIKENESS SEMBLANT MARIONETTE
(— FORMED BY INTERSECTING LINES) KNOT
(— IN PRAYER) ORANT
(— IN WOOD GRAIN) BURL FLAKE
(— MADE OF CORN) KNACK
(— MADE OF 3 LINES) TRIGRAM TRIANGLE
(— OF SPEECH) IMAGE IRONY TROPE APORIA CLIMAX FLOWER SCHEME SIMILE VISION ZEUGMA ANALOGY IMAGERY CHIASMUS DIALLAGE METAPHOR METONYMY OXYMORON SYLLEPSIS ABSCISSION
(— OUT) SUS DOPE SUSS BOTTOM
(—S OF SPEECH) COLORS
(— UP) ITEM
(— USED AS COLUMN) ATLAS TELAMON CARYATID
(— USED AS MAGIC SYMBOL) PENTACLE
(ANATOMICAL —) ECORCHE
(ARTIFICIAL —) GOLEM
(BIBLICAL —) ANGEL CHERUB
(BIZARRE —) GROTESQUE
(CARVED —) GLYPH FIGURINE
(CENTRAL —) HERO
(CIRCULAR —) HOOP
(CLAY —) HANIWA
(COMIC —) BILLIKEN
(CONSPICUOUS —) MARK
(CRESCENT-SHAPED —) LUNE
(DANCE —) SWING TRACE SQUARE PURPOSE ASSEMBLE PROMENADE
(DOMINANT —) CAPTAIN
(DUMMY —) MANNEQUIN
(FEMALE —) ORANTE
(FOLDED PAPER —) FLEXAGON
(GEOMETRICAL —) BODY CONE CUBE LUNE PRISM RHOMB SOLID CIRCLE GNOMON ISAGON ISOGON OBLONG SECTOR SPHERE SQUARE DIAGRAM ELLIPSE LOZENGE PELCOID POLYGON RHOMBUS SECTION HEXAFOIL SPHEROID TRIANGLE RECTANGLE POLYHEDRON PARALLELOGRAM
(GREEK —) KOUROS
(GROTESQUE —) MAGOT BABOON MAXIMON
(HAVING FULL ROUNDED —) ZAFTIG ZOFTIG
(IDEAL —) EIDOLON
(IMAGINARY —) BOGEYMAN
(IMPORTANT —) PANJANDRUM
(INCISED —) INTAGLIO
(JAPANESE — ON GRAVE) HANIWA
(MATH —) SINE COSINE
(MUMMYLIKE —) USHABTI
(MUSICAL —) IDEA LICK OSTINATO
(ODD —) MAUMET
(OVAL —) SWASH ELLIPSE
(PAPER —) FLEXAGON
(PREHISTORIC —) CHACMOL CHACMOOL
(QUADRILLE —) POULE
(QUEER —) GIG
(RHETORICAL —) COLOR COLOUR
(RHYTHMIC —) SNAP
(SCULPTURED —) CANEPHOR
(SHADOW —) SKIAGRAM
(SKATING —) SPIRAL BRACKET COUNTER
(SPINDLE-SHAPED —) FUSEE FUZEE
(STUFFED —) DUMMY
(SYLLOGISTIC —) SCHEMA
(SYMBOLIC —) MORAL EMBLEM
(TAILOR'S —) MANNEQ MANNEQUIN
(TRIANGULAR —) TRIQUET
(UNDRAPED —) NUDE
(WINGED —) ANGEL EIDOLON
(WORSHIPPING —) ORANT
(PL.) DATA SPILING
(PREF.) EID(O)
(SUFF.) HEDRON
FIGURED FIGURY FACONNE
FIGUREHEAD DUMMY FRONT SCROLL
FIGURINE TANAGRA CRIOPHORE
FIGWORT BARTSIA PILEWORT PAULOWNIA PENSTEMON BLUEHEARTS

FIJI
BAY: MBYA NATEWA NGALOA SAVUSAVU
CAPITAL: SUVA
EASTERN GROUP: LAU
ISLAND: ELD KIA ONO AIWA KIOA KORO MALI NGAU VIWA WAIA AGATA MANGO MOALA NAIAU RAMBI MAMOLO MATUKU MBENGA MBULIA NAIRAI NAVITI NGAMEA OVALAU TOTOYA YASAWA YENDUA KAMBARA KANDAVU LAKEMBA TAVEUNI VITILEVU
MOUNTAIN: NARARU MONAVATU
NIECE OR NEPHEW: VASU
POINT: VUYA
TOWN: BA MAU MBA MOMI NADI REWA SUVA TUVU NANDI THUVU ETUMBA LABASA NALOTO NAMOLI NARATA NASALA NAVOLA SAGARA LAUTOKA VATUKOULA

FIJIAN VITIAN
FILAGO GIFOLA
FILAMENT BRIN DOWL HAIR HARL NEMA PILE SILK CHIVE CHORD FIBER FIBRE FILUM TWIRE CIRRUS ELATER HEATER MANTLE STRAND THREAD CIRRHUS FIMBRIA FLIMMER RHIZOID TEXTILE PARANEMA PHACELLA STERIGMA PARAPHYSIS
(— MATERIAL) TUNGSTEN
(— OF FEATHER) BARB DOWL DOWLE
(— OF MINERAL) STRINGER
(— OF SILK) BRIN
(—S OF FLAX OR HEMP) HARL
(TWISTED —S) STRAND
(PL.) HACKLE
FILAMENTOUS BYSSOID STRINGY HAIRLIKE
FILANDERS BACKWORM
FILARIASIS MUMU
FILBERT HAZEL COBNUT HAZELNUT
(SIEVE OF —S) PRICKLE
FILCH BOB FUB NIM ROB BEAT DRIB FAKE PILK PRIG SMUG SNIP FETCH LURCH PILCH SNAKE SNEAK STEAL CLOYNE PILFER SMOUCH STRIKE CABBAGE PURLOIN
FILE BOX ROW BARB DECK LINE LIST RANK RASP RATE RISP ROLL SLIP STUB EMERY ENTER FLOAT FOUND GRAIL INDEX LABEL RIFLE TRACK TRAIN ACCUSE ANSWER BEFOUL CARLET DEFILE FILACE RASCAL RUBBER STRING TOPPER ARCHIVE ARRANGE CHOILER CONDEMN DOSSIER EXHIBIT GRAILLE QUANNET TICKLER DRAWFILE
(— DOWN SAW TEETH) JOINT
(— OFF) DEFILE
(— OF SIX SOLDIERS) ROT
(— USED BY COMBMAKERS) GRAIL TOPPER GRAILER GRAILLE
(— WITH COURT OF LAW) BOX
(COARSE —) RAPE
(CURVED —) RIFFLER
(KIND OF —) INDIAN
FILE BOX SOLANDER
FILEFISH LIJA UNIE TURBOT UNICORN BALISTID FOOLFISH PLECTOGNATH
FILET DEBONE
FILIAL PIUS SONLY
FILIBUSTER FLIBUTOR STONEWALL
FILIGREED LACED
FILING RASION LIMATION
(PL.) LEMEL SCOBS LIMAIL
FILIPENDULA ULMARIA
FILIPINO MORO KALINGA KANKANAI
FILL EKE HIT PAD BUNG CLOY CRAM FEED GLUT HOLD LADE LINE MEET PANG QUAR SATE STOP TEEM BELLY BLOAT BULGE CHOKE ESTOP FLOCK GORGE KEDGE PITCH PRIME STORE STUFF CHARGE FULFIL INFUSE OCCUPY QUERRE SUPPLY AGGRADE DISTEND ENLARGE EXECUTE FILLING FRAUGHT FULFILL IMPLETE INFLATE INVOLVE PERFECT PERFORM PERVADE PLENISH SATIATE SATISFY SUFFUSE COMPLETE COMPOUND FREQUENT PERMEATE
(— COMPLETELY) SATURATE
(— CUP TO BRIM) BRIM CROWN BUMPER
(— FULL) FARCE STUFF
(— HORSES' TEETH) BISHOP

(— IN) NOG KILL STOP SLUSH INFILL BALLAST
(— IN CHINKS) LIP
(— INTERSTICES) BLIND
(— IN WITH RUBBLE) HEART
(— LEATHER WITH OIL) FAT
(— OUT) BUNCH SWELL
(— THE BASES) LOAD
(— TO EXCESS) CROWD FLOOD CONGEST SURFEIT
(— TO OVERFLOWING) FLOW THWACK
(— UP) STOP BRICK CHOKE CLOSE ESTOP STOAK FULFIL IMPACT STODGE PLENISH
(— UP HOLE) STIFLE
(— WITH) SWILL
(— WITH ALE) RACK
(— WITH ANXIETY) ALARM ALARUM
(— WITH CARGO) STOW
(— WITH CLAY) CAT PUG
(— WITH FEAR) APPAL APPALL
(— WITH HORROR) ABHOR
(— WITH LIGHT) GLUT
(— WITH LIQUOR) TUN SKINK
(— WITH METAL) BACK
(— WITH MORTAR) GROUT
(— WITH ODORS) EMBALM
(— WITH RUBBISH) BASH
(— WITH TERROR) AMAZE
(ONE'S —) SLITHERS

FILLED BIG ALIVE FLUSH QUICK SATED SOLID GRAVID LOADED CROWDED HAUNTED IMPLETE OPPLETE REPLETE SWOLLEN FREQUENT INSTINCT POPULOUS
(— OUT) BOLD FULL
(— TO EXCESS) FLOWN
(— WITH AIR) INFLATED
(— WITH EXCITEMENT) ABUZZ
(— WITH FEAR) AFRAID
(— WITH INTERSTICES) AREOLAR
(— WITH MOISTURE) FAT
(— WITH PRIDE) YNPRIDID

FILLER GARA BOGUS SILEX SILKA SQUIB BALAAM LIGNIN FILLING LOADING WRAPPER
(— FOR CRACKS) SPACKLE
(QUILT —) BATT BATTING

FILLET BAND BONE GIRT LIST ORLE ORLO SOLE TAPE AMPYX CROWN FACET FILET GORGE LABEL LEDGE MITER MITRE QUIRK SCROD SNOOD STRAP STRIA TIARA VITTA ANADEM BENDEL BINDER CIMBIA COMBLE CORONA DIADEM FASCIA INFULA LISTEL NORSEL POTONG QUADRA REGLET REGULA RIBBON ROLLER TAENIA TURBAN TURBOT ANNULET BANDAGE BANDEAU CLOISON CORONET EYEBROW FACETTE FRONTAL GARLAND LAMBEAU MOLDING TRESSON TRINGLE BANDELET CINCTURE FRONTLET HAIRLACE HEADBAND PLATBAND TRESSOUR TRESSURE UNDERCUT
(— OF HERRING) ROLLMOP
(BEEF —) TOURNEDOS
(PREF.) TAENI(A)(O)

FILLIFORM CATENOID

FILL-IN MODESTY

FILLING GOB FILL MODE PLUG WEFT WOOF INLAY STUFF FILLER STOPPING STUFFING FIBERFILL
(— OF COLUMN FLUTES) CABLING
(— OF GAPS) CONFAB
(— UP) CLOSURE RIPIENO
(BASKET —) SLEW
(DENTAL —) INLAY
(SILK —) SHIKII

FILLIP BLOW FLIP SNAP SPUR TOSS URGE FILIP FLASH FLIRT FLISK IMPEL BUFFET INCITE MOMENT PROJECT STIMULATE
(— ON THE NOSE) SNITCH

FILLY COLT FOAL GIRL

FILM H BRAT HAZE HULL KELL MIST SCUM SKIM SKIN VEIL WEFT BLEAR COVER FLAKE FLICK GLAZE LAYER MYLAR PEARL PLATE SCALE SHOOT SHORT BUBBLE MOTHER PATINA SCRUFF CUTICLE FEATURE PHILOME TAFFETA TOPICAL TRAILER BEESWING FIRECOAT NEGATIVE PELLICLE MICROFILM MONOLAYER
(— OF AIR) PLASTRON
(— OF ICE) VERGLAS
(— OF OIL) SLICK
(— OF OXIDE) TARNISH
(— OF TARTAR) SCALE PLAQUE
(— ON COPPER) PATINA
(— ON PORRIDGE) BRAT
(— ON TEETH) PLAQUE
(— ON WINE) BEESWING
(— OVER EYE) WEB
(— OVER THE EYES) WEB
(DISCARDED —) OUTTAKE
(ORIGINAL —) MASTER
(POLYESTER —) MYLAR
(X-RAY —) BITEWING

FILMING (REALISTIC —) VIDEOVERITE

FILMY FINE HAZY GAUZY MISTY SHEER WISPY CLOUDY CLOUDED TIFFANY FILMLIKE GOSSAMER

FILOSOFO DI CAMPAGNA, IL
(CHARACTER IN —) NARDO EUGENIA LESBINA RINALDO TRITEMIO
(COMPOSER OF —) GALUPPI

FILTER CLAY RAPE SEEP SIFT SILE DRAIN SEITZ SIEVE BOUGIE CANDLE COLATE CONTEX LAUTER MEDIUM PURIFY REFINE STRAIN BAGHOUSE COLATURE FILTRATE INFILTER STRAINER

FILTERER CLARIFIER

FILTH FEN KET DIRT DUNG GORE MUCK NAST SLUT SOIL SUDS ADDLE BILGE DRECK GLEAM GLEET JAKES POUCE SWILL DEFILE FULYIE FULZIE IMMUND ORDURE SORDES SORDOR VERMIN SLOTTER SQUALOR SULLAGE FOULNESS MUCKMENT SNOTTERY WORTHING COLLUVIES
(PREF.) COPR(O)

FILTHINESS MUCOR SQUALOR SULLAGE CENOSITY

FILTHY LOW FOUL MIRY VILE BAWDY DIRTY DROVY DUNGY GROSS LAIRY MUCKY NASTY AUGEAN BAWDRY CRUMBY CRUMMY CRUSTY DIRTEN IMMUND IMPURE SORDID BEASTLY BESTIAL HOGGISH OBSCENE PIGGISH SQUALID UNCLEAN ORDUROUS SLUTTISH

FILTRATE MALLEIN

FILTRATION BAGGING COLATURE
(KIND OF —) GEL

FIN ARM RAG RIB ANAL BURR FANG HAND KEEL SAIL FLASH PINNA CAUDAL FINLET ACANTHA FEATHER FLIPPER PINNULE VENTRAL FORELIMB PECTORAL
(BOMB —) VANE
(PREF.) PTER(O) PTERYG(O)

FINAGLE CHEAT TRICK REVOKE DECEIVE FENAGLE

FINAL LAST UTTER FINIAL LATTER RUNOFF ULTIMA UTMOST DARREIN DERNIER EXTREME FINALIS OUTMOST PARTING SUPREME ABSOLUTE DECISIVE DECRETAL DEFINITE EVENTUAL FAREWELL ULTIMATE
(— STANZA) ENVOI
(NOT —) NISI

FINALE END CODA FINIS ENDING WRAPUP CLOSING

FINALITY END ERGO

FINALLY YET LAST AFINE ATLAST LASTLY

FINANCE TAX BACK BANK FUND GOODS REVENUE TAXATION TREASURE

FINANCIAL FISCAL MONETARY PECUNIARY

FINANCIER BANIAN BANYAN MONEYMAN
(AUTHOR OF —) DREISER
(CHARACTER IN —) FRANK HENRY AILEEN BUTLER EDWARD SEMPLE STENER LILLIAN WINGATE COWPERWOOD

FINBACK WHALE FINNER GIBBAR FINFISH RORQUAL JUBARTAS

FINCH FINK MORO PAPE JUNCO SERIN TERIN BURION CANARY CITRIL LINNET PALILA SISKIN TOWHEE BUNTING CHEWINK PEEWEEP REDHEAD REDPOLL SENEGAL SPARROW TANAGER WAXBILL AMADAVAT COMBASOU FIRETAIL GOULDIAN GROSBEAK HAWFINCH LONGSPUR SNOWBIRD BRAMBLING SEEDEATER
(— FLOCK) CHARM
(SOUTH AMERICAN —) REDSISKIN

FIND GET RUG MEET VAIL CATCH INVENT LOCATE STRIKE ADJUDGE FINDING DISCOVER SCROUNGE
(— FAULT) CARP BARGE BLAME CAVIL GRONT KNOCK PINCH SCOLD NATTER ARRAIGN
(— GUILTY) ATTAINT CONVICT
(— OUT) AFIND CHECK ESSAY LEARN SPELL TROVE DETECT CONTRIVE DECIPHER DISCOVER
(— REFUGE) BIEL BIELD
(— SOLUTION) SOLVE
(— THE SUM) SUMMATE
(— TIME) EEM

FINDER SIGHT SEEKER FOUNDER

FINDING TROVER INQUEST VERDICT
(POLICE —) MO

FINE AOK CRO GAY RUM TAX BEIN BIEN BOTE BRAW CAIN CROP DIRE ERIC FAIR GENT GOOD HUNK JAKE LEVY MOOI NEAT NICE PURE RARE SEPT SLAP TALL TEAR TINE TRIM ABWAB BONNY BRAVE BULLY CHECK DAISY DANDY DELIE DUCKY FRAIL GAUDY GRAND GREAT HUNKY ISSUE KELTY MULCT NIFTY NOBLE RORTY SHARP SHEER SMALL SPALE SWANK SWEET SWELL UNLAW WALLY WHITE AMENDE AMERCE BONNIE BONZER BRAWLY BRIGHT CHEESY CHOICE CLEVER COSTLY CRAFTY DAINTY FACETE FINISH FLUTED GERSUM HERIOT HUNGRY INCONY MELLOW ORNATE PEACHY PRETTY PROPER QUAINT RANSOM SARAAD SCONCE SERENE SILKEN SLIGHT SPIFFY TENDER CLARIFY CONDEMN CORKING CREANCE CUNNING ELEGANT ESTREAT FERDWIT FINICAL FORFEIT FRAGILE GALANAS GALLANT GALLOWS GRADELY GRASSUM IMMENSE MARCHET MERCHET MURDRUM ORFGILD PENALTY PERFECT REFINED SCUTAGE STAVING TENUOUS TOPPING VALIANT WERGILD ABSOLUTE BLOODWIT BUDGEREE CAVALIER CLINKING DELICATE DUSTLIKE FLITWITE FOOTGELD HANDSOME LASHLITE MARITAGE PENALIZE PESHKASH PINPOINT PLEASANT SKILLFUL SPLENDID SUPERIOR WARDWITE WIRESPUN COPACETIC MAGNIFICENT
(— AGAINST SERVANTS) CHECK
(— FOR KILLING) BOTE
(— IN LIEU OF FLOGGING) HIDE
(BLOOD —) ERIC WITE
(FEUDAL —) RELIEF
(OSTENTATIOUSLY —) GAUDY
(PRINTING OFFICE —) SOLACE
(VERY —) BUNKUM SPLENDID
(PL.) SILT FLOUR
(PREF.) LEPT(O)

FINE-DRAW RANTER

FINE-LOOKING SPICY WALLY SPIFFY

FINELY FINE GAILY GAYLY WALLY BRAGLY RARELY SMALLY BRAVELY SMICKLY SWEETLY

FINENESS ALLOY GRAIN TRICK DENIER FINERY PURITY THREAD EXILITY FINESSE DELICACY
(— AS RECKONED BY CARATS) TITLE
(— OF FABRIC) CUT GAGE GAUGE
(— OF METAL) STANDARD
(— OF PITCH) COUNTS

FINERY GAUD WALY ARRAY BRAWS WALLY BAUBLE BAWDRY BEAUTY FEGARY GAIETY GAYETY TAWDRY BRAVERY GAUDERY REGALIA BEAUETRY ELEGANCE FINENESS FOFARRAW FOLDEROL FOOFARAW FRIPPERY ORNAMENT RIBANDRY
(TAWDRY —) FRIPPERY

FINESPUN HAIR THIN TWITTERY

FINESSE ART TACT CHEAT SKILL TRICK PURITY SERENE CUNNING ARTIFICE DELICACY SUBTLETY THINNESS
FINE-TUNE TWEAK
FINFOOT SUNBIRD
FINGER TOY PAUT PLAY DIGIT INDEX PINKY DACTYL HANDLE MEDDLE MEDIUS PADDLE PILFER PINKIE POLLEX ANNULAR DIGITAL MINIMUM MINIMUS PURLOIN DIGITIZE THRIMBLE
(— IDLY) TWIDDLE
(— INFECTION) FELON
(CROOK A — AT) BECKON
(FORE —) INDEX
(LITTLE —) PINKY PINKIE PIRLIE MINIMUS AURICULAR
(RING —) ANNULAR RINGMAN ANNULARY
(THIRD —) RINGMAN
(PL.) HOOKS
(PREF.) DACTYL(IO)(O) DIGITI DIGITO
(SUFF.) DACTYLIA DACTYLOUS
FINGERFLOWER FOXGLOVE
FINGERING DOIGTE
FINGERLING PARR TROUTLET
FINGERNAIL DIGGER
(RELATING TO —) ONYCHOID
(SUFF.) ONYCHA ONYCHES ONYCHIA ONYCHIUM ONYCHUS ONYX
FINGERPRINT DAB ARCH LOOP WHORL LATENT
FINGERPRINTING (KIND OF —) DNA
FINGERROOT FOXGLOVE
FINGERSTALL COT
FINIAL EPI NOB TEE TOP CROP KNOB KNOP KNOT BUNCH CREST CROWN FINAL POPPY PRICKET ORNAMENT PINNACLE
FINICAL NICE FUSSY CHOOSY DAINTY DAPPER JAUNTY PRETTY PRISSY SPRUCE CHOOSEY FINICKY FINIKIN FOPPISH MINCING PERJINK PICKING SMICKER DELICATE
FINICALLY SMICKLY GINGERLY
FINICKY NICE DINKY FIKEY FIKIE PRISSY FINICAL FINIKIN PRECISE
FINISH DO DIE END CHAR EDGE FACE FINE MILL OVER PASS SINK SNUG STOP BLOOM BOUND CEASE CHARE CHEVE CLOSE CROWN ENDUP FEEZE GLACE GLAZE LIMIT SPEED UPPER BOTTOM BUSHEL FULFIL FULLDO PLISSE POLISH SETTLE WINDUP ABSOLVE ACHIEVE DEPETER EXECUTE FLUTING FULFILL PERFECT SURFACE COMPLETE CONCLUDE DEPRETER DRESSING FINALIZE FROSTING TERMINAL
(— CAREFULLY) NEATEN
(— CLOTH) BURL CONVERT
(— FILMING) WRAP
(— METAL) PLANISH
(— OFF) DASH CRUSH ABSOLVE ACCOMPLISH
(— OF FABRIC) CIRE HOLLAND
(— OF PAPER) STIPPLE
(— STONE) COMB BOAST DROVE
(— WITH A SEAM) FELL
(— WORK) FLOOR
(CALENDERED —) CHASING
(DULL —) MAT MATTE
(GLAZED —) GLACE LACKER LACQUER
(PHOTO —) MAT MATT MATTE
(STUCCO —) SPATTER
(SUPERFICIAL —) BLAZONRY
FINISHED BY DID OER PAU ARCH DONE DOWN FINE GONE OVER PAST PURE RIPE SHOT ENDED EXACT KAPUT NAPOO ROUND CLOSED NAPOOH ORNATE PERFECT REFINED ROUNDED STOPPED THROUGH BANKRUPT CLIMAXED GOFFERED LUSTERED POLISHED
(— IN NATURAL COLOR) FAIR
(— WITH NAP) BRUSHED
(ABSOLUTELY —) SUNK
(HIGHLY —) SUAVE
(IMPERFECTLY —) RUDE
FINISHER EYER ENDER CORKER GAFFER BEETLER CEMENTER ENAMELER SOCKDOLOGER
FINISHING CRUSHING
FINITE LIMITED
FINK (PLAY THE —) RATON

FINLAND

CAPITAL: HELSINKI HELSINGFORS
COIN: PENNI MARKKA
DIVISION: IJORE VILLIPURI
GOD: TAPIO JUMALA
ISLAND: ALAND KARLO AALAND HAILUTO VALLGRUND
ISTHMUS: KARELIA
LAKE: JUO MUO KEMI KIVI NASI OULO PURU PYHA SIMO ENARE HAUKI INARI KALLA LAPPA LESTI PUULA LENTUA SAIMAA SOUNNE SYVARI KOITERE NILAKKA PIELINEN
LANGUAGE: AVAR LAPP UGRIC MAGYAR OSTYAK TAVAST SAMOYED ESTONIAN
MEASURE: KANNU TUNNA VERST FATHOM SJOMIL OTTINGER SKALPUND TUNNLAND
MOUNTAIN: HALTIA
NAME: SUOMI
PARLIAMENT: EDUSKUNTA
PROVINCE: HAME KYMI OULU LAPPI VAASA KUOPIO MIKKELI UUSIMAA
RIVER: II KALA OULU SIMO TENO IVALO LOTTA OUNAS SIIKA IIJOKI LAPUAN MUONIO PASVIK TORNIO KITINEN KOKEMAKI
TOWN: ABA ABO KEM KEMI OULU PORI VASA ENARE ESPOO KOTKA LAHTI TURKU VAASA IMATRA KUOPIO MIKKELI TAMPERE HELSINKI
TRIBE: HAME VEPS VEPSE UGRIAN KARJALAISET SUOMALAISET

FINLET PINNULE
FINN FIOUN INGER OSTIAK OSTYAK TAVAST INGRIAN CHEREMIS INGERMAN SWEKOMAN
(PL.) SUOMI
FINNISH
(PREF.) FENNO
FINNOCK HERLING
FINTA GIARDINIERA, LA
(CHARACTER IN —) ONESTI ANCHISE ARMINDA BELFIORE SANDRINA SERPETTA VIOLANTE
(COMPOSER OF —) MOZART
FIORD FJORD INLET
FIORIN KNOTGRASS
FIORITURA ORNAMENT
FIPPLE FLUTE RECORDER
FIR VER LARCH SAPIN BAUMIER LASHORN PINABETE
FIR CLUB MOSS FOXFEET
FIRE CAN FEU LOW AGNI APOY BALE BRIO BURN HEAT KILN LOWE POOP SACK SWAP SWOP ZEAL ARDOR ARSON BLAST BLAZE BREAK BURST EMPTY FEVER GLEED INGLE LIGHT LOGHE LOOSE LOUGH PLUFF SERVE SHOOT SQUIB STOKE AROUSE ENGHLE EXCITE FERVOR IGNITE INCITE KINDLE SMUDGE SPIRIT SPLEEN VULCAN ANIMATE BONFIRE BURNING BURNOUT CHIMNEY DISMISS EMITTER EXPLODE FURNACE GLIMMER INFLAME INSPIRE SMOLDER BACKFIRE BALEFIRE CAMPFIRE DETONATE HELLFIRE ILLUMINE IRRITATE NEEDFIRE SMOULDER VIVACITY PORCELAINIZE
(— A REVOLVER) FAN
(— ON) AFIRE
(— THE CHARGE) HIT
(— TWO ROUNDS) DOUBLE
(— UPON) GUN SPRAY
(BALL OF —) DYNAMO
(CROSS —) GANTLET GAUNTLET
(DAMPENED —) SMOTHER
(FOREST —) BREAK
(LITTLE —) SPONK SPUNK
(MASSED —) ARTILLERY
(PEAT —) GREESAGH
(RUNNING-OUT —) DANDY
(SIGNAL —) BALE BEACON BALEFIRE
(PREF.) EMPYRO IGNEO IGNI PHLOGO PYR(ET)(ETO)(ITI)(O)
(SUFF.) PYRA
FIRE ALARM FIREBOX
FIREARM ARM GUN IRON SHOT TUBE FIRER ORGAN PIECE RIFLE JEZAIL MAGNUM MAUSER MUSKET PISTOL POPPER BOMBARD CARBINE CURRIER DEMIHAG HANDGUN PINFIRE SHOOTER SPANNER ARQUEBUS BROWNING CULVERIN EXPELLER EXPLODER PETRONEL REVOLVER
(PL.) HARDWARE ARTILLERY
FIRE ARROW MALLEOLUS
FIREBACK REREDOS MACARTNEY
FIREBALL BOLIDE
FIRE BEETLE COCUYO CUCUYO ELATER ELATERID
FIREBOAT PALANDER
FIREBRAND BLAZE BRAND BLEERY BOUTEFEU RABBLEROUSER
FIREBRICK QUARLE
(PL.) GROG
FIREBUG BUG ARSONIST
FIRE CARRIER PORTFIRE
FIRECLAY THILL
FIRE COVER CURFEW CURPHEW
FIRECRACKER DEVIL SQUIB BANGER PETARD SALUTE CRACKER SNAPPER FIREWORK WHIZBANG
FIRE-CURED DARK
FIREDAMP GAS FOULNESS WILDFIRE
FIREDART PHALARICA
FIREDOG DOG IRON ANDIRON
FIRE ENGINE RIG TUB MANUAL
FIRE EXTINGUISHER SQUIRT EXTINCTOR
FIRE FIGHTER EXEMPT HOTSHOT
FIREFLY CUCUYO FIREBUG GLOWFLY LAMPFLY FIREWORM GLOWWORM LAMPYRID
FIREGUARD FENDER
FIRELINE GUTTER
FIRELOCK FUSEE FUZEE SPANNER
FIREMAN VAMP FIRER FUELER STOKER TEASER TIZEUR FIREBOY HOSEMAN BAKEHEAD FURNACER
FIREPLACE FOCUS FOGON FORGE FOYER GRATE INGLE TISAR HEARTH CHIMNEY CHEMINEE
(— AND CHIMNEY) STACK
(— STONE) MANTEL
(PORTABLE —) BARBECUE BARBEQUE
FIREPLUG PLUG HYDRANT
FIRER STOKER BLASTER
FIRESIDE SMOKE HEARTH
FIRESTAND HASTER HASTENER
FIRE THORN PYRACANTH
FIREWEED FIRETOP ROSEBAY PILEWEED PILEWORT
FIREWOOD FIRE LENA SLAB WOOD CHUNK FAGOT BILLET BILLOT ELDING FIRING TALWOOD FIREBOTE TALLWOOD TALSHIDE
FIREWORK JET SUN GERB DEVIL GERBE PEEOY SAXON SHELL SQUIB WHEEL FIZGIG MAROON PETARD ROCKET SALUTE SHOWER TRACER CASCADE SERPENT SPARKER TORPEDO VOLCANO FOUNTAIN SPARKLER GIRANDOLE
(PL.) FUN FIRE
FIRE WORSHIPPER PARSI GHEBER GHEBRE PARSEE
FIRING FIRE FUEL COUGH SALVO BURNING DRUMFIRE
FIRKIN VESSEL
FIRM HUI PAT BUFF FAST HARD IRON NASH SURE TAUT TRIG TRIM CHAMP CORKY CRISP DENSE FIRMA FIXED HARDY HOUSE LOYAL RIGID SOLID SOUND STARK STIFF STITH STOUT SWITH TIGHT TOUGH CEMENT HARDEN HEARTY SECURE SETTLE SICCAR SICKER SINEWY STABLE STANCH STEADY STEEVE STOLID STRONG STURDY TRUSTY ADAMANT CERTAIN COMPACT COMPANY CONCERN CONFIRM CONTEXT DECIDED DURABLE STAUNCH UNMOVED CONSTANT FAITHFUL FIDUCIAL OBDURATE RESOLUTE SUBSTANT UNSHAKEN

(— BUT EASILY CUT) SEMISOFT
(NOT —) FUZZY
(PREF.) PAGIO
FIRMAMENT SKY DEEP POLE CARRY ETHER CANOPY HEAVEN EXPANSE EMPYREAN EMPYREUM EXPANSUM
FIRMLY BUFF FAST FIRM HARD SADLY STARK TIGHT HARDLY SQUARE SURELY SOLIDLY SECURELY STRONGLY
FIRMNESS BODY GRIT IRON ETHAN PROOF FIXURE COURAGE FIRMITY GRANITE BACKBONE DECISION FASTNESS SECURITY SOLIDITY STRENGTH TENACITY
(— OF CHARACTER) SAND
(— OF PURPOSE) RESOLVE
FIRN NEVE
FIRST ERST FUST GULE HEAD HIGH MAIN AHEAD ALPHA CHIEF FORME NIEVE PRIMA PRIME PRIMO MAIDEN PRIMAL PRIMUS VIRGIN FIRSTLY HIGHEST INITIAL LEADING PREMIER PRIMARY EARLIEST FOREHAND FOREMOST FORMERLY ORIGINAL PARAVANT PREMIERE PRINCEPS
(— PRIZE) BLUE
(— SERGEANT) TOP
(— STATE) DELAWARE
(PREF.) PRIMI PRIMO PROT(O)
(— IN TIME) ARCH
FIRSTBORN AYNE EIGNE ELDEST
FIRST-CLASS PUCKA GAY TOP BOSS POSH FLASH PRIME PUKKA BUNKUM STUNNING
FIRST-FRUITS ANNATES
FIRSTHAND DIRECT PRIMARY ORIGINAL
FIRST-RATE AOK SLAPUP TIPTOP BOSS BRAG GOOD JAKE MAIN SLAP BULLY DANDY LUMMY PRIME SLEEK SLICK SUPER SWELL BONSER BONZER BOSKER CHEESY FAMOUS TIPTOP BLIGHTY BOSHTER CAPITAL SKOOKUM STELLAR TOPPING CHAMPION CLINKING CLIPPING TOPNOTCH
FIRTH ARM KYLE FRITH INLET COPPICE ESTUARY
FISCAL BURSAL MONETARY
FISH AU ID AKU AWA AYU BIB CAT COD DAB DAP DIB EEL FIN GAR GIG GOO HEN IDE IHI JIG JUG ORF RAY SAR TAI UKU BANK BARB BASS BLAY BOCE BOGA CARP CAST CERO CHUB CHUG CHUM CLOD CRAB CUSK DACE DORY DRAG DRAW DRUM ERSE FUGU GADE GHOL GOBY GRIG HAKE HIND HUCH HUSO JACK JUNK LINE LING LOTE MADO MERO MOLA OPAH PEAL PEGA PIKE POOR POUT PRIM QUAB RAIL RUDD RUFF SCAD SCUP SEER SHAD SOLE SPET SPIN SPOT TILE TORO TUNA ULUA ACARA AHOLE AKULE ANGLE ATULE BEGTI BETTA BINNY BLAIN BLEAK BOLTI BOLTY BREAM BULLY BULTI CABIO CATLA CHIRO CISCO COBIA CONEY DANIO DORAB DOREE DRAIL DRIFT DRIVE ELOPS ERIZO FLOAT FLUKE FOGAS FRIAR GADID GRUNT GUPPY HILSA HUCHO JUREL KILLY LAKER LANCE MANTA MIDGE MINIM MORAY OTTER PERCH PIABA PLATY PORGY POWAN POWER REINA ROACH SAIDE SARGO SAURY SEINE SHARK SKATE SMELT SNOEK SNOOK SPRAT SQUID SULEA SWEEP TENCH TETRA TRABU TRAWL TROLL TROUT TUNNY UMBRA VIUVA VORAZ WAHOO WHIFF AIMARA ALEVIN ANABAS ANGLER BARBEL BARBER BENNET BICHIR BISKOP BLENNY BONITO BOWFIN BUMPER BURBOT CALLOP CANDIL CAPLIN CARANX CARIBE COELHO COTTID CREOLE CUCHIA CUNNER DARTER DASSIE DENTEX FISHET GANOID GINNEL GULPER GUNNEL HAMLET HAPUKU HILSAH HUSSAR INANGA KOKOPU LAUNCE LEDGER LIGGER LOUVAR MAIGRE MARLIN MEDAKA MENISE MILTER MINNOW MOLLIE MOLOID MULLET NONNAT PHOEBE PLAICE POMPON PUFFER PUNECA REDFIN REMORA ROBALO ROUGHY RUNNER SABALO SALELE SALEMA SALMON SAPSAP SARDEL SAUGER SAUREL SERRAN SHINER SIERRA SIMARA SPARID SUCKER TAILER TAIMEN TANDAN TARPON TAUTOG TESTAR TETARD TINOSA TOMCOD TURBOT VENDIS WALLER WEAVER WIRRAH WRASSE ZINGEL ALEWIFE ALFIONA ANCHOVY BACALAO BARBUDO BATFISH BEARDIE BERGYLT BERYCID BOXFISH BRAGGLE BUFFALO BUMMALO CABEZON CANDIRU CAPELIN CAPLING CATFISH CAVALLA CAVALLY CHIMERA CHROMID CICHLID CLUPEID CONVICT CORVINA COWFISH CRAPPIE CROAKER CTENOID CUTLIPS CYCLOID DRABBLE DREPANE DRUMMER EELPOUT ESCOLAR FATHEAD FINFISH GALJOEN GEELBEC GEELBEK GOBIOID GOGGLER GOLDEYE GOURAMI GRAYSBY GROUPER GRUNION GRUNTER GUAPENA GUAVINA GUDGEON GULARIS GURNARD GWYNIAD HADDOCK HAGFISH HALIBUT HARMOOT HERRING HINALEA HOGFISH HOUTING ICEFISH ICHTHUS INCONNU JAWFISH JEWFISH JUGULAR LABROID LAGARTO LONGFIN MACHETE MAHSEER MAYFISH MOJARRA MOONEYE MORWONG OARFISH OLDWIFE OQUASSA PEGASUS PIGFOOT PINTADO PIRANHA POISSON POLLACK POMFRET POMPANO PUPFISH RASBORA RONQUIL SANCORD SARDINE SAUROID SAVELHA SAWFISH SCALARE SCAROID SCHELLY SCULPIN SENNETT SEVRUGA SILURUS SLEEPER SMUTTER SNAPPER SOLDIER SPAWNER STERLET SUNFISH TELEOST TOMTATE TOPKNOT TORPEDO TUBFISH UMBRANA UNICORN VENDACE VIAJACA WAREHOU WAUBEEN WHAPUKA WHAPUKU WHITING ALBACORE ALFONSIN APOGONID ARAPAIMA ATHERINE BAITFISH BALISTID BIGMOUTH BILLFISH BLENNOID BLUEBACK BLUEFISH BOARFISH BONEFISH BRISLING BROTULID BULLHEAD CACKEREL CANCHITO CARANGID CARANGIN CARDINAL CATALINA CATALUFA CHANCITO CHIMAERA CHOANATE CHROMIDE CORACINE CREVALLE CREVALLY CROSSOPT CYPRINID DEALFISH DIPNEUST DITREMID DONCELLA DRAGONET DRUMFISH DUMBFISH ECHENEID ELEOTRID EPISCATE FALLFISH FILEFISH FLAGFISH FLATFISH FLATHEAD FLOUNDER FOOLFISH FROGFISH FUNDULUS GAMBUSIA GEELBECK GILTHEAD GOATFISH GOLDFISH GRAINING GRAYFISH GRAYLING GREYSKIN HAIRFISH HALFBEAK HANDFISH HANDLINE HAPLOMID HARDHEAD HARDTAIL HOMOCERC HORNFISH HORSEMAN JACKFISH JUMPROCK KABELJOU KARMOUTH KELPFISH KINGFISH LADYFISH LUMPFISH MACKEREL MENHADEN MILKFISH MOONFISH PICKEREL PILCHARD PIRARUCU PORKFISH QUERIMAN ROBALITO ROCKFISH ROCKLING ROSEFISH SAILFISH SALANGID SANDFISH SANDGOBY SCIAENID SCOMBRID SCOTSMAN SEERFISH SKILFISH SKIPJACK SOAPFISH STUDFISH STURGEON TALLYWAG TARWHINE TERAGLIN TILEFISH TOADFISH TREEFISH TREVALLY WARMOUTH WEAKFISH WHISTLER WRYMOUTH QUILLBACK SCORPAENO NEEDLEFISH SHEEPSHEAD SHOVELHEAD SHOVELNOSE SILVERSIDES MOUTHBREEDER
(— BROTH) DASHI
(— BY TROLLING) DRAIL
(— FOR EELS) GRIG SNIGGLE
(— FOR SALMON) SNIGGER
(— LIGHTLY) DAP
(— NETTED) LIFT
(— NOT UNDERSIZED) COUNT KEEPER
(— PRODUCT) SURIMI
(— TAPE) SNAKE
(— THROUGH ICE) CHUG
(— UNDERWATER) GOGGLE
(— WITH HANDS) GUMP GUDDLE
(AQUARIUM —) GUPPY RASBORA
(BAKED —) COULIBIAC
(BLIND —) PINKFISH
(CURED —) DUNFISH
(DISH OF RAW —) SEVICHE
(FABLED —) MAH
(FEMALE —) RAUN SPAWNER
(FIGHTING —) PLAKAT
(FRIED —) ESCABECHE
(HAWAIIAN —) AU
(HERALDIC —) CHABOT
(INDIAN —) ROHU
(NUMBER OF —) SCHOOL
(OLD —) MOSSBACK
(PART OF —) EYE FIN JAW ANUS CHEEK NARIS SCALE MAXILLA MANDIBLE OPERCULUM PREMAXILLA
(PULPED —) POMACE
(PUREE OF —) BRANDADE
(QUANTITY OF —) MAZE
(RAW —) SASHIMI
(REFUSE —) CHUM SHACK
(SALTED —) COR
(SMALL —) TIDDLER
(SMOKED —) FUMADO
(SPLIT —) KLIPFISH
(STEWED —) MATELOTE
(THIN —) RACER
(YOUNG —) FRY ALEVIN
(25 LBS. OF —) STICK
(PREF.) ICHTHY(O) ISCI
(SUFF.) CHROMIS ICHTHYS
FISH BASKET POT CAUL CREEL SLATH
FISH BOX TRUNK
FISH BRINER COBBERER
FISH CLEANER GILLER
FISH DRESSER IDLER
FISHER MART EELER PEKAN SABLE SOBOL TAIRA TAYRA MARTEN SEINER WEJACK MARTRIX TRAWLER TROLLER
(SPONGE —) HOOKER
FISHERMAN (ALSO SEE ANGLER) TOTY EELER ANGLER GIGMAN GILLER KEDGER MAIMUL SEINER WORMER ADMIRAL DORYMAN DRAGMAN DRIFTER PRAWNER RODSTER SHANKER SMELTER STRIKER TRAWLER TROTTER TROWMAN PETERMAN PISCATOR SEASONER SHRIMPER
FISHERY FISHING PISCARY SEALERY
FISHGARTH WEIR
FISHHOOK FLY GIG HOOK LARI ANGLE DRAIL KIRBY LARIN SLEEK ANGULE SPROAT KENDALL ABERDEEN BARBLESS CARLISLE LIMERICK
(PART OF —) EYE GAP BARB BEND POINT SHANK
(PL.) PULLDEVIL
FISHING PIKING ANGLING BANKING BASSING GRAINING SNOEKING
(— TOOL) OVERSHOT
FISHING GROUNDS HAAF
FISHING ROD GAD
FISHING TACKLE TEW LEDGER
FISHLINE GIMP TROT SNELL TRAWL DIPSEY LIGGER BOULTER GANGION OUTLINE SETLINE TRIMMER HAIRLINE TROTLINE
FISH LOUSE GISLER
FISHMONGER PESSONER
FISH NEST REDD
FISHNET FLUE SEINE SETNET
FISHPOND STEW VIVER PISCINA VIVARIUM
FISHPOUND MADRAGUE
FISH SPEAR GRANES WASTER LEISTER
FISHTAIL SKID UROSOME
FISHWAY PASS RACEWAY
FISHY DULL FUNNY GLASSY VACANT

FISSION BREAKING CLEAVAGE CLEAVING GAMOGENY SCISSION
FISSURE GAP CHAP CONE FLAW GOOL GULL LEAK LOCH LODE REFT RENT RIFT RIMA RIME SEAM SLIT TEAR VEIN VENT CHASM CHINE CHINK CLEFT CRACK FLAKE GRIKE PIPER PORTA SHAKE SPLIT ZYGON CLEAVE CRANNY DIVIDE LESION RICTUS RIMULA SPRING SULCUS BLEMISH CREVICE FISSURA MOFETTE OPENING SWALLET APERTURE BLOWHOLE CLEAVAGE COLOBOMA CREVASSE INCISURE QUEBRADA SCISSURA TRAVERSE
(— IN BUILDING STONE) DRY
(— IN HEEL) GAUG
(— IN LIMESTONE) GRIKE
(— IN MAST) SPRING
(— IN PLATEAU) ABRA
(— OF LIVER) PORTA
(UNDERGROUND —) SWALLET SWALLOW
(PL.) RHAGADES
(PREF.) RHAGADI
(SUFF.) SCHISIS SCHIST
FISSURED RIMATE CHAPPED CLEFTED FISSATE
FIST JOB PUD DUKE NAVE NEIF NIEF FOIST GRASP INDEX NIEVE CLENCH CLUTCH DADDLE EFFORT MAULER MAULEY PINKER STRIKE ATTEMPT CLUBFIST FISTNOTE PUFFBALL TIGHTWAD
FISTFIGHT SETTO TURNUP
FISTICUFF BOX NEVEL FISTIFY
FISTULA EGILOPS
(PREF.) SYRING(O)
FISTULOUS TUBULAR
FIT GO APT FAY GEE JAG PAN RIG SET SIT ABLE AGUE BOUT FEAT FURY GOOD HARD KINK MEET MESH PANG RIPE SORT SUIT TRIM TURN WELL WHIM ADAPT ADEPT APPLY BESIT CHINK CLICK DIGNE EXIES FADGE FANCY FITLY FRAME FRISK FUROR HAPPY ICTUS MATCH PITCH QUEME QUIRK READY RIGHT SERVE SPASM SPELL START STOUR SWOON TALLY ACCESS ADJUST ANSWER ATTACK BECOME BEHOVE BESORT DUEFUL FINISH FITTEN HABILE HEPPEN LIABLE PROPER SEASON SEEMLY SPLEEN SQUARE STREAK STROKE STRONG SUITED WORTHY ADAPTED BEHOOVE CAPABLE CONCENT CONDIGN CONFORM CORRECT DESPAIR FASHION FITTING HEALTHY PREPARE QUALIFY SEIZURE TANTRUM WIDDRIM ADEQUATE BECOMING DOVETAIL ELIGIBLE GLOOMING IDONEOUS OUTBREAK PAROXYSM PASSABLE SUITABLE SYNCOPES
(— CLOSELY) FAY CHOCK
(— CORNER TO CORNER) BUTT
(— FOR THE GALLOWS) WIDDIFOW
(— IN) GO NESTLE
(— INTO SOCKET) FANG
(— LOOSELY) SLOP
(— NAUTICALLY) RIG
(— OF ANGER) WAX FRAP FUME HUFF RAGE SNIT TIFF FLING RAVERY SPLEEN
(— OF DEPRESSION) HUMP
(— OF ILL HUMOR) DOD PET TIG FUNK POUT TOUT GRUMPS
(— OF ILLNESS) DROW TOUT FLING
(— OF ILL TEMPER) MAD TANTRUM
(— OF LAUGHTER) GIRD KINK
(— OF NERVOUSNESS) TWITCHET
(— OF RESENTMENT) PIQUE SNUFF
(— OF SHIVERING) AGUE GROOSE
(— OF STUBBORNNESS) REEST
(— OF SULKS) GEE STRUM
(— OF SULLENNESS) DOD
(— OF TEMPER) WAX BAIT BIRSE HISSY PADDY TETCH GROUCH SPLEEN SQUALL BRAINGE
(— OF WEEPING) CRY
(— OF YAWNING) GAPE
(— ONE WITHIN ANOTHER) NEST
(— OUT) ARM RIG BUSK BEFIT EQUIP ASTORE CLOTHE OUTFIT APPAREL APPOINT FURNISH HABILLE ACCOUTER
(— RIFLE BARREL) BED
(— TIGHTLY) STUFF
(— TO BE DRUNK) SORBILE
(— TOGETHER) MESH NEST COAPT JOINT COHERE ASSEMBLE
(— UP) RIG
(— WITH COMPACTNESS) BOX
(— WITH FETTERS) GARNISH
(FAINTING —) SWOON SYNCOPE
(RITUALLY —) KOSHER
(PL.) LUNES
(SUFF.) ABLE IBLE
FITCH LINER
FITFUL GERY CATCHY GERFUL GLEAMY CURSORY FLIGHTY RESTLESS UNSTABLE VARIABLE SPASMODIC
FITLY FIT PAT DULY FEATLY GLADLY MEETLY TIDELY APROPOS HAPPILY PROPERLY SUITABLY
FITNESS FORM APTNESS DECENCY DECORUM DIGNITY APTITUDE CAPACITY IDONEITY JUSTNESS PROPERTY CONGRUITY
FITTED APT ABLE ADAPT KEYED SUITED ADAPTED ENGAGED ADJUSTED ASSORTED ELIGIBLE
FITTER TUBER GASMAN
FITTING TO APT CAP DUE LUG PAT BUTT FAIR FEAT FORK HARP JUMP JUST KIND MEET CLEAT HAPPY QUEME WORTH BECOME CLENCH CLEVIS LEADER PROPER SADDLE SEEMLY WASHER ADAPTER CONGRUE PENDANT SERVING SHACKLE SUCTION TACTFUL CONDULET DECOROUS GRACEFUL RIGHTFUL SUITABLE RECEPTACLE
(— FOR MILL-STONE) RIND RYND
(— TIGHTLY) CLOSE
(GREASE —) ZERK
(LIGHT —) PLUG LUMINAIRE
(PIPE —) CROSS ELBOW
(PL.) BRASS COVER REPAREL FITMENTS
FITZGERALD ELLA
FIVE CINQ FUNF CINQUE EPSILON QUINQUE
(— CENTS) JITNEY NICKEL
(— HUNDRED DOLLARS, POUNDS) MONKEY
(— IN CRAPS) PHOEBE
(— OF TRUMPS) PEDRO
(— YEARS) LUSTRUM
(GAME CALLED —S) HANDBALL
(TWO —S) QUINAS
(PREF.) CINQUE LEPT(O) PEN(T)(TA) (TH) QUINQU(E)
FIVES BALL SNACK
FIVESTONES SNOBS
FIX BOX JAM PEG PIN SET CLEW CLUE FAST FIRM GAFF GLUE HOLD HOLE JAMB LOCK MEND MOOR NAIL PICK RELY SEAL SPOT STAY AFFIX ALLOT DEFIX FOUND GRAFT GRAVE IMBED INFIX LIMIT PLACE PLANT POINT POSIT SEIZE STATE STEEK STELL STICK TRYST ADJUST ANCHOR ARREST ASSIGN ASSIZE ATTACH CEMENT CLINCH DEFINE ENROOT ENTAIL FASTEN FICCHE FIXATE FREEZE GROUND IMPALE REPAIR REVAMP SETTLE SQUARE TEMPER APPOINT ARRANGE CALCIFY CONFIRM DELIMIT DESTINE DILEMMA GRAPPLE IMPLANT IMPRESS IMPRINT PREPARE STATION PINPOINT RENOVATE TRANSFIX
(— A FIGHT) RIG
(— A MAST) STEP
(— AMOUNT) AFFEER
(— ATTENTION) NAIL
(— DEEPLY) GRAVE
(— FIRMLY) SEAL FREEZE IMPACT INCUBE RAMPIRE
(— IMMOVABLY) RIVET
(— IN AMAZEMENT) PETRIFY
(— IN MUD) MIRE
(— IN POSITION) SHIP
(— PRICE) ASSIZE CHARGE SETTLE
(— THE MIND) INTEND
(— UP) CLEW CLUE
(— UPON) CHAP AFFIX
(— WORK OF ART) REDO
(GAMBLING —) RIG STCK
FIXATION TIC FETICH FETISH
(SUFF.) PAGUS PEXIA PEXIS PEXY
FIXATIVE FIXER SKATOLE AMBRETTE EUDESMOL HYRACEUM LABDANUM
FIXED PAT PUT SAD SET SOT FAST FIRM FLAT HARD GIVEN SIKER STAID UPSET FINITE FROZEN INTENT MENDED SICKER STABLE STATED STEADY STRONG CERTAIN DORMANT EMPIGHT HABITED LIMITED SETTLED SITFAST STATARY STATIVE STELLED ACCURATE ARRANGED ATTACHED CONSTANT DEFINITE EXPLICIT FASTENED IMMOBILE IRONCLAD MOVELESS RESIDENT RESOLUTE STANDING STUBBORN
(NOT —) FLUID SHIFTY MOVABLE FUGITIVE INSECURE MOVEABLE
(PREF.) APLANO
FIXEDLY SAD FAST FIRM FIXLY INTENTLY
FIXEDNESS FASTNESS
FIXER HYPO PATCH
FIXTURE ANNEX EVENT GUARD FAUCET SHIELD BRACKET CREEPER KNOCKER THIMBLE
(LIGHTING —) SCONCE
(STORE —) GONDOLA
FIZZING FIZZY GASSING
FIZZLE FLOP FUSS BARNEY FAILURE FLIVVER
(— OUT) DIE
FLABBINESS MYATONIA
FLABBY LAX FOZY LASH LIMP WEAK BAGGY FLASH FOGGY FRUSH SAPPY WOOZY CASHIE DOUGHY FEEBLE FLAGGY FLAPPY LIMBER QUAGGY WATERY FLACCID YIELDING
FLABELLUM RHIPIDION
FLACCID LIMP WOOZY FLABBY FLAGGY EMARCID FLACKED YIELDING
FLAG FAG LAG SAG SOD FAIL FANE FLAT HOOK IRIS JACK JADE LECK PINE TIRE TURF WAFT WAIF WILT CREST DROOP FAINT FLAKE SEDGE SLAKE UNION VEXIL WHEFT WHIFF BANNER BOUGEE BURGEE COLORS CORNET EMBLEM ENSIGN FANION GUIDON LEVERS PENCEL PENNON SIGNAL TABARD WIMPLE ANCIENT BEEWORT CALAMUS CATTAIL CURTAIN DECLINE DRAPEAU FANACLE LABARUM PENDANT PENNANT SCOURGE BANDEROL BRATTACH GONFALON HANDFLAG LANGUISH PAVILION STANDARD STREAMER TRICOLOR VEXILLUM WATCHMAN
(— CORNER) UNION
(— OF DENMARK) DANEBROG
(— OF TRANSVAAL) VIERKLEUR
(— OF TRUCE) KARTEL
(— OF U.S.) GRIDIRON
(— ON LANCE) PAVON
(BLUE — WITH WHITE SQUARE) PETER
(CAVALRY —) STANDARD
(KNOTTED —) WAFT
(PIRATE —) ROGER BLACKJACK
(SERPENT-LIKE —) DRACO ANGUIS
(SHIP'S —) DUSTER
(TURKISH —) ALEM
(WATER —) SAG
(PL.) BUNTING
FLAG BEARER GUIDON ANCIENT
FLAGELLANT WHIPPER SCOURGER
(PL.) ALBI
FLAGELLATE MONAS NOCTILUCA
FLAGELLUM WHIP CILIUM RUNNER KONSEAL WHIPLASH
(PREF.) BLEPHAR(O) MASTIG(O)
(SUFF.) KONT
FLAGEOLET PIPE ZUFOLO BASAREE LARIGOT SIBILUS ZUFFOLO MONAULOS
FLAGGING WEAK LANGUID
FLAGITIOUS WICKED CORRUPT HEINOUS CRIMINAL FLAGRANT GRIEVOUS
FLAGON GUN STOUP BOTTLE VESSEL FLACKET FLAGONET REHOBOAM
FLAGRANT BAD RED RANK GROSS ODIOUS STRONG WANTON

WICKED BLATANT GLARING HATEFUL HEINOUS SCARLET VIOLENT SHAMEFUL
FLAGSHIP FLAG ADMIRAL
FLAGSTONE FLAG LECK SLAB FAVUS
FLAIL BEAT FLOG WHIP DRASH FRAIL THRAIL THRASH THRESH SWINGLE SWIPPLE STRICKLE THRESHEL
FLAIR RAY BENT ELAN NOSE ODOR SMELL VERVE GENIUS TALENT LEANING PANACHE
FLAKE CHIP FILM FLAG FLAW RACK SNOW FLANK FLECK FLOCK LAMIN SCALE SLATE SPALL SPAWL STRIP APHTHA HURDLE LAMINA PALING FLAUGHT SHAVING FLOCCULE FRAGMENT
(— OF DIRT) SMUT
(— OF METAL) FLITTER
(— OF SNOW) FLAG
(— OF SOOT) STRANGER
(PREF.) LEPID(O)
(SUFF.) LEPIS
FLAKY SCALY WACKY OFFBEAT SHIVERY
FLAMBE JUBILEE
FLAMBEAU TORCH
FLAMBOYANCE BLARE PANACHE
FLAMBOYANT BAROCK FLORID GARISH ORNATE BAROQUE BUCKEYE FLAMING GORGEOUS
FLAME LOW FIRE GLOW LOWE LUNT ARDOR BLAZE FLARE FLASH GLARE GLEED INGLE LIGHT RESEPH TONGUE BURNING FLAMELET INKINDLE
(ACETYLENE —) CALCIUM
(SMALL —) SPUNK FLAMELET FLAMMULE
(PL.) GLEED
FLAME SCARLET FLORENTINE
FLAME TREE KURRAJONG
FLAMING LIVE AFIRE FIERY FLAMY VIVID AFLARE ARDENT BLAZING BURNING FLARING FLAGRANT
FLAMMA, LA (CHARACTER IN —) AGNES CERVIA BASILIO DONELLO SILVANA
(COMPOSER OF —) RESPIGHI
FLAN PLANCHET
FLANGE BEAD BOSS BEZEL COLLAR COLLET FLANCH SHROUD FEATHER DUCKBILL FOLLOWER
(— OF GIRDER) BOOM
(WITHOUT —) BALD
FLANGER FLAYER GOUGER
FLANK LEER LISK SIDE WING CHEEK SKIRT THIGH BORDER FLITCH
(— OF ARCH) HANCH HAUNCH
(PL.) ILIA
(PREF.) LAPAR(O)
FLANNEL LANA DOMETT SAXONY STAMIN RUBBISH WHITTLE MOLLETON NONSENSE SWANSKIN
FLAP ADO FAN LUG ROB TAB TAG TAP WAP BATE BEAT BLOW CLAP FLIP FLOG FLOP GILL LOBE LOMA SLAM SLAT WAFF WELT ALARM APRON FLACK FLAFF FLICK BALLUP BANGLE LAPPET LIBBET STRIKE TONGUE WAFFLE WALLOP WINNOW AILERON BLINDER CLICKET FLACKER FLAPPET FLICKER FLOUNCE FLUTTER SWINDLE VALANCE AVENTAIL BACKFLAP COATTAIL CODPIECE TURNOVER AGITATION COMMOTION CONFUSION
(— OF BOOTEE) FLY
(— OF GARMENT) LAP
(— OF HAT OR CAP) VALANCE
(— OF HINGE) LEAF
(— ON HOLSTER) FLOUNCE
(— ON SADDLE) SKIRT JOCKEY
(— VIOLENTLY) FLOG SLAT
(CARDIAC —) CUSP
(FLESHY —) GILL
(MUD —) BOOT
(TROUSERS' —) FALL
FLAPPER FLAP WING FLOPPER SNICKET
FLAPPING WAFF WHUTTER
FLARE BELL FLUE BLAZE FLAME FLASH FLECK FUSEE LIGHT SPIRT TORCH FLANCH SIGNAL SPREAD FLICKER TRUMPET OUTBURST
(— ON SHIPBOARD) DUCK
(— UP) ERUPT KINDLE
(RAILROAD —) FUSEE
(PL.) TROUSERS
FLARING BELL FLUE EVASE GAUDY AFLARE FLIPPY FLAMING GLARING SWAGGER BOUFFANT DAZZLING
FLASH DOT BEAT DASH LAIT LAMP LASH LEAM POOL RUSH SHOT STAB WINK BLASH BLAZE BURST FLAME FLARE FLOSH FLUFF GLADE GLAIK GLEAM GLENT GLINT GLITZ LEVIN MARSH SPARK STEAM BOTTLE FILLIP GLANCE QUIVER REPORT BLUETTE FLAUGHT FOULDRE GLIMMER GLIMPSE GLISTEN GLITTER INSTANT LIGHTEN QUICKEN SHIMMER SPARKLE TWINKLE BULLETIN SPLINTER SUNBURST CORUSCATE SCINTILLATION
(— FORTH) OUTRAY
(HOT —) FLUSHING
(NEWS —) FUDGE
FLASHBACK THROWBACK
FLASHING CURB FLASH STEEP ARDENT BRIGHT FLASHY FORWARD LAMPING SHINING CREASING METEORIC SLASHING SNAPPING
FLASHLIGHT BUG GLIM FLASH TORCH PENLITE PENLIGHT
FLASHY GAY FLAT GAUD LOUD BAVIN FIERY GAUDY NOBBY SHOWY SLEEK ZOOTY FLOSSY FROTHY GARISH SLANGY SPORTY STUNTY INSIPID RAFFISH TINHORN DAZZLING FLASHING SPORTING TIGERISH VEHEMENT
FLASK BOX PIG BODY HEAD HELM JACK OLPE SNAP BETTY BULGE DEWAR FRAME GIRBA GOURD BOTTLE FIASCO FLACON GUTTUS HELMET LAGENA AMPULLA BOMBOLA CANTEEN FLASKET MATRASS TICKLER WARBURG CHRISMAL CUCURBIT
(POCKET —) TICKLER
(PREF.) OLPIDI
FLAT DEAD DOWD DULL EVEN FADE FLUE PLAT SLOB TAME ABODE AFLAT BANAL BLAND BLUNT DUSTY HAUGH LEVEL MOLLE MUSTY PLAIN PLANE PRONE ROOMS SEBKA SLAKE VAPID WALSH AGRUFE BORING CALLOW DREARY FLASHY JEJUNE LEADEN PLANAR QUATCH SEBKHA SILENT SIMOUS DECIDED FLIPPER INSIPID INSULSE PLATOID PROSAIC SHILPIT TABULAR UNIFORM DIRECTLY LIFELESS TENEMENT UNBROKEN WATERISH CHAMPAIGN POINTLESS PROSTRATE
(— AND CIRCULAR) DISCOID
(— AND SHORT) CAMUS CAMUSE
(— IN MUSIC) BEMOL MOLLE
(— OF SWORD) PLAT
(MUD —) SLOB SLAKE CORCASS
(NOT —) BRISK
(SALT —) SALINA
(THEATRICAL —) JOG
(PREF.) PLAN(I) PLAT(Y)
FLATBOAT ARK SCOW PULLBOAT
FLATCAR FLAT IDLER LORRY
(ON A —) PIGGYBACK
FLATFISH DAB RAY BUTT DACE KITE SLIP SOLE TONG BREAM BRILL FLUKE QUIFF RHINA WHIFF ACEDIA CARTER PLAICE TURBOT HALIBUT SUNFISH TORPEDO FLOUNDER MARYSOLE
FLATHEAD SALISH
FLATIRON IRON GOOSE STEEL SADIRON
FLATLY
(PREF.) PLANO
FLATNESS BATHOS SILENCE EVENNESS KURTOSIS
(— OF NOSE) SIMITY
FLAT-NOSED CAMUS
FLATTEN BEAT COMB DECK EVEN PLAT CRUSH GRADE LEVEL PLUSH SPLAT BEETLE CLINCH DEJECT SMOOTH SPREAD SQUASH DEPRESS EXPLAIN PANCAKE PLANISH SUBSIDE SURBASE COMPRESS DISPIRIT
FLATTENED ECRASE OBLATE DILATED PLANATE TABULAR
FLATTER BULL CLAW COAX DAUB FAGE FUME PALP SOAP WORD CHARM FLOAT GLOZE HONEY PAINT ROOSE SLEEK SMALM BECOME BUTTER CAJOLE CRINGE FICKLE FLEECH FRAISE GLAVER KITTLE PEPPER PHRASE SAWDER SLAVER SMOOGE SOOTHE STROKE ADULATE BEGUILE BEHONEY BLARNEY FLETHER FLUTTER INCENSE PALAVER SOOTHER SWEETEN WHEEDLE BESLAVER BLANDISH BOOTLICK COLLOGUE
FLATTERER FLOIT COGGER DAUBER EARWIG GLOZER JENKINS PRONEUR SOOTHER BOOTLICK CLAWBACK COURTIER DAMOCLES INCENSER LOSENGER SLAVERER SMOOTHER
FLATTERING SOAPY SMARMY SMOOTH BUTTERY CANDIED COURTLY GLAVERING
FLATTERY BULL BUNK DAUB FLUM MUSH SOAP FRAIK GLOZE SALVE TAFFY BUTTER CARNEY FLEECH GREASE PHRASE SAWDER SLAVER BLARNEY DAUBING EYEWASH FAWNING FLETHER INCENSE PALAVER CAJOLERY ADULATION
FLATULENCE WIND VAPOR
FLATULENT GASSY WINDY TURGID POMPOUS VENTOSE FLATUOUS INFLATED
FLATWARE SILVER
FLATWORM ACOEL FLUKE PLATODE RADIATE POLYCLAD
FLAUNT BOSH SHOW WAVE BOAST SKYRE STOUT VAUNT PARADE DISPLAY FLUTTER TRAIPSE BRANDISH FLOURISH
FLAUNTING GAUDY PURPLE SKYRIN FLAGGERY
FLAVONE CHROMONE
FLAVOR GAMY GOUT MASK ODOR RASA SALT TANG ZEST AROMA ASSAI CURRY DEVIL SAPID SAPOR SAUCE SAVOR SCENT SMACK SPICE TASTE TINGE ASARUM ASSAHY INFUSE RANCIO RELISH SEASON TARAGE FLAVOUR PERFUME SUPTION VARIETY HAUTGOUT PIQUANCY
(DEVELOP —) BREATHE
(DISTINCTIVE —) TACK SMACK
(HIGH —) HOGO
(SHARP —) TWANG
(SPECIAL —) GUST
(UNPLEASANT —) TACK
FLAVORED SPICY TINCT SPICED
FLAVORFUL SAPID SAVOROUS
FLAVORING DIP MOCHA ALMOND CASSIS VANILLA MIREPOIS
FLAVORLESS BLAND STALE SILENT WATERISH
FLAW BUG FIB GAP LIE MAR RUB WEM BANE BLOT CHIP FLEE GALL HOLE RASE RIFT SPOT WIND BOTCH BRACK BURST CHICK CLEFT CRACK CRAZE FAULT FLAKE PLUME SPECK BLOTCH BREACH DEFECT FOIBLE LACUNA LESION BLEMISH BLISTER DEFAULT EYELAST FEATHER FISSURE NULLIFY SUNSPOT VIOLATE WHITLOW FRACTURE FRAGMENT GENDARME WINDFLAW
(— IN CASTING) BUCKLE
(— IN CLOTH) BRACK
(— IN DIAMOND) GENDARME
(— IN MARBLE) TERRACE
(— IN METAL) SNAKE
(— IN PRECIOUS STONE) FEATHER
(— IN STEEL) STAR
(— IN STONE) DRY
(— IN WICK) THIEF
(MORAL —) SMIRCH
FLAWED CRACKED
FLAWLESS CLEAN SOUND PERFECT
FLAX LIN POB TOW CARD FLIX HARL LINE LINT ROCK GRAIN HURDS BREADS BYSSUS KORARI PEANUT

PEBBLE SCUTCH LINSEED FLAXWORT HARAKEKE
(— DISEASE) PASMO
(PREPARE —) RET
(PREF.) BYSSI BYSSO LINO
FLAXEN FLAXY BLONDE
FLAXWEED TOADFLAX
FLAY SKIN SCULP STRIP FLEECE UNCASE CENSURE PILLAGE REPROVE SCARIFY
FLEA LOP SCUD FLECH FLECK PULEX TUNGA CHEGRE CHIGOE VERMIN PULICID SANDBOY
(— INFESTED) PULICOSE
(PREF.) PULI
FLEABANE SKEVISH SCABIOUS WHITETOP
FLEA BEETLE THRIPS
FLEAM BEVEL
FLEAWORT CAMMOCK FLEASEED PSYLLIUM
FLECHE SPIRE SPIRELET
FLECK FLAKE FREAK DAPPLE FLEECE POUNCE STREAK STIPPLE
FLEDERMAUS, DIE (CHARACTER IN —) ADELE FALKE FRANK ALFRED ORLOFSKY ROSALINDE EISENSTEIN
(COMPOSER OF —) STRAUSS
FLEDGED FLUSH FLIGGED
FLEDGLING SQUAB NESTER FLIGGER BIRDLING
FLEE FLY LAM RUN BOLT FLEG LOUP SCUR SHUN TURN ELOPE ELUDE SKIRR SPEED DECAMP ESCAPE RUNOFF VANISH ABANDON ABSCOND FORSAKE SCAMPER LIBERATE SKEDADDLE
(SUFF.) FUGAL FUGE
FLEECE JIB KET TEG BUCK CAST FELL GAFF MORT PLOT ROOK SKIN TEGG TEGS CHEAT FLICK PASHM PLOAT SHAVE SHEAR SHEEP SWEAT PASHIM PIGEON PUSHUM TOISON SHEARING
(— OF MEDIUM GRADE) SUPER
(POOREST PART OF —) ABB
FLEEING FUGIENT HOTFOOT RUNNING FUGITIVE
FLEER GIBE JIBE LEER FLIRE FLOUT SCOFF SNEER
FLEET BAY FAST FLIT NAVY SAIL SKIM SWIM CREEK DRAIN DRIFT EVAND FLOAT FLOTA HASTY INLET POWER QUICK RAPID SWIFT ARGOSY ARMADA FLIGHT HASTEN NIMBLE SPEEDY CARAVAN COMPANY FLOTILLA NAVARCHY WARCRAFT
FLEETING BRIEF BUBBLE CADUCE FLYING VOLAGE CURSIVE FLIGHTY PASSING POSTING SHADOWY VOLATIC CADUCOUS FUGITIVE VOLATILE
FLESH KIN BEEF BODY FELL GAME LAMB LIRE MEAT RACE WEED SLATE STOCK FAMILY MUSCLE SEASON CARNAGE KINDRED MANKIND NATURAL HUMANITY MOONLIGHT
(— ABOUT CHIN AND JAWS) GILL
(— OF CALF) SLINK
(— OF GOAT) CHEVON
(— OF KID) CABRITO
(— OF SHEEP) TRAIK
(— ON LOWER JAW) CHOLLER
(— OUT) CLOTHE
(— UNDER SKIN) FELL
(ANIMAL —) BRAWN
(DEAD —) MURRAIN
(HORSE —) JACK
(LIFELESS —) MUMMY
(PUTREFYING —) CARRION
(SUN-DRIED —) TAPA
(SUPERFLUOUS —) LUMBER
(PREF.) CARNI CRE(O) CREATO KRE(O) SARC(O)
(SUFF.) SARC
FLESHBRUSH STRIGIL
FLESH-COLORED SARCOLINE
FLESH-EATING CARNAL CARNIVOROUS
FLESHER LINING
FLESHINESS FULLNESS CORPULENCE
FLESHLESS LENTEN
FLESHLY CARNAL FLESHY SENSUAL SARKICAL
FLESHY FAT BEEFY LUSTY OBESE PLUMP PULPY STOUT ANIMAL BODILY BRAWNY CARNAL BUNTING CARNOSE SARCOUS CARNEOUS
FLETCH WING FLIGHT
FLEUR-DE-LIS LIS LYS LILY LUCY FLEUR
FLEX BEND
FLEXED PENCHE
FLEXIBILITY WHIP FLUIDITY
FLEXIBLE ACDC LIMP LUSH SOFT BUXOM LIMSY LITHE WANDY WITHY FLOPPY LIMBER LITHER PLIANT SUPPLE DUCTILE ELASTIC FINGENT FLEXILE FLEXIVE LISSOME PLIABLE SPRINGY WILLOWY WINDING WRIGGLE BENDSOME YIELDING
(PREF.) CAMPTO
FLEXURE ARCH BEND BENT CURL FOLD CURVE TWIST SIGMOID WINDING
FLICK PIC FILM FLIP CLICK FLACK FLANK FLECK FLIRT FLISK MOVIE CINEMA
(SKIN —) NUDIE
(PL.) CINEMA
FLICKER FAIL FLIT LICK WINK BLINK FLAME FLARE FLICK FLUNK WAVER BICKER FITTER SHIVER YUCKER BLINTER FLIMMER FLITTER FLUTTER SKIMMER TREMBLE TWINKLE WHIFFLE FLICHTER HIGHHOLE
FLICKERING FLICKY FLUTTER LAMBENT FLEXUOUS UNSTEADY
FLICKERTAIL STATE NORTHDAKOTA
FLIER ACE BIRD KIWI FLYER PILOT AIRMAN AVIATOR LEAFLET CIRCULAR PAMPHLET
FLIGHT FLY GUY HOP LAM BOLT BUNK LAKE PAIR ROUT WING CHEVY FLOCK GLIDE GRICE SCRAP VOLEE CHIVVY EXODUS FUGACY HEGIRA HEJIRA JOYHOP SPIRAL BOUQUET EVASION FLAUGHT FLYOVER MIGRATE MISSION SCAMPER STEPWAY REGIFUGE STAMPEDE SWARMING
(— APPROVAL) AOK
(— OF BALL) HOOK DRIVE SLICE
(— OF BIRDS) VOLARY VOLERY VOLLEY
(— OF FANCY) SALLY
(— OF GEESE) SKEIN
(— OF SNIPE) WISP
(— OF STEPS) RISE TRAP GRECE PITCH SCALE STOOP PERRON STAIRS STEPWAY STAIRWAY
(— OF WILD FOWL) SKEIN
(— OF WOODCOCK) RODING
(ABORTIVE —) ABORT
(HASTY —) TIFT
(HAWK'S —) CAREER
(HIGH —) TOWER
(IN —) ALOFT
(LATE NIGHT —) REDEYE
(SUDDEN —) START STAMPEDE
(UNAUTHORIZED —) BUGOUT
(UPWARD —) SOAR
(PREF.) AERO
(SUFF.) FUGAL FUGE PHOBE PHOBI(A)(AC)(C) PHOBUS
FLIGHTY ANILE BARMY GIDDY LIGHT SWIFT FITFUL GARISH UNFIRM VOLAGE WHISKY FLYAWAY FOOLISH GIGGISH MOONISH ROCKETY FLEETING FREAKISH HELLICAT SKIPPING VOLATILE
(— PERSON) TRIVVET
FLIMFLAM CON
FLIMSINESS INANITY
FLIMSY LIMP THIN VAIN WEAK FRAIL GAUDY JERRY FEEBLE PALTRY SLEAZY SLIGHT SLIMSY HAYWIRE SHALLOW TENUOUS TIFFANY GIMCRACK GOSSAMER JIMCRACK TWITTERY
FLINCH SHY FUNK GAME JARG BLUNK BUDGE FEIGN QUAIL SHUNT START WINCE WONDE BLANCH BLENCH FALTER FLENSE RECOIL SHRINK SCRINGE SCUNNER SQUINCH
FLINCHER VELLINCH
FLINDER FLITTER SMITHERS
FLINDERSIA SILKWOOD
FLINDOSA CUDGERIE
FLING SHY BUZZ CAST DART DASH DING EMIT FLAP FLEG GIBE HURL KICK LASH PECK PICK SLAT TOSS WARP BRAID CHEAT DANCE FLIRT LANCE PITCH SHOOT SLING SNEER SWING THROW WHANG BAFFLE EFFUSE HURTLE LAUNCH PLUNGE REBUFF SPIRIT ENFORCE FLOUNCE REPULSE SARCASM SCATTER SWINDLE SHYLANCE SPANGHEW
(— HEADLONG) RUINATE
(— MISSILES) CHUNK
(— UPWARD) HAUNCH
(HIGHLAND —) WALLOCH
FLINT CORE BLANK CHERT MISER SILEX EOLITH QUARTZ REJECT ESLABON FURISON SCRAPER GRATTOIR GUNFLINT
(PREF.) SILICEO SILICI SILICO
FLINTINESS HEART
FLINTLOCK FUSEE FUSIL FUZEE MUSKET SPANNER FIRELOCK MIQUELET SNAPHAAN
FLINTWOOD WHITETOP
FLIP SKY TAP FLAP SNAP TOSS TRIP FLANK FLICK FLIRT GOAPE SLIRT SMART FILLIP FLITCH GOGAGA LIMBER NIMBLE PLIANT PROPEL
(— OUT) GOAPE
FLIP-FLOP SANDAL REVERSAL
FLIPPANT AIRY FLIP GLIB FLUENT LIMBER NIMBLE
FLIPPER ARM FIN PAW HAND SWELL PADDLE FLAPPER SPRINGER
FLIRT TOY FIKE FLIP MASH TICK VAMP FLICK ROVER SLIRT JILLET MASHER TRIFLE GALLANT PICKEER TWINKLE COQUETTE PHILANDER
FLIRTATION FIKE PASSADE COQUETRY PHILANDER
FLIT DART FLOW SCUD FLECK FLEET FLICK FLIRT FLOAT FLURR HOVER QUICK SCOOT SKIFF SWIFT NIMBLE FLICKER FLUTTER
FLITCH FLICK GAMMON LONGWOOD MIDDLING
FLOAT BOB FLY KIT SEA BOOM BUOY CORK DRAG FLOW FLUX HAWK HONE HOVE LIVE PONT RAFT RIDE SAIL SCOW SOAR SWIM TILT WAFT WAVE BALSA BLADE CAMEL DERBY DRIFT DRIVE FLEET FLOOD FLUSH GRAIL HOVER LADLE QUILL SHOAD SWOON BILLOW BOBBER BUCKET BUNGEY CANNEL DOBBER PADDLE PONTON RADEAU STREEL TOPPER CAISSON DRINGLE FLATTER FLOTTER FRESHEN OROPESA PAGEANT PLANKER PLUMMET PONTOON SLICKER LEVITATE PICKOVER
(— AIMLESSLY) DRIFT
(— DELIGHTFULLY) COWD
(— FOR HERRING NET) BOWL
(— FOR RING BUOY) LEMON
(— LOGS) DRIVE
(— OF REEDS) KELEK LIGGER
(— PAST) GLACE
(— PROPERLY) WATCH
(CANOE —) AMA
(FISHLINE —) BOB CORK BOBBER DOBBER TRIMMER
(PLASTERER'S —) DARBY
FLOATBOARD BLADE FLOAT LADLE
FLOATER STIFF
FLOATING FREE WAFT AWASH LOOSE ADRIFT AFLOAT FLYING NATANT BUOYANT FLYAWAY PENDENT DRIFTING FLUITANT SHIFTING UNFUNDED
FLOCCILATION TILMUS
FLOCK MOB POD BAND BANK BEVY FOLD GAME GANG HERD MANY PACK ROUT SAIL SORT TEAM TRIP WISP BROOD BUNCH CHARM COVEY CROWD DRIFT DROVE FLAKE FLECK GROUP PLUMP SEDGE SHOAL SWARM TRIBE TROOP COVERT FLIGHT GAGGLE HIRSEL MANADA MEINIE RAFTER SCHOOL SCURRY VOLERY COMPANY GOOSERY THICKEN PADDLING

(— OF BIRDS) POD BANK HERD TEAM WISP BROWN COVEY SEDGE SIEGE TRIBE FLIGHT VOLERY
(— OF BITTERNS) SEDGE SIEGE
(— OF DUCKS) PADDLING
(— OF FINCHES) CHARM CHIRM
(— OF GEESE) SKEIN GAGGLE
(— OF HERONS) SEDGE SIEGE
(— OF LARKS) EXALTATION
(— OF LIONS) PRIDE
(— OF MALLARDS) SORD SUTE
(— OF NIGHTINGALES) WATCH
(— OF PARTRIDGE) COVEY
(— OF PEACOCKS) MUSTER
(— OF PIGEONS) KIT LOFT
(— OF PLOVER) WING
(— OF ROOKS) ROOKERY
(— OF SANDPIPERS) FLING
(— OF SHEEP) FOLD HIRSEL
(— OF SHELDRAKE) DOPPING
(— OF SNIPE) WISP
(— OF SWANS) BANK GAME MARK
(— OF TURTLE-DOVES) DOLE
(— OF WIDGEONS) COMPANY
(— OF WILDFOWL) SCRY SKEIN
(— TOGETHER) RAFT
(SMALL —) SPRING
(PREF.) **(— OF WOOL)** FLOCCI

FLOCKING REPAIR

FLOE PAN

FLOG CAT TAN TAW BEAT CANE CHOP HIDE LASH LICK LUMP TOCO WALE WARM WELK WHIP YANK BIRCH EXCEL FIGHT FLAIL HORSE KNOUT LINGE QUILT SAUCE SKEEG SWISH WHANG BREECH COTTON LARRUP LATHER STRIKE SWITCH THRASH WALLOP WATTLE BALEISE BELABOR COWHIDE SCOURGE SJAMBOK TROUNCE CARTWHIP CHAWBUCK SLAISTER URTICATE VAPULATE
(— WATER) SCRINGE

FLOGGER HORSING SWISHER

FLOGGING TOCO TOKO TANNING BIRCHING WHIPPING

FLOOD SEA BORE BUOY FLOW FLUX POUR TIDE EAGRE FLOAT FLUSH SPATE SWAMP SWILL WATER DELUGE EXCESS RAVINE SLUICE SPLASH DEBACLE FLOTTER FRESHET NIAGARA TORRENT ALLUVION CATARACT INUNDATE OVERFLOW SURROUND

FLOODED AWASH AFLOAT

FLOODGATE CLOW DRAG GOLE HATCH SLUICE STAUNCH CATARACT PENSTOCK

FLOODING UP PROUD FLOWAGE DILUVIAL FLOATING

FLOODLIGHT OLIVET

FLOODPLAIN BENCH DAMBO

FLOOR BECK DECK DROP FLAT LAND LOFT PAVE SEAT BOARD FLOAT GRASS PIANO PIECE SOLAR STAGE STORY BELFRY FLIGHT GROUND SOLLAR PLANCHE BARBECUE FLOORING HALFPACE PAVEMENT SUBFLOOR
(— OF COAL MINE) SOLE THILL
(— OF COAL SEAM) SILL
(— OF FORGE) HEARTH
(— OF GLASS FURNACE) SIEGE
(— OF OCEAN) SEABED
(— OF SPORTS RING) CANVAS
(— OF WOOLSHED) BOARD
(FOREST —) SEEDBED
(GROUND —) TERRENO BASEMENT
(OPENWORK —S) GRATINGS
(RAISED —) LEEWAN HALFPACE
(THEATRE —) GALLERY
(THRESHING —) MOWSTEAD
(UPPER —) LOFT

FLOORBOARD FOOTLING
(BOAT'S —) BURDEN
(BOAT'S —S) BURDEN

FLOORING STAGE PARQUET TERRAZZO
(— FOR STACK) RICKSTAND

FLOORMAN CALLBOY

FLOP DOG BOMB SWOP WHOP SQUAB BUMMER TURKEY FAILURE TRAGEDY

FLORA CYBELE FLORULA
(— AND FAUNA) BIOTA

FLORAL TREE LEAF

FLORENCE FLASK BETTY

FLORENCE IRIS ORRIS TREOS

FLORESTAN (WIFE OF —) LEONORA

FLORID FINE HIGH BUXOM FRESH RUDDY ORNATE ROCOCO RUBIED ASIATIC FLOWERY TAFFETA BLOOMING FIGURATE RUBICUND SANGUINE SPLENDID VIGOROUS

FLORIDA

BAY: BISCAYNE APALACHEE WACCASASSA
CAPITAL: TALLAHASSEE
COLLEGE: ROLLINS
COUNTY: BAY LEE DADE GULF LEON POLK BAKER DIXIE HARDEE HENDRY NASSAU ORANGE ALACHUA BREVARD BROWARD MANATEE OSCEOLA VOLUSIA PINELLAS SARASOTA
INDIAN: AIS OCALE UTINA CALUSA CHATOT POTANO TIMUCUA SEMINOLE
ISLANDS: KEYS
KEY: WEST LARGO BISCAYNE
LAKE: DORA APOPKA HARNEY JESSUP NEWNAN LEDWITH ARBUCKLE KISSIMMEE OKEECHOBEE
NATIVE: CONCH CRACKER
RIVER: BANANA INDIAN AUCILLA MANATEE SCAMBIA SUWANEE OCHLAWAHA
STATE BIRD: MOCKINGBIRD
STATE NICKNAME: SUNSHINE
STATE TREE: PALMETTO
TOWN: TICE COCOA MIAMI OCALA TAMPA ORLANDO PALATKA SEBRING TAMARAC SARASOTA PENSACOLA
UNIVERSITY: STETSON
WETLANDS: GLADES

FLORIDIAN CRACKER

FLORIMEL (HUSBAND OF —) MARINEL

FLORIN GULDEN

FLORIPES (BROTHER OF —) FIERABRAS
(HUSBAND OF —) GUY

FLOSS FLUFF SKEIN WASTE CADDIS SLEAVE CADDICE

FLOSSER FANNER

FLOSS-SILK TREE SAMOHU

FLOTSAM JETSAM WILSAM WAFTURE WAVESON DRIFTAGE FLOATAGE

FLOUNCE FLAP HUFF SKIT SLAM FLING FRILL RUCHE PEPLUM RIPPLE ROBING ROUNCE RUFFLE VOLANT FALBALA FALBELO FROUNCE RUCHING FLOUNDER FURBELOW STRUGGLE

FLOUNDER DAB GAD BUTT KEEL POLE ROLL TOSS BREAM FLUKE SLOSH WITCH WRELE GADOID GROVEL MEGRIM MUDDLE PLAICE TOLTER TURBOT WALLOP WALLOW WARSLE BLUNDER FLASKER FLOUNCE PLOUNCE STUMBLE SUNFISH TOPKNOT VAAGMAR ANACANTH FLATFISH FOOLFISH PLUNTHER SANDLING

FLOUR AMYL ATTA DUST CONES HOVIS BINDER CLEARS FARINA FLOWER PATENT POLLEN SICKEN TSAMBA WHITES BOXINGS BRAVURA CRIBBLE CANAILLE
(— OF MALT) SMEDDUM
(COARSE —) THIRD CHISEL BOXINGS CRIBBLE
(COVER WITH —) DREDGE
(FINE —) CONES SUJEE
(LOW-GRADE —) TAIL
(PARTICLE OF —) CHOP
(POTATO —) FROW
(UNSORTED —) ATTA
(PREF.) ALEURO

FLOURISH TAG WAG BOOM BRAG FUSS GROW LICK RIOT RISE SHOW TUCK WAVE ADORN BLOOM BOAST CHEVE GLOSS QUIRK REIGN SHAKE SWASH SWING SWISH TUSCH VAUNT CATTER PARADE PARAPH QUAVER SQUIRL THRIVE BLOSSOM BURGEON CADENZA DISPLAY ENLARGE FANFARE GAMBADE GAMBADO PASSAGE PROSPER ROULADE SUCCEED TRIUMPH WAMPISH ARPEGGIO BRANDISH CURLICUE INCREASE ORNAMENT SKIRMISH
(— OF BAGPIPE) WARBLER
(— OF TRUMPET) MORT SENNET TUCKET

FLOURISHING FAR FRIM FRUM PERT GREEN PALMY PEART VITAL BLOOMY FLORID GOLDEN FLORENT HEALTHY VERNANT THRIVING VEGETOUS PROSPEROUS

FLOURY MEALY

FLOUT BOB GIBE JEER JERK JIBE LOUT MOCK FLEER FLITE FRUMP SCOFF SCOMM SCORN SCOUT SNEER TAUNT DERIDE INSULT BETONGUE

FLOW GO EBB ERN JET PUT RUN SET SUE BORE COMB FLIT FLUX FUSE GUSH HALE LAVA LAVE MELT PASS POUR RAIL ROLL SEND SHED SILE SLIP SOAK SWIG TAIL TEEM TIDE WELL AVALE DRAIN DRIFT EAGRE EXUDE FLEAM FLEET FLOAT FLOOD FLUSH FRESH GLIDE ISSUE QUELL RIVER SCOOT SLIDE SPEND SPILL SPURT SWILL TRILL ABOUND AFFLUX COURSE CURSUS DELUGE GUGGLE GUTTER POPPLE RECEDE RINDLE SPRING STREAM CURRENT DEVOLVE DISTILL DRIBBLE EMANATE FLOWAGE FLUTTER FLUXION ILLAPSE INDRAFT MEANDER SPURTLE TRINKLE TRINTLE ALLUVION BACKWASH CURRANCE CURRENCY DOWNFLOW EMISSION FOUNTAIN GOWITHIT INUNDATE
(— AGAINST) LAP LAVE BATHE
(— BACK) EBB
(— BEYOND BANKS) DEBORD SURROUND
(— DOWN) AVALE
(— IN) INFLOW INFLOOD
(— IN RILLS) DRILL
(— IN RIVULETS) GUTTER
(— IN SPURTS) SALTATION
(— INTERMITTENTLY) HEAD
(— NOISILY) BICKER
(— OF AIR) SIDEWASH
(— OF ELECTRICITY) BOLT OSCILLATION
(— OF LANGUAGE) STRAIN
(— OF METAL) CREEP
(— OF RADIO SIGNAL) BEAM
(— OF SOUNDS) CADENCE
(— OUT) EMIT ISSUE EFFUSE SPREAD EXHAUST RESOLVE
(— OVER) BERUN
(— SLOWLY) SEEP EXUDE GLEET
(— TOGETHER) CONCUR CONFLOW
(— WITH) FLEET
(CONTINUOUS —) LAPSE
(COPIOUS —) HALE RIVER
(LAVA —) COULE COULEE
(RHYTHMICAL —) LILT
(STRONG —) TORRENT
(TIDAL —) BORE AEGIR EAGER EAGRE
(PREF.) RHEO RHYSI
(SUFF.) FLUENCE FLUENT FLUOUS FLUX RRHAGIA RRHEA RRHOEA

FLOWER (ALSO SEE PLANT AND HERB) BUD GAY BEST BLOW FLAG IRIS IXIA PINK POLE POSY ROSE ARROW ASTER BLOOM BLUET BREAK DAISY ELITE FANCY FLOOR GOWAN LILAC PANSY PHLOX TRUSS TULIP TUTTY AZALEA CHOICE CORYMB CROCUS CYMULE DAHLIA DATURA FLORET MAYPOP ORCHID SCILLA SEASON SHOWER SINGLE STEVIA UNFOLD AMELLUS ANEMONE ARBUTUS BLETHIA BLOSSOM BOSTRYX CAMPANA DEVELOP ESSENCE FLEURET FLOSCLE GAZANIA GENTIAN GERBERA IPOMOEA PETUNIA PICOTEE TORENIA BELAMOUR CAMELLIA CYCLAMEN DAFFODIL DIANTHUS GARDENIA GERANIUM HEPATICA HIBISCUS HYACINTH PRIMROSE SNOWDROP SPARAXIS
(— FOR BUTTONHOLE) BOUTONNIERE
(— STATE) FLORIDA

(— WITH 6 SEGMENTS) SEXFOIL
(ART OF — ARRANGING) IKEBANA
(AXIS OF —) CYME SPIKE UMBEL CORYMB MIASMA RACEME
(COTTON —) SQUARE
(DEFORMED —) BULLHEAD
(DOUBLE —) BURSTER
(DRIED —S) BRAYERA
(GLOWING —) TORCH
(IMAGINARY —) AMARANTH
(PART OF —) OVARY PETAL SEPAL STALK STYLE ANTHER CARDEL PISTIL STAMEN STIGMA PEDICEL FILAMENT PEDUNCLE PERIANTH RECEPTACLE
(SHOWY —) ORCHIS
(STRIPED —) BIZARRE
(UNFADING —) AMARANTH
(PL.) SPRAY BOUQUET
(PREF.) ANTH(O) FLORI
(SUFF.) ANTHEMA ANTHEMUM ANTHERA ANTHEROUS ANTHERY ANTHES ANTHOUS ANTHUS FLORAL FLOROUS
FLOWER-BED KNOT BORDER
FLOWER-BUD CAPER CLOVE
FLOWERFLY SYRPHID
FLOWERHEAD CALATHUS
FLOWERING AFLOWER FLOWERY ANTHESIS BLOOMING
FLOWERING GLUME LEMMA
FLOWERLESS ANANTHOUS
FLOWER-LIKE ANTHOID
FLOWER-OF-AN-HOUR SHOOFLY
FLOWER-PECKER KAKAWAHIE
FLOWERPOT POT CACHEPOT
FLOWERY BLOWN BLOOMY FLORID POSIED FLORENT PRIMROSE
FLOWING FAIR FLUX LAVE SIDE AFLOW FLOAT FLUID FLUOR QUICK TIDAL AFFLUX DEFLUX FLUENT FUSILE LIVING COPIOUS CURRENT CURSIVE EMANANT FLUXING FLUXION FLUXIVE RUNNING SLIDING STREAMY DEFLUENT DILUENDO FLUVIOSE
(— AT LOW SPEED) SLACK
(— BACK) EBB
(— IN) INFLUX INFLUENT INFLUXION
(— OF GLAZE) STREAMING
(— OF TIDE) FLOOD
(— OUT) ELAPSE EFFLUENT
(— SMOOTHLY) VOLUBLE PROFLUENT
(— TOGETHER) CONFLUX
(PREF.) **(— OUT)** EFFLUVIO
FLOWOFF RUNOFF
FLU (TYPE OF —) ASIAN
FLUB BOOT ERRATUM
FLUCAN SELVAGE SELVEDGE
FLUCTUATE SWAY VARY VEER YOYO FLEET SWING WAVER BALANCE VIBRATE WAMPISH UNDULATE UNSTEADY VACILLATE
FLUCTUATING WAVY HECTIC LABILE RUBATO ERRATIC FLUXIVE WAYWARD UNSTABLE UNSTEADY
FLUCTUATION CYCLE FADING JIGGLE FLICKER FLUTTER VIBRATO OSCILLATION
(— IN LAKES) SEICHE
(— OF LAKE SURFACE) SEICHE
FLUE NET BARB DOWN OPEN PIPE THIN VENT FLARE FLUFF FLUKE TEWEL FUNNEL TUNNEL UPTAKE CHIMNEY OUTTAKE PASSAGE DOWNTAKE
FLUE-CURED BRIGHT
FLUENCY SKILL
FLUENT GASH GLIB FLUID READY FACILE LIQUID SMOOTH STREAM COPIOUS CURRENT FLOWING FLUIDIC RENABLE VERBOSE VOLUBLE ELOQUENT FLIPPANT
FLUFF FUG FLUE FUZZ LINT OOZE PUFF BEARD ERROR FLOSH FLOSS WHEEL MISTAKE
FLUFFING WHEELING
FLUFFY SOFT DOWNY DRUNK FILMY FLUEY FUZZY LIGHT LINTEN PLUFFY FEATHERY UNSTEADY
(NOT —) CLOSE
FLUID INK SAP MASS RASA BLOOD FLUOR HUMOR JUICE LATEX SERUM SPERM SWEAT WATER FLUENT LIQUID WATERY COOLANT FLOWING FLUIBLE FLUXILE GASEOUS SYNOVIA EMULSION FLOATING FLUXIBLE FORESHOT PERSPERATION
(ANIMAL —) SERUM
(BODY —) CHYLE
(EAR —) PERILYMPH
(EGYPTIAN PRIMEVAL —) NU NUN
(ELECTRIC —) VRIL
(ETHEREAL —) ICHOR
(LIVER —) BILE
(LUBRICATING —) SYNOVIA
(MAMMARY —) MILK
(PLANT —) SERO
(SLIMY —) MUCUS
(SOLDERING —) FAKE
(SUPPURATION —) PUS
(THICK VISCOUS —) GRUME
(WATERY —) LYE SANIES SEROSITY
(WORKING —) AIR
(PREF.) SERO
FLUIDITY LENGTH
(— UNIT) RHE
FLUKE FLUE PALM BLADE GRASP SCALE PLAICE DISTOME PLATODE SCRATCH FLATWORM FLOUNDER BILHARZIA
(— OF ANCHOR) HOOK KILLICK
(— OF WHALE'S TAIL) BLADE
FLUME CHUTE DITCH SHUTE SLUICE
FLUMMERY SOWENS WASHBREW
FLUMMOX ABASH ADDLE CONFOUND EMBARRASS DISCONCERT
FLUNK BUST FAIL SKEW SPIN FLICKER
FLUNKY SNOB TOADY COOKEE JEAMES LACKEY FOOTMAN SERVANT STEWARD
FLUORESCENCE BLOOM
FLUORESCENT PSYCHEDELIC
FLUORINE PHTOR PHTHOR
FLUORITE CAND FLUX FLUOR
FLURRY ADO FIT FACT FRET GUST PIRR SPIT STIR TEAR HASTE SKIFF SKIRL BOTHER BUSTLE SCURRY SQUALL CONFUSE FLUSKER FLUSTER FLUTTER FOOSTER SWITHER WHITHER SPITTING
FLUSH JET EVEN GLOW HUSH JUMP POOL ROSE BLOOM BLUSH COLOR ELATE FLASH FLUSK FRESH KNOCK LEVEL RAISE ROUGE SCOUR START VIGOR AFLUSH EXCITE HECTIC LAVISH MANTLE MORASS REDDEN RUDDLE SLUICE SPRING THRILL ANIMATE BOBTAIL CRIMSON SUFFUSE ABUNDANT AFFLUENT PRODIGAL ROSINESS
(— GAME) SERVE
(— IN SKY) SUNGLOW
(NOT —) FLAT
FLUSHED RED ROSY BEAMY FIERY FLOWN FLORID FLUSHY HECTIC CRIMSON RUBICUND
FLUSTER PAVIE SHAKE BOTHER FLURRY FUDDLE MUDDLE POTHER RATTLE CONFUSE FLUSKER FOOSTER SWITHER BEFUDDLE FLOWSTER FLUSTRUM
FLUTE NAY FIFE FUYE PIPE AULOS CRIMP CUENA PUNGI QUENA STICK STYKE TIBIA TWILL CANNEL DOUCET FLAUTO GEWGAW GOFFER POOGYE ZUFOLO CHAMFER DIAULOS FLAMFEW FLUTING GAUFFER HEMIOPE MAGADIS MATALAN PICCOLO SIBILUS SIFFLOT TONETTE TRANGAM WHISTLE ZUFFOLO FLAUTINO MONAULOS RECORDER
(— OF A COLUMN) STRIGA CHANNEL
(— STOP) VENTAGE
(CHINESE —) TCHE
(EAST INDIAN —) MATALAN
(EUNUCH —) KAZOO
(JAPANESE —) FUYE SHAKUHACHI
(LYDIAN —) MAGADIS
(MOSLEM —) NAY
(PHOENICIAN —) GINGRAS
(PL.) NEHILOTH
(PREF.) AUL(O)
FLUTED QUILLED
FLUTEMOUTH CORNETFISH
FLUTE PLAYER AULETE FLUTER FLUTIST TIBICEN TOOTLER AULETRIS FLAUTIST
FLUTING STRIX FULLER GADROON STRIGIL COULISSE QUILLING
FLUTTER BAT FAN FUG BATE BLOW BUZZ FLAP FLIT FLOW FLUE OOZE PLAY WAFF WAVE FLACK FLAFF FLARE FLECK FLICK FLOSS FLURR HOVER PULSE SHAKE WAVER BANGLE FLAUNT FLURRY RUFFLE SWIVET TREMOR WAFFLE WALLOP WINNOW FLACKER FLAFFER FLASKER FLATTER FLAUGHT FLICKER FLITTER FLUSKER SKIMMER WAGTAIL WHIFFLE FLICHTER SQUATTER VOLITATE
(IN A —) PITAPAT
FLUTTERING AWING FLITTY WHUTTER AFLUTTER FLICKERY
FLUTTERINGLY PITAPAT
FLUTTER-TONGUING GROWL
FLUX FLOW FUSE LASK MELT BORAX FLOAT FLOOD ISSUE RESIN ROSIN SMEAR SMELT FUSION CURRENT EURIPUS FLOWING LEAKAGE OUTFLOW
(— UNIT) WEBER MAXWELL
FLY BEE FAG FAN GAD HOP RUN FIRK FLEA FLEE FLEG FLIT FRIT GNAT KITE KIVU LASH LEAP MELT RACK RAKE SAIL SCUD SMUT SOAR SOLO WHEW WHIR WHIZ WIND WING ZIMB AGILE ALERT EMPID FLEET FLIER FLOAT FLURR FLUSH FLYER GLIDE LATCH MIDGE MUSCA OXFLY PERLA PHORA PILOT POPUP QUICK SEDGE SHARP SKIRL SKIRR STOUR WHAME WHIRR ZEBUB ASILID AVIATE BANGLE BLOWER BOTFLY BREEZE DAYFLY ESCAPE FLIGHT FLYBOY GADFLY GORFLY JARFLY LEPTID MEDFLY MOTUCA NIMBLE PALMER PHORID PUNKIE RANDON ROBBER SEPSID SEROOT SPRING TIPULA TSETSE VANISH VERMIN WINNOW AVIGATE AVOLATE BROMMER CANOPID CHALCID CONOPID FORMATE GRANNOM KNOWING LOVEBUG ORTALID PYRALIS SCIARID TYRPHID AIRPLANE BIBIONID BRACONID COACHMAN DIPTERAN DROPPING EPHYDRID EULOPHID GLOSSINA HORSEFLY HOUSEFLY RUBYTAIL SIMULIID TACHINID TATUKIRA VOLITATE
(— AFTER GAME) RAKE
(— AIMLESSLY) BANGLE
(— ALOFT) SOAR TOWER
(— AWAY) CARRY
(— CLUMSILY) FLIGHTER
(— ERRATICALLY) GAD
(— INTO RAGE) FUFF RARE
(— LOW) DICE DRAG HEDGEHOP
(— NEAR THE GROUND) ACCOST
(— OUT) EXPIRE
(— RAPIDLY) SCUR SKIRR
(— TOO HIGH) SCUD
(— WIDE) MISS
(BITING —) PIUM
(FISHING —) BEE DUN OAK BUZZ GNAT HARL HERL SMUT WASP ZULU ABBEY ALDER BAKER FAIRY NYMPH SEDGE BADGER BOBFLY CADDIS CAHILL CANARY CLARET DOCTOR HACKLE MILLER ORIOLE WILLOW BABCOCK BUTCHER CADDICE COLONEL DROPPER DUBBING GRANNOM HUZZARD SPINNER WATCHED WATCHET BUCKTAIL CATSKILL COACHMAN FERGUSON GOVERNOR STREAMER WOODRUFF WRENTAIL
(KIND OF —) FACE
(MAY —) DUN DRAKE
(POP —) BLOOP BLOOPER
(SHEEP —) FAG KED
(STONE —) SALLY
(PREF.) MUSCI MYI(O)
(SUFF.) MYI(A)(O)
FLYBLOWN BLOWN STRUCK
FLYBOAT FLUTE FLIGHT
FLYCATCHER TODY PEWEE PEWIT CHEBEC COBWEB MILLER PEEWEE PHOEBE PIPIRI RAFTER TYRANT YETAPA ELEPAIO FANTAIL GRIGNET GRINDER PITIRRI TOMFOOL TYRANNI BEAMBIRD FIREBALL FIREBIRD FLYEATER FORKTAIL

GERYGONE KINGBIRD KISKADEE PITANGUA WALLBIRD SCISSORTAIL
FLYER (FLEXIBLE —) SLED
FLY, FISHING (PART OF —) EYE TAG BODY BUTT HEAD HORN TAIL WING CHEEK JOINT HACKLE RIBBING TOPPING
FLYING AWING FLIGHT VOLANT WAVING FLOTANT VOLATIC AVIATION FLOATING
(— MANEUVER) LUFBERY
(— TAIL DOWN) CABRE
(STUDY OF — OBJECTS) UFOLOGY
FLYING DUTCHMAN, THE
(CHARACTER IN —) ERIK SENTA DALAND
(COMPOSER OF —) WAGNER
FLYING FISH SKIPPER VOLADOR
FLYING FOX KALONG PTEROPID
FLYING GURNARD ANGLER BATFISH LATCHET LOPHIID VOLADOR
FLYING LEMUR COBEGO COLUGO KUBONG
FLYING MACHINE AVIATOR AEROSTAT
FLYING PHALANGER CUSCUS SQUIRREL
FLYING SAUCER UFO
FLYING SQUIRREL TAGUAN ASSAPAN
FLYMAN LOFTMAN
FLYSCH MACIGNO
FLYWHEEL FLY FLIER FLYER WHORL WHARVE
FOAL CADE COLT FILLY PODDY SLEEPER
FOAM FOB SUD BARM BEES BOIL FUME HEAD KNIT REAM SCUD SCUM SUDS WORK CREAM FROST FROTH SPUME YEAST BUBBLE FLOWER FLURRY FREATH IMBOST LATHER SEETHE BLUBBER DESPUME MELDROP
(PREF.) APHR(O) SPUMI
FOAMING AFOAM NAPPY YEASTY SPUMOUS MANTLING SPUMANTE
FOAMY BARMY BEADY SPUMY SUDSY FROTHY SPUMOSE
FOB FUB SPUNG POCKET
FOCAL POINT OMPHALOS
FOCUS AIM FIX PUT POINT PURSE TRAIN CENTER CLIMAX DIRECT FASTEN FIXATE HEARTH TEMPLE NUCLEUS CONVERGE FOCALIZE GANGLION
FODDER HAY FEED FOOD SOIL VERT GOOMA MANGE VETCH EATAGE FORAGE FOTHER PODDER SILAGE STOVER FARRAGE PODWARE PROVAND BROWSING ENSILAGE ROUGHAGE
FODDERCAGE TUMBREL
FODDERER FOGGER
FOE ENEMY FIEND RIVAL FOEMAN HOSTILE OPPOSER OPPONENT WRANGLER
(STUBBORN —) WRANGLER
FOG FF DAG RAG DAMP DAZE HAAR HAZE MIST MOKE MOSS MURK PRIG RACK ROKE SMOG SMUR SOUP BEDIM BRUME CLOUD GRASS HUMOR MUDDY SMIRR SPRAY STOUR VAPOR MUDDLE NEBULA SALMON STUPOR FOGGAGE OBSCURE POGONIP SMOTHER BEWILDER MOISTURE
(— OF THE NILE) QOBAR
(FROZEN —) BARBER
(LIGHT —) GAUZE
(SEA —) HAAR HARR
FOGBOW DOG FOGDOG SEADOG MISTBOW FOGEATER
FOGDOG DOG STUBB FOGBOW SEADOG FOGEATER
FOGGINESS CLOUDING
FOGGY DIM DULL HAZY MIRK MOKY MURK ROKY DENSE DIRTY GROSS MISKY MISTY MURKY ROOKY ROUKY SPEWY CLOUDY GREASY GROGGY MARSHY MILKEN SMURRY BRUMOUS MUDDLED OBSCURE CONFUSED NUBILOUS VAPOROUS
FOGHORN SIREN TYFON RIPPER MEGAFOG
FOG-SIGNAL DIAPHONE
FOGY DODO FOGEY DUFFER FOGRAM FOOZLE STODGER MOSSBACK
FOGYISH MUSTY
FOIBLE VICE FAULT FERLY FEEBLE FAILING FRAILTY WEAKNESS
FOIL BACK BALK EPEE FILE FOIN SOIL TAIN BLADE BLANK BLUNT CHEAT ELUDE EVADE FALSE STAIN STUMP SWORD TRACK TRAIL BAFFLE BLENCH BOGGLE CHATON DEFEAT DEFILE FLORET OFFSET OUTWIT STIGMA STOOGE THWART BEGUILE FAILURE FOILING FOLIATE LAMETTA PAILLON POLLUTE REPULSE STONKER TRAMPLE DISGRACE
(— STRIPS) WINDOW
(FENCING —) EPEE BLUNT FLORET FLEURET
(PART OF —) END TIP BELL GRIP HILT BLADE FORTE GUARD POINT BUTTON FOIBLE HANDLE POMMEL MOUNTING
(POINTED —) TANG
(TIN —) TAIN
FOIST WISH FUDGE FATHER SUBORN FOISTER SHOEHORN
FOLD BOW FLY LAP PEN PLY SET WAP BEND COTE CREW CRUE DART FAIL FALX FAUN FELD FLAP FURL HANK HOOD LIRK LOOP RUCK RUGA SWAG TUCK WRAP BREAK CLASP CRIMP CRISP CROZE DRAPE FAULD FLIPE FLOCK FLYPE FRILL GROIN LAYER PARMA PINCH PLAIT PLEAT PLICA PRANK QUILL SINUS YIELD BOUGHT BUCKLE COLLOP CREASE CRISTA CUTTLE DEWLAP DIAPIR DOUBLE ENFOLD FORNIX FRENUM FURDLE GATHER GUSSET HURDLE INFOLD LABIUM LAPPET MANTLE PIPING PLIGHT PUCKER RIMPLE RUMPLE WIMPLE CAPSIZE CRINKLE CRUMPLE EMBRACE ENVELOP FLEXION FLEXURE PINFOLD PLACATE PLICATE REVERSE ROLLING ROULEAU TURNING VALVULA CRIMPING FLECTION FLITFOLD QUILLING SCAPULET SPLENIUM SURROUND PLICATION REPLICATE REFLECTION
(— CLOTH) RAG
(— DOWN) COLLAPSE
(— FOR CATTLE) BAWN
(— IN HOOD) SHOVE
(— INWARD) CRIMP
(— OF MEMBRANE) CRISTA
(— OF SKIN) APRON DEWLAP SHEATH OMENTUM FORESKIN MESENTERY
(— ROCKS) DEFORM
(—S OF TOGA) SINUS
(CARDIAC —) CUSP
(GEOLOGICAL —) DIAPIR CLOSURE EXOCLINE SYNCLINE MONOCLINE
(LOOSE —) LAPPET
(RESTRAINING —) FRENUM FRAENUM
(SCOTTISH —) CAT
(SHEEP —) REEVE
(PREF.) PLEXI PLICATO PLICI PTYCH(O) SINU(ATO) VALVI VALVO
(SUFF.) FARIOUS PLEX PLICATE PLOID
(COVERING —) STEGE STEGITE
FOLDAGE SOC SOKE
FOLDED SHUT DOUBLE FANLIKE PLICATE PLICATED REFLEXED WREATHED
(— AND WAVED) GYROSE
(PREF.) PLICATO
FOLDER KIT BOOK FILE FOLD ATLAS COVER FOLIO BINDER CLEANER HANDOUT LEAFLET STROKER PAMPHLET
FOLDING KNOT
(— OF LEAF) PTYXIS
(— PAPER) ORIGAMI
FOLDOUT GATEFOLD
FOLIACEOUS LEAFY PHYLLOID
FOLIAGE HERB SHADE GREENS LEAVES SHROUD BOSCAGE GILLERY LEAFAGE LEAFERY UMBRAGE FRONDAGE GREENERY
(CARVED —) KNOT
FOLIATED SPATHIC
FOLIATION SEXFOIL TREFOIL CINQFOIL SEPTFOIL
FOLIC ACID PGA
FOLIO CASE ATLAS FOLIUM
FOLK SOULS DAIONE PEOPLE
(— TALES) LORE
(FAIRY —) SHEE SIDHE
(STRANGE —) FRAIM FREMD
(PL.) GENTRY
FOLKLORE (IMITATION —) FAKELORE
FOLKSONG SON TONADA VOLKSLIED
FOLKSY HOMY HOMEY HOMESPUN
FOLKTALE DROLL FABULA MARCHEN
FOLLETTO DUSIO
FOLLICLE CRYPT LACUNA OVISAC CONCEPTACLE
FOLLOW GO PAD SUE TAG COME COPY HUNT NEXT OBEY SEEK SHAG TAIL TAKE TOUT ADOPT AFTER CHASE DODGE ENSUE SNAKE SPOOR TRACE TRACK TRAIL TREAD ADHERE ATTEND DANGLE FOLLER OCCUPY PURSUE RESULT SECOND SHADOW SUIVEZ TAGGLE HOTFOOT IMITATE OBSERVE PROFESS REPLACE SUCCEED VALOUWE PRACTICE SUPPLANT
(— A COURSE) RUN
(— A POINTER'S LEAD) BACK
(— CLOSELY) TAILGATE
(— HOSTILELY) DOG
(— INSIDIOUSLY) DOG
(— IN SUCCESSION) VARY
(— SCENT) ROAD CARRY
(— SLAVISHLY) ECHO
(— SLOWLY) DRAGGLE
(— THROUGH) PRESS
(— TRACK) SLEUTH
(— UP) SUE ATTEND
(— UPON) WAIT
FOLLOWER FAN IST SON APER BEAU ZANY ADEPT CHELA GILLY BILDAR COHORT DRIVEN ENSUER GILLIE GUDGET KNIGHT LACKEY SEQUEL SUITOR SULTER VOTARY ACACIAN ACOLYTE CARRIER DEVOTEE EPIGONE FLATTER GRIFTER POLIGAR PURSUER RETINUE SECTARY SEQUENT SPANIEL SUPPOST TRAILER ADHERENT DISCIPLE FAITHFUL FAVORITE HENCHMAN MYRMIDON OBSERVER OFFSIDER PARTISAN RETAINER SECTATOR SERVITOR SATELLITE PURSUIVANT
(— OF ART) BOHEMIAN
(— OF CELEBRITY) GROUPIE
(CAMP —) BUMMER GUDGET LASCAR
(CRANE —) SPOTTER
(SERVILE —) SLAVE LACKEY ANTHONY
(PL.) FOLK SECTA SEQUACES
(SUFF.) ITE
FOLLOWING LAST NEXT SECT SUIT AFTER FIRST INTOW SUANT TRACE TRAIN BEHIND SEQUEL ENSUANT ENSUING SEQUENT AUDIENCE BUSINESS SECUNDUM SEGUENDO TRAILING VOCATION
FOLLOW-UP FOLO
FOLLY ATE SIN RAGE LAPSE MORIA SOTIE BETISE DOTAGE LUNACY NICETY WANWIT DAFFERY DAFFING FOOLERY FOPPERY IDIOTCY MADNESS MISTAKE SOTTAGE UNSKILL FONDNESS FOOLHEAD IDLENESS LEWDNESS MOROLOGY NONSENSE RASHNESS SURQUIDY UNTHRIFT UNWISDOM WILLNESS WOODNESS SIMPLICITY
FOMALHAUT DIFDA DIPHDA
FOMENT SOW ABET BREW SPUR ROUSE STUPE AROUSE EXCITE INCITE AGITATE FERMENT INSPIRE
FOND TID DAFT DEAR DOTE FAIN FOOL FUND KIND VAIN WEAK CRAZY SILLY STOCK STORE ARDENT BEFOOL CARESS CHOICE DEARLY DOTING FONDLE FONDLY LOVING SIMPLE TENDER AMATORY AMOROUS BEGUILE BROWDEN FONDISH FOOLISH INSIPID

PARTIAL DESIROUS ENAMORED SANGUINE TRIFLING UXORIOUS
(FOOLISHLY —) SPOON SPOONY
(PREF.) **(— OF)** PHIL(O)
(SUFF.) **(— OF)** PHIL(A)(AE)(E)(OUS)(US)

FONDLE PET BABY BILL CLAP COAX DAUT DAWT FOND NECK TICK WALY DAUNT INGLE NURSE WALLY CARESS COCKER CODDLE COSSET CUDDLE CUTTER DANDLE GENTLE KIUTLE MUZZLE PAMPER SLAVER STROKE TANTLE TIDDLE CHERISH FLATTER SMUGGLE TWATTLE BLANDISH CANOODLE

FONDLING NINNY NURSLING

FONDLY DEAR FOND DEARLY FOOLISH

FONDNESS GRA LOVE FANCY FOLLY TASTE DOTAGE NOTION FEELING DEARNESS WEAKNESS
(— FOR WOMEN) PHILOGYNY
(SUFF.) **(— FOR)** ITIS

FONS (FATHER OF —) JANUS
(MOTHER OF —) JUTURNA

FONT BILL FUND PILA BASIN FOUNT SOURCE SPRING LAVACRE PISCINA BENITIER DELUBRUM

FONTANEL MOLD MOULD FENESTRA

FOOD BIT KAI PAP SAP BAIT BITE BUNK CARB CATE CHIH CHOP CHOW CRAM DIET DISH EATS FARE FARM FUEL GEAR GRUB HASH JOCK KAIL KALE MEAT NOSH PECK PLAT PROG SALT SOCK STEW TACK TOKE TUCK BREAD BROMA CARBO CHEER CHUCK FLUFF FORAY GRILL SCAFF SCOFF SCRAN TABLE THING TOMMY TREAT TRIPE APPAST BUTTER DODGER DOINGS EATING FODDER FOSTER LIVING MAIGRE MORSEL MUKTUK PABLUM PANADA PANADE REFETE STOVER SUNKET TACKLE TUCKER VIANDS VIVERS WRAITH ALIMENT FAUSTER HANDOUT INGESTA KEEPING KITCHEN NURTURE PABULUM PASTURE PECKAGE PROVANT PULTURE EATABLES FLUMMERY GRUBBERY NUTRIENT PEMMICAN PROVIANT TRENCHER VICTUALS PROVENDER NOURISHMENT
(— AND DRINK) BOUGE CHEER LOWANCE
(— AND LIQUOR) GEAR
(— AND LODGING) FOUND EASEMENT
(— BANNED DURING PASSOVER) HAMETZ CHAMETZ
(— EATEN AS RELISH) KITCHEN
(— EATEN BETWEEN MEALS) BAGGING
(— FOR ANIMALS) FODDER FORAGE
(— FOR CATTLE) BROWSE TACKLE
(— FROM KELP) KOMBU
(— IN SLICES) LEACH
(— IN STOCK) LARDER
(— NOT RITUALLY CLEAN) TEREPHAH
(— OF DUCK EGGS) BALUT
(— OF RUMINANTS) CUD
(— OF THE GODS) AMRITA AMREETA AMBROSIA
(— OF WHALE) KRILL
(— OF WORKMEN) TOMMY
(— ON TABLE AT ONE TIME) MESS
(— PRESERVATIVE) TINFOIL
(— TO BE CONSUMED ELSEWHERE) TAKEOUT CARRYOUT
(ASIAN —) TEMPEH
(ASIATIC —) TEMPEH
(BABY —) PAP
(BEE —) CANDY
(BREAKFAST —) GRANOLA
(CHINESE —) DIMSUM
(COOKED —) CURY BAKEMEAT
(DAILY —) TUCKER
(EXTRA —) GASH
(FILLING —) STODGE
(FLAVORLESS —) HOGWASH
(GROUND —) DUST
(HAWAIIAN —) POI
(HEAVENLY —) MANNA
(INDIGESTIBLE —) STODGE
(JAPANESE —) TERIYAKI
(KIND OF —) JUNK FINGER
(LIQUID —) LAP SLOP SOUP GRUEL LEBAN LEBEN SUPPING
(LUXURIOUS —) CATE CATES JUNKET
(MADE OF SEVERAL —S) PANACHE
(MIRACULOUS —) MANNA
(RICH —) CHEER
(SEMILIQUID —) SWILL
(SLICED —) PIZZA
(SNACK —) MUNCHIES
(SOFT —) PAP
(STARCHY —) AMYLOID
(TAPIOCA-LIKE —) SALEP
(WATERY —) SLIPSLOP
(WRAPPED —) TAMALE
(PREF.) SITIO SITO TROPH(O)
(SUFF.) PHAGA PHAGE PHAGIA PHAGOUS PHAGUS PHAGY TROPHIA TROPHIC TROPHY
(WANT OF —) ATROPHIA

FOODLESS JEJUNE VICTLESS

FOODSTUFF TRADE CEREAL COOKABLE

FOOFARAW ADO FUSS TODO FRILL BOTHER

FOOL APE ASS BAM BOB COD CON DAW DOR FON FOP FOX FUN GIG KID MUG NIT NUP POT RIG SAP SOT TOY BULL BUTT CAKE CHUB CLOT COLT DINK DOLT DUPE FOND FUTZ GECK GOER GOFF GOOP GOWK GYPE HARE HAVE HOIT JAPE JEST JOKE JOSH MOME MUCK NIZY POOP RACA RACH SIMP TONY TOOT TWIT YOYO ZANY ASINO BLIND BLUFF BUFFO CHUMP CLOWN DALLY FUNGE GALAH GLAIK GOOSE GREEN HORSE IDIOT KNAVE MORON NINNY NIZEY NODDY PATCH PATSY SAMMY SCREW SILLY SNIPE SPOOF STICK STIFF STIRK TOMMY TRICK BUFFLE COUSIN CUCKOO CUDDEN DELUDE DIMWIT DISARD DOTARD DOTTLE FOLEYE FOOTER GAMMON JESTER MOTLEY MUCKER MUSARD NIDGET NIMSHI NINCOM NUPSON SAWNEY SHMUCK STRING TAMPER WITTOL ASINEGO BECASSE BUFFOON CHARLEY CHARLIE COXCOMB DAGONET DECEIVE DIZZARD FATHEAD FOOLISH FRIBBLE GOMERAL GOMERIL HAVERAL JACKASS LACKWIT MADLING MISLEAD NATURAL OMADAWN PINHEAD PLAYBOY SCHMUCK STOOKIE TOMFOOL WANTWIT WITLING ABDERITE BADINAGE DRIVELER FONDLING HOODWINK IMBECILE MONUMENT OMADHAUN TOMNODDY BAMBOOZLE NINCOMPOOP LIGHTWEIGHT
(— AROUND) FUTZ JIVE SKYLARK LALLYGAG
(— AWAY) FRIBBLE
(BORN —) MOONCALF
(LEARNED —) MOROSOPH
(NATURAL —) INNOCENT
(PL.) FOOLERY

FOOLERY GAME FOLLY BARNEY MOTLEY BAUBLERY

FOOLHARDY RASH BRASH FOOLATUM

FOOLISH FAT SOT BETE DAFT DUMB FOND FOOL GAGA GYPE IDLE MADE NICE RASH SOFT VAIN VOID WEAK ZANY BALMY BARMY BATTY BOGGY BUGGY DILLY DIPPY DIZZY DOILT EMPTY FONNE GAWKY GOOFY GOOSY INANE INEPT JERKY LOONY NODDY POTTY SAPPY SAWNY SCREW SEELY SILLY YAPPY ABSURD CUDDEN DOTISH DOTTLE FONDLY GLAKED GOTHAM GOWKIT HARISH INSANE MOMISH MOPISH SHANNY SIMPLE SLIGHT SOFTLY SPOONY STOLID STULTY STUPID TAWPIE UNWISE VACANT ASININE DAMFOOL DOLTISH ETOURDI FANGLED FATUOUS FLIGHTY FOLLIAL FOPPISH GLAIKIT GOOSISH GULLISH IDIOTIC PEEVISH PUERILE SOTTISH TOMFOOL UNWITTY WANTWIT WITLESS ABDERIAN FOOTLING FOPPERLY HEADLESS HEEDLESS HIGHLAND IMBECILE SENSELESS
(PREF.) STULT(I)

FOOLISHLY IDLY FONDLY SIMPLE SIMPLY

FOOLISHNESS JAZZ PUNK FOLLY BARNEY BUNKUM FADDLE LEVITY LUNACY RUBBLE VANITY FATUITY PORANGI BUNCOMBE FONDNESS INSANITY TOMMYROT ABSURDITY SAPPINESS

FOOT FIT PAT PAW PEG PES BASE COOT FUSS GOER HEEL HOOF PIED SOLE TAIL BASIS PIECE BOTTOM CLUTCH GAMMON PATTEN PODIUM RHYTHM TOOTSY TRILBY WALKER FOOTING GAMBONE MEASURE METREME PEDICEL TOOTSIE FOREFOOT
(— OF ANIMAL) PAD PAW HOOF TROTTER
(— OF APE) HAND
(— OF INSECT) TARSUS
(— OF WINE GLASS) MULE
(CHINESE —) CHEK CHIH
(DOUBLE —) DIPODY
(HALF —) SEMIPED
(HOLLOW OF —) VOLA
(LARGE AWKWARD —) CAVE
(METRIC —) IAMB BASIS DIAMB IONIC PAEAN CHOREE DACTYL DIIAMB IAMBUS SYZYGY ANAPEST BACCHIC PYRRHIC SPONDEE TROCHEE ANAPAEST BACCHIUS CHORIAMB DOCHMIUS EPITRITE MOLOSSUS TRIBRACH TRIMACER
(STEWED OX —) COWHEEL
(TUBE —) SUCKER
(WEB —) FOURCHETTE
(PREF.) PED(I)(O) PEDATI PEDICULO PEZO POD(O)
(SUFF.) PED(E) POD(A)(AL)(E)(IA)(IUM)(OUS) PUS

FOOTAGE SETUP

FOOTBALL GRID HURLY ROUGE FOOTER HURLING LEATHER PIGSKIN KICKBALL
(— FORMATION) SHOTGUN WISHBONE
(— LINEMAN) NOSEGUARD
(— LINE SHIFTING) STUNT
(— PASS PATTERN) FLY
(— PATTERN) FLY
(— PLAY) DRAW DELAY SWING KEEPER AUDIBLE REVERSE ROLLOUT SCRAMBLE
(— PLAYER) HUFF LANE RICE BROWN DITKA ELWAY FOUTS SMITH STARR YOUNG AIKMAN BLOUNT BUTKUS CSONKA DEACON DUDLEY GRANGE GREENE MARINO NAMATH NEVERS PAYTON SAYERS SHARPE TAYLOR THOMAS THORPE TITTLE UNITAS DONOVAN DORSETT FLANKER GIFFORD HORNUNG MONSTER MONTANA RIGGINS SIMPSON BRADSHAW SLOTBACK STAUBACH JURGENSEN NOSEGUARD TARKENTON HIRSCHSHELL
(— RECEIVER) WIDEOUT
(— TEAM) JETS RAMS BEARS BILLS COLTS LIONS BROWNS CHIEFS EAGLES GIANTS OILERS SAINTS BENGALS BRONCOS COWBOYS FALCONS PACKERS RAIDERS VIKINGS CHARGERS DOLPHINS PATRIOTS REDSKINS SEAHAWKS STEELERS CARDINALS BUCCANEERS FORTYNINERS
(AUSTRALIAN —) RULES
(KIND OF —) CAMP
(KIND OF — PASS) SPOT SCREEN
(RUSH ON — PLAYER) BLITZ
(SHORT PASS IN —) FLARE

FOOTBOARD CRAMPET CRAMPIT

FOOTBOY PAGE PEDES

FOOTBRIDGE PLANK LIGGER FOOTLOG

FOOTED FITTIT PEDATE
(SUFF.) PEDE PODOUS

FOOTFALL PAD STEP TREAD FOOTSTEP

FOOTGEAR PATTEN FOOTWEAR

FOOTHILL SLOPE

FOOTHOLD TIP HACK STEP FOOTING TOEHOLD BEACHHEAD

FOOTING PAR FOOT TROD BASIS EARTH TRACK HEADING PIECING TOEHOLD FOOTHOLD
FOOTLESS APODAL
FOOTLIGHTS FOOTS FLOATS LIGHTS
FOOTLIKE PEDATE
FOOTMAN SKIP FLUNKY JEAMES LACKEY VARLET DOORMAN FOOTPAD BOTTOMER CHASSEUR HIRCARRA WAGONMAN
FOOTNOTE IBID IBIDEM
FOOTPACE MAT DAIS CARPET HALFPACE PREDELLA
FOOTPAD PAD WHYO PADDER ROBBER FOOTMAN PADFOOT SCOURER LANDRAKER
FOOTPATH LANE TROD JETTY SENDA TRAIL FOOTWAY HIGHWAY PARAPET RAMPIRE SIDEWALK TROTTOIR
(— TO A PASTURE) DRUNG
(RAISED —) CLAPPER
FOOTPICK CASCROM
FOOTPIECE STEP
FOOTPRINT PAD PUG STEP TROD PRICK SPOOR TRACE TRACK TRADE TREAD FOOTING ICHNITE PUGMARK VESTIGE FOOTMARK
(DEER'S —S) SLOT
(HARE'S —) PRICK
(OTTER'S —) SEAL
(PREF.) ICHN(O)
FOOTREST COASTER HASSOCK STIRRUP
(— OF SPADE) TRAMP
FOOTROPE HORSE
FOOTROT HALT
FOOTS SEDIMENT
FOOTSCRAPING SAND
FOOT-SOLDIER KERN PEON KERNE
(PL.) INFANTRY
FOOTSORENESS SURBATE
FOOTSTALK STRIG PODIUM PEDICEL PETIOLE PEDUNCLE
(PREF.) PEDICULO
FOOTSTEP PAD STEP TROD CLAMP VESTIGE FOOTBEAT FORESTEP
(PREF.) ICHN(O)
FOOTSTOOL TUT LOVE MORA STOOL BUFFET SAMBLE CRICKET HASSOCK OTTOMAN FOOTREST
FOOT-WASHING NIPTER
FOOTWAY PATH CATWALK FOOTPATH
(— ALONGSIDE BRIDGE) BANQUETTE
FOOTWEAR CLOG FEET
FOOTYBALL (— PLAYER) SCATBACK
FOP TO ADON BEAU BUCK DUDE DUPE FOOL KNUT PRIG TOFF DANDY FLASH PUPPY MASHER MOPPET VANITY COXCOMB JESSAMY GIMCRACK MACARONI MACAROON MUSCADIN POPINJAY SKIPJACK
FOPPISH APISH DANDY FOPPY SAPPY SILLY DAPPER PRETTY SPRUCE STUPID BEAUISH BUCKISH FANGLED FINICAL FOOLISH DANDYISH SKIPJACK
FOR P IN TO PRO TIL VER TILL SINCE FORWHY BECAUSE FORNENT FAVORING
(— A LONG TIME) YORE
(— CASH) SPOT
(— EXAMPLE) EG VG
(— FEAR THAT) LEST
(— INSTANCE) AS SAY
(— THE EMERGENCY) PRN
(— THE MOST PART) FECKLY GENERALLY
(— TIME BEING) ACTUALLY
(PREF.) PRO
FORAGE ERS OAT RYE CORN GUAR MAST PROG RAID ETAPE FORAY BREVIT RUSSUD ZACATE GOITCHO HAYLAGE PICKEER BOOTHALE SCROUNGE
(— PLANT) ERS
FORAGE-CAP KEPI
FORAGER OUTRIDER
FORAMEN PORE EXOSTOME METAPORE TROCHLEA
FORAMINIFER NUMMULITE
FORAY RAID MELEE CREAGH FURROW INROAD MARAUD RAVAGE RAZZIA SORTIE CHAPPOW HERSHIP PILLAGE SPREAGH SPREATH
FORBEAR LET BEAR HELP HOLD SHUN SIRE AVOID FORGO SPARE WAIVE DEPORT DESIST ENDURE PARENT RETAIN ABSTAIN DECLINE REFRAIN RESPITE ANCESTOR FOREBEAR WITHDRAW
(— PROSECUTION) COMPOUND
(— TO SPEAK) OVERGO
FORBEARANCE MERCY LENITY NONACT PARDON QUARTER MILDNESS PATIENCE
FORBEARING CLEMENT LENIENT PATIENT MERCIFUL TOLERANT
FORBID BAN BAR NIX DEFY DENY FEND TABU VETO WARN DEBAR TABOO BANISH DEFEND ENJOIN IMPEDE OPPOSE REFUSE SHIELD FORFEND FORWARN GAINSAY INHIBIT WITHSAY DISALLOW FORSPEAK PRECLUDE PROHIBIT PROSCRIBE
(— ENTRANCE) SHUT
FORBIDDANCE BAN VETO FORBODE
FORBIDDEN TABU TABOO BANNED DENIED VERBOTEN
(— AS FOOD) TREF TREFA
(SOMETHING —) NONO
FORBIDDING DOUR GRIM HARD BLACK GAUNT STERN FIERCE GLASSY GLOOMY GRISLY ODIOUS STRICT FORBODE GRIZZLY REPULSIVE
(— CLOSED MEETINGS) SUNSHINE
FORCE GAR GAS GUT HAP JAM LID VIM VIS ZIP BANG BEAR BEAT BEND BIRR BODY CLIP CRAM DINT DOOM DRAG EDGE FECK FOSS GRIP GUTS HEAD JAMB JINX MAIN MAKE MANA SNAP SOCK ABATE AGENT ARDOR BRAWL BRING BRUSH CLAMP COACT CRAFT CROWD CRUSH DEMON DRAFT DRIVE EXACT EXERT FOHAT GAVEL IMPEL KARMA MIGHT PAINT PEISE POACH POINT POWER PRESS PRIZE PUNCH REPEL SHEAR SHOVE SINEW STEAM STUFF THROW WAKAN WREST CHARGE COERCE COMPEL CUDGEL DURESS EFFECT EFFORT ENERGY EXTORT HIJACK HOTBED IMPACT IMPOSE JOSTLE MUSCLE OBLIGE POWDER RAVISH SHAKTI STRAIN STRESS WRENCH ABILITY AFFORCE BLUSTER CASCADE COGENCE COGENCY CONCUSS DRAUGHT DYNAMIC IMPETUS IMPRESS IMPULSE LASHKAR OPPRESS REQUIRE SQUEEZE TORMENT VIOLATE WAKANDA ACTIVITY ADHESION AFFINITY BULLDOZE COACTION COERCION DYNAMISM EFFICACY HOTHOUSE MOMENTUM PRESSURE STRENGTH VALIDITY VIOLENCE VIRILITY NECESSITATE
(— AIR UPON) BLOW
(— AN ENTRANCE) RANDOM THRUST
(— APART) SUNDER DISPART
(— BACK) REPEL RAMBARRE
(— BY THREAT) SWAGGER
(— DOWN) CLEW CLUE DETRUDE DISMOUNT
(— IN) INJECT INTRUDE
(— OPEN) BURST JIMMY SPORT RANFORCE
(— OUT) SPEW EJECT ERUPT EVICT EXPEL KNOCK WRING EXTUND EXPRESS
(— PASSAGE) SQUEEZE
(— TO MOVE) STICTION
(— WAY) CROWD WREST WRING
(— WITH LEGAL AUTHORITY) POSSE
(AIR —) LUFTWAFFE
(ALLEGED —) OD
(ARMED —) CREW HEAD POWER CONREY ARMAMENT BATTALIA
(CONCENTRATED —) PITH
(CONFINING —) LID
(CONSTRAINING —) STRESS
(COSMIC —) EVIL
(CREATIVE —) NATURE
(DRIVING —) STEAM SWINGE
(EVOLUTIONARY —) BATHMISM
(EXPLOSIVE —) MEGATON
(HYPOTHETICAL —) FORTUNE
(KIND OF —) LORENTZ
(LACK OF — TO DEFEAT) UNDERKILL
(LIFE —) SHAKTI
(MAIN —) BRUNT
(MILITANT —) SWORD
(MILITARY —) FYRD LEGION WERING BAYONET OCCUPATION ESTABLISHMENT
(MOVING —) SOLICITATION
(NAVAL —) FLEET
(PHYSICAL —) NERVE
(PREPONDERATING —) SWAY
(PROTECTIVE —) CONVOY
(RELIGIOUS —) SANCTITY
(SACRED —) KAMI
(SPIRITUAL —) SOUL
(UNRESTRAINED —) FURY
(UPWARD —) BUOYANCY
(PL.) ARMY WILL COLORS
(SUFF.) **(UNIT OF —)** DYNE
FORCED LABORED ENFORCED FALSETTO SARDONIC SPURIOUS STRAINED SFORZANDO
FORCEFUL RUDE GREAT GUTSY PITHY STIFF STOUT MIGHTY PUNCHY STRONG VIRILE DYNAMIC STHENIC VIOLENT BRUISING ELOQUENT EMPHATIC ENFATICO FORCIBLE VIGOROUS TRENCHANT
FORCEFULNESS PUNCH EMPHASIS
FORCEMEAT FARCE BOUDIN GODIVEAU QUENELLE STUFFING
FORCEPS DOG FURCA TONGS TENAIL BULLDOG CLAMMER PINCERS PINSONS RONGEUR CROWBILL DENTAGRA PINCETTE VULSELLA TENACULUM
(PREF.) FORCI LABID(O)
FORCIBLE VIVE STOUT VALID COGENT MIGHTY POTENT STRONG FORCIVE NERVOUS VIOLENT WEIGHTY EMPHATIC FORCEFUL POWERFUL PREGNANT PUISSANT VEHEMENT VIGOROUS
FORCIBLY AMAIN SADLY HARDLY MAINLY HEAVILY STRONGLY
FORD PASS RACK RIFT WADE WATH DRIFT STREAM CURRENT FORDING PASSAGE PASSING CROSSING
(PAVED —) STEAN STEENING
FORE VAN WAY AFORE AHEAD FRONT PRIOR FORMER FURTHER
FOREARM CUBIT CUBITAL CUBITUS
FOREBEAR ANCESTOR
FOREBODE BODE GIVE OMEN ABODE AUGUR CROAK BETIDE DIVINE BETOKEN MISBODE OMINATE PORTEND PREDICT PRESAGE FORETELL
(— EVIL) CROAK
FOREBODING OMEN BLACK FATAL AUGURY BODING DISMAL GLOOMY ANXIETY BALEFUL BANEFUL DRUTHER OMINOUS PRESAGE BODEMENT SINISTER ABODEMENT PROGNOSTICATION
FOREBODINGLY DIRELY
FOREBRAIN CEREBRUM PROENCEPHALON
FORECAST BODE CAST SCHEME CAUTION FORESEE FORESET PREDICT FOREDEEM FOREDOOM FORETELL PROPHESY ADUMBRATE PREVISION PROGNOSIS PREDICTION PROGNOSTICATION
FORECASTER SEER ORACLE PROPHET
FORECASTLE FOCSLE ISLAND
FORECOURT VESTIBULE
FOREDOOM JINX DESTINY
FOREFACE CUSHION
FOREFATHER AYEL SIRE ELDER PITRI PARENT ANCESTOR FOREBEAR PROGENITOR PRIMOGENITOR
FOREFINGER INDEX
FOREFOOT PAW PUD GRIPE
FOREFOOTING MANGANA
FOREFRONT VAN FRONT VAWARD
FOREGO FORGO WAIVE ESCHEW ABSTAIN NEGLECT PRECEDE

REFRAIN ABNEGATE DISPENSE RENOUNCE
FOREGOING PAST ABOVE ANTERIOR PREVIOUS PRECEDING
FOREGROUND PROSCENIUM
FOREHEAD BROW FRONS FRONT FRONTLET SINCIPUT
(— INDENTATION) STOP
(— MARK) KUMKUM
(HIGH —) LEPTENE
(PREF.) FRONTI FRONTO METOPO
FOREHEARTH SETTLER
FOREIGN UNCO ALIEN FREMD WELSH ALANGE EXILED EXOTIC FRENCH REMOTE UNKIND DISTANT ECDEMIC EPIGENE EXCLUDE FRAMMIT HEATHEN OUTBORN OUTLAND OUTWARD STRANGE BARBARIC EPIGENIC EXTERIOR EXTERNAL FORINSEC OVERSEAS PEREGRIN STRANGER BARBAROUS OUTLANDISH TRAMONTANE
(— TO) DEHORS
(ONE ATTRACTED TO — THINGS) XENOPHILE
(PREF.) ALIENI EXOTO
FOREIGNER ALIEN HAOLE ALLTUD GRINGO PAKEHA GREENER OUTBORN OUTLAND PARDESI ETRANGER OUTSIDER PEREGRIN PORTUGEE STRANGER MLECHCHHA OUTLANDER
(— IN JAPAN) GAIJIN
(— LIVING IN CHINA) TAIPAN
(PREF.) XEN(O)
(SUFF.) XENE XENOUS XENY
FOREIGN-LOOKING EXOTIC
FOREKNOW DIVINE FORESEE FOREWIT
FOREKNOWLEDGE PRESAGE
FORELEG GAMB
FORELOCK TOP BANG QUIFF COTTER TOUPET FORETOP TOPPING FOREBUSH
FOREMAN BOSS BULL CORK JOSS LUNA PUSH CHIEF DOGGY BUNTER GAFFER GANGER LEADER RAMROD SIRDAR TENTER CAPATAZ CAPORAL CAPTAIN FOUNDER HEADMAN MANAGER MANDOER OVERMAN SHOOFLY SKIDDER STEWARD FOREHAND GANGSMAN OVERSEER
(— OF JURY) CHANCELLOR
FOREMOST TOP HEAD HIGH MAIN CHIEF FIRST FORME FRONT GRAND BANNER FORMER LEADING RANKING SUPREME VANMOST CHAMPION
(— PART) VAWARD
FOREORDAIN FATE SLATE DESTINE FORESAY PREDOOM FORECAST
FOREORDINATION FATE
FOREPART FRONT FOREHEAD
(— OF FACE) CHAP
(— OF HEAD) SINCIPUT
(— OF HORSE'S HEAD) CHANFRIN
(— OF SHIP) STEM FORWARD CUTWATER ENTRANCE
FOREPOLE LATH SPILE SPILING
FORERUN HERALD OUTRUN PRECEDE PRELUDE ANNOUNCE FORESHOT
FORERUNNER OMEN SIGN USHER AUGURY HERALD ANCESTOR FOREGOER FOURRIER OUTRIDER PRODROME MESSENGER PRECURSOR
FORERUNNING PRECURSE
FORESADDLE RACK
FORESEE SEE READ DIVINE PURVEY PREVISE PROVIDE ENVISAGE ENVISION FORECAST FOREKNOW PROSPECT PREFIGURE
FORESHADOW HINT FIGURE HERALD BESPEAK FORERUN PATTERN PRELUDE PRESAGE UMBRATE FORETYPE ADUMBRATE
FORESHORE HARD SHORE HARDWAY SEASHORE
FORESHOW BODE ABODE AUGUR BETOKEN PORTEND SIGNIFY FORETELL PROPHESY
FORESIGHT FEAR VISION FOREWIT PRESAGE FORECAST FORELOOK PROSPECT PRUDENCE
(LACKING —) MYOPIC
FORESIGHTED CAGY CAGEY CANNY
FOREST BUSH GAPO MATA RUKH WOLD WOOD FIRTH GLADE GUBAT MATTA MATTO MONTE SYLVA TAIGA WASTE WEALD JUNGLE TIMBER BOSCAGE CALYDON COPPICE CAATINGA WOODLAND
(— CITY) PORTLAND SAVANNAH CLEVELAND
(— FOR DEER) FIRTH
(DENSE —) JUNGLE
(IMMENSE —) MONTANA
(RAIN —) SELVA
(RIVERSIDE —) GAPO
(SHAKESPEAREAN —) ARDEN
(SIBERIAN —) URMAN
(STUNTED —) CAATINGA KRUMMHOLZ
(PREF.) HYL(O) SILVI SYLVI
FORESTAGE APRON
FORESTALL BEAT HELP AVERT DETER LURCH STALL DEVANCE FORERUN OBVIATE PREVENE PREVENT FORSTEAL STAVEOFF ANTICIPATE
FORESTALLER KIDDER GROSSER
FORESTAYSAIL JUMBO
FORESTER FOSTER WALKER MONTERO TINEMAN TREEMAN WOODMAN WOODSMAN
FORETASTE GUST HANSEL TEASER EARNEST HANDSEL ANTEPAST PROSPECT PRELIBATION
FORETELL BODE ERST READ SPAE AUGUR INSEE WEIRD WRITE DIVINE HALSEN HERALD BESPEAK FORESAY PORTEND PREDICT PRESAGE ANNOUNCE FOREBODE FORECAST FORESHOW PROPHESY SOOTHSAY
FORETELLING PROPHECY
FORETHOUGHT CAUTION FORECAST PREPENSE PRUDENCE
FORETOKEN OMEN AUGUR PORTEND PROMISE FORECAST FORESHOW FORESIGN
FOREVER AY AKE AYE EVER ETERN ALWAYS ETERNE ENDLESS ETERNITY EVERMORE
FOREWARN WEIRD PREMONISH
FOREWARNING HINT PORTENT PREMONITION
FOREWING PRIMARY
FOREWORD PROEM PREFACE PREAMBLE
FORFEIT WED FINE LOSE TINE WITE CHEAT CRIME DEDIT FORGO LAPSE FOREGO SCONCE DEFAULT ESCHEAT FORWORK PENALTY FORFAULT
FORFEITURE FINE BLIND MULCT TINSEL ESCHEAT FORFEIT PENALTY
FORGE FOGE MINT TILT WELL CLICK FALSE FEIGN SMITH STOVE HAMMER SMITHY STEADY STITCH STITHY SWINGE CHAFERY FALSIFY FASHION BLOOMERY
FORGED BOGUS SPURIOUS
FORGER SMITH FALSER FALSARY LEVERMAN
FORGERY SHAM FALSUM FICTION BLOOMERY
FORGET LOSE OMIT WANT FLUFF BILEVE UNKNOW UNMIND NEGLECT OVERLOOK
FORGETFUL FLAKY SPACY OBLIVIOUS
FORGETFULNESS SWIM FLUFF LETHE AMNESIA AMNESTY OBLIVION
(PREF.) LETHO
FORGET-ME-NOT MYOSOTE
FORGETTING
(PREF.) LETHO
FORGING HOOP CLICK JACKET
FORGIVE REMIT SPARE ASSOIL EXCUSE PARDON ABSOLVE CONDONE OVERLOOK
FORGIVENESS GRACE PARDON FORGIFT
FORGIVING GRACE HUMANE CLEMENT MERCIFUL MAGNANIMOUS
FORGOTTEN DERELICT UNMINDED
FORINT FLORIN
FORK CROC EVIL HOOK TANG TINE CLEFT CLOFF FURCA GLACK GRAIN GRAIP PRONG TWIST BISECT BRANCH CLITCH CROTCH DIVIDE FEEDER GAFFLE HACKER OFFSET TWISEL BIPRONG FOURCHE FRUGGIN HAYFORK TOASTER CROTCHET EQUULEUS GRAINING PITCHFORK
(— OF BODY) SHARE
(— OF PENNON) FANON
(— OF WINDPIPE) BRONCHUS
(— OVER) PAYOUT
(FISHING —) SPEAR
(MEAT —) TORMENTOR
(THATCHER'S —) GROM
(TUNING —) DIAPASON
(PREF.) FURCI
FORKED BIFID FORKY FURCAL PRONGY DIVIDED FURCATE LITUATE BIFORKED BIRAMOUS BRANCHED FOURCHEE SUBBIFID
FORKING STAR
FORLORN LORN LOST REFT ALONE ABJECT FORFAIRN FORSAKEN HELPLESS HOPELESS PITIABLE WITLOSEN
FORM AME DIG FIG HEW HUE SET BLEE BODY CASE CAST CAUL DOME FLOW GARB IDEA KERN KITE MAKE MODE MOLD PLAN RITE SEAT THEW TURN BENCH BLANK BLOCK BOARD BUILD BUNCH CHART CHECK CRUSH DUMMY EIDOS ERECT FORGE FORMA FORME FRAME GALBE GUISE IMAGE MATCH MEUSE MODEL SHAPE SPELL STAMP THROW USAGE ADJUST CHALAN COUPON CREATE CUSTOM DEVISE DOCKET FIGURE FILLER HANGER INVENT MANNER REMOVE RITUAL SCHEMA SCHOOL SPONGE STRIKE SYSTEM TAILLE AGENDUM ARRANGE COMPOSE CONFECT CONTOUR DEVELOP FASHION FEATURE FORMULA GESTALT IMPANEL INVOICE LITURGY MAKEDOM OUTLINE PATTERN PORTRAY PORTURE PRODUCE PROFILE SPECIES STATURE BILLHEAD CEREMONY COMPOUND CONCEIVE CONTRIVE FORMWORK INSTRUCT LIKENESS MODALITY ORGANIZE SEMBLANCE
(— A HEAD) POME
(— A NETWORK) PLEX
(— A RING) ENVIRON
(— ASSUMED AFTER DEATH) KAMARUPA
(— BRANCHES) BREAK
(— BY CUTTING OFF) ABJOINT
(— CONNECTION) ALLY
(— FOR BELL FOUNDING) SWEEP
(— FOR CONCRETE) BOXING
(— FOR HOLDING BARREL) SQUAW
(— FOR MOLD) JACKET
(— FOR PRESSING VENEERS) CAUL
(— FRUIT) KNIT
(— INTO A CHAIN) CATENATE
(— INTO BALL) CONGLOBE
(— INTO RINGLETS) CRISP
(— LEATHER) CRIMP
(— MOUND) TUMP
(— OF GOVERNMENT) ESTATE KINGSHIP
(— OF PREDICATION) CATEGORY
(— POLITICAL SUCCESSION) CAVE
(— WITH PLASTER) RUN
(— YARN INTO THREAD) CABLE
(ANCESTRAL —) BLASTAEA STEMFORM
(CEREMONIAL —) RITE
(CONVENTIONAL —) AMENITY
(DEXTROROTATORY —) CAMPHOR
(DISPLAY —) MANNEQUIN
(IMPERFECT —) SEMIFORM
(IRREGULAR —) PSEUDOMORPH
(ISOMETRIC —) DIPLOID
(LINGUISTIC —) FOSSIL GERUND
(LITERARY —) KNACK
(LITURGICAL —) SERVICE
(LYRICAL —) SESTINA
(MUSICAL —) RAGA SUITE
(POETIC —) CINQUAIN
(POINTED —) ANGLE
(SCHOOL —) SHELL
(SHOE —) LAST FILLER
(SHORTENED —) ABBREVIATION
(SONG —) BAR

(SPECTRAL —) SHADOW
(SPEECH —) LEXEME IDIOLECT
(SPIRAL OR CIRCULAR —) GYRE
(STRUCTURE —) MORPHOLOGY
(TOP —) GROOVE
(VERB —) FUTURE CONATIVE DEFINITE DURATIVE
(VERSE —) EPODE BALLAD PANTUM SONNET KYRIELLE LIMERICK
(VISIBLE —) RUPA
(WILD —) AGRIOTYPE
(WORD —) ETYMON ANOMALY
(PREF.) IDO MORPH(O) PLASMATO
(SUFF.) FY GEN(E)(ESIA)(ESIS)(ETIC)(IC)(IN)(OUS)(Y) IFY MORPH(A)(AE)(IC)(ISM)(OSIS)(OTIC)(OUS)(Y) PLASIA PLASIS PLASM(A)(IA)(IC) PLAST(IC)(Y) PLASY
(HAVING — OF) IC(AL)
(IN THE — OF) OID(AL)

FORMAL DRY SET BOOK PRIM BUDGE CHILL COURT EXACT STIFF SOCIAL SOLEMN STOCKY ANGULAR BOOKISH LOGICAL NOMINAL ORDERLY OUTWARD PRECISE REGULAR SOLWARD STARCHY STATELY STILTED ABSTRACT ACADEMIC AFFECTED ELEVATED FORMULAR OFFICIAL PUNCTUAL STARCHED WHITETIE

FORMALDEHYDE FORMAL MONOSE HARDENER METHANAL

FORMALISM ACADEMISM

FORMALIST PEDANT SCHOLASTIC

FORMALISTIC COURT ACADEMIC

FORMALITY FORM POMP SASINE STARCH BUCKRAM DECENCY WIGGERY CEREMONY PHARISAISM

FORMALIZE STIFFEN

FORMALLY FORMLY STARCHLY

FORMAT SIZE GETUP SHAPE STYLE

FORMATION FORM RANK SPUR BIOME FLIGHT GROWTH HARROW MASSIF SPREAD POTENCE BOTRYOID
(— ENCLOSING MINE WORKING) GROUND
(— ENCOUNTERED IN DRILLING) STRAY
(— OF BRAIN) FORNIX
(— OF BRANCHES) CANOPY
(— OF CRYSTAL) SHOOT
(— OF JOINT) ANKYLOSIS
(— OF PLANES) JAVELIN
(— OF SCAR) ULOSIS
(— OF WILDFOWL) WEDGE
(— ON TOAD) SPADE
(— RESEMBLING ICICLE) STIRIA
(BATTLE —) HERSE
(BRAIN —) FORNIX
(CLOUD —) NUBECULA
(DANCE —) SET
(DIAGONAL —) HARROW
(DRIPSTONE —) COLUMN
(ECOLOGICAL —) BIOME
(FLIGHT —) SQUADRON
(FOOTBALL —) SHOTGUN WISHBONE
(GEOLOGIC —) BOEL CULM CHICO STRAY MARKER MEDINA CURTAIN MANLIUS MATAWAN POTOMAC TERRAIN AQUIFUGE FERNANDO KOOTANIE KOOTENAI LOCKPORT TOPATOPA YORKTOWN
(GLACIAL —) ARETE
(HABIT —) FIXATION
(INDENTED —) CLEFT
(INFANTRY —) TERTIA ECHELON
(LAND —) BOOTHEEL
(MILITARY —) SNAIL FLIGHT
(MORBID —) GROWTH
(NAVAL —) SCREEN
(POINTED —) BEAK
(THICKET —) MAQUIS
(PREF.) PLASTO
(TAIL —) CERC(O)
(SUFF.) GENESIA GENESIS OSIS POEIA POESIS POIESIS POIETIC

FORMATIVE CREANT PLASTIC DEMIURGIC
(SUFF.) POEIA POESIS POIESIS POIETIC

FORMED BUILT BOOKIT DECIDED MATURED SETTLED WROUGHT TIMBERED
(— AT BASE OF MOUNTAIN) PIEDMONT
(— INTO STEPS) GRADY
(— ON SURFACE OF EARTH) EPIGENE
(IMPERFECTLY —) ABORTIVE
(STURDILY —) BUXOM
(PREF.) APO PLASTO

FORMEE PATE PATTEE

FORMER DIE OLD ERER ERST FERN FORE LATE ONCE PAST ELDER FORME GAUGE GUIDE MAKER OTHER PRIOR BYGONE RATHER WHILOM ANCIENT ANOTHER CREATOR EARLIER FIRSTER FURTHER ONETIME PRIDIAN QUONDAM TEMPLET UMWHILE PRETERIT PREVIOUS PRISTINE SOMETIME STRICKLE UMQUHILE PRECEDING
(PREF.) PROTER(O)

FORMERLY ERE NEE OLD ERST FORE ONCE THEN YORE GRAVE WHILOM WHILST ONETIME QUONDAM SOMETIME UMQUHILE

FORMIDABLE MEAN STOUR FEARFUL ALARMING DREADFUL MENACING TERRIBLE FEROCIOUS REDOUBTABLE
(— PERSON) TARTAR

FORMING
(SUFF.) GENIC GEROUS

FORMLESS ARUPA DOUGHY ANIDIAN CHAOTIC DEFORMED INDIGEST

FORMOSA (SEE TAIWAN)

FORMULA LAW MIX DATE FIAT FORM RULE CANON CREED DHIKR GRAPH INDEX LURRY KEKULE MANTRA METHOD RECIPE THEORY RECEIPT APOLYSIS CLAUSULE DOXOLOGY EXORCISM
(— OF FAITH) KELIMA
(MAGICAL —) CARACT
(OFFICIAL —) PROTOCOL
(WORD —) PATERNOSTER
(PL.) RAKA RAKAH

FORMULARY SYMBOL

FORMULATE PUT CAST DRAW FRAME DEVISE CAPSULE COMPOSE FORMULE PLATFORM

FORMULATED STATED WRITTEN

FORMULATION (— OF A TRUTH) COUNT CREED DOGMA APHORISM APOTHEGM DOCTRINE
(SUFF.) **(SYSTEMATIC —)** ICS

FORMWORK SHUTTERING

FORNIX VAULT PSALIS

FORSAKE DENY DROP FLEE QUIT SHUN ABAND AVOID FORGO LEAVE WAIVE DEFECT DEPART DESERT FOREGO FORHOO FORLET REFUSE REJECT ABANDON DISCARD FORLESE DESOLATE FORHOOIE RENOUNCE WITHDRAW

FORSAKEN LORN FORLORN DESERTED DESOLATE LASSLORN

FORSETE (FATHER OF —) BALDER

FORSOOTH EVEN MARRY QUOTH

FORSWEAR DENY ABJURE REJECT ABANDON PERJURE ABNEGATE MANSWEAR RENOUNCE

FORSYTE SAGA (AUTHOR OF —) GALSWORTHY
(CHARACTER IN —) JON VAL JUNE MONT FLEUR HOLLY IRENE JOLLY MONTY DARTIE JOLYON PHILIP SOAMES ANNETTE FORSYTE LAMOTTE MICHAEL PROFOND PROSPER SWITHIN TIMOTHY BOSINNEY WINIFRED

FORT PA DUN LIS PAH LISS PEEL SHEE SPUR WORK COTTA REDAN SIDHE CASTLE SANGAR SCHERM SCONCE STRONG BASTION BULWARK CITADEL CLOSURE REDOUBT BASTILLE CASTILLO FASTHOLD FASTNESS FORTRESS MARTELLO PRESIDIO
(FAIRY —) LIS LIOS LISS SHEE SIDHE
(HILL —) RATH
(MAORI —) PA PAH
(RUINS OF —) ZIMBABWE
(SMALL —) GURRY FORTIN BASTIDE FORTLET FORCELET

FORTE FORT LOUD STARK METIER STRONG EMINENCY STRENGTH

FORTESCUE COBBLER SCORPION

FORTH OUT AWAY FURTH
(PREF.) E OUT

FORTHCOMING PROXIMATE

FORTHRIGHT BALD BURLY GUTTY CANDID

FORTHRIGHTLY FRANKLY

FORTHRIGHTNESS CANDOR PLUMPNESS

FORTHWITH EFT NOW ANON AWAY BEDENE DIRECT BETIMES FORTHON DIRECTLY

FORTIFICATION BAWN BOMA FORT MOAT WALL REDAN TOWER ABATIS CASHEL CASTLE GLACIS LAAGER BASTION BULWARK CITADEL DEFENCE DEFENSE PARAPET PILLBOX RAMPART RAVELIN REDOUBT FORTRESS MUNITION RONDELLE STRENGTH
(LINE OF —S) TROCHA
(PART OF —) BERM MOAT ANGLE DITCH FLANK GORGE SCARP SLOPE COVERT ESCARP GLACIS PARADE BASTION CURTAIN PARAPET RAMPART SALIENT TENAILLE BANQUETTE TERREPLEIN COUNTERSCARP

FORTIFIED ARMED CONFIRMED

FORTIFY ARM MAN BANK FORT LINE WALL WARD FENCE SPIKE STANK BATTLE IMMURE MUNIFY MUNITE BULWARK COMFORT DEFENSE GARNISH RAMPIRE BASTILLE EMBATTLE FORTRESS RAMFORCE STOCKADE

FORTITUDE GRIT GUTS SAND FIBER FIBRE HEART NERVE PLUCK METTLE BRAVERY COURAGE HEROISM STAMINA BACKBONE PATIENCE STRENGTH
(AUTHOR OF —) WALPOLE
(CHARACTER IN —) TAN HANZ NORA BOBBY BRANT CLARE JERRY PETER ZANTI EMILIO LAUNCE GALLEON JERRARD MONOGUE STEPHEN ZACHARY BROCKETT ROSSITER WESTCOTT CARDILLAC GOTTFRIED AITCHINSON

FORTNIGHT (HALF A —) WEEK

FORTNIGHTLY BIWEEKLY

FORTRESS (ALSO SEE FORT) BURG KEEP KASBA PIECE PLACE ROCCA CASBAH CASTLE ALCAZAR BARRIER BOROUGH CASTRUM CHATEAU CITADEL KREMLIN ZWINGER ALCAZAVA BASTILLE FASTNESS STRENGTH
(AUTHOR OF —) WALPOLE
(CHARACTER IN —) ADAM JOHN KRAFT PARIS ROGUE BENJIE CAESAR JUDITH REUBEN TEMPLE UHLAND WALTER HERRIES SUNWOOD JENNIFER MARGARET ELIZABETH GOLIGHTLY CHRISTABEL
(NORTH AFRICAN —) KABBAH

FORTUITOUS CASUAL CHANCE RANDOM FORTUIT FORTUNEL

FORTUITY LUCK CHANCE

FORTUNATE EDI FAT HAP SRI GOOD SHRI WELL CANNY FAUST HAPPY LUCKY RIGHT WHITE DEXTER EUROUS BLESSED FAVORED WEIRDLY GRACIOUS

FORTUNATELY FAIR HAPPILY

FORTUNE DIE HAP LOT URE BAHI DOOM FALL FARE FATE HAIL LUCK PILE SEEL STAR EVENT GRACE ISSUE LINES SONSE SPEED WEIRD WHATE CHANCE ESTATE MISHAP RICHES WEALTH DESTINY SUCCESS THEEDOM VENTURE ACCIDENT CASUALTY FELICITY STOCKING
(GOOD —) SELE SONSE SPEED THRIFT FURTHER GOODHAP BONCHIEF FELICITY
(ILL —) DOOM THRAW
(PREF.) TYCH(O)

FORTUNES OF RICHARD MAHONY (AUTHOR OF —) RICHARDSON
(CHARACTER IN —) TOM JOHN LUCY MARY ZARA CUFFY OCOCK POLLY SARAH LALLIE MAHONY RICHARD TURNHAM CUTHBERT

FORTUNE-TELLER SEER SIBYL

SYBIL SPAEMAN SORTIARY SPAEWIFE
(PL.) CHALDAEI
FORTY DAYS OF MUSA DAGH
(AUTHOR OF —) WERFEL
(CHARACTER IN —) TER HAIK MARIS SARKIS BEREKET GABRIEL STEPHAN GONZAGUE HAIGASUN HULIETTE KILIKIAN BAGRADIAN NOKHUDIAN
FORUM COURT PLATFORM TRIBUNAL
FORWARD ON TO AID BOG BUG GAY ABET BAIN BOLD FORE FREE HELP PERT SEND SHIP STEP AHEAD ALONG AVANT BARDY BRASH CAGER EAGER FAVOR FORTH FRACK FRECK FRONT HASTY PAWKY PUSHY RANDY READY RELAY REMIT SAUCY SERVE SPACK ULTRA AFFORD ARDENT AVAUNT BEFORE BRIGHT COMING DEVANT FORRIT FORTHY HASTEN NUZZLE ONWARD PROMPT REMAIL ROUDAS SECOND TOWARD ADVANCE BETIMES EARNEST EXTREME FURTHER PROMOTE PUSHING RADICAL SOLICIT ADELANTE ARROGANT FROMWARD IMMODEST IMPUDENT MALAPERT ONCOMING PERVERSE PETULANT TELLSOME TOWARDLY TRANSMIT OBTRUSIVE
(MOST —) HEADMOST
(PREF.) ANTE
(LEANING —) PRONO
FORWARDNESS IMMODESTY
FOR WHOM THE BELL TOLLS
(AUTHOR OF —) HEMINGWAY
(CHARACTER IN —) MARIA PABLO PILAR JORDAN ROBERT ANSELMO
FORZA DEL DESTINO, LA
(CHARACTER IN —) CARLO ALVARO LEONORA CALATRAVA
(COMPOSER OF —) VERDI
FOSSA FOSS FOVEA GALET TRENCH VALLIS FOSSULA FOSSETTE
FOSSE DITCH GRAFF
FOSSIL CYCAD CYSTID DOLITE EOZOON FUCOID ICHITE PINITE AMBRITE BLASTID CHAMITE CRINITE ICHNITE JUNCITE LITUITE NEREITE OVULITE REMANIE TYLOPOD ZOOLITE ZOOLITH AISTOPOD AMMONITE ANCODONT ASTROITE BACULITE BALANITE BIOCHRON BLASTOID BUFONITE CALAMITE CERATITE CONCHITE CONODONT ECHINITE EOHIPPUS FAVOSITE FILICITE FUSULINA GEDANITE GYROLITH MIMOSITE PEUCITES POLYPITE SALIGRAM SCAPHITE SERAPHIM SPONGOID SYNAPSID TARSIOID CARPOLITE TRILOBITE OSTRACODERM
(PREF.) NECR(O) ORYCT(O)
(SUFF.) LITE LITH(IC) LITIC
FOSSILIZE PETRIFY
FOSTER REAR NURSE COCKER HARBOR NUZZLE SUCKLE CHERISH DEPOSIT EMBOSOM GRATIFY INDULGE NOURISH NOURSLE NURTURE BEFRIEND CULTIVATE
FOSTERAGE NURSERY
FOSTER-CHILD DALT DAULT
FOSTERED (ARTIFICALLY —) SPOONFED
FOSTERER NORRY
FOUL BAD BASE EVIL HORY RANK ROIL VILE BAWDY BLACK DIRTY DITCH FUNKY GRIMY GURRY HORRY KETTY LOUSY MUDDY MUSTY NASTY RUSTY SULLY WEEDY CLARTY DEFAME DIRTEN DREGGY FILTHY GREASY IMPURE MALIGN ODIOUS PUTRID ROTTEN SOILED SORDID UNFAIR VIROSE ABUSIVE BEASTLY DEFACED FULSOME HATEFUL ILLEGAL IMBROIN NOISOME OBSCENE PROFANE SLOTTER SMEARED SQUALID TETROUS UNCLEAN VICIOUS AMURCOUS ENTANGLE FECULENT INDECENT MEPHITIC SLOTTERY STAGNANT STINKING TRAUCHLE WRETCHED
(— UP) ERR BOTCH
(BASKETBALL —) HACK
FOULMOUTHED RIBALD ROUDAS ABUSIVE OBSCENE PROFANE
FOULNESS FEDITY PRAVITY
(— OF MOUTH) SABURRA
FOUL-SMELLING FUNKY
FOUL-UP SNAFU
FOUMART POLECAT
FOUND FIX TRY YET BASE CAST REST STAY BEGIN BOARD BUILD ENDOW ERECT PLANT SETUP START ATTACH BOTTOM DEPART GROUND INVENT EQUIPPED PRACTICE PROVIDED SUPPLIED
FOUNDATION BED BASE BODY FIRM FOND FUND GIST ROOT SILL SOLE BASIS FOUND STOCK STOOL ANLAGE BOTTOM CRADLE GROUND LEGACY MATRIX PODIUM RIPRAP BEDDING BEDROCK CHANTRY COLLEGE MORTISE PINNING RADICAL ROADBED SUBBASE WARRANT BACKBONE DONATION MATTRESS MIREPOIX PEDESTAL PLATFORM STANDARD UNDERLAY
(— FOR WIG) CAUL
(— OF BASKET) SLATH SLARTH
(FLOATING —) CRIB
(LACE —) RESEAU
(PRECARIOUS —) STILT
FOUNDATIONER GOWNBOY COLLEGER
FOUNDATION-STOP DIAPASON
FOUNDED FUSILE
FOUNDER FAIL IMAM SINK AUTHOR CASTER DYNAST EPONYM HELLEN YETTER AFOUNDE STUMBLE BELLETER MISCARRY LAMINITIS PATRIARCH
(— OF COLONY) OECIST OIKIST
FOUNDLING WAIF ORPHAN
FOUNT FONS FONT SOURCE
FOUNTAIN URN AQUA FOND HEAD KELD PANT PILA SYKE WELL DIRCE FOUNT GURGE QUELL SURGE ORIGIN PHIALE PIRENE SOURCE SPRING BUBBLER CONDUIT SPRUDEL AGANIPPE SALMACIS UPSPRING WELLHEAD
(— ON SHIP) SCUTTLEBUTT
(INK —) DUCT
(SODA —) SPA
(PREF.) PEGO
(SUFF.) CRENE
FOUNTAINHEAD ORIGIN SOURCE
FOUNTAIN PEN STICK STYLO
FOUR MESS CATER DELTA DALETH FEOWER TETRAD QUARTET QUATRAL MURNIVAL QUADRATE
(— OF ANYTHING) GUNDA
(— OF TRUMPS) TIDDY
(— TIMES A DAY) QD QID
(— YEAR PERIOD) PYTHIAD
(GROUP OF —) TETRAD
(PREF.) QUADR(I)(U) QUADRATO QUATER TESSARA TETR(A)
(— ATOMS OF HYDROGEN) TETRAZ(O)
(— TIMES) QUATER TETRAKIS
(HAVING — PARTS) TETR(A)
FOURCHETTE FORGET SIDEWALL WISHBONE
FOURFOLD FOURBLE QUATERN
FOUR HORSEMEN OF APOCALYPSE (AUTHOR OF —) IBANEZ
(CHARACTER IN —) JULIO CHICHI MARCELO DESNOYER HARTROTT
FOURIERISM SOCIALISM
FOUR-O'CLOCK FRIARBIRD
FOURPENNY BIT JOE FLAG JOEY GROAT
FOURSQUARE FRANK
FOURTEENER SEPTENAR
FOURTH DELTA QUART FARDEL FORPIT FERLING QUARTER QUADRANT
(— HOUR) SEXT
(— OF BAHMANI EMPIRE) TARAF
(— OF CAKE) FARL FARLE
(— OF YEAR) RAITH
(AUGMENTED —) TRITONE
(PREF.) QUART(I) TETART(O)
FOUSSA CIVET GALET
FOVEOLA VARIOLE
FOWL HEN RED COCK GAME GRIG JAVA ROCK SLIP BIDDY CHUCK CLUCK COPPY DUMPY MALAY MANOC MARAN SILKY ANCONA ASHURA BANTAM BRAHMA CAMBAR COCHIN HOUDAN LAMONA LEGBAR POLISH REDCAP SULTAN SUSSEX BUFFBAR CAMPINE CHICKEN CORNISH DORKING FRIZZLE HAMBURG LEGHORN MINORCA OKLABAR POULTRY ROOSTER SPANISH SUMATRA COCKEREL CUBALAYA DELAWARE DUCKWING DUNGHILL GAMECOCK LANGSHAN SHANGHAI SHOWBIRD VOLAILLE
(AGGREGATION OF —) RAFT
(CASTRATED —) CAPETTE
(CRESTED —) TOPKNOT
(GUINEA —) KEET COMEBACK
(MALE —) STAG
(STUFFED —) FARCI
(TAILLESS —) RUMKIN
(5-TOED —) SILKY SILKIE
FOWLER BIRDMAN
FOWLING-PIECE SHOTGUN
FOX DOG KIT PUG TOD ASSE FOOL STAG WILD ADIVE BRANT CAAMA SWIFT TRICK VIXEN ZORRO ARCTIC BAGMAN CANDUC COLFOX CORSAC FENNEC LOWRIE OUTWIT RENARD RUSSEL BEGUILE CHARLEY CHARLIE KARAGAN REYNARD STUPEFY VULPINE CUSTOMER MUSKWAKI OUTAGAMI PLATINUM
(KIND OF —) KIT
FOX-AND-GEESE MERELS
FOXGLOVE POPPY POPDOCK THIMBLE FLAPDOCK POPGLOVE
FOX GRAPE ISABELLA LABRUSCA
FOXHOUND WALKER
FOX HUNTER PINK
FOX-LIKE ALOPECOID
FOXTAIL CAUDA CHAPE COUGH KNEED TWITCH SETARIA GAMELOTE
FOXY SLY WILY COONY SHREWD CUNNING VULPINE DEXTROUS
FOYER HALL LOBBY ANTEROOM
FRACAS BOUT BRAWL MELEE MUSIC BICKER RUMPUS SHINDY UPROAR QUARREL SHINDIG FRACTION INCIDENT
FRACTION BIT CUT PYO FLUX PART BREAK PIECE SCRAP BREACH LITTLE MOIETY DECIMAL GLUTOSE WETNESS
(— OF RADIATION) ALBEDO
(NAPHTHA —) LIGROIN
(PREF.) MER(I)(O)
(SUFF.) MER(E)(IC)(OUS)(Y)
FRACTIONAL ALIQUOT FRACTED PARTIAL
FRACTIOUS MEAN UGLY CROSS UNRULY CRABBED PEEVISH WASPISH PERVERSE SNAPPISH
FRACTURE BUST FLAW REND BILGE BREAK CLEFT CRACK FAULT JOINT BREACH DEFORM HACKLE DIACOPE FISSURE RUPTURE DIACLASE FRACTION
(PREF.) RHEGMA RHEGNO
(SUFF.) CLASE RHEXIS RRHEXIS
FRACTURED SPLIT BROKEN
FRACTURING SLIP STRAIN FAILURE
FRA DIAVOLO (CHARACTER IN —) PAMELA DIAVOLO LORENZO ZERLINA COCKBURN
(COMPOSER OF —) AUBER
FRAGILE FINE FROW WEAK FRAIL FROWY LIGHT SWACK FEEBLE FROUGH INFIRM SLIGHT TENDER BRICKLE BRITTLE FROUGHY SLENDER TIFFANY DELICATE EGGSHELL ETHEREAL FRACTILE SLATTERY BREAKABLE
FRAGILITY DELICACY
FRAGMENT BIT END ORT ATOM BLAD CHIP DRIB FLAW GROT MOIT MOTE PART RUMP SHED SNIP WISP ANGLE BLAUD BRACK BREAK BROKE CATCH CHUNK CLOUT CRUMB FRUST GIGOT PIECE RELIC SCRAP SHARD SHERD SHIVE SHRED SPALL SPELL SPLIT CANTLE FARDEL FILING GOBBET MORSEL REMAIN SCREED SHIVER SIPPET SLIVER CANTLET EXCERPT FLINDER FLITTER FRITTER FRUSTUM

MACERAL MAMMOCK REMANIE REMNANT SEGMENT SHATTER SHAVING SNIPPET AVULSION CHIPPING DETRITUS FRACTION OARTICLE POTSHERD SCANTLET SKERRICK SPLINTER
(— CUT OFF) CANTLE
(— OF BONE) SEQUESTER SEQUESTRUM
(— OF BRICK) BRICKBAT
(— OF DIAMOND) CLEAVAGE
(— OF ICE) CALF
(— OF LAVA) FAVILLA LAPILLUS
(— OF MELODY) LAY
(— OF ROCK) CRAG CLAST AUTOLITH LAPILLUS
(— OF SAIL) HULLOCK
(— OF SOD) TAB
(— OF STONE) SCABBLING
(— OF UNFINISHED WORK) TORSO
(— OF VEIN MATERIAL) SHOAD SHODE
(—S OF CLOUD) SCUD
(—S OF DIAMOND) BORT
(—S OF SAND) FINES
(CAST IRON —) POTLEG
(ICE —S) BRASH
(JAGGED —) BROCK
(LITERARY —) ANALECTA
(LITERARY —S) ANALECTA
(MASS OF —S) BRASH
(PLANT —) SHIVE
(SHELL —S) SHRAPNEL
(WOODY —S FOUND IN FOOD) CHAD
(PL.) BRASH FRUSH SCRAPS CINDERS FITTERS GUBBINS SMATTER FLINDERS LEFTOVER SMITHERS SMITHEREENS

FRAGMENTAL CLASTIC

FRAGMENTARY HASHY SNIPPY SCRAPPY DIVIDUAL

FRAGRANCE BALM ODOR AROMA SCENT SMELL SWEET BREATH FLAVOR FRAGOR BOUQUET INCENSE PERFUME SUAVITY

FRAGRANT NOSY RICH BALMY OLENT SPICY SWEET SAVORY SPICED ODORANT ODOROUS PERFUMY SCENTED AROMATIC FLAGRANT NECTARED ODORIFIC REDOLENT

FRAIL FINE POOR PUNY WEAK CRAZY REEDY SEELY SILLY BASKET BROTEL CROCKY FLIMSY INFIRM SICKLY SINGLE SLIGHT SLIMSY SQUEAL TICKLE TOPNET BRITTLE BRUCKLE FRAGILE SLENDER SLIMPSY UNHARDY DELICATE PINDLING

FRAILTY FAULT FOIBLE INVENT FAILING DELICACY WEAKNESS
(HUMAN —) ADAM

FRAMBESIA PIAN YAWS BUBAS MORULA

FRAME BED BIN BOW BOX FLY GYM MAT SET BAIL BEAM BIER BUCK BULK BUNK CANT CASE CAUM CELL CLAM CRIB CURB DESK DRAG FORM FROG GATE GILL HACK HARP HECK JACK MOLD PORT RACK SASH SLEY SOLE STEP AIRER ANGLE BANJO BLADE BLIND BLOCK BUILD CADRE CHASE CLEAT CRATE CROOK DRAFT EASEL FLAKE FLASK FLEAK FLOAT GRATE HERSE HORSE MOUNT OXBOW PERCH PRESS SCRAY SETUP SHAPE STAND STATE STEAD STOCK STOOL TRAIL BARROW BATTEN BINDER BUCCAN BUCKET CASING CHEVAL COFFIN CRADLE CRATCH CRUTCH DECKLE DREDGE FABRIC FENDER GANTRY GRILLE HANGER HARROW HOTBED HURDLE PERSON PILLAR QUADRA REDACT REEDER SCREEN SETTLE SLEDGE SPIDER SQUARE STAPLE TANGLE TENTER TESTER ARMRACK BREAKER CABINET CARRIER CASEBOX CHASSIS COAMING COASTER CRAMPON CRIMPER DRAUGHT DROSSER FASHION FRAMING FRISKET GALLOWS GARLAND GATEWAY GIGTREE GRATING HAYRACK HOUSING ICEBOAT MACHINE MONTURE OXBRAKE PORTRAY SETTING STADDLE TRANSOM TRESTLE TRIBBLE BARBECUE BOWGRACE CARRIAGE CASEMENT CONCEIVE CONTRIVE DOORCASE GRAFFAGE GRIDIRON GRILLAGE HALBERDS HOGFRAME PLOWHEAD RAILROAD RECEIVER RETAINER SKELETON THRIPPLE TRIANGLE TURNPIKE BRANDRITH OUTRIGGER
(— FOR ARCH) COOM COOMB
(— FOR BEEHIVE) SECTION
(— FOR CANDLES) HEARSE
(— FOR CARRYING STRAW) KNAPE
(— FOR CASK) GANTRY STALDER
(— FOR CATCHING FISH) HATCH
(— FOR CLOTHES DRYING) AIRER
(— FOR CONFINING HORSE) TRAVE TRAVAIL
(— FOR COW'S HEAD) BAIL
(— FOR DRYING FISH) HACK HAIK
(— FOR DRYING SKINS) HERSE
(— FOR FISHING LINE) CADAR CADER
(— FOR GLAZING LEATHER) BUCK
(— FOR HAWKS) CADGE
(— FOR HONEYCOMB) SECTION
(— FOR KILLING PIGS) CREEL
(— FOR LENS) BOW
(— FOR ROLLER BEARINGS) CAGE
(— FOR SMOKING MEAT) BOUCAN BUCCAN
(— FOR STACK) HAYRACK STADDLE
(— FOR WASHING ORE) BUDDLE
(— OF A VESSEL) HULL
(— OF MIND) HAZE SPITE SPIRIT TEMPER FEELING POSTURE
(— OF PIER) JETTY
(— OF SAW) HUSK
(— OF SPINNING MULE) SQUARE
(— OF STRAW) SIME
(— OF TINWORK) MARQUITO
(— ON STAGE) CEILING
(— TO CATCH STARFISH) TANGLE
(— TO CLEAN SHIP'S BOTTOM) HOG
(— TO DRY CLOTHES) AIRER
(— WHICH JOINS) YOKE
(BELL —) SWEEP
(BOBBIN —) BANK
(CARRIAGE —) BRAKE BREAK
(CLOTHES —) AIRER
(COUNTING —) ABACUS
(DIVING —) LUNET LUNETTE
(EMBROIDERY —) TENT TABORET TAMBOUR
(FISHING —) DREDGE
(GLAZIER'S —) FRAIL
(HARNESS —) HEALD
(LOOM —) SLAY SLEY LATHE BATTEN SLEIGH
(MINING —) APRON
(PHOTOGRAPHY —) BUTTERFLY
(PORTABLE —) BIER CACAXTE
(PRINTING —) CHASE PRESS
(SHIP'S —) CANT
(SLUBBING —) BILLY
(STRETCHING —) TENT SLEDGE TENTER
(TANNING —) BEAM
(WINDOW —) CHESS
(2-WHEELED —) GILL
(PL.) PROFILE

FRAMED NATE NATED ENGAGED

FRAMEWORK BED BENT BIER BONE BUCK BULK CAGE CRIB DURN GRID RACK SASH BONES CADRE CHUTE COPSE CREEL FLAKE SHELL STOCK BELFRY BRIDGE BUSTLE CABANE CASING CRADLE DESIGN FABRIC GOCART GUARDS HARROW HEARSE REBATO SHIELD STROMA WATTLE CABINET CARCASS CLIMBER COMMODE DERRICK FRAMING FULCRUM JACKBOX LATTICE PANNIER REBATER RETABLE STADDLE TRESTLE BARBECUE BEDSTEAD BULKHEAD CARRIAGE CRADLING CRIBWORK GRIDIRON GRILLAGE OSSATURE SCAFFOLD SHELVING SHOWCASE SKELETON TEMPLATE
(— AROUND HATCHWAY) FIDDLEY
(— FOR BUILDING SHIP) STOCKS
(— FOR CORNSTACK) HOVEL
(— FOR PEAL OF BELLS) CAGE
(— OF REFERENCE) SCHEMA
(— TO EXPAND SKIRTS) BUSTLE PANNIER
(EMPTY —) HUSK
(FOLDING —) SCREEN
(SCULPTOR'S —) ARMATURE

FRAMING CURB LEAD BELFRY ARMATURE BEDPLATE

FRAMLEY PARSONAGE (AUTHOR OF —) TROLLOPE
(CHARACTER IN —) LUCY MARK FANNY SMITH LUFTON THORNE CRAWLEY ROBARTS SOWERBY DUNSTABLE

FRANC LEU LEY

FRANCE
(PREF.) GALLO

FRANCE

BAY: BISCAY ARACHON
CAPE: HAGUE
CAPITAL: PARIS
CHEESE: BLEU BRIE BONBEL BOURSIN MUNSTER CAMEMBERT MARCILLAT ROQUEFORT
COIN: ECU SOL SOU GROS AGNEL BLANC BLANK FRANC LIARD LIVRE LOUIS OBOLE SAIGA SCUTE BLANCA BLANCO DENIER DIZAIN TESTON AGNEAUX CENTIME TESTOON CAVALIER NAPOLEON
DANCE: GAVOT BRANLE CANARY CANCAN BOUTADE GAVOTTE
DEPARTMENT: AIN LOT VAR AUBE AUDE CHER EURE GARD GERS JURA NORD OISE ORNE TARN AISNE INDRE ISERE LOIRE RHONE YONNE ARIEGE CANTAL CREUSE LOZERE NIEVRE CORREZE GIRONDE MOSELLE
DIVISION, ANCIENT: ARLES PERCHE NEUSTRIA AQUITAINE AQUITANIA
DYNASTY: CAPET VALOIS BOURBON ORLEANS CAPETIAN MEROVINGIAN
FOOD: PATE CREPE CANAPE MOUSSE QUICHE BRIOCHE SOUFFLE ESCARGOT PIPERADE POTAUFEU TOURNEDO
ISLAND: RE YEU CITE CORSE GROIX HYERE OLERON USHANT CORSICA
KING: ODO EUDES PEPIN CLOVIS LOTHAIR
LAKE: ANNECY CAZAUX
MEASURE: POT SAC AUNE LINE MINE MUID PIED VELT ARPEN CARAT LIEUE LIGNE MINOT PERCH PINTE POINT POUCE TOISE VELTE ARPENT HEMINE LEAGUE QUARTE SETIER CHOPINE HEMINEE POISSON SEPTIER BOISSEAU QUARTAUT ROQUILLE QUARTERON
MILITARY ACADEMY: STCYR SAINTCYR
MOUNTAIN: PUY DORE BLANC CINTO FOREZ PELAT COTEDOR MOUNIER VENTOUX VIGNEMALE CHAMBEYRON
MOUNTAIN RANGE: ALPS ECRINS VOSGES CEVENNES PYRENEES MARITIMES
NAME: GAUL GAULE GALLIA
NATIONAL ANTHEM: MARSEILLAISE
NATIVE: CELT GAUL FRANK BASQUE BRETON GASCON NORMAN PICARD CATALAN GALLOIS LORRAIN FRANCIEN LIGURIAN PROVENCAL BURGUNDIAN
PORT: CAEN BREST CALAIS TOULON LEHAVRE BORDEAUX CHERBOURG DUNKERQUE MARSEILLE
PROTESTANT: HUGUENOT
PROVINCE: FOIX ANJOU AUNIS BEARN ALSACE ARTOIS COMTAT POITOU AUVERGNE BRETAGNE BRITTANY LIMOUSIN LORRAINE PROVENCE TOURAINE
RACE TRACK: AUTEUIL LONGCHAMPS
REPUBLIC CALENDAR: NIVOSE FLOREAL VENTOSE BRUMAIRE FERVIDOR FRIMAIRE GERMINAL MESSIDOR PLUVIOSE PRAIRIAL FRUCTIDOR THERMIDOR VENDEMIAIRE
RESORT: PAU NICE CANNES MENTON RIVIERA

RIVER: AIN ILL LOT LUY LYS VAR AIRE AUBE AUDE CHER DRAC EURE GARD GERS LOIR OISE ORNE TARN VIRE ADOUR AISNE AULNE DROME INDRE ISERE LOIRE MARNE MEUSE RHONE RISLE SAONE SEINE SELLE SOMME VIAUR YONNE ALLIER ARIEGE ESCAUT SAMBRE SCARPE VEZERE VIENNE DURANCE GARONNE GIRONDE MAYENNE MOSELLE CHARENTE DORDOGNE
STOCK EXCHANGE: BOURSE
STRAIT: BONIFACIO
TOWN: AY EU AIX DAX GEX PAU AGDE AGEN ALBI ALES AUBY AUCH BRON CAEN LAON LOOS METZ NICE OPPY ORLY RIOM SENS SETE STLO TOUL UZES VAUX VIMY VIRE ARLES ARRAS BLOIS BREST DIJON DINAN DOUAI ERNEE LAVAL LILLE LISLE LYONS NANCY NERAC NESLE NIMES ORNES PARIS REIMS ROUEN SEDAN TOURS TULLE VICHY AMIENS ANGERS CALAIS LEMANS LONGWY NANTES PANTIN RENNES RHEIMS SARLAT SENLIS SEVRES TARARE TARBES TOULON TROYES TULLUM VALOIS VERDUN BAREGES CASTRES LIMOGES ORLEANS ROUBAIX VALENCE BORDEAUX CLERMONT GRENOBLE MULHOUSE ROCHELLE TOULOUSE MARSEILLE STRASBOURG
TRIBE: REMI AEDUI ARVERNI SALUVII ALLOBROGES
VERSE FORM: LAI ALBA AUBADE RONDEL BALLADE DESCORT RONDEAU VIRELAI VIRELAY
WATERFALL: GAVARNIE
WEIGHT: GROS MARC ONCE CARAT LIVRE POUND TONNE TONNEAU ESTERLIN
WIND: MISTRAL
WINE: MACON MEDOC GRAVES CHABLIS POMEROL BORDEAUX BURGUNDY MUSCADET SAUTERNE CHAMPAGNE
WINE DISTRICT: MEDOC ALSACE BORDEAUX BURGUNDY CHAMPAGNE

FRANCESCA DA RIMINI
(CHARACTER IN —) PAOLO FRANCESCA GIANCIOTTO MALATESTINO
(COMPOSER OF —) ZANDONAI
FRANCHISE SOC SOKE VOTE CHASE FERRY HONOR INFANG CHARTER FREEDOM LIBERTY CONTRACT FREELAGE SUFFRAGE TENEMENT
FRANCISCAN MINOR MINORITE
FRANCOLIN COQUI TETUR TITAR REDWING PHEASANT
FRANCOPHILE GALLOMAN
FRANGIBLE BRITTLE
FRANGIPANI SHAKEWOOD
FRANK FREE OPEN RANK BLUFF BLUNT BURLY LUSTY NAIVE PLAIN BRAZEN CANDID DIRECT FORTHY HONEST SALIAN ARTLESS GENUINE LIBERAL PROFUSE SINCERE CAREFREE CAVALIER GENEROUS OUTFRONT STRAIGHT VIGOROUS OUTSPOKEN FOURSQUARE OPENHEARTED PLAINSPOKEN
FRANKENSTEIN (AUTHOR OF —) SHELLEY
(CHARACTER IN —) HENRY ROBERT VICTOR WALTON CLERVAL JUSTINE WILLIAM ELIZABETH FRANKENSTEIN
FRANKFURTER DOG HOTDOG REDHOT CORNDOG
FRANKINCENSE THUS OLIBAN OLIBANUM
FRANKLY FREELY OPENLY PLAINLY CANDIDLY
FRANKNESS CANDOR FREEDOM OPENNESS
FRANKPLEDGE BORROW FRIBORG
FRANSERIA RAGWEED
FRANTIC MAD WOOD RABID INSANE MANIAC FURIOUS LUNATIC VIOLENT DERANGED FEVERISH FRENETIC FRENZIED MANIACAL
FRAPPE ICE GRANITE
FRATERCULA MORMON
FRATERNAL BROTHERLY DIZYGOTIC NONIDENTICAL
FRATERNITY FRAT FRARY HOUSE ORDER FRATRY QUALITY SOCIETY SODALITY
FRATERNIZE FRAT COTTON
FRAUD GYP DOLE FAKE GAFF GAUD GULL JAPE JUNT LURK RUSE SHAM SKIN WILE CHEAT COVIN CRAFT DOLUS FAKER FAVEL GLAIK GUILE HOCUS LURCH SHARK SHIFT SHUCK SWICK SWIKE TRICK BROGUE DECEIT FIDDLE FULLAM HUMBUG INTAKE STUMER WRENCH FLIVVER KNAVERY ROGUERY STUMOUR SWINDLE BOODLING COZENAGE IMPOSTER OPERATOR SUBTLETY TRUMPERY
FRAUDULENT SKIN WILY CRONK COGGED CRAFTY QUACKY ABUSIVE CROOKED CUNNING KNAVISH CHEATING COVINOUS FRAUDFUL GUILEFUL QUACKISH SINISTER SPURIOUS
FRAXINELLA DITTANY RUEWORT
FRAY FRET BROIL BROOM FEAZE MELEE RAVEL AFFRAY BUSTLE CHAUVE FRIDGE TIFFLE CONTEST FRAZZLE
FRAYED WORN FLAGGY RAVELED RAVELLY
FRAZER FINNER
FREAK FIRK FLAM WHIM FANCY HUMOR LUSUS MAVEN MOODS SCAPE SPORT HIPPIE MEGRIM SPLEEN WHIMSY CAPRICE CROTCHET ESCAPADE FLIMFLAM WHIMWHAM MONSTROSITY
(CRAZY —S) LUNES
FREAKISH FREAKY BIZARRE FLIGHTY MAGGOTY WHIMSIC CRANKISH
FRECKLE CHIT EPHELIS FRECKEN LENTIGO SUNSPOT HEATSPOT FERNTICLE FERNTICKLE
FRECKLED FRECKLY FLECKLED
FREE LAX LET MOD RID BOLD EASE LISS OPEN PERT REDD SHED SHUT CLEAN CLEAR FLUID FRANK LARGE LISSE LOOSE READY SCOUR SLAKE SPARE UNTIE ACQUIT DEGAGE DEVOID EXEMPT FACILE FLUENT FREELY GRATIS IMMUNE LOOSEN SOLUTE UNSLIP VACANT VAGILE CLEANSE DELIVER GRIVOIS INEXACT LASKING LIBERAL MANUMIT RELEASE SCIOLTO UNBOUND UNBOWED UNSLAVE UNTWIST WELCOME WILLING ABSOLUTE AUTARKIC BUCKSHEE EASINESS EXPEDITE FACILITY FREEHAND GRIVOISE INDIGENT LAXATIVE LIBERATE UNBRIDLE FOOTLOOSE
(— AND EASY) GLIB CAVALIER FAMILIAR
(— BROOK OF WEEDS) RODE
(— FROM) EX REDD DEVOID DISPATCH
(— FROM ACCUSATION) SACKLESS
(— FROM ACIDITY) DULCIFY
(— FROM AMBIGUITY) HOMELY DECIDED
(— FROM ANXIETY) CONTENT
(— FROM ARTIFICIAL) ARTLESS
(— FROM BIAS) CANDID
(— FROM CARE) EASY CARELESS
(— FROM CHARGE) FDD PURGE FRANCO
(— FROM CONSTRAINT) CASUAL
(— FROM DEDUCTIONS) NET
(— FROM DEFECT) HAIL HALE SOUND
(— FROM DIRT) BRIGHT
(— FROM DOUBT) RESOLVE
(— FROM DRUG ADDICTION) CLEAN
(— FROM ELECTRICAL CHARGE) DEAD
(— FROM ERROR) LEAL SOUND CORRECT ACCURATE
(— FROM EVIL) RESCUE
(— FROM EXTREMES) EQUABLE
(— FROM FLAWS) GOOD
(— FROM FROST) FRESH
(— FROM IMPURITIES) FINE DRESS DEFECATE DEPURATE
(— FROM KNOTS) ENODE ENODATE
(— FROM MARKS) BLANK
(— FROM MICROORGANISMS) ASEPTIC STERILE
(— FROM OBLIGATION) ACQUIT EXCUSE
(— FROM PENALTY) ABSOLVE
(— FROM RESTRAINT) ABANDONED
(— FROM STONES) CHESSOM
(— FROM WHITE) SATURATE
(— OF DIFFICULTIES) AFLOAT
(— OF FAT) ENSEAM
(— OF OVERTONES) PURE
(— OF TAR) WRECK
(— ONE'S SELF) SOLVE
(— PLUNGER) ARM
(— THROW AREA) KEYHOLE
(PREF.) ELEUTHER(O) IMMUNO LIBRO
(— FROM) DE
FREEBASE COCAINE
FREEBOARD QUICKSIDE
FREEBOOTER TORY RIDER ROVER THIEF PIRATE RAIDER BRIGAND CATERAN CORSAIR PINDARI PILLAGER RAPPAREE SNAPHANCE
FREEBORN INGENUOUS
FREEDMAN LEYSING TITYRUS (PL.) LAET
FREEDOM RUN EASE FRITH LARGE UHURU ACCESS STREET APATHIA BREADTH LEISURE LIBERTY LICENCE LICENSE RELEASE AUTONOMY FREELAGE FREENESS IMMUNITY IMPUNITY LARGESSE WITHGATE
(— FROM BIAS) CANDOR
(— FROM CALAMITY) WELFARE
(— FROM CONSTRAINT) ABANDON
(— FROM DANGER) SECURITY
(— FROM ERROR) ACCURACY
(— FROM GUILT) SHRIVE
(— FROM MIXTURE) PURITY
(— FROM NOISE) QUIET
(— OF ACCESS) ENTREE
(— OF ACTION) SWINGE LATITUDE
(— OF MOVEMENT) RANGE
(— OF SPEECH) PARISIA
(— TO PROCEED) HEAD
(— TO RETURN) RECOURSE
(CARELESS —) ABANDON
(LIMITED —) PLAY
(PREF.) ELEUTHER(O)
FREEHOLD BARONY REALTY
FREEHOLDER SWAIN BONDER YEOMAN FRANKLIN
FREEING LIVERY ACQUITAL
FREE LANCE ROUTIER
FREELY FREE LIEF LARGE LARGELY READILY HEARTILY
FREEMAN BUR AIRE BARON CEORL HAULD BONDER CITIZEN FRANKLIN ROTURIER
(POOR —) THETE
FREEMASON FRATER MORGAN NOACHITE
(ONE NOT A —) COWAN
FREESTONE HAZEL
(— STATE) CONNECTICUT
FREETHINKER INFIDEL SKEPTIC AGNOSTIC
FREEZE ICE RIME CATCH CHILL FROST CURDLE FRAPPE HARDEN STARVE STEEVE CONGEAL GLACIATE
FREEZING COLD FREEZY FRIGID FROSTY GLACIAL ICECOLD CRYONICS GELATION (PREF.) CRY(O) KRY(O)
FREIGHT COST LOAD CARGO GOODS ASTRAY BURDEN LADING FRAUGHT HOTSHOT PLUNDER PORTAGE TRUCKAGE
(— CAR) TRUCK
FREISCHUTZ, DER (CHARACTER IN —) MAX CUNO AGATHE HERMIT KASPAR SAMIEL AENNCHEN
(COMPOSER OF —) WEBER
FREMD FRAIM FRAMMIT
FRENCH CREOLE FRANCO GALLIC GALLIAN GALLICAN
(— MIXED WITH ENGLISH) FRANGLAIS
(CANADIAN —) JOUAL
(PREF.) FRANCO GALLO

FRENCH GUIANA **(CAPE OF —)** ORANGE
(CAPITAL OF —) CAYENNE
(RIVER OF —) MARONI
(TOWN OF —) MANA KOUROU
FRENCH HONEYSUCKLE SULLA
FRENCH LAVENDER STECHADOS
FRENCHMAN GAUL PICARD FRENCHY MONSIEUR PARLEYVOO
FRENCH MULBERRY SOURBUSH
FRENCH NUDE ALESAN
FRENCH REPUBLIC MARIANNA MARIANNE
FRENCH SUDAN (SEE MALI)
FRENCHWOMAN GRISETTE
FRENULUM TENDON
FRENUM BRIDLE FRAENUM FRENULUM VINCULUM
FRENZIED MAD AMOK MUST RABID RAMAGE BERSERK FANATIC FRANTIC MADDING FRENETIC FURIBUND POSSESSED
FRENZY AMOK FURY GERE MOON MUST RAGE AMUCK FUROR MANIA MUSTH FURORE RAVING MADNESS OESTRUS SWIVVET DELIRIUM INSANITY
FREQUENCY HERTZ PITCH CREBRITY
FREQUENT USE BANG KEEP HAUNT HOWFF OFTEN THICK AFFECT COMMON HOURLY INFEST RESORT ENHAUNT OFTTIME CREBROUS FAMILIAR PRACTICE ACCUSTOMED
(PREF.) SYCHNO
FREQUENTLY OFT OFTEN HOURLY UNSELDOM
FRESH GAY HOT NEW WET FLIP GOOD RACY SMUG WARM BRISK CRISP GREEN MOIST QUICK RUDDY SASSY SMART SOUND SWEET VIVID CALLER CALVER FLORID LIVELY MAIDEN REDHOT STRONG UNUSED VERNAL VIRENT VIRGIN ANOTHER NOUVEAU UNFADED VERDANT NOUVELLE ORIGINAL SPANKING YOUTHFUL
(NOT —) PALE STALE
(PREF.) CENO
(SUFF.) CENE
FRESHEN PERK BRACE FRESH RENEW BREEZE CALLER REVIVE CHOUNCE PEARTEN REFRESH SWEETEN FRENCHEN
FRESHENER BRACER
FRESHET TIDE FLOOD FRESH SPATE TORNADO
FRESHMAN FOX BEJAN FROSH BEJANT GREENY PENNAL FRESHER
(GERMAN —) PENNAL
FRESHNESS DEW SASS VERD NOVELTY VERDURE VIRIDITY ORIGINALITY
FRET DIK NAG ORP RUB RUX VEX CARK FASH FRAY FUSS GALL GNAW RAGE STEW YIRM CHAFE CRAKE CRISP FLISK GRATE PIQUE WORRY WREAK ABRADE CORSIE CRYSAL HARASS MUCKLE NETTLE PLAGUE REPINE RIPPLE RUFFLE CHRYSAL GRECQUE GRIZZLE MEANDER SCRUPLE SQUINNY ALIGREEK IRRITATE
FRETFUL CROSS GIRNY ORPIT TEATY TEENY TESTY FRETTY PENCEY SULLEN TATCHY TWISTY FRECKET PEEVISH PETTISH SPLEENY CAPTIOUS CRANKOUS FRETSOME FROPPISH PETULANT PINDLING QUERULOUS
FRETTED FRETTY MAGGED
FRETTING FRET EATING
FREY FREYR YNGVI
(FATHER OF —) NJORD
(SISTER OF —) FREYA
FREYA **(BROTHER OF —)** FREY
(FATHER OF —) NJORD
(HUSBAND OF —) ODIN
FRIABLE CRIMP CRISP CRUMP FLAKY FRUSH MEALY SHORT CRUMBY CRUMMY FLUFFY PUTRID CHESSOM CRUMBLY MOLDERY POWDERY RESOLUTE ROTTENLY SHATTERY
(NOT —) SAD
FRIAR FRATE FREER MINIM MINOR BHIKKU FRATER GELONG GOSAIN LISTER BHIKSHU JACOBIN LIMITER SERVITE BREVIGER CAPUCHIN JACOBITE MINORIST MINORITE PREACHER AUGUSTINE CARMELITE CORDELIER MENDICANT BENEDICTINE
FRIARBIRD COLDONG PIMLICO MONKBIRD
FRIAR SKATE DOCTOR
FRICANDEAU GRENADINE
FRICASSEE POTPIE
FRICATIVE BUZZ HISS OPEN YOGH DURATIVE
FRICTION BUZZ DRAG HISS CHAFE WINDAGE
(PREF.) TRIBO
(SUFF.) TRIPSIS
FRICTIONLESS SMOOTH
FRIED FRIT SAUTE
FRIEDCAKE WONDER CRULLER FATCAKE DOUGHNUT
FRIEND AME AMI AMY BOR CAD EME PAX AMIE BHAI CHUM NABS OPPO PARD WINE AMIGA AMIGO BRICK BUDDY INGLE NETOP TROUT AIKANE BELAMY COBBER COUSIN CUMMER GOSSIP INWARD KIMMER PRINCE QUAKER ACHATES COMRADE SOCIETY COCKMATE COMPADRE DEMOPHIL FEDERATE HICKSITE INTIMADO INTIMATE TILLICUM CATERCOUSIN
(— OF BRIDEGROOM) PARANYMPH
(—S NOT SPEAKING) CUTS
(BOSOM —) CONFIDANT
(CLOSE —) PRIVY COBBER COMPADRE
(DIVINE —) SOCIUS
(FAMILIAR —) CRONY GREMIAL SPECIAL
(GIRL —) DOXY DRAG DONEY DOXIE STEADY
(INTIMATE FEMALE —) CUMMER
(PRIVATE —) PRIVADO
(WOMAN —) GIMMER
(PL.) FOLK KITH SOCE FOLKS SOCIETY
FRIENDLESS FORLORN
FRIENDLINESS AMITY AFFINITY BONHOMIE GOODWILL
FRIENDLY COSH EASY GOOD HOLD HOMY KIND TOSH CADGY CHIEF COUTH GREAT HOMEY MATEY THICK AMICAL CHATTY CHUMMY FOLKSY FORTHY HOMELY KINDLY SMOOTH AFFABLE AMIABLE AMICOUS COUTHIE AMICABLE HOMELIKE INTIMATE SOCIABLE NEIGHBORLY
FRIENDSHIP PAX AMITY AMOUR
FRIEZE KELT FRISE CUSHION FALDING FRISADO FRIEZING
FRIGATE ZABRA
FRIGATE BIRD IOA IWA ALCATRAS
FRIGATE MACKEREL BONITO TASSARD
FRIGG FREA FRIJA
FRIGGA **(HUSBAND OF —)** ODIN
(SON OF —) BALDER
FRIGHT COW BOOF FEAR FLEG FRAY ALARM GHAST GLIFF GLOFF PANIC SCARE AFFRAY GASTER GLIFFY SCHRIK TERROR STARTLE SWITHER FRIGHTEN GASTNESS GLIFFING
FRIGHTEN AWE COW FLY SHY SOB BAZE BREE DARE DOSS FEAR FLEG FLEY FRAY FUNK HARE HAZE SHOO AFEAR AFLEY ALARM APPAL BLUFF GALLY GHOST GLIFF HAZEN SCARE SHORE SPOOK AFFRAY ALARUM APPALL BOGGLE BOOGER COWARD FLAITE FLIGHT FRIGHT GALLEY GALLOW AFFREUX FRECKEN SCARIFY STARTLE TERRIFY AFFRIGHT MISTRYST
(— BIRDS) KEEP
(PREF.) TERRI TERRORI
FRIGHTENED RAD EERY FRIT GAST EERIE GHAST WINDY AFEARD AFRAID AGHAST SCARED SCAREY STURTIN GHASTFUL
(EASILY —) TIMID SKITTISH
FRIGHTENING EERY DREAD EERIE GOURY HAIRY FRIGHTY GHASTLY SHIVERY DREADFUL FEARSOME FLEYSOME
FRIGHTFUL WAN DIRE GRIM UGLY AWFUL FERLY HORRID UGSOME AFFREUX DIREFUL FEARFUL GASHFUL GHASTLY HIDEOUS ALARMING DREADFUL ELDRITCH FEARSOME GHASTFUL HORRIBLE HORRIFIC TERRIBLE TERRIFIC
FRIGID DRY ICY COLD BLEAK FISHY ARCTIC FROSTY FROZEN WINTRY GLACIAL FREEZING SIBERIAN
FRIGIDITY GLARE
FRILL DIDO PURL JABOT RUCHE RUFFLE ARMILLA FLOUNCE SPINACH SPINAGE CHITLING CRIMPING FRILLERY FURBELOW
(— OF HAIR) APRON
(PL.) PUFFERY FOOFARAW FRILLERY
FRILLINESS CHICHI
FRILLING RUCHE ROUCHE SWEEPER
FRILLY CHICHI
FRINGE WLO EDGE GILL LOMA RUFF WELT BEARD THRUM BORDER EDGING MARGIN PELMET TASSEL BULLION CREPINE EYELASH FEATHER FIMBRIA MACRAME SELVAGE TRAILER VALANCE WHISKER CILIELLA FRISETTE INDUSIUM PENUMBRA SELVEDGE TRIMMING
(— OF TEETH) PERISTOME
(SOFT —S) THRUM
(PL.) ZIZITH TZITZIS TZITZIT
(PREF.) CROSS(O) FIMBRI(O) LACINI THYSAN(O)
FRINGED JUBATE CILIATE LACINIATE
FRINGEFOOT UMA
FRINGEPOD LACEPOD
FRINGETAIL VEILTAIL
FRINGE TREE SHAVINGS
FRIPPERY FLIPPERY TRINKUMS
(PL.) GAUDERY
FRISK COLT FISK PLAY ROLL SKIP WHID BOUND CAPER SKICE CAREER CAVORT CURVET FRISCO FROLIC TITTUP WANTON FRISCAL FRISKLE
FRISKY GAY PERT FRISK CROUSE FEISTY KIPPER LIVELY WANTON BUCKISH COLTISH JIGGISH PLAYFUL SKITTISH SPORTIVE
FRISON KNUB
FRIT FRETT CALCINE
FRITTER FOOL FRIT TEAR BOLLO DRILL WASTE BANGLE DRIVEL LOUNGE BEIGNET DRIBBLE FLITTER SLATTERN
FRIVOLITY LEVITY FRIBBLE INANITY ITEMING FUTILITY NONSENSE NUGACITY
FRIVOLOUS GAY DAFT VAIN GIDDY INANE LIGHT PETTY SILLY WASHY FLIMSY FRILLY FRIVOL FROTHY FUTILE TOYISH YEASTY FATUOUS FRIBBLE LIGHTLY NIDGETY SHALLOW TRIVIAL GIMCRACK JIMCRACK SKITTISH TRIFLING
FRIVOLOUSNESS FUTILITY
FRIZZ FRIZ CREPE FRIZE FRIZZLE FROUNCE
FRIZZED CRISPY
FRIZZLE CRAPE CREPE
FRIZZLY FUZZY CRIMPY FRIZZY
FRIZZY FUZZY CRIMPY FRIZZLY
FROCK DUD JAM GOWN JUMP SLIP SLOP WRAP LAMMY SMOCK TRUSS TUNIC CLERIC JERSEY LAMMIE MANTLE ROCHET SUKKENYE
FROCK COAT CRISPIN
FROG PAD POD KICK FROSH FROSK FROUD PADDO PADDY RANID RONCO ANURAN PEEPER TOGGLE CHARLIE CRAWLER CREEPER CROAKER CUSHION FRESHER FROGLET PADDOCK PODDOCK QUILKIN BULLFROG FERREIRO FROGGING PLATANNA REPLACER
(— IN LOOM) HEATER
(— OF HORSE'S HOOF) FRUSH CUSHION
(TREE —) HYLA NOTOTREMA
(PREF.) BATRACH(O) RANI
FROG CRAB RANINIAN

FROGFISH ANGLER SLIMER TOADFISH
FROGGER CHASER TRAILER ZOOGLER
FROGGY RANARIAN
FROGHOPPER HOPPER CERCOPID
FROGMOUTH MOPOKE MOREPORK PODARGUE
FROGS (AUTHOR OF —) ARISTOPHANES
(CHARACTER IN —) AEACUS CHARON BACCHUS DIONYSUS HERCULES XANTHIAS AESCHYLUS EURIPIDES
(SUFF.) BATRACH(O)(US)
FROLIC BUM GAY RIG BLOW COLT GAME GELL HAZE JINK LAKE LARK ORGY PLAY PLOY RANT REEK ROMP TEAR CAPER FREAK FRISK MERRY PRANK RANDY ROUSE SALLY SPORT SPREE BUSTER CAVORT CURVET FRATCH GAMBOL PLISKY POWWOW PRANCE ROLLIX SHINDY SPLORE VAGARY WANTON DISPORT GAMMOCK MARLOCK PLISKIE ROLLICK SCAMPER SKYLARK SPANIEL STASHIE WASSAIL CAROUSAL JAMBOREE
FROLICSOME GAY DAFT ROID ANTIC BUXOM CADGY FRISK GILPY LARKY FRISKY LIVELY WANTON ANTICAL JOCULAR LARKING LARKISH PLAYFUL WAGGISH ESPIEGLE FRISKFUL FROLICKY GAMESOME LARKSOME PRANKISH SPORTFUL SPORTIVE
FROLICSOMENESS HEYDAY
FROM A AB DE EX OF FAE FRA FRO VAN VON ASOF THROM AGAINST
(— A DISTANCE) ALOOF
(— BEGINNING TO END) THROUGH
(— ELSEWHERE) ALIUNDE
(— OFF) AFFA
(— SIDE TO SIDE) OVER CROSS ATHWART
(— THIS PLACE) HENCE
(— THIS TIME) HENCE
(PREF.) AP APH APO
FROND FERN TRESS CROSIER FRONDLET
FRONT BOW VAN BROW FACE FORE HEAD PROW THIN AFORE VAUNT BEFORE DEVANT FACADE FACING FORMER OPPOSE SECTOR VAWARD ADVANCE FORWARD FRONTAL FURTHER OBVERSE PALATAL PREFACE RESPECT SLENDER FOREHEAD FOREMOST FOREPART FORESIDE FRONTAGE
(— OF ASTROLABE) WOMBSIDE
(— OF BARN) FOREBAY
(— OF BIRD'S NECK) GUTTUR
(— OF BODY) GROUF
(— OF HEAD) VISAGE FORETOP
(— OF HELMET) VENTAIL
(— OF SHIRT) BOSOM
(— OF WATERWHEEL BUCKET) START
(— UPON) AFFRONT
(PREF.) ANTER(O) PRO
(IN —) FORE PRO(S)(SO)
(IN — OF) ANTE ANTER(O) PRAE PRE
FRONTAL PALL FRONT SINDON TABULA FRONTON METOPIC FRONTLET SUFFRONT
(ALTAR —) TABULA
FRONTIER BOUND COAST FRONT MARCH BORDER BARRIER FRONTURE OUTLYING
(FORTIFIED —) LIMES
FRONTING OBVIOUS
FRONTISPIECE FRONT UNWAN FRONTIS
FRONTLET TIARA FRONTAL CHAMFRON
FRONT PAGE (AUTHOR OF —) HECHT MACARTHUR
(CHARACTER IN —) EARL BURNS GRANT HILDY PEGGY WALTER HARTMAN JOHNSON WILLIAMS
FRONTPIECE GORE
FROST ICE COLD HOAR RIME RIND
(GROUND —) PERMA
(PREF.) CRYMO PAGO RHIGO
(HOAR —) PACHNO
FROSTED GLACE PRUINOSE
FROSTING ICING DIVINITY
FROSTWEED ROCKROSE
FROSTY ICY COLD RIMY CHILL CRISP FRORE GELID GLARY HUNCH BOREAL FRIGID FROREN CHILLING INIMICAL PRUINOUS
(NOT —) OPEN
FROTH FOB BARM FOAM HEAD REAM SCUM SUDS WORK CREAM SPUME YEAST FLOWER FREATH LATHER SPURGE
FROTHER CREOSOTE
FROTHING HUMMING MANTLING
FROTHY BARMY FOAMY LIGHT REAMY SPEWY SPUMY SUDSY FLASHY YEASTY SPUMOSE SPUMOUS WHIPPED SPUMANTE
FROWARD RANK CROSS AWKWARD PEEVISH WAYWARD CONTRARY FROPPISH PERVERSE PETULANT PROTERVE SHREWISH UNTOWARD
FROWN GLUM LOUR GLOOM GLOUT GLUMP LOWER SCOWL GLOWER GLUNCH FROUNCE FRONTLET
FROWNING GLUM GLUNCH
FROWZY BLOUSY BLOWSY BLOWZY RAFFISH FROWZLED SCABROUS SLOVENLY
FROZEN FAST FIXED FRORE FRORY GELID GLARY FRAPPE FROREN GLACIAL
FRUCTIFICATION CONK AECIDIUM BASIDIUM APOTHECIUM
FRUCTOSE ACROSE
FRUGAL EASY MILD CANNY CHARY ROMAN SCANT SPARE MEAGER SAVING SCANTY SCARCE SCOTCH SKIMPY CAREFUL PRUDENT SCRIMPY SLENDER SPARING THRIFTY PROVIDENT PARSIMONIOUS
FRUGALITY SPARE THRIFT ECONOMY PARCITY MANAGERY
FRUGALLY HARD CHARILY SAVINGLY
FRUIT BEL FIG HAW UVA AKEE ATTA BAEL BITO COYO DATE DIKA DROP GEAN JACK LIME NOOP PEAR PLUM POME SEED SLOE SNAP SORB AKENE ANISE APPLE BERRY CLING COUMA DRUPE GENIP GOURD GRAPE GUAVA HAZEL ILAMA LEMON LIMON MANGO MELON OLIVE PAPAW PEACH RIPER SORVA TRYMA ACHENE ACINUS ALMOND BANANA BUTTON CEDRON CEREZA CHERRY CITRON CITRUS COBNUT COCHAL COCONA DAMSON DURIAN EMBLIC EMBOLO GUARRI JUJUBE KEEPER LEGUME LONGAN LOQUAT MAMMEE MARANG MAYPOP MUYUSA NARRAS ORANGE PAPAYA PAWPAW PELLAS POMATO RESULT SAPOTA SQUASH UVALHA WAMPEE WESTME ZAPOTE APRICOT ATEMOYA AVOCADO AZAROLE BILIMBI BLOATER CARAWAY CHAYOTE CHECKER CIRUELA COCONUT CURRANT DESSERT GEEBUNG GENIPAP GHERKIN KUMQUAT MURCOTT PIGFACE PRODUCT RIPENER SERVICE SHALLON SOROSIS SOURSOP TANGELO ACHENIUM BAYBERRY BELLERIC BILBERRY CALABASH CANISTEL CAPSICUM CARDAMUM CITRANGE COCOPLUM CUCUMBER DEWBERRY DOGBERRY EGGFRUIT FOLLICLE FRUITAGE FRUITERY FRUITLET GOLKAKRA INKBERRY LIMEQUAT OSOBERRY PIEPRINT PODOCARP RAMBUTAN SEBESTEN SEEDBALL SHADDOCK SWEETSOP SYCONIUM CARYOPSIS CHERIMOYA NECTARINE PINEAPPLE SAPODILLA TAMARILLO CHERIMOYER CLEMENTINE MANGOSTEEN
(— LIKE APPLE) MEDLAR
(— OF CACTUS) SABRA
(— OF CAPER) CAPOT
(— OF CITRON) ETROG ETHROG
(— OF HEMLOCK) CONIUM
(— OF OAK) ACORN
(— OF PALM) SALAK PUPUNHA
(— OF ROSE) HEP HIP BUTTON
(— ON TREES) HANG
(—S COOKED IN SYRUP) COMPOTE
(AGGREGATE —) ETAERIO DRUPETUM HETAERIO
(ASTRINGENT —) GAB GAUB CHEBULE
(AVOCADO-LIKE —) ANAY
(CANDIED —) CONSERVE
(CARMINATIVE —) BADIAN
(COILED —) STROMBUS
(COLLECTIVE —) SYNCARP
(COMPOUND —) SYNCARP
(DRIED —) PASA CUBEB MUMMY SABAL OREJON CAPSULE EMBELIA
(EARLY —) PRIMEUR HASTINGS
(FALLEN —) SHEDDER WINDFALL
(FIRST —S) ANNATES BIKKURIM PRIMICES
(FLESHY —) SYCONIUM SARCOCARP
(FUZZY —) KIWI
(GOURD —) PEPO
(GRAPEFRUIT-LIKE —) SUHA
(GRAPELIKE —) WAMPEE
(HAWTHORN —) PEGGLE
(IMPERFECT —) SPECH NUBBIN
(MASHED —) FOOL
(MEDICINAL —) DRUPE AIWAIN AJOWAN EMBELIA
(ONE-SEEDED —) AKENE ACHENE
(PALMYRA —) PUNATOO
(PLUMLIKE —) CARISSA CIRUELA
(PRESERVED —) SUCCADE CONFITURE
(PRICKLY —) HEDGEHOG
(SELF-FERTILIZED —) AUTOCARP
(SLICED DRIED —) SNITS SNITZ SCHNITZ
(SPURGE —) TAMPOE
(SUPERIOR —) TOPPER
(UNRIPE OAK —) CAMATA
(WINGED —) SAMARA
(WOODY —) XYLOCARP
(PREF.) CARP(O) FRUCTI FRUGI
(BEAK-LIKE —) RYNCO
(SUFF.) CARP(OUS)(US)(Y)
FRUIT BAT KALONG
FRUIT-BEARING FERTILE
FRUIT DOVE KUKU
FRUITFUL FAT FOODY BATTEL FECUND FRUITY GRAVID FERTILE TEEMFUL UBEROUS ABUNDANT CHILDING FRUITIVE PREGNANT PROLIFIC PLENTEOUS
FRUITFULNESS UBERTY FATNESS
FRUITGROWER FRUITIST
FRUITLESS DRY GELD VAIN ADDLE BARREN FUTILE STERILE USELESS ABORTIVE BOOTLESS
FRUIT PIGEON KUKU LUPE KUKUPA MANUMA MANUTAGI
FRUIT ROT BLET
FRUIT STONE COB PYRENE PUTAMEN
(PREF.) PYREN(O)
FRUMP JUDY
FRUSTRATE BALK BEAT BILK CRAB DASH DISH FOIL LAME BAULK BLANK BLOCK CHECK CROSS ELUDE SMEAR THRAW WRECK BAFFLE BLIGHT BUGGER DEFEAT DELUDE DERAIL KIBOSH OUTWIT SCOTCH THWART ANIENTE DECEIVE FALSIFY PREVENT CONFOUND INFRINGE STULTIFY
FRUSTRATED DISHED MANQUE
FRUSTRATER MARPLOT
FRUSTRATING BOOTLESS
FRUSTRATION FOIL SUCK DEFEAT FIASCO
FRUSTRUM GUTTA
FRUSTULE TESTULE HYPOTHECA
FRY SILE BROOD FRIZZ KRILL SAUTE FRIZZLE GREYFISH
(HANGTOWN —) OMELET
(KIND OF —) HANGTOWN
FRYER FRIER FRIZZER SPRINGER
FRYING PAN FRYPAN SPIDER CREEPER SKILLET
FUCHSIA CORREA KONINI FUCHSIN EARDROPS
FUCHSIN ROSEINE SOLFERINO
FUCHSINE RUBIN RUBINE MAGENTA ROSANILINE

FUDDLE FUZZLE FLUSTER
FUDDLED FAP REE DOPY BOSKY DOPEY SWASH TIPSY WOOZY MAUDLIN TOSTICATED
(— WITH MALT LIQUOR) SWIPEY
FUDGE HUNCH SNUDGE PENUCHE DIVINITY
FUEL GAS OIL POB COAL COKE FIRE PEAT UPLA ARGOL AVGAS ACETOL BUNKER ELDING FIRING NAPALM SHRUFF TIMBER COALITE GASOHOL PABULUM SYNTHOL FIREBOOT FIREBOTE GASOGENE GAZOGENE TRIPTANE
(GAS —) ETHANE
(JELLED —) NAPALM
(ROCKET —) BORANE HYDYNE
FUGITIVE HOT FLEME FLYER FUGIE SCAMP OUTLAW FLEEING LAMSTER REFUGEE RUNAWAY FLEETING RUNAGATE UNSTABLE
(PL.) MANZAS
FUGUE FUGA RICERCAR
(— THEME) DUX
(PART OF —) STRETTA
FULA PEUL PEUHL FELLANI FELLATA
FULANI PEUL PEUHL
FULCRUM BAIT GLUT
(— FOR OAR) ROWLOCK
FULFILL FILL FULL KEEP MEET HONOR ANSWER COMPLY FULFIL REDEEM ACHIEVE PERFORM SATISFY COMPLETE COMPLISH ACCOMPLISH
(— A TERM) EXPIRE
FULFILLMENT PASS EFFECT FUNCTION PERFORMANCE
(— OF GOD'S WILL) KINGDOM
(IMAGINARY —) FANTASY
FULGURATION BLICK
FULL BAD BIG FAT FOW COOL DEEP FAIR GOOD JUST PANG RANK TRIG TUCK AMPLE AWASH BROAD CLEAR FLUSH LARGE LUCKY PIENO PLAIN PLENY ROUND SATED SOLID TIGHT TOTAL WHOLE ENTIRE GOGGLE HONEST STRONG BAPTIZE BRIMFUL COPIOUS DESTROY DIFFUSE FULFILL FULSOME LIBERAL OROTUND PERFORM PLENARY REPLETE TEEMING TRAMPLE WEALTHY ABSOLUTE ADEQUATE BOUFFANT BRIMMING CHOCKFUL COMPLETE EXTENDED FREQUENT PREGNANT RESONANT THOROUGH
(— CLOTH OR YARN) WALK
(— OF AIR) LIGHT
(— OF BLANKS) LACUNOSE
(— OF CHINKS) RIMOSE
(— OF DELAY) MOROSE
(— OF DEVILTRY) HEMPY HEMPIE
(— OF DIRT) FOUL
(— OF EGGS) GRAVID
(— OF ENERGY) STOUT SWANK
(— OF ENTHUSIASM) RARING
(— OF ERRORS) FOUL
(— OF FLAWS) CRAZY
(— OF FUN) FROLIC
(— OF HAPPINESS) SUNSHINY
(— OF INTEREST) AGOG
(— OF IRON) SIDEROSE
(— OF LIFE) SPUNKY ANIMATE
(— OF LOOPS) KINKY
(— OF MATTER FOR THOUGHT) MEATY
(— OF PROMISE) PREGNANT
(— OF RUSHES) SPRITTY
(— OF SAND) ARENOSE
(— OF SLEEP) SOPOROSE
(— OF SMALL OPENINGS) POROUS
(— OF SPIRIT) GENEROUS
(— OF VIGOR) FLUSH GREEN LUSTY ANIMATED SPIRITED
(— OF ZEST) RACY
(NOT —) SCANT
(VERY —) SKELPING
(PREF.) PLENI PLERO
(SUFF.) **(— OF)** IOUS OSE OUS
FULL-BLOODED PLETHORIC
FULL-BLOWN JUICY
FULLBODIED FAT LOFTY HEARTY ROBUST
FULL-BOSOMED BUXOM
FULLER GAG HARDY HARDIE ROLLER TUCKER WALKER BLOCKER CREASER THICKER CLOTHIER
FULL-FACED AFFRONTE AFFRONTY
FULL-FLAVORED BOLD RACY
FULL-FLEDGED ALLOUT ENTIRE SUMMED
FULL-GROWN ADULT RIPE GROWN MATURE SEEDED
FULL-LENGTH UNCUT
FULLLNESS (— OF TONE) VOLUME
FULLNESS BODY FLAIR FLARE FULTH PLENUM FULNESS PLEROMA SATIETY
FULL-SOUNDING ROUND SONOROUS
FULLY ALL DOWN EVEN INLY WELL AMPLY LARGE ENOUGH FAIRLY THRICE WHOLLY CLEARLY LARGELY UTTERLY CLEVERLY ENTIRELY INWARDLY MATURELY
FULMAR HAG NELLY NODDY HAGDON NELLIE MALDUCK MALMOCK STINKER MALLEMUCK
FULMINATE BLOW RAIL FULMINE
FULSOME FAT SUAVE FOULSOME
FUMARIC BOLETIC LICHENIC
FUMAROLE HORNITO
FUMBLE BOOT DROP MUFF MULL PIRL BOBBLE BOGGLE FAFFLE MUMBLE PRODDLE MISFIELD THRUMBLE
FUMBLER STUMER BUNGLER STUMOUR
FUMBLING HALTING
FUME FUFF RAGE REEK STEW EWDER SMOKE STIFE STORM VAPOR SEETHE SNUFFLE FUMIGATE
(— A CASK) STUM
FUMID SMOKY SMOKEY
FUMIGATE SMEEK SMOKE PASTIL CYANIDE PASTILLE
FUMIGATION GASSING
FUMIGATOR AERATOR
FUMITORY FUMARIA FUMEROOT FUMEWORT
FUN GIG GAME GELL JEST JOKE LAKE PLAY BORAK BOURD HUMOR KICKS MIRTH MUSIC SPORT FROLIC GAIETY GAYETY DAFFERY DAFFING GAMMOCK WHOOPEE
(MAKE — OF) JAPE RIDE
(UNRESTRAINED —) HELL
FUNCTION ACT JOB MAP RUN USE DUTY FORM ROLE WORK POWER ACTION AGENCY MATRIX MISTER OFFICE SQUASH CONCEPT FACULTY ISOLATE MAPPING OPERATE PERFORM SERVICE WORKING ACTIVITY BUSINESS MINISTRY PROVINCE
(— EFFECTIVELY) AVAIL
(—S OF JUDGES) ERMINE
(APPARENT —) STUDY
(CHEMICAL —) PARACHOR
(CLERICAL —) DIET
(ECCLESIASTICAL —) DIET
(ESSENTIAL —) DHARMA
(LAVISH —) WINGDING
(MATHEMATICAL —) DEL FORM METRIC INVERSE QUARTIC
(SPECIAL —) CEREMONY
(USEFUL —) PURPOSE
(WORD —) DEIXIS
(SUFF.) CY URE
FUNCTIONAL DYNAMIC
FUNCTIONARY BEADLE FLUNKY CAPTAIN FLUNKEY CHAPRASI
FUNCTIONING ALIVE AFLOAT
FUNCTIONLESS OTIOSE
FUND BOX BANK FOND MASS CHEST KITTY MOUNT SLUSH STOCK STORE ESCROW CHALUKA JACKPOT RESERVE HALUKKAH PECULIUM
(COMMON —) POT POOL
(POLITICAL —S) BARREL
(RESERVE —) REST
(PL.) CAJA PURSE COFFER
FUNDAMENT NOCK TAIL BOTTOM FUNDUS
FUNDAMENTAL NET BASE BASAL BASIC KLANG PRIME VITAL BOTTOM PRIMAL SIMPLE BASILAR BEDROCK ORGANIC PRIMARY RADICAL ABSOLUTE CARDINAL ORIGINAL RUDIMENT SUBSTRAT ULTIMATE PRIMORDIAL RUDIMENTARY
(PL.) ABCS NITTYGRITTY
FUNDAMENTALLY AUFOND
FUNDUS FORNIX
FUNERAL TANGI BURIAL EXEQUY BURYING CORTEGE FUNEBRE FUNERARY MORTUARY
FUNERAL DIRECTOR BLACKMAN
FUNEREAL BLACK FERAL DISMAL SOLEMN FUNEBRE FUNERAL DIRGEFUL EXEQUIAL MOURNFUL SEPULCHRAL
FUNGI MYCOFLORA
FUNGICIDE MANEB NABAM ZINEB CAPTAN FERBAM CALOMEL BORDEAUX DICHLONE
FUNGOID MYCOID FUNGOUS
FUNGOSO (FATHER OF —) SORDIDO
FUNGUS BUNT MOLD SMUT BLACK BRAND ERGOT FUNGE HYPHO MOREL MOULD PHOMA SPUNK SWARD TRUFF VALSA VERPI AGARIC BOLETE FUNGAL MILDEW OIDIUM AMANITA BOLETUS CHYTRID FUNGOID GEASTER LEPIOTA TRUFFLE AECIDIUM CLATHRUS CORNBELL EUMYCETE FUSARIUM HELVELLA MUCEDINE MUSHROOM OOMYCETE OTOMYCES PHALLOID POLYPORE PUFFBALL RHIZOPUS SAPROGEN SPOROGEN TREMELLA TUCKAHOE STINKHORN NEUROSPORA PENICILLIUM
(KIND OF —) PORE
(PLANT —) UREDO
(UNICELLULAR —) BEES EAST YEAST
(PREF.) AGARICI BASIDIO HYDNO MYC(ET)(ETO)(O)
(SUFF.) MYCES MYCET(O) MYCETE(S) MYCOSIS
(— DISEASE) OSIS
FUNK FUNG NESH
FUNKY HIP FOUL PANICKY
FUNNEL CAST STACK TEWEL TRUNK FILLER FUMMEL HOPPER SIPHON SYPHON TUNNEL TUNNER TRUMPET TUNDISH HYPONOME WINDSAIL
(UNDERGROUND —) SWALLET SWALLOW
(PREF.) CHOAN(O)
(SUFF.) CHOANITE CHOANITIC
FUNNY ODD GOOD COMIC DROLL MERRY QUEER COMICAL JOCULAR RISIBLE STRANGE HUMOROUS
(VERY —) SPLITTING SIDESPLITTING
FUR FOX BEAR CALF COON FLIX FLUE FOIN GRAY GREY GRIS MINK PEAN PELF PELL PILE SEAL VAIR BUDGE COYPU CROSS FITCH FLICK GENET GRISE OTTER PAHMI SABLE SCARF SHUBA BADGER BEAVER COUGAR DESMAN ERMINE FISHER GALYAC JACKET MARTIN NUTRIA PELAGE POTENT RABBIT SPRING SUSLIK TANUKI CALABER CARACAL FITCHET FITCHEW FURRURE MINIVER TOPCOAT CACOMIXL ERMINOIS KOLINSKI
(— OF LAMBSKIN AND WOOL) BUDGE
(— OF SABLE) ZIBELINE
(— RESEMBLING PERSIAN LAMB) KRIMMER
(BEAVER —) WOOM CASTOR
(GRAY —) GRAY GREY GRIS GRISE CRIMMER LETTICE
(HERALDIC —) PEAN
(LAMB —) CARACUL KARAKUL
(NUMBER OF — SKINS) TIMBER TIMMER
(RABBIT —) CONY SCUT CONEY FLICK LAPIN HATTER SUSLIK SEALINE SOUSLIK ERMILINE
(SQUIRREL —) SISEL CALABAR
(SQUIRREL OR MARTIN —) AMICE POPEL
(STONE MARTEN'S —) FOIN
(PL.) PELTRY FURRIERY
(PREF.) DORA
FURBEARER PLATINUM
FURBELOW DIDO FRILL FALBALA
FURBISH DO FIG RUB FAKE FINE VAMP CLEAN SCOUR FINIFY

POLISH BURNISH VARNISH RENOVATE
FURCATE FORKY BRANCH FURCAL
FURCULA SPRING FURCULUM
FURCULUM WISHBONE
FURFOOZ GRENELLE
FURIES DIRAE ALECTO ERINYS ERINYES MEGAERA ERINNYES TISIPHONE
FURIOUS MAD GRIM WOOD YOND ANGRY BRAIN GIDDY IRATE LIVID RABID SHARP FIERCE FURIAL FURIED INSANE RENISH STORMY ACHARNE FRANTIC HOPPING MADDING MANKIND PELTING RAGEOUS REDWOOD RUSHING TEARING VIOLENT FRENZIED MAENADIC TOWERING VEHEMENT VESUVIAN WRATHFUL
FURIOUSLY CRAZY ANGERLY TEARING
FURL FOLD HAND ROLL STOW WRAP FRESE TRUSS FARDEL FURDLE TAKEIN
FURLED IN
FURLONG SHOT STADE
FURLOUGH LEAVE BLIGHTY
FURNACE ARC KILN OVEN TANK BENCH CUPEL DRIER DRYER FORGE MOUTH TISAR BURNER CALCAR COCKLE CUPOLA HEATER ATHANOR CHAFERY CRESSET FIREPOT PUDDLER ROASTER BESSEMER BLOOMERY CALCINER CHAUFFER FIREWORK IRONCLAD LIMEKILN PRODUCER REFINERY TRYWORKS
(— DOOR) TWEEL
(ALMOND —) ALMAN
(ARC —) HEROULT
(GLASS-HEATING —) TISAR
(PLUMBER'S —) DEVIL
(PORTABLE —) DANDY CRESSET
FURNACEMAN BUSTLER DROSSER SMELTER IMPROVER REHEATER
FURNISH ARM SOW DECK FEAT FEED FILL FRET FRUB GIVE LEND TRIM VEST ARRAY BESEE ENDOW EQUIP FRAME INDUE PITCH POINT SERVE SPEED STOCK STORE STUFF AFFORD GRAITH INSURE INVEST OUTFIT RENDER SUPPLY ADVANCE APPAREL APPOINT BRACKET GARNISH INSTORE PERFORM PLENISH PRESENT PRODUCE PROVIDE SUFFICE ACCOUTER DECORATE FRUBBISH MINISTER ACCOMMODATE
(— ABUNDANTLY) FREQUENT
(— ANALYSIS) ACCOUNT
(— FULLY) CHARGE
(— REFRESHMENT) EASE
(— WITH) BESEE
(— WITH DRINK) BIRL BYRL
(— WITH MEALS) BOARD
(— WITH NEW PARTS) RETROFIT
(— WITH POWER) QUALIFY
(— WITH STEEP SLOPE) ESCARP
(— WITH STRENGTH) MAN
(— WITH TROOPS) GARRISON
(— WITH WINGS) IMP
FURNISHED ARMED BODEN GARNI
(COMFORTABLY —) BEIN
FURNISHING ADVANCE FITMENT
(PL.) STUFF BAGGAGE PENATES
FURNITURE ADAM BUHL TIRE SAMAN STOOL STUFF GRAITH FITMENT INSIGHT MEUBLES MOVABLE EQUIPAGE ORNAMENT SUPELLEX TACKLING
(— PIECE) ETAGERE
(CHEAP —) BORAX
(SHIP'S —) HARNESS
(STORED —) LUMBER
(STYLE OF —) SHERATON
FURORE FUROR BROUHAHA
FURRED PURED LOADED
FURRING PACKING
FURROW FUR GAP GAW RIB RUT FURR GRIP HINT LINE PLOW RAIN RILL ROUT RUCK SEAM SULK CHASE DRAIN DRILL EARTH FIELD RIGOL SCORE SEUGH STRIA GROOVE GUTTER INDENT SULCUS SUTURE TRENCH BREAKER CHAMFER CHANNEL CRUMPLE FEERING PLOWING QUILLET SCRATCH WINDROW WRINKLE CARRIAGE NOTAULIX THOROUGH VALLECULA
(PREF.) AULAC(O) HOLC(O) LIRELLI SULCI SULCO
FURROWED SEAMED EXARATE FURROWY SULCATE TRENCHED
FURROWING KNOT DRESS
FURRY SHAGGY
FUR SEAL URSAL
FURTHER MO AID YET ALSO HELP YOND ADDED AGAIN FRESH SPEED SUPRA BEYOND EXTEND SECOND ADVANCE DEVELOP FARTHER FORWARD PROMOTE MOREOVER REMANENT ULTERIOR
FURTHERMORE BESIDES FURTHER OVERMORE
FURTIVE SLY PRIVY CLAMMY SECRET SHIFTY SNEAKY HANGDOG MEACHING MYSTICAL SNEAKING STEALTHY THIEVISH CLANDESTINE
FURTIVELY SLILY SLYLY SIDELINS
FURTIVENESS STEALTH
FURUNCLE BOIL
FURY HAG IRE MAD WAX BURN RAGE ANGER BRETH DREAD FUROR IRISH RIGOR WRATH ALECTO BELDAM CHOLER FRENZY FURORE MADNESS MEGAERA WIDDRIM DELIRIUM FEROCITY VIOLENCE WOODNESS TISIPHONE
FURZE FUN FUZZ LING ULEX WHIN GORSE WHINCOW
FUSE RUN CAKE FLOW FLUX FRIT FUZE MELT WELD BLEND FOUND FUSEE FUZEE QUILL SMELT SQUIB SWAGE TRAIN UNITE MINGLE SPITTER COALESCE CONCRETE CONFLATE COPULATE PORTFIRE SAUCISSE COLLIQUATE
FUSED CONNATE
FUSEE FUZEE SPINDLE VESUVIAN VESUVIUS
FUSELAGE BODY
(— MEMBER) LONGERON
FUSIFORM FUSATE SPINDLE
FUSIL **(DIVIDED INTO —S)** PLUMETE
FUSION ZYG FLUX UNION FUSURE CHIASMA FLUXION CYTOGAMY MITAPSIS PLASMOGAMY
(PREF.) ZYG(O)(OTO)
(SUFF.) APSIS
FUSS DO ADO ROW TEW COIL FAFF FIKE FIRK FIZZ FRET ROUT SONG STIR TIME TODO TOUSE TOWSE TRADE WHAUP BOTHER CADDLE DIRDUM FANTAD FETTLE FISSLE FISTLE FIZZLE FRAISE FUFFLE FUSTLE HOORAY HURRAH PHRASE POTHER RACKET SETOUT STROTH TURNUP FOOSTER FRIGGLE FUSSIFY NAUNTLE POOTHER SPUFFLE SPUTTER TAMASHA BUSINESS FOOFARAW SCRONACH
FUSSBUDGET PRIG
FUSSBUDGETY SPOFFISH
FUSSINESS DAINTY FADDLE FIKERY FOOSTER
FUSSING BOTHER
FUSSY BUSY FIKY FIXY DITSY DITZY FUDGY PICKY CHICHI FIDDLY FIDFAD PROSSY SPOFFY SPRUCE STICKY FIDGETY NIGGLING NOTIONAL SPOFFISH SQUEAMISH PERSNICKETY
FUSTET ZANTE FUSTIC
FUSTIAN RANT HOLMES PILLOW BOMBAST TWADDLE CORDUROY MOLESKIN
FUSTIC LIME MORA FUSTET DYEWOOD AMARILLO
FUSTINESS FOIST FROWST
FUSTY FOIST MOLDY MUSTY FOISTY RANCID FROWSTY MALODOROUS
FUTILE IDLE TOOM VAIN OTIOSE USELESS BOOTLESS FECKLESS FOOTLESS FUTILOUS HELPLESS NUGATORY
FUTILITY VANITY NUGACITY VAINESSE
FUTTAH WHATA
FUTURE TOBE LATER SKULD AVENIR COMING ONWARD OPTION TOCOME TOWARD LAVENIR FUTURITY ONCOMING
(— TIME) MANANA
FUZZ LINTERS
FUZZY LINTY LOUSY MUZZY WOOLY WOOLLY
FYTTE PASSUS

G

G GEE GOLF GEORGE
GA AKRA ACCRA INKRA
GAAL **(FATHER OF —)** EBED
GAB GOB YAP BLAB CHIN CHINFEST
GABBLE WAB CANK CHAT CONK JAVER BABBLE GAGGLE HABBLE PATTER RABBLE TATTER YABBLE CLATTER JAUNDER TWADDLE TWITTER SLIPSLOP SLUMMOCK
GABBRO BOJITE NORITE EUCRITE
GABION KISH KEESH BASKET WALING CORBEIL
GABLE GAVEL GOFOL DETAIL DORMER GABLET KENNEL MEMBER PINION AILERON PEDIMENT
GABON **(CAPITAL OF —)** LIBREVILLE
(LAKE OF —) ANENGUE AZINGUO
(MOUNTAIN OF —) MPELE IBOUNDJI
(NATIVE OF —) FANG ADOUMA ECHIRA OKANDE
(RIVER OF —) ABANGA IVINDA OGOOUE NGOUNIE
(TOWN OF —) OYEM BONGO KANGO MITZIC OMVANE MAKOKOU
GABOON OKOUME
GABRIELINO TOBIKHAR
GAD GAR RUN FISK GAUD JAZZ RAKE JINKET GADLING TRAIPSE VIRETOT
(— ABOUT) HAIK ROLL STRAM GALLANT TROLLOP
(BROTHER OF —) ASHER
(FATHER OF —) JACOB
(MOTHER OF —) ZILPAH
GADABOUT GAD GOER GADDER TRAIPSE
GADDI **(FATHER OF —)** SUSI
GADFLY GAD CLEG GLEG BRIZE CLEGG STOUT WHAME BOTFLY BREEZE GADBEE OESTRID TABANID HORSEFLY
(PREF.) ESTRA ESTRI ESTRO OESTR(I)
GADGET DODAD GISMO GIZMO HICKY DINGUS DOODAD GILGUY HICKEY JIGGER JIMJAM WIDGET CONCERN DOFUNNY GIMMICK WHATNOT BUSINESS DOHICKEY GIMCRACK JIMCRACK HOOTNANNY CONTRAPTION THINGAMAJIG WHANGDOODLE
(PL.) GIBBLES GUBBINS GADGETRY
GADI **(SON OF —)** MENAHEM
GADUS MORRHUA
GADWALL RODGE VOLANT GADWELL REDWING SHUTTLE
GAEL CELT KELT SCOT GOIDEL GAEDHEAL
GAELIC ERSE IRISH
GAFF CLIP SPAR SPUR YARD GAFFLE GABLOCK GAFFLET SLASHER GAVELOCK
(— MACKEREL) GAMBEER
GAFFE SLIP
GAFFER STAGEHAND
GAG YAK YUK BOFF GEGG JOKE PONG SCOB YOCK YUCK HEAVE KEVEL SCOBE AGUAJI MUZZLE WHEEZE
(KIND OF —) SIGHT
GAGA **(GO —)** FLIP
GAGARIN YURI
GAGE (ALSO SEE GAUGE) LAY PAWN WAGE GAUGE JEDGE NORMA WAGER FEELER PLEDGE SPIDER SCANTLE STANDARD UDOMETER
GAHAM **(FATHER OF —)** NAHOR
(MOTHER OF —) REUMAH
GAHERIS **(MOTHER OF —)** MORGANSE
GAIETY JOY GALA JEST RANT CHEER MIRTH BAWDRY FROLIC GAYETY LEVITY BAUDERY BEGONIA DAFFERY DAFFING GAYNESS JOLLITY JOYANCE ROLLICK BUOYANCY FESTIVAL HILARITY VIVACITY
(NOISY —) RACKET
GAILY GAY GAYLY BRAVELY LIGHTLY
GAIN BAG DAP GET NET POT WIN BEAR BOOT DRAW GROW HAVE LAND MAKE PELF SACK TILL ADDLE BOOTY CATCH LATCH LUCRE REACH SCORE ARRIVE ATTAIN CHIEVE DERIVE GATHER INCOME OBTAIN PROFIT RACKUP STRAIN CAPTURE CONQUER EMBRACE GAYMENT GETTING HARVEST POSSESS PROCURE REALIZE VANTAGE WINNING CLEANING CONQUEST PURCHASE PERQUISITE
(— ADMISSION) ENTER
(— ADVANTAGE) GLEEK
(— ASCENDANCY) PREVAIL
(— BY EXTORTION) SQUEEZE
(— BY FORTUNE) DRAW HAZARD
(— COMMAND OF) MASTER
(— IN FAVOR) PROPITIATE
(— KNOWLEDGE) EDIFY LEARN
(— OVER) ENGAGE
(— UNDERSTANDING) SMOKE
(— WITHOUT DEDUCTION) CLEAR
(DISHONEST —) MEED
(ESTIMATED —) ESTEEM
(ILL-GOTTEN —) PELF BOODLE
(ILLICIT —) SPLOSH
(MATERIAL —) PUDDING
(UNEXPECTED —) BUNCE
(PL.) PICKING PLUNDER GANANCIAS
GAINFUL LUCROUS GAINSOME
GAINSAY DENY FORBID IMPUGN OPPOSE REFUTE RESIST DISPUTE RECLAIM WITHSAY AGAINSAY CONTRAVENE
GAIT BAT JOG GANG LOPE PACE RACK SKIP STEP TROT VOLT WALK AMBLE AUBIN GOING STALK TRAIN ALLURE CANTER GALLOP LOUNGE SLOUCH SWINGE TODDLE WADDLE WALLOW WAMBLE WOBBLE DOGTROT HICKORY PIAFFER SAUNTER SCUTTLE SHAMBLE SHUFFLE WALKING WAUCHLE
(— OF ILL-BROKEN HORSE) CHACK
(DEFECTIVE —) WINDING
(LIMPING —) HIRPLE
(UNGAINLY —) SLOUCH
(UNSTEADY —) STAGGER
(4-BEAT —) AMBLE
GAITER SPAT VAMP STRAD BONNET BRAGAS COCKER GASKIN GUETRE HOGGER HUGGER LEGGIN PUTTEE GAMBADE GAMBADO LEGGING STARTUP BOOTIKIN CUTTIKIN SPATTERDASH
(PL.) UPPERS GASKINS GAMASHES GRAMOCHES
GAIZE MALMSTONE
GAJO GORGIO
GALABIA ROBE
GALACTITE MILKSTONE
GALACTOSIDE IDEIN IDAEIN
GALAGO LEMUR LEMUROID
GALAHAD **(MOTHER OF —)** ELAINE
GALAL **(FATHER OF —)** ASAPH JEDUTHUN
GALANAS GAINES
GALAOR **(BROTHER OF —)** AMADIS
GALATEA **(DAUGHTER OF —)** LEUCIPPUS
(FATHER OF —) NEREUS
(HUSBAND OF —) PYGMALION
(LOVER OF —) ACIS
(MOTHER OF —) DORIS
(SON OF —) PAPHUS METHARME
GALAX COLTSFOOT
GALAXY NEBULA SPIRAL
(KIND OF —) SEYFERT
(PREF.) GALACT(O)
GALBANUM FERULA GALBAN ALBETAD
GALCHA PAMIR
GALE BLOW GELL HELM WIND GAGEL PERRY STOUR BUSTER EASTER BAYBUSH BURSTER GALEAGE TEMPEST FLEAWOOD GALEWORT NORWESTER
(KIND OF —) NEAR
GALEA MITRA HELMET
GALGA INGUSH
GALIBI CARIBI KALINA
GALINGALE CYPRESS WANHORN CHINAROOT
GALIPOT BARRAS GALLIPOT TACAMAHAC
GALJOEN BLACKFISH
GALL GA GAW BAIT FELL FRET NERVE WRING ANBURY COCKLE HARASS HUTZPA ANBERRY BEDEGAR CHUTZPA GALLNUT HUTZPAH KNOPPER NUTGALL BEDEGUAR CECIDIUM CHUTZPAH FLEASEED IRRITATE OAKBERRY SEEDGALL SPURGALL TACAHOUT
(SAND —) SALT NATRON SANDIVER
(PL.) PURPLES
(PREF.) CHOL(E)(O)
(SUFF.) CHOLIA CHOLY
GALLANT GAY BEAU PROW BLADE BRAVE BULLY CIVIL JOLLY LOVER NOBLE PREUX SHOWY SPARK SWAIN DONZEL ESCORT HEROIC POLITE RUTTER SPARKY SQUIRE SUITOR AMATORY AMORIST AMOROSO AMOROUS CONDUCT GALANTE GREGORY SPARKER STATELY TOPPING YOUNKER BELAMOUR CAVALIER CICISBEO FEMALIST GALLIARD HANDSOME POLISHED
GALLANTRY GAME DRURY DRUERY BRAVERY COURAGE PROWESS CHIVALRY PARAMOUR
GALLBERRY INKBERRY
GALLED RAW
GALLEON CARAC CARRACK GALLOON
GALLERY POY SAP COOP GODS JUBE LOFT PAWN ALURE BOYAU ORIEL PRADO ARCADE BURROW DEDANS NARROW PIAZZA SCHOOL SOLLAR SUBWAY TUNNEL BALCONY GALERIE HEADWAY MIRADOR TERRACE VERANDA BARTISAN BRATTICE CANTORIA CORRIDOR HOARDING PARADISE PERAMBLE SCAFFOLD TRAVERSE VERANDAH BLINDSTORY
(— IN BAZAAR) PAWN
(— IN HOUSE OF COMMONS) VENTILATOR
(— MADE BY INSECT) MINE
(— OF FORT) CASEMATE
(CHURCH —) JUBE LAFT LOFT
(MINE —) BORD BROW SLOVAN
(MINSTREL'S —) ORIEL
(OPEN —) LOGGIA
(UNDERGROUND —) HYPOGEE HYPOGEUM
GALLEY FUST CUDDY DRAKE FOIST STICK BIREME GALIOT HEARTH ZYGITE BASTARD CABOOSE DROMOND GALLIOT HEXERIS KITCHEN LYMPHAD TRIREME UNIREME CAMBOOSE COOKROOM CROMSTER GALLEASS RAMBERGE

(— BOTTOM) SLICE
(CHIEFTAIN'S —) BIRLING BIRLINN
(PHILIPPINE —) CALAN
(VIKING —) AESC DRAKE
GALLEY SLAVE FORSADO SFORZATO
GALLFLY CYNIPID
GALLIMAUFRY HASH OLIO
GALLINACEOUS RASORIAL
GALLINAE RASORES
GALLINAZO VIRU VULTURE
GALLING BITTER
GALLINULE COOT KORA MOHO RAIL GORHEN PUKEKO SKITTY MOORHEN STANKIE SULTANA DABCHICK HYACINTH MANUALII RAILBIRD RICEBIRD SWAMPHEN
GALLIVANT KITE ROAM ROVE GALLANT
GALLNUT
(PREF.) CECIDIO CEDIDO
GALLON GAWN CONGIUS
(— OF ORE) DISH
(EIGHTH —) OCTARIUS
(HALF —) POTTLE
(128 —S) LEAGUER
GALLOON ORRIS
GALLOP FOG RUN AUBIN PRICK CANTER CAREER COURSE TITTUP WALLOP TANTIVY
GALLOWS NUB CRAP DROP FORK TREE BOUGH CHEAT FURCA WIDDY GIBBET WOODIE DERRICK FORCHES JUSTICE POTENCE STIFLER WARYTREE
GALLOWS BIRD HEMPY WIDDY HEMPIE HEMPSEED WIDDIFOW CRACKROPE
GALOOT OAF
GALOSH ARCTIC ZIPPER EXCLUDER OVERSHOE
GALUTH GOLUS GOLAHI
GALVANIC VOLTAIC
GALVANIZE ZINC ZINCIFY SHERADISE
GALVANOMETER DETECTOR REOMETER
GAMBADO BOOT ANTIC CAPER GAITER LEGGING
GAMBESON WAMBAIS
GAMBIA (CAPITAL OF —) BANJUL
(COIN OF —) BUTUT DALASI
(LANGUAGE OF —) JOLA WOLOF FULANI MALINKE
(MONEY OF —) DALASI
(NATIVE OF —) JOLA PEUL WOLOF DIOLAS FULANI MANDINGO SERAHULI
(TOWN OF —) KAUUR MANSA FATOTO BINTANG BRIKAMA KUNTAUR
GAMBIA POD BABLOH
GAMBIER CATECHU
GAMBIT PLOY MANEUVER
GAMBLE BET DICE GAFF GAME NICK PLAY PUNT RISK SPORT STAKE WAGER CHANCE GAMMON HAZARD PLUNGE FLUTTER
(— AGAINST) BUCK
GAMBLER PIKER SPORT CARROW DEALER PLAYER PUNTER HUSTLER PLAYMAN PLUNGER SLICKER THROWER BLACKLEG GAMESTER HAZARDER
GAMBLER, THE (CHARACTER IN —) ALEXEY BLANCHE PAULINE
(COMPOSER OF —) PROKOFIEV
GAMBLING GAMING HAZARDRY
(— CHARGE) VIG VIGORISH
(— DEVICE) PACHINKO
GAMBLING HOUSE HELL TRIPOT
GAMBO GOOSE SPURWING
GAMBOL HOP PLAY ROMP CAPER FRISK KEVEL PRANK CAREER CAVORT FROLIC PRANCE GAMBADO CAPRIOLE
GAMBREL ROOF CAMMOCK SPREADER
GAME COB FUN JEU JIG GAMY LAKE MAIL PLAY DANCE DOZEN GAMEY PARTY SPIEL SPORT WATHE BATTUE DOZENS MORRIS QUARRY RAMSCH VENERY JENKINS KNICKER BREATHER FIGHTING FOREGAME FRONTENIS
(— CALLED FIVES) HANDBALL
(— EASILY WON) LAUGHER
(— FOR FISHERMEN) SKISH
(— LIKE HANDBALL) FIVES
(— LIKE HOCKEY) DODDART
(— NARROWLY WON) SQUEAKER
(— OF CAT) BILLET
(— OF FIVE HUNDRED) EUCHRE
(— OF FOOTBALL) BOWL CAMP
(— OF FORFEITS) KEN
(— OF HOCKEY) BANDY SHINNY
(— OF INSULTS) DOZENS
(— OF MARBLES) TAW BOWL BONCE GULLY KEEPS KNUCKS MIGGLES
(— OF MENTAL SKILL) GO CHESS CHECKERS
(— OF NINEPINS) KAILS KAYLES
(— OF PRISONER'S BASE) CHEVY CHIVVY
(— WITH BOOMERANG) BRIST
(— WITH COUNTERS) DUMPS GOOSE
(— WITH SHUTTLECOCK) TAHYING
(BACKGAMMON —) HIT IRISH
(BALL —) CAT TUT SNOB CATCH RUGBY SOCCER SQUASH TENNIS CRICKET KNAPPAN ONEOCAT BASEBALL FOOTBALL HANDBALL SLUGFEST SOFTBALL BROOMBALL
(BASQUE —) JAI
(CALL THE —) UMP
(CARD —) AS HOC LOO MAW NAP PAM PIT PUT SET BRAG CENT FARO FISH FROG GRAB JASS LANT PINK POOL POPE POST RUFF SANT SKAT SLAM SNAP SOLO STUD VINT BEAST BUNCO BUNKO CARDS CARIE CHICO CINCH COMET CRIMP DECOY GILET GLEEK GRAND LEAST MONTE NODDY OMBER OMBRE PEDRO PITCH POKER PRIME RUMMY SCOPA SLAMM STOPS STUSS TRUMP WHIST BANKER BASSET BIRKIE BOODLE BOSTON BRIDGE CASINO CHEMMY COMMIT ECARTE EIGHTS EUCHRE FARMER FLINCH HEARTS HOWELL LOADUM PANFIL PIQUET QUINZE RAMSCH ROUNCE SLOUGH SMUDGE SPIDER TOURNE AUCTION AUTHORS BELOTTE BEZIQUE CANASTA CASSINO CAYENNE CHICAGO COONCAN GARBAGE HUNDRED JACKPOT PLAFOND PONTOON PRIMERO REVERSI SCOPONE SETBACK TRIUMPH VINGTUN VITESSE BACCARAT BASEBALL BRISCOLA COMMERCE CONQUIAN CONTRACT CRIBBAGE FREAKPOT HANDICAP IMPERIAL NAPOLEON PATIENCE PENCHANT PENNEECH PINOCHLE SHOWDOWN SKINBALL SKINNING SLAPJACK TREDILLE TRESILLO VERQUERE VIDERUFF
(CARNIVAL —) HOOPLA
(CHILDREN'S —) TAG DIBS JACKS KICKBALL PEEKABOO
(CONFIDENCE —) RAMP SCAM STING MURPHY BIGMITT
(COURSE —) GOLF
(COURT —) PELOTA SQUASH TENNIS HANDBALL
(DICE —) FARE TRAY BINGO CRAPS NOVUM RAPHE HAZARD BARBUDI ADDITION BARBOTTE CAMEROON HOOLIGAN
(DRAWN —) SPOIL REFAIT
(DRINKING —) HIJINKS
(EGYPTIAN —) SENT SENIT
(FOLLOW THE —) HUNT
(GAMBLING —) EO TAN FARO HAND KENO PICO BOULE CRAPS MACAO MONTE POKER PROPS RONDO STUSS BRELAN HAZARD RONDEAU ROULETTE
(GENERAL —) HEI HIT HOB NIM TAG TAW TIG BALL BASE BULL BUNT BUZZ CENT DIBS DUCK FARE GOLF HOLE JOWL KENO MALL PALM POLO POOL SLAM SNOB TICK BANDY BINGO BONCE BOULE CHESS CHUBA CHUNK CLOSH DARTS DOLOS FIVES GOOSE HALMA HOUSE IRISH JACKS LOTTO LURCH NOVUM NULLO PITCH PUSSY RUGBY SALTA SALVO SCRUB TOUCH TROCO WHOOP BEAVER BEETLE CAROMS CHIVVY CHUNKY CLUMPS COBNUT COCKAL COOTIE CRAMBO FEEDER GOBANG GRACES HAZARD HOOPLA HUBBUB JEREED KAYLES MERELE PACHIS PELOTA PLUMPS RAGMAN RINGER SEESAW SHINNY SIPPIO SKILLO STICKS TENNIS TIGTAG TIPCAT TIVOLI TRIGON TRUCKS BALLOON BEANBAG BEEBALL BOWLING COBBLER CONKERS CROQUET CURLING DIABOLO DODDART DOUBLES DREIDEL ENDBALL GOGGANS HANGMAN HURLBAT LOGGATS MAHJONG MATADOR MUGGINS NETBALL PALLONE PASSAGE PEEVERS PUSHPIN QUINTET RINGTAW SARDINE SQUAILS STATUES TENPINS TOMBOLA ANAGRAMS BALKLINE BASEBALL CHARADES CHECKERS CHOUETTE DOMINOES DOUBLETS DRAUGHTS DUCKPINS FIVEPINS FOOTBALL FORFEITS GIVEAWAY HARDHEAD KICKBALL KORFBALL LEAPFROG NINEPINS PARCHESI PEEKABOO PETANQUE PURPOSES PUSHBALL PYRAMIDS RINGTOSS ROULETTE ROUNDERS SCRABBLE SKITTLES STOBBALL STOWBALL TRAPBALL VERQUERE PARCHEESI PHILOPENA SHUFFLEBOARD
(GUESSING —) LOVE MORA CANUTE
(INDIAN —) CHUNKY HUBBUB
(INFERIOR —) CHECK
(JAPANESE —) GO
(KIND OF —) VIDEO
(MEXICAN —) FRONTENIS
(NUMBERS —) BUG
(OUTDOOR —) GOLF POLO HURLY ROQUE RUGBY SOCCER CROQUET HURLING BASEBALL FOOTBALL LACROSSE
(PROGRESSIVE —) DRIVE
(PUZZLE —) GLAIK
(QUIZZING —) TRIVIA
(REHEATED —) SALMI SALMIS
(SWINDLING —) BUNCO BUNKO
(SWISS —) JASS
(THREE BOWLING —S) SERIES
(TRAPSHOOTING —) SCOOT
(VIDEO —) ATARI
(WAR —) BARRIERS
(WORD —) GHOST HANGMAN ANAGRAMS
(PL.) LUDI
GAMECOCK STAG STAIG
GAMEKEEPER GAMIE KEEPER WALKER WARNER VENERER WARRENER
GAMESTER DICER PLAYER GAMBLER PLAYMAN SHARPER HAZARDER TABLEMAN
GAMETE OVUM SPERM OOCYTE ZYGOTE GAMETOID OOGAMETE OOSPHERE
GAMETOCYTE GAMONT CRESCENT GONOCYTE
GAMETOPHYTE GERMLING
GAMIN TAD ARAB URCHIN GAVROCHE
GAMMA AGMA
GAMMON BAM
GAMP ORRIS UMBRELLA
GAMUT GAMME RANGE SCALE SERIES COMPASS DIAGRAM
GANDAREWA (SLAYER OF —) KERESASPA
GANDER STEG STAIG GANNER
(— AND GEESE) SET
GANDHARI (HUSBAND OF —) DHRITARASHTRA
GANEF RASCAL
GANESA GUNPUT GANAPATI
GANG MOB SET BAND BUND CORE CREW GING PACK PAIR PUSH TEAM BATCH BUNCH GROUP HORDE SPELL SQUAD CHIURM COFFLE GAGGLE LAYOUT MOHOCK SCHOOL COMPANY
(— MEMBER) WHYO
(— MEMBER) SKINHEAD
(— OF CONVICTS) PUSH
(— OF FISHHOOKS) PULLDEVIL
(— OF MINERS) CORE
(— OF WITCHES) COVEN

(GROUP OF —S) MAFIA
(ROWDY —) TRIBULATION
GANGBUSTERS SOCKO
GANGLING GAWKY RANGY GANGLY
GANGLION TUMOR CEREBRUM
GANGPLANK BROW GANGWAY
GANGRENE NOMA CANKER GANGER SPHACEL NECROSIS MORTIFICATION
(PREF.) NECR(O) SPHACELO
GANGSTER HOOD PUNK WHYO APACHE BANDIT COWBOY GUNMAN GUNSEL CHOPPER
GANGUE MATRIX LODESTUFF VEINSTONE
GANGWAY BROW ROAD SLIP LOGWAY TUNNEL CATWALK COULOIR GATEWAY
GANJA GUNJAH CANNABIS
GANNET BOOBY GAUNT SOLAN PIQUERO SEAFOWL ALCATRAS
GANTRYMAN DROPMAN
GANYMEDE (BROTHER OF —) ILUS ASSARACUS
(FATHER OF —) TROS
(MOTHER OF —) CALLIRRHOE
GAOLER (ALSO SEE JAILER) ADAM ALCAIDE
GAP SAG FLAW GAPE GOWL GULF MUSE NICK SLAP SLOP WANT BREAK BRECK CHASM CHAUM CHAWN CLOVE FRITH MEUSE MUSET NOTCH SHARD SHERD VUIDE BREACH GULLET HIATUS LACUNA SPREAD THROAT VACUUM CLOSING OPENING VACANCY VACUITY APERTURE DIASTEMA ENTREFER INTERVAL MULTIGAP QUEBRADA
(— IN BANK OF STREAM) GAT
(— IN FENCE) SLAP
(— IN FOOTBALL LINE) SLOT
(— IN MEMORY) AMNESIA
(— IN TURF) BUNKER
(— SERVING AS PASS) COL
(VOCAL CORD —) RIMA
(PREF.) CHASMO
GAPE GAN GAP GANT GAUP GAWK GAWP GAZE GOVE GRIN YAWN CHAUN GERNE HIATE STARE RICTUS DEHISCE INHIATE
(PREF.) CHAEN(O)
GAPER COMBER
GAPING GALP AGAPE HIANT CHAPPY CHASMA GAWISH MOUTHED RINGENT ADENOIDAL
GAR HOUND SNOOK AGUJON CHERNA GARFISH GARPIKE BILLFISH GOREFISH GURDFISH HORNBEAK HORNFISH HORNKECK LONGJAWS LONGNOSE
GARAGE HANGAR LOCKUP SIDING GARRIDGE
(ROW OF —S) MEWS
GARAM MASALA SPICES
GARAVANCE CARAUNA GARBANZO
GARB (ALSO SEE APPAREL AND DRESS) COWL GEAR TOGA VEST DRESS GUISE HABIT STOLA APPAREL CLOTHES COSTUME RAIMENT GLADRAGS
(LIGHT —) STRIP
(MUSLIM —) IHRAM
(PARTICOLORED —) MOTLEY
(PLAY —) ROMPERS
(RED —) SCARLET
(SPECIAL —) REGALIA
(UNIVERSITY —) ACADEMICALS
GARBAGE GASH SLOP OFFAL TRASH WASTE GIBLET REFUSE SCRAPS
(— IN — OUT) GIGO
(— IN, — OUT) GIGO
GARBAGEMAN DUSTMAN
GARBLE GELD JUMBLE MANGLE DISTORT GARBLING MUTILATE MISREPRESENT
GARDANT AFFRONTE
GARDEN HAW EDEN KNOT TILL YARD ARBOR GARTH CIRCLE POMACY POMARY QUINTA ROSARY SHAMBA VERGER VIHARA ACADEMY HERBARY OLITORY ORCHARD ROCKERY TOPIARY CHINAMPA FLORETUM HORTYARD KALEYARD LEIGHTON PARADISE PARTERRE POTAGERE ROSARIUM CULTIVATE
(— CITY) CHICAGO
(— PLOT) ERF
(— STATE) NEWJERSEY
(BEER —) BRASSERIE
(SECLUDED —) PLEASANCE
(PREF.) HORT(I) TOPI
(SUFF.) ETUM
GARDENER MALI PONICA TILLER CROPPER PLANNER BOSTANGI
GARDEN HELIOTROPE VALERIAN
GARDENIA TIARA
GARDENING TOPIARY
GARDEN ROCKET RUGOLA ARUGULA EVEWEED
GARDEN-VARIETY AVERAGE
GARDEN WARBLER JACK HAYBIRD BECAFICO FAUVETTE FIGEATER
GARFISH (SEE GAR)
GARGAMELLE (SON OF —) GARGANTUA
GARGANEY TEAL CRICK
GARGANTUA AND PANTAGRUEL
(AUTHOR OF —) RABELAIS
(CHARACTER IN —) JOHN BRIDE BACBUC TRIPPE BADEBEC PANURGE ANARCHUS JOBERLIN GARGANTUA TRIBOULET GARGAMELLE GRANGOSIER HOLOFERNES PANTAGRUEL PICROCHOLE PONOCRATES ENTOMMEURES TROUILLOGAN RAMINAGROBIS
GARGANTUAN HUGE VAST GIANT HOMERIC TITANIC ENORMOUS GIGANTIC HOMERIAN
GARGET MASTITIS
GARGLE GURGLE COLLUTORY
GARGOYLE BOSS
GARIBALDI GOLDFISH
GARISH GAUDY GIDDY SHOWY CRIANT GLARING
GARISHNESS GLARE
GARLAND BAY LEI CROWN TORAN VITTA ANADEM CORONA CRANTS ROSARY WREATH CHAPLET CORANCE CORONAL FESTOON
(PREF.) STEMMATI STEPHAN(O)
GARLIC AJO MOLY RAMP CHIVE PORET ALLIUM PORRET RAMSON
GARMENT GI DUD TOG BACK BRAT COAT GOWN PELL PELT RAIL ROBE SARI SARK SHAG SILK SLIP SLOP SULU VEST WEED ABAYA BUREL BURKA CENTO CLOAK CLOTH COTTE CYMAR DRESS FROCK HABIT HAORI JOSEY JUPON KHAKI MANGA NABOB SHAWL SHIFT SHIRT SIMAR SKIRT STOLE WRIEL ALPACA ATTIRE BARROW BLOUSE BOUBOU BURKHA CAFTAN CAMLET CAPOTE CHAMMA COTTON CYCLAS ERMINE EXOMIS FECKET HUIPIL JACKET JERSEY JUMPER KERSEY KIRTLE MOHAIR MOTLEY SARONG SHORTY SHROUD STROUD TAMEIN ZIZITH AMICTUS BLOUSON BROIGNE BUNTING CAMBLET CASSOCK CHIRIPA CRAWLER CUCULLA CULOTTE DOUBLET FALDING FLOCKET GROGRAM PALETOT PELISSE RAIMENT SHORTIE SURCOAT SWEATER VESTURE WRAPPER BATHROBE BODYSUIT CAMELINE CAPUCHIN CHAUSSES COLOBIUM CORSELET COVERALL DEERSKIN EPIBLEMA GAMBESON GUERNSEY HIMATION INDUMENT PADUASOY PULLOVER SCAPULAR SEALSKIN SLIPOVER SNOWSUIT VESTMENT WEARABLE PETTICOAT REDINGOTE STROUDING
(— OF DERVISH) KHIRKAH
(— OF HERALD) TABARD
(— OF HIGH PRIEST) EPHOD
(— OF PATCHES) CENTO
(ARAB —) ABA
(ARABIAN —) ABA
(BABY'S —) BARROW CRAWLER CREEPER
(BADLY-MADE —) DRECK
(BLUE —) MAZARINE
(BURIAL —) SHROUD
(COARSE —) BRAT STROUD
(DEFENSIVE —) JACK BROIGNE GAMBESON
(ECCLESIASTICAL —) STOLE RHASON ROCHET CASSOCK
(ECCLIASTICAL —) FANON ORALE CHASUBLE
(ETHIOPIAN —) CHAMMA
(HINDU —) SARI SAREE
(INFANT'S —) BARRY BARROW DIAPER BUNTING SLEEPER PANTYWAIST
(INQUISITION —) SANBENITO
(JAPANESE —) HAORI
(LEATHER —) BUFF
(LINEN —) LINE
(LONG —) JIBBA KANZU STOLE JIBBEH MANDYAS PELISSE HIMATION
(MALAY —) SARONG
(MEDIEVAL —) ROCHET CHAUSSES DALMATIC GAMBESON
(MONK'S —) SCAPULAR
(MOURNING —) SABLE
(ONE-PIECE —) BODYSUIT JUMPSUIT
(ONE-PIECE WOMAN'S —) CATSUIT
(OUTER —) BRAT COAT GOWN HAIK HYKE SLOP WRAP FROCK HAORI NABOB PALLA PILCH SMOCK DOLMAN ROCHET CHEMISE GALABIA PALETOT SURCOAT SWEATER HIMATION OVERSLOP
(PADDED —) TRUSS
(PENITENTIAL —) CILICE
(PULLOVER —) DASHIKI
(RED —) SCARLET
(ROMAN —) TOGA
(SLEEVELESS —) ABA CAPE COWL VEST MANTLE CUCULLA GANDURAH
(SQUARE —) KAROSS
(SYRIAN —) ABAYA
(THIN —) GOSSAMER
(TIGHT-FITTING —) HOSE COTTE TRICOT LEOTARD
(WOMAN'S —) IZAR BURKA CYMAR NABOB SIMAR BURKHA CHITON JOSEPH PEPLOS PEPLUM VISITE BLOUSON BURNOUS
(PL.) GEAR COSTUME GARNISH FLANNELS
(PREF.) RHACO
GARNER REAP MOPUP STORE GATHER IMBARN COLLECT
GARNET YAG YIG GRENAT PYROPE ANTHRAX GRANATE OLIVINE VERMEIL ESSONITE MELANITE ROSOLITE YANOLITE CARBUNCLE RHODOLITE UVAROVITE
(SYNTHETIC —) YAG
(YTTRIUM IRON —) YIG
GARNISH LARD TRIM ADORN DRESS EQUIP MENSE STICK FURNISH PARSLEY TOPPING CHUMMAGE DECORATE DUXELLES ORNAMENT
GARNISHED GARNI
(— WITH GRAPES) VERONIQUE
(— WITH VEGETABLES) BOUQUETIERE
GARNISHEE CHECK FACTOR GARNISH
GARRET ATTIC SOLAR SOLLAR MANSARD COCKLOFT
GARRISON WARD STUFF PRESIDY WARNISON
GARROTE STRANGLE
GARRULITY POLYLOGY
GARRULOUS GABBY TALKY WORDY BABBLY TONGUY VOLUBLE
GARTER GARTEN LEGLET ELASTIC STRAPPLE
GARTH CORTILE OUTGARTH
GARUM LIQUAMEN
GAS DAMP XENON FLATUS GENAPP LEAVEN OXYGEN PETROL EXHAUST KRYPTON PROPANE YPERITE AFTERGAS ETHERION FIREDAMP HYDROGEN STANNANE VESICANT
(— CONSTANT) R
(— FUEL) ETHANE
(COLORLESS —) OXAN OXANE KETENE GERMANE STIBINE SILICANE
(EXPLOSIVE —) METHYLAMINE
(KIND OF —) NERVE
(MARSH —) METHANE
(NERVE —) SARIN
(NONCOMBUSTIBLE —) INERT
(POISONOUS —) ARSINE ADAMSITE AQUINITE CYANOGEN PHOSGENE BRETONITE PHOSPHINE

(RADIOACTIVE —) THORON
(TEAR —) ACROLEIN
(VOLCANIC —) MOFETTE
(PREF.) MANO PNEUM(O)(ON) (ONO) PNEUMA PNEUMAT(O)
(CONTAINING —) PYOPNEUMO
(PRESENCE OF —) PHYS(O)
(SUFF.) **(INERT —)** ON
GAS-BURNER BUNSEN
GASCONADE BRAG CROW BOAST BLUSTER
GASEOUS AERIFORM GASIFORM VOLATILE
GASH CUT CHOP LASH BLASH CRIMP GANCH GRIDE SCORE SLASH SLISH SCOTCH SLUICE TRENCH INCISION INCISURE
(— A FISH) RIM
GASKET LUTE CASKET GASKIN GROMMET SCISSIL
GASKIN BRAGAS
GASOLINE AVGAS JUICE PETROL BENZINE NATURAL
GASP FOB BLOW GAPE KINK PANK PANT CHINK CROAK FETCH THRATCH
GASPING CHINK
GASTEROPOD WHELK STROMB UNICORN PTEROPOD
GASTRONOME EPICURE
GASTROPOD SLUG DRILL HARPA OLIVA SNAIL BUCKIE NERITE ABALONE MOLLUSK TOXIFER UNIVALVE VELUTINA PULMONATE PROSOBRANCH
GAT HEATER
GATAM (FATHER OF —) ELIPHAZ
GATE BAB BAR JET HEAD LIFT PORT SASH SLAP TAKE YATE YETT ENTRY HATCH JANUA PURSE SALLY SPRAY STICK TORAN ENAJIM ESCAPE FENDER FUNNEL HARROW INGATE LIGGAT PADDLE PORTAL RUNNER TIMBER TORANA WICKET ZAGUAN BARRIER CLICKET FIVEBAR GATEWAY LIDGATE POSTERN SHUTTER ABOIDEAU ANTEPORT DECUMANA ENTRANCE FOREGATE GURDWARA PENSTOCK TOLLGATE TOWNGATE TRIMTRAM TURNPIKE ELECTRODE
(— OF CASTLE) BAR
(— OF DRYDOCK) CAISSON
(BACK —) POSTERN
(COMPUTER —) AND
(CUSTOMS —) BARRIER
(IRRIGATION —) CHECK TAPON TAPPOON
(LICH —) SCALLAGE TRIMTRAM
(RUNNING —) FUNNEL
(SAW —) FRAME
(SAWMILL —) SASH
(SLALOM —S) HAIRPIN
(SLUICE —) HATCH VALVE
(TEMPLE —) VIMANA
(TIDE —) ABOIDEAU ABOITEAU
(WATER —) SLUICE
(PREF.) PYL(E)
GATEADO DIOMATE
GATEHOUSE BAR LODGE
GATEKEEPER WARDEN CERBERUS GATEWARD PORTITOR STILEMAN
GATEMAN GUARD
GATEPOST DURN HARR HEEL PIER POST SHAFT POSTEL
GATEWAY DAR DOOR GATE LOKE PORT TORU PYLON TORAN TORII BARWAY GOPURA TORANA PROPYLON
(COMPUTER —) PORT
GATHER GET LEK POD WIN BAND BREW CLAN CLOT CROP CULL FURL HERD HIVE HOST PICK REAP RELY TUCK AMASS BANGE BROOM BUNCH FLOCK GLEAN GUESS INFER LEASE PLUCK RAISE SWEEP ACCRUE COMPEL CORRAL DECERP DERIVE GARNER HUDDLE HUSTLE IMBARN MUSTER RAMASS SCRAPE CLUSTER COLLATE COLLECT COMPILE CONGEST CONVENE CONVOKE HARVEST RAMMASS RECRUIT ASSEMBLE CUMULATE SHEPHERD
(— AS ARMY) HOST
(— BY SCRAPING) SCRATCH
(— GRAPES) VINDEMIATE
(— GRASS SEED) STRIP
(— HEADWAY) SET
(— HERBS) SIMPLE
(— IN A HEAP) HATTER
(— IN RAGS) TAT
(— SEWING) GAGE GAUGE
(— UP) KILT
(SUFF.) LEGE
GATHERED KILTED CUMULATE
GATHERER GEDDER TUCKER RUFFLER CHICLERO PLICATOR PUCKERER
GATHERING BEE HUI LED LEK SUM FAIR FEST KNOT SING SIVA LEVEE SHINE TRYST AFFLUX INDABA MUDDLE PLISSE POWWOW RUELLE SMOKER COLLECT COMMERS COMPANY FUNFEST HARVEST HOSTING HUSKING JOLLITY KLATSCH MEETING MOOTING NYMPHAL ROCKING TURNOUT ASSEMBLY CONCLAVE FUNCTION JAMBOREE PANIONIA POTATION RECOURSE SINGSONG SOCIABLE STAMPEDE
(— FOR DANCING) FANDANGO
(— OF ANIMALS) DRIVE
(— OF ARMED MEN) HOSTING
(— OF CLOTH) SHIRR SHIRRING
(— OF FILM) CISSING
(— OF SCOUTS) CAMPOREE JAMBOREE
(— OF TEAM) HUDDLE
(— OF WITCHES) COVEN
(— OF WOMEN) HENPARTY
(— PLACE) LESCHE
(BASUTO —) PITSO
(FORMAL —) HALL
(RELIGIOUS —) SHOUT
(SOCIAL —) BEE FRY BAKE BALL CLUB DRUM STAG WINE BAILE BINGE BINGO DANCE MIXER SHIVOO SMOKER CANTICO COTERIE KLATSCH SHINDIG SQUEEZE BARBECUE CAMPFIRE CLAMBAKE TALKFEST RECEPTION SYMPOSIUM
(STUDENTS' —) KOMMERS
(THREE-DAY —) CURSILLO
(SUFF.) **(FESTIVE —)** FEST
GAU BANT
GAUCHE CLUMSY AWKWARD
GAUD GAY GAUDY FANGLE VANITY TRINKET
GAUDINESS GLARE GLITTER
GAUDY GAY LOUD CHEAP FLARY SHOWY VAUDY BRAZEN FLASHY FLIMSY FLORID GARISH GAWISH SKYRIN TAWDRY TINSEL BRANKIE CHINTZY FLARING GAUDISH GLARING BRUMMAGEM MERETRICIOUS
GAUGE (ALSO SEE GAGE) BORE GAGE MOOT PLUG SIZE TRAM GADGE NORMA RANGE DENTIN FEELER FORMER GABARI DEPTHEN TEMPLET TRAMMEL ESTIMATE INDICANT MEASURER STANDARD SURFACER TEMPLATE MANOMETER
(— FOR SLATES) SCANTLE
(RAIN —) UDOMETER
GAUGER SURVEYOR
GAUL GALLIA
(PL.) PICTONES
GAULISH
(PREF.) GALLO
GAUNT BONY GRIM LANK LEAN SLIM THIN PINED SPARE THIRL BARREN HAGGED HOLLOW MEAGER MEAGRE SHELLY SKINNY HAGGARD SCRAWNY SLENDER DESOLATE RAWBONED CADAVEROUS
GAUNTLET TOP CUFF GLOVE GANTLET GAINPAIN GANTLOPE
GAUR BISON SELADANG
GAUZE LISSE MARLI MARLY UMPLE CYPRUS CYPRESS TIFFANY CARBASUS
GAUZY FILMY
GAVE GIN GUV YAF YAFE
GAVEL HAMMER GAVELAGE
GAVIAL NAKOO LIZARD GHARIAL LORICATE
GAVOTTE MUSETTE
GAWK GAWKY GAWNEY LUMPKIN RAMMACK
GAWKY GOWKIT ANGULAR AWKWARD GAWKISH
GAY MAD AIRY BOON DAFT GLAD GLEG HIGH RORY TRIM WILD BONNY BUXOM GAUDY JOLLY LIGHT MERRY NITID RIANT RORTY SUNNY VAUDY WLONK ALEGER BLITHE CHEERY FLASHY FRISKY FROLIC GARISH JOCUND JOVIAL JOYFUL JOYOUS KIPPER LIVELY SOCIAL SPORTY WANTON BOBBISH CHIPPER FESTIVE GALLANT GIOJOSO GLEEFUL LARKING RACKETY SMICKER SMILING TITTUPY WINSOME CAVALIER DEBONAIR FROHLICH GAMESOME PLEASANT PRIMROSE SPARKISH SPLENDID SPORTIVE
GAY-FEATHER LIATRIS
GAYUMART (SLAYER OF —) ANGROMAINYUS
(SON OF —) SIYAMAK
GAYWINGS MAYWINGS
GAZE EYE PRY CAPE GAPE GOUK GOWK LEER LOOK MOON OGLE PEER PORE SCAN TOOT GLAIK GLARE GLOAT GLORE SIGHT STARE TWIRE VISIE WLITE ASPECT GLOWER REGARD AFTEREYE
GAZELLE AHU GOA ADMI AOUL CORA DAMA MOHR ADDRA ARIEL KORIN MHORR DZEREN GROUSE ALGAZEL CHIKARA CORINNE DIBATAG TABITHA CHINKARA
GAZELLE HOUND SALUKI
GAZETTE COURANT JOURNAL
(— OF CRIMES) HUE
GAZEZ (FATHER OF —) CALEB HARAN
(MOTHER OF —) EPHAH
GE TAPUYAN
GEAN MERRY MURIE MURRY GUIGNE GASKINS
GEAR KIT SPUR TACK TRIM IDLER TOOTH FOURTH GRAITH HYPOID PINION TACKLE CLOBBER GEARING HARNESS REVERSE RIGGING SEGMENT TRILOBE BACKPACK HEADGEAR OVERDRIVE
(— OF DIVER) ARMOR
(CAR —) LOW HIGH FIRST SECOND REVERSE
(CHAFING —) SCOTCHMAN
(DEFENSIVE —) ARMORY
(RUNNING —) CARRIAGE
(TRANSMISSION —) HIGH FIRST SPEED FOURTH SECOND REVERSE
GEARED GIRT
GEARWHEEL UNILOBE WABBLER WOBBLER
GEB KEB SEB
GEBER (FATHER OF —) URI
GECKO FANFOOT TARENTE GEKKONID LACERTID
GEDALIAH (FATHER OF —) AHIKAM
(SLAYER OF —) ISHMAEL
GEE WOW GOSH GOLLY JEEPERS
GEELBEC SALMON TERAGLIN
GEEPOUND SLUG
GEESE SET
GEEZER COOT
GEIGER TREE ALOEWOOD SEBESTEN
GEL JELL JELLY LIVER GELATE ALCOGEL
GELATIN AGAR GLUE COLLIN GLUTIN GLUTOID HAITSAI NORGINE ISINGLASS
GELATINOUS COLLOID MUCULENT COLLOIDAL JELLYLIKE
GELD LIB GELT ALTER CASTRATE
GELDING HORSE SPADE SPADO
GEM GIM JADE ONYX OPAL RUBY SARD AGATE BERYL BIJOU CAMEO JAZEL JEWEL PEARL SPARK STONE TOPAZ ZIMME AMULET BAGUET CRUSTA GARNET IOLITE JASPER PEBBLE PYROPE RONDEL ZIRCON ASTERIA CITRINE DIAMOND DOUBLET EMERALD JACINTH KUNZITE ONEGITE PERIDOT SPARKLE ACHROITE AMATRICE AMETHYST BAGUETTE HYACINTH INTAGLIO MARQUISE ORIENTAL RONDELLE SAPPHIRE SARDONYX HIDDENITE MOONSTONE RUBICELLE

(— CARVED IN RELIEF) CAMEO INTAGLIO
(— ENGRAVED WITH CHARM) ABRAXAS
(— OF IMPERFECT BRILLIANCY) LOUPE
(— REFLECTING LIGHT IN 6 RAYS) ASTERIA
(— STATE) IDAHO
(— SURFACE) BEZEL FACET
(IMITATION —) PASTE
(MYTHICAL —) CARBUNCLE
(TRANSPARENT —) IOLITE
(UNCUT —) ROUGH CABOCHON
GEMALLI (SON OF —) AMMIEL
GEMARIAH (FATHER OF —) HILKIAH SHAPHAN
(SON OF —) MICHAIAH
GEMMA BUD GEMMULE SOREDIUM
GEMMULE SPORE BROODSAC
GEMMY EMERALD
GEMSBOK ORYX KOKAMA GEMSBUCK
GEMSTONE JADE STAR CHEVEE PYROPE SPINEL EMERALD FISHEYE CROSSCUT HYALITHE MORGANITE TANZANITE
(PART OF —) BEZEL CROWN CULET FACET TABLE GIRDLE PAVILION
(SYNTHETIC —) YAG
GENA CHEEK
GENDER SEX KIND CLASS FEMININE
GENE GEN ALLEL ALLELE AMORPH FACTOR LETHAL PRIMER CYTOGENE MODIFIER POLYGENE RECESSIVE
(— MATERIAL) DNA
(GROUP OF —S) OPERON
(SET OF —S) HAPLOTYPE
GENEALOGY PEDIGREE
GENERAL (ALSO SEE SOLDIER) MAIN MOST BROAD GROSS ATAMAN COMMON HETMAN PUBLIC VULGAR CURRENT GENERIC MARSHAL SUMMARY AUFIDIUS CANIDIUS CATHOLIC ECUMENIC ENCYCLIC OVERHEAD PANDEMIC PUFIDIUS STRATEGE BRIGADIER
(PL.) DIADOCHI
(PREF.) CAEN(O) CEN(O) COEN(O) PAN
GENERALITY CREDO GENERALE
GENERALIZATION LAW AXIOM BROMIDE
GENERALIZE WIDEN EXTEND SPREAD BROADEN
GENERALIZED GROSS GLOBAL
GENERALLY ASARULE BROADLY LARGELY OVERALL ROUNDLY MOSTWHAT
GENERALSHIP STRATEGY
GENERATE MAKE SIRE TEEM BEGET BREED IMPEL SPAWN STEAM CREATE FATHER GENDER IMPOSE KITTLE DEVELOP INBREED PRODUCE ENGENDER
(— PUS) DIGEST
GENERATION AGE KIND TIME WORLD STRAIN STRIND DESCENT DIPLOID GETTING KINDRED GAMOBIUM GENITURE SAECULUM THEOGONY TRIPLOID UPSPRING OFFSPRING
(FUTURE —S) POSTERITY
(SPONTANEOUS —) ABIOGENESIS
(SUFF.) GON(E)(IDIUM)(IMO)(IUM)(Y)
GENERATIVE GENIAL GAMETIC GENESIC GENETIC SEEDFUL SEMINAL PROLIFIC
GENERATOR KIPP BUZZER DYNAMO RULING ELEMENT DIPHASER GENERANT OSCILLATOR
GENEROSITY GRACE LARGE BOUNTY GENTRY BREADTH FREEDOM HONESTY COURTESY GOODNESS KINDNESS LARGESSE
GENEROUS BIG FREE OPEN SOFT FRANK HEFTY LARGE NOBLE LIBERAL GRACIOUS HANDSOME INSORDID LARGEOUS MAGNIFIC OPENHANDED
GENEROUSLY LUCKY MANLY KINDLY FRANKLY
GENESIS BIRTH ORIGIN BERESHIT GENETICS
GENET BERBE CIVET DAPPLE VIVERRINE
GENEVA GIN
GENIAL BEIN BIEN WARM DOUCE SONSY DOULCE FORTHY FURTHY HEARTY KINDLY MELLOW MENTAL CHEERFUL GRACIOUS PLEASANT
GENIALITY BONHOMIE
GENICULATE KNEED ELBOWED
GENIE GENIUS HATHOR SANDMAN
GENII XIN JANN
GENIN BUFAGIN
GENIP GINEP JAGUA IRONWOOD
GENIPAP LANA GENIP JAGUA GUENEPE
GENISTA FURZE RETAMA
GENITAL SECRET
(PL.) HARNESS PRIVITY GENITURE
GENITALS
(PREF.) EDE(O)
GENIUS KA FIRE GIFT HAPI KALI TURN ANGEL BRAIN DEMON GENIO KNACK NUMEN DAEMON INGENY INGINE TALENT WIZARD DUSTMAN DUAMUTEF EINSTEIN FRAVASHI PENCHANT SILVANUS
(— OF LANGUAGE) IDIOM
GENOA GEANE
GENOTYPE BIOTYPE LOGOTYPE
GENOUILLERE KNEELET
GENRE EPIC KIND SORT TYPE CLASS STYLE FABLIAU SPECIES CATEGORY
GENS CLAN HOUSE
GENSERIC (BROTHER OF —) GONDERIC GONTHARIS
(FATHER OF —) GODIGISDUS
GENTEEL NICE GENTY GENTIL JAUNTY POLITE STYLISH GRACEFUL
GENTIAN BIT FELWORT AGUEWEED GALLWEED BALDMONEY PENNYWORT
GENTILE ARIAN ARYAN HEATHEN
GENTILITY COUTH POLISH CIVILITY GENTRICE NICENESS
GENTLE MOY CALM DEFT DEWY FAIR HEND KIND MEEK MILD MURE NESH SLOW SOFT SOOT TAME BLAND CANNY LIGHT LITHE MILKY QUIET SMALL SOBER SWEET BENIGN BONAIR CADISH DOCILE FACILE LYDIAN MODEST PLACID REMISS SILKEN SILVER SOFTLY TENDER AFFABLE AMABILE CLEMENT GRADUAL SOAKING SUBDUED DEBONAIR DELICATE DOVELIKE EGGSHELL LAMBLIKE LENITIVE MAIDENLY MANSUETE MODERATE PEACEFUL SARCENET TOWARDLY TRANQUIL
(— AS OF THE WIND) LOOM
GENTLEFOLK GENTRY GENTILITY
GENTLEMAN NIB SIR BABU GENT TOFF BABOO CURIO DORAY SAHIB SENOR GEMMAN MILORD SENHOR SIGNOR YONKER BRAVERY GALLANT GENTMAN MYNHEER CAVALIER MIRABELL SEIGNEUR SEIGNIOR SQUIREEN
(— COMMONER) HAT
(— TRAINING FOR KNIGHTHOOD) DONZEL
(— WITHOUT FORTUNE) STALKO
(COUNTRY —) SQUIRE
(GIPSY —) RYE
(MALAY —) TUAN
(MILITARY —) CADET
(POOR —) BUCKEEN
(WOULD-BE —) SHONEEN
(PL.) HERREN CHIVALRY
GENTLEMAN-AT-ARMS PENSIONER
GENTLEMANLY JAUNTY
GENTLENESS FLESH LENITY AMENITY DOUCEUR CLEMENCY KINDNESS MANSUETUDE
GENTLY SOFT CANNY SOAVE EASILY FAIRLY LIGHTLY EASYLIKE PRETTILY TENDERLY
GENTRY COUNTY GENTRICE SQUIRAGE SZLACHTA
GENUBATH (FATHER OF —) HADAD
GENUFLECTION VENIE KNEELING
GENUINE ECHT GOOD LEAL PURE REAL TRUE VRAI PLAIN PUKKA SOLID ACTUAL ARRANT DINKUM DIRECT HONEST KOSHER PISTIC CURRENT GERMANE GRADELY SINCERE VERIDIC GRAITHLY STERLING RIGHTEOUS
(NOT —) TIN SHAM BOGUS PLASTIC PRETENDED
(SEEMINGLY —) COLORABLE
(SUFF.) **(NOT —)** ASTER
GENUINENESS VERIDITY
GENUS KIND CLASS ANALOG GENDER GENERAL
(— OF ALGAE) DASYA FUCUS BANGIA CHORDA CODIUM HYPNEA NOSTOC PADINA DIATOMA LEMANEA LIAGORA PTILOTA VALONIA ZYGNEMA ANABAENA BRYOPSIS CAULERPA CERAMIUM CHONDRUS CONFERVA CUTLERIA DICTYOTA DUMONTIA GELIDIUM GOMONTIA HALIMEDA LERAMIUM LESSONIA NEMALION OOCYSTIS PALMELLA PORPHYRA STRIARIA TAONURUS ULOTHRIX
(— OF AMOEBA) CHAOS
(— OF AMPHIBIAN) HYLA RANA SIREN PROTEUS AMPHIUMA NECTURUS
(— OF ANT) ATTA ECITON LASIUS PONERA TERMES FORMICA PHEIDOLE TAPINOMA
(— OF ANTELOPE) ORYX KOBUS BUBALIS GAZELLA MADOQUA REDUNCA ANTILOPE EGOCERUS
(— OF APE) PAN PONGO SIMIA
(— OF APHID) ADELGES CHERMES
(— OF ARACHNID) ACARUS GALEODES
(— OF ARMADILLO) DASYPUS XENURUS
(— OF ASCIDIAN) CIONA MOLGULA BOLTENIA PYROSOMA
(— OF ASCLEPIAD) STAPELIA
(— OF AUK) ALCA ALLE
(— OF BABOON) PAPIO
(— OF BACTERIA) VIBRIO EIMERIA ERWINIA GAFFKYA PROTEUS SARCINA BACILLUS BRUCELLA SERRATIA SHIGELLA YERSINIA BORDETELLA
(— OF BADGER) MELES ARCTONYX HELICTIS
(— OF BAMBOO) DENDROCALAMUS
(— OF BARNACLE) LEPAS BALANUS ELMINIUS
(— OF BASIDIOMYCETE) BOVISTA
(— OF BAT) EUDERMA PETALIA DESMODUS DIPHYLLA MOLOSSUS MORMOOPS NOCTILIO NYCTERIS PLECOTUS PTEROPUS VAMPYRUM
(— OF BEAN) ABRUS
(— OF BEAR) URSUS EUARCTOS MELURSUS
(— OF BEAVER) CASTOR
(— OF BEE) APIA APIS BOMBUS ANDRENA TRIGONA COLLETES HALICTUS MELIPONA
(— OF BEETLE) AMARA FIDIA HISPA LAMIA LARIA LYTTA MELOE SAGRA ALTICA ASILUS CLERUS ELATER LYCTUS PTINUS SILPHA ACILIUS ADELOPS AGRILUS ANOBIUM ANOMALA BRUCHUS CARABUS CASSIDA EPITRIX PRIONUS SAPERDA SITARIS ADORETUS AGRIOTES APHODIUS CALOSOMA CATORAMA CYBISTER DYNASTES DYTISCUS EPICAUTA EUMOLPUS HARPALUS LAMPYRIS MEGASOMA PASSALUS POPILLIA SCOLYTUS SPHINDUS TENEBRIO DERMESTES
(— OF BIRD) ARA ALCA APUS CRAX CREX GYPS JYNX MIRO MITU MOHO OTIS PICA RHEA SULA TYTO XEMA AJAJA ANOUS ANSER ARDEA ARGUS ASTUR BUCCO FALCO GAVIA GOURA GUARA GYGIS IRENA JUNCO LARUS LERWA LOXIA MIMUS MITUA MUNIA PIPRA PITTA SITTA TODUS UPUPA VIDUA VIREO ALAUDA ALCEDO ANHIMA ANTHUS AQUILA BONASA BRANTA CAPITO CIRCUS COLIUS CORVUS DACELO ELANUS FULICA GALLUS JACANA LANIUS LEIPOA LIMOSA MARECA MENURA MEROPS MILVUS MONASA NESTOR NUMIDA PASSER PASTOR PERDIX PERNIS PROGNE QUELEA RALLUS SAPPHO SCOPUS SIALIA SPINUS

STERNA SYLVIA TETRAO TRERON TRINGA TROGON TURDUS TURNIX VULTUR ANHINGA APTERYX ARTAMUS BUCEROS CACICUS CAPELLA CARIAMA CERTHIA CHIONIS CICONIA CINCLUS COLINUS COLUMBA COTINGA CUCULUS ELAENIA GALBULA GARRUPA HALCYON HIRUNDO IBYCTER ICTERUS KAKATOE LAGOPUS LOPHURA LYRURUS MALURUS MANACUS MESITES MILVAGO MOMOTUS ORIOLUS PANDION PAROTIA PIRANGA PITYLUS PLAUTUS PLOCEUS PORZANA REGULUS SEIURUS SERINUS STURNUS TANAGRA TIMALIA TOTANUS XENICUS ZENAIDA ACCENTOR ACCIPTER ACREDULA AFROPAVO AGELAIUS AMIZILIA BOTAURUS BUCORVUS BURHINUS CHAETURA COLYMBUS CORACIAS COTURNIX DELICHON DIATRYMA DINORNIS DIOMEDEA DREPANIS EMBERIZA EUPHONIA EURYPYGA FULMARUS GARRULUS GEOSPIZA GERYGONE GLAREOLA GRALLINA GYPAETUS IONORNIS LUSCINIA MACHETES MYCTERIA NEOPHRON NOTORNIS NUMENIUS OREORTYX PENELOPE PHAETHON PITANGUS PLATALEA PLEGADIS PODARGUS PRIONOPS PRUNELLA PUFFINUS RUPICOLA SALTATOR SAXICOLA SCOLOPAX SPEOTYTO SPIZELLA STRUTHIO TRAGOPAN TYRANNUS
(— OF BIVALVES) MYA PINNA ANOMIA MACTRA NUCULA ETHERIA MYTILUS PANDORA COLYMBUS HINNITES PISIDIUM SAXICAVA TRIDACNA XYLOTRYA SPHAERIUM
(— OF BOWFIN) AMIA
(— OF BRACHIOPOD) ATRYPA CRANIA ATHYRIS DISCINA SPIRIFER
(— OF BRYOPHYTE) RICCIA
(— OF BRYOZOAN) BUGULA ESCHARA FLUSTRA RETEPORA
(— OF BUG) ANASA CIMEX EMESA CORIXA TINGIS
(— OF BUTTERFLY) CALIGO COLIAS DANAUS MORPHO PIERIS THECLA EURYMUS JUNONIA KALLIMA LYCAENA PAPILIO STRYMON VANESSA ARGYNNIS HESPERIA LEMONIAS MELITAEA SPEYERIA
(— OF CABBAGE) COS
(— OF CACTUS) CEREUS NOPALEA OPUNTIA HARRISIA
(— OF CANTELOUPE) CUCUMIS
(— OF CAT) FELIS ACINONYX HEMIGALE
(— OF CATTLE) BOS NEAT TAURUS
(— OF CEPHALOPOD) SEPIA SPIRULA
(— OF CETACEAN) INIA
(— OF CHINK) LACUNA
(— OF CHIPMUNK) EUTAMIAS
(— OF CILIATE) COLPODA CHILODON EUPLOTES
(— OF CIVET) FOSSA PAGUMA
(— OF CLAM) ENSIS GEMMA SOLEN SPISULA
(— OF COCKLE) CHIONE
(— OF COCKROACH) BLATTA
(— OF CODFISH) GADUS
(— OF CORAL) ASTREA FUNGIA MAENDRA OCULINA PORITES ACROPORA TUBIPORA
(— OF CRAB) UCA MAIA BIRGUS CANCER GRAPSUS OCYPODE PAGURUS LITHODES PORTUNUS
(— OF CRANE) GRUS
(— OF CRAYFISH) CAMBARUS
(— OF CRICKET) ACHETA GRYLLUS
(— OF CRUSTACEAN) APUS HIPPA JASUS LIGIA MYSIS CYPRIS LIGYDA SELLUS TRIOPS ARGULUS ARTEMIA ASTACUS BOPYRUS CALAPPA CHELURA DAPHNIA EMERITA HOMARUS IDOTHEA LERNAEA NEBALIA SQUILLA CAPRELLA ESTHERIA GAMMARUS LEUCIFER LIMNETIS LIMNORIA NEPHROPS PHRONIMA
(— OF CTENOPHORE) BEROE CESTUM
(— OF CUCUMBER) CUCUMIS
(— OF CURASSOW) CRAX
(— OF DEER) AXIS DAMA PUDU RUSA CERVUS MAZAMA MOSCHUS RUCERVUS
(— OF DIATOM) DIATOMA SYNEDRA MERIDION NAVICULA
(— OF DODO) DIDUS
(— OF DOG) CUON CANIS LYCAON
(— OF DORMOUSE) GLIS
(— OF DRAGONFLY) AESCHNA
(— OF DUCK) AIX ANAS AYTHYA MERGUS NYROCA NETTION SPATULA CLANGULA FULIGULA
(— OF EAGLE) AQUILA
(— OF ECHINODERM) ASTERIAS
(— OF EDENTATE) MANIS
(— OF EEL) CONGER ECHIDNA MURAENA ANGUILLA GYMNOTUS MORINGUA
(— OF FERN) FILIX TODEA ANEMIA AZOLLA DOODIA CYATHEA ISOETES ONOCLEA OSMUNDA PELLAEA WOODSIA ADIANTUM ASPIDIUM ATHYRIUM BLECHNUM CETERACH CIBOTIUM CLEMATIS DAVALLIA LYGODIUM MARATTIA SALVINIA SCHIZAEA VITTARIA
(— OF FIREFLY) LAMPYRIS
(— OF FISH) AMIA ESOX HURO LOTA MOLA RAJA ZEUS ALOSA BADIS BERYX BETTA DORAS ELOPS GADUS GOBIO HUCHO LATES MANTA MUGIL PERCA SALMO SARDA SOLEA UMBRA ALBULA ANABAS APOGON BAIGRE BARBUS BELONE CARANX CLUPEA COTTUS DIODON GERRES GOBIUS HIODON KUHLIA LABRUS LATRIS MOBULA MYXINE NOMEUS PAGRUS PSETTA REMORA SCARUS SPARUS TRIGLA TRUTTA TURSIO WEEVER ABRAMIS ALOPHAS ALOPIAS ARACANA ASPREDO BROTULA CARAPUS CLARIAS DREPANE ECHIDNA GARRUPA GIRELLA GYMNORA LEPOMIS LIMANDA LUCANIA LYCODES OSMERUS PEGASUS PRISTIS SCIAENA SCOMBER SEPIOLA SERIOLA SIGANUS SILLAGO SILURUS SPHYRNA SQUALUS SYNODUS THUNNUS TORPEDO TOXOTES TRIODON XIPHIAS ZOARCES AMEIURUS ANABLEPS ANGUILLA ARAPAIMA ASTYANAX ATHERINA BALISTES BODIANUS CARANGUS CHIMAERA CLADODUS CTENODUS CYPRINUS DAPEDIUS DIPLODUS DIPTERUS DOROSOMA ECHENEIS ETRUMEUS FUNDULUS GADOPSIS GALAXIAS GAMBUSIA GOBIESOX HAEMULON ICOSTEUS KYPHOSUS LEBISTES LUTIANUS MEGALOPS MORMYRUS MUSTELUS NOTROPIS OPHIDION PALOMETA PANTODON PHOCAENA POLYODON PYGIDIUM SERRANUS SQUATINA COREGONUS MYCTOPHUM
(— OF FLAGELLATE) COCOS GONIUM OPHION SYNURA VOLVOX ATTALEA CARYOTA EUGLENA GIARDIA BORASSUS CERATIUM EUDORINA HEXAMITA HYDRURUS
(— OF FLEA) PULEX BOSMINA
(— OF FLY) DACUS MUSCA MYMAR PERLA PHORA ASILUS CEPHUS FANNIA PIMPLA RHYSSA SCIARA TIPULA CALIROA CHALCIS DIOPSIS EPHYDRA HYLEMYA MIASTOR ORTALIS OSCINIS PANORPA TACHINA THEREVA ACROCERA AGROMYZA ANOMALON APHIDIUS BORBORUS CHELONUS CHRYSOPA CHRYSOPS GLOSSINA PSYCHODA SCHEDIUS SIMULIUM STOMOXYS
(— OF FLYING SQUIRREL) BELOMYS
(— OF FOSSIL) AMPYX ERYON ADAPIS ATRYPA BAIERA ERYOPS GEIKIA HYENIA KLUKIA MAMMUT OLENUS ORTHIS RHYNIA ANDRIAS ANTEDON APTIANA ASAPHUS DICERAS EXOGYRA GANODUS HAMITES HYBODUS KNORRIA LESKEYA LESLEYA LOXOMMA MESONYX MOROPUS MYLODON OTOZOUM PHACOPS PHIOMIA PROAVIS PROETUS WALCHIA AGLASPIS AGNOSTUS AMYNODON APHELOPS ARCHELON BIRKENIA BRONTOPS CALIPPUS CALYMENE CAYTONIA CERATOPS CLYMENIA CTENODUS DAPEDIUS DEINODON DIATRYMA DINOHYUS DIPLODUS DIPTERUS ENCHODUS ENCRINUS EODISCUS EOHIPPUS EOSAURUS EUSMILUS GORDONIA GRYPHAEA HALLOPUS HELIGMUS ILLAENUS LANARKIA LEBACHIA LECROSIA LEGUATIA LESTODON LITUITES MACLUREA MARRELLA METOPIAS OLDHAMIA PLACODUS PORTHEUS RUTIODON SMILODON SPIRIFER STEGODON STEGOMUS TAONURUS THELODUS XIPHODON ZAMICRUS CONULARIA
(— OF FOX) ALOPEX VULPES UROCYON
(— OF FROG) RANA ANURA HYLODES
(— OF FUNGUS) FOMES IRPEX PHOMA TUBER VALSA VERPA ALBUGO BREMIA CAEOMA EMPUSA FUMAGO HYDNUM ISARIA OIDIUM PEZIZA TORULA ZYTHIA ACRASIA ACRASIN AMANITA BOLETUS CANDIDA CHALARA CYATHUS ELSINOE ERYSIBE FABRAEA GEASTER LEPIOTA MONILIA NECTRIA OZONIUM PACHYMA PYTHIUM RHIZINA RUSSULA SIMBLUM STEREUM STICTIS STILBUM TYPHULA XYLARIA ACHORION AECIDIUM AGARICUS BOTRYTIS CALVATIA CLATHRUS CLAVARIA COLLYBIA COPRINUS CORYNEUM CYPHELLA CYTTARIA DAEDALEA DIPLODIA ENDOTHIA ENTOLOMA ENTYLOMA ERYSIPHE EXOASCUS FUSARIUM GEASTRUM GNOMONIA GRAPHIUM HELOTIUM HELVELLA LENZITES MERULIUS MYCOGONE PAXILLUS PHOLIOTA PUCCINIA RHIZOPUS RHYTISMA SEPTORIA SORDARIA SPICARIA TAPHRINA TERFEZIA TRAMETES TREMELLA TROCHILA USTILAGO USTULINA VENTURIA CORDICEPS
(— OF GALLFLY) CYNIPS
(— OF GASTROPOD) FICUS HARPA LIMAX OLIVA EBURNA PATELLA TENEBRA SCYLLAEA STROMBUS
(— OF GEESE) CHEN ANSER NETTAPUS
(— OF GNAT) SCIARA
(— OF GOAT) IBEX CAPRA OREAMNOS
(— OF GRASS) POA ZEA AIRA COIX AVENA BRIZA ORYZA STIPA APLUDA ARUNDO BROMUS ELYMUS HOLCUS LOLIUM LYGEUM MELICA MILIUM NARDUS PHLEUM SECALE UNIOLA ZOYSIA BAMBUSA BUCHLOE CHLORIS CYNODON FESTUCA HILARIA HORDEUM LAGURUS LEERSIA MELINIS MOLINIA PANICUM SETARIA SORGHUM ZIZANIA AEGILOPS AGROSTIS ARISTIDA AXONOPUS BULBILIS CENCHRUS DACTYLIS ELEUSINE GLYCERIA GYNERIUM IMPERATA PASPALUM PHALARIS SPARTINA SPINIFEX TRISETUM TRITICUM
(— OF GRASSHOPPER) LOCUSTA
(— OF GUAN) CRAX
(— OF GULL) XEMA LARUS
(— OF HAWK) BUTEO CIRCUS
(— OF HERB) GYP IVA AMMI ARUM BETA GEUM GLAX HEBE LENS MEUM MUSA OLAX RUTA SIDA SIUM ADOXA AJUGA APIOS APIUM CALLA CANNA CAREX CARUM CICER DALEA DRABA ERUCA ERVUM FEDIA GALAX GAURA GILIA GLAUX HOSTA INULA LAPPA LAVIA LAYIA LEMNA LINUM LOASA LOTUS LUFFA MADIA MALVA NAPEA PANAX PARIS PHACA PHLOX PILEA RHEUM RHOEO RUBIA SEDUM TACCA URENA VICIA VIGNA VINCA VIOLA ZIZIA ACAENA ACNIDA ACORUS ACTAEA ADONIS ALISMA ALLIUM ALSINE AMOMUM ANOGRA ARABIS ARALIA ARNICA ASARUM ATROPA BACOPA BAERIA BASSIA BELLIS BIDENS BLITUM BLUMEA

BORAGO CAKILE CALTHA CASSIA CELSIA CICUTA CISTUS CLEOME CNICUS COLEUS CONIUM COPTIS COSMOS CRAMBE CREPIS CRINUM CROCUS CROTON CUNILA CYNARA DAHLIA DATURA DAUCUS DIODIA DONDIA ECHIUM ELODEA ELODES EMILIA EUCLEA FILAGO GALEGA GALIUM GIFOLA GYNURA ISATIS ISMENE KOCHIA KRIGIA KUHNIA LAMIUM LECHEA LUZULA MALOPE MENTHA MIMOSA MONTIA MUCUNA MUILLA NERINE NERIUM NESLIA ONONIS OTHAKE OXALIS PICRIS PISTIA PYROLA RESEDA RESTIO RHEXIA RIVINA RUPPIA SAGINA SALVIA SCILLA SESBAN SESELI STEVIA SUAEDA THALIA TULIPA VIORNA ZINNIA ABRONIA ADLUMIA AETHUSA ALEGRIA ALETRIS ALKANNA ALPINIA ALTHAEA ALYSSUM AMORPHA AMSONIA ANCHUSA ANEMONE ANETHUM ANYCHIA APHANES ARACHIS ARCTIUM ARNEBIA ARUNCUS BABIANA BARTSIA BEGONIA BOEBERA BUTOMUS CACALIA CAJANUS CALYPSO CARLINA CELOSIA CHELONE CIRCAEA CIRSIUM CLARKIA COMARUM CROOMIA CURCUMA CUSCUTA CYTINUS DATISCA DECODON DERINGA DIASCIA DROSERA ELATINE EOMECON EPISCIA ERODIUM FELICIA FICARIA FRASERA FREESIA FUMARIA GAZANIA GERBERA GLECOMA GLYCINE GUNNERA HALENIA HECHTIA HEDEOMA HOMERIA HUGELIA HYPOXIS IRESINE JASIONE KICKXIA KNAUTIA KOELLIA LACTUCA LAPPULA LAPSANA LEWISIA LIATRIS LINARIA LINNAEA LOGANIA LOPEZIA LUNARIA LUPINUS LYCHNIS LYTHRUM MARANTA MEDEOLA MIMULUS MITELLA MOLLUGO MONESES MUSCARI NEMESIA NIGELLA OTHONNA PAEONIA PAPAVER PAVONIA PEGANUM PETUNIA PLUCHEA PRIMULA RORIPPA ROTALIA RUELLIA SALSOLA SAMOLUS SCANDIX SENECIO SESAMUM SHORTIA SILYBUM SINAPIS SOLANUM SONCHUS STACHYS STATICE SUCCISA SWERTIA TAGETES TALINUM TELLIMA THAPSIA THESIUM THLASPI THURNIA TORENIA TORILIS TOVARIA TRILISA URGINEA VALLOTA VERBENA ZEBRINA ACALYPHA ACANTHUS ACHILLEA ACONITUM AGALINIS AGERATUM ALLIARIA ALLIONIA ALOCASIA AMBROSIA AMMOBIUM ANDRYALA ANGELICA ANTHEMIS ANTICLEA APOCYNUM ARCTOTIS ARENARIA ARGEMONE ARISAEMA ASPERULA ATRIPLEX BAPTISIA BARBAREA BARTONIA BERGENIA BERTEROA BETONICA BISTORTA BOLTONIA BORRERIA BRASSICA BRUNONIA BUCHNERA CALATHEA CAMASSIA CAMELINA CANNABIS CAPSICUM CERINTHE CLEMATIS COCHARUS COLLOMIA COLUMNEA COMANDRA COOPERIA CRASSULA CUBELIUM DENTARIA DIANTHUS DICENTRA DIPSACUS DISPORUM DYSSODIA ECHINOPS EPIFAGUS ERANTHIS EREMURUS ERIGENIA ERIGERON ERYNGIUM ERYSIMUM EUCHARIS EUTHAMIA FITTONIA FLAVERIA FLOERKEA FRAGARIA GALACTIA GENTIANA GERARDIA GESNERIA GILLENIA GLAUCIUM GLECHOMA GLORIOSA GLOXINIA GOODENIA GRATIOLA GUZMANIA HELENIUM HELONIAS HEPATICA HESPERIS HEUCHERA HIBISCUS HIPPURIS HOSACKIA HOTTONIA HUDSONIA HYDROLES HYSSOPUS IONIDIUM ISNARDIA JATROPHA JUSSIAEA JUSTICIA KNEIFFIA KOHLERIA LAPORTEA LAVATERA LEONOTIS LEONURUS LEPIDIUM LEPTILON LIMONIUM LOPHIOLA LYCOPSIS MACLEAYA MANFREDA MANTISIA MEDICAGO MEIBOMIA MYOSOTIS MYOSURUS OBOLARIA OENANTHE OPOPANAX ORONTIUM PAROSELA PHACELIA PHORMIUM PHYMOSIA PHYSALIS PHYSARIA PLANTAGO PLUMBAGO POLYGALA POLYMNIA POTERIUM PRUNELLA PSORALEA RAPHANUS RHAGODIA SABBATIA SAMBUCUS SANICULA SARCODES SAROTHRA SATUREIA SCABIOSA SCOLYMUS SESBANIA SESUVIUM SEYMERIA SIDALCEA SILPHIUM SOLIDAGO SPERGULA SPIGELIA SPINACIA STOKESIA TAENIDIA THASPIUM TIARELLA TRIBULUS TRILLIUM TROLLIUS TUECRIUM UVULARIA VACCARIA VALERIAN VANELLUS VERATRUM VERNONIA VERONICA VISCARIA WATSONIA XANTHIUM RUDBECKIA
(— OF HERON) ARDEA EGRETTA
(— OF HORSE) EQUUS CALIPPUS EOHIPPUS
(— OF HYDROZOAN) DIPHYES PHYSALIA
(— OF HYENA) HYAENA CROCUTA
(— OF INSECT) NEPA APHIS EMESA JAPYX SIREX BOREUS CICADA COCCUS CORIXA EMPUSA ICERYA KERMES MANTIS PHASMA PODURA SIALIS THRIPS CHALCIS FORMICA FULGORA LEPISMA ORYSSUS RANATRA STYLOPS VEDALIA BACILLUS CAMPODEA EPHEMERA LABIDURA LACCIFER LECANIUM LYONETIA MACHILIS MANTISPA NERTHRUS REDUVIUS
(— OF ISOPOD) IDOTEA IDOTHEA CIROLANA
(— OF JAY) GARRULUS
(— OF JELLYFISH) CYANEA AURELIA AEQUOREA
(— OF JERBOA) DIPUS
(— OF KELP) AGARUM
(— OF LANGUR) SIMIAS
(— OF LEAFHOPPER) AGALLIA EMPOASCA
(— OF LEECH) HIRUDO HAEMOPIS
(— OF LEMUR) INDRI GALAGO
(— OF LIANA) BAUHINIA
(— OF LICE) APHIS PSYLLA ARGULUS ONISCUS BOVICOLA ERIOSOMA GONIODES LIPEURUS
(— OF LICHEN) CORA USNEA STICTA EVERNIA GRAPHIS LECIDEA LOBARIA PHYSCIA CETRARIA CLADONIA LECANORA PARMELIA ROCCELLA STRIGULA
(— OF LILY) CAMAS CAMASS QUAMASH
(— OF LIMPET) ACMAEA
(— OF LIZARD) UTA AGAMA DRACO GEKKO AMEIVA ANGUIS ANOLIS IGUANA EUMECES LACERTA PYGOPUS SCINCUS ACONTIAS CHIROTES COLEONYX LYGOSOMA RHINEURA
(— OF LOCUST) TETRIX TETTIX
(— OF MACAW) ARA
(— OF MAMMAL) BOS SUS HOMO LAMA ALCES BISON CAPRA TAYRA DUGONG FRISON AELURUS AILURUS BUBALUS GALIDIA GYMNURA LINSANG OTOCYON AUCHENIA CYCLOPES CYNOGALE SURICATA TRAGULUS
(— OF MAPLE) ACER
(— OF MARSUPIAL) DASYURUS MACROPUS POTOROUS TARSIPES
(— OF MARTEN) MARTES MUSTELA
(— OF MEDUSA) SARSIA GERYONIA
(— OF MICROSPORIDIAN) GLUGEA
(— OF MILDEW) ERYSIPHE UNCINULA
(— OF MILLIPEDE) JULUS
(— OF MINT) ICIMUM NEPETA MELISSA PERILLA PHLOMIS ORIGANUM
(— OF MITE) ACARUS ACERIA LEPTUS DEMODEX ACARAPIS
(— OF MOLD) MUCOR FULIGO MELIOLA
(— OF MOLE) TALPA SCALOPS SCALOPUS
(— OF MOLLUSK) ARCA DOTO LEDA LIMA CHAMA DONAX EOLIS FICUS HARPA LIMAX MUREX OLIVA VENUS AEOLIS ANOMIA BANKIA CASSIS CHITON LEPTON LUCINA OSTREA PECTEN PHOLAS PYRULA SEMELE TEREDO TETHYS ACTAEON ASTARTE ATLANTA CARDITA CARDIUM CYPRAEA CYPRINA DOSINIA ETHERIA EXOGYRA LINGULA TELLINA BUCCINUM GRYPHAEA HALIOTIS LIMACINA LUTRARIA MODIOLUS NAUTILUS PINCTADA SCYLLAEA STROMBUS
(— OF MONGOOSE) GALIDIA
(— OF MONKEY) AOTES AOTUS CEBUS ATELES MACACA CACAJAO COLOBUS NASALIS SAIMIRI PITHECIA
(— OF MOOSE) ALCES
(— OF MOSQUITO) AEDES CULEX STEGOMYIA
(— OF MOSS) BRYUM CHILO EUXOA MNIUM SAMIA SESIA TINEA ACTIAS ALYPIA ARCTIA BOMBYX COSSUS DATANA HYPNUM LESKEA PLUSIA PSYCHE SPHINX THYRIS URANIA AGROTIS ALABAMA APATELA ARCHIPS ATTACUS BARBULA CRAMBUS FUNARIA GRIMMIA PHASCUM PRONUBA PYRALIS SESAMIA TORTRIX ZEUZERA ZYGAENA ANDREAEA CATOCALA DAWSONIA DIATRAEA DICRANUM ENDROMIS EPHESTIA EUPREPIA GALLERIA GELECHIA HEPIALUS PLUTELLA PRODENIA PYRAUSTA SATURNIA SPHAGNUM THUIDIUM
(— OF MOTH) CHILO ABRAXAS
(— OF MOUSE) MUS APODEMUS
(— OF MUSKMELON) CUCUMIS
(— OF MUSKRAT) FIBER ONDATRA
(— OF NARWHAL) MONODON
(— OF NEMATODE) ACUARIA ALAIMUS ANGUINA NECATOR
(— OF NUDIBRANCH) GLAUCUS
(— OF OATS) AVENA
(— OF OPOSSUM) MARMOSA
(— OF ORCHID) DISA VANDA BLETIA LAELIA PHAJUS ACINETA AERIDES ANGULOA BRASSIA CORDULA EUCOSIA IBIDIUM ISOTRIA LIPARIS LISTERA MALAXIS POGONIA VANILLA ANGRECUM ARETHUSA BLETILLA CALANTHE CATTLEYA CYTHEREA FISSIPES GOODYERA MILTONIA ONCIDIUM PERAMIUM SERAPIAS SOBRALIA TRIPHORA
(— OF OSTRICH) STRUTHIO
(— OF OTTER) LUTRA
(— OF OWL) BUBO NINOX STRIX KETUPA NYCTEA AEGOLIUS SPEOTYTO
(— OF OXEN) BIBOS
(— OF OYSTER) OSTREA AVICULA
(— OF PALM) NIPA ARECA ASSAI COCOS HOWEA SABAL ARENGA ELAEIS INODES KENTIA RAPHIA RHAPIS ATTALEA BACTRIS CALAMUS CARYOTA CORYPHA ERYTHEA EUTERPE GEONOMA LATANIA LICUALA PHOENIX SERENOA THRINAX BORASSUS HYPHAENE IRIARTEA LODOICEA MAURITIA
(— OF PARASITE) STRIGA CUSCOTA CUSCUTA HYDNORA OLPIDIUM CASSYTHIA
(— OF PARRAKEET) ARATINGA
(— OF PARROT) NESTER AMAZONA KAKATOE
(— OF PEACOCK) PAVO
(— OF PENGUIN) EUDYPTES
(— OF PHALANGER) DROMICIA
(— OF PIGEON) GOURA DUCULA COLUMBA
(— OF PLANT) ALOE ARUM COLA DION FABA IRIS IXIA PUYA SOJA ADOXA AGAVE ASTER BATIS CANNA CHARA DIOON DRYAS INULA NAIAS PIPER RUMEX TRAPA TYPHA XYRIS YUCCA ZILLA ABROMA ACACIA AIZOON ALBUCA ANANAS CACTUS CUPHEA DATURA EXACUM FERULA IBERIS JAMBOS JUNCUS LICHEN LILIUM MAYACA MORAEA NUPHAR PHRYMA RICCIA SILENE SMILAX STRIGA URTICA VISCUM ALONSOA ASTILBE BALLOTA CABOMBA CUCUMIS CYPERUS DIONAEA DROSERA ENCELIA EPACRIS

EPIGAEA EURYALE FAGELIA GLYCINE GODETIA HELXINE HOOKERA ISOETES ISOLOMA KARATAS LYCOPUS MANIHOT MONARDA NELUMBO NITELLA RAOULIA RICINUS STEMONA SYRINGA TRIURUS TURNERA WOLFFIA WYETHIA ZOSTERA ABUTILON ACANTHUS ADIANTUM ANABASIS ANTHYLIS BRASENIA BRODIAEA BROMELIA CALADIUM CAPSICUM CYCLAMEN FORCRAEA FURCRAEA GALTONIA GASTERIA GERANIUM LATHRAEA LATHYRUS MARSILEA MONSTERA NYMPHAEA PANDANUS PEDALIUM PELVETIA PERESKIA SAURURUS SPARAXIS THEVETIA TIGRIDIA TRITONIA VELLOZIA VICTORIA ZINGIBER

(— OF POLYZOAN) LEPRALIA LOXOSOMA

(— OF POPLAR) ALAMO

(— OF PORCUPINE) COENDOU HYSTRIX

(— OF PORPOISE) INIA PHOCAENA

(— OF PRAWN) PALAEMON

(— OF PROTOZOAN) BODO HYDRA MONAS ADELEA AMOEBA ACINETA ARCELLA EIMERIA STENTOR DIDINIUM EUGLYPHA ISOSPORA UROGLENA

(— OF RABBIT) LEPUS

(— OF RACCOON) OLINGO

(— OF RAT) ANISOMYS

(— OF REPTILE) SPHENOGON

(— OF RHIZOPOD) AMOEBA GROMIA LAGENA HATTERIA PELOMYXA

(— OF RODENT) MUS CAVIA DIPUS LEPUS ZAPUS GEOMYS LEMMUS SPALAX CYNOMYS DINOMYS ECHIMYS LEGGADA MERINES NESOKIA ZYZOMYS ALACTAGA ARVICOLA CAPROMYS CITELLUS CRICETUS HAPLODON HYDROMYS LAGIDIUM MICROTUS MYOTALPA ORYZOMYS

(— OF ROTIFER) HYDATINA PEDALION

(— OF RUST) UREDO HEMILEIA UROMYCES

(— OF SALAMANDER) ANDRIAS EURYCEA SIREDON TRITURUS

(— OF SCALE) KERMES LECANIUM

(— OF SCALLOP) HINNITES

(— OF SCORPION) BUTHUS SCORPIO CHELIFER

(— OF SEA ANEMONE) MINYAS ACTINIA

(— OF SEACOW) RHYTINA

(— OF SEA FAN) GORGONIA

(— OF SEAL) PHOCA HYDRURGA MIROUNGA ZALOPHUS

(— OF SEA OTTER) ENHYDRA

(— OF SEA SLUG) ELYSIA

(— OF SEA URCHIN) ARBACIA CIDARIS DIADEMA ECHINUS

(— OF SEAWEED) ULVA FUCUS ALARIA LAMINARIA RHODYMENIA

(— OF SEDGE) FUIRENA SCIRPUS SCLERIA SCHOENUS

(— OF SHARK) LAMNA GALEUS ISURUS ACRODUS ALOPIAS SPHYRNA SQUALUS CLADODUS MENASPIS SQUATINA

(— OF SHEEP) OVIS

(— OF SHELL) PUPA LAMBIS EXOGYRA LATIRUS MALLEUS TROCHUS HAMINOEA MACLUREA OLIVELLA TRIGONIA UMBRELLA

(— OF SHREW) SOREX BLARINA

(— OF SHRIMP) CRAGO CRANGON

(— OF SHRUB) IVA ACER BIXA BRYA HOYA ILEX INGA ITEA MABA OLEA RHUS ROSA SIDA THEA ULEX ALNUS ANONA BIOTA BUTEA BUXUS CATHA DALEA DIRCA ERICA EURYA FICUS HAKEA IXORA LEDUM MALUS OCHNA PADUS RIBES RUBUS SABIA SALIX TAXUS THUJA TREMA UNONA URENA VITEX ABELIA ACAENA ADELIA ALHAGI AMYRIS ANNONA ARALIA ARONIA AUCUBA AZALEA BAPHIA BAUERA BETULA BLUMEA BYBLIS CANTUA CASSIA CELTIS CERCIS CISTUS CITRUS CLEOME CLUSIA COFFEA CORDIA COREMA CORNUS CORREA CROTON DAPHNE DATURA DERRIS DIOSMA DONDIA DRIMYS ECHIUM EVODIA FATSIA FEIJOA GARRYA GNETUM GREWIA GUAREA KALMIA KERRIA LARREA LIPPIA LITSEA LUCUMA LYCIUM MIMOSA MYRCIA MYRICA MYRTUS OCOTEA OLINIA OPILIA PENAEA PERSEA PIERIS PROTEA PTELEA PUNICA QUIINA RAMONA RANDIA ROCHEA ROYENA RUSCUS SALVIA SAPIUM SCHIMA SELAGO SESBAN SORBUS STEVIA STYRAX SUAEDA TECOMA AECULUS AMORPHA ARBUTUS ARDISIA ARMERIA ASIMINA ASSONIA BANKSIA BAROSMA BENZOIN BORONIA BUMELIA BURSERA CALLUNA CARISSA CASASIA CERASUS CESTRUM CLETHRA CNEORUM COLUTEA CORYLUS COTINUS CUNONIA CYRILLA CYTISUS DEUTZIA DOMBEYA DURANTA EHRETIA ENCELIA EPACRIS EPHEDRA EUCHLEA EUGENIA EURSERA FABIANA FUCHSIA GENISTA GMELINA GYMINDA HAMELIA HOVENIA KARATAS LAGETTA LANTANA MAHONIA MERATIA MONIMIA MORINDA MUTISIA MYRRHIS NANDINA NEMESIA OLEARIA OTHONNA PAVETTA PAVONIA PENTZIA PIMELEA PISONIA PURSHIA QUASSIA QUERCUS RAPANEA REMIJIA RHAMNUS RHODORA ROBINIA ROMNEYA RUELLIA SALSOLA SENECIO SKIMMIA SOLANUM SOPHORA SPIRAEA SURIANA SYRINGA TAMARIX TELOPEA XIMENIA XYLOPIA XYLOSMA ZELKOVA ACALYPHA ALANGIUM ALSTONIA ANAGYRIS ATRIPLEX BALOGHIA BAUHINIA BERBERIS BORRERIA BUCKLEYA BUDDLEIA CAMELLIA CAPPARIS CAPSICUM CARAGANA CASSIOPE CASTANEA CODIAEUM COLLETIA CONDALIA CONNARUS COPROSMA CORIARIA CRATAEVA DAVIESIA DENDRIUM DILLENIA DODONAEA DOVYALIS DRACAENA DUBOISIA EMPETRUM EUONYMUS EUPTELEA EXOSTEMA FRAXINUS GALACTIA GOODENIA GORDONIA GUAIACUM HIBISCUS HIRTELLA IONIDIUM JASMINUM JATROPHA JUSTICIA KNIGHTIA KRAMERIA LABURNUM LAVATERA LAWSONIA LEONOTIS MAGNOLIA MAYTENUS MICHELIA MYOPORUM NOTELAEA PALIURUS PAROSELA PHILESIA PHOTINIA PHYMOSIA PLUMIERA POLYGALA POTERIUM PROSOPIS PSORALEA RHAGODIA ROLLINIA RORIDULA RUSSELIA SAMBUCUS SATUREIA SAURAUIA SESBANIA SOLANDRA SORBARIA SPARTIUM TABEBUIA TORRUBIA TRECULIA VARRONIA VERNONIA VERONICA VIBURNUM VOCHYSIA WITHANIA ZIZYPHUS MENZIESIA

(— OF SILKWORM) BOMBYX

(— OF SKUNK) MEPHITIS

(— OF SLOTH) BRADYPUS

(— OF SLUG) DOTO ARION DORIS LIMAX ELYSIA GLAUCUS

(— OF SNAIL) HUA PILA CONUS FUSUS GALBA HELIX MITRA OVULA PHYSA THAIS TURBO CERION EULIMA NATICA NERITA RISSOA TRITON ANCYLUS BITTIUM BULINUS BUSYCON CYMBIUM LATIRUS LITIOPA LYMNARA MELANIA MODULUS PURPURA RANELLA VALVATA VERTIGO VITRINA ZONITES ACHATINA ALOCINMA ELLOBIUM FOSSARIA GYRAULUS HELICINA HELISOMA JANTHINA KATAYAMA LITORINA NERITINA OLEACINA SUCCINEA

(— OF SNAKE) BOA ERYX NAIA NAJA ASPIS BITIS BOIGA ECHIS ELAPS CAUSUS DABOIA ELAPHE HURRIA ILYSIA LIGUUS NATRIX PYTHON VIPERA ATHERIS BOAEDON COLUBER ECHIDNA MEHELYA OPHIDIA ZAMENIS BOTHROPS BUNGARUS CERBERUS CROTALUS DEMANSIA EUNECTES FARANCIA LACHESIS MICRURUS STORERIA TYPHLOPS

(— OF SPIDER) ARANEA LYCOSA MYGALE AGALENA ARGIOPE ATTIDAE NEPHILA PHOLCUS LINYPHIA ULOBORUS

(— OF SPIROCHETE) BORRELIA

(— OF SPONGE) SYCON GEODIA SCYPHA ASCETTA CHALINA GRANTIA SPONGIA SYCETTA LEUCETTA

(— OF SPOROZOAN) NOSEMA

(— OF SQUID) LOLIGO SEPIOLA

(— OF SQUIRREL) SCIURUS

(— OF SUBSHRUB) LECHEA ARMERIA ASCYRUM BEGONIA FELICIA ATRIPLEX COLUMNEA

(— OF SWAN) OLOR CYGNUS

(— OF TAKIN) BUDORCAS

(— OF TAPEWORM) BERTIA LIGULA DAVAINEA HARRISIA

(— OF TAYRA) GALERA GALICTIS

(— OF TELEDU) MYDAUS

(— OF TERN) GYGIS STERNA

(— OF THISTLE) CNICUS CARDUUS

(— OF TICK) ARGAS ARGUS IXODES HYALOMMA

(— OF TOAD) BUFO HYLA PIPA ALYTES XENOPUS ASCAPHUS

(— OF TREE) ACER BIXA BRYA COLA HURA ILEX INGA MABA OLAX OLEA RHUS THEA ABIES AEGLE ALNUS ANIBA BIOTA BUTEA BUXUS CARYA CEIBA CYCAS DURIO EURYA FAGUS FICUS HAKEA HEVEA HOPEA IXORA KHAYA LARIX MALUS MELIA MESUA MORUS NYSSA OCHNA PADUS PICEA PINUS PYRUS SALIX TAXUS THUJA TILIA TOONA TREMA TSUGA ULMUS UNONA VITEX XYLIA ABROMA ACHRAS AKANIA AMOMIS AMYRIS ANDIRA ANNONA ARALIA AUCUBA AZALEA BAPHIA BETULA BOMBAX CANTUA CARAPA CARICA CASSIA CEDRUS CELTIS CERCIS CITRUS CLUSIA COFFEA CORDIA CORNUS DATURA DRIMYS EPERUA EPERVA EUCLEA EVODIA FEIJOA GARRYA GENIPA GINKGO GNETUM GREWIA GUAREA IDESIA ILLIPE LAURUS LITCHI LITSEA LUCUMA LYCIUM MAMMEA MIMOSA MYRCIA MYRICA OCOTEA OLNEYA OSTRYA OWENIA PAPPEA PARITI PERSEA PRUNUS PTELEA QUIINA RANDIA ROYENA SAPIUM SAPOTA SCHIMA SENCIO SESBAN SHOREA SIMABA SORBUS STYRAX TECOMA AGATHIS ARBUTUS ARDISIA ASIMINA ASSONIA BANKSIA BUMELIA BURSERA CANANGA CANELLA CASASIA CATALPA CEDRELA CERASUS CLETHRA COPAIVA CORYLUS COTINUS CUNONIA CUPANIA CYDONIA CYRILLA DOMBEYA ECHINUS EHRETIA EPACRIS EUGENIA FERONIA GMELINA GUAZUMA GYMINDA HAGENIA HALESIA HICORIA HOVENIA HUMIRIA JUGLANS KADELIA KOKOONA LAGETTA LICANIA LINGOUM MACLURA MICONIA MORINDA MORINGA MURRAYA OCHROMA OLEARIA PANGIUM PIMENTA PISONIA PLANERA POPULUS PROTIUM PSIDIUM QUASSIA QUERCUS RAPANEA REMIJIA RHAMNUS ROBINIA SCHINUS SENECIO SEQUOIA SLOANEA SOLANUM SOPHORA SURIANA SYRINGA TAMARIX TECTONA TELOPEA TORREYA TROPHIS VATERIA XIMENIA XYLOPIA XYLOSMA ZELKOVA AESCULUS ALANGIUM ALBIZZIA ALSTONIA ANTIARIS AVERRHOA BALANOPS BALOGHIA BAUHINIA BRABEJUM BROSIMUM BUDDLEIA CABRALEA CAMELLIA CANARIUM CAPPARIS CARAGANA CARPINUS CARYOCAR CASEARIA CASTANEA CASTILLA CECROPIA CINCHONA CODIAEUM CONDALIA CYBISTAX DILLENIA DIPTERYX DODONAEA DOVYALIS DRACAENA DUBOISIA EUCOMMIA EUONYMUS EUPTELEA EXOSTEMA FITZROYA

FRAXINUS FUNTUMIA GARCINIA GARDENIA GORDONIA GUAIACUM HIBISCUS HIRTELLA HOMALIUM HYMENAEA ILLICIUM JATROPHA KANDELIA KNIGHTIA LABURNUM LAPORTEA LAVATERA LECYTHIS LEUCAENA LYSILOMA MAGNOLIA MALLOTUS MAYTENUS MESPILUS MICHELIA MIMUSOPS MYOPORUM NOTELAEA PHOTINIA PISCIDIA PISTACIA PLATANUS PLUMIERA PONCIRUS PROSOPIS QUILLAJA RAVENALA ROLLINIA SAMADERA SAMBUCUS SANTALUM SAPINDUS SAURAUIA SESBANIA SIMARUBA SPONDIAS SWARTZIA TABEBUIA TAXODIUM TORRUBIA TRECULIA VARRONIA VERONICA VIBURNUM VIRGILIA VOCHYSIA
(— OF TUNICATE) SALPA ASCIDIA DOLIOLUM
(— OF TURTLE) EMYS AMYDA CHELUS CHELYS CARETTA CHELONE CLEMMYS TESTUDO TRIONYX ARCHELON CHELONIA CHELYDRA PELUSIOS
(— OF TWINER) STEMONA
(— OF UNIVALVE) DOLIUM
(— OF VINE) ROSA ABRUS ABUTA PISUM TAMUS UNONA VIGNA VITIS AKEBIA CISSUS COBAEA DERRIS ENTADA HEDERA MUCUNA PETREA POTHOS SICANA SICYOS SOLLYA VIORNA ARAUJIA BASELLA BOMAREA BRYONIA ECHITES EMBELIA EPACRIS FALCATA HUMULUS IPOMOEA MIKANIA PISONIA SECHIUM UNCARIA ZANONIA ANAMIRTA ATRAGENE BIGNONIA CLEMATIS COCCULUS DEGUELIA DOLICHOS EUONYMUS JASMINUM KENNEDYA PANDOREA PUERARIA SECAMONE SERJANIA TACSONIA WISTARIA
(— OF WALRUS) ODOBENUS
(— OF WASP) SPHEX VESPA BEMBEX CYNIPS SCOLIA TIPHIA CHRYSIS EUMENES MASARIS MUTILLA ANDRICUS CHLORION ODYNERUS POLISTES POMPILUS SPHECIUS
(— OF WEASEL) MUSTELA
(— OF WEED) CAPSELLA
(— OF WEEVIL) APION HYPERA SITONA CLEONUS CALANDRA CALENDRA CURCULIO
(— OF WHALE) CETE ARETA KOGIA BALAENA ORCINUS ZIPHIUS PHYSETER
(— OF WOLVERINE) GULO
(— OF WORM) DERO SPIO ALARIA EUNICE KERRIA MERMIS NEREIS SYLLIS ACHAETA ACHOLOE ASCARIS DUGESIA EISENIA FILARIA GLYCERA GORDIUS HESIONE LEODICE POLYNOE SABELLA SAGITTA SERPULA SETARIA SPIRURA TUBIFEX ARABELLA ASCAROPS BIPALIUM BONELLIA COOPERIA DOCHMIUS ECHIURUS FASCIOLA GEOPLANA PHORONIS SPADELLA SUBULURA SYNGAMUS SYPHACIA
(— OF ZORIL) ICTONYX
(PREF.) GEN(O)
(SUFF.) IA

GEODE DRUSE

GEOGRAPHER AMERICAN BAKER DAVIS GUYOT RONNE ATWOOD BOWMAN BRYANT SEMPLE DAVIDSON HUTCHINS MITCHELL ROBINSON GROSVENOR HUNTINGTON
ARAB BAKRI
AUSTRIAN KORISTKA PAULITSCHKE
CANADIAN PALLISER
DUTCH BLAEU
EGYPTIAN PTOLEMY
ENGLISH BEKE PEEL KEANE BEAZLEY EVEREST HAKLUYT MARKHAM RENNELL THOMPSON GREENOUGH MACKINDER FRESHFIELD
FRENCH JOMARD RECLUS VALLOT ANVILLE DELISLE DEMANGEON
GERMAN BEHM KOHL BANSE PENCK VOGEL ANDREE BEHAIM CLUVER RATZEL RITTER APIANUS EBELING GERLAND HETTNER KIEPERT KRUMMEL PESCHEL SCHONER BERGHAUS BRUCKNER BUSCHING DRYGALSKI PETERMANN RICHTHOFEN CHRISTALLER
GREEK SCYLAX STRABO MARINUS PYTHEAS DIONYSIUS PAUSANIAS ERATOSTHENES
HUNGARIAN TELEKI
ICELANDIC THORODDSEN
ITALIAN BALBI CODAZZI AMORETTI MARSIGLI
POLISH LELEWEL
PORTUGUESE CORDEIRO
RUSSIAN SEMENOV GERASIMOV KROPOTKIN SHOKALSKI PRZHEVALSKY
SCOTTISH MILL BROWN JOHNSTON
SPANISH COSA
SWEDISH HEDIN

GEOLOGIST AMERICAN DALY DANA HALL KEMP KING REID TARR CROSS GUYOT HAGUE HOBBS LEITH MCGEE ORTON SCOTT SMITH SPURR WHITE ARNOLD ATWOOD BAYLEY DUTTON EMMONS FOSTER HAYDEN HOLMES IRVING JAGGAR LAWSON LESLEY MARCOU MATHER MENARD POWELL SHALER UPJOHN WRIGHT BALLARD BARRELL BRANNER GILBERT HOLLICK IDDINGS JOHNSON MACLURE MERRILL PIRSSON RANSOME RUSSELL TALMAGE VANHISE WHITNEY WRATHER LEVERETT MASURSKY MITCHELL NEWBERRY PUMPELLY SILLIMAN WINCHELL HITCHCOCK JOHANNSEN SALISBURY TWENHOFEL CHAMBERLIN LOUDERBACK WASHINGTON
AUSTRALIAN DAVID MAWSON
AUSTRIAN BECKE HAUER SUESS HAIDINGER HOCHSTETTER MOJSISOVICS
BELGIAN RENARD
CANADIAN BELL ADAMS LOGAN DAWSON TYRRELL WALLACE
DANISH KOCH
DUTCH TROMP
ENGLISH BELT TATE FUCHS JUKES LYELL SMITH SORBY ANSTED BONNEY CLARKE FORBES HOLMES MAWSON SCROPE DAWKINS GREGORY HOLLAND MANTELL BUCKLAND LYDEKKER PHILLIPS SEDGWICK GREENOUGH MURCHISON PRESTWICH STRICKLAND
FRENCH FOUQUE ARCHIAC DAUBREE DELESSE BARRANDE BEAUMONT BERTRAND DOLOMIEU DUFRENOY LAPPARENT
GERMAN BUCH ABICH COHEN DECHEN ROEMER WERNER ZITTEL ALBERTI BISCHOF CREDNER GEINITZ LEONHARD QUENSTEDT KEYSERLING ROSENBUSCH
ICELANDIC THORODDSEN
IRISH OLDHAM
ITALIAN MERCALLI
NEW ZEALAND HAAST
NORWEGIAN BROGGER KJERULF
RUSSIAN OBRUCHEV
SCOTTISH HALL CROLL LYELL GEIKIE HUTTON MILLER RAMSAY OGLIVIE PLAYFAIR MACCULLOCH
SWEDISH ANTEVS TORELL HISINGER NATHORST NORDENSKJOLD
SWISS HEIM DELUC

GEOMETRIC CUBIST CUBISTIC
(— TERM) SECANT

GEOMETRY EUCLID SPHERICS
(KIND OF —) SOLID

GEOPHAGY PICA

GEORGIA

CAPITAL: ATLANTA
COLLEGE: SPELMAN MOREHOUSE
COUNTY: BIBB CLAY COBB COOK HALL TIFT WARE BANKS BRYAN BUTTS DOOLY EARLY FLOYD GRADY PEACH RABUN TROUP WORTH COFFEE COWETA DEKALB ECHOLS ELBERT FANNIN FULTON JASPER LANIER OCONEE TWIGGS WILKES CATOOSA LAURENS LUMPKIN GWINNETT MUSCOGEE
INDIAN: GUALE YUCHI CHIAHA OCONEE YAMASEE
LAKE: LANIER MARTIN HARDING NOTTELY BANKHEAD HARTWELL SINCLAIR
MOUNTAIN: STONE KENNESAW
NATIVE: CRACKER
PRESIDENT: CARTER
RIVER: PEA FLINT ETOWAH OCONEE PIGEON CONECUH SATILLA ALTAMAHA OCMULGEE
STATE BIRD: THRASHER
STATE NICKNAME: PEACH
STATE TREE: LIVEOAK
TOWN: JESUP MACON JASPER OCILLA AUGUSTA CONYERS DECATUR ELLIJAY GRIFFIN VIDALIA MARIETTA MOULTRIE SAVANNAH VALDOSTA WAYCROSS
UNIVERSITY: EMORY GATECH MERCER

GEORGIA (ALSO SEE RUSSIA)

CAPITAL: TIFLIS TBILISI
COIN: RUBLE
LANGUAGE: KARTVELIAN
MOUNTAIN: USHBA SHKHARA TETNULD DIDIABULI RUSTAVELI
MOUNTAIN RANGE: LIKHI KARTLI LOMISI LIKHSKY MESKHET CAUCASUS LOMISSKY MESKHETI KARTLIYSKY KARTALINIAN
PEOPLE: GORJ OSSET GEORGIAN KARTVELI SAKARTVELO
PLAIN: KARTLI COLCHIS KOLKHIDA KARTALINIAN
RIVER: KURA RIONI INGURI KODORI MTKVARI
TOWN: GORI POTI BATUMI KUTAISI RUSTAVI SUKHUMI KHASHURI MTSKHETA
VOLCANO: KAZBEK MKINVARI

GEORGIAN ADZHAR CRACKER
GEORGIA PINE LONGLEAF
GEPHYREAN STARWORM
GER STRANGER
GERAINT (WIFE OF —) ENID
GERANIUM DOVEFOOT FLUXWEED SHAMEFACE
GERANIUM LAKE SPARK NACARAT
GERANIUM PINK BERMUDA
GERBIL JIRD
GERIANOL ISOLATE
GERM BUG CHIT SEED SPARK SPAWN SPERM GERMEN GERMULE MICROBE SEMINAL RUDIMENT SEEDLING SEMINARY SEMINIUM
(— CELL) GONE
(PREF.) BLAST(O) SPERM(A)(ATI)(ATIO)(ATO)(I)(IO)(O)
(SUFF.) BLAST(IC)(Y) SPERM(A)(AE)(AL)(IA)(IC)(OUS)(UM)(Y)
GERMAN BALT HANS ALMAN HEINE JERRY ALMAIN DUTCHY HEINIE TEUTON TEDESCO COTILLON GERMANIC TUDESQUE
(PREF.) TEUTO
GERMANDER POLY BETONY FOXTAIL SOVENEZ SCORDIUM
GERMANE GERMAN APROPOS RELEVANT PERTINENT
GERMANIC GOTHIC GOTHONIC TEUTONIC
GERMAN MEASLES ROSEOLA RUBELLA
GERMAN SHEPHERD ALSATIAN
GERMAN SILVER ALBATA

GERMANY

ANCIENT: ALMAIN ALMAINE
ANCIENT TRIBESMAN: JUTE TEUTON VISIGOTH OSTROGOTH
CANAL: KIEL WESER LUDWIG
CAPITAL: BERLIN
CHEESE: MUENSTER TILSITER LIMBURGER
COAL REGION: RUHR SAAR SARRE
COIN: MARK KRONE TALER GULDEN KRONEN THALER PFENNIG GROSCHEN
DIALECT: KOLSCH KOELSCH BALTISCH HESSISCH

DYNASTY: HOHENSTAUFEN HOHENZOLLERN
FOOD: WURST KNODEL SPATZLE STRUDEL MARZIPAN ROULADEN
HANSEATIC CITY: KOLN LUBECK COLOGNE HAMBURG LUEBECK
ISLAND: USEDOM WOLLIN FEHMARN FRISIAN
LAKE: DUMMER WURMSEE AMMERSEE BODENSEE CHIEMSEE MURITZEE CONSTANCE
LANGUAGE: DEUTSCH
MEASURE: AAM IMI OHM FASS FUSS LAST RUTE SACK STAB CARAT EIMER KANNE KETTE LINIE MAASS METZE RUTHE SIMRI MASSEL MORGEN OXHOFT SEIDEL STRICH JUCHART KLAFTER TAGWERK SCHEFFEL SCHOPPEN STUBCHEN VIERLING
MONEY: NOTGELD OSTMARK
MOUNTAIN: FELDBERG WATZMANN
MOUNTAIN RANGE: ORE ALPS HARZ RHON HARDT HUNSRUCK
NAME: REICH ASHKENAZ GERMANIA DEUTSCHLAND
NATIVE: GOTH SAXON TEUTON
PORT: EMDEN BREMEN HAMBURG ROSTOCK STETTIN
RESORT: EMS BADEN AACHEN
RIVER: ALZ EMS INN EDER EGER ELBE ISAR LAHN LECH MAIN NAAB NAHE ODER OKER REMS RUHR SAAR SIEG ALLER DONAU EIDER FULDA HAVEL HUNTE ILLER LEINE LIPPE MOSEL MULDE PEENE REGEN RHEIN RHINE SAALE SAUER SPREE UCKER VECHT WERRA WESER DANUBE ELSTER KOCHER NECKAR NEISSE RANDOW TAUBER WARNOW ALTMUHL JEETZEL PEGNITZ SALZACH UNSTRUT
STATE: BADEN HESSE LIPPE BAYERN BREMEN HESSEN SAXONY BAVARIA HAMBURG PRUSSIA SAARLAND BRUNSWICK
TOWN: AUE EMS HOF ULM BONN GERA GOCH HAAR HAMM JENA KIEL KOLN LAHR SUHL AALEN AHLEN EMDEN ESSEN FURTH GOTHA HAGEN HALLE HERNE MAINZ MOLLN NEUSS PIRNA TRIER AACHEN ALTENA ALTONA BARMEN BERLIN BREMEN CASSEL DACHAU DESSAU ERFURT KASSEL LINDEN LUBECK MUNICH PLAUEN TREVES BAMBERG BRESLAU COBLENZ COLOGNE COTTBUS CREFELD DRESDEN GORLITZ HAMBURG HANOVER LEIPZIG MAYENCE MUNCHEN MUNSTER POTSDAM ROSTOCK SPANDAU ZWICKAU AUGSBURG CHEMNITZ DORTMUND DUISBURG FREIBURG LIEGNITZ MANNHEIM NURNBERG SCHWERIN WURSELEN WURZBURG DARMSTADT KARLSRUHE MAGDEBURG NUREMBERG OSNABRUCK STUTTGART WUPPERTAL DUSSELDORF HEIDELBERG OBERHAUSEN
UNIVERSITY TOWN: FREIBURG HEIDELBERG
WEIGHT: LOT GRAN LOTE LOTH UNZE LOTHE PFUND STEIN PRUNDE DRACHMA ZENTNER VIERLING
WINE: MOSELLE RIESLING

GERMFREE AXENIC
GERMICIDE KRELOS MERBROMIN
GERMINABLE PREGNANT
GERMINATE BUD HIT CHIP CHIT GERM SHOOT SPIRE SPRIT BRAIRD SPROUT STRIKE PULLULATE
GERMINATION CATCH
GERSHOM **(FATHER OF —)** LEVI MOSES
(MOTHER OF —) ZIPPORAH
GERSHWIN IRA GEORGE
GERYON **(DOG OF —)** ORTHUS
(FATHER OF —) CHRYSAOR
(MOTHER OF —) CALLIRRHOE
(SLAYER OF —) HERCULES
GESAN TAPUYAN CHAVANTE
GESHAM **(FATHER OF —)** JAHDAI
GESTATION GOING BREEDING PREGNANCY
GESTE DEED
GESTICULATE GESTURE
GESTURE CUT FIG BECK BERE GEST SIGN FILIP GESTE HONOR SANNA ACTION BECKON BREATH CUTOFF FILLIP MOTION SALUTE SIGNAL CURTSEY FASHION FLICKER MURGEON ACCOLADE CEREMONY
(— OF DERISION) SNOOK
(— OF DOUBT) SHRUG
(— OF SALUTATION) SALAAM
(AFFECTED —) GAATCH
(HAND —) MUDRA
(HINDU —) NAMASTE
(OBSCENE —) BIRD
(OSTENTATIOUS —) POMP
(THREATENING —) MINT
(USELESS —) FUTILITY
GET COP DIG GIT WIN EARN FALL GAIN GRAB HAVE HENT TAKE TILL AFONG ANNEX CATCH COVER FETCH LATCH DERIVE OBTAIN PUZZLE SECURE ACQUIRE CAPTURE COMPARE CONQUER PROCURE PRODUCE RECEIVE PERCEIVE
(— ABOARD) FLIP
(— ABOUT) BEGO NAVIGATE
(— ALONG) DO GEE FARE FEND AGREE FADGE FODGE SPEED FETTLE
(— AROUND) BYPASS COMPASS FINESSE FLUMMER OUTFLANK
(— AT) ACCESS ATTAIN
(— AWAY) LAM RYNT SLIP EVADE CHEESE ESCAPE
(— BACK) REDEEM RETIRE RECOVER
(— BETTER OF) WAX BEST DING DOWN DAUNT FLING SHEND SHENT STICK STING JOCKEY OVERGO RECOVER OVERCOME SURMOUNT
(— BY ARTIFICE) WIND
(— BY ASKING) KICK
(— BY CUNNING) WHIZZLE
(— BY EXTORTION) GRATE
(— BY FLATTERY) COG
(— CLEAR OF) STRIP
(— DISHONESTLY) FIRK
(— DOWN) ALIGHT
(— DRUNK) SOUSE
(— IN RETURN) REAP
(— LOST) STRAY TRAIK
(— ON) AGE FARE BOARD CHEFE CHEVE FRAME MOUNT SHIFT EXPLOIT
(— ON WELL) LIKE
(— OUT) LEAK SCRAM CHEESE OUTWIN VOETSAK
(— PAST) BEAT HURDLE
(— POSSESSION) CARRY
(— READY) GET BOUN PARE RANK BOWNE BRACE FRAME FETTLE ORDAIN APPAREL
(— RID) CAST DISH DUMP FREE JUNK SHAB TOSS ERASE SHAKE SHIFT SHOOT SLOUGH UNLOAD DELIVER DISCARD EXTRUDE DISPATCH DISSOLVE
(— SURREPTITIOUSLY) SNEAK
(— THE POINT) SAVVY
(— TO BOTTOM OF) FATHOM
(— UNDER CONTROL) RAIM
(— UNDER WAY) ROLL
(— UP) ARISE HUDDUP UPRISE HAIRPIN
(PREF.) **(— OFF)** DE
GETA SABOT
GETHER **(FATHER OF —)** ARAM
GETHSEMANE **(LOCALE OF —)** OLIVET
GETTING **(— ON)** TOWARD
(— OUT OF BED) LEVEE
GET-TOGETHER DO DRINK HOBNOB BAMBOCHE POTLATCH
GET-UP ATTIRE
GETUP SETOUT
GEWGAW DIE TOY WALY KNACK WALLY BAUBLE FANGLE FEGARY JIGGER FLAMFEW TRANGAM TRINKET FOLDEROL GIMCRACK JIMCRACK TRIMTRAM
GEYSER BORE JETTER

GHANA

CAPITAL: ACCRA
COIN: PESEWA
DAM: AKOSOMBO
LAKE: VOLTA BOSUMTWI
LANGUAGE: GA EWE TWI FANTI HAUSA DAGBANI DAGOMBA
MONEY: CEDI NEWCEDI
MOUNTAIN: AFADJATO
NATIVE: GA EWE AHAFO BRONG FANTI ASHANTI DAGOMBA MAMPRUSI
REGION: VOLTA ASHANTI BRONGAHAFO
RIVER: OTI PRA DAKA TANO AFRAM VOLTA ANKOBRA KULPAWN
TOWN: HO WA ODA AXIM FIAN KETA TALA TEMA ACCRA BAWKU ENCHI LAWRA LEGON SAMPA YAPEI DUNKWA KARAGA KPANDU KUMASI NSAWAM OBUASI SWEDRU TAMALE TARKWA WASIPE ANTUBIA DAMONGO MAMPONG PRESTEA SEKONDI SUNYANI WINNEBA AKOSOMBO KINTAMPO TAKORADI
WIND: HARMATTAN

GHARRY SHIGRAM
GHASTLY WAN GASH GRIM PALE BLATE GHAST LURID UNKET UNKID DISMAL GOUSTY GRISLY PALLID CHARNEL DEATHLY FEARFUL GASHFUL GRIZZLY GRUGOUS HIDEOUS MACABRE DREADFUL GRUESOME HORRIBLE SHOCKING TERRIBLE
GHAWAZI BARAMIKA
GHAZEL ODE POEM
GHERKIN CUCUMBER CORNICHON
GHETTO JEWRY JUDAISM
GHIBELLINE WAIBLING
GHOST HAG KER BHUT HANT JUBA WAFF BUGAN CADDY DUFFY DUPPY FETCH GAIST GUEST HAUNT JUMBY LARVA PRETA SHADE SPOOK UMBRA CHUREL IDOLON SOWLTH SPIRIT SPRITE TAISCH ANTAEUS ANTAIOS BOGGART BUGGANE GYTRASH PHANTOM SPECTER SPECTRE VAMPIRE BARGHEST GUYTRASH PHANTASM REVENANT
(PREF.) SPECTRO SPOOKO
GHOSTFISH WRYMOUTH
GHOSTLY EERY EERIE GOUSTY SHADOWY UNCANNY WEIRDLY CHTHONIC GHASTFUL SPECTRAL
GHOST MOTH SWIFT HEPIALID
GHOSTS **(AUTHOR OF —)** IBSEN
(CHARACTER IN —) HELEN JACOB ALVING OSWALD REGINA MANDERS ENGSTRAND
GHOST-WRITER SPOOK
GHOULISH SATANIC
GHUZ OGHUZ
GI DOGFACE SOLDIER
GIAI NHANG
GIANNI SCHICCHI **(CHARACTER IN —)** BUOSO DONATI LAURETTA RINUCCIO SCHICCHI
(COMPOSER OF —) PUCCINI
GIANT ORC ANAK ETEN HUGE OGRE OTUS WATE YMER YMIR AFRIT BALOR CACUS HYMIR JOTUN MIMAS MIMER THRYM TITAN TROLL AFREET ALBION FAFNIR GIGANT GOEMOT PALLAS THJAZI THURSE TITYUS WARLOW ANTAEUS CYCLOPS GOLIATH WARLOCK ASCOPART BELLERUS COLBRAND GIGANTIC GOEMAGOT GOGMAGOG MASTODON MORGANTE ORGOGLIO TYPHOEUS PROCRUSTES
(1-EYED —) CYCLOPS
(100-EYED —) ARGUS
(100-HANDED —) GYGES COTTUS BRIAREUS
(1000-ARMED —) BANA
(PL.) ANAK ANAKIM COTTUS ALOADAE REPHAIM NEPHILIM ZAMZUMMIM
(PREF.) GIGANT(I)(O)
GIANTESS NORN ARGANTE

GIANT FULMAR NELLY STINKER STINKPOT
GIANT GRASS OTATE
GIANT HERON GOLIATH
GIANTISM ACROMEGALY
GIANTLIKE CYCLOPIC CYCLOPEAN CYCLOPIAN
GIANT LILY FIGUE MAGUEY
GIANT PUFFBALL FUZZ FUZZBALL
GIANTS IN THE EARTH (AUTHOR OF —) ROLVAAG
(CHARACTER IN —) OLE PER ANNA HANS OLSA BERET HANSA PEDER
GIARDIA LAMBLIA
GIB JIB SHOE DEMUR SLIPPER
GIBBAR GIBBERT JUBARTAS
GIBBER CHAT CHATTER
GIBBERISH GREEK JABBER JARGON CHOCTAW ABRACADABRA
GIBBET STOB TREE CROOK JEBAT GALLOWS POTENCE EQUULEUS
GIBBON LAR WAWA UNGKA WUYEN CAMPER HULOCK HOOLOCK SIAMANG HYLOBATE
GIBBOUS CONVEX HULCHY HUMPED SACCATE
GIBE (ALSO SEE JIBE) BOB RUB GIRD JAPE JEST JIBE PROG QUIB QUIP SKIT WIPE FLEER FLING FLIRT FRUMP GLEEK KNACK SCOFF SCOMM SCORN SLANT SNEER DERIDE GLANCE HECKLE BROCARD SARCASM RIDICULE
GIBING SNASH
GID DUNT GIDDY STURDY GOGGLES POTHERY VERTIGO
GIDDALTI (FATHER OF —) HEMAN
GIDDINESS LUNACY SOORAWN
GIDDY GAGA AREEL BARMY DITSY DITZY GLAKY INANE LIGHT SILLY SPACY WESTY GIGLET GLAKED GOWKED GOWKIT SHANNY STURDY VOLAGE GLAIKET LARKING HALUCKET HELLICAT SKIPPING
GIDDY-HEADED HELLICAT
GIDEON (FATHER OF —) JOASH
GIDEONI (SON OF —) ABIDAN
GIFT BOX FOY QUO SOP BENT BOON DASH ENAM MEED SAND BONUS BRIBE CAULP CUDDY DONUM FLAIR GRANT KNACK TOKEN BEFANA CADEAU DASHEE DONARY GENIUS GERSUM GIFTIE GIVING HANSEL LEGACY RECADO REGALO TALENT XENIUM APTNESS BEFFANA BENEFIT CHARISM CHARITY DEODATE DONATIO DOUCEUR ETRENNE FACULTY FAIRING GIFTURE HANDSEL PRESENT PROPINE REGALIO SUBSIDY TASHRIF TRIBUTE AMATORIO APTITUDE BENEFICE BESTOWAL BLESSING COURTESY DONATION DONATIVE GARRISON GIVEAWAY GRATUITY MORTUARY OBLATION OFFERING POTLATCH SPORTULA BENEFACTION REMEMBRANCE PHILANTHROPY PRESENTATION
(— FROM HUSBAND TO WIFE) ARRAS
(— OF GOD) GRACE
(— OF MONEY) POUCH GARNISH BAKSHISH BAKSHEESH
(— OF NATURE) DOWER DOWRY
(— RECEIVER) DONEE
(— TO GOD) DEODATE
(— TO ROMAN PEOPLE) CONGIARY
(CHARITABLE —) ALMS ENAM PITTANCE
(COMPULSORY —) SIXENIA
(LIBERAL —) LARGESSE
(NATURAL —) TALENT
(NEW YEAR'S EVE —) ETRENNE HAGMENA HOGMANAY
(SPIRITUAL —) CHARISM CHARISMA
(PL.) OBLATA MISSILES
GIFTBOOK ANNUAL KEEPSAKE
GIG RUN TUB MOZE BANDY BUGGY CHAIR GIGGE CHAISE CLATCH DENNET WHISKY CALESIN TILBURY STANHOPE ENGAGEMENT
GIGANTIC HUGE GIANT MAMMOTH TITANIC COLOSSAL ENORMOUS GIGANTAL ATLANTEAN MONSTROUS BROBDINGNAGIAN
GIGGER TEASELER
GIGGLE TEHEE KECKLE NICKER TEEHEE TITTER SNICKER TWITTER
GIGLET JIG
GIL BLAS
GIL BLAS (AUTHOR OF —) LESAGE
(CHARACTER IN —) GIL BLAS LEWIS PEREZ AURORA MENCIA SCIPIO ANTONIA ARSENIA ROLANDO ALPHONSO DOROTHEA FABRICIO MATTHIAS OLIVAREZ SANGRADO
GILD GILT BEGILD ENGILD ORFGILD
GILDED GILT AURATE INAURATE
GILDER TRACER
GILEAD (FATHER OF —) MACHIR
(SON OF —) JEPHTHAH
GILGAMESH IZDUBAR
GILL JILL QUAD GHYLL PLICA GILLIE LAMELLA BRANCHIA QUADRANT
(—S OF BIVALVE) BEARD
(PL.) GINNERS CHOLLERS BRANCHIAE
(SUFF.) BRANCH(IA)(IATE)
GILLAR PITTO
GILLIE GILLY HENCHMAN
GILLS
(PREF.) BRANCHI(O)
GILLYFLOWER STOCK GILVER GELOFRE GILLIVER
GILT SOW
GILTHEAD CONNER MELANURE
GIMBAL GEMEL JEMBLE
GIMCRACK QUIP BAUBLE FIZGIG GEWGAW JIMJAM TRIFLE TRANGAM TRINKET JIMCRACK WHIMWHAM
GIMLET SCREW WIMBLE PIERCEL PIERCER
GIMMICK GAFF SHTIK SHTICK SCHTICK
GIMP TAR ORRIS GUIMPE GIMPING
GIN MAX CRAB GRIN LACE RUIN TAPE TRAP CLEAN JACKY SNARE SNARL DIDDLE GENEVA JAMBER JAMMER SPRINGE TITTERY TWANKAY EYEWATER HOLLANDS SCHIEDAM SCHNAPPS
(— AND TREACLE) MAHOGANY
(BAD —) RUIN
(DROP OF —) DAFFY
GINATH (SON OF —) TIBNI
GINGER PEPPER RATOON AROMATIC ZINZIBER COLTSFOOT
GINGERBREAD SPICE PARKIN PEPPERCAKE
GINGERLY GINGER WARILY CHARILY EDGINGLY
GINGERROOT HAND RACE
(PL.) ASARUM
GINGHAM CHAMBRAY
GINKGO ICHO
GINSENG SANG FATIL PANAX ARALIA IVYWORT REDBERRY
GIOCONDA, LA (CHARACTER IN —) ENZO CIECA LAURA ALVISE BARNABA GIOCONDA GRIMALDO
(COMPOSER OF —) PONCHIELLI
GIRAFFE OONT CAMEL DAPPLE KAMEEL SERAPH CAMAILE RUMINANT
GIRASOL OPAL
GIRD BELT BIND GIRR GIRT HASP YERK CLOSE SCOFF ENGIRD ENRING FASTEN GIRDLE SECURE ACCINGE ENVIRON CINCTURE SURROUND
GIRDER BEAM GIRD GIRT GIRTH TABLE TRUSS BINDER SUMMER WARREN GIRDING TWISTER BUCKSTAY STRINGER
GIRDING CINCTURE
GIRDLE OBI ZON BARK BELT CEST GIRD HOOP SASH ZONA ZONE CEINT GIRTH MITER PATTE SARPE WAIST BODICE CESTUS CINGLE CIRCLE MOOCHA TISSUE ZODIAC ZONULA ZOSTER BALDRIC BALTEUS CENTRUM CENTURE COMPASS GIRDING SHINGLE CEINTURE CINCTURE CINGULUM SURROUND
(— FOR HELMET) TISSUE
(— OF CASSOCK) SURCINGLE
(— OF DIATOM) HOOP
(BRIDE'S —) CEST CESTUS
(LITTLE —) ZONULE ZONELET
(ROYAL —) MALO
(SACRED —) KUSTI
(PREF.) ZON(I)(O) ZOSTERI ZOSTERO
(SUFF.) PLEURA
GIRDLED RUNG
GIRL BIT GAL HER KIT POP SHE SIS TIB TID TIT BABE BABY BINT BIRD CHIT DAME DEEM DELL GILL JANE JILL JUDY LASS MARY MOPS MORT PERI PUSS SLUT WREN BEAST BUNNY FILLY FLUFF GUIDE KITTY LUBRA QUEAN SISSY SKIRT TIDDY TITTY TOOTS TRULL BURDIE CALICO CLINER CUMMER DALAGA DAMSEL DEEMIE FEMALE FIZGIG GEISHA GIRLIE LASSIE LOVELY MAGGIE NUMBER PIGEON SHEILA SISTER SUBDEB TOMATO CAMILLA COLLEEN CRUMPET DAMOSEL MADCHEN MAUTHER TENDREL BONNIBEL FARMETTE FEMININE GRISETTE MUCHACHA
(— NOT YET 13) PRETEEN
(— OF MEXICAN DESCENT) CHICANA
(AGILE —) YANKER
(AWKWARD —) HOIT
(BEATIFIED —) BEATA
(BEAUTIFUL —) PERI BELLE
(BOISTEROUS —) GILPY GILPEY
(BOLD —) HOIDEN HOYDEN
(CAMP FIRE —) ARTISAN
(CHORUS —) CHORINE CORYPHEE
(CLUMSY —) TAUPIE TAWPIE
(COUNTRY —) MEG JOAN
(DANCING —) ALMA DASI ALMAH KISANG KISAENG BAYADERE DEVADASI
(DANCING —S) GHAWAZI
(DEAR —) PEAT
(DUMPY —) CUTTY
(FLIGHTY —) GOOSECAP
(FLIRTATIOUS —) JADE JILLET
(FLOWER —) NYDIA
(FORWARD —) STRAP
(FROLICSOME —) GILPY
(GANGSTER'S —) MOLL
(GIDDY —) GIG GIGLET GIGLOT JILLET
(GREEK —) HAIDEE
(GYPSY —) GITANA
(HIRED —) BIDDY BIDDIE
(IMPUDENT —) STRAP
(JAPANESE —) GEISHA
(LITTLE —) SIS COOKY SISSY COOKIE LASSOCK
(MISCHIEVOUS —) CUTTY HUSSY
(MODEST —) BLUSHET
(NAIVE —) INGENUE
(NON-JEWISH —) SHIKSE SHICKSA
(PERT —) MINX HUSSY
(PRETTY —) PRIM BUNNY
(PRETTY—) BUNNY
(PRETTY —) CUTEY CUTIE
(ROMPING —) STAG TOMBOY
(SAUCY —) SNIP
(SEDUCTIVE —) LOLITA
(SERVANT —) SLUT
(SHIFTLESS —) MYSTERY
(SILLY —) SKIT
(SINGING —) ALMA ALMEH
(SLENDER —) SYLPH
(SMALL —) PINAFORE
(SPIRITED —) FILLY
(UNATTRACTIVE —) FRUMP
(UNMARRIED —) MOUSME TOWDIE MUSUMEE MADEMOISELLE
(WANTON —) GIG FILLOCK
(WILD —) BLOWZE
(WORKING —) ORISETTE
(WORTHLESS —) HUSSY
(YOUNG —) BUD MODER TITTY MAIDEN MOTHER BAGGAGE COLLEEN FLAPPER GIRLEEN ROSEBUD
(PL.) GIRLERY GIRLHOOD
(PREF.) PUPI
GIRLFRIEND LADY STEADY
(GANGSTER'S —) MOLL
GIRL OF THE GOLDEN WEST
(CHARACTER IN —) DICK JACK RANCE MINNIE JOHNSON RAMERREZ
(COMPOSER OF —) PUCCINI
GIRT CINCT
GIRTH GIRD GIRT TAPE CINCH

GARTH GIRSE GRETH WANTY CINGLE WARROK COMPASS GIRDING SHINGLE WEBBING
GIST JET NET NUB SUM CHAT CORE GITE KNOT MEAT PITH GREAT HEART JOIST POINT SENSE BURDEN KERNEL ESSENCE PURPORT SUMMARY STRENGTH
GITH MELANTHY
GIVE ADD GIE HOB TIP BEAR DEAL DOLE HAND METE SELL TAKE WEVE WHIP YEVE ALLOW AWARD COUGH GRANT REFER YIELD ACCORD AFFORD BESTOW CONFER DEMISE DOTATE FASTEN IMPART IMPOSE IMPUTE RENDER SUPPLY CONSIGN DELIVER FORGIVE FURNISH PRESENT PROPINE BEQUEATH DISPENSE
(— A BOOST) BOLSTER
(— ADHERENCE) ASSENT
(— ADMITTANCE) ACCEPT
(— ADVICE) READ ADVISE
(— AN ACCOUNT) TELL RELATE REPORT
(— AND TAKE) GIFFGAFF
(— ANYTHING NAUSEOUS TO) DOSE
(— A PLACE TO) SITUATE
(— APPROVAL) CONSENT
(— A REASON) ACCOUNT
(— A REMEDY) MINISTER
(— AS CONCESSION) YETTE
(— AS EXPLANATION) ASSIGN
(— ASSURANCE) EFFRONT
(— ATTENTION TO) HEED
(— AUTHORITY) ENABLE EMPOWER ACCREDIT
(— AWAY) PART
(— BACK) REFUND RETURN RESTORE
(— BIRTH) KIT BEAR BORN DROP FIND MAKE BEGET BREED ISSUE WORLD FARROW KINDLE LITTER DELIVER FRESHEN
(— BY WILL) DEVISE
(— CARE) NURSE
(— CLAIM TO) REMISE
(— COUNSEL) AREAD AREED
(— CREDIT FOR) FRIST
(— CURRENCY TO) PASS
(— EAR) HARK HARKEN LISTEN HEARKEN
(— EXPRESSION TO) EMOTE FRAME VOICE
(— FORM) CUT
(— FORTH) WARP YIELD AFFORD CONCEIVE
(— GROUND) RETIRE
(— HEED) LOOK ATTEND
(— IN) BOW RELENT CONCEDE COLLAPSE
(— IN EXCHANGE) SWAP SWOP
(— INFORMATION) WARN
(— IN MARRIAGE) BESTOW SPOUSE
(— INSTRUCTION) LEAR
(— NAME TO) BAPTIZE
(— NOTICE) WARN HERALD APPRISE PUBLISH ANNOUNCE INTIMATE
(— NOTICE TO APPEAR) GARNISH
(— OBLIQUE EDGE) CANT
(— OFF) EMIT SEND SHED EXUDE FLING DIVIDE EFFUSE EVOLVE EXHALE EXPIRE EXCRETE SEPARATE
(— ONE'S SELF OVER TO) ADDICT
(— ONE'S WORD) PROMISE
(— OUT) BOOM LEAK EXUDE ISSUE PETAL EVOLVE EMANATE OUTGIVE
(— OVER) LIN
(— PAIN) AGGRIEVE
(— PLACE) VAIL BACCARE
(— PLEDGE) GAGE
(— PROMINENCE TO) FEATURE
(— RELUCTANTLY) BEGRUDGE
(— SATISFACTION) ABY ABYE ABEGGE
(— SPARINGLY) INCH
(— STRENGTH TO) NERVE
(— SUPPORT) ASSIST ANIMATE
(— TEMPORARILY) LEND
(— TIP) TOUT
(— TONGUE) CRY YEARN
(— UP) PUT BURY DROP PART CHUCK DEMIT DEVOW FORGO LEAVE RAISE REMIT SHOOT SPARE SPEND WAIVE ABJURE ADDICT BETRAY DESERT DEVOTE FOREGO MIZZLE REFUSE RELENT RENDER RESIGN VACATE ABANDON DEPOSIT DESPAIR FLUMMOX FORBEAR FORGIVE REFRAIN RELEASE ABDICATE RENOUNCE
(— VENT TO) EMIT ISSUE DISCHARGE
(— VOICE) BOLT ACCENT
(— WARNING) ALERT
(— WAY) GO FAIL FOLD KEEL MOVE SINK VAIL BREAK BUDGE BURST FAINT SLAKE YIELD BUCKLE FALTER RELENT SWERVE FOUNDER RECLAIM SUCCUMB
(— WITNESS) DEPOSE
GIVE-AND-TAKE SWAP
GIVEN APT DONEE NATHAN PROMPT
(— TO) ALL AFTER
(SUFF.) **(— TO)** ABLE IBLE LEW
GIVER DONOR
(— OF ALMS) ALMONER
(— OF LIFE) APHETA
(NAME —) EPONYM
GIVING DOLE BOUNTY DATION REMISE
(— BY WILL) TESTATION
(— HELP) ADJUTANT
(— MILK) FRESH
(— NO MILK) YELD YELL
(— TROUBLE) CUMBROUS
GIZMO DOODAD GADGET
GIZZARD CROP GIGERIUM
GIZZARD SHAD SKIPJACK
GLABROUS BALD SMOOTH GLABRATE LEVIGATE
GLACIAL (— FORMATION) ARETE
GLACIARIUM RINK
GLACIATE ICE
GLACIATION MINDEL
(— STAGE) RISS WURM
GLACIER BRAE ICECAP STREAM CALOTTE ICEBERG PIEDMONT
(FACING A —) STOSS
(FACING AGAINST —) STOSS
(PREF.) GLACIO
GLACIOLOGY CRYOLOGY
GLACIS ESPLANADE
GLAD GAY FAIN LIEF VAIN CANTY HAPPY PROUD BLITHE FESTUS GLADLY JOCUND JOYFUL JOYOUS GLADFUL GLEEFUL JOCULAR ANIMATED CHEERFUL CHEERING FESTIVAL GLADSOME PLEASING
GLADDEN JOY GLAD BLESS BLISS CHEER EXULT MIRTH BLITHE COMFORT GLADIFY LIGHTEN REJOICE
(PREF.) TERP(I)(SI)
GLADE LAWN LAUND SLADE SHRADD SUNGLADE SUNSCALD
(PREF.) NEMO
GLADIATOR THRAX RETIARY SAMNITE SECUTOR ANDABATA
GLADIOLUS GLAD IRID LILY LEVERS LILIUM GLADIOLA
GLADLY GLAD LIEF FAINLY LIEFLY LOVELY HAPPILY
GLADNESS JOY GLAD GLEE BLISS MIRTH BLITHE FAINNESS GLADSHIP PLEASURE
GLADSOME BLITHE
GLAGA KASA KUSA TALTHIB
GLAMOR SCRY UTIS OOMPH PIZAZZ BRABBLE PIZZAZZ BALLYHOO
GLAMORIZE POT GLORIFY
GLAMOROUS GLAM EXOTIC ALLURING CHARMING
GLAMOUR HALO PAZAZZ PIZAZZ PIZZAZZ PRESTIGE
GLANCE EYE RAY SEE BEAM CAST GLIM LEER PEEK SCRY SKEG VIEW WINK BLENK BLINK BLUSH CAROM FLASH GLEEK GLENT GLIDE GLIFF GLINT GLISK GRAZE PRINK SCREW SIGHT SKIME SLANT SQUIZ TWIRE APERCU ASPECT CARROM GANDER REGARD SCANCE STRIKE VISION EYEBEAM EYESHOT EYEWINK GLIMPSE BELAMOUR GLIFFING OEILLADE
(— OFF) GLACE
(— THROUGH) SAMPLE
(LOVE —) AMORET
(MELANCHOLY —) DOWNCAST
(SHARP —) DART
(SIDELONG —) SHEW SLENT SKLENT
(SLY —) GLEG GLIME GLOAT
GLAND MILT NOIX SETA CLYER CRYPT GONAD LIVER MAMMA ACINUS BREAST KERNEL THYMUS TONSIL ADRENAL CRUMENA NECTARY PAROTID PAROTIS TEARPIT THYROID CONARIUM ENDOCRIN FOLLICLE FOLLOWER GANGLION GLANDULA GLANDULE HOOFWORM PROSTATE SCIRRHUS SPERMARY TESTICLE
(PREF.) ADEN(O) SCIRRH(O)
(SUFF.) ADEN SCIRRHUS
GLANDERS FARCY MALLEUS
GLANDULAR EARTHY INNATE SEXUAL ADENOID PHYSICAL ADENOIDAL
GLANS NUT GLAND
GLARE BEAT GAZE BLARE BLAZE BLOOM FLAME GLAZE STARE GLITTER ICEBLINK RADIANCE
GLARING HARD RANK GLARY AGLARE GARISH BURNING FLARING STARING FLAGRANT
GLASGOW (NATIVE OF —) GLASWEGIAN
GLASS CUP VER CALX FLAT FLUX FRIT JENA MOIL PONY VITA CHARK FACER FLINT GLAZE STOOP STOUP VERRE VITRE CALGON CEMENT CULLET RUMMER SPECKS VITRUM ALEYARD BIFOCAL BRIMMER CHIRPER CRYSTAL PERLITE SCHMELZ TALLBOY VITRITE FROSTING OBSIDIAN SCHOPPEN PERSPECTIVE
(— IN STATE OF FUSION) METAL
(— OF A MIRROR) STONE
(— OF BEER) BREW
(— OF BRANDY) SNEAKER
(— OF SPIRITS) CHASSE
(— OF WHISKY) KELTY RUBDOWN
(— OF WINE) APERITIF
(— STICKING TO PUNTY) COLLET
(BEER —) SHELL SEIDEL PILSNER PILSENER
(BELL-SHAPED —) CUP CLOCHE
(BURNING —) SUNGLASS
(CHEVAL —) PSYCHE
(COLORED —) SMALT SMALTO TINTER SCHMELZ
(COLORED —S) GOGGLES
(CUPPING —) VENTOSE
(CURVED —) LENS
(DESSERT —) COUPE
(DRINKING —) GOBLET RUMKIN PILSNER PIMLICO SCUTTLE TUMBLER SCHOONER
(EUROPEAN ORNAMENTAL —) PELOTON
(EXAMINATION —) SLIDE
(FULL —) BUMPER
(FUSIBLE —) FLUX
(HALF —) SPLIT
(ICE CREAM —) SLIDER
(KIND OF —) CUSTARD CRANBERRY
(LEAD —) STRASS
(LIQUEUR —) PONY PONEY
(LIQUOR —) GUN
(MAGNIFYING —) LOUPE
(MASS OF MOLTEN —) PARISON
(METEORITIC —) TEKTITE MOLDAVITE
(OPALESCENT —) OPALINE
(OPAQUE —) HYALITHE
(ORNAMENTAL —) PELOTON
(PIECE OF —) PANE
(PIECE OF HOT —) BIT
(PULVERIZED —) FROSTING
(REFUSE —) CALX CULLET
(RUBY —) SCHMELZE
(RUSSIAN —) CHARK
(SHERBET —) SUPREME
(SHERRY —) COPITA
(SMOKED —) SHADE
(STAINED —) VITRAIL
(TALL —) RUMMER
(THIN —) MOUSSELINE
(VOLCANIC —) PUMICE PERLITE
(WINDOW —) PANE
(WINE —) FLUTE
(PL.) SHELLS
(PREF.) HYAL(O) VITR(EO)(I)(O)
GLASSBLOWER MUMBLER
GLASS CRAB SPECTER SPECTRE

GLASSES EYEWEAR
(TINTED —) SHADES
GLASSHOUSE STOVE HOTHOUSE
GLASS-LIKE VITRIC
GLASS MENAGERIE (AUTHOR OF —) WILLIAMS
(CHARACTER IN —) TOM JAMES LAURA AMANDA OCONNOR
GLASSWARE AGATA AURENE BURMESE FAVRILE OPALINE STEUBEN VITRICS AMBERINA CORALENE
GLASSWORK GLAZING GLAZIERY
GLASSWORKER GANGMAN GLAZIER SNAPPER GLASSMAN SERVITOR
GLASSWORT KALI KELPWORT SALTWORT SAMPHIRE
GLASSY GLIB FILMY GLAZY GLAZEN GLASSEN HYALINE HYALOID VITREAL VITREOUS
(PREF.) HYAL(O)
GLAUCE (FATHER OF —) CREON
(HUSBAND OF —) JASON
GLAUCUS (FATHER OF —) MINOS ANTHEDON SISYPHUS HIPPOLOCHUS
(MOTHER OF —) MEROPE PASIPHAE
GLAZE DIP LEAD SIZE SLIP GLASS SLEET SMEAR ENAMEL QUARRY CELADON COPERTA EELSKIN GLASSEN GLAZING GLIDDER COUVERTE TIGEREYE
(— OF ICE) GLARE
(POTTERY —) SMEAR
GLAZED FILMY GLACE GLASSEN GLOSSED
GLAZED WARE GLOST
GLAZIER PUTTIER
(TOOL OF —) SPRIG LADKIN
GLEAM RAY BEAM GLOW LEAM WAFT WINK BLENK BLINK BLUSH FLASH GLAIK GLEEN GLENT GLINT GLISK GLIST GLOSE SHINE SKIME SPUNK STARE STEEM TWIRE GLANCE SCANCE FOULDRE GLIMMER GLITTER SHIMMER CORUSCATE SCINTILLA
(— FAINTLY) SHIMMER
(— OF LIGHT) LEAM PINK GLAIK SCANCE
(FAINT —) SCAD
GLEAMING FAW GLOW CLEAR GLINT STEEP ABLAZE BRIGHT GLEAMY ADAZZLE SHINING GLOOMING
GLEAN CULL EARN REAP LEASE DEDUCE GATHER COLLECT SCRINGE
GLEANER STIBBLER
GLEANING CROP GATHERING
(LITERARY —S) ANALECTA ANALECTS
GLEBE SOD CLOD LAND SOIL TERMON KIRKTOWN
GLEE GLY JOY SONG MIRTH SPORT GAIETY DELIGHT ELATION WASSAIL HILARITY MADRIGAL
GLEEFUL GAY MERRY JOYOUS JOCULAR GLEESOME
GLEEMAN SONGMAN MINSTREL
GLEN DEN GILL GLYN GRIFF HEUCH HEUGH KLOOF SLACK SLADE TEMPE CANADA DINGLE POCKET
GLIADIN GLUTIN PROLAMIN
GLIB PAT FLIP SLICK CASUAL GLOSSY OFFHAND RENABLE SHALLOW VOLUBLE FLIPPANT
GLIBLY SLICK
GLIBNESS UNCTION
GLIDE GO SKI FLOW SAIL SILE SKIM SLIP SLUR SOAR SWIM COAST CREEP DANCE FLEET GLACE GRAZE LAPSE MERGE PLANE SCOOP SHIRL SKATE SKIFF SKIRR SKITE SLADE SLEEK SLICK SLIDE SLIPE STEAL GLANCE GLIDER SASHAY SNOOVE ILLAPSE SCRIEVE SCRITHE SKITTER SLITHER AIRPLANE GLISSADE VOLPLANE SEMIVOWEL
(— AWAY) ELAPSE
(— BY) PASS FLEET
(— IN) ILLAPSE
(— OFF) EXIT
(MUSICAL —) PORTAMENTO
GLIDER BIPLANE SCOOTER PARAWING SAILPLANE
(KIND OF —) HANG
GLIDING LAPSE TRAIL SLIDING
(— OF THE VOICE) DRAG
(— OVER) LAMBENT
GLIMMER FIRE GLIM GLOW IDEA LEAM STIM BLINK FLASH GLEAM GLOOM STIME SIMPER BLINTER FLIMMER GLIMPSE GLITTER SHIMMER SPARKLE TWINKLE SUNBLINK
GLIMMERING GHOST AGLIMMER GLOOMING
GLIMPSE ESPY IDEA WAFF WAFT BLINK BLUSH FLASH GLIFF GLINT GLISK SIGHT STIME TINGE TRACE WHIFF GLANCE GLEDGE LUSTER SCANCE GLIMMER INKLING
(BRIEF —) APERCU
(FLEETING —) SHIM SNATCH
GLINT PEEP FLASH GLEAM GLENT GLANCE SPARKLE
GLIS MYOXUS
GLISSANDO GLISS SMEAR GLISSADE
GLISTEN FLASH GLISK GLISS GLIST SHINE GLISTER GLITTER SHIMMER SPANGLE SPARKLE RUTILATE
GLISTENING SHINY AGLISTEN
GLITCH FLAW SNAG
GLITTER FLASH GLARE GLEAM GLEIT GLINT GLITZ GLORE SHEEN SHINE SKYRE STARE BICKER LUSTER SCANCE GLIMMER GLISTEN GLISTER SKINKLE SPANGLE SPARKLE TWINKLE BRANDISH RADIANCE RUTILATE CORUSCATE
(FALSE —) GILT
GLITTERING GEMMY SHEEN SHINY STEEP FULGID SPANGLY AGLITTER GLITTERY RUTILANT BRILLIANT CLINQUANT
GLOAMING EVE DUSK GLOAM GLOOMING TWILIGHT
GLOAT GAZE GLUT TIRE EXULT PREEN
GLOBAL PLANETARY
GLOBE ORB BALL BOWL CLEW CLUE POME AGGER GEOID MONDE MOUND ROUND SPHERE COMPASS GEORAMA GLOBULE GRENADE AQUARIUM ROUNDURE
GLOBEFISH FUGU TOBY TOADO ATINGA BOTETE PUFFER BLAASOP BURFISH OOPUHUE BLOWFISH
GLOBEFLOWER BOLT GOLLAND GOWLAND CORCHORUS
GLOBE THISTLE ECHINOPS
GLOBOSE COCCOID COCCOUS CAPITATE GLOBULAR
GLOBULAR GLOBED ROTUND GLOBATE GLOBOSE GLOBICAL
GLOBULE BEAD BLOB DROP GLOB PEARL BUBBLE BUTTON REGULUS GLOBULET SPHERULE
(— OF TAPIOCA) FISHEYE
GLOBULIN MAYSIN MYOSIN VIGNIN ARACHIN CORYLIN EDESTIN LEGUMIN TUBERIN VICILIN ANTIBODY BIOLOGIC EXCELSIN GLYCININ MUSCULIN ORYZENIN
GLOCKENSPIEL BELL LYRA CARILLON
GLOMERULE GLOME FASCICLE
GLOOM DAMP DUSK MURK CLOUD DREAR FROWN SOMBER DESPAIR DIMNESS GLOOMTH SADNESS DARKNESS MIDNIGHT
GLOOMINESS DUMPS
GLOOMY DUN SAD WAN BLUE COLD DARK DOUR DREE DULL EERY GLUM MIRK MURK ADUSK ADUST BLACK BROWN DOWFF DREAR DUSKY EERIE FERAL GUMLY HEAVY LURID MOODY MORNE MUDDY MUNGY MUSTY MUZZY ROOKY SABLE SORRY STERN SULKY SURLY SWART TRIST CLOUDY DISMAL DREARY DREICH DROOPY DRUMLY GLUMMY MOROSE SOLEMN SOMBER SULLEN TETRIC THRAWN OBSCURE STYGIAN THESTER DARKSOME DESOLATE DOLESOME DOWNBEAT DOWNCAST FUNEREAL GLOOMING LOWERING OVERCAST TRISTFUL PESSIMISTIC
GLORIA HALO GLORY AUREOLE
GLORIFICATION AVATAR
GLORIFY HERY LAUD BLESS DEIFY EXALT EXTOL HERSE HONOR PRIDE WURTH ENHALO KUDIZE PRAISE CLARIFY ELEVATE MAGNIFY DIVINIZE EMBLAZON EULOGIZE PROCLAIM STELLIFY
GLORIOLE HALO AUREOLE
GLORIOUS SRI DEAR DERE MERE SHRI GRAND PROUD BRIGHT EMINENT RENOWNED
GLORY JOY ORE SUN FACE FAME GLOR HALO HORN BLAZE BOAST EXULT HONOR KUDOS PRIDE WULDER AUREOLA CLARITY GARLAND GLORIFY RADIANCE SPLENDOR WORTHING
GLORY-PEA KOWHAI KAKABEAK KAKABILL KOWHAI
GLOSS GILL COLOR DUNCE GLASS GLAZE GLOZE JAPAN SHEEN SHINE BLANCH LUSTER LUSTRE POSTIL REMARK VENEER BURNISH EXPOUND VARNISH FLOURISH PALLIATE POLITURE WHITEWASH
(— OVER) FARD HUSH SALVE SLEEK SOOTHE
GLOSSA LINGUA
GLOSSARY GLOSS CLAVIS
GLOSSIPHONIA CLEPSINE
GLOSSY GLOZE NITID SHINY SILKY SLEEK SLICK SATINY SMOOTH
GLOVE KID CUFF GAGE MITT COFFE BERLIN MITTEN CHEVRON DANNOCK GANTLET GOMUKHI GAUNTLET
(— FOR RUBBING SKIN) STRIGIL
(BISHOP'S —) GWANTUS
(BODY OF —) TRANK
(BOXING —) MUFFLE
(HEDGER'S —) DANNOCK
(HUSKING —) HUSKER
(PART OF —) THUMB TRANK GUSSET BINDING FOURCHETTE
GLOVEMAKER DOMER GLOVER CLASPER FINGERER
GLOVER TRANKER
GLOW ARC LOW AURA BURN FIRE LEAM LOOM LOWE BLAZE BLOOM BLUSH FLAME FLASH FLUSH GLAZE GLEAM GLEED GLORY GLOSS GLOZE SHINE STEAM CORONA KINDLE WARMTH FLUSTER LIGHTEN
(— OF PASSION) ESTUS AESTUS
(— WITH INTENSE HEAT) IGNITE
GLOWER GAZE GLOW GLARE GLOOM GLORE SCOWL
GLOWING HOT RED LIVE ROSY WARM AGLOW FIERY LIGHT QUICK RUDDY VIVID ABLAZE ARDENT ORIENT BURNING CANDENT FERVENT RADIANT SHINING FLAGRANT RUTILANT
GLOWWORM FIREFLY FIREWORM GLOWBIRD LAMPYRID
GLOZE FAWN PAINT SMOOTH FLATTERY
GLUCINUM BERYLLIUM
GLUCOSE AME GLYCOSE DEXTROSE
GLUCOSIDE GEIN APIIN RUTIN TUTIN ADONIN BINDER CORNIN DURRIN FRAXIN FUSTIN IRIDIN PICEIN UZARIN ACACIIN ARBUTIN DAPHNIN DIOSMIN ESCULIN ESTEVIN GITALIN GITONIN GITOXIN HEDERIN HELECIN INDICAN LOGANIN LOTUSIN LUPININ OUABAIN POPULIN ROBININ SALICIN TABACIN TEUCRIN ADONIDIN CARTHAME ERICOLIN GENISTIN GOSSYPIN MORINDIN NARINGIN PARIGLIN PARILLIN PRUNASIN QUINOVIN SAPONINE SCILLAIN SINIGRIN SYRINGIN THEVETIN VERNONIN VIBURNIN VICIANIN
GLUE PAD EPOXY MOUNT STICK BEGLEW CEMENT FUNORI FUNORIN STICKER STICKUM TAUROCOL
(BEE —) PROPOLIS
(WEAK —) SIZE

(PREF.) COLL(A)(O)(OIDIO)(OIDO) GLOEO
(SUFF.) COLL GLIA GLOEA
GLUE-LIKE
(PREF.)
(— SUBSTANCE) GLI
GLUEY GLUISH STICKY STRINGY VISCOUS ADHESIVE
GLUM CLUM DOUR GRUM SURLY GLOOMY GLUMPY MOROSE SULLEN DEJECTED
GLUMALES POALES
GLUME PILE FLIGHT
(FLOWERING —) LEMMA
(PL.) CHAFF
GLUSIDE SACCHARIN
GLUT CLOY FILL GULP QUAT SATE CHOKE DRAFT GORGE BATTEN ENGLUT EXCESS MARROW PAMPER PAUNCH ENGORGE GLUTTON SATIATE SURFEIT SWALLOW OVERFEED SAGINATE SATURATE
GLUTEAL NATAL
GLUTELIN AVENINE ORYZENIN
GLUTENIN AVENIN ZYMOME ZYMOMIN
GLUTINOUS ROPY SIZY ROPEY SLIMY TOUGH STICKY VISCID
(PREF.) GLOEO GLOIO
GLUTTED QUAT GORGED SATIATED
GLUTTER VEER
GLUTTON HOG PIG GLUT GORB GUTS GULCH MIKER GLOTUM HELLUO MACCUS EPICURE GUTLING LURCHER MOOCHER RAVENER SWILLER CARCAJOU DRAFFMAN GOURMAND GULLYGUT
(STUPID —) GRUB
GLUTTONIZE BIZLE BEZZLE
GLUTTONOUS GREEDY GLUTTON HOGGISH GOURMAND
GLUTTONY GULE EDACITY SURFEIT
GLYCERIDE BUTYRIN
GLYCINE SOJA
GLYCOL CARBOWAX
GLYCOPROTEIN MUCIN MUCOID
GLYCOSIDE APIIN CROCIN ACACIIN CYMARIN DIGOXIN GITALIN GITOXIN HEDERIN HYPERIN LOGANIN LOTUSIN SAPONIN ALDESIDE ANDROSIN ANTIARIN HOLOSIDE KETOSIDE
GLYPTOLOGIST JEWELLER
GNARL NOB KNOB KNUR KNARL KNURR SNIRL WARRE DEFORM
GNARLED GNARLY KNARRY KNOTTY CRABBED KNOTTED KNURLED
GNASH TUSK CHAMP CRASH GANCH GRASH GRATE KNASH
GNAT KNAW SMUT MIDGE PUNKY STOUT KNATTE SCIARA SCIARID SCINIPH BLACKFLY DIPTERAN GNATLING
(PREF.) CULIC(I)
GNATCATCHER SYLVIID
GNATHION MENTON
GNAW EAT NAB BITE FRET TIRE CHELE GNARL MOUSE SHEAR ARRODE BEFRET BEGNAW CANKER CHAVEL NATTLE NIGGLE ROUNGE CHIMBLE CHUMBLE CORRODE
GNAWED
(PREF.) BROTO
GNAWING EATING RODENT FRETFUL ARROSION ROSORIAL
GNOME NIS ADAGE NISSE PECHT PYGMY KOBOLD VAKSHA YAKSHI GNOMIDE GREMLIN HODEKEN ERDGEIST
GNOMON COCK INDEX STILE STYLE FESCUE STYLUS
GNOSTIC CLEVER SHREWD KNOWING PERATES EBIONITE MANDAEAN SEVERIAN SIMONIAN SIMONITE
GNU KOKOON BRINDLE
GO BE DO ACT GAE HOP ISH LAY NIM PEP TEE WAG BANG BEAR BING BOWN BUSK DRAW FAND FARE FOND GANG HARK HAUL HUMP MOVE QUIT RAIK ROAM ROLL SEEK SHOT SILE SLAP SNAP STAB STEP TAKE TEEM TOUR WADE WANE WEAR WEND WEVE WIND WISE WORK YEAD YEDE AMBLE BOUND CARRY CHEVE DEMON DRESS FETCH FRAME HAUNT KNOCK LEAVE MOSEY PLUCK REACH SCRAM SHAKE SLOPE SPEED TOUCH TRACE TRACK TRENE TRINE TRUSS WHIZZ YONGE BECOME BETAKE CHIEVE CRUISE DEPART EXTEND QUATCH QUETCH REPAIR RESORT RESULT RETIRE SASHAY STRAKE STRIKE TODDLE TRAVEL WEAKEN JOURNEY SCRITHE DIMINISH WITHDRAW
(— ABOUT) JET BEGO BIGAN
(— ABOUT DEJECTEDLY) PEAK
(— ABOUT GOSSIPING) COURANT
(— AHEAD) HOLD
(— AIMLESSLY) ERR BUMMLE
(— ALONG) PATH
(— ALONG WITH) ACCOMPANY
(— AROUND) SKIRT BYPASS CIRCUE COMPASS ENCOMPASS
(— ASHORE) LAND
(— ASTRAY) ERR MAR WRY MANG WILL MISGO DELIRE FORVAY MISWEND DEROGATE MISCARRY
(— AWAY) AGO HOP OFF BEAT BUNK HIKE NASH PART SHOO VADE CLEAR HENCE IMSHI LEAVE SCRAM SHIFT BEGONE BUGGER DEPART REMOVE VACATE SKIDDOO ELONGATE
(— AWAY AT ONCE) SCRAM
(— BACK) RECEDE RETURN REGRESS RETRACE
(— BACK IN TIME) MOUNT
(— BAD) SOUR
(— BEFORE) LEAD FOREGO PRECEDE ANTECEDE PREAMBLE
(— BEYOND) SURPASS FOREPASS
(— BRISKLY) JUNE
(— BROKE) BUST
(— BY) PASS
(— BY WATER) SAIL
(— COURTING) WENCH
(— DOGGEDLY) PLUG
(— DOWN) SET SINK VAIL DROOP SOUND DESCEND
(— EASILY) AMBLE
(— ERRATICALLY) KICK
(— FAST) HURRY SPLIT BARREL BEELINE
(— FOR) ATTEMPT
(— FORTH) AGO DEPART FORTHGO
(— FORWARD) HUP HUPP ADVANCE AGGRESS PROCEED
(— FOWLING) AUCUPATE
(— FURTIVELY) SLINK SNEAK STEAL
(— HANG) SNICK
(— HEAVILY) LOB LAMPER
(— IN) ENTER INGRESS
(— IN A HURRY) SCUFFLE
(— IN CROWDS) PILE
(— IN HASTE) LEN LAMMAS
(— IN PURSUIT) SUE
(— IN SEARCH) QUEST
(— INTO BUSINESS) EMBARK
(— IT ALONE) SOLO
(— LAME) FOUNDER
(— LEISURELY) BUMMEL JIGGET JIGGIT
(— LIGHTLY) TIPTOE
(— MAD) CRAZE MADDLE
(— NEAR) APPROACH
(— NOISILY) LARUM
(— OFF) MOG DISCHARGE
(— ON) DO GARN LAST PASS PERGE FURTHER PROCEED
(— ON BOARD) BOARD EMBARK ENTRAIN
(— ON FOOT) SHANK
(— ON TO SAY) ADD
(— OUT) EXIT ISSUE SLOCK EGRESS EXEUNT QUENCH SORTIE
(— OVER) KNEE REVOLT SURPASS OVERGANG
(— OVER AGAIN) RENEW REVISE RETRACE
(— PROSPEROUSLY) COTTON
(— QUICKLY) BOP GET HIE BUZZ LAMP PIKE SCAT SPEED
(— RAPIDLY) LAMP SPLIT
(— SHARES) SNACK
(— SIDEWAYS) SIDLE
(— SLOWLY) CRAWL CREEP
(— SLUGGISHLY) SHACK
(— SMOOTHLY) SLIP SKATE
(— STEALTHILY) SHIRK SLINK SNEAK GUMSHOE
(— SUDDENLY) CLAP SCOOT
(— SWIFTLY) SKISE STRIP HIGHBALL
(— THE ROUNDS) PATROL
(— THROUGH) SUFFER
(— THROUGHOUT) COAST
(— THROUGH WATER) SQUATTER
(— TO BED) KIP DOSS FLOP SNUG
(— TO EXCESS) DEBORD
(— TO HARBOR) VERT
(— TOO FAR) OUTREACH
(— TO PIECES) SNURP
(— TO SCHOOL) SCOLEY
(— TO SLEEP) HUSHABY
(— TO WAR) RISE
(— UP) CLIMB AMOUNT ASCEND
(— WEARILY) HAGGLE
(— WELL) COOK
(— WITH) ASSENTTO
(— WITH EFFORT) HIKE
(— WITH IT) FLOW
(— WRONG) MISS FAULT CURDLE MISFARE BACKFIRE
GOAD EGG GAD GIG HAG BAIT BROD BROG DARE EDGE GAUD LASH MOVE PROD SPUR URGE WHIP YERK ANKUS HARRY IMPEL PIQUE PRICK PROGG PUNGE STING VALET INCITE NEEDLE OXGOAD ANKUSHA HOTFOOT INFLAME PROVOKE IRRITATE SLAPJACK STIMULUS
GOADMAN GADMAN GAUDSMAN GOADSTER
GOAL BYE DEN END BASE BUTT DOLE DOOL HAIL HALE MARK METE PORT BOURN FINIS IDEAL SCOOP SCOPE SCORE STING DESIGN OBJECT SIGHTS DESTINY HORIZON TERMINUS OBJECTIVE
(— IN GAMES) HUNK
(FIELD —) BASKET
(REMOTE —) THULE
(UNATTAINABLE —) STAR
GO-ASHORE KOHUA
GOAT BOK TUR IBEX TAHR BEDEN BILLY BOVID EVECK SEROW ALPINE ANGORA AOUDAD CAPRID CHAMAL JEMLAH MAZAME NUBIAN PASANG SAANEN WETHER CHAMOIS AEGAGRUS CAPRIPED MARKHOOR BOUQUETIN
(DOMESTIC —) HIRCUS
(FEMALE —) DOE NANNY DOELING
(MALE —) BUCK BUCKLING
(YOUNG —) KID KIDDY TICCHEN GOATLING
(PREF.) AEG(I)(O) CAPRI EGO
GOAT ANTELOPE GORAL SEROW GOORAL
GOAT CHEESE CHEVRE
GOATEE TUFT
GOATFISH MOANO
GOATHERD DAMON
GOAT-LIKE CAPRINE GOATISH HIRCINE
GOAT MOTH COSSID
GOATSBEARD ROSACEAN
GOATSKIN CRUST CASTOR CHEVRETTE
GOATSUCKER PUCK PEWKE POTOO EVEJAR BULLBAT DORHAWK GRINDER SPINNER DOORHAWK EVECHURR NIGHTJAR PAURAQUE
GOB TAR CLOT GOAF SALT SWAB SWOB WASTE GOBBET SWABBY
GOBBET BIT CHUNK MORSEL
GOBBLE MOP BOLT SLOP EATUP GOFFLE GORBLE
GOBBLEDYGOOK PEDAGESE BAFFLEGAB
GO-BETWEEN AGENT BAWD FIXER MEANS BROKER DEALER PANDAR CONTACT MEDIATOR
GOBLET TASS DINOS GLASS HANAP POKAL SKULL STOOP STOUP BEAKER BUMPER HOLMOS RUMKIN CHALICE SCYPHUS SNIFTER TALLBOY JEROBOAM STANDARD STEMWARE
(PREF.) CALICI
GOBLIN (ALSO SEE HOBGOBLIN) COW HAG NIS PUG BHUT BOGY MARE PUCK BOGEY NISSE OUPHE POOKA BODACH BOGGLE BOOGER CHUREL EMPUSA FOLIOT SPRITE BOGGARD BOGGART BROWNIE

BUGBEAR KNOCKER PADFOOT BARGHEST BOGEYMAN FOLLETTO
GOBY MAPO BULLY BIGHEAD CHALACO GOBIOID GUAVINA GUDGEON MUDFISH BULLHEAD PINKFISH SANDGOBY
GOCART SULKY WALKER STROLLER
GOD (ALSO SEE DEITY) AS EA EL ER RA VE ANU BEL BES COG DAD DES DEV DIS DOD EAR GAR GAW GEB GOG GOL GOM GUM ING KEB LAR LOK MEN MIN ODD ORO SEB SUN TEM TYR ULL UTU VAN AITU AMEN AMON ARES ASUR ATEO ATUA ATYS BAAL BEER BRAN BURE CHAC COCK DEUS DEVA DIEU ESUS FONS FREY GAWD GOSH HAPI HOLY HOTH INTI JOVE KANE KING LIFE LLEU LOKE LOKI LOVE LUGH MARS MIND NABU NEBO NUDD ODIN PTAH SHEN SHIN SOMA SOUL TANE THOR TIKI ULLR UTUG VAYU XIPE YAMA ZEUS ARAWN ASHUR ASURA ATTES ATTIS COMUS DAGDA DEITY DEOTA DUVEL DYAUS DYLAN EBISU ELOAH FREYR GHOST GOLES GOLLY GRAVE GUACA HESUS HIEMS HORUS HOTHR HUACA HYMEN INDRA JUDGE KINGU LADON LIBER LLUDD MAKER MENTU MIDER MOMUS NJORD NUMEN PALES PICUS SILEN TAMUZ THOTH TINIA TRUTH TYCHE URASH WAKEA WODIN WOTAN ZOMBI ADITYA ADONAI ADONAY ANSHAR ANUBIS APOLLO ASEITY AUTHOR CHAMOS CONSUS DEVATA DHARMA ELATHA ELOHIM FATHER FAUNUS GANESA HEAVEN HERMES HOENIR MEZTLI MILCOM MITHRA NEREUS NERGAL OSIRIS PATRON PENEUS PLUTUS PUSHAN SESHAT SOCIUS SOURCE SPIRIT SUTEKH SYLENE TAAROA TAMMUZ TARTAK TERAPH TRITON TRIVIA VARUNA VEDUIS VERITY VISHNU VULCAN WISDOM YAKSHA YAKSHI ZOMBIE ABRAXAS ADRANUS ALPHEUS ANTEROS BELENUS CHEMOSH DAIKOKU DELLING ETERNAL GODHEAD HANUMAN IAPETUS JEHOVAH JUPITER KANALOA MERCURY MITHRAS MUTINUS NEPTUNE NJORTHR PROTEUS PRYDERI REMPHAN ROBIGUS SAVITAR SERAPIS TRIGLAV VATICAN VEJOVIS ZAGREUS ALMIGHTY ASTRAEUS BISHAMON CAMAXTLI DEMIURGE DEVOTION DIVINITY GUCUMATZ INFINITE JIUROJIN KUKULKAN MIXCOATL MORPHEUS POSEIDON SABAZIOS SUMMANUS TANGAROA TERMINUS TUTELARY VEDIOVIS ZEPHYRUS OMNIPOTENT
(— OF AGRICULTURE) PICUS URASH FAUNUS AMAETHON NINGIRSU
(— OF ARTS) SIVA
(— OF ATMOSPHERE) HADAD
(— OF BOUNDARIES) TERMINUS
(— OF COMMERCE) MERCURY
(— OF CORN) CAT
(— OF DAY) HORUS
(— OF DESTRUCTION) SIVA
(— OF EARTH) BEL GEB KEB SEB DAGAN
(— OF EVIL) SET FOMOR FOMORIAN ZERNEBOCK
(— OF FERTILITY) SHANGO
(— OF FIRE) AGNI GIRRU NUSKU RUDRA VULCAN
(— OF FLOCKS) PAN
(— OF HAPPINESS) HOTEI JUROJIN
(— OF HEAVENS) ANU JUMALA
(— OF HOUSEHOLD) LARES PENATES
(— OF JUSTICE) FORSETE FORSETI
(— OF LEARNING) IMHOTEP
(— OF LOVE) AMOR ARES EROS KAMA BHAGA CUPID AENGUS
(— OF MOCKERY) MOMUS
(— OF MOON) SIN ENZU NANNAR
(— OF NATURE) MARSYAS
(— OF POETRY) BRAGE BRAGI
(— OF RAIN) PARJANYA
(— OF REGENERATION) SIVA
(— OF RIDICULE) MOMUS
(— OF SEA) LER VAN AEGIR DYAUS NEPTUNE PROTEUS PALAEMON POSEIDON
(— OF SKY) ANU GWYDION
(— OF SLEEP) HYPNOS HYPNUS MORPHEUS
(— OF SOUTHEAST WIND) EURUS
(— OF STORM) ZU ADAD ADDA ADDU MARUT RUDRA TESHUP
(— OF SUN) RA RE SHU SOL TEM TUM UTU AMON ATEN ATMU ATUM BAAL LLEU UTUG SAMAS SEKER SURYA APOLLO HELIOS SOKARI KHEPERA PHOEBUS SHAMASH PHAETHON TONATIUH
(— OF THUNDER) THOR DONAR PERUN PERKUN PEROUN SHANGO TLALOC HURAKAN TARANIS
(— OF UNDERWORLD) DIS BRAN GWYN YAMA HADES ORCUS PLUTO
(— OF VEGETATION) ATYS ATTIS
(— OF WAR) ER IRA ORO TIU TYR ARES COEL IRRA MARS MENT ODIN THOR MONTU NINIB MEXITL SKANDA CAMULUS MEXITLI NINURTA ENYALIUS NINGIRSU QUIRINUS
(— OF WEALTH) BHAGA KUBERA KUVERA PLUTUS
(— OF WIND) ADAD ADDA ADDU VAYU MARUT AEOLUS BOREAS EECATL
(— OF WISDOM) TAT THOTH
(— WILLING) DV
(ANCIENT GREEK —) CHAOS
(BLIND —) HOTH HOTHR
(EGYPTIAN — OF MUSIC) BES
(FALSE —) BAAL IDOL MAUMET
(FEMALE —) GODDESS
(HAWAIIAN —) AUMAKUA
(HOUSEHOLD —) PENATE
(IMMORTAL —) AKAL
(INFERIOR —) PANISK
(NORSE —) AESIR
(PAGAN —) DEMON
(RAM-HEADED —) AMON KHNUM KHNEMU
(TIMELESS —) AKAL
(TUTELARY —) LAR
(UNKNOWN —) KA
(WOOD —) SILEN SILENUS
(PL.) DI DII KAMI AESIR IGIGI SUPERI PANTHEON TRIMURTI
(PREF.) DEI DEO THE(O)
GODDESS (ALSO SEE DEITY) AI NU ANA ANU ATE AYA DEA DON NUT OPS UNI VAC ANTA BADB BODB CACA DANA DANU ERIS ERUA FRIA HELA HERA JORD JUNO MAIA MEDB NIKE NINA NONA NORN PELE SAGA SATI TARA UPIS ALLAT AMENT ANATH ANTUM ARURU BAUBO CERES CHLOE DEESS DIANA DIANE DIRGA DOLMA DOMNU EPONA FREYA FRIGG HYBLA IAMBE ISTAR KOTYS MAEVE NANAI NINTU PAKHT PALES PARCA SALUS SEDNA SKADI TANIT TYCHE USHAS VENUS VESTA ADEONA AESTAS ANATUM ANUKIT APHAIA ATHENA BELILI BENDIS BOOPIS BRIGIT CYBELE CYRENE EOSTRE FRIGGA GEFJON HELENA HESTIA HYGEIA INNINA KISHAR LIBERA MOTHER NINGAL PEITHO PHOBOS POMONA PRORSA RUMINA SEKHET SELENE SEMELE SKATHI SOTHIS TANITH TEFNUT TRIVIA URANIA VACUNA YDGRUN ANAHITA ANAITIS ARTEMIS ASHERAH DEMETER DERCETO FERONIA FJORGYN GALATER GODHEAD KOTYTTO LARENTA LARUNDA MAJAGGA MAJESTA MINERVA MORNING MORRIGU MYLITTA NEKHEBT NEMESIS PALATUA PARBATI PARVATI SALACIA ADRASTEA AGLAUROS ANGERONA BELISAMA CARMENTA CENTEOTL COCAMAMA DESPOINA DICTYNNA GULLVEIG MORRIGAN NEPHTHYS PARBUTTY PRAKRITI RHIANNON SEFEKHET THOUERIS VICTORIA
(— IN CHARIOT) SELENE
(— OF AGRICULTURE) BAU OPS DEMETER CENTEOTL
(— OF AIR) AURA
(— OF BEAUTY) VENUS LAKSHMI
(— OF BURIAL) LIBITINA
(— OF CHILDBIRTH) LEVANA LUCINA
(— OF DAWN) EOS USAS USHAS AURORA MATUTA
(— OF DEW) HERSE
(— OF DISCORD) ATE ERIS
(— OF EARTH) GE LUA SEB ERDA GAEA GAIA TARI ARURU DIONE JORTH TERRA SEMELE TELLUS THEMIS DAMKINA PERCHTA
(— OF FATE) NONA NORN MOIRA
(— OF FERTILITY) MA ISIS MAMA NERTHUS
(— OF FLOWERS) FLORA CHLORIS
(— OF FORTUNE) TYCHE FORTUNA
(— OF GRAIN) CERES
(— OF HEALING) EIR GULA
(— OF HEALTH) DAMIA HYGEIA VALETUDO
(— OF HEARTH) VESTA HESTIA
(— OF HISTORY) SAGA
(— OF HOPE) SPES
(— OF INFATUATION) ATE
(— OF JUSTICE) DIKE MAAT THEMIS ASTRAEA NEMESIS JUSTITIA
(— OF LEGISLATION) EUNOMIA
(— OF LOVE) ATHOR FREYA VENUS FREYJA HATHOR
(— OF LUCK) FORTUNA
(— OF MAGIC) HECATE
(— OF MARRIAGE) HERA
(— OF MATERNITY) APET
(— OF MERCY) KWANNON
(— OF MOON) SELENE
(— OF MOTHERHOOD) ISIS
(— OF NIGHT) NOX NYX
(— OF OCEAN) NINA
(— OF OVENS) FORNAX
(— OF PEACE) PAX IRENE NERTHUS
(— OF PLEASURE) BES
(— OF PLENTY) OPS
(— OF RAINBOW) IRIS
(— OF SEASONS) DIKE HORA
(— OF THE DEAD) HEL HELA
(— OF THE HUNT) DIANA VACUNA ARTEMIS
(— OF THE MOON) LUNA MOON DIANA SELENA SELENE TANITH ARTEMIS
(— OF THE SEA) INO RAN DORIS BRANWEN EURYNOME
(— OF TRUTH) MAAT
(— OF VEGETATION) OPS CERES COTYS COTYTTO
(— OF VENGEANCE) ARA NEMESIS
(— OF VICTORY) NIKE
(— OF WAR) ENYO ANATH ANATU ANUNIT BELLONA
(— OF WATER) ANAHITA
(— OF WEALTH) LAKSHMI
(— OF WISDOM) ATHENA MINERVA
(— OF YOUTH) HEBE JUVENTAS
(COW-HEADED —) ISIS
(ESKIMO —) SEDNA
(FERTILITY —) ASTARTE
(MARRIAGE —) VOR
(PRESIDING —) QUEEN
(SUBORDINATE —) DEMIURGE
(THUNDER-SMITTEN —) SEMELE KERAUNIA
(3-HEADED —) HECATE
(PL.) HORAE MATRIS POINAE ASYNJUR
GO-DEVIL SLED WEIGHT HANDCAR SCRAPER CULTIVATOR TRAVOIS ALLIGATOR
GODFATHER GOSSIP GODPAPA PADRINO SPONSOR GODPHERE
GODHEAD DEITY GODHOOD DIVINITY
GODLESS WICKED ATHEIST IMPIOUS PROFANE UNGODLY
GODLESSNESS ATHEISM
GODLIKE DEIFIC DIVINE IMMORTAL OLYMPIAN
GODLINESS PIETISM SANCTITY
GODLING DEVATA GENIUS GODKIN GODLET PANISC DEMIGOD PANISCUS
GODLY HOLY WISE PIOUS DEVOUT GRACIOUS
GODMOTHER CUMMER GOSSIP SPONSOR GODMAMMA MARRAINE
GODOWN WAREHOUSE
GODPARENT SPONSOR

GOD'S S
GODSON FILLEUL GODCHILD
GOD TREE CEIBA
GODWIT PICK PRINE BARKER MARLIN SCAMMEL YARWHIP RINGTAIL SHRIEKER SPOTRUMP YARDKEEP YARWHELP
GOFFER QUILL FULLER GAUFFER
GOG (FATHER OF —) SHEMAIAH
GO-GETTER HUSTLER
GOGGLER SCAD
GOGLET COOJA SERAI MONKEY SURAHI GURGLET SURAHEE
GOING FARE GAIT BOUND AGOING WAYING PASSADO SLEDDING
(— ABOUT) AROUND
(— BEYOND OTHERS) ULTRA
(— IN) INEUNT INFARE INGOING
(— ON) FARE AGATE TOWARD
(— OUT) EGRESS
(— UP) ANABASIS
(GET —) BEGIN
(SUFF.) GRESS
GOITER WEN GLANS GOITRE STRUMA BRONCHOCELE
GOITERED ANTELOPE ZENU
GOITROUS STRUMOUS
GOLD OR ORO RED SOL DORE GILT GULL ALTUN AURUM GUILD METAL OCHER OCHRE RIDGE SHINY GOLDEN OBRIZE ORMOLU YELLOW BULLION SPANKER
(— PIECE) TALI
(GREENISH —) AENEUS AENEOUS
(IMITATION —) PINCHBECK
(PREF.) AUR(I) AUREO CHRYS(O) ORI
GOLDBEATER (TOOL OF —) WAGON
GOLDBRICK LOAF SHIRK SLACKER
GOLDCREST MOON TIDLEY MUDDLER TROCHIL
GOLD DUST (PENNY'S WORTH OF —) PESEWA
GOLDEN RED DORE GOLD BLEST DURRY GOLDY SUNNY AUREAL BLONDE GILDEN GILTEN AUREATE AUREOUS HALCYON AURULENT DEAURATE
(— STATE) CALIFORNIA
GOLDEN-AGER RETIREE
GOLDEN ASS (AUTHOR OF —) APULEIUS
(CHARACTER IN —) ISIS MILO FOTIS LUCIUS CHARITES PAMPHILE SOCRATES BYRRHAENA LEPOLEMUS THRASILLUS ARISTOMENES
GOLDEN BOWL (AUTHOR OF —) JAMES
(CHARACTER IN —) ADAM STANT MAGGIE VERVER AMERIGO CHARLOTTE
GOLDEN CHAIN LABURNUM
GOLDEN CLUB TAWKEE TAWKIN TUCKAHOE
GOLDEN EAGLE RINGTAIL
GOLDENEYE CUR GARROT COBHEAD GOWDNIE BULLHEAD IRONHEAD MORILLON WHIFFLER WHISTLER
GOLDEN LION TAMARIN MARMOSET
GOLDEN ORIOLE PIROL WITWALL
GOLDEN PLOVER KOLEA FROGSKIN SQUEALER WHISTLER
GOLDEN RAGWORT LIFEROOT
GOLDENROD BONEWORT SOLIDAGO JIMMYWEED
GOLDENSEAL EYEBALM EYEROOT ICEROOT PUCCOON
GOLDEN SHINER CHUB DACE WINDFISH
GOLDFINCH JACK FINCH GOLDY GOWDY CANARY REDCAP FLAXBIRD GRAYPATE
GOLDFINNY CONNER GOLDNEY CORKWING
GOLDFISH FUNA MOOR COMET CALICO FANTAIL CYPRINID VEILTAIL
GOLD-LEAF ORMOLU
GOLD-OF-PLEASURE FLAX MADWORT OILSEED
GOLDSINNY CONNER CORKWING
GOLDSMITH SONAR AURIFEX
ENGLISH HILLIARD
FRENCH MEISSONIER
GERMAN JAMNITZER
ITALIAN LEONI ROBBIA
WELSH MYDDELTON
GOLF (— CLUB) IRON WOOD BAFFY CLEEK MASHY SPOON WEDGE BULGER DRIVER MASHIE PUTTER BRASSIE MIDIRON NIBLICK
(— COURSE) GREEN LINKS
(— PLAYER) BALL BERG KING KITE VARE BRAID FALDO FLOYD HAGEN HOGAN IRWIN JONES LOCKE LOPEZ MILLS PRICE RAWLS SMITH SNEAD STACY SUGGS ALCOTT CAPONI CARNER GEDDES HAYNIE HILTON LANGER MALLON MILLER MORRIS NELSON PALMER PLAYER VARDON WATSON WRIGHT BERNING BRADLEY COUPLES DEMARET INKSTER SARAZEN SHEEHAN THOMSON TREVINO ZOELLER ANDERSON NICKLAUS ZAHARIAS WHITWORTH BALLESTEROS
(— SCORE) ACE PAR BOGEY EAGLE BIRDIE
(— STROKE) BAFF CHIP HOOK PUTT DRIVE PITCH SLICE
(FREE SHOT IN —) MULLIGAN
(PUTTING TENSION IN —) YIPS
(SHORT — PUTT) GIMME TAPIN
GOLFER TEER
GOLLY GEE WOW GOSH JEEPERS
GOMER (FATHER OF —) JAPHETH
(HUSBAND OF —) HOSEA
GOMUTI EJOO IROK ARENG KITTUL SAGWIRE SAGOWEER
GONAD OVARY GERMEN
GONCALO ALVES KINGWOOD
GONDOLA GON BARGE GUNDALOW
(— GUIDE) POLER
GONE AWAY LOST NAPOO USEDUP
(— BY) AGO DONE PAST AGONE PASSE BEHIND BYGONE
(— OUT OF USE) EXTINCT
(— TO PIECES) HAYWIRE
GONERIL (SISTER OF —) REGAN
GONE WITH THE WIND (AUTHOR OF —) MITCHELL
(CHARACTER IN —) FRANK OHARA RHETT ASHLEY BUTLER WILKES CHARLES KENNEDY MELANIE HAMILTON SCARLETT
GONG BELL CLOCK GANGSA DOORBELL
(SERIES OF —S) BONANG
GONGORISM CULTISM
GONOPHORE MEDUSOID SPOROSAC
GOO GUCK GUNK TRIPE
GOOD BAD BON GAY TOP TRY ABLE BEAU BEIN BIEN BOON BRAW FINE GAIN HEND NICE NOTE PROW SAKE BONNE BONNY BONUM BRAVE BULLY CANNY FRESH GWEED JELLY KAPAI PAKKA PUKKA SEELY SOUND VALID BENIGN BRAWLY BUCKRA DIVINE EXPERT FACTOR FORBYE HONEST MABUTI PRETTY PROFIT PROPER WEALTH BENEFIT COPIOUS CORKING FAIRISH FORTHBY GODLIKE GRADELY HELPFUL LIBERAL SNIFTER STAVING TRAINED UPRIGHT BUDGEREE GRAITHLY INTEREST LAUDABLE PLEASING SALUTARY SKILLFUL SUITABLE
(— FOR NOTHING) NAPOO NAUGHT
(ESPECIALLY —) RARE
(EXCEPTIONALLY —) SLAMBANG
(EXTREMELY —) SLICK
(FAIRLY —) TIDY MIDDLING
(HOLD —) BEAR
(INFINITELY —) HOLY
(MARVELOUSLY —) FANTABULOUS
(MIGHTY —) SKOOKUM
(NO —) DUFF VOID NAPOO NAPOOH VOIDED
(PRETTY —) FAIR TIDY
(RELATIVELY —) SMOOTH
(STRIKINGLY —) RATTLING
(SUPERLATIVELY —) BRAG BEAUTIFUL
(SUPREMELY —) IMMENSE GORGEOUS
(SURPASSINGLY —) SUPERIOR
(VERY —) HOT TOP DANDY DICTY GRAND NIFTY BONZER BOSHTA BOSKER BOSHTER NAILING SPLENDID SWINGING
(PREF.) AGATH(O) BENI EU
GOOD-BYE CIAO LATER BY BYE TATA
GOODBYE TATA
GOOD-BYE ADDIO ADIEU
GOODBYE ADIEU
GOOD-BYE ADIOS
GOODBYE ADIOS
GOOD-BYE LULLABY FAREWELL SAYONARA
GOODBYE (IMPOLITE —) SCRAM
GOOD COMPANIONS (AUTHOR OF —) PRIESTLEY
(CHARACTER IN —) DEAN HUGH NUNN ELSIE INIGO JERRY JIMMY SUSIE TRANT JESIAH OAKROYD ELIZABETH JOLLIFANT LONGSTAFF MCFARLANE JERNINGHAM
GOOD EARTH (AUTHOR OF —) BUCK
(CHARACTER IN —) LIU LUNG NUNG OLAN PEAR WANG CHING HWANG LOTUS
GOOD-FOR-NAUGHT LOSEL
GOOD-FOR-NOTHING STIFF VAURIEN BUM ORRA SLIM SLINK DONNOT KEFFEL RIBALD STUMER BRETHEL FUSTIAN SCROYLE SHOTTEN SKEEZIX SKELLUM SKYBALD VAURIEN WOSBIRD VAGABOND
GOOD FRIDAY PARASCEVE
GOOD-HUMORED SONSY
GOOD-KING-HENRY BLITE ALLGOOD MARKERY MERCURY CHENOPOD
GOOD-LOOKING BRAW FAIR FOXY MOOI BONNY GAWSY COMELY PRETTY SEEMLY EYESOME GRADELY WINSOME GOODLIKE HANDSOME STUNNING
GOODLY BOON PROPER GOODLIKE
GOOD-NATURED SONSY CLEVER AMIABLE
GOODNESS BONTE BONUM MENSK PROOF BONITY BOUNTY SATTVA VIRTUE KINDNESS
GOODS FEE BONA GEAR KIND PELF CARGO STUFF TRADE WORLD WRACK ADVANCE CAPITAL CHATTEL EFFECTS FINANCE HAVINGS INSIGHT TRAFFIC CHAFFERY HIGGLERY PROPERTY
(— BARTERED) DICKER
(— CAST OVERBOARD) JETSAM
(— SUNK IN SEA) LAGAN LIGAN LAGEND
(DRY —) DRAPERY
(HOUSEHOLD —) INSIGHT
(IMPERFECT —) FENT
(INFERIOR —) BRACK
(PIECE —) CUTTANEE
(SECONDHAND —) BROKERY
(SLOW-SELLING —) JOBS
(STOLEN — THROWN AWAY) WAIF
(SURPLUS —) OVERAGE
(VALUABLE —) SWAG
GOOD-SIZED TIDY HEFTY GAWSIE
GOOD-TASTING DAINTY
GOODWIFE GOODY VROUW
GOODWILL GREE PHILANTHROPY
GOODY-GOODY PI MOLLYCODDLE
GOOEY CLARTY
GOOF SAP BOOB FLUB BONER GOOFER
GOOFBALL DOOFUS
GOOGLY BOSEY WRONGUN
GOOK SLIME
GOON HOOD THUG GORILLA MUSCLEMAN
GOOSANDER JACKSAW RANTOCK
GOOSE ELK OIE LAMA NENE ROUT ANSER BRANT BRENT EMDEN HANSA HOBBY ROMAN SOLAN WAVEY CAGMAG CANADA EMBDEN GALOOT GANDER GOSLET HISSER HONKER SOLAND AFRICAN BLACKIE BUSTARD GAGGLER GOSLING GRAYLAG GREASER GREYLAG OUTARDE WIDGEON BALDHEAD BARGOOSE BARNACLE BERNICLE SPURWING TOULOUSE
(— GENUS) ANSER
(MYTHICAL —) GANZA
(PART OF —) BOW EAR EYE TOE WEB BEAN BILL CAPE FOOT KEEL

RUMP WING FLUFF SHANK BREAST COVERT DEWLAP SADDLE FEATHER NOSTRIL SHOULDER SECONDARY
(PREF.) CHEN(O)
GOOSEBERRY BLOB FABE FAPE POHA BRAGAS GOBLIN GOZILL GROZER DOWNING GASKINS GROZART CARBERRY CATBERRY DOGBERRY EATBERRY FEABERRY GOOSEGOG HOUGHTON INDUSTRY KIWIFRUIT
(PL.) THAPES
GOOSE EGG DUCK
GOOSEFOOT BLITE ORACH BASSIA KOCHIA ORACHE QUINOA ALLSEED PIGWEED
GOOSEGIRL GOSSARD
GOOSE GRASS HERIF HARIFFE CLEAVERS
GOOSEHERD GOZZARD GOOSEBOY
GOOSENECK LAMP ROOSTER
GOPHER TUZA GAUFFRE GEOMYID MUNGOFA QUACHIL SALAMICH TUCOTUCO
(— STATE) MINNESOTA
GOPHER BALL HOMER
GOPHERMAN SWAMPER
GOPHERWOOD FUSTIC
GORBODUC (SON OF —) FERREX PORREX
GORDIUS (SON OF —) MIDAS
GORE CLY CLOY GARE HIKE HIPE HOOK HORN PICK PIKE SHOT CRUOR GODET STICK GORING GUSSET
GOREVAN AUBURN
GORGE GAP JAM FILL GASH GAUM GLUT JAMB KHOR RENT SATE BREAK CAJON CANON CHASM CHINE CLUSE DRAFT FARCE FLUME GULLY GURGE KLOOF PONGO POUCH STECH STRID STUFF TANGI CANYON DEFILE NULLAH PIGOUT RAVINE STODGE STRAIT THROAT COULOIR DATIATE DRAUGHT ENGORGE SATIATE SLABBER BARRANCA QUEBRADA
GORGED ACCOLLE
GORGEOUS VAIN GRAND SHOWY COSTLY DAZZLING GLORIOUS SPLENDID
GORGERIN NECK NECKING
GORGIBUS (DAUGHTER OF —) CELIE
GORGING STODGE
GORGON HAG MEDUSA STHENO EURYALE
(MOTHER OF —S) CETO
GORGOPHONE (FATHER OF —) PERSEUS
(HUSBAND OF —) OEBALUS PERIERES
(MOTHER OF —) ANDROMEDA
(SON OF —) ICARIUS APHAREUS LEUCIPPUS TYNDAREUS
GORILLA APE GOON THUG PIGMY PYGMY
GORING CORNUPETE
GORMANDIZE STECH STEGH GUTTLE
GORMANDIZER HELLUO GLUTTON
GORSE ULEX WHIN FURZE GORST
GORY BLOODY
GOSHAWK GOS ASTUR TERCEL
GOSLING GULL
GOSPEL SPELL DHARMA EVANGEL KERUGMA KERYGMA SYNOPTIC
(— OF REDEMPTION) CROSS
(PL.) TEXT
GOSSAMER MOUSEWEB STARDUST
GOSSIP EME GAB GUP PIE WAG AUNT BLAB BUZZ CANT CLAT CONK COZE DIRT DISH NEWS TALK CAUSE CLACK CLASH CLYPE COOSE CRACK FERLY FRUMP GOSSY SIEVE YENTA BABBLE CACKLE CADDLE CALLET CAMPER CLAVER CUMMER FERLIE JANGLE KIMMER NORATE TATTLE TITTLE CLATTER COMPERE GOSTHER HASHGOB NASHGAB SCANDAL TATTLER TRATTLE CAUSERIE CHITCHAT GOSSIPRY QUIDNUNC SCHMOOZE NEWSMONGER SCUTTLEBUTT
(MALICIOUS —) SCANDAL
(OUTPOURING OF —) EARFUL
GOSSIPY BUZZY NEWSY CHATTY
GOTH GOTHIAN SUIOGOTH VISIGOTH
GOTHAM ABDERA
GOTHAMITE ABDERITE
GOTHIC OGIVAL
GOTTERDAMMERUNG
(CHARACTER IN —) HAGEN GUNTHER GUTRUNE SIEGFRIED WALTRAUTE BRUNNHILDE
(COMPOSER OF —) WAGNER
GOUGE DIG PUG BENT SCUFF CHISEL EXTORT FLUKAN GOUGER HOLLOW SCRIBE FLOOKAN SCORPER SELVAGE SELVEDGE STICKING
(— OUT) BULLDOZE
(V-TYPE —) VEINER
GOUGER CHISELLER
GOURD MATE PEPO LUFFA ABOBRA JICARA PATOLA ANGURIA DISHRAG HECHIMA CALABASH CUCURBIT PEPONIDA PEPONIUM
GOURMAND EATER EPICURE GLUTTON GORMAND
GOURMET PALATE EPICURE GOURMAND
GOUT GUT CLOT DROP SPLASH PODAGRA PODAGRY CHIRAGRA ARTHRITIS
(— IN HAND) CHIRAGRA
(SUFF.) AGRA
GOUTTE DROP ICICLE
GOUTWEED AXWEED ASHWEED ACHEWEED AISEWEED BOLEWORT GOATWEED GOUTWORT
GOUTY PODAGRAL PODAGRIC
GOVERN RUN WIN CURB KING LEAD REDE REIN RULE SWAY WALD WARD WIND YEME GUIDE JUDGE REGLE STEER TREAT WIELD BRIDLE DIRECT MANAGE ORDAIN POLICE POLICY TEMPER COMMAND CONDUCT CONTROL PRESIDE REFRAIN DISPENSE DOMINATE IMPERATE MODERATE OVERRULE OVERSWAY POLICIZE REGULATE RESTRAIN
GOVERNED BENT
GOVERNESS ABBESS DUENNA FRAULEIN MISTRESS MADEMOISELLE
GOVERNING REGENT REGITIVE
GOVERNMENT GATE LAND RULE KREIS METRO POWER STATE STEER DURBAR HAVANA POLICY RULING CABINET CZARISM DIARCHY DYARCHY RECTION REGENCY REGIMEN TSARISM CIVILITY ENDARCHY GOBIERNO HEGEMONY ISOCRACY ISOCRYME KINGSHIP STEERING ABSOLUTISM
(— BY FEW) OLIGARCHY
(— BY GOD) THEONOMY
(— BY MANY) POLYARCHY
(— BY MOB) OCHLOCRACY
(— BY SMALL CLASS) OLIGARCHY
(— BY THREE) TRIARCHY
(— BY WEALTHY) PLUTOCRACY
(— BY WOMEN) GYNARCHY GYNOCRACY
(— BY 10) DECARCHY
(— BY 2) DIARCHY DUARCHY
(— NOTE) TBOND
(— OF CEYLON) DISSAVA
(— OF TURKEY) GATE PORTE
(ARBITRARY —) ABSOLUTISM
(BAD —) MISRULE
(CHURCH —) PRELACY
(INDIAN —) CIRCAR SIRCAR
(ITALIAN —) QUIRINAL
(MALAYSIAN —) KOMPENI
(MOROCCAN —) MAGHZEN MAKHZAN
(REGIONAL —) METRO
(RUSSIAN —) KREMLIN
(SWAHILI —) SERKALI
(TURKISH —) PORTE
(PREF.) CRATO
(WITHOUT —) ANARCH(O)
(SUFF.) ARCH ARCHIC ARCHY CRACY CRAT(IC)
GOVERNMENTAL ARCHICAL
GOVERNOR BAN BEY DEY EARL KAID LORD NAIK TUTU VALI BANUS CLEON DEWAN DIWAN HAKIM NABOB NAZIM PACHA PASHA SHEIK SUBAH TUPAN AUTHOR DYNAST GRIEVE LEGATE MOODIR MYOWUN NAIGUE NAIQUE PATESI PENLOP RECTOR REGENT SACHEM SATRAP SHEIKH SHERIF TUCHUN WARDEN CATAPAN DAROGHA LEONATO PODESTA RECTRIX SERKALI SHEREEF TOPARCH TSUNGTU VICEROY WIELDER AUTOCRAT BURGRAVE ETHNARCH HOSPODAR LANDVOGT MISTRESS PENTARCH RESIDENT SUBAHDAR TETRARCH CASTELLAN PRESIDENT PROCONSUL
(— OF ALGIERS) DEY DISAWA
(— OF BURMA) WUN WOON
(— OF EGYPT) MUDIR
(— OF FORTRESS) ALCAIDE ALCAYDE
(— OF SHIRE) ALDERMAN
(— OF TAMMANY) SACHEM
(BYZANTINE —) EXARCH CATAPAN
(CEYLON —) DISAWA
(GERMAN —) LANDVOGT
(GREEK —) ETHNARCH
(JAPANESE —) SHOGUN TYCOON
(PAPAL —) LEGATE
(ROMAN —) TETRARCH
(SELJUK —) ATABEG ATABEK
(SPARTAN —) HARMOST
(TURKISH —) BEY WALI MUDIR KEHAYA
GOVERNOR-GENERAL VALI
GOWDIE SCULPIN
GOWK CUCKOO
GOWN GOR SAC GITE GORE HUKE JAMA RAIL SACK SILK TOGA BANIA DRESS FROCK GOUND HABIT JAMAH MANTO TABBY TOOSH BANIAN BANIYA CAFTAN CAMISE CANDYS CHITON JESUIT JOHNNY KIMONO KIRTLE KITTEL LEVITE MANTUA ARISARD CASSOCK GARMENT JOHNNIE SLAMKIN SULTANA SULTANE WRAPPER CAMISOLE GANDOURA MAZARINE PEIGNOIR
(HAWAIIAN —) MOLOKU MUUMUU
GOYA CURRANT
GOYIM GENTES
GRAB NAB NAP RAP GLAM GOPE GLAUM SCRAB CLUTCH COLLAR CRATCH DIPPER NIPPER NOBBLE SNATCH CRAPPLE GRABBLE GRAPNEL GRAPPLE NIPPERS
GRAB BAG LUCKYDIP
GRABBY ARID
GRABEN TROUGH
GRABWEED BISHOPWEED
GRACE EST ORE BEAT ESTE GARB HELD SWAY ADORN COULE FAVOR HONOR MENSE MENSK MERCY POISE SLIDE THANK VENUS BEAUTY BECOME BEDECK CHARIS POLISH RELISH THALIA AGGRACE CHARISM COMMEND DIGNITY FINESSE GRATIFY MELISMA MORDENT BACKFALL BEAUTIFY BLESSING DECORATE EASINESS ELEGANCE FELICITY GRATUITY LEVATION ORNAMENT
(— OF FORM) FLOW SWAY TOURNURE
GRACEFUL AIRY FEAT GENT BONNY GENTY GRATE COMELY FEATLY FELINE FLUENT GAINLY QUAINT SEEMLY SILKEN VENUST ELEGANT FITTING GENTEEL GRACILE SYLPHID WILLOWY CHARMING DELICATE GRACIOUS LEGGIERO MACEVOLE SWANLIKE SYLPHISH
(PREF.) ABRO HABRO
GRACEFULLY FAIR FEATLY HAPPILY LEGGIERO
GRACEFULNESS JOLLITY ELEGANCE
GRACELESS AWKWARD
GRACES CHARITES
GRACIOUS GOOD HEND HOLD KIND MILD CIVIL GODLY HAPPY LUCKY SUAVE WINLY BENIGN GENIAL GENTLE GOODLY KINDLY AFFABLE CORDIAL WINSOME BENEDICT DEBONAIR GENEROUS HANDSOME MERCIFUL PLEASING SOCIABLE BENIGNANT
GRACIOUSLY FAIR SWEETLY

GRACIOUSNESS GRACE MENSK FACILITY GRATUITY
GRACKLE BEO DAW JACKDAW BOATTAIL TINKLING TROOPIAL
GRADATION HUE CLINE ABLAUT CLIMAX NUANCE GEOCLINE STRENGTH
GRADE CUT BANK CHOP EVEN FORM MARK RANK SIZE STEP GLIDE LEVEL ORDER PLANE SCORE SIEGE STAGE ASCENT DEGREE RATING STAPLE TRIAGE FAILURE INCLINE INSPECT DEMISANG GRADIENT GRADUATE MERIDIAN STANDARD
(— DOWN) FAULT
(— LUMBER) SURVEY
(— OF BEEF) GOOD CUTTER
(— OF LIFE) PLANE
(— OF LUMBER) CULL
(— OF OAK) WAINSCOT
(— OF OFFICER) CORNET
(— ROAD) IMPROVE
(—S ONE THROUGH TWELVE) ELHI
(—S 1 THROUGH 12) ELHI
(ABLAUT —) GUNA
(DESIGNED FOR USE IN —S 1-12) ELHI
(POOR —) DEE
(SUPERIOR —) SUPER
(THIRD —) FAIR
GRADER PLANER CLASSER SCRAPER
GRADIENT GRADE LAPSE SLOPE ASCENT INCLINE DOWNHILL
(SUFF.) CLINAL CLINE
GRADIN GRADINO PREDELLA
GRADUAL EASY FLAT SLOW GRAIL GENTLE LENTOUS STEPWISE PIECEMEAL
GRADUALLY GENTLY EDGINGLY GRADATIM INCHMEAL PIECEMEAL
GRADUATE ALUM GRAD GRADE ALUMNA DIVIDE FELLOW ALUMNUS GRADATE BACHELOR
(EISTEDDFOD —) OVATE
GRADUATED SCALAR MEASURED
GRADUATION CLICK
GRAFT BUD IMP PIE CION WORK GRAFF GRAVY INEYE SCION BOODLE INARCH PAYOLA SPLICE ENGRAFT IMPLANT JOBBERY SQUEEZE TOPWORK APPROACH BOODLING GRAFTING INSITION
GRAFTED ENTE
GRAFTER BOODLER
GRAFTING GRAFTAGE INSITION
(PREF.) GREFFO
GRAIL CUP GRAAL CHALICE SANGRAAL
GRAIN JOT RUN RYE WAY CORN CURN DANA KERN PILE RICE SAND SEED WALE WOOD EMMER FIBER FIBRE FUNDI GAVEL GLEBE GRIST PANIC SCRAP SPARK STUFF TRACE WHEAT ANNONA BARLEY BRAINS CEREAL CURRAN GROATS KERNEL FRUMENT GRANULE PANICLE VICTUAL GRAINING PARTICLE STRAIGHT SWEEPAGE
(— FOR MUSH) KASHA
(— FROM MASH TUN) DRAINS
(— LEFT AFTER HARVEST) GAVEL SHACK
(— MEASURE) THRAVE
(— OF BOARD) BEAT
(— OF CORN) PICKLE
(— OF GOLD) PIPPIN
(— OF WOOD) BATE
(—S OF PARADISE) MALAGUETTA
(CHAFF OF —) BRAN
(COARSE —) THIRD
(COARSELY GROUND —) MEAL GRITS KIBBLE
(DAMAGED —) SALVAGE
(EAR OF —) SPIKE RISSOM RIZZON
(GERMINATED —) MALT
(GROUND —) GRIST
(HANDFUL OF —) REAP
(HULLED —) GRITS GROUT GROATS SHELLING
(HUSKED —) SHEALING SHILLING
(MILLET —) CUSCUS
(MIXED —) MASLIN
(MIXED —S) DREDGE
(PARCHED —) GRADDAN
(REFUSE —) SHAG DRAFF
(SACRIFICIAL —) ADOR
(SHOCK OF —) COP
(STACK OF —) HOVEL
(STORED —) MOW
(STREAKED —) ROEY
(PL.) PICKLES RAGGING
(PREF.) CHONDR(I)(IO)(O) COCC(O) GRANI GRANUL(I)(O) SITIO SITO
(SUFF.) COCCAL COCCIC
GRAIN BEETLE CADELLE
GRAINER DICER BOARDER
GRAINSMAN THROWER DRAFFMAN
GRAIN SORGHUM DURRA SHALLU
GRAM KHESARI
(MILLIONTH —) GAMMA
GRAMMAR DONAT SYNTAX GRAMARY PRISCIAN
(TYPE OF —) TAGMEMIC
GRAMMARIAN PRISCIAN
GRAMPUS ORC ORCA COWFISH DOLPHIN SPRINGER
GRANARY GOLA GUNJ SILO GOLAH GUNGE LATHE GARNER GIRNEL GRANGE HORREUM RESERVE CORNLOFT GRAINERY
GRAND OLD AIRY BRAW EPIC MAIN TALL CHIEF GREAT LOFTY NOBLE PIANO PROUD SHOWY SWELL WLONK ANDEAN AUGUST COSMIC EPICAL FAMOUS GLOBAL KINGLY LORDLY SIGHTY SUPERB SWANKY EXALTER IMMENSE STATELY SUBLIME COSMICAL FOREMOST GLORIOUS GORGEOUS IMPOSING MAJESTIC SPLENDID MAGNIFICENT
(PREF.) BEL
GRAND CANYON STATE ARIZONA
GRANDCHILD OE OY OYE
(GREAT —) IEROE
GRANDDAUGHTER NIECE
GRANDEE DON GRAND OMRAH BASHAW GRANDO MAGNATE
GRANDEUR POMP STATE ESTATE FIGURE PARADE MAJESTY ELEGANCE GRANDEZA HAUTESSE NOBILITY SPLENDOR VASTNESS
GRANDFATHER AIEL NONO BOBBY GRAMP ATAVUS GRAMPS BELSIRE GRANDAD GRANDPA GRANDFER GUIDSIRE
(GREAT —) NONO
(GREAT-GREAT-GREAT —) QUATRAYLE
GRAND HOTEL (AUTHOR OF —) BAUM
(CHARACTER IN —) ANNA OTTO FLAMM GAIGERN PREYSING ELISAVETA FLAEMMCHEN KRINGELEIN GRUSINSKAYA OTTERNSCHLAG
GRANDILOQUENT TALL HEROIC TURGID BOMBAST MAGNIFIC RHETORICAL
GRANDIOSE GRAND COSMIC TURGID SUBLIME COSMICAL IMPERIAL
GRANDISSIMUS (AUTHOR OF —) CABLE
(CHARACTER IN —) KEENE AURORA HONORE JOSEPH PALMYRE AGRICOLA CLOTILDE FUSILIER NANCANOU FROWENFIELD GRANDISSIMUS
GRANDMOTHER GRAM GRAN NANA LUCKY NANNY GRANNY GUDAME LUCKIE BELDAME NOKOMIS BABUSHKA GRANDAME
GRANDMOTHERS (AUTHOR OF —) WESTCOTT
(CHARACTER IN —) JIM EVAN ROSE ALWYN FLORA HENRY NANCY RALPH TOWER CANNON SERENA LEANDER MARIANNE
GRANDPARENT TUTU TUPUNA
(OF —S) AVAL
GRAND SLAM VOLE
GRANDSON NEPHEW NEPOTE
GRANITE MOYITE RUNITE GREISEN SYENITE ALASKITE RAPAKIVI PEGMATITE
(— STATE) NEWHAMPSHIRE
(DECOMPOSED —) GROWAN
(PREF.) PEGMATO SYENO
GRANITEWARE GRAYWARE
GRANNY TUTU BABUSHKA
GRANT AID FEU BOOK BOON CEDE ENAM GALE GIFT GIVE HEAR LEND LOAN MISE SEND STOW YARK ADMIT ALLOT ALLOW AWARD BONUS CHART COWLE FLOAT FUERO LEASE SEIZE SPARE TITHE YETTE YIELD ACCEDE ACCORD AFFORD ASSENT BESTOW BETAKE BETEEM BOUNTY CONFER DESIGN EXTEND FIRMAN IMPART JAGEER NOVATE OCTROI PATENT PERMIT REMISE ADJUDGE APPOINT COLLATE CONCEDE CONSENT DISPONE INDULGE LICENSE PRESENT PROMISE SUBSIDY TRIBUTE APPANAGE BESTOWAL CONTRACT DONATION EXCHANGE MONOPOLY PITTANCE TRANSFER CONCESSION ACKNOWLEDGE
(— AS PROPER) ACCORD
(— FOR EXPENSES) SUPPLY
(— IN REMISSION) PARDON
(— OF LAND) FEU ENAM GALE PATA SASAN CASATE
(— PERMISSION) ALLOW DISPENSE
(— RELIEF) FORGIVE
(— TIME) FRIST
(INDIAN —) ENAM COWLE SASAN JAGEER JAGHIR
(PL.) PORK
GRANTING IF ALTHO REMISE ALTHOUGH ACCORDANCE
GRANTOR LESSOR
GRANULAR CORN OPEN GRAINY
GRANULATE CORN KERN GRAIN SUGAR
GRANULATED CORN GRANULAR
GRANULATION SUGARING
GRANULE GRIT GRANUM LUCULE NODULE BIOBLAST GONIDIUM GRANULET
(— IN PROTOPLASM) PLASTID
(ALTMANN'S —S) BIOPLAST
(ICE —S) FRAZIL
(SUFF.) PLAST
GRAPE UVA EDEN VINE BERRY GRAIN PINOT TOKAY ACINUS AGAWAM ISABEL MALAGA MONICA MUSCAT RAISIN VERDEA WORDEN CATAWBA CONCORD HAMBURG MALMSEY MISSION NIAGARA SULTANA CABERNET DELAWARE GRAPELET HANEPOOT ISABELLA LABRUSCA MALVASIA MORILLON MOUNTAIN MUSCATEL NUCULANE RIESLING SLIPSKIN SYLVANER THOMPSON VINIFERA MUSCADINE
(GARNISHED WITH —S) VERONIQUE
(PREPARED WITH —S) VERONIQUE
(PL.) RAPE UVAE
(PREF.) ACINI UVI UVULO
GRAPEFRUIT POMELO POMOLO POMMELO TORONJA SHADDOCK POMPELMOUS POMPELMOOSE
GRAPE HYACINTH MUSK
GRAPE JUICE MUST SAPA STUM
GRAPENUTS TERRAPIN
GRAPEROOT BERBERIS
GRAPES
(PREF.)
(BUNCH OF —) BOTRY(O) STAPHYL(O)
GRAPES OF WRATH (AUTHOR OF —) STEINBECK
(CHARACTER IN —) AL JIM TOM JOAD NOAH ROSE CASEY MULEY CONNIE GRAVES RUTHIE WINFIELD
GRAPESTONE
(PREF.) ACINI
GRAPEVINE
(PREF.) AMPEL(O)
GRAPH CHART CURVE OGIVE TRACE CONTOUR DIAGRAM PROFILE ISOPLETH
(BOTTOMS OF —S) XAXES
(KIND OF —) FEYNMAN
GRAPHIC PICTORIAL PICTURESQUE
GRAPHITE WAD KISH LEAD WADD KEESH PENCIL PLUMBAGO MODERATOR
GRAPNEL CROW DRAG GRAB CREEP CREEPER GRABBLE GRAPPLE SNIGGER GRABHOOK
GRAPPLE DOG CLOSE GRASP GRIPE LATCH BUCKLE CLINCH GRABBLE

GRAPNEL GRIPPLE SNIGGER SNIGGLE WRESTLE
(— QUARRY) BIND
GRAPPLING IRON CLIP DRAG CLASP CRAMP CORVUS CRAMPER CRAMPON CREEPER GRAPNEL GRAPPLE HARPAGO
GRAPTOLITHA XYLINA
GRASP HUG NAP SEE CLAM CLAW CLUM FAKE FANG FIST GLAM GRAB GRIP HAND HENT HOLD SNAP SPAN TAKE VICE CATCH CINCH CLAMP CLASP CLAUT CLEUK GRIPE GROPE LATCH SAVVY SEIZE SENSE SHAKE SPEND CLENCH CLINCH CLUTCH COLLAR FATHOM GOUPEN RUMBLE SNATCH CLAUGHT COMPASS ENCLOSE GRAPPLE GRIPPLE SMITTLE CONCEIVE HANDFAST HOLDFAST
(— FULLY) SWALLOW
(— MENTALLY) ENVISAGE
(— OF REALITY) EPIPHANY
(PREF.) CHADA
GRASPING HARD NIPPY SNACK GRABBY GREEDY GRIPPY HAVING TAKING BROKING MISERLY PUGGING COVETOUS HANDGRIP AVARICIOUS
GRASS BON FAG FOG POA RAY BENT COIX DISS DOOB GAMA HERB ICHU KANS KUSA MUNJ MUSK RAGI TARE TORE USAR ANKEE BARIT BROME COGON COUCH CROFT DRAWK DRINN FLAWN FUNDI GARSE GIRSE GLAGA GRAMA HARIF HAVER HICHU ILLUK KOGON KUSHA KWEEK MELIC MUHLY PANIC QUILA REESK ROOSA SEREH SPIRE STIPA SUDAN ZORRA BARLEY BHABAR BHARTI DARNEL EMOLOA FESCUE FIORIN GLUMAL KIKUYU QUITCH RAGGEE REDTOP RIPGUT SCUTCH TOETOE TWITCH ZACATE AMOURET CANNACH DOGFOOT ESPARTO EULALIA FESTUCA FINETOP FOXTAIL GALLETA GOLDEYE HERBAGE HORDEUM JARAGUA MATWEED MUSCOVY PANICLE PASTURE PIGROOT SETARIA SORGHUM TIMOTHY TOCUSSO TUSSOCK VETIVER ZACATON AEGILOPS BLUESTEM BROWNTOP CALFKILL CAMALOTE CELERITY COCKSPUR DOGSTAIL DRAWLING DROPSEED EELGRASS ELEUSINE FINEBENT GAMELOTE MANGRASS MATGRASS PASPALUM SANDBURR SANDSPUR SANDSTAY SPANIARD SPARTINA SPINIFEX SWEEPAGE TEOSINTE WHITETOP MARIJUANA
(— AMONG GRAIN) DRAWK
(— FOR STOCK) EATAGE
(— FOR THATCHING) BANGO
(— ON BORDER OF FIELD) RAND
(— READY FOR REAPING) SWATH SWATHE
(— USED FOR MAKING PAPER) ESPARTO
(AROMATIC —) KHUS CUSCUS KHUSKHUS
(BEACH —) STAR
(BERMUDA —) DOOB SCUTCH
(CEREAL —) SORGO SORGHUM
(COARSE —) FAG RISP TATH COGON REESK LALANG SNIDDLE
(COUCH —) CUTCH KWEEK QUITCH SCUTCH STROIL SQUITCH
(CURED —) HAY
(DEAD —) FOG FOGGAGE
(DITCH —) ENALID
(GOOSE —) CLIVERS CLEAVERS
(KIND OF —) COUCH QUACK
(MEADOW —) POA
(NUT —) COCO COCOA
(ORCHARD —) DOGFOOT
(PART OF —) AWN TIP APEX CULM LEAF NODE ROOT STEM BLADE BRACT GLUME SHOOT FLORET FLOWER LIGULE SHEATH TILLER PEDICEL RHIZOME SPIKELET
(PASTURE —) TORE GRAMMA
(POVERTY —) HEATH
(QUAKING —) SHAKER
(REED —) CARRIZO
(REEDLIKE —) BENT DISS
(STORED FORAGE —) HAYLAGE
(SUDAN —) GARAWI
(SWEET —) SORGO
(PREF.) CHORTO GRAMIN(I)(O) HERBI
GRASS-EATING
(PREF.) POE
GRASSERIE JAUNDICE
GRASSHOPPER GRIG CICADA HOPPER QUAKER SAWYER TETTIX ACRIDID CRICKET KATYDID SKIPPER ACRIDIAN LANGOSTA
GRASSLAND HAM LEA RAKH VELD VELDT BOTTOM MEADOW PATANA LEYLAND PASTURE SAVANNA
(ARGENTINE —) CAMPO
(RUSSIAN —) STEPPES
(SWAMPY —) EVERGLADE
(TRACT OF —) PRAIRIE
(PL.) SCHIH
GRASS PEA LANG KHESARI
GRASSQUIT QUAT QUIT CIVITE
GRASS TREE BLACKBOY
GRASSY HERBY
GRATE JAR FRET GRIT RASP CHARK CHIRK DANDY DEVIL GRIDE GRIND RANGE STOVE ABRADE CHAFER SCRAPE SCREAR SCREEK SCROOP GRATING MANGRATE
(FALSE —) DANDY
GRATEFUL KIND SAPID WELCOME THANKFUL
GRATEFULNESS GRATUITY
GRATER RISP
GRATIANO (BROTHER OF —) BRABANTIO
(WIFE OF —) NERISSA
GRATIFICATION GLUT GUST LUXURY RELISH REWARD SATIETY DELICACY GRATUITY PLEASURE TICKLING SATISFACTION
GRATIFIED GLAD PROUD CHARMED CONTENT PLEASED
GRATIFY PAY BABY FEED LUST SATE AMUSE FEAST FLESH GRACE HUMOR MIRTH QUEME SAVOR SERVE SETUP STILL WREAK ARRIDE FOSTER OBLIGE PAMPER PLEASE REGALE SALUTE TICKLE AGGRATE CONTENT DELIGHT FLATTER GLADDEN INDULGE SATISFY PLEASURE
(— THE PALATE) SEASON
GRATIFYING GOOD COMELY DELICATE GRATEFUL
GRATING GRID HACK HARP HECK JACK RACK CRATE CRUDE GRILL HARSH RANGE RASPY TRAIL BAFFLE CRATCH GITTER GRILLE HOARSE RUGGED WICKET BAFFLER ECHELLE ECHELON BABRACOT CATAPULT GRIDIRON METALLIC SCRANNEL STRIDENT PORTCULLIS
(— OVER DRAIN) SIVER SYVER
GRATIS FREE FREELY BUCKSHEE
GRATITUDE THANK THANKS GRATUITY
GRATUITOUS FREE WANTON BASELESS NEEDLESS
GRATUITY FEE TIP BOON DASH VAIL PILON SPIFF SPILL BOUNTY CUMSHAW DASTURI DOUCEUR PRESENT PRIMAGE BAKSHISH BONAMANO BUCKSHEE COURTESY DUSTOORI GRATUITO REAPDOLE BAKHSHISH BAKSHEESH PERQUISITE
(CHRISTMAS —) BOX
(GAMBLER'S —) TOKE
(PL.) LARGESSE
GRAVE BED DRY LOW PIT SAD URN BALK BASS BIER CELL CIST DEEP DELF FOSS GRIT HIGH HOME KIST LAIR LAKE MOLD MOOL RUDE SADE SAGE TOMB URNA DELFT FOSSE GRAFF GROVE HEAVY MOULD SHEOL SOBER STAID STIFF SUANT VAULT BURIAL DEMURE GRIEVE HEARSE SEDATE SEVERE SOLEMN SOMBER SOMBRE STEADY AUSTERE EARNEST FUNERAL PITHOLE SERIOSO SERIOUS SOBERLY CATONIAN DECOROUS MATRONAL SERMONIC SATURNINE
GRAVECLOTHES LINEN CEREMENTS
GRAVEDIGGER RATEL BEDRAL BURIER FOSSOR PITMAN BEDERAL
GRAVEL GRIT ARENA GEEST GRAIL CHESIL RANGLE SAMMEL SHILLA BALLAST CALICHE CHANNEL RATCHEL SHINGLE STANNER BLINDING
(— AND SAND) DOBBIN
(— DEPOSIT) LEAD
(— IN KIDNEYS) ARENA
(LOOSE —) SLITHER
(SCREENED —) HOGGINS
(PREF.) CROCO
GRAVELLY HASKY CHISELLY GLAREOUS
GRAVELY SADLY DEEPLY
GRAVE MOUND TUMULUS
GRAVER BURIN STYLE PLASTIC SCORPER
GRAVESTONE BAUTA PLANK STELA STELE STONE TABLE CIPPUS JUMPER THROUGH
GRAVEYARD CEMETERY
GRAVID HEAVY WOMBED PREGNANT
GRAVIMETER DOODLEBUG
GRAVITATIONAL UNIT SLUG
GRAVITY WEIGHT DIGNITY EARNEST SOBRIETY
(KIND OF —) ZERO
GRAVY JUS SOP BREE FOND LEAR BLANC BUNCE JIPPER
GRAY ASH BAT FOG ASHY BEAR BLAE BLUE DOVE DUSK GREY GRIS GULL HOAR IRON LEAD SALT ACIER CAMEL CRANE HOARY LYART MOUSE STEEL WHITE CASTOR CINDER DENVER FROSTY FRUSTY GREIGE GRISLY ISABEL LEADEN NICKEL NUTRIA PEWTER QUAKER STRING BLUNKET CRUISER GRANITE GRIZARD GRIZZLE GRIZZLY HUELESS MURINUS NEUTRAL PELICAN PILGRIM SARKARA SPARROW ALUMINUM BLONCKET CHARCOAL CINEREAL CINEROUS EVENGLOW FELDGRAU PLATINUM PLYMOUTH
(BROWNISH —) TAUPE
(DARKEST —) BLACK
(GOOSE —) LAMA
(MOLE —) TAUPE
(MOTH —) SHEEPSKIN
(STREAKED WITH —) LYARD
(VIOLET —) GRIDELIN
(PREF.) GLAUC(O) POLI(O)
GRAYBACK DOWITCH GRAYCOAT GREYBACK
GRAYBEARD OLDSTER
GRAY CRANE COOLEN COOLUNG
GRAY DRAB ACIER
GRAYISH NEUTRAL
GRAYLING PINK OMBRE UMBER HERRING UMBRANA BLUEFISH SALMONID
GRAYNESS CANITIES
GRAY PARROT JAKO
GRAYSBY CONY CONEY
GRAY WHALE RIPSACK GRAYBACK HARDHEAD
GRAZE BITE CROP FEED SCUR SKIM AGIST BRUSH GRASS GRIDE RANGE SCAMP SCUFF SHAVE SKIFF SKIRR STOCK BROWSE CREASE FODDER GLANCE RIPPLE SCRAPE SCRAZE PASTURE
GRAZIER PASTURER SQUATTER TREKBOER
GRAZING BIT FEED GRASS COLLOP RASANT FOLDING PASCUAGE
GREASE COOM SAIM SEAM ADEPS BLECK COOMB SMEAR SPICK ARMING AXUNGE CREESH ENSEAM LIQUOR POMATE ALEMITE SAINDOUX
(— IN HARD CAKES) SEAK
(— UP) LARD
(PIG'S —) MORT
(WOOL —) YOK DEGRAS LANOLIN
(PREF.) SEBI
GREASE-HEELS GRAPES
GREASER DOPER
GREASEWOOD CHICO CHEMIZO

GREASY FAT GLET OILY RICH FATTY PORKY YOLKY SMEARY TRAINY CREESHY PINGUID TALLOWY UNCTUOUS
GREAT BAD BIG FAR FAT FIT OLD RAD BARO COOL DEEP DREE FELL FINE GONE GURT HUGE KEEN MAIN MUCH RIAL SOME TALL UNCO VAST VILE AMPLE BURRA CHIEF DANDY FELON GRAND LARGE MEKIL STOUR SUPER SWEET SWELL TOUGH YEDER FIERCE GAPING HEROIC MICKLE NATION STRONG SUPERB CAPITAL EMINENT EXTREME GALLOWS HOWLING IMMENSE INTENSE STAVING TITANIC VIOLENT VOLUMED ALMIGHTY CRACKING ELEVATED ENORMOUS FAVORITE GALACTIC GALAXIAN GIGANTIC HORRIBLE INFINITE PRECIOUS TERRIFIC MONSTROUS MAGNIFICENT
(— LAND) ALASKA
(IMMEASURABLY —) ABYSMAL
(TOO —) OVERDUE
(VERY —) MAIN SORE AWFUL STEEP ARDENT DEADLY IMMANE INGENT MORTAL EXTREME FRANTIC GHASTLY HOWLING SUBLIME DREADFUL MOUNTAIN MONUMENTAL
(PREF.) ARCH MAGN(I) MAHA MEG(A) MEGAL(O)
(HOW —) QUANTI
(SUFF.) MEGALY
GREAT AUK PENGUIN PINWING GAREFOWL
GREAT BARRIER (— ISLAND) OTEA
GREAT BRITAIN (SEE ENGLAND)
GREATCOAT GREGO JEMMY JOSEPH POSTEEN OVERCOAT
GREAT DANE BEARHOUND
GREATER SUPERIOR
(PREF.) MEIZO
GREATER STITCHWORT HEAD SNAPPER HEADACHE SNAPJACK SNAPWORT
GREATER YELLOWLEGS YELPER
GREATEST UTMOST EXTREME MAXIMAL
(— EXTENT) MAX MAXIMUM
(— POSSIBLE) ALL SUPREME
GREAT EXPECTATIONS (AUTHOR OF —) DICKENS
(CHARACTER IN —) JOE PIP ABEL BIDDY DOLGE SARAH ORLICK PHILIP PIRRIP POCKET PROVIS BENTLEY DRUMMLE ESTELLA GARGERY HERBERT JAGGERS MATTHEW HAVISHAM MAGWITCH COMPEYSON PUMBLECHOOK
GREAT GATSBY (AUTHOR OF —) FITZGERALD
(CHARACTER IN —) JAY TOM NICK BAKER DAISY MCKEE GATSBY GEORGE JORDAN MYRTLE WILSON BUCHANAN CARRAWAY CATHERINE WOLFSHIEM
GREAT-GRANDCHILD IEROE
GREAT GRANDFATHER NONO BESAIEL GRANDSIR
GREAT LAKE ERIE HURON ONTARIO MICHIGAN SUPERIOR
GREATLY FAR MUY FELL MUCH AMAIN SWITH FINELY MAINLY STRONG SWYTHE SWEETLY WOUNDLY MIGHTILY
GREAT MOLE RAT ZEMMI ZEMNI
GREATNESS FORCE GRANDEUR GRANDEZA MUCHNESS
GREAT RAGWEED KINGHEAD
GREAT TITMOUSE SHARPSAW
GREAVE JAMB JAMBE JAMBEAU
(PL.) CRAP HOSE GRAVES
GREBE LEAD LOON DIVER GAUNT WITCH DIPPER DOBBER DUCKER FINFOOT HENBILL PYGOPOD ARSEFOOT CARGOOSE DABCHICK DIDAPPER GRUIFORM
GRECE GRICE DEGREE GRISSEN

GREECE

ANCIENT LOCATIONS: ELIS DORIS PYLOS ACHAEA ACTIUM ATTICA DELPHI EPIRUS HELLAS LOCRIS PHOCIS SPARTA THEBES TIRYNS BOEOTIA CORINTH EPEIROS LACONIA MACEDON MEGARIS MYCENAE PAESTUM
ARMY UNIT: TAXIS
BAY: ELEUSIS SALAMIS PHALERON
CAPE: KRIOS MALEA SPADA AKRITAS MATAPAN SIDEROS DREPANON GRAMBYSA TAINARON
CAPITAL: ATHENS ATHENAI
COIN: OBOL HECTE DIOBOL LEPTON STATER DRACHMA DIOBOLON
COLUMN: DORIC IONIC CORINTHIAN
DANCE: PYRRHIC ROMAIKA
DIALECT: COAN ATTIC DORIC ELEAN EOLIC IONIC AEOLIC MELIAN THERAN ACHAEAN ARCADIAN
DISTRICT: ARTA ELIS CANEA CHIOS CORFU CRETE DRAMA EVROS KHIOS PELLA SAMOS ZANTE ACHAEA ACHAIA ATTICA EPIRUS EUBOEA KILKIS KNANIA KOZANE LARISA LESBOS LEUKAS PHOCIS PIERIA SERRAI THRACE XANTHE AETOLIA ARCADIA ARGOLIS BOEOTIA CORINTH KAVALLA LACONIA LARISSA LASETHI MTATHOS PREVEZA RHODOPE CYCLADES IOANNINA KARDITSA KASTORIA MAGNESIA MESSENIA PHLORINA RETHYMNE SALONIKA THESSALY TRIKKALA MACEDONIA
GULF: VOLOS ATHENS MESARA PATRAI PATRAS ARGOLIS CORINTH KAVALLA KNANION LACONIA LEPANTO MESSINI RENDINA SARONIC STRIMON MESSENIA SALONIKA SINGITIC THERMAIC TORONAIC
HOME OF GODS: OLYMPUS
ISLAND: DIA IOS KEA KOS NIO CEOS KEOS MILO SYME SYRA CHIOS CORFU CRETE DELOS KASOS KHIOS LEROS MELOS MILOS NAXOS PAROS PAXOI PAXOS PSARA RODOS SAMOS SARIA SYROS TELOS TENOS THERA THIRA TINOS ZANTE ANAPHE ANDROS CANDIA CERIGO CHALKE EUBOEA EVVOIA GAVDOS IKARIA ITHACA ITHAKI LEMNOS LESBOS LEUKAS LEVKAS PATMOS RHENEA RHODES SIFNOS SKYROS THASOS AMORGOS CIMOLUS CYTHERA KERKYRA KIMOLOS KYTHERA KYTHNOS LEVITHA MYKONOS NISYROS SALAMIS SIPHNOS KALYMNOS MYTILENE SANTORIN SERIPHOS
ISLANDS: IONIAN CYCLADES SPORADES DODECANESE STROPHADES
LAKE: KARLA VOLVE COPAIS KOPAIS PRESPA TOPOLIA KASTORIA TACHINOS VISTONIS
LETTER: MU NU PI XI CHI ETA PHI PSI RHO TAU BETA IOTA ZETA ALPHA DELTA GAMMA KAPPA OMEGA SIGMA THETA LAMBDA EPSILON OMICRON UPSILON
MARKET PLACE: AGORA
MEASURE: PIK BEMA PIKI POUS BARIL CADOS CHOUS CUBIT DIGIT MARIS PEKHE PODOS PYGON XYLON ACAENA BACHEL BACILE BARILE COTULA DICHAS GRAMME HEMINA KOILON ORGYIA PALAME PECHYS SCHENE AMPHORA CHENICA CHOENIX CYATHOS DIAULOS HEKTEUS METRETA STADION STADIUM STREMMA CONDYLOS DAKTYLOS DEKAPODE DOLICHOS MEDIMNOS METRETES PALAISTE PLETHRON PLETHRUM SPITHAME STATHMOS
MOUNTAIN: IDA IDHI OSSA ATHOS PAROS ELIKON PARNON PELION PILION WITSCH HELICON OLYMPUS VURANON KRAGNOVO SMOLIKAS TAYGETOS PARNASSUS
MOUNTAINS: OETA OTHRYS PINDUS RODOPI RHODOPE HYMETTOS TAYGETUS
NAME: ELLAS HELLAS
PENINSULA: ACTE AKTE AKTI MOREA SITHONIA PELOPONNESE
PORT: SYRA CORFU PYLOS SYROS VOLOS MEGARA PATRAI PATRAS KAVALLA KERKYRA PIRAEUS SALONIKA
RIVER: IRI ARDA ARTA AURO AXIOS DOONA EVROS LERNA ALFIOS NESTOS PENEUS PINIOS STRUMA VARDAR ALPHEUS EUROTAS EVROTAS ILISSOS PENEIOS ROUFIAS SARANTA STRIMON ACHELOUS AKHELOOS ALIAKMON KEPHISOS RHOUPHIA
RUINS: DELOS PELLA SAMOS CORINTH ELEUSIS ELEVSIS ACROPOLIS
SEA: CRETE AEGEAN IONIAN MIRTOON
STATE: PHOCIS
TOWN: IOS KEA KOS ARTA ELIS KYME PETA SYME YDRA ADREA AGYIA ARGOS CANEA CHIOS CORFU DRAMA KARYA MELOS NAXOS NEMEA PELLA POROS PSARI PYLOS PYRGI SAMOS SYROS TENOS VAMOS VATHY VOLOS VYRON ZANTE ACTIUM ATHENS CANDIA DAPHNI DELPHI EDESSA ITHACA JANINA KOZANE LARISA MEGARA NIKHIA PATRAS RHODES SERRAI SERRES SPARTA THEBES TIRYNS XANTHE ATHENAI CORINTH ELEUSIS KERKYRA LARISSA MYCENAE PIRAEUS IOANNINA KOMOTINE MARATHON PHARSALA SALONIKA TRIKKALA PERISTERI
VALLEY: NEMEA
VERNACULAR: DEMOTIC
WEIGHT: MNA OKA OKE MINA OBOL LITRA LIVRE MANEH POUND DIOBOL DRAMME KANTAR OBOLOS OBOLUS STATER TALENT CHALCON CHALQUE DRACHMA DIOBOLON TALANTON
WOMEN: THYIAD

GREED AVARICE AVIDITY HOGGERY CUPIDITY RAPACITY
GREEDINESS AVARICE AVIDITY GULOSITY
GREEDY AVID GAIR GORB YELP AVIDE EAGER GUTTY YIVER GRABBY GUNDIE KITISH STINGY GLUTTON GRIPPLE HOODOCK MISERLY PIGGISH COVETOUS ESURIENT GRASPING RAVENOUS LICKERISH
(PREF.) LICHNO
GREEK GREW ATTIC HADJI KOINE METIC ARGIVE IONIAN KLEPHT ACHAEAN ACHAIAN AEOLIAN GRECIAN GRIFFON HELLENE GRECANIC HELLADIC HELLENIC ITALIOTE SICELIOT
(— RESISTANCE GROUP) EDES ELAS
(MODERN —) ROMAIC
(PREF.) GRAECO GRECO HELLENO
GREEN (ALSO SEE COLOR) NEW RAW LEEK NILE VERD VERT CRUDE FRESH LODEN NAIVE CALLOW VIRENT NOUVEAU SINOPLE UNFIRED VERDANT BAYBERRY IMMATURE NOUVELLE VAGABOND VIRIDIAN WEDGWOOD WOODLAND UNTRAINED
(— MOUNTAIN STATE) VERMONT
(COOKED —S) SALAD
(GRAYISH —) RESEDA
(KIND OF —) MOSS KELLY PARIS
(NILE —) BOA
(PALE —) ALOE ALOES
(YELLOWISH —) GLAUZY ABSINTHE GLAUCOUS
(PREF.) CHLOR(O) PRASEO PRASO VERD(O) VIRID(I)
GREEN AMARANTH REDROOT
GREENBACK NOTE FROGSKIN
(PL.) GREEN LETTUCE
GREEN BAY TREE (AUTHOR OF —) BROMFIELD
(CHARACTER IN —) CYON LILY ELLEN GIGON IRENE JULIA SHANE HATTIE WILLIE HARRISON KRYLENKO TOLLIVER
GREENBRIER SMILAX SARSAPARILLA

GREEN CORMORANT SHAG
GREENERY VERDURE
GREENFISH BLUEFISH
GREENHEART BIBIRU BEBEERU
GREEN HERON KIALEE
GREENHORN JAY MUG YAP JAKE PUTT TYRO IKONA GREENY ROOKIE SUCKER INNOCENT SOFTHORN
(— ON WHALER) WAISTER
GREENHOUSE STOVE GREENERY HOTHOUSE ORANGERY COOLHOUSE
GREENISH BERYL SANIOUS
GREENISH-YELLOW RESEDA

GREENLAND
AIR BASE: THULE
BAY: DISKO BAFFIN MELVILLE
CAPE: JAAL GRIVEL WALKER BISMARCK BREWSTER FAREWELL LOWENORN
CAPITAL: GODTHAAB
DISCOVERER: ERIC
MOUNTAIN: FOREL PAYER KHARDYU GUNNBJORN
STRAIT: DAVIS DENMARK
TOWN: ETAH NORD THULE UMANAK GODHAVN IVIGTUT GODTHAAB JULIANEHAB EGEDESMINDE SUKKERTOPPEN HOLSTEINSBORG

GREENLING TROUT BOREGAT BODIERON LORICATE ROCKFISH
GREEN MANSIONS (AUTHOR OF —) HUDSON
(CHARACTER IN —) ABEL RIMA NUFLO
GREEN MONKEY GUENON
GREENNESS VERD VERT VERDURE VERDANCY VIRIDITY
GREEN ONION RARERIPE
GREEN PIKE JACK
GREENROOM FOYER
GREENSHANK TATTLER
GREENSTONE POUNAMU
GREEN SUNFISH REDEYE
GREENWEED WOODWAX
GREEN WOODPECKER ECCLE SPRITE YAFFLE YOCKEL YUKKEL HEWHALL HEWHOLE SNAPPER SPEIGHT YAFFLER POPINJAY WOODHACK WOODWALL
GREET CRY JOY CROW HAIL HALSE ACCOST HERALD SALAAM SALUTE ADDRESS RECEIVE WELCOME
GREETING HOW CIAO HIYA ALOHA GREET HELLO HOWDY KOMBO ACCOST CHEERO SALAAM SALUTE SHALOM ADDRESS CHEERIO COMMEND SLAINTE WELCOME REMEMBRANCE
GREGARIOUS GREGAL SOCIAL
GREGE NUTRIA
GRENADA (CAPITAL OF —) STGEORGES
(ISLAND OF —) CARRIACON
GRENADE EGG TROMBE GRENADO FIREBALL PINEAPPLE
GRENADIER RATTAIL WHIPTAIL
GRENADINE FLORENCE
GRENDEL (SLAYER OF —) BEOWULF
GREREN (— LIGHT) GOAHEAD
GRETCHEN (BELOVED OF —) FAUST
GRETTIR THE STRONG (AUTHOR OF —) UNKNOWN
(CHARACTER IN —) ATLI GEST GLAM GRIM JARL ANGLE BJORN EINAR ASMUND ILLUGI OGMUND OXMAIN SKEGGI STEINN THORIR DROMUND GRETTIR MAKSSON HALLMUND LONGHAIR REDBEARD SNAEKOLL STEINVOR THORFINN THORGILS SLOWCOACH THORBJORN THORSTEINN
GREY (SEE GRAY)
GREYHOUND GREW SALUKI BANJARA SAPLING TUMBLER WHIPPET
GREYISH BEIGE
GRID BOUCAN BUCCAN GRIDDLE GRIDIRON
(CIRCULAR —) DISC DISK
GRIDDLE COMAL GRILL GIRDLE GRILLE BRANDER
GRIDDLE CAKE AREPA LATKE CHAPATTY CORNCAKE FLAPJACK SLAPJACK
GRIDIRON GRID GRILL TRAIL BRANDER BROILER GRIDDLE
GRIEF VEX WOE CARE DILL DOLE DOOL DREE HARM HURT MOAN MOOD PAIN RUTH SORE TEEN TINE AGONY DOLOR GRAME RUING TRIAL WRONG BARRAT DESIRE MISHAP REGRET SORROW STOUND WONDER ANGUISH CHAGRIN EMOTION FAILURE OFFENSE SADNESS THOUGHT TROUBLE WAESUCK WAYMENT DISASTER DISTRESS HARDSHIP
(— STEM) KELLY
(SECRET —) CANKER
(PREF.) DOLORI LYPO
GRIESEN ZWITTER
GRIEVANCE BEEF GRIEF PEEVE BURDEN BYGONE GRAVAMEN HARDSHIP
GRIEVE VEX CARE DOLE DUMP EARN ERME HONE HURT PAIN PINE SIGH WAIL GRAME GRIPE MOURN SORRY WOUND YEARN ATHINK CORSIE LAMENT REPINE SORROW AFFLICT CHAGRIN CONDOLE GRIZZLE TROUBLE WAYMENT COMPLAIN DISTRESS
GRIEVED WOE GRAME SORRY
GRIEVING SORRY
GRIEVOUS SAD DEAR DEEP DERF HARD SORE CHARY DIRTY GRIEF HEAVY SORRY WEARY BITTER DREARY SEVERE SHREWD CAREFUL HEINOUS WEIGHTY DOLOROUS ATROCIOUS
GRIEVOUSLY DERNLY FOULLY SORELY HEAVILY
GRIFFE SPUR
GRIFFIN GRIPE GRYPHON EPIMACUS
GRILL ASK REJA BRACE BROIL DEVIL TRAIL AFFLICT BROILER GRILLADE
GRILLE FACE REJA HAZARD
GRILLROOM GROOM
GRILSE PEAL SEWIN FINNAC GRAWLS BOTCHER FORKTAIL
GRIM DOUR GASH SOUR BLEAK CRUEL GAUNT STERN GRIMLY GRISLY HORRID SEVERE SULLEN TORVID GHASTLY GRIZZLY HIDEOUS MACABRE TORVOUS PITILESS RUTHLESS
GRIMACE MOP MOW MUG POT FACE GIRN IRPE MOUE MUMP YIRN FLEER MOUTH SNEER SNOOT GIMBLE SHEYLE STITCH MURGEON SIMAGRE
GRIMALKIN CAT HAG MOLL CRONE WITCH BELDAM HARRIDAN
GRIME DIRT SMUT COLLY SMOUCH SMUTCH
GRIMME COQUETOON
GRIMNESS TORVITY
GRIMP CLIMB
GRIMY DINGY GRUBBY STAINED SCABROUS
GRIN DRAD GIRN MUMP FLEER RISUS SNEER SIMPER GRIZZLE
GRIND DIG SAP BONE BRAY CHEW FILE GRUN MILL MULL MUZZ SMUG SWOT CRUSH FLOAT FLOUR GRATE GRIDE GRIST QUERN CRUNCH DRUDGE POWDER EMERIZE GRISTLE SWOTTER LEVIGATE
(— COARSELY) KIBBLE
(— DIAMONDS) SKIVE
(— SMALL) BRAY
(— TEETH) GNASH GRATE GRINT GRISBET
(— TO POWDER) TRITURATE
(— WITH WATER) PUG
GRINDER SUB HERO CRASH HOAGY MOLAR HOAGIE MULLER BRUISER TORPEDO PEPPERMILL
GRINDING BREAK MOLAR ABRASION
(— OF CORN) MULTURE
(— OF MEAL) BREAK GRIST
(— OF TEETH) BRUXISM
(PL.) SWARF
GRINDSTONE MANO PAVER STONE
GRIP BITE BURR CLIP FANG FIST HOLD HOLT TAKE VICE CHOKE CINCH CLAMP CLASP GRASP GRIPE PINCH SALLY SEIZE BARREL CLINCH CLUTCH CRADLE FREEZE EMBRACE HANDBAG HOLDING SEIZURE ADHESION FOOTLOCK HANDFAST HANDGRIP HANDHOLD STAGEHAND
(— OF A SWORD) FUSEAU
(— OF BELL ROPE) SALLY
(— TO A SPAR) DOG
GRIPE BEEF CARP CRAB FRIB BITCH CREATE GROUSE HOLLER KVETCH NATTER SNATCH GRIZZLE COMPLAIN
GRIPER GRIZZLER
GRIPES TORMINA
GRIPING GRIPPLE PINCHING
GRIPPER TALON KEEPER NIPPER
GRIPPING STONY STONEY
GRIQUA BASTARD BASTAARD
GRIS-GRIS AMULETS
GRISKINISSA (HUSBAND OF —) ARTAXAMINOUS
GRISLY GRIM GHASTLY GRIZZLY HIDEOUS GRUESOME
GRISON HURON GALICTIS
GRIST PABULUM
GRISTLE CARTILAGE
GRIT SAND GRIND PLUCK SPUNK BOTTOM BRAVERY DECISION GRITROCK RUBSTONE
(— FROM AXLE) SWARF
(PL.) CUTLINGS
GRITH MUND GYRTH
GRITTY SANDY SHARP GRISTY CHISELLY SABULINE SABULOUS
GRIVET TOTA WAAG GEUNON NISNAS
GRIZZLE ROAN
GRIZZLED GRISLY STREAKED
GRIZZLY BEAR (— STATE) CALIFORNIA
GROAN MOAN ROME GRANK GRUNT STECH COMPLAIN
GROANER PUN JOKE
GROAT BIT FLAG GILL HARP
GROATS
(PREF.) ATHERO
GROCER SPICER EPICIER PEPPERER
GROCERY BODEGA PULPERIA
GROG RUMBO TEMPER CHAMOTTE
GROGGERY SHANTY GROGSHOP
GROGGY SHAKY UNSTEADY WAVERING
GROGSHOP SHANTY DOGGERY GROGGERY
GROIN LISK PIER SHARE CLITCH INGUEN GRUNZIE
(PREF.) INGUIN(O)
GROMMET RING BECKET COLLAR EYELET CRINGLE GARLAND
GROMWELL PUCCOON REDROOT SALFERN GRAYMILL
GROOM LAD MAFU NEAT SYCE CURRY DRESS MAFOO PREEN PRIMP STRAP SWIPE TIGER BARBER BATMAN FETTLE FOGGER GUINEA MEHTAR OSTLER HOSTLER MARSHAL COISTREL COISTRIL GROOMLET STRAPPER
GROOMING TOILETTE
GROOVE RUT BEAD DADO GAIN KERF LUCE NOCK PORT RAKE SLOT CANAL CHASE CROZE FLUTE FOSSA GLYPH GORGE GOUGE GUIDE JOINT QUIRK REGAL RIFLE RIGOL SCARF SCORE STRIA SWAGE CREASE CULLIS FULLER FURROW GUTTER KEYWAY RABBET RAGGLE RAGLET REBATE RIFFLE RUNNER SCROBE SULCUS THROAT TRENCH CHAMFER CHANNEL GARLAND KEYHOLE PLOWING SULCATE BOTHRIUM GROOVING PHILTRUM CANNELURE VALLECULA
(— FOR SLIDING DOOR) REGLE
(— IN AUGER) POD
(— IN COLUMN) FLUTE
(— IN HORSE'S TOOTH) MARK
(— IN MASONRY) RAGGLE
(— IN SLUICE) RIFFLE
(— IN STAVES) CROZE
(— IN STONE) JAD
(— IN TIRE) SIPE
(— OF RECORD) TRACK
(— ON UPPER LIP) PHILTRUM
(— ON WEEVIL) SCROBE
(— ON WHALE) SCARF
(—S ON ROCK) LAPIES
(— UNDER COPING) GORGE

(JOINER'S —) SEAM
(RECTANGULAR —) REGLET
GROOVED FLUTED MILLED EXARATE SULCATE
GROOVER FLUTER
GROOVY IN HIP RAD COOL FAROUT SMOOTH STRIATE
GROPE CLAM CLAW FEEL POKE RIPE GLAUM GRAIP FUMBLE GUDDLE GRABBLE GRAPPLE GROPPLE GRUBBLE SCRABBLE
(— AWKWARDLY) FUMBLE
GROSBEAK FINCH HAWFINCH
GROSGRAIN ROYALE
GROSS FAT DULL FOUL LUMP RANK BROAD CRASS FOGGY GREAT GUTTY LARGE MACRO SLUMP THICK WHOLE ANIMAL COARSE EARTHY FILTHY GREASY SORDID STRONG BLOATED FULSOME CLODDISH FLAGRANT INDECENT SLUTTISH
GROSSO MATAPAN
GROTESQUE ANTIC WOOZY ROCOCO BAROQUE BIZARRE CROTESCO FANCIFUL
GROTTO CAVE GROT ANTRE SPEOS CAVERN LUPERCAL
GROUCH BEAR CRAB SULK CRANK GROUSE SOURBALL SOURPUSS
GROUND SEW SOD SUE BASE CLOD DIRT FOLD FOND GIST LAND MOLD REST ROOT SOIL STAY WOLD EARTH FIELD FIRTH FOUND MOULD PLACE SCORE SOLUM TRAIN TUTOR VENUE CREASE MATTER REASON SMACKED FORELAND INITIATE
(— AT TOP OF SHAFT) BANK
(— COVERED WITH RUBBLE) TITI
(— FOR COMPLAINT) BEEF
(— OF FLAG) FIELD
(— OF LACE) FOND
(— OVERLYING TIN DEPOSIT) BURDEN
(BOGGY —) SOG CARR SNAPE
(BROKEN —) HAG
(BURYING —) CEMETERY
(CAMPING —) AUTOCAMP
(COLLEGE —S) CAMPUS
(DUMPING —) TIP TOOM
(FALLOW —) BRISE
(FEEDING —) HAUNT
(FIRM-HOLDING —) LANDFANG
(FISHING —) HAAF
(FROZEN —) TJAELE
(GRASSY —) LAWN CLOWRE
(GRAZING —) HERDWICK
(HARD —) HARDPAN
(HUNTING —) CHASE
(LOW —) INCH SWALE TALAO
(MIDDLE —) LIMBO
(MUDDY —) SLOB
(NEW ENCLOSED —) TINING
(ORIGINAL —) URGRUND
(PARADE —) MAIDAN
(PASTURE —) HIRSEL
(RECREATION —) PARK
(RISING —) HURST HYRST
(SLOPING —) CLEVE
(SOLID —) HILL
(SPONGY —) BOG
(SWAMPY —) PUXY CRIPPLE
(UNCULTIVATED —) JUNGLE
(UNUSED —) AREA
(WET WASTE —) MOOR REESK
(PL.) GROUT STOCK
(PREF.) CHAMAE CHAME GE(O) PEDO SOLI
(ON THE —) HUMI
GROUND BEETLE CARABID
GROUND COVER AJUGA VETCH MYRTLE
GROUNDER COMEBACKER
GROUND HEMLOCK SHINWOOD
GROUND HOG MARMOT
GROUND IVY GILL HEWE HOVE JILL YARROW ALEHOOF CATFOOT GAGROOT MILFOIL TUNHOOF FOALFOOT
GROUNDLESS IDLE FALSE BASELESS
GROUNDLINE SETLINE
GROUNDMAN GRUNT
GROUNDMASS PASTE CEMENT MATRIX
GROUNDNUT GOBBE PEANUT PIGNUT
GROUND PINE FOXTAIL STAGHORN
GROUNDS RATIONALE
GROUNDSEL SIMSON DOGBUSH SENCION SENECIO BINDWEED BIRDSEED
GROUNDSMAN CURATOR
GROUND SQUIRREL GOPHER GRINNY SUSLIK MEERKAT SCIURID SOUSLIK SCIURINE
GROUND THRUSH PITTA
GROUNDWORK BASE FOND FUND BASIS BOTTOM FUNDUS
GROUP MOB SET BAND BEVY BODY CREW DECK FOLD GANG KNOT PAIR RING SECT SORT STEW TEAM TREF ARRAY BATCH BREED BUNCH CASTE CLASS CLUMP COVEY FIRCA FLOCK GENUS GLOBE PLUMP SABHA SKULK SQUAD STACK TALLY WHEEN CIRCLE CLUTCH COHORT FAMILY GRUPPO PARCEL RUBRIC AGGROUP BATTERY BOILING BOUROCK BRACKET CLASSIS CLUSTER COLLEGE COMMUNE COMPANY CONSORT FELLOWS FLUTTER QUOTITY SECTION SEVERAL SOCIETY ALLIANCE CATEGORY CLASSIFY DIVISION FAISCEAU FLOTILLA GROUPING
(— HIRED TO APPLAUD) CLAQUE
(— OF ANGELS) FLIGHT
(— OF ARTIFACTS) CACHE
(— OF ATOMS) CLUSTER RADICAL
(— OF BADGERS) CETE
(— OF BLOOD CELLS) NEME
(— OF BUILDINGS) BLOCK CLUSTER
(— OF CASTINGS) SPRAY
(— OF CATS) CLOWDER
(— OF CELLS) GLAND ISLET LAURA CENTER CORONA EPITHEM SEMILUNE
(— OF CHIMNEYS) STACK
(— OF COMMUTERS) VANPOOL
(— OF COMPUTER JOBS) BATCH
(— OF CRAFTSMEN) ARTEL
(— OF DECOYS) STOOL
(— OF DEITIES) CABEIRI
(— OF DIALECTS) AEOLIC
(— OF EELS) SWARM
(— OF EIGHT) OCTAD OCTET OCTETTE
(— OF EIGHT BINARY DIGITS) BYTE
(— OF FAMILIES) FINE
(— OF FIVE) PENTAD CINQUAIN
(— OF FOUR) MESS QUARTET
(— OF FRIENDS) BUNCH
(— OF FURNISHINGS) ENSEMBLE
(— OF HAITIANS) COMBITE COUMBITE
(— OF HORSEMEN) QUADRILLE
(— OF HOUSES) BOROUGH
(— OF HUTS) BUSTI KRAAL BUSTEE
(— OF ILLUSTRIOUS PERSONS) PANTHEON
(— OF INDIAN STATES) AGENCY
(— OF ISOGLOSSES) BUNDLE
(— OF KINDRED) SIOL
(— OF KINSMEN) AHL
(— OF KITTENS) KENDLE KINDLE
(— OF LAYMEN) COFRADIA
(— OF LIONS) PRIDE
(— OF LISTENERS) AUDIENCE
(— OF MARTENS) RICHESSE
(— OF MILITARY VEHICLES) DEADLINE
(— OF MOLDINGS) DANCETTE
(— OF NERVE CELLS) GANGLIA
(— OF NINE) ENNEAD NONARY
(— OF NUCLEONS) SHELL
(— OF OFFSPRING) CLUTCH
(— OF ORGANISMS) FORM STRAIN
(— OF PARACHUTISTS) STICK
(— OF PERSONS) BAG CLUB KNOT SWAD CROWD DROVE CIRCLE GAGGLE KENNEL
(— OF RETORTS) BENCH SETTING
(— OF RUFFIANS) PUSH
(— OF SCHOLARS) ULAMA
(— OF SCULPTURE) MORTORIO
(— OF SEVEN) HEPTAD SEPTET HEBDOMAD
(— OF SIX) HEXAD SENARY
(— OF SLAVES) COFFLE
(— OF SOILS) LATERITE
(— OF SOLDIERS) DRAFT COHORT
(— OF STARS) ASTERISM
(— OF STRATIFIED BEDS) FACIES
(— OF STUDENTS) SEMINAR
(— OF SYLLABLES) FOOT
(— OF SYMBOLS) FORMULA
(— OF SYMPTOMS) SYNDROME
(— OF TAXA) CLADE
(— OF TEN) DECADE DENARY
(— OF TENTS) CAMP CANVAS
(— OF THEATERS) CIRCUIT
(— OF THREE) TRIO GLEEK TRIAD TRINE TROIKA
(— OF TRAITS) COMPLEX
(— OF TROUT) HOVER
(— OF VERSES) SYSTEM
(— OF WEAPONS) NEST
(— OF WINGS) RUFFLE
(— OF WIRES) DROP
(— OF WORDS) ACCENT GENITIVE
(— OF 10 NOTES) DECUPLET
(— OF 100) SENATE
(— OF 1000) CHILIAD
(— OF 12) DOZEN
(— OF 2 VOWELS) DIGRAM DIGRAPH
(— OF 40 THREADS) BEER BIER
(— OF 60 PIECES) SHOCK
(— TO RAISE CAMPAIGN MONEY) PAC
(ASSISTANCE —) AINI
(ATHLETIC —) TEAM
(ATOMIC —) LIGAND
(AUTHORITATIVE —) CONCLAVE
(AVANT-GARDE —) UNDERGROUND
(CONFUSED —) SNARL
(CORE —) CADRE
(CRIME SYNDICATE —) FAMILY
(ECOLOGICAL —) GUILD
(ETHNIC —) LI ACHANG BALAHI BATTAK ETHNOS CHINGPAW
(ETHNOLOGICAL —) ISLAND
(EXCLUSIVE —) ELECT
(EXPERT —) PANEL
(FAMILY —) GWELY
(GREEK RESISTANCE —) EDES ELAS
(HARMONIOUS —) DOVECOTE
(INTIMATE —) COTERIE
(KINSHIP —) SUSU
(LANGUAGE —) ATALAN
(LARGE —) PASSEL
(LINKED —) NEXUS
(LIVELY —) GALA
(MEMBER OF COMMANDO —) FEDAYEE
(NON-MOSLEM —) MILLET
(PAGAN —) BATAK BATANGAN
(PERFORMING —) COMBO TROUPE ENSEMBLE
(PHILOSOPHICAL —) CENACLE
(POLITICAL —) BLOC PARTY FASCIO COMMONS MACHINE
(SEGREGATED —) GHETTO
(SMALL —) PLUMP
(SOCIAL —) KITH SEPT TRIBE FAMILY INGROUP
(WEALTHY SOCIAL —) JETSET
(PREF.) **(CULTURAL —)** ETHNO
(SUFF.) AD ET OME SOME
GROUPED AGMINATE
GROUPER GAG HIND MERO GUASA HAMEL SCAMP AGUAJI BONACI CHERNA GROPER HAMLET WARSAW BACALAO GARLOPA GARRUPA GOURAMI JEWFISH REDFISH LAPULAPU REDBELLY ROCKFISH SCIRENGA SERRANID
(KIND OF —) WARSAW
(YOUNG —) SNAPPER
GROUPING KIND ARRAY BATTERY KINDRED DIVISION GROUPAGE SODALITY SYNTAGMA
(— OF POTTERY) SERIES
GROUSE CRAB BITCH GANGA GRIPE PEEVE GORHEN GROUCH HOOTER ATTAGEN CHEEPER GAZELLE GORCOCK PINTAIL COMPLAIN MOORBIRD MOORFOWL PARTRIDGE PTARMIGAN
(YOUNG —) POULT SQUEALER
GROUT GROOT LARRY SLUSH GROUTING
GROUTER GUNITER
GROVE CAMP HEWT HOLT MOTT SHAW TOFT TOPE WONG ALTIS BLUFF COPSE GLADE HURST HYRST GARDEN GREAVE GROVET ISLAND OLIVET SCROBE SPRING ACADEMY ARBORET BOSCAGE

COPPICE SPINNEY THICKET WOODING SERINGAL WODELEIE
(— OF ALDERS) CARR
(— OF MANGO TREES) TOPE
(— OF OAKS) ENCINAL
(— OF OSIERS) HOLT
(— OF SUGAR MAPLES) CAMP
(SACRED —) ALTIS SARNA
(SMALL —) SHAW
(PREF.) NAEMOR
(SUFF.) ETUM
GROVEL FAWN ROLL CREEP CRINGE TUMBLE WALLOW WELTER GRABBLE FLOUNDER
GROVELING PRONE WORMY ABJECT HANGDOG REPTILE
GROW AGE BUD GET HIT ICH WAX BOLL COME CROP ECHE ITCH MAKE RISE SEED THEE THRO WEAR EDIFY ISSUE PLANT PROVE RAISE SHOOT SWELL ACCRUE BATTEN BECOME DOUBLE EXPAND EXTEND GATHER SPRING SPROUT THRIVE AUGMENT BROADEN BURGEON DEVELOP DISTEND ENLARGE IMPROVE NOURISH ADOLESCE FLOURISH HEIGHTEN INCREASE MUSHROOM THRODDEN PROLIFERATE
(— ANGRY) STIVER
(— BETTER) IMPROVE
(— COLD) QUENCH
(— DARK) GLOAM GLOOM NIGHT DARKEN DARKLE
(— FAINT) DIE APPAL APPALL
(— FAT) FEED BATTEN
(— IN LENGTH) ELONGATE
(— IRREGULARLY) SCRAMBLE
(— LESS) ABATE SLAKE ASSUAGE DECREASE
(— LIGHT) DAWN
(— LOUDER) SWELL
(— LUXURIANTLY) THRIVE
(— MAD) WOOD
(— MILD) GIVE
(— OLD) AGE OLD SENESCE
(— OVER) INVADE
(— PLUMP) PLIM
(— RAPIDLY) SNOWBALL
(— RICH) FATTEN
(— SOUND) HEAL
(— SPIRITLESS) FLAG
(— STILL) HUSH
(— STRONG) FORTIFY STORKEN
(— THIN) PEAK
(— TOGETHER) JOIN KNIT ACCRETE CONCREW COOSIFY COALESCE
(— TO HEAD) CABBAGE
(— TO STALK) SPINDLE
(— UNDER GLASS) GLASS
(— UNTIDILY) STRAGGLE
(— UP) STEM ACCRUE
(— WEAK) FAINT
(PREF.) **(— TOGETHER)** SYMPHY(O)
GROWING GROWY ONGOING CRESCENT CRESCIVE ACCRESCENT
(— ANGRY) IRASCENT
(— IN AIR) AERIAL
(— IN CLUSTERS) RACEMOSE
(— IN GRAIN FIELDS) SEGETAL
(— IN HEAPS) ACERVATE
(— IN MEADOW) PRATAL
(— IN PAIRS) BINATE
(— IN RUBBISH) RUDERAL
(— IN WATER) AQUATIC
(— ON A STEM) CAULINE
(— OUT) ENATE
(— RAPIDLY) BOOMING
(— THICKLY) HOUSY
(— VIGOROUSLY) THRIFTY
(— WILD) SAVAGE AGRARIAN AGRESTAL
(GOOD FOR —) ARABLE
(SUFF.) PLASIA PLASIS PLASM(A) (IA)(IC) PLAST(IC)(Y) PLASY
(— IN OR ON) COLE COLINE COLOUS
GROWL YAR GNAR GURL GURR NARR RASE ROIN ROME WIRR YARR YIRR GARRE GNARL GNARR GROIN SNARL GOLLAR HABBLE GRUMBLE MAUNDER
GROWLER CLARENCE
GROWLING GROIN SURLY
GROWN THRIVEN
(— COLD) DEAD
(— FROM SEED) MAIDEN
(— HIGH) LOGGY
(— TOGETHER) ADNATE ACCRETE
(FULL —) GREAT MATURE
(WELL —) THRODDY
GROWN-UP ADULT GROWN MATURE
GROWTH FUR WAX BUSH COAT CORN FILM GROW JUBA RISE SPUR SUIT DUVET FLUSH GUMMA MAQUI STAND STOCK STOOL SWELL BUTTON CALLUS CANCER CLAVUS EATAGE EPULIS FRINGE FUNGUS LANUGO SCREEN SPROUT TYLOSE UPCOME WASTME AUXESIS BRACKEN COPPICE ERINEUM FUNGOID MACCHIE SARCOID STATURE TYLOSIS BEARDING CARUNCLE ENDOGENY INCREASE SETATION SWELLING UPSPRING ACCRETION
(— IN EYE) FILM
(— OF BEARD) DOWN
(— OF HAIR) SUIT
(— OF HORN) BUTTON SPIDER
(— OF PLANKTON) BLOOM
(— OF SHOOTS) STOOL
(— OF TREES) MOTTE BOSQUE BOSCAGE COPPICE SHINNERY
(— ON HORSE'S LEG) FUSEE FUZEE
(— ON VESSEL'S BOTTOM) GARR
(ABUNDANT —) FLUSH
(CANCEROUS —) WOLF
(DENSE —) BRUSH FOREST SHINNERY
(DOWNY —) LANUGO
(GREEN —) GREENTH
(HARD —) STONE
(LUXURIANT —) FLOURISH
(ROUGH —) STUBBLE
(RUDIMENTARY —) STUB STUMP
(SIDE —) SPRIG
(SPARSE —) SCRAGGLE
(SUPERFICIAL —) MILDEW
(TRANSPARENT —) DRUSE
(VIGOROUS —) THRIFT
(WOODY —) BURL
(2ND — OF GRASS) FOG
(PREF.) AUXANO AUXO
(SUFF.) PHYTA PHYTE(S) PHYTIC PHYTUM PLASTY TROPHIA TROPHIC TROPHY
(INHIBITION OF —) STASIA STASIS
GROWTH OF THE SOIL (AUTHOR OF —) HAMSUN
(CHARACTER IN —) AXEL ISAK BREDE INGER OLINE OLSEN STROM BARBRO SIVERT ARONSEN ELESEUS REBECCA GEISSLER LEOPOLDINE
GRROVE (— ALONGSIDE MOLDING) QUIRK
GRUB BOB DIG CHOW EATS HUHU MOIL MOOT ROOT ROUT STUB WORM CHUCK GROUT MATHE SCRAN SNOUT WROTE ASSART ESSART GRUGRU MAGGOT MUZZLE ROOTLE NEASCUS PIGROOT FLAGWORM GRUBWORM MUCKWORM SKINWORM
GRUBBY TIRED
GRUBROOT STARWORT
GRUDGE DOWN ENVY DERRY PEEVE SCORE SPITE ANIMUS GROUCH GRUNCH GRUTCH MALICE MALIGN SPLEEN DESPITE EYELAST SIMULTY
GRUDGING JEALOUSY
GRUEL SLOP BLEERY BURGOO CAUDLE CONGEE CROWDY SKILLY SOFKEE BROCHAN CROWDIE LOBLOLLY WANGRACE
GRUESOME UGLY GRISLY GROOLY HORRID SORDID FEARFUL GHASTLY HIDEOUS MACABRE
GRUFF BLUFF ROUGH SURLY CLUMSE SULLEN AUSTERE BEARING BRUSQUE CLUMPST
(PL.) TAILINGS
GRUIFORMES GRALLAE
GRUMBLE CARP GIRN GREX HONE KREX ROIN BLEAT BROCK CROAK DRUNT GROIN GROWL GRUMP GRUNT MUNGE GROUCH GROUSE GRUDGE GRUNCH MUMBLE MUNGER MURMUR MUTTER NOLLER PEENGE REPINE RUMBLE SQUEAL TARROW YAMMER CHANNER CHUNNER CHUNTER GNATTER GRIZZLE GRUNTLE MAUNDER MURGEON QUADDLE SWAGGER COMPLAIN
GRUMBLER GROUCH QUADDLE GROGNARD
GRUMBLING BITCH DRUNT GRIPE GROIN GRUDGE MURMUR MURGEON
GRUMP SULK GRUMBLE COMPLAIN
GRUMPY ILL CROSS DUMPY SURLY GLUMPY GLUMPISH GRUMPISH
GRUNGY DUMPY
GRUNION SMELT
GRUNT OINK BURRO GROIN HUMPH RONCO SARGO GRUMPH RONCHO BURRITO CROAKER GRUNTER GRUNTLE PIGFISH PINFISH TOMTATE KNORHAAN KOORHAAN PORKFISH REDMOUTH RONCADOR
GUACHARO FATBIRD OILBIRD
GUAICURU CADUVEO
GUAM (BAY OF —) AGAT YLIG CETTI AJAYAN UMATAC
(CAPITAL OF —) AGANA
(HARBOR OF —) APRA
(ISLAND OF —) CABRAS
(MOUNTAIN OF —) TENJO LAMLAM
(PENINSULA OF —) OROTE
(TOWN OF —) UPI ARRA ASAN TOTO YONA AGANA LUPOG MAGUA MERIZO UMATAC MALOLOS
GUAMA INGA PACAY
GUAN JACU ORTALIS PHEASANT
GUANA CHANE
GUANABANA SOURSOP
GUANACO LLAMA
GUANCHE CANARIAN
GUANO OSITE
GUAPENA SERRAN SERRANA AGUAVINA
GUARANTEE (ALSO SEE GUARANTY) BAIL BAND SEAL CINCH COVER ASSURE AVOUCH ENGAGE ENSURE INSURE RATIFY SECURE SURETY CAUTION CERTIFY HOSTAGE WARRANT AWARRANT GUARANTY PRESTATE SECURITY WARRANTY
GUARANTEED ASSURED CERTIFIED FOOLPROOF
GUARANTOR ENGAGER GRANTOR GUARAND SPONSOR GUARANTY
GUARANTY (ALSO SEE GUARANTEE) ANDI AVAL PAWN SEAL CAUTIO PLEDGE WARRANT SECURITY WARRANTY
GUARD BOW LEG NIT PAD SEE CARE CURB HERD HOLD KEEP KNOW LOOK REDE SAVE STOP STUB TENT TILE WAIT WEAR WERE WITE YEME ASKAR AWARD BLESS BLOCK CHECK COVER FENCE FORAY HEDGE HINGE PILOT SCREW SKIRT TUTOR WAKEN WATCH ASKARI BANTAY BASKET BRACER BRIDLE BUMPER BUTTON CONVOY DEFEND DRAGON ESCORT FENDER GHAFIR GUNMAN JAILER KAVASS KEEPER MIDDLE POLICE SCREEN SECURE SENTRY SHIELD SHROUD WAITER WARDER YEMING BULWARK CHERISH ESGUARD FRONTAL GHAFFIR GHATWAL GUARDER KEEPING PANDOUR PRESIDY PROTECT SOULACK TRABANT WARDAGE WARRANT CHAPERON DEFENDER GARRISON MUDGUARD OUTGUARD PEDESTAL PILOTMAN PRESERVE SECURITY SENTINEL SHEPHERD SPLASHER WARDSMAN WATCHMAN
(— ON FOIL) BUTTON
(— WHILE IN TRANSIT) RIDE
(AXLE —) HOUSING
(COACH —) SHOOTER
(CONSULAR —) KAVASS
(IMPERIAL —) BOSTANGI BOSTANJI
(KEYHOLE —) LAPPET
(LET DOWN —) NAP
(MOUNTED —) SHOMER
(NECK —) CAMAIL
(ON —) AWARE EXCUBANT
(PRISON —) HACK SCREW CHASER JAILER
(STIRRUP —) TAPADERA

(SWORD —) BOW TSUBA
(WRIST —) BRACER
(PL.) HEAVIES
GUARDED WARY IMMUNE MANNED
GUARDEDLY GINGERLY
GUARDHOUSE BRIG CLINK BULLPEN HOOSEGOW
GUARDIAN HERD ANGEL ARGUS TUTOR YEMER CUSTOS KEEPER MIMING PASTOR PATRON SHOMER WARDEN CORONER CURATOR GARDANT GARDEEN GRIFFIN BARTHOLO BELLERUS CERBERUS CREANCER DEFENDER ECKEHART FRAVASHI GOVERNOR GUARDANT PROTUTOR TUTELARY
(— OF GARDENS) PRIAPUS
(— OF HOME) SIF
(WORLD —) LOKAPALA MAHARAJA
(PL.) SELLI SELLOI
GUARDIANSHIP WARD TUTELA CUSTODY KEEPING TUITION WARDAGE WARDING CUSTODIA GUARDAGE TUTELAGE WARDENRY WARDSHIP
GUARDROOM WARDROOM
GUARDSMAN GUARDEE
GUASA MERO

GUATEMALA

CAPITAL: GUATEMALA
COIN: PESO CENTAVO QUETZAL
DANCE: ELSON GUARIMBA
DEPARTMENT: PETEN IZABAL JALAPA QUICHE SOLOLA ZACAPA JULIAPA ESCUINTLA
GULF: HONDURAS
INDIAN: MAM CHOL ITZA IXIL MAYA XINCA CARIBE QUICHE POKOMAM
LAKE: DULCE GUIJA PETEN IZABAL ATITLAN
MEASURE: VARA CUARTA FANEGA TERCIA CAJUELA MANZANA
MOUNTAIN: AGUA FUEGO PACAYA TACANA ATITLAN TOLIMAN TAJAMULCO
PORT: OCOS BARRIOS LIVINGSTON
RIVER: AZUL BRAVO DULCE LAPAZ BELIZE CHIXOY NEGINO PASION SAMALA CHIAPAS MOTAGUA SARSTUN POLOCHIC
RUINS: TIKAL
TOWN: OCOS COBAN VIEJA CHAHAL CHISEC CUILCO FLORES IZTAPA JALAPA SALAMA SOLOLA TACANA TECPAN YALOCH ZACAPA ANTIGUA CUILAPA JUTIAPA SANJOSE PROGRESO
VOLCANO: AGUA FUEGO PACAYA TACANA ATITLAN TAJUMULCO
WEIGHT: CAJA LIBRA

GUAVA ARACA MYRTAL GUAYABA GUAYABO GOIABADA
GUAYCURU MBAYA
GUDDLE GUMP NOODLE HANDFISH
GUDGEON PIN QUAB CHALDER TRUNNION
GUDRUN (FATHER OF —) HETEL
(HUSBAND OF —) ATLI
GUELDER-ROSE GAITER OPULUS DOGWOOD WHITTEN DOGBERRY SNOWBALL VIBURNUM
GUENDOLEN (HUSBAND OF —) LOCRINE
GUENON GRIVET NISNAS VERVET TALAPOIN TALLAPOI MOUSTACHE
GUEREZA COLOBIN COLOBUS
GUERILLA (VIETNAMESE —) VIETCONG
GUERRILLA COWBOY GORILLA JAYHAWK SKINNER BUSHWACK FELLAGHA KOMITAJI
GUERRILLERO KOMITAJI
GUESS AIM CALL HARP REDE SHOT WEEN AREAD COUNT ETTLE FANCY INFER TWANG DEVISE DIVINE RECKON IMAGINE SURMISE SUSPECT
(— CORRECTLY) TOUCH
(WILD —) STAB
GUEST COME GOER HOST DINER INVITEE VISITOR SYMPHILE VISITANT
(— AT RANCH) DUDE
(UNINVITED —) SHADOW
(PL.) LEVEE COMPANY
(PREF.) XEN(O)
(SUFF.) XENE XENOUS XENY
GUEST-HOUSE GASTHOF
GUESTHOUSE BANDB
GUFA KUFA GOOFAH KUPHAR
GUFFAW GAFF ROAR HEEHAW
GUIDANCE AIM DUCT EGIS AEGIS STEER CONDUCT GUIDAGE HELMAGE LEADING WISSING AUSPICES ENGINERY REGIMENT STEERAGE
GUIDE GUY LAY PIR TIP AIRT BEAD CURB GAGE GATE LEAD PASS REIN RULE SWAY WISE CARRY CHARM DRESS FRAME GAUGE LIGHT MAHDI MOROC PILOT STEER TEACH WEISE ADALID BARKER BEACON BEDWAY CONVOY DIRECT ESCORT FORMER GILLIE GOVERN INFORM LEADER MANAGE MENTOR POPPET CONDUCE CONDUCT COURIER GHILLIE INSPIRE MARSHAL MERCURY PIONEER SHIKARI STERNER TRACKER CALENDAR CICERONE DIRECTOR DRAGOMAN ENGINEER FAIRLEAD LODESMAN PEDESTAL POLESTAR PRACTICO REPEATER SHIKAREE SIGNPOST
(— ON GUN) SIGHT
(MORAL —) LABARUM
(RAILWAY —) ABC BRADSHAW
(SPIRITUAL —) PIR GURU BISHOP DIVINE
(TRAFFIC —) MUSHROOM
(SUFF.) AGOGUE AGOGY
GUIDEBOOK ABC GUIDE WAYBOOK BAEDEKER HANDBOOK ROADBOOK
GUIDELINE SLUG DIRECTIVE PARAMETER
GUIDEPOST GUIDE PARSON WAYMARK WAYPOST SIGNPOST
GUIDERIUS (FATHER OF —) CYMBELINE
GUIDEWAY SLAY SLEY SLEIGH SLIDEWAY SWANNECK
GUIDING POLAR BEHIND HOMING LEADING
GUIDO (WIFE OF —) ALERIA
GUILD HUI GILD HOEY HONG YELD CRAFT HANSA HANSE GREMIO GUIDRY SCHOLA BASOCHE COLLEGE COMPANY MYSTERY
(CHINESE —) TONG
GUILE DOLE WILE CHEAT CRAFT FRAUD TRAIN CAUTEL DECEIT HUMBUG CUNNING FALLACY ARTIFICE
GUILELESS PLAIN CANDID HONEST ARTLESS ONEFOLD IGNORANT INNOCENT SACKLESS UNNOOKED
GUILLEMOT AUK COOT LARY LAVY LOOM QUET TURR URIA ARRIE CUTTY FROWL MURRE SCOUT TOIST TYSTE GRYLLE LUNGIE MAGGIE MARROT SCRABE TINKER DOVEKEY DOVEKIE SEACOOT SKIDDAW TARROCK WILLOCK PUFFINET ROCKBIRD SCUTTOCK SPRATTER
GUILT SIN SAKE WITE BLAME CULPA FAULT PIACLE PLIGHT NOCENCE OFFENSE HAMARTIA INIQUITY
GUILTLESS FREE PURE CLEAN UNSAKED INNOCENT SACKLESS
GUILTY FAULTY NOCENT WICKED CORREAL HANGDOG NOXIOUS PECCANT BLAMEFUL CRIMINAL CULPABLE GUILTFUL
(— OF ERROR) LAPSED
GUINEA MEG BEAN QUID QUEED GEORGE SHINER GEORDIE
(HALF —) SMELT

GUINEA

CAPE: VERGA
CAPITAL: CONAKRY
COIN: FRANC
ISLAND: TOMBO TRISTAO
ISLAND GROUP: LOS
MEASURE: JACKTAN
MONEY: SYLI CAURI
MOUNTAIN: TAMGUE
MOUNTAINS: LOMA NIMBA
NATIVE: SUSU TOMA KISSI FULANI GUERZI MALINKE KOURANKE LANDUMAN
RIVER: NIGER BAFING FALEME SENEGAL KONKOURE TINKISSO
TOWN: BOKE FRIA KADE LABE BENTY BEYLA COYAH KOULE MAMOU DABOLA DALABA DOUAKO FABALA KANKAN KINDIA BOFOSSO CONAKRY DUBREKA FARANAH KONFARA KOUMBIA OUASSOU SIGUIRI KEROUANE
WEIGHT: AKEY PISO UZAN BENDA SERON QUINTO AGUIRAGE

GUINEA-BISSAU (ARCHIPELAGO OF —) BIJAGOS
(CAPITAL OF —) BISSAU
(RIVER OF —) GEBA CACHEU MANSOA CORUBAL
GUINEA FOWL KEEL KEET PEARL MEBACK GALEENY PINTADO COMEBACK GALLINEY
(SOUND OF —) POTRACK
GUINEA GRASS PANIC PANICLE SACATON ZACATON GAMELOTE
GUINEA PEPPER PIMENTO
GUINEA PIG CAVY
(MALE —) BOAR BUCK
GUINEA RUSH ADRUE
GUISE HUE FORM GARB COLOR COVER SHAPE MANNER PERSON APPAREL CLOTHES GUISARD LIKENESS
GUISER MUMMER
GUITAR AX AXE BOX KIT PIPA DOBRO JAMON KITAR SITAR TIPLE CUATRO GIMBRI KITTAR SANCHO SATTAR CITHERN CITTERN MACHETE UKULELE CHARANGO CHITARRA BOTTLENECK
(ACOUSTIC —) DOBRO
(JAPANESE —) SAMISEN SHAMISEN
(KIND OF —) FOLK PEDALSTEEL
(PART OF —) KEY NUT PEG BASE BODY BONE FRET HEAD HEEL HOLE NECK BRACE GUARD WAIST BRIDGE SADDLE STRING ROSETTE FINGERBOARD
GUITARFISH RAY BATOID PURAQUE
GUITGUIT PITPIT
GULANCHA GILO GILOE
GULCH COULE GULLY SLUIT CANYON COULEE RAVINE
GULDEN FLORIN GUILDER
(100,000 —) TUN
GULES MARS RUBY TORTEAU
GULF SINE CHAOS GULPH VORAGE VORAGO
(BOTTOMLESS —) ABYSM ABYSS
GULFWEED SARGASSO
GULL COB COX MEW COBB CONY COOT CULL DUPE FOOL GOLL LARI MALL PINT PIRR SELL SKUA XEME ALLAN ALLEN ANNET BOSUN CHEAT CHUMP COBBE COKES CROCK CULLY HOODY JAGER LARID LARUS PEWIT SCULL SMELT YAGER BONXIE BUBBLE CHOUSE COUSIN JOCKEY PEEWIT PIGEON SIMPLE TEASER TULIAC VICTIM WAGGEL WHILLY CROCKER DECEIVE MEDRICK PICKMAW POPELER SCAURIE SEABIRD SEAFOWL SWARBIE TARROCK TRUMPIE BLACKCAP DIRTBIRD DOTTEREL DUNGBIRD SEEDBIRD
(LIKE A —) LAROID
(YOUNG —) SCAURY SCAURIE
GULLET MAW GULE LANE GORGE GARGLE PECHAN THROAT KEACORN STOMACH SWALLOW WEASAND GURGULIO
(PREF.) ESOPHAG(O) LAEMO LEMO RUMENO
GULLIBLE GOOFY GREEN SIMPLE CULLIBLE
GULLIVER GRILDRIG
GULLY BOX GEO GUT DRAW GULL RAIK RAKE SICK SIKE DONGA DRAFT GOYLE GULCH SLAKE SLUIT ZANJA ARROYO GULLET GULLEY GUTTER NULLAH RAVINE SHEUCH SHEUGH CHIMNEY COULOIR DRAUGHT BARRANCA
GULLYWASHER TORRENT CLOUDBURST
GULP BOLT GAUP GLUT GULL POOP SOPE SWIG GULCH QUILT SLOSH

SWIPE ENGLUT GLUTCH GOBBLE GOLLOP PAUNCH SLABBER SWALLOW SWATTLE SLUMMOCK
(— NOISILY) SLORP
GUM ASA AMRA BLOB FILL GOOM LOAD TUNO ALGIN AMAPA BABUL CUMAY DHAVA ACAJOU ANGICO BALATA BARRAS CHICLE KARAYA TOUART TUPELO CARANNA CARAUNA CHICLET GINGIVA GUMWOOD PERRIER BORRACHA CARABEEN DEXTRINE DRESSING FEVERGUM CALENDULIN
(ACACIA —) GEDDA
(AROMATIC —) MYRRH
(ASTRINGENT —) KINO
(CHEWING —) WAX CHICLE
(FRAGRANT —) BUMBO
(KIND OF —) ESTER XANTHAN
(PERSIAN —) SARCOCOLLA
(RED —) JARRAH
(UNGRADED —) SORTS
(WOOD —) XYLAN
(PL.) ULA
(PREF.) COMMI GUMMI GUTTI
GUM ARABIC KIKAR ACACIA ACACIN
GUMBO MUD OKRA
GUMBOIL PARULIS
GUMBO-LIMBO JOBO BIRCH GOMART MASTIC NEGRITO ALMACIGO ARCHIPIN
GUMDROP GUM JUJUBE
GUMMER BIDDY BIDDIE SCRAPER SCUFFER SCUFFLER SCUPPLER
GUMMY GLUEY CLAGGY MASTIC GUMMOUS
GUMPTION GRIT NOUS NERVE PLUCK SENSE SPUNK SPRAWL
GUMS
(PREF.) GINGIV(O) ULEMO ULO
GUMSHOE TEC
GUM SUCCORY HOGBITE
GUM TREE KARI KARRI TOOART TOUART TUPELO EUCALYPT
GUMWEED GRINDELIA SUNFLOWER
GUN GAT POP BREN HAKE PIAT ROER STEN TUBE BARIL FIFTY FIRER FUSEE FUZEE RAKER REWET RIFLE ARCHIE BERTHA CANNON CHASER CULVER DUCKER HEATER INCHER JEZAIL MINNIE QUAKER RANDOM ROSCOE SPIGOT SWIVEL TUPARA CALIVER FIREARM HACKBUT HANDGUN JINGALL LANTACA MUZZLER AMUSETTE ARQUEBUS CHAUCHAT CULVERIN FIRELOCK GALLOPER OERLIKON PEDERERO REVOLVER SHAGBUSH STERLING TROMBONE
(—FOR DISCHARGING STONES) PERRIER
(AFGHAN —) JEZAIL
(BOAT —) BASE
(KIND OF —) ZIP BURP RIOT STUN HIRED
(LOWER-DECK —) BARKER
(MACHINE —) CHOPPER GATLING
(SPRING —) STEL
(TOP —) ACE
(TOY —) SPARKLER
(TYPE OF —) BURP BOFORS
(PL.) FLAK CHASE ARTILLERY
GUNA RAJAS TAMAS SATTVA
GUNBOAT SKIP BARCA GONDOLA TINCLAD
GUN CARRIAGE PANEL MADRIER GALLOPER
GUNCREWMAN PLUGMAN
GUNDOBAD (BROTHER OF —) GODOMAR CHILPERIC GODEGISEL
(FATHER OF —) GUNDIOCH
GUNDOG POINTER
GUNFLINT STONE
GUNI (FATHER OF —) NAPHTALI
GUNITE SHOTCRETE
GUNK GOO
GUNLOCK ROWET FIRELOCK
GUNMAN HOOD GUNSEL GUNSMAN TORPEDO ENFORCER GANGSTER
GUNNEL BLENNY SWORDICK
GUNNER GUN POPPER FIREMAN SHOOTER ENGINEER
GUNNY TAT BURLAP BAGGING SACKING
GUNNYSACK CORNSACK
GUNPOWDER SULFUR SULPHUR
(— SIZE) PEBBLE
GUNSHOT REPORT
GUNSIGHT VISIE HAUSSE
GUNSTOCK BLANK TIPSTOCK
GUNSTONE OGRESS PELLET
GUNTHER (SISTER OF —) KRIEMHILD
(WIFE OF —) BRUNEHILDE
GUNTRAM (BROTHER OF —) SIGEBERT CHARIBERT CHILPERIC
(CHARACTER IN —) ROBERT GUNTRAM FREIHILD FRIEHOLD
(COMPOSER OF —) STRAUSS
(FATHER OF —) CLOTAIRE
GUNWALE GUNNEL PORTOISE
GUNZ SCANIAN
GUPPY MILLIONS BELLYFISH
GUR GOOR KHAUR JAGGERY VOLTAIC
GURGE EDDY SWIRL
GURGLE GLOX GLUG BRAWL CLUNK QUARK SLOSH BICKER BUBBLE BULLER BURBLE GOLLER GUGGLE RUCKLE
GURGLINGLY TRILLIL
GURJUN YANG
GURNARD CUR TUB PIPER ELLECK ROCHET BATFISH CAPTAIN GRUNTER LATCHET SOLDIER TRIGLID TUBFISH VOLADOR HARDHEAD KNORHAAN LORICATE
GURO KWENI
GURU MENTOR
GUSH JET BOIL FLOW FOAM HUSH RAIL SLOP WALM BELCH SLUSH SMALM SMARM SPATE SPIRT SPURT STOUR SWOSH BURBLE PHRASE SWOOSH WALLOW WHOOSH SLOBBER
(SENTIMENTAL —) SLOSH
GUSHING SLOPPY SMARMY EFFUSIVE
GUSSET GORE INSET MITER MITRE QUIRK PIECETTE
GUST BUB FLAN GALE GUSH WAFF WAFT WIND BLAST FRESH SLANT FLURRY HUFFLE SQUALL FLAUGHT WILLIWAW WINDFLAW WINDBLAST
(— OF RAIN) SKIT
(— OF WIND) FLAM FLAN FUFF GALE GUSH PIRR SCUD TIFT BERRY BLAST BLORE FLAFF THODE SQUALL WINDFLAW
GUSTATION TASTE
GUSTO GUST ZEST VERVE RELISH UNCTION
GUSTY DIRTY PUFFY BLASHY BLASTY FRETFUL GUSTFUL SQUALLY
GUT GIB BOWEL CECUM CLEAN CAECUM CATGUT HOLLOW STRING ELISION GRALLOCH VISCERAL
(FISH —) GIP GILL
(TWISTED —) THARM THERM
(PL.) MOXIE BOWELS COJONES PUDDING ENTRAILS
GUTHRIE ARLO
GUTSY BALLSY PLUCKY SPUNKY
GUTTA SOH DROP PUAN SIAK SUSU DUJAN GERIP SANGE SUNDIK CAMPANA JANGKAR SEMARUM TRENAIL TRUNNEL HANGKANG KETAPANG
GUTTER GRIP REAN SIKE GRIPE GULLY RIGOL SIVER SPOUT SWEAL BOTTOM CANNEL CULLIS GROOVE GUZZLE KENNEL RIGGOT RUNNEL STRAND TROUGH VENNEL CHANNEL CHENEAU GRIZZLE
(— OF STREET) KENNEL
(MINING —) BOTTOM HASSING
(ROOF —) RONE
(PL.) LIMBERS
GUTTERMAN SWAMPER
GUTTURAL GRUM BURRY HARSH THICK
GUY BOD CAT EGG JOE NUT BIRD BOZO DUDE GENT GINK HUSK JACK JOHN STUD BLOKE CABLE COOKY JOKER SCOUT SPOOF STIFF BUFFER COOKIE FELLOW GAZABO GAZEBO GAZOOK GILGUY HOMBRE JASPER JIGGER MALKIN MAUMET MAWKIN KNOCKER BLIGHTER
(FALL —) GOAT CHUMP SCAPEGOAT
GUYANA (CAPITAL OF —) GEORGETOWN
(RIVER OF —) CUYUNI BERBICE DEMERARA MAZARUNI ESSEQUIBO
(TOWN OF —) ITUNI BILOKU ISSANO MACKENZIE
(WATERFALL IN —) MARINA KAIETEUR
GUY MANNERING (AUTHOR OF —) SCOTT
(CHARACTER IN —) GUY MEG LUCY BROWN DANDY HARRY JULIA BERTRAM DINMONT GLOSSIN SAMPSON MANNERING MERRILIES ELLANGOWAN HATTERAICK
GUY ROPE STAY VANG
GUZ GAZ GEZ ZAR ZER GUDGE
GUZERAT KANKREJ
GUZZLE BUM GUM SOT TUN BEND GULL SLOSH SWILL GOOZLE GUDDLE SWATTLE SWIZZLE CHUGALUG
GUZZLER BENDER
GWYNIAD SCHELLY
GYASCUTUS PROCK
GYLE BEER GAIL BREWING
GYMKHANA AUTOCROSS
GYMNASIUM GYM PALESTRA TURNHALL PALAESTRA
GYMNAST SOKOL BENDER TURNER ACROBAT TUMBLER
(FAMOUS —) KORBUT
GYMNASTIC (— SOCIETY) SOKOL
GYNOECIUM BRUSH APOCARP
GYNOPHORE PODOGYN
GYPSUM GYP GYPS YESO GESSO LUDIAN PARGET GYPSITE SATINITE SELENITE ALABASTER
GYPSY FAW ROM CALO APTAL CAIRD GIPSY ROMNI BOSHAS GITANO ROMANY TINKER AZUCENA CZIGANY MOONMAN TINKLER TZIGANE ZINCALO ZINGARO BOHEMIAN EGYPTIAN FLAMENCO ZIGEUNER
(MALE —) ROM
(NON —) GORGIO
(SEA —) BAJAU
(PL.) ROMANESE
GYRATE GYRE SPIN TURN TWIRL WHIRL CURVET INGYRE ROTATE REVOLVE SQUIRREL
GYRATION PRECESSION
GYRATORY GIDDY GYRAL
GYRFALCON JERKIN
GYRON GIRON ESQUIRE
GYROSE SINUATE
GYVE FETTER

H ETA HOW AITCH HOTEL ASPIRATE
HABERDASHER OUTFITTER
HABERDASHERY TOGGERY
HABERGEON HAUBERK
HABILIMENT GARB HABIT APPAREL RAIMENT CLOTHING
(PL.) CLOTHES EQUIPAGE
HABILITATE ENABLE
HABIT LAW PAD SET USE WON COAT GARB GATE SUIT THEW WONT FROCK HAUNT JONES TACHE TRADE TRICK USAGE CUSTOM GROOVE MANNER PRAXIS TALENT CLOTHES FOLKWAY HABITUS WONTING CROTCHET HABITUDE PHYSIQUE PRACTICE PRACTISE ASSUETUDE CONSUETUDE
(— OF GRINDING TEETH) BRUXISM
(BAD —) HANK VICE MISTETCH CACOETHES
(CHARACTERISTIC —) TRICK
(DEPRAVED —) CACHEXY CACHEXIA
(MONASTIC —) SCHEMA
(SPEECH —S) ACCENT
(PL.) DAPS
(PREF.) HEXICO
HABITABLE BIGLY LIVABLE
HABITAT ECE HOME RANGE PATRIA STATION LOCALITY
(NATURAL —) ELEMENT
(PREF.) EC(O) OEC(O) OIKO
HABITATION HOLD TELD TENT ABODE BIELD HABIT HOUSE BIDING WONING DOMICILE DWELLING PANTHEON TENEMENT RESIDENCE
(— SITE) YACATA
(COMMUNIAL —) PUEBLO
(QUIET —) SHADE
(UNDERGROUND —) HOLE
HABITUAL USUAL COMMON HECTIC CHRONIC REGULAR FREQUENT ORDINARY
HABITUATE USE HOWF ENURE FLESH HABIT INURE ADDICT SEASON HACKNEY ACCUSTOM ACQUAINT OCCASION
HABITUATED WONT SEASONED ACCUSTOMED
HABITUDE HABIT SCHESIS
HABITUE DENIZEN COURTIER
HABRONEMIASIS BURSATI BURSATTEE
HACEK WEDGE
HACHALIAH (SON OF —) NEHEMIAH
HACK CAB HAG HEW BOLO CHIP HAKE DEVIL HATCH CABBIE DRUDGE FIACRE HACKLE HAGGLE HODMAN JOBBER MANGLE SCOTCH HACKNEY MATTOCK VETTURA MUTILATE
(LITERARY —) GRUB DEVIL

HACKBERRY EGGBERRY HACKTREE HAGBERRY ONEBERRY
HACKBUT HAGBUT DEMIHAG HACKBUSH
HACK GHARRI SHIGRAM
HACKLE COMB RUFF HECKLE NAPPER RUFFER HATCHEL ROUGHER
HACKNEY HACK MIDGE NODDY
HACKNEY CARRIAGE MIDGE FIACRE JARVEY VETTURA
HACKNEYED HACK WORN BANAL HOARY STALE TRITE CANNED CLICHE COMMON FOREWORN TIMEWORN
HAD D HED HEDDE
(— NOT) HADNA HADNT
HADAD (FATHER OF —) ISHMAEL
HADADEZER (FATHER OF —) REHOB
HADDOCK GADE GADID SCROD DICKEY HADDIE
(DRIED —) CRAIL RIZZAR SPELDING SPELDRIN
HADE UNDERLIE
HADES DIS PIT ADES HELL AIDES ORCUS PLUTO SHEOL SHADES TARTAR ACHERON AIDONEUS TARTARUS
(FATHER OF —) SATURN
(GODDESS OF —) HEKATE
(RIVER IN —) STYX LETHE
(RIVER OF —) STYX
(WIFE OF —) PROSERPINA
HADORAM (FATHER OF —) TOU JOKTAN
HAECCEITY THISNESS
HAEMON (FATHER OF —) CREON PELASGUS
(SON OF —) THESSALUS
HAEMUS (FATHER OF —) BOREAS
(MOTHER OF —) ORITHYIA
(SON OF —) HEBRUS
(WIFE OF —) RHODOPE
HAFF LAGOON
HAFNIUM CELTIUM
HAFT HEFT HOVE HELVE DUDGEON
HAFTER HANDLER
HAG ATE MARE CRONE REBEC RUDAS SHREW SIBYL VECKE WITCH BELDAM HECATE ROUDAS BELDAME HAGGARD HELLCAT HARRIDAN
HAGAR (MISTRESS OF —) SARAH
(SON OF —) ISHMAEL
HAGBOAT HOGGET HOGGIE
HAGFISH HAG BORER VECKE MYZONT SUCKER PLACOID MYXINOID
HAGGARD PALE THIN GAUNT WISHT HAGGED
HAGGI (FATHER OF —) GAD
HAGGITH (HUSBAND OF —) DAVID
(SON OF —) ADONIJAH

HAGGLE CHOP PRIG DODGE BADGER BANTER BOGGLE DICKER HACKER HIGGLE HUCKLE NAGGLE NIFFER PALTER SCOTCH THREEP BARGAIN CHAFFER HUCKSTER
HAGGLER DODGER
HAGGLING BARGAIN CHAFFER
HAGIOGRAPHA KETUBIM
HAGIOSCOPE SQUINT SQUINCH
HAIDA SKITTAGET
HAIL AVE HOY HALE GREET SALVE SPEAK STORM ACCOST BAYETE HAGGLE HALLOO HERALD SALUTE ACCLAIM
(SOFT —) GRESIL GRAUPEL
(PREF.) CHALAZI CHALAZO
HAILSTONE STONE
HAINAI IONI
HAIR FAX JAG RIB WIG BARB CROP FLUE GLIB HEAD KEMP PELF PILE SETA WIRE BEARD CRIMP CRINE FRIZZ FRONT PILUS QUIFF ANGORA BRILLS BRUTUS CRINET FIBRIL FROWZE MERKIN SETULA THATCH TRAGUS CULOTTE ELFLOCK GLOCHIS TOPKNOT WHISKER CAPILLUS COLLETER PALPOCIL TENTACLE TRICHODE TRICHOME VIBRISSA
(— BROWN) ARGALI
(— OF ANIMALS) FUR PELF
(— OF HORSES OR COWS) CERDA
(— OF TERRIER) FALL
(— ON HORSE'S HOOF) CRONET
(— ON LEAF) GLAND
(— ON TEMPLES) HAFFET HAFFIT
(— ON THIGHS) CULOTTE
(— OVER EYES) BROW GLIB EYELASH
(BARBED —) GLOCHIS
(BRAID OF —) QUEUE PIGTAIL
(BUNDLE OF —) LEECH
(CAMEL'S —) DEER
(COARSE —) KEMP BRISTLE
(CURLED —) FRIZZ
(CUTDOWN —) STUMPS
(FALSE —) WIG JANE FRONT PERUKE
(FRIZZED —) FROWZE
(GRAY —) GRIZZLE
(LOCK OF —) TUZ FEAK TATE FLOCK TRESS
(LONG HEAVY —) MANE
(LOOSE —) COMBINGS
(MATTED —) SHAG ELFLOCK
(MOP OF —) MANE SHOCK TOUSLE
(NOSE —) VIBRISSA
(PERSON WITH SHORT —) SKINHEAD
(PLANT —) COLLETER
(ROOT —) FIBRIL
(SNARL OF —) TANGLE
(SOFT —) DOWN LANUGO

(STINGING —) STING STIMULUS
(STINGING —S) COWHAGE
(STRAIGHTEN —) CONK
(STRAY LOCK OF —) TAG
(STYLE —) CORNROW
(TREAT —) CONK
(TUFT OF —) PLUME KROBYLOS
(WAVING LOCK OF —) WIMPLER
(WHITE —) SNOW SNOWS
(PL.) SETAE COWAGE COWHAGE HACKLES
(PREF.) CAPILLI CHAET(I)(O) CHETO COME COMI CRINI HIRSUTO LACHN(O) PIL(I)(O) TRICH(O) TRICHINO VILLI
(SUFF.) CHAETA CHAETES CHAETUS COMA THRICHOUS THRIX TRICHA TRICHI(A) TRICHY
HAIRBREADTH HERMELE WHISKER
HAIR BROWN QUAIL
HAIRBRUSH TOILETRY
HAIRCLOTH HAIR CILICE
HAIRCUT BOB CUT CROP BUTCH SHINGLE DUCKTAIL
HAIRDO AFRO COIF BEEHIVE FRISURE PAGEBOY
HAIRDRESSER WAVER FRISEUR COIFFEUR
HAIRDRESSING FRISURE BANDOLINE
HAIR FRAME PALISADE
HAIRINESS PILOSISM PILOSITY
HAIRLESS BALD PELON CALLOW ATRICHIC DEPILOUS GLABROUS
(— PERSON) PILGARLIC
HAIRLIKE PILIFORM TRICHOID
HAIRLINE WHISKER
HAIRNET KELL SNOOD
HAIRPIECE MERKIN POSTICHE
HAIRPIN ACUS BODKIN SKEWER
HAIRSPLITTING FINE PILPUL
HAIRSTYLE DA AFRO CONK SHAG UPDO BINGLE MOHAWK CORNROW PAGEBOY DUCKTAIL PONYTAIL DREADLOCKS
HAIRWORM GORDIID GORDIOID
HAIRY FAXED MOSEY PILAR ROUGH COMATE COMOUS PILARY PILINE PILOSE CRINITE CRINOSE HIRSUTE PILEOUS VILLOUS UNSHAVEN
(PREF.) DASI DASY HEBE

HAITI

CAPE: FOUX
CAPITAL: PORTAUPRINCE
CHANNEL: SUD STMARC
COIN: GOURDE
DEITY: LOA
GULF: GONAVE
INDIAN: TAINO
ISLAND: VACHE GONAVE TORTUE NAVASSA TORTUGA
ISLAND GROUP: CAYMITES

LAKE: SAUMATRE
MAGIC: OBI OBEAH
MOUNTAIN: NORD CAHOS NOIRES LAHOTTE LASELLE TROUDEAU
NATIONAL HERO: OGE
PLAIN: NORD CAYES JACMEL LEOGANE ARCAHAIE CULDESAC GONAIVES
PRIEST: BOCOR HOUNGAN
RELIGION: OBEAH
RIVER: GUAYAMOUC ARTIBONITE
SPIRIT: LOA BAKA BOKO
TOWN: AQUIN CAYES FURCY LIMBE HINCHE JACMEL JEREMIE LEOGANE SALTROU GONAIVES KENSCOFF

HAKAM CACAM HAHAM CHOCHEM KHAKHAM
HAKE GADE HAIK LING GADOID CODLING HADDOCK WHITING ANACANTH QUODLING
HAKENKREUZLER SWASTIKA
HALBERD BILL PIKE GLAIVE GLEAVE POLEARM PARTISAN
(PART OF —) BEAK BUTT BLADE SPIKE
HALBERDIER DRABANT
HALCYON CALM ALCYON GOLDEN
HALE FIT YELL FRACK FRECK TRAIL ROBUST STRONG HEALTHY VIGOROUS
HALER HELLER
HALF M ARF ELF DEMI HAUF HOVE SEMI SIDE MEDIO HALFEN HALFLY MOIETY MEDIETY
(— AND —) ONE
(— GALLON) POTTLE
(— OF BLADE) FORTE
(— OF DRAW) BRACKET
(— OF EM) EN
(— OF INNING) BOTTOM
(— OF MOLD) VALVE
(FRUIT —S) SLABS
(PREF.) DEMI HEMI SAM SEMI
(ONE AND A —) SESQUI
HALFBACK (OFFENSIVE —) SLOTBACK
HALFBEAK GAR IHI BALAO PIPER BALLYHOO
HALF-BLOOD DEMISANG
HALF BOOT PAC BUSKIN BOTTINE
HALF-BREED BREED METIF METIS SAMBO MUSTEE RAMONA CABOCLO MESTIZO METISSE DEMISANG HARRATIN MIXBLOOD
HALF-CASTE TOPAZ TOPASS
HALF-CONSCIOUSNESS DOVER
HALF-CRAZY FIFISH
HALF CROWN GEORGE ALDERMAN
HALF-DEAD ALAMORT
HALF DENIER MAILE MAILLE
HALF DOBRA PECA
HALF-DRUNK MAUDLIN
HALF-EATEN SEMESE
HALF-FARTHING CUE MITE MINUTE
HALF-GABLE AILERON
HALF GAINER ISANDER
HALF-GROWN HALFLIN
HALF-GUINEA SMELT
HALF-HEARTED LUKEWARM
HALFHEARTED TEPID
HALF HITCH ROLLING
HALF MASK LOUP DOMINO
HALF-MOON LUNETTE DEMILUNE
HALF NOTE MINIM
HALFPENCE GROCERY
HALFPENNY OB MAG MEG DUMP GRAY GREY MAIK MAIL MAKE MEKE OBOL SOUSE STAMP BAUBEE BAWBEE MAILLE HAPENNY PATRICK STUIVER
(COUNTERFEIT —) RAP GRAY
(IRISH —) PATRICK
(THICK —) DUMP
HALF-PIKE SPONTON DEMIPIKE SPONTOON
HALF-PINT CUP JACK CUPFUL
HALF REST SOSPIRO
HALF SOLE TAP
HALF STEP CHROMA
HALFTONE DROPOUT
HALF TURN DEMIVOLT
HALF-WIT ASS DOLT DUNCE HAVEREL TOMFOOL STAUMREL UNDERWIT
HALF-WITTED SOFT DOTTY SIMPLE HALUCKET IMBECILE STAUMREL
HALF-YEARLY BIANNUAL
HALIBUT BUT BUTT FLITCH TURBOT FLATFISH
HALIFAX BALLYHACK
HALIOTIS ABALONE
HALIRRHOTHIUS (FATHER OF —) NEPTUNE
(MOTHER OF —) EURYTE
(SLAYER OF —) MARS
HALL HA AULA HELL IWAN SALA AIWAN ATRIO BALAI BURSA CURIA DIVAN ENTRY FOYER HOUSE OECUS SALLE SALON ATRIUM CAMERA DURBAR EXEDRA GARDEN LESCHE SALOON SCHOOL SENATE TOLSEY TRANCE APADANA CHAMBER DANCERY GALLERY HALLWAY KURHAUS KURSAAL MEGARON PASSAGE VINGOLF ANTEROOM ARCHEION ASSEMBLY BASILICA CHOULTRY COLISEUM CORRIDOR FOREHALL HASTROND HOSPITAL RAADZAAL TOLBOOTH VALHALLA
(— FOR PERFORMANCES) ODEON ODEUM
(— OF JUSTICE) COURT
(— WITH STATUES) VALHALLA
(DINING —) MESS COMMON REFECTORY
(LECTURE —) SCHOLA
(MISSION —) CITADEL
(MUSIC —) GAFF
(TOWN —) CABILDO RATHAUS TRIBUNAL
(UNIVERSITY —) BURSA
HALLMARK CROWN TRAIT SHOPMARK
HALL OF FAME (AVIATION —) ELY SIX BYRD LAHM LEAR LINK LUKE MOSS POST RYAN WADE EAKER GLENN LEMAY PIPER REEVE ARNOLD BOEING CESSNA FOKKER HUGHES LEVIER MARTIN ROGERS SPAATZ SPERRY TOWERS TRIPPE TURNER WALDEN WRIGHT YAEGER CHANUTE EARHART GRUMMAN LANGLEY LOENING SHEPARD TWINING MITCHELL NORTHROP SIKORSKY ARMSTRONG LINDBERGH MCDONNELL RICKENBACKER
(BASEBALL —) OTT COBB DEAN FORD FOXX HOYT KELL KLEM MACK MAYS MIZE RUTH WYNN AARON BANKS BERRA COMBS EVERS FRICK GOMEZ GROVE HAFEY KINER LEMON LOPEZ LYONS PAIGE PLANK RUSIE SPAHN TERRY VANCE WALSH WANER WHEAT YOUNG ALSTON CHANCE CRONIN CUYLER FELLER FRISCH GEHRIG GOSLIN KALINE KOUFAX LAJOIE LANDIS MANTLE MANUSH MCGRAW MUSIAL RICKEY SISLER TINKER WAGNER WILSON WRIGHT YAWKEY APPLING AVERILL BURKETT HORNSBY HUBBARD HUGGINS JOHNSON PENNOCK RUFFING SIMMONS SPEAKER STENGEL TRAYNOR BOUDREAU COMISKEY DIMAGGIO GRIFFITH MACPHAIL MARICHAL MCCARTHY ROBINSON WILLIAMS COVELESKI BRICKHOUSE MARANVILLE
(BASKETBALL —) GALE GOLA PAGE REED WEST COUSY FULKS GREER HAGAN HYATT LUCAS MIKAN ARIZIN BARLOW BAYLOR COOPER FOSTER HANSON HOLMAN KRAUSE MURPHY PETTIT PHILIP RAMSEY ROOSMA SEDRAN TWYMAN WOODEN BECKMAN BRADLEY BRENNAN DEHNERT GRUENIG KURLAND POLLARD SCHAYES SCHMIDT SHARMAN WACHTER BORGMANN ENDACOTT LAPCHICK LUISETTI MACAULEY SCHOMMER MCCRACKEN STEINMETZ VANDIVIER DEBERNARDI DEBUSSCHERE
(BUSINESS —) FORD HAAS LUCE OCHS VAIL GARST HEINZ ROUSE SLOAN BATTEN DISNEY DORIOT DUPONT HILTON KAISER LASKER MELLON MORGAN OGILVY PENNEY SCHIFF SCHWAB EASTMAN SARNOFF WHITNEY CARNEGIE FRANKLIN MCCORMICK VANDERBILT ROCKEFELLER WESTINGHOUSE WEYERHAEUSER
(FOOTBALL —) MIX RAY BELL HEIN HUFF LARY MARA OTTO FEARS GROZA GUYON HALAS HAYES LAYNE LILLY LYMAN MUSSO NEALE RINGO ROYAL BADGRO BLANDA BUTKUS GRANGE HINKLE KINARD MATSON MCAFEE ROONEY THORPE TITTLE TRIPPI UNITAS ALWORTH GILLMAN LUCKMAN MILLNER LOMBARDI MITCHELL WARFIELD JURGENSEN PARSEGHIAN
(GOLF —) BERG FORD HOPE BOROS BURKE DUTRA EVANS HAGEN HOGAN JONES SHUTE SMITH SNEAD ARMOUR COOPER DIEGEL GHEZZI LITTLE NELSON OUIMET PALMER PICARD RUNYAN TRAVIS DEMARET GULDAHL HARBERT MANGRUM REVOLTA SARAZEN ZAHARIAS DEVICENZO
(THEATER —) DREW KERR BROOK HECHT KELLY SIMON PRINCE DUNNOCK CHAMPION KINGSLEY LANSBURY MCARTHUR MEREDITH SONDHEIM STRASBERG YOUNGMANS BLOOMGARDEN
HALLOO HO HOO LOO ALEW BAWL LURE WHOOP ACCOST TALLYHO
HALLOW BLESS HALWE DEDICATE SANCTIFY
HALLOWED HOLY SACRED BLESSED
HALLSTAND HATRACK
HALLUCINATION DWALE ACOASMA ACOUASM ACOUSMA FANTASY PHONEME DELUSION ILLUSION PHANTASY ZOOSCOPY
HALLUCINOGEN ACID
HALLUX TALON
HALLWAY ENTRY FOYER TRANCE
HALMA HOPPITY
HALMALILLE PETWOOD
HALO DOG BURR GLOR NIMB GLORY SHINE AREOLA CIRCLE CORONA GLORIA NIMBUS SUNDOG AREOLET AUREOLE BOROUGH CINCTURE
HALOHESH (SON OF —) SHALLUM
HALT HO HOP ALTO BAIT BALK HOLD LIMP SKID STAY STOP TRIP WAIT BAULK BLOCK BREAK CEASE CHECK HILCH HITCH STAND STICK ARREST BARLEY FREEZE PULLUP SCOTCH STANCE CONTAIN CRIPPLE STATION STOPPAGE
(— GAME) CALL
(— TO DOGS) TOHO
(REFRESHMENT —) DRIVEIN
HALTER EVIL SOLE BRANK NOOSE TRASH WANTY WIDDY WITHE POISER CAUSSON CAVESON JAQUIMA POINTEL BALANCER NECKLACE HACKAMORE
HALTING BODE LAME ZOPPA CRIPPLE LIMPING
HALVE BISECT DIVIDE DIMIDIATE (PL.) HALVERS
HALVING HAPLOSIS
HAM PIG EMOTE GAMMON JAMBON JARRET PESTLE GAMBONE PROSCIUTTO
(— IT UP) EMOTE
(BROTHER OF —) SHEM JAPHET
(FATHER OF —) NOAH
(PICNIC —) CALA CALI
(SON OF —) CUSH PHUT CANAAN MIZRAIM
(PL.) HUNKERS
HAMATUM UNCIFORM
HAMBURGER WIMPY
HAMESUCKEN HAMFARE
HAMITE BORAN BORANA DANAKIL DANKALI
HAMLET KOM BURG DORP TOON TOWN TREF VILL ALDEA CASAL HAMEL SITIO STEAD THORP VICUS ALDEIA BUSTEE THORPE CLACHAN KAMPONG KIRKTON KIRKTOWN
(AUTHOR OF —) SHAKESPEARE
(CHARACTER IN —) OSRIC HAMLET HORATIO LAERTES OPHELIA BERNARDO CLAUDIUS GERTRUDE POLONIUS REYNALDO CORNELIUS FRANCISCO MARCELLUS VOLTIMAND FORTINBRAS ROSENCRANTZ GUILDENSTERN

HAMMEDATHA (SON OF —) HAMAN
HAMMER AX AXE BIT DOG PEG SET CALL COCK DROP HORN MALL MASH MAUL MELL SETT TILT CAVIL KEVEL KNOCK MADGE POUND SMITE THUMP BEETLE BUCKER CLOYER DRIVER FALLER FULLER MALLET MARTEL NOPPER OLIVER PLEXOR SCUTCH SLEDGE TACKER TILTER KNAPPER KNOCKER MALLEUS PLESSOR STRIKER CRANDALL MALLEATE MJOLLNIR SCUTCHER TREMBLER
(— FOR DRESSING STONE) KEVEL
(— OF GUNLOCK) DOG COCK DOGHEAD
(— OUT) ANVIL
(BRICKLAYER'S —) SCOTCH SCUTCH SCUTCHER
(FLATTEN BY —) PEEN
(LEADEN —) MADGE
(MINER'S —) BULLY
(PART OF —) BELL CLAW FACE GRIP HEAD NECK PEEN POLL CHEEK HANDLE
(PAVING —) REEL
(PERCUSSION —) PLEXOR PLESSOR
(PNEUMATIC —) GUN BUSTER
(POINTED —) PICK
(SLATE-CUTTER'S —) SAX
(STEAM —) IMPACTER IMPACTOR
(THOR'S —) MJOLNIR MJOLLNIR
(TUNING —) KEY
(WAR —) MARTEL
HAMMERED BEATEN WROUGHT
HAMMERHEAD PEEN UMBRE CORNUDA UMBRETTE
HAMMERKOP UMBER UMBRETTE
HAMMERLOCK BAR ARMLOCK
HAMMERMAN STRIKER
HAMMOCK SACK HUMMOCK
(— CARRIED BY BEARERS) DANDY
(— SLUNG ON POLE) MACHILA
(WOODEN —) KATEL KARTEL
HAMMOLEKETH (BROTHER OF —) GILEAD
(FATHER OF —) MACHIR
HAMPER BIN COT MAR PED TUB BEAT BIND CLOG CURB FLAT HURT LOAD SLOW TUCK BLOCK CABIN CRAMP CRATE MAUND RUSKY SERON BASKET BURDEN FETTER HALTER HINDER HOBBLE HOPPLE IMPEDE TANGLE BUFFALO CONFINE HANAPER MANACLE PANNIER PERPLEX SHACKLE TRAMMEL ENCUMBER ENTANGLE OBSTRUCT RESTRAIN RESTRICT STRAITEN
HAMPERING STIFLING DIFFICULT
HAMSTER CRICETID
HAMSTRING HOX HOCK LAME HOUGH IMPEDE ENERVATE
HAMUL (FATHER OF —) PHAREZ
HAMUTAL (FATHER OF —) JEREMIAH
(HUSBAND OF —) JOSIAH
(SON OF —) JEHOAHAZ ZEDEKIAH
HANAMEEL (COUSIN OF —) JEREMIAH
(FATHER OF —) SHALLUM
HANAN (FATHER OF —) AZEL ZACCUR MAACHAH IGDALIAH
HANANI (FATHER OF —) HEMAN
(SON OF —) JEHU
HANANIAH (FATHER OF —) AZUR BEBAI HEMAN ZERUBBABEL
(GRANDSON OF —) IRIJAH
(SON OF —) ZEDEKIAH
HANAPER HAMPER
HAND M CAT DAB FAM FIN HAN PAW PUD CLAW DEAL DUKE GIVE GOLL HALF JACK LOOF MAIN MANO MITT PART PASS SPAN CAMAY CLAUT CLEUK FLUSH GLAUM GRASP GRIPE INDEX MANUS NIEVE POWER SHARE STIFF STOCK BRIDGE CLUNCH CLUTCH DADDLE DOUBLE FAMBLE GOWPEN HANDLE MAULEY MINNIE STAGER WORKER CLAWKER FAMELEN FLAPPER FLIPPER POINTER WORKMAN GRAPPLER MORTMAIN
(— COUNTING ZERO) BACCARA BACCARAT
(— DOWN) DEVOLVE TRADUCE BEQUEATH TRANSMIT
(— GESTURES) MUDRA
(— IN POKER) FULL SKIP BLAZE FLUSH SKEET TIGER BICYCLE JACKPOT SKIPPER IMMORTAL STRAIGHT
(— IN WHIST) MORT TENACE
(— ON) BUCK SPREAD
(— ON HIP) AKIMBO
(— OVER) GIVE REACH BETEACH BITECHE DELIVER
(— UP STRAW) SERVE
(— WITH 5 HIGHEST TRUMPS) JAMBOREE
(AT —) NEAR CLOSE
(BABY'S —) SPUD
(BIG AND UNGAINLY —) MAIG
(BRIDGE —) BID DUMMY DOUBLE CHICANE LAYDOWN
(CLENCHED —) FIST
(COLD —S) SHOWDOWN
(CURSIVE —) CIVILITE
(DECK —) HAWSEMAN
(DUMMY —) BOARD
(ELDEST —) EDGE SENIOR
(EUCHRE —) JAMBONE
(EXTRA — IN LOO) MISS
(FRENCH —) COULEE
(GRASPING —) CLAUT
(GREEN —) FARMER JACKEROO
(LEFT —) SINISTRA
(LONE —) JAMBONE
(PART OF —) PAD BALL HEEL PALM DIGIT INDEX THUMB WRIST CARPUS CREASE FINGER PINKIE THENAR MINIMUS BRACELET LIFELINE FINGERTIP FOREFINGER HYPOTHENAR TRANSVERSE
(PERSIAN —) SHIKASTA
(POKER —S) BOARD
(RANCH —) COWBOY
(REEL —) SPINDLER
(RIGHT —) DEXTER
(ROUND —) RONDE
(SECTION —) SNIPE
(SKILLFUL —) DAB
(SLAPPING OF RIGHT —) HIGHFIVE
(SPARE — IN CARDS) CAT JAMBOREE
(UNSKILLED —) DABSTER
(UPPER —) BULGE EMINENCE
(WEAK CARD —) BUST
(PREF.) CHEIR(O) CHIR(O) MANI MANU PALMATI PALMI
(SUFF.) CHEIRIA CHIRIA
HANDBAG BAG CABA NEIF CABAS PURSE SATCHEL ENVELOPE GRIPSACK POCHETTE RETICULE POCKETBOOK
HANDBALL PALM
HANDBARROW BIER HANDY TRUCK BARROW
HANDBELL SKELLAT TANTONY
HANDBILL BILL FLIER FLYER LIBEL DODGER
HANDBOOK VADY GRADUS MANUAL BAEDEKER
HANDBOW STONEBOW
HANDCAR DRAG
HANDCART PRAM DANDY HURLY TRUCK GOCART TROLLY TROLLEY
HANDCUFF CUFF STAY LINKER NIPPER STAYER MANACLE TRAMMEL WRISTER BRACELET HANDBOLT HANDLOCK LIGAMENT SNITCHER WRISTLET
(PL.) IRONS SNAPS DARBIES NIPPERS
HANDEDNESS
(SUFF.) CHEIRIA CHIRIA
HANDER-IN INGIVER
HANDFUL M MAN GRIP LOCK WISP YELM CLAUT GRIPE LITCH GOUPIN GOWPEN HANTLE YAFFLE FISTFUL MANIPLE
(— OF GRAIN) RIP REAP SINGLE SONGLE
(— OF LEAVES) PATRIN
(DOUBLE —) GOWPEN
(LAST — OF HARVEST) KIRN
(SMALL —) PUGIL
HANDFUL OF DUST (AUTHOR OF —) WAUGH
(CHARACTER IN —) JOCK JOHN LAST TODD TONY BEAVER BRENDA MENZIES MESSINGER
HANDGRIP TUFFING
HANDGUN GAT HAKE ROSCOE CALIVER HANDARM ARQUEBUS REVOLVER ARQUEBUSE
HANDICAP START BURDEN DENIAL HAMPER HINDER IMPEDE STRIKE PENALTY ENCUMBER PENALIZE
(SPORTS —) BISQUE
HANDICAPPED CRIMP CRIMPED
HANDICRAFT MYSTERY ARTIFICE MECHANIC HANDCRAFT
HANDICRAFTSMAN ARTISAN
HANDILY HANDY GAINLY
HANDINESS YARAGE
HANDING (— OVER) TRADITION
HANDIWORK MACHINE
(SAILOR'S —) SCRIMSHAW
HANDKERCHIEF WIPE CLOUT FOGLE HANKY ROMAL STOOK WIPER HANKIE MADRAS NAPKIN SUDARY TIGNON BANDANA BELCHER FOULARD KERCHER MANIPLE ORARIUM SNEEZER BANDANNA KERCHIEF MOCKETER MONTEITH MOUCHOIR SUDARIUM VERNACLE VERONICA
HANDLE BOW EAR FAN LUG NIB NOB PAD PIN PLY USE ANSA BAIL BALE BOOL BUTT CROP FEEL FIST GAUM GRIP HAFT HALE HAND HANK HILT KILP KNOB LIFT RAPE RUNG STOP GRASP GRIPE GROPE HELVE MOUNT SHAFT SPOKE STAIL STALE START STEAL STELE STOCK SWING TREAT WIELD BECKET FETTLE FINGER FUSEAU HANGER LIFTER MANAGE MANURE POMMEL ROUNCE TILLER CONDUCT DUDGEON WOOLDER BEERPULL BELLPULL BITSTALK BITSTOCK DISPENSE HANDGRIP HANDHOLD HANDLING MOPSTICK STAGHORN PENHOLDER MANIPULATE
(— AWKWARDLY) FUMBLE THUMBLE
(— BADLY) ILLGUIDE
(— CLUMSILY) PAW FUMBLE
(— IMPROPERLY) GAUM
(— MODISHLY) GALLANT
(— OF AXE) HELVE
(— OF BENCH PLANE) TOAT TOTE
(— OF CANNON) MANIGLION
(— OF DAGGER) DUDGEON
(— OF KETTLE) BAIL
(— OF LADLE) SHANK
(— OF OAR) GRASP
(— OF PLOW) HALE STAFF START STILT PLOWTAIL
(— OF PRINTING PRESS) ROUNCE
(— OF RAKE) STALE
(— OF SCYTHE) TACK SNATH SNEAD THOLE SNATHE SNEATH
(— OF SPOON) STEM
(— OF SWORD) HAFT HILT
(— OF WHIP) CROP
(— RECKLESSLY) FOOL
(— ROUGHLY) MALL MAUL TOWSE MUZZLE GRABBLE MANHANDLE
(— VIOLENTLY) BOUNCE
(CRANK —) WINK
(CROSSBOW —) TILLER
(CURVED —) BOOL BOUL
(DETACHABLE —) KILP
(LIFTING — OF GUN) DOLPHIN
(PUMP —) BRAKE SWIPE
(ROPE —) SHACKLE
(WOODEN —) TREE
(PL.) HALES
HANDLED (EASILY —) BANTAM
HANDLER DOCKHAND
(AIRPLANE —) AIREDALE
(SUFF.) STER STRESS
HANDLEY CROSS (AUTHOR OF —) SURTEES
(CHARACTER IN —) JOHN PIGG HARDY MELLO BELINDA BRAMBER DOLEFUL MICHAEL SWIZZLE JORROCKS FLEECEALL BARNINGTON
HANDLING USE CONTROL
(SEVERE —) KILLING
(SKILLFUL —) CONDUCT
(UNSKILLFUL —) BUNGLING
HANDMAID ANCILLA
HAND-MILL QUERN PEPPERMILL
HANDOUT DOWN
HANDRAIL BAR RAIL MANROPE

BANISTER EASEMENT MOPSTICK TOADBACK
HANDSAW STADDA
HANDSHAKE SHAKE SHRUG
HAND-SHAPED PALMATE
HANDSOME BRAW FAIR FINE MOOI NICE PERT TALL BONNY FETIS FITTY FUSOM LUSTY ADONIC BRAWLY CLEVER COMELY FARAND GOODLY HEPPEN LIKELY PROPER SEEMLY ADONIAN AVENANT ELEGANT FEATISH FEATOUS FEWSOME GALLANT LIBERAL SMICKER GOODLIKE STUNNING VENEREAN WEELFARD
HANDSOMELY FAIRLY HANDSOME
HANDSTONE MANO
HAND STRAP TOGGEL TOGGLE
HANDSTROKE TALLY
HANDWORK MACRAME TOOLING
HANDWRITING PAW FIST HAND WRITE DUCTUS NESHKI NIGGLE SCRIPT SCRIVE BATARDE WRITING BACKHAND HANDWRIT
(ARABIC —) NESKI NASKHI NESKHI
(BAD —) CACOGRAPHY
(CRAMPED —) NIGGLE
HANDY DAB DEFT GAIN NEAT WEME JEMMY LUSTY QUEME READY TIGHT ADROIT CLEVER HEPPEN KNACKY DEXTROUS EXPEDITE HANDSOME SKILLFUL
HANDYMAN MOZO JUMPER GREASER SWAMPER
HANG NUB TOP CRAP DRAG FALL HANK KILT PEND TREE TUCK DRAPE DROOP HOVER KETCH NOOSE SCRAG STRAP SWING TRINE TRUSS TWIST ANHANG APPEND DANGLE DEPEND GIBBET HALTER IMPEND SLOUCH STRING TALTER DOGGONE HANGING LANTERN STRETCH SUSPEND
(— ABOUT) DRING HOVER
(— AROUND) KNOCK HANKER LOITER SLINGE
(— BACK) LAG BOGGLE
(— BEHIND) PLOD
(— CRIMINAL) STRAP TOTTER
(— DOWN) DIP LOP LAVE DROOP DEPEND FESTOON PROPEND
(— HEAVILY) SWAG
(— IN POSITION) SET
(— IN SUSPENSE) POISE
(— LOOSELY) BAG SAG FLAG FLOW LOLL BANGLE DANGLE PAGGLE
(— OF GARMENT) SET
(— ONE'S HEAD) SLINK
(— ON THE LINE) DRIPDRY
(— OUT) LILL
(— OVER) HOVER WAUVE IMPEND WHAUVE
(— PICTURE NEAR CEILING) SKY
(— SOGGILY) TROLLOP
(— VERTICALLY) PLUMB
(— WITH TAPESTRY) TAPIS
(PREF.) CREMO
HANGAR DOCK GARAGE AIRDOCK
HANGER PASSIVE SHABBLE BASELARD WHINYARD
(— FOR CARCASSES) STANG
(COAT —) SHOULDER
(CRANK —) BRACKET
(LACE-MAKING —) WORKER
(SWORD —) CARRIAGE
HANGER-ON BUR CAD BURR SPIV LEECH TOADY CLIENT HANGBY HEELER LACKEY SPONGE LACQUEY PENDING PARASITE
(— OF CELEBRITY) GROUPIE
HANGING FLAG HEMP TURN ARRAS BAGGY DRAPE SWING CELURE DORSEL DOSSER DERRICK DRAPERY PENDENT PENSILE ANTEPORT HANGMENT PARAMENT
(— LOOSE) LOPPY BAGGED
(— LOW) SIDE
(— THREATENINGLY) IMMINENT
(ALTAR —) FRONTAL
(LIMPLY —) FLAGGY SLIMPSY
(WALL —) CEILING DRAPERY TENTURE KAKEMONO
(PL.) TAPIT TAPPET DRAPERY PARAMENT
HANGMAN KETCH HANGER HANGIE TOPMAN DERRICK GREGORY TOPSMAN VERDUGO CARNIFEX SCRAGGER
(HALTER OF —) TOW
HANGMAN'S DAY FRIDAY
HANGNAIL AGNAIL
HANGOUT NEST HAUNT JOINT SCATTER
HANGOVER HOLDOVER RESIDUUM KATZENJAMMER
HANG-UP BAG
HANIEL (FATHER OF —) ULLA
HANK HASP SKEIN BOBBIN SELVAGEE
(— OF FLAX) HEAD
(— OF TWINE) RAN
(— OF YARN) SLIP
HANKER HANK ITCH LONG YEARN LINGER
HANKERING ITCH HANKER
HANKUL ENMUN ONMUN
HANNAH (HUSBAND OF —) ELKANAH
(SON OF —) SAMUEL
HANNIEL (FATHER OF —) EPHOD
HANOCH (FATHER OF —) REUBEN
HANS BRINKER (AUTHOR OF —) DODGE
(CHARACTER IN —) HANS RAFF GLECK HILDA GRETEL BOEKMAN BRINKER MEVROUW
HANSOM CAB SHOFUL SHOWFUL
HANUMAN ENTELLUS
HANUN (FATHER OF —) NAHASH ZALAPH
HAP REDE CHANCE FORTUNE HAPPING
HAPHAZARD CASUAL CHANCE CHANCY RANDOM BUCKEYE SCRATCH CARELESS SCRAMBLY SLAPDASH TUMULTUARY
HAPHAZARDLY ANYHOW SLAPDASH
HAPLESS POOR UNLUCKY
HAPLY HAPS HAPPILY
HAPPEN BE DO GO HAP COME COOK FALL FARE GIVE LUCK PASS RISE TIDE TIME BREAK EVENE EVENT LIGHT OCCUR SHAPE ARRIVE BECOME BEFALL BETIDE CHANCE TUMBLE FORTUNE STUMBLE SUCCEED BECHANCE OVERCOME
(— AGAIN) RECUR
(— TOGETHER) CONCUR
HAPPENING HAP FACT EVENT THING CHANCE TIDING TIMING INCIDENT OCCASION OCCURRENCE
(ACTUAL —) FACT
(UNCANNY —) WEIRD
(UNEXPECTED —) ACCIDENT
HAPPILY FAIN FITLY GLADLY JOYOUSLY
HAPPINESS JOY WIN GLEE SELE SONS WEAL BLISS GLORY MIRTH SOOTH FELICE WEALTH DELIGHT ECSTASY FELICIA RAPTURE UTILITY FELICITY GLADNESS HILARITY
(PLACE OF —) CAMELOT
HAPPY FIT COSH FAIN GLAD GLEG SELI WELY BONNY FAUST FELIX LIGHT LUCKY MERRY PROUD SEELY SONSY SUNNY WHITE BLITHE BONNIE BRIGHT JOYFUL COMICAL GLEEFUL HALCYON JOCULAR PERFECT SEELFUL WEALFUL WEIRDLY BLISSFUL CAREFREE DISPOSED FROHLICH GRACIOUS SUNSHINE
(PREF.) FELICI
HARA-KIRI SEPPUKU
HARALD (FATHER OF KING —) OLAF
HARAN (BROTHER OF —) ABRAHAM
(DAUGHTER OF —) ISCAH MILCAH
(FATHER OF —) CALEB TERAH
(MOTHER OF —) EPHAH
(SON OF —) LOT
HARANGUE RANT ORATE SPOUT CONCIO PATTER SCREED SERMON SPEECH SPRITZ TIRADE ADDRESS DECLAIM EARBASH DIATRIBE PERORATE
HARASS FAG GIG HAG HOX MAG NAG RAG TAW VEX BAIT CARK FRAB FRET GALL GNAW HAKE HALE HARE HAZE HOCK JADE PAIL PUSH RIDE SEEK TIRE TOIL TOSS WORK ANNOY BESET BULLY CHAFE CHASE CHEVY CHIVY CURSE FLISK GRIND GRIPE HARRY HOUND HURRY PRESS TARGE TEASE TRASH WEARY WORRY BADGER BOTHER CHIVVY CHOUSE CUMBER FERRET HASSLE HATTER HECKLE HECTOR HESPEL HOORAY HURRAH INFEST MOLEST MURDER OBSESS PESTER PINGLE PLAGUE POTHER PURSUE AFFLICT AGITATE BEDEVIL DRAGOON HAGRIDE HARRAGE OPPRESS PERPLEX PROVOKE TERRIFY TORMENT TRAVAIL TROUBLE TURMOIL BULLYRAG DISTRACT DISTRESS EXERCISE FORHAILE IRRITATE SPURGALL SUPPRESS PERSECUTE
(— MENTALLY) GRUDGE
HARASSED BESTEAD HARRIED HAUNTED
(— BY) BEFORE
HARASSING WARM
HARBINGER OMEN ANGEL USHER HERALD FORAGER FORAYER FURRIER OUTRIDER PRODROME
(— OF SUMMER) SWALLOW
HARBOR REE BEAR DOCK HOLD PIER PORT BASIN BAYOU CHUCK CREEK HAVEN HITHE SLADE BREACH BUNDER COTHON FOSTER REFUGE OUTPORT PORTLET SEAPORT SHELTER CARENAGE ENHARBOR SHIPRADE
(— A CRIMINAL) RESET
(SUBMARINE —) PEN
HARBOR SEAL DOTANT DOTARD RANGER SEALCH TANGFISH
HARD DRY FIT ILL COLD DEAR DOUR DURE FAST FIRM IRON MEAN NASH OPEN CHAMP CLOSE CORKY HARSH HORNY ROCKY SMART SNELL SOLID SOUND STEEL STERN STIFF STONY STOOR STOUT TIGHT BOARDY BRAWNY COARSE FLINTY GLASSY KITTLE KNOBBY KNOTTY ROBUST RUGGED SEVERE STARKY STINGY STRICT STRONG STURDY UNEATH UNNETH WOODEN ADAMANT ARDUOUS AUSTERE CALLOUS HARDWAY HORNISH ONEROUS SUBDURE CORNEOUS DILIGENT HARDBACK HARDENED IRONHARD OBDURATE PETROSAL RIGOROUS SCLEROID SCLEROSE TOILSOME
(— BY) FORBY FORTHBY
(— TO BEAR) FIERCE
(— TO MANAGE) SALTY
(— TO PLEASE) FINICKY CONCEITY
(— TO REACH) CUMBROUS
(— TO READ) BLIND
(— TO SATISFY) EXIGENT EXIGEANT
(— TO SELL) STICKY
(— TO UNDERSTAND) DIFFUSE
(PREF.) DURO SCLER(O) STERE(O)
HARD-BILL SEEDEATER
HARD-BITTEN GNARLED
HARDEN SET TAW BAKE BEEK CAKE FIRM HARN KERN SEAR BRAZE ENURE FLESH INURE SETUP STEEL STONE BRONZE ENDURE FREEZE OBDURE OSSIFY POTASH SEASON TEMPER CALCIFY EMBRAWN PETRIFY STIFFEN THICKEN CONCRETE ENHARDEN INDURATE SOLIDIFY
(— QUILL) DUTCH
(CASE —) STEEL
HARDENED DRAW HARD LOST SALTED CALLOUS COCTILE CRUSTED FIBROUS INDURATE OBDURATE
HARDENING SET POROMA SCLEROMA OSSIFICATION
(— OF TISSUES) SCLEREMA SCLERIASIS
HARDHACK SPIREA IRONBUSH WHITECAP
HARDHEAD LION BOCHE
HARDHEARTED STERN STONY OBDURATE
HARDICANUTE (FATHER OF —) CANUTE
(HALF-BROTHER OF —) HAROLD
(MOTHER OF —) EMMA

HARDIHOOD PLUCK COURAGE AUDACITY
HARDLY ILL SCANT BARELY RARELY SCARCE UNEATH SCARCELY
HARDNESS SEG GRAIN PROOF RIGOR STEEL DURESS DURITY ADAMANT HARDSHIP SEVERITY SOLIDITY
(— OF CHARACTER) HEART
(— SCALE) MOHS
HARD-OF-HEARING DULL DUNCH DEAFISH
HARDPAN PAN CLAYPAN MOORPAN MOORBAND ORTSTEIN
HARDSCRABBLE ARID
HARDSHIP HARD GRIEF PINCH RIGOR STOUR THRONG UNWEAL SQUEEZE ASPERITY HARDNESS
(PL.) EXTREMES
HARDTACK PANTILE
(— AND MOLASSES) BURGOO
HARD TIMES (AUTHOR OF —) DICKENS
(CHARACTER IN —) JUPE JAMES SISSY JOSIAH LOUISA SLEARY THOMAS SPARSIT STEPHEN GRAGRIND BLACKPOOL BOUNDERBY HARTHOUSE MCCHOAKUMCHILD
HARDWARE TRIM IRONWARE
(COMPUTER —) MONITOR
HARDWOOD ASH HARD BREAKAX LEAFWOOD
HARDWORKING EIDENT
HARDY DOUR HARD WIRY LUSTY MANLY STOUR STOUT TOUGH GARDEN INURED RUGGED STURDY SPARTAN STUBBED GAILLARD GALLIARD STUBBORN
HARE PUG WAT BAWD CONY PUSS SCUT BAWTY CUTTY LEPUS PUSSY MALKIN MAUKIN BELGIAN LEPORID POUSSIE VENISON BAUDRONS KLIPHAAS LEPORINE
(— IN FIRST YEAR) LEVERET
(— TRACK) PRICK
(FEMALE —) DOE
(GREAT —) MANABOZHO
(KIND OF —) VARYING SNOWSHOE
(LITTLE CHIEF —) CONY PIKA
(MALE —) BUCK
(PATAGONIAN —) MARA
(SIBERIAN —) TOLAL
(PL.) FLICK
(PREF.) LAG(O) LEPORI
HAREBELL BLAWORT THIMBLE BLAEWORT BLUEBELL
HAREBRAINED GIDDY WINDY
HARELIP LAGOSTOMA
HAREM SERAI ZENANA ANDERUN HAREMLIK SERAGLIO
(ROOM IN —) ODA ODAH
HAREPH (FATHER OF —) CALEB
(SON OF —) BETHGADER
HARE'S-EAR MODESTY BUPLEVER
HARHAIAH (SON OF —) UZZIEL
HARIJAN PANCHAMA
HARK (— BACK) HOICKS
HARL WHIRL
HARLEQUIN DUCK SQUEALER
(FEMALE —) LADY
(MALE —) LORD
HARLOT PUG DRAB LOON SLUT HIREN PAGAN QUEAN RAHAB STRAP TWEAK WHORE RIBALD TOMBOY DELILAH MERMAID WAGTAIL MERETRIX MISWOMAN STRUMPET
(PREF.) PORN(O)
HARLOTRY PUTAGE BITCHERY
HARM NEY NOY NYE WEM ARME BALE BANE DERE HURT SCAT SORE TEEN WERD ABUSE ANNOY GRAME HERME LOATH QUALM SHEND SPOIL TOUCH WATHE WEMMY WOUGH WOUND WRAKE WREAK WRONG DAMAGE DAMNUM DANGER GRIEVE INJURE INJURY SCATHE SORROW WONDER DESPITE DISEASE FORFEIT IMPEACH TROUBLE UNQUERT BUSINESS DISAVAIL DISSERVE ENDAMAGE MISCHIEF NOCUMENT NUISANCE
(— REPUTATION) DEFAME
(DO —) ENVY
(PREF.) NOCI
HARMFUL BAD EVIL HARM NASTY NOXAL NOCENT NOCIVE NOYFUL UNSELY BANEFUL HURTFUL NOISOME NOXIOUS DAMAGING INIMICAL SINISTER PERNICIOUS
HARMFULNESS VICE MALICE
HARMINE BANISTERINE
HARMLESS SAFE SELI TAME CANNY SEELY SILLY WHITE DOVISH FEARLESS HURTLESS INNOCENT SACKLESS UNHARMED
(MAKE —) DEFANG
HARMONIA (DAUGHTER OF —) INO AGAVE SEMELE AUTONOE
(FATHER OF —) MARS
(HUSBAND OF —) CADMUS
(MOTHER OF —) VENUS
(SON OF —) POLYDORUS
HARMONIC OVERTONE
HARMONICA HARP EUPHON SYRINX AEOLINE PANPIPE ARMONICA ZAMPOGNA MOUTHORGAN
HARMONIOUS HAPPY SWEET COSMIC SILKEN UNITED MUSICAL SPHERAL TUNEFUL BALANCED CHARMING HARMONIC PEACEFUL ACCORDING CONCINNOUS CONCORDANT
(— RELATIONSHIP) SYNC
(PREF.) SYMPHO
HARMONITE RAPPIST RAPPITE
HARMONIUM ORGAN VOCALION
HARMONIZE GO FIT GEE KEY JIBE SORT TUNE AGREE ATONE BLEND CHORD GROUP HITCH RHYME ACCORD ASSORT ATTUNE COTTON COMPORT CONCENT CONCORD CONSORT ORDINATE ACCOMMODATE
HARMONIZING HENOTIC
HARMONY SUIT TUNE CHIME CHORD UNITY ACCORD ATTUNE COSMOS HEAVEN MELODY UNISON BALANCE CONCENT CONCERT CONCORD CONSENT CONSORT KEEPING RAPPORT DIAPASON FABURDEN SYMPATHY SYMPHONY CONGRUITY
(— OF COLORS) TONE
HARNEPHER (FATHER OF —) ZOPHAH
HARNESS TUG GEAR HAME LEAF REIN YOKE BRACE CROWN DRAFT FRONT GEARS SLING TRACE COLLAR FETTLE GULLET INSPAN TACKLE DRAUGHT GEARING GIGTREE LORMERY SIMBLOT TOGGERY DRAWGEAR ENCLOSER HEADGEAR TACKLING TURNBACK
(— FOR LOOM) LEAF HEALD MOUNTING
(— FOR PULLING GUNS) BRICOLE
(DECORATIVE —) CAPARISON
(PART OF —) BIT REIN GIRTH TRACE COLLAR BLINDER CRUPPER BELLYBAND BREECHING CHECKREIN
(WEAVING —) HEADLE HEDDLE
HARNESSED ANTELOPE GUIB GUIBA BOSCHBOK BUSHBUCK
HARNESS MAKER KNACKER WHITTAW
HAROLD I HAREFOOT
HARP ARPA FORK LYRE VINA NABLA NANGA HARPER SABECA CHROTTA DECHORD SAMBUKE AUTOHARP CLARSACH
(— ON) RUBIN
(CELTIC —) TELYN CLARSACH
(FINNISH —) KANTELA KANTELE
(ICELANDIC —) LANGSPIL
(JAPANESE —) KOTO
(JEW'S —) TRUMP
(PART OF —) BASE BODY FOOT NECK BOARD PEDAL PILLAR STRING
(PERSIAN —) SANG
(TRIANGULAR —) TRIGON TRIGONON
HARPER MINSTREL
HARPOON IRON FIZGIG GRAINS FISHGIG HARPAGO STRIKER HARPAGON
HARPOONED FAST
HARPOONER STRIKER
HARP SEAL HARP BEATER SADDLER
HARPSICHORD SPINET CEMBALO CLAVIER CLAVECIN HASPICOL
HARPY HAG AELLO CELAENO OCYPETE PODARGE
HARQUEBUS HAGBUT CALIVER HACKBUT ARQUEBUS
HARQUEBUSIER CARABIN
HARRIDAN HAG
HARRIER HAWK KAHU BEAGLE FALLER MILLER PUTTOCK HARROWER
HARROW COG CHIP DISC DISK DRAG HARO TINE BRAKE BREAK HERSE DREDGE DRUDGE FALLOW LADDER SPADER CUTAWAY LACERATE OXHARROW
HARROWED HAGGARD
HARROWING TINE TINING TEARING
(— OF HELL) ANASTASIS
HARRY DUN HAG BRACE CHIVEY CHIVVY FERRET HARASS CRUCIFY
HARSH ILL ACID BULL DOUR FOUL HARD HASH HASK IRON RUDE SOUR ACERB ACRID ASPER BRUTE CRONK CRUDE GRILL GRUFF HEAVY HUSKY RASPY ROUGH ROUND RUVID SHARP SNELL STARK STERN STIFF STOUR STOUT BRUTAL COARSE FLINTY GRAVEL GRISLY HOARSE RAGGED RASPED RUGGED SEVERE SHREWD STURDY SULLEN TETRIC UNKIND UNRIDE AUSTERE CRABBED RASPING RAUCOUS SQUAWKY VIOLENT ABRASIVE ACERBATE ASPERATE ASPEROUS CATONIAN CLASHING DRACONIC GRAVELLY GRINDING GUTTURAL JANGLING OBDURATE RIGOROUS SCABROUS SCRANNEL STRIDENT STROUNGE STUBBORN TETRICAL UNGENTLE UNKINDLY
(— OF VOICE) STEER
HARSHLY HARD HARSH SHORTLY
HARSHNESS WOLF RIGOR DURESS CATOISM CRUDITY CRUELTY DUREZZA RAUCITY ACERBITY ACRIMONY ASPERITY FELLNESS HARDNESS HASKNESS MORDANCY SEVERITY
HART SPADE VENISON
HARTEBEEST ASSE TORA TORI BUBAL CAAMA KAAMA KONZE LECAMA BUBALIS CONGONI KONGONI SASSABY
HART'S-TONGUE LONGLEAF
HARUM (SON OF —) AHARHEL
HARUMAPH (SON OF —) JEDAIAH
HARUSPEX SEER ARUSPEX ARUSPICE EXTISPEX
HARUZ (DAUGHTER OF —) MESHULLEMETH
HARVEST IN WIN CROP HEAP PICK RABI REAP SLED SNAP FOISON GATHER HAIRST RUBBEE UPROOT COMBINE GRABBLE INGATHER SHEARING
(— OF GRAPES) VENDAGE
HARVESTER COMBINE
HARVEST FISH WHITING MOONFISH STARFISH
HARVEST HOME KIRN MELL HOCKEY HORKEY
HARVESTING SLEDDING
HARVESTMAN CARTER CARTARE
HARY JANOS (COMPOSER OF —) KODALY
HAS S AS HATH
(— NOT) NAS AINT
HASADIAH (FATHER OF —) ZERUBBABEL
HAS-BEEN WUZZER
HASH RAPE MINCE HACHIS MUDDLE RAGOUT
HASHABIAH (COMPANION OF —) EZRA
(FATHER OF —) BUNNI KEMUEL JEDUTHUN MATTANIAH
HASHABNIAH (SON OF —) HATTUSH
HASHISH HEMP ASSIS CHARAS
HASHUBAH (FATHER OF —) ZERUBBABEL
HASID ASSIDEAN
HASKALAH (FOLLOWER OF —) MASKIL
HASP COP HAPS COPSE SPRENT
HASSAR DORAD
HASSOCK TUT BOSS PESS POUF TOIT TRUSH BUFFET TUFFET

HASTE HIE POST RACE RAGE RAPE CHASE FEVER HASTY HURRY SPEED BUSTLE FLURRY SWIVET DISPATCH RAPIDITY STROTHER PRECIPITATION
(HEADLONG —) SPURN
(IN —) HOTFOOT
(IN GREAT —) AMAIN
(WITH —) EXPRESS

HASTEN HIE RAP RUN BUSK DUST FIRK PELL PLAT POST RACE RAPE RUSH SPUR URGE CATCH CHASE DRIVE FLEET HASTE HURRY PRESS PREST SLATE SPEED STEER EXPEDE SCURRY STREAK SWITHE ADVANCE FORWARD HACKNEY HOTFOOT PREVENT QUICKEN SLITHER SWIFTEN WITHHIE DISPATCH EXPEDITE ACCELERATE
(— AWAY) FLEE SHERRY SQUIRR

HASTILY HOTLY RAPELY RASHLY FOOTHOT HOTFOOT HYINGLY HEADLONG

HASTY FAST RAPE RASH BRASH FLEET QUICK FLYING RAPELY CURSORY HOTHEAD HURRIED PEPPERY TEARING HASTEFUL HEADLONG SUBITANE
(TACTLESSLY —) BRASH

HAT DIP FEZ LID NAB ATTE BAKU CADY COIF DISC DISK FELT FLAT HIVE HOOD KNAB MOAB SLOP TILE TOPI BEANY BENJY BENNY BERET BOXER CADDI CORDY DERBY DICER GIBUS JERRY KELLY MILAN MITER MITRE SHAKO SHELL TARAI TERAI TOPEE TOQUE TRUSH ABACOT BEANIE BEAVER BOATER BOWLER BRETON BUMPER CADDIE CASQUE CLAQUE CLOCHE COCKUP COIFFE FEDORA GALERO HELMET PANAMA PILEUS RAFFIA SAILOR SHOVEL SLOUCH TITFER TOPPER TURBAN VIGONE BANDEAU BANGKOK BLOOMER BRIMMER BYCOKET CATSKIN CAUBEEN CHAPEAU FANTAIL HATTING HATTOCK HOMBURG LEGHORN PETASOS PILLBOX PLATEAU PLATTER SALACOT SCRAPER SHALLOW SKIMMER SMASHER STETSON TARBUSH TRICORN BONGRACE CAPELINE GOSSAMER HEADGEAR JIPIJAPA MONTABYN MUSHROOM NABCHEAT RAMILIES REHOBOAM ROUNDLET SOMBRERO TARBOOSH TARBOUCH BORSALINO
(— BLOCKER) ROPER
(— MAKER) MODISTE MILLINER
(— OF MERCURY) PETASUS
(BEAVER —) CASTOR
(CARDINAL'S —) GALERO
(CLERGYMAN'S —) SHOVEL
(COCKED —) BICORNE RAMILIE SCRAPER
(COWBOY —) STETSON
(FABRIC —) TOQUE
(FELT —) DERBY JERRY TARAI TERAI ALPINE BOWLER TRILBY BILLYCOCK
(FLAT-TOP —) TAM
(HARD —) LABORER
(HIGH —) KYL PLUG TILE TOPPER
(IRON —) GOSSAN GOZZAN
(KIND OF —) COSSACK PORKPIE
(MILITARY —) BUSBY BEARSKIN
(OILSKIN —) SQUAM
(OPERA —) GIBUS CLAQUE
(PART OF —) BOW BRIM CROWN PINCH LINING BINDING HATBAND SWEATBAND
(PITH —) TOPI TOPEE
(RED —) GALERO
(SILK —) KYL BEAVER SHINER CATSKIN
(STIFF —) TILE DERBY KELLY BOATER BOWLER SAILOR
(STOVEPIPE —) CAROLINE
(STRAW —) BAKU FLAT HOOD KADY KATY TOYO BENJY BENNY CADDY STRAW BASHER BOATER PANAMA LEGHORN
(TOP —) PLUG TOPPER
(UNBLOCKED —) CONE
(WATERPROOF —) TARPAULIN
(WIDE-BRIMMED —) FLAT BENJY TARAI SMASHER SUNDOWN
(3-CORNERED —) TRICORN

HATBAND BAND WEED WEEPER

HAT BRIM LEAF TARFE TURNUP

HATCH HECK BREED BROOD CLECK CLOCK COVEY GUICHET UNSHELL DISCLOSE INCUBATE

HATCHED (NEWLY —) SQUAB

HATCHERY CHICKERY

HATCHET MOGO HACHE GWEEON THIXLE CLEAVER FRANCISC TOMAHAWK
(PREF.) SECURI

HATCHING CLETCH BREEDING ECLISION

HATCHWAY HATCH SCUTTLE

HATE FIRE TEEN ABHOR SPITE DETEST HATRED LOATHE UNLOVE DESPITE

HATEFUL FOUL LOTH BLACK CURST DIRTY HATEL LOATH CURSED ODIOUS HEINOUS HIDEOUS ACCURSED FLAGRANT ABOMINABLE

HATER ULYSSES

HATH MOOLUM

HATHATH (FATHER OF —) OTHNIEL

HATING
(PREF.) MIS(O)

HAT MONEY TAMPANG

HAT-PLANT SOLA

HATRED DOSA ENVY HATE HELL ONDE HAINE ODIUM SPITE ENMITY RANCOR AVERSION ABHORRENCE
(— OF CHILDREN) MISOPEDIA
(— OF MARRIAGE) MISOGAMY
(— OF MEN) MISANDRY MISANTHROPY
(— OF NEW IDEAS) MISCAINEA
(— OF REASONING) MISOLOGY
(— OF WOMEN) MISOGYNY
(PREF.) MIS(O)

HATTER GADGER HURRER

HATTUSH (FATHER OF —) HASHABNIAH

HAUBERK BYRNIE

HAUGHTILY BIGLY

HAUGHTINESS AIR PRIDE HEIGHT MORGUE ORGUIL DISDAIN HAUTEUR STOMACH HAUTESSE

HAUGHTY DAIN HIGH RANK STAY DIGNE DORTY HUFFY LOFTY LUSTY POTTY PROUD STOUT SURLY TAUNT FEISTY FIERCE HAUGHT QUAINT SNOOTY UPPISH DISTANT HAUTAIN HONTISH PAUGHTY STATELY SUBLIME ARROGANT CAVALIER DEIGNOUS FASTUOUS GLORIOUS IMPERIAL INSOLENT ORGULOUS PRIDEFUL SCORNFUL SNIFFISH SUPERIOR TOPLOFTY PEREMPTORY

HAUL KEP LUG RUG TEW TOW TUG CART DRAG DRAW DRAY HALE HURL JUNK PULL SKID TAKE TOTE TRAM BOUSE DRAVE HEAVE LIGHT ROUSE SNAKE TOUSE TOWSE TRACT TRICE TRAVOY DRAUGHT SCHLEPP CORDELLE HANDBANK
(— AFT) TALLY
(— DOWN) STRIKE
(— IN) GATHER
(— LOGS) TODE SLOOP SWAMP SIWASH HANDBANK
(— OF FISH) TACK DRAVE
(— OF NET) LIFT
(— SAIL) BUNT CLEW CLUE
(— SHIP) SPRING
(— TO DECK) BOARD
(— UP AND FASTEN) TRICE
(— WITH TACKLE) BOUSE

HAULAGE DOOK

HAULAGEWAY GANGWAY

HAULING HALE CARTAGE

HAUNCH HIP HOOK HUCK HANCE HUCKLE
(PL.) GRUG HUNKERS

HAUNT DEN HANT HOME HOWF KEEP NEST WALK GHOST HOWFF SPOOK STALK INFEST KENNEL OBSESS OUTLAY PURSUE REPAIR PURLIEU FREQUENT PRACTICE
(— OF ANIMALS) LIE HOME
(FAMILIAR —) SLAIT

HAUNTED SPOOKY

HAUNTING BESETTING

HAUSTELLATE GLOSSATE

HAUSTORIUM SINK SINKER SUCKER

HAUTBOY OBOE WAIT

HAUTEUR PRIDE HEIGHT MORGUE

HAVE A AN OF OWN HOLD BOAST ENJOY OUGHT WIELD POSSESS
(— ON) WEAR

HAVEN ARK HOPE PIER PORT HITHE HARBOR HAVENET

HAVILAH (FATHER OF —) CUSH JOKTAN

HAVING
(SUFF.) IOUS OSE OUS

HAVOC HOB HELL RUIN WASTE RAVAGE

HAW HOI HECK SLOE WIND WYND BOOTS PEGGLE ALISIER

HAWAII

BAY: POHUE HALAWA KIHOLO MAMALA KAMOHIO KANEOHE WAIAGUA KAWAIHAE MAUNALUA
BEACH: WAIKIKI
CAPITAL: HONOLULU
CHANNEL: AUA KAIWI KALOHI PAILOLO
COUNTY: MAUI KAUAI HAWAII HONOLULU
CRATER: KILAUEA
DESERT: KAU
DISTRICT: KONA PUNA
FISH: ULUA AKULE MOANO
FORMER NAME: SANDWICH
HARBOR: PEARL
HEAD: DIAMOND
ISLAND: MAUI OAHU KAUAI KAULA LANAI NIIHAU MOLOKAI
MOUNTAIN: KAALA KOHALA KAMAKOU MAUNAKEA LANAIHALE
MOUNTAIN RANGE: KOHALA KOOLAU WAIANAE
NATIVE: KANAKA
STATE BIRD: NENE GOOSE
STATE FLOWER: HIBISCUS
STATE NICKNAME: ALOHA
STATE TREE: CANDLENUT
TOWN: EWA AIEA HANA HILO LAIE PAIA KAPAA KEAAU LIHUE MAILI KAILUA KEKAHA PAHALA HONOKAA KAHULUI KANEOHE WAHIAWA WAIANAE WAILUKU HONOLULU PAPAIKOU
TREE: KOA NAIO WILIWILI
VALLEY: MANOA
VOLCANO: KILAUEA HUALALAI MAUNAKEA MAUNALOA

HAWAIIAN KANAKA KAMAAINA

HAWFINCH KATE GROSBEAK

HAWK IO EYAS KITE SELL ALLAN BATER BUTEO CADGE EYESS HOICK HOUGH REACH RIVER STOOP BAWREL FALCON FOOTER HIGGLE KEELIE MERLIN MUSKET OSPREY PALLET PEDDLE RAMAGE RAPTOR RIFLER SHIKRA VERMIN BUZZARD GOSHAWK HAGGARD HARRIER HERONER KESTREL LENTNER STANIEL SWOOPER BRANCHER CARACARA HARROWER LENTINER PASSAGER ROUGHLEG SPARHAWK TALENTER TARTARET MORTARBOARD
(— FIGHT) CRAB
(CAGE FOR —S) MEW
(COUPLE OF —S) CAST
(CROP OF —) GORGE
(FEMALE —) FORMAL FORMEL
(MALE —) JACK TASSEL TERCEL
(SMALL —) ELANET
(UNTAMED —) HAGGARD
(YOUNG —) EYAS NIAS BOWET BOWESS BRANCHER
(PREF.) HIERACO

HAWKER CRIER CRYER BADGER CADGER COSTER DUFFER JOWTER PEDDER PETHER CAMELOT CHAPMAN HIGGLER MERCURY PEDDLER CRATEMAN GLASSMAN HUCKSTER

HAWKEYE STATE IOWA

HAWKING FALCONRY

HAWKMOTH SPHINX

HAWK PARROT HIA

HAWKWEED DINDLE BUGLOSS FIREWEED OXTONGUE

HAWSE BAG JACKASS

HAWSER FAST WARP HEADLINE

HAWTHORN HAW MAY QUICK THORN AIGLET MAYBUSH COCKSPUR MAYBLOOM MAYTHORN QUICKSET
(FRUIT OF —) HAZEL PEGGLE
HAY HEI RIP MATH RAKH RISP FETTLE STOVER WINDLIN SWEEPAGE
(— CUT FINE) CHAFF
(— PUT IN BARN) END
(— SPREADER) TEDDER
(BUNDLE OF —) TRUSS
(PILE OF —) TUMBLE
(ROW OF —) WINDROW
(SECOND-GROWTH —) EDDISH
(SMALL LOAD OF —) HURRY
(SMALL PIECE OF —) TATE
HAYCOCK MOW COIL HOVEL QUILE SHOCK DOODLE HIPPLE LAPCOCK HAYSHOCK
HAYFIELD PARK RAKH MOWING
HAYFORK PIKE PICKEL
HAYLOFT LOFT TALLET SCAFFOLD
HAYMAKER PICKMAN
HAYMOW GOAF HAYLOFT OVERDEN OVERHEAD
HAYRACK HECK HAYRIG THRIPPLE
HAYSTACK COB PIKE RICK HOVEL HAYRICK STACKAGE
HAYSUCK EYSOGE
HAY SWEEP BUCK
HAYWARD MEADSMAN
HAZAN CANTOR CHAZZAN
HAZARD DIE LAY LOT JUMP PAWN RISK WAGE JENNY LOSER PERIL CHANCE DANGER NIFFER BALANCE IMPERIL VENTURE ENDANGER JEOPARDY SANDTRAP
(BILLIARDS —) INOFF
(GOLF —) TRAP BUNKER
(ROAD —) ESS
HAZARDOUS NICE NASTY RISKY CHANCY QUEASY RISQUE UNSAFE UNSURE PARLOUS PERILOUS
HAZARDOUSLY CHANCILY
HAZE FOG URE FILM GLIN MIST REEK SMOG TRUB DEVIL GAUZE HAZLE SMEETH
(— AND SMOKE) SMAZE
HAZEL AGLET AIGLET COBNUT MUFFIN FILBERT HAZELNUT NOISETTE
(— FOR THATCHING) SPRAYS
HAZEL HOE PULASKI
HAZELNUT NIT HAZEL FILBERT
HAZEL TREE AVELLANO
HAZILY DIMLY
HAZINESS HAZE GRAYOUT
HAZO (FATHER OF —) NAHOR
(MOTHER OF —) MILCAH
HAZY DIM ABLUR FOGGY MISTY MUZZY SMOKY THICK VAGUE BLURRY CLOUDY DREAMY OBSCURE SMUISTY NEBULOUS
(NOT —) OPEN
HE A E HI HO HEH HEY HIM HYE SHE ESSO ILLE THON CESTUI
(— DIED) OB
(— GAVE AND DEDICATED) DDD
(— MADE) F FEC
(— PAINTED IT) PNXT
(— READS) LEG
(— WAS NOT FOUND) NEI
HEAD BIT BUT COP DON FAT MIR NAB NOB PEN POW TOP BEAN BOSS CAPE COCO CONK COSP CROP DATU DEAN DOME HELM JOLE JOWL KAID KNOB LEAD LOAF MAKE MASK NOLL PASH PATE POLL RAIS TETE TURN YEAD ALDER ATTIC BLADE BLOCK BONCE CHIEF CHUMP CROWN DATTO MAZER ONION RISER SCALP SHODE SKULL START TIBBY TROPE BELFRY BLANCH CABEZA CENTER CHAULE COBBRA COCKER DAROGA EXARCH GARRET GATHER HEADER KAISER MAHANT MAZARD NAPPER NODDLE PALLET RUBRIC SCONCE CAPITAL CAPTAIN COCONUT COSTARD COSTREL COXCOMB CRUMPET CUPHEAD GENARCH HEADING HEGUMEN NUCLEUS PRELATE TOPKNOT CALABASH CEPHALON DECURION DIRECTOR DUFFADAR FOUNTAIN HEADLINE INITIATE PHYLARCH POINTING TOPPIECE CAPERNOITIE
(— IN PARTICULAR DIRECTION) STEM
(— OF ABBEY) ABBOT
(— OF ALEMBIC) MITER MITRE
(— OF BEAR, WOLF OR BOAR) HURE
(— OF CABBAGE) LOAF
(— OF CEREAL) EAR
(— OF CHAIR) MAKER
(— OF CLOVER) COB SUCKER
(— OF COLUMN) CHAPITER
(— OF COMET) COMA
(— OF CONVENT) ABBESS SUPERIOR
(— OF CRIME SYNDICATE) CAPO
(— OF DANDELION) BLOWBALL
(— OF DRILL BRACE) CUSHION
(— OFF AGAIN) RESUME
(— OF FAMILY) ALDER COARB COMARB GOODMAN
(— OF FISH) JOWL
(— OF GANG) TINDAL
(— OF GOVERNMENT) MUKHTAR
(— OF GRAIN) ICKER
(— OF GUILD) ALDERMAN
(— OF HAIR) SUIT CRINE FLEECE CHEVELURE
(— OF HARPOON) BOMB
(— OF HERRING) COB
(— OF INSTITUTION) WARDEN
(— OF JEWISH ACADEMY) GAON
(— OF LANCE) MORNE MOURNE
(— OF LOOM) JACQUARD
(— OF MONASTERY) HEGUMEN
(— OF MUSHROOM) BUTTON
(— OF MUSICAL INSTRUMENT) SCROLL
(— OF NUNNERY) DAME
(— OF ORDER) MURSHID
(— OF PROJECTILE) OGIVE
(— OF RING) CHATON
(— OF RIVET) BULLHEAD FLATHEAD SNAPHEAD
(— OF SEPT) COARB COMARB
(— OF STATE) CAUDILLO PRINCEPS
(— OF TAPEWORM) SCOLEX
(— OF TREE) COMA
(— OF 10 MONKS) DEAN
(— ON) SQUARE
(— PREMATURELY) BUTTON
(— USED AS TARGET) SARACEN
(— WRAP) SNOOD
(ACADEMIC —) DEAN
(BAKED SHEEP'S —) JAMES JEMMY
(BALD —) PILGARLIC
(BARBED —) FLUKE
(DRAGON'S —) RAHU
(EMPTY —) MONAD
(FLOWER —) DAISY ARNICA BUTTON PINBALL
(FLOWER —S) CURD ANTHEMIS
(FROM — TO FOOT) CANAPE
(LATHE —) POPPET
(NAIL —) ROSEHEAD
(POPPY —) POST
(PRINTED —) BOXHEAD
(SEED — OF FLAX) HOPPE
(SHRUNKEN —) TSANTSA
(PL.) GEONIM
(PREF.) CEPHAL(O) CORY(PH)(PHO) CRANIO
(SUFF.) CEPHALIC CEPHALOUS CEPHALUS CEPHALY PATE
HEADACHE HEAD SODA BUSTHEAD HEADWARK MIGRAINE CEPHALALGY
HEADBAND MITER MITRE VITTA CARCAN DIADEM TAENIA CIRCLET GARLAND CARCANET FOOTBAND STEPHANE
HEADBOROUGH VERGES
HEADCAP SETHEAD CAPELINE
HEADCLOTH ROMAL RUMAL
HEADDRESS FLY TOP TOY APEX COIF FRET HEAD HORN KELL PARE POUF TETE TIRE TOUR AEGIS AMPYX CROWN GABLE LAUTU PASTE POLOS PSHEM SHAKO TIARA TOWER VITTA ALMUCE ATTIRE ATTOUR BONNET CASQUE CORNET FAILLE HENNIN KENNEL KULLAH MOBCAP PINNER TIRING TUINGA BANDORE COMMODE FLANDAN MORTIER PSCHENT STEEPLE TABLITA THERESE TRESSON TUTULUS BILIMENT BINNOGUE BYCOCKET CAPRIOLE COIFFURE HEADGEAR HEADTIRE KAFFIYEH MASKETTE STEPHANE TRESSURE
(— OF DOGES) TOQUE
(— OF GODS) MODIUS
(— OF POPE) REGNUM
(— WITH LONG LAPPET) PINNER
(HIGH —) TOWER STEEPLE FONTANGE
(MEDIEVAL —) BARB
(WIDOW'S —) BANDORE
HEADED KNOTTED
(— OUT) RIZZOMED
(SUFF.) PATED
HEADER BINDER BONDER NOBBER SADDLE KNOBBER HEADSMAN STRETMAN
HEADFAST HEADROPE
HEADFIRST HEADLONG
HEADFOREMOST TOPSAIL
HEADFRAME POPPET GALLOWS
HEADGEAR (ALSO SEE HEADDRESS) HIVE PASTE BONNET BRIDLE HEADWEAR
HEADHUNTER LAKHER TAIYAL ATAIYAL QUIANGAN
HEADING END HEAD STOW LEMMA PILOT TROPE WICKET CAPTION DIPHEAD HEADILY STENTON WITCHET FOREHAND STENTING
(MASTHEAD —) EDITOR
HEADLAND KOP PEN RAS BILL CAPE HEAD MULL NASE NAZE NESS NOOK NOUP PEAK SCAW THRUM FORELAND PROMONTORY
HEADLESS ACEPHALOUS
(PREF.) ACEPHALO
HEADLINE HEAD STAR LABEL BANNER CAPTION DROPLINE SCREAMER STREAMER SCAREMONGER
HEADLONG FULL RANK AHEAD HASTY PRONE STEEP SUDDEN RAMSTAM TANTIVY GADARENE HEADLING RECKLESS PRECIPITATE
HEADMAN BAAS JARL CHIEF DATTO MALIK PATEL POMBO VIDAN ATAMAN CABEZA HETMAN INDUNA LOWDAH LULUAI POTAIL TOPMAN KOMARCH ALDERMAN CABOCEER CAPITANO HEADSMAN KONOHIKI MALGUZAR MOKADDAM PENGHULU PRINCEPS STAROSTA TENIENTE
HEADMASTER HEAD RECTOR REGENT PRECEPTOR
HEADMOST FOREMOST
HEADNOTE SYLLABUS
HEADPHONE
(PL.) CANS
HEADPIECE CAP POT BASKET CASQUE HELMET PALLET TESTER TREMOR BASINET BRASSET CASQUET CHAMFRON TESTIERE
HEADPIN KINGPIN
HEADQUARTERS BASE DEPOT YAMEN AGENCY FONDACO EXCHANGE BATTALION
(MILITARY —) SHAKO PENTAGON
HEADROPE BALK BAULK HEADLINE
HEADSET PHONES
HEADSHIP CHIEFTY
(SPIRITUAL —) KHALIFAT
HEADSPACE OUTAGE
HEADSTALL HALTER BRADOON BRIDOON JAQUIMA
HEADSTOCK POPPET
HEADSTONE STELE
HEADSTRONG RASH COBBY RACKLE STOCKY UNRULY HOTSPUR RAMSTAM VIOLENT WAYWARD PERVERSE STUBBORN
HEADWAITER CAPTAIN
HEADWAY WAY DENT SEAWAY WAYGATE HEADROOM
HEADWORD ENTRY
HEADY BOLD WINY NAPPY HUFFCAP
HEAL CURE HALE KNIT MEND SAIN AMEND COVER LEECH SALVE SOUND WHOLE PHYSIC RECURE SUPPLE TEMPER WARISH CLEANSE GUARISH RECOVER REDRESS RESTORE MEDICATE
(— OVER) INCARN
HEALD CAMB DUPE HAVEL
HEALED WHOLE
HEALER CURER ALTHEA SHAMAN

POWWOWER PRACTITIONER
(SUFF.) IATRIST
HEALING IATRIC POWWOW BALSAMIC CURATION IATRICAL SANATION
(PREF.) IATR(O)
(SUFF.) IATRIA IATRIC(S) IATRIST IATRY
HEALTH SAP HAIL HEAL SONS QUART SALEW LIKING PLEDGE SALUTE SANITY EUCRASY SLAINTE EUCRASIA TONICITY VALETUDE VALIDITY GESUNDHEIT
(— ORGANIZATION) HMO
(GOOD —) PROST PLIGHT PROSIT VERDURE GESUNDHEIT
(ILL —) SICKNESS
(NORMAL —) USUAL
(RESTORE CONDITION OF —) REHAB
(PREF.) HYGE(I) HYGI SALUTI
HEALTHFUL HEALTHY HYGIENIC SALUTARY SANATORY SANITARY
HEALTHY FIT FIER FIRM HALE IRON SAFE SANE SANO TIDY WELL BONNY HODDY QUART SOUND STOUT VALID ENTIRE HEARTY ROBUST BOUNCING LAUDABLE SALUTARY SANITARY VEGETOUS VIGOROUS
(PREF.) SANI
HEALTHY-LOOKING BONNY BONNIE
HEAP COP CUB HOT MOW PIE SOW TON BALE BING BULK DECK DESS HILL HOTT LEET PILE POKE POOK RAFF REEK RUCK SESS TASS TUMP AMASS CLAMP CLUMP COUCH CROWD SHOCK SORUS STACK WOPSE BURROW HIPPLE HOTTER ISLAND JALOPY MEILER OODLES QUARRY RICKLE RUCKLE SCRAPE SORITE TOORIE BOUROCK CUMULUS ENDORSE HAYCOCK HAYRICK HURROCK TOOROCK TUMMELS WINDROW BASURALE CONGERIES ACCUMULATE ACCUMULATION
(— HAY) UNCOCK
(— OF DEAD BODIES) CARNAGE
(— OF GAME) QUARRY
(— OF GRAIN) BING
(— OF MORTAR) BINK
(— OF ORE) PANEL MONTON
(— OF PRODUCE) BURY CLAMP
(— OF REFUSE) BURROW BASURAL
(— OF RUBBISH) GAGING
(— OF SILVER ORE) TORTA
(— OF SLAIN) CARNAGE
(— OF STONES) AHU MAN CAIRN SCRAE SCREE HURROCK MONTJOY
(— OF VEGETABLES) HOG
(— REPROACHES) KICK
(— TOGETHER) AGGEST HOWDER LUMBER CUMULATE
(— UP) HILL SACK AGGEST ACERVATE AGGERATE OVERHEAP
(COMBUSTIBLE —) PYRE
(MANURE —) HOTT MIXEN
(PROMISCUOUS —) RAFF
(STONE —) CAIRN
(PREF.) CUMULI CUMULO SOREDI SORI SORO THOMO
HEAPED COCKED ACERVATE CUMULATE
HEAR EAR LIST OYES OYEZ LEARN LITHE HARKEN LISTEN HEARKEN
(— CONFESSION) SHRIVE
(— DIRECTLY) IMPINGE
(PREF.) ACOU(O) AUDIO
HEARD AUDIBLE
(EASILY —) CLEAR
(VAGUELY —) RUMOROUS
HEARER AUDIENT AUDITOR
HEARING EAR LIST OYER AUDIT SOUND ASSIZE AUDIENCE AUDITION
(DISORDERED —) PARACUSIS
(PREF.) ACOU(O)
(SUFF.) ACOUSIA ACOUSIS ACUSIA ACUSIS
HEARKEN HARK HEAR HEED LIST TEND LITHE ATTEND HARKEN INTEND
HEARSAY REPORT ACCOUNT
HEARSE HACK CATAFALCO
HEART AB COR ANGI CORE GIST HATI PUMP RAAN SOUL YOLK ANGIO BOSOM BOWEL CHEER JARTA QUICK BREAST CENTER CENTRE DEPTHS HASLET MIDDLE NATURE TICKER VISCUS COURAGE EMOTION ESSENCE FEELING
(— OF DIXIE) ALABAMA
(— OF ROTTEN TREE) DADDOCK
(DEAR —) DILIS
(PREF.) ANGI ANGIO CARDI(A)(O) CORDI PHREN(O)
(AROUND THE —) PERICARDI(O)
(SUFF.) CARDIA CARDIUM
HEARTACHE SORROW
HEARTBEAT STROKE
(SUFF.) CROTIC
HEARTBREAK HOUSE (AUTHOR OF —) SHAW
(CHARACTER IN —) DUNN ELLIE MANGAN HESIONE MAZZINI HUSHABYE SHOTOVER UTTERWORD
HEARTBURN PYROSIS
HEART CHERRY GASKINS
HEARTEN BIELD CHEER HEART SPIRIT EMBOLDEN INSPIRIT
HEARTFELT DEAR DEEP REAL TRUE INFELT INWARD CORDIAL GENUINE SINCERE
HEARTH EARD SOLE TEST ASTRE CUPEL EARTH FOCUS FOGON FOYER INGLE SMOKE CHIMNEY
(— GODDESS) VESTA
HEARTH-MONEY FUMAGE
HEARTILY INLY AGOOD DEARLY FREELY WARMLY SHEERLY DINGDONG INWARDLY STRONGLY
HEARTINESS GOODWILL
HEARTLESS SARDONIC
HEARTLESSNESS CYNICISM
HEART OF MIDLOTHIAN (AUTHOR OF —) SCOTT
(CHARACTER IN —) MEG JOHN DAVID DEANS EFFIE MADGE BUTLER GEORGE JEANIE REUBEN GEORDIE PORTEUS STAUNTON ROBERTSON MURDOCKSON
HEARTSEASE PANSY
HEARTSICK (BE —) ACHE
HEARTSORE ACHING
HEARTTHROB DUNT FLAME
HEARTWOOD ALOES HEART SAPAN SPINE GUAYAB BUBINGA DURAMEN TRUEWOOD
HEARTY REAL WARM BUXOM COBBY FRECK HEAVY STOUT DEVOUT ENTIRE ROBUST STANCH BOBBISH CORDIAL EARNEST HEALTHY RAFFING SINCERE HEARTFUL VIGOROUS BOISTEROUS
HEAT HET HOT RUT SUN TAP BOIL FIRE GLOW SALT WARM ARDOR BEATH BROIL CALOR CAUMA CHAFE FEVER PRIDE PROUD STECH TEPOR TRIAL ACHAFE ANNEAL DEGREE DIGEST FERVOR HEATEN IGNITE SCORCH SEASON SIZZLE SPARGE WARMTH CALCINE CALORIC ENCHAFE FERMENT FLUSTER INCENSE INFERNO PASSION SWELTER UPERIZE CALIDITY PRESSURE MICROWAVE
(— GENTLY) SOAK
(— OF BATTLE) PRESS
(— SCRAP IRON) BUSHEL
(— SWEETEN, AND SPICE) MULL
(— TOBACCO) SAP
(ROWING —) REPECHAGE
(SCORCHING —) EWDER
(TRIAL —) REPECHAGE
(PREF.) CALORI PYR(O) THERM(ATO)(O)
(BURNING —) KAUMO
(MODIFIED BY —) COCTO
(SUFF.) THERM(Y)
HEATED WARM FIERCE STEAMY
HEATER GAT GUN FIRE COCKLE PISTOL SMOKER CHAFFER CHOFFER LATROBE
(WATER —) BOILER
HEATH BENT YETH BESOM BRIAR BRIER ERICA ERICAD COMMONS HEATHER RHODORA CRAKEBERRY
(PREF.) ERICO
HEATHCOCK GROUSE
HEATHEN AKKUM PAGAN ETHNIC PAYNIM GENTILE PROFANE SARACEN GENTILIC
HEATHENISM ODINISM OTHINISM PAGANISM
HEATHER BENT GRIG LING BROOM ERICA HEATH HADDER
HEATHERY LINGY
HEATH PEA CARMELE
HEATING BAKEOUT BURNING
HEATLESS ATHERMIC
HEAVE GAG BUNG HEFT HOVE KECK LIFE QUAP FETCH HOIST SCEND SURGE BUCKLE KECKLE POPPLE ESTUATE
HEAVEN SKY HIGH ABOVE BLISS DYAUS ETHER GLORY ASGARD CANAAN HIMMEL SVARGA SWARGA URANUS WELKIN KINGDOM OLYMPUS DEVALOKA EMPYREAL EMPYREAN PARADISE SVARLOKA VALHALLA
(12TH PART OF —) HOUSE
(PL.) ARCH LIFT LANGI HEIGHT REGION SPHERE ELEMENT TENGERE EMPYREAN KAMALOKA
(PREF.) URAN(I)(O) URANOSO
HEAVENLY ABOVE DIVINE ANGELIC BLESSED URANIAN ETHEREAL OLYMPIAN AMBROSIAL
HEAVEN'S MY DESTINATION
(AUTHOR OF —) WILDER
(CHARACTER IN —) BAT HERB BRUSH COREY EFRIM LOUIE MCCOY BURKIN CROFUT GEORGE JESSIE MARGIE MORRIE DOREMUS QUEENIE ROBERTA BLODGETT ELIZABETH
HEAVENWARD ZIONWARD
HEAVER COALY DANNER HEFTER
HEAVILY SOSS CLOIT CLYTE HEAVY PLUMP SADLY SOUSE SWACK
HEAVINESS DOLE HEFT GLOOM POISE WEIGHT GRAVITY
(— OF MIND) GLOOM
HEAVING HEFT SWELL
HEAVY FAT HOT SAD CLIT DEEP DOWF DULL HARD BEEFY BURLY DENSE DOWFF DUNCH GRAVE GREAT GROSS HEFTY HOGGY STIFF THARF THERF THICK WROTH CHARGE CLUMPY CLUMSY COSMIC DOUGHY DRAGGY HEARTY LEADEN LIVERY LOGGER SODDEN STODGY STRONG STUPID WOODEN INSIPID LABORED LIVERED LUMPING MASSIVE ONEROUS OUTSIZE PESANTE WEIGHTY CUMBROUS GRIEVOUS PERSANTE PREGNANT THUMPING PONDEROUS SATURNINE
(— LOOKING) HORSY
(PREF.) BARY GRAVI HADR(O)
HEAVY-FOOTED SOGGY LEADEN INFICETE
HEBDOMAD WEEK
HEBDOMADARY WEEKLY
HEBE (FATHER OF —) JUPITER
(HUSBAND OF —) HERCULES
(MOTHER OF —) JUNO
HEBER (GRANDFATHER OF —) ASHER
(SON OF —) SOCHO
(WIFE OF —) JAEL
HEBREW RABBINIC
HEBRIDES (ISLAND OF —) IONA HARRIS
(ISLAND 0F —) MULL SKYE ULST BARRA ISLAY LEWIS
HEBRON (FATHER OF —) KOHATH
HECATE TRIVIA
(FATHER OF —) PERSES
(MOTHER OF —) ASTERIA
HECKELPHONE OBOE HAUTBOY
HECKLE BAIT GIBE HACK RAZZ HARRY BADGER DERIDE HARASS HECTOR NEEDLE HATCHEL
HECTIC ETIK SEPTIC HECTIVE FEVERISH FRENETIC FRENZIED
HECTOLITER VAT
(5.82 —S) LEAGUER
HECTOR BAIT HUFF BULLY HARRY TEASE WORRY HARASS HECKLE BLUSTER BRAVADO BROWBEAT
(FATHER OF —) PRIAM
(MOTHER OF —) HECUBA
(SLAYER OF —) ACHILLES
(WIFE OF —) ANDROMACHE
HECUBA (DAUGHTER OF —) POLYXENA

(FATHER OF —) DYMAS CISSEUS
(HUSBAND OF —) PRIAM
(SON OF —) PARIS HECTOR HELENUS POLYDORUS
HEDDA GABLER (AUTHOR OF —) IBSEN
(CHARACTER IN —) THEA BRACK DIANA HEDDA EILERT GABLER GEORGE TESMAN ELVSTED JULIANA LOVBERG
HEDDLE CAMB DOUP HAVEL HEALD
(PL.) CAAM
HEDGE BAR HAW HAY HYE OXER SAVE BEARD EDDER FENCE FRITH FUDGE HOVER MOUND QUICK COPPER FRIGHT RADDLE ENCLOSE QUICKSET RUFFMANS SEPIMENT SURROUND THICKSET
(PREF.) SEPI SEPTATO
(SUFF.) SEPTATE
HEDGE BINDWEED CREEPER HELLWEED WOODBINE
HEDGEHOG ORCHEN TENREC URCHIN ECHINUS ERICIUS YLESPIL HEDGEPIG HERISSON
HEDGE LAUREL TARATA
HEDGE MUSTARD BANKWEED FLUXWEED
HEDGE NETTLE STACHYS
HEDGE PARSLEY HOGWEED
HEDGE-PRIEST PATRICO
HEDGE SPARROW DICKY DONEY DICKEY EYSOGE PHILIP CHANTER DUNNOCK HAYSUCK PINNOCK TITLING ACCENTOR
HEDGEWOOD LAYER
HEED EAR CARK COME CURE GAUM HEAR KEEP LOOK MIND NOTE OBEY RECK TEND TENT VISE WARE YEME AWAIT TASTE VALUE ATTEND INTENT NOTICE REGARD REMARK REWARD CAUTION OBSERVE RESPECT SUSPECT THOUGHT OBSERVATION
HEEDFUL WARE ATTENT DILIGENT VIGILANT REGARDFUL
(ANXIOUSLY —) JEALOUS
HEEDFULNESS CARE CAUTION
HEEDLESS DEAF RASH BLIND DIZZY GIDDY BLITHE REMISS UNWARY LANGUID UNHEEDY CARELESS LISTLESS MINDLESS RECKLESS WISTLESS NEGLECTFUL
HEEDLESSLY BLIND HEADLONG
HEEL CAD TIP BUTT CALX FROG JERK HIELD LOUSE SPIKE TALON DOTTLE BUDMASH INCLINE BOOTHEEL
(— IN) SHOUGH
(— OF GATE) HARR
(— OF HORSESHOE) SPONGE
(— OF SWORD BLADE) TALON RICASSO
(— OVER) SEEL TILT CAREEN
(PREF.) CALCANEO TAL(I)(O)
HEEL BEVEL RAND
HEELING ALIST
HEEL PLATE SHOD CLEAT
HEELTAPS LEES DREGS
HEFT WEIGHT
HEFTY HEAVY
HE-GOAT
(PREF.) HIRCO
HEIFER IO QUI QUEE QUEY QUOY BULLER STOCKER
(— IN 2ND YEAR) STIRK
(YEARLING —) BURLING
HEIGH-HO HECH
HEIGHT SUM ACME ALTO APEX FELL HIGH LOFT MOTE PINK TUNE CREST HICHT STATE ALTURE INCHES SUMMIT CEILING COMMAND HEIGHTH STATURE SUPREME ALTITUDE EMINENCE HAUTESSE SIDENESS VERTICAL ACROPOLIS
(— OF AMBITION) EVEREST
(— OF EXALTATION) RUFF RUFFE
(— OF EXCELLENCE) TIPTOP
(— OF FASHION) GO
(— OF INSPIRATION) ESTRO
(— OF PERFECTION) PRIME
(— OF PROSPERITY) GLORY
(— OF ROOM) STUD STUDDING
(— OF SAIL) HOIST
(GREATEST —) NOON SUMMIT ZENITH
(ROCKY —) KNOT
(PREF.) ACR(O) BATHO BATHY BATO HYPS(I)(O)
HEIGHTEN ENDOW EXALT FORCE RAISE ACCENT BOLSTER ELEVATE ENHANCE SUBLIME ESCALATE
(— FLAVOR) PETUNE
HEINOUS SWART CRYING WICKED SCARLET FLAGRANT GRIEVOUS ATROCIOUS
HEIR SCION SPRIG COHEIR HERITOR LEGATEE APPARENT PARCENER
(— APPARENT) ATHELING ETHELING
(CELTIC —) TANIST
(CELTIC CHIEF'S —) TANIST
(FEMALE —) DISTAFF
(PREF.) HEREDI HEREDO
HEIRESS BEGUM PORTIA FORTUNE HERITRIX
HEIRLOOM
(PL.) CIMELIA
HEL (FATHER OF —) LOKI
(MOTHER OF —) ANGURBODA
HELAH (HUSBAND OF —) ASHUR
(SON OF —) TEKOA
HELEB (FATHER OF —) BAANAH
HELEK (FATHER OF —) GILEAD
HELEN (PURSUER OF —) PARIS
HELENUS (FATHER OF —) PRIAM
(MOTHER OF —) HECUBA
(SON OF —) CESTRINUS
(WIFE OF —) ANDROMACHE
HELEZ (FATHER OF —) AZARIAH
HELI (SON OF —) JOSEPH
HELIANTHEMUM SUNROSE
HELICAL SPIRAL
HELICAON (FATHER OF —) ANTENOR
(MOTHER OF —) THEANO
(WIFE OF —) LAODICE
HELICOPTER HOVER COPTER CHOPPER MEDEVAC WINDMILL WHIRLYBIRD
(— TO REMOVE CASUALTIES) DUSTOFF
(ARMED —) GUNSHIP
(MOVE LIKE A —) HOVER
HELIOGRAPH (USE A —) SIGNAL
HELIOPOLIS ON
HELIOS HYPERION PHAETHON
(DAUGHTER OF —) CIRCE PASIPHAE
(FATHER OF —) HYPERION
(MOTHER OF —) THEIA
(SISTER OF —) EOS SELENE
(SON OF —) AEETES PHAETHON
HELIOSIS SUNBURN
HELIOTROPE HELIO BENNET SETWALL GIRASOLE TURNSOLE VALERIAN
HELIPORT SKYPORT
HELIX COIL SPIRAL
HELIXIN HEDERIN
HELL PIT POT HECK PAIN ABYSS AVICI BLAZE DEUCE HADES SHEOL BLAZES NARAKA TARTAR TOPHET TUNKET ABADDON GEHENNA HELLBOX INFERNO TORMENT TARTARUS BARATHRUM PERDITION PANDEMONIUM
(RIVER IN —) STYX LETHE
(PREF.) TARTARO
HELLBENDER TWEEG MENOPOME
HELLE (BROTHER OF —) PHRIXUS
(FATHER OF —) ATHAMAS
(MOTHER OF —) NEPHELE
HELLEBORE POKE BUGBANE ITCHWEED LINGWORT LUNGWORT NOSEWORT POKEROOT VERATRUM EARTHGALL
HELLEN (FATHER OF —) DEUCALION
(MOTHER OF —) PYRRHA
(SON OF —) DORUS AEOLUS XUTHUS
(WIFE OF —) ORSEIS
HELLER HALER HALERZ
HELLERI SWORDTAIL
HELL-FIRE BRIMSTONE
HELLGRAMMITE DOBSON SIALID CLIPPER CRAWLER SPRAWLER
HELLION TERROR
HELLISH HELLY AVERNAL SATANIC STYGIAN DEVILISH INFERNAL TOPHETIC
HELLKITE FIEND
HELLO CIAO HALLO HILLO HULLO HILLOA CHINCHIN
HELM KEY STEER STERN TIMON HELMET TIMBER STEERAGE
HELMET CAP POT CASK HELM HOOD ARMET CREST GALEA MAZER MOUND BARBEL BEAVER CASQUE CASTLE GALERA HEAUME MORION PALLET SALADE SALLET TESTER BASINET CASQUET GALERUM GALERUS AVENTAIL BURGANET BURGONET HEADGEAR KNAPSCAP SCHAPSKA SKULLCAP TARNHELM TESTIERE KNAPSKULL
(— PART) VENTAIL
(CRASH —) SKIDLID
(PITH —) TOPI TOPEE
(PREF.) GALEI
HELMET-SHAPED GALEATE
HELMSMAN PILOT STEER GLAUCUS TIMONEER
HELON (SON OF —) ELIAB
HELP AID BOT ABET AMOI BACK BOOT CAST LIFT STOP AVAIL BOOST FAVOR FRITH HEEZE RESET SPEED START STEAD YELDE ASSIST HELPER RELIEF REMEDY SECOND SUCCOR UPTAKE BENEFIT BESPEED BESTEAD CHEVISE COMFORT FORWARD FURTHER HELPING IMPROVE PRESIDY PROMOTE REDRESS RELIEVE SUPPORT SUSTAIN ADJUMENT BEFRIEND SUFFRAGE
(— FORWARD) FRANK FURTHER
(— IN GROWTH) NOURISH
(— ON) ADVANCE
(— ONWARD) FORWARD
(— OUT) FIRK
(HIRED —) LABOR
HELPER AID CAD FOAL HELP MATE PAGE ANSAR AIDANT BARBOY COOKEE DIENER FLUNKY JUMPER NIPPER TENTER WAITER ADJOINT ADJUNCT ADJUTOR ANCILLA CASHBOY GALOPIN SUMPMAN SWAMPER HELPMATE OFFSIDER SCULLION TROUNCER
(— IN GLASSWORKS) SNAPPER
(BLACKSMITH'S —) STRIKER
(CHIMNEY SWEEP'S —) CHUMMY
(COOK'S —) SLUSHY
(COOPER'S —) TUBBIE
(HORSESHOER'S —) FLOORMAN
(LEGAL —) PARACLETE
(PICKPOCKET'S —) BULKER
(YOUNG —) FOAL
HELPFUL GOOD AIDANT AIDFUL HELPLY SECOND SPEEDY USEFUL ADJUVANT HELPSOME OBLIGING SINGULAR SERVICEABLE
HELPING HELP ORDER AIDANT PORTION SERVING ADJUTORY ADJUVANT
(SECOND —) FOLLOW
HELPLESS NUMB SILLY ABJECT UNABLE AIDLESS FORLORN FECKLESS HAVELESS REDELESS
HELPLESSNESS ADYNAMIA
HELTER-SKELTER TAGRAG PELLMELL
HELVE HELM SHAFT
HELVE HAMMER OLIVER
HEM HUM WLO FELL SLIP WELT HEDGE SPLAY PURFLE TURNUP HEMMING TURNING SURROUND
(— AND HAW) HAVER
(— GLOVE) WRIST
(— IN) BOX LAP GIRD BEBAY BESET IMPALE BESIEGE COMPASS ENCLOSE ENVIRON STRAITEN SURROUND
(— IN FISH) EBB
(— OF SAIL) TABLING
(— OF TROUSERS) CUFF
(PREF.) LIMBI
HEMAM (BROTHER OF —) HORI
(FATHER OF —) LOTAN
HEMAN (FATHER OF —) JOEL ZERAH
(GRANDFATHER OF —) SAMUEL
HEMATITE ORE OLIGIST SANGUINE
HEMDAN (FATHER OF —) DISHON
HEMICRANIA MIGRAINE
HEMIEPES ENOPLION
HEMIMORPHITE CALAMINE
HEMIOLIC SESCUPLE
HEMISTICH SECTION
HEMITHEA (BROTHER OF —) TENES
(FATHER OF —) CYCNUS
(MOTHER OF —) PROCLEA

HEMLOCK BUNK CASH KELK BENNET CICUTA COWBANE DEATHIN SHINWOOD
HEMOPHILIAC BLEEDER
HEMORRHAGE STAXIS APOPLEXY BLEEDING HEMOPTOE PETECHIA
HEMOSTATIC RHATANY ERIGERON
HEMP IFE KEF KIF TOW BANG CARL POOA RINE SANA SUNN ABACA BHANG DACHA DAGGA FIQUE GANJA HURDS MURVA RAMIE SABZI SISAL AMBARY CABUYA FIMBLE LIAMBA NALITA SINAWA AMYROOT CABULLA GAGROOT NIYANDA PANGANE PITEIRA SOSQUIL BIRDSEED CANNABIS CHUCKING LOCOWEED NECKWEED NEPENTHE MARIJUANA
(KIND OF —) ALOE
(REFUSE —) HARDS HURDS
(PREF.) CANNABI
HEMP AGRIMONY EUPATORY HEMPWEED
HEMPEN NOGGEN
HEMP NETTLE IRONWORT
HEMPWEED BONESET DUCKBLIND
HEN FOWL BIDDY CHUCK LAYER BROODY MABYER PULLET SULTAN CLOCKER HOVERER PARTLET LANGSHAN
(— THAT HAS NOT LAID) TOWDIE
(— WITH CHICKENS) CLUCK
(— WITH SHORT LEGS) GRIG
(BROODY —) SITTER
(FATHER OF —) ZEPHANIAH
(FATTENED —) POULARD
(MUD —) COOT
(1-YEAR-OLD —) YEAROCK
HENBANE HEBENON CHENILLE
HENCE AWAY ERGO HYNE THUS AVAUNT HETHEN HEREOUT
HENCEFORTH YET ERGO HENCE
HENCHMAN FELLOW SATRAP SERVANT FOLLOWER RETAINER UNDERLING
HEN COOP CAVY CAVIE
HENGEST (BROTHER OF —) HORSA
(KINGDOM FOUNDED BY —) KENT
(SON OF —) AESC
HEN HARRIER FALLER KATABELLA
(IMMATURE —) RINGTAIL
(MALE —) MILLER
HENHOUSE ROOST
HENNA MENDY ALCANNA ALHENNA CAMPHIRE
HENNIN STEEPLE
HENPECK NAG
HENRY QUAD HAWKIN SECOHM HEINRICH QUADRANT
HENRY ESMOND (AUTHOR OF —) THACKERAY
(CHARACTER IN —) HOLT FRANK HENRY JAMES MOHUN ESMOND RACHEL STUART BEATRIX FRANCIS
HENRY IV-PART I (AUTHOR OF —) SHAKESPEARE
(CHARACTER IN —) JOHN OWEN PETO BLUNT HENRY PERCY POINS EDMUND SCROOP THOMAS VERNON WALTER DOUGLAS HOTSPUR MICHAEL QUICKLY RICHARD BARDOLPH FALSTAFF GADSHILL MORTIMER ARCHIBALD GLENDOWER LANCASTER WESTMORELAND
HENRY IV-PART II (AUTHOR OF —) SHAKESPEARE
(CHARACTER IN —) DAVY DOLL FANG JOHN PETO WART BLUNT GOWER HENRY POINS RUMOR SNARE FEEBLE MORTON MOULDY PISTOL SCROOP SHADOW SURREY THOMAS MOWBRAY QUICKLY SHALLOW SILENCE TRAVERS WARWICK BARDOLPH BULLCALF CLARENCE FALSTAFF HARCOURT HASTINGS HUMPHREY COLEVILLE LANCASTER TEARSHEET WESTMORELAND NORTHUMBERLAND
HENRY V (AUTHOR OF —) SHAKESPEARE
(CHARACTER IN —) NYM GREY JAMY YORK ALICE BATES COURT GOWER HENRY LEWIS EXETER ISABEL PISTOL SCROOP THOMAS BEDFORD BOURBON CHARLES MONTJOY ORLEANS WARWICK BARDOLPH BURGUNDY FLUELLEN GRANDPRE RAMBURES WILLIAMS ERPINGHAM KATHARINE MACMORRIS SALISBURY GLOUCESTER WESTMORELAND
HENRY VIII (AUTHOR OF —) SHAKESPEARE
(CHARACTER IN —) ANNE VAUX BUTTS DENNY HENRY SANDS BULLEN LOVELL SURREY THOMAS WOLSEY ANTHONY BRANDON CRANMER NORFOLK SUFFOLK CAMPEIUS CAPUCIUS CROMWELL GARDINER GRIFFITH NICHOLAS PATIENCE GUILDFORD KATHARINE BUCKINGHAM ABERGAVENNY
HENRY VI-PART I (AUTHOR OF —) SHAKESPEARE
(CHARACTER IN —) JOAN JOHN LUCY HENRY BASSET EDMUND TALBOT THOMAS VERNON ALENCON BEDFORD CHARLES RICHARD SUFFOLK WARWICK WILLIAM BEAUFORT BURGUNDY FASTOLFE GARGRAVE MARGARET MORTIMER REIGNIER GLANSDALE LAPUCELLE SALISBURY WOODVILLE GLOUCESTER PLANTAGENET
HENRY VI-PART II (AUTHOR OF —) SHAKESPEARE
(CHARACTER IN —) SAY CADE DICK HUME IDEN JACK JOHN VAUX BEVIS GOFFE HENRY PETER SMITH EDWARD GEORGE HORNER SCALES ELEANOR HOLLAND MATTHEW MICHAEL RICHARD SIMPCOX STANLEY SUFFOLK WARWICK BEAUFORT CLIFFORD HUMPHREY JOURDAIN MARGARET SOMERSET STAFFORD ALEXANDER SALISBURY SOUTHWELL BUCKINGHAM BOLINGBROKE PLANTAGENET
HENRY VI-PART III (AUTHOR OF —) SHAKESPEARE
(CHARACTER IN —) BONA HUGH JOHN HENRY LEWIS MARCH EDMUND EDWARD EXETER GEORGE OXFORD RIVERS BOURBON NORFOLK RICHARD RUTLAND STANLEY WARWICK CLIFFORD HASTINGS MARGARET MONTAGUE MORTIMER PEMBROKE SOMERSET STAFFORD MONTGOMERY PLANTAGENET WESTMORELAND NORTHUMBERLAND
HEP (NOT —) ICKY
HEPATICA AI TRINITY
HEPATITIS FAVISM JAUNDICE
HEPHAESTUS LEMNIAN
(FATHER OF —) ZEUS
(MOTHER OF —) HERA
(WIFE OF —) CHARIS
HEPHZIBAH (HUSBAND OF —) HEZEKIAH
(SON OF —) MANASSEH
HER A ARE SHE HARE HERS HURE
HERA JUNO
(FATHER OF —) CRONOS KRONOS
(HUSBAND OF —) ZEUS
HERALD BODE LYON USHER BEADLE DECLARE FORERUN PREFACE STENTOR USHERIN BLAZONER PRECURSE PROCLAIM ROTHESAY MESSENGER
HERALDIC FECIAL FETIAL
HERALDRY ARMORY
HERB ANU APE PIA RUE UDO WAD ALOE ANET ANYU ARUM COUS DILL HEMP IRID LEEK MINT MOLY POLY RAPE RUTA SAGE SOLA WOAD WORT YAMP YARB AVENS AWIWI BLITE BRUSH CANNA CHIVE CREAT CROUT DAGGA DAISY DRABA GALAX GAURA GILIA GRASS HOSTA LOASA LUFFA MEDIC MUNGO NANCY ORACH SEDGE SEDUM SENNA SOLAH STOCK SULLA TANSY THYME ZIZIA ALLIUM ARALIA ARNICA AXSEED BAGPOD BAMBAN BANANA BLINKS BORAGE CANCER CATGUT CATNIP CENIZO CICELY CISTUS CLOVER COCASH COLEUS CONIUM COWISH COWPEA CRAMBE ELODEA ENDIVE ERYNGO FENNEL GALAXY GINGER HARMEL HYSSOP KOCHIA KRIGIA KRIGLA LOOFAH LOVAGE RAMTIL RATTLE ROBERT SESAME SESELI SHEVRI WASABI ABRONIA ALPINIA ALTHAEA ALYSSUM AMORPHA AMSONIA ANCHUSA ANEMONE ANGELON ARACHIS BABIANA BABROOT BARTSIA BIRDEYE BLINKER BONESET BUGSEED BUGWEED CHICORY CUDWEED CULVERS DEWDROP DYEWEED EPISCIA ERODIUM FREESIA FROGBIT FUMMORY GERBERA GINSENG GOITCHO GOSMORE GOUAREE GUAYULE GUNNERA HARMALA HEDEOMA HENBANE HERBLET IRESINE ISOLOMA JONQUIL LABIATE LEWISIA LINNAEA MARANTA MIMULUS MUDWEED MUDWORT MULLEIN MUSTARD NAILROD NEMESIA NIEVETA PAVONIA PETUNIA PINESAP PINWEED PUCHERA ROSELLE SAFFLOR SALSIFY SEEDBOX SKIRRET SOWBANE SPIGNEL STACHYS ABELMOSK ABELMUSK ACANTHUS ACONITUM AGERATUM ALOCASIA ALUMROOT AMBROSIA AMMOBIUM ANGELICA ARGEMONE ASPHODEL BEDSTRAW CALATHEA CAPEWEED CARELESS CENTAURY CHENILLE COLLOMIA COSTMARY COWWHEAT CRASSULA CROMWELL DANEWEED DEERWEED DROPWORT ECHINOPS EGGPLANT EREMURUS ERIGERON EUCHARIS FEVERFEW FLEABANE FOWLFOOT GAYWINGS GERARDIA GESNERAD GESNERIA GHETCHOO GLOXINIA GOATROOT GUZMANIA HAREBELL HEPATICA HEUCHERA HIBISCUS HOLEWORT HONEWORT HOROKAKA HUDSONIA IRONWEED LICORICE LOCOWEED MANDRAKE MANFREDA MANYROOT MARDOWRT MARJORAM MARTYNIA MURRNONG PHACELIA PINKROOT PLUMBAGO POKEWEED SACALINE SAINFOIN SALICORN SAMPHIRE SANDBURR SCABIOUS SHINLEAF SMALLAGE SNOWDROP SOAPROOT SOAPWORT STAPELIA SUNDROPS TETRIFOL TOCALOTE WOODRUFF MONEYWORT PUSSYTOES RUDBECKIA SAXIFRAGE SPIKENARD NASTURTIUM PENNYCRESS PERIWINKLE SARRACENIA
(— COUNTERACTING POISON) CANCER
(— OTHER THAN GRASS) FORB
(AROMATIC —) MINT ANISE CLARY CATNIP CAAPEBA CHERVIL DITTANY
(BIENNIAL —) LEEK PARSLEY ANGELICA
(BULBOUS —) LILY CANNA ALLIUM CRINUM GARLIC NERINE SQUILL BABIANA SHALLOT DOGTOOTH SLANGKOP
(FABULOUS —) MOLY PANAX PANACE
(FLOATING —) FROGBIT
(FORAGE —) FITCHES GOITCHO
(MEDITERRANEAN —) CRAMBE
(MYTHICAL —) MOLY
(POISONOUS —) CONIUM HEMLOCK MONKSHOOD
(PL.) POTAGERIE
HERBAGE HAY BITE GRASS GRAZE PICHI ADONIS SACATE ZACATE GRAZING
HERB EVE IVA IVY
HERB GRACE RUE
HERBICIDE IPE DIQUAT DIURON SILVEX DALAPEN DALAPON LINURON MONURON ATRAZINE PARAQUAT PICLORAM PROPANIL SIMAZINE
HERB IMPIOUS DOWNWEED HOARWORT
HERB PARIS TRUE ONEBERRY TRUELOVE
HERB ROBERT JENNY ROBIN ROBERT
HERCULEAN HUGE
HERCULES ERCLES ALCIDES HERSHEF OETAEUS OVILLUS HERAKLES

(BROTHER OF —) IPHICLES
(CAPTIVE OF —) IOLE
(FATHER OF —) JUPITER
(MOTHER OF —) ALCMENA
(WIFE OF —) HEBE MEGARA DEIANIRA
HERCULES ALLHEAL OPOPANAX
HERCULES-CLUB ARALIA IVYWORT RUEWORT SHOTBUSH
HERD BOW GAM MOB BAND CREW GAME GANG HEAD RACE ROUT RUCK TAIL TEAM TRIP DROVE FLOCK HEARD TROOP CAVIYA CHOUSE HIRSEL HUDDLE MANADA MEINIE REMUDA SPREAD THRAVE CREAGHT RANGALE SHEPHERD
(— CATTLE) TAIL WRANGLE
(— OF CATTLE) FLOTE
(— OF COLTS) RAG
(— OF HORSES) RACE HARAS HARRAS REMUDA
(— OF SEALS) PATCH
(— OF WHALES) GAM
(— OF WILD SWINE) SOUNDER
HERDBOY BOUCHAL
HERDER DROVER FEEDER HERDBOY
HERDSMAN AMOS SENN GAUCHO HERDER LOOKER PASTOR HERDBOY LLANERO THYRSIS VAQUERO BEASTMAN DAMOETAS GARTHMAN NEATHERD PASTORAL PASTURER RANCHERO SWANHERD WRANGLER
HERE ICI ADSUM READY WHERE HEREAT HITHER PRESENT
(— AND THERE) ABOUT ABROAD AROUND PASSIM SPARSIM
HEREAFTER BEYOND
HEREDITAMENT LAND
HEREDITARY INBORN INNATE KINDLY LINEAL PATERNAL
HEREDITY (— UNIT) RNA
HEREIN WITHIN
HERESY DOCETISM KETZEREI MISBELIEF
HERETIC BUGGER KETZER ZINDIQ LOLLARD PATARIN PROFANE SECTARY JUDAIZER MISCREANT SABELLIUS MISBELIEVER
(PL.) ACEPHALI
HERETICAL HERETIC HETERODOX MISCREANT
HERETO HITHER
HERETOFORE ERST BEFORE ERENOW EREWHILE FORMERLY
HEREWARD THE WAKE (AUTHOR OF —) KINGSLEY
(CHARACTER IN —) BRAND GODIVA MARTIN WILLIAM ALFTRUDA HEREWARD TORFRIDA LIGHTFOOT
HERITAGE DESCENT HEIRDOM HEIRSHIP PATRIMONY
HERMA MERCURY
HERMAPHRODITE MOPH SCRAT ANDROGYNOUS
HERMAPHRODITIC BISEXED BISEXUAL MONOECIOUS
HERMAPHRODITISM GYNANDRY
HERMAPHRODITUS (FATHER OF —) MERCURY
(MOTHER OF —) VENUS
HERMENEGILD (FATHER OF —) LEOVIGILD
HERMES MERCURY AGORAIOS CYLLENIUS
(FATHER OF —) ZEUS
(MOTHER OF —) MAIA
HERMIA (BELOVED OF —) LYSANDER
(FATHER OF —) EGEUS
HERMIONE (FATHER OF —) MENELAUS
(HUSBAND OF —) PYRRHUS
(MOTHER OF —) HELEN
HERMIT ARME MUNI HANIF MINIM ANCHOR SANTON SULLEN ASCETIC EREMITE RECLUSE TAPASVI ANCHORET MARABOUT SOLITARY
HERMITAGE ASHRAM ASHRAMA RECLUSE
HERNIA BURST RAMEX BREACH RUPTURE MEROCELE
(SUFF.) CELE COELE COELUS
HERO CID KIM RAB AJAX EGIL IDAS KAMI MAUI NALA NATA OFFA RINK YIMA ADAPA BERNE DEBON ETANA FAUST GHAZI HODER HOTHR IRAYA KIPPS MARKO ORSON TASSO TIMON VOTAN EGMONT FIGARO GIDEON GOLIAS HEROIC IASION IOLAUS MAUGIS MINYAS OSSIAN PELHAM PENROD RIENZI ROLAND RUSTAM SIGURD TARZAN USHEEN VATHEK ALCESTE BOGATYR DEMIGOD FAUSTUS GLUSKAP GRINDER INGOMAR JAMSHID MACBETH MANRICO MARMION MAZEPPA ORLANDO OTHELLO PALADIN RAFFLES TANCRED THALABA THESEUS TROILUS ULYSSES VOLPONE WERTHER WIDSITH WIELAND ACADEMUS ARGONAUT CHAMPION FANSHAWE FERUMBAS FRITHJOF GAEDHEAL GILGAMES LAMMIKIN MALAGIGI MORGANTE OROONOKO PALMERIN PARSIFAL PERICLES RASSELAS RODOMONT SUPERMAN TRISTRAM WAVERLEY
(LOVER OF —) LEANDER
(TRIBAL —) JUDGE
HERODIAS (BROTHER OF —) AGRIPPA
(FATHER OF —) ARISTOBULUS
(HUSBAND OF —) HEROD
HEROIC EPIC FELL GREAT NOBLE EPICAL FEATLY EXTREME GALLANT VALIANT FEARLESS HEROICAL HOMERIAN INTREPID SPLENDID
HEROIN JUNK SCAG SKAG SNOW HORSE JONES SMACK STUFF
HEROINE AIDA EMMA MIMI RUTH JULIE MEDEA NORMA SEDNA THAIS ESTHER FEDORA GUDRUN HELENA JUDITH JULIET MARTHA MIGNON PAMELA PHEDRE RAMONA ROMOLA SALOME SILVIA TRILBY UNDINE ERMINIA EVELINA GALATEA GINEVRA GRAINNE HEROESS MONIMIA SHIRLEY ZENOBIA ZULEIKA ATALANTA ISABELLA MARGARET PATIENCE POMPILIA ROSMUNDA SOFRONIA
HEROISM VALOR BRAVERY COURAGE PROWESS
HERON QUA POKE SOCO CRAIG CRANE EGRET FRANK HERNE PADDY QUAWK YABOA AIGRET GAULIN KIALEE KOTUKU QUAKER SQUAWK BITTERN CRABIER GOLIATH HANDSAW QUABIRD SQUACCO BOATBILL GAULDING HERONSEW UMBRETTE
(— FLOCK) SIEGE
HERON'S-BILL ERODIUM
HERPES DARTRE TETTER
HERPES ZOSTER ZONA SHINGLES
HERRING ALEC BRIT CHUB SHAD SILD BLOAT CAPON CISCO DORAB HILSA MARAY MATIE SPRAT KIPPER POLLAN TAILOR ANCHOVY BLOATER CLUPEID NAILROD ROLLMOP SHADINE BLUEBACK BRISLING BUCKLING CROPSHIN GRAYBACK QUODDIES SCUDDAWN STRADINE
(— SEASON) DRAVE
(— UNIT) LAST MAZE
(FEMALE —) RAUN
(LAKE —) KIYI CISCO
(RED —) CAPON SOLDIER
(SMOKED —) BLOATER
(YOUNG —) COB BRIT SILD SILE SILL SOIL WILE BRITT COBBE MATIE SPRAT SARDINE SPERLING
(2, 3 OR 4 —S) WARP
HERS HERN SHISN
HERSE (FATHER OF —) CECROPS
(SISTER OF —) AGRAULOS
(SON OF —) CEPHALUS
HERSELF HI HER SELF ITSELF
HERSEY (— LOCALE) ADANO
HERSHEF ARSAPHES
HESHVAN BUL CHESHVAN
HESIONE (FATHER OF —) LAOMEDON
(HUSBAND OF —) TELAMON
(RESCUER OF —) HERCULES
HESITANCY HANG
(— IN SPEECH) BALBUTIES
HESITANT SHY CAGY CHARY GROPING HALTING RETICENT SUSPENSE
(NOT —) FACILE
HESITATE COY HEM BALK STAY STOP CHECK CRANE DEMUR DOUBT FORCE PAUSE STALL STAND STICK SUSSY WAVER BOGGLE FALTER HANKER LINGER MAMMER RELUCT SCOTCH TARROW TARTLE BALANCE PROFFER SCRUPLE STAGGER STAMMER SWITHER THRIMBLE
(— IN SPEAKING) HACKER
HESITATING JUBUS HALTING BACKWARD DOUBTFUL JUBEROUS TIMOROSO
HESITATION HANG HINK WAND PAUSE STAND STICK SUSSY SWITHER
(SPEECH —) STAMMER
HESPERUS VESPER
HESRON (FATHER OF —) REUBEN
HESSIAN BURLAP
HESTIA (FATHER OF —) KRONOS
(MOTHER OF —) RHEA
HETAERA LAIS THAIS PHRYNE MISTRESS
HETER-
(PREF.) XEN(O)
HETERODOX HERETIC SINISTRAL
HETERODOXY HERESY CACODOXY
HETEROGENEOUS MIXED MOTLEY UNLIKE DIVERSE PIEBALD ASSORTED
HETEROMYS SACCOMYS
HETEROSEXUAL STRAIGHT
HETEROTROPHIC HOLOZOIC
HETEROXENOUS INDIRECT
HETEROZYGOUS CROSS SPLIT IMPURE
HETMAN ATAMAN
HEW CUT HAG CHIP SNAG STUB SHRED SLICE
(— OUT) CARVE
(— STONE) CHAR
HEWER JOEY GETTER GIDEON FACEMAN
HE WHO GETS SLAPPED (AUTHOR OF —) ANDREYEV
(CHARACTER IN —) ALFRED ZINIDA BENZANO BRIQUET JACKSON MANCINI REGNARD CONSUELO
HEX WITCH VOODOO WHAMMY
HEXAGON SEXANGLE
HEXAGONAL HEX DIMETRIC
HEXAGRAM PENTACLE
HEXAMETER MIURUS RHOPALIC
(DACTYLIC —) EPOS HEROIC
HEXOBARBITAL EVIPAL
HEXOSAN MANNAN GLUCOSAN MANNOSAN
HEYDAY MAY HIGHDAY
HEY PRESTO SUDDENLY
HEZEKIAH (FATHER OF —) AHAZ NEARIAH
(MOTHER OF —) ABI
HEZION (SON OF —) TABRIMON
HEZRON (FATHER OF —) PHAREZ REUBEN
HIATUS GAP BREAK CHASM BREACH HIATAL LACUNA
HIBERNATE SHACK WINTER SLUMBER
HIBERNATING LATITANT
HIBERNIA EIRE ERIN IRELAND JUVERNA
HIBERNIAN IRISHMAN IVERNIAN
HIBISCUS ROSELLE
HICCUP YEX YOX HICK HOCKET HOQUET SINGULTUS
HICK BOOR HIND JAKE BACON BUSHMAN CORNBALL CHAWBACON
HICKORY NOGAL PIGNUT BULLNUT SHAGBARK
HICKORY NUT TRYMA PIGNUT BULLNUT KISKITOM
HICKWALL ECCLE HECKLE HICKWAY
HID LATENT
HIDDEN HID SHY DEEP DERN LOST TECT BLIND CLOSE DOGGO DUSKY PERDU PRIVY ARCANE BURIED COVERT INNATE LATENT MASKED MYSTIC OCCULT SECRET VEILED BOSOMED CLOUDED COVERED CRYPTIC OBSCURE RECLUSE SUBTILE ABDITIVE ABSTRUSE CRYPTOUS HIDEAWAY PALLIATE SCREENED SECLUDED SNEAKING CRYPTICAL RECONDITE
(PREF.) CRYPT(O) KRYPT(O)

HIDE HOD WRY BUFF BURY CASE CROP DARK DERN FELL FELT HILL HOOD JOUK LEAN MASK PELL PELT SCAB SKIN SKUG SNUG STOW VEIL WELL BELIE BELLY BLIND CACHE CLOAK CLOUD COUCH COVER DITCH EARTH FLANK GLOSS LAYNE LOSHE MANSE PLANT SHADE SPOIL STASH STEER TAPIS BURROW BUSHEL CASATE EMBOSS ENCASE ENCAVE ENWOMB FOREST HUDDLE IMBOSK LIELOW MANENT PELAGE SCREEN SHADOW SHIELD SHROUD ABSCOND CONCEAL COWHIDE EMBOWEL FLAUGHT OBCLUDE OVERLAY SECLUDE SECRETE SPREADY TAPPICE CARUCATE DISGUISE ENSCONCE HIDELAND HOODWINK PALLIATE PLOWLAND SQUIRREL SUPPRESS CLANDESTINE
(— AS AN EEL) MUD
(— IN WOODS) WOOD BUSHWACK
(— UNDER) BUSHEL
(CALF'S —) DEACON
(DRESSED —S) LEATHER
(HALF OF —) BEND
(HAVING SOFT —) MELLOW
(SHEEP'S —) SLAT
(TANNED —) CROP
(THICKEST —S) BACKS
(UNDRESSED —) KIP
(PL.) JUFTI JUFTS
(PREF.) DERM(AT)(ATO)(O) DORA
(SUFF.) DERM(A)(ATOUS)(IA)(IS)(Y)
HIDE-AND-GO-SEEK BOGLE WHOOP BOGGLE
HIDEAWAY MEW LAIR SHANGRILA
HIDEBOUND BORNE NARROW BIGOTED
HIDEOUS FELL GASH GRIM UGLY AWFUL TOADY DEFORM GRIMLY GRISLY HORRID ODIOUS OGRISH GHASTLY DEFORMED DREADFUL FIENDISH GRUESOME HORRIBLE SHOCKING TERRIBLE MONSTROUS
HIDEOUSLY FOULLY
HIDING DERN MICHING SECRECY ABDITIVE HIDEAWAY
HIDING-PLACE CACHE
HIEMAL WINTRY
HIERACIUM DINALE HAWKWEED
HIERARCHY SATRAPY
HIEROGLYPH CIPHER
(PL.) SIGNARY
HIEROPHANT PRIEST
HIGGLE HUCK HAGGLE
HIGH UP ALT AIRY DEAR HAUT MAIN MUCH RANK TALL ACUTE ALOFT BRENT CHIEF CLOSE DRUNK FIRST GREAT HAUTE LOFTY MERRY NOBLE SHARP SPACY STEEP BOMBED COSTLY RIPPED SHRILL SPACEY STONED ZONKED EMINENT EXALTED HAUGHTY STICKLE SUBLIME TOPPING VIOLENT ELEVATED FOREMOST PIERCING TOWERING WIPEDOUT SPACEDOUT
(— AND MIGHTY) HOGEN
(— IN CHROMA) STRONG
(— IN PITCH) ALT ACUTE
(— IN RANK) MUCH
(— ON DRUGS) STONED
(— PITCH) ORTHIAN
(BE —) FLY
(MOST —) SERENE
(PRETTY —) STIFFISH
(VERY —) TAUNT RAREFIED RARIFIED
(PREF.) ALTI HYPS(I)(O)
(ON —) HYPS(I)(O)
HIGHBORN NOBLE GENEROUS
HIGHBOY TALLBOY
HIGHBRED SOFT REFINED
HIGHBROW EGGHEAD
HIGH-CLASS CLASSY UPSTAGE
HIGH-CLIMBER TOPPER
HIGH-COLORED BLOWSY BLOWZY
HIGH-CROWNED COPATAIN
HIGHER OVER ABOVE SENIOR SUPERIOR
(PREF.) SUPER(O) SUPRA
HIGHEST ACE TOP HEXT FIRST EXTREME MAXIMAL SUPREME BUNEMOST HIGHMOST OVERMOST
(— IN DEGREE) LAST
HIGHFALUTIN PAUGHTY
HIGH-FED BEANY
HIGH-FLAVORED GAMY
HIGH-FLOWN TALL TUMID
HIGH-HANDED BOSSY CAVALIER
HIGH-HAT SNOOT
HIGHLAND RAND CERRO
HIGHLANDER GAEL TARTAN NAINSEL PLAIDMAN REDSHANK TREWSMAN UPLANDER
(PL.) TREWS TARTAN
HIGHLIGHT ADORN HEIGHTEN PINPOINT SALIENCE
HIGHLY THRICE
HIGH-MINDED HAUGHT
HIGHNESS ALTESSE ALTEZZA ALTITUDE
(— OF PRICE) DEARTH
HIGH-PITCHED ACUTE PROUD PIPING TREBLE ORTHIAN SHRIEKY
HIGH-POWERED INTENSE MAGNUM
HIGH-PRICED DEAR
HIGH-RIGGER TOPPER
HIGH-SOUNDING BIG BOMBAST MAGNIFIC SONORANT SONOROUS SOUNDING
HIGH-SPIRITED METTLED CRANK FIERY FIERCE LIVELY GALLANT GINGERY RAMPANT CAVALIER VASCULAR
HIGH-SPIRITEDNESS SPLEEN
HIGH-STRUNG HYPER TENSE NERVOUS
HIGHTAIL (— IT) LEAVE SCRAM
HIGH-TONED TONY DICTY DICKTY
HIGHWAY VIA WAY BELT ITER PATH PIKE ROAD TOBY BOLOS ARTERY CAUSEY COURSE RUMPAD SKYWAY STREET BELTWAY CALZADA FREEWAY RAMPIRE THRUWAY ARTERIAL AUTOBAHN BROADWAY CAUSEWAY CHAUSSEE HIGHROAD MOTORWAY SPEEDWAY
(— ROBBERY) TOBY
(LOCATED OFF THE —) DEVIOUS
(PART OF —) EXIT GORE LANE LOOP RAMP ACCESS BRIDGE ISLAND MEDIAN DIVIDER ROADWAY JUNCTION OVERPASS SHOULDER UNDERPASS INTERSECTION
HIGHWAYMAN PAD RIDER SCAMP BANDIT CUTTER PADDER RODMAN BRIGAND FOOTPAD LADRONE PRANCER RODSMAN TOBYMAN BIDSTAND DAMASTES HIGHTOBY HIJACKER LANCEMAN OUTRIDER BANDOLERO
HIGH-WROUGHT INTENSE
HIKE UP MUSH WALK MARCH RAISE TRAMP RAMBLE ADVANCE INCREASE
HILARIOUS MAD RORTY JOVIAL JOCULAR RAUGHTY CHIRPING GLORIOUS
HILARITY GIG JOY GLEE LAUGH MIRTH GAIETY GAYETY DEVILRY JOLLITY WHOOPEE MERRIMENT
HILKIAH (FATHER OF —) AMZI HOSAH
(SON OF —) ELIAKIM GEMARIAH JEREMIAH
HILL BEN DEN DUN HOE HOW KOP LOW PUY TOR VAN ALTO BANK BERG BRAE BULT BUMP COTE DAGH DENE DOWN DRUM FELL HIGH HONE KNAP LOMA LUMP MESA MOOR MOTE NOUP PAHA TOFT ZION BARGH BUTTE CERRO CLIFF COAST HEUGH KNOCK KNOLL KOPJE MORRO MOUND MOUNT STILL SWELL TELLE WATCH ASCENT BARROW BEACON COBBLE COLLIS COPPLE CUESTA HEIGHT HEUVEL LOMITA SPRUNT STRONE CAELIAN CAPITOL COLLINE DRUMLIN HILLOCK NUNATAK PICACHO SOWBACK VIMINAL AREOPAGY CATOCTIN DRUMLOID FOOTHILL MONTICLE QUIRINAL MONADNOCK
(— OF SAND) DENE DUNE
(— OF STRATIFIED DRIFT) KAME
(— UP) MOLD
(ARABIAN —) TEL
(BROAD-TOPPED —) LOMA
(CONICAL —) LAW PAP PINGO
(CRAGGY —) TOR
(FORTIFIED —) RATH
(HIGH —) BEN
(ISOLATED —) HUM TOFT BARGH BUTTE
(LAST —) STRONE
(LOW —) HOW BAND DENE WOLD KOPPIE SOWBACK
(NIPPLELIKE —) PAP
(NORTH AFRICAN —) JEBEL DJEBEL
(RESIDUAL —) CATOCTIN
(ROUNDED —) DODD HONE MAMELON
(SAND —) DENE
(SHARP-POINTED —) KIP KIPP PIKE
(SMALL —) KNAP KNOLL KOPJE KOPPIE HILLOCK MOLEHILL
(STEEP —) BREW BROW STILL
(STONY —) ROACH
(SUGAR-LOAF —) SPITZKOP
(WOODED —) HOLT HURST
(PREF.) BUNO
HILLARY (CONQUEST OF —) EVEREST
HILLBILLY HOEDOWN
HILL-FORT RATH
HILLOCK HOW LOW NOB BOSS BULT DOWN KAME KNAP KNOB TERP TOFT TUMP BERRY HEAVE HURST KNOCK KNOLL KOPJE MOUND TOMAN BARROW BURROW COPPET HILLET HUMMOCK MAMELON TUMMOCK TUMULUS MOLEHILL
HILLSIDE BENT BRAE COTE EDGE CLEVE FALDA SLADE SLOPE FELLSIDE SIDEHILL
HILLTOP DOD NAB PIKE RISE KNOLL
HILLY KNOBBY
HILT HAFT BASKET POIGNET HANDGRIP
(— OF DAGGER) DUDGEON
(PART OF —) BOW CUT GRIP RING GUARD BUTTON POMMEL CAPSTAN LANGUET QUILLON RICASSO CROSSPIECE COUNTERGUARD
HILUM EYE SCAR HILUS PORTA NUCLEUS CICATRIX
HIM A EN HE HEM HIN LUI MUN
HIMATION PALLION PALLIUM
HIMERUS (FATHER OF —) LACEDAEMON
(MOTHER OF —) TAYGETE
(SISTER OF —) CLEODICE
HIMSELF HIM IPSE SELF HISSEL ITSELF HERSELF HISSELF
HIND ROE CONY HINE HINT CONEY HEARST HINDER VENISON CABRILLA
HIND-BODY ABDOMEN
HINDBRAIN RHOMBENCEPHALON
HINDER BAR DAM KEP LET MAR ROB CLOG HELP SLOW SLUG STAY STOP TENT WARN AFTER BLOCK CHEAT CHECK CHOKE CRAMP DEBAR DELAY DETER EMBAR ESTOP HEDGE SLOTH STYMY THROW TRASH ARREST CUMBER DETAIN FORBID FORLET HAMPER HARASS HINNER IMPEDE IMPEND INJURE RETARD RETRAL SCOTCH TAIGLE UNHELP ABSTAIN DEPRIVE FORELAY IMPEACH INHIBIT OCCLUDE PREVENT TRACHLE ENCUMBER HANDICAP IMPEDITE OBSTRUCT PRECLUDE PROHIBIT POSTICOUS
(PREF.) POSTERO
HINDERED FOUL
HINDERER LETTER
HINDERMOST LAG ACHTER
HINDQUARTER HIND HAUNCH
(HALF —) LEG
(PL.) FOUCH CRUPPER HAUNCHES
HINDRANCE BAR LET RUB BALK CURB REIN SLUG SNAG STAY STOP BLOCK CHECK DELAY HITCH TRASH ARREST CUMBER DENIAL HINDER OBJECT REMORA UNHELP SHACKLE UNSPEED DISCOUNT DRAWBACK HOLDBACK OBSTACLE PULLBACK
HINDU BABU BABOO SUDRA BABHAN BANIAN BANYAN GENTOO JAJMAN KALWAR KHATRI NAYADI

SHUDRA THAKUR VAISYA MUSAHAR VAIRAGI
(— ASCETIC) SADHU
(— ASSOCIATION) SANGH
(— CASTE) TELI VARNA
(— CUSTOM) SATI SUTTEE
(— ENERGY) SAKTI SHAKTI
(— IDOL) SWAMI
(— INTERJECTION) OM AUM
(— PHILOSOPHY) YOGA VEDANTA
(— PRACTICE) PURDAH
(— RITE) PUJA POOJA
(— SAGE) RSI RISHI
(— SCRIPTURE) VEDA
(— SECT) SIKH
(— VARNA MEMBER) SUDRA
(— WORSHIPER) SAKTA
(— WRITING) VEDA
(— WRITINGS) SMRTI TANTRA
(TWICE-BORN —) KSATRIYA
HINDUSTANI URDU HINDI OORDOO DAKHINI
HINDWING BALANCER
HINGE RUN BAND BUTT FLAP HARR TRIM TURN CARDO CROOK GEMEL JOINT MOUNT NODUS SKELL SKEWL TWIST DEPEND GARNET GEMMEL GIMMER HANGLE JIMMER SNIBEL CHARNEL COXCOMB FULCRUM HOLDBACK
(— OF BIVALVE SHELL) CARDO
(— OF HELMET) CHARNEL
(— TOGETHER) SCISSOR
(HALF OF —) FLAP
(PHILATELIC —) STICKER
(PREF.) GINGLYMO
HINGED SWING
(SUFF.) POMATOUS
HINNY BURDON FUNNEL JENNET
HINT CUE TIP ASTE ITEM MINT TANG WIND WINK CHEEP IMPLY INFER POINT SPELL STEER TOUCH TRACE WHIFF ALLUDE BREATH GLANCE OFFICE SMATCH TIPOFF WHEEZE INKLING LEADING MEMENTO POINTER SUGGEST UMBRAGE WHISPER WRINKLE ALLUSION INDICATE INNUENDO INTIMATE TELLTALE
(HUNT —) CLUE
HINTERLAND BLED BACKLAND
HIP HEP MOD COXA HUCK FUNKY PITCH SHOOP HAUNCH HUCKLE TRENDY TUNEDIN HIPBERRY TURNEDON
(— JOINT) COXA THURL
(— OF ROSE) BERRY CHOOP SHOOP
(— OF TARGET) SPOT
(PREF.) COX(O) ISCHI(O) OSPHY(O)
HIPBONE FINBONE PINBONE EDGEBONE SIDEBONE
HIPPARCHUS (BROTHER OF —) HIPPIAS
(FATHER OF —) PISISTRATUS
HIPPARETE (BROTHER OF —) CALLIAS
(FATHER OF —) HIPPONICUS
(HUSBAND OF —) ALCINIADES
HIPPEUS KNIGHT
HIPPIE FREAK
HIPPOCAMPUS ERGOT HIPPO SEAHORSE
HIPPOCOON (BROTHER OF —) TYNDAREUS
(FATHER OF —) OEBALUS
(MOTHER OF —) GORGOPHONE
(SLAYER OF —) HERCULES
HIPPODAMIA (FATHER OF —) ADRASTUS OENOMAUS
(HUSBAND OF —) PELOPS PEIRITHOUS
(SON OF —) ATREUS TROEZEN PITTHEUS THYESTES
HIPPOLYTUS (FATHER OF —) THESEUS
(MOTHER OF —) HIPPOLYTE
(STEPMOTHER OF —) PHAEDRA
HIPPOMENES (FATHER OF —) MEGAREUS
(MOTHER OF —) MEROPE
(WIFE OF —) ATALANTA
HIPPONACTEAN SCAZON
HIPPOPOTAMUS HIPPO ZEEKOE BEHEMOTH BUNODONT
HIPPOTHOE (FATHER OF —) MESTOR
(MOTHER OF —) LYSIDICE
(SON OF —) TAPHIUS
HIPPOTRAGUS OZANNA EGOCERUS
HIPSTER HEPCAT
HIRAH (COMPANION OF —) JUDAH
HIRE FEE JOB HAVE MEED RENT SIGN WAGE LEASE PREST WAGES EMPLOY ENGAGE RETAIN SALARY TAKEON BESPEAK CHARTER CONDUCE CONDUCT FREIGHT STIPEND
(— CATTLE) TACK
HIRED PAID TEEKA TICCA WAGED
HIRELING HACK VENAL HACKNEY MYRMIDON WAGELING MERCENARY PENSIONER PENSIONARY
HIRSUTE HAIRY PILOSE SHAGGY TRESSY
HIS S AS ES IS HISN
HISPID STRIGOSE STRIGOUS
HISS BLOW FUFF HISH HIZZ QUIZ SISS SIZZ GOOSE WHISS FISSLE FIZZLE SIFFLE WHOOSH WHISTLE SIBILATE
(— OF SWORD) SOUGH
HISSING BIRD AFFLATUS SIBILANT
HIST PEACE
HISTONE GLOBIN
HISTORIAN MORONI STORIER ANNALIST
AMERICAN FAY FOX GAY NYE BEER BOYD DODD FEIS FISH GARD HART KANE MAYS SHEA ZINN ADAMS AMORY BEARD BEMIS CURTI ELSON FORCE GIBBS GROSS HAZEN HORAN LEECH MAHAN MARTY MCGEE MOORE MUNRO MYERS SMITH STONE UNGER USHER WROTH ABBOTT ARENDT BARBER BARZUN BECKER BEESLY BOURNE BOWERS BRAUER FISHER GREENE HANSEN LATANE LOWELL MALONE MOTLEY MUZZEY NEVINS OWSLEY PATTEE PAXSON REEVES RHODES ROSZAK SLOANE SPARKS STILES TOLAND TURNER WINSOR ANDREWS BASSETT CHAPMAN CHEYNEY CHIDSEY CLELAND DUNNING GARRATY GAYARRE HEADLEY HULBERT JAMESON LEARNED LENGYEL LOVEJOY MCELROY MORISON PADOVER PALFREY PARKMAN RIDPATH SCHMITT SHANNON TICKNOR TUCHMAN VANLOON VANTYNE BANCROFT BETTMANN BOTSFORD BRODHEAD CHANNING COMMAGER COOLIDGE HILDRETH JOHNSTON MCMASTER PENNIMAN PHILLIPS PRESCOTT ROBINSON STEPHENS THWAITES TRUMBULL BEVERIDGE GROSVENOR MACDONALD PRIESTLEY STEVENSON KUYKENDALL MCLAUGHLIN WESTERMANN OBERHOLTZER ROSTOVTZEFF SCHLESINGER
ARGENTINIAN FUNES LOPEZ MITRE CARBIA
AUSTRIAN BIBI SRBIK ARNETH LORENZ HORMAYR LOSERTH MENGHIN PRIBRAM ASCHBACH HELLWALD WURZBACH SCHREIBER
BELGIAN JUSTE HYMANS GACHARD HASSELT LAURENT PIRENNE
CANADIAN BEGG BRYCE WRONG BIBAUD DENISON GARNEAU BOURINOT CASGRAIN
CHINESE PANKU
COLOMBIAN ACOSTA RESTREPO
CZECH GOLL PALACKY
DANISH HOLM ALLEN BARFOD AAGESEN AAGESON BRANDES MOLBECH WORSAAE PEDERSEN HAMMERICH NEERGAARD
DUTCH BOR BLOK GEYL FRUIN HOOFT JAPIKSE BARLEAUS HUIZINGA
ENGLISH COXE DYER HALL HYDE MUIR OMAN PAUL ROSE STOW TOUT WARD ACTON BIRCH BROWN CARTE DAVIS DIXON DORAN DOYLE EDMER FIRTH FYFFE GOOCH GREEN GROTE GUEST HELPS INNES MERES PARIS SMITH TERRY TOOKE WELLS BARKER BUCKLE BURNET CAMDEN COLOMB CREASY DUTTON FINLAY FISHER FROUDE GIBBON GILDAS HALLAM MILMAN PETRIE POWELL ROSCOE SEELEY STRYPE STUBBS TAWNEY TURNER WARNER WILSON BEAZLEY BOULGER COULTON DOUGLAS FORSTER FREEMAN HASSALL HAYWARD KNOLLES LANGTON LINGARD MITFORD POLLARD RALEIGH SYMONDS TOYNBEE ADOLPHUS CHADWICK GAIRDNER GARDINER GUEDALLA KINGLAKE MACAULAY MAITLAND MARRIOTT OLDMIXON PALGRAVE PHILLIPS PROTHERO STRACHEY ARMSTRONG KINGSFORD ROBERTSON TEMPERLEY TREVELYAN HAVERFIELD
FINNISH FORSMAN
FRENCH FAY SEE DROZ FAIN THOU DURUY FILON FLACH GIDEL GLOTZ GOYAU MABLY MONOD NAUDE RENAN SOREL AULARD BALUZE BEMONT BONNET DANIEL DAUDET GERARD GILSON GUIZOT HAUSER MARTIN MASSON MATTER MIGNET OZANAM ROMIER THIERS VANDAL VERTOT ZELLER BARANTE BLONDEL CHENIER CHERUEL COMINES FAGNIEZ FAURIEL JULLIAN LAGORCE LANFREY LAVISSE LERMINA MADELIN MEZERAY PFISTER RAMBAUD THIERRY DEBIDOUR DUCHESNE GODEFROY HANOTAUX LUCHAIRE MICHELET PARFAICT RULHIERE BEAUCOURT BONNEMERE BOURGEOIS HERICAULT LAMARTINE SEIGNOBOS SIEGFRIED TILLEMONT DESJARDINS GUIGNEBERT ROHRBACHER CHANTELAUZE
GERMAN DAHN HEHN KAPP KOCH LENZ NIEM ALZOG FALKE JAFFE KLOPP KOSER LUDEN MEYER MOSER PERTZ RANKE RIEHL SYBEL VEHSE VOGEL VOIGT WAITZ WEBER ZEUSS ABELIN BELOCH BOHMER HEEREN HEIDEN KUGLER MENZEL ONCKEN PREUSS QUIDDE RITTER SICKEL WUTTKE ANDREAS DROYSEN DUMMLER ECKHART FISCHER FORSTER HAEBLER HELMOLT HETTNER KEUTGEN LEHMANN LINDNER ROTTECK RUVILLE SCHAFER SCHMIDT SCHULTE BRESSLAU DELBRUCK DONNIGES FLEMMING GALLETTI GERVINUS HOETZSCH HOFFMANN KAUFMANN KROMAYER LEDEBOUR SCHLOZER FREIDRICH LAMPRECHT SCHIEMANN SCHMOLLER SLEIDANUS ARCHENHOLZ BAUMGARTEN BIEDERMANN HIRSCHFELD LAPPENBERG MARHEINEKE POSCHINGER TREITSCHKE ZIMMERMANN BRANDENBURG FALLMERAYER GARDTHAUSEN GREGOROVIUS SECKENDORFF
GREEK DURIS GREEN ARRIAN STRABO BIKELAS EPHORUS LAMBROS SOZOMEN TIMEAUS DEXIPPUS EUSEBIUS HERODIAN POLYBIUS XENOPHON CRATIPPUS DIONYSIUS HERODOTUS HESYCHIUS PHILISTUS TIMAGENES ANAXIMENES CLITARCHUS HELLANICUS HIERONYMUS PHYLARCHUS THEOPOMPUS THUCYDIDES ARISTOBULUS MEGASTHENES OLYMPIODORUS AGATHARCHIDES
HEBREW JOSEPHUS
HUNGARIAN FEJER TOLDY PAULER TELEKI FESSLER FRAKNOI MAILATH MANNHEIM MARCZALI SZILAGYI
ICELANDIC SNORRI
IRISH BURY LECKY CHESNEY GILBERT WADDING
ITALIAN AMARI CANTU VOLPE CANALE CIAMPI DENINA EMILIO FEDELE GIOVIO NOVATI VASARI ACCOLTI FERRERO VILLANI VILLARI AMMIRATO CIBRARIO GIANNONE MOLMENTI MURATORI BERTOLINI LIUTPRAND SALVEMINI GUICCIARDINI

MEXICAN ALAMAN PEREYRA CLAVIJERO BUSTAMANTE
NORWEGIAN KOHT LANGE MUNCH DIETRICHSON
PERUVIAN ULLOA
POLISH KUBALA BIELSKI CHODZKO DIUGOSZ LELEWEL SZUJSKI ASKENAZY JABLONSKI BOBRZYNSKI KUCHARZEWSKI
PORTUGUESE GOES MELO LOPES BARROS CASTANHEDA
ROMAN CATO LIVY NEPOS CORDUS FLORUS TROGUS SALLUST TACITUS APPIANUS VALERIUS EUTROPIUS SUETONIUS FENESTELLA
RUMANIAN IORGA KOGALNICEANU
RUSSIAN KAVELIN POGODIN BRUCKNER KARAMZIN MILYUKOV SOLOVIEV TURGENEV VENGEROV DRUZHININ POKROVSKI HRUSHEVSKY KOSTOMAROV
SCOTTISH MILL BOECE BROWN LAING BURTON TYTLER CARLYLE GILLIES NEILSON SPALDING BOBERTSON MACKINTOSH MACPHERSON
SPANISH AVILA LOPEZ XEREZ PINELO PULGAR TORENO DESCLOT GOMARRA HERRERA MARIANA MONCADA FERRERAS LAFUENTE MENENDEZ SEPULVEDA MONTESINOS
SWEDISH DALIN BESKOW GEIJER CARLSON FRYXELL FORSSELL MESSENIUS
SWISS KOPP BLUMER GELZER MULLER STUMPF TSCHUDI SISMONDI GAGLIARDI BURCKHARDT

HISTORICAL GENETIC
HISTORIOGRAPHER SCALD SKALD
HISTORY STORY ANNALS LEGEND RECORD SURVEY ACCOUNT ANCESTRY PROPHECY RELATION
(— OF EXPERIENCES) MEMOIRS
(— OF JAPAN) KOJIKI
(LIFE —) COURSE
(MUSE OF —) CLIO
(PAST —) RECORD
(PERIOD OF JAPANESE —) HEIAN
(PREVIOUS —) BACKGROUND
(TRIBAL —) PHYLOGENY
HISTRION ACTOR
HISTRIONIC ACTORY ACTORISH ACTRESSY
HIT BAT BOP BOX DOT GET HAT JOB PEG PIP WOW BASH BEAN BEAT BELT BIFF BLOW BOFF BONK BUST CHOP CONK DONG FOUR GOLD NAIL PINK POKE PUCK PUNT RUFF SLAM SLAP SLUG SOCK SWAT SWIP TAKE TANK TUNK WART WIPE ANGLE BOFFO CHECK CLOUT CLUNK CROWN FIVER FLICK GOUFF KNOCK PASTE POTCH PRANG PUNTA PUNTO SCORE SLASH SLOSH SMASH SMITE SNICK SOCKO SWIPE TAINT TOUCH VENUE ATTAIN DOUBLE FOURER HURTLE SCLAFF STRIKE VOLLEY ATTAINT BOFFOLA CONNECT MUZZLER SANDBAG SHELLAC WHERRET BLUDGEON BOUNDARY LENGTHER STRICKEN
(— A KEY) STRIKE
(— BALL) CUR FLY DINK DRIVE SHOOL SKITE SNICK
(— BUNT) DRAG
(— GAME) STOP
(— GENTLY) BABY
(— GLANCINGLY) TIP
(— GOLF BALL) CAN BLAST EXPLODE
(— HARD) DUMP SLOG SLUG PASTE SKELP SOUSE DEVVEL STOUSH STONKER
(— IN BOXING) LEADOFF
(— IN FACE) CLOCK
(— IN FIELD HOCKEY) CORNER
(— IN TILTING) TAINT
(— IT OFF) CLICK
(— LIGHTLY) KISS
(— ON BULL'S-EYE) GOLD
(— POORLY) DUB
(— SHARPLY) CLIP
(— SUDDENLY) ZAP
(— TOGETHER) CLASH
(— UPON) FIND
(— WITH FOOT) KICK SPURN
(BASE —) BINGLE DOUBLE SAFETY SINGLE TRIPLE SCRATCH SMOTHER
(BOXING —) SLUG PUNCH
(CRICKET —) SLOG BOUNDARY
(EASILY —) SITTING
(FENCING —) HAI HAY VENUE
(SHARP —) LICK
(SMASH —) SOCKEROO
(SOLID —) LINEDRIVE
HITCH JET TUG WED HALT HIKE ITCH KNOT LIFT PULL CATCH HOTCH SPELL TRACE FASTEN HIRSLE INSPAN MAGNUS SHUFFLE CONTRETEMPS
(— IN ROPE) CATSPAW
(NOSE —) BOZAL
HITCHHIKE HOP THUMB
HITCHHIKER PICKUP
HITCHING KNOT SHRUG
HITHER HERE
HITHERTO YET BEFORE
HITLERITE NAZI
HIT-OR-MISS CASUAL CHANCE HOBNOB CARELESS
HITTER SWATTER
HITTING BATTING SLOGGING
HITTITE HATTI KHATTI TABALIAN
HIVE GUM BIKE SKEP PYCHE STAND STATE STOCK SWARM APIARY ALVEARY BEEHIVE SWARMER
(— PLACED OVER ANOTHER) SUPER
HIVES CROUP UREDO
HLORRITHI THOR THORR
HOAGIE TORPEDO
HOAR GRAY RIME HOARY
HOARD HEAM KEEP POSE SAVE AMASS HUTCH MISER STASH STOCK COFFER MAGPIE MUCKER STOUTH GENIZAH HUSBAND SQUIRREL TREASURE
(— OF SAVINGS) STOCKING
(SECRET —) POSE
(THIEF'S —) PLANT
HOARDER MUCKER STORER HUSBAND
HOARFROST RAG HOAR RIME RIND
HOARINESS HOAR ROOP MUCOR
HOARSE RAW FOGGY GRUFF HEAZY HUSKY RAWKY ROKEY ROUGH ROUPY STOUR CROAKY CROUPY RASPED ROUPIT GRATING RAUCOUS
HOARSENESS FROG ROUP QUACK RAUCITY HASKNESS BARYPHONIA
HOARY AGED GRAY GREY HOAR WHITE FROSTY ANCIENT HOARISH INCANOUS
HOATZIN ANNA HANA HOACTZIN
HOAX BAM COD FUN GAG HUM KID RAG RIG BILK DUPE FAKE GAFF GEGG GUNK JOSH QUIZ RAMP RUSE SELL SHAM SKIT CHEAT FRAUD GREEN SHAVE SPOOF TRICK WINDY CANARD DIDDLE HUMBUG STRING BLAFLUM DECEIVE FLIVVER ARTIFICE
HOB HUB PUNCH MATRIX
HOBAB (BROTHER-IN-LAW OF —) MOSES
HOBBER LEANER
HOBBLE GIMP LOCK SPAN BUNCH HILCH HITCH STILT STUMP HABBLE HIRPLE HOPPLE LANGLE LANKET TOLTER CRAMBLE CRAMMEL CRIPPLE SHACKLE SHAFFLE SPANCEL STAGGER TRAMMEL SIDELINE
HOBBLEBUSH DOGWOOD
HOBBLING LAME
HOBBY BUG FAD HOBBLER PASTIME AVOCATION
HOBBYHORSE HOBBY PLAYMARE
HOBBYIST BUG
HOBGOBLIN (ALSO SEE GOBLIN) COW HAG HOB PUG BOGY PUCK BOGEY BUCCA BUGAN POKER SCRAT SPOOK BOODIE BOWSIE EMPUSA SPOORN BUGABOO RAWHEAD BOGGLEBO COLTPIXY POPLEMAN PUCKEREL WORRICOW
HOBNAIL HOB HUB PUNCH TACKET
HOBNAILED TACKETY
HOBO BO BOE BUM STIFF TRAMP VAGRANT VAGABOND SUNDOWNER
HOCK HAM HOX HEEL ANKLE HOUGH HUXEN SINEW SKINK IMPAWN JARRET CAMBREL GAMBREL HOCKSHIN SUFFRAGO
HOCKEY HURLY HORKEY HURLEY SHINNY CAMMOCK HURLBAT
(— DISK) PUCK
(— PLAYER) DYE ORR ROY HALL HOWE HULL BUCYK DIONE MOORE SHORE CLARKE COWLEY DRYDEN DURNAN GOULET HARVEY MALONE MIKITO MORENZ PILATE PLANTE POLVIN ULLMAN VACHON BOURQUE GRETZKY LAFLEUR LEMIEUX MESSIER RATELLE SAWCHUK WORSLEY CHEEVERS CONACHER ESPOSITO SCHRINER THOMPSON TROTTIER LAROCOQUE MAHOVLICH PERREAULT DELVECCHIO
(— STAR) ORR
(— TEAM) JETS BLUES KINGS BRUINS DEVILS FLAMES FLYERS OILERS SABRES SHARKS CANUCKS RANGERS WHALERS CAPITALS PENGUINS REDWINGS SENATORS CANADIENS ISLANDERS LIGHTNING NORDIQUES BLACKHAWKS MAPLELEAFS NORTHSTARS
(AREA IN FRONT OF — GOAL) CREASE
(ILLEGAL CHECK IN —) SPEARING
(INFRACTION IN —) SPEARING
HOCKEY STICK HOOKY HURLY STICK BULGER SHINNY CAMBUCA CAMMOCK DODDART HURLBAT
HOCUS-POCUS CANTRIP JUGGLERY FAKERY HUMBUG FLIMFLAM QUACKERY
HOD TRAY
(FATHER OF —) ZOPHAH
HODAVIAH (FATHER OF —) HASSENUAH
HOD CARRIER PADDY
HODESH (HUSBAND OF —) SHAHARAIM
HODGEPODGE CHOW HASH MESS OLIO RAFF SALAD BOLLIX JUSSEL MAGPIE MEDLEY MELANGE CHIVAREE CHOWCHOW HOTCHPOT KEDGEREE MISHMASH PASTICHE PORRIDGE SCRAMPUM PATCHWORK
HODOMETER VIAMETER
HOE BROD CHIP CLAT HACK HOWE SHIM CLAUT LARRY THIRD CHONTA HACKER PAIDLE PECKER SARCLE GRUBBER PULASKI SCRAPER SCUFFLE GRIFFAUN STRADDLER
(— HANDLE) STAIL
(HORSE —) NIDGET NIGGET
(PART OF —) BLADE SHANK HANDLE FERRULE
HOECAKE CORNCAKE
HOG BEN SOW BOAR GALT GILT PORK DUROC GRUNT SHOAT BARROW HOGGET HOGGIE OINKER PORKER PORKET YORKER BACONER BUTCHER GRUNTER HOGLING MONTANA BABIRUSA BUNODONT HEREFORD LANDRACE VICTORIA RAZORBACK
(KIND OF —) ROAD
(PREF.) SUI
HOGAN ABODE LODGE TEPEE DWELLING
HOGBACK RIDGE FLATIRON HOGFRAME
HOGCHOKER SOLE
HOGFISH CAPITAN LADYFISH LORICATE SCORPION
HOGGER HUGGER HOGHEAD
HOGGISHNESS GRILL GRYLL
HOGLAH (FATHER OF —) ZELOPHEHAD
HOGNOSE SNAKE ADDER FLATHEAD
HOG PLUM AMRA JOBO
HOGSHEAD CASK CARDEL
HOG'S-MEAT TOSTON HOGWEED
HOG-TIE HAMPER
HOGWASH SLOP DRAFF SWASH SWILL PIGWASH
HOIST FID HEFT KILT LIFT SWAY SWIG WHIM WHIP CRANE ERECT HEAVE HEEZE HEIST HOICK HOOSH HORSE RAISE WEIGH JAMMER

LAUNCH LIFTER TUGGER WHIMSY DERRICK
(— A LOG) CANNON
(— ANCHOR) CAT
(— FISH) BRAIL
(— FLUKES) FISH FANCHER
HOISTED (— TIGHT) ATRIP
HOISTMAN CAGEMAN
HOKUM BLAA BLAH HOKE JUNK
HOLD HOD OWN BULK DEEM FEEL FILL GAOL GAUM GIVE GRIT HANK HAVE HELD HEND HILT HOLE HOLT HOOK JAIL KEEP LOCK NAIL RELY SOFT STOW AFONG AHOLD AHOLT BELAY CARRY CINCH CLAMP CLING GRASP GRIPE LATCH LEASE PAUSE POISE ROCCA STORE WOULD ADHERE ADSORB ARREST CLUTCH DETAIN HANDLE INTERN MANURE OCCUPY REGARD REPUTE RETAIN ADJUDGE CAPTURE CLAUGHT CONFINE CONTAIN ENCLOSE FERMATA GRAPPLE HOLDING RECEIVE SEIZURE SUBSIST SUSPEND COMPRISE FOOTHOLD FOREHOLD HANDFAST HANDHOLD HEADLOCK HOLDFAST PURCHASE THURROCK
(— A BELIEF) SUPPOSE
(— AS PRECIOUS) TREASURE
(— AS TRUE) ACCEPT
(— AT BAY) DOMPT
(— BACK) STAY STOP WELL BELAY LAYNE STINT BOGGLE DETAIN FLINCH HINDER RETIRE SHRINK CONTAIN DETRACT FORBEAR INHIBIT RECLAIM REFRAIN REPRESS SLACKEN HESITATE RESTRAIN SUPPRESS WITHDRAW
(— BACK ON LEASH) TRASH
(— CLOSELY) CRADLE CUDDLE
(— CONSULTATION) ADVISE
(— CORONER'S INQUEST) CROWN
(— DEAR) CHERISH
(— DOWN) PINION CONTAIN
(— FAST) FIX BAIL BITE CLING SNARL CLENCH CLINCH SECURE STABLE
(— FIRMLY) CLIP INSIST
(— FORTH) ORATE SPIEL
(— FROM) ABSTAIN
(— GOOD) APPLY SERVE
(— IN CHECK) REIN GOVERN REPRESS COMPESCE
(— IN CONTEMPT) SMILE DISPRIZE
(— IN PLACE) ANCHOR
(— OF PLASTER) KEY
(— ON COURSE) STEM FETCH STAND
(— ON FINAL NOTE) TENOR
(— ON SHORE) LANDFAST
(— OUT) DREE LAST STAY OFFER EXTEND PROTEND STRETCH SUSTAIN
(— PROTECTIVELY) LAP
(— TIGHTLY) CLIP STICK
(— TOGETHER) BOND COHERE CONSIST
(— UP) ROB BEAR HALT STAY ERECT HEIST IMPEDE UPHOLD RUMPADE SUPPORT SUSTAIN TRADUCE
(— UP BY LEADING STRINGS) DADE
(— UP TO CONTEMPT) FLEER
(— UP TO PUBLIC NOTICE) GIBBET
(SHIP'S —) HOLE HOLL FISHHOLD
(WRESTLING —) CROTCH NELSON KEYLOCK CHANCERY HEADLOCK SCISSORS SIDEHOLD
(PREF.) CHADA
HOLDBACK DAM
HOLDER WYE HAVER STOCK DIPPER SOCKET CRACKER CASSETTE JAGIRDAR
(— FOR CARRYING GLASS) FRAIL
(— FOR COIL) SPOOL
(— FOR CUP) ZARF
(— FOR FLOWERS) FROG JARDINIERE
(— FOR FOOD) COZY COSEY
(— FOR TOOLS) TURRET
(— FOR WHIP) BUCKET
(— OF BENEFICE) ABBE
(— OF GRANT) ENAMDAR
(ALLOTMENT —) CLERUCH
(CANDLE —) SPIDER GIRANDOLE
(FLOWER —) FROG
(LAMP —) BODY
(TAPE —) CASSETTE
(PL.) GRIPPERS
(PREF.) PORTE
HOLDFAST CLINCH HAPTERON
HOLDIKEN HADDIN
HOLDING HAL COPY COTE HOLD TAKE GRASP HONOR HADDIN POFFLE TENANT TENURE TENANCY COMMENDA
(— DIFFERENT OPINIONS) APART
(— FAST) IRON
(— OF LAND) ROOM
(— OF OFFICE) OCCUPATION
(— OF SECURITIES) CARRY
(PL.) FLOCKS PROPERTY
HOLDUP HEIST STICKUP
HOLE CAN CUP EYE GAP PIT TAP BORE BURY LEAK MAIL MUSE PECK PINK POCK PUKA WANT CHINK DITCH FLOSS FOSSE MEUSE SINUS SLACK SPRUE SQUAT TEWEL THIRL THURL BURROW CAVITY CENTER CENTRE CRANNY CRATER EYELET HOLLOW LACUNA OBTAIN OILLET PIERCE POCKET POUNCE WEEPER BLOWOUT BOGHOLE BOTHROS DIBHOLE EYEHOLE KEYHOLE MORTICE MORTISE OILHOLE OPENING PINHOLE POTHOLE SCUTTLE SWALLET VENTAGE ACCEPTER APERTURE BLOWHOLE BOREHOLE COALHOLE CRABHOLE FUMAROLE HANDHOLE KNOCKOUT KNOTHOLE OVERTURE PEEPHOLE POSTHOLE PUNCTURE WELLHOLE WINDHOLE PERTUSION PERFORATION
(— CAUSED BY LEAK) GIME
(— FOR MOLTEN METAL) SUMP
(— FOR WIRE) HUB HUBB
(— IN BANK OF STREAM) GAT
(— IN GARMENT) FRACK
(— IN GUILLOTINE) LUNET LUNETTE
(— IN HEDGE) SMEUSE
(— IN HIDE) BOTHOLE
(— IN KEEL) LIMBER RUFFLE
(— IN KIVA) SIPAPU
(— IN ONE STROKE) ACE
(— IN STREAM BED) DUMP
(— INTO MOLD) GEAT SPRUE
(— IN WIND INSTRUMENT) LILL
(— THREE BELOW PAR) ALBATROSS
(AIR —) SPIRACLE
(BREATHING —) SUSPIRAL
(DEEP —) POT GOURD
(FOX —) KENNEL
(FULL OF —S) POROSE
(GOLF —) CUP DOGLEG
(KIND OF —) OZONE
(MELON —) GILGAI
(RABBIT —) CLAPPER
(SAND —) BUNKER
(SINK —) SOAKAWAY
(SPY —) JUDAS
(TO —) GOBBLE HAZARD
(VOLCANIC —) FUMAROLE
(VOLCANIC STEAM —S) SOFFIONI
(WATER —) DUB CHARCO
(WELL-LIKE —) CASCAN
(PREF.) TREMATO TROGLO
HOLIDAY HOL PLAY TIDE WAKE FERIE FESTA MERRY FIESTA JOVIAL FESTIVE HALEDAY PLAYDAY YEARDAY PASSOVER SHABUOTH WAYGOOSE
(EASTERN —) TET
(HALF —) REMEDY
(PL.) FERIA
HOLINESS PIETY HALIDOM SANCTITY SANCTIMONY
HOLLA SOLA
HOLLAND (ALSO SEE NETHERLANDS) FROGLAND
HOLLANDAISE GULASH GOULASH
HOLLAND BLUE ORION
HOLLANDER DUTCHMAN
HOLLANDS GIN GENEVA
HOLLER HALLO HOLLO HALLOO KYOODLE
HOLLO SOLA
HOLLOW DEN DIP KEX BOSS BOWL CAVE COMB COOM COVE DALK DELL DENT DINT DISH DOCK DOKE FOLD GORE HOLE HOLL HOWE IDLE KEXY KHUD SINK SLOT THIN VAIN VOID WAME BASIN BIGHT CAVUM CHASE CLEFT CUPPY DELVE DOWFF EMPTY FALSE FOSSA GAUNT GOYLE GULCH GULLY HEUCH LAIGH NOTCH SCOOP SINUS SLOCK SWAMP WOMBY ARMPIT BULLAN CAVITY CORRIE DIMPLE HOLLER INDENT KETTLE MATRIX POCKET RECESS SOCKET SUNKEN VACANT WALLOW BOXLIKE CONCAVE UNSOUND VACUITY CAVITARY CHELIDON CORELESS CRUCIBLE FISTULAR FOSSETTE NOTCHING SPECIOUS
(— AMONG HILLS) SWAG SLOCK
(— BETWEEN BREASTS) SLOT CLEAVAGE
(— BETWEEN WAVES) TROUGH
(— IN COIL OF CABLE) TIER
(— IN HILL) COOM CLASH COMBE COOMB CORRIE
(— IN SNOW) IGLOO
(— IN TILE) KEY
(— OF ARM) LEAD ARMPIT
(— OF EAR) ALVEARY
(— OF EYEBALL) ORBIT ORBITA
(— OF FOOT) VOLA
(— OF HANDS) GOUPEN GOWPEN
(— OF HORSE'S TOOTH) MARK
(— OF KNEE) HAM
(— OF ROOF) VALLEY
(— OUT) CUT DIG BORE HOWK KERF CAVERN EXCISE
(LONG —) GROOVE
(NOT —) SOLID FARCTATE
(PASSING —) CRESCENT
(ROUND —) CIRQUE
(SECLUDED —) GLEN
(SPRINGY —) GAW
(WOODED —) GULLY
(PREF.) CAEL(I)(O) CAVI CAVO CEL(O) COEL(I)(O)
(SUFF.) COELOUS COELUS
HOLLOWED HOWKIT CONCAVE SPOUTED
HOLLOW-EYED HAGGARD
HOLLOWNESS VANITY INANITY VACUITY CONCAVITY
HOLLY HOLM HULL ILEX MATE DAHOON HOLLIN HULVER TOLLON YAUPON CATBERRY INKBERRY MILKMAID
HOLLYHOCK HOCK ALTHEA MALLOW
HOLM AIT ISLET ISLAND BOTTOMS
HOLM-OAK ILEX
HOLOFERNES (SLAYER OF —) JUDITH
HOLOTHURIAN TREPANG
HOLY SRI SHRI HUACA SAINT SANTO DEVOUT DIVINE SACRAL SACRED BLESSED PERFECT SAINTLY SINLESS BLISSFUL INNOCENT REVEREND SPIRITUAL SANCTIMONIOUS
(— MAN) SADHU
(— OF HOLIES) ADYT ADYTUM
(ALL —) PANAGIA
(PREF.) HAGI(O) HIERATICO HIER(O) HOSIO SANCTI SANCTO SEMNO
(SUFF.) HIERIC
HOLY BASIL TULCE TOOLSY
HOLY SPIRIT PARACLETE
HOLY STONE BEAR BIBLE
HOLY WOOD LIGNUM
HOMAGE FEE COURT HONOR YMAGE FEALTY MANRED INCENSE LOYALTY MANRENT MANSHIP OVATION SERVICE TREWAGE EMINENCE OBEISANCE
(PAY —) GENUFLECT
(PAY — TO) KNEEL
(SUPREME —) LATRIA
HOME BYE DEN HAM BASE CASA HAME HUNK WIKE ABODE ASTRE BEING DOMUS FOYER HAUNT SMOKE HEARTH HEIMAT BLIGHTY SHELTER DOMICILE FIRESIDE ROOFTREE
(— FOR THE POOR) HOSPICE
(— OF REFUGE) HOSPICE
(— OF THE BLESSED) GIMLE
(AT THE — OF) CHEZ
(FUNERAL —) CHAPEL
(HARVEST —) KERN KIRN MELL HOCKEY
(IN THE — OF) CHEZ
(KIND OF —) MOTOR

(NURSING —) CLINIC
(REST —) FARM HOSTEL
(PREF.) **(RETURN —)** NOST(O)
HOMELAND HAVAIKI BANTUSTAN
HOMELESS ROOFLESS VAGABOND
HOMELIKE HOMEY HAMEIL HAMILT HOMISH HOMESOME
HOMELINESS YEOMANRY
HOMELY FOUL UGLY PLAIN DUDGEN RUGGED PLAINLY EVERYDAY FAMILIAR HOMELIKE
HOME PLATE RUBBER
HOMER KOR CHOMER
HOME RUN SWAT SWOT BLAST DINGER
HOMESICKNESS HEIMWEH NOSTALGIA
HOMESPUN KERSEY RUSSET RAPLOCH
HOMESTEAD TOFT TREF ONSET PLACE WORTH GRANGE TYDDYN FARMERY ONSTEAD STEADING
HOMESTEADER NESTER
HOMETHRUST HAI HAY
HOMEWORK PREP
HOMICIDE DEATH MORTH KILLING
HOMILETIC KERYSTIC
HOMILY PRONE OMELIE POSTIL SERMON
HOMINY SAMP NASAUMP
HOMOEOMERY GERM SEED
(PL.) SPERMATA
HOMOGENEITY SAMENESS
HOMOGENEOUS LIKE SOLID GLOBAL SIMPLE COMPACT MASSIVE SIMILAR
(PREF.) HOL(O) IS(O)
HOMOGENOUS ENTIRE
HOMOLOGUE CYANINE HOMOTYPE
(PREF.) NOR
HOMOPHONY MONODY
HOMORGANIC COGNATE
HOMOSEXUAL GAY FLIT
(— WOMAN) LESBIAN
(FEMALE —) DIKE DYKE
HOMOZYGOUS PURE ISOGENIC

HONDURAS
CAPITAL: TEGUCIGALPA
COIN: PESO CENTAVO LEMPIRA
DEPARTMENT: YORO COLON COPAN VALLE OLANCHO
GULF: FONSECA
INDIAN: MAYA PAYA SUMO ULVA CARIB LENCA PIPIL TAUIRA JICAQUE MISKITO MOSQUITO
ISLAND: ROATAN
ISLANDS: BAY BAHIA
LAKE: CRIBA YOJOA BREWER
MEASURE: VARA MILLA MECATE TERCIA CAJUELA MANZANA
MOUNTAINS: PIJA AGALTA CELAQUE
PORT: LACEIBA TRUJILLO
RIVER: COCO SICO ULUA AGUAN LEMPA NEGRO TINTO WANKS PATUCA SULACO GUAYAPE OLANCHO SEGOVIA SANTIAGO
RUINS: TENAMPUA
TOWN: TELA YORO COPAN LAPAZ ROATAN GRACIAS LACEIBA TRUJILLO YUSCARAN JUTICALPA
WEIGHT: CAJA LIBRA

HONE HO STROP STROKE STRICKLE
HONEST FAIR GOOD JAKE TRUE AFALD FRANK LEGIT ROUND SOUND WHITE CANDID DEXTER DINKUM ENTIRE PROPER RUSTIC SINGLE SQUARE SINCERE UPRIGHT RIGHTFUL STRAIGHT
(BARELY —) SHARP
HONESTLY TRULY DINKUM HONEST INDEED SINGLY SQUARE SQUARELY
HONESTY FAITH HONOR SATIN CANDOR EQUITY LUNARY REALTY VERITY JUSTICE LUNARIA PROBITY BOLBONAC FAIRNESS FIDELITY MOONWORT SATINPOD YEOMANRY
HONEY MEL MELL HINNY HONEYBUN
(— BEVERAGE) MULSE
(COLOR OF —) AMBER
(ROSE-FLAVORED —) RODOMEL
(PREF.) MELI(TTO) MELL(I)
HONEYBEE (ALSO SEE BEE) BEE GYNE KING DRANE DRONE QUEEN DINGAR DRONER EGATES CYPRIAN DEBORAH DESERET KOOTCHA MELISSA STINGER ACULEATE ANGELITO
HONEY BUZZARD PERN
HONEYCOMB COMB FRAME WAXCOMB
(PREF.) CERIO FAVI
HONEYCOMBED FAVOSE FAVEOLATE
HONEYCREEPER IIWI MAMO PALILA DREPANID GUITGUIT
HONEYDEW MANNA MILDEW
HONEY EATER OO IAO TUI MOHO MINER TENUI MANUAO MAOMAO ROSTER BELLBIRD WURRALUH
HONEYED SWEET HYBLAN SUGARY SUGARED HYBLAEAN LUSCIOUS
HONEY GUIDE MOROC
HONEY MESQUITE ALGAROBA HONEYPOD
HONEY PLANT HOYA HUAJILLO
HONEY-STONE MELLITE
HONEYSUCKLE VINE SUCKLE WEIGELA BINDWEED SUCKLING WOODBINE

HONG KONG
BAY: SHEKO REPULSE
CAPITAL: VICTORIA
COIN: CENT DOLLAR
DISTRICT: WANCHAI
GARDENS: TIGERBALM
ISLAND: LANTAO
MOUNTAIN: CASTLE VICTORIA
PENINSULA: KOWLOON
TOWN: KOWLOON

HONING (— DEVICE) OILSTONE
HONK KONK YANG CRONK
HONKER GOOSE
HONOR BAY ORE CLIO FAME FETE HORN KUDO LAUD ADORE CROWN GLORY GRACE HERRY IZZAT MENSE MENSK SPEAK TREAT CREDIT DECORE ENHALO ESTEEM HOMAGE HONOUR LAUREL PRAISE REVERE SALUTE WORTHY DIGNITY EMBLAZE GLORIFY HONESTY MANSHIP RESPECT WORSHIP ACCOLADE DECORATE GRANDEZA TASHREEF
(PL.) ACES
(PREF.) TIMO
HONORABLE DEAR FREE GOOD DIGNE NOBLE OPIME WHITE GENTLE HONEST HONORA LORDLY SQUARE UPRIGHT GENEROUS HANDSOME HONORARY
HONORABLENESS HONESTY
HONORABLY GENTLY
HONORARIUM SALARY DOUCEUR ALTARAGE HONORARY
HONORED GOOD FAMOUS LAUREL LAURELED PRESTIGIOUS
HONORIFIC MAGNIFIC
HOOD HOW COIF COWL GOON HEAD HUDE JACK AMICE ALMUCE BIGGIN BONNET BURLET CALASH CAMAIL CANOPY CAPOTE CUTOFF DOMINO FUNNEL MANTLE RAFFIA BANGKOK BASHLYK CALOTTE CAPUCHE MOBSTER BLINDAGE CALYPTRA CAPUCCIO CAPUTIUM CHAPERON CUCULLUS FOOLSCAP GANGSTER LIRIPIPE LIRIPOOP MAZARINE TROTCOZY NITHSDALE
(— AND CAPE COMBINED) FALDETTA
(— FOR EVENING WEAR) CAPELINE
(— OF BOILER) VOMIT
(— OF CARRIAGE) HEAD
(— OF MAIL) COIF CAMAIL COIFFE
(— OF REFRACTORY MATERIAL) MANTLE
(— OF VEHICLE) TOP CAPOTE
(— ON CUPBOARD) TREMOR
(— ON HORSES) BLINKER
(— OVER DOOR) MARQUISE
(— OVER SIGNAL LIGHT) VISOR
(LENS —) SUNSHADE
(MONK'S —) COWL
(STIRRUP —) TAPADERO
(STRAW —) JAVA
(WOMAN'S —) SURTOUT VOLUPER
HOODED COWLED GALEATE CUCULLATE
HOODED CROW HOODIE GRAYBACK GREYBACK
HOODED MERGANSER SMEW SNOWL SPIKE TADPOLE TOWHEAD MOSSHEAD
HOODED SEAL WIG HOOD HOODCAP
HOODLUM YOB HOOD LOUT PUNK BADDY YOBBO YOKEL BADDIE SKOLLY LURCHER HOOLIGAN LARRIKIN
HOODOO JINX
HOODWINK MOP DUPE FOOL SEEL BLEAR BLIND BLUFF CHEAT BAFFLE CLOYNE DELUDE GAMMON WIMPLE AVEUGLE BEGUILE BLINKER DECEIVE MISLEAD INVEIGLE
HOOEY BUSHWAH
HOOF CLOOF CLOOT COFFIN UNGUIS UNGULA CLOOTIE HOOFLET FOREHOOF
(PREF.) UNGULI
HOOFED UNGULATE
HOO-HA ADO
HOOK DOG GAB JIG PEW TUG CLIP DRAG FLAG GAFF HAKE HUCK KILP MEAK NOCK PEVY PRIN PUGH SETT SKID STAY TACK CATCH CHAPE CLEEK CLICK CRAMP CROME CROOK DRAIL HAMUS ONCIN PEAVY PREEN SARPE SPOON TACHE UNCUS BECKET DETENT HANGLE HINGLE PINTLE TENTER AGRAFFE GAMBREL GRUNTER HAMULUS HITCHER HOOKLET KNUCKLE NUTHOOK PELICAN PENNANT PINHOOK POTHOOK RAMHEAD SNIGGLE SPERKET UNCINUS BOATHOOK CROTCHET GRABHOOK PORTHOOK PULLBACK VULSELLA WEEDHOOK
(— FISH) FOUL HANG SNAG DRAIL HITCH STRIKE SNIGGLE FISHHOOK
(— FOR BACON) COMB
(— FOR KETTLE) KILP HANGLE TRAMMEL
(— FOR POT) DRACKEN POTHOOK SLOWRIE
(— FOR TWISTING HEMP) WHIRL WHIRLER
(BENCH —) JACK
(BOAT —) HITCHER
(BOXING —) CROSS
(BUTCHER'S —) GAFF
(COUPLING —) JIGGER
(KIND OF —) MOUTH
(LONG-HANDLED —) HOCK MEAK
(MUSICAL —) FLAG PENNANT
(PRUNING —) SARPE CALABOZO
(REAPING —) HINK TWIBILL
(SAFETY —) CLEVIS
(SKIDDING —S) GRAB
(2 —S FASTENED AT SHANKS) DOUBLES
HOOKAH KALIAN CHILLUM NARGHILE
HOOKED ADUNC UNCATE UNCOUS ADUNCAL FALCATE HAMATED HAMULAR ADUNCATE ADUNCOUS AQUILINE HAMIFORM UNCINATE
HOOKEDNESS ADUNCITY
HOOKER-OUT STICKMAN
HOOK-SHAPED ANKYROID
HOOKUP CIRCUIT
HOOKWORM STRONGYL
HOOLIGAN ROUGH ROWDY TOUGH APACHE GOONDA LARRIKIN
(SOUTH AFRICAN —) TSOTSI
(PL.) AMALAITA
HOOP RIB BAIL BAND BOND BOOL CLIP GIRD GIRR PASS RING TIRE GARTH GIRTH FRETTE HOOPLE LAGGIN WICKET CIRCLET GARLAND TROCHUS TRUNDLE
(— FOR A SPAR) BANGLE
(— FOR BARREL) BAND GIRD GIRTH
(— FOR LAMPSHADE) HARP
(— FOR ORE BUCKET) CLEVIS
(— FOR WINNOWING GRAIN) WEIGHT
(— NET) TRUNK
(— OF WHEEL) STRAKE
(— TO STRENGTHEN GUN) FRETTE
(HALF —) BAIL BALE
HOOPED RUNG
HOOPLA FANFARE

HOOPOE HOOP UPUPA WHOOP IRRISOR DUNGBIRD PICARIAN
HOOPSKIRT TUBTAIL
HOOP SNAKE WAMPUM
HOOPSTER CAGER
HOOSE HUSK
HOOSEGOW JUG JAIL POKY POKEY
HOOSIER SCHOOLMASTER
(AUTHOR OF —) EGGLESTON
(CHARACTER IN —) BUD PETE JONES MEANS RALPH SMALL WHITE HANNAH MARTHA SANDER SHOCKY WALTER HAWKINS JOHNSON MATILDA PEARSON THOMSON
HOOSIER STATE INDIANA
HOOT CURR WHOO WHOOP WHOOT EXPLODE ULULATE
(— OF REPROACH) FIE
HOOVE BLOAT
HOOVER VACUUM
HOP HIP NIP FLIP JUMP LEAP BOUND HITCH SWINE FLIERS GAMBOL SPRING TITTUP CROWHOP HOPBIND HOPVINE LUPULUS SKIPPER
HOPBUSH AKE AKEAKE
HOP CLOVER SHAMROCK SUCKLING
HOPE WON DEEM SPES TROW COMBE THINK TRUST DESIRE EXPECT PERDUE ESPEIRE THOUGHT SPERANZA VELLEITY
(VAIN —) PIPE WANHOPE
HOPEFUL FOND BUOYANT SANGUINE WENLICHE
HOPEFULNESS OPTIMISM
HOPELESS DULL ALLUP ABJECT FORLORN DOWNCAST
HOPELESSNESS ANOMIE DESPAIR
HOPHNI (BROTHER OF —) PHINEHAS
(FATHER OF —) ELI
HOP HORNBEAM DEERWOOD HARDHACK IRONWOOD
HOPI MOKI MOQUI
HOP-LIKE LUPULINE
HOPPER CURB JACK BUNKER CLOSET HAPPER MACARONI
HOPPLE HOBBLE PASTERN SIDELANG
HOPS SHATTER
(— BETWEEN 2 AND 4 YEARS) OLDS
HOPSCOTCH POTSY HOPPERS PALLALL PEEVERS
HOP TREE RUEWORT WINGSEED
HORDE ARMY CAMP CLAN PACK CROWD GROUP SWARM LEGION THRONG
(INNER —) BUKEYEF
HOREHOUND HENBIT MARVEL WONDER MARRUBE
HORI (FATHER OF —) LOTAN
(SON OF —) SHAPHAT
HORIZON LAYER VERGE COMPASS FINITOR ORTERDE SKYLINE
HORIZONTAL LEVEL LINEAR NAIANT ACLINAL STRAIGHT
HORIZONTALLY FLATLY BARWAYS BARWISE ENDLONG FESSWAYS FESSWISE
HORMIGO QUIRA
HORMONE HGH ACTH KININ CORTIN LUTEIN EQUILIN ESTRIOL ESTRONE GASTRIN INSULIN RELAXIN STEROID THEELIN THEELOL ANDROGEN ECDYSONE ENDOCRIN ESTROGEN FLORIGEN GALACTIN LACTOGEN OESTRIOL SECRETIN CORTISONE
(PITUITARY —) ACTH
HORN BEAK BATON BUGLE CONCH CORNO CORNU SHOOT ANTLER CLAXON KLAXON OXHORN TOOTER ALPHORN ALTHORN ANTENNA BUFFALO CLARONE FOGHORN HELICON HUTCHET OUTHORN PRICKET SHOPHAR UNICORN BEAKIRON BUCKHORN CLAVICOR CORNICLE OLIPHANT SLUGHORN STAGHORN WALDHORN NOISEMAKER
(— NOTE) MORT
(— OF COW) SCUR
(— OF CRESCENT MOON) CUSP
(— OF DILEMMA) PIKE
(— OF DRINK) SLOSH
(— OF YOUNG STAG) BUNCH
(BUDDING —) SHOOT
(DRINKING —) RHYTON
(ENGLISH —) CA
(FRENCH —) CORNO
(GREY —) COLUMN
(HUNTER'S —) HUTCHET WALDHORN
(INSECT'S —) ANTENNA
(IVORY —) OLIFANT
(RAM'S —) SHOPHAR SHOFAR
(RUDIMENTARY —) SLUG
(STUNTED —) SCUR
(PREF.) CORNEO CORNI CORNU
(SUFF.) CERA(S) CEROS CEROUS CERUS CORN
HORNBEAM HARDBEAM HARDHACK HORNWOOD IRONWOOD
HORNBILL TOCK CALAO TOUCAN BUCEROS HOMURAI BROMVOEL PICARIAN YEARBIRD
HORNBLENDE SIDERITE
HORNED FORKED CORNUTE
(PREF.) CERA CERVI CORNEO CORNI CORNU
HORNED DACE CHUB
HORNED POUT CATFISH
HORNED SCREAMER ANHIMA KAMACHI KAMICHI UNICORN
HORNED VIPER WAMPUM CERASTES
HORNET VESPA VESPID STINGER
HORNGELD CORNAGE
HORNLESS NAT NOT MOIL POLL DODDY MULEY POLEY DODDED HUMBLE HUMMEL MAILIE MULLEY POLLED ACEROUS
HORNPIPE MATELOTE
HORN POPPY SQUATMORE
HORNSTONE CHERT KERALITE
HORNSWOGGLE DUPE
HORNTAIL SIREX ORYSSID UROCERID WOODWORM
HORNWORT COONTAIL HORNWEED
HORNWRACK SEAMAT
HORNY WAUKIT CALLOUS CERATOID CORNEOUS KERASINE KERATOID
HORNYHEAD CHUB
HOROSCOPE SCOPE THEME FIGURE GENESIS NATIVITY
HORRIBLE DIRE GRIM UGLY AWFUL BLACK GREAT GRISLY HORRID GEARFUL GHASTLY HIDEOUS HORRENT UNSLOGH DREADFUL GRUESOME HORRIFIC SHOCKING TERRIBLE MONSTROUS
HORRID GRIM UGLY AWFUL ROUGH RUGGED SNUFFY UGSOME WICKED HIDEOUS DREADFUL GRUESOME HORRIBLE SHOCKING
HORRIFIC FEARFUL
HORRIFIED AGHAST GHASTLY HORRENT
HORRIFY APPAL AGRISE DISMAY ENHORROR
HORROR FEAR DREAD TERROR CONSTERNATION
(PL.) JIMJAMS
HORRORS CREEPS
HORSA (BROTHER OF —) HENGIST
HORS D'OEUVRE CANAPE RELISH OUTWORK ZAKUSKA
(PL.) ASSIETTE
HORS D'OEUVRE) TAPA
HORSE BAY COB CUT DUN GEE GRI NAG PAD POT RIP TIT ARAB AVER BARB DOON GOER GROG HACK HAND HOSS JADE MARE MOKE PRAD PROD QUAD RACK RIDE ROAN ROIL SKIN STUD TEAM TURK WEED YAWD ZAIN AIVER ARION ARVAK BEAST BIDET BLACK BROCK CAPLE CAPUL CHUNK CLYDE CREAM CROCK DUMMY EQUID FAVEL GLYDE GRANI HAIRY HOBBY MILER MOREL PACER PINTO PIPER POLER PUNCH RACER ROGUE RUNSY SCREW SHIER SHIRE SKATE SOMER STEED STIFF TACKY WALER WIDGE ALEZAN AMBLER BANKER BOLTER BRONCO BRUMBY BUCKER BUSSER CABBER CALICO CASTER CHASER CHEVAL COLLOP CURTAL CUSSER DAPPLE DOBBIN DRIVER ENTIRE EQUINE FENCER FILLER GANGER GARRON GLEYDE GRULLA HUNTER JUMPER KEFFEL LEADER MAIDEN MORGAN NUBIAN ORLOFF OUTLAW PELTER PLATER POSTER PULLER RACKER ROARER ROUNCY RUNNER SAVAGE SORREL STAGER TARPAN TRACER TURKEY VANNER WARPER WEAVER ALSVINN ALSVITH ARABIAN BARBARY BELGIAN BOARDER CABALLO CHARGER CLICKER CLIPPER COACHER COCOTTE COURSER CRIBBER CRIOLLA CRITTER DRAFTER FLEMISH GALATHE GELDING GIGSTER GRUNTER HACKNEY KNACKER LEEFANG MONTURE MUSTANG NEIGHER PACOLET PALFREY PIEBALD PRANCER PRANKER RATTLER REESTER REFUSER REMOUNT RUNAWAY SADDLER SLEDDER SLEEPER SPANKER STAGGIE STEPPER SUFFOLK SUMPTER TRAPPER TRESTLE TROOPER TROTTER WHEELER ARDENNES BATHORSE BUCKSKIN CHESTNUT CHEVALET COCKTAIL COLICKER CREATURE CYLLAROS DEMISANG DESTRIER EOHIPPUS FOOTROPE FRIPPERY GALLOPER GALLOWAY HRIMFAXI KADISCHI MACHINER OUTSIDER PALOMINO RIDGLING ROADSTER SKEWBALD STALLION STIBBLER TRIPPLER WHISTLER YARRAMAN CLYDESDALE
(— ACT) MANAGE
(— ANCESTOR) EOHIPPUS
(— CERTAIN NOT TO WIN) STIFF
(— ESTABLISHMENT) HARAS
(— LOSING FIXED RACE) STUMER STUMOUR
(— OF ACHILLES) XANTHUS
(— OF ALEXANDER THE GREAT) BUCEPHALUS
(— OF CALIGULA) INCITATUS
(— OF DALE EVANS) BUTTERMILK
(— OF DICK TURPIN) BLACKBESS
(— OF DON QUIXOTE) ROSINANTE
(— OF DUKE OF WELLINGTON) COPENHAGEN
(— OF GENERAL CUSTER) COMANCHE
(— OF GENERAL SHERMAN) RIENZI
(— OF LONE RANGER) SILVER
(— OF MOHAMMED) ALBORAK
(— OF NAPOLEON) MORENGO
(— OF ORLANDO) VEGLIANTINO
(— OF RINALDO) BAYARD
(— OF ROBERT E. LEE) TRAVELLER
(— OF ROY ROGERS) TRIGGER
(— OF SIGURD) GRANI
(— OF STONEWALL JACKSON) LITTLESORREL
(— OF TEX RITTER) WHITEFLASH
(— OF TOM MIX) TONY
(— OF ULYSSES GRANT) CINCINNATI
(— OF UNIFORM DARK COLOR) ZAIN
(— OF WILL ROGERS) SOAPSUDS BOOTLEGGER
(— RACE) WALKOVER
(—S RUNNING BEHIND) RUCK
(— THAT WON'T START) STICK
(ARABIAN —) ARAB KOHL ARABIAN
(BALKY —) JIB JIBBER
(BREED OF —) SHETLAND APPALOOSA PERCHERON CLYDESDALE LIPPIZANER
(BROKEN-DOWN —) JADE CROCK SCREW DURGAN GARRAN
(CALICO —) PINTO
(CASTRATED —) GELDING
(CLUMSY —) STAMMEL
(DECREPIT —) SKATE GLEYDE
(DRAFT —) HAIRY PUNCH SHIRE BEETEWK BELGIAN SUFFOLK PERCHERON
(DROVE OF —S) ATAJO
(EASY-PACED —) PAD
(FALLOW —) FAVEL
(FAMILY —) DOBBIN
(FAMOUS —) SILVER TRIGGER
(FAST —) GANGER
(FEMALE —) MARE FILLY
(FLEMISH —) ROIL
(GOLD —) PALOMINO
(GRAY —) SCHIMMEL

(HIGH-SPIRITED —) STEPPER
(IMAGINARY —) AULLAY
(IMMUNIZED —) BLEEDER
(INFERIOR —) PLUG CAYUSE PLATER
(JUMPING —) LEPPER
(MALE —) STALLION
(NEAR —) HAND
(OLD —) JADE PLUG PROD YAUD AIVER CROCK
(PACK —) BIDET SUMPTER
(PART OF —) EAR EYE JAW RIB FACE HOCK HOOF KNEE LOIN MANE NECK NOSE POLL TAIL BELLY CHEEK CROUP ELBOW FLANK MOUTH THIGH BREAST CANNON GASKIN HAUNCH STIFLE BUTTOCK CORONET FETLOCK FOREARM NOSTRIL PASTERN WITHERS FOREHEAD FORELOCK SHOULDER THROATLATCH
(PIEBALD —) CALICO
(RANGE —) FANTAIL
(ROAN —) SCHIMMEL
(SADDLE —) MOUNT
(SHAFT —) SHAFTER THILLER
(SHAGGY —) ALTAI
(SLUGGISH —) HOG
(SMALL —) NAG TIT BIDET GENET HOBBY CANUCK JENNET GALLOWAY
(STOCKY —) COB
(TEAM OF —S) CARTWARE
(TEAM OF 3 —S WITH LEADER) UNICORN
(TRICK —) SIMON
(TV —) MRED
(UNBROKEN —) BRONCO
(VICIOUS —) LADINO
(WILD —) BRONC FUZZY BRUMBY KUMRAH OUTLAW TARPAN JUGHEAD BANGTAIL FUZZTAIL WARRIGAL
(WINGED —) PEGASUS
(WORN-OUT —) HACK GARRAN KNACKER CROWBAIT
(WORTHLESS —) JADE SHACK KEFFEL
(YOUNG —) TIT COLT FOAL STAG STOT STAGGIE
(2-YEAR OLD —) TWINTER
(3 —S ABREAST) TROIKA
(3 —S ONE BEHIND ANOTHER) RANDEM
(4 —S ABREAST) QUADRIGA
(PL.) MANADA STABLE UNICORN
(PREF.) HIPP(O)
(SUFF.) HIPPUS

HORSE BALM KNOBWEED KNOTROOT RICHWEED
HORSE BLANKET RUG MANTA
HORSE BOY TRACER
HORSE CHESTNUT CONKER
HORSE-CLOTH MANTA
HORSECLOTH HOUSE HOUSING
HORSE DEALER COPER CHANTER COURSER
HORSE-EYE JACK XUREL
HORSE FENNEL SESELI
HORSEFLESH JACK
HORSEFLY BOT GAD CLEG CLEGG STOUT BOTFLY BREEZE GADBEE GADFLY BULLDOG DEERFLY TABANID
HORSEHAIR SETON
HORSELAUGH GUFFAW
HORSELEECH ALUKAH
HORSELOAD SEAM
HORSE MACKEREL TUNNY SAUREL
HORSEMAN RIDER CHARRO COWBOY HUSSAR KNIGHT RUTTER COURIER PICADOR PRICKER CAVALIER GALLOPER
(PL.) HORSE CAVALRY
HORSEMANSHIP CAVALRY
HORSEMINT RIGNUM
HORSE MUSHROOM WHITECAP
HORSE NETTLE SOLANUM
HORSEPLAY HIJINKS
(PANTOMIME —) RALLY
HORSEPOWER SOUP
HORSEPOX GREASE
HORSE-RACE DERBY
HORSE-RADISH MAROR MOROR REDCOLL
HORSE-RADISH TREE BEN BEHN BEHEN
HORSESHOE TIP SHOE PLATE HOBBER LUNETTE
HORSETAIL TAIL PRELE TOADPIPE
HORSETAIL LICHEN TREEHAIR
HORSETAIL TREE AGOHO AGOJO
HORSEWEED COCASH COWTAIL HOGWEED FIREWEED SCABIOUS
HORSEWHIP BEAT CHABOUK
HORTATORY EMOTIVE
HORTICULTURIST (ALSO SEE BOTANIST)
HORUS SEPT SOPT SEPTI HORMAKHU
(FATHER OF —) OSIRIS
(MOTHER OF —) ISIS
HOSACKIA ACMISPON
HOSE LINE VAMP HOSEN GASKIN BROGUES BULLION HOSIERY CHAUSSES HANDLINE HOSEPIPE
HOSEA OSEE
(FATHER OF —) BEERI
HOSHAIAH (SON OF —) AZARIAH JEZANIAH
HOSHEA (FATHER OF —) NUN AZAZIAH
HOSIERY HOSE KNEESOCK KNITWEAR
(— WORKER) LOOPER
HOSPICE IMARET DIACONIA HOSPITAL
HOSPITABLE DOUCE CLEVER DOULCE SOCIAL CORDIAL FRIENDLY
HOSPITAL BEDLAM CRECHE SPITAL COLLEGE LAZARET PESTHOUSE POLYCLINIC
(— AREA) ICU
(— WARD) ICU
(MENTAL —) SNAKEPIT
(MOVABLE —) AMBULANCE
(PRIVATE —) HOME
HOSPITALITY SALT MENSE XENODOCHY
HOSPODAR VOIVOD GOSPODAR
HOST SUM ARMY FYRD WARE CROWD EMCEE HORDE JASON MAKER POWER SWARM WERED LEGION LODGER NATION THRONG BALEBOS COMPANY FYRDUNG SACRING VIANDER LANDLORD PARTICLE MULTITUDE
(— OF INVADERS) HERE
(EUCHARISTIC —) LAMB SACRING
(PL.) SABAOTH
(SUFF.) XENOUS XENY
HOSTA NIOBE FUNKIA
HOSTAGE BORROW PLEDGE SURETY RANSOMER
HOSTEL INN ENTRY HOSTAGE KINGDOM HOSPITAL
HOSTELRY AUBERGE PARADOR
HOSTESS TAUPO LANDLADY CHATELAINE
HOSTILE FOE HARD UGLY ALIEN BLACK ENEMY FREMT HATEL STOUT DEADLY FRIGID INFEST ADVERSE ASOCIAL FIENDLY OPPOSED UNQUERT WARLIKE CONTRARY INIMICAL OPPOSITE
HOSTILITY WAR FEID FEUD HATE ANIMUS ENMITY HATRED RANCOR SCHISM DAGGERS RUPTURE
(PL.) WAR ARMS ARMOR WARFARE
HOSTLER NAGMAN OSTLER HORSEBOY
HOT WARM ADUST CALID EAGER FIERY ARDENT CALIDO ESTIVE FERVID IGNITE STOLEN SULTRY TORRID ANIMOSE ANIMOUS BOILING BURNING CANDENT FERVENT PEPPERY THERMAL CALIENTE CAYENNED FEVERISH SEETHING SIZZLING GANGBUSTERS
(— WATER) SOUP
HOTBED BED NEST HOTHOUSE
HOT-BLOODED VASCULAR
HOTBOX SMOKER STINKER
HOTDOG DOG FRANK WEENIE WEINER WIENER WIENIE FRANKFURTER
(— KIND OF PERSON) FIREBRAND
HOTEL INN SPA DIGS FLOP FONDA HOUSE HYDRO HOSTEL HOTTLE POSADA FLEABAG FONDACO FUNDUCK GASTHOF HOSTELRY
(— AT AIRPORT) AIRTEL
(— NEAR AIRPORT) AIRTEL
(WATERSIDE —) BOATEL
HOTELKEEPER HOTELIER
HOTHAM (FATHER OF —) HEBER
HOTHAN (SON OF —) SHAMA JEHIEL
HOT-HEADED BRAINISH MADBRAIN
HOTHIR (FATHER OF —) HEMAN
HOTHOUSE STEW STOVE PINERY FRUITERY
HOT ROD DRAGSTER
HOTSHOT HONCHO
HOT-TEMPERED PEPPERY CHOLERIC SPITFIRE
HOTTENTOT NAMA TOTTY HOTNOT KOKANA WITBOOI QUAEQUAE
(PL.) BALAO BALAWU
HOUND DOG PIE BAIT HARL HUNT MUTE BESET BRACE BRACH ENTRY HARRY LEASH LIMER SLATE AFGHAN BASSET BEAGLE CANINE HARASS HUNTER JOWLER LEAMER LUCERN SLEUTH TUFTER CURTISE ENTRADA GELLERT REDBONE SKIRTER BARUKHZY BLUETICK BRATCHET COURSING FOXHOUND
(BITCH —) BRACH
(CRY OF —) MUSIC
(EXTINCT —) TALBOT
(KIND OF —) BIZAN IBIZAN
(RELAY OF —S) VANLAY
(SLEUTH —) TALBOT
(SPECTRAL —) SHUCK
(PL.) RACHES
HOUND'S-TONGUE TORYWEED
HOUR URE TIDE TIME CURFEW GHURRY
(CANONICAL —) NONE SEXT PRIME TERCE MATINS TIERCE ORTHROS VESPERS COMPLINE EVENSONG
(HALF —) BELL
(KILOWATT —) KELVIN
(KIND OF —) HAPPY
(LAST —S) DEATHBED
(STUDY —) PREP
(6 —S) QUADRANT
(PREF.) HORO
HOURGLASS (PART OF —) BULB SAND FRAME WAIST
HOURLY HORAL HORARY
HOUSE BOX KEN CASA CRIB DOME DUMP FIRM FLET HALL HELL HOLE HOME RACE ROOF STOW ABODE ADOBE AERIE BAHAY BANDA COVER DACHA DOMUS HOOCH HOOSE JACAL LODGE MEESE PLACE STAGE WHARE BESTOW BIGGIN BOTTLE CAMARA CASITA CASTLE CHEMIS CLOTHE DUPLEX FAMILY HEARTH HOOTCH MAISON PALACE PARISH SINGLE STABLE WIGWAM BASTIDE BIGGING CABOOSE CASSINE EUDEMON FAZENDA HOGGERY HOUSING MESUAGE QUARTER SHELTER AEDICULA BARADARI BUNGALOW DOMICILE DOVECOTE DWELLING HACIENDA MEDSTEAD MESSUAGE TENEMENT NOVITIATE
(— AND LAND) DEMESNE
(— AND 5 ACRES) COTE
(— FOR DOGS) KENNEL
(— FOR WOMEN) HAREM
(— IN BOROUGH) HAW
(— OF A MARABOUT) KOUBA
(— OF CORRECTION) BRIDEWELL
(— OF ILL-FAME) KIP
(— OF KNIGHTS TEMPLARS) PRECEPTORY
(— OF LEGISLATURE) SEANAD CHAMBER ASSEMBLY
(— OF PARLIAMENT) COMMONS LAGTING REICHSTAG
(— OF PROSTITUTION) CRIB BAGNIO BORDEL
(— OF REFUGE) MAGDALEN MAGDALENE
(— OF THIEVES) KEN
(— OF WORSHIP) BETHEL CHURCH
(— WITH TRIANGULAR FRONT) AFRAME
(APARTMENT —) INSULA
(ASTROLOGICAL —) ANGLE
(AUSTRALIAN —) HUMPY
(CHANGE —) DRY
(CHAPTER —) CABILDO
(CHEAP EATING —) SLAPBANG
(CLAY —) ADOBE TEMBE
(COACH —) REMISE

(COMMUNAL —) MORONG
(COUNTRY —) PEN DACHA CASINO GRANGE QUINTA BASTIDE CHATEAU
(COW —) VACCARY
(DAIRY —) WICK
(DISREPUTABLE —) KEN
(EATING —) COOKSHOP
(EMPTY —) SQUAT
(ESKIMO —) IGLU IGLOO TOPEK KASHGA KASHIMA
(FIJI —) BURE
(FORTIFIED —) GARRISON
(FULL —) SRO
(GAMBLING —) BANK HELL RIDOTTO
(GOVERNMENT —) KONAK
(GREEK —) FRAT SORORITY FRATERNITY
(GRINDING —) HULL
(GROUP OF —S) CLUSTER
(HAWAIIAN —) HALE
(LODGING —) INN KIP HOST ENTRY HOTEL HOSTEL
(LOG —) TILT
(MANOR —) HAM HALL COURT PLACE SCHLOSS SEIGNEURY
(MERCANTILE —) HONG
(PLANETARY —) TOWER
(POULTRY —) ARK HENNERY
(PUBLIC —) INN PUB HOWF HOWFF JOINT HOSTEL SHANTY CANTEEN POTSHOP SNUGGERY
(RANCH —) HUT
(RELIGIOUS —) CELL CONVENT KELLION MONASTERY PRESBYTERY
(RENTED —) LET
(REST —) DAK KHAN SERAI
(RETREAT —) CENACLE
(ROOMING —) DOSS FLOP FLEABAG
(ROYAL —) AERIE
(SENATE —) CURIA
(SMALL —) COT HUT BACH CELL CABIN HOVEL SHACK CASITA COTTAGE MAISONETTE
(SOD —) SODDY
(STILT —) CHIKEE CHICKEE
(SUMMER —) TRELLIS
(TENEMENT —) LAND CHAWL
(THATCHED —) BANDA
(TOY —) COBHOUSE
(TURKISH —) KONAK
(TYPE OF —) PREFAB
(PREF.) DOMI ECO OECO OIKO STEG(O)
(SUFF.) OECA OECIA STEGE STEGITE

HOUSEBOAT BARGE HOUSER WANGAN WANIGAN DAHABEAH
HOUSEBREAKER MILL JACOB MILLKEN
HOUSEBREAKING CRACK
HOUSECARL THINGMAN
HOUSECOAT DUSTER
HOUSED (— IN) PUTUPAT
(NOT —) OUTLER
HOUSEFINCH BURION LINNET REDHEAD
HOUSEHOLD HIRED HOUSE FAMILY HOUSAL MEINIE MENAGE FIRESIDE MAINPAST
(— GOD) LAR
(PREF.) EC(O) OEC(O) OIKO
HOUSEHOLDER ASTRER GOODMAN GUIDMAN NAUKRAR FRANKLIN
HOUSEKEEPER HUSSY MATRON
HOUSELEEK JUBARB AYEGREEN HOMEWORT SENGREEN SILGREEN
HOUSEMATE DOMESTIC
HOUSE OF MIRTH (AUTHOR OF —) WHARTON
(CHARACTER IN —) GUS BART JUDY LILY GRYCE PERCY SIMON BERTHA DORSET GEORGE SELDEN TRENOR LAURENCE PENISTON ROSEDALE
HOUSE OF SEVEN GABLES
(AUTHOR OF —) HAWTHORNE
(CHARACTER IN —) MAULE PHOEBE VENNER JAFFREY CLIFFORD HEPZIBAH HOLGRAVE PYNCHEON
HOUSEWARMING INFARE
HOUSEWIFE DAME FRAU FROW WIFE HUSSY VROUW BUSHWIFE HAUSFRAU
(MEAN —) NIP
HOUSEY-HOUSEY BINGO
HOUSING BOX BASE CASE DRUM TRAP BANJO BLIMP GLOBE HOUSE KIOSK BARREL RADOME SHIELD HOUSAGE SHELTER DOGHOUSE PADCLOTH PECTORAL PEDESTAL SHABRACK
(HORSE'S —) BASE
(PLASTIC —) RADOME
(RADAR —) BLISTER
(PL.) HOLSTERS
HOVA IMERINA
HOVEL HUT COSH CREW CRIB CRUE HELM HULK HULL BOTHY CHOZA HUTCH LODGE BOTHIE BURROW CRUIVE PONDOK
HOVELER HOBBLER HUFFLER
HOVEN BLOATING
HOVER BAIT FLIT HANG HOVE LOOM BROOD POISE FLUTTER HOVERER
HOW AS FOO HOO HOWE HOWEER HOWEVER QUOMODO WHEREBY
HOWDAH TOWER AMBARI AMBAREE
HOWEVER BUT THO YET ONLY HOWSO STILL THOUGH
HOW GREEN WAS MY VALLEY
(AUTHOR OF —) LLEWELLYN
(CHARACTER IN —) HUW BETA DAVY IVOR OWEN EVANS IANTO GWILYM IESTYN MARGED MORGAN BRONWEN ANGHARAD GRUFFYDD
HOWITZER HOWITZ LICORN UNICORN
HOWITZER SHELL OBUS
HOWL BAY WAP WOW BAWL GOWL GURL HURL RAVE WAUL WAWL YAWL YOLL YOUT YOWL TIGER WHEWL WRAWL BEHOWL STEVEN ULULATE
(— VOCIFEROUSLY) TONGUE
HOWLER BONER ERROR ARAGUATO
HOWLER MONKEY MONO ARABA HOWLER GUARIBA GUEREBA STENTOR ALOUATTE
HOWLING ULULANT
HOY TJALK BILANDER CRUMSTER
HOYDEN MEG BLOWZE RIGSBY TOMBOY
HREIDMAR (SON OF —) REGIN FAFNER FAFNIR
H-SHAPED ZYGAL
HUAMUCHIL INGA
HUAVE WABI HUABI
HUB HOB BOSS NAVE STOCK CENTER CENTRE FAUCET HUBBLE SOCKET SPIDER OMPHALOS
(— AND SPOKES) SPEECH
HUBBLE UPROAR TELESCOPE
HUBBLE-BUBBLE CALEAN KALIAN CALAHAN
HUBBUB ADO DIN COIL FLAP STIR CLAMOR FRAISE HUBBLE RABBLE RACKET TUMULT BOBBERY CLUTTER BROUHAHA HUBBABOO ROWDYDOW SPLATTER
HUCHEN HUSO
HUCHNOM TATU
HUCKLEBERRY HURT ERICAD CRACKERS
HUCKLEBERRY FINN (AUTHOR OF —) TWAIN CLEMENS
(CHARACTER IN —) JIM TOM DUKE FINN HUCK JANE KING POLLY SALLY SUSAN WILKS JOANNA PHELPS SAWYER WATSON DOUGLAS GRANGERFORD SHEPHERDSON
HUCKSTER BADGER CADGER KIDDER HAGGLER KIDDIER TRUCKER OUTCRIER
HUDDLE RUCK HUNCH CRINGE CROUCH FUMBLE HOWDER HURTLE SCRUMP SHRIMP SHRINK CROODLE SCRINCH SCROOCH SCRUNCH SHUFFLE
HUDIBRAS (AUTHOR OF —) BUTLER
(CHARACTER IN —) RALPHO CROWDERO HUDIBRAS SIDROPHEL
HUE RUD BLEE BLUE COND CYAN CHLOR COLOR GREEN LEMON SHOUT TAINT TINCT CHROMA
(DULL —) DRAB
(SOMBER —) DARK
HUELESS GRAY GREY
HUFF DOD PET BLOW RUFF TIFF DRUNT SNUFF OFFENSE
(— AND PUFF) PANT
HUFFY FUFFY SHIRTY
HUG CLIP COLL COUL MOLD CREEM CRUSH HALSE PRESS CUDDLE HUDDLE HUGGLE STRAIN CHERISH EMBRACE SQUEEZE
HUGE BIG FELL MAIN VAST ENORM GIANT GREAT JUMBO LARGE STOUR HEROIC IMMANE BANGING BUMPING DECUMAN HIDEOUS IMMENSE MASSIVE MONSTER TITANIC COLOSSAL ENORMOUS GALACTIC GIGANTIC MOUNTAIN PYTHONIC SLASHING SWAPPING THUMPING HUMONGOUS THWACKING MOUNTAINOUS
HUGENESS ENORMITY
HUGUENOT CAMISARD
HUGUENOTS, LES (COMPOSER OF —) MEYERBEER
HUISACHE WABI AROMO CASSIE POPINAC OPOPANAX
HUL (FATHER OF —) ARAM
(GRANDFATHER OF —) SHEM
HULDAH (HUSBAND OF —) SHALLUM
HULK CHOP HULL CORSE
HULL HUD POD BODY BULK HULK HUSK PILL BURSE CASCO SWELL
(— OF COTTON BOLL) BUR BURR
(— OF SHIP) BODY HULK BOTTOM
(PART OF —) BEAM DECK KEEL RAIL BATTEN RABBET CEILING FUTTOCK KEELSON GARBOARD PLANKING STRINGER WATERWAY STANCHION SHELFPIECE SPIRKETING
HULLABALOO DIN FLAP FUROR MANIA CLAMOR HUBBUB RACKET BROUHAHA
HUM BUM BLUR BRUM BUZZ HUSS TUNE CHIRM CROON DRONE FEIGN SOUGH SOWFF THRUM HUMBLE TEEDLE FREDDON TRUMPET BOMBINATE
(— OF VOICES) CHIRM
HUMAN BEING BIPED MANLY FINITE FLESHY HUMANE MORTAL MANNISH HOMININE HUMANIST
(— BEING) CYBORG
(— LINKED TO SPACE ENVIRONMENT) CYBORG
(BIONIC — BEING) CYBORG
(PREF.) HOMI HOMIN(I)
HUMAN BEING MAN WIGHT MORTAL PERSON ADAMITE CREATURE RATIONAL
(PREF.) ANTHROP(O)
HUMAN COMEDY (AUTHOR OF —) SAROYAN
(CHARACTER IN —) BESS MARY ARENA HOMER KATEY TOBEY ACKLEY GEORGE GROGAN HUBERT LIONEL MARCUS THOMAS BYFIELD ULYSSES MACAULEY SPANGLER
HUMANE CIVIL KINDLY TENDER MERCIFUL
HUMANELY MANLY
HUMANITARIAN (ALSO SEE PHILANTHROPIST) PUBLIC PHILANTHROPIC
HUMANITY FLESH MENSK WORLD MANHEAD MANHOOD MANSHIP SPECIES ADAMHOOD HUMANISM KINDNESS LENITUDE
HUMBLE LOW BASE HOWE MEAN MEEK MILD MURE POOR TAME VAIL ABASE ABATE BUXOM DEMIT DIMIT LOWER LOWLY PLAIN SILLY SMALL SOBER WORMY ATTERR DEJECT DEMEAN DEMISS EMBASE HONEST MASTER MODEST REDUCE SIMPLE SLIGHT UNPUFF AFFLICT DEGRADE DEPRESS FOOLISH IGNOBLE MORTIFY OBSCURE CONTRITE DISGRACE
(— ONESELF) STOOP GROVEL
HUMBLED SMALL ABASED DEJECTED
HUMBLENESS HUMILITY
HUMBLER INFERIOR
HUMBLING SETDOWN ABJECTION
HUMBLY SIMPLE
HUMBUG BOO FIE GAS GUM HUM KID BOSH BUNK FLAM GAFF GAME GUFF JAZZ SHAM CHEAT FRAUD FUDGE GUILE JOLLY SPOOF SPOOK TRICK BARNEY BLAGUE BUNKUM GAMMON BLARNEY EYEWASH FLUMMER HOGWASH VERNEUK BUNCOMBE FLIMFLAM

FLUMMERY HUCKMUCK IMPOSTER NONSENSE
(SORT OF —) BEE
HUMDINGER ACE PIP DARB LULU ONER BEAUT DILLY DOOZY CORKER DINGER HUMMER SNORTER RIPSNORTER
HUMDRUM IRKSOME PROSAIC BOURGEOIS
HUMERAL VEIL
HUMERUS ARM
HUMID WET DAMP DANK MOIST SOGGY STICKY SULTRY WETTISH HUMOROUS
HUMIDITY
(PREF.) HYGR(O)
HUMILIATE ABASE ABASH SCALP SHAME NIDDER NITHER DEGRADE MORTIFY PUTDOWN UNPLUME DISGRACE
HUMILIATED SMALL ASHAMED
HUMILIATION DUST COMEDOWN DISGRACE
HUMILITY MODESTY MEEKNESS MILDNESS
HUMIN MELANIN
HUMMEL FALTER
HUMMING AHUM BROOL SINGING
HUMMINGBIRD RUBY STAR MANGO SYLPH TENUI TOPAZ AMAZON COQUET HERMIT HUMMER ROSTER SAPPHO COLIBRI EMERALD HUMBIRD JACOBIN RAINBOW SNOWCAP TROCHIL WARRIOR CALLIOPE COQUETTE FIRETAIL FROUFROU MIMOTYPE PICARIAN SAPPHIRE WHITETIP
HUMMOCK HUMP KNOLL CHENIER HAMMOCK TUSSOCK
HUMOR CUE PIN TID WIT BABY BILE CANT COAX MOOD TIFF VEIN WHIM FRAME IRONY TUTOR MEGRIM PAMPER PHLEGM SANIES SOOTHE SPLEEN SPRITE TEMPER FOOLING GRATIFY INDULGE VITREUM VITRINA ARCHNESS DISHUMOR DROLLERY EYEWATER FUMOSITY SANGUINE VITREOUS
(BAD —) BATS THROW
(ILL —) BILE DUDGEON
(KIND OF —) WRY
(QUIET —) DRYNESS
(SLIMY —) HIPPOMANES
(WATERY —) ICHOR
HUMORIST JOKER FUNSTER FUNMAKER FUNNYMAN
AMERICAN NYE LEAF SHAW WARD LEWIS SHUTE SMITH LELAND LOOMIS MASSON ROGERS MARQUIS THOMSON PERELMAN STREETER SULLIVAN SHILLABER
AUSTRIAN SAPHIR
CANADIAN LEACOCK
ENGLISH PAIN WARD SEAMAN
FRENCH RABELAIS
GERMAN RICHTER
IRISH MAHONY
HUMOROUS DROLL FUNNY PAWKY QUEER JOCOSE COMICAL GIOCOSO PLAYFUL WAGGISH PLEASANT SARDONIC
HUMP BOSS HUNK BULGE BUNCH CROUP CRUMP HULCH HUNCH GIBBER GIBBUS HUMMIE GIBBOUS
(— ACROSS ROAD) RAMP
(PREF.) HYB(O)
HUMPBACK LORD CRUMP PUNCH WHALE KYPHOSIS
HUMPBACKED HUMPED HUMPTY GIBBOSE GIBBOUS
(PREF.) CYPH(O) HYB(O)
HUMPBACKED SALMON HADDO HOLIA
HUMPED HULCH HUMPY HUTCH HUMPTY HUNCHY BUNCHED
HUMPHRY CLINKER (AUTHOR OF —) SMOLLETT
(CHARACTER IN —) JERRY LYDIA GEORGE WILSON BRAMBLE CLINKER HUMPHRY JENKINS MATTHEW MELFORD OBADIAH TABITHA DENNISON WINIFRED LISMAHAGO
HUMUS MOR MOLD MULL HUMIN MOULD
HUN AVAR BOCHE BULGAR MAGYAR VANDAL
(KING OF —S) ATLI ETZEL ATTILA
(KING OF THE —S) ATLI ETZEL ATTILA
HUNCH HUMP HUNK HULCH HUNCHET SCRUNCH
HUNCHBACK URCHIN HUMPBACK
HUNCHBACK OF NOTRE DAME
(AUTHOR OF —) HUGO
(CHARACTER IN —) CLAUDE FROLLO PHOEBUS ESMERALDA GRINGOIRE QUASIMODO CHATEAUPERS
HUNDRED RHO CENT CENTUM HUNDER HUNNER CANTRED CANTREF CENTARY
(— THOUSAND) LAC LAKH
(NINE —) SAN SAMPI
(ONE — DOLLARS) BILL
(5 —) D
(PREF.) CENT(I) HECATO HECATOM HECATON HECT(O)
HUNDREDFOLD CENTUPLE
HUNDRED-HANDED BRIAREAN
HUNDREDTH CENTESIMAL
(— OF INCH) POINT
(— OF RIGHT ANGLE) GRAD GRADE
HUNDREDWEIGHT CENT CENTAL CENTENA CENTNER HUNDRED QUINTAL
HUNGARIAN HUN KUMAN MAGYAR
(PREF.) UGRO

HUNGARY

CANAL: SIO SARVIZ
CAPITAL: BUDAPEST
COIN: GARA BALAS FILLER FORINT KORONA
COUNTY: VAS PEST ZALA BEKES FEJER HEVES TOLNA NOGRAD SOMOGY BARANYA
DANCE: CZARDAS
DYNASTY: ARPAD ANGEVIN
FOREST: BAKONY
GYPSY: SZIGANE TZIGANE
KING: BELA GEZA IMRE ARPAD ISTVAN KALMAN MATTHIAS
LAKE: FERTO BALATON VELENCE BLATENSEE
MEASURE: AKO HOLD JOCH YOKE ANTAL ITCZE MAROK METZE HUVELYK MERFOLD
MONEY: PENGO
MOUNTAIN: KEKES BAKONY MECSEK BORZSONY KORISHEGY
MOUNTAIN RANGE: BUKK MATRA MECSEK CARPATHIAN
MUSICAL INSTRUMENT: TAROGATO
NATIVE: HUN SERB CROAT GYPSY MAGYAR SLOVAK UGRIAN
PLAIN: PUSZTA
REGIME: KADAR
RIVER: DUNA MURA RAAB RABA SAJO ZALA BODVA DRAVA DRAVE IPOLY KAPOS KOROS MAROS RABCA TARNA TISZA DANUBE HENRAD POPRAD SZAMOS THEISS ZAGYVA VISTULA BERRETYO
TOWN: ABA ACS OZD VAC BUDA EGER GYOR MAKO PAPA PECS PEST TATA ZIRC KOMLO CEGLED MOHACS SOPRON SZEGED DBRECEN MISKOLC SZENTES DEBRECEN SZEGEDIN
WEIGHT: VAMFONT VAMMAZSA
WINE: EGER TOKAJ TOKAY SZEKSZARD

HUNGER BELL CLEM WANT ACORIA DESIRE FAMINE CRAVING APPETITE
(— PANGS) MUNCHIES
HUNGRY YAP HOWE KEEN LEER YAUP EAGER EMPTY THIRL UNFED HOLLOW JEJUNE PECKISH YAPPISH ANHUNGRY ESURIENT
HUNK DAD DAUD JUNK STUD ADONIS MOUNTAIN
(— OF BREAD) TOMMY
HUNKY STUDLY MUSCULAR ATTRACTIVE
HUNKY-DORY JIMDANDY
HUNT DOG GUN JAG MOB RUN GREW JACK LARK PUMP SEAL SEEK SHOP CHASE CHEVY DRIVE HOUND REVAY STALK TRACK TRAIL BATTUE BEAGLE BREVIT CHEVVY COURSE FALCON FERRET SEARCH SHIKAR VANLAY ENCHASE AUCUPATE PIGSTICK SCROUNGE VENATION
(— BIG GAME) GHOOM
(— DEER) FLOAT
(— DOWN) QUARRY
(— DUCKS) TOLL
(— FOX) CUB
(— HINT) CLUE
(— WITH HAWK) FLY
(— WITH SPEAR) STICK
HUNTER GUN HUNT PINK JAGER BIRDER CHASER GUNNER JAEGER NIMROD THERON ACTAEON BUSHMAN CATCHER COURSER MONTERO SHIKARI SHOOTER SKIRTER STALKER TRAILER VENERER CEPHALUS CHASSEUR FIELDMAN HUNTSMAN TRAILMAN
(— ON SNOW) CRUSTER
(BUFFALO —) CIBOLERO
(MYTHOLOGICAL —) GWYN ORION
(RING OF —S) TINCHEL TINCHILL
HUNTING DRAG HANK AHUNT WATHE SHIKAR VENERY CUBBING GUNNING BEAGLING PURCHASE SHOOTING SURROUND VENATION
(— SIGNAL) SEEK
HUNTRESS DIANA
HUNTSMAN WHIP HUNTER JAEGER ACTAEON CATCHER COURSER MONTERO SCARLET VENATOR VENERER CHASSEUR
HUPHAM (FATHER OF —) BENJAMIN
HUR (GRANDSON OF —) BEZALEEL
(SON OF —) REPHAIAH
HURAM (FATHER OF —) BELA
HURDLE TRAY FLAKE FRITH PANEL STALE STICK DOUBLE RADDLE SLEDGE WATTLE
HURDS TOW
HURDY-GURDY LIRA ROTA LANTUM VIELLE SAMBUKE HUMSTRUM SYMPHONY
HURI (SON OF —) ABIHAIL
HURL BUM BUN CAST CLOD DASH DUST FIRE PASH PELT PICK SLAT SOAK SOCK DRIVE FLING HEAVE LANCE PITCH SLING SMITE SPANG SWING THIRL THROW WHIRL LAUNCH THRILL HURLBAT SWITHER WHITHER JACULATE PRECIPITATE
HURLY-BURLY HURL RACKET UPROAR
HURRAH HAIL HUZZA HOORAY HURRAY BRAVISSIMO
HURRICANE BAGUIO PRESTER FURACANA FURICANE WILDWIND
HURRIED HASTY RAPID THRONG HASTEFUL SNATCHED
HURRY ADO FOG HIE NIP RAP RUB RUN BUSK DASH DUST HUMP PELL PLAT POST RAPE RESE RUSH STIR TEAR TIFT TROT URGE WHIR CHASE CROWD HASTE HYPER LURRY MOSEY PRESS SESSA SKIRT SPEED STAVE STOUR WHIRL BUCKET BUNDLE BUSTLE HASTEN HUSTLE POWDER STROTH TATTER WHORRY HOTFOOT QUICKEN SCUDDLE SKELTER SLITHER WHITHER DISPATCH EXPEDITE SPLUTTER ACCELERATE
(— ABOUT) SCOUR
(— A HORSE) SPUR
(— AWAY) FLEE BUNCH SCREW SKIRT
(— CLUMSILY) TAVE TEAVE
(— NOISILY) SPLUTTER
(— OFF) DUST
(— UP) BUSK
(GO IN A —) ZOOM
HURRYING FLUSTER
HURT CUT HOT NOY DERE FIKE GALL HARM PAIN SCAT ABUSE BLAME GRIEF GRIPE PINCH SORRY SPITE THORN WATHE WOUND BRUISE DAMAGE GRIEVE IMPAIR INJURE INJURY LESION MIFFED MITTLE PAINED PUNISH SCATHE STRAIN STROKE WINGED AFFLICT HURTING OFFENCE OFFENSE SCADDLE MISCHIEF NUISANCE
(— EASILY) FROISSE
(— FEELINGS) CUT TOUCH

(— REPUTATION) LIBEL
(— SEVERELY) KILL
(EASILY —) GINGER
(PREF.) NOCI
HURTFUL BAD ILL EVIL MALIGN NOCENT NOCIVE NOUGHT SHREWD TAKING BALEFUL BANEFUL HARMFUL MALEFIC NOCUOUS NOXIOUS SCADDLE UNQUERT GRIEVOUS HURTSOME SCATHFUL
HURTLE HURL FLING THIRL
HUSBAND EKE MAN WER BOND CHAP FERE KEEP LORD MAKE MATE SAVE SIRE BARON CHURL HOARD HUBBY MATCH STORE MANAGE MASTER MISTER SPOUSE CONSORT GOODMAN GUIDMAN HENPECK PARTNER CONSERVE
(— OF ADULTRESS) CUCKOLD
(— OF SQUAW) SANNUP
(AFFIANCED —) FUTURE
(SUPPLEMENTARY —) PIRRAURU
(PL.) PUNALUA
(PREF.) MARITI
HUSBANDMAN BOND BOOR CARL CLOWN COLON RUSTIC TILLER ACREMAN HUSBAND PLOWMAN TILLMAN AGRICOLE
HUSBANDRY GAINER GAINOR THRIFT ECONOMY MANAGERY
HUSH SH HSH MUM PAX HESH HOOT LULL BURKE SHUSH STILL WHISH WHIST WHUSH HUDDLE BESTILL HUSHABY SILENCE
HUSHED QUIET STILL GENTLE WHISHT
HUSHIM (HUSBAND OF —) SHAHARAIM
HUSK BUR COD HUD KEX SID ARIL BARK BURR COAT COSH HOSE HUCK HULK PILL SEED SHIV SKIN HOOSE SCALE SHACK SHALE SHAUP SHELL SHILL SHOOD SHUCK SHUDE COLDER DEHUSK FLIGHT SLOUGH BOLSTER CARCASS CASCARA
(— OF NUT) SHACK BOLSTER
(— OF OATS) SHUD SHOOD FLIGHT
(CORN —) HOJA
(PL.) BHUSA CHAFF BHOOSA HULKAGE SHELLING
(PREF.) LEMMO LEPO LOPO SILIQUI
(SUFF.) LEMMA
HUSKY HUSK CODDY FOGGY THICK FURRED BUIRDLY HULKING BOUNCING SIBERIAN
HUSSITE TABORITE
HUSSY MINX SLUT BESOM CUTTY GIPSY GYPSY MADAM STRAP HIZZIE LIMMER DROSSEL
HUSTINGS BEMA
HUSTLE FAN PEG HUMP JUMP BLITZ SKELP BUCKET BUNDLE BUSTLE JOSTLE RABBLE RUSTLE SCUFTER
HUSTLECAP PINCH
HUSTLER HUSTLE PEELER BUSTLER FIREBALL
HUT COE COT BARI BUTT COSH COTE CREW CRIB HALE HULK HULL ISBA IZBA SHED SKEO TENT TILT BASHA BENAB BOHIO BOOTH BOTHY CABIN CHAWL CHOZA HOOCH HOVEL HUMPY HUTCH JACAL KRAAL LODGE SCALE SETER SHACK SHIEL TOLDO TOPEK WHARE WURLY BOHAWN BOTHAN CANABA CHALET GUNYAH GUNYEH HOOTCH MIAMIA PONDOK RANCHO REFUGE SAETER SCONCE SHANTY SHELTY WIGWAM WIKIUP BALAGAN BARRACK BOUROCK CAMALIG COTTAGE GOONDIE HUDDOCK HUTMENT SHEBANG YAKUTAT BARABARA CHANTIER RONDAWEL SHIELING THOLTHAN TUGURIUM
(— FOR TEMPORARY USE) CORF
(— IN VIETNAM) HOOCH HOOTCH
(— OVER MINING SHAFT) COE
(ABORIGINAL —) MIMI WURLY GUNYAH MIAMIA WURLEY GOONDIE
(FISHERMAN'S —) SKEO SKIO
(HEATED —) HOTHOUSE
(HERMIT'S —) CELL
(KIND OF —) NISSEN
(NAVAJO —) HOGAN
(POULTRY —) IGLOO
(RITUAL —) SUCCAH SUKKAH
(SAMOYED —) CHUM
(SENTRY —) BOX
(SIBERIAN —) JURT
(SOUTH AFRICAN —) STRUIS
(PREF.) CALIO
HUTCH ARK BUDDLE RABBITRY
HUTIA UTIA JUTIA PILORI
HUZ (FATHER OF —) NAHOR
HUZZAH SHOUT
HWYL FERVOR EXCITEMENT
HYACINTH LILY MUSK LILIUM CROWTOE FLOATER GREGGLE JACINTH BLUEBELL CROWFOOT HAREBELL JACOUNCE
HYACINTH BEAN LABLAB BONAVIST BONNYVIS DOLICHOS
HYACINTHUS (FATHER OF —) AMYCLAS
(MOTHER OF —) DIOMEDE
HYALITE OPAL
HYALOGEN NEOSSIN
HYBRID DZO ZHO MULE ZOBO CROSS GRADE HINNY LIGER COYDOG GALYAK MOSAIC MULISH SPLAKE TURKEN BASTARD BIGENER CATTALO JERSIAN MONGREL PLUMCOT ZEBRASS ZEBRULA ZEBURRO CARIDEER CITRANGE KAFERITA LIMEQUAT ZEBRINNY
(PREF.) NOTH(O)
HYBRIDIZE CROSS
HYDRA POLYP
HYDRANT CHUCK FIREPLUG
(PART OF —) NUT CHAIN BARREL BONNET STANDPIPE CONNECTION
HYDRANTH SIPHON SYPHON
HYDRATE SLAKE
HYDRAULIC
(PREF.) HYDR(I)(O)
HYDRAZINE DIAMIDE
HYDRAZOATE AZIDE
HYDRIA KALPIS
HYDROCARBON ARENE CUMOL FREON GUTTA IDRYL INDAN IRENE TOLAN XYLOL ALKANE ALKYNE ALLENE BUTANE BUTYNE CARANE CETANE CETENE CYMENE DECANE ETHANE ETHENE HEXINE INDANE INDENE MELENE NONENE OCTANE OCTENE OCTINE PICENE PINENE PYRENE RETENE TOLANE TOLUOL XYLENE AMYLENE AZULENE BENZENE CHOLANE CYCLENE DECALIN ETHERIN FULVENE HEPTANE HEPTENE HEPTYNE LYCOPIN MUCKITE MYRCENE OLEFINE PENTINE PENTYNE PHYTANE PROPANE STYRENE TETROLE TOLUENE BIPHENYL CADALENE CADINENE CAMPHANE CARBURAN CEROTENE CETYLENE CHRYSENE CORONENE CUMULENE DECYLENE DIOLEFIN DIPHENYL DOCOSANE DYSODILE EICOSANE ETHYLENE EUDALENE FLUORENE HEXYLENE ILLIPENE ISOPRENE LYCOPENE MENTHENE NONYLENE OCTYLENE PARAFFIN PRISTANE PYRACENE RUTYLENE SABINENE SQUALENE STILBENE
(SUFF.) YLENE
HYDROCHLORIC ACID
(SUFF.) CHLORHYDRIA
HYDROCYANIC PRUSSIC
HYDRODAMALIS RHYTINA
HYDROEXTRACTOR BUZZER WHIZZER
HYDROFLUORIC PHTHORIC
HYDROFOIL FOIL
HYDROGEN HYDRO PROTIUM
(HEAVY —) DIPLOGEN
HYDROGRAPHER AMERICAN MAURY MITCHELL
ENGLISH SMYTH MURRAY
GERMAN NEUMAYER
NORWEGIAN SVERDRUP
HYDROHEMATITE TURGITE
HYDROID POLYP OBELIA ACALEPH ZOOPHYTE
HYDROLEA NAMA
HYDROMEL ALOJA
HYDROMETER SPINDLE
HYDROPERITONEUM ASCITES
HYDROPHOBIA LYSSA RABIES
HYDROPHOBIC LYSSIC
HYDROPHYLLIUM BRACT
HYDROPLANE SKIM GLIDER
HYDROXIDE ALKALI HYDRATE HYDRIDE
HYDROXYL
(SUFF.)
(CONTAINING —) OLIC
HYDROZINCITE CALAMINE
HYENA HINE DABUH SIMIR HYAENID
HYGIENIC SANITARY
HYGRODEIK PAGOSCOPE
HYLAS (FATHER OF —) THIODAMAS
(LOVER OF —) DRYOPE
(MOTHER OF —) MENODICE
HYLLUS (FATHER OF —) HERCULES
(MOTHER OF —) DEIANIRA
(SLAYER OF —) ECHEMUS
(WIFE OF —) IOLE
HYLOZOIST PHYSICIST
HYMEN CHERRY BRIDEGOD MAIDENHEAD
HYMENIUM THECIUM
HYMENOCALLIS ISMENE
HYMN ODE FUGE LAUD SING DIRGE GATHA PAEAN PSALM YASHT YMPNE ANTHEM CARVAL CHORAL HIMENE HIRMOS MANTRA ORPHIC THEODY VESPER CHORALE EXULTET HEIRMOS INTROIT CANTICLE CATHISMA DOXOLOGY ENCOMIUM PSALMODY SEQUENCE TRISAGION TROPARION
(— COLLECTION) MENAION
(MEXICAN —) ALABADO
(VEDIC —) MANTRA
(PL.) HYMNODY
HYMNAL HYMNARY HYMNBOOK
HYPATIA (AUTHOR OF —) KINGSLEY
(CHARACTER IN —) AMAL MIRIAM AUFUGUS HYPATIA ORESTES PELAGIA RAPHAEL VICTORIA HERACLIAN PHILAMMON
HYPE EXCITE PROMOTE PUFFERY INCREASE
HYPER EXCITABLE
HYPERACTIVE MANIC
HYPERBOLE AUXESIS
HYPERCORACOID RADIAL SCAPULA
HYPERCRITICAL NICE CAPTIOUS CRITICAL
HYPERDULIA ADORATION
HYPEREMIA RUBOR
HYPEREMIC CONGESTED
HYPERENOR (BROTHER OF —) EUPHORBUS POLYDAMAS
(FATHER OF —) PANTHOUS
(MOTHER OF —) PHRONTIS
(SLAYER OF —) MENELAUS
HYPERICUM TUTSAN
HYPERION (DAUGHTER OF —) AURORA
(FATHER OF —) URANUS
(MOTHER OF —) GAEA
(WIFE OF —) THEA
HYPERON BARYON
HYPEROPIC FARSIGHTED
HYPERSENSITIVITY ATOPY ALLERGY
HYPHA STOLON
HYPHEN BAND
(PL.) LEADERS
HYPNOTIC AMYTAL BROMAL CHLORAL SECONAL BARBITAL NARCEINE SOPORIFIC
HYPNOTISM DEVIL BRAIDISM HYPNOSIS MESMERISM
HYPNOTIST OPERATOR SVENGALI
HYPO FIXER
HYPOBLAST ENDODERM HYPODERM
HYPOCHONDRIA HIP HYP HYPO MEGRIM
HYPOCHONDRIAC ARGAN HIPPY HIPPIST ATRABILIAR
HYPOCOTYL RADICLE TIGELLA TIGELLUS
HYPOCRISY SHAM POPEHOLY PHARISAISM
HYPOCRITE CANT BIGOT CHEAT FACER FRAUD BLIFIL CAFARD

HUMBUG MUCKER MAWWORM SIMULAR CHADBAND DECEIVER TARTUFFE
HYPOCRITICAL FALSE SLAPE DOUBLE CANTING PLASTER POPEHOLY SPECIOUS
HYPOCYCLOID ASTROID
HYPODERMIS SKIN
HYPOPHARYNX LINGUA LABIELLA
HYPOSTASIS PERSON
HYPOSTATIZE ENTIFY
HYPOSTOME MANUBRIUM
HYPOTENUSE SUBTENSE
HYPOTHESIS SYSTEM THEORY PREMISE WEGENER SUPPOSAL POSTULATE
HYPOTHETICAL IDEAL
HYPOTRACHELIUM GORGERIN
HYPSEUS (DAUGHTER OF —) CYRENE **(FATHER OF —)** PENEUS **(MOTHER OF —)** CREUSA **(WIFE OF —)** CHLIDANOPE
HYPTIS OREGANO
HYRAX DAS CONY CONEY DAMAN WABUR DASSIE WABBER ASHKOKO KLIPDAS HYRACOID
HYRMINA (FATHER OF —) EPEUS **(HUSBAND OF —)** PHORBAS **(SON OF —)** ACTOR
HYRNETHO (BROTHER OF —) AGELAUS CALLIAS EURYPYLUS **(FATHER OF —)** TEMENUS **(HUSBAND OF —)** DEIPHONTES
HYSTERIA MOTHER NERVES PIBLOKTO TARASSIS **(PRONE TO —)** VAPORISH **(RELIGIOUS —)** LATA
HYSTERICAL FRANTIC NERVOUS SHRIEKY

I

I A Y HI HY CHE ICH ISS SHE ITEM UTCH INDIA UTCHY
(— AM) ISE CHAM ICHAM
(— HAD) CHAD
(— WILL) CHILL ICHULLE
(— WOULD) CHUD
IALEMUS (FATHER OF —) APOLLO
(MOTHER OF —) CALLIOPE
IALMENUS (BROTHER OF —) ASCALAPHUS
(FATHER OF —) ARES APOLLO
(MOTHER OF —) ASTYOCHE CALLIOPE
IAMB IAMBIC IAMBUS
(— AND DACTYL) FEET
(DOUBLE —) DIIAMB
IAMUS (FATHER OF —) APOLLO
(MOTHER OF —) EVADNE
IAPETUS (FATHER OF —) URANUS
(MOTHER OF —) GAEA
(SON OF —) ATLAS MENOETIUS
(WIFE OF —) ASIA CLYMENE
IAPYGIANS MESSAPII
IAPYX (BROTHER OF —) DAUNIUS PEUCETIUS
(FATHER OF —) LYCAON DAEDALUS
IASION (BROTHER OF —) DARDANUS
(FATHER OF —) ZEUS JUPITER
(LOVER OF —) CERES DEMETER
(MOTHER OF —) ELECTRA
(SON OF —) PLUTUS
IATROCHEMICAL SPAGYRIC
IATROCHEMISTRY SPAGYRIC
IBANAG CAGAYAN
IBEX KYL TEK TUR ZAC GOAT KAIL BEDEN EVECK IZARD JAELA EVICKE SAKEEN
IBHAR (FATHER OF —) DAVID
IBIS GUARA GANNET HADADA JABIRU TURKEY CICONIID IRONHEAD
IBNEIAH (FATHER OF —) JEROHAM
ICARIUS (BROTHER OF —) TYNDAREUS
(DAUGHTER OF —) ERIGONE PENELOPE
(FAITHFUL DOG OF —) MOERA
(FATHER OF —) OEBALUS
(MOTHER OF —) GORGOPHONE
ICARUS (FATHER OF —) DAEDALUS
(MOTHER OF —) NAUCRATE
ICE YS GEAL FROST GLACE CRYSTAL VERGLAS
(— IN ROUGH BLOCKS) RUBBLE
(ANCHOR —) FRAZIL
(DRIFTING FRAGMENT OF —) PAN CALF
(GROUND —) FRAZIL
(PATCH OF —) RONE
(PINNACLE OF —) SERAC
(RIDGE OF —) HAMMOCK HUMMOCK
(SEA —) GLACON SLUDGE
(SHORE —) FAST
(SLUSHY —) SISH
(SOFT —) SLOB LOLLY
(THIN NEW —) DISH PANCAKE
(THIN OR FLOATING —) FLOE GRUE BRASH
(WATER —) SHERBET
(PREF.) CRYSTALL(I)(O) GLACI(O)
(SUFF.) CRYST
ICE AX PIOLET
ICEBERG BERG GROWLER FLOEBERG
(OFFSHOOT OF —) CALF
ICEBOAT SKEETER
ICE CREAM BISK CREAM GLACE AUFAIT BISQUE NOUGAT TASTER SPUMONI TORTONI
(— BETWEEN WAFERS) SLIDER
(— MOLD) BOMBE
(— TREAT) MALT
ICE CREAM CONE CORNET
ICED COLD GLACE FRAPPE
ICEFISH SALANGID
ICE FLOE PAN
ICEHOUSE IGLU IGLOO
(— WORKER) AIRMAN

ICELAND

BALLAD: RIMUR
BAY: FAXA HUNA
CAPITAL: REIKJAVIK REYKJAVIK
COIN: AURAR EYRIR KRONA
DISH: SKYR SVIO BLOOMGR HAROFISK
EPIC: EDDA SAGA
FIRST SETTLER: ARNARSON
FJORD: BREIDHA
GEYSER: GRYLA
GIANT: ATLI
GLACIER: HOFSJOKULL LANGJOKULL VATNAJOKULL
HERO: BELE ERIC LEIF SIGUROSSON
LAKE: MYVATN THORISVATN
MEASURE: SET ALIN LINA ALMUD TURMA ALMENN ALMUDE FERFET POTTUR FATHMUR FERALIN FERMILA OLTUNNA SJOMILA
MOUNTAIN: JOKUL
PARLIAMENT: ALTHING
REPUBLIC: LYOVELDIO
RIVER: HVITA JOKULSA THJORSA
TOWN: AKRANES AKUREYRI KEFLAVIK KOPAVOGUR
VOLCANIC ISLAND: SURTSEY
VOLCANO: LAKI ASKJA HEKLA ELDFELL
WATERFALL: GULL DETTI GULLFOSS DETTIFOSS
WEIGHT: PUND POUND

ICE-STONE CRYOLITE
ICHABOD (FATHER OF —) PHINEHAS
(GRANDFATHER OF —) ELI
ICHNEUMON URVA NYMSS MEERKAT VANSIRE
ICHOROUS GLEETY
ICHTHYOSIS FISHSKIN
ICHU HICHU STIPA
ICICLE ICARY ICKLE YOKEL TANGLE SHOGGLE SHOOGLE COCKBELL
ICINESS GLARE
ICING ICE PIPING ALCORZA FROSTING MERINGUE
ICON IKON EIKON IMAGE DEESIS
ICONOCLAST DEBUNKER
ICONOSTASIS DIASTYLE
ICTEROHEMATURIA CARCEAG
ICTONYX ZORILLA
ICTUS ACCENT STRESS DOWNBEAT
ICY GELID BOREAL FRIGID WINTRY GLACIAL
ID ES ORF GARDON SYPHILID

IDAHO

CAPITAL: BOISE
COUNTY: ADA GEM BUTTE CAMAS LATAH LEMHI POWER TETON BLAINE BONNER CARNAS CASSIA JEROME OWYHEE BENEWAH KOOTENAI
DAM: OXBOW BROWNLEE
INDIAN: BANNOCK KALISPEL NEZPERCE SHOSHONI
LAKE: BEAR GRAYS PRIEST
MOUNTAIN: RYAN BORAH RHODES TAYLOR BIGBALDY BLUENOSE
MOUNTAIN RANGE: CABINET SELKIRK
NICKNAME: GEM
RIVER: SNAKE LOCHSA SALMON PAYETTE
SPRINGS: SODA HOOPER LAVAHOT
STATE BIRD: BLUEBIRD
STATE FLOWER: SYRINGA
TOWN: ARCO BUHL MALAD NAMPA BURLEY DRIGGS DUBOIS MOSCOW WEISER CASCADE CHALLIS ORIFINO REXBURG POCATELLO

IDAS (BROTHER OF —) LYNCEUS
(FATHER OF —) APHAREUS
(MOTHER OF —) ARENE
(WIFE OF —) MARPESSA
IDDO (FATHER OF —) ZECHARIAH
(SON OF —) AHINADAB
IDE ORFE
IDEA EGG GIG KINK EIDOS IMAGE THING ANONYM DHARMA ECTYPE FIGURE INTENT NOTICE NOTION RECEPT THREAP THROPE BEGRIFF CONCEIT CONCEPT GIMMICK GLIMPSE MAROTTE OPINION PROJECT SPECIES SURMISE THOUGHT GIMCRACK NOTIONAL BRAINCHILD PRECONCEPTION
(—S OF LITTLE VALUE) STUFF
(CENTRAL —) ARGUMENT
(COMMONPLACE —) SHIBBOLETH
(CONSERVATIVE —S) FOGYISM
(DOMINANT —) CLOU
(DULL STUPID —S) STODGE
(FAINT —) GLIMMER
(FALSE —) FALLACY
(FANTASTIC —) VAPOR MAGGOT
(FAVORITE —) HORSE
(FIXED —) TICK
(FUNDAMENTAL —) KEYNOTE
(GENERAL —) HANG
(IRRATIONAL —) FOLLY
(MAIN —) POINT
(MUSICAL —) SENTENCE
(ODD —) FREAK
(OVERWORKED —) CLICHE
(PLATONIC —) ESSENCE
(RECURRING —) BURDEN
(STALE —S) BILGE
(SUPERSTITIOUS —) FREIT
(TRANSCENDENT —) FORM
(TRITE —) PABLUM PABULUM
(PL.) EIDE THOUGHT
(PREF.) IDEO
IDEAL ISM IDEA DREAM AERIAL BEAUTY DOMNEI DREAMY EDENIC MENTAL UNREAL PATTERN PERFECT UTOPIAN ABSTRACT FANCIFUL IDEALITY NOTIONAL QUADRATE ORIFLAMME
(— OF BEAUTY) KALON
IDEALISM IDEOLOGY
IDEALIST IDEIST UTOPIAN FICHTEAN UTOPIAST
IDEALIZE PLATONIZE
IDEALIZED POETICAL
IDENTICAL LIKE SAME SELF VERY ALIKE EQUAL METOO EVENLY PROPER CORRECT IDENTIC NUMERIC SELFSAME
IDENTIFIABLE NAMEABLE
IDENTIFICATION IDENT DOCUMENT EQUATION RECOGNITION
(— METHOD) DNA
IDENTIFIED SIGNATE
IDENTIFIER LINK BIRDER
IDENTIFY PEG TAB MARK NAME RANK SPOT IDENT PLACE TALLY FINGER DISCERN DIAGNOSE PINPOINT
(— WITH) ENTER
IDENTITY SEITY UNITY IPSEITY ONENESS EQUALITY SAMENESS
(— OF PITCH) UNISON
(PERSONAL —) SEITY
IDEOGRAPH CHARACTER
(PL.) KANJI
IDEOGRAPHIC REAL
IDEOLOGICAL MENTAL
IDEOLOGY ISM
IDIOBLAST SPHERE IDIOSOME

IDIOCY ANOIA ANOESIA FATUITY IDIOTRY MOROSIS IDIOTISM
IDIOM CANT ARGOT JUANG DORISM IFUGAO JARGON MEDISM SPEECH AEOLISM ANOMALY GRECISM PAHLAVI PEHLEVI TURKISM DANICISM DORICISM IDIOTISM IONICISM LANGUAGE LOCALISM PARLANCE RURALISM
IDIOMORPHIC EUHEDRAL
IDIOPHONE RATTLE
IDIOSOME SPHERE
IDIOSYNCRASY TIC WAY QUIRK IDIASM RUMNESS
IDIOT FON OAF SOT DAFF DOLT FOOL AMENT BOOBY DUNCE FONNE CRETIN HOBBIL NIDGET NIDIOT DINGBAT DULLARD NATURAL OMADAWN PINHEAD IMBECILE INNOCENT SLAVERER
(AUTHOR OF —) DOSTOEVSKI
(CHARACTER IN —) LEF GANYA AGLAYA PARFEN MYSHKIN NATASYA EPANCHIN ROGOZHIN FILIPOVNA ARDALIONOVITCH
IDIOTIC DAFT DOPY ZANY IDIOT FATUOUS FOOLISH WANTWIT IMBECILE
IDLE COLD DEAD HACK HAKE HANG HULL JAUK LAKE LAZE LAZY LUSK MUZZ ORRA SOFT SORN TICK VAIN VOID DALLY EMPTY ORROW SHOOL SLIVE THOKE WASTE COOTER DAIDLE DANDER DREAMY FOOTER GAMMER LOUNGY OTIANT OTIOSE SLIMSY TEETER TIDDIE TIFFLE TRIFLE TRUANT UNUSED VACANT DRONISH IDLEFUL IDLESET LOAFING SAUNTER SHACKLE SLUMBER SLUTHER UNLUSTY VACUOUS WHIFFLE BASELESS BOOTLESS FAINEANT INACTIVE INDOLENT SHAMMOCK SLAISTER SLOTHFUL TRIFLING WORKLESS
(TO BE —) SLOTH
IDLENESS LAZE RUST SLOTH IDLETY IDLESET IDLESSE IGNAVIA VACANCY VACUITY FLANERIE IDLEHOOD INACTION
(— PERSONIFED) LAURENCE LAWRENCE
(LIVE IN —) MAROON
IDLER BUM GAUM HAKE JAUK KERN LOON DRONE BADAUD BUMBLE DONNOT IDLEBY LUBBER PLAYER QUISBY RODNEY STALKO TRUANT BLELLUM BUCKEEN DAWDLER FAITOUR FRANION IDLESBY LOLLARD LOUNGER LOUTHER LURDANE SLOUNGE TRIFLER DOLITTLE FAINEANT IDLESHIP LAYABOUT LAZARONE UNWORKER WHIFFLER
IDLE WHEEL IDLER RUNNER
IDLY TOOMLY VAGUELY
IDMON (DAUGHTER OF —) ARACHNE
(FATHER OF —) APOLLO
(MOTHER OF —) CYRENE ASTERIA
IDOCRASE EGERAN CYPRINE VESUVIAN
IDOL GOD BAAL ICON JOSS LION TIKI WOOD ZEMI ANITO BESAN EIKON GUACA HOBAL HUACA IMAGE STOCK SWAMI IDOLET IDOLUM MAMMET MAUMET MINION PAGODA POPPET PUPPET TERAPH EIDOLON MAHOMET BAPHOMET MAUMETRY PANTHEUM
(HEATHEN —) DEVIL
(PREF.) EIDOLO IDOLO
IDOLATER AKKUM PAGAN BAALIST BAALITE HEATHEN IDOLIST
IDOLATROUS PAGAN IDOLISH
IDOLATRY BAALISM IMAGERY ADULTERY MAUMETRY
IDOLIZE GOD IDOL ADORE ADMIRE WORSHIP
IDUMAEAN EDOMITE
IDUN (HUSBAND OF —) BRAGI
IDYIA (DAUGHTER OF —) MEDEA
(FATHER OF —) OCEANUS
(HUSBAND OF —) AEETES
(MOTHER OF —) TETHYS
(SON OF —) APSYRTUS
IDYL IDYLL BUCOLIC ECLOGUE
IDYLLIC HALCYON PASTORAL THEOCRITEAN
IDYLLS OF THE KING (AUTHOR OF —) TENNYSON
(CHARACTER IN —) BORS ENID BALAN BALIN ISOLT ARTHUR ELAINE GARETH GAWAIN MERLIN MODRED VIVIEN ETTARRE GALAHAD GERAINT LYNETTE PELLEAS BEDIVERE LANCELOT TRISTRAM GUINEVERE PERCIVALE
IF AN AND GIF GIN THO GEVE IFFEN INCASE SOBEIT THOUGH PROVIDED
(— EVER) ONCE
(— NOT) BUT ELSE NISI
(PREF.) **(AS —)** QUASI
IF WINTER COMES (AUTHOR OF —) HUTCHINSON
(CHARACTER IN —) MARK NONA EFFIE MABEL PERCH SABRE TYBAR BRIGHT FARGUS HAROLD FORTUNE TWYNING
IGAL (FATHER OF —) JOSEPH NATHAN
IGDALIAH (SON OF —) HANAN
IGEAL (FATHER OF —) SHEMAIAH
IGERNA (HUSBAND OF —) UTHER GORLOIS
(SON OF —) ARTHUR
IGNEOUS PLUTONIC
(SOURCE OF — ROCK) MAGMA
(PREF.) PLUTONO
IGNIS FATUUS WISP SPUNKIE WILDFIRE
IGNITE TIND FLASH LIGHT SHOOT SPARK ILLUME KINDLE CALCINE LIGHTEN
IGNITED LIVING BURNING
(CAUSE TO BECOME —) RETROFIRE
IGNITER PUNK SPARKER
IGNITION FIRE LIGHTING
IGNOBLE LOW BASE MEAN VILE ABJECT GRUBBY SORDID CURRISH SERVILE UNNOBLE BASEBORN SHAMEFUL
IGNOBLY BASELY
IGNOMINIOUS BASE VILE INFAMOUS SHAMEFUL
IGNOMINY SHAME REBUKE SCANDAL DISGRACE DISHONOR
IGNORAMUS IDIOT IGNARO SIMPLE AMHAAREZ
IGNORANCE IRONY TAMAS AGNOSY AVIDYA AVIJJA BETISE NICETY RUDITY UNSKILL DARKNESS IDIOTISM NESCIENCE
(BOLD —) BAYARD
(FEIGNED —) IRONY
(PREF.) AGNOIO
IGNORANT LAY DARK NICE RUDE VAIN GREEN GROSS SILLY INGRAM SIMPLE ARTLESS REDNECK SECULAR UNAWARE UNCOUTH UNKNOWN IMPERITE INNOCENT INSCIENT INSCIOUS NESCIENT UNTAUGHT BENIGHTED
(— OF EVIL) INNOCENT
IGNORANTLY SIMPLY
IGNORE BALK BLOW OMIT SINK SNUB VAIN BAULK BLINK ELIDE BYPASS MISKEN SLIGHT DESPISE MISKNOW NEGLECT TUNEOUT CONFOUND OVERJUMP OVERLEAP OVERLOOK OVERPASS
IGOROT BONTOK NABALOI KANKANAI
IGUANA GUANA GUANO LEGUAN
IGUVINE UMBRIAN
IJO DJO BONI BONNY
IKKESH (SON OF —) IRA
ILAIRA (FATHER OF —) LEUCIPPUS
(HUSBAND OF —) CASTOR
(MOTHER OF —) PHILODICE
(SISTER OF —) PHOEBE
ILEUM
(PREF.) ILEO
ILEUS MISERERE
ILIA RHEA
(FATHER OF —) NUMITOR
(SON OF —) REMUS ROMULUS
ILIAD (AUTHOR OF —) HOMER
(CHARACTER IN —) AIAS HELEN PARIS PRIAM ATHENA HECTOR NESTOR ACHILLES DIOMEDES MENELAUS ODYSSEUS PANDARUS AGAMEMNON APHRODITE PATROCLUS ANDROMACHE
ILIONE (BROTHER OF —) POLYDORUS
(FATHER OF —) PRIAM
(HUSBAND OF —) POLYMNESTOR
(MOTHER OF —) HECUBA
(SON OF —) DEIPYLUS
ILIUM TROY
ILK KIN KIDNEY
ILL BAD EVIL ILLY SICK AEGER CRONK CROOK DONCY FUNNY WISHT GROGGY INJURY POORLY SICKLY UNWELL SICKISH VICIOUS MISCHIEF PHYSICAL
(— AT EASE) ASHAMED AWKWARD FAROUCHE
(PREF.) MAL(E) MIS
ILL-ADVISED FOOLISH
ILL-BALANCED LOPSIDED
ILL-BEHAVED UNTHEWED
ILL-BEING ILLTH
ILL-BODING DIRE DISMAL
ILL-BRED HOYDEN CADDISH CHURLISH PLEBEIAN MISLEARED
ILL-CHOSEN UNSORTED
ILL-CONSIDERED HASTY
ILL-DEFINED BLIND VAGUE MONGREL
ILL-DRESSED FRUMPY FRUMPISH
ILLEGAL BLACK LAWLESS UNLAWFUL WRONGOUS ADULTERINE
(NOT —) COLD
ILLEGALITY NONO UNLAW
ILLEGIBLE BLIND
ILLEGITIMACY BASTARDY
ILLEGITIMATE BASE BASTARD BOOTLEG NATURAL NOTHOUS MISBEGOT NAMELESS UNLAWFUL WRONGFUL MISBEGOTTEN
(PREF.) NOTH(O)
ILL-FATED UNHAPPY UNSONCY UNCHANCY
ILL-FAVORED UGLY UNSONCY
ILL-FEELING PIQUE
ILL-FORMED SCRAWLY INFORMED
ILL HUMOR TID BILE DRUNT GRUMP THRAW FANTEE SPLEEN DUDGEON FANTIGUE
ILL-HUMORED FOUL GLUM CROOK DUDDY GRUMPY MOROSE STUFFY SULLEN CROOKED FRETFUL PEEVISH
ILLIBERAL LITTLE NARROW INSULAR BANAUSIC GRUDGING
ILLICIT SLY BLACK ILLEGAL UNLAWFUL
ILLIMITABLE INFINITE

ILLINOIS
CAPITAL: SPRINGFIELD
COLLEGE: AURORA EUREKA OLIVET QUINCY SHIMER
COUNTY: BOND CASS COOK KANE OGLE COLES MACON BUREAU DUPAGE GRUNDY HARDIN MASSAC PEORIA IROQUOIS MACOUPIN SANGAMON
FRENCH SETTLEMENT: CAHOKIA
HILLS: SHAWNEE
INDIAN: FOX SAUK
LAKE: MICHIGAN
NICKNAME: SUCKER PRAIRIE
PRESIDENT: REAGAN
RIVER: OHIO ROCK WABASH ELKHORN MACKINAW SANGAMON
STATE BIRD: CARDINAL
STATE FLOWER: VIOLET
STATE TREE: OAK
TOWN: PANA ALEDO ALTON CAIRO CARMI DIXON FLORA LACON OLNEY PARIS PEKIN ALBION CANTON EUREKA GALENA HARDIN HAVANA HERRIN JOLIET NORMAL OTTAWA PEORIA QUINCY SKOKIE URBANA VIENNA CHICAGO DECATUR GENESEO MENDOTA NOKOMIS TAMPICO KANKAKEE ROCKFORD

ILLINOISIAN SUCKER
ILLIPE BASSIA VIDORICUM
ILLITERATE UNREAD IGNORANT MUSELESS UNTAUGHT
ILL-MADE AWKWARD
ILL-NATURED SHREWD CRABBED

SHREWISH ACID UGLY NASTY SURLY CRABBY SNARLY SULLEN THWART CANKERY PEEVISH
ILLNESS DROW TOUT BRASH CHILL TRAIK MORBUS PLUNGE DISEASE SICKNESS
(IMAGINARY —) HYPOCHONDRIA
(MENTAL —) MANIA MONOMANIA
(MINOR —) HURRY
(MOMENTARY —) DROW
(SUDDEN —) WEED SWEAM
ILL-NOURISHED SHELLY
ILLOGICAL MAD SPURIOUS
ILL-OMENED OBSCENE DISMAL UNLUCKY
ILL-SHAPED WEEDY
ILL-SMELLING FUSTY STINKING
ILL-TEMPERED SURLY ILL FESS MEAN PUXY ACRID CHUFF NURLY RATTY CAMMED CHUFFY CURSED GIRNIE SHRILL SNAGGY RAMPANT ROPABLE VICIOUS CAMSHACH LUNGEOUS SHREWISH VIXENISH MALODOROUS
ILL-TREAT FOB HOIN MISDO AFFRONT
ILLUMINATE FIRE LIMN CLEAR LIGHT ENLIMN ILLUME KINDLE BESHINE CLARIFY EMBLAZE LIGHTEN MINIATE RADIATE EMBRIGHT FLOURISH ILLUMINE LUMINATE
(— FAINTLY) TWILIGHT
ILLUMINATED FIRELIT
ILLUMINATION E GLIM GLORY LIGHT SHINE LIGHTING LUMINARY
(— INCREASE) WOMP
(— UNIT) PHOT
(MANUSCRIPT —) MINIATURE
ILLUMINE SUN FIRE LAMP CLEAR LUMINE ENLIGHT
ILL-USAGE ABUSE
ILLUSION MAYA DEATH DREAM ERROR FAIRY FANCY FLESH TRICK MATTER CHIMERA ELUSION FALLACY FICTION MOCKERY PHANTOM RAINBOW ZOLLNER DELUSION PHANTASM PRESTIGE
ILLUSIVE PHANTOM
ILLUSORY FALSE EVANID FATUOUS PHANTOM TRICKSY APPARENT ILLUSIVE SPECTRAL
ILLUSTRATE INSTANCE
ILLUSTRATION CUT GAY ICON IKON SHOW SPOT INSET FIGURE COMPARE DISIMILE EXEMPLUM INSTANCE VIGNETTE
ILLUSTRATIVE CLASSIC
ILLUSTRATOR ERTE
ILLUSTRIOUS GRAND NOBLE NOTED SHEEN BRIGHT CANDID HEROIC EMINENT EXALTED GLORIED SHINING GLORIOUS HEROICAL LUCULENT MAGNIFIC PRECLARE RENOWNED SPLENDID STARLIKE BRILLIANT REDOUBTABLE
(MOST —) ILMO ILLMO
ILL WILL SPITE ENMITY GRUDGE MALICE MAUGER MAUGRE RANCOR DESPITE AMBITION
ILL-WISHER FOE
ILUS (FATHER OF —) TROS
(MOTHER OF —) CALLIRRHOE
(SON OF —) LAOMEDON
ILVAITE YENITE LIEVRITE
ILYSIA TORTRIX
IMAGE DAP GOD MAP FORM ICON IDOL IKON JOSS MAKE SEAL SIGN SPIT TIKI AGNUS DITTO EPHOD FANCY HERMA IMAGO MEDAL MORAL PAINT PRINT SAMMY SANTO SHAPE SIGIL SWAMI SWAMY TOTEM AGALMA ALRAUN EFFIGY EMBLEM FIGURE MAUMET MODULE POPPET RECEPT REFLEX SHRINE SPHINX STATUE SVAMIN TERAPH VISAGE WEEPER EIDOLON EXPRESS FANTASY GODLING IMAGERY KATCINA PICTURE PROPOSE CONCEIVE DAIBUTSU OPTOGRAM PORTRAIT SURPRINT ZOOMORPH SEMBLANCE SIMILITUDE SIMULACRUM RESEMBLANCE
(— IN CHINESE COSTUME) MANDARIN
(— OF CHRIST) SUDARIUM
(— OF DEITY) SWAMI GODKIN SVAMIN GODLING
(— OF SAINT) BULTO SAINT SANTO GEORGE SANTON
(— OF WOOD) XOANON
(— RECALLED BY MEMORY) IDEA
(CULT —) JOSS
(FALSE —) GHOST GHOSTING
(GOOD-LUCK —) ALRAUN ALRUNA
(HEAVENLY —) FRAVASHI
(LINGERING —) SHADE
(MENTAL —) FANCY IMAGO RECEPT CONCEPT FANTASY SPECIES PHANTASM
(RADAR —) BLIP
(REFLECTED —) SHADOW SPECIES
(SEQUENCE OF —S) REVERIE
(VAGUE —S) FRINGE
(PL.) IMAGERY TERAPHIM
(PREF.) EID(O)(OLO) EIKON(O) ICON(O) IDOLO IKON(O) TYP(I)(O)
IMAGERY ICONISM
IMAGINARY IDEAL AERIAL FEIGNED FICTIVE SHADOWY CHIMERAL CHIMERIC FANCIFUL FICTIOUS MYTHICAL NOTIONAL QUIXOTIC ROMANTIC SCENICAL VISIONAL BARMECIDE
IMAGINATION CHIC BRAIN FANCY FLAME NOTION FANTASY PROJECT THOUGHT
(DROLL —) HUMOR
IMAGINATIVE FORMFUL CREATIVE FANCIFUL POETICAL
IMAGINE SEE WIS REDE WEEN DREAM FANCY FEIGN FRAME GUESS IMAGE THINK DEVISE FIGURE IDEATE INVENT RECKON COMPASS CONCEIT CONJURE FANCIFY FANTASY FEATURE PICTURE PORTRAY PROJECT PROPOSE SUPPOSE SURMISE SUSPECT CONCEIVE DAYDREAM JEALOUSE
IMAGINED FANCIED SUPPOSED
IMAGINER FANCIER
IMAGINING FICTION PHANTOM
IMAGO MOTH
IMAM IMAUM MAHDI
IMBALANCE DRIVE DYSCRASIA
IMBECILE MAD DOTE FOOL AMENT ANILE DAFFY IDIOT CRANKY DOTARD DOTING DOTISH CONGEON FATUOUS
IMBECILITY AMENTIA FATUITY
IMBIBE DRINK SMACK ABSORB SPONGE INHAUST SWALLOW IRRIGATE
(— NOISILY) SLURP
IMBIBING SUCTION
IMBIBITORY SPONGY
IMBRIUS (FATHER OF —) MENTOR
(SLAYER OF —) AJAX
(WIFE OF —) MEDESICASTE
IMBRUE EMBREW INSTEEP
IMBUE SOAK STEW COLOR CROWN EMBUE ENDUE INDUE SCENT STEEP TINCT ENSOUL IMBIBE INFUSE LEAVEN SEASON ANIMATE INGRAIN INSENSE INSTILL SATURATE TINCTURE INOCULATE
IMBUED INSTINCT REDOLENT
IMHOTEP (FATHER OF —) PTAH
(MOTHER OF —) SEKHMET
IMIDE LACTIM SACCHARIN
IMITATE APE COPY ECHO MIME MOCK ZANY ENSUE FORGE IMAGE MIMIC AFFECT ANSWER FOLLOW PARROT SEMBLE COPYCAT EMULATE PAGEANT PATTERN PASTICHE RESEMBLE SIMULATE
(— WITH RECORDED SOUND) LIPSYNC LIPSYNCH
(PREF.) MIMO
IMITATION COPY FAKE FAUX SHAM DUMMY IMAGE MIMIC ALPACA ANSWER BUMPER ECTYPE SHADOW CAMBLET FOULARD IMITANT MIMESIS MOCKAGE MOCKERY CHENILLE PARROTRY PASTICHE POSTIQUE
(— OF COIN) COUNTER
(BURLESQUE —) TRAVESTY
(COTTON —) CAMBRIC
(EXAGGERATED —) BURLESQUE
(UNSUBSTANTIAL —) GHOST
(PREF.) NE
(SUFF.) EEN ETTE
IMITATIVE ARTY MIMIC ARTFUL ECHOIC SHODDY MIMETIC SIMULAR SLAVISH APATETIC EPIGONAL
IMITATOR APE MIME ZANY MIMIC COPIER COPYIST EPIGONE EMULATOR EPIGONUS HOMERIST
(SUFF.) MIMUS
IMMACULATE CLEAN CANDID CHASTE BLOTLESS PRISTINE SPOTLESS UNSOILED
IMMANENCE INBEING
IMMATERIAL MENTAL SLIGHT ETHEREAL FORMLESS SEPARATE TRIFLING
IMMATURE RAW CRUDE GREEN SAPPY SMALL VEALY YOUNG BOYISH CALLOW JEJUNE LARVAL NEANIC TENDER GIRLISH HALFLIN IMPUBIC LADDISH NOUVEAU PUERILE UNBAKED JUVENILE NEPIONIC UNWEANED SHIRTTAIL
IMMATURITY NONAGE
IMMEASURABLE UNTOLD ABYSMAL INFINITE
IMMEDIACY HERE
IMMEDIATE CLOSE DIRECT MODERN PARATE SUDDEN INSTANT PRESENT PROXIMAL SYNECTIC POSTHASTE
IMMEDIATELY PDQ TIT ANON ASAP AWAY FAST JUST ONCE SOON PLUMB RIGHT ASTITE DIRECT PRESTO PRONTO SUBITO DIRECTLY HEREUPON OUTRIGHT STRAIGHT
IMMEDIATENESS INSTANCY
IMMEMORIAL DATELESS
IMMENSE HUGE VAST GIANT GRAND GREAT LARGE UNMEET UNRIDE TITANIC ENORMOUS GIGANTIC INFINITE SLASHING WHOOPING PLANETARY
IMMENSELY ALOT EVER
IMMENSITY VAST IMMANE IMMENSE ENORMITY GRANDEUR HUGENESS
IMMERSE DIP SINK SOAK COVER DOUSE MERGE MERSE SOUSE STEEP DRENCH PLUNGE BAPTIZE BOWSSEN DEMERGE EMBATHE ENSTEEP IMMERGE DISSOLVE
IMMERSED DEEP INNATE
IMMERSION DIP DUNKING MERSION
IMMERSIONIST DIPPER
IMMIGRANT LAG BALT ISSEI JIMMY METIC POMMY GUINEA HALUTZ CHALUTZ INCOMER PILGRIM COMELING
IMMINENCE INSTANCY
IMMINENT TOWARD PENDING PROXIMATE
IMMIX BLEND
IMMOBILE FIXED INERT STILL FROZEN DORMANT GLACIAL TRANCED MOVELESS
(PREF.) ANKYL(O)
IMMOBILIZATION FUSION FIXATION
IMMOBILIZE PIN FREEZE SPLINT STIFFEN
IMMOBILIZED STIFF
IMMODERATE FREE DIZZY UNDUE LAVISH UNMETH EXTREME OVERWEENING
IMMODERATENESS EXCESS
IMMODEST FREE BRAZEN OBSCENE INDECENT PETULANT UNCHASTE SHAMELESS
(NOT —) DELICATE
IMMORAL BAD ILL EVIL IDLE LOOSE WRONG WANTON CORRUPT VICIOUS CULPABLE DEPRAVED INDECENT SLIPPERY
IMMORTAL DIVINE ENDLESS ETERNAL GODLIKE UNDYING ENDURING UNDEADLY
IMMORTALITY AMRITA ATHANASY ETERNITY
IMMOVABLE PAT SET FAST FIRM FIXED RIGID ADAMANT SITFAST CONSTANT IMMOBILE IMMOTIVE OBDURATE

IMMUNE FREE SALTED REFRACTORY
IMMUNITY SOC CHARTER FREEDOM LIBERTY WOODGELD PROTECTION
IMMUNOGLOBULIN IGA IGE IGM UGG
IMMURE MURE WALL CONFINE CLOISTER IMPRISON
IMMUTABILITY ONENESS
IMMUTABLE ETERNAL
IMNAH (FATHER OF —) ASHER
IMOGEN (FATHER OF —) CYMBELINE
(HUSBAND OF —) POSTHUMUS
IMP PUG BRAT LIMB DEMON TERROR URCHIN DEVILET DEVILING DEVILKIN FOLLETTO
(PRINTING-HOUSE —) RALPH
IMPACT HIT JAR BEAT BITE BLOW BUMP DASH DUSH JOLT SLAM BRUNT CLASH FEEZE PEISE POISE PULSE SHOCK SKITE GLANCE STROKE CONTACT IMPULSE COLLISION
(— OF VALUES ON YOUTH) YOUTHQUAKE
(HAVING STRONG —) GUT
IMPAIR MAR BLOT HARM HURT MAIM MANK SOUR WEAR ALLOY CLOUD CRACK CRAZE DECAY ERODE QUAIL SPOIL TAINT ACRAZE DAMAGE DEADEN DEFACE HINDER INJURE LABEFY LESSEN REDUCE SICKEN WEAKEN WORSEN BLEMISH CRIPPLE DISABLE IMPEACH REFRACT SHATTER STRETCH VITIATE DECREASE ENFEEBLE IMBECILE IMPERISH INFRINGE LABEFACT
(— BY INACTIVITY) RUST
(— ESSENTIALLY) RUIN
(— GRADUALLY) WASTE
IMPAIRED HURT STALE CROCKY FLYBLOWN
(— BY AGE) FUSTY
(— IN TONE) BREATHY
(HEARING —) DEAF
(SPEECH —) APHASIC
(PREF.) DYS
IMPAIRMENT ALLAY FAULT SPOIL DOTAGE IMPAIR INJURY LESION BEATING DEFICIT DISEASE EROSION WEARING AKINESIA PAIRMENT
(— OF CONSCIOUSNESS) ABSENCE
IMPALA PALLA PALLAH REDBUCK ROOIBOK ROODEBOK ROOYEBOK
IMPALE BAIT SPIT GANCH GANSH SPEAR SPIKE STAKE STICK STING SKIVER TRANSFIX
IMPALPABLE ELUSIVE
IMPART GIVE SEND SHED TELL BREAK DRILL SHARE YIELD BESTOW COMMON CONFER CONVEY DIRECT IMPUTE INSTIL PARTEN REVEAL DELIVER DIVULGE PURPORT DISCOVER INSTRUCT INTIMATE
(— KNOWLEDGE) TEACH INFORM
(— SECRETS) CONFIDE
(— TONE) TONE
(— ZEST) ANIMATE
IMPARTIAL EVEN FAIR JUST EQUAL LEVEL CANDID NEUTER UNBIASED
IMPARTIALITY CANDOR EQUITY EQUACITY EVENNESS
IMPARTIALLY FAIRLY EQUALLY
IMPASSABLE WICKED INVIOUS PASSLESS ROADLESS TRACKLESS
IMPASSE LOGJAM DEADLOCK
IMPASSION COMMOVE
IMPASSIONED ARDENT FERVID FERVENT FEVERISH PERFERVID
IMPASSIVE STOIC FROZEN STOLID PASSIVE STOICAL APATHETIC PHLEGMATIC
IMPASSIVENESS APATHY MORGUE STOICISM
IMPATIENT HOT ANTSY EAGER HASTY SHARP TESTY FRETFUL PEEVISH RESTIVE TIDIOSE CHOLERIC PETULANT
IMPATIENTLY HASTILY
IMPEACH CALL ACCUSE CHARGE INDICT ARRAIGN CENSURE IMPLEAD TRAVERSE
IMPEACHMENT APPEAL
IMPECCABLE SINLESS
IMPECUNIOUS POOR
IMPEDE BOG DAM GUM JAM LET MAR CLOG GRAB JAMB KILL SLUG SNAG ANNOY BLOCK CHECK CHOKE DELAY EMBAR ESTOP HITCH SLOTH SPOKE BAFFLE FETTER FORBID FORSET HAMPER HARASS HINDER HOBBLE PESTER RETARD STYMIE IMPEACH PREVENT SHACKLE ENCUMBER HANDICAP OBSTRUCT PRECLUDE
IMPEDED FOGBOUND
IMPEDIMENT BAR RUB CLOG SNAG STOP BLEAR BLOCK HITCH SPOKE STICK BURDEN RUBBER SCOTCH BLINDER EMBARGO OBSTACLE OBSTANCY
(— IN SPEECH) HAAR HALT
IMPEDIMENTA STUFF
IMPEDING CATCH HEAVY FOULING
IMPEL PAT PUT BEAR BEAT CALL CAST GOAD HURL MOVE SEND URGE WHIP CARRY DRIVE FEEZE FORCE KNOCK PRESS PRICK PULSE COMPEL EXCITE INCITE INDUCE PROPEL ACTUATE DESTINE INSPIRE INSTINCT MOTIVATE
(— TO GREATER SPEED) GATHER
IMPELLER RUNNER
IMPEND BREW HANG DEPEND OVERHANG
IMPENDING TOWARD PENDENT PENDING IMMINENT MENACING
IMPENETRABLE HARD DENSE MURKY PROOF THICK AIRTIGHT HARDENED
IMPENITENT OBDURATE
IMPERATIVE AMUST VITAL PRESSING MASTERFUL
IMPERCEPTIBLE OCCULT SUBTLE
IMPERFECT ILL HALF POOR AMISS BLIND FUZZY ROUGH BOTCHY FAULTY PLATIC ATELENE STICKIT UNWHOLE VICIOUS INPARFIT MUTILOUS
(PREF.) ATEL(O)
IMPERFECTED INCHOATE
IMPERFECTION BUG RUB WEN FLAW KINK MOLE SLUR VICE WART ERROR FAULT BLOTCH DEFECT FOIBLE BLEMISH CRUDITY DEFAULT DEMERIT FAILING FRAILTY WEAKNESS
(— IN BOTTLE) HEELTAP
(— IN GLASS) STRIA STREAK
(— IN LEATHER) FRIEZE
(— IN SILK) CORKSCREW
(— IN WICK) THIEF WASTER
IMPERFECTIVE ATELIC
IMPERFECTLY ILL HALF AMISS ROUGHLY
IMPERFORATION ATRESIA
IMPERIAL TUFT ROYAL KINGLY PURPLE MAJESTIC
IMPERIALIST KHAKI CAESAR CAESAREAN
IMPERIL RISK EXPONE EMPERIL ENDANGER JEOPARDY
IMPERIOUS BOSSY SURLY LORDLY HAUGHTY DESPOTIC IMPERIAL MASTERLY PRESSING MASTERFUL
IMPERISHABLE ETERNAL UNDYING ENDURING IMMORTAL
IMPERMANENCE ANICCA
IMPERMANENT FLEETING
IMPERMEABLE AIRTIGHT
IMPERSONAL COLD DEADPAN INHUMAN ABSTRACT
IMPERSONALITY UNSELF
IMPERSONATE POSE TYPIFY PERSONIFY
IMPERSONATION GENIUS
IMPERSONATOR APER ACTOR MIMIC CACHINA KACHINA KATCINA
IMPERTINENCE PAWK SNASH AUDACITY
IMPERTINENT GAY FREE PERT RUDE FRESH SASSY SAUCY PUSHING IMPERENT IMPUDENT OBTRUSIVE OFFICIOUS MEDDLESOME
IMPERTURBABILITY ATARAXY ATARAXIA SANGFROID
IMPERTURBABLE COOL PLACID GLACIAL TRANQUIL UNFLAPPABLE
IMPERVIOUS DEAD GASTIGHT HARDENED HERMETIC MOTHPROOF
(— TO HEAT) ADIATHERMIC
(— TO LIGHT) OPAQUE
(SUFF.) PROOF
IMPETUOSITY BIRR ELAN FURY HASTE WRATH FOUGUE POWDER RANDOM SPLEEN
IMPETUOUS HOT RAMP RASH RUDE BRASH EAGER FIERY FRECK HASTY HEADY SHARP ARDENT BROTHE FIERCE FLASHY LAVISH RACKLE STRONG BUCKISH FURIOUS HOTHEAD HOTSPUR RAMSTAM VIOLENT BRAINISH EMPRESSE HEADLONG SLAPDASH VEHEMENT PRECIPITATE
IMPETUS BIRR FARD SEND DRIFT GRACE SWING YMPET BENSEL IMPACT POWDER RAVINE SWINGE SWOUGH IMPULSE MOMENTUM
IMPIGNORATE PAWN
IMPINGE FALL IMPACT ASSAULT CROSSCUT ENCROACH
IMPINGEMENT IMPACT
IMPIOUS UNHOLY ATHEIST ATHEOUS GODLESS UNGODLY DOWNWEED HOARWORT NEFANDOUS NEFARIOUS
IMPISH IMPY ELFISH PUCKISH WARLOCK
IMPLACABLE STOUT DEADLY MORTAL
IMPLACABLY FATALLY
IMPLANT FIX IMP SET SOW HAFT ROOT GRAFT INFIX INLAY ENRACE ENROOT FASTEN INFUSE INSTIL ENFORCE ENGRAFT IMPRESS INSPIRE ENTRENCH INSTINCT
IMPLANTED INBORN INSITE
IMPLEMENT (ALSO SEE TOOL) AX AXE BAT CARD DISC DISK FORK GRAB HACK HONE HOOK LOOM PLOW SPUD SPUR TOOL CROOK DRILL FLINT LANCE SCRUB SHEAR SLICK SPADE SPOON STEEL STICK TRIER AMGARN BEAMER BLADER BROACH COLLAR COOLER DIBBLE DREDGE DRIVER DUSTER EOLITH FLAKER FLUTER HACKER HARROW INVOKE LADDER LIPPER LUNATE MARKER MEALER PACKER PADDLE PALLET PESTLE PLOUGH RIMMER SCREEN SCYTHE SEATER SEEDER SERVER SHEARS SHOVEL SICKLE SLICER SMOOTH BREAKER CHOPPER CLEANER CLEAVER ENFORCE FLESHER FLYFLAP GAROTTE GRUBBER HARPOON HUSTLER KNAPPER MATTOCK NUTPICK SKIMMER SLABBER SLASHER SLEEKER SLICKER SPATTLE SPATULA SPITTLE SPURTLE STAMPER STICKER SWATHER UTENSIL AGITATOR BUSHWACK MEASURER SCUTCHER SEARCHER SHREDDER SKETCHER SPLITTER SPREADER STRIPPER TERRACER THWACKER TOLLIKER TRANCHET TWEEZERS WARKLOOM WORKLOOM NUTCRACKER
(— FOR CUTTING CHEESE) HARP
(— FOR HANGING POT) HALE
(—S OF HUSBANDRY) WAINAGE
(— TO PREVENT MALT FROM OVERFLOWING) STROM
(ANCIENT —) POINT SLICE AMGARN EOLITH NEOLITH RACLOIR PALEOLITH
(BAKER'S —) PEEL
(CLIMBING —) CREEPER
(ESKIMO —) ULU
(GARDENING —) HOE RAKE SEEDER SICKLE
(HEDGING —) TRAMP
(IRRIGATION —) CROWDER
(LOGGING —) TODE
(POTTER'S —) PALLET SPATTLE
(PREHISTORIC —) CELT FLAKER
(SHOVEL-LIKE —) SCOOP
(SOLDERING —) DOCTOR
(TORTURE —) ENGINE
(UPROOTING —) MAKE
(WINNOWING —) FAN
(PL.) GEAR CUTLERY GAINAGE FLAUGHTS
(SUFF.) LABE

IMPLEMENTATION PERFORMANCE
IMPLICATE DIP ENWRAP CONCERN EMBROIL INCLUDE INVOLVE
IMPLICATION CLAIM IMPLIAL INNUENDO
IMPLICIT COVERT
IMPLIED TACIT IMPLICIT
IMPLORATION PETITION
IMPLORE ASK BEG CRY PRAY CHARM CRAVE PLEAD INVOKE OBTEST BESEECH CONJURE ENTREAT SOLICIT PETITION
IMPLOSION INRUSH
IMPLY HINT ARGUE CARRY COUCH INFER EMPLOY ENTAIL IMPORT INDUCE CONNOTE CONTAIN INCLUDE INVOLVE PRESUME SIGNIFY SUGGEST SUPPOSE PREDICATE
IMPOLITE RUDE UNCIVIL
IMPOLITENESS CRUDITY
IMPONDERABLE FRIGORIC
IMPORT SAY WIT BEAR BODY GIST TOUR DRIFT FORCE IMPLY MORAL SCOPE SENSE SOUND SPELL TENOR VALOR AMOUNT CHARGE DENOTE INGATE INTENT MATTER SPIRIT BETOKEN MEANING PRETEND SIGNIFY CARRIAGE INDICATE
(PL.) INWARDS
IMPORTANCE BORE MARK PITH FORCE POISE WORTH CHARGE IMPORT MATTER MOMENT REMARK STRESS STROKE WEIGHT ACCOUNT ESSENCE GRAVITY VALENCY EMPHASIS MAGNITUDE SIGNIFICANCE
IMPORTANCE OF BEING EARNEST (AUTHOR OF —) WILDE
(CHARACTER IN —) JACK ALGIE PRISM CECILY EARNEST ALGERNON WORTHING BRACKNELL GWENDOLEN MONCRIEFF
IMPORTANT BIG KEY DEAR DREE HIGH MAIN REAL GRAVE GREAT HEAVY MAJOR GAPING MIGHTY NEEDLE STRONG URGENT VALOUR CAPITAL CENTRAL CRUCIAL EMINENT MATTERY PIVOTAL SERIOUS WEIGHTY EVENTFUL MATERIAL PRESSING MOMENTOUS OVERBEARING SIGNIFICANT
(— PERSON) LION
(HIGHLY —) VITAL
(MOST —) TOP ULTIMATE
(MOST — ONE OF GROUP) FLAGSHIP
IMPORTER MILLINER
IMPORTUNATE URGENT INSTANT DEVILING EXIGEANT PRESSING
IMPORTUNE BEG WOO BEAT BONE PREY PRIG TOUT URGE PRESS TEASE BESEECH BESIEGE INSTANT SOLICIT TERRIFY INSTANCE
IMPORTUNITY BRASS URGENCY
IMPOSE LAY SET TOP CLAP GIVE LEVY MUMP POLE SORN ABUSE APPLY CLAMP INPUT STAMP TRUMP BURDEN CHARGE ENJOIN ENTAIL FASTEN FATHER IMPONE IMPUTE BLAFLUM DICTATE INFLICT IRROGATE
(— UPON) FOB GAG HUM LAY DUPE SELL CULLY TRAIL BLUDGE DELUDE EXCISE HUMBUG NUZZLE CULLION DECEIVE HOODWINK
IMPOSED BOUNDEN
IMPOSING BIG EPIC BUDGE BURLY GRAND HEFTY NOBLE PROUD AUGUST EPICAL FEUDAL PORTLY HAUGHTY POMPOUS STATELY HANDSOME MAGNIFIC SONORANT SONOROUS
(— UPON) PRACTICE PRACTISE
IMPOSITION BAM COD HUM LEVY SELL TAIL GOUGE IMPOT CHOUSE GAMMON INTAKE TAILLE IMPOSAL ARTIFICE IMPOSURE
(MILITARY —) CESS
(SCHOOL —) PENSUM
IMPOSSIBLE OUT HOPELESS
IMPOST LAY TAX CAST LEVY TAIL TASK TOLL ABWAB ANNALE AVANIA EXCISE GABELLE POUNAMU TALLAGE TONNAGE TRIBUTE CHAPTREL SPRINGER
(PL.) CUSTOMS
IMPOSTOR FOB FAKE GULL IDOL CHEAT FAKER FRAUD GOUGE QUACK BUNYIP FOURBE HUMBUG MUMPER EMPIRIC FAITOUR PROCTOR SHAMMER PHANTASM
IMPOSTURE BAM GAG FAKE HOAX SHAM CHEAT FRAUD TRICK DECEIT HUMBUG JUGGLE ARTIFICE DELUSION JUGGLERY
IMPOTENCE ACRATIA UNMIGHT WEAKNESS
(— THROUGH MAGIC) LIGATURE
IMPOTENCY UNWELTH
IMPOTENT WEAK FRIGID PAULIE UNABLE STERILE UNMIGHTY
IMPOUND FIND POIND POUND INTERN PINFOLD
IMPOVERISH PILL CLOUD BEGGAR IMPOOR SICKEN DEPLETE DEPRESS EMPOVER BANKRUPT POVERISH PAUPERIZE
IMPOVERISHED POOR OBOLARY BANKRUPT INDIGENT
IMPRACTICAL CRAZY FECKLESS
IMPRECATE WISH SWEAR
IMPRECATION DASH OATH PIZE WISH BLAME CURSE DAMME DAMMIT CONSARN ANATHEMA
IMPREGNABILITY STRENGTH
IMPREGNABLE FAST PROOF
IMPREGNATE BIG HOP DOPE FILL LIME MILT BREED IMBUE STOCK STUFF TINCT AERATE CHARGE INFORM INFUSE LEAVEN SEASON SETTLE ASPHALT ENVENOM IMPREGN CHROMATE CONCEIVE CREOSOTE FRICTION FRUCTIFY GRAPHITE MEDICATE PERMEATE SATURATE SILICATE TINCTURE
(SUFF.) **(— WITH)** URET(UM)
IMPREGNATED BRED COATED
IMPRESS FIX BITE COIN DING DINT ETCH GRAB MARK AFFIX BRAND CLAMP CRIMP DRIVE GRAVE GRILL INFIX PRESS PRINT REACH SEIZE STAMP STEAD WRITE AFFECT ENSEAL FASTEN INCUSE INDENT SALUTE STRIKE ANTIQUE ENGRAVE ENSTAMP IMPLANT IMPREST IMPRINT INSENSE AUTOTYPE INSCRIBE NEGATIVE
(— CONSIDERABLY) WOW
(— DEEPLY) DELVE ENGRAVE
(— SUDDENLY) SMITE
(— VERY MUCH) SLAY
(— WITH FEAR) AFFRIGHT
(FAIL TO —) UNDERWHELM
IMPRESSED AGOG BLIND ANTIQUE INDENTED
IMPRESSIBLE WAXY
IMPRESSION CUT HIT AURA CAST CHOP DENT DINT IDEA MARK MOLD SEAL STEP STIR FANCY GOUGE IMAGE MOULD PRINT STAMP STATE ECTYPE EFFECT ENGRAM FIGURE INCUSE OFFSET SIGNET SPLASH STRIKE EOPHYTE ETCHING FANTASY IMPRESS MOULAGE OPINION SEALING SQUEEZE STENCIL TOOLING BLANKING ENGRAMMA NEGATIVE PRESSION PRESSURE STAMPAGE TOOLMARK PHOTOGENE
(— OF DIE) CLICHE
(— ON COIN) CROSS
(— WITHOUT INK) ALBINO
(AUDITORY —) SOUND
(DOUBLE —) MACKLE MACULE
(GENERAL —) REPUTE
(IMMEDIATE —) APERCU
(LATER —) REPRINT
(LUMINOUS —) PHOSPHENE
(MAKE AN — ON) GRAB
(MENTAL —) GRAVING
(STRONG —) HUNCH
(TRANSITORY —) SNAPSHOT
(VIVID —) SPLASH
(PREF.) TYP(I)(O)
(SUFF.) TYPAL TYPE TYPIC TYPY
IMPRESSIONABLE SOFT WAXY WAXEN TENDER PLASTIC PASSIBLE
IMPRESSIONIST LUMINIST
IMPRESSIVE BIG FAT EPIC AWFUL GRAND NOBLE PROUD SOCKO EPICAL SOLEMN PESANTE STATELY TEARING TELLING WEIGHTY FORCIBLE IMPOSING SMASHING SONORANT SONOROUS STUNNING MAGNIFICENT
IMPRESSIVENESS WEIGHT
IMPREST LOAN
IMPRIMATUR SEAL LICENSE APPROVAL SANCTION
IMPRINT DINT ETCH MARK SIGN STEP PRESS STAMP CUTOFF FASTEN STRIKE ENGRAVE ENSTAMP IMPRESS APREYNTE COLOPHON EPIGRAPH PRESSION PRESSURE STAMPAGE
(— ON CHEEK) FASTEN
(PUBLISHER'S —) COLOPHON
IMPRISON JUG LAG NUN BOND GAOL HULK JAIL QUOD SEAL SHOP WARD CROWD EMBAR GRATE COMMIT IMMURE JIGGER PRISON SLOUGH CONFINE INTOWER BASTILLE
IMPRISONED FAST
IMPRISONMENT BAND BOND ARREST CHAINS DURESS PRISON CUSTODY DURANCE
IMPROBABLE FISHY UNLIKE UNLIKELY
IMPROMPTU GLIB MAGGOT SUDDEN OFFHAND
IMPROPER BAD PAH PAW AMISS LARGE SPICY UNDUE UNFELE UNJUST ILLICIT INDECENT PERVERSE TORTIOUS UNSEEMLY WRONGOUS MALODOROUS
IMPROPERLY AMISS
IMPROPRIETY SOLECISM
IMPROVE FIX BEET GAIN GOOD GROW HELP MEND AMEND EDIFY EMEND GRADE MOISE SMART TOUCH BETTER ENRICH PROFIT ADVANCE BENEFIT CORRECT CULTURE ELEVATE PERFECT PROMOTE RECTIFY UPGRADE UPSWING
(— APPEARANCE OF HORSE) BISHOP
(— APPEARANCE OF TEA) FACE
(— CONDUCTIVITY) AGE
IMPROVED BETTER
IMPROVEMENT AMENDS PICKUP POLICY PROFIT REFORM REDRESS UPSWING
IMPROVIDENT PRODIGAL WASTEFUL
(— PERSON) MICAWBER
IMPROVISATION THEME CALYPSO
IMPROVISE JAM COOK FAKE PONG VAMP WING ADLIB FANTASY
(— MUSICALLY) JAM FAKE NOODLE
(— NONSENSE SYLLABLES) SCAT
IMPRUDENCE FOLLY
IMPRUDENT FESS RASH FALSE UNWARY FOOLISH RECKLESS
IMPUDENCE GALL BRASS CHEEK MOUTH NERVE SLACK BRONZE PUPPYISM
IMPUDENT BOLD COXY FACY RUDE BANTY BARDY BRASH FRESH GALLY LIPPY SASSY SAUCY BRASSY BRAZEN CHEEKY STOCKY BIGGETY CHUNKED FORWARD GALLOWS PERKING INSOLENT MALAPERT AUDACIOUS BAREFACED
IMPUDENTLY COOLY COOLLY FRESHLY
IMPUGN DENY FALSE DISPUTE IMPEACH
IMPULSE FIT BIAS RESE SEND URGE DRIVE NISUS SPEND START DESIRE MOTIVE SIGNAL SPLEEN YETZER CALLING CONATUS IMPETUS INSTINCT MOVEMENT STIRRING
(— CARRIER) AXON
(BLIND —) ATE
(ELECTRICAL —) KICK
(SPONTANEOUS —) ACCORD
(SUDDEN —) SPLEEN
(SUPERNATURAL —) AFFLATUS
(PREF.) OSMO
IMPULSION SWING IMPULSE
IMPULSIVE QUICK FITFUL HEADLONG IMPETUOUS
IMPURE DRY FOUL LEWD GROSS HORRY MUDDY FILTHY TURBID UNPURE MONGREL SCABBED UNCLEAN VICIOUS INDECENT MACULATE PRURIENT MACULATED

IMPURITY CRUD DONOR DROSS DOPANT FEDITY ACCEPTER ACCEPTOR FOULNESS
(— IN LINT) SHALE
(— IN MINERAL) GANG GANGUE
(PL.) SCUM GARBLE SLUMMAGE
IMPUTABLE OWING
IMPUTATION SCANDAL
IMPUTE LAY PUT RET ARET EVEN WITE COUNT REFER ARRECT CHARGE FASTEN IMPOSE OBJECT RECKON REPUTE ASCRIBE ENTITLE IMPEACH
IN A I N Y AT TO BAJO INBY INTO UPON ALONG INTIL ATHOME
(— ACCORDANCE) AFTER
(— ADDITION) EKE TOO ALSO ABOVE AGAIN ALONG FORBY STILL BEYOND BESIDES FARTHER FURTHER MOREOVER OVERPLUS THERETIL
(— ADVANCE) AHEAD FORTH BEFORE
(— A FAINT) AWAY
(— ANY CASE) EVER HOWEVER
(— A SERIES) SERIATIM
(— A STATE OF ACTION) ENERGIC
(— BEHALF OF) PRO
(— CASE THAT) AUNTERS
(— CIRCULATION) ABROAD
(— CONNECTION WITH) FORNENT FERNINST
(— EARNEST) AGOOD
(— EXCESS OF) OVER
(— FACT) SOOTH TRULY INDEED ITSELF MERELY VERILY ACTUALLY VERAMENT
(— FAITH) IVADS EFECKS YFACKS
(— FRONT) FORE AFACE FORNE AGAINST PARAVANT
(— FULL) ALONG
(— GOOD SEASON) BETIMES
(— GOOD SPIRITS) BOBBISH
(— GRACEFUL MANNER) ADAGIO
(— JEST) AGAME
(— NO MANNER) NOWISE NAEGATES
(— ONE DIRECTION) ANON
(— ORDER) FOR ATAUNT ATAUNTO
(— PLACE OF) FOR WITH INSTEAD
(— POSSESSION) WITHIN
(— PROGRESS) AFOOT TOWARD
(— PROPER MANNER) DULY
(— RESPECT TO) ANENT
(— RETURN FOR) AGAINST
(— ROTATION) ABOUT
(— SO FAR AS) AS QUA
(— SOLE CONTROL) ABSOLUTE
(— SOOTH) PARFEY PERFAY
(— SPITE OF) FOR ALTHO MALGRE AGAINST DESPITE MALGRADO
(— SUSPENSE) PENDING
(— THE DOING OF) WITH
(— THE FIELD) ABROAD
(— THE FIRST PLACE) IMP IMPRIMIS
(— THE FUTURE) HENCE
(— THE MORNING) MANE
(— THE REAR) AREAR ASTERN
(— THE REGIONS OF UNBELIEVERS) IPI
(— THE SAME PLACE) IBID IBIDEM
(— THE SAME WAY) AS
(— TOWARD) INOWER
(— TRUTH) MARRY SOOTH CERTES INDEED VERILY SOOTHLY FORSOOTH
(— VAIN) WASTELY
(— VIEW OF THE FACT THAT) SEEING
(— WHAT MANNER) HOW QUOMODO
(NOT —) OUT
(PREF.) A IL IM IN INTRO IR
INABILITY (— TO FEED) APHAGIA
(— TO MASTICATE) AMASESIS
(— TO SPEAK) ALOGIA ANEPIA DUMBNESS
(— TO WALK) ABASIA
(— TO WRITE) AGRAPHIA
INACCESSIBILITY FASTNESS
INACCESSIBLE COY REMOTE UNGAIN WICKED SHADOWY
INACCURATE SOUR FALSE LOOSE FAULTY UNJUST INEXACT IMPROPER SLIPSHOD
INACHUS (DAUGHTER OF —) IO
(FATHER OF —) OCEANUS
(MOTHER OF —) TETHYS
(SON OF —) PHORONEUS
INACTION RUST
INACTIVATE MOTHBALL
INACTIVE LAX DEAD DRUG FLAT IDLE LAZY MESO SLOW HEAVY INERT NOBLE SLACK SULKY ASLEEP SEDENT STATIC SUPINE TORPID CESSANT DORMANT PASSIVE RESTIVE COMATOSE COMATOUS DEEDLESS DILATORY FAINEANT SLOTHFUL SLUGGISH THEWLESS THOWLESS QUIESCENT
INACTIVITY SLOTH ANERGY TORPOR ANERGIA ABEYANCE IDLENESS CESSATION SEGNITUDE
INADEQUACY DEFECT FRAILTY SCARCITY
INADEQUATE BAD BARE POOR THIN INEPT SCANT SHORT SLACK FEEBLE STRAIT FOOLISH INVALID SLENDER HIGHLAND INFERIOR MISERABLE
(PREF.) MAL
INADEQUATELY BADLY SLACK SLACKLY
INADVERTENCE LAPSUS
INADVERTENT CARELESS
INAJA JAGUA
INALIENABLE INHERENT
INAMORATA AMORADO AMORETTO
INANE DITSY DITZY DIZZY EMPTY GIDDY JERKY SILLY VAPID JEJUNE VACANT FATUOUS FOOLISH INSIPID PUERILE VACUOUS IMBECILE SLIPSLOP TRIFLING SENSELESS
INANGA MINNOW
INANIMATE DEAD DULL BRUTE INERT DEADLY STOLID STUPID LIFELESS
INANIMITY CONSENSUS
INANITY FATUITY VACUITY
INAPPLICABLE SPURIOUS
INAPPROPRIATE INEPT UNAPT UNDUE FOREIGN UNHAPPY
(SOMETHING —) CAMP
INAPT UNHAPPY BACKWARD FOOTLESS MALAPROPOS
INARTICULATA LYOPOMA
INARTICULATE DUMB LAME THICK
INARTISTIC CRUDE ARTLESS
INATTENTION ABSENCE NEGLECT APROSEXIA
INATTENTIVE DEAF SLACK ABSENT REMISS SUPINE DREAMSY UNTENTY CARELESS DISTRAIT HEEDLESS MINDLESS
INAUDIBLE SECRET
INAUDIBLY INWARDLY SECRETLY
INAUGURATE AUGUR BEGIN SETUP HANDSEL INITIATE
INAUGURATION HANDSEL
INAUSPICIOUS BAD ILL EVIL FOUL ADVERSE OBSCENE OMINOUS UNHAPPY UNLUCKY SINISTER
INAUTHENTIC SPURIOUS
INBORN GENIAL INBRED INNATE NATIVE CONNATE NATURAL HABITUAL INHERENT
INBRED INBORN INNATE
INBREED SELF
INBREEDING ENDOGAMY
INCA INGUA OREJON
INCALCULABLE UNTOLD SUMLESS UNKNOWN
INCA MAGIC FLOWER CANTUT CANTUTA
INCANDESCENCE GLOW
INCANDESCENT BRIGHT
INCANTATION CHARM DAWUT SPELL CARMEN FETISH MANTRA SHAZAM CANTION CHANTRY GREEGREE
INCAPABLE DEAD NUMB UNABLE HANDLESS
INCAPACITATE NAPOO UNFIT NOBBLE UNABLE DISABLE
INCAPACITATED FLAT DISABLED STRICKEN
INCARCERATE JAIL IMMURE CONFINE IMPRISON
INCARNATE BODIED EMBODY CARNATE ENFLESH HUMANIFY PERSONIFY
INCARNATION RAMA IMAGE ADVENT AVATAR GENIUS MNEVIS TERTON HUTUKTU EPIPHANY PERSONIFICATION
INCAUTIOUS RASH UNWARY UNCHARY UNTENTY CAREFREE RECKLESS
INCENDIARY FIREBUG ARSONIST BOUTEFEU
INCENSE CENSE INFLAME KETURAH PROVOKE IRRITATE THYMIAMA
(— INGREDIENT) ONYCHA
(— VESSEL) SHIP
(PREF.) THURI
INCENSE-BOAT NAVICULA
INCENSED RAW HETUP IRATE RILED WROTH WRATHFUL
INCENTIVE BROD GOAD SPUR PRICK MOTIVE IMPETUS IMPULSE INCITIVE STIMULUS MOTIVATION
INCEPTION ORIGIN ANCESTRY
INCESSANT STEADY ENDLESS CONSTANT
INCESSANTLY FOREVER
INCH UNCH PRIME UNCIA
(ABOUT 7 —S) FISTMELE
(100TH OF —) POINT
(4 —S) HANDFUL
(48TH OF —) IRON
(9 —S) SPAN
INCHOATE FORMLESS
INCIDENT GO EVENT LIABLE CAUTION EPISODE PASSAGE SUBJECT ACCIDENT CASUALTY OCCASION OCCURRENCE
(AMUSING —) BAR BREAK
(LITERARY —) BIT
INCIDENTAL BY BYE SIDE STRAY CASUAL EPISODIC GLANCING INCIDENT OCCURRENT
INCIDENTALLY BYHAND OBITER APROPOS BYTHEWAY
INCINERATE COMBUST CREMATE
INCINERATOR BURNER SALAMANDER
INCIPIENCE BUD
INCIPIENT INITIAL GERMINAL INCHOATE
INCISE CHOP RASE LANCE INCIDE CHANNEL ENGRAVE
INCISION CUT GASH SLIT SNIP ISSUE SCORE BROACH SCOTCH STREAK CUTDOWN DIACOPE APLOTOMY CECOTOMY COLOTOMY CULDOTOMY
(SUFF.) TOMY
INCISIVE ACID KEEN CRISP SHARP BITING BRUTAL CUTTING ACULEATE PIERCING TRENCHANT
INCISIVENESS MORDANCY
INCISOR CUTTER NIPPER GATHERER
INCITE EGG HIE HOY PUT SIC TAR ABET BEET BUZZ EDGE FIRE GOAD LASH MOVE PROD SICK SNIP SPUR STIR URGE WHET AWAKE CHIRK EGGON IMPEL PRICK PROKE SPARK SPURN STING TEMPT AROUSE BESTIR ENTICE EXCITE EXHORT FILLIP FOMENT HALLOO INDUCE KINDLE NETTLE PROMPT UPSTIR URGEON ACTUATE ANIMATE COMMOVE INCENSE INSPIRE PROMOVE PROVOKE QUICKEN SOLICIT INCITATE MOTIVATE
(— SECRETLY) SUBORN
(— TO ATTACK) SET HIRR SOOL
INCITEMENT GOAD PROD SPUR STING MOTIVE EGGMENT STIRRING
(— OF LITIGATION) BARRATRY
INCITER FEEDER MONITOR INCENSOR INCENTOR
INCLEMENCY RIGOR CRUELTY TYRANNY ASPERITY HARDNESS SEVERITY
INCLEMENT RAW HARD RUDE SOUR GURLY STARK COARSE RUGGED SEVERE UNFINE UNKINDLY
(NOT —) OPEN CIVIL
INCLINATION DIP GEE MAW PLY SET BENT BIAS BROO CANT CARE DRAG DRAW EDGE FALL GUST HANG LEAN LIKE LIST LOVE LUST MIND SLEW TURN VEIN WILL BEVEL BOSOM DRAFT DRIFT FANCY GRAIN HABIT HIELD HUMOR KNACK LURCH PITCH POISE SLANT

SLOPE STUDY SWING TASTE THEAT TREND AFFECT ANIMUS ANLAGE ASCENT DESIRE DEVICE GATHER GENIUS INTENT LIKING MOTION NOTION PONDUS RELISH SQUINT TALENT YETZER APTNESS CONATUS COURAGE CURRENT DESCENT DRAUGHT FANTASY INKLING LEANING STOMACH VERSANT WILLING APPETITE APTITUDE CLINAMEN DEVOTION GRADIENT PENCHANT TENDENCY VELLEITY VERGENCY WOULDING PROCLIVITY PROPENSITY
(— DOWNWARD) DIP DESCENT HANGING
(— FROM VERTICAL) RAKE
(— OF OARSMAN'S BODY) LAYBACK
(INWARD —) BATTER
(PLEASUREFUL —) RELISH
(PREDOMINATE —) STRENGTH
INCLINE APT BOW DIP KIP TIP WRY BEAR BEND BIAS BREW CANT CAST DOCK DOOK DOOR DROP GIVE HANG HEEL HELD HILL LEAN LIKE LIST PECK PEND RAKE SEEL STAY SWAY TILT TURN BEVEL CLIMB CLINE DROOP FLECT HIELD JINNY OFFER PITCH SHAPE SLANT SLOPE SOUND VERGE AFFECT GLACIS INTEND SHELVE STEEVE UPBROW DECLINE DESCEND GANGWAY PROPEND PROCLINE PROCLIVE
(— SKI) EDGE
(PREF.) CLIN(O)
INCLINED APT FIT SIB BENT CANT FAIN LIEF RIFE VAIN ALIST ARAKE ATILT GIVEN LEANT PRONE READY ASLOPE COUCHE MINDED PROMPT SLOPED SUPINE FORWARD HANGING OBLIQUE PRONATE STUDIED AFFECTED DISPOSED ENCLITIC PREGNANT PROPENSE SIDELING TALENTED
(— TO DRINK) BIBULOUS
(— TO LEARN) WALTY
(READILY —) PROMPT
INCLINING HILLY SHELVY SLOPING CERNUOUS PROPENSE SIDELING
(SUFF.) CLINIC CLINOUS
INCLUDE ADD LAP HAVE TAKE ANNEX COUCH COVER IMPLY EMPLOY ENSEAM RECKON BELOUKE COLLECT CONNOTE CONTAIN EMBRACE IMMERSE INVOLVE RECOUNT SUBSUME COMPRISE CONCLUDE
(— IN LIST) ENGROSS
INCLUDING TO CUM
(— EVERYTHING) OVERALL
INCLUSIVE GRAND CAPABLE CATHOLIC
INCLUSIVELY BROADLY
INCLUSUS RECLUSE
INCOHERENT FUZZY BROKEN RAVING INCHOATE
INCOHERENTLY IDLY
INCOMBUSTIBLE APYROUS ASBESTIC
INCOME GAIN PORT RENT RENTE LIVING PEWAGE PEWING PROFIT SALARY FACULTY INTRADO INTRATE PRODUCE REVENUE STIPEND INTEREST PROCEEDS POCKETBOOK
(— OF BENEFICE) ANNAT
(ANNUAL —) RENTE
(FRENCH —) RENTE
(UNFORESEEN —) GRAVY
INCOMMENSURATE UNEQUAL
INCOMMODE VEX ANNOY MOLEST PLAGUE TROUBLE DISQUIET
INCOMPARABLE ALONE
INCOMPATIBILITY SOLECISM ANTIPATHY
INCOMPATIBLE ALIEN REPUGNANT
INCOMPETENT INEPT UNFIT SLOUCH UNABLE UNMEET FECKLESS HANDLESS HELPLESS SPLITTER
INCOMPLETE WANE BLIND ROUGH BROKEN UNDONE DIVIDED LACKING PARTIAL SKETCHY IMMATURE INCHOATE SEGMENTAL
(GRAMMATICALLY —) PENDANT
(PREF.) ATEL(O) DEMI SEMI
INCOMPLETELY BADLY HALVES
INCOMPOSITE PRIME
INCOMPREHENSIBILITY ACATALEPSY
INCOMPREHENSIBLE PARTIAL COCKEYED
INCONCLUSIVE FUZZY
INCONGRUITY JAR ANOMALY SOLECISM
INCONGRUOUS ALIEN ABSURD ANOMALOUS
INCONNU CONY NELMA CONNIE SHEEFISH
INCONSEQUENTIAL NUGATORY
INCONSIDERABLE WEAK LIGHT PETTY LITTLE
INCONSIDERATE RASH UNKIND ASOCIAL RECKLESS
INCONSISTENCY HOLE
INCONSISTENT ALIEN REPUGNANT
INCONSPICUOUS OBSCURE
INCONSTANCY CHANGE LEVITY
INCONSTANT FICKLE BRUCKLE FLUXILE MOONISH MUTABLE PROTEAN SLIDING VARIOUS FLUXIBLE METEORIC MOVEABLE STRUMPET VARIABLE CHAMELEON MERCURIAL VERSATILE
INCONTESTABLE SURE CLEAN CERTAIN POSITIVE
INCONTINENCE ENURESIS
INCONTINENT LOOSE LAXATIVE
INCONTROVERTIBLE GRAND
INCONVENIENCE FASH BOTHER CUMBER STRESS SQUEEZE DISQUIET
INCONVENIENT UNKED CLUMSY UNBANE UNGAIN AWKWARD UNHANDY ANNOYING UNCHANCY UNTOWARD
INCOORDINATION ASTASIA
INCORPORATE MIX FOLD FUSE JOIN ANNEX KNEAD MERGE UNITE ABSORB EMBODY ENGRAIN ENTRAIN INWEAVE INCORPSE
(— IN WALL) ENGAGE
INCORPOREAL AERY BODILESS ASOMATOUS
INCORRECT BAD ILL OFF FALSE WRONG PECCANT UNRIGHT UNSOUND VICIOUS PERVERSE
(PREF.) CAC(O)
INCORRIGIBLE HARD
INCORRUPTIBLE IMMORTAL
INCREASE UP ADD EIK EKE IMP WAX BUMP ECHE GAIN GROW HELP HIKE HYPE ITCH JACK JUMP MEND MORE MUCH PLUS PUSH RISE SOAR THEE THRO BOOST BUILD BULGE CLIMB CROWD FLUSH FRESH GOOSE HEAVE LARGE RAISE SPURT SWELL ACCENT ACCESS ACCRUE BETTER BIGGEN CHANGE CREASE DEEPEN DOUBLE EXPAND EXTEND EXTENT GATHER GROWTH PUMPUP SPREAD SPRING UPTICK ADVANCE AMPLIFY AUCTION AUGMENT AUXESIS BALLOON DISTEND ELEVATE ENGROSS ENHANCE ENLARGE GREATEN IMPROVE INFLATE MAGNIFY STEEPEN SURCRUE ACCRESCE ADDITION COMPOUND ESCALATE FLOURISH HEIGHTEN LENGTHEN MAJORATE MAXIMATE MAXIMIZE MULTIPLY THRODDEN PROPAGATE PROLIFERATE
(— ACCORDING TO RATIO) SCALEUP
(— AT USURY) OCKER
(— GREATLY) ACCUMULATE
(— HEAT OF KILN) RUSTLE GLISTER
(— IN BUSINESS) UPBEAT
(— IN PAY) FOGY FOGIE
(— IN SIZE) AUXESIS
(— IN STRENGTH) FRESHEN
(— KNOWLEDGE) ENRICH
(— OF DEPTH) OVERFALL
(— OF LOUDNESS) CRESCENDO
(— OF POWER) SURGE
(— OF WEALTH) THRIFT
(— POWER) SOUP
(— PRICE BY BIDDING) CANT
(— RAPIDLY) SOAR MUSHROOM
(— SPEED) JAZZ GOOSE ACCELERATE
(— STITCHES) FASHION
(— SUDDENLY) LEAP
(PRICE —) RIST
(SALARY —) FLOWON
(SHORT-TERM —) BOOMLET
(TEMPORARY —) BULGE
(PREF.) AUXO
(SUFF.) AUXE OSIS
INCREASING GROWING CRESCENT CRESCIVE DILATANT SWELLING CUMULATIVE
(— RAPIDLY) BOOMING
INCREDIBLE TALL STEEP DAMNED FABULOUS COCKAMAMY COCKAMAMIE
INCREDULITY UNBELIEF
INCREDULOUS INFIDEL
INCREMENT DOSE DELTA INCREASE
INCRIMINATE ACCUSE
INCRUST FOUL
INCRUSTATION CRUD MOSS CRUST SCALE TARTAR FOULING FURRING
INCUBATE SIT BROOD CLOCK COVER HATCH
INCUBATION PASSAGE
INCUBATOR FURNACE HATCHER COUVEUSE ISOLETTE
INCUBUS DUSE MARE DUSIO NIGHTMARE
INCULCATE BREED INFIX INCULK INFUSE IMPLANT IMPRESS INSTILL
INCULCATED BRED
INCUMBENT COARB BEARER
INCUR RUN BEAR GAIN WAGE CONTRACT
INCURABLE BOOTLESS HOPELESS
INCURRENT INHALANT
INCURSION RAID ROAD FORAY INFALL INROAD RAZZIA DESCENT HOSTING INBREAK INCURSE ANABASIS INVASION
INCUS AMBOS ANVIL
INDEBTED LIABLE DEBTFUL BEHOLDEN
INDEBTEDNESS DEBT SCORE
INDECENCY IMPURITY PRIAPISM RIBALDRY
INDECENT PAW BLUE FOUL LEWD RANK BAWDY GROSS NASTY SAUCY GREASY IMPURE PAWPAW SMUTTY CURIOUS GRIVOIS IMMORAL OBSCENE IMMODEST IMPROPER SHAMEFUL UNCOMELY
INDECENTLY DIRTY
INDECISION DEMUR DOUBT MAYBE POISE SWITHER
(PSYCHOTIC —) ABULIA
INDECISIVE DRAWN HALTING
(BE —) TEETER
INDECISIVENESS SUSPENSE
INDECOROUS RUDE COARSE FORWARD UNCIVIL IMMODEST IMPOLITE IMPROPER INDECENT UNSEEMLY UNTOWARD GRACELESS TASTELESS
INDEED SO ARU NAY TOO WIS YEA AWAT DEED EVEN IWIS JUST SURE MARRY QUOTH TIENS ATWEEL ITSELF PARDIE SURELY FAITHLY FRANKLY SOOTHLY FORSOOTH VERAMENT
INDEFATIGABLE TIRELESS
INDEFENSIBLE INVALID
INDEFINABLE NAMELESS
INDEFINITE HAZY FUZZY GROSS LOOSE VAGUE DIVERS INEXACT AORISTIC NUBILOUS
INDEFINITELY IN
INDELIBLE FAST FIXED
INDELICATE RAW FREE WARM BROAD GROSS ROUGH COARSE GREASY IMPOLITE IMPROPER UNSEEMLY
INDEMNIFICATION RELIEF
INDEMNIFY PAY REPAY RECOUP SATISFY WARRANT
INDENT JAG BRIT DENT GIMP MUSH NICK CHASE DELVE NOTCH STAMP TOOTH WHEEL BRUISE CRENEL ENGRAIL GAUFFER
INDENTATION CHOP DENT DINT DOKE FOIL KINK SCAR BOSOM BULGE CLEFT CRENA DINGE NOTCH SINUS DIMPLE FURROW

GROOVE INDENT RECESS IMPRESS CRENELLE TOOTHING
(— IN BOTTLE) KICK
(— IN DOG'S FACE) STOP
(— IN SHELL) EYE
INDENTED WAVED CRENATE NOTCHED SINUATE
INDENTURE BIND INDENT ESCALLOP SYNGRAPH
INDEPENDENCE AUTARKY FREEDOM AUTARCHY
(— OF GOD) ASEITY ASEITAS
(POLITICAL —) SWARAJ
INDEPENDENT FREE PROUD SEEKER BIGGITY DIVIDED MUGWUMP SECTARY ABSOLUTE PECULIAR POSITIVE SEPARATE
(STATISTICALLY —) ORTHOGONAL
(PREF.) SELF
INDEPENDENTLY APART
INDESCRIBABLE TERMLESS INEFFABLE
INDETERMINATE AORISTIC FORMLESS INFINITE
INDEX PIE FIST HAND ARNETH ELENCH PIGNET TONGUE POINTER ALPHABET EXPONENT REGISTER
(COMPUTER —) KWIC KWOC

INDIA

ANCIENT NAME: BHARAT
CAPE: COMORIN
CAPITAL: NEWDELHI
CASTE: JAT MAL AHIR GOLA JATI MALI DHOBI SANSI SUDRA VARNA DACOIT DHANUK LOHANA VAISYA AGARWAL BRAHMAN DHANGAR
COAST: MALABAR
COIN: LAC PIE ANNA FELS LAKH PICE TARA ABIDI CRORE PAISA RUPEE
COLLEGE: TOL
DESERT: THAR
DISTRICT: SIBI NASIK PATNA SIMLA ZILLAH MALABAR NELLORE MOFUSSIL
GULF: KUTCH CAMBAY MANNAR
ISLAND: CHILKA
LAKE: WULAR CHILKA COLAIR DHEBAR SAMBAHR
LANGUAGE: URDU HINDI TAMIL TELUGU SANSKRIT
MEASURE: ADY DHA GAZ GUZ JOW KOS LAN SER BYEE COSS DAIN DHAN HATH JAOB KUNK MOOT PARA RAIK RATI SEIT TAUN TENG TOLA AMUNA BIGHA CAHAR COVID CROSA DANDA DRONA GARCE GIREH HASTA PALLY PARAH RATTI SALAY YOJAN ADHAKA ANGULA COVIDO CUDAVA CUMBHA GEERAH LAMANY MOOLUM MUSHTI PALGAT PARRAH ROPANI TIPREE UNGLEE YOJANA ADOULIE DHANUSH GAVYUTI KHAHOON NIRANGA PRASTHA VITASTI OKTHABAH
MOUNTAIN: MERU GHATS KAMET MASTUJ TANKSE KALAHOI SIWALIK VINDHYA SULEIMAN
MOUNTAIN RANGE: SATPURA VINDHYA ARAVALLI HIMALAYA
NATIVE: TODA HINDU TAMIL
PROVINCE: HAR ASSAM BIHAR ANDHRA BENGAL KERALA MADRAS MYSORE ORISSA PUNJAB GUJARAT HARYANA KASHMIR MANIPUR
REGION: MALABAR
RIVER: AI DOR SON TEL KOSI KUSI NIRA REHR SIND BETWA BHIMA DAMOH GOGRA INDUS JAWAI RAPTI SANKH SONAR TAPTI TUNGA CHENAB GANGES KISTNA PENNER SUTLEJ WARDHA CAUVERY CHAMBAL IRAWADI KRISHNA NARMADA NARMEDA HEMAVATI HYDASPES MAHANADI NERBUDDA VINDHYAS
SEAPORT: DAMAN BOMBAY COCHIN MADRAS CALCUTTA
STATE: ASSAM BIHAR KERALA MYSORE ORISSA PUNJAB GUJARAT MANIPUR
STRAIT: PALK
TERRITORY: DIU GOA DAMAN MINICOY AMINDIVI
TOWN: DIU AGRA DAMA GAYA PUNA REWA ADONI AKOLA ALWAR ARCOT BHERA DACCA DATIA DELHI GIROT KALPI PATAN PATNA POONA SALEM SIMLA SURAT TEHRI AJMERE AMBALA BARELI BARODA BHOPAL BOMBAY CHAMBA COCHIN DUMDUM HOWRAH INDORE JAIPUR KANPUR LAHORE MADIRA MADRAS MADURA MEERUT MULTAN MUTTRA MYSORE NAGPUR RAMPUR UJJAIN ALIGARH BENARES BIKANER CALICUT CAWNPUR DINAPUR GWALIOR JODHPUR KARACHI KURNOOL LASWARI LUCKNOW RANGOON RANGPUR AMRITSAR BHATINDA BHATPARA CALCUTTA DINAPORE JABALPUR KOLHAPUR MANDALAY MIRZAPUR PESHAWAR SHOLAPUR SRINAGAR VARANASI
TRIBE: AO GOR BHIL BADAGA SHERANI
WATERFALL: JOG GOKAK CAUVERY
WEIGHT: MOD PAI SER VIS DHAN DRUM KONA MYAT PALA PANK PICE RAIK RATI RUAY SEER TANK TOLA YAVA ADPAD BAHAR CANDY CATTY HUBBA MASHA MAUND PALLY POUAH RATTI RETTI RUTEE TICAL TICUL TIKAL ABUCCO DHURRA KARSHA CHITTAK PEIKTHA

INDIAN LO RED ROJO INJUN TAWNY ABNAKI INDISH REDMAN BHARATI HOSTILE NAIKPOD REDSKIN LONGHAIR MUSKOGEE PENOBSCOT SHAHAPTIAN NARRAGANSET
(— LEADER) NEHRU
(AMERICAN —) AIS AUK FOX HOH KAW OTO REE SAC SIA UTE WEA ZIA ADAI COOS CREE CROW DOEG ERIE EYAK HANO HOPI HUPA IOWA KATO KOSO MOKI MONO OTOE OTTO PIMA PIRO SAUK TANO TAOS TEWA TIOU TOAG UTAH WACO YUMA ZUNI ACOMA ALSEA BANAK BIDAI CADDO CHAUI COMOX CONOY COREE CREEK HANIS HOOPA HUECO HURON JEMEZ KANIA KANSA KAROK KERES KIOWA KOROA KUSAN LENCA LIPAN MAKAH MANSO MIAMI MINGO MODOC MOQUI NAMBE OMAHA OSAGE OSTIC OZARK PECOS PINAL PIUTE PONCA SAMBO SARSI SEWEE SIOUX SITKA SKIDI SLAVE SNAKE SOOKE TETON TEXAS TIGUA TONTO TWANA TYIGH UINTA UNAMI WAPPO WASCO WASHO WIYOT YAMEL YAZOO YUCHI YUROK AGAWAM AHTENA APACHE ATSINA ATUAMI AVOYEL BILOXI CALUSA CAYUGA CAYUSE CHATOT CHERAW CHETCO COOSUC CUPENO DAKOTA DIGGER EYEISH FARAON GILENO HAINAI HAISLA ISLETA KAIBAB KAINAH KANSAS KICHAI KOSIMO KUITSH LAGUNA LENAPE MANDAN MAUMEE MAYEYE METOAC MICMAC MIKMAK MOHAVE MOHAWK MUNSEE NASHUA NATICK NAUSET NAVAHO NAVAJO NEUTER NOOTKA OGLALA ONEIDA OREJON OTTAWA PAIUTE PAPAJO PATWIN PAWNEE PEORIA PEQUOD PEQUOT PIEGAN PODUNK PUEBLO QUAPAW QUERES RIKARI SALISH SAMISH SANTEE SAPONI SATSOP SENECA SHASTA SILETZ SIOUAN SIWASH SKAGIT SOKOKI SUMASS SUMDUM SUTAIO SYLVID TAPOSA TENINO TOHOME TOLOWA TONGAS TUNICA TUTELO UMPQUA WALAPI WAPATO WATALA WAXHAW WEANOC WIKENO WINTUN YAKIMA YAMASI ZUNIAN ABENAKI ALABAMA ALIBAMU AMERIND ANDARKO ANDASTE ARIKARA ATAKAPA AYAHUCA BANNOCK CAHOKIA CALOOSA CATAWBA CHILCAT CHILULA CHINOOK CHOCTAW CHUMASH CHUMAWI CIBECUE CLALLAM CLATSOP COCHITI COLCINE COWLITZ DEADOSE DHEGIHA DWAMISH ESSELEN GOSHUTE HELLELT HIDATSA HUCHNOM HUICHOL INGALIK JUANENO KANAWHA KLAMATH KOASATI KOHUANA KOPRINO KUNESTE KUTCHIN KUTENAI LUISENO MASHPEE MASKOKI MOHEGAN MOHICAN MONACAN MONSONI MONTAUK MOUSONI NANAIMO NASCAPI NATCHEZ NIANTIC NIMKISH NIPMUCK OJIBWAY PACIFID PADUCAH PAMLICO PICURUS QUAITSO SALINAN SANETCH SANPOIL SERRANO SHAPTAN SHAWANO SHAWNEE SIKSIKA SIUSLAW SONGISH SPOKANE SQUAXON STIKINE TAMAROA TESUQUE TIMUCUA TLINGIT TONKAWA TUALATI TULALIP TUTUTNI UGARONO WAILAKI WALPAPI WAMESIT WANAPUM WASHAKI WEWENOC WHILKUT WICHITA WISHOSK WITUMKI WYANDOT YANKTON YAQUINA YAVAPAI YOJUANE YONKALA ABSAROKA ACHOMAWI ACHUMAWI ALGONKIN AMERICAN AMOSKEAG APALACHI ARIVAIPA ARKANSAS ASTAKIWI ATFALATI ATSUGEWI CAHINNIO CAHUILLA CANARSIE CHAWASHA CHEHALIS CHEMAKUM CHEROKEE CHEYENNE CHIMAKUM CHOPTANK CHOWANOC CLACKAMA COLUMBIA COLVILLE COMANCHE COQUILLE COYOTERO DELAWARE DIEGUENO ETCHIMIN FLATHEAD HITCHITI HUNKPAPA ILLINOIS IROQUOIS KALISPEL KAWAIISU KICKAPOO KIKATSIK KLASKINO KLIKITAT KONOMIHU LAMANITE MALECITE MASCOTIN MENOMINI MIKASUKI MINITARI MISSOURI MOGOLLON MUSCOGEE MUSKWAKI NEHANTIC NESPELIM NOTTOWAY OKINAGAN ONONDAGA PAMUNKEY PANAMINT PATUXENT PAVIOTSO PENACOOK PISHQUOW POWHATAN PUYALLUP QUATSINO QUERECHO QUILEUTE QUINAULT ROCKAWAY SAHAPTIN SAULTEUR SAVANNAH SEMINOLE SHIVWITS SHOSHONE SIHASAPA SINGSING SINKIUSE SINKYONE SINTSINK SISSETON SOUHEGAN SQUAMISH SQUEDUNK TLAKLUIT TOBIKHAR TOPINISH TSIHALIS TUSHEPAW TUSKEGEE UMATILLA WABANAKI WACHUSET WAHPETON WETUMPKA YAHUSKIN YAMACRAW DOUSTIONI SQUAWTITS
(BRAZILIAN —) BUGRE
(CANADIAN —) DENE COMOX HAIDA SLAVE TINNE DOGRIB HAISLA LASSIK MICMAC SARSEE BEOTHUK GOASILA KHOTANA KOYUKON CHISEDEC COWICHAN HEILTSUK KIMSQUIT KWAKIUTL LILLOOET SALTEAUX SHUSHWAP
(FEMALE —) SQUAW KLOOCH
(MALE —) BUCK SANNUP SIWASH
(MEXICAN —) MAM OVA CHOL CORA JOVA MAYA MAYO ROTO SERI TECA TECO XOVA AZTEC CHIZO CHORA HUABI HUAVE KAMIA NAHUA OPATA OTOMI YAQUI ZOQUE CAHITA CHOCHO CONCHO EUDEVE KILIWI NEVOME OTONIA PAKAWA TARASC TOLTEC ZOTZIL ACOLHUA AKWAALA AMISHGO CHATINO CHINCHA CHINIPA CHONTAL COTONAM COUHIMI GUASAVE HUASTEC HUAXTEC MAZATEC MISTECA MIXTECA NAYARIT SINALOA TEGUIMA TEHUECO TEPANEC TEPEHUA TZENTAL TZOTZIL ZACATEC ZAPOTEC CHANABAL CHAPANEC CHUCHONA COLOTLAN COMANITO CONICARI GUASAPAR HUASTECO IRRITILA JACALTEC JANAMBRE LACANDON LAGUNERO TARUMARI TECPANEC TEXCOCAN TEZCUCAN TOTONACO TZAPOTEC YUCATECO
(OTHER —) GE ITE ONA URO URU YAO AGAZ ANDE ANTA ANTI AUCA BABU CAME CANA CARA CHUJ COTO CUNA DENE DIAU DUIT INCA ITEN ITZA IXIL MOJO MOXO MURA

MUSO MUZO PEBA PIRO RAMA TAMA TAPE TATU TOBA TRIO TUPI TUPY ULUA ULVA ACROA ARARA ARAUA ARUAC AUETO BAURE BETOI BRAVO BUGRE CAITE CAMPA CANCA CARIB CHANE CHIMU CHITA CHOCO CHOKO CHOLA CHOLO CHONO COCTO COLAN CUEVA DIRIA GUANA GUATO HUARI JAVAH KASKA LENCA MOCOA MOZCA OPATA OYANA PALTA PAMPA PASSE PETEN PINTO PIOJE PIOXE PIPIL POKAN POKOM QUITU SENCI SIUSI SMOOS TAINO UAUPE UMAUA VEJOZ WAURA XINCA YAGUA YAMEO YUNCA YUNGA AGUANO AIMARA AKAVAI AKAWAI AMORUA ANDOKE ANTISI APANTO APARAI APIACA ARAWAK AROACO ATORAI AYMARA BABINE BANIVA BETOYA BORORO BRIBRI BRUNKA CAHETE CAIGUA CANCHI CANELO CARAHO CARAJA CARAYA CARIRI CAUQUI CAVINA CAYAPA CHAIMA CHARCA CHAYMA CHICHA CHISCA CHOCOI CHORTI COCAMA COCOMA COCORA COFANE COLIMA COTOXO CUCAMA CULINO CUMANA DOGRIB DORASK GALIBI GOYANA GUAIMI GUAQUE GUAYMI HUARPE HUBABO IGNERI INCERI IXIAMA JIVARO JUCUNA JUMANA JURUNA KARAYA KEKCHI KUCHIN LENGUA LUCAYO MACUSI MAKUSI MANGUE MANIVA MIRANA MUYSCA NAHANE NASCAN OMAGUA OTOMAC PAPAGO PKOMAM PURUHA QUICHE SABUJA SACCHA SALIBA SALIVA SAMUCU SEKANE SETIBO SIPIBO SUERRE TACANA TAGISH TAHAMI TAMOYO TAPAJO TAPUYA TARUMA TECUNA TICUNA TIMOTE TOTORO TUCANO TUNEBO UIRINA UITOTO VILELA WAIWAI WITOTO WOOLWA YAHGAN YAHUNA YARURO YURUNA ZAPARA ACHAGUA ACKAWOI AKAMNIK ANDAQUI ANGAITE APALAII APINAGE ARECUNA ARHUACO BEOTHUK BILQULA CACHIBO CAINGUA CALIANA CAMACAN CARANGA CARIBAN CARIBEE CARRIER CASHIBO CHARRUA CHIBCHA CHIMANE CHIMILA CHIRINO CHONCHO CHOROTE CHUMULU CHUNCHO CHURAPA CHUROYA CIBONEY CJACOGO COROADO FRENTON FUEGIAN GITKSAN GOAHIVO GOAJIRA GUAHIVO GUARANI GUARANY GUARAYO GUARRAU GUARUAN GUATUSO GUETARE HUANUCO HUATUSO ITONAMA JACUNDA JICAQUE KALIANA KOPRINO KULIANA LUCAYAN MAIPURE MISKITO MONGOYO MORCOTE NICARAO PAMPERO PAYAGUA PEDRAZA PIARROA POKOMAM PUELCHE PUQUINA QUECHUA QUEKCHI RANQUEL SARIGUE SATIENO SHUSWAP SINSIGA SIRIONE TAHLTAN TALUCHE TALUHET TAMANAC TARIANA TARRABA TAYRONA TELEMBI TIMBIRA TIRRIBI TSONECA UARAYCU UCAYALE VOYAVAI WOYAWAY YUSTAGA ZUTUHIL AGUARUNA AHOUSAHT AKIYENIK ALACALUF AMAHUACA APOLISTA ARAQUAJU AWISHIRA BOTOCUDO CAINGANG CALINAGO CANAMARY CANOEIRO CAQUETIO CARIBISI CARIJONA CARIPUNA CAYUBABA CHAMBOIA CHANDALA CHAVANTE CHIQUITO CHIRIANA COLORADO COMIAKIN CONCHUCU CORABECA CUSTENAU GUAYAQUI GUAYCURU JAVITERO KANHOBAL KLASKINO LOROKOTO MACARANI MAYORUNA MISSKITO MOSQUITO NIQUIRAN OCHOZOMA OROTINAN PACAVARA PALENQUE PARUKUTU PINALENO POIGUARA POKONCHI POPOLOCO POTYUARA PUPULUCA QUATSINO QUERENDY QUIMBAYA SHIRIANA SNONOWAS SUBTIABA TADOUSAC TAPACURA TENAKTAK TOCOBAGA TOROMONA TSATTINE TUMUPASA UAREKENA URUKUENA USPANTEC YURUCARE
(SOUTH AFRICAN —) COOLY COOLIE
(SPANISH-AMERICAN —) CHOLO

INDIANA
CAPITAL: INDIANAPOLIS
COLLEGE: BALL BETHEL DEPAUW GOSHEN MARIAN PURDUE WABASH
COUNTY: JAY CASS CLAY KNOX OWEN PIKE RUSH VIGO BOONE FLOYD WELLS JASPER TIPTON DAVIESS PULASKI
INDIAN: MIAMI HAWNEE
LAKE: MONROE MANITOU WAWASEE MICHIGAN
NATIVE: HOOSIER
RIVER: OHIO WHITE WABASH
STATE BIRD: CARDINAL
STATE FLOWER: PEONY
STATE TREE: TULIP
TOWN: GARY PERU PAOLI VEVAY ALBION ANGOLA BRAZIL GOSHEN JASPER KOKOMO MUNCIE SHOALS WABASH

INDIAN BEECH KURUNJ
INDIAN BREAD TUCKAHOE
INDIAN CORN KANGA MAIZE CHOLUM JAGONG MEALIES
INDIAN FIG SABRA
INDIAN FISH FLATFISH
INDIAN GOOSEBERRY EMBLIC
INDIAN HEMP KEF KIF SANA DAGGA SABZI AMYROOT DOGBANE
INDIANIAN HOOSIER
INDIAN JALAP TURPETH
INDIAN LICORICE JEQUIRITY
INDIAN MADDER MUNJEET
INDIAN MALLOW SIDA DAGGA PIEPRINT
INDIAN MILLET JONDLA
INDIAN MULBERRY AL AAL ACH ALROOT
INDIAN PIPE FITROOT EYEBRIGHT WAXFLOWER
INDIAN POKE ITCHWEED HELLEBORE
INDIAN RED BOLE
INDIAN SHOT ALIIPOE
INDIAN TOBACCO GAGROOT LOBELIA PUKEWEED SOURBUSH
INDIAN YELLOW PIOURY PURREE
INDIA-RUBBER BUNGEE BUNGIE
INDIC (— LANGUAGE) URDU VEDIC
INDICATE RUN SAY BODY CITE HINT LOOK MAKE MARK READ SHOW ARGUE INDEX INFER POINT PROVE SPEAK ALLUDE ATTEST BETRAY DENOTE DESIGN EVINCE FINGER IMPORT NOTIFY REVEAL BESPEAK BETOKEN CONNOTE DECLARE DISPLAY POINTTO PORTEND SIGNIFY SPECIFY ADMONISH ANNOUNCE DECIPHER DISCLOSE EVIDENCE MANIFEST OUTPOINT REGISTER SIGNALIZE
(— BY SOUNDING) STRIKE
(— WILLINGNESS) AGREE
INDICATION BECK CLEW CLUE HINT LEAD MARK NOTE SHOW SIGN CURVE INDEX PROOF SCENT TOKEN AUGURY BEACON INDICE REMARK SAMPLE SIGNAL AUSPICE MENTION PROFFER SYMPTOM ALLUSION ARGUMENT EVIDENCE MONITION MONUMENT NOTATION SIGNANCE TELLTALE
(— OF APPROVAL) CACHET
(— OF CONTROL) COLLAR
(— OF LIGHT) AUREOLE
(— OF OFFICE) SEAL
(— OF SOMETHING TO COME) PROGNOSTIC PROGNOSTICATION
(INFALLIBLE —) ORACLE
(OBSCURE —) SHADOW
(VAGUE —) GLIMMER
(PL.) INDICIA
INDICATOR PIN HAND OMEN SIGN FLOAT INDEX LITMUS SHOWER STYLUS TARGET LACMOID POINTER DETECTOR TELLTALE
(— LIGHT ON COMPUTER) CURSOR
(— OF BALANCE) COCK
(— OF HOUR) GNOMON
(DIRECTION —) FLASHER
(ECONOMIC —) LAGGER LEADER
(ELECTRONIC — TUBE) NIXIE
INDICIA POSTAGE
INDICT DITE CRIME PANEL ACCUSE ATTACH CHARGE INDITE ARRAIGN ARTICLE IMPEACH TROUNCE WARRANT
INDICTMENT CHARGE DITTAY
INDIFFERENCE APATHY PHLEGM ATARAXY DISDAIN ATARAXIA COLDNESS EASINESS FROIDEUR STOICISM
INDIFFERENT COLD COOL DEAD DRAM EASY SOSO ALOOF BLASE EQUAL HOHUM SOBER STOIC CASUAL DEGAGE FRIGID SUPINE CALLOUS LANGUID NEUTRAL DETACHED LISTLESS LUKEWARM MEDIOCRE RECKLESS SUPERIOR UPSITTEN APATHETIC
INDIFFERENTIST POLITIC
INDIFFERENTLY DRYLY HUMDRUM
INDIGENCE NEED WANT PENURY BEGGARY POVERTY TENUITY
INDIGENE ENDEMIC
INDIGENOUS DESI NATIVE DOMESTIC HOMEBORN ABORIGINAL
INDIGENT POOR NEEDY BEGGARLY HAVELESS
INDIGESTIBLE STUDGY
INDIGESTION APEPSY APEPSIA DYSPEPSY
INDIGNANT ANGRY WROTH ANNOYED UPTIGHT INCENSED
INDIGNATION IRE RAGE ANGER WRATH DESPITE DISDAIN DUDGEON JEALOUSY
INDIGNITY CUT SLUR SCORN INSULT SLIGHT AFFRONT OFFENCE CONTUMELY
INDIGO ANIL NILL SHOOFLY (PREF.) INDI(CO)
INDIRECT SLY SIDE DEVIOUS OBLIQUE CIRCULAR GLANCING OVERHEAD OVERWART SIDELONG SIDEWAYS SIDEWISE ROUNDABOUT
(— WAY) AMBAGE
INDIRECTION CIRCUITY
INDIRECTLY ROUND SECONDHAND
INDIRECTNESS OBLIQUITY
INDISCREET RASH HASTY SILLY WITLESS CARELESS HEEDLESS
INDISCRETION FOLLY LAPSE FREDAINE
INDISCRIMINATE MIXED MINGLED SWEEPING PROMISCUOUS
INDISCRIMINATELY PELLMELL
INDISPENSABLE CENTRAL NEEDFUL CRITICAL
INDISPOSED ILL MEAN SICK ILLISH UNWELL
INDISPOSITION AIL BRASH MALADY AILMENT SICKNESS
(— TO MOTION) INERTIA
INDISPUTABLE SURE CERTAIN EVIDENT MANIFEST POSITIVE APODICTIC
INDISTINCT DIM DARK DULL HAZY FAINT FUZZY INNER LIGHT MISTY MUDDY SHADY THICK VAGUE BLEARY CLOUDY DREAMY INWARD SLURRY WOOLLY BLEARED BLURRED OBSCURE SHADOWY UNCLEAR NEBULOUS
(— IN SOUND) NEUTRAL
(— IN UTTERANCE) CHOKING
INDISTINCTNESS BLUR CONFUSION
INDITE PEN DITE DRAW
INDIVIDUAL GEE MAN ONE HEAD SORT UNIT BEING MONAD THING PROPER SINGLE SPIRIT VERSAL APOMICT ATAVISM AZYGOTE BIONTIC DIPLOID EIDETIC ISOLATE MONADIC NUMERIC SEVERAL SPECIAL EVERYONE IDENTITY SEPARATE SINGULAR SOLITARY SPECIMEN PERSONAGE
(COLOR-BLIND —) MONOCHROMAT
(COUNTRIFIED —) HOBNAIL
(DESPICABLE —) HEEL
(DULL —) BOEOTIAN
(FOOLISH —) SOP

(HAUGHTY —) POT
(IDENTICAL —) CLONE
(IMMATURE —) ADULTOID
(IMPUDENT —) BOLDFACE
(INDEPENDENT —) MAVERICK
(IRRITABLE —) SNAPPER
(LEADING —) KEY
(MOSAIC —) GYNANDER
(MUTANT —) SALTANT
(PHYSIOLOGICAL —) BION
(PROSAIC —) PHILISTINE
(ROUGH-LOOKING —) BOHUNK
(SKILLED —) ADEPT
(SLOVENLY —) GROBIAN
(STUPID —) HOBBIL
(TRICKY —) BILK
(UNDERSIZED —) KIT KITT
(WINGED —) ALATE
(YOUNG —) KID
(PL.) FRY
INDIVIDUALITY KA SEITY QUALITY SELFDOM HECCEITY IDENTITY SELFHOOD
INDIVIDUALIZE ATOMIZE
INDIVIDUALLY APART APIECE SINGLY PROPERLY
INDIVIDUATION AHANKARA
INDIVISIBLE PUNCTUAL
INDO-CHINESE SERIFORM
INDOCTRINATE BRIEF INSTRUCT
INDO-EUROPEAN ARIAN ARYAN JAPHETIC
INDOLE KETOLE
INDOLENCE SLOTH LANGUOR IDLESHIP MUSARDRY SLUGGING
(— PERSONIFIED) LAURENCE LAWRENCE
INDOLENT IDLE LAZY FAINT INERT SWEER DROWSY OTIOSE SUPINE DRONISH LANGUID WILSOME FAINEANT INACTIVE LISTLESS LOUNGING SLOTHFUL SLUGGISH PICKTOOTH
INDO-MALAYAN (— TREE) SUPA

INDONESIA
CAPITAL: DJAKARTA
COIN: RUPIAH
GULF: BONE TOLO TOMINI
ISLAND: ALOR BALI BURU JAVA CERAM IRIAN SUMBA WETAR BAWEAN BORNEO BUTUNG FLORES KOMODO LOMBOK MADURA PELENG CELEBES SALAJAR SUMATRA SUMBAWA SULAWESI
ISLAND GROUP: ARRU EWAB SUNDA BANJAK NATUNA ANAMBAS MOLUCCA TABELAN SABALANA
LAKE: RANAU TOWUTI
LANGUAGE: BAHASA MALAYAN
MOUNTAIN: BULU NIUT RAJA DEMPO MURJO NIAPA LEUSER SLAMET MENJAPA OGOAMAS SAMOSIR KATOPASA KERINTJI MAHAMERU RINDJANI TALAKMAU
MOUNTAINS: MULLER BARISAN QUARLES SCHWANER
NATIVE: BUGI
PROVINCE: RIAU ATJEH DJAMBI MALUKU LAMPUNG BENGKULU
RIVER: HARI MUSI DIGUL KAJAN PAWAN BARITO KAMPAR KAPUAS MAHAKAM
SEA: JAVA BANDA CERAM TIMOR FLORES ARAFURA CELEBES
STRAIT: SUNDA LOMBOK MAKASSAR
TOWN: PALU MEDAN MALANG MANADO BANDUNG KENDARI MAKASAR SEMARANG SURABAJA PALEMBANG SURAKARTA
VOLCANO: GEDE AGUNG DEMPO RAUNG MARAPI MERAPI SINILA SLAMET SUNDORO TAMBORA KERINTJE RINDJANI
WEIGHT: CATTY OUNCE THAIL

INDONESIAN NESIOT SADANG
INDOORS WITHIN
INDRA SAKKA SAKRA
INDRI BABACOOTE
INDUBITABLE SURE EVIDENT APPARENT MANIFEST UNIVOCAL
INDUCE GET DRAW LEAD MOVE URGE WORK ARGUE BRIBE BRING CAUSE IMPEL INFER TEMPT WEIGH ADDICT ADJURE ALLURE ENGAGE ENTICE IMPORT INCITE INVITE OBTAIN REDUCE SEDUCE SUBORN ACTUATE PREVAIL PROCURE PROVOKE SOLICIT MOTIVATE PERSUADE WIREDRAW
(— BY BRIBERY) FIX
INDUCEMENT BAIT MOTIVE REASON FEATURE PERSUASION
INDUCT STALL INSTAL KNIGHT INITIATE
INDUCTANCE HENRY
INDUCTION EPAGOGE
INDULGE PET BABY CADE CANT FEED GLUT ALLOW HUMOR JOLLY SPOIL TUTOR WALLY WREAK COCKER FOSTER PAMPER PETTLE DEBAUCH GRATIFY
(— IN PRIDE) PRIDE
(— ONESELF) WALLOW WANTON
(— TO EXCESS) PAMPER DEBAUCH SURFEIT
INDULGED CADE
INDULGENCE LAW BINGE FAVOR FOLLY MERCY SPREE EXCESS INDULT PARDON PATENT JUBILEE QUIENAL SURFEIT COURTESY DELICACY EASINESS GLUTTONY POCULARY
(FREE —) SWING
(SEXUAL —) LECHERY
INDULGENT FOND GOOD MEEK MILD SPOONY LENIENT TOLERANT
INDURATE HARDEN INDURE
INDURATED SCLEROID SCLEROUS
INDURATION SCLEROMA
INDUSTRIOUS BUSY DEEDY EIDENT STEADY OPEROSE PAINFUL DILIGENT SEDULOUS VIRTUOUS WORKSOME
INDUSTRY TOIL LABOR SCREEN VIRTUE CERAMICS SEDULITY
INDWELLING IMMANENT INHERENT
INE (WIFE OF —) AETHELBURH
INEBRIATE SOUSE EBRIATED
INEBRIATED DRUNK DRINKY
INEFFACEABLE INBURNT INDELIBLE
INEFFECTIVE DUD WEAK CLUMSY DREEPY FLABBY FUTILE FLACCID HALTING STERILE BUMBLING
INEFFECTIVELY ILL BADLY FEEBLY
INEFFECTUAL WAN DEAD IDLE TAME VAIN VOID JERKY FUTILE SPINDLY USELESS BOOTLESS FAINEANT FIDDLING NUGATORY
INEFFICIENT ILL LAME POOR CLUMSY DOLESS ROTTEN UNABLE SLOUCHY USELESS FECKLESS HANDLESS
INELASTIC DEAD
INELEGANT RUDE HOYDEN AWKWARD
INELOQUENT WANMOL
INEPT DORKY INAPT ABSURD AWKWARD FOOTLESS MALADROIT
INEPTITUDE PIFFLE
INEQUAL ROUGH
INEQUALITY ODDS CAHOT WHELK ANOMALY EVECTION IMPARITY NUTATION
(— OF SURFACE) WAVE
INEQUITABLE HARD
INERADICABLE LASTING INDELIBLE PERMANENT
INERT DEAD DULL LAZY SLOW HEAVY NOBLE SULKY LEADEN SODDEN STUPID SUPINE TORPID PASSIVE INACTIVE INDOLENT LIFELESS SLOTHFUL SLUGGISH STAGNANT THEWLESS THOWLESS
INERTIA TAMAS
INESCAPABLE DEAD NECESSARY
INESTIMABLE SUMLESS PRICELESS
INEVITABILITY FINALITY
INEVITABLE DUE SURE DIRECT CERTAIN FATEFUL FOREGONE
INEXACT FREE ROUGH CLOUDY
INEXHAUSTIBLE INFINITE
INEXORABLE STERN STONY STRICT RIGOROUS
INEXPEDIENCY IMPOLICY
INEXPEDIENT UNWISE
INEXPENSIVE LOW CHEAP DIMESTORE REASONABLE
INEXPERIENCED RAW PUNY CRUDE FRESH YOUNG UNSEEN KITLING STRANGE INEXPERT INSOLENT PRENTICE UNTRADED
INEXPERT ILL RUDE CRUDE GREEN SIMPLE
INEXPLICABLE FELL
INFALLIBLE FAILSAFE SUREFIRE UNERRING FOOLPROOF
INFAMOUS BASE RUDDY BLOODY NOTOUR ODIOUS BLEEDING FLAGRANT NIDERING SHAMEFUL NEFARIOUS OPPROBRIOUS
INFAMY STAIN BAFFLE DEFAME SHONDE DISHONOR IGNOMINY OPPROBRIM OPPROBRIUM
INFANCY CRADLE BABYHOOD
INFANT BABE BABY TINY WEAN CHILD MINOR PREMIE CHRISOM MILKSOP PREEMIE BALDLING BANTLING
(NAKED —) SCUDDY
(NEWLY-BORN —) NEONATUS
(VORACIOUS —) KILLCROP
INFANTILE BABYISH
INFANTRY FOOT FANTERIE FOOTFOLK
INFANTRYMAN GI ASKAR ZOUAVE DOGFACE DRAGOON DOUGHBOY PIOUPIOU SOREFOOT VOETGANGER
INFATUATE FOOL ASSOT BESOT
INFATUATED MAD FOND GAGA GONE ASSOT CRAZY DOTTY ENTETE ENGOUEE FOOLISH BESOTTED
INFATUATION ATE PASH RAVE CRUSH FOLLY BEGUIN
(TRANSIENT —) CRAZE
(SUFF.) (— FOR) MANE MANIA(C)
(— WITH) ITIS
INFECT SMIT TAINT CANKER DEFILE EMPEST ENTACH INFEST POISON CORRUPT DISEASE POLLUTE SMITTLE CONTAMINATE
INFECTED SEPTIC FUNGUSED
(NOT —) BLAND
INFECTION COLD DOSE SMIT FELON TAINT FUNGUS
INFECTIOUS TAKING SMITTLE CATCHING SMITABLE SMITTING VIRULENT
INFEFTMENT SASINE
INFER DRAW PICK READ TAKE EDUCE GUESS JUDGE ALLEGE DECIDE DEDUCE DEDUCT DERIVE DIVINE GATHER INDUCE REASON COLLECT INCLUDE PRESUME SURMISE CONCLUDE CONSTRUE
INFERENCE EDUCT SEQUEL ANALOGY SEQUELA ILLATION SEQUENCE SEQUITUR OBSERVATION PRESUMPTION
INFERIOR BAD BUM DOG ILL JAY LOW OFF SAD EVIL LESS MEAN POOR PUNK SLIM SOUR WAFF BASER BAUCH BELOW CHEAP DOGGY GROSS LOUSY LOWER PETTY PLAIN SCALY SCRUB TACKY TATTY WORRY BEHIND CAGMAG COARSE COMMON CRAPPY FEEBLE FEMALE IMPURE LESSER MEASLY PALTRY PEDARY PUISNE PUISNY ROTTEN SECOND SHABBY SHODDY WOODEN BADDISH CRIPPLE HUMBLER NAGGISH POPULAR SCRUBBY SUBJECT ABNORMAL ANTERIOR DEROGATE ORDINARY PARAVAIL TERRIBLE
(PREF.) DEMI INFRA SUB
(SUFF.) ASTER EEN
(— ONE) LING
INFERIORITY LESSNESS MEANNESS
INFERNAL BLACK AVERNAL BLASTED ETERNAL HELLISH SATANIC SHEOLIC STYGIAN CHTHONIC DAMNABLE DEVILISH PLUTONIC PLUTONIAN
INFERTILE DEAD DEAF DOUR LEAN POOR THIN CLEAR EFFETE STERILE
INFEST COE VEX BESET INFECT PESTER PLAGUE OVERRUN TORMENT
INFESTATION SCALE PLAGUE STRIKE MYIASIS LOAIASIS PEDICULOSIS
INFESTED MITY BLOWN BROOD BUGGY FLUKY FLUKED GRUBBY HAUNTED FLYBLOWN
INFIDEL DEIST KAFIR GIAOUR

PAYNIM ATHEIST SARACEN SKEPTIC AGNOSTIC MISCREANT MISBELIEVER
INFIDELITY PERFIDY ADULTERY TRAHISON
INFIELD CARPET INTOWN DIAMOND
INFILTRATE FILTER CRETIFY COLONIZE
INFILTRATION SEEPAGE ADIPOSIS SATURATION
INFINITE CHAOS COSMIC ENDLESS ETERNAL IMMENSE
INFINITENESS ETERNITY
INFINITESIMAL PUNCTUAL
INFINITIVE SUPINE VERBID
(FRENCH —) ETRE
INFINITY OLAM ANANTA ETERNITY
INFIRM LAME WEAK ANILE CRAZY CRONK SHAKY CRANKY FEEBLE SICKLY UNFIRM UNSURE CASALTY CRAICHY DOWLESS DWAIBLE FRAGILE INVALID SAPLESS UNFEARY DODDERED FIRMLESS INSECURE RESOLUTE UNSTRONG
INFIRMARY SICKBAY
INFIRMITY WOE CRAZE DOTAGE FOIBLE UNHEAL DISEASE FAILING FRAILTY UNMIGHT DEBILITY SICKNESS WEAKNESS
INFIX INLAY INSET ENGRAVE IMPLANT INGRAIN
INFIXED INHERENT
INFLAME RAW BURN FIRE GOAD HEAT STIR ANGER BLAIN FLAME SCALD SHAME AROUSE ENAMOR EXCITE FESTER IGNITE INCEND KINDLE MADDEN RANKLE EMBRASE FLUSTER INCENSE ESCHAUFE
(— WITH LOVE) ENAMOR
INFLAMED RED ANGRY FIERY ABLAZE FRETTY HEATED TORRID FLAGRANT
INFLAMMABLE FIERY ARDENT TOUCHY PICEOUS TINDERY
INFLAMMATION ACNE FIRE ANGER FELON GLEET SCALD SEBEL AGNAIL ANCOME BLIGHT CANKER DEFLUX GREASE IRITIS CATARRH CECITIS CHAFING COLITIS COXITIS FISTULA GONITIS ILEITIS QUITTOR SUNBURN ADENITIS ANGIITIS AORTITIS BURSITIS CHILITIS CYCLITIS CYSTITIS SHINGLES
(SUFF.) ITIS
INFLATE HOVE HUFF KITE PLIM PUFF BLOAT BOLNE HEAVE SWELL DILATE EMBOSS EXPAND HUFFLE INBLOW PUMPUP TUMEFY BLADDER BOMBAST DISTEND FORBLOW OUTSWELL SUFFLATE
INFLATED TRIG BLOWN FLOWN GASSY PUFFY TUMID TURGID BOMBAST BULLATE FUSTIAN OROTUND STILTED SWOLLEN TURGENT BLADDERY OUTBLOWN TOPLOFTY TUMOROUS VANITOUS BOMBASTIC OVERBLOWN PLETHORIC
INFLATION FLATUS CADENCE TYMPANY
INFLECT COMPARE DECLINE
INFLECTION SIGN TONE ARSIS ACCENT FLEXION LATINISM MODULATION
INFLECTIONAL FORMAL
INFLEXIBILITY ACAMPSIA
INFLEXIBLE ACID DOUR FIRM HARD IRON EAGER SOLID STERN STIFF STONY STOUR SEVERE STRICT STUFFY ADAMANT RESTIVE GRANITIC IRONCLAD OBDURATE PREFRACT RESOLUTE RIGOROUS STIFFISH STUBBORN ADAMANTINE
INFLICT DO ADD PUT SET GIVE SEND INFER YIELD IMPOSE RAMROD STRIKE
(— CHASTISEMENT) WREAK
(— HURT) BRUISE
(— INJURY) AGGRIEVE
(— PAIN) LAY CHASTISE
INFLICTION (— OF PUNISHMENT) AUTODAFE
INFLORESCENCE CHAT CYME AMENT ARROW BRUSH SPIKE UMBEL CORYMB FLOWER RACEME SPADIX TASSEL BOSTRYX PANICLE THYRSIS CYATHIUM FASCICLE NUCAMENT
INFLOW INSET AFFLUX INCOME INFLUX INCOURSE
INFLOWING AFFLUENT
INFLUENCE IN WIN BEND BIAS COAX DRAG DRAW HAND HANK HEFT LEAD MOVE PULL PUSH RULE SUCK SWAY BRIBE CHARM CLOUT COLOR ENACT FORCE GRACE IMPEL JUICE MOYEN POWER REACH SPELL VAPOR VOGUE WEIGH AFFECT ALLURE CREDIT EFFECT GOVERN IMPORT INDUCE INFLOW INFLUX MOTIVE OBSESS PONDUS SALUTE SHADOW STROKE WEIGHT ACTUATE ATTINGE ATTRACT BEARING BEWITCH BLARNEY BOSSDOM CAPTURE CONCUSS CONTROL DISPUTE ENCHANT GRAVITY IMPRINT INCLINE INSPIRE MASTERY SUASION TENDRIL DOMINION HEGEMONY INTEREST LEVERAGE MEDICINE PRESTIGE SANCTION STRENGTH CAPTIVATE
(— BY GIFTS) GREASE
(— BY THREATS) INTIMIDATE
(— CORRUPTLY) BRIBE
(— FOR DESTRUCTION) MAELSTROM
(— OF GODS) MANA
(— OF PERSONALITY) MAGNETISM
(— OF THE STARS) BLAS
(— UNREASONABLY) OBSESS
(ATTEMPT TO —) JAWBONE
(BENIGN —) UNCTION
(CONSTRAINING —) STRESS PRESSURE
(CONTROLLING —) SWAY
(CORRUPTING —) SMOUCH SMUTCH
(DEPRESSING —) CHILL
(DIABOLICAL —) DEVILDOM
(DISRUPTIVE —) GREMLIN
(DOMINANT —) GENIUS STREAM
(DULLING —) DAMPER
(ELEVATING —) LIFT
(HARMFUL —) UPAS GRUDGE
(INJURIOUS —) RUST
(MALEVOLENT —) DISASTER
(MALIGN —) TAKING
(PERNICIOUS —) BALE BLAST
(SINISTER —) MALICE
(SOOTHING —) SALVE
(SPIRITUAL —) NUMEN
(SURROUNDING —) AIR AMBIENCE
(UNDER — OF ALCOHOL OR DRUGS) ZONKED
INFLUENCING INFUSIVE
INFLUENTIAL BIG GRAVE POWERFUL
INFLUENZA FLU LEUMA GRIPPE PINKEYE
INFLUX STORM INCOME INFLOW INRUSH ILLAPSE
(— IN A MINE) COURSE
(— OF TIDE) INSET
INFOLD WRAP IMPLY TWINE EMPLOY INWRAP ENVELOP INVOLVE CONVOLVE
INFORM KEN BEEF BLOW FINK NOSE POST SHOP SHOW TELL WARN WISE LEARN PEACH ADVISE ASSURE DELATE DETECT NOTIFY PREACH SNITCH WITTER APPRISE EDUCATE IMPEACH INSENSE PARTAKE POSSESS RESOLVE SIGNIFY SUGGEST ACQUAINT DENOUNCE INFORMED INSTRUCT SPARSILE
(— AGAINST) SHOP RUMBLE DENOUNCE
INFORMAL BREEZY CASUAL CHATTY COMMON FOLKSY TWEEDY INTIMATE SLIPSHOD SOCIABLE NEGLIGENT OFFICIOUS
INFORMANT AUTHOR INFORMER SQUEALER SYCOPHANT
INFORMATION AIR GEN OIL WIT CLEW CLUE DOPE INFO LORE NEWS NOTE TALE WIRE WORD DATUM GRIFF SCOOP SKILL ADVICE INSIDE LIGHTS NOTICE APPRISE PEMICAN READOUT TIDINGS WITTING BRIEFING NOTITION PEMMICAN
(— ON VIDEO SCREEN) DISPLAY
(BODY OF —) DIGEST
(CONDENSED —) PEMICAN PEMMICAN
(INCIDENTAL —) SIDELIGHT
(SECRET —) ARCANUM
(SUFF.) ANA IANA
INFORMED UP HEP WISE AWARE WITTY KNOWING LEARNED
(WELL —) UPON
INFORMER FINK NARK NOSE PIMP SPIV STAG RUSTY SNEAK SPLIT BEAGLE CANARY FINGER SETTER SNITCH TELLER DELATOR STOOLIE TANQUAM APPROVER PROMOTER SQUAWKER SQUEAKER SQUEALER TELLTALE SYCOPHANT WHISTLEBLOWER
INFORTUNE MARS SATURN
INFRACTION BREACH OFFENCE TRESPASS
(— IN HOCKEY) SPEARING
INFRARED ULTRARED
INFREQUENCY SELDOMCY
INFREQUENT RARE SELDOM FUGITIVE SPORADIC UNCOMMON
INFRINGE IMPOSE INVADE TRENCH IMPINGE INFRACT INTRUDE ENCROACH REFRINGE TRESPASS
INFRINGEMENT FOUL BREACH TRESPASS VIOLENCE
INFRINGER PIRATE
INFULA FANON LABEL LAPPET HEADBAND
INFUNDIBULUM FUNNEL PAVILION
INFURIATE ENRAGE ENFELON
INFUSE DRAW MASK IMBUE IMMIT SPOIL STEEP AERATE AERIFY IMMISS INFLOW INFORM INFUND INVEST LEAVEN BREATHE DISTILL ENGRAIN IMPLANT INFOUND INSPIRE INSTILL SUFFUSE SATURATE
(— TEA) TRACK
(— WITH HATRED) TURN
INFUSED SHOT
INFUSION SHADE CARDIN INCOME TISANE HORDEATE
(— OF MALT) WORT GROUT
(BITTER —) RUE
INFUSORIAN LEPOCYTE
INGA GUAVA
INGATE GATE LEDGE TEDGE
INGATHERING HARVEST
INGENIOUS SLY CUTE FAST FEAT FINE ACUTE SHARP SMART WITTY ADROIT BRAINY CLEVER CRAFTY DAEDAL GIFTED KNACKY PRETTY QUAINT SUBTLE CUNNING POLITIC SKILLFUL
INGENUITY ART WIT ENGINE ADDRESS COMPASS ARTIFICE CONTOISE INDUSTRY QUENTISE
INGENUOSITY NAIVETE
INGENUOUS FREE FRANK NAIVE PLAIN CANDID HONEST SUBTLE ARTLESS NATURAL SINCERE INNOCENT
INGENUOUSNESS NAIVETE
INGEST EAT INCEPT ENGLOBE SWALLOW
INGESTION SLURP
INGOT GAD SOW WEDGE LINGOT NIGGOT CROPHEAD
(— OF BRASS) STRIP
(— OF SILVER) SHOE TING SCHUYT
(SILVER —) SYCEE
(SILVER —S) SYCEE
(SOAKING —S) HEAT
INGRAIN GRAIN INFUSE ENFLESH
INGRAINED INWORN
INGRATE SNAKE
INGRATIATE FLATTER
INGRATIATING BLAND SILKY SLEEK SLICK SOAPY SILKEN SMOOTH
INGRATITUDE UNTHANK
INGREDIENT FACTOR AMALGAM BINDING ELEMENT ADJUVANT
(ACTIVE —) ANIMA
(FUNDAMENTAL —) BASIS
(FUSIBLE —) BOND
(MAIN —) BASE
(SALVE —) ALOE
INGRESS ENTRY ENTRANCE
INGROWTH APODEMA
INGUEN GROIN

INHABIT BIG WIN WON COVER DWELL HABIT OCCUPY BEDWELL INDWELL POSSESS POPULATE
INHABITANT INMATE BURGHER CITIZEN DENIZEN DWELLER PEOPLER BORDERER CONFINER DEMESMAN HABITANT INCOLANT INHOLDER
(— OF ALASKA) SOURDOUGH
(— OF BORDER REGION) MARCHER
(— OF CITY) CIT CITIZEN
(— OF EXTREME NORTH) HYPERBOREAN
(— OF INDIA) BHARATA
(— OF JUNGLE) JUNGLI
(— OF MAINE) DOWNEASTER
(— OF MOON) LUNARIAN
(— OF SWISS ALPS) GRISON
(— OF TORRID ZONE) ASCIAN
(— OF VIRGINIA) COOHEE
(— OF WISCONSIN) BADGER
(EARTH —) TERRAN
(OLDEST —) PATRIARCH
(PL.) SIDE WARE
(SUFF.) COLA ITE OT OTE
INHABITING
(SUFF.) COLE COLINE COLOUS
INHALATION SNUFF BREATH
(PREF.) ANEM(O)
INHALE DRAW TAKE SMOKE SNIFF SNUFF ATTRACT BREATHE INHAUST INSPIRE RESPIRE ASPIRATE
(— A DRUG) SNORT
(PREF.) INSPIRO
INHALER SNIFTER
INHARMONIOUS ABSURD RUGGED ABSONANT
INHERE CONSIST INEXIST
INHERENCE INBEING
INHERENT KIND INBORN INNATE INWARD NATIVE PROPER INGENIT NATURAL HABITUAL IMMANENT INTEGRAL INTERNAL RESIDENT
INHERIT HEIR SUCCEED
INHERITANCE KIND ENTAIL HEIRDOM HEIRSHIP HEREDITY HERITAGE LANDFALL VACANTIA
(— OF CATTLE) ERF
(PARTICULATE —) MENDELISM
INHERITED INBORN INNATE CONGENITAL
(SUFF.) CLINOUS CLINY
INHIBIT COOP CURB SNUB CRIMP DETER FORBID STIFLE SUPPRESS
INHIBITED COLD
INHIBITION AKINESIS
INHIBITOR PARGYLINE PHENELZINE
INHIBITORY COLYTIC
INHOSPITABLE STERN DESERT
INHUMAN FELL CRUEL BRUTAL FIERCE IMMANE SAVAGE BESTIAL MANLESS DEVILISH KINDLESS
INHUMANE WANTON
INHUMANITY CRUELTY
INHUME BURY INTER ENTOMB
INIMICAL BAD FROSTY HOSTILE
(— TO LIFE) ANTIBIOTIC
INIQUITOUS ILL DARK WRONG SINFUL WICKED NEFARIOUS
INIQUITY SIN EVIL VICE CRIME GUILT DARKNESS MISCHIEF
INITIAL LETTER VIRGIN ASPIREE PRINCIPAL
(INTERWOVEN —S) CIPHER
(PL.) PERFINS
INITIALLY ATFIRST
INITIATE HEAD MYST OPEN ADEPT ADMIT BEGIN BREAK ENTER EPOPT FOUND START GROUND INDUCE INDUCT INVENT LAUNCH MYSTES ORPHIC BAPTIZE INSTALL INSTATE OPERATE ORPHEAN SYMMIST YTIGGER COMMENCE ESOTERIC INCHOATE ORIGINATE
INITIATION DIKSHA OPENING ENTRANCE
(— OF GROWTH) BUDBREAK
INITIATIVE PEP LEAD GETUP ACTION AMBITION GUMPTION OVERTURE
INJECT DRIVE IMMIT
(— DRUG) SKINPOP
(— DRUGS) SHOOT MAINLINE
INJECTION JAG HYPO SHOT BOOSTER CLYSTER INSERTION
INJUDICIOUS UNWISE
INJUDICIOUSNESS ACRISY
INJUNCTION HEST BEHEST CHARGE IMPOSE RUBRIC BIDDING DICTATE EXPRESS MANDATE PRECEPT
INJURE DO GAS ILL MAR BURN CHEW DERE ENVY GALL HARM HURT MAUL TEAR TEEN WERD ABUSE BLAST CRAZE DIRTY MISDO RIFLE SCALD SHEND SMITE SPOIL STEER WOUND WRONG BRUISE DAMAGE DEFACE DEFECT DEPAIR GRIEVE HINDER IMPAIR INJURY MANGLE NOBBLE PUNISH RANKLE SCATHE SCOTCH STRAIN AFFLICT AFFRONT CONTUSE DAMNIFY DESPITE FORWORK MISBEDE TERRIFY AGGRIEVE DISASTER DISSERVE FORSLACK IMPERISH INTERESS MISCHIEF MISGUIDE MUTILATE PREJUDGE SPURGALL
(— BY ASPERSION) SPATTER
(— BY FALSE REPORT) SLANDER
(— BY GLANCE OF BASILISK) STRIKE
(— BY TREADING UPON) FITTER
(— SCENT) STAIN
(— SERIOUSLY) DO KILL SPOIL
(— SLIGHTLY) ANNOY
(— THE BACK) CHINK
(— WITH GRENADE) FRAG
(DELIBERATELY —) FRAG
(SEVERELY —) WASTE
INJURED HURT LESED BLASTED
(EASILY —) NICE
INJURIOUS BAD ILL EVIL NOCENT NOYANT NOYFUL SHREWD ABUSIVE HARMFUL HURTFUL NOXIOUS SCADDLE DAMAGING GRIEVOUS SINISTER TORTIOUS TORTUOUS WRACKFUL WRONGFUL PERNICIOUS
INJURIOUSLY HEAVILY
INJURY ILL JAM MAR BALE BANE BURN EVIL HARM HURT JEEL LOSS RUIN SCAT TEEN TORT WITE ABUSE BLAME CHAFE CRUSH GRIEF SCALD SCORE SPITE SPOIL TOUCH WATHE WRACK WRONG BREACH BRUISE DAMAGE DANGER IMPAIR LESION SCATHE STRAIN STROKE TRAUMA BEATING DESPITE EXPENSE OFFENSE OUTRAGE PAYMENT SCADDLE SCRATCH SORANCE BUSINESS CASUALTY CREPANCE INTEREST MISCHIEF NUISANCE
(— OF HORSES) TREAD CREPANCE
(— OF PLANTS) SUNSCALD
(— TO REPUTATION) SCANDAL
(CHIEF —) FOCUS
(MALICIOUS —) REVENGE
(SERIOUS —) MAYHEM
INJUSTICE WRONG INJURY INJURIA UNRIGHT HARDSHIP INEQUITY
(GROSS —) INIQUITY
INK BEAT SIGN COLOR ARNEMENT ATRAMENT
(DISPENSER OF —) SQUID
(KIND OF —) RED INDIA
(PRINTER'S —) CYAN
INK-BALL DABBER PUMPET
INKER SLOSHER
INKING PAD TOMPION
INKLE SPINEL
INKLING HOE HINT ITEM SCENT GLIMMER GLIMPSE UMBRAGE
INKSTAND STANDISH
INKWELL FOUNT INKSTAND
INKY BLACK ATRAMENTOUS
INLAID PIQUE CONTISE
(— DECORATION) BUHL BOULE BOULLE
(— WORK) KOFTGARI
INLAND MAUKA INMORE INWARD MIDLAND INTERIOR
INLAY PICK PIKE COUCH HATCH INLET PIQUE SPELL CRUSTA ENAMEL IMPAVE INDENT NIELLO TARSIA ENCHASE ENCRUST INCRUST COMMESSO
INLAYING TARKASHI
INLET ARM BAY CUT GEO RIA VOE COVE DOCK HOPE MERE SLEW WICK BAYOU BRACE CHUCK CREEK FIORD FJORD FLEET HAVEN LOGAN LOUGH STOMA ESTERO HARBOR INFALL SLOUGH TONGUE DOGHOLE INDRAFT SUCTION CALANQUE SEAPOOSE
(— OF THE SEA) EA
(MUDDY —) SUMP
(REGULATED —) SLUICE
(TIDAL —) GAP
INLIER WINDOW
INLYING INNERLY
INMATE FISH LODGER TENANT BEADSMAN DOMESTIC PRISONER
(BEDLAM —) ABRAMMAN ABRAHAMMAN
(RELIGIOUS —) NOVICE
INMOST SECRET RETIRED
INN PUB KHAN STOP VENT ANGEL BANDB FONDA HOTEL MESON SERAI TAMBO VENTA CABACK HARBOR HOSTEL HOSTRY IMARET POSADA PUBLIC SHANTY TABARD ALBERGE AUBERGE BOLICHE CAFENEH CAFENET FONDACO FONDOUK HOSTAGE LOCANDA OSTERIA SOJOURN SURAHEE CHOULTRY GASTHAUS HOSTELRY ORDINARY SERAGLIO WAYHOUSE ROADHOUSE
(KIND OF —) MOTOR
INNARDS GIZZARD INWARDS STUFFING
INNATE BORN KIND INBORN INBRED CONNATE INGRAIN NATURAL INHERENT INSTINCT
(— QUALITY) LARGESS
INNER BEN ENTAL INSIDE INWARD INWITH MENTAL INTERIOR INTERNAL PECTORAL
(— LIGHT) SEED
(PREF.) ENT(O) ESO
(— PARTS OF BODY) BATHY
INNER MONGOLIA (CAPITAL OF —) HOHHOT HUHEHOT
INNERMOST UPPER INMOST MIDMOST INTIMATE
INNERVATE AROUSE
INNINA ISHTAR
INNING END HAND HEAD FRAME
(PL.) KNOCK WICKET
INNKEEPER HOST DUENA TAPPER VENTER GOODMAN HOSTESS HOSTLER PADRONE BONIFACE HOSTELER
(PL.) CAUPONES
INNOCENCE BLUET WHITE CANDOR PURITY SIMPLICITY
INNOCENT SOT DEWY FREE NAIF PURE CANNY CLEAR NAIVE SEELY SILLY WHITE CHASTE DOVISH HONEST SIMPLE CHRISOM LAMBKIN UPRIGHT ARCADIAN HARMLESS IGNORANT PASTORAL PRIMROSE SACKLESS UNGUILTY ZACCHEUS
INNOCUOUS HARMLESS INNOCENT
INNOVATE NOVELIZE
INNOVATION NOVEL NOVELTY
INNOVATOR HERETIC
INNUENDO HINT SLUR SLIPE
INNUMERABLE MYRIAD NUMBERLESS
INO (BROTHER OF —) POLYDORUS
(FATHER OF —) CADMUS
(HUSBAND OF —) ATHAMAS
(MOTHER OF —) HARMONIA
(SISTER OF —) AGAVE SEMELE AUTONOE
(SON OF —) LEARCHUS PALAEMON MELICERTES
INOCULATE SEED PLANT INFUSE ENGRAFT EQUINATE
INOCULATION JAG
INOCULUM STAB STREAK
IN-OFF JENNY
INOFFENSIVE HARMLESS
INOPERATIVE OFF DEAD RESTY SILENT NUGATORY
INOPPORTUNE UNTIMELY
INORDINATE WILD UNDUE ENORMOUS
INORGANIC MINERAL
INOSITOL DAMBOSE
INPOURING INFLUX
INQUEST CROWN QUEST ASSIZE OFFICE INQUIRY
INQUIET UNEASY
INQUILINE GUEST
INQUIRE ASK AXE SEEK QUERY

SPERE DEMAND FRAYNE SEARCH EXAMINE HEARKEN QUESTION
INQUIRER ASKER QUERENT
INQUIRY PROBE QUERY THANK TRIAL DEMAND EXAMEN TRACER DOCIMASY QUESTION RESEARCH SCRUTINY SPEERING
INQUISITION CUSTOM INQUIRY QUAESTIO
INQUISITIVE NOSY PEERY PRYING CURIOUS MEDDLING QUIZZICAL
INROAD RAID BREACH INBREAK INVASION
INSALUBRIOUS NOXIOUS
INSANE MAD WUD DAFT NUTS WILD WOOD BALMY BATTY BUGGY CRAZY DIPPY MANIC QUEER WRONG CRANKY LOCOED SCREWY FLIGHTY FRANTIC FURIOUS LUNATIC WITLESS BUGHOUSE DEMENTED DERANGED DISTRACT
(— ONE) MANIAC
INSANITY RAGE CRACK CRAZE FOLIE MANIA FRENZY LUNACY MADNESS VESANIA DELIRIUM DEMENTIA WOODNESS ACROMANIA PSYCHOSIS
INSATIABLE GREEDY VORACIOUS
INSCRIBE DELVE ENTER WRITE BLAZON DOCKET ENDOSS INDITE LEGEND LETTER SCRIBE SCRIVE SCROLL ASCRIBE ENDORSE ENGROSS DEDICATE DESCRIBE EMBLAZON ENSCROLL INTITULE
INSCRIBED INWRIT WRITTEN DESCRIPT
INSCRIPTION HEAD ELOGY CACHET LEGEND LETTER ELOGIUM EPIGRAM EPITAPH MENTION TITULUS WRITING COLOPHON EPIGRAPH GRAFFITO INSCRIPT SCRIBING
(— ON ROCK) PETROGLYPH
(— ON TOMBSTONE) ELOGE ELOGIUM
(3-LETTER —) TRIGRAM
INSCRUTABLE EQUIVOCAL MYSTERIOUS
INSECT ANT BEE BUG DOR DUN ELF FLY NIT ANER FLEA GNAT GOGO GYNE MOTH PELA PEST PUPA SPIT WASP WETA ZIMB APHID APHIS BICHO BORER FLYER GOGGA GUEST IMAGO LOUSE MINER ROACH SCALE BEETLE BLIGHT CALLOW CICADA CIXIID EARWIG EMBIID HAWKER HOPPER INSTAR MANTIS NITTER PODURA PSOCID SAPPER SAWFLY THRIPS VERMIN WALKER WEEVIL ATTACUS BLATTID BOATMAN BRUMMER BUZZARD CRAWLER CREEPER CRICKET CYNIPID DEALATE DRUMMER EARWORM FIREBUG FIREFLY GALLFLY GIRDLER GRAYFLY HEXAPOD JAPYGID KATYDID PHASMID SANDBOY SCINIPH SKIPPER SPECTRE STAINER STYLOPS TERMITE VAGRANT WEBWORM ALDERFLY ALKERMES BLACKFLY BRACONID DIPTERAN FIREBRAT FULGORID GLOWWORM HOMOPTER HORNTAIL LACEWING LECANIUM MEALYBUG PRONYMPH SEMIPUPA SEXUPARA SPHECOID STINKBUG STYLOPID SYMPHILE
(— STAGE) PUPA IMAGO LARVA
(IMMATURE —) NYMPH
(LOWEST —S) AMETABOLA
(PART OF —) EYE CLAW COXA WING FEMUR TIBIA CERCUS LABRUM PALPUS TARSUS THORAX ABDOMEN ANTENNA OCELLUS MANDIBLE SPIRACLE OVIPOSTOR PROTHORAX TYMPANIUM MESOTHORAX METATHORAX OVIPOSITER TROCHANTER
(PL.) HEXAPODA
(PREF.) ENTOM(O)
(SUFF.) CORIS
INSECTICIDE DDD DDT DIP EPN CUBE FLIT MINEX MIREX NALED SEVIN TIMBO ALDRIN DERRIS ENDRIN RONNEL CALOMEL ISODRIN LINDANE MENAZON OVICIDE PHORATE CARBARYL CHLORDAN CULICIDE DIELDRIN FENTHION NICOTINE ROTENONE SCHRADAN ANTRYCIDE MALATHION PARATHION PYRETHRUM
INSECTIVORE MOLE SHREW AGOUTA DESMAN TENREC MOONRAT ALAMIQUI
INSECURE DICKY EEMIS LOOSE SHAKY INFIRM TICKLE UNFAST UNSAFE UNSURE CASALTY
INSECURITY DANGER
INSEMINATE BREED
INSENSATE SURD FATUOUS
INSENSIBILITY DAMP APATHY STUPOR TORPOR
INSENSIBLE DEAD DULL LOST NUMB BRUTE DENSE MARBLE OBTUSE SEARED STUPID WOODEN DATELESS APATHETIC
INSENSITIVE DEAD BLUNT CRASS STONY OBTUSE STUPID BOORISH
INSEPARABLE WRAPPED
INSERT SLIP SPUD STOP BOTCH DICKY ENROL ENTER FUDGE IMMIT INFER INFIX INLET INSET SETIN STUFF COLLET GUSSET INWORK INWEAVE GATEFOLD INTROMIT SANDWICH SLASHING SUBTRUDE THROWOUT
(— IN SHOE) CUSHION
(— STONE CHIPS) PIN
(— SURREPTITIOUSLY) FOIST
(SKIRT —) GORE
INSERTION FLOWER BEADING
(TAPERED —) MITER MITRE
INSET GODET INSERT
(DRESS —) MOTIF
INSHEATHE EMBOSS
INSIDE IN BEN ATHIN INBYE INNER INWITH KEYHOLE INTERIOR
(— OF ANGLE BAR) BOSOM
(— OF OUTER EAR) BUR BURR
(PREF.) END(O)
INSIDIOUS SLY SNARY COVERT SUBTLE GUILEFUL
INSIGHT KEN SIGHT APERCU THEORY NOSTRIL
INSIGNIA TYPE BADGE ORDER SIGNS COLLAR GEORGE CADUCEUS COMMENDA HERALDRY OPINICUS PONTIFICALS
(HERALDIC —) ARMOR
(MILITARY —) EAGLE
INSIGNIFICANCE NOTHINGNESS
INSIGNIFICANT NULL POOR PUNY DINKY FOOTY PETIT PETTY POTTY SCRUB SMALL HUMBLE NAUGHT PALTRY PUISNE SIMPLE SLIGHT FOOLISH NAUGHTY NIFLING NOMINAL PELTING PIMPING SCRUBBY TENUOUS TRIVIAL BAUBLING INFERIOR PEDDLING PITIABLE SNIPPING TRIFLING TRIPENNY
INSINCERE FALSE DOUBLE HOLLOW FEIGNED LIPDEEP ARTIFICIAL
INSINCERITY ARTIFICE DISGUISE
INSINUATE HINT MINT WIND CRAWL SCREW TWIST ALLUDE GLANCE INFUSE INSTIL WRITHE IMPLANT INNUATE
INSINUATING SNIDE SILKEN SMARMY
INSINUATION HINT INKLING
INSIPID DRY WAW BLAH DEAD FADE FLAT FOND FOZY LASH TAME BANAL BAUCH BLAND FLASH INANE PROSY STALE VAPID WALSH WAUGH FLASHY FRIGID JEJUNE SWASHY THREEP WAIRSH WALLOW EXOLETE FATUOUS INSULSE MAWKISH PROSAIC SAPLESS SHILPIT WEARISH WEERISH LIFELESS UNSAVORY WATERISH
INSIST AVER PRESS ASSERT THREAP CONSIST
(— PEEVISHLY) CRAIK
(— UPON) SOLICIT
INSISTENCE URGENCY INSTANCY
INSISTENT LOUD ADAMANT INSTANT EMPHATIC FRENZIED IMPOSING
INSISTER STICKLER
INSOLE CUSHION SLIPSOLE
INSOLENCE GUM LIP SASS CHEEK MOUTH PRIDE SNASH HUBRIS DISDAIN AUDACITY SURQUIDY CONTUMELY PETULANCE
INSOLENT FACY PERT RUDE WISE BARDY BRASH LUSTY PROUD CHEEKY LORDLY WANTON ABUSIVE DEFIANT PAUGHTY ARROGANT IMPUDENT PETULANT SCORNFUL AUDACIOUS
INSOLUBLE HOPELESS
INSOLVENT BANKRUPT
INSOMNIA AHYPNIA AGRYPNIA
INSOUCIANT CAVALIER
INSPECT SEE SUS VET CASE ESPY LOOK SUSS BRACK CHECK SIGHT VISIT INLOOK PERUSE SURVEY EXAMINE OVERSEE CONSIDER OVERLOOK OVERVIEW
(— CASUALLY) BROWSE
(— COINS) SHROFF
(— MERCHANDISE IN BALTIC) BRACK
(— TROOPS) REVIEW
INSPECTION EYE PRY VIEW CHECK SIGHT REVIEW SURVEY BEDIKAH CHECKUP INSIGHT INSPECT PERUSAL VIDIMUS OVERHAUL OVERVIEW SCRUTINY
(— OF CLOTH) ALNAGE
(— OF TROOPS) REVIEW
(KIT —) RAGFAIR
INSPECTOR SAYER SNOOP BISHOP CENSOR CONNER JUMPER LOOKER VIEWER GRAINER MOOCHER PERCHER SAMPLER SNOOPER VEADORE EXAMINER SEARCHER
(— OF COAL) KEEKER
(— OF COTTON LOOMS) TACKLER
(— OF ELECTRIC LAMPS) AGER
(ECCLESIASTICAL —) EXARCH
INSPIRATION FIRE SIGH POESY ANIMUS SPIRIT SPRITE IMPULSE MADNESS PEGASUS AFFLATUS AGANIPPE INFLATUS
(— IN ORATORY) HWYL
(ORATORICAL —) HWYL
INSPIRE FIRE MOVE CHEER ELATE EXALT SPARK BEACON INBLOW INCUSS INDUCE INFORM INFUSE KINDLE PROMPT ACTUATE ANIMATE EMBRAVE ENFORCE ENLIVEN HEARTEN IMPLANT PREMOVE QUICKEN SUGGEST CATALYZE ENTALENT INSPIRIT MOTIVATE SUFFLATE
INSPIRED AWED VATIC AFFLATED DAEMONIC ENTHEATE VISIONED
INSPIRER SOUL
INSPIRING INFUSIVE SPLENDID STIRRING
(— AWE) FORMIDABLE
INSPIRIT CHEER ELATE HEART ROUSE SPIRIT ANIMATE CHERISH COMFORT ENLIVEN HEARTEN INSPIRE QUICKEN ALACRIFY
INSPISSATE STIFFEN THICKEN
INSPISSATED STIFF THICK
INSTABILITY ANOMY ANOMIE SLIDDER FLUIDITY
INSTALL SEAT CHAIR STALL INDUCT INVEST ENSTOOL POSSESS ENTHRONE INITIATE
INSTALLATION INDUCTION
(— OF MINISTER) INFARE
(FLOATING —) PLATFORM
(MILITARY —) GARRISON
INSTALLMENT KIST SERIAL EARNEST CONTRACT
(— OF SERIAL) HEFT
(— OF WAGES) COMPO
(— SELLER) TALLYMAN
(FIRST —) HANDSEL
(NEXT —) SEQUEL
INSTALMENT (— OF EPIC) RHAPSODY
(— OF SERIAL) HEFT
INSTANCE SEC CASE PINK SAMPLE EXAMPLE PURPOSE ENSAMPLE EXEMPLAR
(EXTREME —) CAPSHEAF
INSTANT POP SEC HINT WHIP WINK BLICK CLINK CRACK FLASH GLENT GLIFF GLISK JIFFY POINT SHAKE SOUND START TRICE WHIFF WIGHT

BREATH FLIFFY MINUTE MOMENT SECOND PRESENT CLIFFING
(PRECISE —) TIME
INSTANTANEOUS PRESTO DIRECTLY
INSTANTANEOUSLY OUTRIGHT
INSTANTLY SLAP SWITH PRONTO SWITHE DIRECTLY MOMENTLY
INSTAR STAGE
INSTEAD EITHER
(PREF.) ANTI PRO
INSTEP WRIST TARSUS
(PREF.) PEDI(O)
INSTIGATE EGG ABET GOAD MOVE SPUR URGE IMPEL SETON ATTICE ENTICE EXCITE FOMENT INCITE INDUCE INVOKE PROMPT SPIRIT SUBORN ACTUATE INCENSE INSTINCT
INSTIGATION MOTION MOTIVE EGGMENT INSTANCE INSTINCT
INSTIGATOR AUTHOR MOTIVE SOURCE MONITOR
INSTILL GRAFT INFIX IMPART INFUSE INSTIL BREATHE IMPLANT
INSTINCT KIND FILLED NATURE CHARGED IMPULSE CAPACITY TENDENCY
INSTINCTIVE INNATE NATURAL INHERENT ORIGINAL
INSTITUTE BEGIN BRING ERECT FOUND RAISE START STUDY FOMENT INVENT KINDLE ORDAIN ACTIVATE
(— MEMBER) PIARIST
INSTITUTION BANK CAMP FOLD CLINIC FRIARY SCHOOL ACADEMY CHARITY COLLEGE GALLERY JUBILEE LIBRARY SHELTER STATION VERITAS SEMINARY ORPHANAGE OBSERVATORY PENITENTIARY
(— FOR HOMELESS CHILDREN) PROTECTORY
(— FOR INSANE) ASYLUM
(CHARITABLE —) SPITTLE DEACONRY HOSPITAL
(DRUIDICAL —) GORSEDD
INSTRUCT KEN REAR SHOW WISE BREED COACH DRILL EDIFY ENDUE GUIDE TEACH TRAIN CHARGE DIRECT GROUND INDUCE INFORM LESSON PREACH REFORM SCHOOL COMMAND EDUCATE INSENSE POSSESS ADMONISH DOCUMENT
(— BEFOREHAND) PRIME
INSTRUCTED SCIENCED
INSTRUCTION LORE ADVICE ASSIZE CHARGE LESSON COUNSEL PRECEPT TUITION WISSING COACHING DOCTRINE DOCUMENT MONITION PEDAGOGY PROPHECY TEACHING TUTELAGE
(COMPUTER —) MACRO
(DIVINE —) LAW
(SACRED —) TORAH
(SERIES OF COMPUTER —S) LOOP
(PL.) BRIEF BRIEFING
INSTRUCTIVE DOCENT DIDACTIC
INSTRUCTOR DON SOAK SCREW TUTOR MENTOR REGENT ACHARYA CRAMMER MONITOR TEACHER BEACHBOY CHAIRMAN ELDERMAN
(RELIGIOUS —) SWAMI
INSTRUMENT (ALSO SEE MUSICAL INSTRUMENT) DEED TOOL WRIT AGENT SLANG THEME FACTUM OCTANT TEREBRA UTENSIL SYNGRAPH
(— FOR ACQUIRING KNOWLEDGE) ORGANON
(— NOT UNDER SEAL) PAROL
(— OF DESTRUCTION) SWORD
(— OF DIVINATION) EPHOD
(— OF TORTURE) BOOT RACK BRAKE BRANK FURCA GADGE WHEEL TUMBREL BARNACLE SQUEEZER SCARPINES PILLIWINKS
(—S OF WAR) ENGINERY
(CALCULATING —) ABACUS
(DETECTING —) SQUID
(FINANCIAL —) ITEM
(KEYBOARD —) MELLOTRON
(LEGAL —) DEED GRANT FACTUM SASINE SCRIPT CHARTER CODICIL DUPLICATE
(METEOROLOGICAL —) LIDAR
(NAUTICAL —) OCTANT
(NAVIGATIONAL —) LORAN TELERAN
(NEGOTIABLE —) HUNDI HOONDEE
(OFFICIAL —) SLANG
(PREHISTORIC —) CELT
(SCIENTIFIC —) HELIOSTAT
(SCIENTIFIC OR OTHER —) AWL FAN HOE KEY MET RAX SAX BROG CLAM COMB DIAL DRAG FILE FORK GAGE HOOK PALM PLOW RACK RING SPAR ARMIL BEVEL BLADE BRACE BRAKE CHAIN CLAMP CORER DATER DOLLY DRILL FLAIL FLOAT FLUKE GAUGE GLASS INDEX KNIFE LADLE LEVER METER MISER PILOT RAZOR SCALE SCOPE SLATE SLICE SLING SPADE SPEAR SPRAY STAMP STEEL SWIFT THROW TONGS TUNER WHISK ABACUS BEATER BEETLE BODKIN BRIDGE CHOWRY CIRCLE DOUCHE ENGINE ERASER FERULE FOLDER GRATER LEAPER MORTAR NEEDLE PALLET PESTLE PICKER PLOUGH PULLER PUMPER RAMMER RASPER RATTLE RUBBER SCALER SCORER SCRIBE SCUTCH SCYTHE SHEARS SQUARE SQUIRT STADIA STRAIK STROBE STYLET STYLUS TACKLE TICKER WIMBLE ALIDADE BELLOWS BREAKER CADRANS CLEAVER COMPASS DIOPTER DOLABRA DOUBLER FISTUCA GRAFTER GRAINER GRAPPLE HATCHEL LAYOVER MASSEUR MEASURE OOMETER OOSCOPE PAVIOUR PELORUS PIERCER PINCERS PRICKER PRINTER PYROPEN QUADRAT SCRAPER SEXTANT SHOCKER SHUTTLE SLITTER SOUNDER SPLAYER SPRAYER STRIGIL SUNDIAL SWINGLE TRAMMEL TRIMMER WHISTLE ANALEMMA ATOMIZER BARNACLE BIRDCALL BLOWPIPE BUTTERIS CALLIPER COALRAKE DECAPPER DETECTOR DIAGRAPH DIPMETER DIVIDERS EQUULEUS ERGMETER EXPLORER FATHOMER GEOPHONE HOROLOGE IMPINGER IRISCOPE ISOGRAPH ISOSCOPE JOVILABE MESOLABE MHOMETER ODOMETER OHMMETER PHOTOMER QUADRANT RECORDER RINGHEAD RUMMAGER SCISSORS SEARCHER SQUEEGEE STILETTO STRICKLE TJANTING TRIANGLE VELLINCH VIAGRAPH YAWMETER
(SURGICAL OR MEDICAL —) GAG HOOK SPUD FLEAM PROBE SCALA SCOOP SNARE SOUND STAFF STYLE BILABE BOUGIE BROACH GORGET LANCET SEEKER TREPAN TROCAR UNGULA VECTIS XYSTER AGRAFFE AIRDENT DILATER FORCEPS HARPOON LEVATOR LIGATOR MYOTOME PELICAN PLUGGER RONGEUR SCALPEL SOUNDER SYRINGE TRACTOR TRILABE TURNKEY ANOSCOPE AURILAVE AXOMETER BISTOURY DIRECTOR DIVULSOR ECRASEUR ELEVATOR EXSECTOR HEMOSTAT KERATOME MYOGRAPH SPECULUM TREPHINE
(VOID —) NULLITY
(PREF.) **(POINTED —)** SCOLO
(WIND —) AEOLO
(SUFF.) LABE METER METR(E)(O)(Y) STAT(IC)
(MUSICAL —) INA
(SURGICAL REMOVAL —) ECTOME
INSTRUMENTAL MEDIATE ORGANIC SERVILE SERVIENT MINISTERIAL
INSTRUMENTALIST KLEZMER SIDEMAN
(SUPPLEMENTARY —) RIPIENO RIPIENIST
INSTRUMENTALITY HAND MEANS AGENCY MEDIUM CHANNEL COUNCIL MINISTRY
(— FOR ACQUISITION OF KNOWLEDGE) ORGANON
(NAVAL —S) BEACH
INSUBORDINATE FACTIOUS MUTINOUS UNWIELDY
INSUBORDINATION MUTINY
INSUBSTANTIAL AIRY PUNY INANE WISPY FROTHY POROUS SLENDER SPECTRAL VAPOROUS INTANGIGLE
INSUBSTANTIALITY FRAILTY
INSUFFICIENCY PAUCITY
(PREF.) OLIG(O)
INSUFFICIENT POOR WANE SHORT SCANTY
INSUFFICIENTLY BARELY FEEBLY THINLY
INSULATE ISLE DEADEN ISLAND ISOLATE
INSULATION LAGGING ISOLATION
INSULATOR NOB KNOB CLEAT TAPLET VITRITE MEGOHMIT STANDOFF
(PL.) STRING
INSULT CAG FIG JOEY RUMP SLAM SLAP SLUR ABUSE CHECK FLOUT FRUMP SLANG INJURE INJURY OFFEND OUTRAY RUFFLE SCRAPE ABUSION AFFRONT OFFENCE OUTRAGE BRICKBAT DISHONOR CONTUMELY
INSULTING RUDE ABUSIVE ARROGANT INSOLENT
INSULTINGLY FOULLY
INSURANCE LINE CHOMAGE COVERAGE INDEMNITY
(— AGENT) TWISTER
(UNEMPLOYMENT —) DOLE POGEY
INSURE COVER ASSURE ENSURE FURNISH
INSURER ABANDONEE
INSURGENT REBEL RISER CHOUAN OAKBOY TAIPING BARRABAS CAMISARD STEELBOY
INSURRECTION RIST MUTINY REVOLT UPROAR OUTBREAK SEDITION UPRISING REBELLION
INSURRECTO GUGU
INTACT SOUND WHOLE ENTIRE MAIDEN
(PREF.) INTEGRI
INTAGLIO ENTAIL DIAGLYPH
(PART OF —) INCAVO
INTAKE (AIRCRAFT ENGINE —) AIRSCOOP
INTANGIBLE VAGUE SUBTLE AERIFORM SLIPPERY
INTEGER SUM NORM TOTITIVE
INTEGRAL FLUX NEEDFUL
INTEGRANT ELEMENT
INTEGRATE FUSE PIECE COMBINE FULFILL ORGANIZE
INTEGRATED FUSED INTEGRAL
INTEGRATION BALANCE HARMONY
INTEGRITY HONOR TRUTH HONESTY JUSTICE PROBITY CHASTITY STRENGTH SINCERITY
INTEGUMENT KEX ARIL PILL SKIN TESTA TUNIC SWATHE CUTICLE ENVELOP EPIDERM EXODERM PRIMINE TUNICLE VELAMEN EPISPERM PERISARC SCABBARD SECUNDINE
(PREF.) SCYT(O)
(SUFF.) DERM(A)(ATOUS)(IA)(IS)(Y)
INTELLECT MIND NOUS HEART INWIT MAHAT SKILL BRAINS NOTICE REASON SPIRITS THINKING
(HIGHEST —) NOUS
INTELLECTUAL BLUE GAON IDEAL BOOKSY MENTAL NOETIC SOPHIC BRAHMIN EGGHEAD GNOSTIC CEREBRAL HIGHBROW LONGHAIR SOPHICAL DIANOETIC SPIRITUAL
(PL.) EGGMASS
INTELLIGENCE AIR CIT SAT CHIT KNOW MIND NEWS NOTE NOUS WORD AGIEL SAVVY SENSE SMART ADVICE BRAINS ESPRIT INGENY NOTICE PSYCHE SMARTS WITTING MENTALITY
(— IN EGYPTIAN LORE) CHU
(— OF PLANET JUPITER) JOPHIEL
(LACKING —) VACUOUS
(LIVELY —) WIT
INTELLIGENT APT GASH PERT ACUTE ALERT SHARP SMART SPACK AKAMAI BRAINY BRIGHT CLEVER MENTAL SHREWD SPRACK WITFUL KNOWING INFORMED LUMINOUS RATIONAL SKILLFUL
(— GROUP) MENTA

INTELLIGENTSIA CLERISY
INTELLIGIBLE CLEAR PLAIN LUMINOUS PELLUCID PERVIOUS REVELANT PERCEIVABLE
INTELLIGIBLY SIMPLY
INTEMPERANCE ACRASY EXCESS ACRASIA OUTRAGE
INTEMPERATE SHRILL SURFEIT
(NOT —) SWEET
INTEND GO AIM FIX CAST MEAN MIND MINT PLAN PLOT TEND ALLOT ALLOW ETTLE TIGHT ATTEND DESIGN RECKON SETOUT BEHIGHT DESTINE FORELAY PRETEND PROPOSE PURPORT PURPOSE FOREMIND MEDITATE PRETENSE
INTENDED ON FIANCEE SUPPOSED
INTENSE HOT ACID COLD DEEP HARD HIGH KEEN BLANK DENSE GREAT HEAVY QUICK SHARP TENSE VIVID ARDENT BRAZEN FIERCE INTENT PITCHY SEVERE STRONG BURNING CHARGED CHRONIC CUTTING EXTREME FERVENT FRANTIC FURIOUS VICIOUS VIOLENT EGYPTIAN GRIEVOUS POWERFUL PROFOUND SEETHING TERRIFIC VEHEMENT
(VIOLENTLY —) RABID
INTENSELY VERY STIFF HIGHLY ACUTELY CURSEDLY FERVIDLY MORTALLY SHREWDLY
INTENSIFICATION
(PREF.) DE
INTENSIFIED ACUTE
INTENSIFY RISE URGE EXALT RAISE ACCENT DEEPEN HEATUP BOLSTER ENFORCE ENHANCE IMPROVE INFLAME MAGNIFY SHARPEN THICKEN CONDENSE HEIGHTEN INCREASE REDOUBLE
INTENSION INTENT MEANING
INTENSITY EDGE HEAT ARDOR DEPTH DRIVE FEVER FIELD VIGOR ACCENT DEGREE DOSAGE FERVOR FRENZY STRESS CURRENT FEROCITY STRENGTH VIOLENCE
(— OF DISEASE) ACUITY
(— OF EMOTION) ARDENCY
INTENSIVE HARD HIGH EXTENDED
INTENSIVELY HARD SOLIDLY
INTENT SET DEEP DOLE FELL HENT MIND RAPT TENT BEADY CAUSE DRIFT ETTLE FIXED HEART PRICK SCOPE TENOR TENSE EFFECT SPIRIT COUNSEL INTENSE PRESENT PURPOSE STUDIED WISTFUL
(CRIMINAL —) DOLE
(EVIL —) DOLUS
INTENTION AIM END GOAL HENT MIND VIEW WILL HEART SCOPE ANIMUS ATTENT DESIGN DEVICE EFFECT INTENT OBJECT REGARD COUNSEL COURAGE EARNEST FORESET MEANING PROPOSE PURPORT PURPOSE SUPPOSE THOUGHT PRETENSE OBJECTIVE
(CRIMINAL —) DOLE
INTENTIONAL SET WILLFUL WILLING WITTING INTENDED
INTENTLY BUSILY WISHLY EAGERLY FIXEDLY
INTER BURY EARTH ENTER GRAVE PLANT ENTOMB INHUME INEARTH
INTERACTION COUPLING
INTERAGENT MEDIUM MIDDLER
INTERBREED CROSS
INTERBREEDING APOGAMY MIXTURE PANMIXY CROSSING
INTERCALATE INSERT
INTERCALATION EMBOLISM
INTERCEPT KEP HEAD KEEP STOP CATCH NORMAL ABSCISS TRAMMEL GAINCOPE INTERPEL RETRENCH
INTERCEPTION CUTOFF
INTERCESSION MOYEN DIPTYCH PLEADING
INTERCESSOR MEANS PLEADER ADVOCATE MEDIATOR
INTERCHANGE CHANGE ANAGRAM COMMUTE PASSAGE PERMUTE COMMERCE EXCHANGE
(— OF OPINION) COUNSEL
(— OF WORDS) SPEECH
(PREF.) TRANS
INTERCHANGEABLE FUNGIBLE
INTERCHANGED CROSS
INTERCOLUMNIATION EUSTYLE SYSTYLE DIASTYLE
INTERCOMMUNICATION LIAISON
INTERCONNECTED SYNDETIC
INTERCONNECTION BONDING
INTERCOURSE GAM DEAL MANG MONG TRADE TRUCK TURGY BAWDRY HOBNOB NEGOCE COITION DEALING MIXTURE QUARTER SOCIETY TRAFFIC BUSINESS COMMERCE CONVERSE RECOURSE RELATIONS
INTERDICT BAN TABU DEBAR TABOO FORBID UTRUBI INHIBIT PROHIBIT SUPPRESS
INTERDICTION VETO
INTEREST BUG DIP FAD USE BENT GOOD HAND HOLD PART CLOSE COLOR DRIVE FAVOR FETCH GAVEL HOBBY RENTE RIGHT STAKE STUDY USAGE USURA USURY BEHALF ENGAGE EQUITY ESTATE FAENUS FERVOR FINGER INCOME USANCE ATTRACT CONCERN RESPECT USAUNCE CONTANGO INCREASE VIGORISH
(— OF HUSBAND) CURTESY
(— ON LAND) CLOSE
(— PAID TO MONEYLENDER) VIG VIGORISH
(ACTIVE —) SYMPATHY
(EXORBITANT —) JUICE
(LEGAL —) EASEMENT
(POLITICAL —) FENCE
(SECURITY —) LIEN
(SPECIAL —) MEAT ANGLE
INTERESTED HIPPED ENGAGED SERIOUS CONCERNED
(— IN) INTO
(UNEASILY —) PRURIENT
INTERESTING FRUITY CURIOUS PIQUANT STORIED ABSORBING
INTERFACE PORT
(COMPUTER —) PORT
INTERFERE CUT MAKE ANNOY BLOCK CHECK HITCH POACH BAFFLE HAMPER HINDER HOBBLE IMPEDE MEDDLE STRIKE TAMPER INTRUDE INTROMIT
(— SLIGHTLY) BRUSH
(— WITH) AIL JOLT MESS CROSS HECKLE BLANKET DISTURB
INTERFERENCE BALK CHOKE THUMP HINDER JOSTLE MEDDLE CONFLICT FREINAGE
INTERFERING CUT
INTERFEROMETER ETALON
INTERFLUVE DOAB
INTERGROWTH PERTHITE
INTERIM BREAK VACANCY
INTERIOR BEN BELLY BOSOM INNER ENTIRE INLAND INWARD INWITH MIDDLE GIZZARD ENTRAILS INTERNAL
(— OF CUPOLA) CALOTTE
(— OF TEMPLE) CELLA
(— OF VESSEL) HOLD
(— PART) MANTLE
INTERJECT POKE ENTER SQUIB INJECT THRUST
INTERJECTION (ALSO SEE OATH) AW ER HA LO BAH BOO COO FIE GAD GEE GIP GUP HAH HAY HEH HEY HOY HUH LAW OOH POW WOW AHEM AHOY ALAS ANAN BOOH CHUT CIAO DAMN DEAR EGAD EVOE FORE GOSH HAHA HAIL HECH HECK HEHE HEIL HELL HOLA JOVE ODSO OOPS OUCH OYEZ PISH POOH POSH RATS SHOO WELL WHEW ADIOS ALACK ARRAH BASTA BEDAD BRAVO BULLY FAITH FANCY FAUGH GOLLY GOODY HALLO HEIGH HOLLA HUZZA MAFEY MARRY MERCY MUSHA OHONE PROST PSHAW RIGHT SUGAR TENEZ ZOWIE ATWEEL BARLEY CRIKEY CRIPES EUREKA HARROW JIMINY OUTCRY PHOOEY PROSIT RIGHTO SHUCKS YIPPEE BEGORRA CARAMBA CRIMINE HEAVENS BEGORRAH GADZOOKS LACKADAY
(— EXPRESSING APOLOGY) OOPS WOOPS
(— INDICATING DISMAY) UHOH
(— OF AGREEMENT) UHHUH
(— OF NEGATION) UHUH
(— TO EXPRESS DISGUST) YUK YECH YUCK YECCH
(— TO EXPRESS FEAR) YIKES
(— TO EXPRESS PLEASURE) YUMYUM
(BIBLICAL —) SELAH
INTERLACE LACE WARP BRAID WEAVE ENLACE PLEACH WATTLE ENTRAIL INWEAVE WREATHE
INTERLACED BRACED FRETTED PLEACHED
INTERLACEMENT KNOT
INTERLACING RETE TWINY
INTERLINING DOUBLER
INTERLOCK KNIT LOCK MESH PITCH ENGAGE FINGER TANGLE DOVETAIL
INTERLOPE INTRUDE
INTERLUDE JIG JEST LETUP COMEDY VERSET TEMACHA TRIUMPH ANTIMASK ENTRACTE ENTREMES RITORNEL VERSETTE PARENTHESIS
(OPERATIC —) RITORNELLO
(QUIET —) LACUNA
(ROMANTIC —) IDYL IDYLL
INTERMEDDLER STRANGER
INTERMEDDLING GESTION
INTERMEDIARY MEAN AGENT MOYENER MEDIATOR TRAMPLER MIDDLEMAN
INTERMEDIATE MEAN MESNE FILLER ISATIN MEDIAL MEDIUM MIDDLE NEUTRAL MIDDLING
(PREF.) MEDI MES(O)
INTERMEDIATOR BROKER
INTERMENT BURIAL BURYING DEPOSIT HUMATION
INTERMINABLE ETERNAL INFINITE TIMELESS UNENDING
INTERMINGLE MIX BRAID COALESCE IMMINGLE INTERMIT INTERMIX
INTERMINGLED AMONG AMONGST
INTERMINGLING
(SUFF.) MIXIS
INTERMISSION REST WAIT BREAK DWELL PAUSE DEVALL RECESS NOONING RELACHE RESPITE INTERVAL SURCEASE VACATION
(— OF FEVER) APYREXIA
(— OF PAIN) SABBATH
INTERMISSIVE CESSANT
INTERMIT CEASE DEFER DEVAUL SUSPEND
INTERMITTENT BROKEN FITFUL PERIODIC
INTERMIX BLEND MEDLEY MINGLE
INTERMIXTURE CROSS INTIMACY
INTERNAL INLY INNER ENTIRE INLAND INNATE INSIDE INWARD DOMESTIC
(PREF.) INTRA
INTERNALLY INLY INSIDE INWARD INWARDLY
INTERNET (CONNECTED TO —) ONLINE
INTERNODE ROSETTE
INTERPELLATION FLOWER
INTERPENETRATED SHOT
INTERPLAY AUSPICE
INTERPOLATE FARCE FARSE FOIST FUDGE INSERT THRUST
INTERPOLATION GAG FARSE
(ACTOR'S —) GAG
INTERPOLATOR DIASKEUAST
INTERPOSE BAR CHOP POKE DEMUR OBJECT STRIKE THRUST THWART MEDIATE STICKLE
INTERPRET MAKE OPEN READ SCAN TAKE AREAD AREED FANCY GLOSS GLOZE RECHE DEFINE DIVINE INTEND CLARIFY COMMENT DECLARE ENGLISH EXPLAIN EXPOUND CONSTRUE DECIPHER SIMPLIFY
INTERPRETATION REDE GLOSS SENSE GOSPEL STRAIN ANAGOGE BARAITA COMMENT DOBHASH EPIKEIA MEANING READING CABALISM EXEGESIS INNUENDO MOONSHEE SOLARISM SOLUTION
INTERPRETER BROKER DUBASH

MUNSHI UNDOER EXEGETE LATINER MUNCHEE CABALIST DRAGOMAN EXPONENT LINKSTER TRUCHMAN
(— OF DREAMS) ONEIROCRITIC
(— OF SCRIPTURE) TROPIST
(PL.) HAHAM SELLI SELLOI CHOCHEM HAKAMIM
INTERRELATED INTIMATE
INTERRELATIONSHIP ACCORD LIAISON COMMERCE
INTERROGATE ASK GRILL TARGE DEBRIEF EXAMINE INQUIRE
INTERROGATION EROTESIS QUESTION
INTERROGATORY EROTETIC
INTERRUPT CUT MAR NIP CHOP STOP TAKE BREAK CHECK CRACK EMBAR ARREST DERAIL DERANGE DISRUPT FORBREAK INTERMIT INTERPEL OBSTRUCT
INTERRUPTED BROKEN CHOPPY SNATCHY
INTERRUPTER BUZZER
INTERRUPTION BLIP CESS JUMP STOP BLOCK BREAK CHECK DWELL LAPSE PAUSE BREACH HIATUS HOCKET HOQUET ISLAND OUTAGE CAESURA CUTBACK DIASTEM BLOCKING BREAKAGE SOLUTION STOPOVER
(— OF SOUND) BLIP BLEEP
(WITHOUT —) FLUSH
INTERRUPTOR TIKKER BREAKER CHOPPER RHEOTOME
INTERSECT CUT CROSS BISECT INCISE CROSSCUT
INTERSECTING SECANT CRUCIAL COMPITAL
INTERSECTION LEET CHINE CROSS CURVE CHIASMA CROSSING CROSSWAY JUNCTION
INTERSESSION WINTERIM
INTERSEXUAL EPICENE
INTERSEXUALITY GYNANDRY
INTERSPACE SPACE POCKET
INTERSPERSE DOT SALT SHED MEDDLE THREAD CHECKER INTERSOW SPRINKLE
INTERSTICE GAP PORE SEAM CHINK GRATE SPACE AREOLA AREOLE RIFFLE CELLULE VACUITY
(PL.) CANCELLI
INTERSTRATIFY INTERBED
INTERTWINE KNIT LACE WARP PLAIT TWINE FELTER TANGLE WAMPLE WARPLE WRITHE ENSNARL COMPLECT IMPLEACH INTERTEX
INTERTWINED INWOUND
INTERTWIST RADDLE
INTERVAL GAP LAG CENT GULF REST SAND SEXT SPOT STEP BLANK BREAK COMMA CYCLE FIFTH LAPSE PRIME QUINT SIXTH SPACE SWING TENTH THIRD BREACH DECIMA DEGREE DIESIS DITONE FOURTH MERLON SECOND SLATCH SYSTEM ADVANCE DIASTEM DISCORD HEADWAY HEMIOLA INTERIM PASTIME RESPITE SCHISMA SETTIMO STADIUM TRITONE DIAPASON DIAPENTE DISTANCE ELEVENTH ENTRACTE FONTANEL INTERACT MICROTONE PARENTHESIS
(— BETWEEN FINGERS) SUBVOLA
(— BETWEEN ROPE STRANDS) CONTLINE
(— OF BRIGHTNESS) FLICKER
(— OF CALM) LULL
(— OF EASE) REPRIEVE
(— OF FAIR WEATHER) SLATCH
(— OF HARSH WEATHER) SNAP
(— OF ROPE STRANDS) CONTLINE
(— OF SEMITONE) APOTOME
(— OF TIME) WINDOW
(AT REGULAR —S) SPACED
(MUSICAL —) TONE FIFTH NINTH SIXTH TENTH THIRD FOURTH OCTAVE SECOND UNISON SEVENTH TRITONE MEANTONE
(REST —) SOB
(SHORT —) STREAK
(TIME —) HEADWAY
INTERVALE BOTTOM
INTERVENE CHOP STEP STRIKE MEDIATE OBVIATE STICKLE INTERCUR
INTERVENING MESNE MIDDLE MEDIANT
(PREF.) INTER
INTERVIEW BUZZ CONTACT AUDIENCE CONGRESS
INTERWEAVE MAT PLAT CRISP PLAIT PLASH PLEACH RADDLE TANGLE WATTLE ENTWINE TEXTURE TRELLIS COMPLECT ENTANGLE IMPLEACH INTERTEX
INTERWEAVING BREDE CROWN INTIMATE
(— OF INITIALS) CIPHER
INTERWOVEN INWOVEN IMPLICIT INTIMATE
(— WITH COLORS) PIRNIT
INTESTINAL INNER ENTERAL ENTERIC SPLANCHNIC
INTESTINE GUT ROPE BOWEL INNER THARM INWARD MIDDLE THAIRM
(PORTION OF —) JEJUNUM
(PL.) VISCUS INGANGS CHITLINS
(PREF.) COL(O) ENTER(O)
INTHROW RIDGE
INTIMACY LIAISON PRIVACY AFFINITY CHUMMERY GOSSIPRY INTRIGUE MUTUALITY
(UNDUE —) LIBERTY
INTIMATE PAL SIB BOON GRIT HINT HOME HOMY KIND NEAR NEXT PACK TOSH BOSOM CHIEF CLOSE GREAT HOMEY PALLY PRIVY THICK ALLUDE ENTIRE FRIEND HOMELY INTIME INWARD NOTICE SECRET STRAIT STRICT THRANG THRONG CHAMBER CLOSEUP GREMIAL INNERLY INNUATE KEYHOLE PRIVADO PRIVATE SIGNIFY SPECIAL SUGGEST UPCLOSE COCKMATE ESPECIAL FAMILIAR FREQUENT FRIENDLY INDICATE INTIMADO
(INGRATIATINGLY —) PALSY
(MOST —) MIDMOST
(PL.) FOLKS
INTIMATELY INLY NEAR TOSH WELL COZILY CLOSELY INWARDLY
INTIMATION CUE HINT ITEM WARN WIND SCENT NOTICE OFFICE GLIMMER INKLING CIRCULAR INNUENDO MONITION
INTIMIDATE COW HAZE ABASH BULLY COWER DAUNT DETER PSYCH HECTOR PSYCHE TERRIFY BROWBEAT BULLDOZE BULLYRAG FRIGHTEN
INTO IN INTIL WITHIN
(PREF.) IL IM IN INTRO IR
INTOLERABLY PLAGUY
INTOLERANCE BIGOTRY
INTOLERANT CLOSED BIGOTED
INTONATION FALL CHANT ITALICS
(LOCAL —) TWANG
(MONOTONOUS —) SINGSONG
INTONE CANT SING TONE CHANT CHAUNT ENTUNE MODULATE CANTILLATE
INTOXICANT BOZA HASH BHANG CHARAS MESCAL PEYOTE COCAINE HASHISH HASHEESH MARIJUANA
INTOXICATE FOX TIP TOX CORN FLAW GOOF SOAK TODDY FUDDLE MUDDLE SOZZLE SPRING TIPSIFY DISGUISE OVERTAKE SPRINKLE
INTOXICATED CUT FAP LIT WET HIGH LUSH RIPE SHOT SOSH TOFT TOSY BOSKY BUFFY DRUNK FRESH FRIED FUNNY HEADY LACED NAPPY PIPED TIGHT BLOTTO BOILED GROGGY LOADED LOOPED MELLOW PIPPED QUAINT SCREWY SKEWED SLEWED SLOPPY SODDEN SOSHED SOZZLE STEWED TANKED UPPISH UPPITY WASTED ZONKED EBRIATE EXALTED FLECKED JINGLED POTSHOT SCREWED SLOPPED SMASHED SPIFFED SQUIFFY UNSOBER WRECKED BESOTTED COCKEYED DELEERIT ELEVATED OVERSEEN OVERSHOT PLEASANT SQUIFFED TEMULENT TOXICATE WIPEDOUT
INTOXICATING HARD HEADY STARK HUFFCAP
INTOXICATION WINE FUDDLE IVRESSE LOCOISM DISGUISE EBRIOSITY TEMULENCE
(— OF ANIMALS) DUNZIEKTE
INTRACTABLE BAD HARD SALTY STACK SURLY FIERCE KITTLE SULLEN THWART UNRULY CRABBED HAGGARD RESTIVE ROPABLE WAYWARD CHURLISH INDOCILE MUTINOUS OBDURATE PERVERSE SHREWISH
INTRADA ENTREE
INTRADOS SOFFIT
INTRANSITIVE NEUTER
INTREPID BOLD BRAVE HARDY HEROIC PRETTY SAVAGE DOUGHTY VALIANT RESOLUTE
INTREPIDITY GAME VALOR COURAGE
INTRICACY KNOT INTRIGUE
INTRICATE HARD MAZY BLIND DAEDAL IMPLEX KNOBBY KNOTTY SUBTLE TANGLY TRICKY COMPLEX CRABBED CURIOUS GORDIAN PERPLEX PUZZLED SINUOUS INVOLUTE INVOLVED ANFRACTUOUS
(ARTIFICIALLY —) CONTRIVED
INTRIGUE PLOT ANGLE CABAL CLOAK STORY AFFAIR AMOUNT BRIGUE DECEIT SCHEME CONNIVE FACTION FINAGLE JOBBERY TRINKET TRINKLE ARTIFICE CHEATING COLLOGUE PRACTICE PRACTISE STRATEGY TRIPOTER
INTRIGUER JESUIT SCHEMER DESIGNER TRINKETER
INTRIGUING EXCITING SCHEMING
INTRINSIC REAL TRUE INBORN INBRED INNATE INWARD NATIVE GENUINE NATURAL ABSOLUTE IMMANENT INHERENT INTERNAL INTIMATE
INTRINSICALLY PERSE PROPERLY
INTRODUCE READ DEBUT ENTER FRONT IMMIT INFER PLANT START USHER BROACH HERALD INDUCE INDUCT INFUSE INJECT INSERT INVECT INVOKE LAUNCH PREFER FORERUN IMPLANT INSTILL INVEIGH PRECEDE PREFACE PRELUDE PRESENT SHUFFLE SPONSOR TROTOUT ACQUAINT INNOVATE INTROMIT WIREDRAW
(— AIR INTO) AERATE
(— AS FIRST ACT) INITIATE
(— FROM WITHOUT) IMPORT
(— SURREPTITIOUSLY) FOIST
INTRODUCTION LASSU PROEM PRONE INTRADA INTROIT ISAGOGE MENTION PREFACE ENTRANCE EXORDIUM PREAMBLE PROLOGUE PRELUSION
(— INTO STOMACH) GAVAGE
(— OF DRAMA) PROTASIS
(— OF NEW PRODUCT) ROLLOUT
(— OF NOVELTY) CHANGE
(MUSICAL —) INTRO INTRADA OVERTURE
(SUFF.) PHORESIS
INTRODUCTORY EXORDIAL ISAGOGIC LIMINARY PROTATIC SYSTATIC PRELUSIVE PRELIMINARY
INTROIT REQUIEM
INTRORSE ANTICAL
INTROSPECTION INLOOK REFLEX
INTRUDE JET ABATE BARGE CRASH POACH BOTHER CHISEL INGYRE INJECT INVADE IRRUPT THRUST AGGRESS OBTRUDE ENCROACH INFRINGE TRESPASS
INTRUDER INTRUS INCOMER INVADER STRANGER
INTRUSION INVASION
INTRUSIVE NOSY FRESH NOSEY SPURIOUS
(PREF.) XEN(O)
INTUITION HUNCH PRESAGE INSTINCT
INTUITIONIST EIDETIC
INULIN ALANTIN
INUNDATE FLOW DROWN FLOOD INUND SWAMP DELUGE OVERFLOW SUBMERGE SURROUND
INUNDATED AWASH
INUNDATION FLOW FLOOD SPATE

WATER DELUGE ALLUVIO FRESHET ALLUVION FLOODAGE OVERFLOW
INURE URE BREAK ENURE STEEL HARDEN SCHOOL SEASON ACCUSTOM INDURATE ACCLIMATIZE
INVADE ASSAIL INTRUDE ENCROACH INTRENCH TRESPASS
INVADER HUN PICT
INVADING INGRUENT
INVAGINATION GULLET
INVALID BAD BUM NULL CHRONIC NUGATORY
INVALIDATE UNDO AVOID BREAK CANCEL INFIRM IMPROVE INVALID VITIATE
INVALUABLE COSTLY PRECIOUS PRICELESS
INVARIABLE STEADY UNIFORM CONSTANT
INVARIABLENESS ONENESS
INVARIABLY EVER ALWAYS
INVASION RAID INROAD DESCENT INBREAK INJURIA
(— BY BACTERIA) SEPSIS
INVECTIVE ABUSE HOKER SATIRE RAILING DIATRIBE REPROACH
INVEIGH RANT INVECT DECLAIM DENOUNCE
INVEIGLE COAX ROPE WILE CHARM DECOY SNARE ALLURE ENTICE SEDUCE
INVENT COIN FIND FORM MINT VAMP FEIGN FRAME FRUMP CREATE DESIGN DEVISE IDEATE CONCOCT CONJURE CONTRIVE DISCOVER
INVENTED MADE
INVENTION FANCY DEVICE FINDAL NOTION FANTASY FICTION FIGMENT FORGERY WITCRAFT
(DRAMATIC —) IBSENISM
INVENTIVE ADROIT FERTILE CREATIVE MECHANIC ORIGINAL PREGNANT
INVENTIVENESS WIT ARTIFICE
INVENTOR TALOS COINER FINDER FRAMER MINTER CREATOR MINTMAN ENGINEER ARTIFICER
AMERICAN HOE LEE BELL COLT EADS FELT GRAY HALL HOWE HUNT IVES LAND LINK LOWE MOOG OLDS OTIS PAGE READ VAIL WOOD ADAMS ALLEN BLAKE BOWIE BROWN COWEN DAVIS DOLBY EARLE ELLIS EVANS FIELD FITCH GIBBS HYATT LEWYT LIBBY LOCKE MCKAY MOODY MOREY MORSE NOYES PERKY PRATT PUPIN RUBIC TESLA WHITE BENDIX BISELL BITTER BORDEN BORTON BOYDEN BOYKIN CAHILL CHURCH CLYMER CURTIS DURYEA EDISON FARBER FOLMER FRENCH FULTON GARAND GAYLEY GORDON GORRIE HAMLIN HAYNES HORGAN HOUDRY HUGHES HUSSEY JANNEY JATVIK JUDSON KALMUS LOOMIS PITNEY PORTER SAXTON SHOLES SINGER SPANEL SPERRY TIMKEN TUPPER WARING WESSON WILCOX WILSON WRIGHT ACHESON APPLEBY BABBITT BETHELL BIGELOW BRADLEY CARRIER CORLISS CURTISS EASTMAN GATLING GODFREY HAMMOND HOLLAND JACUZZI JENKINS KNOWLES LANSTON PERKINS PULLMAN SCHICCK SELLERS STEVENS TAINTER THURBER WHITNEY ZAMBONI BACHRACH BERLINER BIRDSEYE BOGARDUS BUSHNELL DAHLGREN DEFOREST ELLSBERG ERICSSON EVINRUDE GILLETTE GOODYEAR HALSTEAD WATERMAN ABPLANALP BURROUGHS BUTTERICK DRAWBAUGH HONEYWELL HOTCHKISS INGERSOLL MCCORMICK HERRESHOFF WESTINGHOUSE
AUSTRIAN PORSCHE KEMPELEN WELSBACH
BELGIAN SAX BAEKELAND
CANADIAN ABBOTT FESSENDEN
CHINESE TSAI
DUTCH BORDEN COSTER DREBBEL
ENGLISH KAY MOON WATT DUNNE MAXIM MILLS SMITH AYRTON BRAMAH BRUNEL DONKIN GURNEY HOLDEN LISTER PITMAN WALLIS BABBAGE BESEMER BUDDING BURGESS DELARUE GAUDENS MORLAND MURDOCK SIEMANS STARLEY CROMPTON OUGHTRED STURGEON ACKERMANN APPLEGATH ARKWRIGHT ARMSTRONG HEATHCOAT WHITWORTH CARTWRIGHT HARGREAVES STEPHENSON TREVITHICK WHEATSTONE
FRENCH LYOT COANDA FOUCHE GIRARD LENOIR MONIER PROGIN LAENNEC LUMIERE CHRETIEN DAGUERRE DELSARTE JACQUARD CHASSEPOT CHARDONNET MONTGOLFIER
GERMAN FOCKE BUNSEN DIESEL DREYSE MAUSER WANKEL DAIMLER SIEMENS FLETTNER BAUERSFELD
GREEK CTESIBIUS ARCHIMEDES
IRISH BRENNAN
ITALIAN MARCONI
NORWEGIAN KRAG
SCOTTISH GED BARR WATT BAIRD DUNLOP MILLER GREGORY NEILSON TWADDELL MACINTOSH SYMINGTON
SWEDISH DALEN NOBEL POLHEM
SWISS ZWICKY PICCARD SCHWEPPE VETTERLI
INVENTORY BILL LIST STOCK ACCOUNT INVOICE TERRIER ANAGRAPH DATABASE REGISTER SCHEDULE
INVERSE
(PREF.) OB
INVERSION WALDEN CHIASMUS ENTROPION
(— OF STITCHES) PURL
INVERT CANT TURN REVERT REVERSE
INVERTASE SUCRASE
INVERTEBRATE INSECT MOLLUSC MOLLUSK
INVERTED AWKWARD
INVEST DON DUB PUT BELT FUND GARB GIFT GIRD GIRT GOWN LOCK SINK VEST WRAP BELAY BLOCK ENDOW ENDUE FEOFF INDUE CLOTHE EMBODY ENROBE FORSET OCCUPY ORDAIN BESIEGE COMPASS ENFEOFF ENVELOP INSTATE OBSERVE BENEFICE BLOCKADE SURROUND
(— IN ARMOR) EMPANOPLY
(— ONESELF) COVER ASSUME
(— WITH) INFEFT
(— WITH AUTHORITY) SCEPTER ACCREDIT
(— WITH ENERGY) CATHECT
(— WITH HONOR) DIGNIFY
(— WITH SOVEREIGN DIGNITY) ENTHRONE
(SUFF.) **(— WITH ATTRIBUTES OF)** FY IFY
INVESTED GARTERED
(— WITH AUTHORITY) REGENT
INVESTIGATE SPY SUS SIFT SUSS CHECK PROBE SOUND STUDY EXCUSS FATHOM SEARCH DISCUSS EXAMINE EXPLORE INQUIRE INDAGATE SCRUTATE
(— QUICKLY) SKIP
INVESTIGATION CHECK PROBE TRIAL EXAMEN PILPUL SEARCH DELVING INQUEST INQUIRY LEGWORK ZETETIC ANALYSIS QUESTION RESEARCH SCRUTINY SOUNDING
INVESTIGATOR SNOOP TRIER SLEUTH GUMSHOE SPOTTER FIELDMAN
(NARCOTICS —) NARC NARK
(PRIVATE —) SHAMUS
INVESTING AMBIENT
INVESTITURE VESTURE INDUMENT
INVESTMENT DOG FLIER CUTICLE CATHEXIS PANNICLE
(— OF TOWN) SIEGE
(RISKY —) SPECULATION
INVETERATE BLACK SWORN ROOTED CHRONIC HARDENED
INVIDIOUS ENVIOUS HATEFUL
INVIGORATE PEP BRACE CHEER RAISE RENEW VIGOR VIVIFY COMFORT ENFORCE ENLIVEN FORTIFY INNERVE INSINEW REFRESH INSPIRIT
INVIGORATING BRISK CRISP FRESH TONIC VITAL HEARTY LIVELY BRACING CORDIAL VEGETANT
INVIOLABILITY SANCTITY
INVIOLABLE SACRED SECURE STYGIAN
INVIOLATE SACRED
INVISIBLE HID BLIND SECRET UNSEEN VIEWLESS SIGHTLESS
(PREF.) APHAN(O) CRYPT(O) KRYPT(O)
INVITATION BID CALL CARD INVITE BIDDING CALLING
(— TO CONTEND) DARE
(— TO RIDE) GETIN GETON HOPIN HOPON CLIMBON
INVITE ASK BID WOO BEAR CALL LURE PRAY TOLL CLEPE COURT LATHE TEMPT TRYST ALLURE DESIRE ENTICE INDITE ATTRACT CONVITE PROVOKE REQUEST SOLICIT
INVITING ADORABLE HOMELIKE
INVOCATION WISH DAWUT NANDI BISMILLAH
INVOICE BILL BRIEF CHALAN FACTURE MANIFEST BORDEREAU
INVOKE WISH CLEPE EVOKE APPEAL ATTEST OBTEST CONJURE ENTREAT PROVOKE SOLICIT INVOCATE
(— EVIL) BESHREW IMPRECATE
INVOLUCRE HULL HUSK CUPULE CALYCLE CALYCULE EPICALYX
INVOLUNTARY FORCED REFLEX HELPLESS
INVOLUTE INVOLVED
INVOLUTED SCREWY
INVOLUTION ATRESIA
INVOLVE DIP LAP MIX MIRE WRAP BROIL CARRY COUCH IMPLY RAVEL DIRECT EMPLOY ENGAGE ENTAIL HANKLE INWRAP TANGLE COMPORT CONCERN CONNOTE EMBRACE EMBROIL ENSNARE ENTWINE ENVIRON IMMERSE INCLUDE ENCUMBER ENTANGLE INTEREST
(— IN DIFFICULTY) STEAD
INVOLVED IN DEEP GONE INTO BLIND KNOTTY COMPLEX ENGAGED PLAITED IMPLICIT INVOLUTE CONCERNED ANFRACTUOUS
INWARD ENTAD INNER INWITH BENWARD INNERLY HOMEFELT INTRINSIC
(PREF.) IL IM IN INTRO IR OB
INWICK INRING
IO (BROTHER OF —) PHORONEUS
(FATHER OF —) INACHUS
(SON OF —) EPAPHUS
IODINE (SOURCE OF —) KELP
(PREF.)
(REMOVAL OF —) DESIODO
IOLAUS (COMPANION OF —) HERCULES
(FATHER OF —) IPHICLES
(MOTHER OF —) AUTOMEDUSA
(WIFE OF —) MEGARA
IOLE (FATHER OF —) EURYTUS
(HUSBAND OF —) HYLLUS
IOLITE IBERITE PELIOMA
ION ACID ADION ANION CATION ISOMER KATION LIGAND AMPHION HYDRION OXONIUM SPECIES ZWITTERION
(— DURATION) LIFETIME
(FATHER OF —) XUTHUS
(MOTHER OF —) CREUSA
(SON OF —) GELEON ARGADES HOPLETES AEGICORES
(PREF.) IONTO
(SUFF.) **(CHARGED —)** ONIUM
IONIA (GULF OF —) ARTA
IONIAN (— ISLAND) CORFU
IONIZATION BURST
IOPHON (FATHER OF —) SOCRATES
(MOTHER OF —) NICOSTRATE
IOTA JOT TAD WHIT GHOST TITTLE SCRUPLE SCINTILLA
IOU SCRIP MARKER

IOWA
CAPITAL: DESMOINES
COLLEGE: COE DORDT LORAS CORNELL PARSONS GRINNELL WARTBURG
COUNTY: IDA LEE SAC CASS LINN PAGE POLK TAMA ADAIR BOONE CEDAR EMMET FLOYD LUCAS SIOUX BREMER KEOKUK OBRIEN DUBUQUE KOSSUTH MAHASKA OSCEOLA
LAKE: CLEAR STORM SPIRIT
NICKNAME: HAWKEYE
PRESIDENT: HOOVER
RIVER: CEDAR SKUNK BIGSIOUX MISSOURI
STATE BIRD: GOLDFINCH
STATE FLOWER: WILDROSE
STATE TREE: OAK
TOWN: ADEL AMES LEON ALBIA MASON ONAWA OSAGE PERRY SIOUX ALGONA ELDORA KEOKUK LEMARS MARION SIBLEY VINTON ANAMOSA OTTUMWA WATERLOO DAVENPORT

IOWAN HAWKEYE
IPECAC ITOUBOU
IPHIANASSA (FATHER OF —) PROETIUS
(HUSBAND OF —) BIAS
(MOTHER OF —) ANTIA
IPHICLUS (BROTHER OF —) HERCULES
(FATHER OF —) PHYLACUS AMPHITRYON
(MOTHER OF —) ALCMENA
(SON OF —) PODARCES PROTESILAUS
(WIFE OF —) CLYMENE
IPHIDAMAS (FATHER OF —) ANTENOR
(MOTHER OF —) THEANO
(SLAYER OF —) AGAMEMNON
IPHIGENIA (BROTHER OF —) ORESTES
(FATHER OF —) AGAMEMNON
(MOTHER OF —) CLYTEMNESTRA
(SISTER OF —) ELECTRA
IPHIMEDIA (HUSBAND OF —) ALOEUS
(SON OF —) OTUS EPHIALTES
IPHINOE (FATHER OF —) PROETUS
(MOTHER OF —) ANTIA
(SISTER OF —) LYSIPPE IPHIANASSA
IPHIS (FATHER OF —) LIGDUS
(MOTHER OF —) TELETHUSA
(WIFE OF —) IANTHE
IPHITUS (BROTHER OF —) CLYTIUS
(FATHER OF —) EURYTUS
(SISTER OF —) IOLE
(SLAYER OF —) HERCULES
IPIL VESI
IPOMOEA NIL NILL BATATAS MANROOT TURBITH TURPETH SCAMMONY
IPSEITY SELFHOOD
IRA (FATHER OF —) IKKESH
IRACUND IREFUL
IRAD (FATHER OF —) ENOCH
(GRANDFATHER OF —) CAIN
(SON OF —) MEHUJAEL

IRAN
CAPE: HALILEH
CAPITAL: TEHRAN TEHERAN
COIN: PUL ASAR CRAN LARI RIAL BISTI DARIC DINAR LARIN SHAHI TOMAN STATER ASHRAFI KASBEKE PAHLAVI
DESERT: KERMAN
FORMER NAME: PERSIA
GOVERNORSHIP: ILAM YAZD SEMNAN ZANJAN HAMADAN LORESTAN
LAKE: NIRIS NIRIZ TASHT TUZLU URMIA SAHWEH SISTAN MAHARLU NEMEKSER URUMIYEH
LANGUAGE: ZEND PAHLAVI
MEASURE: GAZ GUZ MOV ZAR ZER CANE FOOT GAREH JERIB KAFIZ MAKUK QASAB ARTABA CHARAC CHEBEL GARIBA GHALVA OUROUB CAPICHA CHENICA FARSAKH FARSANG MANSION MISHARA PAIMANEH PARASANG SABBITHA STATHMOS
MOUNTAIN: CUSH KUSH HINDU KHOSF ARARAT HAMUNT BINALUD KHORMUJ SABALAN DEMAVEND
MOUNTAIN RANGE: ELBURZ SIAHAN ZAGROS JAGATAL
PEOPLE: LUR KURD MEDE SART KAJAR MUKRI PERSE TAJIK HADJEMI PERSIAN
PORT: JASK BUSHIRE PAHLEVI
PROVINCE: FARS GILAN KERMAN TEHRAN ESFAHAN KHORASAN KORDESTAN
RIVER: MAND MUND SHUR ARAKS JAGIN KARUN RABCH SEFID BAMPUR GORGAN HALIRI TIGRIS KARKHEH MASHKEL SAFIDRUD ZAYENDEH EUPHRATES
STRAIT: HORMUZ
TOWN: FAO KOM QUM AMOL ARAK SARI YAZD AHWAZ KHVOY NIRIZ RASHT RESHT ABADAN DEZFUL GORGAN KASVIN KERMAN MASHAD MESHED SHIRAZ TABRIZ TAURIS HAMADAN ISFAHAN SANANDAJ
WEIGHT: SER DRAM DUNG ROTL SANG SEER ABBAS ARTEL MAUND PINAR RATEL BATMAN DIRHEM GANDUM KARWAR MISCAL NAKHOD NIMMAN ABBASSI TCHEIREK

IRANIAN TAT SART GALCHA SHUGNI BACTRIAN BARTANGI
(— SOVEREIGN) SHAH

IRAQ
CAPITAL: BAGDAD BAGHDAD
COIN: DINAR DIRHAM
DISTRICT: BASRA KURDISTAN
FORMER NAME: MESOPOTAMIA
MOUNTAINS: ZARGOS KURDISTAN
OASIS: MANIYA
PEOPLE: ARAB KURD
PORT: FAO BASRA
RIVER: ZAB TIGRIS EUPHRATES
TOWN: ANA HIT AFAQ AMARA BAIJI BASRA ERBIL HILLA MOSUL NAJAF HILLAH KIRKUK TIKRIT KARBALA

IRASCIBILITY BILE CHOLER
IRASCIBLE WARM ANGRY CROSS FIERY GASSY HASTY IRATE SHARP TECHY TESTY CRANKY CRUSTY IREFUL ORNERY SPUNKY TETCHY TOUCHY ANGULAR BILIOUS FRETFUL IRACUND PEEVISH TINDERY TOUSTIE WASPISH CAPTIOUS CHOLERIC PETULANT SNAPPISH STOMACHY
IRATE MAD SORE ANGRY HEATED CHOLERIC WRATHFUL
IRE FURY ANGER STEAM WRATH
IREFUL ANGRY HETUP JEALOUS

IRELAND
BAY: MAL CLEW SLIGO BANTRY DINGLE GALWAY TRALEE DONEGAL DUNDALK KILLALA BLACKSOD DROGHEDA
CAPE: CLEAR
CAPITAL: TARA DUBLIN BELFAST
COIN: RAP REAL
COUNTY: CORK DOWN LEIX MAYO CAVAN CLARE KERRY LOUTH MEATH SLIGO ANTRIM ARMAGH CARLOW GALWAY OFFALY TYRONE ULSTER DONEGAL KILDARE LEITRIM WEXFORD WICKLOW KILKENNY LIMERICK MONAGHAN FERMANAGH LONDONDERRY
ISLAND: ARAN TORY SALTEE RATHLIN
LAKE: DOO KEY REE TAY CONN DERG ERNE MASK CARRA GOWNA LEANE RAMOR BODERG COOTER ENNELL DROMORE OUGHTER SHEELIN
MEASURE: MILE BANDLE
MONEY: PUNT
MOUNTAIN: OX CAHA ANTRIM GALTEE KEEPER MOURNE MULREA DONEGAL ERRIGAL KENNEDY KIPPURE WICKLOW LEINSTER
MOUNTAIN RANGE: GALTY STACKS COMERAGH
OTHER NAME: EIRE ERIN BANBA IERNE IRENA ULSTER BOGLAND HIBERNIA INISFAIL
PEOPLE: CELT ERSE GAEL CELTIC HIBERNIAN
PERTAINING TO: CELTIC GAELIC
POINT: CAHORE CARNSORE
PORT: COBH
PROVINCE: ULSTER MUNSTER CONNACHT LEINSTER CONNAUGHT
RIVER: LEE BANN DEEL ERNE NORE SUIR BOYNE CLARE FEALE FLESK FOYLE LAUNE BANDON BARROW LIFFEY KENMARE MUNSTER SHANNON
TOWN: CORK NAAS TRIM ADARE CAVAN ENNIS OMAGH SLIGO ARMAGH CARLOW DUBLIN GALWAY LURGAN TRALEE LIMERICK TIPPERARY

IRENE (FATHER OF —) JUPITER
(MOTHER OF —) THEMIS
IRENIC CALM HENOTIC PEACEFUL
IRENICA AITESIS
IRI (FATHER OF —) BELA
IRIDESCENCE LUSTER LUSTRE REFLET
(— ON METAL) TARNISH
IRIDESCENT SHOT IRISED IRIDINE IRISATE OPALINE PAVONINE
IRIS EYE SET FLAG LILY LUCE LUCY SEGG AZURE IREOS ORRIS SEDGE FLAGON LEVERS LILIAL LILIUM SHADOW SUNBOW ALCAZAR BABIANA FLAGGER GLADDON FLAGLEAF
(FATHER OF —) THAUMAS
(MOTHER OF —) ELECTRA
(PREF.) IRIDICO IRIDIO IRID(O)
IRISH ERSE EIRANN IRISHRY MILESIAN HIBERNIAN
(— KING) RIG
(ILLITERATE —) KEELMAN
(MEMBER OF — REPUBLICAN ARMY) PROVO
(PREF.) HIBERNO
IRISHMAN MAC PAT CELT GAEL KELT SCOT GREEK IRISH PADDY YREIS TEAGUE GRECIAN IRISHER MILESIAN ORANGEMAN
(LEARNED —) OLLAMH
IRISH MOSS SLOKE CHONDRUS
IRISHWOMAN HARP
IRK BORE ITCH ANNOY WEARY BOTHER
IRKSOME DULL WARM WEARY HUMDRUM OPEROSE PAINFUL TEDIOUS ANNOYING TIRESOME
IRKSOMENESS TEDIUM
IROKO ODUM ODOOM MUVULE KAMBALA
IRON BIT DOG IRE AIRN MARS WIRE ANGLE ANVIL BASIL BRAND DRAIL DRIFT FLOSS HORSE NEGRO PRESS SPIKE STEEL WAVER ANCONY BEATER CALKER CAUTER FERRUM GAGGER GOFFER JAGGER OSMUND CAUTERY COBIRON CRAMPER FERRITE FURISON GAMBREL GAUFFER PRICKER SADIRON FLATIRON TRICOUNI
(— FOR CLOSING STAVES) HORSE
(— FOR STRIKING COINS) PILE
(— OF MILLSTONE) RIND RYND
(— ORE) LIMNITE
(— PIECES) POTLEG
(— PLATE) TRAMP
(— SHORTAGE) ANEMIA
(— SUPPORTING SPIT) COBIRON
(— TO SUPPORT BEAM) TORSEL
(ANGLE —) LATH STIFFENER
(BASKETWORK —) BEATER
(BOOM —) WITHE WYTHE
(BRANDING —) BURN
(CAST —) METAL YETLIN SPIEGEL YETLING PROMETAL SEMISTEEL
(CLIMBING —) GAFF SPUR CREEPER
(CRUDE CASTING OF —) PIG
(DRIVING —) CLEEK
(GLASSBLOWING —) BAIT

(GOLF —) WEDGE JIGGER MASHIE MIDIRON NIBLICK
(GRAPPLING —) CRAMPON CRAMPOON
(HATTER'S —) SLUG
(LEG —S) SLANGS
(MASS OF WROUGHT —) BLOOM
(METEORIC —) SIDERITE
(PASTY —) SPONGE
(PIG —) SPIEGEL KENTLEDGE
(PRIMING —) DRIFT
(PUDDLING —) RABBLE
(RUSSIAN —) SABLE
(SHEET —) TERNE
(SOLDERING —) COPPER
(SPECULAR —) HEMATITE
(TAILOR'S —) GOOSE
(TAMPING —) DRIVER
(8 PIGS OF CAST —) FODDER
(PL.) GARTERS
(PREF.) FERRI FERRO SIDER(O)
(SUFF.) SIDERITE
IRONBARK MUGGA
IRON BROWN NEGRO
IRONCLAD ARMORED IRONSIDE
IRON, GOLF (PART OF —) TOE FACE GRIP HEAD HEEL NECK NOSE SOLE HOSEL SHAFT
IRON GRAY BAT
IRON HAT GOSSAN
IRONIC DRY WRY ACERB ACERBIC SATIRIC SARCASTIC
IRONICAL BLAND CRUEL PAWKY
IRON-LIKE MARTIAL
IRON MAN TALUS
IRONMONGERY HARDWARE
IRON-OXIDE RED TARRAGONA
IRONSMITH FERRER
IRONSTONE DOGGER SIDERITE
IRONWEED FLATTOP VERNONIA WINGSTEM
IRONWOOD TITI COLIMA MOPANE MOPANI PURIRI WAMARA CYRILLA JOEWOOD AXMASTER BURNWOOD FIREWOOD
IRONWORKER LOHAR MOSCHI
IRONWORT SIDERITE
IRONY SATIRE ASTEISM SARCASM RIDICULE
IROQUOIS HURON MINGO CAYUGA MENGWE
IRRADIATE XRAY EMBEAM
IRRATIONAL MAD REE SURD WILD BRUTE SILLY ABSURD RAVING STUPID BESTIAL FOOLISH
IRRECONCILABLE HOSTILE FRONDEUR
IRREDUCIBLE BASIC
IRREGULAR ODD DUMB WILD BUMPY EROSE FANCY MIXED WOPSY ATYPIC CATCHY FITFUL PATCHY RAGGED RUGGED SPOTTY UNEVEN UNLIKE WEEWAW ANAXIAL ATACTIC BAROQUE CATERAN CRABBED CROOKED CURSORY DEVIOUS DIFFORM ERRATIC FRECKET MUTABLE SCRAWLY SNATCHY UNEQUAL WAYWARD ABNORMAL ATYPICAL DOGGEREL INFORMAL PINDARIC SCRAGGLY SCRAMBLY UNLAWFUL UNSTABLE UNSTEADY VARIABLE AMORPHOUS SCRAMBLING PROMISCUOUS
(— IN SHAPE) BAROQUE
(HAVING — EDGE) EROSE
(PREF.) AMETR(O) ANOM ANOMAL(O)
IRREGULARITY SNAG DEFECT RUFFLE ANOMALY ACCIDENT
(— IN YARN) SLUB SNICK
IRREGULARLY UNDULY
IRRELEVANT INEPT
IRRELIGIOUS PAGAN WICKED HEATHEN IMPIOUS PROFANE SENSUAL
IRREMEDIABLE HELPLESS HOPELESS
IRREPROACHABLE SPOTLESS
IRRESISTIBLE KILLING MESMERIC OPPOSELESS
IRRESISTIBLY FATALLY
IRRESOLUTE FICKLE INFIRM UNSURE WANKLE DOUBTFUL UNSTABLE
IRRESPONSIBLE WILDCAT CAREFREE FECKLESS SKITTISH
IRRESPONSIVE LEADEN
IRRETRIEVABLE HOPELESS
IRREVERENCE IMPIETY
IRREVERENT ATHEIST AWELESS IMPIOUS PROFANE
IRREVOCABLE DEAD
IRREVOCABLY FATALLY FINALLY
IRRIGATE FLOAT WATER SYRINGE
IRRIGATION KAREZ
IRRIGATOR FLOATER
IRRITABILITY BATE NERVES SPLEEN ERETHISM SORENESS VAGOTONY SENSITIVITY
IRRITABLE BAD EDGY BIRSY CROOK FIERY FUSSY HASTY HUFFY JUMPY MUSTY NAGGY RASPY TESTY TETTY TILTY TOITY CRANKY GROWLY NETTLY PATCHY SNUFFY SPUNKY STOCKY TEETHY TETCHY TOUCHY BILIOUS CRABBED FRATCHY FRETFUL HORNETY HUFFISH KICKISH PECKISH PEEVISH SPLEENY TEDIOUS TWITCHY WASPISH CHOLERIC LIVERISH PETULANT SNAPPING SNAPPISH STOMACHY SPLENETIC
IRRITANT PHOSGENE
IRRITATE BUG EAT GET IRE IRK NAG RUB TAR TEW TRY VEX BURN CRAB FIRE FRET GALL GOAD GRIG GRIT ITCH NARK RASP RILE ROIL SOUR TEEN ANGER ANNOY CHAFE EAGER FRUMP GRATE GRILL GRIPE PEEVE PIQUE STING TARRY ABRADE BOTHER FRIDGE GRAVEL HARASS HECTOR NETTLE PUTOUT RUFFLE AFFRONT INCENSE INFLAME NERVOUS PROVOKE STOMACH ACERBATE
IRRITATED RILY SORE HUFFY RAGGY MUFFED SHIRTY EMPORTE FRATCHED SOREHEAD
(EASILY —) TESTY
IRRITATING ACRID HARSH PESTY CORSIE ELVISH GRAVEL FRETFUL GALLING IRKSOME PUNGENT RASPING ANNOYING FRETSOME GRAVELLY NETTLING SCRATCHY SPITEFUL STINGING TIRESOME MADDENING NETTLESOME
IRRITATION AGRO FRET TEEN AGGRO BIRSE PIQUE STEAM NEEDLE RUFFLE TEMPER WARMTH ANTPRICK FLEABITE PINPRICK VEXATION
IRRUPTION BREAK INROAD INBREAK INBURST ERUPTION INVASION
IRU (FATHER OF —) CALEB
IS S YS BEES
(— NOT) NIS AINT ISNT
ISAAC (FATHER OF —) ABRAHAM
(MOTHER OF —) SARAH
(SON OF —) ESAU JACOB
(WIFE OF —) REBEKAH
ISABELLA (BROTHER OF —) CLAUDIO
(HUSBAND OF —) BIRON VILLEROY VINCENTIO
(LOVER OF —) ZERBINO
(SLAYER OF —) RODOMONT
ISABELLE (GUARDIAN OF —) SGANARELLE
(HUSBAND OF —) VALERE
ISAIAH ESAY ESAIAS
(FATHER OF —) AMOZ
ISANDER (BROTHER OF —) HIPPOLOCHUS
(FATHER OF —) BELLEROPHON
(SISTER OF —) LAODAMIA
ISCAH (BROTHER OF —) LOT
(FATHER OF —) HARAN
(SISTER OF —) MILCAH
ISCHEMIA ANEMIA
ISCHIAL SCIATIC
ISEULT (FATHER OF —) HOEL ANGUISH
(HUSBAND OF —) MARK
(LOVER OF —) TRISTAN
ISFENDIYAR (BROTHER OF —) BISHUTAN
(FATHER OF —) GUSHTASP
(SLAYER OF —) RUSTAM
(SON OF —) BAHMAN
ISHBAK (FATHER OF —) ABRAHAM
(MOTHER OF —) KETURAH
ISHBOSHETH (FATHER OF —) SAUL
ISHI (SON OF —) ZOHETH
ISHIAH (FATHER OF —) IZRAHIAH
ISHMAEL (FATHER OF —) AZEL ABRAHAM JEHOHANAN NETHANIAH
(MOTHER OF —) HAGAR
(SON OF —) ZEBADIAH
ISHMAIAH (FATHER OF —) OBADIAH
ISHPINGO CINNAMON
ISHSHAKKU PATESI
ISHTAR NINNI
ISHUAH (FATHER OF —) ASHER
ISHUI (FATHER OF —) SAUL
(MOTHER OF —) AHINOAM
ISINGLASS AGAR LEAF MICA PIPE KANTEN CARLOCK
ISIS (BROTHER OF —) OSIRIS
(FATHER OF —) SATURN
(MOTHER OF —) RHEA
ISLAM ABBASID
(— CALL TO PRAYER) AZAN
ISLAMIC (— CUSTOM) SUNNA
ISLAND CAY ILE CALF CAYO HOLM INCH ISLE JAVA POLO ENNIS MALTA MAYDA AVALON ITHACA OGYGIA REFUGE RIALTO CIPANGO JAMAICA MADEIRA TOWHEAD BLEFUSCU CALAURIA DOMINICA GUERNSEY LILLIPUT LUGGNAGG
(— IN EVERGLADES) HAMMOCK
(— OF REIL) INSULA
(ARTIFICIAL —) CRANNOG
(CORAL —) ATOLL
(FABLED —) MERU UTOPIA
(FLOATING —) HOVER
(FLYING —) LAPUTA
(FORTIFIED —) CRANNOG
(LEGENDARY —) BRAZIL OBRAZIL
(LITTLE —) AIT KAY KEY ISLET
(LOW —) KEY
(ROCKY —) SKERRY
(SANDY —) BEACH BARRIER
(SMALL —) CAY EYET EYOT ISLE ISLET NUBBLE SANDKEY
(PREF.) NESO
ISLANDER KANAKA ISLEMAN INSULARY
ISLE CAY IZLE ISLET SKERRY
ISLET OE AIT CAY KEY EYOT HAFT HOLM ILOT MOTU ROCK ISLOT STACK NUBBLE
ISMENE (FATHER OF —) OEDIPUS
(MOTHER OF —) JOCASTA
(SISTER OF —) ANTIGONE
ISOBAR MEIOBAR MESOBAR PLEIOBAR
ISOGRAM ISOPLETH
ISOLATE SPORE ENISLE ISLAND DISSECT SECLUDE COLONIZE INSULATE PRESCIND SEPARATE SEQUESTER
ISOLATED LONE POCKET UNIQUE OUTLYING SOLITARY STRANDED SECESSIVE
ISOLATION HERMITRY LONENESS SOLITUDE SEQUESTER
ISOMER PYRAN TOSYL XYLENE ETHANOL CUMIDINE DECOSANE DODECANE CARBOLINE
ISOMERIC ISO ALLO
ISOMETRIC ALLO CUBIC REGULAR TESSULAR
ISOPLETH GEOTHERM
ISOPOD SLATER ASELLUS BOPYRID GRIBBLE EPICARID
ISOTOPE MUON IONIUM THORON ACTINON CARRIER PROTIUM TRITIUM
ISOTYPE COTYPE SYNTYPE
ISPAGHUL SPOGEL
ISPAHAN HERAT HERATI

ISRAEL

CAPITAL: JERUSALEM
COIN: AGORA AGURA POUND PRUTA PRUTAH SHEKEL
COLLECTIVE FARM: KIBBUTZ
DESERT: NEGEV
FORMER NAME: CANAAN PALESTINE
GULF: AQABA
LAKE: HULEH TIBERIAS
MEASURE: CAB HIN KOR LOG BATH EPHA EZBA OMER REED SEAH CUBIT EPHAH HOMER KANEH QANEH
MOUNT: TABOR
MOUNTAIN: NAFH SAGI HARIF

MERON RAMON ATZMON CARMEL
PLAIN: ESDRAELON
RIVER: FARIA MALIK SOREQ JORDAN QISHON SARIDA YARKON LAKHISH
SEA: DEAD GALILEE
SEAPORT: EILAT ELATH ASHDOD TELAVIV
TOWN: ACRE RAMA EILAT HAIFA HOLON JAFFA JENIN JOPPA RAMLE SAFAD BATYAM HEBRON NABLUS JERICHO NATANYA TELAVIV TULKARM NAZARETH

ISRAELI SABRA
(— AIRPORT) LOD
(— STUDY CENTER) ULPAN
ISRAELITE JEW SAINT HEBREW JACOBITE
(PL.) ZION
ISSUE END ISH COME EMIT FALL FLOW GIVE GUSH HEAD MISE REEK TERM VENT ARISE COUNT EVENT FRUIT LOOSE OUTGO SETON SOURD UTTER EFFECT EFFUSE EGRESS EMERGE ESCAPE EXITUS MUTTON RESULT SEQUEL SETTER SPRING UPPING BALLOON DEBOUCH DESCENT DRIZZLE EMANATE ESSENCE EXSURGE OUTCOME PROCEED PROGENY REDOUND REFLAIR SUCCESS EXPEDITE FONTANEL INCREASE ISSUANCE KINDLING OUTGOING
(— AND ORDER) BID
(— SLOWLY) EXUDE
(— SPASMODICALLY) BELCH
(— SUDDENLY) SALLY
(— WITH FORCE) SPOUT
(BOND —) CONSOL
(FAVORABLE —) SPEED FORTUNE
(FINAL —) FATE UPSHOT UTMOST
(NEW —) REMAKE
(NUMEROUS —) SPAWN
(REAL —) CRUX
ISSUED OUT
ISSUING EMANANT JESSANT MANATION
ISTHMUS BALK STRAIT TARBET
ISTLE PITA IXTLE JUAMAVE GUAPILLA
IT HE HIT MUN ESSO TAGGER
(— FOLLOWS) SEQ SEQU
(— HAS BEEN SWORN) JURAT
ITALIAN ITALIC AUSONIAN MACARONI
ITALIANA IN ALGIERI, L'
(CHARACTER IN —) ELVIRA TADDEO LINDPRO ISABELLA MUSTAPHA
(COMPOSER OF —) ROSSINI
ITALITE VESBITE
ITALY AUSONIA HESPERIA SATURNIA

ITALY

CAPE: TESTA CIRCEO LICOSA LINARO COLONNE FALCONE PASSERO RIZZUTO SANVITO TEULADA VATICANO
CAPITAL: ROMA ROME
CHEESE: ROMANO FONTINA RICOTTA BELPAESE PARMESAN TALEGGIO
COIN: LIRA LIRE TARI GRANO PAOLI PAOLO SCUDO SOLDO DANARO DENARO DUCATO SEQUIN TESTONE ZECCHINO
FAMILY: ASTI ESTE AMATI CENCE DORIA BORGIA MEDICI SFORZA
FOOD: PASTA PIZZA SCAMPI GNOCCHI LASAGNE POLENTA RAVIOLI RISOTTO SPUMONI TORTONI CAPONATA LINGUINE MACARONI PEPERONI
GULF: GAETA GENOA OROSEI SALERNO TARANTO CAGLIARI ORISTANO
ISLAND: ELBA LERO CAPRI LEROS PONZA GIGLIO ISCHIA LINOSA SALINA SICILY USTICA ALICUDI ASINARA CAPRAIA GORGONA LEVANZO PANAREA PIANOSA SICILIA VULCANO FILICUDI SARDINIA
ISLANDS: EGADI LIPARI TUSCAN PELAGIE PONTINE TREMITI
LAKE: COMO ISEO NEMI GARDA ALBANO LESINA LUGANO VARANO BOLSENA PERUGIA MAGGIORE BRACCIANO
MEASURE: PIE ORNA CANNA PALMA PALMO PIEDE PUNTO SALMA STAIO STERO BARILE MIGLIE MIGLIO MOGGIO RUBBIO TAVOLA TOMOLO BOCCALE BRACCIO SECCHIO GIORNATA POLONICK QUADRATO
MOUNTAIN: ETNA ROSA VISO AMARO BLANC CORNO SOMMA CIMONE BERNINA VESUVIUS
MOUNTAIN RANGE: ALPS ORTLES APENNINES MARITIMES
NATIVE: ITALO LATIN OSCAN ROMAN SABINE TIRANO TUSCAN LOMBARD SIENESE LIGURIAN VENETIAN
NATIVE:) PISAN PISANO
PASS: FREJUS BERNINA BRENNER SPLUGEN
PORT: BARI POLA ZARA GENOA TRANI ZADAR RIMINI SALERNO TRIESTE
PROVINCE: ASTI COMO ENNA PISA AOSTA CUNEO FORLI LECCE NUORO PARMA PAVIA RIETI SIENA UDINE FOGGIA MATERA MODENA PADOVA RAGUSA TRENTO VERONA BRESCIA PISTOIA SASSARI VITERBO
REGION: CARSO APULIA LATIUM MARCHE MOLISE PUGLIA SICILY UMBRIA ABRUZZI LIGURIA TUSCANY VENETIA CALABRIA CAMPANIA LOMBARDY PIEMONTE SARDINIA
RESORT: LIDO SANREMO TAORMINA
RIVER: PO ADDA AGRI ANIO ARNO LIRI NERA RENO SELE TARO ADIGE CRATI MANNU OGLIO PARMA PIAVE SALSO STURA TIBER TIRSO ANIENE BELICE MINCIO OFANTO PANARO RAPIDO SANGRO SIMETO TANARO TEVERE TICINO BIFERNO BRADANO CHIENTI METAURO MONTONE OMBRONE PESCARA RUBICON SECCHIA TREBBIA VOLTURNO
SEA: IONIAN ADRIATIC LIGURIAN
STRAIT: MESSINA OTRANTO BONIFACIO
TOWN: BRA RHO ACRI ALBA ASTI BARI COMO DEGO ELEA ENNA ESTE FANO GELA IESI LODI NARO NOLA PISA POLA ROMA ROME ACQUI ANZIO AOSTA ASOLA AVOLA CAPUA CUNEO EBOLI FIUME FORLI GENOA IMOLA LECCE LUCCA MASSA MILAN MONZA OSTIA PADUA PARMA PAVIA RIETI SIENA TEANO TRENT TURIN UDINE VELIA ALCAMO AMALFI ANCONA ANDRIA AREZZO CEFALU FAENZA FOGGIA GENOVA MANTUA MESTRE MILANO MODENA NAPLES NAPOLI NOVARA RIVOLI SPEZIA TRENTO VARESE VENICE VERONA BERGAMO BOLOGNA BOLZANO BRESCIA CARRARA CASERTA CATANIA COSENZA CREMONA FERRARA FIRENZE GORIZIA IMPERIA LEGHORN LIVORNO MARSALA MESSINA PALERMO PERUGIA PISTOIA POMPEII RAVENNA TARANTO TRIESTE BRINDISI CAGLIARI FLORENCE PIACENZA SORRENTO SYRACUSE
VOLCANO: ETNA SOMMA VULCANO VESUVIUS STROMBOLI
WATERFALL: FRUA TOCE
WEIGHT: CARAT LIBRA ONCIA POUND CARATO DENARO LIBBRA OTTAVA
WINE: SOAVE CHIANTI MARSALA ORVIETO

ITCH EWK EACH REEF RIFF YEUK YEWK YUKE PSORA TICKLE ITCHING SCABIES PRURITUS CACOETHES VANILLISM
(PREF.) ACARI ACARO PSOR(O)
ITCHING ITCHY YEUKY PRURIENT PRURITUS URTICANT
ITCHY SCRATCHY
ITEM ANA JOB TOT ENTRY PIECE POINT THING DETAIL PARCEL ARTICLE SEVERAL PARTICULAR
(— IN SERIES) COURSE
(— OF PROPERTY) CHATTEL
(— OF VALUE) ASSET
(APPENDED —) ADDENDUM
(CHOICE —) PLUM
(COLLECTOR'S —) SPOIL
(DECORATIVE —) CONCEIT
(DESIRED —S) WISHLIST
(LUXURY —) BOUTIQUE
(NEWS —) FACTOID DISPATCH
(OFF-BRAND —) GENERIC
(UNPUBLISHED —S) ANECDOTE
(VALUELESS —) BEAN
(PL.) CHECKAGE
ITEMIZE DETAIL
ITERATE ECHO REPEAT REITERATE
ITERATION PLEONASM
ITHIEL (FATHER OF —) JESAIAH
ITHRA (SON OF —) AMASA
(WIFE OF —) ABIGAIL
ITHRAN (FATHER OF —) DISHON
ITHREAM (FATHER OF —) DAVID
(MOTHER OF —) EGLAH
ITHURIEL'S-SPEAR GRASSNUT
ITINERANT ERRANT ROADMAN RUNNING AMBULANT STROLLER STROLLING PERIPATETIC
ITINERARY DIET JOURNAL WAYBILL
(— OF ROYAL PROGRESS) GEST
ITINERATION EYRE
ITS HIS
ITSELF IT HERSELF
ITSY-BITSY WEE
ITTAI (FATHER OF —) RIBAI
ITYS (FATHER OF —) TEREUS
(MOTHER OF —) PROCNE
ITZA PETEN
IULUS ASCANIUS
IVANHOE (AUTHOR OF —) SCOTT
(CHARACTER IN —) JOHN BRIAN GIRTH ISAAC LUCAS ROBIN WAMBA CEDRIC ROWENA ULRICA MAURICE REBECCA RICHARD WILFRED REGINALD BEAUMANOIR
IVATAN BATAN
IVORY EBURE DENTINE ELEPHANT
(DUST OF —) EBURINE
(WALRUS —) RIBZUBA RIBAZUBA
IVORY BLACK ABAISER

IVORY COAST

CAPE: PALMAS
CAPITAL: ABIDJAN
DAM: BANDAMA
LANGUAGE: DIOULA
MOUNTAIN: NIMBA
PEOPLE: ABE AKAN ATLE KOUA KROU MANDE ABOURE LAGOON MALINKE VOLTAIC
RIVER: KOMOE BANDAMA CAVALLY SASSANDRA
TOWN: MAN DALOA TABOU BOUAKE GAGNOA KORHOGO SASSANDRA

IVORY GULL SNOWBIRD
IVORY NUT ANTA TAGUA JARINA
IVORY PALM TAGUA COROJO COROZO
IVORY TREE PALAY
IVY TOD GILL HOVE IVIN JILL PICRY ARALIA HEDERA HIBBIN ALEHOOF ARALIAD IVYWORT BINDWEED FOALFOOT
(— LEAGUER) ELI
(PREF.) HEDERI
IWW WOBBLY
IXION (FATHER OF —) PHLEGYAS
(SISTER OF —) CORONIS
(WIFE OF —) DIA
IYNX (FATHER OF —) PAN
(MOTHER OF —) ECHO
IZHAR (FATHER OF —) KOHATH
IZMIR SMYRNA

J

J JAY JIG JULIETT
JAALAM (FATHER OF —) ESAU
JAAL GOAT BEDEN JAELA
JAASIEL (FATHER OF —) ABNER
JAAZANIAH (FATHER OF —) AZUR SHAPHAN JEREMIAH
JAB GAG GIG JAG JOB POKE STAB STICK
JABAL (BROTHER OF —) JUBAL
(FATHER OF —) LAMECH
(MOTHER OF —) ADAH
JABBER YAP CHAT YACK JAVER BURBLE GABBER GABBLE JOBBER NATTER YABBER YATTER CHATTER
JABESH (SON OF —) SHALLUM
JABIRU STORK CICONIID
JABOT RUFFLE
JACANA PARRA
JACARANDA BROWN DATE TALLYHO
JACARE CAIMAN CAYMAN
JACHIN (FATHER OF —) SIMEON
JACINTH LIGURE
JACK DIB FLAG JACA CRICK DICKY KNAVE NANCA COLORS KATHAL SCALET SETTER WENZEL MATADOR BLOCKING JACKFISH POLIGNAL SOURJACK TURNSPIT UPLIFTER
(— IN BOWLS) BABY MARK KITTY MASTER MISTRESS
(— IN CARDS) PAM PUR TOM BOWER CNAFE KITTY KNAPE KNAVE MAKER KNIGHT VARLET WENZEL VARLETTO
(— OF CLUBS) PAM NODDY BRAGGER MATADOR
(— OF SAME SUIT) NOB
(— OF TRUMPS) TOM JASS JASZ BOWER HONOR PLAYBOY
(PIANO —) HOPPER STICKER SAUTEREAU
(ROASTING —) TURNSPIT
(SPINNING —) BEAT
JACKAL DIEB JACK KOLA THOS CANID CANINE DRAGON SILVER THOOID SIACALLE
JACKAROO RINGNECK
JACKASS JACK
JACKASS FISH MORWONG TERAKIHI
JACK BEAN OVERLOOK
JACK CREVALLE TORO
JACKDAW DAW KAE JACK SHELL CADDOW CARDER CHOUGH KADDER CADESSE DAWCOCK DAWPATE GRACKLE
JACKER SLIPMAN TORCHER
JACKET SAC COAT ETON JACK JUMP JUPE SACK VEST ACTON COVER DICKY JUPON PARKA POLKA SHRUG WAMUS BANIAN BASQUE BIETLE BLAZER BOLERO CARACO CORSET DOLMAN FECKET GANSEY JERKIN JERSEY JUMPER RAILLY REEFER SACQUE SADDLE SLEEVE SLIVER SONTAG TABARD TEMIAK WAMPUS WARMUS ZOUAVE BEDGOWN CANEZOU LOUNGER NORFOLK PALETOT PALTOCK PEACOAT RISTORI SPENCER SURCOAT SWEATER CAMISOLE CARDIGAN CHAQUETA HANSELIN JIRKINET MACKINAW OVERSLOP PENELOPE SEALSKIN CARMAGNOLE ROUNDABOUT WINDBREAKER WINDCHEATER
(— FOR TURKEY) APRON
(— LINED WITH STEEL) PLACCATE
(— OF BOOK) DUSTCOVER
(— OF INDIA) BANIAN BANIYA
(— UNDER ARMOR) ACTON TRUSS HAQUETON
(CROCHETED —) SONTAG
(DINNER —) TUXEDO
(ETON —) BUMFREEZER
(HOODED —) GREGO ANORAK GRIEKO
(HUSSAR'S —) PELISSE
(KIND OF —) MAO NEHRU SAFARI
(LADY'S —) BRUNSWICK
(LIFE —) MAEWEST
(LOOSE —) VAREUSE
(MALAY —) BAJU BADJU KABAYA
(MILITARY —) TUNIC
(PART OF —) FOB HEM DART FLAP SEAM VENT GORGE LAPEL BUTTON COLLAR INSEAM PIPING POCKET REVERS SLEEVE ARMHOLE OUTSEAM BUTTONHOLE
(PEASANT'S —) SAYON
(UNDRESS MILITARY —) SHELL
(WORK —) BAWNEEN
JACKFRUIT JACA KATHAL SOURJACK
JACKHAMMER SINKER PLUGGER
JACKKNIFE DIVE JACK PIKE BARLOW
JACKMAN SHELLMAN
JACK-OF-ALL-TRADES DOCTOR TINKER GIMCRACK
JACK-PUDDING ZANY CLOWN BUFFOON
JACKS DIBS
JACKSCREW CRICK
JACKSMELT PEIXEREY
JACKSNIPE GID JED JACK PEERT SCAPE SNIPE SNIGHT CHOROOK CREAKER JUDCOCK SQUATTER
JACKSTAY JACK HORSE PARREL JACKROD RAILWAY
JACKSTRAW SPILIKIN
JACK TREE NANGKA
JACOB ISRAEL
(BROTHER OF —) ESAU
(DAUGHTER OF —) RACHEL DEBORAH
(FATHER OF —) ISAAC
(MOTHER OF —) REBEKAH
(SON OF —) ACER LEVI ASHOR JOSEPH
JACOB'S LADDER POLEMONIUM
JACQUARD FACONNE
JADA (BROTHER OF —) SHAMMAI
(FATHER OF —) ONAM
JADE YU DUN TIT HACK JAUD MINX PLUG SLUT TIRE HUSSY QUEAN TRASH BEJADE HARASS RANNEL AXSTONE HILDING POUNAMU
(DIRTY —) SLAISTER
JADED BLASE FORGONE SHOPWORN DISJASKIT
JADEITE YU
JAEGER LARI SKUA ALLAN BOSUN LARID SHOOL BONXIE TEASER TULIAC TRUMPIE DIRTBIRD DUNGBIRD
JAEL (HUSBAND OF —) HEBER
(VICTIM OF —) SISERA
JAFFIER (WIFE OF —) BELVIDERA
JAG BUN JOG BARB GIMP JAUG LOAD SOSH TOOT SKATE TOOTH INDENT
JAGELLO (WIFE OF —) HEDWIG
JAGGED JAGGY HACKLY RAGGED RUGGED SCRAGGY SHAGGED SNAGGED INDENTED SCRAGGLY TATTERED
JAGGERY GUR GOOR GOUR KHAUR KHAJUR KITTUL
JAGUAR CAT OUNCE TIGER PANTHER UTURUNCU
JAHANGIR (FATHER OF —) AKBAR
JAHATH (FATHER OF —) LIBNI SHIMEI SHELOMOTH
JAHAZIAH (FATHER OF —) TIKVAH
JAHAZIEL (FATHER OF —) HEBRON ZECHARIAH
JAHDO (FATHER OF —) BUZ
(SON OF —) JESHISHAI
JAHLEEL (FATHER OF —) ZEBULUN
JAHZEEL (FATHER OF —) NAPHTALI
JAI ALAI PELOTA
(— BASKET) CESTA
(— COURT) FRONTON
JAIL CAN GIB JUG PEN BOOB CAGE COOP CRIB DUMP GAOL HELL HOLD HOLE KEEP LAKE LOCK NICK SLAM STIR WARD CHOKY CLINK GRATE KITTY LIMBO LODGE POKEY TENCH TRONK BUCKET CARCEL COOLER ENJAIL JIGGER LIMBUS LOCKUP TOLZEY FREEZER FURNACE GEHENNA KIDCOTE PINFOLD SLAMMER TOLLERY BASTILLE CALABOZO HOOSEGOW IMPRISON MILLDOLL TOLLHALL BRIDEWELL CALABOOSE
(— TERM) JOLT
JAILBIRD CON LAG TERMER PRISONER
JAILER ADAM GAOLER KEEPER WARDEN ALCAIDE TURNKEY INCLUDER
JAIR (FATHER OF —) KISH
(SON OF —) ELHANAN MORDECAI
JAKAN (FATHER OF —) EZER
JAKE FINE HICK FELLOW
JAKES AJAX GONG
JALAP MECHOACAN
JALON (FATHER OF —) EZRA
JALOPY HEAP BUGGY CRATE CLUNKER
JAM DIP CRAM JAMB BLOCK CHOKE CROWD CRUSH JEELY STICK JEELIE KONFYT THRONG JACKPOT PRESERVE MARMALADE
(— FOR LACK OF LUBRICATION) SEIZE
(TRAFFIC —) GRIDLOCK
JAMAICA (CAPITAL OF —) KINGSTON
(RELIGIOUS ADHERENT OF —) RASTA RASTAMAN
(RIVER OF —) BLACK COBRE MINHO
(TOWN OF —) MAYPEN PORTANTONIO SPANISHTOWN
JAMAICA COBNUT OUABE PIGNUT
JAMAICA DOGWOOD BABASCO BARBASCO FISHWOOD
JAMAICAN (— MUSIC) SKA
JAMAICAN RAINBIRD TOMFOOL
JAMAICA VERVAIN GERVAO
JAMAICIN BERBERINE
JAMB DURN ALETTE HAUNCH REVEAL DOORPOST
(PL.) COVING
JAMBOREE BASH
JAMES JEM JIM JIMMY SEAMAS SHAMUS
(BROTHER OF —) JOHN JESUS JOSES
(COUSIN OF —) JESUS
(FATHER OF —) CLOPAS
(MOTHER OF —) MARY SALOME
JAMIN (FATHER OF —) RAM SIMEON
JAMMAICA PEPPER ALLSPICE
JANAKA (DAUGHTER OF —) SITA
JANAMEJAYA (FATHER OF —) PARIKSHIT
JANE EYRE (AUTHOR OF —) BRONTE
(CHARACTER IN —) EYRE JANE JOHN MARY REED ADELE DIANA ELIZA GRACE POOLE BERTHA BESSIE EDWARD ELLIOT INGRAM LEAVEN RIVERS TEMPLE VARENS BLANCHE FAIRFAX GEORGIANA ROCHESTER
JANGLE CLAM SQUABBLE
JANGLING HARSH JANGLY AJANGLE
JANISSARY CREOLE RABIRUBIA

JANITOR DURWAN PORTER SERVITOR
JANIZARY SOLAK SOLACH
JANNA (FATHER OF —) JOSEPH
(SON OF —) MELCHI
JANSENIST RIGORIST
JANUARY ENERO
(— IN SPANISH) ENERO
JANUS IANUS BIFRONT
JAOB JOW
JAPAN NIPPON YAMATO CIPANGO

JAPAN
ABORIGINE: AINU
BAY: ISE MUTSU OTARU ARIAKE ATSUMI SENDAI SURUGA TOYAMA WAKASA UCHIURA
CAPE: TOI ESAN MINO NOMA SHIO SOYA SUZU ERIMO KYOGA RURUI MUROTO NOJIMA TODOGA SHIRIYA ASHIZURI SHAKOTAN
CAPITAL: TOKIO TOKYO
COIN: BU RIN SEN YEN OBAN KOBAN OBANG TEMPO ICHEBU ITZEBU KOBANG
FORMER CAPITAL: EDO
ISLAND: IKI SADO AWAJI BONIN HONDO KURIL REBUN HONSHU KIUSHU KURILE KYUSHU RYUKYU CIPANGO LOOCHOO RISHIRI SKIKOKU HOKKAIDO IKISHIMA OKIGUNTO OKUSHIRI TSUSHIMA YAKUJIMA
ISLAND GROUP: OKI GOTO BONIN VOLCANO
LAKE: OMI BIWA TOYA TOWADA CHUZENJI KUTCHAWA SHIKOTSU INAWASHIRO
MEASURE: BU JO SE BOO CHO KEN TAN HIRO SHAKU TSUBO
MOUNTAIN: ZAO FUJI ASAHI ASAMA YESSO ASOSAN ENASAN HIUCHI KIUSIU YARIGA FUJISAN HAKUSAN KUJUSAN TOKACHI FUJIYAMA
PORT: UBE OTARU YAHATA YAWATA
PREFECTURE: MIE GIFU NARA OITA SAGA AICHI AKITA CHIBA EHIME FUKUI GUMMA HYOGO IWATE KOCHI KYOTO SHIGA AOMORI KAGAWA MIYAGI NAGANO TOYAMA NIIGATA OKINAWA SAITAMA TOTTORI NAGASAKI WAKAYAMA YAMAGATA TOKUSHIMA
SEA: SUO AMAKUSA
STRAIT: KII BUNGO OSUMI NEMURO TANEGA TOKARA TSUGARU TSUSHIMA
STREET: GINZA
TOWN: OME TSU GIFU KOBE KURA MITO NAHA NARA OITA OTSU SAGA UEDA AKITA ATAMI CHIBA FUKUI KIOTO KOCHI NIKKO OSAKA OTARU SAKAI UJINA URAWA CHOSHI MATSUE NAGOYA SASEBO SENDAI TAKADA TOYAMA FUKUOKA NIIGATA OKAYAMA OKAZAKI SAPPORO HAKODATE KAMAKURA KANAZAWA KAWASAKI KUMAMOTO NAGASAKI YOKOHAMA YOKOSUKA HIROSHIMA
VOLCANO: ASO USU FUJI ASAMA ASOSAN HAKUSAN FUJIYAMA
WATERFALL: KEGON
WEIGHT: MO FUN KIN KON RIN SHI KATI KWAN NIYO CARAT CATTY MOMME PICUL KWAMME HIYAKKIN

JAPAN CEDAR SUGI
JAPANESE JAP JAPONIC
(— ART OF SELF-DEFENSE) AIKADO
(— CONGLOMERATE) ZAIBATSU
(— STYLE OF PAINTING) YAMATO
(ABORIGINAL —) AINU
(OF — CULTURAL PERIOD) YAYOI
(PERIOD OF — HISTORY) HEIAN
JAPANESE APRICOT UME
JAPANESE CHERRY SAKURA
JAPANESE DEER SIKA
JAPANESE GELATIN AGAR
JAPANESE IRIS SHADOW
JAPANESE PERSIMMON KAKI
JAPANESE PLUM KELSEY
JAPANESE PORGIE TAI
JAPANESE QUINCE JAPONICA
JAPANESE VELVET BIRODO
JAPE GAUD JOKE BEGUNK
JAPHETH (BROTHER OF —) HAM SHEM
(FATHER OF —) NOAH
(SON OF —) JAVAN
JAPHIA (FATHER OF —) DAVID
JAPONICA ASTILBE
JAQUENETTA (LOVER OF —) ARMADO
JAR TUN CELL JANG JARG JOLT JURR OLLA BANGA BOCAL CADUS CRUSE KADOS SHOCK DOLIUM HUSTLE HYDRIA IMPACT JUDDER KALPIS PANKIN PINATA PITHOS TINAJA CANOPUS CONCUSS POTICHE PSYKTER STAMNOS TERRINE MARTABAN STINKPOT
(— FOR LIQUOR) GREYBEARD
(— VIOLENTLY) STAVE
(BELL —) CLOCHE
(BULGING —) OLLA
(EARTHENWARE —) CAN NAN CROCK GAMLA PIPKIN PITHOS TERRINE
(PHYSICIST'S —) LEYDEN
(POROUS —) GURGLET
(SQUAT —) KORO
(STONE —) STEEN STONE CROPPA
(STRAWBERRY —) PLANTER
(WATER —) KANG BANGA CHATTI CHATTY GUMLAH HYDRIA
(2-HANDLED —) AMPHORA
(PREF.) DOLIO URCEI
JARASANDHA (FATHER OF —) BRIHADRATHA
(SLAYER OF —) BHIMA
JARDINIERE POT
JARED (SON OF —) ENOCH
JARGON CANT JIVE RANE SLUM ARGOT IDIOM LINGO SLANG LINGUA LINSEY PATOIS PATTER PIDGIN SHELTA SIWASH CHINOOK CHOCTAW DIALECT JARGOON PALAVER BARRIKIN KEDGEREE PARLANCE POLYGLOT SCHMOOZE SHOPTALK GOBBLEDEGOOK GOBBLEDYGOOK GOGGLEDEGOOK
(— OF TINKERS) KENNICK
(THIEVES' —) FLASH
(TINKER'S —) KENNICK
(UNINTELLIGIBLE —) BARAGOUIN
JARHA (MASTER OF —) SHESHAN
JARIB (FATHER OF —) SIMEON
JARRING JARG RUDE SOUR HARSH ROUGH DARING STRIDENT
JASHUB (FATHER OF —) BANI ISSACHAR
JASMINE BELA MALATI PIKAKE JESSAMY WOODBINE
JASON (VESSEL OF —) ARGO
(WIFE OF —) MEDEA
JASPER JASPIS MORLOP DIASPER BASANITE CREOLITE WEDGWOOD
JATAYU (FATHER OF —) GARUDA
(SLAYER OF —) RAVANA
JAUNDICE AURIGO GULSACH ICTERUS JANDERS YELLOWS JAUNDERS GRASSERIE
(PREF.) ICTER(O)
JAUNDICED ICTERODE
JAUNT TRIP SALLY JAUNCE VAGARY JOURNEY
JAUNTILY AIRILY BOUNCILY
JAUNTING CAR SIDECAR OUTSIDER
JAUNTY PERK PERT TRIM COCKY PERKY SASSY DAPPER JANTEE SHANTY FINICAL PERKING DEBONAIR

JAVA
INDONESIAN NAME: DJAWA
ISLAND: BALI LOMBOK MADURA
MEASURE: PAAL
MOUNTAIN: GEDE MURJO RAOENG SEMERU SLAMET SEMEROE SOEMBING
PORT: BATAVIA SURABAJA TJILATJAP
RIVER: SOLO LIWUNG BRANTAS
TOWN: BOGOR DESSA KEDIRI MALANG BANDUNG BATAVIA JAKARTA SEMARANG SURABAJA
WEIGHT: POND TALI

JAVA ALMOND PILI CANARI KANARI TALISAY
JAVA COTTON KAPOK
JAVA HEAD (AUTHOR OF —) HERGESHEIMER
(CHARACTER IN —) TAOU YUEN RHODA EDWARD GERRIT JEREMY NETTIE VOLLAR AMMIDON DUNSACK WILLIAM
JAVAN (FATHER OF —) JAPHETH
JAVANESE KRAMA KROMO
JAVANESE SKUNK TELEDU
JAVA PLUM DUHAT JAMBUL LOMBOY JAMBOOL
JAVA SPARROW MUNIA PADDY RICEBIRD
JAVELIN COLP DART PILE ACLYS PILUM SPEAR JAREED LANCET ASSAGAI HARPOON HURLBAT JAVELOT ACONTIUM GAVELOCK
JAW JIB BEAK CHAP CHAW CHOP JOWL WANG ANVIL CHAFT CHEEK CHOKE SCOLD CHAWLE FEELER JAWBONE MAXILLA MANDIBLE
(— OF FORCEPS) BEAK
(— OF SPIDER) FANG
(— OF VISE) CHAP
(—S OF BIRD) BILL
(FALSE —) CLAMP
(RECEDING NOSE AND UNDERSHOT —) LAYBACK
(PL.) MAW BITS THROAT
(PREF.) **(UNDER —)** GENYO
(SUFF.) GNATHA(E) GNATHI(A)(C)
(SM) GNATHOUS GNATHUS
JAWBONE JOWL WANG MAXILLA CHAWBONE
(PREF.) MAXILLI MAXILLO
JAWBREAKING CRACKJAW
JAY JAYPIET SIRGANG BLUECOAT MEATBIRD
JAYHAWK RAID
JAYHAWKER KANSAN
JAZERANT GESSERON
JAZZ BOP HYPE JIVE BEBOP HOTCHA RICKYTICK
(— DATE) GIG
JEALOUS YELLOW EMULOUS ENVIOUS
JEALOUSY ENVY YELLOWS EMULATION ZELOTYPIA
JEAN FROCKING
JEAN-CHRISTOPHE (AUTHOR OF —) ROLLAND
(CHARACTER IN —) ADA JEAN GRAZIA KRAFFT LOUISA MICHEL COLETTE LORCHEN OLIVIER STEVENS MELCHIOR GRUNEBAUM
JEANPAULIA BAIERA
JEATERAI (FATHER OF —) ZERAH
JECHOLIAH (HUSBAND OF —) AMAZIAH
(SON OF —) UZZIAH AZARIAH
JEDAIAH (FATHER OF —) HARUMAPH
JEDIAEL (FATHER OF —) SHIMRI MESHELEMIAH
JEDIDAH (HUSBAND OF —) AMON
(SON OF —) JOSIAH
JEEP PEEP SEEP BANTAM
JEER BOB BOO MOB GECK GIBE GIRD JAPE JEST JIBE MOCK SKIT WIPE FLIRT FLOUT FLUTE FLYTE FRUMP GLAIK LAUGH SCOFF SCOMM SNEER TAUNT CHIACK DERIDE BARRACK RIDICULE
JEERING BIRD FLOUT DERISIVE
JEEVES VALET
JEHALELEL (SON OF —) AZARIAH
JEHIEL (BROTHER OF —) JEHORAM
(FATHER OF —) HOTHAN HACHMONI JEHOSHAPHAT
(SON OF —) GIBEON OBADIAH SHECHANIAH
JEHIZKIAH (FATHER OF —) SHALLUM
JEHOADDAN (HUSBAND OF —) JOASH
(SON OF —) AMAZIAH
JEHOAHAZ (FATHER OF —) JEHU JOSIAH JEHORAM
(SON OF —) JEHOASH
JEHOASH (FATHER OF —) AHAZIAH JEHOAHAZ
JEHOHANAN (SON OF —) ISHMAEL
JEHOIACHIN (FATHER OF —) JEHOIAKIM

JEHOIADA (FATHER OF —) PASEACH
(SON OF —) BENAIAH
(WIFE OF —) JEHOSHEBA
JEHOIAKIM (FATHER OF —) JOSIAH
(SON OF —) JEHOIACHIN
JEHONADAB (FATHER OF —) RECHAB
JEHONATHAN (FATHER OF —) UZZIAH
JEHORAM (BROTHER OF —) AHAZIAH
(FATHER OF —) AHAB JEHOSHAPHAT
(SLAYER OF —) JEHU
(WIFE OF —) ATHALIAH
JEHOSHAPHAT (FATHER OF —) ASA AHILUD NIMSHI PARUAH
(SON OF —) JEHU JEHORAM
JEHOSHEBA (FATHER OF —) JORAM
(HUSBAND OF —) JEHOIADA
(SON OF —) JOASH
JEHOVAH JAH LORD JAHVE YAHWEH
(— WITNESS) PIONEER
JEHOZABAD (FATHER OF —) OBEDEDOM
(MOTHER OF —) SHOMER SHIMRITH
JEHOZADAK (FATHER OF —) SERAIAH
(SON OF —) JESHUA
JEHU (FATHER OF —) HANANI JOSIBIAH JEHOSHAPHAT
(SON OF —) JEHOAHAZ
(VICTIM OF —) JEHORAM
JEHUDI (FATHER OF —) NETHANIAH
JEHUSH (FATHER OF —) ESHEK
JEJUNE DRY ARID MEAGER INSIPID
JEKAMIAH (FATHER OF —) SHALLUM
JELL COME FIRM
(INCENDIARY —) NAPALM
JELLY GEAL JEEL JELL GELEE CULLIS JUJUBE ALCOGEL FISNOGA GELATIN JELLIFY FLUMMERY HYDROGEL QUIDDANY MARMALADE
(AGAR-AGAR —) KANTEN
(CALF'S-FOOT —) SULZE
(FRUIT —) ROB
(INFLAMMABLE —) NAPALM
(MEAT —) ASPIC
(PREF.) GELATI
JELLYFISH JELLY QUARL CARVEL MEDUSA ACALEPH AURELIA BLUBBER MEDUSAN SLOBBER SUNFISH SCYPHULA SEACROSS STROBILA SEANETTLE
(PART OF —) ARM BELL MOUTH MARGIN STOMACH TENTACLE UMBRELLA MANUBRIUM
(PREF.) MEDUSI
JELLYLIKE SLABBY
JEMIMA (FATHER OF —) JOB
JEMMY BETTY JIMMY
JEMUEL (FATHER OF —) SIMEON
JENNET ASS
JENNY ASS MULE BETTY JINNY
JEOPARDIZE STAKE EXPOSE HAZARD IMPERIL ENDANGER
JEOPARDY RISK PERIL DANGER HAZARD
JEPHTHAH (FATHER OF —) GILEAD
JEPHUNNEH (SON OF —) CALEB
JEQUIRITY BEAN EYEN RUTTEE
JERAH (FATHER OF —) JOKTAN
JERAHMEEL (FATHER OF —) MAHLI HEZRON HAMMELECH
JERBOA GERBIL JUMPER
JERED (FATHER OF —) MAHALALEEL
(SON OF —) ENOCH
JEREED TZIRID
JEREMIAD LAMENT TRAGEDY
JEREMIAH (DAUGHTER OF —) HAMUTAL
(FATHER OF —) HILKIAH
(SON OF —) JAZANIAH
JEREMOTH (SON OF —) ELAM HEMAN MUSHI ZATTU
JERIMOTH (DAUGHTER OF —) MAHALATH
(FATHER OF —) BELA DAVID HEMAN MUSHI AZRIEL BECHER
JERIOTH (HUSBAND OF —) CALEB
JERK BOB GAG JET NUD TIT BOUT CANT DINK DORK FIRK GIRD HIKE JERT JIRT JOLT JOUK KICK NERD PECK PUTZ SNAP SNIG YANK YERK BRAID CHUCK DWEEB FLIRT HITCH HOICK SCHMO SLIRT SNAKE SPANG SPASM SURGE TWEAK TWICK FILLIP JIGGER SCHMOE SHMUCK SWITCH TWITCH WRENCH FLOUNCE SACCADE SADSACK SCHMUCK SPANGHEW SCHLEMIEL
JERKED MEAT TASAJO
JERKILY HITCHILY
JERKIN SAYON JACKET
JERKY NERVY SHARP CHOPPY ELBOIC FLICKY FLINGY HITCHY JIGGETY CHOPPING PALMODIC RATCHETY SACCADIC
JEROBOAM REHOBOAM
(FATHER OF —) JOASH NEBAT
(WIFE OF —) ANO
JEROHAM (FATHER OF —) PASHUR
(SON OF —) ADAIAH AZAREEL AZARIAH ELKANAH IBNEIAH
JERSEY FROCK SHIRT GANSEY TRICOT ZEPHYR MAILLOT SINGLET CAMISOLE GUERNSEY
JERUSALEM ZION ARIEL SOLYMA AHOLIBAH
JERUSALEM ARTICHOKE TUBER CANADA GIRASOL
JERUSALEM CHERRY SOLANUM
JERUSALEM DELIVERED (AUTHOR OF —) TASSO
(CHARACTER IN —) HUGH OTHO SWENO ARMIDA OLINDO ALADINE ERMINIA GODFREY RINALDO TANCRED ARGANTES BOUILLON CLORINDA SOLIMANO SOPHRONIA
JERUSALEM OAK AMBROSIA
JERUSALEM SAGE PHLOMIS SAGELEAF
JERUSALEM THORN CASCOL RETAMA
JERUSHA (FATHER OF —) ZADOK
(HUSBAND OF —) UZZIAH
JESAIAH (BROTHER OF —) PELATIAH
(FATHER OF —) HANANIAH
JESHAIAH (FATHER OF —) JEDUTHUN REHABIAH
(MOTHER OF —) ATHALIAH
JESHARELAH (FATHER OF —) ASAPH
JESHER (FATHER OF —) CALEB
(MOTHER OF —) AZUBAH
JESIAH (FATHER OF —) UZZIEL
JESSAMINE JASMINE WOODBINE
JESSE (FATHER OF —) OBED
(SON OF —) DAVID
JESSICA (FATHER OF —) SHYLOCK
(HUSBAND OF —) LORENZO
JEST BAR BOG COD COG FUN GAB JOE TAX BULL GAME GAUD GIRD JAPE JOKE JOSH PLAY QUIP QUIZ RAIL SKIT BOURD BREAK CHAFF CLOWN DROLL FLIRT GESTE GLEEK SPORT THING BANTER GLANCE JAPERY RAILLY TRIFLE DICTERY GAMMOCK JOLLITY WAGGERY DROLLERY RAILLERY
(— SPITEFULLY) SLENT
JESTER FOOL MIME BUFFO CLOWN DROLL IDIOT JAPER JOKER PATCH WAMBA DISOUR MOTLEY YORICK BADCHAN BOURDER BUFFOON DIZZARD DROLLER JOCULAR JUGGLER PICADOR SCOFFER SCOGGIN TOMTRAM MERRYMAN OWLGLASS PLEASANT RAILLEUR TRINCULO
JESTING DROLL JAPERY SCOPTIC WAGGISH
(COARSE —) RIBALDRY
(RUDELY —) INFICETE
JESUI (FATHER OF —) ASHER
JESUIT PAULIST TERTIAN IGNATIAN LOYOLITE
JESUS GEE GIS IHC IHS JHS YHS JESU WISDOM
(SAYINGS OF —) AGRAPHA
JET SST BOLT NOIR TAIL TANG BREAK DUMBY DUMMY JETTO SALLY SCOOT SPOUT SPRAY SPURT AIRBUS CANDLE DELUGE DOUCHE GAGATE SQUIRT FANTAIL JETTEAU SPATTER SPURTER FOUNTAIN SOFFIONE UPSPRING
(— OF FLAME) TONGUE
(— OF METAL) BREAK
(— OF VOLCANIC STEAM) STUFA
(KIND OF —) JUMP LEAR PLASMA
(SMALL —) SQUIB
(SUBSONIC —) AIRBUS
JET-BLACK BUGLE
JETHER (FATHER OF —) EZRA JADA GIDEON
(SON-IN-LAW OF —) MOSES
(SON OF —) AMASA
JETHRO (DAUGHTER OF —) ZIPPORAH
(SON-IN-LAW OF —) MOSES
JETTING SALIENT
JETTISON DUMP DITCH JETSAM
JETTY JET PEN DIKE PIER GROIN JUTTY BRIDGE OVERHANG
JEUSH (FATHER OF —) ESAU BILHAN REHOBOAM
(MOTHER OF —) AHOLIBAMAH
JEW SAINT ESSENE JUDEAN LITVAK SEMITE SMOUCH SMOUSE TOBIAD BARABAS GRECIAN KARAITE MARRANO APIKOROS CONVERSO GALICIAN JUDAHITE LANDSMAN SEPHARDI
(—S OUT OF ISRAEL) DIASPORA
(BALKAN —) LADINO
JEWEL GEM JOY DROP OUCH BIJOU REGAL STONE BROOCH GEORGE TRIFLE CRAPAUD GARLAND POUNDER
(MATCHING SET OF —S) PARURE
(PL.) BULSE PERRIE
JEWELER GEMMARY LAPIDARY
JEWELRY ICE JUNK OUCH PARURE COLLARET LAPIDARY
(CHEAP — MATERIAL) OROIDE
(MOCK —) LOGIE
(PIECE OF —) GAUD
JEWELS OF THE MADONNA
(CHARACTER IN —) GENNARO MALIELLA RAFFAELE
(COMPOSER OF —) WOLFFERRARI
JEWELWEED CEROLINE EARJEWEL SNAPWEED
JEWFISH MERO GUASA WARSAW PERCOID JUNEFISH MULLOWAY SERRANID
JEWISH JUDAIC SEMITIC
(— BODY) VAAD
(— COMMUNITY) KEHILLAH
(— QUARTER) MELLAH
(— SCHOOL) ALJAMA
(PREF.) JUDAEO JUDEO
JEW OF MALTA (AUTHOR OF —) MARLOWE
(CHARACTER IN —) JACOMO MARTIN ABIGAIL BARABAS MATHIAS CALYMATH ITHAMORE LODOWICK BELLAMIRA BERNARDINE
JEWRY GHETTO JUDAISM
JEW'S-HARP HARP TROMP TRUMP GEWGAW FLAMFEW TRANGAM GUIMBARD
JEW'S MALLOW DESI
JEZANIAH (FATHER OF —) HOSHAIAH
JEZEBEL GILLIVER
(FATHER OF —) ETHBAAL
(HUSBAND OF —) AHAB
(SLAYER OF —) JEHU
JEZER (FATHER OF —) NAPHTALI
JEZOAR (FATHER OF —) ASHER
(MOTHER OF —) HELAH
JEZREEL (FATHER OF —) HOSEA
JIB GIB BALK BAULK DEMUR GIGUE STICK GIBBET SPITFIRE
JIBE (ALSO SEE GIBE) FIT GEE KAY GAFF GIBE JAPE JERK MOCK SKIT AGREE FLIRD MARCH SNACK SQUARE THRUST
JIBSAM (FATHER OF —) TOLA
JIDLAPH (FATHER OF —) NAHOR
JIFFY SEC JIFF BRAID FLISK WHIFF GLIFFY GLIFFING
JIG BUCK FRISK GIGUE SQUID GARLIC JIGGER JIGGET JITTER LOCATOR
(— FOR WASHING ORE) HUTCH
(FISHING —) PILK
JIGGER SHOT DANDY PIQUE DOODAD GADGET JIGMAN VATMAN CHIGGER
JIGGLE DIDDLE JUGGLE TEETER
JIHAD WAR JEHAD STRIFE CRUSADE
JILT GUNK KICK SACK BEGOWK BEGUNK MITTEN

JIMMY PRY OPEN BETTY JAMES JEMMY
JIMNA (FATHER OF —) ASHER
JIMSONWEED DATURA DEWTRY JIMSON FIREWEED STRAMONY
JINGLE TUNE CHIME CHINK CLINK DINGLE RICKLE TINKLE CHINKLE CLERIHEW DINGDONG JINGLING
(MEANINGLESS —) SPORT
JINGLING SMIT JANGLE RIGADIG TINKLING
JINGO WARRIOR WARMONGER
JINGOISM CHAUVINISM
JINKER WHIM
JINN DJIN JANN AFRIT EBLIS GENIE AFREET DJINNI SHAITAN
(PL.) JINNI
JINNI MARID AFREET ALUKAH GENIUS YAKSHA YAKSHI JINNIYEH
JINRIKIMAN KURUMAYA
JINRIKISHA GOCART KURUMA RICKSHAW
JINX HEX JONAH HOODOO WHAMMY
JIPIJAPA CHIDRA PANAMA PALMILLA TOQUILLA
JITTERBUG TRUCKING
JITTERY EDGY JUMPY TENSE SPOOKY AJITTER ILLATEASE
JIVARO JIBARO SHUARA XIBARO
JIVE BOP ROCK
JIVER HEPCAT
JOAB (BROTHER OF —) ASAHEL ABISHAI
(MOTHER OF —) ZERUIAH
(SLAYER OF —) BENAIAH
(UNCLE OF —) DAVID
(VICTIM OF —) ABNER
JOAH (FATHER OF —) ASAPH JOAHAZ ZIMMAH OBEDEDOM
(SON OF —) EDEN
JOAHAZ (SON OF —) JOAH
JOAN JUG JONE
(— OF ARC) PUCELLE
JOANNA (FATHER OF —) RHESA
(HUSBAND OF —) CHUZA
JOASH (FATHER OF —) AHAB BECHER AHAZIAH SHEMAAH JEHOAHAZ
(SON OF —) GIDEON
(VICTIM OF —) ZECHARIAH
JOB LAY TUT CHAR CRIB FIST SHOP TURN BERTH CHORE FIRST PLACE BILLET HOBJOB HUSTLE JOBSITE SWEATER BUSINESS POSITION
(EASY —) BLUDGE
(FATHER OF —) ISSACHAR
(HIGH-PAYING EASY —) PLUM
(KIND OF —) NOSE
(SMALL —) CHORE JOBBLE
JOBAB (FATHER OF —) JOKTAN
JOBBER BRAGER DEALER FLUNKY BROGGER COURSER
JOB'S TEARS COIX ADLAI ADLAY
JOCHEBED (HUSBAND OF —) AMRAM
(SON OF —) AARON MOSES
JOCKEY JOCK RIDER ROPER WASTER CHANTER EQUISON TURFITE SKIPJACK
(— FOR POSITION) DICE
(DISC —) DEEJAY
JOCOSE JOCO LEPID JOCULAR PLAYFUL
JOCOTE MOMBIN
JOCOTE DE MICO BARBAS
JOCULAR GAY AIRY GLAD JOKY DROLL FUNNY HAPPY JOLLY MERRY WITTY BLITHE ELATED JAPISH JOCOSE JOCUND JOKISH JOVIAL JOYFUL JOYOUS LIVELY BUOYANT COMICAL FESTIVE GLEEFUL PLAYFUL WAGGISH ANIMATED CHEERFUL DEBONAIR GLADSOME HUMOROUS JOCATORY JOKESOME LAUGHING MIRTHFUL BURLESQUE
JOCULARITY FUN WAGGERY
JOCUND BUDGE MERRY JOCANT JOCULAR
JOE JO
(HALF —) JOANNES JOHANNES
JOED (FATHER OF —) PEDAIAH
JOEL (BROTHER OF —) NATHAN
(FATHER OF —) NEBO SAMUEL ZICHRI PEDAIAH PETHUEL IZRAHIAH
(SON OF —) HEMAN
JOELAH (FATHER OF —) JEROHAM
JOE-PYE WEED EUPATORY
JOEWOOD JOEBUSH BARBASCO IRONWOOD
JOG BOB HOD JAG JIG JOT MOG KICK LOPE POKE SHOG SPUD STIR TROT WHIG DUNCH HOTCH MOSEY NUDGE TWEAK DIDDLE JITTER JOGGLE JUNDIE
(— ALONG) FADGE FODGE
(— AWKWARDLY) DODGE
(— WITH ELBOW) DUNCH
JOGGER LOPER LAYBOY RUNNER
JOGGLE HOTCH JUGGLE SHOGGLE SHOOGLE
JOGLI (SON OF —) BUKKI
JOHA (FATHER OF —) BERIAH
JOHANAN (FATHER OF —) JOSIAH KAREAH TOBIAH AZARIAH ELIOENAI HAKKATAN
(SON OF —) AZARIAH
JOHANNES JOE PECA
JOHN IAN JEAN JOCK JONE JUAN SEAN JOHANN SEAGHAN GIOVANNI
(BROTHER OF —) JAMES
(FATHER OF —) ZEBEDEE ZACHARIAS
(MOTHER OF —) SALOME ELISABETH
JOHN BROWN'S BODY (AUTHOR OF —) BENET
(CHARACTER IN —) CLAY JACK LUCY LUKE DUPRE SALLY SOPHY SPADE VILAS ELLYAT MELORA SHIPPY WINGATE WEATHERBY BRECKINRIDGE
JOHNNYCAKE CORNCAKE
JOIADA (FATHER OF —) ELIASHIB
JOIAKIM (FATHER OF —) JESHUA
JOIN ADD COP FAY MIX OUP PAN TAG TIE UNY ALLY COPE FAIR FUSE GAIN GLUE KNIT LINK MEET MELL SEAM SOUD TAIL TEAM YOKE ANNEX BLEND ENTER FRANK GRAFT JOINT MERGE TENON UNITE WRING ACCEDE ADJECT ADJOIN ASSIST ATTACH CEMENT COCKET COMMIT CONCUR ENGAGE INDENT JOGGLE MARROW MINGLE PIECEN RELATE RELIDE SPLICE STITCH STRIKE COMBINE CONJOIN CONNECT CONTACT INJOINT JOINING MORTISE SHACKLE ACCOUPLE COALESCE COMPOUND COPULATE DOVETAIL JUNCTION ACCOMPANY COMPAGINATE
(— BATTLE) JOUST ENGAGE
(— BY SEWING) STITCH SUTURE
(— CLOSELY) FAY AFFY WELD GRAFT
(— IN COMBAT) BUCKLE
(— IN MARRIAGE) WED TACK HITCH COUPLE
(— MECHANICALLY) DOCK
(— THE PARTS OF) PIECE
(— TOGETHER) CLOSE COAPT FRANK HITCH COUPLE ENGLUE ENJOIN ASSEMBLE COAGMENT COALESCE
(— UP) ACCEDE
(PREF.) ARTIO
JOINED JOINT ALLIED DIRECT SEAMED ACCOLLE ADJUNCT APPINED EMBOITE ADJUGATE COMBINED CONJUNCT COPULATE INTEGRAL
(PREF.) GAM(ETO)(O) ZEUCTO ZEUGLO
JOINER SNUG WRIGHT JOINTER
JOINING BAR JOIN SEAM BRIDE CLOSE SPLICE BETWEEN JOINDER ADDITION JUNCTION JUNCTIVE JUNCTURE SYNECTIC
JOINT BED HAR HIP JAY BUTT COXA FISH HEAD HELL HOCK JOIN KNEE LITH LOCK SEAL SEAM TUCK ANKLE BRAZE BUILD CARDO CHASE ELBOW MITER MITRE PLACE SCAPE SCARF SPALD UNION UNITE WRIST BOXING COMMON HAUNCH MUTUAL SCARPH SPLICE STIFLE SUTURE TOGGLE UNITER ARTHRON ARTICLE COGGING DIGITAL FETLOCK FLEXURE ISCHIUM JOINING KNUCKLE SCATTER SHIPLAP SIAMESE CONJOINT CONJUNCT COUPLING DIACLASE DOVETAIL FLASHING JOINTURE JUNCTURE SUBJOINT SUFFRAGO TROCHOID VARIATOR
(— ABOVE HOCK) STIFLE
(— OF APPENDAGE) SEGMENT
(— OF BIRD'S WING) FLEXURE
(— OF FLAIL) CAPEL
(—OF INSECT LEG) PHALANX
(— OF MEAT) BARON SADDLE
(— OF SHIP) CHASE
(— OF STEM) NODE
(ANKLE —) COOT
(ELBOW —) NOOP
(FLEXIBLE —) HINGE
(GROOVED —) RABBET
(HIP —) COXA THURL
(MASONRY —) JOGGLE
(MINING —) CLEAT SLINE
(QUARRYING —) CUTTER
(SCARF —) BOXING
(THE —) STIR PRISON
(UNIVERSAL —) CARDAN
(VERTICAL —) BUILD
(WHEEL-LIKE —) TROCHITE
(PREF.) ARTHR(O) ARTI CO CONDYL(O) HARMO HOM(O)
JOINTED ARTHROUS
JOINTED CHARLOCK KRAUT RUNCH
JOINTER JOINER SKIMMER
JOINT FIR EPHEDRA
JOINT GRASS PASPALUM
JOINTLY
(PREF.) CO COL COM CON COR
JOINTURE DOWER
JOIST GEEST LEDGE BRIDGE RAGLIN DORMANT SLEEPER CARRIAGE
(PL.) PIGGIN JOISTING
JOJOBA PIGNUT SHEEPNUT
JOKE BAR DOR FUN GAB GAG GIG JOE KID ROT WIT YAK YUK FOOL GAFF GAME GAUD GEGG JAPE JEST JOSH LICE NOTE QUIP QUIZ TYPE YOCK YUCK BREAK CRACK FLIRT GLEEK GRIND LAUGH PRANK RALLY SPORT TRICK BANTER JAPERY PLISKY WHEEZE JOKELET WAGGERY CHESTNUT
(— COLLECTION) ANA
(PRACTICAL —) BAR FUN GAG RIG HOAX REAK SHAVIE HOTFOOT
(STALE —) GROANER CHESTNUT
(PL.) JAPERY
JOKER BUG DOR WAG CARD CLOWN GRIND SLAVE FARCER FOOLER GAGGER JOKIST FARCEUR GIMMICK FUNNYMAN HUMORIST JOKESTER
JOKESTER WAG WIT
JOKIM (FATHER OF —) SHELAH
JOKING JOSH BANTER JOCOSE
(PRACTICAL —) GAME
JOKSHAN (FATHER OF —) ABRAHAM
(MOTHER OF —) KETURAH
(SON OF —) DEDAN SHEBA
JOKTAN (FATHER OF —) EBER
JOLLIFICATION RAG RANT BEANO JOLLY SINDIG
JOLLITY MIRTH GAIETY HILARITY JOLLITRY
JOLLY GAY KID BOON BUXOM GAWSY MERRY RORTY SONSY WALLY BLITHE CROUSE JOVIAL STRING JOCULAR RAUGHTY DISPOSED
JOLLY BOAT YAWL DANDY
JOLT JAR JET JIG JOG JOT JUT BELT BUMP DIRD DIRL HIKE JOWL JUMP KICK SHOG JAUNT HOTTER IMPACT JOGGLE JOSTLE JOUNCE JUMBLE
JOLTING JERKY BUMPITY HOTTERY
JONA (SON OF —) PETER
JONADAB (COUSIN OF —) AMNON
(FATHER OF —) SHIMEAH
(UNCLE OF —) DAVID
JONAH JINX JONAS HOODOO
(FATHER OF —) AMITTAI
JONAN (FATHER OF —) ELIAKIM
JONATHAN (BROTHER OF —) JOHANAN
(COMPANION OF —) DAVID
(FATHER OF —) SAUL ASAHEL JOIADA KAREAH ABIATHAR
(SON OF —) MEPHIBOSHETH

JONES HABIT HEROIN ADDICTION
(ARCHITECT —) INIGO
JONQUIL JONK LILY DAFFODIL
JORAM (FATHER OF —) TOI AHAB JEHOSHAPHAT

JORDAN
CAPITAL: AMMAN
COIN: DINAR
GULF: AQABA
MOUNTAIN: BUKKA DABAB ATAIBA MUBRAK
REGION: PEREA BASHAN PERAEA
RIVER: HOR JORDAN YARMUK
TOWN: AQABA ARIHA IRBID KARAK ZARQA ZERKE NABLUS JERICHO

JORIM (FATHER OF —) MATTHAT
JOSE (FATHER OF —) ELIEZER
JOSEPH JOSEY GIUSEPPE
(FATHER OF —) HELI JACOB JUDAH MATTATHIAS
(MOTHER OF —) RACHEL
(SON OF —) IGAL JESUS
(WIFE OF —) MARY ASENATH
JOSEPH ANDREWS (AUTHOR OF —) FIELDING
(CHARACTER IN —) ADAMS BOOBY FANNY PETER JOSEPH PAMELA POUNCE THOMAS WILSON ANDREWS GOODWILL SLIPSLOP
JOSEPHINE BLUSH PHENY
JOSEPH VANCE (AUTHOR OF —) DEMORGAN
(CHARACTER IN —) JOE BONY JANEY NOLLY SIBYL VANCE JOSEPH LOSSIE THORPE VIOLET BEPPINO DESPREZ PHEENER RANDALL SPENCER PERCEVAL CHRISTOPHER MACALLISTER
JOSES (BROTHER OF —) JESUS
(FATHER OF —) ELIEZER
JOSH GUY KID RIB JEST JOKE CHAFF STRING
JOSHAVIAH (FATHER OF —) ELNAAM
JOSHBEKASHAH (FATHER OF —) HEMAN
JOSHI JOTI JOTISARU
JOSHUA JESUS
(FATHER OF —) NUN JOZADAK
JOSIAH (FATHER OF —) AMON ZEPHANIAH
(MOTHER OF —) JEDIDAH
JOSIBIAH (SON OF —) JEHU
JOSTLE JOG JOLT JOSS PUSH SHOG CROWD ELBOW HUNCH JUNDY SHOVE HURTLE HUSTLE JOGGLE JUNDIE JUSTLE SHOULDER
JOSTLING SCRAMBLE
JOT ACE DOT ATOM IOTA MARK MITE TARE WHIT GRAIN MINIM POINT TWINT WIGHT TITTLE SCRUPLE SMIDGEN SYLLABLE
(— DOWN) NICK
JOTHAM (FATHER OF —) GIDEON UZZIAH
(MOTHER OF —) JERUSHAH
JOTTING TOT
JOTUNN GEIRROTH
JOUNCE HIKE JOLT JAUNT
JOURNAL TOE BOOK DIARY PAPER BLAZER SERIAL DAYBOOK DIURNAL GAZETTE GUDGEON JOURNEY CASHBOOK NOCTUARY TRUNNION
(SEA —) LOGBOOK
JOURNAL BEARING RHODING
JOURNALISM NEWSWRITING
JOURNALIST SCRIBE WRITER BYLINER DIARIAN
AMERICAN BLY DIX NEW BAER BAUM CAIN CAPA CERF CHEW COBB CONY CROW DALY DANA DREW EDEL EDGE GELB HOWE HUIE HUNT IDOE KENT LOEB MOTT OTIS OWEN PAGE PAUL PECK POST PRAY PYLE RAAB REED REID ROSS SANN SNOW WALN WEBB WEED WIND ADAMS ALSOP BACHE BAKER BEACH BEALS BEEBE BENET BRANN BROUN CANBY CREEL DUANE EARLY ELSER FISKE FLYNN GREEN GUILD HABER HARTE HOPPE HOUSE IRWIN JAMES KEOGH KROCK LAHEY LASKY LEWIS LOCKE MCCOY MEANS MOLEY MOORE MORSE NOVAK NOYES OGDEN OHARA OMARR PAINE PIATT POORE PRIME QUINN RALPH REEDY ROWAN ROYKO SAXON SCALI SIDEY SOBOL STONE STOWE SWING SWOPE TIEDE TOWLE TWAIN UPTON UTLEY WALSH WHITE WILLE YOUNG ZEVIN ALLSOP ASBURY BAILEY BIERCE BIRNIE BISHOP BLIVEN BONSAL BOWERS BOWLES BUGBEE BURMAN CAPUTO CHILDS CROUSE DECTER FOWLER GILDER GILMER GODWIN GRAHAM GRAVES GREENE HAMILL HARSCH HARVEY HASKIN HATTON HERSEY HICKOK HOWARD HOWELL KEIRAN KENNAN KNEBEL LAFFAN LAWSON LELAND LUBELL MANNES MANTLE MARDEN MEDILL MILLER MILLIS MOLLOY MORRIS MORTON MOWRER NELSON NEWELL PEGLER REDMAN RESTON RIDDER RUNYON SAFIRE SAVAGE SEAMAN SEATON SELDES SHIRER STREIT TAYLOR TERKEL TILTON TOLAND TUCKER TURNER WALKER WALTER WARMAN WIESEL WILCOX WILSON YARMON ANTHONY AXTHELM BARRETT BIGELOW BOMBECK BRENNAN BULLARD CARROLL CONNIFF DANIELS DREIFUS EASTMAN EDWARDS FARRELL FEARING FISCHER FREEMAN FRENEAU GALLICO GARRETT GERVASI GIBBONS GREELEY GUNTHER HALLOCK HASSARD HELOISE KENDALL LOSSING MANNING MARQUIS MELONEY OCONNOR OURSLER OVERTON POLLARD PRINGLE RANDALL RAYMOND REDPATH RITCHIE RUSSELL SANBORN SERVISS SMALLEY STANTON VANLOON VEILLER VILLARD WELLMAN WHEELER WOLFERT YARDLEY BROWNELL BUCHWALD CREELMAN JOHNSTON LAWRENCE LIPPMANN MCINTYRE MCKELWAY MEREDITH PULITZER ROBINSON STARRETT STEFFENS STILLMAN STODDARD SULLIVAN THOMPSON TOWNSEND WESTCOTT WHITLOCK WILLIAMS BENEFIELD BERNSTEIN MACDONALD MARCOSSON MCCORMICK MOREHOUSE PATTERSON WATTERSON WOOLLCOTT CHAMBERLIN WEITZENKORN
ARGENTINIAN AVELLANEDA
AUSTRALIAN DONALD WARNER FAWKNER PATERSON MOOREHEAD
AUSTRIAN BAHR SEIDL HEVESI SAPHIR CASTELLI
BRAZILIAN BANDEIRA
CANADIAN LAUT RYAN BROWN DAFOE BOWELL BRIAND DUNTON HEWITT RASKIN PAASSEN WHITMAN DECELLES SINCLAIR FRECHETTE
CZECH CAPEK NERUDA HAVLICEK
DANISH PALUDAN JORGENSEN GOLDSCHMIDT
DUTCH SCHIMMEL
ENGLISH LOW MEE BELL FOOT FYFE GORE HARE LANE LUCY MAIS SALA SIMS TOYE ARRAN BANKS BLAKE COTES CROWE DICEY DORAN GIBBS LEMON LEVIN LEWIS LOCKE MIALL MOULT SCOTT SHIEL STEAD STEED WERTH ARKELL ARNOLD BAINES BANGOR BARKER BEGBIE BENHAM BOADEN BROOKS BUCKLE CANTON CASTLE CHIROL DARWIN DILLON DIVINE FORBES GARVIN GIBBON HANNAY MACKAY MANNIN MAYHEW MORLEY MURRAY NORMAN REEVES SQUIRE TRAILL WATSON BENTLEY BOLITHO BURGESS BYWATER CARLILE CHORLEY COBBETT DURANTY ENNEVER GILLOTT HAMMOND HASKELL HERBERT HORABIN LEHMANN MEYNELL MITFORD ROBERTS SHORTER SPENDER STANLEY WALLACE BAERLEIN CARSWELL CHISHOLM COCKBURN COURTNEY FLETCHER HOBHOUSE LAWRENCE LOCKHART MONTAGUE MORRISON ROBINSON SLOCOMBE STEEVENS STRACHEY TOWNSEND WOODFALL BLANCHARD COLERIDGE COLQUHOUN CRANKSHAW GREENWOOD LESTRANGE MACDONELL MONYPENNY THORNBURY BALLANTYNE BRAILSFORD CHATTERTON CHESTERTON FONBLANQUE HUDDLESTON MASSINGHAM THURSFIELD HOLLINGSHEAD
FRENCH BLUM KARR MACE PUJO BULOZ CAPUS CLAIR DUPUY GOSSE GRIMM HAMEL HAVES HERVE MEYER MILLE SOREL STEEG VERON BABEUF BERTIN BODARD CARNOT CARREL DAUDET DELORD DUCAMP FONTAN FRERON GOZLAN HEBERT LEROUX MAZADE NISARD PICHON ROMIER SARCEY SCHWOB UZANNE BRISSOT CARRERE CHARMES GENOUDE HAUREAU LARBAUD LINGUET MATHIEU MICHAUD MIRBEAU NALECHE RECOULY REINACH REYBAUD SCHERER SIMONDS TABOUIS TILLIER VIARDOT CALMETTE CLARETIE DUJARDIN GIRARDIN GUEROULT JOUVENEL MAZELINE NEFFTZER PELLETAN PERTINAX PROUDHON QUILLARD RENAUDOT RIVAROLI VEUILLOT BAINVILLE CAILLAVET CAVAIGNAC DESCHAMPS MIRECOURT ROCHEFORT SAUERWEIN VACQUERIE BARTHELEMY DESMOULINS LACRETELLE MONTLOSIER TASCHEREAU TAILLANDIER MONTALEMBERT
GERMAN LONS BUSCH GIDAL THOMA BECKER DREYER EISNER GEROLD GORRES GROSSE GUBITZ HARDEN ZENGER BARTELS FRANZOS GUTZKOW HAMMANN KALISCH MARTENS BERNHARD FRAENKEL ROHRBACH LIEBNECHT SCHUCKING STREICHER BEUMELBURG POSCHINGER
HUNGARIAN BAJZA HERZL BALAZS HUSZAR MORICZ RAKOSI
INDIAN ABBAS MEHTA
IRISH BELL LYND WEST CONNOR LESLIE OBRIEN OKELLY PIGOTT DESMOND OCONNOR ROLLESTON
ITALIAN NENNI ANCONA MONETA FALLACI MORAVIA BATTISTI ALBERTINI FEDERZONI
JAPANESE HEARN INUKAI FUKUZAWA KAWAKAMI
NEW ZEALAND BALLANCE
NORWEGIAN FINNE VINJE BRATTELI
PARAGUAYAN BENITEZ
PERUVIAN CANDAMO
RUSSIAN KATKOV SHUKOV CHERNOV NOVIKOV DOBROLYUBOV
SCOTTISH BELL DENT REID BLACK CALER MUNRO FORBES CHALMERS CARRUTHERS
SOUTH AFRICAN WOODS
SWEDISH MYRDAL THORILD STRANDBERG
SWISS DROZ FAZY MEYER MURET GIROUD DUCOMMUN
WELSH EVANS CUDLIPP
JOURNEY BE GO JOG RUN WAY DIET EYRE FARE FORE GAIT GANG GATE HIKE JUMP RACE RAIK RIDE ROAD STEP TOUR TREK TRIP TURN WENT BROAD COVER DRIVE JAUNT REISE SITHE TRAIK TRAIL TURUS WEENT COMINO ERRAND FLIGHT HEGIRA JUNKET TRAVEL VAGARY EMBASSY ENTRADA EXCURSE JORNADA JOURNAL MEANDER PASSAGE STRETCH TRAVAIL TROUNCE WALKING WAYFARE GODSPEED PROGRESS PILGRIMAGE
(— BY SEA) VOYAGE
(— DOWNSTREAM) DESCEND
(DAY'S —) DIET
(DESERT —) JORNADA
(FATIGUING —) TRAIK
(LONG —) TREK
(PART OF —) LEG
(TEDIOUS —) TRANCE
(PL.) PERIPATETICS
JOURNEYING CRUISE
JOURNEYMAN YEOMAN

JOUST PLAY TILT JOSTLE JUSTLE TOURNEY
JOUSTER TILTER
JOVIAL GAY BOON JOVY BULLY JOLLY MERRY GENIAL HEARTY MELLOW WANTON BACCHIC HOLIDAY JOCULAR CONVIVIAL RANTIPOLE
JOVIALITY JOLLITY ROLLICK HILARITY
JOWL CHOW CHAULE
(PL.) CHOPS
JOY JO WIN GLEE LIST PLAY BLISS CHEER DREAM EXULT MIRTH REVEL GAIETY HEYDAY DELIGHT ECSTASY ELATION JOYANCE RAPTURE REVELRY FELICITY GLADNESS HILARITY PLEASURE
JOYFUL GAY GLAD BEAMY JOLLY BLITHE FESTUS JOCUND JOVIAL JOYANT JOYOUS GAUDFUL GLADFUL GLEEFUL JOCULAR GLADSOME
JOYFULLY FAIN FAINLY GLADLY JOYOUSLY
JOYLESS DESOLATE LUSTLESS UNBLITHE
JOYOUS GAY GLAD JOLLY MERRY YOUSE BLITHE JOVIAL FESTIVE GIOJOSO GLEEFUL JOCULAR SMILING FRABJOUS FROHLICH SUNSHINY
JOYOUSNESS HILARITY
JOYRIDE SPIN
JOY STICK CONTROL
JOZABAD (FATHER OF —) JESHUA
JOZACHAR (VICTIM OF —) JOASH
JUBAL (FATHER OF —) LAMECH
(MOTHER OF —) ADAH
JUBILANT ELATED JOYFUL EXULTANT
JUBILATION JOY JOYANCE JUBILEE
JUDA (FATHER OF —) JOSEPH HANANIAH
(MOTHER OF —) JOANNA
JUDAH (FATHER OF —) JACOB
(MOTHER OF —) LEAH
(SON OF —) ONAN
JUDAHITE JEW
JUDAISM JEWISM HEBRAISM
JUDAS TREE CERCIS
JUDEA JEWRY
JUDEO-SPANISH JUDESMO JUDEZMO LADINO
JUDE THE OBSCURE (AUTHOR OF —) HARDY
(CHARACTER IN —) SUE DONN JUDE FAWLEY RICHARD ARABELLA DRUSILLA BRIDEHEAD PHILLOTSON
JUDGE (ALSO SEE JURIST) DAN JUS SEE WIG CADI CAID CAZY DEEM DOOM HOLD IMAM JUEZ JURY KAZI QADI RATE RULE SCAN AWARD COUNT COURT DAYAN GAUGE HAKIM INFER JUDEX MINOS OPINE PUNEE TRIER WEIGH BREHON CENSOR CRITIC DANIEL DECERN DEEMER DICAST DOOMER INTEND JUDGER JURIST OPINER PUISNE SAMSON SAMUEL SETTLE SQUIRE ACCOUNT ADJUDGE ALCALDE ARBITER BENCHER BRIDOYE CENSURE DISCERN FLAGMAN FOUJDAR HELIAST JURYMAN JUSTICE MUNSIFF PODESTA REFEREE SCABINE SHAMGAR SUPPOSE APPRAISE CENTENAR CONCLUDE CONSIDER DEEMSTER DEMPSTER DIRECTOR DOOMSMAN DOOMSTER ESTIMATE FOREDEEM JEPHTHAH JUDGMENT JUDICATE LINESMAN MINISTER MITTIMUS ORDINARY QUAESTOR RECORDER REGICIDE SCABINUS STRADICO
(— OF UNDERWORLD) AEACUS
(PREF.) KRIT(O)
JUDGMENT ACT EYE BOOK DEEM DOME DOOM REDE VIEW ARRET AWARD FANCY JUISE SENSE SIGHT SKILL TASTE ADVICE ASSIZE DECREE ESTEEM JUWISE OUSTER STEVEN ACCOUNT CENSURE CONCEIT HOLDING OPINION THOUGHT VERDICT WITTING DECISION ESTIMATE JUDICIAL JUDICIUM SAGACITY SAPIENCE SENTENCE THINKING PREJUDICE OBSERVATION
(PREF.) GNOMO
JUDICATORY SYNOD
JUDICIOUS SAGE WISE POLITIC PRUDENT CRITICAL JUDICIAL MODERATE SENSEFUL SENSIBLE WISELIKE
JUDITH (FATHER OF —) BEERI
(HUSBAND OF —) ESAU
JUDITH PARIS (AUTHOR OF —) WALPOLE
(CHARACTER IN —) ADAM EMMA JOHN CARDS DAVID PARIS STANE JUDITH REUBEN WALTER WARREN DOROTHY FRANCIS GAUNTRY GEORGES HERRIES SUNWOOD WILLIAM FORESTER JENNIFER CHRISTABEL FERNYHIRST
JUDO (— EXERCISES) KATA
(— LEVEL) DAN
(— PRACTICE) RANDORI
(— SCHOOL) DOJO
(EXPERT LEVEL IN —) DAN
(EXPERT LEVEL OF —) DAN
JUG CAN EWER JACK JUST OLLA ASCUS ASKOS BUIRE GAMLA GOTCH JORUM JUBBE STEAN BOGGLE CROUKE GOGLET GOMLAH HYDRIA CREAMER PITCHER CRUISKEN LECYTHUS LEKYTHOS OENOCHOE PROCHOOS
(— FOR BEER) GROWLER
(— WITH SPOUT) BUIRE DOLLIN
(ALE —) TOBY
(BEER —) BOCK
(BULGING —) GOTCH
(CREAM —) POURER POURIE
(LEATHER —) JACK BOMBARD
(ONE-HANDLED —) URCEUS
(SPOUTLESS —) OLPE
JUGATED BAJOIRE
JUGGERNAUT IDOL
JUGGLE TRICK BAFFLE FUMBLE CONJURE SHUFFLE
JUGGLER HARLOT CONJURER JONGLEUR TREGETOUR
JUGGLERY GUILE HANKYPANKY HOCUSPOCUS LEGERDEMAIN
JUGHEAD SAP
JUGLONE NUCIN
JUGULARES DERIPIA
JUGUM FIBULA JUGULUM
JUICE JUS SEW BREE BROO FOND OOZE PULL SUCK ANIMA BLOND BLOOD CLOUT GRAVY HUMOR LASER MOBBY PERRY CASIRI CREMOR JIPPER LIQUOR SUCCUS CAMBIUM AGUAMIEL HYPOCIST VERJUICE INFLUENCE
(— OF COCONUT) MILK
(— OF TREE) SAP LYCIUM JELUTONG
(— OF UNRIPE FRUIT) OMPHACY
(APPLE —) CIDER
(CANE —) SLING
(CASSAVA —) CASSAREEP CASSARIPE
(CONCENTRATED —) SIRUP SYRUP
(DRIED —) ALOE KINO
(ETHEREAL —) ICHOR
(FERMENTED —) SURA GRAPE
(FRUIT —) ROB ROHOB
(GRAPE —) MUST SAPA STUM
(INSPISSATED —) HYPOCIST
(INTOXICATING —) SOMA
(LETTUCE —) THRIDACE
(MEAT —) BLOND
(POPPY —) CHICK MECONIUM
(TOBACCO —) AMBEER AMBIER
(VITAL —) SAP
(PL.) ESSENCE HUMIDITY
(PREF.) CHYL(I)(O) MYRO OPO
(SUFF.) CIDAL CIDE
JUICY FAT FRIM FRUM NAISH SAPPY FRUITY SUCCOSE WATERISH
JUJUBE BER ELB TSAO LOTUS LOTEBUSH LOTEWOOD ZIZYPHUS
JUKEBOX PICCOLO NICKELODEON
JULIUS CAESAR (AUTHOR OF —) SHAKESPEARE
(CHARACTER IN —) CATO CASCA CINNA CLITO PORTA VARRO BRUTUS CAESAR CICERO CIMBER DECIUS JULIUS LUCIUS MARCUS STRATO CASSIUS FLAVIUS LEPIDUS MESSALA PUBLIUS ANTONIUS CLAUDIUS LIGARIUS LUCILIUS MARULLUS METELLUS OCTAVIUS PINDARUS POPILIUS TITINIUS CALPURNIA DARDANIUS TREBONIUS VOLUMNIUS ARTEMIDORUS
JUMBLE PI PIE ROG HASH MESS MUSS RAFF BOTCH BOLLIX BUMBLE FUDDLE GARBLE HUDDLE JABBLE JUMPER JUNGLE MEDLEY MOMBLE MUDDLE PALTER RAFFLE WELTER WUZZLE CLUTTER CONFUSE EMBROIL GOULASH SHUFFLE DISORDER MISHMASH PASTICHE RHAPSODY SMACHRIE
(— OF SOUNDS) LURRY
JUMBLED CRAZY HASHY JUMBLY MEDLEY HUDDLING MACARONIC
JUMP HOP LEP NIP DART JETE LEAP LUTZ SKIP SKIT STEN STOT TUMB BOUND CAPER FENCE HALMA SALTO SAULT SPANG SPEND START STOIT VAULT DOUBLE FOOTER HURDLE INSULT LAUNCH SPRING SPRUNT STARRE WALLOP CISEAUX CROWHOP SALTATE SKYLARK BALLONNE
(— ABOUT) SKIT CAPER
(— FROM AIRCRAFT) BAIL BALE
(— IN FENCING) BALESTRA
(— ON HORSEBACK) LARK
(— ON SKATES) AXEL SALCHOW
(— TO CONCLUSION) SALTUS
(ELECTRICAL —) ARC
(PL.) ALLEGRO
JUMPER LAMMY SWAGE BARKER LEPPER HANDYMAN
JUMPING SALIENT SALTANT
JUMPING-JACK PANTINE
JUMPING JACK PANTINE
JUMPY ITCHY NERVOUS
JUNCO SNOWBIRD
JUNCTION HIP FROG JOIN NODE SEAM CLOSE CROWN RAPHE UNION FILLET INFALL CONTACT JOINING MEETING UNITION ABUTMENT JUNCTURE CONSERTION
(— OF EARTH AND SKY) HORIZON
(— OF STREAMS) GRAINS
(— OF THREADS) FELL STOP
(— ON TOOTH) CERVIX
(ROAD —) TOLL
JUNCTURE PASS SEAM PINCH CRISIS STRAIT ARTICLE BRACKET JOINING OPHRYON EXIGENCY JOINTAGE JOINTURE OCCASION QUANDARY
JUNEBERRY SHADBLOW SHADBUSH SERVICEBERRY
JUNE BUG DOR BUZZARD DUMCLOCK
JUNGLE BUSH RUKH SHOLA BOONDOCK
(AUTHOR OF —) SINCLAIR
(CHARACTER IN —) ONA JACK DUANE JONAS CONNOR JURGIS MARIJA RUDKUS ANTANAS ELZBIETA STANISLOVAS
JUNGLE BENDY WEENONG
JUNGLE BOOK (AUTHOR OF —) KIPLING
(CHARACTER IN —) KAA KHAN AKELA BALOO HATHI SHERE BULDEO MESSUA MOWGLI TABAQUI BAGHEERA BANDARLOG
JUNIOR PUNY CADET YOUNG PUISNE YOUNGER
JUNIPER CADE EZEL GORSE GORST RETEM SAVIN SABINE
JUNK CRAM GEAR GOOK TOPE DRECK REFUSE SCULCH DISCARD PLUNDER TONGKANG
(WORTHLESS —) SLUM
JUNKET TRIP KNACK JINKET SAFARI
JUNKMAN TATTER SCRAPMAN SCAVENGER
JUNO MONETA PRONUBA
JUNO AND THE PAYCOCK
(AUTHOR OF —) OCASEY
(CHARACTER IN —) JACK JUNO MARY BOYLE JERRY JOXER DEVINE JOHNNY BENTHAM CHARLIE TANCRED
JUNTO CABAL
JUPITER JOVE STATOR FORTUNE MUSHTARI TERMINUS

(SATELLITE OF —) LEDA
(PREF.) JOVI ZENO
JUPITER'S BEARD JOUBARB SENGREEN
JUR LWO LUOH
JUREL RUNNER CREVALLE HARDTAIL
JURGEN (AUTHOR OF —) CABELL
(CHARACTER IN —) LISA HELEN JURGEN MERLIN SEREDA ANAITIS CHLORIS DESIREE DOLORES DOROTHY KOSHCHEI GUENEVERE
JURIDIC LEGAL
JURISDICTION SOC BAIL SOKE FUERO HONOR REALM VERGE ABBACY BANDON BEYLIK DANGER DIWANI RIDING SPHERE DEANERY DEWANEE DROSTDY EMIRATE FOUDRIE KHANATE BAILIERY CHAPELRY FOUJDARY LIGEANCE PASHALIC PROVINCE
(— OF BISHOP) SEE
(COERCIVE —) SWORD
(MORMON —) KEYS
(REMOVE FROM —) ELOIN
(SUFF.) DOM
JURISPRUDENCE LAW BYRLAW REPORTS
JURIST JUDGE MUFTI BREHON LAWYER DOTTORE
AMERICAN DAY JAY LEE BEAN BOND BORK DANA DANE DYER GOFF GRAY HALL HAND HUNT KENT NOTT POPE REED RUSK SHAW TAFT TAIT WARE ZANE ADAMS BETTS BLACK BLAIR BROWN CASEY CHASE DAVIS DAWES DUANE EATON FIELD FREAR GRIER LAMAR LIMAN LOGAN MIKVA MOODY MOORE PAINE RANDA SMITH STONE STORY TANEY TYLER WAITE WAYNE WEARE WHITE WYTHE YATES BAYLOR BREWER BURGER BURTON BUTLER BYRNES CATRON CLARKE COOLEY CRATER CURTIS DANIEL DARROW DONLON DULLES FOLGER FORTAS FULLER GASTON GIBSON HARLAN HOLMES HUDSON HUGHES JEROME KENYON LANDIS LOWELL LURTON MARTIN MEDINA MILLER MINTON MORRIS MURPHY NELSON PARKER PECORA PETERS PITNEY POWELL SCALIA SEWALL SHIRAS SIRICA STRONG SUMNER SWAYNE UPSHUR VINSON WARREN WILBUR BALDWIN BRADLEY CARDOZO CLAYTON CUSHING DOUGLAS DRAYTON GRIFFIN JACKSON JOHNSON JUSTICE LINDSEY MCKENNA PARSONS ROBERTS SANBORN SANFORD SHERMAN STEVENS STOWELL TRIMBLE VOELKER WHARTON WHEATON ANDERSON BLACKMUN BRANDEIS CLIFFORD GOLDBERG GRISWOLD GROSSCUP KIRCHWAY LAWRENCE MACVEAGH MARSHALL MATTHEWS MCKINLEY MITCHELL PENFIELD ROSENMAN RUTLEDGE SEDGWICK STAFFORD WALWORTH WOODBURY ELLSWORTH GREENLEAF GROESBECK HOPKINSON PENDLETON REHNQUIST SHARSWOOD UNDERWOOD WHITTAKER YOUNGDAHL BLATCHFORD CELEBREZZE MCREYNOLDS POINDEXTER TROWBRIDGE WASHINGTON FRANKFURTER VANDEVANTER
ARGENTINIAN CALVO DRAGO ALBERDI QUESADA CASTILLO
AUSTRIAN GROSS UNGER GLASER ZELLER REDLICH LAMMASCH RINTELEN SCHMERLING
BELGIAN NYS PICARD LAURENT DESCAMPS GERLACHE
BOLIVIAN SILES SAAVEDRA
BRAZILIAN PESSOA BARBOSA BARROSO PECANHA
CANADIAN CARON JETTE ARMOUR DAVIES MULOCK STUART DOHERTY LACOSTE FOURNIER HAULTAIN NEWCOMBE RICHARDS ROBINSON THOMPSON HALIBURTON FITZPATRICK
CHILEAN EGANA DONOSO
COSTA RICAN CARRILLO
CUBAN URRUTIA
CZECH HACHA
DUTCH GEER ASSER LODER GROTIUS OPZOOMER BYNKERSHOEK
ENGLISH MAY AMOS CAVE COKE HALE HOLT KING REID ANSON BOWEN BRYCE GROVE HURST IMPEY JAMES MAINE PRATT SCOTT TWISS VINER ABBOTT ATKYNS AUSTIN BARNES CARSON DAVIES FINLAY GATLEY HENLEY HEWART HUGHES MERSEY NORTON PALMER SANKEY SELDEN AMULREE BRACTON DARLING DENNING GODFREY HOLLAND JENKINS MOULTON PLOWDEN RUSSELL WIDGERY CAMPBELL CHALMERS HAILSHAM JEFFREYS CALDECOTE FORTESCUE HERSCHELL LITTLETON OPPENHEIM BLACKSTONE FITZHERBERT
FRENCH ADAM GIDE MOLE DOMAT FLACH WEISS CASSIN COCHIN DEMETZ DONEAU DUGUIT GOHIER HOTMAN MERLIN PITHOU DECAZES HENAULT LECONTE NOGARET RENAULT CUJACIUS DUMOULIN GODEFROY PASQUIER PORTALIS AGUESSEAU BEAUMANOIR EPREMESNIL LAFERRIERE
GERMAN UZ BAR FALK GANS HUGO KAHL POST WACH ZORN CROME FRANK HANEL KRAUS MOSER SPAHN TEMME WITTE AEGIDI AHRENS FICKER GERBER GNEIST HITZIG KELSEN LABAND MEZGER PREUSS BOCKING COCCEJI GOLDAST GOSCHEL HEFFTER KOSTLIN RICHTER THIBAUT WICHERT ANCILLON DERNBURG EICHRODT FISCHART GEFFCKEN HABERLIN HEDEMANN HUFELAND ALTHUSIUS EBERMAYER FEUERBACH HINSCHIUS KIRCHMANN PUFENDORF HEINECCIUS KOHLRAUSCH GOLDSCHMIDT KANTOROWICZ MITTERMAIER HOLTZENDORFF
GREEK POLITES
INDIAN SAPRU
IRISH BALL MORRIS OHAGAN MACNEILL ODALAIGH FITZGIBBON
ITALIAN AZO FIORE ROCCO ACCORSO ALCIATI CARRARA GRAVINA MANCINI ORLANDO TANUCCI BARTOLUS BULGARUS GAROFALO IRNERIUS ANZILOTTI ROMAGNOSI FILANGIERI PIERANTONI
JAPANESE ADACHI
MEXICAN IGLESIAS
NEW ZEALAND STOUT BULLER MANING
NORWEGIAN FALSEN HAGERUP
PANAMANIAN PORRAS
PARAGUAYAN BAEZ
PERUVIAN CORNEJO
ROMAN GAIUS LABEO CELSUS FRONTO PAULUS ULPIAN SABINUS SALVIUS PAPINIAN PROCULUS SCAEVOLA SULPICIUS TRIBONIAN MODESTINUS GREGORIANUS
RUSSIAN KAVELIN MARTENS MUROMTSEV MEYENDORFF VINOGRADOFF POBEDONOSTSEV
SCOTTISH HOME CRAIG FORBES ERSKINE GIFFORD JEFFREY LORIMER BROUGHAM
SPANISH GALVEZ PINELO AGUSTIN
SWEDISH UNDEN
SWISS DUBS MUSY HILTY HUBER LARDY MEILI BLUMER DELOLME
URUGUAYAN BRUM
JUROR JURAT ASSIZER JURYMAN CENTUMVIR
JURY ARRAY PANEL QUEST ASSIZE JURATA COUNTRY EMPANEL INQUEST
(— COUNTY) VISNE
JURYMAN DICAST JURIST ASSIZER
JURY-RIGGED HAYWIRE
JUST ALL DUE EVEN FAIR FLOP LEAL MERE ONLY TRUE EQUAL FIRST LEVEL NOBUT ROUND VALID ZADOC CANDID GIUSTO HONEST JUSTIN JUSTUS MERELY SQUARE EQUABLE LEESOME MERITED UPRIGHT ACCURATE LIEFSOME RATIONAL RIGHTFUL SKILLFUL UNBIASED
(— AS) AFTER
(— HOVE CLEAR) ATRIP
(— IN TIME) SONICA
(ONLY —) HARDLY SCARCELY
JUSTAUCORPS JUSTICO
JUSTICE LAW DOOM RIGHT SKILL DHARMA EQUITY REASON HONESTY SHALLOW SILENCE DEEMSTER JUDGMENT JUSTITIA JUSTNESS RECORDER
(— OF PEACE) BEAK SQUIRE
(AUTHOR OF —) GALSWORTHY
(CHARACTER IN —) HOW RUTH DAVIS FROME JAMES FALDER WALTER CLEAVER COKESON WILLIAM HONEYWILL
(RETRIBUTIVE —) NEMESIS
(PREF.) DICAEO
JUSTIFIABLY FAIRLY
JUSTIFICATION CALL COLOR EXCUSE APOLOGY DEFENCE WARRANT APOLOGIA
JUSTIFIED FAIR JUST
JUSTIFY AVOW CLEAR PROVE SALVE DEFEND EXCUSE HONEST DERAIGN EXPLAIN RECTIFY SUPPORT WARRANT DARRAIGN MAINTAIN SANCTION UNDERPIN VINDICATE
JUST-IN-TIME KANBAN
JUSTLY WELL TRULY EVENLY FAIRLY EQUALLY HANDILY SQUARELY
JUSTNESS SQUARE FITNESS JUSTICE ACCURACY
JUSTUS JESUS
JUT HANG BULGE JETTY JUTTY BEETLE EXTEND IMPEND EXTRUDE
JUTE PAT DESI PAUT DAISEE ARAMINA CHINGMA
JUTTING HANGING
JUVENILE TEEN YOUNG JEJUNE PUERILE YOUTHFUL
JUXTAPOSED ADJACENT
JUXTAPOSITION BALANCE CONTACT CONTRAST NEARNESS

K KA KAY KILO KING
KAABA CAABA ALCAABA
KABAYA BADJU CABIE
KABELJOU KOB
KABISTAN KUBA
KABOB KEBOB SHASLIK
KABUKALLI CUPIUBA
KACHA (FATHER OF —) BRIHASPATI
KACHARI BODO
KACHIN SINGFO SINGPO CHINGPAW
KADAGA COORG
KADAMBARI (FATHER OF —) CHITRARATHA
(MOTHER OF —) MADIRA
KAFFIR KATI XOSA FINGO TEMBU CAFFRE INFIDEL TAMBUKI WAIGULI
(— BOY) UMFAAN
KAGU GRUIFORM
KAHODA (SON OF —) ASHTAVAKRA
KAIKAWAKA CEDAR
KAIKAWUS (FATHER OF —) KAIQUBAD
(WIFE OF —) SAUDABAH
KAIKEYI (HUSBAND OF —) DASHARATHA
(SON OF —) BHARATA
KAIKHUSRAU (FATHER OF —) SYAWAUSH
(MOTHER OF —) FARANGIS
KAINGIN SWIDDEN
KAKI TRIUMPH
KAKU (GRANDFATHER OF —) ZOHAK
(SLAYER OF —) MINUCHIHR
KALAPOOIAN LAKMIUT
KALE COLE KAIL COLLARD SPROUTS BORECOLE
KALEVALA (AUTHOR OF —) UNKNOWN
(CHARACTER IN —) KULLERVO ILMARINEN VAINAMOINEN LEMMINKAINEN
KALI (HUSBAND OF —) SIVA SHIVA
KALMASHAPADA (FATHER OF —) SUDASA
KALMUCK ELEUT UIRAD KHOSHOT
KALPA EON AEON
KALUMPIT ANAGEP
KAMA (DAUGHTER OF —) TRISHA
(FATHER OF —) DHARMA
(MOTHER OF —) LAKSHMI SHRADDHA
(SON OF —) ANIRUDDHA
(WIFE OF —) RATI PRITI
KAMAHI BIRCH TOWAI
KAMALA WURRUS ROTTLERA
KAME AS ESKAR ESKER
KAMICHI SCREAMER
KAMPUCHEA (SEE CAMBODIA)
KANA IROFA IROHA
KANGAROO ROO EURO BILBI FLIER FLYER TUNGO BOOMER FOSTER WOILIE DIDELPH POTOROO WALLABY BETTONGA BOONGARY FILANDER FORESTER WALLAROO
(FEMALE —) DOE GIN
(YOUNG —) JOEY
KANGAROO APPLE GUNYANG POROPORO
KANGAROO RAT JERBOA BETTONG POTOROO
KANHOBAL CONOB
KANKANAI IGOROT
KANS KUSA GLAGA KUSHA GLAGAH
KANSA (FATHER OF —) UGRASENA
(SLAYER OF —) KRISHNA
KANSAN JAYHAWK

KANSAS

CAPITAL: TOPEKA
COLLEGE: BAKER TABOR BETHANY STERLING WASHBURN
COUNTY: ELK GOVE LINN LYON NESS RENO GEARY PRATT ROOKS TREGO BARTON COFFEY NEMAHA NEOSHO BOURBON LABETTE ATCHISON
FORT: RILEY SCOTT
INDIAN: KANSA KIOWA PAWNEE WICHITA COMANCHE
LAKE: CHENEY KIRWIN NEOSHO MILFORD
MOUNTAIN: SUNFLOWER
NATIVE: JAYHAWK
NICKNAME: JAYHAWKER SUNFLOWER
PRESIDENT: EISENHOWER
RIVER: SALINE SOLOMON ARKANSAS MISSOURI
STATE BIRD: MEADOWLARK
STATE FLOWER: SUNFLOWER
STATE TREE: COTTONWOOD
TOWN: ALMA GOVE HAYS IOLA COLBY DODGE HOXIE LAKIN LEOTI SEDAN LARNED SALINA ABILENE CHANUTE LIBERAL ULYSSES WICHITA

KAOLIANG SORGHUM
KAOLIN PIPECLAY
KAPOK CEIBO FLOSS
KARAISM ANANISM
KARAKA KOPI
KARA KIRGHIZ BURUT BOUROUT
KARATAS PITA
KARATE (— SCHOOL) DOJO
(EXPERT LEVEL IN —) DAN
(EXPERT LEVEL OF —) DAN
(KOREAN —) TAEQUONDU
KAREN SGAU SGAW
KARENNI PADAUNG
KARMA FATE
(BAD —) DEMERIT
KARNA (FATHER OF —) SURYA
(MOTHER OF —) KUNTI PRITHA
(SLAYER OF —) ARJUNA
KARTTIKEYA (FATHER OF —) RUDRA SHIVA
KASKA NAHANE
KAT KHAT QUAT CAFTA
KATE KAI
KATHERINE (HUSBAND OF —) PETRUCHIO
KAUNAS KOVNO
KAURI COWRIE BERAIROU
KAUSHALYA (HUSBAND OF —) DASHARATHA
(SON OF —) RAMA
KAVA AVA AWA YAQONA KAVAKAVA YANGGONA
KAW AKHA
KAYANUSH (BROTHER OF —) FARIDUN PURMAYAH

KAZAKHSTAN (ALSO SEE RUSSIA)
CAPITAL: ALMATY ALMAATA
COIN: RUBLE
DESERT: BARSUKI KARAKUM KYZYLKUM
LAKE: ALAKOL TENGIZ ZAYSAN BALKHASH SILETITENIZ SELETYTENGIZ
LANGUAGE: KAZAKH KIPCHAK QIPCHAQ
MOUNTAIN: KHANTENGRI
MOUNTAIN RANGE: ALTAI ULUTAU TIENSHAN CHINGIZTAU DZUNGARIAN TARBAGATAY
NAME: KAZAK KAZAKH
PENINSULA: MANGYSHLAK
PLATEAU: USTYURT
RIVER: URAL YAIK ISHIM TOBOL IRTYSH SYRDARYA
SEA: ARAL CASPIAN
TOWN: OMSK YAIK RUDNY URALSK ALMAATA TROITSK CHIMKENT ORENBURG KARAGANDA QARAGHANDY PETROPAVLOVSK SEMIPALATINSK
VALLEY: FERGANA

KAZOO BAZOO GAZOO ZARAH HEWGAG MIRLITON
KEEL FIN BACK SEEL BARGE CARINA CRISTA RADDLE SERRULA
(— OF BIRD'S MANDIBLE) GONYS
(AFTERPART OF —) SKAG SKEG
(PREF.) CARINI
KEELBILL ANI
KEELBIRD ANI
KEEN DRY FLY GAY SHY YAP ACID DEAR FINE GAIR GLEG HIGH HOWL NUTS PERT TART TEEN WAIL WARM WILD ACUTE ALERT BREME BRIEF BRISK EAGER QUICK SHARP SMART SNELL SPICY VIVID ARGUTE ASTUTE BITTER CAOINE GREEDY LIVELY SEVERE SHREWD SHRILL CUNNING HAWKING MORDANT PARLISH PARLOUS PUNGENT SERIOUS THIRSTY OBSERVANT SAGACIOUS TRENCHANT PERSPICACIOUS
(PREF.) OXY
KEENER HOWLER
KEENLY KEEN FELLY DEARLY ACUTELY
KEENNESS EDGE ACUITY ACUMEN PUNGENCY
(— OF SIGHT) ACIES
KEEN-SCENTED NASUTE NOSEWISE
KEEN-SIGHTED EAGLE
KEEP HUG HAVE HOLD SALT SAVE STOW WAIT WITE BLESS ROCCA WITIE COFFER DETAIN REDUIT CONFINE CONTAIN DEFORCE HUSBAND KEEPING OBSERVE RESERVE WARRANT CONSERVE MAINTAIN PRESERVE RESTRAIN WITHHOLD
(— ABREAST) FOLLOW
(— A COURSE) CAPE
(— AFLOAT) BUOY
(— AN EYE ON) STAG
(— APART) DOTTLE ISOLATE SEPARATE
(— A SMALL SHOP) CRAME
(— ASUNDER) PART
(— AT A DISTANCE) ESTRANGE
(— AWAY) ABSENT
(— AWAY FROM) ABHOR AVOID
(— A WOUND OPEN) TENT
(— BACK) DAM HAP ROB STAY ARREAR DETAIN RETARD RESERVE
(— COMPANY WITH) GANG MOOP CONSORT
(— FOR SALE) STOCK
(— FREE) ESCHEW
(— FROM BOILING OVER) KEEL
(— FROM BURNING) REDD
(— GUARD) SENTINEL
(— HIDDEN) HOARD SECRETE
(— IN) CAGE
(— IN CIRCULATION) WIND
(— IN EXCITEMENT) ALARM ALARUM
(— IN MIND) RETAIN
(— IN ORDER) TARGE
(— IN STOCK) CARRY
(— IN THE TRACK) GATHER
(— OFF) FEND WEAR EXPEL FENCE SHIELD
(— OUT) BAR EXPEL
(— POSSESSION) HARBOR
(— SCORELESS) BLANK
(— SECRET) HUSH WHIST
(— STRAIGHT) DIRECT
(— TABS ON) FINGER
(— TIME) GO
(— TOGETHER) WHIP
(— TO ONESELF) BOSOM

(— UNTIL YEAR OLD) HOG
(— UP) SUBSIST SUSTAIN CONTINUE
(— WAITING) DELAY
(— WARM) STIVE STOVE FOSTER
(— WATCH) BARK TOUT WAIT BEWAKE
(PREF.) SOZ(O)
(— OFF) ALEXI
KEEPER NAB KEEP SCREW TUTOR YEMER CUSTOS GAOLER JAILER LIFTER LOOKER PARKER PASTOR RAHDAR RANGER WARDEN BAILIFF CURATOR GEARMAN PIKEMAN PROVOST BEARWARD DEERHERD DOLLYMAN ELDERMAN FEWTERER GUARDANT GUARDIAN HOUNDMAN TRAITEUR WARRENER
(— OF CATTLE) HAYWARD
(— OF DOGS) FEWTERER
(— OF ELEPHANT) MAHOUT
(— OF INN) PUBLICAN
(— OF LOCK) NAB
(— OF PRISON) GAOLER JAILER WARDEN ALCAIDE PROVOST
(DOOR —) DURWAN
KEEPING CARE WARD TRUST CHARGE CUSTODY STORAGE DETAINER
KEEPSAKE DRURY TOKEN GIFTBOOK SOUVENIR
KEEVE TUB VAT KIEVE
KEG CAG PIN TUB CADE CASK KNAG WOOD ANKER BARRICO COSTREL
KELOID SCAR
KELP KILP LEAG VAREC WRACK GIRDLE SEAWEED BELLWARE
KELPIE NIX BARB
KELT SLAT LIGGER
KENAF DA GOMBO MESTA AMBARI KANAFF PAPOULA STOKROOS
KENILWORTH (AUTHOR OF —) SCOTT
(CHARACTER IN —) AMY HUGH TONY GILES JANET SMITH ALASCO DICKIE DUDLEY EDMUND FOSTER SLUDGE SUSSEX VARNEY WALTER GOSLING MICHAEL RALEIGH RICHARD ROBSART WAYLAND DOBOOBIE ELIZABETH LAMBOURNE LEICESTER TRESSILIAN FLIBBERTIGIBBET
KENNEL STALL VENERY VENISON DOGHOUSE
KENO HOUSE
KENTISH (— UNIT) YOKE

KENTUCKY
CAPITAL: FRANKFORT
COLLEGE: BEREA ASBURY CENTRE BRESCIA URSULINE
COUNTY: BATH BELL BOYD HART TODD ADAIR BOYLE TRIGG WOLFE ESTILL MENIFEE MAGOFFIN
INDIAN: SHAWNEE CHEROKEE IROQUOIS
LAKE: CUMBERLAND
RIVER: DIX OHIO SALT BARREN
STATE BIRD: CARDINAL
STATE FLOWER: GOLDENROD
STATE NICKNAME: BLUEGRASS
STATE TREE: TULIP
TOWN: INEZ BEREA CADIZ DIXON HYDEN MCKEE PARIS CORBIN HARLAN HAZARD GLASGOW GREENUP PADUCAH DANVILLE COVINGTON LEXINGTON OWENSBORO

KENYA
BAY: FORMOSA
CAPITAL: NAIROBI
COIN: SHILLING
LAKE: MAGADI RUDOLF NAIVASHA VICTORIA
LANGUAGE: LUO KIKUYU SWAHILI
MEASURE: WARI
MOUNTAIN: ELGON KENYA KULAL NYIRU MATIAN LOGONOT
PEOPLE: LUO MERU BANTU KAMBA KISII LUHYA MASAI NANDI KIKUYU OGADEN BALUHYA HAMITIC HILOTIC TURKANA KIPSIGIS
RIVER: LAK ATHI TANA KEIRO TURKWELL
TOWN: MERU KITUI NAROK KIPINI KISUMU MOYALE NAKURU NAYUKI ELDORET MALINDI MOMBASA

KERATIN HORN
KERCHIEF CURCH DORAG ROMAL RUMAL ANALAV CYPRUS MADRAS NAPKIN PEPLUM CYPRESS KERCHER PANUELO THERESE BABUSHKA BANDANNA HEADRAIL KAFFIYEH KINGSMAN
KERESAPA (BROTHER OF —) URVAKHSHAYA
(FATHER OF —) THRITA
KERF CARF SKAFF GROOVE UNDERCUT
KERI QRI KERE
KERMANSHAH COCONUT
KERMES GRAIN
KERNEL NUT BUNT CORE KERN MEAT PITH BERRY GOODY GROAT ACINUS ALMOND CARNEL PICKLE NUCLEUS PICHURIM
(CORN —S) HOMINY
(UNHUSKED —S) CAPES
(PL.) NIXTAMAL
(PREF.) CARY(O) KARY(O)
KEROGEN SAPROPEL
KEROSINE PARAFFIN
KERSENNEH ERS ERVIL
KERSEY WASHER ORDINARY
KESTREL FANNER KEELIE STANIEL STANNEL STANYEL STANCHEL WINDHOVER
KETA CHUM
KETCH SAIC
KETONE IRONE ACETOL ARMONE CARONE CARVOL COTOIN HEXONE IONONE QUINOL ACETOIN ACETONE ACYLOIN BENZOIN CAMPHOR CARVONE DYPNONE FLAVONE JASMONE MUSCONE PHORONE SHOGAOL THUJONE ACRIDONE ANTHRONE BAECKEOL BUTANONE BUTYRONE CHALCONE CHALKONE CHROMONE DEGUELIN EXALIONE FENCHONE MENTHONE PROPIONE PULEGONE ROTENONE STEARONE TAGETONE THIENONE VALERONE XANTHONE
KETTLE LEAD STEW DIXIE BOILER CANNER FESSEL MARMIT MASLIN TRIPOD VESSEL CALDRON SKILLET STEWPOT CALABASH FLAMBEAU
KETTLEDRUM NAKER ATABAL KETTLE TIMBAL TYMBAL TIMBALE TYMPANY
KEVEL CAVEL HAMMER KNAPPER
KEWPIE DOLL
KEX KECKSY
KEY CAY KAY CLEW CLUE CRIB FLAT ISLE JACK KING NOTE PLUG PONY BASAL DITAL INDEX SCREW TASTO WREST BUTTON CHIAVE CIPHER CLAVIS COTTER OPENER SAMARA SPLINE WINDER DIGITAL LANGUET PASSKEY SPEAKER LATCHKEY TONALITY
(— FOR TUNING HARP) WREST
(— OF KEYBOARD INSTRUMENT) CHIP MANUAL
(— OF LIFE) ANKH
(— OF ORGAN) TASTO DIGITAL
(— OF PIANO) IVORY NATURAL
(— OF SPINET) CHIP
(— ON WOODWIND INSTRUMENT) LANGUET SPEAKER
(—S OF CARILLON) CLAVECIN
(— UP) STRING
(ARITHMETICAL —) ADDITIVE
(ASH —) PIGEON
(FALSE —) GLUT
(FEATHER —) FIN STOP SPLINE FEATHER
(KIND OF —) CHURCH
(PART OF —) BOW BLADE WARDING SHOULDER SERRATION
(SKELETON —) GILT TWIRLER
(TELEGRAPH —) BUG TAPPER
(WHITE —) NATURAL
(PREF.) CLAVI CLEID(O) CLEIST(O)
(SUFF.) CLEISIS CLISIS
KEYBOARD MANUAL CELESTA CELESTE CLAVIER PEDALIER
(PRACTICE —) DUMBPIANO
(TYPEWRITER —) QWERTY
(PREF.) CLAVI
KEY-DESK CONSOLE
KEYHOLE KEY SLOT LOCKHOLE
KEYNOTE A B D E KEY MESE TONIC FINALIS
KEYSTONE KEY QUOIN VERTEX SAGITTA VOUSSOIR
(— STATE) PENNSYLVANIA
KEYWAY SPLINE KEYSLOT
KEZIA (FATHER OF —) JOB
KHA KA KHMU KACHE LAMET
KHALAT SEERPAW
KHAN CAN CHAM HAWN SERAI TACON CHAGAN KHAKAN
KHAS-KURA NEPALI PAHARI PARBATI GORKHALI
KHATTISH HATTIC
KHEDIVE QUITEVE
KHELLIN VISAMMIN
KHOTANA KOYUKON
KHUSKHUS CUSCUS VETIVER
KIANG ONAGER CHIGETAI HEMIONUS
KIBBLE GIG KETTLE
KIBBLER CRACKER
KICK BOOT FICK FLEG FLIG FOOT FUNK HEEL HOOF LASH PORR POTE PUNT RUSH SHIN TRIP TURF YERK ANGLE BUNCH FLING KEVEL PAUSE PUNCH SCENE SKELP SPANG SPURN CHARGE CORNER FITTER KICKER KICKUP OBJECT SPIRAL VOLLEY DROPOUT FOUETTE KICKOFF DROPKICK PLACEKICK
(— ABOUT) SPARTLE
(— AS A HORSE) FLING WINCE
(— AT GOAL) SHOOT
(— HEELS UP) SPURN
(— IN) ANTEUP
(— ON SHINS) HACK SHINNER
(— OUT) SPUR
(— OVER) CATCH
(BALLET —) BRUSH
(KIND OF —) SQUIB
(SOCCER —) CORNER
(SWIMMING —) THRASH
KICKBACK RECOIL
KICKER TEDDER WINCER
KICKOFF (BEFORE —) PREGAME
KICKSHAW TIDBIT TITBIT
KID COD FUN POD RIB TUB FAWN FOOL GOAT JIVE JOKE JOSH CHAFF CHILD FAGOT HORSE JOLLY KIDDY SPOOF TEASE KIDLET SQUIRT DECEIVE EANLING FATLING TICCHEN YOUNGER CHEVEREL YEANLING
(UNDRESSED —) SUEDE
(WHIZ —) BRAIN GENIUS EINSTEIN
KIDDING JOKE SPOOFERY
KIDNAP STEAL ABDUCT HIJACK PANYAR SPIRIT
KIDNAPER PLAGIARY SNATCHER SPIRITER
KIDNAPING SNATCH PLAGIUM PLAGIARY
KIDNAPPED (AUTHOR OF —) STEVENSON
(CHARACTER IN —) ALAN BRECK COLIN DAVID RIACH SHUAN BALFOUR RANSOME CAMPBELL EBENEZER HOSEASON RANKEILLOR
KIDNEY NEAR NEER REIN TYPE CLASS NEPHRON
(PL.) REINS ROGNONS
(PREF.) NEPHR(O) RENI RENO
(SUFF.) NEPHRITIS NEPHROSIS
KIDNEY BEAN FRIJOLE
(PL.) FASELS
KIER KEEVE PUFFER
KIESELGUHR DOPE GUHR
KILL DO BAG END GET ICE MOW OFF OUT PIP ZAP BANE BOLO COOK COOL DOIN DOWN FELL MORT NECK SLAY TAME WING BLAST BRAIN CROAK CULLE FETCH FORDO GANCH MISDO NAPOO QUELL SABER SCRAG SHOOT SMITE SNUFF SPEED SPEND SPILL SPOIL STALL STICK SWELT SWORD WASTE CORPSE DEADEN DIDDLE FAMISH FINISH HANDLE IMPALE MARTYR MURDER POISON RUBOUT STARVE UNLIVE ACHIEVE BUTCHER DESTROY EXECUTE FLATTEN HATCHET KILLING MORTIFY SMOTHER STONKER SUICIDE DEATHIFY DISPATCH

DISSOLVE IMMOLATE JUGULATE STILETTO
(— ANIMALS) CONTROL
(— BY STONING) LAPIDATE
(— BY SUBMERSION) STIFLE
(— CALF AFTER BIRTH) DEACON
(— CATTLE) PITH
(— EVERY TENTH) DECIMATE
(— GAME) SATCHEL
(— OFF) ENECATE
(— SMALL GAME) BARK
(— TIME) GOOF
(— WITH GRENADE) FRAG
(DELIBERATELY —) FRAG
KILLDEER PLOVER KILLDEE DEERKILL
KILLED KILT WINGED SKITTLED
(FRESHLY —) GREEN
KILLER GUN BRAVO GUNMAN SLAYER TORPEDO MURDERER THRESHER
(SUFF.) CIDAL CIDE
KILLER WHALE ORCA DOLPHIN GRAMPUS
KILLIFISH KELLY KILLY MINNOW COBBLER GUDGEON MAYFISH MUDFISH PANCHAX FUNDULUS ROCKFISH SACALAIT STUDFISH SWAMPINE MUMMICHOG
KILLING FELL KILL MORT QUELL TUANT MURDER CLEANUP HANGING CLEANING DISPATCH FELICIDE HOMICIDE MANSLAUGHTER
(MERCY —) EUTHANASIA
KILLJOY NARK GLOOM LEMON GRINCH SOURPUSS
KILN BING KEEL LEHR OAST CULLE DRIER GLAZE STOVE TILER COCKLE CUPOLA TILERY FURNACE CALCINER LIMEKILN
KILOGRAM (— OF MARIJUANA) KEY
(— OF MARIJUANA OR HEROIN) KEY
(— OF NARCOTIC) KEY
(907 —S) NETTON
KILOMETER LI CLICK KLICK
KILORAD KRAD
KILOWATT-HOUR KELVIN
KILT QUELT PIUPIU FILIBEG PHILIBEG PETTICOAT
KILTER SKEET
KIM (AUTHOR OF —) KIPLING
(CHARACTER IN —) ALI KIM OHARA ARTHUR HURREE LURGAN MAHBUB BENNETT KIMBALL CREIGHTON MOOKERJEE
KIN SIB KATI KITH CATTY CUNNE FLESH FAMILY AFFINITY RELATION
KIND ILK KIN LOT BOON CAST FAIR FORM GOOD HAIR HEND LIKE MAKE MEEK MILD MODE MOLD NICE RATE SELY SOFT SORT SUIT TRIM TYPE WING BREED BROOD CLASS GENRE GENUS GESTE ORDER SPICE STAMP BENIGN BLITHE FACILE GENDER GENTLE GOODLY HUMANE KIDNEY KINDLY MANNER MISTER NATURE SPEECE STRAIN STRIPE TENDER CLEMENT EDITION FASHION FEATHER FLESHLY LENIENT QUALITY REGIMEN SPECIAL SPECIES SPECKLE FRIENDLY GENEROUS MANSUETE OBLIGING BENIGNANT INDULGENT OFFICIOUS PERSUASION
(— OF) A
(— OF PEOPLE) FOLK
(DIFFERENT IN —) DIVERS
(DISTINCTIVE —) BRAND
(OF EVERY —) ALKIN
(PREF.) GEN(O)
KINDLE BEET BLOW FIRE LUNT MOVE TAKE TEND TIND FLAME LIGHT QUICK SPARK SPUNK ACCEND ALIGHT DECOCT ENFIRE EXCITE IGNITE ILLUME EMBLAZE ESPRISE INCENSE INFLAME SOLICIT KINDLING
KINDLINESS CANDOR
KINDLING FIRE BAVIN FAGOT TWIGS TINDER IGNITION
KINDLY FAIR GAIN KIND NESH AGREE COUTH HENDE NAISH BENIGN BLITHE COUTHY GENIAL HOMELY AMIABLE BENEFIC INNERLY FAVOROUS GENEROUS GRACIOUS QUEMEFUL TOWARDLY
KINDNESS LOVE ALOHA FAVOR BOUNTY CANDOR LENITY BENEFIT SERVICE CLEMENCY EASINESS GOODNESS HUMANITY LENITUDE MILDNESS
KIND OF
(SUFF.) EE
KINDRED KIN SIB KIND KITH BLOOD FLESH HOUSE FAMILY KOBONG NATION STRIND COGNATE KINFOLK KINSMEN RELATED SIBSHIP AFFINITY COGNATION CONGENIAL CONGENEROUS
KINE KYE COWS CATTLE
KINETIC ACTUAL
(— POTENTIAL) L
KING RI SO ASA BAN DAM LOT LUD PUL REX REY RIG ROY AGAG AMON ATLI BALI BELI BIJA BORS BRAN BRES CRAL CZAR JEHU KRAL LEIR MARK NUDD NUMA OMRI OTTO PHUL RAJA RIAL SIRE TSAR TZAR WANG YIMA ARDRI BALOR BELUS CONOR CREON DAGDA DAHAK EGLON ETZEL GYGES HEROD HIRAM HOGNI HOSEA IPHIS IXION JOASH LAIUS LLUDD LYCUS MESHA MIDAS MINOS NADAB NEGUS NORSE NUADA PEKAH PRIAM RAJAH SAMMY SWAMI ZIMRI ZOHAK AEOLUS AGENOR AILILL ALARIC ALBOIN ALONSO ALOROS ARIOCH BLADUD CODRUS DIOMED DUNCAN ELATHA FINGAL FRODHI FROTHI GOEMOT INKOSI KABAKA LEMUEL LYCAON MEMNON MINYAS NESTOR NODONS OENEUS OGYGES PELEUS PELIAS SAUGHT SHESHA SVAMIN TEUCER URIENS UZZIAH VASUKI ADMETUS AHAZIAH AMAIMON AMYCLAS ANGEVIN ARDRIGH ARTEGAL ATHAMAS BAGINDA BELINUS BUSIRIS CACIQUE CEPHEUS CROESUS ELIDURE EPAPHUS EPOPEUS ETHBAAL EURYTUS GUNTHER HYGELAC INACHUS JAMSHID JEHOASH JEHORAM KINGLET LAERTES LATINUS LEONTES MENAHEM MONARCH PANDION PHINEUS POLYBUS REGULUS ROMULUS ROYALET SMERDIS SOLOMON VOLSUNG ACRISIUS ADRASTUS AEGYPTUS ALBERICH AMRAPHEL ASNAPPER BAHMANID BRENNIUS CLAUDIUS COPHETUA ELDORADO ETEOCLES ETHELRED GILGAMES GOEMAGOT GOGMAGOG GORBODUC HEZEKIAH HROTHGAR JEHOAHAZ JEROBOAM KINGLING LAOMEDON LISUARTE MANASSEH MELIADUS MENELAUS ODYSSEUS ORCHAMUS OSNAPPAR OVERKING PADISHAH PEKAHIAH PENTHEUS RAMESSID REHOBOAM RODERICK RODOMONT ROITELET SARPEDON SHEPHERD SISYPHUS TANTALUS GILGAMESH
(— AND QUEEN OF TRUMPS) BELLA
(— CHANGED TO WOLF) LYCAON
(— OF ARMS) GARTER NORROY
(— OF BEASTS) LION
(— OF DWARFS) ALBERICH
(— OF FAIRIES) OBERON
(— OF JUDAH) ASA
(— OF TRUMPS) HONOR
(— WITH 10 WIVES) HEROD
(IRISH —) RI RIG ARDRI ARDRIGH
(NEIGHBOR OF —) QUEEN BISHOP
(POLYNESIAN —) ALII ARII ARIKI
(PREF.) REGI
KING ARTHUR (MOTHER OF —) IGRAINE
KINGBIRD PIPIRI PETCHARY
KINGBOLT KING KINGPIN MAINPIN
KING CRAB LIMULID LIMULUS PANFISH
KINGDOM WEI ELAM REALM REIGN WORLD ESTATE MONERA MORVEN REGION REGNUM SAXONY MITANNI
(ANCIENT IONIAN —) EPIRUS
KINGFISH BARB CERO HAKE HAKU MINK OPAH TOMCOD CHENFISH SCIAENID TOMMYCOD
KINGFISHER HALCYON PODITTI TOROTORO
KING JOHN (AUTHOR OF —) SHAKESPEARE
(CHARACTER IN —) JOHN BIGOT ESSEX HENRY JAMES LEWIS MELUN PETER ARTHUR BLANCH ELINOR GURNEY HUBERT PHILIP ROBERT DEBURGH LYMOGES BRETAGNE PANDULPH PEMBROKE CHATILLON CONSTANCE SALISBURY FAULCONBRIDGE
KING LEAR (AUTHOR OF —) SHAKESPEARE
(CHARACTER IN —) KENT LEAR CURAN EDGAR REGAN ALBANY EDMUND OSWALD GONERIL BURGUNDY CORDELIA CORNWALL GLOUCESTER
KINGLET REGULI
KINGLY REGAL ROYAL REGNAL BASILIC IMPERIAL MAJESTIC PRINCELY
KING-OF-ARMS NORROY
KING PARAKEET WELLAT
KINGPIN TOPBANANA
KING'S EVIL CRUELS CREWELS CRUELLS
KING'S HENCHMAN, THE
(CHARACTER IN —) EADGAR AELFRIDA AETHELWOLD
(COMPOSER OF —) TAYLOR
KINGSHIP STOOL THRONE KINGDOM ROYALTY DEVARAJA KINGHOOD
KING SOLOMON'S MINES
(AUTHOR OF —) HAGGARD
(CHARACTER IN —) GOOD JOHN JOSE ALLAN HENRY KHIVA TWALA CURTIS GAGOOL GEORGE IGNOSI UMBOPA FOULATA SCRAGGA INFADOOS SILVESTRE VENTVOGEL QUATERMAIN
KING'S PEACE GRITH
KING'S ROW (AUTHOR OF —) BELLAMANN
(CHARACTER IN —) DRAKE ELISE JAMIE NOLAN RANDY RENEE TOWER CASSIE GORDON LOUISE MCHUGH PARRIS SANDOR PERDOFF MONAGHAN CASSANDRA WAKEFIELD
KING'S SCHOLAR TUG
KING VULTURE PAP PAPA
KININ KALLIDIN
KINK NIB SNICK BUCKLE DOGLEG KINKLE
(— IN ROPE) GRIND
KINKAJOU POTTO HEYRAT APOROSO
KINKING FLUTING
KINKY NAPPY ENCOMIC KINKLED
KINO BIJA BIJASAL
KINSHIP SIB BLOOD NASAB STOOL ENATION KINDRED SIBNESS SIBSHIP AFFINITY AGNATION RELATION PROPINQUITY
KINSMAN KIN SIB ALLY BLOOD AFFINE AGNATE COUSIN FRIEND BROTHER GOTRAJA KINDRED WINEMAY BANDHAVA RELATION RELATIVE COLLATERAL
KINSWOMAN SISTER KINDRED RELATIVE
KIOSK STALL STAND
KIP SKIP GRASSER KIPSKIN UPSTART
KIRGHIZ QYRGHYZ
KIRGIZ (MOUNTAIN RANGE IN —) ALAI
KIRIBATI (CAPITAL OF —) TARAWA BAIRIKI
(FORMER NAME OF —) GILBERTISLANDS
(ISLAND OF —) BERU MAKIN ABAIANG ABEMAMA NONOUTI TABITEUEA
KIRN MELL
KISH (FATHER OF —) JEHIEL
(SON OF —) SAUL
KISMET FATE
KISS BA LIP NEB BASS BUSS PECK PREE MOUTH POGUE SLAKE SMACK BEKISS CARESS SALUTE SLAVER SMOOCH SMOUCH OSCULATE
(— OF PEACE) PAX

(— WETLY) SLOBBER
(STOLEN —) SMOORICH
KISSING LIPWORK
KIT CHIT DUFFEL KITTEN OUTFIT POCHETTE
(LUMBERMAN'S —) TURKEY
(MESS —) CANTEEN
KITCHEN BUT GALLEY CABOOSE CUISINE KITCHIE COOKROOM
(— CONTAINER) CANISTER
(SHIP'S —) CABOOSE
KITCHEN-GARDEN OLITORY
KITE LAP CHIL CYTE HAWK GLEDE CHILLA DRACHE DRAGON ELANET FALCON PREYER SENTRY MILVINE PUDDOCK PUTTOCK FORKTAIL HELLKITE
KITH COUSINRY
KITTEN KIT KITTY KITTLE CATLING KITLING
KITTIWAKE GULL WAEG ANNET KITTY PICKUP HACKLET TARROCK TIRRLIE
KITTY CAT POT BADRANS BAUDRONS
KIVA ESTUFA
KIWI APTERYX
(BROWN —) ROA
KLAMATH WEED AMBER GOATWEED
KLANG PHONE
KLIPSPRINGER KAINSI KLIPBOK
KLONDIKE CANFIELD SOLITAIRE
KLUTZ BOOB
KNACK ART FEAT FEEL GATE GIFT HANG CATCH QUIRK SKILL TRICK TALENT SLEIGHT WRINKLE INSTINCT
(— FOR DISCOVERY) NOSE
KNACKER CLAPPER
(PL.) BONES
KNAPSACK WALLET MOCHILA MUSETTE SNAPBAG SNAPSACK
KNAPWEED SWEEP BLUETOP FLATTOP BALLWEED BELLWEED BOLEWEED BULLWEED BUNDWEED CENTAURY CLUBWEED CROPWEED HARDHEAD IRONHEAD IRONWEED KNOTWEED MATFELON
KNAVE BOY ELF LAD NOB PAM PUR TOM JACK BOWER CHEAT DROLE MAKER NODDY ROGUE TIGER VIPER COQUIN FRIPON HARLOT KNIGHT PICARO RASCAL VARLET WENZEL CAMOOCH CUSTREL PEASANT VILLAIN BEZONIAN COISTREL SWINDLER VARLETTO
(— OF CLUBS) PAM
KNAVERY ROPERY CATZERIE PATCHERY RASCALITY
KNAVISH ROGUISH SCAMPISH
KNAWEL KNOTWEED KNOTWORT
KNEAD ELT TEW MOLD POST BRAKE STOCK PETRIE MASSAGE
(— HIDES) STOCK
KNEADING (— MACHINE) BRAKE
KNEADING-TROUGH HUTCH
KNEE GENU HOCK CROOK KNAPPER SLEEPER SUFFRAGO
(— HOLLOW) HAM
(— OF COMPOSING STICK) SLIDE
(PREF.) GENU GONY
KNEECAP CAP ROTULA PATELLA
(PL.) MARROWBONES
KNEE-JERK AUTOMATIC
KNEEL SIT KNEE COUCH SHIKO KOWTOW
KNEELER SPRINGER
KNEELING SHIKO BENDED
KNEEPAN ROTULA PATELLA
KNELL BELL RING TOLL KNOLL STROKE
KNICKERBOCKERS PLUSFOURS
KNICKKNACK TOY CURIO KNACK TRICK GEWGAW NOTION PRETTY BIBELOT GIMCRACK TCHOTCHKE
KNICKNACK CURIO
KNIFE DAH DIE PIN SAX ULU BOLO BUCK MOON SAEX SHIM SHIV SNEE SPUD TANG BOWIE BURIN CHIVE CUTTO FACON GULLY KNIVE KUKRI PANGA SHANK SHAVE SKEAN SLICE BARLOW BARONG CAMPIT CARVER COLTER COUTEL CUTTLE CUTTOE DAGGER DOCTOR JIGGER PANADE PARANG PAVADE PORKER PULLER RIMMER SICKLE SLICER TREVET TRIVAT WORKER BREAKER CATLING CHOPPER COUTEAU FIPENNY KIOTOME MACHETE PALETTE SCALPEL SEVERER SKINNER SLASHER SNICKER STICKER SUNDANG TICKLER WHITTLE BELDUQUE BILLHOOK CALABOZO JOCTELEG SERPETTE THWITTLE YATAGHAN SNICKERSNEE
(— FOR BREAKING FLAX) BEATER
(— FOR LEATHER) PIN
(— FOR RUBBER DOUGH) DOCTOR
(BLACKSMITH'S —) BUTTERIS
(BOWIE —) TOOTHPICK
(BURMESE —) DAH DAO DOW
(CURRIER'S —) CLEANER
(ENGRAVER'S —) CRADLE
(ESKIMO —) ULU
(MORO —) BARONG
(PART OF —) NEB TIP WEB BACK EDGE HEEL HILT BLADE CHOIL GUARD POINT RIVET FULLER HANDLE POMMEL BOLSTER QUILLON ROCASSO
(SHOEMAKER'S —) BUTT
(SURGICAL —) LANCET CATLING SCALPEL BISTOURY EXSECTOR
(TANNER'S —) GRAINER
(WHALER'S —) SPADE
KNIFE-PLEATED KILTED
KNIGHT N DUB ELF SIR ADUB GANO TULK EQUES EQUIS HORSE LANCE RIDER THANE TOLKE CABALL ERRANT KEMPER PENCEL RITTER ROGERO GENILON PALADIN YOUNKER ALMANZOR BACHELOR BANNERET CAVALIER COLVILLE GANELONE IRONCLAD ISENBRAS PALMERIN RUGGIERO
(— IN CHESS) HORSE
(— OF ROUND TABLE) GAN KAY BORS OWEN GARETH GAWAIN MODRED CARADOC CRADOCK GALAHAD GANELON EGLAMORE LANCELOT PALMERIN PERCIVAL TRISTRAM
(BOASTFUL —) KAY
(CARPET —) DAMMARET
(MERCENARY —) FREELANCE
(NEIGHBOR OF —) ROOK BISHOP
(ROMAN —) MAECENAS
KNIGHT-ERRANT KEMPER PALADIN
KNIGHTHOOD CAVALRY
KNIGHTS (AUTHOR OF —) ARISTOPHANES
(CHARACTER IN —) CLEON DEMUS NICIAS AGORACRITUS DEMOSTHENES
KNIPHOFIA TRITOMA
KNIT SET BIND KNOT PLAIT PURSE UNITE WEAVE COMPACT CONNECT WRINKLE CONTRACT
(— STOCKINGS) SHANK
(KIND OF —) WEFT
KNITTED FLAT WOVEN
KNITTING PURL
(— OF BONES) POROSIS
KNITTING LOOP STEEK
KNITTING NEEDLE WIRE
KNOB BOB BUR NOB NUB BEAD BOLL BOSS BURR CLUB DENT HEAD HEEL KNOP KNOT KNUB LIFT NODE NOOP PULL SNUG STUD TORE BERRY BULLA BUNCH FORTE GEMMA KNURL NATCH ONION PLOOK PLUKE BUTTON CROCHE EMBOSS NOBBLE NUBBLE PIMPLE PISTON POMMEL FERRULE HORNTIP KNOBBLE BELLPULL DOORKNOB DRAWSTOP OMPHALOS
(— OF HAIR) TOORIE
(— OF ROCK) BUHR BURR KNUCKLE
(— ON BILL OF SWAN) BERRY
(— ON BUTT OF CANNON) GRAPE
(— ON CHAIR) POMMEL
(— ON DEER'S ANTLER) OFFER CROCHE
(— ON ROPE) MOUSE
(TY —) VOL
(PREF.) CONDYL(O) TYL(O)
KNOBBED NODOSE TOROSE BULLATE TUBEROUS TYLOTATE
KNOBBY GOUTY NODAL KNOTTY TOROSE WHELKY GOUTISH KNOBBLY SCRAGGED
KNOCK CON DAD HIT JOW JUT POP PUN RAP WAP BANG BASH BEAT BUMP CALL CHAP CHOP DASH DAUD DING DUMP DUNT HACK JOLT JOWL KNAP NOCK NOIT PINK PLUG POLT POSS PUSH ROUT SLAM SLAY SNOP TANK TIRL WHAP WHOP CLOUR CLUMP KNOIT POUND SMITE SNOCK STAVE STRAM THUMP BOUNCE DUNTLE KNATCH KNETCH STOTER CANVASS PINKING
(— ABOUT) RUMBLE
(— DOWN) MOW DROP DUMP FELL FLOOR GRASS LEVEL SMITE SOUSE HURTLE RAFFLE UNPILE CLOTHESLINE
(— FOR A LOOP) FLOOR
(— OFF) SECURE
(— ON HEAD) MAZER MAZARD
(— OUT) OUT SAP CONK COOL KAYO FLATTEN STIFFEN
(— UNCONSCIOUS) COLDCOCK
(— WITH THE HORNS) DISH
(IGNITION —) PING
KNOCKER CROW RISP HAMMER WHACKER
(DOOR —) CROW HAMMER RAPPER
KNOCK-KNEED VARUS VALGUS
KNOCKOFF COPY
KNOCKOUT KO KAYO CRUSHER NOBBLER
(PRETENDED —) DIVE
KNOLL NOB HIGH KNAP KNOB KNOW TOFT HEAVE HURST HYRST MOUND SHOAL COPPLE BOUROCK HUMMOCK
KNOP NOB KNOB KNOSP KNAPPE
KNOT BOB BOW BUN FAG NIB NOB NUB PIN TIE BEND BURL BURR CHOU CLOD CLOT CLUB HARL KILL KNAG KNAR KNOB NODE NOIL NURL SLUG SNUB TRUE WAFT WALL BUNCH CLOVE CROWN DUNNE GNARL GNARR HALCH HALSH HATCH HITCH KNURL MOUSE NODUS NOEUD SNARL SNICK SWIRL TWIST WARRE BOUGHT BUTTON CLINCH CROCHE FINIAL GRANNY MASCLE SORTIE TANGLE BOWKNOT BOWLINE CHIGNON COCKADE GORDIAN MAYBIRD CICISBEO DRAWKNOT GRAYBACK KNITTING SLIPKNOT TRUELOVE CLOVEHITCH SHEEPSHANK
(— IN CLOTH) FAG NEP BURL
(— IN COTTON FIBERS) NEP
(— IN SIGNAL FLAG) WAFT WEFT WHEFT
(— IN WOOD) NUR PIN BURL BURR KNAG KNAR KNUR NURR SNUB GNARL KNAUR KNURL KNURR
(— IN YARN) SLUG SNICK
(— OF HAIR) BOB BUN COB PUG CLUB KNURL CHIGNON
(— OF RIBBONS) FAVOR
(EMBROIDERY —) PICOT
(KIND OF —) LOVER LOVERS
(LOVE —) AMORET
(ORNAMENTAL —) BOW
(SHOULDER —) WING
(WALL —) WALE
(PREF.) NODI
KNOTGRASS LIGNUM HOGWEED PIGWEED BINDWEED BIRDWEED DOORWEED KNOTWEED KNOTWORT PINKWEED POLYGONY WIREWEED
KNOTTED KNIT NOUE TIED NOWED NODOSE SWIRLY CRABBED NODATED SCRAGGY
KNOTTY HARD CRAMP GOUTY NODAL COMMON CRAGGY GNARLY KNAGGY KNOBBY KNURRY NODOSE NODOUS COMPLEX GNARLED GOUTISH JOINTED KNARRED KNOTTED SCABROUS
KNOTWEED LIGNUM ALLSEED HOGWEED JUMPSEED POLYGONY POLYGONUM
KNOW CAN CON KEN WIS WIT WOT CITE HAVE SABE WEET WIST WOTH SAVVY SKILL COGNIZE
(— NOT) NOOT
(—S NOT) NOTE

(DID NOT —) KENDNA
(DO NOT —) KENNA
KNOWABLE SENSABLE
KNOW-HOW CRAFT MOXIE SMART SMARTS SAVVY SKILL
KNOWING FLY HEP HIP SLY FOXY GASH INON ONTO SPRY WISE AWARE CANNY DOWNY JERRY LEERY SPACK WITTY EXPERT SCIENT SCIOUS SHREWD WITFUL WITTER GNOSTIC SAPIENT WISEUP
(— SUPERFICIALLY) SCIOLOUS
(SUFF.) GNOSIA GNOSIS GNOSTIC GNOSY
KNOWINGLY CANNILY SCIENTER SHREWDLY WITTERLY
KNOW-IT-ALL MAVIN SAVANT
KNOWLEDGE CAN WIT BOOK KITH KNOW LAIR LEAR LORE NOTE INWIT JNANA SAVVY SKILL VIDYA ADVICE AVIDYA CLERGY GNOSIS NOESIS NOTICE WISDOM CUNNING DIANOIA HEARING KNOWING MEANING SCIENCE WITTING DAYLIGHT DOCTRINE EPISTEME LEARNING LETTRURE NOTITION PRUDENCE SAPIENCE SCIENTIA COGNIZANCE
(— OF ALL THINGS) OMNISCIENCE
(— OF SPIRITUAL TRUTH) GNOSIS
(ABSOLUTE —) PANSOPHY
(EXPERT —) SKILL
(FAMILIAR —) HANG
(GENERAL —) GROUNDING
(INWARD —) INWIT
(LATER —) AFTERWIT
(MYSTERIOUS —) ARCANUM
(PIECEMEAL —) SMATTER
(PRACTICAL —) INSIGHT
(PRIVATE —) PRIVITY
(PUBLIC —) LIGHT
(SLICK —) ANGLE
(SLIGHT —) INKLING SMATTER
(SPIRITUAL —) GNOSIS
(SUPERFICIAL —) SCIOLISM
(SUPERIOR —) MASTERY
(SUPREME —) PRAJNA
(SYSTEMATIZED —) SCIENCE
(UNIVERSAL —) PANSOPHY
(PREF.) EPISTEMO GNOSIO
(SUFF.) GNOSIA GNOSIS GNOSTIC GNOSY ICS SOPH(ER)(IC)(IST)(Y)
KNOWLEDGEABLE KNOWING SKILLED STUDIED
KNOWN EVER COUTH COMMON
(ACTUALLY —) SPECIOUS
(ALSO — AS) AKA
(GENERALLY —) PUBLIC
(LITTLE —) FAMELESS
(NOT —) DARK SILENT
(OTHERWISE — AS) ALIAS
(PUBLICLY —) EXOTERIC
(UNMISTAKABLY —) STATED
(WIDELY —) COMMON
KNOW-NOTHING SAM
KNUCKLE KNUCK JARRET
(PREF.) CONDYL(O)
KNUCKLEBONE DIB DOLOS TALUS COCKAL SHACKLE
KNUCKLEHEAD SAP DUMDUM
KNURL MILL NULL DWARF SNARL
KNURLING NULLING REEDING KNULLING
KOALA BEAR BAALU BALOO SLOTH KOOLAH WOMBAT CARBORA PHALANGER
KOANGA (CHARACTER IN —) JOSE PEREZ SIMON KOANGA PALMYRA MARTINEZ
(COMPOSER OF —) DELIUS
KOBOLD NIS GNOME NISSE HODEKEN HUTCHEN
KOEL KOIL KOKIL RAINBIRD
KOHATH (FATHER OF —) LEVI
(SISTER OF —) JOCHEBED
KOHL COHOL ALCOHOL
KOHLRABI BROMATIUM
KOKAN LAMPATIA
KOKO LEBBEK
KOKOON GNU
KOKUM GARCINIA
KOKUMIN BAN
KOLA COLA BICHY GOORANUT
KOLAIAH (SON OF —) AHAB
KOMATIC SLED
KOMATIK SLED
KOMBU KOBU KAMBOU CHAKOBU
KOMMETJE WALLOW COMITJE
KONAK YALI
KOOK NITWIT DINGBAT DINGALING
KOOKABURRA KOOKA JACKASS
KOOKY CRAZY OFFBEAT
KOPECK KAPEIKA
KORAH (FATHER OF —) ESAU IZHAR ELIPHAZ
(MOTHER OF —) AHOLIBAMAH
KORAKAN RAGI RAGGI RAGGY
KORAN KITAB QURAN ALCORAN
(SECTION OF —) SURA SURAH
KORE DESPOINA
(FATHER OF —) IMNAH
KOREA (SEE NORTH KOREA OR SOUTH KOREA)
KOREC MIRA
KORINA LIMBA
KOS COAN
KOSHER (NOT —) TREF
KOSIN KOUSSIN TAENNIN BRAYERIN
KOSO PANAMINT
KOULAN GOUR
KOVANSHCHINA (CHARACTER IN —) ENNA IVAN MARFA ANDREY DOSIFEY GOLITSYN KHOVANSKY
(COMPOSER OF —) MUSSORGSKY
KOWHAI GOAI PELU LOCUST SOPHORA
KOWTOW KNEEL SHIKO
KOYUKON TENA KHOTANA
KRAAL CRAW MANYATTA ZIMBABWE
KRAIT ADDER KORAIT BUNGARUM
KRATER KELEBE
KRAUNHIA WISTARIA
KREIS CIRCLE
KREUTZER SONATA (AUTHOR OF —) TOLSTOY
(CHARACTER IN —) LIZA VASYLA POZDNISHEF TRUKHASHEVSKY
KRIEMHILD (BROTHER OF —) GERNOT GUNTHER GISELHER
(FATHER OF —) GIBICH
(HUSBAND OF —) ATTILA SIEGFRIED
KRIS CREASE CREESE DAGGER
KRISHNA VASUDEVA
(BROTHER OF —) BALARAMA
(FATHER OF —) VASUDEVA
(FOSTER FATHER OF —) NANDA
(FOSTER MOTHER OF —) YASHODA
(MOTHER OF —) DEVAKI
(UNCLE OF —) KANSA
KRISTIN LAVRANSDATTER
(AUTHOR OF —) UNDSET
(CHARACTER IN —) ULF IVAR GAUTE MUNAN SIMON SKULE ERLEND JOFRID NAAKVE AASHILD HALVARD KRISTIN LAVRANS RAMBORG ULVHILD BJORGULF JARDTRUD NIKULAUS RAGNFRID ANDRESSON BJORGULFSON IVARSDATTER LAVRANSDATTER
KRONE CROWN CORONA
KRU KROOBOY KROOMAN
KRUMMHORN CREMONA CROMORNE
KSHATRIYA THAKUR
KUA MAKUA MAKWA
KUBA BUSHONGO KABISTAN
KUDZU VINE KOHEMP
KUI KHONDI
KU KLUXER KLUXER KLUCKER KLANSMAN
KUKURUKU IKPERE
KULANAPAN POMO
KUMAN POLOVTZY
KUMBUK ARJAN ARJUN
KUMMEL ALLASCH
KUMQUAT NAGAMI
KUNTI (FATHER OF —) PANDU SHURA
(SON OF —) BHIMA KARNA ARJUNA YUDHISHTHIRA
KURRAJONG CALOOL LACEBARK
KURUKH ORAON
KUSA DARBHA
KUSHAIAH (SON OF —) ETHAN
KUSIMANSEL MANGUE
KUTCHIN LOUCHEUX
KUWAIT (— NATIVE) ARAB
(CAPITAL OF —) ALKUWAIT
(OIL FIELD OF —) WAFRA BAHRAH BURGAN SABRIYA MINAGISH RAUDHATAIN
(OTHER NAME OF —) KOWEIT KUWEIT
(TOWN OF —) MAGWA AHMADI HAWALLI ABDULLAH FAHAHEEL
KVASS ALE BEER QUASH
KWENI GURO
KYANITE DISTHENE
KYOODLE YAP
KYPHOSIS HUMPBACK

KYRGYZSTAN (ALSO SEE RUSSIA)
CAPITAL: FRUNZE BISHKEK PISHPEK
COIN: SOM
LAKE: ISSYKKUL
MOUNTAIN: VICTORY KHANTENGRI
MOUNTAIN RANGE: ALAY KIRGIZ ZAALAY CHATKAL FERGANA TIENSHAN TRANSALAY KOKSHAALTAU KUNGEYALATAU TERSKEYALATAU
NAME: KYRGYZ KIRGHIZIA KIRGIZIYA
RIVER: CHU NARYN SYRDARYA
TOWN: OSH TOKMAK BISHKEK KYZYLKIYA PREZHEVALSK
VALLEY: CHU TALAS FERGANA

KYURINISH LESGHIN LEZGHIAN

L

L EL LIMA FIFTY
LAADAH (FATHER OF —) SHELAH
(GRANDFATHER OF —) JUDAH
LAADAN (FATHER OF —) GERSHOM
LAAGER LEEGTE LEAGUER
LABAN (DAUGHTER OF —) LEAH RACHEL
(FATHER OF —) BETHUEL
(SISTER OF —) REBEKAH
LABDACUS (FATHER OF —) POLYDORUS
(MOTHER OF —) NYCTEIS
(SON OF —) LAIUS
LABDANUM MYRRH
LABEL TAG BILL FILE MARK FICHE STAMP TALLY TITLE DIRECT DOCKET TICKET ENDSEAL LAMBEAU STICKER
(— ON SUIT OF CLOTHES) ETIQUET
LABELLUM LIP LABEL PETAL
(PART OF —) HYPOCHIL
LABIAL ROUND
LABIATE HOREHOUND
LABIUM LIP LABRUM
LABOR ADO FAG TUG WIN CARK MOIL TASK TAVE TILL TOIL WORK BEGAR DELVE GRAFT GRIND HEAVE PAINS SWEAT SWINK TEAVE TREAD WHILE YAKKA CORVEE DRUDGE EFFORT HAMMER STRIVE BULLOCK FATIGUE MANUARY OPIFICE PROCURE SERVICE SLAVERY TRAVAIL TROUBLE TURMOIL BUSINESS DRUDGERY EXERTION GROANING INDUSTRY LABORAGE STRUGGLE
(— ARDUOUSLY) BILDER
(— HARD) THRASH THRIPPLE
(— LEADER) DEBS
(— UNDER) SUFFER
(DAY'S —) DARG JOURNEY
(DIFFICULT —) DYSTOCIA
(EXCESSIVE —) STRAIN
(FORCED —) BEGAR CORVEE
(HARD —) HARD BULLWORK
(HIRED —) TOGT
(IMPOSED —) TASKAGE
(MENTAL —) HEADWORK
(ROUTINE —) SCUTWORK
(SEVERE —) AGON
(UNPAID —) CORVEE
LABORATORY LAB SHOP KITCHEN OFFICINA WORKSHOP PHYTOTRON
LABOR CAMP GULAG
LABORED HEAVY FORCED SWEATY STRAINED
LABORER (ALSO SEE WORKER AND WORKMAN) BOY BHAR ESNE HIND JACK JOEY MOZO PEON TOTY BAGDI CHURL GUASO HUNKY NAVVY PALLI PINER STIFF BALAHI BEGARI BOHUNK COALER COOLIE DAYMAN DILKER DOCKER FELLAH FLUNKY FOGGER HEAVER HODMAN HOLEYA JIBARO LUMPER RAFTER TASKER WAYMAN WORKER BRACERO BYWONER CREWMAN DAYSMAN DIGGORY DIRGLER DRAINER DVORNIK GRECIAN HARDHAT HOBBLER MANUARY MAZDOOR PICKMAN PIONEER PIPEMAN PLOWMAN SANDHOG SCOURER SHIPPER SMASHER SOUGHER SPALLER STOCKER SWINKER TOTYMAN WORKMAN BIJWONER CHAINMAN COTTAGER DOLLYMAN FARMHAND FLOORMAN GANGSMAN HOLDSMAN SPADEMAN SPALPEEN STRAPPER TIDESMAN ROUSTABOUT
(DOCK —) SEAGULL
(INEXPERIENCED —) GREENER
(LOWLY —) GRUNT
LABORIOUS HARD HEAVY STIFF TOUGH SWEATY UPHILL ARDUOUS OPEROSE SLAVISH TOILFUL DILIGENT LABOROUS TOILSOME
LABRADOR TEA LEDUM GOWIDDIE
LABRYS AX AXE
LABURNUM AWBER
LABYRINTH MAZE CIRCUIT MEANDER
LABYRINTHINE TORTUOUS BYZANTINE
LAC LACCA LACQUER
LACE VAL BEAT BEST FOND GOTA LASH PEAK FILET LACIS LIVEN ORRIS POINT SCREW SPRIG WEAVE BLONDE CADDIS CORDON DEFEAT EDGING GRILLE LACING LASHER THRASH TUCKER VENISE ALENCON ALLOVER BULLION CURRAGH CUTWORK FOOTING GALLOON GUIPURE HONITON LATCHET MACRAME MALINES MECHLIN MELANGE NANDUTI TAMBOUR TATTING TORCHON TROLLEY ARGENTAN BOBBINET BONEWORK BOOTLACE BRUSSELS DENTELLE ILLUSION LACEWORK LIMERICK PEARLING STAYLACE COLBERTINE NEEDLEPOINT
(— EDGING) PUNTILLA
(— IN PLACE OF COLLAR) RUCHE
(— MAKER) TWISTHAND
(— PATTERN) TOILE
(KIND OF —) CLUNY
(KNOTTED —) TATTING
LACEBARK LAGETTO DAGUILLA LACEWOOD
LACE BUG TINGITID
LACEDAEMON (DAUGHTER OF —) CLEODICE
(FATHER OF —) ZEUS JUPITER
(MOTHER OF —) TAYGETE
(SON OF —) HIMERUS
(WIFE OF —) SPARTA
LACERATE REND TEAR GANCH ENGORE HARROW MANGLE SCARIFY FRACTURE
LACERATION RIP TEAR WOUND
LACERTA LIZARD
LACEWING NEUROPTERAN
LACEWOOD SYCAMORE
LACEWORK DENTELLE
LACHRYMOSE SAD TEARY WEEPY MAUDLIN
LACINARIA LIATRIS
LACING LACET LINGEL ECHELLE LANGUET
(RAWHIDE —S) BABICHE
LACINIATION DAG
LACK FAIL LANK LIKE LOSS MAIM MISS NEED VOID WANE WANT FAULT MINUS DEARTH DEFECT INLAIK ABSENCE BLEMISH DEFAULT FAILURE PAUCITY REQUIRE VACANCY SCARCITY SOLITUDE WANTROKE
(— CONFIDENCE) DOUBT
(— FAITH) DIFFIDE
(— HARMONY) DISAGREE
(— OF APPETITE) ANOREXIA
(— OF CLARITY) DARKNESS
(— OF CONFIDENCE) MISTRUST
(— OF COORDINATION) ASYNERGY DYSERGIA
(— OF DEVELOPMENT) AGENESIS
(— OF EARNESTNESS) ITEMING
(— OF EFFUSIVENESS) RESERVE
(— OF EMOTION) APATHY
(— OF ENERGY) ATONY ANERGY ATONIA
(— OF FLAVOR) SILENCE
(— OF FORESIGHT) MYOPIA
(— OF HARMONY) DISCORD DISUNITY
(— OF INTENTION) ACCIDENT
(— OF INVOLVEMENT) DISTANCE
(— OF ORDER) ATAXY ATAXIA DISARRAY
(— OF PATRIOTISM) INCIVISM
(— OF REFINEMENT) CRUDITY
(— OF SENSE) FOLLY
(— OF SENSE OF SMELL) ANOSMIA
(— OF STEADINESS) LEVITY
(— OF SYMPATHY) DYSPATHY
(— OF VIGOR) LANGUOR
(— OF VITALITY) ANEMIA ADYNAMIA
(— OF WIND) CALM
(— OF WORTH) IMMERIT
(— STRENGTH) DROOP
LACKADAISICAL LANGUID LISTLESS
LACKEY SKIP SLAVE LAPDOG LACQUEY STAFFIER
LACKING BUT SHY BARE FREE SANS WANT ALACK GNEDE MINUS SHORT ABSENT BARREN DEVOID WITHIN WANTING DESOLATE INDIGENT
(PREF.) LONCH(O)
LACKLUSTER DULL FISHY CLOUDY GLASSY
LACONIA (CAPITAL OF —) SPARTA
LACONIAN SPARTAN
LACONIC CURT SHORT CONCISE POINTED SPARTAN SUCCINCT
LA CORUNA GROIN
LACQUER LAC DOPE DUCO JAPAN CHATON LACKER URUSHI VARNISH
LACRIMAL
(PREF.) DACRY(O)
LACTATION (— PERIOD) NOTE
LACTONE CUMARIN LIMONIN MECONIN DIKETENE
LACTOSCOPE PIOSCOPE
LACUNA GAP BREAK HIATUS
LACUSTRINE LAKISH
LAD BOY BUB MAN BOYO CARL CHAP DICK HIND JOCK LOON LOUN SNAP BILLY BUCKO CADDY CHIEL GROOM YOUTH BURSCH CADDIE CALLAN FELLOW LADDIE LADKIN MANNIE NIPPER SHAVER CALLANT MUCHACHO SPRINGER STRIPLING
(AWKWARD —) GROMET GRUMMET
(MISCHIEVOUS —) GAMIN
(MY —) AVICK
(SERVING —) GILLIE GOSSOON
LADDER STY STEE JACOB SCALE AERIAL BANGOR ESCAPE PULEYN GANGWAY POLEYNE POMPIER
(— IN HOSE) RUN
(— TO LOFT) TRAP
(FIREMAN'S —) STICK
(FISH —) FISHWAY
(JACOB'S —) CHARITY
(REVOLVING —) POTENCE
(ROPE —) ETRIER
LADDER-LIKE SCALAR
LADDIE JOCKEY LATHIE LADDOCK LADDIKIE
LADE BAIL LAVE LADEN TRUSS BURDEN ONLOAD FRAUGHT
(— INTO COOLER) STRIKE
LADEN HEAVY BELAST LOADED FRAUGHT FREIGHT GESTANT
LA-DI-DA TOOTOO EXTREME
LADING LOAD CARGO BURDEN FREIGHT
LADINO SPANIOL
LADLE DIP JET GAWN SKEP CLATH CYATH KEACH STOOP DIPPER LADING CUVETTE CYATHUS KYATHOS POTSTICK
(— FOR MOLTEN METAL) SHANK
(— OUT SOUP) SLEECH
(— WITH HANDLES) CYATH SHANK CYATHUS KYATHOS SKIPPET

(BRINE —) LOOT
(LARGE —) SCOOP
(PREF.) ARYTENO
LADRONE TULISAN LATHERIN
LADY BIBI BURD DAMA DAME RANI DONNA HANUM BEEBEE DOMINO FEMALE KADINE KHANUM RAWNIE SAHIBA SENORA LADYKIN MADONNA SENHORA BELAMOUR SINEBADA
(— OF HIGH RANK) BEGUM
(— OF HOUSE) GOODWIFE
(BEAUTIFUL —) CLEAR
(LEADING —) PREMIERE
(TURKISH —) KHANUM
(YOUNG —) DEB MISS DAMSEL MAIDEN DAMOZEL DEBUTANTE
(PL.) LADYHOOD
LADYBUG VEDALIA
LADYFISH WRASSE PUDIANO BONEFISH BONYFISH DONCELLA
LADYISH TENPOUNDER
LADYLIKE FEMALE
LADYLOVE LADY DELIA MINION MISTRESS
LADY'S-COMB NEEDLES
LADY'S-MANTLE DEWCUP PADELION
LADY'S-SLIPPER DUCK YELLOW NERVINE YELLOWS UMBILROOT
(PREF.) CYPRI CYPRO
LADY'S-SMOCK SPINK
LADY WINDERMERE'S FAN
(AUTHOR OF —) WILDE
(CHARACTER IN —) LORTON ERLYNNE AUGUSTUS MARGARET DARLINGTON WINDERMERE
LAEL (SON OF —) ELIASAPH
LAERTES (FATHER OF —) ARCESIUS
(MOTHER OF —) CHALCOMEDUSA
(SON OF —) ULYSSES
(WIFE OF —) ANTICLEA
LAG DRAG DRAW SLOG DELAY TRAIL HOCKER LAGGER LINGER LOITER STRING DRIDDLE LAGGING
(— IN PRODUCTION) SLIPPAGE
(KIND OF —) JET
LAGGARD SLOW TARDY LAGGER TORTOISE
LAGGING TARDY JACKET DEADING LAGGARD CLEADING DRAWLING FOREPOLE
LAGNIAPPE TIP GIFT BONUS EXTRA PILON PRESENT
LAGOMORPH HARE PIKA RABBIT
LAGOON HAFF POOL BAYOU LIMAN LAGUNA SALINA
LAHAD (FATHER OF —) JAHATH
LAHMI (BROTHER OF —) GOLIATH
LAID (— ACROSS WALL) INBOND
(— DOWN) THETIC THETICAL
(— WASTE) BARE
LAIR DEN LAY FORM HOLD SHED COUCH EARTH HAUNT LODGE MEUSE SQUAT HARBOR KENNEL SPELUNK
(— OF FOX) KENNEL
(— OF OTTER) HOLT HOVER
(— OF WILD BOAR) SOUNDER
LAISH (SON OF —) PHALTIEL
LAISSE TIRADE
LAITY FOLK LAYMEN PEOPLE
LAIUS (FATHER OF —) LABDACUS
(SON OF —) OEDIPUS
(WIFE OF —) JOCASTA
LAKE LAY SEA VLY BAHR JAIL JHIL LAGO LLYN LOCH MERE MOAT SHOR TANK TARN VLEI VLEY BAYOU CHOTT JHEEL LERNA LIMAN LOUGH SPARK TUBIG LAGOON NYANZA STROND ANCYLUS CARMINE LAKELET TURLOUGH
(CASHEW —) AUBURN
(DRY —) PLAYA
(FENNY —) BROAD
(MOUNTAIN —) TARN
(RELATING TO —S) LIMNAL
(SALT —) SHOT CHOTT SHOTT SALINA SALINE
(SHALLOW —) PLAYA
(SMALL —) GURGES MARIGOT
(TEMPORARY —) PINAG
(YELLOW —) PINK
(PREF.) LIMN(I)(O)
(SUFF.) LIMNION
LAKE CARP DRUM LAKER
LAKE-DWELLING CRANNOG
LAKE HERRING KIYI CISCO GRAYBACK
LAKE TROUT POGY TOGUE
LAKE WHITEFISH POLLAN
LAKME (CHARACTER IN —) LAKME GERALD NILAKANTHA
(COMPOSER OF —) DELIBES
LAKSHMANA (FATHER OF —) DURYODHANA
(SLAYER OF —) ABHIMANYU
LAKSHMI SRI SHREE
(HUSBAND OF —) VISHNU
LALAPALOOZA ONER
LAMA ELK AUCHENIA
LAMB BUM PET PUR CADE DEAR DUPE ELIA LOME SOCK YEAN AGNUS PESAH PODDY AGNEAU COSSET HIEDER LAMBIE LAMKIN PESACH SUCKER WASTER WEANER CHILVER EANLING FATLING HOGLING PASCHAL PERSIAN RUFFIAN TWAGGER BAAHLING LAMBLING PASSOVER YEANLING
(— AND WHEAT) KIBBE
(SCYTHIAN —) BAROMETZ
(SHOULDER OF —) BANJO
(SIDE OF —) CONCERTINA
LAMBASTE BEAT WHIP CREAM SCOLD SCORE CENSURE SQUABASH
LAMBENT BRIGHT RADIANT
LAMBREQUIN MANTLING
LAMBSKIN LAMB BAGDAD BAGHDAD SALZFELLE
LAMB'S QUARTERS MUCKWEED
LAMB'S WOOL WASSAIL
LAME BUM GAME HALT LAHN GAMMY GIMPY GRAVEL TINSEL CRIPPLE CRIPPLY HALTING HIPHALT GORGERIN SPAVINED
(— A HORSE) STUB NOBBLE
(— WITH HORSESHOE NAIL) ACCLOY
LAMEBRAIN CLOD KNUCKLEHEAD
LAMECH (DAUGHTER OF —) NAAMAH
(SON OF —) NOAH JABAL JUBAL TUBALCAIN
(WIFE OF —) ADAH ZILLAH
LAMELLA PLICA FOLIUM FORNIX
LAMELLAR SPATHIC
LAMELLIBRANCH PELECYPOD
LAMENESS HALT
LAMENT CRY WEY CARE DOLE HONE HOWL KEEN MEAN MOAN PINE SIGH TEAR WAIL WALY WEEP CROON DUMKA GREET KINAH MOURN PLAIN QINAH BEHOWL BEMOAN BEWAIL BEWEEP COMMOS KOMMOS PLAINT REGRET REPINE SORROW SQUAWK THREAP YAMMER BEMOURN CONDOLE DEPLORE EJULATE ELEGIZE GRIZZLE REGRATE THRENOS WAYMENT COMPLAIN CORONACH MOURNING THRENODY ULLAGONE WELLAWAY
LAMENTABLE YEMER FUNEST RUEFUL DOLEFUL PITIFUL PITIABLE PLAINFUL YAMMERLY
LAMENTATION KEEN MOAN WAIL DOLOR LINOS RUING TANGI LAMENT PLAINT REGRET SORROW THRENE PLANGOR TRAGEDY WAYMENT WILLAWA CORONACH MOURNING PATHETIC WAILMENT WELLAWAY LAMENTING
LAMINA FILM LAME LAMP LEAF OBEX BLADE FLAKE LAMIN PLATE SCALE SHELL TABLE FOLIUM CAPSULE
LAMINATE LEAFY FLAGGY
LAMINATED BUILT FOLIATE TABULAR
LAMINATION SLABBING
LAMINITIS FOUNDER
LAMMAS DAY GULE TERM
LAMMERGEIER AREND OSSIFRAGE
LAMP ARC EYE SEE DAVY GLIM INKY JACK SLUT ALDIS ARGAND ASTRAL BULLET HELION LAMPAD TARGET ILLUMER LAMPION LAMPLET LANTERN LUCERNE LUCIGEN SUNLAMP SUNSPOT AEOLIGHT CIRCLINE GASLIGHT SIDELAMP TORCHERE PHOTOFLASH PHOTOFLOOD
(— FOR FIREPLACE) KYLE
(CHIMNEYLESS —) TORCH
(DARKROOM —) SAFELIGHT
(IRON —) CRUSIE
(KIND OF —) POLE
(MAKESHIFT —) BITCH
(NIGHT —) VEILLEUSE
(PART OF —) CAP CORD HARP SHELL FINIAL NIPPLE SOCKET SWITCH WASHER NECKWING
(SAFETY —) DAVY GEORDIE
(STAGE —S) BATTEN
(TYPE OF —) GOOSENECK
(4-CORNERED —) CHILL
(PL.) CLUSTER
(PREF.) LYCHNO
LAMPBLACK LINK SOOT
LAMPETIA (FATHER OF —) APOLLO HELIOS
(MOTHER OF —) NEAERA
(SISTER OF —) PHAETHUSA
LAMP HOLDER HUSK
LAMPLIGHTER LEERIE
LAMPOON PIPE SKIT GESTE LIBEL SQUIB IAMBIC SATIRE BERHYME PASQUIN COCKALAN RIDICULE SATIRIZE PASQUINADE
LAMPOONER PASQUIL PASQUIN
LAMPREY EEL PRIDE LAMPER MYZONT RAMPER SAYNAY SUCKER LAMPERN
LAMP RING CRIC
LAMPSHADE GLOBE
(PART OF —) RIB RING SHADE SPIDER
LAMPSTAND TORCHERE
LAMPWARE (— STYLE) TOLE
LAMPWICK MATCH
LANATE WOOLY LANOSE WOOLLY
LANCE PIC CANE DART SHAFT SPEAR STAFF BROACH ELANCE GLAIVE GLEAVE LANCET ROCKET LANCELET SPICULUM
(KING ARTHUR'S —) RON
LANCE GUARD VAMPLATE
LANCE HEAD MORNE SOCKET
LANCELET AMPHIOXUS
LANCER LANCE SOWAR UHLAN
LANCE REST QUEUE FEWTER
LANCET FLEAM FLEEM LANCELET
LANCEWOOD YAYA CIGUA CANELA YARIYARI
LAND ERD ERF NOD RIB AGER DIRT FOLD GALE GISH GORE JODO MARK SITE SOIL EARTH EJIDO ETHEL FIELD GLEBE JUGER PLANT SHORE SOLUM ALIGHT ASSART FUNDUS GROUND COMMONS COUNTRY DEMESNE ELLASAR HOLDING LANDING LIBRATE QUILLET TERRENE ALLODIAL BOOKLAND COMMONTY FARMLAND FLEYLAND FOLKLAND POMERIUM PRAEDIUM
(— A PLANE) GREASE
(— BETWEEN FURROWS) SELION
(— BETWEEN RIVERS) DOAB
(— BORDERING SEA) SHORE
(— CLEARING) KAINGIN
(— CONVERTED TO TILLAGE) TWAITE THWAITE
(— HAVING VALUE OF POUND PER YEAR) LIBRATE
(— IN CONACRE) MOCK
(— IN GRASS) LAYER
(— LEFT FALLOW) ARDER
(— MEASURE) RIG
(— OF BLISS) GOKURAKU
(— OF GIANTS) UTGARTHAR
(— OF MANSION) DEMESNE
(— OF OPPORTUNITY) ARKANSAS
(— OF PLENTY) GOSHEN
(— OF REGION) MOLD MOULD
(— PLOWED IN A DAY) JORNADA
(— RECOVERED FROM SEA) INTAKE INNINGS
(— REGULARLY FLOODED) SALTING
(— SURROUNDED BY WASTE) HOPE
(— UNIT) URE KIPUKA MECATE MORGEN MANZANA VIRGATE
(ALLUVIAL —) BATTURE
(ANCESTRAL —) ETHEL
(ARABLE —) LEA LEY LAINE

(ARID —) DESERT STEPPE
(BOTTOM —) SLASH CALLOW STRATH
(CHURCH —) GLEBE TERMON
(CHURCH —S) CROSS
(CLEAR —) BUSHHOG
(CLEARED —) ASSART
(COMMON —) EJIDO EXIDO STRAY
(CONTINENTAL —) MAIN
(CULTIVATED —) FARM ARADA TILTH CULTURE FEERING WAINAGE LABORAGE METAIRIE
(ENCLOSED —) CLOSE INTAKE
(FREEHOLD —) MULK
(GRAVELLY —) GEEST GRAVES
(GRAZING —) GRASS HIRSEL HIRSLE FEEDING
(HEATHY —) ROSLAND
(HERITABLE —) ODAL UDAL
(IMAGINARY —) FAERIE COCKAYNE LILLIPUT
(LEASED —) TACK
(LONG STRIP OF —) SLANG SPONG
(LOW —) BOG FEN GALL INKS CARSE BOTTOM
(LOW RICH —) CARSE
(NATIVE —) SOD KITH BLIGHTY BIRTHDOM HOMELAND
(OBDURATE —) TILL
(ON —) ASHORE
(PARCEL OF —) FEU LOT MOCK
(PASTURE —) HA ALP FEED HOGA WALK GRASS VELDT LEASON SCATHOLD SCATLAND
(PLATEAU —) HIGHVELD
(PLOWED —) ARADA FALLOW FURROW BREAKING
(PRIVATE —) SEVERAL
(PROMISED —) CANAAN
(PURE —) JODO SUKHAVATI
(RECLAIMED —) POLDER THWAITE
(RESOWN —) HOOKLAND
(ROUGH —) BRAKE
(SAVANNAH —S) LALANG
(SCRUBBY —) SCROG SCROGS
(SMALL PARCEL OF —) SUERTE
(SWAMPY —) WOODSERE
(TIMBER —S) STICKS
(WASTE —) HEATH
(WESTERN —) HESPERIA
(WET —) SOAK SWAMP SWANG
(WOODED —S) STICKS
(PL.) ACRES SUCKEN LAENDER NOVALIA
(PREF.) CHERSO CHOR(O)
(SUFF.) GAEA GEA

LANDBOOK TERRIER
LAND-CRAB HORSEMAN
LANDED PRAEDIAL
LANDFORM CUSP CUESTA
LANDHOLDER LAIRD COSCET TALUKDAR
LANDHOLDING BARONY
LANDING BANK VTOL YARD STAITH LANDAGE ARRIVAGE FOOTPACE HALFPACE LANDFALL
(— IN WATER) SPLASHDOWN
(ABRUPT —) PANCAKE
(BOAT —) SLIP
(CRASH —) PRANG
(SMOOTH —) GREASER
LANDING PLACE GHAT HARD SCALE PALACE ARRIVAGE
LANDING STAGE MEAR STAGE STAIR STAITH STELLING
LANDLADY WIFE DUENA PADRONA GOODWIFE
LAND-LOCK EMBAY
LANDLOCK EMBAY
LAND-LOCKED MEDITERRANEAN
LANDLORD HOST LEASER LESSOR GOODMAN PADRONE ZAMINDAR
LANDMARK COPA DOLE DOOL MARK MERE BAKEN BOUND CAIRN MARCH MEITH SENAL CIPPUS SEAMARK
LANDMASS BULGE
LANDOWNER THANE BONDER SQUIRE CACIQUE EFFENDI FREEMAN BHUMIDAR FRANKLIN ZAMINDAR
(PL.) GAMORI GEOMOROI
LANDSCAPE VIEW BOCAGE PAYSAGE SCENERY LANDSKIP
LANDSLIDE SLUMP LANDFALL LANDSLIP
LANDSLIP SLIDE
LANDSMAL MAL NYNORSK
LAND SPRING LAVANT
LANDVOGT BAILIFF
LANE GUT WAY GANG LOAN LOKE PASS RACE VEIN WIND WYND ALLEY CHASE DRANG DRONG ENTRY BOREEN VENNEL LANEWAY LOANING TWITTEN DRIFTWAY
(AIR TRAFFIC —) CORRIDOR
(FREE-THROW —) PAINT
(NARROW —) CHAR CHARE TEWER BOREEN RUELLE
(OCEAN —) SEAWAY
LANGOUSTINE PRAWN
LANGUAGE (ALSO SEE DIALECT) BAT KWA LIP CHIB CODE LEED RUNE TALE TESO LEDEN LINGO SLANG VEDIC LANGUS LINGUA SPEECH TONGUE YABBER ACCENTS CABLESE DIALECT IDIOLECT LEGALESE PARLANCE PILIPINO
(— AKIN TO SHAN) THAI
(— COMBINATION) SPANGLISH
(— ENDING) ESE
(— FAMILY) URALIC
(— IN SURINAME) SRANAN
(— THAT CONDEMNS) ABUSE
(— VARIETY) BASILECT
(ARTIFICIAL —) RO IDO NEO ARULO NOVIAL VOLAPUK ESPERANTO
(BANTU —) TSWANA KIRUNDI UMBUNDU TSHILUBA
(BIBLICAL —) ARAMAIC
(COMPUTER —) ADA BAL RPG ALGOL BASIC COBOL PROLOG SNOBOL FORTRAN
(ENGLISH WITH YIDDISH —) YINGLISH
(FIGURATIVE —) IMAGERY
(FLORID —) SILLABUB
(FOOLISH —) STUFF FLUMMERY
(FOUL —) SMUT ORDURE
(GYPSY —) CALO
(IMPUDENT —) SNASH
(INCOMPREHENSIBLE —) CHOCTAW
(INDO-ARYAN —) SINHALA
(INTERNATIONAL —) ANGLIC
(KIND OF —) MACHINE
(LATIN —) GRAMMAR HUMANITY
(NONSENSICAL —) BANTER
(OBSCENE —) BAWDY BAWDRY
(OF — OR BEHAVIOR) ETIC
(OF — STRUCTURE) EMIC
(OF A —) EMIC
(ORDINARY —) PROSE
(OVERPRETENTIOUS —) BOMBAST
(PERT —) SAUCE
(PIDGIN —) SABIR CAVITENO FANAKALO
(PLAIN —) CLEAR
(PROPAGANDISTIC —) NEWSPEAK
(SECRET —) ARGOT
(SHOWY —) FLUBDUB
(SIGN —) ASL AMESIAN
(SLEAZY —) SMARM
(SPECIFIC —) GA GE HO MO VU AIS AKA ATA EDO EFE EPE EVE EWE FAN FON FOX FUL GEG HET ICA IJO ILA KAI KAU KOL KOT KRU KUI LAB LAI LAZ MON MRU SIA TWI UDI YAO ZIA AFAR AGAO AGAU AGNI AHOM AINU AKAN AKIM ALUR AMBO ANDI ANTA ARUA AVAR BARI BEJA BIAK BODO BONI BORA BUBE BUGI BULU CARA CHAM CHIN CHOL CHUJ COOS CORA COTO CREE CROW CUNA DENE DOBU DYAK EFIK EKOI ERIE EYAK FANG FIJI FULA FUNG GARO GEEZ GHEG GOLA GOLD HARE HEHE HOPI HOVA HULA HUPA IBAN IDJO IJAW IXIL KADU KAFA KAMI KAVI KAWI KELE KOCH KOMI KONO KOTA KUKI KURI LAHU LAKH LAPP LASI LATI LAZI LESU LETT LUBA MANX MAYA MOLE MORO NAGA NAMA NIAS NIUE NUBA NUPE OGOR PALA PALI PEGU PEUL PUME RAMA SAHO SERB SERI SGAW SHAN SIUS SORB SULU SUMO SUMU SUSU TAAL TIAM TIBU TINO TODA TSHI TUPI TUPY VEPS VOTE XOSA ZULU ALEUT ALSEA ARAUA AUETO AZTEC BAJAU BALTI BANTU BASSA BATAK BATTA BAURE BEMBA BHILI BICOL BILIN BONNY CAMPA CARIB CAYUA CHANE CHIMU CHOCO CHOPE COFAN COIBA COMAN CUEVA CUMAN CUNZA CZECH DAFLA DAYAK DIERI DINKA DUALA DUTCH DYULA EMPEO FANTI FINGO FUNJI GAFAT GALLA GANDA GETAN GETIC GOLDI GONDI GREBO GREEK GUAMO GUATO GURMA GYPSY HABAB HAIDA HAIKH HATSA HAUSA HINDI HUABI HUARI HURON HUSKY HYLAM IGALA ILOKO IRAYA IRISH JAKUN JATKI JUANG JUTIC KABYL KAMBA KAMIA KANDH KAREN KAROK KHASI KHMER KHOND KHUZI KIOWA KISSI KIWAI KOINE KOLIS KONDE KONGO KORKU KORWA KOTAR KUMUK KUMYK KUSAN KWOMA LAMBA LAMUT LANGO LATIN LENCA LENDU LHOKE LHOTA LIMBA LIMBU LUIAN LUNDA MAGHI MAHRA MAHRI MALAY MALTO MAORI MAZUR MBUBA MEDIC MENDI MIKIR MODOC MOSSI MUONG MURMI MURUT NAHUA NOGAI NORSE NYORO ORAON ORIYA OROMO OSAGE OSCAN PALAU PAMIR PELEW PEUHL PLATT PUNIC RONGA SAKAI SAMAL SANTO SAXON SCOTS SERER SHILH SHINA SHONA SICEL SIKEL SLAVE SOTHO SOYOT SUOMI SWAZI TAINO TAMIL TELEI TONGA TURKI UDISH UIGUR URIYA UZBEK VOGUL WAYAO WELSH WOLOF YAKUT YUNCA ZERMA ABIPON ABKHAS ACAWAI ACHOLI ADIGHE ADZHAR AFGHAN AHTENA ALTAIC ANDAKI ANDHRA ANDOKE ANGAMI APACHE APANTO APIACA ARABIC ARANDA ARAONA ARAWAK ARUNTA ATAROI AVANTI AYMARA BAGOBO BAHASA BAITSI BAKELE BANIVA BASQUE BASUTO BEAVER BHOTIA BHUMIJ BIHARI BILAAN BILOXI BOHUNK BONTOC BORORO BRAHUI BRETON BRIBRI BUKAUA BULGAR BURIAT CAGABA CANITA CARAJA CARIAN CARIRI CAUQUI CAVINA CAYAPA CAYUGA CAYUSE CEBUAN CHAGGA CHAIMA CHANGO CHOCHO CHOKWE COCAMA CONIBO COPTIC CREOLE DAKOTA DANISH DOGRIB DYERMA ESKIMO EUDEVE FRENCH FULANI FULNIO FUTUNA GADDAN GALCHA GALIBI GATHIC GENTOO GERMAN GILAKI GILIAK GILYAK GOTHIC GUAIMI GUETAR GUINAU GULLAH GURIAN HAINAN HANTIK HARARI HATTIC HEBREW HERERO HIBITO IBANAG IBIBIO IFUGAO IGNERI IGOROT INDIAN INDOIS INNUIT INUPIK ISINAI ISLETA IVATAN KABARD KACHIN KAFFIR KAIBAL KALMUK KAMASS KANAKA KANURI KATIRI KEKCHI KHALKA KHAMTI KHARIA KHOWAR KIKUYU KILIWA KODAGA KODAGU KOIARI KOIBAL KOLAMI KOREAN KORYAK KOTIAK KPELLE KUNAMA KURNAI KURUKH KYURIN LADINO LAGUNA LAHNDA LAHULI LENAPE LEPCHA LIBYAN LIUKIU LIVIAN LUSHAI LUVIAN LUWIAN LYCIAN LYDIAN MAGAHI MAGYAR MANCHU MANOBO MBONDO MBUNDA MEDIAN MEGREL MICMAC MINOAN MISHMI MISIMA MOHAWK MONTES MUYSCA MYSIAN NEPALI NEWARI NINGPO NOOTKA NUBIAN NYANJA OJIBWA ONEIDA OORIVA OSTIAK OTOMAC OVAMPO PAHARI PAIUTE PALAIC PAPAGO PAPUAN PASHTO PAZAND POLISH PUSHTO PUSHTU RASHTI REJANG ROMANY SAFINE SAKIAN SALISH SAMOAN SANGIL SANGIR SARCEE SASSAK SAVARA SEDANG SEKANI SELKUP SELUNG SEMANG SENECA SENUFO SESUTO SHARRA SHASTA SILETZ SINDHI SLOVAK SOMALI SONRAI SUBIYA SURHAI SUSIAN TARTAR TAVGHI TELEGU TELEUT TETTUM THONGA TIPURA TUNGUS VANNIC VOTYAK YANKEE YARURA YORUBA ZAREMA ABENAKI ACHAGUA AEQUIAN AKWAALA AKWAPIM ALABAMA ALTAIAN AMANAYE AMHARIC

AMORITE AMUESHA APINAYE ARAMAIC ARAPAHO ARAUCAN ARECUNA ARGOBBA ARICARA ARMORIC ASHANTI ASURINI ATACAMA ATAKAPA AUSTRAL AVESTAN AXUMITE BAGHELI BAGIRMI BAINING BAKONGO BALANTE BALUCHI BAMBARA BANGALA BANNACK BASHKIR BENGALI BEOTHUK BERBERI BHOTIYA BHUTANI BOSNIAN BRITISH BULANDA BUNDELI BUNYORO BURMESE BUSHMAN CALIANA CALINGA CARRIER CASHIBO CATALAN CATAWBA CAWAHIB CHACOBO CHARRUA CHATINO CHEBERO CHECHEN CHIBCHA CHIMILA CHINOOK CHIRINO CHIWERE CHONTAL CHOROTI CHUKCHI CHUMASH CHUROYA CHUVASH CIBONEY CIMBRIC CLALLAM COCHIMI CORNISH COTONAM COWLITZ CYMRAEG DAGBANE DAGOMBA DANAKIL DANKALI DARGHIN DEUTSCH DHEGIHA DRAVIDA ENGLISH ESCUARA ESSELEN EUSKERA FINNISH FLEMISH FOOCHOW FRIESIC FRISIAN GAULISH GOAJIRO GUAHIBO GUARANI GUAYAKI GURUNSI GYARUNG HAITIAN HANUNOC HIDATSA HITTITE HUASTEC HUCHNOM HUICHOL HURRIAN IBERIAN ILOKANO ILONGOT INGALIK IPURINA ITALIAN ITELMES ITONAMA JACUNDA JAGATAI KAKHYEN KALINGA KALMUCK KAMASIN KANAUJI KANNADA KASHUBE KASSITE KIKONGO KIPCHAK KIRANTI KIRGHIZ KIRUNDI KLAMATH KOASATI KONKANI KOYUKON KUBACHI KULAMAN KURDISH KUTCHIN KUTENAI LAMPONG LATVIAN LESGHIN LINGALA LOATUKO LUGANDA MAGADHI MAHICAN MALINKE MALTESE MAPUCHE MARATHI MASKOKI MERCIAN MEXICAN MINAEAN MINGREL MISKITO MITANNI MOABITE MOCHICA MONUMBO MORATTY MORISCO NAHUATL NICOBAR OJIBWAY OSMANLI OSSETIC PAHLAVI PALAUNG PANJABI PARBATE PERMIAK PERMIAN PERSIAN PICTISH PRAKRIT PUNJABI PUQUINA QUECHUA QUERCHI SABAEAN SALINAN SAMBALI SAMNANI SAMNITE SAMOYED SANDAWE SANTALI SANTANA SEMITIC SERBIAN SHAWANO SHAWNEE SHILLUH SHIPIBO SHUSWAP SIAMESE SIRIONO SIUSLAW SOGDIAN SONGHAI SONGISH SORBIAN SPANIOL SPANISH STIKINE SUBANUN SVANISH SWAHILI SWEDISH TAGALOG TIBETAN TUAMOTU TURKISH UMBRIAN UMBUNDU VISAYAN WALLOON WENDISH YENISEI YIDDISH ZABERMA ZONGORA ABANEEME ACHINESE ACHUMAWI AKKADIAN AKSUMITE ALACALUF ALBANIAN ALFURESE AMAHUACA AMERICAN AMMONITE ANGOLESE ANNAMESE ANZANIAN APALACHI ARMENIAN ASSAMESE ASSYRIAN ATJINESE AWISHIRA BACTRIAN BALINESE BARBACOA BECHUANA BHOJPURI BISCAYAN BOSNISCH BOTOCUDO CAHUILLA CAINGANG CANARESE CANOEIRO CAQUETIO CARELIAN CARIJONA CAYUBABA CHALDEAN CHAMORRO CHEHALIS CHEMAKUM CHEYENNE CHINGPAW CHIQUITO CHITRALI COCONUCA COLUMBIA COMANCHE CORAVECA CROATIAN CUSTENAU DELAWARE DIEGUENO EGYPTIAN ELAMITIC ETHIOPIC ETRUSCAN FALISBAN FORMOSAN FRANKISH FULFULDE GALICIAN GALLEGAN GEORGIAN GERMANIC GORKHALI GUAICURU GUJARATI HADENDOA HAWAIIAN HITCHITI ILLINOIS ILLYRIAN IROQUOIS JAPANESE JAVANESE KANARESE KANAWARI KANKANAI KASHMIRI KASUBIAN KERMANJI KIMBUNDU KOLARIAN LANDSMAL LANUVIAN LIGURIAN LIHYANIC LILLOOET LIVONIAN LUSATIAN MADURESE MAHRATTI MAKASSAR MALAGASY MANDINGO MARSHALL MASOVIAN MAYATHAN MAZOVIAN MONGOLIC MUSKOGEE NUMIDIAN NYAMWEZI ONONDAGA OSSETIAN PAMPANGO PHRYGIAN PILIPINO POLABIAN PORTUGAL PRUSSIAN RABBINIC ROMANIAN SABELLIC SANSKRIT SAWAIORI SCOTTISH SCYTHIAN SEBUNDOY SEECHELT SHAMBALA SHIRIANA SHOSHONE SICILIAN SKIPETAR SLAVONIC SOUTHRON SQUAMISH SUBARIAN SUBTIABA SUMATRAN SUMERIAN TAHITIAN TALMUDIC TAMASHEK THRACIAN TURCOMAN VENETIAN VOLSCIAN WOGULIAN YUGOSLAV YUKAGHIR CANAANITE MONGOLIAN
(STRONG —) FRENCH
(SWAHILI —) KISWAHILI
(UNCLEAN —) SEWERAGE
(UNIVERSAL —) PASILALY
(WELSH —) CYMRAEG
(PL.) BALTIC FINNIC MAHORI SEMITIC SUDANIC ILLYRIAN
(PREF.) GLOSS(O) GLOTT(I)(O) KI
(SUFF.) ESE GLOT

LANGUE D'OC LEMOSI LIMOSI

LANGUET LANGUID LANGUAGE

LANGUID WAN LANK DOWIE FAINT DREAMY FEEBLE SICKLY SUPINE TORPID CARELESS FLAGGING HEEDLESS INDOLENT LISTLESS SLUGGISH

LANGUISH DIE FADE FALL FLAG PINE WILT DROOP DWINE FAINT QUAIL SWOON SICKEN WITHER DECLINE

LANGUISHING FADE SICK LANGUID LOVESICK

LANGUOR KEF KIF BLAHS ENNUI MALAISE DEBILITY LASSITUDE

LANGUR DOUC MAHA LOTONG LUTONG SIMPAI WANDEROO

LANK LEAN THIN GAUNT LANKY SLANK MEAGER MEAGRE SCRANKY SLUNKEN

LANKY LEAN RENKY SLINK GANGLY GANGLING

LANOLIN LANUM DEGRAS

LANSEH DUKU LANSA LANZON

LANTANA OREGANO

LANTERN (ALSO SEE LAMP) BUAT BOUET BOWET CROWN DARKY LIGHT CUPOLA LOUVER PHAROS SCONCE THOLUS CIMBORIO LANTHORN LUMINARIA
(— ON ROOF) FEMEREIL
(DARK —) DARKY ABSCONCE ABSCONSA
(ELEVATED —) PHAROS
(OPTICAL —) EPISCOPE

LANTERN FISH INIOME

LANTERN FLOUNDER MEGRIM

LANTERN FLY FULGORID

LANTERN PINION RUNDLE TRUNDLE

LANYARD CORD WAPP GILGUY LANIARD BACKROPE

LAODAMIA (BROTHER OF —) ISANDER HIPPOLOCHUS
(FATHER OF —) ACASTUS BELLEROPHON
(HUSBAND OF —) PROTESILAUS
(MOTHER OF —) HIPPOLYTE
(SLAYER OF —) ARTEMIS
(SON OF —) SARPEDON

LAODICE (FATHER OF —) PRIAM
(HUSBAND OF —) HELICAON
(MOTHER OF —) HECUBA

LAOIGHIS LEIX

LAOMEDON (DAUGHTER OF —) HESIONE
(FATHER OF —) ILUS
(MOTHER OF —) EURYDICE
(SON OF —) PRIAM CLYTIUS

LAOS
CAPITAL: VIENTIANE
COIN: KIP
MEASURE: BAK
MOUNTAIN: BIA LAI LOI SAN COPI KHAT ATWAT KHOUNG TIUBIA
PEOPLE: LU KHA LAO MEO YAO THAI
RIVER: NOI DONE KHONG MEKONG NAMHOU SEBANG
TOWN: NAPE PAKSE XIENG PAKLAY THAKHEK SAVANNAKHET LUANGPRABANG
WATERFALL: MEKONG

LAP LEP LIP BARM FOLD GORE LICK SLAP SLOD SOSS SUCK WASH WELT SKIVE LAPPER LAPPET LICKUP SHOVEL INTERLAP
(— IN STEEL) SPILL
(— OF STRAKES) LAND
(KIND OF —) PACE
(LOSE A —) RISE ARISE STAND

LAPACHOL TECOMIN

LAPBOARD PANEL

LAPDOG MESSAN MESSET SHOUGH

LAPEL LAPPET REVERE REVERS

LAPIDARY STONER GEMMARY LAPIDIST

LAPIDOTH (WIFE OF —) DEBORAH

LAPILLUS RAPILLO
(PL.) CINDER

LAPIS LAZULI AZURE

LAP-JOINTED CLINCH

LAPP LAPPISH LAPPONIC

LAPPED FOLIATED

LAPPET LAP PAN BARBE FANON LABEL CORNET INFULA PINNER
(PREF.) LACINI

LAPSE DROP FADE FALL HALT SLIP ERROR FAULT FOLLY SPACE TRACT EFFLUX HIATUS LAPSUS DELAPSE ESCHEAT FAILURE PASSAGE PROCESS RELAPSE RESOLVE SLIDING ABEYANCE CADUCITY
(— INTO WRONGDOING) STUMBLE
(— OF MEMORY) BLACKOUT
(MENTAL —) ABERRATION
(PL.) LACHES

LAPSED CADUCOUS

LAPSING CADUCOUS

LAPSTRAKE CLINCH

LAPTOP PORTABLE

LAPWING WEEP WYPE PEWIT PEEWEE PEEWIT PLOVER TIRWIT HORNPIE PEEWEEP PIEWIPE TEUCHIT FLOPWING PEESWEEP TEEWHAAP TERUTERU

LARBOARD PORT BABURD

LARCENY THEFT FELONY ROBBERY BURGLARY STEALAGE

LARCH ALERCE LARICK SPRUCE JUNIPER EPINETTE TAMARACK

LARD MORT SAIM ADEPS DAUBE ENARM FLARE FLECK FLICK AXUNGE ENLARD INLARD NEUTRAL SAINDOUX

LARDED PIQUE CADUCE CADUCOUS

LARDER CAVE PANTRY SPENCE BUTTERY LARDINER

LARGE BIG BULL DEEP FEAT GOOD LONG MAIN ROOM TALL AMPLE BULKY BURLY GRAND GREAT GROSS HUSKY JOLLY LARGY MACRO MAXIM RENKY ROUND SMART SPACY WALLY GAWSIE GOODLY HEROIC MAXIMA STRONG TRABAL BOWERLY CAPITAL COPIOUS FAIRISH FEARFUL HEALTHY HULKING LASKING LIBERAL MASSIVE OUTSIZE SIZABLE BOUNCING CHOPPING OUTSIZED PLUMPING SENSIBLE SWACKING
(— AND HOLLOW) CAVAL
(— AND ROUND) SIDE
(— IN DIAMETER) STOUT
(APPALLINGLY —) HIDEOUS
(EXTRA —) MAXI
(EXTREMELY —) GIANT DECUMAN GIGANTIC
(FAIRLY —) SMART
(INDEFINITELY —) NTH INFINITE
(MODERATELY —) FAIR TIDY PRETTY
(UNUSUALLY —) HEAVY SKELPIN SKELPING
(VERY —) HUGE JUMBO ROYAL BOXCAR BUMPER INGENT NATION GOLIATH INTENSE BEHEMOTH SLAPPING SPANKING SWINGING WHACKING HUMONGOUS
(PREF.) MACR(O) MEGA MEGAL(O)
(HOW —) QUANTI

LARGE-FOOTED MEGAPOD
LARGE-FRAMED ROOMY
LARGE-LETTERED UNCIAL
LARGELY BIG HARD BIGLY
LARGENESS BULK MICKLE BREADTH FREEDOM GIANTISM LARGEOUR
LARGE-SCALE EPIC
LARGEST BEST MAXIMUS
LARIA BRUCHUS
LARIAT ROPE LASSO NOOSE RIATA CABESTRO
LARK GAME ROMP ANTIC PRANK FROLIC PEEWEE SCHEME GAMMOCK LAVROCK LAYROCK SKYLARK CALANDER LAVEROCK
LARKA KOLS HO
LARKSPUR LOCOWEED
LARNITE BELITE
LARRIGAN PAC
LARRIKIN NUT ROWDY HOODLUM
LARVA BOT BLOW BOTT CRAB GRUB HUHU SLUG TURK WOLF WORM ALIMA ASCON BARDY BRUKE ERUCA LEECH OTTER REDIA SYCON CORBIE COSSID DRAGON EPHYRA GRUGRU HOPPER LEPTUS LEUCON LOOPER MAGGOT MEASLE PEDLAR TORCEL WABBLE WORMIL WOUBIT ATROCHA BUDWORM CADELLE CREEPER DIPORPA FIGWORM FLYBLOW GORDIAN HYDATID HYPOPUS PEDDLER PLANULA PLUTEUS PREPUPA VELIGER WIGGLER ACTINULA ANTIZOEA ARMYWORM BOLLWORM BOMBYCID BOOKWORM CASEWORM CERCARIA COENURUS CYRTOPIA DEUTOVUM DROPWORM EPHYRULA FIREWORM FURCILIA GEOMETER GILTTAIL GLOWWORM GNATWORM LEAFTIER LEAFWORM MEALWORM MUCKWORM NAUPLIUS PILIDIUM ROOTWORM SCYPHULA SEMIPUPA SILKWORM SKINWORM SPANWORM SPRAWLER STAGWORM SUBIMAGO TORNARIA VERMICLE WASPLING WIREWORM WOODGRUB WOODWORM
LARVACEA ATREMATA COPELATA
LARVAL NEPIONIC
LARYNGITIS CROUP
LARYNX
(PREF.) LARYNG(O)
LASCIVIOUS LEWD NICE SALT HORNY RANDY LUBRIC WANTON BLISSOM FLESHLY GOATISH PAPHIAN PRURIENT SALACIOUS
LASCIVIOUSNESS LECHERY ASELGEIA LUXURITY LUBRICITY
LASERWORT SILPHIUM
LASH CUT BEAT FIRK FLOG JERK LACE WELT WHIP WIRE YERK LEASE LEASH SCORE SKEEG SLASH THONG TRICE WHALE CANVAS CILIUM LAINER LAUNCH STRIPE SWINGE SWITCH FLYFLAP KURBASH SCOURGE
(— BOWSPRIT) GAMMON
(— OUT) THRASH
(— TOGETHER) RACK
LASHER THONGMAN
LASHING YARK YERK GAMMON LISTING MOUSING SEIZING SLATING FRAPPING
(PL.) OODLES OODLINS SLITHERS
LASS TIB GILL PRIM TRULL DAMSEL KUMMER LASSIE DAMOZEL LASSIKY TENDREL MUCHACHA
(COUNTRY —) JENNY
LASSITUDE BLAHS COPOS STUPOR LANGUOR MALAISE LETHARGY
LASSO LASH LAZO ROPE RIATA LARIAT CABESTRO
LAST ABY LAG DURE GOON HOLD KEEP RIDE SAVE ABIDE FINAL SERVE ABEGGE ENDURE LATEST LATTER REMAIN ULTIMA UTMOST DARREIN DERNIER EXTREME PERDURE SUPREME CONTINUE EVENTUAL HINDMOST LATEMOST REARMOST TERMINAL ULTIMATE AFTERMOST
(— BUT ONE) PENULT
(— OUT) SPIN STAY
(AT —) FINALLY
(THE —) OMEGA
(PREF.) ESCHATO POSTREMO ULTIMO
LAST DAYS OF POMPEII (AUTHOR OF —) BULWER LYTTON
(CHARACTER IN —) IONE BURBO JULIA NYDIA DIOMED ARBACES CLODIUS GLAUCUS SALLUST APAECIDES
LASTING FIXED LASTY DURANT DURING STABLE ABIDING DURABLE DUREFUL CONSTANT ENDURING LIVELONG REMANENT STANDING
(— FOR LONG PERIOD) AEONIC AEONIAL
(— FOR ONE DAY) DIARY DIURNAL
LASTINGNESS STAY DURATION
LAST OF THE MOHICANS
(AUTHOR OF —) COOPER
(CHARACTER IN —) CORA WEBB ALICE DAVID GAMUT MAGUA MUNRO NATTY UNCAS BUMPPO DUNCAN HAWKEYE HEYWARD MONTCALM CHINGACHGOOK
LAST PURITAN (AUTHOR OF —) SANTAYANA
(CHARACTER IN —) JIM IRMA ROSE ALDEN BOBBY EDITH MARIO PETER WEYER BOWLER OLIVER DARNLEY HARRIET SCHLOTE BUMSTEAD
LAST SUPPER CENA COENA MAUNDY
LAT STAMBHA
LATCH FLY PIN HASP RISP SHUT CATCH CHAIR CLICK CLINK SNECK SNICK KEEPER CLICKET
LATCHET DAG TAB SANDAL LANGUET
LATCHING LASKET
LATCHKEY CLICKET PASSKEY
LATE LAG NEW DEEP RIPE SLOW TARDY RECENT TARDIVE UMWHILE ADVANCED LATEWARD SOMETIME UMQUHILE
(— COMER) CUNCTATOR
(— IN DEVELOPING) SEROTINOUS
LATE GEORGE APLEY (AUTHOR OF —) MARQUAND
(CHARACTER IN —) JOHN MARY APLEY AMELIA GEORGE ELEANOR HORATIO MONAHAN OREILLY WILLIAM WILLING BOSWORTH PRENTISS CATHARINE
LATELY LATE ALATE NEWLY
LA TENE MARNEAN
LATENT HIDDEN MASKED ABEYANT DORMANT PASSIVE LATITANT QUIESCENT
(PREF.) CRYPT(O) KRYPT(O)
LATER POI SIN ANON POST SYNE AFTER ELDER NEWER BEHIND FUTURE LATTER PUISNE ANOTHER INFERIOR UMQUHILE
(PREF.) HYSTERO INFRA META POST
LATERAL SIDE
(PREF.) PLEUR(O)
LATERALLY SIDELONG
LATERITE CABOOK KUNKUR
LATEST LAST LATTER FARTHEST FURTHEST
LATEX GUTTA SORVA ANTIAR SENAMBY
LATH BAT LAG SLAT SPAIL SPALE SPELL SWALE REEPER SPLENT SPLINT STOOTH LATHING FOREPOLE LATHWORK
LATHE LAY SLEY TURN LAITH THROW BEATER WISKET
(— FOR CYLINDERS) BROAD
(— OF LOOM) LAY
(TURNING —) THROW
(WATCHMAKER'S —) TURN TURNS MANDREL
LATHER FOAM SUDS FROTH FREATH SAPPLES
LATHERED SOAPY
LATIGO STRAP
LATIN ROMAN HISPERIC LATINITY SCATTERMOUCH
(— COMPOSITION) VULGUS
LATIN-AMERICAN LATIN LADINO LATINO HISPANIC
LATINUS (DAUGHTER OF —) LAVINIA
(FATHER OF —) FAUNUS
(SON-IN-LAW OF —) AENEAS
(WIFE OF —) AMATA
LATITUDE SCOPE SPACE WIDTH EXTENT HEIGHT
(HELIOCENTRIC —) LIMIT
LATONA (DAUGHTER OF —) DIANA
(FATHER OF —) COEUS
(MOTHER OF —) PHOEBE
(SON OF —) APOLLO
LATRIA ADORATION
LATRINE BOG REAR PRIVY TOILET BOGGARD
LATTER LAST FINAL RECENT SECOND PRESENT
(— PORTION) AUTUMN
LATTICE MESA GRATE HERSE TWINE GRILLE PINJRA UMBREL GRATING CANCELLI
(— OF POINTS) SATIN
(MOVING —) APRON
(PREF.) CLATHR
LATTICED CLATHRATE
LATTICE PLANT LACELEAF
LATTICEWORK ARBOR GRATE GRATING ESPALIER TUKUTUKU

LATVIA
CAPITAL: RIGA
COIN: LAT RUBLIS KAPEIKA SANTIMS
MEASURE: STOF KANNE STOFF STOOF VERST ARSHIN KULMET SAGENE VERCHOC KROUCHKA POURVETE
NAME: LATVIJA LETTLAND LETTONIE
NATIVE: LETT
PEOPLE: LETT
RIVER: AA OGRE DVINA GAUJA VENTA SALACA LIELUPE
TOWN: CESIS LIBAU DVINSK LIBAVA TUKUMS JELGAVA LIEPAJA REZEKNE DUNABURG VALMIERA DAUGAVPILS
WEIGHT: LIESPFUND

LAUAN KALUNTI
LAUD EXTOL PRAISE ADVANCE APPLAUD COMMEND GLORIFY MAGNIFY EMBLAZON EULOGIZE MACARIZE
LAUDATION PUFF EULOGY PRAISE PANEGYRIC
LAUDATORY SNEER EPENETIC PRAISING
LAUDER ESTEE
LAUGH YAK YUK GAFF YOCK YUCK CHUCK FLEER LEUGH RISUS ARRIDE NICKER TITTER CHORTLE GRIZZLE SNICKER SNIGGER SNIRTLE TWITTER LAUGHTER
(— CONTEMPTUOUSLY) SNORT DERIDE
(— GLEEFULLY) CHECKLE
(— HYSTERICALLY) CHECKLE
(— IN AFFECTED MANNER) GIGGLE
(— IN COARSE MANNER) FLEER GUFFAW
(— LIKE HEN) CACKLE
(— LOUDLY) GAFF GUFFAW
(— MOCKINGLY) FLEER
(— OUT LOUD) CRACKUP
(— QUIETLY) GULE SMUDGE CHUCKLE SNIRTLE
(BELLY —) BOFF BOFFOLA
(LOUD —) GAUSTER
LAUGHABLE ODD RICH COMIC DROLL FUNNY MERRY QUEER WITTY AMUSING COMICAL RISIBLE STRANGE WAGGISH FARCICAL HUMOROUS LAUGHING PLEASANT SPORTIVE RIDICULOUS
LAUGHING RIANT RIDENT IRRISION MIRTHFUL
(— MATTER) MOWS
LAUGHING GULL PEWIT
LAUGHING JACKASS KOOKABURRA
LAUGHING OWL WEKAU WHEKAU
LAUGHINGSTOCK GUY BUTT JEST JOKE SONG SPORT DERISION RIDICULE
LAUGHTER JOKE MIRTH RISUS SNIRT CACKLE LAWTER SPLEEN HILARITY RISIBILITY
(HYSTERICAL —) CACHINNATION

(**VULGAR —**) HAWHAW
(PREF.) GELOTO
LAUNCE LANT LANCE SMELT AMMODYTE SANDLING
LAUNCH PUT BURST DRIVE LANCE ELANCE STRIKE BAPTIZE PINNACE PROMOTE STEAMER TELSTAR VIBRATE CATAPULT
(**— HOSTILELY**) DIRECT
LAUNCHER (**ROCKET —**) BAZOOKA
LAUNCHING BLASTOFF
LAUNDER TYE WASH TRUNK SLUICE STRAKE LAUNDRY
LAUNDRESS TRILBY LAVENDER
LAUNDRY WASH BAGWASH LAVATORY WASHATERIA WASHETERIA
(**PUBLIC —**) STEAMIE
LAUREL BAY IVY LAURY UNITE WICKY DAPHNE KALMIA MALLET MYRTLE CAJEPUT IVYWOOD WOEVINE BREWSTER CALFKILL
(**GROUND —**) ARBUTUS
LAUREL OAK ACAJOU
LAURIC PICHURIC
LAURUSTINE VIBURNUM
LAUSUS (**FATHER OF —**) NUMITOR MEZENTIUS
(**SISTER OF —**) ILIA
(**SLAYER OF —**) AMULIUS
LAUTVERSCHIEBUNG SHIFT
LAVA AA ASHES SPINE COULEE LATITE SCORIA VERITE FAVILLA LAPILLO MALPAIS ASPERITE ORENDITE PAHOEHOE
(**MUD —**) MOYA LAHAR
(**SCORIACEOUS —**) AA SLAG
(**SLAGGY —**) SCORIA
LAVABO LAVATORY
LAVAGE LAVATION LAVEMENT
LAVALAVA SULU
LAVAN KALUNTI
LAVATORY LOO BASIN CHALET CLOSET LAVABO OFFICE LATRINE LAVETTE WASHROOM CLOAKROOM
LAVE LIP WASH BATHE SPLASH
LAVENDER BEHN ASPIC BEHEN SPICK SPIKE INKROOT LAVANDIN STICHADO
LAVENGRO (**AUTHOR OF —**) BORROW
(**CHARACTER IN —**) JOHN MOLL ARDRY HERNE PETER ISOPEL JASPER BERNERS FRANCIS LEONORA TAGGART LAVENGRO SAPENGRO SLINGSBY WILLIAMS WINIFRED PETULENGRO
LAVER SION SLAKE SLOKE LOUTER PHIALE AMANORI CISTERN CANTHARUS
LAVINIA (**FATHER OF —**) LATINUS
(**HUSBAND OF —**) AENEAS
(**MOTHER OF —**) AMATA
LAVISH FREE LASH LUSH FLUSH LARGE SPEND SPORT WASTE COSTLY WANTON COPIOUS OPULENT PROFUSE GENEROUS LUCULLAN PRODIGAL SQUANDER WASTEFUL REDUNDANT MUNIFICENT
LAVISHNESS WASTE FINERY LAVISH
LAW ACT FAS IUS JUS LAY LEX ADAT DOOM JURE RULE CANON DROIT NOMOS TORAH BYELAW BYRLAW DECREE DHARMA EQUITY BROCARD DANELAW DERECHO HALACHA HALAKAH JUSTICE PRECEPT SETNESS STATUTE JUDGMENT JUDICIAL ROGATION STATEWAY TANISTRY ORDINANCE
(**—S OF MANU**) SUTRA SUTTA
(**— VIOLATOR**) SCOFFLAW
(**BEDOUIN —**) THAR
(**DIETARY —S**) KASHRUTH
(**ELEMENTARY —**) BROCARD
(**EQUAL —**) ISONOMY
(**ISLAMIC —**) ADA BAI ADAT SHERI SHARIA SHERIAT
(**JEWISH —**) MISHNA MISHNAH
(**KIND OF —**) LEASH
(**MARRIAGE —**) LEVIRATE
(**MOSAIC —**) TORAH
(**OPPOSING —**) ANTINOMY
(**PROPOSED —**) BILL
(**UNIVERSAL —**) HEAVEN
(PL.) LORS
(PREF.) JURIS LEGI LEGO NOM(O) THESMO
(SUFF.) LEGE NOMY
LAW-ABIDING LAWFUL
LAWBREAKER FELON HOUGHER
LAWFUL DUE JUST LEAL TRUE VERY LEGAL LEGIT LICIT LOYAL VALID KINDLY LEEFUL ENNOMIC LEESOME INNOCENT LIEFSOME RIGHTFUL
LAWGIVER MINOS MOSES SOLON LAWYER LAWMAKER
LAWLESS LEWD UNRULY ILLEGAL MOBBISH ANARCHIC
LAWLESSNESS ANOMY ANOMIE ANARCHY
LAWMAKER LEGIFER
LAWN ARBOR GRASS LINON SWARD UMPLE CYPRUS BATISTE QUINTIN TIFFANY
LAWSUIT LIS CASE SAKE SECTA ACTION BRABBLE
LAWYER (ALSO SEE JURIST) JET PEAT AVOUE PATCH SHARK BREHON JURIST LAWMAN LEGIST SQUIRE WRITER COUNSEL MUKHTAR TEMPLAR DEFENDER LEGISTER TRAMPLER BARRISTER MOUTHPIECE PETTIFOGGER
(**PALTRY —**) PETTIFOGGER
(**UNSCRUPULOUS —**) SHYSTER
LAX DULL FREE LASH LAZY LINK SLOW SWAG WIDE LARGE LOOSE RELAX SLACK TARDY REMISS BACKWARD INACTIVE DISSOLUTE NEGLIGENT
LAXATIVE LAX LASK CASCARA APERIENT HYDROMEL LAPACTIC RELAXANT SOLUTIVE TARAXACUM
LAXITY LASCHETY LATITUDE
LAY LIE SET CLAP LAIC LEWD SLEY SONG WAGE BIGHT CIVIL COUCH DITTY LATHE LEDGE QUIET STAKE STILL COMMON HAZARD IMPOSE IMPUTE MELODY APPEASE ASCRIBE LAYDOWN POPULAR SECULAR SIRVENTE TEMPORAL
(**— ASIDE**) DOFF DOWN DUMP SHUCK DEPOSE DIVEST DEPOSIT PIGEONHOLE
(**— AWAY**) STORE
(**— BARE**) BARE NAKE TIRL TIRVE DENUDE DETECT OPPOSE UNCOVER DENUDATE
(**— CLAIM**) ASSERT BESPEAK ARROGATE
(**— CROSSWISE**) COB
(**— DOWN**) ABDICATE PRESCRIBE
(**— EGGS**) BLOW WARP LEDGE OVIPOSIT
(**— FLAT**) SQUAT ADPRESS
(**— HOLD OF**) FANG GRIP HENT TAKE GRIPE LATCH ATHOLD ATTACH COLLAR COMPRISE
(**— IN**) EMBED
(**— IN BIGHTS**) JAG
(**— IN COIL**) FLEMISH
(**— IN PLEATS**) FOLD
(**— IT ON**) COAT
(**— LOW**) STREW STRIKE
(**— OFF**) FORE IDLE STOP
(**— OF LOOM**) BEATER
(**— ON**) APPLY INFLICT
(**— OPEN**) BREAK CHINE EXPOSE UNMASK
(**— OUT**) FRAY PLAT ARRAY RANGE SPELD SPEND BEWARE DESIGN EXTEND SPREAD STREAK STREEK CHECKER DEVELOP STRETCH CONTRIVE
(**— PRONE**) LEVEL
(**— RUBBLEWORK**) SNECK
(**— SIEGE**) INVEST
(**— SMOOTH**) EVEN
(**— SNARE FOR RABBITS**) HAY
(**— STONE**) PAVE
(**— STRAIGHT**) COMB
(**— TYPE**) CASE
(**— UP**) HEAP HIVE ADDLE HOARD HUTCH STOCK TREASURE
(**— WASTE**) PEEL WEST HARRY HAVOC HARASS RAVAGE DESTROY DESOLATE FORWASTE
LAYABOUT IDLER
LAYBOY JOGGER
LAYDOWN LAYOUT SPREAD
LAYER BED FLY HEN LAY BARK CAKE COAT DASS FACE FILM FLAP FOLD LAIR LOFT RIND SEAM SKIN WEFT ZONA CHESS COUCH COVER CRUST CUTIS FLAKE FLASH LEDGE SCALE CARPET COURSE FASCIA FILLER FOLIUM INTINE LAMINA LISSOM STREAK BLANKET COATING CUTICLE EPICARP FEATHER FLAVEDO GANGMAN INLAYER LAMELLA PACKING PHELLEM PROPAGO PROVINE STRATUM SUBCOAT SUPPORT ECTOCYST ECTOSARC ENDOCYST ENDODERM EPIBLAST EPIBLEMA EPISPORE EPITHECA INTERBED MOLLISOL PERIOPLE PERISARC SUBCRUST PERIPLAST PHELLODERM
(**— IN FUNGI**) HYMENIUM
(**— OF ATMOSPHERE**) MESOSPHERE OZONOSPHERE
(**— OF BLOOD VESSEL**) EXTIMA EXTERNA
(**— OF CELLS**) EXINE CORTEX EXTINE CAMBIUM PHELLEM TAPETUM PERICYCLE
(**— OF CLAY**) GLEY VARVE SELVAGE SELVEDGE
(**— OF CONCRETE**) RAFT
(**— OF EARTH**) SPIT
(**— OF EYE**) RETINA
(**— OF FAT**) LEAF FINISH
(**— OF FELT**) BAT BATT
(**— OF FIBER**) LAP
(**— OF FINE MATERIAL**) CUSHION
(**— OF FOREST GROWTH**) SUBSTORY OVERSTORY
(**— OF FUEL**) FIREBED
(**— OF GLASS**) CASING
(**— OF IRIS**) UVEA
(**— OF MEAT**) SPINE
(**— OF MORTAR**) SCREED
(**— OF NERVE FIBERS**) ALVEUS
(**— OF ORGANIC MATTER**) FLOOR
(**— OF PLASMA**) BUFFCOAT
(**— OF ROCK**) CAP SHELF SHELL SLATE FOLIUM SEPTUM BLISTER SKULLCAP
(**— OF ROOTS**) SOLE
(**— OF SEDIMENT**) WARP
(**— OF SHALE**) BONE
(**— OF SHEEPSKIN**) FLESHER
(**— OF SHOE HEEL**) LIFT
(**— OF SILT**) VARVE
(**— OF SKIN**) DERM DERMA EPIDERM
(**— OF SOIL**) SOLUM CALLOW CASING HARDPAN HORIZON
(**— OF STONES**) DASS DESS
(**— OF TANBARK**) HAT
(**— OF TISSUE**) BED DARTOS FASCIA SEROSA ELASTICA EPIBLEMA PERIDERM
(**— OF TOBACCO LEAVES**) HANGER
(**— OF TURF**) FLAW KERF
(**— OF WHITE MATTER**) CAPSULE
(**— OF WOOD**) CORE
(**BONY —**) LAMELLA CEMENTUM
(**BOTTOM —**) BEDDING
(**FLAT —**) BED FLAP FLAKE
(**FROZEN —**) PERMAFROST
(**GERM —**) MESODERM
(**IMPERVIOUS —**) LINING
(**OUTER —**) HUSK
(**THIN —**) SCRAPE
(**UNDERLYING —**) SUBSTRATUM
(**UPPER —**) SURFACE
(PREF.) LAMELLI LAMIN(I) PTYCH(O) STRATI
(SUFF.) CLINAL CLINE LAMIN
(**— OF SKIN**) DERMIS
(**GERM —**) BLAST(IC)(Y)
LAYERING LAP GOOTEE STOOLING
LAYMAN LAIC CLERK IDIOT DEACON SECULAR DEFENSOR EXHORTER EXOTERIC FAMILIAR STRANGER WORLDMAN
LAYOFF FURLOUGH
LAYOUT MISE DUMMY SETOUT
(**— OF CARDS**) TABLEAU
LAZARETTO SPITAL SPITTLE
LAZARUS (**SISTER OF —**) MARY MARTHA
(**SISTER OF —**) MARTHA
LAZINESS LAZE SLOTH SLOUCH OISIVITY

LAZULITE SIDERITE
LAZY ARGH IDLE LASS DOXIE DRONY FAINT INERT LINGY LUSKY RESTY SLOAN SLOTH CLUMSY LIMPSY LURDAN LUTHER ORNERY SWEERT TRAILY CLUMPST DRONISH LUSKISH PEAKISH SLIVING DROGHLIN FAINEANT FECKLESS INDOLENT LITHERLY OSCITANT SLOTHFUL SLUGGARD THOWLESS TRIFLING SHIFTLESS
LAZY EYE AMBLYOPIA
LEA LAY GRASS LAYER LAYLAND LEALAND
LEACH TAP LETCH SOFTEN
LEAD GO TEE VAN WIN BEAR DADE GIVE GROW HAVE HEAD HERD LEED SLIP TAKE TEEM WORK BLAZE BOUND BRING CARRY GREBE GUIDE MAYNE PILOT PRESA SOUND START TRAIN TREAT CONVEY DEDUCE DIRECT ESCORT INDUCE INDUCT LEADER SATURN BEGUILE CAPTAIN CONDUCE CONDUCT LEADING MARSHAL PIGTAIL PIONEER PLUMBUM PLUMMET LEADSMAN MANUDUCE MANUDUCT SQUIRREL
(— A BAND) BATON
(— AND SUPPORT) DADE
(— ASIDE) CHAR SINGLE
(— ASTRAY) ERR MANG TURN WARP BEFOOL BETRAY ENTICE WANDER WILDER DEBAUCH MISLEAD MISWEND PERVERT SOLICIT TRADUCE BEWILDER INVEIGLE MISGUIDE
(— AWAY) CHAR ABDUCT DIVERGE
(— BACK) REDUCT
(— FORCIBLY) ESCORT
(— IN CARD GAME) SNEAK WHITECHAPEL
(— IN RACE) LAP
(— IN SINGING) PRECENT
(— INTO ERROR) ABUSE DELUDE
(— MONOXIDE) MASSICOT
(— ON) TRAIL
(— PASSIVE EXISTENCE) VEGETATE
(— POISONING) PLUMBISM
(BLACK —) WAD WADD GRAPHITE
(COLOR —) PLOMB
(DEEP-SEA —) DIPSY DIPSEY
(MOCK —) BLENDE
(OVERLAPPING —) DRIP
(PLUMBING —) BLUEY
(SYMBOL FOR —) PB
(WHITE —) KREMS CERUSE
(PREF.) GALENO MOLYBD(O) PLUMB(I)(O)
(SUFF.) AGOGUE AGOGY
LEAD-COLORED WAN BLAE
LEADEN HEAVY INERT PLUMBEAN
LEADER BO BOH COB DUX HOB MIR CAST COCK DUCE DUKE HEAD HOBB JEFE NAIG NAIK OMDA SOUL TYEE CHIEF DOYEN ELDER FIRST MAHDI MOSES OMDEH PILOT SEYID TRACE ARCHON CALIPH DESPOT HEADER HONCHO RECTOR SAYYID TYCOON ACREMAN ADVISER CAPTAIN CONDUCT DEMAGOG DRUNGAR FOREMAN FUEHRER INDUCER PRIMATE ACCENTOR CAUDILLO DIRECTOR FUGLEMAN HEADSMAN HERETOGA LODESMAN PANDARUS STRATEGE AYATOLLAH PENDRAGON PROTAGONIST
(— OF ARMY) VAIVODE VOIVODE
(— OF DACOITS) BOH
(— OF FLOCK) PATRIARCH
(— OF GUISERS) SKUDLER
(— OF MINING GANG) CORPORAL
(— OF MUTINEERS) ELECTO
(— OF REVOLT) ANARCH
(BAND —) BATONEER
(CHOIR —) CANTOR PRECENTOR
(CHORUS —) CHORAGUS
(COSSACK —) ATAMAN HETMAN
(FASCIST —) RAS
(HOLY —) MAHATMA
(INTELLECTUAL —) BRAIN
(MINING —) CORPORAL
(MOB —) MOBOCRAT
(MUSLIM —) MAHDI
(POLITICAL —) SACHEM
(PRAYER —) IMAM
(RELIGIOUS —) AGA AGHA LAMA SHEIKH
(SCOUT —) AKELA SIXER
(SPIRITUAL —) GURU SADDIK GUARDIAN
(TAMMANY —) SACHEM
(SUFF.) ARCH ARCHIC ARCHY
LEADERSHIP LEAD AEGIS MANRED CONDUCT IMAMATE LEADING MANRENT CHIEFDOM GUIDANCE HEADSHIP HEGEMONY
(— BY TALENTED) MERITOCRACY
LEADING BIG BEST COCK DUCT HEAD LEAD MAIN AHEAD CHIEF FIRST BANNER PREMIER STELLAR GUIDANCE PROMINENT
(— OUTWARD) EMISSARY
(— TO NOTHING) IDLE
LEAD MONOXIDE MASSICOT
LEADSMAN SOUNDER
LEADWORK PLUMBAGE PLUMBING
LEADWORT CROWTOE PLUMBAGO
LEAF PAD BACK BARB BUYO FLAG FLAP FOIL FOLD GEAR PAGE PALM STUB BLADE BLANK FLIER FLYER FOLIO FROND GRASS GUARD LEAVE SCALE SEPAL SIGHT SPILL TEPAL BONNET CADJAN CARPEL COUPON FOLIUM FRAISE FULZIE NEEDLE PEPPER DAMIANA FOLDOUT HARNESS LEAFLET TREFOIL WITNESS PHYLLADE PHYLLOME MICROPHYLL
(— FAT) FLICK
(— FROM AXIL) BRACT
(— OF BOOK) PAGE FOLIO INSET PLATE FLYLEAF
(— OF CALYX) BARB
(— OF CORN) HUSK
(— OF COROLLA) PETAL
(— OF DOOR) VALVE
(— OF HEDDLES) GEAR
(— OF PALM) FAN OLA PAN CHIP OLLA FROND LATANIER
(— OF SPRING) BACK
(—S OF CORIANDER) CILANTRO
(BETEL —) PAN SIRIH
(BIBLE —) COSTMARY
(DEAD —) FLAG
(EXTRA —) INSERT
(HOLLOW —) PHYLLODE
(PART OF —) RIB TIP APEX BASE LOBE STEM VEIN BLADE SINUS LAMINA MARGIN MIDRIB PETIOLE LEAFSTALK
(RUDIMENTARY —) CATAPHYLL
(SPRING —) WRAPPER
(STRAWBERRY —) FRAISE
(THIN —) LAMELLA
(TOBACCO —) LUGS STRIP CUTTER WRAPPER
(WASTE GOLD —) SKEWING
(PREF.) FOLI(O) PETAL(I)(O) PHYLL(I)(O)
(SUFF.) FOLIATE FOLIOUS PETALOUS PHYLL(A)(OUS)(UM)(Y)
LEAFAGE FOLIAGE
LEAFHOPPER HOPPER JASSID THRIPS HOMOPTER
LEAFLET FLIER PINNA TRACT MAILER FOLIOLE STUFFER
(—S DROPPED FROM AIR) BUMF
(PAIR OF —S) JUGUM
(PL.) SENNA CAROBA
LEAFLIKE PHYLLINE
LEAFMOLD KOLINSKY
LEAFSTALK HAFT CHARD PETIOLE
LEAFY GREEN LEAVY FOLIATE FOLIOSE FRONDOSE
LEAGUE BOND BUND BANDY BOARD GUEUX HANSA PARTY UNION WHEEL CIRCUIT COMPACT ALLIANCE SYSTASIS COALITION
(— OF NATIONS) GENEVA
(BUSH —S) STICKS
(MINOR —) BUSHES
LEAGUED FEDERATE
LEAH (DAUGHTER OF —) DINAH
(FATHER OF —) LABAN
(HUSBAND OF —) JACOB
(SISTER OF —) RACHEL
(SON OF —) LEVI JUDAH REUBEN SIMEON ZEBULUN ISSACHAR
LEAK BLAB BLOW SEEP WEEP GEYZE SPUNK INLEAK SIGGER SPRING ZIGGER LEAKAGE MELTERS SCREEVE
(— IN ELECTRIC CIRCUIT) FAULT
LEAKAGE ESCAPE SEEPAGE
(— OF ELECTRICITY) CREEPAGE
(— OF GAS) SLIP
(— OF WIND) RUNNING
LEAKING ALEAK DRIBBLE NAILSICK
LEAKY LEAK UNTIGHT GIZZENED
LEAL FAITHFUL
LEAN BEAR BEND BONY HANG HEEL LANK PEND POOR PRIN RACY RELY REST SEEL STAY SWAY THIN TOOM EMPTY GAUNT HIELD LANKY LEANY SLANK SOUND SPARE STOOP HOLLOW MEAGER RECUMB SKINNY SPRING UPLEAN ANGULAR FATLESS HAGGARD INCLINE SCRAGGY SCRAWNY SLUNKEN STRINGY MACILENT SCRAGGED SCRANNEL
(— FOR SUPPORT) ABUT
(— FORWARD) PROCLINE
(— OVER) WHAUVE
(PREF.) CLIN(O)
LEANDER (LOVE OF —) HERO
LEANDRE (FATHER OF —) GERONTE
(LOVER OF —) LUCINDE
LEANER HOBBER
LEANING AGEE BIAS DRIFT FLAIR TREND PENCHE HANGING ACCLINAL ENCLITIC FROMWARD PROPENSE PROCLIVITY PROPENSITY
(— BACKWARD) SUPINE
(STRONG —) GENIUS PENCHANT
LEANNESS LANK POVERTY SPARENESS
LEAN-TO SHED LINTER OUTSHOT SKILLION
LEAP FLY HOP POP BEND DART DIVE FALL GIVE JUMP LOPE LOUP RAMP RISE SKIT WIND BOUND BREAK CAPER DANCE EXULT FLIER FLYER FRISK LUNGE PRIME SALTO SAULT SCOPE SCOUP SPANG STEND VAULT BOUNCE BREACH CURVET INSULT LAUNCH SPRENT SPRING SPRUNT WALLOP REBOUND SALTARY SALTATE SUBSULT BUCKJUMP LEAPFROG SPANGHEW UPSPRING
(— BACK) RESULT SPRUNT
(— FOR JOY) EXULT
(— IN DANCING) STOT
(— LIGHTLY) SKIP
(— OF HORSE) CURVET BALOTADE CAPRIOLE CROUPADE
(— OF WHALE) BREACH
(— OUT) SALLY
(— OVER) FREE OVER SKIP CLEAR HURDLE
(— UPON) ASSAIL POUNCE
(BALLET —) FISH JETE ASSEMBLE CABRIOLE FISHDIVE ELEVATION ENTRECHAT
(FENCING —) VOLT VOLTE
(FROLICSOME —) CAPER
(SKATING —) AXEL
(SUICIDAL —) BRODIE
(PL.) ALLEGRO
(PREF.) SCIRTO
LEAPING GAMBOL SPRING RAMPANT SALIENT SALTANT
LEAR (DAUGHTER OF —) REGAN
LEARCHUS (BROTHER OF —) MELICERTA
(FATHER OF —) ATHAMAS
(MOTHER OF —) INO
LEARN DO CON GET SEE WIT ARAL FIND HAVE HEAR LEAR LERE EDIFY GLEAN STUDY RECORD REALIZE RECEIVE DISCOVER ASCERTAIN
(— FROM EXPERIENCE) ASSAY
LEARNED BLUE SEEN LERED LORED DUCTUS BOOKISH CLERKLY CUNNING ERUDITE STUDIED TUITIVE ACADEMIC CLERGIAL LETTERED OVERSEEN POLYMATH PROFOUND SCIENCED
(— GROUP) LITERATI
(— MAN) OLLAV
(AFFECTEDLY —) INKHORN
(SOMETHING TO BE —) LIRIPIPE
LEARNEDLY CLERKLY
LEARNER PUPIL NOVICE SCHOLAR TRAINEE PRENTICE ABECEDARIAN
(LATE —) OPSIMATH
LEARNING ART WIT BOOK LEIR

LERE LORE CLERGY WISDOM APPRISE CUNNING GRAMMAR INSIGHT LETTERS WISTING BOOKLEAR BOOKLORE DOCTRINE HUMANISM LETTRURE MATHESIS PEDANTRY
(— LATE IN LIFE) OPSIMATHY
(SUFF.) MATHY
LEASE FEU FEW LET SET FARM HIRE RENT TACK COWLE DIMIT FIRMA LISSE DEMISE POTTAH RENTAL ASSEDAT CHARTER SETTING BACKTACK SUBLEASE
(— AGAIN) SUBLET
LEASEHOLDER LIVIER
LEASH LEAD LYME SLIP LEASE TRASH COUPLE STRING SWINGE
(— OF HOUNDS) HARL
(DOG —) SLIP TRASH TIRRET
(HAWK'S —) LOYN LUNE TIRRET CREANCE
LEASING LOCATIO
LEAST LEST MINIMAL MINIMUM MINIMUS
(AT —) HURE
LEAST FLYCATCHER CHEBEC
LEAST SANDPIPER PEEP OXEYE STINT
LEATHER ELK KID BEND BOCK BUFF CALF CAPE HIDE NAPA ROAN SEAL ADUST ALUTA BALAT FLANK NIGER RETAN SUEDE BULGAR CASTOR CHAMMY CHROME LIZARD ORIOLE OXHIDE PEBBLE RUSSET SHAMMY SKIVER TURKEY BELTING BUFFING CANEPIN CHAMOIS COWHIDE COWSKIN DEGRAIN DOGSKIN DONGOLA HEADCAP HOGSKIN KIDSKIN MURRAIN PANCAKE PECCARY PERSIAN SAFFIAN ANTELOPE BUCKSKIN BULLNECK CABRETTA CALFSKIN CAPESKIN CHEVEREL COLTSKIN CORDOBAN CORDWAIN DEERSKIN GOATSKIN KANGAROO LAMBSKIN SHAGREEN SHEEPSKIN
(— FOR DRESSING FLAX) RIBSKIN
(— FROM SHEEPSKIN) ROAN
(— SHREDS) MOSLINGS
(— STRIP) RAND
(ARABIAN —) MOCHA
(ARTIFICIAL —) KERATOL PEGAMOID
(BOARDED —) BOX
(BOOKBINDING —) ROAN
(CORDOVAN —) CORDOBAN CORDWAIN
(GOAT —) MOROCCO MAROQUIN
(GRAINED —) ROAN
(KIND OF —) NAPA
(MOROCCO —) LEVANT MAROQUIN
(PATCH OF —) CLOUT
(PRUSSIAN —) SPRUCE
(RUSSIAN —) YUFT BULGAR RUSSIA JUCHTEN
(SHEEPSKIN —) BOCK BUCK NAPA MOCHA
(SOFT —) OOZE ALUTA
(SUPERIOR —) BUFF
(THICK —) BUTT
(UNTANNED —) RAWHIDE
(WASH —) LOSH LOSHE
(PREF.) SCYT(O)
LEATHERBACK LUTH
LEATHERFISH LIJA FOOLFISH
LEATHERJACKET FILEFISH ZAPATERO
LEATHERLEAF CASSANDRA
LEATHERNECK GYRENE MARINE
LEATHERWOOD DIRCA WICOPY BURNWOOD FIREWOOD IRONWOOD LEADWOOD ROPEBARK
LEATHERWORKER TAWER BEDDER CHAMAR MADIGA FLUFFER CHUCKLER
LEAVE GO GET LET BUNK DROP FADE FLEE HOOK LEAF PART QUIT VADE VOID WALK AVOID CONGE FAVOR FORGO GOOUT GRACE SHOVE SPLIT WAIVE BUGGER BUGOFF DEPART DESERT DEVOID FORLET PERMIT RETIRE SECEDE STRAND VACATE FORLEIT FORLESE FORSAKE LARGESS LIBERTY LICENSE FAREWELL PATIENCE UNTENANT PERMISSION SABBATICAL
(— ALONE) FORBEAR DESOLATE
(— BEHIND) LET PLANT DISTANCE OUTSTRIP
(— BRIGHT TRAIL) STREAM
(— BY WILL) BEQUEATH
(— COVER) BREAK
(— HASTILY) SCUR SKIP SKIRR
(— HURRIEDLY) CUT BLOW BOLT FLEE JUMP SCAT SKIP
(— IN ISOLATION) MAROON
(— IN SAFEKEEPING) CHECK
(— NOTHING TO BE DESIRED) SATISFY
(— OF ABSENCE) ABSIT EXEAT LIBERTY FURLOUGH
(— OFF) CEASE DEVAL PETER BILEVE CHEESE DESIST SURCEASE
(— OUT) BATE OMIT SKIP SLIP ELIDE
(— PORT) SAIL CLEAR
(— QUICKLY) SCREW
(— SECRETLY) STEAL
(— SUDDENLY) KITE
(— UNDONE) PRETERMIT
LEAVED
(SUFF.) PHYLLOUS
LEAVEN ZYM ZYMO RAISE YEAST INFUSE RAISING SOURING
(PREF.) ZYM(O)
LEAVENING EMPTINGS
LEAVES PATRIN FOLIAGE LEAFAGE LEAFERY
(— OF BAOBAB TREE) LALO
(— OF ORCHID) FAHAM
(— OF TOBACCO) LEAF FLYINGS SECONDS
(— ON STEM AFTER WITHERING) INDUVIAE
(— USED AS STYPTIC) MATICO
(— USED FOR TEA) MANUKA
(BOILED — OF POTHERB) CHARD
(DRIED —) LAUHALA
(FALLEN —) DUFF
(MEDICINAL —) COCA FILE BUCCO BUCKU FARFARA FUMARIA
(PALM —) ATAP ATTAP CADJAN CAJANG
(TEA —) SOUCHONG
(WITHERED —) PININGS
(SUFF.) **(HAVING —)** CLEMA PHYLLOUS
(NUMBER OF —) MO
LEAVE-TAKING VALE ADIEU CONGEE PARTING WAYGANG FAREWELL WAYGOING
LEAVING BIT ORT TAG
(PL.) RAFF SNUFF REFUSE RESIDUE RESIDUUM
(PREF.) LIPO

LEBANON
CAPITAL: BEIRUT BEYROUTH
COIN: LIVRE PIASTRE
MOUNTAIN: ARUBA HERMON SANNINE KENISSEH
PLAIN: ELBIKA
RIVER: JOZ LYCOS DAMOUR LITANI HASBANI LEONTES ORONTES KASEMIEH
SEAPORT: TYRE SAIDA SIDON BEIRUT
TOWN: SUR TYRE ALEIH HALBA SAIDA SIDON ZAHLE JUNIYE ZAHLAH QARTABA TRIPOLI MERJUYUN
VALLEY: BEQAA

LEBBEK KOKO KOKKO SIRIS
LEBKUCHEN LEKACH
LECHER GOAT LECH LETCH LUXUR SATYR PALLIARD
LECHEROUS LEWD SALT PRIME RANDY WANTON BOARISH CODDING GOATISH LUSTFUL SATYRIC LIKEROUS SCABROUS SPORTIVE STUPROUS SALACIOUS
(PREF.) LUBRI
LECHERY LUXURY
LECTERN DESK EAGLE LUTRIN LATERAN LATTERIN
LECTION GOSPEL EPISTLE READING PERICOPE PROPHECY
LECTIONARY LEGEND
LECTOR LISTER READER
LECTURE JOBE CREED FORUM HOMILY LECTOR LESSON SERMON ADDRESS EARBASH HEARING PRELECT READING JOBATION ORDINARY
LECTURER DOCENT LECTOR READER DRYASDUST
LED (EASILY —) DUCTILE
LEDA (DAUGHTER OF —) HELEN CLYTEMNESTRA
(FATHER OF —) THESTIUS
(HUSBAND OF —) TYNDAREUS
(SON OF —) CASTOR POLLUX
LEDGE BEAD BERM DESS LINE STEP ALTAR BENCH CLINT LINCH SHELF SNOUT BEARER OFFSET SETTLE STANCE CHANNEL LEDGING RETABLE
(— BEHIND ALTAR) GRADIN GRADINE
(FIRESIDE —) STOCK
LEDGEMAN BREAKER
LEDGER BOOK SLAB LIEGER JOURNAL OVERLIER
LEDGER BOARD RIBBON
LEE LEW LEEWARD
LEECH GILL HARPY LEACH APODAN SANGSUE BDELLOID HELMINTH
(PREF.) BDELL(A) HIRUDINI
(SUFF.) BDELLA
LEEK FOUAT ALLIUM PORRET SCALLION SENGREEN ROCAMBOLE
(— COLORED) PRASINE
(PREF.) PRASEO PRASO
LEEK GREEN RESEDA
LEER LEAR LOOK OGLE FLEER LEERY SKIME SMIRK TWIRE
LEERFISH GARRICK
LEES LAGS ADDLE DRAFF DREGS DROSS GROUT AMURCA BOTTOM DUNDER MOTHER SORDOR ULLAGE GROUNDS EMPTINGS SEDIMENT WINEDRAF
LEEWAN SOFA DIVAN
LEEWARD DOWNWIND
LEEWARD ISLANDS (ISLAND OF —) KURE ARUBA NEVIS NIHOA LAYSON MIDWAY NECKER ANTIGUA MONTSERRAT
LEEWAY ROOM ROPE DRIFT
LEFT G CAR KAY GAWK NEAR PORT OTHER TOWARD DESERTED SINISTER
(— BEHIND) RELICT
(— EYE) OL OS
(— HELPLESS) STRANDED
(— OVER) ODD ORRA REMAINDER
(BE — ON BASE) DIE
(TURN —) HAW
(PREF.) LAEV(O) LEV(O) SINISTR(O)
LEFT HAND MG MS SM SIN GAUCHE
(— PAGE) VERSO
LEFTHANDED CAR GAUCHE AWKWARD DUBIOUS OBLIQUE KITHOGUE SOUTHPAW
LEFT-HANDER SOUTHPAW
LEFTIST RAD RADICAL
LEFTOVER END ORT REMNANT SURPLUS REMAINDER
(— YARN) THRUMS
(TOBACCO —) TOPPER
(PL.) SCRAN ANALECTS
LEG ARM GAM PEG PIN CRUS GAMB JAMB LIMB TRAM BOUGH GAMBE JAMBE REACH SHANK STICK STUMP BENDER GAMBON GAMMON LEGLET MOGGAN OVIGER PESTLE PLANTA PROLEG WALKER FORELEG TRESTLE FORELIMB
(— OF CRUSTACEAN) PODITE
(— OF HAWK) ARM
(— OF LAMB) GIGOT WABBLER WOBBLER
(— OF TABLE) BALUSTER
(— OF WHEELBARROW) STILT
(—S OF ARTIFICIAL FLY) HACKLE
(— USED FOR FOOD) PESTLE
(ARTIFICIAL —) PYLON
(FURNITURE —) CABRIOLE
(HAVING CREASELESS —S) STOVEPIPE
(LAST —) HOMESTRETCH
(MILK —) WEED
(TROUSER —) SLOP
(WIRE —S) SLING
(WOODEN —) PEG STUMP TIMBER
(PL.) PROPS TONGS STAMPS STICKS

(PREF.) SCEL(O)
(SUFF.) SCELES
(LOWER —) CNEMA CNEMIA CNEMIC CNEMUS
LEGACY ENTAIL LEGATE BEQUEST HERITAGE WINDFALL
LEGAL LEAL LICIT SOUND VALID LAWFUL SQUARE JURIDIC RIGHTFUL
(DOING — WORK) PROBONO
LEGALISM NOMISM SCRIBISM
LEGALISTIC COURT
LEGATE ENVOY DEPUTY EXARCH LEGATUS CONSULAR LEGATARY PANDULPH
LEGATION MISSION
LEGATO SMOOTH
LEGEND EDDA MYTH POSY SAGA TALE FABLE STORY TITLE THREAP CAPTION CUTLINE HAGGADA
(MAP —) KEY
(PREF.) MYTHO
LEGENDARY FABLED FICTIOUS
LEGERDEMAIN JUGGLERY PRESTIDIGITATION
LEGERDEMAINIST JUGGLER
LEGGING SPAT COCKER BOTTINE GAMBADO JAMBEAU BALATONG BOOTIKIN CHIVARRA
(LEATHER —) STRAD
(PL.) CHAPS SHANKS BROGUES COGGERS GAMASHES LEATHERS OVERALLS
LEGIBLE FAIR READABLE
(NOT —) OBSCURE
LEGION HOST TERZO TERZIO
LEGIONARY ANT DRIVER FORAGER
LEGISLATION DYSNOMY LAWMAKING
LEGISLATOR SOLON LAWGIVER LAWMAKER
LEGISLATURE DIET COURT THING LAGTING RIKSDAG LANDRATH RIGSRAAD
LEGITIMATE JUST TRUE VERY LEGAL LEGIT LOYAL HONEST KINDLY KOSHER LAWFUL REABLE SQUARE NATURAL LEGITIME
LEGITIMATELY FAIRLY MULIERLY
LEGPIECE JAMBEAU
LEGUME DAL POD URD DAHL DHAL GUAR PULSE LENTIL LOMENT PEANUT PODDER COCHLEA LEGUMEN PODWARE SOYBEAN STROMBUS
LEHUA OHIA
LEIPOA LOWAN MEGAPOD PHEASANT
LEISHMANIASIS UTA ESPUNDIA
LEISTER SPEAR WASTER
LEISURE TIME TOOM VOID OTIUM RESPITE VACANCY VACATION
LEISURELY SLOW SOODLY TIMELY TOOMLY GRADUAL PICKTOOTH
LELEX (FATHER OF —) NEPTUNE POSEIDON
(MOTHER OF —) LIBYA
(SON OF —) MYLES
LEMAN UNDERPUT
LEMMING CRICETID
LEMMUS MYODES
LEMNISCUS FILET FILLET LAQUEUS
LEMON DOG DUD CEDRA CHLOR LEMONY CEDRATE FAILURE KUMQUAT
LEMONADE COOLER
LEMON GRASS TANGLAD
LEMON SOLE MARYSOLE
LEMON VERBENA ALOYSIA
LEMUR LORI MAKI VARI AVAHI INDRI KOKAM LORIS POTTO SIFAC ADAPID AYEAYE COBEGO COLUGO GALAGO KUBONG MACACO MAHOLI MONKEY SIFAKA APOSORO MEERKAT NATTOCK PRIMATE SEMIAPE TARSIER AMPONGUE BABAKOTO MONGOOSE PRIMATAL TARSIOID
LEND OCKER PREST SECOND ADVANCE IMPREST
(— AT INTEREST) GAVEL
(— ITSELF) ALLOY
LENDING (— AGENCY) MOUNT
LENGTH LUG DREE TOWT PITCH SCOPE SIDTH COURSE EXTENT TOWGHT FOOTAGE DISTANCE LEGITUDE SIDENESS
(— ATHWARTSHIP) ABURTON
(— OF BRIDGE) BAY
(— OF CABLE) SCOPE SHACKLE
(— OF CHAIN) SHOT
(— OF CLOTH) CUT BOLT YARD
(— OF FIBER) STAPLE
(— OF FISHING LINE) CAST
(— OF GEAR TOOTH) FACE
(— OF HAIR) KNOT
(— OF HAIR IN FISHING LINE) IMP
(— OF LIFE) LONGEVITY
(— OF LINE) LOYN
(— OF METAL) SHAPE
(— OF MOUTH) GAPE
(— OF NET) LEAD
(— OF PISTON STROKE) TRAVEL
(— OF ROPE) DRIFT SPOKE BRIDLE COURSE STOPPER
(— OF SERVICE) STANDING
(— OF SHOEMAKER'S THREAD) END
(— OF SOUND) QUANTITY
(— OF THREAD) STITCH
(— OF TILE) GAUGE
(— OF TIMBER) BALK FLITCH
(— OF TIME) DURATION
(— OF TRIP) GATE
(— OF WALL) PANE
(— OF WINDMILL ARM) WHIP
(— OF YARN) KNOT TAPE CHASE SKEIN
(— UNIT) FERMI
(— 0F ORGAN PIPE) FOOTAGE
(AT FULL —) ALONG
(CONTINUOUS —) STRETCH
(FOCAL —) FOCUS
(PROJECTING —) SPONSON
(UNIT OF —) PIC PIK ROD FOOT INCH KILO PIKE REED VARA WRAP YARD FERMI METER SHAKU POLLEX FURLONG PLETHRON
(UTMOST —) EXTREME
(PREF.) MEC(O)
LENGTHEN EKE LONG DILATE EXPAND EXTEND LENGTH AMPLIFY DISTEND PRODUCE PROLONG STRETCH ELONGATE INCREASE PROTRACT
(— BY INTERPOLATION) FARSE
LENGTHENING HOLD ECTASIS DIASTOLE
LENGTHWISE ALONG ALENGTH ENDLONG ENDWAYS ENDWISE VERTICAL
LENGTHY LONG LARGE PROLIX LONGFUL EXTENDED
LENIENCY FAVOR MERCY LENITY CHARITY CLEMENCY LENIENCE
LENIENT LAX EASY KIND MILD SOFT FACILE GENTLE HUMANE LENITIVE
LENITIVE MILD MITIGANT SEDATIVE
LENITY MERCY HUMANITY KINDNESS LENITUDE
LENO GAUZE
LENS EYE CROWN GLASS OPTIC FLASER PEBBLE READER APLANAT BIFOCAL CONCAVE CONTACT DOUBLET ACHROMAT EYEGLASS EYEPIECE HYPERGON LENTICLE LUNETTES MENISCUS MAGNIFIER PANTOSCOPE
(JEWELER'S —) LOUPE
(KIND OF —) FRESNEL
(WITHOUT —) APHAKIA
(PREF.) PHAC(O)
LENT CAREME IMPREST
LENTICULAR PHACOID
LENTIGO FRECKLE
LENTIL LENS LINT TILL LENTILE LENTICLE
(PREF.) PHAC(O)
LEOFRIC (FATHER OF —) LEOFWINE
(WIFE OF —) GODIVA
LEONORE (GUARDIAN OF —) ARISTE
(SISTER OF —) ISABELLE
LEONTOCEBUS MIDAS
LEOPARD PARD TIGER PARDAL WAGATI LIBBARD PAINTER PANTHER PARDALE CATAMOUNT
(SNOW —) IRBIS OUNCE
LEOVIGILD (SON OF —) ERMENEGILD
(WIFE OF —) GOISWINTHA
LEPCHA RONG RONGPA
LEPER LAZAR MESEL LAZARUS
LEPIDOMELANE ANNITE
LEPIDOPTERA GLOSSATA
LEPIDOPTERIST AURELIAN
LEPIDOSIS SCALING
LEPRECHAUN ELF SPRITE LURACAN
LEPROSY LEPRA MESEL SCALL ALPHOS LAZARY MESELRY
LEPROUS MESELY MESELED
LEPTON MITE MUON
LEPTOSPIROSIS JAUNDICE
LERP LAAP
LESBIAN FEM DIKE DYKE FEMME EROTIC SAPPHIC TRIBADE SAPPHIST
LESBIANISM SAPPHISM
LESION PIT GALL HIVE SORE CRATER ESCHAR LEPRID ANTHRAX CHANCRE FISSURE LEPROMA BEESTING ERUPTION LEUKEMID TERTIARY
LESOTHO (MONEY OF —) LOTI MALOTI

LESOTHO
CAPITAL: MASERU
COIN: RAND
FORMER NAME: BASUTOLAND
LANGUAGE: SOTHO SESOTHO
MONEY: LOTI SENTE MALOTI LICENTE LISENTE
MOUNTAINS: MALUTI
PEOPLE: BASOTHO
RIVER: ORANGE CALEDON
TOWN: LERIBE MASHAI MORIJA PITSENG QUTHING SEKAKES MAFETENG
WATERFALL: MALETSUNYANE

LESPEDEZA SERICEA
LESS FEW MIN MENO FEWER MINOR LESSER SMALLER WANTING
(— BY A COMMA) MINOR
(PREF.) HYPO MEIO MIMIO MIO
(— THAN NORMAL) HYPO
LESSEE FARMER TERMOR HUURDER TACKSMAN
LESSEN CUT EBB BATE DOCK EASE FAIK FRET KILL LESS SINK WANE ABATE BREAK LOWER MINCE SMALL TAPER BUFFER DEADEN DEJECT IMPAIR INLESS MINIFY MINISH NARROW REBATE REDUCE WEAKEN AMENUSE ASSUAGE CURTAIL DEPLETE DEPRESS ELEVATE LIGHTEN RELIEVE SHORTEN CONTRACT DECREASE DEROGATE DIMINISH DISCOUNT EMBEZZLE MITIGATE MODERATE PALLIATE
(— FORCE) GELD
(— IN VALUE) SHRINK CHEAPEN
(— SENSITIVITY) DULL
(— STRENGTH) WEAR
(— TENSION) RELAX
(— VELOCITY) DEADEN
LESSENING LETUP PERDITION
(— OF PRISON TERM) REMISSION
(— PAIN) PAREGORIC
LESSER PETIT MINUTE SMALLER INFERIOR
(PREF.) MINI MI(O)
(SUFF.) **(— ONE)** ET ETTE
LESSER CELANDINE PILEWORT
LESSON TAX LEAR TASK STUDY EXAMPLE LECTURE PRECEPT READING DOCUMENT LIRIPOOP RECITATION
(DIFFICULT —) SOAK
(TORAH —) PARASHAH
LESSOR SETTER
LEST UNLESS ANANTER ANAUNTERS
LET LAT SET HIRE ALLOW LEASE LEAVE LETTEN PERMIT SUFFER TENANT
(— BAIT BOB) DIB
(— BECOME KNOWN) SPILL
(— BURN) BISHOP
(— CONTINUE) DRILL
(— DOWN) VAIL DEMIT DIMIT LOWER STOOP STRIKE SUBMIT
(— DOWN ROCK FACE) ABSEIL
(— FALL) DROP VAIL AVALE AWALE DEPOSE
(— FLY) PEG BOLT FIRE WING
(— GO) DROP FAIK QUIT DEMIT BILEVE DEMISE DISMIT UNHAND DISCARD UNSEIZE
(— HIM TAKE) SUM
(— IN) IMMIT INLET IMMISS ADHIBIT

(— IT BE REPEATED) REPET
(— IT STAND) STET
(— KNOW) ACQUAINT
(— LAND) GAVEL
(— LOOSE) FREE SLIP LIBERATE
(— OUT) BLAB TEAM WAGE ALTER BREAK SPILL ARRENT BROACH
(— SLIP) BALK BAULK CHECK FOREGO
(— UP) EBB EASE ABATE
LETDOWN DRAG DOWNER HANGOVER
LETHAL FATAL DEADLY MORTAL
LETHARGIC LOGY INERT DROWSY SLEEPY TORPID DORMANT PASSIVE COMATOSE COMATOUS SLUGGISH SLUMBROUS
LETHARGY COMA LOGY SLOTH STUPOR TORPOR SLUMBER HEBETUDE INACTION SOPITION
(FEELING OF —) BLAHS
LETO LATONA
LETT BALT
LETTER EF EL EM EN EX HE MU NU PE PI XI AIN AYN BEE CEE CHI DAK DEE EDH ESS ETA ETH GEE HET JAY KAY LIL MEM NUN PEE PHI PSI RHO SIN TAU TAV TAW TEE VEE WAW YOD YOK ZED ZEE ALEF ALIF AYIN BETA BETH BILL BULL CHIT DEAD HETH IOTA KAPH RESH SHIN SORT TETH YODH YOGH ZETA AITCH ALEPH ALPHA BLIND BREVE CAPON DELTA DEMIT FAVOR GAMMA GIMEL GRAPH KAPPA KNOWN KOPPA OMEGA SADHE SIGMA STAVE STIFF THETA ZAYIN ACCENT ADVICE ANSWER BILLET CADJAN CARTEL CHARTA COCKUP DALETH FAVVER ITALIC LAMBDA LAMEDH MEDIAL SAMEKH SCRIPT SIGLUM SUNNUD SYMBOL VERSAL CODICIL COLLINS CONTROL DIGAMMA DIPLOMA EPISTLE EPSILON KAREETA MISSIVE OMICRON SPECIAL UPSILON AEROGRAM ASCENDER ENCYCLIC MONITORY NUNDINAL PASTORAL
(— OF DEFIANCE) CARTEL
(— OF PERMISSION) EXEAT
(—S DIMISSORY) APOSTOLI
(—S OF MARQUE) MART
(ANGLO-SAXON —) EDH ETH THORN
(AUTHORIZING —) BREVE
(BEGGING —) SCREEVE
(BLACK —) GOTHIC
(BREAD AND BUTTER —) COLLINS
(CAPITAL —) CAP UNCIAL CAPITAL FACTOTUM MAJUSCULE
(FRIENDLY —) SCREED
(INITIAL —) BLOOMER
(LOVE —) POULET
(LOWERCASE —) MINISCULE
(OBSOLETE —) EPISEMON
(OFFICIAL —) BRIEF
(PAPAL —) BULL TOME BREVE ENCYCLIC
(PRIVATE —) BOOK
(SHORT —) CHIT LINE NOTE BILLET LETTERET
(SILENT —) MUTE
(SMUGGLED —) KITE
(SUBSCRIPT —) SUBFIX
(WORD —) LOGOGRAM
(PL.) MAIL APOSTOLI
(PREF.) EPISTOLO
LETTER BOX APARTADO
LETTER CARRIER CORREO MAILMAN POSTMAN
LETTERER SKETCHER
LETTERING FAC WRITE INCUSE CALLIGRAPHY
(— ON TV SCREEN) CRAWL
(TV —) CRAWL
LETTERPRESS TEXT CAPTION
LETTING FIRMA LOCATIO
LETTING-OUT DROPPING
LETTISH LATVIAN
LETTUCE COS BIBB GRASS SALAD KARPAS SALLET ICEBERG ROMAINE FIREWEED MILKWEED
LETUP (WITH NO —) ONEND
LETUSHIM (FATHER OF —) DEDAN
LEUCIPPE (BROTHER OF —) CALCHAS
(FATHER OF —) MINYAS THESTOR
(SISTER OF —) THEONOE
(SON OF —) TEUTHRAS
LEUCIPPUS (BROTHER OF —) APHAREUS
(DAUGHTER OF —) PHOEBE HILAIRA
(FATHER OF —) OENOMAUS PERIERES
(MOTHER OF —) GORGOPHONE
(WIFE OF —) PHILODICE
LEUCITE LENAD
LEUCITITE ITALITE SPERONE ALBANITE CECILITE
LEUCOCYTE POLY NEOCYTE HEMAMEBA MONOCYTE OXYPHILE
LEUCOMA ALBUGO WALLEYE
LEUCORRHEA WHITES
LEUCOTHEA (FATHER OF —) ORCHAMUS
(MOTHER OF —) EURYNOME
LEUKEMIA CHLOROMA LEUKOSIS
LEVANT EASTERN WORMSEED
LEVANTINE SCATTERMOUCH
LEVEE DIKE DYKE WALL WEIR DURBAR STOPBANK
LEVEL BONE EVEN FAIR FLAT GLAD LUTE PLAT RAZE SHIM VIAL COUCH EQUAL FLUSH GRADE PLAIN PLANE POINT SLICK SOLID CHARGE DOUBLE EVENLY FIELDY NIVEAU SLIGHT SMOOTH STRIKE TUNNEL FLATTEN GALLERY GANGWAY REGULAR DEMOLISH LEVELLER SUBGRADE
(— AFTER PLOWING) BUSH
(— AND SCATTER) GELD
(— A RAFTER) EDGE
(— OFF) HAMMER BULLDOZE
(— OF SOCIETY) STRATUM
(— OF STAGE) STUDY
(— PLACE) PLANILLA
(COMMON —) PAR
(ENERGY —) SINGLET
(EXPERT — OF KARATE) DAN
(EYE —) EYELINE
(HIGHER —S) BRASS
(HIGHEST —) SUMMIT
(LOWEST —) FLOOR BOTTOM HARDPAN
(MINING —) KIP HEAD GALLERY GANGWAY
(NOT ON THE —) ALOP
(ON THE —) TRUE
(STRATIGRAPHIC —) HORIZON
(TOP —) HIGH CEILING
(PREF.) PLAN(I)
LEVELED BENT
LEVELER DIGGER
(PL.) ACEPHALI
LEVELING EGALITE EGALITY
LEVER KEY PRY BEAM GAUL HOOK HORN JACK SWAY TREE BRAKE FLAIL FLIRT HELVE PEDAL PINCH PLUTO PRIZE SPOON STANG STANK SWIPE THROW BINDER CLUTCH COUPER DETENT FEELER GAFFLE HAMMER HEAVER HOPPER LOWDER PORTER ROCKER TAPPET TILLER BALANCE BOOTLEG CROWBAR POINTER RAMHEAD SHIPPER SWINGLE TREADLE TRIGGER TUMBLER BACKFALL GAVELOCK SELECTOR THROTTLE
(— ARM) NIGGER
(— FOR CROSSBOW) GAFFLE GARROT
(— FOR TURNING RUDDER) HELM TILLER
(— IN KNITTING MACHINE) JACK
(— IN TIMEPIECE) PALLET
(— LIKE CANTHOOK) PEAVY PEAVIE
(— OF GIN) START
(CONTROL —) JOYSTICK
(GEARSHIFT —) STICK
(LUMBERMAN 'S —) PEAVY PEAVEY
(ORGAN —) BACKFALL KNEESTOP KNEESWELL
(SPINNING —) BOOTLEG
(SPOKELIKE —) SWINGLE
(THROTTLE —) GUN
(WEAVING —) LAM LAMM SWELL BINDER TIPPLER
LEVERAGE PRY PRIZE
LEVI (FATHER OF —) JACOB ALPHAEUS
(MOTHER OF —) LEAH
(SON OF —) KOHATH MERARI GERSHON
LEVIGATE DUST
LEVITATE RISE FLOAT
LEVITY FOLLY HUMOR GAIETY FLIPPANCY WHIFFLERY
LEVOROTATORY LAEVO LEVOGYRE NEGATIVE
LEVY CUT TAX CESS MISE REAR LEVEL RAISE ASSESS EXTEND EXTENT IMPOSE IMPOST UPTAKE IMPRESS TRIBUTE DISTRAIN DISTRESS SHIPPAGE
(— A TAX) GELD GELT TAIL STENT
(— DISTRESS) DRIVE
(IRISH —) MART
LEVYING EXACTION
LEWD NICE BAWDY FOLLY PRIME RANDY HARLOT IMPURE LACHES LUBRIC RAKISH WANTON HIRCINE LEERING LUSTFUL OBSCENE RAMMISH RIGGISH SCARLET SENSUAL WHORISH PRURIENT SLUTTISH UNCHASTE SALACIOUS
LEWDNESS FOLLY RAKERY LECHERY HARLOTRY PUTANISM LUBRICITY SCULDUDDERY
LEXICOGRAPHER AMERICAN GOVE ALLEN EVANS GOULD CARHART MATHEWS WEBSTER WHEELER BARNHART BARTLETT WORCESTER
BRAZILIAN MORAES
ENGLISH WYLD COLES DYCHE ROGET SCOTT SMITH BAILEY BLOUNT CRAGIE FARMER FLORIO FOWLER MURRAY ONIONS WALKER BRADLEY CAWDREY JOHNSON MINSHEU WITHALS BULLOKAR COCKERAM COTGRAVE AINSWORTH COCKERELL PARTRIDGE STORMONTH RICHARDSON
FRENCH LITTRE ROBERT BEAUJAN GODEFROY LAROUSSE FURETIERE
GERMAN ERMAN MURET SACHS FLUGEL SCHNEIDER
GREEK POLLUX SUIDAS PAMPHILUS
ICELANDIC BLONDAL
ITALIAN CESARI CALENUS FANFANI FACCIOLATI FORCELLINI
NEW ZEALAND PARTRIDGE
POLISH LINDE
SCOTTISH GRANT MURRAY OGILVY
LEXICON CALEPIN WORDBOOK
LIABILITY DEBT DEBIT CHARGE TRIBUTE OBLIGATION
LIABLE APT ABLE OPEN GUILTY EXPOSED OBVIOUS ONEROUS SUBJECT AMENABLE INCIDENT
(— TO MISCHANCE) RISKY
(— TO SIN) PECCABLE
(NOT —) EXEMPT IMMUNE
(SUFF.) ABLE IBLE
LIAISON BOND AFFAIR AFFAIRE LINKING INTIMACY INTRIGUE
LIANA CIPO BEJUCO GUARANA BUSHROPE
LIANG TAEL
LIAR LEAR ANANIAS BOUNCER CRACKER CRAMMER PROCTOR WARLOCK WERNARD FABULIST
LIBATION AMBROSIA
LIBEL DEFAME MALIGN VILIFY SLANDER
LIBELOUS FAMOUS SCANDALOUS
LIBER PHLOEM
LIBERAL WET FAIR FREE GOOD OPEN WHIG BROAD FRANK LARGE NOBLE SOLUTE JANNOCK PROFUSE ADVANCED CATHOLIC GENEROUS HANDSOME LARGEOUS PRODIGAL SEPARATE MUNIFICENT
(CANADIAN —) GRIT
(NOT —) CHARY SPARE
LIBERAL ARTS MUSES
LIBERALITY LARGE BOUNTY BREADTH CHARITY FREEDOM HONESTY LARGESS
LIBERALLY LARGE BROADLY
LIBERATE FREE QUIT FRITH REMIT UNGYVE UNWRAP DELIVER MANUMIT RELEASE UNSLAVE UNFETTER UNTHRALL
LIBERATION LIB FREEDOM RELEASE DELIVERY KAIVALYA DISCHARGE
(— OF SPORE) ABSCISSION

LIBERIA
CAPITAL: MONROVIA
CUSTOM: SANDE
HILLS: BOMI
MEASURE: KUBA
MOUNTAIN: UNI NIETE NIMBA WUTIVI
MOUNTAINS: BONG SATRO
PEOPLE: GI KRU KWA VAI VEI GOLA KROO KROU TOMA BASSA GIBBI GISSI GREBO KPELLE KROOBY KRUMAN KROOBOY MANDINGO
RIVER: CESS LOFA MANO LOFFA MANNA MORRO CESTOS DOUOBE STJOHN STPAUL CAVALLY SANPEDRO
TOWN: GANTA GRIBO REBBO HARPER ZORZOR NANAKRU TAPPITA BUCHANAN MARSHALL SASSTOWN

LIBERTINE ROUE PUNKER PANURGE STRIKER LOTHARIO LOVELACE STRINGER
LIBERTY MAY SOC EASE LARGE LEAVE SCOPE ACCESS LEEWAY SCOUTH STREET FREEDOM LARGESS LICENSE WITHGANG
(— OF ACTION) PLAY SWING
(— OF CHOICE) FREEWILL
(— OF ENTRANCE) INGRESS
(— OF GOING OUT) ISH
(— OF TURNING PIGS INTO FIELDS) SHACK
(— TO BUY AND SELL) TOLL
(— TO HUNT) CHASE
(AT —) FREE IDLE
(PARTIAL — OF HAWK) HACK
(SEXUAL —) INTIMACY
(UNDUE —) HEAD
LIBERTY CAP PILLEUS
LIBIDINIZATION EGOISM
LIBIDINOUS FLESHY FLESHLY
LIBNI (FATHER OF —) MAHLI GERSHON
LIBRA AS PONDUS
LIBRARIAN AMERICAN COLE DANA HILL HUNT KOCH LANE DEWEY EAMES EVANS GREEN MUDGE POOLE SHERA SMITH WROTH CUTTER FOLSOM HUMMEL JEWETT MEARNS PUTNAM WINSOR CARLSON EDMANDS MUMFORD SONNECK VANNAME WELLMAN BARTLETT BOSTWICK COGSWELL HAVILAND MACLEISH SAUNDERS SPOFFORD HENDERSON YARMOLINSKY
CANADIAN READY
ENGLISH BOND COXE DIBDIN LARKIN PANIZZI PATMORE THOMPSON
FRENCH DUPUY OMONT BONNECHOSE TASCHEREAU
GERMAN EBERT BURGER
PERUVIAN ULLOA
SPANISH MACHADO
LIBRARY DEN AMBRY BIBLE MUSEUM BHANDAR BOOKERY ATHENEUM
LIBRETTO BOOK WORD TESTO TEXTBOOK

LIBYA
ALPHABET: TIFINAGH
CAPITAL: BENGASI BENGAZI TRIPOLI
COIN: DIRHAM
DESERT: FEZZAN MURZUK MURZUCH
GULF: SIDRA SIRTE
MEASURE: SAA BOZZE DONUM JABIA TEMAN BARILE MISURA MATTARO
MOUNTAIN: BETTE
OASIS: JALO KUFRA SEBHA FEZZAN GIOFRA TAZERBO GIARABUB
SEAPORT: HOMS DERNA SIDRI TOBRUK BENGAZI
TOWN: BRAK DERJ HOMS BARKA DERNA SEBHA SIDRI UBARI ZAWIA ELMARJ GARIAN MURZUQ REMADA TOBRUK MISURATA
WEIGHT: KELE UCKIA GORRAF TERMINO KHAROUBA

LICE CREEPERS
(FISH —) EPIZOA
LICENSE TAG CHOP GALE HEAD EXEAT LEAVE SLANG SWING BANDON CAROON FIRMAN INDULT PATENT PERMIT READER TICKET CAROOME CERTIFY CROTTLE FACULTY FREEDOM INDULTO LIBERTY LICENCE PLACARD WARRANT ESCAMBIO IMMUNITY MORTMAIN PASSPORT TEZKIRAH
(— FOR CART) CAROOME
(— PLATE) NUMBER
(PEDDLER'S —) SLANG
LICENTIOUS GAY LAX FREE LEWD WILD FRANK LARGE LOOSE FILTHY RIBALD UNRULY WANTON CYPRIAN FLESHLY IMMORAL LAWLESS LIBERAL UNYOKED
LICENTIOUSNESS DIRT LICENSE
LICHEN RAG MOSS MANNA USNEA ARCHIL CORKIR KORKIR ORCHIL CROTTAL CROTTLE CUDBEAR EVERNIA OAKMOSS PARELLA ARCHILLA CAPEWEED LECANORA LUNGWORT PARMELIA ROCKHAIR TREEHAIR WARTWORT
LICIT LEGAL LAWFUL LEEFUL
LICK LAP LIKE SUCK MOUTH SLAKE CONQUER
LICKER-IN TUMBLE
LICKING LAMBENT GRUELING
LICKSPITTLE LACKEY
LICORICE POMFRET SWEETROOT
LICORICE PILL CACHOU
LICYMNIUS (FATHER OF —) ELECTRYON
(MOTHER OF —) MIDEA
(SISTER OF —) ALCMENA
(SLAYER OF —) TLEPOLEMUS
(WIFE OF —) PERIMEDE
LID DIP BRED DECK TYMP COVER BRIDLE EYELID POTLID CLAPPER CLICKET CLOSURE SCUTTLE SHUTTER COVERCLE OPERCULUM
(SUFF.) POMATOUS
LIE FIB GAB KIP LAY LIG LIN SIT YED CRAM FALL FLAW LIGG REST RIDE WHID DEVIL DWELL FABLE FEIGN LEASE STAND STORY BOUNCE FITTEN PALTER RAPPER RESIDE SPRAWL VANITY YANKER BOUNCER CONSIST CRACKER CRAMMER CRUMPER FALSITY GRABBLE LEASING PLUMPER TWISTER UNTRUTH WHACKER WHISKER WHOPPER MENDACITY TARADIDDLE PREVARICATE
(— AHEAD) AWAIT
(— ALONGSIDE) ACCOST
(— AROUND) COMPASS
(— AT ANCHOR) HOVE
(— AT FULL LENGTH) STRETCH
(— CONCEALED) DARKLE
(— CONTIGUOUS) CONFINE
(— DETECTOR) POLYGRAPH
(— DORMANT) SLEEP
(— DOWN) LEAN COUCH CHARGE
(— FLAT ON BELLY) GROVEL
(— HEAD TO WIND) TRY
(— HIDDEN) LURK MICHE TAPPISH
(— IN AMBUSH) HUGGER
(— IN BED) KIP THOKE
(— IN WAIT) AWAIT LOWER AMBUSH FORELAY
(— IN WATER) DOUSE DROWN
(— LOW) TAPPICE
(— NEXT TO) ADJOIN
(— OPPOSITE TO) SUBTEND
(— OVER) COVER
(— PRONE) GROVEL GRABBLE
(— PROSTRATE) STREEK
(— QUIET) SNUDGE
(— SNUG) CUDDLE
(— UNEVENLY) SAG
(— WITH SAILS FURLED) HULL
(BIG —) CAULKER
(IMPUDENT —) BOUNCE
(MONSTROUS —) STRAMMER
(PREF.) **(— HID)** LANTHAN(O) LANTHO

LIECHTENSTEIN
CAPITAL: VADUZ
CASTLE: GUTEMBURG
MOUNTAIN: RHATIKON
RIVER: RHINE SAMINA
ROMAN NAME: RHAETIA
TOWN: HAAG BALZER SCHAAN NENDELN
TRIBE: ALAMANNI

LIED BALLAD
LIEF DEAR LEAVE LEEVE LIEVE FREELY GLADLY BELOVED
LIEN MORTGAGE
LIEU STEAD
LIEUTENANT LUFF ZANY LOUEY JAYGEE KEHAYA CAIMAKAM QAIMAQAM TENIENTE WOODVILE SHAVETAIL
(— JUNIOR GRADE) JAYGEE
LIFE IT VIE ZOE HIDE JIVA PUFF SNAP TUCK VALE ANIMA BEING BLOOD DEMON HEART LIFER QUICK SWEAT BIOSIS BREATH CANDLE COURSE ENERGY SPIRIT SPRITE LIFELET LIFEWAY VITALITY VIVACITY
(— AFTER DEATH) FUTURITY
(— IN HEAVEN) GLORY
(— IN SOCIETY) SAMSARA SANSARA
(— OF FURNACE LINING) CAMPAIGN
(— OF THE SEA) HALIBIOS
(ACADEMIC —) ACADEMIA
(ANIMAL —) FLESH
(ANIMAL AND PLANT —) BIOS BIOTA BIOLOGY EDAPHON
(CLOISTERED —) VEIL
(EARLY —) YOUTH
(ETERNAL —) GRACE
(HOME —) DOMESTICITY
(INTELLECTUAL —) JIVATMA
(LOCAL —) BIOTA
(MONASTIC —) CLOISTER
(MORAL —) DAENA
(MOSS —) BRYOLOGY
(PLANT —) BIOS BIOTA FLORA BOTANY
(PUBLIC —) WORLD
(ROBUST —) JUICE
(SIGN OF —) PULSE
(SINGLE —) CELIBACY
(TERRESTRIAL —) GEOBIOS
(WAY OF —) BAG SCENE FASTLANE
(WITHOUT —) AZOIC
(PREF.) BI(O) EMBIO PSYCH(O) VIT(A)(O)
(NOT —) ABIO
(SUFF.) BIA BIONT BIOSIS BIOTIC BIOUS BIUM BIUS BY PSYCHE
LIFE BELT SAFETY
LIFEBLOOD BLOOD SWEAT
LIFE-FORCE KUNDALINI
(YOGI —) KUNDALINI
LIFE FOR THE TSAR, A
(CHARACTER IN —) SOBININ SUSANIN ANTONIDA
(COMPOSER OF —) GLINKA
LIFELESS ARID BLAH DEAD DULL FLAT AMORT HEAVY INERT VAPID ANEMIC TORPID SAPLESS DESOLATE GRIPLESS INACTIVE
(PREF.) ABIO
LIFELESSLY DEADLY INERTLY
LIFELESSNESS ANEMIA
LIFELIKE VIVE QUICK EIDETIC NATURAL ANIMATED SPEAKING
LIFE PRESERVER FLOAT NEDDY
LIFESAVER HERO
LIFETIME AGE DAY WORLD LIVING LIFEDAY DURATION LIFELONG
(— OF FLOWER) ANTHESIS
LIFE WITH FATHER (AUTHOR OF —) DAY
(CHARACTER IN —) DELIA GULICK CLARENCE MARGARET
LIFEWORK (ARTIST'S —) OEUVRE
LIFT WIN BOOM BUOY CAST COCK HEFT JACK REAR TOSS WEVE ARSIS BOOST BREAK ELATE HEAVE HITCH HOICK HOIST HOOSH MOUNT PRESS RAISE SPOUT STEAL WEIGH BUCKET CLEECH SNATCH TAKEUP ELEVATE ENHANCE HEELTAP NAUNTLE BOOKLIFT CHAIRWAY ELEVATOR LEVITATE
(— HAT) DOFF
(— IN PAWNSHOP) SPOUT
(— IN VEHICLE) SETDOWN
(— IN WEIGHT LIFTING) SQUAT
(— OF WAVE) SCEND
(— OF WEIGHTS) SNATCH

(— ONESELF) SOAR
(— QUICKLY) PERK
(— UP) HOVE CRANE ERECT EXALT EXTOL HORSE WEIGH ADVANCE ELEVATE NAUNTLE
(— WITH BLOCK AND TACKLE) BOUSE
(KIND OF —) SKI
(SKI —) GONDOLA
LIFTED ARRECT SUBLIME
LIFTER GAGGER SERVER HOISTER HOISTMAN
LIFTING HIKE UPTAKE
LIFT VALVE POPPET
LIGAMENT BAND BOND ARTERY FRENUM PAXWAX STRING ZONULE ARMILLA LIGATURE
(PREF.) DESM(A)(IDI)(IDIO)(O) SYNDESM(O)
LIGAMENTOUS DESMOID
LIGATE BAR
LIGATURE ASH CLAM PLICA DIGRAM PNEUMA STIGMA BANDAGE DIGRAPH FUNICLE LIGAMENT LIGATION
(— OE) ASH
LIGGER TRIMMER
LIGHT BUG DAY GAY HAP LAW SHY SUN AIRY EASY FAIR FALL FINE FIRE FLIT FLUX GLIM LAMP LEET LUNT MILD SLUT SOFT BAVIN BLAZE CORKY FANAL FILMY FLAME FLEET FUFFY LEGER LOUGH MERRY PITCH QUICK SHEER SPILL WHITE BEACON BRIGHT CHAFFY FLOATY FLOSSY FLUFFY FROTHY GENTLE HAPPEN ILLUME KINDLE LANCET LUSTER LUSTRE MARKER PASTEL PHAROS SIGNAL SLUSHY STINGY STRIKE STROBE SUTTLE VOLAGE BENGOLA BUOYANT CRESSET FRAGILE GLITTER LAMBENT SFOGATO SMITHER SUMMERY TORTAYS TRIVIAL UNGRAVE BACKFIRE DAYLIGHT DELICATE DIAPHANE ELECTRIC EXPEDITE FEATHERY GASLIGHT GOSSAMER LEGGIERO LUMINARY PALOUSER SUNLIGHT SUNSHINE
(— AND BRILLIANT) LAMBENT
(— AND FIRE ON HORSE'S MANE) HAG
(— AND FREE) FLYAWAY
(— AND QUICK) VOLANT
(— CANDLES) TOLLY
(— DISPLAY) LED
(— FROM NIGHT SKY) AIRGLOW
(— IN WINDOW) LANCET
(— OF MORNING) AURORA
(— ON TV SCREEN) SNOW
(— UP) FLASH GLOZE ILLUME RELUME GLORIFY
(— UPON) STRIKE
(BRIGHT —) GLARE GLEAM
(BURST OF —) FLASH
(CIRCLE OF —) HALO NIMBUS
(EMIT —) LASE
(EMIT COHERENT —) LASE
(FAINT —) GLIMMER SCARROW
(FEEBLE —) TAPER GLIMMER
(FITFUL —) SHIMMER
(GREEN —) GOAHEAD
(HARBOR —) BUG
(INDICATOR —) BEZEL
(INDICATOR — ON SCREEN) CURSOR
(INNER —) SEED
(KIND OF —) KLEIG KLIEG
(LASER — EMITTER) LIDAR
(NEBULOUS —) CHEVELURE
(NEW —) SEPARATE
(NIGHT —) MORTAR
(PARKING —S) DIMMERS
(PATCH OF —) CURSOR
(PERSIAN GOD OF —) MITHRAS
(REFLECTED —) SKYME
(SHIP'S —) FANAL
(SMALL —) TAPER
(STUDIO —) KLIEG
(TRAFFIC —) BLINKER
(WAVERING —) FLICKER
(PL.) BUFF
(PREF.) LUCI LUMIN(I)(O) PHOS PHOT(O)
LIGHT-COLORED BLONDE
LIGHTED LUMINOUS
LIGHTEN ALAY CLEAR LEVIN LIGHT RAISE ALLEGE BLEACH ENCLEAR FOULDRE MOLLIFY SWEETEN THUNDER LEVIGATE
LIGHTENING BREAK
(— OF HAIR) FROSTING
LIGHTER KEEL SCOW ACCON BARGE CASCO PRAAM WHERRY DROGHER GABBARD GONDOLA PONTOON CHOPBOAT
LIGHTERMAN KEELER KEELMAN
LIGHT-FOOTED SPRY
LIGHT-GREEN
(PREF.) CHLOR(O)
LIGHT-HEADED IDLE BARMY LIGHT LIVELY CARRIED GLAIKET SKITTISH
LIGHT-HEARTED GAY GLAD GIDDY BUOYANT WINSOME CAREFREE DEBONAIR VOLATILE
LIGHTHEARTEDNESS BUOYANCY
LIGHTHOUSE FANAL LIGHT MINAR BEACON PHAROS LANTERN
(PREF.) PHARO
LIGHT IN AUGUST (AUTHOR OF —) FAULKNER
(CHARACTER IN —) DOC JOE GAIL LENA ALLEN BROWN BURCH BYRON GROVE HINES LUCAS BOBBIE BURDEN JOANNA EUPHEUS CHRISTMAS HIGHTOWER
LIGHTLESS APHOTIC
(PREF.) APHOTO
LIGHTLY LIGHT AIRILY FAIRILY HOVERLY LEGGIERO SLIGHTLY
LIGHT-MINDED BLITHE ETOURDI
LIGHTNESS CHEER VALUE GAIETY LEVITY AIRINESS BUOYANCY LEGERETE LEGERITY
(— OF MOVEMENT) BALLON
LIGHTNING BOLT FIRE LAIT LEVIN FULMEN METEOR FOULDRE SULPHUR THUNDER FIREBALL FIREBOLT WILDFIRE
LIGHT-O'-LOVE COCOTTE LEVERET
LIGHT-TEXTURED FOZY
LIGHTWOOD FATWOOD
LIGIA LIGYDA
LIGNEOUS WOODY XYLOID
LIGNIN LIGNOSE XYLOGEN
LIGNITE JET
LIGNUM VITAE GUAYACAN POCKWOOD
LIGROIN BENZINE CANADOL
LIGULA LANGUET
LIGULE STRAP LIGULA
LIKE AS ALA DIG DOTE LIST LOVE ALIKE ENJOY EQUAL FANCY SAVOR TASTE ADMIRE AFFECT BELIKE LIKELY MATTER PLEASE SEMBLE SIMILE THEWAY CONCEIT SIMILAR SEMBLANT SUITABLE SEMBLABLE
(— A GLAND) ADEMOSE ADENOUS
(— BETTER) PREFER
(— HAIR) CRINITE
(VERY —) SIAMESE
(PREF.) HOME(O) HOMOE HOMOI SYM
(SUFF.) AR EOUS ESQUE IC(AL) INE IS ISH ISTIC LY ODE OID(AL) SOME
LIKELIHOOD APTNESS
LIKELY APT FAIR LIKE READY LIABLE PROOFY SEEMLY GRADELY SMITTLE APPARENT FEASIBLE POSSIBLE PROBABLE PROSPECTIVE
(MOST —) BELIKE
LIKEN EVEN LIKE REMENE SEMBLE COMPARE ASSEMBLE CREDIBLE RESEMBLE SIMILIZE
LIKENESS DAP BLEE ICON IDOL MAKE SECT BLUSH DUMMY GLIFF IMAGE MORAL SHAPE EFFIGY FIGURE STATUE ANALOGY KINSHIP PATTERN PICTURE RETRAIT EQUALITY HOMOLOGY PARALLEL PORTRAIT SEMBLANCE SIMILARITY
(— OF ORIGIN) ISOGENY
(DISTORTED —) CARICATURE
(PERFECT —) SPIT
LIKENING SIMILE
LIKEWISE EKE TOO ALSO ITEM EITHER EQUALLY LIKEWAYS
(— NOT) NOR
LIKHI (FATHER OF —) SHEMIDAH
LIKING GOO GRA PAY GOUT GUST LIKE LIST LUST FANCY FLAIR GUSTO HEART SHINE SKILL SMACK TASTE THEAT SWALLOW AFFINITY APPETITE FONDNESS PENCHANT
(ECCENTRIC —) FOIBLE
(MENTAL —) PALATE
(SUFF.) (— FOR) PHIL(A)(AE)(E)(IA) (ISM)(IST)(OUS)(US)
LIKUTA
(PL.) MAKUTA
LILAC LILAS MAUVE LAYLOCK
LILACIN SYRINGIN
LILIOM (AUTHOR OF —) MOLNAR
(CHARACTER IN —) WOLF JULIE MARIE FICSUR LILIOM LOUISE MUSKAT LINZMAN HOLLUNDER
LILLIPUTIAN TINY
LILY ALOE IXIA KELP SEGO AZTEC CALLA CLOTE AUGUST LILIUM VALLEY COCUISA MONOCOT ASPHODEL LILYWORT MARTAGON NENUPHAR
(AFRICAN —) AGAPANTHUS
(CLIMBING —) GLORIOSA
(PALM —) TI
(SEA —) CRINOID
(WATER —) CANDOCK CAMALOTE
(PREF.) LIRIO
(SUFF.) CRINUS
LILY OF THE VALLEY LILIUM MUGGET MUGUET MUGWET LILYWORT SHINLEAF
LIMA BEAN HABA LIMA
LIMB ARM LEG CLAW FOOT KNOT LITH TRAM WING ARTUS BOUGH SPALD SPAUL SWAMP BRANCH MEMBER PODITE FEATURE FLIPPER FORCEPS PLEOPOD NECTOPOD
(PREF.) MEL
(SUFF.) (CONDITION OF —) MELIA
LIMBA AFARA FRAKE
LIMBER BAIN FLIP LIMP LUSH AGILE LINGY LITHE LISSOM SEMMIT SUPPLE SWANKY BRUSHER BRUTTER KNOTTER LIMMOCK PLIABLE FLEXIBLE FLIPPANT
LIME CALX LIMA CEDRA CEDRAT CHUNAM CITRON FUSTIC
(— IN BRICK) BOND
(KIND OF —) KEY
(WILD —) COLIMA
(PREF.) CAL(AREO)(I)(IO)(O)
LIMEN THRESHOLD
LIMESTONE CAM HUM CALP CAUK CAUM LIAS LYAS MALM CHALK POROS ROACH CLUNCH KUNKUR MARBLE OOLITE CIPOLIN SCAGLIA DOLOMITE PISOLITE TRAVERTINE
(— REGION) KARST
(DECOMPOSED —) ROTTENSTONE
LIME TREE LIME TEIL LINDEN
LIMEY TAR
LIMIT CAP END FIX BIND BUTT FINE HOLD LINE LIST MARK MERE PALE TAIL BLOCK BOUND COAST GAUGE HEDGE SCANT STENT STINT VERGE BORDER BOURNE DEFINE EFFLUX EXTENT FINISH FINITE HAMPER LENGTH MODIFY NARROW PALING SCRIMP TROPIC UPSHOT ASTRICT CLOSURE COMPASS CONFINE CONTENT HORIZON MAXIMUM MEASURE OUTSIDE BOUNDARY CONTRACT DEADLINE IMPRISON LIMITARY LIMITATE OUTGOING OUTREACH RESTRAIN RESTRICT SOLSTICE TERMINUS PARAMETER
(— EFFECT) ALLAY
(— IN A FOREST) BAIL
(— MOTION) HOLD
(— OF STATUTE) PURVIEW
(— OF VISION AT SEA) KENNING
(EXTREME —) HEIGHT
(LOWER —) FLOOR
(TAKE TO THE —) TAX
(UPPER —) CEILING
(UTTER —) EXTREME
(PL.) AMBIT CANCELS ENVIRONS PERIMETER
(PREF.) ORI
LIMITATION TAIL FRAME STINT DENIAL CLOTURE RESERVE
(— OF DEBATE) CLOTURE
(— OF INHERITANCE) TAIL
(— OF WANTS) STOICISM
(PL.) SWADDLE
LIMITED MILD TAIL BORNE BRIEF SHORT SMALL FINITE NARROW STINTY STRAIT BOUNDED SPECIAL

CONFINED DEFINITE LIMITARY PAROCHIAL SECTARIAN MEASURABLE PROVINCIAL RESTRICTED
(— IN APPEAL) CHICHI
(— IN SCOPE) MODERATE
LIMITING DEFINITE ADJECTIVE EXCLUSIVE
(— LINE) RUBICON
LIMITS (NEAR OUTER — OF PLAY) DEEP
LIMMA DIESIS
LIMMU EPONYM
LIMO (KIND OF —) STRETCH
LIMON (BROTHER OF —) SCEPHRUS
(FATHER OF —) TEGEATES
(MOTHER OF —) MAERA
LIMONENE CINENE CARVENE CITRENE
LIMONITE BOGORE BOGIRON PEAIRON
LIMONIUM STATICE
LIMOUSINE LIMO BERLIN SALOON SUBURBAN
LIMP HIP HOP CLOP GIMP HALT HIMP HOIT SOFT THIN HENCH HILCH HITCH LINGY LOOSE LOPPY SLAMP STILT FLABBY FLIMSY HAMBLE HIMPLE HIRPLE HOBBLE LENNOW LIMBER LIMPSY FLACCID LIMMOCK SHAFFLE UNSMART DRAGGLED DROOPING CLAUDICATION
LIMPET CHINK OPIHI SHELL ACMAEA LIMPIN FLIDDER
LIMPID PURE CLEAR LUCID BRIGHT CRYSTAL PELLUCID
LIMPING HALT LAME GIMPY LIMPY ZOPPA HALTING
LIMPLY LANKLY
LINAGE SPACE
LINALOOL LICAREOL
LINCHPIN FORELOCK
LINCOLN (IN-LAW OF —) TODD
LINCTUS LOOCH LOHOCH LOHOCK
LINDEN LIN LIME LYNE TEIL TILIA TILLET LINWOOD BASSWOOD DADDYNUT WOODLIND
LINE BAR BOX FIX RAY ROW TAW BOFF CASE CEIL COLA CRIB DASH FACE FILE GAME GAPE LACE LARD LATH LEAD LING MAIN MARK RACE RANK RULE STOP TAUM WHIP AGONE FAINT FEINT FLEET HATCH LIGNE LINEA METER RANGE SCORE SPIEL STRIA TOUCH TRACE TRAIL TRAIN TWIST BINDER CABURN CEVIAN CREASE DEGREE DOUBLE EARING GASKET ISOBAR ISOHEL ISOPAG ISOTAC METIER NETTLE SECANT SECOND SPRING STREAK STRING STRIPE AZIMUTH BABBITT CATLINE CONTOUR CREANCE ENVELOP GUNLINE HIPLINE ISOCHOR ISOGRAM ISOHYET ISONEPH ISORITH ISOSTER ISOTOME KNITTLE MARLINE NACARAT SCRATCH WINDROW BALKLINE BISECTOR BOUNDARY BUSINESS CHAMPAIN DATELINE DEADLINE DIAGONAL DIAMETER DRAGLINE DRUMLINE FISHBACK GANTLINE GEODESIC GIRTLINE HAIRLINE HANDLINE HEXAPODY ISOGLOSS ISOGONIC ISOPHANE ISOPHENE ISOPLERE ISOTHERE ISOTHERM LANDWIRE LIFELINE MARTINET SLIPBAND STRINGER SUBCLONE SUBSTILE SUBSTYLE UPSTROKE PERPENDICULAR
(— AROUND STAMP) FRAME
(— AS CENTER FOR REVOLVING) AXIS
(— HEARTH) FIX FETTLE
(— IN GLASS) STRING
(— IN HAT) HEADLINE
(— MINESHAFT) TUB
(— OF ACTION) LAY
(— OF BATTLE) FRONT
(— OF BUSINESS) WAY
(— OF CELLS) ANNULUS
(— OF CLIFFS) SCARP BREAKS
(— OF COLOR) SLASH STREAK
(— OF DANCERS) CHAIN
(— OF DESCENT) SIDE STEM STIRP STOCK PHYLUM STRAIN ANCESTRY BREEDING
(— OF DETERMINANT) COLUMN
(— OF DEVELOPMENT) STREET
(— OF DEVOLUTION) ENTAIL
(— OF FAMILY) STEM
(— OF FIBERS) CHRYSAL
(— OF FIRE HOSE) LEAD
(— OF FLOTATION) BEARINGS
(— OF FORTIFICATION) LIMES ENCEINTE
(— OF HAY) WAKE WALLOW
(— OF HEALTH) HEPATICA
(— OF HIGH TIDE) LANDWASH
(— OF HOUSES) BLOCK
(— OF INTERSECTION) GROIN BUTTOCK
(— OF JUNCTION) MEET SEAM
(— OF LIGHTNING) STREAK
(— OF MERCHANDISE) NAMEPLATE
(— OF MERCURY) HEPATICA
(— OF PERSONS) QUEUE CORDON STICKLE
(— OF PORES) HATCHING
(— OF SOLDIERS) RAY FILE RANK WAVE CORDON
(— OF STITCHING) BASTING
(— OF TACK) PITCH
(— OF TALK) SPIEL
(— OF TIMBERS) BOOM STOCKADE
(— OF TREES) SCREEN
(— OF TYPE) SLUG KICKER
(— OF UNION) SUTURE
(— ON A LETTER) SERIF
(— ON BOOK COVER) BAND
(— ON COAT) GORGE
(— ON DOLPHIN) STOP
(— ON HIGHWAY) BARRIER
(— ON WEATHER MAP) ISOBAR
(— THAT CUTS ANOTHER) SECANT
(— TO BIND CABLES) CABURN
(— TO FASTEN SAIL) EARING GASKET
(— TO RAISE FLAG) LANIARD LANYARD
(— TO START RACE) TRIG
(— TOUCHING ARC) TANGENT
(— UP) LAY QUEUE
(— WITH BRICKS) GINGE
(— WITH PANELLING) WAINSCOT
(— WITH STONES) STEEN STEYN
(— WITH TIMBER) CRIB
(ANCHOR —) RODING
(BEARING —) CUT
(BOTTOM —) NET
(BOUNDARY —) MERE FENCE BORDER ISOGLOSS
(BOUNDING —) SIDE BOUNDARY PERIMETER
(BRIEF —) ITEM
(COASTAL —) SEAMARK
(CONNECTING —) LIGATURE
(CONTINUOUS —) STRETCH
(CONTOUR —) ISOBASE ISOCHASM ISOTHERM
(CURVED —) ARC SLUR SWEEP
(CUTTING —) SECANT
(DEMARCATION —) BOMBLINE
(DIAGONAL —) BIAS
(DIVIDING —) EDGE MIDRIB DIVISION FRONTIER
(ELECTRIC —) HIGHLINE
(ENCIRCLING —) RIM
(FACIAL —) TRAIT
(FINISHING —) TAPE WIRE
(FISHING —) TOME TROT FLEET SNELL SNOOD LEADER LEDGER NORSEL BACKING BOULTER OUTLINE SPILLER SPILLET TRIMMER BLOWLINE CORKLINE FISHLINE SNAGLINE TROTLINE
(HORIZONTAL —) LEVEL
(IMAGINARY —) AGONE HINGE GROOVE ISOBAR ISOGAM ISOHEL ISOPAG HORIZON ISOBASE ISOBATH ISOGRIV ISOHYET ISOLINE ISOTACH ISOBRONT ISOCHASM ISOCHEIM ISOCHLOR ISOCHORE ISOCRYME ISOGLOSS ISOPHOTE ISOPLETH ISOSTERE ISOTHERM
(INCISED —) SCORE
(INCLINED —) CANT
(LIMITING —) RUBICON
(LONGITUDINAL —) MERIDIAN
(MEDIAN —) RAPHE
(METRICAL —) EIGHT STAFF STICH DIMETER SAPPHIC STICHOS MONOMETER OCTAMETER PENTAMETER
(MINESHAFT —) BRATTICE
(MUSICAL —) ACCOLADE
(NAUTICAL —) EARING LACING GESWARP MARLINE PAINTER RATLINE DOWNHAUL MESSENGER
(ONE-TENTH OF —) GRY
(PERPENDICULAR —) CATHETUS
(PLOTTED —) ADIABAT
(RADIATING —) BEAM
(RAILROAD —) STEM STUB
(RAISED —) RIDGE
(SPECTRUM —) GHOST DOUBLET SINGLET TRIPLET MULTIPLET
(STARTING —) SCRATCH
(STRAIGHT —) CHORD BEELINE STRAIGHT
(SUPPLY —) AIRLIFT UMBILICAL
(SURVEYING —) WAD BASE CHAIN
(THEATRICAL —S) FAT
(THIN —) THREAD
(TOW —) CORDELLE
(TRANSPORTATION —) FEEDER CARRIER
(WAVY —) SQUIGGLE
(ZIGZAG —) DANCETTE
(42 —S) LENGTH
(PREF.) LINEO STICHO
(SUFF.) STICH(OUS)
(STRAIGHT —) TRIX
LINEAGE GET KIN KIND RACE TEAM BIRTH BLOOD SPACE STIRP STOCK FAMILY HAVAGE NATION PARAGE SOURCE SPRING STRAIN DESCENT KINDRED PROGENY SUCCESS ANCESTRY PEDIGREE PARENTAGE
LINEAL DIRECT
LINEAMENT LINE TRACT TRAIT FEATURE
LINEAR RUNNING
LINECUT ZINCO
LINED MASONED
LINEMAN END GUARD CENTER TACKLE FORWARD WIREMAN CHAINMAN
LINEN LIN BUCK LAWN CRASH IRISH TOILE BARRAS DAMASK DIAPER NAPERY RAINES SENDAL BATISTE DORNICK HOLLAND LOCKRAM TABLING BARANDOS OSNABURG PLATILLA
(— CLOSET) LOCKER
(— FOR SHIRTS) SARKING
(— TO COVER CHALICE) PALL
(CHINESE —) KOMPOW
(COARSE —) HARN BARRAS
(FINE —) LAKE LAWN BYSSUS DAMASK DIAPER RAINES
(HOUSEHOLD —) NAPERY TABLING
(SCRAPED —) LINT
(SHADE OF —) ECRU
(SPANISH —) CREA
(TWILLED —) SILESIA
(PREF.) BYSSI BYSSO LINO
LINER SHIP BASKET SCRIBER STEAMER
LINES
(PREF.)
(TWO CROSSED —) CHIASMO CHIASTO
LINET (BROTHER OF —) LIONES
(HUSBAND OF —) GARETH
LINEUP SHOWUP
LING BURBOT DRIZZLE STOKVIS
LINGA DILDO
LINGCOD CULTUS
LINGER LAG HANG HOVE LING STAY CLING DALLY DELAY DEMUR DWELL HAUNT HOVER PAUSE TARRY DRETCH HANKER LOITER TAIGLE TARROW DRINGLE
LINGERER LUNGIS LAGGARD
LINGERIE FRILLIES PRETTIES
LINGERING SLOW DELAY MOROSE TARDANT DRAGGING
LINGO BAT CANT JARGON LINGUA PATTER DIALECT
LINGUA GLOSSA TONGUE
LINGUAL GLOSSAL
LINGUIST (ALSO SEE PHILOLOGIST)
LINGUISTIC GLOTTIC
LINGUISTICS GRAMMAR PHILOLOGY
LINIMENT EIK EMBROCHE OPODELDOC
LININ PLASTIN
LINING FUR BACK COAT BAIZE BRASS FACING PANNEL BABBITT

BUSHING CEILING FURRING FURRURE THIMBLE TINNING TUBBING CLEADING DOUBLING DOUBLURE FIREBACK SHEETING UNDERLAY WAINSCOT PERCALINE
(— FOR ROOF) SARKING
(— FOR WALL) FIRRING FURRING
(— FOR WELL) STEENING STEYNING
(— OF BEARING) JEWEL
(— OF CYLINDER) BUSH
(— OF FURNACE) BASQUE FIREBACK
(— OF HAT) TIP CAUL
(— OF SMELTING LADLE) SCULL
(MINESHAFT —) CRIB
(WOODEN —) LAG BRATTICE
(SUFF.) PLEURA

LINK JAR TIE TOW JOIN KNIT LUNT SHUT YOKE CLEEK COMMA NEXUS COPULA COUPLE FASTEN FETTER TOUGHT CODETTA CONNECT COUPLER ENCHAIN INVOLVE LIAISON SHACKLE CATENATE IDENTIFY VINCULUM COLLIGATE
(— ARMS) CLEEK
(— FOR TWO COMPUTERS BY PHONE) MODEM
(— IN NETWORK) LEG
(COMPOUND —) SWIVEL
(WOODEN —) LAG

LINKAGE BOND CELL COUPLING LINKWORK
LINKED CONNEX CATENATE INTEGRAL
LINKING HOOKUP ANNECTANT
(— DEVICE) LINCHPIN
LINKMAN LINKBOY LIGHTMAN
LINKS MACHAIR
(BOGGY —) MACHAIR
LINNET FINCH TWITE LENARD LINTIE REDPOLL REDFINCH
LINSANG CIVET ZINSANG
LINSEED LINGET
LINSEY-WOOLSEY WINCEY
LINT FLY FLUE FLICK CADDIS CADDICE CHARPIE CARBASUS
(SCRAPED —) XYSTUS
LINTEL CAP CLAVY HANCE CLAVEL DARNER SUMMER SQUINCH TRANSOM BRESSUMMER
(— OF FIREPLACE) MANTEL
LINUS (BROTHER OF —) ORPHEUS
(FATHER OF —) APOLLO OEAGRUS ISMENIUS
(MOTHER OF —) CALLIOPE PSAMATHE
LION CAT LLEW MORNE SHEDU SIMBA LIONEL LIONET LEOPARD
(MOUNTAIN —) PUMA COUGAR
(PREF.) LEON LEONT(O)
LION MONKEY LEONCITO
LION-TAILED MONKEY MACACO MACAQUE WANDEROO
LIP BLOB BRIM EDGE MASK PUSS SASS APRON CHOPS GROIN MOUTH SPOUT TUTEL LABIUM LABRUM ROUTER CHILOMA LABELLUM UNDERLIP
(— DISEASE) PERLECHE
(— OF BELL) SKIRT
(— OF COROLLA) GALEA
(— OF FLOWER) HELM
(— OF ORCHID) SLIPPER
(— OF PITCHER) BEAK
(— OF VESSEL) SPOUT
(—S OF MOOSE) MUFFLE
(CHAD WOMAN WITH DISTENDED —S) UBANGI
(FLAT —) APRON
(LOWER —) JIB FIPPLE
(PL.) LABRAS CUSHION
(PREF.) CHEIL(O) CHIL(O)
(SUFF.) CHIL(IA)(O)(US)
LIPARITE RHYOLITE
LIPASE PIALYN
LIPIDE FAT CERIDE ADIPOID STERIDE TETHELIN
LIPLIKE LABIAL
LIPOCHROME LUTEIN
LIPOID FAT ADIPOSE
LIPOMA STEATOMA
LIPOPROTEIN HDL LPL
(PLASMA —) VLDL
LIPPED LABIATE
LIPPIA WRIGHT ALOYSIA
LIP PLUG LABRET TEMETA
LIPPY STIMPART
LIPS
(PREF.) LABIO
LIQUEFACTION (— OF GEL) SOLATION
LIQUEFIED FUSILE POTATE REMISS RESOLVED
LIQUEFY RUN FUSE MELT RELENT LIQUATE DISSOLVE ELIQUATE
LIQUEUR EAU OUZO RAKI AURUM CREME NOYAU CHASSE GENEPI KUMMEL PASTIS PERNOD RACKEE STREGA ANESONE CORDIAL CURACAO PERSICO RATAFIA RATIFIA ABSINTHE ADVOCAAT ALKERMES AMARETTO ANGELICA ANISETTE CALVADOS MANDARIN PRUNELLE VESPETRO MARASCHINO BENEDICTINE
(PL.) EAUX
LIQUID AQUA BREE BLASH DRINK FLUID LEACH MOIST ACETAL FLUENT FURANE AEROSOL BUCKING CINEOLE EYEWASH FLOWAGE VINASSE BLACKING EFFLUENT EFFUSION EXCITANT FURFURAN LEACHATE LIBATION SOLUTION
(— AFTER SALT CRYSTALLIZATION) BITTERN
(— IN CELL) EXCITANT
(— UNIT) TUN CHENG SHENG SHING POTTLE MUTCHKIN PUNCHEON
(ACID-RESISTANT —) GROUND
(COLORING —) HENNA
(COOKING —) BREE BROO BROTH STOCK
(DISABLING —) MACE
(DISTILLED —) SPIRIT
(FILTHY —) ADDLE
(INSULATING —) ASKAREL
(MAY BE —) ASSETS
(OILY —) ANILINE CHLORAL PICAMAR CARDANOL CREOSOTE
(PERFUMED —) COLLEN COLOGNE
(REFUSE —) SCOURAGE
(REFUSE —S) SEWAGE
(SIZING —) GLAIK
(STERILIZED —) JOHNIN
(STINKING —) CACODYL
(SYRUPY —) HONEY
(TANNING —) LIME
(THICK —) DOPE GLOP SIRUP SYRUP
(THICK, STICKY —) GLOP
(VISCOUS —) TAR SCHRADAN
(VOLATILE —) ETHER ALCOHOL DILUENT LIGROIN
(WEAK —) BLASH SLIPSLOP
(PREF.) LATICI
LIQUIDATE SINK SLAY SETTLE
LIQUIDATION CLEANUP
LIQUOR ALE BUB DEW GAS LAP OKE PAD POT RUM SUP TAP WET BEER BREE FIRE FIZZ GEAR GROG LUSH PURL SUCK SWIG TAPE TIFF BOGUS BUDGE CEBUR DRINK GLASS HOOCH JUICE KEFIR MOBBY NAPPY PERRY PISCO SAUCE SHRAB SHRUB SICER SKINK STICK BOTTLE CASSIS CHICHA DIDDLE DOCTOR FOGRAM FUDDLE GATTER GENEVA GUZZLE HYDROL KIRSCH MAOTAI MASTIC MESCAL POTTLE ROTGUT SAMSHU STRUNT TIPPLE WHISKY BITTERN BRACKET BRAGGET GROCERY PHLEGMA SPUNKIE SUCTION TAPLASH TEQUILA WAIPIRO WHISKEY ABSINTHE BRAGWORT EYEWATER HYDROMEL MEDICINE OKOLEHAO POTATION RUMBOOZE FIREWATER
(— CABINET) TANTALUS
(— CASE) GARDEVIN
(— FROM MUST) ARROPE
(— FROM PEARS) PERRY PERRIE
(— FROM WOOL-SCOURING) SUD SUDS
(— MIXED WITH WINE) DOCTOR
(— SALE) ABKARI
(— TAKEN IN SODA WATER) CINDER
(ACID —) VERJUICE
(ALCOHOLIC —) GIN ARAK HOOCH ARRACK BRANDY SAMSHU AQUAVIT BITTERS SNOOTFUL
(ALCOHOLIC —S) ARDENT
(BITTER —) TIRE
(CHEAP —) SMOKE
(COLORLESS —) GLYCID GLYCOL GLYCIDOL GUAIACOL
(CRAB APPLE —) WHERRY
(DISTILLED —) DEW SOTOL GRAPPA PHLEGM SCHNAPPS
(DRUGGED —) HOCUS
(HARD —) BOOZE
(INTOXICATING —) GROG LOAD LUSH TAPE BUDGE GUZZLE KUMISS HASHISH MOONSHINE
(MALT —) ALE BUB BEER STOUT ENTIRE PORTER STINGO
(MOTHER —) HYDROL BITTERN
(POT —) BREWIS
(RICE —) SAMSHU
(SPIRITUOUS —) DEW GROG MOBBY STRUNT WAIPIRO KAOLIANG
(STRAIGHT —) SHORT
(STRONG —) RUG TUBA VINO HOGAN RUMBO STINGO
(TAN —) OOZE
(TANNING —) LAYAWAY TAILING
(WATERED —) BLASH
(WEAK —) BULL SLIPSLOP
LIRA LIRE ZWANZIGER
(ONE-TWENTIETH —) SOLDO
LIRIPIPE TIPPET
LISSOME LITHE LIMBER NIMBLE SUPPLE SVELTE FLEXIBLE
LIST TIP BILL FILE HEEL LEET NOTE POLL ROLL ROON ROTA SWAG BRIEF CANON GISTS INDEX PANEL SCORE SCRIP SCROW SLATE AGENDA CENSUS COLUMN DETAIL DOCKET ERRATA HUDDLE LEGEND PURREL RAGGER RAGMAN RECORD ROSTER SCREED SCROLL SERIES CATALOG CITATOR COMPILE DIPTYCH ITEMIZE LISTING NOTITIA WAYBILL CALENDAR CINCTURE HANDLIST PLATBAND REGISTER SCHEDULE SYNONYMY TITULARY
(— OF BOOKS) CANON
(— OF CANDIDATES) LEET SLATE TERNA
(— OF CAPABILITIES) REPERTOIRE
(— OF CHURCH DATES) ORDO
(— OF CONTESTANTS) DRAW SEEDING
(— OF CRIMINAL CONVICTIONS) RECORD
(— OF DISEASES) NOSOLOGY
(— OF INGREDIENTS) FORMULA
(— OF JURORS) TALES
(— OF MAP SYMBOLS) LEGEND
(— OF PASSERS WITHOUT HONORS) GULF
(— OF RATES) TARIFF
(— OF SAINTS) CANON
(— OF SECURITIES) PORTFOLIO
(— OF THEATRICAL PARTS) CAST
(COMPUTER —) MENU
(GENEALOGICAL —) BEGATS
(IMPRESSIVE —) ARRAY
(LEGAL —) TABLEAU
(LONG —) LITANY
(MAKE A —) CATALOG
(OBITUARY —) NECROLOGY
(PRAYER —) BEADROLL
(WINE —) CARD
(PL.) CAREER BARRACE
LISTEL QUADRA
LISTEN HARK HEAR LIST TEND TENEZ ATTEND HARKEN INTEND WHISPER
(— TO) DIG EAR HARK HEAR CATCH ATTEND
LISTENER AUDITOR OTACUST
LISTENING PRICK AUDIENT HEARING
(— DEVICE) BUG
(PREF.) ACOU
LISTER SULKY RIDGER
LISTERA OPHRYS
LISTING AGEE ITEM FRAME PARADE LASHING
(— OF JURORS) ARRAY
LISTLESS DOPY DULL WOFF DOWFF FAINT MOONY DONSIE SUPINE LANGUID UNLISTY UNLUSTY CARELESS INDOLENT THOWLESS TONELESS UNHEARTY
LISTLESSLY DAVIELY
LISTLESSNESS ACEDIA APATHY UNLUST VACUITY

LISUARTE (DAUGHTER OF —) ORIANA
(FATHER OF —) ESPLANDIAN
LITANY AITESIS ROGATION
LITE LOCAL LOWCAL
LITERAL VERBAL TEXTUAL
LITERALLY SIMPLY
LITERARY BLUE BOOKISH LITERATE
(— MATERIAL) KITSCH
(— WORK) PREQUEL
(SUFF.) **(— STYLE)** ESE
LITERATE LETTERED
LITERATI CLERISY
LITERATURE FICTION LETTERS CLAPTRAP
(— CLANDESTINELY DISTRIBUTED) SAMIZDAT
(CLANDESTINE —) SAMIZDAT
(EROTIC —) EROTOLOGY
(OBSCENE —) SCATOLOGY
(RUSSIAN SUPPRESSED —) SAMIZDAT
(SACRED —) VEDA SRUTI
(WISDOM —) CHOKMAH HOKHMAH
LITHE BAIN SPRY WIRY SWACK CLEVER LIMBER LISSOM SILKEN SUPPLE SVELTE WANDLE LISSOME FLEXIBLE

LITHUANIA
CAPITAL: VILNA WILNA VILNIUS
COIN: LIT LITAS MARKA CENTAS FENNIG OSTMARK AUKSINAS SKATIKAS
FORMER CAPITAL: KOVNO KAUNAS
NAME: LITVA LIETUVA
PEOPLE: BALT LETT ZHMUD LITVAK YATVYAG
RIVER: NEMAN NERIS RUSNE VENTA DUBYSA LIELUPE NEMUNAS PREGOLYA
TOWN: MEMEL VILNA JELGAVA VILNIUS KAPSUKAS KLAIPEDA SIAULIAI

LITHUANIAN BALT ZHMUD
LITIGANT SUER SUITOR
LITIGATE LAW PLEAD CONTEST
LITIGATION LAW LIS MOOT SUIT LAWING PLEADING PLEASHIP
LITMUS LAKMUS TURNSOLE
LITOTES MEIOSIS
LITTER DIG PIG BIER RAFF REDD BREED CABIN CLECK DOOLY DRECK HAULM MULCH SEDAN TRASH DOOLIE FARROW GOCART KINDLE KITTEN MAHMAL REFUSE CLUTTER LETTIGA LOUSTER MAMMOCK NORIMON RUBBISH RUMMAGE SCAMBLE BRANCARD CARRIAGE KINDLING MUNCHEEL PAVILION STRETCHER
(— FOR LIVESTOCK) BEDDING
(— OF PIGS) FAR FARE FARROW
(— ON PACK ANIMAL) CACOLET
(CAMEL —) KAJAWAH
(FOREST —) DUFF
(MOLE —) CACOLET
(SENT TO MECCA) MAHMAL
LITTERBUG SLOB
LITTERED FOUL
LITTLE FEW LIL PEU WEE CURN LITE POCO TINY VEEN CHOTA CRUMB SMALL TASTE WHONE BITTIE DAPPER LEETLE MINUTE PETITE PICKLE PUSILL KENNING MODICUM THOUGHT FRACTION SNIPPING
(— BY LITTLE) EDGINGLY INCHMEAL
(— LESS THAN) ABOUT
(— MUSICALLY) POCO
(— ONE) RUNT BUTCHA POPPET
(A —) SOMEWHAT
(INDEFINITELY —) NTH
(PREF.) OLIG(O) PARVI PAUCI PUSILL(I) STEN(O)
(SUFF.) ISK KIN STENOSIS ULE
(— ONE) CLE ELLA ETTE IE ILLA
LITTLE DEMON (AUTHOR OF —) SOLOGUB
(CHARACTER IN —) SASHA LIUDMILA PYLNIKOV PEREDONOV RUSTILOVA NEDOTYKOMKA
LITTLE DORRIT (AUTHOR OF —) DICKENS
(CHARACTER IN —) AMY JOHN CASBY FANNY FLORA ARTHUR DORRIT EDWARD PANCKS CHIVERY CLENNAM MEAGLES WILLIAM BLANDOIS PLORNISH BARNACLES
LITTLE MINISTER (AUTHOR OF —) BARRIE
(CHARACTER IN —) DOW ROB ADAM GAVIN MICAH NANNY BABBIE OGILVY DISHART MCQUEEN RINTOUL WEBSTER MARGARET
LITTLENESS ATOMITY
LITTLE WOMEN (AUTHOR OF —) ALCOTT
(CHARACTER IN —) JO AMY MEG BETH DEMI JOHN BHAER DAISY FRITZ KIRKE MARCH BROOKE CARROL LAURIE MARMEE LAURENCE THEODORE
LITTORAL COAST
LITURGY FORM RITE ABODAH MAARIB MINHAG NEILAH MINCHAH MYSTERY HIERURGY SHAHARIT
LIVE BE USE WIN KEEP LEAD STAY ALERT ALIVE DWELL EXIST GREEN HABIT LEEVE QUICK SHACK VITAL HARBOR LIVELY LIVING REMAIN RESIDE BREATHE INHABIT SUBSIST CONTINUE CONVERSE VIGOROUS
(— AT ANOTHER'S EXPENSE) COSHER
(— BY BEGGING) CADGE SKELDER
(— BY STRATAGEMS) SHARK
(— FROM DAY TO DAY) EKE
(— IN CONTINENCE) CONTAIN
(— IN LUXURY) STATE
(— IN PEACE) COEXIST
(— IN SAME PLACE) STALL
(— ON) SURVIVE
(— RIOTOUSLY) JET
(— TEMPORARILY) CAMP
(— THROUGH) PASS TIDE
(— TOGETHER) AGREE COHABIT
(— WELL) BATTEN
LIVE-BOX CAR
LIVE-FOREVER LULANG ORPINE
LIVELIHOOD BEING BREAD LIVING LIFEHOOD
LIVELINESS PEP BRIO FIRE FIZZ LIFE PUNCH SPUNK BOUNCE ESPRIT GAIETY SPIRIT ENTRAIN SPARKLE ACTIVITY VITALITY VIVACITY
LIVELONG LEELANG ENDURING
LIVELY GAY TID AIRY BRAG CANT FAST FESS GLEG KECK LIVE PERT RACY SPRY TAIT TRIG VITE VIVE WARM YARE AGILE ALERT ALIVE BONNY BRISK BUXOM CANTY CHIRK COBBY CORKY CRISP DESTO FRESH FRISK JAZZY KEDGE KINKY MERRY PAWKY PEART PEPPY POKEY RUDDY SASSY SMART VIVID WHICK ACTIVE BLITHE BOUNCY BRIGHT CHEERY CHIRPY COCKET CROOSE CROUSE DAPPER FIERCE FRISCH GINGER JOCUND KIPPER LIVING NIMBLE QUIVER SEMMIT SPARKY SPRACK TROTTY VEGETE WHISKY WIMBLE ALLEGRO ANIMATE ANIMOSE BOBBISH BUCKISH BUOYANT GIGGISH GIOCOSO JOCULAR KINETIC LEBHAFT POINTED ROUSING SPIRITY SPRINGY TITTUMY TITTUPY WINCING ANIMATED BOUNCING CHIRRUPY FRISKFUL FRISKING GALLIARD SANGUINE SKITTISH SMACKING SPANKING SPIRITED SPORTIVE STEERING STIRRING TRIPSOME VEGETOUS VOLATILE SPARKLING
(— PERSON) SWINGER
(BE —) SWING
(TO BE —) SWING
LIVEN LACE CHEER ANIMATE
LIVE OAK ENCINA
LIVER MAW FOIE HEPAR VISCUS PUDDING
(— ATROPHY) LUPINOSIS
(— OF LOBSTER) TOMALLEY
(PREF.) HEPATICO HEPAT(O)
LIVER-COLORED HEPATIC
LIVERPOOL (NATIVE OF —) SCOUSE SCOUSER LIVERPUDLIAN
LIVERWORT HEPATICA MOSSWORT
LIVERY SUIT CLOTH LIVRE UNIFORM CLOTHING
LIVESTOCK FEE WARE STOCK STORE STUFF CHATTEL BESTIALS FATSTOCK
LIVE WIRE HUSTLER
LIVID HAW WAN BLAE BLUE
LIVING KEEP ALIVE BEING BREAD GOING QUICK VITAL WHICK AROUND LIVELY VIABLE ZOETIC ANIMATE SUPPORT ANIMATED BENEFICE
(— IN THE WORLD) SECULAR
(— IN WAVES) LOTIC
(— NEAR THE GROUND) EPIGEAN
(— ON BANKS OF STREAMS) RIPAL RIPARIAN
(— THING) QUICK
(BARE —) CRUST
(ECCLESIASTICAL —) BENEFICE
(PREF.) ONT(O) VIVI
(— ORGANISMS) BIO
(SUFF.) **(— IN OR ON)** COLE COLINE COLOUS
LIVING-ROOM PARLOR
LIVRE FRANC
LIXIVIATE LEACH
LIXIVIUM LYE
LIZARD DAB EFT GOH UMA UTA DABB GILA IBIT SEPS TEGU TEJU URAN AGAMA ANOLE BLUEY DRACO GECKO GUANO SKINK SNAKE SWIFT TEIID TOKAY TWEEG VARAN AMEIVA ANGUID ARBALO DRAGON GOANNA HARDIM IGUANA LACERT LEGUAN MOLOCH TEIOID WORRAL ZONURE BUMMAJO CAUDATE CHEECHA DIAPSID MONITOR REPTILE SAURIAN SCINCID SCINCUS TUATARA TUCKTOO BASILISK KAKARIKI MOKAMOKA SCINCOID SCORPION SLOWWORM TEGUEXIN WHIPTAIL ZONUROID CHAMELEON CHUCKWALLA PLEURODONT
(PREF.) LACERTI SAUR(O)
(SUFF.) SAUR(A)(IA)(IAN)(US)
LIZARD FISH ULAE INIOME SOAPFISH SPEARING
LLAMA ALPACA VICUNA GUANACO
LLUDD NUDD
LO SEE ECCE
LOACH DOJO BEARDIE MUDFISH
LOAD BUN JAG LUG TON BUCK CARK CRAM DECK DRAW FILL HAUL LADE LAST LUMP PACK RAKE SEAM STEM STOW TOTE TURN BARTH CARGO DRAFT PITCH PRIME STACK TRUSS TURSE BURDEN CHARGE COMBLE DEMAND FODDER FOTHER HAMPER LADING LOADEN THRACK WEIGHT BALLAST CARLOAD DERRICK DRAUGHT ENDORSE FRAUGHT FREIGHT ONERATE OPPRESS BACKPACK CARRIAGE ENCUMBER HEADLOAD SHIPLOAD PLANELOAD
(— A DIE FOR CHEATING) COG
(— FABRICS) WEIGHT
(— OF COAL) KEEL
(— OF HAY OR CORN) HURRY
(— OF LAMBS) DECK
(— OF LOGS) PEAKER BUNKLOAD
(— OF WOOL) TOD
(— ON BACK) ENDORSE INDORSE
(— SHIP) STEM
(— TO CAPACITY) SATURATE
(— TO EXCESS) ENCUMBER
(ELECTRIC —) DEMAND
(EXCESSIVE —) SURCHARGE
(HORSE —) SEAM SUMAGE
(LAST — OF GRAIN) WINTER
(SMALL —) JAG JAGG JOBBLE
(PL.) BUSHEL
LOADER CHARGER
LOADING LADING MARGIN ARRASTRE
(— PLACE) PIER
LOADSTONE MAGNET SIDERITE LODESTONE
LOAF BAP BUM COB AZYM HACK HAKE HULL LAKE MIKE SLIM SORN BANGE BREAD BRICK DRING MOUCH SHOOL SLIVE SLOSH BLUDGE BROGUE CADDLE DIDDLE GEORGE HALLAH RODNEY SLINGE WASTEL HOOSIER MANCHET SHACKLE SLOUNGE SOLDIER OBLATION PANHAGIA QUARTERN SHAMMOCK

(— AROUND) HULL HOWFF SLOSH RODNEY GOLDBRICK
(— OF BREAD) COB BATON FADGE MICHE TOMMY HALLAH TAMMIE
(BROWN —) GEORGE
(KIND OF —) DELI
(ROUND —) BUN COBURG
(SMALL —) BAP COB NACKET
(SUGAR —) TITLER
LOAFER BUM CAD YOB BEAT GRUB STIFF BUMBLE BUMMER CADGER KEELIE SLOUCH SLOVEN BLUDGER COASTER FAITOUR HOODLUM SLINKER SOLDIER COBERGER HOOLIGAN LARRIKIN LAYABOUT SEASONER
LOAFING IDLE MIKE
LOAM RAB LAME MALM MARL SLIP LOESS REGUR CLEDGE
LOAMY MELLOW
LOAN DHAN LEND LENT PREST CREDIT DONATE MUTUUM ADVANCE FIXTURE IMPREST
LOANBLEND HYBRID
LOATH LOTH LAITH LEATH SWEER DAINTY BACKWARD
LOATHE UG HATE SHUN ABHOR LAITH WLATE AGRISE DETEST DESPISE SCUNDER SCUNNER NAUSEATE
LOATHING NAUSEA REVOLT DISGUST SCUNNER
LOATHLY LAIDLY
LOATHSOME FOUL UGLY VILE POCKY LAIDLY UNLIEF HATEFUL LOATHLY MAWKISH OBSCENE TETROUS WLATFUL DEFORMED NAUSEOUS WLATSOME NEFANDOUS ABOMINABLE
LOB ARC
LOBBY HALL FOYER NARTHEX PASSAGE TAMBOUR ANTEROOM COULISSE
LOBBYIST PROMOTER
LOBE ALA FIN LAP AXIS LIST MALA ALULA EXITE FIBER FIBRE FLUKE GALEA LOBUS THECA TOOTH UVULA EARLAP FILLET FOLIUM GLOSSA INSULA LAPPET LIGULE LOBING MANTLE VANNUS VERMIS AROLIUM AURICLE HEMAPOD LACINIA LOBULUS AMYGDALA EPICHILE GLABELLA LABELLUM PALPIFER PHYLLOID SQUAMULE
(— OF ANTHER) THECA
(— OF LEAF) LACINIA PINNULA PINNULE SEGMENT
(— OF WHALE'S TAIL) FLUKE
(PREF.) (— OF BRAIN) LEUC(O)
LOBED CUT LOMATINE
(SUFF.) FID FIDATE
LOBLOLLY LOUT MIRE PINE GRUEL
LOBSTER CRAY HOMARD DECAPOD SHEDDER CRAWFISH CRAYFISH LANGOSTA MACRURAN
(— ENCLOSURE) CRAWL
(— LESS THAN 10 INCHES LONG) JOE
(FEMALE —) HEN
(NORWAY —) SCAMPO
(SMALL —) PAWK NANCY
(UNDERSIZED —) SHORT
LOBSTER POT COY CRAIL CREEL TRUNK FISHPOT
LOBULARIA KONIGA
LO-CAL LITE
LOCAL HOME NATIVE LIMITED TOPICAL VICINAL REGIONAL EPICHORIC
(NOT —) AZONIC
(PREF.) TOP(O)
LOCALE AREA SITE LOCAL PLACE SCENE
LOCALITY SPA HAND PLAT SPOT LOCUS PLACE POINT SITIO SITUS STEAD HABITAT LATITUDE POSITURE SITUATION
(BARREN —) GALL
(BEAUTIFUL —) XANADU
(GUARDED —) POST
LOCALIZE SITUATE POSITION
LOCATE SITE SPOT PITCH PLACE BESTOW BILLET SETTLE SITUATE PINPOINT
(— AT INTERVALS) SPOT
(— WATER) DIVINE
LOCATED SET FIXED SEATED SITUATED
(— OFF THE HIGHWAY) DEVIOUS
LOCATING SYSTEM SOFAR
LOCATION FALL HOME PLOT SEAT PLACE SITUS WHERE UBIETY AMENITY STATION HOMESITE STANDING
(ESSENTIAL —) EYE
(FOREST —) CHANCE
(GEOGRAPHIC —) SEAT
(MINING —) MYNPACHT
(NATURAL —) HABITAT
(SUFF.) TOPE TOPY
LOCH LOUGH LOCHAN
LOCK COT KEY FEAK FRIB HOLD TRIM YALE CHUBB CLASP SASSE TRESS DUBBEH ENLOCK LUCKEN DAGLOCK EARLOCK KEYLOCK PINLOCK SPANNER DEADLOCK FORELOCK
(— IMPROPERLY) BIND
(— IN RIVER) SASSE
(— OF HAIR) COT TAG TUZ COTT CURL FEAK TATE FLAKE FLOCK FLUKE QUIFF TRESS TANGLE COWLICK EARLOCK FRIZZLE SERPENT WIMPLER FORELOCK SIDELOCK
(— OF WOOL) TAG COTT FRIB FLOCK STAPLE HASLOCK
(— UP) JAIL STOW ENCAGE CABINET
(CANAL —) COFFER CHAMBER
(DIRTY —) FRIB
(MATTED —) COT COTT DAGLOCK
(MUSKET —) ROWET
(PART OF —) REWET STRIKE
(WHEEL —) REWET
LOCKED FAST LUCKEN
LOCKER HUTCH ASCHAM
LOCKERMAN NIBBLER SCOTCHER SNIBBLER
LOCKET BRELOQUE
LOCKJAW TETANUS TRISMUS
LOCKNUT JAMNUT KEEPER
LOCKOUT SHUTOUT
LOCKS MOP
LOCKSMITH LOCKYER
LOCKUP JUG BRIG GAOL JAIL LOCK LOGS STIR CHOKY CLINK TRONK COOLER HOOSEGOW ROUNDHOUSE
LOCOMOTION FLYING LATION
LOCOMOTIVE HOG PIG PUG BOGY GOAT HOGG MULE SHAG TANK BOGIE DINKY DUMMY MOGUL PILOT DIESEL DOCTOR DOLLIE DONKEY ENGINE LOADER PUSHER SMOKER YARDER BOBTAIL BOOSTER SHUNTER STEAMER CALLIOPE CHOOCHOO COMPOUND DOLLBEER
(— WITHOUT CARS) WILDCAT
(EXTRA —) HELPER
(PART OF —) CAB ROD BELL DOME HOSE LAMP STEP BRACE HINGE PILOT TRUCK BOILER JACKET TENDER COUPLER SANDBOX WHISTLE CYLINDER HANDRAIL INJECTOR SANDPIPE HEADLIGHT RESERVOIR DRIVEWHEEL SMOKESTACK
LOCOMOTOR ATAXIA TABES
LOCOWEED LOCO LEGUME PEAVINE CRAZYWEED
LOCRINE (DAUGHTER OF —) SABRINA
(FATHER OF —) BRUTE BRUTUS
LOCULUS THECA
LOCUS PLACE EVOLUTE SURFACE SYNAPSE CONCHOID ENVELOPE HOROPTER
LOCUST WETA BRUKE CICAD HONEY ACACIA CICADA QUAKER SKIPPER TETRIGID VOETGANGER
LOCUST TREE CAROB ACACIA LOCUST ROBINIA ALGAROBA
LODE LEAD REEF VEIN LEDGE COURSE FEEDER QUARRY SCOVAN COUNTER
LODOLETTA (CHARACTER IN —) ANTONIO FLAMMEN LODOLETTA
(COMPOSER OF —) MASCAGNI
LODESTONE MAGNET SIDERITE TERRELLA
LODGE DIG HUT INN LIE BEAT CAMP HOST KEEP ROOM STAY STOW TENT BOWER CABIN COUCH COURT GROVE GUEST HOGAN HOTEL HOUSE HOWFF LAYER LOGIS STICK TARRY ALIGHT BESTOW BILLET BURROW COSHER GESTEN GRANGE HOSTEL RESIDE SETTLE BARRACK LODGING QUARTER SOJOURN EMBOLIZE HARBINGE
(— AND EAT) COSHER
(— FOR SAFEKEEPING) DEPOSIT
(— IN COURT) BOX
(DRUID —) GROVE
(LOCAL —) COURT
(SPORTSMAN'S —) SHEAL
LODGEPOLE PINE TAMARACK
LODGER INMATE ROOMER TENANT
LODGING BED CRIB FERM GIST HAFT HOST NEST GEAST LOGIS HARBOR HOSTEL LIVERY HOSPICE HOUSING COUCHANT GUESTING
(— FOR SOLDIERS) CASERN
(— OF MARABOUT) KOUBA
(CHEAP —) DOSS
(TEMPORARY —) SHELTER
(VILE —) KENNEL
(PL.) PAD DIGS DIGGINGS
LODGINGHOUSE INN KIP GITE STOP HOTEL LOGIA LOCANDA PENSION HOSTELRY
LODICULE SQUAMULA SQUAMULE
LOESS LIMON
LOFT BALK FLAT GOLF JUBE LAFT ATTIC SOLAR GARRET SOLLAR HAYLOFT COCKLOFT SCAFFOLD TRAVERSE
(— GOLF BALL) PITCH
(HAY —) TALLET TALLIT
LOFTIEST SUPREME
LOFTINESS PRIDE HEIGHT DIGNITY MAJESTY EMINENCE GRANDEUR HIGHNESS CELSITUDE
(— OF SPIRIT) MAGNANIMITY
LOFTSMAN LINESMAN
LOFTY AIRY HIGH LOFT TALL BRENT ELATE GRAND GREAT NOBLE PROUD SKYEY STEEP WINGY AERIAL ANDEAN HAUGHT TOPFUL TOWERY UPWARD WINGED ANDESIC ARDUOUS EMINENT EXCELSE HAUGHTY SUBLIME ARROGANT ELEVATED GENEROUS MAJESTIC OLYMPIAN TOWERING
LOG NOG BUNK CLOG DRAG SKID CHOCK CHUCK CHUNK PIECE STICK STOCK BATTEN BILLET PEAKER PEELER SADDLE SAWLOG BACKLOG DAYBOOK DEADMAN DEGRADE JOURNAL LOGBOOK DEADHEAD
(— AS ANCHOR) DEADMAN
(— AS RAFTER) VIGA
(— BINDING A RAFT) SWIFTER
(— CAR) BUNK
(— FASTENED TO TRAP) DRAG
(— SUPPORTING MINE ROOF) NOG
(— WITHOUT BARK) BUCKSKIN
(— WITH SPIKES IN END) DEADENER
(ENCLOSED —S) BOOM
(FLOATING —S) DRIVE
(LOAD OF —S) PEAKER
(PILE OF —S) DECK ROLLWAY
(SAWED —) BOULE
(SLABBED —) CANT
(SMALL —) LOGGET
(SPLIT —) PUNCHEON
(STRIPPED —) BATTEN
(SUNKEN —) DEADHEAD
LOGANIN MELIATIN
LOGARITHM DENSITY
(— SYMBOL) PF PH PK RH
(NEGATIVE —) PH
LOGBOOK LOG JOURNAL
LOGE BOX BOOTH LODGE STALL
LOGGER RIDER BOWMAN DECKER FALLER GOPHER HOOKER LIMBER MARKER SCORER CHOPPER FROGGER GRABBER SPOTTER CATTYMAN
LOGGIA LODGE BALCONY MIRADOR
LOGIC NYAYA LOGICS CANONIC WITCRAFT
(— OF DISCOVERY) HEURETIC
LOGICAL SANE RAISONNE RATIONAL
LOGISTILLA (SISTER OF —) ALCINA MORGANA

LOGMAN CHASER CHOPPER
LOGO LABEL EMBLEM
LOGOGRAM IDEOGRAM
LOGOMACHY (ONE ENGAGED IN —) DEBATER
LOGOS WORD
LOGOTYPE SIG
LOG PERCH DARTER HOGFISH ROCKFISH
LOGROLLING BIRLING
(— TOURNAMENT) ROLEO
LOGWOOD BRAZIL ADMIRAL DYEWOOD BLUEWOOD HYPERNIC CAMPEACHY
LOGY DROWSY GROGGY
LOHAN RAKAN
LOHENGRIN (CHARACTER IN —) ELSA HENRY ORTRUD FREDERICK GOTTFRIED LOHENGRIN TELRAMUND
(COMPOSER OF —) WAGNER
(FATHER OF —) PARSIFAL
(WIFE OF —) ELSA
LOIN LEER LISK ALOYAU LUNYIE
(— STEAK) FILET FILLET TOURNEDOS
(PORK —) GRISKIN
(2 UNCUT —S) BARON
(PL.) REINS FILLET SADDLE
(PREF.) LUMB(O) OSPHY(O)
LOINCLOTH IZAR MALO MARO DHOTI LUNGI PAGNE PAREU MOOCHA PANUNG DHOOTIE
LOIS (DAUGHTER OF —) EUNICE
(GRANDSON OF —) TIMOTHY
LOITER LAG CLUG FOOL HAKE HANG HAWM HAZE HOVE LOUT MIKE MUCK SLUG COOSE DELAY DRAWL KNOCK MOUCH SHOOL SIDLE TARRY COOTER DAWDLE LAGGER LINGER MUCKER STRAKE TAIGLE PROJECT SHAFFLE LALLYGAG LOLLYGAG SCOWBANK SLAMMOCK SLUMMOCK HANGAROUND
LOITERER DRONE IDLER LAGGER LAGGARD LURCHER
LOITERING SLIMSY LAGGARD
LOKAPALA MAHARAJA
LOKI (DAUGHTER OF —) HEL
(FATHER OF —) FARBAUTI
(MOTHER OF —) NAL LAUFEY ANGRBODHA
(SLAYER OF —) HEIMDALL
(WIFE OF —) SIGYN ANGURBODA
LOLITA NYMPHET
LOLL FUG IDLE LAZE LOUT FROWST LOLLUP LOUNGE SOZZLE SPRAWL RECLINE SCAMBLE SCOWBANK
LOLLAPALOOZA LULU ONER
LOLLIPOP LOLLY SUCKER SUCKABOB
LOLO NOSU
LONDON SMOKE COCKAGNE
(— DISTRICT) SOHO CHEAPSIDE
(BRIDGE IN —) TOWER ALBERT PUTNEY CHELSEA WATERLOO
(DISTRICT OF —) SOHO ACTON ADELPHI ALSATIA BRIXTON CHELSEA MAYFAIR
(MONUMENT IN —) GOG MAGOG NELSON CENOTAPH VICTORIA
(RIVER OF —) THAMES
(STREET OF —) BOND FLEET CANNON SAVILE DOWNING WARDOUR HAYMARKET
(SUBURB OF —) KEW FINCHLEY
LONDONER FLATCAP
LONE LANE SOLE ALONE APART SINGLE SOLITARY
(— STAR STATE) TEXAS
LONELINESS ONENESS VACANCY SOLITUDE
LONELY LORN ONLY SOLE VAST ALONE UNKET UNKID WISHT ALANGE DEAFLY SULLEN DEAVELY FORLORN LONEFUL SOLEYNE DESOLATE SECLUDED SOLITARY
(PREF.) EREM(O)
LONESOME ALONE DOLEY LONELY LANESOME SOLITARY
LONG HO DIE FAR FIT YEN ACHE DREE HANK HONE ITCH LANG SIDE TALL WILN WISH YAWN CRAVE DREAM GREEN LATHY LONGA MOURN STARK WEARY YEARN ARIGUE ASPIRE DESIRE DREICH HANKER HUNGER LINGER LONGUS PROLIX STOUND THIRST LENGTHY TEDIOUS WEILANG GEMINATE INFINITE
(— AGO) FERN LANGSYNE
(— AND SLENDER) REEDY SQUINNY
(— AND UNIFORM IN WIDTH) LINEAR
(— FOR) CARE HONE COVET CRAVE TASTE ASPIRE DESIRE SUSPIRE
(— RESTLESSLY) ITCH
(— SINCE) YORE
(EXTRA —) MAXI
(TEDIOUSLY —) MORTAL
(PREF.) DOLICH(O) LONGI LONGO MACR(O) MEC(O)
LONG-BILLED CURLEW SMOKER
LONGBOAT SLOOP
LONG-BODIED RACY RANGY
LONGERON SPAR
LONGEVITY VIVACITY
(— CHARACTER) SHOU
LONGING YEN ENVY ITCH LUST PINE WISH BRAME YEARN DESIRE HANKER TALENT THIRST ATHIRST CRAVING THIRSTY WILLING WISHFUL WISTFUL APPETENT APPETITE CUPIDITY HOMESICK PRURIENT
LONGINGLY WISTLY
LONGITUDE (PLANET'S —) EPOCH
LONGITUDINALLY ENDLONG
LONG-LASTING CHRONIC
LONG-LEGGED RANGY
LONGLEGS STILT
LONGLINE BULTOW
LONG-LIVED LONGEVE MACROBIAN
LONGSHOREMAN DOCKER HOBBLER WHARFIE DOCKHAND STEVEDORE ROUSTABOUT
LONG-STANDING OLD
LONG-SUFFERING MEEK PATIENT ENDURING PATIENCE
LONG-TAILED MACRURAL
LONG-TAILED WHIDAH REDBILL
LONG TOM SKIPPER
LONG-WINDED PROLIX PROSAIC
LOOK LA LO AIR EYE KEN SEE SPY CAST GAWK GAZE GIVE GLOM HEED KEEK LATE LUCK MARK MIEN POKE SEEM SWAP VIEW WAIT ACIES BLUSH DEKKO FAVOR FLASH GLEAM GLEER GLIFF GLINT SCREW SIGHT SQUIZ VIZZY WLITE APPEAR ASPECT EYEFUL GANDER GLANCE REGARD REWARD VISION EYESHOT EYEWINK INSIGHT SEEMING DISCOVER LANGUISH OEILLADE
(— ABOUT) BELOOK SPECTATE
(— AFTER) TENT ATTEND FATHER FETTLE PROCURE
(— AMOROUSLY) SMICKER
(— ASKANCE) GLIM LEER SKEW BAGGE GLENT GLEDGE SKLENT
(— AT) DIG SEE GLOM LAMP VIEW VISE GLISK ADVISE BEHOLD REGARD REWARD CONSIDER SPECTATE
(— BACK) RETROSPECT
(— CLOSELY) PRY ESPY SCAN
(— CROSS-EYED) SHEYLE
(— DOWN UPON) SNOB DESPISE
(— DULLY) BLEAR
(— EVERYWHERE) COMB
(— FIXEDLY) GAZE KYKE GLORE STARE
(— FOR) SPY FOND SEEK AWAIT GROPE EXPECT PROPOSE RESPECT
(— FORWARD) EXPECT FORESEE ENVISAGE ENVISION
(— GLANCINGLY) BLINK
(— GLOOMY) SCOWL
(— IN SNEAKING MANNER) SNOOP
(— INTENTLY) GLOSE VISIE GLOWER EYEBALL
(— INTO) SOUND SEARCH
(— JOYOUS) SMILE
(— LIKE) IMITATE
(— OBLIQUELY) GLIME GOGGLE SQUINT
(— OF DERISION) FLEER
(— OF PLANETS) ASPECTS
(— ON) SPECTATE
(— OUT) FEND MIND CHEESE JIGGERS OUTLOOK
(— OVER) SCAN TOISE BROWSE SURVEY EXAMINE
(— SEARCHINGLY) COMB PEER PORE TOOT
(— SLYLY) PEEP GLINK
(— SOUR) GLUNCH
(— STEADFASTLY) GLOAT
(— SULKY) LUMP
(— SULLEN) LOUR LOWER
(— TO) RESPECT
(— UPON AS) ACCOUNT
(— WILDLY) GLOP WAUL WHAWL
(— WITH FAVOR) SMILE
(AMOROUS —) SMICKER
(ANGRY —) SCOWL
(BRIEF —) GLIM GLINT GLIMPSE
(CLOSE —) VISIE
(LOVING —) BELGARD
(OBLIQUE —) SQUINT
(QUICK —) SCRY GLENT
(SEARCHING —) SCRUTINY
(SEVERE —) FROWN
(SIDELONG —) GLEE GLIME
(SLY —) GLEG GLIME TWIRE
(SULLEN —) GLOOM GLOUT GLUNCH
(TENDER —) LANGUISH
(WANTON —) LEER
(PL.) DAPS
(PREF.) **(— THROUGH)** PERSPECTO
LOOKER BEAUTY HERDSMAN SEARCHER
LOOKER-ON BEHOLDER
LOOK HOMEWARD ANGEL
(AUTHOR OF —) WOLFE
(CHARACTER IN —) BEN GANT LUKE DAISY ELIZA HELEN JAMES LAURA EUGENE GROVER OLIVER LEONARD MARGARET
LOOKING (— ASKANCE) SQUINT
(— BACKWARD) REVIEW RETROSPECT
(— OBLIQUELY) SQUINT
(— UP) ROSY
LOOKING BACKWARD (AUTHOR OF —) BELLAMY
(CHARACTER IN —) WEST EDITH LEETE JULIAN BARTLETT PILLSBURY
LOOKOUT HUER TOUT SCOUT WATCH BANTAY CONNER TOOTER FUNERAL OUTLOOK ATALAYAN BANTAYAN BARTIZAN COCKATOO PROSPECT TOWERMAN WATCHOUT OBSERVATORY
LOOM BEAM BULK HULK LEEM DOBBY FRAME GLOOM BEETLE DOBBIE DRAWLOOM HANDLOOM JACQUARD OVERPICK
(— ATTACHMENT) LAPPET
(PREF.) HIST(O)
LOOM AXLE ROCKTREE
LOOM BAR EASER DAGGER
LOOMFIXER TACKLER
LOOM HARNESS LEAF HEADLE SIMBLOT MOUNTING
LOON DIVER IMBER WABBY COBBLE DUCKER GUNNER WHABBY PYGOPOD
LOONY MAD DAFT CRAZY INSANE WEIRDO FOOLISH
LOOP BOW EYE LUG NOB TAB TAG ANSA BEND COIL FAKE HANK KINK KNOB KNOP LEAF LINK LOUP PURL BIGHT BRIDE CHAPE COQUE GUIDE KINCH LACET LATCH NOOSE PEARL PICOT SHANK STRAP TERRY WITHY BECKET BILLET BUCKLE FOLIUM HANGER HOLDER KEEPER KINKLE PARRAL SPIRAL STAPLE STITCH TWITCH COCKEYE COUPURE CRINGLE CRUPPER GROMMET KNUCKLE LATCHET SEGMENT ANTINODE COURONNE
(— AND THIMBLES) CLEW CLUE
(— BY ICESKATER) SPOON
(— FOR HOISTING) SLING
(— FOR REINS) TERRET TERRIT
(— FOR REMOVING TUMORS) SNARE
(— IN KNITTING) STEEK
(— IN MINER'S ROPE) SLUG
(— IN NEEDLEWORK) BRIDE
(— OF INTESTINES) KNUCKLE
(— OF IRON) OOLLY
(— OF ROPE) FAKE BIGHT FLAKE KINCH NOOSE ANCHOR BECKET PARRAL SNORTER SNOTTER
(— OF SCABBARD) FROG
(— OF TUBING) SCROLL
(— ON ARMOR) VERVELLE

(— ON SAIL) LASKET
(— ON SPINNING FRAME) BAND
(— ON SWORD BELT) HANGER
(HANGING —) FESTOON
(HARNESS —) COCKEYE
(HEDDLE —) DOUP
(KIND OF —) LIPPES
(ORNAMENTAL —) PICOT
(SHOULDER —) EPAULET
(SURGICAL —) CURET CURETTE
(TIGHT —) KINK KINKLE
(TWISTED —) KINK
(PREF.) FUNDI
LOOPER INCHWORM SPANWORM
LOOPHOLE LOOP CATCH CHINK MEUSE EYELET OILLET WICKET BARBICAN PORTHOLE
LOOSE GAY LAX EASY EMIT FREE GLAD LASH LIMP OPEN SOFT UNDO WIDE WILD BAGGY CRANK FRANK LARGE LIGHT RELAX SLACK UNTIE VAGUE WASHY ADRIFT FLUFFY LIMBER SLOPPY SOLUTE SPORTY SUBURB UNBIND UNGIRT UNLASH UNTIED WOBBLY ABSOLVE CHESSOM FLYAWAY IMMORAL MOVABLE RELAXED SETFREE SHOGGLY STRINGY UNBOUND UNHITCH UNTIGHT DIFFUSED DISCINCT FLOATING INSECURE LAXATIVE SHATTERY UNSTABLE
(— AN ANCHOR) TRIP
(— ARROW) BOLT
(MORALLY —) FRANK
(PREF.) LAXI
LOOSE-JOINTED LANKY SHACKLY
LOOSELY SLACK LARGELY SLACKLY
LOOSEN LAX BREAK SLACK UNTIE LAXATE LIMBER UNBEND RESOLVE SLACKEN UNGRIPE UNLOOSE UNSCREW DISHEVEL UNSTRING
(— ANCHOR) TRIP
(— ROCK) GAD
LOOSENESS SLACK LAXITY LATITUDE
(PREF.) LYO
LOOSENING START SOLUTIVE SOLUTORY
(PREF.) LYS(I)
LOOSESTRIFE KILLWEED PEATWEED PEATWOOD PRIMWORT
LOOSING
(SUFF.) LYSE LYSIS LYST LYTE LYTIC LYZE
LOOT SACK SWAG BOOTY HARRY SPOIL STEAL THEFT BOODLE MARAUD HERSHIP PILLAGE PLUNDER SNAFFLE
LOOTING SACK
LOP DOD LAP CLIP DODD OCHE SNED SNIG SNIP TRIM SHRAG SHRED SHRUB STUMP TRASH TWINE SHROUD SNATHE TRASHIFY TRUNCATE
(— OFF) COW DOD CROP DODD HEAD SNAG SNED PRUNE SHRED TRUNK DEFALK AMPUTATE
LOPE SHAG
LOPPED
(PREF.)
(— OFF) TRUNCATO
LOPPER CLABBER
LOPPINGS SHROUD
LOQUACIOUS GABBY FUTILE SPEECHFUL
LOQUACITY PRATE PRATTLE FUTILITY
LOQUAT BIWA NISPERO
LORAL FRENAL
LORD BEL DAM DEN DON GOD HER LOR MAR SID SIR DION DOMN EROS HERR LAUK LOSH NAIK SIRE TUAN ANGUS ARAWN BARON LAFEU LIEGE LUDDY NIGEL OMRAH RABBI SAHIB SWAMI THANE DOMINE DUMAIN KYRIOS PRABHU SAYYID SIGNOR TANIST THAKUR CAMILLO CERIMON JACQUES JEHOVAH MARCHER OGTIERN VAVASOR BHAGAVAT DESPOTES DRIGHTEN GRANDPRE LORDLING MARGRAVE OVERLORD PALATINE SEIGNEUR SEIGNIOR SUPERIOR SUZERAIN THALIARD
(— OF DARKNESS) HYLE
(— OF UNIVERSE) ORMAZD ORMUZD
(— OF WORLD) LOKINDRA
(FEUDAL —) DAUPHIN VAVASOR SUZERAIN
(JAPANESE —) KAMI
(JUDAIC —) ADONAI
(MUSLIM —) OMRAH
LORD CHANCELLOR WOOLPACK
LORD JIM (AUTHOR OF —) CONRAD
(CHARACTER IN —) JIM DAIN BROWN STEIN WARIS MARLOW DORAMIN
LORDLINESS PRIDE
LORDLY PROUD SUPERB ARROGANT DESPOTIC
LORDOSIS SWAYBACK
LORDSHIP NAVY DYNASTY ERECTION SEIGNORY SIGNORIA
LORE LEAR LORUM MASTAX LEARNING
LORGNETTE STARER
LORICA LORIC SHEATH SHIELD
LORIKEET PARROT WARRIN CORELLA WEROOLE
LORIS KOKAM LEMUR SLOTH LEMUROID
LORN ALONE
LORNA DOONE (AUTHOR OF —) BLACKMORE
(CHARACTER IN —) FRY TOM ALAN JOHN RIDD ANNIE DOONE DUGAL ENSOR LORNA CARVER FAGGUS JEREMY REUBEN BRANDIR STICKLES HUCKABACK
LORRY RIG DRAG RULLY TRUCK CAMION ROLLEY TIPPER JAGANNATH JUGGERNAUT
LORY LOORY CORELLA LORIKEET
LOSE LET TIN AMIT DROP TINE WANT FORGO LAPSE LEASE TRAIL GAMBLE MISLAY FORBEAR FORFEIT FORLESE SLATTER
(— AT CARDS) BUST
(— BET) WRONG
(— BRILLIANCE) FAINT
(— BY DEATH) BURY
(— BY GAMING) GAME
(— BY STUPIDITY) BLUNDER
(— CONTROL) BLOW CRACK
(— COURAGE) DREEP TAINT
(— DELIBERATELY) THROW
(— FLAVOR) FOZE APPAL APPALL
(— FORCE) COLLAPSE
(— FRESHNESS) FADE WILT WITHER
(— HEART) JADE FAINT QUAIL COLLAPSE
(— HOPE) DESPAIR DESPOND
(— IT) SNAP
(— LUSTER) TARNISH
(— MOISTURE) GUTTATE
(— NERVE) CHICKEN
(— OFFICE) FALL
(— ONE'S BREATH) CHINK
(— ONE'S WAY) STRAY
(— ONE'S SKILL) SLIP
(— POWER) FAIL DISSOLVE
(— SELF-POSSESSION) ABASH
(— SPIRIT) JADE
(— STRENGTH) GO FADE FAIL PALL WEAKEN LANGUISH
(— SUPPORT) ERODE
(— UNDER HORIZON) SINK
(— VISION) DAZZLE
(— WARMTH) COOL CONGEAL
(— WEIGHT) ENSEAM
(— ZEAL) QUENCH
LOSER ALSORAN
LOSING (BEGIN — STREAK) GOCOLD
LOSS ACE BATH COST HARM LEAK LOST MISS LAPSE QUALM WASTE BURIAL DAMAGE DAMNUM DEFEAT INJURY TINSEL AVERAGE DEBACLE DEFICIT EXPENSE JACTURE LEAKAGE LEESING MISTURE REPRISE AMISSION BREAKAGE CLEANING MISSMENT PERDITION SACRIFICE
(— BY EVAPORATION) ULLAGE
(— BY SIFTING) ULLAGE
(— IN WORKING) SLIPPAGE
(— OF ABILITIES) COLLAPSE
(— OF ABILITY TO WRITE) AGRAPHIA
(— OF ACTIVITY) AKINESIA
(— OF APPETITE) ASITIA ANOREXIA
(— OF BRILLIANCY) ECLIPSE
(— OF CARGO) AVERAGE
(— OF CONSCIOUSNESS) SWOON ABSENCE APOPLEXY BLACKOUT FAINTING
(— OF ELASTICITY) SET
(— OF ELECTRICITY) EFFLUVE
(— OF EXPRESSION) AMIMIA
(— OF FEELING) APOPLEXY ANESTHESIA ANAESTHESIA
(— OF FORTUNE) RUIN DECAY
(— OF GOOD NAME) IGNOMINY
(— OF GOODS) SHRINKAGE
(— OF HAIR) DEFLUX ALOPECIA PTILOSIS
(— OF HONOR) ATIMY
(— OF HOPE) DESPAIR
(— OF MEMORY) AMNESIA BLACKOUT
(— OF PRESTIGE) DISHONOR
(— OF SCENT) CHECK
(— OF SENSE OF SMELL) ANOSMIA
(— OF SIGHT) ANOPSY ANOPSIA
(— OF SIZE) WANE
(— OF SOUND) APOCOPE SYNCOPE APHERESIS
(— OF SPEECH) ALALIA APHASIA APHONIA
(— OF VOICE) ANAUDIA APHONIA
(— OF VOWEL) APHESIS
(— OF WILL POWER) ABULIA
(AT A —) ASEA
(CONTRACT —) LESION
(TAKE A — ON) EAT
(SUFF.) ZEMIA
LOST ASEA GONE LORN TINT ATSEA STRAY WASTE ASTRAY BUSHED HIDDEN NAUGHT FORFEIT FORLORN MISSING CONFUSED OBSCURED BENIGHTED
(— IN THOUGHT) PREOCCUPIED
LOST HORIZON (AUTHOR OF —) HILTON
(CHARACTER IN —) HUGH BRIAC CHANG HENRY CONWAY LOTSEN BARNARD CHARLES ROBERTA BRINKLOW MALLISON PERRAULT RUTHERFORD
LOST LADY (AUTHOR OF —) CATHER
(CHARACTER IN —) IVY BLUM NIEL FRANK OGDEN PETERS HERBERT ELLINGER POMMEROY CONSTANCE FORRESTER
LOT BAG CUT HAP PEW CHOP CROP DEAL DOLE DOOM DRAW FALL FATE HEAP PACK PART PILE REDE SKIT SLEW SLUE SORS SORT BATCH BLOCK BREAK BUNCH CAVEL FIELD GRACE GRIST GROSS LINES SHARE SHOOT SIGHT SITHE STAND TEEMS TROOP WEIRD AMOUNT BARREL BOODLE BUNDLE CHANCE DICKER FARDEL HANGUP OODLES PARCEL TICHEL BOILING DESTINY FEEDLOT FORTUNE OODLINS PORTION SANDLOT BACKYARD CABOODLE JINGBANG MOUTHFUL RIMPTION WOODLAND
(— OF PERSONS) BOODLE
(— OF TEA) BREAK
(— OF 60 PIECES) SHOCK
(BUILDING —) ERF
(BURIAL —) LAIR
(FATHER OF —) HARAN
(GREAT —) SWAG
(MISCELLANEOUS —) RAFT
(SISTER OF —) ISCAH MILCAH
(UNCLE OF —) ABRAHAM
(VACANT —) COMMON COMMONS
(PREF.) CLERO SORTI
LOTAN (FATHER OF —) SEIR
LOTION WASH EYEWASH EYEWATER LAVATORY
(HAND — INGREDIENT) ALOE
LOTOPHAGUS EATER
LOTS MANY HEAPS TEEMS BUSHEL HODFUL
LOTTERY AMBO LOTTO SWEEP TERNO RAFFLE TOMBOLA
LOTTO KENO BINGO TOMBOLA
(— GAME) HOUSE
LOTUS LOTE LOTOS PADMA NELUMBO WANKAPIN
(SACRED —) PADMA
LOTUS TREE SADR ZIZYPHUS
LOUCHEUX KUTCHIN
LOUD HARD HIGH MAIN CRUDE

FORTE GAUDY GREAT HEAVY SHOWY STARK STOUR WIGHT BRASSY BRAZEN COARSE CRIANT FLASHY GARISH HOARSE VULGAR BLATANT CLAMANT HAUTAIN VIOLENT BIGMOUTH FRENZIED PIERCING SLAMBANG STREPENT STRIDENT VEHEMENT STREPITANT
(NOT —) LOW SOFT
(RATHER —) MEZZOFORTE
LOUDHAILER BULLHORN
LOUDLY BOST ALOUD FORTE STARK
LOUDNESS STRESS SONORITY MAGNITUDE
(— UNIT) PHON SONE
(UNIT OF —) PHON
LOUDSPEAKER WOOFER SPEAKER TWEETER BULLHORN SQUAWKER
LOUD-SPOKEN RANDY
LOUIS LUIGI LODOWIC

LOUISIANA
CAPITAL: BATONROUGE
COLLEGE: LSU TULANE DILLARD GRAMBLING
COUNTY: CADDO ACADIA PARISH TENSAS LAFOURCHE
CULTURE: TCHEFUNCTE
DIALECT: CREOLE
FESTIVAL: MARDIGRAS
INDIAN: ADAI WASHA ATAKAPA
LAKE: IATT CLEAR LARTO BORGNE SALINE DARBONNE MAUREPAS
MOUNTAIN: DRISKILL
NATIVE: CAJUN CREOLE ACADIAN
NICKNAME: CREOLE PELICAN
PARISH: WINN CADDO ACADIA IBERIA SABINE TENSAS ORLEANS RAPIDES OUACHITA CALCASIEU
RIVER: RED AMITE BOEUF SABINE TENSAS OUACHITA
STATE BIRD: PELICAN
STATE FLOWER: MAGNOLIA
STATE TREE: CYPRESS
STREAM: BAYOU
TOWN: JENA MANY HOMER HOUMA EDGARD GRETNA MINDEN MONROE RUSTON BASTROP VIDALIA BOGALUSA TALLULAH NEWORLEANS

LOUISIANIAN CAJUN ACADIAN
LOUNGE HAWM LOAF LOLL SORN SOSS BANGE TRAIK DACKER FROUST FROWST GLIDER LOLLUP LOPPET RIZZLE SLINGE SOZZLE LAMMOCK SAUNTER SLOUNGE
LOUNGER IDLER SLOUNGER
LOUPE LENS
LOUR FROWN
LOUSE BOB BUG SOW CRAB CRUMB BOOGER BRAULA COOTIE GISLER PALMER SISTEN VERMIN MORPION PUCERON GRAYBACK
(FISH —) GISLER ARGULUS
(PLANT —) APHID APHIS
(WOOD —) SOW ISOPOD SLATER
(YOUNG —) NIT
(PREF.) ONISCI PEDICUL(I)(O)
LOUSEWORT RATTLE SNAFFLES
LOUSINESS PEDICULOSIS
LOUSY SEEDY CRAPPY CRUMMY PEDICULOUS
LOUT HOB LOB LUG YOB BOOR CHUB COOF GAUM GAWK HOOD JAKE LOON NOWT SWAB SWAD BOOBY CHUMP CUDDY GNOFF LOOBY LOURD ROBIN THRUM WHAUP YAHOO YOBBO YOKEL BOHUNK CLUNCH GOBBIN HOBLOB LOURDY LUBBER LUNGIS SLOUCH TRIPAL BUMPKIN GROBIAN HALLION HAWBUCK HOODLUM LOBCOCK PALOOKA LOBLOLLY
(COUNTRY —) KERN BUMPKIN
LOUTISH SWAB HULKY SLOOMY BOORISH HULKING VILLAIN BOEOTIAN CLOWNISH
LOUVER SLAT LOUVRE LUFFER DIFFUSER FEMERELL
(PL.) SHUTTER
LOVABLE AMABEL CUDDLY AMIABLE ADORABLE DOVELIKE LOVESOME ENDEARING
LOVABLENESS DEARNESS
LOVAGE SMELLAGE
LOVE GRA LOO AMOR EROS KAMA LIKE ALOHA AMOUR CUPID DRURY FANCY HEART MINNE AFFECT TENDRE CHARITY EMBRACE FEELING PASSION DEVOTION KINDNESS LOVEHOOD PARAMOUR
(— IN RETURN) REDAME
(— OF COUNTRY) PATRIOTISM
(— OF CRUELTY) SADISM
(— OF MANKIND) PHILANTHROPY
(— OF MARVELOUS) TERATISM
(— OF THE ARTS) VIRTU
(— OF WOMEN) PHILOGYNY
(— TO EXCESS) IDOLIZE
(— TOWARD DEITY) BHAKTI
(ARDENT —) PASSION
(CHRISTIAN —) CHARITY
(EXCESSIVE —) IDOLATRY
(INTENSE —) FIRE
(MY —) MACHREE
(NATURAL —) STORGE
(SELF-GIVING —) AGAPE
(SENTIMENTALLY IN —) SPOONY
(UNLAWFUL —) LEMANRY
(PREF.) ERO(TO)
(SUFF.) PHIL(A)(AE)(E)(IA)(ISM)(IST)(OUS)(US)
LOVED DEAR BELOVED
(MUCH —) SWEET
LOVE-DRUG DAGGA
LOVE FEAST AGAPE
LOVE KNOT AMORET
LOVELINESS BEAUTY
LOVELOCK EARLOCK
LOVELY DREAMY LOVING TENDER AMIABLE AMOROUS ADORABLE LOVESOME
LOVEMAKING AMOUR
LOVER GRA LAD MAN BEAU CHAP AMANT AMOUR DRURY LEMAN ROMEO SPARK SWAIN AMADIS AMANTE MARROW MINION SQUIRE ADMIRER AMORIST AMOROSO CELADON GALLANT PATRIOT SPARKER SPECIAL SPRUNNY AMORETTO BELAMOUR CASANOVA CICISBEO PARAMOUR STREPHON INAMORATO
(— BOY) ROMEO
(MODEL —) LEILAH
(SILLY —) SPOON
LOVE SEAT CAUSEUSE
LOVE'S LABOR'S LOST (AUTHOR OF —) SHAKESPEARE
(CHARACTER IN —) DULL MOTH BOYET MARIA ARMADO DUMAIN ADRIANO BEROWNE COSTARD MERCADE ROSALINE FERDINAND KATHERINE NATHANIEL HOLOFERNES JAQUENETTA LONGAVILLE
LOVING DEAR FOND TENDER AMATORY AMOROUS
(PREF.) PHIL(O)
(SUFF.) PHIL(A)(AE)(E)(OUS)(US)
LOW BAS BOO LAW MOO BASE BASS KEEN MEAN NEAP OPEN ORRA ROUT SLOW VILE WEAK BLORE DIRTY GROSS HEDGE LAICH PUTID SHORT SMALL SNIDE THIRD CALLOW EARTHY FILTHY GENTLE GRUBBY HARLOT HUMBLE LIMMER MENIAL ORNERY RASCAL RIBALD SECRET SHABBY SILKEN TURPID VULGAR BESTIAL IGNOBLE RAFFISH REPTILE SLAVISH SUBMISS HOLSTEIN SOUTERLY
(— AS OF A VOWEL) OPEN
(— DOWN) SIDE
(— IN LIGHTNESS) DULL
(— IN PERCEPTION) CRUDE
(— IN PITCH) GRAVE
(— IN PRICE) MODERATE
(— IN QUALITY) HEDGE
(— IN SATURATION) GRAYISH
(— IN SPIRITS) BLUE DOWN GLOOMY DOWNCAST
(— IN TONE) SOFT SUBMISS
(— IN WATER) RACE
(— NUMBERS) MANQUE
(— POINT) TROUGH
(IMMEASURABLY —) ABYSMAL
(PREF.) CHAMAE CHAME TAPIN(O)
LOW-BORN PLEBEAN VILLAIN PLEBEIAN
LOWBORN WAFF
LOWBRED BASTARD PLEBEIAN
LOWCAL LITE
LOW-DOWN BUCKASS
LOWER CUT DIP LOW BASE BATE DOWN DROP DUCK FELL SINK VAIL ABASE ABATE ALLOY AVALE BELOW BLAME COUCH COWER DECRY DEMIT DOUSE FROWN GLOOM LEVEL SCOWL STOOP BEMEAN DEBASE DEJECT DEMEAN EMBASE GLOWER HUMBLE JUNIOR LESSEN MODIFY NETHER REDUCE SETTLE STRIKE SUBDUE SUBMIT BENEATH DECLASS DEGRADE DEPRESS SHORTEN DIMINISH DOWNWARD INFERIOR MODERATE
(— BANNER) VAIL
(— BY HALF STEP) FLAT
(— IN ESTEEM) CHEAPEN DEROGATE
(— IN PITCH) FLAT SHADE
(— ONESELF) SINK BEMEAN DESCEND
(— PRICES) BEAR
(— SAIL) AMAIN
(— SLIGHTLY) SHADE
(— THE HEAD) STOOP
(PREF.) BATH(O)(Y) CATO INFERO INFRA NERTERO
(— IN STATUS) INFRA
(MAKE —) DE
LOWERING DIP DUCK DOWLY HEAVY LAPSE BEETLE SULLEN PEJORATION
(— OF BODY) FONDU
(— OF LAND) ABLATION
LOWEST LAST LEAST EXTREME LOWMOST PRIMARY PARAVAIL NETHERMOST
(— CLASS) LAG
(— POSSIBLE) KNOWDOWN
LOWING MUGIENT
LOWLAND LAICH POLDER LALLAND DOWNLAND
(— BESIDE RIVER) INKS
(BARREN —) LANDES
LOWLANDER SAXON ZHMUD SASSENACH
LOWLIER LESS
LOWLIFE SCUM AMEBA
LOWLINESS (— OF MIND) HUMILITY
LOWLY LOW BASE SILLY HUMBLE BASEBORN
LOW-LYING CALLOW LALLAN INFERIAL SUBJECTED
LOW-MINDED BASE MEAN
LOWNESS LOWTH
(— OF PITCH) GRAVITY
(— OF SPIRITS) GLOOM SPLEEN MEGRIMS
LOW-PITCHED GRUFF
LOW-SPIRITED HIPPED DEJECTED
LOW SUNDAY QUASIMODO
LOX (PARTNER OF —) BAGEL
LOY SLICK
LOYAL FAST FEAL FIRM HOLD LEAL REAL TRUE LIEGE PIOUS SOUND ARDENT HEARTY LAWFUL SECRET STANCH CONSTANT FAITHFUL STALWART YEOMANLY
(BE — TO) OBEY
(REMAIN —) STANDBY
LOYALIST TORY
LOYALLY SURELY
LOYALTY ARDOR FAITH FEALTY HOMAGE LEALTY REALTY SPIRIT REALITY DEVOTION FIDELITY CONSTANCY NATIONALISM
LOZENGE TAB JUBE COIGN QUOIN CACHOU JUJUBE MASCLE PASTIL QUARRY ROTULA RUSTRE TABLET TABULE TROCHE CREMULE DIAMOND TABELLA PASTILLE ROSEDROP
(— OF CEMENT) WAFER
LOZI ROZI BAROTSE
LSD ACID
LUBBER LOUT SWAB LOOBY SLOUCH LOBCOCK LILBURNE
LUBBERLY AWKWARD
LUBRICANT DOPE GREASE AQUADAG UNGUENT
LUBRICATE OIL DOPE GLIB GREASE LUBRIFY
LUBRICATOR OILER OILCAN
LUCARNE LUCOMBE
LUCE GED

LUCENT BRIGHT LUCIBLE
LUCERNE LEGUME ALFALFA
LUCIA DI LAMMERMOOR
(CHARACTER IN —) LUCY EDGAR HENRY ARTHUR ASHTON BUCKLOW RAVENSWOOD
(COMPOSER OF —) DONIZETTI
LUCIANA (SISTER OF —) ADRIANA
LUCID SANE CLEAR AERIAL BRIGHT LIMPID CRYSTAL DILUCID LITERATE LUCULENT LUMINOUS
LUCIDITY SANITY CLARITY
LUCIFER DEVIL MATCH PHOSPHOR
LUCK HAP CESS EURE SONS SPIN GRACE ISSUE CHANCE THRIFT FORTUNE HANDSEL SUCCESS VENTURE HAMINGJA
(BAD —) ACE DOLE DEUCE HOODOO UNLUCK AMBSACE MISCHANCE
(BAD — TO YOU) YLAHAYLL
(GOOD —) HAP SONCE SONSE FORTUNE THEEDOM
(ILL —) UNHAP DIRDUM DISGRACE MISHANTER
(RELATING TO —) ALEATORY
(STROKE OF —) MANNA
(UNEXPECTED —) BUNCE
LUCKILY HAPPILY
LUCKY HOT CANNY HAPPY JAMMY SEELY SONSY CHANCY LUCKLY LUCKFUL ONAROLL GRACIOUS PROVIDENTIAL
LUCRATIVE FAT GOOD GAINFUL
LUCRE GELT SWAG DROSS MOOLA
LUCREZIA BORGIA (CHARACTER IN —) ALFONSO GENNARO LUCREZIA
(COMPOSER OF —) DONIZETTI
LUD (FATHER OF —) SHEM
LUDICROUS AWFUL COMIC DROLL ABSURD COMICAL FOOLISH HIDEOUS RISIBLE FARCICAL BURLESQUE
LUDO UCKERS
LUFF DERRICK
LUFFA LOOFAH SPONGE
LUG EAR HUG TUG WAG SNUG SPUD TOTE ZULU PATCH WALTZ SCHLEP
LUGE SLED
LUGGAGE BAGS SWAG TRAPS HATBOX BAGGAGE CARRYON TRUSSERY
(AIRPLANE —) CARRYON
LUGGAGE-CARRIER GRID
LUGGAGE CASE IMPERIAL
LUGGAR JAGGAR JUGGER LAGGAR
LUGGER CAT TOUP ZULU FIFIE
LUGUBRIOUS BLACK TEARY BALEFUL DOLEFUL DOLOROUS LACHRYMOSE
LUGWORM LOB LUG LOBWORM SANDWORM
LUIGINO TEMIN
LUISA MILLER (CHARACTER IN —) WURM LUISA MILLER WALTER RODOLFO FREDERICA
(COMPOSER OF —) VERDI
LUKEWARM LEW LUKE TEPID WLACH
LULL CALM DRUG FODE HUSH ROCK CROON HUSHO LETUP SLACK STILL LACUNA SOPITE HUSHABY HUSHEEN
LULLABY LULL BALOO BALOW LULLAY HUSHABY HUSHEEN ROCKABY
LULLING DROWSY CIRCEAN
LULU PIP DARB ONER BEAUT DOOZY CORKER DOOZER SNORTER HUMDINGER
LUMBER BURR DEAL RAFF NANMU STOCK STRIP CUMBER FINISH FLITCH RAFFLE REFUSE SAMCHU SHORTS TIMBER DEGRADE DUNNAGE GUMWOOD RUMMAGE TRUNDLE STEPPING
(INFERIOR —) SAPS SCOOT
LUMBERING AWKWARD LUMBERLY LUMBROUS
LUMBERJACK JACK AXMAN LOGGER TOPPER TIMBERER
(COMPETITION FOR —S) ROLEO
LUMBERMAN PINER DOGGER SCORER CHOPPER GIRDLER TIMBERER
LUMINAIRE LAMP
LUMINANCE HELIOS
LUMINARY STAR LIGHT CANDLE PLANET
LUMINESCENCE FLAME
LUMINOSITY FIRE GLOW LIGHT VALUE
LUMINOUS LIGHT LUCID SHINY BRIGHT LUMINANT
LUMMOX BOZO GALOOT LOBSTER PALOOKA
LUMP BAT BOB COB CUB DAB DAD FID GOB JOB LOB NIB NOB NUB WAD BLOB BURL CLAG CLAM CLOT COOL COWL DUNT GLOB JUNK KNOB KNOT NIRL PONE SWAD TOKE BLOOM BUNCH CHUCK CHUNK CLAUT CLUMP CLUNK GLEBE HUNCH KNOLL KNURL MOUSE SLUMP STONE WEDGE WODGE CLUNCH DOLLOP GOBBET HUBBLE HUDDLE LUMPET NUBBLE NUGGET CLUMPER CLUNTER PUMPKNOT
(— IN CLOTH) BURL
(— IN GLASS) YOLK
(— OF BLACK LEAD) SOP
(— OF BLOOD) CLOD
(— OF CLAY) BAT
(— OF COAL) NUBBLING
(— OF DOUGH) DIP
(— OF FAT) KEECH
(— OF GLASS) BLOOM
(— OF IRON) OOLLY
(— OF LAVA) BOMB
(— OF LINT) SLUG
(— OF MEAT) OLIVE
(— OF METAL) MASS SLUG
(— OF ORE) ROCK HARDHEAD
(— OF RUBBER) THIMBLE
(— OF SALT) SALTCAT
(— OF WOOD) CHUMP
(— OF YEAST) BEE
(— ON HORSE'S BACK) SITFAST
(— ON SKIN) MILIUM
(LARGE —) BLAD DOLL HUNK
(LITTLE —) NODULE KNOBBLE
(ROUNDED —) CLOT
(PREF.) THROMB(O)
LUMPFISH GROSS PADDLE SUCKER
LUMPISH STODGY CHUCKLE
LUMPSUCKER PADLE PADDLE SEAOWL
LUMPY GOBBY CHUNKY CLOGGY CLUNCH COBBLY STODGY BUNCHED NODULAR NODULOSE
LUNACY MOON FOLLY MADNESS DELIRIUM INSANITY
LUNARIA SATINPOD
LUNARY VOLVELLE
LUNATIC NUT GELT LOONY WACKO BEDLAM MADMAN MANIAC WEIRDO CRAZOID FANATIC FRANTIC CRACKPOT MOONLING MOONSICK MOONSTRUCK MOONSTRICKEN
LUNCH CUT BAIT CRIB TIFF BEVER PIECE SNACK BRUNCH NACKET TIFFIN UNDERN BAGGING ELEVENS DEJEUNER DRINKING ELEVENER LUNCHEON NUNCHEON COLLATION
(— ORDER) BLT
(DAIRY —) CREMERIE
(MINER'S —) SNAP
LUNCHEON CRIB LUNCH STULL TIFFIN DEJEUNE DINETTE NOONMEAT
LUNCHROOM EATERY
LUNETTE OUTWORK
LUNG PULMO DRAGON LONGUE
(PREF.) PNEO PNEUM(A)(ATO)(O)(ON)(ONO) PULMO PULMON(I)
LUNGE FOIN PASS SPAR POINT VENUE CHARGE ALLONGE
LUNGFISH CYCLOID DIPNOAN MUDFISH SIRENOID
LUNGS LIGHTS VISCUS BELLOWS
(PERTAINING TO —) PULMONIC
LUNKHEAD DOLT DOPE JUGHEAD
LUNULE ALBEDO
LUO DHOLUO
LUPIN ARSINE
LUPINE SUNDIAL
LURCH JOLL STOT SWAG PITCH STOIT CAREEN STOITER STUMBLE SWAGGER
(LEAVE IN THE —) DITCH
LURCHING DRUNKEN ROLLING
LURE CON JAY BAIT HOOK ROPE TOLL WISE DECOY DRILL FEINT SLOCK SNARE SNOOK SPOON SQUID STALE TEMPT TROLL ALLURE CAPPER CLARET ENTICE ENTRAP RABATE SEDUCE TREPAN VELURE ATTRACT GUDGEON INVEIGH PHANTOM PITFALL WOBBLER BUCKTAIL INVEIGLE LUREMENT
(— INTO GAMBLING) HUSTLE
(— OF CARRION) TRAIN
(— WILDFOWL) STOOL
LURI ALUR
LURID RED PURPLE SULTRY CRIMSON GHASTLY
LURK DARE LOUT COUCH LOWER SKULK SLINK SNEAK AMBUSH DARKLE
LURKING LURKY GRASSANT LATITANT
LUSCIOUS FOND RICH SWEET CREAMY DULCET DELICATE
LUSH SOT RICH DRUNK GREEN LUSTY MOIST TOPER SAVORY FERTILE OPULENT PROFUSE THRIVING
LUST HELL ITCH KAMA BLOOD PRIDE DESIRE LIBIDO LIKING LUXURY NICETY PASSION COVETISE CUPIDITY CARNALITY
(SUFF.) LAGNIA
LUSTER NAIF GLASS GLINT GLOSS SHEEN SHINE WATER LUSTRE POLISH REFLET BURNISH GLIMPSE GLISTER LUSTRUM NITENCY FULGENCE LUSTRATE RADIANCY SPLENDOR
(— OF FIBER) BLOOM
(BRONZE-LIKE —) SCHILLER
LUSTERLESS MAT WAN DEAD DULL FISHY STARY
LUSTFUL HOT GAMY GOLE LEWD RANK SALT CADGY LUSTY PRIME RANDY RUTTY WANTON BEASTLY CODDING FLESHLY FULSOME GOATISH JEALOUS RAMMISH RUTTISH LIKEROUS SALACIOUS
LUSTFULNESS SATYRISM
LUSTILY CRANK HOTLY
LUSTING ITCHY
LUSTRATION ABHISEKA
LUSTROUS CLEAR DOGGY NITID BRIGHT GLOSSY ORIENT SHEENY SILKEN SILVER SHINING SPLENDID
LUSTY BRAG CANT BURLY CRANK FLUSH FRACK FRANK FRECK GUTSY HARDY JUICY RANDY STIFF STOUT GAWSIE ROBUST STURDY LUSTFUL LUSTICK BOUNCING PHYSICAL SKELPING SPORTIVE VIGOROUS
LUTE TAR BIWA LAUD DOMRA NABIA NABLE REBAB REBEC SAROD CITOLE ENLUTE LORICA LUTING SCREED VIELLE ANGELOT BANDORE DICHORD DYPHONE MANDOLA MANDORE MINIKIN PANDORE THEORBO VIHUELA ANGELICA ARCHLUTE PENORCON TAMBOURA TEMPLATE TRICHORD
LUTER DAUBER PASTER
LUTJANID JEWFISH

LUXEMBOURG
CAPITAL: LUXEMBOURG
HIGHEST POINT: BURGPLATZ
LOWLAND: BONPAYS GUTLAND
MEASURE: FUDER
MOUNTAIN RANGE: ARDENNES
PLATEAU: ARDENNES
RIVER: OUR SURE SAUER ALZETTE MOSELLE
TOWN: BOUS EICH ROODT WILTZ PETANGE VIANDEN DIEKIRCH DUDELANGE ETTELBRUCK DIFFERDANGE

LUXURIANT GOLE LUSH RANK RICH FRANK PROUD LAVISH WANTON OPULENT PROFUSE RAMPANT TEEMING PAMPERED PRODIGAL
LUXURIANTLY FATLY
LUXURIATE BASK REVEL FROWST WALLOW WANTON
LUXURIOUS HIGH LUSH NICE POSH

RANK SOFT GAUDY PLUSH SWANK CAPUAN DELUXE GILDED PALACE SILKEN SWANKY WANTON APICIAN ELEGANT DELICATE LUCULLAN PRODIGAL REGALADO SENSUOUS TRYPHENA TRYPHOSA SUMPTUOUS
LUXURIOUSLY HIGH DELUXE
LUXURY FRILL FINERY OUTRAGE DELICACY ELEGANCE PLEASURE RICHNESS PRINCELINESS
LUXURY-LOVING DELICATE
LUZON (— VOLCANO) TAAL
LYCANTHROPE WEREWOLF
LYCAON (DAUGHTER OF —) CALLISTO
(FATHER OF —) PELASGUS
LYCEUM PLATFORM
LYCHNIS FIREBALL NONESUCH
LYCIUM RUSOT
LYCOPODIUM MOSS FOXTAIL CROWFOOT STAGHORN
LYCURGUS (BROTHER OF —) POLYDECTES
(FATHER OF —) DRYAS EUNOMUS
(SON OF —) OPHELTES
LYCUS (BROTHER OF —) AEGEUS PALLAS IPHINOE
(FATHER OF —) PANDION
(MOTHER OF —) PYLIA
(WIFE OF —) DIRCE
LYDIA MAEONIA
LYE LEY BOUK BUCK STRAKE LESSIVE LIXIVIUM SOAPLEES
LYING FLAT FALSE LEASE CRETISM LEASING MENTERY ACCUBATION MENDACIOUS
(— APART) DISSITE
(— AT BASE OF MOUNTAINS) PIEDMONT
(— CLOSE) QUAT
(— DOWN) DOWN LODGED CUMBENT DORMANT COUCHANT
(— HID) LATITANT
(— IDLE) INACTIVE
(— ON BACK) SUPINE
(— ON FACE) PRONE PROCUMBENT
(— ON GROUND) REPENT REPTANT
(— OPEN) PATENT
(— OVER) JACENT
(— UNDER GRASS) LEA
LYING-IN INLYING CHILDBED GROANING
LYMPH CHYLE VIRUS
(PREF.) CHYL(O)
(SUFF.) CHYLIA
LYMPHAD GALLEY
LYMPHANGITIS WEED FILLING
LYMPHATIC LACTEAL
LYMPHOGRANULOMA BUBO
LYMPHOMATOSIS FISHEYE
LYNCEUS (BROTHER OF —) IDAS
(FATHER OF —) AEGYPTUS APHAREUS
(WIFE OF —) HYPERMNESTRA
LYNCH HANG DEWITT
LYNX LOSSE OUNCE PISHU BOBCAT GORKUN LUCERN CARACAL LUCIVEE WILDCAT CARCAJOU
LYRE ASOR HARP LYRA SHELL CHELYS KINNOR KISSAR TRIGON CITHARA TESTUDO BARBITON PHORMINX TRICHORD TRIGONON
LYREBIRD LYRETAIL PHEASANT
LYRIC LAY LIED HOKKU LAEAN MELIC GHAZEL TENSON CANCION CHANSON DESCORT MADRIGAL
(HAVING — AND DRAMATIC QUALITIES) SPINTO
(LOVE —) ALBA
(PL.) SONG
LYRICAL ODIC MELIC
LYSIPPE (FATHER OF —) PROETUS
(HUSBAND OF —) MELAMPUS
(MOTHER OF —) ANTIA
(SISTER OF —) IPHINOE IPHINASSA
LYTTA WORM

M EM EMMA MIKE METRO
(WRONG USE OF —) MYTACISM
M-1 GARAND
MAACAH (HUSBAND OF —) DAVID
(SON OF —) ABSALOM
MAACHAH (FATHER OF —) NAHOR URIEL TALMAI
(HUSBAND OF —) JEHIEL MACHIR REHOBOAM
(MOTHER OF —) REUMAH
(SON OF —) HANAN ABIJAH ACHISH ABSALOM SHEPHATIAH
MAADAI (FATHER OF —) BANI
MA'AM MARM MISTRESS
MAARIB ARBIT ARBITH
MAASEIAH (FATHER OF —) ADAIAH BARUCH SHALLUM
(SON OF —) AZARIAH ZEDEKIAH ZEPHANIAH
MAATH (FATHER OF —) MATTATHIAS
MAAZ (FATHER OF —) RAM
MACA ENIMAGA
MACABRE SICK SCARY HORRIBLE
MACACA PITHECUS
MACADAMIZE METAL
MACAO (CHINESE NAME OF —) AOMEN
(ISLAND OF —) TAIPA COLOANE
MACAQUE KRA BROH BRUH MACAC TOQUE MACHIN MONKEY RHESUS RILAWA WANDEROO
MACARIA (FATHER OF —) HERCULES
(MOTHER OF —) DEIANIRA
MACARIZE LAUD
MACARONI FOP DANDY DITALI
MACARONIC SKEW
MACAROON AMARETTO
MACAW ARA ARARA PARROT MARACAN ARACANGA COCKATOO
MACAW-TREE MACOYA MACAHUBA
MACBETH (AUTHOR OF —) SHAKESPEARE
(CHARACTER IN —) ROSS ANGUS BANQUO DUNCAN HECATE LENNOX SEYTON SIWARD FLEANCE MACBETH MACDUFF MALCOLM MENTEITH CAITHNESS DONALBAIN
MACE CROC MALL MAUL POKER VERGE MALLET SPARTH CATTAIL
(PART OF —) HEAD HILT SPIKE FLANGE HANDLE
(REED —) DOD DODD
(ROYAL —) SCEPTER SCEPTRE
MACE-BEARER BEADLE VERGER MACEMAN
MACERATE RET SOUR STEEP
MACHAON (BROTHER OF —) PODALIRIUS
(FATHER OF —) AESCULAPIUS
(MOTHER OF —) CORONIS
MACHETE BOLO GULOC PANGA PARANG CURTAXE CUTLASH CUTLASS
MACHI (COMPANION OF —) CALEB JOSHUA
(SON OF —) GEUEL
MACHIAVELLIAN CRAFTY CUNNING GUILEFUL
MACHINATE TAMPER
MACHINATION ARTIFICE INTRIGUE SCHEMERY
MACHINE (ALSO SEE DEVICE AND ENGINE) GIN HOG JIG SAW AGER BABY COMB GEAR JACK LIFT MULE PUMP RASP TRAY WHIM WINK ADDER AWNER BALER BENCH BILLY BOARD BRAKE BREAK COPER CRANE DEVIL EDGER ERNIE FRAME FUDGE FUGAL JENNY JERRY JOLLY LATHE LAYER METER MIXER MOWER NAVVY RAKER RESAW ROVER SCREW SETUP SHEEN SIZER STAMP SULKY TRONE VINER WILLY BARKER BEADER BEAMER BEATER BEETLE BENDER BILLER BINDER BOLTER BUCKLE BUMPER BUTTER CANTER CAPPER CARDER CONCHE COOLER CREWER DECKER DOFFER DONKEY DRAPER DREDGE DUSTER ENGINE FLAKER FOLDER FOOTER FORMER GADDER GAPPER GLAZER GRADER GRATER GUMMER HEADER HEMMER HOBBER HOGGER HOOPER HULLER HUSKER IRONER JIGGER JORDAN KICKER LEGGER LIFTER LINTER LOGGER MAILER MANGLE MILLER MITRER NAPPER NETTER NIBBER NIPPER PACKER PEGGER PINNER PLATER PUMPER RIPPER ROSSER ROTARY ROUTER SANDER SCUTCH SEALER SEAMER SHAKER SHAPER SHAVER SINGER SKIVER SLICER SORTER SPACER STOCKS STOKER TEDDER TENTER TWINER VANNER WASHER WELDER WILLOW ABRADER AUTOMAT AVIATOR BACKHOE BATCHER BELLOWS BLENDER BLUNGER BOTTLER BRANNER BREAKER CANDROY CAPSTAN CHIPPER COMBINE CRUSHER DIBBLER DRESSER EMULSOR ENCODER ENROBER ERECTOR EXOSTRA FLANGER FLOSSER FREEZER GARNETT GLASSER GRAINER GRINDER GROOVER GROUTER HUMIDOR IRONMAN JOINTER KNITTER KNOTTER MACHINA MANGLER MATCHER MITERER PERRIER PLODDER PLUCKER POTCHER PRINTER QUILLER REPRESS RIVETER ROASTER SAMMIER SCALPER SHEARER SHEETER SIROCCO SLABBER SLASHER SLITTER SLOTTER SLUBBER SLUGGER SMASHER SPALLER SPEEDER SPINNER SPONGER SPOOLER SPRAYER STACKER STAMPER STAPLER STEAMER STEMMER STICKER TENONER TEREBRA TOOTHER TRAMPER TREATER TRIMMER TRUSSER TWILLER TWISTER TYPOBAR WHIPPER WHIZZER AERIFIER AIRCRAFT BROACHER CALENDER CANCELER CARTONER CLINCHER COLLATOR COMPRESS DUNGBECK ELEPHANT EXPLODER EXTRUDER FILATORY FINISHER FLYWINCH FORKLIFT GATHERER HARDENER HAYMAKER HERCULES HUMMELER IMPACTER KILLIFER MORTISER MOULINET ODOGRAPH OROGRAPH PROFILER PULSATOR SCHIFFLI SCUTCHER SHREDDER SOFTENER SPLITTER SPREADER SPRIGGER SQUEEZER STITCHER STRANDER STRIPPER SURFACER TEMPERER THREADER THRESHER THROSTLE TRAVELER TRISPAST TUNNELER UPSETTER WINNOWER ADDRESSER
(ANCIENT MILITARY —) BALISTA BALLISTA
(BETTING —) PARIMUTUEL
(POLITICAL —) APPARAT
(STAGE —) PAGEANT
MACHINE-GUN POMPOM MITRAILLEUSE
MACHINE GUN STINGER CHAUCHAT
MACHINERY MINT TOPCAP SUCCULA APPARATUS
MACHINE SHOP TURNERY
MACHINIST FRILLER THINNER MACHINER
MACHIR (FATHER OF —) AMMIEL MANASSEH
MACHISMO MACHO
MACHNADEBAI (FATHER OF —) BANI
MACKEREL CERO CHAD PETO SCAD TINK BLINK OPELU SNOEK TUNNY BONITO SAUREL TINKER BLINKER BLOATER SCOMBER TASSARD ALBACORE HARDHEAD SCOMBRID SEERFISH
(— ABOUT 8 OR 9 INCHES) TINK TINKER
(KING —) CERO
(PICKLED —) SCALPEEN
(POOR BONY —) SLINK SLINKER
(SNAKE —) ESCOLAR
(YOUNG —) SPIKE
(PREF.) SCOMBRI
MACKLE SLUR SHAKE MACULA
MACROGAMETE OVUM
MACROSCOPIC GROSS
MACROSPECIES LINNEON
MAD FEY AWAY GITE GYTE HYTE WOOD YOND ANGRY BATTY BRAIN CRAZY DIPPY FOLLE MANIC RABID WACKO WACKY BEDLAM FRENZY INSANE MANIAC WOODEN BERSERK BONKERS FANATIC FRANTIC FURIOUS LUNATIC MADDING MADDOCK MANKIND REDWOOD WITLESS DELIRANT DEMENTED DISTRACT INFORMAL MANIACAL MINDLESS RAVENING POSSESSED
(GET —) SEERED

MADAGASCAR
CAPITAL: ANTANANARIVO
FORMER NAME: MALAGASYREPUBLIC
ISLAND GROUP: ALDABRA
LAKE: ITASY ALAOTRA
MEASURE: GANTANG
NATIVE: HOVA SAKALAVA
PEOPLE: HOVA COTIER MARINA
RIVER: IKOPA MANIA SOFIA MANGOKY MANGORO ONYLAHY
TOWN: IHOSY MANJA TULEAR MAJANGA NOSSIBE TSIVORY TAMATAVE ANTISIRABE

MADAI (FATHER OF —) JAPHET
MADAM MEM MUM BAWD MAAM PANI DONNA MADAME SENORA SENHORA SIGNORA GOODWIFE MISTRESS SINEBADA
MADAMA BUTTERFLY
(CHARACTER IN —) SUZUKI CIOCIOSAN PINKERTON SHARPLESS
(COMPOSER OF —) PUCCINI
MADAME BOVARY (AUTHOR OF —) FLAUBERT
(CHARACTER IN —) EMMA LEON BOVARY DUPUIS HOMAIS CHARLES HELOISE ROUAULT LHEUREUX RODOLPHE BOULANGER
MADAR YERCUM
MADCAP RASH
MADDEN ENRAGE INCENSE INFLAME DISTRACT
MADDENED ENRAGED FRENZIED
MADDER GAMENE LIZARY ALIZARI GARANCE MUNJEET TANAGRA GARANCIN SPURWORT WOODRUFF
MAD-DOG SKULLCAP MADWEED HOODWORT
MADE SET BUILT COMPACT PREPARED TIMBERED
(— FLUID BY HEAT) FUSILE
(— LATELY) NEW
(— OF DISSIMILAR PARTS) MIXED

(— OF FLAX) LINEN
(— OF GRAIN) OATEN CEREAL
(— OF IVORY) EBURNEAN
(— OF SILVER) ARGENT
(— OF STONE) STONEN
(— OF TWIGS) VIRGAL
(— SHORT) CURTAL
(— TART) EUCHRED
(— TO ORDER) BESPOKEN
(— TRANSLUCENT) AJOURE
(— UP) ACCRETE
(— WITH CEDAR) CEDARN
(CUNNINGLY —) SLY
(PREF.) (— OF) DIA
(SUFF.) (— OF) INE
MADE-BEAVER SKIN CASTOR
MADEIRA ISLANDS (ISLAND OF —) GRANDE DEZERTE
(TOWN OF —) FUNCHAL
(WINE OF —) BUAL TINTA MALMSEY SERCIAL VERDELHO
MADELON POLIXENE
MADHGOUSE SCRUM
MADHOUSE ASYLUM BEDLAM
MADHUCA BASSIA ILLIPE
MADLY WOOD CRAZY
MADMAN GELT WACKO BEDLAM MANIAC CRAZOID FURIOSO LUNATIC WOODMAN
MADNESS MAD FURY MOON WOOD FOLIE FOLLY FUROR MANIA BEDLAM FRENZY LUNACY DEWANEE ECSTASY MOONERY WIDDRIM DELIRIUM DEMENTIA PIBLOKTO WILLNESS WOODNESS WOODSHIP
(PREF.) LYSSO MANIC
(SUFF.) MANE MANIA(C)
MADONNA LADY VIRGIN
MADREPORE FUNGID
MADRIGAL ENSALADA
MADRONA LAUREL MANZANITA
MADTOM TADPOLE
MADWORT ALYSSUM BUGLOSS
MAENAD FROW BASSARID BACCHANTE
(PL.) BACCHAE
MAFIA MOB GANG CLIQUE
MAFIC FEMIC
MAFURA ROKA ELCAJA
MAGANI BAGANI
MAGAZINE MAG BOOK DRUM FLAT IGLOO SLICK STORE RETORT ALMACEN JOURNAL CASSETTE
(BLACKWOOD'S —) MAGA
(FASHION —) ELLE
(OLD MUSIC —) ETUDE
(SCIENCE FICTION —) FANZINE
MAGDALEN MAUDLIN
MAGGOT MAD GRUB MAWK WORM METHE GENTLE WARBLE WORMIL MADDOCK SKIPPER MUCKWORM
MAGGOTY MAWKISH
MAGIC JUJU MAYA RUNE CRAFT FAIRY GOETY SPELL TURGY GOETIC TREGET VOODOO ALCHEMY CANTRIP CONJURY DEVILRY GLAMOUR GRAMARY MAGICAL SORCERY BRUJERIA HECATEAN WIZARDRY NECROMANCY
(BLACK —) GOETY GOETIC MALEFICE
(PERSONAL —) CHARISM CHARISMA
(WHITE —) TURGY
MAGICAL WIZARD WONDER HERMETIC NUMINOUS THEURGIC
MAGIC FLUTE, THE (CHARACTER IN —) PAMINA TAMINO PAPAGENA PAPAGENO SARASTRO MONOSTATOS
(COMPOSER OF —) MOZART
MAGICIAN MAGE BOKOR MAGUS UTHER CUNJAH GOETIC GOOFER GUFFER MAGIAN MERLIN WABENO WIZARD CHARMER GWYDION KOSCHEI WARLOCK WIELARE WISEMAN CONJURER FETISHER SORCERER THEURGIC TROLLMAN ARCHIMAGE
MAGIC MOUNTAIN (AUTHOR OF —) MANN
(CHARACTER IN —) HANS NAPHTA BEHRENS CASTORP CAUCHAT CLAVDIA JOACHIM ZIEMSSEN KROKOWSKI PEEPERKORN SETTEMBRINI
MAGISTERIAL LOFTY PROUD AUGUST CURULE LORDLY HAUGHTY STATELY ARROGANT DOGMATIC
MAGISTERY MASTERY
MAGISTRACY AMT PRYTANY
MAGISTRATE BEAK FOUD EPHOR JUDGE JURAT MAYOR PRIOR REEVE AMTMAN ARCHON AVOYER BAILIE BAILLI CENSOR CONSUL FISCAL KOTWAL SYNDIC ALCALDE BAILIFF BURGESS DUUMVIR ECHEVIN EPHORUS JUSTICE NOMARCH PODESTA PRAETOR PREFECT PROVOST STEWARD SUFFETE TRIBUNE ALABARCH ALDERMAN CAPITOUL DEFENSOR DEMIURGE DICTATOR GOVERNOR MITTIMUS PHYLARCH PRYTANIS RECORDER STRADICO STRATEGE HUNDREDER CORREGIDOR
(— IN CHANNEL ISLANDS) JURAT
(— OF ANCIENT ROME) EDILE AEDILE
(— OF INDIA) COTWAL KOTWAL
(— OF MECCA) SHERIF SHEREEF
(— OF VENICE AND GENOA) DOGE
(MOHAMMEDAN —) CADI CADY SHERIF
(SCOTCH —) PROVOST STEWARD
MAGMA ICHOR
MAGMATIC JUVENILE
MAGNANIMITY HEIGHT FREEDOM
MAGNANIMOUS BIG FREE GREAT LARGE LOFTY NOBLE HEROIC EXALTED GENEROUS
MAGNATE BARON MOGUL TITAN BASHAW TYCOON
MAGNESIA PULVIL
MAGNET FIELD ADAMAS MAGNES ADAMANT SOLENOID TERRELLA LODESTONE
MAGNETIC (— FIELD MEASURER) SQUID
MAGNETISM IT DEVIL OOMPH
MAGNETITE LOADSTONE LODESTONE
MAGNETIZE TOUCH SATURATE
MAGNETOMETER DOODLEBUG
MAGNIFICATION POWER
MAGNIFICENCE GITE POMP FLARE GLORY STATE PARADE JOLLITY ROYALTY GRANDEUR SPLENDOR
MAGNIFICENT RIAL GRAND NOBLE PROUD ROYAL AUGUST LAVISH IMMENSE POMPOUS STATELY SUBLIME GLORIOUS GORGEOUS MAGNIFIC PALATIAL PRINCELY SPLENDID
MAGNIFICENT OBSESSION
(AUTHOR OF —) DOUGLAS
(CHARACTER IN —) BRENT HELEN JOYCE NANCY WAYNE DAWSON HUDSON ROBERT ASHFORD MERRICK
MAGNIFY LAUD BLESS ERECT EXALT PRAISE ADVANCE DISTEND ENLARGE GLORIFY GREATEN INCREASE MAXIMIZE MULTIPLY
MAGNIFYING
(PREF.) MICR(O)
MAGNIFYING GLASS LOUPE READER
MAGNILOQUENT TURGID BOMBAST
MAGNITUDE BULK MASS SIZE DATUM LEVEL SOLID EXTENT FIGURE PERIOD EXTREME CONSTANT FUNCTION INFINITE
MAGNOLIA YULAN BIGBLOOM CUCUMBER MAURICIO
(— STATE) MISSISSIPPI
MAGOG (FATHER OF —) JAPHETH
MAGPIE MAG PIE PIET PYAT CISSA KOTRI MADGE NINUT MARGET NANPIE PIANET PIEMAG SIRGANG HAGISTER MARGARET PHEASANT PIENANNY CHATTERBOX
MAGPIE LARK PEEWEE GRALLINA
MAGPIE ROBIN DAYAL DHYAL
MAGUEY AGAVE MESCAL CANTALA
MAGYAR SZEKEL SZEKLER
MAHALAH (MOTHER OF —) HAMMOLEKETH
(UNCLE OF —) GILEAD
MAHALATH (FATHER OF —) ISHMAEL JERIMOTH
(HUSBAND OF —) ESAU REHOBOAM
MAHALI (FATHER OF —) MERARI
MAHATMA SAGE ARHAT
MAHAZIOTH (FATHER OF —) HEMAN
MAH-JONGG WOO
MAHLAH (FATHER OF —) ZELOPHEHAD
MAHLI (FATHER OF —) MUSHI MERARI
MAHLON (DAUGHTER OF —) NAOMI
(SON OF —) ELIMELECH
(WIFE OF —) RUTH
MAHOE EMAJAGUA
MAHOGANY SIPO ALMON CAOBA CEDAR ROHAN ACAJOU AGUANO SAPELE THITKA ALBARCO AVODIRE BAYWOOD GUNNUNG MADEIRA RATTEEN TABASCO BANGALAY HARDTACK TANGUILE
(INDIAN —) TOON
(PHILIPPINE —) BAGTIKAN
MAHONIA ASHBERRY ODOSTEMON
MAHOUND MACON
MAHUA FULWA MOWHA MOWRA MADHUCA PHULWARA
MAHUANG EPHEDRA
MAHWA ILLIPE ILLUPI
MAIA (FATHER OF —) ATLAS
(MOTHER OF —) PLEIONE
(SON OF —) MERCURY
MAID MAY AYAH GIRL LASS MEDE SLUT CHINA WENCH WOMAN MAIDEN SLAVEY TWEENY VIRGIN ANCILLA GENERAL MAIDKIN PHYLLIS PUCELLE WENCHEL BONIBELL BRANGANE HANDMAID SUIVANTE TIREMAID
(— IN WAITING) DAMSEL DAMOZEL
(— OF-ALL-WORK) SLAVEY GENERAL
(— OF HONOR) MARIE
(KIND OF —) METER
(KITCHEN —) SCOGIE
(LADY'S —) AYAH ABIGAIL TIREMAID
(NURSE —) BONNE
(OLD —) TABBY SPINSTER
(WAITING —) ABIGAIL SUIVANTE
MAIDEN MAY BIRD BURD DAME GIRL MAID DALAGA DAMSEL FROKIN MEISJE COLLEEN CYDIPPE DAMOZEL MADCHEN DAUGHTER
(— WITH BASKET ON HEAD) CANEPHOR
(MOUNT IDA —) OREAD
(MUSLIM —) HURI HOURI
(WEAVING —) ARACHNE
(PREF.) PARTHENO
MAIDENHAIR GINGKO ADIANTUM
MAIDENLY VIRGIN GIRLISH VIRGINAL
MAIDEN PINK SPINK DIANTHUS
MAIDSERVANT LASS BIDDY BONNE SKIVVY ANCILLA LISETTE
MAIEUTIC HEBAMIC
MAIGRE BAR SCIAENID WEAKFISH
MAIL BAG DAK HOOD POST ARMOR MATTER AIRMAIL JACKPOT MAILBAG ORDINAR POSTAGE POSTBAG SEAPOST TAPPALL ORDINARY
(IMPROPERLY ADDRESSED —) NIX NIXY NIXIE
(JUNK —) CATALOG
(KIND OF —) HATE VOICE
MAILBAG BAG POUCH POSTBAG
MAILBOX POST PILLAR POSTBOX
MAILLECHORT ARGENTON
MAILLOT SWIMSUIT
MAILMAN POSTMAN BREVIGER
MAIM LAME BREAK TRUNK HAMBLE MANGLE MAYHEM SCOTCH CRIPPLE MUTILATE TRUNCATE
(— AN ANIMAL) LAW MANK
MAIMED GAMMY SPAVINED
(PREF.) PERO
MAIMING MAYHEM
MAIN HIGH LINE MOST CHIEF GRAND GREAT OCEAN PRIME SHEER MIGHTY CAPITAL LEADING CARDINAL FOREMOST

MAINE
CAPITAL: AUGUSTA
COLLEGE: BATES COLBY BOWDOIN

COUNTY: KNOX WALDO KENNEBEC AROOSTOOK PENOBSCOT SAGADAHOC PISCATAQUIS
INDIAN: ABNAKI
LAKE: GRAND SEBEC SEBAGO RANGELEY SCHOODIC MOOSEHEAD CHESUNCOOK
MOUNTAIN: BIGELOW CADILLAC KATAHDIN
NATIVE: MANIAC
RIVER: SACO KENNEBEC AROOSTOOK KENNEBAGO PENOBSCOT
STATE BIRD: CHICKADEE
STATE FLOWER: PINECONE
STATE NICKNAME: LUMBER PINETREE
STATE TREE: PINE
TOWN: BATH ORONO AUBURN BANGOR BELFAST HOULTON KITTERY MACHIAS BOOTHBAY LEWISTON OGUNQUIT PORTLAND SKOWHEGAN

MAINLAND
(PREF.) EPEIRO
MAINLY BROADLY CHIEFLY LARGELY
MAINSTAY KEY ATLAS SINEW STOOP PILLAR BACKBONE RELIANCE
MAIN STREET (AUTHOR OF —) LEWIS
(CHARACTER IN —) ERIK HUGH WILL CAROL MILFORD VALBORG KENNICOTT
MAINTAIN AVER AVOW BEAR FEND FIND HOLD KEEP LAST SAVE ADOPT ARGUE CARRY CLAIM ESCOT SALVE ADHERE ALLEGE ASSERT AVOUCH DEFEND INTEND RETAIN THREAP UPHOLD UPKEEP CONFIRM CONTEND DECLARE DISPUTE JUSTIFY NOURISH SUBSIST SUPPORT SUSTAIN CONTINUE PRESERVE
(— AS TRUE) AVOUCH SOOTHE
(— POSITION) STALL
(— SOLEMNLY) VOW
(— WITHOUT REASON) ARROGATE
MAINTAINER FOUNDER RETAINER
MAINTENANCE KEEP LIVING UPKEEP ALIMONY CUSTODY FINDING KEEPING PREBEND SERVICE
(— OF POPULATION) BALANCE
MAITHILI TIRHUTIA
MAIZE CORN GRAIN CEREAL INDIAN JAGONG STAPLE MEALIES DJAGOONG
(— CRUSHED WITH PESTLE) STAMP
MAJAGUA HAU BARU BOLA MAHO MOJO BURAO GUANA MAHOE PURAU BALIBAGO CORKWOOD EMAJAGUA
MAJESTIC HIGH AWFUL GRAND LOFTY REGAL ROYAL AUGUST KINGLY SUPERB STATELY SUBLIME ELEVATED IMPERIAL MAESTOSO SPLENDID
MAJESTY DIGNITY AUGUSTUS GRANDEUR KINGSHIP
MAJOON BANG BHANG
MAJOR BEY DUR DURUM SHARP CAPITAL GREATER MAGGIORE
MAJOR BARBARA (AUTHOR OF —) SHAW
(CHARACTER IN —) LOMAX SARAH CUSINS BARBARA CHARLES STEPHEN ADOLPHUS BRITOMART UNDERSHAFT
MAJORCA (SEAPORT IN —) PALMA
MAJORITY BODY BULK FECK MOST CORPSE SUBSTANCE
(ABSOLUTE —) QUORUM
MAJOR LEAGUE BIGS
MAKARAKA IDDIO
MAKARI KOTOKO
MAKE DO CUT GAR LET MAY FORM GIVE LEVY BRAND BUILD CAUSE COVER FETCH FORGE FRAME SEIZE SHAPE STAMP AUTHOR COBBLE CREATE GRAITH INDUCE RENDER CONFECT FASHION IMAGERY IWURCHE PERFORM PRODUCE CONTRIVE GENERATE
(— A BLUNDER) GOOF
(— ACKNOWLEDGMENT) CONFESS
(— ACTIVE) ENERGIZE
(— A DIFFERENCE) SKILL
(— A DRINK LAST) NURSE
(— ADVANCES) SOLICIT IMPORTUNE
(— AGAIN) RENEW
(— AMENDS) ABYE ATONE ABEGGE ANSWER REDEEM EXPIATE REDRESS
(— A MESS OF) PIE
(— ANGRY) GRAMY WRATH
(— A RUG) HOOK
(— AS PROFIT) GROSS
(— ATTRACTIVE) GILD
(— A VISIT) COSHER
(— AWAY WITH) ABOLISH EMBEZZLE
(— BARE) STRIP DENUDE
(— BELIEVE) LET PRETEND
(— BETTER) AMEND HEIGHTEN
(— BLUE) HIP
(— BRIGHT) ENGILD ILLUME CLARIFY
(— BRISK) PERK
(— BROWN) TAN
(— BY STAMPING) MINT
(— CANDLE) DIP DRAW
(— CERTAIN) ASSURE ENSURE
(— CHANNEL IN) THROAT
(— CHEERFUL) SOLACE
(— CHOICE) OPT CHOOSE SELECT
(— CLAMMY) ENGLEIM
(— CLEAR) DECLARE DEVELOP DISCUSS EXHIBIT EXPOUND LIGHTEN DESCRIBE
(— COLD) REFREID
(— COMPLETE) SPHERE
(— CONSPICUOUS) ENNOBLE
(— CONTENT) SATISFY
(— CULTIVABLE) EMPOLDER
(— CUT PRIOR TO LAYERING) TONGUE
(— DEMANDS) POSTULATE
(— DESTITUTE) BEREAVE
(— DIFFERENT) ALTER CHANGE
(— DIRTY) MOIL GRIME
(— DISPLAY OF) AFFECT DISCOVER
(— DRUNK) FOX SOUSE FUDDLE SOZZLE
(— DRY) HAZLE HAZZLE
(— EARLIER) ADVANCE
(— EFFERVESCENT) AERATE
(— EFFIGY) GUY
(— EFFORT) PUSH
(— END OF) SNIB FETCH
(— ENDURING) ANNEAL
(— EQUAL) WEIGH EQUATE
(— EVEN) GLAZE LEVEL WEIGH SQUARE
(— FACES) GIMBLE MURGEON
(— FALSE PRETENSES) SHAM
(— FAST) FIX BAIL FAST GIRD KNIT MAKE STOP BELAY HITCH BUCKLE FASTEN SECURE
(— FAT) BATTEN
(— FIRM) FIX BRACE FASTEN
(— FIT) APTATE STRIKE
(— FOOLISH) DAFF GREEN NUGIFY STULTIFY
(— FOOL OF) DOR BORE DOLT DORRE BEGOWK DOODLE
(— FOOTSORE) SURBATE
(— FOR) HEAD
(— FROTHY) MILL
(— FULL) FARCE FULFILL
(— FUN OF) GUY KID GAFF JAPE JEST JOSH RIDE DROLL GLAIK SCOUT SMOKE
(— FUSS OVER NOTHING) FAFF
(— GLAD) FAIN
(— GLASS) FOUND
(— GLOSSY) SLEEK
(— GLOW) FURNACE
(— GOLDEN) ENDORE
(— GOOD) ABET SUPPLY RESTORE SUPPORT RETRIEVE
(— GRINDING NOISE) GRINCH
(— GURGLING SOUND) CROOL
(— HAPPY) BLESS ENJOY REFORM BEATIFY SATISFY FELICIFY
(— HARD) TAW STEEL ENDURE HORNIFY
(— HARDY) FASTEN
(— HEADWAY) STEM WALK ENFORCE
(— HEALTHY) SANIFY
(— HELPLESS) STAGGER
(— HOLY) BLESS SACRE HALLOW SANCTIFY
(— HORSE SEEM YOUNGER) BISHOP
(— ILL) MORBIFY
(— IMMOBILE) FREEZE
(— IMPACT) ASSAIL
(— INCURSION) HARRY
(— INSIGNIFICANT) MICRIFY
(— INTO BUNDLE) FARDEL
(— INTO LAW) ENACT
(— INVALID) DAMASK
(— JOINT) SYPHER
(— KNOWN) BID OUT GIVE WISE AREAD BEKEN BREAK KITHE SOUND SPEAK BEWRAY BROACH COUTHE DENOTE DESCRY EXPOSE INFORM REVEAL SPREAD CONFESS DECLARE DELIVER DIVULGE PUBLISH SIGNIFY UNCOVER ANNOUNCE DECIPHER DISCLOSE DISCOVER INDICATE PROCLAIM PROMULGE
(— LESS) MINISH
(— LESS DENSE) THIN RAREFY
(— LESS SEVERE) MITIGATE
(— LIABLE) DANGER
(— LOVE) WOO COURT SPOON GALLANT
(— LUKEWARM) WLECCHE
(— LUSTERLESS) FLATTEN
(— MANIFEST) EVINCE EXPLAIN
(— MELANCHOLY) HYP
(— MELODIOUS) ATTUNE
(— MELODY) DREAM
(— MENTION) SPEAK
(— MERRY) JET GAUD CHEER SPORT FROLIC SHROVE DISPORT REHAYTE
(— METALLIC SOUND) CHINK
(— MISTAKE) ERR BOOB GOOF
(— MONOTONOUS NOISE) DRONE
(— MORAL) ETHICIZE
(— MUCH OF) DAWT DANDLE
(— MURMURING NOISE) BUM
(— NEAT) FEAT SMUG TIDY GROOM
(— NEST) TIMBER
(— NEW AGAIN) RENOVATE
(— NONMAGNETIC) DEGAUSS
(— NUMB) DAZE ETHERIZE
(— OFF) BAG BOLT HOOK ANNEX HEIST MOSEY SLOPE SPIRIT SCARPER
(— ONE) UNE
(— ONE'S WAY) AIRT BORE TRADE PLY FRAME
(— OPEN) AIR PATEFY
(— OUT) FARE FILL GLEAN SKILL DISCERN DECIPHER
(— OVER) TURN ALIEN CHANGE RECOCT DELIVER REFORGE
(— PALE) CHALK
(— PLEASANT) SWEETEN
(— POIGNANT) SAUCE
(— PREGNANT) ENWOMB
(— PROGRESS) GAIN STEM GATHER
(— PROUD) WLENCH
(— PUBLIC) BLOW BLAZE BREAK BLAZON DELATE DIVULGE FANFARE PUBLISH BULLETIN
(— QUIET) ALLAY QUIET APPEASE
(— RATTLING NOISE) TIRL
(— READY) DO BUN GET BOUN BOWN BUSK YARK BELAY BOWNE DRESS PREST PRIME FETTLE GRAITH ADDRESS APPAREL DISPOSE PREPARE
(— RECORD OF) REFER
(— REFERENCE) MENTION
(— RESISTANCE) REBEL
(— RESOLUTE) STEEL
(— RETURN FOR) REQUITE
(— RICH) FREIGHT IMBURSE
(— ROSY) FLUSH
(— RUSTLING SOUND) FISSLE FISTLE
(— RUTTING CRY) FREAM
(— SCANTY LIVING) EKE
(— SERIES OF NOTES) TINKLE
(— SHIFT) SCAMBLE
(— SIGN OF CROSS) BLESS
(— SMALL) MICRIFY BELITTLE
(— SMALLER) MINIFY COMPRESS
(— SMOOTH) SLAB GLAZE SLEEK GENTLE HAMMER SCRAPE LEVIGATE
(— SOFT) NESH GENTLE

(— SOGGY) SOP
(— SOUR) FOX WIND
(— SPIRITLESS) MOPE
(— SPORT OF) LARK
(— SPRUCE) PERK SMARTEN
(— STRAIGHT) ADDRESS
(— STRONG) STEEL FASTEN FORTIFY
(— STUPID) MOIDER STULTIFY
(— SUITABLE) ADAPT
(— SURE) SEE INSURE
(— THIN) EMACIATE
(— TIDY) RED REDD
(— TIPSY) FLUSTER
(— TRANSITION TO) MODULATE
(— TRIM) SMUG
(— UNEVEN) RUFFLE RUMPLE
(— UP) UP COOK FORM SPELL INDITE SETTLE ANALYZE COMPACT COMPOSE COMPUTE CONCOCT CONFECT FASHION COMPOUND COMPRISE DISPENSE
(— UP ACCOUNTS) BREVE
(— USELESS) SPIKE SPOIL
(— USE OF) FEE BUSK APPLY AVAIL BROOK SERVE SPEND EMPLOY EXECUTE IMPROVE UTILIZE
(— VIBRANT SOUND) CHIRR
(— VOID) ABATE ANNUL
(— WAR) WARRAY
(— WET) DRAGGLE
(— WHISTLING NOISE) WHEW
(— WHITE) BLANCH BLEACH CANDIFY
(— WORSE) IMPAIR PEJORATE
(PREF.) POETICO POETO
(SUFF.) EN FECT FEIT FIC(AL)(ATE)(ATION)(ATIVE)(ATOR)(ATORY)(E)(ENCE)(ENT)(IAL)(IARY)(IENT) FIER FIQUE FY IFY POEIA POESIS POIESIS POIETIC

MAKE-BELIEVE BORAK DUMMY ASSUMED PRETENCE
MAKER DOER JACK KNAVE SMITH FACTOR FORGER FORMER WORKER WRIGHT CREATOR DECLARER OPERATOR
(— OF ARROWS) FLETCHER
(— OF BARRELS) COOPER
(— OF POTS) POTTER
(— OF SADDLETREES) FUSTER
(— OF SONGS) BULBUL
(— OF TALLOW) CHANDLER
(DRIP-COFFEE —) MACCHINETTA
(SUFF.) STER STRESS

MAKESHIFT JURY RUDE JERRY TOUSY BEWITH CUTCHA KUTCHA APOLOGY JACKLEG STOPGAP RESOURCE TIMENOGUY
MAKEUP FACE BUILD GETUP HABIT PAINT ROUGE SETUP SHAPE FACIES FORMAT ANATOMY CONSIST FEATURE EYELINER PHYSIQUE TRAVESTY MAQUILLAGE
MAKING FACT
(SUFF.) FACIENT FACT(ION)(IVE)(ORY) FIC FICATION
MALABAR BAY
MALABAR ALMOND KAMANI ALMENDRO
MALACCA CANE
MALACEAE POMACEAE PYRACEAE
MALADJUSTMENT SCAR
MALADROIT ILL INEPT AWKWARD UNHANDY BUNGLING
MALADY AMOK EVIL MORB CAUSE GRIEF ONCOME AILMENT DISEASE ILLNESS DISORDER MISCHIEF SICKNESS
(SUFF.) (— ARISING FROM) ITIS
MALAGASY LEMURIAN
MALAGASY REPUBLIC (SEE MADAGASCAR)
MALAGIGI (COUSIN OF —) RINALDO
MALAISE UNEASE
MALAPROPISM SLIPSLOP
MALAR JUGAL
MALARIA AGUE MIASMA SHAKES QUARTAN PALUDISM
(— PARASITE) VIVAX
MALARIAL PALUDAL PALUDOSE PALUDOUS

MALAWI

CAPITAL: LILONGWE
COIN: KWACHA TAMBALA
FORMER CAPITAL: ZOMBA
FORMER NAME: NYASALAND
HIGHLANDS: SHIRE
LAKE: NYASA
LANGUAGE: YAO CEWA BANTU NGONI TONGA NYANJA TUMBUKA
MOUNTAIN: MLANJE
PEOPLE: YAO BANTU CHEWA NGURU NYANJA
RIVER: SHIRE
TOWN: DOWA CHOLO MZUZU NCHEU ZOMBA KARONGA BLANTYRE LILONGWE
VALLEY: RIFT

MALAY AMOK ASIL AMUCK BAJAU ILOCO JAKUN MANOBO ILOKANO
MALAYAN (— TREE) TERAP
MALAY APPLE OHIA JAMBO KAVIKA

MALAYSIA

CAPITAL: KUALALUMPUR
COIN: SEN TRA TRAH RINGGIT
ISLAND: ARU GOA KAI OBI OMA ALOR BALI GAGA JAVA MUNA MURU SULU AMBON BANDA BOHOL BUTON CERAM LUZON MISOL PANAY SANGI SUMBA TIMOR WETAR BANGKA BOEFON BOEROE BORNEO BUTUNG FLORES LOMBOK MADURA PELENG SANGIR TALAUR WAIGEU AMBOINA CELEBES JAMDENA MINDORO MOROTAI PALAWAN SALAJAR SALWATI SUMATRA SUMBAWA BELITONG DJAILOLO TANIMBAR
ISTHMUS: KRA
LANGUAGE: TAGALOG
MONEY: DOLLAR RINGGIT
MOUNTAIN: BULU NIUT RAJA MURJO NIAPA LEUSER SLAMET BINAIJA RINDJANI
PEOPLE: ATA BAJAU SEMANG BISAYAN TAGALOG VISAYAN
RIVER: KUTAI PERAK BARITO PAHANG
STATE: KEDAH PERAK SABAH JOHORE PAHANG PENANG PERLIS MALACCA SARAWAK
TOWN: IPOH DAVAO ILOILO KANGAR KUPANG MANADO KUANTAN KUCHING MALACCA SANDAKAN SEREMBAN
WEIGHT: TAEL WANG TAMPANG

MALCHAM (FATHER OF —) SHAHARAHIM
(MOTHER OF —) HODESH
MALCHIAH (FATHER OF —) HARIM PAROSH RECHAB
MALCHIEL (FATHER OF —) BERIAH
MALCHIRAM (FATHER OF —) JEHOIACHIN
MALCHISHUA (FATHER OF —) SAUL
MALCONTENT FRONDEUR
MALDIVES (CAPITAL OF —) MALE
(MONEY OF —) LAARI RUFIYAA RUFIYAN
MALE HE DOG HIM MAN TOM BUCK BULL COCK JACK ADULT MANLY SPEAR JOHNNY MANFUL MASCLE VIRILE LALAQUI MANKIND MANLIKE MANNISH PURUSHA
(— OF ANIMALS) TOM BUCK BULL JACK STUD STALLION
(EFFEMINATE —) NANCE
(GELDED —) GALT
(SWAGGERING —) GREASER
(YOUNG —) GROOM
(PREF.) ANDR(O)
(SUFF.) ANDRIA ANDROUS ANDRY
MALECITE ETCHEMIN
MALEDICTION BAN WISH CURSE MALISON ANATHEMA
MALEFACTOR BADDY FELON BADDIE CULPRIT CRIMINAL EVILDOER
MALEFIC TAKING
MALEFICENT BALEFUL
MALELEEL (FATHER OF —) CAINAN
MALEO MEGAPOD
MALE ORCHIS CUCKOO CROWTOE CULLION PURPLES RAGWORT CROWFOOT
MALEVOLENCE SPITE ENMITY GRUDGE HATRED MALICE RANCOR SPLEEN MALIGNITY
MALEVOLENT ILL EVIL FELL MALIGN HATEFUL HOSTILE SPITEFUL RANCOROUS
MALFEASANCE MISCONDUCT MALPRACTICE
MALFORMATION CURL ERROR HEMITERY MONSTROSITY
(— OF CARNATION) TWITTER
(— OF FRUIT) CATFACE
MALFORMED SHAMBLE
MALFUNCTION GLITCH

MALI

ANCIENT CITY: TIMBUKTU
CAPITAL: BAMAKO
FORMER NAME: FRENCHSUDAN
LAKE: DO DEBO GAROU KORAROU
LANGUAGE: DOGON DYULA MANDE MARKA PEULH BAMBARA MALINKE SENOUFO SONGHAI
MOUNTAIN: MINA MANDING
PEOPLE: MOOR PEUL TUAREG BAMBARA MALINKE SONGHAI SENOUFO
RIVER: BANI BAGOE BAKOY NIGER BAOULE AZAOUAK SENEGAL
TOWN: GAO SAN KATI KITA NARA BAMBA KAYES MOPTI NIONO NIORO SEGOU SIKASSO

MALICE DOLE ENVY HAIN PIQUE SPITE VENOM VIRUS ENMITY GRUDGE RANCOR SPLEEN DESPITE AMBITION MALIGNITY MALEVOLENCE
MALICIOUS SHREW SNIDE TEENY BITTER DOGGED MALIGN WANTON HATEFUL HEINOUS LEERING SPITOUS VICIOUS CANKERED NARQUOIS SINISTER SPITEFUL VENOMOUS VIPEROUS
MALIGN ILL FOUL ABUSE LIBEL WRONG BEWRAY DEFAME REVILE VILIFY ASPERSE DEPRAVE HURTFUL SLANDER TRADUCE BLASPHEME
MALIGNANCY FEROCITY
MALIGNANT EVIL ATTRY BLACK FELON FERAL SWART ATTERY MALIGN BALEFUL ENVIOUS HATEFUL HELLISH PEEVISH REPTILE VICIOUS WARLOCK CANKERED SHREWISH SPITEFUL VENOMOUS VIPEROUS VIRULENT WRATHFUL RANCOROUS
(NOT —) BENIGN INNOCENT
MALIGNITY GALL LIVER VENOM VIRUS HATRED MALICE RANCOR DESPITE
MALINGER MIKE DODGE SHIRK SKULK
MALINGERER SCONCER
MALL MART WALK ALLEE
(SHOPPING —) GALLERIA
MALLARD TWISTER
(FLOCK OF —S) SORD SUTE PADDLING
MALLEABLE MILD SOFT DUCTILE PLASTIC BATTABLE
MALLEIN MORVIN
MALLEMUCK MOLLIE MALMARSH
MALLET MALL MAUL MELL GAVEL BEATER BEETLE DRIVER HAMMER DRESSER FLOGGER STRIKER PLOWMELL
(— FOR BREAKING CLODS) BILDER
(CURRIER'S —) MACE
(HATTER'S —) BEATER
(PAVER'S —) TUP
(PREF.) MALLEI MALLEO SPHYRA
MALLEUS HAMMER OSSICLE PLECTRUM
MALLOTHI (FATHER OF —) HEMAN
MALLOW MAW DOCK HOCK ALTEA KOKIO MALVA MAUVE TAUPE CHEESE ESCOBA GEMAUVE ABUTILON PIEPRINT
MALLUCH (FATHER OF —) BANI
MALMSEY MALVASIA MALVOISIE
MALNUTRITION CACHEXY CACHEXIA CACOTROPHY
MALODOROUS GAMY HIGH NOSY OLID RANK FETID SMELLY VIROSE VIROUS NOISOME
MALPRACTICE (UNDERHAND —S) SKULDUGGERY

MALT WORT
(GROUND —) GRIST
(REMAINS OF —) DRAFF
MALTA (ANCIENT NAME OF —) MELITA
(CAPITAL OF —) VALLETTA
(ISLAND OF —) GOZO COMINO
(MONEY OF —) LIRA
(TOWN OF —) QORMI RABAT HAMRUN SLIEMA XAGHRA ZABBAR BIRKIRKARA
MALTASE GLUCASE
MALTESE CROSS (LIKE A —) PATE PATEE PATTEE
MALTHA BREA
MALTHOUSE MALTING
MALTOSE AMYLON
MALTREAT MAUL ABUSE DIGHT DEFOUL DEMEAN HESPIL HUSPEL MISUSE THREAT BEDEVIL MISGUIDE MANHANDLE
MALTREATMENT ABUSE
MALVA DOCK MALLOW
MAMAMU MU
MAMBA COBRA ELAPOID
MAMMA MA MOM MAMA WIFE MOMMA WOMAN MOTHER
MAMMAL OX ASS BAT CAT COW DOG FOX PIG YAK BEAR BOAR COON DEER GOAT HARE LION LYNX MINK MOLE PUMA SEAL ZEBU BEAST BISON CAMEL COATI COYPU GENET HORSE HYENA LEMUR LLAMA MOOSE OKAPI OTTER PANDA RATEL SABLE SHEEP SHREW SKUNK SLOTH SWINE TAPIR TIGER WHALE ZORIL ALPACA ANIMAL BADGER COUGAR CULPEO DESMAN DUGONG FISHER FOUSSA GOPHER GRISON JAGUAR MARTEN MONKEY OCELOT OLINGO TENREC VICUNA WALRUS WOMBAT BUFFALO CARIBOU DOLPHIN ECHIDNA GIRAFFE GLUTTON GUANACO HIPPOID HUANACO MANATEE OPOSSUM PECCARY POLECAT PRIMATE RACCOON SUCKLER SURICAT TARSIER TYLOPOD WILDCAT AARDVARK AARDWOLF ANTELOPE BANXRING CACOMIXL CREODONT ELEPHANT FALANAKA HEDGEHOG KINKAJOU MAMMIFER PANGOLIN PINNIPED REINDEER SQUIRREL PRONGHORN RHINOCEROS
(EXTINCT —) STEGODONT
MAMMALIA MASTOZOA
MAMMEE ABRICO ABRICOT
MAMMILLA PAP TEAT NIPPLE
MAMMOTH HUGE LARGE GIGANTIC
MAMRE (BROTHER OF —) ANER ESHCOL
MAN BO HE BOY GEE GUY HIM LAD TAO WAT WER BUCK CHAL CHAP COVE DICK EARL GENT GOME HOMO JACK JONG MALE RINK TULK BERNE BIMBO BIPED BLOKE CHURL COVEY CULLY FORCE FREKE GROOM GUEST HEART HOMME HORSE JOKER SEGGE SWAIN WIGHT BIMANE CHIELD CUFFIN FELLOW HOMBRE MANTZU WEPMAN BIMANUS HOMONID KINSMAN MANKIND
(— AFFECTING FOREIGN WAYS) MACARONI
(— DRESSED AS WOMAN) BESSY MALINCHE
(— IN DEBT) DYVOUR
(— IN GAMES) PIECE
(— IN PRIVATE STATION) IDIOT
(— IN TUG-OF-WAR) ANCHOR
(— LEADING 12TH NIGHT) BEAN
(— OF ALL WORK) MOZO
(— OF AUTHORITY) AGHA SEIGNIOR
(— OF BEAUTY) APOLLO
(— OF BRASS) TALOS
(— OF COURAGE) LION
(— OF GREAT WEALTH) NABOB
(— OF HIGH RANK) CHAM KHAN THAKUR GRANDEE
(— OF POWER) MAGNATE
(— OF SUBSTANCE) IDLEMAN
(— OF THE COMMON PEOPLE) JACK
(— OF VIGOR) WYE
(— OF VIOLENCE) RABIATOR
(— OF WAR) ANDREW CARAVEL CRUISER
(— TO MAN) SINGLE
(ARTIFICIAL —) GOLEM
(ATTRACTIVE —) FOX HUNK
(BACKGAMMON —) BLOT BUILDER
(BALD —) PILGARLIC
(BEST —) BRIDEMAN PARANYMPH
(BIG —) COB BRUISER MUGWUMP
(BLESSED —) BEATUS
(BRISK —) SPARK
(CASTRATED —) SPADO EUNUCH
(CHIEF —) FOREMAN OPTIMATE
(CHURLISH —) NABAL BODACH
(CLEANING —) BUSBOY
(COMMON —) CARL STREET YEOMAN
(COVETOUS —) HUNKS
(CRAFTY —) FOX
(CRUEL —) OGRE BRUTE
(DISAGREEABLE —) GLEYDE
(DISCREET —) PRUDHOMME
(DISLIKED —) CUT
(DISSOLUTE —) RAKE
(ECCENTRIC —) GEEZER
(EDUCATED —) EFFENDI
(EFFEMINATE —) DILDO FAIRY NANCE PUNCE SISSY JESSIE COCKNEY MEACOCK MIDWIFE MILKSOP ANDROGYN MOLLYCODDLE
(END —) BONES BRAKE
(ENLISTED —) GI SNIPE AIDMAN AIRMAN KEEPER STORES ARMORER STRIKER SONARMAN
(ENTIRE —) EGO
(EXTINCT —) TEPEXPAN
(FAITHFUL —) TRUEMAN
(FANCY —) PONCE
(FASHIONABLE —) TOUPET ELEGANT FOPLING GALLANT
(FIRST —) ASK ADAM ASKR TIKI FOREMAN
(FLASHILY-DRESSED —) LAIR
(FOPPISH —) BLOOD
(FREE —) LIBER
(GRAY-HAIRED —) GRIZZLE
(GREAT —) VAVASOR
(HARDHEARTED —) KNARK
(HAUGHTY —) BASHAW
(HOLDUP —) FOOTPAD
(HOLY —) SADHU SAINT SANNYASI
(HONORS —) WRANGLER
(IDEAL —) SUPERMAN
(IMMORAL —) REP
(INEFFECTUAL —) DUFFER
(INSANE —) FURIOSO
(LADY'S —) FOPLING DAMMARET
(LAME —) BACACH
(LEARNED —) ULEMA LAMDAN OLLAMH PUNDIT SAVANT SOPHIST
(LECHEROUS —) SATYR
(LEWD —) BROTHEL
(LIAISON —) COURIER
(LITERARY —) GIGADIBS
(LITTLE —) MANNET SHRIMP MANNIKIN
(LUSTFUL —) GOAT
(MAINTENANCE —) CAMPMAN
(MARRIED —) HUSBAND BENEDICT
(MECHANICAL —) ROBOT
(MEDICINE —) PEAI DOCTOR SHAMAN ANGAKOK
(MEEK —) MOSES
(MIGHTY —) SAMSON
(ODD-JOB —) JOEY
(OLD —) HAG OLD BOOL CUFF GAFF CRONE DOBBY UNCLE BODACH DUFFER FATHER GAFFER NESTOR GERONTE STARETS ECKEHART VELYARDE PATRIARCH
(OLD-CLOTHES —) POCO
(ONE-ARMED —) WINGY
(ONE-EYED —) ARIMASP
(ONE-FOOTED —) MONOPODE
(OVERFASTIDIOUS —) DUDE
(PARTY —) SIDESMAN
(POOR —) PAUPER
(PRIMITIVE —) URMENSCH
(PRINCIPAL —) HERO TOPARCH
(RASH —) HOTSPUR
(RICH —) DIVES NABOB CROESUS
(RIGHT-HAND —) HENCHMAN
(RIGHTEOUS —) SADDIK
(SERVING —) GARCON
(SOUND-EFFECTS —) CRAWK
(STERN —) GRIMSIRE
(STRAIGHT —) STOOGE
(STRONG —) KWASIND
(STRONG-ARM —) HOOD GORILLA
(STUPID —) SUBMAN
(SWAGGERING YOUNG —) GREASER
(THICKSET —) GRUB KNAR SPUD
(TOUGH —) KNAR
(UNEMPLOYED —) BATLAN
(UNKNOWN —) INCOGNITO
(UTILITY —) JUMPER
(VICIOUS —) YAHOO
(WEAK —) WIMP
(WELL-BUILT —) HUNK
(WHITE —) BOSTON BUCKRA PAKEHA CACHILA
(WHITE — LIVING WITH ABORIGINE) COMBO
(WILD —) WOODMAN WOODWOSE
(WISE —) NAB HAKAM MAGUS SABIO SOLON SOPHY NESTOR WIZARD SOLOMON TOHUNGA
(WIZENED —) GNOME
(WOMANISH —) JENNY
(WRETCHED —) CAITIFF
(YOUNG —) BOY LAD JONG PUNK YOUTH BOCHUR DAMSEL EPHEBE KNIGHT BOUCHAL BUCKEEN YOUNKER BOYCHICK COCKEREL SPRINGAL
(PREF.) ANDR(O) ANTHROP(O) HOMI(NI)
(SUFF.) ANDRIA ANDROUS ANDRY ENGRO VIR(ATE)
MAN-ABOUT-TOWN JOHNNY CLUBMAN FLANEUR
MANABOZHO MICHABOU WINABOJO
MANACLE BAND BOND DARBY HAMPER TIRRET SHACKLE HANDCUFF HANDLOCK
(PL.) IRONS CHAINS
MANAGE DO GET MAN RUN BEAR BOSS COPE CURB FEND HACK HOLD KEEP LEAD MAKE RULE TEND TOOL WIND WORK BROOK CARRY DIGHT FORTH FRAME GUIDE MAYNE ORDER SHIFT SPEND STEER SWING WIELD CONVEY DEMEAN DEVISE DIRECT FETTLE GOVERN HANDLE INTEND MANURE TEMPER AGITATE CONDUCT DISPOSE EXECUTE FINAGLE HUSBAND MINSTER OFFICER OPERATE SOLICIT STEWARD CONTRIVE ENGINEER NEGOTIATE
(— AWKWARDLY) FOOZLE
(— CLUMSILY) KEVEL
(— SKILLFULLY) MANIPULATE
(— SUCCESSFULLY) HACK
(— TO BEAR) AFFORD
(— WITH CARE) NURSE
MANAGEABLE EASY YARE BANTAM DOCILE WIELDY DUCTILE FLEXIBLE YIELDING
MANAGEMENT CARE HEEL WORK CHARGE CONDUCT CONTROL ECONOMY GESTION RUNNING CARRIAGE DEMEANOR ENGINERY MANAGERY MANEUVER REGIMENT STEERAGE STEERING
(DELICATE —) NICETY
(DOMESTIC —) MENAGE HUSBANDRY
(GOOD —) EUTAXY
(SKILLFUL —) PRACTICE PRACTISE
MANAGER BOSS DOER EXEC AGENT DAROGA DEPUTY PURSER SYNDIC AMILDAR CURATOR ERENACH HUSBAND STEWARD WIELDER AUMILDAR DIRECTOR DISPOSER ENGINEER HERENACH INSTITOR
(— OF ENTERTAINERS) ROADIE
(— OF FARM) HIND GRIEVE
(ASSISTANT —) CAPORAL
(MINE —) CAPTAIN
(POLITICAL —) FUGLEMAN
(STAGE —) REGISSEUR
(SUFF.) EER
MANAHATH (FATHER OF —) SHOBAL
MANAKIN PIPRA
MAN-AT-ARMS KNIGHT
MANATEE DUGONG SEACOW COWFISH HOGFISH MERMAID LAMANTIN MUTILATE SIRENIAN

MANBARKLAK JARANA KAKARAL
MANCALA WARI
MANCHE **(— CAPITAL)** STLO
MANCHU SHERRY
MANCHURIA **(CHINESE NAME FOR —)** MANCHOW
(PENINSULA OF —) LIAOTUNG
(PROVINCE OF —) JILIN LIAONING HEILONGJIANG
(RIVER OF —) AMUR LIAO YALU ARGUN USSURI SUNGARI
MANDAEAN SABAEAN
MANDANE **(FATHER OF —)** ASTYAGES
(HUSBAND OF —) CAMBYSES
(SON OF —) CYRUS
MANDARIN TOWKAY CHINESE
MANDARIN ORANGE SATSUMA
MANDATE BREVE ORDER BEHEST CHARGE DECREE FIRMAN BIDDING COMMAND PRECEPT PROCESS MANDAMUS MANDATUM WARRANTY
(— OF GOD) JUDGMENT
MANDATORY OBLIGATORY
MANDIBLE BEAK JOWL SETA RAMUS JAWBONE GNATHITE
(— PART) MALA
MANDINGO MANDE MALINKE WANGARA
MANDOLIN OUD MANDORA
MANDRAKE ALRAUN DUDAIM
MANDREL ROD BALL STUD SLEEVE CHEMISE SPINDLE TRIBLET
MANDRICARDO **(BELOVED OF —)** ANGELICA
(FATHER OF —) AGRICAN
(SLAYER OF —) ORLANDO
MANDRILL MAIMON MORMON
MANE JUBA MONE CREST PITRI ENCOLURE
MAN-EATER
(PL.) ANTHROPOPHAGI REQUIN REQUIEM
MANEGE TRAIN
MANEUVER PLAY TURN WISE GAMBIT JOCKEY MANURE PESADE VRILLE FINAGLE FINESSE ARTIFICE DEMARCHE ENGINEER EXERCISE STRATEGY WINDLASS
(— GENTLY) EASE
(— IN AUTO RACING) SLINGSHOT
(— IN SPACE) DOCK
(— IN SURFING) CUTBACK
(— OF MOTORCYCLE OR BICYCLE) WHEELIE
(AERIAL —) BUNT LOOP SPIN FISHTAIL WINGOVER
(BICYCLE —) WHEELIE
(BULLFIGHTING —) VERONICA
(ILLEGAL —) GAME
(KIND OF —) HEIMLICH VALSALVA
(ROADWAY —) UTURN
(ROCK-CLIMBING —) LAYBACK
(SKIING —) SNOWPLOW
(VEHICLE —) WHEELIE
(WRESTLING —) ESCAPE BUTTOCK
MANEUVERABLE YAR YARE
MANEUVERING FINESSE FLANKING FOOTWORK
MANEUVRE **(DRESSAGE —)** PESADE
MANGE ITCH REEF SCAB CANKER DARTARS SCABIES
MANGER BIN BUNK CRIB HECK STALL CRATCH
MANGLE MAR HACK IRON MOUTH BRUISE GARBLE HACKLE IRONER MAGGLE MURDER MAMMOCK LACERATE MUTILATE
MANGO DIKA AMHAR AMINI BAUNO AMCHOOR CARABAO PAHUTAN
(POINT OF —) NAK
MANGOSTEEN SANTOL GARCINIA
MANGROVE BACAO GORAN MANGLE MYRTAL BACAUAN CERIOPS COURIDA HANGALAI LANGARAI
MANGUE CHOLUTECA CHOROTEGA
MANGY SCABBY ROINISH SCABETIC
MANHANDLE MAUL MESS ROUGH SCRAG WORKOVER
MANHATTAN ROBROY
MANHATTAN TRANSFER
(AUTHOR OF —) DOSPASSOS
(CHARACTER IN —) BUD GUS JOE HERF JOHN RUTH STAN CONGO ELLEN EMERY EMILE HARRY JIMMY SUSIE GEORGE MCNIEL NELLIE OKEEFE PRYNNE BALDWIN HARLAND MERIVALE PEARLINE THATCHER GOLDWEISER OGLETHORPE
MANHOOD ADAMHOOD
MANIA RAGE CRAZE FUROR FRENZY DELIRIUM HYSTERIA INSANITY CACOETHES
MANIAC KILLER MADMAN FANATIC LUNATIC
(KIND OF —) EGO
MANIFEST HAVE NUDE OPEN RIFE SENE SHOW APERT CLEAR FRANK GROSS KITHE NAKED OVERT PLAIN PROVE SPEAK SUTEL ARRANT ATTEST COUTHE EVINCE EXTANT GRAITH LIQUID OSTEND PATENT PHANIC APPROVE BETOKEN CONFESS DECLARE EVIDENT EXHIBIT EXPRESS OBVIOUS SIGNIFY VISIBLE APPARENT DISCLOSE DISCOVER INDICATE PALPABLE PROCLAIM
(NOT —) LATENT
(PREF.) PHANER(O) PHANTA(SMO) PHANTO
MANIFESTATION ACT SON BEAM COMA SIGN GLINT AVATAR COMING EFFECT OSTENT ADVANCE DISPLAY EXPRESS OUTSIDE SHOWING EPIPHANY MANIFEST
(BARELY PERCEPTIBLE —) SCINTIL
(BRIEF —) GLEAM
(DIVINE —) SPIRIT SHEKINAH
(HORRIBLE —) CHIMAERA
(MORAL —) SOUL
(VAGUE —) GLIMMER
(SUFF.) PHANE PHANOUS PHANT PHANY
MANIFESTLY WITTERLY
MANIFESTO PLACARD
MANIFOLD MANY TURRET VARIOUS FELEFOLD MANYFOLD MULTIPLE MULTIPLEX REPLICATE
(SUFF.) PLOID
MANIKIN ECORCHE PANTINE PHANTOM HOMUNCIO HOMUNCLE MANNIKIN
MANILA HEMP ABACA
MANIOC CASSAVA CATELLA MANDIOCA
MANIPLE BAND FANON ORALE FANNEL COMPANY HANDFUL SUDARIUM
MANIPULATE COG RIG COAX COOK DIAL FAKE HAND STIR TOOL CROOK HUMOR KNEAD SHAPE TREAT WIELD CHIVVY GOVERN HANDLE JOCKEY MANAGE WANGLE MASSAGE SHUFFLE
(— BY DECEPTIVE MEANS) RIG
(— DISHONESTLY) RIG SHUFFLE
(— FRAUDULENTLY) FIDDLE
MANIPULATION PASS JUGGLERY MANAGERY
MANITO ORENDA POKUNT MANITOU TAMANOAS
MANITOBA **(CAPITAL OF —)** WINNIPEG
(RIVER OF —) RED SEAL SWAN NELSON ROSEAU SOURIS PEMBINA CHURCHILL SASKACHEWAN
(TOWN OF —) CARMAN BRANDON DAUPHIN KILLARNEY SWANRIVER
MANKIND MAN FLESH SHEEP WORLD BIMANA SPECIES HUMANITY UNIVERSE MORTALITY
MANLIKE MALE MANLY MANNISH HOMINOID
MANLINESS ARETE VIRTUS MANSHIP
MANLY BOLD MALE HARDY MANNY DARING VIRILE MANLIKE
MAN-MADE SYNTHETIC UNNATURAL CULTURAL SYNTHETIC
MANNA TREHALA WINDFALL
MANNER AIR BAT JET LAT WAY FORM GAET GARB GATE KIND MAKE MIEN MODE RATE SORT THEW TOUR WISE WONE GUISE LATES SHAPE STYLE TENUE TRICK COURSE CUSTOM METHOD MISTER STRAIN ADDRESS AMENITY FASHION QUALITY QUOMODO CARAPACE DEMEANOR LANGUAGE
(— OF APPROACH) ABORD
(— OF DOING) ACTION
(— OF HANDLING) HAND
(— OF MAKING ANYTHING) FACTURE
(— OF PERFORMING) HAND
(— OF SITTING) ASANA
(— OF SPEAKING) SLUR SOUGH ACCENT GRAMMAR PARLANCE
(— OF SWIMMING) STROKE
(— OF WALKING) STEP
(AFFECTED —) AIR
(AMUSING —) DROLLERY
(ARROGANT —) BRAG HAUTEUR
(CHARACTERISTIC —) TOUCH
(EMOTIONAL —) STRAIN
(FORBIDDING —) SHELL
(FORMAL —) STARCH
(GRAND —) PANACHE
(HABITUAL —) SONG
(LIVELY —) JAZZ
(OUTWARD —) TOUR FRONT
(RESTRAINED —) RESERVE
(SECRET —) STEALTH
(SMOOTH —) JAPAN
(SWAGGERING —) SIDE PANACHE
(UNUSUAL —) SINGULARITY
(USUAL —) HABIT
(PL.) ADDRESS CORNERS HAVINGS BREEDING
(SUFF.) WISE
(AFTER THE — OF) FASHION
(IN A —) LY
(IN THE — OF) IC(AL)
MANNERED CUTE CUTESY MORATE THEWED
MANNERISM TIC POSE TRICK IDIASM
(EXAGGERATED —) CAMP
(PL.) DAPS
MANNERLY CIVIL POLITE
MANNERS MORES HAVANCE HAVINGS PSANDQS BEAUETRY BREEDING
MANNITOL MANNITE PUNICIN
MANOAH **(SON OF —)** SAMSON
MAN-OF-WAR CARAVEL
MAN-OF-WAR FISH PASTOR
MANON **(CHARACTER IN —)** MANON GRIEUX LESCAUT BRETIGNY
(COMPOSER OF —) MASSENET
MANON LESCAUT **(CHARACTER IN —)** MANON GRIEUX GERONTE
(COMPOSER OF —) PUCCINI
MANOR HAM HOF BURY HALL TOWN VILL BARONY ESTATE COMMOTE MANSION LORDSHIP TOWNSHIP
MANPOWER BRAWN LABOR
MANROOT IPOMOEA
MANROPE LIMMER
MANSERVANT (ALSO SEE SERVANT) LAD MOZO GROOM VALET ANDREW BUTLER TEABOY
MANSFIELD PARK **(AUTHOR OF —)** AUSTEN
(CHARACTER IN —) TOM MARY WARD FANNY HENRY JULIA MARIA PRICE YATES EDMUND NORRIS THOMAS BERTRAM CRAWFORD RUSHWORTH
MANSION DOME SEAT HOTEL HOUSE MANSE SIEGE TOWER CASTLE HARBOR HOSTEL CHATEAU
(— OF THE MOON) ALNATH
MANSLAUGHTER BLOOD FELONY HOMICIDE
MANTEL CLAVY CLAVEL
MANTELET MANTA MANTLE MANTLET GALAPAGO
MANTELPIECE BRACE PAREL CLAVEL MANTEL MANTLING
MANTICORE MONTEGRE
MANTIS CAGN RACER REARER MANTOID PROPHET
MANTIS CRAB SQUILLA
MANTIS SHRIMP SQUILL
MANTLE CAPA HOSE PALL REAM ROBE CLOAK CREAM FROCK JABUL LAMBA PALLA TUNIC CAMAIL CAPOTE KHIRKA KIRTLE ROCHET SLAVIN SOLMAN TABARD CHLAMYS CHRISOM CHUDDAR FERIDJI MANTEAU PAENULA

PALLIUM SLEEVES WHITTLE WRAPPER BARRACAN CHRYSOME MANTELET REGOLITH RICINIUM STOCKING
(PREF.) CHLAMYD(O) PHARO
MANTLEROCK REGOLITH
MANTO (DAUGHTER OF —) TISIPHONE
(FATHER OF —) HERCULES TIRESIAS
(HUSBAND OF —) RHACIUS
(SON OF —) OCNUS MOPSUS AMPHILOCHUS
MANTRA OM DHARANI GAYATRI MANTRAM SAVITRI
MANTUA MANTY SEMAR
MANTZU MIAOTZE
MANUAL VADY COACH GREAT TUTOR PORTAS CAMBIST CEMBALO DIDACHE MANUARY BOMBARDE HANDBOOK KEYBOARD ORDINARY PORTHORS SYNOPSIS
(MAGICIAN'S —) GRIMOIRE
(NAVIGATION —) BOWDITCH
MANUAO IAO
MANUBRIUM HYPOSTOME
MANUFACTORY ARSENAL
MANUFACTURE COIN FAKE MAKE FORGE PERFORM PRODUCE WORKING BOOKWORK
(— OF LIQUOR OR DRUGS) ABKARI
(ILLEGAL —) COINING
MANUFACTURED STORE
MANUFACTURER BRAND MAKER WRIGHT DISKERY SPINNER SUPPLIER
(ORIGINAL EQUIPMENT —) OEM
MANUMIT FREE DELIVER RELEASE LIBERATE
MANURE HOT MIG DUNG LIME MUCK SAUR SOIL TATH FECES GUANO MIXEN FULZIE SEASON SLEECH COMPOST FOLDING GOODING POUDRET DRESSING WORTHING
MANURED BONED
MANUS HAND
MANUSCRIPT CODEX FLIMSY MATTER SCRIPT UNCIAL CURSIVE PANDECT PAPYRUS PINTURA WITNESS EXEMPLAR PARCHMENT
MANX CAT RUMPY
MANX SHEARWATER CREW PUFFIN SCRABE SCRABER
MANY TEN ALOT FELE LOTS MUCH SERE SLEW FORTY GREAT MAINT MOULT SCADS OODLES TWENTY ENDLESS JILLION SEVERAL VARIOUS BEAUCOUP MANIFOLD COUNTLESS
(BEING —) NUMEROUS
(GOOD —) HANTLE
(GREAT —) MORT RAFF SWITH
(PREF.) MULT(I) PLURI POLY
(HOW —) POSO QUOT
MANYATTA KRAAL
MANY-COLORED POLYCHROME BONT
MANY-HANDED BRIAREAN
MANYPLIES FARDEL OMASUM MANIFOLD PSATERIUM
MANYROOT RUELLIA
MANY-SIDED VERSATILE VARIOUS
MAO NEHRU
MAOCH (SON OF —) ACHISH
MAORI (— IMAGE) TIKI
(— LAW) UTU
(— VILLAGE) PA PAH KAINGA
(NOT —) PAKEMA
MAP KEY CARD DICE PLAT PLOT CARTE CENTO CHART DRAFT INSET QUART STILL DRAUGHT GRAPHIC CARTGRAM GATEFOLD PLATFORM CARTOGRAM
(— OF HEAVENS) HOROSCOPE
(CELESTIAL —) PLANISPHERE
(PREF.) CARTO CHARTO
MAPAU MAPLE MATIPO TARATA PIRIPIRI
MAPLE MAZER DOGWOOD SYCAMORE WINGSEED
(FLOWERING —) ABUTILON
(GROVE OF —) SAPBUSH
MAQUILLAGE MAKEUP
MAR BLOT SCAR SMIT SNIP BLOOM BOTCH SHEND SPILL SPOIL BLOTCH DEFACE DEFEAT DEFORM EFFACE IMPAIR INJURE MANGLE BLEMISH DISGRACE
MARABOU STORK ARGALA MORABIT ADJUTANT
MARANAO LANAO
MARASMUS MARCOR ATHREPSIA
MARAUD RAID DACOIT PICKEER PILLAGE
MARAUDER TORY BANDIT BUMMER LOOTIE PIRATE CATERAN LADRONE
(PL.) BLACKS
MARAUDING BANDITRY OUTRIDING
MARBLE MIB MIG PEA POT TAW ALLY BOOL BOWL DUCK DUMP MARL AGATE AGGIE ALLEY BONCE COMMY IMMIE IVORY LINER PUREY RANCE DOGGLE MARMOR MARVEL MIGGLE PARIAN PEEWEE STEELY CARRARA CIPOLIN GLASSIE GRIOTTE KNICKER PARAGON PITCHER SHOOTER BROCATEL DOLOMITE KNUCKLER
(— WORKER'S TOOL) BURIN
(BLACK —) JET
(IMITATION —) SCAGLIOLA
(SIENA —) BROCATELLO
(PL.) TAW BOWLS PLUMPS HUNDRED
MARBLED MIRLY
MARCH FILE HIKE LIDE MARK MUSH SLOG ROUTE TRACE TRINE TROOP WALTZ DEFILE DOUBLE PARADE REVIEW DEBOUCH STRETCH FOOTSLOG PROGRESS
(— BEHIND) COVER
(— IN FRONT OF) LEAD
(— OBLIQUELY) INCLINE
(DAY'S —) ETAPE
(START OF —) HUP
(PL.) FRONTIER
MARCHING (— UP) ANABASIS
MARCHIONESS MARCHESA MARQUISE
MARCOT GOOTE
MARCOTTAGE GOOTEE
MARE SEA YAD YADE YAUD GILLIE GILLOT GRASNI HUNTRESS
MARE'S-TAIL HIPPURID
MARGARET MEG META MARGET MARGOT GRETCHEN
MARGARINE BUTTERINE
MARGATE PORGY
MARGAY TIGER
MARGIN HEM RIM VAT BANK BRIM BROW CURB EDGE FOLD HAIR INCH LIMB LIST RAND BRINK EAVES MARGE VERGE BORDER FRINGE LABRUM LACING CUSHION DRAUGHT MARGENT SELVAGE HAIRLINE
(— OF CARAPACE) DOUBLURE
(— OF CIRCLE) LIMB
(— OF LIP) PROLABIUM
(— OF PAGE) BACK
(— OF SAFETY) LEEWAY
(— OF SEA) STRAND
(— OF SHELL) LABRUM LIMBUS
(— OF SUPERIORITY) LEAD
(— OF WING) TERMEN
(—S OF HERD) SWING
(NARROW —) ACE NECK WHISKER
(SEA —) COAST
MARGOSA NIM NEEM NEEMBA
MARGRAVE RUDIGER MARKGRAF
MARIA (FATHER OF —) OCTAVIO PETROBIUS
(HUSBAND OF —) PETRUCHIO
MARIANA SILYBUM
MARIGOLD GOLD GULL SAMH AZTEC BOOTS GOLDE GOOLS HELIO BACLIN BUDDLE GOLDCUP GOLDING GOLLAND KINGCUP MARYBUD TAGETES
MARIJUANA BOO POT HERB WEED DAGGA GANJA GRASS GANJAH MOOCAH CANNABIS CARNABIS LOCOWEED MARYJANE PANAMARED SINSEMILLA
(BUTT OF — CIGARETTE) ROACH
(CHEMICAL IN —) THC
(KILOGRAM OF —) KEY
(ONE OUNCE OF —) LID
(ONE WHO SMOKES —) POTHEAD
(ONE WHO TAKES —) POTHEAD
(OUNCE OF —) CAN LID
(PUFF ON — CIGARETTE) TOKE
MARINA DOCK BASIN BOATEL
MARINADE SOUSE
MARINE JOLLY GALOOT GULPIN GYRENE TOPMAN MARINAL HALIMOUS MARITIME NAUTICAL AEQUOREAL THALASSIC THALASSIAN
(PREF.) ENALI(O) THALASS(O) THALASSI(O) THALATTO
MARINER MARINE SAILOR SEALER SEAMAN BUSCARLE SEAFARER WARRENER
(PL.) SEAFOLK
MARINHEIRO ACAJOU
MARIONETTE PUPPY POPPET PUPPET
MARITAL INTIMATE HUSBANDLY
MARITIME MARINE HALIMOUS NAUTICAL
MARJORAM ORIGAN ORIGANE AMARACUS
MARK AIM END HOB HUB MOT POP BELT BLOT BUOY BUTT CHOP CLIP DELE DINT FAZE FIST GOAL KEEL LINE MIND NOTE RIST SCAR SEAR SIGN SMOT SMUT SPOT TEND TEXT TICK VIRE WAND WIND BADGE BOTTU BRAND BREVE CHANT CHECK CLOUD DATUM DITTO DRAFT FLECK FRANK GHOST GRADE HACEK HILUM KNIFE LABEL MARCH MARCO MEITH NOKTA POINT PRINT PROOF ROVER SCART SCOPE SCORE SCUFF SPOOR STAMP SWIRL TOKEN TOUCH TRACE TRACK TRACT WATCH WHITE ACCENT ALPIEU BEACON BESPOT BLOTCH BUTTON CARACT DAGGER DAPPLE DENOTE DIRECT INDICE LETTER MARKER NOTICE OBJECT SMUTCH STREAK STRIKE STROKE SUCKER SYMBOL TARGET UPSHOT WICKER WITTER BETOKEN CEDILLA CHARBON COCKSHY DEMERIT DIAMOND DRAUGHT EROTEME EXCUDIT FINMARK IMPRESS IMPRINT INSIGNE KENMARK SCARIFY SERRATE SIGNARY SPECKLE STRIATE SYMPTOM VESTIGE WAYMARK BRACELET CROWFOOT DATEMARK DIASTOLE DISPUNCT EVIDENCE FOOTMARK FOOTSTEP IDENTIFY IDEOGRAM MONUMENT NOTATION
(— A BIRD) BAND
(— AFTER ASSAY) TOUCH
(— AS PAID) RECEIPT
(— AS SPURIOUS) ATHETIZE
(— BOUNDS) STAKE
(— BY BURNING) CHAR
(— BY CUTTING) SCRIBE
(— BY PLOWING) STRIKE
(— CROSSWISE) CRANK
(— DENOTING CORRUPT PASSAGE) OBELUS
(— DIRECTIONS) ADDRESS
(— IN ARCHERY) CLOUT HOYLE ROVER WHITE
(— IN BOOK) PRESSMARK
(— IN CANON) LEAD
(— IN CURLING) TEE COCK
(— INDICATING CONTRACTION) CORONIS
(— INDICATING DIRECTION) ARROW
(— IN QUOITS) MOT
(— OF ACKNOWLEDGEMENT) ACCOLADE
(— OF CADENCY) MARTLET
(— OF CONDEMNATION) THETA
(— OF DISGRACE) STAIN STIGMA
(— OF DISHONOR) ABATEMENT
(— OF DISTINCTION) BELT
(— OF ESTEEM) LAUREL GARLAND
(— OFF) DIVIDE STRIKE SUBTEND
(— OFF LAND) FEER PHEER
(— OF OFFICE) SEAL
(— OF OWNERSHIP) SWANMARK
(— OF PURITY) HALLMARK
(— OF RANK) PIP
(— OF REFERENCE) OBELISK
(— OF SERVITUDE) YOKE
(— OF SIGNATURE) CROSS
(— OF SUPERIORITY) BELL
(— OF WEAVER) KEEL
(— ON ANIMAL'S FACE) BLAZE STRIPE
(— ON CHART) VIGIA
(— ON DICE) PIP

(— ON EXAM) PASS
(— ON FEATHER) BAR SPANGLE
(— ON FOREHEAD) KUMKUM
(— ON PENNSYLVANIA BARNS) HEXAFOOS
(— ON SHEEP) SMIT BUIST
(— ON SHIP) SURMARK
(— ON SKIN) PLOT CREASE
(— ON STAMP) CONTROL
(— OUT) RUN CANCEL DELINE AIRMARK APPOINT COMPART DESCRIBE
(— OVER GERMAN VOWEL) UMLAUT
(— OVER LETTER N) TILDE
(— OVER LONG VOWELS) MACRON
(— RIGS) FEER
(— SHEEP OR CATTLE) BASTE BUIST DEWLAP
(— TIME) BEAT COUNT
(— TO BE ATTAINED) BOGEY BOGIE
(— TO GUIDE VESSELS) MYTH
(— TO SCARE DEER) SHEWEL
(— TRANSVERSELY) LADDER
(— UNDER LETTER C) CEDILLA
(— UNDER SIGNATURE) PARAPH
(— WITH LINES) HATCH CAMLET
(— WITH POINTED ROLLER) GRILL
(— WITH RED) RUBRICATE
(— WITH RIDGES) RIB
(— WITH STRIPES) WALE STREAM
(— WITH TAR) BASTE
(ACCENT —) VERGE
(ANGULAR —) HOOK
(AVERAGE —) CEE
(BALLOT —) SCRATCH
(BOUNDARY —) DOOL MEAR MERE TERM WIKE MEITH STAKE LANDMARK
(CADENCY —) BRISURE
(CANCELLATION —) BUMPER KILLER
(CIRCULAR —) SEAL
(CON MAN'S —) DUPE
(CURLY —) TWIDDLE
(DIACRITICAL —) TIL BREVE GRAVE HACEK TILDE MACRON TITTLE
(DIRTY —) SMIRCH
(DISTINCTIVE —) BADGE INDICIA
(DISTINGUISHING —) ITEM COCARDE EARMARK INSIGNE
(DOUBLE-DAGGER —) DIESIS
(EASY —) YAP SMELT PIGEON
(EIGHTH —) URE
(EXACT —) NICK
(EXCLAMATION —) SCREAMER
(IDENTIFICATION —) MOLE CREST SPLIT SIGNET WATTLE EARMARK KENMARK LUGMARK COLOPHON
(LOW-WATER —) DATUM
(MAGICAL —) SIGIL
(MERIDIAN —) MIRE
(MUSICAL —) PRESA CORONA
(NAVIGATION —) PERCH
(PARAGRAPH —) PILCROW
(POOR —) DEE
(PRINTER'S —) PARALLEL
(PROOFREADER'S —) STET CARET DELE
(PUNCTUATION —) DASH STOP BRACE BREVE COLON COMMA HYPHEN PERIOD BRACKET DIERESIS ELLIPSIS DIACRITIC SEMICOLON PARENTHESIS
(RANDOM —) ROVER
(RED —) HICKEY
(SCORING —) TALLY
(SECTARIAN —) BOTTU TILAKA
(SERVICE —) COMSAT
(SKATE —) CUSP
(SMALL ROUND —) DOT
(SURVEYOR'S —) PICKET
(TRAMP'S —) MONICA MONNIKER
(WHITE —) RACHE
(PL.) POINTING
(PREF.) STIGONO

MARKED FAR GREAT SCORED SEVERE SPOTTY COLORED EMINENT MARCATO POINTED SCARRED SPECKED SPOTTED
(— BY COLORED RINGS) AREOLATE
(— BY FURROWS) RIVOSE
(— BY INTELLIGENCE) ABLE
(— BY PROSTRATION) ALGID
(— BY REFINEMENT) ELEGANT
(— BY RIDGES) SERRIED
(— BY SHREWDNESS) ADROIT
(— BY SIMILARITY) AKIN
(— BY SIMPLICITY) ATTIC
(— BY WAVY LINES) GYROSE
(— OUT) DISTINCT
(— SPOTS OR LINES) MACULATE
(— UP) FOUL
(— WITH BANDS) ZONATE
(— WITH SMALLPOX) FRETTEN
(— WITH SPOTS OR LINES) NOTATE
(— WITH WHITE) BAUSOND
(EXTREMELY —) INTENSE

MARKEDLY BYOUS

MARKER HOB HUB IOU DOLE FLAG MARK SPAD STUMP TYPER BUTTON GUIDON HOBBLE HUBBLE TABBER DAYMARK SCRIBER
(BRIDGE —) PYLON
(STONE —) STELE

MARKET CURB GUNJ MART PORT SALE SOOK SOUK VEND VENT CHEAP CROSS GUNGE HALLE PASAR PRICE TRONE TRYST BAZAAR BOURSE MERCAT OUTLET PARIAN RIALTO STAPLE POULTRY CHEAPING DEBOUCHE EMPORIUM EXCHANGE MACELLUM
(CATTLE —) TRISTE
(KIND OF —) BEAR BULL FLEA OPENAIR
(MEAT —) SHAMBLES
(OLD CLOTHES —) RAGFAIR

MARKETABLE SUK SUQ SOUK STAPLE SALABLE VENDIBLE

MARKET-DAY NUNDINE

MARKETING (SYSTEM OF —) ADMASS

MARKETPLACE SUK SUQ SAUK SOOK SOUK TRON AGORA CHAWK CHOWK HALLE PLAZA BAZAAR RIALTO EMPORIUM

MARKET-TOWN BORGO

MARKING EYE HOOD COLLAR CLOUDING SCARRING SCRIBING
(— OF WOOD) CURL GRAIN
(— ON FEATHER) SPANGLE
(— ON MARS) CANAL
(—S ON STEEL) DAMASK
(ANIMAL —) SADDLE SHIELD
(CATTLE —) JINGLEBOB
(CRESCENT-SHAPED —) LUNULA LUNULE
(DROP-SHAPED —) GUTTA
(POSTAL —) INDICIA OVERPRINT
(RINGLIKE —) ANNULUS
(STRIPED —) STRAKE

MARKKA FINMARK

MARKSMAN SHOT MARKER PLUFFER SHOOTER SHOTMAN SHOOTIST

MARL MALM MARLITE

MARLI MARIE

MARLIN AU AGUJA

MARLINESPIKE FID JAEGER PRICKER STABBER

MARMALADE CHEESE SQUISH CODINIAC

MARMALADE TREE CHICO MAMEY MAMMIE SAPOTE ZAPOTE

MARMOSET MICO TITI SAGOIN JACCHUS OUITITI QUIRCAL SAIMIRI TAMARIN WISTITI ORABASSU

MARMOT BOBAC PAHMI GOPHER SUSLIK SCIURID SIFFLEUR WHISTLER

MARMOTA ARCTOMYS

MAROON AZTEC ENISLE PICNIC STRAND CIMARRON

MARQUEE TENT CANOPY MARQUISE

MARQUETRY INLAY

MARQUISE NAVETTE

MARQUISETTE LENO

MARRAM SEAREED MATGRASS MATWWEED

MARRANOS ANUSIM

MARRED CUPPY SCABBY SLURRED SPECKED

MARRIAGE MUTA DAIVA HYMEN KARAO UNION BEENAH BRIDAL BUCKLE SPLICE SPOUSE EXOGAMY NUPTIAL PUNALUA SPOUSAL WEDDING WEDLOCK CONUBIUM LEVIRATE OPSIGAMY
(— AFTER DEATH OF FIRST SPOUSE) DIGAMY
(— AT ADVANCED AGE) OPSIGAMY
(— BELOW POSITION) HYPOGAMY
(— CONTRACT) KETUBAH
(— OUTSIDE FAMILY) EXOGAMY
(— PORTION) TOCHER
(— VOW) IDO
(— WITH AN INFERIOR) MESALLIANCE
(— WITHIN GROUP) ENDOGAMY
(COMMUNAL —) HETAIRISM
(SECOND —) BIGAMY
(PREF.) GAMO
(SUFF.) GAM(AE)(IST)(OUS)(Y) GAMETE

MARRIAGEABLE NUBILE

MARRIED COVERT WEDDED ESPOUSED
(NOT —) SOLE

MARROW KEEST MARIE MERCH MERGH MEDULLA
(PREF.) MEDULLI MYELINO MYEL(O) MYELO
(SUFF.) MYELIA MYELITIS

MARRY TIE WED FAST WIFE WIVE CLEEK HITCH MATCH BUCKLE CROTCH ENSURE MARROW SPLICE HUSBAND NUPTIAL WEDLOCK DESPOUSE
(— OFF) BESTOW
(— UNSUITABLY) MISYOKE
(PREF.) GAMETO GAMO
(SUFF.) GAM(AE)(IST)(OUS)(Y) GAMETE

MARS ARES MAMERS MARMAR MAVORS MASPITER TEUTATES
(FATHER OF —) JUPITER
(MOTHER OF —) JUNO
(SON OF —) REMUS ROMULUS
(PREF.) AREO

MARSH BOG FEN HAG CARR DANK FELL FLAM FLAT HOPE JHIL MASH MIRE OOZE QUAG ROSS SOIL SUDS TARN VLEI VLEY WASH WHAM FLASH GLADE JHEEL LIMAN SLACK SLASH SLUMP SWAMP MORASS PALUDE PUDDLE CIENAGA CORCASS POCOSIN PONTINE QUAGMIRE STROTHER TURLOUGH
(SALT —) SALT SEBKA SALINA SALINE
(PREF.) ELO HELO LIMN(I)(O) PALUDI

MARSHAL ARRAY ORDER MUSTER PARADE JERONIMO MARECHAL MOBILIZE
(— FACTS) HASH

MARSHALL ISLANDS (CAPITAL:) MAJURO
(COIN:) DOLLAR
(ISLAND:) JALUIT MAJURO ENIWETOK KWAJALEIN
(LANGUAGE:) ENGLISH JAPANESE MARSHALLESE
(PEOPLE:) MARSHALLESE

MARSH BOG QUAG

MARSHBUCK SITUTUNGA

MARSH ELDER JACKO

MARSH FEVER HELODES

MARSH GAS METHANE

MARSH HARRIER PUDDOCK PUTTOCK

MARSHLAND MAREMMA

MARSHMALLOW MALLOW WYMOTE

MARSH MARIGOLD BOOTS CAPER CRAZY GOOLS DRAGON GAMOND GOWLAN COWSLIP ELKSLIP GOLDCUP KINGCOB KINGCUP MARYBUD DRUNKARD

MARSH PENNYWORT PENNYROT WATERCUP

MARSH PINK SABBATIA

MARSH TEA LEDUM

MARSH TREFOIL BUCKBEAN

MARSH WREN LONGBILL

MARSHY BOGGY FOGGY MOORY MOSSY PONDY SNAPY SPEWY CALLOW MARISH PLASHY QUAGGY QUASHY SLUMPY HELODES MOORISH PALUDAL QUEACHY PALUDINE WATERISH

MARSILEA NARDOO

MARSUPIAL KOALA QUOLL CUSCUS POSSUM QUOKKA WOMBAT BETTONG DASYURE OPOSSUM POTOROO KANGAROO BANDICOOT PETAURIST

MARSUPIUM POUCH
MART STAPLE EMPORIUM
MARTEN FOIN PEKAN SABLE SOBOL FISHER MARTRIX MUSTELID MUSTELIN
(GROUP OF —S) RICHESSE
(SUFF.) ICTIS
MARTENSITE SORBITE
MARTHA (BROTHER OF —) LAZARUS
(CHARACTER IN —) JULIA NANCY LIONEL MARTHA HARRIET PLONKETT
(COMPOSER OF —) FLOTOW
(SISTER OF —) MARY
MARTIAL BELLIC WARLIKE WARRIOR BELLICAL MILITARY
(— ART) TAEKWONDO
MARTIAL ARTS BUDO JUDO KENDO AIKIDO KARATE JUJITSU
(— SCHOOL) DOJO
(— TRAINEE) NINJA
(PERSON TRAINED IN —) NINJA KARATE KUNGFU
MARTIN MARTLET SWALLOW MARTINET
MARTIN CHUZZLEWIT (AUTHOR OF —) DICKENS
(CHARACTER IN —) GAMP MARK MARY SETH JONAS MERCY SARAH GRAHAM MARTIN TAPLEY ANTHONY CHARITY PECKSNIFF CHUZZLEWIT
MARTINI GIBSON
(KIND OF —) VODKA
MARTINMAS TERM
MARTYR STEPHEN WITNESS SUFFERER
MARTYRDOM MARTYRY PASSION
MARVEL MARL MUSE FERLY SELLY ADMIRE WONDER MAGNALE MIRACLE MONSTER PORTENT PRODIGY SELCOUTH ADMIRATION
MARVELOUS FAB SUPER SUPERB EPATANT MIRIFIC STRANGE FABULOUS WONDROUS MIRACULOUS
MARVY RAD COOL
MARX BROTHERS (ONE OF —) CHICO HARPO ZEPPO GROUCHO
MARY MOLL POLL MAMIE MAURA MOLLY MIRIAM MARILLA
MARY JANE MARIJUANA

MARYLAND
BATTLESITE: ANTIETAM
CAPITAL: ANNAPOLIS
COLLEGE: HOOD GOUCHER STJOHNS
COUNTY: KENT CECIL TALBOT CALVERT HARFORD ALLEGANY SOMERSET
INDIAN: CONOY NANTICOKE
LAKE: PRETTYBOY
MOUNTAIN: BACKBONE
NATIVE: WESORT TERRAPIN
NICKNAME: COCKADE OLDLINE
RIVER: CHESTER POTOMAC CHOPTANK PATUXENT
STATE BIRD: ORIOLE
STATE TREE: OAK
TOWN: BELAIR DENTON EASTON ELKTON TOWSON LAPLATA ABERDEEN BETHESDA POCOMOKE BALTIMORE

MARYSOLE CARTER LEADER CARTARE
MARZIPAN MARCHPANE
(— BASE) ALMOND
MASAI WAKWAFI WAKWAVI
MASCEZEL (BROTHER OF —) GILDO
MASCOT BILLIKEN
MASCULINE MALE BUTCH DOGGY MACHO RUDAS VIRILE LALAQUI MANLIKE
(EXAGGERATEDLY —) MACHO
(PREF.) ANDR(O) MASCULO
(SUFF.) ANDRIA ANDROUS ANDRY
MASCULINITY (EXAGGERATED —) MACHISMO
(EXAGGERATED AWARENESS OF —) MACHISMO
MASH PAP BEER CHAP MASA MASK MESH SLOP CHAMP CREEM SMASH SMUSH MUDDLE STILLAGE
(FATHER OF —) ARAM
MASHED CHAPPED DAUPHINE
MASHER FLIRT BEETLE
MASJID MOSQUE
MASK FACE HIDE JEST LOUP SLUR VEIL BLOCK BLOOP CLOAK COVER GRILL GUISE LARVE POINT VIZOR DOMINO GRILLE MUZZLE SCREEN VEILER VIZARD BECLOUD CONCEAL CURTAIN MASKOID ANTEMASK DEFILADE DISGUISE MASCARON PRETENSE
(— OUT) CROP
(GAS —) CANARY
(HALF —) LOO LOUP DOMINO
(KIND OF —) SKI
(PHOTOGRAPHIC —) MATTE
(PL.) AREITO
MASKED LARVATED VIZARDED
MASKED BALL (CHARACTER IN —) HORN ANGRI AMELIA RENATO TOMASI ULRICA ARMANDO RIBBING SAMUELE ARVIDSON GUSTAVUS RICCARDO ANCKERSTROEM
(COMPOSER OF —) VERDI
MASKER GUISARD MASQUER
MASKING MUMMERY MUMMING COLORING
MASKLIKE PERSONATE
MASLIN MESTLEN MASHLOCH MUNGCORN MASSELGEM
MASNADIERI, I (CHARACTER IN —) CARLO AMALIA FRANCESCO MASSIMILIAN
(COMPOSER OF —) VERDI
MASON LAYER BUILDER MASONER COMACINE KNOBBLER LAMMIKIN SCUTCHER
MASONRY ASHLAR MANTLE RUSTIC BACKING BLOCAGE MOELLON NOGGING ISODOMUM QUOINING ROCKWORK EMPLECTON RUBBLEWORK
(UNDRESSED —) RAGWORK
MASQUE MASK COMUS DEVICE ANTIMASK DISGUISE
MASQUER REX
MASQUERADE BALL MASK GUISE DOMINO MASQUE PARADE MASKERY DISGUISE
MASQUERADER RAGSHAG
MASQUERADING CARNIVAL

MASS BAT BED GOB SOP TOD WAD BODY BULK CLOD GOUT HEAP HEFT KNOT LEAD LUMP MOLE OBIT STOW SWAD AMASS BATCH BLOOM CLAMP CLASH CLUMP CROWD CRUST DIRGE GLOBE GORGE GROSS MATTE MISSA PRESS SLUMP SOLID SPIRE STORE WODGE COMMON GOBBET NUGGET PROPER VOLUME WEIGHT BOUROCK CONGEST DENSITY MASKINS MESKINS MYSTERY REQUIEM SALOMON CALAPITE CONGERIE ENDOSOME FLOCCULE MOUNTAIN MYCETOMA SOULMASS ACCUMULATION
(— IN THE WHITE NILE) SUDD
(— OF BACTERIA) SLIME BAREGINE SYMPLASM
(— OF BLOSSOMS) BLOW
(— OF BLUBBER) MELON
(— OF BRANCHES) SPRAY
(— OF BUBBLES) FOAM
(— OF BUSHES) SHAG
(— OF CARPELS) SOREMA
(— OF CELLS) COMB CANCER MORULA CUMULUS STALACE PULVINUS
(— OF CLOUDS) BANK
(— OF COAL) JUD
(— OF COLORS) BLOB
(— OF COTTON) FUSSOCK
(— OF CURED RUBBER) LOAF
(— OF DEBRIS) SLIDE
(— OF DOUGH) DUMPLING
(— OF FIBERS) KAPOK
(— OF FILAMENTS) FLOCCUS MYCELIUM
(— OF FILTH) GORE
(— OF FRAGMENTS) BRASH
(— OF GAS) PROMINENCE
(— OF GOLD) BONANZA
(— OF HAIR) GLIB TOUPET
(— OF HYPHAE) MEDULLA
(— OF ICE) BERG CALF FLOE FLAKE PATCH ICICLE STURIS GROWLER ICEBERG FLOEBERG
(— OF INSECTS) CACHE
(— OF IRON) BALL BLOB CORE BLOOM INDUCTOR
(— OF LAVA) BOMB SPINE
(— OF LEAVES) FOLIAGE
(— OF LIMESTONE) HUM
(— OF LOOSE BOULDERS) CLATTER
(— OF METAL) SOW INGOT BUTTON
(— OF MOLTEN GLASS) GOB BLOOM GATHER PARISON
(— OF MUD) CLASH
(— OF ORE) BACK SLUG BUNNY SQUAT REGULUS
(— OF PEOPLE) CROWD HORDE
(— OF POMACE) CHEESE
(— OF ROCK) DOME NECK HORSE LEDGE NAPPE SCALP SNOUT INLIER SARSEN BOULDER FOOTWALL
(— OF SAND) PAAR
(— OF SOAP) CURD
(— OF SPORES) SORUS
(— OF SUGAR) FONDANT
(— OF SUGAR CRYSTALS) STRIKE
(— OF TISSUE) COLLAR GANGLION NUCELLUS
(— OF TREES) THICKET
(— OF WATER) HEAD
(— OF YARN) COP BALLOON
(— OF YOLK) LATEBRA
(— OVERHANGING) CORNICE
(—S OF DRIFTWOOD) EMBARRAS
(— TOGETHER) HUDDLE
(ALPINE —) FLYSCH
(AMORPHOUS —) JUMBLE SYMPLASM
(BILLOWY —) CLOUD
(BUSHY —) SHOCK
(COMPACT —) BRIQUET
(CONCENTRATION OF MOON —) MASCON
(CONFUSED —) COT JUMBLE JUNGLE PILEUP CLUTTER RUMMAGE SHUFFLE
(DISORDERLY —) SCRAMBLE
(EGG —) BUNION CULTCH SPONGE
(FATTY —) BEAN HEADSKIN
(FECAL —) SCYBALUM
(FLATTISH —) DAB
(FLUFFY —) PUFF
(FLUID —) FLUOR
(GLASSY —) SLAG
(GLOBULAR —) MOORBALL
(INDISTINCT —) SMUDGE
(IRREGULAR —) CUB
(LIVING —) BLASTEMA
(MOIST —) PULP
(MOUNTAIN —) OROGEN
(NUCLEAR —) SHIELD
(OVERSPREADING —) PALL
(PART OF —) INTROIT
(PEAR-SHAPED —) BOULE
(POROUS —) FILTER
(PROJECTING —) BOSS
(PULPY —) SQUELCH
(RECTANGULAR —) BRICK
(ROOT —) SOLE
(ROUNDED —) COB NOB KNOB BOLUS KUGEL BULLET RONDLE
(SEDIMENTARY —) GOBI
(SHAPED —) PAT LOAF
(SHAPELESS —) JELLY
(SLIPPERY —) SIND SLUD SLUDDER
(SLUSHY —) POSH
(SOFT —) MASH MOXA MUMMY
(STICKY —) CLAG
(SWOLLEN —) CERE
(TANGLED — OF HAIR) MOP KNURL
(TUFTY —) FLOC
(UNCTUOUS —) LANOLIN
(UNIT OF —) DALTON
(UPRIGHT —) COLUMN
(PL.) MEINY MEINIE TRENTAL POPULACE
(PREF.) ONCO
(SUFF.) IUM OME
MASSA (FATHER OF —) ISHMAEL

MASSACHUSETTS
CAPE: ANN COD
CAPITAL: BOSTON
COLLEGE: SMITH AMHERST SIMMONS WHEATON WILLIAMS RADCLIFFE WELLESLEY
COUNTY: DUKES ESSEX BRISTOL NORFOLK SUFFOLK BERKSHIRE NANTUCKET BARNSTABLE
INDIAN: NAUSET POCOMTUC
ISLAND: DUKES NANTUCKET

LAKE: ONOTA QUABBIN ROHUNTA WEBSTER
MOUNTAIN: BRODIE POTTER ALANDER EVERETT GREYLOCK
MOUNTAIN RANGE: BERKSHIRE
POND: WALDEN
PRESIDENT: BUSH KENNEDY
RIVER: NASHUA CHARLES CONCORD QUABOAG TAUNTON CHICOPEE DEERFIELD MERRIMACK
STATE BIRD: CHICKADEE
STATE FLOWER: MAYFLOWER
STATE NICKNAME: BAY OLDBAY OLDCOLONY
STATE TREE: ELM
TOWN: AYER LYNN OTIS ATHOL BARRE LENOX AGAWAM DEDHAM GROTON LOWELL NAHANT NATICK REVERE SAUGUS WOBURN HOLYOKE IPSWICH PEABODY TAUNTON BROCKTON CHICOPEE COHASSET SCITUATE UXBRIDGE YARMOUTH CAMBRIDGE NANTUCKET WORCESTER PITTSFIELD SPRINGFIELD
UNIVERSITY: CLARK TUFTS HARVARD BRANDEIS

MASSACRE SLAY POGROM CARNAGE SCUPPER WIPEOUT BUTCHERY SLAUGHTER
MASSAGE ROLF WISP KNEAD FACIAL MODIFY PETRIE SHAMPOO SHIATSU TRIPSIS BLANDISH LOMILOMI ANATRIPSIS MANIPULATE
(— OF DEEP MUSCLES) ROLFING
(— WITH FINGERS) SHIATSU SHIHTZU
(MUSCLE —) ROLF ROLFING
(ONE WHO —S) ROLFER
MASSAGER MASSEUR VIBRATOR
MASSECUITE GUR FILLMASS
MASSED DENSE
MASSENA QUAIL COPPY
MASSIVE BIG BEAMY BULKY GROSS HEAVY LUSTY MASSY SOUND STERN STRONG HEALTHY HULKING VOLUMED TIMBERED MONUMENTAL
MAST BUCK MAIN POLE SPAR OVEST STICK STING DRIVER JIGGER MIZZEN ARTEMON ASHERAH MASTAGE PANNAGE SPANKER FOREMAST JURYMAST MAINMAST SHIPMAST MIZZENMAST
(FALLEN —) SHACK
(SIXTH —) DRIVER
MASTAX TROPHI
MASTER DON HER JOE MAS RAB SAB SIR ARCH BAAS BEAK BEST BOSS COCK FACE HERR JOSS KING LORD MIAN SIRE TUAN BWANA LEARN MARSE MASSA RABBI SAHIB SWAMI SWAMY SWELL BRIDLE BUCKRA CASTER DEACON DOMINE HUMBLE MAITRE PATRON RECTOR RHETOR SIRCAR WAFTER CAPTAIN CONQUER DOMINIE DOMINUS EFFENDI MAESTRO NAKHODA OGTIERN PADRONE RABBONI AMAISTER BARGEMAN BEMASTER KINGFISH LANDLORD MAGISTER OVERCOME SLOOPMAN SURMOUNT VANQUISH
(— OF CEREMONIES) EMCEE VERGER COMPERE CHAIRMAN
(— OF CRAFT) KAHUNA
(— OF HOUSEHOLD) BALABOS GOODMAN
(— OF REVELS) ALYTARCH
(— OF WHALER) SPOUTER
(FENCING —) LANISTA
(INFERIOR —) KNIFER
(PREF.) ARCH
MASTER-AT-ARMS JAUNTY JAUNTIE
MASTER BUILDER (AUTHOR OF —) IBSEN
(CHARACTER IN —) ALINE HILDA BROVIK RAGNAR SOLNESS
MASTERFUL BOSSY LORDLY VIRILE HAUGHTY ARROGANT MAGERFUL PEREMPTORY
MASTER OF BALLANTRAE
(AUTHOR OF —) STEVENSON
(CHARACTER IN —) CHEW DASS BALLY BURKE HENRY JAMES TEACH ALISON DURRIE GRAEME FRANCIS SECUNDRA MACKELLAR DURRISDEER
MASTERPIECE GEM TOPPIECE
MASTERSTROKE COUP
MASTERY GREE GRIP GRIPE COMMAND MAISTRY OVERHAND
MASTHEAD FLAG HIGHTOP
MASTICATE GUM CHAW CHEW
MASTICATORY PAN BUYO
MASTIC BULLY JOCUM JOCUMA
MASTIC TREE ACOMA AUSUBO COCUYO COCULLO LENTISK
MASTIFF ALAN MASTY BANDOG TIEDOG
MASTIGONEME FLIMMER
MASTITIS CLAP WEED GARGET
MAST TREE ASAK
MASTURBATE ABUSE
MASTURBATION ONANISM FROTTAGE
MASTWOOD POON KAMANI
MAT COT RUG TOD BASS FLAT FLET FOOT HAIR MOSS NIPA PACE RAFT SHAG TAUT DOILY KILIM TATTY COTTER FELTER FOOTER PAUNCH PETATE TARGET TATAMI THATCH COASTER CUSHION DOORMAT KAITAKA MATTING FOOTPACE FROSTING MATTRESS SPANDREL
(— BORDER) TANIKO
(BOWLING —) FOOTER
(FIBER —) IE BASS
(PALM-LEAF —) YAPA
(PICTURE-FRAME —) FLAT
(POLYNESIAN —) LAUHALA
(SCOURING —) BEAR
(TABLECLOTH —) GARDNAP
(PL.) DUNNAGE
MATACHIN BOUFFON
MATACO CORONADO
MATADOR MAT ESPADA CAPEADOR
(— MOVEMENT) PASE
MATCH GO CAP VIE BOUT COPE EVEN FERE LUNT MAKE MATE MEET MILL MOTE PAIR PEEL PEER SIDE SUIT AGREE AMATE EQUAL FIRER FUSEE FUZEE MOUSE PARTY RIVAL SPUNK TALLY VENUE VESTA ASSORT BESORT CANCEL COMMIT FELLOW KIPPIN MARROW QUADER RUBBER SAMPLE SWATCH COMPEER EXAMPLE IGNITER ILLUMER KINDLER KIPPEEN LIGHTER LUCIFER PARAGON PAREGAL PATTERN PENDANT SINGLES APPROACH BONSPIEL BREATHER CONGREVE EUPYRION FOURSOME INFLAMER LOCOFOCO PARALLEL PORTFIRE REANSWER VESUVIAN VESUVIUS SEMIFINAL PREMINIARY QUARTERFINAL
(— AT DICE) MAIN
(— FOR FIRING CANNON) MOUSE
(— IN POKER) SEE CALL
(BOXING —) SPAR FIGHT PRELIM SLUGFEST
(CURLING —) SPIEL BONSPIEL
(DANCING —) KANTIKEY
(DISHONEST —) CROSS
(GOLF —) NASSAU FOURSOME
(LARGE-HEADED —) FUZEE
(SCOLDING —) FLYTE FLYTING
(SHOOTING —) TIR SHOOT
(SLOW —) LUNT SMIFT SQUIB
(TILTING —) CAROUSEL CARROUSEL
(UNEQUAL —) DISPARAGE
(WORTHY —) ROLAND
(PL.) LIGHTS
MATCHED INSYNC ASSORTED
MATCHING MARROW SUITABLE
(NOT —) ODD
MATCHLESS ALONE UNIQUE NONESUCH PEERLESS
MATCHMAKER SHADCHAN
MATE CAWK FERE METE PAIR PEER BILLY BREED BUDDY BULLY CHINA CLASP CULLY DICKY MATCH PARTY TALLY YERBA BUNKIE COBBER FELLOW FUTURE MARROW PAREIL SPOUSE BROTHER COMPEER COMRADE CONSORT HUSBAND PARAGON NEIGHBOR PIRRAURA
(— WELL) NICK
(BOATSWAIN'S —) BUFFER
(GUNNER'S —) LADY
(SECOND —) DICKY
MATERIAL FINE MOLD COMPO GAUZE GOUGE HYLIC METAL MOULD PASTE PLASS STUFF THING TRADE BORROW CARNAL CYANUS FABRIC GRAITH HOGGIN MATTER PAPREG PUBLIC THINGY APPAREL FOOTING SUBJECT TEXTILE UNIDEAL WEIGHTY ADDITIVE CORPORAL ECONOMIC EQUIPAGE RELEVANT SENSIBLE SNOODING TANGIBLE THINGISH OBJECTIVE PHENOMENAL
(— ELIMINATED) CULLAGE
(— FOR FERMENTING) GUILE
(— FOR OYSTER BEDS) CULCH CULTCH
(— IN GRAIN) DOCKAGE
(— IN MAKING CEMENT) ADDITION
(— IN NEEDLEWORK) INKLE
(— OF CORDED SILK) CRYSTAL
(— OF SCREENINGS) HOGGIN HOGGING
(— REMOVED BY SAW CUT) KERF
(—S FOR MAKING GLASS) FRIT
(— USED IN WAXING) BALL
(— WEIGHED) DRAFT DRAUGHT
(ABSORBENT —) DOPE
(ALLUVIAL —) SHINGLE
(ANCIENT —) MURRA MURRHA
(ARTISTIC —) KITSCH
(BAGGING —) HOPSACK
(BITUMINOUS —) KEROGEN
(BONY —) COSMINE
(BUILDING —) LATH ADOBE BRICK STAFF SWISH TABBY TAPIA SILLAR CONCRETE
(BUILDING —S) TIGNUM
(CLAY —) TAPIA
(CLAYEY —) GOUGE
(COLORING —) TINCTION
(COMBUSTIBLE —) KINDLING
(CONSTRUCTION —) BREEZE
(CORE —) NIFE
(CUSHIONING —) AIRFOAM
(DEPOSITED —) FOOTS
(DIAMOND —) BORT
(DOWNY —) FLUE
(DRESS —) FOULE VOILE PEELING COTILLON EOLIENNE
(DYEING —) SUMAC SUMACH
(EMBOSSED —) CLOQUE
(EMROIDERY —) ARRASENE
(EXCAVATED —) SPOIL
(FACING —) ENAMEL
(FILLING —) FIBERFILL
(FISSIONABLE —) STUFF
(FOUNDATION —) UNDERLAY
(GLUTINOUS —) GELATIN
(GRANULAR —) BASIS
(HARD —) CARBIDE
(HEAT-RESISTANT —) ALSIFILM
(ILLUSTRATIVE —) ART
(INSECTICIDAL —) SCABRIN
(INSULATING —) KERITE PECITE BLANKET LAGGING OKONITE MEGOTALC
(LEFTOVER —S) ARISINGS
(LOOSE —) SAND GRAVEL DETRITUS
(MINING REFUSE —) ATTLE
(MINUTE —) SESTON
(MOLDING —) PREPREG
(NUTRITIVE —) FUEL
(OPAQUE —) MASK
(ORGANIC —) EXINITE
(PAPER-THIN —) FOIL
(PATCHING —) BOTCH
(PETRIFIED —) GEMSTONE
(POLISHING —) RABAT
(POWDERED —) FINES
(PRIMORDIAL —) BLASTEMA
(RAW —) STOCK STAPLE
(REFRACTORY —) GROG BULLDOG CASTABLE
(RESIDUAL —) CEMENT
(RESOURCE —) SWIPE
(REVERSIBLE —) DAMASK
(SEDIMENTARY —) SILT
(SILK —) HONAN PEKIN FOULARD SARCENET
(SLIMY —) GLIT SWARF
(SMOKING —) KEF KIF
(STIFF —) CANVAS

(STIFFENING —) BOXING
(TANNING —) BADAN SYNTAN
(THIN SLICE OF —) WAFER
(TILE-STRENGTHENING —) WEB
(TRASHY —) SLUSH
(TWEEDY —) HOMESPUN
(TYPE-HIGH —) BEARER
(UNPUBLISHED —) INEDITA
(UNSOLICITED —) SLUSH
(UPHOLSTERY —) LAMPAS
(VOLCANIC —) EJECTA TEPHRA
(WATERPROOF —) KERATOL
(WORTHLESS —) GARBLE
(WOVEN —) LAPPET
(PL.) STOCK STUFF
(PREF.) HYL(O)
(SUFF.) **(PLASTIC —)** PLASM(A)
MATERIALISM HYLISM SOMATISM
(DIALECTICAL —) DIAMAT
MATERIALISTIC SENSATE SENSUAL BANAUSIC
MATERIALIZE REIFY DESCEND
MATER LECTIONIS GRAPHY
MATERNITY WARD NATUARY
MATGRASS NARD MATWEED
MATH MUTH MONASTERY
(KIND OF —) NEW
MATHEMATICIAN ALGORIST GEOMETER
AMERICAN SEE FINE WEST WEYL AIKEN BEGLE BROWN FISKE GIBBS GODEL HARDY MASON MOORE MUSES POLYA SMITH YOUNG CAJORI HOPPER KASNER KEYSER LEHMER LOOMIS MILLER NEWTON OSGOOD PEIRCE RUNKLE VEBLEN WIENER DICKSON GODFREY METZLER NEUMANN SAFFORD BANNEKER BIRKHOFF BOWDITCH COOLIDGE FRANKLIN WELCHMAN MURNAGHAN HUNTINGTON VONNEUMANN WILCZYNSKI RITTENHOUSE
AUSTRIAN HAGEN DOPPLER PURBACH
BELGIAN LEMAITRE
BRAZILIAN GUSMAO
DUTCH BLAEU VLACQ CEULEN STEVIN HUYGENS SNELLIUS GRAVESANDE MUSSCHENBROEK
EGYPTIAN HYPATIA PTOLEMY
ENGLISH DEE LAMB MUIR PELL ALLEN BONDI BOOLE COTES DIRAC ELLIS HARDY JEANS MURIS ROUTH SHARP SMITH WALES ATWOOD BARLOW BARNES BARROW BRIGGS CAYLEY COCKLE DARWIN DIGGES GUNTER HADLEY HUTTON KELVIN LARMOR NEWTON ROBINS STOKES TAYLOR WALLIS WEDDLE BABBAGE DODGSON HARRIOT LUBBOCK MAKEHAM MASERES PEACOCK RECORDE RUSSELL WHEWELL WHISTON CLIFFORD GLAISHER GOMPERTZ LEYBOURN MACMAHON OUGHTRED RAYLEIGH BRONOWSKI DUNSTABLE GREENHILL NICHOLSON TODHUNTER WHITEHEAD WHITTAKER WOODHOUSE CODDINGTON GELLIBRAND SACROBOSCO SAUNDERSON
FRENCH BIOT FINE LAME LEVY BORDA BOREL CHEZY COMTE LEROY MONGE PRONY RAMUS STURM VIETE BEAUNE BEZOUT BOSSUT CAUCHY FERMAT FERNEL GALOIS JORDAN MOIGNO PASCAL PICARD BOUGUER BROCARD CHARLES CHASLES CHUQUET COURNOT DARBOUX FOURIER GERMAIN GOURSAT HERMITE KOENIGS LACROIX LAPLACE POINSOT POISSON PUISEUX VERNIER ALEMBERT BERTRAND CLAIRAUT CORIOLIS DEMOIVRE GERGONNE HACHETTE HADAMARD LAGRANGE LAGUERRE LEBESGUE LEGENDRE MERSENNE MONTUCIA PAINLEVE POINCARE PONCELET ROBERVAL BRIANCHON CONDORCET DESARGUES DESCARTES LIOUVILLE BURCKHARDT DEPARCIEUX MAUPERTUIS
GERMAN GAUSS HESSE KLEIN MAYER MISES PASCH PFAFF RUNGE WOLFF BALMER CANTOR JACOBI KUMMER MOBIUS MULLER STIFEL APIANUS CLEBSCH FRIESEN HILBERT KASTNER LAMBERT LEIBNIZ PLUCKER RIEMANN WIDMANN ARONHOLD BLASCHKE CLAUSIUS DEDEKIND DROBISCH LEIBNITZ MERCATOR RHATICUS SCHOTTKY SCHUBERT DIRICHLET GRASSMANN KRONECKER LINDEMANN BIEBERBACH EISENSTEIN HINDENBURG PRINGSHEIM TSCHIRNHAUS WEIERSTRASS KONIGSBERGER
GREEK CONON EUCLID PAPPUS DIOCLES PTOLEMY ANTIPHON AUTOLYCUS OENOPIDES SOSIGENES APOLLONIUS ARCHIMEDES DIOPHANTUS PYTHAGORAS DINOSTRATUS
HUNGARIAN BOLYAI
INDIAN ARYABHATA RAMANUJAN
IRISH BALL KELVIN SALMON HAMILTON BROUNCKER
ITALIAN CEVA BALDI FRISI PEANO AGNESI GRANDI CARDANO CREMONA GALILEO PACIOLI RICCATI BELTRAMI BRIOSCHI CAMPANUS MALFATTI BOSCOVICH CAVALIERI FIBONACCI TARTAGLIA BELLAVITIS MASCHERONI TORRICELLI
JAPANESE SEKI
NORWEGIAN LIE ABEL STORMER GULDBERG
POLISH BARTEL CIOLEK WRONSKI
PORTUGUESE NUNES
RUSSIAN KRYLOV LIAPUNOV CHEBYSHEV KOLMOGOROV KOVALEVSKI LOBACHEVSKI
SCOTTISH TAIT IVORY KEILL LESLIE NAPIER BURGESS FORSYTH GREGORY MAXWELL PLAYFAIR STIRLING
SWISS EULER AMSLER CRAMER GULDIN BYRGIUS STEINER BERNOULLI CHRISTOFFEL
MATHEMATICS MATHESIS
MATING NICK COUPLE DIALLEL BREEDING HOMOGAMY PANMIXIA
(RANDOM —) PANGAMY
MATRASS BOLTHEAD CUCURBIT
MATRED (DAUGHTER OF —) MEHETABEL
(FATHER OF —) MEZAHAB
MATRIMONIAL MARITAL NUPTIAL SPOUSAL CONJUGAL
MATRIMONIO SEGRETO, IL
(CHARACTER IN —) FIDALMA PAOLINO CAROLINA ELISETTA GERONIMO ROBINSON
(COMPOSER OF —) CIMAROSA
MATRIMONY WEDLOCK MARRIAGE
MATRIMONY VINE JASMINE JESSAMY BOXTHORN
MATRIX PI BED MAT SORT PLASM SHELL SLIDE DYADIC MASTER MOTHER STRIKE STROMA CALYMMA FORMULA MATRICE PATTERN PROPLASM
MATRON DAME
MATTAN (SON OF —) SHEPHATIAH
MATTANIAH (FATHER OF —) BANI ELAM HEMAN ZATTU
(SON OF —) ZACCUR
MATTE SLURRY REGULUS
MATTED COTTY FELTY PINNY FELTED TAGGED TAUTED WAUKIT STRINGY FELTLIKE CESPITOSE
MATTENAI (FATHER OF —) JOIARIB
MATTER BIT RES BONE CASE GEAR HYLE ITEM RECK WHAT AMPER FORCE PARTY SKILL STUFF THEME TOPIC AFFAIR ARGUFY BEHALF DITTAY IMPORT ARTICLE CONCERN MATERIA SHEBANG SIGNIFY SUBJECT BUSINESS COMETHER MATERIAL
(— ADDED TO BOOK) APPENDIX
(— AROUND THE TEETH) TOPHUS
(— CONSTITUTING PERFUME) ESSENCE
(— DISCHARGED) FLUX
(— EJECTED) CAST
(— FOR PRINTING) COPY
(— IN DISPUTE) ISSUE
(— OF BUSINESS) SHAURI
(— OF CHANCE) LOTTERY
(— OF CONCERN) FUNERAL
(— OF CONSCIENCE) REMORSE
(— OF DISCOURSE) SUBJECT
(— OF FACT) SENSE
(— OF INTEREST) GRIST
(— OF NO IMPORTANCE) TOY
(— TO) CONCERN
(ALLUVIAL —) GEEST
(BRAIN —) ALBA
(CARTILAGINOUS —) GRISTLE
(COLORING —) DYE COLOR CROCK EOSIN MORIN PIURI ALNEIN ANATTO BUTEIN FUSTIC INDIGO ORCEIN PIOURY ANNATTO CARMINE CASTORY CUDBEAR LIGULIN OENOLIN PIGMENT PUNICIN TURACIN XANTHIN ALGOCYAN ALIZARIN BRAZILIN FUSTERIC LAPACHOL SCOPARIN TINCTION TINCTURE
(CORRUPT —) PUS ATTER
(DECAYED ORGANIC —) DUFF
(DECAYING —) DUFF
(DIFFICULT —) PROBLEM
(DISCHARGED —) EXUDATE
(ESSENTIAL —) POINT
(EXPLANATORY —) HAGGADA
(FATTY —) SEBUM
(FECAL —) SIEGE
(FILTHY —) GUNK
(FOREIGN —) SOIL DROSS
(FOUL —) FILTH SORDES
(FRONT —) FOREWORD
(GELATINOUS —) BREAK SPAWN
(GRAY —) GLIOSA CINEREA
(HYPOTHETICAL —) PROTYLE
(INANIMATE —) AJIVA
(INDECENT —) STUFF
(INFECTIOUS —) MIASMA
(INFLAMMABLE —) TINDER
(MINERAL —) FLOAT FLOATS
(NERVE —) CINEREA
(POTENTIAL —) PRAKRITI
(PRIMARY —) PRADHANA
(PRINTED —) BOX DISPLAY
(PRIVATE —) SECLUSION
(PULVERIZED —) ATTRITUS
(READING —) BODY
(SLIMY —) GLAIR
(SMALL —) MINUTIA
(SOFT —) PASH
(SUBJECT —) SCOPE CONTENT
(SUPPURATIVE —) PUS
(TRIVIAL —) JOKE
(TYPESET —) CHASE
(WASTE —) DIRT DRAFF DROSS RAMMEL SEWAGE EXCRETA
(WORTHLESS —) SLAG CHAFF GANGUE GARBAGE
(WRITTEN —) SCRIVE
(PL.) HARNESS SQUARES
(PREF.) HYL(O)
(SUFF.) **(COLORING —)** PHYLL
MATTER-OF-FACT THINGY PROSAIC PROSAICAL DRY PROSE LITERAL PROSAIC
MATTER-OF-FACTNESS PROSE
MATTHAN (GRANDSON OF —) JOSEPH
MATTHEW (FATHER OF —) ALPHAEUS
MATTING MAT TAT BAST BEAR BUMP SIRKI TATTY SAWALI TATAMI COCOMAT RABANNA
MATTOCK MAT BILL HACK MATAX PICKAX TUBBAL TWIBIL GRUBBER
MATTRESS BED MAT TICK DIVAN FUTON QUILT RESAI REZAI PALLET BISCUIT MATRACE PAILLASSE PALLIASSE
(INFLATABLE —) LILO
MATURATE MATTER
MATURE AGE OLD BOLD FULL GRAY RIPE ADULT MANLY RIPEN SHOOT ACCRUE AUTUMN DECOCT DIGEST MELLOW SEASON SEEDED CONCOCT DEVELOP FURNISH PERFECT PROVECT MATURATE
(PREF.) TEL(E)(O)
MATURED ADULT GROWN FORMED HEADED MELLOW SEEDED HOMOGAMY
(SEXUALLY —) HIGH
MATURING (— EARLY) RATHRIPE
MATURITY AGE RIPENESS

MATWEED NARD NARDUS
MATZOTH MATZOS AFIKOMEN
MAUDLIN BEERY MOIST FUDDLED
MAUDLINISM BATHOS
MAUL FAN PAW TUG MALL MELL GAVEL GLAUM BEATER BEETLE BEMAUL MUZZLE SCAMBLE
MAUND MAO MEIN MAHAN
MAUNDER HAVER
MAUNDY NIPTER MANDATE
MAURITANIA (CAPITAL OF —) NOUAKCHOTT
(COIN OF —) KHOUM
(MONEY OF —) OUGUIYA
(RIVER OF —) SENEGAL
(TOWN OF —) ATAR NEMA AGMAR KAEDI OUJAF
MAURITANIAN MOOR
MAURITIUS (CAPITAL OF —) PORTLOUIS
(CHANNEL OF —) QUOIN
(ISLAND OF —) AGALEGA GABRIEL RODRIGUEZ
(RIVER OF —) GRAND POSTE REMPART
(TOWN OF —) VACOAS TRIOLET CUREPIPE SOUILLAC
MAUSOLEUM MOLE TOMB SHRINE TURBEH BARADARI
MAUVE MALLOW PURPLE MAUVINE
MAVEN ADEPT EXPERT
MAVERICK STRAY
MAW MAA CRAW CROP GORGE CROPPY THROAT
MAWKISH CUTE SAPPY SOPPY SOUPY WALSH DRIPPY SICKLY VANILLA
MAXILLA SETA GNATHITE CULTELLUS
MAXILLIPED JAWFOOT GNATHITE
MAXIM SAW SAY DICT ITEM NORM RULE TEXT WORD ADAGE AXIOM GNOME LARGE MOTTO DICTUM SAYING SYMBOL BROCARD DICTATE IMPRESA PRECEPT PROVERB APHORISM APOTHEGM DOCTRINE MORALISM PROTASIS SENTENCE
(PL.) LOGIA
MAXIMUM FULL MOST PEAK CREST EXTREME OUTSIDE SUMMARY ULTIMATE
MAXIXE CARIOCA
MAXWELL LINE WEBER
MAY CAN MUN MOTE MOWE MUST PRIME SHALL HEYDAY HAWTHORN SYCAMORE
(3D OF —) RUDMASDAY
MAYA PRAKRITI
MAYAN COCOM
(— CALENDAR PERIOD) UAYEB UINAL
(— GOD) CHAC CHAAC
MAYAPPLE MANDRAKE
MAYBE MEBBE HAPPEN PERHAPS POSSIBLY
MAY DAY BELTANE
MAYFISH ROCKFISH
MAYFLOWER ARBUTUS
MAYFLY DUN DOON DRAKE NAIAD DAYFLY SPINNER EPHEMERA
MAYHEM FELONY
MAYONNAISE MAYO GOULASH DRESSING
(GARLIC —) AIOLI
MAYOR MAIRE BAILIFF DEMARCH PODESTA PROVOST HIZZONER PALATINE
(BULGARIAN —) KMET
(IRISH —) SOVRAN SOVEREIGN
(SPANISH —) ALCALDE
MAYOR OF CASTERBRIDGE
(AUTHOR OF —) HARDY
(CHARACTER IN —) JOPP SUSAN DONALD NEWSON FARFRAE LESUEUR LUCETTA MICHAEL RICHARD HENCHARD ELIZABETH TEMPLEMAN
MAYORSHIP CHAIR
MAYPOLE SHAFT
MAYPOP MAYCOCK MARACOCK
MAYWEED BALDER COTULA MATHER HOGWEED COMPOSIT DILLWEED
MAZE JUNGLE WARREN CONFUSE BEWILDER LABYRINTH
MAZEPPA (CHARACTER IN —) MARIA ANDREY MAZEPPA KOCHUBEY
(COMPOSER OF —) TCHAIKOVSKY
MAZUMA (ALSO SEE MONEY) LUCRE
MCCOY QUILL
ME I MA US MOI
MEAD MEATHE BRAGGET HYDROMEL METHEGLIN
MEADOW LEA ABEL MEAD VEGA WISH WONG FIELD GRASS LEASE MARSH SWALE WARTH CALLOW PARAMO SAETER SMOOTH POTRERO THWAITE CHINAMPA
(ARTIFICIAL —) CHINAMPA
(FLOODED —) SALTING
(IRISH —) BAAN
(LOW —) ING INCH INGE HAUGH CALLOW
(NORWEGIAN —) SAETER
(PREF.) PRATI
(SUFF.) ING
MEADOW CROWFOOT FROGWORT
MEADOW GRASS POA
MEADOWLAND ALP MOWING MOWLAND
MEADOWLARK ACORN MEDLAR
MEADOW MOUSE VOLE
MEADOW PEA COWPEA
MEADOW PIPIT WEKEEN CHEEPER TIETICK TITLING LINGBIRD TWITLARK
MEADOW SAFFRON UPSTART COLCHICUM
MEADOW SAXIFRAGE SESELI
MEADOWSWEET SPIREA MEADWORT
MEAGER BALD BARE LANK LEAN NICE POOR THIN GAUNT NAKED SCANT SILLY SKIMP SOBER SPARE JEJUNE LEEPIT LENTEN MEAGRE NARROW PILLED SCANTY SLIGHT SPARSE STINGY SCRAGGY SCRANNY SCRIMPY SCRUBBY SLENDER SPARING STARVED STERILE MARGINAL SCRANNEL SCRATCHY MISERABLE
MEAGERLY BARELY SPARELY SPARINGLY
MEAGERNESS ECONOMY EXILITY TENUITY SPARENESS
MEAL AMYL ATTA BAKE CENA CHOW FARM FEED HASH KAIL MEAT MONG NOSH TUCK COENA FLOUR MANGE SCOFF BUFFET COMIDA DINNER FARINA MANGER POLLEN REPAST SPREAD SQUARE SUPPER UNDERN BLOWOUT COOKOUT CRIBBLE MELTITH NAGMAAL NOONING SETDOWN ALMUERZO CORNMEAL EVENMETE MEALTIDE ORDINARY TRENCHER
(— AND WATER) DRAMMOCK
(— FROM CASSAVA ROOT) FARINE FARINHA
(— FROM ORCHID ROOT) SALEP
(— GROUND BY HAND) GRADDAN
(— OF FELLOWSHIP) AGAPE
(— STIRRED WITH MILK) STUROCH
(ACORN —) RACAHOUT
(AFTERNOON —) TEA
(CEREMONIAL —) SEDER
(COARSE —) GRIT GROUT KIBBLE CRIBBLE GURGEONS
(COLLEGE —) HALL
(CORN —) MASA ATOLE NOCAKE
(ELABORATE —) FEAST BANQUET
(EXCESSIVE —) SURFEIT
(FIRST —) ALMUERZO
(FULL —) GORGE
(HASTY —) SNAP CHACK
(HEARTY —) AIT
(HEAVY —) TIGHTENER
(IMPROMPTU —) BITE CHECK
(LIGHT —) BAIT BEVER CHACK CHECK FOURS NUNCHEON
(MIDDAY —) NOON
(MORNING —) BRUNCH
(PERTAINING TO —) PRANDIAL
(PURIM —) SEUDAH
(SCANTY —) PICK
(SMALL —) SNAP MORSEL
(SOLITARY —) SULLEN
(UNSORTED —) ATTA
(PL.) TUCKER
(PREF.) ATHERO
MEALTIDE MELTITH
MEALTIME CHOW MELTETH
MEALY FLOURY FARINOSE PERONATE
MEALYBUG COCCID
MEAN LOW BASE CLAM HARD LEAN MIDS NICE POKY POOR SLIM VILE AGENT ARGUE DINGY DIRTY DUSTY FOOTY GRIMY KETTY LOUSY MANGY MESNE MEZZO MIDST MINGY MOYEN MUCKY NASTY PETIT PETTY RATTY RUNTY SCALD SCALL SCALY SCRUB SEEDY SILLY SMALL SNIDE SNIVY SORRY SOUND SPELL ABJECT BADASS BEMEAN COMMON DENOTE DESIGN DIRTEN FEEBLE FROWZY FRUGAL GRUBBY HUMBLE HUNGRY IMPORT INSECT INTEND LEADEN LITTLE MEASLY MEDIAL MEDIUM MENIAL MIDDLE NARROW ORNERY PALTRY PEANUT PILLED POKING RASCAL SCABBY SCREWY SCUMMY SCURVY SHABBY SLIGHT SNIFTY SNIPPY SORDID SQUALL STRAIT TEMPER YELLOW AVERAGE CAITIFF CHANNEL CHETIVE COMICAL CONNOTE HACKNEY HATEFUL HILDING IGNOBLE MESQUIN MISERLY MOTETUS OBSCURE PEAKING PELTING PIGGISH PIMPING PITIFUL PORTEND REPTILE ROINISH SCABBED SHABBED SIGNIFY VICIOUS BEGGARLY CHURLISH DOGGEREL MEDIOCRE MIDDLING NIGGLING PICAYUNE PITIABLE RASCALLY RIFFRAFF SHAMEFUL SNEAKING TWOPENNY WRETCHED
MEANDER ROVE WIND STRAY TWINE CIRCLE WIMPLE WINDLE SERPENT WINDING STRAGGLE
MEANING WIT HANG DRIFT SENSE SOUND IMPORT INTENT SEMEME PURPORT PURPOSE CARRIAGE INNUENDO SENTENCE STRENGTH REFERENCE SIGNIFICANCE
(BASIC —) EFFECT
(DOUBLE —) WHIM EQUIVOKE
(ESSENTIAL —) CORE CONTENT
(IMPLIED —) EMPHASIS
(LITERAL —) LETTER
(MANIFEST —) FACE
(PRECISE —) VALUE
(REAL —) SPIRIT
(SECONDARY —) OVERTONE
(SECRET —) HEART
(SENSE THE — OF) READ
(SIGNIFICANT —) PITH
(SUBTLE —) OVERTONE
MEANINGFUL RICH PREGNANT
MEANINGFULNESS BODY
MEANINGLESS BANAL EMPTY ABSURD FECKLESS SENSELESS
(— LETTER OR CODE) NULL
MEANLY POORLY SLIGHT COMMONLY
MEANNESS BEGGARY
MEANS MIDS AGENT DRIVE MESNE MOYEN PURSE THEME AGENCY AVENUE ENGINE MATTER MIDDES POCKET STRING WRENCH BALANCE BENEFIT DEMESNE FACULTY FASHION QUOMODO COURTESY
(— OF ACCESS) DOOR AVENUE
(— OF COMMUNICATION) CANAL COMMERCE
(— OF DEFENSE) HORN HEDGE SHIELD BULWARK
(— OF ENTRANCE) INGRESS
(— OF ESCAPE) CHINK SCAPE FLIGHT
(— OF ESTIMATE) GAGE GAUGE
(— OF INFLUENCING) HOLD
(— OF LIVING) ALIMONY
(— OF OFFENSE) ARM
(— OF PROTECTION) SAFETY
(— OF SECURITY) WALL
(— OF SUPPORT) HOLD ALIMENT SUPPORT
(— OF TESTING) CHECK
(— TO END) FULCRUM
(ARTIFICIAL —) MACHINE
(BY THIS —) HEREBY

MEANSPIRITED POOR SUPINE CURRISH BANAUSIC RECREANT
MEANTIME MEAN WHILE WHILES INTERIM
MEANTONE TERTIAN
MEANWHILE WHILST INTERIM MEANTIME
MEANY BRUTE
MEASLES RUBEOLA MORBILLI
(BLACK —) ESCA APOPLEXY
MEASURE (ALSO SEE UNIT AND WEIGHT) AR BU EM EN HO KO LI MO RI SE TU AAM ARE AUM BAG CAB CHO DRA ELL FAT FEN FIT FOU FUN GAD GAZ GUZ HIN HOB IMI KAB KAN KIP KOR KOS LEA LOG LUG MAU MIL MOY PIK RIG RIN ROD SAA SHO TON TUN VAT VOG WEY ACRE ALMA AUNE BARN BATH BEKA BOLL BOUW BUTT CADE CENT CHIH COOM COSS DEPA DOSE DRAA DRAM DYNE EPHA EPHI FALL FANG FOOT FULL GAGE GERA GILL GIRT GOAD GRAM GREX HAND HATT HIDE HOOP HOUR IMMI INCH KNOT KOKU LAST MEAL METE MILE MUID NAIL NOOK OMER PACE PINT PIPE POLL RATE REAM RIME ROOD ROPE ROTL SAAH SACK SALM SEAH SEAM SIZE SKEP SPAN STEP TAKT TAPE TIME TRAM TRUG TSUN VARA WIST YARD ALMUD AMBER ANKER ARDAB ARDEB ARURA BEKAH BIGHA BLANK BODGE BRASS CABAN CABLE CABOT CANDY CARAT CARGA CATTY CAVAN CHAIN CHANG CHING CLOVE COOMB CRANS CUBIT CUMAL CUNIT DENUM DEPOH DIGIT DRAFT DUNAM DUNUM EPHAH GAUGE GERAH GIRTH HOMER HUTCH JUGER LABOR LAGEN LIANG LIBRA LIGNE LIPPY LITER LITRE MEITH METER METRE MINIM MODEL OUNCE PEISE PERCH PLANK POUND QUIRE RASER RHYME SALMA SCALE SCORE SHAKU SHENG SHING SIEVE SLEEP STACK STERE STONE STOOP STOUP THERM TOISE TOVET TRACE VERST YOJAN APATAN ARCHIN ARPENT ARSHIN ASSIZE BARREL BATMAN BEMETE BOVATE BUNDLE BUSHEL CANADA CANTAR CHOMER CHOPIN COLLOP COUDEE COVIDO CUERDA DAVACH DAVOCH DECARE DEGREE DENIER DIPODY DIRHAM DRACHM ENGLER EXTENT FANEGA FATHOM FEDDAN FINGER FIRKIN FIRLOT FLAGON FODDER FORPET FOTHER GALLON GRAMME HALEBI HIDAGE KISHEN LEAGUE MICRON MODIUS MODULE MOGGIO MORGEN NUMBER OITAVA OUROUB OXHIDE QANTAR REASON SAZHEN SETIER SQUARE STERAD STRIKE SULUNG TERMIN THRAVE WINDLE YOJANA ADOULIE AMPHORA ANAPEST ARSHINE BATTUTA BRACCIO BREADTH CADENCE CALIPER CALORIE CENTARE CENTNER CENTRAD CHITTAK COMPASS CONGIUS CONTAIN DECIARE DIOPTER DRACHMA DRAUGHT ENTROPY FARSAKH FARSANG FRUNDEL FURLONG HECTARE HEMINEE KILIARE NOCKTAT QUARTAN QUARTER SCHEPEL SCRUPLE SECCHIO SKEPFUL SKIPPLE SPANGLE SPINDLE STADION STADIUM TERTIAN VIRGATE ALQUEIRE CAPACITY CARUCATE CENTIARE CHETVERT CRANNOCK DACTYLIC DECAGRAM DECIGRAM DESIATIN DIAPASON HOGSHEAD INNOCENT LANDYARD METEWAND MUTCHKIN PARASANG PLOWGANG PLOWGATE SCHOONER SCHOPPEN STANDARD PRECAUTION
(— DEPTH) SOUND
(— FOR DRINKS) JIGGER
(— FOR FISH) COT VOG CRAN LAST DRAFT HAMPER DRAUGHT
(— FOR SHELLFISH) WASH
(— OF BEER) HANDLE
(— OF BUTTER) SPAN
(— OF CHAFF) FAN
(— OF COAL) TEN CORF KEEL CHALDER CHALDRON
(— OF DEVELOPMENT) AGE
(— OF DIAMONDS) BULSE
(— OF DISCREPANCY) LEEWAY
(— OF EELS) BIND STICK
(— OF EFFICIENCY) DUTY
(— OF FURS) MANTLE
(— OF GRAIN) MOY COOP
(— OF HERRINGS) MEASE
(— OF HORSE) HAND
(— OF LIQUOR) FIFTH
(— OF MEDICINE) DOSE DROP
(— OF MERCURY) FLASK
(— OF MINING CLAIMS) MERE
(— OF OUTER SPACE) PARSEC
(— OF PEAS) COP
(— OF RAISINS) FRAIL
(— OF ROTATION) ANGLE
(— OF SILK) DRAMMAGE
(— OF STRAW) KEMPLE
(— OF SUPERIORITY) LEAD
(— OF TIMBER) TON STANDARD
(— OF WAR) BLOCKADE
(— OF WATCHES) LIGNE
(— OF WATERCRESS) HAND
(— OF WEIGHT FOR ARROWS) SHILLING
(— OF WHISKY) CRUISKEN CRUISKEEN
(— OF WOOD) CORD STACK STERE
(— OF WOOL FINENESS) BLOOD
(— OF WORK) POOL
(— OF YARN) LEA RAP CLEW HEER THREAD SPANGLE SPINDLE
(— OUT) BATCH
(ANGULAR —) ARC
(COERCIVE —) SANCTION
(COUNTERFEIT —) SLANG
(DANCE —) TRACE
(DUE —) MANNER
(FULL —) SATIETY COMPLEMENT
(LIQUID —) CUP GILL PINT MINIM QUART GALLON
(OLD LIQUID —) TIERCE
(PHARMACISTS'S —) MINIM
(QUANTITATIVE —) MAGNITUDE
(ROAD —) SCHENE
(RUSSIAN —) VERST SAGENE
(SANCTIONED —) STANDARD
(SIAMESE —) NIOU
(TAKE —S) ACT
(PREF.) METR(O)
(SUFF.) METER METR(E)(O)(Y)
(BY A SPECIFIED —) MEAL
MEASURED NUMEROUS
MEASURE FOR MEASURE
(AUTHOR OF —) SHAKESPEARE
(CHARACTER IN —) ELBOW FROTH LUCIO PETER ANGELO JULIET POMPEY THOMAS CLAUDIO ESCALUS MARIANA VARRIUS ABHORSON ISABELLA OVERDONE FRANCISCA VINCENTIO BARNARDINE
MEASURELESS ENDLESS INFINITE
MEASUREMENT GAGE DEPTH GAUGE LEVEL MEITH METAGE DIALING MEASURE SOUNDING
(— BY LINES) STICHOMETRY
(— FOR TAXATION) HIDE HIDAGE
(— OF CLOTH) ALNAGE
(— OF FINENESS) SET SETT
(CIRCULAR —) RADIAN
(EARTH —) GEODESY
(LUMBER —) LAST
(TIME —) HOROMETRY
MEASURER METER
(— OF LAND) SURVEYOR
MEASURING
(SUFF.) METRY
MEASURING-ROD METEWAND METEYARD METESTICK
MEAT BEEF FISH FOOD LAMB LEAN LIFT PORK FLESH STEAK VIFDA VIVDA BUCCAN CAGMAG CONFIT FLEECE MATTER NUTTON TARGET PECKAGE
(— AND FISH) LAULAU
(— COOKED ON SKEWERS) SATE HASLET HASSLET
(— COOKED WITH SKEWERS) SASSATIE
(— DRIED IN SUN) JERKY CHARQUI PEMMICAN
(— OF CONCH) SCUNGILI
(— OF KID) CAPRETTO
(— ON SKEWERS) YAKITORI
(— WITH VEGETABLES) STEW MULLIGAN
(BOILED —) SOD SODDEN BOUILLI
(BROILED —) GRISKIN GRILLADE
(BUFFALO —) FLEECE
(CANNED —) SPAM
(CHOPPED —) BURGER
(COCONUT —) COPRA
(CURED —) HAM
(CUT OF —) ARM
(DRIED —) MUMMY
(FAT —) SPECK
(FROZEN —) FRIGO
(INFERIOR —) CAGMAG STICKING
(JERKED —) BILTONG CHARQUI
(KIND OF —) MINCE
(LEAN —) MUSCLE
(MINCED —) CHUET JIGOTE RISSOLE SANDERS
(POTTED —) RILLETT
(RABBIT —) LAPAN
(RAGOUT OF —) HARICOT
(ROAST —) BREDE CABOB
(ROLLED —) BIRD
(SALTED —) JUNK MART
(SIDE —) SOWBELLY
(SLICED —) CARPACCIO
(SLICE OF —) BRACIOLA BRACIOLE
(SMALL PIECES OF —) SATAY
(SMOKED —) BUCCAN
(THIN SLICES OF —) PICCATA
MEAT CURER BATHMAN
MEATHEADED DENSE
MEAT HOOK GAMBREL
MEAT JELLY ASPIC
MEATLESS PARVE LENTEN PAREVE
MEAT PIE PASTY
MEATUS BUR BURR ALVEARY
MEATY PITHY
MECATE MCCARTY
MECHANIC JOINER WRIGHT ARTISAN FELTMAN SHOPMAN WORKMAN BANAUSIC OPERATIVE
MECHANICAL FROZEN INHUMAN METALLIC AUTOMATIC
(NOT —) HORMIC
MECHANICALLY BLINDLY
MECHANISM FAN BOND FEED GEAR KITE LIFT MOTE APRON CATCH CROWD FORCE ORGAN SHAKE SLIDE SPARK STEER ACTION BOTTOM CUTOFF INFEED MOTION SICKLE STRIKE AUTOVAC BUILDER CHANNEL CONTROL EJECTOR GIGBACK GRIPPER GUNLOCK HOLDOUT SETTING TRIPPER ACTUATOR ELEVATOR KINETICS RACKWORK ROLAMITE SELECTOR SETWORKS SIGNALER STEERING STOPWORK THROWOUT
(— OF HEREDITY) PANGENESIS
MECHANIZE DESKILL AUTOMATE
MECHLIN MALINES
MECONIN OPIANYL
MEDAL GOLD GONG STAR AWARD MODEL STAMP PLAQUE SILVER MEDALET OSCELLA VERNICLE MEDALLION
(PL.) EXONUMIA
MEDALLION CAMEO TONDO PADUAN PATERA PANHAGIA
MEDAN (FATHER OF —) ABRAHAM
(MOTHER OF —) KETURAH
MEDDLE TIG FOOL MELL MESS MIRD NOSE POKE TOUCH DABBLE FIDDLE FINGER HECKLE POTTER PUTTER TAMPER TANGLE TINKER
(— IRRESPONSIBLY) TRIFLE
MEDDLER SNOOP YENTA SNOOPER BUSYBODY KIBITZER STICKLER STIFFLER BUTTINSKY
MEDDLESOME NOSY FRESH NEBBY
MEDDLING BUSY
MEDEA (AUNT OF —) CIRCE
(BROTHER OF —) ABSYRTUS APSYRTUS
(FATHER OF —) AEETES
(HUSBAND OF —) JASON AEGEUS
(MOTHER OF —) IDYIA
(SISTER OF —) CHALCOPE CHALCIOPE
MEDIA ELASTICA
(ONE OF THE —) PRESS RADIO TELEVISION

MEDIAL MEDIAN MEDIUM MIDDLE AVERGAGE
MEDIAN MEDIAL MESIAL AVERAGE MIDLINE
(— STRIP) MALL TERRACE
MEDIANT THIRD
MEDIATE MEAN REFEREE INTERCEDE
MEDIATING MIDDLE MIDWAY
MEDIATOR MEANS MEDIUM DAYSMAN MIDDLER PLACATER STICKLER MODERATOR
MEDIC DOC HOP DOCTOR NONESUCH SHAMROCK
MEDICAL IATRIC PHYSIC IATRICAL PAEONIAN
(— WORK) ALMONING
(PREF.) **(— TREATMENT)** IATR(O)
MEDICAMENT REMEDY SMEGMA FRONTAL EPULOTIC
MEDICINAL IATRIC PHYSIC MEDICAL THERIAL PHYSICAL SALUTARY THERICAL OFFICINAL
MEDICINE DRUG MUTI PEAI DROPS GRUEL STEEL STUFF TONIC TRADE AMULET ECLEGM ELIXIR MAGUAL PHYSIC POWDER REMEDY SIMPLE ALOETIC ANODYNE ANTACID CORDIAL HEPATIC LUCHDOM MIXTURE NERVINE OPORICE PLACEBO POROTIC PYROTIC SPLENIC AROMATIC DIAPENTE DIGESTER DRUGGERY EARDROPS ECCRITIC EMULGENT LAXATIVE LEECHDOM LENITIVE LOBLOLLY PECTORAL PHARMACY PULMONIC RELAXANT SEDATIVE SPECIFIC STOMATIC CATHARTIC PURGATIVE PRESCRIPTION
(— BOTTLE) VIAL PHIAL
(AMOUNT OF —) DOSAGE
(CHINESE —) SENSO
(COLD —) CONTAC
(QUACK —) NOSTRUM
(SHIP'S —) LOBLOLLY
(SYSTEM OF —) AYURVEDA
(UNIVERSAL —) PANACEA
(PL.) GALIANES
(PREF.) IAMATO IATRO PHARMACO
MEDICINE MAN PEAI DOCTOR KAHUNA PIACHE POWWOW SHAMAN SINGER ANGEKOK TOHUNGA CONTRARY POWWOWER
MEDICK SNAIL
MEDIEVAL OLD GOTHIC
MEDIOCRE BUSH HACK MEAN SUCH MEDIUM AVERAGE INFERIOR MIDDLING MODERATE PASSABLE
MEDITATE CAST CHEW MUSE BROOD GLOAT STUDY THINK WEIGH PONDER RECORD BETHINK COMMENT IMAGINE PREPEND REFLECT REVOLVE COGITATE CONSIDER PURPENSE RUMINATE
MEDITATION MOYEN STUDY THINK ZAZEN DHYANA MUSING REVERIE THOUGHT HIGGAION
(PLACE OF —) ZENDO
MEDITATIVE MUSING MUSEFUL PENSIVE RUMINANT
MEDITERRANEAN MIDLAND
MEDIUM BATH EVEN LENS MEAN ETHER JUICE MIDST MOYEN ORGAN BALIAN BISTER BISTRE DIGEST MIDDLE MIDWAY ORACLE SLUDGE TEMPER PSYCHIC VEHICLE MEDIOCRE SHOWCASE CONTINUUM
(— FOR DISCUSSION) PLATFORM
(— OF DIVINE REVELATION) ORACLE
(— OF EXCHANGE) CURRENCY
(— OF EXPRESSION) VOICE
(— OF TRANSMISSION) AIR AIRWAVE
(CULTURE —) AGAR STAB BROTH HYRAX SLANT CULTURE BOUILLON
(ENVELOPING —) SWATH
(PAINTING —) TEMPERA
(PLANT GROWTH —) PERLITE
(REFINING —) ALEMBIC
MEDIUM, THE (CHARACTER IN —) FLORA MONICA
(COMPOSER OF —) MENOTTI
MEDLAR MESPIL LAZAROLE
MEDLEY OLIO BABEL REVUE JUMBLE CHIVARI CLANGOR FARRAGO GOULASH MELANGE MIXTURE BROUHAHA KEDGEREE MACARONI MISHMASH RHAPSODY SLAMPAMP VARIORUM CHARIVARI MACEDOINE
(— OF TUNES) QUODLIBET
MEDOC WINE LAFITTE
MEDREGAL BONITO
MEDULLA PITH MARROW
MEDULLA OBLONGATA BULB
MEDUSA JELLY QUARL GORGON BLUBBER GERYONID
(FATHER OF —) PHORCYS
(MOTHER OF —) CETO
(SLAYER OF —) PERSEUS
(PL.) BRACT
MEEK LOW DAFT MURE LOWLY GENTLE HUMBLE NEBBISH PACIFIC LAMBLIKE YIELDING
MEEKNESS MANSUETUDE
MEERSCHAUM PIPE GRAVEL KIEFEKIL SEPIOLITE
MEET FIT KEP SEE COPE FACE FILL HENT NOSE ABIDE CLOSE CROSS FRONT GREET INCUR OCCUR PIECE TOUCH ANSWER BATTLE BEMEET COMBAT CONCUR FULFIL INVENT SEMBLE CONTACT CONTEST CONVENE CONVENT COUNCIL FULFILL RUNINTO SATISFY ASSEMBLE CONFRONT CONVERGE GAINCOPE
(— A BET) SEE
(— A NEED) SUFFICE
(— AT END) BUTT
(— FACE TO FACE) AFFRONT
(— FORCIBLY) SMITE
(— SQUARELY) ENVISAGE
(— VIOLENTLY) CHECK HURTLE
(— WITH) GET SEE BUMP FIND STRIKE
(ATHLETIC —) GALA GYMKHANA
MEETING MOD FEIS MOOT CLOSE FORUM SABHA SHINE STOUR SYNOD TRYST ACCESS AUMAGA CAUCUS CHAPEL CLINIC HUDDLE POWWOW SEANCE CABINET CHAPTER COLLEGE CONTACT CONVENT COUNCIL JOLLITY MOOTING OCCURSE REVIVAL SEMINAR SITTING SYNAXIS ASSEMBLY CONGRESS CONSULTA DELEGACY ECCLESIA EXERCISE JUNCTION OSCULANT TERTULIA WARDMOTE CONCOURSE COLLOQUIUM
(— FULLY ATTENDED) PLENUM
(— OF BARDS) GORSEDD
(— OF NEIGHBORS) HUSKING
(— OF SCHOLARS) LEVY
(— OF WITCHES) ESBAT SABBAT SABBATH
(— OF WORSHIPERS) SERVICE
(— STANDARDS) FIT
(ANGLO-SAXON —) GEMOTE
(APPOINTED —) RENDEVOUS
(ENDWISE —) ABUTMENT
(EVENING —) SOIREE
(FORBIDDING CLOSED —S) SUNSHINE
(GENERAL —) PRIME
(NOT —) PARALLEL
(POLITICAL —) CAUCUS
(PRIVATE —) CONCLAVE
(RACE —) REGATTA
(SECRET —) CABAL CONSULT CONCLAVE
(SOCIAL —) CLUB JOLLY HOBNOB
(SPORTS —) GYMKHANA
(TOWN —) TUNMOOT
MEETINGHOUSE MORADA
MEETING PLACE AMBALAM CENACLE TINWALD
MEGALOMANIAC MONARCHO
MEGAPHONE VAMPHORN
MEGAPODE MALEO LEIPOA
MEGARA (FATHER OF —) CREON
(HUSBAND OF —) HERCULES
MEGAREUS (FATHER OF —) HIPPOMENES
(MOTHER OF —) OENOPE
(SON OF —) EUIPPUS
(WIFE OF —) IPHINOE
MEGILP GUMPTION
MEGINNING (— OF ACTIVITY) DAYONE
MEHETABEL (HUSBAND OF —) HADAD
(MOTHER OF —) MATRED
MEHIR (FATHER OF —) CHELUB
MEHTAR BUNGY BHUNGI
MEHUJAEL (FATHER OF —) IRAD
MEIOSIS LITOTES REDUCTION
MEISTERSINGER VON NURNBERG, DI (CHARACTER IN —) EVA HANS VEIT DAVID FRITZ SACHS POGNER KOTHNER WALTHER STOLZING MAGDALENE BECKMESSER
(COMPOSER OF —) WAGNER
MELAMPUS SEER
(BROTHER OF —) BIAS
(FATHER OF —) AMYTHAON
(MOTHER OF —) IDOMENE
(SON OF —) MANTIUS ANTIPHATES
(WIFE OF —) LYSIPPE
MELANCHOLIA ATHYMY ATHYMIA SADNESS
MELANCHOLIC HYPPISH
MELANCHOLY WO LOW SAD WOE BLUE DRAM DULL DUMP MARE ADUST BLUES DEARN DOWIE DREAR DUSKY GLOOM SORRY WISHT GLOOMY SOMBER SOMBRE SORROW SPLEEN SULLEN YELLOW CHAGRIN DOLEFUL DUMPISH ELEGIAC SADNESS SPLEENY THOUGHT ATRABILE LIVERISH TRISTFUL
MELANESIAN DOBUAN KANAGA KANAKA EFATESE
MELANGE OLIO GOMBO GUMBO SMORGASBORD
MELANIPPUS (FATHER OF —) THESEUS HICETAON
(LOVER OF —) COMAETHO
(MOTHER OF —) PERIGUNE
(SON OF —) IOXUS
MELANISM PHAEISM
MELANTERITE INKSTONE
MELANTIUS (SISTER OF —) EVADNE
MELATOPE EYE
MELCHI (FATHER OF —) ADDI JANNA
MELCHIAH (SON OF —) PASHUR
MELD SET SAMBA SPREAD BOLIVIA DECLARE
MELEA (FATHER OF —) MENAN
MELEAGER (FATHER OF —) OENEUS
(MOTHER OF —) ALTHAEA
MELECH (FATHER OF —) MICAH
MELEE BRAWL MEDLEY RUMBLE DOGFIGHT PELLMELL WINGDING
MELIA (FATHER OF —) OCEANUS
(SON OF —) ISMENUS TENERUS AEGIALEUS PHORONEUS
MELIBOEA (FATHER OF —) AMPHION
(HUSBAND OF —) NELEUS
(MOTHER OF —) NIOBE
MELIORATE MITIGATE
MELISMA JUBILUS
MELL KIRN
MELLIFLUOUS SUGARED HYBLAEAN
MELLOW AGE OMY HAZE LUSH MALM PLUM RICH RIPE SOFT FRUSH RIPEN FLUTED GOLDEN MATURE
MELLOWED BEERY
MELODIOUS SOFT SOOT TUNY SWEET TUNED ARIOSO DULCET MELODIC MUSICAL SIRENIC SONGFUL TUNABLE TUNEFUL CANOROUS CHARMING NUMEROUS SOUNDFUL
(EXCESSIVELY —) SIRUPY SYRUPY
MELODRAMA HAM SOAP TANK
MELODY AIR HUM LAY ARIA LILT NOTE TUNE CANTO CHANT CHARM DREAD MELOS MIRTH NIGUN CANTUS CHORAL GHAZEL MONODY NIGGUN STROKE CANZONA CANZONE CHORALE DESCANT HARMONY MEASURE MELISMA PLANXTY ROSALIA CARILLON CAVATINA DIAPASON VOCALISE
(— COMPASS) AMBITUS
(MOURNFUL —) DUMP
(PASTORAL —) MUSETTE
(SIMPLE —) PLAINSONG
(SYNAGOGAL —S) CHAZANUT HAZANUTH
MELON PEPO GOURD MANGO CASABA CITRON DUDAIM

MAYCOCK CUCURBIT HONEYDEW PEPONIDA PEPONIUM
(KIND OF —) CRANSHAW CRENSHAW
MELT FLY RIN RUN BLOW FADE FLOW FLUX FUSE THAW DEICE FOUND LEACH SMELT SWEAL SWELT TOUCH GUTTER RELENT SOFTEN DISTILL FORMELT RESOLVE DISCANDY DISSOLVE ELIQUATE COLLIQUATE
(— AWAY) SWEAL
(— DOWN) RENDER
(— IRREGULARLY) DROZE
MELTED RUN FONDU FUSED FUSILE
MELTING SOFT FUSILE FUSION
MELTWATER OUTWASH
MELVILLE (BOOK BY —) OMOO
MEMBER LIMB LITH PART BRANCH FELLOW FILLET GIRDER SOCIUS AMANIST COMPART ERANIST FAIRING ALBRIGHT AULARIAN BRIDLING
(— OF ANSAR) HELPER
(— OF BALLET) FIGURANT
(— OF BAND) SIDEMAN
(— OF BODYGUARD) HUSCARL
(— OF BROTHERHOOD) ESSENE SENUSSI
(— OF CHURCH) BROTHER PARISHIONER
(— OF CLAN) CHILD CALEBITE
(— OF CLERGY) DEFENSOR
(— OF COAST GUARD) SPAR
(— OF COUNCIL) CONSUL HEEMRAAD
(— OF COURT) DICAST EPHETE
(— OF CREW) HAND IDLER LAYER DRIVER STROKE BOWSMAN FORETOP BRAKEMAN SHAREMAN
(— OF CULT) ANGEL AMIDIST
(— OF FACULTY) COUNSEL LECTURER
(— OF FAMILY) FETII
(— OF FRATERNAL ORDER) ELK SHRINER FORESTER KIWANIAN
(— OF FRATERNITY) GREEK
(— OF FRENCH ACADEMY) IMMORTAL
(— OF GANG) HENCHMAN
(— OF GENTRY) SEIGNEUR
(— OF GIRL SCOUTS) BROWNIE
(— OF GREEK ARMY) EVZONE
(— OF GUILD) COMACINE HOASTMAN
(— OF HOUSEHOLD) FAMILIAR
(— OF HUNTING PARTY) STANDER
(— OF INN OF COURT) ANCIENT BENCHER
(— OF IRISH REPUBLICAN ARMY) PROVO
(— OF ITALIAN ARMY) ALPINO
(— OF KNOW-NOTHING PARTY) SAM
(— OF LEGISLATURE) SOLON DEPUTY DELEGATE
(— OF LITERARY GROUP) FELIBRE
(— OF LOWEST CLASS) LUMPEN
(— OF MIDDLE CLASS) BURGHER
(— OF PARLIAMENT) CONTENT THINGMAN
(— OF PRIMROSE LEAGUE) KNIGHT
(— OF RELIGIOUS ORDER) DAME FRIAR EUDIST FRAILE FRATER HERMIT JESUIT SISTER ALEXIAN BEGUINE BRINSER DERVISH HUSSITE SEPARTE SERVANT SERVITE CENOBITE EXORCIST HUMANIST PENITENT SALESIAN THEATINE
(— OF RETINUE) SEQUEL SEQUENT
(— OF RUSSIAN ARISTOCRACY) BOIAR BOYAR BOYARD
(— OF SAME GENUS) CONGENER
(— OF SECRET ORGANIZATION) DEMOLAY
(— OF SECRET SOCIETY) BOXER DANITE
(— OF SECT) BABI SHIA BABEE DRUSE HASID KHOJA SHIAH AUDIAN BEREAN BRAHMO CATHAR DIPPER DOPPER IBADHI JUMPER KHLYST SHIITE SMARTA WAHABI AISSAWA AJIVIKA AUDAEAN CAINITE CHASSID DREAMER EMPIRIC EUCHITE IBADITE ISAWIYA ISMAILI RAPPIST SENUSSI SEVENER AQUARIAN CALIXTIN DARBYITE DUKHOBOR EBIONITE FAMILIST GLASSITE LABADIST MANDAEAN SADDUCEE SEVERIAN SHAFIITE SIMONIAN STUNDIST
(— OF STAFF) ATTACHE
(— OF STATE) CITIZEN
(— OF STOCK EXCHANGE) BOARDMAN
(— OF TEAM) SPARE BOBBER KICKER
(— OF TRIBE) LEVITE JUDAHITE LAMANITE
(— OF UPPER CLASS) EFFENDI
(— OF VARNA) SUDRA SHUDRA
(— OF WHITE RACE) HAOLE
(— OF WINDOW) APRON
(— OF YOUTH GANG) HOMEBOY
(—S OF CLASS) FRY
(—S OF PROFESSION) FACULTY
(—S OF SECT) SKOPTSY
(—S OF TRIBUNAL) ACUERDO
(ARCHITECTURAL —) FAN ARCH FLAT SILL SPAN GABLE SOCLE STILE STILT CORBEL FASCIA CONSOLE CORNICE
(CHURCH —) GREEK LATIN DANITE DUNKER KIRKER TUNKER AZYMITE BAPTIST BEGHARD BROTHER DUNKARD KIRKMAN SECEDER ARMENIAN BRYANITE CATHOLIC DISCIPLE DOWIEITE JACOBITE
(CHURCH —S) FAITHFUL
(EVERY —) ALL
(FEEBLEST —) WRIG
(FULL —) GREMIAL
(OLDEST —) FATHER
(OVERHANGING —) BRACKET
(POLITICAL —) CADET ENDEK SHIRT GUELPH HUNKER LEADER APRISTA LEFTIST LIBERAL ABHORRER BUCKTAIL DEMOCRAT HERODIAN LABORITE
(PROJECTING —) TENON
(SECRET —) CRYPTO
(SENIOR —) DOYEN
(TENSION —) HANGER
(TERMINAL —) TOE
(SUFF.) AD CRAT
(— OF A CLASS) ANDER MER(E)(IC)(IS)(OUS)(Y)
MEMBERS
(SUFF.)
(— OF THE FAMILY) IDAE
(— OF THE SUBFAMILY OF) INAE
MEMBERSHIP SEAT GARTER GUILDRY
MEMBRANE RIM WEB CAUL COAT DURA FELL HEAD TELA GALEA HYMEN VELUM AMNION AMNIOS EXTINE INTINE MENINX MOTHER MUCOSA PLEURA RETINA SEPTUM SEROSA TIMBAL TUNICA TYMPAN BLANKET CAPSULE CHORION CHOROID CUTICLE DECIDUA EPICYTE HYALOID OOLEMMA PERIOST PUTAMEN STRATUM VELAMEN ECTODERM ENDOCYST ENVELOPE EPENDYMA EPISPORE EXOLEMMA INDUSIUM INTEXINE LABELLUM PATAGIUM PELLICLE STRIFFEN ALLANTOIS PERIPLAST PERIOSTEUM PERITONEUM
(— OF BRAIN) MATER
(— OF EGG) POTAMEN
(— OF EYE) SCLERA SCLEROTIC
(— OF GRAIN) INTINE
(— OF ORANGE) ZEST
(NICTITATING —) HAW
(TYMPANIC —) TYMPAN MYRINGA DRUMHEAD DRUMSKIN
(PL.) ADNEXA ANNEXA MENINGES
(PREF.) CHORI(O) HYMEN(O) MENING(O) MYRINGO VEL(I)
(SUFF.) YMENITIS
MEMBRANOUS HUSKY SKINNY HYMENOID SCARIOSE SCARIOUS
MEMENTO RELIC TOKEN MEMORY TROPHY KEEPSAKE REMINDER SOUVENIR
MEMINNA PEESOREH
MEMNON (FATHER OF —) TITHONUS
(MOTHER OF —) AURORA
(SLAYER OF —) ACHILLES
MEMOIR ELOGE RECORD HISTORY MEMORIAL
MEMORABLE GRAND SIGNAL CLASSIC NOTABLE MEMORIAL NAMEABLE NOTEWORTHY
MEMORANDA (SET OF —) TICKLER
MEMORANDUM BILL CHIT MEMO NOTE SLIP BRIEF JURAT CAHIER CIPHER DOCKET MEMOIR MINUTE TICKET JOTTING MEMORIAL NOTANDUM PROTOCOL BORDEREAU DIRECTIVE
MEMORIAL AHU AGALMA CAHIER FACTUM MEMOIR MEMORY RECORD TROPHY DENKMAL MEMENTO MENTION EBENEZER MONUMENT REMEMBRANCE
MEMORIZE LEARN MANDATE REMEMBER
MEMORY MIND EPROM HEART IMAGE STORE RECALL RECORD MEMENTO STORAGE MEMORIAL SOUVENIR
(— CHIP) DRAM
(— ON COMPUTER CHIP) RAM ROM
(— SUBDIVISION) PAGE
(BAD —) FORGETTERY
(COMPUTER —) RAM ROM PAGE CACHE STACK SCRATCHPAD
(MECHANICAL —) ROTE
(OF POOR —) FLUFFY
(PAINFUL —) SCAR
(PROGRAMMABLE —) EPROM
(SMALL COMPUTER —) SCRATCHPAD
(STORED COMPUTER —) FIRMWARE
(PREF.) MNEM(I)(O)
(SUFF.) MNESIA(C) MNESIS MNETIC
MEN THEY ORANG INNUIT MANHEAD MANHOOD MANKIND MENFOLK HUMANITY
(BLESSED —) BEATI
MENACE BOAST IMPEND THREAT BOGEYMAN MINATORY THREATEN
MENACING STOUT SURLY FIERCE TOWARD MINATORY MINACIOUS
MENAHEM (FATHER OF —) GADI
(VICTIM OF —) SHALLUM
MEN-AT-ARMS CHIVALRY
MEND DO FIX BEET DARN HEAL HELP KNIT STOP TINK AMEND CLOUT EMEND GRAFT MOISE PATCH COBBLE DOCTOR FETTLE RANTER REFORM REPAIR SOLDER SPETCH TINKLE IMPROVE INWEAVE REDRESS RIGHTLE
(— BY ADDING FEATHERS) IMP
(— CLUMSILY) BOTCH
(— MEN'S CLOTHES) BUSHEL
MENDACIOUS FALSE DISHONEST
MENDACITY LYING DECEIT FALSITY UNTRUTH
MENDER TINKER KETTLER BEATSTER
MENDICANCY BEGGARY
MENDICANT NAGA DANDI FAKIR FRIAR UDASI BEGGAR BHIKKU FAKEER FRATER GOSAIN AJIVIKA BAIRAGI EUCHITE VAIRAGI PANDARAM SANNYASI PASSIONIST
MENDING COBBLE
MENEL NELL
MENELAUS (BROTHER OF —) AGAMEMNON
(FATHER OF —) ATREUS PLISTHENES
(MOTHER OF —) AEROPE
(SISTER OF —) ANAXIBIA
(WIFE OF —) HELEN
MENHADEN POGY PORGY BUNKER CHEBOG SHINER ALEWIFE BUGFISH BUGHEAD CLUPEID ELLFISH FATBACK OLDWIFE SAVELHA SHADINE WHITING BONYFISH HARDHEAD
MENHIR BOUTA GORSEDD PEULVAN CATSTONE HAGIOLITH
MENIAL FAG BASE LOON PAGE KNAVE DRIVEL HARLOT POTBOY VARLET SERVILE SLAVISH BANAUSIC SCULLION SERVITOR
MENILITE OPAL
MENISCOID CRESCENT
MENNONITE HOOKER AMISHMAN AMMANITE HUTERITE
MENOETIUS (BROTHER OF —) ATLAS PROMETHEUS
(FATHER OF —) ACTOR

(MOTHER OF —) AEGINA
(SON OF —) PATROCLUS
MENOPAUSE CLIMAX
MENSTRUATE FLOW
MENSTRUATING SICK
MENSTRUATION FLOW CURSE FLUOR CRAMPS PERIOD COURSES
(FIRST —) MENARCHE
(PREF.) MENO
(SUFF.) (— CONDITION) MENIA
MENSTRUUM SOLVENT
MENTAL IDEAL GENIAL INWARD MINDLY PHRENIC PSYCHIC CEREBRAL
MENTALITY MIND SENSE ACUMEN REASON SPIRIT PSYCHISM
MENTHA LABIATE
MENTHANE TERPANE
MENTHOL CAMPHOR
MENTION CALL CITE HINT MIND MING MINT NAME CHEEP CLEPE SPEAK TOUCH MEMBER NOTICE SPEECH MEANING SPECIFY SUGGEST CITATION INSTANCE MEMORATE REHEARSE REMEMBER REFERENCE REPETITION
(— BY NAME) NEMN NEMME NEMPNE
(— CASUALLY) DROP
(— FIRST) PROMISE
(— PUBLICLY) PLUG
(HONORABLE —) ACCESSIT
MENTOR GURU TEACHER CICERONE
MENTUM PERULA
MENU CARD CARTE
(COMPUTER —) DISPLAY
MEONOTHAI (FATHER OF —) OTHNIEL
MEPACRINE ATABRIN ATABRINE
MEPERIDINE DEMEROL
MEPHIBOSHETH (BROTHER OF —) ARMONI
(FATHER OF —) SAUL JONATHAN
(MOTHER OF —) RIZPAH
(SON OF —) MICHA
MEPHISTOPHELIAN SATANIC
MEPROBAMATE MILTOWN
MERAB (FATHER OF —) SAUL
(HUSBAND OF —) ADRIEL
MERARI (FATHER OF —) LEVI
MERCAPTAN THIOL
MERCEDARIAN NOLASCAN RANSOMER
MERCENARY HACK VENAL JACKAL HESSIAN PINDARI HIRELING WAGELING
MERCER SILKMAN
MERCERIZE SCHREINER
MERCHANDISE LINE CARGO CHEAP GOODS STUFF WARES ARTWARE CHAFFER SHIPPER TRAFFIC CHAFFERY SALEWARE
(CHEAP SHODDY —) BORAX
(RETURNED —) COMEBACK
MERCHANT ARAB SETH SETT TELI WALLA BADGER BANIAN DEALER FACTOR KITELY NEPMAN RETAIL SELLER TAIPAN TRADER ANTONIO CHAPMAN GOLADAR HANSARD HOWADJI CHANDLER HUCKSTER MARCHAND POVINDAH SOUDAGUR STOREMAN
(COAL —) HOASTMAN
(GRAIN —) LAMBADI
(GREAT —) TAIPAN
(HINDU —) BUNIA BUNNIA
(WINE —) VINTNER
MERCHANT OF VENICE (AUTHOR OF —) SHAKESPEARE
(CHARACTER IN —) GOBBO TUBAL PORTIA ANTONIO JESSICA LORENZO NERISSA SALANIO SALERIO SHYLOCK BASSANIO GRATIANO LEONARDO SALARINO STEPHANO BALTHASAR LAUNCELOT
MERCIFUL KIND MILD HUMANE RUEFUL TENDER CLEMENT LENIENT MILDFUL PITIFUL SPARING GRACIOUS QUEMEFUL
MERCILESS GRIM CRUEL SHARP BLOODY FIERCE SAVAGE WANTON PITILESS
MERCURY HG AZOCH AZOTH DRAGON HERMES SPIRIT CHIBRIT MARKERY TEUTATES QUICKSILVER
(FATHER OF —) JUPITER
(MOTHER OF —) MAIA
MERCY LAW ORE HORE PITY RUTH GRACE GRITH BLITHE LENITY CHARITY QUARTER CLEMENCY LENIENCY COMPASSION
(— TO ANTAGONIST) QUARTER
(PREF.) MISERI
MERE BARE NUDE ONLY PURE PUTE SOLE VERY NAKED SHEER SINGLE
(PREF.) PSIL(O)
MEREL PIN
MERELY BUT JUST ONLY BARELY PURELY SIMPLY SINGLY SOLELY ALONELY UTTERLY ENTIRELY SCARCELY
MEREMOTH (FATHER OF —) BANI URIAH
MERETRICIOUS CHEAP GAUDY GILDED TAWDRY PUNKISH
MERGANSER SMEE SMEW HARLE SNOWL SPIKE HERALD SAWNEB WEASER BRACKET GARBILL JACKSAW RANTOCK SAWBILL TADPOLE TOWHEAD TWEEZER WHEEZER EARLDUCK MOSSHEAD SHELDRAKE
MERGE FUSE JOIN MELD SINK BLEND ENTER GLIDE UNIFY UNITE VERGE MINGLE COALESCE COMMERGE CONFLATE LIQUESCE
MERGING BLEND FUSION
MERICARP COCCUS
MERIDIAN (THOSE LIVING UNDER SAME —) ANTOECI
MERIDIONAL NOON NOONTIDE
MERINGUE KISS
MERINO DELAINE
MERISTEM PERIBLEM
MERIT DUE EARN MEED PUNY BROOK FOUND THANK WORTH DESERT PRAISE VIRTUE WRIHTE DEMERIT DESERVE PUDDING
(— CONSIDERATION) COUNT
(POSSESSING —) WORTHY
MERITED JUST
(NOT —) INDIGN
MERITOCRACY ELITE
MERITORIOUS CAPITAL MERITORY THANKFUL VALOROUS
MERL BLACKIE
MERLIN (MISTRESS OF —) VIVIAN VIVIEN
MERLON COP
MERMAID ARIEL NIXIE SIREN MERROW MERWOMAN
MERMAN SEAMAN MANFISH
MERODACH (FATHER OF —) EA
(WIFE OF —) ZARPAINT
MEROPE (BROTHER OF —) PHAETHON
(FATHER OF —) ATLAS OENOPION PANDAREUS CRESPHONTES
(HUSBAND OF —) POLYBUS SISYPHUS POLYPHONTES
(MOTHER OF —) PLEIONE CYPSELUS HARMOTHOE
(SISTER OF —) AEDON CLEOTHERA
(SON OF —) AEPYTUS
MEROPODITE FEMUR MEROS
MEROZOITE AGAMETE
MERRILY GAILY GAMELY LIGHTLY LUSTICK JOYOUSLY
MERRIMENT FUN JOY GALE GLEE JEST UTAS DERAY MIRTH FROLIC SPLEEN DAFFERY DAFFING FESTIVE JOLLITY WAGGERY HILARITY
MERRY GAY BOON CANT GLAD GOLE BONNY BUXOM CADGY CRANK DROLL JOLLY LIGHT LUSTY MURRY SUNNY VOGIE VOKIE BLITHE COCKET FROLIC JOCANT JOCOSE JOCUND JOVIAL JOYOUS LIVELY FEASTLY GLEEFUL HOLIDAY JOCULAR LUSTICK RAFFING WINSOME CHIRPING DISPOSED FESTIVAL GAMESOME GLEESOME LAUGHING PLEASANT SPANKING SPORTFUL SPORTIVE CONVIVIAL
(RIOTOUSLY —) SATURNALIAN
(UNREASONABLY —) DAFT
MERRY-ANDREW AIRY ZANY ANTIC DROLL JESTER BUFFOON
MERRY-GO-ROUND CAROUSEL TURNABOUT ROUNDABOUT
MERRYMAKING ALE MAY RAG KIRN PLOY REVEL GAIETY JUNKET RACKET SPLORE WHOOPEE CARNIVAL FESTIVITY
MERRYTHOUGHT WISHBONE
MERRY WIDOW (CHARACTER IN —) ZETA HANNA MIRKO DANILO GLAWARI
(COMPOSER OF —) LEHAR
MERRY WIVES OF WINDSOR
(AUTHOR OF —) SHAKESPEARE
(CHARACTER IN —) NYM ANNE FORD HUGH JOHN PAGE CAIUS EVANS ROBIN RUGBY FENTON PISTOL SIMPLE QUICKLY SHALLOW SLENDER WILLIAM BARDOLPH FALSTAFF
MERUS PALM
MESA HILL LOMA BENCH MESILLA PLATEAU TERRACE CARTOUCH
MESADENIA CACALIA
MESCAL PEYOTE PEYOTL WOKOWI MEXICAL CHALLOTE
MESCALERO FARAON
MESECH (FATHER OF —) JAPHET
MESENTERY CROW RUFFLE
MESH NET MASK MOKE CHAIN PITCH SHALE ACCRUE ENGAGE MASCLE SCREEN INTERLOCK SCREENING
(— IMPROPERLY) BUTT
(IN —) DIRECT
MESHA (FATHER OF —) CALEB SHAHARAIM
(MOTHER OF —) HODESH
MESHED ENGAGED
MESHEZABEEL (FATHER OF —) ZERAH
(SON OF —) PETHAHIAH
MESHILLEMOTH (FATHER OF —) IMMER
MESHULLAM (FATHER OF —) BERECHIAH BESODEIAH ZERUBBABEL
(SON OF —) SALLU
MESHULLEMETH (FATHER OF —) HARUZ
(HUSBAND OF —) MANASSEH
(SON OF —) AMON
MESOCARP FLESH
MESOMORPHIC SOMAL SOMATIC ATHLETIC
MESON RHO KAON MUON PION OMEGA BARYTRON MESOTRON
MESOPODIUM PETIOLE
MESOPOTAMIA (— REGION) SUMER
(TREE OF —) HOMA
MESOTONIC TERTIAN MEANTONE
MESQUITE HONEY KEAWE PACAY CASHAW ALGAROBA HONEYPOD IRONWOOD MOSQUITO
MESS JAG JAM MIX MUX PIE SOP CLAT FIST HASH JAMB MUCK MULL MUSS SLUB SOSS STEW SUSS BOTCH CAUCH JAKES STREW SWILL BOLLIX BUNGLE CADDLE CLATCH JUMBLE MUCKER PICKLE PUDDLE SOZZLE TUMBLE EYESORE MAMMOCK MULLOCK SCAMBLE SLOTTER COUSCOUS DISORDER LOBLOLLY SHAMBLES SLAISTER
(— AROUND) JUKE
(— OF FOOD) SAND
(— OVER) ABUSE
(GREASY —) GAUM
(SLOPPY —) SLOBBER SLAISTER
(WATERY —) SLOSH
MESSAGE CHIT MODE SAND SEND WIRE WORD RUMOR TELEX BREVET CIPHER ERRAND GOSPEL LETTER SCROLL BLINKER BODWORD DEPECHE EMBASSY MISSION SENDING TIDINGS AEROGRAM CREDENCE DISPATCH GRAFFITO MAILGRAM VOICEMAIL
(— BY FLAGS) HOIST
(— FROM GOD) ANGEL
(CHRISTIAN —) EVANGEL
(CIPHER —) SCYTALE
(COMPLIMENTARY —) RECADO
(INDICATING — IS RECEIVED) WILCO
(SECRET —) PRIVATE
(SEND —) TELEX
(SEQUENCE OF —S) QUEUE
MESSALIAN EUCHITE
MESSENE (FATHER OF —) TRIOPAS
(HUSBAND OF —) POLYCAON

MESSENGER BODE PEON POST SAND SEND TOTY VAUX ANGEL ENVOY MUMMU VISOR BEADLE BROKER BUNENE CHIAUS HERALD LEGATE NUNCIO PIGEON RUNNER APOSTLE CARRIER CASHBOY CONTACT COURANT COURIER EXPRESS FORAGER FORAYER MALACHI MERCURY MESSAGE MISSIVE NAMTARU PATAMAR TOTYMAN TROTTER TRUMPET EMISSARY FOREGOER HIRCARRA LOBBYGOW NUNCIATE ORDINARY PORTATOR APPARITOR
(— OF APSU AND TIAMAT) MUMMU
(— OF GOD) ANGEL
(— OF SHAMASH) BUNENE
(— OF THE GODS) HERMES MERCURY
(MOUNTED —) COSSID ESTAFET
(RELIGIOUS —) APOSTLE
(UNDERWORLD —) NAMTARU
MESSIAH CHRIST WOVOKA
(MUSLIM —) MAHDI
MESSINESS YUCK
MESSMATE YUBA
MESSUAGE HAW TOFT MEESE MIDSTEAD
MESSY GOOEY SLOPPY SOZZLY STICKY
MESTIZO CHOLO LADINO CURIBOCA MAMELUCO
MESTOR (DAUGHTER OF —) HIPPOTHOE
(FATHER OF —) PERSEUS
(MOTHER OF —) ANDROMEDA
(WIFE OF —) LYSIDICE
METAL ORE TIN BODY DIET GOLD IRON LEAD ZINC BARIUM CESIUM CHROME COBALT COPPER INDIUM LATTIN NICKEL ORMOLU OSMIUM RADIUM SILVER SODIUM BISMUTH CADMIUM CALCIUM HAFNIUM IRIDIUM LITHIUM MERCURY RHENIUM RHODIUM THORIUM TUTANIA URANIUM YTTRIUM ALUMINUM ANTIMONY CHROMIUM DEADHEAD PLATINUM RUBIDIUM SCANDIUM TANTALUM TINCTURE TITANIUM TUNGSTEN VANADIUM
(— IN MASS) BULLION
(— IN PLATES) LATTEN
(— IN SHEETS) LEAF PLATE
(— STRIP) SPLINE
(BABBITT —) LINING
(BASE —) BILLON
(COARSE —) MATTE
(DECORATED —) TOLE
(GROUND —) BRONZING
(HEAVIEST —) OSMIUM
(IMPURE MASS OF —) REGULUS
(LIGHTEST —) LITHIUM
(LIQUID —) MERCURY
(MASS OF —) INGOT
(MOLTEN —) TAP SQUIRT
(OLD POT —) POTIN
(ORNAMENTED —) NIELLO
(PERFORATED —) STENCIL
(PIECE OF CRUDE —) SLUG
(POINTED —) NAIL
(POROUS —) SPONGE
(PRECIOUS —) ORE GOLD PLATE SILVER PLATINUM
(SEMIFINISHED —) SEMIS
(SHEET —) LATTEN DOUBLES KALAMEIN
(TYPE —) QUAD QUADRAT
(UNREFINED —) PIGIRON
(WASTE —) GATE SPRUE
METALLIC HARD THIN TINNY
METALLOPHONE SARON
(BALINESE —) GANGSA
METALLURGIST AMERICAN HUNT HOLLEY PETERS SHIMER
ENGLISH PERCY MUSHET THOMAS HADFIELD
FRENCH HEROULT
METALOPHONE (BALINESE —) GANGSA
METALWARE TOLE LORMERY GRAYWARE PONTYPOOL
METALWORK ZOGAN
METALWORKER BARMAN FOONER FORKMAN FOUNDER SUDSMAN
METAMERE SOMITE SEGMENT MEROSOME
METAMERIC SEGMENTAL
METAMORPHIC
(PREF.) BLAST(O)
METAMORPHOSE TURN SHAPE INDENIZE TRANSMEW
METAMORPHOSIS METABOLE PETALODY PHYLLODY SEPALODY
(SUFF.) ODY
METANIRA (HUSBAND OF —) CELEUS
(SON OF —) DEMOPHON TRIPTOLEMUS
METAPHOR IMAGE TROPE FIGURE KENNING
METAPHORICAL FIGURAL FIGURATE TROPICAL
METASTOMA LABIUM
METATE QUERL
METE DEAL DOLE GIVE ALLOT AWARD MATCH SERVE MEASURE APPORTION
METEMPSYCHOSIS SAMSARA
METEOR STAR ARGID CETID COMID DRAKE LUPID LYRID URSID ANTLID AUGUST BOLIDE BOOTID CORVID CYGNID DRAGON HYDRID LEONID LIBRID LYNCID LYRAID PHASMA PISCID TAURID AQUARID AQUILID ARIETID AURIGID CAMELID CANCRID CEPHEID CORONID GEMINID MEATURE ORIONID PEGASID PERSEID POLARID PRODIGY COLUMBID CRATERID DRACONID ERIDANID FIREBALL FORNAXID HERCULID LACERTID SAGITTID SCORPIID SHOTSTAR TOUCANID VIRGINID
(SUFF.) ID
METEORITE BAETYL BOLIDE ANDRITE ATAXITE EUCRITE AEROLITE AEROLITH BAETULUS BAETYLUS IREOLITE SIDERITE SKYSTONE
METEOROLOGIST AMERICAN EDDY ESPY WARD ROTCH FERREL MARVIN CLAYTON REDFIELD CARPENTER
AUSTRIAN FALB HANN PERNTER
ENGLISH REID SHAW DINES GALTON GLAISHER
FRENCH MOREUX PELTIER
GERMAN DOVE FICKER WEGENER BRUCKNER NEUMAYER
NORWEGIAN MOHN SVERDRUP
RUSSIAN TILLO
SCOTTISH MILL BUCHAN
SWEDISH MALMGREN
SWISS WILD DELUC
METEOROLOGY AEROLOGY
METER IONIC METRE SEVEN ALCAIC RHYTHM CADENCE GAYATRI MEASURE SUBMETER VIAMETER YAWMETER
(CUBIC —) STERE
(MILLIONTH OF —) MICRON
(NETHERLANDS —) ELL
(SQUARE —) ARE CENTIARE
(VEDIC —) GAYATRI
(10,000 —S) GREX
(10 CUBIC —S) DEKASTERE
METHADONE AMIDONE
METHANE FORMENE
METHANOL WOODINE CARBINOL
METHAQUALINE QUAALUDE
METHEGLIN MEAD
METHOD ART WAY DART FORM GARB GATE KINK LINE MIDS MODE REDE RULE SORT ORDER STYLE TRACK USAGE COURSE ENGINE MANNER STEREO SYSTEM FASHION PROCESS TACTICS WRINKLE ADJUVANT STANDARD
(— OF ANGLING) HARLING
(— OF APPEALING) DHARNA DHURNA
(— OF COLORING TEA) FACING
(— OF CONSTRUCTION) JACAL
(— OF CULTIVATION) JUM JOOM STUMPING
(— OF DIETING) BANTING
(— OF DISTILLATION) DESCENT
(— OF ELECTION) SCRUTINY
(— OF FATTENING POULTRY) GAVAGE
(— OF INDUCTION) CANON
(— OF INSTRUCTION) SCHOOL
(— OF INVESTIGATION) ORGANON ORGANUM
(— OF MILKING) NIEVLING
(— OF MURAL DECORATION) KHASI
(— OF PROCEDURE) GAME
(— OF SELECTING POPE) SCRUTINY
(— OF TRACKING) DOVAP
(— OF TREATMENT) SCOPE
(CLEVER —) KINK KINKLE
(FIXED —) FORMULA
(MEDICAL —) CUSHION
(OUTMODED —) ARCHAISM
(PAINTING —) GOUACHE
(PRINTING —) AQUATONE
(SCIENTIFIC —) BACONISM
(SURVEYING —) STADIA
(USUAL —) COURSE PRACTICE
METHODICAL TRIG EXACT FORMAL SEVERE ORDERLY REGULAR ORDINARY ORDINATE
METHODIST JUMPER WESLEYAN SWADDLING
METHODIZE ORDER REGULATE
METHODOLOGY TECHNIC
METHUSAEL (FATHER OF —) MEHUJAEL
(SON OF —) LAMECH
METHUSELAH (FATHER OF —) ENOCH
METHYLAL FORMAL
METICULOUS FUSSY NARROW STICKY CAREFUL FINICAL FINICKY PARTICULAR
METION (BROTHER OF —) CECROPS
(FATHER OF —) ERECHTHEUS
(MOTHER OF —) PRAXITHEA
METONYM SYNONYM
METRICAL MEASURED
(— QUANTITY) MATRA
METRICS PROSODY
METRONOME (PART OF —) BOX KEY CASE PIVOT SCALE SHAFT WEIGHT PENDULUM
METROPOLIS CITY SEAT CAPITAL
METROPOLITAN EPARCH EXARCH
METTLE PITH SAUL PRIDE SPUNK GINGER SPIRIT COURAGE SMEDDUM
METTLESOME FIERY PROUD SKEIGH SPUNKY STUFFY FLIGHTY GINGERY SPIRITED
MEUSE
(PREF.)
(RIVER —) MOSA
MEW PEN WOW CAGE CAST COOP GULL MEWL MOLT SHED MEUTE MIAOU MIAOW SEAGULL HIDEAWAY INTERMEW SEEDBIRD CONFINEMENT
MEWER WRAWLER
MEWL WRAWL
MEWS ALLEY COURT STREET STABLES
MEXICAN AZTEC
(AMERICAN OF — DESCENT) CHICANO
MEXICAN-AMERICAN PACHUCO
MEXICAN ELM MEZCAL
MEXICAN ONYX TECALI
MEXICAN PERSIMMON CHAPOTE
MEXICAN POPPY ARGEMONE
MEXICAN TEA BASOTE APASOTE FISHWEED WORMSEED

MEXICO

CAPITAL: MEXICOCITY
COIN: PESO TLAC ADOBE CLACO TLACO AZTECA CENTAVO PIASTER
LAKE: CHAPALA
MEASURE: PIE VARA ALMUD BARIL JARRA LABOR LEGUA LINEA SITIO FANEGA PULGADA
MOUNTAIN: BUFA BLANCO CUPULA PEROTE ORIZABA
PENINSULA: BAJA YUCATAN
PEOPLE: MAM CHOL CORA MAYA MIXE PIMA SERI TECO XOVA AZTEC NAHUA OPATA OTOMI ZOQUE EUDEVE MIXTEC TOLTEC NAYARIT TEPANEC TOTONAC ZACATEC ZAPOTEC TEZCUCAN TOTONACO ZACATECO
RIVER: BRAVO LERMA BALSAS GRANDE PANUCO TABASCO GRIJALVA SANTIAGO
STATE: LEON NUEVO COLIMA

OAXACA SONORA CHIAPAS DURANGO HIDALGO NAYARIT SINALOA TABASCO YUCATAN CAMPECHE QUINTANA VERACRUZ
TOWN: LEON LAPAZ TEPIC ARIZPE COLIMA JALAPA JUAREZ MERIDA OAXACA PARRAL POTOSI PUEBLA CANANEA DURANGO GUAYMAS MORELIA ORIZABA PACHUCA TAMPICO TORREON CULIACAN ENSENADA MAZATLAN MONCLOVA SALTILLO TLAXCALA VERACRUZ
VOLCANO: COLIMA TOLUCA JORULLO PARICUTIN POPOCATEPETL
WEIGHT: BAG ONZA CARGA LIBRA MARCO ADARME ARROBA OCHAVA TERCIO QUINTAL

MEZAHAB (DAUGHTER OF —) MATRED
MEZEREON DAPHNE
MEZZANINE ENTRESOL
MIAO HMONG
MIAROLITIC DRUSY
MIASMA REEK MALARIA MAREMMA
MIB MIGGLE
MIBSAM (FATHER OF —) SIMEON ISHMAEL
MICA DAZE TALC GLIST SLUDE BIOTITE GLIMMER ALURGITE FUCHSITE PHENGITE MUSCOVITE PHLOGOPITE
MICAH (FATHER OF —) UZZIEL MERIBBAAL
(SON OF —) ABDON
MICAH CLARKE (AUTHOR OF —) DOYLE
(CHARACTER IN —) JACOB MICAH SAXON CLANCY CLARKE GERVAS JOSEPH REUBEN DECIMUS STEPHEN LOCKARBY MONMOUTH TIMEWELL
MICAIAH (FATHER OF —) IMLAH
MICE (BREEDING PLACE FOR —) MURARIUM
MICHA (FATHER OF —) MEPHIBOSHETH
(SON OF —) MATTANIAH
MICHAEL MIKE MICKY MICHEL MIGUEL
(FATHER OF —) IZRAHIAH JEHOSHAPHAT
(SLAYER OF —) JEHORAM
(SON OF —) OMRI SETHUR
MICHAH (FATHER OF —) UZZIEL
MICHAIAH (FATHER OF —) URIEL GEMARIAH
(HUSBAND OF —) REHOBOAM
(SON OF —) ABIJAH
MICHAL (FATHER OF —) SAUL
(HUSBAND OF —) DAVID PHALTI

MICHIGAN

BAY: SAGINAW THUNDER KEWEENAW STURGEON
CAPITAL: LANSING
COLLEGE: ALMA WAYNE ADRIAN ALBION CALVIN OLIVET OWOSSO OAKLAND
COUNTY: BAY CASS IRON LUCE CLARE DELTA IONIA IOSCO ALCONA OCEANA OGEMAW OSCODA OTSEGO GOGEBIC OSCEOLA TUSCOLA KALKASKA
INDIAN: OTTAWA
LAKE: BURT TORCH HOUGHTON
MOUNTAIN: CURWOOD
NATIVE: WOLVERINE
NICKNAME: LAKE WOLVERINE
RIVER: CASS BRULE HURON DETROIT SAGINAW STCLAIR ESCANABA MONTREAL MENOMINEE
STATE BIRD: ROBIN
STATE FLOWER: APPLEBLOSSOM
STRAIT: MACKINAC
TOWN: MIO ALMA CARO HART FLINT IONIA LANSE ADRIAN ALPENA BADAXE OWOSSO PAWPAW WARREN DETROIT LANSING LIVONIA PONTIAC SAGINAW ANNARBOR CADILLAC ESCANABA KALKASKA MANISTEE MUNISING MUSKEGON CHEBOYGAN KALAMAZOO

MICIPSA (FATHER OF —) MASINISSA
MICONIA TAMONEA
MICOPLASMA PPLO
MICROBAR BARYE
MICROBE GERM
MICROBIOLOGIST AMERICAN NATHAN
FRENCH LWOFF
SWISS ARBER
MICROCEPHALIC PINHEAD
MICROFICHE FICHE FILMCARD
MICROFILM COM
(SHEET OF —) FICHE
MICROMETER MU BIFILAR
(— CALIPER) MIKE
MICRON MU
MICRONESIA (CAPITAL:) PALIKIR
(COIN:) DOLLAR
(ISLAND:) KOSRAE ULITHI WOLEAI POHNPEI MORTLOCK
(PEOPLE:) TRUKESE POHNPEIAN
(STATE:) YAP CHUNK KOSRAE POHNPEI
(TOWN:) TOL WENU
MICRONESIAN KANAGA NAURUAN
(— ISLAND) NUI GUAM ROTA TRUK MAKIN NAURU WOTHO MAJURO
MICROORGANISM BUG GERM AZOFIER BUTYRIC MICROBE BACILLUS MYCOPLASMA
MICROPHONE BUG MIKE PARABOLA
(KIND OF —) LAVALIERE
(REMOVE CONCEALED —) DEBUG
(SHIELD FOR —) GOBO
MICROPYLE FORAMEN
MICROSCOPE GLASS SCOPE
(PART OF —) ARM BASE CLIP KNOB LENS LIMB TUBE STAGE FILTER HOLDER APERTURE EYEPIECE CONDENSER DIAPHRAGM NOSEPIECE OBJECTIVE ADJUSTMENT
MICROSCOPIC SMALL MINUTE
MICROSECOND (HUNDREDTH OF —) SHAKE
MICROSPECIES JORDANON
MICROSPOROPHYLL STAMEN
MICROTONE SRUTI SHRUTI
MICROTUS ARVICOLA
MICROWAVE ZAP NUKE
MIDBRAIN MESENCEPHALON
MIDDAY NOON UNDERN MIDNOON NOONDAY MERIDIAN NOONTIME
MIDDEN BASURAL SAMBAQUI
MIDDLE MEDIO MESNE NAVEL CENTER MEDIAL MEDIAN MESIAL CENTRAL MEDIATE MEDILLE
(— OF SAIL) BUNT
(— OF SHIP) WAIST
(— OF WINTER) HOLL HOWE
(— WAY) VIAMEDIA
(PREF.) MEDI(O) MES(O) MESIO MEZZO
MIDDLE-AGED MIDDLING
MIDDLE EAST (— NATIVE) WOG
MIDDLEMAN BUTTY BROKER DEALER FOGGER JOBBER LUMPER BUMAREE BUMMAREE BUTTYMAN HUCKSTER REGRATER
MIDDLEMARCH (AUTHOR OF —) ELIOT
(CHARACTER IN —) FRED TYKE WILL CALEB CELIA GARTH JAMES RIGGS VINCY BROOKE EDWARD JOSHUA CHETTAM LYDGATE RAFFLES TERTIUS CASAUBON DOROTHEA LADISLAW NICHOLAS ROSAMOND BULSTRODE FEATHERSTONE
MIDDLER PLATEMAN
MIDDLETONE HALFTONE
MIDDLING FAIR MEAN SOSO NEUTRAL MEDIOCRE MEETERLY
(PL.) DUNST FARINA SHARPS SIZINGS SEMOLINA WEATINGS
MIDGE GNAT SMUT PUNKY MIDGET MINGIE PUNKIE WEEVIL
MIDIAN (FATHER OF —) ABRAHAM
(MOTHER OF —) KETURAH
MIDMOST
(PREF.) MESATI
MIDNIGHT NOON NOONTIDE
MIDPOINT BASION PORION STOMION GNATHION
MIDRIB COSTA SHAFT MIDVEIN
(— OF LEAF) PEN
MIDRIFF APRON SKIRT
(PREF.) PHREN(O)
MIDSHIPMAN WART MIDDY PLEBE REEFER SNOTTY OLDSTER
MIDST DEPTH CENTER MIDDLE MIDWARD
(PREF.) **(IN THE —)** INTER
MIDSUMMER DAY JOHNSMAS
MIDSUMMER NIGHT'S DREAM
(AUTHOR OF —) SHAKESPEARE
(CHARACTER IN —) MOTH PUCK SNUG EGEUS FLUTE SNOUT BOTTOM COBWEB HELENA HERMIA OBERON QUINCE THESEUS TITANIA LYSANDER DEMETRIUS HIPPOLYTA STARVELING MUSTARDSEED PHILOSTRATE PEASEBLOSSOM
MIDWAY MEDIO GAYWAY HALFWAY
MIDWIFE BABA DHAI GAMP HOWDY LUCKY COMMER CUMMER GRANNY HOWDIE KIMMER LUCINA LUCKIE GRANNIE HEBAMME
MIEN AIR BROW PORT VULT ALLURE ASPECT DEMEAN MANNER OSTENT BEARING DEMEANOR PORTANCE
MIFF TICKOFF
MIFFED IRKED
MIG MIB DUCK
MIGHT ARM BULK MOTE FORCE MOUND POWER SHOULD STRENGTH
(PREF.) CRATO
MIGHTILY HEFTILY
MIGHTINESS (HIGH —) HOGEN
MIGHTY FELL HIGH KEEN MAIN MUCH RANK RICH VAST FELON GREAT HEFTY STERN STOOR POTENT STRONG VIOLENT ENORMOUS FORCEFUL POWERFUL PUISSANT SAMSONIC
(PREF.) DEIN(O) DIN(O) MEG(A)(AL)(ALO)
MIGNON (CHARACTER IN —) MIGNON MEISTER SPERATA WILHELM LOTHARIO
(COMPOSER OF —) THOMAS
MIGNONETTE WELD WOLD RESEDA LUTEOLA
MIGRAINE MEGRIM
MIGRANT MOVER
MIGRATE RUN FLIT TREK DRIFT FLIGHT COLONIZE
MIGRATION TREK EXODUS FLIGHT EELFARE EMOTION PASSAGE DIASPORA
MIGRATORY PEREGRINE
(NOT —) RESIDENT SEDENTARY
MIKADO DAIRI
MIKIR ARLENG
MIKLOTH (FATHER OF —) JEHIEL
(MOTHER OF —) MAACHAH
MILCAH (FATHER OF —) HARAN ZELOPHEHAD
(HUSBAND OF —) NAHOR
MILD LEW MOY CALM COLD EASY FAIR LENT MEEK NESH PLUM SOFT TAME WARM BALMY BLAND BUXOM GREEN LIGHT LITHE MELCH MELSH MILKY NAISH QUIET BENIGN FACILE GENIAL GENTLE HUMBLE KINDLY REMISS SMOOTH AFFABLE AMIABLE CLEMENT LENIENT SARSNET VELVETY BENEDICT DOVELIKE FAVONIAN LENITIVE MERCIFUL SARCENET SARSENET SOOTHING TRANQUIL
(— CLOSELY) JIB
(PREF.) LENI
MILDEW OIDIUM
MILDLY FEEBLY GENTLY
MILDNESS MILD LENITY SUAVITY CLEMENCY HUMILITY KINDNESS
MILE (GO —S) DEGREE
(NAUTICAL —) KNOT KAIRI
(ONE-EIGHTH —) FURLONG
(SEA —) NAUT
(SIXTY —S) DEGREE
(THIRD —) LI
(3 —S) HOUR LEAGUE
MILESTONE MILLIARY
MILETUS (FATHER OF —) APOLLO
(MOTHER OF —) ARIA DEIONE
(SON OF —) BYBLIS CAUNUS
(WIFE OF —) CYANEE
MILFOIL AHARTALAV
MILIEU CLIMATE TERRAIN AMBIENCE

MILITANT WARRISH FIGHTING
(ONE WITH — ATTITUDE) HAWK
MILITARISTIC PRUSSIAN
MILITARY MARTIAL WARLIKE MILITANT SOLDIERY
(— OBJECTS) MILITARIA
(— POST) THANA
(— SCIENCE) LOGISTICS
MILITIA FYRD ARRAY MILICE
MILITIAMAN CHOCO UHLAN LUMPER TRAINER FENCIBLE SHIRTMAN
(TURKISH —) TIMARIOT
MILK COW LAC FUZZ LAIT PAIL SKIM BLEED JUICE MILCH MULCT BOTTLE ELICIT RAMMEL STROKE SUCKLE EXPLOIT
(— CLOSELY) JIB
(— DRY) STRIP
(— OUT) EMULGE
(— PAN) LEAD
(— PRODUCT) KHOA
(— SICKNESS) TIRES
(BREAST —) SUCK DIDDY
(COW'S —) MESS
(CURDLED —) SKYR TYRE TAYER LOPPER CLABBER TATMJOLK
(FERMENTED —) KUMISS MATZOON
(NEW —) RAMMEL
(PINT OF —) PINTA
(SOUR —) SKYR WHIG BONNY BLEEZE BLINKY CLABBER JOCOQUE
(WATERY —) BLASH
(PREF.) GALACT(O) LACT(I)(O)
(SUFF.) GALACTIA
MILK CART KIT PRAM BUNGEY
MILKFISH AWA BANGOS SABALO SAVOLA BANDENG SABALOTE
MILKING (— PARLOR) BAIL
(— TIME) MEAL
MILKLESS PARVE PAREVE
MILKMAN KITTER CHALKER
MILK PAIL TRUG LEGLEN
MILK SHAKE FRAPPE
MILK SNAKE ADDER
MILKSOP SOP MOLLY SISSY COCKNEY MEACOCK
MILK-SUGAR LACTOSE
MILKWEED ANGLEPOD
MILKWOOD MELKHOUT
MILKWORT SENECA SENEGA CENTAURY GAYWINGS POLYGALA
MILKY MILCHY LACTARY LACTEAL OPALOID LACTEOUS
MILKY WAY GALAXY
(PREF.) GALACT(O)
MILL FULL MILN REED STAR BREAK FLOUR KNURL QUERN CHERRY FANNER STAMPS BLOOMER MOLINET PUGMILL SMUTTER ARRASTRA ARRASTRE BUHRMILL SPINNERY TRAPICHE WALKMILL
(CHOCOLATE —) MOLINET
(FULLING —) STOCKS
(SHINGLING —) FORGE
(SUGAR —) CENTRAL TRAPICHE
(PREF.) MOLARI MYL(O)
MILLBOARD TARBOARD
MILLDAM WEIR WARREN WARRANT
MILLED GRAINED
MILLENARIAN CHILIAST
MILLENIUM CHILIAD
MILLER MILLMAN STOCKER MULTURER NILLWARD
MILLER'S-THUMB BLOB CULL CABOT CHABOT COTTOID MUDDLER BULLHEAD
MILLET BUDA KODA KOUS MOHA ARZUN BAJRA CHENA CUMBU DUKHN DURRA GRAIN HIRSE KODRA MILLY PANIC PROSO TENAI WHISK BAJREE DHURRA HUREEK JONDLA JOWARI MILIUM RAGGEE DAGASSA PANICLE ZABURRO BIRDSEED KADIKANE
(PREF.) MILIO
MILLHAND CROPMAN
MILLIGRAM (200 —S) CARAT
MILLILITER MIL
MILLIMETER LI
(THOUSANDTH OF —) MICRON
MILLINER ARTISTE MODISTE
MILLING GRAINING
MILLION CONTO QUENT
(THOUSAND —S) GILLION MILLIARD
(10 —) CRORE
(1000 —) MILLIARD
(PL.) GUPPY
(PREF.) MEGA
MILLIONTH
(PREF.)
(ONE —) MICR(O)
MILLIPEDE JULID POLYPOD DIPLOPOD PILLWORM RINGWORM WIREWORM
MILLISECOND SIGMA
MILL ON THE FLOSS (AUTHOR OF —) ELIOT
(CHARACTER IN —) BOB TOM KENN LUCY DEANE GLEGG GUEST JAKIN WAKEM MAGGIE PHILIP PULLET STEPHEN STELLING TULLIVER
MILLPOND DAM MILLDAM BINNACLE MILLPOOL
MILLRACE LADE LEAD LEAT FOREBAY TAILRACE MILLSTREAM
MILLRYND INK
MILLSTONE RYND STONE BEDDER LEDGER LIGGER RUNNER
(LOWER —) METATE
(UPPER —) MANO
(PL.) RUN
MILLSTREAM DAM LADE FLEAM
MILLWORKER DOGGER
MILO SORGHUM
MILPA LADANG
MILQUETOAST CASPAR
MILT MILK SEED SPLEEN
MILTONIST DIVORCER
MIMAS (FATHER OF —) THEANO
(MOTHER OF —) AMYCUS
(SLAYER OF —) MEZENTIUS
MIME ACTOR MIMER MIMIC
(PL.) MIMIAMBI
MIMEOGRAPH RONEO
MIMIC APE HIT COPY ECHO MIME MINT MOCK ECHOER MOCKER MONKEY BUFFOON COPYCAT IMITATE PAGEANT
(PREF.) MIM(EO)(O)
MIMICKING TAKEOFF SIMULANT IMITATIVE
MIMICRY APERY MIMESIS MOCKAGE MOCKERY
MIMOSA AROMA ACACIA CASSIE ALBIZZIA HUISACHE TURMERIC
MINCE CHOP SHEAR FINICK
MINCED HACHE
MINCEMEAT GIGOT MINCE
MINCING NIMINY FINICAL MINIKIN MIGNIARD SKIPJACK
MINCINGLY FINE GINGERLY
MIND CIT CHIT HEAD HEED LOAF MOOD NOTE NOUS OBEY RECK SOUL BESEE BRAIN PHREN SENSE SKULL WATCH ANIMUS MATTER NOTICE PSYCHE REGARD COURAGE SENSORY SUBJECT THINKER THOUGHT
(CONSCIOUS —) SENTIENT
(INFINITE —) GOD
(RIGHT FRAME OF —) TUNE
(STATE OF —) BAG
(YEAR'S —) MINNING
(PREF.) MENTI NOO PHREN(O) PSYCH(O)
(SUFF.) **(CONDITION OF —)** THYMIA
MINDFUL HEEDY MINDLY HEEDFUL OBSERVANT
MIND READER MENTALIST
MINE BAL DIG PIT DELF HOLE HUEL MEUM BARGH DELFT DELPH METAL STOPE WHEAL COYOTE GOPHER GROOVE RESCUE BONANZA BORASCA COALPIT MINERAL OPENCUT TORPEDO GOLCONDA MYNPACHT PROSPECT
(— BY BLASTING) SHOOT
(— IRREGULARLY) GOPHER
(— PASSAGE) SLUM
(COAL —) ROB COALPIT COLLIERY
(KIND OF —) CLAYMORE
(MILITARY —) FOUGADE FOUGASSE CAMOUFLET
(OLD —) GWAG
(RICH —) GOLCONDA
(TIN —) STANNARY
(UNPRODUCTIVE —) DUFFER SHICER BORASCA
MINER PECK PICK PYKE BARER DOGGY ARTIST BUCKER CUTTER DAMMER DELVER DIGGER GANGER GETTER HAGGER JUMPER MATTER PELTER REEFER SNIPER STOPER TINNER TOPMAN VANNER COLLIER CRUTTER DIRGLER FEIGHER GEORDIE GROOVER HITCHER HUTCHER LEADMAN PICKMAN PIKEMAN PIONEER PLUGMAN ROCKMAN SNUBBER ENTRYMAN HEADSMAN STRIPPER WINZEMAN
(— WHO WORKS ALONE) HATTER
MINERAL JET GEET HOST MINE SPAR TALC BERYL BLOOM EARTH EMERY FLUOR GLEBE GUEST LENAD SQUAT TRONA ACMITE ALAITE AUGITE BARITE BARYTE BLENDE CASTOR CERITE COCKLE CURITE DAVYNE EGERAN EHLITE ERRITE GALENA GARNET GLANCE GYPSUM HALITE HAUYNE HELVIN HUMITE ILLITE IOLITE LABITE MIXITE NATRON NOSEAN NOSITE PINITE RUTILE SALITE SILICA SPHENE SPINEL ADAMINE ADAMITE ADELITE ALTAITE ALUMITE ALUNITE AMOSITE ANATASE APATITE ATOPITE AXINITE AZORITE AZULITE AZURITE BAUXITE BAZZITE BELLITE BIOTITE BISMITE BITYITE BOHMITE BOLEITE BORNITE BRUCITE CALCITE CELSIAN CYANITE DIAMOND DICKITE DUFTITE EDENITE EPIDOTE ERIKITE ERINITE EUCLASE FLOKITE GAGEITE GAHNITE GEDRITE GLADITE GOTHITE GUMMITE HELVITE HESSITE HOPEITE HOWLITE HULSITE IHLEITE ILVAITE INESITE INYOITE ISERITE JADEITE JARLITE JOSEITE KEMPITE KERNITE KOPPITE KOTOITE KYANITE LANGITE LARNITE LAURITE LAUTITE LEHIITE LEIFITE LEONITE LEPTITE LEUCITE LOWEITE MARTITE MELLITE MULLITE OKENITE OLIVINE PALAITE PENNINE PETZITE PYRITES RATHITE REALGAR RETZIAN RHAGITE RINKITE ROMEITE ROSSITE SENAITE SODDITE SVABITE SYLVITE THORITE TURGITE ULEXITE UTAHITE UVANITE VAUXITE VOGLITE VRBAITE WARBITE WIIKITE ZEOLITE ZINCITE ZOISITE ZORGITE ZUNYITE AIKINITE ALLANITE ALLUVIAL ALUNOGEN AMBONITE ANAUXITE ANCYLITE ANDORITE ANKERITE ARIEGITE ARMENITE ARTINITE ASBOLITE AUGELITE AUTUNITE AWARUITE BADENITE BAKERITE BARARITE BARYLITE BAVENITE BETAFITE BEYERITE BILINITE BIXBYITE BLAKEITE BLOEDITE BOOTHITE BORACITE BOWENITE BRAGGITE BRAUNITE BRAVOITE BROMLITE BRONZITE BROOKITE BRUSHITE CALCSPAR CARBOCER CEROLITE CHIOLITE CHLORITE CHROMITE CIMOLITE CINNABAR CLEVEITE COHENITE COLUSITE COOKEITE COSALITE CREEDITE CROCOITE CRYOLITE DANALITE DAPHNITE DATOLITE DELTAITE DENDRITE DIALLAGE DIASPORE DIGENITE DIOPSIDE DIOPTASE DIXENITE DOLOMITE DYSODILE EGUEIITE ELIASITE ELPIDITE EMBOLITE ENARGITE EPSOMITE ERIONITE EUCOLITE EULYTINE EULYTITE EUXENITE EVANSITE FASSAITE FAYALITE FELDSPAR FERSMITE FIBROITE FLINKITE FLUORITE FOOTEITE FUCHSITE FUSINITE GEMSTONE GENTHITE GIBBSITE GINORITE GOETHITE GOYAZITE GRIPHITE GROTHINE GROUTITE GYROLITE HANKSITE HANUSITE HARTTITE HATCHITE HAUERITE HAUYNITE HEMATITE HOMILITE HUGELITE IDOCRASE INDERITE IODYRITE JALPAITE JAROSITE JEZEKITE KALINITE KAMACITE KASOLITE KEHOEITE KLEINITE KOKTAITE KOLSKITE KRAUSITE LAGONITE LAVENITE LAZULITE LAZURITE LEVYNITE LEWISITE LIMONITE LINARITE LOMONITE LOWIGITE MARSHITE MEIONITE

MELILITE MELONITE MESITITE MESOLITE MIERSITE MIMETITE MISENITE MOLYSITE MONAZITE MONETITE MORAVITE MOSESITE NADORITE NASONITE NEPOUITE NOCERITE NOSELITE OXAMMITE PEGANITE PETALITE PIMELITE PINNOITE PISANITE PODOLITE PORODINE PRICEITE PRIORITE RINNEITE ROSELITE SAGENITE SALEEITE SALESITE SAPONITE SASSOLIN SCAWTITE SHANDITE SHARPITE SHORTITE SIDERITE SMALTITE SMITHITE SODALITE SPADAITE SPURRITE STANNITE STIBNITE STILBITE STOLZITE STRUVITE STURTITE SZMIKITE TAGILITE TANGEITE TEALLITE TENORITE TILASITE TITANITE TRIPLITE TROILITE TYROLITE TYSONITE URANOTIL VEGASITE VOLTAITE VOLTZITE WEHRLITE WEISSITE WELLSITE WILKEITE WURTZITE XENOLITE XENOTIME YENTNITE ZARATITE MILLERITE MUSCOVITE NEPHELINE NICCOLITE PHENACITE TANZANITE WILLEMITE STISHOVITE
(BLACK —) JET GEET CERINE YENITE KNOPITE NIOBITE ALLANITE GRAPHITE HIELMITE ILMENITE ONOFRITE MAGNETITE SAMARSKITE
(BLUE —) MOLYBDENITE
(BRIGHT —) BLENDE
(BROWN —) CERINE EGERAN GUILDITE JAROSITE
(FIBROUS —) ASBESTOS
(GRAY-WHITE —) TRONA HOPEITE
(GREEN —) AMESITE GAHNITE ILESITE PRASINE PREHNITE SMECTITE
(MOTTLED —) SERPENTINE
(ORANGE —) SANDIX
(RADIATED —) ASTROITE
(RADIOACTIVE —) CURITE
(RARE —) CYMRITE EUCLASE TYCHITE BARYLITE
(RED —) GARNET RHODOCHROSITE
(SOFT —) TALC KERMES
(TRANSPARENT —) MICA POLLUX ABRAZITE SODALITE
(WHITE —) BARITE HOWLITE STILBITE
(YELLOW —) TOPAZ PYRITES PENTLANDITE
(YELLOWISH-GREEN —) EPIDOTE ECDEMITE
(PREF.) ORYCT(O)
(SUFF.) CLASE INE ITE LITE LITH(IC) LITIC XENE

MINERALOGIST AMERICAN HUNT KUNZ BRUSH KRAUS EGLESTON WHITLOCK CLEAVELAND
AUSTRIAN BORN BECKE WULFEN HAIDINGER TSCHERMAK
ENGLISH BROOKE CLARKE GREGOR MILLER PHILLIPS
FRENCH HAUY ROME DAUBREE FRIEDEL LACROIX LAUMONT DOLOMIEU DUFRENOY BRONGNIART
GERMAN MOHS COHEN RASPE DECHEN KOBELL WERNER ZIRKEL KARSTEN NEUMANN AGRICOLA LEONHARD QUENSTEDT
ITALIAN SELLA BRUGNATELLI
RUSSIAN FERSMAN
SWEDISH GAHN HISINGER SEFSTROM CRONSTEDT BLOMSTRAND

MINERAL TAR MALTHA
MINERAL WATER SELTZER
MINERVA MENFRA
MINESWEEPER ALGERINE
MINGLE MIX FUSE JOIN MELL MOLD MONG MOOL ADMIX BLEND MERGE TWINE COMMIX FELTER HUDDLE JUMBLE MEDDLE MEDLEY COMBINE COALESCE CONFOUND
(PREF.) MISCE
MINGLED FUSED MIXED MEDLEY CONFUSED PELLMELL
(PREF.) MYXTI
MINGLING MIX PELLMELL
(— OF VOWELS) CRASIS
(PREF.) MIXO
(SUFF.) MIXIS
MINIATURE BABY SMALL LITTLE POCKET MINIKIN
MINIM HALFNOTE
MINIMAL BASAL LIMINAL MARGINAL
MINIMIZE DECRY MINCE LESSEN MINIFY SMOOTH SCISSOR BELITTLE DISCOUNT
MINIMUM BARE BEDROCK
(— OF CAPITAL) SHOESTRING
(— OF VISION) STIME STYME
MINING WORK MINERY SPATTER GROOVING
(KIND OF —) PLACER
MINION PEAT SATAN MIGNON DARLING MINIKIN CREATURE SATELLITE
MINIONETTE EMERALD
MINISTER PRIG AGENT CLERK DEWAN ELDER ENVOY HAMAN PADRE VIZIR ATABEG DEACON DIVINE GALLAH HELPER PANDER PARSON PASTOR PESHWA PRIEST VIZIER BROTHER DOMINIE OFFICER PESHKAR PREFECT PALATINE PREACHER SECRETARY
(— OF FINANCE) DEWAN
(— TO) TEND SERVE INTEND
(— TO PASSIONS) PANDER
(— WITHOUT SETTLEMENT) STIBBLER
(PRIME —) PADRONE
(WAR —) SERASKIER
MINISTRANT
(PL.) SELLI SELLOI
MINISTRATION SERVICE TENDANCE
MINISTRY SERVICE
MINIUM SANDIX
MINIVER LASSET
MINK FAG HURON NORSE VISON JACKASH KOLINSKY MUSTELIN PLATINUM

MINNESOTA
CAPITAL: STPAUL
COLLEGE: BETHEL STOLAF WINONA BEMIDJI HAMLINE AUGSBURG CARLETON
COUNTY: LYON PINE TODD ANOKA MOWER AITKIN DAKOTA ISANTI ITASCA MCLEOD NOBLES ROSEAU WASECA WILKIN CHISAGO WABASHA CROWWING HENNEPIN OTTERTAIL
INDIAN: SIOUX OJIBWA CHIPPEWA
LAKE: LEECH ITASCA BEMIDJI SUPERIOR
MOUNTAIN: EAGLE MISQUAH
MOUNTAIN RANGE: CUYUNA MESABI MISQUAH
NICKNAME: NORTHSTAR
RIVER: SAUK RAINY STCROIX
STATE BIRD: LOON
STATE TREE: REDPINE
TOWN: ADA ELY MORA ANOKA EDINA FOLEY AUSTIN CHASKA DULUTH MILACA NEWULM WADENA WASECA WINONA BEMIDJI FOSSTON HIBBING IVANHOE MANKATO BRAINERD PIPESTONE

MINNESOTAN GOPHER
MINNOW PINK BANNY GUPPY HITCH MINIM MINNY BAGGIE MENNON DOGFISH FATHEAD GULARIS PHANTOM PINHEAD PINKEEN BONYTAIL CYPRINID FLATHEAD GAMBUSIA MOONFISH SATINFIN
(PL.) MENISE
MINOR FLAT LESS MOLL WARD PETIT PETTY INFANT LESSER SLIGHT
(PERIOD OF BEING A —) NONAGE
MINORESS CLARE CLARISSE
MINORITY FEW NONAGE INFANCY
MINOS (DAUGHTER OF —) ARIADNE PHAEDRA
(FATHER OF —) JUPITER LYCASTUS
(MOTHER OF —) EUROPA
(SLAYER OF —) COCALUS
(SON OF —) ANDROGEOS DEUCALION
(WIFE OF —) PASIPHAE
MINSTER CHADBAND
MINSTREL BARD LUTER BADHAN HARPER JOCKEY BADCHAN GLEEMAN JOCULAR PARDHAN PIERROT SONGMAN JONGLEUR
MINSTRELSY GLEE DREAM
MINT NEW COIN NANA SAGE AJUGA BASIL ORGAN THYME HYSSOP SAVORY STRIKE ALLHEAL BALLOTA CAPMINT LABIATE MONARDA OLITORY OREGANO PERILLA PHLOMIS POTHERB STACHYS BERGAMOT CALAMINT IRONWORT LAMPWICK LAVENDER MARJORAM SAGELEAF SELFHEAL SKULLCAP PATCHOULI PATCHOULY PENNYROYAL PEPPERMINT
MINTER MONEYER
MINTING COINING
MINUCHIHR (DAUGHTER OF —) NAUDAR
(FATHER OF —) IRAJ
MINUET MINAWAY
MINUS LESS WANTING
MINUTE FINE NICE TINY CLOSE MINIM PRIME SMALL ATOMIC MOMENT NARROW INSTANT SCRUPLE DETAILED
(LAST —) DEADLINE
(ORIGINAL —) PROTOCOL
(24 —S) GHURRY
(PL.) ACTA
MINX JADE PEAT SLUT SNIP HUSSY HUZZY LIMMER SNICKET
MIRACLE SIGN ANOMY MARVEL WONDER PRODIGY THEURGY
(SITE OF —) CANA
(PREF.) THAUMA(TO)
MIRACLE PLAY GUARY
MIRACULOUS MARVELOUS
(NOT —) NATURAL
MIRAGE SERAB CHIMERA FLYAWAY LOOMING ILLUSION TOWERING
MIRANDA (FATHER OF —) PROSPERO
(LOVER OF —) FERDINAND
MIRE BOG DUB CLAY GLAR LAIR MOIL SLOB SLUB SLUE SLUR ADDLE CLART EMBOG FANGO GLAUR LATCH SEUGH SLAKE SLOSH SLUSH SQUAD STALL SLOUGH SLUDGE SLUTCH CLABBER GUTTERS SLUBBER LOBLOLLY WORTHING
MIREILLE (CHARACTER IN —) RAMON OURRIAS VINCENT MIREILLE
(COMPOSER OF —) GOUNOD
MIRIAM (BROTHER OF —) MOSES
MIRITI PALM ITA BURITI MORICHE
MIRLITON KAZOO
MIRO TOMTIT
MIRROR APE FLAT BERYL GLASS IMAGE STEEL STONE PEEPER PSYCHE REFLEX SHINER SHOWER CONCAVE HORIZON REFLECT DIAGONAL SPECULUM
(— BETWEEN WINDOWS) PIERGLASS
(PREF.) CATOPTRO
MIRTH GLEE CHEER DREAM SPORT GAIETY BAUDERY DISPORT JOLLITY HILARITY
(CONTEMPTUOUS —) SPORT
(VIOLENT —) SPLEEN
MIRTHFUL CADGY MERRY RIANT FESTIVE GLEEFUL JOCULAR DISPOSED LAUGHFUL CONVIVIAL
MIRY OOZY PUXY LAIRY MUCKY SLAKY CLAGGY CLASHY LUTOSE MIPISH POACHY SLABBY GUTTERY SLOUGHY
MISADVENTURE GRIEF ACCIDENT CALAMITY CASUALTY DISASTER MISHANTER
MISANTHROPE CYNIC HATER TIMON
(AUTHOR OF —) MOLIERE
(CHARACTER IN —) ORONTE ALCESTE ARSINOE ELIANTE CELIMENE PHILINTE
MISANTHROPIC CYNICAL
MISANTHROPY CYNICISM TIMONISM
MISAPPLIED ABUSIVE
MISAPPLY ABUSE CROOK WREST DISUSE MISUSE
MISAPPREHEND MISTAKE

MISAPPREHENSION ILLUSION
MISBECOME MISSIT MISSEEM
MISBEHAVE MISUSE MISBEAR MISFARE MISHAVE MISLEAD MISGUIDE
MISBEHAVIOR MALVERSATION
MISBELIEF MISCREED
MISCALCULATE DUTCH MISCAST MISCOUNT
MISCALL BECALL MISNAME
MISCARRIAGE FAIL MISHAP FAILURE ABORTION (PREF.) ECTRO
MISCARRY FAIL WARP ABORT MISGO FOUNDER MISFARE MISGIVE BACKFIRE
MISCARRYING ABORTIVE
MISCELLANEOUS CHOW ORRA SUNDRY ASSORTED CHOWCHOW
MISCELLANY ANA VARIA MEDLEY WHATNOT CHOWCHOW GIFTBOOK
MISCHANCE CALAMITY CASUALTY DISASTER
MISCHIEF HOB ILL BALE BANE EVIL HARM HURT JEEL WRACK INJURY MURCHY SORROW WONDER DEVILRY KNAVERY MALICHO SCADDLE DEVILTRY MALLECHO
MISCHIEF-MAKING URCHIN
MISCHIEVOUS BAD SLY ARCH IDLE PIXY ROYT ELFIN HEMPY PIXIE ROYET ELFISH ELVISH GALLUS HEMPIE IMPISH NOCENT NOYANT SHREWD SULLEN WICKED GALLOWS HARMFUL KNAVISH LARKISH MOCKING NAUGHTY PARLISH PLISKIE PUCKISH ROGUISH SCADDLE UNHAPPY UNLUCKY WAGGISH LITHERLY LUNGEOUS SPORTIVE SPRITISH VENOMOUS WANSONSY
MISCHIEVOUSNESS ROGUERY
MISCONCEPTION DELUSION ILLUSION
MISCONDUCT CULPA DOLUS OFFENCE OFFENSE DISORDER MALFEASANCE
MISCONSTRUCTION STRAIN
MISCONSTRUE MISJUDGE
MISCREANT KNAVE
MISDEED ILL MISS SLIP AMISS UNWORK DEFAULT FORFEIT OFFENCE OFFENSE DISORDER **(CATCH A —)** DETECT
MISDEMEANOR SIN CRIME FAULT DELICT OFFENCE OFFENSE DISORDER
MISDIRECT PERVERT MISGUIDE
MISER CUFF SKIN CHUFF CHURL FLINT GRIPE HAYNE HUNKS NABAL PIKER SCRAT SCRIB CODGER HUDDLE NIPPER PELTER SCRIMP SNUDGE WRETCH DRYFIST GOBSECK NIGGARD SCRAPER SCROOGE CHINCHER GATHERER HAPTERON HARPAGON HOLDFAST MUCKERER MUCKWORM PINCHGUT CURMUDGEON
MISERABLE WOE EVIL GRAY PUNK SOUR DAWNY DEENY DUSTY MISER WOFUL YEMER ABJECT CHETIF CRUMBY CRUMMY ELENGE FEEBLE PRETTY UNSELY WOEFUL BALEFUL FORLORN PITIFUL SCRUFFY UNHAPPY WANSOME FORSAKEN PITIABLE SCRANNEL UNTHENDE WRETCHED
MISERABLES, LES (AUTHOR OF —) HUGO **(CHARACTER IN —)** JEAN JAVERT MARIUS COSETTE EPONINE FANTINE VALJEAN JONDRETTE MADELEINE PONTMERCY THENARDIER FAUCHELEVANT
MISERERE SUBSELLA
MISERLINESS AVARICE MISERISM SNUDGERY TENACITY
MISERLY WOE GARE MEAN NEAR GRIPPY KNIVEY STINGY CHINCHE PELTING WANSITH SCRAPING SNUDGERY
MISERY WO WOE BALE RUTH GNEDE GRAME WREAK THREAT ANGUISH MISEASE TRAGEDY CALAMITY DISTRESS WANDRETH WOWENING
MISFIRE SKIP SNAP
MISFORTUNE ILL BLOW DOLE DREE EVIL HARM RUTH TEEN CROSS CURSE HYDRA SCATH TRAIK DAMAGE DIRDUM MISERY MISHAP RUBBER SCATHE SORROW UNHEAL UNLUCK WANHAP WROATH AMBSACE MALHEUR MISCARE MISFALL MISFATE MISLUCK REVERSE TRAGEDY TROUBLE UNSELTH UNSPEED CALAMITY DISASTER DISGRACE DISTRESS MISCHIEF ADVERSITY MISCHANCE
MISGIVING DOUBT QUALM
MISGOVERN MISRULE
MISGUIDED WET
MISHAEL (BROTHER OF —) ELIZAPHAN **(FATHER OF —)** UZZIEL
MISHAM (FATHER OF —) ELPAAL
MISHANDLE BUNGLE
MISHAP SLIP GRIEF SHUNT SITHE UNHAP WANHAP FORTUNE MISTIDE ACCIDENT CASUALTY MISCHIEF PRATFALL **(MINOR —)** GLITCH
MISHEARING OTOSIS
MISHIT DUFF
MISHMA (BROTHER OF —) MIBSAM **(FATHER OF —)** ISHMAEL
MISHMASH OLIO BOTCH GOULASH
MISINFORM MIZZLE
MISINTERPRET WARP WREST WRITHE MISREAD PERVERT MISCOUNT
MISJUDGE MISDEEM MISWERN
MISLAY LOSE DISPLACE MISPLACE
MISLEAD COG ERR BUNK DUPE GULL HOAX HYPE JIVE BLUFF CHEAT FALSE SHUCK BETRAY DELUDE SEDUCE WILDER CONFUSE DEBAUCH DECEIVE MISLEAR INVEIGLE MISGUIDE BAMBOOZLE BLUNDER MISLEAD MISRULE ILLGUIDE MISGUIDE
MISLEADING JIVE BLIND FALSE CIRCEAN TORTIOUS
MISMANAGE MULL BLUNK
MISOGYNIC CYNICAL
MISPLACE MISLAY MISPUT MISSET DISPLACE
MISPLACED LOST MALPOSED
MISPLAY BLOW DUFF ERROR FLUFF FUMBLE
MISPRINT LITERAL
MISPRONOUNCE MISCALL STUMBLE
MISQUOTE GIVE
MISREPRESENT SKEW ABUSE BELIE COLOR MISUSE DISTORT FALSIFY SLANDER MISCOLOR
MISREPRESENTATION FRAUD CALUMNY DAUBERY GARBLING
MISS ERR HIP SHE FAIL LACK LOSE SKIP SLIP SNAB FORGO HANUM MISSY PANNA SKIRT DESIRE KUMARI FRAULEIN MISTRESS OVERLOOK OVERSLIP SENORITA **(CLOSE —)** SHAVE **(NARROW —)** SHAVE
MISSEL BIRD MAVIS SHIRL DRAINE JAYPIE MISTLE SHRITE SYCOCK CHERCOCK
MISSHAPE DEFORM
MISSHAPEN UGLY BLOWN DEFORM THRAWN DEFORMED UNSHAPED MALFORMED (PREF.) DYSMORPHO
MISSILE ABM GUN SAM BALL BIRD BOLT DART MIRV NIKE SHOT PLUMB SHAFT STONE BULLET EXOCET ROCKET SEEKER BOMBARD FIREPOT GRENADE MISSIVE OUTCAST PROJECT AERODART BRICKBAT MINUTEMAN PROJECTILE SIDEWINDER **(— DEPOT)** SILO **(ANTIBALLISTIC —)** ABM **(BALLISTIC —)** ICBM ATLAS **(DEFECTIVE —)** DUD **(SURFACE-TO-AIR —)** SAM (PL.) MITRAILLE (PREF.) TELI
MISSING LACK WANT ABSENT WANTING **(— OF CUE)** FLUFF (PREF.) E
MISSION SAND TASK CHARGE ERRAND SORTIE VISITA MESSAGE BUSINESS DEVOTION LEGATION NUNCIATURE **(— OF MERCY)** RESCUE
MISSIONARY APOSTLE COLPORTER

MISSISSIPPI

CAPITAL: JACKSON
COLLEGE: RUST ALCORN BELHAVEN MILLSAPS TOUGALOO
COUNTY: TATE HINDS JONES LAMAR LEAKE PERRY YAZOO ALCORN ATTALA COPIAH JASPER PANOLA TIPPAH TUNICA CHOCTAW NESHOBA NOXUBEE ITAWAMBA YALOBUSHA
INDIAN: TIOU BILOXI TUNICA CHOCTAW NATCHEZ CHICKASAW
LAKE: ENID SARDIS BARNETT GRENADA OKATIBBEE
MOUNTAIN: WOODALL
NATIVE: MUDCAT TADPOLE
NICKNAME: BAYOU MAGNOLIA
RIVER: LEAF PEARL YAZOO BIGBLACK
STATE BIRD: MOCKINGBIRD
STATE FLOWER: MAGNOLIA
STATE TREE: MAGNOLIA
TOWN: IUKA MARKS BILOXI LAUREL PURVIS TUNICA TUPELO WINONA BELZONI CORINTH GRENADA NATCHEZ WIGGINS GULFPORT MERIDIAN KOSCIUSKO

MISSIVE NOTE BILLET LETTER EPISTLE MESSAGE MISSILE
MISSLE BUS

MISSOURI

CAPITAL: JEFFERSONCITY
COLLEGE: AVILA DRURY TARKIO LINCOLN WEBSTER STEPHENS
COUNTY: RAY COLE DENT IRON LINN ADAIR BARRY HENRY MACON RALLS TANEY GRUNDY PETTIS PLATTE DAVIESS NODAWAY
INDIAN: OSAGE
LAKE: OZARKS TABLEROCK
MOUNTAIN: TAUMSAUK
NATIVE: PUKE PIKER
NICKNAME: SHOWME BULLION
PLATEAU: OZARK
PRESIDENT: TRUMAN
RIVER: OSAGE
STATE BIRD: BLUEBIRD
STATE FLOWER: HAWTHORN
STATE TREE: DOGWOOD
TOWN: AVA EDINA ELDON HAYTI LAMAR MACON MILAN ROLLA BUTLER GALENA KAHOKA NEOSHO POTOSI BETHANY BOLIVAR CAMERON LEBANON MOBERLY PALMYRA SEDALIA STLOUIS HANNIBAL SIKESTON

MISSPEAK ERR
MISSTATEMENT ERRATUM
MISSTEP TRIP
MIST DAG FOG MUG URE DAMP DRIP DROW FILM HAAR HAZE MOKE RACK ROKE SCUD SMUR BRUME CLOUD DRISK GAUZE STEAM MIZZLE NEBULE SEREIN SERENE SMEETH **(COLD —)** DROW BERBER **(DRIZZLING —)** SMUR DRISK SMIRR SMURR **(SMOKY —)** SMOG **(WHITE —)** HAG (PL.) SMOKES (PREF.) NEBULI NIMBI
MISTAKE ERR BALK GAFF GOOF MISS SLIP TRIP ERROR FAULT FLUFF GAFFE LAPSE BARNEY BOBBLE ESCAPE MISCUE SLIPUP STUMER BLOOMER BLOOPER BLUNDER CONFUSE DEFAULT JEOFAIL STUMOUR WRONGER CONFOUND MISPRINT MISPRISE **(CLERICAL —)** TYPO **(STUPID —)** BUBU BONER CLANGER (PL.) ERRATA
MISTAKEN WET WRONG ASTRAY

VICIOUS OVERSEEN OVERSHOT TORTIOUS
(NOT —) RIGHT
MISTER DON REB HERR SENOR SENHOR SIGNOR GOODMAN SIGNIOR GOVERNOR MONSIEUR
MISTFLOWER EUPATORY
MISTILY FOGGILY
MISTINESS FILM HAZE
MISTLETOE MISSEL ALLHEAL GADBUSH
MISTREAT BANG ABUSE SHAFT BATTER SAVAGE VIOLATE
MISTRESS MRS PUG TOY AMIE BIBI DAME DOLL DOXY LADY MISS PURE AMIGA AMOUR DOLLY DONNA DUENA FANCY LEMAN LUCKY MADAM NANCY WOMAN BEEBEE MINION MISSIS MISSUS NEAERA PARNEL SAHIBA SENORA TACKLE WAHINE BEDMATE DELILAH HERSELF HETAERA KITTOCK LEVERET METREZA PADRONA SENHORA SIGNORA SULTANA CAMPASPE DESPOINA DULCINEA FARMWIFE GOODWIFE GUDEWIFE HAUSFRAU LADYLOVE LANDLADY MIGNIARD PARAMOUR PECULIAR SINEBADA TIMANDRA COURTESAN INAMORATA
(— OF CEREMONIES) FEMCEE
MISTRUST MISTROW SURMISE DISTRUST JEALOUSE JEALOUSY MISDOUBT
MISTY HAZY MOKY BLEAR DAGGY FILMY FOGGY MISKY MOCHY MOOTH MURKY RAWKY ROKEY ROUKY BLURRY CLOUDY GREASY MIZZLY SMURRY STEAMY BRUMOUS OBSCURE NEBULOUS NUBILOUS VAPOROUS
MISUNDERSTAND MISKNOW MISTAKE
MISUNDERSTANDING MALENTENDU
MISUSE ABUSE ABUSION PERVERT MALTREAT
MITE BIT ATOM CENT DITE DRAM ATOMY BICHO SPECK ACARID ACARUS CHIGOE LEPTUS MINUTE SMIDGE ACARIAN BDELLID CHIGGER DEMODEX SMIDGEN ARACHNID DIBRANCH FARTHING HANDWORM ORIBATID SANDMITE
(TEXAS CITRUS —) SPIDER
(PREF.) ACAR(I)(O)
MITER MITRE TIMBER TIMBRE
MITERWORT COOLWORT
MITICIDE ACARICIDE PHOSPHAMIDON
MITIGATE BALM COOL EASE HELP ABATE ALLAY DELAY MEASE RELAX REMIT SLAKE ASLAKE LENIFY LESSEN MODIFY PACIFY SOFTEN SOOTHE SUCCOR TEMPER ASSUAGE COMMUTE CUSHION ELEVATE MOLLIFY QUALIFY RELEASE RELIEVE SWEETEN PALLIATE ALLEVIATE
(— PAIN) PLASTER
MITIGATING LENITIVE
MITIGATION REMORSE
MITOCHONDRION SARCOSOME
MITT MUFF
MITTEN BOOT CUFF MITT MUFF LOOFIE MUFFLE NIPPER MUFFLER
MIX BOX BEAT CARD DASH FUSE JOIN KNIT MELL MENG MESS STIR ADMIX ALLOY BLEND BRAID IMMIX KNEAD MISCE TWINE BLUNGE CAUDLE COMMIX CRUTCH GARBLE JUMBLE MEDDLE MEDLEY MINGLE MUDDLE PERMIX STODGE TEMPER WUZZLE BLUNDER SHUFFLE SWIZZLE CONFOUND LEVIGATE SCRAMBLE
(— AND STIR WHEN WET) PUG
(— AT RANDOM) SHUFFLE
(— CONFUSEDLY) BROIL
(— FLOCKS) BOX
(— LIQUORS) BREW
(— PLASTER) GAGE GAUGE
(— TEA) BULK
(— WINE) PART
(— WITH WHITE) LOAD
(— WITH YEAST) BARM
(— WOOL OF DIFFERENT COLORS) TUM
(CONCRETE —) SOUP
(LIQUOR —) SODA QUININE SELTZER
MIXABLE MISCIBLE
MIXED CHOW IMPURE MEDLEY MOTLEY PIEBALD STREAKY CHOWCHOW
(— BLOOD) MESTIZO
(— CHALICE) KRASIS
(— UP) HAYWIRE
(NOT —) SINCERE
(PREF.) MIXO
MIXER HOG BANBURY MUDDLER PICKLER
(CEMENT —) BOXMAN
(CONCRETE —) PAVER
(FOOD —) BEATER
MIXTURE AIR MIX BODY BREW DASH FEED HASH MANG MELD MONG MULL OLIO PUER SOUP STEW ALGIN ALLOY BLEND BLENT BROMO DOUGH GUMBO SALAD STUFF FOURRE GARBLE GUNITE LIGNIN MASLIN MEDLEY MELLAY MINGLE MOTLEY TEMPER AMALGAM COMPOST CUSTARD FARRAGO FILICIN FORMULA GOULASH HEADING KOGASIN MELANGE MISTION MISTURA MIXTION MONGREL OLLAPOD RECEIPT TIMBALE ALKYLATE BLENDURE DRAMMOCK EMULSION POSSODIE POWSOWDY SOLUTION MACEDOINE MENAGERIE MISCELLANY SALMAGUNDI SMORGASBORD
(— ADDED TO WINE) DOSAGE
(— ATTRACTIVE TO PIGEONS) SALTCAT
(— FOR CAKE) BATTER
(— FOR DRESSING LEATHER) DUBBIN DUBBING
(— OF ALE AND OATMEAL) STOORY
(— OF ALKALOIDS) ADONIDIN JABORINE
(— OF BARKS) TONGA
(— OF CEMENT AND STONE) BUMICKY
(— OF CLAY AND CHALK) MALM
(— OF CLAY AND ROCK) BODY
(— OF CLAY AND SAND) LOAM
(— OF DRUGS) SPECIES
(— OF ELEMENTS) DIDYMIUM
(— OF FEEDS) MASH
(— OF IMPURE ARSENIDES) SPEISS
(— OF OATS AND BARLEY) DREDGE
(— OF PRINCIPLES) EUONYMIN
(— OF PROTEINS) CROTIN
(— OF SALTS) SOYATE
(— OF SAND AND STONES) CHAD
(— OF SAWDUST AND GLUE) BADIGEON
(— OF SHALE AND SANDSTONE) HAZLE
(— OF SLAG AND ORE) BROWSE
(— OF VINEGAR AND HONEY) OXYMEL
(— OF VITAMINS) BIOS
(— OF WHITE AND BLACK) GRIZZLE
(— OF WINE, HONEY AND SPICES) CLARY
(— TO ADULTERATE LIQUORS) FLASH
(— TO DOCTOR WINE) GEROPIGA
(— TO WHITEN BREAD) HARDS
(— USED AS A FERMENT) BUB
(— USED AT SEDER) HAROSET CHAROSES
(ACUTE —) ACUTA
(AERIFORM —) GAS
(CARVER'S —) COMPO
(CAULKING —) BLARE
(CHEMICAL —) SYNGAS
(CLAY —) COB SLIP
(COATING —) COLOR
(CONFUSED —) MESS CHAOS FUDDLE SOZZLE
(CRUMBLY —) STREUSEL
(EXPLOSIVE —) DUALIN FIREDAMP
(FOOD —) FILLING
(FREEZING —) CRYOGEN
(GILDING —) ASSIETTE
(HYDROCARBON —) ABIETENE
(ITALIAN CONDIMENT —) TAMARA
(JUMBLED —) BOTCH PASTICHE
(MECHANICS' —) PUTTY
(PLASTIC CEMENT —) CLOY
(PRESERVATIVE —) STUFF
(SEASONED —) STUFFING
(SMOKING —) CHARAS CHURRUS
(TANNING —) PURE
(THICKENING —) ROUX
(UNPALATABLE —) DRAMMOCK
(WATERY —) SLURRY
(WELDING —) THERMIT
(SUFF.) CRASE CRASIS CRASY
MIZZAH (FATHER OF —) REUEL
(GRANDFATHER OF —) ESAU
MIZZEN DANDY
MIZZONITE DIPYRE
MKS UNIT JOULE
MNEMONIC MEMORIAL
MOAN HONE MOON REEM WAIL CROON GROAN MOURN MUNGE QUIRK SOUGH MUNGER
MOANING SOUGH DIRGEFUL
MOAT FOSS DITCH FOSSE GRAFF RUNDEL
MOB CREW GANG HERD RAFF ROUT COHUE CROWD HURRY MAFIA PLEBE PLEBS MOBILE RABBLE TUMULT VOULGE DOGGERY CANAILLE RIFFRAFF VARLETRY CLAMJAFRY
(PREF.) OCHLO
MOBCAP MOB
MOBILE THIN FLUID ROVING MOVEABLE
(— ARTIST) CALDER
(FREELY —) THIN
MOBSTER HOODLUM
MOBY DICK (AUTHOR OF —) MELVILLE
(CHARACTER IN —) AHAB STUBB ISHMAEL FEDALLAH QUEEQUEG STARBUCK
MOCCASIN PAC CONGO TEGUA SHOEPACK
(— WITH LEGS) LARRIGAN
(PL.) SHANKS
MOCCASIN FLOWER NERVINE
MOCHA BARK
MOCHICA YUNCA
MOCHILA MACHEER KNAPSACK
MOCK DO BOB DOR GAB MOW COPY DEFY GECK GIBE GIRD JAPE JEER JEST JIBE PLAY QUIZ BOURD DORRE ELUDE FLEER FLIRT FLOUT FRUMP HOKER KNACK MIMIC RALLY SCOFF SCORN SCOUT SLEER SPORT TAUNT BEMOCK DELUDE DERIDE ILLUDE NIGGLE IMITATE MURGEON RIDICULE
MOCKER MOWER GIRDER BOURDER FLOUTER SCORNER RAILLEUR
MOCKERNUT BULLNUT
MOCKERY DOR GAB MOW GLEE JEER BOURD DORRE FARCE FLOUT GLAIK SCOFF SPORT BISMER HETHING LUDIBRY MOCKADO MOCKAGE DERISION ILLUSION RIDICULE SCOFFERY
(GOD OF —) MOMUS
MOCKING GAB ACID SPORT SCOPTIC IRRISORY NARQUOIS SARDONIC TRUMPERY
MOCKINGBIRD MIMUS MOWER MOCKER
MOCK ORANGE SYRINGA PHILADELPHUS
MOCOA COCHE
MOD HEP HIP YEYE TRENDY
MODE CUT JET TON WAY FORM GATE MOOD RAGA TONE TWIG WISE FERIO FINAL GENUS MODUS STATE STYLE VOGUE ACTING BAROCO CESARE COURSE DATISI FAKOFO FANGLE FESAPO MANNER METHOD BAMALIP CALEMES CAMENES DABITIS DARAPTI DIBATIS DIMARIS DIMATIS DISAMIS FAPESMO FASHION FERISON FESTINO CELARENT DOKMAROK FELAPTON FRESISON TONALITY
(— OF BEHAVIOR) THEW HABITUDE
(— OF BEING) CATEGORY
(— OF CONDUCT) LAW
(— OF DRESS) HABIT TENUE
(— OF DRESSING HAIR) MADONNA
(— OF EXPRESSION) IRONY
(— OF MORAL ACTION) CONDUCT
(— OF PARTITIONING) CANT

(— OF PROCEDURE) ORDER SYSTEM
(— OF RULE) REGIME
(— OF SPEECH) ACCENT LATINISM PARLANCE
(— OF STANDING) STANCE
(— OF STRUCTURE) BUILD
(PREVAILING —) GARB
(TEMPORARY —) VOGUE
MODEL WAX COPY FORM MOLD NORM CANON DUMMY IDEAL LIGHT MOULD NORMA SHAPE DESIGN FUGLER GABARI MODULE PRAXIS SOURCE BOZZETO DIORAMA EXAMPLE GABARIT MODULET PARAGON PATTERN PICTURE SAMPLER CALENDAR ENSAMPLE EXEMPLAR EXEMPLUM FORMULAR FUGLEMAN MAQUETTE MODELLER MODULIZE PARADIGM PROPLASM SPECIMEN TYPORAMA MANNEQUIN PLANETARIUM
(— MATERIAL) BALSA
(— OF EARTH) TERRELLA
(— OF FOOT) CAST
(— OF HUMAN BODY) FORM MANIKIN
(— OF PERFECTION) PARAGON
(— OF SOLAR SYSTEM) ORRERY
(— OF STATUE) ESQUISSE
(INFERIOR —) JALOPPY
(MATHEMATICAL —) SPACE
(PRELIMINARY —) MAQUETTE PROPLASM
(PREF.) TYP(I)(O)
MODERATE BATE COOL CURB EASE EASY EVEN MEEK SOFT ABATE ALLAY ALLOY LIGHT LOWER MEZZO MODER REMIT SLACK SLAKE SOBER SWEET ARREST BRIDLE DECENT GENTLE LESSEN MEANLY MIDWAY MODEST MODIFY REMISS SEASON SOFTEN SUBMIT TEMPER CENTRAL CHASTEN CONTROL SLACKEN ATTEMPER CENTRIST MEETERLY MIDDLING MITIGATE MODERATO ORDINATE PALLIATE PASSABLE CONTINENT ABSTEMIOUS MEASURABLE REASONABLE
(— IN BURNING) SOFT
(— OF THE WIND) LOOM
MODERATELY GEY FAIR MEAN MEANLY MEETLY PRETTY MIDWISE MEETERLY MIDDLING
MODERATENESS CLEMENCY MODICITY
MODERATION MEAN STAY MINCE SPARE MANNER MEDIUM REASON COMPASS MEDIETY MODESTY SOBRIETY ABATEMENT IMMODESTY
MODERATO MASSIG
MODERATOR ANCHOR ANCHORMAN
MODERN NEW LATE RECENT NEOTERIC SPACEAGE
MODERNE ARTDECO
MODEST COY MIM SHY DEFT MURE NICE PURE SNUG BLATE DOUCE LOWLY QUIET SMALL CHASTE DEMURE HUMBLE PUDENT SIMPLE VIRGIN CLERKLY PUDICAL DISCREET MAIDENLY PUDIBUND RESERVED RETIRING SHAMEFUL VERECUND VIRTUOUS
MODESTY AIDOS PUDOR NICETY DECENCY PUDENCY SHYNESS CHASTITY FOREHEAD HUMILITY PUDICITY
MODICUM DROP BREAK SPICE PENNORTH SCANTLING SEMBLANCE PENNYWORTH
MODIFICATION BOB ECAD FORM SALT CHANGE ENGRAM FACIES SANDHI SINGLE UMLAUT ENGRAMMA
(— OF A REMEDY) TINCTION
(GLOTTAL —) STOP
MODIFIED VARIANT
MODIFY EDIT VARY ALTER AMEND HEDGE TOUCH BUFFER CHANGE DOCTOR MASTER TEMPER ARABIZE COMPARE FASHION MASSAGE QUALIFY ATTEMPER DENATURE GRADUATE MODERATE FAUCALIZE
(— ARTICULATION) COLOR
(— COLOR) TONE
MODILLION ANCON MODEL TRUSS CARTOUCH
MODISH CHIC MODY SOIGNE TIMISH TONISH STYLISH
MODISHNESS CHIC
MODRED (FATHER OF —) ARTHUR
(MOTHER OF —) MARGAWSE
MODULATE SINK INFLECT QUALIFY
MODULATION ACCENT CHANGE CADENCE BUNCHING PASSAGIO
MODULE LEM UNIT COMPONENT
(KIND OF —) LUNAR
(LUNAR EXCURSION —) BUG LED
MOGUL NABOB NAWAB RULER VICEROY PADISHAH
MOHAIR MOIRE
MOHAMMED MAHOMET MAHOUND MUDEJAR PROPHET
(SITE OF — TOMB) MEDINA
(UNCLE OF —) ABBAS
MOHAMMEDAN MOSLEM PAYNIM MAHOMET
MOHAMMEDANISM TURBAN TURKERY MAUMETRY
MOHAWK NICKER
MOHR MHORR GAZELLE
MOHUR MOOR AHMEDI
MOIETY MEDIETY
MOIST WET DAMP DANK DEWY NESH UVID DABBY GIVEY GREEN HUMID JUICY MADID MOCHY SAMMY SAPPY SLACK SOAKY SOCKY SPEWY SWACK WASHY WEEPY CLAMMY MOISTY STICKY WETTISH HUMOROUS MUCULENT
(PREF.) HUMI(DI) HYGR(O) UDO
MOISTEN DIP WET DAMP MOIL BASTE BATHE BEDEW JUICE LATCH LEACH STEEP WOKIE DABBLE DAMPEN HUMECT HUMIFY IMBRUE MADEFY SPARGE TEMPER HUMIDIFY IRRIGATE IRRORATE
(— LEATHER) SAM SAMMY
MOISTURE DEW WET BREE DAMP DANK ROKE HUMOR MOIST WATER PHLEGM AQUOSITY HUMIDITY
(— DEFICIENT) XERIC
(— FROM SKIN) SWEAT
(— IN STONE) SAP
(— ON BEARD) BARBER
(CONDENSED —) BREATH
(REMOVE CONDENSED —) DEFOG
(PREF.) HUMI(DI) HYGR(O) UDO
MOJARRA SHAD PATAO
MOKI MOGUEY MOKIHI
MOKSHA MUKTI
MOLAR WANG FORMAL MOLARY GRINDER
(PREF.) MYL(O)
MOLASSES DIP LICK CLAGGUM THERIAC TREACLE LONGLICK
(PREF.) MELASSI
MOLD DIE FEN PIG PLY SOW CALM CAST CURB FORM MULL MUST SOIL TRAP BLOCK CHAPE CHILL FRAME INGOT MODEL MOULD MUCOR PLASM PRINT SHAPE SHARE STENT STINT VALVE COFFIN GABARI INFORM LINGET MATRIX SQUARE BASTARD FASHION FESTOON MATRICE RILLETT SANDBOX SKILLET TEMPLET COQUILLE FUMAGINE HOODMOLD PROPLASM TEMPLATE WHISKERS PENICILLIUM
(— FOR METAL) SOW SKILLET
(— OF ASPIC) DARIOLE
(— OF SHIP) SWEEP
(— THAT ATTACKS HOPS) FEN
(CHEESE —) CHESSEL
(SLIME —) MYCETOZOAN MYXOMYCETE
(PREF.) PLASM(ATO)(O)
(SUFF.) PLASIA PLASIS PLASM(A) (IA)(IC) PLAST(IC)(Y) PLASY
MOLDAVITE TEKTITE
MOLDBOARD REEST
(— SURFACE) WREST
MOLDED FICTILE
MOLDER ROT MURL DECAY ERODE CAPPER MANGLE MOSKER FIGURER PLASTER PLASTIC
MOLDINESS MUST FINEW MUCOR VINEW
MOLDING BEAD COVE CYMA DADO GULA KEEL LIST OGEE OVAL CABLE FILET GORGE LABEL LEDGE ROVER STAFF BANDLE BASTON BILLET CASING COLLAR CONGEE COVING FILLET LISTEL MULLER REGLET SQUARE ZIGZAG ANNULET BEADING CABLING CHAPLET CORNICE DOUCINE ECHINUS EYEBROW FINGENT HIPMOLD LOZENGE MOULAGE NECKING SURBASE TONDINO TRINGLE ASTRAGAL BAGUETTE BANDELET CASEMATE CASEMENT CINCTURE CYMATION CYMATIUM DANCETTE DOGTOOTH FUSAROLE HOODMOLD KNURLING MOULDING NAILHEAD NECKMOLD ARCHIVOLT BOLECTION
(CONCAVE —) GORGE CONGEE SCOTIA CAVETTO
(CONVEX —) REED CABLE OVOLO THUMB TORUS BASTON REEDING ASTRAGAL FUSAROLE
(OGEE —) TALON
(OUTSIDE —) BACKBAND
(PL.) TORI LEDGMENT

MOLDOVA (ALSO SEE RUSSIA)
CAPITAL: CHISINAU KISHINEV
COIN: RUBLE
MOUNTAIN: VYSOKAYA BALANESTI
NAME: MOLDAVIA BESSARABIA
PLAIN: BUGEAC
RIVER: PRUT DANUBE IALPUG COGALNIC DNIESTER
STEPPE: BALTI
TOWN: BALTI TIRASPOL

MOLDY FUSTY HOARY MUCID MUGGY MUSTY VINNY FOISTY MOULDY FOUGHTY
MOLE COB UNT COBB MAIL OONT PIER PILE TAPE WANT JUTTY MOODY NEVUS TALPA TAUPE ANICUT MOUDIE HYDATID SLEEPER TALPOID MOLDWARP MOONCALF SORICOID STARNOSE UROPSILE ZANDMOLE
(PREF.) TALPI
MOLE CRICKET CHANGA
MOLECULE ACID ATOM BASE AMMINE CHIRAL DIPOLE HEXANE HYDROL LIGAND PRIMER HYDRONE SPECIES TEMPLATE OCTAPEPTIDE
(CLUSTER OF —) CAP
(PROTEIN —) BIOGEN
MOLEHILL TUMP HOYLE WANTHILL
MOLE RAT SEMNI ZEMMI ZOKOR SLEPEZ SPALACID ZANDMOLE
MOLEST GALL HAUNT TEASE BOTHER HARASS HECKLE INFEST PESTER MISLEST TROUBLE
MOLID (FATHER OF —) ABISHUR
(MOTHER OF —) ABIHAIL
MOLL FLANDERS (AUTHOR OF —) DEFOE
(CHARACTER IN —) MOLL JEMMY ROBIN FLANDERS
MOLLIFIER SLAVE
MOLLIFY HUSH ALLAY RELAX ADULCE GENTLE PACIFY RELENT SOFTEN SOOTHE TEMPER ASSUAGE DULCIFY SWEETEN ATTEMPER MITIGATE UNRUFFLE
MOLLIFYING MILD SUPPLING
MOLLUSK ARK CLAM CONE PIPI SPAT BORER CHAMA CHANK CHINK CLAMP CONCH COWRY DORIS DRILL MUREX PINNA SNAIL VENUS AEOLID BAILER BUBBLE CERION CHITON COCKLE COURIE DOLIUM JINGLE LEPTON LIMPET MUSSEL NERITA OYSTER PECTEN PHOLAD PURPLE SEMELE STROMB ABALONE ADMIRAL ASTARTE BIVALVE CARDITA DECAPOD JUNONIA MOLLUSC PIDDOCK SALPIAN SCALLOP TOHEROA TREPANG TROPHON DUCKFOOT FIGSHELL HALIOTIS NAUTILUS PTEROPOD SAXICAVA STROMBUS UNIVALVE VERMETUS SHELLFISH NUDIBRANCH PERIWINKLE

(— TRIBE) NAIADES
(LARVAL —) VELIGER
(YOUNG —) SPAT
MOLLYCODDLE BABY MOLLY WANTON INDULGE MILKSOP
MOLOSSUS (FATHER OF —) PYRRHUS
(MOTHER OF —) ANDROMACHE
MOLT MEW CAST MUTE SHED MOULT DISCARD EXUVIATE INTERMEW
MOLTEN FUSED
MOLTING BROKEN ECDYSIS
MOLUCCAS (ISLAND OF —) ARU KAI OBI BURU LETI SULA AMBON BABAR BANDA CERAM WETAR BATJAN TIDORE MOROTAI TERNATE TANIMBAR HALMAHERA
MOLUS (BROTHER OF —) EVENUS
(DAUGHTER OF —) MOLIONE
(FATHER OF —) ARES MARS
(MOTHER OF —) DEMONICE
MOLYBDENUM (EXCESS OF —) TEART
MOMBIN JOCOTE
MOMENT MO GIRD HINT SAND TICK AVAIL BLINK BRAID CLINK CRACK GLIFF GLISK JIFFY SHAKE SNIFT SPURT STOUN TRICE VALUE FILLIP GLIFFY MINUTE PERIOD SECOND STOUND WEIGHT YAWING ARTICLE INSTANT INSTANCE MOMENTUM TWINKLING
(— FOR LEGERDEMAIN ACTION) TEMPS
(— OF STRESS) CRISE
(APPROPRIATE —) PLACE
(CRITICAL —) BIT INCH CORNER
(DECISIVE —) CRISIS
(EXACT —) BIT POINT
(OPPORTUNE —) KAIROS
(PRECISE —) NICK
(SCHEDULED —) TIME
MOMENTARY MOMENTAL TRANSIENT
MOMENTOUS FELL GRAVE EPOCHAL FATEFUL WEIGHTY EVENTFUL PREGNANT
MOMENTOUSNESS GRAVITY
MOMENTUM WAY FORCE SPEED IMPETUS
MON PEGUAN TALAING
MONACO (NATIVE OF —) MONEGASQUE

MONACO
ANCIENT NAME: MONOECUS
CAPITAL: MONACO MONACOVILLE
DYNASTY: GRIMALDI
LANGUAGE: FRENCH
PEOPLE: MONEGASQUES
PRINCE: LOUIS ALBERT HONORE ANTOINE CHARLES RAINIER FLORESTAN
RIVER: VESUBIE
SECTION: MONTECARLO LACONDAMINE MONACOVILLE

MONAD ATOM JIVA AMEBA HENAD MONAS
MONADIC UNARY
MONADNOCK BARABOO
MONARCH KING QUEEN DANAID DIADEM PRINCE DANAINE EMPEROR AUTOCRAT
MONARCHIAN PRAXEAN
MONARCHICAL KINGLY
MONARCHY KINGDOM
MONASTERY WAT ABBEY BADIA LAURA RIBAT TEKKE TEKYA FRIARY MANDRA VIHARA BONZERY CERTOSA CONVENT KHANKAH MINSTER MONKERY CLOISTER LAMASERY
(ALGERIAN —) RIBAT
(BUDDHIST —) TERA KYAUNG BONZERY LAMASERY
(CARTHUSIAN —) CERTOSA
(HINDU —) MATH
(MOSLEM —) TEKKE TEKYA KHANKAH
(PREF.) MANDRI
(SUFF.) MINSTER
MONASTIC MONKLY MONKISH ABBATIAL CENOBIAN MONACHAL
MONASTICISM MONKERY MONKISM
MONDAY LUNDI
MONETARY EXPLICIT PECUNIARY NUMISMATIC
MONEY (ALSO SEE COIN) AES BOX DIB FAT FEE FEI GET OOF ORO SAP TIN WAD BUCK CASH COAT COIN COLE CRAP CUSH DUBS DUST FUND GATE GELT GILT GOLD HOOT JACK JAKE KALE LOOT LOUR MALI MINT MOSS MUCK PELF ROLL SALT SAND SHAG SOAP SWAG BEANS BLUNT BRASH BRASS BREAD BUNCE BUNTS CHINK CHIPS CLINK DARBY DIMES DOUGH DUMPS FUNDS GREEN GRIGS IMPUT LOLLY LUCRE MEANS MOOLA MOPUS OCHER PURSE RHINO ROCKS ROWDY SCADS SHINY SMASH SPUDS STIFF STUFF SUGAR ARGENT BARATO BARREL BOODLE CHANGE CUNYIE DANARO DINERO DOREMI FARLEU FARLEY FEUAGE FLIMSY FUMAGE GRAITH HANSEL KELTER MAZUMA POCKET SHEKEL SILLER SILVER SPENSE SPLOSH STAMPS STEVEN STUMPY TALENT WAMPUM WISSEL ADVANCE CABBAGE CHATTEL CHINKER COUNTER CRACKER CRUSADE DEPOSIT FALDAGE GUNNAGE OOFTISH SCRATCH SPANKER SPECIES STOCKER CRIMPAGE CURRENCY DEMIMARK INCOMING INTEREST SPENDING STERLING STOCKING XERAPHIN SPONDULIX WAMPUMPEAG SPONDULICKS WHEREWITHAL
(— BET) COMEBACK
(— DUE) DEVOIRS
(— FOR LIQUOR) WHIP
(— HOLDER) TILL
(— LENT) LUMBER
(— MANAGER) GUNSLINGER
(— OF ACCOUNT) ECU ORA
(— PAID TO BIND BARGAIN) ARLES
(— TAKEN IN) DRAWING
(ADDITIONAL —) BONUS
(AVAILABLE —) CAPITAL
(BAD —) SMASH
(BAR —) BONK TANG
(BASE —) SHICE
(BRIBE —) SOAP BOODLE
(COINED —) SPECIE
(COUNTERFEIT —) BOGUS QUEER BOODLE DUFFER SHOWFUL SLITHER
(EARNEST —) ARLES ARRHA DEPOSIT HANDSEL HANDGELD HANDSALE
(EXPENSE —) DIET
(EXTORTED —) PROTECTION
(FERRY —) NAULUM
(HARD —) SPECIE
(HAT —) TAMPANG
(HAVING NO —) FLYBLOWN
(INVESTED —) STOCK
(KIND OF —) NEAR
(LARGE SUM OF —) NUT
(NEAR —) ASSETS
(ON THE —) EXACTLY
(PAPER —) BUCK GREEN SCRIP CABBAGE CURRENCY FROGSKIN
(PASSAGE —) SHIPHIRE
(PLEDGE —) EARNEST
(PRIZE —) PEWTER
(PROTECTION —) ICE
(PUSH —) SPIFF
(READY —) CASH DARBY PREST READY STUFF STUMPY
(REFUNDED —) DRAWBACK
(SHELL —) PEAG HAWOK WAKIKI WAMPUM
(SILVER —) SYCEE
(SMALL SUM OF —) SPILL
(STANDARD BANK —) BANCO
(SUBSISTENCE —) BATTA
(SYSTEM OF — TRANSFER) GIRO
(TRAVELLING —) VIATICUM
(WIRE —) LARI LARIN LARREE
(10 DOLLARS IN —) SAWBUCK
MONEYBAG FOLLIS
MONEY BELT ZONE
MONEY BOX TILL CHEST PIRLIE
MONEY-CHANGER SARAF SHROFF CAMBIST ARGENTER
MONEY-CHANGING AGIO AGIOTAGE AGIO
MONEY DRAWER TILL SHUTTLE
MONEYED RICH WEALTHY
MONEYLENDER BANYA CHETTY USURER LOMBARD MAHAJAN MARWARI SHYLOCK BUMMAREE
MONEYMAKING BANAUSIC
MONEYWORT MANG MYRTLE PRIMWORT
MONGER DEALER
MONGOL HUN KALKA BALKAR BURIAT DAGHUR SHARRA BERBERI KALMUCK KHALKHA SILINGAL
(PL.) HU
MONGOLIA (CAPITAL OF —) ULANBATOR ULAANBAATAR
(DESERT IN —) GOBI
(MONEY OF —) MONGO TUGHRIK
(RIVER OF —) ORHON DZAVHAN KERULEN SELENGE
(TOWN OF —) ONON MUREN DARHAN BULAGAN CHOIREN TAMTSAK ULANBATOR CHOYBALSAN
MONGOOSE MUNG URVA CIVET MUNGO MONGOE MEERKAT VANSIRE
MONGREL CUR DOG FICE FIST MUTT CROSS FEIST LIMER POOCH SCRUB HYBRID PYEDOG BASTARD CURRISH PIEBALD DOGGEREL
MONIKER NAME ALIAS
MONILIALES HYPHO
MONIMIA (GUARDIAN OF —) ACASTO
(HUSBAND OF —) CASTALIO
(LOVER OF —) POLYDORE
MONISM HENISM ONEISM
MONITION TUITION
MONITOR CRT MARKER MENTOR LANTERN PREFECT
MONITOR LIZARD IBID IBIT URAN VARAN WARAL GOANNA WORRAL MONITOR KABARAGOYA
MONK BO FRA COWL LAMA MARO ARHAT BONZE CLERK FRATE FRIAR PADRE YAHAN ARAHAT BHIKKU CULDEE GALLAH GETSUL GOSAIN MONACH SANTON VOTARY CALOYER CLUNIAC GALLACH JACOBIN STARETS STUDITE ATHONITE BACHELOR BASILIAN MARABOUT MONASTIC OLIVETAN SANNYASI TALAPOIN TRAPPIST BALDICOOT CELESTINE THELEMITE BERNARDINE CISTERCIAN
(CHIEF —) ABBOT
(PL.) AGAPETI ACOEMETI
MONKEY APE CAY KRA PUG SAI TUP BEGA BROH BRUH DOUC KAHA MONA MONK MONO SAKI SIME TITI TOTA WAAG ZATI ARABA CEBID DIANA JACKO JOCKO KAHAU MUNGA OATAS PATAS PONGO PUGGY SAJOU TOQUE UNGKA BANDAR COAITA COUXIA GRISON GRIVET GUENON HOWLER LANGUR MACACO MARTEN MIRIKI MONACH NISNAS OLINGO OUBARI PINCHE RILAWA SAMIRI SIMIAN SIMPAI TEETEE VERVET WARINE WEEPER WISTIT BHUNDER COLOBIN GUARIBA GUEREZA HANUMAN KALASIE LUNGOOR MACAQUE MEERKAT MOUSTOC OUAKARI PRIMATE ROLOWAY SAIMIRI SAPAJOU STENTOR TAMARIN ARAGUATO CAIARARA CAPUCHIN DURUKULI ENTELLUS LEONCITO MANGABEY MARMOSET MARTINET MUSTACHE ORABASSU PRIMATAL TALAPOIN TCHINCOU WANDEROO BRACHYURA MALBROUCK
(HOWLER —) ALOUATTA
(KIND OF —) GREASE VERVET COLOBUS
(LIKE A —) PUGGISH
(PREF.) PITHEC(O)
MONKEY BREAD BAOBAB ADANSONIA
MONKEY FLOWER MIMULUS
MONKEYPOT LECYTH KAKARALI LECYTHIS SAPUCAIA
MONKEY PUZZLE BUNYA PINON PINION

MONKEYSHINE DIDO SINGERIE
(PL.) HORSE
MONKFISH MONK LOTTE RHINA SQUATINA
MONKISH CENOBIAN MONASTIC
MONK PARROT LORO
MONKSHOOD ATIS ACONITE ACONITUM NAPELLUS MOUSEBANE
MONO MONACHI
MONOACETATE ACETIN
MONOCARPELLARY SIMPLE
MONOCHORD MAGAS MAGADIS UNICHORD
MONOCHROME CAMAIEU MONOTINT
MONOCLE QUIZ LORGNON EYEGLASS
MONOCLINOUS PERFECT
MONOECISM SYNOECY SYNOEKY
MONOGRAM IHS JHS YHS CIPHER HERALD CHRISMON
(LITERARY —) GBS RLS TSE
MONOGRAPH STUDY MEMOIR BULLETIN DISCOURSE
MONOLITH MENHIR PILLAR
(CIRCLE OF —S) CROMLECH
MONOLITHIC GLOBAL
MONOLOGIST DISEUSE
MONOLOGUE MONOLOGY SOLILOQUY
MONONUCLEOTIDE AMP
MONOPHTHONGAL PURE
MONOPHTHONGIZE SMOOTH
MONOPHYSITE AGNOETE AGNOITE JACOBITE
(PL.) ACEPHALI
MONOPLANE TAUBE PARASOL
MONOPODE SKIAPOD
MONOPOLIZE LURCH ABSORB CONSUME ENGROSS
MONOPOLY REGIE TRUST CARTEL APPALTO
(GOVERNMENT —) REGIE
MONOSACCHARIDE OSE DIOSE HEXOSE KETOSE MONOSE GLYCOSE HEPTOSE PENTOSE PYRANOSE
MONOTONOUS ARID DEAD DULL FLAT WASTE DREARY SAMELY SODDEN ADENOID HUMDRUM INSIPID IRKSOME ONENOTE TEDIOUS BORESOME DRUDGING SAMESOME SINGSONG UNVARIED VEGETABLE
MONOTONY DRAB DRYNESS HUMDRUM DULLNESS SAMENESS
MONOTREME ECHIDNA DUCKBILL
MONOXENOUS DIRECT
MONSIEUR BEAUCAIRE (AUTHOR OF —) TARKINGTON
(CHARACTER IN —) BEAU MARY NASH VALOIS CARLISLE MIREPOIX PHILLIPE MOLYNEAUX WINTERSET CHATEAURIEN
MONSOON VARSHA
MONSTER OGRE BILCH LARVA MORMO RAHAB TERAS UNMAN ELLOPS GERYON MAKARA SHRIMP TYPHON BICORNE CHIMERA CYCLOPS DIDYMUS DIPYGUS ECHIDNA GRENDEL GRIFFIN GRIFFON PRODIGY SLAPPER UNBEAST WARLOCK JANICEPS LINDWORM MOONCALF TARASQUE TYPHOEUS UROMELUS LEVIATHAN
(— WITH 100 EYES) ARGUS
(— WITH 100 HANDS) BRIAREUS
(FABULOUS —) OGRE KRAKEN WIVERN TANIWHA
(FEMALE —) HARPY LAMIA SCYLLA
(HALF-BULL HALF-MAN —) MINOTAUR
(HERALDIC —) SATYRAL
(IMAGINARY —) CHIMERA
(INVISIBLE —) BUNYIP
(LOCH —) NESS NESSIE
(MAN-DEVOURING —) OGRE LAMIA
(MYTHICAL —) HARPY SCYLLA SPHINX CHIMERA WARLOCK MINOTAUR
(SEA —) ORC BELUE PHOCA KRAKEN PISTRIX ZIFFIUS WASSERMAN
(SUPERNATURAL —) LARVA
(TWO-BODIED —) DISOMUS
(WATER —) NICKER
(9-HEADED —) HYDRA
(PREF.) TERAT(O)
(SUFF.) PAGUS
MONSTRANCE SUN
MONSTROSITY FREAK DIPYGUS MONSTER ABORTION IMMANITY MOONCALF TERATISM
(SUFF.) DYMUS
MONSTROUS VAST ENORM GIANT FIENDLY FLAMING HIDEOUS TITANIC BEHEMOTH COLOSSAL DEFORMED ENORMOUS FLAGRANT GIGANTIC PYTHONIC SLAPPING NEFARIOUS PRODIGIOUS
MONTAGNARD SEKANI

MONTANA
CAPITAL: HELENA
COLLEGE: CARROLL
COUNTY: HILL TETON TOOLE CARBON CUSTER FERGUS MCCONE WIBAUX BIGHORN PONDERA RAVALLI CHOUTEAU FLATHEAD MISSOULA
INDIAN: CROW ATSINA SALISH ARAPAHO KUTENAI SIKSIKA SHOSHONE
LAKE: HEBGEN FLATHEAD FORTPECK MEDICINE
MOUNTAIN: AJAX BALDY COWAN SPHINX TORREY GRANITE HILGARD TRAPPER GALLATIN PENTAGON SNOWSHOE
MOUNTAIN RANGE: CRAZY LEWIS POCKY BIGBELT
NICKNAME: BIGSKY MOUNTAIN TREASURE
RIVER: MILK TONGUE KOOTENAI MISSOURI
STATE BIRD: MEADOWLARK
STATE FLOWER: BITTERROOT
TOWN: BUTTE HAVRE MALTA TERRY CIRCLE CONRAD HARDIN HELENA HYSHAM SCOBEY BOZEMAN CHINOOK CHOTEAU EKALAKA FORSYTH GLASGOW ROUNDUP BILLINGS MISSOULA

MONTANIST PHRYGIAN

MONTENEGRO
CAPITAL: CETINJE
COIN: PARA FLORIN PERPERA
LAKE: SCUTARI SHKODER
MOUNTAIN: DURMITOR
NAME: ZETA ILLYRIA CRNAGORA TSERNAGORA
PORT: BAR ULCINJ ANTIVARI DULCIGNO
RIVER: IBAR ZETA DRINA MORACA
TOWN: NIKSIC CETINJE TITOGRAD PODGORICA

MONTEZUMA AZTEC
MONTH AB AV BUL MAY PUS SOL ZIF ZIW ABIB ADAR AHET AOUT APAP ASIN ELUL IYAR JETH JULY JUNE KUAR MAGH MOON TYBI AGHAN APRIL ASARH CHAIT ENERO IYYAR MAIUS MARCH NISAN PAYNI RABIA RAJAB SAFAR SAWAN SEBAT SHVAT SIVAN SIWAN TEBET THOTH TIZRI UINAL AUGUST BHADON CHOIAK JUMADA JUNIUS KARTIK KISLEV KISLEW KISLEY MECHIR MESORE NISSAN NIVOSE PAOPHI PHAGUN SAPHAR SHABAN SHABAT SHEVAT TAMMUZ TEBETH TISHRI VEADAR ABAGHAN APRILIS BAISAKH BYSACKI CHAITRA CHISLEV ETHANIM FLOREAL HESHVAN JANUARY MARTIUS OCTOBER PACHONS PHALGUN RAMADAN SARAWAN SHAABAN SHAWWAL THAMMUZ VENTOSE BRUMAIRE DECEMBER DULKAADA FEBRUARY FERVIDOR FRIMAIRE GAMELION GERMINAL MESSIDOR MUHARRAM NOVEMBER PLUVIOSE POSEIDON PRAIRIAL SEXTILIS ZULKADAH SEPTEMBER
(— OF ISLAMIC YEAR) RABI SAFAR
(IN NEXT —) PROXIMO
(IN PRECEDING —) ULTIMO
(PRESENT —) INSTANT
(SIX —S) SEMESTER
(SYNODIC —) LUNATION
(PREF.) MENO
(SUFF.) MESTER
MONTHLY MENSAL
MONTMORILLONITE SMECTITE
MONUMENT VAT WAT LECH TOMB CROSS STONE TABUT TITLE BILITH DOLMEN HEARSE HEROON MEMORY RECORD TROPHY ARCHIVE CHAITYA CHHATRI CHORTEN DENKMAL FUNERAL TRILITH BILITHON CENOTAPH MEMORIAL MONOLITH TROPAION
(— IN CHURCH) SACELLUM
(— OF BALEARIC ISLANDS) TALAYOT
(— OF BALEARIC ISLES) TALAYOT
(— OF HEAPED STONES) CAIRN
(— WITHIN CHURCH) SACELLUM
(PILLARLIKE —) SHAFT STELA STELE
MONUMENTAL EPIC
MOO LOW
MOOCH BUM CADGE SPONGE
MOOCHER MIKER CADGER GRAFTER SKELDER SPONGER FREELOADER
MOOD CUE FIT TID MIND TIFF TIFT TONE TUNE VEIN WHIM DEVIL FRAME FREAK HEART HUMOR SPITE PLIGHT SPIRIT SPLEEN SPRITE STRAIN TALENT TEMPER CAPRICE FANTASY FEATHER JUSSIVE ATTITUDE OPTATIVE
(— IN LOGIC) BARBARA
(— OF BAD TEMPER) MAD DORTS
(— OF DEPRESSION) FUNK LETDOWN
(CROSS —) FRUMPS
(FRIVOLOUS —) JEST
(GROUCHY —) DODS
(IRRITABLE —) GRIZZLE
(PENSIVE —) MELANCHOLY
(SULKY —) PET
(SULLEN —) STRUNT SULLENS
MOODY SAD GLUM SULKY BROODY GLOOMY MOROSE SULLEN MOODISH PENSIVE
MOOLA DOUGH
MOOLAH GELT MONEY
MOON BUAT LAMP LUNA MAHI DIANA LUNET LUCINA PHOEBE CHANDRA CYNTHIA LEWANNA LUNETTE MOONLET FOGEATER MENISCUS SATELLES
(AREA ON —) MARE TERRA
(FULL —) PLENILUNE
(LARGE MASS ON —) MASCON
(NEW —) PRIME
(PART OF COURSE OF —) MANSION
(SING TO THE —) BAY
(WANING —) WANIAND
(PREF.) LUNI MENI SELEN(I)(O)
MOON AND SIXPENCE (AUTHOR OF —) MAUGHAM
(CHARACTER IN —) AMY ATA DIRK TIARE BLANCHE CHARLES COUTRAS STROEVE STRICKLAND
MOONBLIND LUNATIC
MOONEYE HIODONT
MOONEYE CISCO BLOATER
MOON-EYED LUNATIC
MOONFISH OPAH SUNFISH JOROBADO
MOONFLOWER ACHETE
MOONLIGHT FLESH MOONGLOW
MOONRAT GYMNURE
MOONSET MOONDOWN MOONFALL
MOONSHINE BREW MOON SHINE SHINNY BOOTLEG BLOCKADE
MOONSTONE (AUTHOR OF —) COLLINS
(CHARACTER IN —) CUFF EZRA JOHN BLAKE BRUFF CANDY LUKER RACHEL GABRIEL GODFREY ROSANNA FRANKLIN JENNINGS SPEARMAN VERINDER ABLEWHITE BETTEREDGE HERNCASTLE MURTHWAITE
MOONSTRUCK MAD LOONY LUNATIC
MOONWORT LUNARY HONESTY
MOOR FEN BENT FELL MOSS POST BEACH BERTH HOVEL TURCO COMONTE MARRANO MOGRABI

MOORMAN MORESCO MORISCO COMMONTY
(INFERTILE —) LANDE
MOOR COCK GORCOCK MUIRCOCK
MOORED GIRT
MOORING DOCK MOORAGE
MOORLAND ROSLAND OUTFIELD
MOOSE BELL ELAND CERVID ORIGNAL
(YOUNG —) CALF
MOOSEWOOD DIRCA
MOOT MUTE STIR PORTMOOT
MOP BOB SOP SWAB MALKIN MERKIN MOPPET SCOVEL
(— FOR CLEANING CANNON) MERKIN
(— OF HAIR) TOUSLE
(BAKER'S —) MALKIN MAWKIN
MOPANE IRONWOOD
MOPE MOON MUMP PEAK POUT SULK BOODY BROOD GLOOM
MOPING FUSTY DUMPISH
MOPOKE FROGMOUTH
MOPSUS SEER
(FATHER OF —) AMPYCUS RHACIUS
(MOTHER OF —) MANTO CHLORIS
MORA LOVE TIME LIMMA SEMEION
MORAL TAG PURE CIVIL ETHIC EPIMYTH ETHICAL UPRIGHT HONORARY
(MAN OF —S) AESOP
(PL.) THEW
MORALIST ETHICIAN
MORALISTIC DIDACTIC
MORALITY MORALS VIRTUE
MORALIZING PI
MORASS BOG FEN FLOW MOSS ROSS SUMP FLUSH MARSH SLACK POLDER SLOUGH QUAGMIRE
MORAY PUSI ELGIN HAMLET MURAENA
MORBID SICK MORBOSE PECCANT
MORDANT HANDLE SPIRIT CAUSTIC STRIKER SCATHING
MORDECAI (FATHER OF —) JAIR
(WARD OF —) ESTHER
MORE MO MAE PIU OTHER HELDER
(— OR LESS) HALFWAY
(— THAN) BUT OVER ABOVE RISING PLUSQUAM
(— THAN ADEQUATE) AMPLE
(— THAN ENOUGH) TOO
(— THAN HALF) BETTER
(— THAN ONE) SEVERAL
(— THAN ONE OR TWO) SUNDRY
(— THAN SUFFICIENT) ABUNDANT
(— THAN THIS) YEA
(LITTLE —) ADVANTAGE
(ONE —) ANOTHER
(PREF.) MALLO PLEIO PLEO PLIO
(— THAN) PLU SUPER
MOREEN TABBY
MOREL HELVELLA MORIGLIO
MORELLO MOREL GRIOTTE MULBERRY
MOREOVER EFT EKE TOO ALSO MORE AGAIN EITHER BESIDES FARTHER FURTHER THERETO LIKEWISE OVERMORE
MOREPORK OWL PEHO RURU MOPOKE MOPEHAWK
MORGUE LIBRARY MORTUARY
MORION CABASSET
MORMON COHAB SAINT DANITE PATRIARCH
(— STATE) UTAH
MORMONE CALCITONIN
MORNING GAY MORN MATIN MORROW UNDERN COCKCROW MORNTIME
(IN THE —) MANE
MORNING GLORY NIL KOALI TWINER GAYBINE IPOMOEA MANROOT PILIKAI BINDWEED SCAMMONY MOONFLOWER
(— GROWING AMONG GRAIN) BEAR
MORNING-GOWN PEIGNOIR
MORNING STAR VENUS DAYSTAR LUCIFER MERCURY BARTONIA
MORO LUTAO SAMAL YAKAN ILLANO JOLOANO MARANAO
MOROCCO MAROQUIN

MOROCCO

CAPE: NUN NOUN
CAPITAL: RABAT
COIN: OKIA RIAL OKIEH DIRHAM MOUZOUNA
DISTRICT: ERRIF
FRENCH NAME: MAROC
MEASURE: KALA SAAH FANEGA IZENBI TOMINI
MOUNTAIN: TOUBKAL
MOUNTAIN RANGE: RIF ATLAS
PEOPLE: MOOR BERBER KABYLE MOSLEM MUSLIM
PORT: SAFI CEUTA RABAT SAFFI AGADIR TETUAN LARACHE MAZAGAN MELILLA MOGADOR TANGIER
PROVINCE: CEUTA MELILLA
RIVER: DRA SOUS WADI SEBOU TENSIFT MOULOUYA
TOWN: FES FEZ SAFI OUJDA RABAT AGADIR MEKNES KENITRA TANGIER TETOUAN MARRAKECH CASABLANCA
WEIGHT: ROTL ARTAL ARTEL GERBE RATEL KINTAR QUINTAL

MORON FOOL AMENT IMBECILE
MORONITY MOROSIS
MOROSE SAD ACID GLUM GRUM SOUR MOODY RUSTY SURLY CRUSTY GLOOMY SEVERE STINGY SULLEN CRABBED CROOKED PEEVISH STROUNGE SATURNINE SPLENETIC
MOROSELY CRUSTILY
MOROSENESS ASPERITY
MORPHEME BASE ETYMON COGNATE
MORPHINE SNOW
MORPHOLOGICAL FORMAL
MORRIS MILL MERELS
MORSE WALRUS
MORSEL BIT NIG ORT TIT BITE GNAP SNAP SCRAN TIDBIT BUCKONE MORCEAU NOISETTE PARTICLE SKERRICK
(— OF CHEESE) TRIP
(— OF CHOCOLATE) BUD
(— OF SEASONED MEAT) GOBBET
(CHOICE —) TIDBIT TITBIT
(PREF.) PSOMO
MORTAL BEING DYING FATAL HUMAN VITAL DEADLY FINITE LETHAL BRITTLE DEATHLY DEATHFUL
(FIRST —) YAMA
MORTALITY FLESH MURRAIN
MORTALLY DEADLY FATALLY
MORTAR DAB COMPO DAGGA GROUT LARRY ROYAL SORKI SWISH CANNON CEMENT HOLMOS MINNIE POTGUN BEDDING COEHORN DAUBING PERRIER POUNDER PUGGING SOORKEE
(— AND PESTLE) DOLLY DOLLIE
(— EXTRUDED BETWEEN LATHS) KEY
(— FOR ROCKETS) TROMBE
(— FOR SALUTES) CHAMBER
(— MADE WITH STRAW) BAUGE
(ANTISUBMARINE —) SQUID
(INFERIOR —) SLIME
(SMALL —) HOBIT ROYAL TINKER
(THIN —) LARRY
MORTARBOARD CATERCAP TRENCHER
MORTAR BOAT PALANDER
MORTGAGE DIP LAY BOND LIEN ENGAGE MONKEY OBLIGE WADSET WEDDEED THIRLAGE
(KIND OF —) ARM
MORTGAGOR REVERSER
MORTIFICATION ENVY SHAME SPITE CHAGRIN GANGRENE NECROSIS VEXATION
MORTIFIED ASHAMED
MORTIFY ABASE ABASH SHAME SPITE DEMEAN HUMBLE CHAGRIN CRUCIFY MACERATE
MORTISE GAIN COCKET
(SIDE OF —) CHEEK
MORTUARY MORGUE FUNERARY SAWLSHOT SEPULCHRAL
MORWONG TARAKIHI
MOSAIC BUHL BOULE INLAY AUCUBA BOULLE EMBLEM MUSIVE SCREEN FRISOLEE INTARSIA TERRAZZO
(— PIECE) SMALTO TESSARA
(POTATO —) CRINKLE
(WOOD —) TARSIA INTARSIA
MOSCOW (NATIVE OF —) MOSCOVITE
MOSEL (— FEEDER) SAAR
MOSES (BROTHER OF —) AARON
MOSEY ROAM ANKLE SAUNTER
MOSLEM MOOR HADJI HAFIZ HANIF ISLAM MALAY SALAR PAYNIM SHIITE TURBAN ISLAMIC MOORMAN SANGGIL SARACEN ISLAMITE SANGUILE
(— SCHOLAR) ALIM ULAMA ULEMA
(— SECT) SUNNI
MOSQUE JAMI MOSCH DURGAH MASJID MESKED
MOSQUITO GNAT AEDES CULICID GAMBIAE SKEETER ANOPHELE DIPTERAN
(PREF.) CULIC(I) EMPID(O)
MOSS FOG MNIUM USNEA HYPNUM MUSKEG AEROGEN FOXFEET GULAMAN HAIRCAP PILIGAN TORTULA CROWFOOT MOSSWORT SPHAGNUM STAGHORN
(— HANGING FROM TREE) WEEPER
(PL.) MUSCI
(PREF.) BRY(O) MUSC(I)(O) SPHAGNI SPHAGNO
MOSSBUNKER MENHADEN
MOSSHORN STEER
MOSSI MOLE MORE
MOSSI-GURUNSI GUR
MOSS PINK PHLOX
MOSSTROOPER RIDER
MOSSY OLD FOGGY HOARY MUSCOSE
MOST BEST MOSTLY FARTHEST
(PREF.) PLEISTO
MOSTLY MOST FECKLY CHIEFLY MOSTDEAL
MOT JEST ZINGER
MOTE ATOM ATOMY FESCUE MOATHILL
(PL.) DUST
MOTEL COURT
MOTH IO GEM NUN PUG DART HAWK LUNA MOTE PAGE ACREA APPLE ATLAS EGGAR EGGER FLAME GAMMA IMAGO MORMO PISKY PLUME SAMIA SWIFT THORN USHER WITCH ANTLER BAGONG BUGONG BURNET COSSID DAGGER DATANA HERALD HUMMER JUGATE LACKEY LAPPET MILLER MOODER MUSLIN PLUSIA PRALID QUAKER RUSTIC SPHINX THISBE TINEID TISSUE TUSSUR VENEER ARCTIAN ARCTIID BAGWORM BUDWORM CRAMBID CRININE DELTOID DRINKER EMERALD EMPEROR EUCLEID FESTOON FIGWORM FOOTMAN FRENATE HOOKTIP NOCTUID PEGASUS PSYCHID PYRALIS SLICKER STINGER SYLINID TINEOLA TORTRIX TUSSOCK URANIID VAPORER ZYGENID AEGERIID ARMYWORM BOMBYCID CATOCALA CECROPIA CINNABAR COCHYLIS FISHTAIL FORESTER GEOMETER GOLDTAIL GRISETTE HAWKMOTH HEPIALID KNOTHORN MOTHWORM PHYCITID PLUTELLA SPHINGID SPRAWLER WAINSCOT SATURNIID PALMERWORM
(— BREEDER) AURELIAN
(VERY SMALL —) MICRO
(PREF.) PHALAENO SETO
MOTH BALL REPELLER
MOTHER INA MOM DAME MAMA MERE MADRE MAMMA MAMMY MATER MINNY MODUR MITHER MULIER MUTTER VENTER GENETRIX
(— OF GOD) THEOTOKOS
(— OF THE GODS) RHEA
(DIVINE —) MATRIGAN
(GREAT —) AGDISTIS
(NOURISHING — OF MAN) CYBELE
(OF THE SAME —) UTERINE
(SEVEN —S) MATRIS
(SIDE OF —) ENATE
(PREF.) MADRE MATR(I)(O) METRO
MOTHERLAND COUNTRY
MOTHERLY MATERNAL MATRONAL
MOTHER-OF-PEARL NACRE PEARL ABALONE

MOTIF SPRIG DESIGN DEVICE MOTIVE SCALLOP APPLIQUE MORESQUE
MOTILE ZO ZOO
MOTION WAY FARD FEED GIRD MOVE SIGN WHID HURRY PAVIE APPORT MOMENT MOTIVE TRAVEL UNREST IMPULSE ACTIVITY MOVEMENT OVERTURE
(— ASEA) SCEND
(— OF AIR) AIRFLOW
(— OF CONTEMPT) FICO
(— OF HORSE) AIR
(— TO) ALLATIVE
(ABRUPT —) CHOP
(BACKWARD —) STERNWAY
(CAM —) COULIER
(CIRCULAR —) GYRE COMPASS
(CONFUSED —) GURGE
(DANCE —) CAPER
(DIZZY —) SWIMBEL
(EXPRESSIVE —) GESTURE
(FORWARD —) HEADWAY
(GLIDING —) SWIM SKITTER
(HASTY —) WAFF
(HEAVING —) ESTUS AESTUS
(HURRIED —) HUSTLE
(ILLEGAL —) BALK BAULK
(IRREGULAR —) SWAG
(JERKING —) BOB LIPE JIGGLE
(LATERAL —) DRIFT
(QUIVERING —) TREMOR
(RAPID —) SCOUR BRATTLE
(REARING —) PESADE
(RECIPROCATING —) SEESAW
(ROCKING —) SHOOGLE
(ROTARY —) SWAY BACKSPIN SIDESPIN
(SHOWY —) FANFARE
(SIDEWAYS —) CRAB
(SLOW —) CRAWL
(SPINNING —) ENGLISH
(SUNWISE —) DEASIL
(SWEEPING —) WHISK
(SWIMMING —) FLUTTER
(TREMULOUS —) SHAKE
(UNDULATING —) WAVE
(UNSTEADY —) WABBLE WOBBLE
(UPWARD —) HEAVE
(VIGOROUS —) SKELP
(VIOLENT —) JERK RAPT BENSEL
(WAVERING —) SHAKE
(WAVING —) WAFF
(WHIRLING —) SWIRL
(PREF.) CIN(E)(EMATO)(EMO)(ET)(ETO) KIN(E)(EMATO)(EMO)(ET)(ETO) KINESI MOTI MOTO PHORO
(SUFF.) CINESIA KINESIA KINESIS KINETIC
MOTIONLESS DEAD ASLEEP STATIC IMMOBILE STAGNANT STIRLESS
MOTION PICTURE PIC CINE FILM FLICK MOVIE BIOPIC CINEMA TALKIE CHEAPIE SMELLIE FLICKERS TELEFILM PHOTODRAMA
(PL.) SILENTS
(PREF.) CINE(MATO)(MO)(T)(TO)
MOTIVATE PROPEL ACTUATE ANIMATE INSPIRE
MOTIVATED COVERT
MOTIVATION DRIVE
MOTIVE GOAD SAKE SPUR CAUSE MOTIF SCORE ACTUAL DESIRE OBJECT REASON REGARD SPRING ATTACCO IMPULSE PATTERN RESPECT RINCEAU SUBJECT INSTANCE STIMULUS
(— FOR OBEDIENCE) SANCTION
(ALLEGED —) PRETEXT
(CHIEF —) MAINSPRING
(PRINCIPAL —) MAINSPRING
MOTLEY MIXED MEDLEY RAGTAG MOTTLED PIEBALD UNKEMPT
(PREF.) PARTI PARTY
MOTMOT HOUTOU SAWBILL PICARIAN
MOTOR AUTO TOOT TOUR MOVER ENGINE BOOSTER ROTATOR TURBINE EFFERENT OUTBOARD
MOTORBIKE MOPED
MOTORBOAT KICKER LAUNCH AUTOBOAT RUNABOUT HYDROFOIL
MOTORCAR LIMO COUPE MOTOR SEDAN JALOPY FLIVVER JALOPPY STEAMER CABRIOLET DOODLEBUG LIMOUSINE KNOCKABOUT
(MINIATURE —) KART
(MINIATURE — FOR RACING) KART
(RACING —) KART
MOTORCYCLE BIKE CYCLE MOPED MOTOR STEED TRICAR CHOPPER AUTOETTE DIRTBIKE MINIBIKE TRICYCLE PIPSQUEAK
(PART OF —) HORN SEAT TANK TIRE BRAKE GUARD LEVER LIGHT VALVE WHEEL CLUTCH FENDER SADDLE SIGNAL CALIPER EXHAUST MUFFLER TOOLBOX HANDGRIP THROTTLE GEARSHIFT TAILLIGHT TENSIONER CARBURETOR TACHOMETER SPEEDOMETER
(SMALL —) MINIBIKE
MOTORIST AUTOIST
(SELFISH —) ROADHOG
MOTORMAN CARMAN WATTMAN TROLLYMAN
MOTORTRUCK DRAY LORRY CAMION BOBTAIL FLATBED
MOTTLE CHECK TABBY SPONGE
MOTTLED JAZZ PIED CHINE PINTO TABBY CALICO MARLED MOTLEY RUMINATE SPLASHED
MOTTO MOT LOGO WORD ADAGE AXIOM POESY CACHET DEVICE EUREKA LEGEND REASON IMPRESA EPIGRAPH
(— IN A RING) POSY
(— OF CALIFORNIA) EUREKA
(— OF MAINE) DIRIGO
MOUE FACE
MOUFLON MUSIMON
MOULDER CRUMBLE
MOULDING (HOLLOW —) SCOTIA
(ZIGZAG —) DANCETTE
MOULIN CHIMNEY
MOUND AHU COP HOW LAW LOW BALK BANK BOSS BUND BUTT GOAL HILL HUMP KNOW MOLE POME TELL TEPE TERP TUFT TUMP AGGER BERRY DHERI ESKAR ESKER KNOLL MONDE MOTTE MOUNT PINGO RAISE STUPA TOMAN BARROW CAUSEY MEILER RIDEAU ANTHILL BOUROCK HILLOCK MAMELON BACKSTOP BARBETTE SNOWBANK TEOCALLI
(— ABOUT A PLANT) TUMP
(— FOR MEMORIAL) CAIRN
(— IN BUILDING MATERIAL) DIMPLE
(— OF DETRITUS) WASH
(— OF ICE) DOME
(— OF WOOD TO BE CHARRED) MEILER
(ANCIENT —) TEL TELL
(BURIAL —) LAW LOW TOR TOLA BERRY GUACA HUACA BARROW KURGAN TUMULUS
(FORTIFIED —) DUN
(GLACIAL —) KAME
(KING'S —) POME
(MILITARY —) BARBETTE
(PALISADED —) MOTTE
(VOLCANIC —) HORNITO
(PREF.) BUNO
MOUND BIRD MEGAPODE
MOUNT BEN STY BACK HEAD RIDE RISE SCAN ARISE BIPOD BOARD CLIMB GETON HEAVE HINGE SCALE SPEEL SPIRE SWARM ASCEND ASPIRE BREAST MORIAH CHARGER COLLINE HAIRPIN HARNESS BESTRIDE MOUNTAIN MOUNTING MOUNTURE SURMOUNT
(— A HORSE) FORK LIGHT WORTH
(— BY STEPS) SCAN
(— HIGH) SOAR
(— NEAR TROY) IDA
(— ON PIN) STICK
(— ON WINGS) SOAR
(— UP) ACCRUE
(— UP TO) RUNTO
(STEREOTYPE —) CORE
MOUNTAIN BEN KOP BERG CIMA DAGH FELL KLIP KNOB MONS MONT NEBO PICO PIKE JEBEL MOUNT RANGE BARROW BUNDOC GILEAD GUNONG HEIGHT PISGAH HELICON MONTURE NUNATAK MONADNOCK
(— INHABITED BY SPIRIT) GUACA HUACA
(— MASS) OROGEN
(— PASS) GHAT GHAUT
(— STATE) MONTANA
(— TRACT) DUAR
(AT BASE OF —) PIEDMONT
(BUDDHIST SACRED —) OMEI
(FABLED —) KAF MERU
(GREEK —) OSSA PELION HELICON OLYMPUS MAENALUS
(HIGH —) ALP
(ROUND —) REEK
(SMALL —) NOB KNOB BUTTE
(SNOW —) JOKUL
(SUBMARINE —) GUYOT SEAMOUNT
(PREF.) MONTI ORE(O) ORI ORO
MOUNTAIN ASH SORB SORBUS DOGBERRY MOZEMIZE ROUNTREE WINETREE
MOUNTAIN BEAVER SEWELLEL
MOUNTAIN BINDWEED SOLDANEL
MOUNTAIN CAP SCALP
MOUNTAIN CLIMBER CRAGSMAN
MOUNTAIN CRANBERRY FOXBERRY
MOUNTAINEER WASIR WAZIR HEIDUC HAYDUCK HILLMAN ORESTES MONTESCO TIERSMAN
(PL.) GUTI GUTIANS
MOUNTAIN GOAT IBEX MAZAME
MOUNTAIN LAUREL IVY HEATH ERICAD KALMIS LAUREL IVYWOOD CALFKILL
(THICKET OF —) SLICK
MOUNTAIN LINNET TWITE
MOUNTAIN LION PUMA COUGAR
MOUNTAIN MAHOE EMAJAGUA
MOUNTAIN MISERY TARWEED
MOUNTAINOUS RANGY ALPINE VICIOUS
MOUNTAIN PARSLEY FLUELLEN
MOUNTAIN RANGE KAF QAF TIER SIERRA SAWBACK DINDYMUS
MOUNTAIN SICKNESS VETA
MOUNTAINSIDE FELLSIDE
MOUNTAINTOP MAN DOME
MOUNTAIN WOOD ROCKWOOD
MOUNTEBANK ANTIC BALADIN BALADINE IMPOSTOR OPERATOR
MOUNTED CARDED SADDLE ASTRIDE EASELED EQUITANT
MOUNT ETNA MONGIBEL
MOUNTING MOUNT SCAPE ASCENT FLIGHT MONTANT SOAKING ASPIRANT INCABLOC MOUNTURE
(— OF GEM) CHASE
(STYLE OF —) SETTING
MOURN DOLE KEEN SIGH WAIL PLAIN BEWAIL GRIEVE LAMENT SORROW GRIZZLE
MOURNER WAILER WEEPER
(HIRED —) SALLIE SAULIE
(PROFESSIONAL —) MUTE BLACK KEENER
MOURNFUL SAD BLACK MINOR SORRY WEEPY RUEFUL TRISTE DERNFUL FUNEBRE SIGHFUL WAILFUL DEJECTED DIRGEFUL ELEGIOUS FUNEREAL MAESTIVE MESTFULL PLANTFUL YEARNFUL PLAINTIVE
MOURNING DOLOR SHIVA DISMAL SORROW WIDOWED
(— CLOTH) RADZIMIR
MOURNING BECOMES ELECTRA
(AUTHOR OF —) ONEILL
(CHARACTER IN —) ADAM EZRA ORIN BRANT DAVID HAZEL NILES PETER MANNON LAVINIA CHRISTINE
MOUSE MURINE MYGALE RODENT SHINER VERMIN ARVICOLE CRICETID MYOMORPH
(COMPUTER —) TRACKBALL
(LIKE A —) MURIFORM
(MEADOW —) VOLE
(STRIPED —) KUSU
(PREF.) MURI MY(O) SMINTHO
(SUFF.) MYS
MOUSEBIRD COLY
MOUSE-COLORED DUN
MOUSE DEER PLANDOK
MOUSE GRAY SAKKARA SPARROW
MOUSELIKE MURINE
MOUSETRAP TIPE
MOUSING KEEPER
MOUSY DRAB
MOUTH OS GAB GAM GOB JIB MUG MUN NEB ORF ROW YAP BEAK BEAL BOCA HEAD MUSS PUSS

SHOP TRAP YAWN BAZOO BOCCA BRACE CHOPS CODON STOMA TUTEL GEBBIE KISSER MUZZLE RABBLE RICTUS SUCKER THROAT CLAPPER FLUMMER ORIFICE OSTIOLE STOMACH LORRIKER PAVILLON
(— AND THROAT) COPPER WHISTLE
(— OF CANYON) ABRA
(— OF GLASS FURNACE) BOCCA
(— OF HARBOR) BOCA
(— OF PERITHECIUM) OSTIOLE
(— OF RIVER) BEAL BOCA LADE ENTRY FIRTH INFLUX OSTIUM ESTUARY OSTIARY OUTFALL
(— OF SHAFT) BRACE
(— OF TRUMPET) BELL CODON PAVILLON
(— PARTS OF ARTHROPOD) TROPHI
(AWAY FROM —) ABORAL
(KILN —) KILNEYE KILNHOLE
(SORE — OF SHEEP) ECTHYMA
(TOWARD —) ORAD
(TOWARD THE —) ORAD
(WRY —) MURGEON
(PL.) ORA
(PREF.) BUCCO ORI ORO OSCULI STOM(A)(AT)(ATO)(O)
(SUFF.) STOMA(TA)(TE)(TOUS) STOME STOMI(A) STOMOUS STOMUM STOMY

MOUTHFUL GAG GOB SUP GNAP SWIG GOLEE GOBBET

MOUTH-ORGAN HARP HARMONICA

MOUTHPART BILL

MOUTHPIECE BAR BEAK BOCAL MOUTH FIPPLE SYRINX PROPHET
(— OF BAGPIPE) MUSE
(— OF OTHERS) FUGUEMAN
(— OF PIPE) STEM

MOUTHWASH GARGLE COLLUTORIUM

MOUTH-WATERING SALIVANT

MOVABLE FREE LOOSE MOBILE PORTABLE REMUABLE
(PL.) MEUBLES

MOVE GO ACT AWE FIG GEE GET WAG BOOM BORE BUCK BUMP CALL DRAW FIRK FLIT GOAD HEAT KNEE MAKE PIRL ROLL SILE SPUR STEP STIR SWAY WORK ANKLE BLITZ BUDGE CARRY CAUSE CROWD DRAFT HEAVE IMPEL LIGHT MARCH MUDGE QUECH REMUE ROUSE SHAKE SHIFT TOUCH GAMBIT HANDLE HUSTLE INCITE INDUCE KINDLE MOTION PROMPT QUITCH REMBLE SASHAY STRAKE ACTUATE AGITATE ANIMATE DISTURB DRAUGHT FLUTTER INSPIRE MIGRATE PROVOKE AMBULATE BULLDOZE CATAPULT DEMARCHE DISLODGE DISPLACE MOTIVATE
(— ABOUT) ROLL WEND DISPACE SHUFFLE CONVERSE LOCOMOTE
(— ACROSS) THWART
(— ACROSS SCREEN) CRAWL SCROLL
(— ACTIVELY) YANK
(— AIMLESSLY) GAD POKE BOGUE
(— ALONG) SHOG
(— APART) ABDUCT SPREAD
(— A RESOLUTION) FIRST
(— ASIDE) SKEW
(— AS IN STUPOR) DAVER
(— ASUNDER) SINGLE
(— AT TOP SPEED) LICK
(— AWAY) CUT MOG DECAMP RECEDE
(— AWKWARDLY) HODGE HIRSEL LARRUP SHAMBLE SLUMMOCK
(— BACK) FADE ARSLE RECUR RECEDE RETIRE RETREAT
(— BACKWARD AND FORWARD) GIG SWAY DARTLE DIDDLE SHUFFLE SHUTTLE
(— BOOM OR SAIL) JIB
(— BRISKLY) FAN HALE STIR FRICK FRIKE FRISK KNOCK SQUIRT TRANCE TRAVEL WHIPPET
(— BY FITS AND STARTS) JIFFLE
(— BY JERKS) HITCH JIGGET JIGGLE JINKLE
(— BY SMALL SHOCKS) JOG
(— BY WHEELS) ROLL TRUNDLE
(— CHESS PIECE) DEVELOP
(— CLUMSILY) HOIT JOLL PAUT BARGE KEVEL HIRSEL LUMBER TOLTER GALUMPH STUMBLE
(— COMPUTER VIDEO DISPLAY) SCROLL
(— DIAGONALLY) CATER
(— DOWN) SILE STOOP DECLINE DESCEND
(— FORCIBLY) SHOVE
(— FORWARD) BREAK ADVANCE PROGREDE
(— FROM SIDE TO SIDE) WAG
(— FURTIVELY) LEER GLIDE SLINK SLIVE SNEAK STEAL
(— GRADUALLY) EDGE
(— GRATINGLY) SCRAPE
(— HAPHAZARDLY) BUCKET
(— HASTILY) SCUR SKIRR
(— HAUGHTILY) SWOOP
(— HEAVILY) LUG LUMP FLUMP LUMBER
(— IN AGITATION) SEETHE
(— IN AWKWARD MANNER) GANGLE
(— IN CIRCLES) MILL PURL
(— IN MARBLES) FULK
(— IN ON) NEAR
(— IN RIPPLES) CURL
(— IN SHAMBLE) SHUFFLE
(— IN SHUFFLING MANNER) MOSEY
(— IN SMALL DEGREES) INCH
(— INWARDLY) ENMOVE
(— IN WATER) SQUELCH
(— IN WAVES) LAP CRINKLE
(— JERKILY) JAG BUCK FLIP KICK FLIRT BUCKET TWITCH
(— LANGUIDLY) MAUNDER
(— LAZILY) HULK
(— LEISURELY) AMBLE
(— LIGHTLY) BRUSH FLUFF
(— LOOSELY) SLOP
(— NERVOUSLY) DITHER
(— NIMBLY) KILT LINK WHIP DANCE
(— OFF) FIRK RYNT MOSEY MORRIS
(— ON) MOG VAMP AVAUNT SUCCEED WHIGFARE
(— OUT) BLOW
(— OUT OF SIGHT) SINK
(— QUICKLY) BOB FIG CLIP DUCK FIRK FLAX FLIT GIRD JINK KITE SCUR WHAP WHEW WHID WHOP YANK FLASH GLENT SKEET SKIRR SKITE SPANK SQUIB STAVE STOUR THROW NIDDLE STRIKE WALLOP SKIMMER
(— QUIETLY) SLIP
(— RAPIDLY) BANG BOLT BUZZ HEEL HURL SKIR THUD CHASE GLINT SCOUR CAREER GIGGIT HURTLE WHIRRY AGITATE CLATTER HIGHTAIL
(— RESTLESSLY) FIG GAD FIKE ITCH CHURN SQUIB JIFFLE KELTER
(— SHAKILY) HOTTER
(— SIDEWAYS) SKID SLEW SLUE
(— SIDEWISE) CRAB EDGE SIDLE SLENT
(— SINUOUSLY) WRIGGLE
(— SLOWLY) LAG MOG INCH PANT PAUT SLUG BOGUE CRAWL CREEP DRAWL FUDGE SHLEP SLOOM SNAIL HAGGLE LINGER SCHLEP SCHLEPP TRINTLE
(— SMOOTHLY) SLIP DRIFT FLOAT GLIDE SLEEK GLISSADE
(— SPIRALLY) GYRATE
(— STEADILY) FORGE
(— STEALTHILY) GLIDE SLINK SMOOT SNAKE
(— STIFFLY) CRAMBLE CRAMMEL
(— SUDDENLY) BOLT LASH YERK GLENT START FLOUNCE STARTLE
(— SWIFTLY) CUT FLY BOOM HARE LEAP RAKE SCUD SPIN BREEZE COURSE WUTHER SWIFTEN
(— THROUGH AIR) FLY
(— TO AND FRO) FAN FLOP DODGE SHAKE WIGWAG AGITATE
(— TO ANOTHER PLACE) ADJOURN
(— TO LEEWARD) DRIVE
(— TREMULOUSLY) WAPPER
(— TRIPPINGLY) WALTZ WAPPER
(— UNEASILY) FIDGET
(— UNSTEADILY) BICKER BUMBLE FALTER HOBBLE WABBLE WAMBLE WELTER WOBBLE BLUNDER STAGGER STUMBLE
(— UP AND DOWN) BOB HOWD SEESAW TEETER
(— UPWARD) ARISE ASCEND GRADUATE
(— VESSEL) KEDGE
(— VIGOROUSLY) FLOG STRAY
(— VIOLENTLY) DASH FLOG HURL LASH LEAP SWASH AGITATE COMMOVE
(— WAVERINGLY) FLEET
(— WEAKLY) FLAG
(— WITH BEATING MOTION) FLAP
(— WITH EFFORT) ACHE WADE
(— WITH LEAPS) SKIP SPRING
(— WITH NOISY ACTIVITY) BUSTLE
(— WITH POMP) SWEEP
(— WITH SHORT TURNS) ZIGZAG
(CHESS —) KEY COOK NECK PLOY GAMBIT KEYMOVE
(STRATEGIC —) TACK
(SUCCESSFUL —) SCORE
(SUDDEN —) GAMBADE

MOVED MOSSO ANIMATE FRANTIC INSTINCT
(— BY LOVE) AMOROUS
(EASILY —) FLESHLY SKINLESS

MOVEMENT EDDY MOTO PLAY STIR CARRY CAUSE FLICK FLISK FLOAT FRONT GESTE MUDGE TREND UKIYO ACTION CURSUS ENTREE MOMENT MOTION PIAFFE SPRAWL STROKE CURRENT FURIANT GAMBADO GESTURE KINESIS PIAFFER UKIYOYE BUSINESS CHARTISM FEMINISM FUTURISM HASKALAH STIRRING PERIPATETICS
(— BY ORGANISMS) TAXIS
(— FOR POLITICAL UNION) ENOSIS
(— FROM POINT TO POINT) PASSAGE
(— IN BULLFIGHT) SUERTE
(— OF AIR) SPIRIT
(— OF CHORUS) STROPHE
(— OF CLOUDS) CARRY
(— OF COMPUTER BITS) SHIFT
(— OF EYES) NYSTAGMUS
(— OF HAND) PASS
(— OF HORSE) LEVADE PIAFFE
(— OF LEG) STEP
(— OF LOOM) MOUSING
(— OF NEEDLE) STITCH
(— OF PLANTS) NUTATION
(— OF PROTOPLASM) CYCLOSIS
(— OF QUADRILLE) TRENISE
(— OF ROPE) SURGE
(— OF SHIP) STERNWAY
(— OF SHUTTLE) SHOOT
(— OF TIDE) LAKIE
(— OF TROOPS) LIFT
(— OF WATER) BOBBLE
(— TO AND FRO) SHUTTLE
(— TOWARD GOAL) STRIDE
(AGITATED —) WORKING
(ART —) CUBISM
(AVANT-GARDE —) UNDERGROUND
(BACKWARD —) BACKUP BACKLASH BACKWASH
(BALLET —) PLIE BATTU FRAPPE FOUETTE FLICFLAC
(BOBBING —) BOBBLE
(BODILY —) ACTION
(BOWEL —) LAXATION
(BOWING —) LEG
(BOXING —) SPAR
(BRISK —) SNAP
(BROWNIAN —) PEDESIS
(CAVALRY —) CARACOLE
(CIRCULAR —) CYCLING
(CLEVER —) PAW
(CONFUSED —) MILLING
(CONVULSIVE —) SPASM
(DANCE —) FRIS BRISE CLOSE GIGUE GLIDE LASSU SPIRAL BATTERIE
(DARTING —) FLIRT
(DECISIVE —) UPCOME
(DOWNWARD —) DECLINE
(DROLL —) GAMBADE GAMBADO
(ENLIGHTENMENT —) HASKALAH
(EXPANSION —) BOOM
(EYE —) REM SACCADE
(FANTASTIC —) GAMBADO
(FENCING —) VOLT
(FLAPPING —) FLAFF
(FLUCTUATING —) PLAY

(FORWARD —) SWEEP ADVANCE PROGRESS INCESSION PROCESSION
(FROLICKING —) FRISK GAMBOL
(GRADUAL —) CREEPISM
(GRAZING —) SKIFF
(GREEK UNDERGROUND —) EAM
(GYMNASTIC —) KIP SWING DISMOUNT
(HUMOROUS —) BURLA
(IMPATIENT —) FLOUNCE
(INCIPIENT —) MINT
(INDEPENDENCE —) SWADESHI
(INVOLUNTARY —) REFLEX
(JAPANESE ART —) YAMATO YAMATOE
(JERKING —S) BALLISM
(JERKY —) SNATCH
(JERKY EYE —) SACCADE
(LATERAL —) LEEWAY
(MASS —) STAMPEDE
(MASSAGE —) SCIAGE
(MILITARY —) BOUND MANEUVRE
(MUSICAL —) AIR DUET BURLA DUMKA LARGO ADAGIO ENTREE FINALE PRESTO ANDANTE PRELUDE SCHERZO POSTLUDE SARABAND SYMPHONY ALLEMANDE INTERMEZZO
(NOISELESS —) WHID
(OBLIQUE —) GLANCE
(OSCILLATING —) HUNT
(PAINTING —) FAUVISM TACHISM TACHISME VORTICISM
(POETRY —) IMAGISM
(POLITICAL —) LEFTISM GAULLISM
(QUADRILLE —) POULE
(QUICK —) PAW DART WHID WHIP YERK GLENT SHAKE GLANCE
(RATIONALISTIC —) DEISM
(REELING —) STAGGER
(RELIGIOUS —) JOCISM BABIISM PIETISM STUNDISM
(RETROGRADE —) SLIP CREEP
(RETURN —) BACKHAUL
(RHYTHMIC —) DANCE
(ROCKING —) HOWD
(ROWING —) HOICK
(SKATING —) MOHAWK CHOCTAW
(SKILLED —) SUERTE
(SNATCHING —) CLUTCH
(SPASMODIC —) JUMP HICCUP SPRUNT HICCOUGH
(SPRINGY —) LILT
(STAGGERING —) WAMBLE
(STEALTHY —) SLINK
(SUDDEN —) HITCH SPANG START FLICKER
(SWAYING —) SWAG
(SWEEPING —) SWINGE
(SWIFT —) SWOOSH
(TERRORIST —) NIHILISM
(THEOLOGICAL —) ARIANISM
(TUMULTUOUS —) HORROR EMOTION
(TURNING —) CARACOLE
(UNEXPECTED —) LUNGE
(UNSTEADY —) WABBLE WOBBLE
(UP AND DOWN —) SEESAW
(UPWARD —) BULGE SCEND
(UPWARD — OF VESSEL) SCEND
(WALKING —) AMBLE
(WATCH —) EBAUCHE BAGUETTE
(WAVING —) WAFT
(ZIGZAG —) TACK MEANDER
(PREF.) KINESI KINETO KIN(O)
(SUFF.) CINESIA KINESIA KINESIS KINETIC

MOVEMENTS
(SUFF.)
(PERFORMANCE OF —) PRACTIC PRAXIA PRAXIS

MOVER MOTIVE CLIPPER
(KIND OF —) PEOPLE

MOVIE (ALSO SEE MOTION PICTURE) PIC FILM FLICK BIOPIC FLICKS SLEEPER MELODRAMA
(— WITH BLOODSHED) SHOOTEMUP
(ANIMATED —) TOON CARTOON
(BIOGRAPHICAL —) BIOPIC
(CRIME —) FILMNOIR
(SUCCESSFUL —) MEGAHIT
(PL.) PICTURES

MOVIES (DEVOTEE OF —) CINEPHILE

MOVING WAY HIGH ASTIR GOING QUICK AFLOAT MOVENT ANIMATE CURRENT AMBULANT FLITTING PATHETIC POIGNANT TOUCHING AFFECTING
(— ABOUT) AROUND AMBULANT
(— AIMLESSLY) ERRANT
(— BACKWARDS) CRAB
(— DOWN LINE) ACTIVE
(— FORWARD) ADVANCE
(— HAPHAZARDLY) AFLOAT
(— IN MANY DIRECTIONS) DIFFUSE
(— JERKILY) ATWITCH
(— RAPIDLY) STICKLE SKELPING
(— SLOWLY) SOFT GLACIAL TEDIOUS
(— TO AND FRO) AGITATED
(NOT —) STICKY STABILE

MOVINGLY PATETICO

MOW CUT BARB GOAF SKIM TASS CRADLE SCYTHE SICKLE DESECATE
(— BEANS) THROAT
(— FOR STORING GRAIN) TOSS
(— OF CORN) CANSH
(HAY —) TASS

MOWER MEADER
(FOREMOST —) LORD

MOWING MATH MOWTH SHEAR
(SECOND —) AFTERMATH

MOXIE GALL SPIRIT

MOZA (FATHER OF —) CALEB ZIMRI

MOZAMBIQUE (CAPE OF —) DELGADO
(CAPITAL OF —) MAPUTO
(LAKE OF —) CHUALI NHAVARRE
(MONEY OF —) METICAL
(RIVER OF —) SAVE MSALU RUVUMA LIMPOPO LUGENDA ZAMBEZI
(TOWN OF —) MAUA TETE BEIRA MAPAI ZUMBO CHEMBA MANICA NAMAPA PAFURI CHIMOIO NAMPULA

MOZZETTA CAMAIL

MR HERR SIGNOR SIGNIOR SIGNORE

MR MIDSHIPMAN EASY (AUTHOR OF —) MARRYAT
(CHARACTER IN —) EASY JACK AGNES MESTY WILSON REBIERA GASCOIGNE MIDDLETON

MRS MME FRAU MISS PANI HANOUM SENORA SENHORA SIGNORA GOODWIFE

MRS DALLOWAY (AUTHOR OF —) WOOLF
(CHARACTER IN —) PETER SALLY SETON SMITH WALSH HOLMES KALMAN WILLIAM BRADSHAW CLARISSA DALLOWAY SEPTIMUS

MRS WARREN'S PROFESSION
(AUTHOR OF —) SHAW
(CHARACTER IN —) FRANK PRAED VIVIE CROFTS GEORGE SAMUEL WARREN GARDNER

MUCH FAR FELE MICH REAL WELL GREAT HEAPS MOLTO MOULT SIZES MICKLE MUCHLY ABUNDANT BEAUCOUP MUCHWHAT
(— CALLED FOR) LEEFTAIL
(PRETTY —) GAILY GAYLY
(SO —) ALL SUCH TANTO INSOMUCH
(TOO —) TROP TROPPO
(VERY —) ALL BADLY GREAT HEAPS LOADS SWITHE SWYTHE APLENTY GEYLIES GREATLY
(PREF.) ERI MULT(I) POLY SYCHNO
(HOW —) POSO QUANTI

MUCH ADO ABOUT NOTHING
(AUTHOR OF —) SHAKESPEARE
(CHARACTER IN —) HERO JOHN PEDRO URSULA VERGES ANTONIO CLAUDIO CONRADE FRANCIS LEONATO BEATRICE BENEDICK BORACHIO DOGBERRY MARGARET BALTHASAR

MUCILAGE GUM MUCUS MUCAGO

MUCILAGINOUS MALACOID

MUCK CACK SOIL

MUCOID BLENNOID

MUCUS SNOT MUCOR BUBBLE MUCAGO PHLEGM SNIVEL PITUITE
(PREF.) BLENN(I)(O) MUC(I)(O)(OSO) MYX(O)
(SUFF.) MYXA

MUD DAB FEN CLAY DIRT DUBS FANC GLAR LAIR MIRE MOIL SAUR SIND SLAB SLEW SLOB SLOP SLUB SLUD SLUE SLUR SUMP CLART FANGO GLAUR GUMBO SLAKE SLIME SLOSH SLUSH SPOSH SQUAD WAISE PELOID SLOUGH SLUDGE CLABBER GUTTERS MURGEON SLOBBER SLODDER SLUDDER SLUTHER SULLAGE
(LACUSTRINE —) GYTTJA
(LIQUID —) SLUSH
(OF DRIED —) CUTCHA
(THIN —) SLUR
(PREF.) LIMI LIMO PEL(O) TELMAT(O)

MUDAR AK AKUND ASHUR MADOR YERCUM AKMUDDAR

MUDCAP ADOBE

MUD CAT FLATHEAD

MUDCAT STATE MISSISSIPPI

MUDDLE MIX BALL DOZE HASH MASH MESS MULL MUZZ SOSS ADDLE SNAFU BEMUSE BURBLE FANKLE FOITER FUDDLE HUDDLE JUMBLE MAFFLE MIZZLE MOFFLE MUCKER POTHER PUDDLE TANGLE BECLOUD BEDEVIL BLUNDER CONFUSE EMBROIL FLUSTER POOTHER STUPEFY BEFUDDLE BEWILDER CONFOUND DISORDER FLIUNDER

MUDDLED ADDLE BEERY FOGGY FUZZY MUSED MUZZY DRUMLY GROGGY BESOTTED CONFUSED

MUDDY DEEP FOUL GLET OOZY ROIL SICK DIRTY DROVY DUBBY GUMLY ROILY SLAKY CLAGGY CLARTY CLASHY DREGGY DROUMY DRUMLY GROUTY LIMOUS PUDDLY SALLOW SLABBY SLOBBY SLOPPY SLUBBY SLUDGY TURBID CLATCHY GUTTERY MUDDIFY MUDDISH SLOUGHY CLABBERY LUTULENT SLOBBERY
(— BY STIRRING) STUDDLE

MUDFISH BOWFIN KOMTOK

MUDFLAT PLAYA

MUDFLOW LAHAR MUDSPATE

MUDGUARD WING CUTTOO SPLASHER

MUDHOLE PULK SLOUGH LOBLOLLY

MUD MINNOW DOGFISH MUDFISH

MUD PUPPY DOGFISH

MUERMO ULMO

MUEZZIN CRIER

MUFF ERR BLOW BOBBLE MUFFLE SNUFFKIN

MUFFIN COB GEM SINK COBBE HAZEL SINKER MANCHET PIKELET POPOVER

MUFFLE MOB MOP PAD DAMP DULL MUTE NOSE WRAP BUMBLE DEADEN MUZZLE SHROUD STIFLE ENVELOP
(— A BELL) CLAM
(— THE HEAD) MOBLE

MUFFLED DEAD DEAF DULL CLOSE THICK HOLLOW INWARD MOBBED WRAPPED

MUFFLER SCARF MUFFLE SILENCER

MUFTI JURIST CIVVIES

MUG TOT BOCK CANN FACE PUNK THUG STEIN KISSER NOGGIN PEWTER SCONCE SEIDEL CANETTE GODDARD TANKARD BLACKPOT PANNIKIN SCHOPPEN
(ALE —) TOBY
(LIQUOR —) CAN GUN
(TWO-HANDLED —) SCONCE

MUGGER GOA HAM

MUGGING YOKING

MUGGINS SNIFF

MUGGY FOZY MUNGY PUGGY STICKY MUGGISH PUTHERY

MUGWORT BULWAND MUGWEED

MUISCA CHIBCHA

MUISHOND ZORIL ZORILLE

MULATTO PARDO GRIFFE GRIQUA GRIFFIN TERCERON

MULBERRY AL AAL ACH AUTE KOZO MORE WAUKE ALROOT MURREY MORELLO SOURBUSH SYCAMINE
(PREF.) MOR(I)

MULBERRY FIG SYCAMORE

MULCT ROB FINE CHECK AMERCE SCONCE FORFEIT PENALTY

MULE BUCKER HYBRID ACEMILA IRONMAN JARHEAD JUGHEAD RATTAIL SUMPTER CENCERRO HARDTAIL QUADROON QUATERON

(DROVE OF —S) ATAJO MULADA
(MOHAMMED'S —) ALBORAK
MULE ARMADILLO MULITA
MULE DRIVER SKINNER
MULE SHOE PLANCHE
MULETEER ASSMAN ARRIERO
MULE TRAIN (— DRIVER) WAGONER
MULISH BALKY STUPID STUBBORN OBSTINATE
MULL CHAW BOSOM STUDY FETTLE MULMUL PONDER STEATIN COGITATE MEDITATE
MULLAH ULAMA ULEMA
MULLEIN TORCH AGLEAF ICELEAF DOVEWEED FELTWORT FOXGLOVE HAGTAPER LUNGWORT VERBASCO
MULLER DAMPENER
MULLET BOBO LISA LIZA BOURI GARAU KANAE MOLET HARDER MULLOID GOATFISH MUGILOID SPRINGER
(UNPIERCED —) STAR
MULLIGRUBS COLIC
MULLION MONIAL
MULLOWAY JEWFISH KINGFISH SCIAENID
MULTICOLORED PIED CALICO
MULTIFARIOUS MANIFOLD
MULTIFARIOUSNESS VARIETY
MULTIFORM DIVERSE
MULTILINGUAL POLYGLOT
MULTIPLE DECUPLE PARALLEL SEPTUPLE MULTIPLEX
MULTIPLICAND FACIEND
MULTIPLICATION INCREASE DUPLATION
MULTIPLICITY MULTEITY
MULTIPLIER FACIENT COFACTOR
MULTIPLY VIE BREED LAYER DOUBLE INVOLVE ENGENDER INCREASE MANIFOLD PROPAGATE PROLIFERATE
(— BY ITSELF) SQUARE
MULTIPLYING
(PREF.) POLY
MULTITUDE SEA ARMY CRAM HEAP HIVE HOST ROUT RUCK CLOUD CROWD FLOTE MEINY POWER SHOAL SWARM HIRSEL HOTTER LEGION MAMPUS MEINIE NATION THRONG SMOTHER PLURALITY
(PL.) FLOCKS
MULTITUDINOUS LEGION MYRIAD MANIFOLD NUMEROUS
MULTIVALENT POLYAD
MULTURE THIRL THIRLAGE
MUM CLUM DARK MUMMER
MUMBLE CHEW MOUP MUMP BROCK CHELE MOUTH CHAVEL FAFFLE FUMBLE HOTTER HUMMER MAFFLE MOFFLE PALTER DRUMBLE FLUMMER GRUMBLE
(— PEEVISHLY) WITTER
MUMBLER MAFFLER
MUMBLETY-PEG KNIFE
MUMMER ACTOR GUISER GUISARD
MUMMERY MORRIS HODENING PUPPETRY
MUMMICHOG MUDFISH
MUMMY CONGO MUMMIA SKELET
(PREF.) MOMIO
MUMMY BROWN BAY SNUFF TAMARACK
MUMMY CASE SLEDGE
MUMPS BRANKS PAROTITIS
MUNCH CHEW NOSH CHUMP MANGE MUNGE
MUND GRITH
MUNDA KOLARIAN
MUNDANE WORLD EARTHLY FLESHLY SECULAR TERRENE SUBSOLAR
MUNG BEAN MUG GRAM MONGOE BALATONG
MUNIA MAYA PADDA
MUNICIPAL TOWN CIVIL
MUNICIPALITY CITY TOWN CABILDO
MUNIFICENCE BOUNTY ROYALTY LARGESSE
MUNIFICENT ROYAL LIBERAL MUNIFIC PROFUSE MAGNIFIC PRINCELY OPENHANDED
MUNITION
(PL.) ARMAMENT ORDNANCE
MUNJ MOONJA MANJEET
(CULMS OF —) SIRKI SIRKY
MUNTIACUS CERVULUS
MUNTJAC KAKAR RATWA KIDANG
MURAL TOPIA FRESCO
MURCIA (RIVER OF —) SEGURA
(TOWN OF —) MULA LORCA TOTANA
MURDER HIT OFF BANE KILL SLAY BLOOD BURKE DEATH SCRAG FELONY RUBOUT KILLING MURDRUM MURTHER THUGGEE HOMICIDE MASSACRE THUGGERY THUGGISM PATRICIDE
(FEATURING —) SNUFF
(PREMEDITATED —) HIT
MURDERER BANE CAIN KILLER ASSASSIN
MURDER IN THE CATHEDRAL
(COMPOSER OF —) PIZZETTI
MURDEROUS FELL GORY CRUEL FELON BLOODY CARNAL SAVAGE DEATHFUL SANGUINARY
MURKINESS HAZE GLOOM
MURKY DARK BLACK DIRTY MIRKY MUDDY CLOUDY PUDDLY
MURMUR COO HUM BRUM BURR CLUM CURR HUZZ MUSE BRAWL BROOL GRANK INKLE MOURN RUMOR SOUCH SOUGH BABBLE BURBLE GRUDGE GRUTCH HUMMER MUTTER PIPPLE REPINE RUMBLE CROODLE MURGEON WHIMPER WHISPER WHITTER COMPLAIN
(— AGREEABLY) CHIRM
(— AMOROUSLY) COO
(— OF PAIN) MOAN
(— OF STREAM) PURL
(CONFUSED —) BABBLE
(DEEP —) BROOL
MURMURING BUZZ BRABBLE MURGEON RUMOROUS
MURRAH SURTI
MURRAIN PLAGUE
MURRAL DALAG
MURRE TINK ARRIE LUNGIE STRANY TINKER ROCKBIRD
MURREY SANGUINE
MUSA SABA
MUSANG POWCAT POLECAT
MUSCA FLY
MUSCADINE BULLACE SCUPPERNONG
MUSCAT (SEE OMAN)
MUSCLE EYE PEC BOWR LIRE THEW FLESH MOUSE PSOAS SINEW BENDER BICEPS CORACO FLEXOR LACERT PENNON RECTUS SOLEUS TENSOR AGONIST AMBIENS CANINUS DELTOID DILATOR ERECTOR EVERTOR FLECTOR GLUTEUS ILIACUS LEVATOR MUSCULE NASALIS OBLIQUE ROTATOR SCALENE SCALLOP TRICEPS VAGINAL ABDUCTOR ADDUCTOR ADJUSTER ANCONEUS ARRECTOR ATOLLENT BIVENTER DIDUCTOR EXTENSOR GEMELLUS GRACILIS INVERTOR MASSETER MENTALIS OBLIQUUS OMOHYOID OPPONENS PALMARIS PATHETIC PECTORAL PERONEUS PROCERUS PRONATOR RETENTOR SCALENUS SERRATUS SPINALIS SPLENIUS TEMPORAL TIBIALIS HAMSTRING OBTURATOR SARTORIUS
(— MASSAGE) ROLF ROLFING
(HAVING LUMPY —S) LOADED
(THIGH —) HAMSTRING
(PL.) BRAWN THEWS
(PREF.) INO MUSCUL(O) NERVI NERVO
(SUFF.) EUS MYA MYARIA
MUSCLE-BOUND (NOT —) SPRY
MUSCLE SUGAR INOSITE INOSITOL
MUSCOVITE MICA
MUSCOVY DUCK PATO SCOVY
MUSCULAR ROPY HEFTY HUSKY THEWY BRAWNY ROBUST SINEWY STRONG TOROSE NERVOUS ATHLETIC
MUSCULATURE DETRUSOR
(SUFF.) **(HAVING —)** MYA MYARIA
MUSE CLIO DUMP MESE MULL NETE REVE AMUSE AOIDE DREAM ERATO MNEME STUDY THINK HYPATE MELETE PONDER THALIA URANIA EUTERPE REFLECT CALLIOPE COGITATE CONSIDER MEDITATE POLYMNIA RUMINATE MELPOMENE POLYHYMNIA TERPSICHORE
(— OF ASTRONOMY) URANIA
(— OF COMEDY) THALIA
(— OF EPIC POETRY AND ELOQUENCE) CALLIOPE
(— OF HISTORY) CLIO
(— OF LOVE POETRY) ERATO
(— OF MIMIC ART) POLYHYMNIA
(— OF POETRY AND DANCE) TERPSICHORE
(— OF THE FLUTE) EUTERPE
(— OF TRAGEDY) MELPOMENE
(PL.) PIERIDES
MUSETTE OBOE
MUSEUM MOMA MUSEE PRADO LOUVRE
(— IN NEW YORK CITY) MET MOMA FRICK CLOISTERS GUGGENHEIM
(— PIECE) RELIC
(PREF.) MUSEO
MUSH SAMP KASHA SLUSH MUSHER SEPAWN SOFKEE POLENTA SAGAMITE SCRAPPLE
(LIKE —) SOGGY
MUSHI (FATHER OF —) MERARI
MUSHROOM FAT CEPE FLAT GROW DEATH ENOKI MITRA MOREL AGARIC BEAVER BUTTON FUNGUS AMANITA BLEWITS BOLETUS BROILER LEPIOTA SHITAKE MUSHRUMP SHIITAKE WHITECAP ENOKIDAKE CHAMPIGNON SHAGGYMANE CHANTERELLE TEONANACATL
(— HUNTER) MYCOPHILE
(PART OF —) CAP GILL RING STEM STALK STIPE VOLVA PILEUS ANNULUS MYCELIUM
(PREF.) MYC(O) MYCET(O)
MUSHY SOFT SOPPY
MUSIC RAG DRAG FUNK GLEE JAZZ NOME ROCK BEBOP CANOR CHIME DREAM GIMEL GYMEL MURKY NOISE SWING DREHER FUSION MUSICA DESCANT FORLANA LANCERS LANDLER MUSICAL MUSICRY FALSETTO FANDANGO GUARACHA
(— FOR ENTRANCE) ENTREE
(— OF LOUISIANA) ZYDECO
(— OF SOUTHERN LOUISIANA) ZODICO ZYDECO
(— OF WEST INDIES) REGGAE
(— SUNG IN UNISON) PLAINSONG
(BACKGROUND —) MUZAK
(BAGPIPE —) PIBROCH
(CALYPSO —) GOOMBAY
(CHURCH —) ANTIPHON ANTIPHONY
(CONCERTED —) ENSEMBLE
(COUNTRY —) BLUEGRASS
(DANCE —) DISCO
(EVENING —) DREAM SERENA
(IDENTIFYING —) SIG
(INDIAN —) RAGA
(JAMAICAN —) SKA REGGAE
(JAPANESE COURT —) GAGAKU
(JAZZ —) SKIFFLE
(JAZZ OR FOLK —) SKIFFLE
(KIND OF —) POP RAP SOUL TEXMEX COUNTRY JAZZROCK SOFTROCK TECHNOPOP
(LATIN-AMERICAN —) SALSA
(LIVELY —) GALOP FURLANA
(MOD —) RAP
(MORNING —) AUBADE
(NEGRO —) SOUL
(NIGHT —) TAPS
(OLD — MAGAZINE) ETUDE
(PASSAGE OF —) MORCEAU
(PATTERN OF HINDU —) RAGA TALA
(PIECE OF —) ARIA HYMN MASS TRIO ALBUM ETUDE FUGUE MOTET OPERA RONDO SONATA ARIETTA CANTATA CHORALE PRELUDE QUARTET CONCERTO ENSEMBLE MADRIGAL NOCTURNE OPERETTA ORATORIO RHAPSODY SONATINA SYMPHONY SIMPHONIA
(PIPED —) MUZAK
(PLAY — WELL) COOK
(RECORDED BACKGROUND —) MUZAK
(RESOUNDING —) HIGGAION

(ROCK —) PUNK BIGBEAT BUBBLEGUM
(ROUGH —) CHARIVARI
(SAD —) MESTO
(SENTIMENTAL —) SCHMALZ SCHMALTZ
(STACCATO —) SECCO
(SYNCOPATED —) RAGTIME
(TYPE OF —) SERIAL SERIALISM MINIMALISM
(UNSOPHISTICATED —) FUNK
(VOCAL STYLE OF —) DOWOP DOOWOP
(WEST INDIAN —) REGGAE
(WRITE —) NOTATE COMPOSE
(ZULU —) KWELA
MUSICAL LYRIC SWEET LIQUID LYRICAL TUNABLE TUNEFUL CANOROUS HARMONIC NUMEROUS
(— CLOSING) CODA
(— DIRECTION) BIS PIU ADUE ARCO BRIO FINE MENO MUTA POCO ANIME ASSAI DOLCE GRAVE GUSTO LARGO LENTO MEZZO MOLTO MOSSO OSSIA PRIMO SECCO SEGNO SEGUE SOPRA TACET TEMPO TUTTI ADAGIO ARIOSO DOPPIO FREDDO MARCIA PRESTO RUBATO SEMPRE SIMILE SUBITO TENUTO TROPPO VELOCE VIVACE AGITATO ALLEGRO AMABILE ANIMATO ATTACCA FURIOSO GIOCOSO MARCATO MORENDO PIETOSO SORDINO TREMOLO DOLOROSO MAESTOSO MODERATO SALTANDO SEMPLICE SPICCATO CRESCENDO GLISSANDO OBBLIGATO SOSTENUTO SPIRITOSO
(SUFF.) **(— DEVICE)** INA INE
(— INSTRUMENT) INA
MUSICAL INSTRUMENT AX AXE GLY GUE KIN OUD QIN TAR UKE ZEL ALTO ASOR BELL CRUT DRUM GLEE GLEW GORA HARP HORN KORA KOTO LIRA LUTE LYRE OBOE ROTE SANG SAWM TAAR TUBA VINA VIOL ANVIL AULOS BANJO BLOCK BUGLE CELLO CHENG CRWTH CUICA DOMRA FLUTE GORAH GOURA GUDOK GUIRO GUSLA GUSLE KAZOO MBIRA NABLA ORGAN RAMKI REBAB REBEC ROCTA RUANA SAROD SHAWM SHELL SHENG TARAU TELYN TRUMP VEENA VIOLA ZANZE ZINKE BALAFO BONANG CABASA CITOLE CORNET CROUTH CYMBAL DOUCET FIDDLE GENDER GLARIN GUITAR GUSLEE JARANA RAPPEL REBECK RIBIBE SABECA SANCHO SANTIR SPINET TABRET TREBLE TYMPAN URHEEN VIOLET VIOLIN ZITHER ALTHORN ANGELOT ANKLONG ARGHOOL BAGPIPE BANDORE BANDURA BASSOON BAZOOKA CELESTA CHEKKER CHIKARA CITHARA CLARINA CLAVIER CLAVIOL DICHORD DOLCIAN DOLCINO DULCIAN FISTULA FLUTINA GAMELIN GITTERN HELICON KANTELE MAGADIS MARIMBA OCARINA PANDURA PIBCORN RACKETT SAMISEN SARANGI SARINDA SAXHORN SERPENT SISTRUM SORDONO THEORBO TRUMPET UKULELE URANION VIHUELA ADIAPHON AKALIMBA AUTOHARP AUTOPHON BARBITON BERIMBAU BOUSOUKI BOUZOUKI CALLIOPE CASTANET CLARINET CORNPIPE CRESCENT DULCIMER DYOPHONE EUPHONON FIDICULA FLAUTINO HORNPIPE HUMSTRUM KRUMHORN LAPIDEON MARTENOT MELODION NEGINOTH NEHILOTH PENORCON PHONIKON PSALTERY SCHWEGEL SERINGHI SOURDINE SYMPHONY TAMBOURA TAROGATO TRIANGLE TRICHORD TROMBONE VIRGINAL ZAMBOMBA ACCORDION BOMBARDON SAXOPHONE DIDGERIDOO DIDJERIDOO MELLOPHONE PEDALSTEEL TETRACHORD VIBRAPHONE
(AFRICAN —) KORA MBIRA
(ANCIENT —) ASOR LUTE LYRE CRWTH REBEC
(BALINESE —) GANGSA
(STRINGED — OF INDIA) SARANGI
(PL.) BRASS FAMILY STRINGS PERCUSSION
MUSICALITY HARMONY
MUSIC HALL GAFF MELODEON
MUSICIAN BARD WAIT ASAPH LINOS VIOLA BOPPER BUSKER MUSICO PLAYER VIOLER VIOLIN BANDMAN BOPSTER CELLIST GAMBIST ORPHEUS TWANGER VIOLIST KORAHITE MARIACHI MINSTREL MUSICKER THRUMMER TWANGLER CITYBILLY MINNESINGER
(FOLK —) FOLKY FOLKIE
(JOB OF —) GIG
(NOISY —) RANTER
(WEST AFRICA —) GRIOT
(WEST AFRICAN —) GRIOT
(WORK AS —) GIG
(PL.) ENSEMBLE WAITSMEN
MUSING PENSIVE MUSARDRY
MUSK MOOST CATTAIL MIMULUS AMBRETTE FIXATIVE
(PREF.) MOSCHI
MUSK DEER CERVID KASTURA
MUSKEG BOG FEN
MUSKELLUNGE LONGE MUSKIE
MUSKET FUSIL FUZIL MATCH DRAGON JINGAL BUNDOOK CALIVER ENFIELD GINGALL BANDHOOK BISCAYAN BISCAYEN CULVERIN ESCOPETA SNAPHAAN TOPHAIKE MATCHLOCK
MUSKET BALL GOLI
MUSKETEER FUSILEER STRELITZ
(THREE —S) ATHOS ARAMIS PORTHOS
MUSKET FORK GAFFLE
MUSK MALLOW ABELMOSK
MUSKMELON MANGO ATAMON WUNGEE SPANSPEK CANTALOUPE
MUSKOGEE CREEK SEMINOLE
MUSK OX OVIBOS
(WOOL OF UNDERCOAT OF —) QIVIUT
MUSKRAT SQUASH ONDATRA MUSQUASH
MUSK SHREW SONDELI
MUSK TURTLE STINKER STINKPOT
MUSKWOOD CAOBA
MUSKY MOSCHATE
MUSLIM LAZ ALIM SIDI SWAT TURK ARAIN HAFIZ IBADHI KAZAKH TURBAN ABBADID AYYUBID BAGIRMI BASHKIR IBADITE KHAKSAR MUDEJAR SUNNITE ALAOUITE ISLAMIST ISLAMITE QADARITE SIFATITE
(— BEADS) TASBIH
(— BROTHERHOOD) TARIQA
(— CALL TO PRAYER) AZAN
(— CHIEF) RAIS REIS
(— DOCTRINE) TAWHID
(— FOUNDATION) WAKF WAQF
(— JUDGE) CAID QAID
(— LEADER) MAM
(— MYSTIC) SUFI
(— OFFICIAL) OMRAH
(— PLAY) TAZIA
(— PRACTICE) PURDAH
(— PRINCIPLE) TAQIYA
(— SCHOLARS) ULAMA ULEMA
(— SECT) SUNNI WAHHABI MURJIITE
(— TOMB) TABUT
(— TREE) TUBA
(— WOMAN OF RANK) BEGUM
(EDUCATED —) MULLAH
(PL.) SHIA SHIAH SUNNI
MUSLIN BAN MULL DORIA SWISS GURRAH MULMUL SHALEE SHILLA TANJIB BETEELA FACTORY JAMDANI ORGANDY STENTER COTELINE SEERHAND TARLATAN
(PL.) COSSAS
MUSQUASH MUSKRAT ONDATRA
MUSS FUFFLE RUMPLE GLOMMOX UNDRESS
MUSSEL CLAM UNIO NAIAD ANODON JINGLE LACERT MUCKET PALOUR BIVALVE GLOCHID MYTILID UNIONID BULLHEAD DEERHORN
(PREF.) CONCH(O) MYTILI MYTILO
MUSSELCRACKER BISKOP
MUSSULMAN MOSLEM
MUST BIT BUD BUT MAN MAY MUN BOOD MAUN MOTE SAPA STUM DULCE GOTTA OUGHT SHALL
(— BE TAKEN) SUM
(— NOT) MAUNNA
MUSTACHE WALRUS VALANCE WHISKER
MUSTACHE MONKEY MOUSTOC
MUSTANG PONY BRONCO SPHINX
MUSTARD ZEST CRESS SENVY SINEWY AWLWORT CADLOCK KEDLOCK SINAPIS CHADLOCK CHARLOCK FLIXWEED AUBRIETIA
(— PLANT) WASABI
(PREF.) SIN
MUSTARD GAS YPERITE
MUSTARD PLASTER SINAPISM
MUSTELUS GALEUS
MUSTER LEVY ENROL RAISE SPUNK GATHER HOSTING MARSHAL RECRUIT
(— OUT) DEMOB
MUSTINESS FUST MUST
MUSTY HOAR FUNKY FUSTY HOARY MOLDY MUCID RAFTY VINNY FOISTY FROWZY RANCID FOUGHTY FROWSTY COBWEBBY
MUTABLE FICKLE MUTATORY VARIABLE
MUTATE SPORT
MUTATION SHIFT SPORT CHANGE MUANCE SILKIE ANAGRAM VARIANT SALTATION
(VOWEL —) UMLAUT
MUTE PAD DUMB ECHO LENE SURD BLACK MEDIA WHIST DAMPER MUFFLE SILENT STIFLE TENUIS SORDINE SOURDINE
(— AT FUNERAL) SALLIE
(— FOR TRUMPET) DERBY
MUTED DULL SORDO STILL DISCREET SOURDINE
MUTENESS SILENCE DUMBNESS
MUTILATE MAR HACK MAIM BREAK GARBLE HAMBLE INJURE MANGLE MARTYR MITTLE CONCISE CASTRATE EMBEZZLE
(— AN ANIMAL) LAW
MUTILATION STRIP CONCISION
MUTINEER PANDY MUTINADO
MUTINOUS UNRULY
MUTINY REVOLT STRIFE REBELLION
MUTINY ON THE BOUNTY
(AUTHOR OF —) HALL NORDHOFF
(CHARACTER IN —) BYAM BLIGH PEGGY ROGER GEORGE ROBERT TEHANI BURKITT ELLISON MAIMITI STEWART TINKLER WILLIAM FLETCHER MILLWARD MORRISON MUSPRATT CHRISTIAN
MUTISM ALALIA
MUTTER CROOL MOTRE HOTTER HUMMER MUMBLE MURMUR PATTER THROAT CHANNER CHUNNER CHUNTER GRUMBLE MAUNDER TOOTMOOT MUSSITATE
MUTTERING GROWL
MUTTON BRAXY VIFDA VIVDA MOUTON BRAXIES
(LEG OF —) CABOB WABBLER WOBBLER
MUTTONBIRD OII
MUTTONFISH SAMA ABALONE EELPOUT MOJARRA
MUTTONHEAD DOLT
MUTUAL COMMON RECIPROCAL
(PREF.) CO INTER
MUZZLE GAG NOSE MOUTH SNOUT FOREFACE GUNPOINT
(— FOR FERRET) COPE
(— OF CANNON) CHOPS
MUZZLE-LOADER CAPLOCK MUZZLER
MYALGIA COURBATURE
MYALL YARRAN WARRIGAL

MYANMAR
BAY: BENGAL HUNTER HEANZAY
CAPITAL: RANGOON
DIVISION: PEGU MAGWE ARAKAN KARENNI SAGAING MANDALAY IRRAWADDY TENASSERIM

FORMER CAPITAL: AVA
GULF: MARTABAN
MEASURE: LY DHA GON LAN MAU NGU SAO TAO TAT BYEE DAIN PHAN SEIT TAUN TENG THAT SALAY SHITA THUOC LAMANY PALGAT TRUONG CHAIVAI OKTHABAH
MONEY: KYAT
MOUNTAIN: POPA NATTAUNG SARAMATI VICTORIA
MOUNTAINS: CHIN NAGA DAWNA KACHIN KARENNI PEGUYOMA
NATIVE: AO VU WA AOR LAI LAO MON PYU TAI CHIN KADU KUKI LOLO MIAO NAGA SEMA SGAU SGAW SHAN THAI KAREN KHMER LHOTA BIRMAN BURMAN KACHIN RENGMA PALAUNG ARAKANESE
PLATEAU: SHAN
PORT: AKYAB BASSEIN HENZADA MOULMEIN
RIVER: HKA NMAI PEGU MEKONG SALWIN SHWELI KALADAN MALIKHA MYITNGE SALWEEN SITTANG CHINDWIN INDAWGYI IRRAWADDY
SEA: ANDAMAN
TOWN: YE AVA PEGU AKYAB BHAMO KARBE KATHA MINBU PAPUN PROME TAVOY HSENWI HSIPAW LASHIO MAYMYO MONYWA SHWEBO BASSEIN HENZADA PAKOKKU RANGOON MANDALAY MOULMEIN
WEIGHT: TA CAN MAT MOO PAI VIS BINH DONG KYAT RUAY VISS BAHAR BEHAR CANDY TICAL TICUL ABUCCO PEIKTHA

MY ANTONIA **(AUTHOR OF —)** CATHER
(CHARACTER IN —) JIM JAKE LENA OTTO WICK ANTON CUZAK FUCHS LARRY BURDEN CUTTER ANTONIA DONOVAN HARLING LINGARD MARPOLE AMBROSCH SHIMERDA
MYCELIUM SPAWN MYCELE TAPESIUM
MYCTERIA TANTALUS
MY DEAR MACHREE
MYDRIATIC PHENYLEPHRINE
MYIASIS STRIKE
MYNA APER MINA MYNAH GRACKLE
MYNES **(BROTHER OF —)** EPISTROPHUS
(FATHER OF —) EVENUS
(WIFE OF —) BRISEIS
MYOCOMMA FLAKE
MYRIAD HOST TOMAN COUNTLESS
MYRIAPOD JULID POLYPOD PAUROPOD MILLIPEDE
MYRRH STACTE
MYRRHA **(SON OF —)** ADONIS
MYRTLE MYRT LILAC BALTIC JAROOL ARRAYAN JAPONICA RAMARAMA
MYSELF SELF MYSEN HERSELF
MYSID SHRIMP
MYSOST PRIMOST
MYSTERIES OF PARIS **(AUTHOR OF —)** SUE
(CHARACTER IN —) FLEUR SARAH CICELY MURPHY WALTER FERRAND GEORGES JACQUES RODOLPH CHOUETTE CLEMENCE HARVILLE POLIDORI MACGREGOR RIGOLETTE
MYSTERIES OF UDOLPHO **(AUTHOR OF —)** RADCLIFFE
(CHARACTER IN —) EMILY DUPONT MORANO MONTONI LUDOVICO STAUBERT VILLEFORT LAURENTINI VALANCOURT
MYSTERIOUS DIM DARK DEEP EERY SELI EERIE SABLE WAKON ARCANE EXOTIC MYSTIC OCCULT SECRET CRYPTIC PUCKISH UNCANNY UNCOUTH ABSTRUSE ESOTERIC NUMINOUS SIBYLLIC CRYPTICAL
MYSTERIOUSLY DARKLY EERILY HEIMLICH
MYSTERY MIST RUNE CABALA ENIGMA SECRET ARCANUM PROBLEM SECRECY
(— STORY) WHODUNIT
(— WRITER FIRST NAME) ERLE ELLERY
(RELIGIOUS —) SACRAMENT
(PREF.) MYST(ERI)(ERIO)(ICO)
MYSTIC SUFI OCCULT ORPHIC SECRET EPOPTIC ESOTERIC
MYSTICAL MISTY MYSTIC ANAGOGIC TELESTIC
MYSTICALLY GHOSTLY
MYSTICISM CABALA SUFIISM
MYSTIFY BEAT BEFOG BOTHER MUDDLE PUZZLE BECLOUD CONFUSE BEWILDER
MYSTIQUE AIR AURA
MYTH SAGA FABLE LEGEND MYTHOS ALLEGORY
MYTHICAL FABLED FABULOUS FICTIOUS
MYTHOMANIAC LIAR

N

N EN NU NAN NOVEMBER
NAAM (FATHER OF —) CALEB
NAAMAH (BROTHER OF —) TUBALCAIN
(FATHER OF —) LAMECH
(MOTHER OF —) ZILLAH
(SON OF —) REHOBOAM
NAARAH (HUSBAND OF —) ASHUR
NAASSENE OPHITE
NAB HAT NIB GRAB HEAD KNAB NAIL CATCH SEIZE ARREST CLUTCH COLLAR NIBBLE NOBBLE SNATCH CAPTURE APPREHEND
NABAL (WIFE OF —) ABIGAIL
NABALOI IBALOI IGOROT
NABK NUBK NABAK NEBUK NABBUK NEBACK NEBBUK NEBBUCK
NABOB DIVES NAWAB NOBOB DEPUTY VICEROY GOVERNOR PLUTOCRAT
(— DEPUTY) NAWAB
(PL.) NABOBRY
NACELLE CAR BOAT BASKET CHASSIS COCKPIT SHELTER
NACHSCHLAG SPRINGER AFTERNOTE
NACKET BOY CAKE LUNCH NOCKET
NACRE PEARL SHELLFISH
NADAB (FATHER OF —) AARON SHAMMAI
(MOTHER OF —) ELISHEBA
NADIR BATHOS BEDROCK
(OPPOSED TO —) ZENITH
NAG CUT RAG TIT BAIT CARP FRAB FRET FUSS GNAW JADE MOKE PLUG PONY PROD RIDE SNAG TWIT YAFF ANNOY COBRA HOBBY HORSE SCOLD SKATE SNAKE STEED TEASE BADGER BERATE BOTHER DOBBIN GARRAN GLEYDE HAGGLE HARASS HECKLE HECTOR KEFFEL PADNAG PESTER PLAGUE ROUNCY WANTON HACKNEY HENPECK TORMENT DINGDONG HARANGUE IRRITATE PARAMOUR CATAMARAN
(AMBLING —) HOBBY
NAGA SEMA COBRA KABUI LHOTA SNAKE
NAGGING NIGGLING
NAGKASSAR SURIGA
NAGOR TOHI ANTELOPE REEDBUCK
NAHANE KASKA
NAHATH (FATHER OF —) ZOPHAI
NAHBI (FATHER OF —) VOPHSI
NAHOOR SHA SNA SHEEP URIAL BHARAL OORIAL
NAHOR (BROTHER OF —) HARAN ABRAHAM
(FATHER OF —) SERUG
(SON OF —) TERAH
(WIFE OF —) MILCAH
NAHSON (FATHER OF —) AMMINADAB
(SISTER OF —) ELISHEBA
(SON OF —) SALMON
NAHUATL AZTEC CAZCAN MEXICA
NAHUM ELKOSHITE
NAIAD NAIS NYMPH MUSSEL HYDRIAD
NAIF BABE
NAIL CUT FIX HOB NAB PIN TEN BOSS BRAD BRAG BROD CLAW CLOY DUMP HOOF PILE SLUG SPAD STUB STUD TACK TRAP AFFIX CATCH CLOUT DRIVE GROPE PLATE SCALE SEIZE SPEED SPICK SPIKE SPRIG TALON BULLEN CLENCH CLINCH COOLER CORKER DETAIN FASTEN GARRON HAMMER SECURE SINKER TACKET TENTER TINGLE UNGUIS UNGULA CAPTURE CLINKER FASTENER HOLDFAST ROSEHEAD SPARABLE SPIKELET TENPENNY TRICOUNI
(— BITING) ONYCHOPHAGIA
(— GROWTH) ONYCHAUXIS
(— OBLIQUELY) TOE
(HEADLESS —) SPRIG
(HOOKED —) TENTER TENTERHOOK
(INGROWN —) ONYXIS ACRONYX
(MARKING —) SPAD SPEED
(OLD HORSESHOE —) STUB
(SHOEMAKER'S —) CLOUT SPARABLE
(TOED —) TOSHNAIL
(PREF.) GOMPHO HELO ONYCH(O) UNGUI
(SUFF.) ONYCHA ONYCHES ONYCHIA ONYCHIUM ONYCHUS ONYX
NAILROD STICKWEED
NAIVE OPEN RACY FRANK GREEN CANDID JEJUNE SIMPLE ARTLESS NATURAL CHILDISH INNOCENT UNTAUGHT WIDEEYED CHILDLIKE GUILELESS INGENUOUS PRIMITIVE UNTUTORED UNWORLDLY
(— GIRL) INGENUE
NAIVETE GREENNESS SIMPLICITY
NAKED BALD BARE MERE NUDE OPEN CLEAR EXACT PLAIN STARK ADAMIC BARREN CUERPO SCUDDY SIMPLE EXPOSED LITERAL OBVIOUS MANIFEST STARKERS STRIPPED SMOCKLESS UNADORNED UNCLOTHED UNCOVERED
(PREF.) GYMN(O) NUDI
NAKED OAT PILLAS PILCORN PILKINS
NAKEDWOOD MABI SNAKEWOOD
NAKHI MOSO MOSSO
NAKONG SITUTUNGA
NAMAYCUSH CREE FISH LAKER LONGE LUNGE TOGUE TROUT LONGUE SISCOWET
NAMBY-PAMBY WET INANE SILLY VAPID CODDLE INSIPID KEEPSAKE
NAME DUB FIX NOM SET CALL CITE FAME NAIL NOMB NOUN READ TERM ALIAS CLAIM CLEPE COUNT ETHIC NEVEN NOMEN POINT QUOTE STYLE TITLE ACCUSE ADDUCE APPEAL GOSSIP MONICA REPUTE SELECT ALLONYM APPOINT BEHIGHT DECLARE ENTITLE EPITHET MENTION MONIKER SPECIFY VOCABLE CATEGORY CHRISTEN COGNOMEN IDENTIFY IDENTITY INDICATE MONICKER NOMINATE ENUMERATE PATRONYMIC NOMENCLATURE
(— OF NEWSPAPER) MASTHEAD
(— OF PLACE) TOPONYM
(— TABLET) FACIA
(— WRITTEN BACKWARDS) ANANYM
(ADDED —) AGNAME AGNOMEN
(ALTERNATIVE —) BUNCH
(ANCESTOR'S —) EPONYM
(ANOTHER —) ALIAS
(ASSUMED —) PEN ALIAS ONOMASTIC PSEUDONYM SOBRIQUET
(BAD —) CACONYM
(DAY —) AHAU
(DERIVATION OF —) EPONYMY
(FAMILIAR —) NICKNAME
(FAMILY —) SURNAME
(FIRST —) FORENAME PRAENOMEN
(GENERIC —) PRAENOMEN
(GOOD —) HONOR CREDIT
(PEN —) PSEUDONYM
(POPULAR DOG —) FIDO LADY SHEP SPOT ROVER
(REGISTERED —) AFFIX
(TECHNICAL —) ONYM
(UNSUITABLE —) MISNOMER
(WELL-SUITED —) EUONYM
(PREF.) NOMEN ONOMATO
(SUFF.) NOMEN NYM ONYM
NAMED DIT CITED HIGHT NEMPT DUBBED YCLEPT ONYMOUS YCLEPED
NAMELESS BAS
(— ONE) WHO
NAMELY FOR VIZ SCIL NOTED TOWIT FAMOUS SCILICET
NAMEPLATE MASTHEAD
(AUTOMOBILE —) MARQUE
NAMESAKE EPONYM JUNIOR HOMONYM
NAMIBIA (BAY OF —) WALVIS
(CAPITAL OF —) WINDHOEK
(DESERT OF —) KALAHARI
(PEOPLE OF —) NAMAS BANTUS BUSHMEN HEREROS OVAMBOS
NANA (AUTHOR OF —) ZOLA
(CHARACTER IN —) NANA ROSE HUGON LOUIS SATIN FONTAN GEORGE HECTOR MIGNON MUFFAT SABINE XAVIER ESTELLE STEINER BEUVILLE DAGUENET FAUCHERY PHILIPPE DECHOUARD
NANDI BANANDE MUNANDI KIPSIKIS
NANDU RHEA
NANISM DWARFISM
NANNAR SIN
NANNY GOAT NURSE
(ORIENTAL —) AMAH
NANTICOKE TOAG
NAOMI MARA
(DAUGHTER-IN-LAW OF —) RUTH
NAOS CELLA SHRINE TEMPLE
NAP GIG KIP NOD RAS CALK CAMP DOWN DOZE FUZZ LINT OOZE PICK PILE RUFF SHAG WINK COVER DOVER FLUFF GRASP SEIZE SLEEK SLEEP STEAL CATNAP DROWSE SIESTA SNOOZE DROPOFF EMERIZE RECLINE SLUMBER
(TO RAISE —) TEASE
NAPE NOD CUFF NECK NUKE POLL NUCHA NUQUE SCRAG SCUFT SCURF NODDLE SCRUFF TURNIP NIDDICK
(PREF.) NUCH(I)
NAPERY LINEN DAMASK DOILIES NAPKINS
NAPHTALITE ENAN AHIRA
NAPHTHA NEFTE PETROLEUM
NAPKIN CLOTH DOILY TOWEL DIAPER NAPERY KERCHIEF SUDATORY HANDCLOTH SERVIETTE
NAPLES BISCUIT LADYFINGER
NAPLESS BARE HARD
NAPOLELEON (AIDE TO —) NEY
NAPOLEON (— III) LOUIS BOUSTRAPA
(BATTLE OF —) ULM ACRE JENA WATERLOO
(BIRTHPLACE OF —) CORSICA
(BROTHER-IN-LAW OF —) MURAT
(GAME LIKE —) PAM
(ISLAND OF —) ELBA HELENA CORSICA
(MARSHALL OF —) NEY
(MOTHER OF —) HORTENSE
(PLACE OF VICTORY FOR —) LODI LIGNY
NAPPE DECKE
NAPPY ALE DISH DOWNY HEADY KINKY WOOLY LIQUOR SHAGGY STRONG WOOLLY COTTONY FOAMING VILLOUS
NARC TMAN
NARCISSUS LILY PLANT CRINUM EGOIST FLOWER LILIUM JONQUIL POLYANTHUS
(FATHER OF —) CEPHISSUS

(LOVED BY —) ECHO
(MOTHER OF —) LIRIOPE
(TRUMPET —) DAFFODIL
NARCOTIC (ALSO SEE DRUG) KAT KEF BANG DOPE DRUG HEMP JUNK BHANG DAGGA ETHER OPIUM HEROIN OPIATE ANODYNE COCAINE CODEINE HASHISH METOPON NARCEIN HYPNOTIC MORPHINE TAKROURI DIACODION MARIJUANA SOPORIFIC CHLORODYNE
(— AGENT) GAZER
(— DOSE) LOCUS
(— ORGANIZATION) DEA
(— OVERDOSE) OD
(— PLANT) DUTRA MANDRAKE
(INJECT —) SHOOTUP
(SALE OF —S) SCORE
(SMALL AMOUNT OF —) SNIFTER
(PL.) JUNK STUFF
NARCOTICS JUNK HEROIN
NARCOTINE OPIANE
NARD SPICE ANOINT RHIZOME MUSKROOT SPIKENARD
NARDOO ARDOO NARDU CLOVER
NARGIL COCONUT
NARGILEH PIPE HOOKA HOOKAH NARGHILE
NARK SPY VEX NOTE ANNOY TEASE OBSERVE INFORMER IRRITATE
NARRA NAGA ASANA APALIT
NARRATE SPIN TELL BRUIT STATE STORY DEPICT DETAIL DEVISE RECITE RELATE REPORT DISCUSS RECOUNT STORIFY DESCRIBE REHEARSE
NARRATION TALE FABLE STORY DETAIL ACCOUNT HAGGADA RECITAL SYNAXAR ALLEGORY DELIVERY DIEGESIS HAGGADAH
NARRATIVE EPIC JOKE MYTH SAGA TALE CONTE DRAMA FABLE PROSE STORY COMEDY JATAKA LEGEND ACCOUNT EPISODE HISTORY MEMOIRS MIDRASH NOVELLA PARABLE RECITAL ALLEGORY ANECDOTE APOLOGUE ARETALOGY HAGIOLOGY
(— OF VOYAGE) PERIPLUS
(— POEM) EPIC EPOS SAGA
(BRIEF —) ANECDOTE
(PL.) ACTA EXEMPLA
NARRATOR TESTO TELLER RELATOR SAGAMAN TALESMAN RACONTEUR
NARROW JERK LEAN MEAN NEAR POKY SLIT TRUE BORNE CLOSE CRAMP PINCH RIGID SCANT SHARP SMALL SOUND TAPER ANGUST BIASED LINEAR LITTLE MEAGER STRAIT STRICT TWITCH BIGOTED ERICOID LIMITED PRIMARY SLENDER THRIFTY CONDENSE CONTRACT PAROCHIAL PROVINCIAL
(— DOWN) CONFINE
(— DOWN STAVES) BUCK
(— INLET) RIA
(— IN OUTLOOK) SUBURBAN
(— IN PRINCIPLE) STRAITLACED
(NOT —) CATHOLIC
(VERY —) HAIRBREADTH
(PREF.) AUGUSTI DOLICH(O) STEN(O)
(SUFF.) STENOSIS
NARROWED LISTED INSWEPT CONTRACT ANGUSTATE
NARROWING CAP CHOKE INTAKE STENOSIS
NARROWLY WIDE STRAITLY
NARROW-MINDED REDNECK BORNE PETTY
NARROWNESS BIAS BIGOTRY LOCALISM PAROCHIALISM
NARSINGA TRUMPET
NARTHECIUM ABAMA
NARTHEX HALL STOA ENTRY FOYER LOBBY PORCH PORTICO PRONAOS VESTIBULE
NARWHAL MONODON
NASAB NUSUB KINSHIP
NASAL NOSY NARINE RHINAL TWANGY ADENOID STRINGY
(PREF.) NASIO RHIN(O)
NASCENCY BIRTH ORIGIN GENESIS BEGINNING
NASEBERRY SAPODILLA
NASHGAB OAF GOSSIP
NASI OFFICER PATRIARCH
NASICORN RHINOCEROS
NASTIKA ATHEIST
NASTURTIUM CAPUCINE NOSEWORT RADICULA STURSHUM STURTION
NASTY BAD PAH FOUL MEAN UGLY DIRTY SNIDE FILTHY HORRID ODIOUS RIBALD SCUZZY BAGGAGE BEASTLY DEFILED HARMFUL OBSCENE SQUALID UNCLEAN INDECENT NAUSEOUS SPITEFUL STITEFUL DANGEROUS MALICIOUS OFFENSIVE
NAT NOT DEMON SPIRIT
NATA (WIFE OF —) NANA
NATAL INBORN INNATE NATIVE GLUTEAL CONGENIAL
NATAL BROWN MAHAL
NATAL PLUM AMATUNGULA
NATANT AFLOAT FLOATING SWIMMING
NATATORIUM BATH POOL
NATCHEZ STINKER STINKARD
NATION BENI FOLK GEAT HOST LAND LEDE RACE VOLK AEDUI CASTE CLASS FANTE FANTI REALM STATE TRIBE FANTEE GEATAS PEOPLE WAGOGO ARVERNI COUNTRY SOCIETY LANGUAGE COMMUNITY MANDATORY MINISTATE MULTITUDE
(— SYMBOL) FLAG CREST
(HEBREW —) JACOB
(LARGE —) COLOSSUS
(PREF.) ETHN(O)
NATIONAL CITIZEN FEDERAL GENTILE GENTILIC
(— DEMOCRACY) ENDEX
NATIONALISM JINGOISM PHYLETISM
NATIONALIST CHINA (SEE TAIWAN)
NATIONALITY FLAG
NATIVE (ALSO SEE PEOPLE AND TRIBE) ABO ITE RAW SON TAO BORN FREE GOOK HOME KIND LIVE NEIF WILD INNER NATAL PUNTI EPIROT GENIAL INBORN INNATE KINDLY MOTHER NORMAL SIMPLE VIRGIN CITIZEN DENIZEN DZUNGAR ENDEMIC GENUINE NATURAL PAISANO POLISTA DOMESTIC GRASSCUT HABITUAL HOMEBORN HOMEMADE INHERENT LANDSMAN ORIGINAL PRIMEVAL PRISTINE RESIDENT YAMMADJI ABORIGINE CONGENIAL INGRAINED INHERITED INTRINSIC ORIGINARY TAWNYMOOR ABORIGINAL
(— BEAR) KOALA
(— BEECH) FLINDOSA
(— MINERAL) LIVE
(— OF ALBANIA) SKIPETAR
(— OF ANJOU) ANGEVIN
(— OF BENGAL) KOL
(— OF CANADA) HABITANT
(— OF CHINA) CELESTIAL
(— OF FENS) SLODGER
(— OF FLORIDA KEYS) CONK CONCH
(— OF GALLOWAY) GALWEGIAN GALLOVIDIAN
(— OF GLASGOW) GLASWEGIAN
(— OF ILLINOIS) SUCKER
(— OF IRELAND) BOGTROTTER
(— OF LIVERPOOL) SCOUSE
(— OF LONDON) COCKNEY
(— OF LOW CLASS) TAO
(— OF MADAGASCAR) HOVA
(— OF MALAYA) INFIEL
(— OF MANCHESTER) MANCUNIAN
(— OF MARITIME PROVINCES) BLUENOSE
(— OF N. CAROLINA) TARHEEL
(— OF NEW GUINEA) BOONG
(— OF NEW SOUTH WALES) CORNSTALK
(— OF PHILIPPINES) GUGU
(— OF SCOTLAND) GEORDIE
(— OF SOUTHERN ILLINOIS) EGYPTIAN
(— OF TYNESIDE) GEORDIE
(— OF W. AUSTRALIA) GROPER
(— PLANT) INDIGINE
(— WHO TEACHES) CATECHIST
(BORN AND BRED AS A —) CREOLE
(FREE —) TIMAWA
(UNCIVILIZED —) MYALL
(SUFF.) ESE ITE OT OTE
(— OF) ER IER YER
NATIVE SON (AUTHOR OF —) WRIGHT
(CHARACTER IN —) JAN MAX MARY BORIS MEARS BESSIE BIGGER DALTON ERLONE THOMAS BRITTEN BUCKLEY
NATIVITY BIRTH JATAKA GENESIS GENITURE HOROSCOPE
NATTERJACK NEWT TOAD
NATTY CHIC NEAT POSH TIDY TRIG TRIM NIFTY SMART SPICY DAPPER JAUNTY SPIFFY SPRUCE FOPPISH VARMINT
NATURAL RAW AFRO BORN EASY FOOL HOME KIND OPEN RACY REAL WILD NAIVE USUAL CANCEL CASUAL COMMON CONJON CRETIN DIRECT EARTHY HOMELY INBORN INBRED INNATE KINDLY MOTHER NATIVE NORMAL PHYSIC ARTLESS GENUINE QUADRUM REGULAR INHERENT LIFELIKE ORDINARY PHYSICAL UNCOINED PRIMITIVE REALISTIC UNASSUMED UNFEIGNED
(— LOGARITHM) LN
(— TALENT) DOWER FLAIR
(NOT —) DYED AFFECTED
(PREF.) PHYSICO PHYSI(O)
NATURALIST AMERICAN LEA COPE DALL LONG MUIR SNOW WARD FLAGG HYATT LEIDY LUCAS MASON ORTON PEALE SETON TEALE ABBOTT AKELEY BARTON DELONG FOSSEY GODMAN HOLDER MORTON NELSON PORTER SAVAGE STORER WALKER WILKES WILSON AGASSIZ ANDREWS BACHMAN BUCKLEY DITMARS FUERTES GIBBONS HOLLAND HOLLING MERRIAM PEATTIE SCUDDER WALCOTT COOLIDGE HALDEMAN HOLBROOK JENNINGS SCHWATKA BURROUGHS INGERSOLL SUBLETETE RAFINESQUE SCHOOLCRAFT
AUSTRALIAN BANFIELD
DANISH BERGSOE WINSLOW
DUTCH CAMPER HOEVEN HOMBERG SWAMMERDAM LEEUWENHOEK
ENGLISH RAY BELL BAKER BANKS BATES BRADY FORBE GOSSE LEACH NORTH BAILEY DARWIN HUDSON SLOANE BORLASE CATESBY DUGMORE EDWARDS NEEDHAM PENNANT WALLACE BRODERIP BURCHELL LYDEKKER STEBBING SWAINSON BOWERBANK JEFFERIES CARRUTHERS TEGETMEIER WILLIAMSON ATTENBOROUGH
FRENCH BELON CHENU BUFFON CUVIER BAILLON DAUBENY DUMERIL GERVAIS LAMARCK LESUEUR ORBIGNY PEIRESC POUCHET POUPART REAUMUR ADDANSON AUDEBERT BONPLAND DESHAYES LACEPEDE RONDELET CASTELNAU DAUBENTON BROUSSONETT
GERMAN OKEN WIED JAGER LIBAU SEITZ MULLER PALLAS MARTIUS NEUWIED SCHWANN SIEBOLD STELLER CHAMISSO ERXLEBEN HUMBOLDT JUNGHUHN SCHUBERT EHRENBERG KIELMEYER BURMEISTER KEYSERLING TREVIRANUS ESCHSCHOLTZ SOEMMERRING SCHLAGINTWEIT
ITALIAN REDI RISSO BONELLI BROCCHI FABRONI FONTANA SCOPOLI AMORETTI MARSIGLI ALDROVANDI SPALLANZANI VALLISNIERI
NORWEGIAN ASBJORNSEN
RUSSIAN EICHWALD FEDCHENKO CHIKHACHEV
SCOTTISH BROWN BAIKIE FORBES HERDMAN JARDINE THOMSON RICHARDSON MACGILLIVRAY

SPANISH COBO AZARA MUTIS
SWEDISH ARTEDI FORSKAL ZETTERSTEDT
SWISS HEER HUBER BONNET GESNER AGASSIZ TSCHUDI SAUSSURE TREMBLEY CLAPAREDE POURTALES RUTIMEYER
NATURALIZE ADAPT ADOPT ACCUSTOM ACCLIMATE ENDENIZEN HABITUATE
NATURALLY SN NATCH KINDLY GENIALLY
NATURALNESS EASE NAIVETE
NATURE ILK BENT BIOS CAST CLAY FORM HAIR KIND MAKE MOOD RACE SORT TRIM TYPE COLOR OUSIA SHAPE STATE TENOR ANIMAL DHARMA FIGURE HEAVEN KIDNEY PHYSIS STRIPE ESSENCE FEATHER INBEING QUALITY SPECIES PRAKRITI UNIVERSE CHARACTER QUALIFICATION
(— DIVINITY) NYMPH
(— GOD) PAN
(— GODDESS) CYBELE ARTEMIS
(— OF GOD) DIVINITY
(— PRINT) PHYTOGRAPH
(— SPIRIT) NAT
(— WORSHIP) PHYSIOLATRY
(APPARENT —) STUDY
(BY ITS VERY —) IPSOFACTO
(CONCEALED —) LATENCY
(COURSE OF —) TAO
(DIVINE —) DEITY
(EMOTIONAL —) HEART
(ESSENTIAL —) ESSE FORM GENIUS
(GOOD —) BONHOMIE
(HUMAN —) FLESH MANHEAD MANKIND
(INHERENT —) GENIUS
(INNER —) SOUL
(INTRINSIC —) BOTTOM
(MORAL —) ETHNOS
(OF THE SAME —) HOMOGENEOUS
(ORGANIC —) BIOS
(PERT. TO —) COSMO
(ROUGH —) SPINOSITY
(SENSUAL —) BLOOD
(SPECIAL —) IDIOM
(SPIRITUAL —) INTERNAL
(TRIFLING —) FRIVOLITY
(TRUE —) ESSE PROPRIETY
(TRUE — OF THINGS) WHERE
(ULTIMATE —) ESSENCE
(UNREGENERATE —) ADAM
(PREF.) PHYSI(O)
(SUFF.) **(HAVING — OF)** IC ICAL
(OF — OF) EOUS
NATURIST NUDIST
NAUGHT NIL EVIL ZERO AUGHT NAGHT OUGHT CIPHER NOUGHT WICKED NOTHING USELESS WORTHLESS
NAUGHTY BAD PAW SAD EVIL WRONG PAWPAW SHREWD WICKED OBSCENE WAYWARD IMPROPER
NAUPATHIA SEASICKNESS
NAURU (CAPITAL OF —) YAREN
(DISTRICT OF —) BOE EWA AIWO IJUW BAITI BUADA NIBOK UABOE YAREN ANABAR ANETAN MENENG ANIBARE
(FORMER NAME OF —) PLEASANTISLAND
(TOWN OF —) ANNA ORRO ANABAR RONAWI YANGOR
NAUSEA PALL QUALM DISGUST NAUSITY LOATHING SICKNESS ANTIPATHY DIZZINESS
NAUSEATE TURN TWIST WLATE REVOLT SICKEN DISGUST SCUNNER STOMACH DISTASTE SCOMFISH
NAUSEATED ILL SICKISH QUALMISH SQUEAMISH
NAUSEATING NASTY WAUGH QUEASY BILIOUS FULSOME BRACKISH STAWSOME LOATHSOME REVOLTING SICKENING
NAUSEOUS NASTY FULSOME OFFENSIVE
NAUSICAA (FATHER OF —) ALCINOUS
(MOTHER OF —) ARETE
NAUSITHOUS (FATHER OF —) NEPTUNE POSEIDON
(MOTHER OF —) PERIBOEA
(SON OF —) ALCINOUS
NAUTICAL (ALSO SEE NAVIGATION) NAVAL MARINE NAUTIC MARINAL OCEANIC TARRISH MARITIME NAVIGABLE
(— FLAG) CORNET PENNON
NAUTILUS MOLLUSK ARGONAUT ARGONAUTA
(— COMMANDER) NEMO
NAVAHO DINE NAVAJO LONGHAIR
(— GROUP) OUTFIT
(— RITE) WAY
NAVAL SEA MARINE NAUTICAL NAVIGABLE
(— DEPOT) BASE
(— FORCE) NAVY FLEET ARMADA SQUADRON
(— JAIL) BRIG
NAVAL OFFICER AMERICAN ROE CONE DALE DYER HART HULL HUSE KING LAND LEVY LUCE MAYO SIMS ALLEN AMMEN BARRY BEALE CAPPS CLARK DAVIS DEWEY DUERK EVANS FISKE FITCH FOOTE GRANT JONES LEAHY LEARY MAHAN MAURY PERRY PRATT ROWAN STARK WALKE BARNEY BENSON BIDDLE BREESE CARNEY CONNER EBERLE GREENE HALSEY HEWITT HOWELL KEARNY KIMMEL KNIGHT MCCAIN MOORER MORRIS NIMITZ PALMER PORTER RODMAN SCHLEY SEMMES TALBOT TOWERS TUCKER WILKES WORDEN BRISTOL BULLOCH CHESTER CUSHING DALGREN DECATUR ELLIOTT GLEAVES GRAVELY GRIDLEY HOLLINS HOPKINS KIMBALL KINKAID MOFFETT NIBLACK SCHENCK SIGSBEE STEWART TRUXTUN WHIPPLE WILLSON WINSLOW YARNELL ZUMWALT BUCHANAN CAPERTON CHADWICK CHAUNCEY FARRAGUT GHORMLEY INGRAHAM LAWRENCE PAULDING PERCIVAL RICKOVER ROBINSON ROUSSEAU SHUBRICK SPRUANCE STANDLEY STIRLING THATCHER GLASSFORD PILLSBURY SCHROEDER SELFRIDGE BAINBRIDGE GREENSLADE MACDONOUGH WAINWRIGHT GOLDSBOROUGH
BELGIAN GERLACHE
BRAZILIAN MELLO
CANADIAN GARNEAU
DANISH HOLM JUEL AMDRUP ADELAER
DUTCH TROMP RUYTER ALMONDE DEWINTER HELFRICH
ENGLISH BALL BYNG HOOD HOPE HOWE LUCE MEUX ALLIN ANSON BAYLY BLAKE BLIGH BOYLE BROKE DRAKE EVANS FOLEY HARDY HAWKE KEYES LEAKE LYONS NOBLE PARRY TRYON AYLMER AYSCUE BEATTY BENBOW BOWERS BURNEY CARDEN COFFIN COLOMB FENNER FISHER FRASER GORDON HALSEY HERVEY HORNBY JERRAM LAWSON LAYTON LITTLE MADDEN MONSON NELSON OSBORN PARKER RODNEY SYFRET VERNON WILSON ADDISON BARCLAY BEDFORD BELCHER CRADOCK DOUGLAS GAMBIER HARWOOD HAWKINS JACKSON MCCLURE MORESBY NASMITH SEYMOUR ANDERSON BEAUFORT BOSCAWEN BROTHERS COCHRANE JELLICOE TRELAWNY TYRWHITT BACKHOUSE BERESFORD CALLAGHAN CHATFIELD COLLINSON FREMANTLE GRENVILLE NARBROUGH NICHOLSON CODRINGTON CUNNINGHAM SOMERVILLE TROUBRIDGE FITZMAURICE MOUNTBATTEN
FRENCH BART LOTI BELLOT DARLAN FORBIN GRASSE COURBET DUPERRE ESTAING FARRERE GUICHEN MOUCHEZ CORBIERE FLEURIAS FLEURIEU MUSELIER NOAILLES CASABIANCA
GERMAN SPEE KONIG HIPPER MULLER RAEDER BEHNCKE CANARIS CAPELLE DOENITZ LUCKNER TIRPITZ JACHMANN LANGSDORFF
GREEK KANARES MIAOULES
HUNGARIAN HORTHY
ITALIAN DORIA LAURIA JACCHINO RICCARDI
JAPANESE ITO KATO TOGO URIU KONDO OKADA SAITO YONAI NAGANO NOMURA FUCHIDA SHIMADA YOSHIDA KAMIMURA SUETSUGU
NORWEGIAN TORDENSKJOLD
PERUVIAN GRAU
PORTUGUESE CASTRO
RUSSIAN GREIG KOLCHAK MAKAROV ALEKSEEV APRAKSIN GORSHKOV KUZNETSOV BELLINGHAUSEN
SCOTTISH BARTON
SPANISH ULLOA GRAVINA MENENDEZ
SWEDISH LINDMAN EHRENSVARD
NAVARRAISE, LA (CHARACTER IN —) ANITA ARAQUIL GARRIDO ZUCCARAGA
(COMPOSER OF —) MASSENET
NAVE HOB HUB NEF APSE BODY FIST PACE AISLE NATHE NIEVE CENTER
NAVEL NOMBRIL OMPHALOS UMBILICUS
(PREF.) OMPHAL(O) UMBILI(CI)
(SUFF.) OMPHALUS
NAVIGABLE BOATABLE PORTABLE
NAVIGATE KEEL SAIL DRIVE GUIDE SKIFF STEER AVIATE COURSE CRUISE DIRECT MANAGE TRAVEL CONDUCT CONTROL JOURNEY OPERATE TRAVERSE ASTROGATE
NAVIGATION HOMING VOYAGE NAUTICS PASSAGE SAILING TRAFFIC CABOTAGE SHIPPING
(— MEASURE) TON KNOT SEAM FATHOM
(— SYSTEM) LORAN TACAN SHORAN
(SYSTEM OF —) DACCA DECCA
NAVIGATOR FLYER NAVVY PILOT AIRMAN AVIATOR COPILOT LABORER AERONAUT SEAFARER SPACEMAN NEPTUNIAN NEPTUNIST
DANISH BERING
DUTCH BERING HARTOG BARENTS HOUTMAN LEMAIRE HEEMSKERK
ENGLISH FOX COOK ADAMS BYRON DIXON DRAKE BAFFIN BARLOW BUTTON CLERKE HUDSON SOMERS WALLIS BARLOWE GILBERT GOSNOLD RALEIGH WEDDELL CAVENDISH FROBISHER LANCASTER VANCOUVER CHANCELLOR WILLOUGHBY
FRENCH CARTIER BETHENCOURT BOUGAINVILLE
GERMAN BEHAIM KOTZEBUE
GREEK EUDOXUS PYTHEAS
ICELANDIC ERICSON
ITALIAN ZENO CABOT VESPUCCI
NORWEGIAN ERIC
PORTUGUESE CAM DIAS DIAZ GAMA CUNHA ZARCO CABRAL DAGAMA GARCIA QUEIROS GILIANES MAGELLAN FERNANDES
RUSSIAN LUTKE GOLOVNIN KRUSENSTERN
SPANISH CANO GALI NINO SOLIS PINZON TORRES BERMUDEZ FERNANDEZ
NAVITE BASALT
NAVVY HAND WORKER LABORER NAVIGATOR
NAVY FLEET SHIPFERD
(— BOARD) ADMIRALTY
(— OFFICER) CPO AIDE MATE BOSUN CHIEF ENSIGN ADMIRAL ARMORER CAPTAIN COMMANDER COMMODORE
(— RADIO OPERATOR) SPARKS
(— VESSEL) PT SUB CARRIER CRUISER FLATTOP DESTROYER SUBMARINE TRANSPORT
NAWAB NABOB RULER VICEROY
NAY NO NAI NEI NOT DENY EVEN

NYET FLUTE NEVER DENIAL REFUSE REFUSAL NEGATIVE
NAZARD STOP NASAT
NAZE NASE HEADLAND
NAZI BROWN HITLERITE
(— SYMBOL) FYLFOT SWASTIKA
NAZIM VICEROY GOVERNOR
NEAERA (DAUGHTER OF —) AUGE EVADNE LAMPETIS PHAETHUSA
(FATHER OF —) PEREUS
(HUSBAND OF —) ALEUS STRYMON
(SON OF —) CEPHEUS LYCURGUS AMPHIDAMAS
NEANDERTHAL CAVEMAN
NEANIC IMMATURE YOUTHFUL
NEAR AD AT BY IN GIN KIN NAR AKIN BAIN DEAR FAST GAIN HARD HEND INBY MEAN NEXT NIGH ABOUT ANEAR ANENT ASIDE CLOSE EWEST FORBY HANDY HENDE JUXTA MATCH NUDGE ROUND SHORT TOUCH ALMOST AROUND BESIDE CLIMAX HEREBY NARROW STINGY TOWARD WITHIN ADVANCE AGAINST FORTHBY SIMILAR THRIFTY VICINAL ADJACENT APPROACH IMMINENT INTIMATE CONTIGUOUS
(— AKIN) GERMANE
(— POINT) PP
(— THE BEGINNING) EARLY FORMER
(— THE EQUATOR) LOW
(— THE MOUTH) ADORAL
(— THE SURFACE) EBB FLEET
(— THE WIND) HIGH AHOLD
(CONVENIENTLY —) HANDSOME
(PREF.) AC AD AF AG AL AP AS AT BY ENGY EPH EPI JUXTA PERI PLESI(O) PROS
NEARBY AROUND GAINLY LOCALLY ADJACENT
(ONES —) THESE
NEARER HITHER
(— FRANCE) CISALPINE
(— ROME) CISALPINE
(— THE REAR) AFTER
(PREF.) **(— IN TIME)** CIS CITRA
NEAREST NEXT EWEST CLOSEST NEARMOST PROCHAIN PROXIMAL IMMEDIATE PROXIMATE
(— THE STERN) AFTERMOST
(PREF.) PROXIMO
NEARIAH (FATHER OF —) ISHI SHEMAIAH
NEARLY GAIN JUST LIKE MOST MUCH ABOUT CLOSE ALMOST FECKLY WELLNIGH VIRTUALLY PRACTICALLY
NEARNESS AFFINITY VICINITY PROPINQUITY
NEARSIGHTED MYOPIC PURBLIND
NEAT GIM NET COSH COWS DEFT DINK FEAT FEEL FEIL GENT JIMP MACK NICE OXEN PRIM PURE SMUG SNOD SNUG TIDY TOSH TRIG TRIM BULLS CLEAN CLEAR COMPT CRISP DINKY DONCY DONSY DOUCE EXACT FEATY FETIS GENTY JEMMY NATTY NIFTY PREST QUEME SMART SMIRK SPICK TERSE TIGHT ADROIT BOVINE CATTLE CLEVER DAINTY DAPPER DIMBER DONSIE HEPPEN MINION POLITE QUAINT SPANDY SPRUCE BANDBOX CONCISE FEATOUS ORDERLY PERJINK PRECISE REFINED SHAPELY TRICKSY UNMIXED MENSEFUL SKILLFUL STRAIGHT TASTEFUL DEXTEROUS SHIPSHAPE UNDILUTED WHOLESOME
NEATLY SNUG DEFTLY FAIRLY FEATLY SMARTLY SPRUCELY
NEATNESS MENSE DEFTNESS ELEGANCE SPRUCERY
NEATNIK (NOT A —) SLOB
NEB EAR NIB TIP BEAK BILL NOSE POINT SNOUT
NEBAIOTH (FATHER OF —) ISHMAEL
NEBAT (SON OF —) JEROBOAM
NEBO (FATHER OF —) MARDUK MERODACH
(WIFE OF —) TASHMET

NEBRASKA
CAPITAL: LINCOLN
COLLEGE: DANA DOANE DUCHESNE HASTINGS
COUNTY: GAGE LOUP OTOE DEUEL DUNDY KEITH SARPY CHERRY COLFAX FURNAS HOOKER NEMAHA VALLEY BUFFALO ANTELOPE BOXBUTTE KEYAPAHA
INDIAN: OTO OMAHA PONCA PAWNEE
PRESIDENT: FORD
RIVER: LOGAN DISMAL PLATTE ELKHORN NIOBRARA
STATE BIRD: MEADOWLARK
STATE FLOWER: GOLDENROD
STATE NICKNAME: BLACKWATER CORNHUSKER TREEPLANTERS
STATE TREE: ELM
TOWN: ORD ALMA COZAD OMAHA PONCA TRYON WAHOO GERING MULLEN NELIGH PENDER TEKAMAH OGALLALA REDCLOUD THEDFORD
UNIVERSITY: CREIGHTON

NEBRIS FAWNSKIN
NEBULA SKY CRAB SPOT VAPOR BALAXY GALAXY SPIRAL PLANETARY
NEBULIZE ATOMIZE
NEBULOUS DIM DARK HAZY FOGGY MISTY MUDDY VAGUE WISPY CLOUDY MYSTIC TURBID CLOUDED EVASIVE SHADOWY UNCLEAR DREAMLIKE
NECESSARILY NEEDS NEEDLY PERFORCE
NECESSARY NEEDY PRIVY VITAL FRIEND TOILET KINSMAN NEEDFUL FORCIBLE INTEGRAL OBLIGATE BEHOVEFUL ESSENTIAL INTRINSIC
(PL.) ALIMENT MISTERS
NECESSITATE FORCE IMPEL COMPEL DEMAND ENTAIL OBLIGE REQUIRE CONSTRAIN
NECESSITY USE CALL DUTY FATE FOOD LACK MUST NEED TASK WANT DRINK ANANKE BEHOOF BESOIN MISTER MUSCLE NEEDBE URGENCY PERFORCE REQUIREMENT
(— OF MOVING) ZUGZWANG
(BY —) PRESENTLY
(OF —) PERFORCE
(PL.) BREAD
(PREF.) DEONTO
NECK COL NUB PET CAPE CRAG CROP HALS KISS WAKE BEARD CHOKE CRAIG HALSE SCRAG SPOON SWIRE TRAIL BEHEAD CARESS CERVIX COLLET COLLUM FONDLE STRAIT CHANNEL EMBRACE ISTHMUS SQUEEZE TUBULUS LALLYGAG
(— ARTERY) CAROTID
(— MUSCLE) SCALENUS
(— OF BOTTLE) THROTTLE
(— OF LAMB) TARGET
(— OF VOLCANO) CORE
(BACK OF —) NOD NAPE NUCH NUQUE SCRUFF NIDDICK
(BOW —) HAWSE
(PERT. TO —) JUGULAR CERVICAL
(RED —) ROOINEK
(PREF.) CERVIC(I)(O) COLLI DER(O) TRACHEL(O)
(SUFF.) DERUS
NECK AND NECK TIE EVEN CLOSE
NECKBAND BAND COLLAR COLLET SHIRTBAND
NECKCLOTH BOA TIE RUFF AMICE CHOKE SCARF STOLE CHOKER CRAVAT BURDASH NECKTIE PANUELO STARCHER BARCELONA SOLITAIRE STEINKIRK
NECKERCHIEF GIMP RAIL FOGLE BELCHER FOULARD NECKLET KERCHIEF NECKATEE NECKCLOTH NECKENGER
NECKING COLLAR GORGERIN
NECKLACE BEE LEI TORC BEADS CHAIN NOOSE CARCAN CHOKER COLLAR GORGET SANKHA TAWDRY TORQUE BALDRIC CHAPLET RIVIERE SAUTOIR LAVALIER NEGLIGEE ESCLAVAGE
(PREF.) MONILI
NECKLET (FEATHER —) MARABOU MARABOUT
NECKLINE COWL SCOOP
NECK RUFF FRAISE QUELLIO
NECKTIE BOW TIE ASCOT SCARF CHOKER CRAVAT GRAVAT OVERLAY
(— PARTY) HANGING LYNCHING
(PART OF —) EDGE SEAM TACK APRON SHELL FACING MARGIN POCKET HEMMING TIPPING NECKBAND INTERLINING
(STRING —) BOLO
(WOMAN'S —) TAWDRY
NECKWEAR ASCOT
NECROMANCER GOETIC MAGICIAN
NECROMANCY GOETY MAGIC GRAMARY SORCERY WIZARDRY EGROMANCY
NECROPOLIS CEMETERY
NECROPSY AUTOPSY
NECROSIS MORTIFICATION
NECTAR HONEY AMRITA AMBROSIA
NECTAR BIRD EATER HONEY SUNBIRD
NECTARINE PEACH BRUNION NECTRON NECTARIN
NECTARY SPUR GLAND NECTARIUM
NEDABIAH (FATHER OF —) JECONIAH
NEDDER ADDER
NEDDY HORSE DONKEY
NEE BORN
NEED ASK NUD LACK TAKE THAR WANT CRAVE DRIVE THARF BEHOOF BEHOVE BESOIN DEMAND DESIRE EGENCE MISTER STRAIT BEHOOVE NEEDHAM POVERTY REQUIRE URGENCY DISTRESS EXIGENCY MISCHIEF EMERGENCE EXTREMITY NECESSITY
NEEDED NECESSARY
NEEDFIRE WILDFIRE
NEEDFUL VITAL INTEGRAL ESSENTIAL NECESSARY REQUISITE
NEEDLE RIB SEW VEX YEN ACUS DARN GOAD TIER WIRE ANNOY BLUNT POINT SHARP SPIKE STRAW STYLE BODKIN DARNER HECKLE STYLUS OBELISK PRICKER PROVOKE SPICULE TUMBLER
(— HOLE) EYE
(— SORTER) HANDER
(COMB. FORM) ACU
(PART OF —) EYE HOLE CROWN POINT SHANK
(PINE —) SPILL
(PINE —S) PININGS
(SHAPED LIKE A —) ACEROSE
(PL.) TWINKLES
(PREF.) ACU RAPHI RAPHIDI
NEEDLE BUG NEPID RANATRA
NEEDLEBUSH URY PINBUSH
NEEDLEFISH GAR SNOOK AGUJON BELONID LONGJAW
NEEDLE GUN RIFLE DREYSE
NEEDLELIKE ACUATE ACERATE ACEROSE ACEROUS ACIFORM ACICULAR BELONOID SPLINTERY
NEEDLEMAN TAILOR
NEEDLE-POINTED ACEROSE
NEEDLESHAPED ACIFORM ACETIOUS
NEEDLESS AMOK
NEEDLESTONE NATROLITE
NEEDLEWORK SEWING SAMPLER SEAMING TATTING KNITTING WOOLWORK HEMSTITCH INSERTION STITCHERY EMBROIDERY STITCHCRAFT
NEEDY BARE POOR INDIGENT NEEDSOME HUNGARIAN PENNILESS PENURIOUS NECESSITOUS
NEEP NEPE TURNIP
NE'ER-DO-WELL LOSER BUM PELF SKELLUM SCHLEMIEL SHIFTLESS WORTHLESS RAPSCALLION
NEFANDOUS IMPIOUS EXECRABLE
NEFARIOUS BAD WICKED HEINOUS IMPIOUS FLAGRANT HORRIBLE INFAMOUS ATROCIOUS
NEFERT (HUSBAND OF —) AMENEMHAT
NEGATE DENY SUBLATE
NEGATION NAY NOT EMPTY DENIAL REFUSAL ANNULMENT NONENTITY
(PREF.) DIS

NEGATIVE NA NE NO CON NAE NAY NIT NIX NON NOR NOT NUL DENY FILM VETO MINUS NEVER NAYWARD STAMPER APOPHATIC PRIVATIVE
(— PREFIX) IL IM IN IR UN DIS NON
(— PRINCIPLE) YIN
(PHOTOGRAPHIC —) CLICHE
(PREF.) INEQUI
NEGATOR NAYSAYER OPPONENT
NEGLECT DEBT FAIL HANG OMIT SHUN SLIP FAULT FORGO SHIRK SLOTH WAIVE BYPASS CESSER FOREGO FORGET IGNORE LACHES LOITER PERMIT SLIGHT DEFAULT DISOBEY FAILURE OVERSEE RESPECT FORSLACK OMISSION OVERLOOK OVERSLIP RECKLESS DISREGARD MISLIPPEN OVERSIGHT PRETERMIT MISPRISION
(— OF DUTY) INCIVISM
NEGLECTED TACKY SHABBY UNDONE DORMANT OBSOLETE
NEGLECTFUL LAX REMISS CARELESS DERELICT HEEDLESS RECKLESS DISSOLUTE NEGLIGENT
NEGLIGEE ROBE MANTEAU MATINEE UNDRESS PEIGNOIR NIGHTGOWN DISHABILLE
NEGLIGENCE CULPA LACHES DEFAULT LASCHETY DISREGARD OVERSIGHT
NEGLIGENT LAX LASH SOFT SLACK CASUAL OVERLY REMISS CARELESS DERELICT DISCINCT RECKLESS SLOVENLY YEMELESS DISSOLUTE NEGLECTFUL
NEGLIGIBLE FAT
NEGOTIATE DEAL SELL BROKE FLOAT TREAT TROKE TRUCK TRYST ADVISE ASSIGN CONFER DICKER DIRECT MANAGE PARLEY SETTLE ARRANGE BARGAIN CHAFFER CONDUCT CONSULT DISCUSS ENTREAT CONCLUDE ENTREATY TRANSACT TRANSFER TEMPORIZE
NEGOTIATION DEAL DICKER PARLEY TREATY PASSAGE ENTREATY PRACTICE
NEGRITO ATA ATI ITA AETA AKKA BATWA BLACK KARON SEMANG TAPIRO ABENLEN BAMBUTE
NEGRITUDE SOUL
NEGRO FON JUR LUO LWO SUK AKIM ALUR BENI BINI BONI EGBA FONG IRON MADI MOKE NUBA NUPE SIDI BENIN BLACK BONGO CUFFY DINKA DJUKA FULUP FUZZY HATSA MUNGO SEPIA SEREC SMOKE TEMNE GULLAH HUBSHI AKWAPIM DAHOMAN GEECHEE QUASHIE SANDAWE SHELLUH SHILLUK BECHUANA ETHIOPIAN MANGBATTU
(— BLOOD) TARBRUSH
(GOLD COAST —) GA FANTI
(LIBERIAN —) KRU VAI VEI GREBO ICROO KRUMAN KROOBOY
(MALE —) BUCK
(OLD —) UNCLE
NEHEMIAH (ADVERSARY OF —) TOBIAH
(FATHER OF —) AZBUK HACHALIAH
NEHUSHTA (FATHER OF —) ELNATHAN
(HUSBAND OF —) JEHOIAKIM
(SON OF —) JEHOIACHIN
NEIGH NIE NYE WHI HINNY NICKER WHINNY WIGHER WHICKER
NEIGHBOR BOR ADJOIN BORDER FELLOW NEIPER ACCOLENT BORDERER CONFINER UCALEGON
(PL.) KITH CONFINES
(SUFF.) GETON
NEIGHBORHOOD WAY AREA HAND ZONE VENUE BARRIO LOCALE REGION PURLIEU SECTION DISTRICT ENVIRONS PRESENCE PROCINCT VICINAGE VICINITY BAILIWICK COMMUNITY PROXIMITY TERRITORY VOISINAGE
(SQUALID —) SLUM
NEIGHBORING NIGH NEARBY CONFINE VICINAL ACCOLENT ADJACENT
NEIGHBORLY FOLKSY FOLKSEY AMICABLE
NEITHER NOT NATHER NITHER NOWDER
(— RIGHT NOR WRONG) ADIAPHOROUS
NELEUS (BROTHER OF —) PELIAS
(DAUGHTER OF —) PERO
(FATHER OF —) NEPTUNE
(MOTHER OF —) TYRO
(SON OF —) NESTOR
(WIFE OF —) CHLORIS
NELLORE ONGOLE
NEMA EELWORM FILAMENT NEMATODE ROUNDWORM
NEMATOCYST CNIDA DESMONEME PENETRANT
NEMATODE EELWORM ROUNDWORM
NEMESIS BANE FATE UPIS AGENT AVENGER PENALTY
NEMUEL (BROTHER OF —) ABIRAM DATHAN
(FATHER OF —) ELIAB SIMEON
NENTSI SAMOYED SAMOYEDE
NEOPHYTE TYRO EPOPT NOVICE ROOKIE AMATEUR CONVERT BEGINNER PROSELYTE YOUNGLING
NEOPLASM TUMOR GROWTH TUMOUR SARCOMA NEWGROWTH
NEOTERIC NEW LATE FRESH NOVEL MODERN RECENT
NEP KNOT CATNIP CATMINT CLUSTER

NEPAL
CAPITAL: KATMANDU KATHMANDU
COIN: MOHAR RUPEE
MOUNTAIN: EVEREST
MOUNTAIN RANGE: HIMALAYA
NATIVE: KHA AOUL LIMBU MURMI NEWAR GURKHA GORKHALI
RIVER: KALI KOSI MUGU SETI BABAI BHERI RAPTI SARDA GANDAK KARNALI NARAYANI
TOWN: ILAM MUGU GALWA JUMLA PATAN BIRGANJ POKHARA BHADGAON LALITPUR BHAKTAPUR BIRATNAGAR

NEPENTHE DRUG PLANT POTION ANODYNE
NEPHEG (FATHER OF —) DAVID IZHAR
NEPHELE (DAUGHTER OF —) HELLE
(HUSBAND OF —) ATHAMAS
(SON OF —) LEUCON PHRIXUS
NEPHELINE LENAD MINERAL SOMMITE ELEOLITE
NEPHEW OY OYE NEVE VASU NEFFY NEVOY NIECE NEPOTE BENVOLIO
NEPHRIC RENAL
NEPHRITE YU JADE AXSTONE POUNAMU TREMOLITE
NEPTUNE LER PAN SEA GREEN OCEAN PLATE SEAGOD
(BROTHER OF —) PLUTO JUPITER
(CONSORT OF —) SALACIA
(DISCOVERER OF —) GALLE
(EMBLEM OF —) TRIDENT
(FATHER OF —) SATURN
(MOTHER OF —) RHEA
(SISTER OF —) JUNO
NER (NEPHEW OF —) SAUL
(SON OF —) ABNER
NERD CLOD DINK DORK DRIP JERK WONK DWEEB TWERP
(COMPUTER —) WEENIE
NEREID NYMPH NEREIS THALIA THETIS CYMODOCE
NEREIDES (FATHER OF —) NEREUS
(MOTHER OF —) DORIS
NERGAL (BROTHER OF —) NINAZU
(FATHER OF —) ENLIL
(MOTHER OF —) NINLIL
NERI (FATHER OF —) MELCHI
(SON OF —) SALATHIEL
NERIAH (FATHER OF —) MAASEIAH
(SON OF —) BARUCH SERAIAH
NERISSA (HUSBAND OF —) GRATIANO
NERO TYRANT FIDDLER
(MOTHER OF —) AGRIPPINA
(SUCCESSOR TO —) GALBA
(VICTIM OF —) LUCAN SENECA
(WIFE OF —) OCTAVIA
NERONE (CHARACTER IN —) MAGO NERO SIMON FANUEL RUBRIA ASTERIA
(COMPOSER OF —) BOITO
NERVE RIB BEND CORD GALL GRIT GUTS LINE SAND VEIN BALLS BRASS CHEEK CHORD CRUST PLUCK PUDIC SINEW SPUNK STEEL TENON VAGUS VIGOR APLOMB COSTAL DARING DENTAL ENERGY FACIAL HUTZPA LUMBAR RADIAL SACRAL STRING AXILLAR CHUTZPA COELIAC COURAGE HUTZPAH SAPHENA SCIATIC SPINDLE ABDUCENS AUDACITY BOLDNESS CERVICAL CHUTZPAH COOLNESS EFFERENT EMBOLDEN GUMPTION STRENGTH TEMERITY AUTONOMIC ENCOURAGE EYESTRING ACCELERATOR
(— CELL) ANAXON NEURON DIAXONE DENDRAXON
(— CENTER) BRAIN CORTEX PLEXUS
(— CONNECTOR) SYNAPSE
(— FIBERS) PONS
(— NETWORK) RETIA PLEXUS
(— SLEEP) NEURO HYPNOTISM
(TYPE OF AFFERENT —) EXCITOR
(PL.) HORRORS JITTERS
(PREF.) NEUR(I)(O)
(SUFF.) NEURA(L) NEURE NEURIA NEURIC
NERVE CELL DIAXON
NERVELESS DEAD WEAK BRAVE INERT UNNERVED FOOLHARDY POWERLESS
NERVOUS EDGY TOEY ANTSY FUSSY GOOSY HYPER JUMPY TENSE TIMID WINDY WIRED FIDGET SINEWY SPOOKY TOUCHY UNEASY FEARFUL FRETFUL JITTERY RESTIVE SCADDLE NEUROTIC TIMOROUS EXCITABLE SENSITIVE TREMULOUS TWITTERLY
(— MALADY) APHASIA NEURITIS
(— SEIZURE) TIC ANEURIA
NERVURE RIB COSTA NERVE NEURON CUBITAL
NERVY BOLD RASH JERKY PUSHY BRAZEN SINEWY STRONG FORWARD JITTERY IMPUDENT INTREPID VIGOROUS EXCITABLE
NESS RAS CAPE SKAW SUFFIX HEADLAND
NEST BED DEN EST JUG WEB AERY BIKE BINK DRAY DREY EYRY HOME LAIR NIDE REDD SHED TRAP ABODE AERIE BROOD EYRIE HAUNT HOUSE NIDUS SWARM CLUTCH COLONY CUDDLE HOTBED NIDIFY RESORT WURLEY CABINET LODGING RETREAT VESPIARY WITHYPOT LARVARIUM PENDULINE RESIDENCE TERMITARY
(— OF ANIMALS) BED
(— OF ANT) FORMICARY
(— OF BOXES) INRO
(— OF EGGS) CLUTCH
(SQUIRREL'S —) CAGE DRAY DREY
(PREF.) CALIO NIDI OECO
(SUFF.) OECA OECIA
NESTER FLEDGLING
NESTLE JUG LAP LIE PET NEST SNUG FITIN NICHE SPOON BURROW CUDDLE FIDGET NUZZLE PETTLE SETTLE SNUDGE CHERISH SHELTER SNUGGLE SNUZZLE
NESTLING BABY BIRD EYAS NEST POULT SQUAB CUDDLE RETREAT BIRDLING NIDULATE FLEDGLING
NEST OF GENTLEFOLK (AUTHOR OF —) TURGENEV
(CHARACTER IN —) LIZA FYODOR PANSHIN VARVARA KALITINE PAVLOVNA LAVRETSKY
NESTOR SAGE SOLON LEADER ADVISER ADVISOR COUNSELOR PATRIARCH
(FATHER OF —) NELEUS
(MOTHER OF —) CHLORIS
(SON OF —) ANTILOCHUS
(WIFE OF —) ANAXIBIA EURYDICE
NESTORIAN WISE
NET BAG GIN HAY LAM POT WEB CAUL FIKE FLAN FLEW FLUE FYKE GAIN HAAF KELL LACE LAUN LAWN LEAD LEAP MESH MOKE NEAT PURE RETE SALE SEAN TOIL TRAP TRIM WEIR BRAIL CATCH CLEAN

CLEAR DRIFT GAUZE LACIS PITCH POUND SCOOP SEINE SEIZE SNARE SNOOD TRAWL TRINK TULLE YIELD BAGNET BASKET BRIGHT COBWEB ENMESH ENTRAP FABRIC GROUND LEADER MALINE MASILE PANTER PROFIT RAFFLE SAGENE SAPIAO TOWNET TUNNEL DRAGNET ENSNARE FLYTAIL LAMPARA MALINES NETWORK PROTECT RETICLE RINSING SCRINGE SHELTER SPILLER STALKER TRAINEL TRAMMEL MESHWORK SALAMBAO BUCKSTALL RETICULUM
(PREF.) DICTY(O) DIKTYO(N) RETI RETINO

NETHANEEL **(BROTHER OF —)** DAVID
(FATHER OF —) ZUAR JESSE OBEDEDOM
(SON OF —) SHEMAIAH

NETHANIAH **(FATHER OF —)** ASAPH ELISHAMA
(SON OF —) JEHUDI ISHMAEL

NETHER DOWN BELOW LOWER UNDER NEDDER DOWNWARD INFERIOR INFERNAL

NETHERLANDS
CANAL: ORANJE JULIANA DRENTSCH
CAPITAL: AMSTERDAM
CHEESE: EDAM GOUDA LEYDEN
COIN: CENT DOIT RYDER FLORIN GULDEN STIVER DUCATON ESCALIN GUILDER STOOTER
ISLAND: TEXEL MARKEN AMELAND VLIELAND
MEASURE: EL AAM AHM AUM ELL KAN MUD VAT ZAK DUIM LOOD MIJL ROOD ROPE VOET ANKER CARAT ROEDE STOOP WISSE BUNDER KOPPEN LEGGER MAATJE MUDDLE MUTSJE STREEP SCHEPEL MINGELEN OKSHOOFD STEEKKAN
NAME: HOLLAND
NATIVE: DUTCH DUTCHMAN
PROVINCE: DRENTHE LIMBURG UTRECHT ZEELAND FRIESLAND GRONINGEN GELDERLAND OVERIJSSEL
RIVER: EEMS LECK MAAS WAAL YSEL DONGE HUNSE YSSEL DINTEL DOMMEL KROMME MEAUSE SCHELDT
TOWN: EDE ASSEN BREDA HAGUE AALTEN ARNHEM LEIDEN ZWOLLE HAARLEM TILBURG UTRECHT AALSMEER ENSCHEDE NIJMEGEN AMSTERDAM EINDHOVEN GRONINGEN ROTTERDAM
WEIGHT: ONS LAST LOOD POND BAHAR GREIN KORREL WICHTJE ESTERLIN

NETHERWORLD HADES SHADES

NETLIKE MESHY NETTY RETIARY RETICULAR

NETTING BAR CAUL LING MESH TULLE SCREEN DEEPING FISHNET FOOTING BOBBINET WIREWORK

NETTLE VEX FRET LINE ANNOY CNIDA ETTLE PEEVE PIQUE STING HENBIT ORTIGA RUFFLE SPLICE URTICA AFFRONT BLUBBER BLUETOP KNITTLE PROVOKE STINGER IRRITATE CLOWNHEAL GLIDEWORT PELLITORY SMARTWEED
(— RASH) HIVES UREDO URTICARIA
(— TREE) LOTUS GYMPIE
(WHITE DEAD —) ARCHANGEL
(PREF.) CNID(O)

NETTLERASH HIVES

NETWORK WEB CAUL FRET GRID KELL MAZE MESH MOKE RETE CHAIN LACIS BRIDGE COBWEB CRADLE PLEXUS RESEAU SAGENE SYSTEM DRAGNET DIPLEXER GRIDIRON KNITTING WATTLING RETICULUM
(— OF BLOOD VESSELS) RETE TOMENTUM
(— OF CRACKS) CRACKLE
(— OF LINES) RETICLE
(— OF REFRACTORY MATERIALS) MANTLE
(— ON MAP) GRATICULE
(COMPUTER —) LAN
(NUCLEAR —) SKEIN
(PL.) RETIA

NEUME PES VIRGA CLIVIS PNEUMA PODATUS PUNCTUM VIRGULA CLIMACUS QUILISMA SEQUENCE TORCULUS SCANDICUS

NEURAL DORSAL NERVAL NEURIC

NEURALGIA SCIATICA COSTALGIA

NEURILEMMA
(PREF.) LEMMO

NEURITE AXON AXONE

NEURITIS SCIATICA

NEUROGLIAL
(PREF.) GLI(O)

NEUROLOGIST **AMERICAN** BEARD DERCUM PRINCE COLLINS CORNING MERRITT MITCHELL
AUSTRIAN FREUD
ENGLISH ASH GOWERS JACKSON
FRENCH RAYMOND DEJERINE
GERMAN NISSL GUDDEN MOBIUS ALZHEIMER
ITALIAN GOLGI
PORTUGUESE MONIZ
SCOTTISH FERRIER

NEUROTIC DRUG NERVOUS
(— CONDITION) LATAH

NEUTRAL GRAY INERT SWEET AMORAL MIDDLING NEGATIVE UNBIASED COLORLESS IMPARTIAL
(— IN COLOR) SOBER
(OPTICALLY —) INACTIVE

NEUTRALIZE KILL ANNUL BLUNT ERASE CANCEL ABOLISH BALANCE CORRECT DESTROY NULLIFY VITIATE NEGATIVE OVERRIDE SATURATE FRUSTRATE

NEUTRINO LEPTON

NEVADA
CAPITAL: CARSONCITY
COUNTY: NYE ELKO LANDER STOREY WASHOE MINERAL PERSHING
INDIAN: WASHO PAIUTE
LAKE: MUD MEAD RUBY TAHOE WALKER PYRAMID WINNEMUCCA
PEAK: BOUNDARY
RIVER: REESE TRUCKEE HUMBOLDT
STATE BIRD: BLUEBIRD
STATE FLOWER: SAGEBRUSH
STATE NICKNAME: SILVER SAGEBRUSH
STATE TREE: ASPEN
TOWN: ELY ELKO RENO EUREKA FALLON NELLIS PIOCHE SPARKS TONOPAH LASVEGAS LOVELOCK

NEVE ICE FIRN SNOW NEPHEW GLACIER

NEVER NAY NIE NOT NARY NARRA NIVER NOWHEN

NEVER-NEVER DREAMLAND

NEVERTHELESS BUT YET STILL ALWISE THOUGH ALGATES HOWBEIT HOWEVER WHETHER NATHELESS NONETHELESS

NEVUS MOLE SPOT TUMOR NAEVUS SPIDER SPILUS FRECKLE LENTIGO SPILOMA BIRTHMARK

NEW HOT NEO NEU RAW LATE MINT NOVA FRESH GREEN MOIST NOVEL YOUNG MODERN RECENT REDHOT UNUSED VIRGIN ANOTHER FOREIGN STRANGE UNTRIED UPSTART INITIATE NEOTERIC ORIGINAL YOUTHFUL BEGINNING
(— BUT YET OLD) NOVANTIQUE
(BRAND —) SPICK
(COMB. FORM) NEO
(LOVE OF WHAT IS —) NEOPHILIA
(PREF.) CAEN(O) CEN(O) NE(O) NOV(I)(O)
(SUFF.) CENE

NEWBORN YEANLING

NEW BRUNSWICK **(CAPITAL OF —)** FREDERICTON
(COUNTY OF —) KINGS QUEENS SUNBURY MADAWASKA
(MOUNTAIN OF —) CARLETON
(TOWN OF —) BURTON MONCTON BATHURST GAGETOWN

NEW CALEDONIA **(— BIRD)** KAGU
(CAPITAL OF —) NOUMEA
(ISLAND OF —) HUON BELEP DEPINS LOYALTY WALPOLE
(SEAPORT OF —) NOUMEA

NEWCASTLE GOTHAM

NEWCOMER CADET SETTLER COMELING FRESHMAN JACKEROO MALIHINI RINGNECK GREENHORN IMMIGRANT KIMBERLIN
(— IN EAST) GRIFFIN GRIFFON

NEWCOMES **(AUTHOR OF —)** THACKERAY
(CHARACTER IN —) ANN KEW JOHN BRIAN CLARA CLIVE ETHEL JAMES ROSEY ALFRED BARNES BINNIE HOBSON RIDLEY THOMAS NEWCOME PULLEYN FARINTOSH MACKENZIE

NEW DEAL **(— AGENCY)** CCC NRA NYA TVA WPA

NEWEL POST VICE SPINDLE

NEW ENGLAND **(— INHABITANT)** YANK YANKEE JONATHAN
(— SETTLER) PILGRIM PURITAN

NEW-FANGLED UPSTART

NEWFANGLED MODERN

NEWFOUNDLAND **(— CAPE)** RAY RACE BAULD
(— HOUSE) TILT
(— INHABITANT) OUTPORTER
(CAPITAL OF —) STJOHNS
(ISLAND OF —) BELL FOGO GROAIS MIQUELON
(RIVER OF —) GANDER HUMBER EXPLOITS
(TOWN OF —) GANDER HOWLEY WABANA CORNERBROOK

NEW GUINEA
BAY: ORO MILNE HOLNICOTE GOODENOUGH COLLINGWOOD
CAPITAL: PORTMORESBY
COIN: KINA
GULF: HUON PAPUA
ISLAND: BUKA MANUS MUSSAU
ISLAND GROUP: CRETIN NINIGO SAINSON SOLOMON
MONEY: KINA TOEA
MOUNTAIN: ALBERT VICTORIA
NATIVE: ARAU BOONG KARON PAPUAN
PORT: LAE DARU WEWAK MADANG
RIVER: FLY HAMU SEPIK KIKORI PURARI AMBERNO
TOWN: LAE WAU DARU SORON AITAPE KIKORI RABAUL SAMARAI

NEW HAMPSHIRE
CAPITAL: CONCORD
COLLEGE: DARTMOUTH
COUNTY: COOS BELKNAP GRAFTON MERRIMACK
LAKE: SQUAM OSSIPEE SUNAPEE UMBABOG WINNIPESAUKEE
MOUNTAIN: MORIAH PAUGUS WAUMBEK CHOCORUA MONADNOCK
MOUNTAIN RANGE: WHITE
NOTCH: CRAWFORD FRANCONIA
PRESIDENT: PIERCE
RIVER: SACO ISRAEL BELLAMY SOUHEGAN MERRIMACK PISCATAQUA
STATE NICKNAME: GRANITE
TOWN: DOVER KEENE EXETER NASHUA HANOVER LACONIA OSSIPEE

NEW HEBRIDES **(CAPITAL OF —)** VILA
(ISLAND OF —) EPI TANA EFATE MAEWO MABRIM MALEKULA

NEW JERSEY
CAPITAL: TRENTON
COLLEGE: UPSALA
COUNTY: ESSEX OCEAN SALEM UNION BERGEN CAMDEN MERCER MORRIS SUSSEX WARREN PASSAIC MONMOUTH
INDIAN: DELAWARE
PRESIDENT: CLEVELAND
RIVER: DENNIS HAYNES MANTUA RAMAPO MULLICA PASSAIC RARITAN COHANSEY TUCKAHOE
STATE BIRD: GOLDFINCH
STATE FLOWER: VIOLET

STATE NICKNAME: GARDEN
STATE TREE: REDOAK
TOWN: LODI SALEM CAMDEN NEWARK NEWTON NUTLEY RAHWAY TOTOWA BAYONNE CLIFTON HOBOKEN HOHOKUS MATAWAN NETCONG ORADELL PARAMUS PASSAIC TEANECK TENAFLY TRENTON WYCKOFF CARTERET FREEHOLD METUCHEN PATERSON SECAUCUS WATCHUNG HACKENSACK
UNIVERSITY: RUTGERS PRINCETON

NEWLY ANEW AGAIN AFRESH LATELY FRESHLY NEWLINS RECENTLY
NEWMARKET MICHIGAN SARATOGA GRABOUCHE

NEW MEXICO

CAPITAL: SANTAFE
COUNTY: LEA EDDY LUNA MORA QUAY TAOS OTERO CATRON CHAVES DEBACA HIDALGO SOCORRO VALENCIA
CULTURE: MIMBRES
INDIAN: SIA TANO TEWA TIWA ZUNI JEMEZ PECOS APACHE NAVAHO NAVAJO PUEBLO
MOUNTAIN: WHEELER
RIVER: UTE GILA PECOS SANJOSE
STATE BIRD: ROADRUNNER
STATE FLOWER: YUCCA
STATE NICKNAME: SUNSHINE LANDOFENCHANTMENT
STATE TREE: PINON PINYON
TOWN: JAL MORA AZTEC BELEN RATON CLOVIS DEMING GALLUP GRANTS ARTESIA SANTAFE SOCORRO CARLSBAD LASVEGAS TUCUMCARI ALAMOGORDO

NEWNESS NOVITY
NEWS BUZZ DOPE UNCA UNKO WORD CLASH FERLY ADVICE BUDGET CRACKS FERLIE GOSPEL NOTICE REPORT EVANGEL KHUBBER TIDINGS WITTING NOUVELLE KNOWLEDGE SPEERINGS
(— AGENCY) AP UP DNB INS UPI TASS ANETA DOMEI REUTERS
(— BEAT) SCOOP
(— INTERRUPTION) UPDATE
(— ITEM) FACTOID
NEWSBOY NEWSY CAMELOT CARRIER PAPERBOY
NEWSCASTER ANCHORMAN
NEWSMONGER GOSSIP TATTLER NOVELANT NOVELIST QUIDNUNC REPORTER
NEWSPAPER RAG NEWS DAILY ORGAN PAPER PRESS SHEET TIMES ARRIBA HERALD SERIAL SUNDAY COURANT DIURNAL GAZETTE JOURNAL MERCURY TABLOID TRIBUNE NEWSPRINT
(— EDITION) EXTRA FINAL
(— SECTION) ROTO METRO
(— USED BY PICKPOCKET) STIFF
(FEEBLE —) SQUEAK
(SECTION OF —) ROTO
(PL.) PRESS
NEWSPAPERMAN HEARST PRESSMAN
NEWSPERSON REPORTER
NEWSSTAND BOOTH KIOSK STALL STAND BOOKSTALL
NEWSWORTHY NEWSY
NEWT ASK EFT ESK EVET EBBET EFFET LIZARD TRITON AXOLOTL CRAWLER CREEPER REPTILE MANKEEPER
NEW YEAR'S DAY NAURUZ NOROOSE NOWROZE
NEW YEAR'S EVE HAGMENA HOGMANAY

NEW YORK

AVENUE: PARK FIFTH MADISON FLATBUSH
BAY: JAMAICA PECONIC MORICHES
BOROUGH: BRONX KINGS QUEENS BROOKLYN MANHATTAN
BUILDING: RCA PANAM CHRYSLER FLATIRON
CANAL: ERIE GOWANUS
CAPITAL: ALBANY
COLLEGE: BARD CCNY IONA PACE FINCH UNION HUNTER VASSAR WAGNER ADELPHI BARNARD CANISIUS HAMILTON SKIDMORE
COUNTY: ERIE BRONX ESSEX KINGS TIOGA WAYNE YATES BROOME CAYUGA NASSAU ONEIDA OSWEGO OTSEGO PUTNAM QUEENS SENECA ULSTER CHEMUNG GENESEE NIAGARA STEUBEN SUFFOLK CHENANGO DUTCHESS HERKIMER ONONDAGA RICHMOND ROCKLAND SARATOGA SCHUYLER
INDIAN: CAYUGA MOHAWK ONEIDA SENECA MOHICAN MONTAUK IROQUOIS ONONDAGA
ISLAND: FIRE LONG ELLIS STATEN FISHERS LIBERTY SHELTER GOVERNORS MANHATTAN
LAKE: ERIE CAYUGA GEORGE ONEIDA OTISCO OTSEGO OWASCO PLACID SENECA CONESUS HONEOYE ONTARIO SARANAC SCHROON SUCCESS SARATOGA
MOUNTAIN: BEAR MARCY
MOUNTAINS: TACONIC CATSKILL ADIRONDACK
NICKNAME: EMPIRE GOTHAM
PRESIDENT: FILLMORE VANBUREN ROOSEVELT
PRISON: TOMBS ATTICA SINGSING
RIVER: TIOGA HARLEM HOOSIC HUDSON MOHAWK OSWEGO GENESEE NIAGARA
SQUARE: TIMES UNION HERALD MADISON
STATE BIRD: BLUEBIRD
STATE FLOWER: ROSE
STATE NICKNAME: EMPIRE EXCELSIOR
STATE TREE: SUGARMAPLE
STREET: WALL BOWERY BROADWAY
SUBWAY: BMT IND IRT LEX
TOWN: RYE OVID ROME DELHI ILION ISLIP NYACK OLEAN OWEGO UTICA ATTICA AUBURN CARMEL COHOES ELMIRA GOSHEN ITHACA MALONE ONEIDA OSWEGO TAPPAN WARSAW ARDSLEY BABYLON BATAVIA BUFFALO CONGERS ENDWELL GENESEO HEWLETT MAHOPAC MASSENA MERRICK MINEOLA MONTAUK ONEONTA PENNYAN POTSDAM SUFFERN SYOSSET WANTAGH YAPHANK YONKERS BETHPAGE CATSKILL HERKIMER KINGSTON OSSINING SYRACUSE TUCKAHOE ROCHESTER
UNIVERSITY: LIU NYU ADELPHI COLGATE CORNELL FORDHAM HOFSTRA YESHIVA COLUMBIA
WATERFALL: NIAGARA

NEW YORK CITY (BOROUGH OF —) BRONX QUEENS BROOKLYN MANHATTAN STATENISLAND
(COUNTY OF —) BRONX KINGS QUEENS RICHMOND
(ISLAND OF —) WARD ELLIS RANDALL WELFARE
(PARK OF —) GRANT BRYANT BATTERY CENTRAL
(SUBWAY OF —) BMT IND IRT

NEW ZEALAND

BAY: OHUA HAWKE LYALL AWARUA CLOUDY GOLDEN FITZROY PEGASUS POVERTY RANGAUNU
CAPE: EGMONT FAREWELL PALLISER
CAPITAL: WELLINGTON
GULF: HAURAKI
ISLAND: OTEA STEWART PUKETUTU
LAKE: OHAU HAWEA TAUPO PUKAKI PUPUKE TEANAU TEKAPO WANAKA BRUNNER ROTORUA WAKATIPU
MOUNTAIN: COOK FLAT OWEN CHOPE LYALL MITRE OTARI EGMONT STOKES AORANGI PIHANGA TUTAMOE TYNDALL ASPIRING EARNSLAW
NATIVE: ATI ARAWA MAORI RINGATU
PENINSULA: MAHIA OTAGO
RIVER: MOKAU ORETI WAIPA CLUTHA TAIERI TAMAKI WAIHOU WAIROA MATAURA WAIKATO WAITAKI CLARENCE MANAWATU WANGANUI RANGITIKEI
STRAIT: COOK FOVEAUX
TOWN: LEUIN ORETI OTAKI TAUPO CLUTHA FOXTON NAPIER NELSON OAMARU PICTON TIMARU DUNEDIN MANUKAU RAETIHI ROTORUA AUCKLAND HAMILTON KAWAKAWA CHRISTCHURCH
VOLCANO: RUAPEHU NGAURUHOE TONGARIRO
WATERFALL: BOWEN HELENA STIRLING SUTHERLAND

NEW ZEALANDER KIWI ENZED DIGGER
NEXT POI NEAR SYNE THEN UNTO WISE AFTER EWEST FIRST LATER NEIST RIGHT BESIDE COMING SECOND TIDDER TOTHER CLOSEST NEAREST DIRECTLY PROCHAIN PROCHEIN UPCOMING ADJOINING IMMEDIATE
(— AFTER) THEN FOLLOWING
(— IN ORDER) EKA
(— MONTH) PROXIMO
(— OF KIN) GOEL
(— TO LAST) PENULT
(PREF.) **(— IN ORDER)** EKA
NEXUS TIE BOND LINK CHAIN
NGAIO KIO KAIO NAIO TREE
NHANG GIAI
NIAM-NIAM ZANDE AZANDE AZANDI ZANDEH AZANDEH BABUNGERA
NIB NEB PEN BEAK BILL KINK TEAT POINT PRONG SCORER
NIBBLE EAT NAB NIB NIP BITE GNAW KNAB KNAP MOOP MOUP NOSH PECK PICK CHAMP GNARL MOUSE PIECE SHEAR ARRODE BROWSE CHAVEL NATTLE PICKLE PILFER CHIMBLE GNABBLE GNATTER KNABBLE SNAGGLE
NIBELUNGENLIED (AUTHOR OF —) UNKNOWN
(CHARACTER IN —) UTA ETZEL HAGEN IRING GERNOT HUNOLD LUDGER BLOEDEL GUNTHER ORTLIEB BRUNHILD DANKWART DIETRICH GISELHER KRIEMHILD SIEGFRIED HILDEBRAND
NIBLICK BLASTER
NICANOR (WIFE OF —) CLEOPATRA

NICARAGUA

CAPITAL: MANAGUA
COIN: PESO CENTAVO CORDOBA
DEPARTMENT: LEON BOACO RIVAS CARAZO ESTELI MADRIZ MASAYA ZELAYA MANAGUA
ISLAND: OMETEPE
LAKE: MANAGUA
MEASURE: VARA CAHIZ MILLA SUERTE TERCIA CAJUELA ESTADAL MANZANA
MOUNTAIN: MADERA MOGOTON
PORT: CORINTO
RIVER: COCO TUMA WANKS GRANDE ESCONDIDO
TOWN: LEON BOACO RIVAS MASAYA OCOTAL SOMOTO GRANADA MANAGUA JINOTEGA MATAGALPA CHINANDEGA
WEIGHT: BAG CAJA TONELADA

NICCOLITE ARITE KUPFERNICKEL
NICE APT FIT FEAT FINE GOOD JUMP KIND NEAT NYCE PURE TRIM CANNY EXACT FUSSY NIECE SWEET BONITA BONITO DAINTY GENTIL MINUTE PEACHY QUAINT QUEASY SPICED STRICT SUBTLE TICKLE CORRECT ELEGANT FINICAL GENTEEL MINCING PERJINK PICKING PRECISE PRUDISH REFINED DECOROUS DELICATE EXACTING PLEASANT PLEASING

TICKLISH PARTICULAR SCRUMPTIOUS
(TOO —) SUPERFINE
(PREF.) **(PERTAINING TO —)** NICENO
NICELY JUMP
NICETY HAIR QUIDDIT DELICACY JUSTNESS QUIDDITY CRITICISM CURIOSITY PRECISION
(PL.) PERJINKITIES
NICHE BAY WRO APSE CANT COVE NOOK SLOT AMBRY HERNE HOVEL NIECE NITCH PLACE ALCOVE ANCONA BOXING COVERT CRANNY EXEDRA GROOVE MIHRAB RECESS RINCON EDICULE HOUSING RETREAT ROUNDEL AEDICULA CREDENCE TOKONOMA HABITACLE PIGEONHOLE TABERNACLE
NICHOLAS NICKLEBY (AUTHOR OF —) DICKENS
(CHARACTER IN —) BRAY HAWK KATE FRANK GRIDE NOGGS RALPH SMIKE NEWMAN SQUEERS VINCENT CRUMMLES MADELINE MULBERRY NICHOLAS NICKLEBY WACKFORD CHEERYBLE MANTALINI
NICIPPE (FATHER OF —) PELOPS
(HUSBAND OF —) STHENELUS
(MOTHER OF —) HIPPODAMIA
(SON OF —) EURYSTHEUS
NICK CUT JAG MAR NAG NOB CHIP DENT DINT HACK NACK SLAP SLIT CHEAT CHICK GOUGE NITCH NOTCH PRICK SCORE SLACK SNICK TALLY TRICK ARREST RECORD DEFRAUD
(— OF TIME) GODSPEED
NICKEL JIT COIN JITNEY NIMBUS
(ALLOY OF —) INVAR KONEL MONEL
(CONTAINING —) NICCOLIC
(SYMBOL OF —) NI
(WOODEN —) SLUG
NICKELODEON JUKEBOX
NICKEL-SILVER PAKFONG PAKTONG PACKFONG
NICKER NEIGHER
NICKNAME DUB TAG DOEG NICK ALIAS AGNAME BYNAME BYWORD HANDLE MONICA TONAME AGNOMEN CRACKER EKENAME MISNAME MONIKER NICKERY COGNOMEN MONARCHO MONICKER TARTUFFE SOBRIQUET
NICKNAMING PROSONOMASIA
NICOMEDE (HALF-BROTHER OF —) ATTALE
(STEPMOTHER OF —) ARSINOE
NICOSTRATA (FATHER OF —) LADON
(HUSBAND OF —) ECHENUS
(SON OF —) EVANDER
NICOSTRATUS (BROTHER OF —) MEGAPENTHES
(FATHER OF —) MENELAUS
(MOTHER OF —) HELEN
NICOTINIC ACID NIACIN
NICTATE WINK BLINK CLOSE TWINK TWINKLE NICTITATE
NIDDICK NAPE
NIDE NID NEST BROOD LITTER
NIDGE NIG SHAKE QUIVER
NIDGET HOE FOOL IDIOT
NIDIFY NEST
NIDOR ODOR AROMA SAVOR SCENT SMELL
NIDUS NEST
NIECE OY OYE NEPHEW
NIELLO TULA
NIEPA NIOTA KARINGHOTA
NIEVE FIST HAND NEIF SERF NATIVE
NIFTY FINE GOOD KEEN SMART STYLISH
NIGER JOLIBA KWORRA RAMTIL
(CAPITAL OF —) NIAMEY
(MOUTH OF —) NUN
(NATIVE OF —) PEUL HAUSA DJERMA FULANI SONGHA TOUBOU TUAREG
(OASIS IN —) KAOUAR
(REGION OF —) AIR
(RIVER OF —) DILLIA
(TOWN OF —) SAY GAYA TERA BAGAM FACHI GOURE MADAMA MARADI TAHOUA ZINDER

NIGERIA
CAPITAL: LAGOS
COIN: KOBO NAIRA
NATIVE: ARO EBO EDO IBO IJO VAI BENI EBOE EFIK EJAM EKOI NUPE BENIN HAUSA FULANI YORUBA
PLATEAU: JOS
PORT: LAGOS CALABAR
PROVINCE: ISA OYO KANO NUPE ONDO IJEBU OGOJA WARRI OWERRI ADAMAWA
RIVER: OLI GANA YOBE BENUE NIGER KADUNA SOKOTO GONGOLA HADEJIA KOMADUGU
STATE: IMO OYO KANO OGUN ONDO BENUE BORNO KWARA LAGOS BAUCHI SOKOTO ANAMBRA GONGOLA
TOWN: ABA ADO EDE IFE ISA IWO JOS BIDI BUEA KANO OFFA YOLA AKURE ENUGU IKEJA LAGOS MINNA ZARIA BAUCHI IBADAN ILESHA ILORIN KADUNA MUSHIN OWERRI TAKOBA CALABAR ONITSHA OSHOGBO ABEOKUTA
TREE: AFARA

NIGGARD CARL CHURL CLOSE MISER NIGON PIKER SCART TIGHT NIGGER SCRIMP SCRUNT STINGY CHINCHE DRYFIST NITHING SCROOGE PINCHGUT PUCKFIST SCRIMPER EARTHWORM PINCHBECK PINCHFIST PUCKFOIST SKINFLINT PINCHPENNY
NIGGARDLY MEAN CLOSE NIRLY STINT NARROW NIDING NIGHLY NIRLED SCANTY SCREWY SKIMPY SORDID STINGY STRAIT CHINCHE COSTIVE MISERLY NITHING PENURIOUS PARSIMONIOUS
NIGGERFISH CONY HIND CONEY GROUPER GUATIVERE
NIGGLE DOUBT
NIGGLER NITPICKER
NIGGLING PETTY PICAYUNE
NIGH AT NEAR ANEAR ANIGH CLOSE ALMOST NEARLY ADJACENT
NIGHT PM EVE DARK NUIT SOIR DARKY DEATH NACHT NOCHE SLEEP DARKMANS DARKNESS
(— AND DAY) NYCHTHEMERON
(CHILDREN OF —) ERINYS FURIES ERINNYES
(COMB. FORM) NYCTI
(DEPTH OF —) HOLL
(GODDESS OF —) NOX NYX
(LAST —) YESTREEN
(NORSE —) NATT NOTT
(PERT. TO —) NOCTURNAL
(STAY OUT ALL —) PERNOCTATE
(PREF.) NOCT(I)(O) NYCT(I)(O)
NIGHT APE DURUKULI
NIGHT BELL (CHARACTER IN —) ENRICO SERAFINA PISTACCHIO
(COMPOSER OF —) DONIZETTI
NIGHT BLINDNESS NYCTALOPIA
NIGHTCAP HOW COWL DOWD HOUVE PIRNY BIGGIN PIRNIE DORMEUSE SUNDOWNER
NIGHTCLUB CAFE CLUB SPOT AGOGO BOITE DISCO BISTRO NITERY CABARET DANCERY NIGHTERY
NIGHTDRESS SLOP WILYCOAT WYLIECOAT
NIGHTFALL EEN EVE DARK DUSK EVEN SHUTTING TWILIGHT
(OCCURRING AT —) ACRONICAL
NIGHTGOWN SLOP TOOSH NIGHTY BEDGOWN NIGHTIE WYLIECOAT
NIGHTHAWK PISK CUIEJO BULLBAT
NIGHTINGALE JUG BULBUL FLORENCE PHILOMEL ROSSIGNOL
(— SOUND) JUG
(SWEDISH —) LIND JENNY
(PL.) WATCH
NIGHTJAR PUCK POTOO EVEJAR DERHAWK SPINNER WHEELER MOREPORK POORWILL NIGHTHAWK
NIGHT LAMP VEILLEUSE
NIGHTMARE ALP HAG MARA MESS DREAM FANCY FIEND VISION INCUBUS CACODEMON CAUCHEMAR EPHIALTES
(— CAUSER) MARE
NIGHTMARE ABBEY (AUTHOR OF —) PEACOCK
(CHARACTER IN —) EMILY FATOUT FLOSKY GLOWRY STELLA TOOBAD CELINDA CYPRESS ASTERIAS LISTLESS SCYTHROP GIROUETTE MARIONETTA CHRISTOPHER
NIGHTSHADE HERB DWALE MOREL TOMATO HENBANE MORELLE PETUNIA SANDBUR SOLANUM MANDRAKE TROMPILLO
NIGHT'S LODGING (AUTHOR OF —) GORKY
(CHARACTER IN —) LUKA BARON PEPEL SAHTIN BUBNOFF NATASHA ALYOSCHKA KVASCHNYA KOSTILIOFF WASSILISSA
NIGHT WATCHMAN CHARLEY CHARLIE
NIGHTWEAR PJS JAMMIES PAJAMAS
NIHIL NIL NICHIL NOTHING
NIHILIST ANARCHIST SOCIALIST
NIKE VICTORY
(BROTHER OF —) BIA ZELUS CRATOS
(FATHER OF —) PALLAS
(MOTHER OF —) STYX
NIL ZERO NILGAI IPOMOEA NOTHING

NILE
ARABIC NAME: ALBAHR
AS GOD: HAPI
BIRD: IBIS WRYNECK
BOAT: BARIS CANGIA NUGGAR DAHABEAH
CAPTAIN: RAIS REIS
DAM: ASWAN
FALLS: RIPON
FISH: BAGRE SAIDE BICHIB DOCMAC MORMYRID MORMYROID
ISLAND: RODA PHILAE
LATIN NAME: NILUS
NATIVE: MADI NILOT
NEGRO: JUR LUO LWO SUK
PLANT: SUDD LOTUS
REGION: NUBIA
SOURCE: TANA TSANA
TOWN: QUS ABRI ARGO IDFU ISNA QINA ASYUT CAIRO REJAF SAITE ROSETTA
TRIBUTARY: ATBARA KAGERA
VALLEY DEPRESSION: KORE

NILE GREEN BOA
NILGAI NIL NYLGAU ANTELOPE NEELGHAU
NIMBLE FLY DEFT FLIP FLIT GLEG LISH SPRY SWAK YALD YARE AGILE BRISK FLEET LIGHT NIPPY QUICK SWACK TRICK WIGHT YAULD ACTIVE ADROIT CLEVER FEIRIE LIMBER LISSOM LIVELY PROMPT QUIVER SPRACK SUPPLE VOLANT WANDLE DELIVER LISSOME SWIPPER FLIPPANT TRIPPING CITIGRADE SENSITIVE SPRIGHTLY
(PREF.) PRESTI
NIMBLENESS HASTE AGILITY SLEIGHT LEGERITY DEXTERITY LIGHTNESS
NIMBLE-WITTED VOLABLE
NIMBUS AURA HALO NIMB CLOUD GLORY SHINE VAPOR GLORIA AUREOLA AUREOLE
NIMIETY EXCESS
NINAZU (BROTHER OF —) NERGAL
(FATHER OF —) ENLIL
(MOTHER OF —) NINLIL
NINCOMPOOP ASS BOOB DOLT FOOL POOP NINNY NINCOM WITLING BLOCKHEAD SIMPLETON
NINE IX NIE NYE TEAM COMET POTHOOK
(— A.M.) UNDERN MIDMORN
(— ANGLED FIGURE) NONAGON
(— DAYS DEVOTION) NOVENA
(— FOLD) NONUPLE
(— HEADED MONSTER) HYDRA
(— HUNDRED) SAN
(— INCHES) SPAN
(— OF CLUBS OR DIAMONDS) COMET
(— OF DIAMONDS) BRAGGER
(— OF TRUMPS) DIX MENEL SANCHO
(— YEAR CYCLE) JUGLAR

(GROUP OF —) ENNEAD
(MUSIC FOR —) NONET
(PREF.) ENNE(A) NON(A) NOVEM NOVEN
NINEBARK ROSACEAN SEVENBARK
NINEHOLES BUMBLEPUPPY
NINEPIN KAIL SQUAIL SKITTLE SKITTLES
(PL.) BOWLS KEELS KAYLES NINEPEGS
NINETEENTH LARIGOT
NINETIETH NONAGESIMAL
NINETY KOPPA
NINEVEH (FOUNDER OF —) NINUS
NINE WORLDS HEL ASGARD ALFHEIM MIDGARD NIFLHEIM VANAHEIM JOTUNNHEIM MUSPELLSHEIM SVARTALFAHEIM
NINLIL (HUSBAND OF —) ENLIL
(SON OF —) NERGAL NINAZU
NINNI ISHTAR
NINNY DOLT FOOL LOUT DUNCE GOOSE IDIOT NONNY PATCH SAMMY SPOON FONDLE NOODLE SAPHEAD FONDLING BLOCKHEAD NIDDICOCK PEAKGOOSE SIMPLETON
NINON SHEER
NINSUN (SON OF —) GILGAMESH
NINTH (EVERY —) NONAN ENNEATIC
(PREF.) NON(A)
NINTU (DAUGHTER OF —) UTTU
(HUSBAND OF —) ENKI
(SON OF —) NINSAR
NINURTA (FATHER OF —) ENLIL
NINUS (FATHER OF —) BELUS
(SON OF —) NINYAS
(WIFE OF —) SEMIRAMIS
NIOBATE TODDITE SIPYLITE COLUMBATE
NIOBE HERB HOSTA FUNKIA
(BROTHER OF —) PELOPS
(FATHER OF —) TANTALUS
(HUSBAND OF —) AMPHION
(SISTER-IN-LAW OF —) AEDON
NIOBIC COLUMBIC
NIOBIUM COLUMBIUM
NIP CUT SIP VEX BITE BUMP CLIP DRAM GIVE KNIP NIPE PECK SNUB TANG TAUT TUCK BLAST CHEAT CHECK CHILL CLAMP DRAFT FROST PINCH SEIZE SEVER SNAPE SNEAP THIEF BENUMB BLIGHT CATNIP TIPPLE TWITCH WITHER SARCASM SQUEEZE WETTING COMPRESS FROSTBITE VELLICATE
NIPA PALM ATAP ATTAP DRINK
NIPPER BOY LAD CLAW CRAB GRAB HAND BITER CHELA MISER THIEF CUNNER URCHIN GRIPPER INCISOR BRAKEMAN
NIPPERS DOG NIP BITS NIPS TONGS GRATER PLIERS TURKIS FORCEPS PINCERS OSTEOTOME
NIPPLE BUD DUG PAP TIT BEAN TEAT DIDDY DUMMY SPEAN NIBBLE PILLAR MAMILLA PAPILLA THELIUM
(— POINT) THELION
(PREF.) EPITHELI(O) MAMM(I)(ILLI) MAST(O) PAPILLI PAPILLO THEL(O)
NIPPLEWORT BALLOGAN WARTWEED WARTWORT
NIPPY BOLD SHARP
NIREUS (FATHER OF —) CHAROPUS
(MOTHER OF —) AGLAIA
(SLAYER OF —) EURYPYLUS
NIRVANA EDEN EMPTINESS
NIS NIX NISSE GOBLIN KOBOLD BROWNIE
NISAN ABIB
NISEI (— SON OR DAUGHTER) SANSEI
NISUS POWER EFFORT IMPULSE ENDEAVOR
(DAUGHTER OF —) SCYLLA
(FATHER OF —) PANDION HYRTACUS
(MOTHER OF —) IDA
NITER NITRE PETER PETRE POTASH SALTPETER
NITHER BLAST DEBASE SHIVER TREMBLE
NITID GAY BRIGHT GLOSSY SPRUCE SHINING LUSTROUS NITIDOUS
NITO AGSAM
NITON RADON
NITRATE SALT ESTER COTTON AZOTATE
(PREF.) NITR(O)
NITRIC AZOTIC
NITRIDE BORAZON
NITRITE AZOTITE
NITROGEN GAS AZOTE ALKALIGEN
(PREF.) AZ(O)
NITROGLYCERIN TNT SOUP NITRO SIRUP SYRUP GLONOIN GLONOINE
NITWIT DAW NIT BOOB DINK DOLT DOPE KOOK DRONGO DINGBAT DIZZARD DINGALING SIMPLETON
NIX NO HARD NECK NICKER NOBODY SPIRIT SPRITE UNDINE NOTHING
NJAVE ADJAB DIAVE
NJORD (DAUGHTER OF —) FREYA
(SON OF —) FREY
(WIFE OF —) SKADHI
NO NA NE NAE NAH NAW NAY NIT NIX NUL BAAL BAIL BALE NEIN NONE NYET NAPOO AIKONA NAPOOH NOGAKU
(— MORE) NAPOO
(— ONE) NIX NEMO
(— POINTS IN TENNIS) LOVE
(PREF.) NULLI
NOADIAH (FATHER OF —) BINNUI
NOAH NOE
(DOVE OF —) COLUMBA
(FATHER OF —) LAMECH ZELOPHEHAD
(GRANDFATHER OF —) METHUSALEH
(GRANDSON OF —) ARAM MAGOG
(GREAT-GRANDSON OF —) HUL
(MEXICAN —) COXCOX
(RAVEN OF —) CORVUS
(SON OF —) HAM SEM SHEM JAPHETH
(WINE CUP OF —) CRATER
NOB NAB BLOW HEAD NAVE KNAVE SWELL HANDLE TIPTOPPER
NOBEL PRIZE (— IN CHEMISTRY) LEE BERG BERG CECH CRAM HAHN HOFF KLUG KUHN LEHN OLAH TODD UREY ALDER ASTON BOSCH BROWN COREY CURIE DEBYE DIELS EIGEN ERNST FLORY FUKUI HABER HUBER KARLE LIBBY NATTA PREGL SMITH SODDY SYNGE TAUBE TAUBE ALTMAN CALVIN HARDEN HASSEL KARRER LELOIR MARCUS MICHEL MULLIS NERNST PERUTZ PRELOG RAMSAY SANGER SANGER SUMNER WERNER WITTIG BERGIUS BUCHNER GIAUQUE GILBERT GILBERT HOFFMAN KENDREW KENICHI MOISSAN NORRISH ONSAGER OSTWALD POLANYI RUZICKA SEABORG SEMENOV WALLACH WIELAND WINDAUS HAUPTMAN LANGMUIR MITCHELL MULLIKEN PEDERSON TISELIUS HERSCHBACH MERRIFIELD DEISENHOFER
(— IN ECONOMICS FOGEL MILLER DOUGLASS
(— IN ECONOMICS) ARROW KLEIN KLEIN LEWIS OHLIN SIMON SIMON SOLOW STONE TOBIN TOBIN ALLAIS DEBREU DEBREU FRISCH MYRDAL SHARPE KUZNETS SCHULTZ SCHULTZ STIGLER STIGLER BUCHANAN FRIEDMAN HAAVELMO LEONTIEF MARKOWITZ MODIGLIANI
(— IN LITERATURE) PAZ BOLL BUCK COLA GIDE MANN SHAW AGNON BUNIN CAMUS ELIOT HESSE HEYSE LEWIS PERSE SACHS SIMON YEATS ANDRIC BELLOW ELYTIS ELYTIS EUCKEN FRANCE MAFOUZ MILOSZ MILOSZ NERUDA ONEILL SARTRE SINGER SINGER TAGORE BECKETT BRODSKY CANETTI CENETTI GOLDING GOLDING KIPLING LAXNESS MARQUEZ MAURIAC MISTRAL MONTALE ROLLAND RUSSELL SEIFERT SOYINKA WALCOTT BJORNSON CARDUCCI FAULKNER GORDIMER LAGERLOF MORRISON CHURCHILL HEMINGWAY PASTERNAK STEINBECK LAGERKVIST MAETERLINCK
(— IN MEDICINE) DAM CORI DALE HESS KATZ KOCH ROSS ROUS VANE WALD ARBER BLACK BLOCH BOVET BROWN BUMET CHAIN COHEN CRICK CURIE DOISY ELION EULER GOLGI HENCH HUBEL HUBEL JERNE KREBS KREBS KROGH LOEWI LURIA LYNEN MINOT MONIZ MONOD NEHER OCHOA SHARP SNELL SNELL TATUM YALOW BARANY BEADLE BEKESY BISHOP BORDET CARREL CLAUDE DOMAGK ECCLES ENDERS FISHER FLOREY GASSER GILMAN GRANIT HOLLEY HUXLEY KOCHER KOHLER KOSSEL LORENZ MURRAY PALADE PAVLOV RICHET SPERRY SPERRY THOMAS VARMUS WIESEL WIESEL AXELROD BEHRING DAUSETT FIBIGER HERSHEY HODGKIN KHORANA LAVERAN NATHANS NICOLLE ROBERTS RODBELL SAKMANN SCHALLY THELLER DELBRUCK MILSTEIN TONEGAWA BERGSTROM GOLDSTEIN HITCHINGS BENACERRAF MCCLINTOCK MCCLINTOCK MONTALCINI SAMUELSSON
(— IN PEACE) ORR THO HULL KING MOTT PIRE ROOT SATO TUTU ASSER BAJER BALCH BEGIN DAWES FRIED GOBAT LANGE PASSY SADAT ADDAMS ANGELL BRANDT BRIAND BUNCHE BUTLER CASSIN CREMER DUNANT MENCHU MONETA MYRDAL NANSEN QUIDDE ROBLES WALESA WALESA WIESEL WILSON BORLAUG BUISSON DEKLERK JOUHAUX KELLOGG LUTHULI MANDELA PAULING RENAULT SANCHEZ THERESA BRANTING CORRIGAN ESQUIVEL ESQUIVEL SAKHAROV GORBACHEV KISSINGER ROOSEVELT SODERBLOM SCHWEITZER HAMMARSKJOLD AUMGSANSUUKYI
(— IN PHYSICS) LEE BOHR BORN HESS LAMB LAUE MEER MOTT NEEL RABI RYLE TAMM TING WIEN YANG BASOV BETHE BLOCH BOTHE BRAGG BRAUN CURIE DALEN DIRAC ESAKI FERMI FITCH GABOR HERTZ HULSE KUSCH PAULI RUSKA SEGRE SHULL ALFVEN BARKLA BINNIG CRONIN CRONIN FOWLER FOWLER GENNES GLASER HEWISH LANDAU MULLER PERRIN PLANCK RAMSEY ROHRER RUBBIA STRUTT TAYLOR TAYLOR TOWNES WIGNER WILSON YUKAWA BARDEEN BEDNORZ CHARPAK DEHMELT GELLMAN GLAEVER GLASHOW KAPITSA KENDALL LORENTZ MARCONI RICHTER SHAWLOW EINSTEIN FRIEDMAN KLITZING LEDERMAN ROENTGEN SCHWARTZ SIEGBAHN BROCKHOUSE BLOEMBERGEN STEINBERGER CHANDRASEKHAR CHANDRASEKHAR
NOBILITY RANK ELITE GRACE GENTRY STATUS DIGNITY KWAZOKU PEERAGE QUALITY STATION BARONAGE SZLACHTA ELEVATION
(MEMBER OF TATAR —) MURZA
(ROMAN —) RAMNES
NOBLE DON ALII DOGE DUKE EARL EDEL EPIC FAME FREE GENT GOOD GRAF HIGH JARL JUST KAMI KUGE LORD PEER PURE RIAL ARIKI ATHEL BARON BROAD BURLY COUNT DUCAL ERECT ETHEL FURST GRAND GREAT HIRAM KHASS LOFTY MANLY MORAL MURZA PROUD ROYAL STATE AUGUST COUSIN DAIMIO EPICAL FLAITH GENTLE GESITH HAUGHT HEROIC JUNKER KINGLY LORDLY LUCUMO MANFUL SIRDAR SUPERB THAKUR WORTHY YONKER ACERBAS CACIQUE GALLANT GLAUCUS GLORIED GRANDEE HIDALGO LIBERAL MAGNATE MARQUIS PATRICK STAROST STATELY STEWARD SUBLIME TOISECH VOLPONE PANGLIMA PRINCELY
(MINOR —) VIDAME
NOBLEMAN DUKE EARL EMIR LORD

PEER SOUL BARON COUNT ORLOV PARIS THANE COUSIN MILORD ORLOFF THAKUR YONKER GRANDEE HIDALGO MAGNATE MARQUIS STAROST VOLPONE YOUNKER ADELIGER ALDERMAN ALMAVIVA BELARIUS MARCHESE MARQUESS LANDGRAVE MAGNIFICO
NOBLE-MINDED MANFUL LIBERAL
NOBLENESS HONOR DIGNITY
(— OF BIRTH) EUGENY
NOBLEWOMAN LADY MILADY DUCHESS PEERESS BARONESS COUNTESS
NOBODY NIX NEMO NONE NADIE NOMAN SCRUB SCARAB NOTHING JACKSTRAW
NOCENT GUILTY HARMFUL HURTFUL NOXIOUS CRIMINAL
NOCTURNAL NIGHT NOXIAL NIGHTLY NIGHTISH MOONSHINE
(— ANIMAL) COON POSSUM OPOSSUM
(— BIRD) OWL
(— CARNIVORE) RATEL
(— MAMMAL) BAT LEMUR
(— SIGNS) ZODIAC
NOCTURNE LULLABY UHTSONG PAINTING SERENADE
NOD OK BOB BOW ERR NAP NID NIP BECK BEND DOZE NAPE SIGN SLIP SWAY WINK DROOP LAPSE ASSENT BECKON DODDLE DROWSE NODDLE NUTATE SALUTE SIGNIFY
(— OFF) DOZE
NODDING DROWSY NUTANT ANNUENT CERNUOUS DROOPING NUTATION
NODDLE HEAD PATE BRAIN SKULL
NODDY AUK FOOL JACK NOIO TERN KNAVE NINNY DROWSY FULMAR NOODLE SLEEPY HACKNEY TOMNODDY SIMPLETON
NODE BOW BUMP KNOB KNOT LUMP PLOT JOINT NODUS POINT TUMOR BULBIL NODULE DILEMMA GRANULE KNUCKLE FOLLICLE PHYTOMER SWELLING TUBERCLE
(— OF GRASS) KNOT
(— OF POEM) PLOT
(— OF STEM) JOINT
NODULE BOB AUGE BUMP KNOT LUMP MASS NODE YOLK FLINT GEODE PHYMA MILIUM BLISTER CATHEAD GRANULE LEPROMA NABLOCK SARCOID AMYGDALE AMYGDULE COALBALL TUBERCLE WHITEHEAD
(— OF FLINT) CORE
(CHALCEDONY —) ENHYDROS
(PL.) BEADING
NOEL XMAS CAROL NOWEL NATALIS CHRISTMAS
NOGAH (FATHER OF —) DAVID
NOGGIN ALE CUP MUG NOG PEG PIN BEAN GILL HEAD PAIL PATE DRINK GOGGAN NAGGIN NOODLE
NO-GOODNIK SCALAWAG
NOHAH (FATHER OF —) BENJAMIN
NOIL FIBER PINION
NOISE (ALSO SEE SOUND) ADO AIR BUM DIN GIG HUM POP ROW BANG BOOM BRAY BUMP BURR CLAM COIL HOOT KLOP MUSH PEAL RALE RASH REEL RERD ROTE ROUT SLAM ZING ALARM BABEL BLARE BLAST BLOOP BRAWL BRUIT BURLE CHANG CHIRM CLICK DREAM GRASS JERRY KNOCK LARRY LARUM LEDEN PLASH QUONK REERE RERDE RUMOR SLORP SNORE SOUND STEER SWISH WHANG BICKER CACKLE CLAMOR DUNDER GOBBLE GOSSIP HUBBUB NORATE OUTCRY PUDDER RACKET RANTAN RATTLE REPORT SPLASH SQUAWK STEVEN STRIFE TUMULT UPROAR BLUSTER BRATTLE CLITTER CLUTTER CRACKLE ORATION SCANDAL SPATTER STREPOR STRIDOR FLICFLAC QUONKING TINTAMAR CONFUSION
(— OF DISAPPROVAL) RASPBERRY
(EARTHQUAKE —) BRONTIDES
(ELECTRIC —) GRASS
(EXPLOSIVE —) REPORT
(LOUD —) THUNDER
(RESOUNDING —) WHAM WHANG
(SCRAPING —) SCROOP
(PREF.) **(— OF FALLING OBJECT)** KER
NOISELESS QUIET STILL SWEET TACIT SILENT APHONIC CATLIKE
NOISEMAKER BELL HORN GRAGER RATTLE CLAPPER SQUEAKER
NOISETTE HAZEL HAZELNUT
NOISING (— ABROAD) AIR
NOISOME FOUL OLID RANK FETID NASTY PUTRID RANCID HARMFUL HURTFUL NOXIOUS NUISOME ODOROUS STINKING OFFENSIVE MALODOROUS
NOISY LOUD CLASHY CREAKY BLATANT DINSOME FRANTIC MOILING RACKETY RIOTOUS ROUTOUS BRAWLING CLATTERY SONOROUS STREPENT HILARIOUS RATTLEBAG SCAMBLING BOISTEROUS
NOLL HEAD NODDLE NOODLE
NOMA CANKER
NOMAD ARAB BEJA LURI MOOR SAKA SHUA ALANI GYPSY IGDYR JAREG ROVER SHUWA NOMADE ROAMER ROVING SEMITE SLUBBI TUAREG BAZIGAR BEDOUIN SARACEN SCENITE SHORTZY SHUKRIA SOLUBBI TOUAREG KABABISH SCYTHIAN SHINWARI AMALEKITE MIGRATORY PEREGRINE
(— PEOPLE) ALANI
(ETHIOPIAN —) GALLA
(PL.) AKHLAME
NOMADIC ERRATIC VAGRANT VAGABOND FOOTLOOSE ITINERANT
NOMBRIL NAVEL
NOM DE PLUME PENNAME TELONISM PSEUDONYM
NOME ELIS NOMOS MELODY NOMARCHY PROVINCE
NOMENCLATURE LIST NAME TERM ONYMY NAMING GLOSSARY REGISTER CATALOGUE
NOMINAL PAR BASIC PAPER FORMAL SLIGHT UNREAL TITULAR TRIVIAL PLATONIC TRIFLING
(— RECOGNIZANCE) DOE
NOMINATE CALL LEET NAME ELECT NEVEN SLATE SELECT APPOINT ENTITLE PRESENT PROPOSE SPECIFY DESIGNATE POSTULATE
NOMINY SPEECH RIGMAROLE
NONAGE NEANT INFANCY MINORITY PUPILAGE
NONAGENARIAN OLDSTER
NONAGREEMENT DISSENT
NON-ALCOHOLIC SMALL
NO NAME (AUTHOR OF —) COLLINS
(CHARACTER IN —) NOEL CLARE FRANK GARTH KIRKE NORAH ANDREW GEORGE WRAGGE BARTRAM BYGRAVE LECOUNT MAGDALEN VANSTONE
NON-ARAB SHANGALLA
NONASPIRATE LENE
NONBELIEVER PAGAN ATHEIST AGNOSTIC
NONCE NANES NONES NOANCE PRESENT PURPOSE OCCASION
NONCHALANT COOL GLIB ALOOF CASUAL JAUNTY CARELESS DEBONAIR NEGLIGENT
NON-CHRISTIAN PAYNIM INFIDEL
NONCITIZEN TENSOR PEREGRINUS
NONCLERICAL LAY LAIC
NONCOMBUSTIBLE APYROUS
NONCOMMITTAL NEUTRAL
NONCONFORMIST REBEL NONCON BEATNIK DEVIANT FANATIC HERETIC SECTARY BOHEMIAN RECUSANT DISSENTER
(— IN ART) FAUVE
NONCONFORMITY HERESY ADHARMA DISSENT NEGLECT REFUSAL RECUSANCE RECUSANCY
NONCONTINUOUS DISCRETE
NON-CONVERGENCE ABERRATION
NONDESCRIPT BLAH DRAB DULL
NONDISCLOSURE FRAUD
NONDO LOVAGE ANGELICO
NONDUALISM ADVAITA
NONE NO UN NAE NIN ZIP NANE NARY NEEN NONES
(PREF.) NULLI
NONEGO NOTSELF
NONELASTIC BROAD
NONENTITY ZERO AUGHT CIPHER NOBODY NOUGHT NOTHING NULLITY NEGATION
NONESSENTIAL CASUAL FRILLY UNNEEDED EXTRINSIC
(— IN RELIGION) ADIAPHORON
NONESUCH APPLE MODEL PARAGON PATTERN PARADIGM MATCHLESS NONPAREIL UNRIVALED
NON-EXISTENCE ABSENCE NOTHING
NONEXISTENT NULL NAPOOH NOUGHT NONBEING BARMECIDE
(PRACTICALLY —) FAT
(PREF.) NULLI
NONFEASANCE BREACH
NON GRATA UNWELCOME
NONGYPSY GAJO
NONINJURY AHIMSA
NON-JEW GOI GOY
NONJUROR USAGER
NON-LATIN SAXON
NONLEGATO DETACHE DETACHED
NON-MOSLEM GENTILE
NONMOTILE
(PREF.) APLANO
NONNASAL ORAL
NO-NO TABU TABOO
NONPAREIL BEST ONER POPE TYPE PARAGON PERFECT SUPREME UNEQUAL NONESUCH PEERLESS UNRIVALED
NONPAYMENT DISHONOR
NONPLUS SET FAZE POSE STOP BLANK FLOOR POSER STICK STUMP TRUMP BAFFLE GRAVEL PUZZLE RATTLE CONFUSE MYSTIFY PERPLEX STAGGER QUANDARY DULCARNON EMBARRASS
NONPLUSSED BLANK FOOLISH
NONPOISONOUS SAFE EDIBLE
NON-POLYNESIAN PAKEHA
NONPROFESSIONAL BUM LAY LAIC AMATEUR
NONSENSE BAH GAS GUP PAH ROT BILK BLAA BLAH BOSH BUFF BULL BUNK COCK CRAP FLAM FLUM GAFF GOOK GUFF JIVE JUNK PISH POOH PUNK TOSH BALLS BEANS BILGE BLASH DROOL FOLLY FUDGE HAVER HOOEY NERTS SPOOF STITE STUFF TRASH TRIPE WAHOO BABBLE BETISE BLAGUE BUNKUM DRIVEL FADDLE FOLDER FOOTLE IDIOCY KIBOSH LINSEY MALARK NAVERS PIFFLE RUBBLE SQUISH TRIVIA BLARNEY BLATHER EYEWASH FARRAGO FLANNEL INANITY LOCKRAM MALARKY RHUBARB RUBBISH TOSHERY TRIFLES TWADDLE BUNCOMBE CLAPTRAP COBBLERS DISHWASH FALDEROL FLIMFLAM FLUMMERY GALBANUM MACARONI MOROLOGY PISHPOSH PISHTOSH SKITTLES SPLUTTER TOMMYROT TRUMPERY ABSURDITY FRIVOLITY MOONSHINE POPPYCOCK SILLINESS BALDERDASH CODSWALLOP JABBERWOCK TARADIDDLE JABBERWOCKY GOBBLEDYGOOK
(— CREATURE) GOOP SHOO SNARK SHIMOO
(SENTIMENTAL —) SLAVER
NONSENSICAL ABSURD
NONSURFER HODAD
NONUSER (— OF DRUGS) STRAIGHT
NON-VIOLENCE AHIMSA
NOODLE BEAN FOOL HEAD NIZY NOLL PATE MOONY NINNY NIZEY NODDY PASTA PASTE SAMMY BOODLE GUDDLE NODDLE NOGGIN DAWCOCK LOKSHEN NOGHEAD NOUILLE BLOCKHEAD SIMPLETON CAPERNOITIE
(— DISH) PANSIT RAVIOLI KREPLACH
(JAPANESE — SOUP) RAMEN
(STUPID —) BOODLE

(PL.) MEIN FARFEL FERFEL LASAGNA LASAGNE LOKSHEN FETTUCINI
NOOK IN BAY OUT WRO CANT COVE GLEN HERN HOLE NALK NUCK NUIK ANGLE HALKE HERNE NEUCK NICHE ALCOVE CANTLE CORNER CRANNY RECESS CREVICE NOOKERY RETREAT
(FIREPLACE —) INGLE
NOON M APEX DINE NOWN SEXT DINNER MIDDAY UNDERN MIDNOON MERIDIAN
NOONDAY (— REST) NAP SIESTA MERIDIAN
NOOSE TIE TOW BOND DULL FANK GIRN HEMP LACE LOOP ROPE TRAP BIGHT CATCH GRANE HITCH HONDA KINCH LASSO LATCH LEASH SNARE SNARL WIDDY CAUDLE CHOKER CLINCH ENTRAP HALTER LARIAT SPRING TETHER TIPPET TWITCH CHOCKER ENSNARE EXECUTE LANIARD LANYARD SPRINGE NECKLACE SQUEEZER TWITCHEL
(— FOR HAULING LOG) CHOKER CHOCKER
(— FOR SNARING FISH) DULL
(— IN A CORD) KINCH
(HANGMAN'S —) SQUEEZER
NOOTKA AHT AHOUSAHT MOATCAHT MOOACHAHT
NORATE NOISE RUMOR GOSSIP
NORAX (FATHER OF —) HERMES MERCURY
(MOTHER OF —) ERYTHEA
NORDIC ARIAN ARYAN
NORI AMANORI
NORITE GABBRO OLIGOSITE
NORM PAR MODE RULE TYPE CANON GAUGE MODEL NORMA DHARMA MEDIAN AVERAGE MODULUS PATTERN STANDARD TEMPLATE
NORMA MOLD RULE GAUGE MODEL SQUARE PATTERN TEMPLET STANDARD TEMPLATE
(CHARACTER IN —) NORMA ADALGISA POLLIONE
(COMPOSER OF —) BELLINI
NORMAL PAR FULL HOME JUST MEAN SANE WISE CLEAR ERECT USUAL FORMAL NATIVE SCHOOL AVERAGE NATURAL NEUTRAL REGULAR TYPICAL ORDINARY STANDARD CUSTOMARY
NORMANDY (BEACH IN —) OMAHA
(CAPITAL OF —) ROUEN
(RIVER IN —) EURE ORNE SEINE
NORN FATE URTH WURD WYRD NORNA SKULD URDHR URTHR VERDHANDI VERTHANDI
NORSE ICELANDIC
NORSEL BAND LINE ORSEL FILLET NOSSEL ORSELLER
NORTH SEPTENTRION
(PREF.) ARCT(O)

NORTH AMERICA

(ALSO SEE SPECIFIC COUNTRIES)
ISLAND: LONG BANKS PARRY BAFFIN BERMUDA VICTORIA ANTICOSTI ELLESMERE GREENLAND NEWFOUNDLAND
LAKE: ERIE HURON NIPIGON ONTARIO MANITOBA MICHIGAN REINDEER SUPERIOR WINNIPEG ATHABASCA NETTILING
MOUNTAIN: WOOD LOGAN WALSH ROBSON STEELE TOLUCA LUCANIA PARICUTIN TAJUMULCO POPOCATEPETL
NATION: CANADA MEXICO UNITEDSTATES
RIVER: GILA MILK JAMES LIARD OSAGE PEACE PEARL PECOS SNAKE YUKON BALSAS BRAZOS FRASER HUDSON MOBILE NEOSHO PANUCO PLATTE POWDER SABINE TANANA KLAMATH KOYUKUK POTOMAC SUSITNA CIMARRON COLUMBIA DELAWARE MISSOURI NIOBRARA PENOBSCOT PORCUPINE RIOGRANDE STLAWRENCE MISSISSIPPI

NORTH CAROLINA

CAPE: FEAR LOOKOUT HATTERAS
CAPITAL: RALEIGH
COLLEGE: ELON CATAWBA DAVIDSON
COUNTY: ASHE DARE HOKE HYDE NASH PITT WAKE AVERY DAVIE GATES ROWAN SURRY BERTIE BLADEN CRAVEN ONSLOW YADKIN YANCEY CATAWBA PAMLICO CURRITUCK
INDIAN: ENO COREE CHERAW MORATOK PAMLICO CHOWANOC HATTERAS
MOUNTAIN: HARRIS MITCHELL
PRESIDENT: POLK JOHNSON
RIVER: HAW TAR NEUSE CHOWAN LUMBER PEEDEE YADKIN ROANOKE
SOUND: BOGUE CROATAN PAMLICO
STATE BIRD: CARDINAL
STATE FLOWER: DOGWOOD
STATE NICKNAME: TARHEEL OLDNORTH TURPENTINE
STATE TREE: PINE
TOWN: BOONE SYLVA BURGAW DOBSON DURHAM LENOIR SHELBY SPARTA EDENTON HICKORY ROXBORO TARBORO GASTONIA CHARLOTTE
UNIVERSITY: DUKE

NORTH DAKOTA

CAPITAL: BISMARCK
COLLEGE: JAMESTOWN
COUNTY: DUNN EDDY SLOPE STARK WELLS DICKEY DIVIDE GRIGGS KIDDER OLIVER TRAILL PEMBINA ROLETTE
INDIAN: MANDAN ARIKARA HIDATSA
MOUNTAIN: WHITEBUTTE
RIVER: RUSH CEDAR HEART JAMES SOURIS DESLACS SHEYENNE WILDRICE
STATE BIRD: MEADOWLARK
STATE FLOWER: PRAIRIEROSE
STATE NICKNAME: SIOUX FLICKERTAIL
STATE TREE: ELM
TOWN: MOTT CANDO FARGO MINOT ROLLA AMIDON LAKOTA LINTON MOHALL BOWBELLS NAPOLEON

NORTHERN PIKE ARCTIC BOREAL NORLAND NORTHEN
(— BEAR) POLAR RUSSIA
(— CONSTELLATION) URSA ANDROMEDA

NORTH KOREA

CAPITAL: PYONGYANG
COIN: JUN WON CHUN HWAN
PROVINCE: CHAGANG KANGWON TANGGANG
RIVER: NAM YALU IMJIN TUMEN TAEDONG
TOWN: HAEJU HEIJO KEIJO ANDONG ANTUNG HYESAN JUSHIN POCHON SAINNI WONSAN HAMHUNG HUICHON HUNGNAM KAESONG KANGGYE SARIWON SINUIJU CHONGJIN

NORTHMAN DANE
NORTH STAR STATE MINNESOTA
NORTHWEST TERRITORY
(CAPITAL OF —) YELLOWKNIFE
(DISTRICT OF —) FRANKLIN KEEWATIN MACKENZIE
(RIVER OF —) BACK KAZAN DUBAWNT COPPERMINE
(TOWN OF —) RAE INUVIK DISCOVERY SNOWDRIFT

NORWAY LEVANGER

CAPE: NORDKYN NORDKAPP
CAPITAL: OSLO
COIN: ORE KRONE
COUNTY: AMT OSLO FYLKE TROMS BERGEN TROMSO FINMARK HEDMARK OPPLAND OSTFOLD NORDLAND ROGALAND TELEMARK VESTFOLD
DANCE: GANGAR HALLING SPRINGAR SPRINGLEIK
FJORD: OSLO SOGNE HARDANGER TRONDHEIM
INLET: IS KOB RAN ALST ANDS BOKN NORD OFOT SALT SUNN TYRI VEST FIORD FJORD FOLDA LAKSE SOGNE BJORNA HADSEL HORTENS TRONDHEIM
ISLAND: VEGA BOMLO DONNA FROYA HITRA HOPEN SENJA SMOLA ALSTEN AVEROY BOUVET HINNOY KARMOY KVALOY SOLUND SOROYA VANNOY GURSKOY LOFOTEN MAGEROY SEILAND JANMAYEN SVALBARD RINGVASSOY
LAKE: ALTE ISTER MJOSA SNASA FEMUND ROSTAVN TUNNSJO ROSTVATN
MEASURE: FOT MAL POT ALEN MAAL KANDE FATHOM SKIEPPE
MOUNTAIN: SOGNE KJOLEN NUMEDAL BLODFJEL SNOHETTA TELEMARK USTETIND JOTUNHEIM
PARLIAMENT: LAGTING STORTING ODELSTING
PLATEAU: DOURE FJELD HARDANGER
RIVER: OI ENA ALTA OTRA RANA TANA BARDU BEGNA GLAMA LAGEN ORKLA OTTER RAUMA REISA GLOMMA LOUGEN NAMSEN PASVIK DRAMSELVA
TOWN: GOL NES BODO MOSS ODDA OSLO VOSS BJORT FLORO HAMAR MOLDE SKIEN SKJAK BERGEN HORTEN LARVIK NARVIK ALESUND ARENDAL DRAMMEN SANDNES STAVANGER
WATERFALL: VETTI SKYKJE VORING
WEIGHT: LOD MARK PUND SKAALPUND BISMERPUND

NORWEGIAN (FORM OF —) BOKMAL
(LITERARY FORM OF —) NYNORSK
NOSE CAP NEB NIZ PRY PUG SPY BEAK BOKO CONK NASE GROIN LORUM NASUS SCENT SMELL SNIFF SNOOP SNOOT SNOUT TRUNK BEEZER CYRANO DETECT GNOMON MUFFLE MUZZLE NOZZLE PECKER ROOKIE SEARCH SNITCH SOCKET ADVANCE PERFUME SMELLER DISCOVER INFORMER OLFACTOR PERCEIVE PROBOSCIS SCHNOZZLE
(— A LOG) SNIPE
(— BAG) MORRAL
(— CARTILAGE) SEPTUM
(— DISEASE) OZENA OZOENA
(— DIVE) VRILLE
(— FLUTE) PUNGI POOGYE
(— INFLAMMATION) CORYZA RHINITIS
(— MEDICINE) ERRHINE
(— OF AIRPLANE) PROW
(— OF ANIMAL) GROIN
(— OPENING) NARE
(— OUT) EDGE
(— PARTITION) VOMER
(— PIECE) NASAL
(— RING) PIRN
(BLUNT —) SNUB
(FLAT —) PUG SNUB
(PREF.) NAS(I)(O) NASUTI RHIN(O)
(SUFF.) RHINA RHINE RHINIA RHINOUS RHINUS RRHINE RRHINIA
NOSEBAND BOSAL MUSROL CAVESSON
NOSEBLEED EPISTAXIS RHINORRHAGIA
NOSEGAY BOB ODOR POSY POESY SCENT TUTTY BOUQUET CORSAGE PERFUME
NOSH SNACK
NOSINESS CURIOSITY
NOSING CURB
NOSTALGIA LONGING YEARNING
NOSTALGIC RETRO ELEGIAC OLDTIMEY ELEGIACAL
(FASHIONABLY —) RETRO
NOSTOLOGY GERIATRICS
NOSTRADAMUS SEER PROPHET PHYSICIAN
NOSTRIL ALA NARE NARIS THIRL THRILL BLOWHOLE
(PERT. TO —) NARIAL NARINE

(PL.) NARES NARIS SNUFFERS
(PREF.) NARI
NOSTRUM ELIXIR SECRET
NOSU LOLO
NOSY BEAKY PRYING CURIOUS FRAGRANT INTRUSIVE
NOT NA NE NAE NAY NOR PAS BAAL BAIL BALE NICHT SHORN SORRA NOUGHT POLLED SHAVEN NEITHER HORNLESS NEGATIVE
(— ANY) NO NUL NANE NARY NONE NAIRY NOKIN STEAD
(— AT ALL) NEVER LITTLE NOWAYS NOWHIT NOWISE
(— FINAL) NISI
(— THE SAME) OTHER ANOTHER DIFFERENT
(— TO BE REPEATED) NR
(— WANTED) DETROP SUPERFLUOUS
(ALMOST —) SCARCELY
(COULD —) NOTE
(PREFIX MEANING —) IL IM IN IR UN NON
(PREF.) A ANTI DIS E IL IM IN IR NON UM UN
NOTABLE VIP FINE FABLED FAMOUS GIFTED NOTARY SIGNAL UNIQUE EMINENT STORIED SUBLIME DISTINCT ESPECIAL EVENTFUL HISTORIC MEMORABLE NOTORIOUS NOTEWORTHY
NOTARY NOTAR GRAFFER GREFFIER NOTEBOOK OBSERVER OFFICIAL SCRIVENER
NOTARY PUBLIC TABELLION
NOTATION HOLD MEMO NOTE ENTRY SYSTEM MARKING
(— OF DANCING) ORCHESOGRAPHY
(MUSICAL —) TABLATURE
(PHONETIC —) ROMIC
NOTATOR NOTER RECORDER
NOTCH CUT DAG DAP GAP HAG JAG JOG PEG COPE DENT DINT GAIN GIMP KERF MUSH NICK NOCK SLAP SLOT SNIP STEP WARD CRENA GABEL GRADE HILUM SCORE SHARD SHERD SWICK TALLY CRENEL CROTCH DEFILE DEGREE HOLLOW INDENT JOGGLE RAFFLE RECORD SCOTCH CRENATE GUDGEON SERRATE INCISION UNDERCUT
(— BETWEEN HILLS) SLAP
(— ON VERTEBRAE) HYPANTRUM
(— TO FELL TREE) UNDERCUT
NOTCHED EROSE JAGGY RAGULE RAGULY SERRATE CRENATED SERRATED
NOTE BON DOG IOU JOT KEY SEE TEN UNE BILL CARD CENT CHIT ESPY FAME FLAT GOOD HEED MARK MEMO NAME NOIT SIGN SOLE SONG TENT TONE TUNE VIEW CHECK FIVER GLOZE LABEL PRICK SHORT SIXTH SOUND STIFF TENTH TOKEN TRAIT TWANG ATTEND BILLET DEGREE EXCUSE FIGURA FLIMSY LETTER MELODY MINUTE NOTICE POLICY RECORD REGARD REMARK RENOWN REPORT SECOND STRAIN TENNER BETOKEN COMMENT DISCORD MESSAGE MISSIVE NATURAL OBSERVE PUNCTUS REDBACK ANNOTATE BLUEBACK BRADBURY BREVIATE DISPATCH EMINENCE MARGINAL PERCEIVE POSTFACE TREASURY GREENBACK POSTSCRIPT
(— FROM TRAIN) BUTTERFLY
(— OF ASSAULT) WARISON
(— OF HUMOR) TRAIT
(— OF SCALE) DO FA LA MI RE SI SO TI UT ARE SOL
(— OF SNIPE) SCAPE
(— OF WARNING) WATCHWORD
(— ON SHOPHAR) TEKIAH
(—S ON HUNTING HORN) SEEK
(— TO RECALL DOG) FORLOIN
(ALTERED —) ACCIDENTAL
(BANK —S) CABBAGE
(BASS —) DRONE
(BIRD'S —) JUG CHIRP
(BUGLE —) MOT
(EDITOR'S —) STET
(EIGHTH —) UNCA QUAVER
(EMBELLISHING —) ORNAMENT
(ESCAPE —) ECHAPPEE
(EXPLANATORY —) ANAGRAPH SCHOLIUM ANNOTATION
(FUNDAMENTAL —) ROOT
(GRACE —) NACHSCHLAG
(HALF —) MINIM
(HARSH —) BLOB
(HIGH-PITCHED —) BEEP
(HIGHEST —) ELA
(LEADING —) SUBTONIC
(LONG —) LARGE
(LOVE —) POULET
(LOWEST —) KEY GAMUT
(MARGINAL —) TOT QUOTE POSTIL APOSTIL
(MUSICAL —) ALT RAY HALF MESE MIND BREVE GAMUT SHARP TONIC WHOLE EIGHTH ALAMIRE MEDIANT PUNCTUS QUARTER CROTCHET DOMINANT LICHANOS PARAMESE SUBTONIC PIZZICATO SUBDOMINANT APPOGGIATURA
(NONHARMONIC —) CAMBIATA
(POUND —) BRADBURY
(PROMISSORY —) DOG GOOD HUNDI CEDULA ASSIGNAT
(QUARTER —) CROTCHET SEMIMINIM
(SIXTEENTH —) DEMIQUAVER SEMIQUAVER
(SIXTY-FOURTH —) HEMIDEMISEMIQUAVER
(THIRTY-SECOND —) SUBSEMIFUSA DEMISEMIQUAVER
(TREASURY —) TBILL
(TWO —S) DUPLET
(WARBLING —) CHIRL
(WHOLE —) SEMIBREVE
(WRONG —) CLINKER
(100-POUND —) CENTURY
(PL.) ANA GAMUT STRAIN NUMBERS TIRALEE MARGINALIA
NOTEBOOK LOG DIARY NOTARY RECORD STREET JOURNAL
NOTECASE WALLET POCKETBOOK
NOTED COUTH FAMED GREAT NAMELY EMINENT INSIGNE RENOWNED DISTINGUE
NOTEPAPER BOUDOIR
NOTEWORTHY BIG SOLEMN EMINENT NOTABLE SALIENT SPECIAL BODACIOUS MEMORABLE OBSERVABLE
NOTHING NIL NIX ZIP FREE LUKE NADA NILL RIEN WIND ZERO AUGHT BLANK NIHIL SQUAT ZILCH CIPHER NAUGHT NOBODY NOUGHT TRIFLE NULLITY SCRATCH USELESS BAGATELLE DIDDLYSQUAT
(— BUT) ALL
(— DOING) NAPOO NAPOOH
(— MORE THAN) MERE
(— OTHER THAN) ONLY
NOTHINGNESS NOT NADA ZERO NOUGHT VACUITY NIHILITY
NOTICE AD BAN SEE SPY CALL ESPY GAUM GOME HEED IDEA KEEP MARK MIND NEWS NOTE PIPE RIDE SIGN SPOT TWIG ALARM AWAIT COUNT EDICT FLOAT NOTAM ORDER QUOTE ADVICE ALLUDE BILLET ESPIAL NOTION PERMIT READER REGARD REMARK REWARD AFFICHE ARTICLE DISCERN MENTION OBSERVE PLACARD PROGRAM WARNING BULLETIN MONITION PERCEIVE WITTERING
(— UNEXPECTEDLY) CATCH
(ADVANCE —) HERALDRY PREMONITION
(COMMENDATORY —) PUFF BLURB
(DEATH —) OBIT OBITUARY
(FAVORABLE —) RAVE
(FINAL —) OBIT OBITUARY
(LEGAL —) CAVEAT
(MARRIAGE —) BANS BANNS
(OFFICIAL —) EDICT SUMMONS BULLETIN CITATION
(PUBLIC —) BAN EDICT BULLETIN SPOTLIGHT
NOTICEABLE CRUDE GROSS FLASHY MARKED SIGNAL EVIDENT NOTABLE POINTED SALIENT HANDSOME PALPABLE STRIKING OBTRUSIVE PROMINENT CONSPICUOUS OUTSTANDING
(UNDESIRABLY —) CONSPICUOUS
NOTIFICATION DRUM NOTE AVISO NOTICE SUMMONS
(PUBLIC —) SIGN
NOTIFY ALL BID CRY JOG CITE PAGE TELL WARN ADVISE INFORM NOTICE SIGNAL APPRISE DECLARE FRUTIFY PUBLISH ACQUAINT INTIMATE
NOTION BEE GEE BUZZ IDEA IDEE KINK MAZE OMEN VIEW WHIM FANCY FREIT IMAGE SENSE THING WARES BELIEF CEMENT DESIRE DONNEE GADGET MAGGOT NOTICE THEORY VAGARY WHIMSY BROMIDE CONCEIT CONCEPT FANTASY INKLING MAROTTE OPINION THOUGHT WHIMSEY WRINKLE CATEGORY FOLKLORE PHANTASY SUPPOSAL WHIMWHAM INTENTION SENTIMENT WHIRLIGIG
(FALSE —) IDOL
(FANCIFUL —) VAPOR REVERY REVERIE
(FIXED —) TICK
(FOOLISH —) VAPOR VAPOUR
(PUERILE —) BOYISM
(SUPERSTITIOUS —) FREET FREIT
(VISIONARY —) ABSTRACTION
(WRONG —) FALLACY
(PL.) SMALLS SMALLWARE
NOTORIETY FAME ECLAT GLORY HONOR RUMOR RENOWN REPUTE PUBLICITY
NOTORIOUS BIG KNOWN ARRANT COMMON CRYING FAMOUS NOTARY STRONG EVIDENT NOTABLE NOTOIRE APPARENT FLAGRANT INFAMOUS MANIFEST EGREGIOUS
NOTORNIS TAKAHE
NOTUS (BROTHER OF —) EURUS BOREAS ZEPHYRUS
(FATHER OF —) AEOLUS ASTRAEUS
(MOTHER OF —) EOS
NOTWITHSTANDING BUT FOR THO YET EVEN WITH ASIDE ALGATE MAUGER MAUGRE THOUGH AGAINST ALGATES DESPITE HOWBEIT HOWEVER ALTHOUGH NATHLESS WHATRECK
NOUGAT NUT CANDY NUTSHELL
NOUGHT BAD NIL NOT NOWT ZERO NOCHT WRONG NOTHING USELESS WORTHLESS
NOUMENAL ONTAL ONTIC
NOUN MANE WORD THING SUPINE NOMINAL CONSTRUCT INCREASER
(INDECLINABLE —) APTOTE
(KIND OF —) COMMON PROPER DIPTOTE REGULAR TRIPTOTE MONOPTOTE
(QUOTATION —) HYPOSTASIS
(VERBAL —) GERUND
NOURISH AID FEED FOOD GROW BREED NORSH NURSE TRAIN BATTLE BREAST FOISON FOSTER NORICE REFETE SUCCOR SUCKLE SUPPLY CHERISH DEVELOP EDUCATE NURTURE NUTRIFY PROVIDE SUPPORT SUSTAIN MAINTAIN CULTIVATE REPLENISH STIMULATE
(PREF.) NUTRI
NOURISHING ALMA RICH ALIBLE BATTLE HEARTY STRONG NUTRIENT ALIMENTAL HEALTHFUL NUTRITIVE WHOLESOME NUTRITIOUS
NOURISHMENT DIET FARE FETE FOOD KEEP MEAT MANNA FOISON FOSTER ALIMENT PABULUM PASTURE NUTRIMENT REFECTION
(— FOR MIND) PABULUM
(PREF.) THREPSO
NOURONIHAR (FATHER OF —) FAKREDDIN
(LOVER OF —) VATHEK
NOUS MIND REASON ALERTNESS INTELLECT
NOUVEAU RICHE PARVENU UPSTART
NOVA SCOTIA (CAPITAL OF —) HALIFAX
(COUNTY OF —) DIGBY HANTS PICTOU
(STRAIT OF —) CANSO

(TOWN OF —) TRURO PICTOU SYDNEY ARICHAT BADDECK DARTMOUTH
NOVA SCOTIAN ACADIAN BLUENOSE
NOVEL HOT NEW BOOK EPIC RARE FRESH PROSE RECIT ROMAN STORY DARING RECENT SERIAL THRILL FICTION ROMANCE STRANGE UNUSUAL NEOTERIC ORIGINAL THRILLER UNCOMMON NARRATIVE PAPERBACK
(BRIEF —) CONTE
(PREF.) CAEN(O) CEN(O)
NOVELIST (ALSO SEE AUTHOR)
NOVELTY FAD NEWEL RENEW CHANGE NEWNESS PRIMEUR WRINKLE CURIOSITY FRESHNESS
NOVEMBER 1 SAMUIN SAMHAIN
NOVEMBER 11 MARTINMAS
NOVICE DUB HAM BOOT COLT PUNK PUNY TIRO TYRO CHELA GOYIN PUPIL ROOKY YOUTH DRONGO RABBIT ROOKIE TYRONE ACOLYTE AMATEUR CONVERT GRIFFIN LEARNER STARTER STUDENT YOUNKER BACHELOR BEGINNER FRESHMAN INEXPERT NEOPHYTE ARCHARIOS GREENHORN NOVITIATE TENDERFOOT ABECEDARIAN
(MILITARY —) CADET
NOVITIATE FUCHS NOVICERY PROBATION
NOW NOO YET ARAH HERE AHORA ARRAH NONCE SINCE TODAY EVENOO EXTANT ANYMORE CURRENT INSTANT PRESENT FORTHWITH PRESENTLY
(— AND THEN) SOMETIMES STOUNDMEAL
(BUT —) ERSTWHILE
(FROM — ON) EVERMORE
(JUST —) ENOW FRESH
NOWADAYS ANYMORE
NOWEL DRAG
NOX NYX
(BROTHER OF —) EREBUS
(FATHER OF —) CHAOS
NOXIOUS BAD ILL EVIL FETID DEADLY NOCENT NOYOUS PUTRID BALEFUL BANEFUL DAMPISH HARMFUL HURTFUL NOCUOUS NOISOME SCADDLE TEDIOUS VICIOUS INFAMOUS VIRULENT INJURIOUS MIASMATIC OFFENSIVE PESTILENT POISONOUS PERNICIOUS
(— AIR) MALARIA
(MORALLY —) UNWHOLESOME
NOZZE DI FIGARO, LE (CHARACTER IN —) FIGARO BARTOLO BASILIO SUSANNA BARBARINA CHERUBINO MARCELLINA
(COMPOSER OF —) MOZART
NOZZLE BIB JET TIP BEAK BIBB NOSE ROSE VENT GIANT SNOUT SPOUT TWEER GROVEL OUTLET MONITOR NIAGARA ORIFICE SHUTOFF ADJUTAGE ROSEHEAD VERMOREL NOSEPIECE
(BLAST FURNACE —) TUYERE
(MINING —) GIANT
NUANCE SHADE NICETY FINESSE GRADATION VARIATION
NUB EAR HUB JAB JAG KEY NOB CORE CRUX GIST HANG KNOB KNOT KNUB LUMP NECK PITH SNAG HEART NUDGE POINT KERNEL NUBBIN EXECUTE
NUBBIN EAR STUB STUMP
NUBIA WRAP CLOUD SCARF
NUBIAN NUBA BARABRA HADENDOA
(— MUSICAL INST.) SISTRUM
NUBILOUS FOGGY MISTY VAGUE CLOUDY OBSCURE
NUCHA NAPE NECK NUKE NUCHE
NUCLEAR ELEMENTARY
NUCLEATE SEED
NUCLEOLUS
(PREF.) PYREN(O)
NUCLEON MESON BARYON MESOTRON
NUCLEOSIDE VICINE INOSINE CYTIDINE ADENOSINE
NUCLEOTIDE GTP
(SEQUENCE OF —S) EXON
NUCLEUS HUB CELL CORE GERM KERN PITH ROOT SEED CADRE FOCUS HEART MIDST SPERM UMBRA CENTER COLONY DEUTON KARYON KERNEL MIDDLE ISOTOPE NIDULUS HABENULA MEROCYTE MESOPLAST
(— OF ATOM) DEUTERON
(— OF CELL) KARYON
(— OF STARCH GRAIN) HILUM
(— OF SUNSPOT) UMBRA
(ATOMIC —) SPECIES
(CELL —) SYNCARYON HEMIKARYON
(PREF.) (— OF CELL) CARY(O) KARY(O)
NUCLIDE ISOTONE
NUDE BARE LOOSE MODEL NAKED SEASAN STATUE UNCLAD DENUDED EXPOSED PICTURE PAINTING STARKERS STRIPPED UNDRESSED
(FRENCH —) ALESAN
(NOT —) DECENT
(RUN —) STREAK
NUDGE JOG NOG NUB WAG GOAD JOLT KNUB LUMP PEST POKE POTE PROD PUSH BLOCK CHUCK DUNCH ELBOW
NUDIBRANCH SEASLUG
NUDISM NATURISM GYMNOSOPHY
NUDIST ADAMITE NUDIFIER GYMNOSOPH
NUDITY SCUD
NUDNICK PEST
NUDNIK PEST
NUGATORY IDLE NULL VAIN EMPTY PETTY FUTILE HOLLOW INVALID TRIVIAL USELESS TRIFLING FRUSTRATE WORTHLESS
NUGGET EYE LOB GOLD HUNK LUMP MASS SLUG PRILL YELLOW
NUISANCE BANE BORE EVIL HARM HURT PAIN PEST STING INJURY PLAGUE TERROR VEXATION ANNOYANCE
NUKE ZAP DESTROY DEVASTATE
NULL NIL VOID EMPTY INEPT IRRITE INVALID NULLIFY USELESS VACUOUS NUGATORY FRUSTRATE
NULLAH GORGE GULLY NULLA NALLAH RAVINE
NULLIFY BEAT FLAW LAME NULL UNDO VETO VOID ABATE ANNUL ELIDE ERASE LAPSE CANCEL DEFEAT NEGATE OFFSET REPEAL REVOKE ABOLISH COUNTER DESTROY ABROGATE EVACUATE STULTIFY FRUSTRATE
NULLIFYING DIRIMENT
NULLITY NIHILITY
NUMB DEAD DRUG DULL STUN DAZED FUNNY STONY ASLEEP BENUMB CLUMSY DEADEN STUPID TORPID STUNNED STUPEFY ENFEEBLE HEBETATE HELPLESS RIGESCENT TABETLESS
NUMBED ASLEEP
NUMBER SUM BAND BODY COPY CURN DRAW FECK HERD HOST LOTS MAIN MANY MESS MORT SLEW SURD TALE TELL COUNT DATUM DIGIT FOLIE GRIST GROUP INDEX ISSUE SCADS SCORE STAND TOTAL WHOLE ADDEND AMOUNT BUNDLE CIPHER ENCORE FACTOR FIGURE FILLER HIRSEL MYRIAD POLICY RECKON SCALAR TICHEL CHIFFER COMPUTE DECIMAL DIVISOR FOLIATE INTEGER NUMERIC SEVERAL CARDINAL FRACTION NUMERATE QUANTITY CALCULATE MAGNITUDE MULTITUDE MULTIPLIER MULTIPLICAND
(— BETWEEN 4 AND 10) MAIN
(— OF ARROWS) END
(— OF ATOMS) CHAIN
(— OF BEASTS) HERD
(— OF BOMBS) STICK
(— OF BRICKS) CLAMP
(— OF CATTLE) SOUM
(— OF FUR SKINS) TIMBER
(— OF HANKS OF YARN TO POUND) COUNT
(— OF HAWKS) CAST
(— OF HONEYBEES) CLUSTER
(— OF LINKED MINES) GIRANDOLA GIRANDOLE
(— OF NEEDLES) GAGE GAUGE
(— OF PERSONS) STABLE
(— OF POEMS) EPOS
(— OF SHEARERS) BOARD
(— OF TEA CHESTS) BREAK
(— OF THREADS PER INCH) PITCH
(— OF TRICKS) BOOK
(— OF WORDS) FOLIO
(—S GAME) BUG
(— THROWN IN CRAPS) POINT
(BALLET —) ENTREE
(CARDINAL —) ONE TWO ALEF ALEPH THREE
(CHOSEN —) FEW
(COMPLEX —) IMAGINARY
(CONSIDERABLE —) WHEEN HATFUL FISTFUL
(DESCRIBABLE —) SCALAR
(EXCESS —) ADVANTAGE
(EXCESSIVE —) SPATE
(EXTRA —) ENCORE
(GOLDEN —) PRIME
(GOOD —) THRAVE THREAVE
(GREAT —) LAC HEAP HOST LAKH MORT BREAK HIRST MEINY POWER SHOAL SIGHT SWARM LEGION MYRIAD INFINITE INFINITY THOUSAND MULTITUDE MULTIPLICITY
(GREAT —S) FLOCKS
(GREATER —) MO
(INDEFINITE —) LAC STEEN SUNDRY THRAVE JILLION SEVERAL THREAVE UMPTEEN
(IRRATIONAL —) SURD
(LARGE —) ARMY FECK HERD HOST LUMP PECK SLEW ARRAY CROWD FORCE POWER SCADS SHEAF SPATE STACK STORE WORLD GALLON GOOGOL HIRSEL HIRSLE LEGION MELDER BILLION JILLION PLURALITY
(LARGE —S) STRENGTH
(LEAF —) FOLIO
(LEAST WHOLE —) UNIT
(ODD —S) IMPAIR
(OF ANIMALS) PACK
(OPPOSITE —) COUSIN
(ORDINAL —) FIRST THIRD SECOND
(PUT ON SERIAL —) FOLIO
(SMALL —) FEW CURN CURRAN HANDFUL PAUCITY SPATTER
(SUNSCREEN —) SPF
(TOTAL —) AMOUNT
(VAST —) HORDE
(WHOLE —) ALL DIGIT INTEGER
(ZERO —) NOTHING
(PL.) STRENGTH
(PREF.) ARITHMETICO ARITHM(O) LOGARITHMO NUMERO
(SUFF.) ARITHM PLY
(— TERMINATION) TEEN
(— THAT FILLS) FUL FULL
(ORDINAL —) ETH
NUMBERED MENE
NUMBERING TALE COUNT FOLIATION
NUMBERLESS MYRIAD
NUMBERS
(PREF.)
(ODD —) PERISSO
NUMBFISH TORPEDO
NUMBING WARELESS
NUMBLES UMBLES INNARDS NOMBLES VISCERA ENTRAILS
NUMBNESS STUPOR TORPOR STUPIDITY
(PREF.) NARC(O)
NUMBSKULL OAF
NUMEN DEITY GENIUS SPIRIT VESTAL DIVINITY
NUMERAL (ALSO SEE NUMBER) SUM WORD DIGIT CIPHER FIGURE LETTER CHAPTER NUMERIC
(— STYLE) ROMAN ARABIC
(CLOCK —) CHAPTER
NUMERATIVE PEN SEGREGATIVE
NUMERICAL SCALAR
NUMEROUS BIG LOTS MAIN MANY RANK RIFE GREAT LARGE STOUR DIVERS GALORE LEGION MYRIAD SUNDRY UNRIDE COPIOUS

CROWDED ENDLESS FEARFUL FERTILE PROFUSE SEVERAL TEEMING UMPTEEN ABUNDANT FREQUENT MANIFOLD MULTIPLE POPULOUS THRONGED EXTENSIVE MULTIFOLD NUMBERFUL PLENTIFUL **(— AND POWERFUL)** MAIN
(MODERATELY —) FAIR
(VERY —) EXCESSIVE
(PREF.) MYRI
NUMIDIA (BIRD OF —) DEMOISELLE
(CITY OF —) HIPPO
(KING OF —) JUGURTHA
NUMITOR (GRANDSON OF —) REMUS ROMULUS
NUMSKULL NUM DAFF DOLT FLAT BOOBY DUNCE LACKWIT BONEHEAD BLOCKHEAD LAMEBRAIN NUMBSKULL
NUN BIRD SMEW CLARE CLERK MONIAL PIGEON SISTER TERESA VESTAL VOWESS CLUNIAC CONFINE DEANESS DEVOTEE EXTERNE MINCHEN MONKESS RECLUSE TEATINE THEATIN BASILIAN CHAPLAIN CLARISSE PRIORESS TITMOUSE URBANIST URSULINE VISITANT VOTARESS ANGELICAL CARMELITE LORETTINE PRIESTESS RELIGEUSE TRAPPISTINE
(— BIRD) MONASE TITMOUSE
(— HEADDRESS) WIMPLE
(— HOOD) FAILLE
(— MOTH) TUSSOCK
(— ORDER) MARIST TRAPPIST DOMINICAN LORETTINE
(CHIEF —) ABBA ABBESS MOTHER
(LATIN —) VESTA
(SON OF —) JOSHUA
NUNCIATE NUNCIO ANNOUNCER MESSENGER
NUNCIO ENVOY NUNCE LEGATE NUNTIUS DELEGATE MESSENGER
NUNCUPATE DECLARE DEDICATE INSCRIBE PROCLAIM DESIGNATE PRONOUNCE
NUNCUPATIVE ORAL SPOKEN UNWRITTEN
NUNNERY ABBEY NUNRY CONVENT CLOISTER MINCHERY
(HEAD OF —) ABBESS
NUPSON FOOL SIMPLETON
NUPTIAL BRIDAL GENIAL THORAL MARITAL WEDDING ESPOUSAL HYMENEAL MARRIAGE
(PL.) SPOUSAL WEDDING ESPOUSAL HYMENEALS WIFETHING
NUQUE NAPE NECK
NURISTANI KAFIRI
NURSE LPN SIP AMAH AYAH BABA CARE DHAI FEED NANA NUSS REAR SUCK TEND BONNE MAMMY NANNY NORSH ATTEND BAYMAN CRADLE FOMENT FOSTER GRANNY KEEPER NANNIE NORICE NUZZLE SISTER SITTER SUCKLE UMFAAN CHERISH FURTHER NOURISH NURTURE PROMOTE CULTIVATE ENCOURAGE NURSEMAID
(— A GRIEVANCE) SULK
(— OF HIAWATHA) NOKOMIS
(— OF ULYSSES) EURYCLEA
(— OF ZEUS) AMALTHEA CYNOSURA
(— SHARK) GATA
(GULLIVER'S —) GLUMDALCLITCH
(WET —) DHAI DHOLL
NURSEMAID AYAH BONNE
NURSERY RACE CRECHE HOTBED BROODER FOSTERAGE
NURSLING BABY NORRY NURRY FOSTER FOUNDLING
(PREF.) THREMMATO
NURTURE CARE DIET FEED FOOD REAR TEND BREED NURSE TRAIN COCKER CRADLE FOSTER NUZZLE CHERISH EDUCATE SUPPORT BREEDING NORTELRY TRAINING EDUCATION ESTABLISH NUTRIMENT
(PREF.) TROPH(O)
NUSAIRI ANSARIE
NUT ACA BEN BUR COB GUY JOU NIT TAP ANTA BURR COLA CORE DOLT FOOL FROG HEAD KOLA LORE MAST NITE PILI PITH SEED TASK ACORN BETEL BONGA BUNGA CRANK FLAKE FRUIT GLANS HAZEL HICAN JUVIA PECAN TRYMA ALMOND BONDUC BRAZIL CASHEW FELLOW HICCAN ILLIPE KERNEL PEANUT PIGNON PINION PYRENE CASTANA FILBERT HICKORY PROBLEM APPLENUT BEECHNUT BREADNUT CHESTNUT GOORANUT LARRIKIN CAPOTASTO CHINKAPIN ECCENTRIC MACADAMIA PHILOPENA
(— COAL) ANTHRACITE
(— GRASS) SEDGE
(— OF VIOLIN BOW) FROG
(— PINE) PIGNON PINOON PIGNOLIA
(CASHEW —) SEDGE ANACARD
(CONSORT OF —) GEB KEB SET
(DAUGHTER OF —) ISIS NEPHTHYS
(FALLEN —S) SHACK
(KIND OF —) PEA
(PALM —) BETEL LICHI BABASSU COCOANUT COQUILLA
(PERT. TO —) NUCAL
(RIPE —) LEAMER
(RUSH —) CHUFA
(SON OF —) RA OSIRIS
(PL.) MASTAGE
(PREF.) CARY(O) KARY(O) NUCI
NUT-BEARING NUCIFEROUS
NUTCRACKER XENOPS CRACKER PILLORY MEATBIRD NUTCRACK NUTHATCH NUCIFRAGA NUTPECKER
NUTHATCH SITTA TOMTIT XENOPS JARBIRD SITTINE TITMOUSE NUTJOBBER
NUTHOOK BEADLE CONSTABLE
NUTLET NUCULE PYRENA PYRENE GYROLITH
NUTMEG SEED TREE SPICE BEAVER CALABASH NOTEMIGGE NOTEMUGGE
(— COVERING) MACE
(— STATE) CONNECTICUT
(PREF.) MYRISTICI
NUTRIA FUR COYPU GREGE NEUTRIA RAGONDIN
NUTRIENT STARTER
(PLANT —S) SIDEDRESS
(PL.) FOOD HEMOTROPHE
NUTRIMENT DIET FOOD KEEP VIANDS ALIMENT PABULUM SUPPORT NOURISHMENT
NUTRITION EUTROPHY TROPHISM
(IMPERFECT —) DYSTROPHY DYSTROPHIA
(PREF.) TROPH(O)
(SUFF.) TROPHIA TROPHIC TROPHY
NUTRITIOUS BATTLE BAITTLE TROPHIC
NUTRITIVE ALIBLE
NUTS KEEN BALMY BUGGY CRAZY INSANE ENTHUSIASTIC
NUT-SHAPED NUCIFORM
NUTSHELL SHELL INCLUDER
NUTTY BATS GAGA LOCO NUTS RACY ZANY BATTY BUGGY CRAZY QUEER SPICY FRUITY LOVING SPRUCE AMOROUS FOOLISH PIQUANT ZESTFUL DEMENTED PLEASANT ECCENTRIC FLAVORFUL
NUX VOMICA SNAKEWOOD
NUZZLE DIG PET ROOT NURSE SNUFF BURROW CARESS FONDLE FOSTER NESTLE NUDDLE NURTURE SNOOZLE SNUGGLE SNUZZLE
NYCTEUS (BROTHER OF —) LYCUS
(DAUGHTER OF —) ANTIOPE
(FATHER OF —) HYRIEUS
(MOTHER OF —) CLONIA
NYE EYAS NEST NIDE BROOD FLOCK
NYLON
(PL.) HOSIERY
NYMPH FLY GIRL MAIA MITE MUSE PINK PIXY PUPA TICK AEGLE DRYAD HOURI LARVA NAIAD NIXIE OREAD SIREN SYLPH BYBLIS CYRENE DAMSEL DAPHNE HELICE HESTIA KELPIE MAIDEN NEREID SPRITE SYRINX UNDINE CORYCIA ERYTHEA HESPERA LIRIOPE OCEANID CALLISTO CYNOSURA EURYDICE MARPESSA PROSOPON BUTTERFLY HAMADRYAD
(— BELOVED BY PAN) SYRINX
(— BELOVED OF NARCISSUS) ECHO
(— CHANGED TO BEAR) CALLISTO
(— OF FOUNTAIN) EGERIA SALMACIS
(— OF HILLS) OREAD
(— OF MEADOWS) LIMONIAD
(— OF MESSINA STRAIT) SCYLLA
(— OF MT. IDA) OENONE
(CITY —) POLIAD
(LAKE —) NAIAD LIMNIAD
(OCEAN —) SIREN GALATEA OCEANID SEAMAID
(QUEEN OF —S) MAB
(RIVER —) NAIS NAIAD
(SEA —) MERROW NEREID CALYPSO GALATEA MERMAID
(WATER —) NAIS EGERIA LURLEI UNDINE APSARAS HYDRIAD JUTURNA RUSALKA EPHYDRIAD
(WOOD —) DRYAD NAPEA ARETHUSA
(PL.) HYADS THRIAI CAMENAE
(PREF.) NYMPHO
NYMPHAEA CASTALY CASTALIA
NYMPHET LOLITA
NYMPHOMANIAC (BOVINE —) BULLER
NYNORSK LANDSMAL LANDSMAAL
NYROCA AYTHYA
NYSSA TUPELO
NYSTAGMUS TIC WINK
NYX NOX NIGHT
(— PERSONIFIED) NIGHT
(BROTHER OF —) EREBUS
(DAUGHTER OF —) DAY ERIS LIGHT
(HUSBAND OF —) CHAOS
(SON OF —) CHARON

O

O HO OH OCH ZERO CIPHER OMICRON
OAF AUF BOOR CLOD DOLT FOOL LOUT CLOWN DUNCE IDIOT KLUTZ OUPHE YOKEL MUCKER NASHGAB PALOOKA POMPION BLOCKHEAD FOUNDLING SCHLEMIEL SIMPLETON
OAHU **(— BAY)** KAHANA
(— BIRD) JIBI
OAK CLUB CORK HOLM ILEX BRAVE BRIAR EMORY HOLLY ROBLE ROBUR ACAJOU BAREEN CERRIS ENCINA KERMES STRONG TOUMEY VALOMA AMBROSE BELLOTA BELLOTE DURMAST EGILOPS KELLOGG PALAYAN TURTOSA BEEFWOOD BLUEJACK CHAMPION CHAPARRO FLITTERN WAINSCOT BLACKJACK CHINKAPIN QUERCITRON
(— BARK) CRUT
(— FRUIT) MAST ACORN CAMATA BELLOTE
(JERUSALEM —) AMBROSE
(WHITE —) ROBLE
(YOUNG —) FLITTERN
(PREF.) DRY(O) QUERCI
OAKUM OCCAM
OAKWOOD MESA
OAR AIR BOW PLY ROW PALM PEEL POLE ALOOF BLADE ROWER SCULL SPOON SWAPE SWEEP YULOH PADDLE PALLET PROPEL OARSMAN PROPELLER
(— BLADE) PALM PEEL WASH
(— FULCRUM) LOCK THOLE OARLOCK ROWLOCK
(BOW —) GOUGER
(HANDLE OF —) GRASP
(INBOARD PORTION OF —) LOOM
(PART OF —) GRIP LOOM BLADE SHAFT
(STERN —) SCULL SKULL
(PREF.) COPE(O) REMI
OARLOCK LOCK THOLE ROWLOCK
OARS CREW
OARSMAN OAR REMEX ROWER BOWMAN STROKE BENCHER SCULLER WATERMAN
OASIS BAR OJO SPA MERV SIWA WADI WADY SPRING
OAST HOST KILN OVEN COCKLE OASTHOUSE
OAT AIT WOT FEED FOOD PIPE POEM SKEG SONG AUCHT CHEAT GRAIN HAVER PEARL ANGORA EGILOPS
(— HUSK) SHOOD FLIGHT
(— RENT) AVENAGE
(EDIBLE PORTION OF —) GROATS
(FALSE WILD —S) FATUOID
(HUSKED —) SHEALING
(NAKED —) PILLAS PILCORN
(UNTHRASHED —) OATHAY
(WILD —S) HAVERGRASS
(PL.) CORN GRAIN HAVER GROUTS PROVENDER WHITECORN
OATCAKE CAPER HAVERCAKE SOURBREAD
OATEN AITEN
OATH OD ADS BAN DAD DOD GAD GAR GOL GOR GUM ODD SAM VOW BOND CRUM CUSS DARN DRAT ECOD EGAD GEEZ GOSH HECK JEEZ JING NIGS OONS SANG SLID SLUD WORD BEDAD BEGAD BEGOB BLIMY CURSE DAMME DEUCE GOLLY HOKEY MORDU PARDY SACRE SFOOT SLIFE SNIGS SWEAR YERRA ADSBUD APPEAL CRACKY CRIKEY CRIPES CRUMBS FEALTY JABERS JERNIE NEAKES PARDIE PLEDGE RAPPER SBLOOD SLIGHT STRUTH ZOUNDS BEGORRA BEGORRY BEJESUS BYRLADY CORBLEU GADSLID GEEWHIZ GEEWIZZ JEEPERS JIMMINY MORBLEU ODSFISH ODZOOKS PROMISE THUNDER ANATHEMA BEJABERS BODYKINS CRICKETY GADZOOKS JURAMENT PITIKINS SANCTION SEREMENT SNIGGERS SPLUTTER AFFIDAVIT BEJABBERS BLASPHEMY DODGASTED EXPLETIVE PROFANITY SACRAMENT SLIDIKINS SWEARWORD
OATMEAL OATS STODGE YELLOW POTTAGE DRAMMOCK PORRIDGE
(— BREAD) ANACK JANNACK
(— CAKE) PONE SCONE
OATS **(MIXED ROLLED —)** GRANOLA
(PREF.) AVENO
OBADIAH ABDIAS
(FATHER OF —) AZEL JEHIEL SHEMAIAH
(SON OF —) ISHMAIAH
OBAL **(FATHER OF —)** JOKTAN
OBCLUDE HIDE OCCLUDE
OBDURATE FIRM HARD BALKY HARSH INERT ROCKY ROUGH STARK STONY DOGGED INURED MULISH RUGGED SEVERE STURDY SULLEN ADAMANT CALLOUS HARDENED PERVERSE STUBBORN IMPASSIVE UNBENDING
OBEAH OBI OBIA CHARM FETISH VOODOO
OBECHE ARERE AYOUS SAMBA
OBED **(FATHER OF —)** BOAZ JARHA SHEMAIAH
(MOTHER OF —) RUTH
(SON OF —) JESSE AZARIAH
OBEDEDOM **(FATHER OF —)** JEDUTHUN
OBEDIENCE ORDER FEALTY CONTROL SERVICE DOCILITY OBEISANCE
OBEDIENT BENT RULY TALL TAME BUXOM DOCILE PLIANT DEVOTED DUTEOUS DUTIFUL HEEDFUL MINDFUL ORDERLY SUBJECT AMENABLE BIDDABLE YIELDING ATTENTIVE OBSERVING SERVIABLE TRACTABLE
(— TO THE HELM) HANDY
OBEDIENTIARY PRIOR
OBEDIENT PLANT DRAGONHEAD
OBEISANCE BOW LEG JOUK BINGE CONGE HONOR SALAM CONGEE CRINGE CURTSY FEALTY HOMAGE SALAAM CURTSEY DEFERENCE HUMBLESSO REFERENCE
OBELISK MARK PYLON SHAFT DAGGER GUGLIA GUGLIO NEEDLE OBELUS PILLAR AGUGLIA MONUMENT HAGIOLITH
OBELUS DAGGER OBELISK
OBERON KING POEM FAIRY OPERA SATELLITE
(CHARACTER IN —) HUON PUCK FATIMA OBERON TITANIA SHERASMIN
(COMPOSER OF —) WEBER
(WIFE OF —) TITANIA
OBESE FAT FOZY BEEFY PLUMP PUDGY PUFFY PURSY STOUT FLESHY PORTLY PYKNIC ROTUND TURGID ADIPOSE PORCINE PURSIVE BLUBBERY LIPAROUS CORPULENT
OBESITY FAT FATNESS LIPOSIS ADIPOSIS FOZINESS ADIPOSITY
OBEY EAR HEAR HEED MIND DEFER YIELD COMPLY FOLLOW OBEISH SUBMIT CONFORM EXECUTE OBSERVE OBTEMPER
(— HELM) STEER
OBFUSCATE DIM BEFOG CLOUD DARKEN MUDDLE OBFUSK CONFUSE MYSTIFY OBSCURE PERPLEX STUPEFY BEWILDER
OBI OBE SASH CHARM OBEAH FETICH FETISH GIRDLE
OBIT MASS REST DEATH NOTICE OBITAL DECEASE RELEASE SERVICE OBITUARY NECROLOGY OBSEQUIES
OBITUARY NECROLOGY
OBJECT AIM END TAP BALK BEEF CARE CARP FINE GOAL IDEA ITEM KICK MAIN MIND PASS SAKE WHAT ARGUE CAVIL DEMUR GRIPE PINCH POINT SCOPE SIGHT TELOS THING AFFAIR DESIGN EMBLEM ENTITY FIGURE GADGET INTENT MATTER MOTIVE OPPOSE TARGET ARTICLE DINGBAT DISLIKE DISSENT MEANING PROTEST PURPOSE QUARREL REALITY RECLAIM NOUMENON TENDENCY CHALLENGE INTENTION SPECTACLE
(— HAVING FLAWS) SPOIL
(— OF ABHORRENCE) ANATHEMA
(— OF AMBITION) MAIN
(— OF ART) VASE CURIO VIRTU ANTIQUE BIBELOT FIGURINE
(— OF CONTEMPT) SCORN
(— OF CRITICISM) BUTT
(— OF DERISION) SCOFF
(— OF DEVOTION) IDOL TOTEM FETISH
(— OF DISGUST) UG
(— OF DREAD) BOGY BOGEY BOGIE BOGGIE BUGBEAR
(— OF INTEREST) SIGHT
(— OF KNOWLEDGE) SCIBILE
(— OF LAUGHTER) JEST
(— OF LOATHING) SCUNNER
(— OF LOVE) FLAME
(— OF PILGRIMAGE) CAABA KAABAH
(— OF PRIDE) GLORY
(— OF PURSUIT) SHADOW
(— OF RELIANCE) STAY
(— OF REVERENCE) MANITO
(— OF RIDICULE) FUN GAME
(— OF SCORN) GECK SCOFF BYWORD HISSING DERISION
(— OF TERROR) BUG BUGABOO BUGBEAR
(— OF THOUGHT) CONSTRUCT
(— OF WONDER) ADMIRATION
(— OF WORSHIP) GOD IDOL JUJU MUMBOJUMBO
(— TO BE TILTED AT) QUINTAIN
(ALLURING —) DELILAH
(BELOVED —) MINION DARLING MISTRESS
(BIZARRE —) GROTESQUE
(BULKY —) WODGE
(CELESTIAL —) QUASAR
(CONICAL —) ACORN
(CONSPICUOUS —) LANDMARK
(CONTAMINATED —S) FOMITES
(CURVED —) BELLY
(CYLINDRICAL —) BOLE
(DECORATIVE —) BIBELOT
(DESIRABLE —) GRAIL
(FACTORY-MADE —S) ARTWORK
(FLAT —) DISCUS
(HEAVY —) WEIGHT
(MINUTE —) ATOM MITE
(PALTRY —) TRINKET
(POINTED —) SPIKE
(ROUND —) COB RONDEL TRINDLE TRUNDLE
(SACRED —) URIM ZOGO GUACA HUACA SHRINE CHURINGA
(SILLY —) INANITY

(SMALL —) PIRLIE
(STRANGE —S) CURIOSA
(STUDY OF FLYING —S) UFOLOGY
(TEACHING —S) REALIA
(TRANSCENDENTAL —) ENTITY
(TRIVIAL —) GUBBINS
(ULTIMATE —) TELOS
(UNIDENTIFIED FLYING —) BOGEY
(VILE —S) SCUM
(WORTHLESS —) SPLINTER
(PREF.) (FILTHY OR DIRTY —) RHYPARO RHYPO

OBJECTION OB BAR BUT BEEF CRAB FUSS KICK CAVIL DEMUR DOUBT BOGGLE CHESON NIGGLE QUARREL QUIBBLE SCRUPLE DEMURRAL QUESTION CHALLENGE CRITICISM EXCEPTION

OBJECTIONABLE VILE AWFUL HORRID GHASTLY UNLUSTY UNLIKELY FRIGHTFUL OBNOXIOUS OFFENSIVE
(BE —) SUCK

OBJECTIVE AIM END FAIR GAME GOAL HOME REAL SAKE OUTER ACTUAL AMORAL ANIMUS DESIGN MOTIVE TARGET THRUST PURPOSE DETACHED TANGIBLE UNBIASED DIRECTION INTENTION POSITIVAL QUAESITUM ULTIMATUM

OBJECTOR (CONSCIENTIOUS —) CONCHY CONCHIE

OBJETS D'ART VIRTU

OBJURGATE BAN JAW DAMN RAIL ABUSE CHIDE CURSE DECRY BERATE REBUKE REPROVE UPBRAID VITUPER EXECRATE CASTIGATE

OBLATE MONK OFFER DEDICATE MONASTIC

OBLATION CORBAN OFLETE SACRED CHARITY ANAPHORA DEVOTION OFFERING SACRIFICE

OBLIGATE COMMIT STRICT

OBLIGATED BOUND LIABLE BEHOLDEN

OBLIGATION DUE IOU TIE VOW BAIL BAND BOND CALL DEBT DUTY KNOT LOAD LOAN MUST NOTE OATH ONUS SEAL CHECK OUGHT SCORE ARREAR BURDEN CHARGE CONSOL CORVEE CUSTOM FEALTY PLEDGE ANNUITY BONDAGE PROMISE TRIBUTE CONTRACT HYPOTHEC SECURITY WARRANTY AGREEMENT LIABILITY
(— NOT TO MARRY) CELIBACY
(— TO RENDER RENT) CUSTOM
(— TO SECRECY) SEAL
(LABOR —) CORVEE
(MORAL —) BOND DUTY
(PL.) STRINGS

OBLIGATORY BINDING BOUNDEN FORCIBLE IMPOSING LIGATORY INCUMBENT MANDATORY

OBLIGE PUT HOLD PAWN DRIVE FAVOR FORCE COMPEL ENGAGE PLEASE GRATIFY REQUIRE CONCLUDE MORTGAGE OBLIGATE CONSTRAIN ACCOMMODATE

OBLIGED FAIN BOUND DEBTED BOUNDEN DEBTFUL FAVORED PLEASED PLEDGED BEHOLDEN GRATEFUL OBSTRICT BEHOLDING OBLIGATED

OBLIGING KIND BUXOM CIVIL CLEVER TOWARD AMIABLE FAVOROUS AGREEABLE COURTEOUS FAVORABLE OFFICIOUS

OBLIQUE AWRY BIAS SIDE SKEW ASKEW BEVEL CROSS SLANT ASLANT ASWASH LOUCHE SQUINT THWART ASKANCE AWKWARD CROOKED EMBELIF EVASIVE SCALENE SIDLING SLOPING DIAGONAL INCLINED INDIRECT SIDELONG SIDEWAYS SIDEWISE SLANTING TORTUOUS INDICULAR UNDERHAND
(— IN MINING) CLINIC
(— STROKE) SLASH SOLIDUS
(— WORK) SWASHWORK
(PREF.) LECHRI(O) LOX(O) PLAGI(O)

OBLIQUELY AGEE AWRY BIAS AGLEE ASIDE ASKEW AWASH SLANT SLOPE ASLANT ASWASH ASKANCE ASQUINT EMBELIF BIASWISE SIDELONG SIDEWAYS SIDEWISE

OBLIQUITY BIAS DIRT SWEEP DIRTINESS

OBLITERATE INK BLOT DELE RASE RAZE WIPE ANNUL BLACK COVER ERASE SMEAR CANCEL DELETE EFFACE SPONGE ABOLISH DESTROY EXPUNGE OUTRAZE SCRATCH OVERSCORE

OBLITERATION BLOT RASURE ERASURE NEGATION SYNIZESIS

OBLIVION LETHE LIMBO PARDON AMNESTY NIRVANA SILENCE OUBLIANCE

OBLIVIOUS AMORT BLISSFUL HEEDLESS OBLIVIAL FORGETFUL

OBLONG CHITON EVELONG AVELONGE EVENLONG ELONGATED
(ROUNDED —) ELLIPSE

OBLOQUY ABUSE BLAME ODIUM INFAMY CALUMNY CENSURE REPROOF CONTEMPT DISGRACE DISHONOR OBLICQUE

OBNOXIOUS FOUL PERT VILE CURST CURSED FAULTY HORRID LIABLE ODIOUS RANCID SEPTIC HATEFUL INVIDIOUS OFFENSIVE REPUGNANT VERMINOUS
(— PERSON) CREEP

OBOE PIPE REED WAIT AULOS SHAWM SURNAI SURNAY HAUTBOY MUSETTE PIFFERO CHIRIMIA HAUTBOIS SCHALMEY SZOPELKA CHALUMEAU HECKELPHONE
(— DI CACCIA) TENOROON FAGOTTINO
(BASS —) RACKETT
(PREF.) AUL(O)

OBOLE MAIL MAILLE

OBSCENE PAW FOUL LEWD NAST BAWDY GROSS NASTY ROCKY COARSE FILTHY IMPURE RIBALD SMUTTY VULGAR XRATED KNAVISH PROFANE RAUNCHY IMMODEST INDECENT LOATHSOME OFFENSIVE REPULSIVE SALACIOUS
(— CULT) AISCHROLATREIA

OBSCENITY DIRT FILTH RIBALDRY SCULDUDDERY
(PREF.) COPR(O)

OBSCURATION COVER ECLIPSE

OBSCURE DIM FOG BLOT BLUR DARK DEEP HARD HART HAZY HIDE PALE SLUR VEIL BEDIM BEFOG BLACK BLANK BLEND BLIND CLOUD COVER DUSKY FAINT FOGGY GLOOM INNER LOWLY MIRKY MISTY MUDDY MURKY SHADE SMEAR STAIN VAGUE BEMIST CLOUDY DARKEN DARKLE DEADEN DELUDE GLOOMY HUMBLE MYSTIC OCCULT OPAQUE REMOTE SHADOW SOMBER SUBTLE BECLOUD BENIGHT CLOUDED CONCEAL CONFUSE CRABBED CRYPTIC ECLIPSE ENCRUST ENVELOP OBLIQUE OVERLAY OVERTOP SHADOWY SLUBBER TARNISH UNCLEAR UNKNOWN UNNOTED ABSTRUSE DARKLING DISGUISE DOUBTFUL FAMELESS MYSTICAL NAMELESS NUBILOUS OBSTRUSE ORACULAR OVERSILE CALIGINOUS
(MAKE —) BECLOUD
(PREF.) APHAN(O)

OBSCURED HAZY HIDDEN BLINDED CLOUDED DUSKISH DARKSOME DISGUISED INFUSCATE

OBSCURITY FOG MIST CLOUD GLOOM SHADE CALIGO SHADOW DIMNESS OPACITY PRIVACY SILENCE DARKNESS TENEBRES BLINDNESS SECLUSION
(DELIBERATE —) OBLIQUITY
(PL.) MURLEMEWES

OBSECRATE BEG PRAY BESEECH ENTREAT PETITION

OBSEQUIES MASS OBIT PYRE WAKE RITES SERVICE FUNERALS

OBSEQUIOUS SLICK MENIAL SUPPLE COURTLY DEVOTED DUTEOUS DUTIFUL FAWNING SERVILE SLAVISH VERNILE CRINGING OBEDIENT OBEISANT TOADYING ASSIDUOUS ATTENTIVE COMPLIANT
(— PERSON) LIMBERHAM

OBSEQUY RITE EXEQUY RITUAL FUNERAL CEREMONY

OBSERVANCE ACT FORM RITE RULE FREET HONOR CUSTOM REGARD KEEPING CEREMONY PRACTICE ADHERENCE ATTENTION DEFERENCE INDICTION SOLEMNITY
(— OF PROPRIETIES) DECORUM BREEDING ETIQUETTE
(RELIGIOUS —) NOVENA SACRAMENT
(REVERENTIAL —) PUJA
(SUPERSTITIOUS —) FREET FREIT
(PL.) FUNERAL CEREMONY

OBSERVANT ALERT EYEFUL CAREFUL HEEDFUL MINDFUL DILIGENT VIGILANT WATCHFUL REGARDFUL PERCEPTIVE

OBSERVATION EYE SPY HEED IDEA NOTE RAOB VIEW SIGHT WATCH ESPIAL LOGION NOTICE REGARD REMARK AUSPICE AUTOPSY COMMENT CONTACT DESCANT OPINION EYESIGHT GAZEMENT SCHOLION SCHOLIUM ASSERTION ATTENTION ESPIONAGE COGNIZANCE PERCEPTION
(— BY BALLOON) PIBAL
(BASED ON —) EYEBALL
(ECOLOGICAL —S) ANNUATION
(PRELIMINARY —) PROEM
(STALE —) GROANER

OBSERVATIONISM SCHAULUST

OBSERVATORY LICK TOWER LOOKOUT PALOMAR

OBSERVE LO EYE SEE SPY ESPY HEED HOLD KEEP LOOK MAKE MARK MIND NARK NOTA NOTE OBEY SPOT TENT TOUT TWIG VIEW WAIT YEME ABIDE QUOTE SMOKE STUDY UTTER WATCH ADHERE ADVERT ATHOLD BEHOLD DETECT DEVISE FOLLOW NOTICE NOTIFY REGARD REMARK SURVEY COMMENT DISCERN EXPRESS MENTION PROFESS RESPECT WITNESS PERCEIVE PRESERVE SPECTATE ADVERTISE CELEBRATE SOLEMNIZE
(— CLOSELY) SMOKE
(— DULLY) BLEAR
(— FOOTBALL POSITION) KEY
(— OPPOSING POSITION) KEY

OBSERVER O BIRDER CORNER WATCHER AUDIENCE INFORMER ONLOOKER BYSTANDER SCRUTATOR SPECTATOR

OBSESS RIDE BESET HAUNT HARASS INVEST OBSEDE BESIEGE HAGRIDE POSSESS PREOCCUPY

OBSESSED CRAZY DOTTY HAPPY HIPPED BESOTTED

OBSESSION TIC CRAZE MANIA SIEGE MAGGOT ECSTASY FIXATION IDEEFIXE
(SUFF.) (— WITH) ITIS

OBSIDIAN CORE LAVA IZTLE IZTLI LAPIS

OBSOLETE OLD DEAD PAST DATED PASSE BYGONE EFFETE ABOLETE ANCIENT ARCHAIC CLASSIC DISUSED EFFACED EXTINCT OUTWORN OUTDATED OUTMODED OVERWORN DISCARDED

OBSTACLE BAR DAM LET BOYG BUMP DRAG HUMP JUMP OBEX SNAG STAY STOP BLOCK CHECK CLAMP CRIMP FENCE HITCH HYDRA SPOKE STICK STILE ABATIS BUNKER FRAISE HOCKET HURDLE LOGJAM OBJECT RETARD ANSTOSS BARRIER CHICANE FIVEBAR STOPPER BLOCKADE MOLEHILL BARRICADE CONDITION HINDRANCE ROADBLOCK TURNAGAIN
(— TO VIRTUE) SLANDER
(GOLF —) HAZARD
(INSURMOUNTABLE —) IMPASSE

OBSTETRICIAN ACCOUCHEUR

OBSTETRICS TOCOLOGY TOKOLOGY MAIEUTICS MIDWIFERY

OBSTINACY BRASS CONTUMACY
OBSTINATE SET SOT DOUR FIRM SULY BALKY FIXED ROWDY RUSTY STIFF STOUT TOUGH ASSISH CUSSED DOGGED KNOBBY MULISH STEEVE STUFFY STUPID STURDY SULLEN THRAWN UNRULY ASININE BULLISH CRABBED FROWARD PEEVISH RESTIVE WILLFUL CROTCHED OBDURATE PERVERSE PREFRACT RECUSANT RENITENT STOMACHY STUBBORN FORERIGHT PIGHEADED STONEWALL TENACIOUS
(— IN THE WRONG) PERVERSE
(— ONE) MULE
(NOT —) SUPPLE
OBSTREPEROUS LOUD WILD NOISY RORTY UNRULY RAUGHTY CLAMOROUS
OBSTRUCT BAR DAM DIT GAG JAM CLOG COOP CRAB DITT FILL FOUL JAMB STOP TRIG TRIP BESET BLANK BLOCK CHAIN CHECK CHOKE CROSS DELAY HEDGE THROW ARREST CUMBER FORBAR HAMPER HOBBLE IMPEDE OPPOSE PESTER RETARD STIFLE THWART WAYLAY WINDER BARRIER FORELAY OCCLUDE BLOCKADE EMBOLIZE ENCUMBER FLOUNDER OBTURATE OPPILATE BARRICADE EMBARRASS INCOMMODE
OBSTRUCTION BAR DAM GAG LET RUB BOOM BUMP CLOG SLUG SNAG STAY STOP BLOCK CHOKE GORCE HITCH SPOKE HAMPER TAPPEN THWART BARRACE BARRAGE BARRIER BLINDER CHOKAGE EMBOLISM OBSTACLE STOPPAGE AMBUSCADE EMPHRAXIS OCCLUSION
(— IN OILWELL) BRIDGE
(— IN RIVER) GORGE
(— IN TEAT) SPIDER
(— IN VALVE) GAG
(— OF BLOOD VESSEL) EMBOLISM
(— OF PINE LEAVES) TAPPEN
(— OF TONE) VEIL
(INNER —) LOAD
(LEGISLATIVE —) STONEWALL FILIBUSTER
OBTAIN BEG BUM BUY EKE GET PAN WIN EARN FANG FIND GAIN HENT REAP ANNEX CADGE CATCH ETTLE REACH AREACH ARECHE ARRIVE ATTAIN BORROW DERIVE EXPEDE SECURE SPONGE ACHIEVE ACQUIRE CAPTURE CHEVISE COMPASS DEMERIT EXTRACT POSSESS PREVAIL PROCURE RECEIVE SUCCEED PURCHASE SCROUNGE
(— BY CHANCE) DRAW
(— BY HEAT) EXCOCT
(— BY REQUEST) IMPETRATE
(— BY THREAT) EXTORT
(— CONTROL) ENGROSS
(— DISHONESTLY) CROOK SHARP FLEECE NOBBLE SKELDER
(— MONEY FROM) BLEED
(— PERMISSION) CLEAR
OBTAINABLE GOING GETTABLE AVAILABLE DERIVABLE SECURABLE
OBTAINED (— AT SCENE OF CRIME) LATENT
(— DIRECTLY) FIRSTHAND
(WRONGFULLY —) HOT EXTORTED
OBTEST PLEAD
OBTRUDE DIN JET SORN EJECT EXPEL GLARE FLAUNT IMPOSE MEDDLE THRUST INTRUDE INTERFERE
OBTRUSIVE FRESH PUSHY GARISH BLATANT FORWARD PUSHING BUMPTIOUS INTRUSIVE
OBTUND DULL BLUNT QUELL DEADEN
OBTURATOR MUSHROOM
OBTUSE DIM DULL BLINK BLUNT CRASS DENSE THICK BOVINE OPAQUE STUPID STUBBED BOEOTIAN HEBETATE PURBLIND
(NOT —) ACUTE
OBVERSE FACE FRONT CONVERSE
(— OF COIN) MAN HEAD
OBVIATE PREVENT PRECLUDE FORESTALL
OBVIOUS LOUD OPEN BROAD CLEAR CRUDE FRANK GROSS NAKED OVERT PLAIN SLICK STARK LIABLE PATENT BLATANT EVIDENT EXPOSED GLARING SHALLOW SUBJECT VISIBLE APPARENT DISTINCT MANIFEST PALPABLE BAREFACED PROMINENT
(NOT —) DEEP INNER ARCANE HIDDEN MASKED OCCULT SECRET SUBTLE DELICATE DOUBTFUL PROFOUND INEVIDENT
OBVIOUSNESS PATENCY
OBVOLUTE CONTORTED OVERLAPPING
OCA OKA TUBER OXALIS SORREL SOURSOP
OCARINA CAMOTE
OCCASION SEL BOUT CALL GIVE HINT NEED SELE SITH TIDE TIME TURN BREAK BREED CASUS CAUSE CHARE EVENT INFER NONCE RAISE SITHE SLANT STOUR WHILE YIELD AFFAIR AUTHOR CHANCE COURSE EXCUSE PERIOD REASON STOUND CHESOUN INSPIRE OPENING PRETEXT QUARREL CEREMONY ENGENDER EXIGENCY FUNCTION INCIDENT INSTANCE CONDITION ENCHEASON HAPPENING
(— GRIEF) GRIEVE
(— OF EXCITEMENT) ALARM ALARUM
(DEFINITE —) TIDE
(EXCITING —) BLAST
(FAVORABLE —) ADVANTAGE
(FESTIVE —) UTAS BEANO HOLIDAY SHINDIG BEANFEAST MERRYMAKING
(HAPPY —) SIMHAH SIMCHAH
(SOCIAL —) COFFEE
(SPECIAL —) CEREMONY
OCCASIONAL ODD ORRA STRAY ANTRIN CASUAL DAIMEN SCARCE POPPING EPISODIC FUGITIVE SPORADIC IRREGULAR
OCCASIONALLY EVERY ATTIMES BETIMES SOMETIME SOMETIMES
OCCASIVE SETTING WESTWARD
OCCIDENTAL WEST PONENT WESTERN HESPERIAN WESTERNER
OCCLUDE SHUT SORB CLOSE ABSORB OBSTRUCT
OCCLUSAL MORSAL
OCCLUSION CORONARY ARTICULATION
(SUFF.) CLEISIS CLISIS
OCCULT MAGIC ARCANE HIDDEN LATENT MYSTIC SECRET VOODOO ALCHEMY CRYPTIC ECLIPSE UNKNOWN ESOTERIC MYSTICAL SIBYLLIC CONCEALED RECONDITE SIBYLLINE
(— SCIENCE) ESOTERICS
(PREF.) CRYPT(O) KRYPT(O)
OCCULTATION ECLIPSE
OCCULTISM MAGIC CABALA MYSTERY
OCCUPANCY POSSESSION
OCCUPANT HOLDER INMATE RENTER TENANT CITIZEN DWELLER RESIDENT INCUMBENT
(— OF THEATER GALLERY) GOD
(SUFF.) ITE
OCCUPATION ART JOB LAY USE CALL GAME LINE NOTE PLOY TOIL WORK BERTH CRAFT GRAFT TRADE BILLET CAREER EMPLOY METIER RACKET SPHERE TENURE THRIFT CALLING CONCERN CONTROL MYSTERY PURSUIT QUALITY SERVICE ACTIVITY BUSINESS FUNCTION INDUSTRY INVASION PLUMBING VOCATION
(— OF MIND) ABSORPTION
(PLEASURABLE —) RECREATIO
(PROFITABLE —) THRIFT
(SUBORDINATE —) HOBBY AVOCATION
(TEDIOUS —) DRAG
OCCUPIED BUSY FULL HELD KEPT RAPT TOOK INUSE ACTIVE INTENT ENGAGED ABSORBED CAPTURED
(— WITH) INTO
(FULLY —) ENGROSSED
(NOT —) IDLE
OCCUPY LIE SIT USE BUSY FILL HAVE HOLD KEEP TAKE WARM AMUSE BELAY BESET DWELL ABSORB BETAKE EMPLOY ENGAGE EXPEND FULFIL OBTAIN TENANT COHABIT CONCERN CONTAIN ENGROSS ENTREAT IMPROVE INHABIT INVOLVE OVERSIT PERVADE POSSESS SWALLOW DISSOLVE GARRISON INTEREST POPULATE POURPRISE
(— AS SUBSTITUTE) SUPPLY
(— ILLEGALLY) JUMP
(— ONESELF) TIRE TRADE ENTREAT
(— QUARTERS) CAMP
(— THOUGHTS) OBSESS
OCCUR BE GO COME COOK FALL GIVE MAKE MEET PASS RISE SORT ARISE BREAK CLASH EXIST INCUR LIGHT APPEAR ARRIVE BEFALL BETIDE CHANCE HAPPEN PROCEED TRANSPIRE
(— AGAIN) RECUR REPEAT
(— BY CHANCE) LIGHT
(— TO) CROSS ENTER STRIKE
OCCURRENCE GO HAP CASE FACT ITEM NOTE REDE EVENT WEIRD EPISODE PASSAGE INCIDENT JUNCTURE OCCASION ENCOUNTER FREQUENCE HAPPENING
(CHANCE —) ADVENTURE CONTINGENT
(COMMON —) USE FREQUENCY
(FREQUENT —) COMMUNITY
(HALLUCINATORY —) FREAKOUT
(SIMULTANEOUS —) SYNCHRONY COINCIDENCE
(SUDDEN —) ZAP STROKE OUTCROP
(SUPERNATURAL —) MIRACLE
(UNEXPECTED —) SUDDEN BLIZZARD BOMBSHELL
(UNFORTUNATE —) CASUALTY
(UNUSUAL —) ODDITY
OCCURRING (— AT NIGHTFALL) ACRONICAL
(— AT REGULAR INTERVALS) HORAL
(— AT TWILIGHT) CREPUSCULAR
(— BY TURN) ALTERNATE
(— CASUALLY) SPORADIC
(— EVERY EIGHT DAYS) OCTAN
(— EVERY FOURTH YEAR) PENTETERIC
(— FREQUENTLY) COMMON
(— INFREQUENTLY) OCCASIONAL
(— IN USUAL PLACE) ENTOPIC
(SELDOM —) RARE INFREQUENT
OCEAN SEA BLUE BRIM DEEP MAIN POND BRINE DRINK ARCTIC INDIAN EXPANSE NEPTUNE PACIFIC ATLANTIC ANTARCTIC
(— FLOATING MATTER) ALGAE LAGAN FLOTSAM
(— ROUTE) LANE
(— SPRAY) IRONWOOD CREAMCUPS
(— SWELL) SEA
(DEEP PART OF —) HADAL
(OF THE DEEP —) HADAL
(ON THE —) ASEA
(PERTAINING TO — DEPTHS) HADAL
(RELATING TO — BELOW 6000 METERS) HADAL
(PL.) ALOT
OCEANIA MALAYA AUSTRALIA MELANESIA POLYNESIA
(REPUBLIC IN —) FIJI
(SACRED OBJECT OF —) ZOGO
OCEANIC NAVAL MARINE PELAGIC NAUTICAL AEQUOREAL
OCEANOGRAPHER (ALSO SEE HYDROGRAPHER)
OCEANUS TITAN
(DAUGHTER OF —) DORIS OCEANID EURYNOME
(FATHER OF —) URANUS OURANOS
(MOTHER OF —) GAEA GAIA
(SISTER OF —) TETHYS
(SON OF —) NEREUS
(WIFE OF —) TETHYS
OCELLUS EYE EYELET STEMMA EYESPOT
OCELOT CAT TOGER LEOPARD WILDCAT
OCHER RUD SIL KEEL OAKER OCHRE

TIVER ABRAUM RADDLE ALMAGRA TANGIER
(BLACK —) WAD WADD
(RED —) RUD KEEL TIVER ABRAUM REDDLE RUBRIC RUDDLE KOKOWAI
(YELLOW —) SIL SPRUCE
OCOTILLO COACHWHIP CANDLEWOOD
OCRAN (SON OF —) PAGIEL
OCREA OCHREA SHEATH
OCTAHEDROID HYPERCUBE TESSERACT
OCTAVE UTAS UTIS EIGHT EIGHTH OTTAVA EIGHTVO HUITAIN DIAPASON SHEMINITH
(— FLUTE) FLAUTINO
(— OF THE SEVENTH) FOURTEENTH
(— SINGING) MAGADIZE
(DIMINISHED —) SEMIDIAPASON
(FATHER OF —) ARGANTE
(TRIPLE —) TRIDIAPASON
OCTAVIA (BROTHER OF —) AUGUSTUS
(HUSBAND OF —) ANTONY
OCTAVO EIGHTS
OCTET OCTAVE OCTUOR HUITAIN OTTETTO
OCTOPUS HEE POLYP POULP PREKE SQUID CUTTLE CATFISH POLYPOD POLYPUS SCUTTLE DIBRANCH OCTOPEAN DEVILFISH
(— ARM) TENTACLE
(AUTHOR OF —) NORRIS
(CHARACTER IN —) DYKE TREE HILMA LYMAN HOOVEN MAGNUS SARRIA BEHRMAN CARAHER DELANEY DERRICK PRESLEY RUGGLES VANAMEE ANNIXTER SHELGRIM CEDARQUIST GENSLINGER
(SECRETION OF —) INK
OCTOROON METIS MESTEE MUSTEE MESTIZO METISSE OCTAROON
OCTROI TAX GRANT PRIVILEGE
OCTUPLE EIGHTFOLD
OCUBY RUM
OCULAR OPTIC VISUAL OCULARY OPTICAL ORBITAL EYEPIECE
OCULUS MUNDI OPAL
OCYRRHOE (FATHER OF —) CHIRON
(MOTHER OF —) CHARICLO
ODD AUK AWK OUT RUM FELL LEFT LONE ORRA RARE ANTIC CRAZY DIPPY DITSY DROLL EERIE EXTRA FLAKY FUNKY FUNNY IMPAR KINKY OUTRE QUEER SPACY UNKET UNKID WEIRD FLAKEY FREAKY IMPAIR QUAINT SINGLE SPACEY UNEVEN UNIQUE AZYGOUS BAROQUE BIZARRE COMICAL CURIOUS ERRATIC STRANGE UNEQUAL UNUSUAL FANCIFUL FREAKISH PECULIAR SINGULAR UNPAIRED BURLESQUE ECCENTRIC FANTASTIC GROTESQUE LAUGHABLE SQUIRRELY UNMATCHED WHIMSICAL
(— JOBMAN) JOEY
(PREF.) AZYGO IMPARI
ODDBALL GEEK KOOK SPOOK WEIRDO DINGBAT CRACKPOT
ODDITY GIG QUIP JIMJAM ANOMALY RUMNESS QUIZZITY PECULIARITY
(PL.) PURLICUES
ODDMAN UMPIRE ARBITER FLOATER REFEREE
ODDS BISK EDGE CHALK PRICE BISQUE DISCORD DISPUTE QUARREL HANDICAP VARIANCE ADVANTAGE DISPARITY
(— AND ENDS) ORTS STEW BROTT REFUSE SCRAPS GIBLETS SECONDS FEWTRILS REMNANTS SHAKINGS ETCETERAS FRAGMENTS
(AT —) ACROSS
(EXTRAVAGANT —) POUNDAGE
(FAVORABLE —) PERCENTAGE
ODE HYMN POEM SONG LYRIC PAEAN PSALM GHAZEL MONODY ODELET CANZONA CANZONE EPICEDE CANTICLE PALINODE PINDARIC SERENATA STASIMON EPICEDIUM EPINICION PARABASIS
(— OF LAMENTATION) THRENE THRENODY
ODED (SON OF —) AZARIAH
ODENATHUS (WIFE OF —) ZENOBIA
ODEON HALL ODEUM GALLERY THEATER
ODIN OTHIN WODAN WODEN WOTAN
(BROTHER OF —) VE VILI
(CREATED BY —) ASK EMBLA
(DAUGHTER-IN-LAW OF —) NANNA
(DESCENDANT OF —) SCYLD
(FATHER OF —) BOR BORR
(HALL OF —) VALHALLA
(HORSE OF —) SLEIPNER SLEIPNIR
(MANSION OF —) GLADSHEIM
(MOTHER OF —) BESTLA
(PALACE OF —) SYN
(RAVEN OF —) HUGIN MUNIN
(RING OF —) DRAUPNIR
(SHIP OF —) NAGLFAR SKIDBLADNIR
(SON OF —) TYR THOR VALI BALDR BALDER
(SPEAR OF —) GUNGNIR
(SWORD OF —) GRAM
(THRONE OF —) HLIDSKJALF
(WIFE OF —) FRIA RIND FRIGG RINDR FRIGGA
(WOLF OF —) GERI FREKI
ODIOUS FOUL LOTH UGLY VILE LOATH INFAND ODIBLE HATABLE HATEFUL HEINOUS HIDEOUS DAMNABLE FLAGRANT INFAMOUS ABHORRENT INVIDIOUS OBNOXIOUS OFFENSIVE REPUGNANT
ODIUM HATRED STIGMA DISLIKE AVERSION DISFAVOR DISGRACE DISHONOR ANTIPATHY
(PUBLIC —) ENVY
ODOACER (FATHER OF —) EDECON
ODOMETER ODOGRAPH VIAMETER WAYWISER HODOMETER PEDOMETER
ODONTALGIA TOOTHACHE
ODOR AIR FUME FUNK NOSE OLID TANG WAFF WAFT AROMA EWDER FETOR FLAIR FUMET NIDOR SCENT SMACK SMELL SNUFF SPICE STINK BREATH FLAVOR FOETOR HODURE REPUTE STENCH BOUQUET ESSENCE FUMETTE NOSEGAY PERFUME VERDURE PUNGENCE EFFLUVIUM EMPYREUMA FRAGRANCE REDOLENCE
(— FROM FLOWERS) FUME
(— OF GAME) FUMET
(— OF HAY) NOSE
(BAD —) EWDER FROWST STENCH
(DISGUSTING —) STINK
(FOUL —) FIST MEPHITIS
(FRESH —) YMUR
(PUNGENT —) SPICE
(SPICY —) BALM
(STUDY OF —S) OSMICS
(UNPLEASANT —) PONG
(PREF.) OSM(O)
(SUFF.) OSMA OSPHRESIA
ODORIFEROUS BALMY OLENT ODOROUS FRAGRANT
ODOROUS FOUL BALMY OLENT SMELLY NOISOME ODORANT AROMATIC FRAGRANT NIDOROSE NIDOROUS PERFUMED REDOLENT SCENTFUL SMELLFUL
ODYSSEUS ULYSSES
(ADVISER OF —) ATHENA
(DOG OF —) ARGOS
(FATHER OF —) LAERTES SISYPHUS
(FRIEND OF —) MENTOR
(ISLAND OF —) ITHACA
(SON OF —) TELEGONUS TELEMACHUS
(WIFE OF —) PENELOPE
ODYSSEY (AUTHOR OF —) HOMER
(CHARACTER IN —) ARETE CIRCE HELEN AEOLUS NESTOR EUMAEUS ALCINOUS MENELAUS NAUSICAA ODYSSEUS PENELOPE DEMODOCUS EURYCLEIA TEIRESIAS POLYPHEMUS TELEMACHUS
OEAX (BROTHER OF —) PALAMEDES
(FATHER OF —) NAUPLIUS
(MOTHER OF —) CLYMENE
OEBALUS (FATHER OF —) TELON
(SON OF —) ICARIUS HIPPOCOON TYNDAREUS
(WIFE OF —) GORGOPHONE
OECIST OEKIST COLONIZER
OEDIPUS OEDIPAL
(BROTHER-IN-LAW OF —) CREON
(DAUGHTER OF —) ISMENE ANTIGONE
(FATHER OF —) LAIUS
(FOSTER MOTHER OF —) PERIBOEA
(MOTHER OF —) JOCASTA
(SON OF —) ETEOCLES POLYNICES
(WIFE OF —) JOCASTA
OEIL-DE-BOEUF OCULUS
OEILLADE OGLE ELIAD EYLIAD GLANCE ILLIAD
OENEUS (DAUGHTER OF —) GORGE DEIANIRA
(FATHER OF —) PORTHEUS
(SON OF —) TOXEUS TYDEUS MELEAGER
(WIFE OF —) ALTHAEA
OENOCHOE JUG EWER OLPE PROCHOOS
OENOMAUS (DAUGHTER OF —) HIPPODAMIA
(FATHER OF —) ARES MARS
(MOTHER OF —) STEROPE
(SON OF —) LEUCIPPUS DYSPONTEUS HIPPODAMUS
OENOMETER VINOMETER
OENONE (FATHER OF —) CEBREN
(LOVER OF —) PARIS
(SON OF —) CORYTHUS
OENOPION (DAUGHTER OF —) MEROPE
(FATHER OF —) DIONYSUS
(WIFE OF —) HELICE
OESTRID FLY
(— LARVA) BOT
OESTRUS RUT FURY HEAT STING DESIRE ESTRUS FRENZY IMPULSE STIMULUS
OEUVRE OPUS WORK
OF A O BY DE OFF VAN VON FROM HAVE TILL WITH ABOUT
(— AGE) AE
(— ALL) AVA ALDER ALLER
(— COURSE) NATCH
(— DEATH) M
(— EACH) ANA PER SING
(— THIS DAY) HODIERNAL
(— THIS MONTH) HM
(SUFF.) AL AR ILE INE ISH ISTIC ITIC ITIOUS ORIOUS ORY
OFF BY AFF FAR ODD WET AFAR AGEE AWAY DOFF DOWN GONE LESS ALONG ASIDE RIGHT WONKY WRONG ABSENT CUCKOO DEPART REMOTE DISTANT FURTHER REMOVED SEAWARD TAINTED ABNORMAL OPPOSITE
(— GUARD) TARDY
(— THE PATH) ASTRAY
(— THE SUBJECT) AFIELD
(— THE WIND) ROOM ROOMWARD
(FAR —) DISTANT
(PREF.) AP APH APO DE
OFFAL GURRY WASTE REFUSE CARRION DOGMEAT GARBAGE LEAVING RUBBISH GRALLOCH
(— OF FISH) GURRY STOSH
(MILLING —S) GRIT
OFFBEAT ODD FLAKY
OFF-BEAT KOOKY
OFFBEAT KOOKY SPACY WACKY WEIRD KOOKIE SPACEY
OFFBREAK GOOGLY
OFF-CENTER ECCENTRIC EXCENTRIC
OFF-COLOR BLUE RISQUE SUGGESTIVE
OFFENCE (— AGAINST STATE) SEDITION
OFFEND CAG ERR PET SIN VEX GALL HARM HUFF HURT MIFF RASP RASS ABUSE ANGER ANNOY GRATE GRILL PIQUE SHOCK SPITE TOUCH WRONG AGUILT ATTACK GRIEVE INJURE INSULT NETTLE REVOLT AFFRONT DEFAULT DISDAIN MORTIFY OUTRAGE PROVOKE REGRATE STOMACH UMBRAGE VIOLATE CONFRONT DISTASTE IRRITATE TRESPASS DISOBLIGE DISPLEASE
OFFENDED HUFF MIFF SORE AVERTED FROISSE INJURED INSULTED
OFFENDER SINNER CULPRIT

MISDOER PECCANT HABITUAL OFFENDANT
(FIRST —) STAR
OFFENDING PECCANT
OFFENSE PET SIN HUFF LACK SLIP WITE ABUSE CRIME ERROR FAULT GRIEF GUILT MALUM PIQUE SNUFF ATTACK BIGAMY DELICT FELONY PIACLE PRITCH REATUS STRUNT AFFRONT DEFAULT DEMERIT DUDGEON LARCENY MISDEED OUTRAGE SCANDAL UMBRAGE PECCANCY TRESPASS EXTORTION INDECORUM INDIGNITY THEFTBOTE
(— AGAINST LAW) MALUM DELICT DELICTUM
(— AGAINST MORALITY) EVIL CRIME
(SLIGHT —) PECCADILLO
OFFENSIVE BAD ACID EVIL FOUL HARD UGLY BILGY CRUDE DIRTY FETID GROSS NASTY SLIMY YUCKY COARSE FROWZY GARISH HORRID RANCID RIBALD ROTTEN ABUSIVE BEASTLY FULSOME HATEFUL HIDEOUS NOISOME PECCANT RASPING SCARLET DREADFUL INVADING MEPHITIC SHOCKING STINKING UNSAVORY LOATHSOME OBNOXIOUS REPUGNANT REVOLTING SCANDALOUS
(— SIGHT) EYESORE
OFFENSIVENESS ODIUM
OFFER GO BID PUT BODE GIVE HAND LEND PLEA POSE SHOW TAKE TEND DEFER HEAVE PARTY SHORE START ADDUCE AFFORD ALLEGE DELATE INJECT OBLATE OPPOSE PREFER SUBMIT SUPPLY TENDER ADVANCE BIDDING COMMEND EXHIBIT PRESENT PROFFER PROPINE PROPOSE SUGGEST OVERTURE PROPOSAL VOLUNTEER
(— A STAKE) SET
(— EXCUSE) ALIBI
(— FOR SALE) HAWK EXPOSE
(— INDUCEMENT) INVITE
(— IN EXCUSE) PLEAD
(— IN OPPOSITION) OBJECT
(— IN SACRIFICE) IMMOLATE
(— OF MARRIAGE) PROPOSAL
(— PROOF) APPROVE
(— PUBLICLY) JACTITATE
(— RESISTANCE) FEND
(— TO VERIFY) AVER
(— UP) APPEAL
(LAST —) ULTIMATUM
(PUBLIC —) SALE
(SOLEMN —) PLEDGE
(UNACCEPTED —) POLLICITATION
OFFERING BID ALMS BALI DALI DEAL GIFT HOST SOMA DOLLY ENTRY CORBAN NUZZER OFLETE PIACLE PRESENT RETABLO TRIBUTE ANATHEMA DEVOTION DONATION LIBATION OBLATION PESHKASH PIACULUM SACRIFICE
(— TO GOD) CORBAN DEODATE
(— TO HOUSEHOLD DEITIES) BALI
(EUCHARISTIC —) ANAPHORA
(PEACE —S) PACIFICS
(RELIGIOUS —) OBLATION
(SACRIFICIAL —) HOLOCAUST
(THEATRICAL —) FLUFF
(PL.) HIERA ALTARAGE INFERIAE
OFF-GLIDE EXIT VOCULE DETENTE
OFFHAND AIRY CURT GLIB SOON ADLIB BLUSH HASTY ABRUPT BREEZY CASUAL BRUSQUE READILY CARELESS CAVALIER GLANCING INFORMAL EXTEMPORE IMPROMPTU UNSTUDIED
OFFICE HAT JOB SEE BOMA DUTY NONE PART POST ROLE ROOM SHOP TASK TOGA WIKE WORK PLACE STINT TRUST WIKEN YAMEN ABBACY AGENCY BUREAU CHARGE DAFTAR DIWANI DUFTER METIER MISTER BULLPEN CAMARIN CENTRAL DEWANEE DROSTDY EDILITY MYSTERY SERVICE STATION SURGERY AEDILITY CAPACITY CUTCHERY ENSIGNCY FUNCTION KINGSHIP MINISTRY POSITION PROVINCE WOOLPACK BAILIWICK BANKSHALL SITUATION
(— BOY) CHOKRA
(— CHIEF) BOSS MANAGER
(— OF BISHOP) LAWN
(— OF JUDGE) BENCH ERMINE
(— OF PROFESSOR) CHAIR
(— OF ROMAN CURIA) DATARY DATARIA
(— OF RULER) REGENCY
(— OF THE DEAD) DIRGE
(— WORKER) CLERK STENO TYPIST SECRETARY
(BRANCH —) WING
(CASHIER'S —) CAISSE
(CLERICAL —) CASSOCK
(DIVINE —) AKOLUTHIA
(ECCLESIASTICAL —) FROCK BENEFICE EXORCIST
(HIGH —) DIGNITY
(LITURGICAL —) SEXT SERVICE
(MAGISTRATE'S —) KACHAHRI
(MORNING —) ORTHRON ORTHROS
(NAVAL —S) BEACH
(PAY —) WANIGAN
(POLICE —) NICK
(PRIESTLY —) SACERDOCY
(PRINTING —) CHAPEL IMPRIMERY
(RECORD —) CHANCERY
(RESIGN AN —) DEMIT
(TIMEKEEPER'S —) PENNYHOLE
(SUFF.) ATE CY DOM SHIP URE
OFFICEHOLDER IN WINNER OFFICIAL PLACEMAN
OFFICER (ALSO SEE OFFICIAL) COP TAB AIDE EXEC EXON FLAG HOLD NASI SWAB VOGT AGENT CHIEF CRIER DEWAN DIWAN GRAND GRAVE GROOM JURAT SEWER TAXOR USHER ALCADE BEADLE BEAGLE BEDRAL BUTLER CENSOR DEPUTY DIRECT ENSIGN GAILLI GEREFA HERALD KOTWAL LAWMAN LICTOR MANAGE ORATOR PARNAS REDTAB SYNDIC TINDAL ADJOINT AGISTOR ALNAGER ASSIZER BAILIFF COMMAND CONDUCT CORONER DUUMVIR EPAULET FEDERAL FEODARY GAVELER GENERAL JEMADAR KLEAGLE LOBSTER MUSTANG NAPERER PANTLER PATROON REGIDOR SANCTUM SCHEPEN SHERIFF SPEAKER STEWARD WHIPPER WOODMAN ADJUTANT ALDERMAN ALGUACIL ANDREEVE BANNERET CHAFFWAX COFFERER CURSITOR DOORWARD FORESTER GOVERNOR GRASSMAN MERESMAN MINISTER PALATINE PURVEYOR QUESTEUR REPORTER TIPSTAFF VISCOUNT WOODWARD CONSTABLE DIKEGRAVE FINANCIER INTENDANT MODERATOR PAYMASTER SCHOOLMAN TAHSILDAR
(— OF CHURCH) ABBOT ELDER DEACON SEXTON ANTISTES DEFENSOR LAMPADARY SACRISTAN
(— OF COURT) MACER MASTER BAILIFF FEODARY FILACER CURSITOR DEMPSTER EXAMINER SERGEANT ASSOCIATE BYRLAWMAN SURROGATE
(— OF FORESTS) AGISTER AGISTOR
(— OF KING'S STABLES) AVENER
(— OF TABLE) SEWER
(BARDIC —) DRUID
(CAVALRY —) CORNET
(CHIEF —) NASI DEWAN DAROGA PARNAS PRESIDENT
(CHIEF EXECUTIVE —) CEO
(CHURCH —) SEXTON
(COLLEGE —) RECTOR
(COURT —) REEVE SUMMONER
(CUSTOMS —) GAGER SHARK GAUGER JERQUER DOUANIER SEARCHER SURVEYOR TIDESMAN
(FOREST —) RANGER
(GREEK —) STRATEGOS STRATEGUS
(JAPANESE —) SHIKKEN
(KIND OF —) PETTY
(LAW —) GANGBUSTER
(MASONIC —) EAST KING DEACON STEWARD
(MILITARY —) NAIG NAIK COMES MAJOR SUBAH ENSIGN NAIQUE RANKER SARDAR SIRDAR CAPTAIN COLONEL GENERAL JEMADAR MARSHAL SUBADAR WARRANT COMMANDER RABSHAKEH SHAVETAIL
(MINOR —) CHINOVNIK
(MONASTERY —) CELLARER
(MUNICIPAL —) SCHOUT VARLET
(NAVAL —) CPO EXON MATE SWAB BOSUN ENSIGN PURSER YEOMAN ADMIRAL CAPTAIN MUSTANG SPOTTER YOUNKER COXSWAIN SUNDOWNER MIDSHIPMAN
(PAPAL —) DATARY
(POLICE —) COP PIG PEON RURAL COPPER EXEMPT JAVERT KOTWAL ROZZER RUNNER SBIRRO ALYTARCH SEARCHER THANADAR DETECTIVE ROUNDSMAN
(PRESIDING —) CHAIRONE CHAIRPERSON
(PRISON —) SCREW WARDER
(PUBLIC —) JUDGE FISCAL NOTARY PODESTA
(ROMAN —) LICTOR
(SHERIFF'S —) FANG BEAGLE BAILIFF BULLDOG HUISSIER
(SHIP'S —) MATE FANTOD
(STAFF —) TAB AIDE REDTAB ADJUTANT
(TOLL —) SCAVAGER
(TURKISH —) AGA AGHA MUTE VIZIR VIZIER BIMBASHI BINBASHI
(UNIVERSITY —) DEAN REGENT PROVOST
(WARRANT —) MACHINIST
(PL.) BRAID BRASS STAFF
OFFICIAL (ALSO SEE OFFICER) AGA BEG DEY VIP AMIN BOSS KUAN KWAN TRUE AGENT AHONG AMALA AMBAN AMEEN AMLAH CLERK EDILE EPHOR GYANI HAJIB HOMER JURAT LIMMU LINER MAYOR NAZIR OMRAH REEVE SAHIB AEDILE ARCHON ATABEG BASHAW CENSOR CONSUL EPARCH EPONYM FISCAL FORMAL GABBAI GRIEVE HAZZAN HERALD LAWMAN MASTER NOTARY PANDIT PREVOT RABMAG SATRAP SCRIBE SEALER SINGER TAOTAI TAOYIN TRONER VERGER WARDEN WEDANA ALMONER APOSTLE ASIARCH BURGESS CERTAIN JEMADAR LANDRAT MARSHAL MOORMAN PRISTAW REFEREE STALLAR STARTER SUBASHI VAIVODE ALDERMAN APPROVED CARDINAL CELLARER CUSTOMER DOGBERRY GOVERNOR LINESMAN MANDARIN PROVIDER PRYTANIS VESTIARY VISCOUNT WHIFFLER EXECUTIVE MAJORDOMO OMBUDSMAN SELECTMAN MAGISTRATE
(— APPROVAL) VISA VISE
(— DECREE) WRIT UKASE
(— OF CARTHAGE) SUFFETE
(BLUNDERING —) DOGBERRY
(EISTEDDFOD —) DRUID
(GAME —) REF UMP SCORER UMPIRE REFEREE
(MUSLIM —) OMRAH
(PALACE —) PALADIN
(POMPOUS —) BUMBLE
(PRETENTIOUS —) PANJANDRUM
(UNIVERSITY —) PROCTOR
(PL.) KEYS PHAR OMLAH
OFFICIATE ACT FILL SERVE SUPPLY PERFORM CELEBRATE
OFFICIATOR DEICIDE
OFFICIOUS BUSY COOL PERT SAUCY FORMAL FORTHY PUSHING ARROGANT IMPUDENT INFORMAL MEDDLING OFFICIAL INBEARING PRAGMATIC
OFFING OFF FUTURE PICTURE
OFFISH CLAMMY UPSTAGE
OFFSCOURINGS MUD SCURF
OFF-SEASON LAYOFF
OFFSET SLAB STEP ALTAR CRIMP ERASE POISE CANCEL CONTRA JOGGLE REDEEM SETOFF BALANCE COUNTER LATERAL RETREAT SETBACK PROPAGULE
(— ON BULB) SPLIT
OFFSHOOT GET PUP ROD SON LIMB SPUR BOUGH ISSUE SCION SHOOT

SPRIG BRANCH FILIAL GROWTH MEMBER OFFSET SPROUT ADJUNCT APOPHYSIS FILIATION OUTGROWTH RAMIFICATION
(— OF LAKE) BAYOU
(— OF RELIGIOUS ORDER) REFORM
OFFSHORE DEEPWATER
OFFSPRING BOY FRY IMP KID KIN SON BRAT BURD CHIT HEIR SEED SLIP BIRTH BREED BROOD CHILD FRUIT ISSUE SCION SPAWN BEGATS DUSTEE EMBRYO FOSTER GRIQUA JUMART PROLES RESULT STRAIN STRIND MORISCO NISHADA OUTCOME PRODUCE PRODUCT PROGENY YOUNGER CHILDREN DAUGHTER DEMISANG GENITURE INCREASE KINDLING BAIRNTEAM MUSTAFINA
(— OF EUROPEAN-INDIAN) MAMELUCO
(— OF FAIRIES) CHANGELING
(— OF NEGRO AND MULATTO) GRIFFE
(— OF STALLION AND ASS) HINNY FUNNEL
(— OF WITCH) HAGSEED HOLDIKEN
(MYTHICAL —) JUMART
(PREMATURE —) CASTLING
(WITHOUT —) ATOKAL ATOKOUS
(PREF.) GEN(O) GON(O) PAEDO PEDO PROLI
(SUFF.) ITE TOKOUS
OFF-THE-RACK READYMADE
OF HUMAN BONDAGE (AUTHOR OF —) MAUGHAM
(CHARACTER IN —) CAREY EMILY ERLIN FANNY NORAH PRICE SALLY WEEKS LAWSON LOUISA NESBIT PHILIP ROGERS THORPE ATHELNY CLUTTON HAYWARD MILDRED WILLIAM CRONSHAW WILKINSON
OFICINA WORKS OFFICE FACTORY
OFLETE WAFER OBLATION OFFERING
OF MICE AND MEN (AUTHOR OF —) STEINBECK
(CHARACTER IN —) SLIM CANDY SMALL CROOKS CURLEY GEORGE LENNIE MILTON
OFTEN OFT AFTEN OFTLY COMMON EFTSOONS FREQUENT REPEATED
(VERY —) CONTINUALLY
OF TIME AND THE RIVER (AUTHOR OF —) WOLFE
(CHARACTER IN —) ANN GANT JOEL WANG BASCOM ELINOR EUGENE PIERCE ROBERT WEAVER COULSON FRANCIS HATCHER MORNAYE PENTLAND
OGDOAD EIGHT OCTOAD OGDOAS OCTONARY
OGEE (ALSO SEE MOLDING) CYMA GULA TALON MOLDING
OGIVAL HEATER
OGLE EYE GAZE LEER LOOK MASH STARE GLANCE EXAMINE MARLOCK SMICKER OEILLADE
OGRE ORC BOYG BRUTE DEMON FIEND GHOUL GIANT HUGON TYRANT YAKSHA BUGABOO BUGBEAR MONSTER WINDIGO
OGRESS PELLET GUNSTONE
OGTIERN LORD MASTER
OGYGIAN ANCIENT PRIMEVAL
OH OU OW ACH OUCH

OHIO
CAPITAL: COLUMBUS
COLLEGE: KENT HIRAM KENYON XAVIER ANTIOCH OBERLIN DEFIANCE
COUNTY: ERIE PIKE ROSS DARKE MIAMI STARK GALLIA HARDIN SUMMIT LICKING CUYAHOGA HAMILTON
INDIAN TRIBE: ERIE WYANDOT
NATIVE: BUCKEYE
NICKNAME: BUCKEYE
PRESIDENT: TAFT GRANT HAYES HARDING GARFIELD HARRISON MCKINLEY
RIVER: MIAMI MAUMEE SCIOTO CUYAHOGA MUSKINGUM
STATE BIRD: CARDINAL
STATE FLOWER: CARNATION
STATE TREE: BUCKEYE
TOWN: ADA ENON LIMA TROY ADENA AKRON BEREA CADIZ NILES XENIA CANTON DAYTON ELYRIA LORAIN MENTOR TOLEDO CHARDON COLUMBUS SANDUSKY CLEVELAND

OIL BEN FAT ILE ULE BALM CHIA DIKA FUEL ZEST BRIBE CRUDE JUICE OLEUM SMEAR STOCK TRAIN ULYIE ULZIE ACEITE ANOINT BINDER BUTTER CARDOL CHRISM CREESH EUPION GREASE LIQUOR SAFROL SMOOTH ZACHUN CEDRIUM ESSENCE LANOLIN MYRRHOL PHLOROL RETINOL VETIVER BERGAMOT COUMARAN ERIGERON GINGEROL PHTHALAN SDRAVETS TETRALIN CARVACROL LUBRICATE PETROLEUM
(— BEETLE) MELOE MELOID
(— CAKE) SEEDCAKE
(— CAN) OILER
(— CASK) RIER
(— FROM ORANGE FLOWERS) NEROLI
(— FROM RESIN) RETINOL
(— IN PAINTS) TUNG
(— LAMP) LUCIGEN
(— OF TURPENTINE) CAMPHENE CAMPHINE
(— PALM) OILBERRY
(— PAN) SUMP
(— PLANT) SESAME
(— ROCK) SHALE LIMESTONE
(— TREE) EBOE POON TUNG MAHWA
(— VESSEL) DRUM OLPE CRUET CRUSE TANKER CRESSET
(— WELL) DUSTER GASSER GUSHER WILDCAT
(AROMATIC —) SPIKENARD
(BUTTER —) GHEE
(COAL —) PHOTOGEN
(CONSECRATED —) CHRISM
(FISH —) GURRY
(FIXED —) COCUM KOKAM KOKUM
(FLOWER —) ABSOLUTE
(FRAGRANT —) ATAR NARD OTTO ATTAR OTTAR CAFFEOL BERGAMOT CAFFEONE GERANIOL
(FUEL —) DERV
(INFERIOR —) MIDDLING
(KIND OF —) CASTOR
(KIND OF COOKING —) CORN COPRA OLIVE
(LINSEED —) CARRON LINOLEUM
(MINERAL —) NAPHTHA KEROSENE
(ORANGE —) NEROLI
(ORANGE-FLOWER —) NEROLI
(PINE —) FROTHER
(PUNGENT —) CAJUPUT
(REMAINING FUEL —) RESID
(RESIDUAL —) RESID
(SESAME —) GINGILI SIRITCH
(SOLID —) KIKUEL
(VEGETABLE —) MACASSAR
(VULCANIZED —) FACTICE
(WHALE —) SPERM TRAIN
(WOOL —) YOLK
(PREF.) ELAEO ELAIO ELEO OLEI OLEO
OILBIRD FATBIRD GUACHARO
OIL CAKE POONAC RESIDUE
OILFISH ESCOLAR
OILILY SLEEK
OILSEED TIL TEEL SESAME LINSEED RAPESEED
OILSKIN OIL OILER SQUAM OILCASE OILCOAT SLICKER
OILSTONE HONE SHALE WHETSTONE
OIL WELL GUSHER
OILY FAT GLIB LIMY BLAND FATTY LOEIC OLEIC SLEEK SOAPY SUAVE GREASY OILISH OLEOSE OLEOUS SMARMY SMOOTH SUPPLE PINGUID SERVILE SLIPPERY UNCTUOUS COMPLIANT PLAUSIBLE
(PREF.) LIPAR(O)
OINTMENT UNG BALM MULL NARD PASTE SALVE SMEAR BALSAM CERATE CEROMA CHARGE CHRISM GREASE POMADE REMEDY UNGUENT EYESALVE POPULEON REMOLADE SPIKENARD WHITFIELD
(— OF GODS) AMBROSIA
OJIBWAY CHIPPEWA SAULTEUR CHIPPEWAY
OKA OCHA OQUE OQUI OCQUE
OKAPI GIRAFFINE
OKAY OK YES HUNK OKEH HUNKY APPROVE CORRECT SANCTION AUTHORIZE SAYTHEWORD
(JAPANESE —) HAI
OKIA OKET OUNCE
OKINAWA (CAPITAL OF —) NAHA

OKLAHOMA
CAPITAL: OKLAHOMACITY
COLLEGE: CAMERON LANGSTON PHILLIPS
COUNTY: KAY COAL LOVE ADAIR ATOKA CADDO GREER OSAGE ALFALFA OKFUSKEE OKMULGEE
INDIAN TRIBE: WACO WICHITA TAWAKONI
LAKE: EUFAULA OOLOGAH
MOUNTAINS: OUACHITA
NATIVE: OKIE SOONER
NICKNAME: SOONER
RIVER: RED GRAND WASHITA ARKANSAS CANADIAN CIMARRON
STATE FLOWER: MISTLETOE
STATE TREE: REDBUD
TOWN: ADA JAY ALVA ENID HUGO ALTUS MIAMI PONCA TULSA ELRENO GUYMON IDABEL LAWTON MADILL TALOGA VINITA ANTLERS SAPULPA SHAWNEE ANADARKO FORTSILL MUSKOGEE

OKRA GOBO OKRO BAMIA BENDY GOBBO GOMBO GUBBO GUMBO OCHRA BENDEE MALLOW BANDAKA BANDICOY BANDIKAI
OLD AGY ELD AGED AULD COLD WOLD YALD ANILE HOARY MOSSY STALE WOULD EFFETE FORMER FOROLD INFIRM MATURE SENILE SHABBY VETUST AGEABLE ANCIENT ANTIQUE ARCHAIC ELDERLY FORWORN OGYGIAN UMWHILE DECREPIT MEDIEVAL OBSOLETE DODDERING GERIATRIC HACKNEYED SENESCENT VENERABLE
(— AND MELLOW) CRUSTY
(— BAILEY) GAOL JAIL PRISON
(— CLOTHESMAN) POCO
(— FAITHFUL) GEYSER
(— HAND) LONGTIMER
(— MAID) SPINSTER THORNBACK
(— MAN) ANTIQUITY WHITEBEARD
(— SOD) EIRE ERIN IRELAND
(— SQUAW) DIVER HOUND MOMMY CALLOO CALLOW COWEEN DUCKER QUANDY OLDWIFE SCOLDER COCKAWEE LONGTAIL SHARPTAIL SOUTHERLY
(— WOMAN) HAG CRONE GAMMER
(BEING LESS THAN 13 YEARS —) PRETEEN
(GROWING —) SENESCENT
(OF —) WHILOM ERSTWHILE
(PREF.) PALAE(O) PALAI(O) PALE(O) SENI
(— AGE) GER(I)(O) GERATO GERONT(O) PRESBY(O)
(— MAN) GER(I)(O) GERONT(O) PRESBY(O)
OLD AND THE YOUNG (AUTHOR OF —) PIRANDELLO
(CHARACTER IN —) COSTA MAURO SALVO SELMI AURITI GIULIO AURELIO CORRADO MORTARA ROBERTO CAPOLINO DIANELLA FLAMINIO GERLANDO IPPOLITO NICOLETTA LAURENTANO
OLD BAY STATE MASSACHUSETTS
OLD CURIOSITY SHOP (AUTHOR OF —) DICKENS
(CHARACTER IN —) KIT DICK FRED NELL BRASS QUILP SARAH CODLIN JARLEY MARTON THOMAS BARBARA NUBBLES SAMPSON SWIVELLER CHRISTOPHER
OLD DOMINION STATE VIRGINIA
OLDEN ANTIQUE
OLDER MORE ALDER ELDER SENIOR ANCESTOR
OLDEST
(PREF.) EO
OLD-FASHIONED MOSSY RETRO

CORNBALL SCHMALTZY NEANDERTHAL CORNY DOWDY FUSTY PASSE FOGRAM FOGRUM QUAINT STODGY ANCIENT ANTIQUE ARCHAIC ARRIERE ELDERLY VINTAGE FRUMPISH OBSOLETE CRINOLINE PRIMITIVE RINKYDINK OLDFANGLED
(FASHIONABLY —) RETRO
OLD FRANKLIN STATE TENNESSEE
OLD LINE STATE MARYLAND
OLD MAID (AUTHOR OF —) WHARTON
(CHARACTER IN —) JOE TINA DELIA JAMES LOVELL CLEMENT RALSTON SPENDER CHARLOTTE
OLD MORTALITY (AUTHOR OF —) SCOTT
(CHARACTER IN —) JOHN BASIL EDITH HENRY JENNY MAUSE CUDDIE MORTON BALFOUR FRANCIS GRAHAME OLIFANT BOTHWELL DENNISON EVANDALE HEADRIGG MARGARET BELLENDEN CLAVERHOUSE
OLD-TIMER SOURDOUGH
OLD WIVES' TALE (AUTHOR OF —) BENNETT
(CHARACTER IN —) JOHN CYRIL POVEY BAINES CHIRAC GERALD SAMUEL SCALES SOPHIA HARRIET FAUCAULT CONSTANCE CRITCHLOW
OLD-WOMANISH ANILE
OLEANDER LAUREL NERIUM DOGBANE ROSEBAY
OLEFIN ALKENE
OLEIC RAPIC RAPINIC
OLEORESIN GUM ANIME APIOL ELEMI TOLUS BALSAM GURJUN IRIDIN COPAIBA GALIPOT LABDANUM TACAMAHAC
OLFACTION NOSE SMELL OSMESIS SMELLING ESPHRESIS
OLIGARCHIC FEUDAL
OLIGARCHY KREMLIN
OLIGOCLASE SUNSTONE
OLIMPIA (HUSBAND OF —) BIRENO OBERTO
OLINDO (HUSBAND OF —) SOFRONIA
(SAVIOR OF —) CLORINDA
OLIO STEW MEDLEY FARRAGO MELANGE MIXTURE MISHMASH MACEDOINE PASTICCIO POTPOURRI
OLIPHANT HORN ELEPHANT
OLIPRANCE ROMP SHOW FROLIC JOLLITY
OLIVE OLEA MORON BRUNET LIERRE OLIVER OXHORN PIMOLA RESEDA BAROUNI CITRINE MISSION MORILLON OLEASTER
(— FLY) DACUS
(AMERICAN —) DEVILWOOD
(OVERRIPE —) DRUPE
(PREF.) DRUPI
(—OIL) ELAEO ELAIO ELEO
OLIVER NOLL HAMMER HOLLIPER
(BROTHER OF —) ORLANDO
(WIFE OF —) CELIA
OLIVER TWIST (AUTHOR OF —) DICKENS
(CHARACTER IN —) BILL JACK NOAH ROSE TOBY BATES FAGIN HARRY MONKS NANCY SALLY SIKES TWIST BEDWIN BUMBLE CORNEY EDWARD MAYLIE OLIVER CHARLEY CRACKIT DAWKINS GRIMWIG LEEFORD BROWNLOW CLAYPOLE LOSBERNE SOWERBERRY
OLIVET PEARL
OLIVIA (HUSBAND OF —) SEBASTIAN
OLIVINE PERIDOT
OLLA JAR JUG OLE POT OLAY PUCHERA PUCHERO
OLLA PODRIDA HASH OLIO MEDLEY POTPOURRI
OLM PROTEUS SALAMANDER
OLOGY ISM SCIENCE
OLYMPIAN CELESTIAL
OLYMPIAS (FATHER OF —) NEOPTOLEMUS
(HUSBAND OF —) PHILIP
(SLAYER OF —) CASSANDER
(SON OF —) ALEXANDER
OLYNTHUS ASCULA
OMAGUA CAMBEVA
OMAH SASQUATCH
OMAN (CAPITAL OF —) MASQAT MUSCAT
(LANGUAGE OF —) ARABIC BALUCHI
(MOUNTAIN OF —) SHAM HAFIT HARIM NAKHL TAYIN AKHDAR
(NATIVE OF —) ADNAN QAHTAN BALUCHI
(TOWN IN —) SUR NIGWA MASQAT MATRAH SALALAH
OMAR (FATHER OF —) ELIPHAZ
OMASUM BOOK BOUK BIBLE FARDEL MANYPLIES
OMBER SOLO UMBRE HOMBRE MEDIATOR QUADRILLE
OMEGA END LAST
OMELET AMLET AMELET FOOYUNG FOOYOUNG FRITTATA
OMEN BODE LUCK SIGN ABODE AUGUR BODER FREET FREIT GUEST TOKEN WEIRD WHATE AUGURY HANDEL HANSEL AUSPICE PORTENT PRESAGE PRODIGY WARNING CEREMONY FOREBODE SOOTHSAY HARBINGER
OMENTUM WEB CAUL ZIRBUS EPIPLOON
OMINOUS DIRE DOUR GRIM BLACK DOOMY FATAL BODING DISMAL SHREWD AUGURAL BALEFUL BANEFUL BODEFUL DIREFUL DOOMFUL FATEFUL MENACING SINISTER THUNDERY PROPHETIC PORTENTOUS
OMISSION OUT BALK BAULK CHASM SALTUS DEFAULT ELISION FAILURE MISPICK NEGLECT SILENCE PASSOVER OVERSIGHT
(— OF A LETTER) APOCOPE
(— OF SYLLABLES) SYNCOPE
(TACIT —) SILENCE
OMIT CUT LET BALK BATE DROP EDIT KILL MISS PASS SKIP SLIP ABATE ELIDE OBMIT SPARE BELEVE CANCEL DELETE EXCEPT FORGET IGNORE DISCARD EXPUNGE NEGLECT DISCOUNT OVERLEAP OVERLOOK OVERSKIP OVERSLIP DISREGARD PRETERMIT
OMITTED VIDE
OMMATIDIUM FACET FACETTE
OMNIBUS BUS BUSS BARGE HERDIC JOGGER PIRATE AUTOBUS MOTORBUS KITTEREEN
OMNIPOTENT GOD ABLE DEITY GREAT ARRANT MIGHTY ALMIGHTY POWERFUL UNEQUALED UNLIMITED
OMNIPRESENCE UBIQUITY
OMNISCIENT WISE LEARNED POWERFUL PANSOPHIC
OMOPLATE SCAPULA
OMPHALE (FATHER OF —) IARDANUS
(HUSBAND OF —) TMOLUS
(SON OF —) TANTALUS
OMPHALOS HUB BOSS KNOB NAVEL CENTER UMBILICUS
OMRI (FATHER OF —) BECHER MICHAEL
(SON OF —) AHAB
ON O AN IN TO LIT ONE SUR ATOP AWAY OVER UPON ABOUT ABOVE AHEAD ALONG ANENT ABOARD WITHIN FORWARD
(— ACCOUNT OF) IN FOR
(— A HATCH) ABROOD
(— ALL SIDES) ABOUT AROUND
(— AND ON) EVER FOREVER TEDIOUS
(— EARTH) BELOW
(— END) TOGETHER
(— FOOT) UP AFOOT TOWARD FOOTBACK
(— HAND) ALONG
(— HIGH) ALOFT
(— THE CONTRARY) BUT RATHER
(— THE MOVE) AFOOT
(— THE OTHER HAND) BUT AGAIN HOWEVER ALTHOUGH
(— THE OTHER SIDE) OVER ACROSS
(— THE WAY) AWAY AGATE
(— TIME) PROMPT
(— TOP OF) ATOP ABOVE ALOFT
(— WHAT ACCOUNT) WHY
(FATHER OF —) PELETH
(PREF.) IL IM IN IR SUPER
ONAGER ASS GOUR KULAN KOULAN ONAGRA ALACRAN CATAPULT SCORPION
ONAM (FATHER OF —) SHOBAL JERAHMEEL
(MOTHER OF —) ATARAH
ONAN (FATHER OF —) JUDAH
ONCE ANE EEN ERST AINCE ONCET WHILE YANCE FORMER WHILOM QUONDAM UMWHILE FORMERLY SOMETIME UMQUHILE WHENEVER ERSTWHILE
(— MORE) YET ANEW AGAIN ENCORE ITERUM
(AT —) PRESTO
ONDATRA FIBER
ONE J AE AN HE UN ACE AIN ANE ANY EIN MAN OON TAE UNA UNE WON YAE YAN YEN YIN YOU SAME SOLE SOME TANE TEAN THIS TONE TOON UNAL UNIT WHON WONE ALONE ALPHA UNITY WOONE ABOARD FELLOW PERSON SINGLE UNIQUE UNITED CERTAIN NUMERAL PRONOUN SIMPLUM UNBROKEN SINGLETON UNDIVIDED UNMARRIED
(— AFTER ANOTHER) ABOUT TANDEM SERIALLY SERIATIM
(— BORN A SERF) NEIF NEIFE
(— BY ONE) APIECE SINGLY OVERHEAD
(— CONDEMNED WRONGFULLY) CALAS
(— CURIOUS TO KNOW ALL) QUIDNUNC
(— DETESTED) WARLING
(— DEVOTED TO PARTICULAR ART) IST
(— EASILY TRICKED) CULLY
(— ENGAGED IN MARAUDING) LOOTIE
(— ENROLLED IN ARMY) DRAFTEE
(— FOLLOWED BY 100 ZEROES) GOOGOL
(— GIVEN TO DEVILTRY) HELLION
(— HELD IN CONTEMPT) FINK
(— HIGHEST IN RANK) SUPREME
(— INSTRUCTED IN SECRET SYSTEM) EPOPT
(— LATE) SERO
(— MANAGING ENTERTAINERS ON ROAD) ROADIE
(— NOT A REGULAR MASON) COWAN
(— OF PAIR) FELLOW DOUBLET
(— OF TRIPLETS) TRILLING
(— OVERZEALOUS) HYPER
(— SENT FORTH) APOSTLE
(—S NEARBY) THESE
(— TENTH) TITHE
(— THAT IRKS OR ANNOYS) PAIN
(— THAT UNDERGOES CHANGE) MUTANT
(— THOUSAND) MIL
(— TWENTY-FOURTH) CARAT
(— UNKNOWN) QUIDAM
(— VERSED IN LITERATURE) SAVANT
(— WHO BRINGS MEAT TO TABLE) DAPIFER
(— WHO DISPLAYS FASTIDIOUSNESS) EPICURE
(— WHO DOCTORS SOMETHING) COOK
(— WHO EXCELS) ACE
(— WHO FABRICATES) SMITH
(— WHO FOLLOWS ARMY) SUTLER
(— WHO FORSAKES FAITH) APOSTATE
(— WHO FRUSTRATES PLAN) MARPLOT
(— WHO HAS ATTAINED PERFECTION) SIDDHA
(— WHO IS AWAY) ABSENTEE
(— WHO IS DISMISSED) PUSHOUT
(— WHO IS STRANGE OR ECCENTRIC) WEIRDO
(— WHO LOADS SHIP) BUNKER
(— WHO MAKES LIVING BY TRICKERY) CADGER
(— WHO MANAGES) GERENT
(— WHO REGULATES GUN) TRAINER
(— WHO REMOVES NUISANCE) ABATOR

(— WHO REPRESENTS NEWEST) NEO
(— WHOSE MIND IS IMPAIRED BY AGE) DOTARD
(— WHO TESTS) CONNER
(— WHO USES DRUGS) DRUGGY DRUGGIE
(— WHO WANTS TO BE SOMEONE ELSE) WANNABE
(— WITH FIRST-HAND INFORMATION) INSIDER
(APPEALING —) GAS
(BLESSED —) BHAGAVAT
(CONSPICUOUS —) STANDOUT
(EVIL —) WOND SHAITAN SHEITAN
(EXTRAORDINARY —) DOOZY DOOZER
(LITTLE —) BUTCHA PICKANINNY
(LOVED —) MINION
(MOST IMPORTANT —) FLAGSHIP
(NOT —) NARY
(SUPERIOR —) LAMA
(SWEET —) HONEYCOMB
(TIMELESS —) AKAL
(TIRESOME —) DRIP
(PREF.) HENO MON(O) UNI
(— AND A HALF TIMES) SESQUI
(— AND THE SAME) HOM(O)
(— ANOTHER) ALLELO
(— BILLIONTH) NANO
(— MILLIONTH) MICR(O)
(— TRILLIONTH) PICO
(SAME —) AUT(O) AUTH(I)
(SUFF.) **(— BELONGING)** AN EAN IAN
(— BELONGING TO) IE ING
(— BELONGING TO A GROUP) ID
(— BELONGING TO A LINE) ID
(— HAVING) ANDER
(— HAVING TO DO WITH) IE
(— OCCUPATIONALLY CONNECTED WITH) ER IER YER
(— OF A KIND) ING
(— OF A QUALITY) IE
(— SKILLED) AN EAN IAN
(— THAT ADVOCATES A DOCTRINE) IST
(— THAT DABBLES) IST
(— THAT DOES) ER IER YER
(— THAT HAS) ER IER YER
(— THAT MAKES) IST
(— THAT OPERATES) IST
(— THAT PERFORMS) ER IER IST YER
(— THAT PRACTICES) IST
(— THAT PRODUCES) ER IER IST YER
(— THAT SPECIALIZES) IST
(— THAT STUDIES) IST
(— THAT YIELDS) ER IER YER
(LESSER —) IDIUM
(LITTLE —) IE
(SMALL —) IDIUM IUM
ONEGITE AMETHYST GEMSTONE
ONE-LINER JEST JOKE
ONENESS UNION UNITY CONCORD ONEHOOD UNICITY UNITUDE IDENTITY SAMENESS AGREEMENT
ONE-NIGHT STAND GIG
ONE-NOTE MONOTONOUS
ONE-RAYED MONACT
ONEROUS HARD HEAVY ARDUOUS ONEROSE WEIGHTY EXACTING GRIEVOUS LABORIOUS
ONESELF
(PREF.) SUI
(BY, FOR, PERT. TO —) AUT(O) AUTH(I)
ONE-SIDED ECCENTRIC UNILATERAL
ONETIME FORMER FORMERLY ERSTWHILE
ONFALL ONSET ATTACK ASSAULT
ON-GLIDE TENSION ENTRANCE
ONION BOLL CEPA LEEK LILY SYBO CIBOL INGAN PEARL ALLIUM LILIUM PORRET BERMUDA CEBOLLA HOLLEKE PICKLER SHALLOT AYEGREEN RARERIPE SCALLION VALENCIA
(ROPE OF —S) REEVE
(SEASONED WITH —S) LYONNAISE
(SPRING —) SYBO CIBOL SYBOE SYBOW
(STRING OF —S) TRACE
ONKOS TOPKNOT
ONLOOKER BOOK EYER GAZER WITNESS AUDIENCE BEHOLDER OVERSEER BYSTANDER SPECTATOR
ONLY ALL BUT JUST LONE MERE ONCE SAVE SOLE AFALD ALONE ARRAH FIRST MERED NOBUT OLEPY ANERLY BARELY MERELY NOBBUT SIMPLE SINGLE SINGLY SOLELY ALLENARLY EXCEPTING
(— THIS) MERE
(BEING —) SIMPLE
ONMUN HANGUL HANKUL
ONOMATOPOEIA
(PREF.) KE(R)
ONOMATOPOEIC ECHOIC IMSONIC MIMETIC IMITATIVE
ONRUSH BIRR SHAKE ATTACK TIDEWAY
ONSET DASH DINT FALL FARD RESE RUSH BRAID BREAK BRUNT FAIRD FRUSH START STORM STOUR VENUE ACCESS AFFRET ATTACK CHARGE COURGE IMPACT INSULT ONDING ONFALL POWDER THRUST ASSAULT BRATTLE BEGINNING ENCOUNTER ONSLAUGHT
ONSETTER CAGER HITCHER
ONSLAUGHT LASH BLAST ONSET ATTACK ASSAULT DESCENT SISERARA SALIAUNCE
ONSTEAD ONSET FARMHOUSE HOMESTEAD
ONTARIO **(CANAL IN —)** TRENT RIDEAU
(CAPITAL OF —) TORONTO
(LAKE IN —) SIMCOE
(TOWN IN —) EMO GALT LONDON OTTAWA WINDSOR HAMILTON KINGSTON KITCHENER
ONTO ATOP ABOARD
ONTOGENY DEVELOPMENT
ONTOLOGY METAPHYSICS
ONUS DUTY LOAD BLAME BURDEN CHARGE WEIGHT INCUBUS
ONWARD AWAY AHEAD ALONG FORTH UPWARD FORTHON FORWARD TOWARDS FORERIGHT
ONYX ONIX NICOLO TECALI ONYCHIN JASPONYX SARDONYX
(MEXICAN —) ALABASTER
OOCYTE PROGAMETE GAMETOCYTE
OODLES HEAP LOTS MANY TONS RAFTS SCADS SLEWS LASHINGS SLITHERS ABUNDANCE
OOGONIUM NUCULE OOCYST OOGONE
OOLAK WOLLOCK
OOLITE PISOLITE ROESTONE
OOLONG TEA
OOMPH PEP VIGOR ENERGY
OOPAK TEA
OORALI CURARE
OORIAL SHA SHEEP URIAL
OOTHECA OVISAC
OOZE OZ BOG MUD SEW SOP DRIP EMIT LEAK MIRE SEEP SLEW SLOB SLUE WEEP EXUDE GLEET MARSH SLIME SWEAT WEEZE EXHALE SICKER SLEECH SLOUGH SLUDGE SQUASH SQUDGE STRAIN SCREEVE TEICHER TRANSUDE PERCOLATE
(— OUT) SEW SPEW SPUE
(PREF.) STACTO
OOZING WEEPY SQUDGY SEEPAGE SPEWING WEEPING
OOZY OASY SEEPY WASHY SLEECHY ULIGINOUS
OPACATE DIM DARKEN
OPACITY BODY
(— OF CORNEA) ONYX NEBULA LEUCOMA
OPAH CRAVO SUNFISH KINGFISH MARIPOSA MOONFISH
OPAL GEM NOBLE RESIN FIORITE GIRASOL HYALITE ISOPYRE GIRASOLE JASPOPAL MENILITE SEMIOPAL CACHOLONG GEYSERITE
OPALESCENT OPALED OPALINE IRISATED
OPALEYE GREENFISH
OPAQUE DIM DARK DULL DENSE MUDDY SHADY THICK VAGUE OBTUSE STUPID CLOUDED OBSCURE ABSTRUSE EYESHADE
OPEN GO CAP DUP LAX OPE AIRY AJAR BARE FAIR FLUE FREE GIVE NEAR PERT UNDO VIDE AGAPE APERT BEGIN BLOWN BREAK BROAD BURST CHINK CLEAR CRACK FLARE FRANK FRESH JIMMY LANCE LOOSE MUSHY NAKED OVERT PLAIN RELAX SPALD SPLAT SPLAY START UNBAR UNPEG UNTIE UNZIP APPERT CANDID DIRECT ENTAME EXPAND EXPOSE FACIAL FORTHY GAPING HONEST LIABLE OUVERT PATENT PUBLIC SINGLE SPREAD UNBOLT UNDRAW UNFOLD UNFURL UNGLUE UNLOCK UNROLL UNSEAL UNSHUT UNSPAR UNSTOP UNTINE UNWINK UNWRAP VACANT ARTLESS BLOSSOM DISPART FIELDEN OBVIOUS OUTLINE SINCERE THROUGH UNCLOSE UNHINGE APPARENT COMMENCE DISCLOSE EXPLICIT EXTENDED INITIATE MANIFEST OUTFRONT PERVIOUS RESERATE UNFASTEN CHAMPAIGN OSTENSIBLE
(— AIR) ALFRESCO
(— AND CLEANSE) WILLOW
(— A VEIN) BROACH
(— CLOTH) SCUTCH
(— COUNTRY) VELDT WEALD
(— EYES OR LIPS) SEVER
(— THE WAY) INVITE PIONEER
(— TO PURSUIT) FAIR
(— UP) START DEVELOP DISPART DISCLOSE
(— VIOLENTLY) SPORT
(— WIDE) YAWN EXPAND STRETCH
(— WIDELY) GAPE
(BARELY —) AJAR
(FULLY —) WIDE AGAPE YAWNING
(HALF —) MID AJAR
(SLIGHLY —) AJAR
(TOO —) OVERBARISH
OPENBILL OPENBEAK
OPENED APPAUME ECHAPPE
OPENER KEY KNOB LATCH SESAME APERIENT
(— IN POKER) PAIR JACKS
(FURROW —) SHOE STUBRUNNER
(OYSTER —) HUSKER
OPENHANDED FREE LIBERAL GENEROUS RECEPTIVE
OPENING OS CUT EYE GAP YAT ANUS BOLE BORE DAWN DOOR DROP FENT FLUE GATE HOLE LOOP PASS PORE PORT PYLA RIFT RIMA SLAP SLIT SLOT SPAN VENT VOID YAWN YEAT BLEED BRACK BREAK CHASM CHINK CLEFT CROSS DEBUT GRILL HILUM INLET LIGHT MOUTH SCOOT SINUS START THIRL WIDTH ADITUS AVENUE BREACH CASING CHANCE GRILLE HIATUS INTAKE LACUNA MEATUS OILLET OUTLET PORTAL SLUICE SPREAD AIRPORT CREVASS CREVICE DISPLAY FISSURE ORIFICE OUTCAST SWALLET APERIENT APERTURE BUNGHOLE CREVASSE ENTRANCE OVERTURE PLUGHOLE SCISSURE TEASEHOLE
(— BELOW PENTHOUSE) GALLERY
(— FOR ESCAPE) MUSE MEUSE
(— FOR SLEEVE) SCYE
(— FROM SEA) INDRAFT
(— IN ANTHER) STOMIUM
(— IN DECK) SCUTTLE
(— IN EARTH) GROTTO CHIMNEY
(— IN EARTH) MOFETTE
(— IN EARTH) SWALLOW
(— IN FLOOR OR ROOF) HATCH SKYLIGHT
(— IN GARMENT) FENT ARMHOLE
(— IN LOCK TUMBLER) GATING
(— IN MINE) EYE ADIT RAISE SHAFT WINZE WINNING
(— IN MOLD) POUR
(— IN PICTURE FRAME) SIGHT
(— IN PILLAR OF COAL) JENKIN JUNKING
(— IN ROCK) GRIKE
(— IN SALMON TRAP) SLAP
(— IN SEA CAVE) GLOUP
(— IN SKIRT) PLACKET
(— IN SPONGE) APOPYLE
(— IN STAGE) DIP

(— IN TENNIS COURTS) GRILLE HAZARD GALLERY
(— IN TROUSERS) SPARE
(— IN VAULT) LUNET LUNETTE
(— IN WALL) BOLE DREAMHOLE
(— OF BALL) PROMENADE
(— OF BUD) ANTHESIS
(— OF EAR) BUR BURR
(— OF ESOPHAGUS) CARDIA
(— OF EYE) PUPIL
(— OF GEYSER) CRATER
(— OF HOCKEY GAME) BULLY
(— OF PRAIRIE) BAY
(— OF SHELL) GAPE
(— OF SKIRT) SPARE
(— OF STOMACH) PYLORUS
(— THROUGH BULWARKS) GANGWAY GUNPORT SCUPPER
(— TO ASH PIT) GLUT
(— WIDE) DEHISCENT
(— WITH LID) SCUTTLE
(— WITHOUT TREES) BLANK
(ARCHED —) ALCOVE ARCADE
(CHECKERS —) ALMA DYKE FIFE CROSS CENTER SOUTER BRISTOL GLASGOW PAISLEY WHILTER DEFIANCE SWITCHER
(CHESS —) DEBUT GAMBIT DEFENCE DEFENSE
(EROSIONAL —) FENSTER
(FISTULOUS —) SYRINX
(FUNNELLIKE —) CHOANA
(GRILL —) GUICHET
(JAR —) PITHOIGIA
(MOUTHLIKE —) STOMA OSTIUM
(NARROW —) VISTA
(SMALL —) PORE SLOT CHINK STOMA CRANNY EYELET LACUNA CATHOLE CREVICE DOGHOLE FORAMEN GUICHET PINHOLE QUARREL FENESTRA
(WINDOWLIKE —) SPLITE FENESTRA
(PREF.) APERTO CHASMO TREMATO
(SUFF.) PORA PORE PYL(E) STOMA(TA)(TE)(TOUS) STOME STOMI(A) STOMOUS STOMUM STOMY TREMA(TA)

OPENLY BARELY FREELY BROADLY FRANKLY PUBLICE ROUNDLY STRAIGHT

OPEN-MINDED LIBERAL

OPENMOUTHED GAPING GREEDY RAVENOUS CLAMOROUS

OPENNESS CANDOR FREEDOM PATENCY DAYLIGHT FRANKNESS ROUNDNESS

OPENWORK LATTICE TRACERY CAGEWORK FILIGREE FRETTING FRETWORK

OPEN-WORKED AJOURISE

OPERA AIDA FAUST LAKME MANON NORMA THAIS TOSCA BOHEME CARMEN DAPHNE ERNANI LOUISE MIGNON OTELLO RIENZI SALOME ELEKTRA FIDELIO BURLETTA FALSTAFF IOLANTHE LOKACOLO PARSIFAL TRAVIATA WALKYRIE LOHENGRIN PAGLIACCI RHEINGOLD RIGOLETTO SIEGFRIED TROVATORE
(— DIVISION) SCENA
(— GLASS) GLASS JUMELLE LORGNET LORGNETTE
(— HAT) GIBUS CLAQUE
(— SONG) ARIA
(— STAR) DIVA
(COMIC —) BUFFA BURLETTA
(HORSE —) WESTERN
(KIND OF —) SOAP
(SOAP —) SUDSER
(SPANISH —) ZARZUELA
(TV OR RADIO —) SOAP
(16TH CENTURY —) PASTORALE

OPERA GLASSES JUMELLE LORGNETTE

OPERANT EFFICIENT OPERATIVE

OPERATE GO ACT CUT MAN RUN PUSH TAKE WORK DRIVE MULES STEER AFFECT EFFECT MANAGE CONDUCT PROCEED FUNCTION
(— BY HAND) MANIPULATE
(— GUNS) SERVE
(— MINE) FLUSH
(— MOTOR VEHICLE) VROOM
(— RADIO) BLOOP
(CAUSE TO —) POWERUP

OPERATIC LYRIC

OPERATING GOING ATWORK
(FULLY —) AFLOAT

OPERATION DEED PLAY BLAST ACTION AGENCY EFFECT OSTOMY VIRTUE PROCESS CREATION EXERCISE FACELIFT FUNCTION PRACTICE EXECUTION INFLUENCE PROCESSUS
(ARTHMETIC —) PROOF
(FRAUDULENT —) SCAM
(MILITARY —S) CAMPAIGN
(REGULAR —S) ECONOMY
(SURGICAL —) CECOPEXY
(UNDERCOVER —) STING
(SUFF.) **(— FOR OPENING)** STOMY

OPERATIONAL LIVE

OPERATIONS
(SUFF.) ICS

OPERATIVE EYE HAND ARTIST LIVING ARTISAN OUVRIER MECHANIC DETECTIVE EFFECTIVE

OPERATOR DEL DOER AGENT BAKER DEWER NABLA PILOT QUACK BEAMER BILLER BOLTER BUMPER BUSMAN CAPPER DEALER DEGGER DRIVER DUNGER DYADIC GAGGER JOCKEY KICKER RAGGER TRADER AVIATOR BREAKER CENTRAL CHEESER DENTIST FACIENT GLASSER JOGGLER MANAGER OPERANT SURGEON IDENTITY MOTORMAN CONDUCTOR
(INFERIOR —) PLUG
(LOGICAL —) NOT
(RADIO —) HAM CBER SPARKS SPARKER
(TRUCK —) GIPSY GYPSY
(SUFF.) STER STRESS

OPERCULUM LID FLAP ONYCHA OPERCLE APTYCHUS COVERING EYESTONE MANDIBLE

OPERETTA ZARZUELA

OPEROSE BUSY IRKSOME DILIGENT LABORIOUS

OPHELIA (BROTHER OF —) LAERTES
(FATHER OF —) POLONIUS

OPHELTES (FATHER OF —) LYCURGUS
(NURSE OF —) HYPSIPYLE

OPHIDIAN ASP EEL SNAKE CONGER REPTILE SERPENT

OPHIR (FATHER OF —) JOKTAN

OPHITE CAINIAN CAINITE

OPHIUROID ARGUS SANDSTAR

OPHRAH (FATHER OF —) MEONOTHAI

OPHTHALMOLOGIST OCULIST

OPIATE DOPE DRUG HEMP DWALE OPIUM DEADEN ANODINE HYPNOTIC NARCOTIC SEDATIVE DORMITARY PAREGORIC SOPORIFIC

OPIFICER OPIFEX WORKMAN ARTIFICER

OPINE DEEM JUDGE THINK PONDER BELIEVE SUPPOSE OPINIATE

OPINION CRY EYE MOT BOOK DOXY FAME IDEA MIND VIEW WEEN DOGMA FANCY FUTWA GUESS HEART INPUT SENSE SIGHT TENET THINK VARDI VARDY VOICE ADVICE ASSENT BELIEF DEVICE DICTUM ESTEEM GROUND NOTION REPUTE SCHISM CENSURE CONCEIT CONCEPT CONSENT COUNSEL DIANOIA FEELING HOLDING MEASURE SEEMING THINKSO THOUGHT TROWING VERDICT DECISION DOCTRINE JUDGMENT SUFFRAGE PREJUDICE SENTIMENT PERSUASION
(COLLECTION OF —S) SYMPOSIUM
(EXAGGERATED —) BIGHEAD
(EXPRESSION OF —) VOTE
(FAVORABLE —) BROO ESTEEM
(MOHAMMEDAN —) FUTWA
(SET OF PROFESSED —S) CREDO
(UNORTHODOX —) HERESY
(WRONG —) CACODOXY
(PREF.) DOXO
(SUFF.) DOX(Y)

OPINIONATED DOGMATIC CONCEITED OBSTINATE PRAGMATIC

OPINIONATIVE ENTETE

O PIONEERS (AUTHOR OF —) CATHER
(CHARACTER IN —) LOU CARL EMIL IVAR FRANK MARIE OSCAR AMEDEE BERGSON SHABATA TOVESKY ALEXANDRA LINDSTRUM

OPIUM HOP MUD DOPE DRUG OPIE POST CHANDU CHANDOO MECONIUM TOXICANT
(— ALKALOID) CODEIN CODEINE MORPHINE NARCOTIN NARCOTINE PAPAVERIN
(— POPPY) NEPENTHE
(OF —) THEBAIC
(RESIDUE IN — PIPE) YENSHEE
(TINCTURE OF —) LAUDANUM
(PREF.) MECON(O) OPIO

OPIUMISM THEBAISM

OPOSSUM QUICA YAPOK POSSUM YAPOCK MARMOSE OYAPOCK SARIGUE VULPINE MARSUPIAL PHILANDER TACUACINE
(— SHRIMP) MYSID MYSOID
(FAMOUS —) POGO

OPPONENT FOE ANTI ENEMY PARTY RIVAL ALOGIAN NEMESIS OPPOSER ADVERSARY ASSAILANT
(— OF GOV CLINTON) BUCKTAIL
(— OF WAR) PEACENIK
(BOORISH —) BOEOTIAN
(FORMIDABLE —) TIGER
(IMAGINARY —) WINDMILL

OPPORTUNE FIT PAT HAPPY LUCKY READY TIMELY APROPOS FITTING TIMEFUL SUITABLE FAVORABLE

OPPORTUNELY TIMELY APROPOS HAPPILY

OPPORTUNIST CREEPER

OPPORTUNISTIC SHUFFLING

OPPORTUNITY GO MAY OPE SEL EASE HENT MEAN MINT ROOM SELE SHOT TIDE TIME SIGHT SLANT SPACE ACCESS CHANCE SEASON SQUEAK LEISURE OPENING RESPITE VANTAGE APPROACH FACILITY OCCASION ADVANTAGE
(— FOR ACTION) OPENING
(— OF ACTIVITY) SCOPE
(— TO PROCEED) WAY
(FAVORABLE —) SHOW TIME

OPPOSE PIT VIE WAR BUCK COPE DEFY FACE HEAD MEET NOSE STEM WARN WEAR ARGUE BLOCK CHECK CLASH CROSS FIGHT FRONT OCCUR REBEL REBUT REPEL BATTLE BREAST COMBAT DEFEND NAYSAY OBJECT OBTEND OPPUGN REPUGN RESIST THWART WITHER CONTEST COUNTER GAINSAY OBVIATE REVERSE WITHSET CONFLICT CONFRONT CONTRARY CONTRAST FRONTIER OBSTRUCT TRAVERSE ENCOUNTER WITHSTAND ANTAGONIZE
(— BY ARGUMENT) REBUT
(— ONE IN AUTHORITY) REBEL DEFORCE

OPPOSED ANTI ALIEN AVERSE ADVERSE AGAINST COUNTER HOSTILE CONTRARY ABHORRENT ANTARCTIC REPUGNANT
(PERSISTENTLY —) RENITENT

OPPOSER GAINSAYER

OPPOSING RENITENT RELUCTANT
(PREF.) COUNTER

OPPOSITE TO ANENT POLAR ACROSS ANENST AVERSE FACING WITHER ADVERSE COUNTER FORNENT INVERSE OBVIOUS REVERSE ANTIPODE CONTRARY CONTRAST CONVERSE ANTIPODAL REPUGNANT RECIPROCAL
(— MIDDLE OF SHIP'S SIDE) ABEAM
(— OF TRUTH) DEVIL
(— THE ALTAR) WEST
(— THE SUN) ANTISOLAR
(PREF.) ANTI ENANTIO
(DO THE —) DIS

OPPOSITION CON FLAK ATILT CLASH FLACK STOUR STATIC SYZYGY THWART DISCORD TENSION CLASHING CONTRAST DISTANCE OBSTACLE POLARITY ANIMOSITY COLLISION HOSTILITY RENITENCY
(— TO GOD) ANTITHEISM

(ELECTRICAL —) IMPEDANCE
(PREF.) **(IN —)** CONTRA
OPPRESS SIT HOLD LADE LOAD PEIS RACK RAPE RIDE SWAY THEW CROWD CRUSH GRIND GRIPE HEAVY PEISE POISE PRESS WEIGH WRONG BETOIL BURDEN DEFOIL DEFOUL EXTORT HARASS HARROW NIDDER NITHER RAVISH SUBDUE THREAT AFFLICT DEPRESS INGRATE OVERLAY REPRESS SQUEEZE TRAMPLE CONFRONT DISTRESS ENCUMBER PRESSURE SUPPRESS OVERPOWER OVERTHROW OVERWEIGH OVERWHELM
(— WITH DREAD) HAGRIDE
(— WITH HEAT) SWELTER
OPPRESSED SERVILE
OPPRESSION ROD GRIPE PRESS BURDEN THRALL MIZRAIM DULLNESS PRESSURE EXTORTION GRIEVANCE LASSITUDE
OPPRESSIVE HOT DIRE DOWY HARD CLOSE DOWIE FAINT HARSH HEAVY BITTER LEADEN SCREWY SEVERE SMUDGY SULTRY TORRID URGENT WEIGHT ONEROUS SLAVISH GRIEVOUS GRINDING RIGOROUS
OPPRESSIVELY STRAIT
OPPRESSIVENESS LANGUOR
OPPRESSOR CSAR CZAR NERO TSAR TZAR EGLON TYRANT INCUBUS
OPPROBRIUM ENVY ABUSE ODIUM SCORN SHAME INFAMY INSULT CALUMNY DISDAIN OFFENSE SCANDAL DISGRACE DISHONOR REPROACH CONTUMELY
OPS (ASSOCIATE OF —) CONSUS
(CONSORT OF —) SATURN
(DAUGHTER OF —) CERES
(FESTIVAL OF —) OPALIA
(PERSONIFICATION OF —) FAUNA TERRA TELLUS
OPT CULL PICK WISH ELECT CHOOSE DECIDE OPTATE SELECT
(— ABRUPTLY) PLUMP
OPTIC EYE OCULAR VISUAL
OPTICAL VISIBLE
(— APPARATUS) LENS GLASS ALIDAD ALIDADE OPTOMETER PERISCOPE TELESCOPE
(— DEVICE ON RIFLE) SNIPERSCOPE
OPTIMIST POLLYANNA UTOPIANIST
OPTIMISTIC GLAD ROSY SUNNY JOYOUS UPBEAT BULLISH HOPEFUL ROSEATE EUPEPTIC SANGUINE EXPECTANT
OPTION UP CALL DOWN CHOICE SPREAD REFUSAL STRADDLE PRIVILEGE
OPTIONAL ELECTIVE VOLUNTARY PERMISSIVE
OPULENCE LUXE
OPULENT FAT LUSH RICH WELI AMPLE FLUSH PLUSH SHOWY LAVISH MONEYED PROFUSE WEALTHY ABUNDANT AFFLUENT LUXURIANT PLENTIFUL SUMPTUOUS
OPUS WORK ETUDE STUDY
(OVERLABORED —) LUCUBRATION
OQUASSA QUASKY
OR NE ARE AUT ERE ORE GOLD OSSIA OTHER TOPAZ EITHER YELLOW
ORACHE SALTBUSH GREASEWOOD
ORACLE SEER TRIP SIBYL TRIPOD TRIPOS DIVINER AUTOPHONE
ORACULAR OTIC VATIC ORPHIC DELPHIC VATICAL DELPHIAN PYTHONIC PROPHETIC
ORAL ALOUD PAROL VOCAL BUCCAL PAROLE SONANT SPOKEN VERBAL UTTERED UNWRITTEN NONCUPATIVE
ORALE FANON
ORANGE KING MOCK CERES CHILE CHILI CHINO FLAME GENIP HEDGE JAFFA NAVEL OSAGE TENNE AURORA BODOCK BRAZIL COPPER MIKADO NAVAHO SUNTAN TEMPLE TITIAN UVALHA COWSLIP FLORIDA LEATHER MACLURA NARTJIE PAPRIKA PONCEAU PUMPKIN RANGPUR SEVILLE TANGELO TANGIER BERGAMOT BIGARADE CHINOTTI CLAYBANK FLAMINGO HONEYDEW JACINTHE MANDARIN MARATHON MOROCCAN POMANDER SUNBURST VALENCIA BUCCANEER CARNELIAN PERSIMMON TANGERINE
(— BLOSSOM INGREDIENT) GIN
(— GRASS) KNITWEED PINEWEED
(— HAWKWEED) FIREWEED HIERACIUM
(— MEMBRANE) ZEST
(— MILKWORT) CANDYWEED
(— PIECE) LITH SEGMENT
(— ROCKFISH) FLIOMA
(— SEED) PIP
(— TREE) SATSUMA
(BROWNISH —) SPICE
(LARGE —) KING
(MOCK —) SERINGA
(OSAGE —) HEDGE BODOCK
(SOUR —) CURACAO BIGARADE CHINOTTO
(SWEET —) CHINA CHINO
(YELLOW —) SAFFRON
ORANGEBIRD TANAGER
ORANGE HAWKWEED PAINTBRUSH
ORANGELEAF KARAMU
ORANGEMAN MARKSMAN
ORANGEWOOD OSAGE
ORANG LAUT BAJAU
ORANGUTAN APE MIAS ORANG PONGO SATYR SATIRE SATURY PRIMATE SALTIER SATYRUS WOODMAN WOODSMAN
ORAON KURUKH
ORARION STOLE
ORATE PLEAD SPEAK SPIEL SPOUT ADDRESS DECLAIM LECTURE BLOVIATE HARANGUE DISCOURSE SPEECHIFY
ORATION EULOGY HESPED SERMON ADDRESS CONCION HARANGUE SUASORIA OLYNTHIAC PANEGYRIC PHILIPPIC
(— OF CICERO) PHILIPPIC
(FUNERAL —) ELOGE ELOGY MONODY ELOGIUM ENCOMIUM
ORATOR RHETOR DEMAGOG SPEAKER STUMPER CICERONE BOANERGES DEMAGOGUE PLAINTIFF SPOKESMAN
ORATORICAL ELOQUENT RHETORICAL
ORATORIO ELIJAH RORATORIO
ORATORY CHAPEL SACRARY ORACULUM SPEAKING ELOCUTION ELOQUENCE PROSEUCHE
(EXAGGERATED —) RHETORIC
ORB EYE SUN BALL MOON STAR EARTH GLOBE MOUND ORBIT CIRCLE PLANET SPHERE CIRCUIT ENCLOSE ENCIRCLE SURROUND FIRMAMENT
ORBED LUNAR ROUND GLOBATE
ORBIT AUGE PATH APSIS CYCLE TRACK CIRCLE SOCKET SPHERE CIRCUIT ELLIPSE EYEHOLE ECCENTRIC
(POINT IN —) APSIS APOGEE EPIGEE SYZYGY PERIGEE
ORC OGRE ORCA GIANT WHALE GRAMPUS
ORCHARD HOLT TOPE ARBOR GROVE ARBOUR GARDEN HUERTA OLIVET VERGER ARBUSTUM FRUITERY PEACHERY POMARIUM SUGARBUSH
(— GRASS) DOGFOOT COCKSFOOT
ORCHESTRA BAND GROUP CHAPEL CAPELLE CONSORT GAMELAN KAPELLE ENSEMBLE GAMELANG SYMPHONY SINFONIETTA PHILHARMONIC
(— BELLS) GLOCKENSPIEL
(— CIRCLE) PARQUET PARTERRE
(SECTION OF —) BRASS WINDS WOODS STRINGS WOODWINDS PERCUSSION
ORCHESTRATE SCORE ARRANGE COMPOSE
ORCHESTRION HARMONICON APOLLONICON
ORCHID FAAM FAHAM PETAL VANDA CYMBID DUFOIL LAELIA PURPLE AERIDES ANGULOA BOATLIP CALYPSO CULLION FLYWORT LYCASTE POGONIA VANILLA ARETHUSA CALANTHE DENDROBE GYNANDER LABELLUM ONCIDIUM RAMSHEAD SATYRION CORALROOT HABENARIA PUTTYROOT TWAYBLADE SNAKEMOUTH
(KIND OF —) VANDA
ORCHIS CROWTOE CROWFOOT CRAKEFEET
ORDAIN LAW PUT DEEM DOOM LOOK MAKE SEND WILL WITE ALLOT ENACT JAPAN ORDER SHAPE WIELD WRITE DECREE PRIEST ADJUDGE APPOINT ARRANGE BEHIGHT COMMAND DESTINE DICTATE FORTUNE INSTALL PREPARE PRESCRIBE
ORDEAL FIRE GAFF TEST AGONY TRIAL CALVARY GAUNTLET
(— TREE) AKAZGA TANGHIN TANGUIN
ORDEAL OF RICHARD FEVEREL
(AUTHOR OF —) MEREDITH
(CHARACTER IN —) TOM LUCY BERRY CLARE MOUNT ADRIAN AUSTIN BLAIZE CAROLA HARLEY RIPTON FEVEREL RICHARD BAKEWELL THOMPSON GRANDISON DESBOROUGH MONTFALCON
ORDER BAN BID ILK RAY SAY TAX BOON CALL CASE CHIT FIAT FORM ORDO RANK RULE SAND SECT STOP SUIT TELL TIFF TRIM WILL WORD ALIGN ARRAY CHIME CLASS DIGHT EDICT GENUS GRADE GUIDE HAVOC PRESS QUIET RANGE SHIFT STATE TAXIS WHACK ASSIGN AVAUNT BEHEST BILLET CEDULA CHARGE COSMOS CURFEW DECREE DEGREE DEMAND DIKTAT DIRECT ENJOIN FIRMAN FOLLOW GRAITH HOOKUM INDENT KILTER MANAGE METHOD NATURE ORDAIN POLICE POTENT SERIES SETTLE SYNTAX SYSTEM ADJUDGE ARRANGE BESPEAK BIDDING BOOKING COMMAND COMPOSE DISPOSE EMBARGO FLOATER MANDATE PRECEPT PROCESS SOCIETY CATEGORY KODASHIM METHODIZE ORDINANCE PRESCRIBE
(— BACK) REMAND
(— OF ANGELS) CHOIR QUIRE MIGHTS THRONES DOMINIONS PRINCIPALITIES
(— OF BATTLE) BATTALIA
(— OF BELLS) CHANGE
(— OF COURT) SIST VACATUR
(— OF CRUSTACEANS) ISOPODA
(— OFF) TURN
(— OF HOLY BEINGS) HIERARCHY
(— OF SUCCESSION) SEQUENCE
(— OF WORSHIP) AGODUM
(— TOBACCO LEAF) CASE
(— TO LEVY MONEY) PRECEPT
(— TO RETURN) RECALL
(CIVIL —) EUNOMY
(COSMIC —) TAO RITA
(GOOD —) EUTAXY
(IN —) SOAS
(KIND OF —) GAG
(KNIGHTHOOD —) DANNEBROG
(LACKING —) AMISS MESSY MUSSY ROUGH CHAOTIC UNKEMPT CONFUSED
(LEGAL —) SIST STET WRIT DAYWRIT SUMMONS SENTENCE SUBPOENA
(LOWER — OF MAN) ALALUS
(MARCHING —S) ROUTE
(MINOR CHURCH —) BENET
(MONASTIC —) SAMGHA SANGHA ACOEMETI
(PROPER —) TRAIN
(RECURRENT —) ROTATION
(TAKE —S) WAITRESS
(TRAIN —) FLIMSY
(TURKISH —) MEDJIDIE
(UNIVERSAL —) KIND
(WRITTEN —) CHECK DRAFT BILLET DRAUGHT
(PREF.) **(REVERSE —)** OB

(SUFF.) TACTIC TAXIS TAXY
(— OF ANIMALS) INI
ORDERED BANDBOX BESPOKE REGULAR SCRAPED COHERENT
(WELL —) TRIM
ORDERLINESS METHOD SYSTEM CLARITY DECORUM
ORDERLY AIDE DULY NEAT PEON RULY SNOD TIDY TRIM CRISP SOWAR SUWAR BATMAN BURSCH COSMIC FORMAL MODEST ORDENE GRADELY REGULAR SHAPELY DECOROUS GALLOPER GRAITHLY OBEDIENT PEACEABLE SHIPSHAPE
ORDINANCE LAW DOOM FIAT RITE BYLAW EDICT ASSIZE DECREE RECESS CONTROL MANDATE SETNESS STATUTE WORKING DECRETUM JUDICIAL REGIMENT TAKKANAH DIRECTION
ORDINANT DIHELY DIHELIOS DIHELIUM
ORDINARY LAY LOW SOS BEND FESS LALA MEAN PALE PALL RUCK BANAL CHIEF CROSS NOMIC PLAIN PROSE USUAL CANTON COMMON FILLET FLANCH MODERN NORMAL PAIRLE SIMPLE VULGAR AVERAGE MUNDANE NATURAL PROSAIC ROUTINE SALTIRE SAUTIER TRIVIAL VANILLA VULGATE EVERYDAY FAMILIAR HABITUAL MEDIOCRE MIDDLING PLEBEIAN RUMTYTOO WORKADAY QUOTIDIAN SHAKEFORK
ORDINATE ORDER ORDAIN APPOINT ORDERLY REGULAR MODERATE TEMPERATE
ORDNANCE LAW ARMS GUNS ARMOR ORGUE FALCON MINION PETARD PEDRERO RABINET SERPENT WEAPONS BASILISK PETERERO ARTILLERY
ORDO ORDER ALMANAC DIRECTORY
ORDURE
(PREF.) SCAT(O) SCORI
ORE (ALSO SEE MINERAL) TIN CHAT DISH DRAG FELL GOLD IRON LEAD MINE POST PULP ROCK CRAZE CRUDE FAVOR GLORY GRACE HONOR MANTO MERCY METAL PRILL COPPER CUPRITE FLOATER RESPECT SEAWEED SMEDDUM URANITE CLEMENCY KNOCKING CARBONATE REVERENCE
(— CRUSHER) DOLLY
(— DEPOSIT) LODE SCRIN BONANZA
(— LAYER) SEAM STOPE
(— LOADING PLATFORM) PLAT
(— MASS) SQUAT
(— NOT DRESSED) WORK
(— WITH STONE ADHERING) CHAT CHATS
(BEST —) CROP
(BROKEN —) DIRT
(CONCENTRATED —) MIDDLINGS
(COPPER —) BORNITE HORNITE ATACAMITE MALACHITE
(CRUDE —) HEADS
(CRUSHED —) PULP SCHLICH
(CUBE —) SIDERITE
(EARTHY-LOOKING —) PACO
(HORSEFLESH —) BORNITE
(IMPURE —) SPEISS HALVANS
(IRON —) OCHER OCHRE MINION IRONMAN LIMNITE MINETTE OLIGIST TURGITE HEMATITE LIMONITE SIDERITE TACONITE BLACKBAND JACUTINGA
(LEAD —) BOOZE GALENA ARQUIFOUX
(LUMP OF —) HARDHEAD
(MANGANESE —) WAD WADD
(MERCURY —) GRANZA CINNABAR
(SOLID —) RIB
(TIN —) ROWS CRAZE SCOVE WHITS FLORAN TINSTUFF
(URANIUM —) COFFINITE
(WORTHLESS —) SLAG DROSS MATTE
(ZINC —) SMITHSONITE
OREAD PERI NYMPH

OREGON
CAPITAL: SALEM
COLLEGE: REED PACIFIC LINFIELD PORTLAND WILLAMETTE
COUNTY: LINN CROOK CURRY WASCO CLATSOP KLAMATH MALHEUR WALLOWA YAMHILL UMATILLA
INDIAN: ALSEA MODOC WASCO CAYUSE CHETCO KUITSH TENINO KLAMATH TAKELMA YAQUINA
LAKE: ABERT WALDO CRATER HARNEY MCNARY KLAMATH MALHEUR
MOUNTAIN: HOOD WALKER WILSON ELKHORN GRIZZLY JACKASS RAINIER TIDBITS
MOUNTAIN RANGE: BLUE COAST CASCADE
RIVER: ROGUE IMNAHA OWYHEE POWDER UMPQUA BLITZEN KLAMATH SILVIES COLUMBIA DESCHUTES
STATE BIRD: MEADOWLARK
STATE FLOWER: GRAPE
STATE NICKNAME: BEAVER SUNSET WEBFOOT VALENTINE
STATE TREE: FIR
TOWN: BEND MORO VALE NYSSA CONDON EUGENE FOSSIL MADRAS ASTORIA HEPPNER COQUILLE PORTLAND CORVALLIS

OREGON TRAIL (AUTHOR OF —) PARKMAN
(CHARACTER IN —) SHAW HENRY QUINCY FRANCIS PARKMAN CHATILLON DESLAURIERS
OREN (FATHER OF —) JERAHMEEL
ORE-PRODUCING QUICK
ORESTES (COMPANION OF —) PYLADES
(FATHER OF —) AGAMEMNON
(FRIEND OF —) PYLADES
(MOTHER OF —) CLYTEMNESTRA
(SISTER OF —) ELECTRA IPHIGENIA
(WIFE OF —) HERMIONE
ORGAN CUP GILL LIMB PART CHELA FLOAT GREAT HEART MEANS PAPER REGAL SERRA ELATER FEEDER FEELER HAPTOR MEDIUM SPLEEN SUCKER CLASPER CONSOLE JOURNAL ARMATURE EFFECTOR ISOGRAFT MAGAZINE MELODEON MELODICA MYCETOME OOGONIUM EQUIPMENT HARMONIUM NEWSPAPER PORTATIVE
(— GALLERY) LOFT
(— OF HEARING) EAR
(— OF SCORPION) PECTEN
(— OF SENSE) SENSE SENSORY
(— OF SIGHT) EYE
(— OF SILKWORM) FILATOR
(— OF SPIDER) CRIBELLUM SPINNERET
(— OF TOUCH) TACTOR TACTUS
(— PIPE) REED FLUTE SCHWEGEL
(— STOP) ECHO HARP OBOE SEXT TUBA VIOL ACUTA DOLCE FLUTE GAMBA ORAGE QUINT TENTH VIOLA BIFARA CURTAL CYMBAL DECIMA DULCET FUGARA GEDACT NASARD OCTAVE SCHARF TIERCE TROMBA BASSOON BOMBARD BOURDON CELESTE CLARION CREMONA DOLCIAN DOUBLET DULCIAN FAGOTTO GEDECKT MELODIA PICCOLO POSAUNE SERPENT TERTIAN TRUMPET TWELFTH VIOLINA BOMBARDE CARILLON CLARINET DIAPASON DIAPHONE DULCIANA GEMSHORN REGISTER TENOROON TROMBONE WALDHORN BOMBARDON CORNOPEAN DOUBLETTE HARMONICA PRINCIPAL SAXOPHONE CLARABELLA
(— VIBRATO) TREMOLO
(ADHESIVE —) SUCKER
(BRISTLELIKE —) SETA
(CHINESE —) SANG CHENG
(CIRCUS —) CALLIOPE
(HAND —) SERINETTE
(INTROMITTENT —) VERGE
(KIND OF —) REED
(OLFACTORY —) NOSE
(PLANT'S —) HOLDFAST
(PORTABLE —) REGAL
(RESPIRATORY —) LUNG
(SMALL —) REGAL
(STINGING —) NEMATOCYST
(SWIMMING —) OAR CTENE
(VOCAL — OF BIRDS) SYRINX
(WASTE —) KIDNEY
(PREF.) **(INTERNAL —)** VISCER(I)(O)
ORGANELLE LYSOSOME
ORGANIC VITAL INBORN NATURAL INHERENT
ORGANISM WOG BODY ECAD GERM GUEST PLANT AEROBE ANIMAL EMBRYO SYSTEM DIPLONT DISEASE MACHINE PLANONT SUSCEPT HEMAMEBA PATHOGEN PLANKTER MESOPHILE POLYMORPH
(— CHARACTERISTIC) MIXIS
(COLD-BLOODED —) POIKILOTHERM
(COMPOUND —) STOCK
(FOSSIL —) EOZOON
(MINUTE —) AMEBA MONAD SPORE
(MODIFIED —) ECAD
(PELAGIC —S) NEKTON
(POLITICAL —) LEVIATHAN
(SIMPLE —) MONAD
(SMALL AIRBORNE —S) AEROPLANKTON
(PL.) BENTHON BENTHOS HAYSEED NEUSTON PLEUSTON
(PREF.) BIO ONT(O)
(SUFF.) ACEAN ONT PHORA
(SIMPLE —) MONAS
ORGANIZATION ART BIG ITO CLUB FIRM KLAN CADRE FIDAC FORUM HOUSE MAFIA SETUP AUMAGA CHURCH OUTFIT SURVEY SYSTEM CHARITY COMPANY CONCERN DEMOLAY ECONOMY GIDEONS MENORAH SOCIETY CONGRESS PATRONAGE STRUCTURE
(— OF ACTORS) COMPANY
(— OF DEALERS) AUCTION
(— OF EXPERIENCE) SCHEMA
(— WITH MANY BRANCHES) OCTOPUS
(ARMY —) LANDSTORM
(AUXILIARY —) AID SYNODICAL
(COLLEGE —) FRAT ALUMNA ALUMNI ALUMNUS SORORITY
(COMMUNIST —) COMECON
(HARMONIOUS —) ORCHESTRATION
(HEALTH —) HMO
(JEWISH —) ITO MENORAH
(MARDI GRAS —) KREWE
(MUSICAL —) BAND COMBO CAPELLE KAPELLE ENSEMBLE ORCHESTRA
(POLICE —) GESTAPO
(POLITICAL —) PARTY VEREIN HETAERIA HETAIRIA APPARATUS
(SAMOAN —) AUMAGA
(SECRET —) WOW BPOE ELKS MOOSE MASONS MIDEWIN
(SOCIAL —) POLICE
(WAR VETERANS —) AVC DAV GAR SAR VFW FIDAC AMVETS
(WOMEN'S —) DAR WAF WRC WCTU SORORITY
(YOUTH —) KOMSOMOL
ORGANIZE FORM EDIFY FOUND MODEL ORDER RALLY DESIGN EMBODY ARRANGE MODULIZE REGIMENT UNIONIZE BLUEPRINT INSTITUTE INTEGRATE STRUCTURE COORDINATE
ORGANIZED FORMED ORGANIC TOGETHER
(BADLY —) INCONDITE
ORGANIZER PROMOTER
ORGANZA GAZAR
ORGIASTIC BACCHIC SATURNALIAN
ORGY LARK RITE ROMP BINGE REVEL SPREE FROLIC SHINDY REVELRY WASSAIL CAROUSAL CEREMONY SATURNALIA
(PL.) ORGIACS DEBAUCHERIES
ORIANA (FATHER OF —) LISUARTE
(HUSBAND OF —) MIRABEL
(LOVER OF —) AMADIS
ORIBI OUREBI ANTELOPE BLEEKBOK PALEBUCK
ORIEL BAY CHAPEL DORMER RECESS WINDOW BALCONY GALLERY MIRADOR PORTICO CORRIDOR
ORIENT DAWN EAST ADAPT BUILD PEARL PLACE SHEEN ADJUST

LEVANT LOCATE LUSTER RISING GLOWING INCLINE RADIANT SUNRISE LUSTROUS SPARKLING
ORIENTAL ASIAN PEARL BRIGHT INDIAN ORTIVE RISING EASTERN SHINING INDOGEAN LUSTROUS PELLUCID PRECIOUS BRILLIANT LEVANTINE
ORIENTATION ASPECT PHORIA STRIKE COLORING LOCALITY
ORIFICE BUNG HOLE PORE PORT VENT INLET MOUTH STOMA TREMA BLOWER CAVITY OUTLET RICTUS SIPHON THROAT CHIMNEY EARHOLE FORAMEN OPENING OSCULUM OSTIOLE APERTURE FUMAROLE INTROITUS
(— IN VOLCANIC REGION) FUMAROLE
(— OF INFUNDIBULUM) LURA
(BREATHING —) SPIRACLE
(VOLCANIC —) BLOWER
(PREF.) TREMATO
(— OF STOMACH) PYLOR(O)
(SUFF.) PYL(E) TREMA(TA)
ORIGANUM ORGANY MARJORAM ORGAMENT
ORIGILLE (FATHER OF —) MONODANTE
(LOVER OF —) GRIFONE
(SISTER OF —) BRANDIMARTE
ORIGIN NEE GERM KIND RISE ROOT SEED BIRTH CAUSE RADIX START STOCK FATHER GROWTH NATURE PARENT SOURCE SPRING EDITION GENESIS LINEAGE UPSTART NASCENCE UPSPRING BEGINNING INCEPTION OFFSPRING PARENTAGE PROVENANCE
(— ON EARTH) EPIGENE
(FOREIGN —) ECDEMIC
(POINT OF —) POLE
(PREF.) **(ANCIENT —)** PALAE(O) PALAI(O) PALE(O)
(SUFF.) GENY
ORIGINAL NEW HOME SEED FIRST FRESH NOVEL PRIME STOCK FONTAL MASTER MOTHER NATIVE PRIMAL PRIMER SAMPLE PIONEER PRIMARY RADICAL SEMINAL CREATION NASCENCY PRISTINE AUTHENTIC AUTOGRAPH BEGINNING INVENTIVE OFFSPRING PRIMITIVE
(NOT —) DERIVED
(PREF.) ARCH(AE)(AEO)(E)(EO)(I)
ORIGINALITY INGENUITY
ORIGINATE COIN COME DATE GROW HEAD MAKE MOVE OPEN REAR RISE SIRE ARISE BEGIN BIRTH BREED CAUSE ENDOW FOUND HATCH RAISE START AUTHOR CREATE DERIVE DESIGN DEVISE FATHER INVENT PARENT SPRING CAUSATE DESCEND EMANATE PIONEER PROCEED PRODUCE COMMENCE CONCEIVE CONTRIVE DISCOVER GENERATE INITIATE INSTITUTE
ORIGINATION MAKING DESCENT GENESIS BREEDING ORIGINAL COSMOGONY ETYMOLOGY
ORIGINATOR AUTHOR FATHER CREATOR INVENTOR GENERATOR PROGENITOR
ORIOLE PIROL BUNYAH LARIOT LORIOT CACIQUE FIGBIRD PEABIRD FIREBIRD GOLDBIRD HANGBIRD HANGNEST TROUPIAL
ORION RIGEL ALGEBAR
(BELT OF —) ELLWAND
(FATHER OF —) HYRIEUS POSEIDON
(GUIDE OF —) CEDALION
(HOUND OF —) ARATUS
(SLAYER OF —) ARTEMIS
ORITHYIA (DAUGHTER OF —) CHIONE CLEOPATRA
(FATHER OF —) ERECHTHEUS
(MOTHER OF —) PRAXITHEA
(SON OF —) ZETES CALAIS
ORKNEY ISLANDS (CAPITAL OF —) KIRKWALL
(ISLAND OF —) HOY POMONA ROUSAY SANDAY STRONSAY
ORLANDO (BELOVED OF —) ROSALIND
ORLE ORLET BORDER FILLET WREATH BEARING CHAPLET TRESSURE
ORLOP DECK ARLOUP
ORMENUS (FATHER OF —) CERCAPHUS
(SON OF —) AMYNTOR
ORMER ABALONE
ORMOLU GILT GOLD ALLOY BRASS VARNISH
ORNAMENT BOB DUB FLY FOB GAY JOY PIN POT TAG TEE TOY URN BALL BOSS CURL CUSP DICE ETCH FALL FRET FROG GAUD GEAR HUSK KNOP LEAF NULL OUCH RULE STAR TOOL TRIM WALY WING ADORN BRAID BULLA CHASE CROSS CROWN DECOR EXORN FUSEE GRACE GUTTA HELIX HONOR INLAY KNOSP LUNET MENSK MENSO OVOID PATCH POPPY PRUNT SPANG SPRAY SPRIG STALK TRAIL TRICK WALLY AMULET ANKLET ATTIRE BEDAUB BEDECK BILLET BRANCH BROOCH BUTTON CIMIER COLLAR DIAPER DOODAD EDGING EMBOSS ENRICH FALLAL FINERY FLORET FLOWER GORGET INSERT LABRET LUNULA NIELLO OFFSET PAMPRE PARURE PATERA ROCOCO ROSACE RUNTEE SETOFF TABLET TAHALI TEMPLE TIRADE AGREMEN AKROTER AMALAKA BIBELOT BUCRANE CIRCLET COCARDE CORBEIL CROCKET DIGLYPH EARPLUG ECHINUS EMBLEMA ENGRAVE ENHANCE FRIGGER FURNISH GADROON GARNISH NETSUKE RINCEAU ROSETTE SEXFOIL STRIGIL TORSADE TREFOIL TRINKET ACCOLADE ANAGLYPH APPLIQUE BRELOQUE DECORATE FLOURISH GIMCRACK LAVALIER MORESQUE NOSERING PALMETTE ROCAILLE SUNBURST SWASTIKA POPPYHEAD
(— FOR HEAD) MIND TARGET
(— ON CHAIR) SPLAT
(— ON GLASS) PRUNT
(— ON SHIP) BADGE APLUSTRE
(ARCHITECTURAL —) GUTTA
(CHILD'S —) GAY
(CLAW-LIKE —) GRIFFE
(CRYSTAL —) SPAR
(DRESS —) FROG LACE JABOT SEQUIN SPANGLE
(EXTRAVAGANT —) GROTESQUE
(FANTASTIC —) ANTIC
(GLITTERING —) SPANG
(HAIR —) POMPOM TETTIX
(HEAD —) TIARA TEMPLE
(HORSE COLLAR —) HOUNCE
(JAPANESE —) NETSUKE
(JEWELRY —) RONDEL
(LIP —) LABRET
(MATCHING SET OF —S) PARURE
(MUSICAL —) TURN MORDENT BACKFALL PRALLTRILLER
(PENDANT —) BOB BULLA ANADEM BANGLE TASSEL EARRING LAVALIER
(ROCK-CRYSTAL —) ALMOND
(ROOF —) ANTEFIX
(ROOFING —) ANTEFIX
(SCROLL—) ROCAILLE
(SHIP-SHAPED —) NEF
(SHOULDER —) EPAULET
(SPIRAL —) SCROLL
(STOCKING —) CLOCK
(SUPERFLUOUS —) FRILL FURBELOW
(TAWDRY —) GINGERBREAD
(PL.) FIGGERY KNAVERY AGREMENS
ORNAMENTAL FANCY CHICHI FRILLY LILYTURF BLUEBEARD NASTURTIUM SEMPERVIVUM
ORNAMENTATION BOSS FOIL ACORN DECOR ADORNO BABERY CHICHI CILERY DICING BARBOLA CUSPING ECHELLE LACWORK STYLING ACANTHUS APPLIQUE FROUFROU HEADWORK PURFLING ROCAILLE STAFFAGE TRESSURE
(CHEAP —) TINSEL
(EXTRAVAGANT —) ROCOCO
(MUSICAL —) GRUPPO GRUPPETTO SCHLEIFER
ORNAMENTED FIGURY FOILED ORNATE TAWDRY ADORNED FLOUNCY FROSTED TREFLEE WROUGHT GOFFERED SINNOWED ELABORATE STELLATED
ORNAMNET (NECK —) GORGET
(WATCHCHAIN —) BRELOQUE
ORNATE GAY FINE FANCY FUSSY GIDDY SHOWY DRESSY FLORID FLOSSY PURPLE SUPERB AUREATE BAROQUE FLOWERY TAFFETA MANDARIN OVERRIPE SPLENDID ELABORATE UNNATURAL
(EXTREMELY —) GIDDY
ORNERY CONTRARY
ORNITHOLOGIST AUDUBON BIRDMAN
AMERICAN CORY OBER ARBIB BEEBE COUES MINER STONE BAILEY BREWER BUTLER CASSIN KEELER MILLER STROUD TORREY WILSON XANTUS AUDUBON BRASHER CHAPMAN FORBUSH FUERTES HENSHAW NUTTALL RIDGWAY SHUFELDT TOWNSEND
CANADIAN NASH
ENGLISH DIXON GOULD CLARKE LATHAM SHARPE HOSKING KIRKMAN
FRENCH LEVAILLANT
GERMAN NAUMANN REICHENOW KLEINSCHMIDT
INDIAN ALI
NEW ZEALAND BULLER
OROMO GALLA
OROONOKO (WIFE OF —) IMOINDA
OROTUND FULL CLEAR SHOWY MELLOW STRONG POMPOUS RESONANT SONOROUS BOMBASTIC
ORP FRET WEEP
ORPAH (HUSBAND OF —) CHILION
(SISTER-IN-LAW OF —) RUTH
ORPHAN PIP WAIF WARD FOUNDLING STEPCHILD
ORPHANED ORBATE
ORPHEUS (BIRTHPLACE OF —) PIERIA
(FATHER OF —) APOLLO OEAGRUS
(MOTHER OF —) CALLIOPE
(WIFE OF —) EURYDICE
ORPHREY BAND BORDER
ORPIMENT ORPIN HARTAL SPIRIT ARSENIC HARTAIL ZARNICH
ORPINE SEDUM LIVELONG BAGLEAVES EVERGREEN
ORRA ODD IDLE ORROW WORTHLESS
ORRIS GIMP IRIS LACE BRAID ORRICE GALLOON
ORSINO (WIFE OF —) VIOLA
ORT BIT END TAG CRUMB SCRAP MORSEL REFUSE TRIFLE LEAVING REMNANT FRAGMENT LEFTOVER
ORTHOCLASE ADULARIA AMAZONITE
ORTHODOX GOOD GREEK SOUND USUAL PROPER CANONIC CORRECT ACCEPTED CATHOLIC STANDARD CUSTOMARY
ORTHODOXY PIETY TRUTH SOUNDNESS
ORTHOGRAPHY WRITING
ORTHOPTERON WALKER
ORTNIT (BROTHER OF —) WOLFDIETRICH
ORTOLAN BIRD RAIL SORA BUNTING BOBOLINK WHEATEAR
ORTSTEIN HARDPAN
ORYX BEISA PASANG PASENG GAZELLE GEMSBOK ANTELOPE LEUCORYX
OS BONE ESKAR ESKER MOUTH OPENING ORIFICE
OSAGE ORANGE HEDGE OSAGE BODOCK BOWWOOD
OSCILLATE LOG WAG HUNT ROCK SWAY VARY SQUEG SWING WAVER WEAVE SHIMMY FEATHER VIBRATE FLUCTUATE
OSCILLATION HOWL WAVE SHOCK SEICHE SHIMMY SQUEAL FLUTTER LIBRATION VIBRATION
(— OF EARTH'S AXIS) NUTATION
(SUDDEN —) SURGE
OSCULATE BUSS KISS
OSCULATION TACNODE
OSCULATORY PAX

OSIER ROD WAND EDDER SALIX SKEIN SPLIT WITHY BASKET SALLOW WICKER WILLOW DOGWOOD WILGERS REDBRUSH
(— CAGE) TUMBREL
(— WILLOW) TWIGWITHY
OSIRIS HERSHEF UNNEFER
(BROTHER OF —) SET SETH
(CROWN OF —) ATEF
(FATHER OF —) GEB KEB SEB
(MOTHER OF —) NUT
(SISTER OF —) ISIS
(SON OF —) HORUS ANUBIS
(WIFE OF —) ISIS
OSMANLI TURK TURKISH
OSPREY GLED HAWK OSSI GLEDE PYGARG BALBUSARD OSSIFRAGE
OSSATURE SKELETON OSSEMENTS
OSSE DARE ATTEMPT PRESAGE PROMISE VENTURE PROPHESY RECOMMEND UTTERANCE
OSSEOUS BONE BONY SPINY LITHIC OSTEAL
OSSIAN (FATHER OF —) FINN
OSSICLE BONE INCUS ADORAL STAPES ALVEOLE BONELET MALLEUS SCUTELLA
OSSIFICATION OSTOSIS UROSTEON METOSTEON SIDEBONES
OSSIFIED SCLEROUS
OSSUARY URN TOMB GRAVE VAULT OSSARIUM
OSTEND SHOW REVEAL EXHIBIT MANIFEST
OSTENSIBLE NOMINAL SEEMING APPARENT SPECIOUS
OSTENT AIR MIEN SIGN TOKEN DISPLAY PORTENT
OSTENTATION DOG POMP PUFF SHOW CLASS ECLAT FLARE GLITZ PRIDE STRUT SWANK VAUNT PARADE VANITY DISPLAY FLUTTER PAGEANT PORTENT PRESAGE FLOURISH FRIPPERY PRETENCE PRETENSE SHOWINESS SPECTACLE
OSTENTATIOUS ARTY LOUD VAIN GAUDY SHOWY SWANK FLASHY SPORTY SWANKY TURGID FLAUNTY GLARING OBVIOUS POMPOUS SPLASHY SPLURGY FASTUOUS ELABORATE
OSTERIA INN TAVERN
OSTIOLE PORE MOUTH STOMA OPENING ORIFICE APERTURE
OSTRACISM TABU TABOO PETALISM
OSTRACIZE BAN BAR CUT SNUB EXILE BANISH PUNISH REJECT ABOLISH BOYCOTT CENSURE EXCLUDE BLACKBALL PROSCRIBE
OSTRACON SHELL FRAGMENT POTSHERD
OSTRICH EMU RHEA NANDU BREVIPEN STRUCION
(— FEATHER) BOO
(JERKED —) BILTONG
(PREF.) STRUTHI(O)(ONI)
OSTYAK KHANTY
OSWALD (FATHER OF —) ETHELFRITH
(SLAYER OF —) PENDA
OSWEGO TEA BALM

OTAHEITE TAHITI
(— APPLE) HEVI MACUPA MACUPI
OTALGIA EARACHE
OTARIOID SEAL SEALION
OTHELLO MOOR
(AUTHOR OF —) SHAKESPEARE
(CHARACTER IN —) IAGO BIANCA CASSIO EMILIA MONTANO OTHELLO GRATIANO LODOVICO RODERICO BRABANTIO DESDEMONA
(ENSIGN OF —) IAGO
(FRIEND OF —) IAGO
(LIEUTENANT OF —) CASSIO
(WIFE OF —) DESDEMONA
OTHER HE MO HER HIM ELSE MORE OTRA ALTER FORMER NOTHER SECOND TIDDER TOTHER ALTERUM FURTHER DISTINCT DIFFERENT
(— THAN) SAVE
(PL.) LAVE REST LUTRA
(PREF.) ALL(O) HETER(O)
OTHERNESS ALTERITY
OTHERS THEM THEY
OTHERWISE OR NOT ELSE ENSE ALIAS SECUS ALITER EXCEPT BESIDES ELSEHOW ELSEWAYS
OTHERWORDLY FEY SPACY
OTHERWORLDLY EERIE
OTHNI (BROTHER OF —) CALEB
(FATHER OF —) KENAZ SHEMAIAH
(WIFE OF —) ACHSAH
OTIC AURAL AUDITORY ORACULAR AURICULAR
OTIONIA (FATHER OF —) ERECHTHEUS
(MOTHER OF —) PRAXITHEA
(SISTER OF —) PANDORA PROTOGONIA
OTIOSE IDLE LAZY VAIN ALOOF FUTILE OTIANT REMOTE STERILE USELESS INACTIVE INDOLENT REPOSING
OTOLITH SAGITTA LAPILLUS OTOSTEON
OTOLOGIST AURIST
OTTAVINO PICCOLO
OTTER DOG FUR PUP FISH NAIR PELT BITCH HURON LOUTRE SIMUNG TACKLE ANNATTO PERIQUE MAMPALON MUSTELIN PARAVANE
(— TAIL) POLE
(DEN OF — S) HOLT
(SEA —) KALAN
OTTOMAN (ALSO SEE TURKEY) POUF SEAT SOFA TURK COUCH DIVAN SQUAB STOOL FABRIC OTHMAN POUFFE SULTANE FOOTSTOOL
(— COURT) PORTE
(— GOVERNOR) PASHA
(— LEADER) OSMAN
(— PROVINCE) VILAYET
(— STANDARD) ALEM
(— SUBJECT) RAIA RAYAH
OUABE HOGNUT
OUAKARI ACARI UKARI MONKEY UAKARI
OUBLIETTE DUNGEON
OUCH OH OW ADORN BEZEL CLASP JEWEL NOUCH BROOCH FIBULA NOUCHE BRACELET NECKLACE ORNAMENT

OUGHT BIT BUD BUT MOW BOOD BOOT MOTE MUST ZERO SHALL BELONG CIPHER NAUGHT NOUGHT SHOULD BEHOOVE
OUISTITI WISTITI MARMOSET
OUNCE URE OKET OKIA ONCA ONCE ONZA OKIEH UNCIA CHEETAH LEOPARD WILDCAT
(CHINESE —) LIANG
(EIGHT —S) CUPFUL
(HALF —) SEMUNCIA
(ONE-16TH OF —) DRAM
(ONE-20TH OF —) EASTERLING
(ONE-8TH OF —) DRAM
OUPHE ELF OOF OUF GOBLIN
OUR UR ORE URE WER WIR HORE NOTRE UNSER
(— LORD) NS
(— SAVIOR) NSIC
(PREF.) NOSTRI
OURICURY LICURI LICURY CABECUDO
OUR MUTUAL FRIEND (AUTHOR OF —) DICKENS
(CHARACTER IN —) JOHN WEGG WREN BELLA BETTY FANNY HEXAM JENNY JESSE SILAS BOFFIN EUGENE HARMON HIDGEN JULIUS LIZZIE WILFER BRADLEY CHARLEY CLEAVER HANDFORD WRAYBURN HEADSTONE HENRIETTA NICODEMUS ROKESMITH
OURSELVES USSELF USSELS USSELVEN
OUR TOWN (AUTHOR OF —) WILDER
(CHARACTER IN —) JOE WEBB EMILY GIBBS HOWIE SIMON WALLY GEORGE CROWELL NEWSOME REBECCA STIMSON GORUSLOWSKI
OUSIA NATURE ESSENCE SUBSTANCE
OUST BAR BUMP FIRE SACK CHUCK EJECT EVICT EXPEL BANISH DEBOUT REMOVE CASHIER DISCARD DISMISS SUSPEND DISSEIZE FORJUDGE ELIMINATE
OUSTING AMOTION
OUT EX AWAY DOWN HORS DATED FORTH ABSENT BEGONE ISSUED OOTWITH OUTWARD EXTERNAL PUBLISHED
(— AT ELBOWS) SCRUFFY
(— LOUD) BOST
(— OF) EX FROM DEHORS OUTWITH
(— OF BREATH) BLOWN
(— OF COMMISSION) BUNG
(— OF DATE) OLD DOWDY PASSE OUTWORN TIMEWORN OVERDATED
(— OF DOORS) ABROAD FOREIGN THEREOUT
(— OF EXISTENCE) AWAY
(— OF KILTER) ALOP AWRY CRANK BROKEN
(— OF ONE'S MIND) FEY DAFT DELEERIT
(— OF ORDER) AMISS KAPUT FAULTY DEFICIENT
(— OF PLACE) AMISS INEPT
(— OF PLAY) DEAD FOUL
(— OF SIGHT) DOGGO INVISIBLE
(— OF SORTS) CROOK CROSS HUMPY NOHOW SEEDY ROTTEN COMICAL PEEVISH

(— OF THE WAY) BY BYE ASIDE BLIND CLEAR CLOSE AFIELD GEASON REMOTE
(— OF THIS LIFE) HYNE
(— OF TUNE) FALSE SCORDATO
(FARTHER —) UTTER
(NOT —) SAFE
(PREF.) E ECT(O) EXO PRO
(— OF) EC
OUTAGE VENT ULLAGE HEADSPACE
OUT-AND-OUT RANK STARK PATENT REGULAR TEETOTAL THOROUGH GROSS PLUMB SHEER SWORN UTTER ARRANT DIRECT WHOLLY REGULAR ABSOLUTE COMPLETE CRASHING OUTRIGHT
OUTBID OVERCALL
OUTBREAK FIT ROW RASH RIOT BURST SALLY EMEUTE PLAGUE REVOLT RUCKUS TUMULT UPROAR BOUTADE OUTCROP RUCTION BLIZZARD ERUPTION OUTBURST EXPLOSION
(— OF DISEASE) PANDEMIC
(— OF EMOTIONALISM) HYSTERIA
(— OF SELF-INDULGENCE) LOOSE
(— OF TEMPER) MOORBURN
(REVOLUTIONARY —) PUTSCH
(SUDDEN —) SPURT
(VIOLENT —) STORM
OUTBUILDING BARN SHED LODGE PRIVY BARTON GARAGE HEMMEL LEANTO OUTHOUSE SKEELING SKILLING BACKHOUSE
OUTBURST BOUT CROW FLAW FUME GALE GUST RAGE TEAR TIFF AGONY BLAST BLAZE BLURT BREAK BRUNT BURST FLARE FLASH GEARE SALLY SPATE START STORM ACCESS BLOWER BLOWUP ESCAPE FANTAD FANTOD GOLLER TIRADE TUMULT VOLLEY BLOWOUT BOUTADE OUTCROP PASSION TANTRUM TORRENT ERUPTION EXPLOSION
(— OF ANGER) FIT GERE GEARE TATTER
(— OF APPLAUSE) OVATION
(— OF BIRD) SONG
(— OF FEELING) PASSION
(— OF ORATORY) SQUIRT
(— OF SPEECH) STRAIN
(— OF TEMPER) FUFF TIFF BLOWOUT
(— OF WORDS) VOLLEY
(SPACE —) SUPERNOVA
OUTCAST EXILE LEPER RONIN SHREW ABJECT PARIAH WRETCH AOUTLET ISHMAEL MISSILE OUTWALE CASTAWAY CHANDALA REJECTED VAGABOND DIALONIAN
(HOMELESS —) ARAB
(JAPANESE —) ETA RONIN
(PYRENEES —) CAGOT
OUTCOME END OUT FATE TERM CLOSE EDUCT EVENT HATCH ISSUE LOOSE PROOF UPSET BROWST EFFECT EXITUS OUTLET PERIOD RESULT SEQUEL UPSHOT EMANATE PROGENY SUCCESS FATALITY AFTERMATH
(UNPREDICTABLE —) CRAPSHOOT

OUTCROP CROP REEF LEDGE BASSET INLIER BLOSSOM BLOWOUT OUTBREAK OUTBURST
OUTCROPPING BULT SCABROCK
OUTCRY CAW CRY HUE YIP BAWL BRAY DITE GAFF HOWL REAM ROAR SCRY UTAS YARM YELL ALARM BOAST DITTY NOISE OUTAS SHOUT STINK WHAUP BELLOW CLAMOR HOLLER RACKET SCREAM SHRIEK STEVEN TUMULT CALLING EXCLAIM PROTEST SCREECH SHILLOO COMPLAINT PHILLILEW
(PUBLIC —) STINK
OUTDATED PASSE CRINOLINE
OUTDISTANCE DROP SKIN OUTGO SURPASS OUTSTRIP
OUTDO CAP COB COP COW POT TOP BANG BEAT BEST BURN FLOG WHIP EXCEL OUTGO REVIE TRUMP WORSE DEFEAT EXCEED OUTACT NONPLUS OUTPACE SURPASS OUTMATCH OUTSHINE OVERCOME
OUTDOOR OPENAIR
OUTDOORS FORTH OUTBY OUTBYE OUTSIDE
OUTER BUT OVER ALIEN ECTAD ECTAL UPPER UTTER FOREIGN OUTSIDE OUTWARD EXTERIOR EXTERNAL FORINSEC
(PREF.) ECTO EPH EPI EXO
OUTER MONGOLIA (SEE MONGOLIA)
(COIN OF—) MONGO TUGRIK
OUTERMOST FINAL UTTER UTMOST EVEREST EXTREME OUTWARD FARTHEST REMOTEST
OUTFACE DEFY RESIST SUBDUE CONFRONT OVERCOME
OUTFIELDER GARDENER OUTSCOUT
(THROW BY —) PEG
OUTFIT KIT RIG TOG DRAG GANG GARB REAR REEK SUIT TEAM UNIT DRESS EQUIP GETUP HABIT TROUP ATTIRE CONREY DUFFEL FITOUT LAYOUT CLOTHES FURNISH SHEBANG EQUIPAGE FURNITURE GRUBSTAKE
(BRIDE'S —) TROUSSEAU
(CHINESE —) SAMFU SAMFOO
(INFANT'S —) LAYETTE
(SEWING —) HOUSEWIFE
(SPARE —) CHANGE
OUTFLANK OUTWING OVERWING
OUTFLOW FLUX DRAIN ISSUE OUTGO EFFLUX ESCAPE SPRING OUTPOUR
(SEWAGE —) EFFLUENT
OUTGO EXIT EXCEL ISSUE OUTDO EFFLUX EGRESS EXCEED OUTLAY OUTLET OUTRUN OUTCOME PRODUCT SURPASS OUTSTRIP
OUTGROWTH ALA BUD JAG ARIL FOOT HAIR LEAF MOSS SPUR CLAMP FRUIT HILUM HYPHA SCALE SPINE ACULEA COCKLE CUPULE FIBRIL ENATION FEATHER ISIDIUM VERRUCA APPENDIX CARUNCLE EPIDERMA FLOCCULE HAPTERON INDUSIUM OFFSHOOT CARBUNCLE EMERGENCE FLOCCULUS PROPAGULE ROSTELLUM OSTEOPHYTE
(PLANTS —) OVULE
OUTGUESS PSYCH PSYCHE
OUTHOUSE SHED SKEO BIFFY LODGE PRIVY BIGGIN LINHAY OUTHUT LATRINE SKEELING SKILLION
(PL.) STEADING
OUTING OUT SKIP STAY TRIP JUNKET PICNIC COOKOUT HOLIDAY CLAMBAKE VACATION WAYGOOSE EXCURSION WAYZGOOSE
OUTLANDER ALIEN PARDESI
OUTLANDISH ALIEN KINKY OUTRE EXOTIC REMOTE BIZARRE FOREIGN STRANGE UNCOUTH PECULIAR BARBAROUS FANTASTIC GROTESQUE UNEARTHLY
(AMUSINGLY —) CAMPY
OUTLAST ELAPSE SURVIVE OVERBIDE
OUTLAW BAN BAR CACO HORN TORY EXILE EXLEX FLEME RONIN ARRANT BADMAN BANDIT BANISH BRUMBY COWBOY DACOIT UNLEDE BANDIDO ISHMAEL FUGITATE FUGITIVE PROHIBIT PROSCRIBE PROSCRIPT
(IRISH —) WOODKERN
(JAPANESE —) RONIN
(PL.) MANZAS
OUTLAWED ILLEGAL ILLICIT LAWLESS
OUTLAWRY BAN EXILE UTLAGARY
OUTLAY COST MISE OUTGO EXPENSE PENSION
OUTLET BORE DRIP EXIT VENT ISSUE EGRESS ESCAPE EXITUS FUNNEL OUTAGE OPENING FUMEDUCT OVERFLOW SINKHOLE AVOIDANCE
(— FOR COASTAL SWAMP) BAYOU
(— FOR SMOKE) FEMERALL
(— OF CARBURETOR) BARREL
(— OF SPRING) EYE
(AIR —) GRILL GRILLE
(ELECTRIC —) POINT
(REGULATED —) SLUICE
(RETAIL —) MINILAB
OUTLIER KLIP KLIPPE
OUTLINE MAP BOSH EDGE ETCH FLOW FORM LINE PLAN PLAT BRIEF CHALK CHART DRAFT FRAME MODEL SHAPE TRACE AGENDA APERCU DESIGN DOODLE FIGURE FILLET LAYOUT SCHEMA SCHEME SCROLL SKETCH SURVEY CAPSULE CONTOUR CROQUIS DIAGRAM DRAUGHT ELEMENT EXTRACT FEATURE GABARIT ISOTYPE PROFILE SUMMARY CONTORNO DESCRIBE ESQUISSE SKELETON SYLLABUS SYNOPSIS DELINEATE GUIDELINE TREATMENT
(— HASTILY) SPLASH
(— OF ANIMAL'S BODY) UNDERLINE
(— OF A SCIENCE) GRUNDRISS
(— OF COLUMN) ENTASIS
(— OF PLAY) SCENARIO
(— SHARPLY) ITALICIZE
(CURVING —) SWING
(DOUBLE —) FRINGE
(SHADOWY —) GHOST
OUTLIVE OUTLAST OUTWEAR SURVIVE OVERBIDE
OUTLOOK MIND VIEW FRONK FRONT VISTA ASPECT CLIMATE LOOKOUT PURVIEW FRONTAGE OUTSIGHT PROSPECT MENTALITY
(BRASH —) FACE
(MEDICAL —) PROGNOSIS
(SELF-CONFIDENT —) SWAGGER
OUTLYING OUTBY FORANE OUTBYE OUTLAND
OUTMANEUVER HAVE OUTPLAY
OUTMODED COLD DATED KAPUT PASSE RUSTY BYGONE EFFETE ANTIQUE ELDERLY VINTAGE OBSOLETE
OUT-OF-DATE RINKYDINK
OUT-OF-DOOR GIPSY GYPSY
OUTPLAY HAVE
OUTPOST STATION FOREPOST OUTGUARD
OUTPOURING FLOW GALE GUSH FLOOD RIVER SPATE EARFUL LAVISH STREAM OUTFLOW TORRENT FUSILLADE
OUTPUT CUT GET CROP MAKE EXPEL GRIST POWER YIELD ENERGY UPCOME TURNOUT
(IRRELEVANT —) NOISE
OUTRAGE RAPE ABUSE INSULT OFFEND RAVISH ABUSION AFFRONT OFFENSE VIOLATE VIOLENCE INDIGNITY
OUTRAGEOUS ENORM GROSS OUTRE DAMNED UNHOLY HEINOUS OBSCENE UNGODLY FLAGRANT INFERNAL SHAMEFUL SHOCKING ATROCIOUS DESPERATE MONSTROUS
OUTRANK CAMP PREFER SURPASS
OUTRE ODD BIZARRE STRANGE ECCENTRIC
OUTREACH CHEAT EXCEED EXTEND OUTWIT SEARCH DECEIVE SURPASS OVERREACH
OUTRIDER HAYDUK HEIDUK HEYDUCK
(PL.) SWING
OUTRIGGER BOOM PROA BUMKIN RIGGER SPIDER
OUTRIGHT RUN BALD CLEAN TOTAL WHOLE DIRECT ENTIRE OPENLY WHOLLY ABSOLUTE COMPLETE DIRECTLY ENTIRELY
OUTRIVAL WIN EXCEL OUTDO DEFEAT ECLIPSE SURPASS
OUTRUN BEAT COTE NICK PASS OUTGO EXCEED ATRENNE FORERUN OUTFOOT PREVENT
OUTRUSH GUST
OUTSET START OFFSET SETOUT BEGINNING THRESHOLD
OUTSHED SKIPPER
OUTSHINE BLIND EXCEL OUTDO STAIN DAZZLE DEFACE DISTAIN SURPASS OVERSHINE
OUTSIDE BUT OUT BOUT FREE RIND OUTBY UTTER AFIELD OUTFACE SURFACE EXTERIOR EXTERNAL
(— BOUNDS) ALOGICAL
(— OF) BESIDE
(— OF COCOON) FLOSS
(COMB. FORM) ECTO
(JUST —) FRINGE
(MERE —) SHELL
(PREF.) EC ECT(O) EXO EXTERO EXTRA EXTRO
OUTSIDER ALIEN OUTMAN BOUNDER ISHMAEL CIVILIAN EXOTERIC STRANGER EXTRANEAN FOREIGNER PHILISTER
(PL.) OUSTITI
OUTSKIRTS SIDE SKIRTS PURLIEU SUBURBS ENVIRONS PURLIEUS OUTSHIFTS
OUTSMART SLICK
OUTSPOKEN BOLD FREE LOUD APERT BLUFF BLUNT BROAD FRANK NAKED PLAIN ROUND VOCAL CANDID DIRECT ARTLESS EXPRESS EXPLICIT
(ROBUSTLY —) RABELAISIAN
OUTSTANDING ACE BIG ARCH RARE SOME AMONG FAMED NOTED SMASH SOCKO BANNER FAMOUS GIFTED HEROIC MARKED SIGNAL SNAZZY UNPAID EMINENT PALMARY SALIENT STELLAR SUBLIME SUPREME TOPPING FABULOUS INSPIRED PREMIERE SEASONED SKELPING SLAMBANG SMACKING STANDOUT TOWERING BEAUTIFUL PRINCIPAL PROMINENT UNSETTLED MONUMENTAL NOTICEABLE PREEMINENT
OUTSTAY TARRY
OUTSTRETCHED STENT EXPANDED EXTENDED
OUTSTRIP CAP TOP WIN BEST COTE LEAD LOSE PASS EXCEL OUTDO STRIP EXCEED OUTRUN DEVANCE SURPASS DISTANCE OVERCOME TRANSCEND
OUTVIE SURPASS OUTSTRIP
OUTWARD ECTAD OUTER OVERT DERMAD EXODIC EXTERN FORMAL EXTREME VISIBLE APPARENT EXTERIOR EXTERNAL OBSOLETE OUTFORTH EXTRINSIC
(GROWING —) ENATE
OUTWARDS BUT OVER
OUTWEIGH WEIGH OUTPOISE OVERBEAR OVERSHADE PREPONDERATE
OUTWIT FOX POT BALK BEST DISH FOIL HAVE BLOCK CHECK CROSS ELUDE BAFFLE EUCHRE FICKLE JOCKEY OVERGO THWART STONKER OUTGUESS OUTSHARP CROSSBITE OVERREACH CIRCUMVENT
OUTWORK BRAY JETTY FLECHE TENAIL BULWARK RAVELIN BARBICAN HORNWORK TENAILLE HORSESHOE
OUTWORKER BONDAGER
OUTWORN WAPPENED
OUZEL PIET AMSEL COLLY OUSEL OWZEL DIPPER THRUSH WHISTLER
OVAL O ELLIPSE STADIUM VESICAL VULVATE AVELONGE NUMMULAR VULVIFORM

OVARY CORAL GONAD GERMEN OARIUM OOPHORON (PREF.) OOPHOR(O) OV(I) OVARI(O) OVATO
OVATION HAND APPLAUSE
OVEN OON UMU KILN LEAR LEER LEHR OAST BAKER BENCH GLAZE GLOOM HANGI KOHUA TANUR TILER CALCAR MUFFLE CABOOSE FURNACE KITCHEN TANDOOR
(— FORK) FRUGGAN FRUGGIN
(— MOP) SCOVEL
OVENBIRD BAKER FURNER HORNERO TEACHER ACCENTOR
OVER BY BYE OER TOO ALSO ANEW ATOP BACK DEAD DONE GONE PAST UPON ABOVE AGAIN ALOFT ATOUR ATURN CLEAR ENDED EXTRA VAULT ABROAD ACROSS AROUND BEYOND DESSUS EXCESS UPWARD SURPLUS THROUGH FINISHED
(— AGAINST) FORNENT
(— AND ABOVE) ATOP ATOUR BESIDES
(ALL —) NAPOO NAPOOH SURTOUT
(PREFIX) SUR SUPER SUPRA (PREF.) EPH EPI HYPER OB PERI SUPER SUR
OVERABUNDANCE WASTE EXCESS SURPLUS PLETHORA
OVERABUNDANT LUXURIANT
OVERACT HAM EMOTE OUTDO BURLESQUE
OVERACTING HAM
OVERADORNED FLORID
OVERALL (BABY'S —) CRAWLER
OVERALLS SLIP CHAPS JEANS TONGS DENIMS
OVERANXIETY WORRY
OVERARCH COVE
OVERAWE COW ABASH BULLY DAUNT BUFFALO CONCUSS BROWBEAT
OVERBEARING HIGH PROUD LORDLY OVERLY HAUGHTY ARROGANT BULLYING DOGMATIC INSOLENT PRUSSIAN SNOBBISH IMPERIOUS MASTERFUL
OVERBLOUSE SHELL
OVERBLOWN RECHERCHE
OVERBURDEN COVER HOIST PESTER CONGEST OVERLAY ENCUMBER STRIPPING SURCHARGE
OVERBUSY FUSSY PRAGMATIC
OVERCAREFUL METICULOUS
OVERCAST DIM SEW BIND DARK DULL GLUM GREY WHIP CLOUD HEAVY SERGE CLOUDY DARKEN GLOOMY LOWERY CLOUDED NUBILOUS
OVERCHARGE GYP RUSH SOAK CROWD GOUGE STICK STING BURDEN EXCISE OPPRESS EXTORTION
OVERCOAT MINO BENNY GREGO JEMMY SHUBA BANGUP CAPOTE RAGLAN SLIPON TABARD TOPPER ULSTER PALETOT SPENCER SURTOUT TOPCOAT BALMACAN BENJAMIN COONSKIN TAGLIONI COTHAMORE GREATCOAT INVERNESS
OVERCOATING DUFFEL DUFFLE
OVERCOME DO AWE GET MOW WAR WIN BEAT BEST DING LICK LOCK MATE POOP SACK SUNK TAME WAUR CHARM CRUCH DAUNT DROUK DROWN FORDO MOPUP STILL STOOP THROW APPALL BEATEN BUSHED CRAVEN DEFEAT EXCEED EXPUGN FOREDO HURDLE MASTER MOIDER OUTRAY PLUNGE SUBDUE VICTOR CONFUTE CONQUER DEPRESS ENFORCE RECOVER SMOTHER CONVINCE OUTSTRIP SUPERATE SURMOUNT SURPRISE PROSTRATE
(— DIFFICULTIES) SWIM
(— WITH FATIGUE) FORDO FOREDO
(— WITH WEARINESS) HEAVY
(BE — BY HEAT) SWELTER
(EASILY —) WEAK
OVERCONFIDENT SECURE POSITIVE
OVERCROWD PESTER CONGEST SURCHARGE
OVERDAINTY TAFFETA
OVERDECORATED GARISH
OVERDEVELOPED GAUDY
OVERDO EXCEED EXHAUST FATIGUE PERCOCT OVERCOOK OVERWORK BURLESQUE
OVERDONE FUSTIAN EXUBERANT
OVERDOSE OD SICKENER
OVERDRESS SAC SACK DIZEN SACQUE POLONAISE
OVERDRESSED FLOSSY
OVERDRIED SLEEPY
OVERDUE BACK LATE TARDY UNPAID ARREARS BELATED DELAYED EXCESSIVE
OVEREAGER ANTSY FEVERISH FEVEROUS
OVEREAT GORGE SLOFF SATIATE GOURMAND
OVERELABORATE NIGGLE LABORED
OVEREMPHATIC MOUTHY
OVERENRICHED OPULENT
OVEREXACT PRECISE
OVEREXCITED HIGH
(GET —) GOAPE
OVEREXERT TORLE STRAIN TORFEL OVERPLY
OVEREXPOSURE (— TO SUN) HELIOSIS
OVERFASTIDIOUS SPRUCE
OVERFED RANK FULSOME
OVERFEED CRAM
OVERFLOW REE COME FLUX REAM SLOP SWIM TEEM VENT BRIME FLOAT FLOOD SPATE SPILL ABOUND DEBORD OUTLET SPILTH OVERRUN REDOUND BOILOVER EXUNDATE INUNDATE OUTSWELL SUBMERGE CATACLYSM
(— FROM MOLD) SPEW SPUE
OVERFLOWING FLOW AWASH FLOAT DELAVY DELUGE ALLUVIO COPIOUS FRESHET PROFUSE INUNDANT EXUBERANT LANDFLOOD SUPERFLUX
OVERFRIENDLY PALSY PALSYWALSY
OVERGARMENT SMOCK BLOUSE DUSTER
OVERGROWN FOZY RANK GAWKY BRANCHY FULSOME SPRATTY SPRITTY
OVERHAND WHIP
OVERHANG JUT BEND EAVE RAKE BULGE JETTY BEETLE SHELVE TOPPLE FANTAIL OVERLAP PROJECT SUSPEND
OVERHANGING BEETLE SHELVY HANGING PENDENT PENSILE BEETLING IMMINENT OBUMBRANT PENTHOUSE PRECIPITOUS
OVERHASTY RASH
OVERHAUL EXAMINE OVERHAIL RENOVATE FOREREACH
OVERHEAD COST ABOVE ALOFT BURDEN ONCOST UPKEEP EXPENSE OVERTOP
OVERHEARTY ROBUST
OVERHEAT PARBOIL SCOUTHER
OVERINDULGE PAMPER DEBAUCH
OVERINFUSE STEW
OVERLAP LAP RIDE SYPHER SHINGLE IMBRICATE INTERSECT
OVERLAPPING JUGATE RIDING EQUITANT OBVOLUTE IMBRICATE
(— IN FUGUE) STRETTA STRETTO
OVERLAVISH BAROQUE
OVERLAY CAP LAP CEIL COAT WHIP APPLY COUCH COVER GLAZE PATCH PLATE CEMENT CRAVAT SPREAD STUCCO VENEER ENCRUST OPPRESS OVERLIE SMOTHER APPLIQUE TEMPLATE
(— WITH GOLD) BEAT GILD
OVERLOAD CRAM GLUT STUFF SWAMP CHARGE ENCUMBER SURCHARGE
OVERLOADED PLETHORIC PLETHOROUS
OVERLOOK BALK MISS OMIT PASS SKIP SLIP WINK BLINK ELIDE FORGO ACQUIT EXCUSE FOREGO FORGET IGNORE MANAGE OVERGO ABSOLVE COMMAND CONDONE FORGIVE INSPECT MISKNOW NEGLECT CONFOUND DOMINATE DISREGARD DISSEMBLE
OVERLOOKER GAITER
OVERLOOKING (INTENTIONAL —) AMNESTY
OVERLORD LIEGE DESPOT ISWARA SATRAP TYRANT ISHVARA SUZERAIN TYRANNIZE
OVERLY CAP TOO
OVERLYING JESSANT BROCHANT INCUMBENT
OVERMAN CHIEF LEADER ARBITER FOREMAN REFEREE OVERSEER SUPERMAN
OVERMANTLE (— TREATMENT) TRUMEAU
OVERMASTER GET
OVERMATCH BEST DEFEAT EXCEED SURPASS VANQUISH
OVERMODEST PRIM PRUDISH
OVERMUCH TOO EXCESS SURPLUS EXCESSIVE (PREF.) HYPER
OVERNICE FEAT FUSS SAUCY DAINTY QUAINT SPRUCE FINICKY PRECISE DENTICAL PRECIOUS SQUEAMISH
OVERPAINT CLOBBER
(— ENAMEL) CLOBBER
OVERPLAY HAM
OVERPOWER AWE BEAT ROUT RUSH CRUSH DROWN QUELL SWAMP WHELM COMPEL DEFEAT DELUGE ENGULF MASTER OVERGO SUBDUE WRIXLE CONQUER CONTROL OPPRESS REPRESS CONVINCE OUTSCOUT SCUMFISH SURPRISE
(— WITH HEAT) SWELT
(— WITH LIGHT) DAZZLE
OVERPOWERING DIRE FIERCE KILLING DAZZLING STUNNING DESPERATE MONSTROUS
OVERPRAISE FLATTER OVERSELL
OVERPRECISE MIM PRISSY FINICKY CLERKISH NIGGLING PRECIEUSE
OVERREACH DO POT DUPE GRAB CHEAT COZEN CHOILE GREASE NOBBLE OUTWIT OVERGO DECEIVE
OVERREADY FORWARD
OVERREFINED QUAINT PRECIOUS
OVERRIDE SUPERSEDE
OVERRIPE FRACID SQUSHY SQUUSHY
OVERRIPENESS SEED
OVERRULE NIX VETO GOVERN ABROGATE OVERCOME
OVERRULING GREAT PREDOMINANT
OVERRUN TEEM BESET CRUSH SWARM DELUGE EXCEED INFEST INVADE OVERGO RAVAGE SPREAD DESTROY
OVERSEAS OUTREMER
OVERSEE TEND WATCH DIRECT HANDLE MANAGE SURVEY EXAMINE INSPECT NEGLECT DISREGARD SUPERVISE
OVERSEER BAAS BOSS CORK JOSS EPHOR GRAVE REEVE BISHOP CENSOR DRIVER GAFFER GRIEVE KEEKER MIRDHA TINDAL WARDEN BAILIFF CAPATAZ CAPORAL CURATOR FOREMAN HEADMAN KANGANI MANAGER MANDOER MAYORAL OVERMAN PRISTAW TAPSMAN BANKSMAN CHAPRASI DECURION MARTINET SURVEYOR VILLICUS
(— OF MACHINERY) TENTOR
(— OF MINE) CAPTAIN
(SPIRITUAL —) PASTOR PRIEST
OVERSENSITIVE TICKLISH
OVERSENTIMENTAL SOFT SLOPPY
OVERSHADOW DIM CLOUD COVER DWARF SHADE TOWER DARKEN EFFACE ECLIPSE OBSCURE UMBRAGE UPSTAGE BESCREEN DOMINATE OVERCAST
OVERSHOE GUM BOOT GUME ARCTIC GAITER GALOSH GOLOSH PATTEN RUBBER SANDAL FLAPPER EXCLUDER FOOTHOLD PANTOFLE
OVERSIGHT EYE CARE HOLE SLIP ERROR FAULT GAFFE LAPSE

WATCH CHARGE BLUNDER CONTROL JEOFAIL MISTAKE OMISSION TUTELAGE DIRECTION
(LEGAL —) JEOFAIL
OVERSKIRT PEPLUM PANNIER
OVERSMART FLIP
OVERSOFT QUASHY
OVERSPREAD FOG CAST CLOT DECK PALL BATHE BREDE CLOUD COVER SMEAR STREW CLOTHE DELUGE DOODLE INDUCE SCATTER SUFFUSE BESPREAD
OVERSTATE MAGNIFY EXAGGERATE
OVERSTEP PASS EXCEED SURPASS TRANSGRESS
OVERSTEPPING FOOTFAULT
OVERSTIMULATED HYPER
OVERSTOCK SURCHARGE
OVERSTRAINED EPITONIC
OVERSUPPLIED RANK
OVERSUPPLY GLUT
OVERT OPEN PATENT PUBLIC OBVIOUS APPARENT MANIFEST
OVERTAKE PASS ATAKE CATCH ATTAIN BEFALL DETECT ENSNARE OVERHIE FOREHENT OVERHAUL
(— BY DARKNESS) BENIGHT
OVERTASK DRIVE
OVERTAX HOIST EXCEED STRAIN STRESS
OVERTHROW TIP CAST DASH DOWN FALL FELL FOIL FOLD HURL RAZE ROUT RUIN RUSH WALT WEND ALLAY CRUSH EVERT FLING LEVEL QUASH UPSET WORST WRACK WRECK DEFEAT DEJECT DEPOSE REPUTE SLIGHT TOPPLE TUMBLE UNSEAT WRITHE AFFLICT CONQUER CONVELL DESTROY DISMISS RUINATE SUBVERT UNDOING UNHORSE WHEMMLE CONFOUND DEMOLISH OVERCOME OVERTURN REVERSAL SUPPLANT VANQUISH CHECKMATE CONFUSION OVERWHELM
(— BY TRIPPING) CHIP
OVERTONE PARTIAL HARMONIC
OVERTOP COW OVERREACH
OVERTURE OFFER PROEM ADVANCE OPENING PRELUDE APERTURE PROPOSAL SINFONIA VORSPIEL
(INDECENT —) ASSAULT
OVERTURN TIP CAVE COUP KEEL TILT WALT WELT TERVE THROW UPEND UPSET WELME WHALM WHELM SLIGHT TIPPLE TOPPLE WELTER CAPSIZE DESTROY PERVERT REVERSE SUBVERT WHEMMLE
(— A WATCHMAN) BOX
OVERWEENING MISPROUD PRESUMPTUOUS
OVERWEIGHT OUTGANG
OVERWHELM BOWL BURY SINK SLAY AMAZE COVER CRUSH DROOK DROUK DROWN FLOOD FLOOR SEIZE SPATE SWAMP CUMBER DEFEAT DELUGE ENGULF OBRUTE PLUNGE QUELME QUENCH ASTOUND BESIEGE BOMBARD CONFUTE CONQUER ENGROSS FLATTEN IMMERSE INFLOOD OPPRESS SMOTHER ASTONISH DISTRESS DOMINATE INUNDATE OVERCOME SUBMERGE AVALANCHE
OVERWHELMED ACCABLE
OVERWORK HOIN TIRE TOIL SWEAT STRAIN SURMENAGE
OVINE OVIN OVILE SHEEP SHEEPLIKE
OVIPOSITOR TEREBRA
OVOID OVATE OBOVOID
OVOLO OVAL THUMB BOLTEL
OVULE EGG NIT GERM SEED EMBRYO OVULUM GEMMULE SEEDLET
OVUM EGG OVAL SEED SPORE OOSPERM OOSPHERE
OWAIA TREE BOBO
OWE DUE OWN REST AUGHT OUGHT SHALL POSSESS ATTRIBUTE
OWED DUE
OWER DEBTOR
OWING INTHEHOLE
OWL ULE BUBO LULU MOMO RURU SURN TYTO UTUM JENNY MADGE NINOX PADGE SCOPS STRIX TAWNY WEKAU AZIOLA HOOTER HOWLET KETUPA MUCARO RAPTOR STRICH VERMIN WHEKAU BOOBOOK HARFANG KATOGLE WAPACUT WOOLERT BILLYWIX COQUIMBO MOREPORK
(— CALL) HOOT
(CRY OF —) HOOT WHOO TUWHIT TUWHOO
(LIKE AN —) STRIGINE
(YOUNG —) UTUM OWLET
(PREF.) STRIGI
OWL PARROT KAKAPO
OWN AIN OWE AVOW FESS HAVE HOLD HOWE MEET NAIN SELF ADMIT AUGHT OUGHT MASTER CONCEDE CONFESS POSSESS PROSPER ACKNOWLEDGE
(PREF.) **(ONE'S —)** IDIO
OWNER BEL MALIK WALLA HOLDER DOMINUS HERITOR ODALLER PROPRIETOR
(— OF ESTATE) ALIRD
(— OF FISHING PLANT) PLANTER
(— OF SLAVES) PATRON
(— OF YACHT) AFTERGUARD
(PLANTATION —) COLON
(SHEEP —) NABAL
OWNERSHIP ODAL UDAL AUGHT TITLE CORNER SEIZIN SEIZURE SEVERAL TENANCY DOMINIUM PROPERTY COMMUNITY POSSESSION
OX YAK ANOA AVER BEEF BUFF BULL GAUR MUSK NAWT NEAT NEWT NOWT OWSE REEM RUNT STOT URUS ZEBU AIVER BISON BUGLE GAYAL SANGA STEER TOLLY TSINE BOVINE MITHAN ROTHER BANTENG BUFFALO KOUPREY TWINTER SELADANG TALLOWER
(CAMBODIAN —) KOUPREY KOUPROH
(HORNLESS —) MOIL
(KIND OF —) MUSK
(SMALL —) RUNT
(TAME —) COACH
(WILD —) URE ANOA BUFF GAUR REEM URUS BISON BUGLE BANTIN BANTENG BUFFALO SELADANG
(YEARLING —) STIRK
(YOUNG —) STOT
(PREF.) BOVI BU
OXBLOOD KAZAK COPTIC KAZAKH
OXBOW INCIDENT (AUTHOR OF —) CLARK
(CHARACTER IN —) GIL DREW ROSE CANBY CROFT GRIER JOYCE MAPEN TYLER CARTER DAVIES DONALD GERALD MARTIN OSGOOD RISLEY TETLEY FARNLEY KINKAID
OXEN NOWT OWSEN CATTLE
OXEYE BOCE GOLD ASTER CLOUD DAISY GOLDE DUNLIN PLOVER TARPON
OXFOOT (STEWED —) COWHEEL
OXFORD DOWN SHOE CLOTH OXONIAN SLIPPER
OXGANG OSKEN BOVATE OXGATE OXLAND PLOWGANG
OXIDATION RUST
OXIDATIVE AEROBIC
OXIDE EARTH FLOSS CADMIA HAFNIA MOILES ZAFFER CALCINE GUMMITE KERNITE LIMONITE DJALMAITE
(— OF CALCIUM) LIME
(— OF IRON) RUST COLCOTHAR MAGNETITE
OXLIP PAGLE PAIGLE PRIMULA MILKMAID PRIMROSE PRIMWORT
OXSHOE CUE
OXYGEN GAS OZONE OXYGENIUM
(LIQUID —) LOX
(PREF.) OXO
OXYGENATE AERATE VENTILATE
OXYGENATOR GILL
OYSTER COPIS COUNT PINNA PLANT SHELL COTUIT HUITRE NATIVE REEFER BIVALVE MOLLUSK PANDORE RATTLER SHARPER BLUEPOINT GREENGILL LYNNHAVEN
(— BED) PARK STEW LAYER SCALP CLAIRE SCALFE OYSTERAGE
(— CATCHER) OLIVE PYNOT TIRMA KROCKET PIANNET REDBILL SCOLDER SHELDER PILWILLET SKELDRAKE
(— CRAB) PINNOTERE
(— FOSSIL) OSTRACITE
(— MEASURE) WASH
(— PLANT) SALSIFY
(— SHELL) HUSK TEST SHUCK
(— SMALLER THAN QUARTER) BLISTER
(— SOLD BY POUND) COUNT
(IRISH —) POWLDOODY
(ROCK —) CHAMA
(VEGETABLE —) SALSIFY
(YOUNG —) SET SPAT
(2,3, OR 4 —S) WARP
(PREF.) OSTRE(I)(O)
OYSTER CATCHER SEAPIE
OYSTERFISH TAUTOG TOADFISH
OZARK STATE MISSOURI
OZEM (BROTHER OF —) DAVID
(FATHER OF —) JESSE
OZNI (FATHER OF —) GAD
OZOCERITE MALTHA NEFTGIL
OZONE AIR

P PAPA PETER
PA DAD PAW FORT PAPA DADDY FATHER VILLAGE STOCKADE
PABULUM FOOD FUEL PROG CEREAL ALIMENT SUPPORT NUTRIMENT
PAC BOOT SHOE MOCCASIN
PACA CAPA CAVY LAVA LABBA AGOUTI RODENT
PACE FIG PAD RIP WAY BEMA CLIP GAIT LOPE PASS PELT RACK RATE STEP TEAR TROT WALK AMBLE BRAWL CANTO SLINK SPACE SPEED STEEK SWING TEMPO TRACE TREAD CANTER GALLOP STRAIT STRIDE CHANNEL CHAPTER DOGTROT MEASURE PASSAGE SCUTTLE
(FAST —) ROMP
(RAPID —) CLIP CRACKER
(SLOW —) JOG CRAWL CREEP
(PL.) MANAGE
PACER HORSE AMBLER SPANKER TRIPPLER
PACHISI LUDO UCKERS PARCHESI
PACHYDERM BABAR HIPPO RHINO ELEPHANT
PACIFIC CALM MEEK MILD IRENE IRENIC PLACID SERENE PEACEFUL TRANQUIL PEACEABLE
(— ISLAND PINE) IE KOU IEIE LEHUA
PACIFIER DUMMY COMFORTER
PACIFIST BOLO
PACIFY PAY CALM EASE LULL STAY ABATE ALLAY AMESE MEASE PEASE QUELL QUIET STILL PECIFY SERENE SETTLE SOFTEN SOOTHE APPEASE ASSUAGE MOLLIFY PLACATE QUALIFY STICKLE MITIGATE ALLEVIATE RECONCILE
PACK JAM PUN WAD BALE CADE CRAM DECK FILL GANG JAMB LADE LOAD PAIR ROUT STOW SWAG TAMP TOTE TUCK COUCH CRAME CROWD DRESS FLOCK HORDE SKULK SOMER STEVE STORE STUFF TRUSS BARREL BODDLE BOODLE BUDGET BUNDLE CARTON DUFFLE EMBALE ENCASE FARDEL HAMPER IMPACT PARCEL STEEVE THWACK TURKEY WALLET PANNIER PORTAGE RUMMAGE SUMPTER KNAPSACK
(— ANIMAL) ASS MULE BURRO CAMEL HORSE LLAMA DONKEY PACKER
(— BUILDER) GOBBER
(— JURY) WATER
(— LOOSELY) HOVER
(— OF BEARS) SLOTH
(— OF CARDS) STOCK
(— OF DOGS) CRY KENNEL
(— OFF) WAG SHANK TURSE
(— OF FOXES) GROUP SKULK
(— OF HOUNDS) CRY HUNT MUTE
(— ROAD) PACKWAY
(— TIGHTLY) STIVE
PACKAGE PAD BALE BOLT PAIR DUMMY TRUSS BINDLE BUNDLE PACKET PARCEL SAMPLE SEROON DORLACH
(— OF CIGARETTES) DECK
(— OF GOLDBEATER'S SKINS) SHODER
(— OF LEAF) BOOK
(— OF PEPPERS) ROBBIN
(— OF STAMPS) KILOWARE
(— OF VELLUM) KUTCH
(— OF VENEER) FLITCH
(— OF WOOL) BAG PAD BUTT FADGE
(YARN —) CONE CHEESE
PACKAGING (— MATERIAL) SARAN
PACKED THICK THRONGED CONGESTED SPOONWISE
PACKER BALER LINER ROPER CANNER
PACKET BOAT BOOK DECK ROLL SCREW BUNDLE PARCEL SACHET
(— OF A DRUG) BAG
(— OF VELLUM) CUTCH KUTCH
(FIVE DOLLAR DRUG —) NICKEL
PACKHORSE SOMER JAGGER PACKER SUMPTER
PACKHORSEMAN JAGGER
PACKING CUP RAGS GAUZE PAPER STRAW WASTE GASKET GROMMET STOWAGE STOPPING
(— MATERIAL) BALINE GASKET
(CLAY —) LUTE
(SEND —) EXPEL
PACKINGHOUSE MEATWORKS
PACKMAN HAWKER
PACKSACK KYACK
PACKSADDLE BAT BARDEL APAREJO
PACT MISE ACCORD CARTEL PACTUM TREATY BARGAIN COMPACT LOCARNO ALLIANCE CONTRACT COVENANT AGREEMENT CONCORDAT
PAD MAT WAD WAY BLAD BOSS DIGS FROG LURE MUTE PATH PUFF ROAD ROLL SHOE WALK WASE BLOCK INKER PERCH PILCH QUILT STENT STINT STUFF TABBY TRAMP BASKET BUFFER BUSTLE DAUBER HOLDER JOCKEY NUMNAH PADDLE PADNAG PANNEL PILLOW SPONGE TABLET TRUDGE VELURE WREATH BOLSTER BOMBAST CUSHION FOOTPAD PILLION SASHOON
(— FOR HORSE'S BACK) SADDLE
(— IN CRIB) BUMPER
(— OF ROPE) PUDDING PUDDENING
(— OF STRAW) SUNK WASE
(— ON HORSE'S FOOT) FROG
(— WORN AT THE WAIST) TOURNURE
(BOXER'S —) GUMSHIELD
(ETCHER'S —) DABBER
(FENCING —) PLASTRON
(HAIR —) RAT MOUSE TOQUE
(INKING —) INKER TOMPION
(KIND OF —) TOUCH
(MEDICAL —) PLEDGET
(PERFUMED —) SACHET
(POLISHING —) RUBBER VELOUR VELOURS
(POOR —) HUT SHACK
(PROTECTIVE —) SHIELD
(SADDLE —) PANEL PILLOW PILLION
(PREF.) TYL(O)
PADADE CALLITHUMP
PADAUK CORAIL
PADDER MANGLE
PADDING TABBY CADDIS BOLSTER BOMBAST BUSHING CADDICE FILLING PACKING ROBBERY WADDING MAHOITRE STUFFING
PADDLE OAR ROW SPUD WADE ALOOF CANOE SLICE SPANK BUCKET DABBLE PETTLE PUNISH STRIKE THRASH TODDLE SPANKER SPURTLE LUMPFISH
(— BOX) WHEELHOUSE
(— FOR FLOUR) SLICK
(TAILOR'S —) BEATER
PADDLEBOAT PEDALO
PADDLEFISH GANOID DUCKBILL STURGEON POLYODONT SPADEFISH SPOONBILL
PADDOCK LOT FROG PARK CLOSE FIELD SLEDGE GARSTON LOANING BIRDCAGE
PADDYMELON QUOKKA PADMELON
PADISHAH SULTAN PADASHA POTSHAW
PADLOCK LOCK FASTEN SECURE CLOSING FASTENER HORSELOCK
(— LINK) SHACKLE
PADRE MONK CLERIC FATHER PRIEST CHAPLAIN
PADRONA LANDLADY MISTRESS
PADRONE BOSS CHIEF MASTER PATRON LANDLORD INNKEEPER
PAEAN ODE HYMN SONG PRAISE OUTBURST TRIUMPHAL
PAGAN ATA BUID BATAK BUKID APAYAO BAGOBO BANGON BILAAN BONTOC ETHNIC PAYNIM SABIAN ALANGAN DUMAGAT GENTILE HEATHEN INFIDEL SARACEN SUBANUN UNGODLY IDOLATOR
(— OF INDIA) GENTOO
PAGANDOM PAYNIM
PAGE BOY CALL LEAF MOTH SIDE CHILD FACER FOLIO GROOM SHEET DONZEL ERRATA SUMMON VARLET BUTTONS CALLBOY FUNNIES PAVISER SERVANT CHASSEUR HENCHMAN ICHOGLAN
(— BOTTOM) TAIL
(BLANK —S) CANCEL
(FACING —S) SPREAD
(LADY'S —) ESCUDERO
(LAST FEW —S) BACK
(LEFTHAND —) VERSO
(NEWSPAPER —) OPED
(RIGHTHAND —) RECTO OUTPAGE
(TITLE —) TITLE UNWAN RUBRIC
(PL.) ODDMENTS
PAGEANT JEST POMP SHOW ANTIC PARADE RIDING TABLEAU TAMASHA TRIUMPH AQUACADE CAVALCADE SPECTACLE WATERWORK
PAGEANTRY POMP PARADE HERALDRY SPLENDOR
PAGER BEEPER
PAGIEL (FATHER OF —) OCRAN
PAGLIACCI (CHARACTER IN —) BEPPE CANIO NEDDA TONIO SILVIO
(COMPOSER OF —) LEONCAVALLO
PAGODA PON TAA HOON WATT TEMPLE VARELLA
(PART OF —) TEE ROOF TOPE STUPA FINIAL BALCONY
PAHOUIN FAN FANG
PAHUTAN PAHO
PAID EVEN RESOLUTE
(— IN COIN) DRY
(— IN FULL) SATISFIED
PAIL CAN COG PAN SOA SOE BEAT BOWK GAWN MEAL STOP TRUG BOWIE COGUE CRUCK DANDY ESHIN SKEEL STOOP BLICKY BUCKET COGGIE HARASS KETTLE LEGLEN NOGGIN PIGGIN SITULA THRASH COLLOCK
(MILK —) KIT SOE TRUG ESHIN LEGLEN
(ON WHEELS) DANDY
(PART OF —) EAR RIM BODY CURL HANDLE
(POTTERY —) SEAU
(SMALL —) KIT BLICKY BLICKIE
(WOODEN —) COG COGUE LUGGIE PIGGIN
PAIN GYP ACHE AGRA BALE CARE CARK DOLE FRET GRUE HARM HURT PANG SITE SORE TEEN TINE WARK AGONY BEANS CRAMP DOLOR GRIEF GRIPE PINCH PINSE SCALD SMART STING STOUN THRAW THROE WOUND WRING BARRAT GRIEVE MISERY SHOWER STITCH TWINGE AFFLICT ALGESIS ANGUISH EARACHE HURTING MYALGIA OFFENCE PENALTY

TORTURE TRAVAIL TROUBLE AGGRIEVE DISTRESS FLEABITE
(— IN BACK) NOTALGIA SCIATICA
(— IN HAND) CHIRAGRA
(— IN SIDE) STEEK
(— IN THE NECK) PEST
(— OF MIND) AGONY
(— RELIEVER) OPIATE ANODYNE ASPIRIN TYLENOL
(FILL WITH —) YEARN
(SHARP —) WRING
(STOMACH —) GRIPES GNAWING
(WRENCHING —) TORSION
(PL.) FASH LABOR WHILE EFFORT TROUBLE
(PREF.) ALG(IO)(O) DOLORI NOCI PENO
(SUFF.) AGRA ALGIA ALGIC ODYNE ODYNIA

PAINFUL BAD ILL DIRE EVIL FELL SAIR SORE SOUR TART ANGRY CRUEL SHARP SORRY BITTER STICKY TENDER THORNY BALEFUL GRIPING HURTFUL IRKSOME LABORED PENIBLE PUNGENT EXACTING TERRIBLE TORTUOUS DIFFICULT HARROWING
(PREF.) MOGI

PAINLESS EASY

PAINSTAKING BUSY LOVING NARROW CAREFUL PENIBLE DILIGENT EXACTING STUDIOUS ASSIDUOUS ELABORATE

PAINT BICE BLOT COAT DAUB DRAW FARD GAUD LIMN PENT PICT SOIL COLOR FEIGN FUCUS GRAIN ROUGE STAIN BEDAUB DAZZLE DEPICT ENAMEL FRESCO OPAQUE SHADOW SKETCH BESMEAR PORTRAY PRETEND SCUMBLE AIRBRUSH DECORATE DEPEINCT DESCRIBE DISGUISE URFIRNIS CALCIMINE
(— A PIPE) SOIL
(— FACE OR BODY) FUCUS PARGET
(— HASTILY) SQUIGGLE
(— IN DOTS) STIPPLE
(— SKETCHILY) SPLASH
(— THROUGH PATTERN) STENCIL
(— WITH COSMETICS) POP POT FARD
(PREF.) PICTO

PAINTBRUSH WICKAWEE NOSEBLEED
(PART OF —) HAIR CRIMP HANDLE BRISTLE FERRULE

PAINTED PINTO FUCATE PASTOSE PINTADO FUCOIDAL GOFFERED
(— BEAUTY) VANESSA
(— BUNTING) POP NONPAREIL
(— CUP) WICKAWEE PAINTBRUSH
(— WAKE-ROBIN) SARA

PAINTER BRUSH FAUVE ARTIST DAUBER PICTOR PANTHER SIGNIST SIGNMAN WORKMAN BRUSHMAN LUMINIST MURALIST NAZARENE STIPPLER DECORATOR TACTILIST
(PL.) ECLECTICS
AMERICAN AHL COX GAG LOW MAX RAY RIX AMES BAER BEAL COLE DABO DANA DEHN DINE DOVE GRAY HART HAYS HELD HOWE HURD KOCH KOST LOEB LUKS NEAL NEEL PAGE PETO POOR REID THON UFER WEIR WEST WOOD ABBEY AGATE AIKEN ALDIS AVERY BACON BAKER BARSE BEARD BEAUX BETTS BOGGS BROOK BROWN BRUSH BUNCE CHASE CHILD CRANE CURRY DAVIS DEWEY EATON ENNIS FIENE FLAGG FOOTE GILES GOLUB GORDY GORKY GRANT GROLL GROSZ HEALY HENRI HICKS HOMER INMAN IPSEN JONES LAHEY LUCAS MARSH MINOR MOORE MORAN MYERS ODGEN OKADA PEALE PERRY POONS POORE RYDER SHINN SLOAN SMITH SOYER TRYON UPTON WALDO WAUGH WEBER WEEKS WHITE WOOLF WYANT WYETH YOUNG BENSON BENTON BLYTHE BOGERT BOHROD BOUCHE BROWNE CADMUS CHAPIN CHURCH COLMAN COOPER COPLEY COTTON CRANCH CURRAN DANIEL DANNAT DAVIES DEARTH DECAMP DEMUTH DEWING DUNLAP DURAND DURRIE EAKINS FERRIS FISCHL FORBES FOSTER FOWLER GUERIN HAGGIN HARVEY HASSAM HAYDEN HEATON HERTER HOPPER INGHAM INNESS JARVIS JOUETT KINNEY KNATHS KNIGHT LAWSON LEUTZE LEVINE LOOMIS MARTIN MAURER MAYHEW MEIERE MILLER MOSLER MURPHY NEAGLE NOLAND NOURSE OAKLEY PARTON PEARCE PIPPIN POWELL QUIDOR RIVERS ROTHKO SAMPLE SAVAGE SINGER STELLA STUART SYMONS TANGUY TANNER TAUBES TURNER VEDDER WARHOL WRIGHT ZORACH ADDISON ALLSTON AUDUBON BANVARD BELLOWS BINGHAM BRINLEY CAMERON CARLSON CARROLL CASSATT CHAPMAN CHRISTY CORBINO COUDERT CROPSEY DOUGHTY EDWARDS ELLIOTT FASSETT FREEMAN GARNSEY GIFFORD GRIFFIN GROPPER HARDING HARNETT HIBBARD HIGGINS HUBBARD HUBBELL JOHNSON KARFIOL KENDALL KENSETT LAFARGE LATHROP MACEWEN MATHEWS MCENTEE METCALF MUNSELL NAEGELE OKEEFFE OLITSKI PARRISH PEIXOTO PROCTOR RATTNER SAMARAS SCUDDER SIMMONS SMIBERT SPENCER STIMSON TWOMBLY TWORKOV WATROUS WIGGINS ALAJALOV ATCHISON BARTLETT BECKWITH BICKNELL BILLINGS BOUGHTON BRACKMAN BRADFORD BREVOORT BRIDGMAN CORNWELL COSTIGAN DUVENECK FAULKNER HAMILTON HARRISON HOVENDEN HUTCHENS JOHANSEN KRONBERG LOCKWOOD MATTESON MELCHERS PHILLIPS REINHART RICHARDS ROCKWELL ROSSITER SHATTUCK SPEICHER TRUMBULL WHISTLER WILMARTH WOODBURY ALEXANDER ARMSTRONG BEMELMANS BERDANIER BERNSTEIN BIERSTADT BITTINGER BLAKELOCK DAUGHERTY DEKOONING HALLOWELL HAWTHORNE KUNIYOSHI REMINGTON ROTHERMEL SCHREIBER TWACHTMAN VANDERLYN WENTWORTH BLASHFIELD BURCHFIELD CLINEDINST EILSHEMIUS FARNSWORTH HIRSHFIELD HUNTINGTON MACCAMERON WHITTREDGE BERNINGHAUS DELLENBAUGH PRENDERGAST BLUMENSCHEIN BRECKENRIDGE DAINGERFIELD CROWNINSHIELD
ARGENTINIAN CENTURION
AUSTRIAN ALT KLIMT EHRLICH FUHRICH AMERLING HAUSMANN DANHAUSER DEFREGGER KOKOSCHKA FRIEDLANDER PETTENKOFEN
BELGIAN CLAYS ENSOR FOLON NAVEZ VIGNE BEIFVE KEYSER WIERTZ GALLAIT GUFFENS LALAING PAUWELS STEVENS WAPPERS WAUTERS WILLEMS BAERTSON LAERMANS MAGRITTE BROUCKERE EVENEPOEL TONGERLOO BRAEKELEER CHAMPAIGNE VERBOECKHOVEN
BRAZILIAN VOLPI
CANADIAN AZIZ CARR COTE KANE MILNE FORBES HARRIS LISMER OBRIEN VARLEY WALKER WATSON BORDUAS KURELEK MORRICE COLVILLE
CHILEAN MATTA
CHINESE SHUBUN
COLOMBIAN BOTERO
CZECH KUPKA MANES MUCHA BROZIK
DANISH JUEL BLOCH CARLSEN DAISGAARD MARSTRAND WIEGHORST WILLUMSEN ZAHRTMANN ABILDGAARD ECKERSBERG
DUTCH BOL DOU BECK BEGA CORT CUYP GOES GOGH HAAS HALS HEDA HEEM KALF LAAR LELY LOOY MAES MEER NEER AELST APPEL BAUER BOSCH BOUTS BRUYN CODDE DAVID GOYEN HELST HOOCH KETEL MARIS METSU NEEFS OVENS STEEN VELDE VROOM WITTE BACKER DECKER EGMONT ESCHER FLINCK GELDER HEYDEN KESSEL KEYSER MANDER MESDAG MIERIS MULIER OSTADE POTTER RUYSCH SCOREL TOOROP WEENIX AERTSEN AERTZEN ASSELYN BERCHEM BEYEREN CRABETH DOUFFET HOBBEMA ISRAELS KONINCK LASTMAN LIEVENS LOMBARD PATINIR POURBUS VANGOGH VERMEER WYNANTS AGRICOLA DOESBURG DUJARDIN EECKHOUT GOLTZIUS HUYSMANS JONGKIND KOEKKOEK LAIRESSE MOREELSE RUYSDAEL TERBORCH BLOEMAERT CORNELISZ FABRITIUS HOEFNAGEL HONTHORST HOUBRAKEN MIEREVELT MONDRIAAN MOUCHERON REMBRANDT STEENWILK WOUWERMAN BACKHUYSEN BERCKHEYDE CAMPHUYSEN EVERDINGEN GESELSCHAP LINGELBACH BREKELENKAM HONDECOETER POELENBURGH TERBRUGGHEN HOOGSTRAETEN
ENGLISH COX EGG FRY BIRD BONE COLE COPE EAST ETTY EVES GILL HAAG HOOK HUNT JOHN LEAR NASH OPIE SWAN TAIT WARD WEIR BLAKE BROCK BROWN CRANE CROME CUNEO DAVIS DOYLE FRITH FURSE LEWIS LOWRY LUCAS MOORE ORPEN STARK STEER STONE TONKS UWINS WATTS WELLS ABBOTT ASHTON BARKER BOXALL BROOKS BROWNE CARTER CHALON COATES COOPER COSWAY COTMAN COWPER COZENS CROFTS DEWINT DOBSON FILDES GIRTIN GLOVER HACKER HAYDON HOLMES KNIGHT LAVERY LAWSON LEADER MARTIN MAYTER MCEVOY MULLER NEWTON OLIVER OULESS ROMNEY SEVERN SMIRKE STUART STUBBS TURNER VARLEY WALKER ANSDELL BAYLISS BEECHEY BOMBERG CALVERT CAMERON CLAUSEN COLLIER DANIELL DICKSEE GILBERT GUEVARA HERBERT HODGSON HOGARTH HOLIDAY HOLROYD LINNELL MILLAIS MORLAND POYNTER RIVIERE RUSSELL SOLOMON ZOFFANY ARMITAGE ATKINSON AUMONIER BEAUMONT BRANGWYN CALDERON CALLCOTT CORBOULD CRESWICK EASTLAKE FIELDING HILLIARD LANDSEER LEIGHTON MUNNINGS REDGRAVE REYNOLDS RICHMOND RICKETTS ROSSETTI STOTHARD TOPOLSKI WATERLOW WHISTLER AMSHEWITZ BEARDSLEY BONINGTON BOURGEOIS COLLINSON CONSTABLE GREENAWAY NORTHCOTE STANFIELD THORNHILL BROCKHURST KENNINGTON WATERHOUSE WOOLDRIDGE ROTHENSTEIN GAINSBOROUGH
FINNISH EDELFELT
FLEMISH VOS BLES BRIL EYCK GOES BALEN CLAUS CLEVE COXIE ORLEY CAMPIN COQUES CRAYER MABUSE MASSYS RUBENS WEYDEN BLOEMEN BREUGEL BROUWER BRUGHEL CANDIDO TENIERS VANDYCK VANEYCK BRUEGHEL CHRISTUS CRAESBEECK
FRENCH ZO ARP BIDA CAIN DORE DUFY ETEX GROS HEIM HUET LAMI TROY BIARD CAZIN CHERY CORNU COROT DAVID DEGAS DENIS DOYEN DUPRE FRERE JONAS LEGER LHOTE MANET MONET MOROT PATER PUVIS REDON STAEL VEBER VOUET BAUDRY BERARD BERAUD BOILLY BONNAT BONVIN BOUDIN BOUTON BRAQUE BRETON BUFFET CALLOT CARREY CARZOU CHABAS CHERET CHERON CLOUET CORMON COTTET COUDER COUSIN COYPEL DAUBAN DERAIN DONGEN DOUCET DUBUFE FAVORY FORAIN FORBIN FRIESZ GERARD GEROME GERVEX GIGOUX

GRANET GREUZE GUERIN HEBERT HELION HENNER INGRES LAHIRE LATOUR LEBLON LEBRUN LELEUX LEPINE LORJOU MARTIN MERSON MILLET MIRBEL MOREAU MULLER RENOIR SEURAT SIGNAC STELLA TISSOT TROYON VANLOO VERNET VIBERT WEERTS BALTHUS BARRIAS BESNARD BONHEUR BONNARD BOUCHER BOUCHOR BOURDON CABANEL CEZANNE CHARDIN CHARLOT COGNIET COURBET COUTURE DAMERON DORIGNY DROUAIS DUCHAMP FERRIER FLANDIN FOUQUET GARNIER GAUGUIN GENDRON GLEIZES HARTUNG HEDOUIN HERSENT JEANRON LAFOSSE LANCRET LANSYER LAURENS LEBOURG LEGRAND LEHMANN LEMOYNE LESUEUR LORRAIN MAIGNAN MARQUET MATISSE MICHAUX MIGNARD MORISOT NATTIER PICABIA POUSSIN PRUDHON RESTOUT ROUAULT SOUTINE UTRILLO VALADON WATTEAU BELLANGE BERCHERE CARRIERE CHARTRAN CONSTANT DAGUERRE DALAUNAY DAUBIGNY DESCAMPS DETAILLE DROLLING ESPAGNAT FLANDRIN GALIMARD JOUVENET KLINGSOR LANDELLE LATOUCHE LEFEBVRE LENEPVEU LEPRINCE OZENFANT PARROCEL PISSARRO ROUSSEAU SCHEFFER STEINLEN VUILLARD WILLETTE BOULANGER CHATILLON CHENAVARD COUBERTIN DEBUCOURT DEHODENCQ DELABORDE DELACROIX DELAROCHE DESPORTES FALGUIERE FRAGONARD GERICAULT GLEISPACH GUILLEMET HENNIQUIN LAURENCIN METZINGER SCHUSSELE BARTHOLOME BOUGUEREAU BOULLONGNE BRASCASSAT CHASSERIAU DESBROSSES GUILLAUMET GUILLAUMIN HARPIGNIES JACQUEMART MEISSONIER BRACQUEMOND CARMONTELLE LARGILLIERE DESVALLIERES LOUTHERBOURG
GERMAN DIX MAX ADAM DIEZ HESS JANK LENZ MARC MARR SOHN UHDE VEIT ANTES BEGAS BEHAM BINCK BRUYN DURER EBERS EMELE ERNST FOLTZ FRIES FUGER GRAFF GROSZ HOFER KNAUS KUEHL LEIBL MACKE MENGS MEYER MUCKE NEHER NOLDE OESER PECHT PENCZ STUCK THOMA VOGEL BECKER BRACHT BRAITH BUHLER BURGER EBERLE ECHTER FITGER FRIESE GEBLER GUSSOW HECKEL HENSEL HERLIN HERTEL HEYDEN HUBNER KELLER KOBELL KRAFFT KRUGER LANGER LOFFTZ MAREES MENZEL MULLER RETHEL WERNER BALDUNG BARTELS BLECHEN CORINTH CRANACH FLICKEL GENELLI HOFMANN HOLBEIN KLINGER KOPSICH KRELING LENBACH LESSING LINDNER LOCHNER PRELLER RICHTER SCHWIND STEUBEN AGRICOLA AMBERGER BECKMANN CARSTENS DETTMANN FIORILLO GEBHARDT GRUTZNER HABERLIN HENDRICH KAULBACH KIRCHNER KOLLWITZ KUGELGEN KULMBACH ROTTMANN SCHIRMER SCHREYER ZEITBLOM ACHENBACH AINMILLER ALTDORFER BENDEMANN BLEIBTREU BURGKMAIR CORNELIUS ELSHEIMER ENGELHARD FRIEDRICH GRUNEWALD HABERMANN KNACKFUSS KRIEGHOFF MEYERHEIM MODERSOHN PASSAVANT TISCHBEIN ALDEGREVER BAUMEISTER CAMPHAUSEN HECKENDORF HILDEBRAND SCHONGAUER SCHROEDTER WOHLGEMUTH ZIMMERMANN CHODOWIECKI HASENCLEVER HILDEBRANDT HUCHTENBERG MORGENSTERN SCHRAUDOLPH LINDENSCHMIT ROTTENHAMMER WINTERHALTER
GREEK GYSIS AETION NICIAS ZEUXIS APELLES PAUSIAS EUPOMPUS ARISTIDES EUPHRANOR MELANTHUS PAMPHILUS TIMANTHES AGATHARCUS PARRHASIUS POLYGNOTUS PROTOGENES SPYROPOULOS
GUATEMALAN MERIDA
HUNGARIAN LOTZ ZICHY VADASZ WAGNER SZINYEI MUNKACSY
IRISH BARRY DANBY BURTON FORBES LAVERY PETRIE MACLISE COSTELLO MULREADY ODOHERTY
ISRAELI AGAM RUBIN
ITALIAN CHIA FETI MOLA RENI ROSA TURA VAGA BACCI BALLA CAFFI CAMPI CARPI CARRA COSSA COSTA DANTI DOLCI FERRI FETTI FOPPA GATTI GENGA IORIS LIPPI LOTTO LUINI MELZI PALMA PENNI PIERO PISIS PRETI RICCI SANTI SARTO SPADA VANNI VINCI ABBATE ALBANI ALLORI AVANZO BATONI CALCAR CESARI CIARDI COSIMO CRESPI FRANCO GAULLI GIOTTO GUUIDO MORONI NITTIS PASINI PISANO PREDIS RICCIO ROMANO SACCHI SIRONI SODOMA SOLARI SUARDI TITIAN VASARI VERRIO AMIGONI APPIANI BARBARI BAROCCI BARTOLI BASSANO BELLINI BERNINI BOLDINI BRUMIDI CENNINI CHIRICO CIGNANI CORTONA FALCONE FRANCIA GIORGIO GOZZOLI MARATTI MARTINI MORELLI MUZIANO OGGIONO PALIZZI PERUZZI RAPHAEL ROBERTI STROZZI TIBALDI TIEPOLO UCCELLO VECELLI ZUCCARO BACICCIO BAGLIONI BARBIERE BOCCIONI BONFIGLI CAGLIARI CARDUCCI CARRIERA CASANOVA CASTELLO CIPRIANI COGHETTI CORENZIO GRIMALDI MAGNASCO MAINARDI MANTEGNA MICHETTI MONTAGNA POCCETTI PONTORMO SALVIATI SEVERINI UBERTINI VAROTARI VERONESE VIVARINI ASPERTINI BECCAFUMI CAMUCCINI CANTARINI CAVALLINI CORREGGIO FRANCESCA GHISLANDI MAZZOLINO PIAZZETTA SCHIAVONE SEGANTINI BELTRAFFIO BOCCACCINO BORGOGNONE BOTTICELLI CAMPAGNOLA CARAVAGGIO LORENZETTI MODIGLIANI PROCACCINI SIGNORELLI SQUAREIONE TINTORETTO VERROCCHIO ZUCCARELLI ANGUISCIOLA CASTIGLIONE GENTILESCHI PRIMATICCIO ALBERTINELLI BALDOVINETTI FRANCESCHINI MICHELANGELO PARMIGIANINO PINTURICCHIO
JAPANESE KANO OKYO BUSON IWASA KORIN SAITO SOSEN TORII GOSHUN KOETSU KYOSAI SESSHU JAKUCHU JOSETSU SOTATSU UTAMARO HARUNOBU KIYOMASU KIYONAGA KIYONOBU MORONOBU TOYOKUNI HIROSHEGE KIYOMITSU TSUNETAKA
LITHUANIAN SOUTINE
MEXICAN CANTU MERIDA OROZCO RIVERA TAMAYO SIQUEIROS CASTELLANOS
NORWEGIAN DAHL GUDE KROHG MUNCH LERCHE MUNTHE SINDING FEARNLEY WERENSKIOLD
POLISH BENDA GERSON MATEJKO GROTTGER CHELMINSKI MARCOUSSIS WYSPIANSKI
PORTUGUESE FONSECA
RUSSIAN BAKST REPIN BENOIS BERMAN GRABAR BURLIUK CHAGALL ROERICH LARIONOV LEVITSKI MALEVICH CHELISHEV KANDINSKI LISSITZKY RODCHENKO AIVAZOVSKI BOGOLYUBOV BASHKIRTSEV VERESHCHAGIN
SCOTTISH BONE DYCE FAED HILL ALLAN DAVIE GRANT PATON SCOTT AIKMAN ARCHER BARKER BROUGH DUNCAN GEDDES GORDON GRAHAM HARVEY LAUDER LEITCH MANSON MURRAY PETTIE RAMSAY WILKIE DOUGLAS GUTHRIE LORIMER MACBETH NASMYTH RAEBURN THOMSON CHALMERS MACTAGGART MACWHIRTER ORCHARDSON
SPANISH ARCO CANO DALI GOYA GRIS MAZO MIRO MOYA SERT GRECO HAMEN MACIP CEREZO COELLO PAREJA RIBERA RINCON VARGAS ALVAREZ HERRERA IRIARTE MADRAZO MORALES MURILLO ORRENTE PACHECO PICASSO RIBALTA ZULOAGA CESPEDES PRADILLA ZAMACOIS ZURBARAN VELASQUEZ ZUBIAURRE BERRUGUETE
SWEDISH DAHL ZORN BERGH ROSLIN LARSSON FAGERLIN LUNDGREN HELLQUIST JOSEPHSON LILJEFORS
SWISS KLEE LIPS MIND WITZ ASPER DIDAY ITTEN MEYER BODMER CALAME FUSELI GLEYRE HODLER MANUEL BOCKLIN BUCHSER DISTELI LIOTARD PETITOT VAUTIER KAUFFMANN
WELSH JOHN

PAINTING ART OIL PAT DAUB PATA DRAFT MURAL PIECE TABLE WATER CANVAS CROUTE FRESCO MINERY TITIAN BODEGON CAMAIEU CARTOON COMBINE DAUBING GRADINO GRAPHIC HISTORY PAYSAGE FROTTAGE PREDELLA SEAPIECE SYMPHONY AQUARELLE MINIATURE TABLATURE
(— EQUIPMENT) OIL BRUSH EASEL PAINT CANVAS PALLET
(— IN COLLOIDAL MEDIUM) TEMPERA
(— OF EVERYDAY LIFE) GENRE
(— OF FOLIAGE) BOSCAGE
(— ON PLASTER) SECCO FRESCO
(— ON VELVET) THEOREM
(— SCHOOL) ASHCAN
(— WITH OPAQUE COLORS) GOUACHE
(ACTION —) TACHISM
(CIRCULAR —) TONDO
(EGG —) TEMPERA
(JAPANESE INK —) SUMIE
(JAPANESE STYLE OF —) YAMATO
(PREHISTORIC —) PICTOGRAM PICTOGRAPH
(RELIGIOUS —) PIETA TANKA
(SCENIC —) SCAPE
(SMALL —) TABLET
(TEMPERA —) SECCO
(THREE PANEL —) TRIPTYCH
(PL.) GENRE
(SUFF.) CHROMY

PAIR DUO TWO ZYG CASE DIAD DUAD DUAL DYAD MATE SIDE SPAN TEAM TWIN YOKE BRACE MARRY MATCH TWAIN UNITE COUPLE GEMINI COUPLET DOUBLET JUMELLE TWOSOME
(— OF FILMS) BIPACK
(— OF HORSES) SPAN
(— OF MILLSTONES) RUN
(— OF SHOTS) BRACKET
(— OF TONGS) GRAMPUS GRAPPLE
(— OF WINGS) SHEARS
(— ROYAL) PARIAL
(KIND OF —) COOPER
(ONE OF —) IMPAIR NEIGHBOR
(ONE OF A —) MATE
(PL.) GEMELS
(PREF.) GEMINI ZYG(O)(OTO)
(SUFF.) ZYGOUS

PAIRED GEMEL MATED JUGATE ZYGOUS JUMELLE
PAISLEY PRINT SHAWL DESIGN FABRIC
PAIUTE DIGGER
PAJAMAS JAMMIES SHALWAR SLEEPER
PAKHT (HUSBAND OF —) PTAH

PAKISTAN

BAY: SOYMIANI
CANAL: NARA ROHRI
CAPE: FASTA JADDI JIWANI
CAPITAL: ISLAMABAD
COIN: ANNA PAISA RUPEE
DAM: TARBELA

LANGUAGE: URDU PUSHTU SINDHI BALUCHI BENGALI PUNJABI
MOUNTAIN: TIRICHMIR
MOUNTAIN RANGE: MAKRAN KIRTHAR HIMALAYA SULAIMAN
NATIVE: BENGAL PATHAN SINDHI BALUCHI PUNJABI
PORT: CHALNA KARACHI
PROVINCE: SIND PUNJAB
RIVER: NAL BADO RAVI ZHOB DASHT INDUS CHENAB GANGES JAMUNA JHELUM KUNDAR PORALI
STATE: DIR SWAT KALAT KHARAN CHITRAL KHAIRPUR
TOWN: DACCA CHALNA KHULNA LAHORE MULTAN QUETTA KARACHI SIALKOT LYALLPUR PESHAWAR SARGODHA
WEIGHT: SEER TOLA MAUND

PAKTONG TUTENAG
PAL BO ALLY CHUM JACK PARD BILLY BUDDY BUTTY CHINA CRONY LOUKE COBBER COPAIN DIGGER FRIEND COMRADE PARTNER COMPANION
PALACE SALE CHIGI COURT SERAI STEAD CASTLE ELYSEE LOUVRE PALAIS ALCAZAR EDIFICE LATERAN MANSION PALAZZO TRIANON VATICAN ZWINGER BASILICA SERAGLIO WHITEHALL
(— OF SATAN) PANDEMONIUM
(FAIRY —) SHEE SIDHE
PALADIN HERO PEER ANSEIS ASTOLF KNIGHT CHAMPION DOUZEPER
PALAL (FATHER OF —) UZAI
PALAMEDES (BROTHER OF —) OEAX SFORZA ACHILLES
(FATHER OF —) NAUPLIUS
(MOTHER OF —) CLYMENE
(SLAYER OF —) CORINDA
PALAMON (RIVAL OF —) ARCITE
(WIFE OF —) EMELYE
PALANQUIN JAUN JUAN KAGE KAGO DANDI DOOLI DOOLY PALKI SEDAN DOOLIE LITTER PALKEE TONJON NORIMON
PALATABLE SAPID SPICY TASTY DAINTY SAVORY MOREISH DELICATE LUSCIOUS PLEASING SAPOROUS AGREEABLE DELICIOUS TOOTHSOME
PALATAL SOFT FRONT VELAR GUTTURAL
PALATALIZED MOUILLE
PALATE TASTE VELUM RELISH GOURMET URANISCUS
(SOFT —) UVULA
(PREF.) URAN(O)(OSO)
PALATIAL LARGE ORNATE STATELY SPLENDID
PALATINE CAPE OFFICER PALADIN PALATIAL
PALAVER GASH SLUM TALK CAJOLE DEBATE GLAVER JARGON PARLEY CHATTER FLATTER WHEEDLE CAJOLERY FLATTERY
PALE DIM WAN ASHY BLOC FADE GREY GULL LILY PALL SICK THIN WHEY ASHEN BLAKE BLATE BLEAK CLOSE FAINT FENCE GREEN LIGHT LINEN LIVID LURID MEALY STAKE STICK VERGE WHITE ANEMIC BLANCH CHALKY CHANGE DOUGHY FALLOW FEEBLE PALLID PASTEL PICKET REGION REMISS SICKLY SILVER WATERY WHITEN DEFENSE GHASTLY HAGGARD INSIPID OBSCURE SHILPIT DELICATE WATERISH
(— BY COMPARISON) STAIN
(IN —) HAURIENT
(PREF.) LIRO PALLIDI POLI(O)
PALEA PALET SQUAMELLA
PALENESS WAN PALLOR ACHROMA
PALEONTOLOGIST AMERICAN HAY GABB HALL LULL MEEK BERRY GOULD MARSH CLARKE FOSTER GRABAU HORNER OSBORN BEECHER GREGORY MERRIAM WALCOTT KNOWLTON SPRINGER WILLIAMS SCHUCHERT WACHSMUTH WILLISTON
AUSTRIAN SUESS HOERNES MOJSISOVICS ETTINGSHAUSEN
ENGLISH TATE CAUTLEY MANTELL DAVIDSON WOODWARD BOWERBANK PARKINSON
FRENCH BOULE GAUDRY LARTET BARRANDE TEILHARD
GERMAN ZITTEL BEYRICH QUENSTEDT
SCOTTISH FALCONER
SOUTH AFRICAN BROOM
PALESTINE (SEE ISRAEL)
(CITY OF ANCIENT —) DAN
PALETOT COAT JACKET OVERCOAT GREATCOAT
PALFREY HORSE PALFRY
PALIMPSEST TABLET PARCHMENT
PALINDROMIC SOTADIC SOTADEAN
PALING PALE FENCE FLAKE LIMIT PALIS STAKE PICKET FENCING BLENCHING
PALISADE HAY BOMA PALE PEEL CLIFF FENCE RIMER STAKE FRAISE HURDIS PICKET BARRIER ENCLOSE FORTIFY HURDIES STACKET TAMBOUR ESPALIER
(MILITARY —) CIPPUS
(PL.) BAIL BARRIER
PALL FOG BORE CLOY PALE SATE CLOAK CLOTH FAINT QUALM STALE WEARY MANTLE NAUSEA SHROUD DISGUST SATIATE ANIMETTA MORTCLOTH
PALLET BED COT PAD COUCH QUILT PADDLE BLANKET MATTRESS PLANCHER
PALLIARD BEGGAR LECHER RASCAL VAGABOND
PALLIATE EASE HIDE MASK VEIL ABATE CLOAK COLOR COVER GLOSS GLOZE LITHE BLANCH LESSEN REDUCE SMOOTH SOFTEN SOOTHE CONCEAL CUSHION SHELTER DISGUISE MITIGATE
PALLID WAN ASHY PALE PALY BLEAK MEALY WASHY WAXEN WHITE SALLOW GHASTLY BLOODLESS COLORLESS INNOCUOUS
PALL-MALL MAIL
PALLOR ASH WAN PALE ASHES PALENESS
PALLU (FATHER OF —) REUBEN
(SON OF —) ELIAB
PALM ADY DOM ITA ATAP BRAB BURI BUSU COCO DATE DOUM FLAT HIDE JARA KOKO LOOF NIOG NIPA PAWN SAGO SLIP TARA ARCHA ARECA ARENG ASSAI ATTAP BONGA BUNGA CARRY COCOA COYOL CURUA DATIL FOIST HOWEA INAJA JAGUA LOULU MACAW MERUS NIKAU RATAN SABAL SALAK TECUM TUCUM UNAMO YAGUA YARAY ANAHAO ASSAHY BACABA BURITI CHONTA COHUNE COROJO COROZO GEBANG GOMUTI GRUGRU JAMBEE JUPATI KENTIA KITTUL LAWYER LONTAR NIBONG PACAYA RAFFIA ROTANG THENAR TOOROO TROPHY APRICOT BABASSU BACTRIS CARANDA CONCEAL COQUITO ERYTHEA GEONOMA MORICHE PALMYRA PUPUNHA SAGWIRE TALIPOT TROOLIE URUCURI JACITARA LATANIER MACAHUBA PIASSAVA
(— FERN) PONJA
(— FOOD) NUT COCO DATE NIPA SAGO SURA ASSAI TAREE TODDY COCONUT
(— JUICE) SURA
(— LEAF) OLA OLLA CAJAN FROND
(— LILY) TI
(— OFF) COG FOB TOP SHAB FOIST TRUMP
(— OF HAND) FLAT LOOF VOLA TABLE THENAR
(— OUT) APPAUME
(BETEL —) ARECA BONGA PUGUA PINANG
(CLIMBING —) RATTAN
(FEATHER —) HOWEA GOMUTI URUCURI
(KIND OF —) SAGO
(SLAPPING OF —S) SKIN
(SPINY —) PEACH GRIGRI GRUGRU
(PREF.) CYCAD(I)(O) PALMATO PALMI PALPI PALPO
PALMARY CHIEF PALMAR SUPERIOR
PALMATE FLAT BROAD LOBED WEBBED
PALMER LOUSE FERULE STROLL TRAVEL VOTARY WANDER FOISTER PILGRIM
PALMETTO CABBAGE PALMITO BIGTHATCH
(— STATE) SOUTHCAROLINA
PALMISTRY CHIROMANCY
PALMODIC JERKY
PALMYRA BRAB TALA LONTAR RONIER TADMOR BASSINE
(QUEEN OF —) ZENOBIA
PALP FEEL TOUCH CAJOLE FEELER HANDLE PALPUS FLATTER TENTACLE
PALPABLE BALD RANK PLAIN PATENT AUDIBLE EVIDENT OBVIOUS TACTILE APPARENT DISTINCT MANIFEST TANGIBLE CORPOREAL
PALPATE FEEL
PALPATION THROB TOUCH WALLOP DIPPING PITAPAT
PALPEBRA EYELID
PALPITATE PANT QUAP THROB FLACKER FLICKER FLUTTER PULSATE
PALPITATION BEAT DUNT PANT FLICKER FLUTTER PULSATION SALTATION THROBBING
(— OF HEART) THUMB
PALSIED SHAKY SHAKING PARALYZED TOTTERING TREMBLING TREMULOUS
PALSY PARLESIE PARALYSIS
PALTER FIB LIE BABBLE HAGGLE MUMBLE PARLEY TRIFLE BARGAIN CHAFFER CHATTER QUIBBLE SHAFFLE
PALTIEL (FATHER OF —) AZZAN
PALTRY BALD BARE BASE MEAN ORRA PUNY SCAB VILE WAFF CHEAP FOOTY MINOR PETTY SCALD SCALL SCRUB SILLY TRASH CHETIF FLIMSY JITNEY SHABBY SLIGHT TRASHY WOEFUL HILDING PELTING PIMPING PITEOUS PITIFUL ROYNISH RUBBISH SCABBED SCRUBBY TRIVIAL PICAYUNE PICKLING PIDDLING TRIFLING
PALUDAL MARSHY
PAMELA (AUTHOR OF —) RICHARDSON
(BROTHER OF —) PHILOCLEA
(CHARACTER IN —) JACOB DAVERS JERVIS JEWKES PAMELA ANDREWS SWYNFORD
(FATHER OF —) BASILIUS
PAMPA PLAIN PRAIRIE
PAMPAS (— CAT) KODKOD PAJERO
(— DEER) MAZAME
PAMPER PET BABY CRAM DELT GLUT POMP HUMOR SPOIL TUTOR WALLY CARESS COCKER CODDLE COSHER COSSET CUDDLE CUITER DANDLE FONDLE MAUNGE POSSET TIDDLE CHERISH COCKNEY FORWEAN GRATIFY INDULGE SATIATE SMOODGE SAGINATE
PAMPHLET JACK LEAD FLIER QUIRE SHEET TRACT FOLDER BOOKLET CATALOG LEAFLET NOVELET BROCHURE CHAPBOOK CIRCULAR WORKBOOK CATALOGUE NEWSLETTER
PAN FIT TAB VLY MELL PART PRIG VLEI WASH AGREE BASIN BATEA COVER GRAND ROAST SHEET UNITE CENSER FRACHE LAPPET PANKIN PATINA SPIDER VESSEL CRANIUM CREAMER HARDPAN PORTION ROASTER SKILLET SUBSOIL PANNIKIN RIDICULE
(— FOR COALS) BRAZIER
(— OF BALANCE) BOWL BASIN SCALEPAN
(— WITH 3 FEET) POSNET
(EARTHENWARE —) PANCHEON
(EVAPORATING —) ROOM COVER TACHE SALTPAN
(FRYING —) GRIDDLE
(GOD —) FAUNUS

(IRON —) YET FRACHE
(LONG-HANDLED —) PINGLE
(MILK —) LEAD
(OIL —) SUMP
(PREF.) PATELLI PATELLO
PANACEA CURE BEZOAR ELIXIR REMEDY SOLACE CUREALL GINSENG HEALALL NEPENTHE CATHOLICON
PANACHE STYLE

PANAMA
CAPITAL: PANAMA
COIN: BALBOA
COUNTY: DARIEN HERRERA
CROP: ABACA CACAO
GULF: DARIEN SANBLAS CHIRIQUI MOSQUITO
ISLAND: COIBA
LAKE: GATUN
MEASURE: CELEMIN
MOUNTAIN: CHICO GANDI COLUMAN SANTIAGO
MOUNTAIN RANGE: VERAGUA
PENINSULA: AZUERO
PORT: CRISTOBAL
PROVINCE: COCLE COLON CHIRIQUI VERAGUAS
RIVER: CHEPO SAMBU TUIRA BAYANO PANUGO CHAGRES
TOWN: COLON DAVID AZUERO BALBOA PANAMA PENONOME SANTIAGO
TREE: YAYA MARIA QUIRA ALFAJE CATIVO

PANAMA HAT JIPIJAPA
PANAMINT KOSO
PANCAKE BLIN FLAM AREPA CREPE FADGE FLAWN KISRA LEFSE TOURT BLINTZ FRAISE FROISE CRUMPET FLAPPER FLIPPER FRITTER HOTCAKE PIKELET CORNCAKE FLAPJACK FLIPJACK
(PL.) LEFSEN
PANCREAS BUR NUT
PAND PAWN DRAPERY
PANDA WA WAH BEARCAT
PANDAREUS (DAUGHTER OF —) AEDON MEROPE CLEOTHERA
(FATHER OF —) MEROPS
(WIFE OF —) HARMOTHOE
PANDARUS (BROTHER OF —) BITIAS
(FATHER OF —) LYCAON ALCANOR
PANDAVA BHIMA
PANDECT COMPENDIUM
PANDEMONIUM DIN HELL CHAOS NOISE BEDLAM TUMULT UPROAR DISORDER CONFUSION
PANDER BAWD PIMP BULLY CATER BROKER MICHER PURVEY RUFFIAN WHISKIN PROCURER BAWDSTROT
PANDION (BROTHER OF —) PLEXIPPUS
(DAUGHTER OF —) PROCNE PHILOMELA
(FATHER OF —) CECROPS PHINEUS ERICHTHONIUS
(MOTHER OF —) CLEOPATRA
(SON OF —) BUTES LYCUS NISUS AEGEUS PALLAS ERECHTHEUS
(WIFE OF —) PYLIA
PANDORA BANDORE
(BROTHER OF —) PROMETHEUS
(HUSBAND OF —) EPIMETHEUS
PANDOWDY PIE DESSERT
PANDU (BROTHER OF —) DURYODHANA
(FATHER OF —) DHRITARASHTRA
PANE GLASS GLAZE LOZEN PANEL QUIRK SHEET SHOCK SLASH QUARRY QUARREL SECTION PORTLIGHT
PANEGYRIC ELOGE ELOGY EULOGY PRAISE ORATION TRIBUTE ENCOMIUM LAUDATION
PANEL FIN PAN JURY SKIN BOARD GROUP LABEL TABLE ABACUS ASSIZE COFFER HURDLE MIRROR PADDLE PILLOW ROSACE TABLET TYMPAN CAISSON CONSOLE FLIPPER LACUNAR DECORATE MANDORLA MEDALLION
(— IN FENCE) LOOP
(— IN GARMENT) LAP STEAK
(CIRCULAR —) ROUNDEL
(GAUZE —) SCRIM
(GLAZED —) LAYLIGHT
(LEGAL —) ARRAY
(REAR — ON STATION WAGON) LIFTGATE
(RECESSED —) ORB COFFER LACUNAR
(SUNKEN —) CAISSON CASSOON
(3-PART —) TRIPTYCH
PANELLING WAINSCOT
PANFISH SCUP
PANG ACHE CRAM FILL GIRD PAIN STAB TANG AGONY PINCH PRONG SPASM STANG STOUN STUFF THROB THROE SHOWER STOUND TWINGE ANGUISH TRAVAIL
(PL.) GNAWINGS
PANGLOSS (PUPIL OF —) CANDIDE
PANGOLIN MANID MANIS ANTEATER EDENTATE TANGILIN
PANGS MUNCHIES
(HUNGER —) MUNCHIES
PANGWE FAN FANG
PANHANDLE BEG CADGE SKELB SKILDER
(— STATE) WV WVA
PANIC FEAR FRAY FUNK WILD ALARM AMAZE CHAOS SCARE FRIGHT SCHRIK TERROR SWITHER CONSTERNATION
PANICKY FUNKY ALARMED
PANICLE JUBA WHISK ANTHELA
PANNIER BAG PED SERON BASKET CAJAVA CURAGH DORSEL DORSER DOSSAL DOSSER PANTRY CORBEIL CURRACK KAJAWAH KEDJAVE
PANOPE (FATHER OF —) NEREUS
(MOTHER OF —) DORIS
PANOPEUS (BROTHER OF —) CRISUS
(COMPANION OF —) AMPHITRYON
(DAUGHTER OF —) AEGLE
(FATHER OF —) PHOCUS
(MOTHER OF —) ASTERIA
PANOPLY POMP ARMOR ARRAY UNIFORM
PANORAMA VIEW RANGE SCENE SWEEP VISTA NEORAMA PICTURE SCENERY CYCLORAMA POLYORAMA
PANPIPE SICU SIKU QUILL ANTARA SYRINX ZAMPOGNA
PANSY FANCY PENSE VIOLA KISSES PENSEE VIOLET TRINITY FANTASQUE HEARTEASE
(PREF.) VIOL
PANT FAB ACHE BEAT BLOW FUFF GAPE GASP HECH LONG PANK PECH PEGH PINE PIPE PUFF TIFT FLAFF HEAVE QUIRK STECH SUGGE THROB YEARN ANHELE ASPIRE FRIESE PANTLE PULSATE
PANTAGRUEL (COMPANION OF —) PANURGE
(FATHER OF —) GARGANTUA
(MOTHER OF —) BADEBEC
PANTALOONS PANTS TROUSERS
PANTDRESS CULOTTE
PANTHEA (HUSBAND OF —) ABRADATUS
PANTHEIST AMALRICIAN
PANTHEON AESIR TEMPLE ROTUNDA VALHALL VALHALLA
PANTHER CAT PARD PUMA COUGAR JAGUAR LEOPARD PAINTER PANTILE
(KIND OF —) GRAY
PANTIES SCANTIES
PANTILE TILE IMBREX BISCUIT HARDTACK
PANTING ANHELOSE ANHELOUS
PANTOGRAPH EIDOGRAPH POLYGRAPH
PANTOMIME PLAY PANTO DUMBSHOW
PANTOMIMIST MUMMER
PANTRY CAVE STUE AMBRY COVEY CUDDY CLOSET LARDER SPENCE BUTLERY BUTTERY PANNIER PANTLER SERVERY SPICERY CUPBOARD
PANTS CORDS JEANS LEVIS BRIEFS SLACKS DRAWERS JODHPUR BREECHES BRITCHES KICKSIES KNICKERS SNUGGIES TROUSERS
(— THAT REACH TO MID-CALF) CLAMDIGGER
(— WITH WIDE BOTTOMS) BELLS
(KIND OF —) TAP CAPRI
(LEATHER —) CHAPS LEDERHOSEN
(WIDE-LEGGED —) PALAZZO
PANUELO COLLAR RUFFLE KERCHIEF NECKCLOTH
PANURGE (COMPANION OF —) PANTAGRUEL
PANZER TANK
PAOLO (LOVER OF —) FRANCESCA
PAP DUG TIT POBS TEAT NIPPLE EMULSION FLUMMERY
PAPA PA DAD PAP PAW POP SIN BABA EVIL DADDY LOVER PAPPY BABOON FATHER POTATO PRIEST HUSBAND VULTURE
PAPAL (ALSO SEE POPE) POPAL PAPANE POPELY APOSTOLIC
PAPAW PAPA ASIMEN PAPAIO ASIMINA CORAZON JASMINE
PAPAYA PAPAW LECHOSA
PAPER LIL WEB BILL BOND BLANK BROKE ESSAY STUDY THEME ASTHMA BINDLE CARTEL PAPIER REPORT RETREE VESSEL CHEVIOT EXHIBIT JOURNAL WRITING YOSHINO DOCUMENT MONOGRAPH NEWSPRINT ONIONSKIN PARCHMENT VALENTINE
(— FOLDER) STROKER
(— MAKER) WASHERMAN
(— NAUTILUS) ARGONAUT
(— PULP) WATERLEAF
(— QUANTITY) PAGE REAM QUIRE SHEET BUNDLE
(— SIZE) SIXMO
(ABSORBENT —) BLOTTER TOWELLING
(ADVERTISING —) FLIER FLYER SHOPPER
(ALBUMINIZED —) SAXE
(BUILDING —) FELT
(BUNDLE OF —S) DUFTER DOSSIER
(CHINESE —) INDIA
(COMMERCIAL —) PORTFOLIO
(DAMAGED —) BROKE CASSE SALLE RETREE
(DEFECTIVE —) BROKES
(DIPLOMATIC —) NOTE
(DRAWING —) TORCHON
(FOLDED —) SADDLE AIRPLANE
(FRILLED —) PAPILLOTE
(GIVING AUTHORITY) POWER
(GLOSS —) GILL
(HARD —) PELURE
(HEAVY —) FELT
(LAVATORY —) BUMF
(LINING —S) SKIPS
(METAL-COATED —) FOIL
(NEGOTIABLE —) STIFF
(OFFICIAL —) TARGE HOOKUM DOCUMENT
(PARCHMENT —) VELLUM PERGAMYN
(PHOTOGRAPHIC —) SEPIA
(SIZE OF —) CAP COPY DEMI NOTE POST POTT TOWN ATLAS CROWN FOLIO JESUS LARGE LEGAL ROYAL SIXMO ALBERT BILLET CASING LETTER MEDIUM THIRDS BASTARD CABINET EMPEROR THEOREM ELEPHANT FOOLSCAP IMPERIAL
(SMALL PIECES OF —) CHAD
(STRIP OF —) TAPE
(STRONG —) MANILA MANILLA
(THIN —) FLIMSY PELURE TISSUE ONIONSKIN
(THROWN —) CONFETTI
(TOILET —) BUMF
(TRANSPARENT —) GLASSINE
(UNCUT —) BOLT
(WALL —) TENTURE
(WATERMARKED —) BATONNE
(WRAPPING —) SKIP KRAFT SEALING SCREENING
(WRITING —) FLAT LINEN WEDDING
(PREF.) PAPYRO
PAPERBARK CAJEPUT MILKWOOD
PAPERBOARD BENDER VENEER CARDBOARD CHIPBOARD PULPBOARD
PAPER FACTOR JUVABIONE
PAPERWORK BUMF BUMPH
PAPIER-MACHE FLONG
PAPILLA CERAS DEIRID NIPPLE PAPULA MAMMULA THELIUM
(PL.) CERATA
PAPILLOMA ANGLEBERRY

PAPIO MORMON
PAPIST TORY PAPANE CATHOLIC POPELING
PAPPUS DOWN STIPE AIGRETTE PARACHUTE THISTLEDOWN
PAPPY PA DAD PAW PAPA SOFT MUSHY PULPY FATHER SUCCULENT
PAPRIKA PIMENTO PIMIENTO
PAPUA **(BAY OF —)** DYKE MILNE ACLAND HOLNICOTE
(CAPITAL OF —) PORTMORESBY
(MONEY OF —) KINA
(RIVER OF —) FLY KIKORI PURARI
(TOWN OF —) LAE BUNA DARU WEWAK GOROKA KIKORI MADANG SAMARAI
PAPUAN ARAU BIAK HULA KATE BUANG EKARI KIWAI KWOMA SIVAI SULKA BAITSI BANARO IATMUL KEREWA KOIARI ARAPESH BAINING
PAPULE WHELK PIMPLE
PAPYRUS REED PAPER SEDGE BIBLOS GLUMAL SCROLL BULRUSH
(— STRIP) ORIHON
PAR BY NORM EQUAL NORMAL AVERAGE EQUALITY
(ONE OVER —) BOGIE
(ONE UNDER —) BIRDIE
(TWO UNDER —) EAGLE
PARA FODDA PERAU PARRAH
PARABASIS ODE
PARABLE MYTH TALE FABLE STORY APOLOG BYWORD MASHAL SAMPLE BYSPELL PROVERB ALLEGORY APOLOGUE FORBYSEN LIKENESS SIMILITUDE
PARABOLA ARC CURVE ANTENNA
PARACETAMOL PANADOL
PARACHUTE SILK CHUTE BROLLY DROGUE BALLUTE PATAGIUM STREAMER
(— OF DOWN) PAPPUS
(FOLDED —) PACK
(SEND BY —) DROP
(SMALL —) BALLUTE
PARACHUTIST PATHFINDER
(PL.) STICK
PARACLETE AIDER HELPER PLEADER ADVOCATE CONSOLER COMFORTER
PARADE JET TOP POMP SHOW WALK MARCH STRUT FLAUNT MUSTER REVIEW STROLL CORTEGE DISPLAY EXHIBIT MARSHAL CEREMONY EXERCISE FLOURISH GRANDEUR SPLENDOR PAGEANTRY
(— GROUND) MAIDAN
(— OF BULLFIGHTERS) PASEO
(— OF WORDS) FLOURISH
(UNSUBSTANTIAL —) PAGEANT
PARADED AFFICHE
PARADISE EDEN JODO BLISS JENNA AIDENN GOLOKA HEAVEN PARVIS ELYSIUM NIRVANA
(— OF INDRA) SVARGA SWARGA
(— TREE) ACEITUNA STAVEWOOD
PARADOX KOAN ANTINOMY
PARADOXURE MUSANG PALMCAT PALMCIVET
PARAFFIN ALKANE
PARAGON GEM HERO PINK TYPE IDEAL MODEL PEARL APERSEE PATTERN PEROPUS PHOENIX NONESUCH NONPAREIL
(— OF KNIGHTHOOD) PALADIN
PARAGRAPH ITEM SIGN CAPUT PAUSE CLAUSE NOTICE RUBRIC ARTICLE INITIAL PILCROW SECTION CAUSERIE MATERIAL PEELCROW PERSONAL SUBLEADER
(— MARK) PILCROW
(UNIMPORTANT —S) BALAAM

PARAGUAY
CAPITAL: ASUNCION
COIN: GUARANI
DEPARTMENT: GUAIRA ITAPUA OLIMPO CAAZAPA BOQUERON
LAKE: VERA YPOA YPACARAI
LANGUAGE: GUARANI
MEASURE: PIE LINE LINO VARA LEGUA LINEA CORDEL CUADRA CUARTA FANEGA
PLAIN: CHACO
RIVER: YPANE ACARAY PARANA CONFUSO
TOWN: LUQUE PILAR CAACUPE CAAZAPA TRINIDAD CONCEPCION VILLARRICA
WEIGHT: QUINTAL

PARAGUAY TEA MATE
PARAKEET CONURE PARROT WELLAT ROSELLA ARATINGA KAKARIKI POPINJAY ROSEHILL GREENLEEK
PARALLEL EVEN LIKE ALONG EQUAL MATCH SECOND EXAMPLE FRONTAL PARAGON PENDANT ANALOGUE LIKENESS MULTIPLE QUANTITY
(PREF.) ORTH(O) PAR(A)
PARALLELEPIPED CUBOID
PARALLELISM PARITY ANALOGY
PARALLELOGRAM RHOMB OBLONG SQUARE RHOMBUS RHOMBOID RECTANGLE
PARALYSIS CRAMP PALSY POLIO SHOCK PARESIS DIPLEGIA PARAPLEGIA POLIOMYELITIS
(SUFF.) LYSE LYSIS LYST LYTE LYTIC LYZE
PARALYZE DARE DAZE STUN PALSY SCRAM ASTONY BENUMB CONGEAL IMPALSY PETRIFY TORPEDO TORPEFY
(— WITH EMOTION) TRANSFIX
PARALYZED NUMB PALSIED CRIPPLED
PARAMEDIC EMT
PARAMORPHINE THEBAINE
PARAMOUNT ABOVE CHIEF RULER SOVRAN CAPITAL SUPREME DOMINANT SUPERIOR SUZERAIN SOVEREIGN
PARAMOUR DOLL PRIM PURE LEMAN LOVER WOMAN WOOER AMORET FRIEND MASTER MINION FRANION GALLANT HETAERA RUFFIAN SERVANT SPECIAL SULTANA STALLION BOYFRIEND
PARAPET BUTT WALL BAHUT REDAN BARBET BONNET FLECHE PARPEN TRENCH BULWARK PLUTEUS RAILING RAMPART BARTIZAN ENVELOPE TRAVERSE
PARAPH RUBRIC
PARAPHERNALIA GEAR EQUIPAGE APPARATUS EQUIPMENT TRAPPINGS
PARAPHRASE FARSE REWORD TARGET TARGUM PREFACE THARGUM VERSION TRANSLATE
PARASITE BUG BUR FLY BURR MOSS SPIV TRYP CHARK DRONE LEECH SHARK TOADY VIRUS FEEDER FUNGUS GNATHO SHADOW SPONGE SUCKER THRIPS BLEEDER BYWONER SPONGER TAGTAIL DICYEMID ENTOZOON EPIPHYTE HANGERON SLAVERER INFESTANT POTHUNTER SACCULINA SPARGANUM SYCOPHANT TOADEATER TUBHUNTER
(— ON TROUT) SUG
(PL.) ECTOZOA ENTOZOA DRIFTWOOD
(PREF.) **(VEGETABLE —)** PHYT(I)(O)
PARASITIC CYTOZOIC TRENCHER BIOPHILOUS
(— JAEGER) SHOOI DIRTBIRD
PARASOL SHADE AOGIRI SHADOW ROUNDEL TIRESOL KITTYSOL SUNSHADE UMBRELLA
(— MUSHROOM) LEPIOTA
(PREF.) UMBELL(I)
PARATROOPER SKYMAN
PARAVANE OTTER
PARBOIL CODDLE
PARBOILED LEEPIT
PARCEL DAK LOT DAWK DEAD DEAL DOLE METE PACK PART WISP BULSE BUNCH GROUP PIECE BUNDLE DIVIDE FARDEL PACKET PASSEL CONACRE PACKAGE PORTION COMMODITY
(— OF DIAMONDS) SERIES
(— OF GROUND) LOT PICK CLOSE SOLUM SUERTE CONACRE PENDICLE
(— OF HEMP FIBER) PIG
(— OF JEWELS) BULSE
(— OUT) ALLOT
PARCH DRY FRY BURN COOK SEAR ROAST TOAST PEARCH RIZZER SCORCH BRISTLE BRUSTLE GRADDAN SHRIVEL TORREFY TORRIFY
(PREF.) TORRE XER(O)
PARCHED ARID HUSK SERE ADUST FIERY GIZZEN TORRID THIRSTY SCORCHED
PARCHING URENT
PARCHMENT LARK FOREL CHARTA MEZUZAH PAPYRIN SCYTALE DRUMHEAD SHEEPSKIN PALIMPSEST
(— PAPER) DOCKET PERGAMYN
(FINE —) VEL VELLUM
(PIECE OF —) MEMBRANE
(ROLL OF —) PELL SCROLL
PARD PAL CHUM TIGER FRIEND LEOPARD PANTHER PARTNER COMPANION
PARDON FREE CLEAR COVER GRACE MERCY REMIT SPARE ACQUIT ASSOIL EXCUSE SHRIVE ABSOLVE AMNESTY CONDONE FORGIVE OVERLOOK REPRIEVE TOLERATE EXCULPATE
PARDONABLE VENIAL VENIABLE EXCUSABLE
PARDONER QUESTOR QUAESTOR
PARE CUP CHIP COPE FLAY PEEL SKIN FRIZZ SHAVE SKELP SKIVE SLIPE SPADE CHISEL REDUCE REMOVE RESECT CURTAIL FLAUGHT WHITTLE
(— LEATHER) SKIVE
(— SOD) BURNBEAT
(— STAVES) BUCK
(— STONE) BOAST
PAREGORIC ANODYNE MITIGATING
PAREL PARELL APPAREL CLOTHING ORNAMENT
PARENCHYMA AMYLOM MESOPHYL
PARENT DAD DAM MAMA PAPA SIRE DADDY ELDER MATER PATER AUTHOR FATHER MOTHER ORIGIN FORBEAR GENITOR ANCESTOR BEGETTER FILICIDE GUARDIAN
PARENTAGE KIND BIRTH BROOD FAMILY ORIGIN PROGENY ENGENDURE
PARENTHESIS HOOK ASIDE PAREN BRACKET TOENAIL INNUENDO INTERVAL INTERLUDE
(PL.) HOOKS CURVES
PAREVE NEUTRAL
PARGET COAT GYPSUM PARIET PLASTER DECORATE WHITEWASH
PARGO MUTTONFISH
PARHELION DOG SUN SUNDOG
PARIAH LEPER PAREA ISHMAEL OUTCAST
PARIAN CHINA MARBLE PORCELAIN
PARIETAL SOMAL SOMATIC
PARI-MUTUEL TOTE TOTALIZER
PARING CHIP FOIL SHRED SPECK GUBBIN PARURE PEELING
(FISH —S) GUBBINS
(PL.) BOXING
PARIS ALEXANDER
(— AIRPORT) ORLY
(FATHER OF —) PRIAM
(MOTHER OF —) HECUBA
(PALACE IN —) ELYSEE LOUVRE TUILERIES
(RIVER OF —) SEINE
(STOCK EXCHANGE IN —) BOURSE
(SUBWAY IN —) METRO
(WIFE OF —) OENONE OENONE
PARISH CURE HOUSE TITLE CHARGE SOCIETY PECULIAR OUTPARISH
(— HEAD) PASTOR PRIEST MINISTER
(— MEETING) VESTRY
PARISIAN LUTETIAN
PARISINA **(BELOVED OF —)** HUGO
(HUSBAND OF —) AZO
PARISON BLOW GATHERING
PARITY ANALOGY EQUALITY LIKENESS GRAVIDITY
PARK HAY PEN HOLE STOP WAIT GREEN LEAVE CIRCLE DAPHNE GARDEN PRATER COMMONS DIAMOND PADDOCK TERRACE PARADISE TETRAGON

(AMUSEMENT —) FUNFAIR
(KIND OF —) THEME
PARKA PARCA ANORAK JACKET PULLOVER
PARKING (KIND OF —) VALET
PARKLEAVES TUTSAN
PARLANCE TALK IDIOM SPEECH DICTION DISCOURSE
PARLAY WAGER DOUBLE
PARLEY DODGE PARLE SPEAK TREAT UTTER CONFER INDABA PALTER PAROLI DISCUSS PALAVER PARLING PARLANCE DISCOURSE TEMPORIZE NEGOTIATION
PARLIAMENT DIET RUMP TING COURT SENAT CORTES FANTAN MAJLIS SAEIMA COUNCIL ESTATES KNESSET LAGTING RIKSDAG TYNWALD CONGRESS CONVERSE STORTING VOLKSRAAD SANDHEDRIN
(— HOUSE) DAIL SEANAD
(GREEK —) BOULE
(SCAND. —) THING
PARLIAMENTARIAN APRONEER
PARLOR BEN BOOR HALL SALON FOREROOM LOCUTORY SNUGGERY SOLARIUM
(COUNTRY —) SPENCE
(MILKING —) BAIL
PARLORMAID MATRON
PARLOUS KEEN RISKY CLEVER SHREWD CUNNING CRITICAL PERILOUS DANGEROUS HAZARDOUS
PARMASHTA (FATHER OF —) HAMAN
PARMESAN GRANA
PARNACH (SON OF —) ELIZAPHAN
PAROCHIAL PETTY NARROW PAROCHIAN SECTARIAN
PARODIST SPOOFER
PARODY RIB SKIT PUTON SPOOF SATIRE SENDUP TRAVESTY BURLESQUE IMITATION
PAROLE FAITH PLEDGE LICENSE PROMISE
PARONOMASIA PUN AGNOMINATION
PARONYCHIA FELON PANARIS WHITLOW NAILWORT
PAROTITIS MUMPS
PAROXYSM FIT KINK PANG AGONY COLIC QUIRK SPASM STORM STOUR THROE ACCESS ATTACK FRENZY ORGASM RAPTUS SHOWER RAPTURE EPITASIS AGITATION
PARR PAR SAMLET SCEGGER SKEGGER BRANDLIN BRANDLING
PARROT ARA HIA KEA COPY ECHO JAKO KAKA LORO LORY POLL VAZA ARARA CAGIT MACAW MIMIC POLLY AMAZON CAIQUE CONURE KAKAPO REPEAT TIRIBA CORELLA GRASSIE ITERATE LORILET COCKATOO LORIKEET LOVEBIRD PARAKEET PICARIAN POPINJAY BROADTAIL COCKATEEL BUDGERIGAR
(PREF.) PSITTAC(I)
PARROT FISH LORO SCAR LANIA LAUIA SCAUR VIEJA COTORO SCARUS LABROID MUDFISH OLDWIFE BLUEFISH
PARRY FEND STOP WARD AVOID BLOCK DODGE EVADE FENCE PRIME QUART SIXTE OCTAVE PARADE QUINTE SECOND THWART TIERCE COUNTER DEFLECT EVASION
PARSE PACE PEARCE ANALYZE DIAGRAM DISSECT CONSTRUE ANATOMIZE
PARSEGHIAN ARA
PARSHANDATHA (FATHER OF —) HAMAN
PARSI ZOROASTRIAN
(— HOLY BOOK) AVESTA
(— PRIEST) MOBED DASTUR
PARSIFAL (CHARACTER IN —) KUNDRY TITUREL AMFORTAS KLINGSOR PARSIFAL GURNEMANZ
(COMPOSER OF —) WAGNER
PARSIMONIOUS GARE MEAN NEAR NIGH CLOSE MINGY NIPPY SCANT SPARE TIGHT FRUGAL NARROW SCARCE SCOTCH SKIMPY SORDID STINGY STRAIT MISERLY SCRIMPY SPARING COVETOUS GRASPING GRUDGING SCREWING WRETCHED MERCENARY NIGGARDLY PENURIOUS RETENTIVE ABERDONIAN
PARSLEY ACHE CUMIN UMBEL CICELY CONIUM ELTROT KARPAS CHERVIL HOGWEED FLUELLIN
PARSLEY CAMPHOR APIOL APIOLE
PARSNIP TANK WYPE UMBEL CONIUM MADNEP CADWEED HOGWEED SKIRRET BUNDWEED QUEENWEED
(WATER —) SIUM
PARSON RECTOR CROAKER PATRICO PERSONA MINISTER PREACHER GUIDEPOST
(COUNTRY —) RUM
(PL.) PARSONRY
PARSONAGE GLEBE MANSE RECTORY PASTORATE PASTORIUM
PARSON BIRD POE TUI KOKO TUWI POEBIRD POYBIRD
PART DEL END LOT PAN DEAL DOLE FECK GRIN HAET HALF HAND NECK PANE ROLE ROVE SECT SHED SIDE SOME TEAR TWIN AUGHT PARTY PIECE QUOTA SEVER SHARE SHODE SNACK SPLIT TWAIN BEHALF CANTON CLEAVE DEPART DETAIL DIVIDE FEEDER FINGER MEMBER MINUTE MOIETY PARCEL PORTIO QUORUM SECTOR SINGLE SUNDER UNYOKE DISJOIN ELEMENT FEATURE FRUSTUM PORTION SECTION SEGMENT SEVERAL ALIENATE DISSEVER DIVISION ELIQUATE FRACTION LIRIPIPE
(— HAIR) SHADE
(— OF ANIMAL'S TAIL) DOCK
(— OF BEEF) CHUCK SKINK
(— OF BLAST FURNACE) BOSH BELLY
(— OF BOW) PEAK
(— OF CAM WHEEL) LOBE
(— OF CANNON) CHASE
(— OF CHAIR) SPLAT
(— OF COMPASS) FLY
(— OF CONCERTO) CEMBALO
(— OF CONFIRMATION SERVICE) ALAPA
(— OF CROSSBOW) LATH
(— OF DIAMOND) BEZEL
(— OF FLEECE) LEECH
(— OF FOWL'S COMB) BLADE
(— OF FURNACE) HEARTH
(— OF GUN SHIELD) APRON
(— OF HARBOR) FAIRWAY
(— OF HAWK'S BEAK) CLAP
(— OF HIDE) RANGE
(— OF HOOKAH) CHILLUM
(— OF HORSE) FOREHAND
(— OF JOINT) TABLE
(— OF MASS) INTROIT
(— OF POETIC FOOT) ARSIS
(— OF PORK LOIN) GRISKIN
(— OF RIVER) FRESH
(— OF SADDLE TREE) FORK
(— OF STAIR TREAD) NOSING
(— OF STAMEN) ANTHER
(— OF SWORD) FORTE
(— OF SWORD BLADE) FOIBLE
(— OF TEMPLE) CELLA
(— OF THROAT) GULA FAUCES
(— OF TONGUE) DORSUM
(— OF TURTLE) CALIPEE
(— OF VIOLIN BOW) BAGUET
(— OF WHEEL) SPEECH
(— THAT REVOLVES) ROTOR
(— THE LEGS) STRADDLE
(— WITH) CEDE GIVE LOSE SELL LEAVE DONATE ABANDON
(— WITHIN) INSIDE
(ACCOMPANYING —) BURDEN OBBLIGATO
(ARTIFICIAL —) PROSTHESIS
(ASSIGNED —) QUOTA
(ASSUMED —) FIGURE
(BAGLIKE —) SAC
(BEST —) FAT YOLK CREAM FLOWER MARROW
(BRISTLELIKE —) SETA
(BROADEST — OF PLANK) TOUCH
(CENTRAL —) HUB BODY CORE HEART KERNEL
(CHOICE —) ELITE
(CLEAR — OF LIQUID) SWIM
(CLOSING —) HEEL
(COARSE — OF FLAX) HURDS
(CONCLUDING —) WRAPUP
(CONICAL —) BULLET
(CONNECTING —) NECK PONS UNION
(CURVED —) START
(DEPRESSED —) HOLLOW
(DISTANT —S) FARNESS
(DUPLICATE —) SPARE
(EDIBLE — OF CLAM) CHEEK
(EIGHTH — OF CIRCLE) OCTANT
(ESSENTIAL —) PITH
(ESSENTIAL —S) STAMINA
(FIFTH —) QUINTUS
(FINAL —) LAST SHANK EPILOG
(FIRST —) FRONT PRIME VAUNT INITIAL BEGINNING
(FOURTH —) FARDEL FORPIT FERLING
(FRONT —) VAUNT BREAST FORESIDE
(FURTHEST —) TIP
(GREATER —) HEFT SUBSTANCE
(HARDEST —) BRUNT
(HIGHEST —) CROP CROWN HEIGHT
(HUNDREDTH —) CENTESM
(IMPAIRING —) ALLOY
(IN —) HALVES
(INDETERMINATE —) PERCENTAGE
(INNERMOST —) FUND
(INNERMOST —S) PENETRALIA
(INSTRUMENTAL —) HAND CONTINUO
(INTERLACED —) TWINE
(INTRODUCTORY —) PROTASIS
(LARGE —) FORCE
(LATERAL — OF HEAD) CHEEK
(LATTER —) HEEL SHANK
(LEAST —) STITCH
(LESS DESIRABLE —) RIDDLINGS
(LEVEL —) FLAT
(LOWER —) SECONDO
(LOWER — OF ROBE) BASES
(LOWEST —) FOOT BOTTOM GROUND DESCENT
(MAIN —) BODY BULK SUBSTANCE
(MATERIAL —) GIST
(MIDDLE —) DEEP CENTER
(MIDDLE — OF NIGHT) HOWE
(MINOR —) BIT COG
(MINUTE —) PRICK TITTLE
(MISSING —) LACUNA
(MOST IMPORTANT —) EYE FOREHAND
(MOST SERIOUS —) DICKENS
(NARROW —) STRAIT THROAT
(OF HORSE'S THIGH) GASKIN
(OVERDUE —) ARREAR
(PRINCIPAL —) BODY MAIN GROSS
(PRIVATE —) THING MEMBER
(PROJECTING —) ARM JAG JET JOG APSE LOBE SPURN
(PROTUBERANT —) BOSS BULGE
(REJECTED —S) CHANKINGS
(REMAINING —) BUTT DREG HEEL
(REMOTEST —) EXTREMITY
(RINGLIKE —) ANNULUS
(ROOTLIKE —) RADICLE
(ROTATING —) ROTOR
(ROUNDED —) BULB
(SAWLIKE —) SERRA
(SECRET —) RECESS
(SLENDER —) NECK
(SMALL —) BIT ATOM FLOW TITHE DETAIL MINUTE SNIPPET
(SMALLEST —) ATOM WHIT MINIM
(SOFT — OF BREAD) CRUMB
(SOFT — OF VEIN) LEATH
(SOLO —) CALL
(STAMEN —) ANTHER
(STATIONARY —) STATOR
(STILL — OF WATER) KELD
(SWINGING —) FLAIL
(TELLING —) POINT
(TENTH —) TITHE
(THIN —) LEAF
(THIN — OF WALL) ALLEGE
(THIRD —) THIRDENDEAL
(TOP —) HEADPIECE
(TWELFTH —) INCIA POINT UNCIAL
(UPPER —) CHIEF RIDGE OVERPARTY
(UPPERMOST —) TOP PEAK CHIEF UPSIDE TOPSIDE

(VAUDEVILLE —) OLIO
(VITAL —) HEART
(WINGLIKE —) ALA
(WORST —) DEPTH
(WORTHLESS —) DREGS
(24TH —) CARAT
(360TH —) DEGREE
(PREF.) MER(I)(O) PARTI
(SUFF.) MER(E)(IC)(IS)(OUS)(Y) TOMA TOME TOMIC TOMOUS TOMY

PARTAKE BITE PART SHARE DIVIDE PARTEN PARTICIPATE
(— OF) EAT USE HAVE SHARE TASTE TOUCH IMPART

PARTAN CRAB

PARTED PARTITE

PARTHAON (FATHER OF —) AGENOR
(MOTHER OF —) EPICASTE
(SON OF —) OENEUS
(WIFE OF —) EURYTE

PARTHENIA (HUSBAND OF —) ARGALUS

PARTHENIUS (BROTHER OF —) PANDION
(FATHER OF —) PHINEUS
(MOTHER OF —) CLEOPATRA

PARTHENOGENETIC AGAMIC AGAMOUS

PARTIAL HALF PART SEMI BIASED UNFAIR COLORED HALFWAY UNEQUAL HARMONIC INCLINED PARTISAN PROPENSE SKELETON FAVORABLE SEGMENTAL PARTICULAR RESPECTIVE
(PREF.) DEMI MER(I)(O) MES(O) SEMI

PARTIALITY BIAS FAVOR RESPECT AFFECTION SPECIALTY

PARTIALLY HALF HALFWAY HALFWISE

PARTICIPANT BOOK ACTOR PARTY MEMBER PARTNER DUETTIST PARTABLE PARTISAN
(SUBORDINATE —) STOOGE
(PL.) FIELD

PARTICIPATE JOIN SIDE ENTER SHARE ENGAGE ENLIST IMPART COMPETE PARTAKE
(— IN) GO HAVE JOIN STAY STAND TASTE COMMON STICKLE

PARTICIPATION HAND PLOT SOCIETY INTEREST
(COMMON —) COMMUNITY

PARTICIPATOR
(SUFF.) STER STRESS

PARTICIPLE VERBID

PARTICLE ACE BIT DOT FIG GRU JOT PSI RAY ATOM BETA CORN CROT CURN DUST GRUE HAET IOTA KNIT MITE MOTE SNIP SPOT STIM WHIT ALPHA BOSON FLAKE FLECK GHOST GRAIN MESON OMEGA POINT PRION QUARK SHRED SIGMA SPECK STARN STIME THRUM TWINT FILING GEIGER LEPTON MOMENT PANGEN PARTON RIZZOM SMIDGE SMITCH TITTLE VIRION AMICRON FERMION GEMMULE GRANULE NUCLEUS PHOTINO PSYCHON SINGLET SMIDGIN TACHYON ACCEPTER GRAVITON NEUTRINO SMIDGEON SYLLABLE MICROSOME POSITRINO SCINTILLA
(— IN BLOOD) EMBOLUS
(— IN INTERNAL EAR) OTOCONIUM
(— OF FIRE) SPARK
(— OF GOLD) COLOR
(— OF QUARKS) HADRON
(— OF SOOT) ISEL IZLE SMUT AIZLE
(—S IN BEER) FLOATERS
(—S OF GRAIN) CHOP
(— TO BIND QUARKS) GLUON
(ATOMIC —) ION MUON BARYON HADRON LEPTON ELECTRON
(BINDING —) GLUON
(COLLECTION OF CHARGED —S) PLASMA
(COMBINING —) ACCEPTOR
(ELECTRIFIED —) ION ANION PROTON POSITRON THERMION
(ELEMENTARY —) MUON NEUTRON NEUTRINO
(FINE ICY —S) SLEET
(GROUP OF —S) MESON
(HYPOTHETICAL —) QUARK
(JAGGED —) SPLINTER
(KIND OF —) ETA TAU
(LEAST POSSIBLE —) MINIM
(LINGUISTIC —) SERVILE
(MASSLESS —) GLUON
(MESON —) UPSILON
(MINUTE —) JOT ORT RAY ATOM GRAIN SPECK RAMENT GRANULE MOLECULE RAMENTUM CORPUSCLE
(NEGATIVE —) NOR NOT
(NUCLEAR —S) FALLOUT
(PHYSICS —) QUARK POSITRON
(POSITIVELY-CHARGED —) CATION KATION
(PROTEIN —) PRION
(QUARK —S) HADRON
(SMALL —) NIP BLEB CORN MOTE CRUMB GRAIN SPECK PROTON AMICRON GRANULE SPRINKLE SUBMICRON
(SUBATOMIC —) PION LAMBDA
(TINY —) ATOMY
(ULTIMATE —) PSYCHON
(UNCHARGED —) LAMBDA
(PL.) DUST FINES SWARF SIZINGS CUTTINGS FURFURES
(SUFF.) PLAST
(— OF A KIND) ID

PARTI-COLORED PIED FANCY MOTLEY PARTED PIEBALD BUTTERFLY HARLEQUIN

PARTICULAR AND ATOM FIXY ITEM NICE SELF SOME FUSSY PARTY POINT THING CHOOSY DAINTY DETAIL MINUTE MOROSE REGARD SINGLE STICKY ARTICLE CAREFUL CERTAIN CORRECT FINICKY PRECISE PRIVATE RESPECT SEVERAL SPECIAL UNUSUAL CLERKISH CONCRETE ESPECIAL PECULIAR PICKSOME PRECIOUS SINGULAR SUBALTERN RESPECTIVE
(NOT —) INCURIOUS

PARTICULARLY ONLY EXTRA SINGLY SPECIAL EXPRESSLY SPECIALLY

PARTING DEATH GOODBYE FAREWELL
(— AS OF HAIR) SHED

PARTISAN PIKE SIDER STAFF BIASED FACTOR FAUTOR MARIAN ZEALOT CALOTIN DEVOTEE GUISARD PARTNER ADHERENT CRISTINO ESPOUSER FAVORITE FENNOMAN FOLLOWER HENCHMAN JACOBITE MOSSBACK SIDESMAN STALWART URBANIST HIGHFLIER MAZZINIST OCHLOCRAT OLIVERIAN SECTARIAN TERRORIST
(NOT —) CATHOLIC
(PL.) FOLLOWING
(SUFF.) CRAT

PARTITION BAR CUT DAM FIN FLAG SEPT WALL SHOJI SPEER STAGE WITHE BAFFLE DIVIDE PARPAL PARPEN SCONCE SCREEN SEPTUM BARRIER CLOISON ENCLOSE GRATING PINFOLD PORTION SCANTLE BRATTICE BULKHEAD CLEAVAGE DIVISION STOPPING TRAVERSE DASHBOARD DAYABHAGA ICONOSTAS MESENTERY STOOTHING
(— BETWEEN STALLS) TRAVIS TREVIS TRAVISS
(— IN CHIMNEY) WITH WITHE
(— IN CORAL) TABULA
(— IN COTTAGE) SPEER HALLAN
(— IN FRUIT) REPLUM
(— IN LOUDSPEAKER) BAFFLE
(— IN WATERWHEEL) WREST
(— OF ESTATE) BOEDELSCHEIDING
(— OF LATH AND PLASTER) STOOTHING
(HORIZONTAL —) STAGE
(MINING —) SOLLAR BRATTICE STOPPING
(PL.) CANCELLI

PARTLET HEN WOMAN PERTELOT

PARTLY WHAT PARCEL PARTIM HALFLINGS
(PREF.) SEMI

PARTNER BOY PAL ALLY HALF MATE PARD WIFE BUDDY BUTTY PARTY FELLOW MARROW SHARER COMRADE CONSORT HUSBAND CAMARADA COPEMATE SIDEKICK YOKEMATE
(— OF DUMMY) VIVANT
(DANCING —) GIGOLO CAVALIER
(ROMANTIC —) SQUEEZE
(PREF.) CO

PARTNERS INOUT ONOFF TOFRO COMEGO HEMHAW HITRUN HUECRY PROCON BILLCOO DOTDASH DOWNOUT EBBFLOW FARWIDE FIVETEN HAMEGGS HIGHDRY HIGHLOW INSOUTS KITHKIN PATMIKE PUTTAKE TOUCHGO YINYANG AMOSANDY BECKCALL GIVETAKE HANDFOOT HIDESEEK HILLDALE MUCKMIRE MUTTJEFF ODDSENDS RICKRACK ROCKROLL SHOWTELL SPICSPAN TIMETIDE ALASALACK BACKFORTH BALLCHAIN FACTFANCY HITHERYON KNIFEFORK LOSTFOUND READWRITE ROOMBOARD THICKTHIN TRIEDTRUE BAGBAGGAGE BITSPIECES BLACKWHITE FUSSBOTHER HALEHEARTY HOOTHOLLER NOOKCRANNY SPITPOLISH SWITCHBAIT TARFEATHERS ALIVEKICKING ROMULUSREMUS STARSSTRIPES ASSAULTBATTERY

PARTNERSHIP HUI AXIS FIRM HOUSE FUSION CAHOOTS COMPANY CONSORT SOCIETY SOCIETEIT
(MUTUALLY BENEFICIAL —) SYMBIOSIS

PARTRIDGE HUN BIRD KYAH YUTU LERWA RUDGE TITAR CHUKAR REDLEG SEESEE CHEEPER PATRICK SHRIMPI TINAMOU BOBWHITE FRANCOLIN FRENCHMAN TETRAONID
(— NOISE) JUCK
(SAND —) TEHOO
(YOUNG —) CHEEPER SQUEALER

PARTRIDGEBERRY BOXBERRY COWBERRY EYEBERRY ONEBERRY SNOWBERRY TWINBERRY

PARTS
(PREF.)
(SIDE —) ALI

PART-SONG MADRIGAL

PART-TIME PARCEL

PARTURITION EUTOCIA TRAVAIL CHILDBED DELIVERY DYSTOCIA
(SUFF.) TOKY

PARTY DO BAL BEE CRY TEA CAMP CLAN DRUM GALA SECT SIDE BINGE BLAST BRAWL BUNCH CABAL COVEY CRUSH FESTA GROUP LEVEE MIXER COMITE FIESTA FROLIC FRONDE GERMAN INFARE JUNKET PERSON SETOUT SHINDY SHOWER BLOWOUT CANTICO COMPANY FACTION GREGORY PATARIA SHINDIG CLAMBAKE DRINKING FENNOMAN POTLATCH POUNDING SOCIABLE SQUANTUM TERTULIA CONCISION INCLINING MERRIMENT
(— GIVEN AT HOME) HUDDLE
(AFTERNOON —) TEA RECEPTION
(BEACH —) CLAMBAKE
(BOISTEROUS —) BASH HOOLEY BLOWOUT JAMBOREE
(BRIDAL —) SEND SHOWER
(DANCING —) HOP GERMAN CANTICO HOEDOWN RIDOTTO FANDANGO
(DRINKING —) SPREE KNEIPE MOLLIE POTATION SYMPOSIUM
(DRUNKEN —) BLIND
(EVENING —) BALL SOIREE GREGORY ROCKING TERTULIA
(FISHING —) HUKILAU
(HUNTING —) FAID
(INFORMAL —) SOCIABLE TERTULIA
(IRISH —) HOOLEY
(LARGE —) ROUT
(MASQUERADE —) GUISE RIDOTTO
(MEMBER OF YOUTH —) YIPPIE
(MEN'S —) STAG SMOKER
(MILITARY —) COMMANDO
(NOISY —) BEANO SHIVOO
(POLITICAL —) SAM SIDE WAFD

HOOKS LABOR CAUCUS FRONDE SWARAJ ZENTRUM MINSEITO KENSEIKAI SQUADRONE OPPOSITION
(POPULAR —) HOOKS
(ROWDY —) BASH BLAST BLOWOUT WINGDING
(SCOUTING —) ESPIAL
(SEARCH —) QUEST
(SPINNING —) ROCKING
(SUPPLY —) BRIGADE
(TEA —) DRUM TEMPEST
(THIRD —) STRANGER
(TYPE OF —) MIXER
(WILD —) WINGDING WHINGDING
(WORKING —) SQUAD
PARUAH (SON OF —) JEHOSHAPHAT
PARULIS GUMBOIL
PARVENU SNOB ARRIVE UPSTART ARRIVIST MUSHROOM ARRIVISTE
PARVIS PARADISE
PARZIFAL (FATHER OF —) GAMURET
(MOTHER OF —) HERZELOIDE
PASACH (FATHER OF —) JAPHLET
PASCH PACE PAQUE EASTER PASSOVER
PASCHAL LAMB CANDLE SUPPER PASSOVER
PAS DE DEUX DUET
PASE FAROL NATURAL VERONICA
PASEAH (FATHER OF —) ESHTON
PASEAR WALK AIRING EXCURSION PROMENADE
PASHA DEY EMIR BASHAW PASAHAW
PASHTO AFGHAN
PASIPHAE (BROTHER OF —) AEETES
(CHILD OF —) ARIADNE PHAEDRA
(DAUGHTER OF —) ARIADNE PHAEDRA
(FATHER OF —) HELIUS
(HUSBAND OF —) MINOS
(MOTHER OF —) PERSA
(SISTER OF —) CIRCE
PASQUEFLOWER BADGER GOSLING APRILFOOL
PASQUINADE PIPE SQUIB SATIRE LAMPOON PASQUIL
PASS BY GO COL DIE END FIG GAP SAG USE ABRA BEAL CEDE CHIT COMP COVE DREE DROP FALL FARE FLIT FOIN GATE GHAT GULF HALS HAND HAVE JARK LANE LEAD PACE RIDE ROLL SEEK SILE SLAP SLIP STEP WADE WALK WEAR WEND WIND ALLOW CANTO DREIE ENACT FLEET GHAUT GORGE HALSE HURRY KOTAL LAPSE LITHE LUNGE NOTCH OCCUR ORDER PAPER PUNTA REACH RELAY SHAKE SHOOT SMITE SPEND STRIP TRADE UTTER WASTE WHELM YODEL BILLET CHALAN CONVEY COUPON DEFILE DEMISE ELAPSE EXCEED HAPPEN PASSUS PERMIT RAVINE SPIRAL TICKET TRAVEL TWOFER ABSOLVE ALLONGE APPROVE BREATHE DESCEND DEVOLVE DIFFUSE ENTREAT LATERAL OVERGET PASSAGE UNDERGO JUNCTURE REBOLERA PURWANNAH SAFEGUARD
(— A BALL) FEED HEEL
(— ABRUPTLY) LEAP
(— ALONG) BANDY DERIVE
(— AWAY) DIE SET FLEE VADE WING DEPART EXPIRE PERISH FORFARE FORTHGO OVERDRIVE
(— BACK AND FORTH) FIG CRISSCROSS
(— BAD COIN) SMASH
(— BETWEEN HILLS) BEAL SLAP SLACK
(— BEYOND) TURN OVERSHOOT
(— BY) COTE OMIT SKIP VADE WEND APASS CLEAR FORGO FOREGO IGNORE OVERGO INTERMIT OVERHEAVE
(— DISCONTINUOUSLY) SKIP
(— FURTIVELY) SNEAK
(— GRADUALLY) FADE
(— IDLY) TRIFLE
(— IMPERCEPTIBLY) SHADE
(— IN BULLFIGHT) SUERTE
(— IN POKER) BREATHE
(— IN SCRUTINY) PERUSE
(— INTO USE) ENURE INURE
(— JUDGMENT ON) DEEM DECERN SENTENCE
(— LIGHTLY) BRUSH SKATE SKITTER
(— OFF) SHAM FOIST
(— ON) LEAK PACE DELATE TRANSMIT PROPAGATE
(— ONE'S LIFE) TRADE
(— OUT) CONK DEBOUCH EXHAUST
(— OVER) DO HIP BALK FREE SKIM SKIP SLIP COVER CROSS ELIDE FLEET SCOUR SWEEP TRANCE OVERHIP TRANSIT INTERMIT OVERLOOK OVERPOST PROGRESS TRAVERSE
(— OVER LIGHTLY) SKIM SWEEP OVERSKIP
(— OVER QUICKLY) SCUD FLEET
(— QUICKLY) FLIT SPIN SPEED STRIKE
(— THE NIGHT) LIE LODGE
(— THROUGH) CROSS REEVE TRACE DIVIDE OVERGO PIERCE SUFFER EXCURSE PERVADE OVERPASS OVERRIDE PERMEATE PROGRESS PENETRATE
(— THROUGH A BLOCK) REEVE
(— THROUGH HOLE) REEVE
(— THROUGH NARROW WAY) THRID THREAD
(— TIME) DRIVE SPEND TRADE
(— UNHAPPILY) DREE
(— UP) REJECT DECLINE DISREGARD
(— WITH DIFFICULTY) WADE
(— WITH VIOLENCE) RAKE
(CUSTOMS —) CARNET
(FENCING —) FOIN BOTTE LUNGE PUNTA
(FOOTBALL —) FLY FLARE FORWARD LATERAL PITCHOUT
(FORWARD —) AERIAL
(FREE —) PAPER
(FREE —S) PAPER
(HIGH —) CHIP
(HILL —) SLAP
(HOCKEY —) CENTER
(KIND OF —) SPOT OUTLET
(LONG — IN FOOTBALL) BOMB
(MOUNTAIN —) COL GAP NEK SAG GATE GHAT SLIP CLOVE GHAUT KLOOF KLOOT KOTAL POORT SWIRE SWIRL BEALACH
(NARROW —) ABRA GULF CLOSE SLYPE DEFILE
(SHORT — IN FOOTBALL) FLARE
(SUDDEN —) LUNGE
PASSABLE FIT FAIR SOSO TOLLOL GENUINE ADEQUATE MEDIOCRE MODERATE POSSIBLE TRAVELED PERMEABLE TOLERABLE
(PREF.) BATO
PASSABLENESS INDIFFERENCE
PASSABLY SEEMLY
PASSAGE CUT GAT GUT ROW VIA WAY WRO ADIT BELT BORD DOOR EXIT FARE FLUE FORD GANG GATE HALL ITER LANE PACE PASS PAWN RACE RAMP SLIP SLUM VENT WELL AISLE ALLEY ALURE BAYOU BEARD BOGUE CANAL CHOPS CHUTE CLOSE CREEK CRUSH DRAFT DRIFT DRIVE ENTRY FLYBY FORTE GLADE GOING GORGE INLET JETTY MEUSE PATCH PORCH SHUNT SLYPE SOUND ACCESS ADITUS APORIA ARCADE ATRIUM AVENUE BRIDGE BURROW BYPASS CAREER COURSE DEFILE DROMOS EGRESS ELAPSE FAUCES HIATUS MEATUS PARODE RELIEF SCREEN SLUICE STRAIT TRAJET TRANCE TRAVEL TUNNEL VOYAGE ARCHWAY BALTEUS CHANNEL CHAPTER CHIMNEY CONDUIT COULOIR COUPURE DIAZOMA DOGTROT DRAUGHT ESTUARY EXCERPT FISTULA FRAUGHT GALLERY GANGWAY GATEWAY ISTHMUS JOURNEY MANHOLE OFFTAKE OUTTAKE PARADOS PROCESS TRANSIT APPROACH AQUEDUCT CITATION CLOISTER COMMERCE DEBOUCHE DELETION PARADIGM PERICOPE SENTENCE SHIPPING SINUSOID SPILLWAY
(— ACROSS) TRAVERSE
(— ACROSS WATER) WAFT
(— BACK) REGRESS
(— BETWEEN WALLS) SLYPE
(— FOR MOLTEN METAL) SPRVE RUNNER
(— IN BOOK) WHERE EXCERPT
(— IN CRUIVE) SLAP
(— IN JEWISH SCRIPTURE) PARASHAH
(— OF POETRY OR MUSIC) MORCEAU
(— OF THREAD) FLOAT
(—S OF LITERATURE) BEAUTIES
(— TO STOMACH) SWALLOW
(— TO TOMB) DROMOS SYRINX
(AIR —) FLUE THIRL WINDWAY THIRLING VENTIDUCT
(ANATOMICAL —) ITER
(CENSORED —) CAVIAR
(CONTINUOUS —) LAPSE
(COVERED —) OPE PAWN PEND
(DIFFICULT —) APORIA
(LITERARY —) TEXT QUOTE EXCERPT SNIPPET QUOTATION
(MINE —) RUN ADIT HEAD ROOF SLUM DRIVE LEVEL SHAFT THIRL AIRWAY STENTON UNDERCAST
(MINUTE —) PORE
(MUSICAL —) CUE CODA LINK BREAK FORTE INTRO STAVE ARIOSO FUGATO LEGATO PRESTO REPEAT CADENZA CODETTA FANFARE STRETTO FLOURISH RITENUTO SPICCATO STACCATO SYMPHONY VOCALISE PIZZICATO RITARDANDO RITORNELLO
(NARROW —) GUT HASS ALLEY CREEP GORGE JETTY NOTCH SLYPE SMOOT DEFILE GULLET NARROW STRAIT
(OPENING —) INTRO INTRODUCTION
(SECRET —) BOLTHOLE
(SECURE — OF) CARRY
(SUBTERRANEAN —) POSTERN
(SWIFT —) FLIGHT
(THROUGH —) TRANCE
(UNDERGROUND —) SUBWAY
(VAULTED —) PEND
(VOCAL —) SPRECHSTIMME
(WATER —) TICKLE TICKLER
(PREF.) MEATO
(SUFF.) PLANIA PORA PORE
PASSAGE HAWK TARTARET PASSENGER
PASSAGE TO INDIA (AUTHOR OF —) FORSTER
(CHARACTER IN —) AZIZ ADELA CECIL MOORE RONALD STELLA GODBOLE HEASLOP QUESTED FIELDING
PASSAGEWAY (ALSO SEE PASSAGE) BORD FLUE GANG HALL LANE PACE PASS PEND PORT RACE SHED SLIP WENT YAWN AISLE ALLEY ALURE CHUTE DRIFT DRONG ENTRY GOING LUMEN RAISE SHOOT SMOOT STULM ACCESS AIRWAY AVENUE COURSE DINGLE FUNNEL GUTTER INTAKE MANWAY RUELLE RUNWAY TRANCE ZAGUAN DOORWAY GALLERY SLIPWAY TWITTEN WALKWAY WAYGATE CALLEJON CORRIDOR HATCHWAY
(CLEARED — IN CROWD) HALL
(COVERED —) ARCADE CLOISTER
(LOCKED —) CANAL
(MINE —) BORD BOARD DRIFT SLANT STULM WINZE
(NARROW —) SLIP AISLE SMOOT BOTTLENECK
(SLOPING —) RAMP
(UNDERGROUND —) CATACOMB
PASSANT PAST CURRENT CURSORY PASSING EPHEMERAL
PASSE AGED PAST WORN DATED FADED BELATED OBSOLETE OUTMODED
PASSED GONE
PASSENGER FARE INSIDE FERRYMAN TRAVELER WAYFARER
(— WHO AVOIDS PAYING FARE) NIP STOWAWAY
(— WITHOUT TICKET) HARE
(AIRPLANE —) BIRDMAN
(UNBOOKED —) CAD
(PL.) WAYBILL
PASSEPARTOUT SPANDREL

PASSERBY PASSER PASSANT BYPASSER SAUNTERER
PASSERINE OSCINE PERCHER TANAGER
PASSIFLORA TACSO
PASSING DEATH DYING ELAPSE CURSORY DIADROM PASSADO RUNNING SLIDING ELAPSING FLEETING ENACTMENT EPHEMERAL WAYFARING
(— BETWEEN) INTERCURRENT
(— BY) COTE
(— INTO EACH OTHER) FONDU
(— OF HOURS) TIME
(— OF TIME) EFFLUX
(SLOWLY —) LAG
PASSION IRE WAX BATE FIRE FURY HEAT LOVE LUST PASH RAGA RAGE TEAR TIDE WILL ZEAL ANGER ARDOR BLOOD BRAME CHAFE DEVIL ERROR FLAME LETCH MANIA RAJAS SPUNK WRATH AFFECT CHOLER DESIRE FERVOR MOTHER PELTER SATTVA SPLEEN TALENT WARMTH EARNEST EMOTION EROTISM FEELING OUTRAGE VULTURE APPETITE DISTRESS VIOLENCE PADDYWACK
(— FOR DOING GREAT THINGS) MEGALOMANIA
(— FOR MUSIC) MELOMANIA
(ANGRY —) FUNK
(ANIMAL —) KAMA
(EXALTED —) ALTITUDES
(PREF.) PASSI PATH(O)
(SUFF.) **(— FOR)** MANE MANIA(C)
PASSIONATE HOT FOND WARM WILD FIERY GUTSY QUICK WHITE ARDENT FERVID FIERCE FUMOUS IREFUL STORMY SULTRY TORRID AMOROUS FLAMING PEPPERY THERMAL VIOLENT CHOLERIC FRENETIC VASCULAR VEHEMENT WRATHFUL DIONYSIAN IRASCIBLE
PASSIONATELY HASTILY FERVIDLY
PASSIONFLOWER MAYPOP BULLHOOF
PASSIONLESS COLD FREDDO APATHETIC
PASSIVE INERT STOIC PATHIC STOLID SUPINE PATIENT FEMININE INACTIVE SIGNLESS YIELDING APATHETIC
PASSIVENESS QUIETISM
PASSIVITY INERTIA
PASSOVER PESAH PHASE PASQUE PESACH
(— FESTIVAL) SEDER
(JEWISH —) EASTER
PASSPORT CHOP PASS CONGE CONGEE DUSTUK DUSTUCK FURLOUGH TESCARIA TEZKIRAH SAFEGUARD
PASSUS PACE PART PASS STEP CANTO DIVISION
PASSWORD SIGN WORD TOKEN DUSTUK TESSERA WATCHWORD
PAST BY AGO WAS GONE YOND YORE AFTER AGONE APAST ASIDE ENDED SINCE BEHIND BYGONE FOREBY PRETER ANOTHER FOREGONE PRETERIT COMPLETED
(LONG —) HIGH
(RECENTLY —) OTHER
(TIME IN THE —) LANGSYNE
(TIME NOT LONG —) YESTERDAY
(PREF.) PRETER RETRO
PASTA ORZO ZITI PENNE NOODLE TUFOLI FUSILLI LASAGNA RAVIOLI LINGUINE LINGUINI MACARONI RIGATONI MANICOTTI SPAGHETTI FETTUCELLE TORTELLINI MOSTACCIOLI PERCIATELLI TAGLIATELLE
(— BITS) PASTINA
(TUBULAR —) ZITI
(WAY TO COOK —) ALDENTE
PASTE HIT PAP BEAT BLOW DIKA DUFF GLUE MISO PACK PATE CREAM DOUGH FALSE GESSO HENNA PUNCH STICK ATTACH BATTER CERATE FASTEN GROUND PANADA RASTIK STRASS BUCKETY CLOBBER COLOGNE DRAWOUT FILLING GORACCO GUARANA STICKUM BADIGEON BARBOTINE
(— FOR CAULKING) BLARE
(— FOR LINING HEARTHS) BRASQUE
(— FOR SHOES, BOOTS) CLOBBER BLACKING
(— FROM SESAME SEEDS) TAHINI
(— OF CLAY) BATTER
(— OF SESAME SEEDS) TAHINI
(— TO FILL HOLES IN WOOD AND STONE) BADIGEON
(ALIMENTARY —) PUREE FEDELINI SCUNGILLI SPAGHETTI
(AROMATIC —) PASTILE
(CHICK-PEA —) HOMMOS HUMMUS
(COLORING —) HENNA
(DRIED —) GUARANA
(EARTHY —) ENGOBE
(FISH —) BAGOONG
(MEDICATED —) ELECTUARY
(PORCELAIN —) PATE
(POTTER'S —) BARBOTINE
(TOBACCO —) GORACCO
(WEAVER'S —) SOWENS BUCKETY
PASTEBOARD CARD SHAM CARTON FLIMSY TICKET MATBOARD
PASTEDOWN LINING
PASTEL WOAD LIGHT CRAYON PICTURE DELICATE
PASTEL BLUE OADE WOAD
PASTEN HOBBLE TETHER PASTOUR SHACKLE
PASTILLE CACHOU CANDLE LOZENGE
PASTIME GAY TOY GAME PLOY HOBBY SPORT GOSSIP OLEARY SAILING PASTANCE AMUSEMENT DIVERSION ABRIDGMENT
PASTOR HERD ANGEL RABBI CURATE KEEPER PRIEST RECTOR DOMINIE VICAIRE GUARDIAN MINISTER SHEPHERD
PASTORAL POEM DRAMA RURAL RUSTIC BUCOLIC CROSIER IDYLLIC NOMADIC ROMANCE ARCADIAN THEOCRITEAN
PASTORALIST SQUATTER
PASTRY PIE FLAN HUFF PUFF SOCK TART TUCK CORNET DANISH ECLAIR ABAISSE BRIOCHE CANNOLI CARCAKE STRUDEL BAKEMEAT EMPANADA NAPOLEON TALMOUSE TURNOVER APPLEJACK
(— COOK) PASTLER
(— DOUGH) PHYLLO
(— SHELL) BOUCHEE DARIOLE TIMBALE TALMOUSE
(— STRIPS) LATTICE
(— WHEEL) JAGGER
(KIND OF —) PUFF
(SWEET —) DOUCET
(PL.) PIROZKI PIROSHKI
PASTURAGE FEED GANG GATE STRAY COLLOP EATAGE FORAGE HERBAGE SHEEPGATE
PASTURE ALP FOG HAG HAM ING LEA PEN TYE BENT FEED GAET GANG GATE GISE GIST HAFT HALF HEAF HOGA INGE KEEP PARK RAIK AGIST DRIFT EJIDO GRASS GRAZE LAYER LEASE RANGE VELDT INTAKE MEADOW OUTRUN SAETER COWGATE FOGGAGE GRAZING HERBAGE LEALAND POTRERO VACCARY VICTUAL HERDWICK OUTFIELD SHEEPWALK
(— GRASS) TORE GRAMA
(— IN STUBBLE) SHACK
(— LAND) RAKE TACK LEASOW
(HILL —) HOGA
(MOUNTAIN —) SETER SAETER SHIELING
(SHEEP —) HEAF EWELEASE
(SHETLAND I. —) SETER
(SUMMER —) AGOSTADERO
(WET —) SLINK
PASTURELAND BENT SOUM
PASTURING RELIEF PANNAGE
PASTY PIE PATE SLAB PATTY DOUGHY FRACID SAMBOUSE
PAT APT DAB DIB TAP TIG BLOW CLAP GLIB JUMP PALP TICK CHUCK FITLY FIXED IMPEL THROW CARESS DABBLE PRETTY SMOOGE SOOTHE STRIKE STROKE TIMELY APROPOS CHERISH FITTING PATAPAT READILY SUITABLE PERTINENT SEASONABLE
PATAGIUM TEGULA TIPPET SCAPULA PARACHUTE PTERYGODE
PATAGONIA (DEITY OF —) SETEBOS
(RODENT OF —) CAVY MARA
(TREE OF —) MANIU ALERCE ALERSE
PATAGONIAN HARE MARA
PATAMAR COURIER PATTAMAR MESSENGER
PATAYAN YUMAN
PATCH BIT EKE FLY BOUT LAND MEND SKIP SPOT SWAB SWOB VAMP BLAZE BODGE CLOUT CLUMP COVER FRIAR FUDGE PIECE SAVER SCRAP SPECK SPLAT BLOTCH COBBLE COOPER DOLLOP GORGET MOUCHE PARCEL REVAMP SOLDER SPETCH SWATCH TINKLE CLAMPER CLOBBER INWEAVE PELIOMA REMNANT
(— AS ORNAMENT) MOUCHE
(— CLUMSILY) BOTCH CLOUT CLAMPER
(— IN NEWSPAPER) FUDGE
(— OF COLOR) CLOUP DAPPLE SPLASH SPECULUM
(— OF DARK HAIR) SMUT
(— OF DIRT) MIRE
(— OF FEATHERS) BIB CAP PTERYLA
(— OF ICE) RONE
(— OF LAND) RODHAM
(— OF LEATHER) SPECK
(— OF LIGHT) GLADE
(— OF PRINT) FUDGE
(— OF RUFFLED WATER) ACKER
(— OF SALIVA) SIXPENCE
(— OF TIRE) BOOT
(— ON BIRD'S BEAK) CERE
(— ON BIRD'S WING) SPECULUM
(— ON BOAT) TINGLE
(— ON HORSE) SNIP
(— ON PRINTED PAGE) FRIAR
(— ON THROAT) GORGET
(— TOGETHER) CONSARCINATE
(— UP) HEAL JUMP MEND FUDGE SHUFFLE
(BALD —) AREA
(BLURRED —) FOG
(BOGGY —) LATCH LETCH
(CABBAGE —) KALEYARD
(ISOLATED —) POCKET
(KIND OF —) OIL
(LIVID —) PELIOMA
(OOZY —) SPEW SPUE
(OPEN — IN FOREST) CAMPO
(RANK —) DALLOP DOLLOP
(SHOULDER —) FLASH
PATCHOULI PACCIOLI PATCHLEAF
PATCHWORD WASTEWORD
PATCHWORK OLIO BOTCH CENTO CENTON JUMBLE SCRAPS PATCHERY FRAGMENTS PASTICCIO
PATE PIE TOP HEAD BROWN PASTE PASTY PATTY BADGER NODDLE NOGGIN COSTARD COXCOMB
PATELLA CAP PAN DISH VASE ROTULA KNEECAP KNEEPAN WHIRLBONE
PATEN ARCA DISC DISH DISK PLATE PATINA PLATEN VESSEL
PATENT ARCA BALD OPEN BERAT BROAD OVERT PLAIN SUNNUD CHARTER EVIDENT LICENSE OBVIOUS APPARENT ARCHIVES MANIFEST PALPABLE PRIVILEGE
PATENTED BREVETE
PATER FATHER PRIEST
PATERFAMILIAS MASTER
PATERNAL FATHERLY
PATERNITY FATHER ORIGIN
PATESI ISHSHAKKU
PATH ARC PAD RIG RUN RUT TAN WAY BERM FARE GATE LANE LEAD LINE LODE RACE RACK ROAD TRIG TROD WALK ALLEY BYWAY GOING JETTY ORBIT PISTE ROUTE SPACE TRACK TRACT TRADE TRAIL BOSTAL BYPASS CAMINO CASAUN CIRCLE COMINO COURSE GROOVE SLEUTH SPHERE SWATHE TRENCH CHANNEL ERGODIC FAIRWAY FOOTWAY HIGHWAY LANDWAY MEANDER PASSAGE RODDING SIDEWAY TARIQAT TOWPATH TRAFFIC TRUNDLE WAYGATE BORSTALL CENTRODE CROSSCUT

DRIFTWAY TRAILWAY TWITCHEL CROSSWALK
(— BETWEEN HEDGES) TWITCHEL
(— CUT IN MOWING) SWATH SWATHE
(— FOLLOWED BY ENERGY) ERGODIC
(— MADE BY ANIMAL) PIST PISTE
(— OF CELESTIAL BODY) ORBIT
(— OF CLOUDS) RACK
(— OF ELECTRIC CURRENT) CIRCUIT
(— OF MOVING POINT) CURVE LOCUS
(— OF RACE) STRIP
(— OF SUN) ECLIPTIC
(— UP STEEP HILL) BOSTAL BORSTAL BORSTALL
(BRIDLE —) SPURWAY
(BURIAL —) LICHWAY
(CLOSED —) CIRCUIT
(FORTIFICATION —) RELAIS
(GARDEN —) ALLEE
(NARROW —) BERM RACK TRIG RODDIN TROCHA RODDING
(PHILIPPINE FOOT —) SENDA
(STEEP —) SLIDDER
(STONE-PAVED —) STEEN
(SUFI —) TARIQAT
(WINDING —) ESS
(WINDING —S) AMBAGES
(PREF.) HODO ODO
(SUFF.) ODE OID
PATHAN TURI AFRIDI SIVATI BAJOURI BANGASH PAYTHAN DANGARIK
PATHETIC SAD SILLY TEARY TENDER FORLORN PITIFUL DOLOROSO PATETICO PITIABLE POIGNANT STIRRING TOUCHING AFFECTING
PATHFINDER (AUTHOR OF —) COOPER
(CHARACTER IN —) CAP DAVY MUIR MABEL NATTY BUMPPO DUNHAM JASPER MACNAB CHARLES WESTERN SANGLIER ARROWHEAD CHINGACHGOOK
PATHIC MORBID VICTIM PASSIVE CATAMITE DISEASED SUFFERER SUFFERING
PATHOGEN VIRUS
PATHOLOGICAL
(SUFF.)
(— CONDITION) IA
PATHOLOGIST AMERICAN OPIE ROUS SLYE EWING MOORE SMITH WELCH MOHLER FLEXNER HEKTOEN PRUDDEN WARTHIN WHIPPLE RICKETTS GOODPASTURE
AUSTRALIAN POPPER
CANADIAN WESBROOK
DANISH FIBIGER
ENGLISH ADAMI BOYCE PAGET ANNETT FLOREY WRIGHT SPILSBURY
GERMAN HENLE KLEBS TRAUBE ZENKER VIRCHOW COHNHEIM RECKLINGHAUSEN
IRISH STOKES
ITALIAN GUARNIERI
PATHOS BATHOS SNIVEL POIGNANCY
PATHWAY (ALSO SEE PATH) RUN LANE PATH RACK SLADE COURSE RAMBLA RAMBLE RODDIN BORSTAL RODDING
(RAISED —) CAUSEY CAUSEWAY
PATIENCE CALM THILD BEARANCE STOICISM COMPOSURE ENDURANCE FORTITUDE
PATIENT CASE CURE MEEK SOBER BOVINE PASSIVE ENDURING THOLEMOD SUFFERANT
(— OF ASYLUM) BEDLAM
(BE —) BEAR
(HYDROPATHIC —) WATERER
(MEDICAL —) CURE
PATIO COURT ATRIUM COURTYARD
PATOIS CANT GOMBO GUMBO CREOLE JARGON PATTER DIALECT GUERNSEY
(FRENCH —) JOUAL
PATOLA SARI GOURD
PATRIARCH JOB ABBA ENOS LEVI NASI NOAH PAPA POPE ALDER ELDER JACOB PITRI DESPOT JOSEPH NESTOR ABRAHAM ANCIENT VETERAN VENERABLE
(ETHIOPIAN —) ABUNA
PATRICIAN NOBLE EMPEROR PATRICK NOBLEMAN GENTLEMAN
PATRIMONY PORTION ANCESTRY HERITAGE LONGACRE
PATRIOT LOVER AMATEUR
PATRIOTIC PUBLIC ENVELOPE NATIONAL
PATRIPASSIAN NOETIAN
PATROCLUS (FATHER OF —) MENOETIUS
(MOTHER OF —) PERIAPIS POLYMELE STHENELE
(SLAYER OF —) HECTOR
PATROL GUARD SCOUT WATCH STOOGE PATROLE PROTECT
PATROLMAN COP GUARD FLATFOOT INSPECTOR
PATRON GOER BUYER GUEST STOOP AVOWRY CLIENT FATHER FAUTOR JAJMAN ACCOUNT PADRONE PATROON PROCTOR SPONSOR ADVOCATE CHAMPION CUSTOMER DEFENDER GUARDIAN MAECENAS
(PL.) FOLLOWING
PATRONAGE AEGIS FAVOR AVOWRY CUSTOM FAVOUR ACCOUNT AUSPICE FOMENTO HEARING AUSPICES BUSINESS PADROADO
(— AND CARE) AUSPICE
(— TO RELATIVES) NEPOTISM
(POLITICAL —) PAP
PATRONAL TITULAR
PATRONIZE USE DEIGN FAVOR DEFEND FATHER PROMOTE PROTECT EMPATRON FREQUENT
PATRON SAINT (OF CRIPPLES) GILES
(OF ENGLAND) GEORGE
(OF FISHERMEN) PETER
(OF FRANCE) DENIS
(OF GOLDSMITHS) ELOY
(OF IRELAND) PATRICK
(OF LAWYERS) IVES
(OF NORWAY) OLAF
(OF PAINTERS) LUKE
(OF SAILORS) ELMO
(OF SCOTLAND) ANDREW
(OF SPAIN) SANTIAGO
(OF THIEVES) DISMAS
(OF WALES) DAVID
PATROON TRACT CAPTAIN SUPPORTER
PATTEE FORMY FORMEE
PATTEN BASE CLOG FOOT SHOE SKATE STAND STILT CHOPIN GALOSH RACKET SANDAL CREEPER RACQUET SUPPORT CIOPPINO SNOWSHOE
PATTER RAP CANT TALK TIRL ARGOT LINGO HAPPER JARGON BLATHER BLATTER CHATTER DIALECT
PATTERING PITAPAT
PATTERN CUT FUR SET BASE CAST COMB COPY FORM GIMP IDEA LAUE MOLD NORM PLAN SEME STAR WAVE BISON BYSEN CHECK DECOR DISME DRAFT EPURE GUIDE IDEAL INLAY MODEL MOIRE MOULD NOTAN PLAID SEMEE SHAPE WATER BASKET BURELE CANVAS CHECKS DESIGN DIAPER ENTAIL ETOILE FABRIC FIGURE FLORAL FORMAT FORMER LACERY MAGPIE MATRIX MIRROR MODULE MUSTER ONDULE PATRON POUNCE RANDOM RECIPE SAMPLE SQUARE STRIPE SYSTEM ALLOVER CHEVRON EXAMPLE FACONNE FILLING FOLKWAY GESTALT GRIZZLE HOBNAIL MEANDER MEANING MULLION PARAGON PROJECT SAMPLER SLEIGHT STENCIL TEMPLET CALENDAR DENTELLE DYNAMICS FILIGREE HATCHING ILLUSION OVERSHOT PARADIGM PLATFORM STRICKLE PROTOTYPE
(— AFTER) COPY
(— IN BRAIN) GYRATION
(— OF BEHAVIOR) HABIT DISPLAY
(— OF CADENCE) CURSUS
(— OF HINDU MUSIC) TALA
(— OF LARGE SQUARES) DAMIER
(— OF SCARS) KELOID
(— OF SEPARATE OBJECTS) SEME
(— OF STRESS) SUPERFIX
(— OF TARTAN) SET SEET SETT SETTE
(— OF THOUGHT) GROUPTHINK
(— ON PAPER) BURELAGE
(— ON STAMP) GRILL GRILLE
(—S ON SILK) ARMURE
(— USED BY SILVERSMITHS) WORK BOROON
(CHARACTERISTIC BEHAVIOR —) BIT
(CROSS-BARRED —) PLAID
(FABRIC —) PAISLEY
(FACIAL —) BLAZE
(FOOTBALL —) FLY
(FRET —) KEY
(GARMENT —) SLOPER
(HAT —) BLOCK
(KNITTING —) ARGYLE
(MASONRY —) SPICATUM
(MELODIC —) RAGA
(METRIC — OF HINDU MUSIC) TALA
(PORCELAIN —) FITZHUGH
(RUG —) AINALEH
(SCANNING —) RASTER
(SHOE —) FORME
(SKATING —) EDGE
(SOCIAL —) FAMILISM
(SPEECH —) IDIOLECT
(SPOTTED —) SEME
(SQUARED FABRIC —) TATTERSALL
(STRIPED —) BARRE
(SYMBOLIC —) MANDALA
(TAILOR'S —) PROTRACTOR
(TATTOO —) MOKO
(TREE —) HOM HOMA
(WEAVING —) DRAW
PATTERNED GOFFERED
PATTY TABLET BOUCHEE PRALINE PATTYPAN VOLAUVENT
(— SHELL) DARIOLE TALMOUSE CROUSTADE
PATTYPAN SQUASH CYMLING
PATULOUS OPEN SPREAD DISTENDED
PAUCITY LACK DEARTH FEWNESS EXIGUITY SCARCITY
PAUL PAOLO
(ASSOCIATE OF —) DEMAS SILAS TITUS ARTEMAS BARNABAS
PAULDRON POLLET EPAULET PALERON POLDRON POLLETTE
PAULINA (HUSBAND OF —) CAMILLO ANTIGONUS
PAULLU (BROTHER OF —) MANCO HUASCAR
PAULOPOST DEUTERIC
PAULOWNIA KIRI
PAUNCH TUN KITE KYTE BELLY PENCH RUMEN ABDOMEN STOMACH GUNDYGUT POTBELLY
PAUNCHY BLOATED
PAUPER BEGGAR INDIGENT ROUNDSMAN
PAUPERISM BEGGARY
PAUSANIAS (FATHER OF —) CLEOMBROTUS
PAUSE HO HEM HALT HANG HOLD LULL REST RUFE STAY STOP WAIT ABIDE BREAK CEASE CHECK COMMA DELAY DEMUR DEVAL DWELL HOVER LETUP LIMMA POISE SELAH TARRY TENOR BREACH BREATH CORONA CUTOFF FALTER HANKER HIATUS PERIOD STANCE CAESURA FERMATA RESPITE VIRGULE BREATHER INTERVAL
(— BEFORE HURDLE) DWELL
(SUDDEN —) CHECK
(PL.) LIMMATA CAESURAE
PAUT PAW POKE POWT STAMP FINGER
PAVANE DANCE PADUAN PASSAMEZZO
PAVE LAY TAR PATH STUD TILE COVER FLOOR CAUSEY COBBLE QUARRY SMOOTH OVERLAY PREPARE RUDERATE MACADAMIZE
(— WITH STONES) STEEN CAUSEY
PAVED COBBLED
PAVEMENT SARN SLAB HEARTH PAEPAE TARMAC ASPHALT MACADAM MADADAM TELFORD ASAROTUM FLAGGING FLOORING

PATHMENT PEDIMENT PITCHING SIDEWALK TROTTOIR WASHBOARD
PAVER CUBER PAVIOR
PAVID TIMID AFRAID FEARFUL
PAVILION BASE FLAG TELD TENT FOLLY KIOSK PINNA ROYAL STAND CANOPY ENSIGN HOWDAH LITTER PANDAL PALLION COVERING GLORIETTE
(— ON ELEPHANT) HOUDAH HOWDAH
PAVILLON CHINOIS CRESCENT
PAVING FLAG SETT BLOCK BRICK DALLE PAVER STEAN STEEN STONE COBBLE TARMAC ASPHALT TELFORD PITCHING FLAGSTONE
(SQUARE —) MITCHEL
PAVIS COVER PAVADE PAVOIS SHIELD PROTECT
PAW PAT PUD TOE CLAW FOOT GAUM GRAB HAND MAUL PATY PAUT PORT FLAIL PATTE TRICK CLUTCH FUMBLE HANDLE PATTEE CRUBEEN FLIPPER FORELEG FOREFOOT
PAWKY SLY ARCH BOLD CANNY SAUCY CRAFTY LIVELY SHREWD CUNNING FORWARD SQUEAMISH
PAWL COG DOG BOLT HAND SEAR STOP TENT TRIP CATCH CLICK DETENT FINGER PALLET TONGUE CLAWKER RATCHET
PAWN DIP POP WED FINE GAGE HOCK SOAK VAMP WAGE SPOUT SWEAT ENGAGE LUMBER OBLIGE PIGNUS PLEDGE WADSET COUNTER HOSTAGE PEACOCK CHESSMAN MOSKENEER TRIBULATION
(PL.) PHALANX
PAWNBROKER MOUNT UNCLE BROKER LUMBERER MONEYLENDER
PAWNEE PANEE SKIDI WATER ALMOND BISCUIT PLEDGEE
PAWNIE PAWN PEACOCK
PAWNSHOP PAWN SPOUT LUMBER LOMBARD POPSHOP
(UNLICENSED —) TIDDLYWINK
PAX BOARD PEACE TRUCE FRIEND TABLET
PAXWAX WHITLEATHER
PAY DO BUY FEE POP TIP ANTE FOOT FORK GIVE MEET RENT SOLD WAGE BATTA CLEAR COUGH DOUSE PLANK PUTUP REMIT SCREW SHEPE SOUND WAGES YIELD ANSWER BETALL DEFRAY IMPEND PONYUP REWARD SALARY SETTLE COMMUTE DEADRAY HALVANS IMBURSE REQUITE SATISFY SOULDIE STIPEND TRIBUTE RECOMPENSE
(— ATTENTION) DIG SEE COME GAUM HARK HEED TENT ADVERT REGARD AUDIENT
(— COURT TO) NUT SUE GALLANT
(— DOWN) DOUSE
(— FLIRTATIOUS ADVANCES) QUEEN
(— FOR) ABY BUY BYE COUP ABIDE COVER ESCOT STAND ABEGGE
(— FOR LIQUOR) BIRL
(— HEAVY PENALTY) SMART EXPIATE
(— HOMAGE) CHEFE CHEVE CHIVE SALAAM ADULATE
(— IN ADVANCE) IMPRESS
(— MONEY) PINGLE
(— OFF) LIFT SINK ACQUIT
(— OF SOLDIER) SAWDEE
(— OUT) VEER BLEED SPEND STUMP EXPEND DISBURSE
(— PART OF) DEFRAY
(— PENALTY) ABY ABYE
(— TAXES) GILD
(— UP) ANTE QUIT SETTLE LIQUIDATE
(— WITH IOU) VOWEL
(ADVANCE —) IMPREST
(DAILY —) DIET
(EXTRA —) BATTA BONUS KICKBACK
(SMALL —) SCREW
PAYABLE DUE C4RTAL
PAYEE HOLDER ENDORSER
PAYMASTER BAKSHI BUKSHI PURSER BUKSHEE PAGADOR
PAYMENT CRO DUE FEE TAX BILL CENS DOES DOLE DUTY ERIC FEAL FINE GALE GILD HIRE LEVY MAIL MISE TACK TOLL BONUS CANON CLAIM GAVEL MAILL MENSE MODUS PREST PRICE YIELD ANGILD BOUNTY CHARGE LINAGE LOBOLA OUTLAY PAYOLA PLEDGE REBATE RETURN REWARD TARIFF ADVANCE ALIMONY ANNUITY BENEFIT CUSTOMS DEPOSIT FOOTAGE GARNISH PANNAGE PENSION PRIMAGE SOLUTIO STIPEND SUBSIDY SUBSIST TREWAGE TUITION CASUALTY FOREGIFT GRATUITY KICKBACK MALIKANA MARITAGE MONEYAGE TREASURY WOODGELD HEADPENNY MALGUZARI
(— BY CLERGYMAN) SYNODAL
(— FOR INJURY) UTU
(— FOR LABOR) MEED
(— FOR OFFENSE) ENACH
(— FOR RELEASE) LOOSING
(— FOR RERUN) RESIDUAL
(— FOR USE) RENT
(— IN ADVANCE) PREST
(— IN GOODS) TRUCK
(— IN KIND) SPECIE
(— OF DEBT) SOLUTION
(— OF FEE) FEAL
(— OF MINERS) FOOTAGE YARDAGE
(— ON DELIVERY) COD
(— TO SECURE FAVOR) PAYOLA
(ADVANCE —) ANTE
(DEMAND —) DUN BILL
(EVADE —) BILK DEFAULT
(FIXED —) FARM MODUS
(HOMICIDE'S —) KELCHIN
(INSURANCE —) PREMIUM
(PARTIAL —) INSTALMENT INSTALLMENT
(PERIODICAL —) GALE GAVEL
(RENT —) GALE
(SECRET —) PAYOLA
PAYNIM PAGAN PANIME HEATHEN INFIDEL PAGANDOM
PAYOFF FIX SOP BRIBE CLIMAX PROFIT REWARD DECISIVE RECKONING
PDQ ASAP IMMEDIATELY
PEA DAL TUR DHAL GRAM LANG SEED ARHAR CHICK CICER GANDUL LEGUME PIGEON PODDER CARMELE CATJANG KHESARI PODWARE TANGIER GARVANRO MARROWFAT
(— DOVE) ZENAIDA
(— HARVESTER) VINER
(— PETAL) KEEL
(—S AND BEANS) PULSE
(EARLY —S) HASTINGS
(PARCHED —S) CARLS CARLINS
(PL.) POIS GRAIN
(PREF.) PISI
PEABIRD ORIOLE WRYNECK
PEACE PAX CALM EASE FINE LIOS LISS REST AMITY FRITH GRITH LISSE QUIET TRUCE REPOSE SAUGHT SHALOM CONCORD HARMONY REQUIEM SERENITY
(— MAKER) TREATY
(— OF MIND) ATARAXIA
(GODDESS OF —) IRENE
(SYMBOL OF —) DOVE TOGA OLIVE
(PREF.) PACI
PEACEABLE FAIR SOME CIVIL DOUCE QUIET STILL GENTLE SILVER ORDERLY PACIFIC SOLOMON AMICABLE SACKLESS
PEACEFUL CALM SOME SOBER STILL IRENIC PLACID SILVER HALCYON ORDERLY PACIFIC
PEACE PIPE CALUMET
PEACH BLAB PAVY CLING PAVIE SNEAK SPLIT TRUMP ACCUSE BETRAY CARMAN CROSBY FOSTER INDICT INFORM OREJON PEENTO SALWEY BRUNION ELBERTA PERSIAN PIENTAO WHITTLE CRAWFORD ISABELLA RARERIPE ROSEWORT NECTARINE VICTORINE
(— STATE) GEORGIA
(— STONE) PUTAMEN
PEACHBLOW FAKIR
PEACHY FINE DANDY
PEACOCK MAO PAON PAVO PAWN POSE PEKOK STRUT PAJOCK PAVONE POWNIE PEAFOWL PHASIANID
(— TAIL) TRAIN
(CONGO —) AFROPAVO
(EYELIKE SPOT ON —) OCELLUS
PEACOCK BITTERN SUN
PEACOCK BUTTERFLY IO
PEACOCK FISH WRASSE
PEACOCK FLOWER FLAMBEAU POINCIANA
PEA CRAB PINNOTERE
PEAG TAX TOLL BEADS PAAGE PEACK PEAGE PEDAGE WAMPUM
PEAI PIAY PIACHE
PEA JACKET PEACOAT
PEAK ALP BEN NAB NOB PAP PIC TOP TOR ACME APEX BEAK CIMA CUSP DENT DOLT DOME KNOB KNOT PICO PIKE TOLT BLOOM CREST CROWN PIQUE PITCH PITON POINT SLINK SNEAK SPIRE STEAL STUMP CLIMAX CUPULA SHASTA SHRINK SUMMIT ZENITH EPITOME MAXIMUM PICACHO CENTROID
(— OF ANCHOR) PEE
(— OF CAP) SCOOP
(— OF ENERGY) NUCLEUS
(ICE —) SERAC
(ISOLATED —) TOLT
(SHARP —) HORN AIGUILLE
(SNOW-CAPPED —) DOME CALOTTE
(PREF.) ACR(O)
PEAKED WAN PALE THIN DRAWN PIKED SHARP COPPED SICKLY SLIMSY POINTED SLIMPSY
PEAKEDNESS KURTOSIS
PEAL CLAP RING TOLL CHIME CRACK GRILSE SHOVEL MINNING RESOUND SUMMONS THUNDER CARILLON
(— OF THUNDER) CLAP REEL
PEANUT BUR FLAX MANI MEAN PETTY PINDA GOOBER LEGUME PINDAL ARACHIS BEENNUT ARACHIDE EARTHPEA GRASSNUT KATCHUNG VALENCIA MONKEYNUT
(— DISEASE) TIKKA
PEA POD COB PYSE QUASH PESCOD
(POORLY FILLED —) POP
(UNRIPE —) SQUASH
PEAR BOSC BURY DIEGO MELON NELIS SABRA BEURRE BURREL COLMAR PANINI SECKEL WARDEN WINTER KIEFFER PEPERIN PRICKLY AMBRETTE BERGAMOT BLANQUET MUSCATEL TASAJILLO
(PRICKLY —) TUNA NOPAL OPUNTIA
(PREF.) PIRI PIRO PYRI
PEAR HAW THORN
PEARL GEM MABE TERN GRAIN NACRE ONION PICOT UNION BOUTON OLIVET ORIENT BAROQUE BLISTER PARAGON BDELLIUM CATARACT MOONBEAM MARGARITE
(— WEIGHT) TANK
(IMITATION —) OLIVET
(IRREGULAR —) SLUG
(KIND OF —) MOBE
(MOCK —) OLIVET
(PIERCED —) WIDOW
(SEED —) ALIOFAR
(SMOKED —) MITRAILLE
(PREF.) PERLI
PEARL BLUE METAL
PEARL BLUSH ROSETAN
PEARL FISHERS, THE (CHARACTER IN —) LEILA NADIR ZURGA NOURABAD
(COMPOSER OF —) BIZET
PEARL MILLET KOUS BAJRA CUMBU DUCHN DUKHN KOUSE JONDLA DAGASSA
PEARLSIDES ARGENTIN
PEARLWEED SAGINA POVERTY SEALWORT
PEARLY NACRY NACROUS MARGARIC PRECIOUS
PEARLY EVERLASTING LIVELONG MOONSHINE
PEAR-SHAPED FULL MELLOW ROUNDED PYRIFORM
PEASANT TAO BOND BOOR HERA HIND KERN KONO KOPI PEON RAYA RYOT SERF BAIRU BOWER CHURL

KNAVE KULAK RAYAH SWAIN CARLOT COTMAN COTTAR FARMER FELLAH RASCAL RUSTIC BONDMAN LABORER PAISANO VILLAIN CHOPSTICK CONTADINO
(— CLASS) JACQUERIE
(— OF INDIA) RYOT KISAN RAIYAT
(ARABIC —) FELLAH
(IRISH —) KERN KERNE
(ITALIAN —) CONTADINO
(RUSSIAN —) KULAK MUZHIK MUZJIK
PEASANTS (AUTHOR OF —) REYMONT
(CHARACTER IN —) KUBA ROCH ANTEK HANKA SIMON YAGNA YANEK BORYNA NASTKA TERESA MATTHEW MATTHIAS DOMINIKOVA
PEASCOD (UNRIPE —) SQUASH
PEASE CROW TERN
PEASHOOTER TRUNK BLOWER PISTOL BLOWGUN
PEAT GOR PET SOD VAG COOM FUEL MIST MOOR MUCK MULL TURF COOMB YARFA LAWYER MINION YARPHA DARLING FAVORITE
(— BOG) CESS YARPHA
(— CUTTER) PINER
(— SPADE) SLADE TUSKAR TWISCAR
(DRIED — FOR FUEL) VAG
(LAYER OF —) FLAW
PEA TREE KATURAI
PEATY KETTY
PEBA PEVA ARMADILLO
PEBBLE DIB FLAX JACK PLUM CHUCK SCREE STONE BANTAM COGGLE GIBBER GRAVEL QUARTZ SHILLA SYCITE CHUCKIE CRYSTAL SHINGLE STANNER JACKSTONE
(PL.) BEACH DREIKANTER
(PREF.) CALCULI CHALICO PSEPH(O) THRIO
PEBBLY BEACHY
PECAN NOGAL PACANE
PECCADILLO FAULT OFFENSE MISCHIEF
PECCANT FAULTY MORBID CORRUPT SINNING DISEASED
PECCARY HOG SWINE JAVALI WARREE TAGASSU TAYASSU JAVELINA TAYASSUID
PECK DAB DOT JOB NIP BEAK BILL CARP FOOD GRUB HOLE JERK KISS PYKE PITCH PRICK STOCK THROW HATFUL NIBBLE PEGGLE PICKLE PIERCE STROKE CHIMBLE
(1-4TH OF —) LIPPY FORPET FORPIT LIPPIE
PECKER BILL NOSE COURAGE SPIRITS
PECTEN COMB MARSUPIUM
PECTORAL SANDPIPER JACK PERT PEERT BROWNY BROWNIE CHOROOK CREAKER FATBIRD HAYBIRD KRIEKER SQUATTER TRIDDLER JACKSNIPE
PECULATE STEAL MISUSE EMBEZZLE
PECULIAR ODD VERY QUEER WEIRD PROPER QUAINT UNIQUE CURIOUS PRIVATE SEVERAL SPECIAL STRANGE UNUSUAL SEPARATE SINGULAR SPECIFIC
(— TO ONESELF) PRIVATE
(PREF.) IDIO
PECULIARITY KINK IDIOM QUIRK TRAIT TRICK TWIST IDIASM ODDITY AEOLISM ANOMALY FEATURE IRISHRY CROTCHET HEADMARK MANNERISM PROPRIETY SINGULARITY
(— IN BOWL) BIAS
(— OF SPEECH) IDIOLOGISM
(CROTCHETY —) FIKE
PECUNIARY POCKET MONETARY FINANCIAL
PED BASKET HAMPER PANIER
PEDAGOGUE TUTOR PEDANT DOMINIE SQUEERS TEACHER THWACKUM
PEDAGOGY SCHOOL DIDACTICS EDUCATION
PEDAHEL (FATHER OF —) AMMIHUD
PEDAHZUR (SON OF —) GAMALIEL
PEDAIAH (BROTHER OF —) SALATHIEL
(DAUGHTER OF —) ZEBUDAH
(FATHER OF —) PAROSH
(SON OF —) JOEL
PEDAL LEVER SWELL TREADLE FOOTFEED PEDALIAN THROTTLE
(— COUPLER) TIRASSE
(BICYCLE —) RATTRAP
(KIND OF —) WAWA WAHWAH
(PIANO —) CELESTE
(PIANO SOFTENING —) CELESTE
PEDAL POINT DRONE
PEDANT PRIG DUNCE TUTOR DORBEL PURIST TASSEL ACADEME PEDAGOG GAMALIEL DRYASDUST OLOFERNES
PEDANTIC BLUE STODGY BOOKISH DONNISH ERUDITE INKHORN TEACHING SCHOLASTIC
PEDDLE HAWK SELL CADGE SHOVE TRANT TRUCK HIGGLE MEDDLE PIDDLE RETAIL COLPORT
(— OVERPRICED TICKETS) SCALP
PEDDLER ARAB SMOUS BADGER BODGER CRAMER JAGGER JOWTER MUGGER STROLL WALKER YAGGER CHAPMAN NIGGLER PACKMAN ROADMAN SANDBOY SWADDER TROGGER TRUCKER HUCKSTER BOXWALLAH DUSTYFOOT
(— OF DOPE) FIXER
(— OF DRESS PIECES) DUDDER
(— OF FISH) RIPIER RIPPIER
(— OF SHAM JEWELRY) DUFFER
(BOOK —) COLPORTEUR
(ITINERANT —) SMOUS SMOUSE SMOUSER STROLLER
(MOHAM. —) BORA
(STREET —) CAMELOT
(WARES OF —) TROGGIN
PEDESTAL ANTA BASE BASIS BLOCK SOCLE STAND PILLAR PODIUM ROCKER AKROTER SUPPORT PADMASANA ACROTERIUM
(— PART) DADO
PEDESTRIAN PED DULL FOOT SLOW HIKER FOOTER HOOFER WALKER FOOTMAN PROSAIC PLODDING WINGLESS PONDEROUS VOETGANGER PERIPATETIC
PEDICAB TRISHAW
PEDICEL RAY STEM SCAPE STALK PEDUNCLE FOOTSTALK
PEDIGREE STEMMA DESCENT LINEAGE ANCESTRY PETEGREU PUREBRED
PEDIMENT FRONTAL FRONTON FASTIGIUM
PEDIPALP
(PL.) LABIUM
PEDOMETER ODOGRAPH WAYWISER
PEDRERO PERRIER PETRARY
PEDUNCLE STEM SCAPE STALK STIPES PEDICEL EYESTALK HYPOCARP
(PL.) CRURA
PEEK PEEP PIKE GLANCE GLIMPSE
PEEKABOO PEEP BOPEEP PEEPEYE
PEEL BARK HARL HULL HUSK PARE RIND SKIN FLAKE FLIPE SCALE SLIPE STAKE STRIP CORTEX SHOVEL SPITTLE UNDRESS BARKPEEL ORANGEADO
(— OFF) HARL CRAZE FLAKE SHUCK
(BAKER'S —) PALE SPITTLE
(ORANGE OR LEMON —) ZEST ORANGEAT
PEELER CRAB BOBBY CORER HUSTLER SHEDDER SPUDDER PILLAGER
PEELING RIND SKIN PARING PARURE
PEEN PIN PYNE RIVET
PEEP PIP PRY SPY COOK JEEP KEEK KOOK PEEK PEER PINK PULE SKEG STEP TOOT TOTE TOUT CHEEP CHIRP DEKKO GLINT PIPIT SNOOP TWEET DEGREE GLANCE SQUEAK SQUINNY PEEKABOO
(— SHOW) RAREE
PEEPER EYE TOM FROG KEEK VOYEUR
PEEPHOLE PEEP JUDAS EYELET CREVICE
PEEPING NOSY PRYING
PEEPING TOM VOYEUR
PEER PRY DUKE EARL FEAR GAZE LOOK LORD MATE PEEP PINK TOOT TOUT BARON EQUAL GLINT GLOZE MATCH NOBLE RIVAL STARE STIME THANE TWIRE APPEAR FELLOW OLIVER PINKER COMPERE
PEERAGE RANK DEBRETT DIGNITY BARONAGE NOBILITY TENEMENT
PEER GYNT (AUTHOR OF —) IBSEN
(CHARACTER IN —) ASE BOYG GYNT PEER ANITRA HEGSTAD SOLVEIG
PEERING SQUINNY
PEERLESS SUPREME MATCHLESS NONPAREIL UNRIVALED
PEESWEEP FINCH PEWIT LAPWING PEEWEEP
PEEVE IRK ANNOY GRUDGE NETTLE IRRITATE
PEEVISH SOUR CROSS DORTY PENSY SNACK TECHY TEENY TESTY TETTY THRAW TIFFY WEMOD CRUSTY FRANZY GIRNIE HIPPED PATCHY SNARLY SNUFFY SULLEN TATTER TOUCHY TWARLY TWAZZY TWITTY UPPISH UPPITY VAPORY CRABBED FRATCHY FRECKET FRETFUL FROWARD GROUCHY PETTISH SPLEENY TEDIOUS TIFFISH WASPISH CAPTIOUS PERVERSE PETULANT PHRAMPEL PINDLING SANSHACH TWANKING FRAMPOLD,PETULANT
PEEVISHLY CRUSTILY
PEEVISHNESS PET BILE PETULANCE
PEEWEE BOOT RUNT TINY PEWEE MARBLE LAPWING
PEG FIX HOB HUB NOB NOG PIN TEE HOBB KING KNAG PLUG SCOB SHAG SKEG STEP CLEAT DOWEL DRINK NOTCH PERCH PITON PRONG SPELL SPILE SPILL STAKE THOLE THROW TOOTH WADDY DEGREE DOWELL FAUCET MARKER NORMAN PICKET REASON SPIGOT TAPOUN TIPCAT PINNING PRETEXT SCOLLOP SPERKET SUPPORT TRENAIL
(— FOR PLAYING GAME) CAT SPILIKIN
(— FOR SADDLES) SPERKET
(— OF FAUCET) SPIGOT
(— OF STRINGED INSTRUMENT) CHEVILLE
(— OUT) DIE FAIL
(BELAYING —) KEVEL
(IRON —) PITON
(THATCH —) SCOB
PEGA REMORA
PEGALL BASKET PACKALL
PEGASUS QUAVIVER HYPOSTOME
PEG TOP PIRY PEERY PEERIE
PEG WOFFINGTON (AUTHOR OF —) READE
(CHARACTER IN —) PEG RICH VANE HARRY MABEL CIBBER COLLEY CHARLES TRIPLET POMANDER WOFFINGTON BRACEGIRDLE
PEIGNOIR GOWN DRESS KIMONO NEGLIGEE
PEISE BLOW FORCE PASSE POISE POIZE IMPACT WEIGHT BALANCE POISURE
PEKAH (FATHER OF —) REMALIAH
(SLAYER OF —) HOSHEA
PEKAHIAH (FATHER OF —) MENAHEM
(SLAYER OF —) PEKAH
PEKAN WEJACK
PEKING MAN SINANTHROPUS
PELAGE FUR COAT HAIR PILAGE
PELAGIC MARINE AQUATIC OCEANIC PELAGIAN
PELAIAH (FATHER OF —) ELIOENAI
PELALIAH (FATHER OF —) AMZI
PELATIAH (FATHER OF —) BENAIAH HANANIAH
PELEG (BROTHER OF —) JOKTAN
(FATHER OF —) EBER
PELET (FATHER OF —) JAHDAI AZMAVETH
PELETH (FATHER OF —) JONATHAN
(SON OF —) ON
PELEUS (BROTHER OF —) TELAMON
(FATHER OF —) AEACUS
(HALF-BROTHER OF —) PHOCUS
(MOTHER OF —) ENDEIS

(SON OF —) PELIDES ACHILLES
(WIFE OF —) THETIS ANTIGONE
PELF GAIN BOOTY LUCRE MONEY SPOIL TRASH PILFER PILFRE REFUSE RICHES WEALTH COMPOST
PELIAS (BROTHER OF —) NELEUS
(DAUGHTER OF —) ALCESTIS
(FATHER OF —) POSEIDON
(MOTHER OF —) TYRO
(SON OF —) ACASTUS
(WIFE OF —) ANAXIBIA PHYLOMACHE
PELICAN DOVE ALCATRAS ONOCROTAL
(— STATE) LOUISIANA
PELISSE POSTIN POSTEEN
PELL BEAT PELE PELT HURRY PEELE HASTEN
PELLAGRA MAIDISM PELAGRA
PELLEAS (BELOVED OF —) MELISANDE
(BROTHER OF —) GOLAUD
PELLEAS ET MELISANDE
(CHARACTER IN —) ARKEL GOLAUD YNIOLD PELLEAS ALLEMONDE GENEVIEVE MELISANDE
(COMPOSER OF —) DEBUSSY
PELLES (DAUGHTER OF —) ELAINE
PELLET BB WAD BALL CAST PILL SHOT BOLUS PRILL STONE BEEBEE BULLET FECULA OGRESS PILULE CASTING GRANULE PALLION TRATTLE BUCKSHOT GUNSTONE HAILSTONE
(RAIN —S) HAIL
(SNOW —S) GRAUPEL
(PL.) SHOT
PELLICLE FILM SCUM SKIN CRUST CUTICLE EPISTASIS
PELLINORE (SLAYER OF —) GAWAIN
(SON OF —) TORRE DORNAR LAMEROK PERCIVAL AGGLOVALE
PELLITORY BERTRAM BERTRUM WALLWORT
PELL-MELL RUSH MELPELL DISORDER HEADLONG
PELLOCK PALACH PORPOISE
PELLUCID CLEAR BRIGHT LIMPID ORIENT CRYSTAL
PELMA TRACK
PELMET CORNICE VALANCE PALMETTE
PELOPONNESUS (CITY OF —) SPARTA
(PEOPLE OF —) MOREOTE
(RIVER GOD OF —) ALPHEUS
PELOPS (FATHER OF —) TANTALUS
(SON OF —) ATREUS TROEZEN PITTHEUS THYESTES
(WIFE OF —) HIPPODAMIA
PELORIA EPANODY
PELOTA (— BASKET) CESTA
PELT FUR KIT BEAR BEAT BLOW CAPE CAST CLOD COON DASH FELL HIDE HURL KITT PELL PUSH RACK SKIN BESET CHUNK FITCH HURRY SABLE SLASH SPEED STONE WHACK BADGER BEAVER FISHER PELTER PEPPER SERVAL SPRING BETHUMP COONSKIN
(— OF SEAL, WITH BLUBBER) SCULP
(— WITH MISSILES) BUM SQUAIL
(— WITH STONES) LAPIDATE
(BEAVER —) BLANKET
PELTAST SOLDIER TARGETEER
PELTATE SCUTATE
PELTER SKEET
PELTING SLASHING
PELTRY FURS SKINS
PELUDO POYOU ARMADILLO
PELVIS
(PREF.) PELVI(O) PELYCO PYEL(O)
(SUFF.) PELLIC
PEN BIC CAN COT CUB GET HOK MEW PAR PIN STY BOLT CAGE COOP CROO CROW FAUD FOLD JAIL STUB WALK YARD BUGHT CRAWL CREEP CUBBY HUTCH KRAAL POINT QUILL STYLE WRITE BOUGHT CORRAL CRUIVE FASTEN FLIGHT HURDLE INDITE RECORD STYLUS ZAREBA CONFINE WARKLOOM
(— BRAND) CLIC
(— CATTLE) STANCE
(— FOR CATTLE) CUB LOT CREW CRUE LAIR REEVE
(— FOR ELEPHANTS) KRAAL
(— FOR HOGS OR SLAVES) CRAWL
(— OF CUTTLEFISH) GLADIUS
(— POINT) NEB NIB STUB
(— UP) FRANK STIVE
(AUTHOR'S —) STYLE STYLUS
(BALLPOINT —) BIRO
(FOUNTAIN —) STICK
(KIND OF —) POISON
(MUSIC —) RASTRUM
(REED —) CALAMUS
PENALIZE CHECK
PENALTY BETE CAIN COST DOOM FINE LOSS PAIN BEAST JUISE MULCT AMENDE AMERCE SOLACE FORFEIT NEMESIS SURSIZE BLOODWIT HARDSHIP SCAFFOLD
(DRINKING —) KELTIE
PENANCE TAP SORE SHRIFT SORROW REMORSE SUFFERING
(DO —) ATONE
PEN CASE PENNER POPPET
PENCEL FLAG PENNON STREAMER PENNONCEL
PENCHANT BENT TASTE FOIBLE GENIUS LIKING LEANING FONDNESS
PENCIL PEN RED WAD BLUE LEAD WADD LINER SHEAF SKETCH STYLUS POINTEL CHARCOAL KEELIVINE
(PART OF —) CASE LEAD POINT ERASER FERRULE SHOULDER
(SLATE —) CAM CALM SKAILLIE
(PL.) STATIONERY
(PREF.) PENCILLI PENICILLI
PENCILWOOD MORDORE
PEND HANG
PENDANT BOB JAG DROP FLAG JAGG PEND TAIL AGLET BULLA GUTTA POINT AIGLET LUSTER PALAOA PLAYER TABARD TARGET TASSEL EARDROP LANGUET SUPPORT LAVALIER
PENDENNIS (AUTHOR OF —) THACKERAY
(CHARACTER IN —) BELL AMORY EMILY FANNY FOKER HELEN HENRY LAURA ARTHUR BOLTON GEORGE JEMIMA BLANCHE FRANCIS ALTAMONT COSTIGAN CLAVERING PENDENNIS WARRINGTON THISTLEWOOD
PENDENT LOP BAGGED ICICLE HANGING PROMISS
PENDICLE POFFLE
PENDING NISI
PENDULOUS LOP SLOUCH HANGING NODDING PENSILE CERNUOUS DROOPING
PENDULUM SWING PENDLE SWINGEL SWINGLE VIBRATILE
(INVERTED —) NODDY
PENELOPE (FATHER-IN-LAW OF —) LAERTES
(FATHER OF —) ICARIUS
(HUSBAND OF —) ULYSSES ODYSSEUS
(MOTHER OF —) PERIBOEA
(SON OF —) TELEMACHUS
(SUITOR OF —) AGELAUS
PENEPLAIN STRATH ENDRUMPF
PENETRABLE PERVIOUS
PENETRATE CUT DIG DIP SEE BITE BORE DIVE GORE PASS PINK SINK STAB WADE BREAK DRILL DRIVE ENTER IMBUE PROBE SEIZE THIRL CLEAVE FATHOM FICCHE GIMLET INVADE PIERCE RIDDLE SEARCH STRIKE THRILL WIMBLE DISCERN PERVADE PERCOLATE PERFORATE
(— MENTALLY) ENTER
(— ONE'S MIND) SOAK
PENETRATED (EASILY —) MELLOW
PENETRATING ACID KEEN ACUTE LEVEL NASAL SHARP ASTUTE DEADLY SHREWD SHRILL SUBTLE GIMLETY INGOING INTRANT KNOWING PUNGENT PERCEANT PIERCING REACHING TRENCHANT
PENETRATION DEPTH ACUMEN FATHOM INROAD INGOING INSIGHT SEEPAGE INCISION INVASION SAGACITY
(IMAGINATIVE —) INSIGHT
PENEUS (DAUGHTER OF —) DAPHNE
(FATHER OF —) OCEANUS
(MOTHER OF —) TETHYS
(SON OF —) HYPSEUS
PENGUIN AUK DIVER GENTU ADELIE ARCTIC DIPPER GENTOO JOHNNY PINWING BREVIPED MACARONI ROCKHOPPER
(PL.) IMPENNES
(PREF.) SPHENISCI SPHENISCO
PENGUIN ISLAND (AUTHOR OF —) FRANCE
(CHARACTER IN —) MAEL CLENA CRRES DRACO OLIVE PYROT TALPA AGARIC KRAKEN TRINCO VISIRE EVELINE BOSCENOS CLARENCE GREATANK JOHANNES OBEROSIA CHATILLON MARBODIUS
PENINNAH (HUSBAND OF —) ELKANAH
(SON OF —) SAMUEL
PENINSULA CAPE MULL NECK INDIA BILAND BYLAND ISLAND PENILE CHERSONESE
PENIS
(PREF.) BALAN(I)(O) PHALL(O) POSTH(E)(IO)(O)
PENITENCE RUE REGRET SORROW PENANCE PENANCY REMORSE
PENITENT RUER SORRY HUMBLE WEEPER MOURNER STANDER CONTRITE
(— OF 3RD STAGE) KNEELER
PENITENTIARY JUG PEN JAIL STIR TENCH PRISON PENITENT
PENMAN CLERK AUTHOR SCRIBE WRITER
PENMANSHIP HAND SCRIPT PENSHIP WRITING
PENNANT FANE FLAG WHIP COLOR ROGER BANNER BURGEE CORNET ENSIGN PENCIL PENNON PENSIL PINION PINNET MEATBALL REPEATER STREAMER
PENNILESS POOR BROKE NEEDY SKINT BANKRUPT INDIGENT STRAPPED PLACKLESS
PENNON FLAG VANE WING ANVIL BANNER PENCIL PENOUN PINION FEATHER GONFANON
PENNON SPAR PEGGYMAST

PENNSYLVANIA
CAPITAL: HARRISBURG
COLLEGE: JUNIATA URSINUS LYCOMING
COUNTY: ELK ERIE PIKE YORK BERKS BUCKS PERRY TIOGA LEHIGH CAMBRIA JUNIATA LUZERNE VENANGO WYOMING LYCOMING
MOUNTAIN RANGE: POCONO ALLEGHENY
NATIVE: AMISH DUTCH
PRESIDENT: BUCHANAN
RIVER: LEHIGH CLARION JUNIATA LICKING TOWANDA CALDWELL DELAWARE SCHRADER ALLEGHENY SCHUYLKILL MONONGAHELA SUSQUEHANNA
STATE BIRD: GROUSE
STATE FLOWER: LAUREL
STATE NICKNAME: KEYSTONE
STATE TREE: HEMLOCK
TOWN: ERIE ETNA PLUM YORK AVOCA MEDIA EASTON EMMAUS SHARON ALTOONA EPHRATA HERSHEY READING TOWANDA BRYNMAWR SCRANTON SHAMOKIN BETHLEHEM CHARLEROI GETTYSBURG PITTSBURGH
UNIVERSITY: PITT DREXEL LEHIGH TEMPLE BUCKNELL DUQUESNE VILLANOVA

PENNY DY AES MEG RED SOU WIN GILL WING WINN BROON BROWN OULAP PENCE COPPER FOLLIS SALTEE STIVER BROWNIE REDCENT STERLING
(— DREADFUL) HORRIBLE
(DUTCH —) STIVER
(HALF —) HALFLIN
(OLD SCOTCH —) TURNER
(PL.) PENCE FOLLES

PENNYCRESS FANWEED STINKWEED
PENNY-PINCHING STINGY
PENNYROYAL PULIOL HEDEOMA HILLWORT TICKWEED SQUAWWEED
PENNYWEIGHT DWT PENNY WEIGHT STERLING
PENNYWORT ROTGRASS
PENROD (AUTHOR OF —) TARKINGTON
(CHARACTER IN —) CRIM JONES SARAH PENROD MARJORIE SCHOFIELD
PENSION WAGE PAYMENT STIPEND SUBSIDY TRIBUTE GRATUITY MALIKANA
PENSIONER COD RETIREE
PENSIVE MESTO MOODY PENSY SOBER DREAMY MUSING PENCEY WISTFUL THOUGHTY MELANCHOLY
PENT CAGED PENNED CONFINED ENCLOSED RESERVOIR
PENTACLE STAR HEXAGRAM PENTAGRAM
PENTAD QUINTAD
PENTASTICH POEM UNIT STANZA STROPHE
PENTATEUCH TORAH THORAH
PENTECOST SHABUOTH WHITSUNDAY
PENTHESILEA (SLAYER OF —) ACHILLES
PENTHEUS (FATHER OF —) ECHION
(GRANDFATHER OF —) CADMUS
(MOTHER OF —) AGAVE
PENTHIA STARLIGHT
PENTHOUSE CAT PENT ROOF SHED AERIE ANNEX HANGAR LOOKUM SHADOW PLUTEUS BULKHEAD SKEELING SKILLION APPENTICE
PENTOSAN ARABAN
PENTOSE APIOSE RIBOSE
PENTYL AMYL
PENUMBRA AURA
PENURIOUS MEAN POOR BARREN SCANTY STINGY MISERLY WANTING INDIGENT HIDEBOUND NIGGARDLY
PENURY WANT BEGGARY BORASCO POVERTY SCARCITY INDIGENCE PRIVATION
PEON HAND PAWN SERF SLAVE PELADO THRALL FOOTMAN LABORER PEASANT SOLDIER CONSTABLE
PEONY PINY MOUTAN
PEOPLE (ALSO SEE NATIVE AND TRIBE) ARO FUL LOG MEN PUL TAT VAI YAO AKRA ASHA BENI BUGI CHIN CHUD EMIM FOLK FULA GARO GENS HERD HIMA HUMA IRON LAND LEDE LOLO LUBA LURI NOSU PHUD PHUL PHUT RACE RAIS REMI SAFI SARA SEBA SERE TEMA THEY TODA TOMA TULU USUN VITI VOLK WARE AFIFI AVARS BENIN BONGO CATTI CHAGA COURS DEMOS DUALA EDONI ELYMI FOLKS FULAH GENTE GOMER HAUSA JACKS KAREN LAITY LANAO LENDU LUREM MARSI MASAI NOGAI ORANG PUNAN QUADI RAMBO ROTSE SACAE SALAR SAURA SHAKA STOCK TAURI VOLTA WARUA WORLD ABABUA ACHUAS AFSHAR AISSOR ANGAMI ANGLES ARUNTA AVIKOM BAHIMA BAKELE BAKUBA BALUBA BELTIR BOSHAS BULLOM CIMBRI COMMON DAOINE GENTRY GILAKI GILEKI HAUSSA HERERO HERULI KANWAR KPUESI KRUMAN MANTZU MINYAE MOSCHI NATION OVAMPO PAMIRI PUBLIC RAMUSI RUTULI SAFINI SAMBAL SATRAE SEMANG SHARRA TADJIK TAGAUR TELUGU TUNGUZ TURSHA VENETI VOLCAE WACAGO WAHIMA YNDOYS YUECHI ZAMBAL ACHANGO ASTOMOI BAGANDA BAGARRA BAKALAI BANGALA BANGASH BAROTSE BUNYORO DARDANI DENIZEN DURZADA FALISCI GAETULI GENERAL GEPIDAE GOAJIRO GUHAYNA INHABIT IRISHRY ISSEDOI ITALICI KINDRED KURANKO MAKONDE MESHECH MITANNI NABALOI PICENES PICTAVI PUKHTUN ROHILLA SAMBURU SENONES SILURES SUKKIIM TIRURAI VESTINI WABUNGA WACHAGA WAKAMBA WANGONI POPULATE
(— HAVING DISTINCT LANGUAGE) TONGUE
(— OF FASHION) FLOSS
(— OF GOOD BREEDING) GENTRY GENTILITY
(— WITH SIMILAR INTERESTS) MAFIA
(ABORIGINAL —) JAKUN KHMER KODAGU SEKHWAN
(ANCIENT —) CARA CHAM JUNG ELYMI GETAE HURRI ICENI SACAE SERES SICULI DARDANI FALISCI FIRBOLG KIPCHAK SEQUANI SILURES
(BEAUTIFUL —) GLITTERATI
(BIBLICAL —) ALUR IBAD IBAN MAGOG IBANAG SOMALI GADDANG
(CAVE-DWELLING —) HORITE
(COMMON —) DEMOS PLEBE VULGAR VULGUS TILIKUM SNOBBERY
(EXTINCT —) KOT CHONO COFAN COREE CHANGO CHATOT GUINAU HIBITO SAPONI SHIRINO
(FOREST —) SAKAI SAORA SAURA
(GROUP OF —) CAUCUS
(HONORABLE —) HONESTY
(LOWEST CLASS OF —) CANAILLE
(MARITIME —) LAMUT
(MOUNTAIN —) HUZUL HUTZUL
(NOMADIC —) SHUA HORDE IGDYR IHLAT SHUWA HABIRU SHAGIA SARACEN SHAMMAR SHORTZY SHUKRIA
(OLD —) ANCIENTRY
(ORDINARY —) LAYFOLK
(PAGAN —) IRAYA HANUNOO SUBANUN
(POWERFUL GROUP OF —) MAFIA
(PRIMITIVE —) DAFLA IRULA KADIR KURUKH CHENCHU
(WHITE —) ALBICULI
(PL.) MAKHZAN
(PREF.) DEM(O) ETHN(O) PLEBI POPULI
PEOPLED ABAD SETTLED POPULATE
PEORIA MASCOUTEN
PEP GO VIM ZIP DASH MOXIE VERVE VIGOR BOUNCE ENERGY GINGER ANIMATE QUICKEN ACTIVITY
(— UP) ENLIVEN
PEPLUM GOWN SKIRT TUNIC PEPLOS OVERSKIRT
PEPO GOURD MELON SQUASH PUMPKIN PEPONIDA PEPONIUM
PEPPER CAVA IKMO ITMO KAVA SIRI BETEL CHILI MANGO PIPER SIRIH MATICO TOPEPO CAYENNE PAPRIKA PIMENTA RELIENO JALAPENO KAVAKAVA
(JAVA —) CUBEB
(MEXICAN HOT —) SERRANO
(RED —) LADYFINGER
(PREF.) PIPERI PIPERO
PEPPER-AND-SALT JASPER
PEPPERGRASS CRESS CANARY ANOUNOU COCKWEED
PEPPERMINT MENTHE LABIATE
PEPPER TREE MOLLE HOROPITO PIMIENTO
PEPPERWORT DITTANDER
PEPPERY HOT FIERY SAUCY SPICY TOUCHY PIQUANT PUNGENT SPIRITED STINGING
PEPPY RAHRAH GINGERY
PEPTIDE KININ AMANITIN
PEPTIDOGLYCAN MUREIN
PEPTONE ASCARON
PER BY THE EACH THROUGH
PERADVENTURE HAP DOUBT MAYBE CHANCE MAPPEN MAYHAP HAPPILY PERHAPS POSSIBLY
PERAMBULATE ROAM WALK RAMBLE STROLL PERAMBLE TRAVERSE
PERAMBULATION WEND
PERAMBULATOR BUGGY WAGON BASSINET VIAMETER WAYWISER PEDOMETER
PERATE OPHITE
PERCEIVE SEE ESPY FEEL FIND GAUM HEAR KNOW LOOK MIND NOTE SCAN TWIG SCENT SENSE SMELL TASTE TOUCH BEHOLD COTTON DESCRY DIVINE FIGURE NOTICE REMARK SURVEY COGNIZE DISCERN OBSERVE REALIZE SENSATE COMPRISE DESCRIBE UNDERNIM RECOGNIZE
(—CRITICALLY) SAVOR
PERCENTAGE CUT AGIO PART SHARE PROFIT PORTION RAKEOFF SCALAGE CONTANGO DEFLATOR PROPORTION
(INSURANCE —) FRANCHISE
(MINING —) LEY
PERCEPT IDEA
PERCEPTIBLE PUBLIC NOTABLE TACTILE VISIBLE APPARENT PALPABLE SENSIBLE TANGIBLE TRACTABLE PERCEIVABLE
(— BY TASTE) SAPID
(FAINTLY —) SHADOWY
(HARDLY —) FAINT
(PREF.) ESTHETO
PERCEPTION RAY BUMP GAUM TACT SAVOR SCENT SENSE SIGHT ACUMEN VISION CLOSURE FEELING GLIMMER NOSTRIL BEARINGS DELICACY OUTSIGHT COGNITION SENSATION SENTIMENT
(DIM —) GLIMMER
(MENTAL —) TACT TOUCH SENSATION
(NICE —) TASTE
(SPIRITUAL —) WISDOM
(UNREAL —) HALLUCINATION
PERCEPTIVE ACUTE QUICK SHARP SUBTLE KNOWING PIERCING SENTIENT SENSITIVE
PERCH BAR BAS LUG PEG ROD SIT BASS JOUK MADO OKOW PERK PIKE POLE POPE RUFF SEAT BARSE BEGTI BEKTI BLOCK LIGHT REACH ROOST RUFFE STAFF STANG ALIGHT ANABAS BUGARA CALLOP COMBER PERCID SANDER SAUGER SETTLE ZANDER ZINGEL ALFIONE HOGFISH STATION ROCKFISH MARTENIKO TRUMPETER MADEMOISELLE
(KIND OF —) NILE
(LOFTY —) AERIE
(2-YEAR OLD —) EGLING
(PREF.) PERCI
PERCHANCE HAPLY MAYBE AUNTERS FORTUNE PERHAPS POSSIBLY
PERCHER STAKER
PERCHTA BERTHA
PERCOLATE MELT OOZE PERK SEEP SIFT SILT SIPE SOAK WEEP DRILL EXUDE LEACH EXHALE FILTER STRAIN
PERCOLATION SIPING SEEPAGE LEACHING
PERCOLATOR SIPER BIGGIN CAFETIERE DISPLACER
PERCUSSION (ALSO SEE DRUMS) BLOW IMPACT STROKE TOMTOM PNEUMATIC
(— IN MASSAGE) TAPOTEMENT
PERDITA (FATHER OF —) LEONTES
(MOTHER OF —) HERMIONE
PERDITION HELL LOSS RUIN BOWWOWS BALLYWACK DAMNATION
PEREGRINATE TOUR WALK TRAVEL WANDER JOURNEY SOJOURN TRAVERSE
PEREGRINE ALIEN NOMAD EXOTIC ROVING PILGRIM STRANGE IMPORTED
PEREGRINE FALCON SAKER GENTLE TASSEL TERCEL
PEREGRINE PICKLE (AUTHOR OF —) SMOLLETT
(CHARACTER IN —) TOM VANE PIPES SALLY EMILIA HAWSER PICKLE APPLEBY GRIZZLE GAMALIEL GAUNTLET HATCHWAY HORNBECK TRUNNION PEREGRINE CADWALLADER
PEREMPT QUASH DEFEAT DESTROY
PEREMPTORY FLAT FINAL UTTER

EXPRESS HAUGHTY ABSOLUTE DECISIVE DOGMATIC POSITIVE ESSENTIAL MASTERFUL

PERENNIAL HERB CAREX LIANA PEONY SEDUM BANANA CENTRO BLUEWEED CONSTANT ENDURING KNAPWEED TOADFLAX CONTINUAL EVERGREEN PENNYWORT PERPETUAL RECURRENT

PERESH (FATHER OF —) MACHIR
(MOTHER OF —) MAACHAH

PERFECT ALL AOK BACK BORN CURE FILL FINE FULL HOLY HONE PURE SURE TOAT EXACT FINAL FULLY IDEAL PLAIN RIGHT RIPEN SHEER SOUND TOTAL UTTER WHOLE ENTIRE EXPERT FINISH MATURE POLISH REFINE SPHERE TIPTOP CERTAIN CONCOCT CONTENT CORRECT CROWNED DEVELOP GEMLIKE IMPROVE PLENARY PRECISE SINLESS SPHERAL TYPICAL COMPLETE COPYBOOK FLAWLESS INFINITE INTEGRAL REPLENISH
(— IN RIGHTEOUSNESS) HOLY
(— SCORE) MAX
(NOT —) IMMATURE
(PREF.) TEL(E)(EO)

PERFECTA EXACTA

PERFECTED EXACT SUMMED FINISHED PERQUEIR

PERFECTION ACME BEST PINK BLOOM IDEAL BEAUTY FINISH PLENTY PARAGON FINALITY FINENESS FULLNESS MATURITY RIPENESS ERUDITION
(STATE OF —) SIDDHI
(TO —) NINE
(TYPE OF —) PARAGON

PERFECTIVE TELIC

PERFECTLY SPAN QUITE IDEALLY PERQUEIR

PERFIDIOUS FALSE SNAKY DISLEAL SNAKISH DISLOYAL SPITEFUL FAITHLESS

PERFIDY DECEIT TREASON FALSEHOOD FALSENESS TREACHERY

PERFORATE EAT DOCK HOLE DRILL PRICK PUNCH SIEVE THIRL PIERCE POUNCE RIDDLE THRILL PINHOLE PUNCTURE PENETRATE TEREBRATE
(— A STAMP) CENTER

PERFORATED OPEN CRIBROSE FENESTRAL PUNCTURED

PERFORATION BORE HOLE THIRL TORET BROACH EYELET STIGMA TRESIS FORAMEN PINHOLE SEPTULA STENCIL FENESTRA DIABROSIS PERTUSION
(SUFF.) TRESIA

PERFORATOR (SURGICAL —) TROCAR

PERFORM DO ACT CUT KIP CHAR FILL FULL HAVE KEEP LAST MAKE PLAY SHOW STEP CHARE DIGHT ENACT EXERT FETCH PUTON THROW ACQUIT COMMIT EFFECT FULFIL RENDER ACHIEVE EXECUTE EXHIBIT EXPLOIT FUNGIFY FURNISH IWURCHE OPERATE PRESENT PRESTATE PROSECUTE
(— AWKWARDLY) BOGGLE
(— BADLY) BOLLIX
(— BRILLIANTLY) STAR SPARKLE
(— CLUMSILY) THUMB BUNGLE
(— FANCY STUNTS) HOTDOG
(— FULLY) END
(— HASTILY) SKIMP SCAMP,
(— HURRIEDLY) SLUR
(— IN DANCING) FIGURE
(— PERFECTLY) DOTOAT
(— POORLY) CLUTCH
(— SLUTTISHLY) SOZZLE
(— SUCCESSFULLY) CUTIT
(FAIL TO —) CHOKE
(FAIL TO — EFFECTIVELY) CHOKE

PERFORMANCE ACT JOB DEED FEAT GALA HAND SHOW TEST WORK CAPER SLANG SPORT STUNT ACTING ACTION BALLET EFFECT HORARY MASQUE ACCOUNT ACROAMA BENEFIT BOOKING CONCERT EXPLOIT MATINEE MUMMERY RELEASE SHOWING FAREWELL FUNCTION PRACTICE STERACLE OPERATION
(— FOR ONE) SOLO
(— OF DUTY) FEASANCE
(— OF OBLIGATION) SOLUTIO
(— VARIATIONS) COUNTER
(— WITH SENTIMENTALITY) DROOL
(ARAB —) FANTASIA
(BOISTEROUS —) KNOCKABOUT
(BRILLIANT —) BRAVURA
(CHRISTMAS EVE —) GOMBAY
(CLUMSY —) BUNGLE
(DISORDERLY —) SCRAMBLE
(DRAMATIC —) TOPENG PANTOMIME
(FIRST —) OPENING PREMIERE
(HILARIOUS —) HOOT
(INEPT —) BOMB
(MUSICAL —) LESSON RECITAL DIVISION
(NO —) RELACHE
(PAST —) FORM
(RENEWED —) REVIVAL
(SHORT —) SPOT
(STAGE —) SCENE
(SURGICAL —) OPERATION
(TRAVELLING —) SLANG
(TRIAL —) AUDITION
(VOCAL —) SPRECHSTIMME
(VULGAR —) BLOWOFF
(WRONG —) MISPRISION
(SUFF.) LOG(ER)(IA)(IAN)(IC)(ICAL)(IST)(UE)(Y

PERFORMER ACT DOER GEEK MOKE STAR ACTOR SHINE ARTIST DANCER KINKER LEADER PLAYER WORKER ACROAMA ACROBAT ARTISTE GAMBIST HORNIST HOTSHOT SOLOIST EXECUTOR SPARKLER HAMFATTER HEADLINER
(— ON SEVERAL INSTRUMENTS) MOKE
(— WITH NEGRO DIALECT) HAMBONE
(BURLESQUE —) GRINDER
(CIRCUS —) LEAPER
(INFERIOR —) HAM SHINE
(SUFF.) ANT ENT

PERFUME ATAR BALM FUME MUSK NOSE OTTO AROMA ATTAR CENSE CIVET MYRRH SCENT SMELL SPICE CARVOL CHYPRE EMBALM FLAVOR IONONE BOUQUET CARVONE DIAPASM ESSENCE INCENSE JASMINE NOSEGAY ODORIZE SWEETEN BERGAMOT MARECHAL ORANGERY PATCHOULI
(— BASE) MUSK CIVET NEROL NEROLI
(— CENTER) GRASSE
(POWDERY —) PULVIL

PERFUNCTORY CURSORY CARELESS SLIPSHOD SLOVENLY APATHETIC

PERGOLA ARBOR BOWER RAMADA BALCONY TRELLIS

PERHAPS HAPS MAYBE ABLINS BELIKE HAPPEN MAPPEN MAYHAP ABLINGS AIBLINS LIGHTLY PERCASE YIBBLES POSSIBLY PERCHANCE

PERI ELF FAIRY SPRITE

PERIAPT CHARM AMULET

PERICARP BUR BOLL BURR BLADDER

PERICHOLE, LA (CHARACTER IN —) ABDRES PIQUILLO PERICHOLE
(COMPOSER OF —) OFFENBACH

PERICLES (AUTHOR OF —) SHAKESPEARE
(CHARACTER IN —) BOULT CLEON DIANA GOWER MARINA THAISA CERIMON DIONYZA ESCANES LEONINE PERICLES PHILEMON THALIARD ANTIOCHUS HELICANUS LYCHORIDA SIMONIDES LYSIMACHUS
(FATHER OF —) XANTHIPPUS
(MISTRESS OF —) ASPASIA
(MOTHER OF —) AGARISTE
(SON OF —) PARALUS XANTHIPPUS
(TEACHER OF —) ZENO DAMON

PERICLYMENUS (BROTHER OF —) NESTOR
(FATHER OF —) NELEUS POSEIDON
(MOTHER OF —) CHLORIS MELIBOEA

PERICOPE LESSON

PERICRANIUM HEAD BRAIN

PERIDOT OLIVINE

PERIDOTITE PICRITE EULYSITE JOSEFITE SAXONITE WEHRLITE

PERIERES (FATHER OF —) AEOLUS
(MOTHER OF —) ENARETE
(SON OF —) APHAREUS LEUCIPPUS
(WIFE OF —) GORGOPHONE

PERIGEE EPIGEUM

PERIGYNIUM UTRICLE

PERIL RISK WERE WATHE CRISIS DANGER HAZARD MENACE SCYLLA THREAT THRONG TRANCE DISTRESS JEOPARDY CHARYBDIS

PERILOUS KITTLE DOUBTFUL DREADFUL INFAMOUS DANGEROUS HAZARDOUS

PERIMETER RIM CIRCUIT OUTLINE BOUNDARY PERIPHERY

PERIOD GO AGE DOT END EON ERA AEON DATE LIFE RACE SPAN STOP TERM TIDE TIME YEAR AVAIL CLOSE CYCLE EPACT EPOCH LABOR LAPSE PATCH POINT SPACE SPELL STAGE CUTOFF GHURRY HEMERA MOMENT PARODY PICTUN SEASON STOUND ACCOUNT DICOLON FLORUIT PASTIME SESSION STADIUM STRETCH DURATION INDUCIAE INSTANCE LIFETIME SENTENCE
(— ENDING FROST) FRESH
(— FOR WHICH ENJOYED) TENURE
(— IN DEVELOPMENT) STAGE
(— OF ACTION) GO BOUT
(— OF DECLINE) SUNSET EVENING
(— OF DRYNESS) DROUTH DROUGHT
(— OF DUTY) WATCH
(— OF FAIR WEATHER) SLATCH
(— OF FESTIVITY) WAKES
(— OF FIVE YEARS) LUSTRE PENTAD LUSTRUM QUINQUENNIUM
(— OF GLOOM) DEAD
(— OF GRACE) DAY
(— OF HAPPINESS) MILLENNIUM
(— OF HEAT) CALLING
(— OF HUMID WEATHER) SIZZARD
(— OF IMMATURITY) SWADDLE
(— OF INSTRUCTION) LESSON
(— OF ISOLATION) QUARANTINE
(— OF LEAVE) SABBATICAL
(— OF LIFE) AGE ELD SPAN
(— OF MILITARY SERVICE) HITCH
(— OF MOTILITY) SWARMING
(— OF MOURNING) SHIVA SHIBAH
(— OF NEW MOON) SYZYGY
(— OF PERFORMING) STANZA
(— OF PLAY) HALF CHUKKER QUARTER
(— OF RAINFALL) FLUVIAL
(— OF RECREATION) HOLIDAY VACATION
(— OF REMISSION) JUBILEE
(— OF REST) SMOKO BREATHER
(— OF REVOLUTION OF HEAVENLY BODY) ORB
(— OF SERVICE) TOUR
(— OF TIME) DAY HOUR WEEK YEAR MONTH DECADE MINUTE SECOND
(— OF WORK) SHIFT SPELL STINT
(— OF 10 YEARS) DECADE
(— OF 100 YEARS) AGE CENTURY
(— OF 1000 YEARS) CHILIAD MILLIAD
(— OF 14 MINUTES, 24 SECONDS) CENTIDAY
(— OF 2 MONTHS) DIMESTER
(— OF 2 YEARS) BIENNIUM
(— OF 20 TUNS) KATUN
(— OF 20 YEARS) KATUN
(— OF 260 DAYS) TONALMATL
(— OF 4 YEARS) QUADRENNIUM
(— OF 5 DAYS) PENTAD
(— OF 5 YEARS) LUSTRE LUSTRUM
(— OF 50 YEARS) JUBILE JUBILEE
(— OF 7 DAYS) HEBDOMAD
(— OF 7 YEARS) SEPTENARY
(— PRECEDING IMPORTANT EVENT) EVE
(CLASS —) HOUR
(CONTINUOUS —) RUN
(CULTURAL —) HORIZON
(DEFINITE —) MOMENT

(DISTINCTIVE —) EPOCH
(DULL —) SLACK
(EVOLUTIONAL —) HEMERA
(GEOLOGICAL —) JURA KAROO EOCENE ALGOMAN HORIZON NEOCENE CAMBRIAN DEVONIAN JURASSIC SILURIAN TERTIARY TRANSVAAL
(HAPPY —) MILLENIUM
(HYPOTHETICAL —) ACME
(JAPANESE —) MEIJI
(JAPANESE CULTURAL —) JOMON
(LONG —) EON AEON CYCLE
(MEETING —) SESSION
(MENSTRUAL —) TERMS
(OCCASIONAL —) SNATCH
(OF JAPANESE —) JOMON
(OF JAPANESE CULTURAL —) YAYOI
(PENITENTIAL —) LENT
(RECOVERY —) REHAB
(RECURRING —) EMBER
(SHORT —) BIT FIT BLINK SHAKE SPELL SPURT SNATCH
(TELEVISION RATINGS —) SWEEP
(WAITING —) MORATORIUM
(WET —) PLUVIAL
(SUFF.) (OF A —) CHRONOUS

PERIODIC ERAL ANNUAL CYCLIC ETESIAN REGULAR FREQUENT SEASONAL
(NOT —) LOOSE ACYCLIC

PERIODICAL DAILY ORGAN PAPER SHEET ANNUAL DIGEST REVIEW ETESIAN FANZINE JOURNAL REGULAR TABLOID DREADFUL EXCHANGE MAGAZINE EPHEMERIS PICTORIAL

PERIODICALLY TERMLY

PERION (SON OF —) AMADIS

PERIPATETIC ROVING RAMBLING ITINERANT

PERIPHERAL DEEP OUTER DISTAL DISTANT EXTERNAL MARGINAL

PERIPHERY LIP RIM BRIM DOME EDGE AMBIT LIMIT SKIRT AREOLA BORDER BOUNDS FRINGE AMBITUS CONTOUR SUBURBS SURFACE CONFINES PERIMETER

PERIPHRASTIC AMBAGIOUS

PERISCOPE ALTISCOPE HYPOSCOPE OMNISCOPE

PERISH DIE FADE FALL RUIN TINE TYNE QUAIL SPILL SWELT WASTE DEPART EXPIRE STARVE DESTROY FORFARE MISCARRY
(— GRADUALLY) FADE

PERISHABLE SOFT DYING CADUKE BRITTLE FUGITIVE

PERISHED MUSHY

PERISTOME FRINGE

PERITE SKILLED

PERITHECIUM ALVEOLA

PERITONEUM RIM SIPHAC

PERIWIG FLASH GALERA PERUKE TOUPEE GALERUM PERWICK CHEVELURE

PERIWINKLE PERY PIRE WINK PERRY SNAIL MYRTLE WINKLE DOGBANE PINPATCH SENGREEN BLUEBUTTON

PERJINK NEAT TRIM PRECISE

PERJURE FORSWEAR

PERJURED MANSWORN

PERK BRISK FRILL PERCH PREEN PRINK FRESHEN SMARTEN

PERKY AIRY PERT COCKY JAUNTY CHIPPER

PERMANENCE STAY STABILITY

PERMANENT FIXED STABLE ABIDING DURABLE LASTING STATIVE CONSTANT ENDURING REMANENT STANDING INDELIBLE

PERMANENTLY KEEPS

PERMEABLE POROUS PERVIOUS

PERMEATE FILL SEEP SOAK BATHE IMBUE DRENCH INFORM INVADE ANIMATE PERVADE DOMINATE SATURATE PENETRATE

PERMEATED SHOT

PERMEATION SATURATION

PERMIAN DYAS DYASSIC

PERMISSIBLE FREE VENIAL POSSIBLE CONGEABLE
(NOT —) NEFAS

PERMISSION MAY FIAT LIEF PASS CONGE DARST FAVOR GRACE GRANT LEAVE ACCESS ACCORD PERMIT CONSENT LIBERTY LICENSE SANCTION
(— TO ACT) POWER
(— TO BE ABSENT) ABSIT
(— TO PRINT) IMPRIMATUR
(— TO PROCEED) GOAHEAD
(— TO USE) LOAN
(LETTER OF —) EXEAT
(WRITTEN —) PASS

PERMISSIVE TOLERANT CONCESSORY

PERMIT LET CHIT CHOP GIVE LEVE PASS ADMIT ALLOW CONGE EXEAT FAVOR GRACE GRANT LEAVE SERVE ACCORD BETEEM CEDULA DUSTUK ENDURE ENTREE SUFFER CONCEDE CONSENT DUSTUCK FACULTY LICENSE PLACARD POMPANO WARRANT DISPENSE
(— NEGATIVELY) TOLERATE
(— TO ENTER) INTROMIT
(— TO TAKE) SOAK
(CUSTOMS —) CARNET

PERMITTED FREE LOOT LICIT ALLOWED INNOCENT SUPPOSED
(— BY LAW) LEGAL

PERMUTATION BARTER CHANGE EXCHANGE

PERNICIOUS BAD ILL EVIL FATAL QUICK SWIFT DEADLY MALIGN WICKED BALEFUL BANEFUL HARMFUL HURTFUL NOISOME NOXIOUS RUINOUS

PERNIO CHILBLAIN

PERO (BROTHER OF —) NESTOR
(FATHER OF —) NELEUS
(HUSBAND OF —) BIAS
(MOTHER OF —) CHLORIS
(SON OF —) ASOPUS

PEROPUS PARAGON

PERORATION EPILOG PERIOD CLOSING PURLICUE

PEROXISOME MICROBODY

PERPEND JUMPER PARPEN PONDER REFLECT THROUGH

PERPENDICULAR SINE ERECT PLUMB SHEER ABRUPT NORMAL APOTHEM UPRIGHT BINORMAL CATHETUS EVENDOWN VERTICAL
(MUTUALLY —) ORTHOGONAL

PERPENDICULARITY APLOMB

PERPENDICULARLY BOLT SHEER SHEERLY

PERPETRATE DO PULL COMMIT EFFECT PERFORM

PERPETUAL ETERN ENDLESS ETERNAL CONSTANT INFINITO UNENDING CONTINUAL PERENNIAL

PERPETUALLY EVER ALWAYS FOREVER

PERPETUATE CONTINUE ETERNIZE MAINTAIN

PERPLEX CAP MAR SET VEX BEAT CLOG DOIT DOZE FIKE MAZE STUN AMAZE BESET BLAIK STUMP TWIST BAFFLE BOGGLE BOTHER BUNKER CUMBER DARKEN FEAGUE FICKLE GRAVEL HAMPER HARASS HOBBLE KITTLE MAMMER MITHER MOIDER MUDDLE PLAGUE POTHER POTTER PUTTER PUZZLE RAFFLE RIDDLE TWITCH WILDER WRIXLE BEDEVIL BUMBAZE CONFUSE DIFFUSE EMBROIL FLUMMOX MYSTIFY NONPLUS PLUNDER STAGGER STUMBLE TORMENT BEWILDER CONFOUND SURPRISE WINDLASS BAMBOOZLE

PERPLEXED ASEA MAZY ATSEA ANXIOUS NONPLUS PUZZLED CONFUSED TROUBLED INTRICATE TOSTICATED

PERPLEXING HARD MAZY SPINY CRABBY KNOBBY KNOTTY CARKING COMPLEX CRABBED QUISCOS BAFFLING

PERPLEXITY FOG KNOT WERE BRAKE FOITER HOBBLE PUCKER PUZZLE TAKING TANGLE ANXIETY NONPLUS STICKLE TROUBLE POSEMENT SURPRISE CONFUSION LABYRINTH PUZZLEMENT
(MENTAL —) STUDY
(RELIEVE OF —) CLEAR

PERQUISITE FEE TIP LOCK PERK VAIL GOUPIN GOWPEN INCOME ADJUNCT APANAGE VANTAGE CONQUEST GRATUITY
(PL.) PICKING

PERRIER PEDRERO

PERRINIST LIBERTINE

PERSE BLUE
(DAUGHTER OF —) CIRCE PASIPHAE
(FATHER OF —) OCEANUS
(HUSBAND OF —) HELIOS
(SON OF —) AEETES PERSES

PERSECUTE VEX BAIT ANNOY CHASE HARRY HOUND WRACK WRONG HARASS PESTER PURSUE AFFLICT CRUCIFY DRAGOON OPPRESS TORMENT TORTURE

PERSECUTED JOB REFUGEE

PERSECUTOR TORQUEMADA

PERSEPHONE KORE DESPOINA PRAXIDIKE
(DAUGHTER OF —) CORA KORE
(FATHER OF —) ZEUS JUPITER
(HUSBAND OF —) HADES PLUTO
(MOTHER OF —) CERES DEMETER

PERSES (BROTHER OF —) AEETES
(DAUGHTER OF —) HECATE
(FATHER OF —) CRIUS HELIOS
(MOTHER OF —) PERSE EYRYBIA
(SISTER OF —) CIRCE PASIPHAE

PERSEUS RESCUER CHAMPION
(FATHER OF —) ZEUS JUPITER
(GRANDFATHER OF —) ACRISIUS
(MOTHER OF —) DANAE
(STAR OF —) ATIK ALGOL
(VICTIM OF —) MEDUSA
(WIFE OF —) ANDROMEDA

PERSEVERANCE GRIT MOXIE STAMINA INDUSTRY PATIENCE TENACITY CONSTANCY PERSISTENCE

PERSEVERE PEG CANK KEEP PLUG TORE ABIDE STICK HANGIN INSIST REMAIN PERSIST CONTINUE

PERSEVERING BUSY HARD STILL PATIENT RESOLUTE SEDULOUS ASSIDUOUS INSISTENT

PERSIA (SEE IRAN)

PERSIAN MEDE FARSI PERSE GILAKI HAJEMI IRANIC DURZADA HADJEMI IRANIAN MEMNONIAN
(— RED DEER) MARAL

PERSICARY REDLEG REDLEGS REDSHANK HEARTEASE HEARTWEED PEACHWORT

PERSIFLAGE BANTER RAILLERY

PERSIMMON KAKI SIMON SIMMON ZAPOTE CHAPOTE HYAKUME TRIUMPH
(— TREE) GAB GAUB LOTUS

PERSIST HOLD KEEP LAST URGE ADHERE ENDURE INSIST REMAIN PREVAIL SUBSIST CONTINUE PERSEVERE

PERSISTENCE GUTS
(SUFF.) STASIA STASIS

PERSISTENCY TENACITY

PERSISTENT SET DREE FIRM HARD GREAT STOUT TOUGH DOGGED DREECH GRITTY HECTIC SLEUTH DURABLE RESTANT RESTIVE CONSTANT ENDURING HOLDFAST OBDURATE RESOLUTE SEDULOUS STUBBORN ASSIDUOUS OBSTINATE PERENNIAL PRIMITIVE RELENTLESS

PERSISTING
(PREF.) MENO

PERSON BOD CAT EGG EGO GUY MAN ONE BABY BODY CHAL CHAP COVE DUCK FISH FOOD FORM GINK HOOK LEDE LIFE NABS PRIG SELF SOUL BEING BLOKE BOSOM CHILD COOKY GHOST HEART HUMAN PARTI PARTY PIECE STICK THING WATCH WIGHT ANIMAL BUGGER ENTITY FELLOW GALOOT GAZABO JOHNNY KIPPER NUMBER SINNER SISTER SPIRIT SPRITE ARTICLE BLISTER WAGTAIL SPECIMEN TILLICUM
(— ACTING FOR ANOTHER) PROXY
(— ASSOCIATED WITH WORK) WALLAH
(— BEARING HEAVY BURDEN) CAMEL
(— BEHIND THE TIMES) FOGY FOGEY

(— BRINGING GOOD LUCK) MASCOT
(— FROM WHOM FAMILY IS DESCENDED) STIRPS
(— INTERESTED IN FOOD FADS) FOODIE
(— MEANLY CLAD) SCARECROW
(— NAMED) NOMINEE
(— NOT IN THE KNOW) LAME
(— NOT OF NOBLE BIRTH) ROTURIER
(— OF AGE) COOT FALDWORTH
(— OF CONSEQUENCE) BIGGIE BIGWIG TALLBOY
(— OF COURAGE) SPARTAN
(— OF ENERGY) LIVEWIRE
(— OF HONOR) MENSCH
(— OF INFLUENCE) CAPTAIN HEAVYWEIGHT
(— OF INTEGRITY) MENSCH
(— OF MEAN BIRTH) GUTTERBLOOD
(— OF NO REFINEMENT) SLOB
(— OF RANK) STATE MAGNATE EMINENCE MAGNIFICO PERSONAGE
(— OF WEAK MIND) FOOL
(— OF WISDOM) SOLOMON
(— OPPOSED TO CHANGE) LUDDITE
(— PREJUDICED AGAINST ELDERLY) AGIST AGEIST
(— PRETENDING INTELLIGENCE) PSEUD
(— RESEMBLING ANOTHER) SOSIA
(—S IN AMBASSADOR'S SUITE) COMES
(— TO BE IMITATED) EXEMPLAR
(— TOO STRONG FOR ASSAILANT) TARTAR
(— TO SERVE WRIT) ELISOR
(— TRYING TO ATTRACT ATTENTION SHOWBOAT
(— WANTING TO BE SOMEONE ELSE) WANNABE
(— WHO DOESN'T FIT IN) GEEK
(— WHO HOARDS) SQUIRREL
(— WHO IS UP-TO-DATE) SWINGER
(— WHO LOCATES ANTIQUES) PICKER
(— WHO PERFORMS MENIAL TASKS) DOGSBODY
(— WHO TAKES AMPHETAMINES) PILLHEAD
(— WHO TAKES CAPSULES) PILLHEAD
(— WHO TALKS EXCESSIVELY) MOTORMOUTH
(— WITH MENTAL TWIST) CRANK
(— WITH MILITANT ATTITUDE) HAWK
(— WITH NERVOUS DISORDERS) NEUROTIC
(— WITHOUT EQUAL) NONPAREIL
(— WITHOUT STAMINA) JELLYFISH
(— WITH QUEER IDEAS) ROZUM
(— WITH SHORT HAIR) SKINHEAD
(ABJECT —) SLAVE CRAWLER
(ABSENT-MINDED —) MUSARD
(ACTIVE —) GOER
(ADMIRABLE —) GEM PIPPIN RIPPER
(AFFECTED —) POSEUR MINNICK GIMCRACK
(AFFECTEDLY INTELLECTUAL —) PSEUD
(AGGRESSIVE —) SHOVER HOTSHOT
(AMUSING —) COMIC
(ANNOYING —) FIEND NUDNICK
(ANTIQUATED —) MUMPSIMUS
(ARABIZED —) MOZARAB
(ARROGANT —) HUFF TENGU
(ATTRACTIVE —) DISH CUTEY CUTIE KILLER KNOCKOUT
(AVARICIOUS —) YISSER
(AWKWARD —) PUT GAWP HICK MUFF RUBE SLAM STAG STEG KLUTZ STIFF GALOOT GUFFIN TUMFIE HOOSIER LOBSTER SCHLEPP KITHOGUE SHLEPPER SLOMMACK SPELDRIN
(BAD —) UNSEL
(BALD —) BALLARD BALDHEAD SKINHEAD BALDICOOT
(BANISHED —) WRETCH
(BAPTIZED —) MEMBER ILLUMINATO
(BASE —) CUT RASCAL CAITIFF HILDING PUTTOCK
(BELOVED —) FLAME HEARTROOT
(BIG-BELLIED —) GORBELLY
(BLACK —) BLECK
(BOASTFUL —) BLOWER GASCON
(BOISTEROUS —) TEARER
(BOORISH —) GOOP
(BORING —) SCHMO
(BRUTAL —) RUFFIAN
(BUSTLING —) STIRABOUT
(CALLOW —) GORLIN SMARTY GOSLING
(CANONIZED —) SAINT
(CARELESS —) HASH TASSEL
(CASTRATED —) SPADO
(CERTAIN —) QUIDAM
(CHARMING —) SMASHER
(CHATTERING —) MAGPIE
(CHICKENHEARTED —) HEN
(CHILDISH —) BAUBLE WHIMLING
(CHUNKY —) JUNT
(CHURLISH —) TIKE TYKE
(CIRCLE OF —S) COTERIE
(CLEVER —) BIRD WHIZ WHIZZ MERCURY
(CLOWNISH —) BUFFOON HOBNAIL VILLAIN
(CLUMSY —) DUB LOB BOOB GAWK SLOB TIKE TYKE JUMBO KLUTZ STAUP STIFF DUFFER KEFFEL LUMMOX HODMADOD
(COARSE —) COW STIRK BABOON MUCKER
(COAXING —) WHILLY WHEEDLE
(COLD —) ICICLE
(COMBATIVE —) DRAGON GAMECOCK
(COMMONPLACE —) MUT MUTT BROMIDE
(CONCEITED —) IT HUFF COXCOMB PRAGMATIC
(CONFUSED —) FOOSTERER
(CONSERVATIVE —) HUNKER SQUARE MOSSBACK
(CONSPICUOUS —) LIGHT
(CONTEMPTIBLE —) YAP CRUD HEEL PUKE SCAB SKIN SWAB CATSO SHRUB SKITE SKUNK SNIPE TWERP INSECT SHICER STINKER BLIGHTER WHIFFLER PETTITOES
(COWARDLY —) WIMP FUGIE SISSY SLINK SQUIB
(CRAFTY —) TOD FILE SHARK JESUIT
(CRAZED —) NUT NUTTER PSYCHOPATH MESHUGGENAH
(CRINGING —) SNAKE SNOOL FLUNKY SPANIEL
(CRUEL —) LAMB FIEND MALISON
(CUNNING —) PIE
(CURIOUS —) RUBBERNECK
(DAINTY —) MIMMOCK
(DARK —) MOOR OUSEL OUZEL MELANO NIGNOG
(DEAD —) DEFUNCT DECEASED DECEDENT
(DEBAUCHED —) RAKEHELL
(DECREPIT —) CROCK WITHERLING
(DEDICATED —) OBLATE
(DEFORMED —) CRILE CALIBAN HODMADOD
(DENSE —) DUFFER
(DEPENDENT —) JUNKIE
(DEPRAVED —) SKATE
(DERANGED —) PSYCHE
(DESPICABLE —) SCAB HOUND SLAVE CAITIFF
(DESTITUTE —) PAUPER
(DEVILISH —) SHAITAN
(DIMINUTIVE —) BANTY MIDGE BANTAM MIDGET NIFFNAFF
(DIRTY —) SWEEP DRIVEL HOWLET
(DISABLED —) DUCK CRIPPLE INVALID
(DISAGREEABLE —) GOOP PILL QUAT SKITE RATBAG
(DISGRUNTLED —) SOREHEAD
(DISHONEST —) ROGUE ROTTER BEZONIAN
(DISLIKED —) WARLING
(DISREPUTABLE —) RIP QUANDONG
(DISSOLUTE —) RIBALD ROUNDER STRIKER
(DOLEFUL —) MISERY
(DOLTISH —) BLOCK SWINE
(DRUG-ABUSING —) BURNOUT
(DRUNKEN —) LUSH TUMBREL TUMBRIL
(DULL —) LOB BORE DODO DRIP GOON GOOP GRUB LUMP MOME MOPE SLOB CLUNK DROUD PRUNE SCHMO STICK STOCK LURDAM LACKWIT LOBCOCK NUDNICK OPACITY DEADHEAD
(DULL-WITTED —) DOPE GUMP DUNCE
(DUMB —) MUTE
(DUMPY —) HODDYDODDY
(DUPED —) GULL
(DWARFISH —) AGATE CROWL SHURF
(DYING —) MORIBUND
(ECCENTRIC —) COON GINK KOOK TIKE TYKE GAZABO GAZEBO FANTAST ODDBALL
(EDUCATED —) SCHOLAR LITERATE
(EFFEMINATE —) SOFTY SQUAW CODDLE SOFTIE WANTON BADLING SOFTLING SMOCKFACE
(ELDERLY —) SENIOR SOAKER GRAYHEAD GERIATRIC
(EMACIATED —) FRAME WASTREL SKELETON
(EMPTY-HEADED —) NITWIT
(ENERGETIC —) DYNAMO
(ENROLLED —) MEMBER
(ENTERTAINING —) COMEDIAN
(ENTHUSIASTIC —) FANATIC
(ESSENTIAL —) LINCHPIN
(EVIL —) QUED SCUM QUEDE SHREW
(EXALTED —) PERSONAGE
(EXPERIENCED —) EXPERT SOAKER STAGER
(EXPERT —) ACE DAB
(EXTORTIONATE —) SCREW
(EXTRAORDINARY —) ONER BUSTER
(FADED —) SHARGAR SHARGER
(FAINT-HEARTED —) HEN
(FAMOUS —) DON NOTORIETY
(FANTASTIC —) KICKSHAW
(FARSIGHTED —) PRESBYOPE
(FASHIONABLE —) GIMCRACK
(FASTIDIOUS —) MIMMOCK DELICATE
(FAT —) GURK BLIMP FATSO QUILT SQUAB STOUT
(FATUOUS —) GOOP
(FAWNING —) COGGER SPANIEL
(FEEBLEMINDED —) FEEB IDIOT MORON IMBECILE
(FEROCIOUS —) LAMB
(FICKLE —) ROVER MOONCALF
(FILTHY —) HOGG
(FINE —) WHIPPA
(FLABBY —) HUDDERON
(FLAKY —) SPACECADET
(FLASHY —) KID FLASHER
(FLIGHTY —) FLIBBERTIGIBBET
(FOOLISH —) FOP GIT BOZO COOT GUMP HOIT JERK PUTZ BOOBY SOFTY BAUBLE DOODLE DOOFUS DOTARD DRIVEL HOWLET TURKEY GOSLING GUBBINS HAVEREL BUBBLEHEAD
(FORCELESS —) DRIP
(FORGETFUL —) SPACECADET
(FOUL —) DREVILL
(FRANK —) TELLTRUTH
(FRIVOLOUS —) HOBBYHORSE FEATHERBRAIN
(FUSSY —) FAD FADDLE GRANNY SPOFFY GRANNIE
(GAY —) GRIG HUZZA
(GIDDY —) SCATTERBRAIN
(GLOOMY —) SATURNIST
(GOOD-FOR-NOTHING —) KET PELF TASSEL WASTER WANHOPE WASTREL
(GOSSIPING —) SHULER SHUILER
(GOSSIPY —) BIGMOUTH QUIDNUNC NEWSMONGER
(GOSSIPY, TALKATIVE —) YENTA
(GRASPING —) SHYLOCK
(GRAVE —) SOBERSIDES
(GREEDY —) GORB GANNET GRASPER PUTTOCK
(GROTESQUE —) GUY GOLLIWOGG PUNCHINELLO
(GRUMPY —) SOURBELLY
(GULLIBLE —) JAY BOOB GULPIN LOBSTER FLATHEAD SHLEMIEL WOODCOCK
(GYPSY —) CHI CHAI
(HANDLESS —) SAMMY
(HARD —) MALISON

(HARD-HEADED —) NUT
(HATEFUL —) TOAD
(HEAVY —) STODGER
(HEAVY-SET —) LUMP
(HETEROSEXUAL —) STRAIGHT
(HOLY —) SAINT
(HOT-TEMPERED —) SPARK
(HUMPBACKED —) LORD
(HUNGRY —) HUNGARIAN
(HYPOCRITICAL —) PHARISEE
(IDENTICAL —) SELF
(IDLE —) BUMMLE RAGABASH SLUGGARD
(IGNORANT —) BABE BOOB PORK IDIOT IGNARO
(ILL-BRED —) BOOR CHURL CLOWN
(ILL-MANNERED —) GRUB SKUNK
(ILL-NATURED) PATCH CROSSPATCH
(ILL-NATURED —) CRAB HUNKS PATCH
(ILL-TEMPERED —) CRAB ETTERCAP TAISTREL
(ILLUSTRIOUS —) HERO
(IMMATURE —) BUD SQUAB GORLIN
(IMMORAL —) REP PERDU IMPURITAN
(IMPASSIVE —) BLOCK
(IMPERTINENT —) PAUK PAWK SNIP
(IMPETUOUS —) HOTHEAD
(IMPISH —) SPRITE
(IMPORTANT —) NIB POT LION HONOR MOGUL NABOB KINGPIN MUGWUMP SOMEBODY
(IMPOTENT —) SPADO
(IMPRACTICAL —) IDEALIST
(IMPUDENT —) SAUCE SQUIRT SAUCEBOX
(INACTIVE —) SLUGGARD
(INANE —) SHAUP
(INCOMPETENT —) BOZO SCHLEP
(INCONSTANT —) ROVER
(INDECISIVE —) INVERTEBRATE
(INEPT —) DWEEB KLUTZ
(INEXPERIENCED —) BABE INGENUE BEGINNER
(INFAMOUS —) NITHING
(INFERIOR —) BATA SHRUB SHABBLE
(INFLEXIBLE —) RAMROD
(INFLUENTIAL —) MOGUL
(INSCRUTABLE —) SPHINX
(INSENSITIVE —) LOG PACHYDERM
(INSIGNIFICANT —) DAB MUT MUTT NERD NURD QUAT BILSH CREEP DWEEB JOKER SHURF SPRAT SQUIB ABLACH PEANUT NEBBISH PINKEEN WHIFFET GNATLING GRILDRIG PIGWIGEON
(INSINUATING —) WHILLY
(INSURED —) LIFE
(INTRACTABLE —) BUCKIE TARTAR HAGGARD HARDCASE
(IRASCIBLE —) TOUCHWOOD
(IRRESPONSIBLE —) PLAYBOY FLYBYNIGHT
(IRRITATING —) BOT
(ISOLATED —) ISOLATO
(LAME —) VULCAN
(LANK —) TANGLE GANGEREL WINDLESTRAW
(LARGE —) CHUNK WHIPPA SKELPER STODGER STRAPPER
(LASCIVIOUS —) SUCCUBUS
(LAST — IN CONTEST) MELL
(LAZY —) BUM DAW HOIT POKE IDLER TRAIL LORDAN LURDAN BLELLUM LAZYLEGS SLUGABED SLUGGARD
(LEAN —) RIBE TANGLE SHARGER THINGUT
(LEARNED —) CLERK ERUDIT ACHARYA SCHOLAR LITERATO WISEACRE LITERATUS
(LECHEROUS —) SATYR
(LEFT-HANDED —) SINISTRAL
(LETHARGIC —) ZOMBI ZOMBIE
(LEWD —) WANTON GAMESTER
(LIGHTHEADED —) BEEHEAD
(LISTLESS —) MOPE
(LITERATE —) SCHOLAR
(LITTLE —) SMOLT SMOUT
(LIVELY —) GRIG BIRKIE HEMPIE WHISKER
(LONG-HAIRED —) HIPPY HIPPIE
(LOUD-VOICED —) STENTOR
(LOW —) PACK SCUM RASCAL BEASTMAN
(LOW-BORN —) GUTTERBLOOD
(LOW SOCIETY —) MUDSILL
(LUBBERLY —) OAF
(LUMBERING —) PUMPKIN TUMBREL TUMBRIL
(LUMPISH —) DROUD
(LUSTY —) BILCH BILSH
(MAD —) MADLING
(MALICIOUS —) SERPENT
(MARRIAGEABLE —) PARTI
(MARRIED —) WIFE SPOUSE HUSBAND MATRIMONY
(MEAN —) RIP SCAB CHURL HOUND MISER SKATE SNEAK SHICER BASTARD DOGBOLT BEZONIAN HUCKSTER STINKARD EARTHWORM
(MEDDLESOME —) BREVIT HESSIAN
(MENTALLY DEFICIENT —) AMENT
(MENTALLY UNBALANCED —) MATTOID
(MISCHIEVOUS —) IMP LIMB PEST TOOL HEMPIE HELLION WHIPSTER
(MISERABLE —) SNAKE SWELP WRETCH
(MISERLY —) SKATE SCROOGE PINCHGUT PINCHBACK
(MONSTROUS —) WAMPUS
(MORAL —) PURITAN
(MORALLY ILL —) SICKO SICKIE
(MOST DISTINGUISHED —) FLOWER
(NAIVE —) JERK CLUCK GUNSEL INGENUE INNOCENT
(NASTY —) BLEEDER
(NEGLECTED —) TACKY TACKEY
(NIMBLE —) MERCURY
(NOISY —) YAP HOWLET
(OBJECTIONABLE —) CUR COYOTE FOUTER
(OBNOXIOUS —) CREEP
(OBSTINATE —) DONKEY STIFFNECK
(ODD —) GIG CURE GEEZER QUIZZY RATBAG CAUTION
(ODD-LOOKING —) QUIZ
(OFFENSIVE —) TICK SKITE SHOCKER STINKER HEDGEHOG
(OLD —) OLDY OLDIE
(OLD-FASHIONED —) FRUMP
(OPINIONATIVE —) PRAGMATIC
(ORACULAR —) PONTIFF
(ORDINARY —) PUNTER
(OVER-LEARNED —) PEDANT
(OVERGROWN —) FUSTILUGS
(OVERSLENDER —) SPINDLING
(PALTRY —) PELTER
(PAMPERED —) WANTON
(PASSIONATE —) FUME
(PATIENT —) JOB
(PECULIAR —) BIRD CASE
(PEEVISH —) GRIZZLER SPLENETIC
(PERNICKETY —) FIKE
(PERT —) PIE FLIRT
(PLODDING —) STODGE
(POLISHED —) SMOOTHY SMOOTHIE
(POMPOUS —) PUFFIN POMPIST
(POT-BELLIED —) GORREL
(PRE-EMINENT —) STAR
(PRIGGISH —) PRUDE
(PRIVATE —) JUDEX
(PROMISING —) HOPEFUL
(PROSAIC —) PHILISTINE
(PRYING —) POKER PEEPER SMELLER
(PUDGY —) FATSO FATTY PODGE PUDGE ROLYPOLY
(PUGNOSED —) CAMUS CAMUSE
(PUNY —) SCART SHILP SHRIMP TITMAN
(PURITANICAL —) WOWSER
(QUEER —) RUM SKITE SKYTE GEEZER
(QUEER-LOOKING —) JIGGER
(QUERULOUS —) GRUMP JACKDAW
(QUICK-TEMPERED —) SPUNKIE WILDCAT SPITFIRE
(RAGGED —) ROTO SHAGRAG TATTERWAG
(RAPACIOUS —) SHARK CATERER
(RAWBONED —) SCRAG
(RECKLESS —) MADCAP RAMSTAM RANTIPOLE HELLBENDER
(RED-HAIRED —) BRIQUE
(REFRACTORY —) BUCKIE
(RELENTLESS —) HARDFACE
(REMARKABLE —) PHENOMENON
(RESOLUTE —) STALWART
(RESTLESS —) RAMPLER RAMPLOR RANTIPOLE
(RETICENT —) CLAM
(RICH —) MONEYBAGS
(RIDICULOUS —) GOOF HARE MONIMENT MONUMENT
(RIOTOUS —) ROARER
(ROBUST —) STRAPPER
(ROUGH —) TOWSER
(ROUGH-LOOKING —) RULLION
(RUDE —) HICK PORK RULE CHURL CLOWN GROBIAN
(RUSTIC —) COON KERN KERNE HAYSEED HOMESPUN
(SAINTLY —) SADDIK
(SANGUINE —) OPTIMIST
(SAUCY —) PIET
(SCRAWNY —) SCART SCRAG
(SECRETIVE —) OYSTER
(SELF-ASSERTIVE —) PUSHER
(SELF-CENTERED —) HEEL DEVIL FLANEUR
(SELF-RIGHTEOUS —) PHARISEE
(SELFISH —) HOGG
(SENSUAL —) SWING CARNALIST
(SENTIMENTAL —) MARSHMALLOW
(SEXY —) DISH
(SHAMEFUL —) BISMER
(SHIFTY—) SLICKER
(SHORT —) CRILE FADGE KNURL STUMP
(SHOWY —) FLASH FLASHER HOTSHOT
(SHREWD —) FILE YEPE HARDHEAD SNOLLYGOSTER
(SICK —) SICK MALADE PATIENT AEGROTANT
(SICKLY —) INVALID
(SILENT —) MUM MUMCHANCE
(SILLY —) FOP CAKE DITZ GUMP SOFT DOBBY GOOSE SOFTY SPOON CUCKOO NIMSHI SOFTIE GOOSECAP LIRIPIPE LIRIPOOP SOFTHEAD
(SILLY OR CRAZY —) DINGBAT
(SIMPLE —) DRIP LAMB IDIOT TURKEY PIGWIGEON
(SINGULAR —) ODDITY
(SKINNY —) SCRAE SCARECROW
(SLATTERNLY —) SLATE
(SLIM —) SWABBLE
(SLOTHFUL —) SLOWBELLY
(SLOVENLY —) HASH SLOB SLORP TRAIL STREEL SLOMMACK STREELER
(SLUGGISH —) LUMP DOLDRUM DRUMBLE LOBCOCK
(SLY —) COON SLYBOOTS SNECKDRAW SNICKDRAW
(SMALL —) GRIG TICH TICK AGATE DWARF SPRAT INSECT MORSEL POPPET SACKET GNATLING MUNCHKIN
(SOLEMN —) OWL
(SOPHISTICATED —) WELTKIND
(SPIRITED —) SPUNK SPUNKIE
(SPIRITLESS —) MOPE STICK
(SPITEFUL —) HELLCAT ETTERCAP
(SPRUCE —) SPRUSADO
(STIFF —) POKER STICK
(STINGY —) CHURL HAYNE STINGY
(STOCKY —) STUMP
(STOLID —) CLAM THICKSKIN
(STRANGE —) WAMPUS
(STRANGE OR ECCENTRIC —) WEIRDO
(STRAY —) WAIF
(STUBBORN —) BUCKY STOUT BUCKIE
(STUMPY —) SPUD SQUAB
(STUNTED —) URF SCRUNT SHARGAR
(STUPID —) ASS DIP DUB JAY MUT BETE BOOB DODO DOLT DOPE DRIP GAUM GAWP GOOF GUMP HASH HOIT JERK MOKE MUTT NERD PUTZ BLOCK BUCCA CLUCK CLUNK CUDDY DUMMY DUNCE HOBBY JUKES LOACH MORON SHEEP STIFF STIRK STOCK STUPE SUMPH SWINE THICK WAMUS ZOMBI BOODLE DAWKIN DIMWIT DODUNK DONKEY DOOFUS DUFFER DUMDUM GANDER GILLIE GRANNY GUNSEL LUMMOX LURDAN NITWIT NOODLE SACKET SHMUCK STUPEX TUMFIE TUMPHY TURKEY ZOMBIE AIRHEAD

BLUNTIE DULLARD FATHEAD FUSSOCK HOWFING JACKASS JUGHEAD MUDHEAD PINHEAD SAPHEAD SCHMUCK SCHNOOK BONEHEAD BULLHEAD DOTTEREL DUMBBELL FLATHEAD GAMPHREL IRONHEAD MEATHEAD MOLDWARP MUMPHEAD STUNPOLL THICKWIT HODMANDOD MUMCHANCE THICKHEAD BUBBLEHEAD
(STUPID, FOOLISH —) YOYO
(STURDY —) LUMP CHUNK STALWART
(SUAVE —) SMOOTHIE
(SUBMISSIVE —) SLAVE
(SULKY —) GLUMP GRUMP SUMPH GROUCH
(SUPERLATIVE —) SMASHEROO
(SURLY —) CRUST HUNKS
(TACITURN —) OYSTER
(TALKATIVE —) GASSER BLELLUM BIGMOUTH
(TALL, AWKWARD —) GAMMERSTANG
(TENDER —) LAMBKIN
(THICKSET —) NUGGET
(THIN —) RAKE WRAITH BEANPOLE
(THIRD —) GOOSEBERRY
(THOUGHTLESS —) AIRLING SKIPPER BIRDBRAIN
(TIMID —) MOUSE RABBIT NEBBISH MILQUETOAST
(TIMID OR MEEK —) NEBBISH
(TINY —) KEEROGUE
(TIRESOME) PILL
(TIRESOME —) BORE PILL BROMIDE
(TOUGH —) STUD
(TRADITIONAL —) SQUARE
(TREACHEROUS —) JUDAS SNAKE VIPER GUNSEL SERPENT
(TRICKY —) SLYBOOTS
(TROUBLESOME —) COW PEST HELLION HESSIAN
(TRUSTWORTHY —) TRAIST STANDBY
(TRUSTY —) TROJAN
(TYRANNICAL —) SATRAP
(UNAPPRECIATIVE —) INGRATE
(UNATTRACTIVE —) DRIP GOON GRUB NERD NURD SCUG CREEP DWEEB
(UNBENDING —) STIFF
(UNCHASTE —) SHORTHEELS
(UNCIVILIZED —) VISIGOTH
(UNCOUTH —) APE PUT STIFF YAHOO BABOON SLOMMACK ROUGHNECK
(UNDERSIZED —) DURGAN SPARROW
(UNEMOTIONAL —) ICEBERG
(UNFAITHFUL —) INFIDEL
(UNGAINLY —) CLATCH
(UNGRACIOUS —) NEANY MEANIE
(UNHANDY —) FOUTER
(UNHAPPY —) UNSEL
(UNIMPORTANT —) MINNOW NOTHING SCHNOOK NONENTITY
(UNIQUE —) ONER
(UNKNOWN —) INCONNU STRANGER
(UNLUCKY —) SHLIMAZEL SCHLIMAZEL
(UNMARRIED —) MAIDEN SINGLE AGAMIST BACHELOR CELIBATE SPINSTER
(UNPLEASANT —) NERD NURD SCUMBAG
(UNPRACTICAL —) MUFF
(UNREASONABLE —) DUFFER
(UNRULY —) TURK
(UNSCRUPULOUS —) CATSO KNAVE
(UNSOPHISTICATED —) JAY HICK NYAS HAYSEED CORNBALL INNOCENT
(UNTHANKFUL —) INGRATE
(UNTIDY —) SLOVEN STREEL SLAISTER
(UNUSUALLY INTELLIGENT —) WHIZKID WHIZZKID
(UNWANTED THIRD —) GOOSEBERRY
(UNWIELDY —) FUSTILUGS
(USELESS —) POOP SWAB UNSEL BAUCHLE
(VALOROUS —) HERO
(VENOMOUS —) SPITPOISON
(VIGOROUS —) SNEEZER
(VIOLENT —) DRAGON BANGSTER SPITFIRE
(VIRILE —) STUD
(VORACIOUS —) HUNGARIAN
(VULGAR —) MUCKER
(WANTON —) RIG FLIRT WHIPSTER
(WASTEFUL —) SCATTERGOOD SPENDTHRIFT
(WEAK —) WIMP SCART SHILP SOFTY PUSSYCAT WHIMLING
(WEAK-MINDED —) SAPHEAD TOTTYHEAD
(WEAK-WILLED —) PUTTY
(WEAK OR INEFFECTUAL —) WIMP
(WEALTHY —) MONEYBAGS
(WELL-BORN —) FREE
(WHITE —) FAY OFAY GRIFFIN EUROPEAN PALEFACE
(WICKED —) DEVIL SATAN SHREW UNLEAD UNLEDE SATANIST
(WILD —) HELLICAT RANTIPOLE
(WILY —) PIE
(WITHERED —) RUNT
(WITLESS —) WITHAM WITTOME SLABBERER
(WITTY —) WITSHIP SPARKLER
(WORNOUT —) HUSHEL
(WORTHLESS —) GIT YAP FILE GEAR HOIT JADE LOON SCUM TOOT CRUMB LOREL LOSEL SCOUT SHAND BAUBLE BUGGER FELLOW FOUTRA SHICER BUDMASH GULLION BLIGHTER VAGABOND PHARMAKOS
(WRETCHED —) MISER MISERY
(YOUNG —) CUB KID COLT LAMB CHILD HEMPY SMOLT SMOUT SPRIG YONKE GUNSEL HEMPIE JUNIOR CHICKEN CHOOKIE GRISTLE LAMBKIN JUVENILE STRIPLING (PL.) FRY PERSONNEL (PREF.) PROSOP(O) (SUFF.) **(FEMALE —)** INE

PERSONABLE COMELY SHAPELY HANDSOME
PERSONAGE DON DUSE NIBS BLOKE FIGURE SHOGUN TYCOON
(EXALTED —) STATE
(GREAT —) MOGUL SOPHI SOPHY SUFFEE
(GROTESQUE —) PUNCHINELLO
PERSONAL SELF PRIVY DIRECT PRIVATE CHATTELS CORPORAL INTIMATE
(— EFFECTS) DUNNAGE
(PREF.) IDIO
PERSONALITY EGO AURA DRAW SELF SOUL BEING ETHOS HEART EGOITY FIGURE CONTROL FACULTY DEMIURGE PRESENCE SELFHOOD SELFNESS
(OF IMPATIENT —) TYPEA
PERSONATE ACT FEIGN MIMIC MASKED PERSON TYPIFY PRESENT
PERSONATION (SHAM —) IDOL
PERSONIFICATION SOUL GENIUS
(— OF DIVINE VIRTUE) EON
(— OF JUSTICE) THEMIS
(— OF PRINCIPLES) AVATAR
PERSONIFY EMBODY INCARNATE PERSONIZE
PERSONNEL BLOOD STAFF KITCHEN PHYSIQUE
PERSPECTIVE ANGLE OPTICS DISTANCE TELESCOPE
PERSPICACIOUS KEEN ACUTE ASTUTE SHREWD
(MAKE —) CLEAR
PERSPICACITY WIT ACUMEN
PERSPICUOUS CLEAR LUCID PLAIN PRECISE VISIBLE MANIFEST LIGHTSOME
PERSPIRATION DEW SUDOR SUINT SWEAT HIDROSIS OLIGIDRIA SUDORESIS
PERSPIRE PUG MELT BREAN SWEAT SWELTER TRANSPIRE
PERSUADE CON GET WIN COAX GAIN MOVE RULE SNOW TICE URGE WISE ARGUE BRING EDUCE SUADE SWADE WEISE ADVISE ARGUFY ASSURE CAJOLE ENGAGE ENTICE INDUCE REMOVE SUBORN CONVERT DISPUTE ENTREAT IMPRESS PREVAIL SATISFY CANOODLE INFLUENCE
(— SUCCESSFULLY) SELL
PERSUADED PLIABLE GULLIBLE RESOLVED SENSIBLE
PERSUASION KIND SORT BELIEF OPINION SUASION JUDGMENT
(AUTHOR OF —) AUSTEN
(CHARACTER IN —) ANNE CLAY MARY CROFT ELLIOT LOUISA WALTER BENWICK CHARLES RUSSELL WILLIAM HARVILLE MUSGROVE ELIZABETH FREDERICK HENRIETTA WENTWORTH
PERSUASIVE COGENT WINNING INDUCTIVE PLAUSIBLE PROTEPTIC (PREF.) PITHANO
PERT BOLD CHIC FESS FLIP KECK SPRY TRIM ALERT ALIVE BARDY BRISK COCKY DONSY KISKY PEART PERKY PIERT QUICK SASSY SAUCY SMART TAUNT CHEEKY CLEVER COCKET COMELY DAPPER FRISKY SWASHY THWART BOBBISH PAUGHTY INSOLENT PETULANT
(— TALK) CHELP
PERTAIN BE LIE BEAR COME LONG BELIE TOUCH AFFEIR BEFALL BELIMP BELONG RELATE RETAIN CONCERN
(— TO) RINE
PERTAINING (— TO ABDOMEN) ALVINE
(— TO AFFAIRS OF STATE) PRAGMATIC
(— TO AGRICULTURE) GEORGIC
(— TO AIR) AURAL PNEUMATIC
(— TO ALL NATURE) PAMPHYSIC
(— TO ANIMALS) ZOIC
(— TO ANKLE) TARSAL
(— TO APOLLO) PYTHIAN PAEONIAN
(— TO APOSTLE) PETRINE
(— TO APPETITES) ORECTIC
(— TO ARMPIT) AXILLAR
(— TO ARMY) MARTIAL STRATONIC
(— TO ARROW) SAGITTAL
(— TO ART) TECHNICAL
(— TO ATHENA) PALLADIAN
(— TO BACK) DORSAL TERGAL
(— TO BATH) BALNEAL
(— TO BEAM) TRAGAL
(— TO BEARD) BARBAL
(— TO BED) THORAL
(— TO BEES) APIAN APIARIAN
(— TO BELLY) ALVIN ALVINE VENTRAL VENTRIC
(— TO BIBLICAL LAW) LEVITIC
(— TO BIRDS) AVIAN AVINE ORNITHIC VOLUCRINE
(— TO BIRTH) NATAL
(— TO BISHOP) LAWN
(— TO BITTER TASTE) PICRIC
(— TO BLACK SEA) PONTIC
(— TO BODIES AT REST) STATIC
(— TO BODY) SOMAL SOMATIC
(— TO BONE) OSSAL OSTEAL
(— TO BOSOM) GREMIAL
(— TO BRACELET) ARMILLARY
(— TO BRANCHES) RAMOUS
(— TO BREAD) PANARY
(— TO BREADMAKING) PANARY
(— TO BREAKFAST) ENTACULAR
(— TO BREAST) PECTORAL
(— TO BREASTBONE) STERNAL
(— TO BRISTLES) SETAL
(— TO BROTHEL) STEWISH
(— TO BUNCH) COMAL
(— TO CALF) VITULINE
(— TO CALF OF LEG) SURAL
(— TO CART) PLAUSTRAL
(— TO CARTHAGINIANS) PUNIC
(— TO CARVING) GLYPHIC
(— TO CAVE) SPELEAN SPELUNCAR
(— TO CHAIN) CATENARY
(— TO CHAMBER) CAMERAL
(— TO CHARIOTEER) AURIGAL
(— TO CHEEK) MALAR
(— TO CHESS) SCACCHIC
(— TO CHILDREN) PUERILE
(— TO CHINA) SINIAN SINISIAN
(— TO CITY) CIVIC URBAN
(— TO CLAN) SEPTAL
(— TO CLAY) BOLAR
(— TO CLOTHES) VESTIARY VESTURAL
(— TO COAST) ORARIAN
(— TO COINS) NUMMARY NUMISMATIC
(— TO COLOR) CHROMATIC
(— TO COMB) PECTINAL

(— TO CONSTRUCTION) TECTONIC
(— TO CONTESTS) AGONISTIC
(— TO CORK) SUBERIC SUBEROUS
(— TO COUGH) TUSSAL TUSSIVE
(— TO COURT) AULIC JUDICIAL JUDICIARY
(— TO CROCKERY) PIG
(— TO CROWN) CORONAL
(— TO DANCING) SALTATORY TRIPUDIAL
(— TO DAUGHTER OR SON) FILIAL
(— TO DAWN) EOAN
(— TO DEFENSE) PHYLACTIC
(— TO DESERTS) EREMIC
(— TO DIAPHRAGM) PHRENIC
(— TO DIGESTION) PEPTIC
(— TO DINNER) CENATORY PRANDIAL
(— TO DIVINATION) MANTIC
(— TO DOVE) COLUMBINE
(— TO DREAMS) ONEIRIC ONIROTIC
(— TO DRINKING) BIBITORY
(— TO DUNG) STERCORAL
(— TO EARTH) GEAL TELLURIC TERRANEAN
(— TO EARTHQUAKE) SEISMAL SEISMIC
(— TO EAST) EOAN
(— TO EGGS) OVAL
(— TO ESSENCE) BASIC
(— TO EUNUCH) SPADONIC
(— TO EVENING) VESPER
(— TO EYELIDS) BLEPHARAL
(— TO FACE) PROSOPIC
(— TO FAIR) NUNDINAL
(— TO FAITH) PISTIC
(— TO FEET) PEDAL PEDARY
(— TO FERMENTATION) ZYMIC ZYMOTIC
(— TO FIELDS) AGRARIAN
(— TO FINGERS) DIGITAL
(— TO FISH) PISCINE
(— TO FISHING) HALIEUTIC
(— TO FLEAS) PULICENE PULICOSE
(— TO FLESH) SARCOUS
(— TO FLOCK) GREGAL
(— TO FLOOD) DILUVIAL DILUVIAN
(— TO FLOWERS) FLORAL ANTHINE
(— TO FOREARM) CUBITAL
(— TO FOREHEAD) METOPIC
(— TO FORM) MORPHIC
(— TO FOX) VULPINE
(— TO FRANCE) GALLICAN
(— TO FRESH WATER) LIMNETIC
(— TO FROGS) ANURAN RANINE
(— TO FRUIT) POMONAL POMONIC
(— TO FUNERALS) EXEQUIAL
(— TO FUNGUS) MYCETOID
(— TO FURNACE) FORNACIC
(— TO GALLOWS) PATIBULARY
(— TO GARDEN) HORTULAN
(— TO GARRISON) PRESIDIAL
(— TO GENTILES) ETHNIC
(— TO GLASS) VITREOUS
(— TO GOATS) CAPRIC
(— TO GOVERNMENT) ARCHICAL POLITICAL
(— TO GRANDPARENTS) AVAL
(— TO GRINDING) MOLINARY
(— TO GROIN) INGUINAL
(— TO GROUND) SOLARY
(— TO GROVE) NEMORAL
(— TO GULLS) LARINE
(— TO GUMS) ULETIC GINGIVAL
(— TO HAIR) PILAR CRINAL PILARY
(— TO HAND) CHIRAL MANUAL
(— TO HARE) LEPORINE
(— TO HAWKS) ACCIPITRINE
(— TO HEAD) CEPHALIC
(— TO HEALTH) HYGEIAN
(— TO HEAP) ACERVAL
(— TO HEART) CARDIAC
(— TO HEAT) CALORIC THERMAL THERMIC
(— TO HEAVEN) EMPYREAL EMPYREAN
(— TO HIPS) SCIATIC
(— TO HOLIDAY) FERIAL
(— TO HORIZON) MUNDANE
(— TO HORSE) EQUINE HIPPIC CABALLINE
(— TO HOSPITALITY) XENIAL XENIAN
(— TO HOUSE) DOMAL
(— TO HUNGER) FAMELIC
(— TO HUNTING) VENATIC VENERIAL CYNEGETIC
(— TO INCH) UNCIAL
(— TO INTELLECT) NOETIC
(— TO INTESTINES) ALVIN ALVINE
(— TO JAW) MALAR GNATHAL GNATHIC
(— TO JOURNEY) VIATIC
(— TO KIDNEY) RENAL NEPHRIC
(— TO KNOWLEDGE) GNOSTIC
(— TO LAKES) LACUSTRINE
(— TO LAP) GREMIAL
(— TO LAUGHING) GELASTIC
(— TO LAUGHTER) RISORIAL
(— TO LEARNING) PALLADIAN
(— TO LEG) CRURAL
(— TO LICE) PEDICULAR
(— TO LIFE) VITAL ZOETIC
(— TO LINE) FILAR
(— TO LIPS) LABIAL
(— TO LIVER) HEPATIC JECORAL
(— TO LIVERPOOL) LIVERPUDLIAN
(— TO LOINS) LUMBAR
(— TO LOVE) EROTIC AMATORY
(— TO LUCK) ALEATORY
(— TO LUNGS) PULMONIC PNEUMONIC PULMONARY
(— TO MANCHESTER) MANCUNIAN
(— TO MANKIND) COMMON ANTHROPIC
(— TO MARBLE) MARMORIC
(— TO MARKET) NUNDINAL
(— TO MARRIAGE) MARITAL HYMENEAL
(— TO MARS) AREAN MAMERTINE MAVORTIAL
(— TO MARSHES) PALUDAL PALUDIC
(— TO MASS) MOLAR
(— TO MASTER) HERILE
(— TO MEADOWS) PRATAL
(— TO MEAL) PRANDIAL
(— TO MECCA) MECCAWEE
(— TO MEDICINE) IATRIC IATRICAL
(— TO MEMORY) MNESTIC MNEMONIC
(— TO MIDDAY) MERIDIAN
(— TO MILK) LACTARY LACTEAL
(— TO MILL) MOLINARY
(— TO MIND) MENTAL PHRENIC PSYCHIC PSYCHICAL
(— TO MIRROR) SPECULAR
(— TO MOISTURE) HYGRIC
(— TO MONEY) PECUNIARY
(— TO MOON) LUNAR SELENIC SELENIAN
(— TO MORNING) MATIN MATINAL MATUTINAL
(— TO MOTION) GESTIC KINETIC
(— TO MOUNTAINS) MONTANE
(— TO MOUTH) ORAL OSCULAR STOMATIC
(— TO MUSCLE) SARCOUS
(— TO MUSES) PIERIAN
(— TO MUSIC) HARMONIC
(— TO MYSTERIES) TELESTIC
(— TO NAME) ONOMASTIC
(— TO NAMES) ONOMASTIC
(— TO NAVEL) OMPHALIC
(— TO NECK) JUGULAR
(— TO NEPHEW) NEPOTAL
(— TO NET) RETIARY
(— TO NEW ZEALAND) ZELANIAN
(— TO NIGHT) NOCTURNAL
(— TO NOSE) NASAL RHINAL
(— TO NUT) NUCAL
(— TO NUTRITION) TROPHIC
(— TO OAK) QUERCINE ROBOREOUS
(— TO OCEAN) PELAGIC OCEANOUS THALASSIC
(— TO OCEAN DEPTHS) HADAL
(— TO OLD AGE) SENILE GERATIC GERONTIC
(— TO OPEN SKY) SUBDIAL
(— TO PALACE) PALATINE
(— TO PALM) VOLAR
(— TO PARISH) PAROCHIAL
(— TO PARLOR) BEN BOOR
(— TO PARROTS) PSITTACINE
(— TO PASTURES) PASCUAL
(— TO PAWNBROKER) AVUNCULAR
(— TO PEACOCK) PAVONINE
(— TO PEARL) MARGARIC
(— TO PERSPIRATION) SUDORIC
(— TO PICTURE) ICONIC
(— TO PIGS) PORCINE
(— TO PINE) WARRYN
(— TO PLAGUE) LOIMIC
(— TO PLEASURE) HEDONIC
(— TO POETRY) MUSAL IAMBIC
(— TO POISON) TOXIC
(— TO POTTERY) CERAMIC
(— TO PRIESTS) SACERDOTAL
(— TO PRISON) CARCERAL
(— TO PULSE) SPHYGMIC
(— TO PUNISHMENT) PENAL PUNITIVE
(— TO PURIFICATION) LUSTRAL
(— TO QUEEN) REGINAL
(— TO RAIN) HYETAL PLUVIAL
(— TO RAINBOW) IRIDAL
(— TO REGISTER) MATRICULAR
(— TO REMOTE PLACE) FORANE
(— TO RESONANCE) SYNTONIC
(— TO RING) ARMILLARY
(— TO RISING) ORTIVE
(— TO RIVER) AMNIC POTAMIC RIVERINE FLUMINOSE
(— TO RIVER BANK) RIPARIAN
(— TO ROAD) VIATIC
(— TO ROCK) PETREAN SAXATILE
(— TO ROD) BACULINE
(— TO RUBBISH) RUDERARY
(— TO SABLES) ZIBELINE
(— TO SAIL) VELIC
(— TO SALVATION) SOTERIAL
(— TO SANDARAC) THYINE
(— TO SATURDAY) SABBATINE
(— TO SEAL) PHOCINE SIGILLARY SPHRAGISTIC
(— TO SEAM) SUTURAL
(— TO SEASHORE) LITTORAL
(— TO SEAWEED) ALGOUS
(— TO SENSE OF TASTE) GUSTATIVE
(— TO SEVEN) SEPTIMAL
(— TO SEWING) SUTORIAL SUTORIAN
(— TO SHEEP) VERVECINE
(— TO SHEPHERDS) PASTORAL
(— TO SHERIFF) VICONTIEL
(— TO SHIN) CNEMIAL
(— TO SHIP) NAVICULAR
(— TO SHOPMAN) APOTHECAL
(— TO SHOULDER) ALAR SCAPULAR
(— TO SIGHT) VISUAL
(— TO SIGNS) SEMIC SEMANTIC
(— TO SILVER) LUNAR ARGENTAL
(— TO SISTER) SORORAL
(— TO SKIN) DERIC DERMAL CUTICULAR
(— TO SLAVES) SERVILE
(— TO SLEEP) SOMNIAL MORPHETIC
(— TO SMELLING) OLFACTORY
(— TO SNAKE) ANGUINE
(— TO SNORING) RHONCAL RHONCIAL
(— TO SNOW) NIVAL
(— TO SOFT PALATE) VELAR
(— TO SOIL) DAPHIC
(— TO SOLE) VOLAR
(— TO SONG) MELIC
(— TO SPECTACLE) THEORIC
(— TO SPEECH) PHEMIC
(— TO SPINAL CORD) MYELIC
(— TO SPRING) VERNAL
(— TO STARS) ASTRAL STELLAR SIDEREAL
(— TO STATE AFFAIRS) PRAGMATIC
(— TO STEPMOTHER) NOVERCAL
(— TO STOMACH) GASTRIC
(— TO STONE) LITHIC
(— TO STORKS) PELARGIC
(— TO SULPHUR) THIONIC
(— TO SUMMER) ESTIVAL AESTIVAL
(— TO SUN) SOLAR HELIAC
(— TO SUNDAY) DOMINICAL
(— TO SUNDIAL) SCIATHERIC
(— TO SUPPER) CENATORY
(— TO SURFACE OF ANYTHING) FACIAL
(— TO SWALLOWS) HIRUNDINE
(— TO SWEAT) SUDORIC
(— TO SWIMMING) NATATORY
(— TO SWINEHERD) SYBOTIC
(— TO TAIL) CAUDAL
(— TO TAILOR) SARTORIAL
(— TO TANNING) SC
(— TO TEACHER) MAGISTERIAL
(— TO TEARS) LACRIMAL LACHRYMAL
(— TO TEMPO) AGOGIC
(— TO THE BEAUTIFUL) ESTHETIC AESTHETIC
(— TO THIEVING) KLEPTISTIC

(— TO THIGH) CRURAL
(— TO THREAD) FILAR
(— TO THROAT) GULAR JUGULAR
(— TO THUNDER) FULMINEOUS
(— TO TILE) TEGULAR
(— TO TIN) STANNIC
(— TO TITHES) DECIMAL
(— TO TITMICE) PARINE
(— TO TOMB) TOMBAL
(— TO TONGUE) GLOSSAL LINGUAL
(— TO TORTOISES) CHELONIAN
(— TO TOUCH) TACTILE
(— TO TOWER) TURRICAL
(— TO TREES) DENDRAL ARBOREAL
(— TO TWENTY) VICENARY
(— TO UNCLE) AVUNCULAR
(— TO UNDERGROUND WATER) VADOSE PHREATIC
(— TO VESSEL) VASAL
(— TO VIRGIN) PARTHENIAN
(— TO VISION) OCULAR
(— TO VOW) VOTAL
(— TO WAGON) PLAUSTRAL
(— TO WALLS) MURAL PARIETAL
(— TO WAR) POLEMICAL
(— TO WASPS) VESPAL VESPINE
(— TO WAX) CERAL
(— TO WEAVING) TEXTORIAL
(— TO WEIGHT) BARIC PONDERAL PONDERARY
(— TO WELL) PHREATIC
(— TO WHALES) CETIC
(— TO WHEAT) VULGARE
(— TO WHEELS) ROTAL
(— TO WHETSTONES) COTICULAR
(— TO WIFE) UXORIAL
(— TO WILL) VOLITIVE
(— TO WIND) EOLIAN PNEUMATIC
(— TO WINE) VINIC VINOUS
(— TO WINE-MAKING) OENOPOETIC
(— TO WINGS) ALAR PTERIC EXRUPEAL PTEROTIC
(— TO WINTER) HIEMAL
(— TO WISDOM) PALLADIAN
(— TO WOMANKIND) MULIEBRAL
(— TO WOODPECKERS) PICINE
(— TO WOODS) SYLVAN NEMORAL
(— TO WORMS) VERMICULAR
(— TO WOUNDS) VULNERAL
(— TO WRIST) CARPAL
(— TO YESTERDAY) PRIDIAN
(— TO YEW) TAXINE
(SUFF.) **(—TO)** AL AR ORIOUS ORY
PERTINACIOUS FIRM STIFF DOGGED ADHERING STUBBORN OBSTINATE
PERTINENCE RELEVANCE
PERTINENCY FORCE
PERTINENT APT FIT PAT HAPPY COGENT PROPER TIMELY ADAPTED APROPOS GERMANE POINTED TELLING INCIDENT MATERIAL RELATIVE RELEVANT
PERTLY CROUSE
PERTURB BITE GRATE UPSET WORRY DISMAY AGITATE CONFUSE CONTURB DERANGE DISTURB TROUBLE
PERTURBATION DISMAY FLIGHT POTHER UNEASE POOTHER STICKLE TROUBLE TURMOIL EVECTION AGITATION
PERTURBED UNEASY
PERTUSSIS COUGH CHINCOF CHINCOUGH

PERU
CAPITAL: LIMA
COIN: SOL LIBRA DINERO CENTAVO
DEPARTMENT: ICA LIMA PUNO CUSCO CUZCO JUNIN PIURA TACNA ANCASH LORETO TUMBES
DESERT: SECHURA
ISLAND: CHINCHA
LAKE: TITICACA
LANGUAGE: AYMARA QUECHUA
MEASURE: TOPO VARA GALON CELEMIN FANEGADA
MONEY: INTI
MOUNTAIN: HUAMINA COROPUNA HUASCARAN
PERIOD: RECUAY
RIVER: NAPU RIMAC SANTA TIGRE MORONA YAGUAS YAVARI CURARAY MARANON PASTAZA UCAYALI AMAZONAS APURIMAC HUALLAGA URUBAMBA
TOWN: ICA LIMA PUNO CUZCO PAITA PISCO PIURA TACNA CALLAO TUMBES IQUITOS AREQUIPA CHICLAYO TRUJILLO
VOLCANO: MISTI YUCAMANI
WEIGHT: LIBRA QUINTAL

PERUKE WIG FLASH GALERA TOUPEE GALERUM PERIWIG WIGGERY
PERUSAL SIGHT LECTURE SCRUTINY
PERUSE CON READ SCAN STUDY HANDLE SEARCH SURVEY EXAMINE INSPECT
(— QUICKLY) SKIM
PERUVIAN BARK CALISAYA CINCHONA
PERVADE FILL BATHE IMBUE DRENCH INSTIL OCCUPY THREAD INSTILL PERMEATE TRAVERSE
PERVADED STIFF
PERVASIVE POIGNANT
PERVERSE AUK AWK CAM CAR AWRY WOGH WRAW CROSS DONSY GAMMY THRAW WROTH CUSSED DIVERS LOUCHE THRAWN THWART WICKED WILFUL WRAIST AWKWARD CRABBED CROOKED DIVERSE FORWARD FROWARD OBLIQUE PEEVISH WAYWARD CAMSHACH CRANKISH STUBBORN
PERVERSELY AUK AWK AWRY ATHWART OVERWART
PERVERSION WREST ABUSION
(— OF TASTE) MALACIA
PERVERT WRY DRAW RACK RUIN SKEW TURN WARP ABUSE CROOK GLOSS TWIST UPSET WREST DEBASE DETORT DIVERT GARBLE INVERT MISUSE POISON VOYEUR WRENCH WRITHE CONTORT CORRUPT DEGRADE DEPRAVE DEVIATE DISTORT MISTURN SUBVERT TRADUCE VITIATE MISWREST
PERVERTED BAD WICKED ABUSIVE AWKWARD CORRUPT TWISTED VICIOUS
PERVERTER WRESTER
PERVIOUS LEACHY PERVIAL PERVADING
PES NEUME TENOR PODATUS
PESKY VERY PLAGUY ANNOYING DEVILING EXTREMELY
PESO DURO CONANT DOLLAR CAROLUS PATACAO
PESSIMISM WELTSCHMERZ MISERABILISM
PESSIMIST ALARMIST JEREMIAH WORRYWART
PESSIMISTIC GLOOMY ALARMED BEARISH CYNICAL DOWNBEAT
PEST BOT BANE GNAT TICK WEED APHIS MOUSE MYZUS TRAIK INSECT MENACE PLAGUE SCHELM SORROW VERMIN HASSLER NUDNICK SCOURGE MEALYBUG SANDMITE BUTTINSKY
(GARDEN —) APHID
PESTER DUN HOX NAG RAG RIB TIG HAKE ANNOY DEVIL TEASE WORRY BADGER BOTHER HARASS INFEST MOLEST BEDEVIL TORMENT TROUBLE OBSTRUCT PERSECUTE
PESTHOUSE LAZARET LAZARETTO
PESTICIDE ALAR BIOCIDE FUMIGANT
PESTILENCE LUES PEST DEATH QUALM PLAGUE MURRAIN EPIDEMIC MORTALITY
PESTILENT FATAL DEADLY VEXING NOXIOUS
PESTLE MIX BRAY GRIND PESTL PILUM STAMP BEETLE BRAYER MULLER PISTIL CHAPPER POUNDER STAMPER
PET TOY CADE COAX DAUT DEAR DUCK HUFF LAMB NECK PEAT SNIT SOCK SULK TIFF DRUNT DUCKY HUMOR QUIET SPOIL SPOON TETCH CARESS CODDLE COSHER COSSET CUDDLE DANDLE DAUTIE DAWTIE FADDLE FANTAD FANTOD FONDLE GENTLE PAMPER PETKIN SMOOCH SQUALL STROKE WANTON CHERISH DARLING INDULGE PINKENY TANTRUM TIDLING UMBRAGE WHITHER CANOODLE FAVORITE TIDDLING PADDYWACK
(— NICKNAME) DEARIE
PETAL ALA HELM HOOD LEAF WING BANNER
(— IN PEA FLOWER) VEXILLUM
(— OF IRIS) STANDARD
(FLOWER —S) ALAE
(UPPER —) HOOD BANNER
(PL.) COROLLA
PETALIA NYCTERIS
PETARD PITTARD FIREWORK
PETATE BANIG
PETECHIA STIGMA
PETER P FADE FAIL PEAK SAFE WANE CEASE PEDRO PIERS PIERRE SIGNAL DWINDLE
(— OUT) FIZZLE
(BROTHER OF —) ANDREW
(FATHER OF —) JONAS
PETER GRIMES (CHARACTER IN —) ELLEN PETER GRIMES ORFORD BALSTRODE
(COMPOSER OF —) BRITTEN
PETER IBBETSON (AUTHOR OF —) DUMAURIER
(CHARACTER IN —) DEANE MADGE MIMSY PETER LINTOT GREGORY PLUNKET IBBETSON PASQUIER
PETERMAN YEGG
PETER PAN (AUTHOR OF —) BARRIE
(CHARACTER IN —) PAN HOOK JOHN NIBS SMEE PETER WENDY TINKER DARLING MICHAEL TOOTLES MARGARET SLIGHTLY
PETHAHIAH (FATHER OF —) MESHEZABEEL
PETHEUL (SON OF —) JOEL
PETIOLE STEM SPINE STALK STIPE PODEON PEDUNCLE PHYLLODE LEAFSTALK
PETITE SMALL LITTLE MIGNON MIGNONNE
PETITION ASK BEG SUE BILL BOON PLEA PRAY SUIT VOTE WISH APPLY ORATE PLEAD APPEAL DESIRE INVOKE MOTION PLACIT PRAYER STEVEN ADDRESS BESEECH ENTREAT IMPLORE ORATION SOLICIT ROGATION SUFFRAGE
(MAKE —) SUE
(PL.) PRECES
PETITIONER BEGGAR ORATOR SUITOR BEADSMAN APPLICANT ENTREATER PLAINTIFF
PETO WAHOO
PETREL BILL TITI CAHOW MITTY NELLY PRION WITCH FULMAR SPENCY TEETEE ASSILAG GLUTTON KAEDING PINTADO SEABIRD SEAFOWL STINKER ALLAMOTH FORKTAIL STINKPOT ALLAMOTTI MALLEMUCK NIGHTHAWK
PETRIFY DAZE APPAL SCARE APPALL DEADEN STONIFY STUPEFY FRIGHTEN LAPIDIFY FOSSILIZE GORGONIZE
PETRIFYING STONY GORGON
PETROL GAS GASOLINE
PETROLATUM VASELINE
PETROLEUM OIL CRUDE PETROL NAPHTHA
(— INDUSTRY) OILDOM
(CRUDE —) MAZOUT
PETRUCHIO (WIFE OF —) KATHERINE
PE-TSAI PECHAY
PETTED CADE DANDILY
PETTICOAT BAJO GORE KILT SLIP SOUS DICKY GREEN JUPON PAGNE SOUSE KIRTLE LUHINGA PLACKET WHITTLE BALMORAL BASQUINE WILYCOAT UNDERSKIRT
(— OF TARGET) GREEN
PETTIFOG FOG CAVIL BICKER
PETTIFOGGER FOGGER SHYSTER LEGULEIAN
PETTINESS NAGGLE PARVINIMITY
PETTING COLLING
PETTISH DORTY HUFFY FRETFUL PEEVISH PLAINTIVE
PETTY TIN BASE JERK MEAN ORRA PUNY VAIN BANAL GRIMY MINOR PETIT PUNEE SMALL MEASLY MINUTE PALTRY PEANUT POKING

PUISNE PUSILL SNIFTY TWOBIT KITLING PIMPING TRIVIAL TWATTLE CHILDISH FIDDLING INFERIOR NIGGLING NUGATORY PEDDLING PICAYUNE PIFFLING SNIPPETY TRIFLING PAROCHIAL
(PREF.) MICR(O)
(SUFF.) **(— ONE)** EEN

PETULANCE PROCACITY

PETULANT PERT CROSS SAUCY SHORT TESTY TIFFY FEISTY SULLEN WANTON WILFUL CRABBED FRETFUL FROWARD HUFFISH PEEVISH WASPISH PERVERSE SNAPPISH

PEULTHAI (FATHER OF —) OBEDEDOM

PEUMUS BOLDU

PEW BOX PUE BOUT DESK PFUI PUGH SEAT SLIP BENCH BUGHT STALL BOUGHT
(— ATTACHMENT) KNEELER

PEWEE PEWIT PEEWEE PEEWIT

PEWIT PEESWEEP

PEWTER CUP BIDRI BIDRY ETAIN MONEY PUDER BIDERY TRIFLE PEAUDER SADWARE TUTENAG
(— MARK) TOUCHMARK

PEYOTE HIKULI MESCAL

PFENNIG PENNING

PHAEDRA (AUTHOR OF —) RACINE
(CHARACTER IN —) ARICIA OENONE PHAEDRA THESEUS HIPPOLYTUS THERAMENES
(FATHER OF —) MINOS
(HUSBAND OF —) THESEUS
(MOTHER OF —) PASIPHAE
(SISTER OF —) ADRIADNE
(SON OF —) ACAMAS DEMOPHON

PHAETON DUKE FAETON SPIDER STANHOPE

PHAETON BUTTERFLY BALTIMORE

PHALANGER TAIT ARIEL TAPOA CUSCUS TAGUAN OPOSSUM PENTAIL SQUIRREL

PHALAROPE LOBIPED COOTFOOT LOBEFOOT WHALEBIRD

PHALERA BEAD BOSS DISK STUD CAMEO

PHALTI (FATHER OF —) LAISH

PHANTASM DREAM FANCY GHOST VAPOR FIGURE SHADOW SPIRIT FANTASY PHANTOM SPECIES SPECTER SPECTRE

PHANTASMAL EERIE UNREAL SPECTRAL

PHANTASUS (BROTHER OF —) ICELUS MORPHEUS PHOBETOR THANATOS
(FATHER OF —) HYPNOS SOMNUS
(MOTHER OF —) NYX

PHANTASY FANCY FANTASY PHANTASIA

PHANTOM IDOL BOGEY BOGLE DUMMY GHOST IMAGE PHASM SHADE SHAPE UMBRA BOGGLE DOUBLE FANTOM IDOLON IDOLUM SHADOW SPIRIT BUGBEAR EIDOLON ELUSIVE FANTASY FEATURE SPECIES SPECTER ILLUSORY ADAMASTOR SIMULACRUM

PHANUEL (DAUGHTER OF —) ANNA

PHARAOH ALE FARO PHARO TYRANT BUSIRIS

PHARAOH'S HEN VULTURE

PHAREZ (BROTHER OF —) ZARAH
(FATHER OF —) JUDAH
(MOTHER OF —) TAMAR

PHARISEE MUGWUMP NICODEMUS

PHARMACEUTICAL MERCURIAL
(SUFF.) **(— PRODUCT)** EIN EINE IN INE

PHARMACIST CHEMIST DRUGGIST DISPENSER APOTHECARY

PHARMACY FERMACY DRUGSTORE

PHAROS CLOAK LIGHT TORCH BEACON LANTERN

PHARYNGEAL FAUCAL

PHARYNX MASTAX PROBOSCIS
(PREF.) LAEMO LEM(O)

PHASE EFT END LEG FAZE SIDE ANGLE FACET GRADE STAGE ASPECT AVATAR BACKLASH PASSOVER DICHOTOMY
(INITIAL —) BUD
(LOWEST —) BATHOS
(TRANSITORY —) STREAK

PHASM FANTOM METEOR PHASMA PHANTOM

PHEASANT CHIR GUAN ARGUS CHEER KALIJ MINAL MONAL COUCAL GROUSE LEIPOA MAGPIE MONAUL MOONAL PUKRAS KALLEGE FIREBACK ITHAGINE RINGNECK TRAGOPAN MACARTNEY
(BREEDING PLACE FOR —S) STEW
(BROOD OF —S) NID NYE NIDE
(YOUNG —) POULT

PHEASANT CUCKOO COUCAL

PHEASANT DUCK PINTAIL MERGANSER

PHEASANT FINCH WAXBILL

PHEASANT'S-EYE ROSARUBY

PHEBE (HUSBAND OF —) SILVIUS

PHELLEM CORK SUBER

PHENOBARBITOL LUMINAL

PHENOCRYST INSET

PHENOL BHT LACCOL THYMOL ALOESOL CREOSOL DURENOL EUGENOL ORCINOL CHAVICOL RESORCIN CARVACROL

PHENOMENA
(SUFF.) ICS

PHENOMENON FIRE ANOMY COLOR EVENT IMAGE ARTHUS EFFECT METEOR MIRAGE SHADOW ISOTOPY MIRACLE PARADOX PROCESS SYMPTOM ASTERISM PRAKRITI SIDERISM SUNQUAKE LANDSPOUT
(ATMOSPHERIC —) METEOR
(LUMINOUS —) FIREDRAKE
(METEOROGICAL —) STORM

PHENYLSALICYLATE SALOL

PHERES (BROTHER OF —) AESON AMYTHAON
(DAUGHTER OF —) IDOMENE PERIAPIS
(FATHER OF —) CRETHEUS
(MOTHER OF —) TYRO
(NEPHEW OF —) JASON
(SON OF —) ADMETUS LYCURGUS

PHIAL CUP FIAL VIAL CRUET BOTTLE VESSEL

PHILABEG KILT FILIBEG

PHILANDER FOOL WOLF DALLY FLIRT SMOCK

PHILANTHROPIC HUMANE

PHILANTHROPIST DONOR SHARER ALTRUIST HUMANITARIAN
AMERICAN DIX CASE DUKE FELS HOGG HOLT LICK LOEB MOTT RICE SAGE URIS VAUX YALE AVERY BACHE BRUCE DEPEW EVANS FRICK GERRY GETTY GRATZ HEINZ LENOX LEWYT MILLS ODGEN PEROT PRATT SMITH TRASK TULLY COOPER CRERAR DEDMAN EUSTIS FOLSON GEORGE GIRARD GURLEY HAYDEN HEARST LAMONT LASKER LEHMAN LOWELL MELLON MILLER MORGAN MURPHY PEPPER PHIPPS PUTNAM ROBERT SCHIFF STRAUS TAPPAN TULANE COCHRAN CORNELL DOREMUS FARNHAM GILBERT GRELLET HOPKINS LATHROP LAZARUS MILBANK PARRISH PEABODY RUTGERS RYERSON SHEPARD STEWART WARBURG CARNEGIE CORCORAN HARKNESS HARRIMAN LEWISOHN PHILLIPS ROBINSON STERLING JUILLIARD MEYERHOFF ROSENWALD SHEFFIELD CRITTENTON GUGGENHEIM SULZBERGER VANDERBILT ABERCROMBIE ROCKEFELLER
AUSTRIAN FRANKL
CANADIAN MCGILL
ENGLISH FRY GUY COBBE CORAM CORRY KYRLE MAYER SHARP WAUGH GURNEY KENYON SLOANE COWDRAY HIBBERT MONTAGU PEARSON RYLANDS CHRISTIE KINNAIRD MACAULAY SOMERSET FAITHFULL MONTEFIORE OGLETHORPE SHAFTESBURY WHITTINGTON WILBERFORCE
FRENCH MANCE GIRARD MARBEAU MONTYON MICHELIN MIRAMION
GERMAN FALK HIRSCH MULLER FLIEDNER
INDIAN JEEJEEBHOY
IRISH RICE GONNE MADDEN
ITALIAN KRIM
RUSSIAN NOVIKOV
SCOTTISH DALE HERIOT FINDLAY GUTHRIE
SWEDISH NOBEL
SWISS DUNANT

PHILANTHROPY CHARITY ALMSGIVING

PHILEMATOLOGY KISSING

PHILEMON (WIFE OF —) BAUCIS

PHILIP PIP PHILP SPARROW

PHILIPPIC SATIRE SCREED TIRADE ABUSIVE DIATRIBE

PHILIPPINES

ARCHIPELAGO: SULU
CAPITAL: BAGUIO MANILA
COIN: PESO PISO PESETA CENTAVO SENTIMO
FIBER: ERUC ABACA BUNTAL
ISLAND: CEBU BATAN BOHOL LEYTE LUZON PANAY SAMAR NEGROS MASBATE MINDORO PALAWAN ROMBLON MINDANAO
LAKE: TAAL LANAO
LANGUAGE: MORO BICOL IBANAG ILOCANO TAGALOG VISAYAN
MEASURE: LOAN BRAZA CABAN CAUAN CHUPA GANTA APATAN BALITA QUINON
MOUNTAIN: APO IBA MAYON PULOG BANAHAO
NATIVE: ATA ATI ITA TAO AETA ATTA ETAS MORO SULU BICOL TAGAL VICOL IGOROT TIMAUA BISAYAN TAGALOG FILIPINO
PROVINCE: ABRA CEBU SULU ALBAY CAPIZ DAVAO LANAO RIZAL BATAAN CAVITE IFUGAO ILOILO TARLAC SURIGAO
RIVER: ABRA AGNO MAGAT PASIG AGUSAN LAOANG CAGAYAN MINDANAO PAMPANGA
TOWN: IBA AGOA BOAC CEBU JOLO MATI ALBAY DAVAO DIGOS LAOAG PASAY VIGAN APARRI BAGUIO CAVITE ILAGAN ILOILO MANILA BACOLOD BASILAN DAGUPAN CALOOCAN
TREE: DAO IBA TUA TUI ACLE ANAM ATES BOGO DITA IPIL GUIJO LAUAN LIGAS ALUPAG ANAHAU ARANGA ANONANG APITONG TINDALO ALMACIGA AMPALAYA
VOLCANO: APO TAAL MAYON BULOSAN CANLAON
WEIGHT: CATTY FARDO PICUL PUNTO LACHSA QUILATE CHINANTA

PHILISTINE BOOB GIGMAN MUCKER BABBITT GITTITE BOEOTIAN BARBARIAN BOURGEOIS HYPOCRITE
(— CITY) GATH
(PL.) PULESATI PURASATI CAPHTORIM

PHILOLOGIST LAVENGRO LINGUIST
AMERICAN BUCK COOK HART TODD WOOD ADLER BROWN CHILD CURME GIBBS HEMPL MARCH MARSH BENDER BRIGHT MARDEN PRINCE REEVES CHOMSKY EMERSON GEROULD GUDEMAN HOPKINS KENNEDY LEARNED SHELDON WHITMAN HARRISON TRUMBULL GREENOUGH KORZYBSKI BLOOMFIELD STURTEVANT
AUSTRIAN MINOR MULLER KARAJAN REINISCH SCHONBACH
COLOMBIAN CUERVO MARROQUIN
CZECH HANKA GEBAUER JUNGMANN DOBROVSKY
DANISH RAFN RASK VERNER HEIBERG MOLBECH THOMSEN JESPERSEN WESTERGAARD
DUTCH KATE KERN BRINK VRIES VREESE WINKEL HEINSIUS HEREMANS UHLENBECK HUYDECOPER VALCKENAER HEMSTERHUIS
ENGLISH WYLD ASTON EARLE ELLIS NARES SAYCE SKEAT TOOKE CONWAY CRAGIE GOWERS MORRIS

MURRAY ONIONS THORPE WERNER WRIGHT ALLEGRO GARNETT GOMPERZ SKINNER WEEKLEY BOSWORTH CHADWICK STEPHENS WEYMOUTH COLERIDGE DONALDSON FURNIVALL
FINNISH SETALA CASTREN
FRENCH ADAM BREAL DOLET EGGER HENRY LEBAS MEYER RENAN BRUNOT LAMBIN WAILLY BRACHET BURNOUF MEILLET LEFEBVRE VAUGELAS CHABANEAU QUICHERAT HOVELACQUE DARMESTETER
GERMAN AST ABEL BIRT BOPP DIEZ FICK HIRT JULG KERN MOGK PAUL POTT WOLF BERGK BLANC BLASS BOCKH EBERT GREIN GRIMM HAASE HAGEN HAUPT HEYNE HEYSE JUSTI KLOTZ KRAPF KRAUS KROLL LEHRS MEYER NIESE PAULY ZEUSS BECKER BEKKER BENFEY CHRIST FREUND FRISCH HENZEN JACOBI JACOBS KELLER KOCHLY MARTIN MULLER PASSOW REISKE VAHLEN VIETOR ADELUNG BARTSCH BERNAYS BRANDIS BURSIAN CORSSEN CREUZER CURTIUS DINDORF DUNTZER GERLAND KIEPERT KORTING LEPSIUS LESKIEN MATZNER OSTHOFF RIBBECK RITSCHL RUHNKEN SANDERS SCHERER SIEVERS WEIGAND WELCKER WISSOWA ZARNCKE ZUPITZA AUFRECHT BEHAGHEL BISCHOFF BOTTIGER BRUGMANN FOERSTER GRAEVIUS HOFFMANN HUMBOLDT MASSMANN SCHRADER THIERSCH WEINHOLD WESTPHAL XYLANDER ACIDALIUS BAUMSTARK BERNHARDY BUSCHMANN ETTMULLER FRISCHLIN GABELENTZ HOLTZMANN KIRCHHOFF KOSCHWITZ STEINTHAL TRAUTMANN HOLTHAUSEN MULLENHOFF STREITBERG THURNEYSEN VOLLMOLLER BARTHOLOMAE
HUNGARIAN REVAI HUNFALVY DOBRENTEJ ENDLICHER
ICELANDIC JONSSON EGILSSON MAGNUSSON VIGFUSSON
ITALIAN ASCOLI MONACI NOVATI OVIDIO COMPARETTI CASTELVETRO CASTIGLIONE
NORWEGIAN AASEN BUGGE KONOW MUNCH
POLISH ZAMENHOF ROZWADOWSKI
PORTUGUESE COELHO
RUMANIAN HASDEU
RUSSIAN GROT VOSTOKOV SCHIEFNER
SCOTTISH GRANT BAIKIE MURRAY
SPANISH MENENDEZ
SWEDISH IHRE LUNDELL AHLQUIST SODERWALL ZACHRISSON
SWISS MAHLY ISELIN

PHILOLOGY SEMITICS

PHILOMACHUS MACHETES

PHILOMELA STOP FILOMEL
(FATHER OF —) PANDION
(RAVISHER OF —) TEREUS
(SISTER OF —) PROCNE
(SLAIN BY —) ITYS
(VICTIM OF —) ITYS

PHILOSOPHER WIT SAGE CYNIC STOIC ARTIST IONIAN LEGIST DOTTORE ELEATIC ERISTIC SCHOLAR SOPHIST SUMMIST THINKER ZETETIC ACADEMIC EPOCHIST MAGICIAN VIRTUOSO ACADEMIST ALCHEMIST DIALECTIC PHYSICIAN SCHOOLMAN
AMERICAN AYER HOOK HUME LADD MEAD MORE ADLER ALBEE BOWEN BOWNE DEWEY EDMAN FANON FISKE JAMES LEWIS MOORE PAINE PERRY QUINE ROYCE UPHAM WATTS DRAPER HARRIS HICKOK HOFFER HYSLOP JAEGER KALLEN LANGER NOZICK PEIRCE SNIDER BARRETT CALKINS EMERSON HOCKING HOWISON LOVEJOY MARCUSE NEWBOLD CALLAHAN WILLIAMS ALEXANDER SANTAVANA SANTAYANA
ARAB AVICENNA
ARABIAN GHAZZALI
AUSTRIAN BUBER EXNER DEUBLER MEINONG STEINER ZIMMERMANN RATZENHOFER
BELGIAN MERCIER DELBOEUF
BRAZILIAN MAGALHAES
CANADIAN MURRAY STEWART SCHURMAN
CHINESE MOTI LAOTZU MENCIUS CONFUCIUS
CZECH MASARYK SMETANA
DANISH SIBBERN HOFFDING KIERKEGAARD
DUTCH BOLLAND ERASMUS HEYMANS SPINOZA OPZOOMER
EGYPTIAN ORIGEN PLOTINUS
ENGLISH AYER CASE JOAD MILL MORE RYLE WARD BACON BROAD COTES DUNNE GREEN GROTE HOOKE HULME JONES LAIRD LEWES LOCKE MOORE PALEY STOUT SULLY BAYNES BIDDLE BUTLER FOWLER GODWIN GURNEY HOBBES LATHAM MCCABE NEWTON NORRIS OCKHAM TAYLOR AINSLIE BALFOUR BENTHAM BRADLEY COLLIER HALDANE HARTLEY HERBERT HODGSON INGELBY JACKSON RUSSELL SPENCER STEPHEN STEWART WHEWELL CONGREVE CORNFORD COURTNEY CUDWORTH GLANVILL HOBHOUSE MUIRHEAD SCHILLER SIDGWICK BOSANQUET MACKENZIE WHITEHEAD CUMBERLAND HUTCHINSON SHAFTESBURY
FINNISH WESTERMARCK
FRENCH DROZ WEIL ALAIN BAYLE CAMUS COMTE GUYAU HELLO JANET LEROY LIARD MABLY RAMUS REVEL SIMON TAINE BERARD BONALD COUSIN GILSON GOBLOT LEROUX MARCEL PASCAL QUESNE RAYNAL SARTRE VALERY ABAUZIT ABELARD BARTHEZ BERGSON BURIDAN CABANIS CHARRON DAMIRON DIDEROT FOURIER GERANDO HOLBACH MAISTRE MILHAUD REYNAUD ROMAINS ALEMBERT BOURDEAU BOUTROUX CHARTIER FOUCAULT FOUILLEE GASSENDI GILLOUIN GOBINEAU JOUFFROY LAFFITTE MARITAIN MEYERSON ROUSSEAU TEILHARD VACHEROT VOLTAIRE BALLANCHE CONDILLAC CONDORCET DESCARTES HELVITIUS LACHELIER SCHWEITZER MONTESQUIEU LAROMIGUIERE
GERMAN BIEL HAYM KANT KRUG MARX OKEN PREL BAUER CARUS COHEN DREWS ENGEL FRIES GROOS HEGEL LIPPS LOTZE MARBE MEYER RIEHL STEIN UTITZ WAITZ WOLFF BENEKE CARNAP CAROVE EUCKEN FICHTE GABLER GEIGER GEYSER GRUPPE HEINZE HERDER JACOBI KRAUSE KRONER LASSON MAIMON MESSER MULLER PRANTL RITTER SIMMEL STUMPF ULRICI ZELLER ZIEHEN BRUCKER BRUNNER CRUSIUS DEUSSEN DILTHEY DRIESCH DUHRING ECKHART ERDMANN FECHNER HAECKEL HENNING HERBART JUNGIUS KNUTZEN LASAULX LAZARUS LEIBNIZ PAULSEN STIRNER STRAUSS VOLKELT CARRIERE CASSIRER DROBISCH EBERHARD FORTLAGE HARTMANN HERTLING LASSWITZ LEIBNITZ MICHELET MICHELIS PANNWITZ REINHOLD SPENGLER AVENARIUS BILFINGER CORNELIUS DIETERICI EHRENFELS FEUERBACH GOCLENIUS HEIDEGGER LEISEGANG NIETZSCHE SCHELLING THOMASIUS TIEDEMANN VAIHINGER VORLANDER BAUMGARTEN HILLEBRAND KEYSERLING ROSENKRANZ FRAUENSTADT MENDELSSOHN SCHOPENHAUER TRENDELENBURG SCHLEIERMACHER
GREEK BION ZENO CEBES DAMON LYCON PLATO CRATES EUCLID PHAEDO PYRRHO STRATO THALES CRANTOR DEMONAX EUDEMUS PROCLUS TIMAEUS ALCMAEON APULEIUS CRATYLUS DIODORUS DIOGENES EPICURUS MELISSUS MENIPPUS NUMENIUS PHAEDRUS PORPHYRY SOCRATES ARCHELAUS ARISTOTLE CARNEADES CHARMIDES CLEANTHES CRITOLAUS DAMASCIUS EPICTETUS EUBULIDES FAVORINUS HIEROCLES LEUCIPPUS MENEDEMUS PANAETIUS PANTAENUS PHILOLAUS ANAXAGORAS ANAXARCHUS ANAXIMENES ARCESILAUS ARISTIPPUS CHRYSIPPUS DEMOCRITUS EMPEDOCLES HERACLITUS IAMBLICHUS METRODORUS PARMENIDES PHERECYDES POSIDONIUS PROTAGORAS PYTHAGORAS SIMPLICIUS SPEUSIPPUS XENOCRATES XENOPHANES ANAXIMANDER ANTISTHENES ARISTOXENUS CLITOMACHUS DICAEARCHUS CALLISTHENES PHILOSTRATUS THEOPHRASTUS
HUNGARIAN ERDELYI LAKATOS
INDIAN GHOSE IQBAL KRISHNAMURTI
IRISH BERNARD ERIGENA BERKELEY MOLYNEUX
ISRAELI BUBER
ITALIAN NIFO VERA VICO ABANO BRUNO CONTI CROCE FERRI ARDIGO FICINO PAPINI VANINI AQUINAS CANTONI CARDANO FERRARI FRANCHI GENTILE MAMIANI TELESIO UBERWEG GIOBERTI GUARDINI ALGAROTTI CESALPINO CAMPANELLA FIORENTINO POMPONAZZI BONAVENTURA MACHIAVELLI PICCOLOMINI
JAPANESE SUZUKI
NORWEGIAN MONRAD
POLISH LIBELT WRONSKI LUTOSLAWSKI
PORTUGUESE ACOSTA
ROMAN CICERO SENECA BOETHIUS CORNUTUS PLOTINUS AUGUSTINE LUCRETIUS
RUSSIAN BERDYAEV CHICHERIN
RUSSIAN) PLEKHANOV
SCOTTISH BAIN HOME HUME MILL REID SETH CAIRD FLINT FRASER VEITCH FERRIER STEWART WALLACE BREWSTER FERGUSON HAMILTON STIRLING HUTCHESON CALDERWOOD MACKINTOSH
SPANISH VIVES BALMES ORTEGA SUAREZ UNAMUNO AVERROES MAIMONIDES
SWEDISH BOSTROM ATTERBOM SWEDENBORG
SWISS WYSS AMIEL HILTY PREVOST HABERLIN

PHILOSOPHER'S STONE ADROP MICROCOSM

PHILOSOPHIC SAGE

PHILOSOPHICAL DEEP

PHILOSOPHY YOGA ETHICS GOSPEL MAGISM SYSTEM TAOISM APRISMO COSMISM DUALISM INQUIRY MIMAMSA SANKHYA SCEPSIS ACTIVISM HINDUISM HUMANISM IDENTISM IDEOLOGY LEGALISM OCCAMISM STOICISM ABSURDISM NOUMENISM SOCRATISM VEDANTISM
(— OF LIFE) LIGHTS
(NATURAL —) PHYSIC

PHILTER DRUG CHARM WANGA FILTER POTION AMATORY

PHINEHAS **(FATHER OF —)** ELI ELEAZAR
(GRANDFATHER OF —) AARON

PHINEUS **(BROTHER OF —)** CADMUS CEPHEUS
(FATHER OF —) BELUS AGENOR
(MOTHER OF —) ANCHINOE TELEPHASSA
(SISTER OF —) EUROPA
(WIFE OF —) IDAEA CLEOPATRA

PHLEBOTOMIZE BLEED VENESECT

PHLEBOTOMUS TATUKIRA

PHLEGM FLEM GLEET MUCUS WATER FLEUME PITUITE MOUSEWEB

PHLEGMATIC CALM COOL DULL

SLOW INERT MUCOID SLEEPY WATERY VISCOUS COMPOSED SLUGGISH APATHETIC IMPASSIVE
PHLEGYAS (DAUGHTER OF —) CORONIS
(FATHER OF —) ARES MARS
(MOTHER OF —) CHRYSE
(SLAYER OF —) APOLLO
(SON OF —) IXION
PHLOEM BAST LIBER LEPTOME
PHLOGISTIC FIERY HEATED BURNING FLAMING
PHLOMIS SAGELEAF
PHLOX CYME FLOX ALBION BEACON COBAEA
PHOCUS (FATHER OF —) AEACUS ORNYTION
(HALF-BROTHER OF —) PELEUS TELAMON
(MOTHER OF —) PSAMATHE
(SON OF —) CRISIUS PANOPEUS
(WIFE OF —) ANTIOPE
PHOEBE FEBE FIVE MOON DIANA PEWEE ARTEMIS
(BROTHER OF —) CASTOR POLLUX POLYDEUCES
(DAUGHTER OF —) LETO
(FATHER OF —) URANUS LEUCIPPUS TYNDAREUS
(MOTHER OF —) GAEA LEDA
(SISTER OF —) HELEN CLYTEMNESTRA
PHOEBUS SOL SUN APOLLO PHOIBUS
PHOENICIA (COLONY OF —) CARTHAGE
(GODDESS OF —) TANIT BALTIS TANITH ASTARTE
(KING OF —) AGENOR
(TOWN OF —) ACRE TYRE SIDON SAREPTA
PHOENIX FUM FUNG
(BROTHER OF —) CILIX CADMUS THASUS PHINEUS
(FATHER OF —) AGENOR AMYNTOR
(MOTHER OF —) CLEOBULE TELEPHASSA
(PUPIL OF —) ACHILLES
(SISTER OF —) EUROPA
PHOLAS PIDDOCK
PHONE CALL DIAL RING CALLUP RINGUP
PHONEME MORPH TONEME LARYNGAL
PHONEMIC BROAD
PHONOGRAM LOGOGRAM SINOGRAM
PHONOGRAPH VIC PHONO VICTROLA
(— RECORD) DISK PLATTER
PHONY FAKE JIVE SHAM BOGUS FAKER FALSE BRUMMY BUNYIP PHONEY PLASTIC IMPOSTOR SPURIOUS
PHORONEUS (DAUGHTER OF —) NIOBE
(FATHER OF —) INACHUS
(MOTHER OF —) MELIA
(SISTER OF —) IO
(SON OF —) APIS IASUS AGENOR PELASGUS
(WIFE OF —) CERDO LAODICE
PHOSPHATE EHLITE FLOATS APATITE CABOCLE CACOXENE GRIPHITE MONAZITE
PHOSPHORESCENCE BRIMING MARFIRE
PHOSPHORESCENT PHOSPHOR NOCTILUCOUS
PHOTISM SYNOPSY
PHOTO PIC
(— FINISH) MAT MATT MATTE
(ART —) SEPIA
PHOTOENGRAVER ZINCOGRAPHER
PHOTOENGRAVING HALFTONE HELIOGRAPH
PHOTOGENE AFTERIMAGE
PHOTOGRAPH MUG PIC FILM LENS SNAP CARTE IMAGE PANEL PHOTO PINUP PRINT SHOOT STILL CANDID GLOSSY MOSAIC RETAKE SCENIC STEREO AIRVIEW MONTAGE PICTURE TINTYPE LIKENESS PORTRAIT POSITIVE SNAPSHOT TABLETOP CYCLOGRAM MAMMOGRAM
(— OF RENAL EXCRETION) RENOGRAM
(— SIZE) PANEL
(X-RAY —) SKIAGRAM
(PL.) PIX
PHOTOGRAPHER PHOTOG LENSMAN CAMERIST CAMERAMAN PAPARAZZO SHUTTERBUG
PHOTOGRAPHY STEREO CALOTYPE PHOTOGENY
(— SESSION) SHOOT
(KIND OF —) KIRLIAN
PHOTOMETER LUCIMETER
PHOTOMONTAGE COLLAGE
PHOTON BOSON TROLAND
PHRASE CRY HIT MOT SET CRIB FUSS HAVE IDEA TERM WORD COMMA COUCH IDIOM LABEL LEMMA POINT STATE STYLE TOPIC TROPE BYWORD CLAUSE CLICHE DITTON DORISM GRUPPO HOBNOB NOTION PNEUMA PRAISE SAVING SLOGAN ATTACCO DICTION EPITHET PASSAGE CONCEIVE DIVISION DORICISM FLATTERY IDEOGRAM IRISHISM LATINISM LEITMOTIV
(— DIFFERENTLY) TURN
(— UNCTUOUSLY) DROOL
(CANT —) SHIBBOLETH
(JAZZ —) RIFF
(MUSICAL —) RIFF POINT ATTACCO SUBJECT
(PET —) SHIBBOLETH
(PITHY —) LACONISM LACONICISM
(REDUNDANT —) CHEVILLE
(STOCK —) CANT
(TRITE —) CLICHE
(WELL-TURNED —) STROKE
PHRASEOLOGY CANT STYLE DIALECT DICTION WORDING LOCUTION PARLANCE
PHRATRY CLAN
PHRENETIC PYTHIAN FRENETIC
PHRENIC MENTAL
(PL.) PSYCHOLOGY
PHRIXOS (FATHER OF —) ATHAMUS
(MOTHER OF —) NEPHELE
(SISTER OF —) HELLE
PHRONTIS (BROTHER OF —) ARGUS MELAS CYTISSORUS
(FATHER OF —) PHRIXUS
(HUSBAND OF —) PANTHOUS
(MOTHER OF —) CHALCIOPE
(SON OF —) EUPHORBUS HYPERENOR POLYDAMAS
PHRYGIA (GOD OF —) ATYS ATTIS SABAZIOS
(KING OF —) MIDAS
PHRYNIN BUFIDIN
PHTHISIS DECAY
PHUVAH (FATHER OF —) ISSACHAR
PHYLACTERY FILACTERY
(PL.) TEFILLIN TEPHILLIN
PHYLE TRIBE
PHYLLO FILO
PHYLOMACHE (DAUGHTER OF —) ALCESTIS
(FATHER OF —) AMPHION
(HUSBAND OF —) PELIAS
(SON OF —) ACASTUS
PHYLUM HOKA CLASS HOKAN NADENE BRYOZOA ANNELATA ANNELIDA CHORDATA DIVISION LIGNOSAE PORIFERA
PHYMA TUMOR
PHYSALIS POP POPPER TOMATILLO
PHYSETER CATODON
PHYSIC CURE HEAL FISIC PURGE TRADE REMEDY MEDICAL NATURAL RELIEVE DRUGGERY
PHYSICAL ILL LUSTY SOMAL BODILY CARNAL DISTAL NATURAL SOMATIC CORPORAL CURATIVE EXTERNAL MATERIAL CORPOREAL
(PURELY —) BRUTE
PHYSICIAN ASA DOC PILL CURER GALEN HAKIM LEECH MEDIC QUACK ARTIST BAIDYA DOCTOR FELLOW HEALER INTERN MEDICO DOTTORE EMPIRIC SURGEON ALIENIST RESIDENT SAWBONES SUNDOWNER
(— OF GODS) PAEAN
(— OF THE GODS) PAEAN
(PREF.) IATRO JATEO JATO
(SUFF.) IATRIST
AMERICAN ILG LEE RAY BARD COIT DICK DREW FITZ HARE HOLT KING LUST MUDD PARK ROCK ROUS SALK SIMS APGAR APPEL BIGGS BRILL BRUSH CABOT COHEN CROHN DRAKE FLINT GOLER GUION KNOPF KOLFF LILLY LOEWI LOGAN MARAT MINOT SMITH SPOCK TONER TULLY TYSON WHITE BARKER BATTEY BENNET BROOKS CARTER CLARKE DEVITA ENDERS FISHER FOSTER GESELL GORGAS GORRIE HEISER HOOKER HORNER HOSACK JACOBI JARVIK JOSLIN KEELEY KNIGHT KOPITS LAZEAR MILLER MIRKIN MORGAN MORROW MURPHY ODWYER PARRAN PINCUS SCHICK STILES STILLE STORER STRONG TILTON WALKER WATSON WELLER ALVAREZ CAMMANN CHAPMAN DARLING DICKSON FRANCIS GERHARD GILBERT HAGGARD HEPBURN HOPKINS JACKSON JANEWAY ROBBINS TROLAND TRUDEAU WHIPPLE BARTLETT BILLINGS BOYLSTON CHANNING FISHBEIN GUERNSEY GWATHMEY HAMILTON KIRTLAND KNOWLTON MITCHELL PETERSON RICHARDS ROCKWELL SHATTUCK SPALDING TOWNSEND WOODWARD BLACKWELL BRAZELTON STERNBERG CLENDENING GOLDBERGER STEPHENSON WATERHOUSE ZAKRZEWSKA CASTIGLIONI WIGGLESWORTH
ARAB AVICENNA ABDALLATIF
ARGENTINIAN BUNGE
AUSTRIAN BARANY BREUER MESMER OPPOLZER ENNEMOSER ROKITANSKY
BELGIAN WIER HEYMANS
BRAZILIAN CHAGAS KUBITSCHEK
CANADIAN CRAIK DAFOE FISET GRANT OSLER REEVE WIGLE ASHTON MCCRAE BANTING RODDICK SHULMAN DRUMMOND GRENFELL MACPHAIL
CZECH VANCURRA
DANISH GRAM WORM LANGE FINSEN BARTHOLIN
DUTCH GRAAF EIJKMAN BOERHAAVE INGENHOUSZ
ENGLISH BUDD DALE GOOD HAKE HALL HUME MEAD PAVY ROSS SNOW BARRY BRUCE CAIUS DOVER DOYLE DRAKE FLUDD JAMES JONES JURIN LOWER PAGET ACLAND BRIGHT BROWNE CLARKE DARWIN DOBELL FLOREY GARROD HARVEY HAVERS HORDER HUNTER JENNER MANSON PARKES RINGER SLOANE TREVES WILLIS ADDISON ALLBUTT BENNETT CHAPMAN CONOLLY COPLAND DEARDEN FALKNER GLISSON HODGKIN LINACRE NABARRO PRINGLE SIMPSON SKINNER STANTON STEPTOE WHARTON ANDERSON ANDREWES BARNARDO BASHFORD BIRKBECK BUCHANAN CULPEPER GRENFELL HEBERDEN PRICHARD SYDENHAM ARBUTHNOT BLACKMORE BROADBENT LANKESTER RADCLIFFE FOTHERGILL SUMMERSKILL
FRENCH SUE CLOT DENIS DUPRE HAYEM PINEL ROGET WIDAL ANDRAL ASTRUC AUZOUX BERARD FERNEL LEPINE LITTRE MARTIN NIEPCE PLANTE VAQUEZ BAILLON BECHAMP CHARCOT DAVAINE DUMERIL GRASSET LAENNEC LAVERAN LEBOYER LECLUSE MANTOUX MENIERE NICOLLE PECQUET QUESNAY VINCENT BOUCHARD DUCHENNE LANDOUZY LEVADITI BOUILLAUD BROUSSALS GUILLOTIN LAMETTRIE BAILLARGER BRETONNEAU CASSEGRAIN LANCEREAUX POISEUILLE SCHWEITZER BROUSSONETT NOSTRADAMUS
GERMAN ERB BINZ EBEL GALL KOCH MUCH REIL ZINN BLOCH CARUS FAUST FRANK LINGG OSANN REMAK BRUCKE CORDUS DOBLIN DOMAGK KERNER KORTUM LEYDEN MEIBOM NORDAU OERTEL OLBERS

PEUCER AGRIPPA BASEDOW BERENDT JASPERS KAMPFER NEISSER BRUNFELS ERXLEBEN FLEMMING HARTMANN HOFFMANN HUFELAND ZIEMSSEN DOLLINGER FORSSMANN HAHNEMANN NICOLAIER NOTHNAGEL SCHONLEIN DETTWEILER FRIEDREICH LANGERHANS WASSERMANN
GREEK GALEN RUFUS AETIOS CTESIAS SORANUS ALCMAEON DEMOCEDES ORIBASIUS PRAXAGORAS ASCLEPIADES DIOSCORIDES HIPPOCRATES ERASISTRATUS PAPANICOLAOU
IRISH JOYCE STOKES GOGARTY SIGERSON
ITALIAN REDI BOTTA GOLGI ASELLI FARINI MAZZEI BAGLIVI BELLINI CARDANO GALVANI BACCELLI LOMBROSO SCALIGER BLANDRATA CESALPINO FRACASTORO MONTESSORI TOSCANELLI VALLISNIERI
NORWEGIAN HANSEN
PARAGUAYAN BARBERO
PORTUGUESE EGAS
RUMANIAN BABES
RUSSIAN DAHL VERESAEY VORONOFF
SALVADORAN MOLINA
SCOTTISH LIND MOIR BLANE BROWN ARNOTT BRIDIE BUCHAN CHEYNE CULLEN FERGUS FORBES MANSON BRUNTON CANTLIE JAMESON MACLEOD SIMPSON GRAINGER ARBUTHNOT ARMSTRONG PITCAIRNE CHRISTISON MACALISTER RUTHERFORD ABERCROMBIE
SPANISH CHANCA NEGRIN SERVETUS
SWEDISH BARANY MUNTHE ZANDER ACHARIUS
SWISS GOLL HESS AMMAN PEYER KOCHER ROLLIER ZWINGER PARACELSUS
VENEZUELAN VARGAS

PHYSICIST HYLOZOIST
AMERICAN CHU AMES CREW GUNN GUTH HALL HESS HULL IVES KAHN LAMB LAND LANE MORE PAGE RABI ROOD ROSA TING TUVE WOOD YANG ZINN ALTER BACHE BARUS BAUER BETHE BLOCH BOLEY COHEN DUANE EWELL FERMI FITCH HENRY KARLE KUSCH LEMON LYMAN MAYER PUPIN SEGRE STERN SWANN YALOW BEDELL BRIGGS CONDON COOPER CRONIN FRANCK GERMER GLASER KARMAN LOOMIS MAIMAN MORLEY NIPHER PIERCE SLOANE TELLER TOLMAN TOWNES VARIAN WIGNER WRIGHT ALLISON ALVAREZ BABCOCK BARDEEN BURGESS CARHART COMPTON FEYNMAN GLASHOW GODDARD GODLOVE LECONTE NICHOLS PENZIAS PURCELL RANDALL RENWIEK RICHTER ROWLAND SZILARD WHEELER ANDERSON BLODGETT BRATTAIN BRIDGMAN DAVISSON EINSTEIN HASTINGS HAUPTMAN LAWRENCE MILLIKAN SHOCKLEY STRATTON THOMPSON VANALLEN VANVLECK WINTHROP ZWORYKIN BITTINGER GOODSPEED HUMPHREYS INGERSOLL LAURITSEN MICHELSON RAINWATER SCHWINGER HOFSTADTER MENDENHALL RENTSCHLER RUTHERFURD SCHRIEFFER TROWBRIDGE CHAMBERLAIN OPPENHEIMER
ARGENTINIAN CERNUSCHI
AUSTRIAN HESS MACH RABI DOPPLER MEITNER PRECHTL BOLTZMANN SCHRODINGER SCHROEDINGER
BELGIAN PLATEAU
CANADIAN TORY HILLIER DEMPSTER HERZBERG
DANISH BOHR OERSTED MOTTELSON
DUTCH WAALS ZEEMAN HUYGENS LORENTZ ZERNIKE HARTSOEKER KAMERLINGH VANDERMEER MUSSCHENBROEK
ENGLISH EVE BORN LAMB LEES MOTT ASTON BOYLE BRAGG DEWAR DIRAC DYSON FUCHS GROVE JEANS JOULE LODGE NICOL SALAM AITKEN BARKLA CANTON DALTON DARWIN FRISCH KELVIN STOKES ANDRADE BARRETT BULLARD CROOKES DANIELL FARADAY FLEMING GILBERT GUTHRIE HARTREE MICHELL MOSELEY SIEMENS THOMSON TYNDALL APPLETON BLACKETT CHADWICK HAUKSBEE POYNTING RAYLEIGH SCHUSTER STURGEON CALLENDAR CAVENDISH COCKCROFT HEAVISIDE JOSEPHSON GLAZEBROOK RICHARDSON RUTHERFORD WHEATSTONE
FRENCH BIOT HIRN NEEL ARAGO CORNU FABRY JAMIN MALUS PAPIN PETIT PITOT WEISS BRANLY CARNOT CLAUDE COTTON DULONG FIZEAU FORTIN JOLIOT NIEPCE NOLLET PERRIN RAOULT SAVART VIOLLE BABINET BEUDANT BLONDEL BROGLIE CHARLES COULOMB FIZERAU FOURIER FRESNEL JOUBERT KASTLER MASCART PELTIER REAUMUR SAUVEUR AMONTONS ARSONVAL DESPRETZ FOUCAULT LANGEVIN LIPPMANN MARIOTTE POUILLET REGNAULT BECQUEREL BRILLOUIN CAILLETET GUILLAUME LISSAJOUS CHARDONNET
GERMAN MIE OHM BORN DOVE KORN LAUE LENZ REIS WIEN BETHE BOTHE BRAUN BUDDE DEBYE ERMAN HERTZ HOLTZ JOLLY KUNDT MAYER STARK VOIGT WEBER BALMER ELSTER GEIGER HANKEL JENSEN KOENIG LAMONT LENARD LUMMER MAGNUS NERNST PLANCK RIECKE RITTER ZEUNER AEPINUS BEDNORZ BRODHUN CHLADNI FECHNER GEHRCKE HITTORF LAMBERT NEUMANN PLUCKER PRANDTL QUINCKE REGENER RUDOLPH SCAEFER SEEBECK TOEPLER WULLNER CLAUSIUS EINSTEIN GUERICKE ROENTGEN SCHUMANN FEDDERSEN GOLDSTEIN HALLWACHS KIRCHHOFF MOSSBAUER SCHEIBLER STEINHEIL WIEDEMANN BARKHAUSEN FAHRENHEIT KOHLRAUSCH PRINGSHEIM SCHWEIGGER SIEDENTOPF SOMMERFELD LICHTENBERG
GREEK CTESIBIUS
HUNGARIAN WIGNER
INDIAN BOSE SAHA RAMAN
IRISH JOLLY KELVIN STONEY WALTON ANDREWS TOWNSEND FITZGERALD
ITALIAN RIIS FERMI PORTA RIGHI VOLTA ALDINI NOBILI RUBBIA BORELLI CAVALLO GALILEI GALVANI MELLONI VENTURI AVOGADRO BECCARIA BELTRAMI BLASERNA FERRARIS GRIMALDI PALMIERI BOSCOVICH PACINOTTI TORRICELLI
JAPANESE ESAKI YUKAWA TOMONAGA
NORWEGIAN GIAEVER BJERKNES HANSTEEN
POLISH INFELD WROBLEWSKI
RUSSIAN TAMM BASOV FRANK LANDAU KAPITZA LEBEDEV SAKHAROV CHERENKOV PROKHOROV
SCOTTISH KERR TAIT WATT BLACK DEWAR EWING NOBLE WILSON MAXWELL RANKINE STEWART BREWSTER
SWEDISH EDLEN ALFVEN EDLUND NILSON ANGSTROM SIEGBAHN ARRHENIUS BENEDICKS
SWISS WILD BLOCH EULER PAULI ARGAND LARIVE PICTET MUELLER PICCARD PREVOST ALLAMAND
WELSH GROVE

PHYSIC NUT TUBA CURCAS PIGNON TARTAGO
PHYSICS **(— PARTICLE)** QUARK
PHYSIOCRAT ECONOMIST
PHYSIOGNOMY MUG FACE PHIZ VIZNOMY PORTRAIT VISENOMY
PHYSIOLOGIST **AMERICAN** IVY KEYS LUSK HOUGH CANNON DALTON GASSER HARVEY HOWELL CARLSON SCHALLY COURNAND ECKSTEIN ERLANGER HARTLINE MEYERHOF GUILLEMIN HENDERSON OSTERHOUT
ARGENTINIAN HOUSSAY
AUSTRALIAN ECCLES
AUSTRIAN STEINACH
BELGIAN HEYMANS
CANADIAN BEST
CZECH PURKINJE
DANISH KROGH
DUTCH DONDERS EINTHOVEN
ENGLISH DALE HILL KATZ BEALE HALES LOWER ADRIAN DARWIN FOSTER HUXLEY RIVERS WALLER BAYLISS EDWARDS HERRING HODGKIN BARCROFT MARSHALL STARLING ELLIOTSON SHERRINGTON
FINNISH GRANIT
FRENCH BERT MAREY RICHET BEAUNIS BERNARD FLOURENS MAGENDIE DUTROCHET POISEUILLE
GERMAN FICK VOIT BUDGE GOLTZ KUHNE REMAK WUNDT HENSEN HERING LUDWIG MULLER PREYER WAGNER BEHRING BURDACH PFLUGER SCHWANN VERWORN WARBURG MEISSNER MEYERHOF VALENTIN HELMHOLTZ BLUMENBACH HEIDENHAIN
ITALIAN BOVET MOSSO MANTEGAZZA
RUSSIAN CYON PAVLOV
SCOTTISH HALDANE MACLEOD
SWEDISH EULER GRANIT HOLMGREN
SWISS HESS

PHYSIOLOGY BIONOMY ZOONOMY
PHYSIOTHERAPY PATTERNING
PHYSIQUE BODY BUILD COOST HABIT FIGURE STRENGTH
PHYSOCARPUS NEILLIA OPULASTER
PHYSOSTIGMINE ESERE ESERINE
PHYTOMER PHYTON PODIUM
PI JUMBLE CONFUSE PREACHY CONFUSION
PIA PI GABI GABGAB MARMOT
PIACLE SIN CRIME GUILT OFFENSE
PIAN YAWS FRAMBESIA
PIANETTE PYNOT PIANINO
PIANFORTE CEMBALO
PIANIST CEMBALIST CLAVIERIST
PIANO SOFT FLOOR GRAND GRANT STORY FLUGEL GENTLY SOFTLY SPINET SQUARE CLAVIAL CLAVIER GIRAFFE PIANOLA QUIETLY UPRIGHT MELOTROPE
(— SOFTENING PEDAL) CELESTE
(AFRICAN —) KALIMBA
(KIND OF —) THUMB
(PART OF —) ARM KEY LEG LID DESK FALL HEEL LYRE PROP CHEEK PEDAL STRING KEYSLIP KEYBOARD
(STYLE OF JAZZ —) STRIDE
(THUMB —) KALIMBA
PIASSAVA IYO JARA BAHIA PIACABA
PIASTER KURUS
PIATTI CYMBALS
PIAZZA PORCH SQUARE BALCONY GALLERY PORTICO VERANDA PIAZZETTA
PIC PEAK LANCE PHOTO PIQUE PICADOR
PICA M EM LINE
PICARD PYKAR
PICARO KNAVE ROGUE TRAMP BOHEMIAN VAGABOND
PICAROON ROGUE PICARO PIRATE CORSAIR WRECKER
PICAYUNE PIC PETTY MEASLY PALTRY TRIVIAL PISTAREEN
PICCADILL RABATA REBATE REBATO
PICCOLO BUSBOY JUKEBOX FLAUTINO OTTAVINO
PICHICIAGO ARMADILLO CHLAMYPHORE
PICK NAP NIB OPT BILL CULL GAFF HACK LIFT PIKE PILK SHOT WALE

ADORN BEELE BREAK CAVIL ELECT FLANG LEASE PILCH PLUCK PRIDE PRIME CHOICE CHOOSE GATHER PICKAX PUDDLE TWITCH BARGAIN CASCROM DIAMOND DRESSER MANDREL
(— APART) TOW
(— KNOTS FROM) BURL
(— OUT) CULL SPOT TAKE WELE CRONE GLEAN GARBLE SELECT
(— POCKETS) FIG FILE FOIST TOUCH
(— TOBACCO) STRIP
(— UP) SHARK
(FILLING —) ABB
PICKAX PIX BEDE BILL PIKE GURLET TUBBER TWIBIL TWIBILL
PICKED PICK TRIM PIKED CHOSEN DAINTY PEAKED SELECT ADORNED POINTED
(PREF.) LECTO
PICKER COD HOPPER
(BERRY —) HURTER
(PEA —) VINER
PICKEREL JACK SNAKE DUNLIN SAUGER SLINKER WALLEYE
PICKERELWEED TULE WAMPEE
PICKER-UP FINDER
PICKET PEG PALE POST TERN FENCE STAKE FASTEN PALING TETHER ENCLOSE FORTIFY OUTPOST PICQUET PALISADE OUTPICKET
PICKLE BOX ALEC BIND DILL MESS PECK ACHAR BRINE GRAIN MANGO SAUCE SOUSE ATSARA CAPERS DAWDLE HIGDON KERNEL KIMCHI MUDDLE NIBBLE PIDDLE PILFER PLIGHT TRIFLE CONDITE CONFECT GHERKIN TROUBLE VITRIOL MARINADE
(FISH —) ALEC
PICKLED DRUNK OILED UNSOBER MURIATED POWDERED MARINATED
PICKLOCK LOCK PICKER
PICK-ME-UP TONIC BRACER SCREW PICKUP
PICKPOCKET DIP FIG GUN NIP BUNG FILE WIRE DIVER FILER FOIST BULKER BUZZER CANNON DIPPER FIGBOY HOOKER NIPPER RATERO FOISTER MOBSMAN CLYFAKER CUTPURSE KNUCKLER BUZZGLOAK
(HELPER OF —) STALL BULKER
PICKUP BRUSH TRUCK ARREST BRACER ANACRUSIS
PICKWICK PAPERS (AUTHOR OF —) DICKENS
(CHARACTER IN —) BOB SAM MARY ALLEN EMILY TRACY ALFRED HUNTER JINGLE PERKER SAWYER TUPMAN WARDLE WELLER WINKLE BARDELL RACHAEL SLAMMER ARABELLA AUGUSTUS CLUPPINS ISABELLA PICKWICK NATHANIEL SMORLTORK SNODGRASS
PICNIC FRY BALL GIPSY GYPSY BURGOO FROLIC JUNKET MAROON OUTING SHOULDER SQUANTUM SUMMERING WAYZGOOSE
(PRINTERS' —) WAYGOOSE WAYZGOOSE
PICOT LOOP PEARL PERLE
PICOTAH SWEEP PACOTA
PICTOGRAPH GLYPH PICTOGRAM
PICTORIAL GRAPHIC
PICTURE GAY MAP OIL COPY DAUB ICON IKON LIMN SIGN VIEW DECAL FRAME IMAGE LINER PAINT PHOTO PIECE PINAX PRINT SCENE SHAPE STAMP STORY TABLE CACHET CANVAS CHROMO CUTOUT DEPICT EMBLEM MARINE PASTEL SEMBLE SHADOW STEREO TABLET CUTAWAY DIORAMA DIPTYCH EMBLEMA ETCHING EXHIBIT FASHION FEATURE GOUACHE GRAPHIC HISTORY MIZRACH PAYSAGE PORTRAY PORTURE RETRAIT SCENERY TABLEAU VANDYKE AIRSCAPE AUTOTYPE DESCRIBE DROLLERY ENVISION IDEOGRAM KAKEMONO LANDSKIP LIKENESS MAKIMONO MONOTINT OVERDOOR PAINTING PANORAMA PORTRAIT PROSPECT RITRATTO SEASCAPE SINGERIE SKYSCAPE TRIPTYCH VIGNETTE ENCAUSTIC
(— IN BOOK) GAY
(— IN 3 COMPARTMENTS) TRIPTYCH
(— MAT) SPANDREL
(— OF MONKEYS) SINGERIE
(— ON ROLLER) KAKEMONO MAKIMONO
(— PUZZLE) REBUS JIGSAW
(—S IN BOOKS) BABY
(— WOVEN IN SILK) STEVENGRAPH
(COMIC —) DROLLERY
(RELIGIOUS —) TANKA
(STEREOSCOPIC —) ANAGLYPH
(THREE-DIMENSIONAL —) HOLOGRAM
(PREF.) PINAC(O)
PICTURE OF DORIAN GRAY
(AUTHOR OF —) WILDE
(CHARACTER IN —) ALAN GRAY VANE BASIL HENRY JAMES SIBYL DORIAN WOTTON CAMPBELL HALLWARD
PICTURESQUE VIVID EXOTIC QUAINT SCENIC GRAPHIC IDYLLIC ROMANTIC PICTORIAL
PICUL TAN PICO PIKOL
PIDDLE PICK PLAY DAWDLE PICKLE PUTTER TRIFLE
PIDDLING JERK MEASLY PALTRY TRIVIAL USELESS FOOTLING TRIFLING JERKWATER
PIDDOCK DACTYL PHOLAD PHOLAS
PIDGIN LANGUAGE SABIR
PIE PAI FLAM FLAN HEAP MESS PATE PILE TART DOWDY FLAWN PASTY PATTY TORTA TOURT AFFAIR BRIDLE CHEWET MAGPIE PASTRY TOURTE COBBLER SMASHER STRUDEL BAKEMEAT CRUSTADE FLAPJACK PANDOWDY SURPRISE TURNOVER SMASHOVER
(CUSTARD —) QUICHE
(GREEK —) SPANAKOPITA SPANOKAPITA SPANAKOPITTA
(MEAT —) FLOATER
(MINCE —) SHREDPIE
(PL.) BAKEMEAT
PIEBALD PIE PIED PIET MIXED PIETY PINTO CALICO MOTLEY SKEWBALD
PIECE BAT BIT COB CUT DAM FIG JOB LAB LOG MAN TUT GIRL MIND PART PISE PLAY BLYPE DAGON DRAMA DWANG FLOOR PEZZO SCRAP SHARD SHERD SHRED SLICE SNODE STEEK STUCK THROW COLLOP FARDEL FUGATO GOBBET PARCEL STITCH CANTLET EXAMPLE FLINDER FLITTER MORCEAU OPINION PICTURE PORTION SEGMENT DUOLOGUE EMBOLIUM FANDANGO PAINTING
(— AT END) HEELPIECE
(— FOR TWO) DUET DUOLOGUE
(— IN CHECKERS) DAM
(— IN ORGAN) THUMPER
(— LEFT) STUB
(— OF ARMOR) JAMB JAMBE
(— OF BAD LUCK) DIRDUM
(— OF BLANKET) DAGON
(— OF BLUBBER) BIBLE
(— OF CLOTH) REMNANT
(— OF DECEPTION) BEGUNK
(— OF DECORATED METAL) NIELLO
(— OF EIGHT) PIASTRE
(— OF FALSE HAIR) JANE
(— OF FIBER) NOIL
(— OF FIRED CLAY) TILE
(— OF FOOD) MORSEL
(— OF GOOD FORTUNE) GODSEND
(— OF GROUND SURROUNDED BY WASTE) HOPE
(— OF HARD WOOD) MOOT
(— OF LAND) ERF HAM LOT BUTT GORE PANE PARK PLOT CROFT LEASE PATCH SPONG SQUAT ESTATE GARDEN HUERTA RINCON SECTION CLEARAGE METAIRIE PROPERTY SOLIDATE PENINSULA
(— OF LIGHT ORDNANCE) ASPIC
(— OF LINEN) AMIT AMICE
(— OF LOG) SLAB
(— OF MAST) TONGUE
(— OF MATZOTH) AFIKOMEN
(— OF MEAT) EYE HEEL RAND COLLOP EPIGRAM
(— OF METAL) JAG COIN JAGG SPRAG
(— OF MISCHIEF) LARK
(— OF MONEY) COG SOU SHINER
(— OF NEEDLEWORK) SAMPLER
(— OF NEWS) NOVEL
(— OF NONSENSE) FUDGE TRIMTRAM
(— OF ORE) CHAT
(— OF PROPERTY) CHOSE SUBJECT
(— OF SAIL) HULLOCK
(— OF SCENERY) FLAT
(— OF SEPARATED LAND) BUTT
(— OF SKIN) BLYPE
(— OF SKIN FOR GLOVE) TRANK
(— OF SLATE) SLAT
(— OF SOAP) BALL
(— OF SOMETHING EDIBLE) STULL
(— OF TIMBER) FISH COULISSE FOREHOOK
(— OF TOAST) SLINGER
(— OF TOBACCO) FIG
(— OF TRACK) LEAD RUNBY
(— OF TRICKERY) CROOK CANTRIP
(— OF TURF) FLAG DIVOT SCRAW SHIRREL
(— OF WOOD) KIP LATH APRON BOARD CHUMP CHUNK PLANK SPOON WADDY BILLET COMMON STOWER TIMBER LIPPING
(— OF WORK) JOB CHAR TURN
(— OF WRITING) SCREED SCREEVE
(— OUT) EKE
(—S OF MACARONI) DITALI DITALINI
(— SPLIT OFF) SPLINT
(— TO PREVENT SLIPPING) CLEAT
(ARTILLERY —) DRAKE SAKER LANTACA
(BACKGAMMON —) BLOT STONE
(BROAD —) SHEET
(BROKEN —) BRACK MAMMOCK FRACTION
(BUTTING —) HURTER
(CHESS —) PIN KING PAWN ROOK QUEEN BISHOP CASTLE KNIGHT OFFICER
(DRAMATIC —) SKIT
(DREAMY —) REVERIE
(END — OF BUCKET) CANT
(FLAT —) FLAP FLAKE
(FUR —) PALATINE
(GOLD —) SLUG TALI
(IN —S) LIMBMEAL
(IRREGULAR —) SNAG
(KIND OF —) PERIOD
(LARDED — OF MEAT) DAUB
(LARGE —) HUNK MOLE STULL DOLLOP
(LEFT-OVER —) SCRAP
(LITERARY —) CAMEO
(LITTLE —) STNEKI SCANTLING
(LONG —) STRIP
(MAH JONGG —) TILE
(MISCELLANEOUS —S) ODDS
(MOVABLE — IN VIOLIN BOW) NUT
(MUSICAL —) ITEM CHORO DANCE ETUDE CHASER LESSON ALLEGRO ANDANTE BLUETTE CANZONA CANZONE CONCERTO DUOLOGUE ENTRACTE OVERTURE PASTORAL RHAPSODY BAGATELLE INVENTION DIVERTIMENTO
(NARROW —) LABEL STAVE STRIP
(ODD — OF CARPENTRY) DUTCHMAN
(PIANO —) NOVELETTE
(PROJECTING —) TANG
(ROTATING —) CAM ROTOR SPINDLE
(SAMPLE —) SWATCH
(SHAPELESS —) DUMP MAMMOCK
(SIDE —) RIB JAMB JAMBE
(SINGLE —) LENGTH
(SLENDER —) SPILL SLIVER
(SMALL —) BIT BOB NOB PEA CHIP SNIP TATE CRUMB PATCH PRILL SCRAP SPECK MORSEL SIPPET DRIBLET FLITTER PALLION SPLINTER
(SMALL — OF FLESH) GIGOT
(SMALL — OF WOOD) KIP
(SMALL —S) MATCHWOOD
(STRENGTHENING —) DWANG HURTER
(TAPERING —) GORE GUSSET
(THICK —) JUNK HUNCH
(THIN —) SHIM FLAKE SHIVE SLICE

(WEDGESHAPED — OF WOOD) GLUT SHIM
(100-REAL GOLD —) ISABELLA
(25-CENT —) CUTER
(4-DOLLAR GOLD —) STELLA
(PL.) MATERIAL NOBLEMEN
PIECEWORK SETWORK TUTWORK TASKWORK
PIECEWORKER JOBBER
PIECRUST BREAD COFFIN ABAISSE
PIED PINTO SHELD MAGPIED PIEBALD
PIED ANTELOPE BONTEBOK
PIEDFORT PATAGON
PIED WAGTAIL COB COBB PEER PILE PILLAR WAGGIE WASHER WATERIE SEEDBIRD WASHDISH WASHTAIL
PIEPLANT RHUBARB RHAPONTIC
PIER COB ANTA BELT COBB DOCK MOLE PILE QUAY TILT GROIN JETTY JOWEL JUTTY LEVEE STILT WHARF BRIDGE BUNDER MULLION STAGION PIEDROIT STELLING
(— CAP) SUMMER
(HALF —) RESPONSE
PIERCE CUT DAB DAG DEG DIG JAB JAG RIT BARB BEAR BITE BORE BROB BROD CLOY DART DIRL GORE HOLE HOOK LACE LACK PASS PINK POKE PROB PROG RIVE ROVE STAB STOB TAME TANG WHIP BREAK DRIFT DRILL ENTER GOUGE GRIDE LANCE PERCH PITCH POACH PREEN PROBE PRONG SHEAR SNICK SPEAR SPIKE STEEK STICK STING THIRL ATTAME BROACH CLEAVE DAGGER EMPALE FICCHE GIMLET IMPALE LAUNCH PRITCH RIDDLE SEARCH SKEWER STITCH STRIKE THRILL THRING THRUST WIMBLE ASSAGAI JAVELIN ENTHRILL LACERATE PUNCTURE PENETRATE
(PREF.) FORAMINI
PIERCED AJOURE CRIBRAL PERTUSE CRIBROSE PERFORATE
PIERCING SHY FELL HIGH KEEN LOUD TART ACUTE CLEAR EAGLE SHARP SNELL ARROWY BITTER BORING SHREWD SHRILL SNITHE SNITHY CUTTING GIMLETY POINTED PUNGENT DRILLING INCISIVE PERCEANT POIGNANT POUNCING STABBING STICKING PENETRATIVE
PIERHEAD MOLEHEAD
PIET PYOT DIPPER MAGPIE
PIETIST LABADIST
PIETISTIC DEVOUT
PIETY HONOR LOYALTY PIETISM DEVOTION SANCTION GODLINESS
PIFFLE BUFF FOLDEROL
PIG (ALSO SEE HOG, SWINE) COW FAR HAM HOG SLIP SLOB BACON BONAV BROCK CHEAT CHUCK GRICE INGOT PIGGY SHOAT APEREA BONHAM COCHON FARROW GUSSIE HOGGIE PORKET PORKIN SUCKER TITMAN WEANER BONNIVE GLUTTON GRUMPHY HOGLING PIGLING ROOKLER GRUNTLING
(— OUT) GORGE
(BROOD OF —S) TEAM
(CASTRATED —) BARROW
(CASTRATED MALE —) BARROW
(EIGHT —S) FODDER
(FEMALE —) SOW
(MALE —) BOAR
(PART OF —) EAR EYE HAM BUTT HOCK JOWL LOIN POLL TAIL TEAT FLANK SNOUT PICNIC FATBACK FOREFOOT SHOULDER SPARERIB TENDERLOIN
(SMALLEST — OF LITTER) DOLL TITMAN ANTHONY DILLING TANTANY TANTONY
(SUCKLING —) ROASTER
(UNDERSIZED —) RUNT TITMAN TEATMAN
(YOUNG —) ELT FAR SLIP GRICE GURRY
(YOUNG—) SHOAT SHOTE
(YOUNG —) BONEEN BONHAM SQUEAKER
(YOUNG FEMALE —) GILT
(PREF.) HYO
(SUFF.) CHOERUS
PIG DEER BABIRUSA
PIGEON DOO NUN OWL TOY BARB CLAY DOVE JACK KING KITE LUPE RUFF RUNT SPOT BALDY DOWVE FRILL HOMER KOKLA PIPER SQUAB WONGA CULTER CULVER CUSHAT DODLET DRAGON FEEDER HELMET JEWING MAGPIE MANUMA MAUMET MODENA POUTER PRIEST ROCKER SHAKER TRERON TURBIT TURNER WATTLE ANTWERP CARNEAU CARRIER CROPPER FANTAIL FINIKIN JACINTH JACOBIN MALTESE PINTADO SWALLOW TIPPLER TUMBLER BALDHEAD CAPUCHIN FINIKING HORSEMAN MANUTAGI RINGDOVE SASSOROL SQUABBER SQUEAKER SQUEALER FRILLBACK TOOTHBILL
(CLAY —) BIRD GYROPIGEON
(FLIGHTLESS —) SOLITAIRE
(STOOL —) PIG NARK
(YOUNG —) SQUAB
PIGEON BLOOD GARNET
PIGEON HAWK MERLIN
PIGEONHOLE BOX SLOT LABEL SHELVE ANALYZE CELLULE CLASSIFY CUBBYHOLE
(PL.) STOCK
PIGEON HOUSE COT DOOKET DOVECOT COLUMBARY
PIGEON PEA DAL TUR TARE ARHAR DAHIL GANDUL TURNER TURNOR CATJANG
PIGEON WOODPECKER FLICKER
PIGGERY PIGS PIGSTY HOGGERY POTTERY SWINERY CROCKERY
PIGGIE TOE
PIGGIN HANDY PIPKIN
PIGHEADED WILLFUL PERVERSE STUBBORN OBSTINATE
PIGHTLE PIKLE PICKLE PIDDLE PIGTAIL
PIG IRON GRUNDY
PIGLET PORKLING
PIGLIKE SUIFORM SUILINE SWINISH
PIGMENT (ALSO SEE DYE, COLOR) BLUE HEME BROWN COLOR EARTH GREEN HUMIN MORIN MUMMY PAINT STAIN TONER BRONZE CEROID CERUSE IDAEIN LITHOL MALVIN ORANGE PURPLE SIENNA VIOLET BEZETTA GOUACHE PAINTRY PUCCOON STAINER TURACIN ALTHAEIN COLORANT EXTENDER GOSSYPOL MELANOID PAINTURE TINCTURE UROPHEIN VERDITER
(— FOR WOODWORK) KOKOWAI
(— IN BUTTERFLY WING) PTERIN
(BLACK —) ABAISER MELANIN
(BLUE —) BICE SMALT CYANIN ALTHEIN CERULEUM MARENNIN
(BLUE-GREEN —) LEUCOCYAN
(BROWN —) MUMMY SEPIA UMBER BISTER FUSCIN ASTERIN SINOPIA
(BROWNISH-YELLOW —) SIENNA
(GRAPE —) ENIN OENIN
(GREEN —) VERDITER
(MADDER-ROOT —) RUBIATE
(ORANGE-RED —) REALGAR
(PLANT —) CYANIN
(RED —) HAEM LAKE ARUMIN PATISE SANDYX AMATITO KOKOWAI PUCCOON SCARLET SINOPIA CAPSUMIN URORUBIN URRHODIN VERMILION
(RED-VIOLET —) TURACIN
(WHITE —) CERUSE ANATASE LITHOPONE
(YELLOW —) MORIN FLAVIN PURREE ETIOLIN FISETIN GAMBOGE PUCCOON CAROTENE DIATOMIN GALANGIN GENTISIN MASSICOT ORPIMENT UROBILIN
(PREF.) CHROM(AT)(ATO)(I)(IDIO)(O)
PIGMENTATION COLOR LENTIL ARGYRIA LENTIGO JAUNDICE NIGRITIES
(SKIN —) ARGYRIA
(SUFF.) CHROMIA
PIGNUS PAWN PLEDGE
PIGNUT ARNOT ARNUT HOGNUT
PIGS' FEET CRUBEEN PETTITOES
PIGSKIN SADDLE FOOTBALL
PIGSNEY EYE DARLING
PIGSTY FRANK CRUIVE HOGCOTE HOGGERY PIGGERY SWINESTY
PIGTAIL BRAID PLAIT QUEUE COLETA
PIGWASH SWILL
PIGWEED QUINOA BEETROOT CARELESS GOOSEFOOT
PIK DRA PICKI PICKL ENDAZE ENDASEH
PIKA CONY HAIR HARE LEPORID LAGOMORPH
PIKE GED DORE DORY GADE GEDD JACK LUCE TANG TOUG TUCK HAKED LUCET SNAKE SNOOK STING VOUGE SALMON SAUGER JAVELIN WALLEYE BLOWFISH GLASSEYE JACKFISH NORTHERN PARTISAN PICKEREL POULAINE TURNPIKE MUSKELLUNGE
PIKELET CRUMPET
PIKEMAN PIKE WATTLEBOY
PIKE PERCH FOGASH PERCID SANDER SAUGER ZANDER
PIKER TRAMP VAGRANT TELLTALE TIGHTWAD VAGABOND
PILASTER ANTA PIER RIDGE ALETTE ALLETTE RESPOND TELAMON
PILCHARD FUMADO ALEWIFE SARDINE MENHADEN
PILCORN OAT
PILDASH **(FATHER OF —)** NAHOR
(MOTHER OF —) MILCAH
PILE COP FUR LOT NAP PIE TIP BALE BANK BING BULK BUNG BURR COCK DASS DECK DESS DOWN HACK HAIR HEAP LEET LOAD PEEL PIER POLE POOK PYRE REEK RUCK SESS SHAG SPUD AMASS CANCH CLAMP CROWD FAGOT POINT SPILE SPIRE STACK STILT TOWER CASTLE FAGGOT FENDER FILLER GALGAL PILLAR RICKLE RUCKLE FORTUNE JAVELIN PYRAMID REACTOR SPINDLE CROWBILL INCREASE SANDPILE
(— CROSSWISE) COB
(— CURD) CHEDDAR
(— OF BRICKS) HACK CLAMP
(— OF CLOTH) LAY
(— OF HAY) RICK SHOCK DOODLE HAYCOCK HAYRICK
(— OF ICE) HUMMOCK
(— OF LOGS) DECK
(— OF PLATES) BUNG
(— OF REFUSE) DUSTHEAP
(— OF SALT FISH) BULK
(— OF SEALSKINS) PAN
(— OF SHEAVES) SESS
(— OF SHEETS) LIFT
(— OF STONES) ISLAND STONAGE WARLOCK
(— OF TOBACCO) BULK
(— OF WOOD) STRAND
(— TO BE BURNT) PYRE
(— UP) BIG BULK CORD RICK COMPILE ACCUMULATE
(— WHEAT SHOCKS) STITCH
(IRON —) SPINDLE
(LITTLE —) HOT HOTT
(LOOSE —) RICKLE
(ROCK —) HOODOO
(SMALL —) COCK CANCH
(PL.) FIG DRIFT
PILEA ADICEA
PILEATED WOODPECKER LOGCOCK WOODCOCK
PILE DRIVER TUP FISTUCA HERCULES IMPACTER
(— DOLLY) FOLLOWER
(— WEIGHT) RAM TUP MONKEY
PILEUS CAP MITRA PILEOLUS
PILEWORT CRAIN CRANE FICARY FIGWORT CELANDINE
PILFER NIM NIP ROB CRIB HOOK PALM PELF PICK PILK PRIG SMUG SNIG FILCH MICHE MOOCH PILCH PROWL SHARP SLOCK STEAL SWIPE FINGER MAGPIE MOOTCH NIBBLE PICKLE SMOUCH SNITCH CABBAGE MANAVEL PLUNDER PURLOIN SNAFFLE UNHITCH PETTIFOG SCROUNGE
PILFERER PRIG PIKER TAKER SLOCKER FINGERER SLOCKSTER
PILFERING CRIB MICHING PICKING THIEVISH

PILGRIM HADJ HAJI HADJI HAJJI PALMER PELERIN PEREGRIN WAYFARER
(MUSLIM —) HADJ
PILGRIMAGE TRIP TURUS VOYAGE JOURNEY
(— TO MECCA) HADJ
(BRETON —) PARDON
PILGRIM BROWN FRIAR
PILGRIM'S PROGRESS (AUTHOR OF —) BUNYAN
(CHARACTER IN —) POPE PAGAN PIETY SLOTH PLIANT SIMPLE CHARITY DESPAIR HOPEFUL SINCERE APOLLYON FAITHFUL GOODWILL PRUDENCE WATCHFUL CHRISTIAN FORMALISM HYPOCRISY IGNORANCE KNOWLEDGE OBSTINATE DISCRETION EVANGELIST EXPERIENCE PRESUMPTION
(LAND IN —) BEULAH
PILING SPILING STOCKADE
(PL.) STARLING
PILL PIL ROB BALL BARK GOLI PEEL POOL CREEK CACHOU EXTORT TABLET UNHAIR DESPOIL DIURNAL GLOBULE GRANULE PARVULE PILLULE PREFORM BASEBALL GOOFBALL BLACKBALL CIGARETTE
(AROMATIC —) CACHOU
(LARGE —) BALL BOLUS
(LITTLE —) PILULA PILULE
(SLEEPING —) GOOFBALL
(SMALL —) MICRODOT
PILLAGE LOOT PEEL PILL PREY SACK BOOTY FORAY HARRY REAVE RIFLE SPOIL HARROW MARAUD PICORY RAPINE RAVAGE DESPOIL PICKEER PLUNDER RANSACK ROBBERY BOOTHALE EXPILATE PURCHASE SPOLIATE DEVASTATE
PILLAGER PEELER PILLER ROBBER SACKER SPOILER SNAPHANCE
PILLAGING EXECUTION PREDATORY
PILLAR COG HERM JAMB PACK PIER PILE POST PROP STUD TERM JAMBE NEWEL SHAFT STELA STELE STOCK STONE STOOP STUMP CIPPUS COLUMN HERMES PILLER STAPLE BEDPOST DEADMAN TRESTLE TRUMEAU BOUNDARY MASSEBAH PEDESTAL RESPONSE STANCHION
(— CAPPED WITH SLAB) BILITH
(— IN LARGE DOORWAY) TRUMEAU
(— IN MINE) STOOK STUMP
(— OF COAL) SPURN STOOK STOOP
(—S OF HERCULES) ABILA CALPE
(— SUPPORTING ARCH) RESPONSE
(— SURMOUNTED BY HEAD) HERMES
(BUDDHIST —) LAT
(CHANGED TO —) OLENUS
(EARTH —) HOODOO
(MAN-LIKE —) TELAMON
(ROCK —) STACK GENDARME
(SACRED —) ASHERAH
(SEMITE —) MASSEBAH
(STONE —) CIPPUS
(TEMPORARY —) DEADMAN
(UPRIGHT —) STANDARD
(4-SIDED —) OBELISK
(PL.) CRURA
(PREF.) CION(O) STELO STYL(I)(O)
(SUFF.) STELE STYLAR STYLE STYLI(C) STYLOUS
PILLARIST STYLITE
PILLAS PILCORN PILKINS
PILLBOX SCATULA
PILLBUG ISOPOD KEESLIP MILLEPED PILLWORM CHEESELIP
PILLED BALD SHAVEN TONSURED
PILLION PAD PILLOW SADDLE CUSHION
PILLORY CANG THEW JOUGS TRONE CANGUE CRUCIFY HALSFANG
PILLOW COD BOTT DAWN PEEL PILE REST FLOAT WANGER BOLSTER CUSHION FUSTIAN HEADING OREILLER PULVINAR
(PREF.) PULVILLI PULVINI
PILLOWCASE COD BEAR PILL SHAM PILLIVER
PILLOWY PULVINAR
PILM DUST
PILON BONUS LAGNIAPPE
PILOSE HAIRY HIRSUTE PILEOUS
PILOT ACE SPY JOCK KIWI COACH GUARD GUIDE STEER AIRMAN ESCORT MANAGE THAMUS AVIATOR CAPTAIN CONDUCT HOBBLER LODEMAN SHIPMAN WINGMAN AIREDALE GOVERNOR HELMSMAN NAVIGATE NAVIGATOR PALINURUS WHEELSMAN COWCATCHER
(AUTHOR OF —) COOPER
(AUTOMATIC —) GEORGE
(CHARACTER IN —) TOM GRAY ALICE JONES MERRY COFFIN DILLON EDWARD HOWARD MANUAL MUNSON CECILIA PLOWDEN RICHARD GRIFFITH DUNSCOMBE KATHERINE BARNSTABLE CHRISTOPHER BORROUGHCLIFFE
(DUD —) PRUNE
(UNLICENSED —) HOBBLER
PILOT BIRD PLOVER
PILOT FISH ROMERO JACKFISH AMBERFISH
PILOTHOUSE TEXAS CHARTHOUSE CONNINGTOWER
PILUM PESTLE JAVELIN
PIMENTA MYRTAL
PIMENTO PIMENTA ALLSPICE PIMIENTO
PIMP MACK BULLY CADET FAGOT PONCE SNEAK MACRIO PANDER MACKMAN RUFFIAN INFORMER PROCURER PURVEYOR SCOUNDREL SOUTENEUR
PIMPERNEL BURNET WAYWORT EYEBRIGHT MARGELINE WINCOPIPE
PIMPLE GUM NOB PAP WEN ZIT BURL KNOB PUSH QUAT SPOT BLAIN BOTCH HICKY PLOOK PLOUK PLUKE WHELK BLOTCH BOUTON BUTTON PAPULA PAPULE TETTER BUBUKLE PUSTULE PIMGENET WHEYWORM
(— ON NOSE) RUMBUD
(PREF.) CHALAZI CHALAZO PAPULI PAPULO
PIN FID FIX HOB HUB LAG LEG NOG PEG PEN ACUS APEX AXLE BANK BOLT LILL MOOD PEEN POST PRIN PROP PYNE RUNG STUD DRIFT HUMOR KAYLE POINT PREEN SPILL THOLE BOBBIN BODKIN BROACH BROOCH CALIGO COTTER CURLER FASTEN HATPIN JOGGLE NORMAN PINNET SKEWER SPIGOT TEMPER TENPIN TOGGEL TONGUE TRIFLE BAYONET CONFINE ENCLOSE GUDGEON HAIRPIN IMPOUND LOCKPIN PUSHPIN SPINDLE TAMPION TANGENT TUMBLER WOOLDER FORELOCK PINNACLE
(— FOR FITTING PLANKS) SETBOLT
(— IN AXLETREE) LINCHPIN
(— IN RIFLE) TIGE
(— OF DIAL) STYLE GNOMON
(— OF LANTERN PINION) RUNDLE
(— OF WATCH) DART
(— ON CLAVICHORD KEY) TANGENT
(— TO HOLD BEDCLOTHES) BEDSTAFF
(— USED AS TARGET) HOB
(BELAYING —) CAVIL
(BOWLING —) DUCKPIN HEADPIN KINGPIN SLEEPER
(BOWLING —S) DEADWOOD
(CARPENTRY —) DOWEL
(COUPLING —) DRAWBOLT
(ENGAGING —) BAYONET
(HAIR —) BARRETTE
(HEADED —) RIVET
(JEWELED —) PROP
(NECKTIE —) TIETAC TIETACK
(OAR —) THOLE
(ORNAMENTAL —) AGLET AIGLET
(PIVOT —) PINTLE
(SMALL —) LILL MINIKIN MICROPIN
(SPLIT —) COTTER FORELOCK
(SURVEYOR'S —) ARROW
(TAPERED —) DRIFT
(TIRLING —) RISP
(WOODEN —) DOWEL SPILE TRENAIL
(PL.) LEGS KAILS DEADWOOD
(PREF.) PERONEO PERONO
PINACOID BASE HEMIDOME
PINAFORE BRAT SLIP TIDE TIDY TIER TYER DAIDLY PINNER SAVEALL SLIPPER GABERDINE
PINBALL BAGATELLE
PINBALL MACHINE PACHINKO
PINCASE POPPET
PINCE-NEZ NIPPER LORGNON NOSEPINCH
PINCER CLAW
PINCERS TEU TEW CLAM CHELA TUARN PLIERS TURKIS WYNRIS FORCEPS MULLETS NIPPERS PINCHER PINSONS TWEEZERS
PINCH NAB NIP TAD TOP VEX WRY BITE CLAM HURT POOK PUSH STOP TAIT TATE TUCK CHACK CRIMP GRIPE HINCH PUGIL SNUFF SQUAT STEAL STINT TAPER THEFT TWEAK WRING ARREST CLUTCH COLLAR EXTORT HARASS NARROW SNITCH STRAIT STRESS TWITCH SCRINCH SQUEEZE JUNCTURE PRESSURE SHORTAGE STRAITEN VELLICATE
(— OF SNUFF) SNEESH SNEESHIN
(— WITH COLD) NIRL
(— WITH HUNGER) CLAM CLEM
PINCHBECK SHAM CHEAP SPURIOUS PRETENDED
PINCHED CHITTY WASTED HAGGARD PUNGLED SQUINCH
PINCHING CHACK
PINCHPENNY CARL MISER NIGGARD NIGGARDLY
PINDARIC ODE WILD
PINE IE ARA LIM ACHE CHIL CHIR FADE FLAG HALA HONE IEIE KAIL WANT AGGAG DROOP DWAIN GRIEF KAURI MATAI MATSU MOURN OCOTE PINON THUJA WANZE WEARY WRIST YEARN APACHE AROLLA DUSTER FAMINE GRIEVE HUNGER LAMENT PANDAN SHRINK SORROW STARVE TOATOA TORFEL WITHER CYPRESS DAISING DWINDLE FORPINE FOXTAIL JEFFREY LAUHALA TARWOOD TORMENT TORTURE AKAMATSU AUSTRIAN GALAGALA LANGUISH LOBLOLLY LONGLEAF PINASTER STAGHORN TANEKAHA VANQUISH
(— AWAY) PEAK DROOP DWINE SNURP WANZE WINDER FORPINE MACERATE
(AUSTRALIAN —) BEEFWOOD
(GROUND —) FOXTAIL
(KIND OF —) MUGHO JEFFREY
(PITCH —) THYME
(PREF.) PINI PITYO
PINEAPPLE BOMB NANA PINA PINO PITA ANANA ANANAS ABACAXI GRENADE
PINE FINCH SISKIN
PINE MARTEN SABLE
PINE NEEDLE SHAT SPILL PINING ALFILARIA
(PL.) TWINKLES
PINE TREE STATE MAINE
PINFEATHER PEN STUMP STIPULE
PINFISH CHUB SPOT JIMMY PORGY SARGO
PINFOLD POUND
PING KNOCK
PING-PONG SHIFT BOUNCE
PINGRASS ALFILERIA
PINGUIN MAYA ANANAS AGUAMAS PINUELA HUIPILLA
PINGUITUDE FATNESS OBESITY OILINESS
PINING SICK LANGUOR HOMESICK LOVELORN
PINION NOIL WING PINON QUILL PENNON SARCEL SECURE LANTERN PINACLE SHACKLE TRUNDLE FLIGHTER WALLOWER
PINION WHEEL MOBILE
PINITOL SENNITE MATEZITE
PINK JAG PIP CYME DAWN DECK FADE MICE PING STAB WINK ADORN BLINK CORAL ELITE MOVED SWELL WOUND AURORE BISQUE CHERUB FIESTA HEIGHT MINNOW POUNCE SHRIMP SILENE TATTOO ZEPHYR ANNATTO ARBUTUS BEGONIA BERMUDA BLOSSOM CAMPION EXTREME

PARAGON REVEREE SANDUST TUSSORE CONFETTI COQUETTE DECORATE DIANTHUS GILLIVER LIMEWORT RADIANCE RECAMIER
PINKED JAGGED
PINKIE PIRLIE
PINKROOT REDROOT WORMWEED STARBLOOM
PINNA EAR EARFLAP PINNULE APHLEBIA AURICULA PAVILION
PINNACE BARK CROWN WOMAN BARQUE PINNAGE MISTRESS
PINNACLE IT PIN TOP ACME APEX CREST CROWN IDEAL SERAC SPIRE THUMB FINIAL HEIGHT SUMMIT GENDARME
(ICE —) SERAC
(ROCKY —) TOR HOODOO AIGUILLE GENDARME
PINNATE WINGED
PINNER PINDER FLANDAN STICKER
PINNIPED SEAL
PINNULE FIN
PINOCHLE BINOCLE GOULASH AIRPLANE
(— SCORE) MELD
PINPILLOW PIMPLO
PINPOINT ISOLATE
(— OF LIGHT) GLEAM
PINT O GULL PINNET SWIGGER OCTARIUS
(FOURTH —) GILL JACK
(HALF —) CUP NIP GILL JACK CUPFUL NIPPERKIN
(9-10THS —) MUTCHKIN
PINTADO CERO PIED SIER SEARER SIERRA SPOTTED KINGFISH
PINTAIL DUCK SMEE SPIKE SPRIG GROUSE SMETHE CRACKER LADYBIRD LONGNECK PIKETAIL
PINTANO PILOT COCKEYE CHIRIVITA
PINTID EMPEINE
PINTO PAINT
PINTO BEAN ROSILLO
PINUP CHEESECAKE
PINWEED
(PL.) LECHEA
PINWHEEL WINDMILL
PINWORM NEMA OXYURID
PIN WRENCH SPANULE
PINZA EZIO
PION MESON
PIONEER BLAZE GUIDE MINER GROPER HALUTZ SETTLE CHALUTZ EXPLORE EARLIEST EMIGRANT ORIGINAL RAWHIDER VOORTREKKER
PIONEERS (AUTHOR OF —) COOPER
(CHARACTER IN —) JOHN GRANT HIRAM JONES NATTY BUMPPO LOUISA OLIVER TEMPLE EDWARDS RICHARD DOOLITTLE EFFINGHAM ELIZABETH CHINGACHGOOK
PIOUS PI HOLY WISE FROOM GODLY MORAL SEELY DEVOUT DIVINE INWARD PIETIC CANTING DUTIFUL GODDARD PITEOUS SAINTED SAINTLY FAITHFUL REVERENT RELIGIOUS
PIP DIE CHIP ECHO KILL PAIP PEEP SEED SPOT SPECK ACINUS DEFEAT PIPPIN BLACKBALL
PIPAL BO FIG
PIPE TD BIN GUN HUB TAP TEE BONG BUTT CALL CANE DALE DRIP DUCT FLUE HOSE LINE MAIN MUTE PULE REED TILE TUBE WEEP WORM BLAST BRAIL BRIAR BRIER CANAL CANEL CINCH CRANE CROSS CUTTY HOOKA PROBE PUNGI QUILL RIDER RISER SPOUT STAND STRAW TEWEL TRUMP TRUNK VOICE BRANCH BURROW CALEAN CASING DUCTUS DUDEEN FAUCET FILLER GEWGAW HEWGAG HOGGER HOOKAH KINURA NIPPLE NOTICE NOZZLE OFFLET OFFSET POOGYE RANKET SLEEVE SLOUCH SLUICE SUCKER TROWEL TUBULE TUNNEL UPTAKE WEEPER CHANNEL CHANTER CHIBOUK CONDUIT DUCTURE FISTULA HYDRANT SERVICE SPARGER SPINDLE SUCTION TALLBOY TWEEDLE WHISTLE CALIDUCT DOWNTAKE GALOUBET LAMPHOLE MIRLITON NARGHILE NARGILEH PENSTOCK SEMIDOLE SUSPIRAL TELLTALE THRIBBLE
(— AS NAVIGATION AID) SPINDLE
(— BENDER) HICKEY
(— BOWL) STUMMEL
(— FOR CONDUCTING WATER) LEADER
(— JOINT) TURNOUT
(— OF ORE) BUNNY
(— OF PAN) SYRINX
(— OF QUEEN BEE) TEET
(— ON BAGPIPE) DRONE CHANTER
(— SUPPORT) CRADLE
(— TAB) TACK
(— TO MUFFLE TRUMPET) SORDINE
(— USED IN WELL) STRING
(— WITH SOCKET ENDS) HUB
(BOWL AND STEM OF —) STUMMEL
(CEREMONIAL —) CALUMET
(CLAMMING —) BRAIL
(CLEAN A —) REAM
(CONNECTING —) HOGGER
(FLUE —) LABIAL
(HEATING —) CALIDUCT
(IRISH —) DUDEEN
(KIND OF —) UILLEANN
(MUSICAL —) BODY GEWGAW FISTULA SORDINE HORNPIPE SCHWEGEL
(OATEN —) OAT
(ORGAN —) FLUE KINURA LABIAL ERZAHLER SCHWEGEL TREMOLANT
(ORGAN —S) MONTRE
(PART OF —) BIT BOWL STEM SHANK SHAPE SADDLE MOUTHPIECE
(PEACE —) CALUMET
(PROJECTING —) BRACKET
(RESIDUE IN OPIUM —) YENSHGEE
(SEWER —) SLANT
(SHEPHERD'S —) REED LARIGOT CHALUMEAU
(SNAKE-CHARMER'S —) PUNGI
(TOBACCO —) GUN CLAY BRIAR BRIER CUTTY HOOKA STRAW CALEAN DUDEEN HOOKAH BULLDOG CHIBOUK CHILLUM CORNCOB BILLIARD CALABASH MEERSCHAUM
(TOY —) HEWGAG
(VERTICAL —) STACK LAMPHOLE
(WATER — FOR ENGINE) SLOUCH
(4 LENGTHS OF —) FOURBLE
(PREF.) AUL(O) SIPHON(O) SOLEN(O) SYRING(O) TUBI TUBO TUBULI TUBULO
PIPECLAY CAM CALM CAUM
PIPED DRUNK JETTED
PIPEFISH EARL LONGJAW NEEDLEFISH
PIPELAYER YARNER
PIPESTEM STOPPEL STOPPLE
PIPETTE PIPET TASTER
PIPEWORT HATPIN WOOLWEED
PIPING HOSE SOFT VERY CRYING ROULEAU WAILING WEEPING TRANQUIL
PIPING CROW CASSICAN FLUTEBIRD
PIPIRI PITIRRI
PIPISTRELLE BAT NOCTULE
PIPIT PEEP TEETAN WEKEEN CHEEPER SKYLARK TIETICK TITLARK TITLING WAGTAIL LINGBIRD TWITLARK
PIPPIN PIP APPLE PEPPIN RIBSTON
PIPSISSEWA EVERGREEN WINTERGREEN
PIQUANCY SALT ZEST JUICE FLAVOR GINGER TARTNESS
PIQUANT BOLD RACY JUICY NUTTY SALTY SHARP SPICY TASTY ZESTY LIVELY SEVERE CUTTING PEPPERY PUNGENT POIGNANT STINGING
(SHARPLY —) ZINGY
PIQUE FRET GOAD PEAK PICK PIKE PYKE TICK ANNOY PRISE SNUFF SPITE STING HARASS MALICE NETTLE PRITCH STRUNT CHIGGER OFFENSE PROVOKE UMBRAGE IRRITATE MARCELLA
PIRACY CAPTURE PIRATISM
PIRAGUA CANOE DUGOUT PIROGUE PETTIAGUA
PIRANHA PIRAI CARIBE PIRAYA
PIRARUCU PAICHE ARAPAIMA
PIRATE CAPER ROVER ROBBER VIKING CATERAN CORSAIR PICKEER SCUMMER ALGERINE MAROONER PICAROON BUCCANEER SALLEEMAN
(— FLAG) ROGER BLACKJACK
PIRENE (FATHER OF —) ASOPUS ACHELOUS
(MOTHER OF —) METOPE
(SON OF —) CENCHRIAS
PIRIPIRI BIRK BIRCH MAPAN
PIRL SPIN TWINE TWIST REVOLVE
PIRN QUILL BOBBIN PIRNIE SPINDLE
PIROGUE CANOE PERIOQUE
PIROPLASM BABESIA
PIROSHKI PIROGEN
PIROUETTE TURN
PISCINA POOL TANK BASIN SACRARY LAVATORY SACRARIUM
PISE CAJON PISAY
PISHOGUE CHARM SPELL SORCERY WITCHERY
PISMIRE ANT EMMET
PISOLITE PEASTONE
PISTACHIO FISTIC PISTICK
PISTIL CHIVE CARPEL UMBONE POINTEL
(PL.) GYNECIUM
(PREF.) GYN(AE)(AEO)(E)(EO)(O) GYNAECO GYNANDRO GYNECO
(SUFF.) GYN
PISTILLATE FEMALE
PISTOL DAG GAT GUN POP ROD BULL COLT DAGG IRON TACK FLUTE RIFLE STICK BARKER BUFFER BULDER BULLER CANNON DRAGON HEATER POTGUN RIFFLE ROSCOE BULLDOG DUNGEON SHOOTER TICKLER DERINGER PETRONEL REPORTER REVOLVER PEPPERBOX
(TOY —) SPARKLER
PISTON BUCKET FORCER PALLET SUCKER EMBOLUS PLUNGER
(— HUB) SPIDER
PIT PET POT PUT BURY CIST DELF DELL DISC DISK FOSS HELL HOLE KHUD KIST LAKE MINE PLAY PUTT SEED SILO SINK SUMP SWAG TURN WEEM WELL ABYSM ABYSS CRYPT DELFT DITCH FOSSA FOVEA FROST GRAVE LEACH MATCH PITCH PORUS SLACK SLUIG TREAD AREOLE BORROW BUNKER KERNEL OPPOSE RADDLE WALLOW ABADDON ALVEOLA AMPULLA BOTHROS CHARPIT FOSSULA FOXHOLE HANDLER LATRINE MEGARON PINHOLE VARIOLE WINNING CESSPOOL CYPHELLA DOWNFALL FAVEOLUS FENESTRA POCKMARK PUNCTULE WELLHOLE
(— FOR BAKING) IMU UMU
(— FOR OFFERINGS) BOTHROS
(— OF STOMACH) MARK WIND ANTICARDIUM
(— OF THEATER) GROUND PARTERRE
(— ON COCKROACH HEAD) FENESTRA
(— ON LICHENS) LACUNA CYPHELLA
(— SACRED TO DEMETER) MEGARON
(AUTHOR OF —) NORRIS
(BITTER —) STIPPEN
(BOTTOMLESS —) ABYSS ABADDON BARATHRUM
(CHARACTER IN —) PAGE WESS LAURA CURTIS GRETRY JADWIN SHELDON CORTHELL CRESSLER DEARBORN
(COAL —) HEUCH HEUGH WINNING
(COOKING —) IMU
(FODDER —) SILO
(MAORI —) RUA
(MIRY —) SLUIG
(RIFLE —) SANGAR
(ROOFED —) CIST KIST
(SALT —) VAT PEZOGRAPH
(SAND —) BUNKER
(SMALL —) AREOLE LACUNA STAPLE
(TANNING —) LIME LAYER LEACH HANDLER LAYAWAY SUSPENDER
(PREF.) BOTHR(I)(IO)(O) FOVEI
PITA PITO YUCCA ARGHAN

PITCH GO DIP FIT KEY LAB MEL PIC TAR BUCK CANT CHAT CODE COOK DING FALL FORK HURL PECK PICK PLUG RAKE TELL TONE TOSS ABODE BOOST BUNCH CHUCK FLING LABOR LURCH PLANT SLENT SLOPE SPIEL THROW TWIRL BINDER CAREEN DIRECT ENCAMP FILLER LENGTH MALTHA MANJAK PLUNGE SQUARE TOTTER TUMBLE VOLLEY WICKET CURRENT NARRATE ALKITRAN OVERHANG
(— AT A MARK) LAG
(— FROM FIR TREES) ALKITRAN
(— INSIDE) JAM
(— INTO TROUGH OF SEA) SEND
(— OF BIRD OF PREY) PLACE
(— OF HELIX) JAW
(— TENT) TELD
(— TENTS) CAMP
(ABOVE —) SHARP
(AUCTION —) SETBACK
(BASEBALL —) CURVE STRIKE CRIPPLE SPITTER FADEAWAY KNUCKLER SPITBALL BRUSHBACK
(BELOW —) FLAT
(COBBLER'S —) CODE
(FULL —) VOLLEY
(GLANCE —) MANJAK MANJACK
(HIGH —) BLOOPER
(HIGHEST —) PRIDE
(IDENTITY IN —) UNISON
(MINERAL —) BITUMEN
(PREF.) MISERI
PITCH APPLE COPEI CUPAY
PITCHBLENDE CLEVEITE
PITCHED SET
(PREF.) **(— BELOW BASS)** CONTRA
PITCHER JUG JACK OLLA PILL PRIG BUIRE CROCK CRUET GALON GORGE GOTCH AFTABA CROUKE GALLON HURLER POURIE STRAIN URCEUS CANETTE CHUCKER FLINGER GROWLER STARTER STOPPER TWIRLER URCEOLE AIGUIERE ASCIDIUM OENOCHOE SOUTHPAW MOUNDSMAN
(— AND CATCHER) BATTERY
(— FOR BEER) GROWLER
(— OF ORCHID) BUCKET
(— SHAPED LIKE MAN) TOBY
(— WITH ONE HANDLE) URCEUS
(BULGING —) GOTCH
(EARTHEN —) GEORG GORGE
(KIND OF —) RELIEF
(RELIEF —) FIREMAN
(RELIEF —S) BULLPEN
(REMOVE — FROM BASEBALL GAME) DERRICK
(WIDEMOUTHED —) EWER
PITCHER PLANT BISCUIT FLYTRAP FEVERCUP FOXGLOVE WATERCUP NEPENTHES SKUNKWEED
PITCHFORK EVIL PICK PIKE PICKEL SHEPPECK PITCHPIKE
(THATCHER'S —) GROOM
(PL.) HARD
PITCHHOLE CAHOT
PITCHMAN VENDER SALESMAN
PITCH PINE THYME
PITCH PIPE TUNER EPITONION
PITCHSTONE RETINITE
PITCHY BLACK
PITEOUS MEAN PALTRY PITIFUL MERCIFUL MOURNFUL PIERCING
PITFALL PIT FALL TRAP SNARE DANGER TRAPFALL
PITH JET PUT SAP CORE GIST MEAT PULP PUTT SOLA HEART VIGOR ENERGY KERNEL MARROW ESSENCE EXTRACT MEDULLA NUCLEUS PAPYRUS STRENGTH
(PREF.) MEDULLI METR(O) PULPE PULPI PULPO
PITH HELMET TOPI TOPEE
PITHINESS BREVITY
PITHON (FATHER OF —) MICAH
PITH TREE AMBATCH
PITHY CRISP MEATY SAPPY TERSE STRONG CONCISE LACONIC MARROWY SUCCINCT
PITIABLE SAD POOR SEELY WOFUL RUEFUL WOEFUL FORLORN PITIFUL
PITIFUL MEAN MEEK RUTH SILLY SORRY PALTRY RUEFUL TENDER HANGDOG RUESOME RUTHFUL MERCIFUL PATHETIC
PITILESS GRIM CRUEL STERN STONY BRASSY SAVAGE RUTHLESS UNPITIED MERCILESS
PITMAN GEORDIE
PITTANCE BIT ALMS DOLE GIFT MITE SONG TRIFLE BEQUEST
PITTED FOVEATE OPPOSED PUNCTATE ALVEOLATE
PITTER STONER
PITTHEUS (DAUGHTER OF —) AETHRA
(FATHER OF —) PELOPS
(PUPIL OF —) THESEUS
PITURI BEDGERY PITCHERY
PIT VIPER- MOCCASIN
PITY RUE ACHE MEAN MOAN PETE PITE RUTH MERCY PIETY REIVE SCATH BEMOAN PATHOS MERCIFY REMORSE WAESUCK CLEMENCY SYMPATHY COMPASSION
PIVOT TOE AXIS CRUX SLEW SLUE TURN HEART HINGE CENTER SLOUGH WORDLE GUDGEON TRAVERSE TRUNNION
PIVOTAL KEY POLAR CENTRAL TROCHOID
(— POINT) KNUCKLE
PIVOTING DISHRAG
PIVOTMAN CENTER
PIVOT STAND PEDESTAL
PIXILATED DAFT DAFFY DOTTY DRUNK FLAKY KOOKY PIXIE BEMUSED PUCKISH TOUCHED CONFUSED WHIMSICAL
PIXY ELF FAIRY PYGMY ROGUE IMPISH RASCAL SPRITE PUCKISH ROGUISH
PIZE OATH PISE CURSE
PLACABLE WEAK QUIET PACABLE PEACEFUL YIELDING FORGIVING
PLACARD BILL POST TITLE POSTER TICKET AFFICHE REDLINE STOMACHER
PLACATE CALM GENTLE PACIFY PLEASE SOOTHE APPEASE FORGIVE
PLACE L DO BIT FIX PUT SET AREA HOLE LIEU PLAT PLOT POSE POST RANK ROOM SEAT SITE SITU SPOT STEL STEP STOW TEXT VICE YARK BEING ESTER ESTRE HOUSE JOINT LOCUS PLAZA POINT POSIT SCENE SITUS STALL STATE STEAD STELL STOUR WHERE BESTOW CHARGE GROUND IMPOSE INVEST LAYOUT LOCALE LOCATE OFFICE POSSIE RECKON ROOMTH ALLODGE ARRANGE DEPOSIT KITCHEN STATION ABDITORY ALLOCATE DIGGINGS EMPORIUM LOCATION POSITION
(— ALONE) ISOLATE
(— ALTERNATELY) STAGGER
(— APART) ENISLE
(— BEFORE) APPOSE PREFIX
(— BETWEEN) INTERPOSE
(— BY FORCE) PILT
(— CROSSWISE) THWART
(— DEDICATED TO GOD) TEMENOS
(— EXACTLY) PINPOINT
(— FISH IN SALTING BIN) KENCH
(— FOR CATTLE) CAMP
(— FOR DUMPING RUBBISH) SHOOT
(— FOR GAMES) GYMKHANA
(— FOR HAWKING) RIVER
(— FOR MILKING) LOAN
(— FOR MILKING COWS) LOAN
(— FOR MORTAR AND BRICK) FROG
(— FOR PHEASANTS) STEW
(— FOR PRAYERS) IDGAH
(— FOR RABBITS) WARREN
(— FOR RECEPTION) RECEIPT
(— FOR RUBBISH DEPOSITS) LAYSTALL
(— FOR SEETHING) STEW
(— FOR SLEEPING) BED BUNK DOSS FLOP LAIR LIBKIN
(— FOR STROLLING) PROMENADE
(— FOR TORTURE) CATASTA
(— FOR TRAINING HORSES) LONGE
(— FROM WHICH JURY IS TAKEN) VENUE
(— IN) INNEST
(— IN COMPACT MASS) STOW
(— IN LINE) RANK
(— IN OFFICE) INVEST
(— IN ORDER) ARRAY ENRANK
(— IN WATERFALL) LEAP
(— MUCH FREQUENTED) RESORT
(— OF ABODE) LIBKEN
(— OF ACTION) GROUND
(— OF AMUSEMENT) GAFF
(— OF ASSEMBLY) AGORA CURIA KGOTLA SYNAGOG
(— OF BEAUTY) TEMPE
(— OF BLISS) PARADISE
(— OF BLOODSHED) ACELDAMA
(— OF BURIAL) AHU KIL KILL LAIR GRAVE LAYSTOW CATACOMB CEMETERY GOLGOTHA LAYSTALL
(— OF BUSINESS) BANK AGENCY KNACKERY
(— OF CARNAGE) SHAMBLES
(— OF CONCEALMENT) DEN BOMA BLIND STALE HIDING HIDEOUT HIDEAWAY
(— OF CONFINEMENT) BRIG CAGE COOP LIMBO PRISON BULLPEN
(— OF CONFUSION) BABEL TROYTOWN
(— OF CREMATION) GHAT GHAUT
(— OF CRUCIFIXION) GOLGOTHA
(— OF DEPARTED SPIRITS) SHEOL
(— OF DEPRAVITY) SODOM
(— OF DESTRUCTION) ABADDON
(— OF DETENTION) BAGNIO
(— OF DWELLING) WANE
(— OF EMPLOYMENT) SHOP
(— OF ENTERTAINMENT) INN JOINT DANCERY HANGOUT HOSTELRY
(— OF EXERTION) ARENA
(— OF EXILE) PATMOS
(— OF FABRICATION) MINT
(— OF HAPPINESS) CAMELOT
(— OF HONOR) HEAD PRECEDENCE
(— OF IDYLLIC BEAUTY) XANADU
(— OF JUNCTION) SYMPHYSIS
(— OF MISERY) HELL
(— OF NETHER DARKNESS) EREBUS
(— OF NOISE) BABEL
(— OF PLEASURE) OASIS
(— OF PROTECTION) PORT SCUG
(— OF QUARANTINE) LAZARET LAZARETTO
(— OF REFUGE) ARK BAST HOLD ASYLUM ADULLAM HIDEOUT
(— OF RESIDENCE) SOIL DOMICILE
(— OF RESORT) PURLIEU
(— OF REST) OASIS REPOSE
(— OF RESTRAINT) LIMBO PINFOLD
(— OF REVERENCE) MECCA
(— OF SACRIFICE) ALTAR
(— OF SAFETY) GRITH HAVEN WARRANT
(— OF SECLUSION) PRIVACY
(— OF SECURITY) GRITH ASYLUM CORRAL HARBOR GARRISON
(— OF SHELTER) LEW HOLD JOUK COVER
(— OF SUBMISSION) CANOSSA
(— OF THE DEAD) HELL
(— OF TORMENT) GOLGOTHA
(— OF TRADE) MART
(— OF WORSHIP) HEIAU BETHEL CHAPEL CHURCH DESERT SHRINE TEMPLE GURDWARA SYNAGOGUE TABERNACLE
(— SIDE-BY-SIDE) JUXTAPOSE
(— SIDE BY SIDE) APPOSE
(— SPAWNING) REDD
(— STRUCK BY LIGHTNING) BIDENTAL
(— UNDER RESTRICTIONS) PROCLAIM
(— WHERE FOOD IS KEPT) LARDER
(— WHERE MEAT IS SMOKED) BUCAN BUCCAN
(— WHERE OUTCASTS GATHER) HELL
(— WHERE ROADS CROSS) LEET
(— WHERE STREAM IS RAPID) SHARP
(— WHERE TROOPS HALT OVERNIGHT) ETAPE
(— WHERE 4 OR MORE WAYS MEET) CARFAX
(ABIDING —) GRANGE
(BARE —) GALL SCAR SCAUR
(BOGGY —) SLACK SLUMP
(BORING —) DULLSVILLE

(BREEDING —) NIDUS LOOMERY SEMINARY PELICANRY
(BUSHY —) SCROG
(CHAFED —) GALL
(CHIEF —) HEADSHIP
(CIRCULAR —) ORBELL
(CONCEALED —) HIDE
(CONFINED —) CRIB
(CONSECRATED —) HIERON
(COOKING —) GALLEY
(DARK —) GLOOM
(DEEP —) GULF DEPTH GULPH
(DELIGHTFUL —) ELYSIUM
(DILAPIDATED —) DUMP
(DISTASTEFUL —) FLEABAG
(DOME-SHAPED —) IGLOO
(DRINKING —) BOOZER MUMHOUSE
(DRY —) SEARING
(DWELLING —) BY BYE DEN SEE BAWN HAFT HIVE HOME ABODE BEING HOUSE HOWFF SOJOURN HABITACLE
(EATING —) CAFE GRUBBERY
(EMPTY —) BLANK SPACE
(ENCLOSED —) BIN HAY WORTH SEVERAL CLOISTER
(ESSENTIAL —) EYE
(EXOTIC —) XANADU
(FAMILIAR —) KITH
(FAULTY — IN THREAD) TRAP
(FILTHY —) STY
(FIRST —) BLUE LEAD STRAIGHT
(FLAT —) PLAT
(FORTIFIED —) LIS LISS CASTLE FASTNESS
(GARRISONED —) PRESIDIO
(GATHERING —) SHOP AGORA FOYER JOINT LESCHE
(GRASSY —) LAUND
(HALLOWED —) SHRINE
(HALTING —) MARAH
(HIDING —) MEW CACHE HIDEL HOARD STASH COVERT HIDDELS RETREAT STOWAWAY
(HIGH —) EMINENCE
(HIGHEST —) TOP
(HOLLOW —) GULF HOLE HOLL SCOOP CAVITY ALBERCA SINKHOLE
(IDYLLIC —) XANADU BRIGADOON
(IMAGINARY —) FANTASYLAND
(INHABITED —) ABADI
(LANDING —) GHAT HARD HITHE LEVEE SCALE BUNDER PALACE HELIPORT
(LEVEL —) PLANILLA
(LODGING —) CAMP LOGIS BIDING BILLET LIBKEN
(LONELY —) SOLITUDE
(LOOKOUT —) TOOT
(LURKING —) HOLD HOLE HOARD HULSTER
(LYING —) LAY LAIR
(MARKET —) AGORA TRONE MARKET RIALTO
(MARSHY —) SLEW SLOO SLUE SLUMP SLOUGH
(MEETING —) CLUB PNYX COURT FORUM GUILD TRYST TOLSEL TOLZEY AMBALAM KLAVERN TINWALD
(MIDDLE —) MEDIUM
(MUDDY —) SOIL
(NARROW —) NOOK STRAIT
(NESTING —) JUG NIDARY
(OPEN —) ENAJIM
(OTHERWORLDLY —) EMPYREAN
(PARTICULAR —) ROOM
(PASSING —) TURNOUT
(POLLING —) BOOTH
(PRECIPITOUS —) STEEP
(PRIVATE —) SECRET
(RAVELED —) FRAY
(REMOTE —) JERICHO
(RESTING —) LAY CAMP FORM GIST LAIR PARAO CRADLE
(ROCKY —) ROCHER
(SACRED —) HAREM HIERON CHAITYA SANCTUM
(SALTING —) SALADERO
(SECRET —) LAIR ADYTUM CORNER CRANNY
(SECURE —) REDOUBT
(SHADY —) GLOOM SWALE FRESCADE UMBRACLE
(SHELTERED —) NOOK SCUG SUCCOR
(SLEEPING —) ROOST
(SORE —) RAW
(SPAWNING —) REDD
(STARTING —) JUMPOFF
(STEEP —) PITCH
(STOPPING —) HALT MANZIL
(STORAGE —) DEPOT HOARD LODGE SPICERY STORAGE STOWAGE DOCKYARD
(STRONG —) STRENGTH
(SUNKEN —) SWALE
(SWAMPY —) FLUSH SOUGH
(THIRD —) SHOW
(TIGHT —) JAM JAMB
(UNEVEN —) RUB
(WALLOWING —) SOIL
(WATCH —) TOOTHILL
(WATERING —) ABREUVOIR
(WATERY —) SOIL FLUSH
(WEAK —) BLOT
(WET —) DANK
(WORN —) ABRASION
(WRETCHED —) DEN MISERY
(PL.) LOCI
(PREF.) CHOR(O) LOCO TOP(O)
(DRY —) XER(O)
(TAKES — OF) PRO VICE
(SUFF.) ESE THESIS THESTE THETIC TOPE TOPY
(— FOR) ARIUM ORIUM ORY
(— OF) ARY
(— OF DOING) ERY
(— OF GROWING, BREEDING) ERY
(— OF KEEPING) ERY
(— OF SELLING) ERY

PLACEBO SOP TOADY VESPERS PARASITE
PLACED FIXED BESTEAD
(— ON ITS SIDE) LAZY
PLACEHOLDER VARIABLE
PLACE-NAME TOPONYM
PLACENTA MAZA REPLUM
(PREF.) MAZ(O)
PLACENTAL MAZIC
PLACID CALM COOL EVEN MEEK MILD SOFT DOWNY QUIET SUANT SUENT GENTLE SEDATE SERENE SMOOTH PACIFIC TRANQUIL THROBLESS
PLACKET FENT SLIT SPARE WOMAN CLOSING PETTICOAT
PLAGAL MODE
(PREF.) HYPO
PLAGIARISM CRIB PLAGIUM
PLAGIARIST TAKER COPYIST
PLAGIARIZE CRIB LIFT STEAL
PLAGUE DUN IMP POX VEX FRAB FRET GNAW PEST TWIT BESET CURSE DEATH DEUCE HARRY QUALM TEASE TRAIK WEARY WORRY WOUND BOTHER BURDEN HAMPER HARASS INFEST PESTER PESTIS SORROW WANION DESTROY MURRAIN PERPLEX SCOURGE TORMENT TORTURE TROUBLE BEPESTER HANDICAP OUTBREAK PESTILENCE
(PREF.) LEMO LOIMO PESTI PESTO
PLAGUY VERY PESKY VEXING MURRAIN PESTFUL INFERNAL
PLAICE FLUKE FLATFISH FLOUNDER
PLAID CALM FAKE MAUD PLOD TARTAN BRACKEN BRECHAN
(KIND OF —) GLEN
PLAIN DRY LOW BALD BARE CHOL EASY EVEN FLAT OPEN PLAT RIFE VEGA WALD WOLD BLAIR BLUNT BROAD CAMPO CORAH FIELD FRANK GREEN GROSS LAUND LEVEL LLANO MOURN NAKED PAMPA PROSE ROUND SEBKA SECCO SILLY SMALL SOBER TALAO UNORN BEMOAN BEWAIL CHASTE CUESTA GRAITH HOMELY HONEST HUMBLE LENTEN MACHAR MAIDAN PARAMO PUSZTA RUSTIC SABANA SEVERE SIMPLE SINGLE SMOOTH ARTLESS EVIDENT GENUINE IDAVOLL LEGIBLE OBVIOUS POPULAR SAVANNA TERRACE UNARTED VANILLA APPARENT CAMPAIGN DISTINCT EVERYDAY EXPLICIT FAMILIAR HOMEMADE HOMESPUN ITHAVOLL PALPABLE PIEDMONT SEMPLICE STRAIGHT
(— AMONG TREES) LAUND
(— OF ARGENTINA) PAMPA
(— OF RUSSIA) STEPPE
(ALKALI —S) USAR
(ALLUVIAL —) APRON CARSE HAUGH
(ARCTIC —) TUNDRA
(DESOLATE —) CHOL
(HEATHY —) LANDE
(LOW-LYING —) MACHAR MACHAIR
(LUNAR —) MARE
(MARSHY —) BLAIR
(NOT —) MEALYMOUTHED
(SALINE —) SEBKA SEBKHA
(SALT —) SALADA
(SLOPING —) HOPE CUESTA CONOPLAIN
(SMALL GRASSY —) CAMAS CAMASS QUAMASH
(TREELESS —) BLED TUNDRA SAVANNA SAVANNAH
(UNOCCUPIED —) DESERT
(PL.) VIZCACHA
(PREF.) LITI PEDI(O) PLAN(I)
PLAIN CHANT CF
PLAINCLOTHESMAN SPLIT
PLAINLY FAIR BARELY FAIRLY FLATLY SIMPLY BROADLY FRANKLY DIRECTLY
PLAINNESS PROSE INNOCENCE
PLAINSMAN LLANERO
PLAINSONG GROUND
PLAINT WAIL PLANT LAMENT COMPLAINT
PLAINTEXT CLEAR
PLAINTIFF SUER USEE ACTOR ORATOR PURSUER QUERENT
PLAINTIVE SAD CROSS PINING DOLENTE ELEGIAC FRETFUL MOANFUL PEEVISH PETTISH DOLOROSO MANGENDO PETULANT WAILSOME SORROWFUL
PLAIN-VANILLA BASIC
PLAIT CUE PLY KNIT PAIR PLAT RUFF TURN WALE WAND BRAID BREAD CRIMP FETCH FITCH PEDAL PINCH QUEUE QUILL QUIRK TRACE TRESS WEAVE BORDER DOUBLE GATHER GOFFER PLEACH PLIGHT RUMPLE TUSCAN WIMPLE WRITHE CRIMPLE FROUNCE PIGTAIL SCALLOM COMPLECT
(— FOR HAT) DUNSTABLE
(— OF STRAW) MILAN TRACE
(SERIES OF —S) KILTING
PLAITED PLISSE DEVIOUS PLICATE
PLAITING PLISSE LEGHORN NATTIER
PLAN AIM ART LAY WAY CARD CAST COUP DART FOOT GAME HANG IDEA MIND MOOD PLAT PLOT REDE WENT ALLOW BRIEF CHART DARTY DRAFT DRIFT ETTLE FRAME HOBBY MODEL REACH SHAPE TRACE ADVICE AGENDA BEREDE BUDGET CIPHER DECOCT DESIGN DEVISE ENGINE FIGURE INTEND LAYOUT METHOD MODULE ORDAIN PROJET SCHEMA SCHEME SURVEY THEORY ARRANGE CONCERT CONCOCT COUNSEL DRAWING FORELAY NOSTRUM OUTLINE PATTERN PROGRAM PROJECT PURPOSE THOUGHT COGITATE CONSPIRE CONTRIVE ENGINEER FORECAST FOREGAME LANDSKIP MEDITATE PLATFORM PRACTICE SCHEDULE SKELETON STRATEGY BLUEPRINT CALCULATE
(— AHEAD) FORECAST
(— OF FUTURE PROCEDURE) PROGRAM
(— ON A FLOOR) EPURE
(— TOGETHER) CONCERT
(CUNNING —) WHEEZE
(GROUND —) TRACE GRUNDRISS
(INSURANCE —) TONTINE
(KIND OF —) KEOGH
(KIND OF RETIREMENT —) KEOGH
(5-YEAR —) PIATILETKA
PLANARIAN PLATODE TRICLAD FLATWORM PLATYHELMINTH
PLANE BEAD DADO FACE FLAT HOLL MILL AXIAL CHUTE CROZE FACET GLIDE HOULE HOWEL LEVEL MESON SHOOT STICK TABLE WHISK AEQUOR AIRBUS BEADER HOLLOW REEDER ROUTER

SMOKER SNIBEL COURIER INSHAVE JOINTER NONSKED SURFACE WITCHET BULLNOSE DECLINER LEEBOARD MERIDIAN RECLINER SYCAMORE TRAVERSE
(— CURVE) ROSE
(— HANDLE) TOAT TOTE
(— OF CLEAVAGE) BACK
(— OF EARTH'S ORBIT) ECLIPTIC
(— OF ROCK) BED
(—S OF GUNNERY FIRE) SHEAF
(ENEMY —) BANDIT
(INCLINED —) RAMP SLIP
(MOLDING —) HOLL HOULE HOLLOW
(PERSPECTIVE —) TABLE
(RABBET —) PLOW RABAT PLOUGH REBATE FILLETER
(SLOPING —) CUESTA
PLANER JOINTER SURFACER
PLANER TREE HORNBEAM SYCAMORE
PLANET ORB SUN BODY IRIS JOVE MARS MOON STAR EARTH GLOBE HYLEG PLUTO SHREW VENUS WORLD SATURN SPHERE URANUS VULCAN ALMUTEN ANARETA BENEFIC FORTUNE JUPITER MERCURY NEPTUNE PRIMARY CHASUBLE LUMINARY RECEPTOR TERRELLA WANDERER
(— IN A NATIVITY) ALMUTEN
(BENEVOLENT —) FORTUNE
(CONTROLLING —) LORD
(FICTIONAL —) ORK KRYPTON
(HYPOTHETICAL —) VULCAN
(INNER —) MARS EARTH VENUS MERCURY
(MALEFICENT —) SHREW
(MINOR —) VESTA PALLAS PSYCHE
(RULING —) DOMINATOR
(SMALL —) IRIS ASTEROID TERRELLA
PLANETARIUM ORRERY
PLANETOID UNDINE ASTEROID
PLANE TREE CHINAR PLATAN COTONIER PLANTAIN SYCAMORE
PLANET-STRICKEN SIDERATED
PLANISPHERE ASTROLABE METEORSCOPE
PLANK CLAM HOOD PATA PLAT RAIL SOLE WAIR BOARD CLAMP PATTA SHIDE SWALE THEAL DAGGER FLITCH PLANCH ROOFER STRAKE CLAPPER CROSSER DEPOSIT MADRIER RIBBAND STEALER FOREPOLE GARBOARD STRINGER
(— AS PROTECTION) SHOLE
(— OVER BROOK) CLAM
(—S IN BRIDGE) CHESS
(—S LESS THAN 6 FT.) DEAL
(— 6 FT. X 1 FT.) WARE
(CURVED —) SNYING
(ROUGHHEWN —) SLAB
PLANK DRAG RUBBER
PLANK END STUB
PLANKING GORE RACK HATCH SWALE STRAKE CEILING LAGGING BERTHING BRATTICE GARBOARD WATERWAY
PLANKSHEER WATERWAY
PLANKTON KRILL DIATOM SESTON
(GROWTH OF —) BLOOM
PLANNED PREPENSE
(AS —) ONTRACK
PLANNING (KIND OF —) ESTATE
(TECHNIQUE FOR —) PERT
PLANOMILLER SLABBER
PLANT AJI BED SET SOW ACHE ALGA ARUM BURY CROP FAST HERB HIDE MORE RAPE SALT SEED SEGO SLIP TREE WORT ABACA AGAVE AJWAN ARGEL AVENS CAMAS CAROA CHIVE CLOTE CLOVE CUMIN EARLY FANCY GRAFT HEATH INTER INULA JALAP KEIKI ORACH PITCH PUTIN SEDUM SHRUB YERBA ACACIA AJOWAN AKELEY ALASAS ANNUAL BEDDER CACOON CALALU CARROT CLOVER COKERY COSMEA COTTON CUMMIN DERRIS DIBBLE ESCAPE FICOID FORCER GALAXY GROWTH KARREE LENTIL LIGGER MALLOW MANUKA MEDICK MESCAL ORPINE PEPINO SESAME SETTLE SPRING ULLUCU YARROW ABANDON ALKANET ALYSSUM BREWERY BUGLOSS CARAWAY CARDOON CHERVIL CONCEAL CUTTING DAGGERS ENCELIA GENTIAN GINSENG HAEMONY IMPLANT JIKUNGU LETTUCE PALMIET PICKERY RAMBONG SAWMILL ABUTILON AGERATUM AGRIMONY ANGLEPOD BIENNIAL BLUEBELL CAMOMILE CONSOUND DRAWLING DYEHOUSE EMERGENT ENGINERY FOXGLOVE FUMEROOT GASWORKS GERANIUM GROMWELL HAWKWEED HONEWORT JAPONICA KNAPWEED LARKSPUR CHAMOMILE SPIKENARD PHILODENDRON
(— BY SPADING) SPIT
(— DEEPLY) HEEL
(— DISEASE) NECROSIS
(— FIRMLY) BRACE
(— GROWING IN WATER) BILDERS HYDROPHYTE
(— GROWTH MEDIUM) PERLITE
(— IN ROWS) DRILL
(— LIFE) BIOS BIOTA
(— NOT ATTACKED) NONHOST
(— NUTRIENTS) SIDEDRESS
(— OF MEADOWS) POOPHYTE
(— OF THE DEAD) ASPHODEL
(— OUTGROWTH) OVULE
(— ROOTED IN GROUND) LIANA LIANE
(— SUPPORTING PARASITES) SUSCEPT
(— TEMPORARILY) SHEUCH
(— TREE) MOTCH
(— WITH A SPADE) SPIT
(— WITH NO DISTINCT MEMBERS) THALLUS
(— WITH THREE PISTILS) TRIGYN
(— WITH THREE STAMENS) TRIANDER
(— 2ND CROP) ETCH
(AIR —) FLOPPERS
(ANCIENT —) CYCAD
(AQUATIC —) ALISMA NUPHAR SUGAMO TAWKEE AMBULIA AWLWORT FROGBIT DUCKWEED PONDWEED PICKERELWEED
(AROMATIC —) MINT NARD BASIL CUMIN TANSY THYME AMOMUM CUMMIN CARAWAY DITTANY ALBAHACA CALAMINT LAVENDER SPIKENARD
(AUSTRALIAN —) LILAC STYLO LIGNUM LANCEPOD
(BULBOUS —) GALTONIA
(CENTURY —) PITA
(CLIMBING —) VETCH LAWYER RUNNER ULLUCE ULLUCU CORALITA
(COMPOSITE —) SUCCORY HAWKWEED SNEEZEWEED
(CONSECRATED —) HAOMA
(CREATED —) BARAMIN
(CREEPING —) IPECAC KAREAO KAREAU PENNYWORT
(CROSSBRED —) HYBRID
(CRUSHING —) BREAKER
(DWARF —) CUMIN STUNT
(DYE —) WAD ANIL WOAD WOLD WOALD MADDER
(E. INDIAN —) JATI
(ETIOLATED —) ALBINO
(FIBER —) ALOE FLAX HEMP PITA CAJUN RAMIE SISAL
(FLOWERING —) HOP ROSE DAISY HOLLY POPPY ORCHID VIOLET HAWTHORN LARKSPUR POLYGALA PRIMROSE SNOWDROP
(FORAGE —) RAPE ALFALFA DAINCHA
(FOSSIL —) CALAMITE
(GERMINATING —) SPIRE
(GRAIN —) TEFF
(HEDGE —) ESPINO
(HEMP —) FIMBLE
(IMMATURE —) KEIKI
(LEAFLESS —) ULEX DODDER RESTIAD TRIURID
(MALE —) MAS MACRANDER
(MARSH —) CALL FERN RUSH CALLA JUNCUS BULRUSH CATTAIL BUCKBEAN MARSHMALLOW
(MEDICINAL —) ALOE HERB ERICA ARNICA CATNEP CATNIP IPECAC SIMPLE ACONITE BONESET GENTIAN LOBELIA CAMOMILE
(MEDICINIAL —) SENNA
(NON-FLOWERING —) FERN
(NURSERY —) SEEDLING
(PEPPER —) ARA
(PHILIPPINE —) ABACA
(PISTILLATE —) FEMALE
(POISONOUS —) COWBANE DEATHIN HENBANE MANDRAKE SAMNITIS NIGHTSHADE
(POTTED —) BONSAI LANTANA
(POWER —) HYDRO
(PRICKLY —) BRIAR BRIER CACTUS CARDON NETTLE TEASEL TEAZEL PRICKFOOT
(PUNGENT —) PEPPER
(RAPIDLY-GROWING —) FILLER
(REEDY —) SPRIT
(RENDERING —) KNACKERY
(ROSACEOUS —) AVENS
(SENSITIVE —) MIMOSA
(SIBERIAN —) BADAN
(SPINOUS —) KANTIARA
(STAMINATE —) HUSBAND
(SUBMERGED —) ENALID
(SUCCULENT —) ALOE HERB GASTERIA HAWORTHIA HOUSELEEK
(SWORD-LEAVED —) LEVERS
(THALLOPHYTIC —) LICHEN
(TRAILING —) ARBUTUS
(TUFTED —) DRYAS
(TWINING —) SMILAX WINDER CLIMBER BINDWEED SCAMMONY
(UNIDENTIFIED —) HORDOCK
(WATER —) LIMU LOTUS AQUATILE STARFRUIT
(WEEDY —) DOCK KNAWEL
(YOUNG —) SET SPRINGER
(PL.) FLORA
(PREF.) BOTAN(O) PHYT(I)(O)
(SUFF.) AD CHORE COCCUS OECIA PHYTA PHYTE(S) PHYTIA PHYTIC PHYTUM
PLANTAGENET ANGEVIN
PLANTAIN COCK PALA ABACA ALISMA FINGER PISANG WABRON BENTING NETLEAF RIBWORT SITFAST BALISIER BUCKHORN FIREWEED FLEAWORT ISPAGHUL PLANTANO RATSBANE RIBGRASS ROADWEED WAYBREAD
PLANTAIN EATER TOURACO SPLITBEAK
PLANTAIN LILY HOSTA FUNKIA
PLANTATION PEN HOLT WALK FINCA GROVE BOSKET BOWERY COLONY ESTATE SHAMBA SPRING YERBAL CAFETAL FAZENDA NOPALRY PINETUM THICKET ARBUSTUM HACIENDA TRAPICHE VINEYARD
(HEMP —) LATE
(WILLOW —) SALICETUM
PLANTED LISTED
PLANTER SNAG COLON SOWER FARMER SETTLER PLANTATOR
PLANTING GROVE SATION
PLANTING STICK DIBBLE
PLANT LOUSE APHID PSYLLID PUCERON HOMOPTER
PLANTS
(SUFF.) ACEAE ALES INEAE
PLAQUE CHIP PINAX PLATE PLATEAU SARCOID NAMEPLATE STOMACHER
PLASH LIP DASH BLASH PLOSH PLOUT PLEACH PUDDLE SPLASH SPATTER SPECKLE
PLASMA LATEX PLASM
PLASTER CAST CEIL DAUB HARL LEEP LOCK TEER CLEAM GATCH PARGE SLICK SMALM STAFF TOPIC TREAT CHARGE CHUNAM CLATCH GAGING MORTAR PARGET SPARGE STOOTH STUCCO BLISTER MALAGMA DIACULUM DIAPALMA SINAPISM VESICANT CATAPLASM
(— BETWEEN LATHS) CAT
(— OF PARIS) GESSO GYPSUM
(— WITH COW DUNG) LEEP
(COARSE —) GROUT
(COVER WITH —) CEIL
(MEDICAL —) SALVE TOPIC TREAT CHARGE SPARADRAP
(MUSTARD —) SINAPISM
(2 COATS OF —) RENDERSET

PLASTERBOARD GYPSUM DRYWALL
PLASTERED DRUNK SOUSED SWACKED
PLASTERER DAUBER DAUBSTER PARGETER SPREADER
PLASTERING KEY SETWORK ROUGHCAST
PLASTIC ABS FOAM LOID RICH SIRUP LABILE PLIANT ACETATE CATALIN CRYSTAL DUCTILE FICTILE ORGANIC PERSPEX CREATIVE FLEXIBLE LAMINATE MELAMINE PHENOLIC TECTONIC UNCTUOUS FORMATIVE
(—S BASE) RESIN
(FLEXIBLE —) SARAN
PLASTICIZER CAMPHOR
PLASTRON DICKEY CALIPEE
PLAT BED FLAT FOOD PLAN PLOT SLAP BRAID LEVEL PLACE PLAIN PLAIT BUFFET WATTLE ARRANGE FLATTEN PLATEAU QUADRAT
PLATANIST SUSU
PLATANUS PLANE COTONIER SYCAMORE
PLATBAND IMPOST LINTEL EPISTYLE
PLATE BAT CAP CUT DIP DOD EAR FIN GIB WEB ANAL BACK BASE BRIN CASE CAST CURB DIAL DISK DROP FISH GILL GONG GULA HOME HOOF LAME LEAF MOLD NAIL ORAL RETE ROSE SHOE SHUT SLAB SOLE STUD TACE TRAY AMPYX ANODE BASAL BELLY BLADE CHAIR CLAMP CLEAT CLOUT FACIA FENCE FLOOR FLUKE FORCE GLAND GUARD GULAR LAMEL PATEN PYGAL SCALE SCUTE SHEET SHOLE SLICE STAMP STAVE STRAP TABLE TASSE TERNE TRAMP UNCUS WATER ADORAL BAFFLE BRIDGE BUCKLE CASTER CIRCLE CLICHE COLLAR COPPER COSTAL CRUSTA DAMPER DASHER EPIGNE FASCIA FILLER FOLIUM FRIZEL GENIAL GNOMON GORGET GUSSET LABIAL LAMINA LOREAL MASCLE MATRIX MENTAL MENTUM MOTHER PALLET PATTEN PLATEN RADIAL SCREEN SCUTUM SEPTUM SERVER SHEATH SHROUD SPLINT STAPLE TARSUS TEGMEN TURTLE TYMPAN VESSEL BESAGNE BOLSTER BRACKET BRACTEA BUCCULA BUCKLER CHARGER CLYPEUS COASTER CORNULE CORONET CRYSTAL DOUBLER ETCHING FRIZZLE FRONTAL GRAVURE HUMERAL INKBLOT MORDANT MYOTOME NEPTUNE PETALON PRIMARY ROSTRAL ROUNDEL SPANGLE STEALER STEELER TERGITE TESSERA VENTRAL ASSIETTE BEDPLATE BIQUARTZ BRACHIAL CELLOCUT DIASCOPE DRAWBACK ELECTRUM EPIGYNUM EPIPROCT EPISTOME FIREBACK FLOUNDER SKEWBACK STAPLING STRINGER SUBPLATE SURPRINT
(— COVERING KEYHOLE) DROP
(— COVERING MIDDLE EAR) TEGMEN
(— IN AIRPLANE WING) SPOILER
(— IN BATTERY) GRID
(— IN ORGAN PIPE) LANGUET
(— IN STEAM BOILER) SPUT DASHER
(— OF BALEEN) BLADE
(— OF BLAST FURNACE) TYMP
(— OF CTENOPHORE) COMB
(— OF GELATIN) BAT
(— OF GLASS) SLIDE
(— OF JAW) AURICLE
(— OF PRECIOUS METAL) BRACTEA
(— OF SOAP FRAME) SESS
(— OF SUNDIAL) GNOMON
(— ON FIREPLACE) BLOWER
(— ON LANCE SHAFT) VAMPLATE
(— ON PLOW) MOLDBOARD
(— ON SADDLE) SIDEBAR
(— ON SATCHEL STRAP) OLIVE
(— ON SHOE SOLE) SEG
(— ON THROAT OF FISH) GULAR
(— ON WATERWHEEL) SHROUD
(—S OF CARDING MACHINE) ARCH
(—S OF GUN CARRIAGE) FLASK
(— TO SUPPORT BEAM) TASSEL TORSEL
(ARMOR —) SPLINT AILETTE PALLETTE
(COLLECTION —) BROD
(COMMUNION —) PATEN
(DEEP —) MAZARINE
(DERMAL —) SCUTE
(DORSAL —) ELYTRUM ALINOTUM
(EARTHEN —) MUFFIN
(FASHION —) SWELL
(FIREPLACE —) IRONBACK
(FLAT —) APRON
(GOLD — ON FOREHEAD) PATA PATTA
(GROOVED TRAM —) GULLY GULLEY
(GUARD —) SHELL
(HINGED —) SHUT
(HOME —) DISH
(HOT —) GRILL GRILLE
(INSCRIBED —) TABLET
(IRON —) CLOUT STAVE LATTEN MARVER LAPSTONE SKEWBACK MOLDBOARD TURNPLATE TURNSHEET
(LARGE —) DOUBLER
(LOCK —) SELVEDGE
(MELTED —) SOUP
(METAL —) ROVE CHROME
(NAME —) FACIA
(PERFORATED —) DOD GRID WORTLE PINNULE
(PITCHER'S —) SLAB MOUND
(RIMLESS —) COUPE
(SIEVE —) LATTICE
(SIFTING —) TROMMEL
(SKELETAL —) SCLERITE
(THIN —) LAME LAMP LAMINA LAMELLA
(THIN TIN —) TAIN LATTEN TAGGERS
(WALL —) PAN RASEN TORSEL
(WOODEN —) TRENCHER
(PREF.) ELASM(O) LAMELLI LAMIN(I) PLAC(O)
(SUFF.) **(COVERING —)** STEGE STEGITE
PLATEAU PLAT PUNA FJELD KAROO KARST TABLE CAUSSE HAMADA MESETA NIVEAU PARAMO SABANA UPLAND ANASAZI PLATFORM
(PL.) BARRENS
PLATEHOLDER CASSETTE
PLATE-LIKE PLACOID
PLATEN ROLL
PLATER VATMAN CLAIMER COLLARMAN
PLATFORM TOP BANK BEMA DAIS DECK DRIP DROP DUCK FLAT GHAT HEEL KITE PACE PLAT STEP WING ALTAR APRON BENCH BLIND BLOCK CHAIN DUKAN FLAKE FLOAT HEIAU SOLEA STAGE STAND STOEP STOOL STOOP STULL STUMP TOLDO ARBOUR AZOTEA BRIDGE DESIGN GANTRY HURDLE ISLAND MACHAN PAEPAE PALLET PERRON PILLAR PODIUM PULPIT RUNWAY SETTLE SLEDGE ALMEMAR BALCONY BATTERY CATWALK ESTRADE FORETOP GALLERY LANDING LOGEION PADDOCK PATTERN ROLLWAY ROSTRUM SKIDWAY SOAPBOX TRIBUNE BARBETTE FOOTPACE HUSTINGS SCAFFOLD STALLAGE MORTARBOARD
(— FOR ACTORS) LOGEION THEOLOGIUM
(— FOR ALTAR) PREDELLA
(— FOR DRYING FISH) FLAKE
(— FOR PUBLIC SPEAKING) BEMA PODIUM TRIBUNE
(— FOR STORING FOOD) WHATA
(— IN CHURCH) SOLEA
(— IN SYNAGOGUE) ALMEMAR
(— IN TEMPLE) DUKAN
(— IN TREE) MACHAN
(— OF GALLOWS) DROP
(— ON RUNNERS) SLEDGE
(— ON STEAMER) SPONSON
(— ON TOP OF HOUSE) AZOTEA
(— ON WHEELS) SKID DOLLY FLOAT
(— TO SUPPORT MINERS) STULL
(BOARDING —) RAMBADE
(GUN —) BARBET SPONSON BARBETTE
(LEADSMAN'S —) CHAIN
(MINE —) STULL SOLLAR SOLLER
(MOHAMMEDAN STONE —) MASTABA
(MOUNTED —) SKID
(NAUTICAL —) FORETOP MAINTOP ROUNDTOP
(ORE —) BUDDLE
(RAILROAD —) DOCK DOCKEN TRAINWAY
(RAISED —) DAIS PYAL STAND STOEP STOOL STOOP EXEDRA LISSOM PANTALAN
(ROCK —) STANCE
(SLEEPING —) KANG
(STAIRCASE —) HALFPACE HATHPACE
(WOOD —) PLANCHER
PLATING ARMOR SKIRT
PLATINUM COSTLY PLATINA
PLATITUDE CLICHE TRUISM BROMIDE DULLNESS STALENESS TRITENESS
PLATONIST IDEIST
PLATOON SQUAD VOLLEY PELOTON PLOTTON
PLATTER DISH DISK LANX ASHET GRAIL PLATE RECORD CHARGER TRENCHER
PLATY MOON MOONFISH
PLATYPUS DUCKBILL DUCKMOLE MALLANGONG
PLAUDIT APPLAUD APPROVAL ENCOMIUM
(PL.) PRAISE APPLAUSE
PLAUSIBILITY COLOR
PLAUSIBLE FAIR OILY SNOD SLEEK GLOSSY SMOOTH AFFABLE POPULAR CREDIBLE PROBABLE PROVABLE SPECIOUS SUITABLE OSTENSIBLE
PLAY FUN JEU JIG RUN RUX TOY AUTO BEAR COME DAFF DEAL DICE DRAW FAIR GAME JEST LAKE MOVE MUCK PLEE PUNT ROMP SPIN TUNE WAKE CARRY CHARM DALLY DRAMA ENACT FLIRT FROST HORSE SHOOT SOTIE SOUND SPIEL SPORT STUCK WREAK YEDDE ACTION COMEDY COQUET DANDLE DIVIDE FILLER FROLIC GAMBLE GAMBOL GAMING GHOSTS MUSERY NUMBER PIDDLE ROLLIX TRIFLE CONSORT CUTBACK DISPORT EXECUTE EXPLOIT GUIGNOL HISTORY HOLIDAY MIRACLE PAGEANT PASSION PERFORM PRELUDE STAGERY VENTURE BURLETTA MORALITY SKITTLES MELODRAMA
(— ABOUT) SPANIEL
(— A DOMINO) SET POSE
(— AGAINST) BUCK
(— AN INSTRUMENT) BOW BLOW SWAY FINGER TWEEDLE
(— A PART) DO ACT ENTER GAMMON GUIZARD
(— A PIPE) CHARM
(— AT COURTSHIP) FLIRT
(— BAGPIPE) SKIRL DOODLE DOUDLE
(— BY STROKES) STRIKE
(— FANFARE) FLOURISH
(— FAST AND LOOSE) PALTER
(— FIRST CARD) LEAD
(— FLORIDLY) DIVIDE
(— FOR TIME) STALL
(— GOLF BALL) DRIVE
(— IMPOSTER) MUMP
(— IN MUD) MUDLARK
(— IN POOL) BURST
(— IN STREAKS) FORK
(— IN TRIGGER) CREEP
(— JAZZ) BLOW
(— LEGATO) SUSTAIN
(— LOCATION) SET
(— LOOSELY) WAVE
(— LOUT) SWAB SLUBBER
(— MEAN TRICKS) SHAB
(— NERVOUSLY) FIDGET
(— OF COLORS) IRIS
(— OF FOAM) HOOD
(— OF LIGHT) GLORY

(— ON WORDS) PUN CLENCH CLINCH PARAGRAM CALEMBOUR PARONOMASIA
(— THE BUFFOON) DROLL
(— THE BULLY) BLUSTER
(— THE FOOL) HOIT
(— THE HYPOCRITE) FACE
(— THE TOADY) SUPE
(— TRICKS) COD JAPE JINK
(— TRUANT) KIP WAG JOUK MICHE MOOCH MOUCH PLUNK TRONE MOOTCH
(— UNSKILLFULLY) STRUM FOOZLE
(— WITH) DANDLE
(AMOROUS —) GAME
(BOISTEROUS —) ROMP
(BRIDGE —) COUP ECHO SIGNAL SQUEEZE
(END —) SHAKE
(FARCICAL —) SOTIE
(FOOTBALL —) DOWN KEEP DELAY SWING KEEPER SAFETY AUDIBLE COUNTER CUTBACK ROLLOUT SPINNER
(IN —) ALIVE
(JAPANESE —) NOH
(MASKED —) GUISE
(MIRACLE —) AUTO GUARY MIRACLE
(ONE-PERSON —) MONODRAMA
(RAPID CHESS —) SKITTLES
(SHORT —) ONELINER
(USED IN —) LUSORY
(PL.) THEATER VANGELI

PLAYA BEACH SEBKA SALINA SEBKHA

PLAYBOY RAKE ROMEO LOTHARIO LIBERTINE

PLAYBOY OF THE WESTERN WORLD (AUTHOR OF —) SYNGE
(CHARACTER IN —) QUIN KEOGH MAHON SHAWN PEGEEN CHRISTY FLAHERTY MARGARET CHRISTOPHER

PLAY-BY-PLAY DETAILED

PLAYER IT CAP END BACK DUCK SIDE ACTOR BLACK COLOR GUARD BANKER BUSKER FEEDER STAGER STROLL TENTER ALTOIST FIELDER FORWARD GAMBLER STRIKER TRIFLER TURQUET BUDGETER GAMESTER HORNSMAN STROLLER
(— IN CHESS) BLACK WHITE
(— IN CHOUETTE) CAPTAIN
(— OF JAZZ) CAT
(— WHO CUTS CARDS) PONE
(— WHO IS IT) HE
(— WHO SCORES ZERO) DUCK
(— WITH LOWEST SCORE) BOOBY
(BACKGAMMON —) TABLER
(BASEBALL —) SHORT SACKER CATCHER FIELDER LEADOFF PITCHER BACKSTOP
(BASKETBALL —) PIVOT CAGEMAN HOOPMAN HOOPSTER PIVOTMAN
(BOWLING —) LEAD
(CARD —) EAST HAND PONE WEST BLIND DUMMY NORTH OMBRE SOUTH JUNIOR SENIOR BRAGGER DECLARER
(CRICKET —) LEG BOWLER INNING
(CROQUET —) MALLET
(DICE —) SHOOTER
(FLUTE —) AULETE
(FOOTBALL —) END BACK GUARD SLANT BUCKER CENTER TACKLE BLOCKER FLANKER GRIDDER SNAPPER FULLBACK HALFBACK SCATBACK SLOTBACK
(INEPT CHESS —) PATZER
(KEY —) PIVOT
(LACROSSE —) HOME COVER POINT ATTACK STICKMAN
(LEAPFROG —) BACK
(POKER —) AGE
(RUGBY —) SCRUM HOOKER
(SOCCER —) CAP INNER BOOTER
(STUPID —) HAM
(TENNIS —) SMASHER
(TWO OR MORE —S) PLATOON
(UNSKILLFUL —) DUB
(VOLLEYBALL —) SPIKER
(WEAK —) RABBIT
(PL.) CAST

PLAYFUL SLY ELFIN LUDIC MERRY FRISKY GAMBOL JOCOSE LUSORY TOYISH WANTON COLTISH GIOCOSO JIGGISH JOCULAR TOYSOME GAMESOME HUMOROUS LARKSOME SPORTFUL SPORTIVE KITTENISH
(EXTRAVAGANTLY —) MAD
(IRRESPONSIBLY —) MISCHIEVOUS

PLAYFULLY SCHERZANDO

PLAYFULNESS FUN BANTER GAMMICK GAMMOCK

PLAYGROUND OVAL CLOSE TOTLOT PLAYSTOW PLAYSTEAD

PLAYHOUSE HOUSE MOVIE CINEMA THEATER

PLAYING FROLIC LAKING
(— CARD) ACE JACK KING TREY DEUCE QUEEN TAROT
(— CARDS) DECK
(— LIGHTLY) LAMBENT

PLAYING FIELD PADANG

PLAYLET SKIT

PLAYTHING DIE TOY HOOP KNACK PLAIK SPORT BAUBLE LAKING SUCKER TRIFLE PLAYOCK

PLAYWRIGHT AUTHOR DRAMATIST PLAYMAKER
AMERICAN ADE LEA BABE BAUM DALY DELL EYEN HART HOYT INGE KERR LOOS RABE RICE ROOT SHAW UHRY AKINS ALBEE BARRY COHAN DAVIS DOBIE FITCH FRIEL GREEN HECHT HWANG LEWIS LOGAN LORTZ MAMET ODETS RIGGS RIVES SIMON SMITH STEIN WILDE YOUNG ABBOTT BARAKA BARKER BARRAS BEAHAN BOLTON BOOTHE BROOKS COMDEN CROUSE FLAVIN FRINGS GOLDEN HEGGEN HOWARD HUGHES KRASNA LAWSON LERNER LUDLAM MEGRUE MILLER NUGENT OBOLER ONEILL THOMAS TOTTEN WALKER WALTER WEXLEY WILDER ZINDEL ANDREWS BEHRMAN BELASCO BISSELL BLOSSOM BURROWS CARROLL COLLIER HELLMAN HOPWOOD HURLBUT KAUFMAN LEBLANC LINDSAY MOELLER NICHOLS PEABODY RICHMAN RYSKIND SAROYAN SHELDON SHEPARD SHIPMAN SHULMAN SPEWACK TEBELAK VEILLER ANDERSON BOGOSIAN CARLETON CHODOROV COLLISON CONNELLY KINGSLEY KIRKLAND MITCHELL SCHISGAL SCHWARTZ SHERWOOD TOTHEROH WILLIAMS BALDERSON CHAYEFSKY ISHERWOOD MACARTHUR MIDDLETON MOREHOUSE NICHOLSON STALLINGS BOUCICAULT TARKINGTON WEITZENKORN
AUSTRALIAN CHAMBERS
AUSTRIAN BLEI COLLIN MULLER NISSEL WERFEL NEUMANN ZEDLITZ CASTELLI WILDGANS SCHONTHAN SCHNITZLER GRILLPARZER HOFMANNSTHAL
BELGIAN CLAUS GHELDERODE MAETERLINCK
CANADIAN BOLT COOK ROSE SLADE COULTER DOHERTY HERBERT TREMBLAY
CZECH HAVEL KLIMA JERABEK JIRASEK
DANISH EWALD TANDRUP BERGSTROM BUCHHOLTZ OEHLENSCHLAGER
DUTCH FEITH HOOFT COSTER EMANTS VONDEL BREDERO
ENGLISH BAX FRY GAY KYD LEE BART BEHN BELL FORD HILL LEVY LONG NASH ROWE SHAW SIMS TATE TUKE BARRY BROME BYRON DUKES FIELD FOOTE HOOLE JONES KEEFE LEMON LEWIS LILLO LODGE MILNE MOORE MUNRO ORCZY ORTON PEELE SMITH STORY UDALL WOODS ALBERY BOADEN BROPHY CANNAN CASTLE CIBBER COWARD COWLEY CROWNE DAVIES DEKKER DENNIS DIBDIN DRYDEN DURFEY GRAHAM GREENE GRILLO HOWARD JONSON KENNEY LYTTON MANLEY MORTON MUNDAY NABBES PINERO PINTER PORTER PUDNEY ROWLEY SETTLE STEELE STOREY TAYLOR TREECE WESKER WILSON ABLEMAN ACKLAND AMBROSE BAGNOLD BARNETT BARRETT BENNETT BURNAND CHAPMAN CHETTLE EDWARDS FLECKER GILBERT HARWOOD HEYWOOD HOUSMAN JERROLD JOHNSON MARLOWE MARMION MARSTON MERRICK MITFORD MOTTEUX NICHOLS OSBORNE PLANCHE PRESTON SHIRLEY SIMPSON SITWELL SOWERBY TRAVERS WEBSTER BEAUMONT CLIFFORD CONGREVE DAVENANT ETHEREGE FIELDING FITZBALL FLETCHER HAMILTON HOLCROFT HOUGHTON JELLICOE JOHNSTON KNOBLOCK LONSDALE MORRISON PHILLIPS RATTIGAN ROBINSON SHADWELL THEOBALD THURSTON TOURNEUR VANBRUGH WILLIAMS ZANGWILL BOTTOMLEY BRIGHOUSE GOLDSMITH GREENWOOD ISHERWOOD KILLIGREW MANKOWITZ MASSINGER MIDDLETON MONCRIEFF MONKHOUSE SIEVEKING SOUTHERNE VANDRUTEN WYCHERLEY BROADHURST CARTWRIGHT DRINKWATER GALSWORTHY PHILLPOTTS SHAKESPEARE
ESTONIAN TAMMSAARE
FINNISH KIVI CHORELL TAVASTSTJERNA
FRENCH BLUM HUGO JOUY KOCK PYAT VADE BELOT BLOCH CAMUS CAPUS CARRE CEARD COLLE CUREL DUCIS DUMAS FABRE FEVAL FLERS GENET GIONO JARRY PIRON VIGNY WOLFF ACHARD AUGIER BAYARD BECQUE BELLOY BRIEUX COLLIN COOLUS COPEAU DONNAY DOUCET FAVART HALEVY LESAGE MAIRET MARCEL MONVEL MOREAU PAGNOL PARODI PICARD RACINE RAYNAL RENARD ROTROU SARDOU SARTRE SCRIBE SOUMET ANCELOT ANOUILH BARBIER BERNARD BORNIER BOUILLY BOUVIER CLAUDEL COCTEAU DENNERY FERRIER FEYDEAU GRESSET HERVIEU IONESCO LABICHE LAPLACE LARIVEY LAVEDAN LEGOUVE MAURIAC MEILHAC MEURICE MOLIERE MORTIER NUITTER PONSARD PREVOST ROSTAND SANDEAU SARMENT SEDAINE VILDRAC ANDRIEUX BARRIERE BATAILLE BEAUVOIR BENJAMIN CROISSET DANCOURT DUMANOIR FAUCHOIS MARIVAUX MONTEPIN QUINAULT VOLTAIRE BENSERADE BERNSTEIN BOURSAULT CORNEILLE DELAVIGNE DUVEYRIER LEMERCIER VACQUERIE CAMPISTRON CLAIRVILLE DESTOUCHES BEAUMARCHAIS
GERMAN BAB BABO BEER KIND LENZ BLOEM ERNST HALBE JOHST LAUBE SORGE UNRUH ZWEIG ANGELY BRECHT DREYER GOETHE HEBBEL KAISER KLEIST KORNER REUTER TOLLER WEISSE BARLACH BENEDIX BRONNEN GUTZKOW KLINGER LESSING RAUPACH REDWITZ VULPIUS BRENTANO GRYPHIUS HOCHHUTH KATZEBUE KOTZEBUE LISSAUER SCHILLER WEDEKIND WOLZOGEN BEYERLEIN GANGHOFER IMMERMANN SUDERMANN UECHTRITZ WILBRANDT ZUCKMAYER AUFFENBERG BLUMENTHAL FEUCHTWANGER
GREEK ALEXIS SOPHRON THESPIS CRATINUS PHILEMON RHINTHON AESCHYLUS EURIPEDES SOPHOCLES ANTIPHANES PHRYNICHUS PHERECRATES ARISTOPHANES
HUNGARIAN TOTH DOCZI JOKAI VAJDA MOLNAR ZILAHY BESSENYEI KISFALUDY SZIGLIGETI
ICELANDIC KAMBAN LAXNESS SIGURJONSSON
IRISH BEHAN COLUM KEANE KELLY SYNGE WILDE WILLS YEATS ERVINE MARTYN OCASEY TREVOR WELDON BECKETT DUNSANY GREGORY

GRIFFIN LEONARD MATURIN OKEEFFE SHEILDS ORIORDAN SHERIDAN BICKERSTAFFE
ITALIAN FO BETTI CECCHI GIRAUD ALFIERI ARETINO BENELLI CARRERA GIACOSA GOLDONI MARENCO PELLICO TORELLI RUCELLAI SABATINI CHIARELLI NICCOLINI METASTASIO PIRANDELLO
JAPANESE CHIKAMATSU
MEXICAN GAMBOA FUENTES
NORWEGIAN BOJER IBSEN HEIBERG BJORNSON KIELLAND
POLISH ASNYK FREDRO SZUJSKI ZAPOLSKA ZEROMSKI ZULAWSKI NALKOWSKA WYSPIANSKI BELCIKOWSKI BOGUSLAWSKI KORZENIOWSKI
PORTUGUESE SILVA BIESTER
ROMAN SENECA NAEVIUS PLAUTUS TERENCE PACUVIUS
RUMANIAN BEIN BLAGA
RUSSIAN ADAMOV KRYLOV CHEKHOV KAPNIST KIRSHON TOLSTOI BULGAKOV CHIRIKOV FONVIZIN POTEKHIN SUMBATOV ABLESIMOV BOBORYKIN OSTROVSKY KNARITONOV YUSHKEVICH KHMELNITSKI LAZHECHNIKOV
SCOTTISH BEITH BARRIE BRIDIE DAVIDSON ROBERTSON
SOUTH AFRICAN FUGARD
SPANISH CRUZ LARRA ROJAS RUEDA CANETE ENCINA ESPRIU ZAMORA ALARCON ARRABAL MACHADO MORATIN CALDERON DIAMANTE MARTINEZ CERVANTES FERNANDEZ
SWEDISH WEISS BESKOW EDGREN BLANCHE HEDBERG MESSENIUS LAGERKVIST STREINDBERG
SWISS ILG FAESI
WELSH ABSE EVANS HUGHES WILLIAMS LLEWELLYN

PLAZA PLACE PLEIN SQUARE ZOCALO
(— DE TOROS) BULLRING
(— GIRL) ELOISE

PLEA BAR BID PLY MOOT NOLO SUIT ALIBI CLAIM PLEAD ABATER APPEAL EXCUSE REFUGE APOLOGY CONTEND DEFENCE LAWSUIT PRETEXT QUARREL DILATORY ENTREATY PLACITUM PRETENSE

PLEACH PLAIT PLASH INTERLACE

PLEAD BEG SUE MOOT PLEA PRAY PRIG SHOW URGE COUNT ORATE ALLEGE APPEAL ASSERT PLAYTE PURSUE ENTREAT IMPLORE SOLICIT WRANGLE ADVOCATE LITIGATE
(— FOR) SOLICIT PETITION

PLEADER ACTOR VAKIL PATRON SUITOR VAKEEL COUNTOR ADVOCATE

PLEADING PLEA PAROL ANSWER PAROLE ADVOCACY COGNOVIT DEMURRER INTENDIT MEMORIAL

PLEASANT FUN GAY BEEN BIEN BRAW FAIR FINE GLAD GOOD HEND JOLI NEAT TRIM WEME AMENE BIGLY BONNY CANNY COUTH CUSHY DOUCE DRUNK DUCKY GREEN HAPPY HENDE HODDY JOLLY LEPID LISTY LUSTY MERRY NUTTY QUEME SMIRK SUAVE SWEET TIPSY WALLY WETHE COMELY DAINTY DULCET GENIAL KINDLY PRETTY SAVORY SMOOTH AFFABLE ELEGANT FARRAND JANNOCK LEESOME WINSOME DELICATE GLORIOUS GRATEFUL HEAVENLY LIEFSOME LIKESOME LOVESOME THANKFUL TOWARDLY GEMUTLICH
(PREF.) HEDY

PLEASANTLY FAIR WINLY FAIRLY AFFABLY SWEETLY GENIALLY LIKINGLY

PLEASANTNESS GAIETY NAAMAN AMENITY SUAVITY JOCUNDITY

PLEASANTRY WIT JEST JOKE SPORT BANTER JESTING JOLLITY WAGGERY

PLEASE PAY GAME LIKE LIST LUST SUIT WANT WISH AGREE AMUSE BITTE CHARM ELATE FANCY HUMOR QUEME SAVOR TASTE ARRIDE KITTLE OBLIGE REGALE SOOTHE TICKLE AGGRATE APPLESE CONTENT DELIGHT GLADDEN GRATIFY PLACATE REJOICE SATISFY
(— FORWARD) FS
(— THE PUBLIC) TAKE

PLEASED FAIN FOND GLAD APAID HAPPY PROUD BUCKED CONTENT GLADSOME
(BE —) GAME

PLEASING AMEN COOL GLAD GOOD LIEF NICE SOFT AMENE DICTY NIFTY SOOTH SWEET CLEVER COMELY DREAMY FACILE FLASHY GAINLY LIKING LUSTLY MELLOW PRETTY AMIABLE BLESSED CORKING DARLING LIKABLE LIKEFUL TUNABLE WELCOME CHARMING DELICATE FAVOROUS FETCHING GRACEFUL GRACIOUS GRATEFUL HEAVENLY INVITING LIKESOME PLACABLE PLAUSIVE SPECIOUS PLAUSIBLE PERSONABLE
(— TO EAR) HARMONIC
(— TO EYE) EESOME
(— TO HEAR) FAIR
(VERY —) SNAZZY

PLEASURABLE GOOD JOLLY ANIMAL MIRTHFUL

PLEASURE JO EST FUN JOY BANG BOOT EASE ESTE GREE KAMA LIST LUST PLAY WILL BLISS KICKS MIRTH SAVOR SOOTH TASTE DAINTY DEDUIT GAIETY GAYETY LIKING LUXURY NICETY VOLUPT COMFORT DELIGHT GRATIFY JOLLITY JOYANCE VOLUPTY DELICACY FRUITION GLADNESS HILARITY VOLUPTAS
(— BY INFLICTING PAIN) SADISM
(INTERJECTION TO EXPRESS —) YUMYUM
(SELFISH —) LECHERY
(STOLEN —) STOUTH STOWTH
(PL.) DELICIAE

PLEASURE SEEKER FRANION

PLEAT SET FOLD KILT POKE RUCK FLUTE FRILL PINCH PLAIT PRANK GUSSET SUNRAY

PLEATED PLICATE SUNBURST

PLEBE PLEBS FRESHMAN

PLEBEIAN LOW BASE PLEB SNOB COMMON HOMELY VULGAR IGNOBLE LOWBORN POPULAR BASEBORN EVERYDAY HOMESPUN INFERIOR MECHANIC ORDINARY ROTURIER RUPTUARY

PLEBISCITE VOTE DECREE

PLECTRUM PICK SPUR QUILL UVULA MALLEUS POINTEL PLECTRON
(— OF HARP) FESCUE

PLEDGE LAY VAS VOW WAD WED AFFY BAND CLAP EARL GAGE HAND HEST HOCK OATH PASS PAWN WAGE WOID WORD FAITH SIKER SPOUT STAKE SWEAR SWEAT TOKEN TROTH TRUTH WAGER ARREST BORROW COMMIT ENGAGE IMPAWN IMPONE LUMBER PAROLE PIGNUS PLEVIN PLIGHT SICCAR SICKER VADIUM WADSET BARGAIN BETROTH CAUTION CREANCE EARNEST HOSTAGE PROMISE BOTTOMRY MORTGAGE SECURITY SPONSION VADIMONY
(— IN DRINKING) PROPINE
(— ONESELF) UNDERTAKE

PLEDGED HIGHT SWORN ASSURED ENGAGED PIGNORATE
(— TO MARRY) SURE

PLEDGET DOSSIL PENICIL

PLEIADES MAIA MEROPE ALCYONE CELAENO ELECTRA STEROPE TAYGETA

PLEIN-AIRIST LUMINIST

PLEISTHENES (FATHER OF —) ATREUS
(MOTHER OF —) AEROPE
(SON OF —) MENELAUS AGAMEMNON

PLENARY FULL ENTIRE PLENAL PERFECT ABSOLUTE COMPLETE

PLENITUDE PLENITY PLEROMA FULLNESS PLETHORA ABUNDANCE

PLENTEOUS RICH COPIOUS FERTILE AFFLUENT FRUITFUL GENEROUS ABOUNDING EXUBERANT

PLENTIFUL OLD FULL RANK RICH RIFE AMPLE HEFTY LARGE ROUTH SONSY STORE ENOUGH FOISON GALORE LAVISH SONSIE COPIOUS FERTILE LIBERAL OPULENT PROFUSE UBEROUS ABUNDANT FRUITFUL NUMEROUS EXUBERANT

PLENTIFULLY RIFE FREELY GALORE APLENTY

PLENTY WON BAIT COPY MANY RAFF SONS AMPLE CHEAP COPIA FOUTH PRICE ROUTH SONSE TEEMS FOISON OODLES SCOUTH UBERTY LASHINGS
(— OF) GALORE
(GREAT —) ABUNDANCE

PLEON TELSON ABDOMEN

PLEONASM ITERATION MACROLOGY TAUTOLOGY

PLETHORA RASH EXCESS PLENUM PLURISY FULLNESS PLEURISY POLYEMIA PROFUSION REPLETION

PLETHORIC TUMID TURGID SWOLLEN INFLATED

PLEURISY EMPYEMA

PLEURON SCAPULA

PLEXUS RETE GLOMUS NETWORK PROPLEX GENIPLEX

PLIABLE WAXY WEAK LITHY WAXEN DOCILE LIMBER PLIANT SEMMIT SUPPLE BOWABLE FICTILE FINGENT FLEXILE PLASTIC WINDING CUSHIONY FLEXIBLE COMPLIANT

PLIANCY FLEXURE FACILITY

PLIANT APT FLIP SWAK AGILE BUXOM LITHE SWACK YOUNG DOCILE LIMBER SUPPLE WANDLE DUCTILE FLEXILE PLASTIC PLIABLE SLIPPER WILLOWY APPLIANT FLEXIBLE SUITABLE WORKABLE SEQUACIOUS

PLICA FOLD TRICHOMA

PLICATE FOLD PLEAT FOLDED FANLIKE PLAITED

PLIERS BENDER FLEXOR GRATER FLECTOR PINCERS

PLIGHT PLY FOLD ARRAY BRAID DRESS PLAIT POINT STATE WOVEN ATTIRE ENGAGE PICKLE PLEDGE PLISKY STRAIT TAKING BETROTH MISCHIEF QUANDARY

PLIGHTED ASSURATE

PLIM PLUM STOUT SWELL INFLATE PLIABLE

PLIMSOLL (WHITE —S) MUTTONDUMMIES
(PL.) RUBBERS

PLINTH ORLE ORLO BLOCK SOCLE ABACUS PATAND QUADRA SUBBASE FOOTSTALL SCAMILLUS

PLISTHENES (FATHER OF —) ATREUS
(MOTHER OF —) CLEOLA
(SON OF —) MENELAUS AGAMEMNON
(WIFE OF —) AEROPE ERIPHYLE

PLOD JOG GRUB PLOT SLOG STOG TOIL TORE TROG VAMP POACH TRAMP TRASH DRUDGE SLOUCH TRUDGE PLUNTHER
(— ALONG) PEG TORE
(— THROUGH MUD) SLOUGH

PLODDER GRUB DIGGER SLOGGER

PLOIARIA EMESA

PLONK WINE

PLOP FLUMP PLUMP HEAVILY
(— DOWN) SIT

PLOT BREW CAST MARK PACK PLAN PLAT CABAL DRIFT FRAUD GLEBE GRAPH GREEN HATCH MODEL PLECK SCALD STORY STUDY WATCH ACTION BRIGUE CLIQUE DESIGN DEVISE GARDEN MALIGN MYTHOS SCHEME SHAMBA TAMPER AGITATE COLLUDE COMPACT COMPASS CONJECT CONNIVE CONTOUR DRAUGHT FEEDLOT LAZYBED MACHINE PRETEND QUADRAT QUARTER

SWIDDEN ARGUMENT COGITATE CONSPIRE CONTRIVE INTRIGUE PRACTICE PROTRACT SEMINARY MACHINATE
(— OF GRASS) SONK
(— OF LAND) ERF LOT PLAT SHOT FORTY MILPA PATCH PLECK SPLAT COMMON PARCEL SCHERM SHAMBA HAGGARD LAZYBED SEVERAL
(— OF 1-2 ACRE) ERF
(— SECRETLY) WHISPER
(GARDEN —) BED ERF QUINTA QUARTER
(UNPRODUCTIVE —) HIRST
PLOTTER PACKER HATCHER JACOBIN SCHEMER DESIGNER ENGINEER
PLOUK KNOB PIMPLE
PLOVER DROME KOLEA OXEYE PILOT SANDY STILT KILDEE QUAILY TURNIX COLLIER COURSER DOTTREL LAPWING MAYCOCK OWLHEAD PAPABOT WRYBILL BULLHEAD DOTTEREL DULWILLY HILLBIRD KILLDEER RINGNECK SPURWING SQUEALER TOADHEAD WHISTLER WIREBIRD SANDERLING
PLOW EAR ERE BOUT DISK FOIL HINT LIST MOLE PLOD RIVE ROVE SLUG STIR SULK SULL TILL BREAK FLUNK SPLIT SULKY THROW ARAIRE BUSTER DIGGER DIPPER FALLOW FURROW GOPHER JUMPER LISTER PLOUGH RAFTER ROOTER RUTTER SULLOW BACKSET BREAKER HUSBAND SCOOTER SULCATE TWISTER FIREPLOW FURROWER GANGPLOW SNOWPLOW TURNPLOW
(— CROSSWISE) THORTER
(— HANDLE) STILT
(— LIGHTLY) SKIM RIFFLE
(— PART) PINHEAD
(— WITH SPACE BETWEEN FURROWS) RIB RIVE
(MOTORIZED —) TRACTOR
(PL.) OUTSIGHT
PLOWBOY YOKEL
PLOWING ARDER EARTH ARDURE ARATION CARUAGE STIRRING
PLOWLAND CARUE CARVE TILTH CARUCATE TEAMLAND
PLOWMAN PLOWER TILLER ACREMAN
PLOWSHARE LAY SLIP SOCK LAVER REEST SHARE JUMPER
(— BONE) VOMER PYGOSTYLE
(PREF.) VOMERO
PLOY BENT BOWED SPORT RAMBLE TACTIC PURSUIT ACTIVITY ESCAPADE
PLUCK GO PUG ROB TUG BOUT CROP CULL DRAG GAME GRAB GRIT PELT PICK PILL POOK PULL RACE RASE RASH SAND TUCK ARBER ARBOR BREAK DRAFT HANGE MOXIE NERVE PILCH PLOAT PLUME RANCH SMITE SPUNK STEAL STRIP AVULSE DECERP EVULSE FLEECE GATHER PIGEON PLITCH PLOUGH QUARRY SNATCH SPIRIT TWINGE TWITCH COURAGE DEPLUME PLUNDER BOLDNESS DECISION DEMOLISH GAMENESS GUMPTION VELLICATE PURTENANCE
(— APART) DIVELLICATE
(— AS A STRING) TIRL PINCH
(— FEATHERS) STUB
(— LEAVES) BLADE
(— OF SHEEP OR CALF) RACE GATHER
(— UP COURAGE) CHEER
(— WOOL BY HAND) ROO
PLUCKED PLUMED PIZZICATO
PLUCKY GAMY SANDY BANTAM GRITTY SPUNKY FIGHTING
PLUG BUG FID PEG PIN TAP TOP WAD BLOW BONE BOTT BUNG FILL JADE ROOT SHOT SLOG STOP SWAT SWOT BOOST DOWEL DUMMY PILOT PUNCH SHACK SKATE SPILE STUFF SWEAT BOUCHE BOXING BULLET COMEDO DOSSIL DOTTLE FIDDLE SPIGOT BOUCHON BUSHING CHAMBER CHUGGER FERRULE STOPPER STOPPLE DRIVECAP FUSEPLUG PELELITH STOPCOCK
(— FOR CANNON) TAMPION
(— IN GRENADE) BOUCHON
(— IN ORGAN PIPE) STOPPLE TAMPION
(— OF CLAY) BOTT
(— OF OAKUM) FID
(— OF VOLCANO) CORE
(— TO HOLD NAIL) DOOK
(— UP) CLAM STOP ESTOP RAMFORCE
(FIRE —) HYDRANT
(FISHING —) BUG
(LIP —) LABRET
(NOSE —) TEMBETA TEMBETARA
(WASTE —) WASHER
(WATER —) HYDRANT
PLUG-IN JACK
PLUG-UGLY THUG ROWDY TOUGH RUFFIAN ROUGHNECK
PLUM GAGE JOBO RISE ISLAY JAMAN PRUNE SWELL BEAUTY CHENEY DAMSEL DAMSON KELSEY MUSSEL SAPOTE APRICOT BULLACE BURBANK FORTUNE ORLEANS QUETSCH PRUNELLO ROSACEAN ROSEWORT VICTORIA WINDFALL
(COCO —) ICACO
(JAVA —) DUHAT JAMBUL JAMBOOL JAMBOLAN
(WILD —) SKEG SLOE ISLAY
(PREF.) PRUNI
PLUMAGE ROBE RUFF FLUFF HACKLE SHROUD FEATHER FLOCCUS JUVENAL PENNAGE FEATHERS PARADISE PTILOSIS
PLUMB BUNG SHEER BOTTOM BULLET SINKER EXACTLY PLUMMET UTTERLY ABSOLUTE COMPLETE DIRECTLY ENTIRELY VERTICAL
PLUMBAGO LUSTER LUSTRE GRAPHITE LEADWORT
PLUMB BOB PLUMMET
PLUMBISM SATURNISM
PLUMB LINE MERKHET
PLUM CURCULIO TURK WEEVIL
PLUME PEN TIP TUFT CREST EGRET PRIDE PRUNE DEPRIVE DESPOIL FEATHER PANACHE AIGRETTE
(— ON HELMET) CREST PANACHE
(— ON HORSE) PLUMADE
(— ON TURBAN) CULGEE
(EGRET —) OSPREY
(MILITARY —) PANACHE
PLUME NUTMEG SASSAFRAS
PLUMMET LEAD FLOAT PLUMB WEIGHT
PLUMMING BRONZING
PLUMP FAT BOLD FAIR FLOP FULL PLOP SLAP SOSS TIDY BLUNT BONNY BUXOM CLUMP FLUMP FUBBY FUBSY GROUP JOLLY PLUNK PUDGY SAPPY SLEEK SMACK SONSY SQUAB STOUT THICK BONNIE CHUBBY CRUMBY CRUMMY DIRECT FATTEN FLATLY FLESHY FODGEL GAWSIE PLUNGE PUBBLE ROTUND ZAFTIG ZOFTIG BLUNTLY BUNTING CLUSTER DISTEND FULSOME RIBLESS THRODDY CHOPPING FLESHFUL
(— AND ROSY) BUXOM
(— AND ROUND) CHUBBY
(NOT —) ANGULAR
(PLEASINGLY —) ZAFTIG ZOFTIG
PLUM POCKET FOOL
PLUMULE BLASTUS FEATHER GEMMULA GEMMULE GEOBLAST ACROSPIRE
PLUNDER GUT ROB BOOT FANG JUNK LOOT PILL POLL PREY RAID RAPE REIF RIPE RUMP SACK SWAG BEROB BOOTY CHEAT GAINS HARRY PLUCK PREDE RAVEN REAVE RENNE RIFLE SCOFF SHAVE SPOIL STRIP BEZZLE BOODLE CREACH DACOIT FLEECE FORAGE HARROW MARAUD PANYAR PROFIT RAPINE RAVAGE DESPOIL ESCHEAT FREIGHT PILFERY PILLAGE RANSACK SACKAGE SPREAGH SPULZIE BOOTHALE FREEBOOT SPOLIATE
PLUNDERER THIEF BANDIT BUMMER PEELER POLLER RAPTOR ROBBER VANDAL ROUTIER SPOILER MARAUDER RAPPAREE
PLUNDERING PREY SACK MARAUD RAPINE ESCHEAT HERSHIP PURCHASE RAVENOUS SPECHERY SPOILFUL SPOILING PREDATORY
PLUNGE BET DIG DIP CAVE DIVE DOOK DUCK DUMP JUMP PURL PUSH RAKE RISK SINK SOSS BURST DOUSE FLING PITCH PLUMP SOUSE SWOOP FOOTER GAMBLE HEADER LAUNCH SPLASH THRUST WALLOP BRAINGE DEMERGE IMMERSE PLOUNCE SUBMERGE
(— DEEPLY) WHELM
(— INTO) CLAP ENGULF IMMERGE
(— INTO WATER) ENEW
(BETTING —) RAKER
(GAMBLING —) RAKER
PLUNGER RAM SWAB FORCE DUCKER POMMEL BLUNGER STRIKER
PLUNGING FLING
PLUNK DIVE PLONK PLUCK PLUMP DOLLAR SUPPORT SUDDENLY
PLUNTHER PLOD FLOUNDER
PLURAL
(SUFF.) IM
PLURALIST TOTQUOT
PLURALITY MAJORITY MORENESS TRIALITY
(PREF.) POLY
PLURALIZER ESS
PLUS AND GAIN WITH EXTRA BESIDES SURPLUS ADDITION INCREASE POSITIVE
PLUSH EASY BEAVER VELOUR SUPERIOR
PLUSHY SWANK SWANKY
PLUTEUS WAGON PARAPET
PLUTO DIS HADES ORCUS
(BROTHER OF —) JUPITER NEPTUNE
(FATHER OF —) SATURN
(WIFE OF —) PROSERPINE
PLUTOCRAT NABOB RICHARD
PLUTONIC HYPOGENE INTRUSIVE VULCANIAN
PLUTUS (ASSOCIATE OF —) TYCHE EIRENE
(FATHER OF —) IASION
(MOTHER OF —) CERES DEMETER
PLY RUN BEAT BEND BIAS CORD CORE DRAM FOLD MOLD SAIL URGE ADAPT APPLY EXERT LAYER STEER TWIST WIELD YIELD COMPLY DOUBLE HANDLE TRAVEL EXERCISE
(— NEEDLE) SEW
(— WITH DRINK) BIRL ROSIN
(— WITH DRUGS) HOCUS
(— WITH QUESTIONS) HECKLE
(OF ONE —) SINGLE
PLYWOOD (LIKE —) LAMINAR
PNEUMA NEUM SOUL NEUME BREATH SPIRIT
PNEUMATIC HAMMER GUN
PNEUMATOCYST FLOAT
PNEUMONIA PULMONITIS
POACH PUG ROB COOK DROP POKE PUSH SINK BLACK DRIVE FORCE POTCH STEAL BLEACH PLUNGE INTRUDE
POACHED EGGS MOONSHINE
POACHER BLACK POGGE SPOACH LURCHER STALKER WIDGEON BALDPATE BULLHEAD
(SALMON —) REBECCA REBEKAH
(PL.) BLACKS
POALES GLUMALES
POCAHONTAS (HUSBAND OF —) ROLFE
POCHARD DUCK SMEE DIVER POKER SCAUP DUNAIR DUNKER DUNBIRD REDHEAD WHINGER GOLDHEAD WHINYARD
POCHETTE KIT VIOLIN HANDBAG
POCKET BOX CLY FOB PIT CLAY KICK POKE PRAT BASIN BURSE MEANS POUCH PURSE STEAL ACCEPT BECKET CASING CANTINA PLACKET SWALLOW TROUSER ENVELOPE ISOLATED MONETARY PROFONDE SUPPRESS CONDENSED MINIATURE

(— A WRONG) PURSE
(— IN BOOK BINDER) STATION
(— OF NET) BOWL
(BILLIARD —) POT HOLE HAZARD
(KIND OF —) BESOM HACKING KANGAROO
(MAGICIAN'S —) PROFONDE
(NOODLE —S) KREPLACH
(ORE —) CHURN BONANZA
(SMALL —) FOB
(TROUSER —) PRAT BECKET
(WATCH —) FOB
(WATER —) TINAJA ALBERCA
(PL.) KREPLACH
(PREF.) PERO

POCKETBOOK BAG KICK SKIN PURSE INCOME READER WALLET HANDBAG LEATHER BILLFOLD NOTECASE

POCKET GOPHER TUZA QUACHIL

POCKETING COUP

POCKETKNIFE BARLOW PENKNIFE PIGSTICKER

POCKMARK PITHOLE

POD BAG COD GAM KID POP SAC BALL BEAN BOLL HULL HUSK POKE SWAD BOLLY BURSE CAROB FLOCK POUCH QUASH SHAUP SHELL SHUCK SNAIL WHAUP CHILLI LEGUME PESCOD SCHOOL HARICOT PEASCOD SILIQUA PEASECOD PODOCARP POTBELLY SEEDCASE TAMARIND
(— FORMING) KID
(— OF LEGUME) KID
(— OF MESQUITE) HONEYPOD
(BABLAH —S) NEBNEB
(CASSIA —) PUDDINGPIPE
(COILED —) STROMBUS
(EXPLOSIVE —) SANDBOX
(SUBTERRANEAN —) EARTHNUT
(UNRIPE —) SQUASH
(PL.) PIPI SUNT BABUL GARAD BABLAH GARRAT COWHAGE GONAKIE ALGAROBA DIVIDIVI
(PREF.) SILIQUI

PODALIRIUS (BROTHER OF —) MACHAON
(FATHER OF —) ASCLEPIUS

PODARCES (BROTHER OF —) PROTESILAUS
(FATHER OF —) IPHICLUS

PODDED BOLLED

PODIUM DAIS FOOT WALL LECTERN

PODOCARP YACCA

PODWARE PODDER

PODZOL SPODOSOL

POEM GEM LAI LAY ODE DUAN EPIC GEST IDYL JOSE MELE POSY RUNE SONG CENTO DIRGE DITTY EDYLL GESTE HAIKU IWEIN METER STAFF VERSE AMHRAN AUBADE BALLAD CACCIA CARMEN CYCLIC DIXAIN EPOPEE EROTIC ESTRIF HEROID MELODY MONODY NOSTOS PIYYUT SESTET SONNET TENSON TERCET BUCOLIC CANTARE CANTATA CANZONE DESCORT DIZAINE ECLOGUE ELEGIAC FLITING GEORGIC SOTADIC TRIOLET VIRELAI VIRELAY VOLUSPA ACROSTIC AMOEBEUM BRINDISI CANTICLE DINGDONG DOGGEREL INVICTUS LIMERICK MADRIGAL TELESTIC THEOGONY TRISTICH TROCHAIC VERSICLE MONORHYME ROUNDELAY
(— ABOUT DEBATE) ESTRIF
(— ABOUT SHEPHERDS) ECLOGUE
(— GREETING DAWN) AUBADE
(— OF LAMENTATION) ELEGY
(— OF RETRACTION) PALINODE
(— OF 10 LINES) DIZAINE
(— OF 14 LINES) SONNET
(AMATORY —) EROTIC SONNET
(EPIC —) EPOS EPOPEE LUSIAD THEBAID
(HOMELY —) DIT
(IRISH —) AMHRAN
(JAPANESE —) HAIKU RANKA TANKA SENRYU
(LITURGICAL —) VIDDUI VIDDUY SELIHOTH
(LOVE —) AMORETTO
(LYRIC —) LAI LAY ODE ALBA EPODE GHAZEL RONDEL CANZONA PARTIMEN
(MUSICAL —) RONDO
(PART OF —) PASSUS
(PASTORAL —) IDYL IDYLL BUCOLIC
(PERSIAN —) GHAZAL
(RELIGIOUS —) HYMN
(RURAL —) GEORGIC
(SACRED —) PSALM YIGDAL
(SATIRICAL —) IAMBIC KASIDA
(SHORT —) DIT DITTY EPILOG RONDEL SONNET CANZONE EPIGRAM RONDEAU EPILOGUE EPYLLION
(TONE —) BALLADE
(WELSH —) CYWYDD
(PL.) AZAHROT MAKINGS
(SUFF.) STICH

POET OG RSI BARD FILE FILI FIRI LARK MUSE SCOP SWAN ARION LAKER LINOS LINUS LYRIC MAKAR MAKER ODIST RISHI SAYER SCALD SKALD FINDER GNOMIC IBYCUS LAKIST LYRIST SHAPER SINGER DICHTER ELEGIAC EPICIST IDYLIST IMAGIST MUSAEUS ORPHEUS PROPHET CONCRETE FERAMORZ GEORGIAN LAUREATE LUTANIST MINSTREL SONGSTER TROUVERE MINNESINGER
(INSPIRED —) PROPHET
(IRISH —) FILI
(MEDIOCRE —) RIMER RHYMER
(MINOR —) BARDIE
ALBANIAN FISHTA
AMERICAN BLY LOW POE AGAR AGEE BURR CARY CONE DALY HEAD KEMP MARX NASH READ REED SAXE SILL SNOW TABB TATE TOWN VERY WARE ADAMS AIKEN AKINS ALLEN AUDEN BACON BEERS BENET BOGAN BROWN CLAPP CLARK COLES CORSO CRANE DAMON DRAKE ENGLE FAUST FICKE FIELD FINCH FITTS FROST GUEST HAYNE HECHT HOVEY JOLAS MOODY OPPEN PIATT POUND PRIME RIDGE RILEY SIMIC STORY TOWNE WELBY WILDE WYLIE ARNOLD BARLOW BRALEY BRANCH BROOKS BRYANT BURTON CARMER CAWEIN CHENEY CIARDI CLARKE COATES COFFIN CRANCH CULLEN CUTTER DARGAN DUNBAR FISHER GIBRAN GILDER GIORNO GUINEY HOLMES HOOPER KEELER KILMER LANIER LEDOUX LOWELL MILLAY MILLER MONROE MORGAN MORTON NORTON OSGOOD PARKER SAVAGE SEEGER SEXTON SHANGE THOMAS TIMROD TOOMER VIORST WILCOX WRIGHT AINSLIE BABCOCK BRODSKY CARRUTH CHIVERS CROWELL EMERSON FEARING FRENEAU HALLECK HILLYER JEFFERS KNOWLES LAFARGE LAZARUS LIFSHIN LINDSAY MARKHAM MIFFLIN MOULTON PARSONS PATCHEN PEABODY PROCTOR ROBERTS RUSSELL SHAPIRO SHERMAN STEDMAN TAGGARD THAXTER VIERECK WAKOSKI WATTLES WHITMAN BERRYMAN BRAINARD CARLETON CONKLING CORNFORD CUMMINGS DINSMOOR FISHBACK FLETCHER GINSBURG HAGEDORN MACLEISH NEIHARDT PETERSON PHILLIPS PROKOSCH ROBINSON RUKEYSER SANDBURG SCOLLARD SPOFFORD STERLING STODDARD TEASDALE THOMPSON TIETJENS TRUMBULL WHEATLEY WHITTIER AUSLANDER COOLBRITH DICKINSON GUITERMAN HENDERSON HOLLANDER HOPKINSON KREYMBORG OPPENHEIM TUCKERMAN WURDEMANN COATSWORTH LONGFELLOW BRAITHWAITE RITTENHOUSE
ARAB TARAFA
ARGENTINIAN ASCASUBI ECHEVERRIA
AUSTRALIAN GORDON TURNER
AUSTRIAN VOGL KAFKA BACHER FRANKL GRAZIE WERFEL NEUMANN ZEDLITZ CASTELLI WILDGANS WURZBACH ZINGERLE HAMERLING HOFMANNSTHAL
BELGIAN CLAUS GILKIN GIRAUD EEKHOUD ELSKAMP HASSELT CAMMAERTS RODENBACH VERHAEREN MAETERLINCK
BRAZILIAN GAMA COSTA AZEVEDO BANDEIRA GUIMARAES MAGALHAES
BULGARIAN VAZOV BOTYOV
CANADIAN FISET PRATT SCOTT SMITH BIRNIE CARMAN MACKAY MCCRAE FERLAND JOHNSON LAMPMAN SERVICE CAMPBELL CRAWFORD DRUMMOND FRECHETTE MACDONALD
CHILEAN NERUDA MISTRAL
CHINESE LU TU CHAO LIPO TUFU POCHUI MEISHENG
COLOMBIAN ARBOLEDA
CUBAN VALDES
CZECH CECH GOLL ERBEN FRIDA HALEK HANKA JEBAVY KVAPIL MACHAR NERUDA SEIFERT
DANISH BOYE RODE EWALD HAUCH KINGO PLOUG ARREBO JENSEN RAHBEK BLICHER CLAUSEN HOSTRUP KAALUND WINTHER BAGGESEN BODTCHER INGEMANN JACOBSEN AARESTRUP GRUNDTVIG JORGENSEN GERSTENBERG
DUTCH CATS GOES KATE POOT BEETS BERGH EEDEN FEITH HAREN HOOFT DECKER EMANTS LENNEP LOGHEM VERWEY VONDEL BELLAMY BREDERO HELMERS TOLLENS BARLEAUS SECUNDUS ACHTERBERG BILDERDIJK HEEMSKERCK HUYDECOPER BROEKHUIZEN
ECUADORIAN OLMEDO
ENGLISH BAX GAY MAY MEW PYE BELL BIGG COOK CORY DYER GALE GRAY HAKE HALL HILL HOOD HUNT KOPS LEAR NOEL OWEN POPE ROWE TATE VAUX ADAMS AUDEN BASSE BLAKE BLUNT BROWN BRYAN BYROM BYRON CAREW CAREY CLARE COOKE DIXON DONNE DOYLE GOOGE GOULD GOWER GREEN JONES KEATS KEOWN LEWIS MASON MERRY MILNE MINOT MONRO MOORE MYERS NADEN NOYES PAYNE PEELE PERCY PRAED PRIOR SMART SMITH SWAIN WATTS WAUGH WELLS WHITE WOLFE WOODS WYATT YOUNG ABBOTT ANSTEY ARNOLD AUSTIN BAILEY BARKER BARLOW BARNES BARTON BINYON BOWLES BRETON BRONTE BROOKE BROWNE BUTLER CANTON CAPERN CARTER CLOUGH CORBET COTTON COWLEY COWPER CRABBE DANIEL DAVIES DENHAM DOBELL DOBSON DOMETT DOWSON DRYDEN EUSDEN FENTON GIBSON GLOVER GODDEN GODLEY GRAVES GREENE HARVEY HAWKER HAYLEY HEMANS HOWARD JONSON KENYON LANDON LANDOR LARKIN LYTTON MACKAY MARTIN MASSEY MCLEOD MILMAN MILNES MILTON MORRIS MUNDAY NESBIT ROGERS SAVAGE SCOGAN SEWARD SISSON STRODE SYMONS TAYLOR THOMAS TREECE TRENCH WALLER WARNER WARREN WARTON WATSON WITHER WOLCOT WOTTON AINSLIE BAMFORD BARCLAY BLUNDEN BRIDGES CAEDMON CAMPION CHAPMAN CHAUCER COKAYNE COLLINS COPPARD CRASHAW DARYUSH DOUGHTY DRAYTON ELLIOTT FAUSSET FLATMAN FLECKER FRAUNCE FREEMAN GIBBONS GIFFORD GRIGSON HERRICK HEWLETT HOPKINS HOUSMAN INGELOW KENNEDY KIPLING LAYAMON LYDGATE MANNYNG MARLOWE MARVELL MEYNELL MONTAGU NEWBOLT NICHOLS PATMORE PEACOCK PHILIPS POMFRET PROCTER QUARLES SASSOON SEYMOUR SHELLEY SITWELL SKELTON SKIPSEY SOUTHEY SPENDER SPENSER SYMONDS TICKELL TREVENA VAUGHAN WEBSTER WOOLNER AKENSIDE BEAUMONT BETJEMAN BLAGMIRE BRANFORD

BRERELEY BROWNING BUCHANAN
CAMPBELL CHALONER CYNEWULF
DAVENANT FALCONER GASCOYNE
GREVILLE HAMILTON HOCCLEVE
LANGLAND LOVELACE MACNEICE
MOULTRIE OVERBURY ROSSETTI
SHADWELL STERLING SUCKLING
TENNYSON THOMPSON TRAHERNE
WHISTLER ALDINGTON
ARMSTRONG BARNFIELD
BLANCHARD BOTTOMLEY
CALVERLEY CAMBRIDGE CHALKHILL
CHURCHILL CLEVELAND COLERIDGE
CONSTABLE GASCOIGNE
GOLDSMITH HABINGTON
LANGHORNE MASEFIELD
MONKHOUSE ROSCOMMON
SACKVILLE SHENSTONE
SOUTHWELL SWINBURNE
SYLVESTER UNDERHILL WHITEHEAD
BLOOMFIELD BOURDILLON
BRATHWAITE CHATTERTON
DRINKWATER FITZGERALD
MONTGOMERY SOMERVILLE
WORDSWORTH ABERCROMBIE
SHAKESPEARE TURBERVILLE
CHAMBERLAYNE OSHAUGHNESSY
FINNISH MANNINEN RUNEBERG
ARWIDSSON TAVASTSTJERNA
FRENCH NAU AIDE BAIF CHAR FORT
GHIL GRAS KAHN LABE VIAU ARENE
BOREL CARCO DIERX DORAT DUCIS
GACON GREGH GUYAU HARDY
LEGER LOUYS MAROT MURET
PERET PIRON RETTE SCEVE SULLY
TASTU VIGNY AICARD ARAGON
ARTAUD AUGIER AUTRAN BARTAS
BELLAY BERTIN BRETON BRUNET
COPPEE DANIEL DEREME DUPONT
ELUARD FRANCE GUERIN HUGUES
JAMMES LEBRUN MORICE MUSSET
PARODI PRADON RACINE REBOUL
RICARD RICTUS SAMAIN THIARD
VALERY VILLON ANCELOT AUBANEL
BARBIER BOCCAGE BOILEAU
BONNARD BORNIER BOUCHOR
BOURGET BRIZEUX CARRERE
CAZALIS CHENIER CLAUDEL
COCTEAU DELTEIL FEYDEAU
GAUTIER GILBERT GRESSET
HENRIOT HEREDIA JODELLE
LAPRADE MATHIEU MAYNARD
MISTRAL MOLINET PONSARD
REGNIER RIMBAUD RONSARD
ROSTAND SCARRON SEGRAIS
VICAIRE VILDRAC AJALBERT
ANDRIEUX BEAUVOIR BERANGER
BERGERAT BERTRAND BOUILHET
CHARTIER CHAULIEU COLLERYE
CORBIERE GRECOURT GRINGORE
LAFORGUE MALHERBE MALLARME
PEROCHON PERRAULT QUILLARD
QUINAULT RABELAIS ROUSSEAU
VERLAINE BELMONTET BOUFFLERS
CHAPELAIN CREBILLON DELAVIGNE
DESCHAMPS LAMARTINE
LEMERCIER MONTREUIL
PRUDHOMME ARLINCOURT
BARTHELEMY BAUDELAIRE
BOISROBERT CHENEDOLLE
DESPORITES MALFILATRE
CHANTAVOINE GRANDMOUGIN
DESHOULIERES
GERMAN UZ BAUM BOIE DACH
HUCH KLAJ LENZ RIST VOSS AYRER
BOHME BRANT BUSCH FRANK
GLEIM HARDT HEBEL HEINE HERTZ
HOLTY LANGE LOGAU OPITZ RAABE
RILKE SACHS SORGE STEIN UNRUH
WEBER BECKER BRECHT BROGER
BURGER DEHMEL FOLLEN GEORGE
GOETHE GOTTER GRABBE HAMMER
HEBBEL HERDER HESSUS JORDAN
KARSCH KERNER KLEIST KNEBEL
KOBELL KORNER LEFORT MORIKE
MULLER TIEDGE TOLLER UHLAND
ULRICH WALDIS WEISSE WERNER
ALLMERS BARLACH BARTHEL
BOTTGER BROCKES BUCHNER
FONTANE FORSTER GELLERT
HARRIES HENRICI KALBECK
KASTNER KOPSICH MALTITZ
NEUMARK NOVALIS REDWITZ
RUCKERT VISCHER WALTHER
WIELAND BAUMBACH BIERBAUM
BRENTANO CLAUDIUS ECKSTEIN
FLEMMING FREIDANK GERHARDT
GRYPHIUS HAGEDORN HOFFMANN
JUNGHANS KAUFMANN LISSAUER
MAHLMANN OVERBECK SCHEFFEL
SCHILLER SCHUBART STOLBERG
WERNICKE ACIDALIUS BECHSTEIN
BULTHAUPT HAUPTMANN
HOLDERLIN IMMERMANN
KIRCHBACH KLOPSTOCK
MOSENTHAL NIETZSCHE
RODENBERG WILBRANDT
BODENSTEDT CREIZENACH
FASTENRATH HARDENBERG
KOSEGARTEN MATTHISSON
WECKHERLIN FREILIGRATH
KOLBENHEYER SCHNECKENBURGER
GREEK ION BION AGIAS ARION
HOMER ELYTIS ERINNA HESIOD
IBYCUS NONNUS PALLES PIGRES
PINDAR SAPPHO AGATHON
ALCAEUS ARCHIAS BIKELAS
CORINNA EUPOLIS HERODAS
ISYLLUS LESCHES MOSCHUS
MUSAEUS PALAMAS RHIANUS
SOLOMOS THESPIS ANACREON
COLUTHUS DIAGORAS HIPPONAX
NICANDER PANYASIS PHILETAS
PISANDER STASINUS THEOGNIS
TYRTAEUS AESCHYLUS EUPHORION
LYCOPHRON SIMONIDES
SOPHOCLES TERPANDER
TIMOTHEUS PARTHENIUS
PHOCYLIDES SEFERIADES
THEOCRITUS ASCLEPIADES
BACCHYLIDES HERMESIANAX
STESICHORUS CHRISTOPOULOS
HINDU BHARTRIHARI
HUNGARIAN ADY TOTH AMADE
ARANY GARAY REVAI SZASZ JOZSEF
MADACH PETOFI BALASSA
CZUCZOR KOLCSEY MAILATH
BACSANYI GYONGYOSI KISFALUDY
VOROSMARTY
ICELANDIC EGILSSON
GUNNARSSON JOCHUMSSON
THORODDSEN HALLGRIMSSON
SIGURJONSSON
INDIAN GHOSE OQBAL TAGORE
BILHANA
IRISH FILI BANIM COLUM DAVIS
JOYCE KEANE MOORE TIGHE TYNAN
WILDE WILLS WOLFE YEATS
ANSTER BROOKE CLARKE DARLEY
DEVERE FIGGIS GRAVES HEANEY
MAGINN MANGAN PEARSE SKRINE
BARRETT DRENNAN DUNSANY
HIGGINS MACGILL STARKEY
CAMPBELL FERGUSON FLECKNOE
KAVANAGH LEDWIDGE MCCARTHY
STEPHENS ALLINGHAM LARMINNIE
MACDONAGH
ISRAELI BIALIK
ITALIAN REDI ROSA VIDA ZENO
BELLI BERNI BETTI BONDI BOSSI
CASTI DANTE GUIDI MOLZA MONTI
PORTA PRAGA PRATI PULCI TASSO
CIAMPI GIUSTI GROSSI MAMELI
MARINI PARINI POERIO REVERE
ALEARDI ALFIERI ARIOSTO BERCHET
BOIARDO FOLENGO FRUGONI
GUARINI MANZONI MARRADI
MAZZONI MONTALE PASCOLI
ZANELLA ALAMANNI BACCELLI
BIBBIENA CARDUCCI CHIARINI
COSTANZO FILICAIA GUERRINI
LEOPARDI MARTELLI NENCIONI
PETRARCH RUCELLAI TANSILLO
ARNABOLDI BARBERINI BROFFERIO
CALZABIGI CESAROTTI CHIABRERA
MARINETTI QUASIMODO RAPISARDI
ANGIOLIERI CANNIZZARO
FIRENZUOLA METASTASIO
PINDEMONTE BRACCIOLINI
CRESCIMBENI FORTEGUERRI
JAPANESE BASHO AKAHITO
MASAOKA NOGUCHI
LITHUANIAN MAIRONIS
MEXICAN PAZ
NEW ZEALAND DUGGAN
NICARAGUAN DARIO
NORWEGIAN MOE KRAG IBSEN
AANRUD HANSEN GARBORG
BJORNSON WELHAVEN
PAKISTANI FAIZ
PERSIAN HAFIZ SAADI ANVARI
DAKIKI HATIFI NIZAMI FIRDAUSI
PERUVIAN CHOCANO
POLISH POL ASNYK LANGE POTOCKI
SZUJSKI UJEJSKI WITTLIN ZALESKI
KLONOWIC KRASICKI ZEROMSKI
ZULAWSKI GASZYNSKI KARPINSKI
KRASINSKI BRODZINSKI
DANILOWSKI KONOPNICKA
LOBODOWSKI MALCZEWSKI
MICKIEWICZ SARBIEWSKI
WIERZYNSKI WYSPIANSKI
KOCHANOWSKI LENARTOWICZ
SZYMONOWICZ
PORTUGUESE DEUS MELO QUITA
BOCAGE CAMOES CASTRO
GONZAGA QUENTAL RESENDE
RIBEIRO CASTILHO FERREIRA
JUNQUEIRO PALMEIRIM
NASCIMENTO
ROMAN CATO OVID CINNA LUCAN
VARRO ACCIUS BAVIUS ENNIUS
HORACE LIVIUS VERGIL VIRGIL
AVIENUS MARTIAL NAEVIUS
STATIUS TERENCE AFRANIUS
CATULLUS LUCILIUS SEDULIUS
TIBULLUS VALERIUS LUCRETIUS
PROPERTIUS
RUMANIAN BLAGA TZARA
EMINESCU ALEXANDRI ALECSANDRI
THEODORESCU
RUSSIAN FET MEI BELY BLOK
BUNIN BUGAEV ESENIN IVANOV
MAIKOV RYLEEV BALMONT
BRYUSOV GNEDICH GUMILEV
KAPNIST KOLTSOV NIKITIN PUSHKIN
NEKRASOV POLONSKI TYUTCHEV
BESTUZHEV DERZHAVIN
KHERASKOV KHOMYAKOV
LERMONTOV LOMONOSOV
PASTERNAK ZHUKOVSKI
BARATYNSKI BATYUSHKOV
EVTUSHENKO MAYAKOVSKI
PLESHCHEEV BOGDANOVICH
VOZNESENSKY YEVTUSHENKO
SCOTTISH ADAM AIRD GRAY HOGG
LANG MURE THOM AYTON BRUCE
BURNS JACOB LOGAN SCOTT
SHARP SMITH YOUNG AYTOUN
DUNBAR GRAHAM HERVEY LEYDEN
MALLET MICKLE MILLER MURRAY
NICOLL POLLOK RAMSAY SPENCE
WILSON BAILLIE BARBOUR
BARCLAY BEATTIE CLELAND
DOUGLAS GRAHAME KENNEDY
LINDSAY MACBETH PRINGLE
TENNANT THOMSON ANDERSON
CAMPBELL COCKBURN DAVIDSON
DRUMMOND HAMILTON HENRYSON
MACNEILL MAITLAND ALEXANDER
BELLENDEN BLACKLOCK
FERGUSSON GILFILLAN
MACDONALD STEVENSON
BALLANTINE CUNNINGHAM
MACDIARMID MOTHERWELL
MONTGOMERIE
SOUTH AFRICAN BREYTENBACH
LANGENHOVEN
SPANISH CRUZ MENA RUIZ VEGA
DURAN LORCA RIOJA CANETE
CETINA ESPRIU GARCIA VIRUES
ALCAZAR BECQUER GALLEGO
GONGORA HERRERA IRIARTE
JIMENEZ MORATIN SALINAS
AGUILERA BALBUENA CORONADO
FIGUEROA MANRIQUE VILLEGAS
CERVANTES ALEIXANDRE
CASTILLEJO CIENFUEGOS
ESPRONCEDA SANTILLANA
VILLAMEDIANA
SWEDISH DALIN BESKOW CREUTZ
LIDNER TEGNER WALLIN DALGREN
EKELUND LEOPOLD RYDBERG
SJOWALL ATTERBOM BELLMANN
BORJESON BOTTIGER BRINKMAN
KELLGREN LAGERLOF LENNGREN
LEVERTIN NICANDER ADLERBETH
KARLFELDT MARTINSON
MESSENIUS FAHLCRANTZ
LAGERKVIST STAGNELIUS
STRANDBERG WENNERBERG
OXENSTIERNA
SWISS ILG AMIEL FAESI MEYER
BODMER GESSNER LAVATER
FROHLICH LEUTHOLD SPITTELER
SYRIAN GIBRAN
TURKISH NABI FUZULI
URUGUAYAN FIGUEROA
WELSH DAVID HUGHES SYMONS
THOMAS VAUGHAN WILLIAMS
YUGOSLAVIAN POPA

POETASTER BARDET BAVIAN BAVIUS POETITO BARDLING VERSEMAN SONNETEER
POETIC ODIC LYRIC STILTED PEGASEAN POEMATIC
POETICAL (NOT —) PROSE
POETRY EPOS SONG BLANK MELIC POEMS VERSE EPOPEE POESIS SONIOU DOGGREL KALEVALA
(FINNISH —) RUNES
(GOD OF —) BRAGI
(HEROIC —) EPOS
(KIND OF —) CONCRETE
(MUSE OF —) ERATO THALIA EUTERPE CALLIOPE
(PASSAGE OF —) MORCEAU
POGGE BULLHEAD
POGROM RIOT PILLAGE MASSACRE
POGY POGIE MENHADEN
POI (— INGREDIENT) TARO
POIGNANT APT HOME KEEN ACUTE SHARP SMART BITING BITTER MOVING SEVERE URGENT CUTTING INTENSE POINTED PUNGENT SATIRIC INCISIVE PIERCING PRESSING STINGING STRIKING TOUCHING AMAREVOLE
POINCIANA DELONIX FLAMBEAU GULMOHAR FLAMBOYER
POINSETTIA BANNER FIREFLOWER
POINT AIM DOT JOT NAK NEB NIB NUB PEG PIN RES WAY APEX BACK BOKE CHAT CUSP FORK GAFF GAME GOOD HEAD HOLD ITEM KNOT LACE LOOK NAIL PEAK PICK PILE PINT SPOT STOP WHET BEARD CHALK DIGIT FOCUS INDEX LEVEL MUCRO PITCH PRICK PUNCH PUNCT PUNTA PUNTO REFER STAND TEACH THING TOOTH ALLUDE BROACH CRAYON CUSPIS CUTOFF DEGREE DIRECT FLECHE JUGALE MATTER NOSING PERIOD THESIS TITTLE VERTEX ZYGION APICULA ARTICLE BENEFIT CACUMEN CRUNODE ESSENCE GATEWAY PUNCTUM PUSHPIN SHARPEN TANJONG TRAGION ANNOUNCE PUNCTULE STRIPPER PARTICULAR
(— AIMED AT) SCOPE
(— AT ISSUE) BEEF CRUX
(— AT WHICH LEAF SPRINGS) AXIL
(— BEHIND EAR) ASTERION
(— FOR PHONOGRAPH RECORD) STYLE
(— IN CAPSTAN) STRIPPER
(— IN CONSONANT) DAGHESH
(— IN DEBATE) ISSUE
(— IN GAME) SHY
(— IN ORBIT OF PLANET) AUGE APSIS APOGEE SYZYGY APOJOVE PERIGEE APASTRON APHELION
(— IN ORBIT OF SPACECRAFT) PERILUNE
(— IN QUESTION) ISSUE
(— IN SEVEN-UP) GIFT
(— IN SOME GAMES) PUNT
(— NEAREST EARTH) PERIGEE
(— OF A BORDER) VANDYKE
(— OF ANCHOR) BILL
(— OF ANTLER) PRONG
(— OF ANVIL) HORN
(— OF CELESTIAL SPHERE) ANTAPEX
(— OF CHIN) BUTTON
(— OF CONTACT) EPHAPSE
(— OF CRESCENT MOON) CUSP
(— OF CURVE) SPINODE
(— OF CUTTING) STYLE
(— OF DECLINE) EBB
(— OF DEVELOPMENT) STAGE
(— OF DIVERGENCE) AXIL
(— OF ECLIPTIC) LAGNA SOLSTICE
(— OF ENERGY) CHAKRA
(— OF EPIGRAM) STING
(— OF FAITH) ARTICLE
(— OF HONOR) PUNDONOR
(— OF INTEREST) CLOU
(— OF INTERSECTION) FOOT STAURION
(— OF JAVELIN) SAGAIE
(— OF JUNCTION) MEET BREGMA LAMBDA
(— OF LABEL) LAMBEAU
(— OF LACE) TAG
(— OF LAND) ODD CAPE SPIT MORRO HEADLAND
(— OF LEAF) MUCRO
(— OF LIFE) HYLEG
(— OF LIGHT) GLINT SPANGLE
(— OF LIGHTNING ROD) AIGRETTE
(— OF LIPS) CHEILION
(— OF MANGO) NAK
(— OF ONSET) BRINK
(— OF ORIGIN) HIVE SOURCE FOUNTAIN
(— OF PEN) NEB NIB
(— OF PETAL) LACINULA
(— OF REFERENCE) STYLION
(— OF ROCK) NUNATAK
(— OF STAG'S HORN) START
(— OF STORY) KNOT
(— OF STYLUS) CUTTER
(— OF SUPPORT) BEARING
(— OF TEMPERATURE) SOLIDUS
(— OF TIME) DATE INSTANT JUNCTURE
(— OF TOOTH) CUSP
(— OF UMBRELLA) FERRULE
(— OF VIEW) EYE ANGLE FRONT SLANT COLORS CORNER GROUND RESPECT FUTURISM
(— OF VIOLIN BOW) HEAD
(— OF WEAPON) ORD BARB
(— ON AUGER OR BIT) SPUR
(— ON BACKGAMMON BOARD) FLECHE
(— ON BILLIARD TABLE) SPOT
(— ON CURVE) TACNODE
(— ON JAW) GONION
(— ON STAG'S HORN) BROACH
(— ON SUNDIAL) NODE
(— OUT) SHOW DIGIT INFER ASSIGN DIRECT ENSIGN FINGER MUSTER NOTIFY REMARK PRESAGE INDICATE
(APPROPRIATE —) PLACE
(ASTROLOGICAL —) INGRESS DESCENDANT
(AT THAT —) THEN THERE
(BARBED —) FORK
(BLUNT —) MORNETTE
(CARBON —) CRAYON
(CARDINAL —) EAST WEST HINGE NORTH SOUTH
(CARDINAL —S) CARDINES
(CENTRAL —) OMPHALOS
(CHIEF —S) SUM
(CHRONOLOGICAL —) ERA EPOCH
(COMPASS —) E N S W NE NW SE SW ENE ESE NNE NNW SSE SSW WNW WSW AIRT AIRTH RHUMB COURSE
(CRITICAL —) JUMP
(CROWNING —) CAPSHEAF CAPSTONE
(CRUCIAL —) CRUX
(CULMINATING —) HEAD COMBLE
(DOUBLE — OF CURVE) ACNODE CRUNODE
(END —) TERMINUS
(ESSENTIAL —) MAIN
(EXACT —) TEE
(EXCESS —S) LAP
(EXCLAMATION —) BANG SCREAMER
(EXTREME —) END
(FARTHEST —) APOGEE SOLSTICE
(FINAL —) UPCOME
(FIXED —) ABUTMENT
(GET THE —) SEE
(GLAZIER'S —) SPRIG
(HALFWAY — IN CRIBBAGE) CORNER
(HEBREW —) SHEVA
(HIGHEST —) TIP ACME APEX AUGE NOON PEAK CREST FLOOD APOGEE CLIMAX CULMEN HEIGHT PERIOD SUMMIT VERTEX ZENITH EVEREST MAXIMUM MERIDIAN SOLSTICE
(HIGHEST SAFE —) REDLINE
(KNOTTY —) CRUX NODUS
(LAST —) END
(LATERAL —) ALARE
(LOW —) TROUGH
(LOWEST —) NADIR BOTTOM BEDROCK
(LOWEST — OF HULL) BILGE
(MAIN —) JET SUM GIST
(MEDIAN —) HORMION
(NICE —) PUNCTILIO
(NO —S) LOVE
(ONE'S STRONG —) FORTE
(PEDAL —) DRONE
(PIVOTAL —) KNUCKLE
(PRECISE —) NICK
(PROJECTING —) CRAG PEAK BEARD
(SELLING —) HOOK
(SHARP —) JAG PRICK PRICKLE
(SIGNIFICANT —) MILESTONE
(SINGLE —) ACE
(SKULL —) TYLION
(SORE —) NERVE
(STARTING —) BASE ORIGIN SCRATCH
(STATIONARY —) SPINODE
(STRIKING —) SALIENCE
(STRONG —) FORTE
(TAPERING —) ACUMEN
(TENNIS —) LET CHASE BISQUE
(TENTH OF —) MOMENT
(TERMINAL —) GOAL BOURN BREAK AIRPORT
(TOP —) TUFT
(TO THE —) BLUNT COGENT
(TURNING —) CARDO EPOCH CRISIS
(UNIPLANAR —) UNODE
(UTMOST —) EXTREME SUBLIME
(VANTAGE —) TOWER
(VOWEL —) SERE SEGOL SEGHOL
(WEAK —) BLOT
(PREF.) KENTRO MUCRONI PUNCTATO PUNCTI PUNCTO STIGMATI STIGMEO STIGMO
POINT-BLANK BLUNT PLAIN POINT DIRECT WHOLLY EXPRESS DIRECTLY
POINT COUNTER POINT (AUTHOR OF —) HUXLEY
(CHARACTER IN —) JOHN LUCY MARK BURLAP ELINOR GILRAY PHILIP RACHEL SIDNEY WALTER WEBLEY BIDLAKE CARLING EVERARD QUARLES RAMPION BEATRICE MARJORIE SPRANDRELL TANTAMOUNT
POINTED SET ERDE HOME ACUTE EXACT FIXED PEAKY PIKED TANGY TERSE ACUATE FITCHE LIVELY OXEOTE PEAKED PECKED PICKED SPIRED ANGULAR FITCHEE LACONIC PRECISE SPICATE ZESTFUL ACICULAR ACULEATE COPATAIN CULTRATE DIACTINE PUNCTUAL STELLATE ACUMINATE
(PREF.) OXY
POINTEDNESS BARB
POINTER TIP YAD COCK HAND WAND ARROW DUBHE INDEX POINT FESCUE FINGER GUNDOG INDICE SILKER STYLUS FLUSHER INDICANT SIGNITOR
(— IN GREAT BEAR) DUBHE DUBBHE
(— ON ASTROLABE) ALMURY
(— ON GAUGE) ARM
(BUILDER'S —) RAKER
(TEACHER'S —) FESCUE
(PL.) MEN GUARDS YADAYIM
POINTLESS DRY ILL DULL FLAT INANE SILLY VAPID FRIGID STUPID INSIPID WITLESS MUTICOUS
POINTSMAN TRAPPER LATCHMAN SWITCHMAN
POISE PEE CALM HEAD REST SWAY TACT BRACE PEIZE APLOMB OFFSET PONDER BALANCE BEARING DIGNITY OPPRESS POISURE DELIVERY EASINESS SERENITY
(— RECIPROCAL) RHE
POISED SET FACILE HOVERING NERVELESS
(BE —) LIBRATE
POISER HALTER
POISON FIG GAS BANE BIKH DRAB DRUG GALL TUBA VERY ATTER TAINT TOXIN VENOM VIRUS ANTIAR DERRIS INFECT RANKLE TOXIFY TOXOID ACONITE BABASCO CORRUPT ENVENOM FLYBANE MINERAL PERVERT PHALLIN TANGHIN VITIATE ACQUETTA DELETERY RATSBANE VENENATE SAXITOXIN
(— IN DEATH CUP) PHALLIN
(ARROW —) HAYA INEE URALI URARE URARI ANTIAR ANTJAR CURARE CURARI DERRIS OURARI OUABAIN

(FISH —) AKIA CUBE TIMBO DERRIS HAIARI BABASCO BARBASCO
(RAT —) ANTU
(VIRULENT —) BIKH TANGHIN
(PREF.) PHARMACO VENENI VENENO VIRU
POISONED BUCKEYED TOXICATE VENENATE VENOMOUS
POISONER SEPSIN CANIDIA VENEFIC VENOMER
POISON HEMLOCK BUNK CICUTA
POISONING PYEMIA UREMIA ARGYRIA GASSING JIMMIES BOTULISM MYCETISM PLUMBISM CROTALISM FLUOROSIS ICHTHYISM LATHYRISM SATURNISM SELENOSIS INTOXICATION
(ANTIMONY —) STIBIALISM
(LEAD —) SATURNISM
POISON IVY CLIMATH MARKERY MERCURY MARKWEED
POISON OAK YEARA
POISONOUS ATTRY TOXIC ATTERY VENENE VIROSE VIROUS BANEFUL NOISOME NOXIOUS DELETERY MEPHITIC TOXICANT VENENATE VENOMOUS VIRULENT MALIGNANT
(PREF.) TOX(I)(IC)(ICO)(O)
POISON SUMAC BURTREE DOGWOOD
POISON TOBACCO HENBANE
POISONWOOD BUMWOOD
POITREL ARMOR PECTRON
POKE BAG DAB DIG DUB HIT JAB JOG PUG PUR TIG WAD BROD PAUT PORR PROD PROG RAUK RUCK SACK SOCK STAB STIR NIDGE POACH PROKE PROTE PUNCH ROUSE STEER STOKE COWBOY DAWDLE INCITE PIERCE POCKET POUNCE POUTER PUGGLE PUTTER WALLET PRODDLE
(— ABOUT) ROKE ROUT RUMMAGE
(— AROUND) ROOT SCROUNGE
(— FUN) COD
(— LIGHTLY) POTTER PUTTER
(— WITH FOOT) SCUFF
(— WITH NOSE) SNUZZLE
POKE-IN STRANDER
POKELOKEN BOGAN LOGAN
POKER DART DRAW FLIP POIT PORR POTE STUD BLUFF BOGIE CURATE GOBLIN STOKER ACEPOTS FRUGGAN LOWBALL PASSOUT POCHARD SHOTGUN BASEBALL COALRAKE JACKPOTS MISTIGRI SHOWDOWN
(— ACTION) RAISE
(— CHIP) JETON JETTON
(— HAND) RUNT FLUSH SKEET KILTER PELTER STRAIGHT
(— PLANT) TRITOMA
(FORM OF —) DRAW STUD
(HOT —) SALAMANDER
POKEWEED POKE POCAN SCOKE COAKUM GARGET FOXGLOVE INKBERRY REDBERRY
POKEY STIR
POKY DEAD DULL JAIL SLOW DOWDY POKEY POKING SHABBY STODGY STUFFY STUPID CRAMPED TEDIOUS
POLAK BALSA POLLACK

POLAND
CAPITAL: WARSAW
COIN: DUCAT GROSZ MARKA ZLOTY FENNIG HALERZ KORONA
DANCE: POLKA MAZURKA KRAKOWIAK POLONAISE
GENTRY: SZLACHTA
LAKE: GOPLO MAMRY SNIARDWY
MEASURE: CAL MILA MORG PRET LINJA SAZEN STOPA VLOKA WLOKA CWIERK KORZEC KWARTA LOKIEC GARNIEC
MOUNTAIN: RYSY TATRA SUDETEN
NAME: POLONIA SARMATIA
NATIVE: SLAV MARUR SILESIAN
PARLIAMENT: SEJM SEYM SENAT
PROVINCE: OPOLE KIELCE
RIVER: BUG SAN ALLE BRDA GWDA LYNA NYSA ODER STYR BIALA BZURA DRANA DWINA NOTEC SERET WARTA WISTA NEISSE NIEMEN PILICA PRIPET PROSNA STRYPA WIEPRZ VISTULA WISTOKA DNIESTER
TITLE OF ADDRESS: PAN PANI PANIE
TOWN: LWO KOLO LIDA LODZ LVOV OELS BREST BYTOM CHELM POSEN RADOM SRODA TORUN VILNA GDANSK GDYNIA GRODNO KRACOW KRAKOW LUBLIN POZNAN TARNOW WARSAW ZABRZE BEUTHEN BRESLAU CHORZOW GAROCIN GLIWICE LEMBERG LITOUSK WROCLAW GLEIWITZ KATOWICE SZCZECIN TARNOPOL
WEIGHT: LUT FUNT UNCYA KAMIAN CENTNER SKRUPUL

POLAR ARCTIC EMANANT PIVOTAL DIRECTRIX
POLARIS ALRUCABA
POLARITY (WITHOUT —) ASTATIC
POLE BAR LAT LEG LUG POL POY ROD SKY XAT BEAM BIND BROG COPE FALL HOOK KENT MAST NEAP PALO PERK PIKE PROP SKID SPAR TREE UFER CABER FOCUS MASUR MAZUR PERCH QUANT REACH SHAFT SPEAR SPOKE STAFF STANG STILT STING STODE SWAPE SWIPE BEACON BORITY CROTCH FLOWER IMPOSE JUFFER KILHIG RICKER RISSLE RYPECK SPONGE STOWER TONGUE BARLING HEAVENS TOWMAST ALESTAKE FLAGPOLE FOOTPICK POLANDER STANDARD
(— AS EMBLEM OF SOVEREIGNTY) KAHILI
(— AS HOLDFAST FOR BOATS) RYPECK
(— FOR BEARING COFFIN) SPOKE
(— FOR PROPELLING BOAT) POY
(— FOR TOSSING) CABER KEBAR
(— HOLDING SAIL) BOOM MAST SPRIT
(— MARKING SAND DUNE) BALIZE
(— OF TIMBER WAGON) NIB JANKER
(— OF VEHICLE) NEAP
(— ON TWO WHEELS) JANKER
(— SEPARATING HORSES) BAIL
(—S LIVING OUTSIDE POLAND) POLONIA
(— USED AS SIGN) ALEPOLE ALESTAKE
(— WITH BIRD DECOY) STOOL
(BOAT —) SPRIT
(CARRIAGE —) NIB BEAM
(COUPLING —) REACH
(FIR —) UFER UPHER JUFFER
(FISHING —) WAND
(FORKED —) CROTCH
(LOGGING —) JANKER KILHIG KILLIG
(LONG —) PEW
(MANGROVE —) BORITY
(MINE —S) LAGGING
(NEGATIVE —) CATHODE
(PUNT —) QUANT STOWER
(RANGE —) FLAG
(SACRED —) ASHERAH
(SHEPHERD'S —) KENT
(SPRINGY —) BINDER
(STABLE —) BAIL
(STOUT —) KILHIG RICKER
(WATER-RAISING —) SWEEP
(SUFF.) KONT
POLEAX STAFF POLEARM
POLECAT FITCH SKUNK ZORIL FERRET FICHAT WEASEL FOUMART FOULMART PERWITSKY SARMATIER
(— PELT) FITCH
POLE FLOUNDER SOLE
POLEHEAD TADPOLE
POLESTAR STAR GUIDE POLARIS LODESTAR
POLICE MAN FUZZ HEAT GUARD WATCH GOVERN CONTROL JEMADAR OCHRANA POLIZEI PROTECT TOXOTAE OPRICHNIK
(— CAR) PANDACAR
(— FINDING) MO
(— OFFICER) ROZZER
(— STATION) NICK
(SECRET —) CHEKA
POLICEMAN COP JOE KID NAB PIG BOGY BULL FLIC FUZZ GRAB JACK JOHN PEON SLOP TRAP ZARP BOBBY BOGEY BULKY BURLY GAZER PEACE RURAL SCREW SEPOY ASKARI BADGER BOBBIE COPPER FISCAL FLATTY HARMAN JOHNNY PEELER REDCAP ROZZER RUNNER SHAMUS SMOKEY CRUSHER FOOTMAN GHAFFIR GUMSHOE JEMADAR OFFICER SHOOFLY TROOPER ZAPTIAH ZAPTIEH BARGELLO BLUECOAT DOGBERRY FLATFOOT GENDARME MINISTER PATROLMAN
(CANADIAN —) MOUNTY MOUNTIE
(CLUB OF —) BILLY STAFF SPONTOON TRUNCHEON
(MILITARY —) REDCAP SNOWDROP
(MOUNTED —) SOWAR
(PL.) FINEST
POLICE STATION THANA BARGELLO KOTWALEE
POLICY WIT DEAL FRONT ORDER GOVERN NUMBER TICKET WISDOM AUTARKY COUNSEL CUNNING FLOATER LEFTISM LOTTERY TONTINE VOUCHER ACTIVISM ARTIFICE SAGACITY STATEWAY PLURALISM
(CHOSEN —) COURSE
(SOVIET — OF DISCUSSION) GLASNOST
(PL.) APRISMO
POLISH BOB LAP MOP RUB RUD BUFF DUCO FILE POLE CLEAN COUTH FRUSH GLAZE GLOSS GRACE RABAT ROUND SHINE SLICK STONE AFFILE BARREL LUSTER PUNISH REFINE RUMBLE SHAMMY SLIGHT SMOOTH STREAK BEESWAX BURNISH CHAMOIS FURBISH LACQUER PERFECT PLANISH VARNISH ELEGANCE LEVIGATE SIMONIZE URBANIZE SARMATIAN
(— WITH WAX) SIMONIZE
(FINGERNAIL —) ENAMEL
POLISHED FINE COMPT COUTH ROUND SHINY SLICK TERSE BUFFED FACETE GLOSSY INLAND POLITE SMOOTH ELEGANT GALLANT GENTEEL POLITIC REFINED CULTURED
(NOT —) BLIND
POLISHER EMERY BUFFER GLAZER WAGWAG WIGWAG DOLLIER GLOSSER LAPIDARY SMOOTHER
POLISHING SANDING FROTTAGE LIMATION
(— MATERIAL) RABAT
POLITE NEAT TIDY TRIM BLAND CIVIL SUAVE GENTLE HUMANE SMOOTH URBANE COURTLY GALLANT GENTEEL DELICATE DISCREET LUSTROUS ATTENTIVE COURTEOUS
POLITENESS FINISH TASHRIF CIVILITY COURTESY ELEGANCE URBANITY GENTILITY
POLITES (FATHER OF —) PRIAM
(MOTHER OF —) HECUBA
POLITIC WARY WISE SUAVE ARTFUL CRAFTY CUNNING TACTFUL DISCREET PROVIDENT
POLITICAL (— ASSN.) VEREIN
(— PARTY) GOP TORY WHIG LABOR
POLITICIAN BOSS STATIST WARWICK PIPELAYER STATESMAN
POLITY SERFISM
POLIXENES (SON OF —) FLORIZEL
POLL COW DOD NOT POW ROB CHUB COLL DODD HEAD NAPE NOTT PASH CROWN SKULL STRIP CENSUS FLEECE PARROT CANVASS DESPOIL PILLAGE PLUNDER POLLARD
(KIND OF —) EXIT
POLLACK LOB GADE LAIT GADID LYTHE BILLET LAITHE SAITHE BADDOCK SILLOCK WALLEYE BLUEFISH COALFISH GRAYFISH LORICATE MOULRUSH
POLLARD CHU COW DOD BRAN POLL STAG SHEEP CHEVAN

DODDLE DOTARD BOLLING LOPPARD WOODSERE
POLLARD TREE DOTARD RUNNEL
POLLED NOT NOTT POLEY HORNLESS
POLLEN DUST MEAL FLOUR FARINA POWDER BEEBREAD
(— BEARER) ANTHER
(— BRUSH) SCOPA
(— TUBE) SPERMARY
POLLER VOTER BARBER POLLSTER
POLLEX THUMB
POLLINATE SELF FECUNDATE FECUNDIZE FERTILIZE
POLLINATING SIBBING
POLLIWOG TADPOLE
POLLOCK PODLER
POLLSTER HEADCOUNTER
POLLUTE FOIL FOUL SOIL BLEND DIRTY SMEAR TAINT BEFOUL DEFILE INFECT MUDDLE RAVISH ADULTER DEBAUCH PROFANE SLOTTER VIOLATE CONTAMINATE
POLLUTED FOUL DRUNK TURBID CORRUPT
POLLUTING FILTHY
POLLUTION STAIN SULLAGE FOULNESS IMPURITY
POLLUX POL HERCULES
(BROTHER OF —) CASTOR
(MOTHER OF —) LEDA
POLO (PERIOD IN —) CHUKKER
POLONAISE POLACCA FACKELTANZ
POLONIUS CORAMBIS
(DAUGHTER OF —) OPHELIA
(SON OF —) LAERTES
POLT BLOW THUMP STROKE
POLTERGEIST GHOST SPIRIT
POLTROON IDLER COWARD CRAVEN WRETCH DASTARD COWARDLY SLUGGARD
POLUTANT PCB
POLYA RNA
POLYANDRIUM CEMETERY
POLYBUS (FATHER OF —) ANTENOR
(MOTHER OF —) THEANO
(WIFE OF —) MEROPE PERIBOEA
POLYDAMAS (BROTHER OF —) EUPHORBUS HYPERENOR
(COMPANION OF —) HECTOR
(FATHER OF —) PANTHOUS
(MOTHER OF —) PHRONTIS
POLYDORE (BROTHER OF —) CASTALIO
POLYDORUS (FATHER OF —) PRIAM CADMUS HIPPOMEDON
(MOTHER OF —) HECUBA HARMONIA
(SLAYER OF —) POLYMNESTOR
(SON OF —) LABDACUS
(WIFE OF —) NYCTEIS
POLYESTER (— BRAND) DACRON
POLYGALA GAYWINGS
POLYGON DECAGON HEXAGON NONAGON HEPTAGON PENTAGON CHILIAGON MULTANGLE
POLYGRAPH KEELER
POLYHEDRON BEAD PRISM PRISMATOID
POLYMER DIMER HYDROL MANNAN MUREIN HEXAMER OLIGOMER
(— UNIT) MER

POLYNESIA
CHESTNUT: RATA
IMAGE: TIKI
ISLAND: COOK LINE SAMOA TONGA EASTER ELLICE PHOENIX
ISLE: MOTU
KING: ALII ARII ARIKI
LANGUAGE: UVEA TAGALOG
MOUND: AHU
NATIVE: ATI MAORI KANAKA NIVEAN TONGAN NESOGAEAN
PRINCIPLE: TIKI
WOMAN: WAHINE

POLYNESIAN MAORI KANAKA TONGAN FUTUNAN
POLYNICES (BROTHER OF —) ETEOCLES
(FATHER OF —) OEDIPUS
(MOTHER OF —) JOCASTA
(WIFE OF —) ARGIA
POLYNOMIAL CUBIC
POLYP CORAL HYDRA TUMOR ZOOID ISOPOD HYDRULA OCTOPOD
POLYPARY ZOARIUM
POLYPHONY ORGANUM FABURDEN COUNTERPOINT
POLYPIDOM CORMUS
POLYSACCHARIDE LEVAN GELOSE GLUCAN GLYCAN INULIN IRISIN MANNAN AMYLOSE DEXTRAN FUCOSAN HEXOSAN POLYOSE GALACTAN GLYCOGEN LICHENIN SECALOSE SINISTRIN
POLYTYPE CAST
POLYXENA (FATHER OF —) PRIAM
(MOTHER OF —) HECUBA
POLYZOAN POLYP CESTODE RADIATE
POMACE MUST RAPE POMMY STOCK STOSH CHEESE
POMADE CIDER POMATUM LIPSTICK OINTMENT
POMANDER CASE POUNCET
POMATO TOPATO
POME BALL APPLE GLOBE JUNEBERRY
POMEGRANATE GRENAT GRENADE BALAUSTA
POMELO SHADDOCK GRAPEFRUIT
POMERANIA (CAPITAL OF —) STETTIN
(CITY IN —) THORN TORUN ANKLAM
(ISLAND IN —) RUGEN USEDOM
(PROVINCE IN —) POMORZE
POMFRET BULLY HENFISH
POMME DE TERRE POTATO
POMMEL BOB FIB NOB BEAT HORN KNOB PAIK PAKE TORE NEVEL BRUISE BUFFET CRUTCH FINIAL PLUMMET
POMP BRAG FARE WEAL BOAST PRIDE STATE ESTATE PAMPER PARADE RIALTY SCHEME SPRUNK BOBANCE DISPLAY PAGEANT PANOPLY SPLURGE CEREMONY EQUIPAGE GRANDEUR SEMBLANT SPLENDOR
POMPANO DART JUREL ALLICE CARANX PERMIT ALEWIFE COBBLER OLDWIFE CARANGID MACKEREL
(— CLAM) COQUINA
POMPOSITY TUMOR TUMOUR BIGHEAD BIGNESS BOMBAST
POMPOUS BIG BUG BUDGE JELLY LARGE SHOWY TUMID WIGGY ASTRUT AUGUST TURGID BLOATED BOMBAST FUSTIAN OROTUND STILTED SWOLLEN TURGENT BEWIGGED INFLATED MAGNIFIC SWELLING TOPLOFTY IMPORTANT PONTIFICAL PORTENTOUS
PONCEAU GRANAT
PONCHO MANGA RUANA
POND (ALSO SEE POOL) LAY LUM DELF DIKE MOAT PULK SLEW STEW TANK VLEI VLEY CANAL DECOY DELFT LACHE LETCH STANK WAYER CLAIRE LAGOON LAGUNA LAGUNE LOCHAN PUDDLE SALINA SLOUGH SPLASH STAGNE MULLETRY
(— DRY IN SUMMER) TURLOUGH
(— FOR OYSTERS) CLAIRE
(— MAN) JACKER
(ARTIFICIAL —) AQUARIUM
(DIRTY —) SOAL
(FISH —) VIVER GURGES PISCINA
(FISH STORING —) STEW
(SMALL —) KHAL
(STAGNANT —) DUB
(PREF.) LACO LIMN(I)(O)
PONDER CON CAST CHAW MUSE PORE ROLL TURN BROOD STUDY VOLVE WEIGH ADVISE EXPEND REASON RECORD REMORD BALANCE COMPASS EXAMINE IMAGINE PERPEND REFLECT REVERIE REVOLVE APPRAISE COGITATE CONSIDER MEDITATE
PONDERABILITY WEIGHT GRAVITY
PONDEROUS DULL SLOW BULKY GRAVE HEAVY SOGGY AWKWARD WEIGHTY UNWIELDY IMPORTANT
PONDEROUSNESS HEFT
POND HEN COOT
PONDMAN JACKER
PONDOKKIE HUT HOVEL
PONE CAKE LUMP WRIT PAUNE PUDDING SWELLING
PONGEE PAUNCHE SHANTUNG
PONGID APE
PONIARD STAB BODKIN DAGGER STYLET POINADO
PONOCRATES (PUPIL OF —) GARGANTUA
PONT FERRY FLOAT BRIDGE FERRYBOAT
PONTIANAC JELUTONG
PONTIC DUMMY
PONTICELLO BREAK MAGAS
PONTIFF POPE BISHOP PRIEST PONTIFEX
PONTIFICAL AARONIC
PONTIL PUNTY
PONTOON FLOAT RHINO BRIDGE
PONY CAB RAW TAT CAVY TROT YABU BIDET DALES GRIFF PAINT PINTO POWNY TACKY TRICK WELCH WELSH BASUTO BHUTIA BRONCO CAYUSE EXMOOR GARRAN SHELTY TANGUN TATTOO ENGLISH HACKNEY MANIPUR MUSTANG SHELTIE FORESTER GALLOWAY SHETLAND
(— NEW TO RACING) GRYFON GRIFFIN GRIFFON GRYPHON
(STUDENT'S —) CRIB TROT BICYCLE
(USE A —) CRIB
(PL.) DALES
POODLE SHOCK BARBET
POOH TUSH POWWAW
POOK HEAP PICK PULL PLUCK STACK
POOKA PUCK GOBLIN SPECTER
POOL (ALSO SEE POND) CAR DIB DUB LAY LUM PIT POL POT POW BANK BOOK CARR DIKE DUMP FARM FLOW JHIL LAKE LIDO LINN LLYN LUMB MERE PANT PEEL PLUD POLK POND PULE PULK RING SINK SLEW SOIL SWAG TANK TARN WEEL BAYOU BOWLY DECOY FLASH FLUSH FRESH JHEEL KITTY LETCH LOUGH MEARE PLASH PLUMB SLACK STANK STELL STILL THERM TRUNK CARTEL CHARCO FLODGE LAGOON LASHER PLUNGE PUDDLE SILOAM SPLASH STABLE CARLINE CATHOLE CUSHION JACKPOT PLASHET SNOOKER STAGNUM INTERLOT QUINIELA
(— AT JERUSALEM) BETHESDA
(— BELOW WATERFALL) LIN LINN LLYN
(— IN BOG) HAG HAGG
(— OF MONEY) KITTY
(— WITHOUT OUTLET) STAGNUM
(— WITH SALMON NETS) STELL
(ARTIFICIAL —) CUSHION
(AUCTION —) CALCUTTA
(BATHING —) JACUZZI
(BETTING —) EXACTA PERFECTA TRIFECTA
(DIRTY —) SUMP
(FISH —) TRUNK STEWPOND
(MEMBER OF —) STENO
(MOUNTAIN —) TARN
(MUDDY —) LETCH
(SWIMMING —) BATH LIDO PISCINA NATATORY NATATORIUM
(PREF.) LIMN(I)(O) STAGNI
POON DILO PEON PUNA DOMBA KEENA TAMANU SIRPOON MASTWOOD
POONGHIE RAHAN PRIEST PUNGYI PHONGHI TALAPOIN
POOP DOCK FIRE GULP TOOT CHEAT COZEN STERN BEFOOL ISLAND DECEIVE EXHAUST HINDDECK OVERCOME
POOR BAD OFF SAD BASE EVIL FOUL LEAN LEWD PUNK SICK SOUR THIN DINKY EXILE FOOTY GROSS JERRY KETTY SCALY SEELY SILLY SOBER SORRY UNORN FEEBLE HUMBLE HUNGRY LEADEN MEAGER MEAGRE MEASLY PILLED PORAIL PRETTY SCANTY SHABBY STREET SUBPAR CODFISH HAPLESS NAUGHTY SCRAWNY SCRUBBY SQUALID TRIVIAL UNLUCKY INDIGENT ORDINARY PRECIOUS SCRANNEL SNEAKING TERRIBLE UNTHENDE PENNILESS PENURIOUS

(— BOY) HERO
(— MAN) PAUPER
(PREF.) MAL(E) PTOCHO
POORHOUSE MEASONDUE
POORLY ILL BADLY SADLY BARELY FEEBLY SIMPLY SLIGHT SHABBILY
(PREF.) DYS
POOR SOLDIER FRIARBIRD
POORTITH POVERTY
POOR WHITE (AUTHOR OF —) ANDERSON
(CHARACTER IN —) JIM JOE TOM HUGH CLARA MCVEY SARAH STEVE HUNTER SHEPARD WAINSWORTH BUTTERWORTH
POP GO DOT GUN HIT TRY BLOW DART HOCK JUMP PAWN SODA BREAK CLOOP CRACK KNOCK SHOOT ATTACK EFFORT FATHER POPPER STROKE THRUSH ASSAULT ATTEMPT CONCERT EXPLODE INSTANT REDWING BACKFIRE SUDDENLY
POPDOCK FOXGLOVE
POPE LEO JOHN PAPA PAPE PAUL PIUS RUFF CAIUS FELIX GAIUS PETER URBAN ADRIAN BISHOP CLETUS EUGENE JULIAN LUCIUS PUFFIN SHRIKE SIXTUS VICTOR CLEMENS GREGORY HADRIAN BENEDICT BONIFACE INNOCENT PONTIFEX FISHERMAN
(SPECIFIC —) LEO PAUL PIUS URBAN GREGORY
(PREF.) PAPI PAPO POPO
POPERY POPEISM PAPISTRY
POPE'S-EYE NUT NOIX
POPGUN SCOOT PENGUN POTGUN PLUFFER
POPINJAY PARROT PAPINGO
POPLAR ABBEY ABELE ALAMO ASPEN BAHAN LIARD BALSAM POPPLE BAUMIER ABELTREE WHITEBARK
POPLIN TABINET
POPOLOCA CHOCHO
POPPPYCOCK BUNK
POPPY HEAD BLAVER CANKER COPROSE EARACHE PONCEAU REDWEED ARGEMONE BALEWORT BOCCONIA HEADACHE DANNEBROG SQUATMORE COQUELICOT
(CORN —S) SOLDIERS
(PREF.) MECON(O)
POPPYCOCK BOSH BULL PISH FOLLY STUFF HAVERS HUMBUG HOGWASH
POPPYFISH POMPANO
POPPY SEED MAW MOHNSEED
POPULACE MOB MASS CROWD DEMOS PLEBS MASSES MOBILE PEOPLE PUBLIC COUNTRY MULTITUDE
(PREF.) DEM(O) OCHLO
POPULAR LAY POP COMMON GOLDEN PUBLIC SIMPLE VULGAR CROWDED DEMOTIC VULGATE APPROVED FAVORITE PEOPLISH PLEBEIAN GANGBUSTERS
(EXTREMELY —) HOT REDHOT
POPULARITY VOGUE CLAPTRAP
(— OF BUSINESS) GOODWILL
POPULATE MAN BREED PLANT WORLD PEOPLE INHABIT
POPULATION DEME COLONY FLOTSAM KINDRED TOPODEME UNIVERSE
(— OF A SPECIES) MORPH
(PREF.) DEM(O)
POPULUS SALIX
PORATHA (FATHER OF —) HAMAN
PORBEAGLE LAMNA SHARK LAMNID LAMNOID
PORCELAIN JU KO TING CHINA MURRA SPODE BISQUE MURRHA NANKIN BISCUIT CELADON DRESDEN NANKEEN NANKING MANDARIN STEATITE WORCESTER
(FINE —) SPODE
(JAPANESE —) KUTANI
(VARIETY OF —) CAEN KUAN ARITA HIZEN IMARI KYOTO AMSTEL PARIAN SEVRES BUDWEIS DRESDEN LIMOGES MEISSEN SWANSEA COALPORT HAVILAND KAKIEMON CHANTILLY
PORCH HOOD STOA LANAI STOEP STOOP INGANG PARVIS PIAZZA PORTAL RAMADA BALCONY GALERIE GALILEE NARTHEX PASSAGE POIKILE PORTICO PRONAOS VERANDA ANTENAVE SOLARIUM TRANSEPT VESTIBLE
(FRONT —) ANTICUM
PORCUPINE QUILL URSON CAWQUAW COENDOU ERECTER ERICIUS PORKPEN HEDGEHOG HEDGEPIG
(PREF.) HYSTRICO
PORCUPINE ANTEATER ECHIDNA
PORCUPINE FISH ERIZO ATINGA BURFISH DIODONT
PORCUPINE GRASS SPINIFEX
PORE GAZE GLOSE GLOZE STARE STOMA STUDY TRYPA BROWSE PONDER ALVEOLA CINCLIS OSTIOLE TUBULUS BAJONADO JOLTHEAD LENTICEL POROSITY
PORGY TAI SCUP PARGO PLUMA POGGY BESUGO BRAISE MAMAMU PAGRUS SPARID MARGATE PINFISH MENHADEN SPADEFISH
PORK HAM HOG PIG LARD BACON BRAWN MONEY SWINE BALDRIB LARDOON MIDDLING
(— AND SALMON) LAULAU
(— CHOP) BALDRIB GRISKEN
(— SHOULDER) HAND
(DEEP-FRIED —) CUCHIFRITO
(FRIED CUBE OF —) CUCHIFRITO
(SALT —) BACON SPECK SOWBELLY
PORKFISH SISI CATALINETA
PORKY FAT GREASY
PORNOGRAPHIC LEWD ADULT CURIOUS OBSCENE
PORNOGRAPHY SMUT CURIOSA ESOTERICA
POROUS OPEN LIGHT LEACHY CELLULAR
PORPHYRY ELVAN EURITE ELVANITE GRORUDITE
PORPOISE WHALE PALACH PUFFER COWFISH DOLPHIN HOGFISH PELLOCK PULLOCK SNUFFER CETACEAN GAIRFISH
PORRECT EXTEND TENDER PRESENT
PORRET LEEK ONION PORETT SCALLION
PORRIDGE KHIR MUSH POBS SAMP ATOLE BROSE GROUT GRUEL BURGOO CROWDY SEPAWN SKILLY SOWENS TARTAN BROCHAN BURGOUT OATMEAL POBBIES POLENTA POTTAGE FLUMMERY SAGAMITE
(PREF.) POLTO
PORRINGER TASTER TRINKET
PORT GATE GOAL LEFT MIEN WICK WINE CARRY CREEK HAVEN HITHE SALLY SCALE STATE APPORT HARBOR INPORT REFUGE AIRPORT BEARING DIGNITY LIBERTY OUTPORT ANTEPORT DEMEANOR LARBOARD MALTOLTE PORTHOLE PRESENCE
PORTABLE LAPTOP MOBILE MOVABLE BEARABLE
PORTAGE PACK CARGO CARRY TARBET FREIGHT TONNAGE HAULOVER
PORTAL DOOR GATE ENTRY PORCH DOORWAY ENTRANCE
PORTAMENTO DRAG GLIDE SCOOP SLIDE PORTATO GLISSADE
PORTCULLIS BAR SHUT HERSE ORGUE SARASIN CATARACT SARRASIN
PORTE GATE
PORTE-MONNAIE PURSE
PORTEND BODE AUGUR DIVINE EXTEND BESPEAK BETOKEN PREDICT PRESAGE DENOUNCE FOREBODE FORECAST FORETELL
PORTENT AYAH LUCK SIGN SOUND TOKEN AUGURY MARVEL OSTENT WONDER AUSPICE PREDICT PRESAGE PRODIGY CEREMONY DISASTER SOOTHSAY PROGNOSTIC
PORTENTOUS AWFUL GRAVID BODEFUL DOOMFUL FATEFUL OMINOUS POMPOUS DOOMLIKE DREADFUL INFLATED SINISTER
PORTER ALE BEER MOZO CADDY HAMAL STOUT TAMEN BADGER BEARER CADDIE COOLIE DARWAN DURWAN ENTIRE KHAMAL REDCAP SUISSE DROGHER DVORNIK HUMMAUL JANITOR PITCHER REMOVER BADGEMAN BUMMAREE CARGADOR CHAPRASI LODGEMAN PORTITOR RECEIVER
(— AND STOUT) COOPER
(JAPANESE —) AKABO
(MEAT —) PITCHER
(MEXICAN —) TAMEN
PORTFOLIO BLAD
PORTIA (HUSBAND OF —) BRUTUS
(LOVER OF —) BASSANIO
(MAID OF —) NERISSA
PORTIA TREE MAHO BENDY MAHOE
PORTICO ANTA STOA WALK XYST ORIEL PORCH XYSTA ZAYAT EXEDRA PARVIS PIAZZA SCHOOL XYSTUS BALCONY DISTYLE GALLERY NARTHEX PARVISE PRONAOS TERRACE VERANDA PORTICUS POSTICUM VERANDAH PENTASTYLE TETRASTYLE
PORTION BIT CUP CUT DAB JAG LAB LOT PAN BLAD DALE DEAL DOLE DOSE FATE FECK JAGG PART SIZE WHAT DOWER PIECE RATIO SHARE SLICE SNACK TASTE WHACK CANTLE CANTON COLLOP DETAIL GOBBET MATTER PARCEL RASHER REGION EXCERPT PARTAGE SCANTLE SECTION SEGMENT TODDICK TRANCHE FRACTION FRAGMENT PITTANCE QUANTITY SCANTLET FODDERING SOMETHING
(— DRUNK) DRAFT DRAUGHT
(— OF ACTOR'S PART) LENGTH
(— OF ARROW) BREAST
(— OF BIRD SONG) TOUR
(— OF BREAD) TOKE
(— OF BREAD OR BEER) CUE
(— OF CITRUS RIND) ALBEDO
(— OF ESTATE) LEGITIM
(— OF FARMLAND) BEREWICK
(— OF FLOODPLAIN) BANCO
(— OF FODDER) JAG
(— OF FOOD) HELP GOBBET HELPING
(— OF HIDE) HEAD
(— OF LAND) BLOCK PATTI INTAKE DIVISION DONATION
(— OF LIQUOR) STICK DIVIDEND
(— OF LITURGY) ANAPHORA
(— OF MAST) HOUSING HOUNDING
(— OF PASTURE) BREAK
(— OF POEM) STRAIN
(— OF RUG) GRIN
(— OF SERPENT'S BODY) TRAIN
(— OF STEM) BOON
(— OF STORY) SNATCH
(— OF STREAM) LAVADERO
(— OF TEA) DRAWING
(— OF TIME) SPAN DISTANCE
(— OF TOBACCO) CUD
(— OF TONGUE) BLADE
(ADDITIONAL —) RASHER
(ALLOTTED —) MOIRA SCANTLING
(BRIDE'S —) DOWRY
(CLOTTED — OF BLOOD) CRUOR
(COARSER —) BOLTINGS
(EARLY —) SPRING
(INHABITED — OF EARTH) ECUMENE
(LARGE —) SKELP
(LATTER —) AUTUMN EVENING
(MAIN —) CORPSE
(MARRIAGE —) DOT DOTE TOCHER
(MINUTE —) GRAIN
(MOST VALUABLE —) CHIEF
(PERCEPTIBLE —) KENNING
(REPRESENTATIVE —) SAMPLE
(SIGNIFICANT —) CHAPTER
(SIZABLE —) DUNT
(SMALL —) BIT DAB DOT DRAM DROP SOSH TAIT TATE CHACK SPICE SPUNK SHADOW KENNING MODICUM REMNANT SCANTLE SMIDGEN SOUPCON SCANTLET
(SMALL — OF LIQUOR) DOLLOP HEELTAP
(TRIFLING —) SMACK
(SUFF.) (BY A SPECIFIC —) MEAL
PORTLY FAT FULL AMPLE GAUCY

GAWCY GAWSY STOUT GAUCIE GOODLY STATELY SWELLING OVERBLOWN
PORTMANTEAU BAG HOOK VALISE POCKMANKY
PORTRAIT BUST ICON IKON IMAGE IMAGO MODEL PIECE PINUP KITKAT STATUE VISAGE PORTRAY RETRAIT RETRATE LIKENESS RITRATTO VERONICA MINIATURE
(— ON COIN) EFFIGY
PORTRAIT OF A LADY (AUTHOR OF —) JAMES
(CHARACTER IN —) MERLE PANSY RALPH ARCHER CASPAR EDWARD GEMINI ISABEL OSMOND ROSIER GILBERT BANTLING GOODWOOD TOUCHETT HENRIETTA STACKPOLE WARBURTON
PORTRAY ACT GIVE LIMN LINE BLAZE ENACT IMAGE PAINT CIPHER CLOTHE DEPICT FIGURE SHADOW FEATURE IMITATE PICTURE DECIPHER DESCRIBE RESEMBLE

PORTUGAL
BAY: SETUBAL
CAPE: ROCA MONDEGO ESPICHEL
CAPITAL: LISBON
COIN: JOE REI PECA REAL CONTO COROA DOBRA INDIO ESCUDO MACUTA PATACA TESTAO VINTEM CENTAVO CRUSADO MOIDORE EQUIPAGA
COLONY: MACAO TIMOR ANGOLA GUINEA PRINCIPE
DISTRICT: BEJA FARO BRAGA EVORA HORTA PORTO VISEU LEIRIA LISBOA
ISLAND: TIMOR
ISLANDS: MADEIRA
MEASURE: PE ALMA BOTA MEIO MOIO PIPA VARA ALMUD BRACA FANGA GEIRA LEGOA LINHA MILHA PALMO ALMUDE CANADA COVADO QUARTO ALQUIER ESTADIO FERRADO SELAMIN ALQUEIRE TONELADA
MOUNTAIN: ACOR GEREZ MARAO MOUSA PENEDA ESTRELA MONCHIQUE
RIVER: SOR TUA LIMA MINO MIRA SADO SEDA TAGO TEJO DOURO MINHO SABAR TAGUS VOUGA ZATAS CAVADO CHANCA TAMEGA ZEZERE MONDEGO GUADIANA
TOWN: BEJA FARO OVAR BRAGA EVORA HORTA PORTO VISEU GUARDA OPORTO COIMBRA FUNCHAL SETUBAL BRAGANCA
UNIVERSITY: COIMBRA
WEIGHT: GRAO ONCA LIBRA MARCO ARROBA OITAVA ARRATEL QUINTAL
WINE: PORT

PORTUGUESE
(PREF.) LUSO
PORTULACA MOSS PURSLANE
PORWIGLE TADPOLE
POSADA INN
POSAUNE TROMBONE
POSE ASK SET SIT HOARD MODEL OFFER PLANT STICK BAFFLE STANCE NONPLUS PEACOCK POSTURE PRESENT PROPOSE POSITION PRETENSE PROPOUND QUESTION MANNERISM
POSEIDON NEPTUNE EARTHSHAKER
(BROTHER OF —) ZEUS
(FATHER OF —) KRONOS
(MOTHER OF —) RHEA
(WIFE OF —) AMPHITRITE
POSER FACER POSEUR PUZZLE STAYER STICKER STUMPER TWISTER EXAMINER STICKLER BANDARLOG
POSH RITZY SWANKY SWAGGER
POSING OPPOSAL
(— TECHNIQUE) PLASTIQUE
POSIT FIX PUT SET PLACE AFFIRM ASSUME
POSITING PONENT
POSITION LAY LIE HANG LINE POSE RANK SITE CENSE COIGN PLANT POINT POSTE SIEGE SITUS STAND STATE STEAD ASSIZE FIGURE HEIGHT OCTAVE OFFICE STANCE UBIETY VALGUS POSTURE STATION ATTITUDE CAPACITY DOCTRINE LOCATION STANDING VOCATION PLACEMENT SITUATION
(— IN AUTO RACE) POLE
(— IN DISCOURSE) POINT
(— OF AFFAIRS) STATUS
(— OF BODY) AKIMBO
(— OF FEAR) GAZE
(— OF HEAVENLY BODY) HARBOR
(— OF VESSEL) GAUGE HEIGHT
(— OF WEAPON) PORT READY PRESENT
(— WITH NO ESCAPE) IMPASSE
(— WITH NO RESPONSIBILITY) SINECURE
(BALLET —) POINTE
(CHESS —) ZUGZWANG
(COMMANDING —) PRESTIGE
(CRICKET —) GULLY GULLEY
(CRITICAL —) PASS
(DEFENSIVE —) WARD OUTWORK
(DIFFICULT —) SPOT
(DISTINGUISHED —) HONOR
(EMBARRASSING —) FIX HOLE LURCH CORNER
(ESTABLISHED —) TOEHOLD
(FENCING —) CARTE SIXTE SIXTH QUARTE TIERCE SACCOON SECONDE SEPTIME
(FIRST —) PRIMACY
(FOREMOST —) HEAD LEAD STEM
(FORTIFIED —) HEDGEHOG
(FRONT —) FOREHEAD
(HABITUAL —) SET
(HINDMOST —) REAR
(HORIZONTAL —) LEVEL
(INCLINED —) SLOPE
(INITIAL —) ANLAUT
(MEDIAL —) INLAUT
(MIDDLE —) MEAN
(NATURAL —) LEVEL
(NEAR —) NEIGHBORHOOD
(OBLIQUE —) SHEER
(OFFICIAL —) RANK
(OPPOSITE —) OPPOSITION
(RELATIVE —) RANK PLACE TERMS BEARING FOOTING STANDING
(SEATED —) SESSION
(SKIING —) SNOWPLOW
(SOCIAL —) CASTE STATE VALOUR
(SYMBOLIC —) HASTA
(UNFORTUNATE —) PREDICAMENT
(SUFF.) TOPE TOPY
POSITIONAL SITUAL
POSITIVE POS POZ COOL DOWN FLAT PLUS SURE BASIC SHEER UTTER ACTIVE DIRECT THETIC GENUINE HEALTHY ABSOLUTE CONCRETE DECISIVE DEFINITE DOGMATIC EXPLICIT INHERENT RESOLUTE SIGNLESS THETICAL
(THREE —S) KROMOGRAM
POSITIVELY BUT POS FLAT PLUS QUITE FAIRLY INDEED STRICTLY
POSITIVISM COMTISM CERTAINTY DOGMATISM
POSITRON LEPTON
POSSESS GET OWE OWN HAVE HOLD WALD BOAST BROOK OUGHT REACH WIELD MASTER OBTAIN OCCUPY BEDEVIL ENVELOP FURNISH INHABIT INHERIT INSTALL INSTATE SMITTLE ACQUAINT DOMINATE INSTRUCT
POSSESSED MAD CALM COOL OUGHT CRAZED JERUSHA ENTHEATE
(— BY EVIL SPIRIT) DEMONIAC
(AUTHOR OF —) DOSTOEVSKI
(CHARACTER IN —) BLUM DASHA FEDKA MARIE MARYA PYOTR YULIA SHATOV DROZDOV LIPUTIN NIKOLAI STEPHAN VARVARA KIRILLOV LIZAVETA LYAMSHIN PETROVNA SHIGALOV LEBYADKIN STAVROGIN VIRGINSKY KARMAZINOV TIMOFYEVNA VERHOVENSKY
POSSESSION AVER HAND HOLD YHTE AUGHT GRASP STATE CLUTCH CORNER HAVIOR SASINE SEISIN SEIZIN WEALTH CONTROL COUNTER DEMESNE DEWANEE FINGERS KEEPING MASTERY SEIZURE TENANCY CONQUEST DEFIANCE PROPERTY OCCUPANCY OCCUPATION
(— BY INSPIRATION) ENTHUSIASM
(— OF COMMON FEATURES) AFFINITY
(— OF KNOWLEDGE) SCIENCE
(— WITH QUIET ENJOYMENT) SEISIN SEIZIN
(BURDENSOME —) ELEPHANT
(COMMON —) COMMUNION COMMUNITY
(DEAREST —) EWELAMB
(EXCLUSIVE —) MONOPOLY
(LOST — OF BALL) TURNOVER
(OUTDOOR —S) OUTSIGHT
(PETTY —S) SPRECHERY
(RELIGIOUS —) POWER
(SATISFACTORY —) ENJOYMENT
(TEMPORAL —S) WORLD
(TEMPORARY —) LEND
(PL.) ALLS STORE STUFF WRACK DOMAIN ESTATE GRAITH PROPER CAPITAL FORTUNE HAVINGS LIVINGS
POSSET CURDLE PAMPER POWSOWDY BALDUCTUM MERRYBUSH
POSSIBILITY MAY MAYBE POSSE CHANCE PROSPECT QUESTION
(— OF REFORM) RECLAIM
POSSIBLE ABLE RIFE MAYBE LIKELY EARTHLY ELIGIBLE FEASIBLE PROBABLE PROBABLY POTENTIAL CONTINGENT PRACTICABLE
(BARELY —) OUTSIDE
POSSIBLY MAPPEN LIGHTLY PERHAPS PERCHANCE PERADVENTURE
POSSUM TAIT FEIGN PRETEND
POST DAK SET TIE BITT BOMA CAMP CRIB DAWK DOLE FAST FORT MAIL META POLE ROOM SPOT SPUD STOB STUD TREE BERTH CHEEK CLOSH CRANE NEWEL PLACE SETUP SPILE SPRAG STAKE STAND STILT STING STOCK STODE STOOP STULP STUMP BILLET CIPPUS COLUMN CROTCH FENDER GIBBET INFORM OFFICE PICKET PILLAR SAMSON SCREEN STAPLE STOOTH STOWER TRUNCH ASHERAH BOLLARD COURIER GARETTA PLACARD POSTAGE POSTBOX QUARTER STATION STUDDLE UPRIGHT BANISTER DEADHEAD LEGPIECE MAKEFAST PRESIDIO PUNCHEON QUINTAIN STRADDLE STANCHION
(— AS RACE MARKER) META
(— ON PIER) FAST BOLLARD DEADHEAD
(BOUNDARY —) TERM STOOP TERMINUS
(CHIMNEY —) SPEER
(CUSTOMS —) CHOKEY
(DECK —) BITT
(DOOR OR GATE —) DURN
(ECCLESIASTIC —) BENEFICE
(FENCE —) DROPPER
(HANGING —) GIBBET
(INDIAN MILITARY —) TANA TANNA THANA
(MILITARY —) FORT GARRISON
(MOORING —) BITT DOLPHIN
(OBSERVATORY —) CUPOLA
(SACRED —) ASHERAH
(SIGN —) PARSON
(PREF.) STELO
POSTAGE POST INDICIA STAMPAGE
POSTAGE-FREE FRANCO
POSTAGE STAMP DUE HEAD STICKER
POSTBOY YAMSHIK YEMSCHIK POSTILION
POSTCARD (— COLLECTOR) DELTIOLOGIST
POST CHAISE JACK POCHAY POSCHAY
POSTER BILL CLAP SIGN SNIPE CLAPPE AFFICHE PLACARD SHOWING STICKER STREAMER
POSTERIOR BACK REAR CAUDAL DORSAL POSTIC RETRAL ADAXIAL BUTTOCKS
(PL.) WHEERIKINS
(PREF.) OPISTH(O) UR(O)
POSTERIORLY RETRAD

POSTERITY SEQUEL KINDRED FUTURITY
POSTERN SIDE CLOCKET KLICKET PRIVATE POSTICUM
POSTHOUSE YAM MUTATION
POSTICHE WIG SHAM SWITCH TOUPEE PRETENSE SPURIOUS
POSTIL HOMILY COMMENT
POSTILION COURIER POSTBOY YAMSHIK
POSTLUDE SORTIE SORTITA EPILOGUE
POSTMAN MAIL CORREO MAILBAG MAILMAN
POST OFFICE BOMA CORREO POSTHOUSE
POSTPONE OFF STAY WAIT DEFER DELAY FRIST REFER REMIT WAIVE FUTURE LINGER RELONG RETARD ADJOURN DEGRADE OVERSET PROLONG RESPECT SUSPEND CONTINUE PROROGUE REPRIEVE WITHHOLD
POSTPONED DEFERRED
POSTPONEMENT MORA STAY DELAY RESPECT RESPITE DEFERRAL
POSTRIDE COURIER POSTILION
POSTSCRIPT EKE ENVOI ENVOY
POST SUPPORT CROWFOOT
POSTULANT NOVICE
POSTULATE AXIOM CLAIM POSIT ASSERT ASSUME DEMAND THESIS PERHAPS PREMISE PETITION PRINCIPLE
POSTULATION PREMISE
POSTURE SET POSE SEAT SITE ASANA FRONT HEART PLACE SHAPE SQUAT STATE LOUNGE SLOUCH STANCE BEARING CROWHOP STATION STATURE ATTITUDE CARRIAGE POSITION
(— IN BED) DECUBITUS
(— OF DEFENSE) GUARD
(DANCE —) HOLD
(KNEELING —) SHIKO
POSY POESY TUTTY FLOWER BOUQUET NOSEGAY ANTHOLOGY
(SMALL —) FLORET
POT BAG CAN COOP FOOL JUST LEAD OLLA PINT POOL RUIN VASO CREWE CROCK CRUSE DIXIE KITTY SHANT SHOOT ALUDEL CHATTY CHYTRA JORDAN JORDEN KETTLE MARMIT MASLIN MONKEY OUTWIT PINGLE PIPKIN POCKET POSNET BRAISER CHAMBER CUVETTE DECEIVE POTSHOT SEETHER SKILLET YETLING FAVORITE JACKSHEA PRESERVE MARIJUANA
(— FOR CATCHING FISH) COOP
(— FOR MEDICINE) GALLIPOT
(— OF BRASS) LOTA MASLIN
(— OF DRINK) SHANT
(— STICKER) DUMPLING
(— WITH 3 FEET) POSNET
(BOILING —) STEW
(BULGING —) OLLA
(BUSHMAN'S —) JACKSHAY JACKSHEA
(CHAMBER —) JERRY JORDAN JORDEN COMMODE JEROBOAM
(CHIMNEY —) CAN TUN
(EARTHEN —) OLLA CROCK CHATTY PIPKIN
(FLOWER —) PLANTER
(INDIAN —) LOTA LOTAH
(LEATHER —) GISPIN
(LOBSTER —) COY TRUNK
(LONG-HANDLED —) PINGLE
(MELTING —) CREVET CRUCIBLE
(ORNAMENTAL —) PLANTER
(PART OF —) EAR LIP RIM ANTE BASE BODY FOOT NECK SPOUT HANDLE
(PEAR-SHAPED —) ALUDEL
(SMALL ROUND —) LOTA LOTAH
(TEA —) TRACK
(THREE-LEGGED —) TRIVET
(12-GALLON —) DIXY DIXIE
POTABLE DRINK BEVERAGE POTATORY
POTAGE SOUP BROTH
POTAMOGETON PONDWEED PONDGRASS
POTASH KALI SALINE PEARLASH POLVERINE
(— FACTORY) ASHERY
POTASSIUM K KALIUM POTASS
(— DICHROMATE) CHROME
POTASSIUM BICARBONATE SALERATUS
POTASSIUM NITRATE GROUGH
POTATION POT DRAM DRAFT DRINK LIBATION
POTATO PAP YAM CHAT PAPA SPUD YAMP FLUKE IDAHO RURAL TATER TUBER BATATA CAMOTE KUMARA LUMPER MURPHY PRATEY SKERRY BURBANK EPICURE SOLANUM BLUENOSE
(— BALL) NOISETTE
(— CHIP) CRISP
(— MASHER) RICER CHAPPER
(—S AND CABBAGE) COLCANNON
(— SLICES) LATTICE
(— STATE) IDAHO MAINE
(BAKING —) IDAHO
(FRENCH FRIED —) CHIP
(FRENCH FRIED —S) GAUFRETTES
(JAPANESE —) IMO
(KIND OF —) COUCH
(MASHED —ES) MASH
(STEWED —S) STOVIES
(WITH —S) PARMENTIER
(PL.) WARE CHUNO
POT BEARER POTIFER
POTBELLIED KEDGE PODDY STOMACHY ABDOMINOUS
POTBELLY PAUNCH TUNBELLY
POTBOY GANYMEDE
POTE KICK MOPE POIT POKE PUSH NUDGE PLATE POKER SHOVE THRUST
POTEEN POTHEEN WHISKEY POTWHISKY
POTENCE STUD CROSS GIBBET
POTENCY FORCE POWER VIGOR ORENDA VIRTUE EFFICACY STRENGTH VITALITY OPERATION
(TRANSMUTING —) ALCHEMY
POTENT ABLE MAIN RICH STAY STIFF CAUSAL COGENT CRUTCH MIGHTY STRONG DYNAMIC SUPPORT WARRANT FORCIBLE POWERFUL PUISSANT VIGOROUS VIRTUOUS VIRULENT
POTENTATE KING RULER HUZOOR POTENT PRINCE SATRAP DICTATOR DOMINION SOVEREIGN
POTENTIAL EH LATENT VIRTUAL IMPLICIT INCHOATE POSSIBLE PREGNANT
(— ENERGY) ERGAL
(ACTION —) SPIKE
(EXCESS —) OVERVOLTAGE
POTENTIALITY POSSE POWER DUNAMIS DYNAMIS POTENCY CAPACITY PREGNANCY
POTGUN PISTOL POPGUN BRAGGART
POTHER ADO VEX FUSS STEW STIR WORRY BOTHER BUSTLE HARASS POTTER PUTTER PUZZLE PERPLEX TURMOIL
POTHERB WORT CLARY WERTE GREENS CHERVIL OLITORY POTWORT QUELITE SPINACH TAMPALA
POTHOLE POT RUT KETTLE TINAJA
POTHOOK HAIK HAKE CROOK HANGLE RACKAN SLOWRIE TRAMMEL COTTEREL
POTHOUSE TAVERN ALEHOUSE MUGHOUSE
POTION DOSE DRUG DRAFT DRINK DWALE STUFF DRENCH POISON AMATORY MIXTURE PHILTER PHILTRE NEPENTHE
(PALM —) NIPA
POTIPHERAH (DAUGHTER OF —) ASENATH
POTLATCH GIFT FEAST PARTY POTLACH FESTIVAL
POT MARIGOLD GOLD GOLDE SUNFLOWER
POTPOURRI HASH OLIO STEW MASLIN MEDLEY POTPIE RAGOUT FANTASIA PASTICHE JAMBALAYA SALMAGUNDI BOUILLABAISSE
POTRO COLT
POTSHERD BIT PIG TEST CROCK SHARD SHERD FRAGMENT OSTRACON PANSHARD
POTTAGE SEW SOUP SOWL STEW BERRY BROTH BRUET BREWIS BROWET POTAGE OATMEAL PULMENT
POTTED DRUNK CANNED
(— MEAT) RILLETT
POTTER FAD FUSS MUCK POKE ANNOY DAKER TRUCK BOTHER DABBLE DACKER DAIDLE DIDDLE DISHER DODDER FIDDLE FOOTLE FOTTER JOTTER KUMHAR MUDDLE NANTLE NIGGLE PETTLE POUTER TIDDLE TIFFIE TIFFLE TRIFLE CLOAMER CROCKER DISTURB FIGURER FOSSICK HANDLER NAUNTLE PERPLEX PLOWTER PRODDLE THROWER TROUBLE CERAMIST TERRAPIN
(— OFFICIOUSLY) TEW
(MACHINE OF —) JOLLY
POTTERER TWIRLER
POTTERY POT BANK CHUN DELF GROG WARE BIZEN CROCK DELFT GLOST ROUEN SPODE BASALT FICTIL KASHAN MIMPEI ASTBURY BELLEEK BOCCARO BRISTOL DIPWARE FIGMENT JETWARE KAMARES POTBANK POTWARE POTWORK REDWARE SATSUMA TICKNEY TZUCHOU BUCCHERO CERAMICS FIGULINE GRAYWARE SANTORIN SLIPWARE BROWNWARE
(— CIVILIZATION) MINYAN
(— CULTURE) PUCARA
(— DECOR) MISHIMA
(— DECORATED WITH SCRATCHING) GRAFFITO
(ANCIENT —) KAMARES GRAYWARE
(BLACK —) BASALT BUCCHERO
(BLUE-AND-WHITE —) DELFT
(CHINESE —) KUAN YIHSING
(CRUSHED —) GROG
(HINDU —) UDA
(JAPANESE —) IMARI
(RICHLY COLORED —) MAJOLICA
(TURKISH —) IZNIK
(UNGLAZED —) BISCUIT
POTTERY TREE CARAIPE
POTTINGER COOK POTYCARY
POTTO LEMUR APOSORO KINKAJOU
POTTY CRAZY FOOLISH TRIVIAL SNOBBISH
POUCH BAG COD JAG POD SAC BELL BOTA CYST POCK POKE BULGE BURSA POKKE PURSE BUDGET CAECUM CRUMEN GIPSER PACKET POCKET PURSET SACHET ALFARGA ALFORJA CANTINA CRUMENA GIPSIRE MAILBAG MOCHILA OVICYST SCROTUM SPORRAN SWALLOW BURSICLE PROTRUDE SPEUCHAN MARSUPIUM
(— OF FLY) AEROSTAT
(— ON DEER'S NECK) BELL
(— ON PETAL) SPUR
(PILGRIM'S —) SCRIP
(TOBACCO —) DOSS
(PREF.) PERO PHASCO PHASCOL(O) THYLAC(O)
POUCHED SACCATE
POUCH OF DOUGLAS (PREF.) CULDO
POUF PUFF OTTOMAN
POULAINE PIKE CRAKOW
POULPE POULP CUTTLE OCTOPUS
POULTICE QUILT STUPA STUPE MALAGMA EPITHEME SINAPISM CATAPLASM
POULTRY FOWL HENS DUCKS GEESE PULLEN PEAFOWL PIGEONS PULLERY TURKEYS CHICKENS PULLAILE VOLAILLE
POUNAMU JADE PUNAMU NEPHRITE
POUNCE NAB CHOP CLAP JUMP POKE SWAP SWOP FLECK PRICK PUNCH SOUSE SWOOP TALON EMBOSS PIERCE TATTOO BOBCOAT DESCEND SPRINKLE
(— UPON) TIRE STOOP
POUND L LB BUM DAD LIB PIN PUN SOV BEAT CHAP DRUB FRAM PELT PIND POON POSS PUND QUID SKIT SPCA THUD TRAP TUND CRUSH FRAME KNOCK LABOR LIVRE

NEVEL STAMP THUMP TRAMP WEIGH BATTER BRUISE HAMMER LUMBER NICKER POUNCE PRISON THRASH CONTUND CONTUSE PINFOLD THUNDER LAMBASTE RESTRAIN
(— FINE) BRAY
(— SYMBOL) OCTOTHORP
(FISH —) KEEP MADRAGUE
(ISRAELI —S) LIROTH
(1-8TH OF —) HANDFUL
(100 —S) CENTAL CENTURY
(12 —S OF BUTTER) GAUN
(25 —S) PONY PONEY
(32, 56, OR 75 —S OF RAISINS) FRAIL
(500 —S) MONKEY
POUNDMASTER PINDER PINNER PONDER
POUR JAW RUN TUN YET BIRL BREW DROP EMIT FILL FLOW GOSH GUSH HELD LASH LAVE RAIN TEEM TOOM VENT FLOOD FLUSH HEELD HIELD POWER SLIDE SOUSE SPILL SPOUT SWARM TRILL AFFUSE DECANT SLUICE STREAM CASCADE CHANNEL DIFFUSE SUFFUSE
(— AWAY) STAVE
(— BACK) REFUND
(— BEER OR WINE) BIRL
(— BETWEEN) INTERFUSE
(— CLUMSILY) SLOSH
(— COPIOUSLY) HALE
(— DOWN) RASH SILE SHOWER DESCEND DISPUNGE
(— FORTH) SHED TIDE VENT WELL DISTILL OVERFLOW
(— FREELY) SWILL
(— FROM ONE VESSEL TO ANOTHER) DECANT JIRBLE TRANSFUSE
(— IN) INFUSE INFOUND INHELDE
(— IN DROP BY DROP) INSTIL INSTILL
(— LIKE RAIN OR TEARS) LASH
(— MELTED WAX) BASTE
(— MOLTEN LEAD) YOTE
(— OFF) SLUICE
(— OIL UPON) ANOINT
(— OUT) FILL SEND SHED SKINK STOUR UTTER EFFUSE LIBATE DIFFUND DIFFUSE
(— OVER) PERFUSE SUFFUSE
(— TOGETHER) CONFUSE
(— UNSTEADILY) JIRBLE
(— UPON) AFFUSE
(PREF.) CHYMI
(SUFF.) CHYME
POURBOIRE TIP GRATUITY TRINKGELD
POURER TEEMER INFUSER
POURING AFFUSION EFFUSION INFUSION LIBATION
(SUFF.) ENCHYSIS
POURPOINT GIPON JUPON QUILT DOUBLET
POUT BIB MOP MAID MOUE PUSS SULK BLAIN BOODY GROIN BRASSY BRASSIE CATFISH EELPOUT BULLHEAD PROTRUDE
POUTERIA LUCUMA
POUTING BOUDERIE
POUTY DOUR GLUM MOROSE SULLEN
POVERTY LACK NEED WANE WANT DEARTH PENURY BEGGARY DEFAULT MISEASE TENUITY DISTRESS POORTITH PUIRTITH SCARCITY WANDRETH NECESSITY
(SUFF.) PENIA
POVERTY PLANT HEATH HEATHER LINGWORT
POVERTY-STRICKEN POOR NAKED NEEDY SQUALID SHIRTLESS
POWDER BRAY DUST KISH MILL MULL SAND CHALK CURRY ERBIA FLOUR GRIND HEMOL KOSIN PICRA STOUR CEMENT CHARGE CHINOL DECAMP DERMOL EMPASM ESCAPE FARINA FILITE GERATE KAMALA KERMES KUMKUM MELLON PEYTON PINOLE POUNCE RACHEL SMEETH YTTRIA ALCOHOL BESTREW BROCADE LUPULIN SCATTER SMEDDUM SPACKLE SPODIUM ALGAROTH CATAPASM DYNAMITE FLUMERIN PALEGOLD
(— A SHIELD) GERATE
(— FOR BRONZING) BROCADE
(— FOR EYELIDS) KOHL
(— OBTAINED BY SUBLIMATION) FLOWERS
(— TO MASK SWEAT ODOR) EMPASM EMPASMA
(— USED IN CHOCOLATE) PINOLE
(ABRASIVE —) EMERY
(ANTHELMINTIC —) KOSIN
(ANTIMONY —) KOHL
(ANTISEPTIC —) EUPAD
(APERIENT —) SEIDLITZ
(ASTRINGENT —) BORAL
(BLEACHING —) CHEMIC CHLORIDE
(BROWNISH —) LIGNIN
(CATHARTIC —) KAMALA
(COLORING —) HENNA
(EFFERVESCENT —) SALINE
(FINE —) DUST POUNCE ALCOHOL
(FLUORESCENT —) FLUMERIN
(GOA —) ARAROBA
(GOLD —) VENTURINE
(GRAPHITIC —) KISH
(GRAY —) ANTU
(HAIR —) MUST
(MALT —) SMEDDUM
(PERFUMED —) ABIR PULVIL SACHET
(PINK —) CALAMINE
(POISONOUS —) ROBIN
(PURPLE —) CUDBEAR
(REDDISH —) ABIR KUMKUM SIMMON
(ROSE-COLORED —) ERBIA
(SACHET —) PULVIL
(SILICEOUS —S) SILEX
(SMOKELESS —) FILITE PEYTON CORDITE AMBERITE INDURITE SOLENITE
(WHITE —) CHINOL YTTRIA HYPORIT SCANDIA HALAZONE LANTHANA PARAFORM
(YELLOW —) KOSIN DERMOL MELLON LUPULIN MALARIN SAMARIA TANNIGEN
(PREF.) PUMICI
POWDERED SEME SPICED PICKLED SEASONED
POWDER PUFF PLUFF
POWDER ROOM BATHROOM MAGAZINE
POWDERY MEALY PRUINOSE PULVEROUS
POWER ARM ART JUS ROD SAY SUN VIS BEEF BULK DINT GIFT GRIP HAND HANK HEAP HORN IRON KAMI MAIN MANA MAYA SOUP SWAY WALD WILL AGENT CROWN DEMON DEVIL FORCE GRACE HUACA HYDRO INPUT LURCH MIGHT SINEW SKILL STEAM VALUE VIGOR WAKON WIELD YARAK AGENCY APPEAL BREATH CLUTCH CREDIT DANGER DEGREE DOUGHT EFFORT ENERGY FOISON IMPACT MOLOCH MUSCLE SHAKTI STROIL STROKE SWINGE TALENT VIRTUE WEIGHT ABILITY BALANCE BOSSDOM COMMAND CONTROL DEMESNE DESTINY DUNAMIS DYNAMIS ENTHEOS FACULTY POTENCY VALENCY VOLTAGE WAKONDA ACTIVITY AUTONOMY CAPACITY CLUTCHES COERCION DELEGACY DEMIURGE DISPOSAL DOMINION INTEREST LEVERAGE LORDSHIP SEIGNORY STRENGTH PUISSANCE PREROGATIVE
(— FROM SUPREME BEING) EON AEON
(— OF ACID) BASICITY
(— OF ATTORNEY) PROXY
(— OF ATTRACTION) ALLURE
(— OF CHOICE) LIBERTY
(— OF DETERMINING) VOLITION
(— OF DIVORCE) TAFWIZ
(— OF ENTRY) INGRESS
(— OF GIVING) PROPINE
(— OF HEARING) AUDITION
(— OF IMAGINATION) ESEMPLASY
(— OF KNOWING) JNANASHAKTI
(— OF LIVING) VITALITY
(— OF MANIFESTATION) MAYA
(— OF MOVING AT SEA) YARAGE
(— OF PERFORMING) ART
(— OF RESISTANCE) STAMINA
(— OF RETURNING) REGRESS
(— OF SELF-DETERMINATION) FREEWILL
(— OF SPEECH) TONGUE
(— OF TRANSMUTATION) ALCHEMY
(— OF VISION) KEN
(— OF WINE) SEVE
(—S OF EVIL) HELL
(— TO ATTRACT) DUENDE
(— TO CHARM) DUENDE
(— TO CONVINCE) FORCE
(— TO ENTER) ENTRANCE
(AUTHOR OF —) FEUCHTWANGER
(CHARACTER IN —) REB KARL ISAAC JOSEF MARIE NAEMI ANSELF GABRIEL SIBYLLE LANDAUER MAGDALEN ALEXANDER SELIGMANN WEISSENSEE OPPENHEIMER
(CIVIL —) CAESAR
(COERCIVE —) SWORD
(CURATIVE —) THERAPY
(DIVINE —) MOIRA
(ELEVATING —) LIFT
(EMOTIONAL —) STOMACH
(EXTRAPHYSICAL —) MANA
(FIFTH —) SURSOLID
(FOCAL —) DIOPTRY
(GRIPPING —) HOLD
(GROWTH —) BATHMISM
(HYPOTHETICAL —) FORTUNE
(IMPERSONAL —) WAKAN WAKON WAKANDA
(INHERENT —) VIRTUE
(INTELLECTUAL —) WIT
(LEGAL —) JUS
(MAGIC —) ORENDA
(MAGNETIC —) MAGNES
(MENTAL —) HABITUS
(MILITARY —) SWORDCRAFT
(MORMON —) KEYS
(MOTIVE —) PRINCIPLE
(MYSTERIOUS —) MANA
(NATURAL —) OD
(OCCULT —) MAGIC
(PERSUASIVE —) RHETORIC
(PERUVIAN —) HUACA
(POLITICAL —) DOMINIUM
(RATIONAL —) EYE
(REFLECTIVE —) ALBEDO
(ROYAL —) RIAL
(ROYAL —S) REGALIA
(SACRED —) KAMI
(SECOND —) SQUARE
(SECRET —) MAGIC
(SOLE —) MONOPOLY
(SOVEREIGN —) SWAY THRONE
(SPIRITUAL —) NGAI
(STAYING —) STEEL BOTTOM STAMINA
(STRIKING —) PUNCH
(SUPERNATURAL —) CHARISMA
(SUPREME —) EMPIRE HEAVEN IMPERIUM
(THIRD —) CUBE
(UNLIMITED —) OMNIPOTENCE
(VITAL —) SPIRITS
(ZEST-GIVING —) RELISH
(PREF.) CRATO DYN(A)(AMI)(AMO)
(SUFF.) OD ODIC
(RULING —) CRACY CRAT(IC)
POWERBOAT SEDAN SKIFF GLIDER CRUISER STINKPOT GASOLINER
POWERFUL BIG FAT ABLE DEEP HIGH MAIN RANK RICH VERY FORTE HEFTY HUSKY LUSTY STARK STOUT VALID VIVID WIGHT WILDE COGENT HEROIC MIGHTY POTENT SEVERE STRONG CAPABLE FECKFUL INTENSE POLLENT RICHARD SKOOKUM STAVING VALIANT FORCIBLE PUISSANT VIGOROUS
(PREF.) MEGA
POWERLESS WEAK FEEBLE UNABLE HELPLESS IMPOTENT
POWWOW CHAT PAWAW CONFAB FROLIC COUNCIL MEETING SESSION CONJURER
POX ROUP CANKER PLAGUE VARIOLA
(FOWL —) SOREHEAD
(SHEEP —) OVINIA
POYOU PELUDO ARMADILLO
PRABHU LORD CHIEF WRITER
PRACTICABLE AGIBLE DOABLE

USABLE VIABLE FEASIBLE OPERABLE POSSIBLE
PRACTICAL HARD UTILE ACTIVE ACTUAL THINGY USEFUL OPERARY VIRTUAL WORKING BANAUSIC HOMESPUN PRACTIVE THINGISH DOWNTOEARTH
(— JOKE) WAGGERY
(NOT —) PROFESSORY
PRACTICALLY ALMOST NEARLY REALLY VIRTUALLY
PRACTICE ACT ISM LAW PLY SUE TRY URE USE KEEP LIVE PLAN PLOT ADOPT APPLY ASSAY DRILL FOUND GUISE HABIT HAUNT TRADE TRAIN TREAD USAGE CUSTOM EMPLOY FOLLOW GROOVE OCCUPY PRAXIS RECORD BRUSHUP ENHAUNT KNOCKUP OPERATE PROCEED PROFESS RANDORI USAUNCE ACTIVISM ALARMISM EXERCISE FREQUENT GALENISM REHEARSE OBSERVANCE
(— CHEATING) FOIST
(— DECEPTION) DEACON
(— DILIGENTLY) PLY
(— EXERCISE) DRYRUN
(— FRAUD) SHARK
(— HANDED DOWN) TRADITION
(— HYPOCRISY) CANT
(— OF AN ART) PRAXIS
(— OF MEDICINE) GALENISM
(— QUIETLY) RECORD
(— ROWING) TUB
(— WITCHCRAFT) HEX
(BASEBALL —) FUNGO
(BINDING —) LAW
(CEREMONIAL —) RITE
(COMMUNAL —) SUNNA SCHEME SUNNAH INTRIGUE
(CORRUPT —) ABUSE WHORE
(DIPLOMATIC —) ALTERNAT
(DISHONEST —S) CROSS
(EVIL —) MISUSAGE
(HORTICULTURAL —) CUTTAGE
(MEDICAL —) ALLERGY
(RELIGIOUS —) CULT CULTUS
(SUPERSTITIOUS —) FREET
(TENNIS —) KNOCKUP
(UNDERHAND —) JUGGLING
(VICIOUS —) MOLOCH
(SUFF.) CY ERY ICS ISM
PRACTICED EXPERT VERSED PRACTIC SKILLED VETERAN HACKNEYED
PRACTICING EXERCENT
PRACTITIONER ADEPT DOCTOR HEALER LAWYER NOVICE LEARNER EXERCENT FELDSHER HUMANIST HERBALIST HOMEOPATH NATUROPATH
(SUFF.) ICIAN PATH(IA)(IC)(Y)
PRAD HORSE
PRAENOMEN AULUS CAIUS GAIUS TITUS GNAEUS LUCIUS MANIUS MARCUS SEXTUS SERVIUS SPURIUS MAMERCUS NUMERIUS TIBERIUS
PRAESEPE CRIB CRATCH MANGER BEEHIVE
PRAGMATIC BUSY BUSYBODY DOGMATIC MEDDLING OFFICIOUS PRACTICAL
PRAGMATIST REALIST
PRAIRIE BAY BLED CAMAS PAMPA PLAIN CAMASS MEADOW PLATEAU QUAMASH
(— STATE) ILLINOIS
(AUTHOR OF —) COOPER
(CHARACTER IN —) ASA BUSH INEZ PAUL WADE ELLEN HOVER NATTY WHITE ABIRAM BUMPPO ESTHER BATTIUS ISHMAEL HARDHEART MIDDLETON
PRAIRIE BERRY TROMPILLO
PRAIRIE CHICKEN GROUSE
PRAIRIE DOG GOPHER MARMOT
PRAIRIE WOLF COYOTE
PRAISE CRY LOF FUME HERY LAUD LOSE LOVE PRES ADORE ALLOW ALOSE BLESS CAROL CHANT CRACK DEIFY EXTOL GLORY HERSE HONOR KUDOS PLAUD PRIZE ROOSE SALVE VALUE WURTH ANTHEM BELAUD EULOGY FRAISE HILLEL KUDIZE LOANGE LOVING ORCHID SALUTE TONGUE ACCLAIM ADULATE APPLAUD COMMEND FLATTER GLORIFY MAGNIFY NOSEGAY PLAUDIT PUFFING TRIBUTE WORSHIP ACCOLADE APPLAUSE BLESSING DOXOLOGY ENCOMIUM EULOGIZE PROCLAIM PANEGYRIC
(— BE TO GOD) LD
(— HIGHLY) MAGNIFY
(— INORDINATELY) FUME
(— IN THANKSGIVING) JOY
(— OF ANOTHER'S FELICITY) MACARISM
(— TO GOD ALWAYS) LDS
(EFFUSIVE —) FUSS
(EXAGGERATED —) PUFFERY
(EXCESSIVE —) FLATTERY ADULATION PANEGYRIC
(EXCLAMATION OF —) BRAVO
(EXTRAVAGANTLY —) PUFF
(INSINCERE —) CLART DAUBING
(PUBLIC —) PRECONY
(SING FALSE —S) CHANT
PRAISED JUDAH JUDITH LAURELED
(UNDULY —) BEPUFFED
PRAISEWORTHY WORTHY AMIABLE GLORIOUS LAUDABLE SPLENDID EXEMPLARY
PRAJAPATI KA PITRI
PRAKRIT PALI MAGADHI
PRAM BUGGY CARRIAGE HANDCART PUSHCART STROLLER
PRANCE STIR BRANK CAPER DANCE JAUNT PRANK CANARY CAREER CAVORT CURVET GAMBOL JAUNCE TITTUP TRANCE PRANKLE SWAGGER CAKEWALK
PRANCER HORSE DANCER CAPERER
PRANK JIG RAG RIG DECK DIDO FOLD GAME GAUD JEST LARK PLOY PRAT REAK ADORN ANTIC CAPER FREAK SHINE SKITE TRICK VAGUE BROGUE CURVET FEGARY FIGARY FROLIC GAMBOL SHAVIE VAGARY MARLOCK SPANGLE ESCAPADE FREDAINE PRANCOME RIGWIDDIE SHENANIGAN MONKEYSHINE
(PL.) REX GAMES JINKS
PRANKISH TRICKSY
PRANKSTER JOKER FOOLER
(NUDE —) STREAKER
PRASINE LEEK
PRAT PUSH NUDGE TRICK
PRATE GAB BUCK BUKH BUKK CARO CHAT CLAP CLAT TALK BLATE BOAST CLASH SCOLD BABBLE CACKLE CLAVER JANGLE SQUIRT TONGUE BLATHER BLATTER BLETHER CHATTER CLATTER PALAVER PRATTLE TWATTLE
PRATING GAFF CHATTER
PRATIQUE CUSTOM PRODUCT
PRATTLE GUP CHAT CLACK BABBLE BURBLE CACKLE DRIVEL JANNER JAUNER YATTER BLATTER CHATTER CLATTER GABNASH JAUNDER NASHGAB PRITTLE TRATTLE TWADDLE CHITCHAT BAVARDAGE
PRATTLER RATTLE GABNASH PRATTLEBOX
PRATTLING CHAVISH
PRAWN CARID NIPPER PENEID SHRIMP SQUILLA CARIDEAN CARIDOID CREVETTE MACRURAN LANGOSTINO LANGOUSTINE
(SUFF.) CARIS
PRAWN KILLER SQUILLA
PRAXIS HABIT ACTION CUSTOM PRACTICE
PRAY ASK BEG BID BLESS CRAVE DAVEN SOUGH VOUCH INVITE BESEECH ENTREAT IMPLORE REQUEST WRESTLE INVOCATE
(— FOR) BOON
PRAYA BUND BEACH STRAND
PRAYER ACT AHA AVE CRY VOW BEAD BENE BOON PLEA SUIT VOTE AGNUS ALENU NAMAZ SALAT SHEMA ABODAH APPEAL ECTENE ERRAND LITANY MANTRA MATINS ORISON STEVEN VESPER YIZKOR BIDDING COMPLIN FATIHAH GAYATRI GEULLAH KADDISH MEMENTO ORATION PRECULE PREFACE TAHANUN ANAPHORA APOLYSIS CATHISMA DEVOTION KEDUSHAH MISERERE PETITION SUFFRAGE TEHINNAH REQUIESCAT
(— BEADS) ROSARY
(— BEFORE MEAL) GRACE
(— BOOK) MAHZOR MISSAL SERVICE
(— LEADER) IMAM
(— OF DISMISSAL) APOLYSIS
(— RUG) NAMAZLIK
(— SHAWL) TALLITH
(— STICK) BAHO PAHO
(— TOWER) MINARET
(CANONICAL —S) BREVIARY
(CHIEF MOHAMMEDAN —) NAMAZ
(DAILY —) CURSUS
(DEVOTIONAL —) ANGELUS
(HINDU —) GAYATRI
(INAUDIBLE —) SECRET
(INWARD —) ACT
(ISLAM CALL TO —) AZAN
(JEWISH —) ALENU ABODAH GEULLAH HOSHANA KADDISH
(LAST — OF DAY) COMPLIN
(LONG —) CATHISMA
(LORD'S —) PATERNOSTER
(MUSLIM —) SALAH SALAT KHUTBAH
(MUSLIM CALL TO —) AZAN
(OPENING —) COLLECT
(REPETITIVE —) NOVENA
(SECRET —) BREATHING
(SHORT —) GRACE COLLECT
(SILENT —) SECRET
(TABLE —) GRACE
(PL.) HOURS NORITO TIKKUN CHAPLET
(PREF.) EUCHO
PRAYER-BOOK (JEWISH —) MAHZOR MACHZOR
PRAYING ORISON IMPRECANT
(— FIGURE) ORANT
PREACH EDIFY SOUGH TEACH EXHORT GOSPEL SERMON DELIVER HOMILIZE PREDICATE SERMONIZE
PREACHER KHATIB MAGGID PARSON PASTOR TUBMAN DARSHAN LOLLARD MARTEXT PROPHET ROUNDER TEACHER TUBBIST TUBSTER EXHORTER KOHELETH MINISTER PARDONER PULPITER QOHELETH SERMONER SPINTEXT SWADDLER VARTABED BOANERGES
(PL.) PULPIT
PREACHING SPELL PULPIT SERMON HEARING KERUGMA KERYGMA PROPHECY PULPITRY SPELLING
PREACHY DIDACTIC
PREAMBLE PREFACE WHEREAS
PREARRANGED SET
PREBEND CANONRY
PREBENDARY PROVEND
PRE-CAMBRIAN MOINE EOZOIC ARCHEAN PRIMARY HURONIAN TORRIDONIAN
PRECARIOUS NEAR DICKY RISKY SHAKY CASUAL INFIRM NARROW UNSURE DUBIOUS TRICKLE CATCHING DELICATE INSECURE PERILOUS UNSTABLE DANGEROUS UNCERTAIN
PRECAUTION CARE GUARD CAUTEL SAFEGUARD
PRECEDE LEAD FOREGO HERALD FORERUN PREFACE PREVENT ANTECEDE PREAMBLE
PRECEDENCE PAS LEAD PRIMACY HERALDRY PRIORITY
(RIGHT OF —) PAS
(SOCIAL —) LEVEL
PRECEDENT LEAD SIGN MODEL TOKEN USAGE INSTANCE ORIGINAL SPECIMEN STANDARD AUTHORITY
PRECEDING OLD FORE WEST BEFORE FORMER LEADING ADJACENT PREVIOUS
(— ALL OTHERS) FIRST
(PREF.) ANTE
PRECENTOR CANTOR PSALMIST LETTERGAE
PRECEPT LAW HEST LINE RULE TORA WRIT ADAGE AXIOM BREVE

CANON MAXIM ORDER SUTRA SUTTA TENET TORAH BEHEST DICTATE MANDATE WARRANT DOCTRINE DOCUMENT LANDMARK
PRECEPTIVE DIDACTIC MANDATORY
PRECEPTOR TUTOR MASTER
PRECINCT BEAT AMBIT BOUND CLOSE VERGE DOMAIN HIERON VIHARA COLLEGE LENAEUM SOCIETY TEMENOS BANLIEUE DISTRICT ENVIRONS
(PL.) AMBIT
PRECIOUS CUTE DEAR FINE LIEF RARE VERY CHARY CHERE GREAT HONEY CHICHI CHOICE COSTLY DAINTY GOLDEN PEARLY POSING SILVER TENDER PRECISE AFFECTED ORIENTAL OVERNICE VALUABLE WORTHFUL PRICELESS
PRECIOUSNESS PRICE
PRECIPICE LIN KHUD LINN LLYN PALI CLIFF KRANS SCREE SHEER STEEP KRANTZ CLOGWYN DOWNFALL HEADWALL
PRECIPITATE GEL CURD HURL RAIN RASH HASTY HURRY SHOOT SPEED STEEP ABRUPT COAGEL HASTEN SLUDGE SUDDEN TUMBLE UNWARY DISTILL LYCOPIN SUBSIDE TRIGGER CATALYZE HEADLONG PROCLIVE SEDIMENT SETTLING
(— DYE) STRIKE
PRECIPITATELY HEADLING HEADLONG SLAPDASH
PRECIPITATION HAIL MIST RAIN SNOW HASTE SLEET VIRGA
PRECIPITOUS FULL RASH BRANT BRENT HASTY STEEP ABRUPT CHICHI STEEPY SUDDEN PRERUPT HEADLONG
PRECIS JUNONIA SUMMARY ABSTRACT
PRECISE DRY SET FLAT HARD JUMP JUST NEAT NICE TIDY TRIG TRIM TRUE VERY CLEAN CLOSE EXACT PRESS RIGID SOUND FORMAL NARROW RIGORE STARCH STRICT BUCKRAM CAREFUL CERTAIN CLERKLY CORRECT EXPRESS PERFECT PERJINK STARCHY ABSOLUTE ACCURATE DEFINITE EXPLICIT HAIRLINE PINPOINT PUNCTUAL RIGOROUS
PRECISELY BUT EVEN JUST CLEAN SHARP FINELY JUSTLY STRAIT EXACTLY
PRECISENESS RIGOR RIGOUR PRIMNESS
PRECISIAN PRIG PURITAN
PRECISION NICETY CLARITY ACCURACY DELICACY ELEGANCE JUSTNESS
PRECISIONIST PEDANT
PRECLUDE BAR DENY STOP CLOSE CROSS DEBAR ESTOP FORBID HINDER IMPEDE OBVIATE PREVENT SILENCE CONCLUDE INTERPEL PROHIBIT ANTICIPATE
PRECOCIOUS PRECOX UNRIPE FORWARD PREMATURE RATHERIPE
PRECONCEIVE IDEATE
PRECONCEPTION PRENOTION
PRECONDITION PRIUS
PRECURSOR USHER HERALD INITIAL ANCESTOR PRODROME WAYMAKER HARBINGER HEMIAUXIN PROGENITOR
PREDACITY RAVEN RAVIN
PREDATOR COACTOR
PREDATORY HUNGRY HARMFUL RAVENOUS
PREDECESSOR ANCESTOR FOREGOER
(PL.) OLDERS
PREDELLA FOOTPACE
PREDESTINATION FATE DESTINY ELECTION
PREDESTINE DOOM SLATE FOREDOOM FOREPOINT
PREDETERMINE DESTINE FORECAST
PREDICAMENT BOX FIX JAM NODE SOUP SPOT CLASS LURCH STATE STEAD PICKLE PLIGHT SCRAPE DILEMMA IMPASSE CATEGORY JUNCTURE QUANDARY
PREDICANT FRIAR PREACHER DOMINICAN
PREDICATE BASE FOUND AFFIRM ASSERT PRAISE PREACH COMMEND DECLARE EXTREME PREDICT PROCLAIM
PREDICT LAY BODE CALL DOPE READ REDE SPAE AUGUR WEIRD HALSEN FORESAY PRESAGE FOREBODE FORECAST FORETELL PROPHESY SOOTHSAY AUSPICATE PROGNOSTICATE
(— EVIL) CROAK
PREDICTION DOPE WEIRD AUGURY BODING BODWORD PORTENT PRESAGE BODEWORD FORECAST PROPHECY VATICINE
PREDILECTION BIAS HANG FANCY FAVOR LIKING RELISH FONDNESS
PREDISPOSE BEND INCLINE SUBJECT
PREDISPOSED PRONE PARTIAL TENDING INCLINED
PREDISPOSITION ITCH DIATHESIS
PREDOMINANCE MAJORITY REGNANCY ASCENDANCY
PREDOMINANT GREAT RULING CAPITAL REIGNING SUPERIOR CULMINANT HEGEMONIC
PREDOMINATE RULE DOMINE EXCEED GOVERN PREVAIL
PREE KISS PRIE TEST TASTE TRIAL PRYING SAMPLE PROVING TASTING
PREEMINENT BIG TOP ARCH HIGH STAR FIRST GRAND GREAT PALMARY PASSING STELLAR SUPREME FOREMOST PRECLARE SPLENDID SUPERIOR PARAMOUNT PREPOTENT
(PREF.) ARCH
PREEMPT COLLAR
PREEN PIN PERK PICK TRIM WHET DRESS GLOAT PLUME PRIMP PRINK PRUNE SWELL TRICK BROOCH GODWIT SMOOTH REPLUME
(— WINGS) WHET
PREFABRICATED IDENTIKIT
PREFACE FRONT PROEM USHER HERALD PRESAY EPISTLE PRECEDE PREPOSE EXORDIUM FORETALK FOREWORD PREAMBLE PROLOGUE
PREFATORY PROEMIAL PRELIMINARY
PREFECT WALI EPARC GRAVE EPARCH MONITOR PROVOST GOVERNOR PRESIDENT
PREFECTURE EPARCHY
(CHINESE —) FU
(JAPANESE —) KEN
(TIBETAN —) JONG
PREFER LAY LIKE LOVE BRING ELECT EXALT FAVOR OFFER CHOOSE PROFER SELECT OUTRANK PREFECT PRESENT PROMOTE PROPOSE SURPASS
PREFERABLE LIEF RIGHT RATHER ELIGIBLE
PREFERENCE GOO LIKE FAVOR CHOICE DESIRE LIKING RATHER DRUTHERS FAVORITE FOREHAND PRIORITY PRIVILEGE PROMOTION PRECEDENCE
PREFERMENT DIGNITY
PREFIGURE TYPE IDEATE SHADOW TYPIFY FORERUN FORESEE PREDICT FORESHOW PROPHESY ADUMBRATE
PREFIX DUN DOON PREPOSE
PREGNANCY CYESIS TROUBLE ACCYESIS FETATION OOCYESIS GESTATION
PREGNANT BIG GONE OPEN GREAT HEAVY QUICK READY BAGGED CAUGHT COGENT GRAVID PAROUS ENCEINT FERTILE GESTANT TEEMING WEIGHTY CHILDING FORCIBLE GERMINAL PREGGERS PRESSING
(— WITH HUMOR) RICH
PREHALLUX CALCAR
PREHEND SEIZE
PREHISTORIC OGYGIAN IMMEMORIAL
PREINDICATE PRESAGE FORESHOW
PREJUDICE BIAS DOWN HARM HURT KINK TURN AGISM DERRY AGEISM DAMAGE IMPAIR INJURY SEXISM SCUNDER SCUNNER JAUNDICE PREJUDGE
(— AGAINST ELDERLY) AGISM AGEISM
PREJUDICED BIGOTED INSULAR PARTIAL
PREJUDICIAL BIASED HURTFUL CONTRARY DAMAGING INIMICAL SINISTER
PRELATE CHIEF LEADER PRIEST HIERARCH ORDINARY SUPERIOR MONSIGNOR
PRELIMINARY PRIOR PRELIM PREFACE PRELUDE LIMINARY PREAMBLE PREVIOUS PREFATORY
PRELUDE PROEM VERSET DESCANT FORERUN INTRADA PREFACE ANTELUDE BORSPIEL OVERTURE RITORNEL VERSETTE VORSPIEL
PREMATURE RATH UNRIPE IMMATURE PREVIOUS TIMELESS UNTIMELY
PREMEDITATE FORNCAST PURPENSE
PREMEDITATED SET STUDIED PREPENSE
PREMIER CHIEF FIRST OLDEST LEADING EARLIEST
PREMISE LEMMA MAJOR ASSUME GROUND REASON SUMPTION
PREMISES **(REAR —)** BACKSIDE
PREMIUM USE AGIO BACK AWARD BONUS FANCY PRIZE SHAVE USURY BOUNTY DEPORT REWARD GRASSUM CONTANGO DONATIVE FOREGIFT GIVEAWAY
(UNDERCOVER —) ICE
(UNDERCOVER — FOR SEATS) ICE
PREMIXED INSTANT
PREMONITION OMEN HUNCH VIBES NOTICE BODWORD PRESAGE WARNING BODEWORD FORESCENT
PREMUNE SALTED
PRENATAL INUTERO
PREOCCUPATION HEART INSIGHT FIXATION
PRE-OCCUPIED ABSENTMINDED
PREOCCUPIED DEEP LOST RAPT CRAZY ABSENT FILLED INTENT CRACKED ABSORBED ENGROSSED
PREPARATION DIA FIG GEL BALM DIBS DOPE PREP CREAM FLASH GELEE GLAZE GLOSS JELLY READY ACETUM BLEACH BLUING DERRIS FACIAL LOTION MEGILP NEBULA PEPSIN SIMPLE ADDRESS APPREST CLEANER DIPPING EMANIUM ESSENCE ETHIOPS EXTRACT FITNESS FONDANT LINCTUS MELLITE PLACEBO TRYPSIN VARNISH ABSTRACT CONSERVE COSMETIC FIXATURE GELOSINE INHALANT LAUDANUM MEDICINE RACAHOUT TRAINING MAKEREADY PROVISION
(— CONTAINING HONEY) MELLITE
(— FOR COLORING LIQUORS) FLASH
(— OF GRAPEJUICE) DIBS
(AROMATIC —) ELIXIR
(CHEESE —) FONDU FONDUTA
(CHEESELIKE —) YOGURT CROWDIE YOGHURT
(COSMETIC —) HENNA
(ENZYME —) KOJI
(EYELID —) KOHL
(IMPURE RADIOACTIVE —) EMANIUM
(INTOXICATING —) BOZA GANJA
(MEDICAL —) STUFF
(OPIUM —) LAUDANUM
(SALINE —) LICK
(SLOPPY —) SLIBBERSAUCE
(SWEET —) DULCE
(UNCTUOUS —) CERATE
PREPARATORY PRIMAL PIONEER PRELIMINARY
PREPARE DO FIT FIX GET LAY ABLE BOUN BUSK COOK GIRD MAKE PARE PLOT PREP TILL YARK ATTLE BLEND BOWNE BRACE DIGHT DRAFT DRESS EQUIP FRAME

ORDER PREDY READY TRAIN ADJUST DESIGN GRAITH ORDAIN ADDRESS AFFAITE APPAREL APPOINT CONCOCT CONFECT DISPOSE EDUCATE PRODUCE PROVIDE QUALIFY INSTRUCT
(— BANQUET) COVER
(— BEFOREHAND) PRECONDITION
(— BY BOILING) BREW DECOCT
(— BY HEAT) FRIT
(— CAPON) SAUCE
(— COCAINE) FREEBASE
(— FISH) CALVER
(— FLAX FOR LINEN) RET
(— FOOD) DO COOK
(— FOR BUILDING) FRAME
(— FOR BURIAL) EMBALM
(— FOR DISPLAY) DRESS
(— FOR MARKETING) PROCESS
(— FOR PUBLICATION) EDIT
(— FOR TAKEOFF) STRAPIN
(— HASTILY) RASH
(— HEMP) TAW
(— LAND) CURE
(— ONESELF) ADDRESS
(— TEASEL HEADS) CARP
(— TO DEPART) INSPAN

PREPARED UP APT BUN FIT SET BAAN BOON BOUN BOWN GIRT RIPE YARE ALERT BOUND PREST READY GRAITH CURRIED EQUIPPED TOGETHER
(— WITH GRAPES) VERONIQUE
(HASTILY —) EXTEMPORARY
(INCOMPLETELY —) GREEN
(QUICKLY —) RUNNING

PREPAREDNESS PROCINCT

PREPENSE DESIGN FORETHOUGHT

PREPONDERANCE MAJORITY DOMINANCE

PREPONDERATE EXCEED INCLINE SURPASS DOMINATE OUTWEIGH PERSUADE

PREPOSSESS BIAS PREVENT

PREPOSSESSING WINNING

PREPOSSESSION BENT BIAS FETICH FANTASY PREJUDICE

PREPOSTEROUS RICH INEPT ABSURD FOOLISH LAPUTAN GROTESQUE RIDICULOUS

PREPUCE
(PREF.) POSTH(E)(I0)(O)

PREROGATIVE GRACE HONOR RIGHT ESNECY REGALE FACULTY PECULIAR PRIVILEGE

PRESA LEAD

PRESAGE BODE HINT OMEN OSSE SIGN ABODE AUGUR TOKEN AUGURY BETIDE BETOKEN FORESEE OMINATE PORTEND PREDICT FOREBODE FORECAST FOREDOOM FORETELL INDICATE PREAMBLE PROPHESY

PRESBYTER ELDER PRIEST PRESTER ANTISTES MINISTER

PRESBYTERIAN WHIG CLASSIC WHIGGAMORE

PRESBYTERY CLASSIS SENIORY EXERCISE PARSONAGE CONSISTORY

PRESCIENCE PRESAGE FORESIGHT PREVISION

PRESCIND SEVER DETACH

PRESCRIBE SET TAX ALLOT GUIDE LIMIT ORDER ASSIGN DEFINE DIRECT ENJOIN INDITE ORDAIN APPOINT CONFINE CONTROL DICTATE RESTRAIN

PRESCRIBED SET BASIC THETIC POSITIVE THETICAL FORMULARY

PRESCRIPT LAW COMMAND MANDATE PRECEPT

PRESCRIPTION RX BILL FORM CIPHER RECIPE DICTATE FORMULA RECEIPT

PRESENCE EYE FACE SELF BEING ASPECT BEARING COMPANY ASSEMBLY INSTANCE
(— OF GOD) GLORY
(BODILY —) PERSON
(DIRECT —) IMMEDIACY
(DIVINE —) SHEKINAH SHECHINAH

PRESENT AIM BOX NOW BILL BOON GIFT GIVE HAND HERE MEED NEAR NIGH SAND SHOW BEING CUDDY DOLLY ENTER FEOFF GRANT NONCE OFFER PLACE RAISE READY STAGE THERE ACCUSE ACTUAL ADDUCE ALLEGE AROUND BESTOW BOUNTY BROACH CADEAU CLOTHE CUMSHA DONATE DURANT HANSEL KHILAT LATTER MODERN NEARBY PREFER REGALE REGALO RENDER XENIUM COMMEND CUMSHAW DISPLAY DOUCEUR ETRENNE EXHIBIT EXPOUND FAIRING FURNISH HANDSEL INSTANT LARGESS PERFORM PORRECT PRETEND PROPINE RELEASE RESIANT TASHRIF BLESSING CONGIARY DONATION GRATUITY INSTANCE OFFERING PESHKASH RESIDENT SOULCAKE SPORTULA LAGNIAPPE
(— AS GIFT) DASH
(— FOR ACCEPTANCE) TENDER
(— FORMALLY) SERVE
(— FROM PUPIL TO TEACHER) MINERVAL
(— IN DETAIL) DISCUSS
(— IN MIND) DEAR
(— OF MONEY) BAKHSHISH BAKSHEESH BACKSHEESH
(— ONESELF) APPEAR
(— PROMINENTLY) FEATURE
(— TO SOLDIERS) CONGIARY
(— TO STRANGER) XENIUM
(— TO SUPERIOR) NUZZER
(— TO VIEW) YIELD
(— WITHOUT WARRANT) OBTRUDE
(ALWAYS —) CHRONIC
(BRIDEGROOM'S —) HANDSEL
(CEREMONIAL —) KHILAT
(NOT —) ABSENT
(SMALL —) STOCKINGFILLER

PRESENTATION BILL GALA GIFT SHOW DROLL IMAGE DHARMA MUSTER SCHEMA BILLING DISPLAY EPITOME HOOKUPU MUSICAL PRESENT SPECIES ANALYSIS BESTOWAL DELIVERY DONATION EXPOSURE CANDLEMAS PERFORMANCE
(— IN ART) STUDY
(— TO VIEW) OBJECT

PRESENTIMENT FEELING PRESAGE BODEMENT FOREFEEL PRENOTION PREMONITION

PRESENTLY NOW ANON ENOW SOON SHORTLY DIRECTLY

PRESERVATION FILING SAVING KEEPING SERVATION

PRESERVATIVE SALT BORAX SPICE SUGAR CONSERVE TREATMENT
(FOOD —) TINFOIL

PRESERVE CAN JAR CORN HAIN HOLD KEEP SALT SAVE BLESS GUARD SERVE SPARE SWEET WITIE ATHOLD BOTTLE COMFIT DEFEND EMBALM FREEZE GOGGLE POWDER RETAIN SECURE SHIELD UPHOLD CONDITE FORFEND KYANIZE PROTECT RAISINE RESERVE SUCCADE SUSTAIN CHOWCHOW CONSERVE ENSHRINE MAINTAIN MOTHBALL PARADISE WITHSAVE
(— BY BOILING WITH SUGAR) CANDY
(— BY SALTING) CORN CURE SALT
(— OF GRAPES) RAISINE
(— WOOD) KYANIZE PAYNISE
(GAME —) MOOR SHIKARGAH
(HUNTING —) WALK
(PL.) KONFYT

PRESERVED WET CONFECT BRANDIED POWDERED

PRESERVES JAM JELLY

PRESIDE RULE GUIDE DIRECT MODERATE
(— OVER) KEEP

PRESIDENCY MADRAS PRYTANY

PRESIDENT MIR FOUD PREX PREXY PROXY REEVE DEACON RECTOR PRAESES PREFECT
(— OF COLLEGE) PREX PREXY
(— OF GUILD) DEAN
(— OF LEGISLATURE) SPEAKER
(— OF SUPREME COURT) LAWMAN
(— OF TRADE) DEACON

PRESIGNIFY PRESAGE FORETOKEN

PRESLEY (MIDDLE NAME OF —) ARON

PRESS FLY HUG JAM SIT BEAR BEND CRAM DOME DROP DRUK HORN HUSH IRON JAMB KISS PLOT SERR THEW TUCK URGE VICE YERK ARGUE BESET BRIZZ CHAFE CHIRT CRIMP CROWD CRUSH DRIVE EXACT FORCE KNEAD MIDST PRIZE SCREW SHREW SMASH STAMP STUFF TWIST WEIGH WRING ASSAIL CHISEL CLOSET COARCT CRUNCH GOFFER HARASS JOBBER KVETCH MANGLE NUDDLE PREACE SQUASH STRAIN STRESS THRAST THREAP THREAT THREEP THRIMP THRING THRONG THRUST AFFLICT ARMOIRE ATTEMPT BESEECH BESIEGE CONCISE CRUMPLE EMBRACE ENVIRON FLATBED IMPRESS MACHINE OPPRESS SCROOGE SCRUNGE SQUEEZE THRUTCH AGGRIEVE CALENDER COMPRESS PRESSURE SCROUNGE SQUEEGEE SURROUND
(— AGAINST) CONTACT
(— CLOSE) NUDDLE
(— CLOSELY AND PAINFULLY) MASH
(— DOWN) QUAT
(— FORWARD) DRIVE BREAST
(— FOR WINE) TORCULAR
(— HARSHLY) GRIND
(— IN CHEESE VAT) CHISEL CHIZZEL
(— INTO) THRIMBLE THRUMBLE
(— INTO SERVICE) REQUISITION
(— ON ANVIL) HORN
(— ONWARD) STRETCH
(— OUT) EXTRUDE
(— PAINFULLY) PINCH
(— PAPER) COUCH
(— TOGETHER) PACK KNEAD SERRY IMPACT CONSTRICT
(— UPON) ELBOW DOWNBEAR
(— WITH FOOT) TREAD
(— WITH HEAD OR HORNS) BOX
(— WITH NOSE) NOUSLE NUZZLE
(— WITH VIOLENCE) DRIVE
(PREF.) PIEZO PRESSI
(SUFF.) **(— TOGETHER)** ARCTIA

PRESS AGENT FLACK

PRESS-AGENTRY FLACKERY

PRESSED SERRIED
(— WITH BUSINESS) THRONG
(— WITH LEFTHAND FOREFINGER) BARRED

PRESSES
(SUFF.) **(— CLOSE)** NASTIC

PRESSING RASH ACUTE CRYING URGENT CLAMANT EARNEST EXIGENT INSTANT SQUEEZE CRITICAL PREGNANT NECESSITOUS
(— HARD) SEVERE

PRESSMAN PIG MINDER PROVER PRINTER

PRESSURE JAM HEAD HEAT PEND PUSH SWAY DRIVE FORCE IMAGE PINCH STAMP BURDEN DURESS STRESS THRONG WEIGHT BEARING MERCURY PUSHING SQUEEZE TENSION URGENCY EXACTION EXIGENCY FUGACITY PRESSION
(— GROUP) LOBBY
(— OF CIRCUMSTANCE) NECESSITY
(— OF 1 DYNE) BARAD
(— ON INSTRUMENT STRING) STOP
(— UNIT) TORR MICRON
(LIQUID —) HEAD
(MANUAL —) TAXIS
(OSMOTIC —) TONICITY
(UNIT OF —) TORR OSMOL PASCAL MICROBAR
(VAPOR —) FUGACITY
(PREF.) PIEZO TONO

PRESSURE COOKER STEAMER AUTOCLAVE

PRESSWORK BACKUP

PRESTIDIGITATOR PALMER JUGGLER PYTHONIC

PRESTIGE FACE MANA CASTE IKBAL IZZAT KUDOS PLACE CACHET STATUS STATURE ILLUSION INFLUENCE
(HAVING —) STATUSY

PRESTO QUICKLY SPEEDILY

PRESUME BEAR DARE GROW IMPLY INFER ASSUME EXPECT DARESAY SUPPOSE ARROGATE

PRESUMED PUTATIVE

PRESUMING ARROGANT FAMILIAR

PRESUMPTION GALL JOLLITY OUTRAGE PRESUME AUDACITY SUCCUDRY SURQUIDY
PRESUMPTUOUS BOLD PERT FRESH PROUD WICKED WILFUL FORWARD HAUGHTY ARROGANT ASSUMING FAMILIAR INSOLENT FOOLHARDY
PRESUPPOSE IMPLY POSIT ASSUME EXPECT PREMISE FORETAKE
PRESUPPOSITION PREMISE
PRETA PETA
PRETEND ACT LET FAKE MAKE MOCK SHAM CLAIM FEIGN LETON AFFECT ASPIRE ASSERT ASSUME GAMMON INTEND OBTEND POSSUM RECKON SEMBLE ATTEMPT PORTEND PRESUME PROFESS SUPPOSE VENTURE SIMULATE
(— IGNORANCE) CONNIVE
(— TO) FA
PRETENDED FAKE SHAM BOGUS FALSE IRONIC PSEUDO UNREAL ALLEGED ASSUMED COLORED FEIGNED SEEMING SIMULAR AFFECTED IRONICAL SIMULATE
PRETENDER FOP FAKE IDOL CHEAT COWAN FAKER FRAUD POSER QUACK PSEUDO SEEMER AEOLIST CLAIMANT IMPOSTOR INTENDER TARTUFFE MOUNTEBANK
(— TO LEARNING) SCIOLIST
PRETENDING FICTION
PRETENSE ACT AIR FACE GRIM MASK MIEN PLEA RUSE SCUG SHAM SHOW SIGN WILE CLOAK COLOR COVER FEINT GLOSS GLOZE GUISE STUDY EXCUSE HUMBUG VENEER CHARADE DAUBERY FAITERY FASHION FICTION GRIMACE PRETEXT PURPOSE UMBRAGE ARTIFICE DISGUISE POSTICHE POSTIQUE SEMBLANT
(SUPERFICIAL —) VENEER
PRETENSION AIRS PARADE VANITY PRETEXT
(—S TO KNOWLEDGE) SCIOLISM
(FALSE —) DISSIMULATION
PRETENTIOUS BIG ARTY BRAG HIGH SIDY BRANK FLASH GAUDY PUFFY SHOWY BRAGGY CHICHI GEWGAW GLOSSY PUFFED ROCOCO SHODDY TINSEL BOMBAST POMPOUS STILTED TINHORN TOPPING BRAGGART OVERBLOWN RECHERCHE
PRETENTIOUSNESS SIDE SWANK
PRETERMIT OMIT NEGLACT SUSPEND INTERRUPT
PRETERNATURAL GOUSTY GOUSTIE STRANGE ABNORMAL UNCOMMON UNEARTHLY
(— BEING) MARE
PRETEXT PEG FLAM MASK PLEA RUSE VEIL CLOAK COLOR COVER GLOSS SALVO STALL EXCUSE REFUGE SCONCE APOLOGY UMBRAGE OCCASION PRETENCE PRETENSE
PRETTIFY EYEWASH
PRETTINESS (ARTFUL —) COQUETRY)
PRETTY APT GEY PAT ABLE BRAW CUTE DEFT FAIR FEAT FINE GAIN GENT GOOD JOLI MILD MOOI POOR TRIM BONNY DINKY JOLIE POOTY PURTY QUITE SWEET BONITA DIMBER FINELY INCONY MINION PRATTY RATHER TRETIS CLEMENT CUNNING DOLLISH GENTEEL BUDGEREE PRECIOUS
(— WELL) GAILY GAYLY
PRETTY-PRETTY KEEPSAKE
PREVAIL WIN BEAR BEAT REIGN WIELD INDUCE OBTAIN CONQUER PERSIST SUCCEED TRIUMPH DOMINATE
(— BECAUSE BEYOND CONTROL) RAGE
(— OVER) OVERRIDE OVERRULE SURMOUNT
(— UPON) GET FOLD LEAD ARGUFY ENTICE INDUCE OBTAIN ENTREAT OVERSWAY
PREVAILING RIFE GOING USUAL CURRENT DOMINANT
PREVALENCE RUN
PREVALENT UP RIFE BRIEF COMMON POTENT VULGAR CURRENT GENERAL POPULAR RAMPANT REGNANT CATHOLIC EPIDEMIC POWERFUL
PREVARICATE LIE EVADE STRAY SKLENT WANDER QUIBBLE SHUFFLE WHIFFLE
PREVARICATOR LIAR JESUIT
PREVENT BAR LET HELP KEEP NILL SHUN STAY STOP TENT WARN AVERT CHECK DEBAR DETER ESTOP ARREST DEFEND FORBID FORLET HINDER OUTRUN RETAIN REVOKE SECURE FORFEND FORLEIT IMPEACH INHIBIT OBVIATE OCCLUDE PRECEDE RETRACT RULEOUT ANTEVERT INTERPEL PARALYZE PRECLUDE PROHIBIT WITHHOLD
(— OPPONENT FROM SCORING) CHICAGO
PREVENTION PREFACE ESTOPPEL OBSTACLE PREJUDICE
PREVIEW SNEAK SCREEN FUTURAMA
PREVIOUS HASTY PRIOR BEFORE FORMER RATHER EARLIER LEADING FOREGONE PRECEDING
PREVIOUSLY ERE YET ERST FORE ONCE SUPRA BEFORE ALREADY HASTILY PRIORLY FORMERLY HITHERTO
PREVISION FORESEE FORECAST FORESIGHT
PREY ROB FEED GAME SOYL TIRE BOOTY PREDE RAVEN RAVIN SPOIL QUARRY RAVAGE RAVINE VICTIM CAPTURE PILLAGE PLUNDER ROBBERY SPREATH VULTURE
(— OF HUNTER) GAME
(— UPON) DEVOUR PICAROON DEPREDATE
(HAWK'S —) PELT
PREYER KITE
PRIAM (DAUGHTER OF —) CREUSA POLYXENA CASSANDRA
(GRANDFATHER OF —) ILUS
(SLAYER OF —) PYRRHUS
(SON OF —) PARIS HECTOR TROILUS
(WIFE OF —) HECUBA
PRIAPISM TENTIGO
PRICE LAY ANTE COST FARE FEER FIAR FIER FOOT ODDS PRYS RATE BRIBE CHEAP CLOSE VALUE WORTH CHARGE FIGURE HANSEL TARIFF AVERAGE CATALOG CRANAGE EXPENSE FURNACE HANDSEL PRETIUM STORAGE CARRIAGE FERRIAGE INTEREST
(— FOR KEEPING GOODS) STORAGE
(— FOR PASTURING CATTLE) AGISTMENT
(— OF RECLAMATION) RANSOM
(ESTIMATED —) QUOTATION
(HIGH —) DEARTH
(KIND OF —) RETAIL STICKER
(LOW —) WANWORTH
(PROPER —) VALUE
(REDUCED —) SALE BARGAIN
(RISING —S) BOOM INFLATION
PRICELESS RARE COSTLY UNIQUE UNSALABLE
PRICEY DEAR STEEP
PRICK DOT JAG BROD BROG DROB FOIN GOAD JAGG PECK PING PROG SPUR STAB TANG URGE DRESS ERECT POINT PREEN PUNCH STEEK BROACH GALLOP INTENT LAUNCH POUNCE PRITCH SKEWER STITCH TARGET THRUST TWINGE ACANTHA POINTED BULLSEYE
(— OUT) SPOT
(— PAINFULLY) STING
(— WITH NAIL) CLY CLOY ACCLOY
(PREF.) STIGMATI STIGMEO STIGMO
PRICKED PIQUE
(— UP) ARRECT
PRICKER PROD NEEDLE STABBER
PRICKET DAG SNUFFER SPITTER
PRICKING SMART PUNGENT RETRACT POIGNANT POINTURE PUNCTION
(SUFF.) NYXIS
PRICKLE PIKE SETA BRIAR BRIER SPEAR SPINE THORN BASKET ACANTHA ACULEUS PRINKLE SPICULA STICKLE STIMULUS
(PREF.) ECHIN(O)
PRICKLY BURRY JAGGY SHARP SPINY URCHIN BEARDED SPINOSE SPINOUS STICKLY THISTLY ACULEATE ECHINATE MURICATE SCABROUS SCRATCHY SPICULAR STICKERY STINGING VEXATIOUS
(PREF.) CHIN(O)
PRICKLY ASH RUEWORT
PRICKLY HEAT MILIARIA
PRICKLY PEAR TUN TUNA NOPAL SABRA OPUNTIA PINPILLOW
PRICKLY-POINTED PUNGENT
PRICKLY POPPY ARGEMONE COCKSCOMB
PRIDE HEAT HORN LUST POMP RUFF ADORN CREST GLORY ORGUL PLUME PREEN PRIME WLANK EXCESS HUBRIS METTLE NOSISM VANITY COMPANY CONCEIT DISDAIN EGOTISM GLORIFY HAUTEUR STOMACH SMUGNESS SURQUIDY WLONKHEDE
(— ONESELF) PIQUE
(EXCESSIVE —) SWELLING ARROGANCE
(MASCULINE —) MACHISMO
(SENSE OF MASCULINE —) MACHISMO
PRIDE AND PREJUDICE (AUTHOR OF —) AUSTEN
(CHARACTER IN —) JANE MARY DARCY KITTY LUCAS LYDIA BENNET GEORGE BINGLEY COLLINS WICKHAM CAROLINE DEBOURGH GARDINER CATHERINE CHARLOTTE ELIZABETH FITZWILLIAM
PRIDEFUL FASTUOUS
PRIEST EN ABBE CURA CURE DEAN EZRA IMAM MAGA CLERK COHEN EPULO IMAUM ISIAC MOBED PADRE PATER SABIO SARIP VICAR ZADOK ABACES AMAUTA BHIKKU BISHOP DASTUR DIVINE FALMEN FATHER FLAMEN GALLAH GALLUS GELONG GETSUL GOSAIN JETHRO KAHUNA LEVITE POWWOW SHAMAN ANANIAS ARBACES CALCHAS CASSOCK CHANTER DESTOUR DUSTOOR GALLACH LAOCOON PANDITA PAPALOI PATENER PATRICO PHINEAS POONGEE PRESTER STOLIST TEACHER TOHUNGA BABAYLAN BEROSSOS CHRYSEIS HANANIAH KASHYAPA MINISTER PANDARAM PENANCER PONTIFEX POONGHIE SACERDOS SEMINARY SOGGARTH SYRIARCH TALISMAN VARDAPET ZADOKITE OFFICIANT SHAVELING CHAMBERLAIN
((MISSIONARY —) REDEMPTORIST
(— OF APOLLO) CALCHAS CHRYSEIS
(— OF CYBELE) CORYBANT
(— OF RAMA) KASHYAPA
(— OF RHEA) CURETE
(BABYLONIAN —) BEROSSOS
(BUDDHIST —) LAMA BHIKKU GELONG POONGEE POONGHIE TALAPOIN
(BULGARIAN —) BOGOMIL BOGOMILE
(CELTIC —) DRUID
(CHIEF —) SYRIARCH
(CHIEF — OF SHRINE) EN
(EGYPTIAN —) ARBACES CHOACHYTE
(ETRUSCAN —) LUCUMO
(EUNUCH —) GALLUS
(FRENCH —) PERE SULPICIAN
(GREEK —) PAPA
(GYPSY —) PATRICO
(HIGH —) ELI SARIP DASTUR KAHUNA DESTOUR PHINEAS PONTIFF PRELATE CAIAPHAS HIERARCH JEHOIADA PONTIFEX
(HINDU —) PANDARAM
(IGNORANT —) LACKLATIN
(INCA —) AMAUTA
(INFERIOR —) LEVITE
(LAMAIST —) GETSUL

(MAORI —) TOHUNGA
(MORO —) SARIP PANDITA
(MOSLEM —) ALFAQUI TALISMAN
(NEW —) NEOPHYTE
(PAGAN —) BABAYLAN
(PARISH —) CURA CURE PAPA POPE PARSON PERSON SECULAR
(PERSIAN —) MAGUS
(ROMAN —) EPULO FLAMEN
(TIBETAN —) LAMA
(VAISHNAVA —) GOSAIN
(VOODOO —) BOCOR BOKOR
(PL.) LUPERCI

PRIEST-DOCTOR SHAMAN WABENO

PRIESTESS NUN ENTUM HORSE MAMBO MAMBU BACBUC PYTHIA DIOTIMA MAMALOI PHOIBAD PHITONES PYTHONESS
(— OF APOLLO) PYTHIA PHOEBAD
(— OF THE BOTTLE) BACBUC
(BABYLONIAN —) ENTUM
(VOODOO —) HORSE

PRIESTFISH CHERNA ROCKFISH

PRIESTHOOD SALII SACERDOCY

PRIEST-KING PATESI

PRIESTLY AARONIC LEVITIC SACERDOTAL

PRIG BEG FOP BRAD BUCK NAIL SMUG DANDY FILCH PLEAD STEAL THIEF FELLOW HAGGLE PERSON PILFER TINKER ENTREAT PURITAN QUIBBLE

PRIGGER THIEF

PRIGGISH PRUDISH

PRIM MIM NEAT TRIG TRIM MIMZY DEMURE FORMAL MIMSEY PRISSY PRIVET PROPER STUFFY MISSISH PERJINK PRECISE PRIMSIE STARCHY

PRIMACY CHIEFTY PRIMITY HEADSHIP

PRIMA DONNA DIVA STAR

PRIMARY CYAN MAIN BASIC CHIEF FIRST PRIME CAUCUS DIRECT FONTAL MANUAL MAGENTA RADICAL ARCHICAL CARDINAL HYPOGENE ORIGINAL PRIMEVAL PRINCIPAL
(PREF.) ARCHI PROT(E)(EO)

PRIMATE BISHOP GALAGO LEADER PREMAN PRINCIPAL PREHOMINID

PRIME MAY FANG FILL LOAD MAIN CHIEF COACH FIRST PRIDE TONIC YOUTH CHOICE FLOWER SPRING CENTRAL LEADING LUSTFUL PREPARE DOMINEER ORIGINAL YOUTHFUL PRINCIPAL
(— A PUMP) FANG PHANG
(— OF LIFE) FLOWER

PRIME MINISTER DEWAN DIWAN ATABEG PREMIER
(DEPUTY —) TANAISTE
(IRISH —) TAOISEACH

PRIMER ABC CAP DONAT WAFER READER CORDERY HORNBOOK

PRIMEVAL OLD NATIVE ANCIENT OGYGIAN PRIMARY PRISTINE PRIMITIVE

PRIMING MORSING TWOPENNY CLEARCOLE

PRIMING IRON DRIFT

PRIMING WIRE PICKER

PRIMITIVE DARK CRUDE EARLY FIRST GROSS NAIVE PLAIN PRIME FANTEE GOTHIC PRIMAL SAVAGE SIMPLE ANCIENT ARCHAIC PRIMARY PRISCAN BACKVELD BARBARIC EARLIEST IGNORANT ORIGINAL PRISTINE ABORIGINAL PRIMORDIAL NEANDERTHAL ANTEDILUVIAN
(PREF.) ARCH(AE)(AEO)(E)(EO)(I) PALAE(O) PALE(O)

PRIMNESS STARCH PRUDERY

PRIMORDIAL CRUDE FIRST PRIMARY ARCHICAL EARLIEST PRIMEVAL

PRIMORDIUM BUD ANLAGE BLASTEMA

PRIMP PRIM ADORN PREEN PRINK DOLLUP

PRIMROSE GAY OXLIP SPINK FLOWER SUNCUP COWSLIP FLOWERY PRIMULA SCABISH AURICULA PLUMROCK SCURVISH AFTERGLOW PIMPERNEL POLYANTHUS

PRIMULA OXLIP COWSLIP PRIMWORT

PRINCE MIN RAS DUKE EARL EMIR IMAM KHAN KING KNEZ LORD NASI RAJA RANA RIAL SAID WANG ALDER EBLIS EMEER FURST GEBIR MIRZA PWYLL RAJAH SAYID ARJUNA DESPOT DYNAST SHERIF SOLDAN BHARATA ELECTOR GLAUCUS HELENUS MONARCH TANCRED TOPARCH ZERBINO ARCHDUKE ATHELING CARDINAL FLORIZEL HOSPODAR MAMILIUS OROONOKO RASSELAS SARPEDON PENDRAGON
(— OF ABYSSINIA) RAS RASSELAS
(— OF APOSTATE ANGELS) DEVIL EBLIS
(— OF ARGO) DIOMED DIOMEDES
(— OF BOHEMIA) FLORIZEL
(— OF DARKNESS) DEVIL SATAN
(— OF DEMONS) BEELZEBUB
(— OF DYFED) PWYLL
(— OF SALERNO) TANCRED
(— OF SCOTLAND) ZERBINO
(— SOLD INTO SLAVERY) OROONOKO
(— WITH CHARLEMAGNE) ASTOLF ASTOLFO
(ANGLO-SAXON —) ADELING ATHELING
(ARAB —) SHERIF
(CHINESE —) WANG
(ETRUSCAN —) LUCUMO
(GERMAN —) FURST ELECTOR
(INDIAN —) RAJA RANA RAJAH BHARATA AHLUWALIA
(LYCIAN —) GLAUCUS SARPEDON
(MESHECH —) GOG
(MOHAMMEDAN —) SOLDAN
(MOSLEM —) IMAM SAID SAYID SAYYID SHEIKH SOLDAN
(PETTY —) SATRAP VERGOBRET
(SERVIAN —) CRAL
(SLAVIC —) KNEZ
(TROJAN —) HELENUS
(WIFE OF — VALIANT) ALETA

PRINCE EDWARD ISLAND (BAY OF —) ROLLA EGMONT ORWELL MALPEQUE
(CAPITAL OF —) CHARLOTTETOWN
(TOWN OF —) ABNEY SOURIS TIGNISH MONTAGUE GEORGETOWN SUMMERSIDE

PRINCELY NOBLE ROYAL KINGLY STATELY SOVEREIGN

PRINCE'S FEATHER LILAC PILEWORT

PRINCESS AIDA ELSA OZMA RANI DANAE PALLA RANEE SARAH CREUSA GLAUKE ILDICO MADAME PSYCHE ANTIOPE CORONIS PHYLLIS DRAUPADI MAHARANI
(— CHANGED INTO CROW) CORONIS
(— MOTHER OF ZEUS) ANTIOPA ANTIOPE
(— OF ARGOS) DANAE
(— OF CORINTH) CREUSA GLAUKE
(— WHO SLEW ATTILA) ILDICO
(MOHAMMEDAN —) BEGUM
(THRACIAN —) PHYLLIS
(TYRIAN —) DIDO

PRINCEWOOD CYP BARIA CYPRE CERILLO CANALETE SALMWOOD

PRINCIPAL ARCH BOSS HEAD HIGH LEAD MAIN STAR CHIEF FIRST GRAND GREAT PRIME STOCK AUCTOR CORPUS MASTER STAPLE CAPITAL CAPTAIN CENTRAL CHATTEL DECUMAN DOMINUS PREMIER PRIMARY SALIENT STELLAR CARDINAL ESPECIAL FOREMOST OFFICIAL PRESTANT PRINCELY
(— OF SCHOOL) PRECEPTOR HEADMASTER
(POLITICAL —) PLANK
(PREF.) ARCH PROT(O)

PRINCIPALITY ZUPA ARZAVA ARZAWA ORANGE SATRAPY APPANAGE DESPOTAT PRINCEDOM

PRINCIPE (MONEY OF —) DOBRA

PRINCIPLE JUS LAW RTA TAO BASE FATE RITA RULE SEED YANG AGENT AXIOM BASIS CANON CAUSE DATUM ETHOS PRANA SPARK STUFF TENET ANIMUS ARABIN CNICIN COGITO CORTIN ELIXIR EMBRYO FAGINE GOSPEL ARCHEUS BROCARD BUFAGIN CLYSSUS ELEMENT FORMULA GENERAL PRECEPT QUASSIN RADICAL THEOREM URGRUND DOCTRINE GOSSYPOL INTIMISM LANDMARK NICOTINE SANCTION SPECIFIC TINCTURE
(— ACCEPTED AS TRUE) CANON
(— FROM TOAD) BUFAGIN
(— IN BEECHNUTS) FAGINE
(— OF BLESSED THISTLE) CNICIN
(— OF COTTONSEED) GOSSYPOL
(— OF EXISTENCE) TATTVA
(— OF INDIVIDUATION) AHANKARA
(— OF KEY IN MUSIC) TONALITY
(— OF MENTAL LIFE) PSYCHE
(— OF PARTY) PLANK
(— OF REST) ADHARMA
(— UNDERLYING —) REASON RATIONALE
(COSMIC —) HEAVEN URGRUND PRAJAPATI
(DIVINE —) OVERSOUL
(DOGMATIC —) DICTUM
(ELEMENTARY —) BROCARD
(FEMALE —) YIN SAKTI
(FIRST —) ABC SEED ARCHE
(FUNDAMENTAL —) GROUNDSEL
(GERMINAL —) STAMEN
(GOVERNING —) HINGE
(GUIDING —) SQUARE POLESTAR
(KIND OF —) FICK PETER
(LIFE —) SOUL GHOST PRANA
(MALE —) YANG PURUSHA
(MOHAMMEDAN THEOLOGICAL —) IJMA
(MORAL —) SCRUPLE
(NARCOTIC —) FAGINE
(ONTOLOGICAL —) DHARMA
(POISONOUS —) PICROTOXIN
(PRIMAL —) APEIRON
(PROMINENT —) KEY
(QUICKENING —) LIFE
(RHYTHMICAL —) ACCENT
(SANITARY — S) HYGIENE
(SPIRITUAL —) SOUL
(STOIC —) LOGOS
(SUMMARY OF —S) CREED
(VITAL —) JIVA SPIRIT STAMEN ARCHAEUS

PRINK PERK PRIG WINK ADORN PRICK PRIMP PRUNE BEDECK SMUDGE

PRINT CUT GAY GUM RUN DRUK MARK TYPE FUDGE PORTY PRESS SEPIA STAMP BANNER BORDER CARBON CARBRO ENFACE LETTER STRIKE BROMOIL DROPOUT DUOTYPE ENGRAVE GRAPHIC GRAVURE IMPRESS PUBLISH TRACING VANDYKE VESTIGE WOODCUT AQUATONE CALOTYPE CHLORIDE DRYPOINT HALFTONE INSCRIBE LEIMTYPE MONOTYPE POSITIVE URUSHIYE PHOTOENGRAVING
(— OF WILD MAMMAL) PUG
(— OTHER SIDE) BACK
(— OVER) SURCHARGE
(— PROMINENTLY) SPLASH
(— SECOND SIDE) PERFECT
(— TO RIGHT) ADSCRIPT
(BLOCK —) LINOCUT
(SILK SCREEN —) SERIGRAPH
(UNEDITED —) RUSH

PRINTED FONTED

PRINTER TYPO TWICER PRESSMAN IMPRIMENT
(AID TO —) DEVIL
(KIND OF —) LINE LASER INKJET
(PL.) TYPOTHETAE
AMERICAN DAY GOUDY GREEN RUDGE AITKEN BEADLE DRAPER DUNLAP HUNTER ROGERS SHOLES THOMAS UPDIKE WILSON ZENGER DEVINNE GARNETT ROLLINS BRADFORD WOODWORTH
AUSTRIAN WELSBACH
DUTCH BOMBERG ELZEVIR ENSCHEDE
ENGLISH CAVE DAYE JONES WORDE BLOUNT BOWYER BULMER

BUTTER CAXTON OGILBY RAIKES WALKER AWDELAY COPLAND CROWLEY GRAFTON HANSARD NICHOLS BRADSHAW ROYCROFT WOODFALL BASKERVILLE WHITTINGHAM
FRENCH DIDOT DOLET MOREL COLINES PLANTIN RICHARD ESTIENNE
GERMAN FUST ZELL KONIG LUFFT FROBEN MENTEL ZAINER ZENGER PFISTER RATDOLT AMERBACH GRYPHIUS SCHOFFER BREITKOPF GUTENBERG TAUCHNITZ
ITALIAN BODONI GIUNTA CASTALDI MANUTIUS
JAPANESE HARUNOBU
SCOTTISH SMELLIE BALLANTYNE
SWISS GERING
PRINTER'S DEVIL FLY
PRINTING TIRAGE EDITION VIGOREUX CHARACTER IMPRIMERY
(— CHARACTER) SWUNGDASH
(KIND OF —) DNA
(LAST —) THIRTY
PRION PETREL
PRIONID BEETLE
PRIONODON LINSANG
PRIOR ERE OLD FORE PAST EIGNE ELDER FORMER RATHER ALREADY EARLIER FARTHER ANTERIOR FOREHAND HITHERTO PREVIOUS PRECEDING
(PREF.) ANTE EPH EPI
(— TO) ANTE PRAE PRE SUPRA
PRIORITY PRIVILEGE PRECEDENCE PREFERMENT
(PREF.) PRAE PRE
PRIORY ABBEY NUNNERY CLOISTER PRIORATE
PRISCA (HUSBAND OF —) AQUILA
PRISM BLOCK NICOL CYLINDER SPECTRUM WERNICKE REFRACTOR
PRISMATIC SHOWY BRILLIANT
PRISON GIB JUG PEN BRIG COOP GAOL HELL HOCK HOLD HOLE JAIL KEEP LAKE NICK QUAD QUOD SHOP SLAM STIR WARD BAGNE CHOKY CLINK FLEET GRATE JOINT KITTY LIMBO LODGE POUND RATEL TENCH TRONK VAULT BAGNIO BAILEY BUCKET CARCEL CARCER COOLER JIGGER LUMBER RATTLE BASTILE BOCARDO BULLPEN COLLEGE COMPTER CONFINE COUNTER DUNGEON FREEZER GEHENNA KIDCOTE LUDGATE NEWGATE SLAMMER DARTMOOR HOOSEGOW TOLBOOTH TRIBUNAL CALABOOSE PENITENTIARY
(— CAMP) GULAG OFLAG
(— IN ROME) TULLIANUM
(AUSTRALIAN —) TENCH
(IN —) INSIDE
(MILITARY —) GLASSHOUSE GUARDHOUSE
(POLITICAL —) GULAG
(SUBTERRANEAN —) MASSYMORE
(UNIVERSITY —) CARCER
PRISONER CON POW MUTE LIFER DETENU INMATE REMAND TERMER CAITIFF CAPTIVE CONVICT GAOLBIRD JAILBIRD LONGTIMER
(RELEASED —) EXCON
PRISONER OF ZENDA (AUTHOR OF —) HOPE
(CHARACTER IN —) ROSE SAPT FRITZ FLAVIA RUDOLF MICHAEL DEMAUBAN BURLESDON ANTOINETTE RASSENDYLL TARLENHEIM
PRISONER'S BASE CHEVY CHIVY
PRISSY PRIM FUSSY DAINTY FINICKY PRUDISH PRIGGISH SISSIFIED
PRISTINE NEW PURE FIRST FRESH UNTROD ANCIENT PRIMARY ORIGINAL PRIMEVAL PRIMITIVE UNSPOILED
PRIVACY RECESS SECRET PRIVITY RETREAT SECRECY DARKNESS INTIMACY INTIMITY SOLITUDE SECLUSION
(IN —) ASIDE
(PL.) VERENDA
PRIVATE SNUG ALONE CLOSE GUIDE INNER KHASS PRIVY SHARE CLOSET COVERT INWARD POCKET SECRET STANCH POSTERN SECRECY SEVERAL SOLDIER SQUADDY CIVILIAN DOMESTIC ESOTERIC HOMEFELT INTERNAL INTIMATE PERSONAL SINGULAR UMBRATILE
(BRITISH —) TOMMY
(PREF.) CRYPT(O) KRYPT(O) PRIVI
PRIVATEER CAPER MARQUE PIRATE ALABAMA CORSAIR CRUISER DUNKIRK PICKEER
PRIVATELY ASIDE INWARDLY SECRETLY
PRIVATION LOSS WANT PINCH PENURY PERISH ABSENCE POVERTY HARDSHIP
PRIVET PRIM HEDGE SKEDGE IBOLIUM PRIMWORT PRIMPRINT
PRIVILEGE UP PUT SOC BOTE DOWN HAND STAR TEAM CLAIM ENTRY FAVOR FRANK GRACE HONOR REGAL RIGHT THEAM EXCUSE INDULT MUNITY OCTROI OPTION PATENT WARREN CHARTER FALDAGE FREEDOM LIBERTY MITZVAH PASSAGE GRANDEZA STANDAGE PERQUISITE PREROGATIVE
(— TO USE THINGS) BOTE
(ACQUIRED —) EASEMENT
(POKER —) EDGE
(POOL —) STAR
PRIVILEGED CURULE EXEMPT LICENSED CHARTERED
(— PLACE) WARREN
PRIVY WC AJAX GONG REAR BIFFY DRAFT DUNNY ISSUE JAKES PETTY QUIET SIEGE CLOACA CLOSET OFFICE SECRET DRAUGHT FOREIGN LATRINE PRIVATE DONICKER FAMILIAR INTIMATE OUTHOUSE PERSONAL STEALTHY WARDROBE
(MONASTERY —) REREDORTER
PRIZE CUP FEE GEM PRY BELL BEND GAME GREE PALM PLUM PREY PRIX RATE RISK AWARD BACON BOOTY LEVER PLATE PLUME PRICE PURSE STAKE VALUE WAGER ESTEEM GLAIVE PRAISE PREMIO TROPHY BENEFIT CAPTURE GARLAND PREMIUM ESTIMATE LEVERAGE PURCHASE REPRISAL TREASURE
(— FOR LAST) MELL
(FIRST —) BLUE
(LOTTERY —) LOT TERN
(THEATER —) OBIE
PRIZE CUP PEWTER
PRIZED DEAR CHARY VALUED
PRIZEFIGHT GO BOUT MILL MATCH SCRAP BARNEY
PRIZEFIGHTER BOXER BLEEDER FIGHTER SLUGGER PUGILIST
PRIZE MONEY GUNNAGE
PRO TO FOR FAVORING
PROA PARO PRAU PROW PAROO PRAHU CARACOA
PROBABILISTIC STOCHASTIC
PROBABILITY ODDS SHOW CHANCE PERCENTAGE
(STRONG —) PRESUMPTION
PROBABLE MAYBE LIKELY PROBAL TOPICAL APPARENT FEASIBLE POSSIBLE INTHECARDS
PROBABLY BELIKE LIKELY
PROBATION TEST PROOF TRIAL PAROLE EVIDENCE
PROBATIONER STIBBLER
PROBE PICK SEEK SIFT STOG TENT DELVE ENTER GROPE SOUND FATHOM SEARCH SEEKER STYLET THRUST TRACER ACCOUNT EXAMINE INQUIRY SOUNDER GYROMELE
PROBITY HONESTY INTEGRITY RECTITUDE
PROBLEM NUT SUM WHY BOYG CRUX DUAL ISSE KNOT BLAIK HYDRA POSER APORIA ENIGMA HANGUP BUGBEAR DILEMMA FUNERAL GORDIAN GRUELER TICKLER EXERCISE HEADACHE JEOPARDY QUESTION STICKLER SITUATION
(CHESS —) DUAL MOVER SUIMATE MINIATURE
PROBLEMATICAL DUBIOUS DOUBTFUL PUZZLING UNCERTAIN UNDECIDED
PROBOSCIS NOSE SNOUT TRUMP TRUNK ANTLIA LINGUA SIPHON SYPHON TONGUE ROSTRUM
PROBOSCIS MONKEY KAHA KAHUA
PROCACIOUS PREY SASSY SAUCY
PROCAINE NOVOCAINE
PROCAVIA HYRAX
PROCEDURE BIAS FORM HAVE VEIN DRAFT ORDER TENOR TRACK AFFAIR COURSE METHOD POLITY SYSTEM DRAUGHT PROCESS PRODUCT ACTIVITY PROTOCOL OPERATION
(PRESCRIBED —S) CEREMONY
(ROUNDABOUT —) CIRCUITY
(SECRET —) STEALTH
(STANDARDIZED —) BIT
(SURGICAL —) BYPASS
(UNWISE —) FOLLY
PROCEED DO GO BANG BEAR FAND FARE FLOW FOND HAVE MAKE MARK MOVE PASS ROAM ROLL SEEK STEP TAKE TOOL TOUR WEAR WEND WIND YEAD YEDE YEED AMBLE ARISE DRESS FOUND FRAME ISSUE MARCH REACH TRACE BREEZE INTEND PURSUE RESULT SPRING STRAKE STRIKE TRAVEL ADVANCE AGGRESS DEVOLVE EMANATE FORTHGO PRETEND STRETCH CONTINUE PROGRESS
(— AIMLESSLY) CIRCLE
(— ALONE) SINGLE
(— AWKWARDLY) SHLEP SCHLEP SCHLEPP
(— BY STEPS) RATCHET
(— CLUMSILY) FLOUNDER
(— INSIDIOUSLY) SAP
(— LINGERINGLY) LOITER
(— OBLIQUELY) CUT
(— RAGGEDLY) HALT
(— RAPIDLY) RAKE STRETCH
(— SECRETLY) MINE
(—S FROM GAMBLING) MOTZA MOTSER
(— SLOWLY) INCH
(— SUCCESSFULLY) COOK
(— THROUGH) PLAY
(— UNSTEADILY) DRIDDLE
(— WITH) PLAY
(— WITH DIFFICULTY) STRUGGLE
(— WITH LITTLE EFFORT) CRUISE
(PL.) TAKE VAIL AVAILS INCOME PROFITS PROVENT RETURNS PREVENUE
PROCEEDING ACT DEED FARE PLOY STEP AFFAIR AMPARO COURSE DOMENT ISSUANT MEASURE ONGOING PASSANT QUIETUS TEMANET WARRANT CONCURSO INSTANCE PLACITUM PRACTICE
(— BY THREES) TERNARY
(— FROM GOD) DIVINE
(— FROM THE EARTH) TELLURIC
(— STEP-BY-STEP) GRADATORY
(COURT —S) ACTA TRIAL ACTION
(INDIRECT —S) AMBAGES
(PARLIAMENTARY —S) HUSTINGS
(PREVIOUS —) PRECEDENT
(RECORDED —S) ACTA
(SECRET —) COVERTURE
(PL.) ONGOINGS
PROCERITY HEIGHT TALLNESS
PROCESS RUN FANG FOOT TINA WRIT CREST FURCA HAMUS MUCRO SPINA CALCAR CAPIAS CILIUM COURSE CRUNCH FEELER HABEAS INTEND METHOD REPORT ACCOUNT BARBULE FURCULA GOBBING HAMULUS ISOLATE LAMELLA MANDATE SPATULA SUMMONS ACROMION ACTIVITY APPENDIX AUTOTYPE FILAMENT FRENULUM GRAINING INSTANCE MANUBRIUM OPERATION
(— OF BONE) HORN
(— OF CHANGE) ACTION
(— OF CREATING VACUUM) EXHAUST
(— OF DYEING) BATIK HANKING
(— OF METALPLATING) ACIERAGE

(— OF PACKING) GOBBING
(— OF REASONING) ALGEBRA
(— OF SUPPLYING WANTAGE) ULLING
(— ON FISH'S HEAD) LACINIA
(— PAPER) CONVERT
(— TO RECOVER LAND) DADENHUDD
(— TO REGAIN USE) RECYCLE
(ABRUPT —) MUCRO
(ALCHEMICAL —) CIBATION DIPLOSIS
(ARTISTIC —) FROTTAGE
(BRISTLE-LIKE —) STILET STYLET
(CALENDERING —) SWISSING
(CARBON —) AUTOTYPE
(CERAMIC —) FIRING
(COATING —) BLOOMING
(CURVED —) HAMUS
(DEVELOPMENTAL —) ANCESTRY
(EARLIKE —) AURICLE
(FALCONRY —) IMPING
(FINISHING —) BRUSHING CRABBING
(FORKED —) FURCA FURCULA
(HAIRLIKE —) VILLUS
(HELMETLIKE —) CASQUE
(HOOKLIKE —) HAMULUS
(HORNSHAPED —) CORNICLE
(INTELLECTUAL —S) COGITO
(KIND OF —) MARKEY MARKOFF
(KNOBLIKE —) BOSS
(LEGAL —) BAIL SUIT CAUSE ATTAINT INSTANCE
(MATHEMATICAL —) ADDITION DIVISION
(MENTAL —) COMPOUND
(MINING —) STOPING
(MOVIE-MAKING —) SLATING
(NERVE-CELL —) DENDRON
(NERVELIKE —) AXON AXONE
(PHOTOGRAPHIC —) CARBRO
(POINTED —) AWN SPINE STYLUS LANGUET
(PRINTING —) OFFSET GRAVURE STENCIL INTAGLIO
(REORGANIZATION —) HEMIXIS
(SMALL POINTED —) AWN
(SPINNING —) JACKING
(SPINOUS —) ACANTHA
(SPINY —) STYLOID
(TEXTILE —) DECATING
(WEAVING —) HATCHING
(WINGLIKE —) ALA FIN
(PREF.) TYP(I)(O)
(DRY —) XER(O)
(SUFF.) AL ANCE ANT ENCE ESIS IAL ING ISATION ISM IZATION OSIS SIS TH TYPAL TYPE TYPIC TYPY
(— OF BECOMING) ESCENCE

PROCESSED DOWN FINISHED

PROCESSION POMP WALK CORSO DRIVE TRACE TRAIN BRIDAL EXEQUY LITANY PARADE STREAM CORTEGE FUNERAL THIASOS TRIONFO TRIUMPH ENTRANCE MOHARRAM PROGRESS MOTORCADE
(— OF THE HOLY CHRIST) SPIRATION
(BOISTEROUS —) SKIMMITY
(FUNERAL —) EXEQUY EXEQUIES
(IRISH CIVIC —) FRINGES
(MUSLIM —) MOHARRAM MUHARRAM MUHARREM
(SUFF.) CADE

PROCESSOR (KIND OF —) WORD

PROCLAIM BID CRY BAWL DEEM HORN OYES OYEZ SCRY SING TOOT TOUT BLARE BLAZE BOAST CLAIM GREDE KNELL SOUND SPEAK BLAZON BOUNCE DEFAME HERALD INDICT OUTCRY CLARION DECLARE DIVULGE PROTEST PUBLISH TRUMPET ANNOUNCE DENOUNCE RENOUNCE PROMULGATE
(— ALOUD) ROAR
(— PUBLICLY) PRECONIZE
(— WITH BIG TALK) BOUNCE

PROCLAMATION CRY HUE BANS FIAT OYES OYEZ RERD SCRY BANDO BANNS BLAZE EDICT UKASE PLACARD PROGRAM PUBLICATION ANNUNCIATION

PROCLIVITY BENT ANLAGE APETITE APTNESS LEANING TENDENCY

PROCNE (FATHER OF —) PANDION
(HUSBAND OF —) TEREUS
(SISTER OF —) PHILOMELA
(SON OF —) ITYS

PROCONSUL GALLIO PROVOST

PROCRASTINATE LAG TIME DEFER DELAY LINGER ADJOURN POSTPONE PROROGUE TEMPORIZE

PROCRASTINATION DELAY CUNCTATION

PROCREANT FRUITFUL

PROCREATE WIN SIRE BEGET ENGENDER GENERATE OCCASION

PROCREATION INCREASE

PROCREATOR AUTHOR

PROCRIS (FATHER OF —) ERECHTHEUS
(HOUND OF —) LAELAPS
(HUSBAND OF —) CEPHALUS

PROCTOR LIAR PROG ACTOR AGENT PROXY BEGGAR RECTOR MONITOR PROCUTOR

PROCUMBENT HUMIFUSE PROSTRATE

PROCURABLE PARABLE

PROCURATOR PROXY PILATE PROCTOR

PROCURE GET WIN FANG FIND GAIN GIVE HALE BRING INFER TOUCH EFFECT INDUCE OBTAIN ACHIEVE ACQUIRE COMPARE CONQUER CONTRIVE PURCHASE
(— TO COMMIT PERJURY) SUBORN

PROCURER PIMP PROXENET PURVEYOR

PROCURESS AUNT BAWD HACK LENA PANDER COMMODE PINNACE

PROD DAB EGG GIG JAB JOB JOG BROD BROG GOAD HEEL POKE PROG URGE GOOSE HURRY NUDGE PROBE INCITE JOSTLE THRUST IRRITATE
(— THE BUTTOCKS) GOOSE

PRODIGAL PROD FLUSH LARGE COSTLY LAVISH WANTON WASTER PROFUSE SPENDER WASTRIE WASTRIFE PROFLIGATE

PRODIGALITY WASTE WASTRY WASTRIFE PROFUSION

PRODIGIOUS HUGE VAST GIANT AMAZING IMMENSE STRANGE ABNORMAL ENORMOUS GIGANTIC MONSTROUS PORTENTOUS

PRODIGY OMEN SIGN MARVEL OSTENT WIZARD WONDER MIRACLE MONSTER PORTENT CEREMONY

PRODITION TREASON BETRAYAL

PRODUCE DO GO ANTE BEAR FORM GIVE GROW MAKE REAR SHOW TEEM WAGE BEGET BIRTH BREED BRING BROOD BUILD CARRY CAUSE DRIVE FORGE FRAME HATCH ISSUE PUTON RAISE SPAWN THROW TRADE YIELD APPORT CREATE EFFECT GROWTH INCOME INVENT INWORK PARENT SECURE TURNIN ADVANCE ANIMATE COMPOSE DEPROME GIGNATE INSPIRE OUTWORK PRODUCT PROLONG PROVENT CONCEIVE CONFLATE ENGENDER GENERATE INCREASE LENGTHEN OFFSPRING
(— A COPY OF) TYPE
(— AN EFFECT) ACT AFFECT
(— ANEW) REGENERATE
(— AS PROFIT) NET NETT
(— AUDIBLE EFFECT) SOUND
(— BY GREAT EFFORT) GRIND
(— CROPS) CARRY
(— DULL APPEARANCE) CHILL
(— EFFECT) OPERATE
(— FREELY) PULLULATE
(— FRUIT) TEEM
(— HEAT) ENRAGE
(— IN SPECIFIED FORM) FORMAT
(— PAID FOR RENT) CAIN
(— SHARP NOISE) CRINK
(AGRICULTURAL —) PODWARE
(FARM —) HUSBANDRY
(GARDEN —) STUFF TRUCK
(MINING —) LEY
(SUFF.) FER(ENCE)(ENT)(OUS) FIC(AL)(ATE)(ATION)(ATIVE)(ATOR) (ATORY)(E)(ENCE)(ENT)(IAL)(IARY) (IENT) FIQUE GEN(E)(ESIA)(ESIS) (ETIC)(IC)(IN)(OUS)(Y)

PRODUCED (ARTIFICIALLY —) FORCED
(SEXUALLY —) GAMIC
(SUFF.) GENETIC

PRODUCER GASMAN BEARING SHOWMAN DIRECTOR GAZOGENE OUTPUTTER
(— OF COMPUTER SYSTEMS) OEM
(SUFF.) ARIAN EER

PRODUCING IN PROCREANT
(PREF.) EXO
(SUFF.) GENIC GEROUS GON(E) (IDIUM)(IMO)(Y) IGEROUS PARA PAROUS

PRODUCT HEIR ITEM BRAND CHILD FRUIT GROSS OUTGO SPAWN ALCLAD EFFORT FABRIC GROWTH RESULT UPCOME FALLOUT OUTTURN PRODUCE PROGENY TURNOUT OUTBIRTH OFFSPRING
(— MADE IN INDIA) SWADESHI
(— OF ROCK DECAY) LATERITE
(—S OF LAND) ESPLEES
(—S OF ORCHARD) BIKKURIM
(ADDITION —) ADDUCT
(CHEESE AND MILK —S) GERVAIS
(CHOICE —) CAVIAR
(COMPLETED —) TURNOFF
(FISH —) SURIMI
(LEGISLATIVE —) ACT
(MATHEMATICAL —) SQUARE
(MINERAL —) HUTCH
(OXIDATION —) SUBSCALE
(RESIDUAL —) LATERITE
(SECONDARY —) CONGENER
(SURPLUS —S) ARISINGS
(TRANSFORMATION —) BAINITE
(WASTE —) RESIDUENT
(WORTHLESS —) CHAFF
(SUFF.) ADE
(COMMERCIAL —) INE
(MANUFACTURED —) ITE

PRODUCTION WORK FORGE FRUIT GROSS PIECE YIELD GROWTH OUTPUT EDITION GUIGNOL PRODUCE ARTIFICE INDUCTION OPERATION
(— OF MEDIUM) APPORT
(— OF YOUNG) INCREASE
(BEST —S) FAT
(SUCCESSFUL —) HIT
(SUFF.) GENY POEIA POESIS POIESIS POIETIC

PRODUCTIVE FAT RICH LOOSE QUICK ACTIVE BATTLE PAROUS STRONG CAUSING FERTILE GAINFUL HEALTHY TEEMFUL TEEMING CHILDING CREATIVE FRUITFUL GERMINAL PLENTEOUS
(SUFF.) POEIA POESIS POIESIS POIETIC

PROEM PREFACE PRELUDE PROHEIM FOREWORD OVERTURE PREAMBLE

PROETUS (BROTHER OF —) ACRISIUS
(DAUGHTER OF —) IPHINOE LYSIPPE IPHIANASSA
(FATHER OF —) ABAS
(MOTHER OF —) OCALEA
(WIFE OF —) ANTEA

PROFANATION VIOLENCE SACRILEGE

PROFANE LAY NOA BLUE FOUL ABUSE COARSE DEBASE DEFILE DEFOIL DEFOUL UNHOLY VULGAR WICKED GODLESS IMPIOUS POLLUTE SECULAR UNGODLY VIOLATE WORLDLY TEMPORAL UNHALLOW

PROFANITY OATH CURSE CURSING LANGUAGE BLASPHEMY

PROFESS OWN AVOW ADMIT CLAIM AFFECT AFFIRM ALLEGE ASSERT ASSUME FOLLOW PRESUME PRETEND PURPORT PRACTICE
(— TO BE) SUBSCRIBE

PROFESSION ART BAR LAW COAT FEAT GAME WALK CRAFT FAITH FORTE TRADE CAREER CHURCH EMPLOY METIER MISTER CALLING FACULTY QUALITY SERVICE ADVOCACY BUSINESS COACHING FUNCTION PEDAGOGY SOLDIERY VOCATION
(— OF LETTERS) QUILL

(JOURNALISTIC —) PRESS
(SUFF.) SHIP
PROFESSIONAL PRO COLT PAID HIRED EXPERT SKILLED TRAINED FINISHED
PROFESSOR DON PROF HANIF KHOJA LAWYER REGENT ADJOINT ACADEMIC CIVILIAN EMERITUS
PROFESSORSHIP CHAIR FAUTEUIL
PROFFER BID CAP GIVE TEND TENT DEFER DODGE ESSAY OFFER EXTEND OPPOSE PREFER PROFRE TENDER ATTEMPT PRESENT HESITATE
PROFICIENCY SIGHT SKILL ABILITY APTNESS MAITRISE
PROFICIENT ADEPT EXPERT MASTER SALTED VERSED PERFECT SKILLED SKILLFUL
PROFILE FORM FLANK PURFLE SKETCH CONTOUR OUTLINE SECTION PSYCHOGRAPH
(— OF RIVERBED) THALWEG
(— OF RIVER BOTTOM) THALWEG
PROFIT AID GET NET WIN BOOT GAIN MEND NOTE SKIN VAIL AVAIL EDIFY FRAME GRIST LUCRE SCALP SPEED BEHOOF INCOME MAKING PAYOFF RETURN ACCOUNT ADVANCE BENEFIT CLEANUP FURTHER GETTING IMPROVE MILEAGE PLUNDER REVENUE VANTAGE WINNING CLEANING INCREASE INTEREST PERCENTAGE PERQUISITE
(— BY) BROOK
(ILLICIT —) GRAFT
(INORDINATE —) BUNCE
(UNDERCOVER —) SQUEEZE
(PL.) TAKE GRAVY ISSUE AVAILS JALKAR ESPLEES
PROFITABLE FAT GOOD UTILE GOLDEN PLUMMY GAINFUL HELPFUL PAYABLE BEHOVELY ECONOMIC PROVABLE REPAYING VAILABLE REWARDING
PROFITLESS BOOTLESS
PROFLIGATE ROUE ROVE DEFEAT CORRUPT IMMORAL RIOTOUS SPENDER VICIOUS WASTREL DEPRAVED FLAGRANT OVERCOME RAKEHELL WASTEFUL ABANDONED
PROFOUND DEEP HARD WISE ABYSS DEPTH HEAVY OCEAN SOUND THICK PITCHY STRONG ABYSMAL INTENSE ABSTRUSE COMPLETE PREGNANT REACHING THOROUGH
PROFUNDITY ABYSS DEPTH FATHOM DEEPNESS
PROFUSE FREE LUSH SLAB FRANK GALORE LAVISH COPIOUS LIBERAL OPULENT ABUNDANT GENEROUS PRODIGAL SQUANDER WASTEFUL LUXURIANT REDUNDANT UNSPARING
PROFUSELY HEARTILY
PROFUSION RIOT WASTE EXCESS LAVISH FLUENCY OPULENCE REDUNDANCY
PROG FOOD GOAD POKE PROD PROWL TRAMP BEGGAR FORAGE PROCTOR
PROGENITOR BURI MANU ROOT SIRE PITRI STOCK PARENT ANCESTOR
PROGENY BED GET IMP KIN BURD CLAN KIND SEED TEAM BROOD CHILD FRUIT ISSUE STRAIN STRIND INCROSS KINDRED LINEAGE OUTCOME PRODUCT CHILDREN FRUITAGE INCREASE OUTBIRTH OUTCROSS OFFSPRING
(— OF WATER-BUFFALO AND YAK) DZO
(— OF WITCH AND DEMON) HOLD
(INSECT —) SOCIETY
PROGNOSIS FORECAST PROPHASIS
PROGNOSTIC OMEN SIGN TOKEN AUSPICE OMINOUS PRESAGE PROPHECY
PROGNOSTICATE BODE AUGUR SPELL BETOKEN CONJECT PREDICT PRENOTE FOREBODE FORESHOW FORETELL PROPHESY
PROGNOSTICATION RACE PRESAGE FOREBODE FORECAST PROGRESS PROPHECY
PROGNOSTICATOR SEER DOOMER PROPHET HARUSPEX
PROGRAM CARD SHOW FORUM AGENDA DESIGN SCHEME AGENDUM PREFACE CLAMBAKE FESTIVAL GIVEAWAY GUIDANCE JAMBOREE PLAYBILL SCHEDULE SEQUENCE SYLLABUS
(COMPUTER —) DOS EDITOR FIRMWARE SPREADSHEET
(COMPUTER —S) SOFTWARE
(CURRENT AFFAIRS —) REALITES
(EMPLOYEE —) ESOP
(HEALTH —) MEDICAID MEDICARE
(PART OF COMPUTER —) BRANCH
(PARTY —) PLATFORM
(STOCK —) ESOP
(TELEVISION —) SITCOM
PROGRAMMA EDICT DECREE PREFACE PROGRAM
PROGRESS WAY BIRL DENT FARE GAIN GROW MOVE RACE RISE STEM STEP TOUR WEAR WEND WENT BUILD DRIFT FORGE GOING MARCH SWING WEENT ASCENT BUFFET COURSE GROWTH STREEK ADVANCE DEVELOP FOOTING HEADWAY IMPROVE JOURNEY ONGOING PASSAGE PROCESS PROFICIENCY
(— CLUMSILY) SCRAMBLE
(— ERRATICALLY) FLAIL
(— FEEBLY) DODDER
(— INTELLIGENTLY PLANNED) TELESIA TELESIS
(— NOISILY) CHORTLE
(— SLOWLY) CRAWL
(SINGLE —) THROUGH
PROGRESSED FAR
PROGRESSION WAY SWING COURSE GALLOP ADVANCE PASSAGE PROGRESS SEQUENCE
(— OF CHORDS) SWIPE
(MUSICAL —) SKIP
(SMOOTH —) SLIDE
PROGRESSIVE ACTIVE ONWARD FORWARD GRADUAL LIBERAL
(NOT —) SLOW
PROGRESSIVELY STILL
PROHIBIT BAN BAR STOP VETO BLOCK DEBAR ESTOP DEFEND ENJOIN FORBID HINDER OUTLAW FORFEND FORWARN INHIBIT PREVENT DISALLOW PRECLUDE SUPPRESS PROSCRIBE
PROHIBITED HOT TABU TABOO ILLEGAL ILLICIT UNLAWFUL VERBOTEN
PROHIBITING VETITIVE
PROHIBITION BAN NAY NON VETO ORDER BARRIER DEFENCE DEFENSE EMBARGO FORBODE ESTOPPEL
PROHIBITIONIST DRY PUSSYFOOT
PROJECT GAB GAG JET JUT LAP TUT BEAM CAST GAME HURL IDEA PLAN POKE PUSH SAIL SWIM BULGE CHART DRAFT DRIVE IMAGE JETTY JUTTY SETUP SHOOT STICK THROW BEETLE DESIGN DEVICE ESTATE EXTEND FILLIP OUTJUT PROPEL SCHEME SCREEN SHELVE EXTRUDE GOSPLAN IMAGINE KNUCKLE OUTCROP PATTERN BUSINESS CONTRIVE OUTREACH OUTSHOOT OVERHANG PROPOSAL PROTRUDE SPANGHEW
(UNETHICAL —) SCHEME
(VISIONARY —) BABEL
PROJECTILE BALL BOLT CASE SHOT SHAFT TRACER OUTCAST POUNDER FIREBALL SHRAPNEL
(— DESIGNED TO SET FIRE TO HOUSES) CARCASS
(EXPLOSIVE —) BOMB SHELL
(SMALL —S) MITRAILLE
(SUBMARINE —) TORPEDO
(PL.) LEAD SHOT SALVO STUFF
PROJECTING BEETLE SHELVY EMINENT JUTTING OUTSHOT PENDENT SALIENT SNAGGLED PROMINENT OUTSTANDING
(PREF.) PRO
PROJECTION ARM CAM COG DOG EAR FIN GIB JET JOG JUT NAB NAG NUT TAB TOE BEAK BOSS BROW BUHR COAK COCK CROC CUSP HEEL HORN KEEL KICK KINK KNAG KNOB KNOP LOBE RIDE SAIL SNUG SPUD SPUR TEAT WING BULGE CLEAT EJECT ELBOW FENCE FURCA JUTTY PRONG SALLY SCRAG SHANK SHOOT SNOUT SPIKE TOOTH BRANCH CALCAR CORBEL CROSET FUSULA HEARTH ICICLE MENTUM NOSING PALATE RELIEF RELISH TAPPET BREAKER CONSOLE DRAWING EPAULET EYEBROW FETLOCK KNUCKLE LANGUET ORILLON OUTSHOT PRICKER PRICKLE RESSAUT AJUTMENT CASCABEL DENTICLE EMINENCE FOOTLOCK ORILLION OVERHANG OVERSAIL SALIENCE SHOULDER SPROCKET STERIGMA TRUNNION APOPHYSIS OUTTHRUST PROMINENCE
(— CONNECTING TIMBER) COAK
(— EXTENDING BACKWARD) BARB
(— FROM CASTING) SPRUE
(— FROM SHIP'S KEEL) SPONSON
(— IN CLOCK) SQUARE
(— IN ORCHIDS) MENTUM
(— OF FOREHEAD) ANTINION
(— OF JAW) GNATHISM
(— OF PEAT) HAG
(— OF RAFTER) SALLY
(— OF TERRITORY) PANHANDLE
(— ON CANNON) CASCABEL
(— ON CHURCH SEAT) MISERICORD
(— ON FOOTWEAR) STUD
(— ON GUN) CROC LUMP
(— ON HARNESS) HAME
(— ON HORSE'S LEG) FETLOCK
(— ON HORSESHOE) STICKER
(— ON LOCK) FENCE STUMP
(— ON MAST) STOP
(— ON OVARY) STIGMA
(— ON POCKETKNIFE) KICK
(— ON SALMON JAW) GIB
(— ON WHEEL) GUB GROUSER GROUTER
(— OVER AIR PORT) EYEBROW
(CARPENTRY —) TENON
(FIREPLACE —) HOB
(JAGGED —) SNUG
(NARROW —) STRAP TONGUE
(SHARP —) BARB FANG
(SUBMERGED —) KNOLL
(PL.) GRAIN BARLEY
PROJECTOR KINO LANTERN PLANNER SCHEMER BIOSCOPE EPISCOPE VITASCOPE
PROLAMIN ZEIN SEINE GLIADIN HORDEIN KAFIRIN SECALIN
PROLAPSE PTOSIS BLOWOUT FALLING
PROLETARIAN POPULAR
PROLETARIAT MASSES
PROLIFIC BIRTHY BREEDY BROODY FECUND FERTILE PROFUSE TEEMING ABUNDANT FRUITFUL SPAWNING
(BE —) INCREASE
PROLIX LARGE WORDY DIFFUSE LENGTHY PROSAIC TEDIOUS VERBOSE TIRESOME WEARISOME
PROLIXITY REDUNDANCY
PROLOGUE BANS BANNS INDEX PREFACE
PROLONG DREE LENG LONG SPIN DEFER DELAY DRIVE ELONG TWINE DILATE EXTEND LINGER SPREAD DISPACE PRODUCE RESPITE SUSTAIN CONTINUE ETERNIZE LENGTHEN POSTPONE PROROGUE PROTRACT
PROLONGATION BEAK AORTA CONUS STIPE STYLE FERMATA ACROSOME APPENDIX GYNOBASE LABELLUM
PROLONGED GREAT PROLIX DELAYED EXTENDED SOSTENUTO
PROMENADE BUND MAIL MALL PIER PROM WALK CORSO FRONT PASEO PRADO MARINA PARADE PASEAR ALAMEDA GALLERY FRESCADE GALLERIA SEAFRONT BOULEVARD

(CARRIAGE —) TOUR
(GREEK —) STOA
PROMETHEUS (BROTHER OF —)
ATLAS MENOETIUS EPIMETHEUS
(FATHER OF —) IAPETUS
(MOTHER OF —) CLYMENE
PROMETHEUS UNBOUND
(AUTHOR OF —) SHELLEY
(CHARACTER IN —) ASIA IONE EARTH JUPITER MERCURY PANTHEA HERCULES DEMOGORGON PROMETHEUS
PROMINENCE BUR NOB BOSS BURR CUSP KNOB NOOP UMBO AGGER BULLA CREST GRAIN OLIVA SWELL TUBER TYLUS ACCENT CALCAR NODULE TRAGUS BILLING BUTTOCK CONDYLE FASHION HAMULUS KNUCKLE LINGULA AMYGDALA EMINENCY EMPHASIS GLABELLA PULVINAR SALIENCE TUBERCLE MONTICULE PROMONTORY
(PREF.) TUBERCULI TUBERCULO TUBERI
PROMINENT BIG BOLD BEADY BRENT GREAT HEAVY STEEP BEETLE MARKED SIGNAL BLATANT BOLTING CAPITAL EMINENT JUTTING LEADING NOTABLE OBVIOUS SALIENT AQUILINE BEETLING MANIFEST STRIKING NOTICEABLE CONSPICUOUS OUTSTANDING
(SOCIALLY —) SWELL
(UNDULY —) OBTRUSIVE
PROMISCUOUS LIGHT CASUAL RANDOM CARELESS
PROMISCUOUSLY TAGRAG
PROMISE VOW AVOW BAND HEST HETE HOPE HOTE OATH OSSE PASS PLEA SURE WORD FAITH GRANT HIGHT TRUTH ASSURE BEHEST ENGAGE FIANCE HALSEN INSURE PAROLE PLEDGE PLIGHT PROMIT BEHIGHT BETROTH WARRANT CONTRACT COVENANT GUARANTY BETROTHAL OBLIGATION
(— IN MARRIAGE) BETROTH ESPOUSE AFFIANCE
(— OF SUCCESS) LIKELIHOOD
(— RESULTS) PROSPECT
(— TO PAY) NOTE ACCEPT
(— TO TAKE IN MARRIAGE) AFFY
PROMISED VOTARY
(— IN MARRIAGE) SURE HIGHT ENGAGED
(— LAND) CANAAN
PROMISING APT FAIR ROSY BRIGHT LIKELY PROOFY TOWARD GRADELY TOWARDLY
PROMISSORY NOTE IOU HUNDI HOONDI TICKET
PROMONTORY HOE NAB BEAK BILL HEAD MULL NAZE NESS NOOK NOUP PEAK SCAW SKAW TOOT ELBOW MORRO POINT REACH SNOUT SALIENT FORELAND HEADLAND
PROMOTE AID FLOG HELP HYPE LOFT PLUG PUSH AVAIL BOOST EXALT NURSE RAISE SERVE SETON SPEED ASSIST EXCITE FOMENT FOSTER LAUNCH PREFER ADVANCE DIGNIFY ELEVATE FORWARD FURTHER IMPROVE PREFECT PRODUCE PROMOVE SUCCEED SUPPORT INCREASE SUBSERVE
PROMOTER AGENT FRIEND ABETTOR BOOSTER BUBBLER BROACHER HUMANIST PROJECTOR
(SUFF.) ANT
PROMOTION LIFT REMOVE ADVANCE FLACKERY PROMOVAL
(— OF CONSUMER INTERESTS) NADERISM
PROMOTIONAL PROMO
(— PRONOUNCEMENT) PROMO
PROMPT APT CUE MOVE URGE YARE ALERT FRACK PREST QUICK READY SERVE SWIFT WILLY YEDER EXCITE INDITE MATURE NIMBLE SPEEDY SUDDEN ANIMATE FORWARD PROVOKE SUGGEST PUNCTUAL REMINDER
(— TO EVIL) SUGGEST
PROMPTER CUER CALLER MEMORIST ORDINARY SOUFFLEUR
PROMPTING CALL BEHEST BEHIND MOTIVE
(SPIRITUAL —) LEADING
PROMPTITUDE ALACRITY
PROMPTLY UP PAT TID TIT SOON TITE PRONTO YARELY BETIMES PRESTLY QUICKLY DIRECTLY SPEEDILY
PROMPTNESS ALACRITY CELERITY DISPATCH
PROMULGATE SPREAD DECLARE PUBLISH PROCLAIM
PRONAOS ANTICUM
PRONE APT BENT EASY FLAT FREE GRUF BUXOM GIVEN GROOF JACENT LIABLE SUPINE BEASTLY BESTIAL DORMANT SUBJECT ADDICTED COUCHANT DISPOSED DOWNWARD PROPENSE
(— TO TAKE UP FADS) ISMY
(NATURALLY —) PROLIVE
PRONENESS
(SUFF.)
(— TO) ITIS
PRONG NEB NIB PEG PEW BILL FANG FORK HOOK PUGH SPUR TANG TENG TINE TING GRAIN SPADE SPEAN SPRONG FOURCHE TICKLER GRAINING
(— FOR EXTRACTING BUNG) TICKLER
(— FOR FISH) PEW PUGH
(— OF ANTLER) KNAG TIND TINE POINT
(— OF FORK) SPEAN
PRONGHORN CABREE CABRIT MAZAME BERENDO BERRENDO
PRONOUN HE IT ME MY WE YE ANY HER HIM HIS ONE OUR SHE THY WHO YOU OURS THAT THEM THEY THOU WHAT WHOM YOUR THINE WHICH WHOSE ITSELF MYSELF HERSELF HIMSELF OURSELF WHOEVER YOURSELF OURSELVES
(GENDERLESS —) THON
PRONOUNCE SAY PASS ACUTE SPEAK UTTER PREACH RECITE TONGUE ADJUDGE BEHIGHT CENSURE MOUILLE ASPIRATE
(— FREE) ABSOLVE
(— GUILTY) CONDEMN
(— HOLY) BLESS
PRONOUNCED HIGH MARKED DECIDED HOWLING INTENSE MOVABLE
(— AS FRICATIVE) GRASSEYE
(— PALATALLY) MOUILLE
(NOT —) SOFT
PRONOUNCEMENT FIAT CURSE DICTUM DICTAMEN
PRONTO QUICK ATONCE QUICKLY PROMPTLY
PRONUNCIATION BROGUE DICTION ETACISM LIAISON DELIVERY ENCLISIS ORTHOEPY
(BAD —) CACOEPY CACOLOGY LABDACISM
(BROAD —) PLATEASM
(CORRECT —) ORTHOEPY
(FAULTY —) CACOLOGY
(PLEASING —) EUPHONY EUPHONIA
(ROUGH —) BUR BURR
PROOF SAY MARK PULL SLIP TEST ESSAY PREWE REPRO TOKEN TOUCH TRIAL CLENCH GALLEY ORDEAL REASON RESULT REVISE ATTEMPT OUTCOME PROBATE SHOWING UTTERLY VOUCHER WARRANT ANALYSIS CACOLOGY DOCUMENT EVICTION EVIDENCE GOODNESS MONUMENT
(— AGAINST ATTACK) IMPREGNABLE
(— OF WRONGDOING) GOODS
(— SPIRIT OF WINE) SVT
(ABSOLUTE —) APODIXIS
(CLEAR SHARP —) DUPE REPRO
(INDIRECT —) APAGOGE
(PL.) STRING WARRANTY
PROOFREADER MARK CAP DELE STET CARET
PROP LEG BROB BUNT POST REST SPUR STAY STUD TRIG APPUI BRACE PERCH PUNCH RANCE SCOTE SHORE SHOVE SOUSE SPRAG SPURN STAFF STELL STOOP STULL COLUMN CROTCH CRUTCH PILLAR SCOTCH SHORER STAYER UPHOLD BOLSTER FULCRUM PINNING STUDDLE SUPPORT SUSTAIN BUTTRESS CROTCHET DUTCHMAN UNDERLAY UNDERSET
(— AS TRAP) TEEL
(— FOR CART) NEAP
(— FOR ROOF OF MINE) GIB
(— UP) CUSHION SCAFFOLD
(PREF.) FULCI
PROPAGANDA BOLOISM AGITPROP BALLYHOO
PROPAGATE BREED HATCH LAYER EXTEND SPREAD STRIKE DIFFUSE GEMMATE PRODUCE PUBLISH ENGENDER GENERATE INCREASE MULTIPLY POPULATE TRANSMIT PROCREATE
(— BY LAYERING) PROVINE
PROPAGATION BREED BREEDING DIVISION INCREASE LAYERAGE OFFSPRING
(SUFF.) GAM(AE)(IST)(OUS)(Y) GAMETE
PROPEL ROW CALL CAST FIRE FLIP KENT POLE PUSH SEND URGE DRIVE FLICK IMPEL KNOCK PRICK RANGE SPANK THROW HURTLE LAUNCH PROJECT
(— BALL) STROKE
(— BOAT) OAR ROW SET KENT POLE SCULL BUSHWACK
(— BOAT WITH FEET) LEG
(— ONESELF) HAUL
(— PUCK) CARRY
(— SUDDENLY) ZAP
(— WITH FORCE) RIFLE
PROPELLANT LOX
PROPELLER FAN HELIX SCREW AIRSCREW WINDMILL
PROPENSITY YEN BENT ITCH LURCH APTNESS IMPULSE LEANING PRONITY APPETITE FONDNESS INTEREST TENDENCY
PROPER FIT OWN GOOD JUST MEET TRUE WELL PREST RIGHT UTTER COMELY DECENT HONEST LAWFUL MODEST SEEMLY CAPITAL CORRECT FITTING GRADELY SEEMING SKILFUL THRIFTY ABSOLUTE BECOMING CONGREVE DECOROUS FORMULAR IDONEOUS PECULIAR RIGHTFUL SORTABLE SUITABLE VIRTUOUS
(APPARENTLY —) SPECIOUS
(BE — TO) BESEEM
(PREF.) CURIO ORTH(O)
PROPERLY DULY WELL FITLY TRULY ARIGHT FAIRLY FEATLY GLADLY MEETLY RIGHTLY
PROPERTY AVER BONA DHAN TOOL WAIF ASSET AUGHT GOODS GRANT MOYEN STATE STOCK THING WORTH APPEAL DEVISE ESTATE HAVIOR KELTER LIVING MUSHAA REALTY TALENT USINGS WEALTH ACQUEST APANAGE CHATTEL DEMESNE ESCHEAT ESSENCE FACULTY FITNESS HARNESS HAVINGS QUALITY WARISON ALLODIAL CATALLUM HOLDINGS PECULIUM POSSESSION PARAPHERNALIA
(— BELONGING TO WOMAN) STRIDHAN
(— FROM WIFE TO HUSBAND) DOS
(— GIVEN BY WILL) DEVISE
(— OF MATTER AT REST) INERTIA
(— SECURED DISHONESTLY) HARL
(— SEIZED BY FORCE) SPOIL
(ABSOLUTE —) ALODIUM
(BEQUEATHED —) DEVISE
(ENEMY —) HEREM
(LANDED —) DOMAIN ESTATE DEMESNE PRAEDIUM
(MOVABLE —) GEAR CHATTEL EFFECTS CATALLUM
(PERSONAL —) FEE BONA GOODS STUFF INSIGHT PLUNDER
(PRIVATE —) SEVERAL
(RURAL —) FINCA
(STOLEN —) PELF MAINOR STEALTH
(THEATRICAL —S) PROPS

(WITHOUT —) LACKLAND
(SUFF.) ISM
PROPHECY SPAE WEIRD EXHORT PREACH PREDICT BODEMENT FORECAST FORESHOW SOOTHSAY VATICINE SIBYLLISM PROGNOSTIC
PROPHESY OSSE SPAE AREAD AUGUR DIVINE EXHORT PREACH OMINATE PORTEND PREDICT ARIOLATE FORETELL
PROPHET GAD AMOS JOEL SEER ANGEL AUGUR DRUID ELIAS HOSEA JONAH MICAH MOSES NAHUM SILAS SYRUS ARIOLE BALAAM DANIEL ELIJAH HAGGAI ISAIAH MERLIN MORONI NATHAN ORACLE PYTHON SAMUEL EZEKIEL MALACHI SPAEMAN HABAKKUK JEREMIAH
(WEATHER —) PROGNOSTICATOR
(PL.) VATES NEBIIM
(PREF.) VATI
PROPHETE, LA (CHARACTER IN —) JOHN FIDES BERTHA OBERTHAL
(COMPOSER OF —) MEYERBEER
PROPHETESS ANNA ANNE HULDA SIBYL PYTHIA DEBORAH PHOIBAD SEERESS VOLUSPA DRUIDESS SPAEWIFE CASSANDRA PYTHONESS
PROPHETIC FATAL VATIC MANTIC FATEFUL FATIDIC MANTIAN DELPHIAN ORACULAR SIBYLLIC VATICINAL
(— OF DISASTER) APOCALYPTIC
(SUFF.) MANTIC
PROPINE TIP GIFT EXPOSE PLEDGE PROFFER
PROPINQUITY KINSHIP AFFINITY NEARNESS VICINITY PROXIMITY
PROPITIATE MILD ATONE PACIFY APPEASE RECONCILE
PROPITIATORY HILASMIC
PROPITIOUS FAIR KIND HAPPY LUCKY BENIGN DEXTER KINDLY HELPFUL PRESENT FRIENDLY GRACIOUS MERCIFUL TOWARDLY FAVORABLE PROMISING AUSPICIOUS
PROPONENT BACKER ADVOCATE SUPPORTER
PROPORTION END LOT DOSE SIZE CHIME FRAME QUOTA RATIO SCALE SHARE ACCORD DEGREE EXTENT FORMAT QUOTUM ANALOGY BALANCE COMPASS CONTENT MEASURE EURYTHMY QUANTITY SYMMETRY PERCENTAGE
(— OF CATTLE TO GIVEN AREA) SOUM
(— OF MALT IN BREWING) STRAIK
(— OF REFLECTED LIGHT) ALBEDO
(ALLOTTED —) STENT STINT
(EXACT —) SQUARE
(SMALL —) TITHE
PROPORTIONAL TOSCALE
PROPORTIONATENESS CONTOUR
PROPOSAL BID KITE MOVE PLAN PLEA VOEU GRACE OFFER PARTY DEMAND FEELER MOTION MOTIVE PROJECT PROPOSE PURPOSE OVERTURE SCHEDULE SENTENCE PROPOSITION
(— OF HEALTH) TOAST
(FORMAL —) RESOLUTION
(TENTATIVE —) SNIFF
PROPOSE FACE MOVE PLAN POSE SHOW WISH OFFER ALLEGE DESIGN INJECT INTEND MOTION ADVANCE EXHIBIT IMAGINE PROPINE PURPOSE SUPPOSE CONFRONT CONVERSE PROPOUND
(— FOR DISCUSSION) MOOT
(— FOR ELECTION) NOMINATE
(— MARRIAGE) POP
(— RESOLUTION) FIRST
(— TENTATIVELY) SUGGEST
PROPOSITION R FACT AXIOM MODAL OFFER THEME AFFAIR CONNEX MEMBER PORISM GENERAL INVERSE PREMISS PROBLEM PURPOSE THEOREM TYCHISM BUSINESS CONTRARY EMPIREMA IDENTITY IRENICON JUDGMENT NEGATION OVERTURE PROPOSAL PROTASIS SENTENCE SINGULAR SUPPOSAL
(— FOR PEACE) IRENICON
(— IN LOGIC) TERMAL OBVERSE CONTRARY CONVERSE
(— LEADING TO CONCLUSION) PREMISE
(PARTICULAR NEGATIVE —) O
(PRELIMINARY —) LEMMA
(UNIVERSAL NEGATIVE —) E
PROPOUND POSE OFFER POSIT START STATE INVOKE PROPOSE PURPOSE
PROPOUNDER HYLICIST
PROPRIETOR LORD LAIRD MALIK OWNER MASTER PATRON TANIST YEOMAN ESQUIRE PATROON ABSENTEE BONIFACE SQUARSON TALUKDAR YEOWOMAN
PROPRIETY GRACE IDIOM MENSE ESTATE NATURE REASON DECENCY DECORUM ESSENCE FITNESS HOLDING MODESTY CIVILITY PROPERTY ETIQUETTE
PROPROCTOR RECTOR
PROPULSION DRIFT EJECTION
PROPULSIVE ELASTIC
PRORATE ALLOT ASSESS DIVIDE APPORTION
PROROGUE DEFER ADJOURN PROLONG POSTPONE PROTRACT
PROSAIC DRAB DULL FLAT FOOT PROSE PROSY PROLIX STODGY STOLID STUPID FACTUAL HUMDRUM INSIPID LITERAL TEDIOUS SOULLESS TIRESOME WORKADAY
PROSCENIUM FRAME STAGE
PROSCRIBE BAN TABU EXILE LIMIT TABOO FORBID OUTLAW REJECT PROHIBIT
PROSCRIPTION EXILE OUTLAWRY
PROSE CHAT PROSY GOSSIP PROSAIC TEDIOUS SEQUENCE ELOQUENCE
PROSECUTE LAW SUE HOLD URGE CARRY ENSUE ACCUSE CHARGE DEDUCE FOLLOW INDICT INTEND PURSUE IMPLEAD PROCESS
PROSECUTION PURSUANCE
PROSECUTOR DA FISCAL PURSUER SAKEBER PROMOTER QUAESTOR
(PUBLIC —) ACTOR
PROSELYTE CONVERT NICOLAS NEOPHYTE PURSUANT
(JEWISH —) GER
PROSER HAVERER GRATIANO
PROSODY METER METRICS
PROSPECT HOPE VIEW SCENE SPECK VISTA CHANCE CHIEVE FUTURE REGARD SEARCH SURVEY COMMAND EXPLORE FOSSICK HORIZON LOOKOUT OUTLOOK PROJECT RESPECT LANDSKIP OFFSCAPE
(— FOR GOLD) SPECK
(— OF FUTURE) PERSPECTIVE
(— WITHOUT SYSTEM) GOPHER
(FORBIDDING —) DESERT
PROSPECTING LOAMING
PROSPECTIVE VIEW WATCH LOOKOUT EXPECTED
PROSPECTOR SNIPER FOSSICKER SOURDOUGH
(LONE —) HATTER
PROSPECTUS PROGRAM
PROSPER DO DOW FAY HIE LIKE RISE THEE CHEVE CHIVE EDIFY FRAME LIGHT SPEED BATTEN THRIVE BLOSSOM SUCCEED WELFARE FLOURISH
PROSPERITY HAP BOOM GLEE GOOD SEEL SONS WEAL IKBAL SONSE HEALTH THRIFT FORTUNE SUCCESS THEEDOM WELFARE FLOURISH
(GOD OF —) FREY
(INCREASE IN —) FREY UPTICK
PROSPERO (DAUGHTER OF —) MIRANDA
(SERVANT OF —) ARIEL
(SLAVE OF —) CALIBAN
PROSPEROUS UP FAT BEEN BEIN BIEN BOON GOOD FELIX FLUSH HAPPY LUCKY PALMY SONSY EUROUS GILDED SONSIE WELSOM HALCYON HEALTHY THRIFTY THRIVEN WEIRDLY SUNSHINE THRIVING WEALSOME
PROSTITUTE BAG BAT CAT COW DOG MOB AUNT BAWD DOXY DRAB HACK MAUX MISS MUFF PUNK SLUT STEW TART TRUG BROAD CRACK MAWKS PAGAN POULE PROSS STALE WHORE BULKER CALLET CHIPPY DEBASE GIRLIE HARLOT HOOKER LIMMER MUTTON PROSTY RANNEL TOMATO TRADER VIZARD BAGGAGE BROTHEL CRUISER CYPRIAN HACKNEY HETAERA HUSTLER PAPHIAN PINNACE POLECAT PROSSIE PROSTIE PUCELLE SELLARY BERDACHE COMMONER CUSTOMER HACKSTER MAGDALEN MERETRIX OCCUPANT RUMBELOW SLATTERN STRUMPET VENTURER COURTESAN
(PREF.) PORN(O)
PROSTITUTION BORDEL SACKING BORDELLO HARLOTRY PUTANISM
PROSTRATE LOW FELL FLAT GRUF RASE RAZE FLING GROOF PRONE STOOP THROW ATTERR CUMBER FALLEN REPENT WEAKEN FLATTEN DEJECTED HELPLESS OVERCOME PROSTERN DEPRESSED
(— ONESELF) HURKLE
(BECOME —) FALL
PROSTRATION SHOCK KOWTOW COLLAPSE
(BURMESE —) SHIKO
PROSY DRY DULL JEJUNE HUMDRUM INSIPID PROSAIC PROSISH TEDIOUS TIRESOME
PROTAGONIST HERO ACTOR LEADER PALADIN ADVOCATE ANTIHERO CHAMPION
PROTAMINE SALMINE STURINE CLUPEINE
PROTEAN EDESTAN VARIABLE
PROTECT CAP BANK BIEL BIND DIKE FEND FORT HILL KEEP REDE SAVE WARD WEAR BLESS CHAIN CLOUT COURE COVER FENCE GANGE GRATE GUARD HEDGE PAVIS SHADE SHEND UMBER ASSERT BORROW DEFEND SCREEN SHADOW SHIELD WARISH BULWARK CHERISH CUSHION FASCINE FORFEND SECLUDE SHELTER SUPPORT WARRANT BESTRIDE CHAMPION DEFILADE PRESERVE SAFEGUARD
(— AGAINST RAIN) FLASH
(— BY BINDING) KECKLE
(— BY COVERING) HILL
(— BY WINDING WITH WIRE) GANGE
(— FROM INTRUSION) TILE TYLE
(— IRON OR STEEL) BARFF
PROTECTED SAFE SHADY IMMUNE CLOUTED GUARDED SHEATHED SHIELDED
(PREF.) IMMUNO
PROTECTING TUTELAR TUTELARY SECUREFUL
PROTECTION LEE CARE EGIS HOLD WARD WING AEGIS ARMOR BIELD COVER GRITH GUARD SHADE TARGE TOWER AMULET ASYLUM AVOWRY CONVOY ESCORT FENDER REFUGE SAFETY SCONCE SCREEN SHADOW SHROUD AUSPICE CUSTODY DEFENCE HOUSING MANTLET SHELTER TUITION UMBRAGE WARRANT BLINDAGE COVERAGE DEFILADE PASSPORT SECURITY TUTAMENT TUTELAGE WARDSHIP SAFEGUARD
(— FOR SAILOR) HORSE
(— FROM LOSS) INDEMNITY
(— FROM RAIN) OMBRIFUGE
(— FROM SUN) HAVELOCK
(— FROM WEATHER) LEWTH
(— RIGHT) MUND
(ITEM FOR —) MACE
(VALUABLE —) EDMUND
(WISE —) RAYMOND
PROTECTIVE (— SURFACE) LAGGING
PROTECTOR BIB GUARD BRACER FAUTOR KEEPER PATRON REGENT WARRANT DEFENDER GUARDIAN PECTORAL PRESIDENT

(— OF PROSTITUTE) BULLY
(— OF VINEYARDS) PRIAPUS
(CHEST —) BIB
PROTEGE WARD PUPIL SMIKE
PROTEIN ZEIN ABRIN ACTIN OPSIN RICIN SOZIN AVIDIN CASEIN FIBRIN GLOBIN MYOGEN ALBUMIN AMANDIN ELASTIN GELATIN GLIADIN HISTONE HORDEIN KERATIN LIVETIN MUCEDIN PROTEID SERICIN TUBULIN ALEURONE COLLAGEN COLLOGEN FERRITIN GLOBULIN GLUTELIN GORGONIN IPOMOEIN PROLAMIN ELEDOISIN PROPERDIN PROTAMINE
(— IN CEREAL) GLUTENIN
(— PARTICLE) PRION
(POISONOUS —) ABRIN
(RICH IN —S) NARROW
PROTEINASE PAPAIN PEPSIN
PROTEOSE ALBUMOSE ELASTOSE GELATOSE
PROTESILAUS (BROTHER OF —) PODARCES
(FATHER OF —) IPHICLUS
(MOTHER OF —) ASTYOCHE
(SLAYER OF —) HECTOR EUPHORBUS
(WIFE OF —) LAODAMIA POLYDORA
PROTEST AVER BEEF FUSS HOWL KICK BROCK CROAK DEMUR AFFIRM ASSERT BOWWOW EXCEPT HOLLER OBJECT OBTEST PLAINT SQUAWK SQUEAL CONTEST INVEIGH PUBLISH RECLAIM RHUBARB SCRUPLE TESTIFY HARRUMPH PROCLAIM
(— A CHARGE) TESTIFY
(— AGAINST) ABHOR
(— AGAINST INJUSTICE) HARO
(FORMAL —) REMONSTRANCE
(ORGANIZED —) LIEIN
(TINY —) PEEP
PROTESTANT ALASCAN GENEVAN GOSPELER HELVETIC HUGUENOT MORAVIAN SWADDLER
PROTEUS OLM AMOEBA
PROTHESIS CREDENCE PARABEMA
PROTHORAX COLLAR CORSELET MANITRUNK
PROTOCOL PROCEDURE
PROTOPINE FUMARINE
PROTOPLASM PLASMA PLASSON SARCODE OVOPLASM PERIPLAST SOLEPLATE
PROTOPLAST CELL ENERGID
PROTOTYPE IDEAL MODEL FATHER EXAMPLE PATTERN ANTITYPE EXEMPLAR
PROTOZOAN AMEBA FORAM MONAD MONER AMOEBA AGAMETE ARCELLA BABESIA BODONID CILIATE PROTIST RADIATE STENTOR DIDINIUM HYPOZOAN PARAMECIUM
(HYPOTHETICAL —) MONER MONERON
(PL.) MICROZOA
PROTRACT DRAG DRAW DREE PLOT SPIN DEFER DELAY DRIVE TRACT TRAIL TRAIN DILATE EXTEND LINGER SPREAD DETRACT PROLONG CONTINUE LENGTHEN PROROGUE
PROTRACTED DREE LONG DREICH PROLIX LENGTHY DRAGGING EXTENDED
PROTRUDE BUG JUT LILL LOLL PEER POKE POUT BLEAR BULGE BUNCH POUCH SHOOT START STICK STRUT SWELL EXSERT EXTEND EXTRUDE KNUCKLE PROJECT PROTEND HERNIATE OUTPOINT OUTREACH OUTSHOOT
PROTRUDING STEEP ASTRUT BUNCHY GOGGLE BLABBER EMINENT JUTTING OBTRUSIVE
PROTRUDINGLY ASTRUT
PROTRUSION JAG LAP NOB BURR KNOB POUT HERNIA SALIENCE SHOULDER TYLOSOID PROJECTION
PROTUBERANCE BUD HUB JAG NOB NUB WEN BEAN BOLL BOSS BULB BUMP HEEL HUMP JAGG KNAP KNOB KNOP KNOT LUMP NODE PUFF SCAB SNAG STUB UMBO WART BULGE BUNCH CAPUT GLAND GNARL HUNCH KNURL SWELL TORUS TUBER TUMOR BREAST CALLUS HUBBLE PIMPLE POMMEL CRANKLE EXTANCY PAPILLA EMINENCE FLANKARD MAMELEON NODOSITY SWELLING APOPHYSIS PROJECTION
(— AT BASE OF BIRD'S BILL) CERE SNOOD
(— BEARING SPINE) UMBO
(— FROM SWELLING) PUFF
(— IN SIDE OF DEER) FLANKARD
(— ON A CASTING) SCAB
(— ON BONE) CONDYLE EMINENCE
(— ON HAND) MOUNT
(— ON HORSE'S HOOF) BUTTRESS
(— ON MANDIBLE OF GEESE) BEAN
(— ON SADDLEBOW) POMMEL
(— ON SALAMANDER) BALANCER
(— ON TONGUE) PAPILLA
(KNOBLIKE —) CAPUT
(OCCIPITAL —) INION
(RAGGED —) JAG JAGG
(ROUGH —) HUB
(SKIN —) WEN MOLE WART PIMPLE
(PREF.) TORO
PROTUBERANT BULGY BUMPY NODAL PROUD STRUT TUMID BUCKED EXTANT GOGGLE BOTTLED BULGING BUNCHED EMINENT GIBBOUS SALIENT SWOLLEN PROMINENT PROTRUSIVE
(REGULARLY —) CONVEX
PROUD FESS GLAD HIGH IKEY LOFT PERK RANK SIDE VAIN BRANT CHUFF GELLY GREAT JELLY LOFTY NOBLE ORGUL PRIDY SAUCY STEEP STIFF STOUT VOGIE WINDY WLONK COPPED ELATED FIERCE LORDLY ORGUIL PENCEY QUAINT SKEICH SKEIGH UPPISH UPPITY VAUNTY CHUFFED HAUGHTY SUBLIME SWOLLEN TOPPING ARROGANT EXULTANT GLORIOUS IMPOSING INSOLENT ORGULOUS SPLENDID STOMACHY TOPLOFTY OVERBEARING
(TOO — FOR) ABOVE
PROUDLY HIGH
PROVE TRY FAND FOND PREE SHOW TEST ARGUE ASSAY EVICT TAINT TASTE TEMPT ARGUFY EVINCE SUFFER VERIFY BALANCE CONFESS CONFIRM CONVICT DERAIGN IMPROVE JUSTIFY CONCLUDE CONVINCE EVIDENCE INDICATE INSTRUCT MANIFEST
(— FALSE) BELIE BETRAY FALSIFY
(— GUILTY) ATTAINT
(— ONESELF) ACQUIT
(— OUT) SERVE
(— TITLE) DEDUCE
(— VALID) DEFEND
PROVED TRIED EXPERT PROBATE
PROVENCAL LANGUEDOC ROMANESQUE
PROVENDER HAY CORN FEED FOOD OATS STRAW PABULUM PROVAND PROVIANT
PROVERB SAW SAY REDE WORD ADAGE AXIOM CREED GNOME MAXIM SOOTH BALLAD BYWORD DITTON DIVERB MASHAL SAYING SPEECH SYMBOL WHEEZE BYSPELL IMPRESA NAYWORD PARABLE APHORISM FORBYSEN PAROEMIA SCHOLION SCHOLIUM SENTENCE SOOTHSAY
(PREF.) PARAMIO PAROEMIO
PROVIDE DO FIT SEE FEND FILL FIND GIRD LEND LOOK BLOCK CATER ENDOW ENDUE EQUIP SPEED STOCK STORE AFFORD FOISON PURVEY SUBORN SUPPLY COMPARE EXHIBIT FORESEE FURNISH INSTORE PREPARE ACCOUTER APPANAGE DISPENSE PURCHASE
(— AHEAD OF TIME) ADVANCE
(— AMUSEMENT) DISTRACT
(— BY STEALTHY MEANS) SUBORN
(— FOOD) GRUB CATER SCAFF
(— FOR) FEND SERVE CHEVEYS CHEVISE PROVANT
(— STINGILY) SKINCH
(— SUPPORT) ESCOT
(— WITH) BESEE
(— WITH DOWRY) DOT
(— WITH HIP-ROOF) COOT
(— WITH LOAN) ACCOMMODATE
(— WITH MONEY) FUND
PROVIDED IF BODEN FIXED READY SOBEIT PROVISO INSTRUCT PREPARED
PROVIDENCE THRIFT ECONOMY PRUDENCE
PROVIDENT WARY WISE FRUGAL SAVING CAREFUL PRUDENT THRIFTY
PROVINCE LAN AREA NOME WALK AIMAK BANAT FIELD MOUTH NATAL NOMOS REALM SHENG SHIRE SUBAH WORLD BANNAT EMPIRE EYALET MALAGA MONTON OBLAST REGION SIRCAR SPHERE SYSSEL YAMATO DEMESNE DONGOLA EPARCHY MUDIRIA PURVIEW RECTORY VILAYET APPANAGE DISTRICT FUNCTION MUDIRIEH NOMARCHY TERRITORY
(PAPAL —) LEGATION
(ROMAN —) RAETIA RHAETIA
(RUSSIAN —) OBLAST
(SUBDIVISION OF EGYPTIAN —) KISM
(PL.) OUTLAND
PROVINCIAL HICK BORNE CRUDE NARROW RUSTIC STUFFY INSULAR MOFUSSIL SUBURBAN PAROCHIAL PRESIDIAL
PROVINCIALISM LOCALISM
PROVISION BOARD CHECK GRIST FODDER MATTER PURVEY STOVER UNLESS WRAITH APPREST CAUTION CODICIL DOWNSET KEEPING SLEEPER VICTUAL WARNISH WARNISON
(— FOR MAINTENANCE) APANAGE APPANAGE
(—S FOR JOURNEY) VIATICUM
(BOUGHT —S) ACATES ACATERY
(SUBORDINATE —) ITEM
(PL.) CHOW FOOD JOCK KEEP LOAN PROG BOUGE CATES CHUCK SCRAN STORE TERMS TOMMY ANNONA VIANDS VIVRES COMMONS WARNAGE WAYFARE VICTUALS
PROVISO SALVO CAVEAT CLAUSE CAUTION CONDITION
PROVOCATION TEEN APPEAL INCENTIVE
PROVOCATIVE GUTTY SALTY AGACANT PIQUANT IRRITANT APPEALING
PROVOKE BOG EGG GIG IRE TAR VEX BEAR DARE HUFF MOVE PICK STIR TARR TEEN URGE WORK ANGER ANGRY ANNOY EAGER EVOKE FRUMP PIQUE TAUNT TEMPT APPEAL ELICIT EVINCE EXCITE GRIEVE HARASS INCITE KINDLE NETTLE PROMPT SUMMON TICKLE AFFRONT ILLICIT INCENSE INFLAME INSPIRE VROTHER CATALYZE IRRITATE
(— AVERSION) REPEL
PROVOKER GADFLY
PROVOKING AGACANT
PROVOST JUDGE PRIOR REEVE KEEPER WARDEN STEWARD
PROW BOW BEAK SPUR STEM PRORE SNOUT SPERON STEVEN DIVIDER GALLANT VALIANT
(— OF GONDOLA) FERRO
PROWESS FEAT PROW VALOR NOBLEY BRAVERY COURAGE
PROWL OWL PROG ROAM LURCH MOOCH MOUSE RAVEN BREVIT RAMBLE
PROWLER WALKER SLASHER TENEBRION
PROWLIKE PROREAN
PROWLING GRASSANT
PROXIMAL CLOSE
PROXIMATE NEXT CLOSE DIRECT CLOSEST NEAREST PROXIME IMMINENT PROXIMAL
PROXIMITY SHADOW NEARNESS PRESENCE VICINITY PROPINQUITY NEIGHBORHOOD

PROXY VICE AGENT VICAR BALLOT MANDAT PROCTOR
(PL.) ELECTION
PRUDE PRIG COMSTOCK
PRUDENCE CARE METIS ADVICE CAUTEL WISDOM CAUTION COUNSEL SLEIGHT FORECAST FORELOOK
PRUDENT FIT SAFE SAGE WARE WARY WISE CANNY DOOSE DOUCE SOLID SYKER VERTY FRUGAL QUAINT SEKERE SICCAR POLITIC THRIVEN CAUTIOUS DISCREET PROVIDENT
(NOT —) ADVISED
PRUDISH NICE PRIM MIMZY MIMSEY PRIGGISH PUDIBUND VICTORIA
PRUDISHNESS NICETY PUDENCY
PRUNE COW LOP TOP CLIP COLL COUL GELD PLUM SNED SPUR TAME TRIM CLEAN DRESS KNIFE PLUMB PREEN PRIME PURGE SHEAR SHRAG SHRED SHRUB TRASH TWIST DEHORN REFORM SHRIDE SNATHE SWITCH AMPUTATE CASTRATE RETRENCH
(— SEVERELY) DEHORN
(IMPERFECTLY RIPENED —) FROG
PRUNING HOOK SARPE CALABOZO HANDBILL
PRUNING KNIFE SERPETTE
PRUNING SHEARS SECATEUR
PRURIENCE ITCH
PRURIENT ITCHY
PRURITIS ITCH
PRUSSIA PRUCE SPRUCE
PRUSSIAN PRUTENIC
PRY GAG KEEK NOSE NOTE PEEK PEEP PEER TEET TOOT JIMMY LEVER PRIZE SNOOP BREVIT FERRET PIGGLE POTTER PUTTER CROWBAR GUMSHOE LEVERAGE
(— ABOUT) OWL MOUSE SNOOK SCROUNGE
(— INTO) BREVIT
(— INTO AND REPEAT) RAVE
PRYING NOSY NOSEY PEERY CURIOUS PEEPING
PSALM ODE HYMN SONG DIRGE GATHA TRACT ANTHEM CANTATE CHORALE INTROIT MISERERE
(LENTEN —) TRACT
(100TH —) JUBILATE
(95TH —) VENITE
(98TH —) CANTATE
PSALMS HALLEL
(BOOK OF —) PSALTER
PSALTERIUM BOOK LYRA OMASUM PSALTER PSALTERY
PSALTERY GUSLA CITOLE SAUTREE SAUTERIE
PSEUDO FAKE MOCK SHAM BOGUS FALSE FEIGNED SPURIOUS
(PREF.) NE
PSEUDOCARP HIP
PSEUDOLOGIST LIAR
PSEUDONYM ALIAS ANONYM JUNIUS
PSHAW SHA DARN DRAT POOH SUGAR PHOOEY SHUCKS
PSITTACOSIS ORNITHOSIS
PSORIASIS ALPHOS
PSYCHE MIND SELF SOUL
PSYCHIATRIST SHRINK ANALYST ALIENIST
AMERICAN LIDE BERNE BRILL KLINE MEYER SZASZ OLIVER REUBEN SALMON WILDER RADECKI SPITZKA ABRAMSON MENNINGER DUNBARMFRANK
AUSTRIAN ADLER FRANKL
GERMAN PERLS ZIEHEN JASPERS
ISRAELI LEVY
SCOTTISH LAING
SOUTH AFRICAN COOPER
SWISS JUNG BLEULER RORSCHACH BINSWANGER
PSYCHIC (— POWERS) PSI
PSYCHOANALYST FREUDIAN
PSYCHOLOGIST AMERICAN AMES HALL HOLT LADD MEAD SALK BRITT DODGE JANOV LAIRD LEWIN RHINE SEARS SIMON URBAN WELLS ANGELL BORING BRUNER GESELL GINOTT HAINES HUNTER KANNER KOFFKA MASLOW PRINCE STARCH STRONG TERMAN WATSON ALLPORT BALDWIN BATESON CATTELL DOLLARD GODDARD NEWBOLD TROLAND BROTHERS LANGFELD MARSHALL SEASHORE WECHSLER PILLSBURY SCRIPTURE WOODWORTH CARRINGTON HOLLINGWORTH
ARGENTINIAN INGENIEROS
AUSTRIAN ADLER BETTELHEIM
DANISH LANGE
ENGLISH BURT WARD BUCKE ELLIS MYERS OGDEN STOUT SULLY GURNEY MORGAN AVELING BARTLETT MAUDSLEY
FRENCH COUE BINET JANET SIMON BEAUNIS
GERMAN KROH GEISE MARBE STERN WUNDT BENDER KOHLER MULLER PREYER RUBNER ZIEHEN JAENSCH MEUMANN KRONHAUSEN
SCOTTISH BAIN
SWISS JUNG PIAGET
PSYCHOLOGY HORMISM HEDONICS ANIMASTIC FORMALISM
PSYCHOPATH MATTOID
PSYCHOSIS INSANITY PARANOIA SENILITY MELANCHOLIA SCHIZOPHRENIA
PSYCHOTIC MAD CRAZY INSANE
PSYLLA DIMERAN
PSYLLIUM FLEAWORT
PTAH (— EMBODIED) APIS
(ASSOCIATED WITH —) SEKHET
PTARMIGAN RYPE GROUSE LAGOPODE
PTEROCARPUS LINGOUM
PTEROID ALAR
PTEROSAUR DIAPSID
PTERYGIUM WEBEYE
PTERYGOID EXTERNUM
PTERYLA TRACT
PTISAN TEA TISANE
PTOLEMY SOTER
(WIFE OF —) CLEOPATRA
PTOMAINE NEURIN SEPSIN SAPRINE GADININE PUTRESCINE
PTOUS (FATHER OF —) ATHAMAS
(MOTHER OF —) THEMISTO
PUAH (FATHER OF —) ISSACHAR
(SON OF —) TOLA
PUB BAR INN CAFE CAFF BISTRO BOOZER LOUNGE SHANTY TAVERN
PUBBLE FAT FULL PLUMP
PUB-CRAWL BARHOP
PUBERTY
(PREF.) HEBE
PUBES
(PREF.) EPISIO PUBI(O) PUBO
PUBESCENCE DOWN SCURF YOUTH TOMENT TOMENTUM
PUBESCENT HIRSUTE VILLOUS
(PREF.) HEBE
PUBLIC KUNG OPEN TOWN APERT CIVIC OVERT WORLD COMMON SOCIAL VULGAR GENERAL OMNIBUS POPULAR EXTERNAL MATERIAL NATIONAL MULTITUDE
(GENERAL —) GALLERY
PUBLICAN BUNG FARMER KEEPER TAVERNER ZACCHEUS CATCHPOLL
PUBLICATION BOOK ORDO BIBLE FOLIO ISSUE SHEET ANNUAL BLAZON DIGLOT SERIAL WEEKLY ALMANAC BOOKLET ELZEVIR JOURNAL MONTHLY WRITING BIWEEKLY BULLETIN DOCUMENT EMISSION EXCHANGE PRODROME EPHEMERIS PERIODICAL
(KIND OF —) MIMEO NUDIE
PUBLIC HOUSE BAR INN PUB BOOZER PUBLIC SALOON HOSTELRY POTHOUSE
PUBLICIST AGENT SOLON WRITER
PUBLICITY AIR HYPE BLAZE ECLAT BUILDUP PUFFERY RECLAME BALLYHOO BROUHAHA DAYLIGHT FLACKERY HERALDRY PROMOTION
(PROVIDE —) FLACK
PUBLICIZE CRY FLOG HYPE PLUG BLURB BREAK BRUIT HERALD BALLYHOO HEADLINE PROPAGATE
PUBLIC SQUARE PLAZA PLEIN ZOCALO
PUBLISH AIR ASH BLOW CALL EDIT EMIT VEND VENT CARRY ISSUE PRINT SPEAK UTTER BLAZON BROACH DEFAME DELATE EVULGE EXPOSE SPREAD CENSURE DECLARE DIFFUSE DIVULGE GAZETTE PROTEST RELEASE DENOUNCE DISCLOSE EVULGATE PROCLAIM PROMULGE
(— BANNS OF MARRIAGE) CRY SPUR OUTASK
(— IN CHURCH) ASK
(— WITHOUT AUTHORIZATION) PIRATE
PUBLISHER CRIER EDITOR ISSUER PRINTER STATIONER
AMERICAN COX DOW LEA AMES BONI CERF DODD FUNK GINN HOLT HOYT KERN KNOX LOEB LUCE MACY MUIR NAST OCHS ZIFF BOBBS BOEHM BROWN CAREY ENGEL ENOCH FODOR GODEY HECHT HOBBY JONES KNOPF MCRAE SIMON SMITH STERN ZEVIN BOWKER CAPPER CHILDS COVICI CURTIS DUTTON FARRAR FIELDS FORBES GIROUX HARPER HARRIS HEARST HEFNER KEYLOR LAFFAN LESLIE LITTLE MOSHER MUNSEY NIEMAN PAYSON PUTNAM RIDDER RODALE SCHIFF STOKES THOMAS UPDIKE VICTOR WALKER WILSON ZENGER ATTWOOD BINGHAM CAHNERS COLLIER CONNERS DRYFOOS GANNETT GUPTILL LOTHROP MIFFLIN POULSON PRESSER SADLIER SCRIPPS SHUSTER TICKNOR VERONIS WITMARK BANCROFT BARTLETT HOUGHTON PULITZER RINEHART SCHUSTER SCRIBNER WAGNALLS DOUBLEDAY LIVERIGHT MCCORMICK LIPPINCOTT
AUSTRALIAN SHEED MURDOCH THEODORE
CANADIAN SWEET
DUTCH ELZEVIR
ENGLISH DAY BELL BOHN CAPE LANE PAUL ALMON LUCAS MOXON MUDIE UNWIN WARNE WOOLF AITKEN BOOSEY FROWDE HAWKES KNIGHT LINTOT MILLAR NEWNES TONSON TOTTEL BEMROSE BENTLEY BRACKEN CASSELL CHAPMAN DEBRETT DODSLEY JENKINS METHUEN BRITTAIN NEWBERRY QUARITCH RICHARDS WHITAKER HEINEMANN PICKERING RIVINGTON ROUTLEDGE VIZETELLY WHITCHURCH BEAVERBROOK
FRENCH DIDOT HETZEL LEMERRE LITOLFF PLANTIN HACHETTE GALIGNANI
GERMAN COTTA MEYER FROBEN ZENGER PERTHES TEUBNER BAEDEKER SCHIRMER SPRINGER ULLSTEIN BROCKHAUS TAUCHNITZ
IRISH BRACKEN
ITALIAN RICORDI SONZOGNO
SCOTTISH BLACK SMITH CADELL CREECH NELSON CHAMBERS BLACKWOOD CONSTABLE MACMILLAN
SOUTH AFRICAN QOBOZA
WELSH BERRY
PUCCOON GROMYL ALKANET GROMWELL BLOODROOT
PUCE FLEA
PUCK ELF IMP LOB PUG BLOW BUTT DISK POKE POOK DEMON DEVIL FAIRY PEWKE SPORT RUBBER SPRITE STRIKE PUCKREL HOBGOBLIN
PUCKER DRAW FULL RUCK PURSE REEVE RIVEL TIZZY COCKLE COTTER FURROW LUCKEN RUCKLE WRINKLE CONTRACT AGITATION CONSTRICT
PUCKERED PURSY BULLATE COCKLED ROUCHED WRINKLED BULLIFORM
PUCKEREL IMP
PUCKFIST BRAGGART PUFFBALL
PUCKISH PUXY ELFIN IMPISH WHIMSICAL
PUDDING DICK DUFF LINK SAGO BOMBE DOWDY KUGEL MERIT BURGOO FENDER HACKIN HAGGIS HAUPIA JAUDIE SPONGE TANSEY

TARTAN DESSERT ADEQUACY BLOODING HEDGEHOG LIVERING PANDOWDY PLUMDUFF ROLYPOLY STICKJAW WHITEPOT CHARLOTTE
(— CONTAINING KALE) TARTAN
(— INGREDIENT) TAPIOCA
(— OF FLOUR) DUFF
(BOILED —) HOY
(FRUIT —) HEDGEHOG
(HASTY —) MUSH SEPON SUPAWN
(HAWAIIAN —) HAUPIA
(KIND OF —) COTTAGE
(MEAT —) ISING CHEWET HACKIN HACKING
(SUET —) KUGEL
PUDDINGWIFE PUDIANO DONCELLA GLUEFISH
PUDDLE DUB PANT PLUD POOL PULK ROIL SLAB SLOP SOSS SUMP FLUSH PLANT PLASH PUDGE CHARCO FLODGE KENNEL MUDDLE PUDDER SPLASH TAMPER CONFUSE PLASHET SLODDER SPUDDLE BEFUDDLE
(MUD —) DUB SLOP LOBLOLLY
PUDDLEBALL LOOP
PUDDLER'S RABBLE STRIKE
PUDENCY MODESTY DELICACY
PUDGY MIRY BULKY MUDDY PODGY SQUAT CHUBBY SPUDDY ROLYPOLY ROLLABOUT
PUDU VENADA
PUEBLO ANASAZI
PUELCHE PAMPA TEHUELET
PUERILE WEAK SILLY BOYISH JEJUNE TRIVIAL CHILDISH IMMATURE YOUTHFUL

PUERTO RICO
BAY: SUCIA RINCON BOQUERON AQUADILLA
CAPITAL: SANJUAN
ISLAND: MONA CULEBRA VIEQUES
LAKE: LOIZA CARITE CAONILLAS
MEASURE: CUERDA CABALLERIA
RIVER: CAMUY CANAS YAUCO ANASCO TANAMA FAJARDO
TOWN: CAYEY COAMO PONCE ANASCO DORADO MANATI ARECIBO BAYAMON FAJARDO GUAYAMA HUMACAO MAYAGUEZ

PUFF GUF POP BLOW BRAG DRAG FLAM FLAN GASP GUFF GUST HUFF PANT PECH SHOW WAFF WAFT BLURB BLURT ELATE ERUPT EXTOL FLUFF QUIFF SKIFF STECH SWELL WHIFF CAPFUL EXPAND FLATUS BLUSTER EXPLODE GRATIFY INFLATE WHIFFET BRAGGART OVERRATE WINDGALL BOUILLONE
(— FROM SHELL BLAST) BURST
(— OF WIND) FLAM TIFT SCART SLANT FLATUS HUFFLE
(— ON MARIJUANA CIGARETTE) TOKE
(— OUT) BELL BLUB VENT BLOUSE BLUBBER EFFLATE INFLATE
(— OUT SMOKE) EFFUME
(— UP) BLOW HUFF RISE BLOAT HEAVE BLADDER
(— VIOLENTLY) BLAST
(APPLE —) FLAPJACK
(CREAM —) DUCHESSE
(PASTRY —) PROFITEROLE
(SUDDEN —) FLAN FLAW GUST
PUFFBALL FIST FUZZ PUFF SMOKE FUNGUS PUFFIN BULLFICE BULLFIST PUCKFIST SNUFFBOX
PUFFBIRD BARBET MONASE NUNLET DREAMER NUNBIRD BARBACOU
PUFFED BLUB BOLLEN BLOATED SOUFFLE SWOLLEN ARROGANT INFLATED
(— OUT) BAGGY BOUFFANT
(— UP) RANK POBBY ASTRUT BLOATED SWOLLEN TURGENT VENTOSE
(BE — UP) BELL
PUFFER ATINGA BALLER BLOWER SLIMER TAMBOR BURFISH EGGFISH BLOWFISH TOADFISH
PUFFIN LOOM PAPE POPE MARROT MULLET MARROCK WILLOCK COCKANDY PARAKEET TOMNODDY TOMNORRY
(HAWAIIAN —) AO
PUFFY SOFT BAGGY BLOAT FAFFY GUMMY GUSTY PURSY CHUBBY FLUFFY PURFLY PURSIVE SWOLLEN BLADDERY BOUFFANT DROPSICAL
PUG FOX IMP PET BOXER CHAFF GOUGE SPOOR TRACK TRAIL CAMOIS CAMUSE GOBLIN MONKEY MISTRESS PUGILIST FOOTPRINT
PUGENCY TANG
PUGILIST PUG MILLER BRUISER SLOGGER
PUGNACIOUS BELLICOSE
PUG-NOSED CAMUS CAMUSE
PUISNE PUNY LATER PETTY JUNIOR YOUNGER INFERIOR
PUISSANCE ARMY FORCE POWER CONTROL POTENCY PROWESS DOMINION STRENGTH
PUJUNAN MAIDU
PUKKA GOOD REAL GENUINE LASTING COMPLETE SUPERIOR AUTHENTIC
PUKRAS PHEASANT KOKLAS
PULCHRITUDE GRACE BEAUTY
PULE CRY PEEP CHIRP COWRY WHINE SNIVEL WHIMPER
PULING PULY SPINDLY WHINING
PULITZER PRIZE (— IN LETTERS) BOK LEE NYE AGAR AGEE BATE BUCK CARO COLT DOVE DUYN EDEL FEIS GALE GRAU HART INGE LASH LEVY MACK MOTT RICE TATE UHRY VANN WOOD WOUK AIKEN AKINS ALBEE AUDEN BAKER BAKER BEMIS BENET BRUCE BRUCE BULEY CHASE CLAPP CURTI DAVIS DRURY DUGAN FRANK FROST GLUCK HECHT ISAAC ISSAC JAMES KAMOW KIZER KRAMM KUMIN LEECH LUKAS LURIE MABEE MAMET MOSEL NEELY OPPEN PLATH PLATH PUPIN PUSEY SAGAN SIMIC SIMON SMITH STARR TEALE TOOLE TYLER UNGER WELTY WILLS ABBOTT BAILYN BAILYN BECKER BELLOW BRANCH BUTLER BUTLER CATHER CATTON CREMIN CREMIN CROUSE DEGLER DONALD DURANT FERBER FRINGS FULLER GARROW GRAZIA HANDIN HARLAN HENLEY HERSEY HORGAN KAMMEN KENNAN KIDDER KIDDER KINNEL LAPINE LARKIN LOWELL MAILER MAILER MARNET MASSIE MASSIE MCCRAW MILLAY MORRIS NAIFEH NORMAN NORMAN OLIVER ONEILL PULLER RHODES SHAARA SMILEY TAYLOR TAYLOR TERKEL TOLAND ULRICH UPDIKE UPDIKE WALKER WALKER WARNER WILBUR WILDER WILSON WILSON YERGIN ZINDEL ASHBERY BURROWS CHEEVER DILLARD ELLMANN ERIKSON JUSTICE JUSTICE KAUFMAN KENNEDY KENNEDY KINNELL KUSHNER LAFARGE LINDSAY LITWACK LITWACK LOESSER MCFEELY MCFEELY NEMEROV POLLOCK RODGERS SAROYAN SHEEHAN SHEEHAN SHIPLER TUCHMAN VIERECK BOORSTIN FAULKNER HIJUELOS KINGSLEY LELYVELD MACLEISH MARQUAND MCMURTRY MEREDITH MICHENER MORRISON SANDBURG SCHORSKE SCHORSKE SCHUYLER SCHUYLER SHERWOOD SINCLAIR SONDHEIM VANDOREN WOODWARD HEMINGWAY MAHARIDGE MCDOUGALL MCPHERSON SCHENKKAN SILVERMAN STEINBECK HOFSTADTER HOFSTADTER HOLLDOBLER MCCULLOUGH WILLIAMSON WASSERSTEIN
(— IN MUSIC) RAN HUSA IVES TOCH WARD CRUMB KUBIK MOORE PERLE RANDS ROREM ROUSE ALBERT BARBER BOLCOM CARTER HANSON PISTON PORTER POWELL ARGENTO BASSETT COPLAND MARTINO MENOTTI SCHUMAN SOWERBY THOMSON WERNICK ZWILICH ZWILICH COLGRASS DRUCKMAN HARBISON KIRCHNER PETERSON REYNOLDS SESSIONS SESSIONS WUORINEN DELLOJOIO DAVIDOVSKY DELTREDICI SCHWANTNER
PULL IN PU EAR LUG POO POU ROG RUG TIT TOW CHUG CLAW DRAG DRAW DUCT HALE HARL HAUL HOOK RUGG SWIG TIRE TREK TUSH TWIG YANK BOUSE BREAK BUNCH CLOUT DRAFT HEAVE HITCH IMPEL JUICE PLUCK POLLE PROOF TRICE TWEAK ASSUME COMMIT GATHER OBTAIN PLITCH RUGGLE SCHLEP SECURE TWITCH UPROOT WRENCH ATTRACT EXTRACT
(— A BELL) SET
(— ABOUT) TEW SOOL TOSE TOZE MOUSLE
(— APART) RAVE REND TEAR DIVULSE
(— AWAY) AVEL AVELL WREST REVULSE
(— BY EARS) SOLE SOWL
(— DOWN) UNPILE DESTROY DEMOLISH
(— FOR) BACK
(— FORCIBLY) TUG
(— HERE AND THERE) TOOZLE TOUSLE
(— IN PIECES) DIVELLICATE
(— NOSE) SNITE
(— OF DRUM) EAR
(— OFF) CROP DRAW STRIP AVULSE
(— ON CIGARETTE) TOKE
(— ON FISHING ROD) STRIKE
(— ON ROPE) BOWSE
(— OUT) RAX UPROOT EXTRACT OUTBRAID
(— QUICKLY) YANK
(— ROUGHLY) WAP TOWSE WOUSE
(— SUDDENLY) TRICE
(— THE LEG) STRING
(— TOGETHER) KNOT ATTRACT
(— TRIGGER) SQUEEZE
(— UP) LOUK
(— UP BY THE ROOTS) ARACE
(— VIOLENTLY) WHAP WHOP WHANG
(— WITH A TWIST) WRENCH
(— WITH JERK) HOICK SWITCH
(ZIPPER —) SLIDER
PULLDEVIL SCROUGER SCRODGILL
PULLER KNOCKER
PULLER-IN CLICKER
PULLET HEN EAROCK EEROCK EIRACK MABYER POULARD POULAINE
PULLEY RIM CONE DRUM BLOCK FUSEE FUZEE IDLER TRICE WHEEL DRIVEN IDLEBY JOCKEY POLYVE RIGGER SHEAVE SHIVER WHARVE CAPSTAN FERRULE TIGHTER TRUCKLE WHARROW PULLISEE PURCHASE TROCHLEA (PL.) TRISPAST JACKANAPES
PULLOVER JERSEY SWEATER
PULLULATE BUD TEEM BREED SWARM MULTIPLY
PULMONATE LUNGED
PULMONIC PNEUMONIC
PULP MAG PAP PUG CHUM MUSH BROKE JELLY NERVE SLUSH STOCK STUFF MARROW SQUEEZE SQUELCH
(FOOD —) CHYME
PULPIT PEW TUB AMBO BEMA DESK WOOD CHAIR PREACH ROSTRUM TRIBUNE
(— BOARD) TYPE
(— FOR CHOIR BOOKS) ANALOGION
(MOSLEM —) MIMBAR MINBAR
(OPEN-AIR —) TENT
PULPY SOFT SPEWY FLABBY FLESHY SIDDER SIDDOW BACCATE SQUELCHY
PULSATE BEAT BRIM FLAP PANT PUMP THROB COURSE STRIKE PALPITATE
PULSATION BEAT PANT BEATING HEARTBEAT LIFEBLOOD VIBRATION
(— OF ARTERY) ICTUS
PULSE DAL EMP BEAT DOHL TAKT URAD WAVE POUCE STUFF THROB BATTUTA IMPULSE PULSIDGE SPHYGMUS VITALITY (PREF.) PALMO SPHYGMO (SUFF.) CROTIC
PULSING VIBRANT
PULVERIZATION TRIPSIS

PULVERIZE BRAY BUCK DRAG FINE MEAL MULL STUB BRAKE CRUSH FLOUR GRIND POUND BRUISE POWDER ATOMIZE DEMOLISH VANQUISH COMMINUTE MICRONIZE
PULVERIZED FINE POWDERED
PULVERIZER MULLER
PULVERULENT DUSTY CRUMBLY POWDERY
PULVILLUS PAD
PUMA COUGAR PAINTER PANTHER
PUME YARURA
PUMICE LAVA PUMEX PUMIE
(UNCOOLED —) LAVA
PUMMEL FIB BEAT DRUB PAIK SLAT POUND SLATE THUMP POUNCE
PUMP GIN GUN FORK JACK COURT FORCE HEART PLUMB SLUSH DOCTOR DORSAY FORCER SINKER VOLUTE BOOSTER DOWNTON EJECTOR EVACTOR PITWORK SLUDGER SYRINGE TOEPLER BEERPULL ELEVATOR INFLATER INJECTOR PULSATOR PULSOMETER
(— ON SHIPS) DOWNTON
(— UP) AERATE INFLATE
(GAS —) BOWSER
(HAND —) GUN
(MINE —S) SET
(SET OF —S) LIFT
PUMP DOCTOR GRATHER
PUMPER RACKER
PUMPERNICKEL BOMBERNICKEL
PUMPKIN PEPO CHUMP GOURD PEPON QUASH CASHAW CITRUL CUCURB CUSHAW SQUASH QUASHEY CUCURBIT PEPONIDA
PUMPKINSEED RUFF SUNNY FLATFISH FLOUNDER REDBELLY
PUN NICK WHIM ALLUDE CLINCH GROANER QUIBBLE EQUIVOKE PARAGRAM CALEMBOUR PARANOMASIA ANNOMINATION
PUNCH DAB DIG FIB HUB JAB SET BASH BELT BLOW BOFF BUST DECK DING PLUG POKE SETT SLUG SOAK SOCK TIFF BUMBO DOUSE DRIFT FORCE GLOGG PASTE PENCH SHORT SLOSH CANCEL INCUSE PATRIX PAUNCH SHAPER STINGO STRIKE TRACER MATTOIR PERLOIR SANGRIA SHELLAC STARTER EMBOSSER GROUNDER HAYMAKER PRITCHEL PUNCTURE SWATCHEL THICKSET
(CHASING —) TRACER
(DOG OF —) TOBY
(ETCHER'S —) MATTOIR
(HORSESHOE —) PRITCHEL
(KIND OF —) RABBIT
(OVAL —) PLAISHER
(RUM —) RUMBO
(SWINGING —) ROUNDHOUSE
(WIFE OF —) JUDY
PUNCHBOARD PUSHCARD
PUNCH BOWL SNEAKER
PUNCHCARD (GROUP OF —S) DECK
PUNCH-DRUNK PUNCHY SLAPHAPPY
PUNCHED PERTUSE
PUNCHEON CASK PULE SNAP PUNCH
PUNCHER COWBOY SOCKER
PUNCHINELLO CLOWN BUFFOON PUGENELLO
PUNCH PRESS BEAR DROP
PUNCHY POUNCY FORCEFUL
PUNCTILIO PIQUE PUNTO PUNCTO
PUNCTILIOUS NICE EXACT STIFF FORMAL CAREFUL POINTED PRECISE PUNCTUAL
PUNCTUAL DUE EXACT ONTIME PROMPT CAREFUL PRECISE ACCURATE DEFINITE DETAILED EXPLICIT
PUNCTUALLY SHARP
PUNCTUATE MARK STOP POINT EMPHASIZE
(— JAZZ SOLO) COMP
PUNCTUATION MARK DOT DASH STOP BRACE COLON COMMA PRICK SLASH HYPHEN PERIOD STIGME BRACKET VIRGULE ELLIPSIS SEMICOLON
PUNCTURE HOLE PICK PINK PROD STAB DRILL POINT PRICK PUNCH STICK NEEDLE PIERCE PIQURE DEFLATE DESTROY PUNCTUM CENTESIS PINPRICK
(SKIN —) NEEDLESTICK
(SUFF.) NYXIS STIXIS
PUNCTURED CRIBLE
PUNDIT GURU SAGE SVAMI SWAMI CRITIC PANDIT TEACHER
PUNG SLED
PUNGENCY NIP HEAT SALT SNAP ACRIMONY KEENNESS PIQUANCY SALTNESS
PUNGENT HOT TEZ ACID BOLD FELL KEEN RACY RICH SALT TART ACRID ACUTE BRISK NIPPY QUICK SHARP SMART SNELL SPICY TANGY ZESTY BITING BITTER SHRILL SNAPPY CAUSTIC MORDANT PEPPERY PIQUANT POINTED TELLING CAYENNED PIERCING POIGNANT STABBING STINGING
(— QUALITY) ZAP
PUNGI BIN
PUNIC PUNICAL FAITHLESS
PUNISH FIT FIX PAY BUCK CANE COLT COOK CUCK FINE FLOG GATE SORT WIPE ABUSE BIRCH CURSE ORDER SCOUR SHEND SLATE SPILL STOCK STRAP TWINK WREAK AMERCE AVENGE CAMPUS FERULE FOLLOW IMMURE LESSON REFORM SCHOOL STRAFE STRIKE CHASTEN CONSUME CORRECT CORRIGE DEPLETE PENANCE REQUITE SCOURGE CARTWHIP CHASTISE DISTRAIN CASTIGATE
(— BY BLOW ON PALM) PANDY
(— BY COMPENSATION) FINE AMERCE
(— BY CONFINEMENT) GATE
(— BY FINE) MULCT
(— BY LASHING WRISTS) BUCK
(— IN PRISON) ISOLATE
PUNISHING HARD GRUELING
PUNISHMENT GIG FINE LASH PAIN PINE RACK SACK WITE YARD BEANS GRUEL LIBEL PANDY PEINE SMART WRACK WREAK DESERT DIRDUM FERULE LESSON PICKET EXAMPLE GALLOWS GANTLET JANKERS PAYMENT PENALTY PENANCE PENANCY REVENGE SCOURGE HERISSON JUDGMENT PUNITION STOCKING SUPPLICE EXECUTION
(CAPITAL —) SCAFFOLD
(MILITARY —) JANKERS
(SCHOOL —) PANDY
PUNITIVE PENAL PUNITORY
PUNK BAD BOY MUG FUNK JERK MONK POOR PUNG THUG CONCH SPONK SPUNK AMADOU BUNKUM NOVICE HOODLUM RUFFIAN BEGINNER GANGSTER INFERIOR NONSENSE STRUMPET TERRIBLE TOUCHWOOD
PUNKIE MIDGE MIDGET
PUNNING ALLUSIVE BIVERBAL
PUNSCH ARRACK
PUNSTER WAG SPEED
PUNT BET HIT POY KENT KICK QUANT GAMBLE GARVEY SKERRY
PUNTER BIDDER GAMBLER SCALPER SERVITOR
PUNY WEAK DAWNY DEENY DWARF FRAIL PETTY SCRAM WEARY JUNIOR MAUGER NOVICE PUISNE RECENT SICKLY SPROTY MANIKIN PIMPING QUEECHY SHILPIT YOUNGER DROGHLIN INFERIOR PINDLING RECKLING
(— PERSON) TITMAN
PUP PUPPY WHELP
PUPA EGG NYMPH PUPPET TUMBLER WIGGLER FLAXSEED WRIGGLER CHRYSALIS
PUPIL BOY GYTE TYRO WARD BLACK CADET CHILD ELEVE NORRY NURRY RAPIN TUTEE ALUMNA GRADER INFANT JUNIOR SENIOR LEARNER PAULINE SCHOLAR SOJOURN STUDENT ABSENTEE BLUECOAT DISCIPLE RUGBEIAN SCHOOLER
(— AT HEAD OF CLASS) DUX
(— GOING TO UNIVERSITY) ABITURIENT
(— IN STUDIO) RAPIN
(— OF CHRIST'S HOSPITAL) BLUECOAT
(— OF EYE) BLACK PEARL SIGHT
(— WITH SOME AUTHORITY) PREFECT PRAEFECT
(ANGLO-INDIAN —) CHELA
(BOARDED —) SOJOURN
(GERMAN —) ABITURIENT
(PREF.) COR(E)(O)
(SUFF.) CORIA
PUPILAGE (WARDSHIP PEDANTISM
PUPPET BABY DOLL DUPE IDOL MOTE BABBY DROLL DUMMY MAUMET MOTION POPPIN STOOGE WAJANG WAYANG GUIGNOL DROLLERY MARIONET MARIONETTE
(— PLAY) WAJANG
(— SHOW) VERTEP
(— THEATER) BUNRAKU
(PREF.) PUPI
PUPPETEER SARG
PUPPIS STERN
PUPPY FOP PUP DOLL DOUGH WHELP PUPPET
(FEMALE —) GYP
(GREYHOUND —) SAPLING
PURBLIND BISME BISSON
PURCHASABLE VENAL CORRUPT
PURCHASE BUY WIN EARN FISH GAIN KOOP WHIP BOOTY HEDGE PRIZE DUPLEX EFFECT EMPTIO TACKLE ACQUIRE BARGAIN EMPTION PILLAGE PROCURE BARRATRY
(— AND FATTEN CATTLE) HIGGLE
PURCHASER BUYER EMPTOR VENDEE CHAPMAN POULTER SHOPPER CUSTOMER
PURE NET CAST EVEN FAIR FINE FREE FULL GOOD HOLY MERE NEAT PUTE TRUE CLEAN CLEAR FRESH MORAL NAKED SHEER STARK SYCEE UTTER WHITE WHOLE CANDID CHASTE ENTIRE IMMIXT LIMPID PISTIC SIMPLE VESTAL VIRGIN ANGELIC CATHARI GENUINE PERFECT SINCERE ABSOLUTE ABSTRACT COMPLETE DOVELIKE INNOCENT PRISTINE SERAPHIC SPOTLESS VIRGINAL VIRTUOUS SPIRITUAL
(— IN COLOR) ORIENT
(PREF.) KATHARO
PUREE DAL SOUP CREAM BRANDADE
PURFLE ADORN
PURGATIVE PURGE SENNA CALOMEL DIASENE DRASTIC TURPETH ALOEDARY APERIENT CLEANSER ELATERIN EVACUANT CATHARTIC ABSTERSIVE
PURGATORY PAIN SWAMP
PURGE LAX RID FIRE FLUX SOIL CLEAR RHEUM SCOUR DRENCH PHYSIC REMOVE SEETHE SHRIVE SPURGE CHISTKA CLEANSE DETERGE ABSTERGE
PURIFICATION BAPTISM ELUTION LUSTRUM VASTATION
PURIFIED WHITE
PURIFY TRY BOLT FINE PURE WASH CLEAN PURGE SNUFF BLEACH DISTIL FILTER REFINE SETTLE SPURGE WINNOW BAPTIZE CHASTEN CLEANSE EPURATE EXPIATE LAUNDER MUNDIFY SUBLIME SWEETEN DEPURATE EXORCISE FILTRATE LUSTRATE SANCTIFY SCAVENGE SPRINKLE
(— ORE) DILVE
(— SUGAR) CLAY
PURIFYING SMECTIC DEPURANT
PURIRI TEAK BULREEDY IRONWOOD
PURIST PRIG PEDANT STICKLER
PURITAN PRIG SAINT CANTER CROPPY BLUENOSE CATHARAN GOSPELER PRECISIAN ROUNDHEAD
PURITANICAL BLUE STRICT GENTEEL PRECISE
PURITANI, I (CHARACTER IN —) ARTHUR ELVIRA TALBOT WALTON HENRIETTA
(COMPOSER OF —) BELLINI

PURITY PURE ASSAY HONOR WHITE CANDOR SATTVA VIRTUE FINESSE CHASTITY FINENESS PURENESS
(— OF BREED) PEDIGREE
(— OF LUSTER) ORIENT
PURL RIB EDDY KNIT PEARL UPSET RIPPLE TOTTLE CAPSIZE OVERTURN
PURLIEU AREA HAUNT
(PL.) BOUNDS CONFINES ENVIRONS
PURLIN RIB
PURLOIN CAB CRIB WEED ANNEX BRIBE FILCH STEAL SWIPE FINGER PILFER PIRATE CABBAGE SNAFFLE SURREPT ABSTRACT SCROUNGE
PURPLE GAY VIOL LILAC REGAL SHOWY ARGYLE BLATTA BLOODY CROCUS EVEQUE MIGNON ARDOISE FUCHSIA FUCHSIN HEATHEN LOGWOOD PETUNIA PONTIFF PURPURE AMARANTH BURGUNDY CAMERIER CYCLAMEN EGGPLANT EMINENCE IMPERIAL MAUVETTE MULBERRY WISTARIA
(BROWNISH —) PUCE
(DELICATE —) MAUVE
(PALE —) LILAC
(VISIBLE —) RHODOPSIN
(PREF.) PORPHYR(O) PURPUREO PURPURI PURPURO
PURPLE FISH MUREX
PURPLE GALLINULE SULTAN SULTANA HYACINTH
PURPLE LAND (AUTHOR OF —) HUDSON
(CHARACTER IN —) JOHN LAMB ANITA MARCO COLOMA LUCERO MARCOS MONICA SANTOS ANSELMO BARBUDO CALIXTO GANDARA HILARIO ISIDORA PAQUITA PERALTA RICHARD DEMETRIA MARGARITA CARRICKFERGUS
PURPLE LOOSESTRIFE KILLWEED
PURPLE MEDIC ALFALFA
PURPLE RAGWORT JACOBY
PURPLE SANDPIPER REDLEG REDLEGS ROCKBIRD
PURPORT FECK GIST PORT DRIFT SENSE TENOR DESIGN EFFECT IMPART IMPORT INTEND INTENT BEARING MEANING PROFESS PURPOSE COVERING DISGUISE STRENGTH
PURPOSE GO AIM END GOAL IDEA MAIN MEAN MIND MINT PLAN SAKE TALK TEND VIEW WEEN WILL ARTHA CAUSE ETTLE HEART LEVEL POINT SCOPE STUDY THINK DESIGN DEVICE EFFECT INTEND INTENT OBTENT PREFIX REASON SCHEME COMPASS COUNSEL DESTINE EARNEST IMAGINE MEANING PROPOSE THOUGHT DEVOTION FUNCTION PLEASURE PROPOUND DISCOURSE
(ALLEGED —) PRETEXT
(FIXED —) HEART
(INSIDIOUS —) CAUTEL
(MORAL —) ETHOS
(PARTICULAR —) NONCE
(PRESENT —) NONCE
PURPOSEFUL AIMFUL POINTED
PURPOSELESS WASTE RANDOM AIMLESS FECKLESS
PURPOSIVE TELIC HORMIC
PURPURA MUREX PURPLES PELIOSIS
PURPURE GOLP GOLPE PURPLE MERCURY
PURR MURR THRUM WHURL DUNLIN
PURSE BAG CLY JAN BUNG CLAY CLOY FISC KNIT POKE PUSS SKIN BULSE BURSE DUMMY FUNDS MEANS POUCH SPUNG COMMON FOLLIS GIPSER POCKET PUCKER READER SHAMMY ALMONER GIPSIRE LEATHER SPORRAN BUCKSKIN BURSICLE CRUMENAL AUMONIERE POCKETBOOK
(PREF.) BURSI
PURSE CRAB PAGURID
PURSER CLERK BURSAR BOUCHER PINCHGUT NIPCHEESE
PURSING MIMP
(— OF MOUTH) PRIM
PURSLANE PURPIE PUSSLY PIGWEED PUSSLEY PORTULACA
PURSLANE TREE SPEKBOOM
PURSUANCE SUING SEQUENCE
PURSUE BAY RUN SUE HUNT SEEK CHASE CHEVY CHIVY ENSUE HOUND QUEST SLATE STALK TRADE COURSE FOLLOW GALLOP TRAVEL BEDEVIL HOTFOOT CONTINUE PRACTICE
(— ZIGZAG COURSE) TACK
PURSUER FOLLOWER PLAINTIFF QUESTRIST
PURSUIT FAD HUNT SUIT CAPER CAUSE CHASE CHEVY CRAFT HOBBY COURSE SEARCH ASSAULT ACTIVITY ENTREATY PROSECUTION
(— OF PLEASURE) EPICURISM
(— OF WISDOM) PHILOSOPHY
(FAVORITE —) MEAT
PURSUIVANT BUTE MARCH FALCON ORMOND ATHLONE CARRICK ANTELOPE DINGWALL FOLLOWER
PURSY FAT OBESE PUFFY ASTHMATIC
PURULENT PYIC ATTRY ATTERY
PURVEY CATER PANDER SUPPLY FORESEE PROVIDE
PURVEYOR CATER TAKER ACHUAS PROWER CATERER ACHATOUR MANCIPLE
PUS WARE AMPER FESTER MATTER WORSUM QUITTER
(PREF.) PURI PURO PY(O)
(CONTAINING — AND GAS) PYOPNEUMO
PUSH CA DUB JAM JOG JUR PUT BANG BIRR BOIL BOOM BORE BUNT DING DUSH FLOG KENT PICK PILT PING PORR POSS POTE SHOG STOP BLITZ BOOST BRUSH BUNCH CROWD CRUSH DRIVE DUNCH ELBOW GOOSE HUNCH NUDGE PINCH POACH POUSE SCAUT SHOVE SKELP STICK STOVE EXTEND HURTLE HUSTLE JOGGLE JOSTLE POTTER PROPEL THRING THRONG THRUST ASSAULT IMPETUS IMPULSE OPERATE PERPLEX SHUFFLE THRUTCH CONTRUDE INCREASE SHOULDER STRAITEN DISMISSAL
(— ALONG) TUSH
(— APART) SPREAD
(— ASIDE) SHOG
(— BY STICK) KENT POLE
(— FORWARD) BUCKET ADVANCE
(— GENTLY) NUDGE
(— IN HASTE) RUSH
(— INTO) INVADE
(— INTO PROMINENCE) BOOM
(— MONEY) SPIFF
(— ON) BEAR YERK
(— OUT) DEBOUT LAUNCH
(— OUT LIPS) POUT
(— RUDELY) BARGE HORSE HUSTLE
(— TO FULL STRIDE) EXTEND
(— TOGETHER) CONTRUDE
(— UNDERNEATH) SUBDUCT
(— UP) BOOST
(— VIOLENTLY) WHANG
(— WITH ELBOW) ELBOW HUNCH
(— WITH FEET) DIG SCAUT
(— WITH HEAD) BUNT BUTT
(— WITHIN) INVAGINATE
(STRONG —) BEVEL
PUSH BUTTON PUSH PRESSEL
PUSHCART BARROW TROLLEY
PUSHER PLUNGER TRAILER TRAMMER WHEELER
PUSHING OBTRUSIVE PROTRUSIVE
PUSHOVER SNAP SOFTY SUCKER
PUSHY FORWARD AGGRESSIVE
PUSILLANIMOUS WEAK TIMID FEEBLE COWARDLY TIMOROUS
PUSS CAT FACE HARE CHEET CHILD MOUTH RABBIT BAUDRONS
PUSSYCAT SOFTY
PUSTULE NOB BEAL BURL KNOB POCK PUSH QUAT WART ACHOR AMPER BLAIN WHEAL WHELK BLOTCH FESTER PIMPLE TETTER ANTHRAX BLISTER ERUPTION WHEYWORM
PUT DO BET LAY PIT SET BANG BUTT FILL GIVE GROW PILT REST URGE ADAPT APPLY DIGHT DRIVE FOCUS PLACE STALL STATE STEAD STEEK STELL WAGER ASSIGN BESTOW DECAMP IMPOSE INVEST PHRASE REPOSE SPROUT THRUST DEPOSIT EMPLACE EXPRESS INFLICT SUBJECT
(— AN END TO) DATE SNIB ABATE NAPOO SNUFF SPIKE STASH STILL STINT SOPITE STANCH ABOLISH ASSUAGE EXPIATE SATISFY ABROGATE DEMOLISH FINALIZE SURCEASE
(— ANOTHER IN PLACE OF) RELIEVE
(— APART) DISPART
(— ASHORE) MAROON
(— ASIDE) BLOW HAIN SAVE SHUNT REJECT SHUFFLE
(— ASUNDER) PART
(— AT REST) HUSH
(— AWAY) STOW COVER ELONG HUTCH SHIFT RECOND SAVEUP DIVORCE
(— BACK) REMIT REMISE
(— BACK INTO USE) RESTORE
(— BEFORE) PROFER ANTEPONE
(— DOWN) LAY DEMIT QUASH QUELL DEPOSE SQUASH DEPRESS OPPRESS REPRESS SILENCE DIMINISH SUPPRESS
(— EDGE ON) TED
(— EVASIVELY) SHUFFLE
(— FLAX UPON A DISTAFF) DIZEN
(— FORTH) GEM BLOW CAST GIVE PUSH EXERT LANCE PROFER STRETCH
(— FORTH BLOSSOMS) GEM
(— FORWARD) RUN PLEAD TABLE PREFER PRESENT PROPONE PROPOSE SUGGEST OVERTURE
(— GRAIN IN BARN) END
(— IN) ENTER INSERT INTROMIT
(— IN AGONY) THROE
(— IN CHARGE) COMMIT
(— IN CLAIM) PRETEND
(— IN COMPETITION) PIT
(— IN CONDITION) TUNE
(— IN CUSTODY) REMIT
(— IN DANGER) SCUPPER
(— IN DREAD) ADRAD
(— INFORMATION INTO) ADDRESS
(— IN MOTION) AROUSE
(— IN OPERATION) LAUNCH
(— IN ORDER) DO SET REDD SIDE SORT TRIM DIGHT MENSE SHIFT TRICK ADJUST DAIKER GRAITH ORDAIN SETTLE ARRANGE CLARIFY DISPOSE REDRESS INSTRUCT
(— IN PLACE) POSE
(— IN POSSESSION) SEISE
(— IN PRISON) WARD
(— INTO ACTION) SERVE
(— INTO BARN) END
(— INTO CASE) SHEATHE
(— INTO CIRCULATION) EMIT SPRING
(— INTO ECSTASY) ENTRANCE
(— INTO EFFECT) EXECUTE SANCTION
(— INTO IRONS) BOLT
(— INTO RHYTHM) METER METRE
(— LIQUOR INTO CASK) TUN
(— OFF) DAFF DOFF HAFT DEFER DELAY DEMUR FOIST PARRY REMIT REPRY SHIFT TARRY THROW LINGER RETARD SHELVE ADJOURN FORSLOW PROLONG RESPITE POSTPONE PROROGUE PROCRASTINATE
(— ON) DON HYPE APPLY CRACK DRAPE ENDUE MOUNT STAGE ASSUME INVEST ADDRESS
(— ON AIRS) PROSS FINICK REVEST
(— ON ALERT) ALARM
(— ON BOARD) LADE
(— ON COVER) HACKLE
(— ON GUARD) ALERT CAUTION
(— ON HAT) COVER
(— ON PRETENSE) AFFECT
(— ON RECORD) FILE REGISTER
(— ON SALE) SHOP
(— ON SHORT ALLOWANCE) SCRIMP
(— ON STAGE) PRODUCE
(— ON STRING) ENFILE

(— OUT) GET OUT DOUT OUST DOWSE EVICT EXERT OUTED SLAKE SLOCK RETIRE DISMISS EXCLUDE EXTINCT FORJUDGE
(— OUT BATSMAN) SKITTLE
(— OUT OF ACTION) HAMPER
(— RIGHT) AMEND
(— ROAD METAL ON) STEEN
(— SUDDENLY) CLAP
(— SURREPTITIOUSLY) STEAL
(— THROUGH A STRAINER) TAMMY
(— TO FLIGHT) AFLEY FEAZE FLEME GALLY
(— TOGETHER) ADD JOIN BUILD COMPILE COMPOSE CONCOCT CONFECT PREPARE ASSEMBLE COMPOUND
(— TO PROOF) TEST
(— TO RIGHTS) SORT DIGHT
(— TO SHAME) DASH ABASH SHEND UPBRAID
(— TO SLEEP) OPIATE SOPITE SOPORATE
(— TO THE TEST) SEARCH
(— TO TRIAL) TEMPT
(— TO USE) STOW APPLY BESTOW
(— TO WORK) HARNESS
(— UP) ANTE ERECT FLUSH DISPENSE
(— UP HAY) BOTTLE
(— UPON) GAMMON
(— UP WITH) GO BEAR BIDE HACK ABIDE BROOK ENDURE SUFFER COMPORT STOMACH SWALLOW TOLERATE
(— WITH ANOTHER) APPOSE
(SUFF.) STOLE
PUTAMEN PYRENE
PUTCHER PUTLOG PUTCHEN PUTLOCK
PUT-DOWN SLUR
PUT-ON HYPE
PUTREFACTION ROT DECAY SEPSIS (SUFF.) SEPTIC
PUTREFACTIVE SEPTIC (PREF.) SEPTICO
PUTREFIED ROTTEN
PUTREFY ROT ADDLE DECAY SWEAT FESTER POLLUTE PUTRESCE
PUTRESCENT PUTRID ROTTEN
PUTRID FOUL RANK SOUR VILE LOUSY ADDLED RANCID ROTTEN CORRUPT DECAYED FRIABLE VICIOUS DEPRAVED MALODOROUS (PREF.) SAPR(O) SEPTI SEPTO (SUFF.) SEPSIS SEPTIC
PUTT CLOWN BORROW GOBBLE
(SHORT —) GIMME TAPIN
PUTTEE PAT PATA GAITER BANDAGE LEGGING
PUTTER FUSS MESS MUCK POKE TRUCK CADDLE DAWDLE MUCKER MUCKLE PIDDLE TINKER FRIGGLE
PUTTY BEDDING
PUTTYROOT CRAWFOOT
PUTZ CRECHE
PUXY SWAMPY QUAGMIRE
PUZZLE CAP GET SET BEAT CRUX DEAD LICK POSE BEFOG GRIPH POSER QUEER REBUS STICK BAFFLE BOTHER ENIGMA FICKLE FOITER GLAIKS JIGSAW KITTLE RIDDLE CONFUSE MYSTERY MYSTIFY NONPLUS PERPLEX STICKER TAISSLE TANGRAM TRANGAM ACROSTIC BEFUDDLE BEWILDER CONFOUND DISTRACT DUMFOUND ENTANGLE INTRIGUE REMBLERE CROSSWORD METAGRABOLIZE METAGROBOLIZE
(SOPHISTICAL —) SORITES
(TYPE OF —) JIGSAW
PUZZLED ASEA ATSEA PERPLEXED
PUZZLING KNOTTY CURIOUS KNOTTED RIDDLING DIFFICULT PROBLEMATIC
PYCNANTHEMUM KOELLIA
PYCNOGONID SPIDER
PYGARG ADDAX OSPREY
PYGIDIUM PODEX
PYGMALION (AUTHOR OF —) SHAW
(BELOVED OF —) GALATEA
(CHARACTER IN —) HILL LIZA CLARA HENRY ALFRED FREDDY HIGGINS EYNSFORD DOOLITTLE PICKERING
(FATHER OF —) BELUS MUTGO AGENOR
(MURDERED BY —) SICHAEUS
(SISTER OF —) DIDO
(STATUE FASHIONED BY —) GALATEA
PYGMY ELF AKKA AMBA DOKO ACHUA AFIFI ATOMY BATWA DWARF GNOME PIXIE PIGMEW WOCHUA ACHANGO ASHANGO MANIKIN DWARFISH NEGRILLO VAALPENS DANDIPRAT
PYGMY GOOSE GOSLET
PYGMY RATTLESNAKE MASSASAUGA
PYGOSTYLE VOMER
PYKNIC SQUAT STOCKY STHENIC MUSCULAR
PYLADES (COMPANION OF —) ORESTES
(FATHER OF —) STROPHIUS
(MOTHER OF —) ANAXIBIA
(SON OF —) MEDON STROPHIUS
(WIFE OF —) ELECTRA
PYRAMID BENBEN HOPPER TEOCALLI
(— OF CRAYFISH) BUISSON
(DOUBLE —) TWIN ZIRCONOID
(INVERTED —) HOPPER
PYRAMIDAL HUGE ENORMOUS IMPOSING
PYRAMIDICAL TAPER
PYRAMUS (LOVER OF —) THISBE
PYRAZINE ALDINE PIAZIN DIAZINE
PYRE BALE PILE TOPHET BONFIRE BALEFIRE
PYRIDOXIN ADERMIN
PYRITE BALE MUNDIC (PL.) BRAZIL STANNITE FIRESTONE MAGISTRAL MARCASITE
PYROCLES (BROTHER OF —) CYMOCLES
(FATHER OF —) ACRATES
PYROLA LIMONIUM SHINLEAF
PYROMANIAC FIREBUG ARSONIST
PYRONE CUMALIN
PYROPHYLLITE PENCIL
PYROTECHNICS FIREWORKS
PYROXENE ACMITE AUGITE SALITE SAHLITE AEGIRITE DIALLAGE DIOPSIDE WOLLASTONITE
PYROXENITE ARIEGITE MARCHITE OSTRAITE NIKLESITE
PYRRHIC DIBRACH
PYRRHULOXIA GROSBEAK BULLFINCH
PYRRHUS (FATHER OF —) AEACIDES
(MOTHER OF —) PHTHIA
(SON OF —) PTOLEMY SOPATER
(WIFE OF —) ANTIGONE
PYRROLE AZOLE
PYTHON ADJIGER PEROPOD ANACONDA
PYTHONESS WITCH PHITONES
PYTHONIC HUGE INSPIRED ORACULAR MONSTROUS PROPHETIC
PYX BOX CAPSA CASKET CHRISM VESSEL BINNACLE CHRISMAL CIBORIUM
PYXIDIUM CAPSULE

Q

Q KU CUE KUE QUEEN QUEUE QUEBEC
QATAR (CAPITAL OF —) DOHA
(TOWN OF —) RUWAIS UMMSAID
QUA HERON QUABIRD
QUACK PUFF WHACK CROCUS SALVER SUBTLE EMPIRIC IMPOSTOR OPERATOR SANGRADO CHARLATAN
(PREF.) PSEUD(O)
QUACKERY HUMBUG
QUADRAGESIMA LENT
QUADRANGLE QUAD CLOSE COURT TETRAGON
QUADRANT BOW RADIAL SQUARE QUARTER TETRANT ALTIMETER
QUADRATE SUIT AGREE IDEAL QUADER SQUARE PERFECT BALANCED
QUADRIC CONICOID
QUADRILATERAL TRAPEZIA TETRAGRAM
(PL.) TESSARA
QUADRILLE CONTREDANSE
(PL.) LANCERS
QUADRILLION
(PREF.) ASTRA PETA QUEGA
QUADRILLIONTH
(PREF.) FEMTO
QUADROON QUATERON TERCERON
QUADRUPED BABIRUSA
QUADRUPLE FOURBLE FOURFOLD
QUADRUPLED
(PREF.) TETRAKIS
QUADRUPLET FOURLING QUARTOLE
QUAFF QUAX TOOT DRINK QUASS WAUCHT CAROUSE TRILLIL
QUAG BOG MARSH SHAKE QUIVER
QUAGMIRE BOG FEN GOG HAG QUA SOG LAIR PUXY QUAW MARSH MIZZY SWAMP MORASS PUDDLE SLOUGH BOGMIRE PUCKSEY WAGMOIRE
QUAHOG CLAM COHOG VENUS BULLNOSE
QUAIL COW LOWA WEET COLIN COWER DAUNT ORTYX QUAKE SPOIL WASTE BLENCH CURDLE FLINCH SHRINK TURNIX WITHER DECLINE HEMIPOD TREMBLE BOBWHITE
(YOUNG —) SQUEALER
QUAINT DRY ODD TWEE FUNKY NAIVE BIZARRE STRANGE FANCIFUL HANDSOME PICTURESQUE
(— IN APPEARANCE) FUNKY
QUAKE JAR QUOG RESE CHILL QUAIL SEISM SHAKE DITHER QUIVER SHIVER WAMBLE FLUTTER SHUDDER TREMBLE
(PREF.) PALLO

QUAKER ASPEN HERON FRIEND OBADIAH WHACKER HICKSITE TREMBLER BEACONITE BROADBRIM SHADBELLY
(— STATE) PENNA PENNSYLVANIA
QUAKER GRAY ACIER
QUAKING ASPEN QUAKY TREPID SHAKING TREMBLING
QUAKING GRASS BRIZA COWQUAKE WAGWANTS
QUALIFICATION NATURE RESERVE SHADING CAPACITY
QUALIFIED FIT ABLE MEET FITTED FITTEN LIKELY PASSED CAPABLE ELIGIBLE SUITABLE AUTHENTIC
(DULY —) REGULAR
(NOT —) INAPT INHABILE
QUALIFIER MODIFIER
QUALIFY FIT DASH ADAPT ALLAY ALLOY EQUIP HEDGE ENABLE MODIFY SOFTEN TEMPER ABSOLVE CERTIFY ENTITLE LICENSE PREPARE GRADUATE MODERATE RESTRAIN RESTRICT
QUALITIES
(SUFF.) ERY ICS
QUALITY Y BRAN BUMP CHOP COST FEEL GUNA LEAD SORT COLOR GRACE STATE TRAIT ASSIZE BARREL FABRIC STRAIN THREAD TIMBER TIMBRE ADJUNCT CALIBER KINSHIP STATURE ACCIDENT MOVEMENT PROPERTY TONEBRAND
(— OF MIND) CALIBER CALIBRE
(— OF PERSONAL EMOTIONS) PATHOS
(— OF PHOTOGRAPH) CONTRAST
(— OF SOUND) TONE
(— OF TONE) TIMBRE
(— OF VOWELS) LENGTH
(— PECULIAR TO ONESELF) SEITY
(AESTHETIC —) TASTE
(ARTISTIC —) VIRTU
(ATTRACTIVE —) TAKE
(BASIC —) GRAIN
(BASIC —S) STUFF
(CHARACTERISTIC —) TURN
(CHIEF —) SPIRIT
(COLOR —) TONE
(ESSENTIAL —) ALLOY SPECIES SUCHNESS
(GOOD —) THEW
(HEREDITARY —) STRAIN
(IMPECCABLE —) FINISH
(IMPLICIT —) OVERTONE
(INCISIVE —) BITE
(INNATE —) LARGESS
(INTELLECTUAL —) BROW
(MELODRAMATIC —) SENSATION
(MORAL —) THEW
(NATURAL —) TARAGE
(OBJECTIONABLE —) ANILITY

(OF HIGH —) FRANK
(OF HIGHEST —) PRIMO
(OF LOW —) SHLOCK SCHLOCK
(OF POOR —) GROTTY
(PERVASIVE —) AROMA
(PHYSICAL —S) BOTTOM
(POSITIVE —) PLUS
(PRIMAL —) GUNA
(PUNGENT —) SNAP
(RELATIVE —) RATE
(SECONDARY —) OVERTONE
(SPATIAL —) MAGNITUDE
(SPRINGY —) SPINE
(STRUCTURAL —) TEXTURE
(SUBDUED —) SHADE
(SUBTLE —) BOUQUET
(SUPERIOR —) SUPER FINENESS
(TRIED —) TOUCH
(UNESSENTIAL —) ACCIDENT
(UNUSUAL —) SURD
(USEFUL —) ASSET
(WAVY — OF HAIR) FLIX
(SUFF.) ACITY ANCE ANCY CY ENCE ENCY HEAD HOOD ICE ICITY ILITY ITY MENT NESS SHIP TY
(— THAT FILLS) FUL FULL
(CHARACTERIZED BY —) SOME
QUALITY STREET (AUTHOR OF —) BARRIE
(CHARACTER IN —) BROWN LIVVY PATTY SUSAN BLADES PHOEBE THROSSEL VALENTINE
QUALM CALM DROW PALL NAUSEA SQUEAM SCRUPLE
QUALMISH TEWLY SICKISH SQUEAMISH
QUAMOCLIT MOONFLOWER
QUANDARY FIX PUXY PUZZLE TANGLE DILEMMA NONPLUS SWITHER DOLDRUMS JUNCTURE
QUANDONG PEACH
QUANT RYPECK
QUANTIC NONIC OCTIC SEPTIC SEXTIC QUADRIC QUINTIC
QUANTIFIER PREFIX
QUANTITATIVE METRIC
QUANTITY BAG JAG SUM SUP BODY DEAL DISH DOSE FECK JAGG LIFT MASK SOME SOUD WARE BATCH BREAK CLASH GRIST KITTY SIEGE TROOP WHEEN ACTION ADDEND AMOUNT BAGFUL BOTTLE BUDGET DICKER EFFECT FOTHER HANTLE NUMBER PARCEL SCALAR SPINOR THRAVE VOLUME CONTENT FOOTAGE PORTION QUANTUM GLASSFUL KNIFEFUL LADLEFUL PARAMETER
(— OF ARROWS) SHEAF
(— OF BUTTER) CHURNING
(— OF CLOTHES) BUCKING
(— OF COTTONSEED) CRUSH
(— OF CUT TREES) FALL

(— OF DRINK) HOOP DRAFT DRAUGHT
(— OF ELECTRICITY) FARADAY
(— OF EXPLOSIVE) CHARGE
(— OF FISH OR GAME) TAKE CATCH DRAFT DRAUGHT
(— OF GRAIN) GAVEL
(— OF HAY) LOCK TRUSS
(— OF IRRIGATION WATER) DUTY
(— OF LAND) PLOUGHGATE
(— OF LIQUID) DROP JAUP SLASH GOBBET JABBLE
(— OF LIQUOR) HEELTAP
(— OF LUMBER) RUN
(— OF MEAL) MELDER
(— OF METAL) BLOW
(— OF MUD) CLASH
(— OF NARCOTICS) BINDLE
(— OF PAPER) TOKEN
(— OF PRODUCE) BURY
(— OF RAISINS) FRAIL
(— OF THREAD) LEASE
(— OF WOOD) HAG FATHOM
(— PRODUCED) OUTPUT
(DIRECTED —) VECTOR
(EQUAL —) PART
(ESTIMATED —) WEY
(EXCESSIVE —) GLUT SPATE
(FIXED —) CONSTANT
(GREAT —) HOST MORT MUCH RAFT HIRST SHOAL SIGHT STORE BARREL FOREST SLATHER TUMMELS
(INCREASED —) SPATE SPEAT
(IRRATIONAL —) SURD
(LARGE —) ACRE BOLT DEAL FECK HEAP MASS PECK SCAD SLEW FLOOD FORCE GRIST JORUM POWER SCADS SHEAF STACK STORE BUCKET BUSHEL DICKER DOLLOP GALLON MATTER MELDER CLUTHER SKINFUL HECATOMB MOUNTAIN PLURALITY
(LEAST —) BEDROCK
(MINUTE —) DRAM DROP SHADE SCRUPLE PARTICLE
(NOTEWORTHY —) CHUNK
(REGULATED —) QUOTA
(RELATIVE —) DEGREE
(SETTLED —) SIZE
(SIZABLE —) SCUMP
(SLIGHT —) SUSPICION
(SMALL —) ACE BIT SUP TOT CURN DASH DUST HAET HAIR HARL IOTA PEAK SOSH SPOT CANCH PRILL SMACK SPICE SQUIB TOUCH TRACE JOBBLE MORSEL PICKLE SAMPLE SONGLE STIVER CAPSULE CURTSEY DRIBBLE DRIBLET EPSILON HANDFUL MODICUM SMICKET SPATTER TODDICK FARTHING MOUTHFUL PENNORTH SCANTLET SPRINKLE PENNYWORTH SPRINKLING THIMBLEFUL

(UNDIRECTED —) SCALAR
(UNLIMITED —) OCEAN
(VARYING —) SKID
(ZERO —) NOTHING
(SUFF.) **(— THAT FILLS)** FUL FULL SKID
QUANTUM MAGNON PHONON PHOTON ISOSPIN
(— OF ENERGY) PLASMON
QUAPAW KWAPA ARKANSAS
QUARANTINE DETAIN ISOLATE SANCTION
QUARENTENE ROOD FURLONG
QUARK PARTICLE
(PARTICLE TO BIND —S) GLUON
(PROPERTY OF —S) FLAVOR
QUARREL JAR ROW WAP YED BEEF CHIP DEAL FEUD FRAY FUSS JARL JOWL MIFF NIFF ODDS PICK PLEA SPAT TIFF WHID BRACK BRAWL BRIGE BROIL FLITE FLUSK GRUFF HURRY JOWER NOISE PIQUE RUNIN SCOLD SCRAP SHINE STOUR UPSET WRALL AFFRAY BARNEY BLOWUP BREACH BREEZE BRIGUE DEBATE DIFFER DUSTUP FRACAS FRATCH GARROT JANGLE MATTER QUARRY RIPPET SQUARE SQUEAL STRIFE THREAP THREEP THWART BRABBLE BRATTLE DISGUST DISPUTE FACTION OUTCAST PRABBLE RUCTION SIMULTY STASHIE SWAGGER TUILZIE WRANGLE DISAGREE MOORBURN SCRAFFLE SPLUTTER SQUABBLE TRAVERSE
(— IN WORDS) JANGLE
(NOISY —) ROW FRACAS KICKUP
(PETTY —) MIFF SPAT TIFF
QUARRELING BICKER CONTEK CHIDING CONTECK
QUARRELSOME RIXY UGLY ROWTY FEISTY CURRISH SCRAPPY DRAWLING FRAMPOLD FRATCHED PETULANT PHRAMPEL BELLICOSE BUMPTIOUS FRACTIOUS LITIGIOUS CONTENTIOUS
(NOT —) AMICABLE
QUARRELSOMENESS SQUARING WARIANCE
QUARRIED (NOT —) LIVE
(PREF.) ORYCTO
QUARRIER FACEMAN QUARION
QUARRY PIT DELF GAME LODE MEAT CHASE DELFT DELPH PLUCK LATOMY REWARD LATOMIA LOZENGE
(HAWK'S —) MARK
QUARRYMAN SCABBLER SCAPPLER
QUART SHANT WHART
(METRIC —) LITER
(ONE-HALF —) PINT
(TWO —S) MAGNUM
(1-8TH —) GILL
(2 —S) FLAGON
(4 —S) GALLON
QUARTE FOURTH
QUARTER AIRT PART STUD EAVER GRITH TRACT BARRIO BEHALF BESTOW CANTON COLONY FARDEL HARBOR SECTOR TWOBITS CONTRADA FAUBOURG FIERDING STANDARD POBLACION
(— IN BATTLE) GRITH
(— OF A POUND) TRIPPET
(— OF BEEF OR MUTTON) BOUT
(— OF CITY) BLOCK GHETTO
(— OF COMPASS) PLAGE
(— OF FLAG) CANTON
(— OF HOUR) POINT
(— OF HUNDRED) FIERDING
(— OF YEAR) RAITH
(— ONESELF) SORN
(— UPON) LAY
(JEWISH —) ALJAMA
(NATIVE —) MEDINA
QUARTERBACK BOSS
QUARTERING LASKING CHUMMAGE
QUARTER NOTE CROTCHET
QUARTER REST SOSPIRO
QUARTERS BOTHY BILLET BOTHIE LIVERY MENAGE FARDELS CHUMMERY DIGGINGS LODGMENT
(— FOR IMMIGRANTS) HOSTEL
(— OF CREW) FOCSLE FORECASTLE
(— OF SALVATION ARMY) BARRACKS
(GENERAL'S —) PRINCIPIUM
(HIGH —) AERY EYRY AERIE EYRIE
(JUNIOR OFFICERS' —) GUNROOM
(LIVING —) PAD
(MEN'S —) SELAMLIK
(MONASTERY —) FRATRY
(RELIGIOUS —) NOVICIATE NOVITIATE
(TEMPORARY —) CAMP CANTONMENT
(WINTER —) HIBERNACLE
(WOMEN'S —) HAREM SERAGLIO GYNAECEUM
QUARTET FOURSOME
QUARTILE SQUARE TETRAGON
QUARTO FOURS
QUARTZ IRIS ONYX SARD AGATE CHERT FLINT PRASE TARSO TOPAZ JASPER MORION PEBBLE PLASMA SILICA ALENCON CITRINE CRYSTAL RUBASSE SINOPLE AMETHYST BASANITE SARDONYX SIDERITE YENTNITE BUHRSTONE BURRSTONE
QUARTZITE GANISTER SILCRETE
QUASH CASS CRUSH QUELL SPIKE SQUAT SOPITE CASSARE PEREMPT SUPPRESS
QUASI
(PREF.) SEMI
QUASI-ATOM MUONIUM
QUAT FOUR GLUT SQUASH SATIATE UPSTART
QUATERNION TETRAD QUADRATE
QUATREFOIL TRESSURE
(DOUBLE —) EIGHTFOIL
QUAVER QUAP CROMA SHAKE TRILL WAVER CHROMA FALTER QUIVER WABBLE WOBBLE WRIBLE FREDDON VIBRATE
QUAVERY WARBLY UNSTEADY
QUAY KEY POW QUAI LEVEE BUNDER STRAND
QUEACH BOG FEN MARSH THICKET
QUEASINESS KECK SICKNESS
QUEASY NICE SICK SQUEEZY DELICATE NAUSEATED SQUEAMISH
QUEBEC (LAKE OF —) MINTO BIENVILLE MISTASSINI
(TOWN OF —) AMOS HULL AMQUI LAVAL MAGOG PERCE BASSIN VERDUN JOLIETTE MONTREAL LAPRAIRIE
QUEBRACHO BREAKAX AXMASTER IRONWOOD AXBREAKER
QUEBRADA BROOK GULLY RAVINE FISSURE
QUECHUA INCAN KICHUA
QUEEN ENA REG DAME FERS LADY MEDB RANI AEDON BEGUM FIERS RANEE ATOSSA REGINA ROXANA TAILTE TAMARA ARGANTE ATHALIA CANDACE JOCASTE OMPHALE PHEARSE STATIRA TITANIA BRUNHILD GERTRUDE GLORIANA GUINEVER MAHARANI
(— AND KING OF TRUMPS) BELLA
(— CITY) CINCINNATI
(— IN CHESS) FERS LADY FIERS
(— OF CLUBS) SPADILLA
(— OF DENMARK) GERTRUDE
(— OF EGYPTIAN GODS) SATI
(— OF ETHIOPIA) CANDACE
(— OF FAIRY LAND) MEDB GLORIANA
(— OF GEORGIA) TAMARA
(— OF GOTHS) TAMORA
(— OF HEARTS) ELIZABETH
(— OF HEAVEN) HERA
(— OF JUDAH) ATHALIA
(— OF LYDIA) OMPHALE
(— OF SHEBA) BALKIS BILKIS
(— OF SPADES) BASTA LIZZY
(— OF THE ADRIATIC) VENICE
(— OF THE ANTILLES) CUBA
(— OF THEBES) JOCASTA
(— OF THE EAST) ZENOBIA
(— OF THE MAY) MAYLADY MAYQUEEN
(— OF TRUMPS) HONOR
(FAIRY —) MAB ARGANTE TITANIA
(FORMER SPANISH —) ENA
(INDIAN —) RANI SUNK MAHARANI
(MOHAMMEDAN —) BEGUM
(NEIGHBOR OF —) KING BISHOP
QUEEN ANNE'S LACE UMBEL
QUEEN BEE KING
QUEEN ELIZABETH DIANA ORIANA CYNTHIA
QUEENFISH WAHOO CROAKER DRUMFISH
QUEENLY HAUGHTY REGINAL MAJESTIC
QUEENROOT YAWSHRUB
QUEEN'S-DELIGHT YAWSHRUB
QUEENSLAND HEMP SIDA JELLYLEAF
QUEER HEX ODD RUM HARM DICKY DIPPY DROLL FAINT FUNNY GIDDY NUTTY RUMMY COCKLE FIFISH HIPPED QUEASY QUISBY UNIQUE AMUSING COMICAL CURIOUS DISRUPT ERRATIC STRANGE TOUCHED WHIMSIC FANCIFUL OBSESSED PECULIAR
(— THING) QUOZ
QUEERNESS ODDITY
QUEEST RINGDOVE
QUELL DIE CALM FLOW HUSH KILL QUAY SLAY ABATE ALLAY CRUSH QUASH QUIET YIELD PACIFY PERISH REDUCE SOOTHE SPRING STANCH STIFLE KILLING REPRESS SQUELCH SUPPRESS
QUEME QUIM HANDY WHEAM COMELY PLEASE GRATIFY PLEASANT
QUENCH COOL DAMP SIND ALLAY CHECK CRUSH SLAKE SLOCK STILL STANCH STIFLE ASSUAGE SLOCKEN AUSTEMPER
QUENCHED EXTINCT
QUENCHER STANCH
QUENCHING FRITTING
QUENTIN DURWARD (AUTHOR OF —) SCOTT
(CHARACTER IN —) CARL CROYE LOUIS LESLEY PHILIP PIERRE TOISON BALAFRE CHARLES DURWARD EBERSON HERMITE LAMARCK LUDOVIC QUENTIN TRISTAN WILLIAM CRAWFORD HAMELINE ISABELLE HAYRADDIN JAQUELINE MAUGRABIN CREVECOEUR
QUERCINE OAKEN
QUERECHO VAQUERO
QUERELA AUDITA
QUERENT INQUIRER PLAINTIFF
QUERN KERN MILL METATE MILLSTONE
QUERULOUS WHINY FRETFUL PEEVISH NATTERED PETULANT IRRITABLE
QUERY ASK DOUBT DEMAND INQUIRE INQUIRY QUESTION
QUEST ASK BAY GAPE SEEK DEMAND EXAMINE PURSUIT SEEKING VENTURE
QUESTING OUTREACH
QUESTION ASK HOW SPY POSE QUIZ TALK ARGUE DOUBT DREAD QUERY ACCUSE CHANCE CHARGE DEMAND LEADER MATTER PONDER QUAERE REASON SHRIVE EXAMINE INQUIRE INQUIRY PROBLEM PURPOSE SCRUPLE OVERTURE RELEVANT RESEARCH STICKLER CATECHISE
(— AMBIGUOUSLY WORDED) RIDDLE
(— FRETFULLY) RAME
(BAFFLING —) POSER
(BUDDHIST —) KOAN
(CAPTIOUS —) QUIDDIT QUIDDITY
(DIFFICULT —) POSER
(PERPLEXING —) STUMPER
(RHETORICAL —) EROTEMA EROTEME EROTESIS
(UNSOLVED —) CRUX
(ZEN —) KOAN
QUESTIONABLE FISHY QUEER SHAKY UNSAFE BATABLE CLOUDED DUBIOUS DOUBTFUL PROBLEMATIC
(NOT —) DECENT
QUESTIONER APPOSER INQUIRER
QUESTIONING DUBIOUS QUIZZICAL
QUESTION MARK QUERY QUAERE EROTEME

QUESTIONNAIRE POLL INVENTORY
QUETCH STIR TWITCH
QUETZAL QUESAL TROGON
QUEUE CUE COLA LINE BRAID PIGTAIL CROCODILE
QUEY KOY WHY WHEY HEIFER
QUIBBLE COG PUN BALK CARP QUIB QUIP CAVIL DODGE EVADE QUIRK SALVO AMBAGE BAFFLE BICKER HAFFLE PALTER SNATCH BRABBLE CAPTION CHICANE QUIBLET QUIDDIT QUILLET SHUFFLE PETTIFOG QUIDDITY QUILLITY SCRAFFLE CONUNDRUM PREVARICATE
QUIBBLING CHICANERY
QUICA OPOSSUM SARIGUE
QUICK APT RAD YAP FAST FLIT GLEG KECK KEEN LISH LIST PERT RATH RIFE SNAP SOON WHAT WHIT WICK YARE AGILE ALIVE APACE BRISK CHEAP FLEET HASTY MERRY NIFTY NIPPY PREST RAPID READY SHARP SHORT SNACK SNELL SWIFT SWITH TOSTO TRICK VISTO YARRY ACTIVE CLEVER FACILE KITTLE NIMBLE PROMPT PRONTO SNAPPY SPEEDY SUDDEN DARTING SCHNELL SHUTTLE DEXTROUS TRIPPING CITIGRADE
(— AND NEAT) DEFT
(— AS A FLASH) WHIP
(— IN PERCEPTION) ACID
(— IN RESPONSE) GNIB
(— OF MIND) INTELLIGENT
(— TO DETECT) SMOKY
(— TO FLARE UP) GASSY
(— TO LEARN) APT
(— TO MOVE) YARE
(LIGHT AND —) VOLANT
(PREF.) OXY TACHEO TACHISTO TACHO TACHY
QUICKEN PEP MEND STIR WHET HURRY SPEED ACUATE AROUSE HASTEN INCITE KINDLE REVIVE VIVIFY ANIMATE ENLIVEN PROVOKE REFRESH SHARPEN EXPEDITE INSPIRIT ACCELERATE
QUICKENING FLICKER REVIVAL STIRRING
QUICKLY TID TIT ASAP CITO FAST RIFE SOON TIVY WHIP YARE APACE NEWLY RADLY RATHE SHARP SKELP SNACK SNELL SWITH TIGHT WIGHT YEPLY ASTITE BELIVE HOURLY PRESTO PRONTO RASHLY EFTSOON PRESTLY READILY SPEEDILY WIKIWIKI
(— AND WITH FORCE) SWAP
(MORE —) TIDDER TITTER STRETTO
QUICKNESS HASTE SPEED ACUMEN AGILITY SMEDDUM ACTIVITY CELERITY DISPATCH KEENNESS SAGACITY
(— OF DECISION) PROMPTITUDE
(MENTAL —) NOUS SLEIGHT LEGERITY
QUICKSAND FLOW SYRT SYRTIS SWALLOW
QUICK-SELLING LEEFTAIL
QUICKSILVER OREMIX MERCURY TIERRAS HEAUTARIT
QUICK-SPEAKING PROMPT
QUICK-TEMPERED DONCY DONSY PEPPERY IRASCIBLE
QUICK-WITTED APT SHARP SMART NIMBLE KNOWING
QUID FID CHAW CHEW SOVEREIGN
(— OF TOBACCO) CUD FID
QUIDDANY JELLY SYRUP CODINIAC
QUIDDITY QUIBBLE WHATNESS
QUIDNUNC GOSSIP BUSYBODY
QUIESCENCE KAIF REPOSE STASIS DORMANCY
QUIESCENT QUIET LATENT STATIC DORMANT RESTING INACTIVE
QUIET QT ST COY LAY CALM COSH DEAD DUMB EASE EASY HUSH LOUN LOWN LULL REST ROCK SNUG SOFT WEME ACCOY CANNY CIVIL DOWNY LEVEL PEACE PEASE QUATE QUELL QUEME RESTY SALVE SHADY SHUSH SILKY SLEEP SOBER SQUAT STILL SUANT WHIST DREAMY GENTLE PACIFY PLACID RETIRE SAUGHT SEDATE SERENE SETTLE SILENT SMOOTH SOFTLY SOOTHE SOPITE STEADY STILLY HUSHFUL ORDERLY REQUIEM RESTFUL SILENCE COMPOSED DECOROUS PEACEFUL TRANQUIL UNRUFFLE
(— DOWN) DILL
(BE —) SSH
(MAKE —) ALLAY
(STEALTHILY —) SLINKY
QUIETEN SEDATE SOPITE SUBDUE
QUIETISM MOLINISM
QUIETLY LOW FAIR CANNY STILL WINLY EVENLY GENTLY SOFTLY TIPTOE
QUIETNESS REST REPOSE SERENITY
QUIETUDE CALM INERTION
QUIETUS REST DEATH RELEASE
QUILL COP PEN RIB PIRN FLOAT STALK BOBBIN FESCUE PINION SLEEVE BRISTLE CALAMUS PRIMARY TRUNDLE
(— FOR WINDING THREAD) COP
(— OF FEATHER) BARREL
(PORCUPINE —) PEN
QUILLBACK SAILFISH SKIMBACK
QUILLWORT ISOETES FERNWORT
QUILT BEAT GULP WALT WELT WHIP DUVET REZAI CADDOW CHALON PALLET THRASH SWALLOW MATTRESS POULTICE COMFORTER
QUILTING MARCELLA
QUIMPER NICE
QUINCE SKEG COYNE ANGERS SQUINCH JAPONICA
(BENGAL —) BEL BAEL BALE BHEL
QUINCE SEED CYDONIUM
QUININE KINA SPECIFIC
(PREF.) CHIN(O)
QUINK BRANT
QUINONE EMBELIN
QUINSY ANGINA PRUNELLA
QUINTAIN FAN
QUINTE FIFTH
QUINTESSENCE CREAM ELIXIR CLYSSUS OSMAZOME
QUINTILLION
(PREF.) EXA NEBU
QUINTILLIONTH
(PREF.) ATTO
QUINTUPLE QUINARY FIVEFOLD QUINIBLE
QUIP GIBE JAPE JEST JOKE CRACK QUIRK SALLY SCOFF TAUNT RETORT CONCEIT QUIBBLE
QUIRA CAOBA ROBLE HORMIGO VENCOLA MACAWOOD
QUIRE CHOR SEXTERN
(20 —S) REAM
(PL.) INSIDES
QUIRK BEND KINK QUIP TURN CLOCK CROOK TWIST CONCEIT QUIBBLE FLOURISH PAROXYSM MANNERISM PECULIARITY
(— OF BEHAVIOR) TIC
QUIRKY ZANY CRAZY DIPPY DOTTY KINKY
QUIRQUINCHO PICHI PELUDO
QUIRT WHIP ROMAL
QUIS WOODCOCK
QUISLING APOSTATE
QUIT GO DROP NASH PART QUAT AVOID BELAY CEASE DOUSE LEAVE SHIFT SHOOT STASH WHITE BEHAVE CIVITE DESERT DESIST FOREGO RESIGN SECEDE VACATE ABANDON FORSAKE RELEASE UNTENANT
QUITCH COUCH QUICK SCUTCH TWITCH
QUITCLAIM DEED ACQUIT RELEASE DISCHARGE
QUITE SO ALL BUT GEY BRAW EVEN FAIR FREE FULL JUST PLAT WELL CLEAR CLOSE FULLY SHEER STARK CLEVER DAMNED ENOUGH JUSTLY MERELY TOTALLY PERFECTLY
(NOT —) HARDLY
(PREF.) DE
QUITERIA (HUSBAND OF —) CAMACHO
QUITRENT CANON
QUITS EVEN EVENS UPSIDES
QUITTER PUS SLAG PIKER COWARD JUMPER SHIRKER TURNBACK
QUIVER DIRL QUAG QUOG BEVER NIDGE QUAKE SHAKE TRILL WAVER WIVER BICKER COCKER DIDDER DINDLE SHEATH SHIMMY SHIVER TREMOR WAMBLE DORLACH FLUTTER FRISSON SHUDDER TREMBLE TWIDDLE TWINKLE TWITTER VIBRATE FLICHTER WERSLETE
(PREF.) PALLO
QUIVERING ASPEN AGUISH DIDDER DITHER QUAGGLE QUAKING AGITATED ATREMBLE
QUIVER TREE KOKERBOOM
QUIXOTIC ERRANT IMAGINARY VISIONARY
QUIZ ASK GUY EXAM HOAX MOCK CHAFF QUEER EXAMINE QUESTION RIDICULE
QUIZZICAL ODD QUEER QUIZZY CURIOUS WHIMSICAL
QUO KA
QUOD JAIL QUAD PRISON
QUOIN COIN ANGLE GOIGN CORNER LOZENGE KEYSTONE VOUSSOIR
QUOIT CIST DISC DISH DISK LINER DISCUS HOBBER CROMLECH
QUOMODO HOW WAY MEANS MANNER
QUONDAM OLD ONCE WHILE FORMER ONETIME SOMETIME
QUORATEAN KAROK
QUORUM CORAM HOUSE MINYAN MAJORITY
QUOTA PART BOGEY SHARE QUOTIENT PROPORTION
QUOTATION TAG PRICE QUOTE EXTRACT SNIPPET EPIGRAPH
(— DEVELOPED INTO ESSAY) CHRIA
(TRITE —) TAG
QUOTATION MARK GUILLEMET
QUOTE CITE COAT COTE MARK NAME NOTE ADDUCE ALLEGE RECITE REPEAT EXCERPT EXTRACT OBSERVE REHEARSE
(— SARCASTICALLY) FLOUT
QUOTH CO KO CUTH QUAD QUOD SAID SPOKE UTTERED
QUOTIDIAN DAILY TRIVIAL ORDINARY
QUOTIENT QUOTE FRACTION MILLESIMAL
QUO VADIS (AUTHOR OF —) SIENKIEWICZ
(CHARACTER IN —) ACTE NERO PAUL CHILO LYGIA PETER URSUS CROTON EUNICE GLAUCUS VINICIUS PETRONIUS TIGELLINUS
QUTB POLE

R AR ROGER ROMEO
(UVULAR —) BURR
RA RE RAE SHU TEM ATMU BACIS HORUS MENTU KHEPERA SOKARIS
RAAMAH (FATHER OF —) CUSH
(SON OF —) DEDAN SHEBA
RABBAN MASTER TEACHER
RABBET CHECK GROOVE BACKJOINT FILLISTER
RABBI TANA AMORA CACAM HAKAM TANNA MASTER SABORA KHAKHAM TEACHER GAMALIEL SABORAIM
(PL.) AMORAIM TANNAIM
RABBIT BUN REX TAN BUNT CONY JACK POLE RACK BUNNY CAPON CREAM CUNNY DUTCH FRIER LAPIN ANGORA ASTREX CONEEN HAVANA OARLOP PARKER POLISH SILVER TAPETI WOOLER BEVEREN CONYNGE FLEMISH LEPORID SNOWSHOE WARRENER
(— BURROW) CLAPPER
(— FUR) CONY SCUT CONEY FLICK LAPIN FLITCH
(— MEAT) LAPAN
(— SKIN) RACK
(— TAIL) SCUT
(— WARREN) CONYGER
(CASTRATED —) CAPON
(FEMALE —) DOE
(MALE —) BUCK
(RELATIVE —) PIKA
(YOUNG —) KITTEN
(PL.) FLICK WARREN
RABBITFISH SPINY
RABBLE MOB TAG GING HERD RAFF ROUT SCUM FRAPE SCAFF SCUFF TRASH MEINIE RADDLE RAFFLE RAGTAG RASCAL TAGRAG DOGGERY PUDDLER RABBLER RANGALE TRAFFIC BRAGGERY CANAILLE RAGABASH RIFFRAFF VARLETRY RASCALITY CLAMJAMFRY
(DISORDERLY —) HERD
RABBLE-ROUSER FIREBRAND DEMAGOG
RABID MAD RAGING FRANTIC FURIOUS RABIOUS RABITIC FRENZIED RAVENING VIRULENT
RABIES LYSSA MADNESS PIBLOKTO RAVENING
(PREF.) LYSSO RABI
RACCOON COON COATI GUARA TEJON AGUARA MAPACH OLINGO WASHER AGOUARA ARCTOID RATTOON RINGTAIL CRABEATER
(ANIMAL LIKE A —) OLINGO
(HIMALAYAN —) PANDA
RACCOON DOG TANUKI
RACE CAP CUP LOG ROD RUN BENT CONE DASH DRAG GEST HUMP KIND LINE NAME RAIS RAZE RING RINK TEAM TRAM BLOOD BREED BROOD BRUSH CASTE CHEVY CORSO DERBY FLESH HOUSE ISSUE PLATE PURSE RATCH REACH ROUTE SPEED STAKE STAMM STIRP STOCK BROOSE CHEVVY COURSE FAMILY NATION PEOPLE PHYLON RUNOFF SPRING STIRPS STRAIN STRIND BIOTYPE CENTURY CLAIMER CLASSIC HACKNEY HUNDRED KINDRED LINEAGE MATINEE NURSERY PROGENY PROSAPY RACEWAY REGATTA STADIUM FUTURITY HANDICAP MARATHON WALKOVER MOTOCROSS OFFSPRING ORIENTEERING
(— A HORSE) CAMPAIGN
(— AT WEDDING) BROOSE BROUZE
(— FOR BALL-BEARINGS) CONE
(— OF BARLEY) BENT
(— OF GODS) VANIR
(— OF PEOPLE) VANS AMALS VANIR HAZARA SAKAIS YADAVA BAMBUTE FIRBOLG GIANTRY NISHADA RASENNA REPHAIM AMALINGS
(— OF UNDERGROUND ELVES) DROW
(— OF WINDMILL) CURB
(FINAL —) RUNOFF NIGHTCAP
(HORSE —) AGON DERBY PLATE SPRINT MATINEE FUTURITY WALKOVER
(HUMAN —) MAN MANKIND SPECIES MORTALITY
(IMPROMPTU —) BRUSH
(JUMPING —) SCURRY
(LENTEN —S) TORPIDS
(LONG —) ENDURO
(MILL —) LADE
(MOTORCYCLE —) SCRAMBLE MOTOCROSS
(PRELIMINARY —) HEAT
(ROWING —) SCULLS REGATTA
(RUNNING —) MILE RELAY SPRINT HUNDRED HURDLES
(SHORT —) BICKER
(SHORT-DISTANCE —) DASH SCURRY SPRINT
(SKI —) SLALOM DAUERLAUF
(TIDAL —) ROOST
(PL.) FOURS
(PREF.) ETHN(O) GEN(O) PHYL(O)
RACECOURSE LIST OVAL PIST RING TURF EPSOM CAREER CIRCUS CURSUS DROMOS STADIE STRETCH GYMKHANA SPEEDWAY
(PREF.) DROM(O)
(SUFF.) DROME
RACEHORSE DOG PONY PACER RACER CHASER SLEEPER TROTTER BANGTAIL
(— THAT HAS NEVER WON) MAIDEN
(INFERIOR —) PLATER HAYBURNER
(2-YEAR OLD —) JUVENILE
(PL.) RUCK
RACEME STRIG PANICLE
RACEMOSE BOTRYOSE
RACER CRACK SNAKE RUNNER BICYCLIST CINDERMAN
RACETRACK OVAL DROMOS FURLONG AUTODROME
(— INFORMANT) SPIV TOUT TIPSTER
RACEWAY CANAL TRACK GROOVE CHANNEL FISHWAY
RACHEL POWDER
(FATHER OF —) LABAN
(HUSBAND OF —) JACOB
(SISTER OF —) LEAH
(SON OF —) JOSEPH BENJAMIN
RACHIS SPINE SPINDLE
(— OF HOP STROBILE) STRIG
RACHITIS RICKETS
RACIAL GENTILE GENTILIC PHYLETIC
RACING (— BET) WIN SHOW PLACE DOUBLE EXACTA PARLAY TRIPLE PERFECTA QUINELLA TRIFECTA
(AUTO — PROBLEM) SPINOUT
(HORSE —) TURF
(MOTORCYCLE —) MOTOCROSS
RACIST COLOR
RACK GIN RAK RAT TUB BINK BUCK CASE HACK HECK SHOG TACK AMBLE BRAKE DRIER DRYER FLAKE FRAME POKER THROW TOUSE TRAIN WRACK WRECK WRING CIRCLE CRATCH CUDGEL ENGINE NIPPER PULLEY TREBLE WRENCH AFFLICT AGONIZE PENRACK POTTARO TORMENT TORTURE BARBECUE EQUULEUS PINEBANK SAWHORSE
(— ATTACHED TO WAGON) SHELVING OUTRIGGER
(— FOR BARRELS) JIB
(— FOR CHINAWARE) FIDDLE
(— FOR DISHES) BINK
(— FOR FEEDING) HACK HAYRACK
(— FOR FODDER) HECK CRATCH
(— FOR PLATES) CREEL
(— FOR STORAGE) FLAKE
(— IN THRESHER) SHAKER
(DRYING —) CRIB TREBLE
(PLATE —) BINK
(WOODEN —) BUCAN
RACKED WRUNG TORTURED
RACKET BAT DIN GAME RORT BANDY MUSIC RAZOO CLAMOR CROSSE DRIVER HUBBUB HUSTLE RAQUET RATTLE BUSINESS REVELING STRAMASH
(PART OF —) CAP BUTT CORD GRIP HEAD HEEL TAPE YOKE CROWN FLAKE SHAFT HANDLE PALLET STRING THROAT BINDING SHOULDER THROATPIECE
(TENNIS —) SCUFE
RACKETEER HOOD HUSTLER GANGSTER
RACKETT CERVALET CERVELAT
RACKING FIERCE
RACKMAN TOPMAN
RACON BEACON
RACONTEUR STORYTELLER
RACQUET CROSSE GAZELLE
RACY GAMY LEAN SEXY JUICY SALTY SMART SPICY LIVELY RISQUE PIQUANT PUNGENT ZESTFUL SPIRITED MERACIOUS
RAD COOL MARV EAGER MARVY QUICK READY AFRAID ELATED FAROUT WAYOUT RADICAL
RADAR (— BEACON) RACON
(— NAVIGATION SYSTEM) LANAC
(— RECEPTION) ECHO
(— SYSTEM) OBOE
RADARSCOPE PPI HSCOPE
RADDAI (BROTHER OF —) DAVID
(FATHER OF —) JESSE
RADDLE PIT BEAT SCAR RAVEL RUDDLE THRASH SEPARATOR
RADHA (FOSTER SON OF —) KARNA
(HUSBAND OF —) ADHIRATHA
RADIAL RAY TIRE QUADRANT
(PREF.) RADIO
RADIANCE RAY GLOW LEAM GLARE GLEAM GLINT GLORY LIGHT SHINE LUSTER AUREOLA GLITTER SPLENDOR
RADIANT BEAMY SHEEN SHINY ABLAZE BRIGHT GOLDEN LUCENT SHEENY AURORAL BEAMFUL BEAMING FULGENT LAMBENT GLORIOUS LUSTROUS RELUCENT SPLENDID BRILLIANT
(— INTENSITY) J
(PREF.) STILPNO
RADIATE RAY BEAM POUR SHED SHINE EFFUSE SPREAD EFFULGE EMANATE ACTINOID
RADIATED PENCILED STELLATE
RADIATING DIADROM
RADIATION AURA LIGHT INFRARED
(— DOSAGE) REM REP REPP
(— UNIT) LANGLEY
(DEVICE TO GENERATE —) LASER
(ELECTROMAGNETIC —) PUMP
(SOURCE OF —) PULSAR
(UNIT OF —) RAD REM
RADIATOR HEATER EMANATOR
(— FLUID) COOLANT
(SET OF —S) STACK
RADICAL KEY SURD BASAL CRAZY GROUP RADIX ROUGE ULTRA CAPRYL HEROIC CAPITAL CAPROYL DRASTIC EXTREME FORWARD HERETIC JACOBIN LEFTIST

LEVELER LIBERAL PRIMARY CARDINAL LOCOFOCO
(CHEMICAL —) ACYL AMYL CARYL CETYL GROUP ACETYL ADENYL CAPRYL PHENYL PHYTYL HALOGEN LINALYL CARBAMYL QINNAMAL
(NOT —) FORMATIVE DERIVATIVE
(SUFF.) **(ACID —)** OYL
(BIVALENT —) YLENE
RADICALISM EXTREMISM JACOBINISM
RADICCHIO CHICORY CHICKORY
RADICEL ROOTLET
RADICLE (— THAT DEVELOPS IN GRAIN) COME
RADIENT ORIENT
RADIO AIR SET WIRELESS
(— OPERATOR) HAM DEEJAY SPARKS
(— PIONEER) TESLA
(— PROGRAM) TALKSHOW
(— SYSTEM) TBS
(— WAVE EMITTER) QUASAR
RADIOGRAM FLIMSY
RADIOGRAPH EXOGRAPH SKIAGRAM
RADIOISOTOPE TRACER
RADIO-WAVE (— EMITTER) PULSAR
RADISH RUNCH DAEKON DAIKON RIFART CADLOCK CRADLOCK CRUCIFER CROSSWEED
RADIUS RAYON SPOKE SWEEP THROW ADRADIUS
RADIX BASE ROOT ETYMON RADICLE
RADON NITON THORON ACTINON EXRADIO
RADULA RIBBON TONGUE
RAFF LOW IDLE SCUM SWEEP TRASH COMMON JUMBLE LUMBER RABBLE RAFFLE RAGTAG SNATCH RUBBISH
RAFFISH RAKISH TAWDRY RACKETY UNKEMPT
RAFFLE MOVE RAFF JUMBLE RABBLE REFUSE RUBBISH
RAFT COW CRIB MOKI BALSA BATCH FLOAT TABLE DINGEY DINGHY JANGAR MOKIHI PIPERY RADEAU JANGADA ZATTARE CATAMARAN
(— OF INVERTED POTS) GHARNAO
(— OF LOGS) BOOM CRIB
(— WITH CABIN) COW
(BAMBOO —) RAKIT
(FIRE —) CATAMARAN
(LUMBER —) BATCH
RAFT DOG RAKER
RAFTER HIP BALK BLAD FIRM SILE SOIL SPAR SPUR VIGA BAULK BLADE CABER RIDGE BOUGAR BULKER COUPLE CARLINE CHEVRON RAFFMAN SLEEPER
(— OF TURKEYS) FLOCK
RAFTY RAW DAMP FUSTY MUSTY RANCID
RAG JAG LAP TAT HAZE HOAX JAGG SAIL ANNOY CLOUT PRANK SCOLD SCRAP SHRED WIPER GIBBOL LIBBET RAGGLE TAGRAG TATTER FLITTER REMNANT TORMENT RAGSTONE STRAGGLE NEWSPAPER
(— GATHERER) TATTER
(— USED AS CANDLE) SLUT
(CURLING —) CRACKER
(FLAPPING —) WALLOP
(GLAD —S) GARB
(TARRED —) HARDS
(TARRED —S) HARDS HURDS
(PL.) DUDS CADDIS FITTERS RAGGERY FLITTERS
RAGAMUFFIN MUFFLIN BEGGARLY SHABROON TITMOUSE
RAGAU (FATHER OF —) PHALEC
RAGBAG CATCHALL
RAGE GO AWE FAD RAG WAX BAIT BATE BEEF FARE FOAM FRET FUFF FUME FUNK FUNX FURY GLOW GRIM HEAT PELT RAMP RASE RESE TAVE TEAR WOOD ANGER BRETH CHAFE CRAZE FUROR PADDY STORM TEAVE TEVEL VOGUE WRATH FRENZY FURORE PELTER TYAUVE BLUSTER FASHION MADNESS PASSION RUFFIAN TEMPEST INSANITY WOODNESS PADDYWACK
(BE IN A —) RANT
RAGFISH ICOSTEID
RAGGED DUDDY HARSH TATTY FRAYED JAGGED SCOURY UNEVEN SHAGRAG SHREDDY TATTERY SCRAGGLY SCRATCHY TATTERED
RAGGED ROBIN ROBIN CUCKOO
RAGGEE MAND RAGI MARUA MANDUA KORAKAN ELEUSINE
RAGGLE-TAGGLE MOTLEY
RAGING HOT GRIM WILD YOND RABID FIERCE FURIAL FERVENT MADDING PELTING VIOLENT FLAGRANT FURIBUND WRATHFUL
RAGOUT SALMI GOULASH HARICOT TERRINE SALPICON CHIPOLATA PULPATONE
(— OF GAME) SALMI SALMIS
RAGPICKER BUNTER RAGMAN TATTER
RAGWEED HAYWEED HOGWEED AMBROSIA IRONWEED KINGHEAD KINGWEED RICHWEED FRANSERIA
RAGWORT CUSHAG JACOBY BENWEED CAMMOCK SEGGROM LIFEROOT
RAHAM (FATHER OF —) SHEMA
(SON OF —) JORKOAM
RAID BUST RADE ROAD TALA FORAY HARRY PINCH REISE REIVE BODRAG CREACH FORAGE HARASS INROAD MOLEST PANYAR RAZZIA SORTIE BODRAGE BORDRAG CHAPPOW DESCENT JAYHAWK OUTFALL OUTRAKE OUTRIDE OUTROAD SPREATH COMMANDO SPOILING
(— ORCHARDS) SCRUMP SKRIMP SKRUMP
(AIR —) BLITZ
(BOMBING —) PRANG
(CATTLE —) SPREAGH SPREATH
(MAKE A — ON) BUST
(WARLIKE —) HERSHIP
RAIDER REDLEG BUSHWACK
(SEA —) VIKING
RAIL BAN BAR BULL COOT GIRD JEST KOKO LIST MOHO RANT RAVE SKID SORA TRAM WEKA WING CRAKE EASER FENCE GUARD PLATE RAVEL REILE SCOFF SCOLD SLENT STANG STANK STEEL SWEAR BANTER BEDWAY CALLET FENDER RUNNER SKITTY TIKLIN BIDCOCK BILCOCK COURLAN INVEIGH OARCOCK RACKWAY TOPRAIL BULLHEAD CANCELLI CORNBIRD PORTLAST TOADBACK VIGNOLES BRANDRETH BRANDRITH
(— AROUND A WELL) BRANDRETH
(— AT) JEST CURSE SCOFF RATTLE REVILE BETONGUE
(— OF BED) STOCK
(— OF RAILWAY SWITCH) TONGUE
(— ON GUN PLATFORM) TRINGLE
(— ON HAY VEHICLE) THRIPPLE
(— ON SHIP) FIFE
(ALTAR —) SEPTUM
(ARCHED —) HOOPSTICK
(CHAIR —) LEDGE
(FENCE —) RIDER
(GROOVED —) GULLY GULLEY
(PART OF —) BED TIE FROG JOINT SPIKE BALLAST SLEEPER CROSSTIE BASEPLATE FISHPLATE
(SHUNTING —) SWITCH
(PL.) RAILING CANCELLI RAILROAD
(PREF.) RALLI
RAIL CHAIR CARRIAGE
RAILING BAR SEPT GRATE RAVEL FENDER FIDDLE GITTER VEDIKA BARRIER GALLERY PARAPET CANCELLI ESPALIER HANDRAIL PARCLOSE TRAVERSE
RAILLERY GAFF HASH JEST JOKE RAGE CHAFF RALLY SPORT BANTER BLAGUE HOORAY HURRAH SATIRE TRIFLE MOCKERY BADINAGE DICACITY RABULOUS RIDICULE PERSIFLAGE
RAILROAD EL ROAD YARD STEEL COALER FEEDER GRANGER TRAMWAY CEINTURE ELEVATED
(— CAR) IDLER
(— FLARE) FUSEE
RAILROAD CHAIR SADDLE
RAILSPLITTER MAULER
RAILWAY ROAD TUBE COGWAY SUBWAY COGROAD INCLINE TRANVIA WIREWAY ASCENSOR PLATEWAY TRAMROAD FUNICULAR CREMAILLERE
(CARNIVAL —) ROLLERCOASTER
(KIND OF —) COG
(MOUNTAIN —) SWITCHBACK
(UNDERGROUND —) TUBE METRO SUBWAY
RAIMENT RAY GARB CLOTH ATTIRE APPAREL CLOTHES VESTURE CLOTHING DRESSING WARDROBE
(SPLENDID —) SHEEN
(SUFF.) ESTHES
RAIN WET ISLE MIST SMUR ULAN WEET BLASH STORM DELUGE MIZZLE SERENE SHOWER SOAKER DRIZZLE DOWNPOUR SPRINKLE
(— AND SNOW) SLEET
(— CHECK) TARP
(— HEAVILY) TEEM
(— LIGHTLY) SMUR SPIT SPRINKLE
(— OF SPARKS) SHOWER
(— SUDDENLY) PLUMP
(DRIZZLING —) DAG
(FINE —) MIST SEREIN SERENE
(FROZEN —) HAIL GRAUPEL
(GOD OF —) PARJANYA
(HARD —) SLEET
(HEAVY —) PASH SPOUT
(LIGHT —) SEREIN WEATHER HEATDROPS
(SHORT —) SHOWER
(SMALL —) ROKE
(SUDDEN —) SKEW
(WHIRLING —) SKIRL
(WIND-DRIVEN —) SCAT
(PL.) VARSHA
(PREF.) HYET(O) OMBRI OMBRO PLUVI(O)
RAINBIRD KOEL TOMFOOL STORMBIRD
(— OF JAMAICA) HUNTER
RAINBOW ARC BOW ARCH IRIS GAMUT METEOR SUNBOW ILLUSION
(AUTHOR OF —) LAWRENCE
(BROKEN —) WINDDOG WINDGALL
(CHARACTER IN —) TOM ANNA WILL ANTON LYDIA LENSKY URSULA BRANGWEN SKREBENSKY
(PREF.) IRID(O)
RAINBOW FISH GUPPY MAORI
RAINBOW RUNNER SKIPJACK SHOEMAKER
RAINBRINGER KACHINA
RAIN CLOUD NIMBUS
RAINCOAT MAC MACK MINO OILER PONCHO BURSATI OILSKIN SLICKER GOSSAMER MACINTOSH MACKINTOSH
RAINFALL PLOUT SKIFF SKIFT ONDING STEMPLOW
RAIN GAGE UDOMETER
RAINGEAR MAC
RAINMAKER SEEDER
RAINSPOUT RONE
RAINSTORM WET SPATE SCOWTHER
RAIN TREE SAMAN ZAMAN GUANGO ZAMANG ALGAROBA GENISARO MONKEYPOD
RAINY WET KICK FRESH JUICY RAYNE SAPPY WEETY BLASHY DRIPPY HYETAL PLUNGY SPONGY PLUVIAL PLUVINE SHOWERY WEEPING CLUTTERY PLUVIOUS SLATTERY
(— SEASON) VARSHA
RAISE END SET WIN BUMP BUOY GROW HAIN HEFT HIGH HIKE HOVE JACK KICK LEVY LIFT MAKE OVER REAR ROOF STIR TELD TOSS AREAR BLOCK BOOST BREED BUILD CAIRN CHOCK CRANE DIGHT ELATE ENSKY ERECT EXALT FORCE GREET HANCE HEAVE HEEZE HEVEN HOISE HOIST HORSE LEAVE MOUND MOUNT PRICK PUTUP RISER ROUSE VOICE ARRECT ASSIST BETTER CREATE DOUBLE EMBOSS EXHALE GATHER LEAVEN MUSTER NANTLE PREFER REMOVE RISING UPHOLD UPLIFT ADDRESS ADVANCE COLLECT ELEVATE ENHANCE LIGHTEN NOURISH

PRESENT PROMOTE RECRUIT UPSHOOT ANGELIZE HEIGHTEN INSPIRIT RELEVATE
(— A BUMP) CLOUR
(— ALOFT) SPHERE
(— A NAP) MOZE TEASE TEASEL TEAZLE
(— ANCHOR) CAT
(— A NESTLING) FLEDGE
(— A SIEGE) RISE RELIEVE
(— BRIDGE BID) JUMP
(— BY ASSESSMENT) LEVY
(— BY HAND) NOB
(— CLAMOR) BRAWL
(— IN PITCH) SHARP
(— OBJECTIONS) CAVIL BOGGLE
(— ONESELF) CHIN
(— TO A POWER) INVOLVE
(— TO HIGH DEGREE) STRAIN
(— TO 3RD POWER) CUBE
(— UP) BUOY AREAR ELATE EXALT EXTOL ELEVATE CIVILIZE
RAISED HIGH UPSET ARRECT HOGGED BULLATE EXALTED ELEVATED MOUNTANT UPLIFTED UPRAUGHT
(— A SEMITONE) SHARP
RAISIN FIG PASA PLUM LEXIA ZIBEB REYSON CURRANT SULTANA MUSCATEL
(PL.) SPICE
RAISING ATOLLENT
(— OF BELL) SALLY
(— OF CATTLE) GRAZING
(— OF SIEGE) REMOVE
(— OF TONE) ECBOLE
RAJ RULE REIGN
RAJA KING CHIEF RULER PRINCE PANGLIMA
RAJAB MONTH
RAJAH FABRIC
RAJMAHAL CREEPER JITI CHITI JETEE JEETEE
RAJPUT SAMMA SUMRA GAHRWAL RAZBOOCH
RAKE GO HOE RIP WAY COMB PATH RACK RAFF RAVE REAP ROAM ROUE ROVE RUCK BLOOD CLAUT PITCH SCOOP SCOUR SULKY TIGER PLUNGE RABBLE ROLLER SEARCH RANSACK SCRATCH LOTHARIO SCRAPPLE
(— GRAIN) GAVEL
(— UP IN ROWS) HACK
(— WITH GUNFIRE) SCOUR STRAFE ENFILADE
(— WITHOUT TEETH) LUTE
(BUCK —) SWEEP
(CRANBERRY —) SCOOP
(HORSE-DRAWN —) GLEANER
(OYSTER —) GLEANER
(PART OF —) BOW TANG TINE TOOTH HANDLE FERRULE
RAKEHELL RASCAL IMMORAL LIBERTINE
RAKER GUMMER ROOKER
RAKISH SLANG JAUNTY SPORTY WANTON DASHING CARELESS DEVILISH RANTEPOLE RANTIPOLE
RALE RATTLE SIFFLE SIBILUS RHONCHUS
RALLENTANDO DRAG RITARD
RALLY KID DRAG JOKE MOCK RELY STIR BULLY JOLLY QUEER BANTER DERIDE REVIVE COLLECT REBOUND CAMPOREE CLAMBAKE RIDICULE SPEAKING
(KIND OF —) PEP
(POLITICAL —) CLAMBAKE
RAM PUN TIP TUP BUCK CRAM PACK RAME STEM TEAP TOOP ARIES CHOKE CRASH POACH ROGER SLIDE BEETLE CHASER RANCID ROSTRUM BULLDOZER WETHERHOG WETHERTEG
(— OF WAR VESSEL) SPUR
(CASTRATED —) WETHER
(FATHER OF —) HEZRON JERAHMEEL
(SON OF —) AMMINADAB
(PREF.) CRIO
RAMA MELCHORA
(FATHER OF —) DASHARATHA
(MOTHER OF —) KAUSHALYA
(WIFE OF —) SITA
RAMADA ARBOR PORCH
RAMAGE WILD RAMMISH UNTAMED
RAMAGE HAWK BRANCHER
RAMBLE RAKE ROAM ROVE SKIR WALK JAUNT PROWL RANGE TRACE TROLL DODDER RUMBLE STROLL VAGARY WAMBLE WANDER ENRANGE EXCURSE SAUNTER SPROGUE TROUNCE FLAGARIE SCRAMBLE SPATIATE
(— AIMLESSLY) HAZE
(— IN TALK) DODDER
RAMBLING GAD RAISE VAGARY CURSORY DEVIOUS WINDING DESULTORY SCATTERED
RAMBUNCTIOUS RUDE WILD ROUGH UNRULY UNTAMED VIOLENT
RAMBUTAN SOAPWORT
RAMENTUM PALEA PALET SCALE SHAVING
RAMIE BAST HEMP RHEA ORTIGA
RAMIFICATION ARM RAMUS BRANCH OFFSHOOT OUTGROWTH
RAMIFY BRANCH SPRANGLE
RAMMAN ADAD ADDA ADDU
RAMMED EARTH PISE
RAMMEL TRASH RUMMLE RUBBISH
RAMMER TUP HEAD BOSER PUNNER WORMER
RAMONA (HUSBAND OF —) ALESSANDRO
RAMOSE CLADOSE BRANCHED
RAMOTH (FATHER OF —) BANI
RAMP ROB RUN BANK EXIT HOAX RAGE RANK SLIP CREEP STORM WAYON EASING FROLIC GARLIC WAYOFF WAYOUT FOOTPAD SLIPWAY SWINDLE GRADIENT
(AIRPORT —) JETWAY
RAMPAGE RAGE ROMP BINGE SPRAY SPREE STORM RANDAN
RAMPAGEOUS UNRULY GLARING RAMPANT VIOLENT
RAMPANT RANK PROFUSE SALIANT SALIENT SEGREANT
RAMPART BRAY LINE WALL AGGER ARGIN ABATIS VALLUM ABATTIS BULWARK DEFENSE PARAPET RAMPIER BARBICAN MUNITION BARRICADE
RAMPER LAMPREY
RAMPIKE SNAG RAUNPICK ROUNSPIK
RAMROD FORMAL GUNSTICK
RAMSHACKLE RUDE UNRULY RICKETY SHACKLY UNSTEADY
RAMSON RAMP GARLIC BUCKRAM
(PL.) RAMS
RAMSTAM RASH HEADLONG RECKLESS
RAN ARN
(HUSBAND OF —) AESIR
RANCEL SEARCH RANSACK
RANCH RUN FARM TEAR FINCA CHACRA OUTFIT SPREAD WRENCH STATION ESTANCIA HACIENDA
RANCHE NATURAL
RANCHER COWMAN HERDER GRAZIER SHEEPMAN CATTLEMAN
RANCID RAM RANK SOUR FROWY RAFTY RASTY REEST RESTY FROWZY ODIOUS ROTTEN MALODOROUS
RANCOR BILE GALL HATE SPITE ENMITY GRUDGE HATRED MALICE ACRIMONY
RANCOROUS ACRID VENOMOUS MALIGNANT ACRIMONIOUS
(NOT —) GOOD
RAND EDGE ROON RUND BORDER HIGHLAND
RANDAN SPREE RANTAN UPROAR RAMPAGE
RANDOM BANK FORCE LOOSE STRAY CASUAL CHANCE CHANCY AIMLESS RANDALL RENDOUN SHOTGUN UNAIMED VAGRANT ALEATORIC
(AT —) HOBNOB
(SOMEWHAT —) LONG
RANDY LEWD RUDE RUDAS SPREE BEGGAR VIRAGO LUSTFUL RIOTOUS CAROUSAL
RANGE KEN ROW ALLY AREA BEAT GATE GAUT GHAT LINE RAIK RAKE RANK ROAM ROVE SCUM SHOT TOUR WALK ALIGN BLANK CARRY FIELD GAMUT HILLS ORBIT REACH SCOPE SCOUR SHOOT SPACE STAND START STOVE SWEEP SWING VERGE COURSE DANGER EXTEND EXTENT LENGTH RADIUS RAMBLE SCOUTH SPHERE STROLL WANDER BOWSHOT COMPASS DEMESNE EARSHOT GUNSHOT HABITAT HORIZON PURVIEW CLASSIFY DIAPASON EARREACH EYEREACH LATITUDE PANORAMA
(— ABOUT) SCOUR
(— FOR FOOD) FORAGE
(— FOR GAME) QUARTER
(— OF ARROW) FLIGHT
(— OF BRICK) COURSE
(— OF BUILDINGS) CRESCENT
(— OF COLORS) PALETTE SPECTRUM
(— OF COLUMNS) PORTICO COLONNADE PERISTYLE
(— OF FOOD) FARE
(— OF FREQUENCIES) BAND SPECTRUM
(— OF GOVERNANCE) DOMAIN
(— OF GUN) CARRY RANDOM GUNSHOT
(— OF HEARING) EARSHOT
(— OF HILLS) GAUT GHAT HUMP TIER CHAIN GHAUT RIDGE SIERRA SAWBACK BACKBONE
(— OF MOVEMENT) TRAVEL
(— OF ORGANISM) BIOZONE
(— OF PASTURE) GANG
(— OF PLANKS) STRING
(— OF PRINTING TYPES) SERIES
(— OF SIGHT) KEN SCAN EYESHOT KENNING
(— OF TONES) KEY SCALE GRADATION
(— OF VISION) EYE SIGHT KENNING
(— OF WAVELENGTH) BAND
(— OVER) SWEEP
(— TOP) COOKTOP
(— WILDLY) RAMP
(ARCHERY —) BUTTS GREEN
(COOKING —) KITCHENER
(FREE —) SCOUTH SCOWTH LIBERTY
(MOUNTAIN —) CHAIN SERRA SIERRA
(PART OF —) CAP DOOR FLUE HEAD KNOB OVEN RACK TRIM VENT GRATE GUARD GUIDE HINGE PANEL BURNER GASKET HANDLE WINDOW BROILER CONTROL GRIDDLE DRIPPLATE BACKSPLASH
(SHOOTING —) MES GALLERY
(TEMPERATURE —) CONE
RANGE FINDER STADIA MEKOMETER
RANGE POLE PICKET
RANGER ROVER ROBBER MONTERO FIREWARD
RANGOON SHERRY
RANGY OPEN ROOMY SPACIOUS
RANK RAY ROW SEE DANK FOOT FORM FOXY GOLE GREE LINE RAMP RATE ROOM SEED SOUR STEP TIER CENSE CHOIR CLASS FETID FRANK FUSTY GRADE GROSS HONOR LEVEL MARCH ORDER PLACE QUIRE RANGE ROWTY SIEGE SPACE STALL STAND STATE TCHIN TRAIN AFFAIR AGREGE DEGREE ERMINE ESTATE ESTEEM FIGURE LAVISH PARAGE RATING SPHERE STATUS STRONG CALIBER CALLING DIGNITY DUKEDOM EARLDOM FOOTING GLARING RAMMISH RAMPANT STATION WORSHIP ABSOLUTE EARLSHIP ENSIGNCY EQUIPAGE FLAGRANT GENTRICE LADYSHIP PALPABLE STINKING MALODOROUS
(— AND FILE) RUCK RANGALE
(— OF GENTLEMEN) GENTRY GENTILITY
(— OF SERGEANT-AT-LAW) COIF COIFFE
(ACADEMIC —) AGREGE
(BOTTOMMOST —) CELLAR
(HIGH —) PURPLE DIGNITY EMINENCE
(LOWEST —) SCOURING
(MILITARY —) GRADE AIRMAN CORNET CHAOUSH
(NOBLE —) ADELAIDE

(ONE HIGHEST IN —) SUPREMO
(SAME —) KIND
(SOCIAL —) CLASS ESTATE HERALDRY POSITION
(SUFF.) CY HEAD HOOD
RANKLE FRET CHAFE FESTER INJURE RANCOR DESTROY INFLAME
RANSACK RIG DRAG RAKE RIPE SACK SEEK RIFLE DACKER RANCEL SEARCH PLUNDER RUMMAGE
RANSOM FINE RAME REDEEM RESCUE RESGAT EXPIATE
RANSTEAD TOADFLAX
RANT CAVE HUFF RAIL RAND MOUTH REVEL ROUSE SCOLD SPOUT STEVEN BOMBAST CAROUSE DECLAIM FROTHING RODOMONTADE
(— AND RAVE) FAUNCH
RANTAN NOISE
RANTING RANTISM TEARCAT
RANTIPOLE WILD CARROT RAKISH SEESAW ROMPING
RANULA CYST FROGTONGUE
(PREF.) BATRACH(O)
RANUNCULUS MOSS GOLLAND CROWFOOT HEDGEHOG BUTTERCUP
RAOULIA HAASTIA
RAP BOB CON BLOW CHAP GRAB KNAP TIRL TUNK WRAP BLAME CLICK CLINK FLIRT KNOCK STEAL TOUCH BARTER CHARGE HANDLE YANKER
RAPACIOUS CRUEL GREEDY TAKING RAVENING RAVENOUS
RAPACITY RAVEN RAVIN CUPIDITY EXTORTION VULTURISM
RAPE COLE ABUSE COLZA FORCE NAVET NAVEW TOUCH ATTACK CANOLA FELONY RAPEYE TURNIP ASSAULT DESPOIL NAVETTE OPPRESS OUTRAGE PLUNDER RAPTURE STUPRUM VIOLATE COLESEED COLEWORT DISHONOR STUPRATE SUPPRESS
RAPE OF THE LOCK (AUTHOR OF —) POPE
(CHARACTER IN —) ARIEL BETTY PETRE PLUME SPLEEN BELINDA UMBRIEL CLARISSA THALESTRIS
RAPESEED COLZA RAVISON
RAPHA (FATHER OF —) BINEA
RAPHIA JUPATI
RAPHU (SON OF —) PALTI
RAPHUS DIDUS
RAPID GAY FAST CHUTE HASTY MOSSO QUICK ROUND SAULT SHARP SHOOT SHUTE TOSTO WINGY RIFFLE SPEEDY WINGED CURSIVE SCHNELL SKELPIN STICKLE TANTIVY SLAPPING SPEEDFUL OVERNIGHT
(—S IN RIVER) SAULT DALLES RIFFLE STICKLE CATARACT
(MORE —) STRETTO
(PREF.) TACHY
RAPIDITY HASTE SPEED RADEUR CELERITY VELOCITY
RAPIDLY APACE CHEAP FLEETLY HASTILY SPEEDILY QUICKFOOT
RAPIER TUCK TUKE BILBO ESTOC SHARP STOCK VERDUN TOASTER
RAPINE FORCE RAVIN PILLAGE PLUNDER VIOLENCE
RAPINI BROCCOLI
RAPPACCINI (DAUGHTER OF —) BEATRICE
RAPPAREE ROBBER CREAGHT VAGABOND
RAPPEE SNUFF
RAPPEL ABSEIL
RAPPORT ACCORD HARMONY RELATION AGREEMENT
(ESTABLISH —) GROK
RAPSCALLION ROGUE RASCAL VILLAIN HOSEBIRD VAGABOND
RAPT LOST WRAP TENSE INTENT RAVISH TRANCE CARRIED ENGAGED RAPTURE ABDUCTED ABSORBED ECSTATIC
RAPTORES RAPACES
RAPTURE JOY BLISS DELIGHT ECSTASY PAROXYSM RHAPSODY
RAPTUROUS ECSTATIC RHAPSODIC
RARA AVIS PHENIX RARITY WONDER PHOENIX
RARE FINE REAL SELD THIN ALONE EARLY GREAT ANTRIN CHOICE GEASON INCONY SCARCE SEENIL SELDOM SINDLE SPARSE SUBTLE SULLEN UNIQUE ANTERIN CURIOUS TENUOUS UNUSUAL CRITICAL SELDSEEN SINGULAR UNCOMMON RECHERCHE
(PREF.) AREO MANO SPAN(I)(O)
RAREFACTION POROSIS
RAREFIED HIGH THIN SUBTILE ABSTRUSE AETHERED ESOTERIC
RAREFY THIN DILUTE EXTENUATE SUBTILIZE
RARELY SELDEN SELDOM
RARENESS RARITY TENUITY SCARCITY
RARITY SWAN CURIO RELIC RARIETY TENUITY RARENESS
(PL.) CURIOSA
RASCAL BOY CAD DOG IMP LOW RAP BASE DUCK FILE KITE LOON MEAN SHAG SMAK CATSO FILTH GANEF GIPSY KNAVE ROGUE SCAMP SHELM SLAVE SMAIK THIEF VIPER ABLACH BEGGAR BRIBER BUDZAT BUGGER COQUIN HARLOT LIMMER RABBLE RAGGIL RIBALD SCHELM SORROW TINKER BLEEDER CAMOOCH CULLION GLUTTON HALLION HESSIAN NEBULON PANURGE PEASANT RAPTRIL SHELLUM SKEEZIX SKELLUM VILLAIN BEZONIAN BLIGHTER HOSEBIRD LIDDERON PALLIARD PICAROON RAKEHELL RUBIATOR SCALAWAG SPALPEEN TAISTREL VAGABOND WIDDIFOW SCAPEGRACE SCARAMOUCH RAPSCALLION SCARAMOUCHE
RASCALITY FOIST RABBLE KNAVERY ROGUING RASCALRY
RASCALLY BASE MEAN ROOKY ARRANT GALLUS LIMMER GALLOWS KNAVISH RAGGILY SHAGRAG WIDDIFOW
RASE PULL RAIS RAZE ERASE PLUCK INCISE SNATCH
RASH ID CUT BRASH HARDY HASTY HEADY SLASH SLICE DARING SUDDEN UNWARY URGENT BULRUSH HOTSPUR RABBISH RAMSTAM ROSEOLA BLIZZARD CARELESS ERUPTION EXANTHEM HEADLONG HEEDLESS MADBRAIN OVERSEEN PRESSING RECKLESS TEMEROUS IMPETUOUS IMPULSIVE
(SUFF.) ANTHEMA
(SKIN —) ID IDE
RASHER SLICE COLLOP TRIFLE COLOPPE
RASHLY HEADILY HEADLONG
RASHNESS RAGE RESE HASTE ACRISY TEMERITY HEADINESS
RASKOLNIK POPOVETS
RASP RUB FILE RAPE ERUCT GRATE TOOTH RAPEYE RUBBER RUGINE RIFFLER DENTICLE
(SHOEMAKER'S —) FLOAT
RASPBERRY AKPEK BAZOO MOLKA AVARIN RASPIS PLUMBOG ARNBERRY BLACKCAP BOGBERRY CUTHBERT MULBERRY RESPASSE ROSACEAN SALMONBERRY
RASPING HARSH ROUGH STOOR STOUR HOARSE RASION RAZZLY GRATING RAUCOUS GUTTERAL
(PL.) SCOBS
RASPY HARSH GRATING SCREAKY SCRABBLY
RASSE CIVET WEASEL
RASSELAS (AUTHOR OF —) JOHNSON
(CHARACTER IN —) IMLAC PEKUAH NEKAYAH RASSELAS
(MENTOR OF —) IMLAC
(SISTER OF —) NEKAYAH
RAT BUCK DAMN DRAT FINK HEEL NOKI ROTN SCAB VOLE KIORE LOUSE METAD RATON SELVA ZEMMI ZEMNI CRABER MURINE RODENT ROTTAN SLEPEZ VERMIN YUNGAS CUSHION CONFOUND INFORMER MYOMORPH SQUEALER
(— ON) SING
(INDIAN —) KOK
RATAPLAN RATTAN RATTLE
RATCH RASH REND ROCH SPOT NOTCH STREAK RATCHET STRETCH
RATCHET DOG PAWL CLICK DETENT ROCHET
RAT CHINCHILLA ABROCOME
RATE LAY RAG SET CESS CHOP DEEM EARN GAIT GIVE HAND KIND RANK RATA ABUSE CULET CURVE PRIZE RATIO REBUT SCOLD STENT STYLE VALUE ZAKAT ASSIZE GALLOP ACCOUNT BESHREW CARTAGE DESERVE FASHION MILLAGE REPROVE CLASSIFY ESTIMATE QUANTIFY
(— HIGHLY) EXALT PRICE
(— OF ASCENT) GRADE
(— OF CHANGE) GRADIENT
(— OF DRAINAGE) FREENESS
(— OF EXCHANGE) BATTA
(— OF FLOW) FLUX DISCHARGE
(— OF INTEREST) COUPON DISCOUNT
(— OF MOTION) BAT SPEED
(— OF MOVEMENT) PACE TEMPO
(— OF RECKONING) FOOT
(— OF SPEED) BAT AGOGE
(— OF TAX) CENSE
(— OF TRANSFER) FLUX
(— OF TUITION) CULET
(— SCHEDULE) TARIFF
(AT ANY —) HURE
(BIRTH —) NATALITY
RATE BOOK STREET
RATEL BADGER BURIER
RATH CAR HILL REUT RUTH EARLY MOUND QUICK REUTE SWIFT BETIMES CHARIOT YOUTHFUL
RATHER Y BUT GEY ATAD LIKE SOON LOURD QUITE ASTITE ATOUCH BEFORE FAIRLY HELDER KINDLY PRETTY RUTHER SEEMLY SORTOF TIDDER TITTER EARLIER INSTEAD MIDDLING SOMEWHAT
(— THAN) ERE BEFORE
RATIFICATION AMEN RATE SANCTION
RATIFY AMEN PASS SEAL SIGN VISA ENSEAL FASTEN OBSIGN APPROVE CONFIRM SCEPTER CANONIZE ROBORATE SANCTION VALIDATE
RATING RANK CENSE CLASS GRADE WRITER STANDING
RATIO Q PI GAIN RATE SINE SLIP INDEX RESON SETUP SHEAR ASPECT CAMBER DECADE QUOTUM REASON REYSON SECANT AVERAGE PORTION CONTRAST SOLIDITY MULTIPLIER PROPORTION
RATIOCINATION MACH LOGIC THOUGHT REASONING
RATION DOLE ALLOT RATIO ALLOCATE
(— OF BREAD) TOMMY
(ANIMAL —) CHOW
(EXTRA —S) BUCKSHEE
(HOG —) SWILL
(PL.) FOOD BOUCH ETAPE COMMON
RATIONAL SANE LUCID SOBER LOGICAL REASONAL SENSIBLE THINKING
RATIONALISM (GERMAN —) NEOLOGY
RATIONALIZE THOB EXPLAIN
RATITE EMU MOA EMEU KIWI RHEA OSTRICH STRUTHIAN
RAT KANGAROO TUNGO POTOROO SQUEAKER
RATOON SHOOT SPROUT SUCKER
RATTAIL MULE ARREST GRENADIER
RATTAN CANE SEGA ROTAN BEJUCO ROTANG SWITCH RATTOON
RATTLE DIN BIRL BURL REEL RICK TIRL CHINK CLACK CROTAL GRAGER HENPEN HURTLE MARACA RACKLE RICKLE RIFFLE ROTTLE RUCKLE RUTTLE CHACKLE CLACKER CLAPPER CLATTER CLICKET CREAKER GNATTER GROGGER SHATTER SISTRUM

SKELLAT CAIXINHA CHOCALHO COWWHEAT NOISEMAKER
(CRIER'S —) CLAPPER
(IRON —) SKELLAT SKILLET
(PREF.) CROTALI
(SUFF.) CROTIC
RATTLEBRAINED MADCAP
RATTLER LIE ROMBLE RUMBLER
RATTLESNAKE BELLTAIL CASCABEL CASCAVEL CROTALID MASSASAUGA SIDEWINDER
(— PLANTAIN) NETLEAF RATSBANE
RATTLESNAKE ROOT BUGBANE JOYLEAF
RATTLETRAP HEAP GEWGAW JUNKER TRIFLE RICKETY
RATTLING REEL BRISK HUSKY SLAPPING SPLENDID CREPITANT
RATTY NASTY SHABBY UNKEMPT WORTHLESS
RATWA MUNTJAC
RAUCOUS LOUD HARSH COARSE HOARSE SQUAWKY STRIDENT
RAUN ROE ROWN SPAWN
RAUPO CATTAIL
RAVAGE EAT PREY RIOT RUIN SACK FORAY HARRY HAVOC SPOIL WASTE FORAGE DESPOIL DESTROY OVERRUN PILLAGE PLUNDER DEFLOWER DESOLATE POPULATE SPOLIATE
RAVANA (SISTER OF —) SHURPANAKHA
RAVE MAD RAGE RAND WOOD AWEDE BLURB CRUSH RATHE ROUSE STORM TAVER DELIRE TAIVER WANDER
RAVEL FAG RUN FRAY FRET UNDO REYLE SNARL EVENER LADDER RADDLE RUNNER SLOUGH TANGLE CONFUSE INVOLVE PERPLEX RAILING UNWEAVE
RAVELIN RABLIN OUTWORK DEMILUNE
RAVELING LINT
RAVEN DARK BLACK CRAKE RALPH CORBEL CORBIE CORBIN FORAGE RAVINE WAYBIRD
(BRIGHT —) BERTRAM
(SUFF.) CORAX
RAVENING CRUEL RABIES
RAVENOUS GREEDY LUPINE TOOTHY WOLFISH RAPACIOUS VORACIOUS
RAVINE DEN GAP GUT LIN DELL DRAW GILL GULL KHOR KHUD LINN LLYN SIKE WADI BREAK BUNNY CHASM CHINE CLOVE COULE DONGA FLUME GHYLL GLACK GORGE GOYAL GOYLE GRIFF GRIKE GULCH GULLY HEUCH KLOOF NULLA SLADE SLAKE STRID ARROYO CLEUCH CLOUGH COULEE DIMBLE DINGLE DUMBLE GULLET GULLEY HOLLOW NULLAH RAMBLA SHEUGH STRAIT BARRANCA QUEBRADA
RAVING RAVERY DELIRANT FRENZIED DELIRIOUS
RAVISH ROB RAPE ABUSE CHARM FORCE HARRY SPOIL ABDUCT ATTACK DEFILE AFFORCE CORRUPT DELIGHT ENFORCE OPPRESS OUTRAGE OVERJOY PLUNDER POLLUTE VIOLATE VITIATE DEFLOWER ENTRANCE STUPRATE SUPPRESS UNMAIDEN
RAVISHER RAPTER RAVENER
RAVISHMENT ECSTASY RAPTURE TRANSPORT
RAW RA RED ROW BRUT LASH REAR RUDE BLEAK CHILL CRUDE FRESH GREEN HARSH NAKED RAFTY SHARP WERSH BITTER CALLOW COARSE CUTCHA KUTCHA UNRIPE VULGAR WAIRSH NATURAL NOUVEAU UNBOUND VERDANT WEARISH WEERISH IMMATURE RAWBONED UNCOOKED UNEDITED VISCERAL
(— AND COLD) CRIMPY
(PREF.) OMO
RAWBONED RAW BONY LEAN GAUNT LANKY SCRAG SCRAWNY
(— PERSON) SCRAG
RAWHIDE WHIP WHANG COWHIDE COWSKIN GREENHIDE PARFLECHE
RAWNESS CRUDITY
RAY BEAM BETA DORN SOIL WIRE ALPHA BRAND DRESS EQUIP FLAIR FLAKE FLATH GLEAM GLEED MANTA ORDER RAYON ROKER SKATE BATOID CHUCHO OBISPO RADIAL RADIUS RAIOID SEPHEN STREAM TRYGON VISUAL BATFISH COWFISH DEWBEAM DRILVIS FIDDLER HOMELYN PLACOID RAIMENT TORPEDO WAIREPO BRACHIUM MOONBEAM NUMBFISH PLOWFISH PYLSTERT STINGRAY STINGAREE
(— OF LIGHT) GLINT SPEAR GLANCE SUNRAY SUNBEAM
(— OF STARFISH) ARM
(FEMALE —) MAID
(FIN —) SPINE
(KIND OF —) GAMMA
(WITHOUT —S) ABACTINAL
(PREF.) BATO
(ELECTRIC —) NARC(O)
RAYED
(PREF.) ACTIN(IO)(O)
(SUFF.) ACT(INE)
(— WITH IMPAIRMENT) LEXIA
RAYON BEAM RADIUS DUCHESS
RAZE CUT FLAT RUIN ARASE ERASE LEVEL STREW ARRACE EFFACE SCRAPE SLIGHT UNPILE DESTROY SCRATCH SUBVERT UNBUILD DEMOLISH
RAZOR SHIV TUSK MUSSEL RASOIR SHAVER RATTLER SLASHER CUTTHROAT
(PREF.) XYR(O)
RAZORBACK STATE ARKANSAS
RAZORBILL MURRE
RAZOR-BILLED AUK FALK TINK MURRE NODDY SCOOT SCOUT SKOOT TINKER SKIMMER WILLOCK ROCKBIRD
RAZOR CLAM PIROT RASOR SOLEN SPOUT RASOIR
RAZZ BOO KID PAN HARRY TEASE CHIACK HECKLE NEEDLE RIDICULE RASPBERRY
RAZZIA RAID FORAY INCURSION
RAZZING RAZOO
RAZZLE-DAZZLE SHOWBIZ
RE RAY ANENT ACTION MATTER REGARDING
REACH GO GET HIT RAX RUN WIN BEAT COME FIND GAIN HAWK HENT MAKE PUSH REEK REIK RYKE SHOT SORT SPAN SPIT TEND BRACE CROSS FETCH GRASP PERCH RANGE RETCH TOUCH ADVENE ARRIVE ATTAIN DANGER EXTEND FATHOM LENGTH OBTAIN SNATCH STREEK STRIKE ACHIEVE COMPASS CONTACT GUNSHOT OVERGET POSSESS RECOVER STRETCH
(— ACROSS) SPAN OVERSTRIDE
(— AN END) STAY
(— BEYOND) OVERREACH
(— BY EFFORT) ATTAIN
(— BY FIGURING) STRIKE
(— FORTH) EXTEND
(— GOAL) HAIL
(— HIGHER) OUTTOP
(— IN TOTAL) RUNTO
(— OF SIGHT) EYESHOT
(— OF WATER) LODE
(— OUT) UTTER SPREAD STRETCH
(— TO) LINE
(— TOTAL) AMOUNT
(— UNDERSTANDING) AGREE
(— WITH END) ABUT
(EXTREME —) PITCH STRETCH
(TRY TO —) ASPIRE
(ULTIMATE —) PITCH
REACHER INGIVER
REACT ACT BUCK BEHAVE RETROACT
REACTION BELT BUZZ KAHN WOHL START WIDAL FAVISM RECOIL BLOWOFF EMOTION FEELING SETBACK BACKLASH BACKWASH EXCHANGE GUARDING KICKBACK RESPONSE RECEPTION COUNTERBUFF
(— TIME) LATENCY
(ADVERSE —) BACKLASH
(ANGRY —) RISE
(DELAYED —) DOUBLETAKE
(KIND OF —) FEULGEN
(NUCLEAR —) SPALLATION
(VIOLENT —) SONG
REACTIONARY WHITE BOURBON BACKWARD
REACTIVATED AWAKE ACTIVE
REACTIVATOR ACTIFIER
REACTOR PILE CHOKER FURNACE INDUCTOR
(SHUTDOWN OF —) SCRAM
READ GO CON KRI QRI SEE CALL KERE QERI TURN CHOKE JUDGE SOLVE WRITE PERUSE RELATE FORESEE LEARNED LECTION PREDICT ABOMASUM DECIPHER FORETELL INDICATE OVERLOOK
(— ALOUD) LINE DEACON
(— BAR CODES) SCAN
(— HERE AND THERE) BROWSE
(— MECHANICALLY) RETINIZE
(— OF) SEE
(— OFF) DICTATE
(— PROOF) HORSE
(— RAPIDLY) DIP SCAN SKIM GOBBLE
(— SLOWLY) SPELL
(— SYSTEMATICALLY) FREQUENT
(— WITH PROFOUND ATTENTION) PORE STUDY
READER PURSE DIPPER LECTOR LISTER MAFTIR GRANTHI PISTLER DEVOURER
(CHILD'S —) TENPENNY
(CHURCH —) LECTOR ANAGNOST
(PUBLIC —) PRELECTOR
(VORACIOUS —) BIBLIOPHAGIST
(PL.) FOLLOWING
READILY PAT LIEF YERN APTLY PREST YERNE EASILY GAINLY PROBABLY SPEEDILY
READINESS ART EASE GIFT PRESS SKILL BELIEF GRAITH ADDRESS FLUENCY FREEDOM ALACRITY FACILITY GOODWILL
(— TO LEARN) APTITUDE
(IN —) APOISE AGAINST
READING KRI QRE QRI KERE KERI QERI KTHIB KETHIB LESSON LECTION LECTURE PERUSAL SETTING CORALENE
(— ANTIPHONALLY) ALTERNATION
(DOCTOR'S —) EEG EKG
(HEAVY —) TOME
(MARGINAL —) KRI
(PL.) PROCINCT
READING DESK AMBO LECTERN
READING ROOM ATHENEUM
READJUST MEND ADVANCE
(— TYPE) OVERRUN
READY UP APT BUN FIT RAD YAP BAAN BAIN BOON BOUN BOWN FREE GIRT GLIB GNIB RIFE RIPE TALL YARE APERT EAGER FRACK HANDY HAPPY ONTAP PREDY PREST PRIME QUICK SWIFT THERE TIGHT ADROIT APPERT FACILE GRAITH HEARTY PROMPT PREPARE PRESENT RENABLE WILLING CHEERFUL DEXTROUS HANDSOME PREGNANT PREPARED PROVIDED SKILLFUL
(— A COMPUTER) BOOT
(— FOR ACTION) ARM EXPEDITE
(— TO GO) ALLSET
(— WITH WORDS) FLUENT
(MAKE —) PREP
(NOT —) SET BOUND GROOM FORWARD DISPOSED IMPROMPT INCLINED
READY-MADE SALE STORE BOUGHT
REAGENT ETCHANT REACTOR TITRANT ALTERANT REACTIVE NINHYDRIN
REAIA (FATHER OF —) MICAH
REAL BODY FAIR GOOD LEAL LEVY PURE RIAL TRUE VERY VRAI PAKKA PUCKA PUKKA RIGHT ROYAL SOLID SOOTH ACTUAL DINKUM ENTIRE HONEST THINGY CORDIAL GENUINE GRADELY SINCERE THINGAL CONCRETE DEFINITE EXISTENT GRAITHLY POSITIVE THINGISH UNFEIGNED VERITABLE
(EXTERNALLY —) TANGIBLE
(HALF —) PICAYUNE

(NOT —) FACTITIOUS INSUBSTANTIAL
(1-8TH —) TLAC TLACO
REALGAR ARSENIC ROSAKER ZARNICH SANDARAC
REALISM VERITE VERITY REALITY LITERALISM NATURALISM
REALISTIC HARD SOBER VIVID EARTHLY LIFELIKE PROBABLE
REALITY FEAT TRUE BEING SOOTH THING TRUTH ACTUAL DASEIN EFFECT VERITY EARNEST SUBJECT IDENTITY OVERSOUL POSITIVE REALNESS TRUENESS
(LIMITED —) SOMEWHAT
(ULTIMATE —) GOD SOURCE DIVINITY SUBSTANCE
(PL.) REALIA
REALIZATION PASS SENSE CRUSHER FRUITION AWAKENING
REALIZE GET EARN GAIN KNOW FETCH LEARN SENSE EFFECT FULFIL ACQUIRE CONCEIVE RECOGNIZE
(— BEFOREHAND) ANTICIPATE
REALIZED BODILY
(FULLY —) COMPLETE
REALLY ARU WIS ARAH HALF JUST ARRAH TRULY WISHA FINELY INDEED SIMPLY SURELY VERILY ACTUALLY
(NOT —) ILL ALMOST
REALM AREA LAND SOIL BOURN CLIME RANGE REIGN REWME RICHE BOURNE CIRCLE DEMAIN EMPIRE HEAVEN REALTY REGION SPHERE DEMESNE GAELDOM KINGDOM NOTALIA ROYALME TERRENE CLUBLAND DEVILDOM DOMINION ELDORADO GHOSTDOM GIPSYDOM NOTOGAEA
(— OF DARKNESS) PO
(— OF FABULOUS RICHNESS) ELDORADO
(— OF THOR) THRUTHHEIM THRUTHVANG
(MARINE —) NOTALIA TROPICALIA
(VISIONARY —) CLOUDLAND
(ZOOLOGICAL —) NOTOGAEA
(SUFF.) DOM
(— OF ANIMAL LIFE) ALIA
REALTY FEALTY REAUTE ROYALTY
REAM FOAM RIME SEED SKIM CHEAT CREAM FROTH FRAISE RHYMER STRETCH
(PL.) INSIDES OUTSIDES
REAMER BUR BURR SPUD DRIFT RIMER BROACH CHERRY FRAISE RANCER RHYMER RIMMER WIDENER
REANIMATE WAKE RENEW REVIVE RECREATE
REANIMATED AWAKE
REAP BAG CUT REP CROP RIPE GLEAN SHEAR GARNER GATHER SICKLE HARVEST
REAPER LORD COCKER TASKER WINNER CRADLER SHEARER SICKLER
(GRIM —) DEATH
REAPING HOOK SICKLE TWIBIL CROTCHET
REAPPEARANCE RENTREE EMERSION
REAR AFT BACK BUNT HIND HINT JUMP LIFT STEN TOSS BREED BUILD CARVE ERECT JUNCH STEND ACHTER AROUSE CRADLE FOSTER NURSLE SUCKLE APPREAR ARRIERE EDUCATE ELEVATE NOURISH NURTURE UPBRING BUTTOCKS HINDMOST REARWARD
(— CAREFULLY) TIDDLE
(NEARER THE —) AFTER
(TO THE —) BACK BEHIND
(TO THE — OF) ABAFT
REARED (— BY HAND) CADE
(DELICATELY —) SOYLED
REARHORSE MANTIS
REARING CABRE FRESNE PESADE FORCENE RAMPANT
(— UP) STEND
REARRANGE DO ALTER AMEND ADJUST JIGGER REORDER READJUST
REARRANGEMENT WAGNER DIAGENESIS
REARWARD AFT BACKWARD
REASON PEG WAY HOTI NOUS REDE SAKE TALK ARGUE CAUSE COLOR COUNT LOGOS PROOF RATIO SCORE SENSE SKILL THING THINK TOPIC EXCUSE GROUND MANNER MATTER MOTION NOESIS ACCOUNT PREMISE QUARREL SUBJECT TUITION ARGUMENT ENCHESON LOGICIZE VERNUNFT
(— AGAINST) OBJECTION
(— FALSELY) PARALOGIZE
(— FOR PRIDE) BOAST
(LACKING —) INEPT
(SUFFICIENT —) GROUND
(PREF.) RATI
REASONABLE FAIR JUST SANE SOBER NATURAL SKILFUL FEASIBLE MODERATE RATIONAL SENSIBLE
REASONABLENESS EPIKY EPIKIKA FITNESS FAIRNESS SOBRIETY
REASONABLY SOON
REASONER (FALLACIOUS —) SOPHIST
REASONING LOGIC THOUGHT ERGOTISM RATIONAL
(CLUMSY —) ARGAL
(DEDUCTIVE —) SYLLOGISM
(FALLACIOUS —) CIRCLE SOPHISTRY PARALOGISM
REASSEMBLE RELY
REASSEMBLY RALLY
REASSUME REVOKE REPRISE
REAVE ROB REFE SEIZE SPLIT REMOVE DESPOIL PILLAGE PLUNDER UNRAVEL
REB RABBI REBEL MISTER
REBAB GUSLE
REBATE BLUNT CHECK LESSEN REFUND RIBBET DIMINISH DISCOUNT DRAWBACK KICKBACK
REBEC LYRE SAROD RIBIBE RUBIBLE
REBECCA (AUTHOR OF —) DUMAURIER
(CHARACTER IN —) JACK BAKER FRANK GILES MAXIM FAVELL JULYAN CRAWLEY DANVERS BEATRICE DEWINTER
(FATHER OF —) ISAAC
REBEKAH (BROTHER OF —) LABAN
(FATHER OF —) BETHUEL
(HUSBAND OF —) ISAAC
(SON OF —) ESAU JACOB
REBEL REB DEFY KICK RISE TURN ARISE BRAND FAUVE ANARCH CROPPY MUTINE REVOLT FRONDEUR SOLECIST MALCONTENT
(— IN ART) FAUVE
(RELIGIOUS —) APOSTATE
(PL.) REBELDOM
REBELLION MUTINY PUTSCH REVOLT MISRULE UPRISING
REBELLIOUS RUSTY ANARCHIC MUTINOUS AUDACIOUS INSURGENT
REBIRTH REVIVAL
(SPIRITUAL —) REGENERATION
REBOANT AROAR
REBORN REDIVIVUS
REBOUND DAP HOP HANG KISS STOT CANON CAROM STITE BOUNCE CANNON CARROM RECOIL RESILE RESULT BRICOLE REDOUND RICOCHET SNAPBACK
(— ERRATICALLY) KICK
REBOUND CLIP RETAINER
REBUFF NO SLAP SNIB SNUB CHECK FLING NOSER REPEL DEFEAT DENIAL REBUKE REBUTE REFUTE REPULSE SETDOWN
REBUILD MEND
REBUKE NIP WIG BAWL RATE REDD SNEB SNIB SNUB TRIM BARGE BLAME CHECK CHIDE DRESS SAUCE SCOLD SNAPE SNEAP TOUCH DIRDUM GANSEL LESSON PULLUP RATING RATTLE REHETE REMORD THREAP CENSURE CHIDING CORRECT HOTFOOT LECTURE REPROOF REPROVE SARCASM TICKOFF BLESSING BUSINESS CHASTISE KEELHAUL REPROACH SCORCHER THREAPEN UNDERNIM CASTIGATE
REBUS BADGE ENIGMA PUZZLE RIDDLE
REBUT REPEL RECOIL REFUTE REPULSE RETREAT DISPROVE
RECALCITRANT UNRULY RENITENT OBSTINATE RESISTANT
RECALL CITE BRING UNSAY REMAND REMIND RETURN REVOKE UNLOOK BETHINK RECLAIM RETRACE RETRACT REVIVAL UNSHOUT REMEMBER WITHCALL WITHDRAW REPRODUCE
(— FONDLY) CHERISH
(— FROM BANISHMENT) REPEAL
(— OF PURSUERS) RETREAT
RECANT UNSAY ABJURE REVOKE UNSING DISAVOW RETRACT SWALLOW PALINODE RENOUNCE
RECANTATION PALINODE
RECAPITULATE SUM UNITE RECITE REPEAT RECOUNT RESTATE REHEARSE REITERATE SUMMARIZE
RECAPITULATION EPANODOS
RECAPTURE RETAKE RECOVER REPRISAL
RECASTING (— OF LITERARY WORK) RIFACIMENTO
RECEDE DIE EBB BACK FADE STEP VARY RECUR DEPART DIFFER RETIRE SHRINK DECLINE DIGRESS RETREAT CONTRACT DIMINISH ELONGATE WITHDRAW
RECEIPT CHIT RECU RESET APOCHA BINDER RECIPE WARRANT
(PL.) GATE TAKE SALES INCOME ENTRADA
RECEIPTS GATE TAKE
RECEIVE GET BEAR FALL GAIN HAVE HOLD TAKE ADMIT AFONG CATCH GREET GUEST LATCH RESET ACCEPT ASSUME BORROW DERIVE GATHER HARBOR RECULE BELIEVE CONTAIN EMBRACE INHERIT SUSTAIN UNDERFO PERCEIVE
(— A CRIMINAL) RESET
(— A DEGREE) GRADUATE
(— AS GUEST) FANG HOST VANG GREET
(— AS MEMBER) INCEPT
(— AS REWARD) REAP
(— FROM LOTTERY) DRAW
(— INTO RELIGIOUS ORDER) PROFESS
(— PAYMENT) COLLECT
(— SHEETS) FLY
(— STOLEN GOODS) RESET
(— WITH KINDNESS) WELCOME
(— WITH PLEASURE) GRATIFY
(PREF.) RECIPIO
RECEIVER DONEE FENCE PHONE PERNOR SINDICO CYMAPHEN DONATARY REHEATER
(— IN BANKRUPTCY) SINDICO
(— OF INCOME) PERNOR
(— OF PROPERTY) ALIENEE
(— OF STOLEN GOODS) LOCK FENCE
(RADIO —) SET
(SECRET —) TAP
(TELEGRAPH —) INKER INKWRITER
(TELEPHONE —) PHONE CYMAPHEN
RECEIVING PERNANCY
RECENSION REVIEW SURVEY CENSURE CRITIQUE
RECENT HOT NEW LATE PUNY ENDER FRESH GREEN HOURLY LATELY LATTER MODERN CURRENT HOLOCENE NEOTERIC
(MOST —) LAST
(PREF.) CAEN(O) CEN(O) NE(O)
(SUFF.) CENE
RECENTLY ANEW JUST LATE NEWLY LASTLY LATELY FRESHLY LATTERLY
RECENTNESS YOUTH
RECEPTACLE ARK BIN BOX CAN CUP DIP FAT PAN TIN TUB URN VAT BATH BOAT BOWL CASE CELL CIST DOVE DROP FACK FONT HELL HOLD INRO LOOM RACK RECU SAFE SINK TIDY TOUR ARBOR CARRY CREEL KIOSK KITTY RESET SCOOP STEAN STEEN TABLE TORUS BASKET BUCKET BUTLER CARTON CUPULE DIPPER DRAWER HAMPER HOPPER MORTAR PITCHI

POCKET SHRINE TABLET TROUGH ASHTRAY CAPSULE CARRIER CORBULA DUSTBIN ENVELOP HEADBOX LATRINE OMNIBUS OSSUARY PARISON RECEIPT SANDBOX SETTLER SOAPBOX STOWAGE TRAVOIS BURSICLE CANISTER CESSPOOL DUMPSTER FOREBOOT GYNOBASE HONEYPOT LOCKFAST OSSARIUM OVERFLOW PERFUMER SPITTOON STOCKPOT SEPULCHER
(— FOR ABANDONED INFANTS) TOUR
(— FOR BONES) OSSUARY OSSARIUM
(— FOR BROKEN TYPE) HELL
(— FOR BUTTER) RUSKIN
(— FOR COAL) BUNKER
(— FOR CONVEYING) APRON
(— FOR DRY ARTICLES) FAT
(— FOR FOUL THINGS) SINK
(— FOR GLASS BATCH) ARBOR
(— FOR HOLY WATER) FONT
(— FOR ORE-CRUSHING) MORTAR
(— FOR POKER CHIPS) KITTY
(— FOR SACRED RELICS) TABLE SHRINE TABLET SEPULCHRE
(— FOR SAVINGS) SOCK
(— FOR SEWING MATERIALS) TIDY
(— FOR TREASURE) HANAPER
(— FOR TYPE CASES) RACK
(— FOR VOTES) SITULA
(— IN BOTTLE-MAKING MACHINE) PARISON
(— OF CLAY OR STONE) STEAN STEEN
(— OF FLOWER) THALAMUS
(— ON WEIGHING SCALES) PAN
(— OVER ALTAR) DOVE
(CLAY —) BOOT
(DILATED —) GYNOBASE
(ELECTRICAL —) BASEPLUG
(INCENSE —) ACERRA
(OPEN —) TRAY
(PURSELIKE —) BURSICLE
(TAILOR'S —) HELL
(TRASH —) DUMPSTER
(WOODEN —) SEBILLA
(SUFF.) CLINE CLINIC CLINIUM

RECEPTION TEA ROUT COURT CRUSH DIFFA LEVEE SALON TREAT ACCOIL DURBAR RUELLE SOIREE SQUASH ACCUEIL COUCHEE MATINEE OVATION PASSAGE RECEIPT RECUEIL TEMPEST WELCOME ASSEMBLY FUNCTION GREETING PERNANCY REACTION SOCIABLE ACCEPTANCE RECIPIENCE RECIPIENCY
(— AT BEDTIME) COUCHEE
(— OF NATIVE PRINCES) DURBAR
(— OF SOUND) AUDIO
(ARABIC —) DIFFA
(CORDIAL —) WELCOME
(CROWDED —) SQUASH
(FASHIONABLE —) LEVEE SALON
(MORNING —) LEVEE RUELLE
(WEDDING —) INFARE

RECEPTIVE OPEN SENSORY OPENHANDED

RECEPTOR STOCK RECEIVER DOMINATOR

RECERCELEE SARCELLY

RECESS ALA ARK BAY BOX COD CUP PAN BOLE BUNK COVE DEEP HOLE NOOK TRAP AMBRY BOSOM BOWER CANAL CAVUM CLEFT CREEK HAVEN HITCH INLET NICHE ORIEL PRESS SINUS ALCOVE ANCONA CAVERN CENTER CHAPEL CIRQUE CLOSET COFFER CRANNY EXEDRA GROTTO INDENT LOCULE RABBET REBATE BEDSITE CONCAVE CREVICE LOCULUS MANHOLE RETREAT SINKING INTERVAL LOCKHOLE OVERTURE TABLINUM TOKONOMA TRAVERSE VACATION PIGEONHOLE
(— BETWEEN CAPES) BAY
(— FOR FAMILY RECORDS) TABLINUM
(— FOR HINGE LEAF) PAN
(— FOR PIECE OF SCULPTURE) ANCONA
(— FOR URN) LOCULUS
(— IN CHURCH) APSE
(— IN CHURCH WALL) AMBRY AWMRY AUMBRY AUMERY AWMRIE
(— IN COLON) HAUSTRUM
(— IN JAPANESE HOUSE) TOKONOMA
(— IN MOUNTAIN) CIRQUE
(— IN ROCK) HITCH
(— IN SIDE OF HILL) CORRIE
(— IN SIDE OF ROOM) ALA
(— IN WALL) BOLE NICHE ALCOVE
(— ON STAGE) CANOPY
(INMOST —) BOSOM
(PL.) FLASH

RECESSED SUNK SUNKEN

RECESSION BUST RETREAT

RECESSIVE BACKWARD RECEDING RETIRING WITHDRAWN

RECHAB (SON OF —) MALCHIAH JEHONADAB

RECHERCHE RARE CHOICE EXOTIC CURIOUS PRECIOUS UNCOMMON EXQUISITE

RECIDIVIST REPEATER

RECIPE RX FORM RULE FORMULA RECEIPT

RECIPIENT HEIR DONEE ALMSMAN DONATEE DONATORY LAUREATE
(SUFF.) EE

RECIPROCAL CROSS COMMON MUTUAL SECANT SEESAW
(— OF A POISE) RHE
(— OF RADIUS) CURVATURE
(— OF VISCOSITY) FLUIDITY
(PREF.) COUNTER INTER

RECIPROCATE REPAY RETURN REQUITE RETROACT

RECIPROCITY SHU ISOPOLITY MUTUALITY

RECITAL TALE ASHRE CITAL RECIT STORY EXPOSE LITANY PARADE REPEAT TIKKUN READING RELATION REPETITION
(— OF PRAYER) GEULAH HAMOTZI KEDUSHAH
(UNTRUE —) TALE
(SUFF.) LOG(ER)(IA)(IAN)(IC)(ICAL) (IST)(UE)(Y)

RECITATION DHIKR READING RECITAL RHAPSODY

RECITATIVE SCENA CHANSON PARLANDO

RECITE SAY CARP TELL STATE INTONE RECKON RELATE RENDER REPEAT DECLAIM DECLINE DICTATE NARRATE RECOUNT REELOFF REHEARSE
(— AS ELOCUTION EXERCISE) DECLAIM
(— IN MONOTONE) INTONE
(— METRICALLY) SCAN
(— MONOTONOUSLY) CHANT CHAUNT
(— NUMBERS) COUNT
(— PRAYERS) BENSH DAVEN
(— TIRESOMELY) THRUM
(— WITH GREAT EASE) RUSH

RECITER SCALD SKALD ANTERI DISEUR CONTEUR DISEUSE HOMERIST ILIADIST RHAPSODE

RECITING CHARM

RECK RAK CARE DEEM PASS MATTER REGARD CONCERN CONSIDER ESTIMATE

RECKLESS RASH WILD BLIND FOLLE PERDU MADCAP RACKLE SAVAGE GALLOWS RAMSTAM CARELESS HEADLONG HEEDLESS TEARAWAY BLINDFOLD TEMERARIOUS DEVILMAYCARE

RECKLESSLY FAST BLIND RAMSTAM HEADLONG HEADFIRST

RECKLESSNESS BAYARD

RECKON RET ARET CAST DATE ITEM RATE RECK RELY TALE TELL TOTE ALLOT AUDIT CLAIM CLASS COUNT JUDGE PLACE RETTE SCORE TALLY THINK ASSIGN FIGURE IMPUTE NUMBER REPUTE TOTTLE ACCOUNT ASCRIBE COMPUTE INCLUDE PRETEND RECOUNT SUPPOSE SUPPUTE CONSIDER ESTIMATE
(— IN) INCLUDE
(— TOO HIGH) OVERCOUNT

RECKONING TAB BILL NICK POST SHOT TAIL TALE COUNT SCORE TALLY COMPOT LAWING REASON TAILYE TOTTLE ACCOUNT DAYTALE TAILZEE COMPUTUS
(TAVERN —) LAWING

RECLAIM IN TAME ADEEM ASSART OBJECT RECALL REDEEM REFORM RESCUE SUBDUE PROTEST RECOVER RESTORE
(— FOR AGRICULTURE) ASSART
(— FROM SAVAGE STATE) CIVILIZE

RECLAIMANT GOEL

RECLAME FAME

RECLINE LIE LIG LEAN LOLL REST COUCH ACCUMB RECUMB UPLEAN DISCUMB
(— AWKWARDLY) SPRAWL SPRADDLE
(— LANGUIDLY) GAULSH

RECLINING CUMBENT ACCUMBENT RECUMBENT ACCUBATION
(— ON COUCH) ACCUMBENT

RECLUSE NUN MONK CULDEE HERMIT REMOTE ASCETIC EREMITE INCLUSA INCLUSE ANCHORET INCLUSUS SECLUDED SOLITARY SCIOPHYTE SOLITAIRE
(BROWN —) SPIDER
(PL.) SECLUSE

RECLUSIVE HERMETIC

RECOGNITION FAME SPUR HONOR SENSE CREDIT STATUS FEELING KENNING KNOWING AGNITION SANCTION ANAGNOSIS
(— OF ACHIEVEMENT) LAUREL CITATION
(— OF ERROR) RESIPISCENCE
(HONORIFIC —) DISTINCTION
(SUFF.) GNOSIA GNOSIS GNOSTIC GNOSY

RECOGNIZE KEN SEE WIT ESPY FACE KNOW SPOT TELL ADMIT ALLOW BLINK CROWN HONOR KEETH KITHE KYTHE ACCEPT ACKNOW AGNIZE BEKNOW COUTHE REVISE CORRECT DISCERN REALIZE ACCREDIT
(— IN ANY CAPACITY) AGNIZE

RECOGNIZED GOOD CLEAR KNOWN CLASSIC FAMILIAR

RECOIL SHY BALK KICK TURN REBUT SHRUG SHUCK START STRAM BLENCH BOUNCE FLINCH RECULE RESILE RESULT RETORT SHRINK REBOUND REDOUND REVERSE BACKLASH REJOUNCE
(WITHOUT —) DEADBEAT

RECOLLECT RECALL RECORD RETAIN BETHINK COMPOSE RECOVER RECOLETO REMEMBER

RECOLLECTION MIND MEMORY RECALL RECORD MINDING THOUGHT MEMORIAL SOUVENIR ANAMNESIS

RECOMMENCE RENEW REOPEN RESUME REPRISE

RECOMMEND MOVE OSSE PLUG TOUT WISH ADVISE COMMIT PRAISE PREFER COMMEND CONSIGN COUNSEL ENTRUST ADVOCATE RECOMMIT

RECOMMENDATION NAP CHIT VOEU ADVISE COUNSEL TESTIMONY
(PARTY —) COUPON
(SERVANT'S —) CHIT

RECOMPENSE PAY MEED MEND ATONE MENSE QUITS REPAY YIELD AMENDS BOUNTY HADBOT RECOUP REWARD SALARY GUERDON IMBURSE PAYMENT PREMIUM REQUITE RESTORE SATISFY SERVICE

RECONCILE GREE WEAN ADAPT AGREE ATONE ACCORD ADJUST SETTLE SHRIVE REUNITE HARMONIZE

RECONCILED FAIN VAIN SAUGHT

RECONCILIATION ATONE ACCORD SAUGHT REUNION IRENICON
(— OF BELIEFS) SYNCRETISM

RECONDITE DARK DEEP HIGH HIDDEN MYSTIC OCCULT SECRET CRYPTIC CURIOUS OBSCURE RETIRED ABSTRACT ABSTRUSE ESOTERIC

RECONNAISSANCE RECCE RECCO RECCY RECON SURVEY

RECONNOITER CASE SCOUT

RECALL SURVEY EXAMINE PICKEER DISCOVER REMEMBER
RECONSIDER REVIEW FORTHINK
RECONSTRUCT RECAST REPAIR REEVOKE REMODEL RESTORE
RECORD CAN CUT BOOK CARD DATE DISC ITER MARK NICK PAGE ROLL SING SLIP TAPE WICK ALBUM CHART DIARY ENACT ENTER ENTRY FASTI GRAPH JUMBO PRICK QUIPO QUIPU SCORE SIJIL SLATE STYLE TITLE WRITE ANNALS CHARGE DOCKET LEGEND MEMOIR SCROLL SPREAD WARBLE ACCOUNT CALENDS CAPTURE CITATOR DUBBING KALENDS LEXICON MENTION MYOGRAM SHOWING TICKLER TRACING ANAGRAPH ARCHIVES CYLINDER ENTRANCE ERGOGRAM HERDBOOK INSCROLL JUDGMENT KYMOGRAM LAUEGRAM MARIGRAM MELOGRAM MEMORIAL MEMORIZE MONUMENT NOCTUARY ONDOGRAM PANCHART PRESSING REGISTER REMEMBER SCHEDULE STUDBOOK INSCRIPTION OBSERVATION OSCILLOGRAM
(— BY NOTCHES) SCORE
(— OF CAR MOVEMENTS) JUMBO
(— OF DOCUMENT) PROTOCOL
(— OF EVENTS) FASTI
(— OF FOOTPRINTS) STIBOGRAM
(— OF HUMANITY'S FATE) SIJIL SIJILL
(— OF JOURNEY) JOURNAL ITINERARY
(— OF LOAN) CHARGE
(— OF MUHAMMAD'S SAYINGS) HADIT
(— OF MUSCULAR WORK) ERGOGRAM
(— OF PROCEEDINGS) ACTA ITER JOURNAL MINUTES
(COMPUTER —) PRINTOUT
(COURT —) EYRE
(DAILY —) DIARY
(DEMONSTRATION —) DEMO
(FORMAL —) ACT
(HISTORICAL —) STORY
(MAGNETIC —) DISK FLOPPY
(PERSONAL —) BIO VITA RESUME DOSSIER
(PHONOGRAPH —) DISC DISK MONO SINGLE BISCUIT SHELLAC
(PLASTIC MAGNETIC —) DISK
(SHIP'S —) LOG
(TYPE OF —) CD HIFI MONO STEREO MONAURAL
(PL.) LIBER ANNALS ARCHIVE MEMORABILIA
(PREF.) DISC(I)(O)
(SUFF.) GRAM GRAPH(ER)(IA)(IC)(Y)
RECORDED TAPE TAPED ONTAPE
RECORDER VCR FLUTE BOOKER FLAUTO NOTATOR GREFFIER REGISTER FIPPLEFLUTE
(— AND CAMERA) PORTAFAX PORTAPACK
(VIDEOTAPE —) VCR
RECORDING ALBUM ALIVE LABEL VIDEO CUTTING VIDEODISC VIDEODISK
(— AWARD) GRAMMY
(NARRATION —) VOICEOVER
(TELEVISION —) VIDEOTAPE
RECOUNT MING TELL COUNT DEVISE RECITE REGARD RELATE REPEAT SPREAD EXPRESS HISTORY ITERATE NARRATE CONSIDER DESCRIBE REHEARSE REITERATE
RECOUP DEDUCT REGAIN RECOVER INDEMNIFY
RECOUPLING HOOKUP
RECOURSE SUIT ACCESS APPEAL REFUGE RESORT STRING REGRESS RESTAUR RISORSE
(HAVE —) RECUR
RECOVER DOW COUR COWR CURE FIRM HEAL KERE COVER RALLY REACH UPSET BOUNCE RECURE REGAIN RESCUE RESUME RETAKE RETIRE REVERT REVOKE WARISH DELIVER OVERGET OVERPUT OVERSET READEPT RECLAIM RECRUIT REPAREL REPRISE RESTORE RETRIEVE SNAPBACK
(— LOST TERRITORY) REVENDICATE
RECOVERER DIGESTER
RECOVERY CURE RECOUR RECURE REMEDY RETURN SALVAGE COMEBACK SNAPBACK RECLAMATION
(— OF METAL) CUPELLATION
(— PERIOD) REHAB
(FORCIBLE —) RESCUE
RECREANT FALSE CRAVEN YELLOW APOSTATE COWARDLY DESERTER RECRAYED
RECREATE AMUSE EVOKE REVIVE
RECREATION PLAY SPORT SOLACE RENEWAL ACTIVITY DIVERSION PALINGENY
(PERIOD OF —) HOLIDAY VACATION
RECREATIONAL AMUSIVE
RECREATIVE PLAYING
RECREMENT SLAG DROSS SCORIA
RECRUIT BLEU BOOT FRESH RAISE SPROG GATHER INTAKE MUSTER RECREW REPAIR REVIVE RECOVER REFRESH RESTORE ASSEMBLE BEZONIAN CONSCRIPT
(RAW —) ROOKY ROOKIE
RECTAL
(PREF.) ARCHO
RECTANGLE BOX SQUARE CHECKER
(COTTON —) HUIPIL
(CURVILINEAR —) TESSERA
(EQUILATORAL —) SQUARE
(WOVEN —) SINKER
RECTANGULAR OBLONG SQUARE BOXLIKE EMERALD
RECTIFICATION REFORM LIMATION
RECTIFIER DIODE VALVE COLUMN DETECTOR EXCITRON
RECTIFY AMEND EMEND RIGHT ADJUST BETTER DETECT REFORM REMEDY CORRECT IMPROVE REDRESS EMENDATE REGULATE
RECTITUDE DOOM EQUITY JUSTICE PROBITY
RECTOR RULER LEADER PARSON PERSONA INCUMBENT
RECTUM SIEGE TEWEL
(PREF.) ARCHO PROCT(O) RECTO
RECUMBENT IDLE PRONE JACENT CUMBENT LEANING RESTING INACTIVE REPOSING
RECUPERATE MEND RALLY REFETE REGAIN RECOVER RECRUIT RETRIEVE
RECUR ACTUP CYCLE REFER REPEAT RESORT RETURN REOCCUR REVOLVE REAPPEAR
(— CONSTANTLY) HAUNT
RECURRENCE RESORT RETURN ATAVISM REPRISE ITERANCE ITERANCY RECOURSE FLASHBACK
(— OF SOUND) CADENCE
(REGULAR —) RHYTHM
(SUFF.) LY
RECURRENT CYCLIC FREQUENT PERENNIAL
RECURRING ROLLING CONTINUAL
(— ANNUALLY) ETESIAN
(— EVERY THIRD DAY) TERTIAN
(— EVERY 72 HOURS) QUARTAN
(— ON NINTH DAY) NONAN NONANE
(— ON SEVENTH DAY) SEPTAN
(CONSTANTLY —) ETERNAL
(CONTINUALLY —) CONSTANT
(SUFF.) ENNIAL
RECURVED REFLEX ERICOID
RECUTTING FRESHING
RED (ALSO SEE COLOR) GOYA GULY PINK PUCE ROJO ROSY RUBY ANGRY CANNA CORAL FIERY JUDAS ROUGE RUDDY RUFUS ARCHIL AZALEA BLOODY CERISE FLORID FULGID GARNET HECTIC NECTAR ORCHIL ORIENT RAISIN RUBRIC TITIAN TRYPAN VERMIL WANTON CARMINE GLOWING NACARAT PIMENTO RADICAL RUBELLE RUBIOUS STAMMEL VERMILY ARMENIAN AUBUSSON BORDEAUX CARDINAL CHOLERIC COLORADO FLAGRANT MANDARIN MOROCAIN RUBICUND SANGUINE ARTILLERY RUBINEOUS COQUELICOT SANGDEBOEUF
(— AND INFLAMED) BLOODSHOT
(— PLANET) MARS
(ANTIQUE —) CANNA
(BRICK —) TESTACEOUS
(BRIGHT —) TULY CHERRY PUNICIAL VERMILION
(BRILLIANTLY —) FLAMING
(DARK —) CLARET
(EUREKA —) PUCE
(FIERY —) MINIUM
(GRAYISH —) AZALEA
(HERALDIC —) GULES
(IRON OXIDE —) AGATE TARRAGONA
(ORANGE —) NACARAT
(PURPLISH —) LAKE MURREY MAGENTA
(SEE —) GETMAD
(WAX —) COPPER
(YELLOWISH —) MAROON
(PREF.) ERYTHR(O) PHENIC(O) PHOENIC(O) PYRRH(O) PYRRO RHOD(O) RUBE RUBI RUBO RUBRI RUBRO RUFI RUFO
REDACT EDIT
RED ADMIRAL VANESSA
RED AND THE BLACK (AUTHOR OF —) STENDHAL
(CHARACTER IN —) SOREL FOUQUE JULIEN PIRARD DERENAL VALENOD MATHILDE
RED-BACKED SHRIKE POPE
RED BADGE OF COURAGE
(AUTHOR OF —) CRANE
(CHARACTER IN —) JIM HENRY WILSON CONKLIN FLEMING
RED BANEBERRY REDBERRY TOADROOT
RED BAY PERSEA
RED-BELLIED (— TERRAPIN) SLIDER SKILPOT
(— WOODPECKER) CHAB
REDBREAST ROBIN RUDDOCK
RED-BREASTED BREAM FLATFISH FLOUNDER
RED-BREASTED KNOT GRAYBACK GREYBACK
REDBUD CERCIS JUNEBUD
RED CAMPION ROBIN SOLDIER
RED CEDAR SAVIN SABINA JUNIPER
RED CLOVER SAPLING TREFOIL TRIFOLY
RED CURRANT GOYA RIZZLE TIZZAR
REDD RID COMB OPEN LITTER NEATEN REFUSE RESCUE SETTLE ARRANGE DELIVER SMARTEN UNBLOCK UNRAVEL
RED DEER OLEN SPAY STAG
(FEMALE —) HIND
(MALE —) HART STAG
REDDEN RUD FIRE RUBY BLUSH FLUSH LIGHT ROUGE RUDDY BLOODY RUBIFY RUBRIC RUDDLE EMPURPLE
REDDISH REDDY RUDDY RUFUS FLUSHY GINGER RUFOUS COLORADO PYRRHOUS RUBICUND
RED DOG BLITZ
RED DRUM SPOT REDFISH
REDEAR SHELLCRACKER
REDEEM BUY WIN SAVE ALESE CLEAR LOUSE REPRY BORROW OFFSET RANSOM DELIVER FULFILL JUSTIFY RECLAIM WITHBEG AGAINBUY LIBERATE
REDEEMER GOEL SAVIOR
REDEEMING SAVING
REDEMPTION RANSOM REFORM SAFETY SALVATION
REDEYE BASS RUDD VIREO
RED-EYE CATSUP CICADA WHISKY
REDEYE SUNFISH
RED-EYED VIREO REDEYE GRASSET PREACHER
RED-FACED FLUSHED SCARLET
REDFIN DACE SHINER REDHORSE YELLOWFIN
REDFISH SALMON FATHEAD ROSEFISH
RED GOOSEFOOT PIGWEED SOWBANE
RED GROUPER MERO NEGRE REDBELLY
RED GROUSE GORHEN GORCOCK LAGOPODE MOORBIRD MUIRFOWL

RED GUM JARRAH EUCALYPT
RED GURNARD CUR ELLECK ROCHET SOLDIER
RED-HAIRED RUFUS CARROTY
REDHEAD DIVER FINCH POCHARD CARROTTOP KIZILBASH
RED HIND GRAYSBY GROUPER CABRILLA
REDHORSE REDFIN SUCKER
REDIA SPOROSAC
REDIRECT DISPLACE READDRESS
REDISTILL COHOBATE
REDISTRIBUTE FRESHEN REASSIGN
RED LAVER SLOKE
REDNESS RED RUD GLOW HEAT RUDD RUBOR ERYTHEMA RUBEDITY
(— OF NOSE) GROGBLOSSOM
(— OF SKIN) EFFLORESCENCE
(— OF SKY) AURORA
REDO REDACT RESTYLE
(— UNSKILLFULLY) BOTCH
RED OCHER TIVER ABRAUM RUDDLE
REDOLENCE BALM AROMA SCENT
REDOLENT RICH ODOROUS SCENTED AROMATIC FRAGRANT SMELLING
RED OSIER WILLOW REDBRUSH
REDOUBLE REECHO INTENSIFY
REDOUBT FEAR MASK DREAD SCHANZ SCONCE BULWARK
REDOUND TURN ACCRUE BILLOW CONDUCE REFLECT OVERFLOW
RED RASPBERRY CUTHBERT
REDRESS HEAL DRESS REDUB RIGHT AVENGE OFFSET REFORM RELIEF REMEDE REMEDY REPAIR ADDRESS CORRECT RECTIFY REFOUND RELIEVE
RED ROCKFISH TAMBOR
REDROOT PIGWEED
RED ROVER (AUTHOR OF —) COOPER
(CHARACTER IN —) ARK FID DICK HENRY AFRICA DELACY SCIPIO WILDER WYLLYS BIGNALL GRAYSON GERTRUDE RODERICK
RED SAGE LANTANA
RED SALMON SOCKEYE
RED SANDALWOOD CHANDAM
REDSHANK CLEE TEUK SHAKE GAMBET REDLEG YELPER PELLILE TATTLER
REDSKIN RED ROJO TAWNY INDIAN
REDSTART YELPER BRANTAIL FIRETAIL WHITECAP FIREFLIRT
RED STOPPER EUGENIA IRONWOOD
RED-TAILED (— HAWK) REDTAIL
(— TROPIC BIRD) KOAE
RED TAPE CHICHI
RED-TAPISM BEADLEDOM
RED-THROATED LOON WABBY
REDTOP COUCH FIORIN FINETOP FINEBENT FURZETOP BLUEJOINT
REDUCE CUT BATE CLIP DOCK DROP EASE PARE PULL THIN ABASE ABATE ALLAY APPAL BREAK DRAFT ELIDE LOWER QUELL SCANT SHAVE SLAKE SLASH SMELT ATTRIT DEDUCE DEFALK DEJECT DELETE DEPOSE DILUTE HUMBLE LESSEN REBATE REDUCT SHRINK SUBACT SUBDUE WEAKEN ABANDON ABRIDGE ASSUAGE ATOMIZE CHANCER CONQUER CURTAIL DEFLATE DEGRADE DEPLETE DWINDLE ECLIPSE FRITTER INHIBIT RESOLVE RETREAT SCISSOR SHORTEN SUBJECT ABSTRACT ATTEMPER CONDENSE DECREASE DIMINISH DOWNSIZE MINIMIZE
(— ACCORDING TO FIXED RATIO) SCALE
(— ANGLE) CHAMFER
(— BULK) BLEND
(— LUMBER) SIZE
(— PROFITS) SQUEEZE
(— PURITY) ALLOY
(— SAIL) REEF
(— STONE BLOCKS) SPALL SPAWL
(— THE VALUE) DECRY BEGGAR DEPRAVE
(— TO A MEAN) AVERAGE
(— TO ASHES) CREMATE
(— TO CARBON) CHAR
(— TO FINE PARTICLES) ATOMIZE MICRONIZE
(— TO FLAT SURFACE) LEVEL
(— TO INSIGNIFICANCE) DROWN
(— TO LOWER GRADE) BREAK DEMOTE DEGRADE
(— TO NIL) CLOSE
(— TO NOTHING) ANNUL
(— TO PASSIVITY) CHINAFY PROSTRATE
(— TO POWDER) GRIND PULVERIZE
(PREF.) DE
REDUCED SUNK TAIL BROKEN SHRUNK CURTATE DWARFED DEGRADED SHRUNKEN WEAKENED VESTIGIAL
(— TO HELPLESSNESS) PROSTRATE
REDUCING (— EXERCISES) SLIMNASTICS
REDUCTION BUST LETUP SLASH CUTBACK CUTDOWN DOCKAGE SHAVING ANALYSIS DILUTION DISCOUNT DRAWDOWN ABATEMENT SHRINKAGE
(— IN FORCE) RIF
(— IN PITCH) DROP
(— IN PRICE) SAVING CONCESSION
(— OF POWER) SHUTDOWN
(— OF THICKNESS) OFFSET
(— TO ABSURDITY) APAGOGUE
(PREF.) LY(O)
(SUFF.) LYSE LYSIS LYST LYTE LYTIC LYZE
REDUNDANCY EXCESS NIMIETY SURPLUS PLEONASM PLETHORA VERBIAGE MACROLOGY TAUTOLOGY
REDUNDANT WORDY LAVISH PROFUSE SURPLUS VERBOSE SWELLING EXCESSIVE
REDWING POP THRUSH WINDLE GADWALL WINNARD
REDWOOD MAD AMBOYNA BARWOOD FURIOUS SEQUOIA MAHOGANY
RE-ECHO REWORD REBOUND RESOUND REDOUBLE
REED NAL RIE RIX SAG SAX BENT JUNK MILL OBOE PIPE PIRN RODE SLEY TULE ARROW DONAX SPEAR TWILL BENNEL RADDLE SAGGON BASSOON CALAMUS FISTULA WHISTLE WINDING ABOMASUM CLARINET
(— FOR WARPING) WRAITHE
(— FOR WINDING THREAD) PIRN SPOOL
(— IN ORGAN) VIBRATOR
(— OF LOOM) COMB
(— OF MUSICAL INSTRUMENT) TONGUE
(FOXTAIL —) DOD
(GIANT —) DONAX
(MUSICAL —) OAT
(WEAVER'S —) SLAY SLEY RADDLE SLEIGH
(PL.) SPEAR
(PREF.) ARUNDI CALAM(I)(O)
REED BENT CARRIZO
REEDBIRD BOBOLINK
REEDBUCK BOHOR NAGOR REITBOK
REED BUNTING RINGBIRD
REED CANARY GRASS SPIRE DAGGERS
REED END TONGUE
REEDING GADROON MILLING STRIGIL GRAINING
REED MACE RAUPO CATTAIL MATREED
REED ORGAN MELODEON HARMONIUM
REED PIPE MIRLITON
REED WARBLER PITBIRD
REEDY THIN WEAK FRAIL TWILLED
REEF CAY KAY KEY CAYO LODE RYFT SCAR VEIN ATOLL LEDGE SHELF STICK BOILER REEFER SADDLE SKERRY BAGREEF BALANCE BIOHERM MAKATEA TOMBOLO
REEFER CAR COAT STICK JACKET MUGGLES
REEK FOG FUG EMIT FUME HEAP MIST PILE RICK RISE VENT EQUIP EXUDE FETOR ISSUE NIDOR SMEEK SMOKE STEAM VAPOR EXHALE OUTFIT EMANATE
(— WITH CORRUPTION) FESTER
REEL PIRN RANT ROCK SPIN STOT SWAB SWIM TURN GIDDY SPOOL SWIFT TRULL WAVER WHEEL WHIRL WINCE WINCH BOBBIN RECOIL SWERVE TOTTER TUMULT WAGGLE WALTER WELTER WINDER WINDLE WINNLE WINTLE BALLOON STAGGER SWABBLE TITUBATE
(— FOR DRAWING SILK) FILATURE
(— FOR WARP DRYING) BALLOON
(— FOR WINDING YARN) PIRN SWIFT
(— OFF A STORY) SCRIEVE
(— USED FOR YARN) CRIB
(DYEING —) WINCE
(FISHING —) TROW TROLL TRULL WINCH
(HIGHLAND —) HOOLICAN HOOLACHAN
(PL.) REVELS
REELER TWINER
REELING TURN AREEL LURCH FILATURE STAGGERY WAMBLING
REEM MOAN URUS UNICORN
REEVE REE REFE THREAD BAILIFF PROVOST STEWARD OVERSEER
REFECTION MEAL RELIEF REPAST HOGMANAY
(NEW YEAR'S —) HOGMANAY
REFECTORY FRATER FRATRY
REFER DEFER LEAVE POINT ADVERT ALLUDE APPEAL ASSIGN CHARGE COMMIT DELATE DIRECT IMPUTE PREFER RELATE SUBMIT ASCRIBE PERTAIN REJOURN RELEGATE
(— TO) SEE CITE INTEND CONCERN CONSULT MENTION INTIMATE
(— TO SOMETHING REPEATEDLY) HARP
REFEREE ZEBRA BREHON UMPIRE ARBITER AUDITOR
REFERENCE TAB FOLIO REMIT SIGIL APPEAL REGARD RENVOI BEARING MEANING RESPECT ALLUSION HANDBOOK INNUENDO RELATION
(— WORK) OED ATLAS INDEX ROGET ALMANAC LEXICON CATALOGUE GAZETTEER
(BRITISH — WORK) OED
(OBLIQUE —) SQUINT
(SATIRICAL —) GLANCE
REFERENDUM POLL MANDATE
REFINE RUN TRY BOLT EDIT FILE FINE PURE CUPEL EXALT PLAIN SLICK SMELT AFFINE DECOCT EXCOCT FILTER GARBLE SMOOTH CONCOCT ELEVATE PERFECT SUBLIME SWEETEN CIVILIZE HUMANIZE URBANIZE
(— AS GOLD) TEST CARAT
(— PULP) JORDAN
(— SUGAR) CLAY
(— WINE) FORCE
REFINED FINE GENT NEAT NICE TRIE ATTIC EXACT PURED TERSE CHASTE EXCOCT INLAND NIMINY POLITE QUAINT SUBTLE URBANE CLEANLY COURTLY ELEGANT GENTEEL PRECISE SCRAPED AUGUSTAN DELICATE ELEVATED HIGHBRED POLISHED PRECIEUX PRECIOUS SERAPHIC RECHERCHE SOPHISTICATED
(AFFECTEDLY —) FOPPISH
(NOT —) CRUDE
(TOO —) FINESPUN
REFINEMENT COUTH GRACE TASTE NICETY POLISH CULTURE FINESSE DELICACY ELEGANCE POLITURE SUBTLETY URBANITY PRECIOSITY
REFINER TRIER JORDAN SMELTER PURIFIER
REFINERY SMELTER
REFINING HUMAN FINING CULTURE AFFINAGE
REFINISH ANTIQUE
REFLECT COW CHEW MUSE PORE SHOW BLAZE FLASH GLASS GLINT IMAGE SHINE STUDY THINK ADVISE DAZZLE DEBATE MIRROR PONDER RECORD REFLEX RELUCE RETORT RETURN REVISE STEVEN EXPRESS PERPEND REDOUND REFRACT

SHIMMER COGITATE CONSIDER MEDITATE REDOUBLE RUMINATE
(— IRREGULARLY) SCATTER
(— UPON) SPECULATE
REFLECTED DERIVED MIRRORED SPECULAR
REFLECTING
(SUFF.) ESCENT
REFLECTION ECHO FOLD IDEA SKIT BLAME GHOST GLARE GNOME IMAGE DEBATE MUSING PONDER REFLEX RETURN SHADOW CENSURE COUNSEL SPECIES THOUGHT EYESHINE MOONPATH THINKING
(— OF SELF IN ANOTHER'S EYES) BABY
REFLECTIVE PENSIVE THOUGHTFUL
(— POWER) ALBEDO
REFLECTOR DISH FLAT CRITIC HASTER SHINER TAMPER HORIZON DIFFUSER HASTENER SPECULUM
REFLEX COPY IMAGE TROPISM ALLUSION
(NOT —) IDEOMOTOR
REFLUX EBB EBBING REFLOW
REFOREST REBOISE
REFORM MEND AMEND EMEND PRUNE BETTER REBUKE REPAIR CENSURE CORRECT DISBAND RECLAIM RECTIFY REDRESS
REFORMATORY COLLEGE MAGDALEN
REFORMER MOTT APOSTLE UTOPIAN UTOPIST JANSENIST
(DANISH-AMERICAN —) RIIS
(GREAT SOCIAL —) RIIS
REFRACT DIVIDE REFLECT REFRINGE
REFRACTION REBATE REBOUND DIACLASIS
REFRACTOR PRISM
REFRACTORY TOUGH SULLEN UNRULY WANTON ALUNDUM FROWARD MULLITE RESTIVE VICIOUS WAYWARD MUTINOUS PERVERSE STUBBORN CAMSTEERY REBELLIOUS
REFRAIN BOB TAG CURB DOWN KEEP SHUN AVOID FORGO SPARE WONDE BURDEN CHORUS DESIST FOREGO LUDDEN RETAIN THRAIN ABSTAIN FORBEAR LULLABY REFREIT REPRISE TORNADA FABURDEN FALDERAL OVERCOME OVERWORD REPETEND RESTRAIN WITHDRAW TURNAGAIN
(— FROM) CAN HELP AVOID SPARE WAIVE FOREGO RESIGN ABSTAIN
(— FROM EXACTING) REMIT
(— FROM INDULGENCE) ABSTAIN
(— FROM TELLING) LAYNE
(— FROM USING) BOYCOTT
(— OF SONG) BOB TAG DOWN FOOT WHEEL BURDEN CHORUS FALDEROL
(EPODIC —) HEMISTICH
(MEANINGLESS —) DERRY DUCDAME
(RECURRING —) REPETEND
REFRESH FAN COOL REST CHEER FRESH SLAKE CAUDLE REFECT REFETE REGALE REHETE REPOSE REVIVE UNTIRE COMFORT FORTIFY FRESHEN QUICKEN RECRUIT IRRIGATE RECREATE
REFRESHING DEWY BALMY CRISP FRESH TONIC CALLER LIVING BRACING COOLING REFRIGERANT
REFRESHMENT BAIT LUNCH CHARITY NUNCHEON REFRESCO COLLATION
(PL.) FOURS
REFRIGERANT ICE FREON COOLER AMMONIA COOLING CRYOGEN
REFRIGERATE CHILL
REFRIGERATION CRYOGENY
REFRIGERATOR FRIG FRIDGE ICEBOX FREEZER CONDENSER
(— CAR) REEFER
REFUEL TANK FILLUP
REFUGE ARK DIVE HOLT HOME PORT ROCK SOIL BIELD GRITH HAVEN OASIS RESET ASYLUM BILBIE COVERT HARBOR REFUTE RESORT SPITAL SUCCOR ALSATIA CRANNOG RESERVE RETREAT SHELTER UMBRAGE WARRANT BOLTHOLE CRANNOGE FORTRESS HIDEAWAY MAGDALEN RESOURCE SAFEHOLD
(FORTIFIED —) STRONGHOLD
(LAST —) SHEETANCHOR
(PLACE OF —) LAIR
(TAKE —) HOLEUP
REFUGEE REFFO COWBOY FUIDHIR FUGITIVE
REFULGENT BRIGHT SHINING RELUCENT BRILLIANT
REFUND REPAY UPSET REBATE REFOUND RESTORE DRAWBACK KICKBACK
REFURBISH DUST RENEW REVAMP FRESHEN BRIGHTEN RENOVATE
REFUSAL NAY VEE WARN WONT DENIAL MITTEN NAYSAY REPULSE ACCISMUS DECLINAL NEGATION NEGATIVE
(— TO SPEAK) APHRASIA
(SLANG —) NOWAY NODICE
(UNEXPECTED —) REBUFF
REFUSE ASH NAY NIL ORT SUD BALK COOM DENY DUST JUNK KEMP NAIT NILL NITE PELF PELT REDD SCUM SKIM SOIL SUDS WARN BAVIN COOMB CRAWN DEADS DRAST DROSS EXPEL FLOCK NITTE OFFAL RENAY REPEL SCRAN STENT STUFF SWASH SWILL TRADE TRASH WAIVE WASTE COLDER DANDER DEBRIS FORBID LITTER LUMBER MIDDEN NAYSAY PALTRY PELTRY RAFFLE RAMMEL RECUSE REFUGE REJECT SCRUFF SCULCH SHORTS SHRUFF SORDES SORDOR SPILTH BACKING BAGGAGE BROCKLE DECLINE DETRACT DETRECT DISAVOW DISOBEY FORSAKE GARBAGE GUBBINS MULLOCK OFFSCUM OUTCAST PRUNING RUBBISH SOILAGE SULLAGE WITHNAY WITHSAY CRASSIER DENEGATE DISALLOW DISCLAIM GARBLING LEAVINGS RIFFRAFF SWEEPAGE WITHHOLD OFFSCOURING
(— ADMISSION) CLOSE
(— FROM CHARCOAL OR COKE) BREEZE
(— FROM COFFEE BERRIES) TAILINGS
(— FROM CUTTING UP WHALE) GURRY
(— FROM MELTING METALS) SLAG DROSS SCORIA
(— FROM SIFTING COFFEE-BEANS) TRIAGE
(— FROM THRESHING) HUSK COLDER
(— FROM WINE-MAKING) RAPE
(— GREASE) COOM COOMB
(— OF CROP) STOVER
(— OF FLAX) PAB POB HARDS HURDS
(— OF FRUITS) MUST
(— OF GRAIN) PUG BRAN
(— OF GRAPES) MARC
(— OF INSECT) FRASS
(— OF MALT) DRAFF
(— OF MINE) BING DEAD
(— OF OIL MILLS) SHODE
(— OF PLANTS) ROSS
(— OF SILK) STRASS
(— OF SPICES) GARBLE
(— OF WHALE) FENKS GURRY TWITTER
(— OF WOOL) BACKINGS
(— TO APPROVE) VETO
(— TO COMPLY) STONEWALL
(— TO GO) JIB BALK
(— TO MOVE) REEST REIST
(— TO RECOGNIZE) CUT
(— TO SUPPORT) BOLT
(— TO TALK) DUMMY
(BREWERY —) DRAFF
(FISH —) CHUM GUBBINS
(FOOD —) SWILL
(LEATHER —) SPETCHES
(PLANT —) SCROFF
(STREET —) FULLAGE SCAVAGE
REFUTATION DISPROOF ELENCHUS HYPOBOLE REBUTTER
REFUTE DENY AVOID BELIE REBUT REFEL ASSOIL CONFUTE CONVELL CONVICT REPROVE REVINCE CONFOUND DISPROVE INFRINGE REDARGUE
REGAIN READEPT RECOVER RETRIEVE RECAPTURE
(— SOMETHING LOST) RECOUP
REGAL REAL ROYAL KINGLY PURPLE RIGGAL RIGOLE STATELY IMPERIAL MAJESTIC PRINCELY REGALIAN SPLENDID
REGALE FETE FEAST TREAT PLEASE DELIGHT REFRESH
REGALIA KIT ROYALTY
REGALO GIFT BONUS TREAT
REGAN (FATHER OF —) LEAR
(HUSBAND OF —) CORNWALL
(SISTER OF —) GONERIL CORDELIA
REGARD CON CARE DEEM FIND GAUM GAZE GIVE HEED HOLD LIKE LOOK MARK MIND RATE RECK SAKE TELL YEME ADORE COUNT FAVOR HONOR TREAT WEIGH ADDEEM ADMIRE ASPECT BEHOLD ESTEEM FIGURE GLANCE HOMAGE IMPUTE INTEND LIKING MOTIVE NOTICE RECKON REMARK REWARD SURVEY ACCOUNT ADJUDGE CONCERN OBSERVE RESPECT RESPITE CONSIDER ENVISAGE ESTIMATE
(— AS) SEE
(— AS HOPELESS) DEPLORE
(— AS OBJECT OF GREAT INTEREST) LIONIZE
(— AS PROPER) ACCEPT
(— HIGHLY) ADMIRE CONSIDER
(— WITH PROFOUND RESPECT) REVERE VENERATE
(— WITH REPUGNANCE) ABHOR
(ATTENTIVE —) EYE
(MENTAL —) EYE
(PL.) COMPLIMENTS
(SUFF.) SCOPE SCOPIC SCOPUS SCOPY
REGARDED (— WITH AFFECTION) DEAR AFFECTED
REGARDING ABOUT ANENT APROPOS
REGARDLESS DEAF CARELESS HEEDLESS RECKLESS
(— OF THAT) BUT
REGATTA HENLEY LIBERTY
REGEM (FATHER OF —) JAHDAI
REGENCY RULE DOMINION
REGENERATE RENEW REFORM REVIVE RECLAIM GRACIOUS RENOVATE
(NOT —) CIVIL
REGENERATION REBIRTH NEOGENESIS
(GOD OF —) SIVA
REGENT RULER RULING WARDEN SHIKKEN GOVERNOR PANGERANG PROTECTOR
(— DIAMOND) PITT
(— OF NORTH) KUBERA KUVERA
REGIME FASCISM CAFETERIA
REGIMEN CURE DIET KEEP RULE REGIMENT
REGIMENT BUFF RULE COLOR TERCIO GUIDANCE INFANTRY SLASHERS
(BRITISH —) GRAYS GREYS
(COSSACK —) PULK
(FRAMEWORK OF —) CADRE
(INDIA —) PULTON PULTUN
(SPANISH —) TERCIO
(TURKISH —) ALAI
(28TH —) SLASHERS
REGION DO END ERD EYE GAU WON AREA BELT KITH KNOT NECK PART SOIL WONE WOON ZONE CLIME COAST EARTH EXURB INDIA MARCH PAGUS PLACE PLAGE REALM SHIRE TRACT TROAD ALKALI BORDER CENTER DESERT DOMAIN EXTENT GILEAD GROUND GUIANA TATARY CLIMATE CONFINE COUNTRY DEMESNE ENCLAVE IMAMATE KINGDOM MALABAR STATION TARTARY CHIEFDOM CLUBLAND DEMERARA DISTRICT ENVIRONS EPISTOME FLATLAND FORTRESS FRONTIER KRATOGEN LAKELAND LATITUDE NAPHTALI PROVINCE REGIMENT SERICANA STANNARY TERRITORY

(— ABOVE MOUTH) EPISTOMA EPISTOME
(— ADJACENT TO BOUNDARY) MARCH
(— BEYOND ATMOSPHERE) SPACE
(— BEYOND DEATH) CANAAN
(— BORDERING ON HELL) LIMBO
(— FAR AWAY) STRAND
(— IN FIBER) MICELLE
(— NEAR EQUATOR) DOLDRUMS
(— NOTED FOR MANY CONFLICTS) COCKPIT
(— OF AMPLITUDE) ANTINODE
(— OF CHROMOSOME) PUFF
(— OF CLOUDS) WELKIN
(— OF COLD AND DARKNESS) NIFLHEL NIFLHEIM
(— OF DEAD) AMENTI UTGARTHAR
(— OF JAPAN) DO
(— OF MARS) LIBYA
(— OF OCEAN) COUNTRY
(— OF ORIGIN) CRADLE
(— OF PHOTOSPHERE) FACULA
(— OF SHIFTING SAND) ERG
(— OF SIMPLE PLEASURE) ARCADY ARCADIA
(— OF SOURCE OF GOLD) OPHIR
(— OF TISSUE) FIELD
(— OUTSIDE CITY) EXURB
(— WITHOUT LAW) ALSATIA
(— WITHOUT WOODS) WOLD WEALD
(CELESTIAL —S) LANGI
(COASTAL —) LITTORAL
(CULTIVATED —) GARDEN
(DARKISH —S ON MARS) MARE
(DESERT —) ERG HAMADA
(DESERTED —) WASTE
(DESOLATE —) PUNA
(DISTANT —) THULE
(E. INDIAN —) DESH
(ELEVATED —) ALTITUDE
(FOREST —) TAIGA
(FORESTED —) MONTANA
(GEOGRAPHICAL —) BOWL SIDE
(HEAVENLY —) SPHERE
(IDEAL —) JINNESTAN
(INFERNAL —S) ABYSS TARTAR TARTARUS
(LARGE —) COMPAGE
(LIMESTONE —) KARST
(MOUNTAINOUS —) SIERRA
(OPEN —) SAVANNAH
(ORIENTAL —) INDOGAEA
(STAGNANT —) EDDY
(SUPERIOR —) HIGH
(TREELESS —) HIGHMOOR
(UPPER —) HIGH LOFT
(UPPER —S) ETHER
(WOODED —) FOREST
(PL.) DIGGINGS
(PREF.) NESO
(SUFF.) DOM NESE NESIA(N) NESUS

REGIONAL LOCAL SECTIONAL

REGISTER PIE BEAR BOOK FREE LIST MARK PILE POLL READ ROLL STOP ALBUM DIARY ENROL ENTER FASTI GRILL SIJIL SLATE ANNALS BEHAVE ENROLL LEDGER MUSTER RECORD REGEST ALMANAC ASCRIBE CALENDS CATALOG COUCHER DIPTYCH INDORSE KALENDS NOTITIA ROTULET ANAGRAPH ARCHIVES CADASTER CALENDAR GREFFIER INDICATE INSCRIBE MENOLOGY PEDIGREE POLLBOOK TOLLBOOK STROHBASS
(— OF JUDGMENTS) DOCKET
(LOWEST —) CHALUMEAU
(MIDDLE —) CLARINO
(OFFICIAL —) TABLEAU CADASTER

REGISTRAR GUARD BURSAR ACTUARY PATWARI PUTWARI GREFFIER RESIDENT

REGISTRY FLAG STUDBOOK

REGLET FILET BATTEN FILLET RIGLET

REGRATER HUCKSTER

REGRESS EGRESS RETURN ANALYSIS RECOURSE

REGRET REW RUE RUTH GRIEF DESIRE RELENT REPENT SORROW DEPLORE REGRATE REMORSE FORTHINK REPINING

REGRETFUL BAD SORRY REPINING

REGRETTABLE DIRTY DOLOROUS

REGULAR DUE SET EVEN FULL JUST WEAK SOBER SUANT SUENT USUAL FORMAL GIUSTO NORMAL SQUARE STATED STEADY CANONIC CERTAIN CORRECT NATURAL ORDERED ORDERLY ORDINAL PERFECT TYPICAL UNIFORM COMPLETE CONSTANT DECOROUS FORMULAR HABITUAL ORDINARY ORDINATE TESSERAL
(PREF.) SYM

REGULARITY METHOD SQUARE SYSTEM EVENNESS SYNAPHEA
(— OF NATURE) LAW

REGULARLY DULY EVEN ORDERLY PROPERLY STATEDLY

REGULATE SET PACE RATE RULE WIND BOOST FRAME GUIDE ORDER RIGHT SHAPE ADJUST ASSIZE BEHAVE DIRECT GOVERN MASTER RADDLE SETTLE SQUARE TEMPER ARRANGE CONTROL DISPOSE MEASURE MONITOR QUALIFY RECTIFY ATTEMPER MODERATE MODULIZE
(— FOOD) DIET
(— PITCH) KEY STOP

REGULATED ORDENE ORDERED ORDERLY
(NOT —) INCORRECT
(WELL —) ORDERLY

REGULATING BEHIND

REGULATION LAW RULE BYLAW ORDER REGLE USUAL CURFEW ZABETA CONTROL PRECEPT STATUTE VOICING DISPOSAL STEERAGE
(— OF PRICE) ASSIZE
(DORMITORY —S) PARIETALS

REGULATOR GUIDE DISPOSER GOVERNOR
(GROWTH —) GIBBERELLIN

REGULUS MATTE SLURRY KINGLET

REHABIAH **(FATHER OF —)** ELIEZER
(GRANDFATHER OF —) MOSES

REHABILITATE REABLE REPONE RESTORE REINSTATE

REHASH RECHAUFFE

REHEARSAL CALL DRYRUN HEARSAL HERSALL PREVIEW CLAMBAKE NARRATION

REHEARSE TELL TRAIN DETAIL RECITE RELATE DECLINE NARRATE RECOUNT DESCRIBE PRACTICE
(— QUICKLY) RUNOVER

REHEAT FLASH

REHOB **(SON OF —)** HADADEZER

REHOBOAM ROBOAM
(FATHER OF —) SOLOMON
(MOTHER OF —) NAAMAH

REICHSTAG DIET

REIF PLUNDER ROBBERY

REIGN RING RULE REALM RICHE EMPIRE GOVERN KINGDOM PREVAIL REGIMENT REGNANCY
(— IN INDIA) RAJ

REIMBURSE PAY REPAY DEFRAY RECOUP REFUND REBURSE INDEMNIFY

REIN CURB STOP CHECK SWING THONG GOVERN BABICHE LEATHER PLOWLINE RESTRAIN
(PL.) LINES RIBBONS

REINCARNATION AVATAR REBIRTH

REINDEER REIN CERVID TARAND CARIBOU CERVINE CERVOID RANGIFER

REINDEER MOSS SWARD

REINFORCE BAR GUY BACK FACE STAY BRACE FORCE INLAY STUFF SUPER CRADLE DOUBLE GUSSET HARDEN MUSCLE SUPPLY AFFORCE BOLSTER BULWARK ENFORCE GROMMET NERVATE STIFFEN SUPPORT
(— ROAD) SKID

REINFORCED KEYED SPLICED

REINFORCEMENT CREW FUEL STAY BRACE HURTER CUNETTE SPLICING STRAINER
(PL.) SUCCOR SUPPLY

REINVIGORATE QUICK REVIVE RECRUIT RENERVE

REISSUE REPRISE

REITERATE BACK DING REITER REPEAT RESUME ITERATE REHEARSE

REIVER CATERAN

REJECT BEG ORT CAST DEFY DENY DICE FAIL JILT KICK NILL SPIN ABHOR BANDY BELIE BRUSH CHECK EJECT REFEL REPEL SCOUT SPURN WAIVE ABJECT ABJURE DELETE DESERT IGNORE RECUSE REFUSE REFUTE RESPUE RETORT ABANDON CASHIER CONTEMN DECLINE DISCARD DISMISS FORSAKE PROJECT REPROVE REPULSE ABNEGATE ATHETIZE DESELECT DISALLOW DISCLAIM FORSWEAR NEGATIVE RENOUNCE THROWOUT
(— A STUDENT) PLUCK PLOUGH
(— COPY) SPIKE

REJECTED OFFCAST OUTCAST CASTAWAY
(— BY GOD) REPROBATE

REJECTION SACK BRUSH SPURN DENIAL MITTEN REBUFF REFUSAL REPULSE DEFIANCE TURNDOWN
(— AS SPURIOUS) ATHETESIS
(— OF DOCTRINE) HERESY
(INTERJECTION TO EXPRESS —) YUK YECH YUCK YECCH

REJOICE JOY FAIN GAME CHEER ENJOY EXULT GLORY BLITHE PLEASE DELIGHT GLADDEN MAFFICK JUBILATE

REJOICING GLEE MIRTH OVATION FESTIVITY

REJOIN REPLY TAUNT ANSWER REUNITE

REJOINDER REPLY ANSWER COUNTER RESPONSE

REJUVENATE UNOLD

REKEM **(FATHER OF —)** HEBRON

REKINDLE RELUME REVIVE

RELAPSE SINK WEED LAPSE RECIDE RETURN BACKSET SUBSIDE BACKCAST WITHDRAW RECIDIVISM

RELAPSING **(— INTO CRIME)** RECIDIVISM

RELATE SAY ALLY BEAR JOIN READ TELL PITCH REFER SPELL STATE TOUCH ALLUDE ASSERT DELATE DETAIL DEVISE RECITE REPORT REPUTE COGNATE CONCERN DECLARE INVOLVE NARRATE PERTAIN RECOUNT CALABASH DESCRIBE REHEARSE APPERTAIN
(— TO) TOUCH

RELATED KIN SIB AKIN ALLIED AFFINED RELEVANT CONNECTED CONSANGUINE
(— BY FATHER'S SIDE) AGNATE
(— INVERSELY) RECIPROCAL
(— ON MOTHER'S SIDE) ENATE ENATIC COGNATE
(RECIPROCALLY —) CONJUGATE
(PREF.) **(— BY REMARRIAGE)** STEP

RELATING (ALSO SEE PERTAINING)
(— TO) AGAINST
(— TO A RECENT PAST) ERST
(SUFF.) **(— TO)** AL ATIVE IAL IC(AL) ILE INE ISH ISTIC ITIC ITIOUS

RELATION KIN SIB TALE BLOOD FETII AFFINE DATIVE REGARD ACCOUNT BEARING HISTORY KINSHIP KINSMAN RAPPORT RESPECT SCHESIS TELLING AFFINITY HABITUDE RELATIVE TENDENCY REFERENCE REHEARSAL RISHTADAR PROPORTION
(— BETWEEN SPECIES) AFFINITY
(— OF LIKENESS) ANALOGY
(BLOOD —) KIN SIB
(FIXED —) RATIO
(FRIENDLY —S) AMITY
(SYNTACTIC —) FUNCTION
(WORKING —) GEAR

RELATIONSHIP KIN BLOOD ACTION AGENCY AMENITY AMITATE ANALOGY ANGULUS BEARING CONTACT KINDRED KINSHIP LIAISON RESPECT SIBNESS SIBREDE SOCIETY AFFINITY AGNATION CONTRAST GOSSIPRY RELATIVE SYMPATHY COGNATION FILIATION
(BUSINESS —) ACCOUNT
(CLOSE —) BOSOM AFFIANCE INTIMACY BELONGING
(FRIENDLY —) ENTENTE

(HARMFUL —) DISOPERATION
(HARMONIOUS —) SYNC
(INHARMONIOUS —) OUTS
(MARITAL —) BED
(MATHEMATICAL —) PARITY
(MUTUAL —) TERMS SYMMETRY
(SEXUAL —) AFFAIR
(SOCIAL —) FOOTING
RELATIVE KIN ALLY BLOOD AFFINE AGNATE ALLIED COUSIN GERMAN KINDRED KINSMAN APPOSITE COGNATUS RELATION RELEVANT PERTINENT
(PL.) KIN SIB FOLK KINDRED KINFOLK KINNERY KINSFOLK
RELAX LAX VEG GIVE REST ABATE BREAK LOOSE REMIT SLACK DIVERT INKINK LAXATE SOFTEN UNBEND UNGIVE UNKNIT UNWIND DEBLOCK RELEASE RESOLVE SLACKEN UNPURSE MITIGATE UNBUCKLE UNCLENCH WINDDOWN
RELAXANT (MUSCLE —) CURARE CURARI
RELAXATION EASE LAZE REST ATONY CREEP LETUP RELAX SOLACE DETENTE LETDOWN RELACHE BREATHER DIVERSION
(— OF MONASTIC RULES) MISERICORD MISERICORDE
RELAXED LAX LASH LOOSE SLACK SONSY REMISS SONSIE INFORMAL RESOLVED TONELESS UNBENDED UNBRACED GRASPLESS
RELAXING ANIMAL ANODYNE DETENTE
(— POINT) SEAR
RELAY SPELL RELIEF REMUDA AVANTLAY REPEATER
(— OF DOGS) VAUNTLAY
(— OF PALANQUIN BEARERS) DAK
RELEASE LES LET BAIL DROP EMIT FREE LESE LIOS LISS SHED SLIP TRIP UNDO ERUPT EXEEM LEISS LOOSE MUKTI REMIT SLAKE ACQUIT ASSOIL DEMISE EXCUSE EXEMPT LAUNCH MOKSHA REMISE SPRING UNBEND UNTACK UNWORK ABSOLVE APATHIA DELIVER DETENTE DISBAND FREEDOM QUIETUS SOLUTIO UNSTICK DELIVERY DISPENSE DISSOLVE LIBERATE DISCHARGE RELINQUISH
(— AS DOGS) UNLEASH
(— DANCING PARTNER) BREAK
(— EMOTION) ABREAST
(— FROM CENSORSHIP) UNGAG
(— FROM CONFINEMENT) UNMEW UNPEN SPRING STREET
(— FROM DEBT) FREITH
(— FROM MILITARY) INVALID
(— FROM SLAVERY) MANUMIT
(— ON ONE'S WORD) PAROLE
(PRESS —) HANDOUT
RELEASED OFF FREE EXEMPT
RELEGATE DOOM EXILE BANISH COMMIT DEMOTE REJECT DEGRADE
(— TO OBSCURITY) DOWN
RELEGATION (— OF LEGAL DISPUTE) RENVOI RENVOY
RELENT COME MELT ABATE YIELD REGRET REPENT LIQUEFY MOLLIFY SLACKEN
RELENTLESS GRIM HARD HARSH STERN STONY BITTER SAVAGE STRICT AUSTERE PITILESS RIGOROUS
RELEVANCE PRECISION PERTINENCE
RELEVANT APT VALID GERMAN APROPOS GERMANE APPOSITE MATERIAL PERTINENT
RELEVANTLY ADREM
RELIABILITY STEEL CREDENCE
RELIABLE GOOD HARD SAFE SURE TRUE PUKKA SOLID SOUND THERE TRIED TRUST WHITE DINKUM STEADY TRUSTY CERTAIN FAITHFUL SOOTHFUL STRAIGHT
RELIANCE HOPE TRUST CREDIT AFFIANCE MAINSTAY
(— ON FAITH) FIDEISM
RELIC HUACO REMAIN ANTIQUE HALIDOM LEAVING MEMENTO RELIQUE VESTIGE SOUVENIR SURVIVAL
(LIFELESS —) SHELL
(PL.) CORPSE HALIDOM REMAINS
(PREF.) LIPSANO
RELICT WIDOW REMANIE RESIDUAL SURVIVOR EPIBIOTIC
RELIEF AID LAX SOB BOOT BOTE DOLE EASE HELP RELAY SCRUB SPELL SWING ESCAPE REMEDY SUCCOR COMFORT FEEDING REDRESS RILIEVO EASEMENT REPOUSSE
(— FROM SIEGE) RESCUE
(TEMPORARY —) HITCH
(SUFF.) LYSE LYSIS LYST LYTE LYTIC LYZE
RELIEVE ROB BEET EASE FREE HELP LIOS LISS ALLAY LIGHT LISSE LITHE RIGHT SLAKE SPARE SPELL ASSIST LESSEN PHYSIC REMEDY REMOVE RESCUE SOOTHE SUCCOR UNMAZE ASSUAGE COMFORT DELIVER DEPRIVE FRESHEN LIGHTEN REDRESS REFRESH SUCCEED SUPPORT SUSTAIN SWEETEN ALIGHTEN DIMINISH MITIGATE RELEVATE
(— A SAIL) SPILL
(— OF OFFICE) AX AXE
(— OF SIN) CONFESS
RELIEVED THANKFUL
RELIGIEUSE NUN CLERGESS
RELIGION BON DIN LAW SECT BONBO CREED DAENA FAITH OBEAH PIETY SOPHY DHARMA SHINTO SYSTEM TAOISM ELOHISM JAINISM JUDAISM MACUMBA ORPHISM PERSISM RELIGIO SIKHISM SYNAGOG BUDDHISM CAODAISM HINDUISM MAZDAISM PEYOTISM SANTERIA SHAMANISM
(— OF ABRAHAM) HANIFIYA
(— OF TIBET) BON
(— OF WITCHCRAFT) WICCA
(— PRACTICED IN CUBA) SANTERIA
(CHRISTIAN —) WAY
(FALSE —) SUPERSTITION
(GENTILE —) ETHNICISM
(UNORTHODOX —) CULT
RELIGIOSE PIETISTIC
RELIGIOUS PI HOLY EXACT GODLY PIOUS RIGID DEVOUT DIVINE SACRED FERVENT GHOSTLY ZEALOUS SPIRITUAL
(— HOUSE) KELLION
(MORBIDLY —) RELIGIOSE
RELINQUISH LAY LET CEDE DROP QUIT DEMIT FORGO GRANT LEAVE WAIVE YIELD CANCEL DESERT RESIGN ABANDON FORSAKE RELEASE ABDICATE ABNEGATE LINQUISH RENOUNCE
RELIQUARY ARCA CHEF CASKET CHASSE COFFER MEMORY SHRINE STEEPA TABLET CHORTEN HALIDOM MEMORIA FERETORY
RELISH CHOW DASH EDGE GOUT GUST LIKE SOUL SOWL TANG ZEST ACHAR ENJOY GUSTO RELES SAVOR SOWLE SPICE TASTE TRACE ATSARA DEGUST FLAVOR LIKING PALATE SAVOUR BOTARGO OUTWORK STOMACH APPETITE FONDNESS PICCALILLI
(— FOR FOOD) CHAW
(INTELLECTUAL —) TASTE
(MENTAL —) PALATE
(ROMAN —) GARUM
(SALT OR ACID —) ACHAR
RELUCENT RADIANT SHINING GLEAMING
RELUCT TARROW
RELUCTANCE GRUDGE AVERSION ANTIPATHY RENITENCE
(— UNIT) REL
RELUCTANT SET SHY CAGY LOTH NICE CHARY LOATH SWEER THRAW AFRAID AVERSE DAINTY FORCED SWEERT UNFAIN ASHAMED HALTING BACKWARD GRUDGING LOATHFUL RENITENT RETICENT THRAWART
RELY AFFY BANK BASE LEAN LITE REST STAY COUNT RALLY TRUST DEPEND GROUND RECKON REPOSE CONFIDE
(— ON) LIPPEN VENTURE
REMAIN LIE SIT BIDE REST STAY STOP ABIDE CLING DWELL LEAVE STAND TARRY THOLE BELIVE ENDURE MANENT RESIDE SUBSIST SURVIVE CONTINUE
(— ALOFT) HOVER
(— AWAKE) VIGILATE
(— FIRM) INHERE
(— IN DEADLOCK) HANG
(— MOTIONLESS) STAGNATE
(—S IN MASH TUN) GRAINS
(—S IN PIPEBOWL) TOPPER
(—S OF CANE) BEGASS BAGASSE
(—S OF FIRE) EMBER EMBERS
(—S ON STAGE) MANET
(— STATIONARY) FASTEN
(— UNDER HEAT TREATMENT) SOAK
(— UNDISTURBED AFTER HEAT TREATMENT) AGE
(— UNUSED) LIE
(— UPRIGHT) STAND
(ANIMAL —S) SPOILS
(FOSSIL —) EXUVIAE
(FOUL —S) SCURF
(PL.) CHAR DUST ASHES DECAY DRAFF GHOST SHARD SHERD BURIAL DEBRIS FOSSIL RELIEF CARCASS REMNANT RESIDUE RELIQUIAE
(PREF.) MENO
REMAINDER NET HEEL LAVE REST PLUGS ARREAR EXCESS RELIEF BALANCE REMNANT RESIDUE SURPLUS LEAVINGS LEFTOVER RESIDUAL RESIDUUM
(— OF ATOM) CORE
(PL.) GARBLINGS LEFTMENTS
REMAINING OVER BIDING REMNANT LEFTOVER REMANENT RESIDUAL
(PREF.) MENO
REMALIAH (SON OF —) PEKAH
REMARK DIG SAY SEE GIRD HEED NOTE WORD GLOSS STATE TOKEN EARFUL GAMBIT NOTICE REGARD COMMENT DESCANT DISCANT OBSERVE PERCEIVE OBSERVATION
(— BRIEFLY) GLANCE
(ADVERSE —) STRICTURE
(AGGRESSIVE —) SHOT
(AMIABLE —) DOUCEUR
(AMUSING —) GAG
(BANAL —) PLATITUDE
(BITING —) BARB
(CLEVER —) QUIP NIFTY
(CONCLUDING —S) ENVOI
(CRITICAL —) SWIPE BRICKBAT
(CUTTING —) DIG SPINOSITY
(DULL —) BROMIDE
(EMBARRASSING —) BREAK
(EXPLANATORY —) SCHOLION SCHOLIUM
(FOOLISH —) INANITY
(ILL-TIMED —) CLANGER
(INSULTING —) SLUR
(JEERING —) JEST SKIT
(LAUGH-PROVOKING —) GAG
(PITHY —) ONELINER
(SARCASTIC —) HIT GIRD SLANT
(SATIRICAL —) JEST SKIT SGAFT
(SHARP —) SWIPE GANSEL STINGER
(SILLY —) FADAISE
(STAGE —) ASIDE
(STALE —S) BILGE
(TEASING —) NEEDLE
(UNCOMPLIMENTARY —) BRICKBAT
(UNKIND —) BARB
(WITTY —) MOT JEST CRACK ZINGER
REMARKABLE SOME FORBY GREAT SIGNAL STRONG NOTABLE STRANGE UNUSUAL FABULOUS MARKABLE SINGULAR SPANKING STRIKING UNCOMMON BODACIOUS NOTICEABLE PHENOMENAL
(— ONE) LULU
(NOT —) INCURIOUS
REMARKABLY UNCO UNKO JOLLY UNCOW DEUCED UNCOLY SIGNALLY
REMEDIAL BONEHEAD RELEVANT SALUTARY
REMEDILESS BOOTLESS
REMEDY AID BOT BOOT BOTE CURE

GAIN HALE HEAL HELP REDE AZOTH MANDS REDUB SHERE TOPIC PHYSIC RECOUR RECURE RELIEF REPAIR RESIDY URETIC ANTACID CORRECT DRASTIC ICTERIC OTALGIC PLASTER RECTIFY REDRESS RELIEVE ANTIDOTE MEDICINE PHARMACY RECOVERY REMEDIAL SPECIFIC
(— COUNTERACTING POISON) TREACLE ANTIDOTE
(— FOR ALL DISEASES) PANACEA CATHOLICON
(— FOR DIZZINESS) DINIC
(— FOR JAUNDICE) ICTERIC
(— TO REDUCE FEVER) FEBRIFUGE
(CHINESE —) SENSO
(EXTERNAL —) TOPIC
(FAVORITE —) NOSTRUM
(SECRET —) ARCANUM
(SOVEREIGN —) MAGISTERY
(TAPEWORM —) EMBELIA
(TOOTHACHE —) TONGA
(UNIVERSAL —) AZOTH CATHOLICON
(WITHOUT —) BOOTLESS

REMEMBER MEM MIN MEAN MIND MINE MING IDEATE MEMBER RECALL RECORD REMIND RETAIN REWARD BETHINK MENTION RECOLLECT
(— REMORSEFULLY) REMORD

REMEMBRANCE MIN MIND MEMORY RECORD MEANING MINDING MINNING MEMORIAL REMINDER SOUVENIR

REMEMBRANCE OF THINGS PAST (AUTHOR OF —) PROUST
(CHARACTER IN —) MOREL SWANN MARCEL ODETTE RACHEL ROBERT VEDURIN GILBERTE VINTEUIL ALBERTINE DECHARLUS GUERMANTES

REMIND JOG MIN MIND MINE MING IMMIND PROMPT REMEMBER

REMINDER CUE MEMO PROD TWIT TOUCH PROMPT MINDING MONITOR SOUVENIR REFRESHER

REMINISCENCE MEMORY RECALL ANAMNESIS

REMISE RETURN RELEASE REPLACE CARRIAGE

REMISS LAX LAZY MILD PALE FAINT SLACK TARDY BEHIND DILUTED LANGUID CARELESS DERELICT DILATORY HEEDLESS NEGLIGENT

REMISSION CURE LIOS LISS PARDON REMISE LOOSING REMITTAL
(— OF BUSINESS) RECESS
(— OF DEBT) ACCEPTILATION
(PARTIAL —) RELAXATION

REMISSNESS LACHES LASHNESS

REMIT SEND COVER LOOSE RELAX CANCEL EXCUSE PARDON REMAND REMISS RESIGN ABSOLVE FORGIVE RELEASE SUSPEND ABROGATE MITIGATE MODERATE

REMNANT END TAG BUTT DREG FENT REST RUMP RUND RELIC STUMP TRACE REMAIN LEAVING REMAINS SURVIVOR
(— OF CLOTH) FENT
(— OF FOOD) CRUST
(— OF ROCK MASS) KLIP KLIPPE
(— OF VEIL) ANNULUS
(—S OF FILLETS) SCISSEL
(—S OF VEIL) CORTINA
(VESTIGIAL —) SHADOW
(PL.) EPIPLASM

REMODEL MEND RECAST CONVERT

REMONSTRANCE PROOF ADVICE COUNSEL PROTEST REPROOF EVIDENCE

REMONSTRANT ARMINIAN

REMONSTRATE ARGUE OBJECT PROTEST REPROVE COMPLAIN

REMORA CLOG DRAG PEGA SUCKER GUAICAN PEGADOR ECHENEID LOOTSMAN STAYSHIP STOPSHIP SUCKFISH

REMORSE HELL PITY RUTH PRICK REGRET REMORD AYENBITE PENITENCE
(— OF CONSCIENCE) GRUDGE

REMORSEFUL BAD PITIFUL CONTRITE GUILTSICK

REMOTE FAR OFF BACK DEEP FERN HIGH LONG ALOOF HOARY UTTER ALENGE DISTAL ELENGE EXEMPT OTIOSE SECRET DEVIOUS DISSITE DISTANT EXTREME FAILING FARAWAY FOREIGN OBSCURE OUTSIDE ABDITIVE ABSTRUSE ARMCHAIR BACKVELD INTERIOR OUTLYING OUTWORLD SECLUDED SOLITARY OUTLANDISH
(— FROM LIFE) SCHOOLISH
(MOST —) ULTIMA EXTREME HINDMOST ULTIMATE
(PREF.) DIST(O) PALAE(O) PALE(O)

REMOTELY AFAR CLEAN DISTANTLY

REMOTENESS AWAYNESS DISTANCE

REMOTER FARTHER ULTERIOR

REMOVABLE DATIVE REMOTIVE

REMOVAL AX AXE EXILE AMOTION CLEANUP ERASION ABLATION EXCISION EXERESIS OFFGOING REMOTION
(— OF COAL) GETTING
(— OF ICE FROM GLACIER) ATTRITION
(— OF LAND) AVULSION
(DISTANT —) ELOIN ELOIGN
(SUFF.) CENOSIS
(SURGICAL —) ECTOMY

REMOVE GET PUT RID BATE COMB DELE DRAW FILE FLIT FREE LIFT MOVE PARE PEEL PULL QUIT RAZE UNDO VOID WEED APART AUFER AVOID BLAST BRUSH CLEAR EMITY ERASE EVOID HEAVE HOIST LIGHT PLANE RAISE REPEL SHIFT SHUCK SLASH SLIPE STRIP SWEEP WAIVE BANISH CANCEL CHANGE CONVEY DEDUCT DEGREE DEPART DEPOSE EFFACE ELOIGN EXEMPT EXPORT MINISH RELEVE REMBLE SPIRIT ABOLISH AMOLISH DEPRIVE DESCENT DISMISS DISPOST DIVORCE EXCERPT RESCIND RETRACT REVERSE STRANGE SUBDUCT SUBLATE ABSTRACT ASPIRATE DISPLACE DISPLANT ESTRANGE EVACUATE RETRENCH SUPPLANT TRANSFER WITHDRAW ELIMINATE OBLITERATE
(— A FAULT) MEND
(— A STITCH) DECREASE
(— BARK FROM LOG) ROSS
(— BIT BY BIT) SCAMBLE
(— BY CUTTING) ABLATE
(— BY DEATH) SNATCH
(— BY SCRAPING) SHAVE
(— CLOTHING) DOFF STRIP
(— COLOR) BLEACH
(— CONTENTS) GUT
(— CORTEX) DECORTIGATE
(— COVER) UNCAP
(— DEFECTS) SCARF
(— DIRT) BLADE GARBLE
(— EXCESS METAL) CUT
(— FLOATING MATTER) SKIM
(— FROM CHECKER BOARD) HUFF
(— FROM OFFICE) DEPOSE RECALL DISMISS
(— FROM REMEMBRANCE) COVER
(— FROM SHEATH) EVAGINATE
(— GILLS) BEARD
(— HAIR) DEPILATE
(— HUSKS AND CHAFF) GELD
(— IMPURITIES) PURGE
(— INSIDES OF FISH) GIB GIP
(— JUDGE) ADDRESS
(— LOWER BRANCHES) BRASH
(— MAST) UNSTEP
(— ORE) EXTRACT
(— PARTICLES OF GOLD LEAF) SKEW
(— PIECEMEAL) SCAMBLE
(— PITCHER FROM BASEBALL GAME) DERRICK
(— POTATOES) GRABBLE
(— QUEEN BEE) DEMAREE
(— QUIETLY) ABSTRACT
(— ROOTS) GRUB
(— SEED FROM FLAX) RIBBLE
(— SEEDS) STONE
(— SKIN) HULL HUSK
(— SOUND FROM TAPE) BLIP
(— SPROUTS FROM) CHIT
(— STALK FROM) STRIG
(— STAMENS) CASTRATE
(— SURGICALLY) EXTIRPATE
(— TABLECLOTH) DRAW
(— THE TOP OF) COP
(— TO A DISTANCE) ELOIN
(— TO AVOID TAX) SKIM
(— TROUSERS) DEBAG
(— WASTE TO FIBER) GARNETT
(— WOOL) BELLY
(— WORKS OF STOLEN WATCH) CHURCH
(— WRONGFULLY) MISTAKE
(PREF.) DE

REMOVED UP OFF AWAY ALIEN ALOOF APART REMOTE DISTANT SEMOTED ABSTRACT

REMOVER MOVER CROPMAN KNOTTER

REMUDA CAVY CAVAYARD CAVYYARD

REMUNERATE PAY REPAY REWARD GRATIFY SATISFY CONSIDER REIMBURSE

REMUNERATION PAY REWARD SALARY PAYMENT

REMUNERATIVE GAINFUL REWARDING

REMUS (BROTHER OF —) ROMULUS
(FATHER OF —) MARS

RENAISSANCE NARA REBIRTH REVIVAL

RENAL NEPHRIC NEPHRITIC

RENAME ANABAPTIZE

RENCOUNTER CLASH FIGHT DEBATE CONTEST CONFLICT

REND PULL RENT RIVE TEAR TOIL BREAK BURST DIVEL RATCH ROWEL SEVER SPLIT WREST CLEAVE SCREED WRENCH ABSCIND DIVULSE RUPTURE WREATHE DISPIECE DISTRAIN FRACTURE LACERATE SPLINTER
(— AND DEVOUR) TIRE

RENDER DO PAY PUT TRY BEAR DRAW ECHO EMIT MAKE RENT RIND DEFER PRICK REPAY YIELD RECITE REPEAT RETURN DELIVER PRECARY REFLECT REQUITE RESTORE SERVICE TALLAGE TRANSMIT
(— ACID) PRICK
(— AGREEABLE) DULCIFY
(— AS LARD) TRY
(— ASSISTANCE TO SHIP) FOY
(— CAPABLE) ACTIVATE
(— CLEAR) OPEN
(— DEFECTIVE) VITIATE
(— DEFENSELESS) DISARM
(— DESTITUTE) DISFURMSH
(— FIT) ADAPT
(— GODLIKE) DEIFY
(— HEAVY WITH FOOD) STODGE
(— HOMAGE) ATTORN
(— IMMUNE) FRANK VASTATE
(— IMPASSIBLE) STOP
(— IMPERFECT) LAME
(— INEFFECTIVE) VITIATE
(— INSANE) DEMENT DISTRACT
(— KNOTTY) GNARL
(— OBLIQUE) SPLAY
(— OBSCURE) DARKLE
(— OF BOON WORK) PRECARY
(— PLAUSIBLE) GLOSS
(— PURE) EXPURGATE
(— QUIET) ACCOY
(— SENSELESS) STUN ASTONISH
(— SUDDENLY) THROW
(— TURBID) ROIL
(— UNFIT) DENATURE
(— UNSTABLE) UNHINGE
(— VERDICT) PASS
(— VOID) CASS DEFEAT
(— WATERTIGHT) CALK CAULK
(— WEAK) EVIRATE
(— LIABLE) ENGAGE PREDISPOSE
(SUFF.) EN

RENDERED RENDU TRIED

RENDERING RENDU ENGLISH VERSION RENDITION
(— OF SCENE) STUDY

RENDEZVOUS DATE HAUNT TRYST REFUGE HANGOUT MEETING RETREAT
(— FOR SHIPS) DOWN
(— OF WITCHES) SABBAT

RENDING SPLITTING
(— ASUNDER) DIVULSION

RENDITION ACCOUNT CONDUCT DELIVERY
RENEGADE DORAX PERVERT TRAITOR APOSTATE DESERTER RECREANT RENEGADO RUNAGADO RUNAGATE TURNCOAT
RENEGE BEG NIG DENY RENIG DESERT REVOKE RETRACT FAINAIGUE
RENEW NEW REST FRESH RECALL REFORM RENOVE REPEAT RESUME REVIVE INSTORE REBUILD REFRESH REPLACE RESTORE OVERHAUL REJUVENATE
(— MORTAR) REPOINT
(— WINE) STUM
RENEWAL RENEW REVIVAL NOVATION
(SPIRITUAL-) REBIRTH
RENNET LAB RUEN VELL STEEP RENNIN RUNNET EARNING ABOMASUM YEARNING CHEESELIP
RENOUNCE PUT CEDE DEFY DENY QUIT DEVOW FORGO RENAY WAIVE ABJURE DISOWN FORLET FORSAY RECANT REFUSE REJECT RENEGE RESIGN REVOKE ABANDON DECLARE FORLEIT FORSAKE RETRACT WITHSAY ABDICATE ABNEGATE DISCLAIM FORSPEAK FORSWEAR MANSWEAR PROCLAIM RELINQUISH
(— ALLEGIANCE) REVOLT
(— AUTHORITY) REBEL
(— PROMISE) RECEDE
RENOVATE DUST RENEW REVIVE FURBISH REFRESH RESTORE OVERHAUL RENOVIZE
(— HAT) MOLOKER MOLOCKER
RENOWN BAY BRAG FAME ECLAT GLORY KUDOS PRICE RUMOR ESTEEM LUSTER RENONE REPORT EMPRISE SWAGGER WORSHIP PRESTIGE NOTORIETY
RENOWNED FAMED NOBLE NOTED FAMOUS EMINENT RENOMME GLORIOUS MAGNIFIC RENOMMEE
RENT LET SET TAX FARM GALE GAPE HIRE MAIL RACK RIME RIVE SLIT TEAR TOLL TORN WAGE BREAK CANON CENSO CUDDY ENDOW GANCH GAVEL SPLIT BLANCH BREACH BROKEN CENSUS CHASMA CRANNY CUSTOM GAUNCH INCOME SCHISM SCREED STRENT CHARTER CHIEFRY CORNAGE CRACKED CREVICE FISSURE MAILING MOLLAND ONSTAND RENTAGE REVENUE RUPTURE TRIBUTE CHAMPART CHIEFERY HEADRENT STALLAGE VECTIGAL WAYLEAVE LANDGAFOL
(— BY BOAR'S TUSK) GANCH GAUNCH
(— IN LIEU OF SUPPER) CUDDY
(— OF LAND PAID IN KIND) CAIN
(ANNUAL —) CANON
(EARTHQUAKE —) SCARPLET
(GROUND —) CENSO CENSUS
(OATS IN LIEU OF —) AVENAGE
RENTAL KAIN PORT TONNAGE TRIBUTE TUNNAGE
RENTED LETTEN
RENTER FARMER RANTER CHIPPER BOXHOLDER
(— OF GRAZING LAND) AGIST
RENUNCIATION DENIAL APOSTASY DEFIANCE DISAVOWAL REJECTION SACRIFICE
REORGANIZE (— SCIENTIFICALLY) RATIONALIZE
REP CANNELE DROGUET POPELINE
REPAIR DO EIK EKE FIX IMP HEAL HELP MEND TINE AMEND BOTCH DIGHT EMEND HAUNT RALLY REDUB RENEW STORE TRADE UPSET ASTORE BUSHEL COBBLE COGGLE COOPER DOCTOR FETTLE RECURE REDEEM REFORM REMEDY REPASS RESORT RETURN UPKEEP CORRECT INFAINT REDRESS REPAREL RESTORE SERVICE FLOCKING OVERHAUL RETRIEVE REVIVIFY RECONDITION
(— A SOCK) DARN
(— BOAT) CAREEN
(— CLUMSILY) BOTCH
(— FENCE) MOUND
(— ROAD) SKID
(— SHOE) FOX TAP
REPAIRED VAMPED
REPAIRER DOCTOR BOTCHER COBBLER WOFFLER CEMENTER
(SHOE —) JACKMAN BENCHMAN
(TEXTILE —) SMASHER
REPAIRMAN FETTLER
REPARATION BOTE AMENDS REMEDY REWARD DAMAGES REDRESS REPAIRS REQUITAL
(— OF LESIONS) ANAPLASTY
(PL.) ATONEMENT
REPARTEE WIT KNACK REPLY BANTER RETORT RIPOST RIPOSTE BACKCHAT BADINAGE COMEBACK GIFFGAFF
REPAST BAIT FEED FOOD MEAL BEVER FEAST TREAT DRINKING COLLATION
(— BETWEEN MEALS) BEVER BRUNCH BANQUET
(HASTY —) SNACK
(LIGHT —) BAIT VOID VOIDEE COLLATION
REPAY MEED QUIT APPAY TALLY YIELD ACQUIT ANSWER AVENGE REFUND RETORT RETURN REWARD IMBURSE REQUITE RESTORE REIMBURSE
REPEAL ANNUL CANCEL RECALL REVOKE ABANDON ABOLISH RESCIND REVERSE ABROGATE DEROGATE DISENACT RENOUNCE
REPEAT SAY ECHO GAIT RAME RANE SHOW TELL DITTO QUOTE RECUR RENEW RESAY REVIE THRUM ANSWER RENDER RESUME RETAIL SECOND DECLINE DIVULGE ITERATE PRESENT RECYCLE REPLICA REPRISE DINGDONG REDOUBLE REHEARSE REPLICATE
(— BY ROTE) PARROT
(— FROM MEMORY) RECORD
(— GLIBLY) SCREED
(— IN DETAIL) RETAIL
(— INSISTENTLY) PERSIST
(— LORD'S PRAYER) PATTER
(— MONOTONOUSLY) CUCKOO DINGDONG
(— OF PATTERN) GAIT
(— TIRESOMELY) DIN
REPEATED OFTEN CONSTANT FREQUENT PERENNIAL
REPEATEDLY OFT EVERY THRICE
REPEATER GUN RIFLE WATCH PISTOL FLOATER HOLDOVER
REPEL FEND TURN WARD FENCE REBUT DEFEND PUTOFF REBEAT REBUFF REFUSE REFUTE REJECT REPUGN RESIST REVOLT DISGUST PELLATE REPULSE PROPULSE
REPELLANT REPUGNANT
REPELLENT DEET DOPE GRIM MACE HARSH CAMPHOR HATEFUL SQUALID
(INSECT —) DEET
REPELLING HARD SICKLY
REPENT REW RUE MOURN GRIEVE REGRET REPTANT CREEPING FORTHINK
REPENTANCE REW RUE PITY RUTH RUING REGRET SORROW PENANCE REMORSE
REPENTANT ATTRITE PENITENT
REPERCUSSION ECHO TENOR RECOIL REPULSE BACKWASH
REPERTORY REP BOOK LIST INDEX ARSENAL CATALOG
(PERFORMER'S —) REPERTOIRE
REPETITION BIS REP COPY ECHO REPP ROTE PLOCE REVIE TROLL DILOGY REPEAT MENTION RECITAL REPLICA REPRISE IDENTITY ITERANCE ITERANCY NEMBUTSU PALILOGY PARROTRY RECOVERY REDOUBLE REHEARSAL
(— IN REVERSE ORDER) EPANODOS
(— OF HOMOLOGOUS PARTS) MERISM
(— OF SPEECH FORMS) ROTE
(— OF WORD) ANAPHORA BATTOLOGY
(NEEDLESS —) REDUNDANCY
(SUCCESSIVE —) SEQUENCE
(UNINSPIRED —) STENCIL
(UNINTENTIONAL —) DITTOGRAPHY
(PREF.) **(PATHOLOGICAL —)** PALI
REPETITIOUS TATA
REPHAEL (FATHER OF —) SHEMAIAH
REPHAH (FATHER OF —) EPHRAIM
REPHAIAH (FATHER OF —) HUR TOLA BINEA
REPHAIM EMIM
REPINE FRET PINE WEAKEN COMPLAIN
REPINING MURMUR REGRET PLAINTIVE
REPLACE SWAP SWOP RENEW REPAY SHIFT STEAD CHANGE FOLLOW REFUND REMISE REPONE SUPPLY FRESHEN PREEMPT RESTORE SUCCEED DISPLACE SUPPLANT REPLENISH
REPLACEMENT CUT ERSATZ
(— FOR HAND) HOOK
(— OF CONSONANT) LENITION
REPLAY ECHO
REPLENISH CHUNK REFIT RENEW SUPPLY NOURISH PERFECT PLENISH REPLETE RESTORE SUFFICE
REPLETE FAT FULL RIFE SATED STOUT STUFF FILLED GORGED IMPLETE COMPLETE HONEYPOT
REPLETION FULTH FULNESS SURFEIT FULLNESS PLETHORA SATURITY
REPLICA BIS PUP COPY IDEA CHARM CLONE IMAGE REVIE FACSIMILE
REPLICATION ECHO REPLY ANSWER REJOINDER
REPLY CAP JAWAB KNACK RESAY ANSWER REJOIN RETORT RETURN REPLIAL RESOUND RESPOND REPARTEE REPLIQUE RESPONSE SIMILITER
(SECOND —) DUPLY
REPORT CRY POP SAY FAME ITEM NOTE TELL VENT VOTE WORD AUDIT BRUIT COVER CRACK NOISE REFER ROUND RUMOR SCALE SOUND STATE STORY VOICE BREEZE CAHIER CREDIT DELATE DETAIL FINGER GOSSIP RAPORT RECITE RELATE RENOWN REPUTE RETURN RUMBLE SPEECH STEVEN SURVEY THREAP ACCOUNT HANSARD HEARING HEARSAY INKLING KHUBBER NARRATE OPINION PROCESS RECITAL ADVISORY DECISION DESCRIBE HEMOGRAM VERBATIM GRAPEVINE
(— NEWS) COVER
(— OF GUN) CLAP
(— OF INFRACTION) GIG
(— OF PROCEEDINGS) CAHIER
(— OF TIMBER SURVEYOR) CRUISE
(ABSURD —) CANARD
(BELIEVED —) CREDIT
(CASUAL —) FABLE
(COMMON —) CRY FAME SPEECH
(FALSE —) SHAVE CANARD FURPHY SLANDER
(FLYING —) SOUGH
(HONORABLE —) TONGUE
(LAW —) CASE
(MILITARY —) STATE SITREP
(NEWS —) FLASH SCOOP
(NOISY —) RUMBLE
(OFFICIAL —) HANSARD
(POPULAR —) RUMOR RUMOUR
(PUBLIC —) FAME
(UNFAVORABLE —) SKIN
(UNVERIFIED —) VOICE GRAPEVINE
(VAGUE —) BREEZE
REPORTER LEGMAN PISTOL CREEPER NEWSMAN NEWSHAWK PRESSMAN STRINGER PAPARAZZO
(SOCIETY —) JENKINS
(YOUNG —) CUB
REPORTING BEAT COVERAGE
REPOSE RO BED LIE PUT AFFY CALM EASE RELY REST PEACE PLACE POISE QUIET SLEEP REPAST RECLINE EASINESS QUIETUDE SERENITY
(— LAZILY) FROWST
(DREAMY —) KEF
REPOSITORY ARK SAFE AMBRY CAPSA DEPOT HOARD VAULT

ARMORY CASKET MUSEUM VESTRY ARCHIVE CABINET CAPSULE GENIZAH GRANARY HANAPER SPICERY ARCHIVES MAGAZINE TREASURY SEPULCHER STOREHOUSE
(— FOR DEAD) URN
(SECRET —) SECRETAIRE
REPOSOIR REPOSE
REPOSSESS PULL RECOVER
REPREHEND NIP WARN BLAME CHIDE REBUKE CENSURE REPRISE REPROVE CRITICIZE
REPREHENSIBLE ILL AMISS BLAMABLE CRIMINAL CULPABLE SCABROUS
REPREHENSION BLAME REBUKE CENSURE OBLOQUY REPROOF
REPRESENT GIVE LIKE LIMN SHOW TYPE SHADE DEPICT SEMBLE TYPIFY DISPLAY EXHIBIT FASHION PICTURE PORTRAY PROTEST TRADUCE DEFIGURE DESCRIBE RESEMBLE PERSONATE
(— CONCRETELY) THING
(— IN LANGUAGE) ACT BODY DRAW ENACT IMAGE SPEAK BLAZON CLOTHE EMBODY FIGURE SAMPLE BETOKEN EXPRESS DECIPHER
(— ON GRAPH) PLOT
(— ON STAGE) ACT
REPRESENTATION SUN BUST FORM ICON IDEA IDOL IKON SHOW SWAG ANGLE DRAFT FANCY IMAGE INSET LABEL MEDAL TABUT AVOWAL BUDDHA EFFIGY FIGURE FLEECE MODULE OBJECT SCHEMA SCHEME SKETCH SUNRAY WAYANG ANATOMY DIORAMA DRAUGHT DRAWING EPITOME EXPRESS EXTRACT FOLIAGE MAJESTY SCENERY TABLEAU BESTIARY BLAZONRY CREATION EPIPHANY EXTERIOR IDIOGRAM LIKENESS TYPORAMA SIMULACRUM RESEMBLANCE
(— OF SERPENT) BASIL DRAGON BASILISK
(— OF SHRINE OF HUSAIN) TABUT
(— OF VISION) AISLING
(DIPLOMATIC —) DEMARCHE
(FACSIMILE —) TYPORAMA
(FAINT —) SHADOW
(FUNERAL —) CADAVER
(GRAPHIC —) CHART BISECT
(HERALDIC —) LEOPARD LIONCEL
(MENTAL —) FANCY IMAGE
(MINIATURE —) MODEL
(SYMBOLIC —) ALLEGORY
REPRESENTATIVE REP FAIR TYPE AGENT ENVOY VAKIL ASSIGN COMMON DEPUTY EMBLEM LEDGER SAMPLE VAKEEL BURGESS GRIEVER TRIBUNE TYPICAL DECURION DELEGATE EMISSARY EXPONENT FIELDMAN GASTALDO INTIMATE OBSERVER SALESMAN SPECIMEN
(— AT FOREIGN COURT) RESIDENT
(— OF ATMOSPHERE) AERIAL
(— OF CLERGY) PROCTOR
(LEGAL—) SYNDIC
(MANUFACTURER'S —) BLOCKMAN
(POPE'S —) INTERNUNCIO
(PL.) COMMONS
REPRESS CURB HUSH BLUNT BRIDE CHAIN CHECK CHOKE CRUSH DAUNT DROWN QUELL SQUAT BRIDLE COERCE DEADEN REBUKE STIFLE SUBDUE CONTROL DEPRESS INHIBIT REPRIME SILENCE SWALLOW COMPRESS OVERBEAR RESTRAIN RESTRICT RETRENCH REVOCATE STRANGLE SUPPRESS WITHHOLD
REPRESSED SULLEN STIFLED
REPRIEVE DELAY GRACE ESCAPE REPRISE RESPITE SUSPEND POSTPONE
REPRIMAND WIG BAWL CALL CHEW JACK SKIN SLAP SLON SNEB SNIB TASK CHECK CREED SLATE SLOAN SPANK TARGE BOUNCE CARPET EARFUL REBUKE ROCKET STRAFE CENSURE CHAPTER LECTURE REPROOF REPROVE TICKOFF DRESSING WRAGGING
REPRINT COPY DEPRINT OFFPRINT REIMPOSE TAUCHNITZ
REPRISAL PRIZE MARQUE REPRISE REQUITAL RECAPTION
REPROACH ILL TAX BLOT GIBE JIBE LACK NOSE NOTE RAIL SLUR SPOT TEEN TWIT WITE ABUSE BLAME BRAID BRAND CHIDE SCOLD SHEND TAUNT WHITE AYWORD BISMER INFAMY REBUKE REVILE UPCAST VILIFY BLEMISH CENSURE CONDEMN REPROOF REPROVE SLANDER UMBRAID UPBRAID WITHNIM BETONGUE DISHONOR REDARGUE REVILING CONTUMELY OPPROBRIUM REFLECTION
REPROACHFUL BITTER ABUSIVE SHAMEFUL
REPROBATE HARD LOST SCAMP DISOWN RASCAL REJECT SINNER ABANDON CENSURE CORRUPT EXCLUDE REPROVE DEPRAVED DISALLOW HARDENED SCALAWAG SKALAWAG
REPRODUCE BUD HIT COPY BREED SPORE RECITE REPEAT PORTRAY AUTOTYPE MULTIPLY REFIGURE REMEMBER PROCREATE
(— ONESELF) CLONE
REPRODUCTION CAST COPY REVI CLONE IMAGE PRINT ECTYPE RECALL STEREO EDITION ELECTRO EXOGAMY FISSION REPLICA REVIVAL APOMIXIS BLOCKOUT GAMOGAMY HOMOGAMY LIKENESS
(— BY FISSION) SCISSIPARITY
(— OF DESIGNS) SPATTERWORK
(— OF SOUND) AUDIO
(— WITHOUT SEX) MONOGENY
(SUFF.) GAM(AE)(IST)(OUS)(Y) GAMETE GON(E)(IDIUM)(IMO)(IUM)(Y)
REPRODUCTIVE PROLIFIC
REPROOF PROD RATE BLAME CHECK LESSON REBUKE CHIDING LECTURE SETDOWN JOBATION REPROACH REPROVAL SCOLDING TAXATION JAWBATION
(GENTLE —) ADMONITION
REPROVE RAG TAP BAWL FLAY FRIE JOBE RATE SNIB TRIM BLAME CHECK CHIDE CRAWL SCOLD SHEND SHENT SNEAP BERATE CHASTE REBUKE REFORM SCHOOL THREAT CENSURE CONDEMN CORRECT IMPROVE LECTURE UPBRAID WITHNIM ADMONISH CHASTISE KEELHAUL REDARGUE REPROACH UNDERNIM WITHTAKE
REPTILE LOW MEAN WORM GUANA SNAKE VIPER GAVIAL LIZARD MOLOCH TURTLE CRAWLER CREEPER DIAPSID GHARIAL PROTEUS SAURIAN SERPENT TUATARA BASILISK CREEPING CYNODONT DINOSAUR GALESAUR MESOSAUR MOSASAUR PLIOSAUR STEGOMUS SYNAPSID TORTOISE ALLIGATOR CROCODILE PELYCOSAUR PLESIOSAUR
(FLYING —) PTEROSAUR PTERANODON PTERODACTYL PTERODACTYLE
(PART OF —) EYE JAW PIT BODY FANG SCALE TOOTH BUTTON RATTLE SHEATH TONGUE SEGMENT
(PREF.) HERPET(I)(O)
REPTILIAN HERPETIC
REPUBLIC STATE SOVIET POBLACHT
(FRENCH —) MARIANNE
(IDEAL —) ICARIA
(IMAGINARY —) OCEANA
REPUBLICAN RED QUID STALWART SANSCULOT
REPUDIATE DEFY DENY ABJURE DISOWN RECANT REFUTE REJECT DECLINE DISAVOW DISCARD DIVORCE RETRACT DISCLAIM DISVOUCH RENOUNCE
(— DEBTS) NOCHEL NOTCHEL
REPUDIATING NAKIR
REPUGNANCE ENMITY HATRED HORROR DISGUST DISLIKE DISTASTE LOATHING
REPUGNANT ALIEN DIRTY NASTY ADVERSE HATEFUL OPPOSED INIMICAL OPPOSITE ABHORRENT OBNOXIOUS REPULSIVE
REPULSE FOIL ROUT RUSH CHECK FLING REBUT REFEL REPEL SMEAR DEFEAT DENIAL REBUFF REBUTE REFUSE REJECT
REPULSION UG DISLIKE AVERSION
REPULSIVE COLD DAIN EVIL LOTH UGLY VILE LOATH GREASY LAIDLY FULSOME HATEFUL LOATHLY SQUALID SCABROUS UNHONEST
REPURCHASE (— AGREEMENT) REPO
REPUTABLE GOOD HONEST WORTHY CREDIBLE ESTIMABLE
REPUTATION REP FAME LOSE NAME NOTE ODOR PASS GLORY HONOR IZZAT NOISE RUMOR SAVOR VOICE CREDIT ESTEEM RECORD RENOWN SHADOW LAURELS OPINION RESPECT WORSHIP STANDING
(EVIL —) INFAMY
(GOOD —) STANDING
REPUTE FAME ODOR RANK WORD NOISE SAVOR THINK RECKON REGARD STATUS OPINION RESPECT WORSHIP ESTIMATE JUDGMENT POSITION
(ILL —) SLANDER
REPUTED DIT PUTATIVE
REQUEST ASK BEG BOON CALL PLEA PRAY SEEK SUIT TELL WISH CLAIM LIBEL QUEST YEARN APPEAL BEHEST DEMAND DESIRE DIRECT ENCORE INVITE MOTION BESPEAK COMMAND ENTREAT INQUIRY REQUIRE SOLICIT ENTREATY INSTANCE PETITION ROGATION
(— FOR HELP) SOS
(— RECONSIDERATION) RECLAMA
(STRONG —) DUN DEMAND
REQUIEM HYMN MASS REST DIRGE PEACE QUIET REPOSE REQUIN
REQUIN SHARK TOMMY
REQUIRE ASK HAVE LACK NEED TAKE WANT CLAIM CRAVE EXACT FORCE GAVEL COMPEL DEMAND DEPEND DESIRE ENJOIN ENTAIL EXPECT GOVERN MISTER OBLIGE BEHOOVE DICTATE INVOLVE MANDATE SOLICIT STIPULATE
REQUIRED DUE SET SUPPOSED NECESSARY REQUISITE OBLIGATORY
REQUIREMENT CALL MUST NEED LEGAL ORDER BEHEST DEMAND NECESSITY
(VEXATIOUS —) FIKE
(PL.) EXIGENCE EXIGENCY
REQUIRING
(PREF.) END(O)
REQUISITE DUE NEED NEEDY VITAL NEEDFUL ESSENTIAL NECESSARY
REQUISITION ORDER DEMAND INDENT EMBARGO REQUEST
REQUITAL WAR APPAY MERIT REPAY SERVE TALLY YIELD ACQUIT DEFRAY REWARD GRATIFY PAYMENT REVENGE CONSIDER FORYIELD REPRISAL
REQUITE SERVE RECOMPENSE RECIPROCATE
RERAILER DIAMOND
REREAD DOUBLE
RERECORD DUB
REREDOS SCREEN BRAZIER DRAPERY RETABLO FIREBACK REARDOSS
REREMOUSE BAT
RERUN (PAYMENT FOR —) RESIDUAL
RES POINT THING MATTER SUBJECT
RESCIND LIFT ANNUL CANCEL REMOVE REPEAL REVOKE ABOLISH RETRACT RETREAT ABROGATE
RESCRIPT EDICT ORDER DECREE LETTER EPISTLE
RESCUE RID FREE HELP REDD SAVE BORROW RANSOM REDEEM RESKEW SUCCOR WARISH BAILOUT DELIVER RECLAIM RECOVER RELEASE SALVAGE DELIVERY LIBERATE RECOURSE
(— OF PROPERTY) SALVAGE

RESEARCH ARBEIT SEARCH ENQUIRY INQUIRY
RESECT EXCISE
RESEDA LEEK MENNUET MORILLON
RESELL (— AT INCREASED PRICES) SCALP
RESEMBLANCE SWAP PARITY SIMILE ANALOGY AFFINITY LIKENESS PARALLEL VICINITY SIMILARITY
(DIM HAZY —) BLY
(SLIGHT —) BLUSH
RESEMBLE AGREE BRAID FAVOR IMAGE LIKEN APPEAR DEPICT FIGURE RECALL SEMBLE COMPARE IMITATE PORTRAY ASSEMBLE SIMULATE
(SUFF.) ODE OID OPSIS
RESEMBLING LIKE SAME SEMBLE SIMILAR SEMBLANT
(— AN EGG) OVULARIAN
(— COMB) PECTINAL
(— GOOSE) ANSERINE
(— HORSE) EQUOID
(— IVORY) EBURNEAN EBURNEOID EBURNEOUS
(— LADDER) SCALARIFORM
(— SALT) HALOID
(— STAR) STELLATE
(— WALL) MURAL
(SUFF.) ACEOUS AR ARY EOUS FORM FUL IFORM ITIC OIDAL
RESENT HATE MEAN INDIGN MALIGN STOMACH SUGGEST
RESENTFUL HARD HURT BITTER SULLEN ENVIOUS JEALOUS STOMACHY
RESENTMENT HURT DEPIT PIQUE SNUFF SPITE CHOLER ENMITY GRUDGE HATRED MALICE RANCOR DISDAIN DUDGEON OFFENCE OFFENSE STOMACH UMBRAGE JEALOUSY HEARTBURN
(CAUSE —) OUTRAGE
RESERVATION DIBS SALVO SPACE SAVING UNLESS BOOKING CAUTION KEEPING PROVISO RESERVE FORPRISE RESERVAL
(MENTAL —) SALVO SCRUPLE
RESERVE BOOK CAVE FUND HOJU HOLD KEEP SALT SAVE SPARE BACKUP NICETY SEPONE SEPOSE TRIARY BACKLOG CAUTION CONTROL DIGNITY SEPOSIT SHYNESS TENENUE COLDNESS DISTANCE FALLBACK FORPRISE IMMODEST WITHHOLD STOCKPILE
(HOME —S) LANDSTURM
(IN —) ONICE
(MILITARY —) HOJU YOBI TRIARY TRIARII LANDWEHR
(MONETARY —) CUSHION
(PL.) FAT KOKUMIN STRENGTH
RESERVED COY DRY SHY COLD UNCO ALOOF CHARY SAVED BOOKED CLOSED DEMURE MODEST SILENT STANCH COSTIVE DISTANT RETIRED STRANGE RETICENT RETIRING STANDOFF TACITURN WITHHELD
(— FOR ROYAL USE) KHASS
(NOT —) COMMON
RESERVOIR DAM BOSS FONT KEEP LAKE PENT SUMP TANK BASIN FOUNT STANK STORE CENOTE SIPHON SOURCE SYPHON CISTERN CLEARER FAVISSA FOREBAY IMPOUND PISCINA RECEIPT AFTERBAY DEPOSITO FOUNTAIN MAGAZINE STANDAGE
(— OF WEATHERGLASS) STAGNUM
RESET HELP ABODE ALTER RECEPT RESORT SUCCOR RECEIPT REPLANT SHARPEN WELCOME
RESHEPH (FATHER OF —) EPHRAIM
RESIDE BIG WIN BIDE BIGG HOME LIVE STAY TELD WONT ABIDE DWELL LODGE REMAIN CONSIST SOJOURN HABITATE
(— TEMPORARILY) LIE STOP
RESIDENCE DUN WON DOON HALL HOME SEAT SEMI STAY WENE WONE ABODE COURT DAIRI DEMUR HOUSE MAHAL MANSE YAMUN BIDING DUKERY ELYSEE HOSTEL MANOIR TENSER DEANERY DROSTDY EMBASSY SOJOURN CURATAGE DOMICILE DWELLING LEGATION RESIANCE RESIANCY RESIDUUM SEDIMENT SETTLING PREFECTURE
(— FOR STUDENTS) INN
(— OF ARCHBISHOP) PALACE
(— OF CHIEF OF VILLAGE) TATA
(— OF ECCLESIASTIC) MANSE PRIORY DEANERY RECTORY CURATAGE VICARAGE PARSONAGE
(— OF FRENCH PRESIDENTS) ELYSEE
(— OF MANDARIN) YAMEN YAMUN
(— OF MIKADO) DAIRI
(— OF PRIEST) CONVENTO
(— OF SOVEREIGN) PALACE
(— OF SULTAN) SERAGLIO
(FORTIFIED —) DUN
(HILL —) RATH
(OFFICIAL TURKISH —) KONAK
(RURAL —) SEAT FARMSTEAD
(SUMMER —) MAHAL
(TEMPORARY —) STAY
RESIDENT GER FIXED LEGER LIVER INMATE LEDGER STABLE CITIZEN DENIZEN DWELLER PRESENT RESIANT RESIDER RESTING HABITANT INHERENT KAMAAINA MINISTER OCCUPANT
(— AT A UNIVERSITY) GREMIALE
(— OF HAWAII) KAMAAINA
(— OF NEWFOUNDLAND) LIVYER
(— OF WEST. AUSTRALIA) GROPER
(ALIEN —) GER METIC
(CHINESE — OF TIBET) AMBAN
(FOREIGN-BORN —) ALIEN
(OLD —) STANDARD
(TEMPORARY —) TRANSIENT
(SUFF.) ESE ITE
(— OF) ER IER YER
RESIDUAL RELICT REMANIE REMANENT
RESIDUE ASH DREG FOOT GUNK HEEL LAFE LAVE LEES REST SILT SLAG UNIT MAZUT SHARD SHERD BEGASS BORING BOTTOM GRUFFS RELICS BAGASSE CINDERS REMAINS HARDHEAD LEAVINGS LEFTOVER REMANENT RESIDUUM SEMICOKE TAILINGS
(— FROM DISTILLATION) VINASSE
(— FROM FAT) CRAP
(— FROM OLIVES) SANZA
(— FROM REFINING TIN) HARDHEAD
(— IN OPIUM PIPE) YENSHEE
(— IN STILL) BOTTOM BOTTOMS
(— OF COAL) COKE SEMICOKE
(— OF COKE) BREEZE
(— OF COMBUSTION) ASH
(— OF HONEYCOMB) SLUMGUM
(— OF PETROLEUM) MAZUT ASTATKI
(— OF SHINGLES) SPALT
(FRIABLE —) CALX
(INSOLUBLE —) MARC
(SMELTING —) SPEISS
(WORTHLESS —) SNUFF
(PL.) TANKAGE
RESIDUUM TAIL BOTTOM DEPOSIT RESIDUE SEDIMENT
RESIGN QUIT DEMIT FORGO REMIT YIELD PERMIT SUBMIT ABANDON COMMEND DELIVER FORGIVE ABDICATE RENOUNCE RELINQUISH
RESIGNATION PATIENCE DEMISSION SURRENDER
RESILIENCE GIVE LIFE TONE BOUNCE RECOIL SPRING REBOUND BUOYANCY
RESILIENCY TONE
RESILIENT TOUGH BOUNCY LIVELY SUPPLE WHIPPY ELASTIC SPRINGY FLEXIBLE
RESIN ALK LAC BALM BATU BREA HASH TOLU ALKYD AMBER ANIME COPAL CUMAR ELEMI EPOXY GUGAL GUGUL KAURI PITCH ROSEL ROSET SIRUP SYRUP ANTIAR BINDER CHARAS CONIMA DAMMAR GOOGUL GUACIN HARTIN MASTIC STORAX TAMANU ACOUCHI ACRYLIC AMBRITE BENZOIN BISABOL DERRIDE FLUAVIL GAMBOGE IONOMER LADANUM PERSPEX SAGAPEN SHELLAC ALKITRAN ALMACIGA BAKELITE BDELLIUM CACHIBOU CANNABIN COLOPHAN EUOSMITE FORMVAIL GALAGALA GALLIPOT GEDANITE GUAIACUM MALAPAHO MELAMINE OPOPANAX PHENOLIC SANDARAC SCAMMONY
(— DRAWN FROM TREES) CHIP
(— FROM HEMP) CHARAS
(— FROM NORWAY SPRUCE) THUS
(— OF FIR TREE) BLOB
(— PLASTIC) SARAN
(FLEXIBLE —) SARAN
(FOSSIL —) AMBER AMBRITE HARTITE GEDANITE GLESSITE RETINITE
(GRADE OF —) SORTS
(GUM —) ELEMI GUGUL LASER MYRRH ANTIAR BISABOL GAMBOGE BDELLIUM SAGAPENUM
(NARCOTIC —) CHARAS CHURUS
(SYNTHETIC —S) TEFLON
(TURPENTINE —) ALK GALIPOT COLOPHONY
(PREF.) RETIN(O)
(SUFF.) RETIN
RESINOID ALNUIN HELONIN LOBELIN ASCLEPIN CERASEIN CHELONIN TRILLIIN
RESINOUS ROSETY ROSETTY
RESIST BUCK DEFY FACE STAY REPEL STAND DEFEND IMPUGN OPPOSE REPUGN WITHER CONTEST DISPUTE GAINSAY KNUCKLE RESERVE WITHSET OUTBRAVE OUTSTAND
(— AUTHORITY) REBEL DEFORCE
(— SEPARATION) ATTRACT
RESISTANCE DRAG LOAD OHMAGE REBUFF WITHER BALLAST ANTITYPY BLOCKAGE FASTNESS FRICTION HARDNESS OBSTACLE SEDITION
(— OF COTTON FIBERS) DRAG
(— OF KEYS) ACTION
(— THAT EXPLOSIVE MUST OVERCOME) BURDEN BURTHEN
(— TO ATTACK) DEFENCE DEFENSE
(— TO CHANGE) INERTIA
(— TO COLOR CHANGE) FASTNESS
(— TO DISEASE) PREMUNITION
(— TO SLIPPING) BOND
(GREEK — GROUP) EDES ELAS
(PASSIVE —) SATYAGRAHA
(UNIT OF —) OHM
RESISTANT HARD STOUT STABILE STUBBORN
(— TO CHANGE) FAST STICKY
(— TO HEAT) THERMODURIC
RESISTING OBSTANT RELUCTANT
RESISTOR BLEEDER DIVERTOR RHEOSTAT
RESOLUTE BOLD FIRM GRIM BRAVE FIXED HARDY MANLY STERN STIFF STOUT GRITTY MANFUL PLUCKY STABLE STANCH STEADY STUFFY STURDY ANIMOSE ANIMOUS DECIDED CONSTANT FAITHFUL INTREPID POSITIVE STALWART STUBBORN UNSHAKEN
(MAKE —) STEEL
RESOLUTELY TALLY FIRMLY STOUTLY
RESOLUTION VOW SAND THEW NERVE PARTY PLUCK POINT STARCH ACUERDO BESLUIT CENSURE COURAGE MANHEAD MANHOOD PURPOSE RESOLVE THOUGHT ANALYSIS DECISION DIERESIS ENACTURE STRENGTH CONSTANCY
RESOLVE ACT BEND MELT REDE SOIL UNDO LAPSE RELAX SALVE SOLVE SOYLE UNTIE VOUCH ADJUST ADVICE ASSOIL DECIDE DECREE FACTOR INCIDE REDUCE SETTLE STEVEN ABSOLVE ANALYZE APPOINT BETHINK CONSULT PURPOSE CONCLUDE DISSOLVE UNRIDDLE UNTANGLE RECONCILE
(— GRAMMATICALLY) PARSE
(— INTO ELEMENTS) ANALYSE ANALYZE
RESOLVED BENT BOUND INTENT CERTAIN INTENSE RESOLUTE
(HALF —) GOOD
RESONANCE BODY EMPATHY

RAPPORT RESOUND SYNTONY TYMPANY SONORITY VIBRANCY MESOMERISM
RESONANT BIG BRASS RINGY OROTUND RINGING SILVERY VIBRANT CANOROUS PLANGENT SONORANT SONOROUS SOUNDFUL SOUNDING
RESORT GO RUN SPA BEAT DOME HOWF LIDO SEEK TEEM TOUR TURN CAUSE FRAME HAUNT HOWFF JOINT RECUR RESET VISIT ESCORT FINISH REPAIR RETURN REVERT THRONG COMPANY PIMLICO RECOURSE RESOURCE TEETOTUM
(— OF LEARNED) MUSEUM
(— TO) SEEK
(— TO DEVIOUS METHODS) FINAGLE
(— TO EXPEDIENTS) SHIFT
(BATHING —) PLAGE
(DISREPUTABLE —) KEN DIVE
(DRINKING —) DOGGERY
(EVIL —) ROOKERY
(LOW —) KEN DIVE STEW SPITAL
(MEANS OF —) REFUGE
(WORKINGMEN'S —) TEETOTUM
RESOUND DIN DUN ECHO PEAL RING SOUND REECHO EXPLODE REBOUND RESPEAK VIBRATE REDOUBLE
RESOUNDING BRASS REVERB REBOANT EMPHATIC FORCEFUL PLANGENT RESONANT RUMOROUS
(— WITH TALK) ABUZZ
RESOURCE WON BOOT FUND WONE MEANS SHIFT REFUGE RESORT STOPGAP PURCHASE
(PL.) EASE FOND GAIN FUNDS MEANS PURSE SINEW BOTTOM FACULTY FOISONS PURCHASE STRENGTH POCKETBOOK
RESOURCEFUL APT FENDY SHARP SMART ADROIT CLEVER FACILE SHIFTY PLANFUL
RESOURCEFULNESS SENSE SHIFT AGILITY
RESPECT ORE WAY DUTY FACE HEED HORE LOOK MARK DEFER DULIA FRONT HONOR IZZAT PARTY VALUE ASPECT BEHALF DETAIL ESTEEM HALLOW HOMAGE NOTICE REGARD CONCERN OBSERVE RESPITE SUSPECT TASHRIF WORSHIP CONSIDER HABITUDE RELATION VENERATE
(PL.) DEVOIR
RESPECTABLE GOOD NICE SMUG DOUCE DECENT PROPER FRUSANT CULOTTIC
RESPECTFUL AWFUL CIVIL CAREFUL DUTEOUS DUTIFUL HEEDFUL REVERENT
RESPECTIVE SEVERAL
RESPIRATION SIGH EUPNEA ANAPNEA DYSPNEA EUPNOEA ROARING GRUNTING
(PREF.) PNEO PNEUM(A)(O)(ON)(ONO) PNEUMATO SPIRO
RESPIRATOR MUZZLE CUIRASS INHALER
(KIND OF —) DRINKER
RESPIRE BLOW LIVE REST EXHALE REVIVE BREATHE SNUFFLE SUSPIRE
RESPITE SOB REST STAY TRUE DELAY FRIST LETUP PAUSE BARLEY BREATH LAYOFF REGARD REMISE LEISURE RESPECT INTERVAL REPRIEVE SURCEASE
RESPLENDENCE GLORY SHEEN FULGENCE FULGENCY SPLENDOR
RESPLENDENT LUCID SHEEN BRIGHT GILDED ORIENT SILVER AUREATE SHINING GLORIOUS GORGEOUS LUSTROUS SPLENDID SUNSHINY
RESPOND FIELD REACT REPLY ANSWER RETURN TRISAGION
(— TO LURE) STOOL
(— TO PROVOCATION) RISE
(— WARMLY) RISE
RESPONDENT ANSWERER APPELLEE
RESPONSE AMEN ECHO CHORD REPLY SNAFF ANSWER EARFUL VOLLEY INTROIT RESPOND ANTIPHON BEHAVIOR INSTINCT REACTION REANSWER RECEPTION
(— OF KEYS) ACTION
(— OF SHIP) STEERING
(— TO GRAVITY) GEOTAXIS
(INVOLUNTARY —) TIC
(LITURGICAL —) RESPONSORY
(NONCOMMITAL —) ISEE
RESPONSIBILITY BABY BALL CARE DUTY ONUS WITE BLAME GUILT TRUST CHARGE RACKET
RESPONSIBLE GOOD SOLID DIRECT LIABLE AMENABLE
(JOINTLY —) SOLIDARY
RESPONSION REPLY ANSWER
(PL.) SMALLS
RESPONSIVE OPEN SOFT WARM GUILTY MUTUAL NIMBLE SUPPLE TENDER MEETING AMENABLE SENSIBLE
(— TO BEAUTY) ESTHETIC
(— TO STIMULI) SENTIENT
(MUTUALLY —) ANTIPHONIC
(NOT —) IMMUNE
RESPONSIVENESS TOUCH FEELING
(ABNORMAL —) SENSITIVITY
RESPONSORY ANTHEM LIBERA GRADUAL RESPOND
REST BED LAY LIE PUT SET SIT SOB BASE BLOW CALM CAMP EASE HANG HEEL LAIR LAVE LEAN LIOS LISS PROP RELY RIDE RUST STAY STOP COUCH FOUND LEATH LIEBY PAUSE PEACE POISE QUIET RENEW ROOST SLEEP SPELL STAND TRUST WREST ANCHOR BOTTOM FAUCRE FEWTER GROUND INSIST REMAIN REPOSE SETTLE SIESTA STEADY UNTIRE ADHARMA BALANCE BREATHE CAESURA CLARION COMFORT GALLOWS NOONING RECLINE REFRESH RELACHE REMNANT REQUIEM RESIDUE RESPITE SILENCE SLUMBER SOJOURN SUFFLUE SUPPORT SURPLUS AKINESIS INTERVAL QUIETUDE STANDOFF VACATION
(— FOR SPEAR OR LANCE) QUEUE FAUCRE FEWTER
(— FOR SUPPORT) ABUT
(— FOR TYMPAN) GALLOWS
(— HORSE) WIND
(— IDLY) SLUG
(— LAZILY) FROWST
(— ON PLANER) SIDEHEAD
(— ON SUPPORT) BOTTOM
(— UPRIGHT) STAND
(HALF —) MINIM SOSPIRO
(LATHE —) STEADY
(LEG — ON SADDLE) CRUTCH
(MUSKET —) GAFFLE
(NOONDAY —) NAP SIESTA
(QUARTER —) SOSPIRO
(SHORT —) CATNAP
(PREF.) PAULO
RESTATE REHASH
RESTATEMENT SUMMARY
RESTAURANT CAFE DINER GRILL HOUSE PLACE BISTRO BUFFET EATERY AUTOMAT BEANERY CABARET CANTEEN CANTINA OSTERIA TEAROOM HIDEAWAY BRASSERIE CHOPHOUSE TRATTORIA
(— KEEPER) BISTRO TRAITEUR
(SMALL —) CAFF
RESTAURANTEUR (FAMOUS —) SARDI
RESTFUL COOL SOFT QUIET PLACID EASEFUL RELAXED SOOTHFUL TRANQUIL
RESTHARROW WHIN CAMMOCK SITFAST LANDWHIN
RESTHOUSE KHAN SERAI AMBALAM CHHATRI KHANKAH
RESTING DORMANT
(PREF.) STATO
RESTING PLACE (ALSO SEE RESTHOUSE) FORM GIST GITE STAGE CHHATRI DHARMSALA
RESTITUTION AMENDS RETURN RECOVERY
(FINAL —) APOCATASTASIS
RESTIVE ANTSY BALKY FUDGY ITCHY RESTY RUSTY FIDGETY UNRESTY UNWAYED CONTRARY INACTIVE RESTLESS SKITTISH SLUGGISH STUBBORN UNWIELDY
RESTLESS ANTSY FIKIE FUDGY ITCHY FITFUL HAUNTY HECTIC ROVING UNEASY AGITATO ERETHIC FIDGETY FLIGHTY FRETFUL INQUIET RAMPLER RAMPLOR RESTIVE TEWSOME TOSSING UNQUIET UNRESTY VARIANT WAKEFUL FEVERISH FEVEROUS STEERING
(— FLYCATCHER) GRINDER
RESTLESSNESS FIKE STIR FIDGET UNREST DISQUIET ACATHISIA AKATHISIA JACTATION
RESTORATION REPAIR RETURN RENEWAL RESTORE REVIVAL EXCHANGE RECOVERY REMITTER RESTORAL RECLAMATION
RESTORATIVE ACOPON BALSAMIC SALUTARY SANATIVE ANALEPTIC
RESTORE FIX CURE HEAL AMEND BLOCK COVER REDUB REFER RENEW REPAY STORE YIELD ASTORE DOCTOR RECALL REDEEM REFORM REFUND RELATE RENDER REPONE REVERT REVIVE CONVERT ENSTORE INPAINT REBUILD RECLAIM RECOVER RECRUIT RECYCLE REFOUND REFRESH REPLACE REVOLVE DECOHERE REANSWER RECREATE RESTITUE RETRIEVE RESURRECT
(— CONFIDENCE) REASSURE
(— TO CIVIL RIGHTS) INLAW
(— TO FORMER STATE) REHAB
(— TO HEALTH) CURE HEAL MEND
(— TO LIFE) REVIVIFY
(— TO OFFICE) REPONE
(— TO ORDER) STILL
(— YOUTH) REJUVENATE
RESTRAIN BAR BIT DAM BATE BIND BOLT BUCK COOP CRIB CURB DAMP GRAB GYVE HEAD HEFT KEEP REIN SHUT SINK SNEB SNIB SNUB STAY STEM STOP STOW BRANK CHAIN CHECK COART CRAMP DETER GUARD LEASH MINCE POUND REPEL SHUNT SOBER STILL STINT TRASH ARREST BOTTLE BRIDLE CHASTE COERCE DETAIN ENJOIN FETTER FORBID GOVERN HALTER HAMPER HINDER KENNEL OBLIGE REBUKE RETAIN RETIRE REVOKE STIFLE STRAIN TEMPER TETHER ABRIDGE ABSTAIN CHASTEN COHIBIT CONFINE CONTAIN CONTROL ENCHAIN EXCLUDE INHIBIT INJUNCT QUALIFY RECLAIM REFRAIN REPRESS RETRACT SHACKLE SNAFFLE SWADDLE BULLDOZE COMPESCE COMPRESS HANDCUFF IMPRISON RESTRICT SIDELINE WITHDRAW WITHHOLD
(— BY FEAR) OVERAWE
(— HAWK'S WING) BRAIL
(— MOTION) SNUB
(PREF.) ISCH(O)
RESTRAINED SOBER CHASTE MODEST SEVERE ASHAMED DISCREET RESERVED RITENUTO
RESTRAINER YOKE
RESTRAINT BIT BEND CLOG CURB HEFT STAY STOP CHECK CRAMP FORCE LEASH SPARE STENT STINT TRASH ARREST BRIDLE DURESS FETTER STAYER TETHER AWEBAND BONDAGE CONTROL DURANCE EMBARGO MANACLE RESERVE SNAFFLE TRAMMEL HEADREST SOBRIETY
(— OF GOODS) HOCK
(BEYOND —) APE
(WITHOUT —) INSPADES
RESTRICT PEG TIE CURB HOLD BOUND CHAIN COART FENCE HEDGE STINT THIRL COARCT COERCE CORRAL CORSET ENTAIL HAMPER NARROW ASTRICT COHIBIT COMBINE QUALIFY REPRESS SCANTLE SWADDLE CONTRACT DEROGATE DIMINISH RESTRAIN STRAITEN
(— MEANING) MODIFY
RESTRICTED CLOSE CRAMP LOCAL

CLOSED FINITE NARROW STRAIT STRICT OBLIGATE PAROCHIAL
RESTRICTION STENT STINT BURDEN DENIAL BARRIER CONFINE RESERVE SQUEEZE BLACKOUT CABOTAGE RESTRAINT
(LEGAL —) LIEN
(PROPERTY —) EASEMENT
(PL.) BARS SWADDLE
RESTRICTIVE SEVERE BINDING STYPTIC COACTIVE LIMITARY LIMITING CONFINING
RESTY LAZY RESTIVE INACTIVE INDOLENT SLUGGISH
RESULT GO END OUT ECHO FALL FATE FAVE GROW RISE TAKE BACON BRING CHILD ENSUE EVENT FRUIT FUDGE ISSUE PROOF EFFECT EFFORT ENDING EVOLVE FINISH FOLLOW GROWTH RECOIL REVERT SEQUEL SPRING UPCOME UPSHOT ENTRAIN FALLOUT FINDING OUTCOME PROCEED PURPOSE REBOUND REDOUND SUCCEED SUCCESS FRUITAGE SEQUENCE OFFSPRING
(— FAVORABLY) SUCCEED
(— FROM) SUE
(ALGEBRAIC —) DUAL EXPANSION
(AS A —) AGAIN
(INCONCLUSIVE —) DOGFALL
(INEVITABLE —) NEMESIS
(PATHOLOGICAL —S) ALCOHOLISM
(REWARDING —) HAY
(SECONDARY —) SEQUELA
(PL.) AFTERINGS
(SUFF.) ISATION IZATION
RESULTANT CONCEPT OUTCOME PROGENY
RESUME RENEW REOPEN RECOVER SUMMARY CONTINUE PURLICUE REASSUME RENOVATE REOCCUPY
(PL.) EXCERPTA
RESURRECTION RISE RIST UPRIST REBIRTH REVIVAL
RESURRECTION PLANT FERNWORT
RESUSCITATE REVIVE QUICKEN SUSCITE REVIVIFY
RESUSCITATION KATSU RENEWAL REVIVAL
RET RAIT RATE SOAK DEWROT
RETABLE PREDELLA
RETAIL REGRATE HUCKSTER
(— OUTLET) MINILAB
(— STORE) WAREHOUSE
RETAILER DEALER CLOTHIER HUCKSTER
RETAIN HAVE HEFT HOLD KEEP SAVE CATCH ATHOLD CONTAIN RESERVE CONTINUE MAINTAIN PRESERVE
(— MOMENTUM) DRIFT
RETAINER FEE FOOL HEWE LACKEY MENIAL RIBALD SEQUEL YEOMAN HOBBLER HUSCARL JACKMAN LACQUEY PANDOUR SERVANT TRAVERS EMPLOYEE FOLLOWER HENCHMAN MYRMIDON BURKUNDAZ PENSIONER
(ARMED —) GALLOGLASS GALLOWGLASS
(JAPANESE —) SAMURAI
(PL.) FOLK
RETALIATE REPAY AVENGE RETORT REQUITE RECIPROCATE
RETALIATION QUITS MARQUE TALION REPRISAL REQUITAL
(MAKE —) TURN
(VINDICTIVE —) REVENGE
RETALIATORY COUNTER
RETARD LAG CHOP DAMP DRAG SLOW STEM BRAKE DEFER DELAY ELONG STUNT TARDY TARRY THROW TRASH BACKEN BELATE DEADEN DETAIN HINDER INHIBIT SLACKEN ENCUMBER OBSTRUCT PROTRACT RESTRAIN
RETARDANT (FIRE —) BORAX
RETARDATION LAG DRAG DELAY ARREST
RETARDED DARK BEHIND LAGGED SIMPLE OVERAGE
RETARDING LENTANDO
RETCH GAG BOKE KECK HEAVE REACH VOMIT KECKLE RECCHE STRAIN
RETCHING HEFT
RETEM JUNIPER
RETENTION MEMORY RETAIN HOLDING KEEPING RETINUE
(SUFF.) STASIA STASIS
RETIARIUS RETIARY GLADIATOR
RETICENCE RESERVE SECRECY RESTRAINT
RETICENT ABED DARK SNUG CLOSE SECRET SILENT MIMMOUD SPARING BOUTONNE
RETICENTLY HEIMLICH
RETICULATE MESHED NETTED
RETICULE BAG CABAS SACHET WORKBAG CARRYALL RIDICULE
RETICULUM NET MITOME NETWORK MATTULLA
RETINOIC ACID TRETINOIN
RETINOL CODOL
RETINOPHORE VITRELLA
RETINUE CREW GING PORT ROUT SUIT TAIL COURT MEINY SUITE TIRED TRAIN FAMILY REPAIR RETAIN COMPANY CORTEGE SOWARRY EQUIPAGE TENDANCE BODYGUARD
(— OF CAVALRY) SOWARRY
(VILLAINOUS —) BLACKGUARD
RETIRE GO GET DRAW GIVE AVOID LEAVE MICHE REBUT DEPART LOCATE RECALL RECEDE RECESS RECOIL SHRINK SURVEY PENSION REGRADE RETRACT RETREAT WITHDRAW
(— IGNOMINIOUSLY) SLINK
(— IN CRICKET) BOWL
RETIRED QUIET SECRET DEVIOUS OBSCURE OUTGONE PRIVATE RETRAIT SECLUSE SHADOWY ABSTRUSE EMERITUS SECLUDED SOLITARY
(— FROM PLAY) DOWN
RETIREMENT SHADE RECESS RETOUR SECESS PRIVACY PRIVATE RETREAT FIRESIDE SOLITUDE
RETIRING SHY NESH TIMID DEMURE MODEST FUGIENT RESERVED UMBRATIC RECESSIVE
(— ROOM) RECAMERA
RETORT MOT QUIP RISE SNAP VENY QUIRK REPAY REPLY SALLY ANSWER REGEST RETURN RIPOST BOMBOLA CORNUTE CRUSHER PELICAN REFLECT RIPOSTE SQUELCH BACKWORD BLIZZARD COMEBACK MAGAZINE RECEIVER REPARTEE
(CURT —) SNAPHANCE
(GROUP OF —S) SETTING
(PUNNING —) CLINCH
(WITTY —) KNACK ZINGER
RETRACE RECALL FLYBACK RETREAT UNTREAD BACKTRACK
RETRACT BACK UNSAY ABJURE DISOWN RECALL RECANT RECEDE REVOKE SHRINK UNLOOK RESCIND RETREAT SWALLOW PALINODE RENOUNCE WITHDRAW
RETRACTED INNER
RETRACTION PALINODE PALINODY
RETREAT DEN DOME DROP FADE GIVE LAIR NEST ROUT ARBOR AVOID BOWER LODGE NICHE QUAIL QUIET SHADE START ASHRAM ASYLUM BACKUP CASTLE HARBOR RECEDE RECESS REFUGE RESILE RETIRE REVOLT CABINET DESCEND PRIVACY RETIRAL RETRACT SHELTER ANABASIS CRAWFISH DISMARCH FALLBACK FASTNESS NESTLING RECOURSE RECULADE SOLITUDE STAMPEDE WITHDRAW CREEPHOLE KATABASIS
(— FOR FISH) HOD
(FORTIFIED —) REDUIT
(LAST —) REDOUBT
(RELIGIOUS —) ASRAM ASHRAM
(SECURE —) STRENGTH
(SHADY —) ALCOVE
(WINTER —) HIBERNACLE
RETRENCH OMIT EXCISE LESSEN REDUCE ABRIDGE CURTAIL SHORTEN
RETRENCHMENT CUT RAMPART EXCISION RETIRADE LESSENING
RETRIBUTION PAY PAYOFF RETURN REWARD WISSEL MANNAIA PENALTY REVENGE REQUITAL
RETRIBUTIVE VENGEFUL VINDICTIVE
RETRIEVE SHACK RECALL RECURE REGAIN REPAIR RESCUE REVIVE CORRECT RECOVER RESTORE SALVAGE
RETRIEVER LAB FINDER GUNDOG LABRADOR WATERRUG
RETROFLEX DEMAL CORONAL CEREBRAL INVERTED REFLEXED
RETROGRADE RECEDE RETRAL DECLINE INVERSE OPPOSED REGREDE RETREAT BACKWARD DECADENT REARWARD WITHDRAW
RETROGRESS SINK REGRESS BACKSLIDE
RETROGRESSION SINK REGRESS RETREAT FALLBACK
RETROSPECT REVIEW
RETUND DULL TURN BLUNT REFUTE
RETURN EBB GET COME ECHO TURN VAIL RECUR REFER REPAY REPLY VISIT YIELD AIRWAY ANSWER HOMING REMISE RENDER REPAIR REPASS REPORT RESORT RETIRE RETORT RETOUR REVERT CLEANUP PAYMENT REBOUND REDOUND REFLECT REPRISE REQUITE RESTORE REVENUE ATTOURNE DIVIDEND ELECTION EPANODOS FEEDBACK PICKINGS REACCESS REANSWER RECOURSE RECOVERY REDITION REFLECTION RECIPROCATE
(— FOR GOOD) REWARD
(— FROM DEATH) ARISE
(— LIKE FOR LIKE) RETALIATE
(— OF MERCHANDISE) COMEBACK
(— TENNIS BALL) RALLY
(— TO BAD HABITS) LAPSE
(— TO FORMER STATE) RELAPSE
(— TO ORIGINAL CONDITION) RECYCLE
(— TO ZERO) FLYBACK
(GET IN —) REAP
(GROUNDED —) BOND
(TENNIS —) GET BOAST
(TRIFLING —) PEPPERCORN
RETURNING REDIENT REMEANT REDITION
RETURN OF THE NATIVE (AUTHOR OF —) HARDY
(CHARACTER IN —) VYE CLYM VENN DAMON CANTLE JOHNNY DIGGORY NUNSUCH WILDEVE EUSTACIA THOMASIN CHRISTIAN YEOBRIGHT
REUBEN (FATHER OF —) JACOB
(MOTHER OF —) LEAH
REUEL (FATHER OF —) ESAU
(MOTHER OF —) BASHEMATH
(SON OF —) ELIASAPH
REUNE (ONE WHO —S) ALUM ALUMNUS
REUNION COLLEGE ADHESION HERENIGING
(— WITH BRAHMA) NIRVANA
REUNITE RALLY REUNE REJOIN RECONCILE
REUSE RECYCLE
REVEAL BID BARE BLAB HINT JAMB KNOW OPEN SHOW TELL WRAY BREAK EXERT SPEAK SPLIT UNRIP UNTOP UTTER YIELD ACCUSE APPEAR BETRAY BEWRAY DESCRY DETECT EVINCE IMPART OSTEND PATEFY SPRING UNHELE UNLOCK UNMASK UNVEIL UNWRAP BESPEAK CLARIFY CONFESS DEVELOP DISPLAY DIVULGE UNCLOAK UNCOVER UNSHALE UNTRUSS DECIPHER DISCLOSE DISCOVER INDICATE MANIFEST UNBURDEN UNSHADOW UNSHROUD
(— BY SIGNS) EXHIBIT
(— SECRETS) BABBLE
(— UNINTENTIONALLY) BETRAY
REVEILLE DIAN DIANA LEVET ROUSE SIGNAL TRAVALLY
REVEIVER (DISTILLING —) BOLTHOLE
REVEL JOY MASK RANT RIOT BIZLE

COMUS FEAST GLOAT GLORY WATCH BEZZLE FROLIC GAVALL SPLORE TRESCA WALLOW WANTON CAROUSE DELIGHT ROISTER TRESCHE CAROUSAL DOMINEER FESTIVAL WITHDRAW
(NOISY —) JAMBOREE
(PL.) REVELRY
REVELATION TORA TORAH EXPOSE ORACLE REVEAL BATHKOL BATHQOL SHOWING GIVEAWAY OVERTURE APOCALYPSE
(— OF GOD'S WILL) LAW
(SUDDEN —) KICK
REVELER GREEK RANTER RIOTER FRANION PIERROT ROISTER BACCHANT CAROUSER MERRYMAKER
REVELRY JOY ORGY RIOT RIOTISE WASSAIL CARNIVAL CAROUSAL FESTIVAL
REVENANT GHOST WRAITH SPECTER
REVENGE HELL WREAK WROIK AVENGE ULTION REQUITE REQUITAL REVANCHE
(MONTEZUMA'S —) TURISTA
REVENGED EVEN
REVENUE RENT JAGIR MANSE YIELD INCOME ENTRADA FINANCE PROFITS HACIENDA INCOMING
(— FROM WATER RIGHTS) JALKAR
(— REVENUE PAID TO POPE) ANNAT
(CHURCH —) PATRIMONY
(GOVERNMENT —) JAGHIR
(GOVERNMENT —S) JAGIR JAGHIR JAGHIRE
(STATE —) HACIENDA
REVERBERATE DIRL ECHO RING REPEL RETORT REVERB REBOUND REDOUND REFLECT RESOUND
REVERBERATING REBOANT RESONANT SOUNDING
REVERBERATION ECHO REDOUND REBOATION
REVERE ADORE HONOR ADMIRE ESTEEM HALLOW RESPECT WORSHIP VENERATE
REVERED
(PREF.) SEMNO
REVERENCE AWE ORE CULT FEAR DREAD HONOR MENSK PIETY WURTH HOMAGE REGARD WORSHIP DEVOTION VENERANT VENERATE WORTHING
(— FOR ANIMALS) ZOISM
(IRRATIONAL —) FETICH FETISH
(SHOW —) KNEEL
REVEREND SRI SHRI SHREE SVAMI SWAMI PASTOR POTENT STRONG
(PREF.) SEBASTO
REVERENT DEVOUT STRONG AWESOME DUTIFUL
REVERENTIAL PIOUS SOLEMN
REVERIE DUMP DWAM MUSE DREAM DWALM STUDY PONDER MEMENTO MOONING DAYDREAM TRAUMEREI
REVERSAL KNOCK CHANGE DOUBLE SWITCH BACKCAST BACKFLIP OVERTURN THROWBACK TURNABOUT
(PREF.) ALL(O)
REVERSE BACK DOWN FACE FLOP JOLT UNDO ANNUL CHECK UPSET VERSO CHANGE DEFEAT INVERT REPEAL RETURN REVERT REVOKE BACKSET COUNTER INVERSE PUTBACK RETREAT REVERSO SETBACK SNIFTER SUBVERT BACKCAST CONTRARY CONVERSE OPPOSITE OVERRULE OVERTURN RAMVERSE TRAVERSE WATERLOO
(— OARS) SHEAVE
(— OF COIN) PILE TAIL WOMAN
(— OF NOTE) BACK
(— PAGE OF BOOK) VERSO REVERSO
(PREF.) DE DIS DYS
(— ORDER) OB
REVERSED BACK INVERSE REVERTED ROVESCIO
(NOT —) DIRECT
REVERSI QUINOLAS
REVERSION SCRAPS ATAVISM ESCHEAT REMNANT FEEDBACK REVERTAL REVERTER THROWBACK
REVERT ANNUL ADVERT RESORT RESULT RETOUR RETURN REVOKE ESCHEAT RESTORE RECOURSE BACKSLIDE
(— TO A SUPERIOR) FALL
REVETMENT SODWORK
REVIEW HASH VIEW REVIE NOTICE REVISE SURVEY BRUSHUP RECENSE REJUDGE CRITIQUE REVIEWAL REVISION
(— A FLOP) PAN
(— UNSPARINGLY) SLATE
(CRITICAL —) PAN
(ENTHUSIASTIC —) RAVE
(KIND OF —) RAVE
REVIEWER CRITIC
REVILE CALL RAIL ABUSE BLEIR BRAWL REBUT SCOLD SHEND SHENT SLANG MISSAY MISUSE VILIFY INVEIGH MISCALL MISNAME BACKBITE DISGRACE EXECRATE REPROACH CLAPPERCLAW
REVILING ABUSE ABUSION ABUSIVE BLASPHEMY
REVISE EDIT ALTER REDACT REFORM REVIEW CORRECT RECENSE REFLECT REVISIT OVERHAUL
REVISER REDACTOR REFORMER REVIEWER
REVISION REVIEW SURVEY REVISAL REVIEWAL EPANAGOGE
REVITALIZER BRACER
REVIVAL IMAGE PICKUP REBIRTH REPRISE WAKENING
REVIVE DAW EBB WAKE FETCH QUICK RALLY RENEW ROUSE EXHUME GINGER RECALL RELIVE REVERT REVOKE EKPHORE ENLIVEN FRESHEN FURBISH QUICKEN REFRESH RESPIRE RESTORE RECREATE REDIVIVE REKINDLE RENOVATE RETRIEVE
(— FIRE) CHUNK
REVOCATION REPEAL REVERSAL ADEMPTION
REVOICE ECHO
REVOKE LIFT ADEEM ANNUL RENIG CANCEL RECALL RECANT RENEGE REPEAL REVERT ABOLISH COMMUTE FINAGLE RECLAIM RESCIND RETREAT REVERSE ABROGATE REVOCATE
(— A LEGACY) ADEEM
REVOLT ARISE REBEL REPEL START MUTINY OFFEND RELUCT UPRISE UPROAR MUTATION OUTBREAK SEDITION UPRISING JACQUERIE REBELLION
(RELIGIOUS —) APOSTASY
REVOLTING GARISH HORRID BILIOUS FEARFUL HATEFUL HIDEOUS DREADFUL
REVOLT OF THE ANGELS
(AUTHOR OF —) FRANCE
(CHARACTER IN —) MAX ZITA ISTAR ARCADE AUBELS JULIEN SOPHAR MAURICE GILBERTE SARIETTE ESPARVIEU THEOPHILE EVERDINGEN
REVOLUTION GYRE RIOT TOUR TURN CYCLE WHEEL CHANGE ANARCHY CIRCUIT REVOLVE GYRATION MUTATION NOVATION ROTATION SEDITION REBELLION
(RELIGIOUS —) REFORMATION
REVOLUTIONARY RED RADICAL MUSCADIN ROTATING BOLSHEVIK
REVOLUTIONIST JACOBIN REDSHIRT
REVOLVE BIRL GYRE PIRL ROLL SPIN TIRL TURN WELT ORBIT PIVOT THROW TREND TROLL TWINE VERSE WHEEL WHIRL CENTER CIRCLE GYRATE PONDER ROTATE SPHERE SWINGE WAMBLE AGITATE VERSATE CONSIDER OVERTURN REVOLUTE
(CAUSE TO —) TRUNDLE
REVOLVER GAT GUN ROD RIFLE STICK CANNON CUTTER HEATER HOGLEG PISTOL RIFFLE SIXGUN BULLDOG DUNGEON
(PART OF —) ROD BORE BUTT GATE GRIP SPUR BLADE FRAME GUARD LATCH SIGHT SLIDE STRAP BARREL HAMMER HANDLE MUZZLE CHAMBER TRIGGER CYLINDER BACKSTRAP
REVOLVING ORBY VOLUBLE GYRATORY VOLUTION
(PREF.) **(—AROUND)** CIRCUM
REVUE SHOW REVIEW FOLLIES
REVULSION FEAR REACTION
REWARD FEE PAY UTU GREE MEED RENT SPUR WAGE AMEED BOOTY BRIBE CROWN LOWER MERIT PLUME SHEPE YIELD BOUNTY DESERT GERSUM PAYOFF SALARY TROPHY WEDFEE AUREOLE GUERDON PREMIUM RENTAGE SOSTRUM STIPEND WARISON CONSIDER DIVIDEND EXACTION REMEMBER REQUITAL ACKNOWLEDGE
(— FOR GOOD NEWS) ALBRICIAS
(— FOR INFORMATION ON CATTLE THIEVES) TASCAL
(— OF VICTORY) CROWN
(— TO HAWK FOR KILL) QUARRY
(— TO HOUNDS) HALLOW
(ILLUSORY —) CARROT
(UNDERCOVER —) PAYOFF PAYOLA
(UNEXPECTED —) JACKPOT
(PREF.) LUCRI
REWARDED APAID BOUNTIED
REWARDING FAT PREMIANT
(FINANCIALLY —) JUICY
REWRITTEN PALIMPSEST
REZAI ROSEI COVERLET MATTRESS
REZON (FATHER OF —) ELIADAH
RHABDUS SCOPULA
RHADAMANTHUS (FATHER OF —) JUPITER
(MOTHER OF —) EUROPA
RHAPSODIC CONFUSED EFFUSIVE RAPTUROUS
RHAPSODY JUMBLE MEDLEY BOMBAST ECSTASY RAPTURE REVERIE
(— SECTION) LASSU
RHATANY LEGUME
RHEA EMU EMEU NANDU NANDOW RATITE OSTRICH AGDISTIS AVESTRUZ
(DAUGHTER OF —) JUNO CERES VESTA
(FATHER OF —) URANUS
(HUSBAND OF —) SATURN
(MOTHER OF —) GAEA
(SON OF —) PLUTO NEPTUNE
RHEBOK PEELE REHBOC
RHEINGOLD, DAS (CHARACTER IN —) ERDA LOGE FREIA WOTAN FAFNER FASOLT FRICKA HUNDING ALBERICH SIEGMUND SIEGLINDE
(COMPOSER OF —) WAGNER
RHENIUM BOHEMIUM
RHEOMETER STROMUHR
RHEOSTAT DIMMER
RHESA (FATHER OF —) ZOROBABEL
RHESUS BANDAR BUNDER MONKEY BHUNDER MACAQUE
(FATHER OF —) EIONEUS STRYMON
(MOTHER OF —) CALLIOPE
RHETORIC SPEECH BOMBAST PROSAIC ELOQUENCE
(ROLLING —) PERIODS
RHETORICAL FLORID PURPLE AUREATE FORENSIC SWELLING
(FLORIDLY —) AUREATE
RHETORICIAN ORATOR RHETOR
RHEUM GORE TEARS CHOLER SPLEEN
RHINARIUM MUFFLE
RHINE REAN DITCH RUNNEL
RHINESTONE DEWDROP
(PL.) GLITTER
RHINO CASH MONEY PONTOON
RHINOCEROS FOW ABADA BADAK RHINO BORELE KEITLOA UNICORN UPEYGAN NASICORN
RHINOCEROS BEETLE UANG SCARABAEID
RHINOCEROS HORNBILL TOPAU
RHINOPLASTY NOSEJOB
RHIPIDION FLABELLUM
RHIZOID RHIZINA ROOTLET
RHIZOME KAVA NARD ARUKE CAAPI STOCK ARALIA ARNICA ASARUM GINGER IPECAC STOLON BERBERY CALAMUS CULVERS GENTIAN SCOPOLA ZEDOARY ASPIDIUM BARBERRY BERBERIS HELONIAS

KAVAKAVA TRILLIUM TRITICUM VERATRUM
(PL.) INULA GERANIUM
RHODE (FATHER OF —) POSEIDON
(MOTHER OF —) HALIA
(SON OF —) PHAETHON

RHODE ISLAND
CAPITAL: PROVIDENCE
COLLEGE: BROWN BRYANT
COUNTY: KENT BRISTOL NEWPORT
INDIAN: NIANTIC
MOTTO: HOPE
NATIVE: GUNFLINT
NICKNAME: LITTLERHODY
RIVER: PAWTUXET PAWCATUCK BLACKSTONE
STATE FLOWER: VIOLET
STATE TREE: MAPLE
TOWN: BRISTOL NEWPORT WARWICK CRANSTON KINGSTON PAWTUCKET

RHODE ISLAND BENT FURZETOP
RHODE ISLANDER GUNFLINT
RHODESIA (SEE ZIMBABWE)
RHODODENDRON ROSEBAY SPOONHUTCH
(THICKET OF —) SLICK
RHOMB LOZEN WHEEL CIRCLE LOZENGE
RHOMBUS DIAMOND LOZENGE
RHONCHUS RALE SNORE SNORT WHEEZE
RHUBARB ROW FLAP RHEUM HASSEL CITRINE DISPUTE YAWWEED ARGUMENT PIEPLANT
RHYME CHIME CLINK VERSE CRAMBO POETRY RHYTHM TINKLE MEASURE
(— ROYAL) TROILUS
(PL.) RIMUR
RHYOLITE LIPARITE
RHYTHM BEAT STOT TIME CHIME METER PULSE SWING GROOVE CADENCE RAGTIME BACKBEAT MOVEMENT SEQUENCE
(BREEDING —) VOLTINISM
(DISTORTED —) RUBATO
RHYTHMICAL LILTED CADENCED MEASURED NUMEROUS ACCENTUAL
(NOT —) RAGGED
RHYTINA SEACOW
RIA CREEK INLET
RIAL COIN RYEL ROYAL KINGLY SPLENDID
RIALTO MART BRIDGE EXCHANGE
RIANT GAY RIDENT LAUGHING MIRTHFUL
RIATA LASSO LARIAT
RIB FIN KID BULB CORD DIKE JAPE JOKE PURL RIDE SLAT WALE WIFE CORSE COSTA GROIN NERVE OGIVE PEARL RIDGE TEASE VARIX VITTA WHELP BRANCH LIERNE NEEDLE PARODY RIPPLE SCROLL TIMBER TONGUE BRISTLE FEATHER NERVURE PLEURAL STRATUM FORMERET SIDEBONE
(— IN GROINED ROOF) SPRINGER
(— OF INSECT WING) VEIN
(— OF LEAF) NERVE
(— OF SHIP) WRONG
(— OF STOCKING) RIDGE
(— OF VIOLIN) BOUT
(—S OF UMBRELLA) FRAME
(SHORT —S) CROP
(STRENGTHENING —) FEATHER
(VAULTING —) NERVE OGIVE LIERNE TIERCERON
(PL.) SLATS
(PREF.) COST(I)(O) PLEUR(I)(O)
(SUFF.) COSTAL COSTATE PLEURA PLEUROUS
RIBALD LEWD ROGUE COARSE RASCAL VULGAR
RIBALDRY HASH HARLOTRY
RIBAND RIBBON SCROLL
RIBBED RIBBY CORDED COSTATE
RIBBING SPOOFERY
RIBBON BAR BOW FOB PAN BEND COST PADS BRAID CORSE FILET LABEL PADOU PIECE RUBAN SHRED TASTE BENDEL CADDIS CORDON FERRET FILLET LISERE RADULA RECORD RIBAND SHOWER STRING TAENIA TAWDRY TISSUE TONGUE BANDING SAUTOIR TORSADE BANDEROL BOOKMARK FRAGMENT STREAMER TRESSURE PETERSHAM
(— AS BADGE OF HONOR) CORDON
(— AS HEADDRESS) TRESSOUR TRESSURE
(— FOR BORDER) LISERE
(— HANGING FROM CROWN) JESS
(— USED FOR GARTERS) CADDIS CADDICE
(— WORN ON HOSE) FLASH
(COLORED —S) DIVISA
(CORDED —) PETERSHAM
(END OF —S) FATTRELS
(FLOATING —) PAN
(GATHERED —) QUILLING
(KNOT OF —S) SORTIE
(LINGUAL —) TONGUE
(RASPING —) RADULA
(SILK —) CORSE PADOU TASTE
(WATERED —) PADS
(PL.) REINS
(PREF.) TAENI(A)(O)
(SUFF.) TENE
RIBBON FERN PTERIS
RIBBONFISH GARFISH GUAPENA AGUAVINA BANDFISH DEALFISH
RIBBONLIKE TAENIATE TAENIOID TAENIFORM
RIBBON TREE AKAROA HOIHERE HOUHERE LACEBARK
RIBGRASS WINDLES BUCKHORN HARDHEAD PLANTAIN
RIBWORT KLOPS HEADMAN RATTAIL SOLDIER WINDLES HARDHEAD HEADSMAN PLANTAGO
RICCIARDETTO (SISTER OF —) BRADAMANTE
RICE AUS AMAN BORO PADI PAGA RISE SELA TWIG ARROZ BATTY BIGAS CANIN CHITS GRAIN MACAN PADDY PALAY PATNA BRANCH CEREAL CONGEE SIDDHA ANGKHAK MANOMIN RISOTTO
(— BOILED WITH MEAT) PILAF PILAU PILAW
(— COOKED WITH MEAT) RISOTTO JAMBALAYA
(— FIELD) SAWAH
(— IN HUSK) PALAY
(— OF 2ND OR 3RD GRADE) CHITS
(— POLISHINGS) DARAC
(BOILED —) CANIN KANIN
(COLD —) SUSHI
(HUSKED —) CHAL
(INFERIOR —) PAGA
(KIND OF —) DIRTY BASMATI
(LONG-STEMMED —) AMAN
(MOUNTAIN —) SMILO
(SHORT-STEMMED —) AUS
(SPRING —) BORO
(UNCOOKED —) BIGAS
(UNMILLED —) PADI PADDY
(WILD —) MANOMIN
(PREF.) ORYZ(I) RIZI
RICEBIRD BUNTING CACIQUE SPARROW BOBOLINK
RICE FLOWER PIMELEA
RICEGRASS BARIT SACATE ZACATE
RICH FAT ABLE DEEP FAIR HIGH LUSH OOFY WARM GLEBY OPIME PLUMP RITZY ROUND TINNY VIVID BATFUL COSTLY DAEDAL FRUITY HEARTY PLUMMY PLUSHY PODDED SUPERB ULRICA AMUSING BAITTLE COPIOUS FERTILE MONEYED OPULENT PINGUID PLASTIC WEALTHY ABUNDANT AFFLUENT GENEROUS HUMOROUS LUSCIOUS
(— IN FAME) RODERICK
(— IN GIFTS) PREMIOUS
(— IN INTEREST) JUICY
(— IN MALT) HEAVY
(— IN METAL) HIGHGRADE
(— IN RESOURCES) STRONG
(— IN SILICA) ACID
(— IN TIMBRE) GOLDEN
(— MAN) DIVES
(— OF SOIL) PINGUID
(MAN —) NABOB
(NOT —) PLAIN
(OSTENTATIOUSLY —) RITZY
(VERY —) WALLOWING
RICHARD DICCON
RICHARD CARVEL (AUTHOR OF —) CHURCHILL
(CHARACTER IN —) FOX JONES CARVEL DOROTHY MANNERS RICHARD WALPOLE
RICHARD II (AUTHOR OF —) SHAKESPEARE
(CHARACTER IN —) JOHN ROSS YORK BAGOT BUSHY GAUNT GREEN HENRY PERCY EDMUND PIERCE SCROOP SURREY THOMAS AUMERLE HOTSPUR LANGLEY MOWBRAY NORFOLK RICHARD STEPHEN BERKELEY HEREFORD FITZWATER LANCASTER SALISBURY WILLOUGHBY BOLINGBROKE NORTHUMBERLAND
RICHARD III (AUTHOR OF —) SHAKESPEARE
(CHARACTER IN —) ANNE JOHN YORK DERBY HENRY JAMES LOVEL BLOUNT DORSET EDWARD GEORGE MORTON OXFORD RIVERS ROBERT SURREY THOMAS TYRREL WALTER BRANDON CATESBY HERBERT NORFOLK RICHARD STANLEY TRESSEL URSWICK VAUGHAN BERKELEY CLARENCE HASTINGS MARGARET RATCLIFF RICHMOND BOURCHIER ELIZABETH ROTHERHAM BRAKENBURY BUCKINGHAM GLOUCESTER CHRISTOPHER
RICHES GOLD PELF WEAL LUCRE WORTH MAMMON TALENT WEALTH FORTUNE OPULENCE RICHESSE TREASURE
RICHLY HIGH AMPLY FATLY FULLY DEARLY
RICHNESS BODY LUXE SUMEN LUXURY ELEGANCE FECUNDITY
RICHWEED RAGWEED COOLWEED
RICK GOAF GOFE REKE CANCH RICKLE SPRAIN WRENCH CORNRICK
RICKETS RACHITIS
RICKETY SHAKY SHACKY SHACKLY UNSOUND RACHITIC SHATTERY UNSTABLE TOTTERING RAMSHACKLE
RICKMATIC CONCERN BUSINESS
RICOCHET SKIP SKITE GLANCE REBOUND
RICTUS GRIN GRIMACE
RID FREE QUIT SHED SHUT ANOMY CLEAR EGEST REDDE SCOUR SHIFT ACQUIT ANOMIE REMOVE DELIVER
(— OF IMPURITIES) SCORIFY
(— OF INSECTS) BUG
(— OF LICE) CHAT
(— OF WEEDS) CLEAN
(— ONESELF OF) DOFF DEPOSIT DISPATCH
(GET — OF) DITCH ERASE PALMOFF PAWNOFF
RIDDANCE SHUT RELIEF DISPATCH
RIDDER SIFT SIEVE RIDDLE
RIDDLE SIFT BLAIK GRIPH REBUS DEBASE ENIGMA FOITER PUZZLE RUDDLE SCREEN CORRUPT CRIBBLE EXPLAIN GRIDDLE GRIPHUS MYSTIFY PERPLEX PROBLEM CRATEMAN PERMEATE
(— AS GRAIN) REE
(PL.) MURLEMEWES
RIDDLER CRATEMAN
(— OF OLD) SPHINX
RIDE GO NAG RIB BAIT DOSA HACK HURL LAST LIFT PRIG SAIL TOOL CROSS DRIVE TEASE BANTER CANTER DEPEND DODGEM GALLOP JUMBLE NEEDLE NOTICE SADDLE HAYRIDE JOYRIDE OVERLAP SURVIVE TANTIVY BESTRIDE
(— A WAVE) BODYSURF
(— FAST) PRICK POWDER
(— HARD) POUND BUCKET
(— IN HIRED VEHICLE) JOB
(— ON) MOUNT
(— ON A WAVE) BODYSURF
(— ON HORSE) BOOT LARK BURST JOCKEY SCHOOL
(— RECKLESSLY) BRUISE
(— TO HOUNDS) GO
(AMUSEMENT PARK —) SWING
(CYCLE —) SPIN

RIDER TACK ANNEX CROSS HAZER LABEL COWBOY JOCKEY SITTER ALLONGE CODICIL NAGSMAN PRICKER CAVALIER DESULTOR HORSEMAN
(DUKEY —) BRAKEMAN
(DUMMY —) CROSS
RIDERS TO THE SEA (AUTHOR OF —) SYNGE
(CHARACTER IN —) NORA MAURYA BARTLEY MICHAEL
RIDGE AAS ARM BAR FIN RIB RIG RYG BALK BAND BANK BARB BROW BULT BURR BUTT COMB DRUM FRET FULL HACK HILL KEEL LINK LIST PAHA PUFF RAIN REAN ROLL SHIN SPUR WALE WAVE WELT BARGH CHINE COSTA CREST EARTH EAVES GONYS GYRUS JUGUM KNURL LEDGE LINCH RINGE RUDGE SCOUT SHANK SPINE TORUS VARIX WHELP BRIDGE CARINA COLLOP CREASE CRISTA CUESTA CULMEN DIVIDE DORSUM FRENUM RAFTER RIDEAU SADDLE SELION SUMMIT ANNULET APODEMA BREAKER BUCCULA COLLINE COSTULA EYEBROW EYELINE HOGBACK HUMMOCK INTHROW PROPONS RIGGING SOWBACK WINDROW WITHERS WRINKLE YARDANG CATOCTIN CINGULUM FOREDUNE HEADLAND RESTBALK SHOULDER
(— BETWEEN FURROWS) STITCH RESTBALK
(— IN BREASTPLATE) TAPUL
(— IN COAL SEAM) HORSEBACK
(— IN HORSE'S MOUTH) EAR
(— MADE BY PLOWING) HACK SELION
(— MADE BY TOOL) BUR BARB BURR
(— OF BIRD'S BILL) CULM CULMEN
(— OF BRAIN CORAL) COLLINE
(— OF BREASTBONE) KEEL
(— OF CLAY) DOWLE
(— OF EARTH) BALK
(— OF FLESH) COLLOP
(— OF HORSE'S NECK) CREST
(— OF LAND) BULT RAIN SELION STITCH HOGBACK
(— OF SAND IN WATER) REEF SANDBAR
(— OF SCAPULA) SPINE
(— OF SCREW) THREAD
(— OF SNOW) SASTRUGA ZASTRUGA
(— OF UNPLOWED LAND) LINCH LINCHET
(— OF WAVE) CREST
(— ON BOOK) HUB
(— ON CLOTH) WALE
(— ON CROWN OF TOOTH) CINGULUM
(— ON FINGERBOARD OF GUITAR) FRET
(— ON FISH SCALE) CIRCULUS
(— ON FRUITS OF CARROT FAMILY) JUGUM
(— ON GLUMES) CARINA
(— ON MOLLUSK SHELL) COSTULA
(— ON OVULE) RAPHE
(— ON SEA FLOOR) SWELL
(— ON SEASHORE) STANNER
(— ON SHEET METAL) BEAD
(— ON SIDE OF SADDLE) PUFF
(— ON SKIN) WALE
(— ON VIOLIN) NUT
(— PROTECTING CAMP) RIDEAU
(—S ON ROCK) LAPIES
(— WITH SHARP SUMMIT) HOGBACK
(ANATOMICAL —) CARINA
(BEACH —) FULL
(CHEWING —) ENDITE
(CONNECTING —) HAUSE
(CONVOLUTED —) GYRUS
(DRAINAGE —) BREAKER
(GLACIAL —) OS KAME PAHA ARETE ESKAR ESKER SERAC ESCHAR NUNATAK
(HAIRLIKE —) LIRA
(ICE —) SERAC
(ISOLATED —) BARGH
(LONG STONY —) RAND
(MOUNTAIN —) COMB CHINE SIERRA BACKBONE
(NARROW —) DRUM RAZORBACK
(PROJECTING —) HOE SCOUT
(RESIDUAL —) CATOCTIN
(ROCK —) CLEAVER
(SAND —) DUNE ESKER WAVEMARK
(SEEDED —) DRILL
(SHARP-CRESTED —) ARETE ARRIS
(SLIGHT —) PROPONS
(SNOW —) ZASTRUGA
(UNPLOWED —) BALK BAULK
(WOODED —) CHENIER
(PL.) OSAR KNURLING
RIDGED RIDGY SHARP MILLED PORCATE CARINATE
RIDGELING RIG REGALD RIDGIL RIGGOT RIGINAL
RIDGEPOLE ROOFTREE
RIDICULE DO FUN GUY MOB PAN RIG TAX GAME GIBE JEER JEST JIBE JOEY MOCK PLAY QUIZ RAZZ SKIT TROT TWIT BORAK CHAFF CLOWN HORSE IRONY MIMIC MOMUS QUEER RALLY ROAST SCOFF SCOUT SMOKE SNEER TAUNT BANTER DERIDE EXPOSE RAILLY SATIRE BUFFOON LAMPOON MOCKERY SARCASM DERISION RAILLERY SATIRIZE SPOOFERY BURLESQUE
RIDICULOUS DOTTY DROLL FUNNY SILLY ABSURD INSANE COMICAL FOOLISH MOCKING DERISIVE DERISORY FARCICAL INDECENT COCKAMAMY MONSTROUS COCKAMAMIE
RIDING AWHEEL LIVELY OVERLAP PRICKANT SHIVAREE TRITHING CHEVACHIE
(— ACADEMY) MANAGE MANEGE
(— CROP) ROD
(— WHIP) CROP QUIRT
RIDOTTO BALL REDOUTE
RIEM RHEIM RIMPI STRAP THONG
RIENZI (CHARACTER IN —) COLA IRENE PAOLO ORSINI RIENZI ADRIANO COLONNA STEFANO RAIMONDI
(COMPOSER OF —) WAGNER
RIFE EASY FULL RANK QUICK READY ACTIVE FILLED NIMBLE STRONG CURRENT REPLETE ABUNDANT INCLINED MANIFEST NUMEROUS
RIFF BIT SKIM ROUTINE
RIFFLE REEF RIFF WAVE RAPID RIPPLE SHUFFLE WATERFALL
RIFFRAFF MOB RAFF SCUM SCAFF TRASH RABBLE REFUSE RUBBISH CANAILLE POPULACE RAGABASH
RIFLE RIG ROB KRAG LOOT RIPE PIECE YAGER CARBIN JEZAIL JUZAIL RIFFLE SNIDER ARISAKA BULLPUP BUNDOCK BUNDOOK CARABIN CARBINE DESPOIL ENFIELD ESCOPET MARTINI PILLAGE PLUNDER RANSACK SPORTER BANDHOOK REPEATER SPLITTER STRICKLE TAKEDOWN CHASSEPOT
(— BALL CASING) THIMBLE
(— PIN) TIGE
(OPTICAL DEVICE ON —) SNIPERSCOPE
RIFLEMAN JAGER JAEGER
(PL.) RIFLERY
RIFT RIVE BELCH CHASM CRACK SPLIT CLEAVE DIVIDE BLEMISH FISSURE CREVASSE
(— IN TIMBER) LAG
RIG RI FIG REG HOAX JEST JOKE REEK SEMI WIND DRESS EQUIP GETUP PRANK RIDGE SPORT STORM TRICK BANTER CLOTHE GUNTER ROTARY SADDLE SCHEME MARCONI SPUDDER SWINDLE BACKSTAY RIDICULE SEMITRAILER
(DRILLING —) JACKUP
(TRUCKING —) SEMI
RIGADOON DANCE RIGODON
RIGEL REGEL ALGEBAR
RIGGED (FULLY —) ATAUNT
RIGGER CLIMBER SLINGER SCAFFOLD
RIGGING NET GEAR ROOF RIDGE TACKLE APPAREL CLOTHING JACKSTAY TACKLING
RIGHT DUE FEE FIT IUS OFF REE SAY SOC BANG DUTY FAIR FLOP GALE GOOD HAND ITER JUST LIEN REAL RECT REET SANE SLAP SOKE TEAM TRUE WELL CLAIM DRESS DROIT ENTRY EXACT FAVOR FERRY LEGAL RICHT SOUND STRAY TECHT TITLE ACTION ACTUAL ANGARY BALLOT DEMAND DEXTER EATAGE EQUITY PROPER PUTURE ANNUITY APANAGE AUBAINE BENEFIT CORRECT DERECHO DESIRED FACULTY FALDAGE FITTING FOLDAGE FREEDOM GENUINE HAYBOTE LIBERTY LICENSE PRENDER RECTIFY RELIEVE SLAPDAB UPRIGHT WARRANT BANALITY BLOODWIT FIREBOOT FORESTRY HEIRSHIP INTEREST LIFERENT SEIGNORY SLAPDASH STALLAGE STRAIGHT SUFFRAGE SUITABLE THIRLAGE PREROGATIVE
(— AND LEFT) HAY HEY
(— AS COMMAND TO HORSES) REE
(— EYE) OD
(— HAND) MD OPENBAND
(— IN A THING) INTEREST
(— IN WIFE'S INHERITED PROPERTY) CURTESY
(— OF CHOICE) OPTION
(— OF CREDITOR) SECURITY
(— OF EXILE) POSTLIMINY
(— OF EXIT) ISH
(— OF FREE QUARTERS) CORODY
(— OF HOLDING COURT) TEAM
(— OF INQUIRY) SOKEN
(— OF OWNERSHIP) TITLE COMMONTY
(— OF PASTURAGE) FEED STINT EATAGE COWGATE COMMONAGE HORSEGATE
(— OF PRECEDENCE) PAS
(— OF PRESENTATION) ADVOWSON
(— OF PROTECTION) MUND
(— OF RETURNING) REGRESS
(— OF USING ANOTHER'S PROPERTY) EASEMENT
(— OF USING GRASSLAND) EATAGE
(— SIDE) OFFSIDE
(— TIME) TID
(— TO COLLECT REVENUE) DIWANI DEWANEE DEWANNY
(— TO COMMAND) IMPERIUM
(— TO CUT WOOD) VERT GREENHEW
(— TO DECIDE) SAY
(— TO DRAW WATER) HAUSTUS
(— TO DRIVE BEAST) ACTUS
(— TO PASS OVER LAND) ITER
(— TO PAYMENT) RECOURSE
(— TO REJECT) VETO
(— TO SEIZE PROPERTY) ANGARY
(— TO SHOOT FIRST) CAST
(— TO SUE) STANDING
(— TO WORK IN MINE) BEN
(ALL —) HUNK JAKE HUNKY
(EXACTLY —) PAT
(FEUDAL —) CUDDY THIRL MARITAGE THIRLAGE
(FISHING —) PISCARY
(HUNTING —) WARDEN
(INDIAN LEGAL —) HAK HAKH
(JUST —) TOAT TOATEE
(LEGAL —) IUS JUS JURE DROIT ACCESS APPEAL COMMON FISHERY HYPOTHEC
(LEGAL —S) JURA
(MILLER'S —) SOKEN
(MINING —) GALE
(NOT —) AWRY ACUTE
(PROPERTY —) DOMINIUM
(TURN —) GEE
(WIDOW'S —) TERCE TIERCE
(PL.) DIBS JURA
(PREF.) DEXIO DEXTR(O) ORTH(O) RECT(I)
(— HAND) DEXIO DEXTR(O)
RIGHT ANGLE RECTANGLE
(HUNDREDTH OF —) GRAD GRADE
RIGHTEOUS GOOD JUST GODLY MORAL ZADOC ZADOK DEVOUT FITTING PERFECT SKILFUL UPRIGHT INNOCENT VIRTUOUS
RIGHTEOUSNESS DOOM DHARMA EQUITY JUSTICE HOLINESS JUDGMENT JUSTNESS MORALITY RECTITUDE
RIGHTFUL DUE JUST TRUE LEGAL KINDLY LAWFUL PROPER FITTING

RIGHTFULNESS JUSTICE
RIGHT-HANDED RIGHTY DEXTRAL SKILLED DEXTROUS CLOCKWISE
RIGHT-HANDWISE DEASIL DESSIL DEISEAL CLOCKWISE
RIGHTLY RITE FITLY ARIGHT FAIRLY JUSTLY HANDILY PERQUEER SUITABLY
RIGHTS (KIND OF —) MIRANDA
RIGHT WHALE BOWHEAD BALAENID MYSTICETE NORDCAPER
RIGID SET ACID CARK FIRM HARD HIGH FIXED SOLID STARK STERN STIFF STONY STOUT TENSE TONIC TOUGH FORMAL FROZEN MARBLY SEVERE STARCH STICKY STRICT AUSTERE IRONCLAD RIGOROUS STRAIGHT INELASTIC STRINGENT
(— IN SELF-DENIAL) ASCETIC
RIGIDITY FROST RIGOR RIGOUR BUCKRAM SETNESS HARDNESS STIFFNESS
RIGMAREE COIN TRIFLE
RIGMAROLE RANE NOMINY RABBLE RAGMAN SLAMPAMP SLAMPANT AMPHIGORY RIDDLEMEREE
RIGOLETTO (CHARACTER IN —) GILDA MANTUA MADDALENA RIGOLETTO SPARAFUCILE
(COMPOSER OF —) VERDI
RIGOR TYRANNY ASPERITY HARDNESS SEVERITY
RIGOROUS FIRM HARD CLOSE CRUEL EXACT HARSH HEFTY RIGID STERN STIFF TOUGH BITTER FLINTY SEVERE STRAIT STRICT STRONG AUSTERE DRASTIC PRECISE SPARTAN DISTRICT DRACONIC EXACTING IRONCLAD STRAIGHT
(MORALLY —) PURITANIC
(NOT —) INEXACT
(UNDULY —) HARSH
RIKSMAL BOKMAL
RILE VEX ROIL ANGER PEEVE TICKOFF IRRITATE
RILL PURL SIKE CLEFT DRILL PRILL GROOVE RUNLET RILLOCK RIVULET BROOKLET RIVELING TRICKLET ARROYUELO WATERSHUT
RILLSTONE VENTIFACT
RIM HEM LIP BEAD BRIM CURB EDGE SHOE BEZEL BRINK CHIME EAVES FELLY FRAME HELIX SKIRT BORDER CALKER CHOANA FILLET FLANGE MARGIN EXCIPLE
(— HOLDING WATCH CRYSTAL) BEZEL BEZIL
(— OF BASKET) HOOP
(— OF COROLLA) ANNULUS
(— OF CRATER) SOMMA
(— OF EAR) HELIX
(— OF GEM) GIRDLE
(— OF HORSESHOE) WEB
(— OF INSECT'S WING) TERMEN
(— OF JELLYFISH) VELUM
(— OF SANIO) CRASSULA
(— OF TIN) LIST
(— OF WHEEL) FELLY FELLOE STRAKE
(— ON CASK) CHIMB CHIME CHINE
(— ON CLOG) CALKER
(— SURROUNDING FLAGELLUM) CHOANA
(EXTERNAL —) FLANGE
(PROTECTIVE —) BANK
(RAISED —) BOSS
(PREF.) AMBO
RIMA CHINK CLEFT RIMULA FISSURE
RIME RIM HOAR RIND RUNG CRACK CRUST FROST ROUND CRANREUCH
RIMPLE FOLD RIPPLE WRINKLE
RINALDO (BELOVED OF —) ANGELICA
(COUSIN OF —) ORLANDO
(FATHER OF —) AYMON
(HORSE OF —) BAYARD
RIND BARK PEEL PILL RYND SKIN CRUST FROST SWARD CITRON SWARTH
(— OF HAM) SKIN
(— OF MEAT) SPINE
(— OF POMEGRANATE) GRANATUM
(— OF ROASTED PORK) CRACKLING
(PREF.) LEMMO LEPO
(SUFF.) LEMMA
RING GO BEE BOW BUR CUP DEE DIE EKE FAM JOW ORB PIT RIM AMBO BAIL BAND BELL BONG BURR BUZZ CRIC CURB DING DIRL ECHO GYRE HOOP JING LOOP MAIL PASS PEAL RACE RINK RUSH SHUT SING TANG TOLL VIRL WISP AMBON ANLET ARENA BAGUE CAROL CHIME CHINK CLANG CYCLE GRAIN GROUP GUARD GUIDE JEWEL KNELL LUNET PISTE RIGOL ROUND ROWEL TORUS VERGE WAFER WITHE BANGLE BECKET BROUGH BUTTON CIRCLE CIRCUS CIRQUE CLIQUE COLLAR COLLET DINDLE EYELET FAMBLE GIMMER GIRDLE HARROW KEEPER LARIGO LEGLET RINGLE RUNDLE RUNNER SIGNET TORQUE TURRET VIROLE WASHER ANNULUS ARMILLA CIRCLET CIRCUIT CLAPPER COMPASS COUPLER CRINGLE DIAMOND FAMELEN FERRULE GALLERY GARLAND GROMMET GUDGEON MANILLA NUCLEUS PACKING RESOUND ROWLOCK SHACKLE STIRRUP THIMBLE VIBRATE BRACELET BULLRING CINCTURE CORONULE DINGDONG DRAUPNIR DUSTBAND ENCIRCLE FAIRLEAD PACIFIER SONORITY SURROUND TRAVELER
(— AROUND ARTICULAR CAVITY) AMBON
(— AROUND MOON) BROCH
(— AROUND NIPPLE) AREOLA
(— AT EACH END OF CINCH) LARIGO
(— A TREE) FRILL
(— ATTACHED TO JIB) HANK
(— BELLS) FIRE
(— FOR CARRYING SHOT) LADLE
(— FORMING HANDLE OF KEY) BOW
(— FOR SECURING BIRD) VERVEL
(— FOR TRAINING HORSES) LONGE
(— OF ANNULATED COLUMN) BAGUE
(— OF BOILER) STRAKE
(— OF CILIA) TROCHUS
(— OF COLOR) STOCKING
(— OF DNA) PLASTID
(— OF DOTS AROUND EDGE OF COIN) GRAINING
(— OF LIGHT) GLORY
(— OF ODIN) DRAUPNIR
(— OF PILES) STARLING
(— OF RIDING SCHOOL) PISTE
(— OF ROPE) HANK BECKET GARLAND GROMMET SNORTER SNOTTER
(— OF SATURN) ANSA
(— OF SPINES) CORONULE
(— OF STANDING STONES) CAROL
(— OF TWO HOOPS) GEMEL GEMMEL
(— OF WAGONS) CORRAL LAAGER
(— ON BATTLEAX) BUR BURR
(— ON BIRD'S TIBIA) ARMILLA
(— ON DARTBOARD) TREBLE
(— ON DECK) CRANCE
(— ON GUN CARRIAGE) LUNET LUNETTE
(— ON HINGE) GUDGEON
(— ON LAMP) CRIC
(— ON LANCE) BURR
(— ON SPAR) TRAVELER
(— ON UMBRELLA ROD) RUNNER
(— SUPPORTING LAMPSHADE) GALLERY
(— SURROUNDING BUGLE) VIROLE
(— SUSPENDING COMPASS) GIMBAL
(— TO ENCLOSE DEER) TINCHEL TINCHILL
(— UNDER BEEHIVE) EKE
(— USED AS MONEY) MANILLA
(— USED AS VALVE) WAFER
(— WITH GROOVED OUTER EDGE) THIMBLE
(— WITH VIBRATION) DIRL
(BLACKSMITH'S —) BOLSTER
(BRIGHT —) HALATION
(CERVICAL —) TORQUE
(CURTAIN —) EYE
(FINGER —) HOOP
(FLESHY —) ANNULUS
(HARNESS —) DEE BUTTON LARIGO TERRET TORRET TURRET
(HAWK'S —) VERVEL
(INTERLINKED METAL —S) MAIL
(JOINED —) GIMMER GIMMOR
(KIND OF —) MOOD
(LITTLE —) ANNULET
(LUMINOUS —) BROUGH
(MOUNTAINEER'S —) KARABINER
(NECKERCHIEF —) WOGGLE
(NOSE —) PIRN
(OIL —) WIPER
(PACKING —) LUTE
(PART OF —) BAND CLAW PRONG SHANK STONE COLLET SETTING HALLMARK
(PLAITED —) RUSH WISP
(SURGICAL —) CURETTE
(SWIVEL —) TERRET TERRIT
(TAPERING SHANK —) BELCHER
(TARGET —) SOUS SOUSE
(TOOTHED IRON —) HARROW
(TOP OF —) BEZEL BEZIL
(PREF.) CRICO CYCL(O) GYRO
(HAVING OPENED —) SECO
RING AND THE BOOK (AUTHOR OF —) BROWNING
(CHARACTER IN —) PAUL GUIDO PIETRO GIUSEPPE POMPILIA VIOLANTE COMPARINI CAPONSACCHI FRANCESCHINI
RINGDOVE QUIST CUSHAT CUSHIE QUEEST TOOZOO ZOOZOO COWSHOT COWSHUT
RINGED GYRATE ZONATE ANNULAR ANNULOSE
RINGED SNAKE COLUBRID
RINGER CHEER YOUTH COWBOY CROWBAR STOCKMAN
RING FINGER ANNULAR
RINGGIT DOLLAR
RINGHALS COBRA
RINGING BELL BRIGHT FERVID JANGLE CLANGOR OROTUND SINGING DECISIVE RESONANT SONORANT SONOROUS TINNIENT TINNITUS
(— IN THE EARS) TINNITUS
(CHANGE —) CINQUES SINGLES
RINGLEADER FUGLEMAN
RINGLET CURL LOCK TRESS TENDRIL
(— ON FOREHEAD) FAVORITE
(PREF.) CIRR(I)(O)
RING-NECKED TORQUATE
RING-NECKED DUCK DOGY SCAUP MOONBILL RINGBILL BLACKJACK
RING OUZEL AMSEL THRUSH WHISTLER
RING PLOVER SANDY COLLIER KILLDEE DULWILLY RINGNECK
RING-SHAPED ANNULAR CRICOID ANNULARY ANNULATE CIRCULAR
RINGTAIL CACOMIXL CACOMISTLE
RINGWORM TINEA KERION TETTER SERPIGO
RINGWORM BUSH SENNA
RINK ALLEY GLACIARIUM
RINSE NET SIND WASH RANGE RENCH RENSH RINGE SCIND SCOUR SWILL BLUING DOUCHE CLEANSE
RINSING NET SIND FLUSH RESIDUE
RIOT DIN HURL BRAWL REVEL WORRY ATTACK CLAMOR EXCESS JUMBLE MEDLEY RANTAN SPLORE TUMULT ANARCHY CONFUSE DESPOIL REVELRY BLOODWIT CAROUSAL TOHUBOHU
RIOTOUS ROID ROYD WILD NOISY RANDY RANTY HEMPIE RANDIE STORMY WANTON BACCHIC PROFUSE ROARING ABUNDANT BACCHIAN
RIP RIT COOP REAT TEAR BREAK SHARK SHRED SLITE UNSEW BASKET RIPPLE UNSEAM
(— OFF) ROB CHEAT FILCH STEAL DEFRAUD
RIPE FIT BOLD LATE DRUNK READY MATURE MELLOW SIDDER SIDDOW SMELLY DIGESTED FINISHED SEASHORE STINKING SUITABLE
(EARLY —) HASTY RARERIPE
(PREF.) HADR(O)
RIPEN AGE ADDLE AUGUST DIGEST MELLOW CONCOCT CRIMSON

DEVELOP PERFECT COMPLETE MATURATE
RIPENESS MATURITY
RIPHATH (FATHER OF —) GOMER
RIP-OFF GYP THEFT IMITATION
RIPOSTE REPLY RETORT THRUST REPARTEE
RIPPER RIPSAW BOBSLED HUMDINGER
RIPPET FUSS TUMULT UPROAR DISPUTE QUARREL
RIPPING FINE GRAND SWELL CAPITAL TIPPING SPLENDID
RIPPLE CURL FRET PURL RIFF SEED WAVE ACKER CRISP TWINE COCKLE DIMPLE JABBLE LIPPER RIMPLE RUFFLE RUMBLE WIMPLE CRINKLE WAVELET WRINKLE
(— ALONG) DADE
RIPPLING BREAK BULGE JABBLE ARIPPLE
(— OF SEA) LIPPER
(— ON SURFACE) HORROR
RIPSAW RIPPER SPLITSAW
RIPSNORTER SNIFTER HUMDINGER
RISE COME DRAW FLOW GROW HEAD HIGH HIKE HILL HOLT HOVE LIFT PLUM SOAR ARISE BEGIN CANCH CHEER CLIMB ERECT HEAVE HOIST MOUNT OCCUR PITCH PLUFF PROVE RAISE ROUSE SCEND SOURD STAND START SURGE SWELL TOWER YEAST ASCEND ASCENT ASPIRE AURORA BILLOW EMERGE GROWTH HAPPEN HEIGHT ORIGIN RESULT RETORT SOURCE SPRING THRIVE UPDIVE UPREAR UPTICK ADVANCE APPLAUD HUMMOCK REDOUND UPHEAVE UPSHOOT EMINENCE FLOURISH HEIGHTEN INCREASE LEVITATE SCENSION UPSPRING
(— ABOVE) OVERLOOK SURMOUNT
(— ABRUPTLY) SKYROCKET
(— AGAIN) RESURGE
(— AND FALL) LOOM HEAVE WELTER
(— AS PRICE) MEND
(— GRADUALLY) LOOM
(— IN BLISTERS) YAW
(— IN CLOUDS) STOOR
(— IN MINE FLOOR) HOGBACK
(— IN PRICES) BULGE
(— IN VALUE) IMPROVE
(— OF CURVE) CAMBER
(— OF HAWK AFTER PREY) MOUNTY
(— OF SHIP'S LINES) FLIGHT
(— OF WATER) FLOOD
(— PRECIPITOUSLY) SKY
(— RAPIDLY) KITE
(— SHARPLY) BREAK
(— SUDDENLY) BOOM SPRING
(— SWIFTLY) BOIL
(— TO BAIT) TAKE
(— TO GREAT HEIGHT) TOWER
(— TO PEAK) SWELL
(— UP) FUME REAR ASCEND INSURRECT
(CURVED —) HANCE
(GIVE — TO) SPAWN
(SHARP —) HOGBACK
RISE OF SILAS LAPHAM (AUTHOR OF —) HOWELLS
(CHARACTER IN —) TOM COREY IRENE SILAS LAPHAM PERSIS ROGERS PENELOPE BROMFIELD
RISER HEAD RAISE FEEDHEAD INSURGENT
RISHI RSI POET SAGE SAINT DEVARSHI KASHYAPA MAHARSHI
RISIBLE FUNNY GELASTIC LAUGHABLE
RISING BOIL BULL RIST ARISE ARIST ORIENT PUTSCH SOURCE STRAKE UPREST UPWITH MONTANT PUSTULE SURGENT EMERGENT INCREASE MOUNTANT NAISSANT ONCOMING ASSURGENT EXCEEDING
(— ABOVE) SUPERIOR
(— ABRUPTLY) BOLD
(— AGAIN) REORIENT
(— AND FALLING) TIDAL
(— AS A BIRD) ROUSANT
(— AS OF HAWK) SOURCE
(— BY DEGREES) GRADIENT
(— FROM DEAD) RESURRECTION
(— GRADUALLY) SOFT
(— HIGH) AERIAL
(— SHARPLY) ABRUPT
(— STEEPLY) BLUFF
(— TO BREATHE) HAURIANT HAURIENT
(— WITH SUN) COSMICAL
(POPULAR —) EMEUTE
RISK GO RUN SET GAGE JUMP LUCK PAWN PERIL RISCO STAKE STAND THROW WAGER WATHE CHANCE DANGER GAMBLE HAZARD IMPAWN PLIGHT THREAT BALANCE IMPERIL VENTURE ENDANGER EXPOSURE
(PL.) COVERAGE
RISKY BOLD DICEY DODGY CHANCY DARING KITTLE RISQUE PARLISH PARLOUS TECHOUS TICKLISH
RISP BUSH RASP STEM TWIG STALK BRANCH SCRATCH
RISQUE BLUE GAMY RACY SEXY BROAD DARING SCABROUS
RISSOLE CROQUETTE
(PL.) CECILS
RISS-WURM NEUDECKIAN
RISURREZIONE (CHARACTER IN —) DIMITRI KATUSHA SIMONSON
(COMPOSER OF —) ALFANO
RIT CUT RIP RUT REND SLIT TEAR SCRATCH
RITE KEX ASAL BORA BRIS FORM HAKO SOMA BRITH HONOR RIGHT SRADH ABDEST AUGURY EXEQUY FETISH OFFICE PANSIL PIACLE POOJAH RITUAL BAPTISM FUNERAL KATCINA LITURGY MYSTERY OBSEQUY SRADDHA TASHLIK CEREMONY HIERURGY HUSKANAW MORTUARY PIACULUM OBSERVANCE
(FUNERAL —S) EXEQUY EXEQUIES OBSEQUIES
(INITIATION —) BORA
(RELIGIOUS —) SYMBOL
(SECRET —) ORGY
(PL.) CULT SACRA SERVICE
RITUAL FORM RITE SOLEMN AGENDUM HAGGADA LITURGY OBSEQUY SERVICE CEREMONY VISPARAD VISPERED
(PASSOVER —) AGADAH HAGGADA HAGGADAH
(PRAYER —) PUJA
RITUALISTIC SACRAL
RITZY SWANKY HAUGHTY SNOBBISH
RIVAGE BANK RIVE COAST SHORE
RIVAL VIE EVEN PEER SIDE MATCH COMPETE CORRIVE EMULATE PARAGON CORRIVAL EMULATOR OPPONENT
(PREF.) ANT(I) ANTH(O)
RIVALRY VIE GAME STRIFE PARAGON JEALOUSY STRIVING EMULATION
RIVALS (AUTHOR OF —) SHERIDAN
(CHARACTER IN —) BOB JACK LUCY ACRES JULIA LYDIA LUCIUS ANTHONY ABSOLUTE BEVERLEY LANGUISH MALAPROP MELVILLE OTRIGGER FAULKLAND
RIVE RIP PLOW REND STAB TEAR CRACK REAVE SEVER SPLIT WEDGE CLEAVE SUNDER THRUST SHATTER FRACTURE
RIVELING RULLION
RIVER EA LE LEE REE RIO TJI ALPH AVON BAHR GEON ILOG KILL WADI WADY BAYOU CREEK FLOOD GANGA GIHON GJOLL GLIDE HABOR INLET KIANG TCHAI BARCOO GUTTER KHUBUR NYANZA STRAIT STREAM CHANNEL COCYTUS ESTUARY FROEMAN ILISSUS PHARPAR RUBICON SENEGAL AFFLUENT ERIDANUS PACTOLUS STAIRCASE
(— CHANNEL) ALVEUS
(— IN SPIRITUAL) JORDAN
(— NEAR GATE OF HEL'S ABODE) GJOLL
(— OF ATTICA) ILISSUS
(— OF DAMASCUS) PHARPAR
(— OF HADES) STYX LETHE
(— OF LYDIA) PACTOLUS
(— OF PARADISE) GEON GIHON
(— OF QUEENSLAND) BARCOO
(— OF UNDERGROUND) PHLEGETHON
(— OF UNDERWORLD) STYX LETHE ACHERON COCYTUS FLEGETON
(AFRICAN —) NYANZA SENEGAL
(CHINESE —) HO KIANG
(EGYPTIAN —) BAHR NILE
(FULL —) BANKER
(JAVANESE —) TJI
(MINOR —) BAYOU
(SACRED —) ALPH GANGA
(SMALL —) BACHE TCHAI
(TIDAL —) ESTUARY
(PREF.) FLUVI(O) POTAM(O)
(SUFF.) POTAMIA POTAMUS
RIVERBANK RIPA RIPE
RIVERBED LAAGTE BATTURE
(DRY —) WADI WADY
RIVER BLINDNESS ONCHOCERCIASIS
RIVERBOAT COG BARGE FOIST PULWAR
RIVER DUCK TEAL MALLARD WIDGEON GREENWING
RIVERINE (— FISH) HUCHO
RIVERWEED WATERWEED
RIVET STUD CLINK ROOVE PANHEAD FLATHEAD
(— ATTENTION) GRIP
(— HEAD) CUPHEAD
RIVULET RUN BURN GILL LAKE MOTH RILL SIKE BACHE BATCH BAYOU BOURN BROOK GHYLL RITHE RINDLE RUNLET RUNNEL STREAM STRIPE STRYPE CHANNEL RIVERET BROOKLET
RIXY TERN
RIZPAH (LOVER OF —) SAUL
(SON OF —) ARMONI MEPHIBOSHETH
RIZZAR DRY PARCH RASOUR RAZOUR CURRANT HADDOCK
RIZZOM BIT EAR RISOM STALK STRAW RISSOM
RNA POLYA
ROACH HOG BUTT ROCK SPOT BRAISE BLATTID SUNFISH
ROAD LEG PAD TAO VIA WAY BELT BORD CASH DRAG DRUN FARE GAET GANG GATE LINE LODE LOKE PASS PATH PAVE PIKE RADE RAID RIDE RODE ROTE ROUT SLAB SPUR WENT BARGH BLAZE BYWAY CLOSE DRIFT DRIVE DROVE FORAY GAITE GOING METAL PRAYA ROUTE TRACE TRACK BYROAD CAMINO CAREER CAUSEY CHEMIN COURSE DUGWAY FEEDER RIDING ROUGHT RUNWAY SLOUGH STREET TARMAC TRAJET BEELINE CALZADA CARTWAY ESTRADA GANGWAY HIGHWAY LANDWAY OUTGANG PACKWAY PASSAGE RAILWAY RAMPIRE ROADWAY ROLLWAY SKIDWAY TELFORD AUTOBAHN BEALLACH BLACKTOP BROADWAY CHAUSSEE CORDUROY FOOTRILL HORSEWAY OVERPASS RIDGEWAY SPEEDWAY TRACKWAY TRAMROAD TRAVERSE TURNPIKE WAGONWAY ROADSTEAD
(— BORDERING SHORE) PRAYA
(— FOR LOGGING) SKIDWAY CROSSHAUL
(— FOR SPACECRAFT) CRAWLERWAY
(— HAZARD) ESS
(— IN COAL MINE) BORD BOARD FOOTRILL
(— ON CLIFF) CORNICHE
(— SCRAPER) HARL HARLE
(— SURFACE) TELFORD
(ALTERNATE —) DETOUR
(CEMENT OR CONCRETE —) SLAB
(COUNTRY —) BOREEN DRIFTWAY
(DESCENDING —) BAHADA BAJADA
(IMPASSABLE —) SLOUGH IMPASSE
(IMPROVISED —) CASH
(MILITARY OR PUBLIC —) AGGER
(NARROW —) DRANG DRUNG RODDIN
(PAVED —) CALZADA CHAUSSEE
(PRINCIPAL —) ARTERY
(PRIVATE —) LOKE DRIVE DRIVEWAY
(RAISED —) AGGER RAMPIRE CAUSEWAY

(ROMAN —) ITER CAUSEY
(SIDE —) BRANCH SHUNPIKE
(STEEP —) BRAE PATH BARGH SPRUNT
(TEMPORARY —) SHOOFLY
(UNIMPROVED —) DROVE
(ZIGZAG —) SWITCHBACK
(PREF.) ODO VIA
(SUFF.) ODE OID
ROADBED BALLAST BITUMEN
ROADBOOK MAP ITINERARY
ROAD DONKEY ROADER
ROADMAN PEDDLER SALESMAN CANVASSER
ROADMASTER OVERSEER
ROAD RUNNER CUCKOO PAISANO
ROADSIDE HEDGE
ROADSTEAD RAID DOWNS
ROADSTER BUGGY TRAMP DRIVER BICYCLE RUNABOUT RACEABOUT SPEEDSTER
ROADWAY DECK EXIT STREET MACADAM SLIPWAY TRUCKWAY
(— MANEUVER) UTURN
ROAM GO ERR RUN WAG RAKE RAME RAVE ROIL ROLL ROVE WALK GIPSY GYPSY KNOCK RANGE SCAMP SPACE STRAY TAVER VAGUE WAVER BANGLE RAMBLE STROLL SWERVE TAIVER VAGARY WANDER GALLANT PROCEED SQUANDER VAGABOND
(— FURTIVELY) PROWL
ROAMING ERROR NOMADIC ROAMAGE FUGITIVE
(PREF.) PLAN(O)
ROAN HORSE GRIZZLE
ROANOKE WAMPUM
ROAR CRY BAWL BEAL BELL BERE BOOM BRAY CAVE HOWL HURL RAIR RARE RERD ROIN ROME ROOP ROUT YELL BLARE BROOL CRACK RERDE ROUST SHOUT SNORE BELLOW BULDER BULLER CLAMOR GOLLAR GOLLER RUMMES SCREAM SHRIEK STEVEN BLUSTER RUMMISH THUNDER ULULATE
(— AS BOAR) FREAM
(— LIKE WIND) HURL
(— OF SURF) ROTE
(LOW —) BROOL
ROARING RUT LOUD AROAR BRISK ROUST BELLOW BOOMING RIOTOUS THRIVING
ROARING BOY TWIBIL TWIBILL
ROARING GAME CURLING
ROARING MEG CANNON
ROAST RAZZ ROTI SOAK BREDE BROWN PARCH ASSATE CODDLE REMOVE TORREFY TORRIFY BARBECUE RIDICULE
(— IN ASHES) BRY
(KIND OF —) RIB RUMP
(STUFFED —) FARCI
ROASTED ASADO
(NOT —) GREEN
ROASTER BURNER SCORCHER
ROASTING ASSATION
ROASTING JACK TURNSPIT
ROB COP PAD EASE FAKE FLAP MILL NICK PEEL PELF PICK PILL POLL PREY PULL RAMP RIPE ROLL TOBY BENIM BRIBE FLIMP HARRY HEAVE HEIST LURCH PINCH PLUCK PLUME PROWL REAVE RIFLE ROIST SHAKE SPOIL SPUNG STEAL STRUB TOUCH HARROW HIJACK HUSTLE PILFER RAVISH RIPOFF STRIKE THIEVE BEREAVE DEPRIVE DESPOIL PLUNDER RUMPADE SNAFFLE UNPURSE DEFLOWER SPOLIATE
(— HOUSE) MILL
(— OF CHASTITY) DEFILE
(— OF FORCE) COOL
(— OF JOY) DESOLATE
(— OF VIGOR) ETIOLATE
(— WITH VIOLENCE) RAMP
ROBALO FISH PIKE SNOOK SNOWK SERGEANT
ROBBED RUBATO
(NOT —) UNPILLED
ROBBER PAD CROOK FOMOR LARON THIEF BANDIT BRIBER DACOIT FORMOR HOLDUP LATRON RIFLER BRIGAND CATERAN FOOTPAD HEISTER LADRONE MOONMAN PANDOUR PRANCER RAVENER ROUTIER SPOILER TOBYMAN BARABBAS FOMORIAN PILLAGER RABIATOR BANDOLERO
(— ON HIGH SEAS) PIRATE
(— WHO USES VIOLENCE) RABIATOR
(GRAVE —) GOUL GHOUL
(HIGHWAY —) PAD FOOTPAD TOBYMAN
(INDIAN MURDEROUS —) DACOIT
(IRISH —) WOODKERN
(MOUNTAIN —) CHOAR
(NIGHT —) MOONMAN
(SEA —) FOMOR FORMOR FOMORIAN
(WANDERING —) ROUTIER
(PREF.) LESTO
(SUFF.) LESTES
ROBBERY JOB JUMP REIF RIFE HEIST SCREW STALE FELONY HOLDUP STOWTH BRIBERY DACOITY LARCENY PILLAGE PLUNDER REAVERY STICKUP THUGGEE PURCHASE SPOLIATION
(— ON HIGH SEAS) PIRACY
(HIGHWAY —) TOBY
ROBE GOWN TOGA VEST KANZU STOLA CHIMER KIMONO KITTEL MANTLE PEPLOS REVEST ARISAID BUFFALO GALABIA SURCOAT VESTURE PARAMENT WOLFSKIN
(— FOR THE DEAD) HABIT
(— OF HONOR) KHALAT KHILAT KILLUT KELLAUT
(— OF MONARCH) PLUVIAL
(— PRESENTED BY DIGNITARY) KHALAT KHILAT
(— REACHING TO ANKLES) TALAR
(ACTOR'S —) SYRMA
(ARAB —) ABA
(BAPTISMAL —) CHRISOM
(BISHOP'S —) CHIMER CHIMERE
(CIRCULAR —) CYCLAS
(CORONATION —) COLOBIUM DALMATIC
(DERVISH'S —) KHIRKA KHIRKAH
(EMPEROR'S —) PURPLE
(FUNERAL —) SABLE
(JEWISH —) KITTEL
(KING'S —) DALMATIC
(LOOSE —) MANT CAMIS CAMUS CYMAR SIMAR SYMAR MANTUA CHIMERE MANTEAU
(MASQUERADE —) VENETIAN
(MEXICAN —) MANGA
(MONK'S —) HAPLOMA
(OLD-FASHIONED —) SAMARE
(OUTER —) JAMA
(PRIEST'S —) ALB
(ROMAN —) TOGA STOLA
(TARTAN —) ARISAID
(TURKISH —) DOLMAN
(WHITE —) CHRISOM
(PL.) ACADEMICALS
ROBERT DOB POP RAB DOBBIN POPKIN
ROBERT OF LINCOLN BOBOLINK
ROBIN THRUSH PINFISH REDDOCK RUDDOCK TOOTLER WINGFISH REDBREAST
ROBIN GOODFELLOW ELF PUCK FAIRY SPRITE HOBGOBLIN
ROBINIA LOCUST
ROBIN SANDPIPER KNOT DOWITCHER
ROBORANT TONIC
ROBOT GELEM GOLEM AUTOMAT TELEVOX
(LIKE A —) FACELESS
ROB ROY (AUTHOR OF —) SCOTT
(CHARACTER IN —) ROB OWEN DIANA FRANK ANDREW MACFIN MORRIS VERNON TRESHAM WILLIAM CAMPBELL FREDERICK INGLEWOOD MACVITTIE RASHLEIGH HILDEBRAND FAIRSERVICE OSBALDISTONE
ROBUST ABLE FIRM HAIL HALE HARD IRON RUDE BONNY HARDY HUSKY LUSTY RENKY SOUND STARK STIFF STOUR STOUT TOUGH VALID WALLY HEARTY RUGGED SINEWY STRONG STURDY HEALTHY NERVOUS STHENIC VALIANT MUSCULAR PITHSOME STALWART SWACKING VIGOROUS STRAPPING
(NOT —) SLENDER
ROBUSTNESS VALIDITY
ROC BIRD BOMB RUKH ROQUE SIMURG SIMURGH
ROCHET CLOAK SMOCK CAMISIA
ROCK CAP JOW LOG PAY RAG DAZE HOST KLIP REEL RUKH SIAL SIMA SWAY SWIG TOSS BRACK CLIFF FLOOR GREET GRUSS HORSE LEDGE ROACH ROQUE SHAKE SHOWD SKARN STONE TRILL CRADLE FACIES GROUND OOLITE PELITE TOTTER BRECCIA COUNTRY FOLIATE GREISEN CIMINITE PHYLLITE SILTSTONE
(— AROUND DRILL HOLE) COLLAR
(— CHUNK) KNUCKLE
(— DEBRIS) SCREE
(— FRAGMENT) CLAST
(— GROUP FAN) GROUPIE
(— IN ANOTHER ROCK) XENOLITH
(— IN MINE) CAPPING
(— IN SEA) STACK
(— SURFACE) KARREN
(— VIOLENTLY) STAGGER
(ARTIFICIAL —) GRANOLITH
(BALD —) SCALP
(BANDED —) BAR
(BARE —) SCARTH
(BASALTIC —) TEPHRITE
(CAP —) COVER
(COLUMN OF MOLTEN —) PLUME
(COMPACT —) BASEMENT
(CONGLOMERATE —) PSEPHITE
(COUNTRY —) RIDER ROCKABILLY
(CRUSHED —) GREET
(CRYSTALLINE —) ELVAN DUNITE SCHIST DIORITE GREISEN ECLOGITE
(DECAY OF —S) GEEST LATERITE
(DECOMPOSED —) GOSSAN GOZZAN
(DENSE —) ADINOLE
(DISINTEGRATED —) SAPROLITE
(EXTRUSIVE —) DACITE SPILITE ANDESITE CIMINITE
(FELDSPATHIC —) PETUNTSE
(FISSILE —) SHALE SHAUL
(FLUID —) LAVA
(FRAGMENTAL —) PSEPHITE
(FRAGMENT OF —) CLAST
(GABBROITIC —) EUCRITE
(GLASSY —) PITCHSTONE
(GRANULAR —) GABBRO OOLITE DIORITE IJOLITE KOSWITE MYLONITE PSAMMITE QUARTZITE
(GRANULATED —) GRUSS
(GREEN —) OPHITE
(HARD —) WHIN KIMGLE WHINSTONE NOVACULITE
(HIGH —) SCOUT
(IGNEOUS —) BOSS SIAL SIMA TRAP BASALT DUNITE GABBRO URTITE FELSITE GRANITE MINETTE PICRITE SYENITE UNAKITE DOLERITE ESSEXITE RHYOLITE TONALITE
(IMPURE —) CHERT
(INSULAR —) SKERRY
(INSULATED —) SKERRY
(INTRUSIVE —) HORTITE MINETTE MAENAITE
(IRON-BEARING —) GAL
(ISOLATED —) SCAR SCARR SCAUR
(JUTTING POINT OF —) KIP
(MANTLE —) REGOLITH
(METAMORPHIC —) SKARN GNEISS SCHIST BUCHITE GONDITE LEPTITE ECLOGITE HORNFELS LIMURITE
(MICA-BEARING —) DOMITE
(MOLTEN —) MAGMA
(MOON —) KREEP
(MOTTLED —) SERPENTINE
(PLUTONIC —) TAWITE HOLLAITE TURJAITE
(POROUS —) TUFA TUFF ARSOITE
(PROJECTING —) CLINT
(PULVERIZED —) FLOUR
(RARE —) ALNOITE
(ROUGH —) CRAG KNAR SCARTH
(ROUNDED —) ROGNON SHEEPBACK
(SAND —) PSAMMITE
(SEDIMENTARY —) CRAG IRONSTONE SANDSTONE
(SHARP —) NEEDLE AIGUILLE
(SLATY —) PLATE SCHALSTEIN
(SOFT —) MALM

(SOLID —) GIBBER
(STUDY OF —S) LITHOLOGY
(SUBMERGED —) SHELF
(SURROUNDING —) GROUND
(UNDERLYING —) FLOOR
(UPRIGHT —) PILLAR
(VOLCANIC —) TUFA TUFF BASALT DACITE DOMITE LATITE TAXITE PEPERIN ANDESITE ASHSTONE EUTAXITE RHYOLITE TEPHRITE TRACHYTE
(WASTE —) MULLOCK
(WORTHLESS —) GANG GANGUE
(WORTHLESS — MATTER) GANGUE
(PL.) ROCHER
(PREF.) FELSO PETR(I)(O) RHYO RUPI SAXI
(SUFF.) CLAST ITE LITE LITH(IC) LITIC PHYRE PHYRIC

ROCKAWAY CARRIAGE
ROCK BADGER CONY HYRAX
ROCK BASS REDEYE CABRILLA
ROCK-BREAKER
(SUFF.) FRAGE
ROCKBRUSH ROSILLA
ROCK CEDAR SABINO
ROCK CRESS ARABIS SICKLEPOD
ROCK DEBRIS TALUS
ROCK DOVE SOD
ROCK-DWELLING SAXATILE
ROCK ELM WAHOO
ROCKER CRADLE SHOOFLY
ROCKET DRAKE TITAN REBUKE STREAK YELLOW CONGREVE SKYLIGHT STARSHIP FIREDRAKE
(DYER'S —) WELD WOLD WOALD WOULD
(SYSTEM OF SPACECRAFT —S) RETROPACK
ROCKET SALAD ROQUETTE
ROCKFISH BASS JACK RENA REINA VIUVA FLIOMA GOPHER RASHER TAMBOR CORSAIR GARRUPA GROUPER BOCACCIO CHINAFISH GREENLING
ROCK HARE KLIPHAAS
ROCK HIND MERO AGAUJI
ROCKHOPPER PENGUIN
ROCK HOPPER MACARONI
ROCKLING BAUD GADE ROKER SORGHE WHISTLER
ROCK NATIVE SNAPPER
ROCK OIL NAPHTHA PETROLEUM
ROCK PIPIT TIETICK
ROCK RABBIT PIKA HYRAX HYRACOID
ROCKROSE CISTUS PINWEED HUDSONIA ROCKCIST SAGEROSE DAYFLOWER SUNFLOWER
ROCK SALT EMOL AMOLE HALITE
(BLOCK OF —) PIG
ROCK SANDWORT CYME
ROCKSHAFT SHAFT ROCKER WEIGHBAR
ROCK TROUT BOREGAT GREENLING
ROCKWEED TANG FUCUS FUCOID SEATANG SEAWEED
(PREF.) FUCI
ROCK WHITING KELPFISH STRANGER
ROCKWORK ROCAILLE
(ARTIFICIAL —) ROCAILLE

ROCKY DAFT HARD STONY CLINTY OBSCENE PETREAN PETROUS UNCOUTH OBDURATE UNSTABLE DIFFICULT RUPELLARY
(PREF.) TRACHY
ROCKY MOUNTAIN (— GOAT) MAZAME
ROCOCO ORNATE QUAINT BAROCCO BAROQUE OUTMODED
ROD BAR BOW CUE GAD GUY LUG PIN TIE BOLT CALM CAME CANE CORE FALL FORK GOAD GONG LINK MACE POLE RAVE SCOB SNAP STEM STUD WAND WHIP YARD ARBOR BIRCH CATCH DOWEL LYTTA OSIER PERCH POWER PUNCH REACH REBAR ROUND SETUP SHOOT SPELK SPILL SPOKE SPRAG STAFF STANG STEEL STICK STING TEYNE TOMMY TRACE VERGE WIPER BALEYS BROACH CANARY CARBON CENTER CRUTCH ETALON FERULA FINGER GLOWER HANGER PISTOL PITMAN PODGER RADDLE RAMMER SKEWER SPRING STADIA SWITCH TOGGLE WATTLE WICKER BACULUS CROPPIE DRAWROD ELLWAND FEATHER FESTUCA MANDREL PLUNGER POINTER POTHOOK PRICKER PROBANG PROLONG SCALLOM SCEPTER SPINDLE STADIUM STICKER TYRANNY VIRGULA WHISKER WINDING AXOSTYLE BACKSTAY BILBERRY BODSTICK BOWSTAVE DIPSTICK JACKSTAY KINGBOLT REVOLVER STRAINER TRAVELER WEEDHOOK
(— AS SYMBOL OF OFFICE) VERGE
(— BEARING TRAFFIC SIGNAL) STANCHION
(— FOR ALIGNING HOLES) PODGER
(— FOR CARRYING GLASS) FORK
(— FOR DISCIPLINE) YARD FERULA FERULE
(— FOR FASTENING THATCH) SPELK SPRINGLE
(— FOR FIREARM BORE) WIPER
(— FOR GLASS-MAKING) PUNTY FASCET PONTEE PONTIL CROPPIE
(— FOR HOLDING MEAT) SPIT
(— FOR TRANSMITTING MOTION) TRACE
(— IN ARC LAMP) CARBON
(— IN CRICKET) STUMP
(— IN INTERFEROMETER) ETALON
(— IN MINE PUMP) SPEAR
(— IN NERNST LAMP) GLOWER
(— IN SPINNING WHEEL) SPINDLE
(— OF CELLS) NOTOCHORD
(— OF FOUNDRY MOLD) LANCE
(— OF LOOM) SHAFT
(— OF WOOD) SCOB
(— ON DOG SLED) GEEPOLE
(— ON LOGGING TRUCK) RAVE
(— POINTED AT BOTH ENDS) SKEWER
(— SYMBOLIZING AUTHORITY) BACULUS
(— TO BIND A CONTRACT) FESTUCA
(— TO FASTEN SAILS) JACKSTAY
(— TO IMMERSE SHEEP) CRUTCH
(— TO URGE BEAST) GOAD PROD
(— UPSET AT ONE END) SETUP
(— USED AS KEY) TOMMY
(— WITH ENDS AT RIGHT ANGLES) STRAINER
(— WITH SPONGE ON END) PROBANG
(— WITH T-HEAD) TOGGLE
(AXIAL —) VIRGULA AXOSTYLE
(BASKETRY —) OSIER SLATH
(BUNDLE OF —S) DRIVER
(CARTILAGINOUS —) LYTTA COLUMELLA
(CLAMMING —) BRAIL
(CONNECTING —) PITMAN
(CURTAIN —) TRINGLE
(DANCER'S —) CROTALUM
(DIVINING —) TWIG DOWSER
(FISHING —) GAD CALCUTTA
(FLEXIBLE —) RADDLE WATTLE
(FORKED —) CRUTCH
(GEM-CUTTING —) SETTER
(GRADUATED —) STADIA STADIUM
(IRON —) SNAP BETTY
(KNITTING —) NEEDLE
(LEAD —) CAME
(LOGGING —) CANARY
(MEASURING —) JUDGE SPILE STADIA ELLWAND METEWAND METEYARD
(PLIABLE —) WINDING
(SMALL —) LANCE
(STRENGTHENING —) RIB
(SUPPLE —) SWABBLE
(TETHERING —) STAKE
(THIN —) TEYNE SCALLOM
(TIE —) ANCHOR
(UMBRELLA —) STRETCHER
(WITHE —) BILBERRY
(PREF.) BACULI RHABD(O) RHAPIDO VERGI

RODENT RAT CONY DEGU HARE MARA MOCO MOLE PACA PIKA UTIA VOLE CONEY COYPU GUNDI HUTIA JUTIA LEROT MOUSE TUCAN ZOKOR AGOUTI BEAVER BITING CURURO GERBIL GLIRID GNAWER GOPHER JERBOA MARMOT MURINE MUROID RABBIT SOKHOR BLESMOL CHINCHA DIPODID GEOMYID GNAWING HAMSTER LEMMING LEVERET MUSKRAT ABROCOME CAPIBARA DORMOUSE LEPORIDE OCTODONT SEWELLEL SPALACID SQUIRREL TUCOTUCO VISCACHA VIZCACHA ANOMALURE PORCUPINE
RODEO ROUNDUP
RODERICK RANDOM (AUTHOR OF —) SMOLLETT
(CHARACTER IN —) TOM STRAP OAKHUM RANDOM BOWLING MELINDA SNAPPER CRAMPLEY NARCISSA RODERICK WILLIAMS QUIVERWIT
RODLIKE VIRGATE RHABDOID
RODMAN CLASHY CLASHEE CHAINMAN
RODOMONTADE BRAG RANT BOAST BLUSTER BOMBAST BRAGGART
RODOMONTE (BELOVED OF —) DORALICE
(VICTIM OF —) RUGGIERO

ROD-SHAPED RHABDOID VIRGULATE
ROE RA DOE FRY PEA RAA RAE DEER HIND KELK RAUN ROUN ROWN CORAL TRUBU CAVIAR
ROEBUCK GIRL CHEVREUIL
ROGER RAM HODGE ROGUE
ROGUE BOY GUE IMP NYM HEMP KEMP KITE LOON ROAG CATSO CRACK CRANK DROLE GIPSY GREEK GYPSY HEMPY KNAVE SCAMP SHELM BEGGAR BORGER BUGGER CANTER CHOUSE COQUIN CURTAL HARLOT LIMMER PICARA PICARO RASCAL SORROW TINKER BLEEDER ERRATIC FOISTER HALLION LADRONE PANURGE SHARPER SKELLUM SWINGER VILLAIN COMROGUE HEMPSEED PICAROON SCALAWAG SWINDLER WHIPJACK
ROGUE HERRIES (AUTHOR OF —) WALPOLE
(CHARACTER IN —) ALICE DAVID PRESS SARAH STARR DEBORAH DENBURN FRANCIS HERRIES MARGARET MIRABELL OSBALDISTONE
ROGUERY ROPERY KNAVERY LOONERY WAGGERY PATCHERY PRIGGISM TRICKERY TRUANTRY
ROGUISH SLY ARCH HEMPY ROGUY WICKED KNAVISH TRICKSY VAGRANT WAGGISH ESPIEGLE SCAMPISH DISHONEST
ROGUISHNESS KNAVERY ARCHNESS
ROI DE LAHORE, LE (CHARACTER IN —) ALIM SITA SCINDIA
(COMPOSER OF —) MASSENET
ROIL VEX FOUL RILE ANNOY AGITATE BLUNDER DISTURB STUDDLE BEWILDER DISORDER IRRITATE
ROILED TURBID
ROISTER REVEL ROIST SCOUR CAROUSE GALRAVAGE
ROISTERER MUN GREEK HUZZA BUSTER HECTOR RIOTER SCOURER TWIBILL EPHESIAN
ROISTERING HOYDEN
ROKE FOG DAMP MIST REEK ROWK STIR FOGGY SMOKE STEAM VAPOR
ROKELAY ROCOLO
ROLAND (BETROTHED OF —) AUDE
(COMPANION OF —) OLIVER
(HORN OF —) OLIVANT
(SWORD OF —) DURANDAL
(UNCLE OF —) CHARLEMAGNE
ROLE BIT JOB LEAD PART ROTE HEAVY FIGURE CLOTHES BUSINESS FUNCTION LIRIPIPE
(CHIEF —) LEAD
(SECONDARY —) COMPRIMARIO
(SMALL —) CAMEO
ROLL BAP BUN ROW WEB BOLT COIL CURL FILE FLOW FURL LIST MILL PASS REEL ROAM ROTA SWAG WELT WIND WRAP BAGEL BIALY BREAD BUILD DANDY DICKY ENROL FLUTE ROYLE SPLIT TOMMY TRILL TROLL WHELM BILLOW BUNDLE CIRCLE ELAPSE

ENFOLD GOGGLE GROVEL KIPFEL LEGEND MUSTER PONDER RECORD ROSTER ROTATE SCROLL UPWIND VOLUME WAMBLE WANDER WHELVE WINTLE WREATH BISCUIT BOLILLO BRIOCHE CROCKET ENVELOP MANCHET NOTITIA REVOLVE ROTULET ROTULUS ROULEAU STRETCH TERRIER TRINDLE TRUNDLE TWISTER BAGUETTE BROTCHEN CANNELON CONSIDER CRESCENT JACKROLL LAMINATE PORTEOUS REGISTER SEDERUNT SPREADER VOLUTATE
(— A BALL) BOWL
(— ABOUT) WALTER SCAMBLE
(— ALONG) COAST TRUCK
(— AS A SHIP) SEEL LURCH
(— AS STONE) REEL
(— BY) WALK
(— CLOSELY) FURL
(— EYES) WALL WAUL WHAWL GOGGLE
(— GLASS) MARVER
(— INTO A BALL) CLEW CLUE
(— OF BILLS) WAD
(— OF BREAD) BAP SEMMEL TAMMIE
(— OF CLOTH) BOLT DOSSIL WREATH
(— OF COINS) ROULEAU
(— OF DOUGH) TWIST
(— OF DRIED BARK) QUILL
(— OF DRUM) HURRY RATTAN
(— OF DUST) KITTEN
(— OF FIBERS) ROVING
(— OF HAIR) PUFF ROACH ROWEL CROCKET
(— OF HAY) WAKE
(— OF LINT OR LINEN) TENT DOSSIL
(— OF LUGGAGE) SWAG
(— OF MINCED MEAT) RISSOLE
(— OF OFFENDERS) PORTEOUS
(— OF PAPER) SPILL STOMP STUMP
(— OF PARCHMENT) BOOK PELL
(— OF ROULETTE WHEEL) COUP
(— OF SPUN YARN) PRICK
(— OF TOBACCO) CAROT CIGAR PRICK SEGAR CAROTTE
(— OF WALLPAPER) BOLT
(— OF WHEAT BREAD) MANCHET
(— OF WOOL) ROVE ROVING CARDING
(— ON CASTERS) TRUCKLE
(— ON LITTLE WHEELS) TRUNDLE
(— ONWARD) DEVOLVE
(— OVER) COMB JOLL WELTER
(— TOGETHER) CONVOLVE
(— TO RUB DOWN DRAWING) STUMP
(— UP) FURL STOW COLLAR
(— UP SLEEVES) REEVE
(BLANKET —) BINDLE SHIRALEE
(BREAKFAST —) BIALY DANISH
(DANDY —) DANCER
(HOLLOW —) CANNELON
(KIND OF —) KAISER
(LONG —) FLUTE
(ON A —) HOT
(PADDED —) BURLET
(PENNY —) TOMMY
(TWISTED — OF WOOL) SLUB
(WHIP —) BACKREST
(PREF.) HELI(C)(CO)

ROLLED (— IN SUGAR) SANDED
ROLLER FLY BOWL BRAY DRUM JACK LEAD MILL PUCK RUBY WAVE BREAK DANDY FINER GODET INKER RIDER SHELL WAVER WINCH BRAYER BREAST DOFFER DUCTOR FASCIA MANGLE ROWLET RUNNER CARRIER CLEARER MOIETER TRUCKLE HEDGEHOG SQUEEGEE STRIPPER TROUPAND
(— FOR MASSAGER) ROULETTE
(— IN HORSE'S BIT) CRICKET
(— IN ORGAN) TRUNDLE
(— IN STEELWORKS) COGGER
(— TO CLEAR FABRIC) MOIETER
(CARDING —) BREAST WORKER SQUIRREL STRIPPER
(CHINESE —) SIRGANG
(DREDGING —) HEDGEHOG
(DROP —) DUCTOR
(GRINDING —) BREAK
(INKING —) BRAYER
(PLAYER ON — DERBY TEAM) JAMMER
(PRINTING —) DANDY SHELL BRAYER DAMPENER
(ROUND IN — DERBY) JAM
(STONE —) MAMMY TOTER
(SURGICAL —) FASCIA
(TOOTHED —) PRICK PRICKER
(TYPEWRITER —) PLATEN

ROLLER COASTER SWITCHBACK
ROLLER DERBY (ROUND IN —) JAM
ROLLERMAN BRAKER JACKMAN LEVERMAN
ROLLER SKATE PEDOMOTOR
ROLLICK PLAY ROMP CAVORT FROLIC ROLLIX
ROLLICKING GAY WILD MERRY JOVIAL LIVELY
ROLLING CURL GOGGLE WHEELY SWAYING TRILLED LURCHING VOLUTION
(— OF SCROLL) GELILAH
(— OF SHIP) LABOR
(— OF STOMACH) WAMBLE
ROLLTOP TAMBOUR
ROLY-POLY TUBBY ROTUND PUDDING TUMBLER SALTWORT
ROM RO GYPSY ROMANY
ROMAINE COS
ROMAN BRAVE LATIN NOBLE PAPAL ANTIQUA UPRIGHT GOWNSMAN
(— COLLAR) RABAT
ROMAN CATHOLIC ROME ROMAN PAPIST ROMIST JEBUSITE BABYLONIC
ROMANCE WOO GEST ANTAR FANCY FEIGN GESTE KATHA NOVEL STORY AFFAIR ANTARA UTOPIA FANTASY FICTION ROMANZA ROMAUNT
(— LANGUAGE) FRENCH ITALIAN SPANISH
ROMAN-FLEUVE SAGA

ROMANIA

CANAL: BEGA
CAPITAL: BUCHAREST
COIN: BAN LEI LEU LEY
COUNTY: OLT ARAD CLUJ DOLJ GORJ IASI ARGES BACAU BIHOR BUZAU ILFOV MURES NEAMT SALAJ SIBIU TIMIS
DISTRICT: ALBA BANAT BIHOR DOBRUJA DOBROGEA MARAMURES
LAKE: SINOE
MOUNTAIN: BIHOR NEGOI CODRUL RODNEI CALIMAN PIETROSU
OLD NAME: DACIA
PASS: ROSUL
PROVINCE: ARDEAL MOLDAVIA WALACHIA
RIVER: ALT OLT JIUL PRUT ALUTA ARGES BUZDU MOROS MURES OLTUL SCHYL SIRET TIMIS TISZA VEDEA CRASNA DANUBE ARGESUL MURESUL SOMESUL BISTRITA IALOMITA
RIVER PORT: BRAILA GALATI GALATZ
TOWN: ARAD CLUJ IASI BACAU CERNA JASSY NEAMT SIBIU TURNU BRAILA BRASOV GALATI GALATZ LUPENI CRAIOVA FOCSANI PLOESTI SEVERIN CERNAVTI KISHENEF TEMESVAR KOLOZSVAR

ROMANIST MISSARY
ROMANIZATION LATINXUA
ROMANSH LADIN
ROMANTIC AIRY WILD IDEAL ARDENT DREAMY GOTHIC POETIC UNREAL FERVENT FABULOUS FANCIFUL
ROMANY RO ROM GIPSY GYPSY ROMAN
ROMANY RYE (AUTHOR OF —) BORROW
(CHARACTER IN —) DALE JACK BELLE ISOPEL JASPER URSULA BERNERS MURTAGH LAVENGRO SYLVESTER PETULENGRO
ROME (CHAPEL IN —) SISTINE
(FOUNDER OF —) ROMULUS
(HILL IN —) CAELIAN VIMINAL AVENTINE PALATINE QUIRINAL
(OLD PORT OF —) OSTIA
(RIVER IN —) TIBER
ROME HAUL (AUTHOR OF —) EDMONDS
(CHARACTER IN —) BEN DAN JOE RAE SOL LUCY BERRY JACOB KLORE MOLLY WAMPY CALASH GURGET HARROW HECTOR JOTHAM JULIUS SAMSON TINKLE WEAVER WILSON FORTUNE LARKINS TURNESA WILLIAM FRIENDLY CASHDOLLAR BUTTERFIELD
ROMEO AND JULIET (AUTHOR OF —) SHAKESPEARE
(CHARACTER IN —) JOHN PARIS PETER ROMEO JULIET TYBALT ABRAHAM CAPULET ESCALUS GREGORY SAMPSON BENVOLIO LAURENCE MERCUTIO MONTAGUE BALTHASAR
ROMOLA (AUTHOR OF —) ELIOT
(CHARACTER IN —) DINO LUCA TITO BARDO CALVO LILLO MONNA PIERO TESSA MELEMA ROMOLA BRIGIDA NICCOLO BERNARDO BALDASARRE
ROMP REG RIG HEMP LARK PLAY ROIL FRISK SHIRL SPORT TRAIN FROLIC GAMBOL HOORAY HOYDEN HURRAH RIPPET COURANT GAMMOCK RAMMACK RUNAWAY
ROMPERS JUMPER JUMPERS
ROMPING ROYT HEMPY ROYET
ROMULUS (BROTHER OF —) REMUS
(FATHER OF —) MARS
RONCADOR GRUNT CROAKER SCIAENID
RONDO ROTA
RONE BUSH BRAKE GUTTER THICKET
RONG LEPCHA
RONGA THONGA
RONSDORFER ZIONITE ELLERIAN
ROOD RUD REED ROPE CROSS SPAWN STANG CRUCIFIX
ROODLES RANGDOODLES
ROOF TOP ATAP BACK DECK DOME FLAT ATTAP COVER HOUSE RAISE RISER SHELL THACK AZOTEA BONNET CUPOLA SUMMIT TECTUM CHOPPER CRICKET GAMBREL MANSARD RIGGING TECTURE BULKHEAD HOUSETOP SAWTOOTH SEMIDOME PENTHOUSE
(— MEMBER) PURLIN
(— OF CARRIAGE) IMPERIAL
(— OF CAVERN) DOME
(— OF MINING CAGE) BONNET
(— OF MOUTH) PALATE
(— OF NASOPHARYNX) VAULT
(— OF RAILWAY CAR) DECK
(— OF THE WORLD) PAMIR
(— OVER DOOR) APPENTICE
(— OVER STAGE) SHADOW
(— PORTION) MONITOR
(AUTOMOBILE —) FASTBACK
(CLOTH —) CHUTT
(FALSE —) CRICKET
(FLAT —) LEADS AZOTEA TERRACE
(STEEPLY TAPERING —) SPIRE
(THATCHED —) ATAP ATTAP CHOPPER
(TOWER —) SADDLEBACK
(VAULTED —) DOME
(PREF.) STEG(O) TECTI TECTO
(SUFF.) STEGE STEGITE
ROOFING HEALING SHINDLE PANTILING TECTIFORM
ROOFTOP PEAK
ROOK GYP ROC CROW DUPE RUKH CHEAT CRAKE JUDGE TOWER BLACKY CASTLE DEFRAUD CASTILLO SWINDLER
(NEIGHBOR OF —) KNIGHT
ROOKERY ROOST RUMPUS BUILDING
ROOKIE COLT DRONGO NOVICE RECRUIT BEGINNER
ROOM PAD WON AULA CAFE CRIB FARM HALL KILN LIEU PLAY SALA SEAT SLUM WAME WENE WONE ATTIC BERTH CUDDY DIVAN EWERY HOUSE LODGE OECUS PLACE SALLE SCOPE SHACK SOLAR SPACE STALL STOVE STUDY BELFRY BREAST CAMERA CASINO

CHAPEL ESTUFA EXEDRA HAMMAM LEEWAY MARGIN PARVIS SCOUTH SINGLE SMOKER SOLLAR STANCE STANZA STUDIO CABINET CAMARIN CHALMER CHAMBER EPINAOS FREEZER GALLERY HOLDING HYPOGEE KITCHEN LAUNDRY LIBRARY SEMINAR SERVERY SMOKERY SURGERY AEDICULA ASSEMBLY BASEMENT CAPACITY DRYHOUSE HOTHOUSE HYPOGEUM LAVATORY NYMPHEUM PLAYROOM SCULLERY SWEATBOX TABLINUM THALAMUS PRESSROOM
(— ADJOINING SYNAGOGUE) GENIZAH
(— BEHIND FACADE) ATTIC
(— BELOW STAGE) MEZZANINE
(— BETWEEN KITCHEN AND DINING ROOM) SERVERY
(— CONTAINING FOUNTAIN) NYMPHEUM
(— DUG IN CLIFF) HYPOGEE HYPOGEUM
(— FOR ACTION) LEEWAY
(— FOR BATHING) HAMMAM
(— FOR CONVERSATION) EXEDRA LOCUTORY
(— FOR DANCING) CASINO
(— FOR FAMILY RECORDS) TABLINUM
(— FOR KEEPING FOOD) LARDER PANTRY
(— FOR PAINTINGS) GALLERY
(— FOR PIGEONS) LOFT
(— FOR PRIVATE DEVOTIONS) ORATORY
(— FOR PUBLIC AMUSEMENTS) CASINO THEATER
(— FOR STOWAGE) LASTAGE
(— FOR TABLE LINEN) EWERY
(— IN COAL MINE) BREAST
(— IN HAREM) ODA ODAH
(— IN KEEP) DUNGEON
(— IN PREHISTORIC BUILDING) CELL
(— IN REAR OF TEMPLE) EPINAOS
(— IN SIDE OF LARGER ROOM) ALA
(— IN TOWER) BELFRY
(— OF STUDENTS' SOCIETY) HALL
(— ON SHIP) CABIN STOKEHOLD
(— OVER CHURCH PORCH) PARVIS
(— OVER STAGE) SHADOW
(— TO ADVANCE) WAY
(— TOGETHER) CHUM
(— TO LIVE) LEBENSRAUM
(— UNDER BUILDING) CELLAR
(— UNDER ROOF) LOFT
(CHILDREN'S —) NURSERY
(COTTAGE —) END
(DINING —) CENACLE DINETTE REFECTORY TRICLINIUM
(DRAWING —) SALON SALOON
(DRESSING —) SHIFT BOUDOIR CAMARIN VESTUARY WARDROBE TIREHOUSE
(DRYING —) HOTHOUSE
(ESKIMO ASSEMBLY —) KASHGA
(EXHIBITION —) THEATER
(GRINDING —) HULL
(HEATED —) STEW
(HIGH —) AERY EYRY AERIE EYRIE
(HOSPITAL —) WARD
(INNER —) BEN INBY INBYE SPENCE THALAMUS
(INSULATED —) FREEZER
(KIND OF —) REC
(KITCHEN —) SCULLERY
(LECTURE —) AUDITORY
(LIVING —) HOUSE LANAI SALON SERDAB SOLARIUM VOORHUIS
(MONASTERY —) CELL LAVABO
(NARROW —) CRIB
(OCTAGONAL —) TRIBUNA
(PORTER'S —) LODGE
(PRIVATE —) SNUG SCHOLA SANCTUM CONCLAVE GARDEROBE
(PUBLIC —) SALOON
(PUEBLO ASSEMBLY —) ESTUFA
(READING —) ATHENEUM
(RECEPTION —) DIVAN PARLOR KURSAAL MANDARAH
(REFRIGERATED —) COOLER
(RETIRING —) RECAMERA
(ROMAN —) ATRIUM AEDICULA FUMARIUM
(ROUND —) ROTUNDA
(SEA —) BERTH
(SECLUDED —) DEN
(SECRET —) HOLE
(SERIES OF —S) SWEEP
(SITTING —) SEAT SITTER BOUDOIR
(SLEEPING —) DORMER BEDROOM DORMITORY
(SMALL —) ALA CELL SNUG STEW ZETA CUBBY CUDDY LOBBY CLOSET CUBICLE SNUGGERY
(SMOKING —) DIVAN DIWAN TABAGIE
(SORTING —) SALLE
(STEAM —) STOVE
(STORAGE —) CAMARIN MAGAZINE THALAMUS
(SWEATING —) SUDARIUM SUDATORY LACONICUM
(THRONE —) AIWAN
(TOP —) GARRET IMPERIAL
(UPPER —) SOLAR
(VAULTED —) CAMERA
(WRITING —) SCRIPTORIUM
(PREF.) STEG(O)
(SUFF.) STEGE STEGITE

ROOMMATE CHUM ROOMY ROOMIE

ROOMY WIDE LARGE RANGY SPACY ROOMSOME SPACIOUS CAPACIOUS COMMODIOUS

ROOSE RUSE EXTOL PRAISE FLATTER BOASTING BRAGGING

ROOST EVE SIT BAUK JOUK TIDE PERCH GARRET HARBOR LODGING ROOKERY SHELTER

ROOSTER COCK GAME GALLO MANOC GAMECOCK
(CREST OF A —) COMB

ROOT DIG PRY ROI TAP BASE BULB CHAY CHOY GRUB MOOR MOOT MORE PLUG PULL RACE SPUR TAIL CHEER FIBER FRUIT GROOT GROUT HEART IREOS LAPPA RADIX STOCK ALRAUN BOTTOM CARROT CATGUT GROUND MUZZLE ORIGIN SENEGA SETTLE SUMBAL SUMBUL ACONITE ALKANET AZAFRAN BIACURU BONIATA CALUMBA CHICORY COLUMBO CRAMPON GINSENG IMPLANT IPOMOEA NUNNARI PAREIRA RADICAL RUMMAGE TURPETH DEDENDUM EARTHNUT PNEUMATOPHORE
(— BRANCH) TAPOUN
(— CONTAINING STARCH) KOONTI
(— DEEPLY) SCREW
(— OF GINGER) RACE
(— OF ORCHID) CULLIONS
(— OF TARO) EDDO
(— OF TOOTH) FANG
(— OF TREE) TANG SPURN
(— OF WORD) THEME
(— OUT) GRUB STUB STOCK EVULSE DISPLANT SUPPLANT
(—S FOR SEWING CANOES) WATAP WATAPEH
(—S OF ACONITE) BIKH NABEE
(— TUBERCLE) CLOG
(— WORD) ETYMON
(— YIELDING RED DYE) CHAY CHOY CHAYA
(AROMATIC —) ORRIS
(CANDIED —) ERYNGO
(CUSCUS —S) VETIVER
(DRIED —) JALAP ALTHEA SENECA BRYONIA KRAMERIA LICORICE SCAMMONY
(DRIED —S) INULA IPECAC KRAMERIA VERATRUM
(EDIBLE —) YAM BEET EDDO RADISH TURNIP WASABI PARSNIP RUTABAGA TUBERCLE
(FERN —) ROI
(FINE —) STRING
(FRAGRANT —S) VETIVER
(KIND OF —) LATENT
(MASS OF FIBROUS —S) SPONGE
(MEDICINAL —) JALAP LAPPA GINSENG
(PROJECTING —) SPUR
(ROASTED BEET —) BONKA
(STUMP AND —) MOCK
(PL.) CULVERS
(PREF.) RADICI RHIZ(O)
(SUFF.) RHIZA RHIZOUS

ROOTCAP CALYPTRA SPONGIOLE

ROOTED FIXED CHRONIC
(DEEPLY —) BESETTING

ROOTER FAN PLUGGER

ROOTLESS ARRHIZAL

ROOTLESSNESS ANOMIE

ROOTLET VIVER CRAMPON RADICEL RADICLE
(PL.) COME CULMS

ROOTSTOCK PIP ROI RACE TARO CROWN ORRIS CASAVA DANNUM GINGER ORIGIN PANNUM STOLON BISCUIT MISHMEE TURMERIC ORRISROOT

ROPE GAD GUY TIE TOW TUG CEEL COLT CORD FALL FAST GUSS HEMP JEFF JUNK LIFT LINE ROOD SEAL SOAM SPAN STAY TACK TAIL TAUM TOME VANG WARP BRACE BRAIL CABLE CABUL CHECK CHORD LASSO LONGE SHANK STRAP STROP SWEEP TRACE TWIST WANTY WIDDY WITHE CABLET HALTER INHAUL LARIAT LISSOM LIZARD MECATE PINION RAPEYE RUNNER SHROUD SLATCH STRAND STRING TETHER WARROK AWEBAND BEDCORD BOBSTAY CATFALL CRINGLE ENTRAIL HALYARD HAYBAND LASHING LEEFANG OUTHAUL PAINTER PAZAREE PENDANT PIGTAIL SEAMING SERPENT SERVICE STIRRUP SWIFTER BACKBONE BACKSTAY BUNTLINE CABESTRO CORDELLE DOWNHAUL DRAGLINE FOREFOOT FORETACK HALLIARD HAULYARD INHAULER JACKSTAY LIFELINE NECKLACE PASSAREE PROLONGE ROUNDING SEQUENCE THRAMMLE BREECHING
(— A STEER) HEEL
(— COLLAR) PARRAL PARREL
(— CONNECTING NETS) BALK BAULK
(— COVERING) QUILTING
(— FOR FASTENING GATE) CRINGLE
(— FOR FISH) STRINGER
(— FOR TRAINING HORSE) LONGE
(— FOR TYING CATTLE) CEEL SEAL AWEBAND
(— HANDLE) FETTLE SHACKLE
(— HOLDING RAFT TOGETHER) BRAIL
(— JOINT) TUCK
(— OF HAIR) CABESTRO
(— OF ONIONS) REEVE
(— OF STRAW) GAD SIME VINE SIMON SUGAN FETTLE SIMMON SOOGAN
(— OF 10 OR MORE INCHES) CABLE
(— ON DERRICK) TELEGRAF
(— ON FISHING NET) PINION SEAMING
(— ORNAMENTATION) TORSADE
(— PASSING AROUND DEADEYE) STRAP STROP
(—S IN RIGGING) CORDAGE
(— STOLEN FROM DOCKYARD) RUMBO
(— WITH HOOK AND TOGGLE) PROLONGE
(— WITH SWIVEL AND LOOP) TOGGEL TOGGLE
(— WOUND AROUND CABLE) KECKLING
(ANCHOR —) RODE VIOL VOYAL
(BELL —) TYALL HANGER
(CIRCUS —) JEFF
(COWBOY'S —) LASSO NOOSE RIATA LARIAT
(DESCEND BY —) RAPPEL
(DRAFT —) SOAM
(DRAG —) GUSS
(FLAG-RAISING —) HALYARD
(FOOT —) HORSE
(GRASS —) SOGA
(GUIDE —) DRAGLINE
(HANDLE —) FETTLE
(HANGMAN'S —) HEMP TIPPET
(HARNESS —) TRACE HALTER
(HARPOON —) FOREGOER
(MOORING —) HEADFAST
(NAUTICAL —) TIE TYE COLT FANG LIFT STAY VANG BRACE BRAIL SHEET SLING STRAP STROP GILGUY HAWSER INHAUL LACING RATLIN SHROUD BOBSTAY BOWLINE CATFALL GESWARP LANYARD

LEEFANG OUTHAUL PAINTER PAZAREE PENDANT PENNANT PIGTAIL RATLINE SNORTER SNOTTER STIRRUP STOPPER SWIFTER TRIATIC BACKBONE BACKSTAY BUNTLINE DOWNHAUL FORETACK JACKSTAY PASSAREE ROUNDING SELVAGEE WOOLDING TIMENOGUY
(PART OF —) SLATCH
(SHORT —) SHANK
(SHORT CART —) WANTY
(SMALL HANDMADE —) FOX
(SMUGGLER'S —) LINGTOW
(TALLOWED —) GASKET
(TETHERING —) SPANCEL
(TOW —) CORDELLE
(WIRE —) HAULBACK JACKSTAY
(WORN OR POOR —) JUNK
(PL.) CORDAGE
(PREF.) FUN(I) RESTI SPIR(O)
ROPEBAND RABAND
ROPE-DANCER ACROBAT
ROPEDANCER ACROBAT FUNAMBULIST
ROPEMAKER FOLLOWER RATLINER
ROPEWALKER FUNAMBULO
ROPEWAY TRAMWAY WIREWAY CABLEWAY
ROPY SINEWY STRINGY VISCOUS MUSCULAR GLUTINOUS
ROQUE CROQUET
ROQUELAURE CLOAK ROCOLO ROCKLAY
RORIPA RADICULA
RORQUAL SEI FINBACK
ROSACEA ACNE
ROSADER (BELOVED OF —) ROSALYNDE
(BROTHER OF —) TORRISMOND
ROSAMUNDA (FATHER OF —) CUNIMOND
(HUSBAND OF —) ALBOIN
ROSARY BEADS CORONA TASBIH BEADING PSALTER BEADROLL
(— BEAD) AVE GAUD GAUDY
(MOHAMMEDAN —) COMBOLOIO
ROSE ASH GUL KNOT MOSS ROIS BRIAR BRIDE BUCKY FLUSH RHODA CANKER OPULUS POMPON BOURBON BURBANK GLAIEUL HUGONIS LOZENGE MANETTI MONTHLY OPHELIA RAMBLER AGRIMONY COLUMBIA DOGBERRY LOKELANI PEDELION
(COTTON —) CUDWEED
(DWARF —) POLYANTHA
(HYBRID —) NOISETTE
(KIND OF —) MOSS
(PREF.) RHOD(O) ROSEO ROSI ROSO
(SUFF.) RHODIN
ROSE ACACIA ROBINIA
ROSE APPLE JAMBO JAMBOS JAMBOSA
ROSEATE SPOONBILL AJAJA
ROSE-BREASTED (— COCKATOO) GALAH
ROSEBUSH ROSER BALWARRA
ROSE CAMPION LYCHNIS
ROSE-COLORED OPTIMISTIC
(— STARLING) PASTOR TILYER
ROSEFISH BRIM BREAM BERGYLT REDFISH
(YOUNG —) SNAPPER
ROSE HIP CHOOP CHOUP
ROSELLE SORREL SABDARIFFA
ROSEMARY COSTMARY MOORWORT ROSMARINE
ROSE MOSS PURSLANE PORTULACA
ROSENKAVALIER, DER
(CHARACTER IN —) OCHS SOPHIE FANINAL MARIANDL OCTAVIAN MARSCHALLIN
(COMPOSER OF —) STRAUSS
ROSET BRAZIL
ROSETTE CHOU KNOT ROSACE ROSULA COCKADE
ROSEWOOD BUBINGA MOLOMPI JACARANDA PALISANDER
ROSH (FATHER OF —) BENJAMIN
ROSIN FLUX ROSET COLOPHONY
(— SPIRIT) PINOLIN
ROSS SCALP
ROSSER BARKER PEELER SCALPER SLIPPER
ROSTER LIST ROTA SCROLL REGISTER
ROSTRATE BEAKED
ROSTRUM PEW AMBE BEAK BEMA GUARD SNOUT PULPIT ACROTER TRIBUNE
ROSY ROSEN BLUSHY AURORAL HEALTHY HOPEFUL AUROREAN BLOOMING BLUSHFUL RUBICUND
ROT COE RET DOTE DOZE DROP FOUL JOKE LEAK POKE SOUR WROX DECAY SPOIL TEASE BLUING FESTER MOLDER ROTTEN CORRUPT HOOFRUT PUTREFY NONSENSE STAGNATE
(— BY EXPOSURE) RET
(— OF GRAPES) SLIPSKIN
(APPLE —) FROGEYE
(FOOT —) FOUL
(FRUIT —) BLET LEAK
(LIVER —) COE
(PREF.) PYTHO
ROTA LIST ROLL ROSTER ROTULA
ROTARY CIRCLE GYRATORY ROUNDABOUT
(PREF.) ROTO
ROTATE RUN BIRL GYRE ROLL SPIN TURN PIVOT RABAT SCREW WHEEL GYRATE REVOLVE TRUNDLE ROTIFORM TURNOVER ALTERNATE
(— CAMERA) PAN
(— HIPS) GRIND
ROTATING VOLUBLE
(— PIECE) CAM
ROTATION SPIN TURN ROUND TWIRL GYRATION SPINNING WHIRLING
(— ON BALL) STUFF
(DEVICE INDICATING SPEED OF —) TACH
(KIND OF —) FARADAY
(STOP —) DESPIN
ROTCHE BULL RATCH ROTGE DOVEKEY DOVEKIE BULLBIRD
ROTE CRWTH HEART ROTTA REPEAT
ROTIFER POLYP LIPOPOD LORICATE PLOIMATE
ROTIFORM TROCHAL
ROTL RATTEL WEIGHT ROTTOLO
(PL.) ARTAL ARTEL
ROTOGRAVURE ROTO COLOROTO
ROTOR IMPELLER
ROTTED PECKY
ROTTEN BAD FOUL PUNK ROXY SOUR ADDLE DAZED MOSEY PUTID ADDLED AMPERY FRACID MOOSEY PUTRID DECAYED SPOILED DEPRAVED UNSTABLE
(HALF —) DOTED DOATED
(PARTIALLY —) DRUXY
(PREF.) PUTRE PUTRI SAPR(O)
ROTTENSTONE TRIPOLI
ROTTER CAD LOUSE
(INDIAN —) BUDMASH
ROTTING SLEEPY CARIOUS
ROTTLERA KAMALA
ROTULA ROUND TROCHE KNEEPAN PATELLA
ROTUND FAT PLUMP ROUND STOUT CHUBBY SUBROUND
ROTUNDA PANTHEON
ROTURIER PEASANT PLEBEIAN RUPTUARY
ROUE RAKE RAKEHELL DEBAUCHEE
ROUGE RED FARD BLUSH PAINT FUCATE REDDEN RUDDLE CLINKER SCRIMMAGE
(ANIMAL —) CARMINE
ROUGH RU ROW RUF BEAT FOUL GURL HARD HASK LAMB ROID ROYD RUDE THUG WILD ACRID ASPER BLUFF BLUNT BRUTE CHURL CRUDE DIRTY GOBBY GROFF GURLY HAIRY HARSH HEFTY JAGGY LUMPY REWCH ROUCH ROWDY RUGGY RUVID STARK STEER STERN STOUR TOUGH TOUSY WIGHT BORREL BROKEN BRUSHY BURRED CHOPPY COARSE COBBLY CRABBY CRAGGY ELBOIC HACKLY HISPID HOARSE HOBBLY HORRID HUBBLY INCULT JAGGED KEELIE KNAGGY KNOTTY NOGGEN RAGGED RAMAGE RASPED ROBUST RUFFLE RUGGED RUMBLY RUSTIS SEVERE SHAGGY SKETCH STICKY TOOSIE TRYING UNEVEN UNFEEL UNFELE UNFINE UNKIND UNMILD UNRIDE ABUSIVE AUSTERE BOORISH BRISTLY CRABBED HIRSUTE INEQUAL INEXACT JARRING RABBISH RAMMAGE RAPLOCH RAUCOUS RUFFLED SCABRID SCRAGGY STICKLE STICKLY UNCOUTH UNKEMPT VICIOUS ABRASIVE ASPERATE CHURLISH DEPOLISH IMPOLITE LARRIKIN OBDURATE SCABROUS SCRAGGED STUBBORN TACTLESS UNGENTLE UNTENDER MANHANDLE SCABERULOUS
(— EDGES) FASH
(— IT) CAMP SIWASH
(— UP) MESS
(— UP ARROW FEATHERS) SPRANGLE
(MAKE —) SHAG
(PREF.) ASPERI DASI DASY TRACHY
ROUGHAGE FIBER FODDER AVERAGE BALLAST BULKAGE CELLULOSE
ROUGH-AND-READY BURLY TOWSY TOWZIE MAKESHIFT
ROUGHCAST HARL PARGET SPARGE ROUGHHEW SLAPDASH
ROUGH-EDGED JAGGED RAGGED
ROUGHEN CHAP FRET GAIG HACK EMERY FEAZE FLOCK FROST SPRAY TOOTH ABRADE CRISLE STIVER CRIZZLE ENGRAIL SCRATCH SPREAZE ASPERATE SPREATHE UNSMOOTH
(— BRICK WALL) STAB
ROUGHER BULLDOGGER
(PONY —) STRANDER
ROUGH-HOB GASH
ROUGHING IT (AUTHOR OF —) TWAIN CLEMENS
(CHARACTER IN —) HANK MARK SLADE TWAIN YOUNG BRIGHAM ERICKSON
ROUGHLY ABOUT
ROUGH-MILL GASH
ROUGHNECK ROWDY TOUGH MUCKER UNCOUTH BANGSTER
ROUGHNESS GAFF GRAIN SCUFF TOOTH RUFFLE CRIZZLE CRUDITY ACRIMONY ASPERITY
(— OF SEA) LIPPER
(— OF SKIN) GOOSESKIN GOOSEFLESH
(— OF WALL) KEY
ROUGHOMETER VIAGRAPH
ROULADE VOLATA ARPEGGIO
ROULETTE FILET FILLET TROCHOID
(HIGH — NUMBERS) PASSE
(TYPE OF —) RUSSIAN
(1-18 IN —) MANQUE
(13-24 IN —) MILIEU
ROUNCEVAL GIANT LARGE MONSTER GIGANTIC
ROUND BALL BEAT BEND BOLD BOUT FAST FULL GIRO HEAD RICH ROON ROTA TOUR TRIM WALK ABOUT AMPLE BEADY BRISK CATCH DANCE GLOBE HAMBO HARSH LARGE MOONY ORBED PLAIN ROMAN RONDO SPOKE TROLL TUBBY CIRCLE COURSE ENTIRE MELLOW NEARLY ROTUND ROUNDY RUBBER RUNDLE SPHERY SPIRAL STOWER STREAK ZODIAC ANNULAR CIRCUIT SHAPELY CIRCULAR COMPLETE CROSSBAR ENCIRCLE GLOBULAR SONOROUS LABIALIZE
(— EDGES OF TIMBER) BEARD
(— END OF LOG) SNIPE
(— FREQUENTLY GONE OVER) BEAT
(— IN BOWLING) FRAME
(— IN CARDS) GRAND
(— IN ROLLER DERBY) JAM
(— OF ACTIVITIES) SWING
(— OF APPLAUSE) HAND JOLLY SALVO PLAUDIT
(— OF CHAIR) BALUSTER
(— OFF) TOP CROWN FILLET
(— OF KNITTING) BOUT
(— OF LADDER) STAVE
(— OF PLAY) LAP
(— OUT) ORB BELLY INTEGRATE
(— UP) CORRAL WRANGLE SCROUNGE

(FINAL FOUR —S) SEMIS
(PENULTIMATE —) SEMI
(PLUMP AND —) CHUBBY
(SWEDISH —) HAMBO
(TRIAL —) HEAT
(PREF.) GLOBI GLOBO PERI ROTUNDI ROTUNDO TROCH(I)(LEI) (O) VENTR(I)(O)
ROUNDABOUT PLUMP DETOUR ROTARY CURVING DEVIOUS CAROUSEL CIRCULAR INDIRECT TORTUOUS AMBAGIOUS
(— MOVEMENT) WINDLASS
ROUNDED FULL BOMBE BOWLY CONVEX MELLOW ROTUND TERETE WHELKY ARRONDI BUNTING COMPAST CONCAVE GIBBOUS SCUTATE SHAPELY COMPLETE FINISHED HOOPLIKE SONOROUS
(— OUT) PLUM
(PREF.) TERETI
ROUNDEL HEURT PLATE POMME PELLET FOUNTAIN
(— AZURE) HURT
(— GULES) TORTEAU TORTEAUX
(— OR) BEZANT BYZANT
(— PURPURE) GOLP GOLPE
(— SABLE) GUNSTONE
(— SANGUINE) GUZE
(— VERT) POMEY
ROUNDER SOAKER WASTREL INFORMER
ROUNDERS TUT PATBALL TUTBALL
ROUNDHEAD SWEDE CROPPY WEAKFISH
ROUND HERRING SHADINE STRADINE
ROUNDHOUSE BARN POOP LOCKUP
ROUND-MOUTH HAG HAGFISH
ROUNDNESS ROTUND SPHERICITY
(— OF RIBS) SPRING
ROUND POMPANO PERMIT PALOMETA
ROUND ROBIN ANGLER SERIES PANCAKE SEQUENCE
ROUNDSMAN VANMAN SWINGMAN WATCHMAN
ROUNDUP RODEO CAMBER GATHER MUSTER
ROUNDWORM NEMA ASCARID EELWORM GORDIAN HELMINTH NEMATODE STRONGYL
ROUP ROLP ROOP CROAK CLAMOR AUCTION SHOUTING
ROUSE DAW GIG HOP JOG BAIT BEET CALL DRAW FIRK GOAD MOVE RANT RAVE STIR WAKE WHET AMOVE ERECT MOUNT RAISE START STEER UPSET WAKEN ABRADE ABRAID AROUSE BESTIR EXCITE FOMENT KINDLE NETTLE RATTLE REVIVE RUFFLE WECCHE AGITATE ANIMATE DISTURB EKPHORE ENLIVEN HEARTEN INFLAME STARTLE INSPIRIT IRRITATE
(— TO ACTION) HIE ALARM ALARUM BESTIR ALACRIFY
ROUSING LIVELY AWAKENING INCITATION
(— OF GAME) BEATING
ROUSTABOUT LADER FLOORMAN RAZORBACK
ROUT MOB MOW DRUM FUSS HERD BRANT CHASE COHUE CROWD EJECT FLOCK LURCH PASTE SMEAR SMITE SNORE CLAMOR DEFEAT FLIGHT NUMBER RABBLE SOIREE THRONG UPROAR CONFUSE CONQUER DEBACLE SCATTER SHELLAC SPARPLE TEMPEST ASSEMBLY CONFOUND DISTRESS VANQUISH
(BACCHIC —) THIASUS
ROUTE WAY BELT GATE GEST LINE PASS PATH SEND TRACE TRACK AIRWAY CAREER COURSE CUTOFF SKYWAY TRAJET CHANNEL CIRCUIT LANDWAY PASSAGE SHUTTLE CORRIDOR DISTANCE LIFELINE SHORTCUT TRAVERSE
(— MARKED OUT) ITER
(— TO DEFEAT) SKIDS
(CIRCUITOUS —) DETOUR
(MIGRATION —) FLYWAY
(OCEAN —) LANE
(OVERLAND —) LANDBRIDGE
(PREF.) ODO
ROUTH PLENTY ABUNDANT
ROUTINE RUT RIFF ROTA DRILL GRIND HEIGH HOHUM ROUND ROUTE SHTIK TROLL GROOVE SCHTIK SHTICK HARNESS SCHTICK EVERYDAY ORDINARY
(— LABOR) SCUTWORK
(COMPUTER —) BOOTSTRAP
(DOMESTIC —) HOMELIFE
(ENTERTAINMENT —) SHTICK
(SHOW BIZ —) SCHTICK
(THEATRICAL —) SCHTICK
(WEARISOME —) TREADMILL
ROVE RUN RAKE RAVE ROAM GUESS KNOCK RANGE ROWAN SCOUR SPACE STRAY FORAGE MARAUD RAMBLE STROLL WANDER SPATIATE STRAGGLE TRANSCUR
(— ON THE WING) FLIT
ROVER FLIRT HOYLE STAKE STRAY MASHER RANGER VIKING GANGREL SCUMMER MARAUDER SLIVERER TRAVELER WANDERER COLORADAN
ROVING END SLUB NOMAD VAGUE ARRANT ERRANT DEVIOUS NOMADIC RAMPLER VAGRANT GADABOUT RAMBLING RESTLESS SLUBBING VAGABOND MIGRATORY RANTIPOLE
(— IN SEARCH OF KNIGHTLY ADVENTURE) ERRANTRY
ROW LAY OAR RIG SET DUST FILE LINE MUSS PULL RANK RULE TIER ALLEY BRAWL CHESS FIGHT MOUTH NOISE ORDER RAMMY RANGE RINGE SCOLD SCRAP SCULL SWATH TRAIN BARNEY BERATE COURSE DUSTUP GARRAY KICKUP LISSOM PADDLE POTHER RACKET RUCKUS RUMPUS SHINDY STREET STROKE BOBBERY BRULYIE QUARREL RUCTION SHINDIG CATEGORY OUTBURST REMIGATE SQUABBLE
(— BACKWARD) STERN
(— OF ARCHES) ARCADE
(— OF BENCHES) STACK
(— OF BUSHES) HEDGE
(— OF CASKS) LONGER
(— OF CORN, BARLEY, ETC.) RIG
(— OF DRY HAY) STADDLE
(— OF GRAIN) SWATH SWATHE
(— OF GRASS) HACK SWATH
(— OF GUNS) TIRE
(— OF HOUSES) CRESCENT
(— OF LAMPS) BATTEN
(— OF SEATS) BARRERA
(— OF SEED) DRILL
(— OF STAKES) ORGUE
(— OF STAMPS) STRIP
(— OF STONES) CORDON
(— OF TREES) SCREEN ESPALIER
(— OF VEGETABLES) RINGE
(—S OF BALCONY) MEZZANINE
(DISORDERLY —) RAG
(DOUBLE — OF TREES) AVENUE
(SHORT —) SPRINT
(PL.) EPEIRA
(PREF.) STICHO
(SUFF.) STICH(OUS)
ROWAN ASH RAN RED RODDIN
ROWAN TREE CARE SORB WICKY WITCH RODDEN RODDIN WICKEN WIGGEN QUICKEN RANTREE WHITTEN WITCHEN ROUNTREE
ROWBOAT GIG OAR BARK OARS PLAT BARIS COBLE DINGY FUNNY KOBIL SCULL SKIFF BARQUE CAIQUE DINGHY LURKER WHERRY SCULLER
(— SEAT) TAFT
(CLINKER-BUILT —) FUNNY
(FLAT-BOTTOMED —) DORY
(PART OF —) RING SEAT STEM SOCKET THWART GUNWALE OARLOCK PAINTER ROWLOCK TRANSOM
(SMALL —) COG
ROWDY TOU BHOY CASH MONEY RORTY ROUGH TOUGH TOMBOY UNRULY VULGAR HOODLUM RAFFISH BARRATER LARRIKIN STUBBORN ROUGHNECK
ROWDYISM YAHOOISM
ROWEN EDGROW RAWING AFTERMATH ROUGHINGS
ROWENA (FATHER OF —) HENGIST
(GUARDIAN OF —) CEDRIC
(HUSBAND OF —) IVANHOE VORTIGERN
ROWER URGER GALIOT STROKE OARSMAN STERNMAN CAIQUEJEE
(— ON UPPER SEATS) THRANITE
(OUTERMOST —) THALAMITE
(SECOND LEVEL —) ZYGITE
ROWING CREW
(— EQUIPMENT) OARAGE
ROWLOCK LOCK CRUTCH OARLOCK RULLOCK
ROXANA (FATHER OF —) OXYARTES
(HUSBAND OF —) ALEXANDER
ROYAL EASY REAL RIAL ELITE REGAL SMALT AUGUST KINGLY REGIUS SOVRAN SUPERB BASILIC GLORIOUS IMPERIAL IMPOSING MAJESTIC PAVILION PRINCELY
(— MACE) SCEPTER SCEPTRE
ROYAL ANTELOPE MADOQUA KLEENEBOC
ROYAL FERN OSMOND OSMUND
ROYALIST TORY ULTRA REGIAN TANTIVY CAVALIER MUSCADIN
(PL.) CHOUANS
ROYALLY PURPLEY
ROYAL PALM COYAL
ROYALTY LOT ALII GALE BONUS CROWN REGAL REALTY MAJESTY PENALTY LORDSHIP NOBILITY REGALITY
ROYET WILD HARSH UNRULY ROMPING
RUB DUB BARK BILL FILE FRAY FRET FRIG FROT RISP SHAB WIPE CHAFE DIGHT FEEZE FRUSH GRATE GRAZE GRIDE LABOR SCOUR SCRUB SMEAR STONE FRIDGE RUBBER STREAK BEESWAX FRICACE FURBISH MASSAGE
(— AS ANIMALS) SHAB
(— AS A ROPE) SNUG
(— AWAY) ERODE ABRADE
(— BOOT) BONE
(— DOWN) WIPE STRAP
(— ELBOWS) JOSTLE JUSTLE
(— GENTLY) STRIKE STROKE
(— HARD) SCOUR SCRUB
(— HARSHLY) GRIND
(— IN) HARPON
(— LIGHTLY) GRAZE
(— OFF) CROCK ABRADE ABRASE
(— OUT) ERASE EFFACE EXPUNGE
(— ROUGHLY) GRATE
(— SNUFF) DIP
(— THE SKIN OFF) SHAW
(— TOGETHER) FIDDLE
(— VELVET FROM ANTLERS) BURNISH
(— WITH GREASE) DUB
(— WITH NOSE) NOUSLE NUZZLE
(— WITH OIL) ANOINT
(PREF.) TRIBO
(SUFF.) TRIBE TRIPSIS
RUBABOO SOUP
RUBBED TERSE
RUBBER BUNA FOAM PARA BUTYL CREPE RASER ALASKA CAUCHO DAPICO ERASER NIGGER RUNNER BISCUIT BURUCHA EBONITE ELASTIC GUAYULE RAMBONG BORRACHA FRICTION NEOPRENE SERNAMBY SERWAMBY SOVPRENE
(— CITY) AKRON
(HARD —) EBONITE
(RECLAIMED —) SHODDY
(PL.) SHAB
RUBBERIZE FRICTION
RUBBERNECK GAPE CRANE STARE TOURIST SIGHTSEE
RUBBER TREE ULE MILKER RAMBONG
RUBBING CHAFE CARESS ABRASION FRICTION FROTTAGE FRICATION
(SUFF.) TRIPSIS
RUBBISH KET BUNK CRAB CRAP FLAM FLUM GEAR GWAG MULL MUSH PELF PELT PUNK RAFF ROSS TOSH TRAG BILGE BRASH BROCK CRAWM CULCH OFFAL SCOWL

SLUSH STENT STUFF TRADE TRASH TRIPE TRUCK WASTE COLDER DEBRIS GARBLE KELTER LITTER PALTRY PIFFLE RAFFLE RAMMEL REFUSE RUBBLE SCULCH SHRUFF SPILTH BAGGAGE BEGGARY FLANNEL MULLOCK RUMMAGE SLITHER TAFFIKE TRAFFIC FIRETRAP NONSENSE RIFFRAFF TRASHERY TRUMPERY CLAMJAMFRY CLAMJAMPHRIE
(VEGETABLE —) WRACK
RUBBISHY POUCY PALTRY TRASHY BAGGAGE RUMMAGY
RUBBLE BRASH STENT TALUS RAMMEL BACKING MOELLON SLITHER
RUBE JAY BOOR HICK JAKE YAHOO JASPER BUMPKIN BUSHMAN HAYSEED CORNBALL
RUBELLA ROTELN
RUBELLITE SIBERITE
RUBICUND RED ROSY RUDDY FLORID FLUSHED
RUBIGINOUS RUSTY
RUBIK ERNO
RUBLE RO RUBLIS
(ONE-HALF —) POLTINIK
RUBRIC RED NAME CANON CLASS TITLE CONCEPT CATEGORY
RUBRICATE MINIATE
RUBY AGATE BALAS RUBIN PYROPE ANTHRAX SPARKLE VERMEIL
RUBY SPINEL BALAS ALMANDINE
RUCHING COQUILLE
RUCK RUT HEAP PILE RICK SLEW CROWD SQUAT STACK TRASH CREASE FURROW HUDDLE PUCKER RUBBISH WRINKLE
RUCKUS ADO ROW FIGHT FRACAS ROOKUS
RUCTION HURRY RUCKUS QUARREL RUPTION FRACTION
RUDABAH (FATHER OF —) MIHRAB
(HUSBAND OF —) ZAL
(SON OF —) RUSTAM
RUDD REDEYE
RUDDER HELM STEER STERN TIMON HELLIM RUTHER STEERER STEERAGE GOVERNAIL
(— BACK) TALON
(— EDGE) BEARDING
(— OF WINDMILL) TAIL
(DIVING —) HYDROVANE
(PART OF —) STOCK
RUDDERFISH CHOPA OPALEYE
RUDDINESS RUBEDITY
RUDDLE RED BOLE KEEL SMIT ROUGE
RUDDY RED RODE RUDE FRESH VIVID BLOWSY BLOWZY FLORID LIVELY GLOWING RUDDISH BLUSHFUL RUBICUND SANGUINE
(NOT —) PALE
RUDDY DUCK ROOK BOOBY NODDY PADDY SPRIG BOBBER DUNBIRD GREASER PINTAIL SLEEPER SPATTER BLUEBILL BULLNECK HARDHEAD WIRETAIL
RUDE ILL RAW BOLD IRON LEWD WILD BLUFF BLUNT CRUDE GREEN GROSS PLUMP ROUGH STOUR SURLY UNORN ABRUPT BITTER BORREL BRASSY CALLOW CHUFFY CLUMSY COARSE DUDGEN GOTHIC HOMELY HOYDEN INCULT RIBALD ROBUST RUGGED RUSTIC SAVAGE SHAGGY SIMPLE STORMY UNFEEL UPLAND VULGAR ABUSIVE ARTLESS BOORISH CARLAGE CARLISH INCIVIL LOUTISH LOWBRED NATURAL UNCOUTH UNHENDE CHURLISH CLUBBISH HOMESPUN IMPOLITE INSOLENT MECHANIC PETULANT PORTERLY STUBBORN SYLVATIC TACTLESS UNGENTLE UNPOLITE YOKELISH GRACELESS TASTELESS
(— AND BOLD) HOIDEN HOYDEN
(NOT —) MANNERLY
RUDENESS GAFF
RUDIMENT GERM ANLAGE VESTIGE BEGINNING PRIMORDIUM
(FIRST —) PRIMORDIUM
(PL.) ABC ALPHABET ELEMENTS GRAMMATES
RUDIMENTARY BASIC GERMING ABORTIVE INCHOATE ABECEDARY ELEMENTAL EMBRYONIC PRIMITIVE ABECEDARIAN
(MOST —) FIRST
(PREF.) LYO PRO
RUE RU REWE MOURN CATGUT REGRET REPENT SORROW BORONIA HARMALA TENTWORT
RUEFUL SAD RUELY WOEFUL DOLEFUL PITIABLE
RUFF SET APEX FURY PAPE POPE CREST PRIDE REEVE TEASE TEAZE TRUMP COLLAR FRAISE RABATO RUFFLE TIPPET ZENITH ELATION PARTLET PASSION QUELLIO REBATER ROTONDE PICKADIL
(FEMALE —) REE
RUFFED BUSTARD HOUBARA
RUFFED LEMUR VARI
RUFFIAN MUN LAMB PIMP PUNK THUG TORY BRAVO BULLY DEVIL ROUGH ROWDY TIGER TOUGH APACHE BRUTAL COARSE CUTTER CUTTLE MOHAWK MOHOCK NICKER PANDER TOWSER HOODLUM SWEATER TUMBLER HACKSTER HOOLIGAN
RUFFLE VEX BAIT FRET HOOP ROOL RUFF STIR BULLY CRISP FRILL GRAZE JABOT PLEAT ROUGH ROUSE SHIRR ABRADE ATTACK GATHER NETTLE PEPLUM RIPPLE BLUSTER BRISTLE DERANGE FLOUNCE FLUTTER PANUELO STIFFEN SWAGGER TROUBLE DISHEVEL DISORDER DISTRACT FURBELOW IRRITATE QUILLING SKIRMISH
(— THE TEMPER) ROIL
RUFFLED ROUGH UNKEMPT
RUFFLING (— ON THE SURFACE OF WATER) HORROR
RUFUS (FATHER OF —) SIMON
RUG MAT RYA TUG BAKU COZY HAUL MAUD PULL SNUG TEAR WRAP BIJAR HERAT HEREZ HERIZ JURUK KAZAK KHILA KONIA KULAH KUMEH LADIK MECCA MELAS MOSUL NAMDA SENNA SISAL TEKKE TUZLA USHAK YURUK ZOFRA AFSHAR BALUCH KANARA KAROSS KASHAN KIRMAN MOGHAN NAMMAD PERGAM RUNNER SHIRAZ SMYRNA TABRIZ TILPAH TOUPEE WILTON BALUCHI BERGAMA BOKHARA BUFFALO DERBEND DRUGGET FERAHAN GIORDES GOREVAN HAMADAN ISPAHAN SHEERAZ SHIRVAN YARKAND AUBUSSON DOMESTIC FOOTPACE PANDERMA SARABAND SEDJADEH SERABEND WOLFSKIN
(— FOR SADDLE) PILCH
(— OF SKINS) KAROSS WOLFSKIN
(GREEK —) FLOKATI
(KIND OF —) AREA SHAG NAVAJO BRAIDED
(PERSIAN —) HEREZ
(PLAID —) MAUD
(PRAYER —) MELAS MELES GHIORDES NAMAZLIK
(REVERSIBLE —) KILIM
(SCANDINAVIAN —) RYA
(SMALL —) MAT
RUGA FOLD CREASE WRINKLE
RUGBY FOOTER RUGGER FOOTBALL
(— PLAY) SCRUM
RUGGED RUDE WILD HAIRY HARDY ROUGH STIFF COARSE CRAGGY HORRID JAGGED KNAGGY KNOTTY ROBUST SAVAGE STRONG STURDY UNEVEN CRABBED GNARLED OBDURATE SCRAGGED VIGOROUS
RUGGIERO (GUARDIAN OF —) ATLANTE
(SISTER OF —) MARFISA
(SLAYER OF —) TISAPHERNES
(WIFE OF —) BRADAMANTE
RUIN DO MAR POT BANE BANG COOK CRAB DAMN DASH DISH DOOM FALL FATE FELL HELL JACK KILL LOSS RASE RAZE SINK TALA BLAST BOTCH BREAK CRUSH DECAY EXILE GUBAT HUACA LEESE LEISS SHEND SHOOT SMASH SPEED SPILL SPLIT SPOIL SWAMP TRASH WRACK WRAKE WRECK BANJAX BEDASH BLIGHT CANCEL COOPER DAMAGE DEFACE DEFEAT DIDDLE DISMAY FOREDO INJURY JIGGER MANGLE RAVAGE UNMAKE BOWWOWS CORRUPT DESTROY FLATTEN FORLESE FORWORK LEESING PERVERT SCUPPER SHATTER SUBVERT TORPEDO UNDOING BANKRUPT COLLAPSE DEMOLISH DESOLATE DISASTER DOWNFALL
(— AT GAMBLING) SHRUB
(SPIRITUAL —) FALL
(PL.) ASHES DEBRIS RELICS RUDERA ZIMBABWE
RUINATION DOGS
RUINED FLAT GONE LORN BROKE KAPUT BROKEN FALLEN NAUGHT NOUGHT FORLORN BANKRUPT DESOLATE
RUINER MARPLOT
RUINOUS DEADLY BANEFUL DECAYED SHENDFUL WASTEFUL CUTTHROAT
RULE LAW MAN RAJ WIN DASH KING NORM SWAY WALD WARD YARD AXIOM CANON GUIDE JUDGE MAXIM NORMA ORDER POWER REGLE REIGN RICHE RIGHT RULER SPILE STAFF SUTRA SUTTA WIELD ALIDAD CUTOFF DECIDE DECREE DITION DOMINE EMPIRE ENTAIL GNOMON GOVERN MANAGE MASTER METHOD REGNUM REGULA SQUARE VASSAL BROCARD COMMAND CONTROL COUNSEL DICTATE DIETARY FORMULA PLUMMET PRECEPT PRESIDE REGENCY REGIMEN THEOREM DICTAMEN DOCTRINE DOMINATE FUNCTION LEGALISM MODERATE ORDINARY OVERLEAD PERSUADE REGIMENT REGNANCY STANDARD TYRANNIS OBSERVANCE
(— BY UPSTARTS) NEOCRACY
(— OUT) EXCLUDE
(—S OF CONDUCT) ETIQUETTE
(—S OF DUELING) DUELLO
(— TYRANNICALLY) HORSE
(ABSOLUTE —) EMPERY AUTARCHY
(MOB —) OCHLOCRACY
(OPPOSING —) ANTINOMY
(PREF.) ARCH(AE)(AEO)(E)(EO)(I)
RULER (ALSO SEE CHIEF, TITLE, LEADER) DEY GOG JAM MIN OBA AMIR CZAR DAME DUKE EMIR INCA KING LORD OBBA RULE TSAR TZAR ALDER AMEER DECAN EMEER HAKIM MPRET MWAMI NAGID NAWAB SCALE SOPHI STEER SUBAH ZUPAN APHETA ARCHON AUTHOR CAESAR DESPOT DUARCH DYNAST EPARCH FERULE GERENT HERSIR ISWARA KABAKA KAISER MASTER NIMROD PATESI PENLOP RECTOR REGENT SATRAP SAWBWA SHERIF SOLDAN SUFFEE SULTAN TYRANT ADMIRAL ALIDADE BOURBON DEMARCH FAIPULE ISHVARA KHEDIVE MONARCH MORMAER PTOLEMY RECTRIX REGULUS REIGNER TOPARCH TRIARCH WIELDER AUGUSTUS BASILEUS DRIGHTEN EXILARCH GOVERNOR HEPTARCH INTERREX OLIGARCH OVERLORD PADISHAH PENTARCH PHYLARCH REGINALD TARAFDAR WHIPKING
(— IN A NATIVITY) APHETA
(— OF ENCLOSURE) HENRY
(— OF UNIVERSE) PANTOCRATOR
(ALBANIAN —) MPRET
(CHIEF —) PADISHAH
(CURVED —) SWEEP
(DEIFIED —) THEOCRAT
(ELF —) AUBREY
(INCA —) CURACA
(INDIAN —) NIZAM MAHARAJA MAHARAJAH
(JAPANESE —) SHOGUN
(JEWISH —) EXILARCH
(MONGOLIAN —) HUTUKTU
(MOSLEM —) SOLDAN
(NAME MEANING —) INCA
(STRONG —) REGINALD
(SUPREME —) SUZERAIN
(TATAR OR MOGUL —) CHAM

(WHITE —S) SERKALI
(PREF.) ARCH(AE)(AEO)(E)(EO)(I)
(SUFF.) ARCHIC ARCHY
RULING CALL CHIEF REGENT SOVRAN CURRENT HOLDING REGITIVE HEGEMONIC
RUM ODD ROME OCUBY QUEER RUMBO TAFIA TAFFIA BACARDI CACHACA JAMAICA PECULIAR SWITCHEL EXCELLENT
RUMBLE CROWL DICKY GROWL MELEE RUMOR SNORE BUMBLE HOTTER HUMBLE LUMBER WAMBLE GRUMBLE QUARREL
(— AS A GANG) BOP
RUMBLER VOLCANO
RUMBO RUM GROG LIQUOR
RUMEN CUD PAUNCH STOMACH
RUMINANT OX COW YAK BULL DEER GOAT CAMEL LLAMA MOOSE SHEEP STEER TAKIN ALPACA MAZAME VICUNA GIRAFFE QUIDDER ANTELOPE TUBICORN
(SUFF.) MERYX
RUMINATE CHAW CHEW MULL MUSE PONDER CONCOCT REFLECT SAUNTER CONSIDER
RUMINATION MERYCISM
RUMKIN RUMMER
RUMMAGE COMB GRUB POKE ROOT ROUT SEEK BUSTLE FORAGE POWTER TOUSLE UPROAR FOSSICK RANSACK ROMMACK DISORDER SKIRMISH UPHEAVAL
(— ABOUT FOR A PROFIT) FOSSICK
(— SALE) JUMBLE
RUMMY GIN RUM TUNK QUEER CANASTA COONCAN DRUNKARD OKLAHOMA
RUMOR CRY SAW BUZZ FAMA FAME TALK WORD BRUIT MUDGE NOISE SOUGH SOUND STORY VOGUE VOICE BREEZE CANARD FURPHY GOSSIP MURMUR POTGUN RENOWN REPORT RUMBLE CLATTER HEARING HEARSAY INKLING OPINION WHISPER NORATION GRAPEVINE SCUTTLEBUTT
(SCANDALOUS —S) GOSSIP
RUMORED AFLOAT
RUMP ASS FUD ARSE BEAM CULE DOCK DOUP DUFF CROUP NACHE NATCH PODEX STERN BOTTOM CURPIN CROUPON CRUPPER HURDIES KEISTER PLUNDER BANKRUPT BUTTOCKS DERRIERE
(— OF BIRD) UROPYGIUM
(— OF HORSE) CROUP CROUPE
(PREF.) PYG(O)
(SUFF.) PYGAL PYGE PYGIA(N) PYGOUS PYGUS
RUMPF CORE
RUMPLE FOLD MUSS WISP TOUSE TOWSE MOUSLE ROMBLE CRUMPLE SCRUNCH WRINKLE
RUMPUS RAG ROW BRAWL SHINE CLAMOR FRACAS HUBBUB RUCKUS SHINDY TOWROW UPROAR BAGARRE BOBBERY ROOKERY RUCTION ROWDYDOW
RUMSHOP BAR SALOON TAVERN BARROOM TAPROOM DRUNKERY
RUN GO BYE ERN FLY FOG GAD HOP JOG LAM LEG PLY RIN RUB URN BUNK CALL FLEE FLOW FUSE HARE HEAT HEEL HUNT IRNE KITE LEAD LEAP MELT PASS PLAY RACE RAKE RINN ROAM ROVE SCUD TEND TRIG TRIP TROT TURN WALK WEEP WORK ASSAY BLEND BREAK BRUSH CHASE COAST EXTRA GOING HURRY NOTCH POINT SCOUP SPEED SPEND STAND TABLE TRACE BICKER CAREER COURSE ELAPSE ESCAPE EXTEND GALLOP HASTEN LADDER MANAGE RESORT ROTATE SPRENT SPRINT STREAM TUMBLE VOLATA ACCURRE CONDUCT CONTAIN FLUTTER LIQUEFY OPERATE PASSAGE RETREAT SCUTTER SKELTER STRETCH FUNCTION TRANSCUR
(— ABOUT) TIG FISK DISCURRE
(— ACROSS) STRIKE
(— AGAINST) JOSTLE
(— AGROUND) BEACH GRAVEL HURTLE STRAND STRIKE
(— ALONG EDGE OF) SKIRT
(— AS DYE) BLEED
(— AS STOCKING) LADDER
(— AT HIGH SPEED) SCORCH
(— AT THE NOSE) SNIVEL
(— AT TOP SPEED) SPRINT
(— AWAY) FLY GUY FLEE HIKE JINK JUMP SMUG ELOPE SCRAM SMOKE DECAMP SCAMPER SCARPER FUGITATE SKEDADDLE
(— AWAY FROM DEBTS) LEVANT
(— AWAY IN PANIC) STAMPEDE
(— BEFORE A GALE) SCUD
(— BEFORE A JUMP) FEAZE FEEZE
(— BETWEEN) INTERCUR
(— BLINDLY) SKITTLE
(— CLUMSILY) LOPPET TUMBLE
(— COUNTER) BELY BELIE CROSS
(— DOWN) SLUR TRASH OVERRUN
(— HARD) DIG
(— HIGH) FLOOD
(— IN CRICKET) BYE WIDE EXTRA NOTCH
(— IN DROPS) WEEP
(— IN PLACE) IDLE
(— INTO) MEET INCUR
(— ITS COURSE) LAPSE
(— NAKED) STREAK
(— OBLIQUELY) SQUINT
(— OF CLAPBOARDING) STRAKE
(— OFF) BOLT FLEE SCADDLE
(— OF MULE CARRIAGE) DRAW
(— OF SHAD) SPURT
(— OF STAIRS) GOING
(— ON SKIS) SCHUSS
(— OUT) EXCUR ISSUE PETER ELAPSE EXPIRE
(— OVER) HEAT TRAMP OVERFLOW
(— RAPIDLY) KITE RAKE SCUR SCOUR SKIRR SPLIT CAREER
(— SHORT) STRAITEN
(— SOAP) FRAME
(— SPEEDILY) CHASE CAREER
(— SWIFTLY) HARE LEAP SCUD CHEVY CHIVY
(— THE SHOW) EMCEE
(— THROUGH) PIERCE DISCURRE
(— TO) ACCURRE
(— TO EXERCISE HORSE) HEAT
(— TOGETHER) HERD MUDDY CLUTTER
(— TRAINS) BLOCK
(— WILD) GAD ESCAPE STARTLE
(— WILDLY) STARTLE
(— WITH AFFECTED PRECIPITATION) SCUTTLE
(— WITH SKIPS) SCOUP
(— WITH VELOCITY) DART
(BRIEF —) STREAK FLUTTER
(COMMON —) RUCK
(END —) SWEEP
(GLASS FURNACE —) BLAST
(HOME —) DINGER
(MUSICAL —) TIRADE ARPEGGIO
(OBSTACLE —) GYMKHANA
(RAPID MUSICAL —) TIRADE VOLATA
(SAILING —) STRETCH
(SHEEP —) SLAIT STATION
(SHORT —) FAIL BICKER SCURRY FLUTTER RAMRACE SCUTTLE
(SKI —) PISTE SCHUSS LANGLAUF
(WILD —) LAMP
(PREF.) TRECHO TREKO
RUNAGATE APOSTATE FUGITIVE RENEGADE RUNABOUT VAGABOND WANDERER
RUNAWAY ROMP FUGIE RUNNER DECISIVE DESERTER FUGITIVE RUNAGATE
(PREF.) DRAPETO
RUNDI HUTU
RUNDLE DRUM RUNG STEP ORBIT CIRCLE SPHERE WINDLASS
RUNDLET KEG BARREL
RUN-DOWN BAD
RUNDOWN INFO CHECK RECAP SCOOP
RUN-DOWN SEEDY
RUNDOWN REPORT
RUN-DOWN SHODDY SQUALID
RUNDOWN SUMMARY ANALYSIS
RUN-DOWN DERELICT
RUNE WEN WYN AESE WYNN CHARM OGHAM SPELL THORN SECRET MYSTERY
RUNG RIM GREE RIME STEP ROUND SCALE SPELL SPOKE STAFF STAIR STALE STAVE STEAL TREAD WRUNG DEGREE RUNDLE STOWER STREAK CROSSBAR TRAVERSE
(— OF CHAIR) SPELL
(— OF LADDER) RIME STEP RANGE SPOKE STALE RONDLE STREAK
(— OF ROPE WALK) STAKE
(PL.) STILE
RUNIC ALPHABET FUTHARK FUTHORC
RUNIC LETTER THORN
RUNLET RUSH RINDLE RUNNEL STREAM RIVELING
RUNNEL RILL BROOK RHINE RINDLE RUNLET POLLARD RIVULET STREAMLET
RUNNER RUG SOW GOER POST SCUD SHOE SKID BLADE COBIA FLOAT LOPER MILER RACER SABOT SCARF SKATE SLIDE SPRAY TEDGE CURSOR HEELER JOGGER KANARA RENNER STOLON TOUTER CHANNEL COURIER HARRIER NOMINEE SARMENT CURSITOR SKIPJACK TRAILING CANDIDATE
(— FOR GRINDING STONE) MARTIN
(— WHO SETS PACE) RABBIT
(BLUE —) HARDTAIL
(BOOKMAKER'S —) SPIV
(ERRAND —) CAD GOFER GOPHER
(FLUME —) HERDER
(PAIR OF —S) SLOOP
(RACE —) SCUTTLER
(SLED —S) BOB
(SLEDGE —) SLIP
(SLEDGE —S) SLIPES
(SNOW —) SKI
RUNNING RUN CARE EASY RACE FLUID QUICK COURSE LIVING COURANT CURRENT CURSIVE FLOWING HOTFOOT SCUTTER SLIDING FUGITIVE
(— ABOUT) COURANT CURSORY
(— ACROSS) DIAGONAL
(— AT SLOW PACE) JOGGING
(— BETWEEN) INTERCURRENT
(— DOWNWARD) DEFLUENT
(— FROM SIDE TO SIDE) SALLY
(— IN) INCURRENT
(— OF SHIPS TOGETHER) ALLISION
(— OVER) OVERFLOWING
(— SIDEWAYS) LATERIGRADE
(— TOGETHER) SLUR
(— TOWARD) APPULSE
(— VERTICALLY) DOWN
(FIRST —S) HEAD
(NOT —) DEAD
(SMOOTHLY —) SWEET
(PREF.) DROM(O)
(SUFF.) DROMOUS
RUNNING GEAR MOBILE
RUN-OF-THE-MILL SOSO AVERAGE ORDINARY
RUNT BOOR SCRAG SCRUB SLINK STEER STUMP STUNT HEIFER PEEWEE SCRUMP SHRIMP TITMAN URLING BULLOCK SHARGAR SHARGER SLINKER RECKLING
RUNTY MEAN SURLY SCRUBBY SCRUNTY STUNTED DWARFISH
RUNWAY RUN TIP DUCT STRIP TRAIL TARMAC SLIPWAY AIRSTRIP DOLLYWAY
(— OF HARE) FILE
RUPEE DIB CHIP SICCA ROUPIE
(ONE-SIXTEENTH —) ANNA
(TENS OF —S) RX
(10 MILLION —S) CRORE
(100,000 —S) LAC LAKH
RUPERT'S DROP TEAR
RUPIA RUPEE ERUPTION
(HALF —) PARDO PARDAO
RUPTURE BLOW REND RENT BREAK BURST CRACK SPLIT BREACH DIVIDE HERNIA RHEXIS DISRUPT RUPTION DIVISION FRACTION FRACTURE HERNIATE
(SUFF.) RHEXIS RRHEXIS
RUPTURED BROKEN
RURAL RUSTIC BUCOLIC COUNTRY AGRESTIC ARCADIAN LANDWARD MOFUSSIL PASTORAL PLEASANT PRAEDIAL VILLATIC
RUSE HOAX ROSE SHIFT STALL TRICK WREST ARTIFICE TRICKERY

RUSH FLY FOG HIE RIP RIX RUB SAG BANG BENT BOLT CLAP DASH DUSH FALL FLAW GIRD HURL HUSH JUNK KICK LASH LEAP LUSH PASH RACE RACK RASH RESE RISH ROUT SCUD SHOT SLUR SPUR SWIP TEAR TILT WHIP WIND ADRUE CARRY CHASE CHUTE DRASH DRIVE FEEZE FLASH FLUSH FRAIL FRUSH HURRY ONSET PIPES PREEL SCOUR SEAVE SHOOT SPART SPATE SPEED SPRAT SPRIT SPROT START STAVE STORM WHIRL CHARGE DELUGE FESCUE HURTLE JUNCUS POWDER RAMACK RANDOM RAVINE STREAK THRESH THRILL ASSAULT BRATTLE BULRUSH DAILIES DEBACLE JUNCITE RAMMISH RAMRACE SKELTER SMOTHER SWITHER TANTIVY TORNADO VIRETOT WHITHER CATARACT DEERHAIR SALTWEED SPLATTER VANQUISH
(— ABROAD) FLUSH
(— AGAINST) CHARGE
(— AWAY) BOLT FLEE SCUTTLE
(— DOWN) TRACE
(— FOR WEAVING) FRAIL
(— HEADLONG) BOIL RUIN SPURN STAMPEDE
(— OF AIR) WAFT
(— OF LIQUID) HEAD FLUSH
(— OF WATER) FRESH SHOOT SPOUT SWASH
(— OF WORDS) SPATE
(— ON FOOTBALL PLAYER) BLITZ
(— ON PASSER IN FOOTBALL) BLITZ
(— OUT) SALLY
(CLUMP OF —S) RASHBUSS
(COMMON —) FLOSS
(DOWNWARD —) HURL
(FLAT —) SHALDER
(FORCEFUL —) JET
(NOISY —) SCUTTER
(ONWARD —) BIRR SURGE
(PL.) REXEN
(PREF.) JUNCI THRYONO

RUSHED HECTIC
RUSHING HURL SCUD FURIOUS HUDDLING IMPETUOUS
(— OF WIND) GUST
RUSHLIGHT SEAVE
RUSH NUT CHUFA
RUSK ZWIEBACK
RUSSELL'S VIPER DABOIA DABOYA JESSUR KATUKA

RUSSIA (SEE ALSO SPECIFIC REPUBLICS)

CAPITAL: MOSCOW
COIN: KOPEK RUBLE GRIVNA KOPECK
COLLECTIVE FARM: KOLHOZ KOLKHOZ
DISTRICT: KARELIA
FORMER NAME: USSR SOVIET MUSCOVY
FORMER REPUBLIC: UZBEK KAZAKH KIRGIZ LATVIA ARMENIA ESTONIA GEORGIA TADZHIK TURKMEN UKRAINE MOLDAVIA LITHUANIA BYELORUSSIA AZERBAIDZHAN
FORTRESS: KREMLIN
LAKE: ARAL NEVA SEGO CHANY ELTON ILMEN ONEGA BAYKAL LADOGA SELETY TAYMYR TENGIZ ZAYSAN BALKHASH
MEASURE: FUT LOF DUIM FASS LOOF STOF FOUTE KOREC LIGNE OSMIN PAJAK STOFF VEDRO VERST ARSHIN CHARKA LINIYA PALETZ SAGENE TCHAST BOTCHKA CHKALIK GARNETZ VERCHOC BOUTYLKA CHETVERT KROUSHKA
MOUNTAIN: POBEDA BELUKHA
MOUNTAIN RANGE: ALAI URAL CAUCASUS
NAME: CIS
PENINSULA: KOLA CRIMEA KARELIA KAMCHATKA
PORT: EISK ANAPA ODESSA
REPUBLIC: ARMENIA BELARUS MOLDOVA UKRAINE AZERBAIJAN KAZAKHSTAN KYRGYZSTAN TAJIKISTAN UZBEKISTAN TURKMENISTAN RUSSIANFEDERATION
RIVER: IK OB DON ILI KET NER OKA ROS TAZ TYM UFA USA AMGA AMUR KARA LENA NEVA OREL STYR SURA SVIR URAL DESNA ISTRA LOVAT MEZEN NADYM NEMAN ONEGA TEREK TOBOL VOLGA ABAKAN DONETS ENISEI IRTYSH OLEKMA DNIEPER NEMUNAS PECHORA YENISEI
SEA: ARAL AZOV KARA BLACK BAIKAL OKHOTSK
TOWN: BAKU KIEV OMSK OREL PERM RIGA GOMEL ISTRA KASAN KAZAN KYZYL MINSK PENSA PSKOV TOMSK FRUNZE IGARKA KERTCH KURGAN NIZHNI ODESSA ROSTOV SARTOV URALSK ALMAATA BATAISK DONETSK IRKUTSK IVANOVO KALININ KHARKOV RYBINSK TALLINN KOSTROMA ORENBURG SMOLENSK TAGANROG TASHKENT VLADIMIR VORONEZH YAROSLAV
VOLCANO: ALAID SHIVELUCH

RUSSIAN IVAN RUSS SLAV VELIKA MUSCOVITE
(— BRAID) SOUTACHE
(— HEMP) RINE
(— NOT ALLOWED TO EMIGRATE) REFUSNIK REFUSENIK
(— POOL) CARLINE
(LITTLE —) RUSSENE RUTHENE UKRAINIAN
RUSSIAN BANK CRAPETTE
RUSSIAN CALF FUDGE

RUSSIAN FEDERATION (ALSO SEE RUSSIA)

CAPITAL: MOSCOW
COIN: RUBLE
FORT: KREMLIN
ISLAND: KURIL SAKHALIN NOVAYAZEMLYA
LAKE: CHANY ILMEN ONEGA BAIKAL BELOYE BRATSK LADOGA PEIPUS RYBINSK TOPOZERO VYGOZERO
MOUNTAIN: ELBRUS KORYAK SREDINNY NARODNAYA
MOUNTAIN RANGE: URAL ALTAI SAYAN BAIKAL KOLYMA CHERSKY KHIBINY PUTORAN BAIKALIA BYRRANGA CAUCASUS STANOVOY BADZHALSKY DZHUGDZHUR VERKHOYANSK
PENINSULA: KOLA TAIMYR CHUKOTKA KAMCHATKA
PLAIN: KUMA KUBAN KARELIA SIBERIAN
REGION: SIBERIA
REPUBLIC: KOMI MARI TUVA SAKHA BURYAT INGUSH KALMYK UDMURT BASHKIR CHECHEN CHUVASH DAGESTAN KARELIAN MORDOVIAN TATARSTAN NORTHOSSETIAN KABARDINOBALKAR
RIVER: OB DON AMUR KAMA LENA OKA? DVINA VOLGA ANGARA IRTYSH KOLYMA USSURI DNIEPER PECHORA SUKHONA YENISEY VYCHEGDA INDIGIRKA
SEA: KARA BLACK JAPAN WHITE ARCTIC BALTIC BERING LAPTEV BARENTS CASPIAN CHUKCHI OKHOTSK PACIFIC SIBERIAN
SWAMP: VASYUGANE
TERRITORY: ALTAI PRIMORYE KRASNODAR STAVROPOL KHABAROVSK KRASNOYARSK
TOWN: UFA AZOV ORSK PERM GORKY KAZAN MOSCOW ROSTOV SAMARA SARATOV MURMANSK VERONEZH LENINGRAD VOLGOGRAD STALINGRAD CHELYABINSK NOVOSIBIRSK SVERDLOVOSK SAINTPETERSBURG
VOLCANO: KLYUCHEVSKAYA

RUSSIAN OLIVE OLEASTER
RUSSIAN THISTLE SALTWORT TUMBLEWEED
RUSSIAN TURNIP RUTABAGA
RUSSIAN WOLFHOUND BORZOI
RUST CLOWN DROSS ROOST ROUST UREDO AERUGO CANKER CORRODE FERRUGO OXIDIZE
(— OF PLANTS) HEMIFORM LEPTOFORM
(KNOT OF —) TUBERCULE
RUSTAM (FATHER OF —) ZAL
(HORSE OF —) RAKSH
(MOTHER OF —) RUDAPAH
(SON OF —) SOHRAB
(WIFE OF —) TAHMINAH
RUSTIC HOB JAY PUT BOOR CARL CHAW HICK HIND JAKE JOCK RUBE RUDE BACON BUSHY CARLE CHUFF CHURL COLIN DAMON DORIC HODGE ROUGH RURAL RURIC SILLY YOKEL AGREST BORREL BUMKIN COARSE FARMER GAFFER HONEST JOBSON RUSSET SAVAGE SCOLOC SCOLOG STURDY SYLVAN UPLAND ARTLESS BOORISH BORRELL BUCOLIC BUMPKIN BUSHMAN COUNTRY DAPHNIS FIELDEN GEORGIC HAYSEED HOBNAIL HOOSIER LANDMAN PAISANO PEASANT PLOWMAN THYRSIS WAYBACK AGRESTIC ARCADIAN BACKVELD CLOWNISH DAMOETAS GEOPONIC LANDWARD MOSSBACK CHAWBACON CLODHOPPER
(NOT —) CIVIL
(UNCOUTH —) JAKE
(YOUTHFUL —) SWAIN
(PL.) COUNTRYFOLK
RUSTLE TODO FISLE STEAL FISSLE FISTLE HIRSEL REESLE BRUSSEL BRUSTLE CRINKLE REESTLE SKITTER WHISTLE
(— OF SILK) SCROOP
(— UP) SNAVVLE
RUSTLER THIEF WADDY DUFFER WADDIE HUSTLER
RUSTLING ARUSTLE CRINKLY FROUFROU SOUGHING FRICATION SUSURROUS
RUSTY HOARY MOROSE ROOSTY SULLEN CANKERY OUTMODED
RUT RAT BRIM RACK RAIK RUCK TRACK TREAD CREASE FURROW GROOVE STRAKE SULCUS UPROAR CHANNEL OESTRUS WRINKLE
(— IN PATH) GAY
RUTABAGA BAGA SWEDE TURNIP
RUTH BABE PITY MERCY MISERY REGRET SORROW BAMBINO CRUELTY REMORSE SADNESS SYMPATHY
(HUSBAND OF —) BOAZ MAHLON
(MOTHER-IN-LAW OF —) NAOMI
(SON OF —) OBED JESSE
RUTHENIAN RUSSENE RUSSNIAK UKRAINIAN
RUTHLESS FELL GRIM CRUEL BRUTAL PITILESS CUTTHROAT
RUTILE NIGRINE SAGENITE
RUTTER PLOW DRAGOON GALLANT TROOPER
RUTTISH RANK LUSTFUL
RUY BLAS

RWANDA

CAPITAL: KIGALI
LAKE: KIVU
LANGUAGE: KIRUNDI SWAHILI
MOUNTAIN: KARISIMBI
MOUNTAIN RANGE: MITUMBA
PEOPLE: TWA HUTU TUTSI WATUSI
RIVER: KAGERA AKANYARU LUVIRONZA
TOWN: BUTARE GABIRO NYANZA GISENYI
TRIBE: BATWA BAHUTU WATUSI BATUTSI

RYA RUG
RYE RAY RIE ERAY REYE SPELT WHISKY GENTLEMAN
RYEGRASS RAY EAVER DARNEL
RYMANDRA KNIGHTIA
RYND BAIL RHIND MILRIND
RYOT RAYAT FARMER RAIYAT TENANT TILLER PEASANT
RYUKYU ISLANDS (— ISLAND GROUP) AMAMI OKINAWA SAKISHIMA
(OTHER NAME FOR —) LUCHU LOOCHO NANSEI

S

S ESS SUGAR SIERRA
SAARINEN EERO ELIEL
SABBATH SUNDAY SABAOTH SHABBAT SHABBOS
SABER KUKRI SABRE BANCAL BASKET TULWAR ATAGHAN CIMETER TULWAUR YATAGAN ACINACES SCIMITAR
SABICU JIQUE JIQUI
SABINE (BROTHER OF —) CURIACE
SABLE DWALE SAPLE OGRESS SATURN DIAMOND ZIBELINE
(ROUNDEL —) PELLET
SABLEFISH SKIL BESHOW COALFISH SKILFISH
SABOTAGE MASTIC DESTROY
SABRA (FATHER OF —) PTOLEMY
(HUSBAND OF —) GEORGE
(SON OF —) GUY DAVID ALEXANDER
SABRINA (FATHER OF —) LOCRINE
(MOTHER OF —) ESTRILDIS
SABTAH (FATHER OF —) CUSH
SABTECHA (FATHER OF —) CUSH
SAC BAG GUT POD CYST SACK ASCUS BURSA FLOAT POUCH THECA VOLVA ACINUS AMNION SACCUS VESICA AMPULLA BLADDER CAPSULE CISTERN HYGROMA UTRICLE VESICLE BROODSAC FOLLICLE SACCULUS SPERMARY
(SPORE —) ASCUS
(PREF.) THEC(A)(I)(O)
SACAR (FATHER OF —) OBEDEDOM
(SON OF —) AHIAM
SACCHARIN SWEET STICKY SUGARY GLUCOSE GLUSIDE
SACCHAROSE SUCROSE
SACERDOTAL HIERATIC PRIESTLY
SACHEM SAGAMORE
SACK AX AXE BAG BED CAN COT MAT SAC FIRE LOOT MUID POCK POKE BAYON GOOSE HARRY POUCH SPOIL BUDGET POCKET RAVAGE SACKET SACQUE DISMISS PILLAGE PLUNDER RANSACK SACKAGE SACKBAG DESOLATE PACKSACK PEIGNOIR
(— OF PALM LEAVES) BAYONG
(— OF WOOL) SARPLAR
(MAIL —) BUM
(PACK —) KYACK
(SAD —) BOLO JERK SCHMO
(PREF.) THYLAC(O)
SACKBUT SAMBUKE TROMBONE
SACKING SACK GUNNY CROCUS SACKEN HESSIAN POLDAVY SOUTAGE
SACRAMENT RITE BAPTISM MYSTERY NAGMAAL PENANCE
SACRARIUM PISCINA
SACRED HOLY TABU HUACA PIOUS SACRE SAINT SANCT SANTO TABOO DIVINE SACRAL HALLOWED HEAVENLY NUMINOUS REVEREND SACROSANCT
(PREF.) HAGI(O) HIER(O) HIERATICO SACR(I)(O) SEMNO
SACRED FIG PIPAL
SACRED FISH KANNUME
SACREDNESS CHURINGA SANCTITY TJURUNGA
SACRIFICE GIVE HOST LOSS OFFER SPEND YAJNA CORBAN FOREGO VICTIM EXPENSE CHILIOMB IMMOLATE KAPPARAH LITATION OBLATION OFFERING PASSOVER SPHAGION PROPITIATION
(— OF CARGO) JETTISON
(— OF 100 OXEN) HECATOMB
(— OF 1000 OXEN) CHILIOMB
(PL.) HAGIGAH CHAGIGAH
SACRIFICIAL PIACULAR
SACRILEGE PROFANATION
SACRILEGIOUS IMPIOUS
SACRISTAN SEXTON SACRIST
SACRISTY SEXTRY SACRARY VERGERY PARATORY SACRARIUM
SACROSANCT SACRED
SACRUM
(SUFF.) HIERIC
SAD LOW WAN DARK DOWY DRAM BLACK DREAR DUSKY MESTO MOODY SABLE SOBER SORRY WEARY YEMER DREARY SOLEMN SULLEN TRISTE WOEFUL BALEFUL DOLEFUL DUMPISH FORLORN FUNEBRE LUCTUAL MOANFUL SOBERLY UNHAPPY DEJECTED GROANFUL MOURNFUL MOURNING PATHETIC PITIABLE SUBTRIST TRISTIVE UNBLITHE DEPRESSED MELANCHOLY
(PREF.) TRISTI
SADDEN SAD DUMP CLOUD GLOOM GRIEVE ATTRIST CONTRIST DISTRESS
SADDENED BROKEN
SADDENING LUCTUAL
SADDLE PAD RIG SAG TAG LOAD SUNK CHINE PANEL PILCH SELLE STICK BURDEN HEADER RECADO PIGSKIN PILLION
(— AND BRIDLE) TACK
(— COVER) MOCHILA
(— FOR ONE-LEGGED RIDER) SOMERSET
(— STUFFED WITH STRAW) SODS
(— WITH) STICK
(— WORKER) LORIMER
(LIGHT —) PILCH PILLION
(MOTORCYCLE —) PILLION
(PACK —) BAT
(PART OF —) HORN RING SEAT SKIRT CANTLE FENDER JOCKEY POMMEL STRING BINDING LEATHER STIRRUP
(STRAW —) SUNK SUGGAN
(WITHOUT A —) ASELLATE
(PREF.) SELLI
SADDLEBACK JACK JACKBIRD
SADDLEBAG ALFORJA CANTINA SUMPTER TEETSOOK
(PL.) JAGS JAGGS
SADDLE BLANKET CORONA
SADDLEBOW BOW ARSON
SADDLECLOTH HOUSE NAMDA HOUSING PADCLOTH SHABRACK
SADDLEMAKER FUSTER KNACKER
SADDLE MAT FLET
SADDLE PAD PANEL NUMNAH PILLOW
SADDLER CODDER KNACKER LORIMER WHITTAW
SADISM BRUTALITY
SADISTIC SICK CRUEL SADIC BRUTAL
SADLY SAD ALAS UNWINLY
SADNESS DUMP RUTH DREAR DUMPS GLOOM GRIEF UNWIN SORROW DESPAIR
SAD SACK BOLO
SAFAWID SUFI
SAFE RUG CRIB PETE SURE WELL AMBRY SALVA SIKER SOUND SECURE SICCAR HEALTHY SYKERLY COCKSURE SILVENDY
(— FOR MEAT) KEEP
(— TO DEAL WITH) CANNY
SAFEBLOWER PETEMAN
SAFEBREAKER YEGG YEGGMAN PETERMAN
SAFE-CONDUCT JARK COWLE GRITH CONDUCT NAVICERT PASSPORT
SAFECRACKER YEGG BOXMAN PETEMAN PETERMAN TORCHMAN
SAFEGUARD SAVE WARD GUARD HEDGE SALVE DEFEND SAFETY SECURE BASTION BULWARK WARRANT FREEWARD PALLADIUM PRECAUTION
SAFEKEEPING CUSTODY STORAGE
(IN —) ONICE
SAFELY SAFE SICCAR SICKER SURELY SECURELY
SAFETY REFUGE SALUTE SURETY WARRANT SECURITY
(PREF.) SOTERIO
SAFETY ZONE ISLET ISLAND REFUGE
SAFFLOWER KUSUM ALAZOR SAFFRON
SAFFRON CROCUS AZAFRAN CROCEUS
(PREF.) CROCEO CROCO
SAFROLE SHIKIMOL
SAG BAG DIP TIE SWAG CREEP DROOP PLANK SLUMP SAGGON CURTAIN DEFLATE
SAGA EDDA EPIC MYTH TALE RIMUR LEGEND NJALSAGA
SAGACIOUS DEEP ACUTE CANNY SHARP ARGUTE ASTUTE SHREWD CORDATE POLITIC PRUDENT SAPIENT
SAGACITY POLICY WISDOM SMEDDUM YEPHEDE PRUDENCE SAPIENCE
SAGAMORE SACHEM
SAGE RSI WARE WISE WITE CLARY HAKAM IMLAC KATHA RISHI SABIO SOLON SOPHY ABARIS DHARMA NESTOR SALVIA SAULGE SAVANT SHREWD WIZARD EYESEED MAHATMA SAPIENT SOPHIST TOHUNGA WISEMAN DEVARSHI MAHARSHI WISEACRE
SAGEBRUSH SAGE HYSSOP SAGEWOOD ARTEMISIA
SAGENESS SAPIENCE
SAGGER COFFIN SETTER CASSETTE
SAGGING DRAG SWAG PTOSIS
SAGITTA ARROW
SAGITTARIUS ARCHER
SAGO PALM CYCAD
SAGRADA CASCARA
SAGUARO SUAHARO SUWARRO PITAHAYA
SAHIB SRI BWANA
SAHIDIC THEBAIC
SAIBLING TORGOCH
SAID DIT QUOTH STATED RELATED
SAIL JIB LUG RAG BEAT GALE HAUL MAIN SCUN SLAT SWAN SWIM WING DANDY FLEET FLIER FLOAT FLYER JUMBO RAFFE SCALE SHEET ACCOST CANVAS COURSE CRUISE DRIVER JIGGER LATEEN MIZZEN MUSLIN SINGLE ARTEMON LUGSAIL SKYSAIL SPANKER SPENCER TRYSAIL BACKWIND FORESAIL GAFFSAIL HEADSAIL MAINSAIL MOONSAIL NAVIGATE RINGTAIL STAYSAIL STUNSAIL
(— ALONG COAST) COAST ACCOST
(— AROUND) TURN DOUBLE
(— BEFORE THE WIND) SPOON
(— BRISKLY) SPANK
(— BY THE WIND) STRETCH
(— CLOSE TO WIND) PINCH
(— DOWN) AVALE AWALE
(— FASTER) FOOT
(— IN SPECIFIED DIRECTION) STAND
(— OF WINDMILL) ARM AWE EIE FAN VAN EIGHE FLIER FLYER SWEEP SWIFT
(— ON COURSE) HAUL WORK
(— QUIETLY) GHOST
(— RAPIDLY) SCUR SKIRR
(— SWIFTLY) RAMP

(— TO WINDWARD) THRASH
(— WITH WIND ABEAM) LASK
(FRAGMENT OF —) HULLOCK
(LIGHT —) SHADOW
(LOWEST —) COURSE
(PART OF —) CLEW FOOT HEAD LUFF SEAM SLAB TACK LEECH PANEL POCKET WINDOW ZIPPER CRINGLE TABLING TELLTALE HEADBOARD
(REDUCE —) REEF
(SMALL —) ROYAL
(TRIANGULAR —) RAFFE LATEEN BENTINCK
(WIND —) BADGIR
(3-CORNERED —) JIB TRINKET
(PL.) VELA CLOTH KITES LINENS SAILAGE CLOTHING
(PREF.) HISTI(O) ISTIO VELI
SAILBOARD (RIDE A —) WINDSURF
SAILBOAT CAT SAIL SCOW BULLY DANDY NABBY SAPIT SCOUT SHARP SKIFF SLOOP SNIPE CANGIA DINGHY QUODDY SAILER SATTIE CATBOAT SCOOTER SHALLOP SHARPIE SUNFISH KEELBOAT SAILSHIP SKIPJACK TRIMARAN
(PART OF —) JIB BOOM BUNK GATE HEAD HELM KEEL MAST SINK SKEG SOLE BERTH CLEAT FRAME HATCH SALON TRUNK WHEEL WINCH ANCHOR GALLEY JIBTOP LOCKER PULPIT RUDDER SHROUD YANKEE BULWARK COAMING COCKPIT COUNTER GALLOWS PUSHPIT TOPSAIL BACKSTAY BOWSPRIT BULKHEAD FOREDECK FOREFOOT FORESTAY HEADSTAY LIFELINE MAINSAIL MASTHEAD OVERHEAD SPREADER STAYSAIL TAFFRAIL TRAVELER CUBBYHOLE MAINSHEET PORTLIGHT STANCHION STATEROOM COMPANIONWAY
(WITCH'S —) SIEVE
SAILFISH BOHO WOOHOO GUEBUCU LONGJAW VOILIER VOLADOR BILLFISH
SAILOR (ALSO SEE NAVAL OFFICER) GOB TAR HAND JACK SALT SWAB TOTY GUARD KLOSH LAKER LIMEY CALASH CLASHY DAYMAN DECKIE HEARTY MARINE MATLOW SEADOG SEAMAN TARPOT TIERER TOPMAN COLLIER MARINAL MARINER MATELOT SHIPMAN SWABBER WARRIOR YARDMAN CANOTIER COXSWAIN DECKHAND FLATFOOT GALIONJI GUNLAYER LANDSMAN LITHSMAN MASTHEAD SHIPMATE WATERDOG WATERMAN WATERRUG YARDSMAN
(— ON LEAVE) LIBERTYMAN
(CAPTIOUS —) SEALAWYER
(EAST INDIAN —) LASCAR
(INFERIOR —) GREENHAND
(OLD —) SALT SHELLBACK
(SCANDINAVIAN —) KLOSH
(TURKISH —) GALIONGEE
SAILORLIKE TARRISH
SAILOR'S-CHOICE BREAM PIGFISH PINFISH WHITING
SAIL YARD RAE
SAINFOIN ESPARCET
SAINT PIR RSI DADU HOLY QUTB WALI ALVAR ARHAT RISHI SANTO BHAGAT HALLOW PATRON SANTON CANONIZE MARABOUT
(CHINESE —) IMMORTAL
(PATRON —) AVOWRY
(PILLAR —) STYLITE
(PL.) SS
(PREF.) HAGI
SAINT ELMO'S FIRE HERMO CASTOR FUROLE HELENA
SAINT JOAN (AUTHOR OF —) SHAW
(CHARACTER IN —) JOAN DUNOIS ROBERT WARWICK BAUDRICOURT
ST-JOHN'S-BREAD CAROB
ST-JOHN'S-WORT AMBER TUTSAN CAMMOCK
SAINT KITTS & NEVIS (CAPITAL:) BASSETERRE
(ISLAND:) NEVIS SOMBRERO SAINTCHRISTOPHER
SAINTLINESS HOLINESS SANCTITY
SAINT LUCIA (CAPITAL OF —) CASTRIES
(MOUNTAIN OF —) GIMIE
(MOUNTAINS OF —) PITONS CANARIES
(VOLCANO OF —) SOUFRIERE
SAINTLY DEVOUT ANGELIC SAINTED BEATIFIC SAINTISH
(— PERSON) ZADDIK
ST REGIS RANERE
SAINT VINCENT (CAPITAL OF —) KINGSTOWN
(PART OF —) UNION BEQUIA GRENADINES
SAITH COALFISH
SAITHE SILLOC POLLACK SILLOCK
SAJ SAIN
SAKE SAKI SCORE ACCOUNT
(SOURCE OF —) RICE
SAKI BISA MONK COUXIA MONKEY YARKEE
SALA (FATHER OF —) ARPHAXAD
(SON OF —) EBER
SALABLE VENAL SELLING SELLABLE VENDIBLE
SALACIOUS LEWD SALT RUTTISH SCARLET SCABROUS
SALAD SALLET COLESLAW TABBOULEH SILLSALLAT
(CORN —) MACHE FETTICUS
(KIND OF —) CAESAR
(LEBANESE —) TABOULI TABBOULEH
(TYPE OF —) TOSSED
SALADA SALINA
SALAL SHALLON
SALAMANDER EFT OLM SOW BEAR NEWT TWEEG GOPHER LIZARD TRITON AXOLOTL CRAWLER CREEPER DOGFISH MECODONT SALAMICH SHADRACH
SALAMI SAUSAGE
(KIND OF —) GENOA
SALAMMBO (AUTHOR OF —) FLAUBERT
(CHARACTER IN —) NARR GISCO HANNO HAVAS MATHO TAMIT HAMILCAR SALAMMBO SPENDIUS
(COMPOSER OF —) REYER
SAL AMMONIAC SPIRIT SALMIAC
SALARY PAY HIRE SCREW WAGES INCOME PACKET PENSION STIPEND
SALE FAIR VENT BREAK HEDGE TOUCH BOURSE VENDUE AUCTION MOHATRA SELLING HANDSALE KNOCKOUT PORTSALE
(— BY AUCTION) CANT ROUP BLOCK VENDUE OUTROOP
(— BY OUTCRY) ROUP ROWP HAMMER
(— OF OFFICE) BARRATRY
(— OF PERIODICAL) CIRCULATION
(— OF TOBACCO) BREAK
(— ON TRUST) CREDIT
(— TO CONSUMER) RETAIL
(PUBLIC —) AUCTION
(RUMMAGE —) JUMBLE
SALESMAN REP CLERK BAGMAN RUNNER SELLER BOOKMAN DRUMMER OUTRIDER PITCHMAN
(— IN FISH MARKET) BUMMAREE
SALESMANSHIP SELLING
SALESPERSON CLERK
SALESWOMAN WINSTER SHOPGIRL VENDEUSE
SALIENT SPUR BULGE CHIEF ARGINE BASTION SALTANT
SALIENTIA ANURA ANOURA ECAUDATA
SALINA SHOR SALINE
SALINE SALT BRINY SALAR SALTY MARINAL
SALIVA SPIT DROOL WATER DRIVEL SLAVER SPUTUM SPITTLE
(— FLOW) PTYALISM
(PREF.) PTYAL(O) SIAL(O)
SALIVARY SIALIC
SALIVATION PTYALISM SLOBBERS
SALLET SALADE
SALLOW WAN SALE SICK ADUST LURID MUDDY SALIX SAUCH SAUGH PALLID YELLOW
SALLY GRIP JERK PASS QUIP SAIL QUICK START ESCAPE GAMBIT SORTIE GAMBADE OUTFALL OUTLEAP DEMARCHE
SALM (BROTHER OF —) TUR IRAJ
(FATHER OF —) FARIDUN
(MOTHER OF —) SHAHRINAZ
(SLAYER OF —) MINUCHIHR
SALMAGUNDI OLIO SILLSALLAT
SALMON DOG LAX LOX SAM KETA MASU PINK AMOUT COHOE COUNT HADDO HOLIA SMOLT SMOOT SPROD TECON ALEVIN BAGGIT KIPPER LAUREL MYKISS SAMLET SAUQUI SILVER TAIMEN ANADROM ANNATTO BLUECAP BOTCHER CHINOOK DOGFISH GILLING GRAVLAX KAHAWAI KOKANEE NEWFISH QUINNAT REDFISH RUNFISH SAWMONT SHEDDER SOCKEYE BLUEBACK BRANDLIN GOLDFISH GRAVLAKS HUMPBACK LASPRING SALMONID SPRINGER OUANANICHE
(— AFTER SPAWNING) KELT BAGGIT SHEDDER
(— BEFORE SPAWNING) GILLING GIRLING
(— ENCLOSURE) YAIR
(— IN 2ND OR 3D YEAR) SMOLT
(— IN 2ND YEAR) SPROD HEPPER GILLING
(— IN 3D YEAR) PUG MORT
(— ON FIRST RETURN FROM SEA) GRILSE
(BLUEBACK —) NERKA SAUQUI SOCKEYE
(CURED —) KIPPER GRAVLAX GRAVLAKS
(DOG —) CHUM KETA
(FATHER OF —) NAHSHON
(FEMALE —) RAUN BAGGIT
(HUMPBACK —) HADDO HOLIA
(MALE —) GIB BUCK COCK
(MILTER —) EKE
(NEWLY HATCHED —) PINK ALEVIN
(SMALL —) PEAL SKIRLING
(SON OF —) BOAZ
(SPENT —) JUDY SLAT LIGGER RUNFISH
(YOUNG —) FOG PARR PEAL SMOLT GRILSE HEPPER JERKIN SAMLET BOTCHER ESSLING SKEGGER LASPRING SPARLING
SALMONELLOSIS KEEL
SALMONEUS (BROTHER OF —) SISYPHUS
(DAUGHTER OF —) TYRO
(FATHER OF —) AEOLUS
(MOTHER OF —) ENARETE
(WIFE OF —) ALCIDICE
SALOME (FATHER OF —) HEROD
(HUSBAND OF —) PHILIP ZEBEDEE ARISTOBULUS
(MOTHER OF —) HERODIAS
SALON HALL SALOON GALLERY
SALOON CAFE CUDDY DIVAN SALON SHADE BARROOM CANTINA RUMSHOP SCATTER DEADFALL DRINKERY DRUNKERY EXCHANGE BRASSERIE
(RAILWAY —) PULLMAN
SALPA SALP THALIA
SALSIFY GOATBEARD
SALT SAL TAR CORN KERN SAWT BRINY ZIRAM AMIDOL AURATE FOLATE GAMMON HALITE MALATE OLEATE OSMATE POWDER SAILOR SALIFY SALINE URANIN XENATE KAINITE LACTATE MALEATE NIOBATE PHYTATE TROPATE ABIETATE BRACKISH HALINOUS PIMELATE PLUMBITE SELENATE
(— FISH) ROIL
(— OUT) CUT GRAIN
(DOUBLE —) ALUM
(HAIR —) ALUNOGEN
(LUMP OF —) SALTCAT
(METAL —) SILICATE
(MIXTURE OF —S) REH USAR
(OLD —) SEADOG
(POISONOUS —) ARSENATE
(ROCK —) PIG HALITE
(ZINC —) ZIRAM
(PREF.) HAL(I)(O) SALI SALIN(I)(O)
(SUFF.) OATE
SALTATE JUMP
SALTATION LEAP
SALT BOILER WELLER
SALTBUSH BLUEBUSH
SALTCELLAR SALT CELLAR SELLER SHAKER SALTFAT SALTFOOT
SALTED SALEE

SALTICID ATTID
SALT PAN PLAYA
SALTPETER NITER NITRE PETER ANATRON CALICHE PRUNELLA
SALT PIT VAT WICH WYCH
SALT PORK SOWBELLY
SALTWORKS SALINA SALTERN SALTERY SALTPANS
SALTWORT KALI BARILLA SALSOLA KELPWORT
SALTY SALT BRINY SALINE SAVORY HALINOUS
SALU (SLAYER OF —) PHINEHAS
(SON OF —) ZIMRI
SALUBRIOUS BENIGN HEALTHY SALUTARY
SALUTARY GOOD BENIGN HEALTHY HELPFUL BENEDICT
SALUTATION AVE HAIL ALOHA SALUS MIZPAH SALAAM SALUTE REGREET SLAINTE WELCOME DIEUGARD GREETING HAEREMAI
(DRINKING —) SKOAL PROSIT PROFACE WASSAIL
SALUTE CAP HAIL HEIL KISS MOVE YULE CHEER DRINK GREET HALCH HALSE HONOR SALUE SALVO COLORS SALAAM EMBRACE ACCOLADE CONGREET
(— TO DANCING PARTNER) COUPEE
(VICTORY —) VSIGN
SALVADOR BAHIA
SALVAGE SAVE SALVE RECOVERY SCROUNGE
SALVAGER SALVOR
SALVATION BODAI MOKSHA SAFETY NIRVANA KAIVALYA SAVEMENT SOULHEAL
(— APPROACH) MARGA
SALVE SAW TAR SALVO SAUVE NERVAL SUPPLE PLASTER UNGUENT OINTMENT
SALVER TRAY SERVER WAITER PLATEAU
SALVIA CHIA SAGE CLARY MEJORANA MINTWEED
SALVO SALUTE SPREAD PROVISO TRIBUTE STRADDLE
(PL.) LADDER
SAM (FATHER OF —) NARIMAN
(SON OF —) ZAL
SAMARA KEY CHAT
SAMARIA AHOLAH
SAMARITAN CUTHEAN CUTHITE
SAMBA CARIOCA
SAMBAR ELK DEER MAHA RUSA
SAME ID EAD ILK ONE IDEM LIKE MEME SELF VERY DITTO EQUAL SAMEN IDENTIC SELFSAME
(— AS) IQ
(— PLACE) IB
(MUCH THE —) ALIKE
(THAT —) THILK THICKE
(PREF.) AUT(O) AUTH(I) HOM(O)(OI) HOME(O) HOMOE IPSI ISO TAUT(O)
SAMENESS ONENESS EQUALITY IDENTITY MONOTONY
SAMLET PINK
SAMNITES SABELLI
SAMOA (CAPITAL OF —) APIA PAGOPAGO
(COIN OF —) SENE TALA
(ISLAND OF —) OFU TAU ROSE MANUA UPOLU SAVAII OLOSEGA TUTUILA
(MOUNTAIN OF —) FITO SAVAII MATAFAO
SAMOGITIAN ZHMUD
SAMOYED TUBA YURAK BELTIR KAIBAL KOIBAL NENTSI KAMASSIN
SAMPHIRE SALTWEED
SAMPLE DIP SIP CAST PREE CHECK ESSAY TASTE TRIAL CHANCE COUPON FLOWER MUSTER SWATCH TASTER EXAMPLE EXCERPT MONSTER PATTERN SAMPLER TASTING INSTANCE PULLDOWN SPECIMEN
(— OF METAL) DIET
SAMPLING SOUNDING
SAMSON (FATHER OF —) MANOAH
SAMSON ET DALILA (CHARACTER IN —) PRIEST SAMSON DELILAH
(COMPOSER OF —) SAINTSAENS
SAMUEL (FATHER OF —) ELKANAH
(MOTHER OF —) HANNAH
SAMURAI BUSHI RONIN
SAN SAMPI
SANAD SUNNUD
SANBENITO SAMARRA
SAN BLAS TULE
SAN CARLOS ARIVAIPA
SANCTIFICATION HOLINESS
SANCTIFY BLESS SACRE SACRI DEDICATE
SANCTIMONIOUS PI DEVOUT PECKSNIFFIAN
SANCTION AMEN FIAT ALLOW PIETY ASSENT BISHOP RATIFY APPROVE ENDORSE JUSTIFY PASSAGE SUPPORT ACCREDIT APPROVAL CANONIZE COURTESY SUFFRAGE
SANCTIONED CANONICAL
SANCTITY SANTY HALIDOME HOLINESS
SANCTUARY ADYT BAST BEMA FANE HOLY SOIL ABBEY ALTAR BAMAH FRITH GIRTH GRITH SECOS SEKOS TOWER ADYTON ADYTUM ASYLUM CHAPEL HAIKAL REFUGE SENTRY SHRINE SACRARY SHELTER ARCHEION CABIRION DELUBRUM HALIDOME HOLINESS SACRARIUM
(— FOR LAWBREAKERS) ALSATIA
(AUTHOR OF —) FAULKNER
(CHARACTER IN —) LEE RED VAN REBA RUBY DRAKE GOWAN LAMAR TOMMY BENBOW HORACE POPEYE RIVERS SNOPES TEMPLE GOODWIN STEVENS
SANCTUM ADYT ADYTON ADYTUM
SAND DIRT GRIT ARENA GRAIL SONDE GRAVEL ISERINE ISERITE PARTING ASBESTIC BLINDING
(— FOR STREWING ON FLOORS) BREEZE
(— HILL) DENE DUNE
(— IN KIDNEYS) ARENA
(— MIXED WITH GRAVEL) GARD DOBBIN
(— ON SEA BOTTOM) PAAR
(BRAIN —) SABULUM ACERVULUS
(COLOR —) CHIP BEACH
(COLORED —) SMALT
(DEAUVILLE —) STUCCO
(VOLCANIC —) SANTORIN
(WATERY —) QUICKSAND
(PREF.) AMM(O) ARENI PSAMM(O)
SANDAL TIP BAXA FLAT SOCK ZORI TEGUA THONG CALIGA CHARUK PATTEN TATBEB RULLION SCUFFER FOOTHOLD GUARACHE HUARACHO
(JAPANESE —) GETA
(LOOSE —) SLIPSLOP
(RED SILK —) CALCEAMENTUM
(WINGED —) TALARIA
(WINGED —S) TALARIA
SANDAL TREE SANTOL
SANDALWOOD NAIO ALGUM ALMUG MAIRE CHANDAM SAUNDERS
SANDALWOOD TREE ILIAHI
SANDARAC TREE ARAR LIGNUM
SANDBAG CONK SANDCLUB
SAND BANK AIR CHAR MEAL SAND BATCH HURST HYRST KNOCK SHELF SHOAL
SANDBAR BALK LOOP SAND BARRA SHOAL TOMBOLO TOWHEAD
SANDBLASTER FROSTER BLASTMAN
SAND BORER SMELT
SANDBOX TREE ASSACU
SAND COLIC SABURRA
SAND DARTER SPECK
SAND DUNE TOWAN BARCHAN
SAND EEL GRIG SANDFISH
SANDEMANIAN GLASSITE
SANDERLING OXBIRD
SAND FLEA SCREW SCROW SANDBOY
SAND-FLY BUSH TURMERIC
SAND GROUSE GANGA ROCKER ATTAGEN PINTAIL
SAND HOLE BUNKER
SANDIVER NATRON
SAND LAUNCE LANT SMELT WRIGGLE AMMODYTE SANDLING SCRIGGLE
SAND LILY SOAPROOT
SANDMAN DUSTMAN
SANDPAPER TREE CHAPARRO
SANDPIPER JACK KNOT PEEP RUFF STIB WEET OXEYE SNIPE STINT TEREK TIPUP WADER DUNLIN GAMBET OXBIRD PLOVER REDLEG TEETER TILTER TILTUP TRINGA BROWNIE CHOROOK CREEKER FATBIRD FIDDLER HAYBIRD KRIEKER MONGLER MONGREL REDBACK TATTLER TIPTAIL GRAYBACK LEADBACK PEETWEET REDSHANK ROCKBIRD SANDPEEP SHADBIRD SQUATTER SWEESWEE TELLTALE TRIDDLER
(FEMALE —) REEVE
(FLOCK OF —S) FLING
SAND PIT BUNKER
SAND ROCKET FLIXWEED
SAND SHARK BONEDOG
SANDSTONE FAKE FLAG GRES GRIT SAND GAIZE HAZEL ARCOSE ARKOSE DOGGER KINGLE ARENITE HASSOCK CARSTONE COCONINO GANISTER PSAMMITE RUBSTONE SANDROCK
(BLOCK OF —) SARSEN
SANDSTORM BURAN HABOOB TEBBAD
SANDUST VANITY
SANDWICH BLT SUB GYRO HERO BUTTY HOAGY BURGER HOAGIE REUBEN DAGWOOD FALAFEL FELAFEL GRINDER WESTERN
(ITALIAN —) GRINDER
(SUFF.) BURGER
SANDWORT LONGROOT SANDWEED
SANDY DEEP GINGER GRISTY SANDED ARENOSE PSAMMOUS SABULINE SABULOUS
SANDY BROWN LARK
SANE SAFE WISE LUCID RIGHT FORMAL NORMAL HEALTHY PERFECT RATIONAL SENSIBLE
SANGA-SANGA ESSANG
SANGUINARY GORY CRUEL BLOODY CRIMSON SANGUINE
SANGUINE FOND GUZE MURREY HEMATIC HOPEFUL SARDONYX
SANHEDRIN GEROUSIA
SANICLE ALLHEAL SELFHEAL
SANIOUS ICHOROUS
SANITARY HYGIENIC
SANITY SENSE REASON WISDOM BALANCE MARBLES LUCIDITY SANENESS
SAN MARINO (CHURCH OF —) PIEVE
(DISTRICTS OF —) CASTELLI
(MOUNTAIN OF —) TITANO
(SUBURB IN —) BORGO
SANNUP SQUAW
SANSKRIT HINDU
(— SOUND OR SIGN) VISARGA
(— WORK) VEDANGA
SANS SERIF DORIC GOTHIC
SANTA MARIA TREE BIRMA GALBA CALABA
SAN TOME (MONEY OF —) DOBRA
SANTONICA WORMSEED
SAO TOME AND PRINCIPE
(CAPITAL OF —) SAOTOME
(MONEY OF —) DOBRA
(NAME OF —) SAOTHOME SAINTTHOMAS
SAP MUG GOON MINE OOZE RASA SEVE DRAIN HUMBO KEEST LYMPH SAPPER WEAKEN AIRHEAD ALVELOZ FLUXURE JUGHEAD SAPHEAD
(— COURAGE) DAUNT
(— OF RUBBER TREE) LATEX
(FERMENTED PALM —) SURA
(PALM —) TODY TODDY
(POISONOUS —) UPAS
(SUGAR MAPLE —) HUMBO
SAPAJOU SAJOU WARINE
SAPANWOOD BOKOM BRAZIL SIBUCAO
SAPEK DONG
SAPID SIPID FLAVORY
SAPIENT WISE SHREWD KNOWING
SAPI-UTAN ANOA
SAPLING SCOB PLANT SAPLE SPIRE RUNNEL SPRING TILLER STADDLE ASHPLANT SEEDLING SHILLALA SPRINGER
(— AMONG FELLED TREES) WAVER
SAPODILLA GUM CHICA CHICO

DILLY ACHRAS MAMMEE SAPOTA SAPOTE ZAPOTE NISPERO NISBERRY NASEBERRY
SAPONIFYING KILLING
SAPONIN GITONIN SENEGIN CYCLAMIN STRUTHIN
SAPONITE PIOTINE
SAPOTA MATASANO
SAPPHIRE SAFIR TOPAZ ADAMAS ASTERIA ASTRION HYACINTH
SAPPHIRINE GURNARD TUB
SAPPHO (AUTHOR OF —) DAUDET
(CHARACTER IN —) JEAN ROSA FANNY IRENE DEJOIE POTTER CAOUDAL CESAIRE FLAMANT GAUSSIN LEGRAND BOUCHEREAU DECHELETTE LAGOURNERIE
SAPPY FRIM FRUM SAPFUL
SAPSAP PEPEREK
SAPUCAIA COCO COCOA KAKARALI
SAPWOOD SAP BLEA SPLENT SPLINT GUAYABI LISTING ALBURNUM
SARA (— WOMAN) UBANGI
SARABAITES REMOBOTH
SARACEN CORSAIR
SARAH ATOSSA
(FATHER OF —) ASHER
(HUSBAND OF —) ABRAHAM
(SON OF —) ISAAC
SARAKOLLE WAKORE
SARASVATI VAC VACH BENTEN
SARCASM RUB GIBE WIPE FLING IRONY TAUNT RUBBER SATIRE BROCARD RIDICULE SCORCHER
SARCASTIC ACID ACRID WITTY BITING IRONIC ACERBIC CUTTING MORDANT PUNGENT INCISIVE SARDONIC SATIRICAL ACRIMONIOUS
SARCASTICALLY DRILY DRYLY ACIDLY
SARCOCARP FLESH
SARCOPHAGUS TOMB COFFIN
SARCOPSYLLA TUNGA
SARDINE BANG LOUR SARD SILD CLUPEID PILCHARD SARDELLE

SARDINIA
CAPITAL: CAGLIARI
CHEESE: ROMANO PECORINO
COIN: CARLINE
GREEK COLONY: OLBIA
GULF: OROSEI ASINARA CAGLIARI ORISTANO
MOUNTAIN: RASU FERRY LINAS GALLURA LIMBARA SERPEDDI VITTORIA
NAME: SARDEGNA
PROVINCE: NUORO SASSARI CAGLIARI
RIVER: MANNU TIRSO LASCIA SAMASSI COGHINAS FLUMENDOSA
STRAIT: BONIFACIO
TOWN: IERZU NUORO SASSARI THATARI CAGLIARI CARBONIA IGLESIAS

SARDONIC SARCASTIC
SARGASSUM GULFWEED
SARGO ZEBRA
SARI PATOLA TAMEIN
SAROD LUTE
SARONG PAU KAIN COMBOY KIKEPA TAMEIN
SARPEDON (BROTHER OF —) MINOS RHADAMANTHUS
(FATHER OF —) ZEUS JUPITER
(MOTHER OF —) LAODAMIA
SARSAPARILLA NUNNARI SHOTBUSH
SARUCH (FATHER OF —) REU
SASH BAR BELT BENN FAJA GATE TOBE SCARF TAPIS TOWEL VITTA FASCIA GIRDLE BALDRIC BURDASH CHASSIS TUBBECK CASEMENT CORSELET WAISTBAND CUMBERBUND CUMMERBUND
(JAPANESE —) OBI
(WINDOW —) CHESS
SASHAY WALK GLIDE STRUT CHASSE TRAIPSE
SASH BAR MUNTIN ASTRAGAL
SASKATCHEWAN (CAPITAL OF —) REGINA
(LAKE OF —) ROUGE REINDEER ATHABASKA CHURCHILL WOLLASTON
(RIVER OF —) WOOD MOOSE SOURIS FRENCHMAN
(TOWN OF —) BIGGAR CLIMAX ESTEVAN MOOSEJAW ROSETOWN SASKATOON
SASQUATCH OMAH BIGFOOT
SASS LIP GUFF
SASSABY TSESSEBE
SASSAFRAS FILE SALOP SALOOP SAXIFRAX
SASSY FLIP KICKY LIPPY MOUTHY SPUNKY
SATAN ANGEL DEVIL EBLIS FIEND SHREW BELIAL LUCIFER SATANAS SHAITAN DIABOLUS SATANAEL
SATANIC SABLE INFERNAL
SATCHEL SCRIP HANDBAG KEESTER
SATE CLOY GLUT ACCLOY SATIATE SATISFY SATURATE
SATED SAD BLASE
SATEEN VENETIAN
SATELLITE MOON ARIEL LUNET DEIMOS MOONET OBERON PHOBOS ACOLYTE ACOLYTH LUNETTE ORBITER SPUTNIK TELSTAR TRABANT UMBRIEL COURTIER FOLLOWER
(— LAUNCHER) AGENA
(— OF JUPITER) IO EUROPA CALLISTO GANYMEDE
(— OF NEPTUNE) NEREID TRITON
(— OF SATURN) RHEA DIONE MIMAS TITAN PHOEBE TETHYS IAPETUS JAPETUS HYPERION
(— OF URANUS) ARIEL OBERON MIRANDA TITANIA UMBRIEL
(U.S. WEATHER —) ESSA
(WEATHER —) TIROS
SATIATE CLOY FILL GLUT PALL QUAT SADE SATE FLESH GORGE SERVE STALL ENGLUT STODGE RASSASY SATISFY SURFEIT SATURATE
SATIATED SICK BLASE JADED SATED
SATIATING STODGY FULSOME
SATIETY FULNESS SURFEIT CLOYMENT
SATIN SAY RASH ATLAS PANNE CYPRUS MUSHRU COOTHAY CYPRESS SATINET
(SILK —) DUCHESS
SATINFLOWER SAFFRON
SATINPOD HONESTY LUNARIA
SATINWOOD ZANTE HAREWOOD
SATIRE WIT GRIND IRONY IAMBIC LAMPOON SARCASM SOTADIC RIDICULE PASQUINADE
SATIRIC BITTER IRONIC ABUSIVE CAUSTIC CUTTING POIGNANT SLASHING
SATIRICAL IAMBIC INVECTIVE
SATIRIST GRIND NIPPER SATIRE JUVENAL PASQUIN SILLOGRAPH
AMERICAN MENCKEN SANDERS
ENGLISH HONE NIGEL SWIFT WAUGH WOLCOT MARVELL CHURCHILL
GERMAN BORNE MURNER RABENER
GREEK LUCIAN SOTADES
ROMAN HORACE JUVENAL PERSIUS
SPANISH LARRA
SATIRIZE SKIN SKIT GRIND EXPOSE IAMBIZE LAMPOON PASQUIN RIDICULE
(— UNFAIRLY) LIBEL
SATISFACTION CRO FIN PAY UTU EASE GREE BELLY ENACH TREAT AMENDS ASSETH CHANGE REASON COMFORT CONTENT DELIGHT GLADNESS PLEASURE REPLETION
(EXPRESSION OF —) VOILA
SATISFACTORILY SPROWSY CLEVERLY
SATISFACTORY PAT FAIR GOOD JAKE WELL DUCKY HUNKY CLEVER DECENT NOMINAL ADEQUATE LAUDABLE
(VERY —) COPACETIC
SATISFIED SAD FAIN FULL GLAD PAID VAIN APAID CHUFF PROUD ASSURED CHUFFED CONTENT PERFECT GRUNTLED SENSIBLE WILCWEME
SATISFY PAY EVEN FEED FILL MEET SAIR SATE SUIT ADEEM AGREE APPAY QUEME SERVE SLAKE SPEED ANSWER DEFRAY PLEASE STODGE SUPPLY ASSUAGE CONTENT EXPLETE FULFILL GRATIFY GRUNTLE RESPOND SATIATE STAUNCH SUFFICE SATURATE
(— APPETITE) STAY
(— BY PROOF) CONVINCE
(— IN ADVANCE) PREVENT
(— NEEDS) DO ADJUST
SATISFYING DUE COOL AMPLE SQUARE PERFECT REWARDING
SATURATE SOG GLUT SATE SOAK DRAWK IMBUE SOUSE STEEP DRENCH IMBIBE SEETHE SODDEN DRUNKEN INGRAIN PERVADE SATIATE SLOCKEN WATERLOG
(— WITH SYRUP) CANDY
SATURATED SOBBY SOGGY SOPPY SODDEN SPONGY DRUNKEN
SATURATION CHROMA PURITY SATURITY
SATURN (FATHER OF —) URANUS
(MOTHER OF —) GAEA
(RING OF —) ANSA
(SATELLITE OF —) RHEA DIONE MIMAS TITAN TETHYS JAPETUS HYPERION ENCELADUS
(SON OF —) JUPITER
(WIFE OF —) OPS CYBELE
SATURNINE SULLEN SATANIC
SATYAGRAHA GANDHISM
SATYR FAUN LECHER SAUMON SALTIER WOODMAN WOODWOSE
SATYRIASIS TENTIGO
SAUCE MOLE SASS SOWL BERCY CHILE CHILI CREAM CREME CURRY GRAVY PESTO SALSA CATSUP COULIS GANSEL MORNAY PANADA ROBERT KETCHUP MARENGO SOUBISE SUPREME TABASCO VELOUTE BECHAMEL CHAWDRON DRESSING DUXELLES MARINADE MATELOTE POIVRADE RAVIGOTE REMOLADE AVGOLEMONO
(CURRY —) SAMBAL
(FISH —) ALEC BAGOONG
(GARLIC —) AIOLI ROUILLE
(HOT —) SALSA
(ITALIAN —) RAGU PREGO
(KIND OF —) MORNAY NANTUA MARINARA
(KIND OF —) HOLSIN
(SALAD —) DRESSING
(SAVORY —) DIP
(SOY —) TAMARI
(SPAGHETTI —) PESTO
(SPICY —) SALSA
(THICK —) LEAR
SAUCEDISH SAUCER BIRDBATH
SAUCEPAN CHAFER GOBLET POSNET SKILLET STEWPAN PANNIKIN
SAUCER BIRD PATERA PHIALE CAPSULE PANNIKIN
(— OCCUPANT) ET
(FLYING —) UFO DISC
SAUCINESS SAUCE DICACITY
SAUCY BOG ARCH BOLD COXY PERT BRASH DONSY DORTY FRESH LIPPY PAWKY POKEY SASSY SMART BANTAM COCKET COPPED CROUSE THWART FORWARD PAUGHTY FLIPPANT MALAPERT PETULANT SANSHACH
SAUDI ARABIA: (CAPITAL OF —) JIDDAH RIYADH
(COIN OF —) RIYAL HALALA HALALAH
(DESERT REGION OF —) NEFUD DAHANA ALNAFUD
(PLATEAU OF —) NEJD
(TOWN OF —) HAIL HOFUF JIDDA MECCA MEDINA ALHOFUF
(WEIGHT OF —) OKE
SAUL (FATHER OF —) KISH
(SON OF —) JONATHAN
(UNCLE OF —) NER
SAUNTER IDLE ROAM ROVE TOIT AMBLE MOSEY RANGE SHOOL SIDLE STRAY TRAIK BUMMEL DACKER DANDER FAFFLE LINGER LOITER LOUNGE POTTER PUTTER

RAMBLE SOODLE STREEL STROLL TODDLE WANDER SNAFFLE STAIVER STRAVAGE
SAURA MAGA
SAUREL SCAD XUREL GASCON BLUEFISH MACKEREL SKIPJACK
SAURY LONGJAW SKIPPER BILLFISH GOWDNOOK SKIPJACK
SAUSAGE POT LINK SNAG COPPA GIGOT BANGER BOUDIN POLONY SALAMI BOLOGNA BOLONEY BOTARGO CHORIZO PUDDING SAVELOY BLACKPOT CERVELAT DRISHEEN KIELBASA LIVERING ROLLICHE ANDOUILLE CHIPOLATA COTECHINO
(KIND OF —) METT
(VIENNA —) WIENER WIENIE
(PREF.) ALLANT(O) BOTULI
SAUTE PANFRY
SAUTERNE YQUEM
SAVAGE ILL FELL GRIM RUDE WILD BRUTE CRUEL EAGER FELON FERAL STERN BRUTAL FIERCE GOTHIC IMMANE BRUTISH FERVENT HOWLING INHUMAN MANKEEN MANKIND ROPABLE UNCIVIL VIOLENT WILROUN CANNIBAL PITILESS THEREOID WARRAGAL
(PREF.) AGRIO
SAVAGELY FELLY UNMANLY
SAVAGERY FURY FERITY FEROCITY
SAVANNA CAMPO SAHEL SABANA
(— LANDS) LALANG
(— REGION) SAHEL
SAVANT ARTIST SCIENT SCHOLAR VIRTUOSO
SAVE BAR WIN HAIN HELP KEEP SAFE SALT STOP STOW AMASS PUTBY SALVE SKIMP SPARE SPELL DEFEND EXCEPT REDEEM RESCUE SAVING SCRIMP UNLESS BARRING DELIVER HUSBAND SALVAGE WARRANT CONSERVE PRESERVE SALTAWAY SETASIDE
(— FROM OBJECTION) SALVE
(— PENURIOUSLY) SCRAPE SNUDGE
(PREF.) SOZ(O)
SAVIN HEATH SABINE JUNIPER
SAVING FRUGAL THRIFT ECONOMY SPARING THRIFTY PROVIDENT
SAVINGS FAT ADDLINGS
(— CLUB) MENAGE
SAVIOR LORD SAVER SOTER REDEEMER
SAVOR EDGE SALT SAPOR SMACK TASTE DEGUST FLAVOR RELISH RESENT SAVOUR SEASON TASTEN SAPIDITY
SAVORLESS FOND INSIPID WEARISH
SAVORY GUSTY MERRY SAPID TASTY DAINTY SMERVY GUSTFUL GUSTABLE TASTEFUL
SAVVY SABE
(— ABOUT) UPON
SAW SAG SEY WEB BUCK REDE ADAGE FREIT GNOME SCEAR SPOKE CLICHE JIGSAW PITSAW RIPSAW SAYING SCRIBE BACKSAW BUCKSAW CONVERT DRAGSAW FRETSAW HACKSAW HANDSAW HEADRIG HEADSAW PROVERB SLABBER WHIPSAW CROSSCUT SENTENCE
(— INTO LOGS) BUCK
(— LENGTHWISE OF GRAIN) RIP
(— OF SAWFISH) SERRA
(— WITH TWO BLADES) STADDA
(CIRCULAR —) BUR BURR EDGER DAPPER TRIMMER
(COMB-MAKER'S —) STADDA
(CROSSCUT —) BRIAR
(CYLINDER —) CROWN TREPAN TREPHINE
(ENDLESS —) RIBBON
(SURGICAL —) TREPAN
(PREF.) PRI(O) PRION(O) SERRATI SERRATO SERRI
(SUFF.) PRION
SAWAN SRABAN SHRAVAN
SAWBILL MOTMOT
SAWBUCK TENNER
SAWDUST COOM COOMB SCOBS SAWINGS
(PREF.) SCOBI
SAW FERN DYGAL BUNGWALL HARDFERN
SAWFISH RAY BATOID COMBFISH
(PREF.) PRIST(O)
SAWFLY CEPHID SECURIFER
SAW GATE FRAME
SAWHORSE BUCK JACK SETTER SAWBUCK TRESTLE
SAWING
(PREF.) PRISO
SAW KERF SKAFF
SAWMILL RASPER
(— DEVICE) KICKER
(— WORKER) PONDMAN LEVERMAN
SAWYER WETA SAWER PITMAN TOPMAN KNOTTER
SAXHORN ALTO TUBA ALTHORN SAXTUBA BARITONE BARYTONE
SAXIFRAGE BAUERA BENNET SESELI ASTILBE ROCKFOIL SELFHEAL SENGREEN MITERWORT PHILADELPHUS
SAXONIAN MINDEL
SAXOPHONE AX AXE SAX ALTO TENOR SOPRANINO
SAY DEED MEAN MOVE TAKE TELL SPEAK SPELL UTTER AUTHOR QUETHE RELATE REMARK SAYING REHEARSE PRONOUNCE
(— A BLESSING) BENSH
(— AGAIN) REPEAT ITERATE
(— FOOLISHLY) BLABBER
(— FURTHER) ADD
(— GLIBLY) SCREED
(— IN ANSWER) REPLY
(— INDISTINCTLY) MUMBLE
(— IN RETURN) REJOIN
(— NO TO) NAIT NICK
(— OVER AGAIN) REPEAT
(— REPEATEDLY) DECANTATE
(— SPITEFUL THINGS) BACKBITE
(— SUDDENDLY) OUT
(— TOGETHER) CHORUS
(— TOO MUCH) SPILL OVERSAY
(—TRULY) MEAN
(— UNDER OATH) DEPOSE
SAYING DIT SAW SAY TAG DICT ITEM REDE TEXT WORD ADAGE AXIOM CHRIA DITTY FREIT MAXIM SPEAK BALLAD BYWORD DICTUM DIVERB LOGION DICTION PROVERB APOTHEGM SENTENCE SPEAKING
(— LITTLE) DUMB
(—S OF JESUS) AGRAPHA
(—S OF RELIGIOUS TEACHER) LOGIA
(BRIEF —) APHORISM
(CLEVER —) QUIP
(COMMON —) CANT BYWORD
(CONCISE —) EPIGRAM
(CURRENT —) DICTUM
(HABITUAL —) OVERWORD
(NOTEWORTHY —) NOTABILIA
(OBSCURE —) ENIGMA
(PITHY —) GNOME MAXIM APOTHEGM APOPHTHEGM
(QUICK —) JERK
(SENTENTIOUS —) REASON
(SILLY —) FADAISE
(TERSE —) EPIGRAM
(TRUE —) SOOTHSAW
(WISE —) SCHOLIUM
(WITTY —) MOT SALLY DICTERY WITNESS
(WITTY —S) FACETIAE
(PL.) LOGIA
(SUFF.) LOGER LOGIA(N) LOGIC(AL) LOGIST LOGUE LOGY
SCAB RAT ROIN SHAB SNOB CRUST SCALD SCALL CANKER ESCHAR RATTER GREENER RUBBERS BLACKLEG BLACKNEB
(— ON HORSE'S HEEL) MELLIT
SCABBARD CHAPE SHEATH PILCHER
SCABBARD FISH HIKU
SCABBLE SCAB SCALP
SCABBY MANGY SCALD ROINISH SCABIOUS
SCABIES ITCH SCAB PSORA
SCABIOSA KNAUTIA
SCABIOUS SCABIA BLUECAP BUNDWEED PREMORSE
SCABROUS ROUGH SULTRY ASPEROUS
SCAD COIN AKULE XUREL DOLLAR GOGGLER QUIAQUIA
(PL.) ALOT LOTS TONS
SCAFFOLD CAGE PEGMA STAGE BRIDGE GANTRY CATASTA HAYLOFT STAGING HOARDING
(MOVABLE —) GANTRY
SCAFFOLDING DOCK STAGING
SCALARE ANGELFISH
SCALAWAG SCAMP
SCALD BURN LEEP PLOT SCAD BLAST PLOUT SCAUD BLANCH SCALDER AMBUSTION
SCALDFISH MEGRIM
SCALE PIP LEAF PELA PILL STEP TAPE CLIMB FLAKE GAMUT GENUS GULAR MOUNT PALEA PELOG PELOK PELTA POISE SCUTE SHALE SHARD SHELL SHERD SHIVE TRUNK ASCEND CAUDAL CINDER COCCID FORNIX GUNTER IMBREX KELVIN LABIAL LADDER LAMINA LIGULE LOREAL MENTAL NUCHAL OCULAR PERULE RAMENT RONDLE RUSTRE SHIELD SQUAMA STRIGA BALANCE CLINKER ELYTRON FRONTAL FULCRUM HUMERAL LATERAL NUCHALE REAUMUR ROSTRUM VENTRAL VERNIER ANALEMMA BRACHIAL INDUSIUM LECANIUM LODICULE MEALYBUG ODOPHONE RAMENTUM SCRAMBLE SQUAMULE TEMPORAL UROSTEGE
(— DOWN) DEGRADE
(— OF CORNSTALK) SHIVE
(— OF 7 TONES) SEPTAVE
(— ON BUTTERFLY) PLUMULE
(— ON MOTH) PATAGIUM
(— USED BY TAILORS) LOG
(GRADUATED —) RETE
(GREAT —) GAMUT
(KIND OF —) BRIX MOHS RICHTER
(SHAD —) CENIZO
(PL.) CHAFF DANDER
(PREF.) LEPID(O) LEPO PHOLID(O) SQUAM(ATO)(ELLI)(I)(O)(OSO)(ULI)
(MUSICAL —) CHORD(O)
(SUFF.) LEPIS PHOLIS
SCALEBOARD SCABBARD
SCALEPAN BASIN
SCALER CULLER SOOTER
SCALES TRON TRONE BALANCE
SCALETAIL SQUIRREL
SCALLION PORRET
SCALLOP DAG CLAM GIMP MUSH CRENA QUEEN SQUIN PECTEN COQUILLE DOUGHBOY ESCALLOP PECTINID
SCALLOPED INVECTED
(SUFF.) CRENATE
SCALP SCAUP SKELP ATTIRE
SCALPEL BISTOURY
SCALPER PUNTER
SCALY SCABBY SQUAMY LEPROSE PALEATE LEPIDOTE SCABROUS SQUAMOSE
SCALY ANTEATER PANGOLIN
SCAM DUPE BUNCO BUNKO CHEAT STING BAMBOOZLE
SCAMP IMP LAD RIP LIMB SLIM ROGUE SKEMP SKIMP THIEF BOOGER BUGGER FRIPON NICKUM RASCAL SINNER SORREL SORROW URCHIN HALLION HESSIAN PEASANT RAMMACK SKELLUM SLUBBER SNOOZER BLIGHTER SCALAWAG SLYBOOTS SPALPEEN VAGABOND WIDDIFOW SCALLYWAG
SCAMPER DASH LAMP CHEVY SCOUP SCOUR CHIVVY BRATTLE SKITHER SKITTER
SCAN PIPE GLASS METER DEVISE SURVEY EXAMINE
(KIND OF —) CAT
SCANDAL GUP CLASH CRACK ECLAT SHAME CALUMNY OFFENSE SCANMAG SLANDER NANNYGATE WATERGATE
SCANDALIZE SHOCK
SCANDALMONGER CLAT
SCANDALOUS UNHOLY SHAMEFUL
SCANDINAVIAN DANE LAPP NORSE SWEDE VIKING LOCHLIN NORSEMAN NORTHMAN SCANDIAN VARANGIAN
(PL.) OSTMEN
SCANT SHY JIMP LEAN MEET POOR THIN SCAMP SHORT SKIMP SPLAY

BARISH GEASON LITTLE MEAGER MEAGRE SCANTY SKINNY STINGY STINTY SLENDER SCRATCHY
(PREF.) OLIG(O)
SCANTILY BARELY FEEBLY SMALLY SCANTLY SPARSELY
SCANTINESS PENURY PARCITY EXIGUITY SPARSITY
SCANTLING STUD FILET JOIST FILLET BOLSTER RIBBAND STUDDING
SCANTY BARE JIMP LANK LEAN POOR SLIM EXILE GNEDE SCANT SHORT SILLY SKIMP SPARE FRUGAL MEAGER MEASLY SCRIMP SKIMPY SLIGHT SPARSE SCRANNY SCRIMPY SLENDER SPARING EXIGUOUS PENURIOUS
SCAPEGOAT PATSY STOOGE FALLGUY
SCAPEGRACE LIMB RASCAL SCALLYWAG SKAINSMATE
SCAPHOID NAVICULAR
SCAPOLITE DIPYRE
SCAPULA BLADE OMOPLATE SPADEBONE
SCAPULAR CUCULLA
SCAR ARR EYE WEM SEAM SEAR WIPE CHALK FESTER KELOID RADDLE STIGMA TRENCH CHELOID SCARIFY CICATRIX SMALLPOX CICATRICE
(— ON SAWED STONE) STUN
(— ON SEED) HILUM
(— ON TREE) CATFACE
SCARAB ATEUCHUS
SCARCE DEAR RARE THIN SLACK DAINTY GEASON CLASSIC UNCOMMON
(PREF.) SPAN(I)(O)
SCARCELY ILL VIX JIMP SCANT BARELY HARDLY MERELY ONETHE SCARCE SCRIMP WENETH SCANTLY UNEATHS UNNETHE
SCARCITY LACK WANT FAULT SCANT DEARTH FAMINE RARITY PAUCITY
SCARE COW BOOF BREE FAZE FEAR FLEG FLIG FRAY GAST HUSH SHOO ALARM APPAL GALLY GLIFF GLOFF PSYCH SPOOK AFFRAY FRIGHT GASTER PSYCHE SCARIFY STARTLE TERRIFY AFFRIGHT FRIGHTEN
(— BIRDS) KEEP
(— OFF) SCAT
(— WORD) BOO
SCARECROW BOGLE BUCCA MOGGY SEWEL BOGGLE DUDMAN MALKIN MAUMET MAWKIN SCARER SHEWEL BOGGART BUGABOO DEADMAN HODMADOD SHAWFOWL
SCARED SCART SCARY AFRAID GOOSEY STREAKED
SCAREMONGER ALARMIST
SCARF BARB HOOD SASH ABNET ASCOT BARBE CLOUD CYMAR FICHU LUNGI NUBIA PAGRI SHADE STOCK STOLE TABLE THROW CRAVAT PEPLOS REBOZO SCREEN SQUARE TAPALO TIPPET UPARNA BURDASH DOPATTA FOULARD MANIPLE MUFFLER NECKTIE ORARIUM OVERLAY PUGGREE SAUTOIR TALLITH CLAUDENT COINTISE DOOPUTTY LIRIPIPE LIRIPOOP MANTILLA MUFFETEE SLENDANG
(— AROUND HAT) PAGRI PUGGERY PUGGREE PUGGAREE
(— ON BISHOP'S STAFF) ORARION ORARIUM VEXILLUM
(— ON KNIGHT'S HELMET) COINTISE
(ARABIAN —) CABAAN
(FEATHER —) BOA
(PRAYER —) TALLIS TALLITH
SCARFING GRAFTING
SCARIFY LIFT
SCARLET LAC RED PINK TULY GRAIN KERMES
SCARLET HAW HAWTHORN
SCARLET IBIS GUARA
SCARLET LETTER (AUTHOR OF —) HAWTHORNE
(CHARACTER IN —) PEARL ROGER ARTHUR HESTER PRYNNE BELLINGHAM DIMMESDALE CHILLINGWORTH
SCARLET LYCHNIS FIREBALL NONESUCH
SCARLETT (LOVE OF —) RHETT
SCARLET TANAGER REDBIRD FIREBIRD
SCARLIKE ULOID
SCARP CLIFF SCARF ESCARP SCARPLET
SCARY EERIE SPOOKY ALARMING FEARSOME TERRIFYING
SCAT (— SINGER) ELLA
SCATHING MORDANT SCALDING
SCATHINGLY ROUNDLY
SCATOLOGICAL BARNYARD
SCATTER DAD SOW TED FLEE ROUT SALT SCAT SEED SHED SPEW VOID FLING SCALE SCHAL SEVER SHAKE SKAIL SPRAY STREW STROW DISPEL PEPPER SHOWER SKIVER SPARGE SPARSE SPREAD SPRENG WINNOW DIFFUSE DISBAND DISJECT FRITTER RESOLVE SCAMBLE SHATTER SKINKLE SKITTER SLATTER SPARKLE SPARPLE SPATTER SWATTER DISPERSE INTERSOW SEPARATE SPLUTTER SPRINKLE SQUANDER SQUATTER
(— BAIT FOR FISH) TOLE TOLL
(— CARELESSLY) LITTER
(— INK) SPLUTTER
(— OVER) BESTREW
(— WATER) SPLASH
SCATTERED LAX OPEN STRAY DAIMEN SPARSE DIFFUSE SPOTTED BESPRENT FUGITIVE SPARSILE
(PREF.) LAXI
SCATTERING SOWING DIASPORA SCATTERY
SCATTERSHOT SHOTGUN
SCAUP DUCK DOGS DIVER DUCKER DUNBIRD POCHARD BLUEBILL GRAYBACK SHUFFLER
SCAVAGE SCEWING
SCAVENGE CLEANSE GARBAGE
SCAVENGER BUNGY RAKER BHANGI BHUNGI MEHTAR REMOVER SCAFFIE CORYDORA HALALCOR RAMSHORN
SCAZON CHOLIAMB
SCEAT SKEAT STYCA
SCENARIO SCRIPT CONTINUITY
SCENE JOG SET CODA CYKE FLAT SITE TODO VIEW ARENA STAGE BRIDGE LOCALE VISION EPISODE PAGEANT TABLEAU COULISSE EXTERIOR INTERIOR PROSPECT TABLETOP
(— IN OPERA) SCENA
(— OF ACTION) STAGE
(— OF ACTIVITY) BEEHIVE
(— OF CONFUSION) BABEL BEDLAM
(— OF HOSTILITIES) FRONT
(CLOSING —) FINALE
(FILM —) FLASHBACK
(FINAL —) CURTAIN EPILOGUE
(INTRODUCTORY —) INDUCTION
(NIGHT —) NOCTURNE
SCENERY DROP FLAT DECOR CUTOUT NATURE IMAGERY PROFILE
(— CHANGER) TRIP
(PIECE OF —) MASKING
SCENESHIFTER GRIP
SCENT AIR DRAG NOSE ODOR VENT WIND CIVET FAULT FLAIR FUMET RELES SAVOR SMACK SMELL SNIFF SNUFF SPOOR TASTE CHYPRE ESSENCE INCENSE NOSEGAY ODORIZE VERDURE FUMIGATE MARECHAL PASTILLE REDOLENCE
(— OF ANIMAL FOLLOWED BY HOUNDS) FEUTE
(— OF COOKING) NIDOR
(— OF FOX) DRAG
(— OF GAME) FUMET FUMETTE
(— OUT) SMOKE
(FALSE —) RIOT
(LOST —) FAULT
SCENTED OLENT ODORATE PERFUMY ESSENCED
SCEPTER ROD WAND VERGE BAUBLE CEPTER FERULA WARDER
SCHEDULE BOOK CARD HOLD LIST SKED TIME PANEL SCRIP SCROW SETUP SLATE TABLE SCROLL CATALOG TABLEAU CALENDAR REGISTER
(— OF COURT CASES) DOCKET
(— OF DUTIES) TARIFF
(— OF GAMES) SEASON
(TELEVISION —) LINEUP
SCHEDULED DUE
SCHEDULING (TECHNIQUE FOR —) PERT
SCHEELITE TUNGSTEN
SCHEHERAZADE (HUSBAND OF —) SCHAHRIAH
(SISTER OF —) DINARZADE
SCHEMA FORM
SCHEMATIC PLAN
SCHEME AIM GIN LAY WAY WEB CAST DART GAME PLAN PLAT PLOT REDE SWIM ANGLE BABEL CADRE DODGE DRAFT DRIFT KNACK PINAX REACH SCALE SETUP SHIFT TABLE THINK TRAIN BRIGUE BUBBLE CIPHER DESIGN DEVICE DEVISE FIGURE HOOKUP POLICY SCHEMA SYSTEM TAMPER THEORY UTOPIA BUSTOUT COUNSEL DRAUGHT GIMMICK IMAGINE KNAVERY NOSTRUM PROJECT PURPOSE CONSPIRE CONTRIVE FORECAST GIMCRACK IDEOLOGY INTRIGUE MANEUVER PLATFORM PRACTICE TRIPOTER WINDMILL MACHINATE
(— FOR PEACE) IRENICON EIRENICON
(— OF ANCESTRY) PEDIGREE
(— OF RANK) LADDER
(ABORTIVE —) SOOTERKIN
(BETTING —) SYSTEM
(CONFIDENCE —) BUSTOUT
(DECEITFUL —) SHIFT
(DELUSIVE —) BUBBLE
(DIAGRAMMATIC —) PINAX
(FANCIFUL —) WINDMILL
(FAVORITE —) NOSTRUM
(KIND OF —) PONZI
(VERSIFICATION —) METER METRE
(VISIONARY —) BABEL
SCHEMER ARTIST DESIGNER ENGINEER SCHEMIST SLEEVEEN
SCHEMING SCHEMY PLANFUL SPIDERY FETCHING PRACTICE
SCHISM RENT DISUNITY SCISSION SCISSURE
SCHISMATIC HERETIC
SCHIST RAG AMPELITE MICACITE MYLONITE OLLENITE PHYLLITE
SCHIZONT MONONT AGAMONT
SCHIZOPHRENIA CATATONY
SCHLEP LUG
SCHMO JERK
SCHMOOZE CHAT
SCHNAPPER WOLLOMAI
SCHNOZZLE NOSE
SCHOLAR TUG DEMY GAON IMAM CLERK PUPIL DIVINE DOCTOR FELLOW JURIST LAMDEN MASTER PANDIT SABORA SAVANT SCOLOG SHEIKH BIBLIST BOOKMAN DANTIST LATINER LEARNER MAULANA STUDENT BOURSIER DISCIPLE HEBRAEAN HUMANIST ISLAMIST MASORITE TABERDAR THAUMASTE PHILOSOPHER
(— OF QUEENS COLLEGE) TABERDAR
(FOUNDATION —) BOURSIER
(MOSLEM —) ULAMA ULEMA
(PL.) CLERISY LITERATI
AMERICAN LEWIS LOWES POUND BLYDEN CONANT GENUNG KELSEY MILLER NEWELL RIDDLE SARTON BABBITT GUMMERE SEYMOUR GOLDMANN HAMILTON HARKNESS PERCIVAL ROBINSON STERRETT LOUNSBURY
AUSTRIAN SPANN
CANADIAN MACMECHAN
CHINESE YEN
CZECH JIRACEK SAFARIK
DANISH MADVIG GULDBERG
DUTCH COBET BURMAN ERASMUS GROTIUS COORNHERT BILDERDIJK
ENGLISH KER LEE BEDE BYNG LONG BYRON CROFT ELYOT JAMES LEWIS LOWTH MAYOR PALEY ROGET ROWSE YOUNG ALCUIN ALFORD BAXTER BODLEY BRIGHT BROOME

BUTLER COWELL DASENT FARMER GARROD GODLEY GROCYN HARRIS JEVONS MURRAY NECKAM NEWMAN NICOLL YAHUDA ALDHELM ALDRICH BAINTON BUTCHER COGHILL DIODATI DUGDALE HOLLAND HOUSMAN LIDDELL MACKAIL STANLEY CHRISTIE GRIERSON HARRISON MCKERROW PATTISON STRACHAN TUNSTALL TYRWHITT CONINGTON NETTLESHIP
FINNISH LONNROT PORTHAN KOSKENNIEMI
FLEMISH BLOMMAERT
FRENCH BUDE LAMY LUCE AMYOT MAURY PARIS RASHI BAILLY BERARD GAGUIN MAGNIN MENAGE MICHEL BROSSES CAUMONT CHASLES DELISLE LEFRANC LONGNON SOURIAU DEMOGEOT ESTIENNE JAUCOURT BONAPARTE SCALIGER BARTHELEMY TAILLANDIER
GERMAN DIEZ BLEEK HEYNE KLOTZ KROLL LEYEN STAHR FROBEN KOCHLY RAUMER CONRING GOEDEKE GOLTHER HEUSLER LUDWICH MOMMSEN RIBBECK RUHNKEN WILHELM AUFRECHT BERNEKER BUTTMANN HAINISCH PFEIFFER SPANHEIM WEINHOLD KOSCHWITZ CAMERARIUS
GREEK DION GAZA CORAY PALLES DIDYMUS MUSURUS RHIANUS PORPHYRY ATHENAEUS CAECILIUS EUPHORION ZENODOTUS CALLIMACHUS CHRYSOLORAS ERATOSTHENES
HUNGARIAN BEL
ICELANDIC BLONDAL SAEMUND VIGFUSSON
INDIAN PATANJALI
IRISH BALL BUTLER TRENCH MAHAFFY KEIGHTLEY
ITALIAN DONI PRAZ ZENO GNOLI MAFFEI VARCHI ALEANDRO MANUTIUS MARTELLI ROSSETTI MARSILIUS NICCOLINI TIRABOSCHI
JAPANESE NITOBE MABUCHI
MEXICAN GAMA
PERUVIAN MENDIBURU
POLISH CIOLEK CHODZKO RACZYNSKI OSSOLINSKI ZDZIECHOWSKI
PORTUGUESE BRAGA
ROMAN PLINY VARRO AUSONIUS CENSORINUS
RUSSIAN LAVROV CHUKOVSKY LOMONOSOV DRAGOMANOV MANDELSTAM
SCOTTISH LANG BLACKIE GROSART LINDSAY CRICHTON BELLENDEN MACDONALD
SPANISH CARO OCHOA CASTRO VILLENA
SWEDISH MALMSTROM STIERNHIELM
SWISS BODMER BREITINGER PELLICANUS

SCHOLARLY CLERKLY ERUDITE LEARNED ACADEMIC

SCHOLARSHIP ART BOOK BURSE BURSARY DEMYSHIP LEARNING

SCHOLASTIC PEDANTIC

SCHOOL GAM TOL EDDY PREP AGGIE BOOKS ECOLE HEDER LYCEE NYAYA SAKHA TEACH TRADE TRAIN TUTOR ALJAMA CAMPUS CHEDER CHURCH KUTTAB KYAUNG MADHAB MALIKI RABFAK SCHOLA SCHULE SQUEEL TRIPOS ACADEME ACADEMY CRAMMER MADRASA PENSION STUDIUM YESHIVA AUDITORY DOCUMENT EXERCISE EXTERNAT PEDAGOGY SEMINARY
(— FOR JUDO OR KARATE) DOJO
(— FOR SINGERS) MAITRISE
(— OF BLACKFISH) GRIND
(— OF BUDDHISM) CHAN RITSU DHYANA SANRON
(— OF FISH) HERD SCALE SCULL
(— OF HINDU PHILOSOPHY) NYAYA
(— OF OPINION) SECT
(— OF PAINTING) GENRE
(— OF PHILOSOPHY) SECT ACADEMY AUDITORY
(— OF VEDA) SAKHA SHAKHA
(— OF WHALES) GAM POD
(ART —) BAUHAUS LUMINISM
(AZTEC —) CALMECAC
(COMPARATIVE —) FOLKLORE
(DAY —) EXTERNAT
(ELEMENTARY —) GRADES
(HIGH —) HIGH ACADEMY COLLEGE
(KIND OF —) MAGNET
(MARTIAL ARTS —) DOJO
(MOSLEM —) HANAFI KUTTAB SHAFII HANBALI
(PAINTING —) ASHCAN
(REFORM —) BORSTAL
(RELIGIOUS —) ALJAMA YESHIVA
(RIDING —) MANEGE
(SANSKRIT —) TOL
(SCOTCH —) SQUEEL
(SECONDARY —) LYCEE LYCEUM COLEGIO
(WRESTLING —) PALESTRA

SCHOOLBOOK COCKER

SCHOOLBOY SCUG PETTY CLERGION

SCHOOL FOR SCANDAL (AUTHOR OF —) SHERIDAN
(CHARACTER IN —) MARIA MOSES PETER JOSEPH OLIVER ROWLEY TEAZLE CANDOUR CHARLES PREMIUM SURFACE SNEERWELL

SCHOOLHOUSE PORTABLE

SCHOOLING LEARNING

SCHOOLMASTER BEAK CAJI CAXI AKHUN KHOJA KHODJA MASTER PEDANT AKHOOND DOMINIE PEDAGOG ORBILIUS

SCHOOLROOM HOMEROOM

SCHOOL SHARK TOPE TOPER

SCHOOLWORK BOOKWORK

SCHOONER JACK TERN QUART QUINT WUINT PUNGEY BALLAHOO

SCHORL COCKLE

SCHRADAN OMPA

SCHROTHER SHREDDER

SCHUSSBOOMER SKIER

SCHUYT SHOE SCOUT EELBOAT

SCIATICA BONESHAW

SCIENCE ART OLOGY SOPHY MATHESIS SCIENTIA
(— OF ALGAE) ALGOLOGY
(— OF ANIMALS) ZOOLOGY
(— OF AQUEOUS VAPOR) ATMOLOGY
(— OF ARTILLERY) PYROBALLOGY
(— OF ATOMS) ATOMICS
(— OF BEING OR REALITY) ONTOLOGY
(— OF BIOLOGICAL STATISTICS) BIOMETRY
(— OF BREEDING) GENETICS
(— OF CAUSES) ETIOLOGY
(— OF CHARACTER) ETHOLOGY
(— OF CLASSIFICATION) SYSTEMATICS
(— OF CLASSIFICATION OF DISEASES) NOSOLOGY
(— OF COLORS) CHROMATICS
(— OF DISEASES) NOSOLOGY
(— OF DOSES) DOSOLOGY POSOLOGY
(— OF DUTY) DEONTICS DEONTOLOGY
(— OF EARTH'S FORMATION) GEOGONY
(— OF EARTH MEASUREMENTS) GEODESY
(— OF ELECTIONS) PSEPHOLOGY
(— OF ENVIRONMENT) ECOLOGY
(— OF ETHICS) DEONTICS DEONTOLOGY
(— OF EXCHANGE) CAMBISTRY
(— OF FERMENTATION) ZYMOLOGY
(— OF FERNS) PTERIDOLOGY
(— OF FLOW OF MATTER) RHEOLOGY
(— OF FOOTPRINTS) ICHNOLOGY
(— OF FORMS OF SPEECH) GRAMMAR
(— OF FRUIT GROWING) POMOLOGY
(— OF FUNDS MANAGEMENT) FINANCE
(— OF GEMS) GEMMARY GEMOLOGY
(— OF GOD) DIVINITY
(— OF GOVERNMENT) POLITICS
(— OF HEALTH MAINTENANCE) HYGIENE
(— OF HEAT) PYROLOGY THERMOTICS
(— OF HISTORY OF EARTH) GEOLOGY
(— OF HUMAN BODY) SEMATOLOGY
(— OF HUMAN SETTLEMENTS) EKISTICS
(— OF IDEAS) IDEOLOGY
(— OF IMAGINARY SOLUTIONS) PATAPHYSICS
(— OF INSECTS) ENTOMOLOGY
(— OF INTELLECT) NOOLOGY
(— OF INTERPRETATION) HERMENEUTICS
(— OF LANGUAGE) GRAMMAR PHILOLOGY
(— OF LAW) NOMOLOGY
(— OF LIFE) BIOLOGY
(— OF LIFE INFLUENCES) EUGENICS
(— OF LIFE OF TREES) SILVICS
(— OF LIGHT) OPTICS
(— OF LYING) PSEUDOLOGY
(— OF MEANING) SIGNIFICS
(— OF MEASURING TIME) HOROLOGY
(— OF MEDIEVAL CHEMISTRY) ALCHEMY
(— OF MIDWIFERY) TOKOLOGY
(— OF MIND) PSYCHOLOGY
(— OF MOLLUSCS) MALACOLOGY
(— OF MORAL DUTY) ETHICS
(— OF MOSSES) BRYOLOGY
(— OF MOTION) DYNAMICS
(— OF MOUNTAINS) OROLOGY
(— OF MUSCLES) MYOLOGY
(— OF NAVIGATION) NAUTICS
(— OF NUMBERS COMBINATIONS) ALGEBRA
(— OF PERSUADING A GOD) THEURGY
(— OF PLANTS) BOTANY
(— OF QUANTITY) POSOLOGY
(— OF RACIAL IMPROVEMENT) EUGENICS
(— OF REASONING) LOGIC
(— OF RECORDING GENEALOGIES) HERALDRY
(— OF REFRIGERATION) CRYOLOGY
(— OF REMEDIES) ACOLOGY
(— OF RIVERS) POTAMOLOGY
(— OF ROCKS) LITHOLOGY
(— OF SEA) THALASSOGRAPHY
(— OF SERUMS) SEROLOGY
(— OF SMELLS) OSMICS
(— OF SOILS) PEDOLOGY
(— OF SOUND) PHONICS ACOUSTICS
(— OF SPATIAL MAGNITUDES) GEOMETRY
(— OF STRUCTURE OF ANIMALS) ANATOMY
(— OF SUBSTANCES) CHEMISTRY
(— OF SUN) HELIOLOGY
(— OF SYMPTOMS) SEMEIOLOGY
(— OF TEACHING) PEDAGOGY
(— OF TEACHING ADULTS) ANDRAGOGY
(— OF THE EAR) OTOLOGY
(— OF TIDES) TIDOLOGY
(— OF TOUCH DATA) HAPTICS
(— OF VALUES) AXIOLOGY
(— OF VERSIFICATION) PROSODY
(— OF VIRTUE) ARETAICS
(— OF WEIGHT OR GRAVITY) BAROLOGY
(— OF WINES) ENOLOGY OENOLOGY
(— OF WORD MEANINGS) SEMANTICS
(BRANCH OF —) BIONICS
(ESOTERIC —) HERMETICS
(KIND OF —) LIFE
(LEGAL —) LAW
(MILITARY —) STRATEGY
(NATURAL —) STINKS PHYSICS
(PHYSICAL —) PHILOSOPHY
(RELIGIOUS —) THEOLOGY
(SUFF.) LOGER LOGIA(N) LOGIC(AL) LOGIST LOGUE LOGY OLOGY SOPH(ER)(IC)(IST)(Y)
(RELATING TO —) METRIC

SCIENTIST BOFFIN
(KIND OF RUSSIAN —) REFUSNIK REFUSENIK

SCIMITAR SAX SEAX TURK KHEPESH TULWAUR
SCINDAPSUS POTHOS
SCINTILLA ATOM
SCINTILLATE SNAP FLASH GLEAM GLANCE GLITTER SPARKLE TWINKLE
SCINTILLATION SPARKLE SPARKLET
SCION IMP ROD CION CYON HEIR ROOT SLIP GRAFT SPRIG BRANCH SPROUT SARMENT SETLING
SCISSORS SHEARS CLIPPER SECATEUR
(PREF.) FORFICI
SCLERITE TORMA LABIUM PLANTA PLAGULA AXILLARY EPIMERON
SCLERODERMA MORPHEA
SCLEROPROTEIN SPONGIN
SCLEROTIUM ERGOT SCLEROTE TUCKAHOE
SCOFF DOR GAB GALL GECK GIBE GIRD JEER JIBE MOCK RAIL CURSE FLEER FLOUT GLEEK SCARF SCORN SCOUT SNEER TAUNT DERIDE REPROVE RIDICULE
SCOFFER MOCKER ABDERITE
SCOLD JAW MAG MOB NAG RAG ROW WIG YAP BAWL CALL CAMP CANT DING FLAY FRAB FUSS HAZE JACK JOBE JOWL JUMP RAIL RANT RATE REDD RICK SHAW SNAG SNUB TUCK YAFF ABUSE BARGE BASTE BOAST CHIDE DRESS FLIRT FLITE PRATE RANDY SCALD SCORE SHORE SHREW SLANG STORM TARGE VIXEN BERATE BOUNCE CALLET CAMPLE CARPET HAMMER HOORAY HURRAH MAGPIE RATTLE REHETE REVILE TATTER THREAP TONGUE YAFFLE YANKIE CHANNER CHEWOUT REPROVE TRIMMER TROUNCE UPBRAID BALLYRAG BERATTLE BETONGUE CHASTISE CIDESTER DINGDONG RIXATRIX CLAPPERCLAW
SCOLDING JAW HURL JESSE SCOLD DIRDUM JAWING RAKING RATTLE SISERA FLITING HEARING LECTURE RAGGING WIGGING BLESSING CARRITCH JOBATION
SCOLEX HEAD
SCOLYTUS IPS
SCONCE SWAPE APPLIQUE
SCONE FARL FARLE
SCOOP BAIL BALE DRAG INFO ROUT DIDLE GOUGE KEACH SHAUL SKEET BUCKET DIPPER DISHER SHOVEL WIMBLE SCRAPER SCUPPET SKIMMER SKIPPET SCOOPFUL
(— FOR CANNON) LADLE
(— FOR DAMPENING CANVAS) SKEET
(— FOR GRAIN) WECHT
(— UP) LAP LAVE GATHER
(— WITH TONGUE) LAP
(CHEESE —) PALE
(GLASSMAKING —) PADDLE
(JAI ALAI —) CHISTERA
(LONG-HANDLED —) DIDLE
(SURGICAL —) CURET CURETTE
SCOOT ZIP DART SCOUT SKEET SKYHOOT
SCOPE AIM AREA AMBIT POWER RANGE REACH ROUND SCALE SCOOP SWEEP VERGE SCOUTH SPHERE TETHER BREADTH CIRCUIT COMPASS OPERAND PURVIEW CONFINES DIAPASON LATITUDE
(— OF VISION) COMMAND
(FREE —) SWING
SCOPOLINE OSCIN OSCINE
SCORBUTUS SCURVY
SCORCH BURN CHAR PLOT SCAM SEAR ADURE ADUST BROIL PARCH PLAUT REESE SCALD SCAUM SINGE SWEAL SWELT BIRSLE BISHOP DEGREE SMITCH SOTTER SPARCH SWINGE SWITHE BLISTER BRISTLE FRIZZLE SCORKLE SCOWDER SWITHEN SWITHER TORRIFY FIREFANG SCOUTHER SCOWTHER
SCORCHED ADUST LEEPIT
SCORCHER SIZZLER
(PREF.) SIRI(O)
SCORCHING BAKING FIRING ADURENT SCALDING
SCORE ACE CUT LAW RIT RUN CARD DEBT DROP GAME GOAL HAIL HOLE MAKE MARK NICK POST RIDE SLOG CHART CHASE CORGE COUNT EXTRA NOTCH OPERA TALLY COOREE FURROW SAFETY SCOTCH SCRIVE SPADES STRING TARGET TICKET TWENTY CONVERT SCORING SCRATCH SQUEEZE GAMEBALL PARTITUR PLACEKICK
(— FOR ALE) ALESHOT
(— HEAVILY AGAINST) SHELL
(— IN BRIDGE) BOARD BONUS SWING
(— IN CRIBBAGE) GO PEG FIFTEEN
(— IN CRICKET) BLOB CENTURY
(— IN PIQUET) CAPOT REPIQUE
(— IN RUGBY) TRY
(— OF NOTHING) DUCK
(— OF 100) TON
(APTITUDE —) STANINE
(BASKETBALL —) HOOP
(BILLIARDS —) STRING
(BOWLING —) PINFALL
(GOLF —) ACE PAR BOGEY DEUCE EAGLE BIRDIE BUZZARD
(INDEX —) APGAR
(KIND OF —) APGAR
(NO —) LOVE
(ORIGINAL MUSICAL —) URTEXT
(PINOCHLE —) LAST
(TENNIS —) CALL FIVE LOVE DEUCE FORTY FIFTEEN
(THREE —) SHOCK SIXTY
(TIE —) HALVE DEADLOCK
(ZERO —) GOOSEEGG
(PL.) MUSIC
SCORED SULCATE SULCATED
SCOREKEEPER SCORER TALLIER TALLYMAN
SCORER NIB MARKER NOTCHER
SCORIA SCUM SLAG CINDER SULLAGE
SCORIFIER CAPSULE
SCORIFY SMELT
SCORN GECK LOUT HOKER SCARN SPURN BISMER SLIGHT CONTEMN DESPISE DESPITE DISDAIN CONTEMPT DERISION MISPRIZE
SCORNFUL SAUCY SCORNY SNIFFY SNIFTY HAUGHTY FRUMPISH INSOLENT SARDONIC
SCORNFULLY ASKEW ASWASH
SCORPION NEPA ALACRAN STINGER UROPYGI ARACHNID PEDIPALP WHIPTAIL
SCORPION FISH LAPON SERRAN HOGFISH SCULPIN LORICATE RASCACIO
SCORPION FLY PANORPID
SCOT (ALSO SEE SCOTSMAN) CELT JOCK KELT SANDY SAXON SCOTTY BLUECAP SCOTSMAN
(PL.) SAWNY SAWNEY LALLANS
SCOTCH TRIG SCOAT SCOTS SCOTTISH
SCOTCHMAN MAC GAUL SANDY TARTAN SCOTCHY SCOTTIE SCOTSMAN
SCOTER COOT FILK DIVER SCOUT WHILK BASQUE DUCKER SURFER PISHAUG SCOOTER SKUNKTOP
SCOTIA MOUTH
SCOTIST DUNCE
SCOTLAND ALBYN ALBANY ALBION SCOTIA ALBAINN ALBANIA
(NORTHERN —) PICTLAND

SCOTLAND

BAY: SCAPA
CAPITAL: EDINBURGH
COIN: DEMY BODLE GROAT PLACK RIDER BAWBEE
COUNTY: AYR BUTE FIFE ROSS ANGUS BANFF MORAY NAIRN PERTH ARGYLL LANARK ORKNEY BERWICK KINROSS PEEBLES RENFREW SELKIRK WIGTOWN ABERDEEN AYRSHIRE CROMARTY DUMFRIES ROXBURGH SHETLAND STERLING
FIRTH: LORN CLYDE FORTH MORAY SOLWAY PENTLAND
ISLAND: RUM BUTE IONA JURA MULL RHUM SKYE ARRAN BARRA ISLAY LEWIS HARRIS ORKNEY SHETLAND
ISLANDS: ORKNEY HEBRIDES SHETLAND
LAKE: TAY NESS MORAR LAGGAN LINNHE LOMOND KATRINE RANNOCH
LANGUAGE: ERSE LALLAN LALLAND
MEASURE: COP BOLL CRAN FALL MILE PECK PINT ROOD ROPE SPAN CRANE LIPPY FIRLOT AUCHLET CHALDER CHOPPIN MUTCHKIN STIMPART
MOUNTAIN: HOPE ATTOW DEARG NEVIS TINTO WYVIS CHEVIOT MACDHUI
NATIVE: GAEL PICT SCOT
ORDER: THISTLE
REGION: FIFE BORDERS GRAMPIAN
RESORT: OBAN
RIVER: AYR DEE DON ESK TAY DOON GLEN NITH NORN SPEY AFTON ANNAN CLYDE FORTH GARRY TWEED YTHAN AFFRIC TEVIOT TUMMEL DEVERON FINDHORN
SEAPORT: ALLOA LEITH DUNDEE ABERDEEN
TOWN: AYR DUNS OBAN WICK ALLOA BRORA CUPAR ELLON LEITH NAIRN PERTH SALEN TROON DUNDEE GIRVAN HAWICK DUNKELD GLASGOW PAISLEY ABERDEEN DUMFRIES GREENOCK KIRKWALL STIRLING
WATERFALL: GLOMACH
WEIGHT: BOLL DROP TRONE BUSHEL

SCOTSMAN SANDY SAWNY BLUECAP
SCOTTISH SCOTCH SCOTLAND
SCOTTISH TERRIER DIEHARD SCOTTIE VERMINER
SCOUNDREL RAP PIMP SCAB VILE WARY BLECK FILTH KNAVE SCAMP SHREW SMAIK SWEEP THIEF WHAUP BRIBER LIMMER SLOVEN VARLET CATAIAN GLUTTON HALLION NITHING SCROYLE SKELLUM VILIACO VILLAIN WARLOCK BEZONIAN LIDDERON MASCHANT
SCOUNDRELLY VILLAIN
SCOUR ASH BEAT COMB RAKE SCUM SEEK SIND SKIR SCOOR SCRUB SKIRR SWEEP DRENCH SCURRY SLUICE DEGRADE FURBISH BACKWASH STONEFILE
(PL.) SKIT
SCOURER BLOOMER DOLLIER PICKLER
SCOURGE EEL TAW LASH WHIP CURSE FLAIL KNOUT SLASH SWING BALEYS PLAGUE SWINGE SCORPION
SCOURGER WHIPSTER
SCOURING BEAT SCOUR HUSHING SCRUBBING
SCOUT SPY BEAR LION SKIP ROVER SPIAL VISOR ESPIAL GAYCAT DESPISE MARINER PICKEER PIONEER SCOURER WATCHER EMISSARY OUTRIDER OUTSCOUT SCURRIER SKIRMISH
(BOY —) CUB BOBCAT SCOUTER WEBELOS EXPLORER
(CUB — SUBDIVISION) DEN
(GIRL —) DAISY
SCOW ACCON FLOAT GARVEY
SCOWL LOUR FROWN GLARE GLOOM GLOUT LOWER SKIME GLOWER VENNER GLOOMING
SCOWLING FROWNY GLARING
SCRABBLE PAW RAKE GROPE CLAMBER SCRAMBLE
SCRAGGY WEEDY
SCRAM GIT HOP LAM BUNK SCAT BUGGER BUGOFF SODOFF BUZZOFF GETLOST
SCRAMBLE MUSS SPURL SCRAWM SPRAWL CLAMBER LOUSTER SCRABBLE SCRAFFLE SCRATTLE SPRACHLE
SCRAP BIT END JAG ORT PIP CRAP ITEM JAGG JUNK PICK SNAP BRAWL GRAIN PATCH SCRAN

SHRED THRUM WASTE FRACAS TUSSLE DISCARD MAMMOCK ODDMENT REMNANT SNIPPET FRACTION SCRAPPET SKERRICK SNATTOCK
(— FOR PATCHING) SPETCH
(— OF PAPER) SCRIP
(— OF SONG) CATCH
(— OF WRITING) SCRAPE
(FOOD —S) BROCK
(LEAST —) STITCH
(LITERARY —S) ANA
(METAL —) SCISSEL SCISSIL
(RAGGED —) SCART
(PL.) ORTS SCRAN RELICS SCROFF GARBAGE GUBBINGS

SCRAPE LEG RUB CLAW COMB RAZE CLAUT CURET ERADE ERODE GRATE GRAZE GRIDE SCALP SCART SCUFF SHAVE ABRADE HOBBLE RUGINE SCREED SCROOP SPLORE CORRADE CURETTE JACKPOT SCRATCH SNAPPER TROUBLE SCRABBLE
(— ALONG) HARL HARLE SHOOL
(— GOLF CLUB ON GROUND) SCLAFF
(— OFF) SPUD
(— OUT) ERASE HOLLOW
(— SKINS) MOON SCUD FLESH HARASS
(— TOGETHER) RAKE GLEAN MUCKER SCAMBLE
(— WITH FEET) SCAUT
(PREF.) RAMENTI SCAPI

SCRAPED BRIGHT

SCRAPER PAN PIG HARL SLIP CURET GLOVE HARLE QUIRL RASER SPOON DOCTOR FRESNO GRADER GRATER RASPER CURETTE FLANGER LEVELER RACLOIR SLUSHER STRIGIL GRATTOIR SCRAPPLE TERRACER UNHAIRER

SCRAPING HARL GRIDE RASURE
(CRACKER —S) CUSH
(METAL —S) DIET
(PL.) RAMENTA

SCRAPMAN CHIPMAN

SCRAPPER BREAKER FIGHTER

SCRAPPLE PANHAS PONHAWS

SCRAPPY BITTY SNATCHY

SCRATCH RAT RIT CLAW CRAB RACE RAIN RAKE RAPE RASE RAUK RAZE RISP RIST SHAB SLUG STUN CHALK CLAUT CLAWK CURRY FRUSH GRAZE RANCH SCART SCLUM SCORE SCRAB SCRAT SCROB SCRUB SHRUB SKELP TEASE TOUCH BRUISE CANCEL CRATCH RASURE RIPPLE SCORCH SCOTCH SCRAPE SCRAWK SCRAWL SCRAWM SCRAZE SCRIVE TORACE DECLARE EMERIZE EXPUNGE SCARIFY SCRABBLE SCRATTLE SCRIBBLE
(— OUT MORTAR) POINT
(PREF.) RAMENTI

SCRATCHER RASER

SCRAWL SCRAWM SPRAWL SCRATCH SCRABBLE SCRIBBLE SQUIGGLE

SCRAWNY BONY LEAN SLINK WEEDY SCRANK SCRAGGY SCRANKY SCRANNY SCRAGGED
(— PERSON OR ANIMAL) RIBE

SCREAM CRY YAW REME WEAK YARM YAUP YAWL YAWP YOWT SKIRL SHRAME SHRIEK SHRILL SQUALL SQUAWL YAMMER SCREECH YELLOCH SKELLOCH

SCREAMER CHAJA ANHIMA

SCREAMING MEEMIES JITTERS HYSTERIA

SCREECH QUAWK QUOCK SCREAM SCREEK SCRITCH SKREIGH ULULATE SKELLOCH

SCREECH OWL STRICH

SCREED BLAUD TIRADE HARANGUE

SCREEN TRY CAGE GOBO HARP HIDE LAWN MASK PICK REJA SCUG SEPT SIFT TENT VEIL ARRAS BLIND CHEEK CHICK CLOAK CLOSE COVER FIGHT GAUZE GRATE HOARD SHADE SHOJI SIEVE SPEER SPIER TATTY BAFFLE BASKET BORDER CANVAS DEFEND ESCORT HALLAN MEDIUM PURDAH RESEAU SCHERM SCONCE SHAKER SHIELD SHROUD THREAD VOIDER CEILING CONCEAL CRIBBLE CURTAIN FLYWIRE GOGGLES GRIZZLY REREDOS SECLUDE SHELTER SHUTTER TESTUDO TROMMEL BACKSTOP BESCREEN BLINDAGE COVERING DIFFUSER ECLIPSER EXCLUDER HOARDING OCCULTER PARAVENT PARCLOSE PAVISADE SCREENER SPLASHER STRAINER TRAVERSE UMBRELLA
(— ALONGSIDE SHIP) PAVISADE
(— BEHIND ALTAR) REREDOS
(— FOR BATTING PRACTICE) CAGE
(— FOR SHIP'S COMBATANTS) FIGHT
(— FOR SIZING ORE) GRATE TROMMEL
(— FOR THEATER LIGHT) JELLY MEDIUM
(— IN BASKETBALL) PICK
(— OF BAMBOO SLIPS) CHEEK CHICK
(— OF BRUSHWOOD) SCHERM
(— OF FIRE) BARRAGE
(— OF SHIELDS FOR TROOPS) TESTUDO
(— OF TAPESTRY) ARRAS CEILING
(— ON AUTOMOBILE) GRILL GRILLE
(— TO PROTECT LOOKOUTS) DODGER
(— USED BY ARCHERS) PANNIER
(BULLETPROOF —) MANTA MANTEL MANTELET
(CHANCEL —) JUBE
(FIRE —) FENDER
(KIND OF —) TOUCH
(MECHANICALLY ACTUATED —) GRIZZLY
(PAPER —) SHOJI
(PL.) CANCELLI

SCREENED BLIND SECLUDED

SCREENINGS CULM SLACK SLECK

SCREENLAND FILMDOM

SCREENPLAY SCRIPT SCENARIO

SCREW HOB VISE WORM CRICK FEEZE SCROW WREST TEMPER TOGGLE COCHLEA AIRSCREW FLATHEAD SETSCREW THUMBKIN WINDMILL
(KIND OF —) ALLEN MEANTIME
(PART OF —) HEAD ROOT CREST PITCH POINT SHANK THREAD
(PROPELLER —) FAN

SCREWBALL KOOK ZANY FLAKE ECCENTRIC NONSENSICAL

SCREW BEAN MESQUITE SCREWPOD TORNILLA

SCREWDRIVER (KIND OF —) PHILLIPS

SCREWED SQUINCH

SCREWER WORMER

SCREWMAN JACKMAN

SCREW PINE IE ARA HALA IEIE AGGAG PALMA VACOA VACONA LAUHALA PANDANUS

SCREW TREE TWISTY

SCRIBBLE SQUIB DOODLE SCRAWL SCRATCH REMARQUE SCRABBLE SQUIGGLE

SCRIBBLING GRAFFITO
(PL.) GRAFFITI

SCRIBE EZRA CLERK THOTH BOOKER PENMAN SCRIVE SOPHER WRITER GRAFFER MASORET SCRIVAN NOVERINT PENCLERK SCRIPTOR SCRIVANO
(PL.) SOPHERIM

SCRIMMAGE MAUL BULLY ROUGE SCRAP BICKER SPLORE SKIRMISH

SCRIMP HINCH SCREW SKIMP

SCRIP EXONUMIA

SCRIPT BOOK NEUM RONDE SERTA SERTO NASKHI NESKHI SCRITE SOOLOOS THULUTH BASTARDA GURMUKHI HIRAGANA KANARESE MAGHRIBI MAITHILI MEROITIC NASTALIQ SCENARIO
(HINDI —) DEVANAGARI
(KOREAN ALPHABETIC —) HANGUL
(TYPE OF —) RONDE

SCRIPTURE WRIT AGAMA CHING SUTRA SUTTA TANTRA
(HINDU —) VEDA
(PL.) BIBLE GRANTH GRUNTH TANACH TENACH SHASTRA

SCRIVENER PENMAN WRITER GRAFFER SCRIVER NOVERINT TABELLION

SCROFULA EVIL CRUELS STRUMA

SCROLL BEND ROLL LABEL SCRIT AMULET ESCROL LEGEND SCRAWL STEMMA VOLUME VOLUTE EVOLUTE PAPYRUS RINCEAU BANDEROL CARTOUCH MAKIMONO
(— AT END OF HANDRAIL) MONKEYTAIL
(— AT MOUTH OF FIGURE) PHYLACTERY

SCROLL-LIKE TURBINAL

SCROPHULARIA FIGWORT

SCROTUM BAG COD PURSE
(PREF.) OSCHE(O) SCROT(I)(O)

SCROUNGER SCAMBLER

SCRUB FILE ABORT SCOUR SCROG CANCEL COPPET MAQUIS SCODGY CLEANSE SCRUBBER YANNIGAN

SCRUBBY SHRUBBY

SCRUBLAND GARIGUE GARRIGUE

SCRUFF CUFF NAPE SCUFF SCROFF

SCRUFFY DOGEARED

SCRUPLE PASS DEMUR DOUBT FORCE POINT QUALM STAND STICK BOGGLE SCOTCH STRAIN STICKLE STUMBLE

SCRUPULOUS NICE SPICED TENDER CAREFUL FINICKY PRECISE DELICATE QUALMISH

SCRUTINIZE EYE PRY SEE SPY SCAN VIEW AUDIT PROBE SIGHT SOUND VISIT PERUSE SURVEY EXAMINE INSPECT ENSEARCH TRAVERSE

SCRUTINIZING NARROW SCANNING

SCRUTINY EYE SEARCH CANVASS EXAMINE HAWKEYE PERUSAL DOCIMASY
(ELECTION —) CANVAS CANVASS

SCRYER SEER

SCUD RUN RACK RAMP SKID SKIM SKIP SCOOT SPOON

SCUDAMORE (LOVER OF —) AMORETTA

SCUDO FILIPPO

SCUFF SLARE SLIDE SCLAFF SCUFFER SCUFFLE SHUFFLE

SCUFFLE HOE CUFF BUSTLE BUSTUP CLINCH CUFFLE TUSSLE WISTER BAGARRE BRULYIE SHAMBLE SHUFFLE SCRUFFLE

SCULL OAR FUNNY SHELL SKULL WHERRY

SCULLERY SINKROOM

SCULLION GIPPO SCULL SLUSH GALOPIN SWILLER CUSTROUN QUISTRON

SCULPIN COTTID GRUBBY JOHNNY BIGHEAD DRUMMER BULLHEAD BULLPOUT CABEZONE HARDHEAD LORICATE SCALAWAG

SCULPTOR CARVER GRAVER IMAGER MARBLER PLASTIC
AMERICAN FRY BALL GABO HART IVES KECK LADD MEAD RUSH TAFT VOLK WARD ADAMS AKERS ANDRE BEACH BOEHM BROWN CLARK DOYLE EVANS GALLO GOULD HOXLE JONES KELLY KONTI MEARS MILLS PERRY PRATT SEGAL SERRA STONE STORY YOUNG AITKEN BARTHE BENDER BITTER BUFANO CALDER CLARKE COUPER CURTIS DALLIN EAKINS EBERLE ELWELL FRASER FRAZEE FRENCH GRAFLY GRIMES HARVEY HOSMER HUGHES KASKEY KEMEYS KINNEY KITSON LAWRIE LEWITT MILLES MOZIER NAKIAN NEWMAN PALMER POTTER POWERS PUTNAM RIMMER ROGERS ROSZAK RUMSEY SHRADY WALKER WARNER ZORACH BARNARD BISSELL BORGLUM BRENNER BRIGHAM EDSTROM EZEKIEL GELLERT GODDARD GREGORY HANCOCK HARTLEY HOFFMAN JACKSON JAEGERS KENDALL LAESSLE LAURENT LIPPOLD LONGMAN LUKEMAN MACNEIL MANSHIP MARTINY MILMORE NIEHAUS NOGUCHI OCONNOR PROCTOR ROBERTS SCHULER SCUDDER SIEVERS SIMMONS

WHITNEY AGOSTINI ALBRIGHT ATCHISON BARTLETT BREWSTER CONNELLY CRAWFORD DAVIDSON DECREEFT DERIVERA FLANAGAN LACHAISE LENTELLI MCCARTAN MULLIGAN NADELMAN ODONOVAN PARAMINO RINEHART CLEVENGER GREENOUGH HUMPHREYS MACDONALD REMINGTON RUCKSTULL VALENTINE ARCHIPENKO MACMONNIES PAPASHVILY PICCIRILLI ZIOLKOWSKI
ARGENTINIAN ALONZO
ATHENIAN ANTENOR
AUSTRIAN DONNER NATTER TILGNER STRASSER
BELGIAN GEEFS FRAIKIN KESSELS LALAING MEUNIER SIMONIS STAPPEN LAMBEAUX TONGERLOO
CANADIAN HEBERT MACCARTHY
CZECH STRUSA MYSLBEK
DANISH BISSEN JERICHAU WILLUMSEN THORVALDSEN
DUTCH VRIES SLUTER TASSAERT DESJARDINS
ENGLISH BELL CARO FORD GILL JOHN SWAN WARD WOOD ANGEL BACON BAILY BANKS BATES BOEHM COLIN DURST HESSE JONES MOORE RHIND STONE TWEED WATTS ARCHER DOBSON GIBSON JAGGER KENNET LANDAU CHAROUX EPSTEIN FLAXMAN GIBBONS GILBERT STEVENS WOOLNER ARMITAGE ARMSTEAD CHANTREY FRAMPTON HEPWORTH SHERIDAN MACKENNAL KENNINGTON WESTMACOTT THORNYCROFT
FLEMISH BOLOGNE
FRENCH ARP ADAM ETEX RUDE UZES BARYE BOSIO CHAPU CRAUK DALOU DAVID DURET LEMOT PAJOU PILON PUECH RODIN DANTAN DEJOUX DUBOIS DUMONT GOUJON HOUDON ISELIN LEGROS MERCIE MILLET ROCHET ANGUIER BEGUINE BOUCHER CARRIES CHAUDET CLODION COLOMBE COUSTOU DESPIAU FREMIET LEMAIRE LEMOYNE MAILLET MAILLOL PIGALLE PRADIER PREAULT RICHIER CAFFIERI CARPEAUX CAVELIER CHAPLAIN COYSEVOX FALCONET FOYATIER GIRARDON GODEBSKI JOUFFROY LEPAUTRE LIPCHITZ SARRAZIN BARTHOLDI BEAUNEVEU BOURDELLE CLESINGER FALGUIERE INJALBERT LANDOWSKI ROUBILLAC BARTHOLOME CASSEGRAIN CHARPENTIER DELAPLANCHE
GERMAN HAHN KISS LENZ NAHL BEUYS CAUER HAAKE KOLBE KRAFT OESER RAUCH STOSS STUCK WOLFF BANDEL BLASER GEIGER HABICH HAHNEL HALBIG HERTER HOSAUS WAGNER AFINGER BARLACH BELLING KAUPERT KLIMSCH KLINGER KRELING SCHADON SCHAPER EBERHARD EBERLEIN FERNKORN SCHLUTER ZUMBUSCH DANNECKER ENGELHARD LEHMBRUCK MAGNUSSEN RIETSCHEL SIEMERING UECHTRITZ LEINBERGER SCHWANTHALER RIEMENSCHNEIDER
GREEK MYRON CHARES ONATAS SCOPAS AGASIAS BOETHUS BRYAXIS CALAMIS CRITIUS PHIDIAS SCYLLIS AGELADAS CANACHUS CRESILAS DAMOPHON LYSIPPUS PAEONIUS SOCIBIUS AGESANDER ALCAMENES ARCHERMUS BATHYCLES EUPHRANOR LEOCHARES PASITELES TAURISCUS TIMOTHEUS POLYCLETUS POLYCLITUS POLYEUCTUS PRAXITELES AGORACRITUS ATHENODORUS CALLIMACHUS LYSISTRATUS CEPHISODOTUS
IRISH FOLEY MACDOWELL FITZGERALD
ITALIAN VELA BANCO DANTI DUPRE LEONI PORTA RIZZO VINCI CANOVA GIOTTO MARINI PISANO ROBBIA SOLARI ALGARDI BERNINI CELLINI FIESOLE GIORGIO LAURANA MAZZONI QUERCIA TRIBOLO AGOSTINO AMMANATI ANTELAMI BARBIERE BOCCIONI CAMPAGNA CERACCHI CIVITALI GHIBERTI LOMBARDO MARCHESI TENERANI BARTOLINI BEGARELLI BORROMINI DONATELLO SANSOVINO GIACOMETTI MODIGLIANI MONTEVERDE VERROCCHIO DELLAROBBIA MICHELANGELO
NORWEGIAN VIGELAND
POLISH KALISH
ROMAN COSMATI
RUMANIAN BRANCUSI
RUSSIAN ZADKINS ORLOVSKI ANTOKOLSKI
SPANISH CANO MENA SILOE PICASSO CHILLIDA HERNANDEZ BERRUGUETE
SWEDISH ZORN MILLES SERGEL BYSTROM BORJESON FOGELBERG
SWISS HOERBST KISSLING TINGUELY
VENEZUELAN MARISOL
SCULPTURAL PLASTIC
SCULPTURE CAMEO DRAFT GRAVE SCULP BRONZE ENTAIL GISANT SCULPT CARVING DRAUGHT ENGRAVE GRADINO IMAGERY INSCULP STABILE MORTORIO NATIVITY PORTRAIT PREDELLA SCULLION
SCULPTURED GRAVEN GLYPHIC
SCUM BRAT FOAM GALL HEAD REAM SCUD SILT SKIM SKIN DROSS FROTH SCURF SLOAK SLOKE SLUSH SPUME FLURRY MANTLE MOTHER REFUSE RIDDAM SCRUFF BLANKET CACHAZA OFFSCUM LAITANCE PELLICLE SANDIVER SCOURING SCUMMING
(— OF THE PEOPLE) RIFFRAFF
(— ON FUSED GLASS) SANDIVER
(— ON LIQUOR) PELLICLE
(— ON MELTED METAL) SLAG
SCUP BREAM PORGY SPARID SCUPPAUG
SCURF SCALD SCALL DANDER FURFUR SCRUFF DANDRUFF
SCURFY SCALD SCURVY LEPROSE SCRUFFY LEPIDOTE SCABROUS SCABERULOUS
SCURRILITY ABUSE REPROACH
SCURRILOUS LOW FOUL VILE DIRTY GROSS RIBALD VULGAR ABUSIVE SCURRIL INDECENT
SCURRY HIE RUN ZIP BELT CRAB SKIN CURRY HURRY SCOUR SKICE SKURRY SCUFFLE SCUTTER SCUTTLE SKELTER SKITTER
SCURRYING SKITTER
SCURVY SCALD SCUMMY SHABBY ROYNOUS SCORBUCH SCORBUTE UNLIKING
SCUT BUN
SCUTAGE ESCUAGE
SCUTATE CLYPEATE
SCUTCH SCOTCH SWINGLE
SCUTE PLATE SCUTUM SCUTELLA
SCUTELLATION SCALING
SCUTIFORM PELTATE
SCUTTLE HOD CRAB SINK SKEP BEETLE MANHOLE SCUDDLE SCUTTER SCRATTLE
SCUTTLEBUTT CASK RUMOR GOSSIP FOUNTAIN
SCUZZY NASTY
SCYLLA (FATHER OF —) NISUS TYPHON
SCYLLITOL INOSITOL
SCYPHUS PYXIS
SCYTHE SY LEA HOOK MEAK REAP CRADLE
SCYTHIAN LAMB BAROMETZ
SEA MER ZEE BAHR BLUE BRIM FOAM FRET GULF HOLM LAVE MAIN MARE RACE TIDE WAVE BRINE BRINY FLOAT FLOOD LOUGH OCEAN AEQUOR PONTUS SEALET STRAND TETHYS CHANNEL HYALINE NEPTUNE BOSPORUS DEEPNESS SEAFLOOD THALASSA
(— DIVINITY) TRITON
(— GOD) PROTEUS
(— LETTER) PASSPORT
(AT —) LOST PUZZLED
(HEAVY —) POPPLE
(HIGH —) MAIN
(MODERATE —) SEAWAY
(PREF.) HAL(I)(IO)(O) MARI MER PELAG(O) THALASS(I)(IO)(O) THALATTO
SEA ANCHOR DRAG DROGUE
SEA ANEMONE POLYP DAHLIA OPELET ACTINIA VESTLET ACTINIAN ZOANTHID
SEA BASS HANAHILL HUMPBACK SERRANID TALLYWAG
SEA BEAR OTARIOID
SEABIRD HAGDON
SEA BISCUIT BREAD GALETTE PANTILE
SEABOARD COAST
SEA BREAD HARDTACK
SEA BREAM TAI CARP CHAD PORGY ROMAN BRAISE SARGUS SPARID TARWHINE
SEA BREEZE DOCTOR
SEA BUTTERFLY PTEROPOD
SEACOAST BANK SEABOARD SEASHORE
SEA COW SIREN DUGONG MANATEE RHYTINA SIRENIAN
SEA CUCUMBER BALATE TREPANG CUCUMBER SYNAPTID TEATFISH
SEADOG SALT FOGBOW FOGDOG SAILOR
SEA DOVE DOVEKIE ICEBIRD
SEA DRAGON PEGASID QUAVIVER
SEA DUCK DIVER EIDER DIPPER DUCKER SCOTER
SEA EAGLE ERN ERNE PYGARG PYGARGUS
SEA-EAR ORMER ABALONE
SEAFARER SEAGOER
SEAFOOD (— AND STEAK) SURFANDTURF
SEAFOOD)- ON SKEWERS) YAKITORI
SEA FOX THRASHER
SEA GIRDLE CUVY CUTWEED
SEA GULL COB GOR MEW COBB ANNET COBBE POPELER
(AUTHOR OF —) CHEKHOV
(CHARACTER IN —) NINA IRINA TRIGORIN CONSTANTIN
SEA-GYPSY SELUNG
SEA HOLLY ERYNGO ERYNGIUM
SEA HORSE WALRUS HIPPODAME HIPPOCAMPUS LOPHOBRANCH
SEA KALE COLE
SEAL CAN FIX FOB GUM BULL CHOP CORK HARP HOOD JARK LUTE BLANK BULLA CLOSE EAGLE PHOCA SIGIL STAMP SWILE THONG UGRUG URSUK WAFER ASSEAL BEATER CACHET COCKET DOTARD ENSEAL ENSIGN FASTEN GASKET MAKLUK MATKAH OBSIGN PHOCID RANGER SEALCH SECURE SIGNET CONFIRM CONSIGN COWROID ENGLUTE HOODCAP IMPRESS QUITTER SADDLER SEALING SEALKIE SIGNARY WEDDELL ADHESIVE BACHELOR BEDLAMER BRELOQUE CYLINDER MANDORLA PINNIPED SECRETUM SEECATCH SIGILLUM SIGNACLE TANGFISH VALIDATE
(— FOR WATCH CHAIN) ONION BRELOQUE
(— OFF) CAP
(— OVER CORK) CAPSULE
(BEARDED —) URSUK MAKLUK
(CUSTOM-HOUSE —) COCKET
(EARED —) OTARY
(FEMALE —) MATKA
(GOLD —) BEZEL
(HARBOR —) DOTARD RANGER TANGFISH
(HERD OF —S) PATCH
(IMMATURE —) BEDLAMER
(KIND OF —) HAIR MONK WEDDELL
(MALE —) WIG SADDLER BACHELOR SEECATCH
(NEWFOUNDLAND —) SWILE RANGER
(PAPAL —) BULL BULLA
(SHETLAND —) SILKIE
(YEARLING —) HOPPER
(YOUNG —) PUP BEATER JACKET BLUEBACK
(3-YEAR OLD —) TURNER
(PREF.) PHOC(O) SIGILLO

SEA LACE WHIPLASH
SEA LAVENDER INKROOT STATICE
SEALED CLOSE
SEALER CAPPER GASKET
SEA LETTUCE LAVER SLAKE SLOKE SEAWEED
SEA LILY CRINOID
SEA LION OTARY HAIRSEAL PINNIPED PINNIPEDE
SEALSKIN SKIN SCULP MATARA SAFARI
SEALSKIN COAT NETCHA
SEALYHAM TERRIER
SEAM DRY BAND DART FASH FELL PURL REND DEVIL PEARL SPILL FAGGOT INSEAM STREAK SUTURE SEAMLET JUNCTURE OVERSEAM
(— IN INGOT) SPILL
(— IN SHIP'S HULL) DEVIL
(— OF COAL) RIDER SPLIT STREAK
(IRREGULAR —) FASH
SEAMAN SALT JACKY MATLO ARTIST CALASH LUBBER SAILOR MARINER MASTMAN SHIPMAN SHIPPER SMASHER WAISTER YOUNKER DESERTER SEASONER
SEAMARK MEITH
SEAMED SEAMY RUGGED
SEA MILE NAUT
SEA MONSTER ORC PHOCA KRAKEN LEVIATHAN ROSMARINE HIPPOCAMPUS
SEAMOUNT GUYOT
SEAMSTER TAILOR SEMPSTER
SEAMSTRESS SEAMER SEWSTER NEEDLEWOMAN
SEANCE SITTING
SEA NETTLE BLUBBER
SEA OF GRASS (AUTHOR OF —) RICHTER
(CHARACTER IN —) HAL JIM BRICE BROCK HENRY LUTIE SARAH JIMMIE BREWTON CAMERON CHARLEY BREWSTER MCCURTIN CHAMBERLAIN
SEA ONION SCILLA
SEA OTTER KID KALAN
SEA OXEYE SALTWEED SAMPHIRE
SEA PERCH GAPER COMBER TRIPLETAIL
SEA PINK THRIFT SABBATIA
SEAPLANE HYDRO AIRBOAT AEROBOAT
SEA PLANTAIN GIBBALS
SEA POACHER BULLHEAD
SEAPORT PARA PORT GROIN NATAL HARBOR ENTREPOT MACASSAR
SEA PUSS OFFSET
SEAR BURN FIRE SERE FLAME FRIZZ ENSEAR SCORCH SIZZLE FRIZZLE
SEA RAVEN SCULPIN
SEARCH FAN SPY BEAT COMB DRAG DRAW FAND FISH FOND GAPE HUNT LAIT RAKE RIPE ROUT SEEK SIFT WAIT FRISK PROBE QUEST SCOUR SNOOP VISIT DACKER DREDGE FERRET FUMBLE RANCEL SLEUTH ENQUIRE EXPLORE FOSSICK INQUEST INQUIRE INSPECT RANSACK SCRINGE ZETETIC FINECOMB OUTREACH SCRABBLE SCROUNGE SCRUTINY SHAKEDOWN
(— ABOUT) GRUB PROG GROPE
(— AMONG REFUSE) SCAVENGE
(— BY FEELING) GROPE
(— DEEPLY) TENT DELVE
(— DIIGENTLY) SCOUR
(— EVERYWHERE) BUSK SCOUR
(— FOR) FORK HUNT LAIT SNOOK REQUIRE SEEKOUT
(— FOR FOX'S TRAIL) CIPHER
(— FOR GAME) DRAW GHOOM QUEST
(— FOR GOLD) FOSSICK
(— FOR KNOWLEDGE) OUTREACH
(— FOR PARTNER) CRUISE
(— FOR PROVISIONS) FORAGE
(— FOR SMUGGLED GOODS) DACKER JERQUE
(— FOR STOLEN GOODS) RANCEL RANSEL RANZEL
(— FOR WEAPONS) FRISK
(— GROPINGLY) GLAMP
(— INTO) EXQUIRE INDAGATE
(— OUT) FERRET INVENT ROOTLE EXQUIRE INDAGATE
(— SHIP) RUMMAGE
(— SYSTEMATICALLY) COMB
(— THROUGH) TURN
(— UNDERWATER) FISH
(CAREFUL —) RESEARCH
(SYSTEMATIC —) SWEEP
SEARCHER FINDER
SEARCHING HARD CLOSE SHREWD CURIOUS GROPING
SEARED ADUST
SEARING CAUTERY
SEA ROBIN GURNARD WINGFISH
SEA ROVER VIKING SCUMMER
SEASAN NUDE
SEASCAPE MARINE SEAPIECE
SEA SCORPION COBBLER
SEA SERPENT ELOPS
SEASHELL PROP
SEASHORE SEA RIPE CLEVE COAST PLAYA MARINE SEASIDE SEABEACH SEABOARD SEACOAST
SEASICKNESS HILO NAUPATHIA
SEA SNAIL LIPARIAN
SEA SNAKE CHITAL KERRIL
SEASON BEEK CORN DASH FALL PERT SALT SEEL TIDE TIME GRASS INURE SAUCE SAVOR SHEMU SPICE AUTUMN EASTER FLOWER HARDEN HAYING MASTER SPRING STEVEN STOUND SUMMER WINTER BUDTIME FLYTIME HARVEST KITCHEN OATSEED SEEDTIME
(— FOR HERRING FISHING) DRAVE
(— HIGHLY) DEVIL
(— IN THE SUN) HAZE
(— OF JOY) JUBILEE
(— OF MERRYMAKING) CARNIVAL
(CLOSED —) SHUTOFF
(DULL —) SLACK
(EGYPTIAN —) AHET PERT SHEMU
(HAYING —) HAYING HAYSEL
(LENTEN —) CAREME
(RAINLESS —) DRY
(RAINY —) KHARIF VARSHA
(REGULARLY RECURRING —) EMBER
(SPRING —) WARE APRIL GRASS
(THE RIGHT —) TID
SEASONABLE PAT TIDY TIMELY TIDEFUL TIMEFUL VETERAN TOWARDLY OPPORTUNE
SEASONABLY TIMELY APROPOS BETIMES
SEASONED SAGY SALT SALTED INDIENNE POWDERED
(MILDLY —) SWEET
SEASONER SURFACER
SEASONING SALT SPICE SEASON PAPRIKA SPICING OREGANUM
SEA SPIDER PYCNOGONOID
SEA SQUIRT ASCIDIAN
SEA SWALLOW TERN
SEAT BOX CAN SEE SET USH BANK BOSS COSY DAIS FLOP FORM FROG ROOM SILL SLIP SUNK TOIT ASANA BENCH CELLE CHAIR DICKY PERCH SELLA SELLE SETTE SIEGE SLIDE STALL STOOL USHER BOUGHT DODONA EXEDRA HUMPTY INSIDE RUMBLE SADDLE SEATER SEGGIO SETTEE SETTLE THWART BUTTOCK CUSHION GRADINE GRADINO INSTALL OTTOMAN SEATING TABORET TRANSOM BLEACHER ENTHRONE PULVINAR SEGGIOLA SUBSELLA WOOLPACK
(— AT PUBLIC SPECTACLE) PULVINAR
(— FOR CLERGY) SEDILE
(— FOR GRINDER) HORSING
(— FOR PLANE IRON) FROG
(— FOR TWO) SOCIABLE
(— NEAR ALTAR) SEDILIUM
(— OF BIRTH) SIDE
(— OF CHAIR) BOTTOM
(— OF DIGNITY) STATE
(— OF EMOTIONS) CHEST SPLEEN
(— OF FEELINGS) STOMACH
(— OF HARE) FORM
(— OF INTELLECT) HEAD
(— OF KNOWLEDGE) RUACH
(— OF ORACLE) DODONA
(— OF PITY) BOWEL
(— OF POWER) SEE
(— OF REAL LIFE) SOUL
(— OF RESPONSIBILITY) SHOULDER
(— OF RULE) OGDOAD
(— OF THEATRE) STALL
(— OF TURF) SUNK
(— OF UNDERSTANDING) SKULL
(— ON ELEPHANT'S BACK) TOWER CASTLE HOWDAH
(— ONESELF) LEAN PITCH
(— SLUNG ON POLES) HORSE
(— WITH BRAZIER BELOW) TENDOUR
(— WITHIN WINDOW OPENING) CAROL
(AIRPLANE —) DORMETTE
(BACKLESS —) STOOL HASSOCK
(BISHOP'S —) APSE BISHOPRIC FALDSTOOL FALDISTORY SYNTHRONUS
(BUS —) KNIFEBOARD
(CANOPIED —) COSY COZY
(CARRIAGE —) DICKY
(CHIEF —) METROPOLIS
(CHIMNEY —) SCONCE
(CHURCH —) PEW DESK STALL SEDILE
(COACH —) BOOT POOP
(COUNTRY —) TOWER GRANGE QUINTA
(DILIGENCE —) BANQUETTE
(DRAPED —) MUSNUD
(DRIVER'S —) BOX DICKY COCKPIT FORETOP
(ELEVATED —) PERCH
(FIXED —) DAIS
(GARDEN —) ALCOVE
(JUDGMENT —) TRIBUNAL
(KEY —) KEYWAY
(LONG —) BANK FORM BENCH
(MOTORCYCLE —) PILLION
(NIPPLE —) LUMP
(OARSMAN'S —) TAFT
(PORCH —) GLIDER
(RECLINING —) DORMEUSE
(ROMAN —) PULVINAR
(ROWER'S —) THWART
(ROYAL —) SIEGE STEAD THRONE
(STAGECOACH —S) BASKET
(STRAW —) BOSS
(TIER OF —S) TENDIDO
(TURF —) SUNK BUNKER
(UNRESERVED —S) BLUES
(PREF.) EDRI(O)
(SUFF.) HEDRAL
SEA TANGLE FURBELOW
SEATED (— IN MIND) INWARD
SEATING (— AREA) LOGE
SEA TROUT SEWEN SMELT KIPPER HERLING HIRLING BODIERON
(— AFTER SPAWNING) KELT
(YOUNG —) PEAL
SEA TURTLE RIDLEY CHELONID
SEA URCHIN WANA REPKIE ARBACIA CIDARID ECHINID ECHINUS RADIATE ECHINOID
(FOSSIL —) ECHINITE
(PREF.) ECHIN(O)
SEAWALL BULWARK
SEAWARD OFF MAKAI
SEAWEED ORE AGAR ALGA KELP LIMU MOSS NORI OOZE REEK REIT TANG WARE DRIFT DULSE KOMBU LAVER SLAKE SLOKE VAREC VRAIC WRACK DELISK FUCOID FUNORI TANGLE HAITSAI OARWEED OREWEED OREWOOD REDWARE SEATANG SEAWARE CARAGEEN GULFWEED HEMPWEED ROCKWEED SARGASSO SEABEARD WHIPCORD WHIPLASH CORALLINE NULLIPORE
(PL.) LUMUT
(PREF.) PHYC(O)
(SUFF.) PHYCEAE
SEA WOLF (AUTHOR OF —) LONDON
(CHARACTER IN —) HUMP MAUD WOLF DEATH LEACH LOUIS LARSEN JOHNSON BREWSTER HUMPHREY JOHANSEN MUGRIDGE VANWEYDEN
SEA WORM PALOLO SABELLA
SEB (CONSORT OF —) NUT
(SON OF —) OSIRIS
SEBA (FATHER OF —) CUSH
SEBASTIAN (BROTHER OF —) ALONSO
(SISTER OF —) VIOLA
SEBESTEN MYXA
SECANT SEC CHORD
SECCO FRESCO
SECEDE SPLINTER

SECESSIONIST SECESH SEPARATE
SECLUDE TACKLE ENCLOSE ISOLATE RECLUSE CLOISTER SEQUESTER
SECLUDED COY SHY DEEP CLOSE QUIET HIDDEN REMOTE SECRET PRIVATE RETIRED RETRAIT SECLUSE HIDEAWAY MONASTIC SEPARATE SOLITARY UMBRATIC CLAUSTRAL
SECLUSION RECESS SHADOW PRIVACY PRIVITY RETREAT SECRECY SEQUEST SOLITUDE ISOLATION
(— OF WOMEN) PURDAH
SECOND AID SEC ABET BACK BETA TICK OTHER VOUCH ASSIST LATTER MOMENT TARTAN TIDDER TOTHER ANOTHER INSTANT SUPPORT SUSTAIN STICKLER
(— BASE) KEYSTONE
(— IN COMMAND) DEPUTY
(— IN HORSE RACE) PLACE
(— PERSON USE) TUISM
(MAJOR —) TONE
(1000TH OF A —) SIGMA
(60TH OF A —) THIRD
(PREF.) DEUT(O) DEUTER(O) SECUNDI
SECONDARY BY BYE SUB SLACK DONKEY SECOND CUBITAL DERIVED INFERIOR MIDDLING
(PL.) FLAGS
(PREF.) DEUT(ER)(ERO)(O) MES(O)
SECONDHAND USED
SECOND MRS TANQUERAY
(AUTHOR OF —) PINERO
(CHARACTER IN —) RAY HUGH PAULA ARDALE AUBREY ELLEAN CORTELYOU TANQUERAY
SECOND-RATE DIMESTORE COMMON SHODDY INFERIOR
SECOND-RATER PIKER
SECRECY DERN HUSH HIDING SECRET HIDLING HIDLINS PRIVACY PRIVITY SILENCE DARKNESS HIDLINGS SCUGGERY VELATION SECLUSION HUGGERMUGGER
(STATE OF —) CLOSET
SECRET SLY DARK DERN INLY BLIND CABAL CLOSE HUSHY PRIVY QUIET ARCANE CLOSET COVERT HIDDEN INWARD POCKET STOLEN ARCANUM COUNSEL CRYPTIC EPOPTIC FURTIVE MYSTERY PRIVACY PRIVATE PRIVITY RECLUSE RESERVE RETIRED SECRETA UNKNOWN ESOTERIC HIDLINGS HUSHHUSH MYSTICAL SNEAKING STEALTHY TETEATETE HUGGERMUGGER
(PREF.) CRYPT(O) KRYPT(O) SUB
SECRETARY CLERK COPPY BARUCH MUNSHI RAPTOR SCRIBE FAMULUS MUNCHEE MOONSHEE
(SENIOR —) QUEENBEE
SECRETE HIDE CACHE NICHE RESET SECERN SECRET CONCEAL SECLUDE SALIVATE SEPARATE
(— MILK) LACTATE
(— ONESELF) HIVE
(— SALIVA) DROOL
(PREF.) ECCRINO
SECRETION INK LAC GOWL LAAP LERP MILT SPIT WOOL HUMOR LAARP MUCUS SEBUM SEPIA SLIME SPADE CEMENT SALIVA SMEGMA CERUMEN CHALONE FLOCOON HORMONE SPITTLE AUTACOID ENDOCRIN
(— OF MILK) LACTATION
(FATTY —) SEBUM
(GLAND —) SUCCUS
(OILY —) SEBUM
(THICKENED —) GUM
(VISCOUS —) SLIME
(WAXY —) LERP LAARP PRUINA
SECRETIVE SLY CAGY DARK SNUG CAGEY CLOSE COVERT SECRET SILENT INVOLVED
SECRETIVENESS SECRECY SLYNESS
SECRETLY CLOSE DARKLY DERNLY SECRET CLOSELY HIDLINGS INWARDLY
SECRET, THE (CHARACTER IN —) ROSE KALINA SKRIVANEK
(COMPOSER OF —) SMETANA
SECT SET ZEN BABI CLAN CULT JODO KIND SHIN ALOGI BHORA ISAWA PANTH BOHORA DONMEH HERESY SCHISM SCHOOL CATHARI DHUNDIA DOCETAE HASIDIM ISAWIYA KHALSAH RINGATU SECTARY SEQUELA SHAIKHI SHINGON SIVAISM SUBSECT AGNOETAE AHMADIYA AISSAOUA MURJIITE NAASSENE SECTUARY SHAKTISM BUCHANITES
(— MEMBER) DRUSE DRUZE
(LEBANESE —) DRUSE
(MEMBER OF —) KHLYST OPHITE YEZIDI MOLOKAN NUSAIRI LINGAYAT
SECTARIAN CULTIST HERETIC MAZHABI SECTARY SECTIST
SECTARY JESUIT HERETIC SECTIST SECTUARY SEPARATE
SECTION CUT END AREA PACE PART SECT UNIT CAPUT FRUST PIECE SHARE TMEMA BILLET BRANCH BRIDGE CANTON LENGTH MEMBER PASSUS SECTOR ARTICLE CUTTING HEADING SEGMENT TRANCHE ADDENDUM DIVISION FRACTION
(— AROUND HOP KILN) CURB
(— OF A BODY) LAMINA
(— OF AVICENNA'S WORK) FEN
(— OF BLOOM) STAMP
(— OF BUILDING) ENTRY
(— OF FENCE) FLAKE
(— OF FILM) EXPOSURE
(— OF FILTER) LEAF
(— OF FISHING TACKLE) TRACE
(— OF GARMENT) GORE
(— OF GLASS) SHAWL
(— OF HIGH GROUND) DIVIDE
(— OF KORAN) SURA
(— OF LADDER) FLY
(— OF LOG) BOLT FLITCH
(— OF LOOM) LAY
(— OF MELODY) STRAIN
(— OF NET) DEEPING
(— OF NEWSPAPER) LEAD ROTO
(— OF PARLIAMENT) LAGTHING
(— OF PSALTER) CATHISMA
(— OF RHAPSODY) LASSU
(— OF ROOF) SEVERY
(— OF ROOTSTOCK) BIT
(— OF SHIP) STEERAGE
(— OF SONG) STOLLEN
(— OF THREE SHEETS) TERNION
(— OF TORAH) PARASHAH
(— OF TRENCH) BAY
(— OF VIOLIN) BOUT
(— OF WOOD) HAG
(— OF YARN) SLUB
(—S OF SCENERY) BOOK
(CONCLUDING —) ABGESANG
(CONIC —) PARABOLA
(DULL —) LONGUEUR
(LOWEST —) BOTTOM
(MINE —) BORASQUE BORRASCA
(MUSICAL —) CODA EPILOG FINALE
(NARROW —) STRIPE
(NATIVE —) KASBA CASBAH
(ONE-SIXTEENTH OF —) FORTY
(PERCUSSION —) BATTERY
(4-PAGE —) OUTSERT
(SUFF.) TOMA TOME TOMIC TOMOUS TOMY
SECTIONALISM LOCALISM
SECTOR AREA GORE HOUSE
(45-DEGREE —) OCTANT
SECULAR LAIC CIVIL COMMON EARTHLY PROFANE WORLDLY TEMPORAL
SECULARIZE LAICIZE
SECURE FID GET GIB KEY POT RUG SEW WIN BAIL BOLT BOND CAUK COCK COLD EASY FAST FIND FIRM FRAP GAIN GIRD HOOK LAND MOOR NAIL SAFE SEAL SHOT SNUG STAY SURE WARM BELAY BLOCK CINCH CLEAT SLOUR SOUND STRAP TIGHT TRUST ANCHOR ASSURE BECKET BUTTON CLINCH DEFEND ENSURE FASTEN OBTAIN PLEDGE SETTLE SICCAR SICKER STABLE STAPLE TRAIST ACQUIRE BULWARK CONFINE DUNNAGE FORFEND FORTIFY RAMPIRE WARRANT GARRISON PRESERVE
(— AGAINST INTRUSION) TILE
(— AID OF) ENLIST
(— A SAIL) TRICE
(— BAIT) EBB
(— FROM LEAKING) COFFER
(— IN ADVANCE) SCOOP
(— PROMPTLY) SNAP
(— WITH BARS) GRATE
SECURED BOUND SETTLED
SECURELY FAST SAFE SICCAR SICKER STRAIT SURELY SOLIDLY SOUNDLY
SECURITY PUP BAIL BAND EASE GAGE MUNI SEAL WAGE FRITH GRITH GUARD QUIET STOCK BORROW CEDULA EQUITY PLEDGE REFUGE SAFETY SCREEN SEVERE SURETY VADIUM BULWARK CAUTION CUSTODY DEFENSE DEPOSIT FLOATER HOSTAGE SHELTER SLEEPER WARRANT COLONIAL COVENANT FASTNESS GUARANTY HYPOTHEC STRENGTH VADIMONY MUNICIPAL
(— DEVICE) SENSOR
(BELOW AVERAGE —) LAGGARD
(PL.) PERCENTS PORTFOLIO
SEDAN SEDIA JAMPAN SALOON TONJON NORIMON TOMJOHN BROUGHAM
SEDATE CALM COOL DOUCE GRAVE QUIET SOBER STAID SERENE EARNEST SERIOUS SETTLED COMPOSED DECOROUS
SEDATENESS SOBRIETY
SEDATIVE AMYTAL ACONITE CALMANT CODEINE LUPULIN BARBITAL LENITIVE QUIETIVE SOOTHING
SEDENTARY STILL SESSILE INACTIVE
SEDGE SAG LING RAIT REIT STAR CAREX CHUFA TIKUG BHABAR EHUAWA GLUMAL THATCH TOETOE TOITOI BULRUSH MONOCOT PAPYRUS SNIDDLE TUSSOCK GALANGAL JIMSEDGE PIKERUSH
(PREF.) CARIC(O)
SEDGE FLY GRANAM GRANNOM
SEDGE WARBLER WREN MOCKBIRD REEDBIRD
SEDGY SAGGY SEGGY TWILLED
SEDIMENT CARR DREG FAEX FOOT GOBI LEES MULM SILT WARP DRAST DREGS FECES FOOTS MAGMA BOTTOM FECULA SIMMON SLUDGE DREWITE GROUNDS GRUMMEL SAPROPEL SETTLING
(— OF BEER OR ALE) CRAP
(IRON —) CAR CARR
(REDDISH —) SIMMON
SEDITION REVOLT TREASON
SEDITIOUS RIOTOUS FACTIOUS MUTINOUS
SEDUCE DRAW JAPE LOCK DECOY TEMPT WRONG ALLURE BETRAY ENTICE DEBAUCH ENSNARE MISLEAD SUGGEST TRADUCE INVEIGLE
(— WITH THE EYE) LEER
SEDUCER UNDOER LOTHARIO
SEDUCTION LURE BRIBE CHARM
SEDUCTIVE TEMPTING
SEDULOUS BUSY INTENT STUDIED DILIGENT UNTIRING
SEDULOUSNESS INDUSTRY
SEDUM MOSS ORPINE SENGREEN
SEE LO EYE KEN SPY VID DATE ESPY LOOK MIND NOTE PIPE SEAT SEGE SPOT VIDE VIEW BESEE CATCH CHAIR SIEGE SIGHT STOOL TENEZ WATCH ATTEND BEHOLD DESCRY NOTICE QUAERE REMARK SURVEY ARCHSEE DISCERN GLIMPSE OBSERVE WITNESS CATHEDRA CONCEIVE PERCEIVE
(— ABOVE) VS
(— BELOW) VI
(— FIT) CHOOSE
(— INTO) INSEE PENETRATE
(— THROUGH) RUMBLE
(— TO) FIX
(— VISIONS) SCRY
SEED BEN MAW NIB PIP BEAN BOIL CHAT CORN DIKA GERM KOLA LIMA MOTE SETH TARE BEHEN

BERRY CACAO CARAT CARVY GRAIN LUPIN SEMEN SPAWN SPERM SPORE STONE ABILLA ACHENE ACINUS ADZUKI BONDUC CACOON CARNEL FENNEL KERNEL LEGUME LENTIL NICKER NUTLET PIGNON PIPPIN TILLEY ACHIOTE ACHUETE ALPISTE ANISEED BUCKEYE CALINUT FRIJOLE HARICOT HAYSEED SEEDKIN SEEDLET SEMINAL AMBRETTE COKERNUT CYDONIUM DILLSEED FLAXSEED FLEASEED HEMPSEED PIGNOLIA PRINCIPE SEEDLING SEEDNESS PISTACHIO PROPAGULE
(— COATING) TESTA
(— COVER) TESTA
(— OF MAPLE) SAMARA
(AROMATIC —S) ANISE
(COFFEE —) PEABERRY
(COLE —) COLZA
(EDIBLE —) PEA BEAN
(FENUGREEK —) HELBEH
(GRAPE —) ACINUS
(IMMATURE —) OVULE
(MUSTARD —) SENVY SINEWY
(NUTLIKE —) PEANUT
(OILY —) ARGAN ABILLA
(PALM —) COROZO
(POPPY —) MAW MOHNSEED
(SESAME —) JINJILI GINGELLY
(PL.) ANISE COFFEE SESAME ZERAIM IGNATIA LARKSPUR
(PREF.) COCC(O) GON(O) OVULI SEMINI SEMINULI SPERM(A)(ATI) (ATIO)(ATO)(I)(IO)(O) SPOR(I)(IDI)(O) (ULI)
(BEAK-LIKE —) RYNCO
(SUFF.) COCCAL COCCIC SPERM(A) (AE)(AL)(IA)(IC)(OUS)(UM)(Y) SPORA SPORANGE SPORANGIATE SPORANGIUM SPORE SPORIC SPORIDIA SPORIUM SPOROUS SPORY
SEEDCAKE WIG WIGG
SEEDCASE TEST TESTA THECA
SEED COAT ARIL TESTA SPIRICLE
SEEDED ARABLE
SEEDER SEEDMAN
SEEDLING FREE LINER
SEEDS
(PREF.) GRANI
SEEDY MANGY SCUFFY
SEEING SIGHT SIGHTED
(— THAT) SITH SINCE
SEEK ASK BEG SIC WOO BUSK FAND FEEL FISH FOND FORK HUNT LAIT LOOK SICK SIFT COURT DELVE ESSAY FETCH SCOUR APPETE BOTTOM FERRET FOLLOW FRAIST PURSUE SEARCH FORSEEK INQUIRE RANSACK REQUIRE RUMMAGE SOLICIT ENDEAVOR
(— AFTER) SUE SUIT ENSUE EXPLORE
(— AIMLESSLY) PROG
(— FAVOR) WISH
(— FOR) APPETE EXPLORE
(— IN MARRIAGE) WOO PRETEND
(— OUT) COMB ENSEARCH
(— TO ATTAIN) ASPIRE
(— URGENTLY) PRESS
SEEKER TRACER PETITOR ZETETIC SEARCHER
(— AFTER FACTS) GRADGRIND
(— OF KNOWLEDGE) PHILONIST
(JOB —) CHANCER
(PLEASURE —) FRANION
SEEKING SOKE SOKEN ZETETIC
(SUFF.) PETAL
SEEM BID EYE SEE FARE LOOK PEER SOUND APPEAR BESEEM REGARD
(— TO BE) LIKE
(IT —S) SEMBLE
SEEMING GUISE QUASI LIKELY SEEMLY APPARENT SEMBLANT
(PREF.) QUASI
SEEMINGLY QUASI SEEMLY SEEMING
SEEMLINESS GRACE DECENCY DECORUM
SEEMLY FIT TALL CIVIL COMELY DECENT LIKELY MODEST BECOMING DECOROUS GRACEFUL
SEEP LEAK OOZE SIPE EXUDE PERCOLATE
SEEPAGE SEEP SIPAGE SPRING
SEEPY WEEPY
SEER SIR SWAMI MOPSUS ORACLE SCRYER PROPHET CHALDEAN MELAMPUS
SEERBAND TURBAN
SEERESS SAGA SIBYL VOLVA ALRUNE ALBRUNA PHOIBAD
SEESAW PUMP TILT DANDLE TEETER TIDDLE TILTER TITTER TOTTER
SEETHE FRY JUG BOIL CREE ITCH STEW WALL WALM BULLER HOTTER SIMMER BLUBBER ELIXATE FERMENT
SEETHING ASEETHE BOILING HUMMING ITCHING SCALDING
SEGMENT CUT LAP FALL HAND LITH MERE PART BLANK CHORD ELITE FEMUR FURCA SHARE SLICE TMEMA CANTLE GLOSSA LENGTH SAMPLE SYZYGY ARTICLE DIGITUS EXERGUE FESTOON ISOMERE MYOMERE MYOTOME SECTION SETIGER ANTIMERE BRACHIUM COLUMNAL DACTYLUS DIVISION GONOTOME HYPOMERE INTERVAL MESOMERE METAMERE MYOCOMMA NARICORN
(— OF CASK) CANT
(— OF CAULIFLOWER) FLOWERET
(— OF CIRCLE) SECTION
(— OF COMMUNITY) FACIES
(— OF EARTH'S CRUST) GRABEN
(— OF FIBER) BAND
(— OF INSECT'S LEG) FEMUR TROCHANTER
(— OF IRIS) FALL
(— OF LEAF) LACINIA
(— OF MAXILLA) STIPES SUBGALEA
(— OF RATTLESNAKE'S RATTLE) BUTTON
(— OF SPEECH) DOMAIN
(ABDOMINAL —) URITE UROMERE PROPODEON
(BODY —) SOMITE
(HERALDIC —) FLANCH FLANCHE
(INSTRUCTIONAL —) LESSON
(MERE —) SNAPSHOT
(PEASANT —) HERA
(SUFF.) MERE TMEMA TMESIS
(— OF) ILE
SEGMENTAL MERISTIC
SEGMENTATION CLEAVAGE
(SUFF.) TOMA TOME TOMIC TOMOUS TOMY
SEGMENTED INSECTED
SEGNO SIGN
SEGREGATE SHED SEVER INTERN ISOLATE CLASSIFY INSULATE SEPARATE
SEGREGATION APARTHEID
SEGUB (FATHER OF —) HIEL HEZRON
SEIGNORAGE ROYALTY
SEIGNORY LORDSHIP
SEINE NET FARE TUCK TRAIN POCKET SAGENE SPILLER MADRAGUE
(— SIGHT) ILE
SEISIN VESTURE
SEIZE BAG CAP CLY GET HAP NAB NAP BEAK BONE CLAW CLUM FANG GALL GLOM GRAB GRIP GRUP HAND HENT HOOK JUMP KEEP LEVY NAIL RAMP SMUG SNAP SPAN TAKE TIRE YOKE CATCH CESSE CLASP CLEEK CLICK CRIMP DRIVE GRASP GRIPE LATCH PINCH RAVEN RAVIN REACH REAVE SNACK ARREST ASSUME ATTACH CLUTCH COLLAR EXTEND FASTEN FREEZE GOBBLE NOBBLE QUARRY SECURE SNATCH ASSEIZE CAPTURE ENCLASP ENCLOSE FORHENT GRABBLE GRAPPLE IMPOUND POSSESS PREEMPT PREHEND SCAMBLE SWALLOW ARROGATE COMPRISE DISTRAIN SPUILZIE SURPRISE UNDERNIM
(— AND HOLD FIRMLY) TRUSS
(— BAIT) STRIKE
(— BY NECK) SCRAG COLLAR SCRUFF
(— PREY) CHOP
(— SUDDENLY) NAB NIP SWOOP SNATCH
(— UPON) ATTACK INFECT
(— WITH CLAWS) STRAIN
(— WITHOUT RIGHT) USURP
(— WITH TEETH) BITE
(— WITH WHOLE HAND) GLAUM
SEIZIN SASINE VESTURE
SEIZING FANG GRIP MARQUE CAPTION SEIZURE
SEIZURE PIT BITE HOLD RAPE GRIPE ICTUS SPELL ARREST EXTENT PRISAL RAPTUS SNATCH TAKING ANGARIA CAPTION CONCEIT TELLACH DISTRESS STOPPAGE
(— IN RETALIATION) REPRISAL
(DRUG ADDICT'S —) WINGDING
(SUFF.) LEPSIA LEPSIS LEPSY LEPT(IC)
SELDOM RARE SELD RARELY UNOFTEN
SELDOM-SEEN ANTRIN ANTERIN
SELECT ORT TAP TRY CULL PICK SIFT SORT TAKE WALE DRAFT ELECT ELITE PITCH TRIED ASSIGN BALLOT CHOICE CHOOSE CLUBBY DECIDE DESUME EXEMPT PREFER SAMPLE SINGLE WINNOW DRAUGHT EMPANEL EXCERPT EXTRACT OUTLOOK EXIMIOUS HANDPICK SELECTED
(— A CAREER) GOINTO
(— BY LOT) DRAW
(— BY PATTERN) SWATCH
(— JURY) STRIKE
SELECTED DRAFT ELECT FANCY DRAUGHT
SELECTING DRAFT GARBLING
SELECTION BLAD CHAP CULL ITEM PICK CHOICE CHOOSE EXCERPT EXTRACT ELECTION HAFTARAH PERICOPE
(— OF PSALMS) HALLEL
(VERSE —) BLAUD SINGSONG
(SUFF.) ECLEXIS
SELECTIVE CHOOSY ECLECTIC
SELED (FATHER OF —) NADAB
SELENE (SISTER OF —) EOS
SELENIDE ZORGITE
SELF EGO SEL SEN JIVA SELL SOUL DAENA NATURE PERSON PSYCHE
(INNER —) ANIMA
(OWN —) AINSELL NAINSEL
(SUPREME UNIVERSAL —) ATTA ATMAN
(PREF.) AUT(O) AUTH(I) EGO
SELF-ACCUSATION GUILT
SELF-ACTING
(PREF.) AUT(O) AUTOMAT(O)
SELF-AGGRANDIZING IMPERIAL
SELF-ASSERTIVE BRASH PERKY CHESTY BLUSTERY BUMPTIOUS
SELF-ASSURANCE CHEEK APLOMB COOLNESS
SELF-ASSURED COCKY CALM PERKY CONFIDENT
SELF-CENTERED SELFISH
SELF-CENTEREDNESS EGOTISM SELFHOOD
SELF-COMMAND NERVE TEMPER
SELF-CONCEIT NOSISM
SELF-CONCEITED COXY PENSY COCKSY PENCEY
SELF-CONFIDENCE CREST HUBRIS HUTZPA CHUTZPA HUTZPAH JOLLITY OPINION CHUTZPAH
SELF-CONFIDENT COCKSURE FLUSH CHESTY
SELF-CONSCIOUS GAWKY BASHFUL
SELF-CONTAINED ABSOLUTE
SELF-CONTAINMENT CLOSURE
SELF-CONTRADICTORY ABSURD
SELF-CONTROL STAY WILL ENCRATY MODESTY RETENUE PATIENCE
(LOSE —) FLIP
SELF-DECEPTION FLATTERY
SELF-DEFENSE (ART OF—) AIKIDO
(ART OF —) KUNGFU
SELF-DENIAL DENIAL
SELF-DENYING ASCETIC
SELF-DESTRUCTION SUICIDE
SELF-DESTRUCTIVE SUICIDAL
SELF-DETERMINATION FREEDOM AUTONOMY
SELF-DISCIPLINE ASCESIS
SELF-ENRICHMENT GROWTH
SELF-ESTEEM EGO PRIDE CONCEIT SELFNESS
SELF-EVIDENT MANIFEST

SELF-EXALTATION NOSISM ELATION
SELF-EXISTENT BEER INCREATE UNCAUSED
SELF-FERTILIZATION AUTOGAMY
SELF-FULFILLMENT FREEDOM SAMADHI
SELF-GENERATION AUTOGENY
SELF-GLORIFICATION VANITY
SELF-GOVERNMENT SWARAJ
SELF-HEAL ALLHEAL HOOKHEAL HOOKWEED BLUECURLS
SELFHOOD SEITY EGOITY IPSEITY OWNHOOD PROPRIUM SELFNESS
SELF-IDENTITY IPSEITY
SELF-IMPORTANT COXY PURDY CHESTY COCKSY BIGGETY POMPOUS BUMPTIOUS
SELF-INDULGENCE NICETY PLEASURE
SELF-INDULGENT WANTON
SELFISH PIGGISH SELFFUL DISSOCIAL
SELFISHNESS EGO SELF EGOTISM SUICISM PHILAUTY SELFHOOD SELFNESS
(MORBID —) PLEONEXIA
SELF-LOVE CONCEIT PHILAUTY
SELF-ORIGINATION ASEITY
SELF-POLLUTION ONANISM
SELF-POSSESSED COOL ASSURED COMPOSED TOGETHER
SELF-POSSESSION PHLEGM COOL POISE APLOMB COOLNESS SANGFROID
SELF-PRODUCED
(PREF.) IDIO
SELF-REALIZATION FREEDOM ENERGISM
SELF-RELIANT BOLD FREE
SELF-REPROACH GUILT REGRET
SELF-RESTRAINT HO HOO ASCESIS CONTROL RESERVE RETENUE HAVLAGAH
SELF-RIGHTEOUS STUFFY
SELF-SACRIFICING HEROIC GALLANT
SELFSAME SAME VERY SELFSAID IDENTICAL
SELFSAMENESS IDENTITY
SELF-SATISFIED SMUG STODGY ASSURED
SELF-SERVICE
(SUFF.) TERIA
SELF-SUFFICIENCY ASEITY ASEITAS AUTARKY AUTARCHY
SELF-SUFFICIENT ABSOLUTE
SELF-TAUGHT PRIMITIVE
SELF-WILLED SET SENSUAL STUBBLE WAYWARD CONTRARY PERVERSE
SELION BUTT
SELL DO FLOG GIVE VEND CHEAP PITCH SHAVE TRADE UTTER WRITE AFFORD BARTER MARKET PEDDLE AUCTION BARGAIN
(— A HORSE) CHANT
(— AT LOW PRICE) DUMP
(— BELOW COST) FOOTBALL
(— BY AUCTION) CANT ROUP
(— DRUGS ILLEGALLY) PUSH
(— FOR) BRING FETCH
(— FRAUDULENTLY) CHANT CHAUNT
(— IN SMALL QUANTITIES) RETAIL
(BUY AND —) CHOP
SELLER BOOMER BUSKER CADGER VENDOR CHANTER FLESHER CHANDLER
(— OF BEER) PINTPOT
(BEST —) CHARTBUSTER
(WINE —) ABKAR
SELLING (SPECULATIVE —) AGIOTAGE
SELSYN SYNCHRO
SELVAGE EDGE LIST ROON GOUGE FORREL LISTING STICKING
SEMACHIAH (FATHER OF —) SHEMAIAH
SEMANTEME RHEME
SEMANTICS SEMOLOGY
SEMAPHORE FISHTAIL
SEMBLANCE FACE IDOL SHOW SIGN COLOR GHOST GLOSS GUISE IMAGE SCHEME VISAGE PRETEXT SEEMING UMBRAGE LIKENESS SEMBLANT SKERRICK SIMULACRUM
(— OF DIGNITY) FACE
(— OF REALITY) DREAM
(FALSE —) COLORING
SEME SEMY GUTTY HURTY FLEURY GOUTTE GUTTEE BEZANTE
SEME-DE-LIS FLORETTY
SEMEI (SON OF —) MATTATHIAS
SEMELE (BROTHER OF —) POLYDORUS
(FATHER OF —) CADMUS
(MOTHER OF —) HARMONIA
(SISTER OF —) INO AGAVE AUTONOE
(SON OF —) BACCHUS
SEMEN SEED SPERM
(PREF.) GON(O) SPERM(A)(ATI)(ATIO)(ATO)(I)(IO)(O)
(SUFF.) SPERM(A)(AE)(AL)(IA)(IC)(OUS)(UM)(Y)
SEMESTER HALF
SEMI RIG
SEMIDARKNESS DUSK
SEMIDIAMETER RADIUS
SEMIDOME CONCHA
SEMIFLUID SOFT HUMOR
SEMIGLOSS EGGSHELL
SEMILIQUID SLAB
SEMINARY YESHIVA JUVENATE
SEMIOPAQUE HORNY
SEMIPORCELAIN GOMBROON
SEMIRAMIDE (CHARACTER IN —) ASSUR ARSACE SEMIRAMIS
(COMPOSER OF —) ROSSINI
SEMIRAMIS (HUSBAND OF —) NINUS
(MOTHER OF —) DERCETO
SEMITE JEW ARAB HARARI SYRIAN MOABITE SEMITIC SHEMITE ARAMAEAN ASSYRIAN CHALDEAN
SEMITIC JEWISH
(— LANGUAGE) GAFAT
SEMITONE FEINT LIMMA DEMITONE HEMITONE
SEMITRAILER ARTIC
SEMOLINA SUJI SEMOLA
SENAPO (DAUGHTER OF —) CLORINDA
SENATE BOULE SENATO COUNCIL SENATUS GEROUSIA SENATORY
(— AND PEOPLE OF ROME) SPQR
(— DIVISION) PRYTANY
SENATOR SOLON CONSUL FATHER LAWMAKER
(PL.) ANZIANI
SENATORSHIP TOGA
SEND MIT FAST PACK SHIP ELATE ENVOY SCEND THROW RENDER THRILL ADDRESS CHANNEL COMMAND CONSIGN DELIGHT DELIVER FORWARD DISPATCH TRANSMIT
(— ABOUT) TROLL
(— ALOFT) CROSS
(— AWAY) MAND SHIP AMAND BANISH DISBAND DISMISS RELEGATE
(— BACK) ECHO TURN WISE REMIT REMAND REMISE RENVOY RESEND RETURN REFRACT
(— BY MAIL) DROP
(— BY PARACHUTE) DROP
(— BY WIRE) FAX
(— DOWN) DEMIT DIMIT STRIKE
(— FOR) SUMMON
(— FORTH) BEAM BEAR CAST EMIT MAND DIMIT FLING LANCH EFFUSE LAUNCH OUTSEND EXPEDITE FULMINATE
(— FORTH IN RAYS) RADIATE
(— HURTLING) SPIN
(— IN) IMMIT IMMISS INTROMIT
(— MESSAGE) TELEX BLINKER
(— OFF) POST WING
(— OFFICIALLY) ISSUE
(— OFF UNCEREMONIOUSLY) SHANK
(— OUT) BEAM EMIT AMAND SHOOT SPEED DEDUCE DEPORT LAUNCH DIFFUSE EXPEDITE
(— OVERSEAS) TRANSPORT
(— SWIFTLY) SPEED
(— TO JAIL) LAG MITTIMUS
(— TO PERDITION) CONFOUND
(— WITHIN) INTROMIT
(SUFF.) MISE MISS MIT
SENDING SAND
(— OF MONEY) REMITTANCE
(— OUT) EMISSIVE
(— WITHIN) INSERTION INTROMISSION
SEND-UP PARODY TAKEOFF

SENEGAL
CAPITAL: DAKAR
MOUNTAIN: GOUNOU
NATIVE: PEUL SOCE DIOLA FOULA LAOBE SERER WOLOF FULANI SERERE BAMBARA MALINKE TUKULER MANDINGO
RIVER: FALEME GAMBIA SALOUM SENEGAL CASAMANCE
TOWN: BAKEL LOUGA MATAM THIES DAGANA KAOLACK RUFISQUE

SENILE DOLD ANILE DOTARD
SENILITY DOTAGE CADUCITY PROGERIA
SENIOR AINE DEAN SIRE DOYEN ELDER ANCIENT SUPERIOR
SENIORITY AGE ANCIENTY SIGNEURY
SENNACHERIB (FATHER OF —) SARGON
(SON OF —) ESARHADDON
SENNET SPET SIGNET
SENOR DON
SENORITA MISS SRTA SRITA
SENSATION FEEL ITCH SOUR STIR SENSE TABET TASTE TIBBIT VEDANA FEELING ESTHESIS EXPERIENCE
(— OF COLD) RHIGOSIS
(— OF FRIGHT) FRISSON
(— OF HEAT) HOTNESS
(— OF PAIN) ALGESIS
(ANTICIPATORY —) FOREFEEL
(BURNING —) ARDOR
(DARTING —) SHOOT
(IRRITATING —) ITCH
(STRONG —) CREEP
(SUBJECTIVE —) AURA
(TASTE —) GUST BITTER
(TINGLING —) DIRL
(VIBRATING —) FREMITUS
(VISUAL —) PHOSE PHOTOMA
(PREF.) AESTHESIO ESTHESIO
SENSATIONAL GORY BOFFO LURID YELLOW SAFFRON SPLASHY TABLOID THRILLY STUNNING MELODRAMATIC
SENSATIONALISM BLARE SENSISM
SENSE WIT FEEL SALT SMELL LETTER MATTER REASON SCONCE WISDOM FEELING HEARING MARBLES MEANING SMEDDUM CARRIAGE GUMPTION JUDGMENT
(— OF APPREHENSION) ANXIETY
(— OF DUTY) PIETY
(— OF HEARING) EAR
(— OF HUMOR) MUSIC
(— OF MOVEMENT) KINESTHESIA KINESTHESIS KINAESTHESIS
(— OF MYSTERY) MYSTIQUE
(— OF ONENESS) KINSHIP
(— OF OUTRAGE) SHOCK
(— OF PANIC) JITTERS
(— OF RIGHT) GRACE
(— OF SHAME) PUDOR
(— OF SIGHT) VISION
(— OF SMELL) SCENT
(— OF STYLE) PANACHE
(— OF SUPERIORITY) EGOTISM
(— OF TASTE) GUST PALATE GUSTATION
(— OF TOUCH) FEEL TASTE
(— OF WORD) ETYMON
(— ON ONE'S WORTH) PRIDE
(— THE MEANING OF) READ
(COMMON —) NOUS SALT BALANCE GUMPTION
(DISCRIMINATING —) FLAIR
(GOOD —) MATTER
(LACKING —) INEPT
(MAKE —) ADDUP FOLLOW
(MORAL —) CONSCIENCE
(PLAIN —) ENGLISH
(RIGHT —S) MIND
(SOUND —) MATTER
SENSE AND SENSIBILITY
(AUTHOR OF —) AUSTEN

(CHARACTER IN —) JOHN LUCY EDWARD ELINOR STEELE BRANDON FERRARS MARIANNE WILLOUGHBY
SENSE-DATUM SENSUM
SENSELESS MAD COLD DUMB SILLY FRIGID STUPID UNWISE WANTON FOOLISH IDIOTIC PEEVISH SOTTISH UNIDEAED POINTLESS REASONLESS
SENSIBILITY HEART SENSE FEELING DELICACY ESTHESIA JUDGMENT (PL.) FEELINGS
SENSIBLE SANE WISE AWARE PRIVY WITTY ACTUAL FEELABLE MATERIAL PASSIBLE RATIONAL SENSICAL SENTIENT WISELIKE PERCEPTIBLE
SENSITIVE FINE KEEN SORE ALIVE MIFFY QUICK KITTLY LIABLE NIMBLE TENDER TETCHY FEELING NERVOUS PRICKLY ALLERGIC DELICATE EROGENIC SENSIBLE SENTIENT SKINLESS TOUCHOUS
(— TO PAIN) TART
(NERVOUSLY —) TOUCHY
(TOO —) OVERSTRUNG
SENSITIVENESS SENSE TOUCH ALGESIA DELICACY
SENSITIVE PEA HONEYCUP
SENSITIVE PLANT MIMOSA
SENSITIVITY FLESH ANTENNA DELICACY FINENESS
SENSITIZER CYANINE
SENSORY SENSUAL AFFERENT
SENSUAL LEWD BRUTE MUDDY CARNAL FLESHY SULTRY WANTON BEASTLY BESTIAL BRUTISH FLESHLY LESBIAN SWINISH PANDEMIC SENSUOUS
SENSUALITY FLESH LIKING LUXURY ANIMALISM
SENSUOUS SOFT LYDIAN SATINY SENSAL FLESHLY SENSUAL LUSCIOUS SENSIBLE
SENTENCE BAN DIT RAP SAW DAMN DOOM TIME AWARD FUTWA JUISE TENER TROPE ARREST ASSIZE COMMIT DECREE DEPORT JUWISE KERNEL REASON ADJUDGE CENSURE CONDEMN FLOATER IMPRESA LAGGING FOREDOOM JUDGMENT VERSICLE PALINDROME
(— CONTAINING ALL LETTERS) PANGRAM
(— CONTAINING EACH LETTER) PANGRAM
(— INDICATING CHARACTER) MOTTO
(— OF TEN YEARS IN PRISON) DIME
(CONCISE —S) LACONICS
(IMPRISONMENT —) LAG RAP LIFE LAGGING STRETCH
(KIND OF —) CLEFT
(MUSICAL —) PERIOD
(SERVE A —) DOTIME
(SHORT —) CLAUSE
(WITTY —) ATTICISM
SENTENTIOUS CONCISE LACONIC
SENTIENCE SENSE
SENTIENT AWARE FEELING SENSILE SENSIVE SENSEFUL SENSIBLE
SENTIMENT MIND POSY ETHNOS GENIUS HOBNOB NOTION PLEDGE FEELING OPINION
(— IN DRINKING) HOBNOB
(EXCESSIVE —) SCHWARMEREI
(FALSE —) FALSETTO
(SLOPPY —) DRIP
SENTIMENTAL SLAB SOFT CORNY GOOEY GUSHY MUSHY SAPPY SOBBY SOPPY SOUPY TEARY FRUITY SLUSHY SPOONY SUGARY SYRUPY INSIPID MAUDLIN MAWKISH ROMANTIC SCHMALZY SNIVELLY MOONSTRUCK NOVELETTISH
(MORBIDLY —) WERTHERIAN
(OVERLY —) MUSHY
SENTIMENTALISM BATHOS SCHMALZ SCHMALTZ
SENTIMENTALIST SOFTHEAD
SENTIMENTALITY GOO HAM MUSH BLURB SIRUP SYRUP BATHOS
(INTOLERABLE —) TREACLE
(MAUDLIN —) GOO
SENTIMENTAL TOMMY (AUTHOR OF —) BARRIE
(CHARACTER IN —) JEAN AARON LOTTA NYLES TOMMY GRIZEL ELSPETH
SENTINEL WAIT DEINO GUARD WATCH BANTAY PICKET SENTRY WARDEN PICQUET COCKATOO PEPHEDRO WATCHMAN
(MOUNTED —) VEDET VEDETTE
(PL.) GRAEAE GRAIAE
SENTINEL BOX STATION WATCHCASE
SENTRY KITE WATCH SENTINEL
SEPAL ALA LEAF HELMET LEAFLET
SEPARATE CUT TOM COMB CULL CURD DEAL FALL FRAY FREE HAZE PART REDD SERE SIFT SORT TEAR TWIN ASIDE BLEED BREAK CALVE ELONG FENCE FLAKE HEDGE PARTY SCALE SEVER SIEVE SKILL SPLIT TWAIN TWIST ABDUCT ABRUPT ASSORT AVULSE BISECT CLEAVE DECIDE DEPART DETACH DIGEST DIVIDE DIVISI FILTER PROPER REMOTE SCREEN SECERN SECRET SEJOIN SETTLE SINGLE SOLUTE SPREAD SUNDER SUNDRY SWATCH UNLUTE WINNOW ABSCISE ABSCISS BRACKET CONCERN DIALYZE DISALLY DISCERP DISJOIN DISLINK DISPAIR DISPART DIVERSE EXPANSE FISSION ISOLATE SCATTER SCIOLTO SECTION SEJUNCT SEVERAL SWINGLE TAKEOUT ABSTRACT BULKHEAD DECOUPLE DETACHED DIFFRACT DISCRETE DISJOINT DISSEVER DISSOLVE DISTINCT DISTRACT DISUNITE DIVIDANT DIVIDUAL FRACTION LAMINATE LEVIGATE LIBERATE PECULIAR SEVERATE SPORADIC UNMINGLE UNSOLDER UNSTRING RESPECTIVE
(— BY BEATING) SCUTCH
(— BY CROSSWALL) ABJOINT
(— BY PICKING) LEASE LEAZE
(— COINS) JOURNEY
(— COMBATANTS) STICKLE
(— COPIES) DECOLLATE
(— FIBERS) HACKLE
(— FROM HERD) IMPRIME
(— GRAIN FROM CHAFF) FAN CAVE WINNOW
(— HAIR) BLOCK
(— INTO COMPONENTS) STRIP
(— INTO FLOCKS) DRAFT DRAUGHT
(— INTO SHREDS) TEASE
(— ONESELF) ABDICATE
(— ORE) JIG SMELT DILLUE
(— SHEEP) DRAW
(— THREADS) SLEY SLEAVE
(PREF.) APH APO CHORI(ST)(STO) ECCRINO IDIO
SEPARATED FREE ALONE BROKEN REMOTE DISTANT DIVIDED ABSTRACT ISOLATED RESOLVED
(— BY INTERVAL) OPEN
(PREF.) CHORI(ST)(STO) DIALY
SEPARATELY APART SINGLY SUNDRY ASUNDER DIVISIM SEVERAL SUNDERLY ABSOLUTELY
SEPARATING BETWEEN
SEPARATION GAP GULF PART RENT SHED BREAK CHASM SPLIT SCHISM BARRIER DIVORCE ELUTION PARTING ANALYSIS AUTOTOMY AVULSION CREAMING DECISION DIALYSIS DISTANCE DISUNION DIVISION INCISION SHEDDING SOLUTION TWINNING SEQUESTER
(— OF BODY PARTS) ABDUCTION
(— OF COMPONENTS) RESOLUTION
(— OF LEAF) CHORISIS
(— OF MAN AND WIFE) ZIHAR DIVORCE
(— OF METALS) DEPART
(— OF PIGMENT) FLOATING
(— OF SUSPENDED MATTER) PRECIPITATION
(— OF WORD PARTS) TMESIS
(— OF YEAST IN BEER) BREAK
(ABNORMAL —) SOLUTION
(MENTAL —) PRECISION
(ORE —) FLOTATION
(PREF.) DE
SEPARATIST ZOARITE BIMMELER
SEPARATOR RAVEL PARTER CREAMER SETTLER SEVERER SUBSIDER
SEPARATRIX SLASH DIAGONAL
SEPHESTIA (FATHER OF —) DAMOCLES
(HUSBAND OF —) MAXIMUS
(LOVER OF —) MENAPHON
(SON OF —) PLEUSIDIPPUS
SEPIA COCONUT SEPIARY
SEPOY PANDY TELINGA
SEPT KIN
SEPTEMBER 29 MICHAELMAS
SEPTET SEPTUOR
SEPTIC PURULENT
SEPTIOLITE MEERSCHAUM
SEPTIVALENT HEPTAD
SEPTUAGINT LXX
SEPTUM VITTA TABULA MYOTOME PHRAGMA MYOCOMMA
SEPULCHER BIER GRAVE TITLE CENOTAPH MONUMENT MORTUARY
SEPULCHRAL HOLLOW CHARNEL TUMULARY
SEPULTURE BURIAL
SEQUEL SUITE EFFECT SEQUENT BACKWASH SEQUENCE
(UNEXPECTED —) AFTERCLAP
SEQUENCE ROPE SUIT ORDER TRACT TRAIN DOCKET ENTAIL SEQUEL SERIES STRING CADENCE CORONET SEQUENT SUCCESS SPECTRUM STRAIGHT
(— IN ACID) EXON
(— IN MELODY) AGOGE
(— IN NUCLEIC ACID) INTRON
(— OF ARCS) PATH
(— OF BEHAVIOR) ACT
(— OF BILLIARD SHOTS) BREAK
(— OF CARDS) QUART TENACE STRINGER
(— OF CHESS MOVES) DEFENCE DEFENSE
(— OF EVENTS) CYCLE SCENARIO
(— OF MELODRAMA) CHASE
(— OF MESSAGES) QUEUE
(— OF ROCK UNITS) SECTION
(— OF SOUNDS) AFFIX
(— OF 3 NUCLEOTIDES) CODON
(ACTING —) EXTERIOR
(CUSTOMARY —) COURSE
(DNA —) HOMEOBOX
(FILM —) INTERCUT
(KIND OF —) CAUCHY
(LITURGICAL —) CANON
SEQUENT ENSUANT SEQUITUR
SEQUENTIAL SERIATE
SEQUESTER SINGLE ISOLATE RECLUDE
SEQUESTERED LONELY PRIVATE RECLUSE RETIRED SECLUDED SOLITARY
SEQUIN CHICK SPANG VENTIN ZEQUIN CHEQUIN CHEQUEEN VENETIAN ZECCHINO
(PL.) GLITTER
SERAGLIO HAREM SERAI ZENANA
SERAH (FATHER OF —) ASHER
SERAI INN
SERAIAH (BROTHER OF —) BARUCH OTHNIEL
(FATHER OF —) KENAZ NERIAH HILKIAH TANHUMETH
SERAPHIC ANGELIC BEATIFIC
SERBOCROATIAN ILLYRIAN
SERE SEAR SERULE UNGREEN HALOSERE
SERED (FATHER OF —) ZEBULUN
SERENADE AUBADE HORNING ALBORADA NOCTURNE SERENATA
(MOCK —) SHIVAREE
SERENADER WAIT
SERENE CALM EVEN CLEAR LITHE SEDATE SMOOTH HALCYON DECOROUS
SERENITY CALM PEACE REPOSE
SERF BOND THEW CHURL HELOT SLAVE THEOW THETE PENEST SERVUS THRALL BONDMAN COLONUS PEASANT VILLEIN ADSCRIPT PRAEDIAL YANACONA
SERFDOM BONDAGE HELOTRY SERFAGE SERVAGE HELOTISM SERFHOOD SERFSHIP
SERGE SAY SAGATHY

SERGEANT NCO TOP SARGE CHIAUS NONCOM DESKMAN SERVANT TOPKICK HAVILDAR SERIAUNT
SERGEANT-AT-LAW COUNTOR COUNTOUR
SERGEANT FISH LING CABIO COBIA SNOOK BONITO CUBBYYEW
SERGEANT MAJOR PINTANO
SERIAL SEQUENTIAL
SERIALLY SERIATIM
SERIEMA CARIAMA GRUIFORM SCREAMER
SERIES RUN SET ECCA RANK SUIT TIRE CHAIN DRIFT DWYKA ORDER SUITE TALLY TRACE COURSE EOCENE SEQUEL STRING SYSTEM BATTERY CASCADE CATALOG BEADROLL SEQUENCE PROGRESSION
(— GATHERED TOGETHER) SORITES
(— IN LINE) ROW
(— OF ABSTRACTS) SYLLABUS
(— OF ARCHES) ARCADE
(— OF BALLET TURNS) CHAINE
(— OF BALLS) OVER
(— OF BOAT RACES) REGATTA
(— OF CELLS) FILAMENT
(— OF CHARACTERS) CLINE
(— OF CHESS MOVES) COOK
(— OF CLASHES) CLATTER
(— OF COMMUNITIES) SERE
(— OF DANCE MOVEMENTS) ADAGIO
(— OF DRAIN TILES) FIELD
(— OF ELEMENTS) PERIOD
(— OF EVENTS) EPOS ACTION
(— OF EXTRACTS) CATENA
(— OF FORTIFICATIONS) CEINTURE
(— OF GAMES) RUBBER
(— OF IMAGES) DREAM
(— OF LEGENDS) SAGA
(— OF LIPS) GILL
(— OF MASSES) TRENTAL
(— OF MEETINGS) SESSION
(— OF METAL DISKS) PILE
(— OF MILITARY OPERATIONS) CAMPAIGN
(— OF MOVEMENTS) DANCE
(— OF NEIGHBORING LOTS) COTE
(— OF NOTES) GAMUT GLISSADE
(— OF PASSES) FAENA
(— OF PILES) DRIFT
(— OF POEMS) DIVAN DIWAN
(— OF PRAYERS) COURSE SYNAPTE
(— OF RACES) CIRCUIT
(— OF REASONS) ARGUMENT
(— OF RINGS) COIL GIMMAL
(— OF ROOMS) SWEEP
(— OF SHOTS) BURST
(— OF SIMILAR STRUCTURES) STROBILA
(— OF SLALOM GATES) FLUSH
(— OF SLIPS) DOCK
(— OF SOILS) CECIL
(— OF STAIRS) FLIGHT
(— OF STAMPS) SET
(— OF STEPS) STAIR STAIRS
(— OF STITCHES) STAY
(— OF STRAPS) LADDER
(— OF STRATA) KAROO MEASURES
(— OF STROKES) RALLY
(— OF TANKS) SOAPER
(— OF THIRTY MASSES) TRENTAL
(— OF THREADS) BINDER STUFFER
(— OF TONES) SCALE
(— OF TRAVELS) ODYSSEY
(— OF VERSES) ANTIPHON
(— OF WORDS) ACROSTIC ALPHABET
(CARD —) CORONET
(CONNECTED —) CATENA
(CONSECUTIVE —) STREAK
(DANCE —) DOUBLE
(GEOLOGICAL —) ECCA LIAS DWYKA KENAI EOCENE MOLASSE KEEWATIN
(GRADUATED —) SCALE
(IMPRESSIVE —) ARRAY
(RADIOACTIVE —) FAMILY
(PREF.) HIRMO
SERIOUS RUM SAD DEEP HIGH ACUTE GRAVE HEAVY SOBER SOLID STAID DEMURE SEDATE SEVERE SOLEMN SOMBER SOMBRE SULLEN AUSTERE CAPITAL EARNEST SERIOSO WEIGHTY GRIEVOUS
(PREF.) SERIO
SERIOUSLY BAD ILL DOWN SADLY DEEPLY GRAVELY SOLIDLY
SERIOUSNESS EARNEST GRAVITY SADNESS GRAVITAS SOBRIETY
SERMON SPELL SUTRA HOMILY POSTIL ADDRESS FUNERAL KHUTBAH SEREMENT SERMONET PREACHMENT
(MUSLIM —) KHOTBAH KHOTBEH KHUTBAH
SERMONIZE LECTURE
SERMONIZING MORALITY
SEROPURULENT SANIOUS
SEROUS ICHOROUS
SEROW THAR JAGLA SERAU
SERPENT (ALSO SEE SNAKE) AHI SEPS WORM ABOMA ADDER APEPI ATHER OPHIS SIREN SNAKE TRAIN CHITAL DIPSAS DRAGON GERARD HYDRUS PYTHON APOPHIS PRESTER SCYTALE JARARACA OPHIDIAN
(— WORSHIPER) NAASSENE
(FEATHERED —) GUCUMATZ KUKULKAN
(HERALDIC —) REMORA
(NORSE —) GOIN
(SACRED —) AVANYU AWANYU
(SKY —) AHI
(PREF.) COLUBRI OPHI(O) SERPU VIPERI
(SUFF.) OPHIS
SERPENTINE SNAKY SPIRY OPHITE SNAKISH BOWENITE METAXITE SCROLLED MARMOLITE
SERPENT STAR OPHIURAN
SERRANO PERCOID GITANEMUK
SERRATE SAWED ARGUTE RAFFLE NOTCHED SERRIED
SERRATION SERRA DENTILE
SERUG (FATHER OF —) REU
SERUM WHEY FLUID BIOLOGIC
(PREF.) ORO ORRHO SERO
SERVANT BOY FAG KID MAN PUG TAG AMAH BATA COOK DASI DAVY HELP HIND JACK LUCE MATY MOZO ALILA BAGOT BOOTS BOULT DAVUS GILLY GROOM HAMAL MAMMY SEWER SLAVE SOSIA SPEED USHER ABDIEL ANDREW BATMAN BEARER BILDAR BUTLER CHAKAR CLASHY DORINE EWERER FEEDER FERASH FLUNKY GILLIE GRUMIO HAIDUK HARLOT KHAMAL MENIAL PAMELA SIRCAR SKIVVY SLAVEY TEABOY TEAGUE TRANIO VARLET VASSAL VOIDER ANCILLA BOOTBOY BOUCHAL COURIER DUFTERY FAMULUS FEODARY FERRASH FLUNKEY FOOTMAN GENERAL GHILLIE MALCHUS PANDOUR PANTLER PAPELON PIQUEUR PISANIO WASHPOT ASSIGNEE CHAPRASI CROMWELL DOMESTIC FOLLOWER GRASSCUT HENCHMAN HOUSEBOY MANCIPLE MINISTER OUTRIDER PANTHINO PHILOTUS PINDARUS SERGEANT SERVITOR STANDARD TRENCHER VADELECT WARDMAID KITCHENER OBSERVANT
(— IN CHARGE OF BREAD) PANTLER
(— IN CHARGE OF DAIRY) DEY
(— IN OFFICE) DUFTERY
(— OF SCHOLAR OR MAGICIAN) FAMULUS
(— WHO CARVES) TRENCHER
(— WHO CLEARS TABLE) VOIDER
(— WHO RUNS BEFORE CARRIAGE) PIQUEUR
(— WHO SERVES TABLE) SEWER
(ARMED —) PANDOUR
(ARMY —) BATMAN LASCAR
(BENGAL —) MEHTAR SIRCAR
(BODY —) VALET SIRDAR
(BOY —) BOY KNAVE CHOKRA BOUCHAL
(CAMP —) BILDAR
(CLOWNISH —) SPEED LAUNCE
(COLLEGE —) GYP SKIP SCOUT
(FEMALE —) AMA NAN AMAH DASI GIRL LASS MAID MAMMY NURSE WENCH PAMELA SKIVVY ANCILLA HANDMAID MUCHACHA WARDMAID
(GENERAL —) FACTOTUM
(HEAD —) BUTLER TINDAL
(HIGH PRIEST'S —) MALCHUS
(HINDU —) DAS DASI
(HOUSE —) COOK HEWE SEWER DOMESTIC MATRANEE SCULLION
(INDIAN —) AYAH
(KITCHEN —) COOK WASHPOT
(LORD OR KING'S —) THANE
(LYING —) FAG
(MAID —) NAN BONNE
(MAN —) BOY JACK MOZO SWAIN VALET ANDREW GILLIE KNIGHT GHILLIE KHANSAMA MUCHACHO SERVITOR
(MISCHIEVOUS —) TEAGUE
(NON-RESIDENT —) DAILY
(PETULANT —) DORINE
(PHILIPPINE —) BATA ALILA
(SCOTTISH —) JURR
(SOLDIER'S —) PAGE
(TRUSTY —) TROUT
(PL.) FOLK VOLK STAFF FAMILIA NETHINIM
SERVE DO KA ACT AID HOP GIVE HELP LEAP SHEW SLAP STAY TEND TOSS WAIT COVER FRAME HORSE SARRA STAND ANSWER ASSIST FRIEND INTEND SAIRVE SARROW SETTLE SPREAD SUCCOR WAITON ADVANCE ASSERVE BESTEAD CONVENT FORWARD FURTHER SERVICE FUNCTION
(— A DISH) MESS
(— AS ESCORT) SQUIRE
(— AS HOST) GIVE
(— AS SUBSTITUTE) PASS
(— AS WELL AS) AVAIL
(— DRINK) SKINK
(— FOOD) HASH KITCHEN
(— FOR PASTURE) GRAZE
(— OBSEQUIOUSLY) LACKEY LACQUEY
(— PERFECTLY) ACE
(SUFF.) **(— FOR)** ORY
SERVER SALVER TUREEN ACOLYTE MINISTER
SERVICE AID FEE CENS DUTY HELP RITE TIDE YOKE FAVOR MUSAF STEAD DEVOIR EMPLOY ERRAND FACTOR OFFICE YIZKOR BENEFIT BONDAGE CHAKARI CORNAGE FUNERAL LITURGY OBSEQUY RETINUE SERVAGE SERVING BREEDING EQUIPAGE FUNCTION HEADWARD KINDNESS MINISTRY ROUNDING TENDANCE SERVITIUM
(ASSIGNED —) MYSTERY
(BODYGUARD —) INWARD
(BREAKFAST —) DEJEUNER
(CHORAL —) MATIN
(CHURCH —) LAUDS CHAPEL CHURCH HEARING STATION SYNAXIS ASPERGES EVENSONG
(COFFEE —) CABARET
(COMMUNICATION —) TELEX
(COMPULSORY —) ANGARIA
(DOMESTIC —) CHAKARI
(FEUDAL —) BOON AVERA ARRIAGE CORNAGE SEAWARD HEADWARD
(FUNERAL —) HERSE HEARSE
(MILITARY —) ARMS CAMP DUTY ESCUAGE
(MILITIA —) COMMANDO
(RELIGIOUS —) AHA SEDER COMMON
(SECRET —) OGPU
(TENNIS —) ACE LET
SERVICEABLE UTILE USEFUL DURABLE THRIFTY FRIENDLY VAILABLE
SERVICEBERRY SHADBLOW SHADBUSH SASKATOON
SERVICE TREE SORB SORBUS CHECKER SASKATOON
SERVILE BASE BOND ABJECT MENIAL SUPINE VASSAL CAITIFF SLAVISH VERNILE COISTREL CRAWLING CRINGING SERVIENT THEWLIKE
SERVILITY CRINGE
SERVING OBED SMACK DISHFUL HELPING SERVIENT WHIPPING
(SUFF.) ATORY
(— FOR) ORIOUS ORY
SERVITOR FAG GROOM PUNTER SERVANT PUNTSMAN
SERVITUDE USE VIA YOKE BONDAGE PEONAGE SERVICE

SLAVERY SERVITUS THEOWDOM THIRLAGE
SERVOMECHANISM SERVO BOOSTER
SERVOMOTOR RELAY SERVO
SESAME TIL TEEL BENNE BENNI SEMSEM VANGLO GINGILI OILSEED WANGALA AJONJOLI BENISEED SERGELIM
SESBANIA AGATI
SESQUITERPENE CEDROL CLOVENE COPAENE HUMULENE
SESSION DAY BOUT DIET HOUR SEAT COURT CLINIC SCHOOL SEANCE ACUERDO HEARING SEMINAR SITTING CONGRESS SEDERUNT SEMESTER
(COURT —) HILARY
(HAVE A —) SIT
(JAM —) CLAMBAKE
(PL.) ASSIZES
(SUFF.) FEST
SESTERTIUS BRONZE
SESTINA SEXTAIN
SET DO DIP FIX GEL KIT LAY LOT MOB PUT SIC SIT SOT CASE CREW CUBE GAGE GANG GIVE JELL KNIT KNOT NEST PAIR PICK PILT POSE REST SETT SORT STEP STOW BATCH CLASS CLOCK COVEY CROWD FIXED GAUGE GLADE GROUP INFIX PAVER PLACE POSIT READY STACK STAID STAND STEAD STEEK STICK SUITE ADJUST CIRCLE CLIQUE DEFINE FASTEN FINALE FORMAL GLAZED GROUND HARDEN IMPOSE PARCEL SERIES SETTLE SPREAD SQUARE STATED BATTERY BOILING COMPANY COMPOSE CONFIRM COTERIE DEPOSIT DISPOSE ENCHASE FACTION IMPLANT INSTATE PLATOON SERVICE STATION STIFFEN STRATUM EQUIPAGE PANTALON SEQUENCE SOLIDIFY STANDARD
(— ABOUT) FALL FANG GANG BEGIN ADDRESS
(— ACROSS) TRANSVERSE
(— AFLOAT) LAUNCH
(— APART) MARK SHED DEMARK DESIGN DEVOTE EXEMPT SACRED SEPONE SEPOSE APPOINT ISOLATE RESERVE ALLOCATE DEDICATE INSULATE SEPARATE SEQUESTER
(— A PERIOD) DATE
(— A PRICE) ASK
(— ARMOR) GARNITURE
(— ARROWS IN ORDER) FRUSH
(— ASIDE) BAR DISH DROP HAIN SIDE SINK SLIP BURKE KAPUT SEPOSE BRACKET EARMARK PURLOIN RESERVE SUSPEND ABROGATE DISPENSE OVERRIDE OVERRULE REVERSED
(— AS ONE'S SHARE) ALLOT
(— AT DEFIANCE) BEARD
(— AT LIBERTY) FREE RELEASE LIBERATE
(— BACK TO BACK) ADDORSED ADDOSSED
(— BEFORE) PRESENT
(— BOUNDS) PRESCRIBE
(— CLOSE TOGETHER) PAVEED
(— DOG ON) SIC SLATE
(— DOWN) JOT LAY GIVE LAND PLANK SCORE EXPONE DEPOSIT
(— DOWN IN WRITING) SUBSCRIBE
(— DOWN UNDER NAME) TITLE
(— EDGEWISE) SURBED
(— ERECT) COCK
(— FIRMLY) FIRM STEM EMBED IMBED PLANT POSIT
(— FORTH) DRAW ETCH SHOW GIVEN STATE DEPART DEPICT EXPOSE SPREAD ARTICLE DISPLAY ENOUNCE EXHIBIT EXPOUND PRESENT PROPONE PROPOSE PURPOSE PROPOUND
(— FORWARD) PREFER ADVANCE
(— FREE) BAIL EASE REMIT SKILL SOLVE ACQUIT ASSOIL ABSOLVE DELIVER ENLARGE UNLOOSE WINFREE ABSTRICT DISPLACE DISSOLVE EXPEDITE UNVASSAL
(— GOING) INITIATE
(— IN ACCORD) SORT
(— IN ACTION) TRIGGER
(— IN EARTH) STRIKE
(— IN FROM MARGINS) INDENT
(— IN FRONT) PREFER
(— IN MOTION) SOW
(— IN OPERATION) DRIVE
(— IN OPPOSITION) PIT
(— IN ORDER) ARRAY FRUSH PITCH ADIGHT DAIKER FETTLE INFORM ADDRESS
(— IN POSITION) PLANT POSIT STAND STICK POSITION
(— IN ROWS) RANGE
(— INTO) INLAY
(— INTO A GROOVE) DADO
(— LIMITS TO) SPAN BOUND
(— OF ACTORS) CAST
(— OF ANIMALS) TEAM
(— OF ARMS) CONVEYER
(— OF BARS) CONCAVE
(— OF BELIEFS) CREDO
(— OF BELLS) RING CHIME CARILLON
(— OF BOOKCASES) STACK
(— OF BOOKS) PLENARY
(— OF CARDS) DECK PACK
(— OF CARS) DRAG
(— OF CHARACTERS) FIELD
(— OF CHIMES) DOORBELL
(— OF CIRCUMSTANCES) CASE EGIS FRAME
(— OF CONDITIONS) REGIMEN
(— OF CORDS) SIMPLE
(— OF DISHES) GARNISH SERVICE CUPBOARD
(— OF EIGHT) OGDOAD
(— OF EXERCISES) KATA
(— OFF) FOIL MENSE SEVER SHOOT ACCENT BUNDLE BALANCE COMMEND EMBLAZE CONTRAST DECORATE EMBLAZON
(— OF FACTS) BOOK
(— OF FALSE CURLS) FRONT
(— OF FISH NETS) DRIFT
(— OF FIVE) PENTAD QUINTUPLET
(— OF FOLDED SHEETS) QUIRE
(— OF FOUR) WARP QUATENARY QUATERNION QUATERNITY
(— OFF TO ADVANTAGE) ADORN COMMEND
(— OF FURNITURE) SUITE DINETTE
(— OF GARMENTS) SUIT
(— OF GEARS) GEARSET
(— OF HIDES) KIP
(— OF HORSES) STABLE
(— OF HOUNDS) VANLAY VAUNTLAY
(— OF IDEAS) SYSTEM
(— OF JEWELLED ORNAMENTS) PARURE
(— OF LEAVES) COROLLA
(— OF LETTERS) ALPHABET
(— OF MUSICAL INSTRUMENTS) CONSORT
(— OF NETS) SHOT
(— OF NOTES) ACCORD
(— OF OPINIONS) CREDO
(— OF ORGAN PIPES) STOP
(— OF ORGANS) ARMATURE
(— OF ORNAMENTS) PARURE
(— OF PINS) KAILS KNOCKOUT
(— OF POINTS) INTERVAL
(— OF PUMPS) LIFT
(— OF QUADRILLES) LANCERS
(— OF RADIATORS) STACK
(— OF RAYS) PENCIL
(— OF ROOMS) STORY
(— OF RULES) CODE EQUITY DECALOG
(— OF SAILS) CANVAS
(— OF SHELVES) STAGE BUFFET DRESSER WHATNOT
(— OF SKI FASTENINGS) BINDING
(— OF SKINS) SHODER
(— OF STAVES) SHOOK
(— OF STEPS) LADDER
(— OF SYMBOLS) KATAKANA
(— OF TABLES) COMPUTUS
(— OF TEETH) DENTURE
(— OF TEN) DECADE
(— OF THREE) BALE TERN LEASH
(— OF TOOLS) STRING
(— OF TRAMS) JOURNEY
(— OF TWELVE) ZODIAC
(— OF TWENTY) SCORE
(— OF TYPEFACES) FAMILY
(— OF VALUES) CURRENCY
(— OF VARIATIONS) PARTITA
(— OF VATS) SOLERA
(— OF VERSES) STAVE
(— OF VOWELS) SERIES
(— OF WARP THREADS) LEA
(— OF 3 ANIMALS) LEASH
(— ON) TAR SLATE
(— ON END) UPEND
(— ONESELF) GO
(— ON FIRE) SPIT TIND LIGHT ACCEND IGNIFY IGNITE KINDLE ENFLAME INFLAME ENKINDLE
(— OUT) BOUN MAKE BOWNE FOUND SALLY START INTEND STARTLE
(— OVER) COUCH
(— RIGHT) REDD ADJUST SCHOOL SQUARE CORRECT REDRESS
(— SNARE) TAIL TILL
(— SOLIDLY) EMBED
(— STRAIGHT) DRESS
(— THICKLY) STUD
(— TO MUSIC) AIR DITTY
(— TO WORK) YOKE
(— TRAP) TELD
(— TYPE) KEYBOARD
(— UP) RIG ROAR AREAR ERECT PITCH RAISE ROUSE IMPOSE SETTLE INSTALL UPDRESS ACTIVATE ESTABLISH INSTITUTE
(— UP IN COLUMNS) TABULAR
(— UPON) BESET ATTACK AGGRESS BROWDEN
(— UPRIGHT) ERECT STAND ARRECT
(— UPSIDE DOWN) TURN
(— VALUE) APPRAISE
(— WITH BRISTLES) STRIGOSE
(— WITH GEMS) CHASE
(ANTIGEN —) SEROTYPE
(BECOME —) STRIKE
(CHESS —) MEINY MEINIE
(CHROMOSOME —) GENOME COMPLEX
(COMPLETE —) STAND
(CONSTRUCTION —) ERECTOR
(INFINITE —) FAMILY
(MATHEMATICAL —) LATTICE MANIFOLD
(MINIATURE —) DIORAMA
(RADIO —) BLOOPER
(SMART —) TON
(STAGE —) SCENE
(TELEVISION —) TUBE
(UNALTERABLY —) STOUT
(PL.) DECOR
(SUFF.) STOLE THESIS THETE THETIC
SETA STALK WHISK CHAETA SETULA SETULE CROTCHET PODETIUM
SETBACK DASH JOLT SNAG KNOCK LURCH BLIGHT BACKSET LICKING PUTBACK RELAPSE REVERSE BUSINESS COMEDOWN HAYMAKER CONTRETEMPS
(TEMPORARY —) HICCUP
SETH (BROTHER OF —) ABEL CAIN
(FATHER OF —) ADAM
(MOTHER OF —) EVE
(SON OF —) ENOS
SETHUR (FATHER OF —) MICHAEL
SETLINE GEAR TRAWL BULTOW OUTLINE TROTLINE
SETTEE SETTLE OTTOMAN WINDSOR
SETTER SOFA GUNDOG DROPPER FLUSHER SETTLER
SETTERWORT PIGROOTS
SETTING SET FALL PAVE VAIL CHASE MIDST SCENE SETUP CHATON MILIEU FERMAIL MONTURE SITTING INTERIOR MARQUISE MOUNTING SHOWCASE BRILLIANT BRIOLETTE
(— APART) BETWEEN
(— FORTH) RECITAL PRESENTATION
(— FREE) SOLUTION
(— OF GEM) FOIL OUCH CHASE GALLERY
(— OF REED) CAAMING
(— OF WHEELS) CAMBER
(CAMERA —) BULB
(FAMILIAR —) HOME
(MUSICAL —) CREDO BALLAD BALLADE
(SHUTTER —) TIME
(STAGE —) SCENE
SETTLE BED FIT FIX ICE PAY SAG SET SIT TAX BANK BIND CALM DAIS

DEAS FAST FIRM HAFT LEND NEST REST ROOT SEAT SINK SNUG TOIT AGREE CLEAR COUCH ISSUE LIGHT LODGE ORDER PITCH PLACE PLANT QUIET SQUAT STATE STILL ACCORD ADJUST ALIGHT ASSIGN CLINCH DECIDE DECREE ENCAMP LOCATE NESTLE PURIFY RESIDE SCREEN SECURE SOOTHE SOPITE SQUARE ACCOUNT APPEASE APPOINT ARRANGE BALANCE CLARIFY COMPONE COMPOSE CONCERT CONFIRM DEPOSIT DERAIGN INHABIT PIONEER RESOLVE SUBSIDE COLONIZE REGULATE SQUATTLE CONJOBBLE RECONCILE
(— ACCOUNTS) WHACK
(— A FINE) AFFEER
(— AMICABLY) COMPOUND
(— AN ACCOUNT) PONYUP
(— BUSINESS) FEEZE PHEESE PHEEZE
(— DOWN) CAMP SLUMP STEADY DESCEND
(— ITSELF) INVEST
(— LANDS ON A PERSON) ENTAIL
(— ON) POINT
(— UP) PONY PONEY
(— UPON) AFFIX AGREE TIGHT
(— VERTICALLY) SQUASH
SETTLED SAD SET FIRM FIXED QUIET STAID FORMED RANGED SEATED SEDATE SQUARE STAPLE STATED CERTAIN DECIDED EMPIGHT STATARY DECOROUS RESOLVED STANDING SEDENTARY
(NOT —) FARROW
SETTLEMENT AUL DEAL FINE FORK MISE PACT POST BARRIO COLONY DIKTAT MOSHAV WINDUP ACCOUNT BIVOUAC FINANCE MAABARA OUTPOST STATION CLERUCHY DECISION DISPATCH JOINTURE KEVUTZAH PRESIDIO SETTLING SHOWDOWN TOWNSHIP PLANTATION
(— OF JERRY-BUILT DWELLINGS) BIDONVILLE
(— OF MONKS) SCETE SKETE
(— OF SHACKS) FAVELA FAVELLA
(— ON OUTSKIRTS) BIDONVILLE
(COLLECTIVE —) KVUTZA MOSHAV KIBBUTZ
(HARSH —) DIKTAT
(INDIAN —) BUSTEE
(MARRIAGE —) MAHR ARRAS DOWNSET
(NEW ZEALAND —) PA PAH
(RAPID —) BOOM
(UPLAND —) BOOLEY
SETTLER METIC SAHIB LIVYER NESTER GRUELER PEOPLER PILGRIM PIONEER TRIMMER FINISHER GACHUPIN HABITANT SHAGROON SIBERSKI SIBERYAK
(— IN AUSTRALIA) GROPER
(— IN NEW ZEALAND) SHAGROON
(DANISH —S) OSTMEN
SETTLING SIT
(— OF ESTATE) ENTAIL
(PL.) LEES SEDIMENT
SET-TO ROW MELEE BOUT TURN PLUCK FETTLE TURNUP BRANGLE
SETUP SET SITTER ENTRAPMENT
SEVEN SEPT ZETA ZAYIN HEPTAD SEPTET HEBDOMAD SEPTETTE
(— OF DIAMONDS) POPE
(— OF TRUMPS) MANILLA
(GROUP OF —) PLEIAD
(PREF.) HEPT(A) SEPT(I) SEPTEM
SEVENFOLD SEPTUPLE
SEVENTEEN (AUTHOR OF —) TARKINGTON
(CHARACTER IN —) MAY JANE PRATT BAXTER GEORGE JOHNNY WATSON GENESIS PARCHER WILLIAM CLEMATIS
SEVEN-UP PEDRO PITCH SLEDGE
SEVER AX AXE CUT BITE DEAL HACK REND SLIT TWIN SHEAR SHRED CLEAVE CUTOFF DEPART DETACH DIVIDE LOPOFF SAWOFF SUNDER DISALLY DISCERP DISCIDE DISJOIN OUTRIVE DISSEVER PRESCIND SEPARATE SEVERIZE
(PREF.) TEMNO
SEVERAL ODD TEN SERE WHEEN DIVERS SUNDRY DIVERSE VARIOUS DISTINCT MULTIPLE
(PREF.) PLURI POLY
SEVERALLY APIECE SEVERAL
SEVERANCE SUNDER SOLUTION
(— OF RELATIONSHIPS) AIR
SEVERE BAD DRY ACID BLUE DEAR DOUR DURE FIRM HARD IRON KEEN ROID RUDE SALT SIDE SORE TART TAUT ACUTE BREME CRUEL EAGER GRUFF HARSH RETHE RIGID ROUGH SHARP SMART SNELL SOBER SOUND STARK STEER STERN STIFF STOUR TOUGH BITING BITTER BRUTAL CHASTE COARSE FROSTY HETTER SIMPLE SOLEMN STRICT TORVID UNKIND UNMILD ACERBIC ASCETIC AUSTERE CAUSTIC CHRONIC CONDIGN CRUCIAL CUTTING DRASTIC SERIOUS SPARTAN TORVOUS UNCANNY VICIOUS VIOLENT WEIGHTY ACERBATE ACULEATE CATONIAN EXACTING GRIEVOUS GRINDING HORRIBLE IRONCLAD IRONHARD RIGOROUS SCATHING STALWART STRAIGHT TERMINAL TERRIBLE STRINGENT
(MOST —) EXTREME
(VERY —) SPLITTING
SEVERELY BAD HARD BADLY STARK STIFF HARDLY SORELY STRONG HEAVILY ROUGHLY SMARTLY SOUNDLY STITHLY SHREWDLY
SEVERIAN AGNOETE AGNOITE
SEVERING
(PREF.) PRISO
SEVERITY FROST RIGOR CRUELTY TORVITY TYRANNY ACRIMONY ASPERITY FERVENCY HARDNESS RIGIDITY SORENESS VIOLENCE
SEW SUE FELL SEAM SLIP PREEN STEEK NEEDLE STITCH OVERSEW THIMBLE OVERCAST OVERHAND
(— A CORPSE) SOCK
(— LOOSELY) BASTE
(— TO REINFORCE) BAR
(— UP FERRET'S MOUTH) COPE
(— WAVED PATTERN) DICE
SEWAGE SOIL WASTE SOILAGE SULLAGE AFFLUENT DRAINAGE SEWERAGE WASTEWATER
SEWELLEL BEAVER BOOMER
SEWER SINK SIRE DRAFT DRAIN FLEET ISSUE MAKER SHORE CLOACA KILTER TACKER VENNEL BELTMAN COPYIST CULVERT DRAUGHT GULLION JAWHOLE SHIRRER PIQUIERE
SEWING TACK SUTURE SEMPSTRY
(SUFF.) RHAPHY RRHAPHY
SEX KIND SECT GENDER
(FEMALE —) SMOCK
(KIND OF —) SAFE
(MALE —) WEPMANKIN
(PREF.) GEN(O)
SEX APPEAL IT OOMPH
SEXLESS NEUTER EPICENE
SEXT MIDDAY
SEXTANT (PART OF —) ARC ARM DRUM LIMB MARK FRAME GLASS INDEX LEVER HANDLE MIRROR SUNSHADE TELESCOPE
SEXTET SESTET SEXTUOR SESTETTO
SEXTON SAXON BEADLE SHAMUS WARDEN SACRIST SHAMASH SHAMMES VESTURER SACRISTAN
SEXTUPLE SENARY
SEXTUPLET SESTOLE SEXTOLE SESTOLET SEXTOLET
SEXUAL GAMIC CARNAL INTIMATE
(PREF.) GAM(ETO)(O) GON(O)
SEXY FOXY FREUDIAN
SEYCHELLES (CAPITAL OF —) VICTORIA
(ISLAND OF —) MAHE LADIGUE PRASLIN
SGANARELLE (BROTHER OF —) ARISTE
(DAUGHTER OF —) LUCINDE
(WARD OF —) LEONORE ISABELLE
(WIFE OF —) MARTINE
SHA YASHIRO
SHAAPH (FATHER OF —) CALEB JAHDAI
(MOTHER OF —) MAACHAH
SHAB RUBBERS
SHABBINESS WAFFNESS
SHABBY BASE MEAN POKY WORN DINGY DIRTY DOWDY MANGY OURIE POKEY RATTY SCALD SEEDY SORRY TACKY CHEESY FROWZY GROTTY GRUBBY GRUNGY SCABBY SCOURY SCUFFY SCURVY SHODDY SHROVY SLEAZY TAGRAG BUNTING MESQUIN SCALLED SCRUBBY SCRUFFY SCUFFED SHABBED SQUALID PALTERLY SLIPSHOD WAFFLIKE
SHABUOTH PENTECOST
SHACHIA (FATHER OF —) SHAHARAIM
(MOTHER OF —) HODESH
SHACK COE HUT CRIB SHAG HUMPY HUTCH SHANTY
SHACKLE COP TIE BAND BIND BOLT BOND GYVE LOCK STAY BASIL BILBO CLAMP COPSE CRAMP CRANK HUMPY TRASH TRAVE FETTER GARTER HAMPER PINION SHANGY STAYER SWATHE COTTAGE COUPLER FETLOCK MANACLE MOUSING PASTERN SHEBANG SNACKLE TRAMMEL RESTRAIN
(PL.) IRONS
SHACKLER SLOTTER
SHAD BUCK CHAD ALLIS ALOSE TRABU ALLICE TWAITE ALEWIFE ANADROM CLUPEID FLATFISH SAWBELLY
SHADBUSH DOGWOOD SERVICE SERVICEBERRY
SHADDOCK LUCBAN POMELO POMPION PAMPELMOUSE POMPELMOOSE
SHADE EYE CAST DULL SCUG SHED TONE VEIL BLEND COLOR ENNUE GHOST GLIDE GLOOM GRAIN SCAUM SCOUG SWALE SWILL TASTE TINCT TINGE TRACE UMBER UMBRA DEGREE FRESCO SHADOW SHIELD SHROUD SPRITE STRAIN STRIPE TONING CURTAIN ECLIPSE GRADATE HACHURE KENNING PROTECT SECTION SHADING UMBRAGE BONGRACE HALFTONE UMBRELLA
(— OF COLOR) EYE CAST TONE
(— OF DIFFERENCE) NUANCE
(— OFF) GRADUATE
(— OF LINEN) ECRU
(— ON HAT) UGLY
(EYE —) UGLY
(NEUTRAL —) TAUPE
(OVERHANGING —) CANOPY
(WINDOW —) STORE
(PREF.) UMBRI
SHADED OMBRE SHADY DRUMLY SOMBER SOMBRE DARKLING
SHADINESS GLOOM
SHADING FLUTING LAYERING
SHADOW DOG FOX BLOT SCUG TAIL CLOUD SCOUG SHADE TRAIL UMBER UMBRA CLEEKS DARKEN FINGER SHROUD TAILER ISOGYRE PHANTOM SCARROW SUGGEST UMBRAGE UMBRATE PENUMBRA PHANTASM SHEPHERD
(PREF.) SCI(A)(O) SKIA SKIO TENEBRI UMBRI
SHADOWED DARKLING
SHADOWINESS GLOOM
SHADOWLESS ASCIAN WHITEOUT
SHADOWS ON THE ROCK
(AUTHOR OF —) CATHER
(CHARACTER IN —) LAVAL CECILE HECTOR PIERRE AUCLAIR BLINKER CHARRON EUCLIDE SAINTCYR FRONTENAC
SHADOWY MISTY VAGUE GLOOMY GHOSTLY OBSCURE
SHADRACH ANANIAS HANANIAH
SHADY DARK BOSKY BOWERY CLOUDY LOUCHE SHADOW SHADOWY UMBROSE ADUMBRAL
SHAFT BAR NIB ROD AXLE BALK BARB BOLT DART FUST HOLE PILE POLE TRAM WELL ARBOR HEUGH QUILL REACH SCAPE SHANK SHOOT SNEAD SPRAG STAFF STALE STANG STAVE STEAL STELE

STILT STING THILL TRUNK BOLTEL CANNON COLUMN GNOMON SCAPUS STAPLE TILLER TUNNEL UPRISE VAGINA BOWTELL CHIMNEY INCLINE MANDREL SPINDLE CAMSHAFT DOWNCAST ESCONSON HOISTWAY LAMPHOLE MISTREAT SHAFTWAY STANDARD WEIGHBAR WELLHOLE
(— CONNECTING WHEELS) AXLE
(— IN GLACIER) MOULIN
(— IN WATCH) STEM
(— OF CANDLESTICK) BALUSTER
(— OF CARRIAGE) FILL SILL THILL
(— OF CART) ROD TRAM SHARP STANG
(— OF CAVERN) DOME
(— OF CHARIOT) BEAM
(— OF CLUSTERED PIER) BOLTEL
(— OF COLUMN) FUST TIGE SCAPE TRUNK VERGE
(— OF FEATHER) SCAPE SCAPUS AFTERSHAFT
(— OF MINE) PIT WORK GRUFF HEUCH HEUGH RAISE SLOPE STULM WINZE GROOVE STAPLE INCLINE WINNING
(— OF PADDLE) LOOM ROUND
(— OF SPEAR OR LANCE) TREE STALE
(— OF WAGON) STAVE THILL LIMBER
(HARNESS —) HEALD
(HOLLOW —) CANNON
(MAIN —) ARBOR
(ORNAMENTAL —) VERGE
(SCYTHE —) SNEAD
(STAIRWAY —) VICE
(TWISTED —) TORSO
(VENTILATION —) UPCAST UPTAKE WINDHOLE
(PREF.) DORY SCAPI
SHAG PILE
SHAGE (SON OF —) JONATHAN
SHAGGY SHAG SWAG HARSH NAPPY ROUGH SHOCK TATTY TOUSY BRUSHY COMATE RAGGED TOOSIE HIRSUTE SHAGRAG SQUALID SWAGGED THRUMMY VILLOUS TATTERED
(PREF.) DASI DASY LASI
SHAGREEN GALUCHAT
SHAGROON PILGRIM
SHAKE BOB DAD JAR JOG ROG WAG WAP JOLT JOWL PLUM QUAG RESE ROCK SHOG STIR SWAY TOZE WEVE WHAP WHOP HOTCH JAUNT KNOCK NIDGE QUASH SHOCK SWING TRILL DIDDER DITHER DODDER DODDLE EXCUSS GOGGLE HOTTER HUSTLE JOGGLE JOUNCE JUMBLE QUATCH QUAVER QUITCH QUIVER ROGGLE RUFFLE SHIMMY SHIVER TOTTER WAMBLE WANGLE WARBLE WEAKEN WOBBLE AGITATE BRANDLE CHOUNCE CONCUSS ROULADE SHUDDER STAGGER SUCCUSS TREMBLE TWITTER WHIFFLE WHITHER BRANDISH CONVULSE ENFEEBLE
(— A PURSUER) LOSE
(— FEATHERS) ROUSE
(— HERRING) SCUD
(— LIGHTLY) LIFT
(— OFF) ARISE EXCUSS
(— TO SEPARATE) HOTCH
(— UP) JABBLE JUMBLE RATTLE
(WIND —) ANEMOSIS
SHAKER DUSTER SIFTER DREDGER JUMBLER POUNCET SANDBOX
SHAKING ASPEN ASHAKE TREMOR JARRING AGITATED
(— OF AIRPLANE) BUFFET
SHAKTI TARA PRAKRITI
SHAKTIS MATRIS
SHAKUNTALA (FATHER OF —) VISHVAMITRA
(FOSTER FATHER OF —) KANVA
(HUSBAND OF —) DUSHYANTA
(MOTHER OF —) MENAKA
(SON OF —) BHARATA
SHAKY CRANK DICKY QUAKY ROCKY TIPSY TOTTY WONKY WOOZY AGUISH COGGLY CRANKY GROGGY INFIRM WAMBLY CASALTY DWAIBLE DWEEBLE PALSIED RICKETY SHOGGLY TITTUPY TOTTERY COGGLEDY INSECURE
SHALE BAT BASS BONE CLOD FLAG KOLM TILL BLAES FAKES METAL PLATE XALLE KILLAS SHILLET MUDSTONE SLIGGEEN TORBANITE PORCELLANITE KUPFERSCHIEFER
SHALL SE MAY MUN MUST SALL
(— NOT) SANNA SHANT SHANNA
SHALLOON CUBICA
SHALLOT CIBOL ALLIUM ESCHALOT SCALLION
SHALLOW EBB BANK FLAN FLAT FLUE GLIB FLEET INANE SHOAL SILLY SMALL FLIMSY FROTHY LITTLE RIFFLE SLIGHT UNDEEP CRIPPLE CURSORY TRIVIAL MAGAZINY
(PL.) FORD
SHALLOW BECOME A —) SHOAL
SHALLOWNESS INANITY
SHALLUM (FATHER OF —) BANI KORE SHAUL JABESH JOSIAH HOLOHESH NAPHTALI
(NEPHEW OF —) JEREMIAH
(SON OF —) HOLOHESH MAASEIAH JEHIZKIAH
(WIFE OF —) HULDAH
SHALLUN (FATHER OF —) COLHOZEH
SHAM BAM FOB FOX GIG FAKE HOAX MOCK PUFF BLUFF BOGUS CHEAT DUMMY FALSE FEIGN FEINT FRAUD LETON QUEER SHUCK SNIDE ASSUME BRUMMY BUNYIP CHOUSE DECEIT DUFFER HUMBUG PSEUDO SHODDY STUMER FALSITY FORGERY GRIMACE MOCKISH PLASTER PRETEND STUMOUR POSTICHE PRETENSE SPURIOUS BRUMMAGEM PASTEBOARD SIMULACRUM
(PREF.) PSEUD(O)
SHAMAN PEAI CURER MACHI KAHUNA WABENO ANGEKOK TOHUNGA CONTRARY WITCHMAN
SHAMARIAH (FATHER OF —) REHOBOAM
SHAMASH (FATHER OF —) SIN
(SISTER OF —) ISHTAR
(WIFE OF —) AA AYA
SHAMBLE SHALE SHOOL CLOUCH BAUCHLE SCAMBLE SHACHLE SHACKLE SKEMMEL ABATTOIR SHAMMOCK
(PL.) BUTCHERY
SHAMBLING SHACKLY
SHAME SISS ABASH AIDOS SHEND SPITE ASHAME BISMER REBUKE MORTIFY PUDENCY SCANDAL SLANDER CONTEMPT DISGRACE DISHONOR REPROACH SHENDING VERGOYNE VITUPERY
(— BY CENSURE) TOUCH
SHAMED (FATHER OF —) ELPAAL
SHAMEFACED SHY
SHAMEFACEDNESS PUDENCY
SHAMEFUL BASE FOUL MEAN GROSS HONTOUS IGNOBLE FLAGRANT IMPROPER INFAMOUS
SHAMELESS HARD BRASH ARRANT BRAZEN BASHLESS BROWLESS IMMODEST IMPUDENT
SHAMELESSNESS BRASS
SHAMGAR (FATHER OF —) ANATH
SHAMIR (FATHER OF —) MICAH
(GRANDFATHER OF —) UZZIEL
SHAMMA (FATHER OF —) ZOPHAH
SHAMMAH (BROTHER OF —) DAVID
(FATHER OF —) JESSE REUEL
SHAMMAI (FATHER OF —) ONAM REKEM
SHAMMES BEADLE
SHAMMUA (FATHER OF —) DAVID ZACCUR
(MOTHER OF —) BATHSHEBA
(SON OF —) ABDA
SHAMPOO TRIPSIS
(— INGREDIENT) ALOE
SHAMPOOING TRIPSIS
SHAMROCK OCA SEAMROG SHAMROOT
SHAMUS TEC SEXTON DETECTIVE
SHANK BODY CRUS GAMB JAMB TANG FEMUR GAMBE CANNON NIBBLE TARSUS KNUCKLE
(THREAD —) STEM
SHANNY BULLY
SHANTY SLED BOIST HUMPY HUTCH SHACK SHEBANG CHANTIER DOGHOUSE
SHAPE AX ADZ AXE CUT DIE HUE ADZE BEAT BEND CAST COLE COPE DRAW FACE FAIR FORM HACK MOLD NICK BEVEL BLOCK BOAST BUILT COLOR DRAPE DRESS FEIGN FORGE FRAME GUISE HORSE JOLLY LATHE MODEL MOULD SWAGE BROACH CHISEL CUTOUT EFFORM FIGURE FORMER FRAISE HAMMER JIGGER SQUARE CHANNEL CONFORM CONTOUR FASHION FEATURE GESTALT INCLINE OUTLINE PATTERN TONNEAU CONTRIVE LIKENESS
(— BY HAMMERING) SMITH
(— DIAMOND) BRUTE
(— GARMENTS) BOARD
(— LIKE AN EGG) OVOID
(— METAL) SWAGE EXTRUDE
(— OF BUST) TAILLE
(— OF ENVELOPE FLAP) KNIFE
(— ONE'S COURSE) ETTLE
(— ON POTTER'S WHEEL) THROW
(— RIGHTLY) FIT
(— ROUGHLY) BOAST SCABBLE SCAPPLE
(— ROUGHLY WITH CHISEL) BOAST
(— STONE) BROACH SCABBLE
(CLAY —) FLOATER
(CONICAL —) BEEHIVE
(GEM —) BAGUET BAGUETTE
(GLOVE —) TRANK
(LIKE A DOUGHNUT) TORIC
(SPIRALLING —) SWIRL
(SURFACE —) GEOMETRY
(UNBLOCKED —) HOOD
(PREF.) MORPH(O)
SHAPED BUILT FITTED BLOCKED FEATURED
(— LIKE A DOUGHNUT) TORIC
(— LIKE A HORN) LYRATE
(— LIKE ALMOND) AMYGDALOID
(— LIKE ANVIL) INCUS
(— LIKE ARROW) SAGITTAL SAGITTATE
(— LIKE BASIN) PELVIFORM
(— LIKE BEAN) FABIFORM
(— LIKE BERRY) BACCIFORM
(— LIKE BOAT) SCAPHOID NAVICULAR
(— LIKE BUCKLER) SCUTATE
(— LIKE CAKE) PLACENTIFORM
(— LIKE CAP) PILEATE PILEATED
(— LIKE CLUB) CLAVATE CLUBBED
(— LIKE COIN) NUMMULAR
(— LIKE COMB) CTENOID
(— LIKE CONE) CONIFORM
(— LIKE CUP) SCYPHATE
(— LIKE DOME) DOMAL
(— LIKE EAR) AURIFORM
(— LIKE FAN) RHIPIDATE
(— LIKE FEATHER) PINNATE PINNATED PENNIFORM
(— LIKE FIDDLE) PANDURATE
(— LIKE FUNNEL) INFUNDIBULAR
(— LIKE HALBERD) HASTATE
(— LIKE HAMMER) MALLEIFORM
(— LIKE HEART) CORDATE CORDIFORM
(— LIKE HOOK) ANKYROID
(— LIKE HORN) CORNIFORM
(— LIKE HORSESHOE) HIPPOCREPIAN
(— LIKE KEEL) CARINATE
(— LIKE KIDNEY) NEPHROID RENIFORM
(— LIKE LEAF) FOLIATE
(— LIKE LENS) LENTOID PHACOID
(— LIKE LENTIL) PHACOID PHACOIDAL
(— LIKE NEEDLE) ACUATE
(— LIKE ORANGE) OBLATE
(— LIKE PEA) PISIFORM
(— LIKE PEAR) PYRIFORM
(— LIKE PITCHER) ARYTENOID ARYTAENOID
(— LIKE POUCH) BURSIFORM
(— LIKE PULLEY) TROCHLEAR
(— LIKE RING) ANNULAR
(— LIKE ROD) BACILLAR
(— LIKE S) SIGMATE
(— LIKE SAUCER) PATELLATE
(— LIKE SAUSAGE) ALLANTOID
(— LIKE SCIMITAR) ACINACIFORM

(— LIKE SHELL) CONCHATE CONCHIFORM
(— LIKE SHIELD) ASPIDATE CLYPEATE
(— LIKE SICKLE) FALCULAR
(— LIKE SLIPPER) CALCEIFORM CALCEOLATE
(— LIKE SNAKE) ANGUIFORM
(— LIKE SOCKET) GLENOID GLENOIDAL
(— LIKE SPINDLE) FUSOID FUSIFORM
(— LIKE SPUR) CALCARINE
(— LIKE STAR) ASTROID
(— LIKE STRAP) LIGULATE
(— LIKE SWORD) GLADIATE
(— LIKE THREAD) FILIFORM
(— LIKE TURNIP) NAPIFORM
(— LIKE WATCH GLASS) MENISCOID
(— LIKE WEDGE) CUNEAL CUNEATE
(— LIKE WHEEL) ROTATE
(— LIKE X) SALTIRE
(— WITH AX) HEWN
SHAPED)- LIKE BELL) CAMPANIFORM
SHAPELESS DUMPY CLUMPY DEFORM DUMPTY INFORM FORMLESS INDIGEST UNSHAPED AMORPHOUS
SHAPELINESS DELICACY
SHAPELY GENT TIDY TRIM CLEAN TIGHT DECENT FORMAL GAINLY FEATOUS FORMFUL SHAPABLE
SHAPHAT (FATHER OF —) HORI ADLAI SHEMAIAH
(SON OF —) ELISHA
SHAPING DESCENT
SHARAI (FATHER OF —) BANI
SHARAR (SON OF —) AHIAM
SHARD SCAUR SHERD SHRED SLIVER
(PL.) PITCHER
SHARE CUT END LOT RUG CANT DALE DEAL DOLE HAND PART PLOT RENT SCOT SNIP DIVVY ENTER PARTY QUOTA RATIO SHEAR SHIFT SLICE SNACK SNICK SNUCK SPLIT WHACK COMMON COPART DEPART DIVIDE FINGER IMPART RATION SHOVEL PARTAGE PARTAKE PORTION DIVIDEND DIVISION INTEREST PURPARTY PERCENTAGE PROPORTION
(— A BED) BUNK
(— DWELLING) STALL
(— EQUALLY) HALVE
(— IN ACTIVITY) PIECE
(— OF CHURCH REVENUE) PREBEND
(— OF EXPENSES) LAW CLUB
(— OF LAND) DAIL DALE FREEDOM RUNDALE
(— OF PROFIT) LAY
(— OF STOCK) STOCK ACTION
(— QUARTERS) CHUM
(— SECRETS) CONFIDE
(ALLOTED —) DOLE
(ANCESTRAL —) PATTI
(EQUAL —) PROPORTION
(FULL —) SKINFUL
(GREATER —) FECK
(LEGAL —) HAK
(MINING —S) KANGAROOS
(ONE'S —) AFFERE
(PROPORTIONAL —) QUOTA
(SMALL —) MOIETY
(PL.) STOCK
(PREF.) MER(I)(O) MERISTO
(SUFF.) MER(E)(IC)(IS)(OUS)(Y)
SHARECROPPER RENTER BYWONER CROPPER
SHARED JOINT BETWEEN
(PREF.) CO
SHAREHOLDER (THEATRE —) RENTER
SHAREZER (BROTHER OF —) ESARHADDON ADRAMMELECH
(FATHER OF —) SENNACHERIB
SHARING INON
(— OF EXPENSE) CLUB
(— VICARIOUSLY) ARMCHAIR
SHARK FOX GATA HAYE KULP MAKO MANO TOPE GUMMY HOMER HOUND LAMIA TIGER TOMMY TOPER BEAGLE DAGGAR GALEID PALOMA REQUIN WHALER ACRODUS BONEDOG DOGFISH FOXFISH HUNFYSH PLACOID REQUIEM SLEEPER SOUPFIN SQUALID SUNFISH TIBURON TIGRONE TUBARON BULLHEAD HYBODONT ROUSETTE SAILFISH SEAHOUND SKAAMOOG SPEAREYE SQUATINA THRASHER THRESHER PORBEAGLE SEALAWYER SELACHIAN WOBBEGONG SHOVELHEAD
(KIND OF —) LOAN MAKO NURSE
(YOUNG —) CUB SHARKLET
(PREF.) SQUALI SQUALO
SHARP DRY SHY ACID ACRE CHIC CUTE EDGY FELL FINE GAIR GASH GLEG GNIB HARD HIGH KEEN PERT SALT TART ACERB ACRID ACUTE ALERT BRASH BREME BRISK CRISP DOWNY EAGER EDGED FALSE HARSH NASAL NEBBY NIPPY PEERY QUICK SMART SNELL SQUAB STEEP STIFF VIVID YAULD ACIDIC ACUATE ARGUTE ASTUTE BITING BITTER BRIGHT CRISPY DIESIS GLASSY JAGGED PLUCKY SEVERE SHREWD SHRILL SNELLY SNITHE STINGY TOOTHY TWEAKY UNRIDE ANGULAR AUSTERE BRITTLE CAUSTIC CUTTING GINGERY NIPPING PIQUANT POINTED PRECISE PUNGENT SHARPEN SLICING SPINOUS VARMINT VIOLENT HATCHETY INCISIVE POIGNANT ACIDULOUS IRRITABLE ASTRINGENT ACRIMONIOUS
(NOT —) MILD
(SHAPED AS —) OCTOTHORP
(PREF.) ACET(O) ACUT(I)(O) OXY
SHARP-EDGED VORPAL CULTRATE
SHARPEN EDGE FILE FINE HONE KEEN WHET BRISK FROST GRIND POINT RAISE SHARP SLYPE STONE STROP ACCENT AFFILE STROKE ENHANCE QUICKEN SMARTEN EXACUATE HEIGHTEN
(— HORSESHOE) FROST
SHARPENED ACUATE
SHARPENER SHARPER STROPPER
(SCYTHE —) RIP RIFLE
SHARPENING (— OF PITCH) RISE
SHARPER GUE GYP BITE KITE ROOK SKIN SNAP BITER CHEAT CROOK GREEK ROGUE SHARK SHARP BESTER COGGER NICKUM PICARO ROOKER SHARPY BARNARD CATALAN GAMBLER SHARKER SPIELER BLACKLEG DECEIVER PIGEONER SWINDLER
SHARPLY DAB SHARP SNACK ACIDLY ROUNDLY SHEERLY SMARTLY STEEPLY
SHARPNESS WIT EDGE SALT WHET PLUCK ACRITY ACUITY ACUMEN ACIDITY ACERBITY ACRIDITY ACRIMONY ASPERITY EDGINESS PUNGENCY
SHARP-POINTED ACUATE ACULEATE
(PREF.) ACUT(I)(O)
SHARPSHOOTER JAGER DEADEYE VOLTIGEUR TIRAILLEUR BERSAGLIERE
SHARP-SIGHTED SIGHTY LYNCEAN
SHARP-TAILED GROUSE PINTAIL
SHARP-WITTED ACUTE CANNY SNELL SHREWD
SHASHAI (FATHER OF —) BANI
SHASHAK (FATHER OF —) ELPAAL
SHASTRA PURANA SASTRA
(— CLASS) SRUTI
SHATTER BLOW DASH DICE BLAST BREAK BURST CRASH CRAZE CREEM FRUSH SMASH SMOKE SPLIT WRECK SHIVER SPIDER BEGUILE CHATTER CONVELL EXPLODE SMATTER TORPEDO DEMOLISH DYNAMITE SPLINTER
(— CLAY TARGET) KILL
SHATTERED BROKEN BROOZLED DODDERED
SHAUL (FATHER OF —) SIMEON
SHAVE BARB BITE DRAW PARE RAZE GLACE GRAZE SKIVE SCHAWE SCRAPE FLATTEN UPRIGHT
SHAVED POLLED SHAVEN
SHAVEN NOT NOTT PILLED TONSURED
SHAVER PLANE PLANER
SHAVING SHAVE SHRED SPALE SPELL RAMENT RAMENTUM
(LATHE —S) TURNINGS
(PL.) COOM COOMB SCOBS MOSLINGS
SHAWL MAUD WRAP LAMBA MANTA MANTO NUBIA PATTU RUMAL SCARF TOZIE AFGHAN ANGORA KAMBAL PEPLOS PEPLUM PEPLUS PUTTOO SARAPE SERAPE TAPALO TOILET TONNAG ZEPHYR AMLIKAR CHUDDAR PAISLEY WHITTLE WRAPPER ALGERINE CASHMERE EPIBLEMA KAFFIYEH SLENDANG TURNOVER
(COARSE —) KAMBAL
(COTTON —) FARDA
(PLAID —) MAUD
(TASSELED —) TALLITH
SHAWM WAIT SHALM BOMBARD SCHALMEI
(KIN OF —) OBOE
SHE A HE HEO HER SHU ELLE HAEC SCHO
(AUTHOR OF —) HAGGARD
(CHARACTER IN —) JOB LEO SHE HOLLY AYESHA LUDWIG USTANE VINCEY BILLALI MAHOMED KALLIKRATES
SHEAF TIE BEAT BUNG GAIT GERB OMER FLASH GAVEL GERBE GLEAN BATTEN THRAVE DORLACH HATTOCK CAPSHEAF CORNBOLE
(— LEVIED AS TAX) CORNBOLE
(— OF ARROWS) FLASH
(— OF FLAX OR HEMP) BEAT BEET GLEAN
(— OF GRAIN) GAIT GARB HOSE GARBAGE
(LAST — OF CORN) NECK
(LAST — OF HARVEST) KIRN
(PROTECTING —) HATTOCK
(UNBOUND —) REAP GAVEL
SHEAL (FATHER OF —) BANI
SHEALTIEL (SON OF —) ZERUBBABEL
SHEAR COW CUT DOD LIP NOT CLIP CROP NOTT TRIM BREAK FORCE SHARE SHEER SHIRL SLIDE STRIP FLEECE STRESS
SHEARER SNAGGER
SHEARIAH (FATHER OF —) AZEL
SHEARLING SHEARHOG
(PL.) ALPACA
SHEARS LEWIS SNIPS FORFEX SHEARER SNOUTER SECATEUR
(PREF.) FORFICI
SHEARWATER HAG CREW COHOW HAGDON HAGLET PETREL PUFFIN SCRABE PIMLICO SCRABER SEABIRD HACKBOLT
SHEATFISH WELS DORAD WALLER CATFISH SILURID
SHEATH COT HOT BOOT CASE CYST HOSE HOTT ARMOR CHAPE FOREL GAINE OCREA SHADE SHEAF SPILL THECA VOLVA COCOON CONDOM FORREL MYELIN OCHREA QUIVER SLOUGH VAGINA AXILEMMA EPILEMMA SCABBARD STANDARD VAGINULA NEURILEMMA
(— FOR BOOK) FOREL FORRIL
(— FOR FINGER) STALL
(— FOR GAMECOCK'S SPUR) HOT HOTT
(— OF CIGARETTE) SPILL
(— OF PLOW) STANDARD
(— OF TISSUE) PERIBLEM
(MEDULLARY —) CORONA
(PREF.) COLE(O) COLI(O) ELYTR(O)
(SUFF.) LEMMA THECA THECIUM
SHEATHBILL PADDY
SHEATHE CLAD COPPER MUZZLE IMPLATE
SHEATHED THECATE
SHEATHING SKIN ARMOR COPPER FACING SHEATH INLAYER SHIPLAP SLITWORK
SHEA TREE KARITE KARITI
SHEAVE SHEAF SHIVER HATTOCK TRUCKLE
(24 —S OF GRAIN) THRAVE THREAVE
SHEBA (FATHER OF —) BICHRI
SHEBANG HUT

SHEBER (FATHER OF —) CALEB
(MOTHER OF —) MAACHAH
SHEBUEL (FATHER OF —) HEMAN
SHECHANIAH (FATHER OF —) ARAH JEHIEL
(SON OF —) SHEMAIAH
SHED BOX CUB SOW ABRI CAST COTE DROP HELM HULL KILN MOLT PEEL POUR SHUD SKEO SLIP BOOTH HIELD HOVEL MOULT SCALE SHADE SPILL THROW VINEA ZAYAT BELFRY BROACH DINGLE EFFUSE GARAGE HANGAR HEMMEL INFUSE LINHAY MISTAL PANDAL SLOUGH CHOLTRY COTTAGE DIFFUSE DISCARD MUSCULE RADIATE SKIPPER EXUVIATE SKEELING SKILLION WOODSHED PENTHOUSE
(— BLOOD) BROACH
(— DROPS) DRIZZLE
(— FEATHERS OR HORNS) MEW
(— FOR LIVESTOCK) SHIPPEN
(— FOR SHEEP) SHEALING
(— LIGHT) ENLIGHT ENLIGHTEN IRRADIATE
(— OVER MINE SHAFT) COE
(— TEARS) GIVE
(— TO PROTECT SOLDIERS) TESTUDO
(CATTLE —) CUB HELM LAIR BELFRY
(MOVABLE —) SOW BAIL MUSCULE
(READILY —) FUGACIOUS
(TEMPORARY —) PANDAL
(WEATHER —) DINGLE
SHEDDING FALL SPILTH ECDYSIS APOLYSIS
(— TEARS) LACHRYMOSE
SHE-DEMON LAMIA
SHEDEUR (SON OF —) ELIZUR
SHEEN GLAZE SHINE LUSTER LUSTRE SHIMMER
SHEEP SNA TEG DOWN LAMB LONK MUGS SHIP SOAY URIN ZENU ANCON BOVID DUMBA HEDER HUNIA MUGGS OVINE SAIGA SHORN TAGGE AOUDAD ARGALI BARHAL BHARAL BIDENT CHURRO DECCAN DORPER DORSET EXMOOR HIRSEL MARKER MASHAM MERINO MUTTON NAYAUR OXFORD PANAMA PAULAR ROMNEY WETHER WOOLIE WOOLLY BIGHORN BLEATER BRAXIES CHEVIOT CRIOLLA DELAINE DISHLEY FREEZER FRONTER JUMBUCK KARAKUL LINCOLN POLLARD SUFFOLK TARGHEE TWINTER VERMONT BIKANERI COMEBACK COTSWOLD DARTMOOR HERDWICK LONGWOOL LUGHDOAN RUMINANT SHEARHOG SHEARING TALLOWER THRINTER MONTADALE ROMELDALE SHROPSHIRE
(— DIFFICULT TO HANDLE) COBBLER
(— IN 2ND YEAR) HOB TAG TEG TAGGE TWINTER
(— THAT HAS SHED PORTION OF WOOL) ROSELLA
(— TO BE SHEARED) BOARD
(DEAD —) MORT BRAXY MORLING
(FEMALE —) EWE GIMMER SHEDER
(HORNLESS —) NOT NOTT
(LOST —) WAIF
(MALE —) RAM TUP BUCK HEDER DINMONT
(MOUNTAIN —) IBEX
(OLD —) GUMMER
(PART OF —) EAR EYE LEG RIB BACK DOCK FACE LOIN NECK RACK RUMP FLANK SHANK BREAST MUZZLE BRISKET FORELEG PASTERN WITHERS FOREHEAD SHOULDER FORESHANK
(THICK-WOOLED —) MUG
(UNSHORN —) HOG TEG
(WILD —) SHA ARGAL AUDAD RASSE URIAL AOUDAD ARGALI BHARAL SHAPOO BURRHEL MOUFLON
(YOUNG —) HOG HOGG HOGGEREL
(3-YEAR-OLD —) THRINTER
SHEEPBERRY ALISIER VIBURNUM
SHEEPCOTE SHEPPEY
SHEEPDOG PULI KELPIE SHELTY BOBTAIL MALINOIS SHETLAND (PL.) PULIK PULIS
SHEEP FLY FAG
SHEEPFOLD REE COTE FANK KRAAL REEVE STELL BOUGHT BARKARY SHEPPEY SHEEPCOT
SHEEPHERDER SNOOZER STOCKMAN
SHEEPISH SHY
SHEEP LAUREL IVY HEATH WICKY KALMIA LAUREL CALFKILL LAMBKILL
SHEEPLIKE OVINE
SHEEPMAN HOBBER
SHEEP PLANT RAOULIA
SHEEP ROT CAW
SHEEP RUN STATION
SHEEPSHEAD JAMES JEMMY JIMMY PARGO PORGY TAUTOG FATHEAD PERCOID SPAROID
SHEEPSHEARER GUN
SHEEPSKIN ROAN SLAT MOUTON SOLDIER CAPESKIN LAMBSKIN WOOLFELL WOOLSKIN
(— TANNED WITH BARK) BASAN BASIL
(— THAT SWEATS UNEVENLY) SOLDIER
(— WITHOUT WOOL) SLAT
(ROUGH-TANNED —) CRUST
SHEEP SORREL SOURWEED
SHEEP TICK FAG KEB KED KADE
SHEEPWALK SLAIT
SHEER BOLD FINE MAIN MERE PURE BLANK BRANT CRUDE FRANK NAKED STARK STEEP SIMPLE CLOTTED GAZETTE EVENDOWN
(MADE OF — FABRIC) PEEKABOO
SHEET FIN CARD FILM FINE FLAT FOIL LEAF SILL BLANK FLONG FOLIO NAPPE CANVAS CIRCLE DOUBLE FASCIA FENDER FLIMSY SHROUD SINDON BLANKET CHUDDAH CHUDDER FLOGGER FRISKET LEAFLET PALLIUM PAPYRUS WRAPPER AIRSHEET EIGHTEEN FOLLOWER HANDBILL INTERLAY SHEETLET
(— ADDED TO DEED) FOLLOWER
(— ATTACHED TO INVOICE) APRON
(— FOR BRIDGE SCORES) FLOGGER
(— OF CELLULOID) CEL CELL
(— OF CLOUDS) PALLIUM
(— OF DOUGH) STRUDEL
(— OF FIBER) BAT LAP BATT
(— OF ICE) GLARE GLAZE
(— OF IRON) CRAMPET CRAMPIT
(— OF LAVA) COULEE
(— OF LEAD) SOAKER
(— OF LEATHER) BUFFING
(— OF MICA) FILM
(— OF MICROFILM) FICHE
(— OF MUSCLE) PLATYSMA
(— OF PAPER) FLAT FOLIO FRISKET LEAFLET HANDBILL
(— OF PARCHMENT) SKIN FOLLOWER
(— OF RUBBER) DAM
(— OF STAMPS) PANE
(— OF STRAW) YELM
(— OF SUGAR) SLAB
(— OF TISSUE) FASCIA
(— OF TOBACCO) BINDER
(— OF WATER) NAPPE
(— USED FOR MATRIX) FLONG
(HEATED —) CAUL
(METAL —S) LATTENS
(NEWS —) GAZETTE
(ORGANIZATION —) BILL
(PERFORATED —) SIEVE
(PROTECTIVE —) CURTAIN
(THEATRICAL —) SIDE
(THIN —) LAMINA
(THIN —S OF IRON) DOUBLES
(TRANSPARENT —) GELATINE
(WINDING —) SINDON SUDARY (PREF.) PALLIO
SHEETING PERCALE DOMESTIC AMERIKANI
SHEHARIAH (FATHER OF —) JEHORAM
SHEKEL (HALF —) BEKAH
SHEKINAH GLORY
SHELAH (FATHER OF —) JUDAH
SHELDRAKE SHELDER BARGOOSE BERGANDER
SHELEMIAH (FATHER OF —) BANI ABDEEL
(SON OF —) IRIJAH JEHUCAL HANANIAH
SHELEPH (FATHER OF —) JOKTAN
SHELESH (FATHER OF —) HELEM
SHELF BANK BERM BINK DECK DESS STEP TACK BENCH LEDGE SKELF STAGE STOOL MANTEL SCONCE SETTLE SHELVE BACKBAR BRACKET COUNTER PLATEAU CREDENCE CUPBOARD
(— BEFORE STOVE) HEARTH
(— BEHIND ALTAR) GRADINE GRADINO RETABLE
(— IN MINE) BUNNING
(— OF ROCK) CAR LENCH LENCHEON
(ALTAR —) BUTSUDAN
(CONTINENTAL —) PLATFORM
(FIREWORKS —) BALLOON
(RAISED —) SETTLE
SHELL ARD HUD PEN POD BAND CASK CHOU CLAM CONE HARD HOOF HULL HUSK MAIL OBUS PELL PILL PIPI PUKA PUPA SKIN SWAD UMBO UNIO BALAT CHANK CHINK CONCH COPIS CRUMP CRUST DRILL FRITZ GOURD MITER MITRA MUREX ORMER OVULA SCAUP SHALE SHARD SHEAL SHERD SHOCK SHUCK TESTA TIARA TROCA TURBO VALVE VENUS ANOMIA ARCHIE BUCKIE BULLET BURGAU CAPSID CERION COCKLE CONKER COWRIE CRUSTA DENTAL DOLIUM ECLAIR JINGLE LORICA MAROON NOUGAT NUCULA PULLET PURPLE SANKHA SINGLE SLOUGH STROMB TRITON TURBAN VANNET VENTER VOLUTE WINKLE BALANUS BALLOON CARACOL CARCASS COCONUT DARIOLE DISCINA GLADIUS LIMACEL MARINER PAPBOAT PHILINE PROJECT SCALLOP SPICULE SPINDLE SPONDYL TEREBRA THIMBLE TOHEROA TORPEDO TOXIFER TROCHID TRUMPET UNICORN BACULITE BACULOID CARAPACE CONCHITE COQUILLE CYLINDER DUCKFOOT EGGSHELL ENVELOPE ESCALLOP FIGSHELL FOCALOID FRUSTULE HELICINA MERINGUE OLIVELLA PUPARIUM SEASHELL SOLARIUM STROMBUS UNIVALVE VELUTINA VERMETID VERMETUS WARRENER WHIZBANG WOODCOCK
(— CONTAINING MEDICINE) CAPSULE
(— OF DIATOM) FRUSTULE
(— OF OYSTER) HUSK SHUCK
(— OF SHIP) HULK SKIN
(— OF SLUG) LIMACEL
(— OF THE EARTH) SIAL
(—S FROM GUN) STUFF
(— SYSTEMATICALLY) COMB
(ANTIAIRCRAFT —) FLAK ARCHIE
(CARTRIDGE —S) BRASS
(CAST —S) EXUVIAE
(CUSTARD-FILLED —) ECLAIR DARIOLE
(EMPTY —) DOP
(FOSSIL —) DOLITE AMMONITE BACULITE BALANITE CONCHITE
(HOWITZER —) OBUS
(MATHEMATICAL —) HOMEOID
(OYSTER —S) CULCH CULTCH
(PART OF —) EAR LIP RIB TIP APEX WING HINGE SPIRE VALVE WHORL MUSCLE SUTURE ADDUCTOR APERTURE
(PASTA —) TUFOLI
(PASTA —S) MANICOTTI
(PASTRY —) CORNET QUICHE DARIOLE TIMBALE TALMOUSE
(PROTEIN —) CAPSID
(SNAIL —) CONKER HODMADOD
(SPIRAL —) CHANK
(TORTOISE —) HOOF
(VEGETABLE —) DOLMA
(PREF.) CHITINO CHITO CONCH(O) LOPO OECO OSTRAC(O) TESTI
(SUFF.) OECA OECIA OSTRACA
SHELLED VINED
SHELLFISH ORM COCK BUCKY NACRE PIROT BUCKIE LIMPET

WIGGLE MOLLUSK PERIWIG ASTACIAN
(PART OF —) EYE FAN LEG CLAW TAIL SHELL TOOTH FEELER RIPPER TELSON UROPOD ABDOMEN ANTENNA CRUSHER CARAPACE
SHELLING RATTLES
SHELL-LESS OON
SHELL MONEY UHLLO WAKIKI
SHELOMI (FATHER OF —) ABIHUD
SHELOMITH (FATHER OF —) DIBRI ZERUBBABEL
SHELTER CAB HUT LEE LOO ABRI BURY EAVE GIDE GITE HERD HIDE HIVE JOKE JOUK LOWN ROOF SCOG SCUG BARTH BELEE BENAB BERRY BIELD BOIST BOOTH BOTHY BOWER CABIN CLEAD CLOAK COVER EMBAY HAVEN HOARD HOUSE HOVEL HOVER HOWFF HUTCH LEWTH LITHE RESET SCOUG SHADE SHEAL ASYLUM AWNING BELFRY BILBIE BOOLEY BOUGHT BURROW COVERT CRADLE DEFEND DUGOUT GABION GUNYAH HANGAR HARBOR HOSTEL PANDAL REFUGE SCONCE SCREEN SHADOW SHIELD SHROUD SUKKAH BOROUGH CABINET CARPORT CHAMBER DEFENSE EMBOSOM EMBOWER HOUSING NACELLE QUARTER RETREAT ROOFING TABERNA UMBRAGE WANIGAN WICKIUP BESCREEN DOGHOUSE ENSCONCE LODGMENT PALLIATE SECURITY SHIELING SNOWSHED WAYHOUSE PESTHOUSE
(— FOR CATTLE) HELM BOOLY STELL HEMMEL
(— FOR CROP WATCHERS) KISI
(— FOR DANCES) ENRAMADA
(— FOR SENTRY) GUERITE
(— FROM WEATHER) LEWTH
(— OVER BEEHIVE) HOOD
(BIRD HUNTER'S —) BLIND
(BULLETPROOF —) MANTLET MANTELET
(CONCRETE-AND-STEEL —) PILLBOX
(CRAMPED —) HUTCH
(FISH —) CROY
(LEAFY —) LEVESEL
(MINING —) TALPA
(PICNIC —) RAMADA
(PORTABLE —) MANTA CABANA
(ROCK —) KRAPINA
(ROUGH —) JACAL
(TEEPEELIKE —) CHUM
(TEMPORARY —) HALE HOLD CABIN BIVOUAC
SHELTERED LEE LEW COSY COZY LOUN LOWN SNUG BIELD LITHE LOUND LOWND SHADY COVERT
(— SPACE) KILLOGIE
SHELTERED LIFE (AUTHOR OF —) GLASGOW
(CHARACTER IN —) EVA BENA CORA ETTA JOHN DELIA JENNY WELCH BARRON GEORGE JOSEPH PEYTON CROCKER ARCHBALD BIRDSONG ISABELLA
SHELTERING BIELDY SHADING
SHELTERLESS HOMELESS ROOFLESS
SHELUMIEL (FATHER OF —) ZURISHADDAI
SHELVE DISH BURKE SHELF SHUNT TABLE PIGEONHOLE
SHELVES STAGE ETAGERE
SHEM (BROTHER OF —) HAM JAPHET
(FATHER OF —) NOAH
SHEMA (FATHER OF —) ELPAAL
SHEMAIAH (FATHER OF —) JOEL HARIM DELAIAH HASSHUB ADONIKAM OBEDEDOM ELIZAPHAN NETHANEEL SHECHANIAH
(SON OF —) ABDA DELAIAH OBADIAH
SHEMARIAH (FATHER OF —) BANI
SHEMIDA (FATHER OF —) GILEAD
SHEMUEL (FATHER OF —) TOLA
SHENANIGAN ANTIC ESCAPADE
SHENAZAR (FATHER OF —) JECONIAH
SHENG SANG CHENG SHING
(ONE-HUNDREDTH —) CHAO
SHEOL HELL HADES
SHEPHATHIAH (SON OF —) MESHULLAM
SHEPHATIAH (FATHER OF —) DAVID JEHOSHAPHAT
SHEPHERD HERD SHEP TEND COLIN CORIN GADDI GYGES SWAIN FEEDER PASTOR TARBOX CORYDON DAPHNIS DRAFTER GADARIA KURUMBA THYRSIS TITYRUS MELIBEUS MENALCAS PASTORAL SHEEPMAN STREPHON
(GERMAN —) ALSATIAN
SHEPHERDESS DELIA MOPSA PHEBE DORCAS BERGERE GALATEA PASTORA PERDITA AMARYLLIS
SHEPHERD KING, THE
(CHARACTER IN —) ELISA AMINTA TAMIRI AGENORE ALESSANDRO
(COMPOSER OF —) MOZART
SHEPHERD'S-PURSE TOYWORT CASEWEED COCOWORT
SHEPHI (FATHER OF —) SHOBAL
SHERAH (FATHER OF —) EPHRAIM
SHERBET ICE GLACE SHRAB SORBET GRANITA SOUFFLE
SHERD SCARTH
SHERESH (FATHER OF —) MACHIR
(MOTHER OF —) MAACHAH
SHERIFF FOUD FOWD SCULT XERIF DEPUTY GRIEVE SCHOUT SHIRRA BAILIFF SHREEVE SHRIEVE ALGUACIL HUISSIER SHIREMAN VISCOUNT
SHERRY FINO CLOVE JEREZ XERES DOCTOR MANCHU SOLERA OLOROSO RANGOON SHERRIS MONTILLA MANZANILLA
SHERRY BROWN CLOVE
SHESHAI (FATHER OF —) ANAK
SHE STOOPS TO CONQUER
(AUTHOR OF —) GOLDSMITH
(CHARACTER IN —) KATE TONY MARLOW CHARLES LUMPKIN NEVILLE HASTINGS PEDIGREE CONSTANCE HARDCASTLE
SHEVA (FATHER OF —) CALEB
(MOTHER OF —) MAACHAH
SHEVRI SESBAN
SHIATSU MASSAGE
SHICER DUFFER
SHIELD ECU EGIS HIDE PELT AEGIS APRON BIELD BOARD CLOAK COVER FENCE GUARD GULAR MULGA PATCH PAVIS PELTA PYGAL SCUTE SHEND TARGE YELDE ANCILE ANGARA BLAZON CASQUE DEFEND FENDER GUNTUB GYROMA LINDEN MENTAL OCULAR PAUNCH RONDEL SCREEN SCUTUM SECURE TARGET BUCKLER CLIPEUS CLYPEUS CONCEAL LOZENGE PANNIER PAVISSE PRIDWIN PROTECT ROSTRAL ROTELLA ROUNDEL SHELTER SUPPORT TESTUDO CARTOUCH CUCULLUS HIELAMEN INSULATE MARGINAL PRESERVE RONDACHE STERNITE SUNSHADE BREASTING
(— BELOW A DAM) APRON
(— FOR ARCHERS) PANNIER
(— FOR CAMERA) GOBO
(— FOR HORSE) BIB
(— FOR LAMP) BONNET CHIMNEY
(— FOR MICROPHONE) GOBO
(— OF ABORIGINES) MULGA HIELAMEN
(— OF A STIRRUP) HOOD
(— OF CONTINENT) CORE
(— OF HIDE) SKILDFEL
(— OF SOMITE) STERNITE
(— OF TRILOBITE) CEPHALON
(— ON MAST) PAUNCH
(— ON THROAT OF FISH) GULAR
(— OVER BASE OF FAN) CANOPY
(— WITHOUT ARMS) ALBERIA
(BONY —) CARAPACE
(BULLETPROOF —) MANTA MANTLET MANTELET
(HERALDIC —) BLAZON
(KING ARTHUR'S —) PRIWEN PRIDWIN
(LEATHER —) CHAFE
(PART OF —) RIB BOSS ORLE UMBO ANTIA
(SACRED —) ANCILE
(SIBERIAN —) ANGARA
(WICKERWORK —) SCIATH
(PREF.) ASPID(O) CLYPEI CLYPEO PELTATI PELTATO SCUT(I) SCUTATI SCUTELLI
(SUFF.) ASPIS
SHIELDBEARER SQUIRE ESQUIRE PELTAST ESCUDERO SCUTIFER
SHIELD BUG STINKBUG
SHIELD FERN FERNGALE
SHIELDMAKER TYCHIOS
SHIELD-SHAPED PELTATE SCUTATE THYROID
SHIFT JIB BACK CHOP CORE FEND FLIT HAUL MOVE RUSE SHIP TACK TOUR TURN VARY VEER WEND BREAK BUDGE CREEP CYMAR DRIFT HOTCH QUIRK SHIRK SHUNT SIMAR SKIFT SLIDE SMOCK SPELL TRICK BAFFLE CHANGE DENIAL DEVICE DOUBLE PALTER SKYFTE SWERVE SWITCH CHEMISE CUTBACK EVASION FRESHEN SHUFFLE SLEIGHT WHIFFLE ARTIFICE DISLODGE DISPLACE DOGWATCH DOUBLING MUTATION PINGPONG RESOURCE REVIRADO TRANSFER TRAVERSE TURNOVER WINDLASS
(— ABOUT AS THE WIND) LARGE
(— ABRUPTLY) JUMP
(— IN DANCING) BALANCE
(— IN TACKING) JIB
(— ORDER OF BELLS) HUNT
(— RAILROAD EQUIPMENT) DRILL
(— SUDDENLY) FLY CHOP GYBE JIBE
(— WEIGHT) WING
(KIND OF —) STICK
(MINING —) CORE
SHIFTINESS LUBRICITY
SHIFTING FLUID QUICK AMBULANT CHOPPING DRIFTING FLOATING SLIPPAGE VARIABLE VEERABLE
(— BACK AND FORTH) YOYO
SHIFTLESS DRIFTY SOZZLY DRIFTING FECKLESS HAVELESS
SHIFTLESSNESS SLOUCH
SHIFTY GREASY DEVIOUS EVASIVE HANGDOG SLIDING SLIPPERY
SHIITE SHIAH SECTARY SHAIKHI TWELVER
SHILHA SHLU CHLEUH
SHILHI (DAUGHTER OF —) AZUBAH
SHILL STICK BONNET CAPPER BOOSTER
SHILLEM (FATHER OF —) NAPHTALI
SHILLING BOB HOG ORA CHIP HOGG LEVY PREST DEENER HARPER TESTON TEVISS THIRTEEN
(20 —S) POUND
(21 —S) GUINEA
(5 —S) CROWN DECUS
SHILLY-SHALLY HEDGE BACK BOGGLE
SHILSHAH (FATHER OF —) ZOPHAH
SHIM GLUT LINER SHIMMER
SHIMEA (FATHER OF —) DAVID
SHIMEATH (SON OF —) ZABAD JOZACHAR
SHIMEI (BROTHER OF —) CONONIAH ZERUBBABEL
(FATHER OF —) BANI GERA KISH JAHATH GERSHON PEDAIAH JEDUTHUN
SHIMMA (BROTHER OF —) DAVID
(FATHER OF —) JESSE
SHIMMER FLASH GLIMMER SHIMPER SKIMMER
SHIMRI (FATHER OF —) SHEMAIAH
(SON OF —) JEDIAEL
SHIMRITH (SON OF —) JEHOZABAD
SHIMRON (FATHER OF —) ISSACHAR
SHIN SHANK SKINK SWARM CNEMIS SHINNY
SHINBONE TIBIA
(SUFF.) CNEMA CNEMIA CNEMIC CNEMUS
SHINDIG SHINDY SHIVOO
SHINDY ROW BOBBERY
SHINE RAY SUN BEAM BUFF GLOW LAMP LEAM LINK STAR BLARE BLICK BLINK BLOOM EXCEL GLAIK GLARE GLEAM GLEIT GLENT GLINT GLISS GLORE GLORY GLOSS GLOZE SHEEN SKYRE STARE BEACON DAZZLE GLANCE LUSTER

LUSTRE POLISH SCANCE EFFULGE GLIMMER GLISTEN GLITTER RADIATE REFLECT SHIMMER SPARKLE RUTILATE
((— IN DARK) PHOSPHORESCE
(— BRIGHTLY) BEEK FLAME LIGHT
(— FAINTLY) SCARROW
(— UPON) SUN SMITE
SHINER CHUB DACE BREAM MOUSE REDFIN CYPRINID WINDFISH
SHINER-UP PATCHER
SHINGLE SHIM BEACH SHAKE SHIDE SLATE ASTYLL CHESIL KNOBBLE STARTER
SHINGLER NOBBLER
SHINGLES ZONA ZOSTER
(PREF.) ZOSTERI ZOSTERO
SHININESS GLARE GLAZE GLOSS
SHINING GLAD NEAT CLEAR GLARY LIGHT LUCID NITID SHEER WHITE ARDENT ARGENT ASHINE BRIGHT FULGID GLOSSY GOLDEN LUCENT MARBLE NITENT ORIENT SERENE SHEENY SPUNKY STARRY ADAZZLE BURNING FULGENT GLARING GLIMMER LAMPING FLASHING GLEAMING LUCULENT LUSTRANT LUSTROUS NITIDOUS RELUCENT RUTILANT SPLENDID STARLIKE SUNBEAMY SUNSHINY
(— THROUGH) TRANSLUCENT
(PREF.) STILPNO
SHINLEAF PYROLA
SHINNY PEG SHINTY
SHINTO (— SECT) RYOBU
SHINTY CAMANACHA
SHIP (ALSO SEE BOAT AND VESSEL) ARK CAT COG HOY NAO BARK BOAT BOOM GRAB HAND HULK KEEL LADE NAVY PAHI PINE PINK SAIL SEND SNOW TREE WOOD ZULU CHECK LAKER OILER PINTA PRORE RAZEE SCOUT SCREW SKIFF WHELP ANDREW ARGOSY BARKEY BARQUE BOTTOM CARTEL CASTLE CHASER COALER CODMAN DECKER DIESEL GALIOT GALLEY HOLCAD HOPPER LANCHA LATEEN LORCHA MASTER MISTIC MOTHER PACKET PUFFER RUNNER SAILER SALVOR SEALER SMOKER TONNER TRAVEL VESSEL ADMIRAL CARRACK CLIPPER COLLIER CONSORT DROMOND FACTORY FELUCCA FOREIGN FRIGATE FRUITER GABBARD GALLEON GUNBOAT INVOICE MACHINE MULETTA ONERARY PATAMAR PINNACE POLACRE SHALLOP SHIPLET SPITKIT STEAMER BALANDRA BALINGER BILANDER CAPITANA CUNARDER DRUMBLER FLAGSHIP GALLEASS GAYDIANG INDIAMAN JAPANNER LANCHARA MAGAZINE PESSONER PIPPINER REPEATER SAILSHIP SCHOONER SMUGGLER SPANIARD LEVIATHAN BRIGANTINE MERCHANTMAN
(— BUILT FROM NAILS OF DEAD) NAGLFAR
(— FITTED AS CHURCH) BETHEL
(— IN LIQUOR TRADE) COPER
(— OF ARGONAUTS) ARGO
(— OF NORSEMEN) KEEL
(CLUMSY —) TUB HULK
(DEPOT —) TENDER
(ESCORT —) CORVETTE
(FLEET OF —S) ARMADA
(JAPANESE —) MARU
(MALAY —) COUGNAR
(NOVA SCOTIAN —) BLUENOSE
(OBJECT SHAPED LIKE A —) NEF
(PART OF —) BOW CAP GUY RUN BEAM BOOM GAFF JACK LIFT MAST RAIL STAY VANG YARD BRACE CHAIN ROYAL SHEET TRUCK JUMPER RUDDER SHROUD STRAKE BOBSTAY BULWARK BUMPKIN COUNTER FORETOP JIBSTAY MAINTOP NETTING PENDANT RATLINE RIGGING SKYSAIL SPANKER STIRRUP STRIKER SWIFTER TOPMAST BACKROPE BACKSTAY CUTWATER FOOTROPE FOREMAST LIFELINE MAINMAST MAINSTAY STUDDING CROSSTREE FORESHEET MAINSHEET NAMEBOARD WATERLINE MARTINGALE MIZZENMAST TOPGALLANT
(PIRATE —) GALLIVAT
(PRIZE —) CAPTURE
(QUARANTINE —) LAZARET
(RECEIVING —) GUARDO
(REMOTE-CONTROLLED —) DRONE
(SLOW —) BUCKET
(STORE —) FLUTER
(SUPPLY —) COPER COOPER
(UNTRIM —) BALLAHOO
(VIKING —) DRAKE
(PL.) NAVY MARINE SEACRAFT SHIPPING
(PREF.) NAU(TI) NAV(I)
SHIPFITTER FITTER ERECTOR
SHIPHI (SON OF —) ZIZA
SHIPHTAN (SON OF —) KEMUEL
SHIPMASTER PADRONE
SHIPMENT CARLOT RAILING DISPATCH SHIPPAGE
SHIPPING (— UNIT CARLOAD
SHIPSHAPE NEAT TAUT TIDY TRIM CIVIL TIGHT ATAUNT ORDERLY
SHIP-SHAPED (— UTENSIL) NEF
SHIP SWEEPER TOPASS TOPIWALA
SHIPWAY BERTH
SHIPWORM ARTER BORER COBRA TEREDO PILEWORM WOODWORM
SHIPWRECK WRACK NAUFRAGE
SHIPWRIGHT WAYMAN BUILDER
SHIRE DERBY SHEER COUNTY
SHIRK BALK FUNK GOOF MIKE BAULK BLINK BUDGE DODGE EVADE FEIGN FUDGE SKULK SLACK RODNEY FINAGLE SHACKLE SHAFFLE SOLDIER SHAMMOCK
SHIRKER FUNK PIKER SOGER FUNKER ROTTER BLUDGER SLACKER SLINKER SUGARER COBERGER CUTHBERT EMBUSQUE SCOWBANK
SHIRLEY (AUTHOR OF —) BRONTE
(CHARACTER IN —) JOE DONNE EMILY LOUIS MOORE PRYOR SCOTT MALONE ROBERT KEELDAR SHIRLEY CAROLINE HELSTONE HORTENSE SWEETING MATTHEWSON
SHIRR SMOCK
SHIRT TOB TOP JUPE SARK TANK TOBE BLUEY HAIRE JUPON KAMIS SHIFT BANIAN BANIYA CAMISA CAMISE PALAKA PARTLET UNDERGO VAREUSE KAMLEIKA
(— FRONT) DICKY DICKEY
(COLLARLESS —) KURTA KHURTA
(FUR —) PARKA
(HAIR —) HAIRE CILICE
(ROMAN —) SUBUCULA
(SLEEVELESS —) FECKET
(SPORT —) IZOD GUAYABERA
(WORKMAN'S —) FROCK
(WORNOUT —) DICKY
SHIRTING CHEVIOT HARVARD HOLLAND SARKING
SHIRTWAIST BLOUSE GARIBALDI
SHISHA (SON OF —) AHIAH ELIHOREPH
SHISH KEBAB SOUVLAKI SOUVLAKIA
SHITTIMWOOD BOXWOOD
SHIVA (SON OF —) GANESHA KARTTIKEYA
(WIFE OF —) KALI DURGA
SHIVAREE BELLING CHIVARI HORNING SERENADE
SHIVER JAR GIRL GRUE BEVER BREAK CHILL CREEM CREEP FRILL GROWS QUAKE SHRUG SLICE CHIVER DITHER DUDDER GROOSE HOTTER NIDDER NITHER QUIVER SHRIMP SPLINT TREMOR CHITTER FLICKER FRISSON SHATTER SHITHER SHUDDER TREMBLE KAMLEIKA SPLINTER
(THE —S) AGUE
(PL.) SMITHERS SMITHEREENS
SHIVERING AGUED CHILL OURIE TREMOR ASHIVER
SHIZA (SON OF —) ADINA
SHNOOK TWERP
SHOAL BAJO BANK FLAT REEF SPIT BARRA DRAVE FLOTE SCULL SHELF SCHOOL SHALLOW TOWHEAD
SHOAT GURRY SHOOT SHOTT
SHOBAB (FATHER OF —) CALEB DAVID
(MOTHER OF —) AZUBAH BATHSHEBA
SHOBAL (FATHER OF —) SEIR CALEB
SHOBI (FATHER OF —) NAHASH
SHOCK COP JAR BLOW BUMP DINT JOLT RACK SHOG STUN TURN APPAL BRUNT GAVEL GLIFF GLOFF SHAKE STOOK STOUR DISMAY FRIGHT IMPACT JOSTLE JUMBLE REJOLT RICKLE ROLLER STRIKE TRAUMA ASTOUND CANVASS DISGUST HATTOCK HORRIFY STAGGER STARTLE STUPEFY TERRIFY DISEDIFY GLIFFING SURPRISE
(— OF CORN) STOOK STOUT STITCH
(MENTAL —) TRAUMA
(TYPE OF —) HAIR MANE
SHOCK ABSORBER SHOCK BUFFER DAMPER DASHPOT SNUBBER
SHOCKED AGHAST
SHOCKER RICKER STOOKER
SHOCKING GRIM AWFUL LURID HORRID UNHOLY BURNING FEARFUL FEARING GHASTLY HIDEOUS DREADFUL ENORMOUS HORRIBLE DESPERATE SCANDALOUS
SHOD CALCED
SHODDY SOFT CHEAP FOOTY MUNGO RATTY SOFTS TACKY SLEAZY TICKYTACKY
SHOE BAL CUE PAN BOOT BROG CLOG DRAG FLAT HALF SKID SOCK TURN BLAKE DERBY KLOMP MOYLE ROMEO SABOT SCRAE SLING SPIKE STOGA STOGY STRAP ANKLET BEAKER BROGAN BROGUE BUSKIN CALIGA CALIGO CHOPIN COBCAB COCKER CRAKOW CREOLE DORSAY GAITER GALOSH GILLIE KILTIE LOAFER MULLER PATTEN PINSON POLISH SADDLE SANDAL SECQUE BAUCHLE BLUCHER BOTTINE CALCEUS CHOPINE COWHIDE FLIPPER GHILLIE OXONIAN RULLION SHOEPAC SLIPPER SNEAKER WINGTIP BALMORAL BRODEKIN CALCEATE COLONIAL PLATFORM PLIMSOLL SABOTINE SANDSHOE SKEWBACK SLIPSLOP SOLLERET
(— FOR GRINDING) MULLER
(— FOR MULE) PLANCHE
(— IN TRUSS OR FRAME) SKEWBACK
(— NOT FASTENED ON) PUMP
(— OF AN OX) CUE
(— OF A SLEDGE) HOB
(— OF COMIC ACTOR) BAXA
(— OF SUBWAY CAR) PAN
(— REPAIRER) JACKMAN
(—S AND STOCKINGS) FEET
(— STYLE) OPENTOE
(— TO CHECK WHEEL) DRAG SKID
(— USED AS BRAKE) SKATE
(— WITH A LONG TONGUE) KILTY KILTIE
(— WITH POINTED TOE) WINKLEPICKER
(— WORN ON EITHER FOOT) STRAIGHT
(ARMORED —) SABBATON
(BABY'S —) CACK
(DOWN-AT-HEEL —) SHAUCHLE
(HOBNAILED —) TACKET
(LARGE —S) GUNBOATS
(LOW-CUT —) SOCK GILLY ANKLET BUSKIN SLIPPER COLONIAL
(MILITARY —) CALIGA
(OLD —) BAUCHLE
(PART OF —) TIP TOE ARCH FLAP HEEL LIFT SOLE VAMP WELT AGLET SHANK COLLAR EYELET FOXING INSTEP LINING THROAT TONGUE COUNTER OUTSOLE QUARTER MUDGUARD PLATFORM SHOELACE BREASTING
(PIKED —) BEAKER
(RAWHIDE —) HIMMING VELSKOEN
(SPORT —S) NIKES
(SPORTS —S) GILLIES
(STEEL —) SOLLERET
(TENNIS —S) TENNIES SNEAKERS
(THIN —) PINSON SCLAFF
(WINGED —S) TALARIA
(WOODEN —) KLOMP SABOT PATTEN RACKET RACQUET

(WORN —) SCRAE
(PL.) SHEEN SHOON SHUNE SCHONE CASUALS FOOTGEAR
(PREF.) CALCEI
SHOEMAKER SNOB FOXER SOLER ARCHER CHAMAR CODGER COZIER FUDGER GOUGER SOOTER SOUTER VAMPER COBBLER CRISPIN CROWNER SHOEMAN SNOBBER UPPERER CORVISER SNOBSCAT CORDWAINER
SHOEMAKING SNOBBING
SHOESTRING LACE LACET
SHOGI (EXPERT LEVEL IN —) DAN
SHOGUN TYCOON
SHOHAM (FATHER OF —) JAAZIAH
SHOMER (SON OF —) JEHOZABAD
SHOO HOOSH DISPEL
SHOOK PACK BLANK SHAKE
SHOOT DAG GUN IMP PAY POT PUT ROD TIP BANG BOLT BROD CANE CHIT CION DRAW LEAF PLUG SLIP WEFT ARROW BLAST BLAZE BROWN DRILL DRIVE EXPEL FLUSH FROND GEMMA GLEAM LANCE LAYER PLUFF SCION SHEET SOBOL SPEAR SPIRE SPRAY SPRIG SPRIT SPURT SQUIB STICK STOOL TUBER TURIO VIMEN BRANCH FLIGHT FLOWER GERMEN GROWTH HEADER HURTLE LAUNCH LEADER OFFSET RATOON SALLOW SOBOLE SPRING SPROUT STOLON STOUND STOVEN STRIKE SUCKER TILLER TURION BUDLING CHIMNEY DROPPER SCOURGE SPIRING TENDRIL TENDRON THALLUS ANAPHYTE APOBLAST CATAPULT TRAILING
(— A MARBLE) LAG TAW KNUCKLE
(— ASIDE FROM MARK) DRIB
(— AT LONG RANGE) SNIPE
(— A WHALE) STRIKE
(— DOWN) SPLASH
(— DUCKS) SKAG
(— FORTH) JET GLEAM SPIRE DARTLE
(— FROM DEER'S ANTLER) SPELLER
(— INDISCRIMINATELY) BROWN
(— MOOSE OR DEER) YARD
(— OF A TREE) STOW WHIP LANCE BRANCH
(— OUT) JUT CHIT DART ERADIATE
(— SEAL) SWATCH
(—S USED AS FODDER) BROWSE
(— UP) SPIRE SPURT
(FIRST —S) BRAIRD
(FLEXIBLE —) BINE
(LATERAL —) ARM
(ORE —) BONANZA
(PAWNBROKER'S —) SPOUT
(SUGARCANE —) LALO
(TENDER —) FLUSH
(WILLOW —) SALLOW
(PREF.) BLAST(O) SOBOLI STOLONI THALL(I)(O)
(SUFF.) BLAST(IC)(Y) SPERM(A)(AE) (AL)(IA)(IC)(OUS)(UM)(Y)
SHOOTER SCOOT BLASTER GUNSTER PLUFFER SHOTMAN SKEETER
SHOOTING COCKING GUNNING GUNPLAY HUNTING POTTING
SHOOTING STAR METEOR COWSLIP SHOOTER PRIMWORT
SHOP CRIB TOKO BOOTH BURSE STORE TRADE KOSHER PARLOR SHOPPE TIENDA WINKEL ALMACEN APOTHEC BOTTEGA CABARET MERCERY SHEBANG SPICERY TABERNA TURNERY BOUTIQUE COOKSHOP CREMERIE EMPORIUM ESPRESSO EXCHANGE MAGAZINE SHOWSHOP SLOPSHOP TENDEJON WAREROOM PERFUMERY HABERDASHERY
(BARBER —) BARBERY
(BLACKSMITH —) SMITHY
(BUTCHER —) CHARCUTERIE
(DRINKING —) BOUSINGKEN
(DRUGGIST'S —) PHARMACY
(HERB —) BOTANICA
(KIND OF —) HEAD
(LIQUOR —) SALOON
(OLD CLOTHES —) FLIPPERY
(PASTRY —) PATISSERIE
(PAWNBROKER'S —) LUMBER SPROUT
(REPAIR —) GARAGE
(SUTLER'S —) CANTEEN
(WINE —) BODEGA CANTINA
SHOPKEEPER CIT ARAB BAKAL BANIAN CHETTY SOUDAGUR
SHOPLIFT BOOST
SHOPLIFTER BOOSTER
SHORE GIB TOM BANK RIPE RIVE SAND SIDE TRIG BEACH BENCH CLIFF COAST MARGE RAKER RANCE SHOAR WARTH RIVAGE STRAND SEASIDE BUTTRESS DOCKSIDE LANDFALL LANDSIDE SEACOAST
SHOREBIRD AVOCET TATTLER WRYBILL SURFBIRD PHALAROPE SANDPIPER
SHORE CRAB OCHIDORE
SHOREFISH OPALEYE
SHORER BRACER CRIBBER
SHORN NOT NOTT POLLED TONSURED
SHORT AIM LAG LOW SHY BAIN CURT NEAR NIGH SOON BLUFF BRIEF BUNTY CLOSE CRISP CUTTY FUBBY FUBSY PUNCH SQUAB UNDER ABRUPT CRISPY SCANTY SCARCE STUGGY STUNTY SUDDEN ULLAGE BOBTAIL BRUSQUE CURTATE LACONIC SQUIDGY STUBBED SUMMARY SNAPPISH SUCCINCT
(— AND FLAT) CAMUS
(— AND THICK) CHUNKY STOCKY STUBBY STUMPY TRUNCH TRUNCHED
(— AND THICKSET) NUGGETY
(— AS OF WOOL) FRIBBY
(— IN PAYMENT) SHY
(— OF MONEY) HARDUP PUSHED IMPECUNIOUS
(— PERSON OR ANIMAL) PUNCH
(BRIEF —S) MONOKINI
(STOUT AND —) BUNTY CHUFFY PLUGGY THICKSET
(PL.) BERMUDAS
(PREF.) BRACHI(O) BRACHY BREVI
(SUFF.) BRACH(ISTO)(Y)
SHORTAGE WANT CRUNCH FAMINE DROUGHT WANTAGE UNDERAGE
SHORT-BREATHED PURSY
SHORTCHANGE FLUFF SHORT
SHORTCOMING SIN FLAW DEBIT FAULT DEFECT FOIBLE DRAWBACK
SHORT-COUPLED CHUFFY
SHORTCUT CUTOFF
SHORT-EARED OWL MOMO
SHORTEN CUT CLIP STAG ELIDE SLASH REDUCE ABRIDGE CURTAIL EXCERPT SCANTLE CONTRACT DIMINISH RETRENCH ABBREVIATE
(— AND THICKEN IRON) JUMP
(— A SAIL) REEF
(— GRIP) CHOKE
SHORTENED CURTED BOBTAIL CURTATE ABRIDGED
SHORTENING LARD
(— IN PRONOUNCIATION) CORREPTION
(— OF SYLLABLE) SYSTOLE
(— OF WORD) APOCOPE
SHORTEST LEAST
SHORTFALL NEED
SHORTHORN DURHAM TEESWATER
SHORT-LIVED FRAGILE
SHORTLY SOON INABIT DUMPILY DIRECTLY PRESENTLY
SHORT-NAPPED RAS
SHORTNESS BREVITY CURTNESS UNLENGTH
(— OF BREATH) ANHELATION
(— OF SIGHT) MYOPIA
(— OF SOUND) QUANTITY
SHORT-RANGE TACTICAL
SHORT-SIGHTED SANDED PURBLIND
SHORTSIGHTEDNESS MYOPIA
SHORT-TEMPERED CROTCHETY CROTCHETED CRUSTY SNIPPY SNUFFY
SHORT-TERM FLOATING
SHORT-WINDED PURSY PURFLY PURFLED PURSIVE
SHOSHONEAN UTE
SHOT POP SET BLUE CASE JOLT OVER PLUG SETT SLUG BLANK FLIER FLING FLUFF FLYER OUTER PLUFF SHOOT TOWEL WHITE CARTON CENTER CENTRE FOLLOW MUDCAP REBOTE ALIIPOE BOMBARD CUTAWAY DEADEYE GUNSHOT LANGREL PELICAN SIGHTER BLIZZARD BUCKSHOT HAILSHOT LANGRAGE MARKSHOT SCORCHER
(— BEYOND TARGET) OVER
(— FOR CULVERIN) PELICAN
(— IN FIFTH CIRCLE) WHITE
(— IN FOURTH CIRCLE) BLACK
(— IN THIRD CIRCLE) BLUE
(— OF NARCOTIC) FIX
(— STRIKING BULL'S-EYE) CARTON
(— THAT HITS) CLOUT
(ARCHERY —) GREEN
(BADMINTON —) CLEAR
(BASKETBALL —) BOMB JUMPER
(BIG —) VIP
(BILLIARD —) DRAG STAB CAROM MASSE SCREW FOLLOW SAFETY SPREAD BRICOLE SCRATCH
(BOW —) DRAFT
(CAMERA —) PAN INTERCUT
(CROQUET —) SPLIT FOLLOW
(CURLING —) INWICK OUTWICK
(DROP —) DINK
(DUNK —) STUFF
(EASY —) SITTER
(FAULTY —) MISTAKE
(FINAL —) UPSHOT
(FREE —) CORNER MULLIGAN
(GOOD —) SCREAMER
(HIGH —) CHIP
(KIND OF —) MUG
(KIND OF BILLIARD —) BANK CAROM
(PISTOL —) BARK
(POOL —) BREAK
(SHORT —) HYPO
(SIZE OF —) F T BB FF TT BBB DUST BUCKSHOT
(SMALL —) PELLET MITRAILLE
(SNOOKER —) POT
(TENNIS —) ACE LOB DINK SERVE SMASH
(VOLLEY OF —S) BLIZZARD
SHOTGUN DOUBLE TUPARA PEPPERER SCATTERSHOT
SHOULD MOW SUD WANT OUGHT
(— NOT) SHUDNA SHOULDNA SHOULDNT
SHOULDER DOD AXLE CLOD DODD GAIN HUMP SHIP STEP SULD BOUGH PITCH SPALL SPULE VERGE AXILLA EPAULE RELISH SCOTCH SPAULD KNUCKLE RIMBASE SHOUTHER
(— AROUND TENON) RELISH
(— OF BOLT) NAB
(— OF FIREARM STOCK) RIMBASE
(— OF FLY) CHEEK
(— OF LAMB) BANJO
(— OF PORK) HAND PICNIC CUSHION
(— OF RABBIT OR HARE) WING
(— OF ROAD) BERM BERME HAUNCH QUARTER
(— PAIN) OMODYNIA
(BEVELED —) GAIN
(PL.) FOREBOWS
(PREF.) OM(O)
SHOULDER BLADE SPALD SPEAL SCAPULA OMOPLATE
(PREF.) SCAPUL(I)(O)
SHOUT BAY BOO CRY HOY HUE BAWL CALL CROW GAPE HAIL HOCH HOOP HOOT REME ROOT ROUP ROUT SCRY TOOT YELL BRAWL CHEER CLAIM CLEPE CRACK GREDE HALLO HAVOC HOLLO HUZZA REERE WHEWT WHOOP ABRAID BOOHOO CLAMOR GOLLAR GOLLER HALLOO HOLLER HURRAH HUZZAH STEVEN YAMMER ACCLAIM SHILLOO GARDYLOO LULLILOO SCRONACH
(— AS CHILDREN) BELDER
(— DERISIVELY) BARRACK
(— FOR OR AGAINST) BARRACK
(— OF APPROVAL) BRAVO
(— OF ENCOURAGEMENT) HARK
(— OF HIGHLAND DANCER) HOOCH
(— OF JOY) IO
(HIGHLAND DANCER'S —) HOOCH

(HUNTING —) CHEVY
(SEAMAN'S —) AHOY
SHOUTING HUE GLAM ROUP ROUT HOLLO CLAMOR HOLLOA JUBILEE
SHOVE JUT PUT BUNT DUSH FEND MUCK PICK POTE PUSH SHOG SHUN BOOST CROWD DUNCH ELBOW HUNCH SHIVE SHUNT HUSTLE JOSTLE JUSTLE MUSCLE THRUST SCAMBLE
(— CARELESSLY) BUNG
(— IN MARBLES) FULK
SHOVEL FAN VAN CAST PEEL SPUD SCOOP SHOOL SPADE SPOON BLUNGER SCOPPET SCUPPIT SLUDGER DUCKBILL DUCKFOOT STROCKLE
(— FOR COIN) MAIN
(— FOR DRESSING ORE) VAN
(BAKER'S —) PEEL
(BANKER'S —) MAIN
(BRICKMAKING —) CUCKHOLD
(CASTING —) SCUTTLE
(CHARCOAL BURNER'S —) RABBLE
(FIRE —) PEEL SLICE
(GRATED —) HARP
(MINER'S —) BANJO
(PERFORATED —) SKIMMER
SHOVELER SCOOPER WHINGER BLUEWING SHOULERD WHINYARD
SHOW DO SAY SEE WIS BOSH CALL DASH HAVE ITEM LEAD MARK MIEN SCAW SEEM SHEW TENT VIEW WEAR WISE ARGUE ASSAY EXERT FLASH GLOSS GLOZE KITHE PRIDE PROVE SHINE SIGHT SLANG SPORT TEACH ACCUSE ASSIGN BETRAY BLAZON CHICHI COUTHE DENOTE DETECT DEVICE DIRECT ENSIGN ESCORT EVINCE EXPOSE FIGURE FLAUNT GAIETY GAYETY LAYOUT MUSTER OBJECT PARADE REVEAL SCHEME SPREAD SPRUNK VANITY ADVANCE ANALYZE BALLOON BESPEAK BETOKEN BRAVURA BREATHE DECLARE DISPLAY DIVULGE EXHIBIT EXPRESS FASHION MONSTER PRESAGE PRODUCE PROPOSE SELLOUT SHOWING SIGNIFY TAMASHA TRIUMPH COLORING CONCLUDE EVIDENCE FLOURISH FORESHOW INDICATE MANIFEST PRETENCE PROCLAIM SEMBLANT SIDESHOW
(— APPROVAL) CLAP APPLAUD
(— BRIEFLY) FLASH
(— CONTEMPT) SCOFF
(— DISCONTENT) GROUCH
(— DISPLEASURE) POUT
(— DOGS) BENCH
(— ENTHUSIASM) DROOL
(— FORTH) BLAZE CIPHER
(— IN PUBLIC CELEBRATION) PAGEANT
(— ITSELF) APPEAR
(— MERCY) SPARE
(— OFF) FLASH PRANK SPORT SWANK HOTDOG PARADE SWAGGER SHOWBOAT
(— OF INDIA) TAMASHA
(— OF LEARNING) SCIOLISM
(— OF LIGHT) BLINK
(— OF REASON) COLOR
(— OF VANITY) AIR
(— ONESELF) BE
(— POSITION OF) MEITH
(— PROMISE) FRAME SHAPE
(— RESPECT FOR) REGARD
(— REVERSE TREND) REACT
(— SIGNS OF GIVING WAY) WAVER
(— SIGNS OF ILLNESS) GRUDGE
(— SPIRIT) SPUNK
(— THE BOTTOM) KEEL
(— THE SIGHTS) LIONIZE
(— THE TEETH) GIRN GRIN
(— THE WAY) LEAD CONDUCT
(— TO BE FALSE) BELIE DISPROVE
(— UNKINDNESS) WAIT
(— WITHOUT SUBSTANCE) FORM
(ARTFUL —) GRIMACE
(CALL-IN RADIO —) PHONEIN
(CINEMA —) FILM MOVIES PICTURES
(DAZZLING —) RAZZLEDAZZLE
(DUMB —) PANTOMINE
(EXTERNAL —) GLOSS
(FALSE —) COLOR FUCUS BUBBLE TINSEL ILLUSION PRETENCE
(FLEETING —) PAGEANTRY
(FLOOR —) CABARET
(GAUDY —) HOOPLA BRAVERY
(KIND OF —) TRUNK
(MERE —) PHANTOM
(MOMENTARY —) FLASH
(ORNATE —) FLUBDUB
(OSTENTATIOUS —) SPRUNK DISPLAY
(OUTSIDE —) VARNISH
(OUTWARD —) FUCUS VISAGE
(PUBLIC —) EXPO
(PUPPET —) DROLL MOTION WAJANG WAYANG GUIGNOL
(RIDICULOUS —) FARCE
(RUDIMENTARY —) SATURA
(RUN THE —) EMCEE
(SPECIOUS —) GLOZE VARNISH
(STREET —) RAREE
(SUPERFICIAL —) GLOSS VENEER
(TELEVISION —) PILOT
(TRAVELLING —) SLANG
(PREF.) PHAENO PHANER(O) PHANTA PHANTO PHENO
(SUFF.) PHANY
SHOW BOAT (AUTHOR OF —) FERBER
(CHARACTER IN —) KIM ANDY ELLY HAWKS JULIE PARTHY GAYLORD RAVENAL MAGNOLIA SCHULTZY
SHOWCASE ISLAND VITRINE
SHOWER WET HAIL RAIN SCAT SUMP AUGER BATHE BLASH SKITE SOUSE FLURRY PELTER PEPPER SHEWER DRIBBLE SHATTER WEATHER COMMORTH SCOUTHER
(CONCENTRATED —) BARRAGE
(HEAVY —) SUMP
(RAIN —) RASH
(SUDDEN —) SCUD SKIT BRASH PLUMP
SHOWERY BRASHY CLASHY SCATTY
SHOWILY GAILY BRAVELY GAUDILY
SHOWINESS DASH GLARE GLITZ PAZAZZ PIZAZZ GLITTER PIZZAZZ FLOURISH GEWGAWRY SPLENDOR
SHOWING SPRANK SPARKLE
(— OFF) EXHIBITION
(— SAME NATURE) AKIN
(— THROUGH THE SKIN) RAW
(ADVANCE —) PREVIEW
(PUBLIC —) EXPO
(SUPERFICIAL —) FACE
(PREF.) PHAEN(O) PHAINO
SHOWMAN IMPRESARIO
SHOWMANSHIP RECLAME
SHOW-ME STATE MISSOURI
SHOW-OFF HAM HOTDOG CUTUP
SHOWY GAY FINE LOUD NICE RORY VAIN DASHY FLARY FLASH FRESH GAUDY GIDDY GRAND JAZZY NOBBY SPICY SWANK TOPPY VAUDY VIEWY BRANKY BRAZEN BRUMMY CHICHI DRESSY FLASHY FLOSSY GARISH GEWGAW GLOSSY JAUNTY PURPLE SHANTY SKYRIN SPANKY SPORTY TAWDRY DASHING FLAUNTY GALLANT GAUDFUL HOTSHOT POMPOUS SHOWFUL SHOWISH SPLASHY SPLURGY CLAPTRAP FASTUOUS GIMCRACK GORGEOUS ORGULOUS SPARKISH SPECIOUS SPLENDID TRUMPERY CLINQUANT OBTRUSIVE
(NOT —) CIVIL LENTEN DISCREET
SHOYU SOY
SHRED DAG HOG JAG RAG ROND ROON SNIP TEAR WISP BLYPE CLOUT GRATE PATCH SHRAG SHRIP CULPON SCREED SLIVER TARGET FRAZZLE FRITTER MAMMOCK SHATTER FILAMENT
(— FISH) SCROD
(— OF CLOTHES) TACK
(— OF FLESH) TAG AGNAIL
(— OF HAIR) TAIT
(PL.) TAVERS CADDICE TAIVERS
SHREDDED CUT
SHREDDER DEVIL
SHREW ERD JES NAG TANA PRESS RANNY SOREX VIXEN CALLET JUMPER MIGALE TARGER TARTAR TUPAIA VIRAGO BLARINA HELLCAT MUSKRAT PENTAIL SCYTALE TUPAIID SINSRING SORICINE SORICOID UROPSILE XANTHIPPE
(TREE —) BANXRING
(PREF.) HYDRAC(O) SORICI
SHREWD DRY SLY ACID ARCH CUTE FELL GASH SAGE TIDY WARE WISE ACUTE CAGEY CANNY HEADY LOOPY PAWKY POKEY SHARP SMART SWACK ARGUTE ARTFUL ASTUTE CALLID CLEVER CRAFTY SPRACK SUBTLE CUNNING GNOSTIC KNOWING PARLISH PARLOUS POLITIC PRACTIC SAPIENT SAGACIOUS PERSPICACIOUS
(— PERSON) FILE
SHREWDLY SLILY CANNILY ASTUTELY
SHREWDNESS NOUS SAVVY ACUMEN POLICY SLYNESS GUMPTION PRUDENCE SAGACITY CALLIDITY
SHREWISH CURST CURSED SHREWD VIXENISH
SHREWMOUSE MYGALE SCYTALE
SHRIEK CRY YIP YARM YELL CHIRK SKIRL SCREAM SCRIKE SHRIKE SKRIKE SPRAICH
SHRIKE POPE BATARA BOUBOU BRUBRU FISCAL FLASHER FLUSHER LOGHEAD MIGRANT MINIVET TRILLER BELLBIRD FALCONET PUFFBACK WOODCHAT
SHRILL HIGH KEEN THIN ACUTE PIPEY SHARP SHILL SHIRL ARGUTE BRASSY GLASSY PIPING SQUEAK TREBLE HAUTAIN MINIKIN SCREAKY PIERCING STRIDENT
(MAKE — NOISE) POTRACK
(PREF.) OXY
SHRIMP GRIT RUNT APANG CARID MYSID PARVA PRAWN NIPPER PANDLE SCAMPI ARTEMIA BROWNIE CAMARON DECAPOD POLYPOD REDTAIL SPECTER SPECTRE CARIDEAN CRAWFISH CREVETTE MACRURAN
(KIND OF —) TIGER
(SUFF.) CARIS
SHRINE ADYT NAOS GUACA HUACA ISEUM MAZAR SEKOS STUPA ZIARA ADYTON ADYTUM CHASSE DAGABA DAGOBA DURGAH HALLOW HIERON MEMORY SAMADH VIMANA ZIARAT CHAITYA CHAPLET CHORTEN EDICULE FANACLE MARTYRY MEMORIA SACRARY TEMENOS THESEUM AEDICULA DELUBRUM FERETORY FERETRUM GURDWARA LARARIUM MARABOUT PANTHEON VALHALLA RELIQUARY
(— FOR MEDITATION) ZENDO
(— STUDY) NAOLOGY
(PREF.) PASTO
SHRINK COY SHY DARE DUCK FULL FUNK GIVE NIRL PEAK ABHOR ARGHE CLING COWER CRINE QUAIL RELAX RIVEL SHRAM SHRUG SHUCK START WINCE BLANCH BLENCH BOGGLE COTTER CRINGE FLINCH LESSEN RECOIL SCRUMP SETTLE SHRIMP WEAZEN ANALYST CRIMPLE CRUMPLE DWINDLE SCUNNER SHRIVEL COLLAPSE CONTRACT
(— FROM DRYNESS) GIZZEN
SHRINKAGE LOSS SETTLE SHRINK SINKAGE
(— OF TYPE) SQUEEZE
SHRINKING COY SHY TIMID BLETHE CREEPS DASTARD FULLING LOATHFUL TIMOROUS
(— FROM REFERENCE TO SELF) AUTOPHOBY
SHRIVE SHRIFT CONFESS SHRIEVE
SHRIVEL NIRL SEAR WELK BLAST CLING CRINE PARCH RIVEL SHRAM SNERP WIZEN BLIGHT COTTER GIZZEN SCORCH SCRUMP SHRINK WEAZEN WITHER CROZZLE
SHRIVELED WEDE CLUNG CORKY THIRL GIZZEN STARKY PUNGLED SHIRPIT WIZENED WRITHEN SHRAMMED WRIZZLED
SHROPSHIRE SALOP
SHROUD HIDE PALL SARK CLOAK CRAPE DRAPE HABIT SHEET SWIFT

EMBOSK HEARSE KITTEL MUFFLE SCREEN SHADOW SINDON SUDARY BENIGHT CONCEAL CURTAIN INVOLVE SWIFTER CEREMENT
(PL.) PUTTOCK
SHROVETIDE SHROVE GUTTIDE CARNIVAL
SHROVE TUESDAY FASTENS GUTTIDE
SHRUB TI BAY HAW KAT MAY QAT TOD AKIA ALEM BUSH COCA HOYA INGA ITEA KARO KEUR KHAT MUSK ULEX AKALA AKELA ALDER ALISO ARUSA BOCCA BROOM BUAZE CEIBO CUMAY ELDER GOOMA GORSE GOUMI HAZEL HENNA IXORA LEDUM LEMON LILAC MAQUI MARIA MUDAR RETEM SALAL SHROG SUMAC THUJA TOYON ZILLA ABELIA AGRITO AKONGE AMULLA ANAGUA ANILAO ARALIA ARUSHA AUCUBA AUPAKA AZALEA BLOLLY CENIZO CHEKAN CHERRY CISTUS CORREA DAPHNE DHAURI DRIMYS FEIJOA FRUTEX JACATE JOJOBA KARAMU KOWHAI LABRUM LARREA LAUREL MATICO MYRTLE NARRAS PENAEA PITURI RAETAM SAVINE STORAX STYRAX ACEROLA AFERNAN AGARITA AMORPHA ARBORET ARRAYAN ARRIMBY AZAROLE BANKSIA BORONIA BUCKEYE BULLACE CANTUTA CHACATE CHAMISE CHANCHE DEUTZIA EHRETIA ENCELIA EPACRID EPHEDRA FUCHSIA GUMWOOD GUTWORT HOPBUSH HOPSAGE JASMINE JETBEAD JEWBUSH JOEWOOD KUMQUAT LANTANA MAHONIA NUNNARI PAVONIA PEABUSH PEARHAW PIMELEA RHODORA SPIRAEA TARBUSH THEEZAN ABELMOSK ALLTHORN BARBERRY CAMELLIA CARAGANA COMEBACK COPALCHE DRACAENA GOATBUSH GOWIDDIE GRAVILEA HARDHACK HARDTACK HAWTHORN HIBISCUS IRONWOOD KEURBOOM KOROMIKO MOORWORT NINEBARK OCOTILLO OLEASTER OSOBERRY PIPEWOOD PONDBUSH ROSEBUSH ROSEMARY SANDSTAY SANDWOOD SASANQUA SHRUBLET SNOWBALL SNOWBELL SNOWBUSH SOAPBARK STANDARD MISTLETOE POINCIANA PHILADELPHUS
(AROMATIC —) THYME CLUSIA BORONIA HOGBUSH ALLSPICE
(AUSTRALIAN —) GOOMA BUDDAH DRIMYS GEEBUNG WARATAH MILKBUSH SANDSTAY
(CHINESE —) KERRIA
(CLIMBING —) CATCLAWS SOLANDRA
(DESERT —) AFERNAN
(EVERGREEN —) BOX BAGO ILEX TITI BOLDO ERICA FURZE HEATH HOLLY KOSAM PYXIE SALAL SAVIN TOYON BAUERA DAHOON KALMIA LAUREL PEPINO PROTEA RUSCUS SAKAKI ARDISIA BARETTA JASMINE JUNIPER MADRONA MAHONIA CALFKILL CARAUNDA EVONYMUS OLEANDER SASANQUA MANZANITA
(FRAGRANT —) JASMINE HUISACHE MEJORANA MEZEREON ROSEMARY
(HAWAIIAN —) AKALA AKELA ILIMA KOKIO OLONA
(LOW —) AYAPANA
(MEXICAN —) BLUEBUSH
(NEW ZEALAND —) KARO KAWA TUTU KARAMU KIEKIE KAWAKAWA KOROMIKO
(PASTURE —) COWBERRY
(PHILIPPINE —) IPILIPIL
(POISONOUS —) GIF CUBE LITHI SUMAC GIFBLAAR LABURNUM
(PRICKLY —) CAPER COLIMA BRAMBLE CATCLAWS
(SPINY —) ULEX AROMA GORSE JUNCO ESPINO BUMELIA CARISSA CYTISUS GENISTA GOATBUSH GRANJENO GUAJILLO HUAJILLO
(STRONG-SMELLING —) SALTWORT
(STUNTED —) SCRAB SCROG SCRUB
(THORNY —) CHANAR HAWTHORN
(TREELIKE —) ARBUSCLE
(TROPICAL —) INGA MAJO HENNA CAMARA DERRIS MOMBIN OLACAD PERSEA HAMELIA JEWBUSH LANTANA SOAPBARK
(WEST INDIAN —) ANIL RATWOOD MILKWOOD
(XEROPHYTIC —) SAXAUL
(PREF.) THAMN(O)
SHRUBBERY MOGOTE ARBORET
SHRUG SHUG HURKLE SHRINK
SHRUNK WEARISH
SHRUNKEN LANK CLUNG PUNGLED SLUNKEN WIZENED CONTRACT
(— HEAD) TSANTSA
SHTICK ACT BIT GAG GIMMICK ROUTINE
SHUAH (FATHER OF —) ABRAHAM
(MOTHER OF —) KETURAH
SHUAL (FATHER OF —) ZOPHAH
SHUBAEL (FATHER OF —) HEMAN GERSHON
SHUCK HULL HUSK SHACK SHELL SHOCK
SHUCKS DARN DRAT NUTS RATS PSHAW PHOOEY
SHUDDER GRUE CREEP GRISE HIRCH QUAKE SHRUG AGRISE GROOSE HIRTCH HOTTER HURKLE SHIVER FRISSON TREMBLE
SHUDDERING RIGOR
SHUFFLE JANK MAKE MILK SLUR MOSEY SCUFF SHALE SHIFT SHOOL JUGGLE RIFFLE RUFFLE SCLAFF SHOVEL DRAGGLE QUIBBLE SHACKLE SHAFFLE SHAMBLE SLIPPER SLUTHER
(— CARDS DISHONESTLY) PACK STACK
(— DISHONESTLY) PACK
SHUHAM (FATHER OF —) DAN
SHUN FIN SHY BALK FLEE TABU VOID WARE ABHOR AVOID EVADE EVITE SHUNT TABOO ASTART DEVOID ESCAPE ESCHEW REFUSE SHRINK DECLINE FORBEAR FORSAKE
SHUNI (FATHER OF —) GAD
SHUNT AYRTON BRIDGE BYPASS SWITCH
SHUSH HUSH WHISH SUPPRESS
SHUSWAP ATNAH
SHUT FAST HASP MAKE SEAL SHOT SLAM SLOT SPAR TAKE TEEN TINE CLOSE LATCH STEEK STICK CLOSED CABINET OCCLUSE UPCLOSE
(— DOWN) SCRAM
(— EYES) WINK
(— IN) BAR LAP CAGE COPSE EMBAR EMBAY FORBAR PENTIT TACKLE BELOUKE ENCLAVE
(— OFF) SCREEN SECLUDE SEPARATE
(— OUT) BAR DEBAR REPEL SKUNK HINDER DEPRIVE EXCLUDE OCCLUDE OUTSHUT PRECLUDE
(— SUDDENLY) SNAP
(— TOGETHER) CLASP
(— UP) BAR CUB MEW PENT STOP CHOKE FRANK STIVE STOVE CLOSET EMBOSS ENJAIL IMMURE IMPARK CONDEMN CONFINE DUNGEON ENCLOSE IMPOUND INCLUDE OCCLUDE OPPRESS PARROCK RECLUSE SECLUDE CONCLUDE PRECLUDE
(HALF —) PINK
(PREF.) OCCLUSO
SHUTDOWN LAYOFF
(— OF REACTOR) SCRAM
SHUT-EYE NAP SLEEP
SHUTOUT SKUNK
SHUTTER LID DROP SHUT BLIND SHADE CUTOFF DAMPER DOUSER SLUICE AUTOMAT BUCKLER SHUTTLE JALOUSIE
(— IN ORGAN) SHADE
(— OF TRIPTYCH) VOLET
SHUTTERBUG SNAPPER
SHUTTING CLAUDENT
SHUTTLE FLY FLUTE SHUNT BROCHE LOOPER SWIVEL SHITTLE
SHUTTLECOCK BIRD PETECA VOLANT
SHVANDA THE BAGPIPER
(CHARACTER IN —) DEVIL BABINSKY ICEHEART SCHVANDA
(COMPOSER OF —) WEINBERGER
SHY COY JIB MIM SCAR SHAN SHUN SKIT UNKO WILD BLATE CAGEY CHARY DEMUR FLING PAVID SCARE SHUNT SQUAB TIMID UNCOW BOGGLE BOOGER DEMURE MODEST SHANNY SKIEGH TARTLE BASHFUL GAWKISH RABBITY STRANGE TREMBLY UPSTAGE BACKWARD COCKSHOT DAPHNEAN FAROUCHE RETIRING SHEEPISH SKITTISH SWAIMOUS VERECUND WILLYARD
SHYLOCK (DAUGHTER OF —) JESSICA
SHYNESS COYNESS MODESTY RESERVE TIMIDITY
SHYSTER PETTIFOGGER
SIALAGOGUE SALIVANT
SIAM (SEE THAILAND)
SIAMANG APE UNGKA GIBBON
SIB SEPT AYLLU SIBLING SIBSHIP CALPULLI
SIBERIA (GULF IN —) OB
(MOUNTAIN RANGE IN —) URAL ALTAI
(NATIVE IN —) YAKU SAGAI TATAR KIRGIZ TARTAR KIRGHIZ YUKAGIR
(RIVER IN —) OB ILI KET PUR TAZ TYM AMGA AMUR LENA MAYA ONON UCUR ALDAN ISHIM NADYM SOBOL TOBOL ANGARA IRTYSH OLEKMA VILYUY
(TOWN IN —) OMSK CHITA KYZYL TOMSK IGARKA KURGAN BARNAUL IRKUTSK LENINSK YAKUTSK
SIBERIAN SQUILL SCILLA
SIBILANT HISS
SIBLING TWIN SISTER BROTHER
SIBYL SYBIL SIBYLLA VOLUSPA AMALTHEA
SIC SOOL
SICILIAN
(PREF.) SICULO
SICILIAN VESPERS, THE
(CHARACTER IN —) ELENA ARRIGO MONTFORT FREDERICK
(COMPOSER OF —) VERDI

SICILY
CAPE: BOEO FARO PASSARO
CAPITAL: PALERMO
CATHEDRAL: MONREALE
COIN: LITRA UNCIA
GULF: NOTO CATANIA
ISLAND: EGADI LIPARI USTICA
MEASURE: SALMA CAFFISO
MOUNTAIN: EREI ETNA MORO SORI IBREI NEBRODI
NATIVE: ELYMI SICEL SICANI SICULI
OLD NAME: TRINACRIA TRIQUETRA
PROVINCE: ENNA RAGUSA CATANIA MESSINA PALERMO TRAPANI SIRACUSA
RIVER: SALSO TORTO BELICE SIMETO PLATANI
SEAPORT: ACI CATANIA MARSALA MESSINA PALERMO TRAPANI
TOWN: ENNA NOTO RAGUSA CATANIA MARSALA MESSINA TRAPANI SYRACUSE
VOLCANO: ETNA AETNA

SICK BAD ILL BADLY CRONK CROOK MORBID MAWKISH SEASICK UNWHOLE CROPSICK MALADIVE PHYSICAL STREAKED
SICKEN TIRE TURN WEARY SUNDER SUNNER WEAKEN DISGUST SCUNNER SURFEIT NAUSEATE
SICKENING FELL SICKLY FULSOME MAWKISH SICKISH NAUSEOUS VOMITOUS
SICKISH DAUNCY
SICKLE HOOK CROOK
(PREF.) DREPANI FALCI ZANCIO
SICKLY WAN FLUE FOND PALE PUKY SICK DAWNY DONCY FAINT GREEN PEAKY SILLY TEWLY WEARY WERSH WISHT AMPERY ANEMIC CLAMMY CRANKY FEEBLE INFIRM PUKISH PULING WANKLY WEAKLY INVALID LANGUID MAWKISH

PEAKING PEAKISH PIMPING QUEECHY SHILPIT SICKISH WEARISH WEERISH DELICATE DISEASED MALADIVE PINDLING
SICKLY-LOOKING SHILPIT
SICKNESS (ALSO SEE DISEASE) MAL SICK SORE TAKING AILMENT DISEASE ILLNESS MALAISE SURFEIT DISORDER
(INTESTINAL —) TURISTA
(MILK —) SLOWS TIRES
(MOTION —) KINETOSIS
(MOUNTAIN —) PUNA SOROCHE
(SUDDEN —) DWALM
SIDA ILIMA ESCOBA
SIDE CAMP COST EDGE FACE HALF HAND KANT LEAF PANE PART BOARD CHEEK FLANK LATUS PARTY PHASE SITHE BEHALF PTERON ENGLISH PENDANT FORESIDE SIDELONG
(— BY SIDE) ACCOLE ABREAST ACCOSTED PARALLEL
(— OF ATTIC) SKEELING SKILLING SKILLION
(— OF BIRD'S HEAD) LORE
(— OF BOOM JAW) HORN
(— OF BOW) BELLY
(— OF BUILDING) WALL
(— OF CAVITY) WALL
(— OF DECK) GANGWAY
(— OF DITCH) SCARP
(— OF DIVIDERS) LEG
(— OF FACE) CHEEK
(— OF GATE) FOLD
(— OF GEM) BEZEL
(— OF HEAD) HAFFET
(— OF HEARTH) BREAST
(— OF HILL) BRAE SCUG SLOPE
(— OF HOG) FLITCH
(— OF HORSESHOE) BRANCH
(— OF LACE) FOOTING
(— OF LAMB) CONCERTINA
(— OF LOG) RIDE
(— OF NAVE) AISLE
(— OF OPENING) JAW JAMB
(— OF PIG) BACON
(— OF QUADRANGLE) PANE
(— OF RABBET) LEDGE
(— OF RACECOURSE) STRETCH
(— OF RECTANGLE) SQUARE
(— OF ROOF) CATSLIDE
(— OF SHIP) BEAM WALE BOARD BULWARK LARBOARD SEABOARD
(— OF STAGE) WING
(— OF TENNIS RACKET) ROUGH SMOOTH
(— OF THEATER GALLERY) SLIP
(— OF TRIANGLE) LEG
(— OF TYPE) BACK
(— OF VALLEY) COTEAU
(— OF VIOLIN) RIB
(— OF WAGON) RAVE
(— PIECE) RAVE
(— SHELTERED FROM WIND) LEE LEW LEEWARD
(—S OF FIREPLACE) COVING
(—S OF GALLERY) SLIPS
(— WITH) SUFFRAGE
(BACK —) REAR BEHIND BACKSIDE
(BY THE —) ALONG
(DRESSED —) FACE
(FAR —) OFFSIDE
(FLAT —) PANE
(FOR EACH —) ALL
(LEFT —) PORT
(MOUNTAIN —) PUNA VETA SOROCHE
(OUTER — OF SKIN) GRAIN
(RIGHT —) FACE
(RIGHT — OF SWORD) INSIDE
(UNDERNEATH —) BOTTOM
(WINDWARD —) AWEATHER
(PREF.) LATER(I)(O) PLEUR(I)(O)
(— BY —) PAR(A)
(— PARTS) ALI
(BY THE — OF) JUXTA
(ON THIS —) CIS CITRA
(SUFF.) PLEURA PLEUROUS STICH(OUS)
SIDEBAR HOUND
SIDEBOARD ABACUS BUFFET SERVER COMMODE DRESSER CELLARET CREDENCE CREDENZA
SIDE-BY-SIDE ACCOLLE
SIDED
(SUFF.) MER
SIDE DISH OUTWORK
SIDEKICK CRONY
SIDEPIECE BAR BOW JAMB WING CHEEK GUSSET EARPIECE LANDSIDE
SIDES
(PREF.)
(ON ALL —) CIRCUM
SIDESLIP SKID SLIP DRIFT DRILL
SIDESMAN HOGGLER QUESTMAN
SIDESPLITTER RIOT
SIDESTEP BEG AVOID DODGE
SIDETRACK SHUNT
SIDEWALK WALKWAY PAVEMENT TROTTOIR BANQUETTE
SIDEWAYS ASKANT ASKANCE EDGEWAYS EDGEWISE SIDELONG
SIDEWISE ASIDE ASIDEN
SIDING CURB SPUR GARAGE
SIDLE EDGE SLIVE PASSAGE SAUNTER
SIDRA PARASHAH
SIEGE BOUT SEDGE ASSIEGE JOURNEY LEAGUER
(— ENGINE) WARWOLF
SIEGFRIED (CHARACTER IN —) MIME WOTAN FAFNER SIEGFRIED BRUNNHILDE
(COMPOSER OF —) WAGNER
(SLAYER OF —) BRUNHILD
(WIFE OF —) KRIEMHILD
SIERRA CERO SERRA SAWBACK KINGFISH

SIERRA LEONE
CAPITAL: FREETOWN
COIN: LEONE
LANGUAGE: KRIO MENDE TEMNE
MEASURE: LOAD KETTLE
MOUNTAIN: LOMA
NATIVE: VAI KONO LOKO SUSU KISSI LIMBA MENDE TEMNE FULANI GALLINA SHERBRO MANDINGO
RIVER: MOA JONG SEWA MONGO ROKEL ROKKEL SCARCY WAANJE
SEAPORT: HEPEL BONTHE SULIMA
TOWN: BO DARU MANO KISSI LUNGI KENEMA MAKENI

SIESTA NAP MERIDIAN
SIEVA BEAN
SIEVE FRY TRY BOLT BUNT DRUM HARP LAWN PREE SCRY SHOE SIFT SILE SIZE TEMS GRATE RANGE SCALP TAMIS TAMMY TEMSE BOLTER RANGER RIDDER RIDDLE SEARCE SEARCH SEMMET SIFTER WEIGHT BOULTEL CHAFFER CRIBBLE DILLUER PRICKLE TIFFANY TROMMEL COLANDER SEARCHER STRAINER
(— FOR MILK) MILSEY
(PREF.) COSCINO CRIBRI ETHMO
SIF (HUSBAND OF —) THOR
SIFT REE TRY BOLT DUST SCRY RANGE SCALP SIEVE TEMSE DREDGE GARBLE RIDDER RIDDLE SCREEN SEARCE WINNOW CANVASS CRIBBLE DRIBBLE SIFTAGE CRIBRATE
(— FLOUR) DRESS
(— IN) INFILTER
(— IN MINING) LUE
(— MEAL) BUNT
(— SHOT) TABLE
(— WHEAT) SCALP
SIFTER SIEVE BOLTER CASTER SIEVER WINNOWER
SIFTING DRIFT GARBLING
(PL.) BOLTING FANNINGS SIEVINGS
SIGH SOB PECH SIFE SOCK WIND MOURN SIGHT SITHE SOUGH TWANK BEMOAN BEWAIL SORROW SUTHER DEPLORE SINGULT SUSPIRE
SIGHT AIM EYE KEN RAY BONE ESPY FACE GAZE PEEP SEET VIEW FERLY RAISE SCENE SCOPE SICHT TRACK VISIE VIZZY BEHOLD DESCRY OBJECT TICKET VISION DISCERN DISPLAY EYESHOT GLIMPSE MONSTER CONSPECT DISCOVER EYESIGHT GUNSIGHT
(— FOR GUN) BEAD LEAF PEEP SCOPE VISIE VIZZY HAUSSE GUNSIGHT
(— OF COMPASS) VANE
(— ON SURVEYOR'S STAFF) TARGET
(—S OF CITY) LIONS
(— TO SEE IF LEVEL) BONE
(AMAZING —) STOUND
(IMAGINARY —) VISION
(IMPRESSIVE —) PICTURE
(OFFENSIVE —) EYESORE
(OUT OF —) HID
(PITIFUL —) RUTH
(SECOND —) TAISH TAISCH DEUTEROSCOPY
(SORRY —) BYSEN
(STRANGE —) FERLY FERLIE
(SUFF.) OPSIA OPSIS OPSY OPTIC OPTICON ORAMA
SIGHTER ALINER ALIGNER
SIGHTING LANDFALL
(— DEVICE) ALIDADE
SIGHTLY VIEWLY EYEABLE
SIGHTSEE RUBBERNECK
SIGLOS DARIC
SIGN INK AYAH DASH FIRM HINT HIRE MARK NOTE OMEN TYPE BADGE COLON FRANK GHOST GUIDA HAMZA INDEX SEGNO SIGIL SINGE SPOOR STAMP TOKEN TRACE ASSIGN AUGURY CARACT EFFECT EMBLEM ENGAGE ENSIGN FUGLER INDICE MOTION NOTICE PARAPH REMARK SIGLUM SIGNAL SIGNET SIGNUM SYMBOL TITTLE WITTER ALEBUSH AUSPICE CHECKER CHEQUER CONSIGN EARMARK ENDORSE INDICIA INSIGNE KNOWING PORTENT PRESAGE PRODIGY PROFFER SHINGLE SHOWING SIGNARY SURMISE SYMPTOM VESTIGE WARNING CEREMONY INDICANT INSTANCE MONUMENT PROCLAIM SIGNACLE SYLLABIC TELLTALE
(— DOCUMENT) FIRM
(— FOR KEYNOTE) ISON
(— OF A COVENANT) SACRAMENT
(— OF ALEHOUSE) LATTICE
(— OF AN IDEA) EMBLEM
(— OF APPROVAL) CACHET
(— OF CONTEMPT) FIG
(— OF DANGER) SEAMARK
(— OF GLOTTAL STOP) HAMZA HAMZAH
(— OF MULTIPLICATION) DOT
(— OF ZODIAC) LEO RAM BULL CRAB GOAT LION ARIES HOUSE LIBRA TWINS VIRGO ARCHER CANCER FISHES GEMINI PISCES TAURUS VIRGIN BALANCE SCORPIO AQUARIUS SCORPION
(— ON MAP) ICON
(ASTROLOGICAL —) CIPHER
(CHARACTERISITC —) SYMPTOM
(DIACRITICAL —) TILDE UMLAUT
(GLOTTAL STOP —) HAMZA HAMZAH
(MATHEMATICAL —) NAME FUNCTOR
(MUSICAL —) CLEF FLAT REST GUIDA NEUME PRESA SEGNO SHARP SWELL SIMILE FERMATA NATURAL
(OUTWARD —) EVIDENCE
(ROAD —) MERGE
(SANSKRIT —) ANUSVARA
(SHILLING —) SOLIDUS
(SHORTHAND —) DIPHONE
(SLIGHT —) SURMISE
(SUBSCRIPT —) SUBFIX
(SUPERSTITIOUS —) GUEST
(TAVERN —) BUSH ALEBUSH ALEPOLE CHECKER CHEQUER ALESTAKE
(TRAMP'S —) MONICA MONIKER
(VOWEL —) SEGOL SEGHOL
(PL.) INDICIA INSIGNIA
(PREF.) SEMA SEMANT(O) SEMASI(O) SEMATO SEMEIO SEMIO SEMO SYMBOLO
(SUFF.) SEME
SIGNAL OS CUE GUN PST WAG BALK BECK BELL BUZZ CALL COND FLAG GATE HASH SIGN WAFF WAFT WAVE WINK ALARM ALERT BLINK FLARE FUSEE FUZEE LIGHT SHAPE SHORT SPEAK TOKEN WHIFF ALARUM BANNER BEACON BECKON BUZZER ENSIGN HERALD MARKER OFFICE RECALL SIGNET

TARGET WAVING WIGWAG BLINKER CHAMADE COMMAND EMINENT GRIFFIN NOTABLE RETREAT TURNOUT ASSEMBLY CRANTARA DIAPHONE FLAGFALL LOGOGRAM STANDARD STRIKING
(— FISHERMEN) BALK
(— FOR A PARLEY) CHAMADE
(— FOR PLUNDER) HAVOC
(— FOR WHALERS) WAIF
(— IN WHIST) ECHO PETER
(— OF DISTRESS) SOS
(— ON HORN) SEEK BLAST STRAKE
(— ON RADARSCOPE) BLIP
(— TO ATTACK) CHARGE
(— TO BEGIN ACTION) CUE
(— TO RETREAT) RETIRE
(— TO RETURN) RECALL
(— WITH FLAGS) WIGWAG
(AUDIO —) HUM
(BOAT'S —) WAFF WAFT
(DANGER —) RED SEAMARK
(DEATH —) KNELL
(DISTRESS —) FLARE
(FOG —) FOGHORN TORPEDO DIAPHONE
(HUNTER'S —) SEEK PRIZE GIBBET STRAKE
(MILITARY —) FLARE TURNOUT ASSEMBLY
(NAVAL —) SECURE VERYLIGHT
(RADIO —) BEAM
(RAILROAD —) BANJO BOARD FUSEE FUZEE TARGET HIGHBALL SEMAPHORE
(TRAFFIC —) ROBOT
(WARNING —) RED ALARM KLAXON TOCSIN REDFLAG REDLIGHT
(WEATHER —) CONE STORMCONE STORMDRUM
SIGNALIZE MARK
SIGNALLING TICKTACK
SIGNALMAN FLAGS BELLBOY BELLMAN
SIGNATE SENNET
SIGNATORY SIGNEE SIGNER
SIGNATURE BOLT FIRM HAND VISA FRANK SHEET SIGIL THEME SIGNUM TUGHRA SECTION HANDWRIT SIGNATOR
SIGNBOARD SIGN SHINGLE
SIGNET SEAL SIGIL
SIGNIFICANCE WIT BODY PITH SOUND AMOUNT IMPORT INTENT LETTER STRESS WEIGHT BEARING CONTENT GRAVITY MEANING SENTENCE STRENGTH
(DEVOID OF —) JEJUNE
(HIDDEN —) HYPONOIA
(LACKING —) INANE
(MORAL —) ETHOS
SIGNIFICANT REAL RICH GREAT MEATY AUGURAL EPOCHAL OMINOUS POINTED SERIOUS SENSEFUL SPEAKING PERTINENT
SIGNIFICANTLY SENSIBLY
SIGNIFICATION SENSE VALOR VALUE ETYMON IMPORT MOMENT NOTION MEANING CARRIAGE SIGNIFIE
SIGNIFICS SENSIFICS
SIGNIFY BE SAY BEAR GIVE MAKE MEAN NOTE SIGN WAVE AUGUR IMPLY SKILL SOUND SPEAK SPELL TOKEN UTTER AMOUNT ARGUFY ASSERT BEMEAN DENOTE EMPLOY IMPORT INTEND MATTER SIGNAL BESPEAK BETOKEN CONNOTE DECLARE EXPRESS PORTEND PRETEND DESCRIBE INDICATE INTIMATE MANIFEST
SIGNIFYING DOZENS GOADING NEEDLING
SIGNOR BRUSCHINO, IL
(CHARACTER IN —) SOFIA BRUSCHINO FLORVILLE GAUDENZIO
(COMPOSER OF —) ROSSINI
SIGNPOST GUIDE MERCURY WAYMARK HANDPOST
SIGURD (HORSE OF —) GRANI
(SLAIN BY —) FAFNIR
(SLAYER OF —) HOGNI
(VICTIM OF —) FAFNIR
(WIFE OF —) GUDRUN
SIGYN (HUSBAND OF —) LOKI
SIKH AKALI SINGH UDASI MAZHABI
SIKKIM (CAPITAL OF —) GANGTOK
(NATIVE OF —) RONG BHOTIA LEPCHA
(RIVER OF —) TISTA
SIKSIKA SIHASAPA
SILAS MARNER (AUTHOR OF —) ELIOT
(CHARACTER IN —) CASS AARON DOLLY EPPIE NANCY SILAS MARNER DUNSTAN GODFREY LAMMETER WINTHROP
SILENCE GAG MUM CALK CLUM HIST HUSH REST CHOKE FLOOR PEACE QUIET SHUSH SQUAT STILL CLAMOR MUFFLE SETTLE STIFLE WHISHT CONFUTE SQUELCH DUMBNESS PRECLUDE SUPPRESS
(— OF CONSONANT) QUIESCENCE
(CODE OF —) OMERTA
SILENCED STILL
SILENCER SOURDINE
SILENT MUM CLUM HUSH HUST MUET MUTE SNUG CLOSE MUTED STILL TACIT WHIST MUETTE SOPITE SULLEN TIPTOE WHISHT APHONIC UNWORDY ASPIRATE RESERVED RETICENT TACITURN
SILENT DON (AUTHOR OF —) SHOLOKHOV
(CHARACTER IN —) DARIA DUNIA MAURA GREGOR PIOTRA STEPAN AKSINIA DENIKIN MELEKHOV ILINICHKA PROKOFFEY PANTALEIMON
SILHOUETTE SHADE ISOTYPE OUTLINE SKYLINE
SILICA FLINT SILEX SINTER COESITE TRIPOLI TRIDYMITE
SILICATE MICA ALVITE CERITE IOLITE PINITE EUCLASE ILVAITE LOTRITE ZEOLITE CALAMINE ERIONITE WELLSITE
SILICEOUS SHELLY
SILICLE POD POUCH SILICULE
SILICON (THIN SLICE OF —) WAFER
SILICOSIS CON
SILIQUE POD
SILK SAY SOY CRIN ERIA LOVE MUGA ATLAS FLOSS GREGE HONAN JAPAN TABBY BLATTA CRACKS CULGEE DUCAPE FRISON MANTUA PONGEE RADIUM SENDAL SHALEE SHILLA SOUPLE TUSSAH ALAMODE CHIFFON HABUTAI PERSIAN SCHAPPE SQUEEZE TIFFANY TSATLEE TUSSORE YAMAMAI ARMOZEEN ARMOZINE LUSTRINE MILANESE
(— FOR LININGS) SARSNET SARCENET
(— TREE) MIMOSA
(CORDED —) PADUASOY
(HEAVY —) CRIN ARMOZINE
(RAW —) GREIGE MARABOU TAYSAAM TSATLEE MARABOUT
(REFUSE —) BUR BURR
(TWILLED —) SURAH TOBINE FOULARD LOUSINE
(UNDYED —) CORAH
(UNTWISTED —) SLEAVE
(UPHOLSTERY —) TABARET
(WASTE —) KNUB NOIL FRISON
(PREF.) SERI(CEO)(CI)(CO)
SILK COTTON KAPOK
SILK-COTTON TREE BULAK SEMUL SIMAL BOMBAX YAXCHE BENTANG MUNGUBA POCHOTE
SILKEN SILL SERIC SILKY SUAVE SEREAN
SILK GRASS KARATAS
SILK GUM SERICIN
SILK OAK LACEWOOD
SILKSMAN SCALPER
SILK TREE SIRIS
SILKWORM ERI ERIA SINA BOMBYX TUSSAH TUSSORE YAMAMAI BOMBYCID
SILKY GLOSSY SILKEN
SILKY CORNEL REDBRUSH
SILKY TAMARIN MARIKINA
SILL GIRD SOLE PLATE PATAND PATTEN SADDLE MUDSILL DOORSILL
SILLINESS BOSH FOLLY BETISE GOOSERY INANITY PORANGI SIMPLES IDLENESS NONSENSE ABSURDITY SIMPLICITY
SILLY TID BETE DAFT FOND FOOL NICE VAIN APISH BALMY BATTY BUGGY CAKEY DENSE DILLY DITSY DITZY DIZZY GIDDY GOOFY INANE KOOKY LOONY SAPPY SEELY WACKY BLASHY CRANKY CUCKOO DAWISH DOTARD DOTTLE FOOTLE FRUITY GUCKED MOPOKE PAULIE SAWNEY SHANNY SIMPLE SINGLE SKIVIE SLIGHT SPOONY VACANT ASININE FATUOUS FOOLISH FOPPISH FRIBBLE GLAIKET PEEVISH PUERILE SCRANNY SHALLOW UNWITTY ANSERINE FEATLESS FOOTLING FOPPERLY
(BE —) DRIVEL
(PREF.) MORO
SILO (PART OF —) BIN DOME PIPE TANK MELON INTAKE LADDER PUMPKIN UMBRELLA PARACHUTE
SILOXANE SILICON
SILPHIUM LASER
SILT DREGS SLEECH DEPOSIT RESIDUE SULLAGE BULLDUST
SILVER LUNA MOON PINA DIANA PLATE SYCEE WEDGE WHITE ALBATA ARGENT SILLER BULLION VERMEIL ARGENTUM STERLING ARGENTINE
(— INGOT) SYCEE
(— STATE) NEVADA
(DEBASED —) VELLON
(GERMAN —) ALBATA
(GILDED —) VERMEIL
(NICKEL —) PAKTONG
(PREF.) ARGENT(O) ARGYR(O)
SILVER BELL HALESIA BELLWOOD COWLICKS
SILVERFISH SHINER SLICKER FISHTAIL WOODFISH
SILVERING BACKING
SILVERSIDES IAO BRIT TINK BRITT FRIAR SMELT TAILOR TINKER GRUNION ATHERINE PEIXEREY PEJERREY SKIPJACK
SILVERSMITH SONAR
SILVERTIP BEAR
SILVER TREE IRONWOOD
SILVER TREE FERN PITAU
SILVERVINE CATVINE
SILVERWEED TANSY
SILVERWING CINDER
SILVERY WHITE ARGENT SILVER SILVERN
(PREF.) GLAUCO
SILVIA (FATHER OF —) BALLANCE
(LOVER OF —) VALENTINE
SILYBUM MARIANA
SIMAR CYMAR SYMAR ZIMARRA
SIMEON (FATHER OF —) JACOB
(MOTHER OF —) LEAH
SIMILAR AKIN LIKE SAME SUCH ALIKE METOO EVENLY LIKELY SIMILE COGNATE KINDRED SEEMABLE SELFLIKE SUCHLIKE SUITABLE SEMBLANCE
(PREF.) HOL(O) HOM(E)(EO)(O)(OE)(OI)
(SUFF.) **(MAKE — TO)** FY IFY
SIMILARITY SIMILE ANALOGY HOMOLOGY HOMOTAXY LIKENESS PARALLEL SAMENESS
SIMILARLY EQUALLY LIKEWISE
SIMILE ICON IKON IMAGE FIGURE SUIVEZ COMPARE
SIMILITUDE IMAGE FIGURE ANALOGY PARABLE PORTRAIT
SIMMER FRY CREE SILE STEW SIMPER SOTTER TOTTLE
SIMON ZELOTES
(BROTHER OF —) JESUS
(FATHER OF —) MATTATHIAS
(SON OF —) JUDAS
SIMON BOCCANEGRA
(CHARACTER IN —) MARIA PAOLO SIMON ADORNO AMELIA ANDREA FIESCO GABRIELLE BOCCANEGRA
(COMPOSER OF —) VERDI
SIMONY BARRATRY
SIMOOM SAMUM SAMIEL KHAMSIN
SIMPER MINCE SMIRK BRIDLE
SIMPLE LOW BALD BARE EASY FOND MERE NICE ONLY PURE RUDE SNAP VERY WEAK AFALD BLEAK DIZZY GREEN NAIVE NAKED PLAIN SEELY SILLY SMALL SOBER AEFALD CHASTE GLOBAL HOMELY HONEST HUMBLE NATIVE OAFISH

RUSTIC SEMPLE SEVERE SINGLE STUPID VIRGIN ARTLESS ASININE AUSTERE BABYISH FATUOUS FOOLISH ONEFOLD POPULAR SIMPLEX SPECIES ARCADIAN EXPLICIT HOMEMADE HOMESPUN INNOCENT INORNATE SACKLESS SEMPLICE SOLITARY
(VEGETABLE —) GALENIC
(PREF.) APL(O) HAPL(O) LITI
SIMPLE-MINDED SEELY SILLY INNOCENT
SIMPLETON AUF AWF COX DAW FON NUP OAF SAP SOT BABE BABY BOOB CAKE COOT CULL FLAT FOOL GABY GAUP GAWP GOFF GOUK GOWK GOWP GUFF PEAK ROOK SIMP SOFT TONY TOOT ZANY COKES GALAH GOOSE IDIOT IKONA JACOB LOACH NINNY NODDY PRUNE SAMMY SMELT SNIPE SPOON TOMMY BADAUD DAUKIN FONDLE GANDER GAUPUS GAWNEY GOTHAM GREENY GULPIN JOSSER NINCUM NOODLE NUPSON SAWNEY SIMKIN SIMPLE DAWPATE GOMERAL GUBBINS JUGGINS MAFFLIN MUGGINS WIDGEON ABDERITE FLATHEAD FONDLING INNOCENT JEANJEAN JOCRISSE KNOTHEAD MOONCALF MOONLING OMADHAUN PEAGOOSE SILLYTON SOFTHEAD WISEACRE WOODCOCK NINCOMPOOP
SIMPLICITY NICETY PURITY MODESTY NAIVETE ELEGANCE
SIMPLIFY CLARIFY EXPOUND
SIMPLY JUST ALONE FONDLY MERELY PLATLY CRUDELY QUIETLY NATIVELY
SIMULACRUM ICON SHAM IMAGE IMITATION
SIMULATE ACT FAKE MOCK FEIGN MIMIC AFFECT ASSUME SEMBLE SIMULE SKETCH
SIMULATED FAINT FAKED ERSATZ FICTIOUS
SIMULATION ACTING ANALOGUE PRETENCE PRETENSE
SIMULTANEOUS CONJOINT CONJUGATE
SIMULTANEOUSLY ONCE TOGETHER
SIN ERR CULP DEBT ENZU EVIL HELL PAPA VICE BLAME CRIME ERROR FAULT FOLLY GUILT SLOTH WATHE WRONG AGUILT COMMIT FELONY NANNAR OFFEND PIACLE PLIGHT VENIAL FRAILTY OFFENSE HAMARTIA INIQUITY PECCANCY QUEDSHIP TRESPASS
(DAUGHTER OF —) ISHTAR
(DEADLY —) ACEDIA
(ORIGINAL —) ADAM
(SEVEN DEADLY —S) ENVY LUST ANGER PRIDE SLOTH GLUTTONY COVETOUSNESS
(SON OF —) NESKU SHAMASH
(WIFE OF —) NINGAL
(PREF.) HAMARTIO
SINCALINE CHOLINE
SINCE AS AGO FOR FRO NOW GONE SETH SITH SYNE BEING WHERE FORWHY BECAUSE SITHENS WHEREAS INASMUCH SITHENCE
(PREF.) CIS CITRA
SINCERE GOOD REAL TRUE AFALD FRANK CANDOR DEVOUT ENTIRE HEARTY HONEST SIMPLE SINGLE CORDIAL EARNEST GENUINE ONEFOLD UPRIGHT FAITHFUL PRAYERFUL
(NOT —) LIP PLASTIC SYNTHETIC SYNTHETICAL
SINCERELY TRULY SIMPLY SINGLY DEVOUTLY ENTIRELY HEARTILY
SINCERITY FAITH HEART CANDOR VERITY HONESTY REALITY
SINDON CORPORAL
SINE SAGITTA
(VERSED —) SAGITTA
SINECURE SNAP
SINEW THEW BRAWN FIBER FIBRE FORCE NERVE POWER LEADER SINNER TENDON
SINEWY WIRY NERVY THEWY ROBUST FIBROSE FIBROUS NERVOUS STRINGY TENDINAL
SINFONIA SYMPHONY
SINFUL BAD EVIL VILE NEFAS WRONG WICKED PECCANT UNGODLY VICIOUS PIACULAR
SING HUM JIG LIP CANT CARP GALE HYMN LILT TUNE CAROL CARRY CHANT CHIRL CROON DIRGE DITTY DRING FEIGN LYRIC RAISE TOUCH TROLL YEDDE CHAUNT CHORUS DIVIDE INTONE MELODY RECORD RELISH STRAIN WARBLE CHORTLE COUNTER DESCANT GRIDDLE SINGING TWEEDLE CHERUBIM FALDERAL MODULATE SINGSONG VOCALIZE
(— ABOUT) BESING
(— ABOVE TRUE PITCH) SHARP
(— AS A BEGGAR) GRIDDLE
(— BRISKLY) KNACK
(— CHEERFULLY) LILT
(— FLORIDLY) DIVIDE
(— HARSHLY) SCREAM
(— IN A CRACKED VOICE) CRAKE
(— IN CHORUS) CHOIR
(— IN LOW VOICE) CROON
(— IN SWISS MANNER) YODEL
(— LOUDLY) BELT TROLL TROLLOL
(— PRAISES) LAUD
(— ROMANCES) GEST GESTE
(— SECOND PART) SURCENT
(— SOFTLY) SOWF SOWTH
(— TO THE MOON) BAY
(— WITH FLOURISHES) ROULADE
(— WITH MEANINGLESS SYLLABLES) SCAT
SINGAPORE (RIVER IN —) SUNGEI SELETAR
(STRAIT OF —) JOHORE SEMBILAN
SINGE GAS BURN CHAR SEAR SWEAL GENAPP SCORCH SWINGE SCOWDER SWITHEN FIREFANG
SINGER ALTO BARD DIVA LARK SWAN BASSO BUFFA BUFFO SKALD VOICE BULBUL BUSKER CANARY CANTOR LYRIST SONGER BASSIST CHANTER CROONER PRIMOMO SOLOIST SONGMAN SOPRANO TROLLER WARBLER BAYADERE CANTADOR CASTRATO CHANTEUR FALSETTO GRIDDLER MELODIST MONODIST THAMYRIS VOCALIST CITYBILLY
(— OF FOLK SONGS) CANTADOR
(— OF ROCK MUSIC) ROCKER
(— OF THE GODS) GANDHARVA
(BEWITCHING —) SIREN
(COUNTRY MUSIC —) CITYBILLY
(FEMALE —) SONGBIRD
(MENDICANT —) BUSKER
(PRINCIPAL —) PRIMOMO
(PROVENCAL —) MUSAR
(STROLLING —) CANTABANK
SINGING CANT SCAT CHANT LYRIC HYMNODY CANOROUS JONGLERY
(— ANTIPHONALLY) ALTERNATION
(— CAROLS) PLYGAIN HODENING
(— COACH) REPETITEUR
(ALTERNATE —) ANTIPHON
(CANTORIAL —) HAZANUTH HAZZANUT
(JAZZ —) SCAT
(SIMULTANEOUS —) CHORUS
SINGLE ODD ONE LAST ONLY SOLE UNAL AFALD ALONE AEFALD SIMPLE SOLEIN SULLEN UNIQUE VERSAL ALONELY AZYGOUS ONEFOLD SEVERAL SIMPLEX TWOSOME PECULIAR SEPARATE SINGULAR SOLITARY SPORADIC PARTICULAR
(— OUT) CUT NAP SPOT ISOLATE SEPARATE
(PREF.) APL(O) HAPL(O) MANI MON(O) UNI
SINGLE-FOOT RACK
SINGLEHANDEDLY SINGLY
SINGLE-MINDED AFALD ONEFOLD DEDICATED
SINGLENESS UNITY ONENESS
SINGLETON ONER UNIT
(— LEAD) SNEAK
SINGLY SINGLE SOLELY SLONELY
SINGPHO CHINGPAW
SINGSONG CANT SOUGH CHANTING
SINGULAR ODD RARE FERLY QUEER QUAINT SEENIL SINGLE CURIOUS STRANGE PECULIAR
SINGULARISM HENISM
SINGULARITY DOUBLET ONENESS ONLINESS
SINHALESE SINHALA
SINISTER AWK CAR KAY DARK DIRE FELL GRIM DISMAL LOUCHE MALIGN AWKWARD OBLIQUE OMINOUS
SINISTRAL REVERSED
SINK DIP DOP EBB LUM SAG SET SYE BORE DRAU DRAW DROP FADE FAIL FALL GOWT HELD KILL LUMB SILE SWAG AVALE DRAFT DRAIN DROOP DROWN HIELD LAPSE LOWER MERGE POACH SQUAT STOOP SWAMP VERGE CLOACA DEVALL DOLINA DOLINE DRENCH GUTTER JAWBOX PLUNGE PUDDLE RESIDE SETTLE COMMODE DECLINE DESCEND DRAUGHT FOUNDER GULLION IMMERSE RELAPSE SCUPPER SCUTTLE SUBSIDE SWALLOW DECREASE SINKHOLE SOAKAWAY
(— AND FALL) TWINE
(— AS IN MUD) LAIR
(— A WELL) DRILL
(— DOWN) BOG AVALE STOOP DECLINE
(— FANGS INTO) STRIKE
(— FOR MIXING DRINKS) WETBAR
(— INTO OOZE) WASEL
(— NAILHEAD) SET
(— SUDDENLY) SLUMP
(— UNDER TRIAL) QUAIL
SINKBOX BOX SINK BATTERY
SINKER BUR BURR SINK DIPSY DONUT PLUMB BULLET
SINKHOLE SINK PONOR UVALA CENOTE COLLECT
SINKING GONE SINKAGE
(— DOWN) FONDU
SINKIUSE COLUMBIA
SINLESS INNOCENT
SINLESSNESS HOLINESS
SINNER DEBTOR PECCANT
SINNING PECCANT
SINUATE GYROSE
SINUOSITY WRIGGLE
SINUOUS WAVY SNAKEY SINUATE SNAKISH TORTILE WINDING INDENTED SWANLIKE
SINUS BOSOM ANTRUM RECESS LOCULUS TEARPIT
(PL.) ANTRA
SINUSITIS ROUP
SIOUAN OTOE ABANIC DAKOTA SANTEE SAPONI CATAWBA DACOTAH
SIOUX (— FORCE) WAKAN WAKON
SIP BIB NIP SUP BLEB SEEP SLUP SUCK TIFF KEACH NURSE SNACK WHIFF TIPPLE TICKLER DELIBATE
SIPHON CRANE THIEF VALINCH FLINCHER
SIPPING LIBANT
SIPUNCULOIDEA ACHAETA INERMIA
SIR PO DAN DEN DON PAN AZAM BAAS HERR MIAN STIR TUAN BWANA SAHIB SENOR SEYID SIEUR MESSER SAYYID SIGNOR SIRREE BARONET DOMINUS EFFENDI MESSIRE SIGNIOR SIGNORE GOSPODIN GOVERNOR
(PL.) LORDINGS
SIRCAR BANIAN
SIRE KING BEGET THROW FATHER GETTER
SIREN BUMMER HOOTER LIGEIA LIGYDA ENTICER LORELEI MERMAID SIRENIAN
SIRENIAN COWFISH MUTILATE
SIRENOMELUS SYMPUS SYMMELUS
SIRICID UROCERID
SIRIS KOKO LEBBEK
SIRIUS SOTHIS TISHIYA CANICULA
SIRLOIN SEY BACKSEY
SIRMUELLERA BANKSIA
SIRUP WAX LICK GOLDY SYRUP GOWDIE GREENS ORGEAT RUNOFF ANTIQUE CLAIRCE ECLEGMA LIQUEUR MOLASSES QUIDDANY
SIRWASH SIDELINE

SISAL RUG CABUYA SISALANA
SISKIN TARIN ABERDEVINE
SISSIFIED PRISSY
SISSOO TALI SHISHAM
SISSY SIS CISSIE SISTER CHICKEN PANTYWAIST
SISTER NUN SIB SIS GIRL NURSE SISSY SOEUR TITTY WOMAN EXTERN PERSON
(YOUNGER —) CADETTE
(PL.) SISTERN SISTREN
(PREF.) SORORI
SISTERHOOD BEGUINES SORORITY
SISTERLY SORORAL
SISYPHUS (BROTHER OF —) ATHAMAS SALMONEUS
(FATHER OF —) AEOLUS
(MOTHER OF —) ENARETE
(SON OF —) SINON GLAUCUS ORNYTION
(WIFE OF —) MEROPE
SIT SET LEAN SEAT BENCH PRESS ROOST SQUAT WEIGH BESTRIDE
(— ABRUPTLY) CLAP
(— ASTRIDE) CROSS HORSE STRADDLE
(— ERECT LIKE A DOG) BEG
(— FORCIBLY) DOSS
(— IN JUDGMENT) DEEM
(— ON) BROOD COVER
(— OVER EGGS) RUCK BROOD CLOCK
(— UPRIGHT) PERK
SITA (FATHER OF —) JANAKA
(HUSBAND OF —) RAMA SOMA
SITATUNGA NAKONG
SITE AREA PLOT SEAT SITU SOLE SPOT TOFT FIELD PLACE SITUS STAND STANCE BIVOUAC DAMSITE HABITAT STEADING
(— OF BIRD SEXUAL DISPLAY) LEK
(— OF HUNT) DRIVE
(— OF SMELTER) BOLE
(ARCHAELOGICAL —) EXCAVATION
(BUILDING —) STANCE
(EXCAVATION —) DIG
(FORTIFIED —) KAIM KAME
(THRESHING —) SETTING
SITTER DOLLY DOLLIE INSESSOR
SITTING DIET SEAT ASSIS CLUTCH SEANCE SEDENT SEJANT SESSION CONGRESS SEDERUNT
SITUATE PLACE POSITION
SITUATED SET SEATED STATURED
(— OPPOSITE) COUNTER
(GET —) ORIENT
SITUATION JOB LIE CASE CRIB PASS PLOT POST SEAT SITE SPOT BERTH SIEGE SITUS STATE STEAD ASSIZE CHANCE ESTATE OFFICE PLIGHT STATUS EPISODE PICTURE PORTENT POSTURE STATION INCIDENT INSTANCE POSITURE STANDING UBIQUITY
(— BESET BY DIFFICULTIES) SCRAPE
(— IN CRIBBAGE) GO
(— IN FARO) CATHOP
(— IN OMBRE) CODILLE
(— OF PERPLEXITY) HOBBLE STRAIT
(AMUSING —) BAR
(AWKWARD —) SCRAPE JACKPOT
(BAD —) SCENE
(CRITICAL —) CLUTCH
(DIFFICULT —) BOX PUXY BOGGLE NINEHOLES PREDICAMENT
(DISTRESSING —) STYMIE
(EXECRABLE —) ATROCITY
(FAVORABLE —) BREAK
(FINAL — OF ACT) CURTAIN
(HIGH —) AERY AERIE
(HOPELESSLY DOOMED —) RATTRAP
(NECESSITOUS —) BREACH
(PAINFUL —) DISTRESS
(RELATIVE —) BEARING
(TIGHT —) CRUNCH
(TRYING —) COW
(UNPLEASANT —) BUMMER
(UNSATISFACTORY —) DILEMMA
(VEXATIOUS —) HEADACHE
(VILE —) DUNGHILL
(ZODIACAL —) HAYZ
SITZ BATH SITZBAD SEMICUPE
SITZMARK BATHTUB
SIVA RUDRA SHIVA ISVARA SHAMBU BHAIRAVA MAHADEVA NATARAJA
(SYMBOL OF —) LINGA LINGAM
(WIFE OF —) KALI
SIX VAU WAW SICE SISE HEXAD HEXADE SENARY SEXTET STIGMA DIGAMMA SIXSOME
(PREF.) HEX(A) SEX(A)(I) SEXTI
SIXFOLD SEXTUPLE
SIX-FOOTED HEXAPOD
SIXMO SEXTO
SIXPENCE HOG PIG BEND KICK ZACK SIMON SPRAT TIZZY BENDER FIDDLE TANNER TESTON CRIPPLE FIDDLER TESTRIL
SIXTEENTH ANA ANNA
SIXTH
(PREF.) SEXTI
SIXTIETH (— PART OF DAY) GHURRY
SIXTY SAMECH SAMEKH
SIZABLE SNUG HEFTY LARGE HANDSOME
SIZE WAX AREA BIND BULK MARK MASS DRESS GIRTH MOUND PLANK SCALE EXTENT FORMAT GROWTH MICKLE MOISON PICNIC SIZING BIGNESS CONTENT CORSAGE FITTING THIRTEEN TWELVEMO
(— OF BOOK) FOLIO OCTAVO QUARTO
(— OF BULLET) CALIBER
(— OF CARDS) TOWN LADIES
(— OF HOLE) BORE
(— OF HOSIERY) POPE
(— OF PAGE) OCTAVO
(— OF PAPERBOARD) LARGE
(— OF PARTICLE) GRIND
(— OF ROPE) GRIST
(— OF SLATE) PEGGY IMPERIAL
(— OF TYPE) GEM PICA RUBY AGATE CANON ELITE PEARL MINION PRIMER BREVIER DIAMOND EMERALD ENGLISH PARAGON COLUMBIAN
(— YARN) SLASH
(CLOTHING —) LONG SHORT STOUT JUNIOR PETITE
(EXTRA LARGE —) SUPER
(GREAT —) MAGNITUDE
(MEASURED —) SCANTLING
(PAPER —) SIXMO
(RELATIVE —) SCALE
(UNUSUAL —) OUTSIZE
SIZEABLE HEFTY
SIZING DRESSING SLASHING
(— LIQUID) GLAIR
SIZZLE FRIZZ
SKADI (FATHER OF —) THJAZI
(HUSBAND OF —) NJORD
SKAG SCAG HEROIN
SKANDA (BROTHER OF —) GANESHA
(FATHER OF —) SHIVA
(WIFE OF —) DEVAYANI VALLIAMMAN
SKASTING (— JUMP) SALCHOW
SKAT CAT NULL TOURNEE
SKATE BOB RAY TUB RAJA RINK SKIT TINK TUBE FLAIR SCULL BATOID DOCTOR FLATHE PATENT PATTEN ROCKER ROLLER RUNNER SKETCH TINKER CHOPINE FLAPPER PLACOID SKETCHER
(— MARK) CUSP
(FEMALE —) MAID
(PREF.) BATO
SKATER PATTENER SKETCHER
SKEDADDLE LAM RUN BUNK FLEE SCAT SCOOT
SKEET FLEE KELTER KILTER PELTER
SKEIN RAP HANK HASP SCAN BOTTOM SLEAVE SELVAGE
SKEINER RANDER SLIPPER
SKELETIN SPONGIN
SKELETON CUP CAGE MORT RAME ATOMY BONES FRAME LOOFAH SICULA SKELET ANATOMY CARCASS RAWBONE ARMATURE CORALLUM MANDIBLE OSSATURE
(— OF DRAMATIC WORK) SCENARIO
SKELETON KEY GILT SCREW TWIRLER
SKELP SCUD
SKEPTIC DOUBTER INFIDEL ZETETIC APIKOROS APORETIC
SKEPTICAL ACADEMIC APORETIC DOUBTFUL
SKEPTICALLY ASKANCE
SKEPTICISM HUMISM UNBELIEF
SKETCH BIT DASH DRAW LIMN PLAN VIEW VITA DRAFT ENTER PAINT TRACE APERCU DESIGN DOODLE SCHEME SPLASH BOZZETO CROQUIS DRAUGHT DRAWING EBAUCHE ETCHING OUTLINE SCHIZZO ESQUISSE MONOGRAM PROFIELE PROSPECT REMARQUE VIGNETTE
(— BEFOREHAND) INDICATE
(AUTOBIOGRAPHICAL —) VITA
(BIOGRAPHICAL —) ELOGY ELOGIUM
(FIRST —) ESQUISSE
(HERALDIC —) TRICK
(OUTDOORS —) LANDSKIP
(PRELIMINARY —) DRAFT ABBOZZO MAQUETTE
(ROUGH —) NOTE CROQUIS POCHADE ESQUISSE
(SATIRICAL —) SKIT
(THUMBNAIL —) BIO
SKEW ASKEW GAUCHE
SKEWBACK SPRINGER
SKEWBALD PINTO PIEBALD
SKEWED ALOP
SKEWER PIN PROD PROG SPIT STAB PRICK SPEAR TRUSS SKIVER TASTER BROCHETTE
SKEWERER TUBER
SKI SKEE SNOWSHOE
(— DOWN AT HIGH SPEED) SCHUSS
(— DOWNHILL) WEDEL
(— DOWN SLOPE) SCHUSS
(— METHOD) PASSGANG
(— MOVEMENT) RUADE
(— POSITION) VORLAGE
(— RACE) SLALOM
(— RACING) LANGLAUF
(— SITE) VAIL
(— STYLE) WEDELN
(— TURN) TELEMARK
(— WITH ROLLERS) TURFSKI
(CROSS-COUNTRY RACING ON —S) LANGLAUF
(ONE WHO —S) SCHUSSBOOMER
(ONE WHO —S DOWNHILL) SCHUSSBOOMER
(PART OF —) TIP EDGE TAIL SHOVEL BINDING
(RELATING TO — EVENTS) NORDIC
(TYPE OF —) SNOWBOARD
(PL.) BOARDS
SKID DOG DRAG SLEW SLUE TRIG DRIFT DRILL SLOUGH SKIDPAN SLIPPER TRIGGER FISHTAIL SIDESLIP
(— LOGS) SNAKE TWICH TRAVOY TWITCH
(— ON RAIL) SKATE
(AUTOMOBILE —) SPINOUT
(FENDER —) GLANCER
(IRON —) SABOT
(ROTATIONAL —) SPINOUT
SKIDDER SNAKER
SKIDI LOUP
SKIDWAY PIT
SKIER KANONE SNOWBIRD LANGLAUFER SCHUSSBOOMER
(— POSITION) VORLAGE
SKIFF CANOE SHELL SKIFT CAIQUE DINGHY SAMPAN CURRANE SKIPPET JOHNBOAT
SKIING TOURING LANGLAUF
(— TURN) TELEMARK
(CROSS-COUNTRY —) LANGLAUF
(DOWNHILL —) WEDELN
(STYLE OF —) WEDELN
SKIL BESHOW SKILFISH
SKILL ART CAN WIT FEAT FEEL HAND PATE TACT CRAFT DRAFT HAUNT KNACK TRICK ENGINE TECHNE ABILITY ADDRESS APTNESS CUNNING FINESSE MASTERY MYSTERY PROWESS SCIENCE SLEIGHT ARTIFICE CAPACITY CHIVALRY DEFTNESS FACILITY INDUSTRY LEARNING
(— IN COMMUNICATION) ORACY
(DIPLOMATIC —) TACT
(INTELLECTUAL —) INTELLIGENCE
(LACK OF —) INERTIA
(NAVIGATION —) SEACRAFT
(PREF.) TECHNI TECHNO
(SUFF.) ICS SHIP TECHNIC TECHNY
SKILLED OLD SEEN WISE ADEPT ASTUTE MASTER PERITE SCIENT

SKILLY VERSED HOTSHOT PRACTIC EDUCATED SKILLFUL
SKILLET PRIG SPIDER
SKILLFUL APT SLY ABLE DEFT FEAT FILE FINE GOOD HEND PERT TIDY WISE ADEPT CANNY FITTY HANDY HENDE READY SLICK SWEET ADROIT ARTFUL CLEVER CRAFTY DAEDAL EXPERT HABILE SCIENT SKILLY SOLERT SUBTLE CUNNING POLITIC SKILLED DEXTROUS PRACTIVE SLEIGHTY TACTICAL PROFICIENT
SKILLFULLY DEFTLY YARELY CRAFTILY
SKILLFULNESS CRAFT
SKIM TOP RIFF SCUD SCUM SCUN SCUR SILE SKIP FLEET GRAZE SCALE SKIFF SKIRR SKIVE BROWSE RABBLE SAMPLE DESPUME SKITTER
(— ON WATER) SCHOON
SKIMMED FLAT FLET
SKIMMER FALK LARI SKEP SCOOP LINGEL SCUMMER CUTWATER
SKIMMINGS SCRUFF
SKIMP JIMP SLUR SCAMP SKINCH
SKIMPY JIMP CHARY SPARE MEAGER MEAGRE SCANTY STINGY
SKIN KIP KIT BACK BARK CASE CAST DERM FELL FLAY FLEA HIDE HILD KITT MORT PEAU PEEL PELT RIND BALAT BLYPE BRAWN FLOAT GENET SLUFF STRIP SWARD CORIUM PELTRY SWARTH UNCASE CUTICLE DOESKIN ENDERON KIDSKIN LEATHER PELLAGE SKIMMER BUCKSKIN DRUMHEAD LAMBSKIN PARADERM PELLICLE SEALSKIN TEGUMENT VITILIGO WOOLFELL
(— AROUND BIRD'S EYE) ORBIT
(— AROUND NAIL) PERIONYCHIUM
(— BETWEEN TOES) WEB
(— FOR BOOKBINDING) BASAN
(— FOR HOLDING WATER) KIRBEH
(— FOR WATER) KIRBEH
(— OF BACON) SWARD
(— OF BOARDS) CARPET
(— OF FRUIT) PEEL
(— OF GOOSE) APRON
(— OF INSECT) CAST
(— OF PLANT) CORTEX
(— OF POTATO) JACKET
(— OF POULTRY NECK) HELZEL
(— OF RABBIT) RACK CONEY
(— OF SEAL) SCULP
(— OF SHARK) SHAGREEN
(— OF THE HEAD) SCALP
(— OF WALNUT) ZEST
(— OF YOUNG CALF) SLINK DEACON
(— WITH WOOL REMAINING ON IT) WOOLFELL
(BARE —) BUFF
(BEAVER —) PLEW
(BOAR'S —) SHIELD
(CAST —) SPOIL SLOUGH EXUVIAE
(CHAFED OR SORE —) IRE
(CHAMOIS —) FURWA
(DEEP LAYER OF THE —) CUTIS
(DRIED —) PARFLECHE
(FAWN —) NEBRIS
(INNER PART OF THE —) DERMA
(LAMB — PREPARED LIKE FUR) BUDGE
(OUTER —) HUSK
(PENDULOUS FOLD OF —) DEWLAP
(ROUGHTANNED —) CRUST
(SHARK —) SHAGREEN
(SHEEP —) BASIL
(SQUIRREL —) VAIR
(SURFACE —) SCARFSKIN
(THICKENED —) BRAWN
(THIN —) FILM PELLICLE STRIFFEN
(TRUE —) ENDERON
(60 —S) TURN
(PREF.) CUT(I)(O) CUTANEO DERM(AT)(ATO)(O) DERO EPIDERM(O) SCYT(O)
(SUFF.) DERM(A)(ATOUS)(IA)(IS)(Y)
SKIN FLICK NUDIE
SKINFLINT SKIN FLINT MISER PIKER SCREW HUDDLE PELTER SCRAPER SCROOGE SKEEZIX TIGHTWAD CHEESEPARER
SKINK ADDA SCINCID SCORPION
(PREF.) SCINCI SCINCO
SKINNY BONY LEAN THIN SLINK
SKIOLD (FATHER OF —) ODIN
SKIP DAP HIP BALK BOUT FOOT JUMP LEAP SLIP TRIP BOUND CAPER DANCE ELIDE FRISK SALTO SCOON SCOPE SCOUP SKITE SMOKE VAULT GAMBOL GLANCE LAUNCH SPRING GUNBOAT SALTATE SKIPPER SKITTER TRIPPLE PORPOISE RICOCHET
(— SCHOOL) TIB
(MINING —) SLIPE
SKIPJACK FOP SKIP BONITO ALEWIFE SKIPPER
SKIPPER IHI SKIP LAODAH LOWDAH SERANG SHIPPER
SKIRMISH FRAY BRUSH CLASH MELEE SKIRM BICKER HASSLE TUSSLE PICKEER RUNNING FIREFIGHT
SKIRMISHER HUSSAR TIRALLEUR
SKIRMISHING SPARRING
SKIRT CUT HUG LAP BANK BASE COAT ENGI JUPE MIDI MINI SAYA TUBE TUTU COAST JUPON LABIE PAREU PASIN STRIP TREND TWIST BASQUE DIRNDL HOBBLE JUMPER KIRTLE PEPLUM SARONG TAMEIN QUARTER BASQUINE PULLBACK SKIRTING
(— STYLE) ALINE
(ARMOR —) TASSES LAMBOYS
(BALLET —) TUTU
(DIVIDED —) CULOTTE
(HOOP —) CRINOLINE
(HOOPED —) TUBTAIL
(LONG —) MAXI
(TARTAN —) KILT ARISAID
(PL.) DOCK DOCKEN
SKIRTING DADE SKIRT PLINTH
(PL.) BROKES
SKIT BLACKOUT
SKITTAGETAN HAIDA
SKITTISH SHY CORKY GOOSY WINDY FLISKY KITTLE SKEIGH SPOOKY FLIGHTY SCADDLE SKADDLE STARTLY BOGGLISH SKITTERY STARTFUL
SKITTLES BOWLS KAYLES KITTLES SQUAILS
SKIVE PARE
SKUA BONXIE JAEGER TEASER TULIAC SEAHAWK STINKPOT WHIPTAIL
SKULDUGGERY JOUKERY PAWKERY
SKULK DERN JOUK LURK LUSK MICHE MOOCH SCOUT SHOOL
SKULL OAR ROW BEAN POLL CRANY MOOCH SCALP SCAUP VAULT COBBRA MAZARD PALLET SCONCE CRANIUM HARNPAN HEADMOLD PANNICLE
(— BONE) VOMER
(— POINT) TYLION
(BACK OF —) OCCIPUT
(INCOMPLETE —) CALVARIA
(PART OF —) INION
(UPPER HALF OF —) SINCIPUT
(PREF.) CRANI(O)
(SUFF.) CRANIA(L)
SKULLCAP COIF PIXY PIXIE SKULL VAULT BEANIE COIFFE CALOTTE CAPELINE HOODWORT
(ARABIAN —) CHECHIA
(JEWISH —) YAMILKE YARMULKE
(STEEL —) SECRET
SKUNK ANNA ATOC ATOK PUSS HURON SKINK SNIPE ZORIL CHINCHA POLECAT SEECAWK SMELLER CONEPATE CONEPATL MUSTELID PHOBYCAT ZORRILLO
(CARTOON —) LEPEW
(JAVANESE —) TELEDU
SKUNK CABBAGE COLLARD POCKWEED
SKY BLUE HIGH LIFT LOFT POLE TIEN AZURE CARRY DYAUS ETHER LANGI VAULT CAELUS CANOPY HEAVEN REGION WELKIN ELEMENT HEAVENS OLYMPUS TENGERE WEATHER
(ICE —) ICEBLINK
(PREF.) CAELI CAELO COELI COELO URAN(I)(O) URANOSO
SKY-BLUE AZURE
(PREF.) CERULEO
SKYLARK LARK YERK
SLAB BAT CANT CLAM LECH PARE SLAT BLADE BOARD DALLE LINER PANEL PLANK SLATE STELA STELE TABLE WADGE ABACUS FLITCH MARVER MIHRAB PAVIOR RUNNER SHEAVE TABLET FLAPPET PLANCHE SHINGLE PORPHYRY PUNCHEON SLABWOOD
(— BESIDE SINK) BUNKER
(— BY SINK) BUNKER
(— INDICATING MECCA) MIHRAB
(— OF CLAY) BAT
(— OF COAL) SKIP SLIP
(— OF GLASS) PANE
(— OF ICE) SCONCE
(— OF LIMESTONE) BALATTE
(— OF MARBLE) DALLE
(— OF PEAT) SCAD
(— OF SANDSTONE) COMAL
(— OVER BROOK) CLAM
(ARCHITECTURAL —) METOPE
(BROKEN-OFF —) BLAUD
(FLOATING —) ICEPAN SCONCE
(GAME —) BOARD
(GRAVE —) LEDGER LEIDGER
(GRINDING —) MULLER
(HOPSCOTCH —) PEEVER
(MEMORIAL —) LEDGER
(PAINTER'S —) SLANT
(PLASTERER'S —) HAWK
(ROOFING —) SLATE
(SQUARE —) QUARRY
(STONE —) PLANK STELA STELE INKSTONE
SLACK DRY LAX OFF CULM DUFF LASH NESH SLOW SOFT VEER CHECK CRANK FLOWN LOOSE SLAKE TARDY ABATED FLABBY FLAPPY REMISS SUPINE UNGIRT BACKING MAKINGS RELAXED SLACKEN SMEDDUM CARELESS DILATORY INACTIVE SLOBBERY NEGLIGENT
(— IN TRIGGER) CREEP
(— OF ROPE) SLATCH
(— SHEET OF SAIL) FLOW
(— SUDDENLY) SURGE
(COAL —) COOM COOMB
(PL.) BAGS
SLACKEN LAG PAY EASE FLAG SLOW DELAY DOWSE LOOSE QUAIL RELAX REMIT SLACK SLAKE START SURGE ASLAKE EXOLVE RELENT UNBEND
(— SPEED) HANG
SLACKENING LETUP DETENTE LETDOWN SLACKAGE
SLACKER SPIV ROTTER COUCHER SLINKER EMBUSQUE
SLACKNESS LACHES LASHNESS
SLADE SOLE
SLAG SCAR DROSS CINDER DANDER SCORIA SLAKIN THOMAS QUITTER SLACKEN
SLAIN FALLEN
SLAKE ABATE SLACK LESSEN QUENCH REFRESH SATISFY
SLAKING FAT
SLAM CLAP DASH FLUB SLOG SLOT VOLE CLASH GRAND PLANK SLOSH STRAM CHELEM FLOUNCE
SLAMMER JAIL STIR PRISON
SLANDER CANT BELIE LIBEL NOISE SMEAR BEFOUL DEFAME INJURE MALIGN MISSAY VILIFY ASPERSE CALUMNY OBTRECT SCANDAL TRADUCE TRUMPET BACKBITE DEROGATE STRUMPET ASPERSION BESPATTER
SLANDERER JUROR BLAZONER
SLANDEROUS FAMOUS SCURRIL SCURRILE VILIPEND SCURRILOUS
SLANG CANT ARGOT FLASH JARGON DIALECT
(THIEVES' —) FLASH
SLANT TIP BIAS CANT FLUE SKEW TILT BEVEL DRAFT SLOPE SPLAY STOOP FLANCH SKLENT DRAUGHT COLORING DIAGONAL
(PREF.) CLIN(O)
SLANTED CANTED BEVELED COLORED COCKEYED
SLANTING AWRY BIAS CANT SKEW BEVEL SLOPE ASLANT ASLOPE SKLENT SQUINT LOXOTIC OBLIQUE

SLOPING AVELONGE COLORING OVERWART SIDELONG
SLANTINGLY AHOO ASWASH SLANTLY
SLANT LINE VIRGULA VIRGULE
SLANTWISE (PREF.) LECHRI(O)
SLAP BOX DAB BAFF BLIP BLOW CLAP CUFF FLAP LICK PLAT SCUD SLAT SNUB SPAT TACK BLIBE CLINK CLOUT CRACK PANDY POTCH SKEEG SKELP SKITE SMACK SPANK TWANG TWANK BLEEZE BUFFET SCLAFF SLIGHT STRIKE TINGLER WHERRET BACKSLAP
(— HARD) BLAD
(RANDOM —) FLAY
SLAPDASH BUCKEYE
SLASH CAG CUT JAG COUP GASH HASH PANE RACE RASH SLIT TOPS KNIFE MINCE SCORE SKICE SLISH RAMMEL SCORCH STREAK SLITTER DIAGONAL SLASHING
SLASHED JAGGED DECOPED TATTERED
SLASHING ABATIS
SLAT BOW LAG FLAT PALE SLOT WAND BLADE SCLAT SLOAT STAVE RIFFLE SPLINE EUPHROE BEDSTAFF
(— IN SLUICE) RIFFLE
SLATE RAG SLAT FRAME KILLAS TABLET TICKET SHALDER SHINDLE SLATING
(— IN SMALL IRREGULAR PIECES) SCANTLE
(— OF COURT CASES) DOCKET
(BLUE —) SHIVER SKAILLIE
(CLAY —) KILLAS
(EXPOSED PART OF ROOFING —) BARI
(SIZE OF —) PEGGY QUEEN DUCHESS COUNTESS IMPERIAL PRINCESS MARCHIONESS
(SURFACE —) BONE
SLATER HELER HELLIER SLATTER SKIMMITY
(TOOL OF —) STAKE
SLATTERN DAB DAW MAB FROW MAUX SLUT TRUB DOLLY FAGOT MAWKS MOGGY MOPSY BLOUSE CLATCH DOLLOP MALKIN SLOVEN STREEL TRAPES LADRONE TROLLOP HUCKMUCK SLUMMOCK
SLATTERNLY DOWDY BLOWSY DAWISH FROWZY SORDID BLOWZED TRAPISH SLATTERN SLOVENLY
SLAUGHTER WAL FELL KILL SLAM SLAY BUTCH HALAL QUELL BATTUE MURDER STRAGE BUTCHER CARNAGE KILLING SCUPPER SHAMBLE BUTCHERY MASSACRE OCCISION SHECHITA HOLOCAUST
(— ACCORDING TO MOSLEM LAW) HALAL
(— OF LARGE NUMBER) HECATOMB
(WHOLESALE —) QUELL
SLAUGHTERER KILLER SHOHET KNACKER SHOCHET
(HORSE —) KNACKER
SLAUGHTERHOUSE ABATTOIR BUTCHERY MATADERO SHAMBLES
(— WORKER) LIMEMAN
SLAUGHTERING SHEHITA SHECHITA
SLAV VEND WEND CZECH HUNKS HUNKY SLAVE USKOK CROATIAN MORAVIAN POLABIAN
SLAVE BOY DAS ARDU BOND DASI DUPE ESNE MOIL SERF DAVUS HELOT SWINK THEOW ABJECT ALIPIN ALLTUD CUMHAL FORSAR GUINEA HIEROS MAMLUK SLAVEY THRALL VASSAL BONDMAN CAPTIVE CHATTEL FORSADO HACKNEY PEDAGOG SERVANT SLAVISH BONDMAID LORARIUS MAMELUKE MANCIPLE MORGIANA PRAEDIAL SLAVELET THEOWMAN ODALISQUE
(— IN TEMPLE) HIEROS
(— OWNER) PATRON
(— WHO WHIPS OTHERS) LORARIUS
(DEFORMED —) CALIBAN
(FREED —) CLIENT
(FUGITIVE —) MAROON CIMMARON
(GALLEY —) FORSAR FORSADO SFORZATO
(HAREM —) ODA ODAH ODALISK ODALESQUE
(HINDU —) DAS DASI
(REFUGEE —) CONTRABAND
(SLAVE'S —) GIBEONITE
(TEMPLE —) HIERODULE
(PL.) CHIURM COFFLE HELOTRY TOXOTAE
SLAVEDRIVER RUSHER
SLAVER DROOL FROTH DRIVEL DRIBBLE SLABBER SLOBBER SALIVATE
SLAVERY YOKE THRALL BONDAGE HELOTRY MIZRAIM THRALDOM SERVITUDE
SLAVEY DRUDGE
SLAVISH MEAN MENIAL
SLAVONIC (— BEING) VILA
SLAY DOIN KILL SMITE SPILL MURDER STRIKE BUTCHER EXECUTE STRANGLE SLAUGHTER
SLAYER BANE HOGNI KILLER MURDERER
(— OF INFIDELS) GHAZI
(SUFF.) CTONUS
SLEAZY FLIMSY TICKYTACKY
SLED LUGE PUNG TODE JUMBO SCOOT SLIDE SLIPE SLOOP HURDLE JUMPER SLEDGE SLEIGH BOBSLED CLIPPER COASTER DOGBOAT DOGSLED KOMATIK MONOSKI POINTER SLIPPER TRAILER TRAVOIS HANDSLED SKELETON TOBOGGAN
(— RIDER) BOBBER
SLEDGE DAN DRAG DRAY LUGE PULK SLED GURRY PULKA SLIDE SLIPE TRAIL TRAIN TROLL TRUNK SLEIGH KIBITKA KOMATIK PADDOCK TROLLEY TRAINEAU
(— FOR CRIMINALS) HURDLE
(— FOR STRAIGHTENING RAILS) GAG
(LOG —) SLOOP TIEBOY
(MINER'S —) MALLET
SLEDGEHAMMER SMASHER
SLEEK SNOD SOFT CLOSE JOLLY SILKY SLICK TRICK SILKEN SLEEKY SLIGHT SMARMY SMOOTH SVELTE SLEEKIT SOIGNEE SLIPPERY
SLEEKNESS GLOSS
SLEEP BED KIP LIB LIE NAP CALK CAMP DORM DOSS DOZE HALE REST WINK BALMY CRASH DORSE ROOST SWOON DROWSE SIESTA SNOOZE SOMNUS SWEVEN SHUTEYE SLUMBER WINKING
(— BROKEN BY SNORING) GRUFF
(— ON A PERCH) JOUK
(— PROBLEM) APNEA
(DEEP —) SOPOR SWOON STUPOR
(KIND OF —) REM
(LIGHT —) SLOOM
(PRETENDED —) DOGSLEEP
(PROFOUND —) SOPOR
(SHORT —) NAP SIESTA SNOOZE
(PREF.) HYPN(O) SOMNI SOPOR
(DEEP —) NARC(O)
SLEEPER TIE MOLE FENDER DORMANT CROSSTIE DORMEUSE ELEOTRID STRINGER
SLEEPINESS SOPITION
SLEEPING BED ASLEEP DORMANT DORMIENT
(— IN HOLY PLACE) INCUBATION
(— TABLET) DALMANE
SLEEPING CAR PULLMAN
SLEEPLESS LIDLESS WAKEFUL RESTLESS WATCHFUL
SLEEPLESSNESS WATCH INSOMNIA
SLEEPY DOZY HEAVY NODDY PEEPY DROWSY GROGGY MORPHIC SLEEPISH SLUMBERY SOMNIFIC SLUMBEROUS
(— ONE) NODDER
SLEET STORM
SLEEVE ARM BAND POKE ARMLET MANCHE MOGGAN BUSHING CATHEAD CUBITAL HOUSING THIMBLE
(— ON A SHAFT) CANNON
(— ON GUN) BAND
(CANVAS —) DROGUE
(HANGING —) TAB
(LEG-OF-MUTTON —) GIGOT
(LONG —) POKE
(ROOMY —) RAGLAN
(TAPERED —) SKEIN
SLEIGH SLO PUNG SLED BOOBY SLIPE TRAIN BERLIN CUTTER SLEDGE CARIOLE TRAINEAU
(MOTORIZED —) SNOWMOBILE
SLEIGHT ARTIFICE
SLEIPNER (OWNER OF —) ODIN
SLENDER FINE HAIR JIMP LANK LEAN PRIN SLIM THIN DELIE EXILE FAINT LATHY REEDY SLANK SLEEK SMALL SPIRY SWAMP WISPY FILATE SCANTY SEMMIT SLIGHT SPINNY SPIRED STALKY SVELTE TENDER GRACILE LISSOME SLIVERY SPIRLIE SQUINNY TENUOUS THREADY WASPISH ACICULAR ETHEREAL HAIRLIKE PILIFORM SPINDLED ATTENUATE
SLENDERNESS EXILITY TENUITY
SLEUTH TEC DETECTIVE
SLEW LOT ALOT RAFT SLUE STROKE
SLICE CUT BITE CHIP CHOP FLAG FLAP JERK SHED STOW CANCH CAPER GIGOT LEACH SHARE SHAVE SHIVE SKELB SLIPE SLIVE CANTLE COLLOP CORNET CULPON SHIVER SLIVER TARGET THIBLE TRENCH SECTION SHAVING TRANCHE COSSETTE TURNOVER
(— CUT IN PLOWING) FLAG
(— OF BACON) BARD BARDE LARDON RASHER
(— OF BREAD) BUTTY WHANG CROUTE TRENCHER
(— OF CHEESE) KEBBOC
(— OF COAL) SKIP
(— OF FISH) COBBIN
(— OF MEAT) STEAK COLLOP CUTLET SCALLOP TAILZIE
(— OF MEAT OR FISH) PAUPIETTE
(— OF SMOKED SALMON) CORNET
(— OF TOAST) ROUND
(— OF VEAL) FRICANDEAU
(— REMOVED FROM ROADWAY) CANCH
(—S OF APPLES) CHOPS
(—S OF VEAL) GRENADINE SCALLOPINI
(— WITH MOTIONS) SAW
(LARGE —) BLAD DODGE
(POTATO —) SCALLOP
(ROLLED — OF MEAT) ROULADE
(THICK —) SLAB WHANG
(THIN —) CHIP WAFER SECTION
(THIN —S OF MEAT) PICCATA
SLICED CUT
SLICK LOY MAG GLIB OILY SNUG SLEEK CLASSY GLOSSY SMOOTHY SLIDDERY
SLICKER FLOAT SLICK SMOOTH SLEEKER SMOOTHER
SLIDE SCLY SKID SLEW SLIP SLUR BALOP CHUTE COAST COULE CREEP GLIDE HURRY MOUNT SCOOT SHIRL SLADE FINDER SLOUGH SLIDDER SLITHER SLUTHER FADEAWAY GLISSADE SLIDEWAY TOBOGGAN SCHLEIFER
(— A DIE) SLUR
(— ALONG) SHOOT
(— BACK) RELAPSE
(— CARDS) SKIN
(— DOWN) RUSE SLUMP
(— FOR LOWERING CASKS) POLEYNE
(— ON DRUMHEAD) BRACE
(— SIDEWISE) SKID SLUE
(TENT —) EUPHROE
SLIDER REGISTER
SLIDEWAY PULLEY
SLIDING COULE
SLIGHT CUT OFF EASY FINE HURT POOR PUNY SLAP SLIM SLUR SNUB THIN WEAK FILMY GAUZY LIGHT MINOR SCANT SMALL SOBER FLIMSY FORGET LACHES LITTLE MINUTE REMOTE TWIGGY CONTEMN FRAGILE GRACILE NEGLECT NOMINAL SHALLOW SKETCHY SLENDER SLIGHTY THREADY VILLAIN DELICATE MISPRIZE OVERLOOK SCRANNEL VILIPEND

SLIGHTER LESS
SLIGHTEST FIRST LEAST
SLIGHTINGLY LIGHTLY
SLIGHTLY FAINTLY SOMEWHAT
(PREF.) MI(O)
(SUFF.) ESCENT ULOUS
SLIGHTNESS DELICACY GRACILITY
SLIM THIN GAUNT WANDY SLIGHT SLENDER TENUOUS
SLIME GLIT GORE OOZE SLAB SLIP SLUM GLEET SLAKE SLOAK SLOKE SLEECH SLUDGE SCHLICH SLUBBER SLUTHER
(PREF.) MUC(I)(O) MUCOSO MYX(O)
(SUFF.) MYXA
SLIMMER DIETER
SLIMY EELY OOZY SLAB MUCID GLAIRY GLEETY GLETTY LIMOUS MUCOUS SNOTTY SLEECHY MUCULENT
SLINE JOINT
SLING DUST LOOP FLING HONDA SLUNG BRIDGE BRIDLE HALTER SLACKIE
(— FOR HAULING GAME) TUMPLINE
(— OF BRAIDED FIBERS) MA
(PREF.) FUNDI
SLINGER FUNDITOR
SLINGSHOT SLING SLAPPY TWEAKER CATAPULT SHANGHAI
SLINK SLY CAST HINT LEER LOOP LURK PEAK MICHE SHIRK SLING SLUNK SNEAK SLINKY
(— AWAY) SHAG SLOKE FLINCH MIZZLE SHRINK
SLIP DIP IMP NOD SLY BALK CARD CHIT DOCK FALL JINK LOOP RUSE SKEW SKID SLEW SLUR SPEW BEWET BEWIT BONER CHECK DAGGE ERROR FLIER FLYER GLIDE LABEL LAPSE SCAPE SCION SHIFT SHIRL SKATE SKITE SLICK SLIDE SLIPE SLIVE SLUMP STALK SURGE COUPON ENGOBE LAPSUS MISCUE SLOUGH SLURRY TICKET UNSLIP DELAPSE FOUNDER ILLAPSE MISSTEP MORTISE SLIDDER SLUTHER SNAPPER STUMBLE BOOKMARK GERTRUDE GLISSADE HEADBAND QUICKSET SCHEDULE SIDESLIP SLIPPAGE SLIPPING
(— AWAY) GO BILK SKIN WISE EVADE ELAPSE
(— BY) ELAPSE
(— FROM A PLANT) STALLON
(— OFF COURSE) SLEW SLOUGH
(— OF FISH) RAND
(— OF PAPER) ALLONGE
(— OF PARCHMENT) PANEL
(— OF WOOD) SPILL REGLET
(— ON CARELESSLY) SLIVE
(— OUT) TIB
(— SECRETLY) CREEM
(— SMOOTHLY) SWIM
(— UP) BLUNDER
(CERAMICS —) SLOP ENGOBE
(INFANT'S —) GERTRUDE
(KIND OF —) FREUDIAN
(PILLOW —) BIER
(PREF.) CLAD(O)
(SUFF.) CLADOUS
SLIPCASE CASE FOREL FORREL
SLIPKNOT BOW SNITTLE DRAWKNOT
SLIPMAN JACKER
SLIPOVER OVERSLIP
SLIPPER FLAT MULE NEAP PUMP SOCK TURN GLAVE MOYLE ROMEO SCUFF BALLET BOOTEE DORSAY JULIET PANTON PINSON SANDAL SCLAFF SCLIFF BAUCHLE CHINELA CRAKOWE EVERETT SCUFFER BABOUCHE FEWTERER PANTOFLE SCLAFFER SLIPSHOE
(PREF.) CALCEI
SLIPPERINESS SLIDDER
SLIPPERY EELY GLEG GLIB SLID GLARY GLINT SLAPE SLEEK SLICK SOAPY SWACK CRAFTY GLINSE GREASY LUBRIC SHIFTY SLIPPY ELUSIVE EVASIVE GLIDDER SHUTTLE SLIDDRY SLIDING SLITHER GLIBBERY SLABBERY SLICKERY SLIDDERY SLITHERY
(PREF.) LUBRI
SLIPPERY DICK DONCELLA
SLIPSHOD JERRY RAGGED SLOPPY UNKEMPT SLAPDASH SLOVENLY
SLIPSTREAM RACE
SLIPUP FLUFF MISTAKE
SLIT CUT EYE JAG KIN NAG RIT FENT GATE NICK PORT RACE RENT SCAR SLOT VENT CRACK SPARE BOUCHE CRANNY OSTIUM STRENT FISSURE PERTUSE PLACKET SLITTED SLOTTEN WINDWAY APERTURE BOTHRIUM
(— HIND LEG) HARL
(— IN EDGE OF SHIELD) BOUCHE
(— IN ORGAN PIPE) MOUTH
(— IN SKIRT) SPARE
(— IN STONE) GRIKE
(— IN TIRE TREAD) SIPE
(— IN WALL) LOOP
(— MADE BY CUT) KERF
(ORNAMENTAL —) SLASH
SLITHER SLIDE HIRSEL SLIDDER SLUTHER
SLIVER TOP SHAVE SKELF SLICE SPELK SPELL SHIVER DELIVERY SPLINTER
(— OF WOOL) ROLL ROVE
(SPINNING —) END RIBBON DELIVERY
SLOB JOKER SLUDGE SLOBBER SLOMMACK LITTERBUG
SLOBBER SLOP SLUP SMALM SMARM SLAVER SLABBER SLATHER SLIVVER BESLAVER
SLOBBERY SLOBBY SMARMY SLAVERY
SLOE SLA SNAG SLONE
SLOG PLOD SLOSH STRIKE
SLOGAN CRY CACHET CUTTER PHRASE CATCHCRY GRAFFITO SLUGHORN WARDWORD CATCHWORD SHIBBOLETH
SLOOP STAR BOYER COMET SMACK SCHUIT HOOGAARS
SLOP SLAP SOSS SQUAB SWILL SOSSLE SOZZLE HOGWASH SLATTER
(— AROUND) SLAISTER
(PL.) SLIVERS SLIPSLOP SLOPPAGE
SLOPE UP DIP LIE BAND BANK BENT BRAE CANT CAST CURB DROP FALL HANG HILL LEAN PALI RAKE RAMP RISE SIDE SINK TILT BEVEL CLIFF COAST GAMMA HIELD PINCH PITCH SCARP SLANT SLENT SLOOP SPLAY STEEP TALUS VERGE YUNGA ASCENT BAJADA BATTER BREAST BROACH ESCARP GLACIS HADING SHELVE TUMBLE UPBROW UPRISE CUTBANK DESCENT DOWNSET FORESET HANDING INCLINE LEANING PENDANT UPGRADE VERSANT WEATHER BANKSIDE DRIPPING GLISSADE GRADIENT SHOULDER SIDELING SNOWBANK ACCLIVITY ESCARPMENT
(— BACK) BATTER
(— DOWN) SHED
(— OF CUESTA) INFACE
(— OF ROOF) CURB
(— OF STERNPOST) RAKE
(— ON GOLF GREEN) BURROW
(— UPWARD) CLIMB ASCEND BATTER
(DOWNWARD —) HANG DEVALL DECLINE DESCENT HANGING DOWNHILL
(GENTLE —) GLACIS
(MARGINAL —) CESS
(MOUNTAIN —) ADRET
(SKIING —) SCHUSS
(STEEP —) BROW HEADWALL
(TOBOGGANING —) ICEHILL
(SUFF.) CLINAL CLINE
SLOPING CANT DEVEX SLANT SLOPE SLOPY ASLOPE SHELVY DECLIVE SCARPED DOWNHILL SIDELING
(— ABRUPTLY) BOLD
(— BACKWARD) SUPINE
(STEEPLY —) RAPID
(SUFF.) CLINAL
SLOPPINESS BLURB
SLOPPY JUICY MESSY SOPPY SLABBY SOZZLY SPLOSHY SLABBERY SLAPDASH SLATTERN SLATTERY SLIPSHOD WATERISH
SLOSH DOWSE SLASH SLUSH SOUSE SQUDGE SPLODGE
SLOT COVE DROP SCROLL SPLINE KEYHOLE GUIDEWAY
SLOTH AI UNAU TARDO ACEDIA IGNAVY ACCIDIE IGNAVIA BRADYPOD EDENTATE PIGRITIA SLUGGING
SLOTH BEAR BHALU ASWAIL
SLOTHFUL FAT ARGH IDLE LAZY INERT LITHER THOKISH UNLUSTY DELICATE INDOLENT SLUGGISH
SLOUCH LOUCH LARRUP LOLLOP LOUNGE SLIDDER TROLLOP SHAMMOCK SLOUCHER
SLOUCH HAT SMASHER
SLOUGH CORE SHED SLEW SLUE BAYOU RAVEL SHUCK SLONK SLUFF SPOIL SWAMP ESCHAR DISCARD LAMMOCK

SLOVAKIA (ALSO SEE CZECH REPUBLIC)
CAPITAL: BRATISLAVA
COIN: CROWN DUCAT HALER HELLER KORUNA
DANCE: POLKA REDOWA FURIANT
MEASURE: LAN SAH MIRA KOREC LATRO STOPA MERICE STRYCH
MOUNTAIN: GERLACHOVSKY
MOUNTAIN RANGE: ORE TATRA BESKID BESKYDY JAVORNIKY CARPATHIAN NIZKETATRY VYSOKETATRY BIELEKARPATY
NAME: SLOVENSKA
RIVER: UH UZH VAG VAH HRON IPEL WAAG DUNAJ MARCH NITRA SLANA BODROG DANUBE HORNAD MORAVA ONDAVA POPRAD TORYSA LABOREC
TOWN: NITRA BANSKA KOSICE MARTIN PRESOV TRNAVA ZILINA ZVOLEN BYSTRICA NOVADUBNICA PARTIZANSKE

SLOVEN BESOM CLART SLUSH TROLLY GROBIAN HALLION TRACHLE HUDDROUN

SLOVENIA (ALSO SEE YUGOSLAVIA)
CAPITAL: LJUBLJANA
COIN: TOLAR
GULF: VENICE
LAKE: BLED BOHINJ
LANGUAGE: SLOVENE
MOUNTAIN: TRIGLAV
MOUNTAIN RANGE: SAVA DRAVA KARST JULIAN KAMNIK POHORJE SAVINJA HIGHALPS KARAVANKE KARAWANKEN
NAME: SLOVENIJA
PORT: KOPER CAPODISTRIA
RIVER: MURA SAVA SOCA DRAVA
TOWN: CELJE KOPER KRANJ MURSKA SOBOTA MARIBOR NOVOMESTO NOVAGORICA CAPODISTRIA

SLOVENLY DOWDY GAUMY MESSY BLOWZY CLATTY FROWZY GRUBBY SHABBY SLOPPY SLOVEN TRAILY UNTIDY BUNTING RAUNCHY SLIVING SLOUCHY UNSONCY CARELESS HUDDROUN SLIPSHOD SLOBBERY SLUBBERY SLUTTISH TROLLOPY
SLOW BOG LAG LAX LEK WET ARGH DREE DULL LASH LATE LAZY LENT SKID SLUG SOFT SULK BLUNT DUNCH DUNNY HEAVY HOOLY INERT POKEY SLACK SLOTH SWEER TARDE TARDO TARDY UNAPT ARREST BEHIND DRIECH DUMMEL HINDER RETARD SLOOMY SOODLY TRAILY COSTIVE DRONISH HALTING LAGGARD LANGUID SLACKEN SOAKING STRANGE TARDANT TEDIOUS UNREADY DILATORY INACTIVE LATESOME SLUGGISH
(— DOWN) SEIZE
(— DOWN SPACECRAFT) DEBOOST
(— IN BURNING) SOFT
(— IN MOVEMENT) GRAVE INERT SULKY
(— OF LEARNING) DULL
(— OF MIND) STUPID
(— TO LEARN) BACKWARD
(— TO RESPOND) GROSS

(— UP) SLACK SLACKEN
(MODERATELY —) ANDANTE
(MUSICALLY —) LENTO
(PLEASANTLY —) SOFT
(VERY —) LARGO
(PREF.) BRADY TARDI
SLOW-BURNING PUNKY
SLOWED STIFF
SLOWER LATTER CALANDO
SLOWING RELENT LENTANDO RITARDANDO RALLENTANDO
(SUFF.) STASIA STASIS
SLOW LORIS KOKAN
SLOWLY SLOW DULLY GRAVE HOOLY LENTO ADAGIO GENTLY HEAVILY
SLOW-MOVING SLEEPY DORMANT DRAWLING SLUGGISH
SLOWNESS LAG SLOTH LENTOR TARDITY LATENESS
SLOWPOKE SNAIL TURTLE ALSORAN DAWDLER
SLOW-WITTED FAT DENSE STUPID
SLOWWORM HAGWORM
SLUDGE GUNK OOZE SLOB
SLUE SLEW PIVOT SWAMP SLOUGH
SLUG BUST LINE MILL PLOW SHOT SNAG STEW ARION CLUMP LIMAX SNAIL RATTLE STRIKE SNIFTER TREPANG GEEPOUND
(PREF.) LIMACI
SLUGGARD DAW SLOW SLUG DRONE BUZZARD CAYNARD LUGGARD SWINGER SLOWBACK SLUGABED
SLUGGISH LAG DOZY DULL FOUL LATE LAZY LOGY SLOW SOFT BROSY DOPEY DRONY FAINT HEAVY INERT LEADY LOURD RESTY SULKY BOVINE DRAGGY DROWSY JACENT LEADEN SLEEPY SLOOMY SLUGGY SUPINE TORPID COSTIVE DORMANT DRONISH LAGGARD LANGUID LENTOUS LUMPISH RESTIVE DILATORY INACTIVE INDOLENT LOURDISH SLOTHFUL SLOTTERY SLUGGARD
(PREF.) BRADY
SLUGGISHNESS LEAD SLOTH APATHY LENTOR PHLEGM INERTIA LANGUOR
SLUICE CLOW GOOL GOTE GOUT SASSE SLUSH TRUNK CLOUGH FENDER LAUNDER PENSTOCK WASTWEIR
SLUICEGATE ABOIDEAU
SLUICEWAY FLASH
SLUM BUSTI BUSTEE WARREN
SLUMBER DORM DOVE DOZE JOUK REST ROUT SLEEP SLOOM DROWSE
SLUMP FALL FLOP SOSS SLOUCH LETDOWN TROLLOP
SLUR BIND SLIM COULE GLIDE SLIME SCRUFF SLIGHT SLUBBER LIGATURE
(— IN PRINTING) SHAKE
SLURRY SLIP
SLUSH MIRE POSH SIND SLOP FLUSH SLOSH SPOSH STUFF SWASH SWOSH LOPPER SLUDGE SLUTCH SLOBBER SLODDER
SLUSHY SLASHY SLOPPY SLOSHY SLUDGY STICKY SPLASHY SLOBBERY
SLUT MAUX BITCH FILTH QUEAN DOLLOP DRAZEL DRAZIL MALKIN DROSSEL PUCELLE SLAMKIN SLATTERN
SLUTTISH DRABBY SLUTTY SORDID
SLY ARCH CUTE FOXY SLEE SLID SLIM CANNY COONY LEERY LOOPY PAWKY PEERY POKEY SLOAN SNAKY ARTFUL ASTUTE CRAFTY FELINE SUBTLE SUPPLE CUNNING EVASIVE FOXLIKE FURTIVE LEERING POLITIC SUBTILE UNFRANK GUILEFUL SLEIGHTY SNEAKING STEALTHY THIEVISH CLANDESTINE
SLYNESS CUNNING PAWKERY STEALTH ARCHNESS
SMACK BANG BARK BIFF BUSS KISS SALT SCAT SLAP TANG TROW VEIN WHAM BAWLY GOUFF SAVOR SNACK SPANG SPICE TASTE TWANG BARQUE BAWLEY FLAVOR SMATCH SMACKEE SPANKER BRAGOZZO SLAPDASH TINCTURE
(— OF) RELISH
SMACKING SKELPING
SMALL BIT SMA WEE BABY MEAN PINK SEED SLIM TINY WEAK BIJOU BITTY DAWNY DEENY DINKY ELFIN PETIT PETTY PINKY POKEY RUNTY TEENY WEENY BANTAM FRIBBY GRUBBY INSECT LITTLE MIDGET MINUTE NARROW PEANUT PETITE SCANTY SLIGHT SMALLY CAPSULE MINIMAL NAGGISH NANITIC NOMINAL PICCOLO QUEECHY SCRIMPY SLENDER THRIFTY PEDDLING PILULOUS SNIPPETY MINIATURE MINISCULE
(— AND NUMEROUS) MILIARY
(— AND THICK) DUMPY DUMPTY
(— BUT TANGIBLE) CERTAIN
(— PORTION) MODICUM
(CONTEMPTIBLY —) MEASLY
(DAINTILY —) MIGNON
(EXCESSIVELY —) BOXY
(NOT —) GOOD
(VERY —) WEE FINE TINY DWARF MICRO PUSIL PYGMY TEENY MINUTE MINIKIN TIDDLEY DWARFISH
(PREF.) LEPT(O) MICR(O) OLIG(O) PARV(I) PAURO TAPIN(O)
(SUFF.) (— ONE) EL ET IUM LING OCK ULA ULE ULUM ULUS
SMALLAGE MARCH
SMALLCLOTHES SHORTS SMALLS
SMALL CRANBERRY FENBERRY
SMALLER LESS MINOR LESSER
(PREF.) MEIO MI(O) MINI
SMALLEST FIRST LEAST MINIM TITMAN MINIMUS
SMALLHOLDER TOFTMAN
SMALL-MINDED PETTY PICAYUNE
SMALLNESS NANISM EXILITY FEWNESS PAUCITY EXIGUITY SCARCITY
SMALLPOX POX VARIOLA ALASTRIM
(PREF.) VARIOLI VARIOLO
SMALL-SCALE MINI
SMALL-TIME PETTY TWOBIT RINKYDINK INSIGNIFICANT
SMALT ROYAL ESCHEL SMALTZ ZAFFER ASMALTE
SMART NIP YEP BRAW FESS FLIP FOXY GNIB NICE PINK POSH RACY SNAP SPRY SWAG TRIG ACUTE BRISK CLEAN DINKY FLASH HEADY JIMMY KIPPY NIFTY NOBBY NUTTY PEERT PRANK PRIDY RITZY SASSY SAUCY SHARP SLEEK SLICK SMIRK SMOKE SMUSH SPICY SPRIG STING SWANK SWISH TIGHT TIPPY TOFFY TRICK AKAMAI BRAWLY BRIGHT CHEESY CLEVER DAPPER GIGOLO JAUNTY KITTLE PERTLY SHREWD SPANKY SPIFFY SPRINK SPRUCE STOUND SWANKY SWIDGE TIDDLY KNOWING PUNGENT SWAGGER TOFFISH VOGUISH BRUSHING SPIFFING
(— IN APPEARANCE) POSH
(— IN DRESS) CHIC CLASSY DRESSY GALLANT
(AFFECTEDLY —) SMUG
(IMPOSINGLY —) STYLISH
SMART ALECK FLIP SMARTY WISEASS WISEGUY WISEACRE WISENHEIMER
SMART-ALECKY CUTE
SMARTEN FINE PUSS SMUG GROOM PRINK SLICK TITIVATE
SMARTLY SMACK SMART SNACK YEPLY TIDELY
SMARTNESS TON SNAP SMART SPIFF SWISH
SMARTWEED CULERAGE REDKNEES
SMASH GIT BASH BUMP CAVE DASH PASH RUSH SCAT TRAP BREAK CRACK CRASH CRAZE PRANG SOCKO STAVE TRASH WRECK BANJAX CRACKER SHATTER SMASHUP DEBRUISE DEMOLISH OVERHEAD STRAMASH
(— A GAP) BREACH
SMASHED BUNG KAPUT STOVEN BROOZLED
SMASHING CRACKING
SMASHUP STRAMASH
SMATTERING TANG SMACK SMATCH SMATTER
SMEAR DAB RUB BLOT BLUR CLAM DAUB DOPE GAUM GLOB GORM MOIL CLEAM DITCH GLAIR SLAKE SLARE SMALM SMARM SULLY BEDAUB BESLAB DEFILE PLATCH SLAVER SLURRY SMIRCH SMOOCH SMUDGE SPREAD STREAK STRIKE BEPAINT BESMEAR PLASTER POLLUTE SPLOTCH SLAISTER
(— OVER) ENGLUTE
(— WITH BLOOD) GILD
(— WITH EGG WHITE) GLAIR
(— WITH MUD) CLART SLIME
(— WITH SOMETHING STICKY) GAUM GORM LIME
(— WITH TAR) PAY
(— WITH WAX) CERE
SMEAR DAB FLATFISH MARYSOLE
SMEARED FOUL BROSY MUSSY SCOVY BLOODY SMUDGY BLURRED BEGUMMED
SMEARING (— WITH OINTMENT) INUNCTION
SMEARY DAUBY GAUMY
SMEDDUM SMITHUM
SMELL FUNK FUST GUSH NOSE ODOR VENT AROMA FETOR FLAIR SAVOR SCENT SENSE SMACK SNIFF SNOOK SNUFF STIFE TASTE OLFACT RESENT SMEECH BREATHE PERFUME REFLAIR VERDURE
(— AFTER PREY) BREVIT
(— OFFENSIVELY) REEK
(BITING —) TANG
(DAMP FUSTY —) RAFT
(DISAGREEABLE —) GOO PONG STENCH
(HAVING PLEASANT —) SNIFTY
(MUSTY —) FUST
(OFFENSIVE —) FUNK FETOR STINK MEPHITIS
(PLEASANT —) INCENSE
(STRONG —) HOGO
(SWEET —) SWEET
(PREF.) BROM(O) ODIO ODORI ODORO OLFACTO OSM(O) OSMIO OSPHRESIO OZO(NI)(NO)
(SENSE OF —) OSPHRESIO
(SUFF.) OSMA
(SENSE OF —) OSPHRESIA
SMELLY OLID RIPE FETID FUGGY WHIFFY SMELLFUL
SMELT DECOCT INANGA EPERLAN ICEFISH ELIQUATE SALMONID SPARLING SPERLING
(FRY OF —) PRIM
SMEW NUN PIED SMEE DIVER SMETHE
SMIDGEN BIT DAB JOT SKOSH SLOSH
SMIDGEON (— OF TEA) SPOT
SMILAX LILY SARSA LILIUM
SMILE BEAM GRIN FLASH FLEER SMEER ARRIDE SMUDGE SMIRKLE
(— AMOROUSLY) SMICKER
(AFFECTED —) SMIRK
(SELF-CONSCIOUS —) SIMPER
SMILING GOOD BONNY RIANT SMILY BONNIE RIDENT SMIRKY TWINKLY SMILEFUL
SMIRCH SMIT SOIL SMEAR SULLY SLURRY SOILURE TARNISH
SMIRCHED DINGY
SMIRK DRAD YIRN SIMPER SMICKER SMIRKLE SMURTLE
SMITE DUNT FRAP GIRD SLAY FLING SKITE STRIKE
(— WITH LIGHTNING) LEVEN
SMITH MIMIR REGIN BOSSER FORGER SMITHY FARRIER GLUTTER SMITHER STEELER WAYLAND FLOORMAN FORGEMAN PANSMITH
SMITHSONITE CALAMINE
SMITHY FORGE SMIDDY STITHY STUDDIE FARRIERY
SMITTEN EPRISE INLOVE STRICKEN
SMOCK BRAT SLOP CAMIS KAMIS SMOKE JIBBAH JUMPER CHEMISE SMICKET
SMOG FOG HAZE
SMOKE PEW USE BLOW FLAN FOGO FUFF FUME FUNK HAVE LUNT NAVE PIPE REEK ROKE TOVE DRINK

REECH SMEEK SMORE SMUSH STIVE VAPOR WHIFF BREATH BUCCAN POTHER SMEECH SMUDGE INCENSE SMOLDER SMOTHER BACONIZE
(— MARIJUANA) BLAST
(AUTHOR OF —) TURGENEV
(CHARACTER IN —) IRINA TANYA OSININ GRIGORY POTUGIN TATYANA BAMBAEFF SHESTOFF BINDASOFF GUBARYOFF LITVINOFF RATMIROFF KAPITOLINA REISENBACH
(FROST —) BARBER
(HAZE AND —) SMAZE
(OFFENSIVE —) FUNK
(TOBACCO —) BLAST
(PREF.) ATMID(O) CAPNO FUMAR(O) FUMI
SMOKE-AND-MIRRORS DISGUISE
SMOKE BROWN ASPHALT
SMOKEHOUSE FUMATORY
SMOKEJACK STACKMAN
SMOKER STAG FUNKER NICOTIAN
(MARIJUANA —) VIPER
SMOKESTACK STACK FUNNEL TUNNEL CHIMNEY
SMOKE TREE ZANTE FUSTET FUSTIC SCOTINO
SMOKING ROOM DIVAN TABAGIE
SMOKY HAZY ROKY DINGY FUMID REEKY FUMISH FUMOSE REECHY REEKIE SMUDGY SMUISTY
SMOLDER SMUSH SMOTHER
SMOLDERING PUNKY
SMOLT SMELT SMOUT SPROD
SMOOCH PET BUSS KISS NECK SMUDGE LALLYGAG LOLLYGAG
SMOOTH DUB FAT LAP NOT BOSS COMB DRAG EASE EASY EVEN FACE FAIR FILE FLAT GLAD GLEG GLIB HONE IRON LENE NOTT REET SLID SNOD SOFT TRIM BLAND BRENT CLEAR COUTH DARBY DIGHT DOLCE DRESS EMERY FLOAT FRAZE GLARE GOOSE HOWEL LEVEL LITHE NAKED PLAIN PLANE PRESS QUIET SCARF SILKY SLAPE SLEEK SLICK SMOLT SNUFF SOAPY SUANT SUAVE SUENT TERSE ABRASE BUFFED CREAMY EQUATE EVENLY FETTLE FLUENT GLOSSY GREASE GREASY LEGATO LIMBER MANGLE POLITE SCREED SILKEN SLIGHT STREAK STRIKE STROKE SVELTE UNFRET BOULDER ERUGATE FLATTEN SLEEKIT EXPLICIT GLABRATE GLABROUS GLIBBERY GRAZIOSO LEVIGATE SARSENET SLIDDERY SQUEEGEE STRICKLE UNRUFFLE
(— BY BREAKING LUMPS) BILDER
(— MARBLE) GRIT
(— ONESELF UP) PREEN
(— OVER) GLOZE PLASTER
(— TYPE) KERN
(HYPOCRITICALLY —) SLEEK
(PHONETICALLY —) LENE LENIS
(PREF.) HOMAL(O) LEIO LEUR(O) LIO LISS(O) LITI OXY
SMOOTHER GLAZER
SMOOTHLY SLICK EASILY EVENLY GLIBLY SMOOTH SPROWSY SWEETLY POLITELY
SMOOTH-MANNERED URBANE
SMOOTHNESS EASE FLUENCY
SMOOTH-RUNNING SWEET
SMOOTH-TONGUED WHILLY
SMOOTH WINTERBERRY CANHOOP
SMOTHER BURKE CHOKE SMEAR SMOKE SMORE MOIDER SMUDGE STIFLE FLASKER OPPRESS QUEASON QUEAZEN SMOLDER SMUDDER
SMOTHERED ETOUFFE STIFLED
SMUDGE BLUR GAUM SLUR SMUT SOIL SOOT CROCK SMEAR SMOKE SMOOCH SMUTCH SMOLDER SMOTHER SOILURE
SMUDGED BLOTTY SMUTCHY
SMUG SLEEK SMUSH SUAVE SMUDGE
SMUGGLE RUN STEAL BOOTLEG SHUFFLE
SMUGGLER OWLER COYOTE RUNNER SPOTSMAN
(— OF DRUGS) MULE
(— OF IMMIGRANTS) COYOTE
(DOPE —) MULE
(DRUG —) MULE
SMUGGLING OWLING
SMUGLY FATLY
SMUT BUNT COOM PORN BLACK BLECK COLLY COOMB CROCK GRIME SMOOT SMITCH SMUTCH SMATTER COLBRAND
SMUTCH BLOT SMIRCH SMITCH SMOUCH SMUDGE
SMUT GRASS TUSSOCK
SMUTTINESS RAUNCH
SMUTTY BAWDY DIRTY SOOTY SULTRY RAUNCHY BARNYARD FREUDIAN
SMYRNA USHAK
SNACK BIT CUT BAIT BITE GORP NOSH SNAP TAPA BEVER BUTTY CHACK CHECK NACHO SHARE SNICK TASTE GOUTER MUNGEY NACKET SNATCH ZAKUSKA ANTOJITO MUNCHIES NUNCHEON
(— SPOT) TEAROOM
(CHOCOLATE —) OREO
SNAFFLE BIT GAG BRIDOON
SNAG KNAG SNUG STUB POINT GLITCH IMPASSE PLANTER SNAGGLE
(PL.) EMBARRAS
SNAIL HUA PILA SNAG CHINK DRILL HELIX OLIVA OVULA PHYSA SHELL THAIS TURBO WHELK CERION CONKER DODMAN NATICA NERITA NERITE PHYSID PURPLE TRITON WINKLE RISSOID UNICORN VERTIGO ZONITID CASSIDID ESCARGOT HODMADOD JANTHINA LYMNAEID MELANIAN NATICEID NERITOID RAMSHORN SOLARIUM WALLFISH PERIWINKLE
(PREF.) STROMBI STROMBULI
(SUFF.) COCHLEI COCHLI(O) COCHLO
SNAILFLOWER CARACOL
SNAKE (ALSO SEE SERPENT AND REPTILE) ASP BOA BOM ESS NAG APOD BOBA BOID BOMA JUBO NAGA NAJA SEPS SNIG ABOMA ASPIC COBRA CONGO CRIBO DRILL JIBOA KRAIT MAMBA PTYAS RACER SNECK TIGER VIPER BOIGID BONGAR CANTIL CHITAL DABOIA DIPSAS ELAPID GOPHER HISSER JESSUR KERRIL PYTHON ROLLER RUNNER TAIPAN URAEUS WENONA ADJIGER ANILIID BOKADAM CAMOODI CRAWLER CREEPER CULEBRA DIAPSID HAGWORM HOGNOSE LABARIA LANGAHA PRESTER RATTLER REGULUS REPTILE SCYTALE SERPENT SPITTER WALPAPI ANACONDA BONETAIL BUNGARUM CASCAVEL CERASTES CROTALID EGGEATER FLATHEAD HAIRWORM JARARACA KEELBACK MOCCASIN OPHIDIAN RINGHALS SNAKELET VIPERINE
(— OIL) BUNKUM POPPYCOCK
(TREE —) BOOMSLANG
(TWO-HEADED —) AMPHISBAENA
(PREF.) OPHI(O) SERPU
(SUFF.) OPHIS
SNAKEBARK IRONBARK
SNAKEBIRD DARTER PLOTUS ANHINGA DUCKLAR
SNAKEHEAD MURRAL
SNAKELIKE ANGUINE VIPEROUS
SNAKE MACKEREL ESCOLAR
SNAKEMOUTH POGONIA
SNAKEPIECE POINTER
SNAKEROOT STEVIA BABROOT BUGBANE SANGREL SANICLE SAWWORT POOLWORT RICHWEED WHITETOP
SNAKESKIN SPOIL HACKLE SLOUGH
(CASTOFF —S) EXUVIAE
SNAKEWEED BISTORT
SNAP SET ZIP BARK BITE CHOP GNAP HUFF JERK KNAP LIRP PIPE SETT BREAK CLACK FILIP FLICK GANCH KNACK KNICK PHOTO SMACK SNACK BLUDGE SNAPPY SNATCH FASTENER PUSHOVER SNAPHEAD CREPITATE
(— AT) HANCH
(— LIGHTLY) KNICK
(— OFF) SNIP
(— TOGETHER) CRASH
(— UP) SNUP SNAFFLE
(— WITH FINGER) LIRP FILIP THRIP FILLIP
SNAPBACK PASSBACK
SNAPDRAGON BULL SNAPS BULLER BULLDOG DOGMOUTH
SNAPE FLINCH
SNAPPER UKU BRIM JOCU SESI BREAM PARGO VORAZ CUBERA HUSSAR JENOAR LAWYER NATIVE TAMURE ULAULA COCKNEY CRACKER BIAJAIBA CACHUCHO FLAMENCO GNATSNAP LUTIANID WOLLOMAI SCHNAPPER MUTTONFISH SHUTTERBUG
SNAPPING CHACK DOGGISH
SNAPPING BEETLE ELATER SKIPPER SNAPPER ELATERID SKIPJACK
SNAPPING TURTLE LOGHEAD SHAGTAIL
SNAPPISH CRUP EDGY PUXY CROSS SNACK TESTY WASPY CUTTED SNAGGY SNAPPY SNARKY SNIPPY DOGGISH PEEVISH
SNAPPY CRISP JEMMY NIPPY ZIPPY
SNAPSHOT PRINT
SNARE BAG GIN HAY NET PIT SET BAIT BUKE FANG GIRN GRIN HOOK LACE LIME TOIL TRAP WAIT WIRE BRAKE CATCH FRAUD GNARE LATCH LEASH SINEW SNARL SNIRL STALE SWEEK TRAIN COBWEB GILDER PANTER SNATCH SPRINT TREPAN TUNNEL ENSNARE MANTRAP OVERNET PITFALL SETTING SNICKLE SNIGGLE SPRINGE BIRDLIME INVEIGLE LIMEBUSH SPRINGLE TENDICLE MOUSETRAP
(— DEER) WITHE
(— FOR ELEPHANTS) KEDDAH
(— FOR FISH) WEEL
(FISH —) WEEL
SNARL ARR BITE CARL GIRN GNAR GURR HARL HURR NARR TWIT WAFF YARR GNARL GNARR GRILL KNURL RAVEL SNIRL TWINE BOWWOW BUMBLE GAUNCH MUCKER TANGLE VENNER GRIZZLE GRUMBLE
SNARLED SNAFU
SNARLER CYNIC
SNARLING LATRANT
SNATCH HAP NAB NIP RAP GRAB HINT RACE RASE SNAP SNIP WHIP WRAP YERK YUCK BRAID CATCH CLAWK CLICK EREPT GANCH GRASP GRIPE PLUCK SNACK STRIP SWIPE SWOOP TWEAK WHIFT WREST SNITCH STRIKE TWITCH WRENCH CLAUGHT GRABBLE SCAMBLE VULTURE
(— MOMENTARY VIEW) GLANCE
SNAZZY CHIC COOL FANCY
SNEAK BLAB GRUB LEER LOOP LOUT LURK PEAK PIMP SHUG SNIG LURCH MEECH MOOCH SCOUT SHARK SHIRK SKULK SLIDE SLINK SLIPE SLIVE SLOKE SNEAP SNICK SNOOK BLIFIL MICHER WEASEL SLOUNGE SNIGGLE SNEAKSBY
(— AWAY) SLIPE
(— OFF) MAG SHAB MIZZLE
(PRYING —) SNOOP
SNEAKER CREEPER GUMSHOE TENNIES
SNEAKERS TENNIES
SNEAKING HANGDOG PEAKING SLIVING
SNEAKY FURTIVE MEECHING
SNEER SHY FLON GIBE GIRD GIRN GULE JEER JERK JIBE MOCK FLEER FLING FLOUT GLEEK JAUNT SCOFF SCOUT SLARE SLEER SNIFF SNIRT SNORT GIZZEN SNEEST TWITCH WRINKLE RIDICULE
SNEERING FRUMPERY
SNEEZE NEESE NEEZE ARREST
(— AT) CONDEMN DESPISE
SNEEZEWEED ALANT ROSILLA HELENIUM
SNEEZEWOOD NIESHOUT
SNEEZEWORT HARDHEAD PTARMICA

SNEEZING PTARMIC
SNELL SNOOD TIPPET GANGING
SNICK TIP SNECK
SNICKER TEEHEE TITTER SMIRKLE SNIGGER SNIGGLE
SNIDE ORNERY
SNIFF NOSE TIFT VENT WIND SCENT SMELL SNAFF SNIFT SNUFF SNIVEL SNAFFLE SNIFFLE SNOTTER
SNIFTER SLUG BALLOON INHALER
SNIGGER NICKER WHICKER
SNIGGLE BRAGGLE
SNIP CUT CLIP CROP MINX NICK SHRED SNICK SCISSOR
SNIPE JACK NICK WISP SCAPE SNITE WADER WILLET BLEATER BLITTER DOWITCH HUMILITY LONGBILL SHADBIRD WOODCOCK
SNIPER TEASER BUSHWACK
SNIPPET BIT
SNIPPINESS SASS
SNIVEL WHINE BUBBLE SNIFFLE SNIFTER SNOTTER SNUFFLE
SNIVELY TEARY TEARFUL
SNOB SNAB SNOOT FLUNKY SHONEEN SNOBBER
SNOBBERY ELITISM
SNOBBISH RITZY DICKTY OFFISH SNOBBY SNOOTY UPPISH HAUGHTY UPSTAGE
SNOOK SNOOT ROBALO
SNOOKER CON HOODWINK
SNOOP PRY PEEK PEEP PRIER SNEAK BREVIT PIROOT GUMSHOE
SNOOPER CREEP BUSYBODY
SNOOPY CURIOUS
SNOOZE NAP NOD DOVER SLEEP SNOOZLE
SNORE ROUT SNARK SNORK SNORT SNOCKER SNOTTER
SNORING STERTOR RHONCHUS
SNORT BLOW ROUT SNUR TOOT VENT BLURT FNESE SNARK SNEER SNORE SNORK WHOOF EXCLAIM SNIFTER SNOCKER SNORKEL SNORTLE SNOTTER
SNOUT NEB SAW BEAK BILL NOSE WROT GROIN SERRA SNOOT MUFFLE MUZZLE NOZZLE GRUNTLE ROSTRUM (PREF.) PROBOSCI(DI) RHYNCH(O) (SUFF.) RHYNCHUS RHYNCUS
SNOUT BEETLE CURCULIO
SNOUT MITE BDELLID
SNOW CORN DRIP GRUE COVER SPOSH STORM SUGAR WHITE POWDER COCAINE GRAUPEL RAMPART WEATHER SCOUTHER WINDSLAB
(— PELLETS) GRAUPEL
(— SLIGHTLY) SPIT
(— UP) STALL
(DISSOLVING —) FLUSH
(DRIFTED —) WINDLE
(GLACIER —) FIRN NEVE BLIZZ
(HEAVY FALL OF —) PASH
(MELTING —) SLUSH
(MUSHY —) SLOB
(NEW-FALLEN —) MANNA
(PARTLY MELTED —) SLUSH
(WHIRLING —) SKIRL
(PREF.) CHIO CHION(O) NIVI
SNOWBERRY MOXA WAXBERRY
SNOWBIRD JUNCO
SNOW BUNTING OATFOWL SNOWBIRD SNOWFOWL
SNOW COCK JERMONAL
SNOWDRIFT WREATH YOWDEN
SNOWDROP TREE BELLWOOD COWLICKS TISSWOOD
SNOWFALL PASH SKIFF SKIFT FLURRY ONDING
SNOWFLAKE FLAG FLAUCHT
SNOW FLEA PODURAN PODURID
SNOW GOOSE WAVY
(— GENUS) CHEN
SNOWINESS NIVOSITY
SNOW LEOPARD IRBIS OUNCE
SNOWLESS GREEN
SNOW MAIDEN, THE (CHARACTER IN —) LEL BOBYL KUPAVA MIZGIR SPRING BERENDEY BOBYLIKHA SNEGUROCHKA
(COMPOSER OF —) RIMSKYKORSAKOV
SNOWMAN YETI
SNOW MOUNTAIN JOKUL
SNOWSHOE WEB PATIN PATTEN RACKET RACQUET
SNOWSTORM PURGA DRIFTER BLIZZARD
SNOWY NIVAL WHITE NIVEOUS
SNUB AIR RITZ SLAP SNIB FRUMP SNEAP SWANK REBUFF REBUTE SIMOUS SLIGHT SNOUCH SNUBBY SETDOWN
SNUBBING MAIL
SNUBBY PUGGISH
SNUB-NOSED SIMOUS (PREF.) SIMO
SNUFF TOP VENT MUSTY SNIFF SNUSH TABAC COHOBA PULVIL RAPPEE SNEESH STIFLE SNUFFLE BERGAMOT MACCABOY ORANGERY SMUTCHIN
(UP TO —) ABLE
SNUFFBOX MILL MULL
SNUFFBOX BEAN CACOON
SNUFFER PRICK DOUTER TOPPER PRICKER
SNUFFLE SNIVEL SNAFFLE SNIFFLE SNIFTER
SNUG LEW RUG BEIN BIEN COSH COSY COZY NEAT SNOD TAUT TEAT TOSH TOSY CANNY CLOSE COMFY COUTH POVIE QUEME TIGHT PENTIT COUTHIE SNUGGERY SNUGGISH
SNUGGLE SNUG BURROW CUDDLE NESTLE SNUDGE CROODLE SNUZZLE
SNUGLY SHORT COSILY
SO SAE SUCH THAT THIS THUS THISSEN INSOMUCH SUCHWISE THUSWISE
(— AM I) LIKEWISE
(— BE IT) AMEN
(— FAR AS) QUOAD
(— TO SPEAK) FAIRLY
(NOT —) SECUS
(QUITE —) EXACTLY
SOAK RET SOB SOD SOG SOP WET BOWK BUCK SIPE BINGE DROUK DROWN SOUSE STEEP STING TOAST DRENCH EMBAIN IMBIBE IMBRUE SEETHE SODDEN SPONGE INSTEEP MICKERY SWELTER SATURATE
(— A CASK) GROG
(— FLAX) RET RATE
(— IN) SOP FEATHER
(— UP) SOP
SOAKED SOGGY SOPPY SOBBED SODDEN WATERY DRUNKEN SOBBING DRAGGLED
SOAKING BATH SUING SOGGING INFUSION
SOAP SAPO SUDS CHIPS STOCK CASTILE TALLATE WINDSOR SANDSOAP SAVONETTE
(— OPERA) SUDSER
(— SUBSTITUTE) AMOLE
(— UNIT) CAKE
(CAKE OF —) TABLET TABULATE
(LIQUID —) FIT
(PREF.) SAP(O) SAPONI
SOAPBARK QUILLAI SOAPWOOD
SOAPFISH JABON
SOAP PLANT AMOLE PALMILLO SOAPROOT SOAPWEED
SOAPSTONE TALC ALBERENE POTSTONE STEATITE
SOAPSTONER TALCER
SOAPWORT BORITH COWHERB SAPONARY SOAPROOT SOAPWEED
SOAR FLY STY KITE FLOAT MOUNT PLANE SPIRE TOWER ASCEND ASPIRE AIRPLANE
SOARING ALOFT FLIGHT ICARIAN SPIRING ESSORANT
SOB YEX SIKE SNOB SNUB SOUGH BLUBBER SINGULT
SOBBING GREET
SOBER SAD CALM COOL SAGE CIVIL FRESH GRAVE QUIET STAID DOULCE SEDATE SEVERE SOLEMN SOMBER STEADY EARNEST PENSIVE REGULAR SERIOUS UNFOXED DECOROUS MODERATE ABSTEMIOUS
SOBRIETY DRYNESS GRAVITY ABSTINENCE
SOBRIQUET BYNAME HAWKEYE
SO-CALLED ALLEGED
SOCCER FOOTER FOOTBALL
(— NAME) PELE
(— PLAYER) SWEEPER
SOCIABLE COSY CHUMMY CLUBBY FOLKSY SOCIAL AFFABLE AMIABLE INNERLY CLUBABLE FAMILIAR FELLOWLY INFORMAL
SOCIAL TEA DISTAL PUBLIC SOIREE SUPPER SOCIABLE SOCIETAL CONVIVIAL
(— WORKER) ALMONER
SOCIALISM ETATISM MARXISM GUESDISM
SOCIALIST FABIAN NIHILIST
SOCIALISTIC PINK
SOCIALIZE CIVILIZE
SOCIETY BUND HALL HERD SANG GUILD MONDE POLIS SABHA SAMAJ SANGH SOKOL ADMASS MENAGE NANIGO PARISH SYSTEM VEREIN ACADEMY COLLEGE COLORUM COMPANY COUNCIL KINGDOM SOCIETE THIASOS EXCHANGE HETAERIA PRECINCT SOCIETAS SODALITY SORORITY
(— OF RELIGIOUS FANATICS) COLORUM
(CHORAL —) CHOIR
(CLOWN —) KOSHARE KOYEMSHI
(CRAFT —) ARTEL
(CRIMINAL —) MAFIA MAFFIA
(DEBATING —) POP
(GENTEEL —) FASHION
(GYMNASTIC —) SOKOL
(HIGH —) SWELLDOM
(LITERARY —) HALL
(MEMBER OF CRUDE —) LUMPEN
(POLITICAL —) TAMMANY
(RELIGIOUS —) CHURCH
(SECRET —) HUI EGBO HOEY PORO TONG LODGE MAFIA OGBONI PURRAH CAMORRA
(STUDENT —) CORPS
(UTOPIAN —) ANARCHY
(WHITE —) MAN
(PREF.) SOCIO
SOCIETY ISLANDS (CAPITAL OF —) PAPEETE
(ISLAND OF —) TAHITI
SOCINIAN RACOVIAN
SOCIOLOGIST AMERICAN HUNT LYND ODUM ROSS WARD BALCH CAREY BARNES BOGART DEVINE DUFFEY HUNTER SUMNER VEBLEN COLLIER DUGDALE ELLWOOD ETZIONI FRAZIER NEARING STEIZLE WILLARD ZUEBLIN BOGARDUS GIDDINGS YANKELOVICH GOLDENWEISER
ENGLISH KIDD WEBB GLASS GEDDES TOYNBEE
FRENCH TARDE DURKHEIM
GERMAN LANGE WEBER FREYER SIMMEL MICHELS SCHAFFLE THURNWALD
GREEK BARDIS
HUNGARIAN MANNHEIM
ITALIAN LORIA
SCOTTISH GEDDES MCLENNAN
SWEDISH MYRDAL
SOCIOLOGY DEMOTICS
SOCK BOP ONE BIFF BUST HOSE VAMP ANKLET ARGYLE VAMPEY STOCKING
(— OF GOAT'S HAIR) UDO
(INFANT'S —) BOOTEE BOOTIE
(JAPANESE —) TABI
SOCKET BOX CUP PAD POD BUSH CELL HOSE LEAD NOSE SHOE CHAIR POINT SHANK BUCKET BUDGET COLLET EYEPIT NOZZLE POCKET SAUCER SCONCE ALVEOLE COCKEYE FERRULE FUTCHEL GUDGEON THIMBLE TORULUS ALVEOLUS DRAWHEAD
(— FOR BIT) POD
(— FOR CARBINE) BUDGET
(— FOR GEM) OUCH
(— FOR LANCE) PORT
(— FOR LENS) CELL
(— FOR MAST) TABERNACLE
(— FOR MOUTHPIECE) BIRN
(— IN GOLF CLUB HEAD) HOSE HOSEL
(— OF BONE) POT
(— OF GEM) OUCH
(— OF HINGE) PAN
(— OF LOCK) KEEPER

(— OF MILLSTONE) INK COCKEYE
(— OF WATER PIPE) BELL
(BIT —) POD
(PREF.) GLENO TORMO
SOCKEYE NERKA KOKANEE BLUEBACK
SOCLE ZOCCO
SOCRATES (— METHOD) MAIEUTIC
(DISCIPLE OF —) XENOPHON
SOD HUB BEAT DELF FAIL FLAG SCAD SONK TURF DELPH GAZON GLEBE SCRAW SWARD CLOWER TERRON SODDING
SODA POP BARILLA
(— FOUNTAIN) SPA
SODA POP TONIC
SODDEN SAMMY SAPPY SOGGY POACHY DRAGGLED
SODI (SON OF —) GEDDIEL
SODIUM NA SODA NATRIUM
(PREF.) NATR(O)
SODIUM BICARBONATE SODA BICARB
SODIUM BORATE BORAX
SODIUM CARBONATE SODA TRONA NATRON ANATRON BARILLA SALSODA
SODIUM CHLORIDE SALT HALITE
SODIUM THIOSULFATE HYPO
SODOMITE DOG BUGGER SPINTRY BOUGERON
SOEVER SOME
SOFA BOIST COUCH DIVAN SQUAB CANAPE LOUNGE SETTEE CAUSEUSE SOCIABLE
(— IN RESTAURANT) BANQUETTE
SOFFIT GATHER PLAFOND INTRADOS PLANCIER
SOFRONIA (LOVER OF —) OLINDO
SOFT COY TID FEIL LASH LIMP LUSH MILD MURE NASH NESH PLUM SART SLOW TOSY WAXY WEAK BALMY BLAND CUSHY DABBY DOLCE DOWNY FAINT GIVEY HOOLY LENIS LIGHT MALMY MEALY MELCH MUSHY MUTED PADDY PAPPY PIANO PLIFF SILKY SLACK SMALL SOAPY SOOTH SWASH SWEET WAXEN WETHE YAPPY CASHIE CREAMY EFFETE FLAGGY FLOSSY FLUFFY GENTLE LITHER LYDIAN MELLOW PIPING PLACID SAMMEL SIDDER SIDDOW SILKEN SLOPPY SMOOTH SOFTLY SPONGY SPOONY TENDER UNDURE CLEMENT COTTONY CRUMBLY DUCTILE FLESHLY LENIENT SQUASHY CUSHIONY FEMININE FLEXIBLE HOTHOUSE LADYLIKE SARCENET SLUGGISH SQUELCHY TRANQUIL
(— AND BRITTLE) FROWY FROWIE FROUGHY
(— AND FLEXIBLE) FLOPPY
(— AND LIFELESS) DOUGHY
(— IN SOUND) SMALL
(— IN TEXTURE) SUPPLE
(VERY —) SQUASHY
(PREF.) LENI MALAC(O) MOLLI
SOFT-COVER PAPERBACK
SOFTEN CUT CREE MELT SOAK SOFT TAME ALLAY BATCH BREAK FRIZZ LITHE MALAX TOUCH WOKIE DIGEST GENTLE LENIFY PACIFY RELENT SOOTHE SUBDUE SUBMIT TEMPER WEAKEN APPEASE ASSUAGE CUSHION LENIATE MOLLIFY QUALIFY SWEETEN UNSTEEL AMOLLISH ATTEMPER ENFEEBLE HUMANIZE MITIGATE MODULATE PALLIATE PRETTIFY
(— BY BOILING) CREE
(— BY KNEADING) MALAX MALAXATE
(— BY STEEPING) MACERATE
(— COLOR) CUT SCUMBLE
(— FIBERS) BREAK
(— GRADUALLY) SQUAT
(— JUTE) BATCH
(— LEATHER) BREY FRIZ FRIZZ
(— METAL) ALLAY
(— TONE) SURD
SOFTENED ROXY ANODYNE MOUILLE FLEXUOUS
SOFTENER (WATER —) CALGON
SOFTENING LENIENT MALACIA BLETTING
(— OF ARTICULATION) LENITION
SOFTER MANCANDO
SOFTHEARTED TENDER
SOFTLY LOW BAJO SOFT HOOLY FAIRLY GENTLY SWEETLY CREAMILY TENDERLY
SOFTNESS SOFT MOLLITIES
(— IN COAL SEAM) LUM LUMB
(TENDER —) LANGUOR
(SUFF.) MALACIA
SOFT-POINTED HEBETATE
SOFT-SHELLED TURTLE FLAPPER FLIPPER FLAPJACK
SOFT-SOAP CON FLANNEL
SOFT-SPOKEN MEALY
SOFTWARE (COMPUTER —) DRIVER MONITOR
(DESKTOP — DISPLAY WYSIWYG
(OF — DISPLAY) WYSIWYG
SOFTY PUSSYCAT
SOGGY SAD DUNCH SOBBY SODDEN SPONGY WATERY
SOIGNE TRIM SLEEK MODISH
SOIL DAG DUB MUD RAY SOD BLOT BLUR CLAY CLOD DAUB DIRT DUST FOIL FOUL GRIT LAND MIRK MOOL MOSS MUCK MURK MUSS SAUR SILE SLUR SMUT SOOT TASH BULLI CROCK EARTH GLEBE GRIME GUMBO LAYER MUCKY ROSEL SLUSH SMEAR SOLUM SOULE SPARK STAIN SULLY BARING BEDAUB BEFOUL BEMIRE BEMOIL GROUND PODZOL SLURRY SMIRCH SMOOCH SMUDGE SPLASH SUDDLE BEGRIME BENASTY BESMEAR BESMOKE BETHUMB FEWMAND PEDOCAL POLLUTE REGOSOL SEEDBED SLUBBER TARNISH TRACHLE AGROTYPE ALLUVIAL BEDABBLE BESMIRCH BUCKSHOT FLYSPECK LATERITE PEDALFER PLANOSOL RENDZINA WOODCOCK SOLONCHAK CONTAMINATE
(— ABOVE CLAY) KELLY
(— AGGREGATE) PED
(— DEPOSITED BY WIND) ELUVIUM
(— FORMED BY DECAY) GEEST
(— INTERMEDIATE BETWEEN SAND AND CLAY) ROSEL
(— PREPARED FOR SOWING) TILTH
(— REMOVED FROM ORE) BARING
(— WITH GREASE) LARD
(AGGREGATE —) PED
(ALKALINE —) SOLONETZ
(ASHLIKE —) PODSOL PODZOL
(AZONAL —) REGOSOL
(CLAYEY —) GALT MALM MAUM ADOBE SOLOD SOLOTH
(COTTON —) REGUR
(DRY —) GROOT
(FRIABLE —) CRUMB
(GRAVELLY —) ROACH GROWAN
(HARD —) RAMMEL
(INFERTILE —) GALL
(LEACHED —S) LATOSOL
(PEATY —) YARFA YARPHA
(PLUMBER'S —) SMUDGE
(POROUS —) SPONGE
(POTTING —) COMPOST
(PRAIRIE —) BRUNIZEM
(RED —) LATERITE
(SILTY —) GUMBO
(SPRINGY —) WOODSERE
(ZONAL —) SEROZEM SIEROZEM
(PREF.) AGRI AGRO GE(O) PED(O) SOLI
SOILAGE SOIL SMUDGE SOILING
SOILED FOUL BLACK DINGY DIRTY MUSSY SOOTY TARRY SMUDGY SMUTTY SNUFFY THUMBED DRAGGLED SHOPWORN
SOIL-EXPOSING EROSIVE
SOIREE EVENING
SOJOURN LIE BIDE STAY STOP ABIDE ABODE TARRY VISIT RESIDE ALLODGE MANSION STATION
(— ABROAD) PEREGRINATION
SOJOURNER PILGRIM
SOKOL FALCON
SOL SOH SOU ALCOSOL EMULSOID HYDROSOL SOLUTION
SOLA SHOLA PAUKPAN
SOLACE CHEER CHEERER COMFORT CONSOLE SWEETEN SOLATION
SOLAR HELIAC SOLLER HELIACAL SOLARIUM
(— REFLECTOR) HELIOSTAT
(— SYSTEM APPARATUS) ORRERY
SOLAR DISK ATEN ATON
(CENTER OF —) CAZIMI
SOLAR ENERGY
(PREF.) HELI
SOLD SELT BOOKED
(ILLICITLY —) BOOTLEG
SOLDER PALE BRAZE FLOAT SOWDER SPELTER
SOLDERER BROGUER
SOLDERING IRON COPPER DOCTOR
SOLDIER GI SON TAP BLEU BOLO GOUM GUGU KERN LEVY SHOT SWAD TULK WART BERNE CROAT FRITZ GUARD GUFFY KHAKI LANCE LIMEY LINER MINER NIZAM PERDU PIKER PIVOT POILU PONGO SAMMY SWEAT TOLKE TOMMY TOPAS ASKARI BONAGH BUMMER DARTER DIGGER EXPERT GALOOT GUNNER GURKHA HAIDUK HEINIE HOSTER LANCER MARKER PIETON REITER SENTRY SKIEUR SOLDAT SWADDY THRASO WEAPON ZOUAVE BAYONET BILLJIM BLIGHTY BRIGAND CARABIN CATERAN CORSLET DARTMAN DOGFACE DRAGOON FEDERAL FEEDMAN FIGHTER GENETOR GOUMIER HOBBLER INVALID JACKMAN MATROSS ORDERLY PALIKAR PANDOUR PAVISOR PELTAST PIKEMAN PRIVATE REDCOAT REGULAR REISTER SCARLET SLINGER SOLDADO STRIKER TROOPER VETERAN WARRIOR ARQUEBUS BEZONIAN BLUECOAT BUCKSKIN BUFFCOAT CAMELEER CAVALIER DESERTER FENCIBLE FUGLEMAN FUSILIER GALLOPER GENDARME GRAYBACK GRAYCOAT IRONSIDE JANIZARY KHANDAIT LANCEMAN LINESMAN MILITANT MIQUELET MUSTACHE PIOUPIOU RAPPAREE SENTINEL SERVITOR SILLADAR SPEARMAN SWORDMAN TOLPATCH TRANSFER TRIARIAN WARFARER WHIFFLER YARDBIRD CATAPHRACT
(— OF MUSCOVITE GUARD) STRELITZ
(— ON GUARD) SENTRY
(— WITH SIDE WHISKERS) BADGER
(ALBANIAN —) PALIKAR
(ALGERIAN —) ARBI
(AMERICAN —) SAMMY
(ANT —) MAXIM
(ARMY OR MARINE FOOT —) GRUNT
(ASIAN —) GOOK
(AUSTRALIAN —) ANZAC DIGGER BILLJIM
(BOMBAY —S) DUCKS
(BRITISH —) LIMEY TOMMY BLIGHTY LOBSTER REDCOAT ROOINEK
(BRUTAL —) PANDOUR
(CAREER —) LIFER
(CAVALRY —) REITER TROOPER
(COWARDLY —) CAPITANO
(DISBANDED —) REFORMADO
(EGYPTIAN —) GIPPO GIPPY GYPPO GYPPY GYPPIE
(FEMALE —) AMAZON
(FILE OF 6 —S) ROT
(FILIPINO —) GUGU
(FOOT —) KERN PAGE PEON GRUNT PIETON FOOTMAN TOLPATCH
(GERMAN —) HUN FRITZ HEINE KRAUT HEINIE
(GREEK —) EVZONE HOPLITE
(HORSE —) RUTTER CUIRASSIER
(INCOMPETENT —) BOLL
(INDIAN —) PEON JAWAN SEPOY GURKHA
(INEPT —) SADSACK
(INVALID —) FOGY FOGEY
(IRREGULAR —) CROAT CATERAN JAYHAWK SEBUNDY MIQUELET RAPPAREE SILLADAR
(MERCENARY —) RUTTER HESSIAN LANSQUENET LANDSKNECHT
(MOROCCAN —) ASKARI
(MOSLEM —) NIZAM

(MOUNTED —) LANCER DRAGOON GENETOR LOBSTER TROOPER VEDETTE CAVALIER
(NEW —) RECRUIT
(NEW ZEALAND —) ANZAC
(NEW ZEALAND OR AUSTRALIAN—) DIGGER
(OLD —) GROGNARD
(PROFESSIONAL —) SAMURAI
(REVOLUTIONARY —) REDCOAT BUCKSKIN
(ROMAN —) FOEDERATUS
(ROMAN —S OF THIRD LINE) TRIARY TRIARII
(RUSSIAN —) IVAN
(SCOTTISH —) JOCK
(SMALL —) BANTAM
(TERRITORIAL —) TERRIER
(TURKISH —) NIZAM REDIF
(U.S. FOOT —) GRUNT
(UNTRAINED —) YARDBIRD
(PL.) FOOT ELITE TERZO TROOP TERTIA CATERVA ENOMOTY MILITIA VELITES FORAGERS INFANTRY SOLDIERY
AMERICAN DIX LEA LEE ORD POE AMES BELL BUTT CARR CLAY DEAN DRUM FISK FORD HAIG HILL HOOD HULL KNOX LANE LEAR LONG LORD LYON MYER OTIS RENO SHAW WOOD WOOL YORK ALLEN BANKS BATES BEALL BLAIR BLISS BLOCH BRAGG BRETT BROWN BUELL BURNS CANBY CATES CHASE CLARK CORSE CRAIG CROOK CROWE DAVIS DODGE EAKER EARLY EATON ELIOT EWELL GATES GAVIN GETTY GRANT GREEN GREGG HAYNE HAZEN HINES HODGE HOVEY HOWZE IRWIN KUTER LEWIS MCCOY MCRAE MEADE MEIGS MILES MOSBY MOWER OHARA ORTIZ PARKE PATCH POORE PRATT ROYCE SCOTT SHAYS SMITH STARK STONE SWIFT SYKES TERRY UPTON VIELE WYMAN ABRAMS ARNOLD BISBEE BOWLEY BUFORD BUTLER CONWAY CULLUM CUSTER DAYTON DEVERS DOZIER EMBICK EMMONS GAINES GIBBON GIBSON GLOVER GORDON GORGAS GRAVES GREENE GROVES HARDEE HARDIN HARMON HARTLE HOOKER HOWARD HUNTER JADWIN JORDAN KEARNY KENNEY LAWTON MACOMB MAHONE MARION MCCOOK MCLAWS MORGAN MORROW NEWTON OLIVER PATTON PHELPS PILLOW PUTNAM RIPLEY ROGERS SCHAFF SEVIER SHARPE SHELBY SPAATZ STRONG STUART SUMNER SUMTER TANNER TAYLOR THAYER TWIGGS VESSEY WARNER WESSON WILCOX ANDREWS BABCOCK BELKNAP BINGHAM BRADLEY BUCKNER BULLARD CARLSON CASWELL CHAFFEE CLINTON CROWDER CROZIER CUSHMAN DICKMAN EDWARDS FERRERO FLEMING FORREST FREMONT FUNSTON GRANGER HALLECK HANCOCK HARBORD HARDING HASKELL HOUSTON INGALLS JACKSON KRUEGER LEDYARD LEJEUNE LIGGETT LINCOLN MAXWELL MENOHER MERRITT NEVILLE PARROTT PICKETT RAWLINS SHAFTER SHERMAN SLEMMER TORBERT TREMAIN TRIMBLE VANDORN VENABLE WHEELER WINGATE ANDERSON BRERETON BURNSIDE CAMPBELL DONELSON FRANKLIN GAILLARD GOETHALS GRIERSON JOHNSTON MAGRUDER MARSHALL MCDOWELL MCNARNEY MOULTRIE OLMSTEAD PERSHING PRESCOTT REYNOLDS SEDGWICK SHERIDAN SNELLING STILWELL STODDARD SUBLETTE SULLIVAN TOWNSEND VANFLEET AINSWORTH ALEXANDER ARMISTEAD ARMSTRONG BONESTEEL DOOLITTLE DOUBLEDAY FETTERMAN HARTRANFT HUMPHREYS MACARTHUR MCCLELLAN PEMBERTON PETTIGREW QUANTRILL ROSECRANS SCHOFIELD SUMMERALL WILKINSON BEAUREGARD BUFFINGTON EISENHOWER LONGSTREET MCGLACHLIN PLEASONTON WAINWRIGHT BUTTERFIELD
ARGENTINIAN JUSTO
AUSTRALIAN CASEY BLAMEY MACKAY MONASH BENNETT CHAUVEL STURDEE LAVARACK
AUSTRIAN DAUN HESS DANKL HADIK LIGNE GALLAS GYULAI TRENCK BENEDEK GABLENZ ALVINCZY BEAULIEU CLERFAYT RADETZKY PHILIPPOVIC
BOLIVIAN DAZA PANDO CAMPERO BALLIVIAN
BRAZILIAN DUTRA FONSECA PEIXOTO
BULGARIAN SAVOY
CANADIAN BOVEY BISHOP CRERAR HUGHES DENISON LINDSAY
CARTHAGINIAN HANNIBAL
CHILEAN CRUZ BULNES FREIRE IBANEZ PRIETO OHIGGINS
COLOMBIAN REYES HERRAN CORDOBA MOSQUERA
DANISH RANTZAU
DUTCH CHASSE KEPPEL COEHOORN DAENDELS
ECUADORIAN ALFARO FLORES
ENGLISH COX NYE BOLS BYNG DILL DYER GAGE GALE GORT HAIG HEAD HILL LACY LAKE LOWE PILE RICH ROSS SLIM VERE WADE ANDRE BOWER BROCK CAREW CAREY CAVAN CLERY CLIVE CLYDE CRAIG CUTTS GLUBB GOUGH HORNE ISMAY JONES KIRKE MAHON MAUDE MILNE MONCK MOORE NEILL NIXON PLATT SMITH STACK SYKES WARDE AYLMER BLOUNT BROOKE BROWNE BULFIN BURLEY CHURCH CONWAY CREAGH DAWSON DOBELL DUNDAS FORBES FRENCH FULLER GORDON GRAHAM HAKING HARRIS HOWARD INGLIS JARVIS LUGARD MARTEL MILLER MORGAN MURRAY NAPIER NORMAN NUGENT PICTON POPHAM RAGLAN SAVAGE SCOBIE SIDNEY SIMCOE TEMPLE TURNER UFFORD VYVYAN WALLER WARREN WAVELL WEMYSS ALLENBY AMHERST ATHLONE BARDOLF BINGHAM BOUQUET BRANDON BRIDGES BURNABY CADOGAN CAVALLO CHANDOS CLAYTON CLINTON COLLINS DEMPSEY DOWDING FASTOLF MACMUNN MAXWELL METHUEN MORLAND OCONNOR PEREIRA POWNALL ROBERTS STEWART SWINTON TORRENS VENNING VINCENT WANTAGE WINGATE ALDERSON ANDERSON AUCHMUTY BECKWITH BENTINCK BLAKENEY BRADDOCK BRANCKER BROWNING BURGOYNE CALLWELL CAMPBELL CARDIGAN CARLETON CATHCART CHETWODE COLBORNE CONGREVE CROMWELL FERGUSON GLEICHEN GREVILLE HAMILTON HARDINGE HASTINGS HAVELOCK HORROCKS LAWRENCE LIGONIER LINDSELL LOCKHART MAITLAND MONTFORT POYNINGS SHRAPNEL STANHOPE TARLETON ALEXANDER BEAUCHAMP BERESFORD BROWNRIGG CONSTABLE HARINGTON HENDERSON KITCHENER MACDONALD OCTERLONY POTTINGER REPINGTON ROBERTSON WILKINSON WOODVILLE AUCHINLECK CODRINGTON CORNWALLIS DESBOROUGH MACDOUGALL MONTGOMERY SHERBROOKE WELLINGTON BRACKENBURY WINTRINGHAM
FINNISH MANNERHEIM
FRENCH FAY FOY NEY BUAT FOCH JUIN NIEL SAXE AMADE ANDRE CONTI COSSE DOUAY DUMAS FOREY HENRY HULIN JUNOT LALLY LEVIS LOBAU MENOU MINIE MITRY MURAT TRACY BAYARD BELLAY BOUDET CHABOT CHANZY CISSEY CLARKE CLOSSE DAUMAS DAVOUT DEJEAN DROUOT DUCROT DUNOIS FABERT FAILLY FAVRAS FLEURY FOLARD FRIANT GERARD GIRAUD GOBERT JARNAC JOFFRE KLEBER LACLOS LANNES LATUDE LAUNAY LAUZUN MAGNAN MAISON MANGIN MARBOT MASSUE MONCEY MOREAU PETAIN ROVIGO SUCHET TROCHU BAZAINE BOICHUT BOSQUET BOUILLE CATINAT CATROUX CHAMILY CHARRAS CHAUVIN CLAUSEL CLISSON CRILLON CUSTINE DEBENEY DREYFUS FABVIER GAMELIN GASSION GOURAUD GROUCHY GUIBERT JOUBERT JOURDAN LABORDE LASALLE LEBOEUF LECLERC LEJEUNE LUCKNER LYAUTEY MARCEAU MARMONT MAURICE MOLITOR MONTLUC MORTIER NIVELLE RENAULT REYNIER TALLARD TURENNE VALENCE VENDOME WEYGAND AUGEREAU BARATIER BOURBAKI CHAMBRUN CHAUCHAT CHOISEUL CLUSERET CONTADES DEGAULLE DEGOUTTE ESTIENNE GALLIENI GOURGAUD GOURGUES GRAZIANI HARCOURT LAMARQUE LANGLOIS LANREZAC LARMINAT LEFEBVRE LORENCEZ MAUNOURY MONTCALM PICHEGRU TAVANNES VANDAMME AIGUILLON ANDREOSSY BERTHELOT BOISSOUDY BOULANGER CANROBERT DAMPIERRE FAIDHERBE GROSSETTI GUEBRIANT HUNTZIGER LAFAYETTE LALLEMAND LAURISTON MACDONALD MONTHOLON NIVERNAIS PELISSIER SCHOMBERG CHASTELLUX GUILLAUMAT KELLERMANN MONTGOMERY ROCHAMBEAU WESTERMANN CHANGARNIER JACQUEMINOT MONTMORENCY CAULAINCOURT LESDIGUIERES
GERMAN EPP JODL KALB ARNIM BOEHN BULOW KLUCK KUNDT HALDER HAUSEN HUTIER KEITEL MOLTKE PAULUS ROMMEL SEECKT BISSING BLUCHER CAPRIVI FISCHER FRITSCH GROENER JOCHMUS SPEIDEL STEUBEN BERNHARD BLOMBERG GALLWITZ GERHARDT GUDERIAN HAESELER HARTMANN LITZMANN RIEDESEL SCHWERIN ZEITZLER ALDRINGEN HAUSHOFER HEERINGEN HINDERSIN LINSINGEN MACKENSEN MANSFIELD REINHARDT RUNDSTEDT THEILMANN WALDERSEE FRUNDSBERG HINDENBURG KESSELRING LUDENDORFF SCHLEICHER SCHLIEFFEN BRAUCHITSCH FALKENHORST FALKENHAUSEN STAUFFENBERG
GREEK ARATUS KALERGES KONDYLES PANGALOS PELOPIDAS ALCIBIADES HIERONYMUS EPAMINONDAS THEMISTOCLES
GUATEMALAN CHACON ORELLANA
HAITIAN PETION RIGAUD SALOMON GEFFRARD
HUNGARIAN GORGEY HUNYADI DAMJANICH SZECHENYI
IRISH LACY WADE COLLEY ODUFFY CADOGAN COLLINS OREILLY OHIGGINS PAKENHAM ALANBROOKE
IRTISH DILL BARRY CUNNINGHAM
ISRAELI ALLON DAYAN ELAZAR NETANYAHU
ITALIAN BIXIO FANTI CANEVA COSENZ DAVILA DOUHET GORGIA NOBILE ABRUZZI CAPELLO BADOGLIO CAVIGLIA CIALDINI COLLEONI GIARDINO GRAZIANI MARSIGLI RAMORINO BARATIERI CAVALLERO DANNUNZIO GARIBALDI LAMARMORA PICCOLOMINI
JAPANESE ABE OKU TOJO ARAKI KOISO NODZU SAITO TAMAI KODAMA KUROKI DOIHARA FUSHIMI KATSURA HASEGAWA SUGIYAMA TERAUCHI FUKUSHIMA HASHIMOTO HIDEYOSHI TAMASHITA
KOREAN PARK
LEBANESE HADDAD
MEXICAN MEJIA ALDAMA ARISTA

CALLES HUERTA ALMAZAN ALMONTE ALVAREZ AMPUDIA CAMACHO MIRAMON MORELOS OBREGON VALLEJO ZULOAGA CANALIZO CARDENAS ESCOBEDO GONZALEZ GUERRERO ITURBIDE VICTORIA BUSTAMANTE
NEW ZEALAND CHAYTOR FREYBERG
NIGERIAN GOWON
PARAGUAYAN MORINIGO ESTIGARRIBIA
PERSIAN ARTAPHERNES
PERUVIAN BALTA PRADO CACERES GAMARRA PIEROLA CASTILLA IGLESIAS SALAVERRY
POLISH BEM PASEK HALLER PULASKI CHLOPICKI DEMBINSKI KOSCIUSKO PILSUDSKI DOMBROWSKI MALCZEWSKI SOSNKOWSKI KRUKOWIECKI
PORTUGUESE ALMEIDA PEREIRA SALDANHA TEIXEIRA
PRUSSIAN GNEISENAU CLAUSEWITZ
ROMAN SULLA AETIUS ANTONY BURRUS CAEPIO CAESAR GALLUS POLLIO POMPEY SCIPIO AGRIPPA ALBINUS CAECINA CALENUS CASSIUS CHAEREA CRASSUS FANNIUS LEPIDUS PLANCUS AFRANIUS AGRICOLA CEREATIS DENTATUS DUILLIUS LUCULLUS FABRICIUS FLAMINIUS PASKEVICH SERTORIUS CORIOLANUS CINCINNATUS
RUMANIAN ILIESCU ANTONESCU
RUSSIAN CUI BERK GURKO KONEV GLINKA NEVSKI PLATOV ZHUKOV BLUCHER BUDENNY CHAPAEV CHUIKOV DENIKIN KALEDIN KAMENEV KUTUZOV SUVOROV VATUTIN WRANGEL ZHDANOV ALEKSEEV AVERESCU BOBRIKOV BRUSILOV GOLITSYN GORBATOV KAULBARS KORNILOV LINEVICH MILYUTIN SAMSONOV SKOBELEV YUDENICH BAGRATION BENNIGSEN GORCHAKOV LECHITSKI MENSHIKOV CHERNYAIEV CHERNYSHEV DRAGOMIROV KUROPATKIN ROSTOPCHIN TIMOSHENKO VOROSHILOV ROKOSSOVSKY SHAPOSHNIKOV
SALVADORAN REGALADO
SCOTTISH HAIG URRY BAIRD MUNRO ELIOTT RUTHVEN DRUMMOND IRONSIDE MIDDLETON
SOUTH AFRICAN BOTHA SMUTS HERTZOG PRETORIUS
SPANISH CID ALVA ELIO MINA MOLA RADA CROIX GARAY OSUNA ULLOA AVALOS GUZMAN TOLEDO ALMAGRO CORDOBA FARNESE MONCADA NARVAEZ NAVARRO ODONOJU PORTOLA ALVARADO CANTERAC CARVAJAL CASTANOS CASTILLO ESPINOSA MANRIQUE MUNTANER ORELLANA VALDIVIA PEDRARIAS REQUESENS VELASQUEZ CASTELLANOS
SWEDISH HORN TOLL BANER BRAHE ARMFELT LEWENHAUPT TORSTENSON ADLERCREUTZ ADLERSPARRE
SWISS DUFOUR ERLACH JENATSCH
TURKISH BABUR ENVER EVREN ATATURL
URUGUAYAN ORIBE FLORES
VENEZUELAN PAEZ GOMEZ CASTRO FALCON MONAGAS
YUGOSLAV ZIVKOVIC MIHAJLOVIC

SOLDIERLY WARLIKE
SOLDIERY HORSE MILITIA SEBUNDY MILITARY SIBBENDY
SOLE CORK FACE GADE MERE ONLY SLIP SOCK SPUR AFALD ALONE CLUMP LEMON OLEPI PELMA WHOLE GADOID INSOLE ONLEPY PLANTA SINGLE SOLEYN SULLEN THENAR TONGUE UNIQUE ANACANTH FLATFISH HOGCHOKE MARYSOLE SINGULAR SOLITARY
(— A SHOE) SPECK
(— FOR WALKING OVER SAND) BACKSTER
(— OF BIRD'S FOOT) PTERNA
(— OF FOOT) PLAT VOLA PELMA PLANT
(— OF PLANE) FACE
(— OF PLOW) SLADE
(— WITH WOOD) CLOG
(HALF —) SHOULDER
(KIND OF —) DOVER
(TOWARD THE —) PLANTAD
(PREF.) PEDI(O) PELMATO
(SUFF.) PELMOUS
SOLELY SOLE ALONE SIMPLY SINGLY WHOLLY SHEERLY ENTIRELY
SOLEMN DEEP SAGE AWFUL BUDGE SOBER DEVOUT FORMAL RITUAL EARNEST SERIOUS WEIGHTY FUNEREAL PORTENTOUS
(STUPIDLY —) POFACED
SOLEMNITY OBIT RITE SACRE GRAVITY SEVERITY
SOLEMNIZE KEEP SEAL
SOLEMNLY GRAVE HIGHLY
SOLENODONT AGOUTA ALMIQUE
SOLEPIECE SOLE GIRDER
SOL-FA SOLMIZATE
SOLICIT ASK BEG SUE WOO DRUM MOVE SEEK THIG TOUT URGE APPLY COURT CRAVE TREAT ACCOST HUSTLE INVITE INVOKE BESEECH CANVASS ENTREAT IMPLORE INSTANT PROCURE REQUEST APPROACH PETITION
SOLICITATION SUIT QUEST CANVASS INSTANT REQUEST SOLICIT ENTREATY INSTANCE
SOLICITOR AVOUE LAWYER WRITER ADVOCATE ATTORNEY TRAMPLER
SOLICITOUS URGENT CAREFUL CURIOUS JEALOUS DESIROUS CONCERNED
SOLICITUDE CARE CARK FEAR HEED PAIN YEME HEART WORRY ANXIETY CONCERN BUSINESS JEALOUSY
SOLID DRY SAD CONE CUBE FAST FIRM FULL HARD CHAMP CUBIC LEVEL MASSY MEATY SOUND STIFF STOUT THICK TIGHT SECURE STABLE STODGY STRONG STURDY COMPACT CUPRENE UNIFORM CONSTANT GROUNDLY MATERIAL STERLING
(GEOMETRICAL —) CONE CUBE PRISM CONOID CUPROID FRUSTUM POLYHEDRON
(NOT —) BUBBLE
(THEORETICAL —) HYPERCUBE
(PL.) POCHE
(PREF.) STERE(O)
SOLIDARITY CIVILITY
SOLIDIFIED SOLID HARDENED
(READILY —) GLACIAL
SOLIDIFY DRY SET CAKE JELL SHOOT GELATE HARDEN COMPACT CONGEAL STIFFEN CONCRETE
SOLIDITY SADNESS FASTNESS FIRMNESS HARDNESS
SOLIDLY FIRMLY SQUARE STOUTLY GROUNDLY
SOLIDUS BEZANT NOMISMA DIAGONAL HYPERPER
(HALF —) SEMIS
SOLIPSISM EGOISM
SOLITAIRE CLARINO CANFIELD KLONDIKE NAPOLEON PATIENCE SOLITARY
SOLITARY ODD WAF LONE ONLY SOLE ALONE ELYNG LONELY ONLEPY SAVAGE SINGLE SOLEYN SULLEN DERNFUL EREMITE PRIVATE RECLUSE UNCOUTH WIDOWED DESOLATE EREMITIC ISOLATED LONESOME PEGBOARD SECLUDED SEPARATE
(PREF.) EREM(O)
SOLITUDE PRIVACY RETREAT SOLITARY
SOLLERET SABBATON
SOLO ARIA CALL ALONE ARIOSO CAVATINA SPADILLA
SOLOIST (BASS —) SUCCENTOR
SOLOMON SAM KOHELETH
(BROTHER OF —) ADONIJAH
(FATHER OF —) DAVID
(MOTHER OF —) BATHSHEBA
SOLOMON ISLANDS (CAPITAL:) HONIARA
(CAPITAL OF —) HONIARA
(ISLAND:) GIZO SAVO FLORIDA MALAITA RENDOVA CHOISEUL SANJORGE NEWGEORGIA GUADALCANAL SANTAISABEL
(ISLAND OF —) BUKA GIZO SAVO TULAGI FLORISA MALAITA RENDOVA RUSSELL CHOISEUL GUADALCANAL BOUGAINVILLE
SOLOMON'S SEAL LILY SEALWORT
SOLON SAGE GNOMIC GNOMIST SENATOR LAWMAKER
SOLPUGID TARANTULA
SOLSTICE SUNSTAY SUNSTEAD
SOLUBLE FRIM FRUM FIXED SOLUTE SOLVABLE
SOLUTION IT LYE AQUA EUSOL STAIN TINCT ACETUM ANSWER ASSOIL DOCTOR ERASER SALINE EXTRACT EYEWASH LACQUER RESOLVE SOLUTIO WORKING ANALYSIS LEACHATE TINCTURE
(— ADDED FOR GOOD MEASURE) INCAST
(— OF CHESS PROBLEM) COOK
(— OF FERMENTED BRAN) DRENCH
(— OF GUM TRAGACANTH) BED
(ACID —) SOUR
(ALCOHOLIC —) ESSENCE
(ANTISEPTIC —) EUSOL
(COLLOIDAL —) GEL
(CORROSIVE —) OLEUM
(PICKLING —) SOUSE
(PRESERVING —) BOLIN
(SALINE —) BRINE
(SOAP —) NIGRE
(SOLID —) AUSTENITE
(STERILE —) JOHNIN
(TEMPORARY —) QUICKFIX
(VISCOUS —) GLUE
(WATERY —) EAU SAP
SOLVE DO FIX READ UNDO WORK BREAK CRACK LOOSE SALVE ANSWER ASSOIL CIPHER FIGURE REDUCE RIDDLE SOLUTE RESOLVE UNRAVEL DECIPHER DISSOLVE
SOLVENT ETHER SOUND CETANE ELUANT ELUENT SPIRIT TOLUOL ACETONE ALCOHOL BENZINE COUPLER DILUENT REMOVER SPOTTER TOLUENE CARBITOL PICOLINE SOLVABLE STRIPPER TEREBENE TETRALIN MENSTRUUM
(UNIVERSAL —) ALKAHEST
SOLVER (PROBLEM —) HACKER
SOMALI SOMAL SHUHALI
(PL.) ASHA
SOMALIA (CAPITAL OF —) MOGADISHU
(COIN OF —) BESA
(DIVISION OF —) HAWIYA
(MEASURE OF —) TOP CABA CHELA DARAT TABLA CUBITO
(MOUNTAIN OF —) SURUDAD
(MOUNTAIN RANGE OF —) GUBAN
(NATIVE OF —) GALLA HAWIYA ISBAAK SOMALI DANAKIL
(RIVER OF —) JUBA NOGAL SCEBELI
(TOWN OF —) MERCA BERBERA KISMAYU HARGEISA
(WEIGHT OF —) PARSALAH
SOMATIC SOMAL BODILY
SOMBER SAD DERN DULL GRAVE MORNE SOBER GLOOMY LENTEN SOLEMN SOMBRE SULLEN AUSTERE SERIOUS DARKSOME SOMBROUS
SOME ANY ODD AFEW THIS CERTAIN
SOMEBODY QUIDAM SOMEONE
SOMEDAY ONCE
SOMEHOW HOW ONEHOW SOMEWAY SOMEGATE
SOMEONE SUCH
SOMERSAULT FLIP TOPPLE FLIFFUS SPOTTER TWISTER BACKFLIP SOMERSET
SOMETHING WHAT ALIQUID WHATNOT SOMEWHAT
(— ABNORMAL) FREAK
(— ADDED) IMP EXTRA DOCTOR
(— AMUSING) HOOT
(— ATTRACTIVE) DUCK
(— BELIEVED) CREDIT
(— BIG) BOUNCER
(— BRIGHT RED) CORAL
(— CHERISHED) APPLE

(— COMMONPLACE) DROSS
(— CONSECRATED) SACRUM
(— CONTRARY TO LOGIC) ALOGISM
(— CORRUPT) CARRION
(— COUNTERFEIT) DUFFER PINCHBECK
(— DIFFICULT) STINKER
(— DISLIKED) DOGMEAT
(— DONE) GERENDUM
(— EASILY ACHIEVED) GIMME
(— EASY) PIPE CAKEWALK
(— ELABORATE) DEVICE
(— ELUSIVE) FUGITIVE
(— EXCELLENT) DANDY
(— EXCESSIVE) LUXUS
(— EXTRAORDINARY) SNORTER
(— FALSE) HOOEY
(— FAMILIAR) KNOWN
(— FIRST-RATE) CHEESE
(— FLAWED) CRIPPLE
(— FOOLISH) IDIOCY FATUITY
(— FORGOTTEN) CORPSE
(— FORKED) CORNUTE
(— FRAUDULENT) CROSS
(— GIVEN WITHOUT CHARGE) FREEBEE FREEBIE
(— HORRIFYING) SHOCKER
(— IDENTICAL) ISOMORPH
(— ILL-DEFINED) BLOB
(— IN ADDITION TO ORDINARY) BONUS
(— INCOMPLETE) END
(— INFERIOR) DOG CULL LESS CAGMAG
(— INJURIOUS) ENEMY
(— INSIGNIFICANT) STRAW FEATHER SNICKET FRAGMENT
(— INTRICATE) KNOT
(— LARGE) GIANT SMASHER
(— MADE UP) FIGMENT
(— NOTABLE) DEUCE
(— NOT ESSENTIAL) FRILL
(— NOT EXPLAINED) MYSTERY
(— OFFERED FOR LOAN) PREMIUM
(— OF GREAT VALUE) EYETOOTH
(— OF LITTLE VALUE) SHUCK FOUTER FOUTRA MAKEWEIGHT
(— OF NO VALUE) HAW DAMN BAUBEE DOCKEN
(— OR OTHER) ANYTHING
(— OUTSTANDING) BROTH DOYEN GASSER STANDOUT
(— PAINFUL) GAFF
(— PATCHED UP) VAMP
(— POOR) FLUMMERY
(— PRECIOUS) DUMPLING
(— PREJUDICIAL) FOE
(— PROVOKING) DEVIL
(— REPELLENT) SPINACH
(— RISKED) HAZARD
(— SHAPELESS) DUMP
(— SHOWY) FLOSS
(— SHRIVELED) SCRUMP
(— SMALL) DOT SNIP
(— SPECTACULAR) DILLY
(— STICKY) CAB
(— STOLEN) CRIB
(— STRANGE) FANTASIA
(— SUPERLATIVE) DARB
(— TAUGHT) DOCUMENT
(— THAT IS LIGHT) SKIFF SKIFT
(— THAT WHIRLS) GIG
(— TO BIND BARGAIN) EARNEST
(— TRIVIAL) CHIP FLUFF
(— UNDECIDED) ACRISY
(— UNINTELLIGIBLE) GREEK
(— UNPLEASANT) GUCK SOUR
(— UNSPECIFIED) ITEM
(— UNSUBSTANTIAL) FROTH
(— UNTRUE) HOKUM
(— USELESS) CRAP BLANK
(— VILE) DUNG
(— WORTHLESS) BOTH DUST HOKUM DUFFER AMBSACE
(— WRITTEN) SCRIPT

SOMETIME FORMER SOMDEL WHILOM ANCIENT QUONDAM SOMEDEAL SOMEPART SOMEWHEN

SOMETIMES NOW TOO WHILE PERDIE WHILES UMQUHILE OCCASIONALLY

SOMEWHAT BIT ATAD POCO SOME ATOUCH PRETTY RATHER SLIGHT SUMMAT ALIQUID SOMEDEAL
(PREF.) SEMI

SOMEWHERE SOMERS SOMEGATE

SOMITE ZONITE SEGMENT TERGITE GONOTOME MEROSOME MESOMERE SOMATOME

SOMMER ELKA

SOMNIFEROUS OPIATE SOMNIFIC

SOMNUS HYPNUS

SON BEN BOY LAD ANAC FILS FITZ ZONE CHILD KIBEI MOPSY FILIUS JUNIOR REUBEN EPAPHUS EPIGONUS MONSIEUR
(— OF CHIEF) OGTIERN
(— OF KING OF FRANCE) DAUPHIN
(— OF NISEI) SANSEI
(— OF PEER) MASTER
(— OF SUDRA) CHANDALA
(DAVID'S FAVORITE —) ABSALOM
(FIRST-BORN —) HEIR
(FOURTH —) MARTLET
(FREEMASON'S —) LEWIS
(ILLEGITIMATE —) NEPHEW
(NISEI —) SANSEI
(PRIEST'S —) NEPHEW
(YOUNG —) MOPSY
(YOUNGER —) CADET
(YOUNGEST —) CADET BENJAMIN
(PREF.) AP FILI(O)

SONANT VIBRANT

SONAR ASDIC
(— BLIP) ECHO
(KIND OF —) SIDESCAN

SONCHUS DINDLE

SONG AIR DIT FIT JIG LAY UTA CANT DUAN FOLK GATO GLEE LEED MELE NOTE RANT RUNE SANG TUNE BLUES CANSO CAROL CHANT CHARM CROON DILDO DITTY MELOS MOLPE OLDIE PAEAN VOCAL BALLAD BRANLE BUBBLE CANTIC CANZON CARMEN CHANTY CHORUS HIMENE JINGLE MELODY ORPHIC SHANTY STRAIN VINATA WAIATA WARBLE BACCHIC BALLATA CANCION CANTION CHANSON COMIQUE DESCANT MELISMA MELODIA REQUIEM REVERDI ROMANCE SCOLION SONGLET THRENOS BIRDSONG BRINDISI CANTICLE CANZONET COONJINE FLAMENCO JUBILATE PALINODE RHAPSODY SERVENTE SINGSONG ZORTZICO ROUNDELAY
(— ACCOMPANYING TOAST) BRINDISI
(— FOR TWO VOICES) GYMEL
(— IN GREEK DRAMA) STROPHE
(— OF BASQUES) ZORTZICO
(— OF BIRD) LAY KOLLER
(— OF JOY) CAROL PAEAN JUBILATE
(— OF LAMENTATION) THRENE THRENODY
(— OF MINSTREL) YEDDING
(— OF OCEANIA) HIMENE
(— OF PRAISE) HYMN CAROL ANTHEM CHORALE
(—S OF BIRDS) RAMAGE
(— UNACCOMPANIED) GLEE
(— WITH MONOTONOUS RHYME) VIRELAI VIRELAY
(ANDALUSIAN —) SAETA
(ART —) LIED
(BOAT —) JORRAM
(CEREMONIAL —S) AREITO
(CRADLE —) HUSHO
(CUBAN —) GUAJIRA COMPARSA
(DANCE —) BALLAD BAMBUCO
(DRINKING —) BACCHIC SCOLION SKOLION WASSAIL
(EVENING —) SERENA EVENSONG SERENATA
(FOLK —) SON FADO FOLK BLUES DOINA BYLINA CANTIGA JUBILEE STORNELLO
(FUNERAL —) DIRGE MONODY EPICEDE THRENODY
(FUNEREAL —) ELEGY
(GAY —) LILT
(GERMAN —) LIED
(GYPSY —) FLAMENCO
(HAWAIIAN —) MELE
(HEBREW —) ELIELI HATIKVAH
(IMPROMPTU —) SCOLION
(JAPANESE —) UTA
(LOVE —) ALBA CANSO CANZO FANCY TORCH AMORET AUBADE SERENA SERENATA
(MELISMATIC —) DIVISION
(MOCKING —) JIG
(MORNING —) MATIN AUBADE
(MOURNFUL —) DUMP PLAINT ENDECHA
(MYSTIC —) RUNE
(NEW ZEALAND —) WAIATA
(NIGHT —) COMPLIN
(NO —S) UTAI
(NUPTIAL —) HYMEN
(PART —) CHACE TROLL CACCIA CANZONET FROTTOLA MADRIGAL
(PASTORAL —) OAT
(PLAIN —) GROUND
(PORTUGUESE —) FADO
(RELIGIOUS —) HYMN CAROL PSALM SHOUT ANTHEM POLYMNY SIRVENT
(REVOLUTIONARY —) CARMAGNOLE
(ROUND-) TROLL
(SACRED —) MOTET
(SAILOR'S —) CHANTY SHANTY
(SANSKRIT —) GITA
(SINGLE —) CUT
(SINGLE — ON RECORD) CUT
(SPIRITED —) LILT
(STUPID —) STROWD
(VINTAGE —) VINATA
(WORK —) HOLLER
(PL.) ZEMMI AREITO
(PREF.) MELO
(SUFF.) ODE ODIC ODIST ODY

SONGBIRD CHAT IORA LARK WREN MAVIS ROBIN SABIA SHAMA SIREN VEERY VIREO BULBUL CANARY LINNET MOCKER ORIOLE SINGER THRUSH CATBIRD GRASSET TANAGER WARBLER ACCENTOR BENGALEE BLUEBIRD BOBOLINK CARDINAL SONGSTER MEADOWLARK

SONGLIKE ARIOSE

SONG OF BERNADETTE (AUTHOR OF —) WERFEL
(CHARACTER IN —) LOUISE THERESE FRANCOIS PEYRAMALE SOUBIROUS BERNADETTE

SONG OF HIAWATHA (AUTHOR OF —) LONGFELLOW
(CHARACTER IN —) KWASIND NOKOMIS WENONAH HIAWATHA CHIBIABOS MINNEHAHA MUDJEKEEWIS

SONG OF ROLAND (AUTHOR OF —) UNKNOWN
(CHARACTER IN —) ALDA ALORY MILON OGIER BERTHA FERRAU GERARD MEDORO MORGAN OBERTO OLIVER ROLAND SADONE ARGALIA CHARLOT GANELON GODFREY MALAGIS REINOLD ASTOLPHO KARAHEUT BRADAMANT GLORIANDA CHARLEMAGNE MANDRICARDO

SONGSTER SINGER WARBLER

SONG THRUSH MAVIE MAVIS

SON-IN-LAW GENER MAUGH

SONNAMBULA, LA (CHARACTER IN —) LISA AMINA ELVINO TERESA RODOLFO
(COMPOSER OF —) BELLINI

SONNET AMORET
(— PART) SESTET
(LOVE —) AMORET

SONOGRAPHY ULTRASOUND

SONORITY RESONANCE

SONOROUS ROUND SHILL TONOUS OROTUND VIBRANT RESONANT SOUNDFUL SOUNDING RESOUNDING

SONOROUSLY DEEPLY

SONS AND LOVERS (AUTHOR OF —) LAWRENCE
(CHARACTER IN —) LILY PAUL ANNIE CLARA DAWES MOREL ARTHUR BAXTER MIRIAM WALTER LEIVERS WILLIAM GERTRUDE

SONSHIP FILIETY

SONYA (FATHER OF —) MARMELADOV

SOOLOOS THULUTH

SOON ERE ANON CITO TITE EARLY NEWLY RADLY RATHE BELIVE INABIT SUDDEN TIMELY BETIMES ERELONG PRESTLY SHORTLY DIRECTLY SPEEDILY PRESENTLY
(AS — AS POSSIBLE) ASAP

SOONER ERE ERER ERST OKIE FIRST BEFORE TITTER

(**— STATE)** OKLAHOMA
(**— THAN)** OR ERE
SOONEST ERST RATHEST
SOOT COOM IZLE SMUT STUP SUMI BLECK BROOK COLLY COOMB CROCK GRIME SOTIK FULIGO SMOUCH SMUTCH SPODIUM
(**— ON GRATE BAR)** STRANGER
SOOTHE COY DEW BALM CALM COAX DILL EASE HUSH LULL ACCOY ALLAY CHARM DULCE HUMOR QUELL SALVE SLEEK STILL BECALM PACIFY SETTLE SMOOTH SOLACE STROKE SUPPLE ADDULCE APPEASE ASSUAGE COMFORT COMPOSE CONSOLE DEMULCE FLATTER GRUNTLE LULLABY MOLLIFY PLASTER QUALIFY ATTEMPER BLANDISH MITIGATE UNRUFFLE
SOOTHER BALM BALSAM ANODYNE
SOOTHING MILD BALMY BLAND DOWNY DULCE STILL SWEET ANETIC ANIMAL DREAMY DULCET GENTLE SMOOTH ANODYNE BALSAMIC SEDATIVE
SOOTHSAY SORT
SOOTHSAYER SEER AUGUR WEIRD ARIOLE DIVINE PYTHON ARUSPEX DIVINER CHALDEAN HARUSPEX TIRESIAS
SOOTY COLLY REECHY SMUTTY BROOKIE COLLIED
SOOTY ALBATROSS NELLIE QUAKER STINKER BLUEBIRD STINKPOT
SOOTY SHEARWATER TITI
SOP BERRY SIPPET SOAKUP SPONGE SUGARSOP SWEETSOP BREADBERRY
SOPATER (FATHER OF —) PYRRHUS
SOPHER SCRIBE
SOPHISM FETCH ELENCH FALLACY SOPHEME
SOPHIST SOPH DUNCE
SOPHISTICATE GARBLE MONDAINE
SOPHISTICATED WISE BLASE CIVIL SALTY SVELTE URBANE WORLDLY
SOPHISTICATION CHIC
SOPHISTRY DECEIT FALLACY SOPHISM CHICANERY
SOPHOCLES (— TRAGEDY) AJAX
SOPHONISBA (BROTHER OF —) HANNIBAL
(FATHER OF —) HASDRUBAL
(HUSBAND OF —) SYPHAX
SOPORIFIC DWALE DROWSY HYPNIC OPIATE SLEEPY HYPNOTIC NARCOTIC SOMNIFIC
SOPPING SQUASHY
SOPPY JUICY SOAKY
SOPRANO CANARY TREBLE DESCANT CASTRATO
SORA ORTOLAN
SORB OCCLUDE LUSATIAN
SORBIAN WENDISH
SORBOSE ACROSE
SORCERER MAGE BOYLA BRUJO WITCH BOOLYA NAGUAL VOODOO WIZARD KORADJI WARLOCK WIELARE FETISHER MAGICIAN WITCHMAN
(PL.) GOETAE
SORCERESS BRUJA CIRCE LAMIA SIBYL WITCH ARMIDA HECATE BABAJAGA KORRIGAN WALKYRIE
SORCERY OBI MAGIC OBEAH SPELL MAKUTU PISHOGUE PRESTIGE SORTIARY WIGELING WITCHERY WITCHING NECROMANCY
(VOODOO —) OBEAH WANGA OUANGA
SORDES SABURRA
SORDID RAW BASE GAMY MEAN VILE DIRTY DUSTY MUCKY SEAMY CHETIF GRUBBY SODDEN MESQUIN SQUALID CHURLISH
SORDOR LEES
SORE BUM FOX PET BUBA CHAP DEAR GALL KIBE KYLE OUCH SAER BLAIN BOTCH GAMMY AGNAIL BITTER BOUBAS CANKER FESTER MELLIT MORMAL RANKLE TAKING CATHAIR CHANCRE SORANCE SCALDING
(— ON HORSE'S FOOT) MELLIT QUITTER
(ARTIFICIAL —) FOX
(SUMMER —S) CALORIS LEECHES
SO RED THE ROSE (AUTHOR OF —) YOUNG
(CHARACTER IN —) HUGH LUCY MARY VEAL ZACH AGNES SARAH AMELIE DUNCAN EDWARD BALFOUR BEDFORD CHARLES FRANCES LUCINDA MALCOLM MCGEHEE SHELTON VALETTE WILLIAM HARTWELL MIDDLETON TALIAFERRO
SORE MOUTH ORF
SORENESS FROG
(— OF EYES) LIPPITUDE
SORGHUM CANE CUSH MILO BATAD DARSO DURRA SORGO CHOLAM HEGARI IMPHEE KAFFIR SHALLU FETERITA KAOLIANG
SOROCHE PUNA
SORREL OCA OKA ROAN SORE CUCKOO HEARTS OXALIS RUBICAN SOUROCK ALLELUIA STABWORT
SORREL TREE TITI ELKWOOD SOURWOOD
SORROW WO RUE WOE BALE CARE DOLE HARM MOAN RUTH SORE TEEN DOLOR GRAME GRIEF MOURN RUING SARRA UNWIN GRIEVE LAMENT MISERY REGRET STOUND UNLUST ANGUISH CONDOLE DEPLORE PENANCE REGRATE REMORSE THOUGHT TROUBLE WOEFARE CALAMITY DISTRESS DOLEANCE DREARING EGRIMONY MOURNING
(— AUDIBLY) WAIL
(— FOR SIN) ATTRITION
(PREF.) LUCTI
SORROWFUL BAD SAD WAN BLUE GLUM CHARY DREAR TRIST WOFUL DISMAL DOLENT DREARY RUEFUL BALEFUL CAREFUL DOLEFUL LUCTUAL RUESOME UNHAPPY WAILFUL CONTRITE DESOLATE DOLESOME DOLOROSO GRIEFFUL MOURNFUL PITIABLE
SORROWFULLY SADLY WRATH DERNLY HEAVILY
SORRY BAD SAD WOE HURT VEXED UNFAIN PITIFUL CONTRITE PENITENT WRETCHED
SORT ILK KIN LOT BRAN COMB GERE HUMP KIND RANK SIFT SUIT WING WORK BRACK BREED GENUS GRADE SAVOR SPICE ASSORT BARREL DILLUE GARBLE GENDER KIDNEY MANNER MISTER NATURE STRAIN STRIPE FASHION SPECIES SPECKLE VARIETY CLASSIFY SEPARATE
(— CHICKS) SEX
(— COTTON BY STAPLE) STAPLE
(— MAIL) CASE
(— MERCHANDISE) BRACK
(— OF) INAWAY
(— OF PERSON) LIKE
(ATHLETIC —) JOCK
(OUT OF —S) GRUMPY
SORTER SHALEMAN
SORTIE RAID ISSUE SALLY ATTACK OUTFALL
SORTILEGE LOT
SORTING GARBLING
(— ROOM) SALLE
SORTITA ARIA
SORUS AECIUM TELIUM
SORVA BORRACHA
SOT LUSH SOAK DRUNK LOURD TOPER LOURDY BLOTTER DASTARD TOSSPOT DRUNKARD
SOTHO SUTO SESUTO
SOTIK SOOT
SOUFFLE FONDU FONDUE
SOUGH MOAN
SOUGHT QUESITED
SOUL BA AME EGO ALMA ANIMA ATMAN GHOST HEART SHADE BUDDHI DIBBUK NATURE PNEUMA PSYCHE SPIRIT SPRITE NEPHESH PURUSHA INTERNAL
(—S OF THE DEAD) LEMURES
(ANIMAL — IN MAN) NEPHESH
(DISEMBODIED —) KER
(EGYPTIAN IMMORTAL —) BA
(INDIVIDUAL —) JIVA
(LIBERATED —) KEVALIN
(UNIVERSAL —) HANSA
(WANDERING —) DIBBUK DYBBUK
(PREF.) PSYCH(O) THYM(O)
(SUFF.) PSYCHE
SOULFULLY GEISTLICH
SOULLESS TURNIPY
SOU MARQUE STAMPEE
SOUND GO CRY FIT BLOW DING DRIP FAST FERE FIRM FLOG FLOW GLUG GOOD HAIL HALE KYLE NOTE RING SAFE SANE TEST TONE TRIG WISE AFFIX BLAST BUGLE CHEEP DREAM FLICK FRESH GLIFF GLUCK GRIND GROPE HODDY NOISE PLANG PLUMB PROBE RIGHT SLUSH SOLID SPANG SPANK SPEAK SWASH VALID WHOLE BICKER BIRDIE DORSAL ENDING ENTIRE FATHOM FAUCAL HEARTY INTACT LABIAL LAGOON ROBUST SIGNAL SINGLE SONANT SPLASH STABLE STRAIN STURDY HEALTHY HEARING HURLING PERFECT PHONEME PLUMMET SCRATCH SONANCE VOCABLE FLAWLESS FOOTFALL GRINDING GROUNDLY LAUGHTER RELIABLE SEARCHER SYLLABIC WAKELESS
(— A BAGPIPE) DOODLE
(— AS IF BY GUN) ZAP
(— BELL) PEAL RING KNELL KNOLL
(— BY PERCUSSION) STRIKE
(— DRUM OR TRUMPET) TUCK
(— FORTH) BOOM
(— INDEPENDENTLY OF THE PLAYER) CIPHER
(— INDISTINCTLY) SLUR
(— IN GREEK AND LATIN) AGMA
(— IN MIND) FORMAL
(— LESS LOUD) FALL
(— LIKE THUNDER) BRONTIDE
(— LOUDLY) TANG LARUM
(— MELODIOUSLY) CHARM
(— OF BAGPIPE) DRONE
(— OF BEATING) RATAPLAN
(— OF BELL) DING PEAL RING KNELL STROKE DINGDONG TINGTANG
(— OF BIRD) JUG CHURR
(— OF BULLET) ZIP
(— OF CICADA) CHIRR
(— OF CONTEMPT) HUMPH
(— OF CORK) CLOOP CLUNK
(— OF COW) MOO LOWING
(— OF DISAPPROVAL) BOO HOOT BAZOO
(— OF DOG) ARF YIP BARK BOOK WOOF YELP YIPE
(— OF DYING PERSON'S VOICE) TAISCH
(— OF ENGINE) CHUG
(— OF EXPLOSION) BOUNCE
(— OF F) DIGAMMA
(— OF FLUTE) TOOTLE
(— OF FOOTSTEPS) TRAMP
(— OF GLOTTAL STOP) HAMZA HAMZAH
(— OF HEN) CLUCK
(— OF HOG) OINK GRUNT SQUEAL
(— OF HOOF) CLOP
(— OF HORN) BEEP TOOT
(— OF HORSE) NEIGH SNORT BLOWING
(— OF KNOCK) RAP
(— OF PLUCKED STRING) TUM
(— OF POURING LIQUID) GLUG GLUGGLUG
(— OF RAIN) SPAT
(— OF RENDING) SCAT
(— OF REPROACH) FIE
(— OF SCISSORS) SNIP
(— OF SHEEP) BAA BLEAT
(— OF SLAP) SCLAFF
(— OF STEAM ENGINE) CHUFF
(— OF STRAW OR LEAVES) RUSTLE
(— OF SURF) ROTE
(— OF THUNDER) CLAP
(— OF TRUMPET) CLARION
(— OF WIND IN TREES) WOOSH
(— OUT) FEEL
(—S HAVING RHYTHM) MUSIC
(— TO AWAKEN TROOPS) REVEILLE
(ABNORMAL —) BRUIT
(ADVENTITIOUS —) RALE
(BLOWING —) SOUFFLE
(BRAWLING —) CHIDE
(BREATHING —) RALE
(BRONCHIAL —) RHONCHUS
(BUBBLING —) BLATHER

(BUZZING —) Z WHIR WHIRR
(CHARACTERISTIC —) SONG
(CLASHING —) SWASH
(CLICKING —) SNECK
(CONSONANT —) ALVEOLAR
(COOING —) CHIRR TURTUR
(CRACKLING —) RISK
(CRISP —) BLIP
(CRUNCHING —) CRUMP SCRUNCH
(DELICATE —) TINK TINKLE
(DISCORDANT —) JAR BRAY JANGLE
(DISTINCTIVE —) SONG
(DRUMMING —) RATAPLAN
(DULL —) BUFF THUD CLONK CLUNK FLUMP SQUELCH
(ELECTRONIC — APPARATUS) SYNTH SYNTHESIZER
(EXPLOSIVE —) POP BARK CHUG PUFF SNORT REPORT
(FAINT —) PEEP GLIFF WHISHT INKLING
(FINAL —) AUSLAUT
(FINANCIALLY —) SOLID
(FLAT —) PLAP
(GENTLE —) TAP
(GROWLING —) SNARL
(GULPING —) GLUCK
(GUTTURAL —) GROWL
(HARSH —) JAR BRAY BLARE CLASH CRANK TWANG SCROOP DISCORD STRIDOR
(HEAVY —) DUMP
(HIGH-PITCHED —) BLIP TING BLEEP
(HISSING —) FIZZ SIZZ SWISH SIZZLE
(HOARSE —) ROOP
(HOLLOW —) CHOCK THUNGE
(HUMMING —) HUM BURR SUUM DRONE SINGING
(INDISTINCT —) BLUR SURD
(INITIAL — OF WORDS) ANLAUT
(JINGLING —) SMIT
(KNOCKING —) RATTAT
(LAPPING —) SLOOSH
(LIGHT REPEATED —) PITAPAT
(LOUD —) PEAL BLARE CLANG CRASH CLANGOR
(LOW —) WHISPER
(LOW-PITCHED —) BASS
(MEANINGLESS —S) GABBLE
(MEDIAL —) INLAUT
(MENTALLY —) SANE WISE
(MOANING —) SUUM SOUGH
(MOURNFUL —) GROAN
(MUFFLED —) MUFFLE
(MUSICAL —) CHIME
(NASAL —) ANUSVARA
(NON-SIGNIFICANT —) GLIDE
(NONVIBRATORY —) FRICTION
(PLEASING —) EUPHONY EUPHONIA
(QUADRAPHONIC —) QUAD
(RASPING —) BUZZ SKIRR SCROOP
(REPEATED —) ECHO
(RESONANT —) BONG
(REVERBERATING —) PLANG
(RINGING —) CLANG CLANK CLING TWANG RINGLE DINGDONG
(ROARING —) BEAL
(RUSHING —) SWOOSH HURLING
(RUSTLING —) FISSLE FISTLE
(SCRAPING —) GRIDE
(SCRATCHY —) SCRAICH SCRAIGH
(SHARP —) POP PING SNAP CHINK CRAKE KNACK SPANG SQUIRK
(SHORT, HIGH-PITCHED —) BLEEP
(SHRILL —) CHEEP KNACK SKIRL SCREED SQUEAK STRIDOR
(SHUFFLING —) SCUFFLE
(SIBILANT —) HISS SHISH SHUSH
(SLAPPING —) CLATCH
(SLIGHT —) SWISH
(SNORING —) SNORK
(SOBBING —) YOOP
(SPEECH —) SURD DOMAL TENUE VOWEL APICAL PHONEME CEREBRAL
(SPLASHING —) LAP CHUNK FLURR SPLAT SWASH
(SPOKEN —) BREATH
(SQUEAKY —) CREAK
(SQUELCHING —) SQUASH
(STRANGLED —) GLUB GLUG
(SWISHING —) SCHLOOP
(TAPPING —) TACK
(TELEPHONE —) SIDETONE
(TINKLING —) PINK
(TRAMPING —) STUMP
(TREMULOUS —) TRILL
(TRILLING —) CHIRR CHIZZ HIRRIENT
(TUNEFUL —) HARMONY
(UNPLEASANT —) BLOOP
(VIBRATING —) TIRL
(VOWEL —) SHWA SCHWA
(WARNING —) ALARM SIREN ALARUM TOCSIN
(WHIRRING —) BIRR FLURR SKIRR
(WHISPERING —) SUSURRUS
(WHISTLING —) STRIDOR
(PREF.) AUDIO AUDIT ECHO PHON(O) SON(I)(O) SONORI SONORO TONICO TONO
(SUFF.) PHON(E)(IA)(Y) SONANCE SONANT SONOUS TONE TONIA TONIC TONOUS TONY

SOUND-ABSORBENT ACOUSTIC
SOUND AND THE FURY (AUTHOR OF —) FAULKNER
(CHARACTER IN —) HEAD JASON DILSEY SYDNEY CANDACE COMPSON QUENTIN BENJAMIN
SOUNDBOARD BELLY
SOUNDED (NOT —) QUIESCENT
SOUNDER TICKER LEADMAN
SOUNDING RAWIN SONANT INKLING SONDAGE SONATION
(— HARSH) BRAZEN
(— OF BELL) CURFEW
(— OF MUSICAL INSTRUMENT) SPEECH
(— OF ORGAN PIPE) CIPHER
(— WITH REVERBERATIONS) PLANGENT
SOUNDLY FAST TIGHT FIRMLY
SOUNDNESS HEAL SANITY FITNESS SOBRIETY STRENGTH VALIDITY
SOUP BREE KAIL KALE SOPA BRODO BROTH GUMBO POSOL BISQUE BORSCH BURGOO CALALU JOUTES POTAGE POZOLE BILLIBI BILLYBI BORSCHT CALALOO GARBURE MARMITE RUBABOO CALLALOO CALLALOU CONSOMME GAZPACHO MINESTRA MORTREUX AVGOLEMONO MINESTRONE COCKALEEKIE MULLIGATAWNY MULLIGATAWNEY
(— UP) SUPE
(BARLEY —) SMIGGINS
(BEEFSKIN —) SKINK
(CABBAGE —) SHCHI STCHI
(CLEAR —) CONSOMME JULIENNE
(COLD —) SCHAV
(HAWAIIAN NOODLE —) SAIMIN
(JAPANESE NOODLE —) RAMEN
(JELLIED —) GAZPACHO
(LARGE QUANTITY OF —) SLASH
(NOODLE —) SAIMIN
(POTATO —) TATTIECLAW
(SHINBONE —) SKINK
(THICK —) BISK GUMBO HOOSH PUREE BISQUE BURGOO CHOWDER GARBURE POTTAGE HOTCHPOT MORTREWES
(THIN —) BROTH SKILLY
(VEGETABLE —) PISTOU
SOUR AWA DRY YAR ACID ASIM CRAB DOUR FOXY GRIM GRUM HARD TART TURN ACERB ACRID AIGRE EAGER GOURY GRUFF MUSTY TEART ACETIC ACIDIC BITTER CRUETY CURDLE PONTIC RANCID RUGGED SULLEN TORVID ACETOSE ACIDIFY AUSTERE SUBACID ACERBATE VINEGARY
(SLIGHTLY —) BLINK BLINKY ACESCENT
SOURCE FONS FONT HAND HEAD HIVE MINE RISE RIST ROOT SEED FOUNT RADIX SPAWN SURGE AUCTOR AUTHOR BOTTOM CENTER FATHER FONTAL ORIGIN PARENT RESORT STAPLE WHENCE EDITION FOUNTAIN WELLHEAD PROVENANCE
(— OF ADVANTAGE) OYSTER
(— OF AID) RECOURSE
(— OF ANCESTRAL LINE) STOCK
(— OF ANNOYANCE) BOGY BOGIE HARROW BUGBEAR
(— OF ASSURANCE) FORTRESS
(— OF CONCERN) BUGABOO
(— OF CONFIDENCE) ANCHOR
(— OF DANGER) THREAT
(— OF DISPLEASURE) DISGUST
(— OF ENERGY) STEAM TAPAS
(— OF ENLIGHTENMENT) TORCH
(— OF GRATIFICATION) TREAT
(— OF HAPPINESS) SUNSHINE
(— OF HARM) CURSE
(— OF HELP) RESOURCE
(— OF HONOR) CREDIT
(— OF INCOME) TITLE REVENUE
(— OF INFORMATION) CHECK
(— OF INSPIRATION) CASTALIA CASTALIE
(— OF INSTRUCTION) BOOK
(— OF JOY) NUTS
(— OF LAUGHTER) SPLEEN
(— OF LIFE) SPRING
(— OF LIGHT) LAMP
(— OF MERRIMENT) FUN
(— OF MONEY) FUND
(— OF NOURISHMENT) BREAST
(— OF PERPLEXITY) PROBLEM
(— OF POWER) STRENGTH
(— OF QUOTATIONS) QUOTATIVE
(— OF RADIATION) PULSAR
(— OF REGRET) SCATH SCATHE
(— OF STREAM OR RIVER) FILL
(— OF STRENGTH) HORN
(— OF SUPPLY) SHOP FEEDER ARSENAL
(— OF TROUBLE) HEADACHE
(— OF WATER) BRON SPRING
(— OF WEALTH) GOLCONDA KLONDIKE
(— OF WORK OF ART) PROVENANCE PROVENIENCE
(— OF WORRY) HEADACHE
(ABUNDANT —) CORNUCOPIA
(BE THE — OF) SPAWN
(ENCLOSED —) FLOW
(FROM ANOTHER —) ALIUNDE
(GENERATING —) LOINS
(MALIGNANT —) CANCER
(PHYSICAL —) MOTHER
(PRIMARY —) RADIX
(PRIMITIVE —) PRIMORDIUM
(RADIO —) QUASAR
(RICH —) MINE
SOURDOUGH LEAVEN
SOURED FOXY QUARRED
SOURING ACESCENCE
SOURNESS ACIDITY ACERBITY ACRIMONY ASPERITY TARTNESS VERJUICE
SOURPUSS CRAB CRANK GROUCH
SOURSOP CORRESOL GUANABANA
SOURWOOD TITI ELKWOOD
SOUSE DIP DUCK TOSH PLUMP STOOP PLUNGE SOZZLE TOSSPOT
SOUTANE SIMAR ZIMARRA
SOUTH MIDI AUSTER DECANI MIDDAY MERIDIAN
(FARTHER —) BELOW
(PREF.) AUSTR(O) NOT(O)

SOUTH AFRICA

BAY: ALGOA FALSE
CAPE: AGULHAS
CAPITAL: CAPETOWN PRETORIA
COIN: CENT RAND POUND FLORIN KRUGERRAND
LANGUAGE: BANTU HINDI TAMIL TELUGU BUJARATI
MOUNTAIN: AUX KOP KATHKIN INJASUTI
NATIVE: YOSA BANTU NAMAS PONDO DAMARA SWAHILI BECHUANA HOTTENTOT
PROVINCE: NATAL TRANSVAAL
RIVER: MODDER MOLOPO ORANGE KURUMAM LIMPOPO OLIFANTS
TOWN: AUS MARA STAD BENONI DURBAN SEVERN UMTATA KOKSTAD SPRINGS MAFEKING GERMISTON JOHANNESBURG
WATERFALL: HOWICK TUGELA AUGRABIES

SOUTH AMERICA

(ALSO SEE SPECIFIC COUNTRIES)
LAKE: MIRIM POOPO TITICACA MARACAIBO LLANQUIHUE
MOUNTAIN: BAIA ANDES GOIAZ PARIMA ACARAHY TUMUCHUMAC
NATION: PERU CHILE BRAZIL GUYANA BOLIVIA ECUADOR URUGUAY COLOMBIA PARAGUAY

SURINAME ARGENTINA NICARAGUA VENEZUELA
RIVER: NEGRO AMAZON CHUBUT PARANA SALADO ORINOCO RIONEGRO ESSEQUIBO MAGDALENA

SOUTH CAROLINA
CAPITAL: COLUMBIA
COLLEGE: COKER FURMAN LANDER CITADEL CLAFFIN CLEMSON ERSKINE WOFFORD
COUNTY: AIKEN HORRY DILLON JASPER OCONEE SALUDA
FORT: SUMTER
INDIAN: PEDEE SEWEE CUSABO SANTEE WAXHAW CATAWBA SUGEREE WATEREE CONGAREE
ISLAND: EDISTO PARRIS HILTONHEAD
LAKE: MARION MURRAY CATAWBA WATEREE HARTWELL MOULTRIE
MOUNTAIN: SASSAFRAS
NATIVE: WEASEL PALMETTO
NICKNAME: PALMETTO
PLATEAU: PIEDMONT
PRESIDENT: JACKSON
RESERVOIR: SANTEE PINOPOLIS
RIVER: BROAD EDISTO PEEDEE SALUDA SANTEE ASHEPOO TUGALOS WATEREE CONGAREE SAVANNAH
STATE BIRD: WREN
STATE FLOWER: JASMINE
STATE TREE: PALMETTO
TOWN: AIKEN GREER UNION BELTON CAMDEN CHERAW CONWAY DILLON SALUDA SENECA SUMTER BAMBERG LAURENS MANNING BEAUFORT FLORENCE NEWBERRY WALHALLA GREENVILLE SPARTANBURG

SOUTH CAROLINIAN WEASEL PALMETTO

SOUTH DAKOTA
BUTTE: MUD CROW SULLY FINGER SADDLE THUNDER DEERSEARS
CAPITAL: PIERRE
COLLEGE: HURON YANKTON
COUNTY: DAY HYDE BRULE MINER MOODY SPINK SULLY TRIPP CUSTER JERAULD YANKTON MELLETTE
INDIAN: BRULE SIOUX DAKOTA CHEYENNE
LAKE: OAHE BIGSTONE TRAVERSE
MONUMENT: RUSHMORE
MOUNTAIN: BEAR SHEEP TABLE CROOKS HARNEY MOREAU
NICKNAME: COYOTE SUNSHINE
RIVER: JAMES MOREAU CHEYENNE MISSOURI
STATE BIRD: PHEASANT
STATE FLOWER: PASQUE
STATE TREE: SPRUCE
TOWN: LEAD HAYTI HURON LEOLA ONIDA CUSTER DESMET EUREKA KADOKA LEMMON MILLER WINNER STURGIS WEBSTER YANKTON ABERDEEN DEADWOOD SISSETON

SOUTHERLY AUSTRINE
SOUTHERN SUDIC AUSTRAL MERIDIAN SOUTHRON MERIDIONAL
(PREF.) NOTIO
SOUTHERN CROSS CRUX CROSS CROSIER
SOUTHERNER CAVALIER SOUTHRON
SOUTHERN FRANCE MIDI
SOUTHERN ILLINOIS EGYPT
SOUTHERN INDIA DRAVIDA
SOUTHERNWOOD APPLERINGIE

SOUTH KOREA
BAY: KANGHWA
CAPITAL: SEOUL
COIN: WON CHUN HWAN
MONEY: JUN CHON JEON
MOUNTAIN: CHIRI
PROVINCE: CHEJU CHOLLA KANGWON KYONGGI
RIVER: HAN KUM PUKHAN SOMJIN NAKTONG YONGSAN
TOWN: CHEJU MASAN MOKPO PUSAN SUWON TAEGU WONJU CHINJU CHONJU INCHON KUNSAN TAEJON CHONGJU KWANGJU CHUNCHON

SOUTHLAND AUSTER
SOUTH SEA ISLANDER KANAKA
SOUTHWESTER SQUAM
SOUTH YEMEN (CAPITAL OF —) ADEN
(ISLAND OF —) PERIM KAMARAN SOCOTRA
(MONEY OF —) DINAR
(TOWN OF —) SEIYUN MUKALLA
SOUVENIR CURIO RELIC TOKEN FAIRING NICKNACK
SOVEREIGN BEY SIR SOV BEAN CHAM CHIP FREE KHAN QUID SHAH SKIV CROWN JAMES NEGUS NIZAM QUEED RULER CHAGAN COUTER GUINEA KAISER KINGLY MASTER PRINCE SAMORY SHINER SOLDAN SOVRAN SULTAN CROWNED MONARCH ZAMORIN AUTOCRAT DOMINANT IMPERIAL SUFFRAIN SUZERAIN
(DIVINELY —) THEARCHIC
(FELLOW —) COUSIN
(HEAVENLY —) TENNO HEAVEN
(MOSLEM —) SOLDAN
SOVEREIGNTY SWAY CROWN REIGN DIADEM EMPERY EMPIRE THRONE DEMESNE DYNASTY KINGDOM MAJESTY SCEPTER SCEPTRE AUTARCHY DOMINION IMPERIUM MONARCHY REGALITY REGNANCY SOVRANTY
(— OF REASON) AUTONOMY
(JOINT —) SYNARCHY
SOVERIGN DYNAST
SOVIET (ALSO SEE RUSSIA) VOLOST COUNCIL GUBERNIA
(— POLICY OF DISCUSSION) GLASNOST
SOW ELT HOG GILT SEED SHED YELT YILT DRILL PLANT PLUMP STREW CHANNEL GRUMPHY IMPLANT OVERSOW SCATTER ENGENDER INTERSOW SEMINATE
(PREF.) HYO SCROFUL(O)
(SUFF.) CHOERUS
SOWAR SILLADAR
SOW BUG ISOPOD SLATER ISOPODAN
SOWENS SONS SWEENS FLUMMERY WASHBREW
SOWER SEEDER SEEDMAN SEEDSTER SEMINARY
SOWING SATION SEMENCE SEEDNESS
(PREF.) SPOR(I)(IDI)(O)(ULI)
(SUFF.) SPORA SPORE SPORIC SPORIDIA SPORIUM SPOROUS SPORY
SOWN SEME SATIVE SEEDED SEMEED
SOW THISTLE DINDLE GUTWEED HOGWEED MILKWEED
SOY SHOYA SHOYU
(— SAUCE) TAMARI
SOYBEAN SOJA SOYA
SPA BATH CURE EVIAN HYDRO
SPACE GAP AREA BLUE CORD COSO DENT FACE LUNG PALE RANK ROOM SIDE VOID ABYSS BLOCK CHINK CLEFT FIELD PLACE RANGE CANTON HIATUS INDENT MATTER ROOMTH ARRANGE COMPASS FOREIGN GUNNIES LEGROOM ROOMAGE SPACING SPATIUM DIASTEMA DISTANCE EXOCOELE INTERVAL
(— ABOVE EARTH) AIRSPACE
(— AMONG MUSCLES) SINUS
(— AROUND HOUSE) AMBIT
(— AT WHARF) BERTHAGE
(— BEFORE KILN) LOGIE KILLOGIE
(— BEHIND ALTAR) FERETORY
(— BETWEEN ARCHES) SPANDREL SPANDRIL
(— BETWEEN BED AND WALL) RUELLE
(— BETWEEN BRIDGE PIERS) LOCK
(— BETWEEN CASKS) CONTLINE
(— BETWEEN COLUMNS) BAY
(— BETWEEN CONCENTRIC CIRCLES) ANNULUS
(— BETWEEN DECKS) LAZARET
(— BETWEEN DOCKS) SLIPWAY
(— BETWEEN EYE AND BILL) LORE
(— BETWEEN FEATHERS) APTERYLA
(— BETWEEN FLOOR TIMBERS) SPIRKET
(— BETWEEN FLUTINGS) FILET FILLET GORGERIN
(— BETWEEN FURROWS) RIG
(— BETWEEN PAGES) GUTTER
(— BETWEEN RAILROAD TIES) CRIB
(— BETWEEN SAW TEETH) GULLET
(— BETWEEN SHIP'S BOWS AND ANCHOR) HAWSE
(— BETWEEN STRANDS) CANTLINE
(— BETWEEN TEETH) DIASTEMA
(— BETWEEN THUMB AND LITTLE FINGER) SPAN
(— BETWEEN TIMBERS) SPIRKET
(— BETWEEN TWO WIRES) DENT
(— BETWEEN VEINS OF LEAVES) AREOLA
(— DEVOID OF MATTER) VACUUM VACUITY
(— FOR SECRETION) BAG
(— IN CHURCH) KNEELING
(— IN COIL OF CABLE) TIER
(— IN FOREST) GLADE
(— IN MINE) GOB
(— IN THEATER) BOX
(— IN TYPE) CORE
(— OCCUPIED) VOLUME
(— OF THREE DAYS) TRIDUUM
(— OF TIME) DAY PULL STEAD GHURRY STITCH INTERVAL
(— ON BILLIARD TABLE) BALK BAULK
(— ON COIN) EXERGUE
(— OVERHEAD) HIGH
(— OVER STAGE) FLIES
(— TRANSMITTER) TIROS
(— UNDER STAGE) DOCK
(— USED AS LIVING-ROOM) LANAI
(— WITHIN LIMITS) CONTENT
(AD —) LINAGE
(AIR —) CENTRUM
(ARCHITECTURAL —) METOPE PEDIMENT SACELLUM
(BACKGAMMON —) POINT
(BARE — ON BIRD) APTERIUM
(BLANK —) GAP ALLEY LACUNA
(BOUNDLESS —) INFINITE
(BREATHING —) BARLEY
(CLEAR —) FAIRWAY HEADWAY DAYLIGHT
(COUNTER —) BACKBAR
(CRAMPED —) CUBBY
(EMPTY —) AIR BLANK VACUUM CAPACITY
(ENCLOSED —) AREA BOWL HATCH VERGE PARVIS CHAMBER CIRCUIT CLOSURE COMPASS PARVISE PTEROMA CLOISTER CONFINES
(EUCLIDEAN —) FLAT
(FLAT —) HOMALOID
(KIND OF —) HILBERT
(LEVEL —) PLATEA PARTERRE
(NARROW —) SLOT STRAIT
(OPEN —) OUT LAWN ALLEY COURT LAUND TAHUA MAIDAN AREAWAY FAIRWAY LOANING APERTURE DAYLIGHT KNEEHOLE
(OPEN — OF WATER) WAKE
(OVERHANGING —) DOME
(POPLITEAL —) HAM HOCK
(ROOF —) CELL
(RUSSIAN — STATION) MIR
(SEATING —) CAVEA
(SHELTERED —) KILLOGIE
(SMALL —) AREOLA
(STORAGE —) ATTIC
(TRIANGULAR —) SPANDREL
(UNFILLED —) GAP GAPE CAVITY HOLLOW BREAKAGE
(VAULTED —) ALCOVE
(VERTICAL —) HEADROOM
(WORKING —) COUNTER
(PREF.) SPATIO
SPACECRAFT BUS SHIP CAPSULE ORBITER
(CHANNEL SENDING TO —) UPLINK
(PROCESS OF SLOWING DOWN —) DEBOOST

(SLOW DOWN A —) DEBOOST
(SYSTEM OF — ROCKETS) RETROPACK
SPACED MEATIC
SPACER QUAD
SPACEWALK EVA
SPACIOUS ROOM SIDE WIDE AMPLE BROAD RANGY ROOMY GOLDEN BARONIAL SCOPIOUS
SPADE DIG LOY FECK LILY PEEL PICK SPIT SPUD DELVE DIDLE GRAFF SLADE SLANE TRAMP DIGGER PADDLE PATTLE SERVER SHOVEL TUSKAR GRAFTER SCAFFLE SCUPPIT SPADDLE SPITTER TWISCAR
(LONG NARROW —) LOY
(PART OF —) FROG STEP BLADE HANDLE SOCKET SHOULDER
(PEAT —) SLADE SLANE TUSKAR
(PLASTERER'S —) SERVER
(TRIANGULAR —) DIDLE
SPADEFISH POGY PORGY MOONFISH
SPADEFUL SPIT SPITFUL
SPAGHETTI PASTA SLEEVING
(— SAUCE) RAGU PREGO
SPAGNUOLO LADINO

SPAIN

CAPE: AJO NAO GATA CREUS MORAS PALOS PENAS PRIOR DARTUCH ORTEGAL SALINAS TORTOSA ESPICHEL MARROQUI SACRATIF
CAPITAL: MADRID
COIN: COB DURO PESO REAL DOBLA CUARTO DINERO DOBLON ESCUDO PESETA ALFONSO CENTIMO PISTOLE REALDOR DOUBLOON
DIALECT: BASQUE CATALAN GALICIAN
ISLAND: IBIZA PALMA GOMERA HIERRO ALBORAN MAJORCA MINORCA MALLORCA TAGOMAGO TENERIFE
ISLANDS: CANARY BALEARIC
MEASURE: PIE CODO COPA DEDO MOYO PASO VARA ALMUD BRAZA CAFIZ CAHIZ CARGA LEGUA LINEA MEDIO MILLA PALMO SESMA ARROBA CORDEL CUARTA ESTADO FANEGA RACION YUGADA AZUMBRE CANTARA CELEMIN ESTADEL PULGADA ARANZADA FANEGADA
MOUNTAIN: GATA ANETO ROUCH TEIDE ESTATS NETHOU TELENO BANUELO CERREDO PERDIDO ALMANZOR MONTSENY MULHACEN PENALARA
MOUNTAIN RANGE: CUENCA GREDOS MORENA TOLEDO ALCARAZ DEMANDA MONCAYO MALADETA MONEGROS PYRENEES
NAME: ESPANA IBERIA HISPANIA
NATIVE: CATALAN IBERIAN
PORT: ADRA NOYA VIGO CADIZ GADES GADIR GIJON PALOS ABDERA CORUNA MALAGA ALMERIA ALICANTE BARCELONA
PROVINCE: JAEN LEON LUGO ALAVA AVILA CADIZ SORIA BURGOS CORUNA CUENCA GERONA HUELVA HUESCA LERIDA MADRID MALAGA MURCIA ORENSE OVIEDO TERUEL TOLEDO ZAMORA ALMERIA BADAJOZ CACERES CORDOBA GRANADA LOGRONO NAVARRA SEGOVIA SEVILLA VIZCAYA ALBACETE ALICANTE BALEARES PALENCIA VALENCIA ZARAGOZA
REGION: LEON ARAGON BASQUE MURCIA CASTILE GALICIA NAVARRE ASTURIAS CASTILLA VALENCIA
RIVER: SIL TER CEGA EBRO ESLA LIMA MINO TAJO ULLA ADAJA CINCA DOURO DUERO GENIL JALON JUCAR NAVIA ODIEL RIAZA SEGRE TAGUS TINTO TURIA ALAGON ARAGON ERESMA HUERVA JARAMA ORBIGO SEGURA TOROTE ALMERIA ALMONTE ARLANZA BARBATE CABRIEL DURATON GALLEGO HENARES MIJARES PERALES GUADIANA
TOWN: ROA ASPE BAZA ELDA HARO IRUN JAEN LEON LUGO OLOT REUS ROTA SAMA VIGO BAENA BEJAR CADIZ CIEZA CUETA ECIJA EIBAR ELCHE GIJON IBIZA JEREZ JODAR LORCA OLIVA PALMA RONDA SIERO UBEDA XERES YECLA ZAFRA AVILES AZUAGA BILBAO BURGOS DUENCA GANDIA GERONA GETAFE GUADIX HELLIN HUELVA HUESCA JATIVA LERIDA LUCENA MADRID MALAGA MATARO MERIDA MURCIA ORENSE OVIEDO TERMEL TOLEDO UTRERA ZAMORA BADAJOZ CORDOBA DAIMIEL GRANADA JUMILLA LINARES LOGRONO MANRESA SEGOVIA SEVILLA TARRASA VITORIA BADALONA FIGUERAS PAMPLONA SABADELL SANTIAGO TORRENTE VALENCIA ZARAGOZA
WEIGHT: ONZA FRAIL GRANO LIBRA MARCO TOMIN ADARME ARROBA DINERO DRACMA OCHAVA ARIENZO QUILATE QUINTAL CARACTER TONELADA
WINE: RIOJA SHERRY

SPALL CHIP SCALE SPAWL GALLET
SPAN ARCH BEAM PAIR CHORD SPANG SWING BRIDGE EXTEND SPREAD OPENING QUARTER BESTRIDE
(— OF TIME) PIECE
(— WITH FINGERS) SPEND
(UNSUPPORTED —) BEARING
SPANDREL GROIN ALLEGE SPANDLE
SPANGLE AGLET BEGEM PRANK SPANG INSTAR SEQUIN CHEQUEEN SPANGLET ZECCHINO PAILLETTE
SPANGLED POWDERED SPANKLED
SPANIARD DON DIEGO MULADI
(CHRISTIAN —) MOZARAB
SPANIEL TRASY COCKER SUSSEX CLUMBER BLENHEIM PAPILLON SPRINGER WATERRUG
SPANISH ALJAMIA HISPANIC
(PREF.) HISPANO
SPANISH-AMERICAN LADINO CHINO LADINO
SPANISH BAYONET IZOTE YUCCA
SPANISH BROOM SPART RETAMA
SPANISH FLY CANTHARIS
SPANISH HOGFISH LADYFISH
SPANISH JACINTH SCILLA
SPANISH JASMINE MALATI
SPANISH MACKEREL SIERRA
SPANISH PLUM SIRUELAS
SPANISH STOPPER IRONWOOD
SPANK PRAT SCUD SKELP PADDLE THRASH SLIPPER
SPANKER DRIVER MIZZEN
SPANKING SMACKING
SPANNER KEY WRENCH
SPANNING ASTRIDE
SPAR BEAM BOOM CAUK CLUB GAFF MAST RAFT SPUR YARD CABER SPAAD SPATH SPELK SPRIT STODE BOUGAR BUMKIN RICKER STEEVE BASTITE BUMPKIN DERRICK DOLPHIN JIBBOOM RIBBAND BOWSPRIT CRYOLITE LAZULITE OUTRIGGER MARTINGALE
(BITTER —) DOLOMITE
(HEAVY —) CAUK BARITE BARYTE
SPARE BONY FAIK GASH HAIN LEAN NICE SAVE SLIM THIN FAVOR LANKY SPELL LENTEN MEAGER MEAGRE SKIMPY RESERVE SLENDER PRESERVE
SPARGE PIPE WEEPER
SPARING CHARY GNEDE SCANT SPARE DAINTY FRUGAL STINGY ENVIOUS ECONOMIC SPAREFUL PENURIOUS ABSTEMIOUS
(— IN COMMUNICATION) RETICENT
(— OF WORDS) CURT
(NOT —) HANDSOME
(PREF.) PARCI
SPARINGNESS PARCITY SCARCITY
SPARK FUNK IZLE AIZLE GRAIN LIGHT PURSE SPERK SPUNK BLUETTE FLANKER FLAUGHT SPARKLE SPUNKIE SPARKLET SCINTILLA
(—S OF MOLTEN IRON) NILL
(VITAL —) GHOST LIGHT
(PREF.) SCINTILLO
SPARKER IGNITER
SPARKLE FUNK SNAP WINK BLINK FLASH GLENT GLINT SHINE SPARK GLANCE KINDLE SIMPER CRACKLE EMICATE FLANKER GLIMMER GLISTEN GLISTER GLITTER RADIATE SHIMMER SKINKLE SPANGLE TWINKLE OPALESCE SPRINKLE CORUSCATE
SPARKLER TWINKLER
SPARKLING DEWY CRISP QUICK SUNNY BRIGHT SPUNKY STARRY CREMANT DIAMOND SHINING TWINKLY MOUSSEUX SMIRKING SPERLING BRILLIANT OPALESCENT SCINTILLANT
(MAKE —) AERATE
(NOT —) STILL
(SLIGHTLY —) PETILLANT
SPARK PLUG (PART OF —) CAP GAP SHELL GASKET BUSHING TERMINAL ELECTRODE INSULATOR
SPARLING SMELT
SPARROW SPUG DICKY DONEY FINCH HEMPY ISAAC PADDA PADDY SPRIG SPRUG CHIPPY PHILIP SPRONG TOWHEE CHANTER CHIPPIE DUNNOCK FIELDIE HAYSUCK PINNOCK SPADGER SPURDIE TITLENE TITLING TITTLIN ACCENTOR FIRETAIL HAIRBIRD WHITECAP
(PREF.) PASSERI
SPARROW HAWK MUSKET SPARHAWK
SPARSE BALD THIN MEAGER MEAGRE SCANTY THRIFTY
SPARTAN GREEK LACONIC
SPASM PANG CRICK QUALM TONUS CLONUS ENTASIA FLUTTER RAPTURE SPASMUS MYOTONIA PAROXYSM
(— OF EYELID) BLEPHARISM
(— OF FOOT) PODISMUS
(— OF IRIS) HIPPUS
(— OF PAIN) GRIP
(— OF THE IRIS) HIPPUS
(—S OF WHALE) FLURRY
(MUSCLE —) TRISMUS
(TONIC —) HOLOTONY
(PREF.) CLONICO
SPASMODIC FITFUL SNATCHY SPASMIC SPASTIC SPURTIVE
SPAT SEED TIFF BROOD JOWER GAITER LEGGING BOOTHOSE BOOTIKIN
SPATE ONRUSH SLUICE RAINSTORM
SPATHE CYMBA SHEATH
SPATHIC SPARRY SPATHOSE
SPATIAL LOCAL STERIC
SPATIATE ROVE RAMBLE STROLL
SPATTER DASH JAUP BERAY SKIRP SLART SPARK SPURT DABBLE SPLASH SQUIRT BESPAWL BESPETE SHATTER SMATTER SPATTLE SPIRTLE SPLATTER SPRINKLE
(— WITH FOAM) EMBOSS
(— WITH MUD) JAP BEMUD SPARK
SPATTERDASH SPAT BONNET GAITER CUTIKIN LEGGING BOOTHOSE BOOTIKIN
SPATTERDOCK DUCK CLOTE TUCKY WOKAS NUPHAR BONNETS CANDOCK
SPATTERING JAP JAUP SPAT SQUATTER
SPATULA SPAT SLICE THIBLE THIVEL CESTRUM SPATTLE SPLATTER
SPAVIN JACK SPAVIE VARISSE
SPAWN RUD BLOT RAUN REDD RUDD SILE SPORE TODDER GENERATE
(— OF SHELLFISH) SPAT
(OYSTER —) CULCH CULTCH
SPAWNEATER SHINER
SPAWNING SICK MILKY SEEDING
SPAY FIX GELD ALTER DESEX SPADE

CHANGE DOCTOR SPEAVE CASTRATE
SPEAK ASK CUT SAY CANT CARP MEAN MOOT MOVE TALE TALK TELL WORD BREAK MOUTH NEVEN ORATE PARLE SOUND SPELL SPIEL UTTER ACCENT INTONE PARLEY PATTER QUETHE SERMON SPEECH SQUEAK TONGUE ADDRESS BESPEAK DECLAIM DELIVER EXCLAIM PARRALL CONVERSE REHEARSE
(— ABUSIVELY) JAW
(— AFFECTEDLY) MIMP KNACK
(— AGAINST) ACCUSE GAINSAY FORSPEAK
(— ANGRILY) ROUSE CAMPLE
(— AT LENGTH) DISSERT ENLARGE
(— BROKENLY) FALTER
(— CAJOLINGLY) COLLOGUE
(— CONFUSEDLY) HATTER CLUTTER SPLATHER
(— CONSTANTLY) YAP
(— CONTEMPTUOUSLY) SCOFF
(— CRITICALLY) LAUNCH
(— CURTLY) BIRK SNAP
(— EVIL) BLACKEN
(— FAIR) PALP
(— FALSELY) ABUSE
(— FAMILIARLY) HOBNOB
(— FIRST TO) ACCOST
(— FOOLISHLY) PRATE GIBBER JABBER
(— HALTINGLY) HACK HAMMER STAMMER
(— HESITANTLY) STAMMER
(— HOARSELY) CROAK CROUP
(— ILL OF) KNOCK DEPRAVE DETRACT
(— IMPERFECTLY) LISP
(— IMPUDENTLY) CHEEK
(— IMPULSIVELY) BLURT
(— INDISTINCTLY) FUMBLE JABBER MUFFLE MAUNDER SPLUTTER
(— IN DRAWL) DRANT DRAUNT
(— INEPTLY) BUMBLE
(— IN JEST) FOOL
(— IN ONE'S EAR) HARK
(— IN POINTLESS MANNER) DROOL
(— INSOLENTLY) SNASH
(— IN STUMBLING WAY) STUTTER
(— IN UNDERTONE) WHISPER
(— IN WHINING VOICE) CANT
(— LOUDLY) TANG
(— LOW) WHISPER
(— MINCINGLY) NAB MIMP
(— MONOTONOUSLY) DROLL
(— OBSCURELY) RIDDLE
(— OF) CALL NEVEN MENTION
(— ONE'S MIND) SHOUT
(— OUT) LEVEL SHOOT
(— PLAYFULLY) BANTER
(— POMPOUSLY) CRACK
(— PROFUSELY) PALAVER
(— QUERULOUSLY) CREAK
(— RAPIDLY) TROLL GIBBER JABBER SQUIRT CHATTER
(— RESENTFULLY) HUFF
(— RHETORICALLY) DECLAIM
(— SARCASTICALLY) GIRD
(— SHORTLY) JERK
(— SLIGHTINGLY OF) BELITTLE
(— SLOWLY) DRAWL
(— SNARLINGLY) SNARL
(— TARTLY) SNAP
(— TEDIOUSLY) PROSE
(— THROUGH THE NOSE) SNAFFLE
(— TO ONESELF) SOLILOQUIZE
(— TRUTH) SOOTHSAY
(— WITH EMPHASIS) DWELL
(— WITH LIPS CLOSED) MUMBLE
(— WITH THE HANDS) SIGN
(— WITH UNCERTAINTY) QUAVER
SPEAKEASY SHEBEEN
SPEAKER TRIS VOICE BRYTHON LOCUTOR MOUTHER STYLIST EPILOGUE SPEECHER
(— IN POEM) PERSONA
(OBSCENE —) RIBALD
(ORATORICAL —) SPOUTER
(PUBLIC —) ORATOR STUMPER
SPEAKING STEVEN LOQUENT PARLANCE SPELLING
(— ARTICULATELY) MEROP MEROPIC
(— MANY LANGUAGES) POLYGLOT
(— POMPOUSLY) MAGNILOQUENT
(— WITHOUT SOUND) MUSSITATION
(EVIL —) PRATING
(INDISTINCT —) JABBER
(PUBLIC —) PLATFORM
(SUFF.) LOGER LOGIA(N) LOGIC(AL) LOGIST LOGUE LOGY LOQUENCE LOQUENT LOQUY
SPEAR GAD DART FRAM GAFF PIKE GRAIN LANCE REJON SHAFT STAFF VALET AMGARN BORDUN BROACH FIZGIG FRAMEA GIDJEE GLAIVE WASTER ASSEGAI BOURDON HARPOON IMPALER JAVELIN TRIDENT VERUTUM EELSPEAR GAVELOCK LANCEGAY STANDARD WALSPERE
(BROKEN —) TRUNCHEON
(EEL —) ELGER PILGER
(FISH —) GIG GAFF TREN POACH FIZGIG GRAINS FISHGIG LEISTER SNIGGER
(SALMON —) WASTER
(PREF.) DORI ENCHO HASTATO LANCI
SPEARFISH AGUJA GOGGLE MARLIN BILLFISH LONGJAWS
SPEAR GRASS SPANIARD
SPEARHEAD BUNT GAFF SPUD PRONG CORONAL
SPEARMINT MENTHE LABIATE
SPEAR-SHAPED HASTATE
SPEAR THROWER ATLATL WOMMALA WOOMERAH
SPEARWORT BANEWORT
SPECIAL VERY EXTRA KHASS CONCRETE ESPECIAL PECULIAR SPECIFIC REDLETTER
(NOT —) GENERAL
SPECIALIST SWELL EXPERT HERALD LEGIST ALTAIST ARABIST FAUNIST FEUDIST GRECIAN OLOGIST SURGEON AQUINIST ARBORIST BANTUIST BOTANIST ETHICIST GEMARIST GEOGNOST GEOMETER HEBRAIST HOMERIST LATINIST URBANIST PHYSICIST PEDIATRIST PATHOLOGIST
(SUFF.) ICIAN LOG(ER)(IA)(IAN)(IC)(ICAL)(IST)(UE)(Y)
SPECIALIZE MAJOR
SPECIALTY BAG THING
SPECIES FOLK FORM KIND SORT BROOD CLASS EIDOS GENRE ESPECE MANNER MISTER APOMICT FEATHER SPECIAL ANALOGUE GENOTYPE INDIGENE
(— VARIANT) MORPH
(ATOMIC —) DAUGHTER
SPECIFIC EXPRESS SPECIAL TRIVIAL CONCRETE ESPECIAL
SPECIFICALLY NAMELY
SPECIFICATION MENTION
(WRITE —S) SPEC
SPECIFICITY HECCEITY
SPECIFIED SET GIVEN
SPECIFY ASSIGN DESIGN DETAIL ARTICLE EXPRESS MENTION INDICATE NOMINATE PRESCRIBE
SPECIMEN CAST TEST ESSAY FACER MODEL SPICE CHANCE SAMPLE SWATCH EXAMPLE ICOTYPE ISOTYPE NEOTYPE PATTERN SAMPLER ALLOTYPE EXEMPLAR HOLOTYPE HYPOTYPE IDEOTYPE INSTANCE REPRESENTATIVE
(— OF WORK) PIECE
(ADDITIONAL —) COTYPE
(ANATOMICAL —) PREPARATION
(EXCELLENT —) RATTLER
(EXTRAORDINARY —) BENDER
(FEMALE —) GYNETYPE
(FINEST —) PEARL
(LARGE —) ELEPHANT
(MISERABLE —) RAT
(POOR —) APOLOGY
(SMALL —) SPRIG
SPECIOUS GAY FAIR FALSE WHITE FACILE GLOSSY HOLLOW TINSEL PAGEANT PLAUSIVE PROBABLE SPURIOUS PLAUSIBLE MERETRICIOUS
SPECIOUSNESS DISGUISE
SPECK DOT JOT PIN PIP MOTE SPOT TICK WHIT BLACK GLEBE PLECK APHTHA SPECKLE FLYSPECK NUBECULA
(— IN LINEN) SPRIT
(— ON FINGERNAIL) GIFT
(BLACK —) DARTROSE
SPECKLE FLECK GARLE SPECK MIZZLE PECKLE STIPPLE
SPECKLED SHELD FIGGED MAILED MENALD SANDED BLOBBED BRACKET PECKLED SPECKED SPECKLY FRECKLED IRONSHOT IRRORATE JASPERED STIPPLED
SPECTACLE POMP SHOW SPEC BYSEN SIGHT CIRCUS DEVICE OBJECT EYEMARK PAGEANT SPECIES TAMASHA MONUMENT NAUMACHY STERACLE NAUMACHIA
(DEPLORABLE —) OBJECT
(ODD —) TRACK
(POMPOUS —) PAGEANTRY
(SORRY —) BIZEN BYSEN BYZEN
(WATER —) AQUACADE
(PL.) LUDI
(SUFF.) CADE ORAMA
SPECTACLES PAIR SPECS BRILLS LUNETS PEEPER SIGHTS GLASSES GOGGLES WINKERS ANAGLYPH CHEATERS BARNACLES
SPECTACULAR VIEWY PAGEANT
SPECTATOR FAN VIEWER WITNESS BEHOLDER OBSERVER OVERSEER RAILBIRD VIEWSTER SCAFFOLDER
(PL.) DEDANS
SPECTER BUG BOGY MARE BOGIE BOGLE GHOST LARVA POOKA SPOOK TAIPO BOGGLE EMPUSA PHOOKA REDCAP SHADOW SPIRIT SPOORN WRAITH BOGGARD BOGGART BUGBEAR PHANTOM RAWHEAD REDCOWL SPECTRE GUYTRASH PHANTASM PRESENCE REVENANT SPECTRUM
(BROKEN —) GLORY
SPECTRAL SPOOKY GHOSTLY SHADOWY
SPECULATE JOB BEAR RISK STAG GAMBLE PONDER WONDER CONSIDER RUMINATE THEORIZE
(— IN STOCKS) SCALP
SPECULATION THEORY THEORIC VENTURE GAMBLING IDEOLOGY
(ABSTRACT —) IDEOLOGY
(DISHONEST —) BUBBLE
(VAGUE —) MYSTICISM
SPECULATIVE ACADEMIC
SPECULATOR PIKER GAMBLER PLUNGER SCALPER BOURSIER BUMMAREE OPERATOR
SPECULUM METAL MIRROR DILATER DIOPTER DIOPTRIC
SPEECH GOB LIP SAW SAY TAT TOY COAX LEED REDE RUNE TALE DUALA FRUMP GLOZE LEDEN LINGO PARLE SERMO SPEAK SPELL SPIEL SPOKE SQUIB VOICE BREATH DILOGY EPILOG GAELIC GASCON GILAKI JARGON LEDDEN LEMOSI ORISON REASON SALUTE STEVEN TONGUE ACCENTS ADDRESS BROCARD EASTERN MEITHEI ORATION PALABRA VULGATE EPILOGUE GALICIAN HARANGUE LANGUAGE LOCUTION LOQUENCE MORAVIAN PARLANCE QUESTION SONORITY SPEAKING
(— CHARACTERIZED BY SLURRING) SLURVIAN
(— FORM) LEXEME
(— IN GREEK DRAMA) RHESIS
(— IN PLAY) SIDE
(— REDUCER) VOCODER
(ABUSIVE —) REVILEMENT
(AFFECTED —) CANT
(AUSTRALIAN —) STRINE
(BITTER —) DIATRIBE
(BOASTFUL —) BLUSTER
(BOMBASTIC —) SQUIRT HARANGUE
(CHILDISH —) LALLATION
(COARSE —) HARLOTRY
(COCKNEY —) LONDONESE
(CONFUSED —) SPUTTER SPLUTTER
(CONTEMPTUOUS —) FRUMP
(CONVERSATIONAL —) PURPOSE
(DULL IN —) PROSY
(EXTEMPORE —) IMPROMPTU
(IMPUDENT —) SASS
(INCOHERENT —) WORDSALAD

(INDIGENOUS —) VERNACULAR
(INTRODUCTORY —) PROLOGUE PROLOCUTION
(IRRITABLE —) SNAP
(JAVANESE —) KRAMA
(KIND OF —) CUED
(LONG —) MONOLOG
(LONG-DRAWN —) TIRADE
(MISLEADING —) PALAVER
(MOCKING —) TRIFLE
(MONOTONOUS —) DRONE
(NASAL —) RHINOLALIA
(OBSCURE —) ENIGMA
(OFFENSIVE —) INJURY
(PERSUASIVE —) ELOQUENCE
(PERT —) DICACITY
(PRETENTIOUS —) FUSTIAN
(ROUNDABOUT —) CIRCUIT
(SANCTIMONIOUS —) SNUFFLE
(SINGSONG —) CANT
(SLANDEROUS —) EVIL
(SLURRED —) SLURVIAN
(STAGY —) HISTRIONICS
(UNINTELLIGIBLE —) HEBREW
(VAPID —) WASH
(PREF.) LALO LEXI LOG(O) PHON(O)
(SUFF.) ESE LEXIA PHASIA PHEMIA PHEMISM PHEMISTIC PHRASEO PHRASIA PHRASIS
(— DISORDER) LALIA

SPEECHIFIER SPOUTER
SPEECHLESS DUMB MUTE SILENT
SPEECHMAKING SPOUTING
(— TO GAIN APPLAUSE) BUNKUM BUNCOMBE
SPEED BAT HIE REV RIP RUN ZIP FLEE FOOT GAIT HARE HIGH PACE PELT PIKE PIRR POST TEAR TILT ZING BLAST HASTE HURRY SMOKE WHIRL ASSIST CAREER FOURTH HASTEN STREAK QUICKEN WHIZZLE AIRSPEED CELERITY DISPATCH ESCALATE EXPEDITE FASTNESS MOMENTUM RAPIDITY VELOCITY ACCELERATE
(— OF NAUTICAL MILE) KNOT
(— OF PITCH) STUFF
(— OF 100 MILES PER HOUR) TON
(— RELATIVE TO SOUND) MACH
(— UP) HASTEN CATALYZE EXPEDITE
(AT FULL —) AMAIN
(AUTOMOTIVE —) LOW HIGH DRIVE FIRST THIRD FOURTH SECOND REVERSE
(DRIVING —) SWING
(FULL —) RANDOM RANDON
(GOOD —) BONALLY
(HIGH —) CLIP MACH
(UNIT OF —) BAUD
(PREF.) DROM(O) TACHO
SPEEDBOAT HYDRO
SPEEDILY CITO SOON APACE RATHE BELIVE PRESTO BETIMES HYINGLY QUICKLY TANTIVY
SPEEDING HURTLING
SPEEDWELL CATEYE HENBIT FLUELLEN NECKWEED NICKWELL BROOKLIME
SPEEDY FAST SOON HASTY QUICK RATHE SWIFT RAKING SUDDEN POSTING TANTIVY EXPEDITE METEORIC SPEEDFUL SPINNING POSTHASTE

SPELEOLOGIST CAVEMAN
SPELL GO FIT HEX JAG HACK JINX MOJO PULL RUNE SCAT TACK TAKE TIFF TIME TOUR TURN BRIEF CHARM CRAFT CRASH MAGIC PATCH SPACE WANGA WEIRD WHEEL ACCESS GLAMOR GOOFER GRIGRI GUFFER MAKUTU MANTRA PERIOD SNATCH STREAK CANTRIP SORCERY SPELDER CANTRAIP EXORCISM GREEGREE MALEFICE PISHOGUE
(— OF ACTIVITY) BOUT
(— OF EVIL EYE) JETTATURA
(— OF EXERCISE) BREATHER
(— OF INSTRUCTION) LESSON
(— OF LISTLESSNESS) DOLDRUMS
(— OF PROSPERITY) UP
(— OF SHIVERING) AGUE
(— OF WEATHER) SNAP SLANT SEASON
(— OF WEEPING) GREET
(— OF WORK) SLOG
(BREATHING —) BLOW
(BRIEF —) SNATCH
(COLD —) SNAP
(CONTINUOUS —) RUN
(DRINKING —) FUDDLE
(EVIL —) JINX
(FAINTING —) DROW DWALM
(MYSTIC —) RUNE
(NIPPING —) SNAPE
(SHORT —) WINK SPURT SNATCH
(STORMY —) FLAW
(VOODOOISTIC —) WANGA
(WITCH'S —) CANTRIP
SPELLBIND ENCHANT
SPELLBINDING BASILISK
SPELLBOUND HEXED
SPELLING GRAPH WRITING PHONOGRAPHY
(BAD —) CACOGRAPHY
(UNSATISFACTORY —) PSEUDOGRAPHY
SPELT FAR EMMER FITCH SPELTZ
SPELTZ EMMER
SPENCER TRYSAIL
SPEND USE BIRL COST DREE DROP LEAD PASS STOW WARE WEAR DALLY DREIE SERVE SHOOT TRADE BESTOW BEWARE EXPEND LAVISH MOIDER OUTRUN CONSUME DISPEND EXHAUST UNPURSE CONFOUND CONTRIVE DISBURSE
(— FRUITLESSLY) DAWDLE
(— IN IDLENESS) DRONE
(— LAVISHLY) BLUE SPORT DEBAUCH
(— MONEY) MELT
(— RECKLESSLY) BLOW LASH
(— SUMMER) ESTIVATE
(— TIME) DREE FOOL DREIE ENTREAT
(— TIME TEDIOUSLY) DRANT
(— WASTEFULLY) SPILL SQUANDER
SPENDTHRIFT WASTER PANURGE ROUNDER SPENDER WASTREL PRODIGAL PROFLIGATE SCATTERGOOD
SPENSER IMMERITO
SPENT DONE WEARY EFFETE OVERWORN
SPERM SEED SEMINIUM

SPERMACETI SPERM CETACEUM
SPERMOGONIUM PYCNIUM
SPERMOPHILE MARMOT SUSLIK
SPERM WHALE CACHALOT PHYSETER
SPET SIGNET SINNET
SPEW PUKE SPUE VOMIT
SPHAERIUM CYCLAS
SPHAGION HIERA
SPHAGNUM MUSKEG
SPHALERITE JACK BLENDE BLACKJACK
SPHENODON TUATARA HATTERIA
SPHERE ORB AREA BALL BOWL LOKA SHOT FIELD GLOBE ORBIT RANGE REALM SCOPE CIRCLE CROTAL DOMAIN HEAVEN REGION RUNDLE COUNTRY ELEMENT GLOBOID KINGDOM ORBICLE PURVIEW EARTHKIN EMPYREAL EMPYREAN MOVEABLE PROVINCE TERRITORY
(— OF ACTION) AMBIT ARENA WORLD DOMAIN
(— OF ACTIVITY) FIELD FRONT
(— OF AUTHORITY) DIOCESE
(— OF CELLS) BLASTULA
(— OF INFLUENCE) DOMAIN SATRAPY
(— OF LIFE) EARTH WORLD STATION
(— OF OPERATION) AREA AMBIT SCOPE THEATER THEATRE
(— OF WORK) TITLE
(CELESTIAL —) CYCLE ELEMENT
(ENCOMPASSING —) AMBIENT
(HOLLOW —) SHELL
(MAGNETIZED —) EARTHKIN TERRELLA
(METAL —) HAMMER
(SMALL —) ORBICLE SPHERULE
(SUBMERSIBLE —) BENTHOSCOPE
(TINKLING —) CROTAL
(PREF.) GLOBO SPHAER(O) SPHER(O)
SPHERICAL ORBIC GLOBAL ROTUND GLOBATE GLOBOSE ORBICAL SPHERIC GLOBULAR ORBICULAR
(PREF.) GLOBO
SPHEROID QUANTASOME
SPHERULE GLOBULE VARIOLE
SPHINX MUSTANG COLOSSUS HAWKMOTH
(SITE OF —) GIZA
SPICA AZIMECH
SPICCATO PIQUE
SPICE MACE VEIN ZEST AROMA CLOVE EPICE TASTE GINGER NUTMEG PEPPER SEASON STACTE SPICERY SPICING ALLSPICE CINNAMON SEASONER
(ADD — TO) ENLIVEN
(PL.) GARAMMASALA
SPICEBUSH BENZOIN SNAPWOOD
SPICED SPICY POWDERED
SPICKNEL MEW SCLERE BEARWORT
SPICULE OXEA TOXA ASTER CHELA CYMBA DESMA DIACT SIGMA SPINE STYLE ACTINE ANCHOR MONACT SCLERE STYLUS TRIACT TRIPOD TYLOTE CALTROP DIACTIN EUASTER HEXAXON MONAXON PINULUS RHABDUS SPICKLE SPIRULA TETRACT TORNOTE TRIAENE TRIAXON TYLOTUS HEXASTER ISOCHELA OXYASTER POLYAXON SCLERITE SPHERULA SPICULUM STRONGYL TETRAXON TRICHITE TYLASTER
(SUFF.) AENE

SPICY RACY SEXY GAMEY NUTTY SWEET SPICED GINGERY PEPPERY FRAGRANT SPICEFUL
SPIDER BUG COB ARAIN ATTID COBBE COPPE LOPPE NANCY TAINT ANANSI ARRAND EPEIRA HUNTER KATIPO TRIVET WEAVER ARANEID CREEPER DRASSID EPEIRID JAYHAWK KNOPPIE POKOMOO RETIARY SERPENT SKILLET SOLDIER SPINNER ARACHNID ATTERCOP CTENIZID DICTYNID ETTERCAP KARAKURT ORBITELE PHALANGE PHALANGY PHOLCOID SALTICID SOLPUGID TELARIAN ULOBORID VENANTES WANDERER TARANTULA
(PART OF —) EYE CLAW COXA FEMUR TIBIA TARSUS ABDOMEN PATELLA PEDICEL SCOPULA SPINNERET METATARSUS PEDIPALPUS TROCHANTER CEPHALOTHORAX
(PREF.) ARACHN(O)
SPIDER CRAB MAIAN MAIID
SPIDERFLOWER QUARESMA
SPIDER MONKEY SAJOU COAITA SAPAJOU
SPIDERWORT TRINITY
SPIEL LINE SPEECH
SPIELER BARKER
SPIFF (— UP) ENLIVEN
SPIGNEL MEU
SPIGOT TAP SPILE DOSSIL DOZZLE STOPCOCK
SPIKE GAD BARB BROB PICK PIKE PILE SPUR TINE PITON POINT ROUGH SPEAR SPICA SPICK MOOTER PRITCH SPADIX SPIKER TENTER ALICOLE GADLING PRICKER PRICKET TRENAIL TURNPIN SPIKELET STROBILE WHEATEAR
(— A CANNON) CLOY
(— AS CANDLESTICK) PRICKET
(— OF CEREAL) EAR
(— OF FLOWER) SPIRE
(— ON GAUNTLET) GADLING
(BRACTED —) AMENT
(DRIED —S) CANNABIS
(WILLOW —) CATKIN
SPIKED SPICATE SPINDLED
SPIKELET CHAT ALICOLE LOCUSTA SPICULE
SPIKENARD PHU NARD ARALIA SUMBUL ARALIAD IVYWORT SPIGNET SPIGNUT
SPILE TAP SPILL FOREPOLE
SPILL LET DRIP DUMP SHED SLOP TELL FLOSH SCALE SKAIL SPILE SQUAB STAVE JIRBLE PURLER SLATTER SLOBBER TURNOVER
(— FOR LIGHTING PIPES) FIDIBUS
SPIN CUT BIRL DRAW GYRE HURL PIRL PURL REEL SCREW SPONE

TWIRL TWIST WEAVE WHIRL FOLLOW GYRATE VRILLE WAMBLE TWIZZLE TEETOTUM
(— AND MAKE HUM) BUM
(— AROUND) SWING
(— ON BASEBALL) STUFF
(— ON BILLIARD BALL) SIDE
(— OUT) SHOOT
(— SILK) THROW
(— SMOOTHLY) SLEEP
(— UNEVENLY) TWITTER
SPINACH SAVOY EPINARD OLITORY POTHERB
SPINAL CORD AXION NUCHA MYELON
(WHITE MATTER OF —) ALBA NUKE
(PREF.) MYEL(O)
(SUFF.) MYELIA
SPINDLE PIN AXLE HASP PIRN SPIT STEM STUD ARBOR FLOAT QUILL SPIKE SPILL VERGE BOBBIN BROACH CANNON FUSEAU BOLSTER MANDREL SPINNEL TRENDLE WHARROW
(AXLE —) ARM
(FOURTH OF —) HASP
(ONE 24TH OF —) HEER
(PREF.) FUSI
SPINDLE TREE GAITER DOGWOOD PEGWOOD EUONYMUS
SPINDLING SPEARY SPINDLY SPIRLIE
SPINDLY LEGGY PULING
SPINE HORN PIKE PILE SETA SPUR CHINE PRICK QUILL SPEAR SPIKE SPINA THORN ACUMEN CHAETA RACHIS ACANTHA ACICULA FULCRUM GLOCHIS PAXILLA PRICKER PRICKLE ROSTRUM SPINULE STICKLE ACICULUM BACKBONE ILLICIUM PAXILLUS PELELITH SPICULUM SPINELET
(— OF FIN) RAY
(— OF SURGEON FISH) TUCK
(CURVATURE OF —) LORDOSIS
(PREF.) ACANTH(O) RACHI(O) RHACHI(O)
(SUFF.) ACANTHUS CHAETA CHAETES CHAETUS RACHIDIA RHACHIS RRHACHIS
SPINEL BALAS CANDITE ESPINEL GAHNITE VERMEIL PICOTITE SPINELLE CEYLONITE RUBICELLE
SPINELESS SLAVISH
SPINET PIANO ESPINET GIRAFFE OCTAVINA SOURDINE VIRGINAL
SPINNER LURE ROTOR
(THREAD OF LIFE —) CLOTHO
SPINNERET GALEA MAMMULA SPINNER
SPINNING AREEL STROBIC LANIFICE
(— WEB) TELARIAN
SPINNING JENNY MULE JENNY
SPINNING MULE IRONMAN
SPINNING WHEEL TURN CHARKHA CHURRUCK
(PART OF —) BAND FLYER WHEEL BOBBIN DISTAFF SPINDLE TREADLE STANDARD
SPINSTER TABBY VIRGIN
SPINULE
(PL.) CTENII
SPINY PICKED THORNY
(PREF.) ACANTH(O) CENTR(I)(O) ECHIN(O)
SPINY OYSTER SPONDYLE
SPINY RAT OCTODONT
SPIRACLE STOMA STIGMA BLOWHOLE
SPIRAEA MAY ROSACEAN MEADOWSWEET
SPIRAL COIL CURL GYRE SPIN HELIX SCREW SNARE SPIRE BUTTON GURGES LITUUS SCREWY SCROLL SPIRED TWIRLY VOLUTE HELICAL ROLLING SPIROID STROPHE WINDING WREATHY GYROIDAL HELICINE HELICOID
(— OF WIRE) GRID
(LACEWORK —) PURL
(PREF.) GYR(O) HELI HELIC(O)
SPIRANT VAU WAW HISS OPEN DURATIVE
SPIRANTHES IBIDIUM
SPIRE CROWN SHAFT SIKAR SPEAR TAPER TOLLY BROACH FLECHE PRICKET SHIKARA SIKHARA SPIRALE SPIRELET
SPIRE-BEARER SPIRIFER
SPIREME SKEAN SKEIN
SPIRIT GO AME FLY NAG PEP VIM AITU AKUA ALMA ATUA BRIO DASH DOOK ELAN FIRE GALL GIMP HYLE JINN LIFE MARC MARE MIND MOOD SOUL TONE ZEMI ZING AGIEL ARDOR ARIEL ASURA AZOTH CHEER DEMON DHOUL DJINN DOBBY ETHOS FLING GEIST GHOST GORIC GUACA GUSTO HAUNT HEART HOLDA HUACA JINNI LARVA MOXIE NUMEN PLUCK POWER PRETA RALPH SAINT SHADE SHRAB SPOOK SPUNK VERVE ASTRAL ASUANG BOTTOM BREATH CHULPA COURIL DAEMON ESPRIT FAINTS FLECHE FYLGJA GENIUS GINGER INWARD KOBOLD LESHEY METTLE MORALE ORISHA PAZAZZ PECKER PIZAZZ PNEUMA PYTHON SPRAWL SPRITE TAFFIA WRAITH ALCOHOL BRAVERY CONTROL CORDIAL COURAGE ENTRAIN EUDEMON KNOCKER MANITOU PISACHI PIZZAZZ PURUSHA RAPPIST SMEDDUM STOMACH CALVADOS ERDGEIST FAMILIAR FOLLETTO PHANTASM SPIRACLE SPIRITUS
(— DWELLING IN JEWEL) AZOTH
(— DWELLING IN MINES) KNOCKER
(— HAUNTING PRINTING HOUSES) RALPH
(— OF DEAD) CHINDI CHINDEE
(— OF DEATH) CHULPA
(— OF DECEASED) AKH
(— OF ENTERPRISE) ADVENTURE
(— OF FERTILITY) YAKSA YAKSHA YAKSHI
(— OF HOSTILITY) ANIMUS
(— OF LOYALTY) PIETAS
(— OF MAN) AKH
(— OF ONE WHO HAS MET VIOLENT DEATH) PISACHI
(— OF PHYSICAL HEART) AB
(— OF PRIESTHOOD) SACERDOTALISM
(— OF THE AGE) ZEITGEIST
(— OF THE AIR) SYLPH
(— OF TRAGEDY) COTHURN
(— OF UNBAPTIZED BABE) TARAN
(—S OF LOWER WORLD) INFERI
(—S OF THE DEAD) MANES
(— WHICH ACTUATES CUSTOMS) ETHOS
(ANCESTRAL —) ANITO KATCHINA
(ARDENT —) RAK RACK ARRACK
(ASTRAL —) AGIEL ASTRAL JOPHIEL UUCHATON
(AVENGING —) FURY ALECTO ALASTOR MEGAERA
(CHARACTERISTIC —) VIBE
(COMBATIVE —) SWORD
(DISEMBODIED —) KUEI KWEI SOUL GHOST LARVA SHADE ASUANG SPECTER SPECTRE
(DIVINE —) ISVARA ISHVARA
(EARTH —) ERDGEIST
(EFFULGENT —S) ARDORS
(EMANCIPATED —) MUKTATMA
(EVIL —) DEV DIV HAG IMP OKI BAKA BENG BOKO BOLL DEVA DUSE MARA OKEE ASURA BUGAN DAEVA DEMON DEVIL JUMBY OTKON DAITYA DIBBUK DYBBUK LILITH AHRIMAN BUGGANE CASZIEL INCUBUS KANAIMA RAKSHAS SHAITAN SHEITAN SKOOKUM WINDIGO ASMODEUS BAALPEOR BEELPEOR HOBOMOCO SUCCUBUS NIGHTMARE
(FAMILIAR —) FLY GENIUS HARPIER
(FEMALE —) DUFFY DUPPY DUSIO HOLDA UNDINE BANSHEE ATAENSIC BABAJAGA BELFAGOR BELFAZOR
(FIGHTING —) DEVIL
(FOREST —) MIMING
(FULL OF —) CRANK
(FULL OF —S) BRAG
(GOOD —) DEVA EUDEMON
(GOVERNING —) ANIMUS
(GUARDIAN —) ANGEL TOTEM FYLGJA NAGUAL
(HIGH —) GINGER COURAGE
(HIGH —S) CREST GAIETY HEYDAY ELATION
(HOSTILE —S) LEMURES
(HOUSEHOLD —S) LARES PENATES
(HUMAN —) JIVATMA
(IMPISH —) PO
(IMPURE —) FAINTS
(INDIAN —) MANITO
(IN VIGOROUS —S) FIERCE
(LOW —S) DUMP BLUES MEGRIM DISMALS
(MALEVOLENT —) BHUT GORIC LARVA
(MALICIOUS —) DOBBY
(MALIGNANT —) IMP KER GYRE DEMON
(MANLY —) SPLEEN
(MISCHIEVOUS —) KOBOLD TIKOLOSH
(MOUNTAIN —) RUBEZAHL
(MOVING —) SOUL
(MUSICAL —) BRIO
(NATURE —) NAT
(NIGHT —) TENEBRIO
(PARTY —) FACTION
(REFINED —) ELIXIR
(RENEWED —) REFRESHMENT
(RESOLUTE —) SPRAWL
(ROVING —) RAMPLER
(SEA —) TANGIE
(SENSED —) KARMA
(SOOTHSAYING —) PYTHON
(SUPERNATURAL —) FAMILIAR
(SYLVAN —) LESHY SYLVAN
(TRICKSY —) ARIEL
(TUTELARY —S) DIS LARES
(VITAL —) TUCK
(VOLATILE —) ESSENCE
(WATER —) ARIEL KELPY ONDINE UNDINE
(WICKED —) IMP THURSE
(PL.) GENII IGIGI DAUBER
(PREF.) PNEUMAT(O) PSYCH(O) THYM(O)
(SUFF.) THYMIA
SPIRITED BRAG FELL GOGO RACY TALL BEANY BIRKY CRANK EAGER FIERY FLUSH KEDGE KINKY LIFEY PEPPY PROUD SASSY SEEDY SMART SPICY VIVID AUDACE FIERCE GINGER LIVELY METTLE PLUCKY SKEIGH SPRUCE SPUNKY VIVACE ANIMATO DASHING FORWARD HUMMING NERVOUS PEPPERY SPIRITY DESIROUS FRAMPOLD GENEROUS PHRAMPEL SLASHING STOMACHY VASCULAR METTLESOME
SPIRITEDLY GAMELY
SPIRITLESS DEAD DOWF MEAN MEEK POOR TAME AMORT FAINT MILKY MUSTY SEEDY SOGGY VAPID ABJECT ANEMIC CRAVEN DREEPY FLASHY JEJUNE LEADEN MOPISH SODDEN SOFTLY WOODEN HILDING INSIPID LANGUID FECKLESS FLAGGING LISTLESS THEWLESS
SPIRITLESSLY DAVIELY
SPIRITLESSNESS LANGUOR
SPIRITLIKE ETHEREAL
SPIRITS LACE RAKI HOOCH MANES METHS FETTLE PECKER FEATHER LEMURES SAMSHOO WAIPIRO
SPIRITUAL ABOVE DEVOUT INWARD MISTLY GHOSTLY CHURCHLY INTERNAL NUMINOUS SUPERIOR PNEUMATIC
(— LEADER) ZADDIK
SPIRITUALISM SPOOKISM
SPIRITUALITY HEAVEN
SPIRITUALIZE REFINE
SPIRITUOUS HARD
SPIROCHETE BORRELIA
SPIT YEX FUFF RACK FROTH REACH SPAWL BROACH SPITTLE SANDSPIT SPITTING
(— AND POLISH) BULL
(— OF LAND) HOOK
(SUFF.) PTYSIS
SPITE ENVY ONDE DEPIT LIVOR PIQUE VENOM HATRED MALICE MAUGRE RANCOR SPLEEN DESPITE AMBITION
SPITEFUL MEAN CATTY NASTY NEBBY PETTY SNAKY ELVISH MALIGN SULLEN WANTON WICKED CATTISH ENVIOUS PEEVISH

SNAKISH VICIOUS WASPISH CANKERED KNAPPISH VENOMOUS
SPITFIRE CACAFOGO PEPPERBOX
(TYPE OF —) VOLCANO
SPITTING FUFF EMPTYSIS
SPITTING SNAKE RINGHALS
SPITTLE SPIT SPAWL SPUTUM SLOBBER
(PREF.) PTYAL(O)
SPITTLEBUG FROGHOPPER
SPITTOON GABOON PIGDAN SPITBOX CRACHOIR CUSPIDOR
SPIV RORTER
SPLAKE MENDIGO
SPLANCHNIC VISCERAL
SPLASH JAW LAP DASH GLOB GOUT JAUP LOSH LUSH SKIT SOSS SPAT WASH BLASH FLASH FLICK FLOOD FLOSH PLASH PLOUT QUASH SKIRP SLART SLASH SLOSH SLUSH SQUAT SWILK BEDASH DABBLE DOLLOP FLOUSE JABBLE LABBER PLATCH SLUNGE SOZZLE SPLOSH SPRENT SQUIRT PLOUTER SPATTER SPIRTLE SPLODGE SPLURGE SWATTER SPLAIRGE SPLATHER SPLATTER SPLOTHER SPLUTHER SPLUTTER
(— OF COLOR) GOUT
(SLIGHT —) GILP
SPLASHBOARD FENDER SPLASHER
SPLASHING SWASH FLASHY JABBLE DASHING SPATTER SPLUTTER SWASHING
SPLASHY BLASHY GLITZY SLOPPY SPRAWLY
SPLATTER DASH BLASH SPLAIRGE
SPLAY FLAN
SPLAYED FLEW FLUE
SPLAYFOOT FLATFOOT
SPLEEN IRE PIP BILE LIEN MELT MILT RHEUM MALICE STOMACH
(PREF.) LIEN(O) SPLEN(I)(O)
(SUFF.) SPLENIA
SPLEENY PEEVISH
SPLENDID GAY BRAW FINE NEAT RIAL BRAVE GRAND JOLLY NOBLE PROUD REGAL ROYAL SHEEN SHOWY STOUT TOUGH WALLY WLONK CANDID COSTLY SIGHTY SOLEMN SPIFFY SUPERB ELEGANT GALLANT SHINING SUBLIME TEARING BARONIAL CHAMPION CLINKING COLOSSAL GLORIOUS GORGEOUS MAJESTIC ORGULOUS RATTLING SLASHING SPANKING STUNNING TERRIFIC
(CHEAPLY —) TINNY
SPLENDIDLY FINE FINELY SPROWSY
SPLENDOR SUN UMA GITE LUXE POMP BLAZE ECLAT GLARE GLEAM GLORY SHEEN SHINE FULGOR LUSTER LUSTRE PARADE RUFFLE CLARITY DISPLAY JOLLITY PANACHE GRANDEUR RADIANCE SUMPTURE
SPLENETIC SULLEN VAPORY PEEVISH
SPLENIC LIENAL
SPLICE FOOT JOIN SCAB PIECE SCARE SKELB CROTCH PIECEN SPLICING
SPLICER STRAPPER
SPLINE FIN SLAT FEATHER
SPLINT SCOB FANON MATCH SPELK SPELL TASSE SPLENT THOMAS CALIPER SPLINTER
(— FOR FRACTURE) JUNK
SPLINTER BROOM BURST PURSE SHAKE SHIDE SHIVE SKELB SKELF SLICE SPAIL SPALE SPALL SPALT SPEEL SPELK SPELL SPILE SPILL SPLIT SPOON SLIVER SPLEET SPLINT FLINDER SHATTER SLITHER SPLITTER
SPLINTERY SKELVY
SPLINTWOOD ALBURNUM
SPLIT AX AXE CUT RIT BUCK CHAP CONE DUNT GAIG MALL MAUL RASH REND RENT RIFT RIVE SKAG SLAT TEAR BLAST BREAK BURST CHECK CHINE LEAVE SHAKE SHEAR SKIVE SLENT SLIVE SMASH SPALD SPALL SPLAT CLEAVE CLOVEN CREASE DEPART DIVIDE FLAGGY FLERRY GOAWAY SCHISM SPRING SUNDER BIVALVE SHATTER SLITHER CREVASSE SCISSION SCISSURE SPLINTER
(— FISH) SCROD
(— IN BOWLING) BEDPOSTS
(— OFF) SPALL SPAWL SCREEVED
(— TICKET) SCRATCH
(KIND OF —) STOCK
(PREF.) SCHISTO SCHIZ(O)
SPLITTERMAN BOLTER
SPLITTING FLAGGY FISSION SCISSION
(— OF PERSONALITY) DISSOCIATION
(— OF WORD) TMESIS
(READILY —) SCISSILE
(PL.) FILMS
(SUFF.) RHEXIS RRHEXIS
SPLOTCH DAB BLOB DASH HALO SPOT FLICK SMUDGE SPECKLE SPLATCH SPLURGE
SPLURGE BINGE SPEND SPRAY SPREE SPLASH
SPLUTTER FUFF GLUTTER SPATTER SPUTTER SPLOTHER
SPODOPTERA LAPHYGMA
SPODUMENE KUNZITE TRIPHANE
SPOIL MAR MUX ROT BLOT BOOT COOK DAZE FANG FOIL FRAB GAIN KILL MANK PELF PREY ADDLE BITCH BLEND BLUNK BOOTY BOTCH CROSS DECAY LOUSE QUAIL QUEER SHEND SPILL STAIN STRIP TOUCH TRASH WALLY BOODLE BUGGER CODDLE COOPER CORPSE COSSET CURDLE DEFACE DEFORM FORAGE INJURE MANGLE PERISH RAVAGE TIDDLE BAUCHLE BEDEVIL BLEMISH CONNACH CORRUMP CORRUPT ESTREPE INDULGE MULLOCK PILLAGE PLUNDER SPOLIUM TARNISH VIOLATE BANKRUPT CONFOUND DISGRACE MISGUIDE SPOLIATE
(— BY SOAKING) RET RAIT RATE
SPOILED BAD BLOWN DAZED MUSTY CADISH STICKIT BRATTISH
(— BY USE) OVERWORN
(EASILY —) GINGER
SPOILER HARROWER
SPOILERS (AUTHOR OF —) BEACH
(CHARACTER IN —) ROY BILL HELEN CHERRY DEXTRY STRUVE CHESTER MALOTTE MCNAMARA STILLMAN GLENISTER
SPOILFIVE MAW
SPOILS BAG LOOT SKIN SWAG BOOTY FORAY SPOLIA PILLAGE PLUNDER PICKINGS
SPOILSPORT NARK PILL GRINCH LETGAME
SPOILT MARDY
SPOKE RUNG QUOTH SPACK SPAKE LOWDER SPONDIL SPONDYL
(— OF WHEEL) RADIUS
SPOKEN ORAL SAID VERBAL VOICED
SPOKESMAN MOUTH HERALD PROPHET SPEAKER TRUMPET MOUTHPIECE
(— OF DEITY) PROPHET
SPOKEWISE RADIAL
SPOLIATION REIF SPOIL RAPINE PILLAGE PLUNDER SPOILING
SPONGE BOT FORM MUMP POLE SILK SORN SWAB ASCON CADGE GRASS LUFFA SCAFF SHARK SHIRK SHOOL SYCON ASCULA BUMMER COSHER LEUCON LOOFAH MALKIN MOPPET RHAGON ROLLER YELLOW BADIAGA BLEEDER GELFOAM RADIATE SCOURER SCRUNGE SYCONID ZIMOCCA DEADBEAT FREELOAD HARDHEAD HEDGEHOG MANDRUKA OLYNTHUS REDBEARD SCROUNGE SILICEAN SPHERIDA SUBERITE ZOOPHYTE PORIFERAN
(TAKE UP LIKE A —) SORB
(YOUNG —) SEEDLING
(SUFF.) AENE
SPONGER BOT BUM TRAMP BUMMER CADGER SPONGE SCAMBLER SMOOTHER
SPONGINESS FOZINESS
SPONGING TRENCHER
SPONGY FOZY FUZZY POACHY QUAGGY FUNGOUS BIBULOUS
SPONSOR COACH GOSSIP SURETY ENDORSE WITNESS
(— AT BAPTISM) HEAVE
SPONSORSHIP EGIS AEGIS
SPONTANEOUS FREE CARELESS FREEWILL UNBIDDEN UNTAUGHT VOLUNTARY
SPONTANEOUSLY KINDLY SELFLY
SPOOF PUTON
SPOOK GYRE GHOST HAUNT SCARE
SPOOL COB COP PIRN REEL QUILL SPILL SPULE TWEEL TWILL BOBBIN BROACH CHEESE COPPIN CARRIER
(— FOR NETS) GURDY
(HERALDIC —) TRUNDLE
SPOON HORN NECK CUTTY LABIS SHELL COCHLEA JUMBLER MUDDLER SKIMMER SPINNER STIRRER BARSPOON COCHLEAR GOBSTICK
(EUCHARISTIC —) LABIS
(FISHING —) TROLL
(FLATTENED —) SPATULA
(LONG-HANDLED —) LADLE
(SKIMMING —) LINGEL SKIMMER
(SNUFF —) PEN
(PREF.) COCHLEARI LIGUL(I)
SPOONBILL AJAJA SPOONY POPELER CICONIID
(PREF.) PLATALEI
SPOONERISM MARROWSKY
SPOONFUL COCHLEARE
SPOON-SHAPED COCHLEAR SPATULAR
SPOONY SILLY FOOLISH
SPOOR SIGN SPUR PISTE
SPORADIC POPPING ISOLATED
SPORANGIUM THECA OOTHECA
SPORE CYST SEED SPORID TELIUM AGAMETE AKINETE BISPORE ISOLANT ISOLATE OOSPORE SEEDLET SPORULE SWARMER CONIDIUM EXOSPORE GONIDIUM PROPAGULE
(— SAC) ASCI ASCUS
SPORES
(PREF.) CONI(DI)
SPOROCYST ZOOCYST SPOROSAC
SPORT FUN GIG KID MUM RIE RUX SEE TOY ALSO GAME GAUD GLEE JEST JOKE LAKE LARK PLAY PLOY RAGE TAIT BOURD BREAK DALLY DROLL FREAK MIRTH FROLIC LAUGHS POPJOY RACING SHIKAR SKIING BOATING CAMOGIE DISPORT DUCKING FOWLING MARLOCK PASTIME ROLLICK ROUNDER SAILING SPANIEL FALCONRY PLEASURE SKYDIVING MOUNTAINEERING
(— OF HAWKING) RIVER
(BOISTEROUS —) HIJINKS
(JAPANESE —) KENDO AIKIDO
(ONE-ON-ONE) EPEE
(ROUGH —) ROMP
(WATER —S) NAUTICS AQUATICS
(WINTER —) SKIJORING
(PREF.) LUDI
SPORTING VARMINT SPORTIVE
SPORTIVE GAY TAIT LARKY MERRY FRISKY JOCUND LIVELY LUSORY TOYFUL TOYING WANTON COLTISH FESTIVE GAMEFUL JESTING JOCULAR PLAYFUL TOYSOME TRICKSY WAGGISH FROLICKY GAMESOME PLAYSOME PLEASANT SPORTFUL
SPORTIVENESS HELL KNAVERY
SPORTS (— OFFICIAL) REF ZEBRA REFEREE
SPORTSMAN SPORT ATHLETE SHIKARI
SPORTSMANLIKE CLEAN SPORTY
SPORTY FLASH RORTY FLASHY RAKISH
SPORULE GRANULE
SPOT BIT DAB PIP SEE WEM BLOT BLUR CHUB DIRT DRAB FLAW GALL MAIL MOIL MOLE PLOT SCAM SITE SKIP SLUR SMUT SOIL SPAT TICK AMPER BLACK CLOUD FLECK GARLE GOODY GUTTA HATCH JIMMY MACLE PATCH PLACE PLECK POINT ROACH SMEAR SPLAT STAIN SULLY TACHE

TAINT WHERE BLANCH BLOTCH DAPPLE FOGDOG GERATE LOCALE MACULE MAZUCA MOTTLE SMUDGE SMUTCH SPLECK STIGMA BLEMISH CHARBON CHECKER FLECKER FRECKLE GUTTULA MASOOKA OCELLUS OLDWIFE SMATTER SMITTER SPATTER SPECKLE SPLOTCH SPOTTLE STATION STIPPLE TERRAIN FENESTRA LOCALITY MACULATE PUNCTULE SPARKLET SPRINKLE
(— A SHIELD) GERATE
(— IN CLOTH) YAW
(— IN MARBLE) TERRACE
(— IN MINERAL) MACLE
(— IN PAPER) SHINER
(— IN SAW BLADE) BLOB
(— IN STEEL) STAR
(— IN WOOD) WEM
(— IN YARN) MOTE
(— OF INK) MONK
(— OF PAINT) DAUB
(— OF QUICKSAND) SUCKHOLE
(— ON CAT) BUTTON
(— ON CAT'S FACE) LAVALIER
(— ON EGG) EYE
(— ON FINGERNAIL) GIFT
(— ON FOREHEAD) TILAK TILAKA
(— ON HAWK) GOUT
(— ON HORSE) RACE SNIP STAR RACHE
(— ON HORSE'S TOOTH) CHARBON
(— ON INSECT WINGS) BULLA
(— ON MOTH'S WINGS) FENESTRA
(— ON PLAYING CARD) PIP
(— ON SUN) FACULA GRANULE SUNSPOT
(—S IN BOOKS) FOXING
(— WITH MIST) ATOMIZE
(BARREN —) GALL
(BLIND —) SCOTOMA SCOTOSIS
(BROWN —) SPRAIN SPRAING
(CRUSTY —) SCAB
(ESSENTIAL —) EYE
(EYELIKE — ON PEACOCK) OCELLUS
(FERTILE —) OASIS
(FIRM — IN BOG) HAG
(GREEN — IN VALLEY) HAW
(HALLOWED —) BETHEL
(INFLAMED —) AMPER
(LEAF —) TIKKA BLACKARM
(LIVER —S) CHLOASMA
(LIVID —) TOKEN
(LOW —) DIP SWAMP HOLLOW
(MARSHY —) SPEW SPUE
(PAINFUL —) SORE
(PLAGUE —) TOKEN
(RED —) FLEABITE
(RETIRED —) SHADE
(ROUGH — IN WOVEN GOODS) FAG
(ROUND —) BLOB
(SCABBY —) SCALD
(SECLUDED —) ALCOVE CLOISTER
(SHADY —) SWALE
(SKIN —) MOLE BLISTER FRECKLE LENTIGO PETECHIA
(SMALL —) DOT PLECK STIGMA LUNULET SPARKLET
(SOILED —) SLOP
(SORE —) BUBU BOTCH
(SPARKLING —) SPANGLE
(SWAMPY —) FLAM
(TIGHT —) JAM JACKPOT
(WEAK —) GALL HOLE CHINK NERVE
(WORN —) FRAY FRET
(PL.) MOONING
(PREF.) MACUL(I)(O) SPIL(O)
SPOTLESS FAIR PURE WEMLESS INNOCENT
SPOTLIGHT ARC SPOT DEUCE
SPOTTED PIED MARLY SCOVY SHELD CALICO FIGGED HAWKED MACLED MAILED MARLED MIRLED PARDED SPOTTY TICKED BRACKET BROOKED FINCHED GUTTATE MOTTLED PARDINE PIEBALD PINTADO SPARKED SPECKED SPECKLY TIGROID FRECKLED LITURATE MACULOSE SPECKLED STIPPLED
(SUFF.) MACULATE
SPOTTED EAGLE RAY MILLER OBISPO
SPOTTED FLYCATCHER COBWEB RAFTER WALLBIRD
SPOTTED GUM EUCALYPT
SPOTTED JEWFISH GUASA
SPOTTED SANDPIPER TIPUP TILTUP CREEKER TIPTAIL PEETWEET
SPOTTED SPURGE DOVEWEED
SPOTTED WINTERGREEN RATSBANE
SPOTTED WOODPECKER PICUS WITWALL
SPOTTER DOTTER
SPOTTING (— OF LEAVES) HELIOSIS
SPOTTY MEALY PATCHY PLATTY SCABBY SPOTTED
SPOUSE EX FERE MAKE WIFE BRIDE MATCH PARTY FELLOW MARROW CONSORT ESPOUSE HUSBAND
SPOUT JET LIP BEAK DALE GEAT GUSH NOSE SHOE ORATE SPILE SPUME SPURT NOZZLE RIGGOT SPLOIT SPROUT STRONE STROUP BUBBLER FOUNTAIN GARGOYLE
(RAIN —) RONE
SPOUTER VAPORER
(MEDITERRANEAN —) ETNA
SPOUTING BLOW SALIENT
SPRAG PROP TRAILER
SPRAGGER SCOTCHER
SPRAIN RICK CHINK STAVE THRAW THROW WRAMP WREST WRICK STRAIN WRENCH STREMMA
SPRAT SMY BLAY BRIT BRITT SPRET SPRIT GARVIE ALFIONE GARVOCK BRISLING
(—S CAUGHT EARLY IN SEASON) DROVE
SPRAWL LOLL TAVE SPURL SCRAWL GRABBLE SCAMBLE SPARTLE SPELDER SCRAMBLE SPRADDLE SPRANGLE STRADDLE
SPRAWLING SPRANGLY
SPRAY FOG HOSE SCUD SPRY STEW SPREE STOUR SWISH TRAIL TWIST WATER HONEST SHOWER SPARGE SPLASH SPRANG SPRITZ CURTAIN SPAIRGE SYRINGE INHALANT SPRANGLE
(— BEHIND MOTORBOAT) ROOSTERTAIL
(— FROM SMALL WAVES) LIPPER
(— MASH) SPARGE
(— OF GEMS) AIGRETTE
(REDUCE TO —) NEBULIZE
SPREAD BED FAN LAY RUN COAT DRAW FLUE SPAN TEER TELD TUCK VEIN WALK APPLY CLEAM CREEP FLARE KILIM PASTE SCALE SLICE SPEND SPLAT SPLAY STALK STREW WIDEN BUTTER EXTEND FLANGE LARDER LAYOUT MANTLE SETOUT THRUST UNFOLD UNFURL BROADEN CANVASS DIFFUSE DISPLAY DISTEND EXPANSE EXPLAIN FEATHER OPENING SCATTER SLATHER STRETCH DIASPORA DISPENSE DISPERSE HUMIFUSE INCREASE MULTIPLY SPLATHER STRAGGLE
(— ABROAD) TOOT BLAZE DELATE SPRING DIVULGE EMANATE
(— APART) GAPE
(— AS GOSSIP) BUZZ
(— BY REPORT) BLOW NOISE NORATE
(— DEFAMATION) LIBEL
(— FOR DRYING) TED
(— INTO) INVADE
(— LIKE GRAIN) FLOOR
(— NEWS) HORN
(— ON THICK) COUCH SLATHER
(— OUT) FAN FLOW OPEN ROLL SPAN ASPAR BREDE SPLAT SPLAY SPRAY EXPAND FLANGE FRINGE MANTLE OUTLAY SPRAWL UNLOCK DIFFUSE DISPAND DISTENT EXPLAIN FEATHER DIFFUSED SPRADDLE SPRANGLE STRAGGLY
(— OUTWARD) FLARE
(— OVER) LAP DASH COVER SUFFUSE
(— PAINT) KNIFE
(— RAPIDLY) MUSHROOM
(— RUMORS) WHISPER
(— SECRETLY) BUZZ
(— THE NEWS) BRUIT
(— THE WORD) TELL
(— THINLY) BRAY DRIVE TOUCH SCANTY
(— TO) CATCH
(— TO THE WIND) SET
(— WIDE) SPELD SPELDER
(EVENLY —) SUANT
(TAPESTRY-WOVEN —) KILIM
(PREF.) STRATO
(SUFF.) CHORE
SPREADER PLOW PLOUGH SANDER
(HAY —) TEDDER
SPREADING FLAN BUSHY FLANGE PATENT ASPREAD DIFFUSE FLARING SPRAYEY PATULENT PATULOUS SPRANGLY
(— OF LIGHT) HALATION
(— RAPIDLY) RUNNING
(NOT —) ERECT
(SLOW —) CREEPAGE
SPREE BAT BUM JAG BLOW BUST GELL LARK RANT SOAK TEAR TIME TOOT BEANO BINGE BOOZE BURST DRINK DRUNK SOUSE SPRAY BENDER BUSTER HOORAY HURRAH JUNKET RANDAN RANTAN RAZZLE SPLORE BLOWOFF JAMBOREE WINGDING
SPRIG POINT
(—S FOR MOURNING) CYPRESS
SPRIGGER STRIPPER
SPRIGHTLINESS GAIETY AIRINESS ALACRITY BUOYANCY VIVACITY
SPRIGHTLY GAY TID AIRY GNIB PERT WARM ALIVE BRISK CANTY CRISP DESTO MERRY PERKY QUICK ALEGER BLITHE BREEZY JAUNTY LIVELY SPANKY SPRACK WIMBLE CHIPPER DELIVER JOCULAR SPARKLY LIFESOME PLEASANT
SPRING EN AIN BUG EYE FLY HOP JET OJO URN VER WAX BATH BOLT BOUT BUCK BUNT DART FLOW FONT GEON HAIR HEAD JUMP KELD LEAP PERT RISE SEEP SKIP SOAK STEM URNA WALM WARE WELL WIND YOAR ARISE BOUND DANCE FLIRT FOUNT FRESH GIHON GLENT GRASS ISSUE LYMPH PRIME QUELL SALLY SOURD SPEND SPOUT START STEND SURGE THROW VAULT BOUNCE CHARCO DERIVE GAMBOL GEYSER JUMPER LOCKET ORIGIN PIRENE RESORT RESULT SILOAM SOURCE SPRINT VENERO BUDTIME EMANATE ESTUARY FLOUNCE GAMBADO PROCEED REBOUND WRAPPER BACKSTAY BANDUSIA CASTALIA FOUNTAIN SPANGHEW ORIGINATE PRINTEMPS
(— AWKWARDLY) KEVEL
(— BACK) RECOIL RESULT RETORT REBOUND
(— DOWN) ALIGHT
(— FORWARD) LAUNCH
(— FROM) DESCEND
(— IN MARSH) WELLHEAD
(— INTO BEING) AWAKEN
(— OF HORSE) GAMBADO
(— OF THE YEAR) VER VOAR
(— ON SHEARS) BACKSTAY
(— SEASON) APRIL GRASS BUDTIME
(— SUDDENLY) FLY BOUNCE
(— TO FASTEN NECKLACE) LOCKET
(— UP) ARISE SHOOT SPROUT BURGEON UPSPRING
(BOILING —) TUBIG
(CARRIAGE —) ROBBIN
(ERUPTIVE —) WALM GEYSER
(FROM A —) FONTAL
(GUSHING —) CHARCO
(HOT —) SPRUDEL
(INTERMITTENT —) NAILBOURN
(INTERMITTENT —S) GIPSIES GYPSIES
(LAND —) LAVANT
(MECHANICAL —) RESORT RESSORT
(MINERAL —) SPA BALNEARY
(SALT —) LICK SALINE
(WARM —S) THERMAE
(WATCH —) SLEEVE
(PREF.) CREN(O) CROUNO PEGO
(SUFF.) CRENE
SPRING BEAUTY LETTUCE
SPRINGBOARD BATULE TREMPLIN
SPRINGBOK GAZELLE SPRINGER
SPRING CHAPLET JAMMER
SPRINGE TRAP NOOSE SNARE
SPRINGILY BOUNCILY SPONGILY
SPRINGINESS GIVE LIFE

SPRINGING LAUNCH SALIENT
(— BACK) RESULT ELASTIC
(— FROM STEPS) GRADY
SPRINGLIKE VERNAL
SPRING ORANGE STYRAX
SPRINGTAIL PODURA FURCULA PODURID SKIPTAIL
SPRINGTIME VER WARE GERMINAL
SPRINGY WHIPPY ELASTIC FLEXIBLE
SPRINKLE ASH DAG DEG BLOW DAMP DUST SHED SPIT FLASH SHAKE SPURT WATER BEDROP DABBLE POUNCE SPARGE SPRENT SPRINK SQUIRT ARROUSE ASPERGE ASPERSE DRIZZLE RANTIZE SCATTER SKINKLE SKITTER SPAIRGE SPARKLE SPARPLE SPATTER SPATTLE SPERPLE SPURTLE DISPUNGE INTERSOW SPITTING SPRINGLE STRINKLE
(— IN BAPTISM) RANTIZE
(— OF RAIN) SPIT
(— OF SNOW) SCOWDERING SCOUTHERING
(— SEED) SPRAIN
(— TOBACCO) BLOW
(— WITH FLOUR) DREDGE
(— WITH POWDER) DUST
(— WITH SALT) CORN
(— WITH SAND) SAND
SPRINKLED SEEDED SPRENT
(— OVER) BESPRENT
SPRINKLER SPARGER SPRAYER WATERER DAMPENER STRINKLE
(HOLY WATER —) HYSSOP
SPRINKLES JIMMIES
SPRINKLING SEME LACING SPARGE STRANK RANTISM STIPPLE STOURING
(— OF PEOPLE) SALT
SPRINT DASH RACE BICKER SPRENT SPRUNT
SPRITE ELF HOB IMP PUG PIXY PUCK ARIEL BUCCA DOBBY FAIRY HOLDA PIXIE GOBLIN PILWIZ SPIRIT SPOORN UMBRIEL COLTPIXY GLAISTIG WATERMAN
(WATER —) NIX NECK NIXIE NICKER
SPRITELY WIMBLE
SPROCKET WHELP
SPROUT BUD LAD PUT BROD CHIT CHUN CION DRAW TOOT CATCH CHICK SCUTE SHOOT SPEAR SPIRE SPRIT SPURT BRAIRD GERMEN RATOON SIRING STOVEN TELLER TILLER BURGEON COPPICE SPURTER TENDRON BOURGEON PULLULATE
(— OF BARLEY) TAIL
(FIRST —S) BREER BRAIRD BREIRD
(STUMP —) TILLER
(PREF.) BLAST(O) CLAD(O) CYM(I)(O)
(SUFF.) BLAST(IC)(Y) CLADOUS SPERM(A)(AE)(AL)(IA)(IC)(OUS)(UM)(Y)
SPRUCE GIM DEFT JIMP NEAT POSH SMUG SPRY TRIG TRIM BRISK COMPT CRISP DINKY FRESH JEMMY JIMMY NATTY NIFTY SLICK SMART SMIRK SPIFF SPRIG DAPPER PICKED SPONGE SPRUNT SPRUSH FINICAL FOPPISH SMARTEN SMICKER SPRUNNY EPINETTE SPIFFING TITIVATE
(KIND OF —) SITKA
(TRIMMED —) LOBSTICK
SPRUE RUNNER PSILOSIS
SPRUER GATER
SPRY AGILE BRISK QUICK NIMBLE BOBBISH
SPUD SPADE TATER BARKER PADDLE POTATO WEEDER SPUDDER
SPUME EST BEES FOAM FROTH YEAST
SPUNK GUTS GETUP PLUCK SPRAWL SMEDDUM GUMPTION
SPUNKY GAME GUTSY
SPUR ARM GAD GIG EDGE GAFF GOAD KNAG MOVE STUD TANG ARETE DRIVE PRICK PRONG ROWEL SPICA SPURN BROACH CALCAR DIGGER EXCITE FILLIP FOMENT GAFFLE GRIFFE INCITE MOTIVE OFFSET RIPPON SICKLE SPERON WEAPON BICYCLE GABLOCK INCITER LORMERY SCRATCH COCKSPUR GAVELOCK
(— OF BIRDS) SPICA
(— OF COCK) HEEL
(— OF GAMECOCK) GAFF
(— ON HORSESHOE) CALK
(—S OF COCK) WEAPON
(— TO ACTION) GOOSE
(PART OF —) BAND CHAIN ROWEL BUTTON
(PREF.) CALCARI
SPURGE BALSAM INTISY RICINUS SUNWEED CATEPUCE DOVEWEED FLUXWEED MILKBUSH MILKWEED TITHYMAL WARTWEED WARTWORT POINSETTIA
SPURIOUS BAD DOG TIN FAKE SHAM BOGUS FUNNY PHONY QUEER SHICE SNIDE NOTHAL PSEUDO BASTARD NOTHOUS POSTICHE PINCHBECK SYNDIETIC
(PREF.) NOTH(O) PSEUD(O)
SPURN FOOT TACK REPEL SCORN REFUSE REJECT CONSPUE CONTEMN DECLINE DESPISE DISDAIN
SPURRY YARR FRANK COWQUAKE SANDWEED
SPURT JET GILP GIRD GOUT JAUP SPAR SPIN BURST CHIRT FLASH PULSE SALLY SPOUT GEYSER RANDOM SPLURT SPRING SPROUT SQUIRT SPATTER
SPUTTER SPIT FIZZLE SOTTER SPATTER SPLUTTER
SPUTUM SPIT
SPY FLY PRY ESPY MOLE NARK NOSE STAG TOOT TOUT WAIT WORM AGENT CALEB LOWER NINJA PERDU PLANT SCOUT SNEAP SPIAL SPION SPOOK WATCH BEAGLE BEHOLD DESCRY GAYCAT MOUTON PEEPER PERDUE SEARCH SHADOW SPIRAL TOUTER WAITER EXAMINE LURCHER OTACUST SMELLER SPOTTER WATCHER DISCOVER EMISSARY HIRCARRA MOUCHARD
(— ON RACEHORSES) TOUT
(— UPON) LAY
(AUTHOR OF —) COOPER
(BIBLICAL —) CALEB
(CHARACTER IN —) JACK BIRCH HENRY SARAH CAESAR HARPER HARVEY LAWTON PEYTON FRANCES WHARTON ISABELLA JEANETTE THOMPSON DUNWOODIE SINGLETON WELLEMERE
(PLANTED —) STOOGE
(POLICE —) SETTER
SPYBOAT VEDET VEDETTE
SQUAB PIPER SQUABBY SQUEAKER SQUEALER SQUILGEE
SQUABBLE MUSS TIFF BRAWL SCRAP BICKER HASSLE JANGLE SQUALL BOBBERY BRABBLE BRANGLE CONTEND PRABBLE QUARREL SWABBLE
SQUAD CREW DECURY TWENTY PLATOON
(— OF DETECTIVES) HOMICIDE
SQUADRON BLUE SOTNIA SQUADER
(— OF AIRCRAFT) ESCADRILLE
(CAVALRY —) RESSALAH
(THREE —S) WING
SQUALID DINGY DIRTY MANGY NASTY SEEDY FILTHY FROWZY SCUZZY SHODDY SLEAZO SLEAZY SORDID SCABROUS SLOTTERY
SQUALL DROW FRET GUST MEWL ROAR SCAT WAUL BARAT FRESH PERRY SKELP BAYAMO FLURRY SQUAWK BORASCA SUMATRA TORNADO BLIZZARD BORASQUE CHUBASCO
SQUALOR DIRT
SQUAMA ALULA TEGULA
SQUANDER SOT BLOW BLUE BURN GAME LASH WARE SPEND SPILL SPORT WASTE BEZZLE LAVISH MAFFLE MUDDLE PADDLE PALTER PERISH PLUNGE TIPPLE BRANGLE CONSUME DEBAUCH DEBOISE DISPEND PROFUSE SCAMBLE SCATTER SKITTLE SLATHER SWATTER EMBEZZLE MISSPEND SQUATTER
SQUANDERER PRODIGAL
SQUANDERING WASTEFUL
(UNRESTRAINED —) RIOT
SQUARE FIX EDGE EVEN FOUR FULL LAME NERD NURD POST QUAD SUIT AGREE CHECK CROSS FRAME HUNKY NERDY PLACE PLAIN PLAZA SUPER BLOCKY DINKUM ISAGON MICKEY PIAZZA QUARRY ZENZIC ZOCALO CARREAU CHECKER COMMONS EMERALD UPRIGHT QUADRANT QUADRATE SQUADRON TETRAGON
(— A STONE) PITCH
(— FOR BOWLING SCORE) FRAME
(— OF CANVAS) SKATE
(— OF CLOTH) PANE
(— OF DOUGH) KNISH
(— OFF) BUTT
(— OF FRAMING) PAN
(— OF GLASS) QUARREL
(— OF LINEN) PALL
(— OF TARTAN) SET SETT
(— OF TURF) DIVOT QUADREL
(— ON BILLIARD TABLE) CROTCH
(— ON CHESSBOARD) HOUSE POINT
(BUILDINGS FORMING —) INSULA
(CARPENTER'S —) NORMA MITER
(CENTER — IN GAME) TAC
(CHURCH —) PARVIS
(FROM — ONE) ANEW
(KIND OF —) PUNNETT
(LINEN —) SUDARIUM
(NOT —) HEP HIP
(ONE-MILE —) SECTION
(PATTERN OF —S) DAMIER
(WOVEN —) SINKER
(PREF.) QUADR(ATO)(I)(U)
SQUARED HEWN QUARTO SQUARE
SQUARE DANCE TUCKER
SQUARE-DEALING WHITE
SQUARELY BUNG FAIR FULL FLUSH SPANG FAIRLY DIRECTLY SMACKDAB
(— AND SHARPLY) SMACK
SQUARISH BOXY
SQUASH PEPO QUAT GOURD SQUAB CASHAW CUCURB CUSHAW MARROW SIMNEL SQUISH SQUUSH TURBAN CYMLING HUBBARD PUMPKIN CUCURBIT CYMBLING PEPONIUM ZUCCHINI
SQUASH BUG STINKBUG
SQUASHY SWASHY SQUUSHY
SQUAT QUAT RUCK STUB SWAT SWOT COWER DUMPY FUBSY HUNCH PUDGY SQUAB FODGEL HUNKER HURKLE QUATCH STOCKY STUBBY SQUATTY TAPPISH SQUATTLE THICKSET
SQUATINA RHINA
SQUATTER NESTER BYWONER
SQUAW JACK WEBB HOUND WENCH MAHALA SQUARK
SQUAWBUSH SHOVAL
SQUAWFISH CHUB BOXHEAD BIGMOUTH CHAPPAUL
SQUAWK SCRAWK SQUALL SQUARK SQUAWL COMPLAIN
SQUAWROOT CLAPWORT ELOTILLO
SQUEAK GIKE PEEP WEAK CHEEP CHIRK QUEAK SCRAWK SCROOP SQUEAL
SQUEAKING SCRANNEL
SQUEAKY CREAKY
SQUEAL PIP RAT FINK HOWL SING SWEEL SCREAK TATTLE WHISTLE
SQUEALER FINK CANARY
SQUEAMISH HELO NICE NAISH PAWKY PENSY DAINTY DAUNCH PENCEY QUAINT QUEASY SPICED TICKLE WAIRCH WAMBLY FINICAL MAWKISH WEARISH NAUSEOUS OVERNICE
SQUEAMISHNESS NICETY DISGUST MALAISE DELICACY
SQUEEZE EKE HUG JAM NIP CLAM MULL MURE VISE ZEST BIRSE BUNCH CHIRT CREEM CROWD CRUSH PINCH PRESS SQUAB SQUAT WRING GRUDGE QUEASE SCRUMP SCRUZE SQUASH STRAIN THRIMP THRING THRONG TWEEZE

TWITCH SCRINGE SCROOGE SCROUGE SCRUNCH SCRUNGE SQUEEGE SQUINCH COMPRESS CONTRACT PRESSURE SHOEHORN THRIMBLE THRUMBLE
(— FROM) SPONGE
(— IN) FUDGE
(— INTO) THRIMBLE
(— MONEY FROM) SWEAT
(— OUT) PINCH STRAIN
(ECONOMIC —) CRUNCH
(PREF.) PRESSI
SQUEEZED STRETTA STRETTO
SQUEEZER REAMER ALLIGATOR
SQUELCH QUELCH SQUASH SQUISH SQUIDGE SLAPDOWN
SQUELCHER BLIZZARD
SQUETEAGUE DRUM DRUMMER SQUETEE BLUEFISH CHICKWIT WEAKFISH
SQUIB MOTE SKIT FILLER EXPLODER
SQUID PLUG CALAMARI CALAMARY
SQUIFFED DRUNK BLOTTO STONED
SQUIGGLE SCRIGGLE
SQUILL SCILLA SLANGKOP
(PREF.) SCILLI
SQUINT AWRY GLEE GLEG SKEN SKEW BAGGE GLENT GLEDGE GOGGLE SHEYLE SKELLY SQUINCH SQUINNY STRABISM STRABISMUS
SQUINT-EYED GLEE GLEED
SQUINTING LOUCHE
SQUIRE SWAIN DONZEL JUNKER TIMIAS ARMIGER ESQUIRE SQUIRET YOUNKER HENCHMAN SCUTIGER SERVITOR SQUARSON SQUIREEN
SQUIRM CURL WIND TWINE WRING WRITHE WRESTLE WRIGGLE SCRIGGLE SQUIGGLE
SQUIRREL BUN CON BUNT LEAD SCUG BUNNY XERUS BOOMER CHIPPY GOPHER RODENT TAGUAN ARDILLA SCHILLU SCIURID CHIPMUNK EGGEATER GRAYBACK JELERANG RATATOSK CHICKAREE
(— SKIN) VAIR
(FLYING —) TUAN TAGUAN ASSAPAN
(PREF.) SCIURO
SQUIRRELFISH ALAIHI MARIAN MOJARRA SERRANO SOLDIER SANDFISH WELSHMAN
SQUIRREL MONKEY TITI SAIMIRI TAMARIN
SQUIRREL SHREW TANA TUPAIA PENTAIL
SQUIRT CHIRT SCOOT SKITE SLIRT SPIRT SPOUT SPURT SQUIB SQUIT SPLOIT SPRENT SPRITZ SCOOTER SQUITTER
SRI BWANA SAHIB

SRI LANKA
CAPITAL: COLOMBO
COIN: CENT RUPEE
FORMER NAME: CEYLON
GULF: MANNAR
LANGUAGE: SINHALA
MEASURE: PARA PARAH AMUNAM PARRAH
POINT: PEDRO
STRAIT: PALK
TOWN: GALLE KANDY JAFFNA MANNAR MATARA BADULLA COLOMBO PUTTALAM
TREE: HORA PALU

S-SHAPED
(PREF.) SIGMO SIGMOID(O)
ST.CROIX (NATIVE OF —) CRUZAN
STAB DAB DAG JAB JAG JOB DIRK GORE PINK POKE PROB SHIV STOB STOG STUG YERK CHIVE KNIFE POACH PRICK PRONG STICK STOKE BROACH DAGGER PIERCE POUNCE SLIVER STITCH THRUST BAYONET STAGGER PRICKADO STILETTO STOCCADO STOCCATA
(— IN MIDBREAST) SLOT
STABBING THORNY JABBING PUNGENT STICKING
(SUFF.) NYXIS
STABILITY POISE FIXURE BALANCE SADNESS FIRMNESS SECURITY CONSTANCY
STABILIZE FIX SET EVEN TRIM POISE SCHOOL STEADY BALANCE BALLAST STIFFEN
STABILIZER ACARDITE
STABLE BYRE FAST FIRM SURE HARAS HEMEL SOLID SOUND STALL STIFF STOUT TAMBO LINTER LIVERY SECURE SICKER STATIC STEADY STRONG STURDY DURABLE EQUERRY LASTING OXHOUSE SETTLED SHIPPEN STABILE BALANCED IMMOBILE RESIDENT STANDING PERMANENT
(EMOTIONALLY —) TOGETHER
(ROYAL —S) MEWS
(PREF.) MONIMO
STABLEBOY LAD MAFU MAFOO JACKBOY
STABLEMAN OSTLER HOSTLER
STACCATO TUT SECCO DETACHE SALTATO RICOCHET SALTANDO
(NOT —) LEGATO TENUTO
STACK COB MOW SOW BIKE DESS LEET PACK PILE POKE RICK CANCH CLAMP GOAVE POAKE SCROO SHOCK STAKE STALK STOCK COLUMN FUNNEL RICKLE CALENDER STACKAGE
(— BRICKS) CLAMP SCINTLE
(— IN KILN) BOX
(— LUMBER) STICK
(— OF ARMS) PILE
(— OF BRICK) LIFT
(— OF CERAMICS) BUNG
(— OF CHLOROPHYLL) GRANUM
(— OF CORN) SHOCK
(— OF FISH) BULK
(— OF GRAIN) RICK
(— OF HIDES) BED
(— OF PANS) SWEATER
(— OF SHEETS) BOOK
(HAY OR CORN —) HOVEL
(SMALL —) COB CANCH RICKLE
(TILE —) WELL
STACKER CROWDER PITCHER STACKMAN
STACKING (— OF AIRCRAFT) HOLDING
STACKYARD MOWIE MOWHAY HAGGARD
STADIUM BOWL DOME STADE STAGE FURLONG STADION COLISEUM
(PRIVATE SEATS IN —) SKYBOX
(ROOFED —) DOME
STAFF MAN PIN ROD TAU TAW CANE CLUB KENT LIMB MACE MALL MAUL PIKE POLE RUNG TREE VARE YARD BATON CROOK CROSS KEVEL NIBBY PEDUM PERCH STAVE STICK SUITE VERGE BASTON CADUCE CEPTER CLEEKY CROCHE CRUTCH FAMILY FERULE GROUND LITUUS MULETA POTENT PRITCH RADIUS RISSLE TAIAHA THYRSE WARDER BACULUS BOURDON CAMBUCA CROSIER CRUMMIE DISTAFF FESTUCA PALSTER SCEPTER SCEPTRE STADDLE THYRSUS CADUCEUS CRUMMOCK PARTISAN PASTORAL PLOWFOOT TIPSTAFF
(— AT END OF NET) BRAIL
(— OF AUTHORITY) VARE VERGE
(— OF COOKS) BOUCHE
(— OF OFFICIALS) OMLAH
(— WITH CROSSPIECE) POTENT
(BISHOP'S —) BAGLE BACULUS CROSIER CROZIER PASTORAL
(FIELD MARSHAL'S —) BATON
(FORKED —) LINSTOCK
(GRADUATED —) LIMB
(HOTTENTOT —) KIRVI
(MAGICIAN'S —) RHABDOS
(NEWSPAPER —) DAYSIDE
(NUBIAN —) KUERR
(PILGRIM'S —) BURDEN
(PLASTERER'S —) BEATER
(SHEPHERD'S —) KENT CROOK
(SPARTAN —) SCYTALE
(TEACHING —) FACULTY
(THIEVES' —) FILCH
(PREF.) LITUI SCEPTRO
STAG HART ROYAL SPADE STAIG WAPITI BULLOCK KNOBBER POINTER KNOBBLER
(— OF THE 3D YEAR) SPIRE
(— OF 2ND YEAR) BROCKET
(— OF 8 YEARS OR MORE) ROYAL
(— THAT HAS CAST HIS ANTLERS) POLLARD
(DEAD —) MORT
(HORNLESS —) HUMMEL
(TURNED TO —) ACTAEON
(12-POINT —) ROYAL
(3-YEAR OLD —) SPADE
(PREF.) ELAPH(O)
STAG BEETLE LUCANID
STAGE LEG BANK GEST POST STEP TREK APRON DUMMY ETAGE FLAKE GRADE PEGME PHASE POINT SCENE STAIR STATE BOARDS DEGREE HEMMEL PERIOD PHASIS STRIDE CATASTA MANSION ROSTRUM STADIUM INSTANCE PLATFORM SCAFFOLD PROSCENIUM
(— DIRECTION) EXIT ENTER SOLUS
(— FOR DRYING FISH) FLAKE
(— FOR HAY) HEMMEL
(— IN DELIRIUM) TILMUS
(— IN FEVER) FLUSH
(— IN PORCELAIN FURNACE) HOWELL
(— IN TRAVELING) GEST
(— MANAGER) REGISSEUR
(— OF CUPOLA) LANTERN
(— OF DEVELOPMENT) ERA BLOSSOM
(— OF FUNGUS) OIDIUM
(— OF GLACIATION) RISS WURM ACHEN MINDEL
(— OF INSECT) INSTAR
(— OF LIFE) AGE ASRAMA ASHRAMA
(— OF MITOSIS) ANAPHASE PROPHASE
(— OF PERSONALITY) LATENCY
(— OF ROCKET) BOOSTER
(— OF THEATER) SCAENA THEATRON
(— WHERE SLAVES WERE SOLD) CATASTA
(BOTTOMMOST —) CELLAR
(COMIC —) SOCK
(EARLIEST —) PRIME
(FINAL —) CLOSE FINISH STRETCH
(FIRST —) YOUTH SPRING
(FLOATING —) DUMMY
(FLOOD —) CREST
(GEOLOGICAL —) GUNZ GLACIAL SENONIAN
(GLACIATION —) WURM
(INITIAL —) INFANCY
(LANDING —) STAIR BRIDGE STAITH STELLING
(MOVING —) PEGMA PEGME
(PART OF —) FLY ARCH DROP FLAT WING APRON DRAPE BATTEN BORDER BRIDGE CENTER RETURN TEASER CURTAIN ENTRANCE TORMENTOR PROSCENIUM
(RADIO —) STEP
(THIRD —) AUTUMN
(PREF.) SCENO
STAGECOACH DILLY STAGE
STAGEHAND GRIP DAYMAN GAFFER
STAGER SOAKER
STAGGER REEL ROLL STOT DAVER DODGE HODGE LURCH PITCH STITE STOIT DACKER DAIDLE FALTER GOGGLE STAVER STIVER SWAVER TOTTER WALTER WAMBLE WELTER WIGGLE WINTLE MEGRIMS STACHER STACKER STAMMER STOITER STOTTER STUMBLE SWAGGER VANDYKE WAUCHLE TITUBATE
(— BACK) RECOIL
STAGGERBUSH LAMBKILL
STAGGERED STURTAN STURTIN
STAGGERING AREEL
STAGGERS DUNT GOGGLES MEGRIMS STAVERS VERTIGO
STAGHEAD SPIKETOP
STAGING STAGE CRIPPLE DERRICK HURRIES
STAGNANCY STASIS
STAGNANT DEAD DULL INERT STILL STATIC COBWEBBY SLUGGISH STAGNATE STANDING
STAGNATION STASIS TORPOR LANGUOR
STAID SET CIVIL GRAVE SOBER

DEMURE STEADY EARNEST SERIOUS DECOROUS
STAIN DYE LIT WEM BLOT BLUR BUFF DIRT DRAB FILE FOIL HURT MEAL MOLE RUST SCAM SLUR SMAD SMIT SMUT SOIL SPOT TASH BLACK BLEND BRAND CLOUD DIRTY HATCH PAINT PLECK SMEAR SPECK SULLY TACHE TAINT TINGE WEMMY BREATH GIEMSA IMBRUE INFAMY INFECT MACULA SMIRCH SMUDGE SMUTCH SPLASH STIGMA SUDDLE ATTAINT BESTAIN BLEMISH DEPAINT DISTAIN SLUBBER SOILURE SPATTER SPLOTCH STADDLE TARNISH BESMIRCH CARMALUM DISCOLOR DISGRACE DISHONOR FLYSPECK MACULATE PYRONINE TAINTURE
(— BLACK) EBONIZE
(— IN LINEN) MELL
(— ON BRICK) SCUMMING
(— WITH BLOOD) ENGORE
(PREF.) MACUL(I)(O) SPIL(O)
STAINED FOXY RUSTY SMUDGY BLOTCHY SMUTCHY
(— BY DECAY) DOATY
(— WITH BLOOD) BLOODY IMBRUED
STAINED GLASS VITRAIL
STAINER TRACER
STAINLESS PURE CHASTE INNOCENT
STAIR STY GREE RUNG STEP DEGREE COCHLEA ESCALIER
(LANDING —) GHAT GHAUT
(MINING —) LOB
(WINDING —) VICE VISE CARACOL CARACOLE TURNPIKE
(PL.) PAIR PITCH FLIGHT DANCERS ESCALIER
STAIRCASE SCALE ESCALIER
(PART OF —) MOLD POST RAIL NEWEL RISER TREAD NOSING LANDING BALUSTER BANISTER HANDRAIL BALUSTRADE
(SHIP'S —) COMPANIONWAY
(SPIRAL —) SPIRAL CARACOLE
STAIRWAY STOOP GREESE PERRON DESCENT ESCALIER
(— ON RIVER BANK) GHAT
(CURVED —) SWEEP
(SHIP'S —) LADDER
(WINDING —) VICE TURNPIKE
STAITH TIP
STAKE BET HOB LAY SET TAW VIE WAD WED ANTE BENT GAGE MAIN PALE PAWN PEEL POOL PUNT RISK STAB STOB TREE WAGE PITCH SPILE SPOKE SPRAG STOCK STOOP STOUR WAGER BAIKIE CAULIS CHANCE CORNER CROTCH ENGAGE GAMBLE HAZARD IMPONE LOGGAT LOGGET PALING PICKET STOWER TRUNCH WEDFEE STOATER STUCKEN VENTURE INTEREST PALISADE PEASTICK STUCKING
(— HIGHER) REVIE
(— IN PRIMERO) REST
(— SUPPORTING FOUNDATION) PILE
(CART —) RUNG
(COMPULSORY — IN POKER) BLIND
(GAMBLING —) BET MISE WAGER
(POINTED —) SOULE SOWEL PICKET
(SURVEYORS' —) HUB
(TETHERING —) PUTTO
(TINSMITH'S —) TEEST
(PL.) POOL JACKPOT
STAKE-SHAPED SUDIFORM
STALACE COLUMELLA
STALE OLD COLD FLAT HOAR PALL SICK WORN BLOWN DATED DUSTY FROWY HOARY MOLDY MUSTY RAFTY SANDY TRITE FROWZY MOULDY STUFFY EXOLETE FROUGHY INSIPID OVERWORN STAGNANT TIMEWORN
(DAMP AND —) WAUGH
STALEMATE PATT STALE
STALK BUN RAY CORN HAFT MOTE POLE RISP STAM STEG STEM TIGE QUILL SCAPE SHANK SPEAR SPIRE STAKE STALE STEAL STIPE STUMP WRIDE COULIS RATOON STIPES CASTOCK FUNICLE PEDICEL PETIOLE SPINDLE CAUDICLE FILAMENT PEDUNCLE PODETIUM STALKLET STERIGMA PETIOLULE
(— OF BUCKWHEAT) STRAW
(— OF CRINOID) COLUMN
(— OF GRAIN) RESSUM RIZZOM
(— OF GRASS) BENT SPEAR
(— OF HAY) RISP
(— OF MOSS CAPSULE) SETA
(— OF OVULE) FUNICLE
(— OF PLANT) SPINDLE TENACLE
(— OF SPORE) STERIGMA
(— OF SPOROGONIUM) SETA
(— OF STAMEN) FILAMENT
(— OF SUGAR CANE) RATOON
(— OF UMBEL) RAY
(—S OF GRAIN) KARBI STRAW
(CABBAGE —) CASTOCK
(CROSSBOW —) TILLER
(DRY —) KEX KECK BENNET
(FLOWER —) SCAPE
(HOLLOW —) BUN KEX KECK
(PL.) HAULM STRAW WRIDE IWAIWA
(PREF.) CAUL(I)(O) CULMI
STALKLESS SESSILE
STALKY AND COMPANY (AUTHOR OF —) KIPLING
(CHARACTER IN —) JOHN MTURK ARTHUR BEETLE STALKY CORKRAN GILBERT
STALL BAY BIN BOX CUB PEW BULK CRIB SPAR STAW BOOSE BOOSY BOOTH CRAME PITCH STAND STASH CARCER CARREL STANCE TRAVIS WICKET BALAGAN CABINET SHAMBLE SHIPPEN BUTCHERY STANDING TRAVERSE
(— FOR TIME) HAVER STRETCH
(— IN CLOISTER) CAROL
(— IN COAL MINE) BREAST WICKET
(— IN MUD) STOG
(— IN ROMAN CIRCUS) CARCER
(BISHOP'S —) TRIBUNE
(CHURCH —) PEW
(THEATER —) LOGE FAUTEUIL
STALLED STOODED
STALLION SIRE STAG STUD ENTRE HORSE COOSER CUSSER ENTIRE CUISSER STALLAND STONEHORSE
STALWART RUDE STARK STIFF WIGHT STRONG STURDY BUIRDLY VALIANT
STAMEN TAMIN STAMMEL
(PART OF —) ANTHER
(PL.) ANDROECIUM
(PREF.) ANDR(O)
(SUFF.) STEMONOUS
STAMINA GUTS SAND BOTTOM
STAMMER FAM HACK MANT STOT STUT GANCH WLAFF FAFFLE FALTER FAMBLE HACKER HAFFLE HAMMER HOCKER HOTTER MAFFLE MAMMER YAMMER FRIBBLE STUMBLE STUTTER HESITATE SPLUTTER TITUBATE
STAMMERING HACK PSELLISM TRAULISM BALBUTIES
STAMP DIE CHOP COIL DRUB FAKE MARK NIXY PAUT POSS RUFF SEAL SNAP TYPE APPEL BLOCK DOLLY ERROR FRANK LABEL LOCAL NIXIE PRINT PUNCH STOCK STOMP STUNT TENOR TOUCH WRITE ACCENT CACHET CLICHE DOCKER FULLER INCUSE INCUTE INDENT LOCKUP PASTER POUNCE SCRIBE SHAPER SIGNET STRAMP STRIKE CARRIER CHARACT EDITION IMPRESS IMPRINT MINTAGE POUNDER REPRINT SEEBECK SPECIAL SQUELCH STICKER TAXPAID WRAPPER HALLMARK ORIGINAL PRESSURE PUNCHEON
(— AFTER ASSAY) TOUCH
(— BOOK COVER) BLIND
(— FOR CUTTING DOUGH) DOCKER
(— HERRING BARREL) DUNT
(— HIDES) STOCK
(— HOLES) STOACH
(— OUT) SCOTCH
(— WITH DIE) DINK
(BOOKBINDING —) BLOCK FILLET
(CANCELLING —) KILLER
(HALF OF —) BISECT
(HAND —) CANCELER
(OFFICIAL —) CHOP
(POSTAGE —) AIR DUE CAPE FAKE HEAD ERROR LABEL LOCAL BUREAU INVERT AIRMAIL BICOLOR CHARITY CLASSIC REPRINT STICKER ADHESIVE COLONIAL ORIGINAL SPECIMEN PRECANCEL
(REVENUE —) FISCAL TAXPAID
(RUBBER —) YESMAN
(SMART —) APPEL
(PL.) MIXTURE KILOWARE
(PREF.) TIMBRO
STAMP-COLLECTING PHILATELY TIMBROLOGY
STAMPEDE RUSH BLITZ CHUTE DEBACLE STAMPEDO
STAMPER FANCIER STOMPER
STAMPING TITLING
STANCE STATION STANDING
(— OF GOLFER) ADDRESS
(— OF HORSE) GATHER
STANCH FIRM STEM STIFF STOUT HEARTY TRUSTY STAUNCH FAITHFUL RESOLUTE
STANCHION BAIL PITON CROTCH CRUTCH STENCIL STANCHEL STANCHER
STAND GO JIB SET BANK BEAR BIER DESK HALT RACK RANK REST STAY STEL ZARF BIPOD BLOCK ERECT FRAME FRONT KIOSK STALL STICK STONE STOOL CASTER COLORS ENDURE HASTER INSIST PATTEN PILLAR SMOKER STANCE STANZA STOUND STRIKE TEAPOY TRIPOD TRIVET CONSIST DIOPTER EPERGNE FOURBLE LECTERN STATION TABORET TRESTLE TROLLEY ATTITUDE BLEACHER COATRACK CROWFOOT FRIPPERY GUERIDON HASTENER INKSTAND POSITION SCAFFOLD STALLAGE STANDING STANDISH STILLAGE STILLING STILLION
(— AS SPONSOR) FANG HEAVE CHRISTEN
(— AT AN ANGLE) CATER
(— AT ATTENTION) BACK
(— BACK) BACCARE BACKARE
(— BEFORE A FIRE) FOOTMAN
(— BEHIND) COVER
(— BY) SERVE STICKTO
(— CLOSE) CROWD ENVIRON
(— DRINKS) SHOUT TREAT
(— ERECT) ROUSE
(— FAST) SUBSIST
(— FASTENED TO MESS TABLE) CROWFOOT
(— FIRM) STAY
(— FOR) MEAN DENOTE
(— FOR AUCTIONING) BLOCK
(— FOR BARRELS) JIB THRALL
(— FOR COFFIN) BIER
(— FOR COMPASS) BINNACLE
(— FOR CONFINING HEAT) HASTER HASTENER
(— FOR DRESSES) FRIPPERY
(— FOR DRILL PIPE) FOURBLE
(— FOR FINJAN) ZARF
(— FOR TILES) CRISS
(— FOR WRITING MATERIALS) STANDISH
(— GUARD) COVER
(— IDLY) LOAF
(— IN AWE) FEAR
(— OFF) AROINT
(— OF FOREST) GROWTH
(— OF PLANTS) STOOL
(— ON AND OFF SHORE) BUSK
(— ON END) STARE UPEND
(— ON HIGH) TOWER
(— ON TWO FEET) BIPOD DUOPOD
(— OUT) CUT TOOT FLAUNT
(— READY) ABIDE
(— STIFFLY) STRUT
(— STILL) HO HOO HALT STAY
(— TO SHOOT) ADDRESS
(— TREAT) MUG SHOUT
(— UNMOVING) FREEZE
(— UNSTEADILY) STAGGER
(— UP) RARE
(— UP FOR) STICKLE
(— UP STIFF) STIVER
(— UP TO) CONFRONT
(— WITH LEGS APART) STRIDE
(BRANCHING —) TREE
(CAKE —) CURATE
(CHEMICAL —) RINGSTAND

(CONCESSION —) JOINT
(FIRECLAY —) CRANK
(HEARTH —) FOOTMAN
(ONE-NIGHT —) GIG
(PRINTER'S —) BANK FRAME
(PULPIT-LIKE —) AMBO
(RAISED —) PERGOLA
(REVOLVING —) KLINOSTAT
(SCULPTOR'S —) CHASSIS
(SHOOTING —) BUTT
(THREE-LEGGED —) TRIVET
STANDARD PAR ALEM DICK FIAR FLAG GAGE IDEA MARK NORM SIGN TEST TOUG ALLOY BOGEY CANON CHECK DOLLY DRAKE EAGLE GAUGE IDEAL JEDGE MODEL NORMA SCALE STAND STOOL AQUILA ASSIZE BANNER CORNET DOLLIE FILLER NORMAL SOCKET SQUARE STAPLE TIPONI TRIPOD VIOLLE ANCIENT CLASSIC DECORUM DRAPEAU LABARUM MODULUS STANDER BRATTACH GONFALON MOUNTING ORIFLAMB ORTHODOX VEXILLUM
(— IN GATE) STRIKE
(— OF ACCURACY) COCKER
(— OF CONDUCT) LINE GNOMON
(— OF PERFECTION) IDEAL
(— OF PERFORMANCE) BOGY BOGEY BOGIE
(— OF PITCH) DIAPASON
(— OF QUALITY) GRADE
(—S OF BEHAVIOR) ETHICS
(CONVENTIONAL —) PIETY
(LIGHT —) CARCEL
(NOT —) BASTARD
(TURKISH —) ALEM TOUG
(PL.) LIGHTS HOLSTERS
STANDARD-BEARER CORNET ENSIGN ALFEREZ ANCIENT STALLER SIGNIFER STANDARD VEXILLARY
STANDARDIZE FORDIZE MACHINE CALIBRATE
STANDEL STORER
STAND-IN SUB STUNTMAN
STANDING RANK BEING ERECT STATE CREDIT ESTEEM REGULAR RESPECT PRESTIGE STAGNANT PERPENDICULAR
(— ALONE) SEPARATE
(— BY ITSELF) ABSOLUTE DETACHED
(— ERECT) HORRENT
(— FIRM) STABLE
(— INCOORDINATION) ASTASIA
(— IN PROFILE) RAMPANT
(— ON STEPS) DEGRADED
(— OUT) BOLD PROUD EXTANT RELIEF SALIENT PROMINENT
(— OUT CLEARLY) EMINENT
(— POSITION) OFFHAND
(— UPRIGHT) STANDARD
(HIGH —) RANK WORSHIP POSITION
(MODE OF —) STANCE
(SOCIAL —) LEVEL ESTATE FASHION STATION
(PREF.) STAT(O)
(— IN SECOND PLACE BEYOND) DVI EKA
(SUFF.) STASIA STASIS STAT STATIC STATICS
STANDPATTISM TORYISM
STANDPOINT STANCE
STANDSTILL JIB SET HALT REST STAY STAND STANCE
STANZA CALL RANN ENVOI ENVOY STAFF STAND STAVE VERSE BASTON DIXAIN DIZAIN OCTAVE SEPTET SESTET SEXTET SIXAIN STANCE STANZO HUITAIN SESTINA SEXTAIN STROPHE TRIOLET TROILUS CINQUAIN OCTONARY QUATRAIN QUINTAIN RISPETTO SETTAINE TRISTICH TROPARION
(SUFF.) STICH
STAPES STIRRUP
STAPLE LOOP FLOSS STITCH SHACKLE STEEPLE VERVELLE
(PL.) BROKES
STAR COR SUN BEID FIRE LAMP ASTER COMES DWARF EXCEL GIANT MOLET RISHI SHINE STARN ALNATH ASTRAL BINARY COUPLE DOUBLE ETOILE LUCIDA MULLET NITHAM SHINER SPHERE STELLA BENEFIC DINGBAT ESTOILE GEMINID STARLET STARNIE ASTERISK ASTEROID HEXAGRAM MALEFICE PENTACLE SUBDWARF SUBGIANT VARIABLE
(COMPANION —) COMES
(DOG —) ASTA SEPT SOPT TOTO SEPTI LASSIE SIRIUS RINTINTIN
(EVENING —) VENUS HESPER VESPER EVESTAR HESPERUS
(FEATHER —) COMATULA
(FILM —) VEDETTE
(FUTURE —) COMER
(GUIDING —) LOADSTAR LODESTAR
(KIND OF —) BETA
(MORNING —) VENUS DAYSTAR PHOSPHOR
(NEW —) NOVA
(OFFICER'S —) PIP
(OF THE —S) SIDEREAL
(PULSATING —) CEPHEID
(RED —) ANTARES
(SHOOTING —) BOLIDE LEONID METEOR COWSLIP SHOOTER
(SPECIFIC —) YED ADIB ALYA ATIK CAPH ENIF ENIR IZAR KIED MAIA NAOS PHAD SADR VEGA WEGA ACRAB ACRUX AGENA ALCOR ALGOL ALKES ANCHA ARNEB CHARA DABIH DELTA DENEB DUBHE GIEDI GUIAM GUYAM HAMAL HAMUL JUGUM MERAK MIZAR NIBAL NIHAI PHACD PHAET RIGEL SAIPH SPICA TEJAT WASAT WEZEN ZOSMA ADHARA ALHENA ALIOTH ALKAID ALMACH ALTAIR ALUDRA APOLLO ARIDED CASTOR CELENO CHELEB DIPHDA ELNATH ETAMIN GIENAH HYADES KOCHAB LESUTH MAASYM MARKAB MARKEB MARSIC MEGREZ MENKAR MENKIB MEROPE MIRACH MIRFAK MIRZAM NEKKAR PHECDA POLLUX PROPUS RANICH SCHEAT SHEDIR SIRIUS THABIT THUBAN ACUBENS ALBIREO ALCHIBA ALCYONE ALGENIB ALGIEBA ALGORAH ALMAACK ALNILAM ALNITAK ALPHARD ALPHIRK ALSHAIN ANTARES AZIMECH BUNGULA CANOPUS CAPELLA ELECTRA GIANSAR GOMELZA GRUMIUM MEBSUTA MELUCTA MENCHIB MINTAKA MUFRIDE POLARIS PROCYON REGULUS ROTANIM RUCHBAR SCHEDAR SEGINUS SHELLAK STEROPE TARAZED TAYGETA TEGMINE THEENIM ACHERNAR ALPHECCA ARCTURUS ASTERION DENEBOLA GRAFFIAS HERCULES MULIPHEN PRAESEPE SCALOOIN SCHEMALI SHERATAN
(THREE —S) KIDS ELLWAND TRIANGLE
(7 —S OF GREAT BEAR) CAR
(PREF.) ASTER(O) ASTR(I)(O) SIDERO STELLI
(SUFF.) ASTER ID
STAR APPLE CAIMITO
STARCH AMYL ARUM SAGO STIFF TIKOR AMYDON AMYLUM CONJEE FARINA FECULA CASSAVA CURCUMA FAECULA MARANTA TALIPOT AMIDULIN DRESSING FIXATURE GLUCOSAN
(— IN SOLUTION) AMIDIN
(ANIMAL —) GLYCOGEN
(PREF.) AMYL(I)(O)
STARCHED FORMAL
STARE EYE BORE DARE GAPE GAUM GAUP GAWK GAWP GAZE GOVE GYPE KIKE LOOK PORE GLARE GLORE GLOWER GOGGLE EYEBALL
(— DOWN) OUTFACE
(— IDLY) GOVE GOAVE
(— IMPERTINENTLY) OGLE
(— VACANTLY) GOWK
(COLD —) FISHEYE
STARFISH PAD STAR ASTERID RADIATE ASTEROID OPHIURAN
(PART OF —) ARM ANUS DISC SPINE EYESPOT TENTACLE MADREPORITE
STARFLOWER ASTER
STAR FRUIT CARAMBOLA
STARING STEEP ASTARE GOGGLE GOOGLY HAGGARD
STAR JELLY STARSHOT
STARK BUCK CARK FAIR HARD CRUDE HARSH NAKED STIFF STARCH DESOLATE METALLIC
STARLIKE ASTRAL SPHERY
STARLING SALI STARE BEAVER PASTOR TILYER SPREEUW STARNEL STAYNIL CHEPSTER CUTWATER SHEPSTER
STARRED LIZARD HARDIM
STARRING FEATURED
STARRY ASTRAL STARNY STELLED SIDEREAL
STAR SAPPHIRE ASTERIA ASTRION ASTROITE
STAR-SHAPED ASTROID
START DIG SET BOLT BOUN DART DASH HEAD JERK JUMP OPEN TURN WHIP ARISE BEGIN BIRTH BRAID BREAK BUDGE ENTER FLIRT GLENT ONSET RAISE ROUSE STORT THROW ABRADE BOGGLE BROACH FLINCH INTEND OFFSET OUTSET SETOFF SETOUT STRIKE TEEOFF TWITCH GETAWAY OPENERS OPENING STARTLE SUNRISE COMMENCE CONCEIVE INCHOATE OUTSTART
(— A HORSE) WINCE
(— ASIDE) SHY SKIT DODGE
(— A TRIP) EMBARK
(— BACK) RECOIL RESILE
(— BURNING) SPIT KINDLE
(— FERMENTATION) PITCH
(— OF BIRD'S FLIGHT) SOUSE
(— OF FLIGHT) HOPOFF TAKEOFF
(— OF PLAY) ACTONE SCENE1
(— OUT) FRAME INTEND
(— SUDDENLY) SPRING
(— UP) JUMP ASTART ASTERT
(— WITH FEAR) STURT
(FROM THE —) ABOVO
(SUDDEN —) SHY SQUIRT
STARTER KOJI OPENER
(BUNG —) FLOGGER
STAR THISTLE CALTROP CALTHROP
STARTING INCOMING
STARTLE JAR SOHO ALARM SCARE SHOCK START STURT AFFRAY BOGGLE BOOGER FRIGHT FRIGHTEN SURPRISE
STARTLING LURID ALARMING SHOCKING
STARVATION LACK PINE FAMINE
STARVE CLEM FAST FAMINE FAMISH AFFAMISH
STARVED MEAGER MEAGRE STARVEN
STARVED-LOOKING SLINK
STARVELING SHARGAR SHARGER
STARVING CLUNG
STARWORT ASTER ASTROFEL ASTROPHEL
STASH QUIT STOP HOARD STORE
STATE WU LAY PUT SAY CASE ETAT MODE NAME POMP PORT TERM TIFF COVIN ESTER ESTRE POLIS SPEAK STADE TERMS TUATH WHACK AFFIRM AGENCY ASSERT ASSURE CAESAR EFFEIR EMPIRE ESTATE IMPORT NATION PLIGHT POLICY POLITY RENDER RIALTY SOVIET STATUS STEVEN CIVITAS DECLARE DESERET DUKEDOM ENOUNCE EXPOUND EXPRESS KINSHIP PROPOSE SPECIFY STATION TERMINE CEREMONY DEVACHAN DOMINION FRANKLIN HEGEMONY INDICATE KINGSHIP REPUBLIC STATELET PREDICAMENT
(— EXPLICITLY) DEFINE
(— FIRST) PREMISE
(— FORMALLY) ENOUNCE
(— IN NORTH CAROLINA) FRANKLIN
(— OF AFFAIRS) CASE ARRAY STATUS
(— OF ALARM) GAST FEEZE SCARE
(— OF AMAZEMENT) STOUND
(— OF ANGER) FUME
(— OF APATHY) STUPOR
(— OF BEING) MODE
(— OF BEING CUT) SCISSION
(— OF BEING DRAWN) TRACTION
(— OF BEING OVERFULL) PLETHORA
(— OF BEING POISONOUS) TOXICITY
(— OF BEING WORSE) PEJORITY

(— OF BLISS) NIRVANA
(— OF CONCENTRATION) DHARANA SAMADHI
(— OF CONFUSION) FOG FLAP HACK MUSS CHAOS SWIRL HASSLE HUBBUB FLUMMOX TROYTOWN
(— OF CONSECRATION) IHRAM
(— OF COOPERATION) HOOKUP
(— OF DISASTER) SMASH
(— OF DISORDER) HELL MUSS FANTAD ANARCHY
(— OF DISSENSION) SCISSION
(— OF DISTRESS) KATZENJAMMER
(— OF DISTURBANCE) GARBOIL
(— OF DOUBT) MIST
(— OF EAGERNESS) HURRY
(— OF ECSTASY) SWOON
(— OF ENCHANTMENT) SPELL
(— OF ENLIGHTENMENT) BODHI
(— OF EQUALITY) PAR
(— OF EXALTATION) FURY ECSTASY
(— OF EXCITATION) FOMENT
(— OF EXCITEMENT) FRY FLAP GALE HIGH SNIT STEW FEEZE HOIGH DITHER DOODAH HUBBUB FANTEEG FLUSTER KIPPAGE SWELTER FANTIGUE
(— OF EXHAUSTION) GONENESS
(— OF FEAR) FUNK JELLY SCARE
(— OF HAPPINESS) ELYSIUM PARADISE
(— OF HEALTH) EUCRASIA
(— OF HUMILIATION) DUST
(— OF IDEAL PERFECTION) UTOPIA
(— OF IMPERFECTION) SCARCITY
(— OF INACTION) DEADLOCK
(— OF INCIPIENCE) EMBRYO
(— OF INTENSITY) BUILD
(— OF IRRITABILITY) FUME GALL FANTAD
(— OF JOY) JUBILEE
(— OF MELANCHOLY) GLOOM
(— OF MENTAL INACTIVITY) TORPOR
(— OF MENTAL READINESS) ATTITUDE
(— OF MIND) CUE HIP CASE MOOD HUMOR FETTLE CARAPACE
(— OF MISERY) HELL GEHENNA
(— OF NEGLECT) LIMBO
(— OF OPPOSITION) DEFIANCE
(— OF ORDER) HARNONY
(— OF OSTRACISM) COVENTRY
(— OF PERFECTION) SIDDHI
(— OF PERTURBATION) CRISE
(— OF PREOCCUPATION) CARE
(— OF QUIET) PEACE
(— OF READINESS) GUARD
(— OF REALITY) ACT
(— OF REJECTION) GATE
(— OF REPOSE) KEF CALM
(— OF RETIREMENT) GRASS
(— OF REVERIE) DUMP
(— OF SENSITIVITY) NERVES
(— OF SLUGGISHNESS) COMA
(— OF SUBDIVISION) FINENESS
(— OF SUFFERING) PURGATORY
(— OF SUSPENSE) TRANCE
(— OF SUSPENSION) ABEYANCE
(— OF TENSION) FANTEEG STRETCH FANTIGUE
(— OF THE SOUL) BARDO
(— OF THINGS) FARE PASS
(— OF TRANQUILLITY) KEF KIF PEACE
(— OF UNCERTAINTY) FOG FLUX
(— OF UNREST) FERMENT
(— OF WEATHER) FREEZE
(— OF WORRY) TEW SWEAT FANTAD
(— POSITIVELY) AFFIRM
(— PRECISELY) FORMATE
(— UNDER OATH) ALLEGE DEPONE TESTIFY
(AGITATED —) FUSS SNIT STIR CHURN STORM LATHER SWIVET
(BLISSFUL —) NIRVANA
(BUFFER —) GLACIS
(CHINESE —) WU SHU WEI
(DAMAGED —) RUIN RUINS
(DAZED —) DAMP
(DEPRESSED —) GLOOM WALLOW
(DISTURBED —) STIR STORM UNREST
(DOMINANT —) SUZERAIN
(DROWSY —) DOVER
(EMOTIONAL —) FEVER FEELING
(EVIL —) PLIGHT
(FEUDAL —) WEI
(FICTITIOUS —) FABLE
(FILTHY —) DIRT
(FLUSTERED —) JITTERS
(FREE —) SAORSTAT
(GERMAN —) REICH
(GLOOMY —) DUMP
(HIGHEST —) SUPREME
(HOLY —) IHRAM
(HORIZONTAL —) LEVEL
(IMPAIRED —) SHATTER
(INDONESIAN —) NEGARA
(INTERMEDIATE —) LIMBO
(IRISH —) TUATH
(LIQUID —) FLUOR FLUIDITY
(LOWEST —) BEDROCK
(MARRIED —) SPOUSAL
(MENTAL —) EARNEST DELUSION
(MIDDLE —) MEAN
(MIXED —) PI PIE
(MORBID —) HIP IODISM
(MORMON —) DESERET
(NEUTRAL —) BUFFER
(ORDINARY —) NORM
(OVERHEATED —) STEW
(PECUNIARY —) FACULTY
(PERMANENT —) STAY
(PERTURBED —) DEVIL
(PROFOUND —) DEPTH
(PROSPEROUS —) WEAL
(RIGID —) RIGOR
(ROYAL —) MAJESTY
(RUDIMENTARY —) INCHOATION
(SHELTERLESS —) EXPOSURE
(SOCIAL —) LIFE
(SOUTHWESTERN —S) SUNBELT
(SOVEREIGN —) INDEPENDENCY
(SPOTTED —) FOXINESS
(STUPEFIED —) NOD
(SUBORDINATE —) SATELLITE
(SWEATY —) STEW
(SWISS —) CANTON
(TROUBLESOME —) HOWDYDO
(ULTIMATE —) END
(UNCERTAIN —) LIMBO
(UNCONTROLLED —) RANDOM RANDON
(UNCULTIVATED —) FERITY
(UNDECIDED —) PENDENCY
(UNFAVORABLE —) FOULNESS
(VERIFIED —) FACT
(WORST —) PESSIMISM
(PREF.) CRATO TYP(I)(O)
(SUFF.) ANCE ANCY ANDRA ANDRIA ATE ATION CY DOM ENCE ENCY ERY HEAD HOOD ION ISATION ISM ITY IZATION MENT NESS OSIS SHIP TH
(CHARACTERIZED BY —) SOME
(DISEASED —) SIS
(MORBID —) IASIS

STATED GIVEN CERTAIN
(DIRECTLY —) EXPRESS
(DISTINCTLY —) EXPLICIT

STATE DEPARTMENT (— EMPLOYEE) ATTACHE

STATE FAIR (AUTHOR OF —) STONG
(CHARACTER IN —) PAT ABEL WARE EMILY FRAKE HARRY MARGY WAYNE ELEANOR GILBERT MELISSA

STATEHOUSE CAPITOL

STATELINESS STATE DIGNITY MAJESTY GRANDEUR

STATELY DATE BURLY GRAND LARGO LOFTY NOBLE PROUD REGAL STATE STOUT AUGUST COUPON PORTLY SOLEMN SUPERB TOGATE GALLANT BARONIAL IMPOSING MAESTOSO MAJESTIC PALATIAL STATEFUL

STATEMENT SAY BILL VOTE WORD AXIOM BRIEF COUNT DIXIT LIBEL STATE STORY BELIEF DICTUM DOCKET EXPOSE FACTUM RETURN SAYING SPEECH ACCOUNT ADDRESS ANALOGY DISSENT EPITAPH EPITOME FORMULA INVOICE MENTION SHOWING ABSTRACT ANTINOMY ARGUMENT AVERMENT BULLETIN DELIVERY EQUATION EXPLICIT JUDGMENT PROPOSAL SCHEDULE SENTENCE SPEAKING SYNGRAPH SYNOPSIS
(— AS PRECEDENT) AUTHORITY
(— OF FACTS) REPORT
(— OF GRIEVANCE) PLAINT
(— OF OPINION) CHANT
(— OF RELATIONS) THEOREM
(— ON DRUG LABEL) LEGEND
(AUTHORITATIVE —) DICTUM
(CASUAL —) REMARK
(CONCISE —) SCHEME APHORISM
(CONDENSED —) RESUME SYNOPSIS
(DEFAMATORY —) LIBEL
(EXAGGERATED —) STRETCH
(FABRICATED —) CANARD
(FINAL — OF ACCOUNT) AUDIT
(FINANCIAL —) BUDGET
(FOOLISH —) INANITY
(FORMAL —) CITATION
(IRRATIONAL —) ALOGISM
(OBSCURE —) ENIGMA
(PLAINTIFF'S —) BODY
(POMPOUS —) BRAG
(PUBLIC —) OUTGIVING
(SELF-CONTRADICTORY —) PARADOX
(SOOTHING —) SALVE
(UNTRUE —) LIE

STATER COLT TURTLE PEGASUS CYZICENE

STATEROOM BIBBY CABIN

STATESMAN GENRO SOLON FATHER STATIST WARWICK JACOBEAN WEALSMAN
(UNPRINCIPLED —) MACHIAVELLIAN
AMERICAN DIX HAY JAY LEE AMES BURR CASS CLAY FISH GREW HALE HULL OTIS POLK REED ROOT RUSK ADAMS BAKER BLAIR BLAND BORAH DAWES CHASE GENET GERRY GLASS HENRY LODGE MARCY OLNEY WYTHE BARUCH BIDDLE BLAINE BOWLES BROOKE BUNCHE CARTER EVARTS FOSTER GORHAM HURLEY MCKEAN MORRIS NORRIS RODNEY SEWARD SUMNER TOOMBS WALTON ACHESON ALDRICH BARBOUR BULLITT CLINTON CUMMINS DANIELS EVERETT GADSDEN HANCOCK HOUSTON KELLOGG LANSING LAURENS LINCOLN MORRILL SHERMAN STANTON TIMSON WEBSTER FRANKLIN GALLATIN HAMILTON HARRIMAN MILLEDGE PINCKNEY RANDOLPH RUTLEDGE SCHUYLER TRUMBULL DICKINSON ELLSWORTH FULBRIGHT PICKERING WASHINGTON SCHUSCHNIGG BRECKENRIDGE
ARGENTINIAN MITRE ALBERDI CARCANO DORREGO FRONDIZI RIVADAVIA
ATHENIAN SOLON
AUSTRALIAN SEE COOK BRUCE EVATT LYONS PRICE BARTON DEAKIN FISHER HOLDER HUGHES ISSACS LAWSON PARKES SCULLIN NICHOLSON
AUSTRIAN BACH RAAB BRUCK KHESL RAMEK UNGER BADENI GLASER PLENER RENNER SEIPEL TAAFFE BURESCH FIRMIAN HELFERT KAUNITZ KOERBER SCHOBER STADION BELCREDI DOLLFUSS HAYMERLE HUSSAREK LAMMASCH WALDHEIM EGGENBERG BELLEGARDE METTERNICH SCHMERLING BARTENSTEIN GOLUCHOWSKI PILLERSDORF STARHEMBERG
BELGIAN SPAAK DEVAUX HYMANS JACOBS JASPAR MERODE ROGIER ANETHAN NOTHOMB THEUNIS ZEELAND DECHAMPS BEERNAERT DELACROIX SCHOLLAERT VANDERVELDE
BOLIVIAN FRIAS MONTES BALDIVIESO
BRAZILIAN ABREU FEIJO CAXIAS BERNARDES MAGALHAES
BULGARIAN DANEV SAVOY MALINOV TSANKOV LIAPCHEV KARAVELOV STAMBOLOV RADOSLAVOV STAMBOLISKI
BURMESE THANT
CANADIAN KING GOUIN JETTE LEGER SCOTT TACHE VIGER BORDEN BOWELL FISHER FOSTER HUGHES MANION SIFTON TUPPER BALDWIN BENNETT BRODEUR

CARTIER CHAPAIS DOHERTY LAURIER MEIGHEN PEARSON RALSTON TRUDEAU MICHENER THOMPSON MACDONALD MACKENZIE PELLETIER CARTWRIGHT LAFONTAINE DIEFENBAKER FITZPATRICK
CHILEAN CRUZ RIOS EGANA MONTT FREIRE CRUCHAGA OHIGGINS BALMACEDA ALESSANDRI
CHINESE WU HUA KOO YEN KUNG SOONG
COLOMBIAN ZEA HERRAN
COSTA RICAN CASTRO
CUBAN PALMA
CZECH BENES HACHA HODZA KRAMAR RIEGER SVEHLA UDRZAL MASARYK
DANISH HALL ZAHLE BLUHME ESTRUP MONRAD RANTZAU GULDBERG STAUNING NEERGAARD GRIFFENFELD
DUTCH CATS COEN FOCK ASSER DOUSA FAGEL HAREN COLIJN DEWITT KUYPER GROTIUS HEINSIUS KLEFFENS HEEMSKERK KARNEBEEK VANDIEMEN BARNEVELDT BEEREENBROUCK
ECUADORIAN FLORES
EGYPTIAN SADAT ZIWAR
ENGLISH FOX LAW PYM EDEN HOPE HYDE LAMB LONG MORE PEEL PITT VANE WEBB WOOD AMERY BACON BEVAN BURKE CECIL CLIVE ELIOT HEATH HOARE JUXON LEWIS NIGEL PAGET SYKES BLOUNT BRIGHT COBDEN CRIPPS CURZON GEDDES GIBSON GRAHAM HARLEY HATTON HEATON HOLLES MILNER MORELY MORTON SAVILE SELDEN SIDNEY SOMERS TEMPLE WOLSEY ASQUITH BALDWIN BALFOUR CADOGAN CANNING FAWCETT FORSTER GERMAIN GIFFARD GOSCHEN HALDANE HALIFAX HAMPDEN HERRIES LAMBTON NORWICH OSBORNE RAFFLES READING RUSSELL STANLEY STEWART SWINTON WALDOCK WALPOLE WINDHAM WYKEHAM WYNDHAM ADDERLEY ANNESLEY BEAUFORT CARTERET COURTNEY CROMWELL DISRAELI GARDINER GOULBURN HAMILTON HARCOURT HASTINGS MACAULAY MONTFORT ROBINSON STANHOPE VILLIERS ADDINGTON BLEDISLOE CAVENDISH CHURCHILL CUSHENDUN FITZNEALE FITZPETER FORTESCUE GAITSKELL GLADSTONE GLANVILLE GODOLPHIN GREENWOOD GRENVILLE HUSKISSON KIMBERLEY LANSDOWNE LIVERPOOL MACDONALD NORTHCOTE STRAFFORD WAKEFIELD BIRKENHEAD PALMERSTON ROCKINGHAM WALSINGHAM WELLINGTON WHITELOCKE WILLINGDON BOLINGBROKE CHAMBERLAIN FITZWILLIAM SHAFTESBURY SOUTHAMPTON CHESTERFIELD
ESTONIAN PATS STRANDMAN
FINNISH KALLIO TANNER CAJANDER MECHELIN RELANDER STAHLBERG MANNERHEIM
FRENCH BLUM COTY DARU MOLE DUPUY FAURE FAVRE FERRY FOULD MARET MONIS PASSY RIBOT SIMON SUGER SULLY AVENOL BARROT BERNIS BIGNON BRIAND CARNOT CASSIN DOUMER DUPRAT FLEURY FOUCHE GUIZOT LOUBET MELINE NECKER PERIER PETAIN ROUHER THIERS TURGOT COLBERT DECAZES GRAMONT HERRIOT MAISTRE MARIGNY MAUPEOU MAZARIN MOLLIEN NOGARET REGNIER ROUVIER SCHUMAN SEGUIER VILLELE VIVIANI CHOISEUL CONSTANS DALADIER DELCASSE FONTANES FRANCOIS GAMBETTA HANOTAUX LHOPITAL MIRABEAU PAINLEVE POINCARE POMPIDOU PORTALIS BONAPARTE BOURGEOIS CHAMPAGNY CLEMENTEL DALHOUSIE DOUMERGUE FALLIERES LAFAYETTE MILLERAND RICHELIEU VERGENNES BARTHELEMY CLEMENCEAU TALLEYRAND WADDINGTON BASSOMPIERRE CHATEAUBRIAND
GERMAN BLOS CUNO FALK MARX SOLF BEUST JAGOW NOSKE PAPEN BRANDT GERBER KRANTZ LUTHER MAURER MIQUEL MOLTKE WORNER BRUNING CAPRIVI CURTIUS FABRICE GESSLER STEPHAN ADENAUER BISMARCK HAINISCH HERTLING HOLSTEIN KUHLMANN SEVERING SPANHEIM BENNIGSEN ERZBERGER HALLSTEIN MICHAELIS BERNSTORFF FEHRENBACH HILFERDING RICHTHOFEN SCHLEICHER STRESEMANN WINDTHORST ZIMMERMANN SECKENDORFF
GREEK ZAIMES KANARES KORIZES RANGABE RHALLES BULGARIS GOUNARES KONDYLES PANGALOS PERICLES TIMOLEON ARISTIDES DINARCHUS DRAGOUMES HYPERIDES PERIANDER TIMOTHEUS TRIKOUPES TSALDARES TSOUDEROS VENIZELOS ALCIBIADES SKOULOUDES THEMISTIUS THERAMENES DEMOSTHENES THRASYBULUS THEMISTOCLES KOUMOUNDOUROS MAVROKORDATOS MICHALAKOPOULOS
HUNGARIAN DEAK NAGY VASS CSAKY SZELL TISZA BANFFY BAROSS EOTVOS GOMBOS HORTHY LONYAY TELEKI BETHLEN HORVATH HUNYADI KOSSUTH WEKERLE ANDRASSY SZECHENYI MARTINUZZI
ICELANDIC HAFSTEIN SIGURDSSON
INDIAN NOON GUPTA NEHRU SINHA BAJPAI GANDHI SASTRI
IRISH HYDE ANDREWS GRATTAN MCNEILL COSGRAVE DEVALERA MACBRIDE CRAIGAVON
ISRAELI ALLON DAYAN RABIN
ITALIAN BALBO BERTI CIANO CROCE DORIA FACTA LANZA MANIN NITTI ROCCO ROSSI SELLA VOLPI BONGHI CAVOUR CRISPI FEDELE GRANDI PEPOLI RUDINI SFORZA ADRIANI ALFIERI AZEGLIO CADORNA CAIROLI DURANDO GASPERI GRAVINA MAMIANI MANCINI ORLANDO PELLOUX PONTANO SONNINO TANUCCI TITTONI VILLARI ALBERONI CIBRARIO CORRENTI DEPRETIS GIOLITTI LAFARINA LUZZATTI MATTIOLI MENABREA NICOTERA RATTAZZI RICASOLI SALANDRA SCIALOIA ANTONELLI FEDERZONI GARIBALDI GUERRAZZI LAMARMORA MINGHETTI MONTANELLI ZANARDELLI MACHIAVELLI LAMBRUSCHINI
JAPANESE ITO GOTO HARA KATO SATO MUTSU OKUBO OKUMA INOUYE KANEKO KOMURA MAKINO TANAKA HAYASHI ITAGAKI IWAKURA IYEYASU KATSURA SAIONJI HIRANUMA KIYOMORI MATSUOKA NOBUNAGA TERAUCHI YAMAGATA YAMAMOTO HAMAGUCHI HIDEYOSHI MATSUKATA WAKATSUKI
KOREAN RHEE
LATVIAN KVIESIS ULMANIS MEIEROVICS
LEBANESE MALIK
LIBERIAN TUBMAN TOLBERT
LITHUANIAN SMETONA VOLDEMARAS
MEXICAN DIAZ ALAMAN CALLES OBREGON ZULOAGA IGLESIAS
NEW ZEALAND FOX HALL WARD ALLEN VOGEL COATES FORBES FRASER MASSEY SEDDON ATKINSON STAFFORD
NORWEGIAN BULL KOHT FALSEN HAMBRO NANSEN HAGERUP KNUDSEN SVERDRUP MICHELSEN MOWINCKEL NYGAARDSVOLD
PERUVIAN PRADO CORNEJO CADLERON BENAVIDES MENDIBURU
PHILIPPINE ROXAS OSMENA QUEZON ROMULO
POLISH BECK WITOS DMOWSKI ZALESKI ZALUSKI SIKORSKI SKRYNSKI KOSCIUSKO PILSUDSKI PADEREWSKI WOJCIECHOWSKI
PORTUGUESE PAES COSTA POMBAL ALMEIDA ARRIAGA CARMONA MACHADO SALAZAR CARVALHO SALDANHA SANTAREM
PRUSSIAN BULOW
ROMAN CATO CINNA PLINY CAESAR CICERO POMPEY SENECA AGRIPPA LAELIUS RUFINUS CAMILLUS CATILINE GRACCHUS MAECENAS STILICHO FABRICIUS FLAMINIUS SERTORIUS SYMMACHUS CASSIDORUS HORTENSIUS
ROMANIAN CARP MANIU IONESCU CATARGIU MIRONESCU TITULESCU MARGHILOMAN KOGALNICEANU
RUSSIAN BIRON GIERS WITTE BLUDOV CANCRIN KALININ MOLOTOV MUNNICH SIEVERS TOLSTOI AVERESCU CHICHKOV DMITRIEV GOLITSYN IZVOLSKI LAMSDORF LITVINOV POTMEKIN STOLYPIN CALINESCU CHICHERIN GORCHAKOV GOREMYKIN GRIBOEDOV MENSHIKOV SPERANSKI NESSELRODE PROTOPOPOV
SCOTTISH HUME KNOX BEATON GORDON MURRAY JAMESON MAITLAND RANDOLPH HORSBRUGH WARRISTON ELPHINSTONE
SERBIAN GRUIC
SOUTH AFRICAN BOTHA BRAND REITZ SMUTS STEYN KRUGER SPRIGG COGHLAN HERTZOG MERRIMAN
SPANISH LUNA ALAVA GODOY OSUNA PEREZ GALVEZ MANUEL TORENO ABASCAL ALARCON ISTURIZ MENDOZA NARVAEZ SAGASTA SILVELA ENSENADA ESCOSURA MANRIQUE OLIVARES QUINTANA ZORRILLA CALOMARDE ESCOIQUIZ ESPARTERO REQUESENS JOVELLANOS MIRAFLORES
SWEDISH EDEN GEER HORN TOLL BRAHE ESSEN UNDEN HANSSON LINDMAN SANDLER BRANTING FORSSELL EHRENSVARD GYLLENBORG WENNERBERG OXENSTIERNA OXENSTJERNA HAMMARSKJOLD
SWISS ADOR DROZ FAZY KERN MUSY FURER GOBAT MEYER MOTTA BLUMER ESCHER MINGER MULLER DEUCHER BLUNTSCHLI SCHULTHESS
TURKISH INONU SARACOGLU
URUGUAYAN RIVERA
VENEZUELAN VARGAS BOLIVAR MONAGAS BETANCOURT
YUGOSLAV PASIC PROTIC ZIVKOVIC DAVIDOVIC MARINKOVIC PRIBICEVIC

STATICE ARMERIA LIMONIUM

STATION BY BYE FIX ORB RUN SET BASE GARE POST RANK ROOM SEAT STOP BEING BERTH CHOKY DEPOT PLACE POSTE SIEGE STAGE STALL STAND STATE DEGREE LOCATE STANCE CONTROL CUARTEL DIGNITY HABITAT OUTPOST GARRISON PILTDOWN POSITION STANDING TERMINAL TERMINUS TRANSFER
(— IN BASEBALL) BASE
(— IN LIFE) BEING CALLING
(— OF HERON) SEDGE SIEGE
(ANIMAL'S —) LIE
(ASSIGNED —) QUARTER
(CONCEALED —) AMBUSH
(CUSTOMS —) CHOKEY
(EXALTED —) PURPLE
(HEALTH —) SANATORIUM SANITARIUM
(MILITARY —) CAMP
(POLICE —) NICK TANA TANNA THANAH KOTWALEE
(POST —) DAK
(RADIO —S) CHAIN NETWORK
(RAILWAY —) GARE CABIN
(RUSSIAN SPACE —) MIR
(SAILING —) MARINA
(SIGNALLING —) BANTAY BEACON
(SURVEYING —) STADIA
(TELEVISION —) CHANNEL
(TOLL —) CHOKY CHOKEY

(TRADING —) FACTORY
(WAY —) TAMBO
STATIONARY SET FAST FIXED STILL ATREST LEDGER STATIC DORMANT SITFAST STABILE STATARY IMMOBILE
STATIONERY PAPER PAPETERIE
STATION WAGON WOODY WOODIE MICROBUS SUBURBAN
STATISTICIAN ANALYST STATIST
STATOBLAST SPORE
STATUARY IMAGERY
STATUE HERM ICON IDOL IKON TERM BUSTO HERMA IMAGE MOSES AGALMA BRONZE HERMES MEMNON STATUA WEEPER XOANON ILISSUS PASQUIN PICTURE STATURE STATUTE ACROLITH CARYATID MARFORIO MONUMENT PANTHEUM PORTRAIT VICTORIA
(— ENDOWED WITH LIFE) GALATEA
(— OF ATHENA) PALLADIUM
(— OF GIGANTIC SIZE) COLOSSUS
(COLOSSAL —) GOG MAGOG
STATUETTE WAX CLIO EMMY OSCAR WINNIE TANAGRA FIGULINE FIGURINE SIGILLUM
(— AWARD) REUBEN
(AWARD —) GRAMMY
STATURE PITCH GROWTH HEIGHT INCHES WASTME CAPACITY
STATUS RANK SEAT PLACE STATE ASPECT FOOTING STATURE POSITION STANDING SITUATION
(— OF YOUNGER SON) CADENCY
(HIGH —) CACHET
(LEGAL —) CAPUT
(SECONDARY —) BACKSEAT
STATUTE ACT LAW LEX DOOM EDICT ASSIZE DECREE SETNESS SITTING STATUTUM TANZIMAT
(— FAIR) MOP
STATUTORY LEGAL
STAUNCH FAST STOUT TRUSTY FAITHFUL STALWART
STAVE LAG SLAT STAP SHAKE STAFF STOVE VERSE BASTON STANZA WATTLE
(— IN) BILGE BULGE
(SET OF —S) SHOOK
(PL.) LAGGEN LAGGIN STICKS STAVING
STAY DAY GET LIE BASE HOLD LEND PROP REST SIST STOP WAIT ABIDE ABODE APPUI DEFER DELAY DEMUR DWELL LEAVE STINT TARRY THOLE ARREST ATTEND BIDING DETAIN EXPECT GUSSET POTENT REMAIN TIMBER UPHOLD EMBASSY JIBSTAY LAYOVER MANSION SOJOURN SUSPEND BACKSTAY CONTINUE FORESTAY HORNSTAY MAINSTAY MARTINGALE
(— AWAY) SKIP
(— BEHIND) LAG
(— CLEAR) AVOID
(— FOR) AWAIT
(— IN BED) LIEIN SACKIN
(— THE NIGHT) BUNK HOSTLE
(— WITH) STICK
(PRIEST'S —) STATION
(SHORT —) VISIT
(TAILORING —) BRIDLE
(PL.) JUMPS JUPES BODICE
STAY-AT-HOME HOMEBODY HOMESTER
STAYER BONER
STAYLACE AGLET AIGLET
STAYSAIL JUMBO
STEAD LIEU ROOM VICE PLACE BEHALF
STEADFAST PAT SAD FAST FIRM SURE TRUE ROCKY STAID STEER STABLE STANCH STEADY CERTAIN EXPRESS SETTLED STAUNCH VALIANT CONSTANT FAITHFUL RESOLUTE STALWART
STEADFASTLY FIRM FIRMLY INTENTLY
STEADILY SAD FAST STEADY
STEADINESS NERVE BALANCE
STEADING ONSET ONSTEAD
STEADY GUY SAD BEAU EVEN FIRM SURE TRIG TRUE CANNY FRANK LEVEL SOBER STUDY SUANT TIGHT SICCAR SMOOTH STABLE STANCH BALLAST EQUABLE STABILE STATARY STAUNCH CONSTANT DECOROUS DILIGENT FAITHFUL RESOLUTE TRANQUIL UNSHAKEN
(— AT ANCHOR) HOLSOM
STEAK BROIL SHELL FLITCH TUCKET FLANKEN GRISKIN PORTERHOUSE
(CLUB —) CONTREFILET
(KIND OF —) SHELL SKIRT TBONE
(LOIN —) FILET FILLET TOURNEDOS
STEAL BAG CAB CLY COP FOX GYP LAG MAG NAP NIM NIP RAP RIG BONE CHOR COON CRIB FAKE GLOM HOOK KNAP LIFT LURK MAGG MAKE MILL NAIL NICK PEAK PICK PRIG SLIP SMUG ANNEX BOOST BRIBE CLOUT CREEP FETCH FILCH FLIMP FRISK GLIDE HARRY HEIST HOIST LURCH MOOCH MOUCH PINCH PLUCK POACH SCOFF SHAKE SHARP SHAVE SLIDE SNAKE SNARE SNEAK STALK SWIPE TOUCH TRUFF COLLAR CONVEY FINGER HIJACK MOOTCH NOBBLE PILFER RIPOFF SNITCH STRIKE THIEVE TWITCH BESTEAL CABBAGE PLUNDER PURLOIN SCHLEPP SKYUGLE SNABBLE SNAFFLE SURREPT ABSTRACT CRIBBAGE EMBEZZLE LIBERATE MANARVEL PECULATE SCROUNGE SHOPLIFT PLAGIARIZE
(— A GLANCE) GLIME
(— ALONG) SLIME SLINK
(— A WATCH) FLIMP
(— AWAY) LOOP SLINK
(— BY ALTERING BRANDS) DUFF
(— CALVES) NUGGET
(— CATTLE) DUFF RUSTLE
(— COPPER FROM VESSEL'S BOTTOM) TOSH
(— OFF) RUN
(— SLYLY) SCROUNGE
STEALER (CATTLE —) DUFFER ABACTOR
STEALING STALE
(PREF.) KLEPT(O)
STEALTHILY SIDLINS THIEFLY SIDELINS
STEALTHY CATTY PRIVY ARTFUL FELINE TIPTOE CATLIKE FURTIVE SNEAKING THIEVISH
STEAM IRE OAM ROKE STEM ANGER BLAST SMOKE SWEAT VAPOR BREATH POTHER CUSHION TICKOFF
(PREF.) ATM(O) ATMID(O)
STEAMBOAT KICKUP STEAMER
STEAMER CLAM LINER TENDER CUNARDER
STEAMER DUCK RACER LOGHEAD
STEAMSHIP SCREW STEAM STEAMER SEATRAIN SHOWBOAT
(— OF VENICE) VAPORETTO
STEAM SHOVEL NAVVY NAVVIE
STEATIN MULL
STEATITE LARDITE POTSTONE SOAPROCK
STEATOPYGOUS RUMPY
STEED NAG ROIL HORSE MOUNT STEAD PEGASUS SLEIPNER SLEIPNIR
STEEL RAIL BLOOM BRACE FUSIL TERNE WEAPON WHITTLE FLEERISH
(— FOR STRIKING FIRE) ESLABON
(— FOR USE WITH FLINT) FUSIL FURISON FLEERISH
(— INLAID WITH GOLD) KOFT KOFTGARI
(DAMASCUS —) DAMASK
(INDIAN —) WOOTZ
(KIND OF —) MILD PEDAL
(MOLTEN —) HEAT
STEELER BONER
STEELING ACIERAGE
STEELWORKER HOOKER STICKMAN STRANDER STRANNER
STEELYARD BISMAR BISMER DESEMER DOTCHIN STATERA
STEENBRAS BISKOP
STEEP RET SOP BATE BOLD BOWK BREW BUCK DEAR DRAW DUNG ELIX LIME MASH MASK SOAK STAY STEW STEY BLUFF BRANT BRENT HATCH HEAVY HILLY QUICK SHARP SHEER SOUSE STIFF ABRUPT BLUFFY CLIFFY CLIFTY DECOCT IMBIBE INFUSE SPRUNT STEEPY ARDUOUS BRASQUE CLIVOSE INSTEEP PRERUPT STICKLE HEADLONG MACERATE SATURATE SIDELING STIFFISH STRAIGHT PRECIPITOUS
(— IN VERY HOT WATER) PLOT
STEEPED SODDEN
STEEPING SOUSE INFUSION
STEEPLE SPEAR SPIRE
STEEPLEBUSH HARDHACK
STEEPLECHASE CHASE GRIND
STEER COX PLY AIRT BEEF BULL HELM LEAD STEM STOT GUIDE SPADE SPADO STERN TOLLY CANNER RUDDER BULLOCK STOCKER COWBRUTE MOSSHORN NAVIGATE
(— VEHICLE) DRIVE
(FAT —) BEAST
(HORNLESS —) NOT NOTT
(VICIOUS —) LADINO
(WILD —) YAW YEW COWBRUTE
(YOUNG —) STOT STOTT
STEERAGE STERN
STEERER SLUER CAPPER
STEERSMAN COX PILOT WHEEL PATRON SLEWER CANOPUS SHIPMAN STEERER COXSWAIN HELMSMAN SEACUNNY STERNMAN WHEELMAN COCKSWAIN
STEGOMYIA AEDES
STEIN MUG SHANT
STEINBOCK BOUQUETIN
STELE SHAFT EUSTELE OBELISK
STELLAR STARRY
STELLATE ASTROSE
STEM BUN BASE BEAK BEAM BINE BIRN CANE CULM CURB NOSE PIPE PROW RISP ROOT RUNT SHAW STUD ARISE FILUM HAULM SCAPE SCREW SHAFT SHANK SHOOT SPIRE STALE STALK STEAL STICK STIPE STOCK STRAW THEME TRUNK TUBER BRANCH CAUDEX CAULIS DERIVE SCAPUS SPRING CAULOME CONTAIN FULCRUM HOPBINE HOPVINE PEDICEL PETIOLE PLASHER SARMENT SPINDLE STEMLET TIGELLA CAULICLE ENGENDER EPICOTYL FORESTEM PEDUNCLE PIPESTEM TIGELLUM
(— OF ARROW) SHAFT
(— OF BANANAS) COUNT
(— OF GLASS) BALUSTER
(— OF GRAPES) RAPE
(— OF HOOKAH) SNAKE
(— OF MATCH) SHAFT
(— OF MUSHROOM) STIPE
(— OF MUSICAL NOTE) TAIL FILUM VIRGULA
(— OF PIPE) STAPPLE
(— OF PLANT) AXIS RUNT CAULIS
(— OF SHIP) PROW STEMPOST
(— OF TREE) BOLE CAUDEX
(—S OF CULTIVATED PLANTS) HAULM
(BULBLIKE —) CORM
(DRY WITHERED —) BIRN
(EDIBLE —) EDDO
(GRIEF —) KELLY
(MAIN — OF DEER'S ANTLERS) BEAM
(ORNAMENTAL —) STAVE
(PITHY JOINTED —) CANE
(THORNY —) LAWYER
(TWINING —) BINE
(PREF.) CAUL(I) CORM(O) CULMI SCAPI STIRPI
(SUFF.) DENDRON OME
STEMLESS ACAULINE
STEMMA OCELLUS OCELLANA PEDIGREE
STEMMER STRIPPER
STEMWARE CRYSTAL
STENCH FOGO HOGO FETOR SMELL STINK WHIFF FOETOR MEPHITIS
STENCIL THEOREM
(— PROCESS) POCHOIR
STENCILED GOFFERED
STENO TEMP
STENOGRAPHY SHORTHAND
STENOSIS SMALLING

STEP CUT FIT JOG PEG PIP BEMA DESS FOOT GREE LINK PACE PASO PEEP RUNG STAP BRASS CORTE DODGE FLIER FLYER GRECE NOTCH POINT STAGE STAIR TOOTH TRACE TREAD DEGREE GRADIN RUNDLE STRIDE WINDER CURTAIL DESCENT FOOTING GRADINE GRADING COONJINE DEMARCHE DOORSTEP FOOTPACE FOOTSTEP FORESTEP PREDELLA STRATLIN
(— ASIDE) DIGRESS
(— BACKWARD) DODGE
(— BY STEP) GRADATIM
(— DOWNWARD) DESCENT
(— FOR GEM MOUNTING) KITE
(— FORWARD) ADVANCE
(— IN A BEARING) BRASS
(— IN BELL RINGING) DODGE
(— IN DOCK) ALTAR
(— IN SELF-ESTEEM) PEG
(— IN SEQUENCE) PLACE
(— IN SHAFT) STEMPEL STEMPLE
(— IN SOCIAL SCALE) CUT
(— IN TRENCH) BANQUETTE
(— LIVELY) SKELP
(— OF LADDER) RIME RUNG ROUND RUNDLE
(— OF TUSK) TOOTH
(— OUT) DIE
(— PERFORMED BY COMPUTER) OPERATION
(—S OF BOWLER) APPROACH
(— SUPPORTING MILLSTONE) TRAMPOT
(ALTAR —S) GRADUAL
(BALLET —) PLIE FOUETTE SISSONE SISSONNE
(BALLET —S) ALLEGRO
(BOUNDING —) SKIP
(CLUMSY —) STAUP
(DANCE —) DIP PAS SET BUZZ DRAG DRAW FLAT SHAG SKIP BRAWL CHASS COULE GLIDE IRISH STOMP BRANLE CANTER CHASSE DOUBLE INTURN STRIDE BRANSLE BUFFALO FISHTAIL GLISSADE PIGEONWING
(FALSE —) HOB SLIP SPHALM SNAPPER SPHALMA STUMBLE
(FIRST —) STARTER RUDIMENT
(FLIGHT OF —S) GRECE GRICE PERRON GEMONIES
(GLIDING —) CHASSE
(HALF —) HALFTONE SEMITONE
(LIGHT —) PITAPAT
(MINING —) LOB STEMPEL STEMPLE
(POMPOUS —) STRUT
(PRIM —) MINCE
(PROCEED BY —S) RATCHET
(SET OF —S) STILE
(STATELY —) STALK
(PL.) STY GHAT GHAUT STILE LADDER
STEPFATHER FATHER STEPSIRE
STEPLADDER TRAP STEPS
(PART OF —) RAIL REST RUNG SHOE STEP BRACE SPREADER
STEPMOTHER MOTHER HANGNAIL STEPDAME
(RELATING TO —) NOVERCAL
STEPPE PUSZTA
(— REGION) SAHEL
(ARID REGION OF —) POECHORE
STEPPED STOPEN
STEPPENWOLF (AUTHOR OF —) HESSE
(CHARACTER IN —) HARRY MARIA HALLER HERMINE
STEPPING
(SUFF.) GRADE
STEREOISOMER ANOMER EPIMER
STEREOTYPE CAST LABEL CLICHE STEREO TYPECAST
STEREOTYPED CHAIN STAGE TRITE USUAL STEREO IDENTIKIT
STERILE DRY DEAD DEAF GELD POOR AXENIC BARREN GALLED MEAGER MULISH OTIOSE ASEPTIC ACARPOUS BANKRUPT IMPOTENT
(PREF.) STEIRO
STERILITY ATOCIA APHORIA
STERILIZE INSULATE
STERILIZING BURNING
STERLING SOUND
(100,000 POUNDS —) PLUM
STERN GRIL GRIM HARD POOP ASPER CRUEL GRUFF HARSH RIGID ROUGH ROUND STARK STOUR FLINTY GLOOMY GRIMLY SEVERE SHREWD STRICT SULLEN TORVID UNKIND WICKED AUSTERE TORVOUS STEERAGE STERNFUL STRAIGHT
(— OF SHIP) DOCK APLUSTRE
(TOWARD THE —) ABAFT
STERNFAST PROVISO
STERNNESS RIGOR TORVITY SEVERITY
STERNPOST POST STEM MAINPOST
STERNUTATIVE ERRHINE PTARMIC
STERNUTATOR ERRHINE
STEROL AMYRIN STERIN AMBRAIN
STEROPE (FATHER OF —) ATLAS
(MOTHER OF —) PLEIONE
(SON OF —) OENOMAUS
STERTOR SNORE
STEVEDORE STOWER TRIMMER WHARFIE CARGADOR DOCKHAND
STEVENSON, R.L. TUSITALA
STEW JUG FRET ITCH SLUM SNIT SWOT BREDI CIVET CURRY DAUBE SALMI STIVE STOVE SWEAT BRAISE BURGOO HODDLE MUDDLE PAELLA SCOUSE SEETHE SIMMER BROTHEL CALDERA GOULASH HARICOT NAVARIN PUCHERO STOVIES TERRINE BOURRIDE ETOUFFEE FRIJOADA HOTCHPOT MORTREUX MULLIGAN STEWPOND STUFFATA WATERZOOI CARBONNADE RATATOUILLE SLUMGULLION
(— A HARE) JUG
(— IN A SAUCE) DAUBE
(— MADE IN FORECASTLE) HODDLE
(— OF TRAMPS) MULLIGAN
(CAJUN —) ETOUFFEE
(FISH —) STODGE CHOWDER MATELOTE
(GAME —) SALMI
(IN A —) UPSET
(IRISH —) STOVIES
(MUTTON —) NAVARIN
(POT FOR —) OLLA
STEWARD HIND VOGT DEWAN DIWAN GRAFF GRAVE REEVE COMMIS FACTOR FARMER GRIEVE LOOKER SIRCAR SIRDAR BAILIFF CURATOR DAPIFER FLUNKEY GRANGER HUSBAND MAORMOR MORMAOR PESHKAR PROCTOR PROVOST SPENCER SPENDER APPROVER BHANDARI CELLARER CONSUMAH GASTALDO HERENACH KHANSAMA LARDINER MALVOLIO MANCIPLE PROVISOR STEADMAN VILLICUS MAJORDOMO
(JOCKEY CLUB —) STIPE
STEWED SODDEN
STEWING ITCHING
STEWPAN STEW COCOTTE SKILLET
STHENELUS (FATHER OF —) PERSEUS CAPANEUS ANDROGEOS
(MOTHER OF —) EVADNE ANDROMEDA
(SON OF —) EURYSTHEUS
(WIFE OF —) NICIPPE
STHENOBOEA (FATHER OF —) IOBATES
(HUSBAND OF —) PROETUS
STIBNITE SURMA STIBIUM ANTIMONY
STIBOPHEN FUADIN
STICHIC SERIAL
STICK CAT CLA DIP GAD HEW LUG WAN BROG BUFF CHOP CLAG CLAM CLUB CRAB GLUE HANG HURL PALE PALO PICK POLE POTE RICE RUNG STAY TREE YARD BATON BRAIL CAMAN CLAME CLAVE CLEAM CLING CROME DEMUR HURLY PASTE PRICK SPELK STAFF STAKE STANG STAVE STEND STING STOCK STOKE VALET VERGE WADDY ADHERE ATLATL BALLOW BATLER BATLET BATTLE BILLET BROACH BULGER CEMENT CLEAVE CLEEKY COHERE CUDGEL FESCUE HOCKEY INHERE KIERIE KIPPIN LIBBET MALLET RADDLE RAMMER RISSLE STRIKE STRING THIVEL TWITCH BACKSET BATLING CAMMOCK CUMMOCK GAMBREL HURLBAT KILNRIB KIPPEEN MOLINET NOBBLER SHANGAN SPURTLE WOOLDER ASHPLANT BLUDGEON BRINGSEL BRINSELL CATPIECE CATSTICK CRUMMOCK DIPSTICK DUTCHMAN GIBSTAFF GOBSTICK KILNTREE POTSTICK SPREADER
(— AS ARCHERY MARK) WAND
(— AS VIETNAM WEAPON) PUNJI
(— FAST) JAM JAMB SEIZE FITCHER
(— FASTENED TO DOG'S TAIL) SHANGAN
(— FOR ADMITTING TENANTS) VERGE
(— FOR DRIVING OXEN) OXGOAD
(— FOR FIRING CANNON) LINSTOCK
(— FOR KILLING FISH) NOBBLER
(— FOR MAKING FENCE) RADDLE
(— FOR MIXING CHOCOLATE) MOLINET
(— FOR MIXING MORTAR) RAB
(— FOR SNUFF) DIP
(— FOR THATCHING) SPAR GROOM SPELK SPRINGLE
(— IN MUD) STODGE
(— IN OPERATION) FREEZE
(— IT OUT) LAST
(— OF A FAN) BRIN
(— OF CANDY) GIBBY
(— OF CHALK) CRAYON
(— OF ORCHESTRA LEADER) BATON
(— OUT) BUG POKE BULGE SHOOT EXSERT EXTEND EXTRUDE PROTEND
(— REGULATING SLUICEWAY) CATPIECE
(— SEPARATING LUMBER PILES) STICKER
(— TO BEAT CLOTHES) BATLER BATLET
(— TO DISTEND CARCASS) STEND BACKSET
(— TOGETHER) CLOT BLOCK CLING BALTER CEMENT COHERE COAGMENT
(— TO HOLD BOW) TILLER
(— TO HOLD LOG LOAD) DUTCHMAN
(— TO KEEP ANIMAL QUIET) TWITCH
(— TO MARK CROSSING) BROG
(— TO POKE WITH) POTE
(— TO REMOVE HOOK FROM FISH) GOBSTICK
(— TO STRETCH NET) BRAIL
(— TO STUFF DOLLS) RAMMER
(— TO THROW AT BIRDS) SQUAIL
(— TO TIGHTEN KNOT) WOOLDER
(— UP) COCK
(— USED AS POINTER) FESCUE
(BAMBOO —) LATHI LATHEE
(BASKETRY —) LEAGUE
(BENT —) RIFLE
(COLD —) ICICLE
(FIELD HOCKEY —) BULGER CAMMOCK
(FISHING —) GAD
(FORKED —) GROM GROOM
(HOCKEY —) CAMAN HURLY HOCKEY HURLEY SHINNY CAMMOCK CUMMOCK DODDART
(IRON-POINTED —) VALET
(KIND OF —) PUGIL
(KNOBBED —) BILLET
(LACROSSE —) CROSSE
(LARGE —) MOCK
(MARKING —) LEAD
(NOTCHED —) TALLY
(ODD —) JAY
(POLISHING —) BUFF
(PRAYER —) PAHO
(PRINTER'S —) SHOOTER
(RANGE-FINDING —) STADIA
(ROUND —) DOWEL SPINDLE
(STIRRING —) MUNDLE POOLER SPURTLE POTSTICK SWIZZLER
(STOUT —) BAT COSH LOWDER
(TALLY —) TAIL
(THROWING —) ATLATL HORNERAH
(TOBACCO —) LATH
(WALKING —) CANE KEBBY WADDY JAMBEE JOCKEY KEBBIE WHANGEE ASHPLANT GIBSTAFF
(PREF.) RHABD(O)
STICKER HINGE LABEL STRIP

WAFER HOPPER PASTER BLEEDER CROSSER MOPSTICK STICKLER
STICK-IN STRANDER
STICKINESS GAUM TACK ROPINESS
STICKING ADHERENT ADHESION COHESION COHESIVE
STICKLE DEMUR BOGGLE HAGGLE HIGGLE
STICKLEBACK BAGGIE BANDIE HACKLE GHOSTER PINFISH
STICKLER (— FOR FORMALITY) TAPIST
STICKMAN DEALER
STICKS BOONIES BOONDOCKS
STICKUM GLUE PINETAR
STICKY CAB CLAM CLIT ICKY DABBY FATTY GAUMY GLUEY GOOEY GUMMY JAMMY MALMY PUGGY SHORT TACKY TOUGH CLAGGY CLAMMY CLARTY CLINGY CLOGGY GLOPPY PLUCKY SMEARY VISCID VISCOUS ADHESIVE TENACIOUS (PREF.) GLOEO GLOIO
STIFF BUM SAD CARK HARD NASH TRIG BUDGE CLUNG RIGID SOLID STARK STEER STITH STOUR THARF TOUGH BOARDY CLEDGY CLUMSY CLUNCH FORMAL FROZEN PLUGGY STARKY STEEVE STICKY STILTY STOCKY STURDY UNEASY WOODEN ANGULAR BUCKRAM COSTIVE STARCHY STILTED RAMRODDY RIGOROUS STAFFISH **(SOMEWHAT —)** CARKLED (PREF.) ANKYL(O) TORPI TORPORI
STIFFELIO (CHARACTER IN —) LINA STANKAR RAFFAELE STIFFELIO **(COMPOSER OF —)** VERDI
STIFFEN GUM SET SIZE BRACE STARK STIFF STRUT TRUSS HARDEN STARCH STOVER CONGEAL STARKEN **(— PRICE)** HARDEN
STIFFENED FUSED CARKLED
STIFFENER KNEE COUNTER
STIFFENING PUFF DRESS
STIFFNESS KINK RIGOR STARCH BUCKRAM PRIMNESS RIGIDITY SEVERITY **(SYMBOL OF —)** RAMROD
STIFLE DAMP FUNK SLAY CHOKE CRUSH STIVE STUFF MUFFLE QUENCH FLASKER QUERKEN SMOTHER SCOMFISH STRANGLE SUPPRESS THROTTLE
STIFLED DEAF ETOUFFE
STIFLING CLOSE STIVY SMUDGY POTHERY SMOTHERY
STIGMA BLOT FOIL NOTE SLUR SPOT BRAND ODIUM STAIN TAINT BLOTCH BLEMISH
STIGMATIZE BLOT BRAND DENOUNCE
STILBITE DESMINE
STILE STY STICK TIMBER
STILETTO BODKIN STYLET PIERCER POINTEL
STILL BUT COY LAY YET BODY CALM COSH HUSH LOWN LULL WORM ACCOY CHECK QUIET WHIST HOWEER HUSHED PACIFY QUENCH SETTLE SILENT SOOTHE STATIC SUBDUE WITHAL ALEMBIC CORNUTE DORMANT HOWEVER PELICAN SILENCE CUCURBIT RECEIVER RESTRAIN STAGNANT STILLERY SUPPRESS **(— PART)** KELD **(PART OF —)** HEAD TUBE RETORT CONDENSER
STILLAGE SLOP STILLING STILLION
STILL-HUNT STALK
STILLNESS CALM HUSH REST PEACE LANGUOR SILENCE STATION
STILT KAKI POGO TILT LAWYER PATTEN SCATCH YEGUITA LONGLEGS STILTIFY TRIANGLE
STILTED LOFTY STIFF FORMAL POETIC STILTY POMPOUS
STIMULANT COCA STIM INULA BRACER CINDER FILLIP GINGER HARMAL PHYTIN CAMPHOR CARDIAC OUABAIN REVIVER ADONIDIN AMMONIAC EXCITANT INCITANT LOBELINE PEMOLINE STIMULUS SASSAFRAS WHETSTONE
STIMULATE FAN HOP KEY PEP FUEL GOAD HYPE HYPO MOVE SEED SPUR STIR URGE WHET FILIP IMPEL PIQUE PRIME ROUSE SPARK STING AROUSE BESTIR EXCITE FILLIP INCITE SPIRIT TICKLE UPSTIR ANIMATE ENLIVEN INNERVE INSPIRE PROVOKE QUICKEN SHARPEN ACTIVATE FARADIZE IRRITATE MOTIVATE TITILLATE **(FAIL TO —)** UNDERWHELM
STIMULATED (ARTIFICIALLY —) HOPPEDUP
STIMULATING PERT SEXY BRISK BRACING PUNGENT EROGENIC EXCITING GENEROUS INCITANT POIGNANT STIRRING **(— ANGER)** ADRENAL (PREF.) AUXO EXCITO
STIMULATION GINGER IMPETUS **(MENTAL —)** SPRITE
STIMULUS CUE AURA BROD EDGE GOAD HYPO SPUR STIM STING FILLIP MOTIVE SOURCE BAHNUNG IMPETUS OESTRUS STRESSOR
STING NIP BARB BITE BURN FOIN GOAD SOAK TANG ATTER DEVIL PIQUE PRICK SMART STANG TOUCH NETTLE ACULEUS BUGBITE PIERCER IRRITATE STIMULUS
STINGILY STRAIT SCARCELY
STINGINESS PARSIMONY
STINGING KEEN SMART PEPPERY PIQUANT POINTED PRICKLY PUNGENT ACRIMONY ACULEATE NETTLING POIGNANT SCALDING URTICANT
STINGING ANT KELEP
STINGRAY ANGLER OBISPO SEPHEN TRYGON BATFISH LOPHIID STINGER WAIREPO
STINGY DRY DREE GAIN GAIR HARD MEAN NEAR NIGH CHEAP CLOSE MINGY SCALY TIGHT CHEAPO DRIECH GRIPPY HUNGRY MEASLY NARROW SCABBY SCARCE SCRIMY SKIMPY SKINNY SNIPPY STRAIT CHINCHY CHINTZY COSTIVE MISERLY NIGGARD PENURIOUS PARSIMONIOUS
STINK FOGO GOAD NIFF PONG STEW SUCK SMELL SMEECH STENCH MEPHITIS (PREF.) BROM(O)
STINKBIRD HOACIN HOATZIN
STINKER RAT BUMMER
STINKING FOUL HIGH FETID PUTID STINKY MALODOROUS
STINKWOOD DOGWOOD
STINT TASK GRIST PINCH SCANT SNAPE SCRIMP SKINCH STINGY TANTUM SCANTLE **(SHORT —)** SNATCH **(WITHOUT —)** FREELY
STIPE STEM STALK
STIPEND ANN HIRE ANNAT WAGES SALARY PENSION PREBEND PROVEND COMMENDA
STIPENDIARY BEAK
STIPPLE SPONGE
STIPPLED DOTTED
STIPULATE ARTICLE PROTEST PROVIDE COVENANT
STIPULATION IF ANNEX CLAUSE ARTICLE PREMISE PROVISO STRINGS COVENANT (PL.) TERMS
STIPULE SPINE SHEATH STIPEL STIPULA TENDRIL
STIR DO ADO FAN GOG JEE PUG WAG BEET BUZZ CARD FUSS MOVE PEAL POKE RAUK ROKE TODO WAKE AMOVE BUDGE CHURN CREEP ERECT FUROR HURRY MUDGE POACH QUICH RAISE ROUST SLICE SPARK STING STOOR STURT TEASE TOUCH AROUSE AWAKEN BUBBLE BUSTLE COOLER CRUTCH EXCITE FLURRY GINGER HUBBUB JUMBLE KIAUGH MUDDLE PADDLE POUTER QUINCH QUITCH REMBLE REMOVE ROUNCE STODGE SUMMON TATTER ACTUATE ANIMATE BLATHER CLUTTER COMMOVE FLUTTER PROVOKE STARKLE SWIZZLE TROUBLE SPLUTTER **(— ABOUT)** KNOCK **(— CALICO COLORS)** TEER **(— DRINK)** MUDDLE SWIZZLE **(— LIQUID)** ROG **(— SOIL)** CHISEL **(— UP)** FAN MIX BUZZ DRUM FUSS MOVE PROG ROIL TOSS AMOVE AREAR AWAKE ERECT QUICK ROUSE SNURL SPOOK STOKE TARRY BESTIR BOTHER CHOUSE EXCITE INCITE JOSTLE KINDLE PUDDLE RUMBLE TICKLE UPSTIR AGITATE ANIMATE COMMOVE DISTURB PRODDLE PROVOKE STUDDLE TORMENT UNQUEME DISTRACT ENKINDLE **(— UP WITH YEAST)** BARM
STIRRER HOG DOLLY ROUSER RUMMAGER
STIRRING RACY ASTIR DEEDFUL ROUSING THRILLY EXCITING PATHETIC
STIRRUP IRON CHAPELET STEELBOW **(PART OF —)** EYE PAD TREAD BRANCH (PREF.) STAPED(I)(IO)
STITCH BAR RUN SEW KNIT LOOP PURL WHIP CABLE CLOSE POINT PREEN PUNTO STEEK ACCRUE FESTON SUTURE TRICOT CROCHET POPCORN FAGOTING **(— IN)** QUILT **(— OF CLOTHES)** TACK **(KIND OF —)** FLAME **(NEEDLEPOINT —)** BARGELLO **(SWEATER —)** CABLE FAGGOT **(TEMPORARY —)** TACK (PL.) JOURS FILLING PINWORK
STITCHBIRD IHI
STITCHDOWN SEWROUND
STITCHED BROCHE
STITCHER WHIPPER
STITCHING SERGING FAGOTING STOATING WHIPPING (SUFF.) RHAPHY RRHAPHY
STITCHWORT PAIGLE ALLBONE SNAPPER HEADACHE SNAPJACK SNAPWORT
STITHY STUDY SMITHY STIDDY STUDDY
STOAT VAIR ERMINE WEASEL CLUBSTER FUTTERET WHITRACK
STOCK COP DOG KIN ROD CANT CROP FILL FOND FUND SEED SELL STEM TRIP BLOND BLOOD BROTH CASTE CREAM FLESH HOARD ISSUE PLANT STALE STIRP STORE STUFF TALON BUDGET CHOKER COMMON FUTURE KAFFIR SHARES STOVEN STRAIN SUPPLY CAPITAL DESCENT PILLORY PROSAPY PROVIDE REPLETE RESERVE BONEYARD BOUTIQUE CROSSBAR DIESTOCK GILLIVER GUNSTOCK MAGAZINE MERCHANT ORDINARY SECURITY PROVISIONS **(— OF ANCHOR)** CROSS **(— OF BREEDING MARES)** STRUDE **(— OF FOOD)** FARE **(— OF GRAIN)** COP **(— OF INDIVIDUALS)** CLONE **(— OF MORPHEMES)** LEXICON **(— OF WEAPONS)** ARSENAL **(— OF WHIP)** CROP **(— OF WINE)** CELLAR **(— SOLD SHORT)** BEAR **(— UNIT)** SHARE **(FARM —)** BOW **(LANGUAGE —)** SALISH SIOUAN BOROTUKE **(MEAT —)** BLOND BOUILLON **(PLASTIC —)** BISCUIT **(RAILROAD —)** GRANGER (PL.) FOODS CIPPUS HARMAN TIMBER CATASTA KAFFIRS (PREF.) STIPI(T)(TI) STIPULI STIRPI (SUFF.) STIPULAR STIPULATE
STOCKADE BOMA PEEL ETAPE ZAREBA BARRIER TAMBOUR STOCKADO
STOCK EXCHANGE BOURSE COULISSE
STOCKFISH STOCK LUTFISK TITLING SPELDING SPELDRON (PREF.) SALPI
STOCKING HOSE SOCK SHANK

STOCK CALIGA MOGGAN SCOGGER SHINNER BOOTHOSE
(— PATTERN) ARGYLE
(FOOTLESS —) HOGGER HUSHION
(PROTECTIVE —) SPATTEE
(SOLELESS —) TRAHEEN
(PL.) HOSE NYLONS BUSKINS BOOTHOSE
STOCKJOBBING AGIOTAGE
STOCKWORK CARBONA
STOCKY FAT COBBY DUMPY GROSS SQUAT STOUT CHUMPY CHUNKY DUMPTY STUBBY STUGGY STUNTY BUNTING COMPACT HEAVYSET STOCKISH THICKSET
STODGY STUFFY STUGGY BOURGEOIS
STOGIE CIGAR
STOIC STOLID APATHETIC IMPASSIVE
STOKEHOLD FIREROOM
STOKER FIREMAN BLOCKMAN
STOLE BOA FUR STAW ARMIL ORARY ARMILLA ORARION PALATINE
STOLEN HOT BENT INOME STOUN FURTIVE
(— GOODS) MAINOUR
STOLID BEEFY BOVINE CLUMSE STUPID WOODEN CLUMPST DEADPAN PASSIVE
STOLIDITY MORGUE
STOLON WIRE SOBOL SOBOLE SOLENIUM
STOMA PORE OPENING OSTIOLE
STOMACH MAW CROP GUTS KYTE MARY POKE READ TANK WAME WOMB BINGY BROOK GORGE GROUF HEART TUMMY BINGEE BINGEY BONNET CROPPY GEBBIE PECHAN VENTER CONCOCT CRAPPIN GIZZARD ABOMASUM
(— OF ANIMAL) CRAW
(— OF CALF) VELL
(— OF FOWLS) CRAW
(— OF RUMINANT) READ RUMEN BONNET OMASUM PAUNCH ABOMASUM MANIFOLD RODDIKIN RETICULUM
(PIG'S —) JAUDIE
(PREF.) GASTER(O) GASTR(I)(O) RUMENO
(SUFF.) GASTER GASTRIA
STOMACHACHE FANTAD GULLION
STOMACHER GIMP TRUSS ECHELLE PLACARD POITREL FOREPART
STOMACHIC COTO CORNUS BITTERS CALUMBA GENTIAN LUPULIN ANTHEMIS
STOMATITIS NOMA
STONE DAM GEM RAG BOND DUCK FLAG HERD KLIP KNAR MARK PELT ROCK STEN TRIG BAUTA CAPEL CHUCK DRAKE GUARD LAPIS PAVER PITCH SCRAE SCREE SNECK STANE ASHLAR BEDDER BENBEN CEPHAS CHATON CLOSER COBBLE GAMAHE GIBBER HEADER JUMPER LEDGER MARVER METATE MULLER NUTLET PEEVER PINNER RUNNER SUMMER TORSEL ANGRITE CALLAIS DINGBAT DONNOCK DORNICK GLIDDER KNEELER KNICKER PERPEND PITCHER PUTAMEN RATCHEL STANNER SURFACE THROUGH BAETULUS CABOCHON DENDRITE EBENEZER HAGSTONE LAPIDATE LAPILLUS LAPSTONE MACEHEAD MONOLITH NAKHLITE SKEWBACK TOPSTONE
(— ADHERING TO LEAD ORE) KEVEL
(— AS AMULET) HAGSTONE
(— AS IT COMES FROM QUARRY) RUBBLE
(— AS ROAD MARKER) LEAGUE
(— AT DOOR) RYBAT
(— BLOCK) ASSIZE
(— FOR GLASS-ROLLING) MARVER
(— FORMING CAP OF PIER) SUMMER CUSHION
(— FOR MOUNTING HORSE) MONTOIR
(— HARD TO MOVE) SITFAST
(— HEAP) MAN CAIRN
(— IN BLAST FURNACE) DAM
(— IN MEMORY OF DEAD) MONUMENT
(— IN SMALL FRAGMENTS) RATCHEL
(— IN WALL) PARPEN
(— MARKING CENTER OF WORLD) OMPHALOS
(— OF FRUIT) COB PIT PAIP COBBE NUTLET PYRENE PUTAMEN
(— OF PYRAMID SHAPE) BENBEN
(— PROVIDING CHANGE OF DIRECTION) KNEELER
(— RELIC) NEOLITH
(— SET IN RING) CHATON
(—S FROM CRUSHER) TAILINGS
(— SHAPED BY WIND) VENTIFACT
(— SHOT FROM STONE-BOW) JALET
(—S IN WATER) STANNERS
(— TO DEATH) LAPIDATE
(— USED AS MONUMENT) MEGALITH
(— USED IN GAME) DUCK DRAKE
(— WITH INTERNAL CAVITY) GEODE
(ARTIFICIAL —) ALBOLITE
(BINDING —) PERPEND THROUGH PIERPONT
(BOND —) GIRDER KEYSTONE
(BOTTOM — OF ARCH) SPRINGER
(BOUNDARY —) TERM MONUMENT TERMINUS MERESTONE
(BROKEN —) RIPRAP
(BROKEN — USED FOR ROADS) BALLAST MACADAM
(BUILDING —) ASHLAR SUMMER MITCHEL SPERONE
(CARVED —) CAMEO CUVETTE
(CASTING —) TYMP
(CHINA —) PETUNSE
(CLAY —) LECH
(COPING —) SKEW TABLET TABLING CAPSTONE
(CURLING —) HOG HERD GUARD LOOFIE POTLID
(CYLINDRICAL —) TAMBOUR
(DESERT —) GIBBER
(DRUID —) SARSEN
(DRYING —) STILLAGE
(EDGING —) SETTER
(FLAT —) PLAT DRAKE LEDGER
(FOUNDATION —) BEDDER
(GLASSY —) TEKTITE
(GLITTERING —) DAZE
(GRAVE —) BAUTA STELE
(GREEN —) CALLAIS
(GRINDING —) METATE MULLER
(HOLY —) BEAR BAETYL
(HOPSCOTCH —) PEEVER PALLALL
(IMAGINARY —) ADAMANT
(KIDNEY —) NEPHRITE
(LAST — IN COURSE) CLOSER
(LOOSE —) GLIDDER
(MAGICAL —) BAETYL
(MEMORIAL —) BAUTA EBENEZER
(METEORIC —) ANGRITE AEROLITE AEROLITH NAKHLITE
(MIDDLE —) HONEY
(MIDDLE — OF ARCH) KEY
(MONUMENTAL —) LECH
(PAVING —) SET SETT PAVER REBATE PITCHER
(PHILOSOPHER'S —) ADROP MAGISTERY TINCTURE
(POLISHING —) SLEEKSTONE
(PRECIOUS —) GEM OPAL RUBY EWAGE JEWEL TOPAZ ADAMAS LIGURE SHAMIR ASTERIA ASTRION CRAPAUD CUVETTE DIAMOND DIONISE EMERALD GELATIA JACINTH OLIVINE SARDINE SARDIUS AMETHYST ASTROITE HYACINTH PANTARBE SAPPHIRE YDRIADES
(PRECIOUS —S) PERRIE
(REFUSE —) ROACH
(ROCKING —) LOGAN
(SACRED —) BAETYL BAETULUS
(SEMIPRECIOUS —) ONYX SARD MURRA GARNET CITRINE TIGEREYE
(SHARPENING —) HONE WHET
(SHOEMAKER'S —) LAPSTONE
(SMALL ROUND —) JACK PEBBLE PELLET
(SOFTENED —) SAP
(STEPPING —) GOAT SARN
(STRATIFIED —) FLAG SLAB
(TALISMANIC —) GAMAHE
(TRANSPARENT —) PHENGITE
(UNSQUARED —) BACKING
(UPRIGHT —) BAUTA MENHIR MASSEBAH
(PL.) LAPIDES LAPILLI
(PREF.) LAPIDI LAPILLI LITH(O)
(— OF FRUIT) PYREN(O)
(SUFF.) LITE LITH(IC) LITIC
STONEBASS BAFARO WHAPUKU
STONEBOAT DRAY
STONEBOW RODD
STONECHAT CHAT SMICH SAXICOLA WHEATEAR
STONECROP ORPIN SEDUM ORPINE PRICKET WALLWORT
STONE CURLEW BUSTARD
STONECUTTER MASON JADDER LAPICIDE LAPIDARY SCABBLER SCAPPLER SQUAREMAN
STONED HIGH DRUNK RIPPED WRECKED
STONEFLY NAIAD
STONEHAND LOCKUP
STONELIKE LITHOID
STONEMAN IMPOSER
STONE MARTEN FOIN
STONEMASON DORBIE
STONE PARSLEY HONEWORT
STONE PINE PINON AROLLA CEMBRA
STONE ROLLER MAMMY MOMMY TOTER
STONE TOTER CUTLIPS
STONEWALLER STICKER
STONEWARE GRES BASALT JASPER BASALTES CANEWARE CHIENYAO
STONEWORKER MASON
STONINESS LAPIDITY PETREITY
STONY RIGID COBBLY PETROUS LAPIDOSE PETROSAL
STOOGE (THREE —S) MOE CURLY LARRY
STOOL FORM MORA SEAT STAB COPPY CROCK HORSE STOLE TREST BUFFET CREEPY CURRIE TRIPOD TUFFET COMMODE CREEPIE KNEELER SHAMBLE TABORET TRESTLE TUMBREL BARSTOOL STILLAGE
(CLOSE —) TOM
(CUCKING —) THEW
(LOW —) COPPY SUNKIE CREEPIE CRICKET
(3-LEGGED —) BUFFET THRESTLE
STOOLBALL TUTBALL
STOOL PIGEON NARK SNITCH STOOGE STOOLIE DIVULGER
STOOP BOW BEND CURB LEAN LOUT POKE SINK COUCH COURB DEIGN STOPE STULP COORIE CROUCH HUCKLE BALCONY DECLINE DESCEND RUCKSEY SUCCUMB
(— OF HAWK) SOUSE
STOOPING DUCK ASTOOP DESCENT
(PREF.) CYPH(O)
STOP HO BAS COG CUT DAM DIE DIT DOG END HOO KEP LIN MAR NIX SET BALK BODE BUNG CALK CALL COOL DROP EASE HALT HELP HOLD HOOK KILL QUIT REED REST SIST SNUB SOFT STAP STAY STEM STOW TEAT TENT TOHO TRIG VIOL WEAR WHOA ABIDE ABORT AVAST BASTA BELAY BLOCK BRAKE BREAK CAULK CEASE CHECK CHOKE CHUCK CLAMP CLOSE DELAY EMBAR HITCH LEAVE MEDIA PAUSE PEACE POINT QUINT REEST SCOTE SLAKE SPARE SPRAG STAND STASH STEEK STICK STINT VIOLA AEOLIN ANCHOR ARREST ASTINT BIFARA BOGGLE BORROW CHEESE CLAMOR COLLAR DESIST DETAIN DEVALL FREEZE GRAVEL INSTOP LAYOFF MONTRE NASARD PERIOD SCOTCH SQUASH STANCE STANCH STIFLE TENUIS TROMBA BASSOON CAESURA MELODIA MUSETTE OPPRESS SOJOURN SQUELCH STATION TERTIAN TWELFTH ASPIRATA BACKSTOP BOMBARDE PRECLUDE RECORDER STOPOVER STOPPAGE SUPPRESS SURCEASE TENOROON WALDHORN WITHSPAR
(— AS IF FRIGHTENED) BOGGLE
(— BLAST) DAMP
(— FLOW) BAFFLE STANCH
(— FOR FOOD) BAIT
(— FOR HORSE) BLOW

(— FROM FERMENTING) STUM
(— GROWTH) BLAST
(— GUN BREECH) OBTURATE
(— IN EARLY STAGES) ABORT
(— IN SPEAKING) HAW
(— LEAK) CALK CAULK FOTHER
(— LIGHT) RED
(— ROWING) EASY
(— SHORT) JIB
(— SPEAKING) SHUTUP
(— SWINGING) SET
(— UNDESIREDLY) STALL
(— UP) DAM CALK CLOG CLOY FILL PLUG CHINK ESTOP STUFF STANCH OCCLUDE STAUNCH OPPILATE
(— USING) SINK
(— WITH CLAY) PUG
(— WORK) SECURE
(BRIEF —) CALL
(GLOTTAL —) STOD CATCH STOSS PLOSIVE STOSSTON
(HARPSICHORD —) LUTE
(ROUGH —) ASPIRATA
(SUCTION —) CLICK
(TEMPORARY —) PAUSE SUSPEND
(VOICELESS —) TENUIS
(WILL NOT —) RUNON
(PL.) REEDWORK
(PREF.) ISCH(O)
STOPCOCK BIB BIBB BIBCOCK BALLCOCK TURNCOCK
STOPGAP RESOURCE
STOPLIGHT IMPEDER
STOPOVER LAYOVER
STOPPAGE JAM BLIN ALLAY CHECK HITCH LEATH STICK STINT ARREST DEVALL STASIS EMBARGO GASLOCK REFUSAL SHUTOFF STOPPLE ASTYLLEN SHUTDOWN STOPWORK CESSATION
(— OF BLOOD) REMORA
(— OF DEVELOPMENT) ATROPHY
(WORK —) BUND HARTAL LOWSIN STRIKE
(PREF.) ISCH(O) STASI
(SUFF.) STASIA STASIS
STOPPED PILEATA
(— WITH HAND) BOUCHE
STOPPER WAD BUNG CORK PLUG STOP VICE CHECK FIPPLE STANCH BOUCHON CLOSURE SHUTOFF STOPGAP STOPPLE TAMPION STOPCOCK
STOPPERED BOUCHE
STOPPING STAY HOLDUP PHASEOUT STOPPAGE
(GRADUAL — OF OPERATIONS) PHASEOUT
STOPPING-PLACE HALT PULLIN OUTSPAN
STORAGE STORE STOWAGE BESTOWAL
STORAX COPALM STACTE STYRAX LORDWOOD
STORE CAVE CRIB DECK FOND FUND HOLD KEEP MART MASS SAVE SHOP STOW TOKO CACHE DEPOT HOUSE HUTCH STASH STOCK UPLAY BAZAAR CELLAR GARNER GIRNEL RECOND STEEVE SUPPLY TIENDA WINKEL ARSENAL BHANDAR BOOTERY GROCERY HARVEST HUSBAND IMBURSE REPOSIT RESTORE SHEBANG BOUTIQUE EMPORIUM EXCHANGE GARRISON MAGAZINE TENDEJON WAREROOM WARNISON
(— BEER) AGE LAGER
(— CROP) BARN
(— FODDER) ENSILE
(— IN A MOW) GOVE
(— IN LUMBER CAMP) VAN
(— IN MOUND) HOG
(— KEPT BY CHINESE) TOKO
(— OF COMPUTER DATA) PUSHDOWN
(— OF FOOD) LARDER
(— OF WEALTH) FORTUNE
(— POTATOES) HOG
(— UP) FUND POWDER IMBURSE SQUIRREL
(ABUNDANT —) MINE
(BREAD —) PANARY
(HIDDEN —) BIKE
(LARGE —) RAFF ANCHOR
(LIQUOR —) GROGGERY
(MARINE —) DOLLYSHOP
(MILITARY —) DUMP
(MILITARY —S) DUMP MUNITIONS AMMUNITION
(READY-TO-EAT FOOD —) DELI DELLY
(RESERVE —) SLUICE
(RICH —) ARGOSY
(SECRET —) STASH
(SMALL —S) SLOPS
(SUPPLEMENTARY —) RELAY
(PL.) SAMAN SUPPLY
STORE CHEESE CHEDDAR
STOREHOUSE BIKE GOLA CACHE DEPOT ETAPE STORE ARGOSY ARMORY BODEGA GODOWN PALACE PANARY STAPLE VINTRY ARSENAL BHANDAR CAMALIG CAMARIN GRANARY STORAGE ENTREPOT MAGAZINE SADDLERY TREASURE
(— FOR BREAD) PANARY
(— OF KNOWLEDGE) THESAURUS
(RAISED —) WHATA FUTTAH PATAKA
(UNDERGROUND —) PALACE MATTAMORE
STOREKEEPER MERCHANT STOREMAN
STOREROOM CAVE GOLA WARD GOLAH BODEGA CELLAR DINGLE BOXROOM BUTTERY GENIZAH LAZARET POULTRY THALAMUS
(PAWNBROKER'S —) LUMBER
STORESHIP FLUTE
STOREY ETAGE ENTRESOL
STORK WADER ARGALA JABIRU SIMBIL HURGILA MAGUARI MARABOU ADJUTANT CICONIID MARABOUT OPENBEAK OPENBILL
(PREF.) CICONI PELARGO
STORKLIKE PELARGIC
STORKSBILL ERODIUM
STORM RIG WAP BLOW HAIL HUFF RAGE RAMP RAND RAVE WIND BLIZZ BLOUT BRASH DEVIL DRIFT FORCE ORAGE STOUR ATTACK BARBER EASTER EXPUGN WESTER BLUSTER BRAVADO CYCLONE DUSTING EQUINOX GAUSTER PISACHI SHAITAN SNIFTER TEMPEST TORMENT WEATHER BLOWDOWN CALAMITY ERUPTION UPHEAVAL WILLIWAW
(— OF BLOWS) STOUR
(— OF RAGE) PELT
(DUST —) DEVIL DUSTER HABOOB KHAMSIN PEESASH SHAITAN
(FURIOUS —) TEMPEST
(HAWAIIAN —) KONA
(SEVERE —) PEELER SNIFTER
(VIOLENT —) FLAW TUFAN CYCLONE SNORTER
STORM DOOR DINGLE
STORMY FOUL GURL RUDE WILD DIRTY DUSTY GURLY GUSTY STARK WINDY WROTH COARSE RUGGED UNFINE WINTRY FURIOUS NIMBOSE RIOTOUS SQUALLY TROUBLE VIOLENT AGITATED BLUSTERY CLUTTERY ORAGIOUS TEMPESTY BOISTEROUS
STORMY PETREL MITTY WITCH SPENCY
STORY GAG SAW DECK DIDO FLAT LORE REDE TALE TEXT YARN ATTIC CRACK ETAGE FABLE FLOOR KATHA PITCH PROSE RECIT SOLAR SPELL SPIEL STAGE STORE CUFFER FABULA FLIGHT PISTLE SCREED SOLLAR ADVANCE HAGGADA HISTORY MANSARD MARCHEN PROCESS RECITAL ANECDOTE DREADFUL ENTRESOL TREATISE NARRATIVE
(— FROM THE PAST) LEGEND
(— OF BEEHIVE) SUPER
(— OF BUILDING) DECK FLAT ATTIC CHESS ETAGE FLOOR PIANO SOLAR STAGE FLIGHT SOLLAR MANSARD ENTRESOL MEZZANINE
(— OF HEROES) SAGA
(ABSURD —) CANARD
(ADVENTURE —) YARN
(AMUSING —) BAR DROLLERY
(BIRTH —) JATAKA
(CORNY —) GROANER
(DOLEFUL —) JEREMIAD
(EERIE —) CHILLER
(EXCITING —) THRILLER
(FAKE —) STRING
(FALSE —) SHAVE CANARD WHOPPER
(FISH —) YARN
(KIND OF —) WAR
(LIFE —) BIO BIOG
(LONG, INVOLVED —) MEGILLA MEGILLAH
(LOWER —) DOWNSTAIRS
(MADE-UP —) FUDGE
(MONSTROUS —) BANGER
(MORBIDLY SENSATIONAL —) DREADFUL
(MYSTERY —) WHODUNIT
(NEWS —) SIDEBAR
(NEWSPAPER —) LEAD FEATURE
(NOTED WAR —) ILIAD
(OLD —) DIDO
(POMPOUS —) BRAG
(PREPOSTEROUS —) CUFFER
(RIBALD —) HARLOTRY
(SAD —) TRAGEDY
(SATIRICAL —) SKIT
(SHORT —) CONTE NOVELLA
(STALE —) CHESTNUT
(UPPER —) ATTIC GARRET BARBECUE HYPEROON CLERESTORY
(PL.) LEGENDA
STORY BOOK TALEBOOK
STORY OF A BAD BOY (AUTHOR OF —) ALDRICH
(CHARACTER IN —) BEN TOM BILL EZRA PHIL SETH ADAMS BINNY KITTY MEEKS NELLY SILAS CONWAY MARDEN NUTTER PEPPER ROGERS ABIGAIL ALDRICH CHARLEY COLLINS WALLACE WINGATE GRIMSHAW WHITCOMB TREFETHEN GLENTWORTH
STORY OF AN AFRICAN FARM
(AUTHOR OF —) SCHREINER
(CHARACTER IN —) EM ROSE TANT WALDO SANNIE GREGORY LYNDALL BLENKINS BONAPARTE
STORYTELLER LIAR FIBBER CONTEUR DISCOUR DISSOUR
STOUP STOOP BENITIER
STOUT ALE FAT SAD FIRM STUT TRIM BONNY BROSY BULKY BUNTY BURLY COBBY FRACK FRECK GREAT HARDY KEDGE OBESE PLUMP PODDY PUNCH STARK STERN BONNIE FLESHY PORTER PORTLY PRETTY PYKNIC ROTUND SQUARE STRONG STUFFY STURDY BOWERLY REPLETE FORCIBLE PLUMPISH POWERFUL ROBOREAN STALWART THICKSET
(— PERSON) GURK
STOUTHEARTED GOOD VALIANT
STOUTLY FAST HARDILY
STOUTNESS STRENGTH CORPULENCE
STOVE HOD STOW BOGEY CHULA PEACH PLATE CHULHA COCKLE COOKER HEATER PRIMUS BRASERO CHAUFFER FRANKLIN POTBELLY SALAMANDER
(— FOR DRYING GUNPOWDER) GLOOM
(— ON SHIP) GALLEY
(PORTABLE —) SALAMANDER
(RUSSIAN —) PEACH
(WARMING —) KANGRI
STOVER OVENSMAN
STOW BIN BOX SET CRAM LADE MASS CROWD DOUSE STORE BESTOW COOPER STEEVE DUNNAGE RUMMAGE
STOWAGE BURTON REMBLAI RUMMAGE
STOWAWAY HIDER
STOWED IN
STOWER TOPPER
STOWING BINNING GOBBING
STP DOM
STRABISMUS CAST CROSS SQUINT TROPIA ANOPSIA COCKEYE WALLEYE
STRADDLE SADDLE SPREAD STRIDE BESTRIDE SPRADDLE STRIDDLE
STRADDLER HOE
STRADDLING ATOP
STRAGGLE GAD ROVE TRAIL RAMBLE RANGLE SPRAWL STREEL

TAGGLE WANDER DRAGGLE MEANDER SCRAMBLE SPRANGLE
STRAGGLER STRAY BUMMER
STRAGGLING RAGGED RAGGLED SPRAYEY SCRATCHY VAGULOUS
STRAIGHT BOLT FAIR FULL GAIN NEAT BRANT CLEAN DOGGY FLUSH RIGHT SHORT SPANG ARIGHT DIRECT HONEST STRAIT STRICT BOBTAIL REGULAR UPRIGHT DIRECTLY SEQUENCE
(— AHEAD) ANON PLUMP OUTRIGHT
(— ON) ENDLONG
(— SKINNY) INFO
(— UP AND DOWN) SHEER CLEVER EVENDOWN
(NOT —) WRY AWRY CRAZY
(PREF.) EUTHY ITHO ITHY ORTH(O) RECT(I)
STRAIGHTEDGE LUTE RULE RULER STRICKLE
STRAIGHTEN GAG CONK ORDER STENT EXTEND SQUARE UNKINK COMPOSE RECTIFY STRETCH
(— BY HEATING) SET
(— HAIR) CONK
(— NEEDLE) RUB
(— RAILS) GAG
STRAIGHT-FIBERED BROAD
STRAIGHTFORWARD EVEN PLAT APERT FRANK LEVEL NAKED PLAIN ROUND CANDID DEXTER DIRECT HONEST SIMPLE SQUARE JANNOCK SINCERE EVENDOWN HOMESPUN OUTRIGHT STRAIGHT OPENHEARTED
(NOT —) CROOKED PLAITED
(PREF.) LITI
STRAIGHTFORWARDLY SINGLY SQUARE STRAIGHT
STRAIGHT-THINKING CLEAR
STRAIGHTWAY ANON AWAY RIGHT ARIGHT BEDEEN BEDENE DIRECTLY
STRAIN FIT LAG RAX SIE TAX TRY TUG ACHE BEND CALL DASH DRAG HEAT HEFT LAWN NOTE PULL RACK RANN RICK SILE SINE SOLO SONG VEIN WORK BRUNT CHAFE DEMUR DRAIN FORCE HEAVE PRESS RETCH SHADE SHEAR SIEVE STOCK SURGE TAMMY TOUCH WREST WRICK CLENCH EFFORT EXTEND EXTORT FILTER INTEND KVETCH SPRAIN SPRING STREAK STRESS STRIND THRONG DESCANT DISCANT EUPLOID FATIGUE STRAINT STRETCH STROPHE TENSION TORMENT COLANDER DIAPASON DIATRIBE DIHYBRID FILTRATE SUBBREED
(— EYES) GOGGLE
(— FROM TWISTING) TORSION
(— MILK) SIE SYE
(— OF AN ARCH) THRUST
(— OF CHICKENS) ANCOBAR
(— OF EXCITEMENT) RACKET
(— OF RAILING LANGUAGE) DIATRIBE
(— ON BUGLE) MOT
(— ON HORN) RECHASE RECHEAT
(— THROUGH COLANDER) COIL
(CONCLUDING —) CADENCE
(MELANCHOLY —) DUMP
(MUSICAL —) FIT SOLO POINT
(MUSICAL —S) TOUCH
(MUTANT —) SALTANT
(PREF.) STREMMATO
STRAINED PENT TENSE INTENSE LABORED INTENDED
STRAINER CAGE ROSE SILE RENGE SIEVE STRUM TAMIS TAMMY THEAD SEARCE SEARCH CRIBBLE COLATORY COLATURE SEARCHER
(— OF TWIGS) HUCKMUCK
(COFFEE —) GRECQUE
(MILK —) SAY MILSEY MILSIE
(WICKER —) THEAD THEDE
(PREF.) COLI ETHMO
STRAINING CUTE COILED ASTRAIN INTENSE COLATURE
STRAIT CUT GUT BAND BELT FRET KYLE NECK PACE BRAKE CANAL PHARE PINCH SHARD SOUND ANGUST FRETUM NARROW PLUNGE CHANNEL EURIPUS BOSPORUS JUNCTURE
(IN —S) SET
(LAST —) EXIGENT
(NEWFOUNDLAND —) TICKLER
(PL.) CHOPS PRESS EXTREMES
STRAITEN PINCH SCANT STRAIT
STRAITENED CRIMP NARROW CRIMPED
STRAITJACKET CAMISOLE
STRAITLACED STIFF STUFFY BLUENOSED
STRAKE SHEER COURSE RISING STREAK COAMING SAXBOARD
(PL.) TIRE
STRAMONIUM DEWTRY
STRAND PLY TOP BANK CORE FLAT TOWT WISP BEACH BRAID CLIFF PRAYA READY SHORE LISSOM MAROON SINGLE SLIVER STRAIN STRIKE SUTURE HAIRLINE
(— OF FIBERS) ROVING
(— OF HAIR) LICK SWITCH
(— OF PROTOPLASM) BRIDGE
(— OF TEXTILE) ROVE
(PREF.) CROCO
STRANDED AGROUND ISOLATED
STRANDER EDGER
STRANGE ODD RUM EERY FELL FREM NICE RARE UNCO ALIEN EERIE FREMT FUNNY KINKY NOVEL QUEER UNKET UNKID WOOZY ALANGE FERLIE QUAINT UNIQUE UNKENT UNKIND CURIOUS ERRATIC HEATHEN ODDBALL UNHEARD UNKNOWN UNUSUAL FANCIFUL INSOLENT INSOLITE PECULIAR SELCOUTH SINGULAR UNCOLIKE UNCOMMON UNKENNED UNKINDLY MONSTROUS
(— TO SAY) ODDLY
(PREF.) XEN(O)
STRANGENESS ODDITY
STRANGER COME UNCO UNKO ALIEN GUEST FRENNE GANGER INCOME INMATE FUIDHIR INCOMER UNCOUTH MALIHINI OUTCOMER PEREGRIN OUTLANDER
(SUFF.) XENE XENOUS XENY
STRANGLE CHOKE GRAIN GRANE SNARL WORRY STIFLE GARROTE QUACKLE GARROTTE JUGULATE THROTTLE
STRANGLEHOLD CHANCERY STRANGUL
STRANIERA, LA (CHARACTER IN —) ALAIDE ARTURO ISOLETTA VALDEBURGO
(COMPOSER OF —) BELLINI
STRAP BAR TUG BAND BELT CLIP CURB GIRD HASP RIDE RIEM BRACE CHEEK GIRTH GUIGE PATTE RIDER RISER SABOT SLING STROP THONG TRACE VITTA ANKLET BACKER BILLET COLLAR ENARME GARTER HALTER HANGER LAINER LATIGO SANDAL TOGGLE WARROK BABICHE BOWYANG CRIBBER DOLPHIN LANYARD LATCHET LEATHER RIEMPIE STIRRUP TICKLER WEBBING BACKSTAY BRETELLE SQUILGEE TURNBACK WRISTLET
(— AROUND HORSE'S THROAT) CRIBBER
(— AROUND MAST) DOLPHIN
(— FOR SHIELD) GUIGE ENARME BRETELLE
(— IN FLAIL) TAPLING
(— OF BRIDLE) REIN
(— OF SENNIT) BACKER
(— ON HAWK'S LEAD) JESS JESSE SENDAL
(— WITH SLIT END) TAWS TAWSE
(ANKLE —) BRACELET
(CARRYING —) METUMP TUMPLINE
(DOOR —) HASP
(HARNESS —) TRACE
(MINER'S —) BYARD
(SHOE —) BAR
(STIRRUP —S) CHAPELET
(TIE —) SHANK
(U-SHAPED —) STIRRUP
(PL.) LADDER
(PREF.) LIGUL(I)
STRAP FERN LONGLEAF
STRAPHANGER STANDEE COMMUTER
STRAPPER SPLICER
STRAPPING SWANK BOUNCING CHOPPING SLAPPING SWANKING
STRAP-SHAPED LORATE LIGULAR LIGULATE
STRATA EOCENE TERRANE UNDERAIR
(— OF COAL) MEASURES
STRATAGEM JIG COUP LOCK RUSE TRAM TURN WILE ANGLE DRAFT FETCH FRAUD GUILE JOKER KNACK TRAIN TRICK WREST BLENCH DECEIT DEVICE HUMBUG POLICY TRAPAN TREPAN WOIDRE WRENCH FINESSE SLEIGHT ARTIFICE CONTOISE FARFETCH INTRIGUE LIRIPIPE LIRIPOOP PRACTICE PRACTISE QUENTISE STRATEGY TRICKERY MOUSETRAP
(INDIRECT —) FEELER
STRATEGY GAME FINESSE
(MANUFACTURING —) KANDAN
STRATIFICATION BEDDING
STRATIFIED BEDDED VARVED
STRATIFORM LAYERED
STRATONICE (FATHER OF —) DEMETRIUS
(HUSBAND OF —) SELEUCUS
(MOTHER OF —) PHILA
STRATUM BED CAP CUT LAY RIB FAST LAIN SEAM TIER COUCH ELITE FLOOR LAYER LEDGE SHELF TABLE COUCHE GIRDLE GRAVEL LAYING LISSOM PINNEL AQUAFER AQUIFER ENTIRIS FISHBED SUBSOIL UPRIGHT AQUIFUGE FAHLBAND SUBGRADE
(— OF COAL) BENCH
(— OF FIRECLAY) THILL
(— OF PALE COLOR) FAHLBAND
(— OF SANDSTONE) PINNEL
(— OF SOIL) SOD
(— OF STONE) GIRDLE
(SOCIAL —) CUT
(THIN —) SEAM LENTIL
STRAW BAKU GLOY MOTE REED RUSH TOYO WASE HAULM PEDAL SHILF STALK STREW YEDDA FESCUE FETTLE PANAMA RIZZOM SIPPER TUSCAN BANGKOK SABUTAN STUBBLE WINDLIN STRAMMEL
(— CUT FINE) CHAFF
(— FOR MAKING HATS) SENNIT BANGKOK LEGHORN SABUTAN
(— FOR THATCHING) YELM
(— MEASURE) KEMPLE
(— TO PROTECT PLANTS) MULCH
(BROKEN —) BHUSA BHOOSA
(COOKERY —S) PAILLES
(PLAITED —) SENNIT
(WAXED —) STRASS
(PREF.) CARPHO
STRAWBERRY BERRY DUNLAP FRAISE RUNNER HAUTBOY FRUTILLA HAUTBOIS KLONDIKE ROSACEAN
(— JAR) PLANTER
STRAWBERRY BUSH WAHOO EUONYMUS EVONYMUS FISHWOOD
STRAWBERRY FINCH AMADAVAT AVADAVAT
STRAWBERRY SHRUB BUBBY COWBERRY
STRAWBERRY TOMATO PHYSALIS BLADDERCHERRY
STRAWBERRY TREE ARBUTUS
STRAY ERR ODD FALL RAVE ROVE WAFF WAIF WALK DRIFT RANGE TRAIK VAGUE WAVER ESTRAY RANGLE SWERVE VAGARY WANDER WILDER DEVIATE FORLORN STRAYER DIVAGATE MAVERICK STRAGGLE
STRAYING ASTRAY ERRANT ABERRANT VAGATION
STREAK PAY RAY BAND SEAM VEIN WALE FLAKE FLECK FLICK FREAK GARLE GLADE SLASH FACULA SMUDGE STRAIN STRAKE STREAM STRIPE FLECKER SPRAING STIPPLE DISCOLOR TRAVERSE
(— CAUSED BY BLOOD) VIBEX
(— IN FABRIC) CRACK SHINER
(— IN GLASS) SKIM
(— IN HAIR) BLAZE

(— IN SKY) ICEBLINK
(— IN WOOD) ROE
(— OF BLUBBER) BLANKET
(— OF LIGHT) STREAM
(— ON BEAST'S FACE) RACE RATCH
(— ON SURFACE OF SUN) FACULA
(—S FROM PLANE) CONTRAIL
(—S IN ROCK) SCHLIEREN
(— WITH FINE STRIPES) LACE
(BACTERIOLOGICAL —) STROKE
(LOSING —) SLUMP
(RAISED —) WEAL
(THEATRICAL —) HAM
(WHITE —) SHIM
STREAKED ROWY LACED HAWKED SMEARY BRINDLE BROCKED BROOKED FINCHED SPARKED STRIPED WHIPPED BRINDLED IRONSHOT PINROWED
STREAKY ROWY SCOVY STREAKED
STREAM EA PUP RIO RUN BECK BURN FLOW FLUX FORD GILL GOTE KHAL KILL LAKE OOZE POUR PUIT PURL RILL SICK SIKE SILE SPIN TIDE BACHE BATCH BAYOU BOGUE BOURN BROOK CREEK DRILL DRINK FLARE FLASH FLEAM FLOOD FLOSS FLUOR FRESH GHYLL NYMPH PRILL RITHE RIVER SWAMP TCHAI TRAIN ARROYO BANKER BOURNE BRANCH BURNIE CANADA COULEE FILLER FLUENT GUZZLE OUTLET PIRATE RANDOM RUNDLE RUNNEL SLUICE SPRUIT STRAND STRONE CHANNEL CURRENT DRIBBLE FLUENCE FRESHET RIVULET TRICKLE AFFLUENT INFLUENT MILLSTREAM
(— ALONG) SLIDE
(— FULL TO TOP) BANKER
(— OF AIR OR SMOKE) PEW
(— OF ELECTRODES) BEAM
(— OF LAVA) COULEE
(— OF SIRUP) THREAD
(— OF SPEECH) STRAIN
(— OUT) BREAK
(FLOWING —) NYMPH
(HIGH-SPEED —) JET
(MYTHOLOGICAL —S) ELIVAGAR
(SLOW —) OOZE
(SLOW-MOVING —) POW
(SLUGGISH —) LANE
(SMALL —) BECK LAKE SIKE DRAFT RITHE COULEE SICKET SQUIRT STRIPE DRAUGHT GRINDLE
(THIN —) TRICKLE TRICKLET
(TIDAL —) COVE SEAPOOSE
(TRANSIENT —) RILL
(TRICKLING —) DRILL
(TURBID —) DRUVE
(UNDERGROUND —) AAR SWALLET
(VIOLENT —) TORRENT
(WEAK —) DRIP
(PREF.) AMNI FLUVI
(— OF LAVA) RHYACO
STREAMER FLAG VANE FALLAL GARTER GUIDON LAPPET PENCEL PENNON PINNET SCROLL SIMPLE WIMPLE BANDEROL FILAMENT
(— OF MOSS) WEEPER
(— ON HEADDRESS) LIRIPIPE
(PAPER —S) CONFETTI
STREAMING SLUICY ASTREAM CRINITE CYCLOSIS DOWNPOUR
STREAMLET RILL RILLET RUNDLE RUNLET RUNNEL RIVULET
STREAMLINE SIMPLIFY
(— FLOW) LAMINAR
STREAMLINED CLEAN SLEEK
STREET ROW RUE WAY CHAR DRUM GATE PAVE STEM TOBY BLOCK BORGO CALLE CANON CHAWK CORSO DRIVE PASEO AVENUE BOWERY CANYON CAUSEY CIRCLE RAMBLA POULTRY TERRACE THROUGH ARTERIAL BROADWAY BYSTREET CHAUSSEE CONTRADA PROSPECT
(— IN BARCELONA) RAMBLA
(— IN FLORENCE) BORGO
(MAIN —) CHAWK CHOWK TOWNGATE
(NARROW —) CHAR ALLEY CHARE RUELLE
(PRINCIPAL —) ARTERY
(QUIET —) CULDESAC
(SIDE —) HUTUNG
STREETCAR TRAMCAR TRAMWAY ELECTRIC
STREET CLEANER ORDERLY CLEANSER
STREET CLEANING SLOPPING
STREET SCENE (AUTHOR OF —) RICE
(CHARACTER IN —) SAM ROSE FRANK STEVE KAPLIN SANKEY WILLIAM MAURRANT
STREETWALKER BULKER CRUISER
STRENGTH EL ARM VIR BEEF DRAW GRIP GUTS HEAD HORN IRON MAIN THEW BRAWN CRAFT ETHAN FIBER FIBRE FORCE HEART JUICE MIGHT NERVE POWER SINEW VIGOR ENERGY FOISON MAUGHT MUSCLE STARCH VIRTUE ABILITY AFFORCE COURAGE PROWESS STAMINA STHENIA CAPACITY FIRMNESS VALIDITY PUISSANCE
(— OF ACID OR BASE) AVIDITY
(— OF ALE) STRIKE
(— OF CARD HAND) BODY
(— OF CHARACTER) GRISTLE
(— OF CURRENT) AMPERAGE
(— OF GRASP) GRIP
(— OF SOLUTION) TITER TITRE
(— OF SPIRITS) PROOF
(— OF TEA) DRAW
(— OF WILL) BACKBONE
(— OF WINE) SEVE
(SUPERIOR —) PREVALENCE
(PREF.) CRATO DYNAM(I)(O) ISCHY(O)
(SUFF.) DYNAMIA DYNAMOUS
STRENGTHEN IMP ABLE BACK BIND FIRM FRAP HELP PROP SOUD STAY BRACE CLEAT FORCE SINEW STEEL THRAP TONIC TRUSS ANNEAL ASSURE DEEPEN ENDURE ENFIRM ENFORT GABION HARDEN INTEND MUNIFY MUNITE NEEDLE SETTLE STRING STRONG AFFORCE BUCKRAM COMFORT CONFIRM ENFORCE FASCINE FORTIFY NERVATE QUICKEN RAMPIRE SUPPORT THICKEN BUTTRESS ENERGIZE ENTRENCH HEIGHTEN ROBORATE
STRENGTHENED BULLED BRANDIED
STRENGTHENING BRACING ROBORANT
STRENGTHLESS DOWLESS
STRENUOUS HARD EAGER ARDUOUS WILLING VIGOROUS
STREPHON (BELOVED OF —) CHLOE
STREPSIPTERON STYLOPS
STRESS HIT BIRR BRUNT ICTUS PINCH SHEAR ACCENT STRAIN THRONG TENSION CENTROID DOWNBEAT EMPHASIS PRESSURE
(— OF SOUND) LENGTH
(METRIC —) BEAT
(SYLLABIC —) ARSIS
STRESSED TONIC STRONG
STRETCH EKE LAG LIE RAX RUN BEAT DRAW LAST MAIN PASS RACK REAM ROLL RYKE SPAN TEND BOARD BURST FETCH RATCH RETCH SIGHT SPELL STENT SWAGE VERGE EXTEND LENGTH SMOOTH STRAIN STRAKE STREEK DISPLAY DISTEND EXPANSE SPELDER ELONGATE LENGTHEN STRAIGHT
(— CLOTH) TENTER
(— FORCIBLY) RACK
(— FORTH) REACH PORRECT PRETEND PROTEND
(— INJURIOUSLY) SPRAIN
(— IRREGULARLY) TRAIL
(— LEATHER) DRAFT STAKE DRAUGHT
(— METAL) FORM
(— OF ARMS) FATHOM
(— OF BROKEN WATER) RIP
(— OF GROUND) BRECK
(— OF INTERVALE) CARSE
(— OF LAND) SWALE COMMON GALLOP PARCEL COMMONS
(— OF OPEN COUNTRY) RANGE
(— OF ROAD) SIGHT
(— OF SEA) CHOP
(— OF TIME) TIFF
(— OF WALL) CURTAIN
(— OF WATER) GLIDE LEVEL LOGIN FAIRWAY
(— OF WORK) YOKE
(— OUT) GROW SPIN REACH STENT STRUT TWINE INTEND OUTLIE SPRAWL SPREAD SPRING DISTEND OUTSPAN PORTEND ELONGATE
(— ROPE) WARP
(— SPRAWLINGLY) STRAGGLE
(— THE NECK) CRANE
(— THE WINGS) MANTLE
(CONTINUOUS —) RUN
(GRASSY —) DRINN
(LEVEL —) LAWN
(PREF.) TANY TASI TEN(O) TENONT(O) TETANI TETANO TINO
(SUFF.) EURYSIS
STRETCHABLE TENSILE
STRETCHED PROSTRATE
(— OUT) PORRECT PROJECT PROLATE ELONGATE EXTENDED
(TENSELY —) TAUT TORT STIFF
STRETCHER COT STENT GURNEY LITTER ANGAREP TROLLEY ANGAREEB BRANCARD STRAINER
STRETCHING
(SUFF.) ECTASIA ECTASIS
STREW BED SOW CLOT DUST LARD SPEW BESET STRAW STRAY STROW CARPET LITTER SPREAD BESTREW SCATTER SKINKLE SPARKLE
(— WITH BULLETS) SPRAY
STREWED BESPRENT
STREWING SEME
STREWN DOTTED BESPRENT
STRIA CORD STRIOLA DRAGLINE STRIOLET
STRIATE VEIN
STRIATION STREAK STRIGA
STRICKEN STREAKED
STRICKER TIPPLER
STRICKLE SWEEP STRIKER
STRICT HARD TAUT TRUE CLOSE EXACT HARSH RIGID STARK STERN TIGHT GIUSTO SEVERE STRAIT STRONG ASCETIC AUSTERE PRECISE REGULAR DISTRICT RESTRICT RIGOROUS STRINGENT
(NOT —) LAX SCIOLTO
STRICTLY NARROW STRAIT CLOSELY PROPERLY
STRICTNESS RIGOR RIGIDITY RIGORISM SEVERITY
STRIDE LAMP SAIL STEP FLOAT SKELP SPANG STEND STRUT LAMPER STROAM STROKE STROME BESTRIDE POINTING STRIDDLE
(— ALONG) LAMP
(— EXULTANTLY) GALUMPH GALLUMPH
(— LOFTILY) STALK
(— PURPOSEFULLY) SLING
STRIDENT HARD HARSH BRASSY GLASSY SHRILL GRATING RAUCOUS YELLING GRINDING
STRIDULATE CHIRP PITTER
STRIFE TUG WAR WIN BATE FEUD HOLD PLEA BRIGE CHEST FLITE JEHAD JIHAD NOISE STOUR STROW STRUT STURT BARRAT BICKER BRIGUE DEBATE ESTRIF MUTINY STRIVE BARGAIN CONTECK CONTEST DISCORD DISPUTE HURLING QUARREL CONFLICT CONTRAST DISPEACE STRUGGLE CONTENTION
(AUTHOR OF —) GALSWORTHY
(CHARACTER IN —) ENID JOHN ANNIE DAVID EDGAR SIMON ANTHONY FRANCIS HARNESS ROBERTS UNDERWOOD
(CIVIL —) STASIS
STRIGIL COMB SCRAPER
STRIKE GO BAT BOB BOP BOX BUM COB CUE DAD DUB GET HAB HIT JOB JOW LAM LAY PUG RAP WAP ABRE BAFF BEAK BEAT BELT BIFF BILL BLAD BLIP BUFF BUMP CHAP CLUB COIN COPE COSH CUFF DING DINT DONG DUNT FALL FANG FIRK FLAP FLOG FRAP GIRD GOWF GRAB HACK HURT JOWL KILL KNEE LASH LILT LUSH MARK NAIL PAIK PASH PLAT PUCK ROUT SLAM SLAP SLAT SLAY SLOG SLUG SOCK SPAR SPAT SWAP SWAT SWIP TAKE

WHAP WHOP WIPE ZONK ANGLE BATON CATCH CHECK CHIME CHINK CLOUT CLUNK CRACK CRUNT DEVEL DOUSE DOWSE DRIVE DUNCH FETCH FILCH FILIP FLAIL KNOCK PANDY PASTE POKER POTCH SABER SKELP SKITE SLOSH SMACK SMITE SNICK SOUND SPANK SQUAP STAMP STEEK SWACK SWEEP SWIPE SWISH THROW WHALE WHANG ACOUPE AFFECT AFFRAP ALIGHT ATTAIN BATTER BOUNCE BUFFET COURSE DUNDER FETTLE FILLIP HAMMER INCUSE INCUTE KEEPER SLOUGH STOUSH STRICK STRIPE SWITCH THRASH WALLOP BEARING FLYFLAP IMPINGE KNUCKLE PERCUSS STRIKER TURNOUT WHAMPLE WILDCAT STOPPAGE STOPWORK STRAMASH STRICKLE
(— ABOUT) FLOP
(— AGAINST) RAM BANG STUMP ASSAULT COLLIDE
(— AND REBOUND) CAROM
(— A WICKET) BREAK
(— CRICKET BALL) EDGE
(— DOWN) LAY FALL SLAY WEND FLASH FLOOR AFFLICT SIDERATE
(— DUMB) DUMFOUND
(— FEET TOGETHER) HITCH
(— FORCIBLY) GET CLOUT DEVEL SLASH
(— GENTLY) PAT
(— GOLF BALL) HOOK DRIVE SCLAFF
(— GROUND IN GOLF) BAFF DUFF
(— HEAVILY) BASH DUNT DUSH FLOP SLUG CLUMP SLOUGH CLOBBER
(— IN CURLING) WICK
(— LIGHTLY) BOB DAB SPAT FLICK
(— OF LOCK) KEEPER STRIKER
(— ON HEAD) COP NOBBLE
(— OUT) FAN DELE POKE TAKE CROSS ELIDE CANCEL DELETE EXPUNGE OUTLASH EXCUDATE
(— REPEATEDLY) DRUM LICK
(— SHARPLY) CUT SNICK
(— SMARTLY) NAP RAP KNAP
(— TEETH TOGETHER) GNASH
(— TOGETHER) CLASH KNACK
(— UP) LILT YERK RAISE
(— VIOLENTLY) RIP BASH DING PASH SOUSE BENSEL
(— WITH AMAZEMENT) CONFOUND
(— WITH BAT) DRIVE
(— WITH FEAR) ALARM ASTONISH
(— WITH FIST) PLUG NODDLE
(— WITH FOOT) KICK BUNCH SPURN STAMP
(— WITH HAMMER) CHAP JOWL MELL
(— WITH HORNS) BUNT BUTT HOOK
(— WITH SHAME) ABASH
(— WITH SPEAR) STICK
(— WITH STICK) SQUAIL
(— WITH WHIP) JERK LASH QUIRK
(— WITH WONDER) SURPRISE
(BOWLING —S) DOUBLE
(HUNGER —) ENDURA
(LABOR —) STEEK STICK TURNOUT WALKOUT
(LUCKY —) BONANZA
(MINING —) TREND
(THREE —S) TURKEY
(PREF.) PLESSI PLEXI TYPTO

STRIKEBREAKER FINK BLACKLEG

STRIKER BATMAN DRUMMER TURNOUT PULSATOR

STRIKER-OUT SETTER

STRIKING FITTY FRESH SHOWY VIVID DARING SIGNAL STRONG SALIENT SKELPIN TELLING COLORFUL CONFLICT DRAMATIC FRAPPANT KNOCKOUT SENSIBLE SIZZLING SPANKING SPEAKING NOTICEABLE PERCUSSION PHOTOGENIC

STRING LAG BAND BEND CORD FILE LACE MEAN PAIR SLIP TAPE TAUM BRAID BRIDE CHORD POINT SINEW SNEAD STRAP TWINE CORDON STRAND TREBLE MINIKIN LIGATURE RHAPSODY
(— IN BIRD'S EGG) CHALAZA
(— OF BEADS) ROSARY CHAPLET NECKLACE
(— OF CASH) QUAN TIAO
(— OF DRUM) SNARE
(— OF FIDDLE) THARM
(— OF FLAGS) HOIST
(— OF INVECTIVE) TIRADE
(— OF LOCK) KEEPER
(— OF LYRE) MESE NETE TRITE HYPATE PARAMESE PARAMETE
(— OF MUSICAL INSTRUMENT) WIRE CHORD DRONE THAIRM CATLING MINIKIN LICHANOSE
(— OF ONIONS) REEVE TRACE
(— OF PHRASES) CENTO
(— OF PROPOSITIONS) SORITES
(— OF RAILWAY CARS) SET
(— OF SUGAR CRYSTALS) COB
(— OF VEGETABLES) STRAP
(— OF VERSES) LAISSE
(— OF VIOL) MEAN
(— OF WAGONS) RAKE
(— TOBACCO) SEW
(— UP) KILT
(BONNET —) BRIDE
(E —) QUINT
(LEADING —) BAND
(OAKUM —) PLEDGET
(ORNAMENTAL —) CORDON
(PULL —S) PLUCK
(SURGICAL —) LIGATURE
(VIOLIN —) THAIRM VIBRATOR
(WEAVING —) LEASH
(SUFF.) CHORD(AL)

STRING BEAN SNAP HARICOT SNAPPER

STRINGCOURSE LEDGE TABLE CORDON STRING

STRINGENCY RIGOR

STRINGENT HARD RIGID TIGHT SEVERE STRICT EXTREME

STRINGER BALK BAULK

STRINGHALTED CRAMPY

STRINGY ROPY WOOLY SINEWY THONGY WOOLLY GARGETY SINEWED THREADY

STRIP BAR LAG TAG BAND BARE BEAD BELT BEND BUSK DRIP FUSE GAGE GAIR HILD HUSK LIST MALL NAKE NUDE PEEL RAND ROLL SACK SHIM SKIN TIRL TIRR WELT CLEAN DRIVE EXUTE FILET FLAKE FLYPE GAUGE GLEAN GUARD HARRY LABEL LINER LYNCH PANEL PLUME REEVE SHEAR SHRED SKELP SLIPE SPEEL SPOIL STRAP STROP STRUB SWATH UNGUM UNRIG BORDER BOXING BRIDGE COLLAR CULPON DENUDE DEVEST DIVEST FEELER FILLET FLEECE LIBBET MATRIX PANUNG REGLET RUNWAY SCROLL SPLINE STREAK STRIPE TARGET UNBARE UNBARK UNCASE BANDAGE BEREAVE CHANNEL DEPLUME DEPRIVE DESPOIL DISROBE FEATHER FLOUNCE LAMBEAU LANGUET NAILROD PINRAIL PLUNDER UNCLOAK UNCOVER UNDRESS BOOKMARK COSSETTE DISARRAY DISENDOW DISTRUSS FOOTBAND SEPARATE
(— ACROSS SAIL) REEFBAND
(— A PLANT) SPRIG
(— BARK) PILL
(— BINDING STALKS TO WALL) TACK
(— BLUBBER FROM WHALE) FLENSE
(— EAR OF CORN) SILK
(— FOR DRAWING CURVED LINES) SPLINE
(— FOR GUIDING PLASTER) BEAD
(— FOR MAKING TUBE) SKELP
(— HANGING AROUND SKIRT) FLOUNCE
(— IN BASKETMAKING) INSIDES
(— IN BEEHIVE) STARTER
(— IN CANING) SPLENT SPLINT
(— IN TYPEWRITER) DRAWBAND
(— OF ARABLE LAND) RIDGE
(— OF BACON) LARDON LARDOON
(— OF CANVAS) FOOTBAND
(— OF CLOTH) LIST PATA RIND ROON GUARD BANNER DUTCHMAN
(— OF CORK) SPREADER
(— OFF) TIRL FLIPE FLYPE SLIPE
(— OF FABRIC) FLIPPER
(— OF FAT) FATBACK LARDOON
(— OF FEATHERS) PLUCK PLUME
(— OF FIELD HOCKEY AREA) ALLEY
(— OFF SKIN) CASE FLAY
(— OF FUR) GROTZEN
(— OF GRASS) VERGE
(— OF HIDE) SPECK DEWLAP
(— OF LAND) BUTT LAND RAIK RAIN RAKE TANG BREAK CREEK SLANG SLIPE SPONG SCREED SELION STRAKE STRIPE FURLONG ISTHMUS CORRIDOR SIDELING
(— OF LEATHER) LAY RAND WELT APRON RANGE THONG BACKSTAY
(— OF LEAVES) TWIST
(— OF LINEN) SETON
(— OF MASONRY) ARCHBAND
(— OF OFFICE) BREAK
(— OF OSIER) SKEIN
(— OF PALM LEAF) CADJAN CAJANG
(— OF PASTRY) STRAW
(— OF PLANKING) APRON
(— OF PLASTER) SCREED
(— OF PRAIRIE) COVE
(— OF PROVISIONS) FORAGE
(— OF RANK) DEGRADE
(— OF RED CLOTH) COXCOMB
(— OF ROADWAY) LANE
(— OF RUBBER) CUSHION
(— OF SHORE) LITTORAL
(— OF TERRITORY) PANHANDLE
(— OF TURF) PARKING
(— OF UNPLOWED LAND) GAIR HADE HEADLAND
(— OF WATER) INLET
(— OF WOOD) LAG LAT LATH LIST SHAW SLAT WELT CHINK CLEAT STAVE BATTEN INWALE RADDLE REEPER REGLET SPLINE SPLINT FOOTING FURRING STICKER TRACKER FOOTLING SPLINTER
(— ON FOLDING DOORS) ASTRAGAL
(— ON PRINTER'S GALLEY) LEDGE
(— ON SQUASH COURT) TELLTALE
(— ON TIRE) CHAFER
(— SEPARATING LINES OF TYPE) LEAD REGLET
(— WORN ON ARM) MANIPLE
(ARMOR —) SPLENT SPLINT
(BOUNDARY —) PERIMETER
(CAMOUFLAGING —) GARLAND
(COMIC —) FUNNY
(CONSTRUCTION —S) LAGGING
(CORSET —) BUSK
(DEPENDENT —) LAMBEAU
(DIVIDING —) CLOISON
(ELECTROPHORETIC —) ZYMOGRAM
(FASTENING —) TACK
(FRIED —) POPADUM POPPADUM
(HORSESHOE-SHAPED —) BAIL BALE
(IRON IN —S) NAILROD
(LANDING —) RUNWAY
(MARINATED —) FAJITA
(MEDIAN —) MALL
(NARROW —) SEAM SLAT SLIP TAPE REEVE STRAKE
(PAPER —) ORIHON
(PERFORATED —) LAG
(PROJECTING —) FEATHER
(RAISED —) RIDGE
(SPACING —) REGLET
(STRENGTHENING —) BEND
(THATCHING —) LEDGER
(UNPLOWED —) BALK LINCH LINCHET LYNCHET

STRIPE BAR RAY BAND BEND LIST PALE SLAT TRIM WALE WEAL WELT ZONE FLECK PLAGA STRIA STRIP SWATH VITTA WHEAL BORDER CLAVUS COTICE FRENUM LADDER RIBBON STRAKE STREAK STREAM COTTISE SPRAING MUSTACHE TRAVERSE
(— OF CHEVRON) ARC
(— OF COLOR ON CHEEK) FRENUM FRAENUM
(— ON ANIMAL'S FACE) SNIP BLAZE
(— ON FABRIC) CROSSBAR
(— ON MILITARY SLEEVE) SLASH
(— ON ROMAN TUNIC) LATICLAVE
(— ON SHIELD) ENDORSE
(ENCIRCLING —) ZONE
(PURPLE —) CLAVUS
(SET OF —S) BAR

STRIPED BANDY PALED PIRNY RAWED RAYED ROWED WALED ZONED BARRED CORDED LISTED

PIRNED BROCKED TIGROID VITTATE FASCIATE STRIPPED
(— CROSSWISE) BAYADERE
STRIPED BASS ROCKFISH SERRANID
STRIPED MAPLE DOGWOOD
STRIPING HAIRLINE
STRIPLIGHT BORDER
STRIPLING LAD SLIP STIRRA YONKER SPAUGHT YOUNKER SKIPJACK SPRINGAL SHAVELING
STRIPPED BARE NUDE NAKED HUSKED PICKED PLUMED UNPEELED
STRIPPER STEMMER SPRIGGER
STRIPPING STROKINGS
(PL.) JIBBINGS
STRIPTEASE (RELATING TO —) EXOTIC
STRIPTEASER STRIPPER ECDYSIAST
STRIVE AIM HIE TEW TRY TUG DEAL FEND PAIN TOIL WORK BANDY DRIVE EXERT FIGHT FORCE LABOR PRESS BRIGUE BUCKLE BUFFET DEBATE INTEND PINGLE STRAIN STRIKE AGONIZE BARGAIN CONTEND CONTEST DISPUTE ENFORCE SCUFFLE CONTRAST ENDEAVOR PURCHASE STRUGGLE
(— AFTER) SEEK FOLLOW CANVASS
(— AGAINST) RESIST
(— FOR SUPERIORITY) VIE KEMP
(— IN OPPOSITION) RIVAL CONTEND
(— TO EQUAL) EMULATE
(— TO OBTAIN) FOLLOW
(— TO OVERTAKE) ENSUE
STRIVING NISUS HORMIC STRIFT CONATUS CONATION
STRIX SYRNIUM
STROBILE BUR BELL BURR CHAT CONE BRUSH
STROKE BAT COY CUT DAB FIT JOW ODD PAT PET POP RUB BAFF BEAT BLOW CHAP CHOP CLAP COUP CUFF DASH DENT DING DINT DIRD DRAW DUNT EDGE FIRK FLAP FLEG FLIP FLOP FUNG GOWF HAND HURT JERK JOWL KERF LASH LICK NACK PAIK PEAL PECK SHOT SMIT SWAP TILT TIRE TUCK WELT WHAP WIPE BRUSH CHASE DOUSE DOWSE DRAFT FLACK FLICK FORCE HATCH ICTUS MINIM PANDY PULSE SHOCK SLASH SLING SLIVE SLOSH STRIP SWEEP SWING SWIPE THROW TOUCH TRAIT TRICE WHACK CARESS CENTER FONDLE FOOZLE GENTLE GLANCE PLAGUE PLUNGE SMOOTH STRAIK STRAKE STRIKE STRIPE DRAUGHT OUTLASH SOLIDUS VIRGULE APOPLEXY BACKHAND DRUMBEAT FOREHAND INSTROKE SCORCHER
(— IN KEEPING TIME) TACT
(— IN PAINTING) HAND
(— IN PENMANSHIP) MINIM
(— IN TENNIS) LET LOB BOAST CHASE SMASH BRICOLE BACKHAND FOREHAND OVERHAND
(— OF A LETTER) DUCT STEM SERIF POTHOOK CROSSBAR
(— OF ART) TOUCH
(— OF BAD FORTUNE) CLAP
(— OF BELL) JOW BELL JOWL KNELL TELLER
(— OF BOW) SCRAPE
(— OF FORTUNE) CAST BREAK BONZER FELICITY
(— OF LUCK) HIT FLUKE STRIKE TURNUP CAPTION
(— OF MISFORTUNE) SISERARY
(— OF SCYTHE) SWATH SWATHE
(— OF SHEARS) SNIP
(— OF WIT) FLIRT
(— OF WORK) BAT CHAR
(— ON THE PALM) LOOFIE
(— WITH CLAW) CLOYE
(BILLIARDS —) SPOT STUN FLUKE FORCE MASSE HAZARD
(CONNECTING —) LIGATURE
(CRICKET —) CUT GLANCE
(CROQUET —) ROQUET
(CURLING —) INWICK
(CUTTING —) GIRD
(DOUBLE SPINNING —) DRAW
(DRUM —) DRAG
(FINISHING —) NOBBLER
(GOLF —) ODD BAFF BISK HOOK LIKE BLAST SLICE BISQUE FOOZLE SCLAFF APPROACH
(HOCKEY —) JOB SCOOP
(JERKY —) STAB
(LIGHTNING —) BOLT
(MEDICAL —) ICTUS APOPLEXY
(MUSICAL —) TACT
(ORNAMENTAL —) FLOURISH
(QUICK —) FLIP
(SKATING —) EDGE MOHAWK CHOCTAW
(SMART —) FIRK
(SOOTHING —) COY
(SWIMMING —) CRAWL TRUDGEN BUTTERFLY DOGPADDLE SIDESTROKE
(SWINGING —) HEW
(SWORD —) MONTANTO
(PREF.) BOLO PLEGA PLEGO
(SUFF.) BOLA BOLE BOLIC BOLISM BOLIST PLEGIA PLEGY PLEXIA
STROLL JET IDLE ROAM ROVE AMBLE ANTER JAUNT RANGE STRAY TRAIK BUMMEL DACKER DANDER GANDER LOUNGE PALMER RAMBLE SOODLE STROAM STROME TODDLE WANDER SAUNTER TURNOUT SPATIATE STRAVAGE STRAVAIG PERAMBULATE
STROLLER SULKY TRAMP SHULER FLANEUR SHUILER VAGRANT BOHEMIAN PUSHCHAIR
STROLLING FLANERIE FUGITIVE
STROMA ECOID OECOID
STRONG FAT FIT HOT FELL FERE FIRM FORT HALE HANG HARD HIGH IRON KEEN RANK SURE TRIG TRIM ACRID BONNY FORCY FRECK FRESH HARDY HEAVY HOGEN HUSKY JOLLY LUSTY NAPPY NERVY ORPED PITHY SHARP SMART SOLID SOUND STARK STEER STERN STIFF STOUR STOUT SWITH THEWY VALID VIVID WIGHT YAULD ARDENT BRAWNY BUCKRA BUNKUM FEIRIE FIERCE MIGHTY POTENT PRETTY ROBUST RUGGED SECURE SEVERE SINEWY STABLE STANCH STARCH STURDY WIELDY BOARDLY BUIRDLY DOUGHTY DURABLE EXALTED FECKFUL HUFFCAP HUMMING INTENSE LUSTFUL NERVOUS POLLENT SKOOKUM STHENIC ATHLETIC BIDDABLE MUSCULAR REVERENT ROBOREAN SPANKING STALWART STIFFISH VIGOROUS MERACIOUS
(PREF.) TRACHY VALE
STRONGBOX ARCA PETE COFFER DEEDBOX
STRONGEST EXTREME
STRONGHOLD HOLD KEEP PEEL PIECE PLACE TOWER CASTLE WARDER BASTION CITADEL KREMLIN REDOUBT FASTHOLD FASTNESS FORTRESS FRONTIER MUNIMENT STRENGTH
(— ON STEEP PLACE) AERY EYRY AERIE EYRIE
STRONGLY BUT SAD BADLY SWITH FIRMLY STRONG DURABLY FRESHLY HEFTILY SOLIDLY STITHLY STOUTLY HEARTILY
STRONG-SCENTED HIGH RANK
STRONG-SMELLING FOXY
STRONTIUM SULPHATE ACANTHIN
STROP RIP STRAP
STROPHE ALCAIC LAISSE STANZA SAPPHIC
STROPHIC MELIC
STROPHIUS (FATHER OF —) CRISSUS
(MOTHER OF —) ANTIPHATIA
(SON OF —) PYLADES
(WIFE OF —) ANAXIBIA ASTYOCHIA CYDRAGORA
STRUCK (— SHARPLY) SMITTEN
(— WITH AMAZEMENT) AGAZED AGHAST
(— WITH FEAR) AFRAID
STRUCTURAL ORGANIC ANATOMIC TECTONIC
(— UNIT) IDANT
STRUCTURE CAGE FALX FORM MAKE ANNEX BOOTH CABIN FLOAT FRAME GETUP HOUSE KIOSK PEGMA SETUP SHAPE STOCK BRIDGE CAGEOT FABRIC GANTRY GIRDER ISOGEN KELSON PREFAB TIMBER COTTAGE EDIFICE FAIRING FEATURE GATEWAY GESTALT KEELSON MANSION NURAGHE OUTCAST PAGEANT STADIUM TURNOUT ZEUGITE AEDICULA AIRCRAFT AIRFRAME BUILDING BUTTRESS COMPAGES CRIBWORK DOMATIUM ENDOCONE ESCORIAL HEADWORK MOUNTURE NEOMORPH SKELETON STANDARD
(— ALONG WALK) PERGOLA
(— BUILT IN WATER) PIER
(— CONTAINING KILN) HOVEL
(— EXTENDED INTO SEA) JETTY
(— FOR PIGEONS) COTE
(— FRAMING SHIP) KEELSON
(— IN ROCKS) FLASER
(— OF CARTRIDGE) ANVIL
(— OF EYE) LENS
(— OF PRETENSION) PERRON
(— ON ROOF) CUPOLA FEMERELL
(— ON SHIP) BLISTER
(— ON STEAMER) TEXAS
(— OVER MINE SHAFT) HEADFRAME
(— OVER WELL) WELLHEAD
(— PRODUCING SMOOTH OUTLINE) FAIRING
(— SHELTERING INSECTS) DOMATIUM
(— SUPPORTING AIRSHIP PROPELLER) PYLON
(— TO DEFLECT CURRENT) SPUR
(— WITHIN SHELL) ENDOCONE
(ANATOMICAL —) BUD APRON CARINA CRESCENT
(ANTICLINAL —) SWELL
(ARCHED —) FORNIX
(ARTISTIC —) MOBILE
(BELL-SHAPED —) PETTICOAT
(BODILY —) FRAME PHYSIQUE
(BRICK —) KANG HOVEL
(BRISTLELIKE —) ARISTA
(BRONZE AGE —) HENGE
(CABINLIKE —) CABANA
(CLIMBING —) LADDER
(COAL-SHIPPING —) STAITH STAITHE
(COMPLEX —) EMBOLUS
(CONELIKE —) PYRAMID
(CONICAL —) BULLET
(CREMATION —) DARGA
(CROWNLIKE —) CORONA
(CRYSTAL —) POLYTYPE
(CYLINDRICAL —) SILO
(DEADENING —) BAFFLE
(DEFENSIVE —) CAT
(FLATTENED —) TABULA
(FORTIFIED —) CAVALIER
(FRAIL —) SHELL
(GENERAL —) GETUP
(GEOLOGICAL —) CAMBER
(GRAMMATICAL —) SYNTAX
(HIGH —) TOWER
(HOLLOW —) SHELL
(KNEE-LIKE —) GENU
(LATTICEWORK —) TRELLIS
(LENS-SHAPED —) LENTOID
(LOFTY —) BABEL STEEPLE
(LOGICAL —) EIDOS
(MEGALITHIC —) HENGE
(ORGANIZED —) BULK
(ORIENTAL STORIED —) PAGODA
(ORNAMENTAL —) KIOSK
(PLANT —) DISC DISK
(POINTED —) BEAK
(PROTECTIVE —) SHEATH
(PUEBLO —) KIVA
(RAISED —) CIMBORIO
(RAMSHACKLE —) COOP
(RINGLIKE —) ANNULUS
(RODLIKE —) RIB
(RUDE STONE —S) SPECCHIE
(SACRIFICIAL —) ALTAR
(SENTENCE —) SYNTAX
(SHELTERING —) COT
(SHIELDING —) SHELTER
(SICKLE-SHAPED —) FALX
(SLENDER —) HAIR
(SPIRY —) PINNACLE
(STEMLIKE —) STOLON
(STONE —) TAULA
(TEMPORARY —) HUT

(**THEATER —**) SKENE
(**TIERED —**) STAGE
(**UNDERLYING —**) BOTTOM
(**UNSTABLE —**) COBHOUSE
(**VEHICLE —**) MONOCOQUE
(**WATERTIGHT —**) CAMEL COFFERDAM
(**WHITE —**) ALBEDO
(PREF.) MORPH(O)
(**RADIATED —**) ACTIN(O)
(SUFF.) (**— OF A KIND**) ID
(**— UNIT**) EME

STRUDEL (**PASTRY KIN TO —**) STOLLEN

STRUGGLE IT TEW TUG VIE WIN AGON CAMP COPE DEAL FEND FICK FRAB GAME PULL TAVE TOIL AGONY FIGHT FLING HEAVE LABOR STRAY SWORD TEAVE TWEIL WORRY WRELE BATTLE BUCKLE BUFFET BUSTLE COMBAT EFFORT HASSLE JOSTLE JUSTLE PINGLE RELUCT SEESAW SPRAWL SPRUNT STIVER STRIFE STRIVE TERVEE TUSSLE WARSLE WIDDLE AGONIZE CLAMBER CONTEND CONTEST DISPUTE FLOUNCE GRAPPLE SCUFFLE TUILYIE WARFARE WAUCHLE WRESTLE CONFLICT ENDEAVOR FLOUNDER SCRAFFLE SCRAMBLE SLUGFEST SPRANGLE SPRATTLE
(**— ALONG**) HOBBLE
(**— CONVULSIVELY**) SPRAWL
(**— FOR LARGESS**) SCAMBLE
(**— FORTH**) ELUCTATE
(**— ON**) POUND
(**— TO GAIN FOOTING**) SCRABBLE SPROTTLE
(**AGONIZED —**) THROE
(**CLOSE —**) HANDGRIPS
(**CONFUSED —**) MUSS
(**DEATH —**) AGONY
(**HAND-TO-HAND —**) GRAPPLE
(**HAPHAZARD —**) SCUFFLE
(**SPIRITUAL —**) PENIEL
(**UNCEREMONIOUS —**) SCRAMBLE

STRUGGLER LAOCOON

STRUM THRUM

STRUMA GOITER GOITRE

STRUMPET BRIM PUNK BIMBO TRULL WENCH WHORE BLOWEN BULKER STIVER TOMBOY TOMRIG COCOTTE SUCCUBA DOLLYMOP PUNKLING SUCCUBUS VENTURER
(**WORN-OUT —**) HARRIDAN

STRUT JET BRAG COCK POMP SPUR BRANK CORSO MAJOR PRINK RANCE SWANK SASHAY SCOTCH STRIDE STROKE STROOT STRUNT NAUNTLE PEACOCK STEMPLE SWAGGER TRANSOM
(**KIND OF —**) MACPHERSON

STRUTTER HAM

STRUTTING COCKING

STUB BUTT SNAG SPUD STOB STUD CHECK ERGOT GUARD HINGE STUMP SPRUNT

STUBBLE BUN ETCH MANE SHACK ARRISH EDDISH STOVER STUMPS EEGRASS GRATTEN STIBBLE

STUBBORN SOT BALKY ROWDY RUSTY STIFF STOUT STUNT THRAW TOUGH MULISH STURDY THWART BULLDOG PEEVISH PIGGISH RESTIVE WAYWARD WILLFUL OBDURATE PERVERSE STUNKARD THRAWART OBSTINATE PIGHEADED TENACIOUS REFRACTORY

STUBBORNNESS STOMACH ADAMANCY

STUBBY STUB CUTTY SQUAT STOCKY STUMPY STUBBED

STUCCO ALBARIUM

STUCK FAST MIRED INARUT MASHED WEDGED STICKIT STOODED

STUCK-UP BUG FROSTED

STUD SET BOLT BOSS KNOB KNOP KNOT NAIL RACE SLUG SPOT BESET BULLA CLOUT HARAS JOIST WRIST ASHLAR ENSTAR INSTAR STOOTH STRING CONTACT POTENCE QUARTER STUDDLE PUNCHEON STANDARD STUDDERY
(**— FARM**) HARAS
(**— IN BOOT SOLE**) SLUG
(**— IN WATCH**) POTENCE
(**— SHOES**) HOBNAIL
(**— WITH NAILS**) CLOUT
(**INTERMEDIATE —**) PUNCHEON
(**ORNAMENTED —**) AGLET AIGLET

STUDDED BOSSY BILLETY STELLED BILLETTE

STUDDLE POST ROIL

STUDENT BOY DIG WIT COED PLUG PREP SMUG SOPH AGGIE BAHUR BEJAN ELEVE FUCHS GRIND MEDIC PUPIL SIZAR SPOON BOCHER BURSAR BURSCH INTERN JUNIOR JURIST MEDICO OPTIME PREMED PRIMAR PRIMER PUISNE SCOLOG SENIOR ADVISEE CHRONIC CLASSIC DANTEAN EDUCAND ETONIAN FAILURE GOLIARD GRECIAN INTERNE INTRANT LEARNER MIDDLER MOOTMAN OPPIDAN PASSMAN PHARMIC PLUGGER SCHOLAR STUDIER TEMPLAR THEOLOG BOTANIST CABALIST COLLEGER DEMOTIST DISCIPLE EDUCATOR FEMINIST HOMERIST HOSTELER ISLAMIST PREMEDIC REPEATER SECONDAR SUBSIZAR TRANSFER
(**— IN TALMUDIC ACADEMY**) BAHUR
(**— LAST IN CLASS**) SPOON
(**— OF LOW RANK**) TERNAR TERNER
(**— WHO LIVES IN TOWN**) OPPIDAN
(**ABNORMALLY ABSORBED —**) SAP
(**AFTER-DEGREE —**) POSTDOC
(**DAY —**) EXTERN EXTERNE
(**DIVINITY —**) STIBBLER
(**DRUDGING —**) PLUG
(**ENGLISH SCHOOL —**) BLUE SWOT ETONIAN OXONIAN SWOTTER BATTELER
(**GRADUATE —**) FELLOW
(**LAW —**) PUNEE JURIST LEGIST PUISNE TEMPLAR STAGIARY
(**MILITARY —**) CADET
(**MOSLEM —**) SOFTA
(**NON-COLLEGIATE —**) TOSHER
(**PLODDING —**) DIG SMUG
(**WANDERING —**) GOLIARD
(**1ST-YEAR —**) FUCHS
(**3RD-YEAR —**) JUNIOR TERTIAN
(PL.) GOWN CLASS HOUSE SEMINAR
(SUFF.) LOG(ER)(IA)(IAN)(IC)(ICAL)(IST)(UE)(Y)

STUDIED COOL VOULU STUDIOUS

STUDIO LOT SHOT ATELIER BOTTEGA GALLERY

STUDIOUS BOOKY BOOKISH CLERKLY DILIGENT SEDULOUS

STUDY CON BEAT BONE BOOK CASE MUZZ PORE ROOM SIFT STUD GRIND ESTUDY EXAMEN LESSON MUSEUM SCOLEY SURVEY ABBOZZO ACCOUNT ANALYZE CANVASS CROQUIS POCHADE REVOLVE SANCTUM ANALYSIS BOOKWORK CONSIDER EXERCISE MEDITATE SCRUTINY TYPOLOGY
(**— ANEW**) REVISE
(**— BY LAMPLIGHT**) LUCUBRATE
(**— HARD**) DIG MUG SAP BONE CRAM PORE SMUG STEW SWOT
(**— OF ALGAE**) PHYCOLOGY
(**— OF BLINDNESS**) TYPHLOLOGY
(**— OF BRAMBLES**) BATOLOGY
(**— OF CLOUDS**) NEPHOLOGY
(**— OF CODES**) CRYPTOLOGY
(**— OF CREEDS**) SYMBOLICS
(**— OF DREAMS**) ONEIROLOGY
(**— OF EARTHQUAKES**) SEISMOLOGY
(**— OF EXCREMENT**) SCATOLOGY
(**— OF FEVERS**) PYRETOLOGY
(**— OF FLYING OBJECTS**) UFOLOGY
(**— OF GRASSES**) AGROSTOLOGY
(**— OF INSECTS**) ENTOMOLOGY
(**— OF LAKES**) LIMNOLOGY
(**— OF MOUNTAINS**) OROLOGY OREOLOGY
(**— OF MOUTH**) STOMATOLOGY
(**— OF MUSCLES**) MYOLOGY
(**— OF ONESELF**) AUTOLOGY
(**— OF PEACE**) IRENOLOGY
(**— OF PLACE NAMES**) TOPONYMY
(**— OF PRIMITIVE CUSTOMS**) AGRIOLOGY
(**— OF PUNISHMENT**) PENOLOGY
(**— OF RELIGIOUS FEASTS**) HEORTOLOGY
(**— OF SACRED EDIFICES**) NAOLOGY
(**— OF SNOW AND ICE**) CRYOLOGY
(**— OF SOILS**) PEDOLOGY
(**—OF SPORES**) PALYNOLOGY
(**— OF TREES**) DENDROLOGY
(**— OF VALUES**) AXIOLOGY
(**— OF VERSIFICATION**) PROSODY
(**— OF WEAPONS**) HOPLOLOGY
(**— STEADILY**) PLOD
(**— UNDER PRESSURE**) CRAM
(**ART —**) ABBOZZO CROQUIS POCHADE
(**BROWN —**) MEMENTO REVERIE
(**CLAY —**) BOZZETTO
(**LABORIOUS —**) GRIND
(**MUSICAL —**) ETUDE
(**PRELIMINARY —**) SKETCH
(**UNINTERESTING —**) GRIND
(SUFF.) ICS SOPH(ER)(IC)(IST)(Y)

STUDY IN SCARLET (**AUTHOR OF —**) DOYLE
(**CHARACTER IN —**) HOPE JOHN LUCY HOLMES TOBIAS WATSON FERRIER GREGSON LESTRADE SHERLOCK STAMFORD JEFFERSON STANGERSON

STUFF PAD RAM WAD CRAM CRAP GAUM GEAR JAZZ PANG SATE STOP TACK TRIG TUCK WHAT CROWD DUROY FARCE FORCE KEDGE METAL PASTE SQUAB TRADE FABRIC GRAITH KIBOSH MATTER PAUNCH STEEVE STODGE TACKLE TIMBER BOMBARD BOMBAST DRUGGET ELEMENT ENFARCE DIAPHANE MARINATE MATERIAL SPLUTTER WHIPPING
(**— AND NONSENSE**) HAVERS PICKLE PIFFLE
(**— FILLET OF VEAL**) BOMBARD
(**— FULL**) STODGE
(**— OF POOR QUALITY SILK**) RASH
(**— ONESELF**) MAST
(**— POULTRY**) FARCE MARINATE
(**— WITH DRESSING**) QUILT
(**CLAGGY —**) STODGE
(**COTTON —**) CALICO
(**HOUSEHOLD —**) GEAR
(**INFERIOR —**) MOCKADO
(**PALTRY —**) TRASH
(**POOR —**) TRIPE
(**SILKEN —**) TARS TARSE DIAPHANE
(**SLOPPY —**) SLIPSLOP
(**STICKY —**) GOOK
(**TASTELESS —**) GLOP
(**THIN —**) CRAPE
(**THIN SILK —**) LOVE
(**WATERY —**) BLASH
(**WISHY-WASHY —**) BLASH
(**WOOLEN —**) SAY DUROY TWILLY DRUGGET SAGATHY SHALLOON
(**WORSTED —**) BUNTING
(**WORTHLESS —**) GEAR GLOP HOGWASH

STUFFED PANG TRIG BLOAT FARCI STODGY BLOATED BOMBAST
(**— DELICACY**) DERMA

STUFFING PAD TAR FARCE KAPOK STECH STUFF BOMBAST FARCING SAWDUST SALPICON STUFFAGE
(**— FOR MATTRESS**) PULU

STUFFY POKY CLOSE FUBBY FUBSY FUGGY STIVY WOOLY WOOLLY AIRLESS FROUSTY

STULTIFY SOT PUPPIFY

STUMBLE CHIP FALL HAMP PECK STOT TRIP HAMEL LURCH SPURN STOIT STUMP BUMBLE CHANCE FALTER HALPER HAMBLE HAPPEN LUMPER OFFEND STEVEL TUMBLE WAGGER BLUNDER FOUNDER MISSTEP SCAMBLE SNAPPER STAMMER STAMPLE STOITER STOTTER STUMMER FLOUNDER THRUMBLE

STUMBLING HACK HURTING OFFENCE OFFENSE

STUMP CAG GET JOB NOG SET BUTT DOCK GRUB LUMP MORE RUNT SNAG STAB STAM STOB STUB STUD CHUNK ORATE SCRAB SCRAG STICK STOCK STOMP STOOL STOOP STOWL DOTARD NUBBIN SCRUNT SPRONG STOVEN

WICKET DODDARD RAMPICK RAMPIKE SLEEPER STUMMEL BALDHEAD HUSTINGS STUBBLES
(— AND ROOT) MOCK
(— OF TAIL) STRUNT
(CIGAR —) TOPPER
(CRICKET —) STICKS
(DEAD —) RUNT
(TREE —) MOCK STOW STOCK STOOP ZUCHE DOTARD NUBBIN STOVEN DODDARD
(WALNUT —) BUTT
STUMPY SNUB BUNTY SNUBBED
STUN DIN BOWL DAZE ROCK ZONK DAUNT DAVER DEAVE DOVER DOZEN DROWN STONY ASTONY BEDAZE BENUMB DEADEN DEAFEN DEVVEL NOBBLE STOUND WITHER ASTOUND DAMMISH SANDBAG SILENCE STUPEFY STUPEND ASTONISH PARALYZE
(— BY A SHOT) CREASE
STUNNED SILLY STUPENT ASTONIED
STUNNER KNOCKER THUMPER TRIMMER
STUNNING CRASHING SHOCKING
STUNT GAG KIP FEAT NIRL BLAST CANOE CROWL DWARF STINT STOCK BARANI BARONI CRADDY DOLPHIN BACKBEND CATALINA CRUCIFIX PORPOISE PRATFALL SUPPRESS
(PUBLICITY —) HYPE
(SWIMMING —) SHARK SPIRAL
STUNTED URLED GRUBBY RUNTISH SCROGGY SCRUBBY SCRUFFY SCRUNTY WANTHRIVEN
STUPA TOPE CHORTEN
STUPEFACTION STOUND STUPOR
STUPEFIED MAD DAMP DAZED DRUNK MAZED SILLY SOTTED ZONKED BEMAZED BEMUSED DONNERT DOZENED DOZZLED STUPENT BESOTTED DATELESS MINDLESS
STUPEFIER OPIUM
STUPEFY FOX BAZE DAMP DAZE DOZE DRUG DULL GOOF MAZE MULL STUN ZONK BESOT DAUNT DAVER DEAVE DIZZY DOZEN SHEND SMOKE STONY ASTONE ASWEVE BEMUSE BENUMB DUDDLE FUDDLE MOIDER MUDDLE STOUND ASTOUND CONFUSE FORDULL SLUMBER STUPEND ASTONISH BEFUDDLE BEMUDDLE BEWILDER CONFOUND MORPHINE PARALYZE SOMNIATE SOPORATE
STUPEFYING STONY
STUPENDOUS GREAT IMMENSE ENORMOUS MONSTROUS
STUPID FAT JAY BETE DOWF DULL DUMB DUNT FOOL HAZY LEWD NICE NUMB SLOW BLUNT BOOBY BRUTE CRASS DENSE DORKY DOTED DUNNY GLAKY GOOSY GROSS HEAVY INERT MOSSY MUZZY SILLY THICK ASSISH BARREN BOVINE CUCKOO DAWKIN DOITED DROWSY DUMMEL HEBETE LOGGER LURDAN OBTUSE OPAQUE SIMPLE SODDEN STOLID STULTY STURDY SUMPHY TAVERT URLUCH WOODEN ASININE BRUTISH CHUCKLE DOLTISH DONNARD DONNERD DOWFART DUFFING DUMPISH FATUOUS FOOLISH FOPPISH GAWKISH GLAIKIT GULLISH INSULSE LUMPISH LURDANE PEAKISH PINHEAD PROSAIC SOTTISH TAIVERT TOMFOOL VACUOUS WITLESS ANSERINE BAYARDLY BESOTTED BLOCKISH BOBBYISH BOEOTIAN CLODDISH DONNERED DUNCICAL FOOTLESS GAUMLESS HEADLESS IMBECILE STOCKISH PINHEADED SENSELESS
(— PERSON) HOIT NERD JUKES SUMPH LUMMOX TUMFIE KALLIKAK
(PREF.) MORO
STUPIDITY BETISE TORPOR BOBBERY DENSITY DUNCERY FATUITY DULLNESS DUMBNESS HEBETUDE STOLIDITY
STUPOR FOG SOG COMA DAMP DOTE SOPOR SWARF STOUND TORPOR TRANCE NARCOMA LETHARGY NARCOSIS
(PREF.) NARC(O) TYPH(O)
STURDILY BUFF TOUGH
STURDY GID BUFF DUNT RUDE TALL THRO BURLY CRANK FELON HARDY HUSKY LUSTY SOLID SOUND STARK STERN STIFF STOUT VAUDY WALLY FEERIE PLUGGY ROBUST RUGGED RUSTIC SQUARE STABLE STEADY STEEVE STOCKY STRONG STUGGY VIRILE FECKFUL UPRIGHT VALIANT STALWART STUBBORN VIGOROUS YEOMANLY
STURGEON HUSO ELOPS BELUGA GANOID MAMMOSE OSSETER STERLET
STUTTER FAM BUFF HACK MANT STOT STUT GANCH FAMBLE HABBER HABBLE STAMMER
STUTTERER RATTLER
STUTTERING TRAULISM BALBUTIENT
STY PEN QUAT STYE WEST FRANK CRUIVE PIGPEN STITHE HORDEOLUM
STYLE AIR CUT DUB PEN SAY TON WAY CHIC FACE FORM GARB HAND KIND MODE MOLD NAME PILE RATE TWIG VEIN GENRE GETUP GUISE IDIOM SHAPE STATE SWANK TASTE FESCUE FORMAT GNOMON GOTHIC PHRASE STEELE STRAIN STYLUS UMBONE COSTUME DIALECT DICTION FASHION INSTYLE QUALITY EQUIPAGE LANGUAGE MARINISM NARRANTE PULLBACK PHRASEOLOGY
(— HAIR) CORNROW
(— OF ARCHITECTURE) ORDER DRAVIDA GEORGIAN
(— OF COOKING) CUISINE
(— OF DRESS) GUISE
(— OF GEM SETTING) BOX
(— OF HANDWRITING) CHANCERY SCRIPTION
(— OF HAT) BLOCK
(— OF MOUNTING) SETTING
(— OF MUSIC) BOOGIE
(— OF PAINTING) GENRE
(— OF PENMANSHIP) HAND
(— OF PRINTING) CAMAIEU
(— OF SPEAKING) ADDRESS
(— OF SWIMMING) STROKE
(— OF WRESTLING) SAMBO
(AFFECTED —) EUPHUISM
(ARTISTIC —) GUSTO GOTHIC ARTIFICE DANDYISM MANNERISM
(BOOKBINDING —) ALDINE MAIOLI MAJOLI FANFARE GROLIER ETRUSCAN HARLEIAN ROXBURGH
(CUSTOMARY —) GATE
(DECORATIVE —) ARTDECO
(DISTINCTIVE —) CLOTHES
(FAVORED —) GROOVE
(HAIR —) CROP TETE
(INFLATED —) FUSTIAN
(JAZZ —) TAILGATE
(LACKING —) FUNKY
(LATEST —) KICK
(OF PAST —) RETRO
(PRETENTIOUS —) BOMBAST
(PROPER —) WEAR
(THEATRICAL —) LYCEUM
(WRITING —) MINUSCULE
(SUFF.) **(IN THE — OF)** ESQUE
STYLET SPEAR STILET STYLUS TROCAR MANDRIN STILETTE
STYLIDIUM CANDOLEA
STYLISH FLY CHIC DOSS POSH TONY DOGGY NIFTY NOBBY RITZY SASSY SHARP SMART SWELL TIPPY TOPPY CHEESY CLASSY DAPPER DRESSY FLOSSY JAUNTY SWANKY TONISH DASHING DOGGISH GENTEEL KNOWING SWAGGER TOFFISH
STYLOBATE PODIUM
STYLOID BELONOID
STYLUS GAD PEN STYLE CUTTER GREFFE TRACER HARPAGO POINTEL PYROPEN
STYMPHALUS (FATHER OF —) ELATUS
(MOTHER OF —) LAODICE
STYPTIC ALUM AMADOU MATICO BAROMETZ STANCHER
STYRENE STYROL CINNAMOL
STYX (— FERRYMAN) CHARON
(FATHER OF —) OCEANUS
(HUSBAND OF —) PALLAS
(MOTHER OF —) TETHYS
SUAEDA DONDIA
SUAH (FATHER OF —) ZOPHAH
SUAN PAN SOROBAN
SUAVE COOL OILY SMUG SOFT BLAND SOAPY SVELT GLOSSY SILKEN SMOOTH URBANE FULSOME POLITIC DEBONAIR UNCTUOUS
SUAVELY CREAMILY
SUAVITY COMITY URBANITY
SUB GRASS UBOAT
SUBALTERN WART
SUBBASE PLINTH
SUBCINCTORIUM BALTEUS BALTHEUS
SUBCLASS GENDER BRYALES CESTODA CYCLIAE DIGENEA SPECIES AMOEBAEA ANAPSIDA CESTODES COPEPODA GANOIDEI SELACHII
SUBCOMPACT MINICAR
SUBCULTURE HIPHOP
SUBCUTANEOUS DEEP
SUBDEACON MINISTER
SUBDIVIDE CARVE MINCE
SUBDIVISION DEN OBE SEX BEAT CAZA DHER HAPU ITEM TASU BUNDA CORPS CURIA DEKAN DHERI FERAE FORTY HSIEN IOWAN NAHIE OKRUG PHYLE SITIO STAGE TALUK TARAF TURMA UINTA ALBIAN ARENIG BANNER BRANCH BUREAU CERCLE CIRCLE CLAUSE COHORT COLUMN COMMOT DAKOTA DANIAN DOGGER FACIES GUELPH HEMERA IMBREX LENGTH LUDLOW MARKAZ NAHIYE OBLAST ONEIDA SANJAK SECTOR SERIAL SHIRAZ STRAIN SUBAGE TAHSIL TASSOO TEHSIL BUKEYEF CENTURY CHEMUNG CHIRIPA COCHITI COMARCA ECOTYPE ELEMENT EPARCHY EPISODE GENESEE MANIPLE MONTANA ORBITAL PHRATRY RONDOUT SASTEAN SECTION SEEDBED SUBAREA SUBLINE SUBPLAT SUBPLOT SUBRACE SUBZONE SUPPORT TRENTON TRINITY WASATCH WASHITA WENLOCK WICHITA BANOVINA DISTRICT DIVISION DJAGATAY ENDBRAIN FLOTILLA GUBERNIA LOCATION MONTEREY NAUCRARY PARTICLE PRECINCT STOCKTON SUBCASTE SUBORDER SUBSTAGE SUBTRIBE TOWNSHIP PARAGRAPH
(— OF SCOUTS) CREW
(EGYPTIAN —) KISM
(SPARTAN —) ENOMOTY
SUBDOMINANT FOURTH
SUBDUE BOW COW ADAW BEAT BEND QUAY TAME ACCOY ALLAY AMATE CHARM CRUSH DAUNT DOMPT QUAIL QUASH QUELL SOBER STILL ADAUNT BRIDLE CHASTE DEBELL DISMAY EVINCE GENTLE MASTER QUENCH REDUCE SUBACT SUBMIT UNWILD ABANDON AFFAITE CAPTURE CHASTEN CONQUER DAUNTON OVERAWE REPRESS REPRIME SUCCUMB CONVINCE OVERCOME SUPPEDIT SUPPRESS SURMOUNT VANQUISH
SUBDUED MAK SOFT TAME MUTED SOBER STILL UNDER BROKEN CHASTE GENTLE ASHAMED SUBMISS SOURDINE
SUBFAMILY KHOISAN CUSHITIC ACRAEINAE
SUBGROUP BAND FAMILY
SUBHEAD BOXHEAD SIDEHEAD
SUBIMAGO DUN
SUBINDEX SUFFIX
SUBIRRIGATE SUB SUBWATER
SUBIRRIGATION SUBBING
SUBJECT DUX PUT ABLE ALLY BODY BONE ITEM OPEN TEXT HOBBY PLACE STOOP STUDY

TESTO THEMA THEME TOPIC GROUND IMPOSE LIABLE PATHIC REDUCE SACOPE SUBDIT SUBMIT THRALL VASSAL CAITIVE CITIZEN FEODARY FEUDARY OBVIOUS PROBAND SERVILE AMENABLE ELECTIVE INCIDENT INFERIOR OBEDIENT OCCASION SENTENCE SUBJUGAL
(— OF DISCOURSE) NOUN
(— OF FUGUE) GUIDA
(— OF PROPOSITION) EXTREME
(— TO ABUSE) REVILE
(— TO ARGUMENT) MOOT
(— TO BAD TEMPER) MOODY
(— TO CHANGE) MUTABLE FUGITIVE
(— TO CRITICISM) SCOURGE
(— TO FATE) FIE
(— TO PERCOLATION) DISPLACE
(— TO SOME ACTION) TREAT
(CONTROVERTED —) ISSUE
(LOYAL —) LIEGE
(PL.) FOLK
SUBJECTION SLAVERY SERVITUS THIRLING
SUBJECTIVE IMMANENT INSEEING INTERNAL PECTORAL EPISTEMIC
SUBJOIN AFFIX ANNEX
SUBJUGATE COW ENSLAVE
SUBJUGATION BONDAGE SERVITUDE
SUBKINGDOM PHYLUM ANNULOSA CHORDATA
SUBLEADER HEADMAN
SUBLEASE FARMOUT SUBTACK
SUBLET JOB SUBSET CONACRE SUBLEASE
SUB-LIEUTENANT CORNET
SUBLIMATE FLOWER ALCOHOL SUBLIME
SUBLIME BIG FUME GRAND LOFTY NOBLE AUGUST REFINE SOLEMN WINGED DANTEAN ELEVATO EXALTED EMPYREAL EMPYREAN MAGNIFIC MAJESTIC SERAPHIC SPLENDID MAGNIFICENT
(— IN STYLE) MILTONIC
(FALSELY —) TUMID
SUBLIMITY GRANDEUR
SUBLUNARY EARTHLY
SUBMARINE SUB BOAT HERO DIVER EBOAT FRITZ GUPPY HOAGY UBOAT HOAGIE SUBSEA PIGBOAT POORBOY TIDDLER
(GERMAN —) UBOAT
(PART OF —) DECK SAIL PLANE TOWER BRIDGE RUDDER PROPELLER SAILPLANE TURTLEBACK FAIRWEATHER
SUBMEDIANT SIXTH
SUBMERGE BOG DIP BURY DIVE DUNK HIDE SINK SOAK TAKE DROWN SOUSE SWAMP WHELM DELUGE DRENCH ENGULF DEMERGE IMPLUNGE INUNDATE SUBMERSE SURROUND OVERWHELM
SUBMERGENCE ONLAP
SUBMISSION VAIL STOOP PATIENCE
SUBMISSIVE MEEK BUXOM DEMISS DOCILE DUTIFUL PASSIVE SERVILE SLAVISH SUBJECT SUBMISS UNERECT AMENABLE OBEDIENT RESIGNED YIELDING
(— TO WIFE) UXORIOUS
SUBMISSIVENESS SLAVERY
SUBMIT BOW EAT ABOW BEND CAVE LEAN OBEY TAKE VAIL AVALE DEFER HIELD STAND STOOP YIELD ASSENT CRINGE DELATE RESIGN CONSIGN KNUCKLE SUBJECT SUBMISE SUCCUMB TRUCKLE PROPOUND
(— FOR CONSIDERATION) REMIT
(— TAMELY) EAT
(— TO) ABIDE STAND SUFFER
SUBNORMAL OFF SICK ABNORMAL
SUBORDER LARI ALCAE APODA APODI GALLI GRUES ARDEAE COHORT CUCULI SAURIA AGLOSSA ANSERES ARCACEA ASCONES CORACII COSTATA SARCURA SYCONES ACRASIDA ADEPHAGA BATOIDEI COLUMBAE CORACIAE CURSORIA ENOPLINA EUSUCHIA FALCONES FREGATAE SELACHII
SUBORDINARY ENDORSE ROUNDEL
SUBORDINATE SUB SINK PETTY SCRUB UNDER EXEMPT MINION PUISNE SECOND YEOMAN PARTIAL SERVANT SERVILE SUBJECT HENCHMAN INFERIOR MYRMIDON PARERGAL POSTPONE SERVIENT ANCILLARY SUBALTERN
(PREF.) **(— TO)** VICE
SUBORN HAVE BRIBE
SUBOVAL PETALOID
SUBPHYLUM EUCHORDA
SUBPOENA SUMMONS
SUBRACE STOCK
SUB ROSA COVERTLY SECRETLY PROVATELY
SUBSCRIBE SIGN ASSENT ASCRIBE CONSIGN SUBSIGN
(— AGAIN) RENEW
SUBSCRIBER RAILBIRD
SUBSCRIPT INFERIOR
SUBSCRIPTION APPROVAL SIGNATURE ABONNEMENT
SUBSEQUENT AFTER LATER FUTURE PUISNE ENSUING POSTNATE
(PREF.) POST
(— TO) CIS
SUBSEQUENTLY SO LATER SINCE
SUBSERVIENT OILY UNDER VASSAL DUTEOUS SERVILE SLAVISH OFFICIAL
SUBSHRUB STOCK GUAYULE COLUMNEA PERIWINKLE
SUBSIDE DIE EBB LAY LIE ADAW CALM FALL LULL SILE SINK VAIL ABATE ALLAY LAPSE RESIDE SETTLE ASSUAGE RELAPSE UNSWELL WITHDRAW
SUBSIDENCE FALL SETTLING
SUBSIDIARY CHILD DONKEY SUBSIDY ACCESSORY
SUBSIDIZE AID HELP BONUS
SUBSIDY AID BONUS BOUNTY POUNDAGE
SUBSILICIC BASIC
SUBSIST BE LIVE RELY
SUBSISTENCE DOLE BEING LIVING
SUBSISTENT ENTITY
SUBSOIL PAN LECK SOLE SHRAVE RATCHEL
SUBSTAGE CARY GUNZ IOWAN MANKATO STADIAL TAZEWELL
SUBSTANCE FAT SUM BODY CORE FECK GIST GITE MEAT TACK WHAT ADROP AGENT ALLOY ARCHE BEING FOMES GREAT KEEST METAL MOYEN OUSIA PROOF SENSE STUFF THING BOTTOM GADUIN GETTER IMPORT MATTER STAPLE WEALTH AEROSOL AGAROID ANTIGEN COLICIN COLLOID CONTENT ELEIDIN EMANIUM ERGUSIA ESSENCE HYALINE MEANING PURPORT REAGENT SUBJECT SUPTION ACCEPTOR ADDITIVE ADHESIVE ALLERGEN AMBEROID ANTIFOAM BASSORIN HARDNESS MATERIAL PSORALEN
(— CAPABLE OF EXPANSION) DILATANT
(— FORMED IN VINEGAR) MOTHER
(— FROM CRUSHED APPLES) POMACE
(— IN BLOOD) ALEXINE ABLASTIN
(— IN LIGHT BULBS) GETTER
(— IN WOODY TISSUE) LIGNIN
(— OF DENTINE) IVORY
(— OF EXTREME HARDNESS) ADAMANT DIAMOND
(— PRODUCING POISONOUS ATMOSPHERE) GAS
(— SURROUNDED BY FOREIGN TISSUE) ENCLAVE
(— THAT INDUCES MITOSIS) MITOGEN
(— THAT STOPS LOCOMOTION) ARRESTANT
(— TO ADD STABILITY) BALLAST
(— TRANSPORTING GERMS) FOMES
(— USED AS HYPNOTIC) URAL
(— USED IN DETECTING OTHERS) REAGENT
(— WITH MOLDY ODOR) CHARACIN
(ADHESIVE —) GLUE GLOEA PASTE CEMENT STICKER
(AMORPHOUS —) GLASS RESIN LIGNIN PECTIN FERRITE SAPONIN
(AROMATIC —) BALSAM
(ASTRINGENT —) ALUM CATECHU
(BITTER —) ALOIN LININ ILICIN
(BLACK —) SOOT BLECK
(CLEANSING —) LYE
(COLLOIDAL —) ALGIN EXPANDER
(COMBUSTIBLE —) COAL
(CONDENSED —) PITH
(CORROSIVE —) CAUSTIC
(CRYSTALLINE —) LAURIN ALANINE HELENIN ELATERIN
(DARK —) ATRAMENT
(DISSOLVED —) SOLUTE
(ETERNAL —) DHARMA ADHARMA
(FATLIKE —) DEGRAS LIPOID ERGUSIA
(FATTY —) SMEAR SUBERIN
(FERMENTATION —) LEAVEN
(FIBROUS —) COTTON
(FILAMENTOUS —) HARL
(FILMY —) GOSSAMER
(FIRST —) YLEM
(GENERATIVE —) SPERM
(GRINDING —) ABRASIVE
(GROWTH-PROMOTING —) AUXIN
(GUMMY —) GUM GURRY AMYLOID GLACTAN
(HARD ANIMAL —) BONE ENAMEL
(HORNY —) BALEEN CHITIN CHONDRIN
(HYPOTHETICAL —) FLUID INOGEN PROTYL
(IDEAL —) CONTINUUM
(INFLAMMABLE —) BITUMEN
(INSOLUBLE —) CARRIER HYALOGEN
(LIVERLIKE —) HEPAR
(NARCOTIC —) DRUG
(NITROGENOUS —) LACTENIN
(POISONOUS —) ARSENIC PHRYNIN EXOTOXIN
(POWDER OF ANY —) FLOUR
(POWDERY —) STOUR
(PREDOMINATING —) BASE
(RESINOUS —) LAC COPAL CARANNA CARAUNA COPALINE COPALITE
(SELF-DEFENSIVE —) ACRAEIN
(SEMISOLID —) GEL
(SOUR —) ACID
(STICKY —) GOO GOOP SIZE STICK GLUTEN BIRDLIME
(SUBTLE —) SPIRIT
(SWEET —) SUGAR
(SYNTHETIC —) HORMONE
(TRANSLUCENT —) HYALINE CHONDRIN
(UNBREAKABLE —) ADAMANT
(UNCREATED —) ADHARMA
(VISCOUS —) GLAIR GREASE SLUBBER
(VITAL —) KEEST
(WAXY —) CERIN PARAFFIN SUBERINE
(PREF.) HYL(O)
(SUFF.) **(— HAVING FORM)** PHANE
(— PRODUCED THRU PROCESS) STATE
SUBSTANDARD BAD BAUCH
SUBSTANTIAL FAT FIRM MEATY PUKKA STOUT ACTUAL BODILY HEARTY SQUARE STABLE STANCH STUFFY STURDY MASSIVE MATERIAL SUBSTANT TANGIBLE
SUBSTANTIATE BACK CONFIRM SUPPORT VALIDATE
SUBSTANTIVE DIRECT
SUBSTITUTE SUB MOCK TEMP VICE AKORI EXTRA PINCH PROXY VICAR BACKUP BEWITH CHANGE DEPUTY DOUBLE ERSATZ STOOGE COMMUTE REPLACE RESERVE STANDBY STANDIN STOPGAP SUBDEAN SUFFECT SUPPOSE DISPLACE EMERGENT MAKESHIFT SURROGATE
(— FOR SIGNATURE) MARK
(— FOR TEA) TIA FAHAM
(— FRAUDULENTLY) SUPPOSE
(NOT —) FULL
(POOR —) APOLOGY
(SOAP —) AMOLE
(TOOTH —) CROWN

(USE OF GRAMMATICAL —) CATAPHORA
(PREF.) PSEUD(O)
(SUFF.) ETTE
SUBSTITUTING
(PREF.)
(— FOR) PRO
SUBSTITUTION SHIFT CHANGE ERSATZ ENALLAGE EXCHANGE NOVATION REPLACEMENT
(— OF SOUNDS) LALLATION
SUBSTRATUM SUB GROUND SUBBING SUBJECT
SUBSTREAM MATTER
SUBSTRUCTURE PODIUM FOOTING CENTERING
(— OF DOME) THOLOBATE
SUBSUME COVER EXPLAIN INCLUDE
SUBSUMING GENERIC
SUBTENANT VAVASOUR
SUBTERFUGE MASK BLIND CROOK QUIRK SHIFT TRICK WRINK AMBAGE CHICANE ARTIFICE PRETENCE TRAVERSE VOIDANCE
SUBTILE SUBTLE TENUOUS
SUBTILIZE EXALT
SUBTITLE TITLE LEADER CAPTION
SUBTLE SLY FINE NICE WILY WISE ACUTE ARGUTE ASTUTE CRAFTY SHREWD CUNNING FRAGILE SUBTILE CLERGIAL
(FALLACIOUSLY —) SOPHISTIC
(TOO —) FINESPUN
SUBTLETY NICE FRAUD DECEIT NUANCE EXILITY FINESSE QUILLET DELICACY FINENESS QUIDDITY QUODLIBET REFINEMENT
(— IN ARGUMENT) QUILLET
(CRITICAL —) NICETY
SUBTLY FINE SLILY SLYLY
SUBTRACT BATE PULL TAKE SHAVE DEDUCE DEDUCT DETRACT SUBDUCE SUBDUCT SUBTRAY DIMINISH
SUBTRIBE HAPU SENAAH SEMNONES
SUBURB ANNEX BORGO BARRIO PETTAH BANLIEU ENDSHIP FAUBOURG
(POORLY CONSTRUCTED —) SLURB
(PL.) BURBS SKIRTS ENVIRONS OUTPARTS SUBTOPIA SUBURBIA
SUBURBIA VILLADOM
SUBVERSION FALL SABOTAGE
SUBVERSIVE RUINOUS
SUBVERT SAP KILL RAZE RUIN EVERT UPSET GAINSAY OVERSET REVERSE RUINATE OVERTURN
SUBVERTED LOST
SUBWAY BMT IND IRT DIVE TUBE METRO
SUCCEED GO FAY HIT FARE RISE WORK CLICK ENSUE FADGE PROVE SCORE SPEED COTTON FOLLOW MAKEIT OBTAIN PANOUT SECOND THRIVE ACHIEVE INHERIT PREVAIL PROSPER THROUGH TURNOUT FLOURISH SUPPLANT
(— IN REACHING) RECOVER
(— TO THRONE) ACCEDE ASCEND
SUCCEEDING VICE AFTER CHANGE ULTERIOR
SUCCESS DO GO HIT MAX WIN WOW BANG CESS LUCK SMASH SPEED THRIFT EXPLOIT FORTUNE FURTHER PROWESS THEEDOM FELICITY GODSPEED
(— IN A MATCH) GAME
(ACCIDENTAL —) FLUKE
(BRILLIANT —) ECLAT
(ECONOMIC —) BOOM
(FINANCIAL —) SELLER
(NOT LIKELY TO BE A —) NOWIN
(SUDDEN —) KILLING
(UNEXPECTED —) JACKPOT
(WORLDLY —) ARTHA
SUCCESSFUL HOT MADE SOCK BOFFO LUCKY SPEEDFUL THRIVING GANGBUSTERS
(BARELY —) NARROW
(HIGHLY —) RUNAWAY
SUCCESSFULLY GREAT HAPPILY PROUDLY
SUCCESSION RUN SUIT ROUND SUITE TRACK ASSISE COURSE SEQUEL SERIES STREAM STRING HEIRDOM SUCCESS ANCESTRY DIADOCHE MUTATION SEQUENCE
(— OF CHANGES) FLUX
(— OF CHORDS) CADENCE
(— OF CRUSTS) CALICHE
(— OF LUCK) STREAK
(— OF STAGES) CASCADE
(— OF WAVES) CRIMP
(— RULERS) DYNASTY
SUCCESSIVELY AROW
SUCCESSOR HEIR CALIF HERES CALIPH HAERES EPIGONUS
(— OF CHIEFTAIN) TANIST
(— OF MUHAMMAD) CALIF CALIPH
(ECCLESIASTICAL —) COARB COMARB
(PL.) DIADOCHI
SUCCINCT BRIEF PITHY SHORT TERSE CONCISE LACONIC SUMMARY
SUCCINIC DIACETIC
SUCCOR AID HELP RESET SERVE SPEED ASSIST RELIEF RESCUE SUPPLY UPTAKE COMFORT DELIVER PRESIDY RELIEVE SECOURS SUSTAIN BEFRIEND
SUCCORY CHICORY
SUCCULENT FRIM FRUM LUSH JUICY LUSHY PAPPY PULPY SAPPY YOUNG CASHIE FLESHY TENDER WATERISH
SUCCUMB BREAK QUAIL STOOP TRAIK YIELD
SUCH SIC SICK THAT SWICH
SUCHNESS TATHATA
SUCK SOUK SWIG SWOOP SUCKLE
(— DRY) SOAK
(— UP) DRINK ABSORB TIPPLE
(SUFF.) MYZA MYZON
SUCKEN THIRL
SUCKER CHUB FISH GULL CUIUI PATSY SOBOL THIEF CHUPON CUPULE MULLET RATOON REDFIN SOBOLE SPROUT SQUARE STOLON SUPPER TILLER CUTLIPS GONOTYL LOCULUS OSCULUM PEDICEL SCOURGE BOTHRIUM HUMPBACK LOLLIPOP PUSHOVER REDHORSE SURCULUS QUILLBACK
(PREF.) BDELL(O) BOTHR(I)(IO)(O) MYZO STOLONI SURCULI
(SUFF.) BDELLA
SUCKLE FEED MILK SUCK LACTATE NOURISH
SUCKLING SUCKER LACTANT SUCKLER TEATLING
SUCTION INTAKE
(SUFF.) MYZA MYZON
SUCTORIA ACINETAE

SUDAN
CAPITAL: KHARTOUM
DESERT: NUBIAN
LANGUAGE: GA EWE IBO KRU EFIK MOLE TSHI YORUBA MANDINGO
MEASURE: UD
MOUNTAIN: KINYETI
NATIVE: DAZA GOLO NUER SERE DINKA FULAH HAUSA MOSSI NUBIYIN
PROVINCE: DARFUR KASSALA KORDOFAN
REGION: DARFUR KASSALA KORDOFAN
RIVER: NILE PIBOR
TOWN: WAU JUBA KOSTI MEROE ATBARA ALUBAYD KASSALA MALAKAL OMDURMAN
WEIGHT: HABBA

SUDANESE FULA FULAH
SUDAN GRASS GARAVA GARAWI
SUDDEN BRASH FERLY HASTY ICTIC SWIFT ABRUPT FIERCE SNAPPY SPEEDY PRERUPT HEADLONG SPURTIVE SUBITANY SUBITOUS OVERNIGHT PRECIPITATE
SUDDENLY BOB POP BOLT FLOP SLAP AMAIN SHORT SKELP SOUSE ASTART BOUNCE PRESTO SUBITO ASUDDEN UNAWARES HEYPRESTO
SUDDENNESS ATTACK SUDDENTY
SUDORIFIC SWEAT SWEATER HIDROTIC SUDATORY
SUDRA HINDU VELLALA
SUDS BUCK FOAM SAPPLES SOAPSUDS
SUE LAW WOO SUIT IMPLEAD TROUNCE
SUET TALLOW
(PREF.) STEAR(I)(O) STEAT(O)
(SUFF.) STEARIN
SUFFER BYE GET LET BEAR BIDE DREE FIND GAIN HURT PAIN PINE ALLOW DREIE INCUR LABOR PROVE SMART SMOKE STAND THOLE ABEGGE BETEEM ENDURE PERMIT AGONIZE SUPPORT SUSTAIN UNDERGO TOLERATE
(— AGONY) THROE
(— A PENALTY) PAY
(— AT STAKE) SMOKE
(— DEFEAT) BOW
(— FOR) ABY ABYE ABIDE
(— FROM HEAT) SWELTER
(— FROM TIME) AGE
(— GREAT AFFLICTION) GROAN
(— HUNGER) CLEM STARVE AFFAMISH
(— LOSS OF) GIVE
(— PAIN) STOUND ANGUISH
(— PENALTY) SWEAT
(— REMORSE) RUE
(— RUIN) WRECK
(— SHIPWRECK) SPLIT
(— SYNCOPE) FAINT
(— THE CONSEQUENCES) ANSWER
(— THROUGH) PASS
(— TO ENTER) ADMIT
SUFFERABLE PATIBLE
SUFFERANCE PAIN MISERY PATIENCE THOLANCE
SUFFERER MARTYR AMNESIC DOORMAT PATIENT
(SUFF.) PATH(IA)(IC)(Y)
SUFFERING BALE COST DREE HURT PAIN PINE RACK AGONY DOLOR GRIEF SMART WRAKE PATHIC PATHOS THRALL INVALID LANGUOR PASSION PASSIVE TRAVAIL DISTRESS HARDSHIP MARTYRDOM
(— FROM HANGOVER) CHIPPY
(— FROM ILL HEALTH) DOWN
(— OF MIND) CARE
(—S OF CHRIST) AGONY
(SUFF.) PATH(IA)(IC)(Y)
(— OF) ITIS
SUFFICE DO LAST COVER REACH SERVE SATISFY
SUFFICIENCY ENOUGH PLENTY ADEQUACY BELLYFUL ABUNDANCE PLENITUDE
SUFFICIENT DUE FAIR GOOD AMPLE DECENT ENOUGH PRETTY BASTANT ABUNDANT ADEQUATE RELEVANT COMPETENT
(— LEGALLY) RELEVANT
(BARELY —) SCANT SKIMP NARROW SCRIMPY
(BE — FOR) COVER
SUFFICIENTLY DULY WELL ENOUGH
SUFFIX POSTFIX
(SLANG —) AROO
SUFFOCATE CHOKE DROWN SMOOR STIVE STUFF SWELT SLOKEN STIFLE OVERLIE QUACKLE SMOLDER SMOTHER SCUMFISH STRANGLE THROTTLE
SUFFOCATION APNEA APNOEA ASPHYXIA
SUFFRAGE VOTE VOICE TONGUE VERSICLE
SUFFRAGETTE CATT
SUFFUSE DIP FILL BATHE EMBAY TINGE INFUSE MANTLE
SUFFUSION COLOR
SUGAR CANDY DIOSE IDOSE MELIS PIECE SUCRE THIRD ACROSE ALDOSE ALLOSE FUCOSE GULOSE HEXOSE INVERT KETOSE LYXOSE OCTOSE PANELA TALOSE TRIOSE XYLOSE AGAVOSE ALTROSE BASTARD CHITOSE GLUCOSE GLUTOSE GLYCOSE LACTOSE MALTOSE MANNOSE PAPELON PENOCHI PENTOSE PENUCHE SORBOSE SUCROSE SWEETEN TETROSE THREOSE BROWNING CONCRETE CYMAROSE DEXTROSE FRUCTOSE FURANOSE LEVULOSE PYRANOSE RHAMNOSE RHODEOSE SECALOSE TURANOSE

(BROWN —) CARAIBE JAGGARY DEMERARA JAGGHERY
(COARSE —) RAAB PANOCHA
(CRUDE —) GUR HEAD MELADA CONCRETE
(INFERIOR —) BASTARD
(SIMPLE —) OSE
(UNREFINED —) CASSONADE MUSCOVADO
(PREF.) GLUC(O) GLYC(O) LYXO SACCHAR(I)(O) SUCR(O) THREO
(SUFF.) ULOSE

SUGARCANE CANE GRAIN GLUMAL RATOON MATTRESS
(— SAP) LIQUOR

SUGARHOUSE (PART OF —) PURGERY

SUGARLESS DRY

SUGARPLUM KISS

SUGARY FAT SUGAR SWEET OVERRIPE

SUGGEST JOG BEAR GIVE HINT MINT IMPLY OFFER POSIT SPEAK ADVISE ALLUDE HINTAT INDITE INFUSE MOTION PROMPT RESENT SUBMIT CONNOTE DICTATE INSPIRE INDICATE INTIMATE PROPOUND
(— DRINKING) PROPOSE
(— INSIDIOUSLY) INFUSE
(— STRONGLY) ARGUE

SUGGESTIBLE SOFT

SUGGESTION CUE CAST HINT TANG WIND GLIFF TWANG ADVICE BREATH MOTION SMATCH INKLING LEADING POINTER PROFFER REMNANT SOUPCON WRINKLE INNUENDO INSTANCE PROPOSAL

SUGGESTIVE RACY SEXY RISQUE ANICONIC PREGNANT REDOLENT
(— OF MELODY) CANOROUS

SUICIDAL KAMIKAZE

SUIT DO GO APT DOW FIT GEE HIT SET SIT ACTO LIKE LIST PAIR SEEM SORT VINE ADAPT AGREE APPLY BEFIT BESIT CLUBS COLOR DRAPE DRESS FADGE FANCY FRAME HABIT LEVEL MATCH PLEAD QUEME SAVOR SERVE SHAPE STAND SUING TALLY AFFEIR ANSWER BECOME COHERE COMPLY DITTOS EFFEIR HEARTS PRAYER SPADES SPEECH SQUARE BEHOOVE COMPORT COSTUME COULEUR FASHION PURSUIT REQUEST SEERPAW DIAMONDS INSTANCE QUADRATE SKELETON STANDARD TAILLEUR TROPICAL PINSTRIPE
(— AT LAW) ACTO CASE LAWSUIT
(— OF ARMOR) PANOPLY
(— OF MAIL) CATAPHRACT
(DIVER'S —) SCAPHANDER
(KIND OF —) ZOOT
(SWIMMING —) BATHER BIKINI MAILLOT

SUITABILITY (MUTUAL —) DECENCY IDONEITY SYMPATHY

SUITABLE APT FIT PAT ABLE FEAT GAIN GOOD JUMP JUST MEET TALL WELL WEME DIGNE EQUAL FITTY QUEME RIGHT SUITY COMELY FITTEN GAINLY GIUSTO HABILE HONEST LIABLE LIKELY PROPER SUITLY AVENANT COMMODE CONDIGN CONGRUE FITTING IDONEAL PLIABLE SEEMING BECOMING DECOROUS ELIGIBLE FEASIBLE HANDSOME IDONEOUS SORTABLE ACCORDING OPPORTUNE
(— FOR MALE AND FEMALE) UNISEX
(— FOR STAGE PERFORMANCE) ACTING
(EXACTLY —) VERY
(NOT —) UNFIT IMPROPER

SUITABLENESS APTNESS HONESTY APTITUDE PROPERTY

SUITABLY FITLY MEETLY TIDELY APROPOS GRADELY

SUITCASE BAG CAP GRIP CAPCASE DORLACH KEESTER PULLMAN

SUITE SET SUIT TAIL SWEEP SWEET TRAIN SERIES PARTITA RETINUE ENSEMBLE EQUIPAGE
(— OF MOLDINGS) LEDGMENT
(— OF ROOMS) FLAT CHAMBER

SUITED FIT ADAPT SEEMLY ADAPTED ASSORTED CONGENIAL
(POORLY —) CROOK
(SUFF.) **(— FOR)** ILE

SUITING COVERT CHEVIOT SHARKSKIN

SUITOR MAN BEAU SUER SWAIN WOOER GALLANT SERVANT

SUKU WASUKUMA

SULCUS RUT FURROW GROOVE

SULFATE DEX

SULFIDE GLANCE CUBANITE SULFURET COVELLITE

SULFUR BRIMSTONE
(PREF.) THI(O)

SULK DOD PET CHAW CRAB DORT GLUM POUT SULL BOODY FRUMP GLUMP GROUT GRUMP GROUCH SNUDGE THURMUS
(PL.) GEE HUMP GLOUT MUMPS FRUMPS SULLENS BOUDERIE

SULKER MUMPER

SULKINESS DORT GRUMP

SULKING PET BOUDERIE

SULKY BIKE CART CHUFF DODDY DORTY GOURY HUFFY HUMPY CHUFFY GLUMPY GROUTY JINKER SNUFFY STUFFY SULLEN SUMPHY DOGGISH HUFFISH MUMPISH
(NOT —) GOOD

SULLEN DOUR FOUL GLUM GRIM SOUR BLACK CHUFF CROSS DUMPY FELON GRUFF HARSH MOODY RUSTY STERN SULKY SURLY WEMOD CRUSTY DOGGED GLOOMY GLUMMY GLUMPY GLUNCH GROUTY MOROSE MULISH SOMBER SOMBRE STUFFY AUSTERE CRABBED CYNICAL FRETFUL LOURING LUMPISH MUMPISH PEEVISH CHUMPISH CHURLISH FAROUCHE LOWERING PETULANT SPITEFUL STUNKARD

SULLENNESS GEE DORT GLUM MUMPS STOMACH

SULLIED DIRTY SPOTTED

SULLY BLOT BLUR DASH FOUL SLUR SMIT SMUT SOIL CLOUD DIRTY GRIME SMEAR SMOKE STAIN TAINT BEFOUL DARKEN DEFILE SMIRCH SMUTCH ATTAINT BEGRIME BESMEAR BLEMISH CORRUPT DISTAIN ECLIPSE POLLUTE SLUBBER TARNISH BESMIRCH BESPATTER

SULPHATE ALUM BARITE ILESITE LOWEITE SULFATE VITRIOL KRAUSITE

SULPHIDE HEPAR GLANCE ZARNEC SULFIDE ZARNICH CUBANITE
(PL.) MATTE

SULPHUR ORE SPIRIT SULFUR YELLOW QUEBRITH BRIMSTONE

SULPHURIC ACID VITRIOL

SULTAN SOLDAN
(— OF MOROCCO) SHERIF SHEREEF

SULTANATE SULTANY ZANZIBAR

SULTANESS SOWDONES

SULTRY CLOSE FLUSH FAINTY SMUDGY POTHERY PUTHERY SWELTRY FEVERISH

SUM ALL GOB AGIO CASH DRAB DUMP FARM FINE FOOT FUND MASS TALE DEDIT GROSS KITTY SUMMA TOTAL WHOLE AMOUNT DEMAND DYADIC FIGURE NUMBER DECUPLE INGOING MANBOTE SUBSIDY SUMMARY SUMMATE ENTIRETY OCTONION QUANTITY MOUNTANCE OVERDRAFT POLYNOMIAL
(— AND SUBSTANCE) TOUR SHORT UPSHOT
(— AS COMPENSATION FOR KILLING) MANBOTE
(— FOR REENLISTMENT) GRATUITY
(— FOR SCHOLARSHIP) BURSARY
(— IN BASSET) SEPTLEVA
(— OF) SIGMA
(— OF DETERMINANTS) STIRP
(— OF EXPONENTS) DEGREE
(— OF FACTORS) COMPLEX
(— OF GOOD QUALITIES) ARETE
(— OF MONEY) POT BANK PILE COVER PURSE STOCK BUNDLE ACCOUNT DEPOSIT GRASSUM STIPEND
(— OF 25 POUNDS) PONY PONEY
(— OF 3 FARTHINGS) GILL
(— OF 500 POUNDS) MONKEY
(— PAYABLE AT FIXED INTERVALS) FARM
(— RISKED) STAKE
(— UP) ADD TOT FOOT RECAP ASSESS RECKON SUBSUME SUMMATE COMPRISE CONCLUDE PERORATE
(COMPLETE —) SOLIDUM
(ENTIRE —) SOLIDUM
(EXCESS —) BONUS
(FORFEITED —) DEDIT
(GREAT —) PLUNK SIGHT MICKLE
(LARGE —) GOB SCREAMER
(PETTY —) CENT DIME DRAB
(SMALL — OF MONEY) SPILL DRIBBLE DRIBLET SHOESTRING
(TRIFLING —) HAY GROAT
(UNEXPENDED —S) SAVINGS
(VAST —) MINT
(VECTOR —) GRADIENT
(PL.) BATTELS

SUMAC FUSTET KARREE SUMACH ANACARD BURTREE SCOTINO SHOEMAKE

SUMATRA (ISLAND NEAR —) NIAS
(LANGUAGE IN —) NIAS
(MEASURE OF —) PAAL
(MOUNTAIN IN —) LEUSER KERINTJI
(RIVER IN —) HARI MUSI ROKAN DJAMBI
(TOWN IN —) ACHIN KUALA MEDAN NATAL SOLOK DJAMBI LANGSA PADANG RENGAT BENKULEN

SUMBUL SAMBUL MUSKROOT

SUMERIAN ACCADIAN AKKADIAN

SUMITRA (HUSBAND OF —) DASHARATHA
(SON OF —) LAKSHMANA SHATRUGHNA

SUMMARIZE RECAP PRECIS RESUME WRAPUP ABSTRACT

SUMMARY SUM CURT LEAD BRIEF CHART RECAP SCORE SHORT SUMMA TOTAL APERCU DIGEST PRECIS RESUME SUMMAR CHAPTER CONCISE EPITOME EXTRACT MEDULLA OUTLINE RUNDOWN VIDIMUS ABSTRACT ARGUMENT BREVIARY BREVIATE DRUMHEAD HEADNOTE OVERVIEW SUCCINCT SYNOPSIS
(— OF FAITH) SYMBOL
(— OF PRINCIPLES) CREED
(CONCISE —) PRECIS

SUMMATION SUM DIGEST SUMMARY

SUMMER ETE SHEMU SOMER AESTAS SIMMER DORMANT
(OF —) ESTIVAL
(PREF.) ESTIVO

SUMMER CYPRESS KOCHIA

SUMMER FLOUNDER PLAICE

SUMMERHOUSE FOLLY KIOSK MAHAL TUPEK ALCOVE CASINO GAZEBO PAGODA CABINET BELVEDERE

SUMMER HYACINTH GALTONIA

SUMMER TANAGER REDBIRD

SUMMERWOOD LATEWOOD

SUMMIT CAP DOD SUM TIP TOP VAN ACME APEX BALD CRAP DODD HELM KNAP KNOT PEAK ROOF CREST CROWN SPIRE COMBLE CULMEN HEIGHT VERTEX ZENITH CALOTTE SUMMARY SUMMITY PINNACLE MOUNTAINTOP
(— OF TUBE) MOUTH
(— WITHOUT FOREST) BALD
(ROCKY —) KNOT
(ROUND —) DOD DODD
(SNOW-CAPPED —) CALOTTE
(PREF.) APICO CORY(PH)(PHO)
(SUFF.) ACE

SUMMON BAN CRY BUZZ CALL CITE DRUM HAIL SIST BUGLE CHARM CLEPE EVOKE HIGHT KNELL SOUND VOUCH ACCITE ADVOKE BECALL BECKON COMPEL DEMAND SOMPNE VOCATE ACCERSE COMMAND CONJURE CONVENE CONVENT CONVOKE PROVOKE SUMMONS WHISTLE ASSUMMON EXORCISE
(— FOR HIRING) YARD

(— INTO COURT) DEMAND
(— TOGETHER) BAND MUSTER ASSEMBLE
(— UP) FIND GATHER COLLECT
SUMMONER SUMNER LOCKMAN SOMPNER OUTRIDER
SUMMONING CALL ARRAY
(— OF KING'S VASSALS) BAN
SUMMONS CRY CALL BREVE CITAL TICKET BIDDING CALLING STICKER WARNING WARRANT CITATION MONITION VOCATION
(— TO GET UP) REVEILLE
(FALCONER'S —) WO
SUMP SINK STANDAGE
SUMPTUOUS RICH GRAND SHOWY WLONK COSTLY DELUXE SOLEMN SUPERB COSTLEW ELEGANT MAGNIFIC SPLENDID MAGNIFICENT
SUMPTUOUSNESS LUXE DAINTY SUMPTURE
SUN ORB SOL ATEN ATON BASK INTI LAMP STAR SENGE SURYA TITAN SUNLET DAYSTAR IOSKEHA PHOEBUS SAVITAR JOUSKEHA
(— MOON AND STARS) HOST
(MOCK —) PARHELION
(RISING —) HERAKHTI
(PREF.) HELI(O) SOLARO SOLI
(SUFF.) HELION
SUN ALSO RISES (AUTHOR OF —) HEMINGWAY
(CHARACTER IN —) BILL COHN JAKE MIKE BRETT CLYNE PEDRO ASHLEY BARNES GORTON ROBERT ROMERO FRANCES MICHAEL MONTOYA CAMPBELL GEORGETTE
SUNAPEE TROUT SAIBLING
SUNBATHE GETATAN APRICATE
SUNBATHER BAKE
SUNBEAM BANANA
SUN BEAR BRUANG
SUNBIRD MAMO CADET FINFOOT
SUN BITTERN CARLE CAURALE SUNBIRD
SUN BLIND CHICK UMRELLA
SUNBONNET TILT UGLY CRESIE KAPPIE SHAKER
SUNBURN GREENING HELIOSIS
(— REMEDY) ALOE
SUNBURNED BRONZED
SUNBURNT ADUST BROWN TANNED
SUNBURST SUNRAY SUNBREAK SUNSHINE
SUNDAE GEDUNK
SUNDA ISLANDS (GREATER —) JAVA BORNEO CELEBES SUMATRA
(LESSER —) BALI TIMOR
SUNDAY EXAUDI JUDICA GAUDETE TRINITY
(FIFTH — AFTER EASTER) ROGATE
(FIRST — AFTER EASTER) QUASIMODO
(FIRST — IN LENT) QUADRAGESIMA
(FOURTH — IN LENT) LAETARE
(LOW —) QUASIMODO
(SECOND — BEFORE LENT) SEXAGESIMA
(THIRD — AFTER EASTER) JUBILATE
SUNDER PART RIVE TWIN BREAK SEVER TWAIN TWINE DEPART DIVIDE SINDER ASUNDER DISALLY DISJOIN DIVORCE DISSEVER SEJUGATE SEPARATE UNSOLDER
SUNDEW DROSERA EYEBRIGHT
SUNDIAL DIAL GHURRY HOROLOGE SCAPHION SOLARIUM
(PART OF —) DIAL LINE PLATE GNOMON DIAGRAM
SUN DISK ATEN ATON CAKRA CHAKRA
SUNDOG WINDGALL PARHELION
SUNDOWNER HOBO DRINK TRAMP WHALER TUSSOCKER
SUN-DRIED TILED
SUNDROPS SCABISH
SUNDRY DIVERS DIVERSE SEVERAL
SUNFISH SUN HURO MOLA OPAH RUFF BREAM FLIER FLYER ROACH SUNNY KIVVER MOLOID REDEAR REDEYE CRAPPIE CROPPIE PANFISH PERCOID BLUEGILL FLATFISH FLOUNDER HEADFISH MOONFISH PONDFISH WARMOUTH REDBREAST PUMPKINSEED
SUNFLOWER GOLD HELIO CANADA GOLDEN SUNFOIL GIRASOLE TURNSOLE
(— STATE) KANSAS
SUNGLASSES SHADES
SUN-GREBE FINFOOT SUNBIRD GRUIFORM
SUNK SUNKEN
(— TO LOW STATE) ABJECT
SUNKEN SUNK LAIGH HOLLOW
SUNKEN BELL (CHARACTER IN —) MAGDA HEINRICH RAUTENDELEIN
(COMPOSER OF —) RESPIGHI
SUNLESS BLAE
SUNLIGHT GLARE
SUNN SAN SANN DAGGA SANAI JANAPA MADRAS JANAPAN SANNHEMP
SUNNITE IHLAT SUNNI SUNNIAH
SUNNY GOOD SUNSHINE
SUN PARLOR SOLARIUM
SUNRISE ARIST SUNUP ORIENT
(KIND OF —) TEQUILA
(TEQUILA —) COCKTAIL
SUNSET SUNFALL
(— STATE) OREGON ARIZONA
SUNSHADE PARASOL ROUNDEL TIRESOL SOMBRERO
SUNSHINE SUN SHINE SUNLIGHT
(— STATE) FLORIDA
SUNSPOT SPOT FACULA MACULA
SUNSPURGE SUNWEED TURNSOLE WARTWEED WARTWORT
SUNSTROKE HELIOSIS SIRIASIS
SUNTAN MERIDA
SUN TREE HINOKI
SUNWISE DEASIL DESSIL
SUNYATA VOID
SUP EAT DINE SOWP FEAST CONSUME SWALLOW
SUPAWN MUSH
SUPER COOL FINE GRAND GREAT NEATO NIFTY
SUPER-
(PREF.) HYPER
SUPERABOUND OVERFLOW
SUPERABUNDANCE FLOOD EXCESS CATARACT PLEONASM PLETHORA PLEURISY PLURISIE
SUPERABUNDANT RANK LAVISH PROFUSE
SUPERALTAR PREDELLA
SUPERANNUATE RETIRE OVERYEAR
SUPERB GRAND GOLDEN CLIPPING GORGEOUS SPLENDID
SUPERCARGO MERCHANT
SUPERCILIOUS GRAND POTTY PROUD OVERLY SNIFFY SNIPPY SNOOTY SNOTTY SNUFFY HAUGHTY ARROGANT CAVALIER SNIFFISH SUPERIOR
SUPERCLASS AGNATHA
SUPERCONSCIOUSNESS SAMADHI
SUPERCOOL SUBCOOL SURFUSE
SUPERFAMILY APINA APOIDEA BOVOIDEA
(SUFF.) OIDA OIDEA OIDEI
SUPERFICIAL GLIB ECTAL SUPER FACIAL FACILE FLIMSY FORMAL FROTHY GLASSY OVERLY SLIGHT CURSORY OUTSIDE OUTWARD PASSING SHALLOW SKETCHY SLIGHTY SURFACE SURFACY COSMETIC EXTERNAL MAGAZINY SMATTERY DEPTHLESS
SUPERFICIALLY FLEET
SUPERFICIES TERM EXTENT
SUPERFLUITY FAT FRILL LUXUS EXCESS OVERSET SURFEIT PLETHORA REDUNDANCY
(CONFUSING —) FLUTHER
SUPERFLUOUS SPARE OTIOSE USELESS NEEDLESS REDUNDANT
SUPERFRONTAL FRONTLET
SUPERHEATED GASEOUS
SUPERHIGHWAY MOTORWAY
(AVOID —) SHUNPIKE
SUPERHUMAN DEMON DAEMON DIVINE INHUMAN UNHUMAN
SUPERIMPOSE LAY OVERLAY SURPRINT
SUPERIMPOSING DISSOLVE
SUPERINTEND CON CONN GUIDE OVERSEE PRESIDE
SUPERINTENDENCE CARE CONTROL EPISCOPY GUIDANCE
SUPERINTENDENCY EDILITY AEDILITY
SUPERINTENDENT BOSS SUPE EPHOR SUPER EDITOR VENEUR VIEWER WARDEN CAPTAIN CURATOR EPHORUS MANAGER DIRECTOR OVERSEER SURVEYOR SWINGMAN
SUPERIOR JOE AYNE COOL FINE MORE OVER TRIE ABBOT ABOVE CHIEF CREAM EIGNE ELDER ELITE EXTRA FANCY FRANK GREAT LIEGE PRIOR PUKKA SWANK UPPER ABBESS BETTER COCKUP CUSTOS DOMINA FATHER FORBYE MAHANT SELECT SENIOR STRONG FORTHBY PALMARY RANKING ABNORMAL DOMINANT GUARDIAN SINGULAR SPLENDID SUPERIAL MARVELOUS PARAMOUNT
(— IN MANNER) SUPERCILIOUS
(— OF CONVENT) HEGUMEN
(— ONE) LAMA
(— TO) ATOP BEFORE
(PREF.) SUPER
SUPERIORITY DROP GREE PRICE HEIGHT MASTERY PROWESS EMINENCE PRIORITY
(MENTAL —) GENIUS
SUPERLATIVE RAVING CURIOUS ROUSING CRASHING OLYMPIAN PEERLESS SWINGING ULTIMATE
(ABSOLUTE —) ELATIVE
(SUFF.) EST
SUPERLATIVELY CRACKING SWINGING
SUPERMAN OVERMAN OBERMENSCH
SUPERNATURAL FEY ARCANE DIVINE NUMINOUS SUPERIOR MARVELOUS PARANORMAL
(— FORCE) WAKANDA
SUPERNUMERARY ORRA
(PREF.) POLY
SUPERORDER GLIRES
SUPERPOSE APPLY
SUPER-REMEDY CUREALL
SUPERSCRIBE DIRECT
SUPERSCRIPT SUPERIOR
SUPERSEDE REPLACE OVERRIDE SUPPLANT
SUPERSTITION FREIT IDOLATRY ABERGLAUBE
SUPERSTITIOUS FREITY
SUPERTONIC SECOND
SUPERVENE BEFALL FOLLOW
SUPERVISE BOSS GUIDE DIRECT GOVERN HANDLE SURVEY FOREMAN OVERSEE PROCTOR ENGINEER OVERLOOK CHAPERONE
SUPERVISION EYE CARE DUTY HAND CHECK CHARGE OVERSIGHT
SUPERVISOR BOSS BULL EPHOR GUIDE SUPER CENSOR GASMAN RUNMAN SOURER WARDEN DESKMAN PROCTOR ALYTARCH CHAIRMAN FLOORMAN FOREHAND KNIFEMAN LEACHMAN MASHGIAH OVERSEER
(— OF STUDENT DISCIPLINE) HEBDOMADAR HEBDOMADER
SUPINE INERT DROWSY LANGUID SERVILE UPRIGHT CARELESS INACTIVE INDOLENT LISTLESS SLUGGISH
SUPPER CENA MEAL CUDDY HOCKEY PASCHAL
(— AT HOME) EATIN
(HARVEST-HOME —) HOCKEY
(LAST —) MAUNDY
(LORD'S —) NAGMAAL
SUPPING CENATION
SUPPLANT FOLLOW REMOVE REPLACE DISPLACE DISPLANT
SUPPLE BAIN FLIP OILY SOFT WIRY LINGY LITHE SLAMP SWACK AJOINT LIMBER LITHER LUTHER PLIANT SUMPLE SVELTE SWANKY WANDLE LISSOME PLIABLE SPRINGE FLEXIBLE
SUPPLEJACK SOAPWORT
SUPPLEMENT ARM EKE MEND TACK ANNEX SUPPLY BOLSTER CODICIL ADDENDUM APPENDIX BOUNTITH
(PL.) FIXINGS

SUPPLEMENTAL SPECIAL PIGGYBACK
SUPPLEMENTARY ADDED SECOND RIPIENO REMANENT PERIPHERAL
SUPPLENESS WHIP
SUPPLIANT ASKER PLEADING
SUPPLICATE BEG PRAY CRAVE PLEAD INVOKE OBTEST SUPPLY BESEECH ENTREAT IMPLORE REQUEST SOLICIT PETITION
SUPPLICATION CRY VOW BEAD BILL LIBEL VENIE APPEAL LITANY PRAYER CRAVING SYNAPTE ENTREATY PETITION PLEADING ROGATION ROGATIVE SUFFRAGE
SUPPLICATORY EUCTICAL
SUPPLIED (— WITH FOOD) THORN
(AMPLY —) ABUNDANT
(SCANTILY —) BARE
SUPPLIER SOURCE
SUPPLIES STOCK STUFF DUFFEL STORES VICTUAL ESTOVERS ORDNANCE
SUPPLY FEED FILL FIND FRET FUND GIVE HEEL LEND LINE ARRAY CATER ENDUE EQUIP INDUE OFFER SERVE STOCK STORE STUFF YIELD BUDGET DONATE EMPLOY FOISON LAYOUT POCKET RENDER SUBMIT ADVANCE FORTIFY FRAUGHT FURNISH LISSOME PROVIDE ACCOMMODATE
(— ABUNDANTLY) SWILL
(— ARRANGED BEFOREHAND) RELAY
(— EXCESSIVELY) FLOOD
(— FOR AN OCCASION) GRIST
(— FULLY) SATISFY
(— LIQUOR BY SHIP) COPER COOPER
(— OF FOOD) BOARD
(— OF HORSES) RELAY REMUDA REMOUNT
(— OF MONEY) BANKROLL
(— OF POTENTIAL JURORS) TALES
(— OF REMOUNTS) REMUDA
(— OF SOLDIERS) GARRISON
(— OF TIN) SERVING
(— PROVISIONS) PURVEY
(— THE NEED) FOR
(— WITH CLOTHES) INFIT
(— WITH FOOD) FODDER
(— WITH FUEL) STOKE
(— WITH LIQUOR) LUBRICATE
(— WITH MONEY) GILD
(— WITH OXYGEN) AERATE
(— WITH WATER) FANG
(CACHED —) CAVE
(CONSTANT —) STREAM
(EXTRA —) RESERVE
(FRESH —) RECRUIT
(FULL —) PLENTY
(HIDDEN —) HOARD
(INADEQUATE —) DEARTH
(LARGE —) TON PILE
(NEW —) RECRUIT
(OVERABUNDANT —) SURFEIT
(PLENTIFUL —) CHOICE
(RENEWED —) RECRUITAL
(RESERVE —) CUSHION
(RICH —) ARGOSY
(SCANTY —) SCANT
(SECRET —) CACHE
SUPPORT AID ARM BAY BED BOW KAI LEG PEG RIB TIE TOM ABET ABUT AXIS BACK BASE BEAM BEAR BUOY CRIB DADE FEND FIND FIRM FORK FUEL HAVE HELP HOLD JAMB KEEP KILP LIFT POST PROP RACK REST ROCK SALT SIDE STAY STEM STUD TRIG ADOPT AEGIS ANGEL APPUI ATLAS BIPOD BLOCK BRACE BROOK CARRY CHAIR CHEER CHOCK CLEAT CRANK FAVOR FLOAT FRAME OXTER PLUNK POISE RANCE SALVE SHORE SPURN STAFF STAKE STEAD STELL STIPE STOCK STOOP STRUT STULL TOWER VOUCH WEIGH ANCHOR ASSERT ASSIST BARROW BEHALF CHEVAL COLUMN CORSET CRADLE CRUTCH DEFEND DONKEY DUOPOD GARTER PATTEN PILLAR POTENT PULPIT PUTLOG SADDLE SECOND SHIELD SOCKET SPLINT STAYER STEADY SUFFER TASSEL TIMBER TINGLE TORSEL UPHAND UPHOLD UPKEEP UPTAKE WHIMSY ALIMENT ARMREST BACKING BOLSTER COMFORT CONFIRM CRIPPLE DEADMAN ENDORSE ESPOUSE FINDING FULCRUM GROMMET HOUSING JACKLEG JUSTIFY KEEPING KNUCKLE NOURISH NURTURE PABULUM PROTECT RADICAL SPIRALE SPONSOR SQUINCH STADDLE STANDER STIFFEN STIRRUP SUBSIST SUSTAIN THICKEN TRESTLE ADJUMENT ADVOCATE BALUSTER BEFRIEND BESTRIDE BOOKREST BUTTRESS CAPSHORE FAIRLEAD FOOTREST FORESTAY FORTRESS HANDREST HOLDFAST JACKSTAY KEYSTONE MAINSTAY MAINTAIN MOUNTING NEEDLING ORTHOTIC OVERCAST PEDESTAL PEDIMENT STANDARD STILLAGE STOCKING STRENGTH SYMPATHY UNDERLIE UNDERPIN UNDERSET PATRONAGE MAINTENANCE
(— FINANCIALLY) BANKROLL
(— FOR ANVIL) STOCK
(— FOR BELL CLAPPER) BALDRIC
(— FOR CANDLE) STICK
(— FOR CANOPY) BAIL TESTER
(— FOR CATALYST) CARRIER
(— FOR COLUMN) SOCLE
(— FOR CORSET) BUSK
(— FOR HEAVY MACHINERY) BUNTING
(— FOR KNEES) STOOL
(— FOR LAUNCHING SHIP) POPPET
(— FOR LEVER) BAIT
(— FOR LIFE-CAR) BAIL
(— FOR MAST) STEP
(— FOR MILL) LOWDER
(— FOR MINE PASSAGE) OVERCAST
(— FOR OARLOCK) OUTRIGGER
(— FOR PICTURE HOOKS) CORNICE
(— FOR PIPE) CHAPLET
(— FOR PLATFORM) STEMPEL STEMPLE
(— FOR SHAFT) STEMPEL STEMPLE
(— IN A LATHE) DOCTOR
(— IN PAPERMAKING TUB) DONKEY
(— OF COLUMN) SOCLE PLINTH
(— OF COPING) KNEELER
(— OF MOLD CORE) ARBOR ARBOUR
(— OF RAIL) CHAIR BALUSTER
(— THROUGH BIT AND BRIDLE) APPUI
(CRUTCHLIKE —) DEADMAN
(ELBOW-SHAPED —) CRANK
(EMBEDDED —) SPURN
(FIREPLACE —) ANDIRON
(GIVE —) FEED
(INCLINED —) RIDER
(LACKING —) FOOTLESS
(LOSE —) ERODE
(MINING —) CAP FRAME
(PORTABLE —) STOOL
(PRINCIPAL —) BACKBONE
(SHOE —) TREE
(TEMPORARY —) NEEDLING
(UPRIGHT —) POPPET BANISTER
(WHEELED —) CARRIAGE
(PL.) SHIPWAY
SUPPORTED BASED BLOCKED ACCOSTED SUCCINCT
(— BY EVIDENCE) PROBABLE
SUPPORTER ALLY JOCK ATLAS STOOP COHORT DRAGON SATRAP APOSTLE BOOSTER DEVOTEE FAVORER FOUNDER LAUDIAN PATROON PROPPER SUPPORT ADHERENT ASSERTER ERASTIAN ESPOUSER FAVORITE HENCHMAN STALWART UPHOLDER CHURCHITE
(ATHLETIC —) CUP JOCK
(CHIEF —) STOOP PILLAR
(PL.) SECOND
(SUFF.) CRAT ITE
SUPPORTING BEHIND BEARING
SUPPORTIVE ENGAGE
SUPPOSE SAY SEE SET WIS WIT DEEM POSE READ TAKE TROW WEEN ALLOW COUNT ETTLE FANCY GUESS JUDGE OPINE SEPAD THINK ASSUME DEVISE DIVINE EXPECT RECKON BELIEVE CONCEIT DARESAY IMAGINE PRESUME PROPOSE SUPPONE SURMISE CONCEIVE CONCLUDE CONSIDER OPINIATE
SUPPOSED ALLEGED ASSUMED PUTATIVE
SUPPOSING IF
SUPPOSITION IDEA FICTION SURMISE WEENING
SUPPOSITORY BOUGIE CANDLE PESSARY
SUPPRESS LAY DOWN GULP HIDE HUSH SINK SLAY SNUB STOP BLACK BURKE CHOKE CRUSH ELIDE QUASH QUELL SHUSH SMORE SPIKE STILL CANCEL QUENCH SQUASH STIFLE CONTAIN CUSHION INHIBIT OPPRESS REPRESS SILENCE SMOLDER SMOTHER SQUELCH RESTRAIN STRANGLE SUPPRIME VANQUISH
(— A SYLLABLE) ELIDE
(— IN SPEAKING) MINCE
SUPPRESSED BLIND CENSORED
SUPPRESSION ABEYANCE AMEIOSIS BLACKOUT
(— OF VOWEL) ELISION
(— OF WORD SOUNDS) SYNCOPE ECLIPSIS
(PREF.) ISCH(O)
(SUFF.) SCHESIS SCHETIC
SUPPURATE RUN BEAL WHEAL DIGEST MATTER QUITTER MATURATE
SUPPURATING
(PREF.) EMPYO
SUPPURATION PYOSIS BEALING COCTION
SUPPURATIVE DIGERENT
SUPRACLAVICLE SCAPULA
SUPREMACY PALM PRIMACY DOMINION OVERRULE
SUPREME HIGH LAST CHIEF VITAL SUBLIME SUMMARY TOPLESS FOREMOST GREATEST PEERLESS
SURA FATIHA FATIHAH
SURCHARGE PACK
SURCINGLE WANTY ROLLER
SURCOAT JUPON CYCLAS KABAYA
SURD SHARP ATONIC FLATED
SURE COLD SAFE BOUND SECURE SICCAR SICKER STEADY WITTER ASSURED CERTAIN PERFECT COCKSURE POSITIVE UNERRING
SURELY WIS FINE IWIS SURE PARDY REDLY ATWEEL PARDIE
SURENESS SURETY SECURITY
SURETY VAS ANDI BAIL BAND BORROW CAUTION ENGAGER SOVERTY SPONSOR BAILSMAN SECURITY
SURETYSHIP SPONSION
SURF BREACH KALEMA
(— NOISE) RUT ROTE
SURFACE DAY AREA FACE ORLO PLAT RYME SIDE ARISE BOSOM FLOOR STONE SWARF CHROME EMERGE FINISH GROUND SCRUFF ASPHALT BLANKET COUNTER ENVELOP OUTFACE OUTSIDE STRETCH ADHEREND CONCRETE EXTERIOR PLATFORM
(— BESIDE FIREPLACE) HOB
(— BETWEEN FLUTES OF SHAFT) ORLO
(— BETWEEN TRIGLYPH CHANNELS) MEROS
(— IN BEATER) BACKFALL
(— OF A GEM) BEZEL
(— OF ARCH) INTRADOS
(— OF BEAM) BACK
(— OF BODY) FLESH HABIT
(— OF CLOTH) PILE
(— OF COAL) BUTT
(— OF CRICKET FIELD) CARPET
(— OF DIAMOND) SPREAD
(— OF EARTH) DUST GROUND TERRENE PENEPLAIN PENEPLANE
(— OF ESCUTCHEON) FIELD
(— OF GEM) FACET TABLE
(— OF GROUND OVER MINE) DAY
(— OF HAND) PALM
(— OF LIQUID) MENISCUS
(— OF MINE) GRASS
(— OF PARACHUTE) CANOPY
(— OF RECESS) REVEAL
(— OF RIFLE BARREL) LAND
(— OF ROOT) RHIZOPLANE
(— OF SAWED LUMBER) FUR
(— OF SHIELD) FIELD

(— OF TOOTH) TRITOR
(— OF VAULT) GROIN
(— OF WATER) RYME SCRUFF
(— WITHIN EARTH) GEOID
(AIRPLANE CONTROL —) ELEVEN
(BOUNDING —) PERIPHERY
(COBBLESTONE —) PITCHING
(CONCAVE —) LAP
(CONCRETE —) PAD
(CONTROL —) RUDDER
(CONVEX —) EXTRADOS
(CURVED —) BELLY
(DULL —) MAT MATTING
(EXTERNAL —) PERIPHERY
(FLAT —) BED FLAT AEQUOR PAGINA
(FLOOR —) BOWL
(FRONTAL —) METOPE
(GEOMETRIC —) TORE CONOID SPHERE QUARTIC CONICOID CYLINDER HELICOID PARABOLOID
(GLASSY —) HYALINE
(GLOSSY —) GLAZE
(GRASSY —) SWARD
(GROOVED —) DROVE
(HAIRY —) NAP
(HORIZONTAL —) LEVEL
(INCLINED —) CANT DESCENT
(MINERAL —) DRUSE
(PAVED —) FOOTWALK
(PILE —) FRIEZE
(PLANE —) AREA FACET
(PRINCIPAL —) FACE
(PRINTING —) CUT
(PROTECTIVE —) LAGGING
(REFLECTING —) MIRROR HORIZON
(ROAD —) MACADAM CORDUROY
(ROUGH —) KEY CRIZZLE STUBBLE
(ROUGHENED —) MAT FOOTGRIP
(SLIPPERY —) GLARE
(SLOPING —) SHELVING
(STRIKING —) BLADE
(UNDER — OF SKI) PALM
(UNGLOSSY PAINT —) FLAT
(UPPER —) NOTAEUM
(UPRIGHT —) JAMB
(WOOLLY —) NAP
(PREF.) (BENT —) SINU SINUATO
SURFACER SEASONER
SURFBOARD GUN
(LONG —) GUN BIGGUN
SURF DUCK COOT SCOTER
SURFEIT CLOY FILL GLUT SATE STAW STALL STUFF AGROTE ENGLUT SICKEN SATIATE SATIETY SURCLOY SATURATE REPLETION SATURATION
SURFEITED SAD SICK BLASE JADED WEARY REPLETE SATIATED
SURFER GREMMY GREMLIN GREMMIE
(GIRL —) WAHINE
(INEXPERIENCED —) GREMMY GREMMIE
SURF FISH PERCH ALFIONA
SURFING (— MANEUVER) CUTBACK
SURF SCOTER COOT SCOTER SURFER PISHAUG SKUNKTOP
SURF SHINER SPARADA
SURGE JAW GUST TIDE WASH DRIVE GURGE LUNGE SPURT SWELL BILLOW BREACH COURSE ONRUSH SEETHE WALLOW WALTER ESTUATE REDOUND AESTUATE UNDULATE
(— OF ELECTRIC POWER) GLITCH
(SHOREWARD —) SUFF
(TIDAL —) EAGRE
SURGEON (AMERICAN) WOOD COOLEY DEVRIES OCHSNER THEOREK SEAGRAVE SLAUGHTER
SURGEON (ALSO SEE PHYSICIAN AND DOCTOR) LEECH ARTIST INTERN MEDICO OPERATOR SAWBONES
(TREE —) TREEMAN
AMERICAN EVE BULL KEEN LONG MAYO MOTT REED WOOD AGNEW COLEY CRILE FLINT GROSS LAHEY CARREL COOLEY FINNEY KELMAN KOPITS LAWLER MORRIS MORTON SHRADY ASHFORD BLALOCK CUSHING DEVRIES HALSTED HARTLEY HUGGINS KELLOGG LAPLACE OCHSNER THEOREK BEAUMONT MCBURNEY MCDOWELL METTAUER SEAGRAVE SLAUGHTER
CANADIAN BETHUNE BIRKETT
ENGLISH POTT REID BRAID HADEN PAGET BARKER BEDDOE BOWMAN CHEYNE COOPER FAYRER LISTER CHARNLEY ERICHSEN MOYNIHAN ABERNETHY BRIFFAULT CHESELDEN PARKINSON
FRENCH ANEL PARE BOYER BROCA PETIT BECHAMP CHOPART CIVIALE DESAULT NELATON CHAULIAC CHASSAIGNAC
GERMAN GRAEFE ESMARCH BILLROTH FORSSMANN
GREEK AMMONIUS
IRISH MADDEN OMEARA
ITALIAN FABRICIUS
RUSSIAN VISHNEVSKY
SCOTTISH BELL SYME BANKS HUNTER LISTON MACEWEN
SOUTH AFRICAN BARNARD
SPANISH CASTROVIEJO
SWISS KOCHER
SURGEONFISH TANG TANGE DOCTOR MEDICO BARBERO SURGEON SAWBONES
SURGERY KNIFE
(VETERINARY —) ZOIATRIA
(SUFF.) CHIRURGIA
SURGING WALE ESTURE ESTUOUS
SURICATE ZENICK MEERKAT
SURINAM (CAPITAL OF —) PARAMARIBO
(RIVER OF —) ITANY MARONI COPPENAME SARAMACCA COURANTYNE
(TOWN OF —) ALBINA KWATTA TOTNESS LELYDORP
SURINAME (LANGUAGE IN —) SRANAN
SURINAMINE ANDIRINE ANGELINE
SURINAM TOAD PIPA PIPAL
SURLINESS CYNICISM MOROSITY
SURLY BAD ILL GRUM LUNT BLUFF CHUFF CYNIC GRUFF GURLY PURDY ROUGH RUNTY RUSTY CHUFFY CRUSTY GRUFFY GRUMPY MOROSE RUGGED SNARLY SULLEN DOGGISH CHURLISH
SURMISE DEEM REDE GUESS INFER TWANG SURMIT JALOUSE SUSPECT WEENING MISTRUST
SURMOUNT TOP BEAT TIDE CROWN ENSIGN HURDLE MASTER OUTTOP OVERGO SUBDUE CONQUER SURPASS OVERCOME SUPERATE
(— DIFFICULTIES) SWIM
SURMOUNTING ATOP BROCHANT
SURNAME BYNAME SURNOUN COGNOMEN OVERNAME SURSTYLE
SURPASS CAP COB TOP WAR BANG BEAT CAMP COTE DING FLOG FOIL HEAD PASS SHED WHAP WHOP EXCEL OUTDO OUTGO TRUMP ATREDE BETTER EXCEED OUTRAY OUTRUN OUTVIE OUTWIT OVERDO PRECEL ECLIPSE FORPASS OUTPEER OVERTOP PARAGON PRECEDE ANTECEDE DISTANCE DOMINATE OUTCLASS OUTMATCH OUTRANGE OUTREACH OUTSHINE OUTSTRIP OUTWRITE SURMOUNT
SURPASSING BEST FINE ABOVE PASSANT PASSING DOMINANT FRABJOUS TOWERING
(PREF.) PRETER SUPER
SURPLICE SARK COTTA EPHOD STOLA CHRISOM
(PL.) WHITES
SURPLUS ODD OVER PLUS REST EXCESS LUMBER SPILTH VELVET OVERAGE OVERRUN OVERSUM ARISINGS LEFTOVER OVERCOME OVERFLOW OVERMUCH OVERPLUS
SURPRISE CAP SHED SWAN YACH AMAZE SHOCK SNEAK FERLIE WAYLAY WONDER ASTOUND GLOPPEN PERPLEX STARTLE ASTONISH BEWILDER CONFOUND DUMFOUND
(BY —) ABACK
(CRY OF —) ACK
(EXCLAMATION OF —) QUOTHA
(EXPRESS —) MIRATE
(INTERJECTION EXPRESSING —) OOPS WOOPS
(SUDDEN —) KICK
SURPRISING FERLIE STRIKING
SURRA MBORI
SURREJOINDER TRIPLY
SURRENDER HEM LET PUT CEDE CESS DING FALL QUIT TAKE REMIT YIELD ADDICT REMISE RENDER RESIGN SUBMIT ABANDON CONCEDE DELIVER FORSAKE KAMERAD ABDICATE ABNEGATE DEDITION DELIVERY RENOUNCE UNDERLIE CAPITULATE
(— BY DEED) REMISE
(— OF CLAIM) REMISE
SURREPTITIOUS COVERT SECRET BOOTLEG FURTIVE SNEAKING
SURROGATE PROXY DEPUTY SUBSTITUTE
SURROUND HEM LAP ORB BELT DIKE DYKE FOLD GIRD GIRT HOOP WRAP BESET BRACE CLASP EMBAY EMBED FENCE HEDGE IMBED INARM ROUND BECLIP BEGIRD BEGIRT CIRCLE COLLET CORRAL ENFOLD ENWRAP FORSET GIRDLE IMPALE INCASE INVEST SPHERE SWATHE ARROUND BESIEGE BESTAND COMPASS EMBOSOM ENCLAVE ENCLOSE ENFEOFF ENROUND ENVELOP ENVIRON INVOLVE WREATHE CLOISTER ENCIRCLE ENTRENCH STOCKADE
(— WITH BOOM) CRIB
(— WITH CORD) GIRT
(— WITH MORTAR) GROUT
SURROUNDED AMID AMONG AMIDST AMONGST BETWEEN
(— BY WATER) INSULAR
SURROUNDING MIDST ROUND CIRCUM AMBIENT
(PL.) SCENE HARNESS ENVIRONS
(PREF.) CIRCUM PERI
SURROYALS CROWN
SURVEILLANCE WATCH SCRUTINY STAKEOUT OVERSIGHT
(— SYSTEM) AWACS
SURVEY EYE SEE DIAL POLL SCAN VIEW AVIEW STOCK STUDY PERUSE REGARD REVIEW SEARCH CANVASS CAPSULE OVERSEE SURVIEW TERRIER THEORIC EPISCOPY LUSTRATE OVERLOOK OVERVIEW PROSPECT SURVEYAL TRAVERSE RECONNAISANCE
(— RAPIDLY) GLANCE
(— TIMBER) SKYLOOK
(BRIEF —) APERCU
SURVEYING GEODESY GROMATICS
(MINE —) LATCHING
SURVEYOR BOLO ARTIST DIALER DIALLER NOTEMAN CHAINMAN GROMATIC LEVELMAN
SURVIVAL ECHO RELIC RELICT
(ANACHRONISTIC —) LEFTOVER
(USELESS —) SNUFF
SURVIVE LAST GETBY BILEVE OUTLAST OUTLIVE
SURVIVOR RELICT
SURYA (FATHER OF —) ADITI DYAUS
(MESSENGER OF —) PUSHAN
(WIFE OF —) USHAS
SUSCEPTIBILITY CAVIL SENSE EMOTION FEELING FRAILTY
(— TO ILL-HEALTH) DELICACY
SUSCEPTIBLE EASY SOFT LIABLE FEELING PATIENT SENSIBLE TOLERANT
(— TO CHANGE) CASALTY
SUSIAN ELAMITE
SUSLIK SISEL ZIZEL MARMOT
SUSPECT FEAR DOUBT FANCY GUESS SMOKE THINK BELIEVE ENDOUTE JALOUSE MISDEEM SUPPOSE DISTRUST JEALOUSE MISDOUBT MISTRUST
(NOT —) COLD
SUSPECTED SPOTTED SUSPECT
SUSPEND CALL HALT HANG OUST SHUT SIST STAY BREAK CLOSE DEBAR DEFER DEMUR EXPEL POISE REMIT SLING SWING APPEND DANGLE ADJOURN EXCLUDE FLUIDIZE INTERMIT OVERHANG PROROGUE REPRIEVE SCAFFOLD SUSPENSE PRETERMIT

(— ANCHOR) COCKBILL
(— FROM ACTIVITY) SIDELINE
(— IN FLUID) ENTRAIN
SUSPENDED SWING AFLOAT LATENT HANGING PENDANT PENDENT PENSILE HOVERING SUSPENSE
(NOT —) VESTED
SUSPENDER GALLUS GARTER BRETELLE
(PL.) BRACES GALLOWS GALLUSES
SUSPENSE DEMUR POISE
SUSPENSION FOG BREI FUME SIST STAY STOP DELAY DOUBT MAGMA SMOKE BREACH CUTOFF SLURRY AEROSOL FAILURE RESPITE ABEYANCE BACTERIN EMULSION INFUSION SHUTDOWN SUSPENSE WISHBONE
(— OF JUDGMENT) EPOCHE
(— OF NOISE) HUSH
(— OF RESPIRATION) SYNCOPE
(— OF SENTENCE) REPRIEVE PROBATION
SUSPENSIVENESS DRIVE
SUSPENSORY SUPPORT
SUSPICION HINT DOUBT SOUPCON SURMISE SUSPECT UMBRAGE DISTRUST JEALOUSY MISDOUBT MISTRUST TINCTURE
(IRRATIONAL —) PARANOIA
(SNEAKING —) IDEA
SUSPICIOUS SHY CHARY FISHY LEERY PEERY QUEER SMOKY SHODDY JEALOUS SOUPCON SUSPECT DOUBTFUL WAFFLIKE
SUSPICIOUSLY ASKANCE
SUSQUEHANNA CONESTOGA
SUSTAIN ABET BACK BEAR BUOY DURE HELP HOLD LAST PROP STAY ABIDE CARRY FAVOR SINEW SPRAG STAND ASSIST CONVEY ENDURE FOSTER SECOND SUCCOR SUFFER UPHOLD UPSTAY ALIMENT BOLSTER CONTAIN NOURISH OUTBEAR PROLONG SUPPORT UNDERFO BEFRIEND BUTTRESS CONTINUE MAINTAIN PRESERVE SCAFFOLD
(PREF.) CO
SUSTAINED TENUTO SOUTENU
SUSTENANCE GEAR MEAT SALT BREAD FOISON LIVING RELIEF ALIMENT PABULUM TABLING
SUSU GERIP SOOSOO DOLPHIN
SUSURRUS WHISPER
SUTLER PROVANT VIVANDIER
SUTTEE SATI
SUTURE SEW SEAM RAPHE SETON STITCH HARMONY PTERION
(SUFF.) RHAPHY RRHAPHY
SVANTOVIT TRIGLAV
SVELTE CHIC TRIM LITHE SLEEK SUAVE SMOOTH URBANE SLENDER
SVENO (SLAYER OF —) SOLIMANO
SWAB GOB MOP WAD BOSH QTIP SWOB WIPE PATCH DOSSIL SPONGE EPAULET SWABBER SQUILGEE
SWABBIE GOB TAR
SWADDLE BIND SWEEL SWATHE
SWAG DRUM GAME LOOT BOOTY LUCRE MONEY BOODLE FESTOON MATILDA
SWAGE BOSS MOUTH UPSET FULLER JUMPER SHAPER SWAGER SWEDGE FLATTER
(PL.) OLIVER
SWAGGER JET ROY BRAG COCK FACE ROLL BOAST BRANK BRAVE NUTTY STRUT SWANK SWASH BLAGUE BOUNCE GOSTER HECTOR PARADO PRANCE RENOWN RUFFLE SPROSE BLUSTER BRAVADO GAUSTER PANACHE ROISTER SOLDIER DOMINEER TIGERISM
SWAGGERER HUFF SWAG BUCKO FACER TIGER CUTTLE JETTER PISTOL BRAVADO HUFFCAP RUFFLER FANFARON WHIFFLER
SWAGGERING HUFFY FACING GASCON HUFFCAP TEARCAT BLUSTERY TIGERISH
SWAGMAN WHALER DRIFTER DRUMMER TRAVELER
SWAIN BEAU COLIN CUDDY RUSTIC STREPHON
SWAINSONA INDIGO
SWALE SLASH
SWALLOW OFF SUP BOLT DOWN DROP GAUP GAWP GLUT GULP SINK SWIG TAKE CLUNK DRINK GORGE GURGE POUCH QUILT SLOCK SWOOP ABSORB ENGLUT ENGULF GLUTCH GOBBET GOBBLE GODOWN GUZZLE IMBIBE INGEST MARTIN POCKET PROGNE SWELLY CONSUME ENGORGE ARUNDELL WITCHUCK
(— AGAIN) REGORGE
(— GREEDILY) BEND SLUP GORGE GULCH SWILL WORRY INHALE
(— HASTILY) SWAP SWOP GLOUP SLUMMOCK
(— IN AGAIN) RESORB
(— OF LIQUOR) SLUG
(— UP) GULF SWAMP ABSORB DEVOUR
(— WITH GREEDINESS) ENGORGE
(LOSS OF ABILITY TO —) APHAGIA
(NOISY —) SLURP
(WOMAN TURNED INTO —) PROCNE
(PREF.) CHELID(O)
SWALLOWTAIL TROILUS
SWALLOWWORT CELANDINE
SWAMP BOG FEN FLAT FLOW MIRE MOSS SLEW SLUE SOAK SUMP VLEI VLEY WHAM WHIN FLUSH LERNA LETCH MARSH SWALE SWANG URMAN DELUGE DISMAL ENGULF MORASS MUSKEG SLOUGH CIENAGA POCOSIN GREENING INUNDATE QUAGMIRE
SWAMP COTTONWOOD LIAR
SWAMPER BUSHER GOPHER
SWAMPHEN COOT
SWAMP LOOSESTRIFE PEATWEED PEATWOOD
SWAMP MAHOGANY GUNNUNG
SWAMP MILKWEED DAGGA
SWAMPY PUXY BOGGY POOLY CALLOW POACHY QUASHY QUEASY SLUMPY MOORISH PALUDAL ULIGINOUS
SWAMPY CREE MASKEGON
SWAN COB ELK PEN OLOR CYGNET HOOPER SWANNET WHOOPER
(FEMALE —) PEN
(FLOCK OF —S) GAME MARK
(KIND OF —) MUTE
SWANFLOWER SWANWORT
SWANHILD (FATHER OF —) SIGURD
(MOTHER OF —) GUDRUN
SWANK CHIC POSH TONY RITZY
SWANKY POSH SWASH SPIFFY
SWAP CHOP SWOP TRADE TRUCK DICKER EXCHANGE
SWARD SOD TURF SPINE SWARF SWATH SWARTH
SWARM FRY SNY BIKE CAST FARE HIVE HOST KNIT NEST SORT SWIM TEEM CLOUD CROWD FLOCK FLUSH FRACK HORDE SNARL FLIGHT HOTTER RABBLE SWARVE THRONG OVERRUN SUBCAST PULLULATE
(— IN) FILL
(— OF BEES) BIKE HIVE
(— OF INSECTS) BAND FLIGHT
(— OF PEOPLE) BIKE DRIFT
(THIRD — OF BEES) COLT
SWARMING ALIVE ASWARM SWARMY
SWARTBACK SWARBIE
SWARTHY DUN DARK BLACK BROWN DUSKY GRIMY MOORY SWART MORIAN SWARTH BISTRED BISTERED
SWASH SWIG SWILL SWATCH SWABBLE SWASHWAY
SWASHBUCKLER SWASH GASCON SLASHER SWASHER
SWASTIKA FYLFOT GAMMADION GAMMATION HAKENKREUZ
SWAT SWOT DEHGAN STRIKE
SWATH SWIPE STADDLE
SWATHE LAP BIND WRAP SWARF ENWRAP INWRAP SWADDLE WINDROW
SWATTER FLYSWAT
SWAY NOD WAG BEAR BEND BIAS FLAP HIKE LILT ROCK ROLL RULE SHOG SWAB SWAG SWIG TILT TOSS WALD WAVE CARRY CHARM LURCH POWER REIGN SHAKE SWALE SWING WAVER WHEEL AFFECT ALLURE CAREEN DIRECT EMPIRE TOTTER WAGGLE COMMAND SHOGGIE STAGGER SWABBLE SWIGGLE
(— IN WALKING) WADDLE
(SUFF.) CRACY CRAT(IC)
SWAYBACK WARFA LORDOSIS RENGUERA
SWAYING ASWAY ROLLING
SWAZILAND (CAPITAL OF —) MBABANE
(COIN OF —) RAND EMALANGENI
(LANGUAGE OF —) SISWATI
(MONEY OF —) LILANGENI
(RIVER IN —) USUTU KOMATI MHLATUZE UMBULUZI
(TOWN OF —) STEGI GOLLEL MANZINI PIGGSPEAK
SWEAR VOW VUM DAMN SINK SNUM SWAN SWOW TAKE CURSE ADJURE AFFIRM BEDAMN DEPONE DEPOSE OBJURE CONJURE DEJERATE EXECRATE FORSWEAR
(— FALSELY) RAP MOUNT FORSWEAR MANSWEAR
SWEARING JURANT JURATION
(FALSE —) PERJURY
SWEARWORD CUSS
SWEAT DEW WET STEW WASH BREAN MADOR SUDOR SUDATE LAUNDER PARBOIL SWELTER SWIVVET TRANSUDE PERSPIRATION
(— SKINS) STALE
(DYNAMITE —) LEAK
(PREF.) HIDR(O) HYDR(O) SUDORI
(SUFF.) IDROSIS
SWEATBOX HOTBOX
SWEATER FROCK GANSEY JUMPER WOOLLY CARDIGAN SLIPOVER
(CLOSE-FITTING —) POORBOY
(WOMAN'S SHORT —) SHRINK
SWEATHOUSE TEMESCAL
SWEATING TUB ASWEAT SWELTRY SUDATION SUDATORY
SWEATY PUGGY ASWEAT PERSPIRY SUDOROUS SWEATFUL

SWEDEN

CAPITAL: STOCKHOLM
COIN: ORE KRONA SKILLING
COUNTY: KALMAR OREBRO UPPSALA
DIVISION: AMT LAEN SKANE OREBRO UPPSALA GOTALAND JAMTLAND SWEALAND
GULF: BOTHNIA
ISLAND: OLAND GOTALAND
LAKE: SILJA VANERN MALAREN VATTERN DALALVEN STORAVAN HJALMAREN
MEASURE: AM ALN FOT MIL REF TUM FAMN STOP FODER KANNA KAPPE LINJE NYMIL SPANN STANG TUNNA FATHOM JUMFRU KOLLAST OXHUVUD TUNLAND FJARDING KAPPLAND KOLTUNNA
MOUNTAIN: SARV AMMAR OVIKS HELAGS SARJEK
PROVINCE: KALMAR OREBRO GOTLAND HALLAND UPPSALA ALVSBORG BLEKINGE ELFSBORG JAMTLAND MALMOHUS WERMLAND
RIVER: DAL UME GOTA KLAR LULE KALIX PITEA RANEA LAINIO LJUSNE TORNEA WINDEL ANGERMAN
TOWN: UMEA BODEN BORAS EDANE FALUN GAVLE LULEA MALMO PITEA VISBY YSTAD ARVIKA OREBRO LUDVIKA UPPSALA GOTEBORG NYKOPING VASTERAS
WATERFALL: HANDOL TANNFORSEN
WEIGHT: ASS LOD ORT MARK PUND STEN UNTZ NYLAST LISPUND SKEPPUND

SWEDISH CLOVER ALSIKE
SWEEP OAR BUCK DUST RAFF SOOP

SWAY TILT BESOM BROOM DIGHT DRIFT FETCH SCOPE SKIRL SWIPE SWOOP BREADTH CLEANSE PICOTAH SHADOOF STRICKLE
(— A NET) BEAT
(— MAJESTICALLY) SWAN
(— OFF) SLIPE
(— OF SCYTHE) SWATH SWATHE
(— ON CULTIVATOR) SKIN
(CHIMNEY —) CHUMMY SWEEPY RAMONEUR
(HAY —) BUCK
SWEEPBOARD STRICKLE
SWEEPER BESOM BUNGY SWEEP TOPAZ BHANGI BHUNGI MEHTAR PRYLER ROADER SOOPER TOPASS BROOMER TUBEMAN BHUNGINI MATRANEE SCRUBBER
SWEEPING SURGE RASANT SWEEPY
(— FOR FISH) DRAFT DRAUGHT
(— OF CURVE) NUTATION
(PL.) DUST FULVIE FULZIE RIFFRAFF
SWEET DOUX DUMP FOOL SOOT SUCK CREAM DILIS DOUCE DULCE FRESH HONEY MERRY SOOTH SPICY SPLIT BREEZE DULCET FRUITY GENTLE SILKEN SILVER SIRUPY SUGARY DARLING FAIRING HONEYED INSIPID MUSICAL PANDROP SUGARED SWEETLY WINNING WINSOME AROMATIC ENGAGING FLUMMERY LIEBLICH LUSCIOUS NECTARED PLEASANT
(SICKLY —) ICKY
(SLIGHTLY —) SEC
(PREF.) DULCI GLYCERO GLYCO HEDY SUAVI
SWEET BAY BREWSTER MAGNOLIA
SWEETBREAD BUR BURR PANCREAS
(— OF DEER) INCHPIN
SWEETBRIER BEDEGUAR EGLANTINE
SWEET CALABASH KURUBA
SWEET CASSAVA AIPI AIPIM
SWEET CHERRY MAZZARD
SWEET CICELY MYRRH
SWEET CLOVER LOTUS MELILOT
SWEET COLTSFOOT LAGWORT
SWEETEN CANDY HONEY SUGAR SWEET PURIFY ADDULCE CLEANSE DULCIFY FRESHEN MOLLIFY PERFUME MITIGATE
SWEETENER SACCHARIN
SWEET FENNEL FINOCHIO FLORENCE
SWEET FERN FERNGALE
SWEETFISH AYU
SWEET FLAG SEDGE BEEWORT CALAMUS
SWEET GALE GOLD GAGEL BAYBUSH FLEAWOOD GALEWORT GALLBUSH
SWEET GUM AMBER COPALM STORAX BILSTED
SWEETHEART JO BOY GRA HON JOE LAD PET PUG SIS AGRA AMIE BABY BEAU DEAR DOLL DOXY DUCK FAIR GILL GIRL JILL LADY LASS LIEF LOVE MASH MORT POUT AGRAH BULLY BUSSY CHERI COOKY DOLLY DONAH DONEY DONNA DRURY FLAME LEMAN LOVER PUGGY SPARK SWEET COOKIE EMILIA FELLOW FRIEND MOPSEY PIGEON STEADY WAHINE AMOROSA BELOVED PHYLLIS PIGSNEY QUERIDA SPRUNNY SWEETIE TOOTSIE DOWSABEL DULCINEA FOLLOWER LADYBIRD LADYLOVE LIEBCHEN LOVELASS MISTRESS SWEETING TRUELOVE
(— OF HARLEQUIN) COLUMBINE
SWEETIE (— PIE) HON DEAR HONEY DEARIE
SWEETLEAF DYELEAVES SYMPLOCOS
SWEET MARJORAM OREGANO
SWEETMEAT DROP DUMP KISS DULCE FUDGE GOODY PASTE PLATE SPICE TOFFY BONBON BUCAYO COMFIT DRAGEE DREDGE JUNKET ALCORZA BANQUET CARAMEL CARAWAY CLAGGUM CONFECT LOUKOUM PENUCHE SUCCADE CONSERVE HARDBAKE MARZIPAN PASTILLE
(PL.) BALUSHAI CONFETTI
SWEETNESS DULCE HONEY SIRUP SYRUP DULCOR DOUCEUR DULCITY SUAVITY FLORIMEL WORDNESS
SWEET ORANGE CHINA CHINO
SWEET PEA CATGUT LATHYRUS
SWEET PEPPERBUSH CLETHRA SOAPBUSH
SWEET POTATO YAM SWEET BATATA CAMOTE KUMARA OCARINA
SWEET RUSH SQUINANT
SWEET-SMELLING AROMATIC
SWEETSOP ANON ATES ATIS ATTA CORAZON SWEETING
SWEET-SOUNDING MERRY
SWEET-TALK ENAMOR
SWEET VIOLET FINELEAF
SWEET WILLIAM DIANTHUS
SWELL BAG DON NIB NOB BEAL BELL BLAB BLOW BLUB BOLL BULB BULK BUMP BUOY DOME FILL FINE GROW HOVE HUFF HUSH PINK PLIM RISE SWAG TOFF TONY WAVE BELLY BERRY BLAST BLOAT BULGE BUNCH DANDY FLASH NIFTY PLUFF PREEN SMART STOCK STRUT SURGE TULIP BILLOW BOWDEN DILATE EXPAND GROWTH LOVELY SPRING STROUT TUMEFY UPRISE AUGMENT BLUBBER BURGEON DISTEND INFLATE REGULAR SWAGGER OVERBLOW TURGESCE
(— OF GUN MUZZLE) TULIP
(— OF WATER) HUSH SURF FLOOD SURGE
(— OUT) BAG POD BUNT DRAW POUT BOSOM BILLOW SPONGE BALLOON BLADDER
(HEAVY —) RUN SEA
(SEA —) WALLOW BACKWATER
(PREF.) OEDE OEDI TUME
SWELLDOODLE EGGFISH
SWELLED BIAS BLOWN
SWELLFISH BLOWER PUFFER TAMBOR
SWELLING BIG BUR NOB PAP PIN BLAB BOLL BUBO BUMP BURR CLAP COWL CURB FROG FULL GALL KNOB KNOT NODE POKE PONE PUFF AMPER BLAIN BOTCH BOUGE BULGE BUNCH BUNNY CLOUR EDEMA JETTY MOUSE PROUD SURGE SWELL TUBER TUMOR ANCOME ASWELL BOSOMY BUNCHY CALLUS FLATUS GIBBER GROWTH KERNEL PIMPLE RANULA STRUMA SWELTH TURGID WARBLE AMPULLA BOSSING CAPELET CHAGOMA CUSHION GOUNDOU HAPTERE PUSTULE SURGENT TURGENT UREDEMA UROCELE APOSTEME BULLNECK CHEMOSIS DACRYOMA FURUNCLE GLANDULE GOURDING HAPTERON HEMATOMA MUCOCELE NODOSITY PULVINUS PUMPKNOT QUELLUNG SCIRRHUS STYLOPOD VESSICNON TUMESCENCE
(— IN HORSE'S CHEST) ANTICOR
(— IN HORSE'S MOUTH) LAMPAS LAMPASSE
(— IN PLASTER) BLUB
(— OF PLANT TISSUE) GALL
(— OF THE CHEEK) HONE
(— ON ANIMAL'S JOINTS) BUNNY CAPELLET
(— ON HEAD) COWL
(— ON SPLEEN) AGUECAKE
(DISCOLORED —) MOUSE
(EYE —) STY STYE
(ROUNDED —) TUBER
(PREF.) GANGLI GANGLO STRUMI
(SUFF.) EMATOMA PHYMA
SWELTER BAKE BOIL STEW SWELT
SWELTERING STEWY SULTRY SWELTRY
SWERVE BOW CUT LUG YAW BIAS FADE JOUK SKEW VARY VEER WARP SHEER STRAY DEPART DEVIATE DIGRESS DIVERGE INSWING
SWIDDEN CAINGIN KAINGIN
SWIFT CRAN FAST FLIT MAIN VITE FLEET HASTY LIGHT QUICK RAPID SNELL SWITH WIGHT WINDY ARROWY MARLET NIMBLE RAKING SOUPLE SPEEDY STRICT SUDDEN SWIFTY TOTTER WINGED COLLIER DEVELIN FLIGHTY POSTING SWALLOW TANTIVY DEVELING HEPIALID PEGASEAN SCREAMER SCUTTLER SQUEALER SWIFTLET SALANGANE
(PREF.) CITI CYPSELO OCY TACHEO TACHISTO TACHO TACHY
SWIFTLY FAST SWAP APACE SNELL SNELLY LIGHTLY STEEPLY TANTIVY
SWIFTNESS FOOT HASTE SPEED CELERITY FASTNESS VELOCITY
SWIG SCOUR SNORT SWILL SWING SWIGGLE
SWILL SOSS BROCK SLOSH SLUICE HOGWASH PIGWASH SWILLING
SWIM DIP COWD SAIL SOOM SPAN TEEM BATHE CRAWL FLEET FLOAT GLIDE SWARM PLUNGE OVERFLOW
(— IN NEW DIRECTION) MILL
(— IN NUDE) SKINNYDIP
(— IN SHOALS) RUN
(— TOGETHER) SCHOOL
(— TRUNKS) JAMS
(PREF.) NECT(O)
(SUFF.) NECTAE NECTES
SWIMMER NAIAD BATHER NATATOR BUTTERFLYER
SWIMMERET PLEOPOD
SWIMMING ASWIM NATANT FLOTANT NATATION
(— APPARATUS) SCUBA
(— DEVICE) SNORKEL
(— STUNT) MARLIN WALKOVER
SWIMMING POOL POOL THERM PLUNGE THERME PISCINA NATATORY
(— ON LINER) LIDO
SWIMSUIT MAILLOT
SWIN (— IN NUDE) SKINNYDIP
SWINDLE CON GIP GYP JOB RIG BILK BURN DUPE FAKE FLAP HAVE MACE PULL RAMP ROOK ROPE SCAM SWIZ BUNCO BUNKO CHEAT COZEN FLING FOIST GOUGE GRIFT LURCH MULCT PLANT PONZI ROGUE SHARK SHARP SHAVE SHUCK SLANG SPOOF STING SWIZZ UNCLE BOODLE BUBBLE BUCKET CHISEL CHOUSE DIDDLE FIDDLE FLEECE GAZUMP HUSTLE INTAKE NOBBLE SUCKER TREPAN DEFRAUD FINAGLE SKELDER THIMBLE VERNEUK FLIMFLAM BAMBOOZLE
SWINDLER DO FOB GYP LEG BILK FYNK HAWK ROOK SKIN CHEAT CROOK ESROC FAKER GANEF GREEK HARPY KNAVE MACER ROGUE CHIAUS GOUGER INTAKE RINGER ROOKER SALTER SHAVER VERSER BUBBLER GRIFTER HUSTLER MACEMAN MAGSMAN NOBBLER SHARPER SKELDER SLICKER SPIELER BARNACLE BLACKLEG CHISELER FINAGLER GILENYER LUMBERER PIGEONER SHELLMAN TRAMPOSO
(DECOY —) BARNARD
SWINDLING MACE BUNCO BUNKO GRAFT ROOKY SHARK GYPPERY JOUKERY CHEATERY JOOKERIE
SWINE HOG OIC PIG SOW BOAR GALT GILT PORK SUID YILT DUROC ESSEX SWIPE WHITE GUSSIE POLAND PORKER PORKET BUSHPIG LACOMBE OINKERS PECCARY SUFFOLK SUIDIAN CHESHIRE HYOTHERE LANDRACE TAMWORTH
(— AND FOOD) PANNAGE
(— AND MAN) OMNIVORA
(PREF.) HYO
SWINEHERD GURTH HOGMAN EUMAEUS HOGHERD HOGWARD
SWINE-LIKE GADARENE
SWING GO COOK HIKE JUMP LILT SCUP SHOG STOT SWAY SWEE TURN SHAKE SHOWD SLING SWALE TREND DANGLE GYRATE HANDLE SWINGE SWITCH SWIVEL

TOTTER JUMPING SHOGGIE SWINGEL WAMPISH BRANDISH FLOURISH OSCILLATE
(— AROUND) JIB SLEW SLUE SLOUGH
(— A SHIP) SPRING
(— BY BATTER) CUT
(— FROM POSITION) CANT
(— FROM SIDE TO SIDE) JOW
(— FROM THE TIDE) TEND
(— OF PENDULUM) BEAT
(— OF SAIL) GYBE JIBE
(— OF SWORD) MOULINET
(— OUT OF LINE) SWAG
(— THE FOREFEET) DISH
(RHYTHMICAL —) LILT
(WILD —) HAYMAKER
(PREF.) OSCILLO
SWINGER HINGE
SWINGING BANK ASWING SWINGY
SWINGLE SWORD SCUTCH SWIPPLE
SWING SEAT TRANSOM
SWINISH SOWISH HOGGISH PORCINE SUILLINE
SWIPE COP CHOP GLOM SLOG WIPE SNAKE STEAL VULTURE
SWIRL BOIL EDDY GULF HURL PURL WALM GURGE SWALE SWEEL SWORL SWOOSH WREATHE TOURBILLION
(— OF SALMON) BULGE
SWIRLING VORTICAL
SWISH HISH WHIP SMART SWILL WHISH
SWISS SWISSER HELVETIC
(— PINE) MUGHO
SWISS FAMILY ROBINSON
(AUTHOR OF —) WYSS
(CHARACTER IN —) JACK EMILY FRITZ ERNEST FRANCIS MONTROSE ROBINSON
SWITCH GAD TAN LASH TWIG WAND AZOTE BIRCH BREAK SHUNT SWISH CHANGE CUTOUT DERAIL DIPPER FERULA FERULE LARRUP RATTAN SCUTCH SILENT SPRING HICKORY KIPPEEN SCOURGE SQUITCH CRYOTRON HAIRWORK POSTICHE
(— FOCUS) FADE
(AUTO —) DIMMER
(ELECTRIC —) KEY
(RAILROAD —) GATE POINT
SWITCHBOARD (PRIVATE PHONE —) PBX
SWITCH ENGINE GOAT
SWITCHMAN SHUNTER SWITCHER

SWITZERLAND

BAY: URI
CANTON: ZUG BERN JURA VAUD BASEL AARGAU GENEVA GLARUS LUZERN SCHWYZ TICINO VALAIS ZURICH GRISONS THURGAU FRIBOURG OBWALDEN
CAPITAL: BERN BERNE
COIN: FRANC RAPPE RAPPEN ANGSTER DUPLONE BLAFFERT
LAKE: URI ZUG THUN AGERI LEMAN MORAT BIENNE BRIENZ GENEVA LUGANO SARNEN WALLEN ZURICH HALLWIL LUCERNE LUNGERN VIERWALD
MEASURE: IMI POT AUNE ELLE FUSS IMMI MUID PIED SAUM ZOLL LIEVE LIGNE LINIE MAASS MOULE POUCE SCHUH STAAB TOISE PERCHE SETIER STRICH JUCHART KLAFTER VIERTEL
MOUNTAIN: JURA RIGI ROSA BLANC CENIS KARPF LINARD PIZELA BERNINA BEVERIN GRIMSEL PILATUS ROTONDO BALMHORN JUNGFRAU
MOUNTAIN PASS: CENIS FURKA ALBERG MALOJA BRENNER GRIMSEL SIMPLON SPLUGEN LOTSCHEN
NAME: HELVETIA
RIVER: AAR INN AARE THUR BROYE DOUBS LINTH REUSS RHINE RHONE MAGGIA SARINE TICINO PRATIGAU
TOWN: BALE BERN BIEL BRIG CHUR SION AARAU BASEL VEVEY GENEVA GLARUS LUZERN SCHWYZ ZURICH FYZABAD HERISAU LUCERNE LAUSANNE MONTREUX
VALLEY: AAR ZERMATT ENGADINE
WATERFALL: SIMMEN HANDEGG IFFIGEN DIESBACH GIESSBACH STAUBBACH TRUMMELBACH
WEIGHT: PFUND CENTNER QUINTAL

SWIVEL LOPER SWAPE SWIPE CASTER FIDDLE TIRRET TOGGLE TONGUE TRAVERSE TRUNNION
SWIVET STEW
SWIZZLE STIR
SWOLLEN BLUB FULL PLIM RANK BLOWN CHUFF GOUTY GREAT GUMMY POBBY PROUD PUFFY TUMID BOLLEN BRAWNY BULLED GOURDY TURGID BESTRUT BLOATED BLUBBER BULBOUS GIBBOSE GIBBOUS GOURDED GOUTISH STICKLE TURGENT BEPUFFED BLADDERY TUMOROUS
(PREF.) PHYS(O)
SWOON KEEL SWEB SWIM DOVER DROWN DWALM FAINT SLOOM SOUND SWARF SWELT STOUND SWOUND TRANCE ECSTASY SWITHER SYNCOPE SWOONING
SWOONING ASWOON SYNCOPE
SWOOP CHOP DIVE JOUK SWAP SWOP SOUSE STOOP SWOPE POUNCE SOURCE DESCEND
(KIND OF —) FELL
SWOOPING SOUSE
SWORD FOX SAX BILL DIRK FALX GRAM IRON PATA SAEX SEAX SPIT TOOL TUCK TURK BILBO BLADE BRAND DEGEN DIEGO ESTOC GULLY KNIFE KUKRI PRICK RIPON SABER SABRE SHARP STEEL ANDREW BARONG BILBOA CATTAN DAMASK DUSACK FLORET GLAIVE HANGER KHANDA KUKERI MIMING PARANG PINKER PORKER RAPIER SMITER SPATHA TILTER TIZONA TOLEDO WAFTER BALMUNG BRANDON CURTANA CUTLASH CUTLASS ESPADON ESTOQUE FERRARA FLEURET IMPALER JOYEUSE MALCHUS MORGLAY SHABBLE SLASHER SNICKER SPURTLE TOASTER WHIFFLE WHINGER ACINACES BASELARD CAMPILAN CLAYMORE DAMASCUS DURENDAL FALCHION FLAMBERG SCHLAGER SCIMITAR SPADROON SPITFROG WACADASH WHINYARD
(— OF CHARLEMAGNE) JOYEUSE
(— OF CID) TIZONA
(— OF HERMES) HARPE
(— OF LANCELOT) ARONDIGHT
(— OF ROLAND) DURENDAL
(— OF SIEGFRIED) GRAM BALMUNG
(— OF SIR BEVIS) MORGLAY
(— OF ST. GEORGE) ASCALON ASKELON
(— USED BY ST. PETER) MALCHUS
(BLUNT —) WAFTER SCHLAGER
(CELTIC —) SAX SAEX
(CURVED —) SCIMITAR
(DOUBLE-EDGED —) KEN PATA KHANDA SPATHA
(DUELLING —) EPEE SHARP
(DYAK —) PARANG
(FENCING —) EPEE FOIL SABER SABRE RAPIER
(HALF OF —) FORTE
(JAPANESE —) CATAN CATTAN KATANA WACADASH
(LONG —) SPATHA WHIFFLE
(MATADOR'S —) ESTOQUE
(MORO —) BARONG CAMPILAN
(NARROW —) TUCK
(NORMAN —) SPATHA
(PERSIAN —) ACINACES
(POINTLESS —) CURTANA CURTEIN
(RUSTY —) SHABBLE
(SHORT —) DIRK ESTOC KUKRI SKEAN CREESE HANGER CURTAXE WHINGER FALCHION WHINYARD
(THRUSTING —) ESTOC STOCK
(TWO-HANDED —) ESPADON SPADONE CLAYMORE
(WOODEN —) WASTER STRICKLE
SWORD-BEARER VERGER SELICTAR PORTGLAVE
(PL.) ENSIFERI
SWORD DANCER MATACHIN
SWORDFISH AU ESPADA ESPADON XIPHIAS ALBACORA BILLFISH BOATBILL FORKTAIL XIPHIOID SCOMBROID
(PREF.) XIPH(O)
SWORD-LIKE
(PREF.) XIPH(I)(O)
SWORDPLAY SPADROON
(STYLIZED —) KENDO
SWORD-SHAPED ENSATE ENSIFORM GLADIATE
SWORDSMAN BLADE BLADER FENCER SLASHER SWORDER THRUSTER
SWORDSMANSHIP KENDO
SWORDTAIL HELLERI
SWORN AVOWED
SWOT GRI MUG
SYAGUSH SHARGOSS
SYBARITE EPICURE
SYBARITIC SENSUOUS
SYCAMORE MAY DAROO COTONIER LACEWOOD PLANTAIN
SYCEE SHOE
SYCOPHANCY FAWNERY
SYCOPHANT TOADY COGGER FAWNER GNATHO HANGBY TAGTAIL CLAWBACK PARASITE PICKTHANK SATELLITE
SYCOPHANTIC FAWNING SERVILE SLAVISH OBEDIENT TRENCHER
SYCORAX (SON OF —) CALIBAN
SYCOSIS MENTAGRA
SYENITE APPINITE TRACHYTE
SYLLABARY KANA IROFA IROHA KATAKANA
SYLLABIC SONANT CENTROID SONANTIC
SYLLABLE ARSIS BREVE GROUP SHORT DISEME SYLLAB THESIS TRISEME ASSONANT
(— DENOTING ASSENT) OM
(BOBIZATION —) BO CE DI GA GE LO MA NI
(IMPROVISE NONSENSE —S) SCAT
(LAST —) ULTIMA
(LAST — BUT ONE) PENULT
(LONG —) LONG
(MUSICAL —) DI DO FA FI LA LE LI ME MI RA RE RI SE SI SO TA TE TI TO UT SOL
(REFRAIN —) DILDO
(SHORT —) MORA SHORT
(STRONG —) STRESS
(TERMINAL —) ENDING
(UNACCENTED —) OUTRIDE
(UNACCENTED —S) THESIS
(UNSTRESSED —) OUTRIDE
SYLLABUS PROGRAM VIDIMUS HEADNOTE SYNOPSIS PROGRAMME
SYLLOGISM BARBARA ABDUCTION ENTHYMEME
(SERIES OF —S) SORITES
SYLPH ARIEL SYLPHID
SYLVAN WOODY FOREST SILVAN WOODEN WOODISH SYLVATIC
SYLVITE HARDSALT
SYMBIOSIS LICHENISM MUTUALISM NUTRICISM
SYMBOL KEY CODE FISH FOUR ICON IDOL IKON MARK NEUM SEAL SIGN TYPE BADGE CREST CROSS EAGLE IMAGE INDEX PRIME TOKEN CARACT CIPHER EMBLEM ENSIGN FIGURE LETTER PNEUME SHADOW SIGNAL FACIEND MANDALA PALATAL CEREMONY CONSTANT DIRECTOR EXPONENT GUTTURAL IDEOGRAM LIGATURE LOGOGRAM OPERATOR SWASTIKA SYMBOLUM TRISKELE IDEOGRAPH METOBELUS OCTOTHORP ORIFLAMME PICTOGRAPH PHRASEOGRAM
(— AS ROAD SIGN) GLYPH
(— FOR WAVELENGTH) LAMBDA
(— OF AUTHORITY) MACE
(— OF DEATH) CYPRESS
(— OF DISTINCTION) BELT HONOR
(— OF FAITHFUL DEAD) ORANT
(— OF FRANCE) LILY
(— OF LIFE) ANKH
(— OF MONK) COWL
(— OF PHYSICIAN) CADUCEUS
(— OF RAILROAD) HERALD
(— OF RESURRECTION) PHOENIX

(— OF SOMETHING SPIRITUAL) SACRAMENT
(— OF SOVEREIGNTY) ASP URAEUS
(— OF SPRING) KARPAS
(— OF STRENGTH) HORN
(— OF SUN) DISC DISK
(— OF UNIVERSE) MANDALA
(— ON UNCHANGEABLENESS) LEOPARD
(— REPRESENTING THE ABSOLUTE) TAIKIH
(ALGEBRAIC —) EXPONENT
(CLAN —) TOTEM
(CRICKET —) ASHES
(CRUSADERS' —) CROSS
(CURVED —) HOOK
(EFFICIENCY —) ETA
(EGYPTIAN —) ANKH SCARAB
(INFORMATION —) GLYPH
(INTERSECTION —) CAP
(KOREAN —) TAHGOOK
(MAGIC —) CARACT
(MATHEMATICAL —) KNOWN FACTOR OBELUS FACIEND OPERAND PLACEHOLDER
(PHALLIC —) LINGA LINGAM
(PICTOGRAPHIC —) ISOTYPE
(PRINTING —) DIAGONAL
(PRONUNCIATION —) ENG
(RELIGIOUS —) CROSS LABRYS
(UNION —) CUP
(8 POINTS ON CIRCUMFERENCE —) OCTOTHORP
(PL.) KATAKANA
SYMBOLIC GRAPHIC SHADOWY ANICONIC
SYMBOLICAL ALLUSIVE MYSTICAL
SYMBOLISM ICONOLOGY
SYMBOLIZE BODY SIGN TOKEN FIGURE SAMPLE SHADOW SYMBOL TYPIFY BETOKEN EXPRESS PORTEND SIGNIFY RESEMBLE
SYMMETRICAL FORMAL DIMERIC REGULAR SHAPELY SPHERAL BALANCED
(NOT —) SKEW
SYMMETRY MEASURE
SYMPATHETIC AKIN FERE SOFT WARM HUMAN FELLOW KINDLY TENDER PIETOSO SIMPATICO
SYMPATHIZER FABIAN BLACKNEB SHAYSITE
SYMPATHY PITY RUTH FLESH PHILIA CONSENT EMPATHY RAPPORT AFFINITY KINDNESS
SYMPHONY SINFONIA
(BEETHOVEN'S THIRD —) EROICA
SYMPOSIUM POTATION
SYMPTOM MARK NOTE SIGN SHOWER STIGMA INSTANCE PRODROME
(DISEASE —) MERCYISM
SYNAGOGUE SHUL SCHUL ALJAMA PROSEUCHA
SYNAPSIS PAIRING
SYNAPTE ECTENE EKTENE
SYNARTHROSIS SUTURE
SYNCHRO SELSYN
SYNCHRONIZE MESH
SYNCHRONIZER SPEEDGUN
SYNCLINE DOWNFOLD ISOCLINE
SYNCOPATED ZOPPA ABRIDGED
SYNCOPE SWOON COTYPE FAINTING
SYNDICATE HUI GROUP CARTEL COMBINE
(UNIT OF CRIME —) FAMILY
SYNDICATED CANNED
SYNDROME (KIND OF —) FANCONI
SYNECDOCHE MERISM
SYNERGIST BOOSTER SESAMIN
SYNOD SOBOR
SYNODAL SENAGE
SYNONYM ANTONYM HOMONYM EUPHONYM POLYONYM
SYNOPSIS BRIEF TABLE EPITOME OUTLINE SUMMARY ABSTRACT ANALYSIS SCENARIO SYLLABUS ABRIDGMENT
SYNSACRUM SACRARY
SYNTACTICAL FORMAL
SYNTHESIS SUMMA FUSION SYSTASIS
SYNTHESIZER MOOG
SYNTHETASE LIGASE
SYNTHETIC ERSATZ PLASTIC SYSTATIC ARTIFICER
SYPHAX (WIFE OF —) SOPHENISBA
SYPHILIS PIP POX LUES SYPH CRINKUM GRINCOME

SYRIA
CAPITAL: DAMASCUS
COIN: POUND TALENT PIASTER
DISTRICT: ALEPPO HAURAN
LAKE: DJEBOID TIBERIAS
MEASURE: MAKUK GARAVA
MOUNTAIN: HERMON LIBANUS
NAME: ARAM
NATIVE: DRUSE ANSARIE SARACEN ANSARIEH
RIVER: ASI BALIKH BARADA JORDAN KNABUR ORONTES EUPHRATES
TOWN: ALEP HAMA HOMS NAWA BUSRA CALNO DERRA HALAB HAMAH IDLIB JERUD RAQQA ALEPPO BALBEL LATAKIA SELEUCIA
WEIGHT: COLA ROTL ARTAL ARTEL RATEL TALENT

SYRINGA PHILADELPHUS
SYRINGE GUN HYPO ENEMA SCOOT DOUCHE FILLER SQUIRT SCOOTER SERRING
SYRINGIN LILACIN
SYRINX PANPIPE
SYRNIUM STRIX
SYRUP DIBS LICK SIRUP ORGEAT ANTIQUE ECLEGMA FALERNUM QUIDDANY
(FRUIT —) ROB
(STARCH —) GLUCOSE
SYRUPY FRUITY
SYRYENIAN SYRYAN ZYRIAN
(PL.) KAMI KOMI
SYSTEM ISM AREA CREDO FRAME ORDER CIRCLE METHOD SCHEME STEREO SYNTAX COMPLEX DUALISM ECONOMY FAGGERY NAVARHO REGIMEN ENSEMBLE GALENISM OVERRIDE RELIGION UNIVERSE
(— FOR ROMANIZING IDEOGRAMS) PINYIN
(— OF BARS) LATTICE
(— OF BELIEFS) FAITH
(— OF BELL CHANGES) CATERS QUATERS STEDMAN
(— OF CORDS) BRIDLE
(— OF CROSSING THREADS) LEASE
(— OF DIET) BANTING
(— OF ETHICS) SELFISM
(— OF EXCHANGE) KULA
(— OF EXERCISES) AEROBICS
(— OF FAITH) CREED
(— OF GEARS) COMPOUND
(— OF JOINTS) CLEAT
(— OF LANGUAGE SIGNS) SIGNARY
(— OF LAW) EQUITY
(— OF LINES IN EYEPIECE) RETICLE RETICULE
(— OF LOGIC) RAMISM
(— OF MANUAL TRAINING) SLOJD SLOYD
(— OF MARKETING) ADMASS
(— OF MEANING) SEMANTIC
(— OF MEDICINE) AYURVEDA
(— OF MONEY TRANSFER) GIRO
(— OF NUMERALS) ALGORISM
(— OF OCCULT THEOSOPHY) CABALA
(— OF PHILOSOPHY) HUMISM COMTISM HOBBISM SAMKHYA SANKHYA STOICISM
(— OF PHONETIC NOTATION) ROMIC
(— OF PRINCIPLES) CODE
(— OF RAYS) ASTER
(— OF ROCKS) CENOZOIC DEVONIAN SILURIAN
(— OF RULE) REGIME
(— OF RULES) ART
(— OF SOLMIZATION) FASOLA
(— OF SPACES) LACUNOME
(— OF SUPPRESSING LITERATURE) SAMIZDAT
(— OF SYMBOLS) CODE
(— OF TENANCY) CROFTING
(— OF TRANSPORTATION) AIRLINE AIRMAIL
(— OF TRUSSING) CABANE
(— OF VALUES) ETHOS
(— OF WEIGHTS) TROY
(— OF WIRES) HARNESS
(— OF WORSHIP) CULT CULTUS
(— OF WRITING) KANJI BRAILLE ALPHABET
(— TO LOCATE AN OBJECT) LIDAR
(ACOUSTICAL —) SODAR
(AGRICULTURAL —) KOLKOZ KOLKHOS
(ALARM —) BUG
(BANKING —) GIRO
(BETTING —) ALEMBERT PERFECTA QUINELLA MARTINGALE
(COLLOIDAL —) SOL
(COMMUNICATION —) BLOWER CIRCUIT
(COMPUTER —) KLUGE KLUDGE TRSDOS
(COMPUTER DISK OPERATING —) MSDOS PCDOS
(CULTURAL —) ISLAM
(DEFENSE —) SAGE
(DISK OPERATING —) DOS
(DISPERSE —) GEL
(ELECTRICAL —) SELSYN
(ELECTRONIC —) TELETEXT
(GEOLOGICAL —) EOCENE CAMBRIAN DEVONIAN KEEWATIN TERTIARY
(HAULING —) DILLY
(HAVERSIAN —) OSTEON
(IRRIGATION —) KAREZ
(LANGUAGE —) LATINXUA
(LOCATING —) LIDAR
(NAVIGATING —) TACAN
(NAVIGATION —) GEE DECCA LANAC TACAN NAVAID SHORAN NAVARHO OMNIRANGE
(PENAL —) GULAG
(RELIGIOUS —) LAW CULT CULTUS SHIISM SUNNISM DRUIDISM
(RHYTHMIC —) STROPHE GLYCONIC
(ROMANIZING —) PINYIN
(SING-SONG VOWEL —) ABLAUT
(SOCIAL —) CASTE
(STAR —) GALAXY
(TECHNOLOGICAL —) FORDISM
(TELEVISION —) SCOPHONY
(TRIANGULATION —) SOFAR
(TRUCK —) TOMMY
(WORK —) FLEXTIME FLEXITIME
SYSTEMATIC ORDERLY REGULAR METHODIC
SYSTEMATIZE ORDER CODIFY ORGANIZE METHODIZE
SYSTEMATIZED CODED ORGANIC
SYSTEMIC DEMETON

T

T TEE TARE TANGO
TAAL AFRIKAANS
TAB JAG PAN TAG BILL COST FLAP CHECK FLASH PRICE TALLY WATCH EARTAB EARTAG SIGNAL TOEPLATE
TABANID GADFLY
TABARD CHIMER CHIMERE
TABARRO, IL (CHARACTER IN —) LUIGI MICHELE GIORGETTA
(COMPOSER OF —) PUCCINI
TABERNACLE PIX PYX HOVEL SACRARY
TABES WASTING
TABETIC MARCID
TABITHA DORCAS
TABLATURE LYRAWAY PICTURE PAINTING
TABLE KEY PIE PYE RUN BANK BUCK DAIS DESK FORM MESS BELLY BENCH BOARD CANON CHART PINAX PLANK SCALE STALL STAND STONE WAGON COMMON SCHEME SHELVE TABLET TABULA TARIFF TEAPOY TRIPOD VANNER CABARET CAMBIST CONSOLE COUNTER DIAGRAM DIPTYCH DRESSER PROJECT SHAMBLE TABLEAU TESSERA TROLLEY WHIRLER CALENDAR CREDENCE GUERIDON PEDIGREE PEMBROKE REGIMENT SETASIDE SPECULUM STILLAGE TOILETTE VANITORY NIGHTSTAND
(— DECORATION) DOILY
(— FOR BOWING HAT-BODY) HURL
(— FOR GLAZING LEATHER) BANK
(— FOR ORNAMENT) CARTOUCH
(— FOR PHOTOGRAPHIC PLATES) WHIRLER
(— FURNISHED WITH MEAL) SPREAD
(— IN STORE) COUNTER
(— OF ANCESTORS) PEDIGREE
(— OF CONTENTS) INDEX METHOD
(— OF DECLINATIONS) REGIMENT
(— TOP) AMOEBA
(— USED IN FELTING A HAT) BASON
(— WITH BRAZIER BENEATH) TENDOOR TENDOUR
(ARITHMETIC —) TARIFF
(ASTROLOGICAL —) SPECULUM
(BOTANIC —) KEY
(CIRCULAR —) ROUNDEL
(COMMUNION —) ALTAR CREDENCE
(DINING —) MAHOGANY
(DRESSING —) TOILET VANITY TOILETTE
(EUCHARISTIC —) PROTHESIS
(FOLDING —) SERVETTE
(INNER —) HOME
(KIND OF —) PARSONS PERIODIC
(MASSAGE —) PLINTH
(MUSICAL —) DIAGRAM
(NIGHT —) SOMNO
(ONE-FOOTED —) MONOPODE
(PRINCIPAL —) DAIS
(PRINTER'S —) STONE
(PROFUSELY ORNAMENTED —) PEMBROKE
(SECTIONAL STUDY —) CARREL
(SERVING —) WAGON
(SHAKING —) SLIMER
(SMALL —) KURSI STAND TABORET TABOURET
(STONE —) DOLMEN
(TEA —) TEAPOY
(WRITING —) DESK
TABLEAU LAYOUT PAGEANT PICTURE
TABLECLOTH CLOTH COVER CARPET
TABLE D'HOTE DINNER
TABLELAND PLAT PUNA PUNO KAROO TABLE KARROO PLATEAU BALAGHAT
TABLET PAD PAX BRED ALBUM FACIA PIECE PINAX SLATE TABLE ABACUS CAPLET TABULA TABULE TROCHE ASPIRIN CODICIL DIPTYCH PALETTE PREFORM TABLING CARTOUCH CHURINGA TABULATE TRIPTYCH MEDALLION
(— BEARING SYMBOL OF CHRIST) PAX
(— FOR PUBLISHING LAWS) PARAPEGM
(— OVER SHOP FRONT) FACIA FASCIA
(AMPHETAMINE —) BENNY
(DRUG —) QUAALUDE
(MEDICATED —) ASPIRIN JELLOID TABELLA
(MEDICINAL —) DISC DISK TROCHE
(MEMORIAL —) BRASS TABUT
(PAINTER'S —) PALETTE
(SLEEPING —) DALMANE
(SQUARE —) ABACK
(UPRIGHT —) STELA STELE
(VOTIVE —) PINAX
(WRITING —) CODICIL TRIPTYCH
(PREF.) PINA PINAC(O) PLAC(O)
TABLEWARE CHINA FLATWARE HAVILAND
(WOODEN —) TREEN
TABOO KAPU TABU TAPU FORBIDDEN INEFFABLE
TABOR ATABAL TABRET TIMBRE TABORIN TIMBREL
TABULATION SCALE SCHEME TABLING
TABUT TAZIA TAZEEA
TACHOMETER CUTMETER
TACHYGLOSSUS ECHIDNA
TACIT SILENT IMPLICIT
TACITURN DUMB STILL SILENT LACONIC RESERVED RETICENT
TACK LAY BEAT CAST STAY BASTE BOARD FETCH ENTAIL LAVEER TACKET TINGLE SADDLERY
(GLAZIERS' —) BRAD
TACKER GUN SPREADER
TACKLE CAT RIG TAW GEAR SWIG TACK YOKE ANGLE FALLS ATTACK BURTON COLLAR GARNET JIGGER LEDGER RUNNER STEEVE TAGLIA TEAGLE DERRICK HALYARD HARNESS RIGGING FISHFALL PURCHASE TACKLING
(— BY NECK) SCRAG
(— FOR RAISING BOAT) FALLS
(— TO HOIST ANCHOR) CAT
(COMBINATION OF —S) JEER JEERS
(FISHING —) TEW LEGER OTTER LEDGER
TACO FLAUTA TAQUITO
TACT TOUCH ADDRESS CONDUCT DELICACY
TACTFUL POLITIC DISCREET GRACEFUL
TACTFULLY HAPPILY
TACTIC GAME PLOY
TACTICAL THEATER
TACTICS FOOTWORK
TACTLESS BRASH GAUCHE
TAD LAD MOPPET SHAVER SPROUT
TADPOLE POWHEAD BULLHEAD POLEHEAD POLLIWOG POLLYWOG PORWIGLE
TAEL LIANG
TAENNIN KOSIN KOUSIN
TAFFETA TABBY ARMOZEEN FLORENCE
TAFFY GUNDY TOFFY TOFFEE CLAGGUM
TAG HE DAG EAR TAB TIG TAIL TICK AGLET DAGGE LABEL TALLY TOUCH AIGLET EARTAB EARTAG FOLLOW SWATCH TAGGLE TAGRAG TICKET TIGTAG HANGTAG
(— OF A LACE) AGLET AIGLET
(ANGLING —) TOUCH
(ORNAMENTED —S) FANCY
TAGALOG PULAHAN
TAGETES MARIGOLD
TAGRAG SHAGRAG
TAHATH (FATHER OF —) BERED
TAHITI (CAPITAL OF —) PAPEETE
(FORMER NAME OF —) OTAHEITE
(MOUNTAIN IN —) OROHENA
TAHMURATH (BROTHER OF —) YIMA
(FATHER OF —) VIVANGHAO
(SLAYER OF —) AHRIMAN
TAHR KRAS JHARAL
TAHSILDAR TALUKDAR
TAI LI AHOM SHAM THAI PORGY KHAMTI
TAIGA URMAN
TAIL BOB BUN CUE BUNT BUSH CLUB FLAG POLE SCUT BRUSH CAUDA SNAKE START STERN TRAIN TWIST FLIGHT FOLLOW RUMPLE SHADOW SWITCH TAILET TAILLE FANTAIL FOXTAIL RATTAIL
(— OF ARTIFICIAL FLY) TOPPING
(— OF BEAST) QUEUE
(— OF BELL CLAPPER) FLIGHT
(— OF BIRD) FAN
(— OF BIRD OR ANIMAL) CUE POLE START
(— OF BOAR) WREATH
(— OF CART) ARSE
(— OF COAT) DOCK
(— OF COMET) BEARD STREAM STREAMER CHEVELURE
(— OF DEER) FLAG SINGLE SHINGLE
(— OF DOG) FLAG STERN
(— OF FISH) UROSOME
(— OF FLY) WHISK
(— OF FOX) BUSH BRUSH FOXTAIL
(— OF HARE OR RABBIT) BUN FUD BUNT SCUT
(— OF HOOD) LIRIPIPE LIRIPOOP
(— OF HORSE) BOB
(— OF MAN'S TIED HAIR) CLUB
(— OF METEOR) TRAIN
(— OF MUSICAL NOTE) QUEUE
(— OF PUG DOG) TWIST
(— OF SQUIRREL) BUN
(— OF STANZA) CODA
(DRAGON'S —) KETU
(STUMP OF —) STRUNT
(TIP OF —) TAG
(PREF.) CAUD(I)(O) CERC(O) ONCHO UR(O)
(SUFF.) CERCAL CERCY URA URE UROUS URUS
TAILBAND FOOTBAND
TAILBOARD ENDGATE ENDBOARD ENDPIECE
TAILED CAUDATE CAUDATED
(PREF.) UR(O)
(SUFF.) URA URE UROUS URUS
TAILING CHAT
(PL.) SAND TAIL GRUFFS
TAILLE TALLY
TAILLESS ACAUDAL ANUROUS ACAUDATE ECAUDATE
TAILOR SLOP SNIP BUILD DARZI GORER SHRED CUTTER DARZEE FULLER SARTOR SNYDER STITCH BOTCHER CABBAGE SNIPPER TIREMAN CLOTHIER SEAMSTER SEMPSTER SHEPSTER
(ITINERANT —) CARDOOER
TAILORBIRD DARZEE
TAILPIECE QUEUE ANQUERA
TAILRACE AFTERBAY
TAILSPIN FLICKER NOSEDIVE
TAILSTOCK DEADHEAD

TAINO HAITIAN
(— BELIEFS) ZEMIISM
TAINT HAUL HOGO MOIL SMUT SPOT VICE CLOUD STAIN TOUCH DARKEN INFECT REMORD SMIRCH SMUTCH ATTAINT BLEMISH CORRUPT DEBAUCH ENVENOM FLYBLOW FORRUMP POLLUTE TARNISH VITIATE EMPOISON TAINTURE CONTAMINATE
TAINTED BAD OFF GAMY HIGH BLOWN PINDY SAPPY TAINT WEMMY RANCID ROTTEN SINFUL SMUTTY CORRUPT FOUGHTY FLYBLOWN
TAIWAN (CAPITAL OF —) TAIPEI
(ISLAND GROUP OF —) MATSU PENGHU QUEMOY
(MOUNTAIN IN —) TZUKAO YUSHAN HSINKAO
(OTHER NAME OF —) FORMOSA
(RIVER IN —) WUCHI TACHIA CHOSHUI HUALIEN TANSHUI
(TOWN IN —) CHIAL TAINAN TAIPEI CHILUNG KEELUNG PINGTUNG TAICHUNG

TAJIKISTAN (ALSO SEE RUSSIA)
CAPITAL: DUSHANBE STALINABAD
COIN: RUBLE
LAKE: SAREZ KARAKUL ISKANDERKUL
MOUNTAIN: LENIN COMMUNISM
MOUNTAIN RANGE: KURAMA MOGOLTAU TIENSHAN PAMIRALAY TURKESTAN ZERAVSHAN GISSARALAY
NAME: TAJIK TADZHIK TOJIKISTON TADZHIKISTAN
RIVER: PANJ MURGAB VAKHSH AMUDARYA SYRDARYA KAFIRNIGAN
TOWN: NUREK REGAR KHOROG KULYAB KHUDZAND URATUYBE KAYRAKKUM KHUDZHAND LENINABAD TURSUNZADE
VALLEY: PANJ GISSAR HISSAR VAKHSH FERGANA OBIKIIK PYANDZH YAVANSU KAFIRNIGAN KAFIRNIHAN

TAJIN TOTONAC
TAJ MAHAL (SITE OF —) AGRA
TAKE COP HIT NIM NIP NOB BEAR BONE DRAW FANG GLOM HAVE LEAD TACK TEEM TOLL ADOPT AFONG BRING CARRY CATCH CREEL FETCH GRASP GRIPE LATCH SEIZE SNAKE ACCEPT CLUTCH COTTON DERIVE EXTEND FERRET FINGER RECIPE SNATCH TAKING ATTRACT CABBAGE CAPTURE RECEIVE UNPURSE UNDERNIM
(— A BATH) TOSH
(— A CERTAIN POSITION) SIT
(— ACROSS) TRAJECT
(— ACTION) ACT
(— A DIRECTION) STEER
(— A DRINK) PULL SMILE
(— ADVANTAGE) DO ABUSE BLUDGE CLUTCH EXPLOIT
(— AFTER) BRAID FOLLOW
(— AIM) BEAD
(— A LITTLE) DELIBATE
(— A NAP) DOSS
(— APART) UNRIG
(— ASIDE) SINGLE
(— AS ONE'S OWN) ADOPT
(— A STAND) ASSERT
(— AWAY) BATE EASE HENT LIFT TOLL WISP ADEEM BENIM BLEED HEAVE REAVE STEAL ABDUCT CONVEY DEDUCE DEDUCT DEMISE DEPOSE DEVEST DIVEST ELOIGN EXEMPT REMOVE UNVEST ABJUDGE BEREAVE DEPRIVE DETRACT FORTAKE RETRACT SUBDUCE SUBLATE ABSTRACT DEROGATE DIMINISH SUBTRACT
(— BACK) RECALL RECANT RECOUP REGAIN REVOKE RETRACT RECAPTURE
(— BACK TO ONESELF) RESUME
(— BY ASSAULT) STORM
(— BY FORCE) SPOIL
(— BY FRAUD) BOB
(— BY LEVY) ESTREAT
(— BY STEALTH) HOOK SNITCH
(— BY STORM) EXPUGN INVADE SURPRISE
(— CARE) FIX SEE GARE KEEP MIND TEND WARD YEME NURSE BEWARE GOVERN INTEND CUIDADO HUSBAND CHAPERON
(— CENSUS OF) MUSTER
(— CHANCE) DICE RISK
(— CHARGE) ATTEND
(— CHARGE OF) CURE SOLICIT
(— COVER) COOK
(— DAMAGE) BANGE
(— DINNER) DINE
(— DOWN) STOOP STRIKE
(— DRUGS ORALLY) POP
(— EXCEPTION) DEMUR STRAIN
(— FIRE) SPUNK
(— FOOD) EAT DINE GRUB
(— FORCIBLY) USURP
(— FOR GRANTED) BEG ASSUME PRESUME
(— FORM) FORM INFORM
(— FOR ONESELF) CAB
(— FOR RESALE) FLOG
(— FRAUDULENTLY) STEAL STRIKE
(— FRIGHT) BOOGER
(— FROM) DETRACT
(— FROM DEPOSIT) DRAW
(— GOLFING STANCE) ADDRESS
(— GREAT DELIGHT) REVEL
(— HEART) BRACE
(— HEED) RECK TENT
(— HOLD) GET BITE GRAB PINCH SEIZE ARREST BEGRIPE
(— HOLIDAY) LAKE
(— IN) IN EAT SUP BITE HOAX KEEP DOWSE DRINK ABSORB DEVOUR ENFOLD GATHER HARBOR INCEPT INGEST INSORB INSUME INTAKE MUZZLE BEGRIPE EMBRACE INCLUDE
(— IN BY LEAKING) LADE
(— IN LIVESTOCK) AGIST
(— IN SAIL) BRAIL
(— INTO HANDS) TOUCH EMBRACE
(— LEGALLY) ATTACH
(— LEVEL OF) BONE
(— LUNCH) TIFFIN
(— MEALS) BOARD
(— NOTE OF) NB COUNT SMOKE NOTICE WITNESS
(— OATH) ABJURE
(— OFF) OFF ROB DOFF EXIT LIFT VAIL DOUSE SHUCK STRIP DEDUCT
(— OFFENSE) DORT HUFF
(— ON) HIRE ADOPT MOUNT START
(— ONE'S LEAVE) CONGEE
(— ONESELF) BETAKE
(— OUT) DELE KILL EXCERPT AIRBRUSH
(— OUT OF EARTH) EXTER
(— OVER) ABSORB SUBSUME
(— PAINS) BOTHER
(— PART) LEAD FIGHT ENGAGE
(— PLACE) BE DO GO COME GIVE PASS ARISE BEFALL HAPPEN
(— PLEASURE IN) ENJOY ADMIRE
(— PORTION OF) PARTAKE
(— POSITION) STAND
(— POSSESSION) GRIP ANNEX BESET SEIZE SPOIL EXTEND CONQUER INHERIT DISTRAIN
(— REFUGE) HIDE SOIL EVADE HAVEN WATCH
(— ROOT) MARE MORE ENROOT STRIKE
(— SHAPE) JELL
(— SHELTER) HOWF NESTLE SHROUD
(— SUPPER) SUP
(— THE PLACE OF) ENSUE SECOND SUPPLY DISPLACE SUPPLANT
(— THOUGHT) ADVISE
(— TO BE TRUE WITHOUT PROOF) PRESUME
(— TO TASK) JACK CARPET CHAPTER
(— TO WING) FLUSH
(— UNAWARE) DECEIVE
(— UP) SORB ENTER MOUNT ADSORB ASSUME GATHER HANDLE STRIKE ELEVATE
(— UP AGAIN) RESUME
(— UP WITH) ALL
(— WELL OR ILL) RESENT
(— WIND ON OPPOSITE QUARTER) JIBE
TAKEN TON TAIN
(— ABACK) BLANK
(— AWAY) ADEMPT
(— OUT) EXEMPT
TAKEOFF JATO VTOL SPOOF SENDUP SCRAMBLE
(PREPARE FOR —) STRAPIN
TAKEOUT STACK
(FOR —) TOGO
TAKER PERNOR
TAKING HOT TAKY CAPTION ADOPTION PERNANCY PREEMPTION
(— A VOTE) DIVISION
(— BACK) RECAPTION
(— EVERYTHING INTO ACCOUNT) OVERALL
(— LIBERTIES) PRESUMPTUOUS
(— OF LIFE) BLOOD
(— PLACE) AGATE
(— POSSESSION) ENTRY
(PREF.) **(— IN)** END(O)
(SUFF.) LEPSIA LEPSIS LEPSY LEPT(IC)
TALAK AHSAN
TALARI PATACA PATACOON
TALAUS (FATHER OF —) BIAS
(MOTHER OF —) PERO
(SON OF —) ADRASTUS
(WIFE OF —) LYSIMACHE
TALC SPAAD TALCUM AGALITE STEATITE SOAPSTONE
TALE SAW DIDO JEST LEED REDE TELL BOURD CONTE CRACK FABLE RECIT SPELL SPOKE STORY WINDY AITION FABULA LEGEND PISTLE PURANA FABLIAU FICTION HISTORY MARCHEN ROMANCE WHOPPER ANECDOTE FOLKTALE SPELLING TREATISE
(— OF ACHIEVEMENTS) GEST GESTE
(— OF ADVENTURE) CONTE
(— OF CHIVALRY) ROMAN ROMANCE
(— OF FATE) WEIRD
(— OF FOUR) WARP
(— OF GOLD COAST NEGROS) NANCY
(— OF GRIEF) JEREMIAD
(— OF TERROR) HAIRRAISER
(COMIC COARSE —) FABLIAU
(DEVISED —) AITION
(EPIC —) TAIN
(FALSE —) BAM VANITY SLANDER
(FATEFUL —) WEIRD
(FOLK —) NANCY THRENE
(FOLK —S) LORE
(HUMOROUS —S) FACETIAE
(ICELANDIC —) SAGA
(MEDIEVAL —) LAI
(MERRY —) BOURD
(METRICAL —) FABLIAU
(PITIFUL —) SOBSTORY
(POETIC NARRATIVE —) SAGA
(SENSATIONAL —) BLOOD SHOCKER
(SHORT —) LAI CONTE
(PREF.) STORIO
TALEBEARER BUZZER GOSSIP TATTLER TALEPYET TELLTALE
TALEBEARING TALEWISE
TALENT GIFT HEAD NOUS VEIN DOWER DOWRY VERVE CICHAR GENIUS ABILITY CHARISM FACULTY CAPACITY CHARISMA
TALENTED ABLE CLEVER GIFTED
TALE OF TWO CITIES (AUTHOR OF —) DICKENS
(CHARACTER IN —) JOHN JERRY LORRY LUCIE PROSS BARSAD CARTON DARNAY JARVIS SYDNEY CHARLES DEFARGE GASPARD MANETTE STRYVER CRUNCHER EVREMONDE
TALER ORT THALER
TALES OF HOFFMANN
(CHARACTER IN —) ANDRES LUTHER STELLA ANTONIA CRESPEL LINDORF MIRACLE OLYMPIA HOFFMANN SCHLEMIL COPPELIUS GIULIETTA NICALUSSE DAPERTUTTO SPALANZANI PITICHINACCHIO
(COMPOSER OF —) OFFENBACH
TALIPES CLUBFOOT
TALISMAN ANGLE CHARM IMAGE OBEAH SAFFI AMULET GRIGRI

SAPHIE SCARAB TELESM ICHTHUS ICHTHYS GREEGREE
(AUTHOR OF —) SCOTT
(CHARACTER IN —) DAVID EDITH PHILIP KENNETH RICHARD SALADIN BERENGARIA MONTFERRAT PLANTAGENET
TALK GAB GAS JAW JIB RAP SAW SAY YAP BLAT BUCK BUKH CANT CARP CHAT CHIN GAFF GIVE GUFF KNAP MEAN TALE TOVE WORD CRACK FABLE MOUTH PARLE PITCH SPEAK SPELL SPIEL SPOKE TUTEL COMMON GAMMON INDABA KORERO PATTER SERMON SPEECH STEVEN TONGUE YABBER ADDRESS CHINWAG DISCUSS JAWBONE LIPWORK PALABRA PALAVER PARRALL PURPOSE WINDJAM CAUSERIE COLLOQUY CONVERSE LANGUAGE PARLANCE QUESTION SCUTTLEBUTT
(— ABOUT) HASH
(— AT LENGTH) RUNON
(— BACK) SASS
(— BIG) SWANK BOUNCE
(— BOASTFULLY) GAS BLATTER
(— BOMBASTICALLY) BEMOUTH
(— CASUALLY) DISH
(— CONFIDENTIALLY) CUTTER
(— CONFUSEDLY) HOTTER
(— DELIRIOUSLY) RAVE
(— DISMALLY) CROAK
(— DRUNKENLY) SLUR
(— EMPTILY) BLOW
(— EXTRAVAGANTLY) ROMANCE
(— FAMILIARLY) TOVE CONFAB
(— FATUOUSLY) BABBLE
(— FONDLY) COO
(— FOOLISHLY) YAK BLAT FLAP YACK HAVER BABBLE DRIVEL FOOTER FOOTLE GABBLE GIBBER SAWNEY TOOTLE BLATHER BLETHER
(— GLIBLY) PATTER SCREED
(— IDLY) GAB GAS BLAB CHAT CHIN GASH YACK FABLE GABBLE JANGLE RABBIT TATTLE CHATTER GNATTER PRATTLE
(— IMPUDENTLY) SASS
(— INACCURATELY) BLAGUE
(— INARTICULATELY) CHUNNER CHUNTER
(— INCESSANTLY) YANK BURBLE RABBIT WAFFLE CHATTER
(— INCOHERENTLY) BABBLE BURBLE HOTTER MITHER MOIDER
(— INCONSIDERATELY) BLAT
(— INDECISIVELY) WAFFLE
(— INFORMALLY) HOBNOB
(— INSOLENTLY) SNASH
(— INTENDED TO DECEIVE) GAMMON PALAVER
(— IRRATIONALLY) RAVE
(— JARGON) JIVE
(— MONOTONOUSLY) DRONE
(— NEEDLESSLY) PALAVER
(— NOISILY) CLAP BLATTER BRABBLE
(— NONSENSE) GAS ROT BLEAT DROOL FUDGE HAVER
(— OFFICIOUSLY) BLEEZE
(— PEEVISHLY) WITTER
(— PERTLY) CHELP
(— PRIVATELY) COLLOGUE
(— RAPIDLY) GABBLE JABBER GNATTER
(— SCANDAL) HORN
(— SNAPPISHLY) KNAP
(— SPORTIVELY) DAFF
(— SUPERFICIALLY) SMATTER
(— TEDIOUSLY) DINGDONG
(— THOUGHTLESSLY) BLAB
(— TOGETHER) DEVISE
(— VAGUELY) WOOZLE
(— VOLUBLY) CHIN PATTER
(— WEAKLY) DRIVEL
(— WITH) CONTACT
(— WITHOUT MEANING) GABBLE
(— WITTILY) SCINTILLATE
(ABSURD —) BOSH
(ABUSIVE —) HOKER JAWING
(ARROGANT —) GUM BRAG
(BACK —) LIP SASS
(BAWDY —) SCULDUDDRY SCULDUDDERY SKULDUDDERY
(BOASTFUL —) BULL GAFF
(BOMBASTIC —) FLASH
(COMMON —) FAME FABLE NOISE HEARSAY
(CONCEITED —) BLAGUE
(CONTINUAL —) CLACK
(COUNTRY —) CLASH
(DECEPTIVE —) GAMMON
(DIFFUSE —) POTTER
(DRIVELLING —) MAUNDERING
(EMPTY —) GAS BOSH GASH FRASE GLOZE FRAISE BLAFLUM GASSING PRATTLE BALLYHOO GALBANUM MOONSHINE POPPYCOCK PRITTLEPRATTLE
(ENTHUSIASTIC —) JAZZ
(EVASIVE —) FLANNEL
(FALSE —) BALLYHOO
(FAMILIAR —) CONFAB CHITCHAT
(FANTASTIC —) GUYVER
(FLATTERING —) FLANNEL
(FLIP —) SASS
(FOOLISH —) GUP GAFF JIVE BLEAT CLACK FABLE BLETHERS COBBLERS
(FORMAL —) ADDRESS
(FRESH —) LIP
(FRIVOLOUS —) PERSIFLAGE
(FUSSY —) PHRASE
(GENERAL —) RUMOR REPORT RUMOUR
(GLIB —) JIVE
(IDLE —) GAB YAK BLAB BUFF CHAT GAFF GEST GUFF YACK FABLE GESTE BABBLE CLAVER GOSSIP JANGLE CHATTER CLATTER PALAVER TWATTLE BABBLING BATTOLOGY BALDERDASH BIBBLEBABBLE
(IMPUDENT —) PRATE SLACK
(INCOHERENT —) GABBER JABBER
(INFORMAL —) CAUSERIE
(INSINCERE —) JAZZ CROCK BUNKUM MALARKEY
(JESTING —) CHAFF JAPERY
(LIGHT —) TRIFLING
(MEANINGLESS —) SLIPSLOP
(NONSENSICAL —) BLABBER BLATHER FOLDEROL
(ORDINARY —) PROSE
(PIOUS OR SANCTIMONIOUS —) PI
(PUBLIC —) NOISE
(RAPID —) GABBLE JABBER CHATTER CLATTER
(SALES —) PITCH
(SCOLDING —) HARANGUE
(SENSELESS —) TWADDLE
(SILLY —) BLAH BUFF CLART CACKLE FOOTLE TWADDLE
(SMALL —) CHAT BACKCHAT CHITCHAT
(SMOOTH —) GLOZE BLARNEY
(STUPID —) MOROLOGY
(TRIFLING —) PRATTLE CHITCHAT
(UNRESTRAINED —) JAWING
(USELESS —) WASTE
(VIOLENT —) BLUSTER
(WEAK —) SLIPSLOP
(WHINING —) BLEAT
(WILD —) RANT
(WORTHLESS —) PIFFLE
(SUFF.) LALIA LOG(ER)(IA)(IAN)(IC)(ICAL)(IST)(UE)(Y)
TALKATIVE COSY GASH GLIB NAWY BUZZY GABBY TALKY CHATTY CLASHY CRACKY FLUENT FUTILE SOCIAL VOLUBLE BIGMOUTH FLIPPANT TELLSOME LOQUACIOUS
TALKATIVENESS FUTILITY
TALKER YENTA CAMPER POTGUN CAUSEUR SPIELER
(IDLE —) WHIFFLER
(NOISY —) BLELLUM
(PROFESSIONAL —) JAWSMITH
(SENSELESS —) RATTLE
TALKING (IDLE —) GASSING
(LOUD —) NORATION
TALKING-TO EARFUL LECTURE
TALKY GABBY
TALL HIGH LANKY LOFTY RANGY STEEP WANDY CRANEY PROCERE
(— AND FEEBLE) TANGLE
(VERY —) TAUNT
TALLAGE CUTTING
TALLER DOMINANT
TALLNESS PROCERITY
TALLOW SUET SEVUM ARMING TAULCH CHERVICE
(PREF.) SEBI SEBO STEAR(O) STEAT(O)
(SUFF.) STEARIN
TALLY TAB JUMP NICK SUIT AGREE CHECK COUNT SCORE STICK STOCK CENSUS STRING SWATCH TAILYE COMPORT TAILZIE
TALMAI (FATHER OF —) AMMIHUD
TALMUD GEMARA
TALON FANG SERE UNCE CLUTCH POUNCE UNGUIS WEAPON
(— OF TOOTH) HEEL
TALONID HEEL
TALPA TESTUDO
TALTHIB GLAGA GLAGAH
TALUS SCREE RUBBLE ASTRAGAL
TAMANDUA ANTEATER
TAMAR (AUTHOR OF —) JEFFERS
(CHARACTER IN —) LEE WILL DAVID JINNY TAMAR STELLA ANDREWS MORELAND CAULDWELL
(FATHER OF —) DAVID ABSALOM
(HUSBAND OF —) ER ONAN
(MOTHER OF —) MAACHAH
(SON OF —) ZARAH PHAREZ
TAMARACK LARCH LARIX EPINETTE
TAMARIN PINCHE JACCHUS LEONCITO MARIKINA MARMOSET
TAMARIND SAMPALOC
TAMARISK ATLE JHOW HEATH MYRICA
TAMASHEK TUAREG
TAMBOURINE RIKK TAAR DAIRA TAMBO TABOUR TIMBER TABORIN TIMBREL
(PART OF —) HEAD TACK SHELL JINGLE
TAMBURLAINE THE GREAT
(AUTHOR OF —) MARLOWE
(CHARACTER IN —) ALMEDA AMYRAS COSROE ZABINA MEANDER MYCETES ORCANES BAJAZETH CALYPHAS MENAPHON CALLAPINE CELEBINUS SIGISMUND TECHELLES ZENOCRATE THERIDAMAS USUMCASANE TAMBURLAINE
TAME MAN CADE DEAD MEEK MILD PACK ACCOY ATAME BREAK DAUNT MILKY SPAKE CADISH ENTAME GENTLE INWARD MEEKEN UNWIFE AFFAITE AMENAGE CORRECT INSIPID SUBDUED CICURATE DOMESTIC MANSUETE
(— FALCON) MAN RECLAIM
TAMED BROKE GENTLE
TAMENESS MANSUETUDE
TAMER (HORSE —) HIPPODAMIST
TAMIL VELLALA
TAMING OF THE SHREW (AUTHOR OF —) SHAKESPEARE
(CHARACTER IN —) SLY BIANCA CURTIS GREMIO GRUMIO TRANIO BAPTISTA LUCENTIO BIONDELLO HORTENSIO KATHARINA PETRUCHIO VINCENTIO CHRISTOPHER
TAMMUZ (FATHER OF —) NINGISHZIDA
TAMMY TAMIS STAMIN
TAMONEA MICONIA
TAM-O-SHANTER TAM TAMMY
TAMP PUG STEM
TAMPER FIX COOK FAKE FOOL GAFF TOUCH DABBLE FIDDLE MEDDLE MONKEY POTTER PUDDLE PUTTER TEMPER FALSIFY TRINKLE
(— WITH HORSE'S TEETH) BISHOP
TAMPION TOMKIN TAMPOON
TAM-TAM GONG
TAN FAN ARAB BARK ADUST ASCOT DRESS TANKA TAWNY ORIOLE COCONUT EMBROWN LEATHER SUNBURN
(BEACH —) SEDGE
(TROTTEUR —) BAY
(PREF.) TANN(I)(O)
TANACETYL THUJYL
TANAGER YENI LINDO REDBIRD WARBIRD CARDINAL EUPHONIA FIREBIRD ORGANIST
TANBARK BARK TAWN AVARAM TURWAR ALGERIAN ALGERINE
TANCRED (FATHER OF —) OTHO
(LOVER OF —) ERMINIA CLORINDA
(MOTHER OF —) EMMA
TANDAN EELFISH
TANEKAHA TOATOA
TANG NIP BITE FANG ODOR TING VEIN SHANK STING STRAP TASTE

TWANG RELISH TANGLE TONGUE SEATANG FAREWELL
TANGELO UGLI
TANGENCY CONTACT
TANGENT SLOPE
TANGERINE NAARTJE MANDARIN
TANGIBLE ACTUAL TACTILE CONCRETE MATERIAL PALPABLE
TANGIER (NATIVE OF —) TANGERINE
TANGLE COT ELF ORE TAT FANK FOUL HARL SHAG TAUT HARLE KNURL SKEIN SNARL SNIRL THRUM TWINE WOPSE BALTER BURBLE ENTRAP FANKLE HANGER JUNGLE MOMBLE MUCKER RAFFLE SLEAVE TAFFLE TARDLE TAUGHT TEIHTE BRANGLE TAISSLE THICKET FURBELOW SCROBBLE
(PL.) COBWEB
TANGLED AFOUL TOUSY MESHED SNARLY TAUTED IMPLICIT INTORTED INVOLVED CESPITOSE
(— UP) HAYWIRE
TANGLEHEAD PILI
TANGUE TENREC
TANGY BRISK
TANHA TRISHNA
TANK DAM DIP TAL VAT BOSH SUMP BASIN MIXER STANK STEEP TRUNK BLOWUP BOILER HOPPER PANZER TROUGH BATTERY BLOWPIT BREAKER CISTERN FLUSHER PISCINA PLUNGER POACHER SETTLER STEEPER BLEACHER DIGESTOR LANDSHIP SUBSIDER
(— FOR DYE OR SOAP) BECK
(— FOR FISH) STEW TRUNK PISCINA AQUARIUM STEWPOND
(— IN SHIP) FOREPEAK
(— ON CANOE) SPONSON
(ARMORED —) FLAIL PANZER WHIPPET LANDSHIP
(KIND OF —) DRUNK SCUBA THINK SEPTIC
(PAPER MANUFACTURING —) POACHER
(PHOTOGRAPHIC —) CUVETTE
(POTTER'S —) PLUNGER
(RECTANGULAR —) BOWLY
(SALT MANUFACTURING —) GRAINER
(SPEEDY —) WHIPPET
(STORAGE —) CHEST
(SUGAR REFINING —) TIGER BLOWUP
(TANNING —) FLOATER
(PL.) HEAVIES
(PREF.) LACO
TANKAGE AMMONATE
TANKARD GUN MUG JACK FACER STOOP STOUP PEWTER POTTLE TANKER GODDARD
TANKER ULCC VLCC BOWSER
(CRUDE-OIL —) ULCC
TANNED BROWN RUDDY TAWNY REECHY BRONZED
(NOT —) RAW
TANNER EGGER SAMAR BARKER STAKER PERCHER
TANNHAUSER (CHARACTER IN —) VENUS HERMANN WOLFRAM ELISABETH TANNHAUSER
(COMPOSER OF —) WAGNER
TANNING PASTING
(— SOLUTION) PLUMPER
TANSY COSTMARY
TANSY MUSTARD FLIXWEED FLUXWEED
TANSY RAGWORT RAGWEED
TANTALIZE GRIG JADE MOCK TEASE HARASS
TANTALUS (— CAPTIVE) IXION
(DAUGHTER OF —) NIOBE
(FATHER OF —) AMPHION JUPITER THYESTES
(MOTHER OF —) NIOBE PLUTO
(SON OF —) PELOPS
(WIFE OF —) DIONE CLYTIA EUPRYTO TAYGETE
TANTAMOUNT SAME
TANTARA BLARE
TANTRA AGAMA
TANTRUM SNIT HISSY SCENE TIRADE TIRRIVEE WINGDING

TANZANIA
CAPITAL: DARESSALAAM
COIN: SENTI SHILINGI
ISLAND: MAFIA PEMBA ZANZIBAR
LAKE: RUKWA
NATIVE: BANTU SUKUMA MAKONDE SWAHILI
REGION: MARA MBEYA PEMBA PWANI TANGA MWANZA RUVUMA TABORA SINGIDA
RIVER: RUVU WAMI RUAHA KAGERA RUFIJI RUVUMA PANGANI MBENKURU
TOWN: WETE KILWA MBEYA MOSHI TANGA ARUSHA DODOMA IRINGA KIGOMA MTWARA MWANZA TABORA MTAWARA MOROGORO ZANZIBAR
VOLCANO: KIBO KILIMANJARO
WATERFALL: KALAMBO
WEIGHT: FARSALAH

TAO MAN PEASANT
(— PRACTICE) WUWEI
TAP BOB DAB PAT TAT TIP TIT TOP BEAT COCK DRUB FLIP JOWL PENK TICK TIRL TUCK TUNK APPEL FLIRT QUILL SNOCK START TOUCH ALETAP BROACH CANNEL DABBLE FAUCET NATTLE SPIGOT TAPLET BIBCOCK BLENDER DRAWOFF HEELTAP PERCUSS
(— A CASK) QUILL STRIKE
(— A DRUM) TUCK
(— FOR A LOAN) TIG
(— ON SHOE) CLUMP UNDERLAY
(— ON THE SHOULDER) FOB
(— REPEATEDLY) DRUM
(— THE GROUND) BEAT
(FENCING —) BEAT
(MASTER —) HOB HUB
(SMART — OF THE FOOT) APPEL
TAPA KAPA SIAPO KIKEPA
TAPACOLO TURCO
TAPE LEAR FERRET GARTER SCOTCH TAPERY YNKELL BINDING MEASURE TAPELINE TELETAPE
(— CARTRIDGE) CASSETTE
(DEMONSTRATION —) DEMO
(FISH —) SNAKE
(KIND OF —) DUCT REELTOREEL
(LAMP —) WICK
(LINEN —) INKLE
(METALLIC —) GALLOON
(NARROW —) TASTE
(PUT ON —) RECORD
(RED —) WIGGERY
(TV —) VIDEO
TAPE GRASS EELGRASS
TAPEMAN CHAINMAN
TAPER DRAW RISE RUSH DRAFT GAUDY PINCH SCARF SNAPE SWAGE CIERGE DRAUGHT LIGHTER PRICKET SHAMMES TRINDLE DIMINISH ACUMINATE
(— OF A SPRING) DRAW
(— OFF) CEASE TONGUE
(— OF PATTERN) STRIP
TAPERED BARRELED BOATTAIL GRADUATED
(SLIGHTLY —) TERETE
TAPERING SHARP SPIRY SPIRAL SPIRED TERETE SPIRING FUSIFORM SUBULATE ATTENUATE
TAPER ROD PODGER
TAPESTRY ARRAS TAPET TAPIS COSTER DORSER DOSSER CEILING GOBELIN HANGING SUSANEE VERDURE AUBUSSON MORTLAKE
TAPEWORM TAPE LIGULA TAENIA CESTODE CESTOID COENURE HYDATID PLATODE BANDWORM COENURUS DAVAINEA FLATWORM HELMINTH STROBILA
(— LARVA) MEASLE
(PL.) CYSTICA
(PREF.) TAENI(A)(O)
TAPHATH (FATHER OF —) SOLOMON
TAPHOLE TAP FLOSS MOUTH
TAPIOCA CASSAVA
TAPIR ANTA KUDA DANTA TENNU TAPIROID
TAPPED ABROACH
TAPPET CAM WIPER
TAPROOM TAP SALOON BARROOM BUVETTE TAPHOUSE
TAPSTER NICKPOT SKINKER
TAPUYAN GE GES GHES BUGRE GESAN JUYAS CAYAPO GOYANA CAMACAN CARAHOS COROADO TIMBIRA APINAGES BOTOCUDO CAINGANG CHAVANTE
TAR PAY BREA LIMEY BINDER SAILOR SEADOG ALKITRAN CREOSOTE
(BIRCH —) DAGGETT
(MINERAL —) MALTHA
TARA DOLMA
TARADIDDLE LIE
TARANTULA HUNTER JAYHAWK MYGALID
TARAS BULBA (AUTHOR OF —) GOGOL
(CHARACTER IN —) BULBA OSTAP TARAS ANDRII YANKEL KIRDYAGA
TARBOOSH FEZ
TARDIGRADA ARCTISCA
TARDILY SLOWLY
TARDINESS SLOTH TARDITY
TARDY LAG LAX DREE LATE SLOW SLACK DREIGH LAGGED REMISS LAGGING OVERDUE DILATORY LATESOME
TARE TINE VETCH LEAKAGE
(PL.) FILTH
TAREA (FATHER OF —) MICAH
TARES ZIZANY
TARGE BUCKLER
TARGET AIM MOT BUTT MARK WAND CLOUT LEVEL PRICK ROVER SCOOP SCOPE TARGE WHITE BANNER NIVEAU OBJECT SLEEVE COCKSHY INCOMER OUTGOER SARACEN POPINJAY
(— OF KNEELING FIGURE) SQUAW
(— OF LEVELING STAFF) VANE
(— OF RIDICULE) GAME
(— RING) SOUS
(EASY —) SITTER
(PIECE OF —) SCAB
(RAILROAD SWITCH —) BANNER
(STRIKE A —) KEYHOLE
(THROWN —) COCKSHY COCKSHUT
(TOWED —) DROGUE
(UNIDENTIFIED —) SKUNK
TARHEEL STATE NORTHCAROLINA
TARIFF ZABETA AVERAGE TRIBUTE
TARNISH DIM BLOT SMIT SOIL CLOUD DIRTY STAIN SULLY TACHE TAINT BREATH DARKEN DEFILE INJURE SMIRCH ASPERSE BEGRIME BESMEAR BLEMISH OBSCURE BESMIRCH DISCOLOR
TARO COCO DALO EDDO GABE KALO MASI TALO COCCO KAROU TANIA TANYA COCKER TARROW YAUTIA COCOYAM DASHEEN MALANGA COCOROOT EDDYROOT
(— PROODUCT) POI
TAROT NAIB TAROCCO
TARPON SABALO
TARRAGON TARCHON ESTRAGON
TARRY BIDE LENG STAY STOP ABIDE DALLY DEMUR PAUSE ARREST LINGER PITCHY REMAIN SOJOURN
TARSIER LEMUR MALMAG
TARSOMETATARSUS SHANK
TARSUS HAND ANKLE DIGITAL
(BIRD'S —) SHANK
TART ACID FLAN SOUR ACERB BOWLA CUPID EAGER SHARP SNIPPY SUNKET PIQUANT POLYNEE PUNGENT SUBACID TARTLET TURNOVER
TARTAN PLAID
(— PATTERN) SETT
TARTAR ARGAL ARGOL CALCULUS
TARTARIN OF TARASCON
(AUTHOR OF —) DAUDET
(CHARACTER IN —) BAIA BRAVIDA GREGORY BEZUQUET TARTARIN BARBASSOU
TARTNESS ACRITY ACIDITY VERDURE ACERBITY ASPERITY VERJUICE
TARTUFFE (AUTHOR OF —) MOLIERE
(CHARACTER IN —) ARGAS DAMIS ORGON DORINE ELMIRE VALERE CLEANTE MARIANE PERNELLE TARTUFFE
TASHMET (HUSBAND OF —) NEBO
TASK FAG JOB TAX CHAR DARG TOIL CHARE CHORE GRIND KNACK LABOR NULLO STINT CHARGE DEVOIR NIYOGA PENSUM RAMSCH

TOURNE FATIGUE SWEATER TRAVAIL BUSINESS EXERCISE TRAUCHLE
(— AS PSYCHOLOGICAL TEST) AUFGABE
(ASSIGNED —) STENT STINT DEVOIR
(DIFFICULT —) BUGGER
(EASY —) PIPE SNAP SETUP PICNIC CAKEWALK
(EXAMINATION —) QUESTION
(ONEROUS —) CORVEE
(ONE WHO PERFORMS MENIAL —S) DOGSBODY
(ROUTINE —) DRUDGE
TASKMASTER DRIVER TASKER RAWHIDER
(BRUTAL —) LEGREE
TASMANIA (CAPITAL OF —) HOBART
(LAKE IN —) ECHO SORELL
(MOUNTAIN IN —) DROME NEVIS BARRON CRADLE LOMOND HUMBOLDT
(RIVER IN —) ESK HUDN TAMAR GORDON JORDAN PIEMAN DERWENT
(TOWN IN —) BURNIE HOBART
TASMANIAN DEVIL DASYURID
TASMANIAN WOLF HYENA TIGER THYLACINE
TASSEL TAG TUFT LABEL THRUM TARCEL TARGET TOORIE CORDELLE
(PL.) ZIZITH
(PREF.) THYSAN(O)
TASSEL)PL.) TZITZIS TZITZIT
TASTABLE GUSTABLE
TASTE EAT GAB GOO LAP SIP CAST DASH GOUT GUST HINT PREE RASA SALT TANG TEST TINT WAFT ASSAY DRINK FANCY GUSTO HEART PROVE RELES SAPOR SAVOR SHADE SKILL SMACK SNACK SPICE TOOTH TOUCH DEGUST FLAVOR GENIUS LIKING PALATE RELISH SAMPLE SMATCH ATTASTE PREGUST SOUPCON THOUGHT APPETITE JUDGMENT PENCHANT SAPIDITY
(— AFTER SWALLOWING) FINISH
(— COMBINED WITH APTITUDE) FLAIR
(— IN MATTERS OF ART) FANCY
(— OF THE CASK) FUST
(BAD —) GOTHISM
(DECIDED —) PENCHANT
(DELICATE —) BREED
(DISCRIMINATING —) SKILL
(GOOD —) DECORUM ELEGANCE
(OF MIDDLE-CLASS —) POLYESTER
(SLIGHT —) TINCTURE
(SOUR —) FOXINESS
(STRONG —) GOO
(PL.) MERIDIAN
(PREF.) SAPORI
(SUFF.) GEUSIA
TASTEFUL NEAT ELEGANT GUSTOSO
TASTELESS DEAF FLAT FLASH MALMY VAPID WERSH WALLON FATUOUS INSIPID INSULSE WEARISH UNSAVORY GRACELESS
TASTER TRIER
TASTING ASSAY
(— OF MALT) CORNY
TASTY SAPID YUMMY GUSTABLE TASTEFUL PALATABLE DELECTABLE
TA-TA TOODLEOO
TATA BYE CIAO LATER CHEERIO
TATAR KIN JUNG KHAN KITAN SOYOT CHAZAR KHAZAR KHITAN KHOZAR SHORTZY MELETSKI
(PL.) HU
TATER SPUD POTATO
TATOUAY CABASSOU
TATTER JAG RAG TAG SHRED FITTER LIBBET TAGRAG TARGET FLITTER TROLLOP
(PL.) DUDS TAVERS FITTERS RIBBONS TAIVERS FLITTERS
TATTERED DUDDY BEATEN TAGGED FORWORN TATTERY TOTTERED
TATTERSALL WINDOWPANE
TATTING LACE
TATTLE BLAB GASH CHEEP CLASH CLYPE PEACH SNEAK TUTEL GOSSIP QUATCH SNITCH TATTER TITTLE CLATTER
TATTLER LAB CLASH SNIPE FABLER GAMBET GOSSIP TUTLER YELPER STOOLIE TITTLER TELLTALE
TATTLETALE REVEALER
TATTLING LEAKY FUTILE
TATTOO TAT MOKO PINK POUNCE RATAPLAN
TATTOOED PINKED
(— MAN) YUN
TATTOOING MOKO
TAUGHT MAK TEACHED INSTRUCT
(EASILY —) DOCIBLE
TAUNT BOB DIG MOB CHIP GIBE GIRD JAPE JEER JEST MOCK PROG SKIT TWIT CHECK FRUMP GLAIK JAUNT SCOFF SCORN SLANT SLARE SLART DERIDE SNEEST UPCAST SARCASM TWITTER RIDICULE
TAUNTING RAIL SARCASTIC
TAUPE MOLESKIN
TAUROTRAGUS OREAS ORIAS
TA-URT THOUERIS
TAUT SNUG TORT STIFF TENSE TIGHT CORDED
TAUTEN SNUB STIFFEN SWIFTER TENSION
TAUTOG CHUB MOLL LABROID
TAVERN BAR INN BUSH HOWF VENT FONDA MITER MITRE TAMBO BISTRO CABACK KNEIPE BUVETTE CABARET CANTEEN OSTERIA TABERNA GASTHAUS ORDINARY POTHOUSE TAPHOUSE
TAW TER ALLY ALLEY SCORE MARBLE GLASSIE SHOOTER
TAWDRY CHEAP GAUDY NASTY GILDED TINSEL RAFFISH DIMESTORE
TAWNY FUSC BRUSK DUSKY FULVID TANNED FULVOUS JACINTH MUSTELINE
(PREF.) CIRRO FUSCO PYRR(O) PYRRH(O)
TAWNY BROWN TENNE CHAMOIS
TAW-SUG SULU
TAX FET LAY LOT TRY CAST CESS DUTY GELD GELT GILD KAIN LEVY POLL RATE SCAT SCOT SESS TAIL TASK TOLL ABUSE AGIST DONUM FINTA HANSA HANSE LEKIN MAILL OBROK QUINT SCATT STENT TOUST VERGI WATCH ZAKAH ZAKAT ABKARI ASSESS AVANIA BURDEN CEDULA DEMAND EXCISE EXTENT HIDAGE IMPOST JEZIAH KHARAJ MURAGE OCTROI OCTROY PAVAGE PURVEY SENSUS STRAIN SURTAX VINAGE BOOMAGE BOSCAGE CHANCER CHEVAGE CHIVAGE CONDUCT FINANCE GABELLE LASTAGE PATENTE PENSION POLLAGE PONTAGE SCUTAGE STIPEND TAILAGE TERRAGE TOLLAGE TRIBUTE ALCABALA AUXILIUM BONAUGHT CARUCAGE CORNBOLE DANEGELD EXACTION EXERCISE KERNETTY MALTOLTE OBLATION PESHKASH ROMESCOT ROMESHOT STACKAGE SUPERTAX TAXATION WHEELAGE CAPITATION
(— AT HARVESTTIME) CORNBOLE
(— FOR STORING LOGS) BOOMAGE
(— OF ONE-FIFTH) QUINT
(— ON EVERY PLOW) CARUCAGE
(— ON HERRING CATCH) LASTAGE
(— ON LIQUOR) ABKARI
(— ON SALT) GABELLE
(— ON UNBELIEVERS) KHARAJ
(— ON WALLS) MURAGE
(— ON WOOD) BOSCAGE
(— ON WOOL) MALETOTE MALTOLTE
(— TO PETTY PRINCES) KERNETTY
(— TO SYNAGOGUE) FINTA
(— TO TENTH AMOUNT) TITHE
(— UNDULY) STRAIN
(CAPITATION —) JIZYA JIZYAH
(CHINESE —) LEKIN LIKEN LIKIN
(EXCISE —) USERFEE
(EXTRAORDINARY —) AUXILIUM
(FEUDAL —) AID
(IRISH —) BONAGHT
(KIND OF —) SIN
(MOHAMMEDAN —) JEZIAH
(PARISH —) PURVEY
(PHILIPPINES —) CEDULA
(POLL —) TOLL CENSUS
(RUSSIAN —) OBROK
(SPANISH —) ALCABALA ALCAVALA
(TURKISH —) VERGI AVANIA
TAXABLE LISTABLE
TAX COLLECTOR TITHER GABELLER
TAXGATHERER POLLER TAXMAN
TAXI CAB JIXIE CRAWLER
(SMALL —) MINICAB
(THREE-WHEELED —) CYCLO
(3-WHEELED —) CYCLO
TAXICAB CAB HACK CRUISER MOTORCAB
TAXIDERMY NASSOLOGY
TAXING SEVERE GRUELING
TAXON MONERA
TAXONOMIC
(SUFF.)
(— DIVISION) IA
TAXONOMIST LUMPER CLADIST SPLITTER
TAXPAYER FILER
TAYASSU PECARI
TAYGETE (FATHER OF —) ATLAS
(MOTHER OF —) PLEIONE
(SON OF —) EUROTAS LACEDAEMON
TAYRA GALERA
TCHAMBULI CHAMBERI
TEA CHA CHAR CHIA TCHA THAM TSIA ASSAM CAPER CHAIS CONGO FAHAM HYSON MIANG PEKOE STEEP CONGOU KEEMUN OOLONG PTISAN SUNGLO LAPSANG REDROOT TWANKAY AUTUMNAL EARLGREY GOWIDDIE SOUCHONG WORMSEED
(AFRICAN —) CAT KAT QAT KHAT QUAT
(BLACK —) BOHEA CONGO OOPAK CONGOU OOPACK SYCHEE
(COARSE —) BANCHA
(CUP OF —) CUPPA
(GREEN —) TWANKAY
(HIGH-GRADE —) GYOKURO
(INFERIOR —) BOHEA
(KIND OF —) OSWEGO
(MEDICINAL —) TISANE
(MEXICAN —) BASOTE APASOTE
(POOR —) BLASH
(WEAK —) MISERABLE
(PREF.) THEI
TEA BOWL CHAWAN
TEACAKE LUNN SCONE
TEACH ARAL LEAR READ SHOW TECH TENT BREED CARRY COACH EDIFY ENDUE LEARN SPELL TRAIN TUTOR WISSE INFORM PREACH SCHOOL BITECHE EDUCATE EXAMPLE EXPOUND GRAMMAR AMAISTER DISCIPLE DOCUMENT INSTRUCT PUPILIZE
(— TO FIGHT) SPAR
TEACHABLE APT DOCILE DOCIBLE
TEACHABLENESS DOCITY DOSSETY
TEACHER RAB ALIM GURU AKHUN BIDDY CADET GUIDE MOLLA RABBI REBBE TUTOR USHER AKHUND AMAUTA DOCENT DOCTOR DOZENT FATHER MADRIH MAULVI MENTOR MULLAH PANDIT PUNDIT RABBAN READER REGENT RHETOR SUPPLY ACHARYA ALFAQUI DOMINIE MAESTRA MAESTRO MOOLVIE MUNCHEE MURSHID PEDAGOG SHASTRI SOPHIST SPONSOR STARETS TRAINER ALFAQUIN AYUDANTE DIRECTOR EDUCATOR EXTENDER GAMALIEL MAGISTER MELAMMED MISTRESS MOONSHEE MUJTAHID MAHARISHI PEDAGOGUE PRECEPTOR ABECEDARIAN PRIVATDOCENT
(— OF ELOQUENCE) RHETOR
(— OF EMINENCE) MAESTRO
(— OF HIGH LEARNING) SOPHIST
(— OF KORAN) ALFAKI ALFAQUIN
(— OF PAUL) GAMALIEL
(INCA —) AMAUTA
(LANGUAGE —) MUNSHI MOONSHEE
(MOHAMMEDAN —) COJA HODJA KHOJA KHOJAH

(MOSAIC —) SCRIBE
(RELIGIOUS —) STARETS STARETZ
(UNIVERSITY —) SCHOLASTIC
(WALDENSIAN —) GARBE
TEACHING LAW DHARMA DOCENT LESSON LORING ACROAMA TUITION BUDDHISM DIDACTIC DOCTRINE DOCUMENT TUTELAGE
(— ACTIVITY) REALIA
(— OBJECTS) REALIA
(— OF CHRIST) GOSPEL
(PL.) ACOUSMA BROWNISM CACODOXY DIDACTICS
TEAK SAJ DJATI EBONY
TEAKETTLE SUKE SUKEY CHAFER KETTLE POURIE CRESSET
TEAL CRICK BLUEWING GARGANEY SARCELLE
TEAM SET FIVE PLOW SIDE SPAN YOKE DRAFT SWING EQUIPE PLOUGH SEXTET DRAUGHT CARTWARE
(— HARNESSED ONE BEFORE ANOTHER) TANDEM
(— OF CARS) ECURIE
(— OF GLASSWORKERS) SHOP CHAIR
(— OF OXEN) SPAN
(— OF 3 HORSES ABREAST) TROIKA
(— THAT FINISHES LAST) DOORMAT
(— 2 ABREAST, 1 LEADING) SPIKE UNICORN
(ATHLETIC —) CLUB
(BASEBALL —) NINE
(BASKETBALL —) FIVE
(FOOTBALL —) ELEVEN
(2-HORSE —) PODANGER
(3-HORSE —) RANDEM
TEAMSTER CARTER TEAMEO CARTMAN SKINNER TEAMMAN
TEAPOT TRACK TRACKPOT
TEAR HIE RIP RIT RUG TUT CLAW PILL PULL RACE RASE RASH RAVE REND RIVE RUGG SKAG SNAG STUN BREAK CLAUT LARME PEARL RANCH SHARK SLENT SPALT SPLIT SPREE TOUSE CLEAVE HARROW RANCHE RIPPLE SCHISM SCREED WRENCH CHATTER CONVELL DISCIND EYEDROP SCRATCH DISTRAIN FRACTURE LACERATE LACHRYMA TEARDROP
(— APART) REND TEASE DISCERP DIVULSE
(— A STRIP OFF) SCOLD
(— ASUNDER) DIVEL
(— AWAY) AVULSE
(— DOWN) UNPILE DESTROY DEMOLISH
(— IN NEGATIVE) SLUG
(— INTO) LAMBAST LAMBASTE
(— INTO PIECES) DRAW TOLE DEVIL SHRED TEASE LANIATE MAMMOCK
(— INTO SHREDS) HOG DEVIL TATTER
(— OFF) STRIP ABRUPT DISCERP
(— OPEN) PROSCIND
(— TO SHREDS) RIPUP
(— UP BY THE ROOTS) ARACHE
(PL.) DEW BRINE RHEUM EYEWATER
(PREF.) DACRY(O) LACHRYMI LACHRYMO SPARASSO
TEARDROP EYEWATER
TEARFUL SOFT TEARY WEEPY LIQUID WATERY WEEPLY FLEBILE MAUDLIN SHOWERY SNIVELY SNIVELLY
TEARING SCREED
(— AWAY) AVULSION
TEARLESS DRYEYED
TEARPIT CRUMEN LARMIER
TEASE COD FUN MAD RAG RIB ROT TAR TRY TUM VEX BAIT CHIP DRAG FASH FRET GRIG HARE HOCK JADE JIVE JOSH LARK NARK RAZZ RIDE SOOL TARR TOUT TWIT WORK CHAFF CHEEK CHEVY CHIAK CHYAK DEVIL FEEZE RALLY TARIE TAUNT TOOSE WRACK BANTER BOTHER CADDLE CHIVVY HARASS HOORAY HURRAH MOLEST MURDER NEEDLE PESTER PLAGUE HATCHEL NEEDLER TERRIFY TORMENT WHERRET
TEASEL KING TASSEL TEASLE MANWEED
TEASELER GIGGER TEASER
TEASELING MOZING
TEASER COMEON TIZEUR
TEASING CHAFF MERRY BANTER DEVILING QUIZZING
TEAT DUG PAP TIT DIDDY SPEAN NIPPLE SUCKLE
TEA TREE TI MANUKA
TEBAH (FATHER OF —) NAHOR
TEBALIAH (FATHER OF —) HOSAH
TECHIQUE SKILL
TECHNICIAN TECHIE SWITCHER
(MEDICAL —) EMT
TECHNIQUE FEAT GATE WRINKLE COQUILLE INDUSTRY SPICCATO
(BILLIARD —) FOLLOW
(DANCE —) HEELWORK
(DECORATION —) IKAT
(DRAMATIC —) METHOD
(JUMPING —) SCISSORS
(PIANO —) PIANISM
(PLANNING —) PERT
(SOFT —) JUJITSU
(WEAVING —) SPRANG
(WRESTLING —) GLIMA
(WRITING —) CUBISM
(SUFF.) URGE URGIC URGY
TECHNOLOGY FISHERY TECHNIC CERAMICS
TECMESSA (FATHER OF —) TELEUTAS
(HUSBAND OF —) AJAX
(SON OF —) EURYSACES
TECOMIN LAPACHOL
TECTRIX COVERT
TEDDER KICKER
TEDIOUS DEAD DREE DULL LATE LONG POKY PROSY WEARY ALENGE BORING DREECH DREIGH ELENGE MORTAL PROLIX STODGY IRKSOME OPEROSE PREACHY PROSAIC VERBOSE BORESOME DRAGGING TIRESOME WEARIFUL
TEDIUM IRK YAWN ENNUI BOREDOM
TEE COCK TIGHT TOZEE WITTER BULLHEAD
TEEM SNY FLOW SWIM SWARM ABOUND BUSTLE SCRAWL PULLULATE
TEEMER SHOOTMAN
TEEMING BIG ALIVE TUMID FERTILE GUSHING TEEMFUL ABUNDANT BRAWLING PREGNANT SWARMING
TEENAGER TEENY TEENYBOPPER
TEENY SMALL
TEESWATER MUGS MUGGS
TEETER ROCK WAVER JIGGLE QUIVER SEESAW WOBBLE TREMBLE
TEETH CTENII CHOPPERS CRACKERS GRINDERS
(HAVING —) IVORIED
(PETRIFIED —) BUFONITE
(SET OF —) DENTURE
(WHEEL —) COGS
(PREF.) DENT(ATO)(I)(INO)(O)
(SUFF.) ODON
TEETHRIDGE ALVEOLE ALVEOLUS
TEETOTUM TOTUM WHIRLIGIG
TEGETICULA PRONUBA
TEGMENTUM ROOF
TEGULA SQUAMA EPAULET SCAPULA PATAGIUM SQUAMULA
TEGUMENT COAT TEGMEN
TEHUELCHE PATAGON
TEJU TEIOID JACUARU TEGUEXIN
TELAMON ATLAS
(BROTHER OF —) PELEUS
(FATHER OF —) AEACUS
(MOTHER OF —) ENDEIS
(SON OF —) AJAX TEUCER
(WIFE OF —) GLAUCE HESIONE
TELAMONES ATLANTES
TELEDU BADGER STINKARD
TELEGONUS (FATHER OF —) ULYSSES
(MOTHER OF —) CIRCE
(SON OF —) ITALUS
(WIFE OF —) PENELOPE
TELEGRAM TAR WIRE FLASH FLIMSY
TELEGRAPH SEND WIRE CABLE BUZZER TELEGRAM TELOTYPE
(BUSH —) GRAPEVINE
TELEMACHUS (FATHER OF —) ULYSSES
(MOTHER OF —) PENELOPE
(SON OF —) LATINUS
TELENCEPHALON ENDBRAIN
TELEOLOGICAL TELIC FINALIST
TELEOLOGY FINALITY
TELEPHASSA (DAUGHTER OF —) EUROPA
(HUSBAND OF —) AGENOR
(SON OF —) CADMUS PHOENIX
TELEPHONE CALL DIAL RING PHONE BLOWER HANDSET
(KIND OF —) CORDLESS
(PART OF —) PAD BASE CORD DIAL HOLE STOP PLATE CRADLE HANDLE HANDSET PLUNGER SPEAKER EARPIECE RECEIVER MOUTHPIECE TRANSMITTER
TELEPHOTE DIAPHOTE
TELEPHUS (FATHER OF —) HERCULES
(MOTHER OF —) AUGE
(WIFE OF —) ARGIOPE LAODICE ASTYOCHE
TELEPRINTER CREED
TELESCOPE TUBE COUDE GLASS SCOPE TRUNK ALINER FINDER SECTOR ALIGNER BINOCLE TRANSIT PROSPECT SPYGLASS REFRACTOR PERSPECTIVE
(PART OF —) LEG CELL LENS TUBE CLAMP GUIDE MOUNT SCOPE CRADLE DEWCAP SLEEVE TRIPOD DIAGONAL DRAWTUBE EYEPIECE MOUNTING SUNSHADE VIEWFINDER
(SURVEYOR'S —) LEVEL
TELEVISION TV AIR BOX TELLY VIDEO VIDEOLAND SMALLSCREEN
(— AFTERNOON FARE) SOAP
(— BAND) UHF
(— COMEDY PROGRAM) SITCOM
(— PROGRAM) TALKSHOW
(— PROGRAM FOR CHILDREN) KIDVID
(— RATINGS PERIOD) SWEEP
(— SERVICE) PAYTV
(— SET) BOX TUBE BOOBTUBE
(— SHOW) RERUN SITCOM
(— STATION) CHANNEL
(CHILDREN'S —) KIDVID
(EDUCATIONAL —) ETV
(ELEMENT ON — SCREEN) PIXEL
(PERSON FOND OF —) VIDEOPHILE
TELIOSPORE TELEUTO
TELL HIP SAY DEEM MAKE MEAN MOOT READ SHOW TALE AREAD AREED BREAK BREVE COUNT NEVEN PITCH SPELL STORY TEACH UTTER AUTHOR DEVISE IMPART INFORM MUSTER QUETHE RECITE RELATE REPEAT REPORT REVEAL CONFESS DIVULGE NARRATE PARTAKE RECOUNT ACQUAINT REHEARSE
(— CONFIDENTIALLY) CONFIDE
(— CONFUSEDLY) SPLATHER
(— EARNESTLY) ASSURE
(— IN ADVANCE) FORESAY
(— LIES) BELY LIGE BELIE
(— OFF) JAR
(— ON) RAT
(— ROMANCES) GEST GESTE
(— SECRETS) CHEEP CLYPE SPILL BABBLE
(— STRIKINGLY) CRACK
(— TALES) BLAB CANT PEACH
(HOME TO WILLIAM —) URI
TELLER CASHIER SPINNER STORIER TALLIER FABLEIST FABULIST SENACHIE
TELLING REDE PUNGENT POWERFUL STINGING
(— OF SECRETS) BLAB
TELLTALE CLASH TATTLER TITTLER REGISTER
TELL-TALE (— SIGN) TIPOFF
TELLURIDE ALTAITE
TELSON PLEON
TELUGU GENTU GENTOO TELINGA
TEM TUM ATMU ATUM
TEMA (FATHER OF —) ISHMAEL
TEMAN (FATHER OF —) ELIPHAZ
(MOTHER OF —) ADAH
TEMENI (FATHER OF —) ASHUR
(MOTHER OF —) NAARAH
TEMERITY GALL CHEEK NERVE AUDACITY RASHNESS

TEMP STENO
TEMPER CUE MAD BAIT BATE COOL DASH DRAW MOOD MULL NEAL PADD SCOT TONE ALLOY BIRSE BLOOD CREST DELAY FRAME GRAIN HUMOR IRISH SAUCE SOBER TRAMP ADJUST ANIMUS ANNEAL DANDER MASTER MONKEY SEASON SPIRIT SPLEEN STRAIN SUBMIT CHASTEN CLIMATE COURAGE HACKLES QUALIFY STOMACH EBENEZER GRADUATE MITIGATE MODERATE MOORBURN
(— CLAY) TAMPER
(— METAL) ALLAY
(— OF MIND) CUE SPIRIT
(CAPRICIOUS —) SPLEEN
TEMPERAMENT BLOOD GEMUT HEART HUMOR CRASIS KIDNEY NATURE TEMPER STOMACH SANGUINE
TEMPERAMENTAL FITIFIED
TEMPERANCE MEDIETY SOBRIETY
TEMPERATE CALM COOL MILD SOFT GREEN SOBER STEADY TEMPRE MODERATE ORDINATE ABSTINENT CONTINENT LYSOGENIC ABSTEMIOUS
TEMPERATURE SUN HEAT TEMP HOTNESS DEWPOINT
(— FACTOR) WINDCHILL
(— UNIT) KELVIN
TEMPERED HARD MILD SOBER SARCENET
TEMPERING MODULATION
TEMPEST GALE THUD WIND ORAGE STORM TUMULT TORMENT TURMOIL WEATHER
(AUTHOR OF —) SHAKESPEARE
(CHARACTER IN —) IRIS JUNO ARIEL CERES ADRIAN ALONSO ANTONIO CALIBAN GONZALO MIRANDA TINCULO PROSPERO STEPHANO FERDINAND FRANCISCO SEBASTIAN
TEMPESTUOUS WILD GUSTY STERN WINDY RUGGED STORMY VIOLENT STALWART
TEMPLATE CURB NORMA TEMPLET PADSTONE STRICKLE
TEMPLE VAT WAT DEUL FANE NAOS RATH CANDI GUACA HUACA KIACK KOVIL MARAE RATHA CHANDI HAFFET HERION MANDIR SACRUM SHRINE TEOPAN TJANDI VIHARA HERAEUM HERAION TEMPLET TEMPLUM VARELLA OLYMPIUM PANTHEON RAMESEUM TEOCALLI VALHALLA PARTHENON
(— AREA) MANDAPA
(CAVE —) SPEOS
(FIJI —) BURE
(HAWAIIAN —) HEIAU
(JAPANESE —) SHA
(PART OF —) PRONAOS
(SHINTO —) SHA JINJA JINSHA YASHIRO
(STUDY OF —S) NAOLOGY
(TOWERLIKE —) ZIGGURAT
(PREF.) NAO
TEMPLES
(PREF.) TEMPORO
TEMPLET FORMER STRICKLE
TEMPO TAKT TIME AGOGE MOVEMENT
TEMPORAL LAIC CIVIL CARNAL TIMELY EARTHLY PROFANE SECULAR
TEMPORARY ACTING FLYING INTERIM STOPGAP WHILEND EPISODAL EPISODIC TEMPORAL PROVISIONAL
(PREF.) PSEUD(O)
TEMPORIZER DRIFTER POLITIC
TEMPT EGG BAIT FAND FOND LURE TEMP TENT ASSAY COURT ALLURE ASSAIL ENTICE INVITE SEDUCE ASSAULT ATTEMPT SOLICIT SUGGEST
TEMPTATION BAIT TRIAL ATTEMPT TESTING SEDUCTION
TEMPTER DEVIL
TEMPTING ALLURING INVITING
TEMPTRESS SIREN DELILAH
TEN ICRE IOTA CHANG DIKER CHEUNG DECADE DENARY DICKER ARTICLE BRISQUE
(— OF TRUMPS) GAME
(PREF.) DEC(A)(I)(U) DECEM DEK(A)
(SUFF.) TY
TEN'A KOYUKON
TENACE FORK
TENACIOUS FAST ROPEY STIFF TOUGH CLAGGY CLEDGY DOGGED GRIPPY PLUGGY STICKY STRONG VISCID GRIPPLE VISCOUS ADHESIVE GRASPING HOLDFAST RETENTIVE PERTINACIOUS
TENACIOUSNESS TENACY FASTNESS
TENACITY LENTOR COURAGE
TENACULUM CLASP
TENANCY CONACRE JOINTURE
TENANT KMET LEUD SAER BARON CEILE DRENG LAIRD BORDAR COTTAR COTTER DRENGH GENEAT HOLDER INMATE LESSEE MOLMAN RADMAN RENTER SOCMAN VASSAL CHAKDAR COTTIER FEODARY FEUDARY GAVELER HOMAGER SOCAGER SOKEMAN VAVASOR COLIBERT CUSTOMER SERGEANT SUCKENER
(— OF CROWN) THANE
(— OF THE CROWN) THANE
(FARM —) CROFTER
(LIFE —) LIVIER LIVEYER
(NEW —) INCOME INCOMER
TENCH CYPRINID
TEN COMMANDMENTS DECALOG
TEND HOP NOD RUN SET WRY BABY BEND DRAW GROW KEEP MAKE MIND MOVE TENT DRESS GROOM NURSE OFFER SOUND TREND VERGE WATCH AFFECT GOVERN INTEND CHERISH CONDUCE DECLINE INCLINE PROPEND
(— A FIRE) STOKE
(— IN A CERTAIN DIRECTION) LEAD
(— TO) NURSE
(— TO ONE POINT) CONVERGE
(— TOWARD) AFFECT
(— WHILE AT PASTURE) GRAZE
TENDENCY SET BENT BIAS HAND TONE VEIN DRAFT DRIFT DRIVE HABIT KNACK TENOR TREND TWIST ANIMUS COURSE EONISM GENIUS MOTION APTNESS CONATUS DRAUGHT IMPULSE LEANING NITENCY SAMKARA APTITUDE INSTINCT STEERING VERGENCY
(— IN NATURE) KIND
(— TO APPROACH) ADIENCE
(— TO GOOD OR EVIL) PROPENSITY
(— TO STICK TOGETHER) CLANSHIP
(— TO WITHDRAW) ABIENCE
(— TO WRATH) TIDE
(INHERITED —) STRAIN
(SUFF.) **(— TOWARD)** PHIL(A)(AE)(E)(IA)(ISM)(IST)(OUS)(US)(Y)
TENDER RAW TID BEAR COCK FINE FOND FRIM FRUM KIND NESH SOFT SORE TAKE TART TENT WARM CAGER DEFER FRAIL GREEN MUSHY OFFER PAPPY DELATE DRIVER GENTLE GIMPER GINGER HUMANE LOVELY RAISER SILKEN ADVANCE AMABILE AMOROSO AMOROUS CONCHER CRAMPER FLESHLY MASHMAN OBLATIO PATACHE PINNACE PITEOUS PITIFUL PORRECT PROFFER RUTHFUL STENTER CAMELEER COCKBOAT EFFETMAN FEMININE HEATSMAN HERDSMAN LADYLIKE MERCIFUL MORTISER SPREADER
(KIND OF —) LEGAL
(PREF.) ABRO HABRO
TENDERFOOT DUDE INNOCENT CHEECHAKO
TENDERHEARTED HUMAN PITIFUL
TENDERIZER PAPAIN
TENDERLOIN FILET PSOAS FILLET UNDERCUT
TENDERLY FONDLY GENTLY AMOROSO
TENDERNESS CHERTE TENDER DELICACY FONDNESS KINDNESS SYMPATHY TENERITY YEARNING
(— OF FEELING) FLESH
TENDING
(SUFF.) CLINIC CLINOUS
(— TO) ABLE ATIVE ATORY BOND BUND CUND FUL IBLE
TENDINOUS SINEWY
TENDON CORD TAIL CHORD NERVE SINEW TENON LEADER PAXWAX STRING
(PREF.) TENO
TENDRIL CURL CLASP CROOK TWIST CIRRUS WINDER CAPREOL CIRRHUS CLASPER TENTACLE
(PREF.) PAMPINI PAMPINO
TENEMENT LAND RENT TACK CHAWL DECKER LIVING WARREN HOLDING LETTING ROOKERY BUILDING PRAEDIUM
TENES (FATHER OF —) CYCNUS
(MOTHER OF —) PROCLEA PHILONOME
(SISTER OF —) HEMITHEA
(SLAYER OF —) ACHILLES
TENET ISM ADOXY CREDO CREED DOGMA BELIEF GNOMON HOLDING MISHNAH PARADOX DOCTRINE
(PL.) FAITH FAMILISM
TENFOLD DENARY DECUPLE
TENNANTITE FAHLERZ FAHLORE
TENNE TAWNY ORANGE HYACINTH

TENNESSEE
CAPITAL: NASHVILLE
COLLEGE: FISK LANE SIENA BETHEL BELMONT LAMBUTH LEMOYNE MILLIGAN TUSCULUM VANDERBILT
COUNTY: DYER KNOX RHEA COCKE GILES HENRY MEIGS OBION COFFEE GRUNDY MCMINN SEVIER UNICOI BLEDSOE FENTRESS
DAM: WILSON WHEELER
INDIAN: SHAWNEE CHEROKEE CHICKASAW
LAKE: DOUGLAS CHEROKEE REELFOOT WATTSBAR
MOUNTAIN: GUYOT LOOKOUT
MOUNTAIN RANGE: SMOKY
NATIONAL PARK: SHILOH
NATIVE: WHELP
NICKNAME: VOLUNTEER
PRESIDENT: POLK JACKSON
RIVER: ELK DUCK CANEY HOLSTON HIWASSEE CUMBERLAND
STATE BIRD: MOCKINGBIRD
STATE FLOWER: IRIS
STATE TREE: POPLAR
TOWN: ERIN ALAMO ALCOA ERWIN PARIS CAMDEN CELINA JASPER SELMER SPARTA BOLIVAR DICKSON JACKSON MEMPHIS PULASKI GALLATIN KNOXVILLE CHATTANOOGA

TENNIES SNEAKERS
TENNIS (— LET) DOOVER
(— NAME) ASHE ILIE
(— PERSONALITY) ASHE ILIE
(— PLAY) RALLY
(— PLAYER) DOD ASHE BETZ BORG GORE GRAF KING BUDGE BUENO COURT EVERT LAVER LENDL LLOYD MOODY MOORE PERRY SEARS SELES VILAS WILLS WRENN AGASSI AUSTIN BECKER BROUGH BROWNE COOPER DUPONT EDBERG JACOBS LARNED MARBLE STERRY TILDEN CONNORS COURIER DOHERTY EMERSON LENGLEN MALLORY MCENROE NASTASE RENSHAW SAMPRAS VICARIO WHITMAN WILDING ATKINSON BADDELEY CAMPBELL CAPRIATI CHAMBERS CONNOLLY GONZALES HILLYARD NEWCOMBE ROSEWALL WILANDER BJURSTEDT WRIGHTMAN NAVRATILOVA
(— SCORE) ADIN LOVE ADOUT DEUCE FORTY THIRTY FIFTEEN
(— SHOT) AD ACE LET LOB ADIN DINK DROP ADOUT SMASH
(— UNIT) SET GAME MATCH
(ANCIENT —) BANDY
(NAME IN —) WADE
(PERFECT SERVE IN —) ACE
(TABLE —) PINGPONG
TENON COG PIN COAK STUB TUSK LEWIS TOOTH TABLING DOVETAIL LEWISSON
(KIND OF —) TUSK
TENOR PES FECK TONE VEIN

COURSE EFFECT TAILLE TENURE CURRENT PURPORT STRENGTH TENDENCY TENORINO
TENOROON FAGOTTINO
TENOR VIOL VIOLET
TENOR VIOLIN ALTO
TEN-PERCENTER AGENT
TENPINS BOWLS NEWPORT
TENPOUNDER AWA CHIRO MACABI BONEFISH BONYFISH LADYFISH SKIPJACK SPRINGER
TENREC TANGUE CENTETES CENTETID HEDGEHOG HEDGEPIG
TENSE EDGY RAPT TAUT STIFF WIRED AORIST CORDED FLINCH FUTURE INTENT NARROW STRAIT STRICT BRITTLE INTENSE PRIMARY FRENETIC PRETERIT STRAINED SYNTONIC
TENSION BENT HEAT DRIVE STEAM SATTVA SPRING STRAIN STRESS TROPPO BALANCE STRAINT TENSURE ISOTONIA
(STATE OF NERVOUS —) YIPS
TENT AUL TOP HALE PAWL TAWN TELD TILT TIPI CABIN CRAME LODGE TEPEE TOPEK TUPIK CANNAT CANVAS DOSSIL SEARCH TEEPEE WIGWAM BALAGAN CABINET KIBITKA MARQUEE SPARVER TABERNA TENTLET TENTORY ZDARSKY PAVILION SHAMIANA TENTICLE TENTWORK SHOOLDARRY
(— FOR WOUNDS) PENICIL
(— WHERE GOODS ARE SOLD) CRAME
(CIRCULAR —) YURT YOURT YURTA KIBITKA
(GENERAL'S —) PRAETORIUM
(INDIAN —) TEPEE WIGWAM
(SAMOYED —) CHUM
(SOUTH AMERICAN —) TOLDO
TENTACLE HORN SAIL PACLE FEELER BRACHIUM
TENTATIVE GINGERLY
TENT CATERPILLAR WEBWORM
TENTERER RACKER RATCHER
TENTH DIME DISME TITHE DECIMA
(— OF CENT) MILL
(— OF LINE) GRY
(PREF.) DECI
TEN THOUSAND
(PREF.) MYRIA MYRIO
TENTWORT RUE
TENUITY EXILITY DELICACY
TENUOUS SLIM FILMY FOGGY FRAIL SUBTLE TENDER FRAGILE GASEOUS SLENDER SUBTILE ETHEREAL GOSSAMER
(TOO —) FINESPUN
TENUOUSNESS FRAILTY
TENURE FEU SORN TACK TAKE TERM GAVEL JAGIR BARONY CAPITE JAGHIR RUNRIG SOCAGE SORREN ALMOIGN BONDAGE BORDAGE BURGAGE CENSIVE CORNAGE CURTESY FARMAGE JAGHEER SOCCAGE SOREHON COPYHOLD DRENGAGE FREEHOLD OVERLAND SOCMANRY SUITHOLD VAVASORY VENVILLE
(LAND —) RUNRIG SOCAGE RUNDALE SOCCAGE
TEPEE CHUM TENT TIPI HOGAN LODGE TEEPEE WICKIUP
TEPHROSIA CRACCA
TEPID LEW WARM WLACH WLECH LUKEWARM
TEQUISLATEC CHONTAL
TERAH (SON OF —) HARAN NAHOR ABRAHAM
TERATOMA EMBRYOMA
TERCET TRISTICH
TEREBINTH TEIL TURPENTINE
TEREDO BORER WOODWORM
TERENTIA (HUSBAND OF —) CICERO
TERETE CENTRIC
TEREUS (FATHER OF —) MARS
(SON OF —) ITYS
(WIFE OF —) PROCNE
TERGITE TERGUM PYGIDIUM
TERGIVERSATION DECEIT
TERGUM PYGIDIUM
TERM HALF NAME NOME WORD LEASE RHEMA SPEAK STYLE TRYST ABBACY GNOMON HILARY NOTION PARODY EPITHET EXTREME SESSION SUBJECT SUMMAND TERMINE VOCABLE EQUIVOKE HEADWORD MAHALATH POCHISMO SEMESTER TERMTIME
(— IN JAIL) JOLT
(— IN LOGIC) CONSTANT
(— IN PROGRESSION) MEAN
(— OF ABUSE) CUSSWORD
(— OF ADDRESS) SIRRAH MADONNA
(— OF CONTEMPT) SLIPE PILCHER TITIVIL
(— OF DEFERENCE) AHUNG
(— OF ENDEARMENT) HON LOVE PEAT ASTOR CHUCK COCKY HONEY JARTA LOVEY MOPSY MOUSE SUGAR YARTA ASTHORE MACHREE STOREEN POSSODIE POWSOWDY PRECIOUS
(— OF IMPRISONMENT) LAG LAGGING STRETCH
(— OF PROPOSITION) REFERENT
(— OF PUNISHMENT) JOB
(— OF RATIO) EXTREME
(— OF REPROACH) GIB BESOM MINGO RONYON
(— OF RESPECT) SAHIB
(— OF SYLLOGISM) EXTREME ARGUMENT
(—S OF REFERENCE) REMIT
(ARITHMETICAL —) NOME GNOMON
(COURT —) HILARY
(DESCRIPTIVE —) EPITHET
(FINAL —S) ULTIMATUM
(HYPHENED —) COMPOUND
(LITERAL —S) LETTER
(POSITIVE —) PLUS
(SOCIAL —S) FOOTING
(UNIVERSAL —) CONCEPT
(PL.) LAY MEANS
(PREF.) HORO
TERMAGANT JADE RUDAS SHREW VIXEN VIRAGO
TERMINABLE FINITE
TERMINAL JACK LAST POLE ANODE DEPOT IMPUT INPUT MUCRO CATHODE POTHEAD DESINENT
(ELECTRIC —) POLE
TERMINATE CUT END ABUT CALL HALT KILL ABORT BLEED CEASE CLOSE ISSUE LAPSE EXPIRE FINISH FOREDO RESULT INCLUDE TERMINE COMPLETE CONCLUDE DISSOLVE
(— A SESSION) PROROGUE
TERMINATED EXPIATE
TERMINATING FINAL
(— ABRUPTLY) BLIND
(SUDDENLY —) ABRUPT
TERMINATION END ISH DATE TERM ABORT CLOSE EVENT ISSUE ENDING EXITUS EXPIRY FINALE PERIOD UPSHOT TERMINUS
(— OF CHURCH CHOIR) CHEVET
(— OF FURNITURE LEGS) FOOT
(— OF RIGHT) LAPSE
(PROSPEROUS —) SUCCESS
TERMINATIVE FINITIVE
TERMINOLOGY JARGON
TERMINUS END FLAT
(— IN FINGERPRINT) DELTA
(— OF PERIOD) TIME
TERMITE ANAI ANAY KING NASUTE WORKER POLILLA
TERMITOPHILE SYMPHILE
TERN KIP DARR INCA LARI NOIO PIRL PIRR RIXY LARID NODDY PEARL SCRAY SKEER SKIRR STERN CHIRRE KERMEW PICKET GOELAND MEDRICK PIRRMAW RITTOCK SCURRIT SEAFOWL STRIKER TARRACK TERNLET MANUSINA SPARLING TIRRACKE
TERPENE CARENE PINENE BORNANE SANTENE THUJENE CAMPHENE FENCHENE LIMONENE NOPINENE
TERRA GE GAEA TELLUS
(DAUGHTER OF —) RHEA THEA PHOEBE TETHYS THEMIS MNEMOSYNE
(HUSBAND OF —) URANUS
(SON OF —) OCEANUS
TERRACE POY DAIS PNYX STEP XYST BEACH BENCH HEIAU LINCH PATIO OFFSET PERRON LINCHET VERANDA BARBETTE CHABUTRA VERANDAH
(— AT ENTRANCE) PERRON
(LOUNGING —) LANAI
(NATURAL —) MESA
(SEA-FRONT —) PROMENADE
TERRA JAPONICA GAMBIR GAMBIER
TERRAPENE CISTUDO
TERRAPIN EMYD COUNT COODLE POTTER SLIDER TURPIN TURTLE EMYDIAN FEUILLE SKILPOT REDBELLY TORTOISE
(FEMALE —) HEIFER
(MALE —) BULL
TERRARIUM VIVARIUM
TERRELLA EARTHKIN
TERRENE EARTHLY
TERRESTRIAL EARTHY EARTHLY TERRENE PLANETAL SUBLUNAR SUBSOLAR TELLURIC PLANETARY SUBASTRAL
TERRET CRINGLE
TERRIBLE DIRE UGLY AWFUL GHAST LURID DEADLY PRETTY TARBLE TRAGIC TURBLE CHRONIC DIREFUL FEARFUL FERDFUL GHASTLY HIDEOUS ALMIGHTY BHAIRAVA FLEYSOME HORRIBLE TERRIFIC TIMOROUS TRAGICAL
(PREF.) DEIN(O) DIN(O)
TERRIBLY FELLY FIERCE GRISLY CONSARN
TERRIER SKYE LHASA SILKY BOSTON DANDIE RATTER SCOTTY DIEHARD SCOTTIE ABERDEEN AIREDALE RATTONER SEALYHAM VERMINER WIREHAIR
(YORKSHIRE) YORKIE
TERRIFIC FINE SWEET GORGON AWESOME FEARFUL DYNAMITE GORGEOUS
TERRIFIED AFRAID AGHAST GHASTLY
TERRIFY AWE COW HAG BREE DARE FEAR FLAY FLEY APPAL DREAD GALLY SCARE ADREAD AFFRAY AGRISE AWHAPE DISMAY FLIGHT FREEZE FRIGHTEN
TERRIFYING GHASTLY HIDEOUS FEARSOME FLEYSOME TERRIBLE
TERRITORIALISM ITOISM
TERRITORY FEE GOA HAN SOC AREA MARK PALE SOKE BANAT DUCHY FIELD MARCH STATE TUATH BORDER COLONY DOMAIN EMPERY EMPIRE GROUND APANAGE CONFINE COUNTRY DEMESNE DUKEDOM EARLDOM ENCLAVE EPARCHY REGENCY SATRAPY APPANAGE CASTLERY CONFINES CONQUEST DISTRICT DOMINION IMPERIUM LIGEANCE LUCUMONY PARMESAN PASHALIK REGALITY SEIGNORY
(FOREIGN —) POSSESSION
(MONASTIC —) ABTHANE
TERROR AWE FEAR FRAY ALARM APPAL DREAD PANIC AFFRAY ALARUM APPALL FRIGHT HORROR DRIDDER AFFRIGHT DREDDOUR SURPRISE
TERRORISM NIHILISM
TERRORIST GOONDA ALARMIST SICARIUS
TERRORIZE FRIGHTEN
TERROR-STRICKEN AWFUL
TERSE CURT SINEWY COMPACT CONCISE LACONIC POINTED SUMMARY UNWORDY SUCCINCT
TERSENESS BREVITY LACONISM
TERTIARY NEOZOIC PALAEIC
TESSELLATED MOSAIC
TESSELLATION AREOLE
TESSERA TILETTE ABACULUS TESSELLA
TESS OF DURBERVILLES (AUTHOR OF —) HARDY
(CHARACTER IN —) ALEC JACK TESS ANGEL CLARE DURBERVILLE DURBEYFIELD
TEST CON SAY TRY FAND FEEL FOND QUIZ SEMI TASK TENT ASSAY AVENA CANON CHECK ESSAY GROPE ISSUE PROBE

PROOF PROVE SENSE SOUND TASTE TEMPT TESTA TOUCH TRIAL SAMPLE TIENTA APPROOF APPROVE AUSSAGE CONTROL EXAMINE GANTLET PLUMMET TESTATE BIOASSAY EXERCISE GAUNTLET SEROLOGY STANDARD
(— CHEESE) PALE
(— EGGS) CANDLE
(— FOR MESSAGES) POLL
(— FOR WEIGHT AND FINENESS) PYX
(— GROUND) BOSE
(— OF COURAGE) SCRATCH
(— OF CRINOID) CALYX
(— OF GUILT) CORSNED
(— OF ORE) VAN
(ASSAY —) ELISA
(COLLEGE —) MIDTERM
(COLLEGE ENTRANCE —) PSAT
(KIND OF —) AMES ORAL MEANS SWEAT DRAIZE LITMUS SCHICK INKBLOT MANTOUX RORSCHACH
(SEROLOGICAL —) COGGINS
(SEVERE —) CRUCIBLE
(SYPHILIS —) KOLMER
(PREF.) DOCIMO OECO
(SUFF.) OECA OECIA
TESTA TEST LORICA EPISPERM
TESTACEOUS SHELLY
TESTAMENT TEST QUETHE WITWORD COVENANT
TESTAR TETARD
TESTATOR LEGATOR
TESTED FIRED TRIED WEIGHED
TESTER TRIER CONNER PROVER SPARVER DENIERER TESTIERE
(BUTTER —) SEARCHER
TESTES
(SUFF.) ORCHISM
TESTICLE STONE BALLOCK DIDYMUS GENITOR
(PREF.) ORCHI(O) ORCHID(O) ORCHO
TESTICLES
(SUFF.) ORCHISM
TESTIFY SPEAK SWEAR AFFIRM DEPONE DEPOSE WITTEN WITNESS EVIDENCE
(— FALSELY) MOUNT
(— TO) BESPEAK
TESTIMONIAL CHIT SCROLL CHARACTER
TESTIMONY TEST ATTEST AVOUCH PROBATE TESTATE TESTIFY WITNESS EVIDENCE
TESTING ASSAY CRUCIAL SHAKEDOWN
(KIND OF —) DNA
TESTIS BALL GONAD STONE BALLOCK CULLION KNOCKER SPERMARY
(PL.) COBS CODS COJONES DOWSETS
TEST TUBE PROOF TESTER PROBATE
TESTUDINATA CHELONIA
TESTUDO SNAIL GALAPAGO TORTOISE
TESTY DONCY MUSTY TUTTY CRANKY DONSIE PATCHY SPUNKY PEEVISH TETTISH TOUSTIE WASPISH SNAPPISH
TETANIC LOCKJAW SPASTIC TRISMUS
TETANUS LOCKJAW HOLOTONY
TETE-A-TETE CHAT TWOSOME CAUSEUSE
TETHER BAND LEASH STAKE PICKET TEDDER TOGGLE PASTERN CABESTRO
(— A HAWK) WEATHER
TETHYS APLYSIA
(DAUGHTERS OF —) OCEANIDES
(FATHER OF —) URANUS
(HUSBAND OF —) OCEANUS
(MOTHER OF —) TERRA
TETHYUM CYNTHIA
TETRA-
(PREF.) QUATER
TETRACHORD GENUS HYPATON LICHANOS
TETRACTYS TETRAD
TETRAD FOURFOLD
TETRADRACHMA OWL
TETRAGONAL DIMETRIC
TETRAHEDRITE FAHLERZ FAHLORE PANABASE
TETRAHEXAHEDRON FLUOROID
TETRAHYDRIDE GERMANE STANNANE
TETRASACCHARIDE LUPEOSE
TETTER DARTRE
TETTIX ACRYDIUM
TEUCER (DAUGHTER OF —) ASTERIA
(FATHER OF —) TELAMON SCAMANDER
(HALF-BROTHER OF —) AJAX
(MOTHER OF —) IDAEA HESIONE
(WIFE OF —) EUNE
TEUTON GOTH LOMBARD
TEUTONIC GOTHIC GERMANIC GOTHONIC

TEXAS
CAPITAL: AUSTIN
COLLEGE: SMU TCU RICE WILEY BAYLOR
COUNTY: BEE CASS COKE JACK REAL RUSK VEGA WEBB WISE BEXAR DELTA ECTOR ERATH GARZA RAINS FANNIN GOLIAD YOAKUM ZAPATA ZAVALA HIDALGO REFUGIO ATASCOSA
FORTRESS: ALAMO
INDIAN: LIPAN BILOXI KICHAI SHUMAN HASINAI COMANCHE TONKAWAN
LAKE: FALCON TEXOMA AMISTAD
MOUNTAIN: GUADALUPE
NATIVE: TEJANO
NICKNAME: LONESTAR
PRESIDENT: JOHNSON EISENHOWER
RIVER: RED PECOS BRAZOS NUECES TRINITY
STATE BIRD: MOCKINGBIRD
STATE FLOWER: BLUEBONNET
STATE TREE: PECAN
TOWN: GAIL VEGA WACO BRYAN MARFA OZONA PAMPA TYLER BORGER DALLAS DENTON ELPASO KILEEN LAREDO ODESSA QUANAH SONORA ABILENE HOUSTON LUBBOCK AMARILLO BEAUMONT FLOYDADA GALVESTON

TEXAS BUCKTHORN LOTEBUSH
TEXAS FEVER TRISTEZA
TEXT BODY MIQRA PLACE SAKHA TESTO WORDS PURANA SCRIPT SHAKHA TEXTUS TEXTLET ANTETHEM PERICOPE VARIORUM
(— OF ADVERTISEMENT) COPY
(— OF OPERA) LIBRETTO
(— OF PLAY) SCRIPT
(— SET TO MUSIC) ORATORIO
(BIBLICAL —) SCRIPTURE
(REVISED —) RECENSION
(SACRED —) MANTRA
(SHASTRA —) SRUTI SHRUTI
TEXTBOOK DUNCE TUTOR GENETICS
TEXTILE (ALSO SEE FABRIC) SABA STUFF GREIGE MOCKADO SAGURAN SINAMAY TEXTURE TIFFANY
(— MACHINE) WILLOW
(PL.) DRAPE
TEXTURE WEB BONE HAND KNIT WALE WOOF FIBER GRAIN COBWEB FABRIC WEFTAGE FRACTURE
(— OF SOAP) FIT
(— OF STONE) GRIT
THADDEUS OF WARSAW
(AUTHOR OF —) PORTER
(CHARACTER IN —) MARY ROSS SARA DIANA BUTZOU ROBSON VINCENT BEAUFORT EUPHEMIA PEMBROKE SOBIESKI SOMERSET THADDEUS CAVENDISH KOSCIUSKO SACKVILLE TINEMOUTH CONSTANTINE
THAHASH (FATHER OF —) NAHOR
(MOTHER OF —) REUMAH
THAI LAO SIAMESE

THAILAND
CAPITAL: BANKOK BANGKOK
COIN: AT ATT BAHT FUANG TICAL PYNUNG SALUNG SATANG
FORMER NAME: SIAM
ISLAND: PHUKET
ISTHMUS: KRA
LANGUAGE: SHAN
MEASURE: WA KEN NIV NMU RAI SAT SEN SOK WAH YOT KEUP NGAN TANG YOTE KWIEN LAANG SESTI TANAN KABIET KAMMEU CHAIMEU ROENENG CHANGAWN
MOUNTAIN: KHIEO MAELAMUN
MOUNTAIN RANGE: DAWNA BILAUKTAUNG
NATIVE: LAO THAI
PLAIN: KHORAT
RIVER: CHI NAN PING MENAM MEKONG MEPING
TOWN: UBON PUKET RANONG AYUDHYA AYUTHIA BANGKOK LOPBURI RAHAENG SINGORA SONGKLA KHONKAEN KIANGMAI THONBURI
WEIGHT: HAP PAI SEN SOK BAHT HAPH KLAM KLOM CATTY CHANG COYAN PILUL FLUANG SALUNG SOMPAY TAMLUNG

THAIS (CHARACTER IN —) THAIS ATHANAEL
(COMPOSER OF —) MASSENET
THAISA (FATHER OF —) SIMONIDES
(HUSBAND OF —) PERICLES
THALABA (WIFE OF —) ONEIZA
THALER DALER
THALLOGEN AMPHIGEN
THALLOID FRONDOSE
THALLUS FROND THALAMUS THAMNIUM
THAMNOPHIS EUTAENIA
THAMYRAS (FATHER OF —) PHILAMMON
(MOTHER OF —) ARGIOPE
THAN AS NA NE OR TO AND BUT NOR THEN TILL
THANE THEGN BANQUO GESITH ABTHAIN MACDUFF
THANK GRACE MERCY AGGRATE REGRACY REMERCY
THANKFUL GRATEFUL
THANKLESS INGRATE SLOWFUL
THANKS TA DANKE GRACE MERCI MERCY GRACIAS GRAMERCY
THANKSGIVING GLORY DOXOLOGY
THANK-YOU-MA'AM CAHOT
THAT AS AT SE BUT HOW THE THO WHO YAT LEST THAM THIK THON WHAT YOND THICK THILK THOUGH BECAUSE
(— IS) IDEST
(— IS TO SAY) NAMELY
(— ONE) ILLE
(— WHICH HAS TO BE PROVED) IQED
(— YONDER) THON
THATCH NIPA DATCH SIRKI SIRKY STING THRUM CADJAN
(— OVER BEEHIVE) HOOD
THATCHED THACK REEDED
THATCHER HELER CROWDER HELLIER THACKER
THAUMAS (DAUGHTER OF —) IRIS AELLO HARPY OCYPETE
(FATHER OF —) PONTUS NEPTUNE
(MOTHER OF —) GAEA TERRA
(WIFE OF —) ELECTRA
THAUMATURGIST
(PL.) GOETAE
THAUMATURGY MAGIC
THAW GIVE MELT FRESH UNTHAW DEFROST
THE LA LE SE TA THI THAM THEY YARE THERE
(PREF.) AL
THEA CAMELLIA
(FATHER OF —) URANUS
(HUSBAND OF —) HYPERION
(MOTHER OF —) TERRA
THEANO (FATHER OF —) CISSEUS
(HUSBAND OF —) ANTENOR METAPONTUS
(MOTHER OF —) TELECLIA
(SISTER OF —) HECUBA
(SON OF —) ACAMAS AGENOR POLYBUS HELICAON IPHIDAMAS ARCHELOCHUS
THEATER CINE GAFF KINO NABE CAVEA HOUSE LEGIT ODEUM SCENE STAGE CINEMA OZONER ADELPHI COCKPIT GUIGNOL

ORPHEUM THEATRE BIOSCOPE COLISEUM PANTHEON SHOWSHOP SPELLKEN STRAWHAT THEATRON PLAYHOUSE NICKELODEON
(— DISTRICT) RIALTO
(CLASSICAL —) ODEUM
(FULL —) SRO
(HARLEM —) APOLLO
(JAPANESE —) NOH BUNRAKU
(LOCAL —) NABE
(NEIGHBORHOOD —) NABE
(PUPPET —) BUNRAKU
THEATRICAL CAMP HAMMY STAGY DRAMATIC SCENICAL SINGSONG
THEATRICALITY HAM PANACHE
THEBAN LAIUS NIOBE AMPHION CADMEAN JOCASTA OEDIPUS PENTHEUS
THEBE (FATHER OF —) ASOPUS
(HUSBAND OF —) ZETHUS
(MOTHER OF —) METOPE
(SISTER OF —) AEGINA
THECA CUP URN CELL VAGINA CAPSULE PYXIDIUM VAGINULE
THEELIN ESTRONE FEMININ OESTRIN
THEFT CRIB LIFT HEIST PINCH SCORE STALE STEAL FURTUM RIPOFF STOUTH BRIBERY LARCENY MICHERY PICKING PILFERY ROBBERY STEALTH BURGLARY STEALAGE STEALING
(LITERARY —) PIRACY
(PETTY —) CRIB PICKERY
(PREF.) KLEPT(O)
(SUFF.) KLEPT
THEINE CAFFEINE
THEIR ARE HER ORE HORE YARE
THEIRS HERN THEIRN
THEM A EM HI UM HEM MUN HEMEN
THEME DUX BASE IDEA TEMA TEXT DITTY HOBBY LEMMA MOTIF PLACE SCOPE TESTO THEMA TOPIC URLAR MATTER MYTHOS SUBJECT ANTETHEM
(— OF FUGUE) DUX
(HACKNEYED —) CLICHE
(MAIN —) BURDEN
(RECURRING —) BURDEN
(STOCK —) TOPOS
THEMIS (DAUGHTER OF —) DICE IRENE EUNOMIA
(FATHER OF —) URANUS
(HUSBAND OF —) JUPITER
(MOTHER OF —) TERRA
THEMSELVES HEM HEMSELF
THEN SO AND POI THO ANON SYNE ALORS
THENCE AWAY THEN THEREFRO
THEOCRACY KHALSA
THEODELINDE (FATHER OF —) GARIBALD
(HUSBAND OF —) AGO AUTHARI
THEODOLITE TAIPO DIOPTER TRANSIT TRANSEPT
THEOLOGIAN FAQIH ULEMA DIVINE MUJTAHID
AMERICAN COX BROWN HATCH NEVIN SMITH TYLER WOODS BURTON CURRAN ELIADE FOSTER GLUECK KOHLER MACHEN SCHAFF STUART TAYLOR EDWARDS EVERETT HOPKINS MCCLURE MOFFATT NIEBUHR PEABODY SEABURY TILLICH VINCENT MCGIFFERT WORCESTER
AUSTRIAN MOHR RAHNER BRUNNER DENIFLE JELLINEK
BELGIAN BAIUS
BRAZILIAN BOFF
CZECH COMENIUS
DANISH MONRAD MULLER MYNSTER PEDERSEN GRUNDTVIG PONTOPPIDAN
DUTCH HAAR VOET WITS BEKKER JANSEN KUENEN KUYPER GOMARUS ARMINIUS BOGERMAN LIMBORCH SCHOLTEN EPISCOPIUS
ENGLISH BEDE BULL DODD HORT OWEN WARD BLUNT COLET HATCH PALEY PUSEY SWETE WATTS ALCUIN BUTLER FERRAR HARRIS HOOKER NEWMAN PECOCK STERNE WESLEY LANGTON MARBECK MAURICE PEARSON WHATELY WHISTON CARDWELL DRUMMOND PELAGIUS WYCLIFFE CHADERTON GUILLAUME LIGHTFOOT STAPLETON WARBURTON GROSSETESTE CHILLINWORTH
FLEMISH JANSEN
FRENCH BEZE GURY AILLY FAVRE PAJON SIMON CALVIN GERSON GLAIRE GOGUEL JURIEU PASCAL PORREE RICHER SORBON ABELARD AMYRAUT BASNAGE BAUTAIN BOCHART CHARRON FENELON QUESNEL BERENGAR CASAUBON COURAYER SABATIER CASTELLIO BOURDALOUE LICHTENBERGER LABERTHONNIERE
GERMAN ECK ESS ADAM ARND BAUR DUHM EBER GASS HEIM MERX RUPP ZAHN AMMON BAUER BUDDE CALOV EMSER FRANK GOEZE HAUCK HENKE KNAPP KRAUS LANGE MAJOR ROTHE STORR WALCH WEBER WEISS ALSTED ANDREA BAHRDT BENGEL CRAMER DALMAN DIPPEL DORNER EBRARD FICKER GEIGER HEILER HERMES HERZOG HEUSSI HIRSCH MOHLER NATORP PEUCER PLANCK REUSCH SEMLER SPENER UHLICH ZELLER ZIMMER AGRIPPA AMSDORF BOUSSET CASPARI CRUSIUS ECKHART EHRHARD ERNESTI FORSTER GERHARD HAERING HARNACK HOFMANN KOSTLIN LECHLER MOSHEIM MUNSTER NAUMANN NEANDER NIPPOLD RITSCHL STRAUSS TILLICH ULLMANN URSINUS WILHELM BULTMANN CALIXTUS CANISIUS CHEMNITZ COCCEIUS CRUCIGER DIBELIUS DILLMANN EBERHARD EICHHORN FLIEDNER GERHARDT GESENIUS HAUSRATH KAUTZSCH KLIEFOTH MICHELIS MYCONIUS OETINGER OSIANDER REIMARUS SCHENKEL AURIFABER BEYSCHLAG BUSEMBAUM DELITZSCH DOLLINGER FABRICIUS FREIDRICH JABLONSKI MICHAELIS NIEMOLLER OLEVIANUS OLSHAUSEN PFEIDERER BAUMGARTEN BONHOEFFER FANNENBERG MARHEINEKE NEUMEISTER WISLICENUS TISCHENDORF FROHSCHAMMER BRETSCHNEIDER SCHLEIERMACHER
GREEK ALLACCI CLEMENT EUSEBIUS
HUNGARIAN BALLAGI
IRISH DODWELL PLUNKET TYRRELL
ITALIAN OCHINO AQUINAS LOMBARD PERRONE SOCINUS PASSAGLIA BELLARMINE
JEWISH HIRSCH
NORWEGIAN MOE
PORTUGUESE ABARBANEL
RUSSIAN BERDYAYEV SCHMEMANN
SCOTTISH CAIRD EADIE BURNET ALESIUS CAMERON ROLLOCK TULLOCH CAMPBELL CHALMERS FAIRBAIRN CUNNINGHAM RUTHERFORD
SPANISH CANO MOLINA SUAREZ VALDES ENZINAS CARRANZA EYMERICO SERVETUS MALDONADO SEPULVEDA
SWEDISH FRYXELL SODERBLOM FAHLCRANTZ
SWISS KUNG BARTH GODET VINET ISELIN BRUNNER DIODATI ERASTUS LAVATER LECLERC BUCHMANN HEIDEGGER
SYRIAN AETIUS
THEOLOGY KALAM IRENICS DIVINITY POIMENIC POLEMICS
THEONOE (BROTHER OF —) CALCHAS
(FATHER OF —) PROTEUS THESTOR
(MOTHER OF —) LEUCIPPE PSAMATHE
THEORBO LUTE ARCHLUTE
THEOREM DUAL LEMMA CONVERSE
THEORETIC PURE
THEORETICAL BOOK PURE CLOSET THEORIC ABSTRACT ACADEMIC ARMCHAIR NOTIONAL PLATONIC
THEORIST MUSER OPINATOR
THEORIZE SUGGEST
THEORIZING IDEOLOGY
THEORY ISM OVISM EROTIC ETHICS HOLISM LAXISM SYSTEM AGOGICS ANIMISM ATOMISM BAASKAP BIGBANG CAMBISM DUALISM FORMISM HOBBISM PEELISM PLENISM THEORIC TYCHISM ACOSMISM AXIOLOGY DITHEISM DYNAMISM ENERGISM ESTHETIC ETIOLOGY FEMINISM FINITISM GHOSTISM GOBINISM HEDONICS IDEALISM IDEOLOGY MOLINISM MONADISM ONTOLOGY PROGRESS SEMANTIC SEMIOTIC SPERMISM
(— OF GAMES) AGONISTICS
(— OF THE UNIVERSE) SYSTEM
(KIND OF —) DOMINO GALOIS
(METRICAL —) STICHOLOGY
(PHYSICS —) BOHRS
(SUFF.) ISM LOGER LOGIA(N) LOGIC(AL) LOGIST LOGUE LOGY OLOGY
THEOW SERF THRALL THEOWMAN
THERAPEUTICS ACEOLOGY
THERAPY PHYSIATRICS
(SUFF.) PATH(IA)(IC)(Y)
THERAVADA HINAYANA
THERE ERE YARE ALONG VOILA WHERE YONDER THEASUM THITHER
THEREABOUTS NEARBY
THEREAFTER UPON THENCE
THEREFORE SO ERGO THEN ARGAL HENCE FORTHY IGITUR THENCE
THEREON UPON
THEREUPON SO SINCE WITHAL THEREON THEREUP
THEREWITH MIT WITH
THERIACA GALENA
THERMOMETER GLASS HYDRA CELSIUS REAUMUR
(PART OF —) BORE BULB LENS SCALE COLUMN GRADUATIONS CONSTRICTION
THERMOPLASTIC SARAN
THERMOSTAT DETECTOR PYROSTAT
THERSANDER (FATHER OF —) POLYNICES
(MOTHER OF —) ARGIA
(SLAYER OF —) TELEPHUS
THESAURUS TREASURE
THESE THIR THIS THEASUM
THESEUS (FATHER OF —) AEGEUS
(MOTHER OF —) AETHRA
(SON OF —) HIPPOLYTUS
(WIFE OF —) PHAEDRA
THESIS ACT PAPER THEMA DOWNBEAT LOGICISM THESICLE
THESTIUS (DAUGHTER OF —) ALTHAEA
(FATHER OF —) PARTHAON
(MOTHER OF —) EURYTE
(SON OF —) TOXEUS PLEXIPPUS
THESTOR (DAUGHTER OF —) THEONOE LEUCIPPE
(FATHER OF —) IDMON APOLLO
(MOTHER OF —) LAOTHOE
(SON OF —) CALCHAS
THETIS (FATHER OF —) NEREUS
(HUSBAND OF —) PELEUS
(MOTHER OF —) DORIS
(SON OF —) ACHILLES
THEY A HI THO THEI ELLAS ELLOS
(— READ) LEG
THIAMINE ANEURIN
THICK FAT SAD HAZY SLAB BLIND BROAD BURLY BUSHY CLOSE CRASS DENSE FOGGY GREAT GROSS MURKY SOLID SQUAB STIFF STOUT CHUMPY COARSE GREASY LUBBER SLABBY SPISSY STOCKY STODGY TURBID BLUBBER GRUMOUS FAMILIAR LUTULENT MOTHERED
(— OF A FIGHT) PRESS
(— WITH SMOKE) SMUDGY
(SHORT AND —) SQUAT
(11 POINTS —) HEAVY
(PREF.) CRASSI DASI DASY HADR(O) PACHY ULO
(— WITH HAIR) DASI DASY
THICKEN GEL BODY CLOT FULL BREAK KEECH LITHE DEEPEN HARDEN ENGROSS STIFFEN
(— HEDGE) PLASH
THICKENED BODIED BULLED FURRED CALLOUS CLUBBED SPISSATED

THICKENER NAPALM
THICKENING FALX LEAR ROUX SWELL CALLUS CLAVATE LIAISON PLACODE ATHEROMA CLUBBING CRASSULA PYCNOSIS EPHIPPIUM
(— OF ARTERIES) ATHEROMA
(— OF COAL SEAM) SWELLY
(— OF LETTER STROKE) STRESS
THICKET COP BOSK RONE SHAG SHAW BLUFF BRAKE CLUMP COPSE COVER DROKE HEDGE QUICK SHOLA SLICK THICK BOSKET BUSHET COVERT GREAVE JUNGLE MALLEE QUEACH SPINNY BOSCAGE BOSQUET BRUSHET COPPICE CORYLET SPINNEY WOODRIS CHAMISAL FERNSHAW QUICKSET SHINNERY THICKSET SALICETUM
THICK-HEADED OPAQUE
THICKHEADED DULL DENSE
THICKHEADED FLY CONOPID
THICK-KNEE CURLEW DIKKOP BUSTARD
THICKLY STEFLY
THICKNESS PLY BODY LAYER DIAMETER
(— OF CHIP) CUT FEED
(— OF CLOTH) LAY
(— OF METAL) GRIP
(— OF PAPER) BULK CALLIPER UNDERLAY
(ONE — OVER ANOTHER) LAYER
(SECOND —) DOUBLING
THICKSET STUB BEEFY PUNCH SQUAT STOUT THICK CHUMPY CHUNKY HUMPTY PLUGGY ROBUST STOCKY STUBBY STUGGY NUGGETY SQUATTY
THIEF GUN NIP PAD CHOR GILT LIFT MILL PRIG BUDGE CREEP CROOK FAKER GANEF PIKER SNEAK TAKER TILER ANGLER BULKER CANNON CLOYER DISMAS GONOPH HOOKER KALLAN LIFTER MICHER NIMMER NIPPER PICKER PIRATE RATERO ROBBER SNATCH TOSHER WASTER BOOSTER COLLERY FOOTMAN GORILLA GRIFTER HARRIER HEISTER LADRONE LURCHER MEECHER MERCURY PRIGGER PRIGMAN PROLLER PROWLER SNAPPER SPOTTER STEALER THIEVER CLYFAKER CONVEYER CUTPURSE FINGERER HARROWER LARCENER PETERMAN PICAROON PICKLOCK PILFERER PRIGSTER SNATCHER
(— AT A MINE) CAVER
(CATTLE —) ABACTOR BLOTTER PLANTER RUSTLER
(CLEVER —) KID CANNON
(CRUCIFIED —) DISMAS
(FLASHY —) KIDDY
(MOUNTAIN —) CHOAR
(NIGHT —) SCOURER
(PETTY —) HOOKER SLOCKER
(RIVER —) ACKMAN LUMPER
(SNEAK —) LURCHER
(VAGABOND —) WASTER
(WHARF —) TOSHER
(PREF.) KLEPT(O)
(SUFF.) KLEPT
THIEVE MAG NIM
THIEVERY PRIGGERY
THIEVING LAW SHARK PUGGING PROGGERY STEALING
THIEVING MAGPIE, THE
(CHARACTER IN —) NINETTA PODESTA GIANETTO
(COMPOSER OF —) ROSSINI
THIEVISH STEALY FURTIVE KLEPTIC SCADDLE PRIGGISH
THIEVISHNESS PRIGGISM
THIGH HAM HOCK FEMUR FLANK GAMMON
(— PAIN) MERALGIA
(PREF.) CRURO FEMORO MER(O)
(SUFF.) MERUS
THILL FILL SILL BLADE SHAFT LIMBER
THIMBLE SKEIN BUSHEL GOBLET SLEEVE CRINGLE
THIMBLEBERRY MULBERRY
THIN HOE LEW BONY FINE FLUE FUSE LANK LEAN LIMP PRIN RARE SLIM WEAK WHEY EXILE FRAIL GAUNT GAUZY LATHY PEAKY SHEER SLINK SMALL SPARE SWAMP THIRL WASHY WIZEN AERIAL BLASHY DILUTE FLUTED HOLLOW MAUGER MEAGER MEAGRE PEAKED SCRANK SEROSE SEROUS SHELLY SKINNY SLEAZY SLIGHT SPARSE SPINNY SUBTLE TENDER TWIGGY WATERY WEAKEN COVERED FOLIOUS FRAGILE GRACILE HAGGARD SANIOUS SCRAGGY SCRAILY SCRANKY SCRAWNY SHALLOW SHILPIT SLENDER SPIDERY SPINDLY TENUOUS THREADY ARANEOUS CACHETIC EGGSHELL HAIRLINE ICHOROUS MACILENT SCRAGGED SCRANNEL SKINKING VAPORISH WATERISH ATTENUATE SPINDLING
(— AND PINCHED) CHITTY
(— LEATHER) DOLE
(— OUT) HOE CHOP DISBUD FEATHER
(— SEEDLINGS) SINGLE
(— THE WALLS) IRON
(MAKE —) EMACIATE
(PREF.) AREO LEPT(O) MANO TENUI
THINE TUUM
THING JOB RES BABY ITEM SORT WHAT CHEAT CHOSE AFFAIR ANIMAL DINGUS FELLOW GILGUY MATTER ARTICLE DINGBAT MINIKIN SHEBANG WHATNOT THINGLET
(— DONE) FACT ACTUS
(— FOUND) TROVE
(— OBSERVED) OBJECT
(— OF LITTLE ACCOUNT) GEWGAW
(— OF LITTLE VALUE) NIFLE TRIFLE TRINKET
(— OF LITTLE WORTH) STIVER
(— SEEN) REGARD
(—S PROHIBITED) VETANDA
(— TO BE REGRETTED) DAMAGE
(— TO EXHIBIT) BRAVERY
(ADMIRABLE —) GEM
(ANOTHER —) ALIUD
(BIG —) SWAPPER SWOPPER
(CONSECRATED —) ANATHEMA
(CORRECT —) CHEESE
(CREEPING —) SERPENT
(DISAGREEABLE —) STINKER
(EASY —) PIE PUSHOVER
(ENORMOUS —) MONSTER
(ENTIRE —) INTEGRAL
(EXTRAORDINARY —) ONER
(FAIR —) POTATO
(FIT —) CHECKER
(FLAT —) PLAT
(FOOLISH —) FOLLY
(GOOD —) WELFARE
(HOLY —) HALIDOM
(HOLY —S) HAGIA KODASHIM
(IMPORTANT —) ACE
(INSIGNIFICANT —) SCRAT
(INSIGNIFICANT —S) SMATTER
(JEWISH —S) JUDAICA
(LITTLE —S) FEWTRILS
(LIVING —S) BIOTA
(MISSHAPEN —) ABORTION
(NEW —) NEWEL
(OUTMODED —) SNUFF
(PETTY —) SHABBLE
(PRECIOUS —) JEWEL
(PRECISE —) POINT
(REMARKABLE —) UNCO PHENOMENON
(RIDICULOUS —) MONUMENT
(RIGHT —) POTATO
(ROTTEN —) ROTTOCK
(SAD —) RUTH
(SILLY —) TRIMTRAM
(SINGLE —) UNIT
(SINGULAR —) ODDITY
(SMALL —) SNIPPET
(STRAY —) WAIF
(STUNTED —) SCRUNT SNEESHIN
(SURE —) CERT SNIP
(TERRIFYING —) BOGEYMAN
(TROUBLESOME —) PEST TRIAL PLAGUE
(UNEXPECTED —) GODSEND
(UNIQUE —) ONER UNICUM
(UNREAL —) NOMINAL
(UNSPECIFIED —S) JAZZ
(UNSUBSTANTIAL —) PUFF
(WITHOUT EQUAL —) NONPAREIL
(WORLDLY —S) EARTH
(WORNOUT —) SNUFF HUSHEL
(PL.) GEAR REALIA SQUARES
(PREF.) REI
(SUFF.) ORIUM ORY SOME
(— USED) ANT
(— USED FOR) ORIUM
THINGAMAJIG GIZMO
THINGAMY DOODAD
THING-IN-ITSELF THINGY NOUMENON
THINGS
(SUFF.) IA
THINGUMBOB DODAD DINGUS DOODAD JIGGER THINGUM THINGAMAJIG
THINGUMMY GISMO GIZMO THINGAMAJIG
THINK LET SEE WIS WIT DEEM FEEL HOLD MAKE MEAN MINT MULL MUSE READ TROW WEEN ALLOW CENSE FANCY GUESS JUDGE LOUSE OPINE PANSE SEPAD ESTEEM EXPECT FIGURE IDEATE REASON RECKON REPUTE BELIEVE CONCEIT IMAGINE REFLECT SUPPOSE SURMISE COGITATE CONSIDER ENVISAGE
(— BEST) SEEM
(— DIFFERENTLY) DISSENT
(— HARD) YERK
(— HIGHLY OF) RATE
(— IDLY) DREAM
(— ILL) MISDEEM
(— LOGICALLY) DEDUCE
(— OF) MIND PURPENSE
(— OF AS) ACCOUNT
(— OUT) STUDY REASON
(— OVER) BETHINK
(— UP) INVENT
(— UPON) BROOD
(— WELL OF) APPROVE
(— WRONGLY) MISTAKE
THINKER SOPHIST PHILOSOPH PHILOSOPHER
(CHINESE —) LEGALIST
THINKING CONCEIT THOUGHT
(CLEVER —) HEADWORK
THINLY AIRILY SPARSE SPARSELY
THINNESS RARITY EXILITY FINESSE TENUITY EXIGUITY
THINNING BALK BAULK PINCH CLEANING
THIOL MERCAPTAN
THIRD FACE GAMMA TERCE THREE DITONE TERTIA TIERCE
(PREF.) TRIT(O)
THIRDLY TERTIO
THIRD-RATE C3 HEDGE
THIRD-RATER PIKER
THIRST DRY ADRY CLEM DRYTH APOSIA DROUTH THRIST DROUGHT DIPSOSIS POLYDIPSIA
(EXCESSIVE —) POLYDIPSIA
(LOSS OF —) ADIPSIA
(PREF.) DIPS(O)
THIRSTING SITIENT
THIRSTY DRY ADRY ATHIRST DROUGHTY
THIRTEEN (YOUNGER THAN —) PRETEEN
THIS HE SO ESTA ESTO THIK DIESE THILK
THIS ABOVE ALL (AUTHOR OF —) KNIGHT
(CHARACTER IN —) PRUE CLIVE MONTY BRIGGS CATHAWAY PRUDENCE
THISTLE PUHA HOYLE CARDON DASHEL DINDLE FISTLE TEASEL CALTROP CARDUUS CARLINA GUTWEED RAURIKI WARATAH BEDEGUAR CALTHROP COMPOSIT ECHINOPS MILKWEED
(PREF.) CARDO
THITHER TO YON YOND THERE YONDER ULTERIOR YONDWARD
THOAS (BROTHER OF —) EUNEUS
(DAUGHTER OF —) HYPSIPYLE
(FATHER OF —) BACCHUS ANDRAEMON
(MOTHER OF —) GORGE ARIADNE HYPSIPYLE
(SON OF —) SICINUS
(WIFE OF —) MYRINE
THOMIST AQUINIST

THOMSONITE MESOLE MESOTYPE OZARKITE
THONG LORE RIEM BRAIL GIRTH LASSO LEASH ROMAL STRAP THUNK WHANG WHANK LACING LINGEL STRING TWITCH AMENTUM BABICHE LANIARD LANYARD LATCHET RIEMPIE
(— ON JAVELIN) AMENTUM
(HAWK'S —) BRAIL
(PREF.) HIMANTO
THOR THUNAR THUNOR
(FATHER OF —) ODIN
(HAMMER OF —) MJOLLNIR
(MOTHER OF —) JORDH
THORACIC DORSAL
THORAX CHEST TRUNK BREAST PEREION ALITRUNK CORSELET FOREBODY
THORITE ENALITE ORANGITE
THORN BROD BUSH GOAD PIKE STOB STUG BRIAR BRIER DOORN PRICK SPIKE SPINE FUSTIC JAGGER ACANTHA PRICKER STICKER COCKSPUR THORNLET
(PL.) SPEAR HAYBOTE
(PREF.) ACANTH(O) SPINI SPINO(SO) SPINULI SPINULOSO
(SUFF.) ACANTHUS SPINOSE
THORN APPLE HAW METEL STAMONY
THORNBACK RAY DORN ROKER
THORNBILL TOMTIT
THORNY HARD SPINY PRICKLY SCROGGY SPINOUS THISTLY THORNED
THORON RADON
THOROUGH RUN DEEP FIRM FULL SOUND ERRANT HOLLOW STRICT HOTSHOT INGOING REGULAR COMPLETE GROUNDLY INTIMATE PRECIOUS
THOROUGHBRED HOTBLOOD
THOROUGHFARE BUND DRUM ROAD ALLEY AVENUE STREET BIKEWAY HIGHWAY PARKWAY WHITEHALL
THOROUGH-GOING WHOLEHOG
THOROUGHGOING PAKKA ARRANT ERRANT HEARTY PROPER PUREDEE RADICAL ABSOLUTE PROFOUND TRUEBRED
THOROUGHLY BUT FULL GOOD INLY CLEAN FULLY PROOF DEEPLY GAINLY KINDLY PROPER RICHLY RIPELY WHOLLY ROUNDLY SOAKING SOBBING SOGGING SOUNDLY DRIPPING GROUNDLY HEARTILY INWARDLY
(PREF.) E
THOROUGHWORT BONESET
THOSE THEM THEY YOND
THOTH DHOUTI
THOUGH AS AND SET YET ALTHO ALTHOUGH
THOUGHT CARE IDEA MOOD VIEW FANCY TASTE TRACE NOTION PENSEE CONCEIT CONCEPT COUNSEL OPINION SURMISE PEMMICAN RUMINATE
(— EXPRESSED IN WORDS) SENTIMENT
(— OUT) ADVISED
(CAREFUL —) ADVICE ACCOUNT
(CONTROLLING —) KEYNOTE
(DEEP —) MUSE MEDITATION
(FANCIFUL —) CONCEIT
(HIGHEST —) IDEE
(INMOST —) CONSCIENCE
(INNERMOST —S) PRIVITY
(ORIGINAL —) BRAINCHILD
(REASONED —) STUDY
(UNCLEAN —) SEWERAGE
(WELL-EXPRESSED —) STROKE
(PREF.) LOG(O)
THOUGHTFUL EARNEST PENSIVE SERIOUS STUDIED STUDIOUS THOUGHTY
THOUGHTFULNESS GRACE COUNSEL
THOUGHTLESS RASH VAIN DIZZY GLAKY SUPINE VACANT ETOURDI GLAIKET RAMSTAM HEEDLESS RECKLESS
THOUSAND CHI MIL GRAND MILLE CHILIAD
(FIVE —) EPSILON
(SIX —) DIGAMMA
(TEN —) TOMAN
(10 —) MYRIAD
(100 —) LAC LAKH
(PREF.) CHILI(A) KILO MILLE MILLI
(TEN —) MYRIA MYRIO
THOUSANDTH (— OF CUBIC CENTIMETER) LAMBDA
(— OF INCH) MIL
(HUNDRED —) SSU
(PREF.) MILLI
THRACIAN GETE GETAN GETIC THRAX
THRALL SERF GURTH SLAVE CAPTIVE
THRALLDOM BONDAGE SLAVERY THIRLAGE
THRASH DAD LAM PAY TAN BANG BEAT BELT COMB DING DRUB DUST FLAX JERK LACE LICK LOUK MILL PAIL SOCK SOLE SOWL SWAP SWOP TOSE TRIM WALK WHAP WHIP WHOP YERK BASTE BELAM BLESS CREAM CURRY DRASH FLAIL FRAIL LINCH LINGE NOINT PASTE SLATE SLOSH SWACK SWING TABOR TARGE THUMP TOWEL TWINK WHALE WHANG ANOINT BUMFEG CUDGEL FETTLE JACKET LARRUP LATHER MUZZLE RADDLE STOUSH SWINGE TANCEL THREAP THRESH THWACK WALLOP LAMBACK LEATHER SWADDLE TROLLOP TROUNCE BETHWACK BUMBASTE LAMBASTE LAMBSKIN RIBROAST SPIFLICATE
THRASHER THREAPER THRESHER SICKLEBILL
THRASHING LICK TOCO LALDY HIDING WIPING BELTING LAMMING LICKING WARMING WHALING DRUBBING STRAPPING
THRASYMEDES (FATHER OF —) NESTOR
(MOTHER OF —) ANAXIBIA
THREAD BAR END BAVE CHIP CLEW CLUE CORD DOUP FILE FILM GIMP GOLD LACE LINE POIL PURL ROON SILK TRAM WIRE WORM BRIDE CHIVE FIBER FIBRE FLOAT FLOSS HYPHA INKLE LISLE LUREX REEVE SCREW SETON SHIVE SHOOT SHUTE STEEK THRUM TWEER TWIRE TWIST WATAP BOTTOM COBWEB COTTON ENFILE FIBRIL INFILE SINGLE STAMEN STITCH STRAIN STRAND STRING TASLAN TISSUE BABICHE BASTING DOUPING SLUBBER SPIREME TWITTER WARPING ACONTIUM FILAMENT GOSSAMER LIGATURE PICKOVER RAVELING SPINNING SPIRICLE
(— AROUND BOWSTRING) SERVING
(— IN SEED COATING) SPIRICLE
(— LEGS OF RABBIT) HARL HARLE
(— OF SCREW) WORM
(— OF WAX) SWARF
(—S THAT CROSS WARP) WEFT WOOF
(— USED FOR COCOON) BAVE
(BADLY TWINED —) SLUBBER
(BALL OF —) CLEW CLUE CLOWE GLOME
(BUTTONHOLE —S) BAR
(COARSE —) GIRD
(COARSEST — IN LACE) GIMP
(COILED —) COP
(FILLING —) PICK
(FINE COTTON —) LISLE
(FLOATING —) PICKOVER
(HARD —) LISLE
(LINEN —) LINE INCLE INKLE
(LOOSELY TWISTED —S) BUMP
(METAL —) LAME WIRE
(OAKUM —) PLEDGET
(PULLED —) SNAG
(REFUSE —S) BUR BURR
(SHOEMAKER'S —) END LINGEL LINGLE
(SILK —) TRAM TRAME DOUPIONI
(SOFT SHORT —) THRUM
(STRONG —) GOUNAU
(SURGICAL —) SETON
(WARP —) END STAMEN
(WAXED —) TACKER
(WEFT —) PICK SHOT
(40 —S) BEER BIER
(PL.) FLOSS
(PREF.) FILI(CI) MIT(O) NEM(A)(O) NEMAT(O) STAMIN(I)
(SUFF.) NEMA NEME STEMONOUS
THREADBARE BARE SEAR SERE USED TRITE PILLED SHABBY NAPLESS
THREADFIN SEER SEIR SULEA BARBUDO KINGFISH SEERFISH
THREADFISH COBBLER SUNFISH
THREADING SCREW STRINGING
THREADLIKE FILATE FILOSE FILIFORM
THREADWORK MACRAME
(KNOTTED —) MACRAME MACRAMI
THREASHOLD BRINK VERGE
THREAT ATTACK MENACE THUNDER
(BOASTFUL —) BRAVADO
(PL.) MINES
THREATEM (— TO RAIN) SCOWDER SCOUTHER SCOWTHER
THREATEN BODE BRAG FACE MINT BOAST SHORE ATTACK IMPEND MENACE ENDANGER MINATORY OVERHANG
(— TO RAIN) SCOUTHER
THREATENED FRAUGHT
THREATENING BIG GLUM UGLY ANGRY BOAST NASTY SABLE SHORE GREASY BANEFUL BODEFUL OMINOUS RAMPANT MINATORY MINITANT MINACIOUS
(— TO RAIN) HEAVY
THREE TREY GIMEL LEASH TRIAS TERNARY TERNION
(— CENT PIECE) TRIME
(— IN ONE) TRIUNE
(— MILES) LEAGUE
(— OF A KIND) GLEEK BRELAN TRIPLET
(GROUP OF —) TRIO TRIAD TRIPLE TROIKA
(SET OF —) TERN PAIRIAL
(PREF.) TER TERNATI TERNATO TRE TRI(S)
(— DIMENSIONS) STERE(O)
(SUFF.) TERNATE
THREE BLACK PENNIES (AUTHOR OF —) HERGESHEIMER
(CHARACTER IN —) HOWAT JAMES PENNY SUSAN EUNICE JANNAN JASPER POLDER BRUNDON MARIANA LUDOWIKA WINSCOMBE
THREE-CORNERED HAT (AUTHOR OF —) ALARCON
(CHARACTER IN —) LUCAS WEASEL EUGENIO MERCEDES FRASQUITA
THREE-DIMENSIONAL CUBIC CUBICAL
THREEFOLD TERN TRINE TERNAL TREBLE TRINAL TRIPLE TERNARY TRIFOLD TRIPLEX THRIBBLE
THREE-FORKED TRISULC
THREE MUSKETEERS (AUTHOR OF —) DUMAS
(CHARACTER IN —) ATHOS ARAMIS WARDES PORTHOS DEWINTER PLANCHET BONACIEUX CONSTANCE DARTAGNAN RICHELIEU
THREEPENCE JOEY TREY THRIP THRUM TICKEY TICKIE
THREE SISTERS (AUTHOR OF —) CHEKHOV
(CHARACTER IN —) OLGA IRINA MASHA ANDREY SOLENI KULIGIN NATASHA PROSOROV VERSHININ
THREE SOLDIERS (AUTHOR OF —) DOSPASSOS
(CHARACTER IN —) DAN RED ANDY JOHN MABE YVONNE ANDREWS FUSELLI ANDERSON GENEVIEVE CHRISTFIELD
THRENODY DIRGE HEARSE THRENE
THRESH COB BEAT CAVE LUMP WHIP BERRY FLAIL FRAIL SPELT STAMP THRASH
THRESHEL DRASHEL
THRESHER TASKER
THRESHER SHARK FOX FOXFISH WHIPTAIL
THRESHOLD HEAD SILL SOLE DEARN LIMEN DRASHEL DOORSILL
(— OF CONSCIOUSNESS) LIMEN
THRIFT SAVING VIRTUE ECONOMY SEAPINK STATICE THEEDOM PARSIMONY

THRIFTILY NEAR
THRIFTLESS WASTEFUL
THRIFTY CANNY FENDY PUIST FRUGAL SAVING CAREFUL SPARING
THRILL JAG WOW BANG DIRL GIRL KICK RUSH SEND FLUSH SHOOT THIRL DINDLE STOUND TICKLE TINGLE TREMOR ENCHANT FRISSON VIBRATE FREMITUS
(PROVIDING A —) KICKY
(SHARP —) ZING
THRILLING TINGLY VIBRANT PLANGENT TINGLING
THRINTER FRONTER
THRIPID PHYSOPOD
THRIPS BLACKFLY PHYSOPOD
THRIVE DOW GROW LIKE RISE THEE ADDLE FADGE MOISE PROVE THRAM BATTEN BATTLE CATTER CHIEVE PROSPER STORKEN SUCCEED WELFARE FLOURISH THRODDEN
(— IN) LOVE
THRIVING BIEN GRUSHIE ROARING THRIFTY BLOOMING TOWARDLY
THRIVINGLY GAILY GAYLY BRAVELY
THROAT MAW CRAG CROP GOWL GULA HALS HASS LANE GORGE HALSE SWIRE FAUCES GARGET GULLET GUTTUR GUZZLE RICTUS CHANNEL JUGULUM STOMACH SWALLOW WEASAND THRAPPLE THROPPLE THROTTLE
(— AILMENT) STREP
(— OF ANCHOR) CLUTCH
(— OF COROLLA) FAUCES
(— OF FROG) KNEE
(CLEAR —) HARRUMPH
(KIND OF —) STREP
(MOUTH AND —) WHISTLE
(SORE —) HOUSTY PRUNELLA
(PREF.) BRONCH(I)(IO)(O) DER(O) GUTTERO
THROATLATCH FIADOR
THROATY THICK GUTTURAL
THROB ACHE BEAT BELK DRUM DUNT LEAP PANG PANT QUOP WARK FLACK PULSE STANG WARCH STOUND STRIKE STROKE TINGLE WALLOP FLACKER PULSATE VIBRATE FLICHTER PALPITATE
(— IN PAIN) SHOOT
(RAPID —S) FRIMITTS
THROBBING DUNT ATHROB THRILL BEATING PITAPAT VIBRANT PULSATORY
THROE PANG PULL STOUR SHOWER PAROXYSM
(—S OF DEATH) AGONY
THROMBIN PLASMASE
THROMBOPLASTIN COAGULIN CYTOZYME
THROMBOSIS SHOCK CORONARY
THRONE GADI SEAT ASANA GADDI GADHI SELLE SIEGE STALL STATE STEAD STOOL MUSNUD SEGGIO SHINZA TRIBUNE CATHEDRA SEGGIOLA SINHASAN
(— OF GOD) MERCYSEAT
(BISHOP'S —) SEE APSE CATHEDRA
(INDIAN —) GADI
THRONE ROOM AIWAN
THRONG CREW HEAP HOST ROUT CHIRT CROWD FLOCK FRACK HORDE POSSE PRESS SHOAL SWARM RESORT THRAVE THREAT THRIMP THRUST COMPANY TEMPEST THRUTCH SURROUND
(— OF SEAFOWL) SAVSSAT
(CONFUSED —) LURRY
THRONGED ALIVE FREQUENT NUMEROUS
THROTTLE GUN CHOKE SCRAG STIFLE GARROTE STRANGLE THROPPLE
THROUGH BY PER DONE THRU WITH ROUND AROUND
(— AND THROUGH) INGRAIN INGRAINED
(RIGHT —) TILL
(PREF.) DIA PER
THROUGHOUT OVER ABOUT ROUND ABROAD BEDENE BIDENE DURING ENTIRE PASSIM SEMPRE OVERALL THRUOUT
(PREF.) HOL(O)
THROW GO DAB DAD HIP HIT PAT PEG PUT SHY ACES BIFF BUCK BUNG CALE CAST CHIP CLOD COOK CUCK DART DASH DROW DUMP HAIL HANK HIPE HULL HURL HYPE JERK LACE MILL PECK PICK PURL SEND SKIM SLAT SOSS TOSS TURF VANG WARP WURP YEND CHUCK CHUNK DOUSE FLICK FLING FLIRT FLURR HEAVE PITCH SLING SPANG DEVEST ELANCE HAUNCH HURTLE INJECT LAUNCH SLIGHT THRILL BLUNDER BUTTOCK COCKSHY MANGANA UPTHROW VIBRATE CATAPULT JACULATE
(— A BASEBALL PITCH) HANG
(— ABOUT) BOUNCE
(— ASIDE) DEVEST
(— AT HAZARD) NICK
(— AWAY) DICE DOFF BANDY SCRAP WAIVE PROJECT JETTISON SQUANDER
(— BACK) REPEL
(— BASEBALL) BURN
(— BY KICKING) WINCE
(— CARELESSLY) COB
(— DICE) JEFF
(— DOWN) DUSH EVEN PILE FLUMP LODGE ABJECT DETURB THRING FLATTEN
(— FORTH) EJECT
(— FORWARD) LAUNCH
(— HEAVILY) LOB
(— HEEDLESSLY) SLIGHT
(— IN CRAPS) CRAP PASS CRABS BOXCARS NATURAL
(— IN QUOITS) RINGER
(— INTO CONFUSION) CLUB EMBROIL FLUTTER CONFOUND CONVULSE
(— INTO DISORDER) PIE ADDLE BOLLIX DERANGE DISRANK DISRUPT EMBROIL DISARRAY
(— INTO PERPLEXITY) FLUMMOX
(— INTO WASTE) BACK
(— JERKILY) FLIRT
(— LIGHT UPON) ILLUME
(— LIQUID) JAW
(— OF A STEER) DOGFALL
(— OFF) CANT CAST EMIT SLIRT SPILL SLOUGH CONFUSE UNBURDEN
(— OFF COURSE) EMIT SHED DERAIL
(— OF SHUTTLE) SHOT SHOOT SHUTE
(— OF THREES) COCKEYES
(— ONESELF) CLAP
(— OPEN) DISPARK
(— OUT) FIRE HOOF LADE BELCH EJECT ERUPT SPOUT DETURB IGNORE EXTRUDE
(— OVER) JILT
(— QUICKLY) LASH
(— REPEATEDLY) PELT
(— ROUGHLY) WAP
(— SIDEWISE) SHY
(— SILK) THROWST
(— SMARTLY) SLAT
(— STEER) BUST
(— STICKS) SQUAIL
(— STONES) ROCK
(— TOGETHER) HUDDLE
(— UNDER) SUBJECT
(— UP) BARF CAVE PICK VOMIT
(— VIOLENTLY) BUZZ DING PASH SOCK WHAP WHOP SMASH HURTLE WUTHER WHITHER SPANGHEW PRECIPITATE
(— WITH A JERK) JET CANT SQUIRR FLOUNCE
(— WITH GREAT FORCE) BUZZ SWACK
(— WITHOUT VIOLENCE) HURL
(CHEATING — OF DICE) KNAP
(FOOTBALL —) GROUND
(FREE —) FOUL
(LARIAT —) HOOLIAN
(LOWEST — AT DICE) AMBSACE AMESACE
(WRESTLING —) HANK HIPE HYPE BUTTOCK BACKHEEL
(SUFF.) JECT
THROWAWAY DODGER
THROWBACK ATAVISM ATAVIST
THROWER TRAMMER THROWSTER
(SPEAR —) ATLATL
THROWING DARTING
THROWING-STICK ATLATL WOMMERA WOOMERA HORNERAH TROMBASH TRUMBASH
THROWN (— AWAY) CASTAWAY
(— DOWN) DEJECTED
(PREF.) **(— OUT)** RHIPTO
THROWSTER TWISTER
THRUM FUM STRUM THUMB FRINGE
THRUSH POP OMAO SOOR APTHA BREVE FRUSH GRIVE MAVIS OUZEL PITTA SABIA SHAMA SHIRL SPREW UZZLE VEERY APHTHA DRAINE JAYPIE KICKUP MISSEL OLOMAO PULISH SHRITE JAYPIET REDWING WAGTAIL BELLBIRD CHERCOCK FORKTAIL PRUNELLA SHAGBARK THRASHER THROSTLE THRUSHEL THRUSTLE URTICATE WOODCHAT SOLITAIRE MONILIASIS NIGHTINGALE
THRUSHLIKE TURDOID
THRUST DAB DEG DIG DUB JAB JAG JAM JOB POP PUG BANG BEAR BIRR BOKE BORE BUCK BUTT CANT CHOP CRAM DART DASH DUSH FOIN HURL KICK LICK MURE PASS PICK PILT POKE PORR POSS POTE PROD PUSH SEND SINK SPAR STAB STOP TILT VENY WHAP WHOP BREAK DRIFT DRIVE EXERT HUNCH LUNGE POACH POINT PROKE PUNCH SHOOT SPANK STAVE STICK STOKE STUFF THROW DARTLE PLUNGE POUNCE STITCH STRAIN STRESS STRIKE STRIPE BEARING IMPULSE PRESSURE SHOULDER STOCCADO
(— A LANCE) AVENTRE
(— ALONG) SLIDE
(— ASIDE) DAFF SHUFFLE
(— AWAY) DOFF SHOVE DETRUDE ABSTRUDE
(— DOWN) THRING DEPULSE DETRUDE
(— IN) INSERT STRIKE INTRUDE
(— OF ARCH) DRIFT
(— OF EXPLOSION) BLOWOUT
(— ONESELF) CHISEL
(— ONWARD) STAVE
(— OUT) POUT REACH STRUT EXSERT DETRUDE EXTRUDE OBTRUDE PROTRUDE OBTRUSIVE
(— SUDDENLY) STRIKE
(— THROUGH) ENFILED
(— WITH ELBOW) HUNCH
(— WITH GREAT FORCE) BUZZ
(— WITH NOSE) NUDDLE
(— WITH WEAPON) FOIN SHOVE
(DAGGER —) DAG
(FENCING —) PASS VENY BOTTE PUNTO VENUE REMISE REPOST TIMING PASSADO RIPOSTE STOCCADO STOCCATA
(HOME —) HAI HAY
(MATADOR'S —) ESTOCADA
(SARCASTIC —) GIRD
THUD BAFF DUMP PHUT PLOD SWAG DOYST FLUMP POUND BOUNCE SQUELCH
THUG MUG GOON PUNK GOONDA RODMAN GORILLA HOODLUM MOBSTER GANGSTER
(LIKE A —) GOONY
(SOUTH AFRICAN —) TSOTSI
THUJA BIOTA
THUJONE SALVIOL
THULUTH SOOLOOS
THUMB THOOM POLLEX THENAR
(— THROUGH) SKIM
(BALL OF —) THENAR
THUMBHOLE BACKLILL
THUMBSTALL POUCER POUSER
THUMP COB DAD DUB BANG BEAT BLOW BUMP DING DIRD DRUB DUNT KNUB LUMP PAIK PAKE POLT SOSS THUD TUND TUNK YARK YERK BLAFF BLIBE BUNCH CLOUR CLUNK CRUMP KNOCK POUND TABOR THACK WHELK BOUNCE HAMMER PUMMEL THUNGE
THUMPING WHAPPING WHOPPING
THUNDER ROAR SULFUR BRATTLE FOULDRE SULPHUR INTONATE

(PREF.) BRONT(E)(O) CERAUN(O) KERAUN(O)
THUNDERBOLT BOLT FIRE VAJRA FULMEN FOULDRE ARTIFACT FIREBOLT
(SHOOTER OF —S) THOR
(PREF.) CERAUN(O) KERAUN(O)
THUNDERING TONANT
THUNDERSQUALL BAYAMO VENDAVAL
THUNDERSTONE ARTIFACT
THUNDERSTORM HOUVARI TEMPEST TORNADO
THURIBLE CENSER
THUS AS SIC DYCE THUSLY THISWISE THUSGATE
THWACK BLOW DUNT LICK CRUMP SOUSE
THWART BALK FOIL WART BENCH CROOK CROSS SPITE THRAW THROW ZYGON BAFFLE SCOTCH STYMIE SNOOKER CONTRAIR CONTRARY TRAVERSE
THWARTING CROSS CROSSING
THYESTES (BROTHER OF —) ATREUS
(FATHER OF —) PELOPS
(MOTHER OF —) HIPPODAMIA
THYIA (FATHER OF —) CASTALIUS CEPHISSEUS
(SON OF —) DELPHUS
THYINE THUGA THUYA
THYLACINE YABBI
THYME MARUM PELETRE HILLWORT SERPOLET
TI KI TOI TITI
TIAMAT (HUSBAND OF —) APSU
(SLAYER OF —) MARDUK
TIARA MITER REGNUM CIDARIS TIARELLA
TIBBU DAZA TEDA
TIBET (CHINESE NAME:) SITSANG

TIBET
CAPITAL: LASSA LHASA
COIN: TANGA
LAKE: ARU BAM BUM NAM MEMA TOSU JAGOK TABIA DAGTSE GARHUR KASHUN SELING TANGRA YAMDOK KYARING TERINAM TSARING ZILLING JIGGITAI
LANGUAGE: BODSKAD
MOUNTAIN: KAMET SAJUM KAILAS BANDALA
MOUNTAIN RANGE: KAILAS KUNLUN HIMALAYA
NATIVE: BHOTIA BHOTIYA
PEOPLE: NOSU
RIVER: NAK NAU SAK SONG INDUS SUTLEJ MATSANG SALWEEN
TOWN: NOH KARAK LHASA GARTOK TOTLING GYANGTSE SHIGATSE

TIBETAN BALTI DRUPA BHOTIA BHUTIA CHAMPA DROKPA KHAMBA KHAMBU PANAKA SHERPA TANGUT BHOTIYA BHUTANI GYARUNG
TIBIA SHIN SHANK CNEMIS SHINBONE
(SUFF.) CNEMA CNEMIA CNEMIC CNEMUS
TIBOURBOU CORTEZ
TIC FIXATION
(ONE SUBJECT TO —) TIQUEUR
TICAL BAHT
TICK FAG JAR KEB KED BEAT KADE NICK PEAK PICK PIKE CHALK CHICK CRIKE PIQUE STRAP ACARID IXODID PALLET TALAJE TAMPAN ACARIAN ARGASID BEDTICK IXODIAN PINOLIA ARACHNID CARAPATO GARAPATA GARAPATO TURICATA
(— OFF) IRK MIFF RILE STEAM
(— OF TIME) MOMENT
(PREF.) ACAR(I)(O) CROTO
TICKED MACKEREL
TICKET LOT TAG COMP BLANK CHECK DUCAT FICHE TOKEN BALLOT BILLET COUPON DOCKET PIGEON POLICY RETURN BENEFIT ETIQUET CONTRACT DEADHEAD STOPOVER TRANSFER PASTEBOARD
(— GIVEN WITHOUT CHARGE) FREEBEE FREEBIE
(COMMISSION —) SPIFF
(FREE —) PASS FREEBEE FREEBIE
(HOT —) RAGE
(LOTTERY —) BLANK HORSE BENEFIT
(SALES —) TRAVELER
(SEASON —) IVORY
(PL.) PAPER
TICKET WINDOW GUICHET
TICKING KISS TICK BEDTICK
TICKLE AMUSE TEASE EXCITE KITTLE PLEASE THRILL TIDDLE CUITTLE
TICKLISH RISKY GOOSEY KITTLE KITTLY QUEASY TENDER TOUCHY TRICKY KITTLISH
TICKSEED COREOPSIS
TICK TREFOIL BEDSTRAW SAINFOIN TICKSEED
TIDBIT NOSH TRACE SAYNETE BEATILLE KICKSHAW
TIDDLEYWINK SQUAIL
TIDE FLOW NEAP WAVE AGGER EAGRE ROUST SPRING OVERTIDE SEAFLOOD
(— MOVEMENT) LAKIE
(CRIMSON —) BAMA
(KIND OF —) YULE
(PREF.) **(HIGH —)** PLEMYRA
TIDINGS NEWS WORD RUMOR SOUND UNCOW ADVICE MESSAGE
(GLAD —) GOSPEL
TIDY RID COSH MACK NEAT SIDE SMUG SNOD SNUG TAUT TOSH TRIG WEME CHART DONCY DONSY DOUCE NATTY NIFTY QUEME TIGHT DONSIE FETTLE POLITE SPOONY ORDERLY ALLIGATE MACKLIKE MENSEFUL SHIPSHAPE
TIE BOW LAP TYE BAND BEND BIND BOND CAST DRAW KILT KNOT LACE LASH LOCK ROOT WASH WISP YOKE ASCOT BRACE CADGE LEASH NEXUS POINT THRAP THROW TRICE TRUSS ATTACH BUNDLE CONNEX COPULA COUPLE FASTEN LIGATE SECURE DOGFALL FOULARD JAZZBOW NECKTIE SHACKLE SLEEPER SPANCEL TABLEAU CROSSTIE DEADLOCK INTERTIE LIGATURE STANDOFF STRINGER VINCULUM
(— BENEATH) SUBNECT
(— IN TENNIS) DEUCE
(— IN WRESTLING) DOGFALL
(— KNOT) CAST
(— LEGS) HOBBLE
(— ONIONS) TRACE
(— SCORE) PEELS
(— THE SCORE) EQUALIZE
(— TOGETHER) KNIT LEASH CONNECT HARNESS
(— UP) SNUB TRAMMEL LIGATURE TWITCHEL
(— UP SHORT) SNUB
(LEATHER —) WANTY
(MADE-UP —) TECK
(NEEDLEWORK —) BRIDE
(STRING —) BOLO
(PL.) GILLIES
TIE BEAM BALK BAULK BINDER
TIED EVEN FAST KNIT EVENED SQUARE
TIEPIN PROP SCARFPIN STICKPIN
TIE PLATE TURTLE
TIER ROW BANK DECK RANK CHESS STORY WITHE DEGREE PINAFORE
(— OF CASKS) RIDER
(— OF GUNS) TIRE
(— OF SEATS) CIRCLE
(— OF SHELVES) STAGE
TIERCE LEASH THIRD UNDERSONG
TIFF MIFF SPAT TIFT
TIFFIN CONDOR
TIGER SHER SHIR TIGRE TIGERKIN
(PREF.) TIGRO
TIGER CAT CHATI MARGAY
TIGERFOOT IPOMOEA
TIGER SHARK DEMOISELLE
TIGER SNAKE ELAPID ELAPOID
TIGHT WET FULL HARD NEAR PANG SNUG TAUT TIDY TRIG CLOSE DENSE DRUNK STENT TENSE STINGY STRAIT STRICT AIRTIGHT
TIGHTEN JAM CALK FIRM FRAP BRACE CAULK CINCH CLOSE FEEZE SCREW THRAP WRENCH STRAITEN
(— WITH ROPE) SWIFT
TIGHTFISTED NARROW STINGY
TIGHT-LIPPED SILENT
TIGHTLY FAST HARD SHORT STRAIT CLOSELY
TIGHTS MAILLOT LEOTARDS
TIGHTWAD FIST MISER PIKER STIFF
TIKVAH (SON OF —) SHALLUM JAHAZIAH
TILDE TIL WAVE TITTLE
(HAVING A —) CURLY
TILE LUMP SLAT FAVUS KASHI LATER SLATE IMBREX LAPPET PAMENT QUARRY SLATER TEGULA AZULEJO CARREAU CONDUIT PANTILE QUARREL STARTER MAINTILE
(— IN HOPSCOTCH) PEEVER
(— USED IN MOSAIC) ABACULUS
(HEXAGONAL —) FAVUS
(HOLLOW —) BACKING
(HOPSCOTCH —) PEEVER
(LARGE —) DALLE QUARL QUARLE
(MAH JONG —) HONOR SEASON
(ONE-HALF —) HEAD
(PERSIAN —) KASHI
(ROUNDED —) CREASE
(SMALL —) TILETTE
(SQUARE —) QUADREL QUARREL
(TURKISH —) IZNIK
(PREF.) OSTRAC(O) PLINTHI
TILER HELER HELLIER
TILL TO EAR FIT LOB CASH FARM PLOW TEAL TOIL DRESS LABOR UNTIL WHILE FURROW MANURE PLOUGH TILLER WHILST HUSBAND SHUTTLE DUCKFOOT OXHARROW
TILLABLE EARABLE
TILLAGE GAINOR MANURE ARATION CULTURE TILTURE
TILLED GEOM TOILED
TILLER HELM STERN STOOL HUSBAND KILLIFER
TILLING EARTH FALLOW
TILON (FATHER OF —) SHIMON
TILT DIP TIP TOP BANK CANT CAVE COCK HEEL LIST PEAK SWAG TRAP BRASH HEELD HIELD JOUST STOOP TIPUP CASTER TILTER TOPPLE CURRENT TOURNEY ATTITUDE COCKBILL QUINTAIN
(— BRICK) HACK
(— IN WATER) DABBLE
(— OF BOWSPRIT) STAVE
(— OF NOSE) KIP KIPP
TILTED ACOCK ASTOOP
TILT HAMMER OLIVER
TILTING DIP JOUSTING
TIMANDRA (FATHER OF —) TYNDAREUS
(HUSBAND OF —) ECHEMUS PHYLEUS
(MOTHER OF —) LEDA
(SISTER OF —) HELEN CLYTEMNESTRA
TIMBAL DRUM TYMBALON
TIMBER CAP LOG RIB BEAM BIBB BUNK BUNT CLOG DRAM FELL FISH FROG GIRT PUMP RAFF SKID SPAR SPUR TREE WOOD CAHUY CAVEL CRUCK FLOOR GRIPE JOIST KEVEL LEDGE ORGUE PLATE RIDER SISSU SPALE STICK BEARER BRIDGE BUMPER CAMBER CORBEL DAGGER FENDER FOREST KNIGHT LIZARD ROOFER SISSOO SUMMER TIMMER BOLSTER CARLING DEADMAN DIVIDER FALLAGE FUTCHEL FUTTOCK GROUSER PARTNER PITWOOD RIBBAND TRANSOM CORDWOOD COULISSE DOGSHORE FOREHOOK STRINGER STUMPAGE TRIPSILL WOODFALL
(— BETWEEN TRIMMERS) HEADER
(— CUT TO LENGTH) JUGGLE
(— IN MINE) COG STULL LIFTER DIVIDER JUGGLER
(— KEPT DRY) BRIGHT
(— ON SCAFFOLD) LIGGER PUTLOG
(— ON SLED) BUNK
(— PIECE) PUTLOG
(— SAWED AND SPLIT) LUMBER
(— SUPPORTING CAP) LEGPIECE
(— SUSTAINING YARDS) MAST
(— TO PROP COAL) BROB
(CONVEX —) CAMBER
(CURVED —) CRUCK
(CUT —) FELL
(FELLED —) HAG
(FLOOR —) JOIST SUMMER

(FLOORING —) BATTEN
(FOUNDATION —) PILE
(FRAMING —) PUNCHEON
(HORIZONTAL —) REASON
(NORWEGIAN —) DRAM
(PHILIPPINE —) LAUAN
(PRINCIPAL — OF VESSEL) KEEL
(ROOF —) LEVER RAFTER
(ROOFING —S) SILE
(SHIP'S —) CANT KEEL KNEE RUNG SPUR APRON LEDGE WRONG DAGGER HARPIN LACING SCROLL BRACKET FUTTOCK STEMSON DOGSHORE STANDARD
(SHIPBUILDING —S) STOCKS DEADWOOD HARPINGS
(SLABBED —) CANT
(SQUARED —) BALK
(SUPPORT —) SILL GIRDER LEDGER PUNCHEON STRINGER
(SYSTEM OF —S) BOND
(UNCUT —) STUMPAGE
(WEATHERBEATEN —) DRIKI
TIMBERLAND STICKS WOODLAND
TIMBERMAN BRACER
TIMBO CUBE AJARI
TIMBRE TONE CLANG COLOR KLANG COLORING
TIMBREL TABOR TABOUR
TIME DAY ELD BELL BOUT HINT HOUR SELE SITH TIDE WHET ABYSS CHARE EPOCH FLASH FRIST KALPA SITHE SPACE STOUN STOUR TEMPO TEMPS VOLTA WHACK WHILE COURSE KAIROS PERIOD SEASON STOUND TEMPUS CADENCE DEWFALL SESSION MOVEMENT
(— AFTER) POST
(— ALLOWED FOR PAYMENT) USANCE
(— AND — AGAIN) OFTEN
(— BEFORE WITHDRAWAL) FLOAT
(— BEING) NONCE
(— FOR PAYING) KIST
(— FOR PAYMENT) CREDIT
(— GRANTED) FRIST
(— HENCE) MORROW
(— IN GRAMMAR) TENSE
(— IN SERVICE) AGE
(— INTERVAL) WINDOW
(— INTERVENING) INTERIM MEANTIME
(— IN THE PAST) LANGSYNE
(— LONG SINCE PAST) YORE
(— OF BEAUTY) BLOOM
(— OF BEGINNING) SPRING
(— OF CRISIS) EXIGENT
(— OF CURRENCY) TENOR
(— OF DYING) LAST
(— OF ELEVENTH ZONE) SAMOA
(— OF EXPIRY) ISH
(— OF EXUBERANCE) CARNIVAL
(— OF FASTING) LENT
(— OF FEASTING) GUTTIDE
(— OF HAPPINESS) CAMELOT
(— OF HIGHEST STRENGTH) HEYDAY
(— OF INACTIVITY) INTERIM NONTERM
(— OF LIGHT) DAY
(— OF MATURITY OR DECLINE) AUTUMN
(— OF MAXIMUM USE) PEAK
(— OF NEWS STORY) BREAK
(— OF OLD AGE) SUNSET
(— OF QUIET) DEAD
(— OF REST) BREATH SABBATH
(— OF TRIAL) PROBATION
(— OF WOE) WOSITH
(— TO COME) FUTURITY
(ANOTHER —) AGAIN
(AT ANOTHER —) ALIAS
(BRIEF —) TINE FLASH THROW
(BY THE —) AGAINST
(CRITICAL —) PINCH
(EACH —) ONCE
(ENDLESS —) PERPETUITY
(EXTENDED —) TRAIN
(FAST —) LENT
(FIT —) TID
(FIXED —) HOUR STEVEN
(FUTURE —) MANANA
(GAY —) FRISK WHOOPEE
(GOOD —) BALL BASH BEANO JOLLY BARNEY FROLIC HOLIDAY
(HARD —) GYP BUSINESS
(IMMEASURABLY LONG PERIOD OF —) EON AEON
(INFINITE —) ABYSS
(INTERVENING —) MEANTIME MEANWHILE
(KIND OF —) PRIME
(LONG —) AGE YEARS
(MUSICAL —) METER METRE
(OLD —S) ELD
(OPPORTUNE —) SEAL SEEL SEIL SELE
(PAST —) FORETIME
(POINT OF —) MOMENT
(PRESCRIBED —) LIMIT
(QUIET —) SLACK
(RIGHT —) TID
(SECOND —) YET EFTSOON EFTSOONS
(SET —) TRYST
(SHORT —) TIFF SPACE START MINUTE STOUND
(SINGLE —) ONCE
(SPARE —) TOOM LEISURE
(SPECIAL —) OCCASION
(STRICT —) MEASURE
(TRIPLE —) TRIPLA
(UNENGAGED —) LEISURE
(UNIT OF —) AEON
(WORKING —) CORE
(PL.) SYSE
(PREF.) CHRON(O) HORO
(SUFF.) AD CHRONE CHRONOUS SEMIC
TIMEAUS (SON OF —) BARTIMAEUS
TIME CLOCK BUNDY TELLTALE
TIME-HONORED VINTAGE
TIMELESS AGELESS ETERNAL DATELESS ATEMPORAL
TIMELESSNESS ETERNITY
TIMELY PAT DULY TIDY COGENT TIMEFUL TIMEOUS TOWARDLY SEASONABLE TEMPESTIVE
TIME OF YOUR LIFE (AUTHOR OF —) SAROYAN
(CHARACTER IN —) JOE TOM NICK KITTY MCCARTHY
TIMEPIECE DIAL CLOCK TIMER VERGE WATCH GHURRY PENDULE HOROLOGE HOROLOGY
TIMETABLE BRADSHAW SCHEDULE
TIME-WORN RUSTY
TIMID SHY ARGH EERY NESH SELY SHAN BAUCH BLATE EERIE FAINT PAVID SCARE SCARY AFRAID COWARD ASHAMED BASHFUL CHICKEN FEARFUL FRIGHTY NEBBISH NERVOUS RABBITY SCADDLE STRANGE TREMBLY COWARDLY FEARSOME GHASTFUL RETIRING TIMOROSO TIMOROUS PIGEONHEARTED
TIMIDITY SHYNESS TIMERITY FUNKINESS
TIMIDLY SMALL
TIMNA (BROTHER OF —) LOTAN
(LOVER OF —) ELIPHAZ
(SON OF —) AMALEK
TIMOLEON (FATHER OF —) TIMODEMUS
(MOTHER OF —) DEMARISTE
TIMON OF ATHENS (AUTHOR OF —) SHAKESPEARE
(CHARACTER IN —) CUPID TIMON TITUS CAPHIS LUCIUS FLAVIUS PHRYNIA LUCILIUS LUCULLUS PHILOTUS TIMANDRA APEMANTUS FLAMINIUS SERVILIUS VENTIDIUS ALCIBIADES HORTENSIUS SEMPRONIUS
TIMOR (CAPITAL OF —) DILI
(COIN OF —) AVO PATACA
(ISLAND OF —) MOA LETI LAKOR
(LANGUAGE OF —) TETUM
(TOWN IN —) KUPANG ATAMBUA
TIMOROUS ASPEN FAINT MILKY TIMID AFRAID COWISH TREPID FEARFUL FERDFUL MEACOCK NERVOUS FEARSOME SHEEPISH TEMEROUS TIMOROSO
TIMOTHY (COMPANION OF —) PAUL
(WIFE OF —) SIF
TIN SN DIXY JOVE DIXIE KATIN SWELL TINNY KHATIN JUPITER PILLION STANNUM PRILLION TINGLASS
(MESS —) DIXY DIXIE
(RELATED TO —) STANNIC
(ROOFING —) TERNE
(SHEET —) LATTEN LATTIN
(TIE — CAN TO TAIL) TAILPIPE
(PREF.) STANN(I)(O)
TINAMOU YUTU MACUCA YNAMBU TATAUPA MARTINET
TINCAL ALTINCAR
TINCTURE BUFO DRUG COLOR IMBUE SMACK STAIN TAINT TENNE TINCT ARGENT ARNICA ELIXIR SATURN DIAMOND SERICON ARAMAIZE INFUSION LAUDANUM TAINTURE PAREGORIC
TINDER SPUNK AMADOU TENDRE FIREBOX
TINE BAY KNAG SNAG TANG GRAIN OFFER POINT PRONG RIGHT TOOTH GRAINING TINETARE TINEWEED
(ANTLER'S —) RIGHT CROCKET SURROYAL
TIN FOIL TAIN
TINGE DYE EYE HUE CAST DASH HINT TANG TINT WOAD COLOR FLUSH IMBUE PAINT SAVOR SHADE STAIN TAINT TINCT TOUCH SEASON SMUTCH BEPAINT DISTAIN GLIMPSE DISCOLOR TINCTION TINCTURE
TINGED FLORID GILDED
TINGGIAN ITNEG ITANEG
TINGLE SOO BURN DIRL GELL GIRL THIRL DINDLE SWIDGE TINKLE PRINGLE PRINKLE TRINKLE VIBRATE
TINGLY AGOG
TING YAO PORCELAIN
TINHORN ARTY
TINKER PRIG TINK CAIRD FIDDLE FIDGET MUGGER KETTLER PROJECT TRAVELER
TINKLE TINK DINDLE DINGLE TINGLE TRINKLE TWINKLE
TINKLING THIN
TINNER TINKER
TINSEL GAUDY TINSY TINNET CLINQUANT
TINT DYE EYE COLOR ENNUE GRAIN SHADE TINCT TINGE SPRAING
(— IN HORSE'S COAT) BLOSSOM
(— WITH COSMETICS) SURFLE
(CLANG —) TIMBRE
TINTED TINCT
TINWORKS STANNARY
TINY TINE BITSY BITTY DEENY SMALL TEENY TIDDY WEENY ATOMIC BITTIE WEESHY MINIKIN ATOMICAL
TIP CAP DIP END FEE NEB TOP APEX CANT CAVE COCK DUMP HEEL HELD HORN KEEL LEAD LIST PALM PIKE PILE SWAG TILT TYPE VAIL GRIFF HEELD MUCRO POINT POUCH SPIRE SPURE STEER CAREEN CENTER CENTRE TICKLE TIPLET TIPPLE TOPPLE WHEEZE APICULA CUMSHAW DERTRUM DOUCEUR GRIFFIN POINTER PROPINE WRINKLE APICULUS BONAMANO ENTOMION FOOTHOLD GRATUITY BAKSHEESH BACKSHEESH PERQUISITE
(— AT A CASINO) TOKE
(— OF ANTENNA) ARISTA
(— OF BILLIARD CUE) LEATHER
(— OF BIRD'S BILL) DERTRUM
(— OF CHIN) POINT
(— OF CRESCENT) HORN
(— OF ELBOW) NOOP
(— OF FOX'S BRUSH) CHAPE
(— OF SKI) SHOVEL
(— OF SPIDER) BULB
(— OF STAMP) SHOE
(— OF TAIL) TAG
(— OF TOE) POINTE
(— OF TONGUE) CORONA
(— OF UMBO) BEAK
(— OF WHEAT KERNEL) BRUSH
(— OF WHIP) SNAPPER
(— ON ORGAN PIPE) TOE
(— OVER) TOP PURL UPEND OVERSET
(— UP) CANT COUP COWP
(ABRUPT —) MUCRO
(BOW —) HORN
(GAMBLING —) TOKE
(INWARD —) BANK
(LARGE —S) LARGESS LARGESSE

(RACING —) NAP
(RUBBISH —) TOOM
(PREF.) ACR(O) APIC(O)
TIPCART COUPE COCOPAN TUMBREL
TIPCAT CAT PIGGY PUSSY KITCAT PIGGIE
TIPPED BANKED
(EASILY —) CRANK
TIPPER DUMPER THROWER TIPPLER
TIPPET FUR AMICE SCARF STOLE ALMUCE SINDON LIRIPIPE LIRIPOOP PELERINE VICTORINE
TIPPLE BIB NIP POT SOT DRAM GILL BIBBER BIBBLE FUDDLE PUDDLE SIPPLE TIPPLER TOOTHFUL
TIPPLER SOT SOUSE TOAST WINER BIBBER BOLLER BOOZER BUBBER DRAMMER PANURGE POTATOR TUMBLER WHETTER ALESTAKE MALTWORM
TIPPLING POTTING BIBACITY BIBATION
TIPSTER TOUT PROPHET
TIPSY CUT BOSKY DRUNK FRESH MUSED MUZZY NAPPY OILED ROCKY SLUED TIGHT TOTTY TOZIE BUMPSY GROGGY SCREWY SLEWED SPRUNG SQUIFF EBRIOSE EBRIOUS EXALTED SQUIFFY ELEVATED MUCKIBUS OVERSEEN PLEASANT SQUIFFED
TIPTOE CREEP
TIP-TOP SWELL TIPPY REGULAR TOPPING
TIRADE LAISSE SCREED STOUSH JEREMIAD INVECTIVE PHILIPPIC
TIRAS (FATHER OF —) JAPHETH
TIRE DO FAG HAG LAG SAG BORE CORD FLAT FLOG JADE KILL MOIL SHOE LABOR SPARE WEARY CASING HAGGLE HARASS SICKEN TIRING TUCKER BALLOON EXHAUST FATIGUE FRAZZLE TRACHLE WEAROUT CLINCHER FORSPEND
(— OUT) HAG FLOG THEAD BEJADE HARASS OVERWEARY
(BURST —) FLAT BLOWOUT
(KIND OF —) SNOW RADIAL
(SMOOTH —) SLICK
(USED —) REMOULD RETREAD
(WORN —) CARCASS
TIRED SAD TAM BEAT BOEG DEAD TIRY BLOWN WEARY AWEARY BLEARY BUSHED PLAYED POOPED TAVERT FORWORN SHAGGED TAIVERT FATIGATE FORWAKED
TIREDNESS FATIGUE
TIRESIAS (FATHER OF —) EVERES
(MOTHER OF —) CHARICLO
TIRESOME DRY DREE FAGGY ALANGE BORING DREICH PROLIX IRKSOME PROSAIC TEDIOUS BORESOME BROMIDIC ENNUYANT LONGSOME
(BECOME —) CLOY WEAR
TIRHANAH (FATHER OF —) CALEB
(MOTHER OF —) MAACHAH
TIRIA (FATHER OF —) JEHALELEEL
TIRING DRUDGING
TIRL RISP
TIRO TYRO NEOPHYTE
TIRTHANKARA JINA
TIRZAH (FATHER OF —) ZELOPHEHAD
TISAMENUS (FATHER OF —) ORESTES THERSANDER
(MOTHER OF —) HERMIONE
TISANE PTISAN TILLEUL
TISSUE FAT WEB CORK FOIL PITH TELA TEXT FACIA GLEBA GRAFT SUBER TRAMA CALLUS DARTOS DIPLOE FABRIC FASCIA LIGNUM PANNUS PHLOEM SHEATH TEXTUS ADENOID ALBUMEN BINDWEB CAMBIUM CLYPEUS EPITELA EXPLANT HYDROME KLEENEX MESTOME NEURINE PHLOEUM TEXTURE TWITTER ADHESION BLASTEMA DESMOGEN ECTODERM ENDODERM EPIPLOON HISTOGEN HYPODERM ISOGRAFT MERISTEM OSTEOGEN PERIDERM PERIDESM POLYPARY STEREOME
(— IN PLANT) STEREOME
(— IN SEED) PERISPERM
(— OF FUNGUS) CENTRUM
(— OF SILK) SARSNET SARCENET SARSENET
(— OF SKULL) DIPLOE
(— SURROUNDING TEETH) GUM
(ADIPOSE —) FATDEPOT
(BLACK —) CLYPEUS
(BOTANICAL —) TRACE
(CELL —) CORK
(CONNECTING —) WEB STROMA TENDON LIGAMENT MESENCHYME
(CORK —) SUBER
(DEAD —) SLOUGH
(FATTY —) LARD GREASE
(HARD —) BONE
(HYPOTHETICAL —) COAGULIN
(LYMPHOID —) TONSIL
(NERVE —) GANGLION
(SOFT —) FLAB
(VEGETABLE —) ARMOR
(WOOD —) LIGNUM VITRAIN
(PL.) CHIRATA CHIRETTA MESODERM
(PREF.) FASCIO HIST(I)(IO)(O) HIST(O) HYPHO
(FATTY —) ADIP(O)
(FIBROUS —) FIBR(I)(ILLI)(INO)(O)(OSO) IN(O)
TISWIN TESVINO TEXGUINO
TIT TID MESIA TITTY BLUECAP COLETIT MUFFLIN PINNOCK
TITAN BANA LETO MAIA ASURA ATLAS COEUS CREUS CRIOS DIONE THEIA CRONOS CRONUS PALLAS PHOEBE TETHYS THEMIS IAPETUS OCEANUS HYPERION
(AUTHOR OF —) DREISER
(CHARACTER IN —) FRANK PETER AILEEN BUTLER PLATOW FLEMING BERENICE LAUGHLIN STEPHANIE COWPERWOOD
TITANESS TETHYS
TITANIA (HUSBAND OF —) OBERON
TITANIC HUGE GREAT TITAN IMMENSE COLOSSAL GIGANTIC
TITANITE SPHENE GROTHITE LEDERITE LIGURITE
TITANIUM DIOXIDE ANATASE
TITA ROOT MISHMI MISHMEE
TITHE DIME DISME TEIND TENTH DECIMA PREBEND TITHING
TITHING BORGH BORROW DECIME DENARY DECENARY
TITHINGMAN DEAN DECURION TUTTIMAN
TITHONUS (FATHER OF —) LAOMEDON
(MOTHER OF —) STRYMO
TITI ORA TEETEE WISTIT SAIMIRI WISTITI IRONWOOD MARMOSET ORABASSU OUISTITI
TITILLATE AMUSE KITTLE TICKLE
TITILLATING GAMY SEXY GAMEY
TITIVATE PRIMP
TITLARK PIPIT TEETING
TITLE (ALSO SEE LEADER, CHIEF, GOVERNOR, RULER) AGA AYA BAN BEG BEY DAN DOM DUE FRA JAM LAR MIR PAN SAG SIR ABBA ABBE AGHA AMIR ANBA BABU DAME DEVI EMIR FRAY GAON GRAF HAJI HERR KHAN KNEZ LARS NAME PANI SIDI SLUG ABGAR ABUNA AMEER BABOO BEGUM CCOYA CLAIM CROWN EMEER FRATE GHAZI GOODY GRACE HADJI HAJJI HAKAM HANUM HONOR KNIAZ KNYAZ LEMMA MIRZA MPRET NAWAB NEGUS NIZAM PANNA PASHA RABBI RIGHT SINGH SOPHI SOPHY THANE UNWAN BASHAW BEGANI COUSIN DEGREE DEMAND DESPOT DOMINE EPONYM EXARCH HANDLE HUZOOR LEGEND MADAME MASTER MEHTAR MISTER PESHWA PREFIX SHERIF SQUIRE SUFFEE TITULE VIDAME ALFEREZ ALTESSE ALTEZZA BAHADUR BARONET CANDACE CAPTION CONVITO CRAWLER DIGNITY EFFENDI EPITHET ESQUIRE FIDALGO GAEKWAR GRAVITY HEADING HIDALGO INFANTE KHEDIVE MAHARAO MESSIRE RABBONI SHAREEF TITULUS VOIVODE BANNERET BASILEUS COMMENDA CONVIVIO EMINENCE GOSPODIN HIGHNESS HOLINESS HOSPODAR INTEREST LOKINDRA MAGISTER MAHARAJA MAHARANA MAHARSHI MISTRESS MONSIEUR PADISHAH PRINCIPE RAUGRAVE SUBTITLE TAMBURAN TITULADO
(— ACQUISITION) USUCAPT
(— HOLDER) OWNER
(— OF BOOK) QUARE
(— OF MEMBER OF PRIMROSE LEAGUE) KNIGHT
(— OF RESPECT) SIR SRI COJA LIEF MIAN SHRI SIDI BURRA HODJA KHAJA KHOJA MADAM SAHIB SIEUR KHOJAH MADAME MILADY
(BENEDICTINE —) DOM
(MOCK —) IDLESHIP
TITMOUSE MAG NUN TIT MAGG OXEYE PARUS SPICK FUFFIT HEFFEL PUFFER TOMTIT VERDIN BLUECAP BUSHTIT COLETIT COLMOSE GOLDTIT GRIGNET HAGMALL JACKSAW MUFFLIN PINCHEM PINNOCK TINNOCK TITMALL TOMNOUP CHICADEE HACKMALL OVENBIRD REEDLING SHABROON SHARPSAW
TITTER GIGGLE CHORTLE SNICKER TWITTER WHICKER
TITTLE DOT JOT IOTA TITLE MINUTE
TITUBATE REEL STAGGER
TITULAR LEGAL NOMINAL HONORARY
TITUS ANDRONICUS (AUTHOR OF —) SHAKESPEARE
(CHARACTER IN —) AARON CAIUS TITUS CHIRON LUCIUS MARCUS MUTIUS TAMORA ALARBUS LAVINIA MARTIUS PUBLIUS QUINTUS AEMILIUS BASSIANUS DEMETRIUS VALENTINE SATURNINUS SEMPRONIUS
TITYUS (FATHER OF —) TERRA JUPITER
(MOTHER OF —) ELARA
TIU ER EAR TIW TYR ZIO ZIU TIWAZ SAXNOT
TIV MUNCHI
TIZZY FLAP SNIT STEW PUCKER SWIVET SWIVVET
TLAKLUIT ECHE LOOT WISHRAM
TLEPOLEMUS (FATHER OF —) HERCULES
(MOTHER OF —) ASTYOCHIA
(SLAYER OF —) SARPEDON
TLINGIT SITKA KOLUSH SUMDUM CHILCAT CHILKAT STIKINE
TMESIS DIACOPE
TNT TROTYL
TO A AD FOR INTO TILL UNTO UPON
(— A CONCLUSION) OUT
(— BE) IBE
(— BE SURE) EVEN
(— COME) BEHIND
(— COMPLETION) DOWN
(— IT) TOOT SESSA
(— PRESS) DOWN
(— SUCH DEGREE) EVEN
(— THAT TIME) UNTIL
(— THE END) AF
(— THE OPPOSITE SIDE) ACROSS
(— THE REAR) ABAFT ASTERN
(— THIS) HERETO
(— THIS PLACE) HERE HITHER
(— VICTORY) ABU ABOO
(— WHAT) WHERETO
(— WIT) NAMELY INNUENDO SCILICET
(PREF.) AC AD AF AG AL AP AS AT INTRO OB
TOAD PAD AGUA BUFO FROG HYLA PIPA PODE HYLID PADDO PADDY PIPAL PIPID TOADY ANURAN CRAPON PEEPER BUFONID CHARLIE CRAPAUD CRAWLER CREEPER FROGLET GANGREL HOPTOAD PADDOCK PODDOCK PUDDOCK QUILKIN REPTILE SERPENT GANGEREL
(PREF.) BATRACH(O) PHRYN(O)
(SUFF.) BATRACH(O)(US)
TOADFISH SAPO SARPO GRUBBY SLIMER CABEZON FROGFISH LORICATE SCORPION
TOADFLAX FLAX FLAXWEED FLAXWORT FLUELLEN GALLWEED GALLWORT RAMSTEAD
TOAD RUSH SALTWEED

TOADSTONE BUFONITE
TOADSTOOL CANKER FUNGUS
TOADY FAWN SUCK TOAD ZANY COTTON EARWIG FAWNER FLUNKY GREASE HEELER LACKEY MUCKER YESMAN FLUNKEY JENKINS LACQUEY PLACEBO SHONEEN TRUCKLE BOOTLICK CLAWBACK LICKSPIT PARASITE SYCOPHANT
TOADYING GNATHONIC
TOADYISM FLUNKYISM
TOAST WET TOSS BREDE PROST ROUSE SANTE SKOAL TRINQ BIRSLE BUMPER CHEERS HEALTH PLEDGE PROSIT BRISTLE CAROUSE CHEERIO FRIZZLE LEHAYIM PROFACE PROPINE RESPECT SLAINTE WASSAIL BRINDISI SCOUTHER
(— AND ALE) SWIG
(— ONESELF) LEEP
(— TO HEALTH) PROSIT
(DISH WITH —) RAREBIT
(JACOBITE —) LIMP
TOBACCO CANE CAPA HAND LEAF LUGS NAVY POAK POKE QUID ROLL SHAG WEED BACCO BACCY BACKY BROKE CUBAN DARKS FOGUS PETUN REGIE SMOKE SNOUT TABAC TWIST BACKER BRIGHT BURLEY COLORY COWPEN FILLER HAVANA RETURN TOMBAC TUMBAK CAPORAL CRACCUS GAGROOT GORACCO KNASTER LATAKIA NAILROD NICOTIA ORONOKO PERIQUE PIGTAIL SOTWEED UPPOWOC CANASTER HONEYDEW MAKHORKA MARYLAND NICOTIAN ORONOOKO SEEDLEAF VIRGINIA MUNDUNGUS NICOTIANA
(— AND PAPER) MAKINGS
(— CAKED IN PIPE BOWL) DOTTEL DOTTLE TOPPER
(— HAVING OFFENSIVE SMELL) MUNDUNGO
(— IN ROPES) BOGIE
(— JUICE) AMBEER PRAISS
(— MOISTENED WITH MOLASSES) HONEYDEW
(— MOSAIC) WALLOON
(— PASTE) GORACCO
(— ROOM) PRIZERY
(— WORKER) LOOPER LEAFBOY LEAFGIRL
(CAKED —) HEEL
(COARSE —) SHAG SCRAP CAPORAL
(CUT —) CANASTER PICADURA
(DRIED —) TABACUM
(HARD-PRESSED —) NAILROD
(HATING —) MISOCAPNIC
(INDIAN —) GAGROOT PUKEWEED EYEBRIGHT
(INFERIOR —) LUGS
(LADIES' —) CUDWEED
(LOWER LEAVES OF —) FLYING
(MILD —) RETURN
(PERSIAN —) SHIRAZ TUMBEK TUMBEKI
(PERUVIAN —) SANA
(POOR QUALITY —) DOGLEG
(PULVERIZED —) SNUFF
(QUID OF —) CUD
(RAW —) LEAF
(ROLLED —) CARROT
(SMALL PIECE OF —) FIG
(VIRGINIA —) COWPEN VIRGINIA
TOBACCO BROWN TABAC
TOBACCO ROAD (AUTHOR OF —) CALDWELL
(CHARACTER IN —) ADA LOV DUDE RICE ELLIE PEARL BENSEY BESSIE JEETER LESTER
TOBACCO WORM HORNWORM
TOBOGGAN COAST CARIOLE CARRIOLE
TOCHARIAN A AGNEAN
TOCHARIAN B KUCHEAN
TOCSIN ALARUM
TODAY DAY NOW HEUTE NOWADAYS
TODDLE TOT FADGE DADDLE DIDDLE DODDLE PADDLE TOTTLE WADDLE
TODDLER TROT TYKE GANGREL TROTTIE
TODDY TOD TUBA TERRY SAGWIRE
TO-DO FUROR HOOHA SCENE BROUHAHA HULLABALOO ADO FUSS STIR WORK STINK DOMENT HOOPLA FLUSTER FOOSTER FOOFARAW TRAVALLY
TODY ROBIN
TOE TER DIGIT DACTYL HALLUX PIGGIE MINIMUS TOENAIL TRIPPET POULAINE
(— OF BIRD) HEEL
(LITTLE —) MINIMUS
(RUDIMENTARY —) DEWCLAW
(PL.) TUN TAIS TOON
(PREF.) DACTYL(O) DACTYLIO DIGITI DIGITO
TOENAIL
(SUFF.) ONYCHA ONYCHES ONYCHIA ONYCHIUM ONYCHUS ONYX
TOEPLATE SHOD
TOFF NOB GENT
TOFFEE TAFFY HARDBAKE BUTTERSCOTCH
TOGA GOWN ROBE TOGUE TRABEA
TOGETHER ONCE SAME ATONE YFERE BEDENE INSAME JOINTLY ENSEMBLE
(— WITH) AND INTO
(PREF.) CO COL COM CON COR SYM SYN
TOGGERY DUDS
TOGGLE COTTAR COTTER TOGGEL NETSUKE
TOGO (CAPITAL OF —) LOME
(LANGUAGE OF —) EWE TWI MINA HAUSA KABRAIS LOTOCOLI
(MOUNTAIN IN —) AGOU
(NATIVE OF —) EWE MINA CABRAI KABRAI OUATCHI
(RIVER IN —) OTI ANIE HAHO MONO
(TOWN IN —) KANDE ANECHO PALIME SOKODE TSEVIE ATAKPAME
TOHUBOHU RIOT CHAOS DISORDER CONFUSION
TOI (SON OF —) JORAM
TOIL FAG TUG DARG GRUB HACK MOIL MUCK PLOD TASK WORK LABOR SCRAT SLAVE SWINK TWEIL YAKKA BILDER DRUDGE EFFORT HAMMER KIAUGH MITHER MOIDER STRIVE UNRUFE YACKER FATIGUE TRAVAIL TURMOIL DRUDGERY INDUSTRY
TOILER PROLE SLAVE MOILER WORKER
TOILET BOG CAN LOO HEAD JOHN BIFFY DUNNY PRIVY CRAPPER BASEMENT BATHROOM DONNIKER LAVATORY PLUMBING DONNICKER
TOILING WORKADAY
TOILSOME HARD SWEATY ARDUOUS TOILFUL MOILSOME SWEATFUL
TOJOLABAL CHANABAL
TOKAY TUCKTOO
TOKEN BUCK CENT HARP SIGN TYPE BADGE CHECK INDEX SCRIP BEAVER CASTOR COLLAR COPPER COUPON DOLLAR EMBLEM JETTON MARKER OSTENT REMARK SIGNAL TICKET WITTER AUSPICE COUNTER EARNEST INDICIA MEMENTO PRESAGE SYMPTOM TESSERA BUNGTOWN COINTISE EVIDENCE FOOTSTEP FORBYSEN INSTANCE KEEPSAKE MONUMENT SHILLING SIGNACLE
(— OF A COVENANT) SACRAMENT
(— OF LUCK) HANSEL HANDSEL
(— OF POSSESSION) SEISIN
(— OF RESPECT) SALUTE
(— OF SUPERIORITY) PALM
(— OF VICTORY) LAUREL
(CANADIAN —) HARP
(CONFIRMING —) SEAL
(LOVE —) DRURY AMORET
(PORCELAIN —S) PI
(WARNING —) MONUMENT
(PL.) EXONUMIA
TOKHARI KUCHEAN
TOK PISIN CREOLE
TOKYO (— STREET) GINZA
(FORMER NAME OF —) EDO YEDO
TOLA (FATHER OF —) ISSACHAR
TOLD (— PRIVATELY) AURICULAR
TOLERABLE GAY SOSO PRETTY TARBLE LIVABLE PATIBLE BEARABLE PASSABLE PORTABLE
TOLERABLY GAIN GEYAN FAIRLY MEETLY MEETERLY MIDDLING
TOLERANCE MERCY SHERE LEEWAY REMEDY
TOLERANT SOFT BROAD BENIGN PATIENT PLACABLE PERMISSIVE
TOLERATE GO BEAR BIDE HACK HAVE ABEAR ABIDE ALLOW BROOK SPARE STAND STICK THOLE ACCEPT ENDURE PARDON PERMIT SUFFER COMPORT STOMACH SUPPORT SUSTAIN
TOLERATION WITHGANG
TOLKIEN (— CREATURE) ENT AROD
TOLL JOW TAX JOWL PIKE RENT KNELL PEAGE CAPHAR EXCISE OCTROI PEDAGE PESAGE BOOMAGE KEELAGE LASTAGE LOCKAGE MULTURE PASSAGE PICCAGE PIERAGE PONTAGE SCAVAGE SUMMAGE TERRAGE TOLLAGE TRONAGE BERTHAGE STALLAGE WEIGHAGE WHEELAGE
(PL.) CUSTOMS RAHDARI RATTAREE
TOLLHOUSE TOLLERY
TOLLIKER DUMMY
TOLSEN FOOTSTEP
TOLUENE DILUENT
TOLYL CRESYL
TOMAHAWK HATCHET NEOLITH
TOMATO TOM BERRY BURBANK
TOMB PIR BIER CIST MOLE GRAVE GUACA HUACA MAZAR SPEOS TABUT THOLE TURBE BURIAL CHULPA DARGAH DURGAH GALGAL HEARSE HEROON SAMADH SHRINE SYRINX THOLOS TROUGH TURBEH CHULLPA MASTABA OSSUARY TOMBLET TRITAPH CENOTAPH CISTVAEN CUBICULO HALLCIST HYPOGEUM KISTVAEN MARABOUT MASTABAH MONUMENT TREASURY MAUSOLEUM SEPULCHER
(— IN CHURCH) SACELLUM
(— OF MOSLEM SAINT) ZIARA ZIARAT
(CAVE —) SPEOS
(PREHISTORIC —) KURGAN
TOMBAC ORSEDE ORSEDUE
TOMBOY HEMP RAMP GAMINE HOYDEN MADCAP TOMRIG
TOMBSTONE SLAT TITLE THROUGH
TOMCAT GIB TOMMY PODGER THOMAS
TOMCOD GADE GADID SMELT GADOID WHITING TOMMYCOD
TOMENTUM WOOL
TOMFOOLERY HELL HORSE
TOM JONES (AUTHOR OF —) FIELDING
(CHARACTER IN —) TOM BETTY JENNY JONES NANCY BLIFIL GEORGE SOPHIA SQUARE WATERS BRIDGET WESTERN THWACKUM ALLWORTHY BELLASTON PARTRIDGE FITZPATRICK NIGHTINGALE
TOMMY FOOL PODGER REQUIN
TOMMYROT WAHOO BALONEY
TOMMY TALKER KAZOO
TOMORROW MANANA MORROW TOMORN
TOM SAWYER (AUTHOR OF —) TWAIN CLEMENS
(CHARACTER IN —) AMY JOE SID TOM FINN HUCK MARY MUFF BECKY POLLY HARPER POTTER SAWYER DOUGLAS LAWRENCE ROBINSON THATCHER
TOMTATE CAESAR
TON TUN TOUN STYLE
TONALAMATL TZOLKIN
TONALITY KEY
TONE A F DO FA LA MI RE SI SO TI DOH KEY SOH SOL CALL FLAT NOTE COLOR COUAC DRONE FIFTH FORTE PRIME SHARP SIXTH SOUND STYLE TONUS ACCENT DEGREE FOURTH SECOND FORMANT MEDIANT PARTIAL DEMITINT ELEVENTH FORENOTE HARMONIC HEADNOTE PARAMESE PARANETE SONORITY
(— A DRAWING) STUMP

(— DOWN) DRAB TAME SOFTEN SUBDUE
(— OF TETRACHORD) TRITE
(— UP) BRACE
(ACCENTED —) SFORZANDO
(BROKEN —) CRACK
(COMPLEX —) KLANG
(DEEP —) BASS
(DOMINANT —) ANIMUS
(DRAWLING —) DRANT DRAUNT
(HIGH-PITCHED —) PIP
(KEY —) KEYNOTE
(KIND OF —) FUZZ
(LOUD —) FORTE
(LOW —) SEMISOUN
(MONOTONOUS —) DRONE
(SHARP NASAL —) TWANG
(SIGNIFICANT —) ACCENT
(SINGLE UNVARIED —) MONOTONE
(STRIDENT —) COUAC
(WHINING —) GIRN
(PREF.) PHON(O)

TONGA (CAPITAL OF —) NUKUALOFA
(COIN OF —) PAANGA SENITI
(ISLAND GROUP OF —) TOFUA VAVAU HAAPAI NIUAFOO TONGATAPU NIUATOBUTABU
(ISLAND OF —) ONO TOFUA VAVAU HAAPAI
(TOWN OF —) NEIAFU

TONGS SNAPS SERVER FORCEPS GRAMPUS TUEIRON SCISSORS

TONGUE COG GAB CHIB CLAP KALI NEAP PAWL POLE REED CLACK IDIOM LADIN VOICE GADABA GLOSSA KABYLE KALIKA LADINO LANGUE LINGUA SPEECH CLAPPER DIALECT FEATHER ILOKANO LANGUET DOVETAIL LANGUAGE LORRIKER PLECTRUM
(— IN FLOORING) SPLINE
(— OF BELL) CLAPPER
(— OF JEW'S-HARP) TANG
(— OF LAND) DOAB REACH LANGUE LANGUET
(— OF MOLLUSC) RASP RADULA
(— OF OXCART) COPE
(— OF SHOE) FLAP KILTY KILTIE
(— OF VEHICLE) NEAP SHAFT
(BELLOWS —) GUSSET
(CELTIC —) BRETON
(GIVE —) PRATE
(GOSSIPING —) CLACK CLACKER
(PART OF —) BUD UVULA FAUCES LINGUA SEPTUM
(PIVOTED —) PAWL
(ROMANY —) ROMANES
(PL.) GAURA
(PREF.) GLOSS(O) GLOTT(I)(O) LIGUL(I) LINGU(I)(LI)(O)
(SUFF.) GLOSSA GLOSSIA GLOT

TONGUEFISH SOLE

TONGUE-LASH SCOLD

TONGUE-LASHING RAT TOCO BUSINESS

TONGUELESS AGLOSSAL

TONGUE-TIED SILENT

TONIC DO DOH ALOE KEEP PICHI PRIME BRACER SAMBUL SONANT SUMBUL BONESET CALAMUS CALOMBO CHIRATA COLOMBA DAMIANA FUMARIA GENTIAN KEYNOTE NERVINE SALICIN TONICAL ANTHEMIS BARBERRY BERBERRY HELONIAS ROBORANT TRILLIUM PIPSISSEWA

TONICITY MYOTONIA

TONKA BEAN GAIAC CUMARU GUAIAC COUMAROU

TONNA DOLIUM

TONNAGE PORTAGE

TONO-BUNGAY (AUTHOR OF —) WELLS
(CHARACTER IN —) RINK EFFIE FRAPP GROVE MOGGS SUSAN ARCHIE EDWARD GEORGE MANTEL MARION OSPREY GARVELL RAMBOAT BEATRICE NORMANDY NICODEMUS PONDEREVO

TONSIL ALMOND KERNEL ADENOID AMYGDAL AMYGDALA
(PREF.) AMYGDAL(O)

TONSILITIS QUINSY

TONSURE CROWN SHAVE SHEAR CORONA DIKSHA RASURE

TONSURED PEELED PILLED SHAVED

TOO SO ALSO OVER TROP LUCKY OVERLY LIKEWISE
(PREF.) OVER

TOOL (ALSO SEE IMPLEMENT AND INSTRUMENT) AX ADZ AWL AXE BIT BUR DIE DIG GIN GUN HOB HOE KEY LAP LOY RIP SAW SAX TAP TIT VOL ZAX ADZE BORE BRAY BURR CLAW COMB DADO DISC DISK DUPE EDGE FILE FLAY FROE FROG FROW GAGE HACK HAWK HONE LEAF LOOM MAUL MILL PICK RASP ROLL SATE SEAX SLED SNAP SPID SPUD STOP TAMP TIER VISE AUGER BLADE BORAL BORER BRAKE BRAND BREAK BRUSH BURIN CROZE DARBY DOLLY DRIFT DRILL DUMMY EDGER FLAKE FLOAT FLUTE GAUGE GOUGE GUIDE HARDY HOBBY HOWEL KNIFE KNURL LEVEL MAKER MISER MODEL PLANE POINT PRUNT PUNCH QUIRK SABER SABRE SCREW SHAVE SHELL SLICE SLICK SNIPE SPADE SPEAR SPLIT STAKE STAMP STING STOCK STRIG STYLE SWAGE TEWEL TOYLE UPSET VALET WAGON BEADER BEATER BIDENT BIFACE BLADER BODKIN BROACH BUDGER BUFFER CALKER CHASER CHISEL CLEAVE COGGLE COLTER CRADLE CRANNY CUTTER DEVICE DIBBLE DIGGER DOCTOR DRIVER ENGINE FASCET FERRET FILLET FLANGE FLORET FLUTER FORMER FRAISE FULLER GIMLET GLAZER GOFFER GRAVER GUMMER HACKER HAMMER HEMMER HOGGER HOLDER HULLER JIGGER JUMPER LADKIN LASTER LIFTER NIBBER PALLET PARTER PICKAX PICKER PLENCH PLIERS PROPER PUPPET REAMER RIPPER ROCKER RUNNER SANDER SAPPER SCRIBE SCUTCH SEATER SHAPER SHAVER SHEARS SHOVEL SKIVER SLATER SOCKET SQUARE STYLET STYLUS SWIVEL TAGGER TASTER TONGUE TREPAN TURNER TURREL TWILLY VEINER WAGGON WIGWAG WIMBLE WORDLE WORMER YANKEE ABRADER BLOCKER BRADAWL CALIPER CAULKER CHAMFER CHIPPER CHOPPER CLEANER CLEAVER COULTER CREASER DIAMOND DOLABRA DRESSER FISTUCA FLANGER FREEZER FROTTON GRAINER GROOVER GRUBBER GUDGEON JOINTER KNOTTER LOGHEAD MITERER OUSTITI POINTEL POINTER PROFILE RIVETER ROUGHER ROUNDER SCAUPER SCORPER SCRIBER SCRIVER SCURFER SLASHER SLEEKER SLICKER SPLAYER SPUDDER STEMMER STRIKER STROKER TICKLER TREBLET TWIBILL UPRIGHT WRAITHE AIGUILLE BIFACIAL BILLHOOK BOOTJACK BURGOYNE CALLIPER CREATURE CRIPPLER CROSSCUT CROWFOOT DUCKFOOT ELEVATOR EXPANDER FLOUNDER GRAVETTE GRIFFAUN POLISHER PRITCHEL PROPERTY PUNCHEON RAVEHOOK RECAPPER SCRAPPLE SCULPTOR SPLITTER STIPPLER STRICKLE STRINGER SURFACER THWACKER TOLLIKER WARKLOOM WORKLOOM SCRATCHER
(— A BOOK) FINISH
(BORING —) TREPAN
(CHEF'S —) WHISK SPATULA
(PL.) TEW FISH GEAR TRADE CUTLERY GIBBLES PIONERY ENGINERY

TOOLED GOFFERED
(— WITHOUT GILDING) BLIND

TOOLHOLDER TURRET MONITOR

TOOLHOUSE COPHOUSE

TOOLING (— ON BOOK) GOFFERING

TOOLSHED DOGHOUSE

TOON LIM CEDAR TOONWOOD

TOOT BLOW TOWT BINGE BLAST SOUND SPREE TRUMPET

TOOTH BIT COG GAM JAG PEG DENS DENT FANG LEAF RASP SNAG TIND TINE TUSH TUSK CRENA IVORY MOLAR PEARL PRONG RAKER TENON BROACH CANINE CUSPID CUTTER DENTAL INDENT JOGGLE TRIGON TRITOR DENTILE DIVIDER GRINDER INCISOR LATERAL SURDENT UNCINUS ABUTMENT BICUSPID BLEPHARA DENTICLE EYETOOTH GAGTOOTH MARGINAL PREMOLAR SAWTOOTH SPROCKET TOOTHLET TRIGONID CARNASSIAL
(— OF A MOSS) BLEPHARA
(— OF HORSE) DIVIDER
(— OF MOLLUSC) MARGINAL
(— OF PINION) LEAF
(— OF RADULA) UNCINUS
(— ON ROTATING PIECE) WIPER
(ARTIFICIAL —) DUMMY PONTIL
(CANINE —) CUSPID HOLDER LANIARY CYNODONT DOGTOOTH EYETOOTH
(GEAR —) COG GUB DENT ADDENDUM SPROCKET
(HARROW —) TINE
(MOLAR —) WANG
(OF SURFACE OF A —) MESIAL
(PART OF —) GUM NECK PULP ROOT CROWN DENTIN ENAMEL CEMENTUM
(UPPER SURFACE OF —) TABLE
(PREF.) DENT(ATO)(I)(INO)(O)(ODO) ODONT(O)
(SUFF.) DENT(ATE) ODON(T)(TA) (TES)(TIA)(TY) ODUS

TOOTHACHE WORM DENTAGRA

TOOTHED SERRATE VIRGATE SERRATED PECTINATE
(SUFF.) ODON ODUS

TOOTHLESS GUMMY

TOOTHPICK QUILL ARKANSAN

TOOTHSOME SAVORY PALATABLE

TOOTHWORT CROWTOE COOLWORT DENTARIA PEPPERROOT

TOO-TOO ULTRA LADIDA

TOP CAP COP GIG NUN TAP TIP ACME APEX BEAT COCK CULM HEAD HELM ROOF SKIM STOP BLOOM CHIEF COVER CREST CROWN FANCY GIGGE OUTDO PITCH RIDGE SHIRT SPIRE STRIP TOTUM TRUMP UPPER CALASH CAPOTE CULMEN SUMMIT UPWARD VERTEX CACUMEN SPINNER ROUNDTOP SURMOUNT TEETOTUM CULMINATION
(— FOR CHIMNEY OR PIPE) COWL HOOD
(— FOR PEDESTAL) DADOCAP
(— OF ALTAR) MENSA
(— OF AUTOMOBILE) HEAD HOOD
(— OF BIRD'S HEAD) PILEUM
(— OF CAPSTAN) DRUMHEAD
(— OF FURNACE) ARCH
(— OF GLASS) PRETTY
(— OF HEAD) MOLD PATE MOULD SCALP VERTEX
(— OF HELMET) SKULL
(— OF HILL) KNAG KNAP KNOLL
(— OF INGOT) CROPHEAD
(— OF MINING SHAFT) PITHEAD
(— OF MOUNTAIN) MAN
(— OF PLANT OR TREE) CROP
(— OF ROOF) DECK
(— OF SPINDLE) COCKHEAD
(— OF THE LINE) AONE
(— OF THUNDERCLOUD) INCUS
(— OF WAVE) COMB
(— OF WOODEN STAND) CRISS
(—S OF CROP) SHAW
(BLOW ONE'S —) SPEW
(BOOT —) RUFF
(BOX —) COUPON
(CARRIAGE —) CALASH
(PEG —) PEERIE
(RESEMBLING A —) STROBIC
(SITUATED AT —) APICAL
(SPINNING —) PEERY PEERIE
(PREF.) ACR(O)
(SPINNING —) RHOMB(O)

TOPAZ PYCNITE PYCNIUM PHSALITE

TOPCOAT OVERCOAT SIPHONIA

TOPE SOT DHER DHERI STUPA DAGOBA SOUPFIN

TOPER BOUSER CUPMAN POTMAN POTTER SIPPER SOAKER SUPPER

TROUGH BOMBARD POTLING SWILLER TOSSPOT BLACKPOT DRUNKARD MALTWORM
TOPI TIANG
(MATERIAL FOR —) PITH
TOPIC HARE ITEM TEXT HOBBY THEMA THEME BURDEN GAMBIT GROUND MATTER SUBJECT OCCASION
(STOCK —) TOPOS
TOPKNOT TUFT CREST ONKOS TOPPING
TOPMAN COB
TOPMINNOW GUPPY LIMIA GULARIS HELLERI SAILFIN GAMBUSIA MOLLIENSIA
TOP-NOTCH APLUS
TOPOGRAPHIC TERRAIN
TOPPER CAP FEZ HAT LID TAM BERET
TOPPLE TIP TOP TILT LEVEL UPEND TOTTLE
TOPS AONE
TOPSAIL RAFFE RAFFEE
TOPSOIL KELLY
TOPSTONE CAPSTONE
TOPSWARM TOPCAST
TOPSY-TURVY COCKEYED REELRALL
TOQUE ZATI MUNGA MACACO RILAWA MACAQUE
TOQUILLA JIPIJAPA
TOR CRAG
TORCEL BURN BERNE BORNE
TORCH DUCK JACK LAMP LINK LUNT PINE TEAD WASE WISP BLAZE BRAND FLARE LIGHT MATCH FOCKLE LAMPAD MASHAL MUSSAL BRANDON CRESSET GRIDDLE LUCIGEN ROUGHIE TORCHET FLAMBEAU
(KIND OF —) PLASMA
(PREF.) DAD(O) LAMPADE
TORCHBEARER KERYX LINKBOY LINKMAN DADUCHUS TORCHMAN
TOREADOR TORERO CAPEADOR
TORII (PART OF —) NYKI DAIWA KASAGI KUSABI LINTEL GAKUZUKA CROSSPIECE
TORIL CHIQUERO
TORMENT WO RAG TAW TRY WOE BAIT BALE FRET MOIL PAIN PANG PINE RACK SOOL TEAR TUCK CHEVY CURSE DEVIL GRILL HARRY SCALD TEASE TWIST WRING CHIVVY HARASS HARROW HECTOR INFEST NEEDLE PLAGUE TRAVEL AFFLICT ANGUISH BEDEVIL CRUCIFY HAGRIDE HATCHEL MALISON PERPLEX PINDING TERRIFY TORTURE TRAVAIL CRUCIATE DISTRAIN LACERATE MACERATE
(EXTREME —) AGONY
TORMENTED RODE CRUCIATE
TORMENTIL SEPTFOIL
TORMENTING PLAGUY
TORMINA TORSION
TORN RENT BROKEN RAGGED BLASTED LACERATE LACERATED
TORNADO VORTEX CYCLONE TRAVADO TWISTER
TORPEDO FISH SHELL SQUIB BATOID HOAGIE
TORPID FOUL NUMB BROSY INERT SODDEN STUPID TOGGER LANGUID TORPENT COMATOSE COMATOUS SLUGGISH
TORPIFY DAZE ETHERIZE
TORPOR COMA SLEEP SWOON ACEDIA ACCIDIE SLUMBER LETHARGY
(PREF.) NARC(O)
TORQUE BEE SARPE TWIST
TORREFY PARCH
TORRENT FLOW RUSH FLOOD SPATE STREAM NIAGARA CATARACT
(— OF WORDS) BLATTER
TORREYA SAVIN TUMION
TORRID HOT SULTRY AUSTRAL BOILING
TORSALO BERNE
TORSION STRESS DIDROMY
TORSK CUSK
TORT LIBEL WRONG
TORTE DOBOS
TORT-FEASOR ACTOR
TORTICOLLIS WRYNECK
TORTILLA TACO BREAD BURRITO TOSTADO ENCHILADA QUESADILLA
(— CHIP) NACHO
(FRIED —) TACO
TORTOISE EMYD BEKKO GAPER COOTER GOPHER TURTLE EMYDIAN HICATEE MUNGOFA TESTUDO GALAPAGO KASHYAPA SHELLPAD SHELLPOT TERRAPIN
(PREF.) CHEL(O)(Y)
TORTOISESHELL CAREY
TORTUOUS CRANKY SCREWY SINUATE WRIGGLY SINUATED
TORTURE GYP TAW BOOT CARD FIRE PAIN PANG PINE RACK AGONY SCREW TWIST ENGINE EXTORT IMPALE MARTYR AFFLICT AGONIZE ANGUISH BOOTING CRUCIFY PERPLEX TORMENT MARTYRDOM STRAPPADO
(METHOD OF —) FALANGA
TORTURER BOURREAU
TORUS CORK TORE DONUT BASTON BOLTEL BOUTELL BOWTELL DOUGHNUT THALAMUS
TORY BANDIT OUTLAW ROBBER PEELITE TANTIVY ABHORRER LOYALIST
TOSS BUM COB LAB SHY BUNG CANT CAST CAVE DOSS FLAP FLIP HIKE PASS SHAG SLAT TOUT CHAFE CHUCK FLICK FLING FLIRT FLURR HEAVE PITCH TEAVE THROW BETOSS BOUNCE DANDLE TOTTER WALTER WELTER WENTLE BLANKET TURMOIL WAMPISH WHEMMEL
(— ABOUT) VEX SWAB TAVE STREW POPPLE THRASH THRESH TORFLE WAMPISH
(— A COIN) SKY
(— A JACK) LAG
(— ASIDE) BANDY
(— AWAY) BLOW
(— CONTEMPTUOUSLY) SLIGHT
(— HEAD) CAVE GECK BRANK
(— IN BLANKET) CANVASS
(— OFF) SWAP SWOP
(— OF HORSE'S HEAD) CHACK
(— OF THE HEAD) HEEZE
(— ON WAVES) SURGE
(— THE LIMBS ABOUT) SPRAWL
(— TO AND FRO) WALK
(— TOGETHER CONFUSEDLY) SCRAMBLE
(— WITH THE HORNS) DOSS HIKE
TOSSING SURGING
(— OF BULLFIGHTER) COGIDA
TOSTAO TESTON
TOT ADD DRAM
TOTAL ADD SUM TAB TOT DEAD MERE TALE COUNT GROSS MOUNT SLUMP SUMMA UTTER WHOLE ENTIRE GLOBAL OMNIUM SUMMED TOTTLE EMBRACE FOOTING GENERAL PERFECT ABSOLUTE COMPLETE ENTIRETY SURMOUNT TEETOTAL
(REACH THE — OF) RUNTO
(PREF.) HOL(O)
TOTALED KAPUT WRECKED DEMOLISHED
TOTALITY ALL BODY HEAP BEING ALLNESS ECOLOGY ETERNITY HUMANITY INTEGRAL INTERVAL OMNITUDE SUMTOTAL
TOTALLY COLD GOOD QUITE WHOLLY
TOTE ADD LUG LOAD PACK CARRY BURDEN CONVEY
TOTEM HUACA
TO THE LIGHTHOUSE (AUTHOR OF —) WOOLF
(CHARACTER IN —) LILY PRUE JAMES MCNAB ANDREW BANKES RAMSAY BRISCOE CAMILLA CHARLES TANSLEY WILLIAM CARMICHAEL
TOTTER TOT REEL ROCK TOIT WALT SHAKE WAVER COGGLE DADDLE DODDER DOTTER FALTER HOTTER JOGGLE STAVER SWERVE TITTER TOTTLE WAMBLE WANGLE WAPPER BRANDLE FRIBBLE STAGGER TREMBLE WHITHER TITUBATE VACILLATE
(PREF.) LABE
TOTTERING LURCH SHAKY GROGGY CRAMBLY PALSIED RICKETY TOTTERY TITUBANT WAMBLING
TOU (SON OF —) HAMATH
TOUCAN TOCO TUCANA ARACARI
TOUCH GET RAP TAG TIG TIP ABUT BILL DASH FEEL HAND KISS KNEE MEET PALP PEAL PLAY RAKE RINE SCAM TACT TAKE FRAUD GLISK GRAZE GROPE SPICE TAINT TASTE TATTO TINGE TRAIT TREAT AFFECT ATTAIN CARESS FINGER GLANCE HANDLE REGARD SCRUFF SMUTCH STRAIN TACTUS TWITCH ATTAINT ATTINGE CONTACT FEELING PALPATE SOUPCON TACTION FLOURISH TINCTURE
(— A KEY) STRIKE
(— BRIEFLY) GLANCE
(— CARESSINGLY) FLATTER
(— CLOSELY) IMPINGE
(— DEEPLY) PIERCE
(— FOREHEAD —) KNUCKLE
(— GENTLY) DAB TAT TICK BRUSH
(— LIGHTLY) GRAZE SCUFF SKIFF
(— OF BRUSH) HAND
(— OF COLOR) EYE
(— OF PAINT) GLOB
(— OF PEN) STROKE
(— OF PLEASURE) GLISK
(— ON) PERSTRINGE
(— RIGHTLY) NICK
(— UP) TATT
(DELICATE —) STROKE
(FINISHING —) HOODER COPESTONE
(PAINTING —) ACCENT
(SLIGHT —) SKIFF SMATCH
(SPIRITUALISTIC —) RAPPORT
(PREF.) TAC TACTO TANGO THIGMO THIXO
(SUFF.) APHIA
(HAVING A — OF) ISH ISTIC
TOUCHDOWN ROUGE
(MAKE A —) LAND
TOUCHED FEY DOTTY
TOUCHING ABOUT LIBANT TENDER AGAINST CONTACT TANGENT ADJACENT PATHETIC POIGNANT AFFECTING CONTINUOUS
(— LIGHTLY) LAMBENT
(— THE MIND) PUNGENT
TOUCHSTONE TEST TOUCH LYDITE BASANITE STANDARD
TOUCHWOOD FUNK MONK PUNK SPUNK PUNKWOOD
TOUCHY HUFFY MIFFY SNAKY TESTY FEISTY KITTLE SNAKEY SNUFFY SPUNKY TENDER TETCHY GROUCHY NERVOUS PEEVISH PEPPERY STROPPY TEMPERY PETULANT TICKLISH
TOUGH RUM BHOY HARD TAUT WIRY BULLY BUTCH CLUNG HARDY STIFF STOUT WITHY BALLSY KNOTTY SINEWY STARCH STRONG HICKORY BULLYBOY LEATHERY UNTENDER ROUGHNECK TENACIOUS
(NOT —) TENDER
TOUGHEN TAW ANNEAL ENDURE HARDEN TEMPER
(— METAL) PLANISH
TOUGHENED CLUNG
TOUGHIE LULU
TOUGHNESS TUCK FIBER FIBRE STRENGTH TENACITY
TOUPEE RUG DOILY SCALP POSTICHE TOPPIECE
TOUR GIRO TURN SWING TOWER TURUS JUNKET SAFARI JOURNEY INVASION PROGRESS TOURETTE
(— OF DUTY) HERD STATION
(CANARY —) GLUCK GLUCKE
TOURACO LORY LOURIE TURAKOO
TOURBILLON KARRUSEL
TOUR DE FORCE STUNT
TOURIST TOURER TRIPPER VISITANT RUBBERNECK HOLIDAYMAKER
TOURMALINE SHORL SCHORL DRAVITE ACHROITE SIBERITE
TOURNAMENT TILT JERID JEREED JOUSTS TOURNEY BONSPIEL CAROUSEL

TOURNEUR DEALER
TOURNEY PLAY
TOURNIQUET GARROT STANCH TWISTER STANCHER TORCULAR
TOUSLE MUSS SOOL SOWL RUMPLE TOOZLE
TOUSLED TAUTED TOWZIE TUMBLED UNKEMPT
TOUT SPIV BRUIT PLIER BARKER STEERER TIPSTER
TOW CRIB HAUL PULL HURDS STUPE TRACK TRACT CODILLA CORDELLE
(KIND OF —) SKI
TOWAGE TRACKAGE
TOWAI BIRCH KAMAHI
TOWARD AD INTO TORT ANENT ANENST AGAINST FORNENT ADVERSUS GAINWARD
(— CENTER) CENTRAD
(— CENTER OF EARTH) DOWN
(— INTERIOR) INBY INBYE
(— ONE SIDE) ASLANT
(— THE END) SF
(— THE HEAD) ANTERIOR
(— THE MOUTH) ORAD
(— THE REAR) ABACK DORSAD BACKWARD
(— THE RIGHT) DEXTRAD
(— THE SIDE) LATERAD
(— THE STERN) AFTER
(PREF.) AC AD AF AG AL AP AS AT IL IM IN INTRO IR OB PROS
(SUFF.) AD
(GOING —) PETAL
TOWEL CLOUT WIPER DIAPER LAVABO RUBBER
(WORD ON —) HIS HERS
TOWER TOR PEEL PIKE REAR RISE SOAR SPUR TOUR BABEL BROCH HEAVE MINAR MOUNT PYLON SIKAR SPIRE STUPA TEXAS ASCEND ASPIRE BELFRY CASTLE CHULPA DOKHMA DONJON GOPURA ROLLER RONDEL SPRING TURRET BASTIDE CHULLPA DERRICK GIRALDA LANTERN MIRADOR NURAGHE SHIKARA SIKHARA STEEPLE TALAYOT TORREON TOURNEL TRACKER TURRION BARBICAN BASTILLE CLOGHEAD DOMINEER RONDELLE SCRUBBER TOURELLE TOWERLET PEPPERBOX
(— CONTAINING COKE) SCRUBBER
(— FOR SENTINEL) GUERITE
(— OF FORT) SPUR
(— OF MOSQUE) MINARET
(— OF SILENCE) DAKHMA
(— ON SUMMIT) PIKE
(— OVER) DROWN BESTRIDE
(ATTACHED —) DETAIL
(BELL —) CARILLON CAMPANILE
(BIBLICAL — SITE) EDAR
(CONNING —) SAIL
(FRACTIONATING —) STILL
(KIND OF —) MARTELLO
(PYRAMIDAL —) SIKAR VIMANA SHIKARA SIKHARA
(SIEGE —) BRATTICE
(SIGNAL —) BANTAYAN
(WIND —) BADGIR
(PREF.) PYRGO TURRI
TOWERING EMINENT SUPERNAL AMBITIOUS
TOWERMAN LEVERMAN
TOWER MUSTARD CRUCIFER
TOWHEE JOREE CHEWINK CHEEWINK
TOWING TRACKAGE
TOWLINE CORDELLE
TOWN BY BYE HAM WON BURG CAMP CITY STAD TOON WENE WICK BAYAN BORGO BOURH BRUGH BURGH DERBY MACHI PLACE PLECK SIEGE STAND STEAD VILLE CIUDAD HAMMON ORANGE PUEBLO STAPLE BASTIDE BOROUGH CHESTER OPPIDUM QUIVIRA TOWNLET BOOMTOWN BOURGADE ENCEINTE HOMETOWN TOWNSHIP
(DESOLATED —) GUBAT
(DULL —) PODUNK
(FORTIFIED —) BURG BURGH ENCEINTE
(KIND OF —) ONEHORSE
(MILITARY —) CANTONMENT
(MUSHROOM —) CAMP
(MYTHICAL —) QUIVIRA
(SMALL —) SHTETL SHTETEL
(UNFORTIFIED —) BOURGADE
(UNIMPORTANT —) PODUNK
(WALLED —) CHESTER
(PL.) PARGANA
(SUFF.) GRAD
TOWN CRIER BELLMAN
TOWN HALL HALL CABILDO RATHAUS TOLBOOTH STADHOUSE
TOWNSHIP DEME DORP VILL BAYAN TREEN BOROUGH
TOWNSMAN CAD CIT DUDE SNOB TOWNY TOWNEE BURGHER CITIZEN COCKNEY OPPIDAN
(PL.) BURGWARE
TOWROPE TOW CABLET GUNLINE TOWLINE CORDELLE
TOXALBUMIN ROBIN PHALLIN
TOXEMIA BLACKLEG ECLAMPSIA
TOXIC VENOMOUS POISONOUS
TOXIN BOTULIN EXOTOXIN
TOY ARK DIE GAY TOP COCK DOLL FOOL MOVE PLAY YOYO BLOCK CORAL DALLY FLIRT HAPPY KNACK LAKIN PLAID SPORT TRICK WALLY BAUBLE DANDLE DIDDLE DOODLE FADDLE FINGER FIZGIG GEWGAW LAKING PRETTY PUPPET RATTLE SUCKER BLOWOUT CRICKET DREIDEL PLAYOCK TANGRAM TRINKET TUMBLER WHIZZER GIMCRACK KICKSHAW PINWHEEL SKIPJACK SQUAWKER SQUEAKER TEETOTUM WINDMILL ZOETROPE
(— AMOROUSLY) MIRD
(— RACER) SLOTCAR
(— WITH) PADDLE
(— WITH FINGERS) PADDLE
(FLYING —) PIGEON
(MUSICAL —) OCARINA
(OPTICAL —) STROBOSCOPE THAUMATROPE
(SOFT —) GONK
(TOUGH —) GIJOE
TOYING DALLIANCE
TOYON TOLLON CHAMISO
TRABEA TOGA
TRACE RUN TUG WAD CAST ECHO HINT LICK MARK RACK SCAN SHOW SIGN STEP TANG TINT TROD BRING GHOST GLEAM GLIFF GRAIN PRINT RELIC SHADE SPICE SPOOR STAMP STEAD THEAT TINGE TOUCH TRACK TRACT TRAIL TRAIN TRESS DERIVE ENGRAM HARBOR LACING RESENT SHADOW SKETCH SMUTCH STRAIN STREAK SWATHE COCKEYE GLIMPSE KENNING MENTION REMNANT SOUPCON SURMISE SYMPTOM THOUGHT UMBRAGE VESTIGE WHISPER DESCRIBE ENGRAMME FOOTSTEP SKERRICK TINCTURE WAINROPE SIMULACRUM
(— A BEE) COURSE
(— A CURVE) SWEEP
(— A DESIGN) CALK
(— MATHEMATICALLY) GENERATE
(— OF A HARE) FARE
(— ON CHART) PRICK
(— THE COURSE OF) DEDUCE
(HARNESS —) TUG THEAT TREAT
(HAVE A —) SMACK
(MEMORY —) ENGRAM ENGRAMME
(SLIGHT —) GHOST STAIN SMATCH SPARKLE
(SLIGHTEST —) SCINTIL
(PL.) FEUTE
(SUFF.) **(HAVING A —)** ISH ISTIC
TRACER SEEKER OUTLINER SEARCHER
TRACERY FANWORK FROSTING TRAILERY
TRACHEA ARTERY WINDPIPE
(— OF CRANE) TRUMP
TRACHEID HYDROID
TRACHYANDESITE ARSOITE VULSINITE
TRACHYTE PIPERNO
TRACING BAROGRAM POLYGRAM TRAILING
TRACK DOG PUG RAT RUT TAN WAD WAY CLEW CLUE DRAW FARE FOIL FOOT HUNT LANE MARK PAGE PATH PIST RACE RACK RAIK RAIL ROAD SHOE SLOT SPUR TROD VENT BLOCK CHUTE DRIFT FEUTE HOUND LODGE PISTE PLANE SLIDE SPACE SPOOR STEAD SWATH TRACE TRACT TRADE TRAIL TRAIN TREAD BEARER COURSE GROOVE HARBOR LADDER RETURN RUNWAY SIDING SLEUTH STRAIN STREAM SWATHE CHANNEL FOILING FOOTING PATHWAY TANGENT TRAFFIC VESTIGE BACKBONE FOOTSTEP GUIDEWAY TRANSFER TRECKPOT TREKPATH WAGONWAY
(— ALONG CREST) RIDGEWAY
(— BY SMELL) SCENT
(— FOR ROPE) CHANNEL
(— GAME) DRAW
(— OF BLOOD) PERSUE
(— OF DEER) SLOT STRAIN
(— OF GAME IN GRASS) FOILING
(— OF HARE) FILE
(— OF SHIP) WAKE
(— OF WOUNDED BEAST) PERSUE
(— ON PRINTING PRESS) BANK BEARER
(BEATEN —) PISTE
(BRANCH —) SIDELINE
(CYCLING —) VELODROME
(RACING —) SPEEDWAY
(RAILROAD —) LEAD SPUR STUB SIDING TANGENT APPROACH BACKBONE
(RUNNING —) FLAT CINDERS
(SHORT BRANCH —) RETURN
(SIDE —) LIE HOLE
(SKATER'S —) FLAT
(SLIPPERY —) SLIDE
(TEMPORARY —) SHOOFLY
(WINDING —) SERPENTINE
(WORM —) NEREITE
(PREF.) ICHN(O)
TRACKER PUGGI PUGGY TRAILER TRAILMAN
TRACKLESS INVIOUS PATHLESS
TRACKMAN SPIKER
TRACT AREA BEAT DUAR FLAT ZONE CAMPO CLIME COAST DRIVE ESSAY FIELD GRABE HORST PATCH SWEEP TRACK BARONY BUNDLE EXTENT PARCEL REGION ENCLAVE EURIPUS QUARTER ROYALTY TERRAIN TRACTUS BROCHURE CAMPAGNA CAMPAIGN CINGULUM DISTRICT FARMHOLD FORESTRY PAMPHLET PROVINCE TOWNSITE TREATISE
(— KEPT IN NATURAL STATE) PARK
(— OF BARREN LAND) BARREN DERELICT
(— OF BRAIN FIBERS) PEDUNCLE
(— OF GRASSLAND) PRAIRIE
(— OF LAND) CRU DOAB DUAB DUAR GORE MARK BLOCK CHASE CLAIM EJIDO FRITH GRANT LAINE SCOPE SWELL TALUK EIGHTY ESTATE FOREST GARDEN ISLAND POLDER STRATH AIRPORT QUILLET RESERVE TERRAIN BOUNDARY CLEARING DERELICT FARMHOLD INTERVAL SCABLAND SLASHING
(— OF MUDDY GROUND) SLOB
(— OF OPEN UPLAND) DOWN DOWNS
(— OF UNCOVERED ICE) GLADE
(— OF WASTE LAND) HEATH
(BOGGY —) RUNN MORASS
(CLAYEY —) TAKYR
(CLEARED —) JUM JHUM JOOM
(DRY —) SEARING
(FORESTLESS —) STEPPE
(GENITAL —) BEARING
(IRREGULAR —) GORE
(OPEN —) VEGA SLASH
(SANDY —) DEN DENE LANDE
(SHRUBBY —) MONTE
(SWAMPY —) FLOW BAYGALL
(UNOCCUPIED AND UNCULTIVATED —) DESERT
(WATERLESS —) THIRST
TRACTABLE EASY SOFT TAME BUXOM TAWIE DOCILE GENTLE TOWARD DUCTILE FLEXILE PLIABLE AMENABLE FLEXIBLE GUIDABLE OBEDIENT TOWARDLY YIELDING MALLEABLE
TRACTARIANISM PUSEYISM
TRACTION DRAFT DRAUGHT
TRACTOR CAT MULE DRAGON

BOBTAIL CRAWLER PEDRAIL AGRIMOTOR
(TRAILER —) RIG
TRADE CHAP CHOP COUP DEAL SELL SWAP CHEAP CRAFT GRAFT PRICE TREAD TROKE TRUCK BAKERY BARTER CHANGE EMPLOY HANDLE METIER MISTER NIFFER OCCUPY SCORCE SCORSE BARGAIN CALLING CHAFFER FACULTY MYSTERY SCIENCE BUSINESS CABOTAGE EXCHANGE PLUMBING MERCHANDISE
(OLD-CLOTHES —) FRIPPERY
(PETTY —) DICKER
(SUBSIDIARY —) SIDELINE
(SUFF.) ERY
TRADEMARK CHOP LOGO MARK BRAND COUPON
TRADER SART BANYA PLIER BALIJA BANIAN BANYAN CHETTY DEALER MONGER NEPMAN TROKER CHAPMAN MARWARI SANGLEY TRUCKER ASTORIAN CHANDLER KURVEYOR MERCHANT OPERATOR
(HORSE —) JOCKEY
(INEXPERIENCED —) LAMB
TRADESMAN CIT BAKAL COOPER EGGLER SELLER TENSOR ARTISAN FRUITER GOLADAR OCCUPIER UPHOLDER
TRADESWOMAN WINSTER
TRADING CABOTAGE
(COASTAL —) CABOTAGE
TRADITION CABAL STORY SUNNA CABALA SMRITI SUNNAH THREAP HALACHA HALAKAH HEREDITY HERITAGE TRANSFER
(PL.) LEGEND
TRADITIONAL CLASSIC POMPIER
TRADUCE ILL SLUR ABUSE DEFAME MALIGN REVILE VILIFY ASPERSE DETRACT SCANDAL SLANDER
TRAFFIC COUP DEAL MANG MART MONG BROKE TRADE BARTER PALTER TRAVEL CHAFFER DEALING PASSAGE BUSINESS CHAFFERY COMMERCE EXCHANGE NAVIGATION
(— CONE) PYLON
(— IN SACRED THINGS) SIMONY
(— IN SLAVES) MAGONIZE
(— JAM) GRIDLOCK
(DRIVE RUDELY IN —) CUTIN
(ILLEGAL —) CONTRABAND
TRAFFICKER COUPER DEALER
TRAGACANTH GUM
TRAGEDY BUSKIN TRAGIC TROIADES
TRAGIC DIRE DREADFUL THESPIAN
TRAGICOMEDY DRAME
TRAGOPAN MONAL
TRAGUS EARLET
TRAIL PAD PUG DRAG FOIL HARL HUNT NECK PATH PIST SIGN SLOT BLAZE CRAWL DRAIL PISTE ROUTE SPOOR STOCK SWEEP TRACE TRADE TRAIN COMING DAGGLE FOLLOW RUNWAY SHADOW SLEUTH STRAIN TAIGLE TRAPES DRAGGLE TRACHLE TRAFFIC OUTTRAIL STRIGGLE TRAILERY
(— ALONG) STREEL TRAPES
(— BY SMELL) SCENT
(— DOWN) FALL
(— OF A FISH) LOOM
(— OF AIRCRAFT) CONTRAIL
(— OF STAG) ABATURE
(— OUT) STREAM
(— THROUGH MUD) DAGGLE
(DESCENDING —) BAHADA BAJADA
(JOGGING —) PARCOURSE
(MOUNTAIN —) CLIMB
(SKI —) PISTE
(WAGON —) RUDLOFF
(WATER —) WAKE
TRAILBLAZER HARBINGER
TRAILER SEMI COACH BOXCAR CARAVAN FLATBED FROGGER GONDOLA ARTMOBILE
TRAILING (— ON GROUND) PROSTRATE
TRAIN SET DRAG GAIT SECT TILL TIRE TURN ZULU BEARD BREED COACH DRESS DRILL ENTER FOCUS LOCAL RANGE TRACE TRACT TRADE TRAIL TRYNE CONVOY DIRECT GENTLE GROUND INFORM MANURE NUZZLE RAPIDE REPAIR SCHOOL SEASON STRING SUBWAY AFFAITE BRIGADE CARAVAN EDUCATE FREIGHT GEARING LIMITED PEDDLER RATTLER RETINUE SHUTTLE VARNISH CIVILIZE DISCIPLE ELECTRIC EQUIPAGE EXERCISE HIGHBALL INSTRUCT MANIFEST REHEARSE
(— AN ANIMAL) BREAK
(— FINE) GAUNT
(— FOR CONTEST) POINT
(— FOR FIGHTING) SPAR
(— OF ANIMALS) COFFLE
(— OF ATTENDANTS) CORTEGE
(— OF COMET) TAIL
(— OF CONSEQUENCES) CONSECUTION
(— OF EXPLOSIVE) FUSE
(— OF FANCY) REVERY REVERIE
(— OF FEATHERS) TAIL
(— OF GOWN) SACK
(— OF MINING CARS) JAG RUN TRIP
(CAMEL —) KAFILA
(FUNERAL —) CONVOY
(PACK —) CONDUCTA
(RAILROAD —) DRAG HOOK LOCAL PICKUP EXPRESS FREIGHT LIMITED RATTLER
TRAINED GOOD MADE ADEPT BROKE BROKEN
TRAINEE BOOT CADET INTERN
TRAINER FEEDER JINETE LANISTA
TRAINING DRILL THEAT ASCESIS ASKESIS CULTURE NURTURE PAIDEIA BREEDING
(— IN HUMANITIES) CIVILITY
(— OF HORSE) DRESSAGE
(EARLY —) TIROCINIUM
(MANUAL —) SLOID SLOYD
(RELIGIOUS —) SADHANA
TRAIPSE GAD WALK TRAMP SASHAY WANDER
TRAIT ITEM LEAD MARK VEIN ANGLE CHARM KNACK TRACT TRICK AMENITY ELEMENT HALLMARK JAPANISM
(CHARACTERISTIC —) TRICK
(CULTURE —) SURVIVAL
(FOREIGN —) EXOTISM
(GOOD —) THEW
(UNDESIRABLE —) DEMON DAEMON
(WELL-DEFINED —) STREAK
(PL.) CORNERS
TRAITOR RAT JUDAS RUSTY NITHING WARLOCK APOSTATE ISCARIOT PRODITOR QUISLING SQUEALER TRADITOR TREACHER
TRAITOROUS FALSE FELON APOSTATE RENEGADE
TRAJECTORY SPORABOLA
TRA-LA-LA TRALIRA
TRAM TUB DRAM TRAMCAR TRAMMEL TRANVIA
(COAL —) TIP
(SET OF —S) JOURNEY
TRAMCAR TRAM DUMMY PICKUP
TRAMMEL TRAM HAMPER STIFLE COTTEREL
TRAMMER PUTTER
TRAMONTANE ALIEN FOREIGN OVERBERG
TRAMP BO BUM PAD BOOM HAKE HIKE HOBO HUMP PUNK SLOG SWAG VAMP WALK YEGG BIMBO BURLY CAIRD CLAMP JAVEL PIKER ROGUE SHACK STIFF STRAG TRAIK TRAIL TRASH TROMP TROUT BAGMAN GAYCAT JOCKER PICARO STODGE STRAMP STROLL TINKER TRANCE TRAPES TRUANT TRUDGE DRUMMER FLOATER RUFFLER SWAGGER SWAGMAN TRAIPSE TRAMPLE TROUNCE TROWANE VAGRANT YEGGMAN CLOCHARD FOOTSLOG GANGEREL STROLLER TRAVELER VAGABOND SUNDOWNER
(— ABOUT) WAG
(LONG —) HUMP
(PL.) MONKERY
TRAMPING MONKERY
TRAMPLE HOX JAM PUG FARE FOIL FULL HOOF CHAMP POACH SCAUT SPURN STOMP TRAMP TRASH TREAD DEFOIL DEFOUL PADDLE SAVAGE STOACH STRAMP WADDLE OPPRESS OVERRUN SCAMBLE FORTREAD OVERRIDE
(— IN MUD) POACH
TRANCE RAPTUS AMENTIA ECSTASY SAMADHI CATALEPSY
TRANQUIL CALM COOL EASY LOWN MILD SOFT EQUAL QUIET STILL GENTLE PACATE PIPING SERENE CALMATO EQUABLE PACIFIC RESTFUL PEACEFUL
TRANQUILIZE CALM LULL QUIET STILL BECALM PACIFY SERENE SETTLE SOFTEN SOOTHE APPEASE COMPOSE
TRANQUILIZER VALIUM DIAZEPAM
TRANQUILIZING ATARAXIC SOOTHING
TRANQUILLITY KEF LEE EASE REST PEACE QUIET SATTVA SERENE HARMONY ATARAXIA QUIETAGE QUIETISM QUIETUDE SERENITY COMPOSURE
TRANQUILLIZER LIBRIUM RESERPINE
TRANS ANTI
TRANSACT DO PASS AGITATE CONDUCT PERFORM
TRANSACTION DEAL DEED GAGE GAGER ACTION AFFAIR FIDDLE MARGIN SPREAD BARGAIN MOHABAT PASSAGE CONTRACT KNOCKOUT OPERATION PROCEEDING
(— AT LOWER PRICE) DOWNTICK
(GAMBLING —) FLUTTER
(STOCK —) STRADDLE
(PL.) ACTA BUSINESS
TRANSCEND PASS SOAR EXCEED OVERTOP SURPASS
TRANSCENDENTAL ACOSMIC
TRANSCENDING EXQUISITE
(PREF.) SUPRA
TRANSCRIBE COPY BRAILLE DESCRIBE EXSCRIBE
TRANSCRIBED CANNED
TRANSCRIBER COPIER COPYIST
TRANSCRIPT COPY SCORE TENOR DOUBLE APOGRAPH EXSCRIPT
TRANSCRIPTION
(PL.) PAZAND PAZEND
TRANSEPT PLAGE PORCH
TRANSFER CALL CEDE DEED FLIT GIVE JUMP PASS SALE SELL TURN ALIEN CABLE CARRY CROSS DROGH REFER REMIT SHIFT ASSIGN ATTORN CHANGE DECANT DELATE DONATE REMOVE SWITCH CESSION CONNECT CONSIGN DELIVER DEVOLVE DISPONE MIGRATE TRADUCE ALIENATE ANTEDATE CROCKING DELEGATE DELIVERY DONATION EXCHANGE TRANSACT TRANSUME VIREMENT NEGOTIATE
(— A RECORDING) OVERDUB
(— DYE) EXHAUST
(— HEAT) CONVECT
(— HOMAGE) ATTORN
(— MOLTEN GLASS) LADE
(— OF ENERGY) FLOW
(— OF PROPERTY) DEED GIFT GRANT DISPOSAL
(— PIGMENT) FLUSH
(— WITH POWDER) POUNCE
(DECORATIVE —) DECAL
(TEMPORARY —) SECONDMENT
TRANSFERENCE DEMISE EMOTION REMOVAL DELATION DISPOSAL TRANSFER
(— OF TRIBUTARY) CAPTURE
TRANSFIGURE DEIFY CLARIFY
TRANSFIX FIX DART STAB PITCH STAKE STICK SKEWER THRILL BESTICK
TRANSFORM TURN SHIFT TOUCH CHANGE STRIKE CONVERT FASHION PERMUTE RECYCLE CATALYZE DISGUISE HETERIZE
(— ENERGY) ABSORB
(KIND OF —) FOURIER LAPLACE
TRANSFORMATION CHANGE HAIRWORK
(— IN ATOM) REACTION
TRANSFORMER SET DIMMER

JIGGER TEASER TOROID VARIAC BALANCE BOOSTER HEDGEHOG
TRANSFUSE ENDUE INDUE
TRANSGRESS ERR SIN BREAK OFFEND OVERGO DIGRESS DISOBEY VIOLATE INFRINGE OVERPASS OVERSLIP OVERSTEP TRESPASS
TRANSGRESSION SIN SLIP CRIME FAULT SCAPE BREACH DELICT ESCAPE MISDEED OFFENSE DELICTUM OVERLOUP TRESPASS
TRANSGRESSOR SINNER OFFENDER
TRANSIENCE FUGACITY
TRANSIENT FLEET BUBBLE FLIGHTY PASSING FLEETING FUGITIVE MOMENTARY
TRANSIENTLY HOVERLY
TRANSISTOR FET MOSFET
TRANSIT BINOCLE PASSAGE TRANSEPT
TRANSITION CUT JUMP LEAP SEGUE SHIFT FERMENT PASSAGE
TRANSITIVE ACTIVE
TRANSITORINESS CADUCITY
TRANSITORY FLEET CADUCE FLYING BRITTLE PASSANT PASSING SLIDING VOLATIC WHILEND CADUCOUS FLEETING FLITTING TEMPORAL VOLATILE MOMENTARY
TRANSKEI (CAPITAL OF —) UMTATA
(TOWN OF —) BUTTERWORTH
TRANSLATE PUT DRAW MAKE TURN WEND RENDER CONVERT ENGLISH EXPOUND TRADUCE CONSTRUE INTERPRET
TRANSLATION CAB KEY CRIB PONY STEP TROT GLOSS HORSE TARGUM UNSEEN BICYCLE CABBAGE ENGLISH THARGUM TRADUCT VERSION SUBTITLE VERBATIM
(— OF BIBLE) PESHITO
(— OF THE CLASSICS) JACK
(BIBLICAL —) PESHITO PESHITTA PESHITTO
(LOAN —) CALQUE
TRANSLATOR TURNER
TRANSLUCENT CLEAR LUCID LIMPID LUCENT HYALINE
(PREF.) HYAL(O)
TRANSMIGRATION SAMARA SAMSARA SANSARA
TRANSMISSION CHAIN DRIVE ENTAIL DESCENT GEARBOX PASSAGE SENDING TRANSFER CONDUCTION CONVECTION
(— OF DISEASE) CONTAGION
(— OF ESTATE) ENTAIL
(— OF SOUND) AUDIO
(— TO OFFSPRING) HEREDITY
(SUFF.) PHORESIS
TRANSMIT AIR BEAM EMIT SEND CARRY CONVEY DEMISE DERIVE ENTAIL EXPORT IMPACT IMPART RENDER CONDUCT CONSIGN FORWARD TRADUCE TRADUCT TRAJECT BEQUEATH DESCRIBE PROPAGATE
(PREF.) DIAGO
TRANSMITTER TUBA SLAVE SPARK BEACON JAMMER PINGER SENDER VEHICLE RADIATOR
TRANSMITTING ALIVE
TRANSMUTE CHEMIC CHEMICK ENNOBLE PERMUTE EXCHANGE TRANSMUE TRANSUME
TRANSOM PATIBLE TRAVERSE
TRANSPARENCY SLIDE
(— OF DIAMOND) WATER
TRANSPARENT THIN CLEAR FILMY LUCID BRIGHT LIMPID LUCENT CRYSTAL FRAGILE HYALINE HYALOID TIFFANY DIOPTRIC LUCULENT LUMINOUS LUSTROUS PELLUCID
(IMPERFECTLY —) TRANSLUCENT
(PREF.) DIAPHAN(O) HYAL(O)
TRANSPIRE HAPPEN
TRANSPLANT SPOT SHIFT DEPLANT
TRANSPORT DAK JOY ROB BEAR BOAT BUSS DAWK DRAY HAUL PASS PORT RAPE RAPT RIDE SEND SHIP BLISS CANOE CARRY DROGH FERRY FLUTE GILLY BANISH BARREL CONVEY DEPORT GALLOP KURVEY WAFTER ECSTASY EXPRESS FRAUGHT ONERARY RAPTURE TRADUCE TROOPER CABOTAGE CARRIAGE DAYDREAM ENRAVISH PALANDER
(— BY PACKHORSE) JAG
(— FOR CRIME) LAG
(— LOGS) BOB
(— ORE) SLUSH
(PREF.) PEREIO
TRANSPORTATION AIR DAK FARE AIRLIFT BOATAGE FREIGHT MINIVAN TRAJECT TRANSPORT
(AIRPORT —) LIMO
TRANSPORTED RAPT
(— BY GLACIER) ERRATIC
TRANSPOSE ADJOINT CONVERT REVERSE
TRANSPOSITION SHIFT ANSWER ANAGRAM
TRANSUBSTANTIATION METUSIA
(BELIEVER IN —) CAPERNAITE
TRANSUDE SEEP
TRANSVAAL DAISY GERBERA
TRANSVAALER TAKHAAR
TRANSVERSE CROSS FACING THWART OBLIQUE
TRANSVERSELY ATHWART
TRANSVESTISM EONISM
TRANSVESTITE BERDACHE
TRAP COY GET GIN PIT SET FALL GIRN GRIN HOOK LACE LIME NAIL PUTT TIPE TOIL WAIT WEEL BRAKE BRIKE CATCH LEASH PLANT POUND SNARE SPELL STALE SWICK SWIKE TRAIN COBWEB CRUIVE EELPOT ENGINE KEDDAH POCKET QUILEZ SNATCH STAYER WILLOW FLYTRAP PITFALL PITFOLD PUTCHEN PUTCHER RATTRAP SETTING SPRINGE TRAMMEL BIRDLIME COALHOLE DEADFALL DOWNFALL TRAPROCK
(— FOR BIRDS) SCRAPE
(— FOR LARGE GAME) HOPO
(— FOR LOBSTER) POT
(— FOR RABBITS, MICE, ETC) TIPE TYPE
(— FOR RATS) CLAM
(— FOR SALMON) PUTT
(— FOR SMALL ANIMALS) HATCH
(— FOR THE FEET) CALTROPS
(— IN POKER) SANDBAG
(— IN THEATER) SCRUTO
(— INTO SERVICE) CRIMP
(— OF SCAFFOLD) DROP
(FISH —) FYKE KILL LEAP WEEL WEIR CREEL WILLY CORRAL CRUIVE WILLOW
(LOBSTER —) POT
(MOTH —) GYPLURE
(RABBIT —) GATENET
(SAND —) BUNKER
TRAPDOOR DROP SLOT TRAP SCRUTO VAMPIRE TRAPFALL
TRAPPED CORNERED
TRAPPER WIRER VOYAGEUR
TRAPPINGS GEAR JHOOL ARMORY TOGGERY BARDINGS EQUIPAGE HOUSINGS CAPARISON
TRAPSHOOTING SKEET
TRASH ROT BOSH DREK GEAR GOOK JUNK PELF RAFF TOSH TRAG CLART DRECK DROSS DRUSH SPANK STUFF SWASH THROW TRADE TROKE WASTE WRACK BUSHWA CULTCH KELTER KITSCH LITTER PADDLE PALTRY RAMMEL REFUSE RUBBLE SCULCH TROUSE BAGGAGE BEGGARY FULLAGE GARBAGE PEDLARY RUBBISH TOSHERY TRAFFIC BLATHERY CLAPTRAP FLUMMERY MUCKMENT PEDDLERY SKITTLES SMACHRIE TRASHERY TRUMPERY
TRASHY CHEAP FLASH TOSHY TRIPY PALTRY SHODDY SLUSHY BAGGAGE RUBBISH RIFFRAFF RUBBISHY SIXPENNY TRUMPERY
TRAUMA WOUND INJURY STRESS
TRAVAIL PAIN TASK TOIL AGONY LABOR TORMENT
TRAVEL GO BAT BUS FLY GIG WAG FARE GANG HIKE PASS PATH RIVE TOTE TRIP VAMP WEND COVER KNOCK SLOPE THROW TRACK CRUISE TRANCE VOYAGE EXPRESS JOURNEY TRAVAIL TRUNDLE WAYFARE PROGRESS TRAVERSE
(— ACROSS SNOW) MUSH
(— AIMLESSLY) SAUNTER
(— ALONG GROUND) TAXI
(— AROUND) TURN COAST CIRCLE GIRDLE COMPASS
(— AT GOOD SPEED) CRACK
(— AT HIGH SPEED) HELL BARREL SCORCH
(— AT RANDOM) DRIFT
(— AT SPEED OF) DO
(— BACK AND FORTH) SHUNT COMMUTE
(— BY AIRCRAFT) AIR FLY AIRPLANE
(— BY OX WAGON) TREK
(— FAST) STREAK
(— IN A VEHICLE) TOOL
(— IN STATE) PROGRESS
(— IN WATER) SWIM
(— ON FOOT) HIKE SHANK KNAPSACK PERAMBULATE PEREGRINATE
(— ON WATER) SAIL
(— OVER) TRANCE TRAVERSE
(— SPEEDILY) VROOM
(— THROUGH) GO
(— THROUGH AIR) GLIDE
(— THROUGH WOODS) BUSHWACK
(— WITHOUT EQUIPMENT) SIWASH
(DAY'S —) JORNADA JOURNAL JOURNEY
TRAVELER GOER CRAWL FARER GUEST HORSE BAGMAN GANGER KILROY POSTER SAILOR VIATOR CRUISER DRUMMER FOOTMAN HOWADJI LEEFANG PILGRIM SWAGGIE TRAILER TREKKER TRIPPER WAYGOER ARGONAUT EXPLORER MAGELLAN OUTRIDER VOYAGEUR WAYFARER PASSENGER
(COMMERCIAL —) BAGMAN SALESMAN
(COMPANY OF —S) CARAVAN
TRAVELER'S JOY HAGROPE BINDWITH CLEMATIS
TRAVELING ERRANT PEREGRINE
TRAVELING SALESMAN RIDER DRUMMER
TRAVELOGUE (— TECHNIQUE) VOICEOVER
TRAVERSE DO GO SEE BURN DENY KNEE LIFT MAKE PASS SPAN WALK COAST COVER CROSS SHEAR SWEEP THIRL TRACE TRACK CIRCLE COURSE DENIAL OVERGO PERCUR TRAVEL VOYAGE WANDER CHANNEL JOURNEY MEASURE OVERRUN PARADOS PERVADE DESCRIBE NAVIGATE OVERPASS OVERWEND SCRAMBLE UNTHREAD PERAMBULATE
TRAVERTINE ONYX TOPHUS ONYCHITE
TRAVESTY EXODE FARCE PARODY SATIRE CHARADE EXODIUM TRAVEST BURLESQUE
TRAVIATA, LA (CHARACTER IN —) FLORA VALERY ALFREDO BERVOIX DOUPHOL GERMONT GIORGIO VIOLETTA
(COMPOSER OF —) VERDI
TRAVOIS DRAY TRAVOY ALLIGATOR
TRAWL SEINE BOULTER DRAGNET STOWNET TRAWLNET TROTLINE
TRAWLER PAREJA BRAGOZZO
TRAY HOD CASE TILL TRUG BATEA BOARD FLOAT SCALE SLICE SUSAN GALLEY MONKEY SALVER SERVER SERVET VOIDER WAITER BALANCE CABARET COASTER CONSOLE SHALLOW DEJEUNER
(— FOR CRUMBS) VOIDER
(— FOR DRYING FISH) FLAKE
(— FOR MATCH SPLINTS) CAUL MONKEY
(— FOR SHELLFISH) FLOAT
(— FOR TYPE) GALLEY
(— TO CATCH OVERFLOW) SAFE
(CIRCULAR —) ROUNDEL
TREACHEROUS FOUL CATTY DIRTY FALSE PUNIC SNAKY SWACK FELINE FICKLE HOLLOW ROTTEN YELLOW SNAKISH FRAUDFUL IMPOSING PLOTTING SLIDDERY
TREACHERY GUILE SWICK TRAIN

DECEIT FELONY PERFIDY TREASON UNTRUTH DASTARDY DISTRUST TRAHISON TRAITORY
TREACLE DIBS CLAGGUM THERIAC
TREAD FIT PAD BEAT FOOT PATH POST RUNG STEP VOLT CLAMP TRACK TRADE DEFOIL DEFOUL PADDLE CRAWLER FEATHER FOOTING RETREAD TREADER FOOTSTEP
(— CLUMSILY) CLUMP BALTER
(— DOWN SHOE HEEL) CAM
(— HEAVILY) SPURN TRAMPLE
(— OF FOWL'S EGG) GRANDO
(— ON) FOIL
(— TO MUSIC) FOOT
(— WARILY) PUSSYFOOT
(TIRE —) COVER
TREADLE PEDAL CHALAZA
TREASON SEDITION TREACHERY
TREASURE POSE ROON HOARD PRIZE STORE TROVE VALUE BURSAR COFFER FINDAL GERSUM WEALTH ASTHORE FINANCE THESAUR WARISON GARRISON TREASURY VALUABLE
(— STATE) MONTANA
(— TROVE) STASH
(LITTLE —) STOREEN
(PL.) CIMELIA
TREASURE BOX HANAPER
TREASURED DEAR CHARY PRECIOUS VALUABLE
TREASURE ISLAND (AUTHOR OF —) STEVENSON
(CHARACTER IN —) BEN JIM PEW GUNN JOHN BONES HANDS ISRAEL SILVER HAWKINS LIVESEY SMOLLETT TRELAWNEY
TREASURER FISC BOWSER BURSAR FISCAL GABBAI BOUCHER HOARDER SPENDER BHANDARI COFFERER HAZNADAR PROVISOR QUAESTOR RECEIVER
TREASURY FISC FISK KIST CHEST HOARD PURSE COFFER CORBAN FISCAL FISCUS BOWSERY BURSARY CHAMBER CHECKER CHEQUER HORDARY AERARIUM THESAURY TREASURE STOREHOUSE
(PAPAL —) CAMERA
TREAT RUN USE DEAL DOSE HOCK LEAD PLAY BEANO BESEE COVER DIGHT GUIDE LEECH SERVE SETUP SHOUT TRACT TRAIT WRITE DEMEAN DOCTOR GOVERN HANDLE LIQUOR PADDLE REGALO CONDUCT ENTREAT GARNISH ACTIVATE AIRBRUSH
(— A HIDE) DRUM
(— AS EQUAL) EVEN
(— BADLY) ILLGUIDE
(— BY MELTING) RENDER
(— CARELESSLY) BANG BANDY
(— CLOUDS) SEED
(— CONFIDENTIALLY) HUSH
(— CRUELLY) CRUCIFY
(— DAINTILY) PAMPER
(— DIABOLICALLY) BEDEVIL
(— DISCOURTEOUSLY) DISGRACE
(— FIBERS) GILL
(— FLOUR) AGENIZE
(— FONDLY) DANDLE
(— FUR) CARROT
(— GENTLY) FAVOR
(— HAIR) CONK
(— HARSHLY) STICK
(— ILLNESS) POMSTER
(— IMPROPERLY) MISUSE
(— IMPUDENTLY) NOSE
(— INADEQUATELY) SCANT
(— LIGHTLY) SCRUFF
(— LOVINGLY) COAX
(— MALICIOUSLY) SPITE
(— MASH) LAUTER
(— MERCIFULLY) SPARE
(— OF) DISCOURSE
(— OF DRINKS) SETUP
(— ROUGHLY) BANG MUMBLE GRABBLE MALTREAT
(— SILK TO RUSTLE) SCROOP
(— SLIGHTINGLY) LIGHTLY
(— STEEL) HARVEY
(— UNFAIRLY) DO SHAFT STICK
(— UNSKILLFULLY) FOOZLE
(— VIOLENTLY) STRONGARM
(— WITH ABUSE) OUTRAGE
(— WITH ACID) SOUR
(— WITH CARE) CODDLE
(— WITH CONSIDERATION) RESPECT
(— WITH CONTEMPT) HUFF SNUB BLURT FLIRT FLOCK FLOUT FLAUNT BAUCHLE
(— WITH HEAT) FOMENT
(— WITH HONOR) RESPECT
(— WITH INATTENTION) FORGET
(— WITH INDULGENCE) FONDLE
(— WITH INJUSTICE) OPPRESS
(— WITH NEGLECT) PIGEONHOLE
(— WITH PARTIALITY) ACCEPT
(— WITH PRIDE) TRAMPLE
(— WITH RESPECT) HONOR
(— WITH RIDICULE) SCOUT
(— WITH RUDENESS) FRUMP
(— WITH TAR) BLACK
(— WITH TENDERNESS) CODDLE
(NEW YEAR'S EVE —) HAGMENA HOGMANAY
TREATISE AGAMA DONET FAUNA FLORA LIBEL SILVA SUMMA SYLVA TRACT TREAT BOTANY POETRY POMONA SERTUM SYSTEM ALGEBRA ANATOMY BIOLOGY COMMENT DIETARY GEOLOGY GRAMMAR HISTORY PANDECT PHYSICS PINETUM POETICS ZOOLOGY ALMAGEST BROCHURE CALCULUS DIDACTIC ECTHESIS EXERCISE GENETICS GEOMANCY GEOMETRY GERMANIA HORNBOOK LAPIDARY MONUMENT PANTHEON PASTORAL PRACTICE SITOLOGY SPECULUM TRACTATE MONOGRAPH
(SUFF.) ICS LOGER LOGIA(N) LOGIC(AL) LOGIST LOGUE LOGY OLOGY
TREATMENT CURE WORK TREAT USAGE ANIMUS DETAIL FACIAL QUARTER BEHAVIOR DEMEANOR ENTREATY
(— BY MASSAGE) SEANCE
(— BY MUD BATHS) PELOTHERAPY
(— FOR FURS) SECRETAGE
(— FOR WOOLLENS) SPONGING
(— OF DISEASE) ALLOPATHY
(BAD —) MISUSAGE
(COLD —) FREEZE
(COMPASSIONATE —) MERCY
(CONTEMPTUOUS —) SPURN
(CRUEL —) SEVERITY
(DIRE —) DOLE
(HARMFUL —) ABUSE
(HARSH —) SHAFT WHATFOR
(INHUMAN —) CRUELTY
(LUXURIOUS —) DELICACY
(SEVERE —) ROUGH
(PREF.) **(MEDICAL —)** IATR(O)
(SUFF.) PRAXIS
(MEDICAL —) IATRIA IATRIC(S) IATRIST IATRY
TREATY MISE ACCORD CARTEL CONCORD ENTENTE LOCARNO ALLIANCE ASSIENTO PROTOCOL TREATISE CONCORDAT
TREBLE TRIPLE DESCANT MINIKIN SOPRANO TRIPLUM
TREBUCHET DONDINE DONDAINE
TREE TI ACH ADY AMA APA ARN ASH BAY BEL BEN BUR DAK DAR EBO ELM FIG FIR GUM HAW KOA KOU LIN NIM OAK SAJ SAL TAL TUI ULE YEW ACLE AGBA AKEE AMLA ANAM ANAN ANDA ARAR ASAK ASOK ATIS ATLE ATTA AULU AUSU BAEL BAKU BITO BOGO BOOM BREA BURI BURR CADE COLA CRAB DATE DHAK DILO DITA DOON EBOE IPIL JACK KINO KOKO LIME MABI MORA NEEM OHIA OMBU PALA PINE POLE POON SADR SORB SUPA TALA TAWA TCHE TEAK TEIL TITI TOON TREW TUNG TUNO UPAS VERA WOOD YATE YAYA AALII ABETO ABURA ACANA ACAPU ACOMA AFARA AGATI AGOHO AKEKI ALAMO ALANI ALDER ALGUM ALISO ALMON ALMUG AMAGA AMAPA AMBAK ANABO ANJAN APPLE ARACA ARBOR ARECA ARJAN ARJUN ARTAR ASOKA ASPEN ATLEE BABUL BALAO BALSA BALTA BANAK BEECH BEHEN BETIS BIRCH BONGO BOREE BOSSE BUMBO CACAO CARAP CAROB CEBIL CEDAR CEIBO DADAP DHAVA DHAWA DILLY DRYAD DURIO ELDER GABUN GAIAC GENIP GINEP GINKO HAZEL ICICA IXORA JAMBO JIQUE JIQUI KAPOR KAPUR KEENA KOKAN KOKIO KOKUM KONGU KUSAM LANSA LARCH LARIX LEHUA LEMON LICCA LIMBA LINDE LINER LINGO MAHOE MAHUA MAMIE MAPLE MAQUI NARRA NIEPA NURSE OADAL OSAGE OSIER PACAY PAPAW PECAN PIPER RAULI ROBLE ROHAN ROWAN SALAI SAMAN SASSY SCRAG SIMAL SIRIS SISSU STICK SUMAC TABOG TARFA TENIO TERAP TIKUR TIMBO TINGI TOONA TUART ULMUS UMIRI URUCA URUCU UVITO WAHOO YACAL YACCA YULAN ZAMAN ACAJOU AHKROT AKEAKE ALAGAO ALERCE ALERSE ALFAJE ALMOND ALUPAG AMAMAU AMBASH AMUGIS AMUYON ANAGAP ANAGUA ANAQUA ANGICO ANILAO ARALIA ARANGA ARBUTE AUSUBO AZALEA BABOEN BACURY BAHERA BAKULA BALSAM BANABA BANAGO BANANA BANCAL BANIAN BANYAN BARBAS BATAAN BIRIBA BOMBAX BONDUC BONETE BOTONG BRAUNA BUCARE BUSTIC CALABA CAMARA CANELA CANELO CAPUMO CARAPA CASSIA CATIVO CAUCHO CEDRON CHALTA CHERRY CHICHA CHINAR CHOGAK CITRON COBOLA COCUYO CUMBER DATURA DHAMAN DHAURA DHAURI DRIMYS DURIAN ELCAJA EMBLIC EMBUIA FEIJOA FILLER FUSTIC GABOON GINKGO GUAIAC GURJAN GURJUN IDESIA IDIGBO ILIAHI ILLIPE ILLUPI JAGUEY JUJUBE KAMALA KEMPAS KINDAL KITTUL LANSAT LANSEH LAUREL LIGNUM LINDEN LITCHI LOCUST LONGAN MAFURA MALLET MAYTEN MEDLAR MILKER MIMOSA ORANGE PANAMA PAWPAW PIQUIA POPLAR RAMBEH ROHUNA RUNNEL SABICU SABINO SANDAN SANTOL SAPELE SAPOTA SAPOTE SATINE SAWYER SERAYA SINTOC SISSOO SOUARI STYRAX SUMACH SUNDRI TALUTO TAMANU TARATA TEETEE TIKOOR TIMBER TINGUY TOATOA TOTARA TUPELO URUCUM URUSHI UVALHA WABAYO WABOOM WAHAHE WALNUT WAMARA WAMPEE WANDOO WATTLE YACHAN YAGHAN YAMBAN ZAMANG ACHIOTE ACHUETE AILANTO AKEPIRO AMBATCH AMBOINA AMUGUIS AMUYONG ANABONG ANNATTO ANONANG APITONG APRICOT ARARIBA ARAROBA ARBORET ARBUTUS AROEIRA ASSAGAI AVOCADO AVODIRE BANILAD BANKSIA BECUIBA BENZOIN BILLIAN BOLLING BUBINGA BUCKEYE BUISSON CADAMBA CAJAPUT CAJUPUT CANELLA CARAIPE CASTANA CATALPA CAUTIVO CERILLO CHAMPAC CHECHEM CHECKER CHENGAL COCULLO CONIFER CURUPAY CYPRESS DEADMAN DESCENT DETERMA DHAMNOO EPACRID FRUITER GONDANG GRIBBLE GUMIHAN HICKORY HOLLONG HOPBUSH HORMIGO KAMASSI KAMBALA KICKXIA KITTOOL KOKOONA KOOMBAR KUMQUAT LOGWOOD MADRONA MANJACK MARGOSA NAARTJE PARAIBA PEREIRA PIMENTO PULASAN PYRAMID RATWOOD REDWOOD SERINGA SERVICE SHITTAH SPINDLE STOPPER SUNDARI SURETTE TANGELO TANGHIN TARAIRI TARATAH TARWOOD TINDALO TREELET TWISTER URUNDAY VETERAN

WALAHEE WALLABA WEENONG WONGSHY WONGSKY YAMANAI YOHIMBE YOHIMBI ZELKOVA ACEITUNA ALGAROBA ALLSPICE ALMACIGA ALMANDER ALMENDRO ALOEWOOD AMARILLO ARAGUANE ARBOLOCO ARBUSCLE AVELLANO BAKUPARI BASSWOOD BAYBERRY BELLWOOD BINDOREE BITANHOL BLACKBOX BOARWOOD BORRACHA BREADNUT CABREUVA CAMELLIA CAMUNING CARAGANA CARAUNDA CHAMPACA CHESTNUT CHINCONA CHINOTTO CINNAMON COCOPLUM COPALCHE COUMAROU CRABWOOD CUCUMBOL DEADFALL DOMINANT DOTTEREL DOVEWOOD DRACAENA DRUMWOOD ETABALLI FIREFALL FORESTER GAMDEBOO GEELHOUT GENISARO GUACACOA GUAYROTO HALAPEPE HARDTACK HARDWOOD HOLDOVER HORNBEAM HOROPITO IRONWOOD ISHPINGO ITCHWOOD JELOTONG JELUTONG KAJUGARU KINGWOOD KNOBWOOD LACEBARK LEADWOOD LORDWOOD MAHOGANY MANDARIN MILKWOOD MOKIHANA OITICICA OLEASTER ONEBERRY PEDIGREE PICHURIM PINKWOOD RAMBUTAN RASAMALA SANDARAC SANDWOOD SAPUCAIA SASSWOOD SEBESTEN SHAGBARK SHAVINGS SILKWOOD SLOGWOOD SOAPBARK STANDARD SUCUPIRA SWEETSOP SYCAMORE TAMARACK TAMARIND TANEKAHA TREELING TURMERIC ZAPATERO PERSIMMON PISTACHIO SASSAFRAS SATINWOOD SANDALWOOD

(— CUT BACK) DOTARD POLLARD

(— FURNISHING SUPPORT TO VINE) HUSBAND

(— IN STREAM) SAWYER

(— LEFT IN CUTTING) HOLDOVER

(— OF HEAVEN) AILANTO AILANTHUS

(— ON WALL) RIDER

(— OVER 2 FT. DIAMETER) VETERAN

(—S IN FOREST) STAND

(— SYMBOLIZING UNIVERSE) YGDRASIL

(— WITH BRANCHES TRIMMED) LOP LOPSTICK

(AROMATIC —) CLUSIA LABIATE

(AUSTRALIAN —) ASH GUM TOON BELAH BELAR BOREE BUNDY BUNYA GIDIA HAZEL KARRI NONDA PENDA SALLY WILGA BAOBAB DRIMYS GIDGEE GIMLET GYMPIE JARRAH KOWHAI MARARA PEROBA SALLEE DOGWOOD GEEBUNG PEEBEEN BEEFWOOD CARABEEN COOLABAH FLINDOSA GRAVILEA IRONBARK LACEBARK QUANDONG ROSEBUSH SANDSTAY SOAPWOOD TILESEED

(BIG —) SEQUOIA

(BORNEO —) BILIAN

(BURMESE —) PADOUK

(CEYLON —) HORA

(CITRUS —) SHADDOCK

(CLOTHES —) COSTUMER

(CLUMP OF —S) TOLL TUMP STELL

(CONTORTED —) SAXAUL

(CUBAN —) JIQUE JIQUI GUACACOA

(CURSED —) WARYTREE

(DEAD —) RUNT SNAG RAMPIKE

(DEAD —S) DRIKI

(DECAYED —) DOTTEREL

(DWARF —) SCRUB ARBUSCLE

(EVERGREEN —) FIR YEW PINE SUGI TAWA ABIES ATHEL CAROB CEDAR CLOVE HOLLY LARCH LEMON OLIVE THUJA BALSAM BIBIRU COIGUE COIHUE KANAGI KAPUKA LOQUAT ORANGE SPRUCE ARDISIA BEBEERU BILIMBI CONIFER HEMLOCK JUNIPER MADRONA MADRONO EUCALYPT EUONYMUS SAPODILLA SANDORICUM

(FAMILY —) STEMMA DESCENT LINEAGE PEDIGREE

(FRUIT —) CORDON

(GENEALOGICAL —) ARBOR JESSE

(GROWTH OF —S) SYLVAGE

(GUM —) KARI KINO BABUL BALTA BUMBO ICICA KARRI KIKAR GIMLET MALLET STORAX TEWART WANDOO GOMMIER COOLIBAH

(HAWAIIAN —) KOA LEHUA ILIAHI

(INFERNAL —) ZAQQUM

(JAPANESE —) KAYA KIAKI KEYAKI KADSURA KATSURA SATSUMA ZELKOVA

(MANDARIN —) SATSUMA

(MEXICAN —) ULE AMAPA DRAGO EBANO SERON CAPULI CATENA CHILTE CAPULIN COPALCHE

(MYTHICAL —) TUBA

(NEW ZEALAND —) AKE KARO KAWA MIRO PUKA RATA RIMU TAWA TORU WHAU HINAU KAORI KAURI MAIRE MANGI MAPAU MATAI TOWAI AKEAKE KAMAHI KANUKA KAPUKA KARAKA KARAMU KAWAKA KONINI MANUKA PURIRI TARATA TITOKI TOATOA TOTARA WAHAHE AKEPIRO MANGEAO PUKATEA TARAIRI TARWOOD KAWAKAWA KOHEKOHE MAKOMAKO

(ORNAMENTAL —) KABIKI LABURNUM POINCIANA

(PHILIPPINES —) DAO IBA TUA TUI ATLE BOGO DITA IFIL IPIL AGOHO AGOJO ALMON AMAGA ANABO BAYOG BAYOK BETIS DANLI GUIJO LAUAN LIGAS TABOG YACAL ALAGAO ALUPAG AMUYON ANAGAP ANUBIN ARANGA BANUYO BATAAN BATETE BATINO BOTONG DUNGON KATMON LANETE MABOLO MARANG MOLAVE SAGING TALUTO AMUGUIS AMUYONG ANABONG ANOBING ANONANG APITONG BINUKAU CAMAGON DANGLIN MANCONO MAYAPIS TINDALO ALMACIGA BITANHOL KALIPAYA KALUMPIT LUMBAYAO MACAASIM MALAPAHO TANGUILE

(POISONOUS —) GUAO UPAS LIGAS TANGHIN TANQUEN MANCHINEEL

(POLYNESIAN —) MACUDA

(SACRED —) CHAMPAC CHAMPAK

(SALT —) ATLE

(SANDARAC —) ARAR

(SHADE —) ELM DILLY GUAMA HEVEA CATALPA HALESIA INKWOOD JOEWOOD SYCAMORE

(SHOWY —) ASAK ASOK ASOKA

(SMALL —) AKE BOX TCHE ALDER CUMAY DWARF HENNA NGAIO SERON AKEAKE BLOLLY CHANAR JOJOBA KOWHAI ARBORET INKWOOD JOEWOOD KADAMBA STADDLE TREELET EMAJAGUA HARDTACK HUISACHE OLEASTER SNOWBELL SOURWOOD TREELING

(SPINY —) LIME AROMA AROMO HONEY BOOGUM BUCARE BUMELIA CATECHU COLORIN LAVANGA COCKSPUR

(STANDING —) FILLER

(STUNTED —) SCRAB SCRUB SCRUNT

(THORNY —) BEL BAEL BREA LEMON AMBACH SAMOHU AMBATCH

(TIMBER —) ASH DAR ENG FIR SAL ACLE ANDA BAKU COCO CUYA EKKI IPIL PELU PINE TALA TEAK YANG ACAPU ALMON AMAPA AMATE AMBAY ANJAN ARACA ARGAN BANAK BIRCH CAROB CEDAR COCOA CULLA EBONY ERIZO FOTUI HALDU ICICA IROKO KAURI KHAYA KIAKI KOKAN MANIU MAPLE MVULE NARRA ROBLE TIMBO ALERCE ALUPAG BABOEN BACURY BANABA BANCAL CARBON CHUPON CORTEZ DAGAME DEGAME DUKUMA ESPAVE FREIJO GAMARI GUMHAR IMBUIA JACANA LEBBEK MUERMO PADAUK SANDAN SATINE SISSOO AMUGUIS AROEIRA BECUIBA BILLIAN CARAIPI CYPRESS ESPAVEL GATEADO GOMAVEL GUARABU GUAYABI HARPULA HOLLONG KOOMBAR LAPACHO REDWOOD AMARILLO BOARWOOD CABREUVA CARACOLI COCOBOLO CRABWOOD DONCELLA GUATAMBU GUAYACAN MAHOGANY SLOGWOOD SUCUPIRA

(TRAINED —) ESPALIER

(TROPICAL —) CYP AKEE AULU DALI DIKA EBOE EKKI GUAO INGA MABA MAHO MAJO PALM SHEA ACKEE BALSA BONGO COUMA DALLI FOTUI GUAMA GUARA ICICA ILAMA JIGUA MARIA NEPAL NJAVE POOLI TARFA ANUBIN BAKULA BALATA BANANA CASHEW CEDRON CHUPON GENIPA HACKIA ITAUBA LEBBEK LECYTH MAMMEE OBECHE PERSEA ANGELIN ANNATTO CAULOTE COPAIBA DATTOCK EHRETIA EUGENIA GATEADO GUACIMO LAPACHO MAJAGUA MOMBINI SANDBOX SOURSOP SURETTE BEEFWOOD CALABASH CAMUNING CORKWOOD FUNTUMIA MUSKWOOD PATASHTE SWEETSOP TAMARIND MONKEYPOD MANGOSTEEN PRINCEWOOD

(UNARMED —) ALBIZZIA

(VARNISH —) DOON THEETSEE

(XEROPHYTIC —) SAXAUL

(YOUNG —) RUNNEL SPRING TILLER SAPLING SEEDLING SPRINGER

(PL.) BLUFF RINDS SILVA OVERSTORY

(PREF.) ARBORI DENDR(O)

(SUFF.) DENDRON

TREE CREEPER TOMTIT

TREE CYPRESS GILIA

TREE DUCK FIDDLER YAGUAZA

TREE EAR FUNGUS

TREE FROG FERREIRO

TREE MOSS USNEA

TREENAIL NOG GUTTA MOOTER TRUNNEL

TREE PEONY MOUTAN

TREE SHREW TANA BANXRING BANGSRING

TREE SNAKE BOOMSLANG

TREE TOAD HYLA HYLID ANURAN

TREE TOMATO TAMARILLO

TREETOP LAP LOP

TREFOIL CANCH LOTUS CLAVER CROWTOE BEDSTRAW SAINFOIN TICKSEED

TREHALOSE MYCOSE

TRELLIS TRAIL PERGOLA TARLIES ESPALIER

TREMATODE FLUKE MARITA STRIGEID

TREMBLE DARE DIRL RESE BEVER QUAKE SHAKE SLOWS WIVER AGRISE DIDDER DINGLE DITHER DODDER FALTER HOTTER HOTTLE NITHER QUAVER QUIVER SHIMMY THRILL TITTER TOTTER TREMOR TRYMLE WABBLE WOBBLE WUTHER FLICKER SHUDDER STAGGER TWIDDLE WHITHER THRIMBLE

(PL.) TIRE TIRES

(PREF.) TREMELLI TROMO

TREMBLER BUZZER HAMMER VIBRATOR

TREMBLING BEVER SHAKY DITHER TREMOR TREPID AQUIVER DODDERY PALSIED QUAKING QUAVERY QUIVERY TREMBLY TWITTER

TREMBLY WOOZY

TREMENDOUS BIG AWFUL GIANT GREAT LARGE HOWLING TEARING ENORMOUS HORRIBLE TERRIBLE TERRIFIC MONSTROUS

TREMOLO HURRY TRILLO

TREMOR RIGOR SHAKE DINDLE QUIVER THRILL SHUDDER TREMBLE

TREMULOUS ASPEN QUAKY SHAKY PALSIED SHIVERY TREMBLY SHIMMERY TINGLING

TRENCH GAW SAP FOSS GRIP GURT LINE MOAT RILL SICK SIKE TAJO TRIG BOYAU CHASE DITCH DRAIN DRILL FLOAT FOSSE GRAFF GRAFT GRAVE GROOP SEUCH TRINK COFFER FURROW GULLET GUTTER SHEUGH ACEQUIA CUNETTE CUVETTE OPENCUT SLIDDER ENCROACH LOCKSPIT PARALLEL SPREADER THOROUGH TRESPASS

(— BELOW FOREST FIRE) GUTTER

(— FOR BURYING POTATOES) CAMP

(**— FOR DRAIN TILES**) CHASE
(**— FORMED BY BANKING VEGETABLES**) GRAVE
(**— ON HILLSIDE**) SLIDDER
(**ARTIFICIAL —**) LEAT
(**IRRIGATION —**) FLOAT SUGSLOOT
(PREF.) BOTHR(O) BOTHRI(O)
TRENCHANT ACID KEEN EDGED SHARP TUANT INCISIVE
TRENCHER PLATTER ROUNDEL
TRENCHERMAN EATER
TREND BEND BIAS HAND TONE TURN BULGE CURVE DRIFT SENSE SLANT SWING TENOR SQUINT STRIKE CURRENT DOWNSIDE MOVEMENT TENDENCY
(**LOWERING PRICE —**) EASE
TRENDY HIP MOD NOW POP CHIC GROOVY
TREPANG BALATE SWALLO SWALLOW TITFISH TEATFISH
TREPIDATION FEAR ALARM DISMAY
TRESPASS DEBT GILUT POACH BREACH FURTUM INVADE INTRUDE OFFENSE ENCROACH ENTRENCH INFRINGE INTRENCH OVERLOUP
TRESS CURL LOCK TAIL BRAID SWITCH RINGLET WIMPLER
TRES-TINE TRAY ROYAL
TRESTLE MARE HORSE INRUN CHEVALET SAWHORSE
TREVALLY TURRUM
TREWS TROUSERS
TRIACETATE ACETIN EUROBIN
TRIAD MAJOR TRIAS TRINE TRIUNE TERNARY TERNION TRILOGY TRINARY TRINITY TRIMURTI TRIRATNA
TRIAL SAY SHY TRY BOUT DOOM FIRE HACK OYER STAB TEST TURN ASSAY CROSS ESSAY GRIEF ISSUE POINT PROOF TASTE TOUCH WHACK ASSIZE EFFORT EQUITY TRINAL APPROOF ATTEMPT CALVARY DISGUST HEARING PROVING SCRATCH CRUCIBLE EXERCISE JUDGMENT QUAESTIO TENTAMEN PROLUSION
(**— BY BATTLE**) WAGER
(**— BY ORDEAL**) ORDALIUM
(**— FOR HOUNDS**) DERBY
(**— OF SPEED**) DASH
(**— OF STRENGTH**) CRUNCH
(**— ROUND**) HEAT
(**AUTHOR OF —**) KAFKA
(**CHARACTER IN —**) LENI JOSEPH ADVOCATE BURSTNER TITORELLI
(**EXPERIMENTAL —**) TENTAMEN
(**RACING —**) PREP
(**SEVERE —**) ORDEAL CRUCIBLE
(PREF.) PEIRA
TRIANGLE APEX CYMBAL OXYGON TRIGON PYRAMID SCALENE TRINITY TRIQUET DINGDONG ISOSCELE
(**SPHERICAL —**) PENDENTIVE
TRIANGULAR HEATER CUNEATE HASTATE
(**— AREA**) QUIRK
(**— CLOTH**) GORE
(**— INSET**) GODET
(PREF.) TRIGON(O)

TRIBAL GENTILE GENTLIC TRIBULAR
TRIBE (ALSO SEE NATIVE AND PEOPLE) AO GI ATI AUS BOH EVE EWE GOG KHA KIN KRA ROD SUK YAO ADAI AKAN AKHA AKIM AKKA BAYA BONI CLAN DAGO GUHA PURU QUNG RACE RAVI REKI SAHO SEID SHIK SHOR SIOL SOGA SUKU SUSU TOBA TURI TUSH UBII VEPS VILI VIRA YANA AEQUI ANGKA APTAL ARAWA BASSI BATAK BESSI BONGO BROOD CHANG CINEL DADJO DEDAN DIERI FIRCA GIBBI HORDE HOUSE ICENI KAJAR KANDH KEDAR KHOND KIWAI KONGO KOTAR KREPI LANGO MAGOG MARSI MBUBA MENDE MENDI MOSSI MUTER NANDI PHYLE PONDO QUADI SERER SOTIK STAMM SUEVI TAIPI TAULI TCAWI TEKKE TELEI TUATH VEPSE VOLOF WAKHI WARRI WASHO WAYAO YOMUD ADIGHE AGAWAM AMHARA ANAMIM ANTEVA APAYAO ARAINS BANYAI BASOGA BUDUMA BUSAOS CHAMPA CHAWIA CHORAI DOROBO FAMILY HERULI KARLUK KEREWA KHAMTI KONYAK KORANA LOBALE MANGAR MOLALA NATION NERVII PAHARI PHYLON POKOMO RAMNES SHAGIA SICULI SIMEON SUKUMA TAINUI TAMOYO TCHIAM TELEUT THUSHI TUSHIN TYPEES VENETI WABENA WABUMA WAGOMA WAGUHA WAHEHE WARORI WASOGA WAVIRA ZARAMO ZEGUHA ZENAGA ABABDEH ABANTES AIAWONG AKWAPIM AMAKOSA ANOMURA ANTAIVA ARVERNI BAGIRMI BAKATAN BAKONGO BAKUNDA BAMBARA BASONGO CABINDA CHAOUIA CHAUWIA CHONTAL CHUKCHI COLLERY DADAYAG DADSCHO ILLANUN JAZYGES KABINDA KABONGA KHOKANI KOLDAJI KONIAGA KOREISH KUBACHI KURUMBA LLANERO NAIADES PALAUNG PARISII PIMENTO RAURACI SAMBALA SAMBARA SEKHWAN SENONES SEQUANI SHAMMAR SHERANI SHERPAS SHUKRIA SILIPAN SUIONES SUKKIIM TAKELMA TARKANI TURKANA VIDDHAL WAGWENO WAICURI WAMBUGU WAREGGA WASANGO ZONGORA AMAFINGO ANDOROBO ASHANGOS ASSHURIM AWABAKAL BARKINJI BATETELA BOANBURA CHERUSCI CHITRALI GEZRITES JICAQUES KUKURUKU LANDUMAN NEBAIOTH ORUNCHUN PALLIYAN PHASIRON PUPULUCA PURUPURU RAHANWIN SAKALAVA SHINWARI SINGSING SINTSINK TCHUKCHI TENGGRIS USTARANA WANGATTA WAPOGORO WAPOKOMO
(**— OF ISRAEL**) DAN GAD ASHER REUBEN EPHRAIM ISSACHAR MANASSEH
(**CHINESE —S**) HU
(**PRIVILEGED —**) MAGHZEN MAKHZAN
(**SEA GYPSY —**) SELUNG
(PREF.) PHYL(O)
(SUFF.) INI
TRIBROMOETHANOL AVERTIN
TRIBULATION AGONY CROSS MISERY SORROW DISTRESS
TRIBUNAL BAR FEME ROTA VEHM BENCH COURT FEHME FORUM JUNTA VEHME MAJLIS ACUERDO ESGUARD MEJLISS RIGSRET AREOPAGY KANGAROO
TRIBUNE BEMA VELUTUS
TRIBUTARY ARM BOGAN BRANCH FEEDER TYBURN AFFLUENT ANABRANCH
TRIBUTE AID FEE TAX CAIN GELT KUDO LEVY PORT RENT SCAT CANON GAVEL HANSE MAILL SALVO SCATT CHAUTH HERIOT HIDAGE HOMAGE IMPOST CARATCH CHEVAGE CHIEFRY OVATION PENSION SYNODAL TREWAGE AUXILIUM BRENNAGE HEREGELD PESHKASH ROMESCOT ROMESHOT
(**FEUDAL —**) HERIOT
TRICE GIRD BLINK THROW INSTANT
TRICHECHUS MANATUS
TRICHINA NEMATODE
TRICHINIZED MEASLY
TRICHION CRINION
TRICHOME SCALE
TRICHOMONIASIS CANKER ABORTION
TRICK DO BAM BOB COG CON CUN DAP DOR FOB FOX FUB FUN GIN GUM JIG JOB PAW RIG BILK BITE BORE CHAW CHIP DIDO DIRT DUPE FAKE FIRK FLAM FLUM FOOL GAFF GAME GAUD GECK GULL HAVE HOAX HOSE JAPE JEST JINK JOUK JUNT LOCK LURK PASS PAWK PRAT PULL RORT RUSE SELL SKIT SLUR TURN WILE WIPE WOOL ANTIC BLEAR BLINK CATCH CHEAT CONNU CRAFT CREEK CROOK CULLY CURVE DODGE DORRE ELUDE FEINT FETCH FOURB FRAUD GLEEK GRIFT GUILE KNACK PAVIE PLANT PRANK SHIFT SHINE SKITE SLICK STUNT TRAIN TRUFF TWIST WHEEL WREST WRINK BAFFLE BANTER BEGUNK BEJAPE BLENCH BROGUE CAUTEL CHOUSE CRADDY DECEIT DELUDE DOUBLE EUCHRE FOURBE HOCKET HUMBUG ILLUDE JOCKEY JUGGLE MANNER PLISKY POLICY SCONCE SHAVIE SPRING TREPAN VAGARY WHEEZE WINNER CANTRIP CHICANE CONCEIT FICELLE FINESSE FORWARD GUILERY KNAVERY MARLOCK PAGEANT SHUFFLE SLEIGHT WHIZZER ARTIFICE CHALDESE CLAPTRAP CLOWNADE CONTOISE CROTCHET DELUSION DOUBLING FLAGARIE FLIMFLAM GILENYIE INTRIGUE JEOPARDY PRACTICE PRANCOME PRESTIGE QUENTISE SLAMPAMP TRAVERSE TRICKING BAMBOOZLE STRATAGEM
(**— OUT**) FARD FANGLE FINIFY
(**BEGUILING —**) WILE
(**CARD —**) CLUB HEART SPADE STICH DIAMOND WEAVING
(**FRAUDULENT —**) RIG TOP
(**JUGGLING —**) FOIST
(**KIND OF —**) ODD
(**KNAVISH —**) DOGTRICK
(**LOVE —**) AMORETTO
(**MEAN —**) TOUCH
(**MONKEY —**) SINGERIE
(**OLD —**) CONNU
(**PETTY —S**) CRANS
(**SIX —S**) BOOK
(**SMART —**) LIRIPIPE LIRIPOOP
(**STUPID —**) SHINE
(**VEXING —**) CHAW
(**WRESTLING —**) CHIP CLICK FAULX FORWARD
(PL.) DAGS
TRICKER TRUMPER
TRICKERY DOLE GAFF SHAM TRAP TRAY WILE COVIN FRAUD HOCUS SHARK TRAIN CAUTEL COVINE DECEIT JAPERY JUGGLE TREGET DODGERY FALLACY GULLERY JOUKERY KNAVERY PAWKERY SLEIGHT ARTIFICE CHEATING COZENAGE JOOKERIE JUGGLERY PRACTICE TRICKING TRUMPERY SHENANIGAN SHENANIGANS
TRICKILY FOXILY
TRICKINESS PAWKERY
TRICKISH KNAVISH FRAUDFUL
TRICKLE DRIB DRIP DRILL STILL TRILL DISTIL DRIVEL GUTTER SICKER SIGGER STRAIN ZIGGER DISTILL DRIBBLE DRIZZLE DROPPLE TRINTLE
TRICKLET RILL
TRICKSTER GULL SHAM RASCAL TRAPAN SLICKER TRICKER SLEEVEEN TRAMPOSO TREGETOUR
TRICKSY ELFISH QUIRKSEY
TRICKY SLY DEEP BRAID DODGY FIKIE GAUDY ROWDY SNIDE ARTFUL CATCHY LUBRIC QUIRKY SHIFTY SMARTY TWISTY DEVIOUS SLANTER TRICKLE WINDING FLIMFLAM JUGGLING LUBRICAL SHIFTFUL SKITTISH SLIDDERY SLIPPERY TORTUOUS TRICKING
TRICLINIC ANORTHIC
TRICOT JERSEY
TRICYCLE VELO CYCLE TRIKE WHEEL TANDEM TRICAR RANTOON ROADSTER SOCIABLE
TRIDENT SPEAR VAJRA TRISUL TRISULA
TRIED TESTED PROBATE WEIGHED RELIABLE
TRIFECTA TRIPLE
TRIFLE ACE BOB DAB FIG HAW PIN SOU TOY BEAN COOT DOIT FICO FOOL HAIR HOOT JAUK MESS MOCK MOTE PLAY RUSE WHIT DALLY FLIRT FLUKE GLAIK ITEMY NIFLE PLACK POINT SCRAT SPORT TRICK TRUFF BAWBEE BREATH DABBLE DANDLE DAWDLE DELUDE DIBBLE DOODAD DOODLE FADDLE FESCUE FIDDLE FOOTER FOOTLE

FRIVOL GEWGAW MONKEY NIDDLE NIGGLE NIGNAY PADDLE PALTER PETTLE PICKLE PIDDLE PIGGLE PINGLE POTTER PUTTER STIVER TIFFLE VANITY WANTON FEATHER FLAMFEW FRIBBLE NOTHING QUIDDLE THOUGHT TRANEEN TRINKET TRIVIAL WHIFFLE COQUETTE FALDERAL FLIMFLAM FOLDEROL GIMCRACK KICKSHAW MOLEHILL NIFFNAFF NIHILITY NUGAMENT RIGMAREE TRANTLUM BAGATELLE
(— WITH) JANK DANDLE DELUDE NIGGLE
(ATTRACTIVE —) CONCEIT
(LITERARY —) TOY
(MERE —) SONG STRAW
(MEREST —) FIG
(SHOWY —) WALLY
(PL.) NUGAE TRIVIA GIBLETS FEWTRILS NONSENSE

TRIFLER DOODLE PLAYER WANTON FLANEUR FOOTLER FRIBBLE NUGATOR PINGLER TWIDDLER WHIFFLER

TRIFLES
(PREF.) NUGI

TRIFLING AIRY FOND IDLE FUNNY INANE LIGHT PETTY POTTY SILLY SMALL FADDLE FLIMSY FUTILE LEVITY LIMUTE LITTLE PALTRY SIMPLE SLIGHT STRAWY TOYISH FOOLISH FRIBBLE ITEMING NOMINAL PUERILE TRIVIAL TWATTLE COQUETRY FIDDLING FLIMFLAM FRIPPERY IMMOMENT NONSENSE NUGATORY PIDDLING SNIPPING FRIBBLING WHIFFLERY NEGLIGIBLE TOMFOOLERY

TRIFOLIUM CLOVER TREFOIL

TRIG NEAT SNOD TRIM CHIPPER

TRIGGER CAUSE VERGE TRICKER

TRIGGERFISH COCUYO TURBOT OLDWIFE BALISTID FILEFISH OLDWENCH

TRIGON TRINE SABBEKA SACKBUT SAMBUCA TRIGONON

TRIGONOMETRY SPHERICS
(— FUNCTION) SINE COSINE

TRILBY (AUTHOR OF —) DUMAURIER
(CHARACTER IN —) ALICE GECKO SANDY TAFFY BILLEE TRILBY OFERRALL SVENGALI

TRILL BURR FLAP ROLL SHAKE QUAVER THRILL TRILLO WARBLE ROULADE TRILLET
(BEGINNINNG OF A —) RIBATTUTA

TRILLED HIRRIENT

TRILLION
(PREF.) TERA TREG(A)

TRILLIONTH
(PREF.) PICO

TRILLIUM SARA TRUE SARAH TRUMP BENJAMIN TRUELOVE

TRILOBITE EODISCID

TRIM AX AXE CUT DUB GIM LIP LOP MOW NET BARB BEAD BUTT CLIP CROP DEFT DINK FEAT FUSS GASH GIMP HACK JIMP LACE NEAT PICK SNAG SNOD SNUG SPUR STOW TACK TOSH TRIG BRAID BRUSH CLEAN COPSE DRESS FITTY GENTY HEDGE KEMPT KNIFE NATTY PREEN PRIME PRUNE PURGE SAUCY SHAVE SHEAR SHRAG SHRIP SLEEK SMART SMIRK SPRIG STUMP TIGHT TRICK VERGE BARBER DAPPER DONSIE DOUBLE FETTLE PICKED REFORM SHROUD SOIGNE SPRUCE SVELTE SWITCH TRIMLY CHIPPER FEATHER FLOUNCE SCISSOR MANICURE ORNAMENT TRIMMING SHIPSHAPE
(— A BOAT) SIT
(— ENDS OF HAIR) SHIRL
(— HEDGE) DUB
(— HIDES) ROUND
(— MEAT) CONDITION
(— SAIL) FILL
(— SEAMS) FETTLE
(— SHOE) FOX
(— TREES) PRIME SWAMP
(— WITH EMBROIDERY) GIMP PANEL
(FURNITURE —) SKIRT

TRIMLY SMARTLY SPRUCELY

TRIMMED PEEKABOO

TRIMMER FINER BRIDLE TACKER VOLANT ROUNDER SMOCKER SCRATTER

TRIMMING COQ FUR GIMP LACE BRAID CHAPE COQUE FRILL GUARD INKLE JABOT ROBIN RUCHE ERMINE LACING OSPREY PURFLE ROBING BEADING CASCADE FALBALA FURRING GALLOON MARABOU PUFFING ROULEAU BRAIDING EAVESING FALDERAL FOLDEROL FROSTING FROUFROU FURBELOW JEWELING PAILETTE PEARLING PICKADIL PLASTRON SOUTACHE PAILLETTE SPAGHETTI STRAPPING
(— OF KNOTTED THREAD) MACRAME MACRAMI
(FEATHER —) MARABOU MARABOUT
(PLEATED —) RUCHE
(PL.) LOP FLOTS SHORTS FIXINGS LOPPING BRAIDING FRILLIES

TRIMURTI TRINITY

TRINE TRENE TRIGON

TRINIDAD-TOBAGO (CAPITAL OF —) PORTOFSPAIN
(POINT OF —) GALERA
(RIVER OF —) ORTOIRE
(TOWN OF —) TOCO ARIMA COUVA LABREA MORUGA SIPARIA

TRINITARIAN MATHURIN

TRINITROTOLUENE TNT TOLITE TRITON

TRINITY TRIAD TRIAS TRINE TRIUNE GODHEAD TERNARY TRIMURTI TRINUNITY

TRINKET TOY DIDO GAUD MERE BIJOU HEART KNACK TAHLI BAUBLE CHARME DEVICE DOODAD GEWGAW BIBELOT TRANGAM TRANKUM GIMCRACK KICKSHAW TRANTLUM TRINKLET WHIMWHAM TCHOTCHKE
(PL.) TRINKUMS

TRINKETRY KNAVERY

TRIO GLEEK TERCET TERZET TRIUNE TERZETTO
(THREE —S) NONET
(TWO —S) SEXTET

TRIOLEFIN TRIENE

TRIONYX AMYDA

TRIOPAS (DAUGHTER OF —) IPHIMEDIA
(FATHER OF —) NEPTUNE
(MOTHER OF —) CANACE
(SON OF —) ERYSICHTHON

TRIOPS APUS

TRIP HOP JAG JET JOG TIP BOUT CHIP FOOT GAIT GATE KILT LINK RAKE SKIP TOUR TROT TURN BROAD DANCE DRIVE HITCH JAUNT SALLY CRUISE ERRAND FLIGHT HEGIRA OFFEND OUTING RAMBLE SAFARI SASHAY VOYAGE JOURNEY MISSTEP SAILING SETDOWN STUMBLE TRIPPER CAMPAIGN PERIPLUS
(— ALONG) CHIP LINK
(— BY DOG TEAM) MUSH
(— INTO COUNTRY) CAMPAIGN
(— IN WRESTLING) CHIP CLICK
(— UP) SUPPLANT
(HUNTING —) SHOOT
(KIND OF —) EGO
(MAKE A QUICK —) NIP
(PART OF —) LEG
(PLEASURE —) JUNKET
(SHORT —) HOP

TRIPE GOO PAUNCH ROLPENS TRILLIBUB CODSWALLOP

TRIPLE TRINE TREBLE TERNARY TRIFOLD TRIPLEX THRIBBLE TRIFECTA

TRIPLE BOND
(SUFF.)
(CONTAINING —) OLIC

TRIPLET TRIN CODON BRELAN PARIAL TERCET TRIOLE TRIPLE TERZINA TRIOLET HEMIOLIA TRILLING TRIPLING TRISTICH
(— OF BASES) CODON

TRIPLETAIL SAMA CHOBIE FLASHER GROUPER

TRIPLICITY TRIGON

TRIPOD CAT TRIP SPIDER TEAPOY TRIPOS TRIVET TRESTLE

TRIPODY HEMIEPES

TRIPOLI SILEX TRIPEL

TRIPPER DECKMAN

TRIPTOLEMUS (FATHER OF —) CELEUS
(MOTHER OF —) METANIRA

TRISHAW CYCLO PEDICAB

TRISMUS LOCKJAW TETANUS

TRISTAN UND ISOLDE
(CHARACTER IN —) MARK MELOT ISOLDE TRISTAN BRANGANE KURWENAL
(COMPOSER OF —) WAGNER

TRISTE SAD

TRISTRAM SHANDY (AUTHOR OF —) STERNE
(CHARACTER IN —) SLOP TOBY TRIM BOBBY SHANDY WADMAN WALTER YORICK SUSANNAH TRISTRAM

TRITE FADE HACK WORN BANAL CONNU CORNY HOARY MUSTY STALE TIRED VAPID BEATEN COMMON MODERN HACKNEY PERCOCT TRIVIAL BROMIDIC SHOPWORN

TRITENESS BATHOS

TRITERPENOID CERIN

TRITON EFT NEWT TRUMPET
(FATHER OF —) NEPTUNE
(MOTHER OF —) AMPHITRITE

TRITURATE POUND POWDER

TRITURATION TRIPSIS

TRITURUS MOLGE

TRIUMPH WIN CROW PALM INSULT PREVAIL VICTORY CONQUEST
(— OVER) SCALP

TRIUMPHANT VICTOR EXULTANT JUBILANT

TRIUMPHING OVANT

TRIUNGULIN CRAWLER

TRIVET SPIDER TRIPOD TRESTLE TRIPPER BRANDISE

TRIVIAL BALD JERK NICE VAIN BANAL LEGER LIGHT PETTY SILLY SMALL TIDDY FIDFAD FOOTLE PALTRY SLIGHT TOYISH COMICAL PIPERLY PUERILE SHALLOW TIDDLEY DOGGEREL FEATHERY FOOTLING GIMCRACK PIDDLING PILULOUS TRIFLING TRINKETY
(NOT —) SOLID EARNEST

TRIVIALITY FOLLY FROTH NIGNAY TRIFLE INANITY IDLENESS NONSENSE NUGACITY

TROCHANTER SCAPULA

TROCHE ROTULA TABLET CACHUNDE PASTILLE

TROCHEE CHOREE CHOREUS TROCHEUS

TROCHLEA PULLEY

TROCTOLITE GABBRO

TRODDEN TRADED
(MUCH —) BEATEN

TROGLODYTIC SPELEAN

TROGON QUEZAL QUETZAL TOCORORO

TROILUS (BELOVED OF —) CRESSIDA
(FATHER OF —) PRIAM
(MOTHER OF —) HECUBA
(SLAYER OF —) ACHILLES

TROILUS AND CRESSIDA
(AUTHOR OF —) SHAKESPEARE
(CHARACTER IN —) AJAX HELEN PARIS PRIAM AENEAS HECTOR NESTOR ANTENOR CALCHAS HELENUS TROILUS ULYSSES ACHILLES CRESSIDA DIOMEDES MENELAUS PANDARUS AGAMEMNON ALEXANDER CASSANDRA DEIPHOBUS PATROCLUS THERSITES ANDROMACHE MARGARELON

TROJAN PARIS TROIC DARDAN HECTOR ANTENOR
(PL.) TEUCRI

TROLL DROW HARL SPIN TROW ANGLE HARLE MOOCH TRAWL TROLLOL
(— WITH LIVE BAIT) ROVE

TROLLER MOOCHER

TROLLEY CORF BOGEY BOGIE DOLLY TRUCK CRADLE PANTOGRAPH
(OFF ONE'S —) BATS CRAZY

TROLLOP CUT DOXY BITCH DOXIE TROLL TRULL DOLLOP

TROMBONE BONE TRAM BUSINE POSAUNE SACKBUT SLIPHORN
(PART OF —) BOW CUP KEY RIM BELL CROOK FLARE SHANK SLIDE BUMPER FLANGE BALANCER MOUTHPIECE
TRONA URAO
TROOP FARE GANG GING ROUT TURM ROUTE SOLAK STAND TURMA WERED CORNET RISALA ROUGHT SCHOOL THREAT TICHEL TROUPE COMPANY COMITIVA
(— OF ARMED MEN) CREW
(— OF FOXES) SKULK
(— OF WORSHIPPERS) THIASUS
(—S ATTACHED TO SOVEREIGN) GUARDS
(—S IN BATTLE ARRAY) SHELTRON
(—S ON WING OF ARMY) ALARES
(ASSAULTING —S) WAVE
(BOMBAY —S) DUCKS
(CAVALRY —) CORNET
(GIRL SCOUT —) SHIP
(LIGHT-ARMED —S) PSILOI
(MOUNTAIN —) ALPINI
(MOUNTAIN —S) ALPINI
(SCOTTISH —S) JOCKS
(PL.) GIS PARADE
TROOPER BARGIR REITER RUTTER BARGEER
(INDIAN —) SOWAR
TROPARION HIRMOS HEIRMOS TROPARY KATABASIS
TROPE IMAGE EVOVAE SIMILE
TROPHONEMA VILLUS
TROPHONIUS (BROTHER OF —) AGAMEDES
(FATHER OF —) APOLLO ERGINUS
TROPHOZOITE CEPHALIN SPORADIN
TROPHY BAG EMMY HUGO PALM PRIZE SCALP REWARD LAURELS
(WRITING —) HUGO
TROPIC SOLAR TROPHIC
TROPINE HYOSCINE
TROS (FATHER OF —) ERICTHONIUS ERICHTHONIUS
(MOTHER OF —) CALLIRRHOE
(SON OF —) ILUS GANYMEDE ASSARACUS
TROT JOG SPUD TRIG FADGE HURRY PIAFFE
(KIND OF —) TURKEY
TROTH CERTY TROGS TRUTH CERTIE
TROTTER DRIVER CRUBEEN SPANKER
TROUBADOR BARD MINSTREL SORDELLO
TROUBLE ADO AIL DIK HOE ILL IRK MAL MAR VEX WOE BEAT BUSY CAIN CARK EARN FASH FIKE GRAM JEEL MASH MOIL PAIN PINE ROUT SORE STIR TEEN TINE TRAY UNRO WORK ANNOY BESET CROSS DROVE DUTCH GRIEF HAUNT LABOR ROWEL SMITE SPITE STEER STURT SUSSY THRIE TWEAK WHILE WORRY BARRAT BOTHER BURBLE CADDLE CUMBER DITHER EFFORT GRIEVE GRUDGE HARASS HATTER KIAUGH MOLEST POTHER RATTLE RUBBER SORROW SQUALL TAKING THREAT UNEASE UNRUFE WORRIT AFFLICT AGITATE ANXIETY CHAGRIN CONCERN DISEASE DISTURB DRUBBLE EMBROIL FASHERY INFLICT PERTURB PILIKIA SCRUPLE SPUTTER THOUGHT TRACHLE TRAVAIL TRIBBLE TURMOIL BUSINESS DARKNESS DISORDER DISQUIET DISTRESS NOISANCE VEXATION WANDRETH
(— ONE'S SELF) PASS
(EXPRESSION OF —) UHOH
(PL.) CHAGRINS
TROUBLED DRUBLY DRUMLY GRUMLY QUEASY CAREFUL FRETFUL HAUNTED AGITATED HARASSED
TROUBLESHOOTER FIXER
TROUBLESOME DIK ILL SAD BUSY HARD FIKIE PESKY ROWDY SPINY TIGHT PLAGUY SHREWD STICKY THORNY UNEASY BRICKLE HARMFUL ONEROUS PESTFUL PLAGUEY TEWSOME ANNOYING FASHIOUS SPITEFUL UNTOWARD PLAGUESOME
TROUBLESOMENESS BOTHER
TROUBLING CHRONIC
TROU-DE-LOUP TRAPHOLE
TROUGH BOX CUP HOD RUN TOM BACK BOSH BUNK COVE DAIL DALE DISH DORR SHOE SINK TRAY TROW VALE BAKIE CHUTE DITCH LAVER SHOOT SHUTE SLIDE SPOUT STRIP ALVEUS BACKET BUDDLE GUTTER HARBOR HOPPER LAVABO MANGER RUNNER SALTER SINKER SLUICE STRAKE TROGUE VALLEY WALLOW CHENEAU CONDUIT LAUNDER RIFFLER TRENDLE TROFFER LAVATORY PENSTOCK
(— FOR ASHES) BAKIE
(— FOR COOLING INGOTS) BOSH
(— FOR KNEADING) HUTCH
(— FOR PAPER PULP) RIFFLER
(— FOR WASHING ORE) TOM HUTCH STRIP BUDDLE STRAKE
(— IN MONASTERY) LAVABO
(— OF A WAVE) SULK
(— OF CIDER MILL) CHASE
(— OF ROCK) SYNCLINE
(— OF THE SEA) ALVEUS
(ANNULAR —) CUP
(BAKER'S —) HUTCH
(EAVES —) CANAL CHENEAU
(GLACIAL —) DORR
(ORE —) TYE
(SHEEP-DIPPING —) DUP
(WOODEN —) TRUG BAKIE TROGUE
(PREF.) BOTHR(O) BOTHRI(O) PYEL(O)
(SUFF.) SCAPH
TROUNCE MOP FLOG MOPUP THUMP TRAMP WHOMP COURSE CUDGEL DEFEAT CANVASS SHELLAC
TROUNCING LACING WARMING
TROUPE BALLET SERVANTS CUADRILLA
TROUPIAL ORIOLE
TROUSER STROSSER
TROUSERING CASINET
TROUSERS BAGS BELLS CORDS DUCKS JEANS KICKS PANTS SLOPS TONGS TREWS BRAIES CHINOS DENIMS FLARES SHORTS SKILTS SLACKS WHITES BOTTOMS BRACCAE BROGUES CUTOFFS KERSEYS NANKINS SHALWAR SLIVERS STRIDES BLOOMERS BREECHES FLANNELS KICKSEYS MOLESKIN NANKEENS OVERALLS SHINTYAN PANTALOONS INDESCRIBABLES
(— CUT AT KNEE) CUTOFFS
(— WITH CREASELESS LEGS) STOVEPIPE
TROUT CHAR KELT PEAL POGY BROOK BROWN CHARR LAKER LUNGE SCURF SEWEN SEWIN SHARD SQUET SQUIT TRUFF FINNOC KIPPER MYKISS QUASKY SALTER TAIMEN TRUCHA TULADI BOREGAT BROOKIE BROWNIE COASTER HERLING OQUASSA POUNDER RAINBOW SQUETEE SUNAPEE AUREOLUS BODIERON GILLAROO HARDHEAD KAMLOOPS SAIBLING SALMONID SISCOWET
(SMALL —) SCURLING SKIRLING
(YOUNG —) WHITLING
TROUVERE BLONDEL
TROVATORE, IL (CHARACTER IN —) INEZ RUIZ DILUNA AZUCENA LEONORA MANRICO FERRANDO
(COMPOSER OF —) VERDI
TROVE (TREASURE —) STASH
TROW DROW TRUE FAITH BELIEF COVENANT
TROWEL HAWK LEAF PIPE DARBY DERBY FLOAT TAPER TREWEL
(HEARTSHAPED —) HEART DOGTAIL
(MOLDER'S —) LEAF TAPER
(PLASTERER'S —) FLOAT
TROY ILION TROIA TROJA
(FOUNDER OF —) ILUS TROS
(INHABITANT OF —) ILIAN
TROYENS, LES (CHARACTER IN —) ANNA DIDO IOPAS PRIAM AENEAS HECTOR NARBAL ASCANIUS PANTHEUS CASSANDRA CHOROEBUS
(COMPOSER OF —) BERLIOZ
TRUANT HOOKY TRONE TROUT MICHER MEECHER TRIVANT VAGRANT
TRUCE PAX BARLEY TREAGUE INDUCIAE
TRUCK DAN UTE BUNK CORF DRAB DRAG DUCK DUMP GUNK RACK WYNN BOGIE BUGGY DILLY DOLLY GILLY LORRY TROKE BARTER BUMMER CAMION DIESEL DROGUE DRUGGE DUMPER JITNEY PICKUP SLOVEN TIPPER TURTLE CARAVAN FOURGON GONDOLA SKIDDER SLEEPER TROLLEY TRUCKLE TRUNDLE DELIVERY HAULAWAY TRANSFER
(COAL —) DAN
(FIRE —) PUMPER
(KIND OF —) PANEL
(LOGGING —) BUNK BUMMER
(MINING —) CORF SKIP BARNEY
(PART OF —) DECK HOOD STEP TANK TIRE GUARD LIGHT STAKE WHEEL BUMPER GRILLE MIRROR AIRHORN CARRIER EXHAUST MUDFLAP BULKHEAD HEADLIGHT TAILLIGHT COMPRESSOR WINDSHIELD
(TIMBER —) DRUG WYNN
TRUCKING (— RIG) SEMI
TRUCKLE FAWN TOADY SLAVER
TRUCKLING SERVILE
TRUCULENCE BRAG
TRUCULENT MEAN CRUEL HARSH FIERCE SAVAGE SCATHING
TRUDGE JOG PAD HAKE PLOD STOG JAUNT TRACE TRAIK TRAMP TRASH STODGE TAIGLE TRAIPSE
TRUE SO GOOD JUST LEAL PURE REAL VERY VRAI PLUMB RIGHT SOOTH SOUND VERAY ACTUAL FIDELE LAWFUL DEVOTED GENUINE GERMANE PRECISE SINCERE STAUNCH FAITHFUL RELIABLE RIGHTFUL SOOTHFUL UNERRING
(— TO THE FACT) LITERAL
(NECESSARILY —) APODICTIC APODEICTIC
(NOT —) INEXACT
(QUESTIONABLY —) ALLEGED
(SEEMINGLY —) PLAUSIBLE
(PREF.) ALETHO ETYMO EU ORTH(O) VERI
TRUFFLE TRUB TRUFF EARTHNUT
TRUISM SOOTH
TRULL DELL BLOWZE CALLET
TRULY YEA AWAT EVEN FEGS IWIS JUST QUITE SOOTH SYKER TIGHT ATWEEL DINKUM INDEED SIMPLY VERILY INSOOTH SOOTHLY VERAMENT WITTERLY
TRUMP DIS DIX LOW PAM LILY RUFF BASTA BASTO DEECE TROMBE MANILLA MATADOR TRIUMPH SPADILLE
(NOT —S) LAY
(2ND HIGHEST —) MANILLE
TRUMPERY MOCKADO RUBBISH GIMCRACK PEDDLERY
TRUMPET BEME LURE TUBA SHELL TRUMP BOZINE BUCCIN CORNET KERANA LITUUS TROMBA TULNIC ALCHEMY BUCCINA CLARINO CLARION KERRANA SALPINX NARSINGA SLUGHORN SOURDINE WATERCUP
(— OF DAFFODIL) CORONA
(— OF FLOWER) CORONA
(AUSTRALIAN —) DIDGERIDOO DIDJERIDOO
(CONCH —) SHELL
(RAM'S HORN —) SHOFAR SHOPHAR
(PREF.) SALPING(O)
(SUFF.) SALPINX
TRUMPET BELL CODON PAVILON
TRUMPET CALL DIAN DIANA SENNET
TRUMPET CREEPER TECOMA COWHAGE CREEPER FOXGLOVE HELLVINE
TRUMPETER MOKI AGAMI TRUMP TOOTER JACAMIN TUBICEN YAKAMIK
TRUMPETER FISH MOKI MOKIHI
TRUMPETER PERCH MADO

TRUMPETS WATERCUP
TRUMPET-SHAPED BUCCINAL
TRUMPETWOOD IMBAUBA
TRUNCATED ABRUPT STUBBED TRUNKED
TRUNCHEON BATON BILLY WARDER SPONTON PARTISAN SPONTOON
TRUNDLE HURL RUNG TRILL TROLL RUNDLE TRUCKLE WALLOWER
TRUNK BOX BODY BOLE BOOT BULK KIST LICH RUNT STAM STEM STUD CABER PETER SHAFT STICK STOCK TORSO ARIGUE BARREL CAUDEX COFFER LOCKER CARCASS CORSAGE STOWAGE TRUNCUS SARATOGA
(ARTERIAL —) AORTA
(DEAD TREE —) RUNT
(ELEPHANT'S —) SNOUT
(FOSSIL —) CYCAD
(SMALL —) HATBOX
(SPLIT —) PUNCHEON
(SWIM —S) JAMS
(TREE —) BOLE BUTT STICK RICKER
(TREE — OVER 8 INCHES IN DIAMETER) MAST
(TRIMMED TREE —) LOG
(WORSHIPPED TREE —S) IRMINSUL
(PREF.) CORM(O) PROBOSCI(DI)
TRUNKFISH CHAPIN BOXFISH COWFISH
TRUSS TIE BIND GIRD SPAN WARREN DORLACH
(— OF STRAW) WAP
(— UP) KILT
TRUST AFFY HOPE LITE POOL RELY REST TICK TREW TROW FAITH FRIST GROUP TRUTH BELIEF CARTEL CHARGE CORNER CREDIT DEPEND FIANCE LIPPEN OFFICE TICKET BELIEVE BETRUST COMBINE CONFIDE CREANCE CRIANCE JAWBONE SECRECY VENTURE AFFIANCE COMMENDA CREDENCE MONOPOLY RELIANCE
(KIND OF) TOTTEN
(PLACE IN —) ESCROW
TRUSTED FIDUCIAL
TRUSTEE CURATOR FEOFFEE SINDICO VISITOR ASSIGNEE MUTWALLI
TRUSTWORTHINESS HONOR TRUST CREDIT HONESTY CREDENCE AXIOPISTY
TRUSTWORTHY SAFE SURE TRIG SOOTH SOUND SYKER TRIED HONEST SECRET SECURE SICKER STABLE TRUSTY COCKSURE CREDIBLE FIDUCIAL RELIABLE TRUSTFUL
TRUSTY TRIG FECKFUL STAUNCH FAITHFUL RELIABLE
TRUTH TAO UNA SOOTH TROTH WHITE SATTVA VERITY LOWDOWN REALITY VERITAS VERACITY VERIDITY VERIMENT
(— TABLE) MATRIX
(FUNDAMENTAL —) PRINCIPLE
(IDEAL —) CHRIST DHARMA
(IN —) CERTES
(RELATING TO —) ALETHIC
(SELF-EVIDENT —) TRUISM
(ULTIMATE —) LIGHT SUNYATA
TRUTH AND JUSTICE (AUTHOR OF —) TAMMSAARE
(CHARACTER IN —) MARI PAAS KARIN TIINA ANDRES INDREK
TRUTHFUL TRUE VERY SOOTH HONEST VERIDIC
TRUTHFULLY GOSPELLY
TRUTHFULNESS HONESTY VERACITY SINCERITY
TRY GO SAY SHY TAX BASH BURL FAND HACK PASS PENK PREE SEEK SLAP STAB TEST TIRL TURN AFOND ASSAY CRACK ESSAY ETTLE FLING GROPE JUDGE OFFER PROVE SENSE SOUND TASTE TEMPT TOUCH WHACK WHIRL APPOSE ASSAIL FRAIST GRIEVE STRIVE AFFLICT AFFORCE APPROVE ATTEMPT DISCUSS ESPROVE IMITATE STAGGER ENDEAVOR STRUGGLE
(— DESPERATELY) AGONIZE
(— FOR GOAL) SHOT
(— HARD) STRIVE
(— OUT) SAMPLE AUDITION
(— TO ATTAIN) AFFECT
(CASUAL —) FLING
(QUICK —) SLAP
TRYING NASTY ARDUOUS CRUCIAL GRUELING
TRYSAIL SPENCER
TSAR SALTAN (CHARACTER IN —) GUIDON SALTAN MILITRISA POVARIKHA TKACHIKHA
(COMPOSER OF —) RIMSKYKORSAKOV
TSAR'S BRIDE, THE (CHARACTER IN —) IVAN LYKOV MARFA LYUBASHA GRYANZNOY
(COMPOSER OF —) RIMSKYKORSAKOV
TSETSE FLY KIVU GANDI DIPTERAN GLOSSINA
T-SHAPED TAU
TSILTADEN CHILION
TSUBO BU
TSWANA CHUANA SECHUANA
TUAREG IMOHAGH IMOSHAGH
TUATARA GUANA GUANO IGUANA HATTERIA
TUB FAT HOD KID KIT SOE SOW TUN VAT BACK BOWK COOL CORF COWL GAWN KNOP MEAL SCOW TYND TYNE BOWIE ESHIN KEEVE KIVER SKEEL STAND BUCKET KEELER KILLER KIMNEL TROUGH TURNEL BATHTUB BREAKER SALTFAT TANKARD TRUNDLE KOOLIMAN LAVATORY
(— FOR ALEWIVES) HOD
(— FOR AMALGAMATING ORES) TINA
(— FOR BREAD) BARGE
(— OF BUTTER) COOL
(— OF HOGWASH) SWILLTUB
(— USED AS DIPPER) HANDY PIGGIN
(— WITH SLOPING SIDES) SHAUL
(BREWER'S —) BACK KEEVE
(KIND OF —) HOT
(LAUNDRY —) WASHTRAY
(MESS —) KID KIT
(MINING —) CORF
(PICKLING —) SALTFAT
(TANNING —) LEACH
(WATER —) DAN JAILER
(WOODEN —) KIT SOE KIMNEL TRINDLE
TUBA BASS HELICON BOMBARDON
TUBE TAG BEAK BODY BOOT CANE CASE CAST CORE CURL DRUM DUCT HORN HOSE PIPE REED WORM BATON CANAL CORER CROOK CRYPT DRAIN GLAND HEART LINER QUILL SIGHT SKELP SLIDE SPILE SPOUT THECA THIEF TRUMP TUBAL VALVE AUDION BARREL CALCAR CANNEL CANNON COLUMN CORNET DEWCAP FILTER GULLET HEADER NOZZLE OCTODE SLEEVE SUCKER SYRINX THROAT TRIODE TUBING TUBULE TUNNEL UPTAKE VESSEL BLOWGUN CHIMNEY CONDUIT CUVETTE DROPPER FERRULE FISTULA HOUSING OOBLAST OVIDUCT QUILLET ROSTRUM SALPINX SHALLOT SNORTER SNUFFER SOXHLET STOPPLE THIMBLE TUBULUS VENTURI ADJUTAGE BOMBILLA CORNICLE DIATREME DRAWTUBE FAIRLEAD GRADUATE ORTHICON OVARIOLE PENSTOCK PIPESTEM SAUCISSE SIPHONET SLEEVING URCEOLUS ZOOECIUM
(— AT BASE OF PETAL) CALCAR
(— CARRYING BASSOON MOUTHPIECE) CROOK
(— COVERING TRACE CHAIN) PIPING
(— FOR DEPOSITING CONCRETE) TREMIE
(— FOR DRINKING MATE) BOMBILLA
(— FOR LINING WELL) WELLRING
(— FOR OBOE REED) STAPLE
(— FOR STIFFENING STRING) TAG
(— FOR TRANSFERRING LIQUID) SIPHON SYPHON
(— FOR WINDING THREAD) COP
(— FROM SHIP'S PUMP) DALE
(— IN ENGINE CYLINDER) LINER
(— OF BALLOON) APPENDIX
(— OF GUN) BORE BARREL
(— OF RETORT) BEAK ROSTRUM
(— OF SPIRIT LEVEL) BUBBLE
(— OF TOBACCO) CIGARET
(— TO LINE A VENT) BOUCHE
(— TWISTED IN COILS) WORM
(— USED IN WHALING) LULL
(AMPLIFIER —) STAGE
(BONE —) SNUFFER
(BOOB —) TV TELLY
(CAMERA —) VIDICON ORTHICON
(DISCHARGE —) TORUS
(DISTILLING —) TOWER
(ELECTRO —) BULB
(ELECTRODE —) AUDION PENTODE
(ELECTRON —) DIODE DRIVER TRIODE TETRODE KENOTRON KLYSTRON PLIOTRON TRINISCOPE
(ELECTRONIC INDICATOR —) NIXIE
(FIREWORKS —) LEADER
(GLANDULAR —) CRYPT
(GLASS —) SIGHT MATRASS
(GLASSBLOWER'S —) BLOWPIPE
(HONEY —) NECTARY SIPHONET
(INDICATOR —) NIXIE
(KIND OF —) PITOT
(KNITTED —) STOCKING
(LABORATORY —) PIPETTE
(PAPER —) LEADER PASTILLE
(PASTRY —) CORNET
(POLLEN —) SPERMARY
(PRIMING —) AUGET
(RECTIFIER —) IGNITRON
(SILK — OF SPIDER) SPIGOT
(SPEAKING —) BLOWER GOSPORT
(SUCKING —) STRAW
(SURGICAL —) CANNULA
(THERMOMETER —) STEM
(VACUUM —) DIODE KEYER HEXODE HEPTODE DYNATRON MAGNETRON
(PREF.) FISTULI SIPHON(O) SOLEN(O) SYRING(O)
TUBELET CIRCLET
TUBER ANU OCA SET ANYU BULB CLOG COCO ROOT SEED SETT YAMP COCCO SALEP JICAMA PIGNUT POTATO WAPATA WINDER YAUTIA EARTHNUT MURRNONG
(DRIED —S) SALEP
TUBERCLE PEARL NODULE STEMMA CUSPULE VERRUCA
TUBERCULAR PHTHISIC
TUBERCULOSIS CON LUPUS CLYERS DECLINE PHTHISIS SCROFULA
TUBING HOSE TUBAGE
TUBMAN DUCKER
TUBULAR PIPY PIPED TUBATE QUILLED CANNULAR
(NOT —) FARCTATE
(PREF.) SOLEN(O)
TUBULE TRACHEA TUBULET TUBULUS CISTERNA
TUCANO BETOYAN
TUCK TOKE STUFF TRUSS FLANGE
(— AWAY) KEEP SAVE STOW
(— IN) TRUSS TROUSS
(— UP) FAKE KILT
TUCKER CORDER KILTER PLEATER
(— OUT) TIRE
TUESDAY (SECOND — AFTER EASTER) HOCKDAY HOKEDAY
TUFA TOPHUS
TUFF TRASS PEPERINO PORODITE SANTORIN
TUFT COP EAR FAG FOB NOB SOP TOP COMA DOWN KNOB KNOP MOCK TAIT TATE TUFF TUSK TUZZ WISP BEARD BUNCH CREST FLOCK STUPA THRUM WHISK CATKIN CIRRUS DOLLOP PAPPUS PENCIL TASSEL TUFFET CIRRHUS FEATHER FLOCCUS HOBNAIL PANACHE SCOPULA TOPKNOT TOPPING TUSSOCK AIGRETTE FLOCCULE ARBUSCULE
(— OF BRISTLES) BIRSE
(— OF CLOTH) FAG
(— OF DIRTY WOOL) DAG
(— OF DOWN) FRIEZE
(— OF FEATHERS) EAR HORN HULU EGRET
(— OF FILAMENTS) BYSSUS
(— OF FLOWERS) TRUSS

(— OF GRASS) FAG SOP MOCK HASSOCK TUSSOCK
(— OF HAIR) TOP COMA TUZZ BRUSH SWITCH COWLICK FEATHER FLOCCUS SCOPULA TOPKNOT IMPERIAL KROBYLOS
(— OF HAIR ON HORSE'S HOOF) FETLOCK
(— OF HAY) SOP
(— OF MALE TURKEY) BEARD
(— OF WOOL) FOB TUSK TUZZ FLOCK
(— ON BIRD'S HEAD) COP CUCK EGRET
(— ON BONNET) TOORIE
(— ON CHIN) GOATEE
(— ON PINEAPPLE) CROWN
(— ON SEED PLANT) PAPPUS
(— ON SPIDER'S FEET) SCOPULA
(—S OF ROPE YARN) THRUM
(VASCULAR —) GLOMUS
(PREF.) LOPH(O) LOPHI(O)
TUFTED COMOSE TAPPET TAPPIT CRISTATE
TUG LUG PUG RUG TIT TOG CHUG DRAG HALE HAUL PULL TOIL TUCK CHUFF HITCH PLUCK SHRUG TRACE JIGGER RUGGLE TOWBOAT TUGBOAT
TUGBOAT TOW TUG TOWBOAT TRACKER
TUI POE TUA KOKO TUWI POEBIRD
TUITION CUSTODY
TULIP LILY LILIUM BIZARRE BREEDER PICOTEE TURNSOLE
TULIP TREE POPLAR BASSWOOD CUCUMBER
TULIPWOOD AUBURN
TULLE ILLUSION
TULWAR SABER
TUMATAKURU IRISHMAN MATAGORY
TUMBLE TOP COUP WALT LATCH SPILL THROW TIFLE TRACE COTTON GROVEL PURLER TIFFLE TOPPLE WALTER WAMBLE WELTER STUMBLE WHEMMEL
(— OVER) TIPPLE WALLOP
TUMBLE-DOWN RUINOUS
TUMBLER NUT CLICK GLASS LEVER WIPER ROLLER ACROBAT DRUMMER TIPPLER TOPPLER VOLTIGEUR
TUMID TURGID BLOATED BULGING FUSTIAN TURGENT INFLATED TUMOROUS
TUMOR PAP WEN BEAL PIAN WART AMPER BOTCH GUMMA MYOMA NEVUS PHYMA SWELL TALPA AMBURY ANBURY EPULIS GLIOMA GYROMA INCOME KELOID LIPOMA MYXOMA NUROMA RISING WARBLE ADENOMA ANGIOMA CYSTOMA DERMOID DESMOID FIBROID FIBROMA LUTEOMA MYELOMA NEUROMA OSTEOMA OSTEOME SARCOMA TESTUDO THYMOMA ULONCUS ATHEROMA BLASTOMA CHLOROMA CHORDOMA CHORIOMA EMBRYOMA GANGLION GLANDULE HEMATOMA HEPATOMA HOLDFAST LYMPHOMA MELANOMA MELICERA NEOPLASM ODONTOMA PHLEGMON PLASMOMA PSAMMOMA SCIRRHUS SEMINOMA TERATOID TERATOMA WINDGALL CHALAZION PAPILLOMA
(— OF EYELID) GRANDO
(— ON HORSES'S LEGS) JARDE
(KIND OF —) GLOMUS
(PUSTULAR —) BLAIN
(SKIN —) OUCH
(STUDY OF —S) ONCOLOGY
(PREF.) CARCIN(O) GANGLI(O) GANGLO MYOM(O) ONCO SCIRRH(O)
(SUFF.) CELE COELE COELUS OMA ONCUS SCIRRHUS
TUMULT DIN COIL FARE FLAW FRAY FUSS HURL MUSS REEL RIOT ROUT VISE BRAWL BROIL HURLY HURRY LURRY NOISE ROUST STOOR STOUR WHIRL AFFRAY BUSTLE CLAMOR DIRDUM EMEUTE FRACAS HUBBUB MUTINY PUDDER RABBLE RIPPET ROMAGE RUFFLE SHINDY STEERY UPROAR UPSTIR BLUSTER BOBBERY BRATTLE FACTION FERMENT GARBOIL TEMPEST TURMOIL DISORDER SEDITION STIRRING STRAMASH COMMOTION PANDEMONIUM
TUMULTUOUS HIGH LOUD RUDE NOISY ROUGH STORMY FURIOUS HURRIED LAWLESS RIOTOUS VIOLENT AGITATED CONFUSED DRAWLING HURTLING
TUMULUS LOW MOTE TUMP MOUND BARROW BURIAN COTERELL
TUN CASK HAAB
(ONE-THIRD —) TERTIAN
(20 —S) KATUN
TUNA AHI ATUN TUNNY BLUEFIN PELAMYD ALBACORE KAWAKAWA
(KIND OF —) SKIPJACK
TUNE AIR ARIA DUMP FADO LEED LILT NOTE PORT RANT SONG CHARM CHORD DITTY DRANT POINT ATTUNE GROUND MAGGOT STRAIN STRING TEMPER GUAJIRA HALLING MEASURE MELISMA SONANCE ANGLAISE FANDANGO GUARACHA HABANERA QUICKSTEP
(— A HARP) WREST
(— AN INSTRUMENT) STRING
(DANCE —) FURIANT ANGLAISE GALLIARD
(FOLK —) FADO
(HILLBILLY —) HOEDOWN
(IN —) ONKEY
(LIGHT —) TOY
(LITTLE —) CATCH
(LIVELY —) LILT SPRING HORNPIPE
(MELANCHOLY —) DUMP
(SACRED —) CHORAL CHORALE
(TRADITIONAL —) TONE
TUNEBO TAME GUACICO
TUNEFUL TUNY CHANTANT TUNESOME
TUNEFULNESS MELODY
TUNGST-
(PREF.) WOLFRAM
TUNGSTEN W WOLFRAM SCHEELIN
TUNGUS EVENK LAMUT
TUNIC COAT JAMA JUPE VEST AODAI COTTE FROCK GIPON GIPPO JAMAH JUPON PALLA ACHKAN BLIAUT CAMISE CHITON CYCLAS FECKET HARDIE KABAYA KIRTLE TABARD ARISARD BLEAUNT CAMISIA DASHIKI PALTOCK SURCOAT TUNICLE COLOBIUM DAISHIKI GANDOURA SUBTUNIC SUBUCULA SUKKENYE
(— OF MAIL) HAUBERK
(AFRICAN —) DASHIKI DAISHIKI
(HOODED FUR —) SOVIK
TUNICATE SALP SALPA SALPID ASCIDIAN TUNICARY UROCHORD
TUNICLE SACCOS
TUNING ANESIS
TUNING FORK EVEL EVIL FORK TUNER DIAPASE DIAPASON MODULANT
TUNING HAMMER KEY

TUNISIA

CAPE: BON BLANC
CAPITAL: TUNIS
COIN: DINAR
GULF: GABES TUNIS HAMMAMET
ISLAND: DJERBA
LAKE: ACHKEL DJERID BIZERTE
MEASURE: SAA SAH SAAH CAFIZ WHIBA METTAR
PORT: SFAX GABES TUNIS SOUSSE BIZERTE
RIVER: MEDJERDA
TOWN: BEJA DOUZ SFAX SUSA GABES GAFSA THALA MATEUR NABEUL SOUSSE BIZERTE JENDOUBA KAIROUAN TEBOURBA ZAGHOUAN
WEIGHT: SAA ROTL ARTAL ARTEL RATEL UCKIA KANTAR

TUNNEL ADIT BORE CAVE CURL PUKA SINK TUBE DRIFT DRIVE KAREZ STALL BURROW PIERCE
(— IN ROCK) SYRINX
(— INTO AN IGLOO) TOSSUT
(IRRIGATION —) QANAT
(KIND OF —) CARPAL
(PROPOSED —) CHUNNEL
TUNNY TUNA ALBACORE SCOMBRID
(YOUNG —) PELAMYD
TUP TIP TRIP MONKEY BLISSOM
TUR (BROTHER OF —) IRAJ SALM
(FATHER OF —) FARIDUN
(MOTHER OF —) SHAHRINAZ
TURACO LORY
TURANDOT (CHARACTER IN —) LIU CALAF TURANDOT
(COMPOSER OF —) PUCCINI
TURBAN PAT MOAB PATA SASH TUFT LUNGI MITER MITRE PAGRI PATTI TOWEL TUFFE MANDIL WRAPPER KAFFIYEH PUGGAREE SEERBAND TOLIPANE TULIPANT TURBANTO
TURBELLARIA APROCTA
TURBELLARIAN FLATWORM
TURBID FAT RILY DROVY GUMLY MUDDY RILEY ROILY DRUMLY GRUMLY QUALLY FECULENT LUTULENT
TURBIDITY RILE
TURBOT BRET BRILL WHIFF FLATFISH
TURBULENCE CAT FURY UPROAR FERMENT RIOTING
(— IN WATER) BULLER
TURBULENT GURL HIGH LOUD RUDE WILD ROILY ROUGH WROTH RUGGED STORMY UNRULY YEASTY FURIOUS RABBISH RACKETY TROUBLE VIOLENT MUTINOUS SCAMBLING BOISTEROUS
TURCO IN ITALIA, IL (CHARACTER IN —) DAMELEC GERONIO FIORILLA PROSDOCIMO
(COMPOSER OF —) ROSSINI
TURDUS MERULA
TUREEN DISH TERRINE
TURF SOD VAG CESS DELF FAIL FALE FEAL FLAG FLAT FLAW PONE SUNK DELFT SCRAW SPINE SWARD TRUFF FLAUGHT SHIRREL SODDING GREENSWARD
(— CUT BY GOLF STROKE) DIVOT
(— FOR LINING PARAPET) GAZON
(DRIED — FOR FUEL) VAG
(PARED —) BEAT
(ROUGH —) GOR
(SMALL PIECE OF —) TAB
(SMOOTH —) FAIRWAY
(THIN LAYER OF —) FLAW
TURF SPADE SLANE
TURGID ERECT TUMID BLOATED INFLATED PLETHORIC
TURGIDNESS TYMPANY
TURK TURCO TURKO SELJUK CORSAIR OSMANLI OTTOMAN TURQUET KONARIOT
TURKANA ELKUMA
TURKEY BUST FLOP STAG STEG BUSTARD ERECTER ERECTOR FAILURE GOBBLER ALDERMAN
(BRUSH —) VULTURN TALEGALLA
(FLOCK OF —S) RAFTER
(KIND OF —) COLD
(MALE —) TOM
(YOUNG —) POULT

TURKEY

CAPE: INCE BAFRA ANAMUR HINZIR KARATAS KEREMPE
CAPITAL: ANKARA
COIN: LIRA PARA AKCHA ASPER ATTUN REBIA AKCHEH SEQUIN ZEQUIN ALTILIK BESHLIK PATAQUE PIASTER MEDJIDIE ZECCHINO
DISTRICT: PERA BEYOGLU CILICIA
GULF: COS ANTALYA
LAKE: TUZ VAN EGRIDIR BEYSEHIR
MEASURE: DRA OKA OKE PIK DRAA HATT KHAT KILE ZIRA ALMUD BERRI DONUM KILEH ZIRAI ARSHIN CHINIK DJERIB FORTIN HALEBI PARMAK NOCKTAT
MOUNTAIN: AK ALA KARA HASAN HINIS HONAZ MURAT MURIT ARARAT BINGOL BOLGAR SUPHAN ERCIYAS KARACALI
PROVINCE: MUS VAN AGRI BOLU ICEL KARS ORDU RIZE SERT URFA

USAK AYDIN BURSA IZMIR SIIRT ANGORA EYALET
REGION: ANATOLIA
RIVER: DICLE FIRAT GEDIZ HALYS IRMAK KIZIL MESTA SARUS SEIHUN SEYHAN SEYLAN TIGRIS SAKARYA MAEANDER
SEAPORT: ENOS IZMIR MERSIN SAMSUN TRABZON ISTANBUL
TOWN: URFA ADANA BURSA IZMIR IZNIK KONYA MARAS SIIRT SIVAS AINTAB EDESSA EDIRNE ELAZIG MARASH SAMSUN ERZURUM KAYSERI SCUTARI USKUDAR ISTANBUL STAMBOUL
WEIGHT: OKA OKE DRAM KILE ROTL ARTAL ARTEL CEQUI CHEKE KERAT MAUND OBOLU RATEL BATMAN DIRHEM KANTAR MISKAL DRACHMA QUINTAL YUSDRUM

TURKEY BUZZARD AURA BROMVOEL BROMVOGEL GALLINAZO
TURKEY-COCK STAG
TURKEY OAK CERRIS
TURKI KAZAK QAZAQ KAZAKH
TURKISH TURK TURCIC OSMANLI OTTOMAN
TURKISH DELIGHT LOUKOUM

TURKMENISTAN (ALSO SEE RUSSIA)
CAPITAL: ASHKHABAD
COIN: RUBLE
DESERT: KARAKUM KARAKUMY
MOUNTAIN RANGE: KOPETDAG KHAROPETDAG KUGITANGTAU
NAME: TURKMEN TURKMENIA
OASIS: MURGAB TEDZHEN AMUDARYA KOPETDAG
RIVER: OXUS ATREK MURGAB TEDZHEN AMUDARYA
SEA: CASPIAN
TOWN: MARY MERV NEBITDAG CHARDZHOU KRASNOVODSK
TRIBE: TEKKE YOMUT ERSARI

TURKOMAN SEID ERSAR
TURK'S CAP LILY MARTAGON
TURMERIC REA ANGO HALDI OLENA HULDEE AZAFRAN CURCUMA
TURMIT TURNIP
TURMOIL ADO DIN COIL DUST MOIL TOIL TOSS BURLE HURLY HURRY STROW TOUSE WHIRL HASSLE JABBLE POTHER ROMAGE UPROAR WELTER CLUTTER EMOTION FERMENT GARBOIL HURLING MAKADOO RUMMAGE TEMPEST DISPEACE DISQUIET
TURN GO BOW CUT GEE JAR RUN TON WIN AIRT BEND BOUT BOWL CALE CAST CHAR CHOP COCK EDDY GIRO HACK HEAD HINT HURL JAMB KINK PULL PURL QUIP ROLL ROVE SLEW TIRL TOUR VEER VERT VICE WAFT WELT WIND AIRTH ANGLE BLANK CHARE CRANK CRASH CREEK CRICK CROOK ELBOW FEEZE GLINT PIVOT PLUCK PRICK QUIRK SHIFT SPELL SWING SWIRL TARVE TERVE TREND TRILL TROLL TWINE TWIST VERSE VOLTI WHEEL WREST ATTURN BOUGHT CIRCLE COURSE DEPEND DIRECT DOUBLE GRUPPO GYRATE INDENT INTEND INTURN POSSET QUEEVE RESORT RETURN ROTATE SPIRAL STRAIN SWIVEL TOURNE TURKEN VOLUME VOLUTE WIMPLE CONVERT CRANKLE CRINKLE DEFLECT DISTURB FLEXION FLEXURE FLOUNCE INCLINE INFLECT PASSADE REVERSE REVOLVE SERPENT SINUATE TWINGLE TWISTER VERSATE WREATHE CLINAMEN DOUBLING FLECTION TOURNURE TRAVERSE VOLUTION
(— ABOUT) SLEW SLUE SLOUGH WINDLASS
(— AGAINST) CROSS
(— AROUND) GYRE WELT WEND RATCH BEWEND SPHERE
(— ASIDE) ERR WRY DAFF SKEW WARD ABHOR AVERT BLENK DETER EVADE FENCE GLENT SHEER WAIVE BLENCH DEPART DETURN DIVERT SWERVE SWITCH CRINKLE DECLINE DEFLECT DEVIATE DIGRESS DIVERGE PERVERT SCRITHE
(— AT DRINKING) TIRL
(— ATTENTION) ADVERT ADDRESS
(— AWAY) DOFF AVERT CHARE HIELD REPEL AVERSE DESERT DETURN DIVERT REVOLT ABANDON DECLINE REVERSE OVERTURN WITHTURN
(— AWRY) CONTORT
(— BACK) KEP ABORT FLIPE FLYPE RETORT RETURN REVERT REFLECT UNTWIST RENVERSE
(— BACK ON) RUMP
(— BROWN) AUGUST
(— BY TOSSING) FLAP
(— CARD FACE UP) BURN
(— DOWN) DIP DENY VETO
(— DOWNWARDS) SLOPE
(— FOR BETTER) CRISIS
(— FOR INFORMATION) REFER
(— IN ARCHERY) END
(— IN CROQUET) BISK BISQUE
(— IN ROPE) NIP RIDER
(— INSIDE OUT) EVERT FLYPE INVERT
(— INTO ICE) CONGEAL
(— INTO STEEL) ACIERATE
(— INTO VINEGAR) ACETIFY
(— INTO WOOD) LIGNIFY
(— LEAVES OF BOOK) LEAF TOSS
(— LEFT) HAW PORT
(— OF AFFAIRS) GO JOB KICK
(— OF CABLE) BITTER
(— OF DUTY) TOUR SHIFT TRICK
(— OF EVENTS) WENT
(— OF EXPRESSION) CONCETTO
(— OFF) SHUNT DIVERT
(— OF FANCY) GUST
(— OF MIND) FREAK
(— OF STRING) WAP
(— OF TIDE) PINCH
(— OF WIT) FLIRT
(— OF YARN) MOUSING
(— ON) HIT AROUSE
(— ONE'S BACK) TERGIVERSATE
(— ON LATHE) THROW
(— OUT) GO USH BEAR FALL FARE OUST SORT TAKE CHIVE FUDGE LOOSE OUTPUT SUCCEED
(— OUT TO BE) PROVE EXFLECT
(— OUTWARD) EVERT SPLAY
(— OVER) CANT FLAP FLIP KEEL VETTE VOLVE CLINCH DESIGN AGITATE CAPSIZE OVERSET
(— PAGES) LEAF
(— POINT OF) ABATE
(— RAPIDLY) SPIN TIRL GIDDY
(— RIGHT) GEE HAP HUP
(— SAIL YARD) BRACE
(— SIDEWAYS) TRAVERSE
(— SKIS) STEM
(— SOUR) FOX BLINK PRILL BLEEZE CHANGE SOUREN
(— SUDDENLY) FLOP SLUE
(— THE BALANCE) PREPONDERATE
(— TO BUY DRINKS) SHOUT
(— TO DUST) MOULDER
(— TO NEAR SIDE) HAW
(— TO OFF SIDE) GEE
(— TO ONE SIDE) CORNER GOGGLE
(— TO STONE) LAPIDIFY
(— TO THE LEFT) HAW PORT WIND WYND
(— TOWARD WIND) LUFF
(— TO WINDWARD) STAY
(— UP) FACE HAPPEN
(— UP NOSE) FLIRT SNURL
(— UPSIDE DOWN) CANT COUP WHELM INVERT QUELME WHELVE WHEMMLE
(— VESSEL IN CIRCLE) CHAPEL
(— WHEELS) CRAMP
(— YELLOW) FIRE
(BALLET —) PIROUETTE
(COMPLETE —) LAP
(DOWNWARD —) SLIDE
(ECCENTRIC —) CRANKUM
(FORTUNATE —) BREAK
(GOOD —) BOON SERVICE
(HALF —) CARACOLE
(IN —) AROUND
(INWARD —) INTROVERT
(SERIES OF —S) CHICANE
(SERIES OF TIGHT —S) CHICANE
(SHARP —) ZAG DOUBLE WRENCH ZIGZAG HAIRPIN
(SKI —) SWING CHRISTIE TELEMARK
(SUDDEN —) CURL
(TAKE —S) ROTATE
(PL.) ALLEGRO
(PREF.) STREPHO STREPSI STREPT(O) TREPO TROP(IDO)(O) VERSI VERTEBR(I)(O) VERTI
(SUFF.) TROPAL TROPE TROPIA TROPIC TROPY
TURNBUCKLE TURNEL TURNBOUT
TURNCOAT RAT APOSTATE RENEGADE RENEGADO RENEGATE
TURNED SOUR VERSED COCKEYED INFLEXED
(— ABOUT) CONVERSE
(— AWAY) FROWARD
(— AWRY) TORTIVE
(— BACK) EVOLUTE RETRORSE
(— DOWNWARD) ABASED DEFLEXED
(— EDGEWISE) BLIND
(— INWARD) VARUS
(— OUTWARD) SPLAY EXTRORSE
(— TOWARD) ANODIC
(— TOWARD ONE SIDE) AWRY
(— UP) ACOCK URVED RETROUSSE
(— WRONG WAY) AWK
(PREF.) STREPSI
TURNER SLICE BODGER SLIDER TWIRLER
TURNING HEAD WIND TWIST VOLTA WRINK DETOUR ROTARY FLEXION FLEXURE VERSION VOLVENT FLECTION STREPSIS WHEELERY ACESCENCE
(— ASIDE) APOTROPAIC
(— BACK) RETORTION REFLECTION
(— FREELY) VERSATILE
(— OF EYE) CAST
(— SOUR) ACESCENT
(— SUNWISE) EUTROPIC EUTROPOUS
(— TO LEFT) SINISTRAL LAEOTROPIC
(— TO RIGHT) DEXTRO
(— TOWARD STEM) ADVERSE
(— UP) OCCURRENT
(METAL —S) SWARF
(PL.) SCULL
(PREF.) STROPH(O) TROPIDO TROPO
(SUFF.) TROPAL TROPE TROPIA TROPIC(AL) TROPISM TROPOUS TROPY
TURNIP BAGA NAPE NEEP RAPE NAVEW SWEDE RAPEYE TURMUT CRUCIFER RUTABAGA
(KIND OF —) SWEDISH
(PL.) KRAUT RAPPINI
(PREF.) NAPI
TURNIP-SHAPED NAPIFORM RAPACEUS
TURNIX QUAIL HEMIPOD ORTYGAN HEMIPODE
TURNKEY SCREW JAILER LOCKSMAN
TURN OF THE SCREW (AUTHOR OF —) JAMES
(CHARACTER IN —) FLORA MILES PETER QUINT JESSEL
TURNOUT RIG TEAM SETOUT EQUIPAGE TRANSFER
TURNOVER PIE PASTY BRIDIE BRAMBLE CALZONE EMPANADA FLAPJACK
(PL.) PIROJKI PIROSHKI
TURNPIN TAMPION
TURNSOLE HELIO
TURNSPIT HASTLER
TURNSTILE TIRL STILE MOULINE TURNGATE TURNPIKE TOURNIQUET
TURNSTONE PLOVER REDLEG CHICARIC CREDDOCK
TURNTABLE DECK RACER ROTARY NONSYNC PLAYBACK
TURNUS (FATHER OF —) DAUNUS
(MOTHER OF —) VENILIA
(SLAYER OF —) AENEAS
TURPENTINE THUS TURPS SCRAPE THINNER OLEORESIN
(BORDEAUX —) GALIPOT
TURPENTINE TREE PEEBEEN
TURPITUDE EVIL FEDITY

TURQUOISE TURKEY TURKIS CALAITE CALLAIS
TURRET ROUND BELFRY CUPOLA GARRET GAZEBO LOUVER TOURET BARMKIN GUERITE MIRADOR MONITOR BARBETTE BARTIZAN GUNHOUSE PINNACLE TURRICLE BELVEDERE PEPPERBOX
(CORNER —) ROUND
TURTLE EMYD ARRAU CARET CAREY TORUP COODLE COOTER JURARA RIDLEY SLIDER THURGI TURKLE CRAWLER CREEPER EMYDIAN JUNIATA LOGHEAD SNAPPER TORTUGA CHELONID FLAPJACK HAWKBILL MATAMATA SHAGTAIL STINKPOT TERRAPIN TORTOISE THALASSIAN
(— HAVING COMMERCIAL SHELL) CHICKEN
(OLD —) MOSSBACK
(PART OF —) EAR BEAK CLAW SHELL SHIELD CARAPACE PLASTRON
(SEA —) RIDLEY
TURTLEHEAD BALMONY CHELONE CODHEAD
TUSCAN BROWN MECCA MOHAWK
TUSCANY COLCOTHAR
TUSK GAM CUSK HORN TUSH IVORY TOOTH ELEPHANT
(— OF WILD BOAR) RAZOR
(ELEPHANT'S —) SCRIVELLO
TUSSLE TUG SCRAP BICKER TASSEL TOUSLE WARSLE TUILYIE
TUSSOCK HASSOCK
TUT HOOT TOOT HOOTS
TUTELAGE TUTELE YEMSEL NURTURE TEACHING
TUTELARY GENIUS
TUTOR DON ABBE TUTE COACH TRACH DOCENT FEEDER GROUND MASTER MENTOR PEDANT SCHOOL GRINDER TEACHER CRANSIER CREANCER GOVERNOR PANGLOSS PUPILIZE PRECEPTOR REPETITEUR SCHOOLMASTER
TUTTI RIPIENO
TUTU TOOT TUPAKIHI
TUVALU (CAPITAL OF —) FUNAFUTI
(FORMER NAME OF —) ELLICEISLANDS LAGOONISLANDS
(ISLAND OF —) NANUMEA NUKUFETAU NUKULAILAI
TUXEDO TUX SOFA TUCK
TVASHTRI (DAUGHTER OF —) SARANYU
TWADDLE ROT BOSH TOSH FUDGE HAVER BABBLE DRIVEL FOOTLE PIFFLE TOOTLE FADAISE TWATTLE NONSENSE SLIPSLOP TOMMYROT
TWANA COLCINE
TWANG TANG PLUCK PLUNK SNUFFLE TWANGLE TWANKLE
TWANGY NASAL
TWAYBLADE DUFOIL TWIFOIL
(PL.) LISTERA
TWEAK FEAK TWIG
TWEED PATTU PATTOO
TWEEZERS TIT TWIRK TWINGE TWITCH MULLETS PINCERS PINCETTE VOLSELLA
TWELFTH TWALT DOZENTH
(— OF INCH) SECOND
(— OF LIGHT PERIOD) INCH
(— PART) UNCIA
TWELFTH DAY EPIPHANY
TWELFTH NIGHT (AUTHOR OF —) SHAKESPEARE
(CHARACTER IN —) TOBY BELCH CURIO FESTE MARIA VIOLA ANDREW FABIAN OLIVIA ORSINO ANTONIO MALVOLIO AGUECHEEK SEBASTIAN VALENTINE
TWELVE TWAL DOZEN DICKER DODECADE
(PREF.) DODEC(A) DUODECIM
TWELVEMONTH TOWMONT
TWELVER IMAMI
TWELVE-TONE SERIAL
TWELVE-TONE-ROW SET
TWENTIETH VIGESIMAL VINGTIEME
TWENTY KAPH CORGE KAPPA SCORE COOREE
(PREF.) ICOS(A) VIGINTI
TWENTY-FIVE QUARTERN
TWENTY-FOURTH CARAT
TWENTY-ONE PONTOON VANJOHN BLACKJACK
20,000 LEAGUES UNDER THE SEA (AUTHOR OF —) VERNE
(CHARACTER IN —) NED LAND NEMO PIERRE ARONNAX CONSEIL
TWERP DRIP NERD TWIT DRONGO SHNOOK
TWICE BIS DOPPIO
(— A DAY) BID
(— IN TIME) AGAIN
(PREF.) BI BIS DI DIS
TWICE-BORN REGENERATE
TWIDDLE TWEEDLE TWITTER
(— FEET) CUT
(— THE FEET) CUT
TWIG COW CHAT RICE RISP SLIP WAND YARD BIRCH BRIAR BRIER SHRAG SHRED SPRAY SPRIG STICK TWIST VIRGA WAVER WITHE BALEYS BROWSE FESCUE GREAVE SALLOW SPRING SWITCH WATTLE WICKER SCOLLOP TWIGLET ANAPHYTE
(— FOR SNUFF) DIP
(— GROWING FROM STUMP) WAVER
(— IN BIRD SNARE) SWEEK
(—S FOR BURNING) CHATWOOD
(—S FOR WATTLING) FRITLES
(—S MADE INTO BROOM) BESOM
(— WORN AT SACRIFICES) INARCULUM
(BARE —) COW
(BROKEN —S) BRUSH
(CUT —) SARMENT
(DRIED —) CHAD
(LITTLE —) SURCLE
(THATCHING —) SCOLLOP
(WILLOW —) SALLOW ANAPHYTE
(SUFF.) CLEMA
TWIGGED VIRGATE
TWIGGY SPRAYEY
TWILIGHT EVE DIMPS DUMPS GLOAM TWALE DIMMET DIMMIT UGHTEN DUCKISH COCKSHUT EVENFALL EVENGLOW EVENTIDE GLOAMING GRISPING CREPUSCLE
(— OF THE GODS) RAGNAROK
(DARKER PART OF —) DUSK
(MORNING —) DAWN
TWILL WALE CHINO CADDIS RUSSEL CADDICE DUNGAREE
TWILLED CORDED
TWIN DUAL GEMEL SOSIE DIDYMUS JUMELLE SIAMESE TWINDLE DIDYMATE DIDYMOID DIDYMOUS PARASITE TWINLING
(PL.) GEMEL COUPLET
(PREF.) DIDYM(O) GEMINI
(SUFF.) DIDYMUS
TWINE MAT COIL DUNE LACE PIRL WIND WRAP TWIRL TWIST ENLACE INFOLD INTORT ANAMITE ENTWINE SKEENYIE
(HANK OF —) RAN
(PITCHED —) WHIPPING
(PREF.) PLEC(O)
TWINEBUSH PINBUSH
TWINFLOWER LINNAEA
TWINGE ACHE GIRD PANG PULL SHOOT TOUCH TWANG STOUND
(— OF CONSCIENCE) SCRUPLE
(— OF PAIN) GLISK
TWINING VOLUBLE AMPLECTANT
TWINKLE WINK BLINK TWEER TWINK TWIRE BICKER SECOND SIMPER WINKLE SPARKLE
TWINKLE-TOED AGILE
TWINKLING TRICE MOMENT TWINKLY
TWINLEAF HELMETPOD
TWIRL SPIN TIRL DRILL QUERL TRILL TWIRK TWIST WHIRL TRUNDLE TWIDDLE TWIZZLE
(— OF BAGPIPE) WARBLER
TWIST BOB CUE MAT PLY WIN WIP CAST COIL CURL DRAW HURL KICK KINK PIRL RICK SKEW SLEW SLUB SLUE TURN WARP WIND WISP WORK CHINK CRANK CRICK CRINK CROOK CURVE FEEZE GNARL KINCH PLAIT QUIRK QUIRL REEVE SCREW SKELL SNAKE SNIRL SNURL SPIRE SWIRL THRAW THROW TWEAK TWIND TWINE TWIRE TWIRL WINCE WITHE WREST WRICK BOUGHT DETORT EXTORT HANKLE INTORT QUEEVE SLOUGH SPRAIN SQUIRL SQUIRM STRAND TWEEZE WAMBLE WARPLE WASHIN WICKER WIMBLE WRABBE WRITHE CHIGNON CONTORT CRANKLE CRINKLE CROOKLE CRUMPLE DISTORT ENTWINE ENTWIST FLOUNCE GIMMICK SQUINCH TORTURE TWISTER TWISTLE TWIZZLE WREATHE WRIGGLE CLINAMEN CONVOLVE ENTANGLE FOREHARD FORETURN SPRINKLE SQUIGGLE VOLUTION
(— A ROPE) DALLY
(— AWAY) WAIVE
(— BACK) RETORT
(— FORCIBLY) WRING
(— IN A ROPE) GRIND SQUIRM
(— IN GRAIN OF A BOW) BOUGHT
(— IN ONE'S NATURE) KINK
(— OF FACE) STITCH
(— OF HAY) HAYBRAND
(— OF PAPER) SPILL
(— OF PEN IN WRITING) QUIRK
(— OF SPEECH) CRANK
(— OF THE MOUTH) DRAD
(— OF TOBACCO) ROLL PIGTAIL
(— OF YARNS) FORETURN
(— OUT OF SHAPE) BUCKLE CONTORT
(— SHARPLY) FEAK
(— TOGETHER) CABLE RADDLE
(CAUSE TO —) TORQUE
(DOUBLE —) ESS
(PREF.) SPIR(I)(O) STREMMATO STREPHO STREPSI STREPT(O) TORSO TORTI
TWISTED CAM KAM WRY AWRY TORT KINKY SCREW TORSE WELKT WRONG ATWIST GAUCHE HURLED KNOTTY SCREWY SKEWED SWIRLY THRAWN THROWN TURKEN TWISTY WARPED WRITHE CRISPED CROOKED GNARLED KNOTTED SCREWED TORQUED TORTILE TORTIVE WHELKED WREATHY COCKEYED IMPLICIT INTORTED INVOLVED NONPLANE THRAWART WREATHEN
(PREF.) PLEC(O) PLECT(O) STREPSI STREPT(O)
TWISTING DALLY KNECK AJOINT TWIRLY WIGWAG ENTRAIL TWIDDLY SQUIGGLY STREPSIS TORTUOUS
(PREF.) STROPH(O)
TWIT TIT CHECK TAUNT TEASE ETWITE NEEDLE TWITTER RIDICULE
TWITCH TIC TIT FEAK FIRK JERK JUMP PIRN TWIG WINK YANK PLUCK START THRIP TWEAK TWICK TWIRK QUATCH QUETCH QUITCH TWINGE TWITCHEL VELLICATE
TWITCHING TIC JERKS PALMUS WORKING SACCADIC
TWITTER TWIT CHIRM CHIRP GARRE TWINK JARGON WARBLE CHIPPER CHIRRUP CHITTER QUITTER TWITTLE WHITTER
TWO TWA BOTH TWAY TWIN TWAIN BINARY COUPLE DOUBLE
(— LINES) LONGWAYS
(— OF A KIND) BRACE
(IN —) ATWO
(US —) UNC
(PREF.) BI BIS DUO DY(O) TWI
(— EACH) BINI
(IN —) DICH(O)
(MORE THAN —) MULTI
TWO-COLORED BICHROME
(PREF.) DICHRO(O)
TWO-DIMENSIONAL FLAT PLANAR
TWO-DOOR COUPE ROADSTER
TWO-FACED FALSE DOUBLEDEALING JANUS JANIFORM
(PREF.) JANI
TWO-FIFTEEN PM TIME
TWOFOLD DUAL BINAL DUPLE BACKED BIFOLD DOUBLE DUPLEX DIGONAL DIPLOID TWIFOLD DIDYMATE DIDYMOID DIDYMOUS DIPLASIC TWEYFOLD BIFARIOUS
(PREF.) DI DIPHY DIPL(O)

TWO-FOOTED BIPED
TWO-FORKED BIFURCAL
TWO GENTLEMEN OF VERONA
(AUTHOR OF —) SHAKESPEARE
(CHARACTER IN —) JULIA MILAN SPEED LAUNCE SILVIA THURIO ANTONIO LUCETTA PROTEUS EGLAMOUR PANTHINO VALENTINE
TWO-HANDED BIMANAL BIMANOUS
TWO-HEADED
(PREF.) DICRANO JANI
TWO-HORNED BICORN BICORNED
TWOPENCE TUPPENCE
TWO-POINTER BASKET
TWOS POT DEUCE
TWO-UP SWY
TWO WIDOWS, THE (CHARACTER IN —) ANEZKA MUMLAL KAROLINA LADISLAV
(COMPOSER OF —) SMETANA
TWO-WINGED
(PREF.) DIPTER(O)
TYCHICUS (COMPANION OF —) PAUL
TYCOON SHOGUN TAIKUN
TYDEUS (FATHER OF —) EONEUS OENEUS
(MOTHER OF —) PERIBOEA
(SON OF —) DIOMEDES
TYKE KIDDIE
TYMPANUM DRUM TYMPAN EARDRUM EPIPHRAGM
TYNDAREUS (BROTHER OF —) ICARIUS
(DAUGHTER OF —) PHILOPOE TIMANDRA CLYTEMNESTRA
(FATHER OF —) OEBALUS PERIERES
(MOTHER OF —) BATIA GORGOPHONE
(WIFE OF —) LEDA
TYPE CUT ILK CAST KIND MAKE MOLD NORM SORT TAKE BOGUS BROOD IMAGE MOULD PRINT STAMP EMBLEM KICKER KIDNEY LETTER NATURE SHADOW STRIPE SYMBOL TAKING TIMBER BATARDE FASHION PARABLE ANTETYPE EXEMPLAR
(— BLOCK) QUAD
(— OF EXCELLENCE) PARAGON
(— PLACED BOTTOM UP) TURN
(— SET UP) MATTER
(ASSORTMENT OF —) FONT
(DANCE —) LASYA
(DISARRANGED —) PI PIE
(GERMAN —) FRAKTUR
(HEAVY-FACED —) IONIC
(HIGHEST —) PINK
(IDEAL —) CHRIST
(INVERTED —) TURN
(OPPOSITE —) ANTITYPE
(ORIGINAL —) PROTOTYPE
(PART OF —) BACK BALL BODY FACE FOOT NICK SIZE STEM BEARD BELLY BEVEL SERIF SHANK GROOVE COUNTER ASCENDER CROSSBAR SHOULDER DESCENDER
(PHYSICAL —) HABIT
(RACIAL —) DEHWAR
(REMARKABLE —) SPECIMEN
(REPRESENTATIVE —) GENIUS
(SET —) STICK
(SIZE OF —) (SEE SIZE) PICA POINT DIAMOND ENGLISH
(STYLE OF —) AGATE CANON DORIC ELITE GOUDY GREEK IONIC KABEL ROMAN BODONI CASLON CICERO GOTHIC HEBREW ITALIC JENSON MODERN BOOKMAN BREVIER CENTURY ELZEVIR EMERALD FULLFACE GARAMOND
(PREF.) MORPH(O)
TYPEBAR
(PL.) BASKET
TYPEE (AUTHOR OF —) MELVILLE
(CHARACTER IN —) TOM TOBY MARNOO MEHEVI FAYAWAY KORYKORY
TYPEFACE FACE FRAKTUR BOLDFACE SANSERIF
TYPEHOLDER PALLET
TYPESETTER MONO
TYPESETTING FAT PHAT
TYPEWRITER MILL TYPER TYPIST PORTABLE
(PART OF —) BAR KEY BAIL KNOB LOOP STOP GUIDE LEVER PLATE SCALE SHIFT HOLDER MARGIN PLATEN RETURN ROLLER SPACER CONTROL RELEASE SUPPORT CARRIAGE KEYBOARD REGULATOR BACKSPACER
TYPHON (FATHER OF —) TARTARUS
(MOTHER OF —) TERRA
TYPHOON WIND CYCLONE TUFFOON
TYPICAL FAIR TYPAL TYPIC USUAL AVERAGE CLASSIC PATTERN PERFECT REGULAR
(PREF.) EU
(SUFF.) **(— OF)** ISH ISTIC
TYPIFY TYPE IMAGE SHADOW ADUMBRATE EPITOMIZE PERSONIFY REPRESENT SYMBOLIZE
(— BEFOREHAND) FORESHADOW
TYPIFYING GENERIC
TYR ER EAR TIU TYRR
(BROTHER OF —) THOR
(FATHER OF —) ODIN
TYRANNICAL LORDLY SLAVISH ABSOLUTE DESPOTIC OPPRESSIVE
TYRANNIZE OPPRESS DOMINEER OVERLORD
TYRANNOUS ABSOLUTE
TYRANNY ROD DESPOTISM
TYRANT ANARCH DESPOT NIMROD FUEHRER PHARAOH PHALARIS
TYRANT FLYCATCHER PEWEE
TYRE (SITE OF —) SUR
TYRO HAM BABE COLT PUPIL NOVICE RABBIT TYRONE BEGINNER NEOPHYTE
(FATHER OF —) SALMONEUS
(HUSBAND OF —) CRETHEUS
(MOTHER OF —) ALCIDICE
(SON OF —) AESON NELEUS PELIAS PHERES AMYTHAON
TYRRHENIAN ETRUSCAN
TYRRHENUS (BROTHER OF —) LYDUD TARCHON
(FATHER OF —) ATYS HERCULES TELEPHUS
(MOTHER OF —) HIERA OMPHALE CALLITHEA
TYTO ALUCO STRIX

U UNCLE UNION
(PREF.) **(— SHAPED)** HY(O)
UDDER BAG DUG TID EWER ELDER SUMEN VESSEL
UFO (STUDY OF —S) UFOLOGY

UGANDA
AIRPORT: ENTEBBE
CAPITAL: KAMPALA
COLLEGE: MAKERERE
FORMER CAPITAL: ENTEBBE
LAKE: KYOGA ALBERT EDWARD GEORGE VICTORIA
LANGUAGE: ATESO GANDA LUGANDA SWAHILI
MOUNTAIN: ELGON MARGHERITA
MOUNTAIN RANGE: RUWENZORI
NATIVE: ATESO BANTU LANGO ACHOLI ANKOLE BAGISU BAKIGA BASOGA BATORO BAGANDA BUNYORO LUGBARA NILOTIC SUDANIC
PLATEAU: ANKOLE
PROVINCE: BUGANDA
RIVER: ASWA KAFU PAGER KATONGA
SEAPORT: MOMBASA
TOWN: ARUA JINJA MBALE KITGUM MOROTO TORORO ENTEBBE MOMBASA
WATERFALL: KABALEGA

UGH OOF YECH YUCK YECCH
UGLY FOUL AWFUL OUGLE SNIVY UNKED CRANKY DREEPY GORGON GROTTY HOMELY LAIDLY ORNERY CRABBED GRIZZLY HIDEOUS HOUGHLY VICIOUS GRUESOME UGLISOME UNLOVELY MONSTROUS
UGLY-TEMPERED SNARLISH
UGNI BLANC TREBBIANO
UIGHUR JAGATAI
UINTAITE ASPHALT GILSONITE
UITOTAN KAIMO WITOTAN
UKASE ORDER
UKE JARANA

UKRAINE
(ALSO SEE RUSSIA)
BAY: KALAMIT KARKINIT
CANAL: CRIMEAN
CAPITAL: KIEV
COIN: KARBOVANET
GULF: TAGANROG TAHANROH
LAKE: KIEV KANIV LENIN DNIEPER SVITYAZ DNIESTER KAKHOVKA
MARSH: PRIPET PRYPYAT
MOUNTAIN: KAMULA HOVERLYA ROMANKOSH MOHYLABELMAK MOHYLAMECHETNA
MOUNTAIN RANGE: CRIMEAN KARPATY CARPATHIAN
PENINSULA: KERCH CRIMEAN
RIVER: BUG BUH STRY TYSA DESNA INHUL SLUCH TISZA DNIPRO DONETS PRIPET SALHYR ZBRUCH DNIEPER DNISTER PRYPYAT TETERIV VORSKLA DNIESTER
SEA: AZOV BLACK
TOWN: KIEV LVIV LVOV KYYIV ODESSA DONETSK KHARKIV KHARKOV KRYVYRIH CHERNOBYL KRIVOYROG ZAPOROZHYE ZAPORIZHZHYA DNIPROPETROVSK

UKRAINIAN RUSSNIAK
UKULELE UKE TAROPATCH
ULAM (FATHER OF —) ESHEK
ULCER FRET KYLE SORE WOLF BOTCH ISSUE RUPIA ULCUS APHTHA MORMAL TETTER BEDSORE CHANCRE EGILOPS ENCAUMA FISTULA AEGILOPS FONTANEL FOSSETTE ULCUSCLE
(ARTIFICIAL —) ISSUE
(PREF.) CHANCRI HELC(O)
ULCERATING EXEDENT
ULCERATION NOMA CANKER CARIES BEDSORE HELCOSIS
ULCEROUS HELCOID
ULEX LING
ULEXITE TIZA
ULLIKUMMI (FATHER OF —) KUMARBI
ULNA CUBIT CUBITAL CUBITUS
ULTIMATE IT NTH DIRE LAST FINAL ULTIME SUPREME ABSOLUTE EVENTUAL FARTHEST ULTIMITY
ULTIMATELY FINALLY
ULTIMO PAST
ULTRA EXTREME FANATIC FORWARD
(NE PLUS —) IDEAL
ULTRACONSERVATISM TORYISM
ULTRACONSERVATIVE WHITE
ULTRAFASHIONABLE RITZY SWELL SWAGGER
ULTRAMONTANISM CURIALISM
ULTRASOUND SONOGRAPHY
ULUA PAPIO PAPIOPIO
ULULATE HOWL
ULYSSES (AUTHOR OF —) JOYCE
(CHARACTER IN —) BUCK RUDY BLOOM BREEN MOLLY BLAZES BOYLAN COFFEY GERTIE HAINES MARION DEDALUS LEOPOLD PUREFOY STEPHEN MULLIGAN MACDOWELL
(FATHER OF —) LAERTES
(MOTHER OF —) ANTICLEA
(SLAYER OF —) TELEGONUS
(SON OF —) TELEMACHUS
(WIFE OF —) PENELOPE
UMBEL RAY AXIS RADIUS SERTULE UMBELLA SERTULUM UMBELLET
UMBELLIFERONE CUMARIN COUMARIN
UMBER OMER OMBER PARTRIDGE
UMBILICUS NAVEL
(PREF.) OMPHAL(O)
UMBO BEAK UMBONULE
UMBONES NATES
UMBRA DOGFISH MUDFISH NUCLEUS UMBRINE
UMBRAGE PIQUE SNUFF OFFENSE
UMBRELLA BELL GAMP MUSH DUMPY BROLLY CHATTA PAYONG PILEUS CHATTAH GINGHAM ROUNDEL FITTISOL KITTYSOL MUSHROOM TYRASOLE BUMBERSHOOT
(PART OF —) CAP RIB ROD TIP GORE JOINT PANEL SHAFT BULLET HANDLE RUNNER SPRING CLOSURE FERRULE STRETCHER
UMBRELLA BIRD COTINGA COTINGID
UMBRELLA BUSH MILJEE
UMBRELLA PALM KENTIA
UMBRELLA PLANT SEDGE GLUMAL
UMBRELLA TREE WAHOO ELKWOOD MAGNOLIA
UMBRETTE UMBRE HOMBRE UMBRET CICONIID
UMBRIAN IGUVINE
UMBURANA ROBLE
UMLAUT MUTATION METAPHONY
UMPIRE REF UMP JUDGE TRIER ARBITER DAYSMAN ODDSMAN REFEREE OVERSMAN STICKLER BIRLIEMAN BYRLAWMAN
UNABASHED BROWLESS
UNABBREVIATED FULL
UNABLE UNHABILE POWERLESS
UNACCENTED GRAVE LIGHT ATONIC
UNACCEPTABLE DREADFUL
UNACCOMPANIED BARE SOLO ALONE SECCO SINGLE
UNACCOUNTABLE STRANGE
UNACCUSTOMED UNUSED STRANGE INSOLITE WONTLESS
UNACQUAINTED STRANGE UNCOUTH
UNADORNED DRY BALD PLAIN SECCO STARK RUSTIC SEVERE SIMPLE AUSTERE LITERAL INORNATE
UNADULTERATED NET FRANK HONEST VIRGIN GENUINE SINCERE ABSOLUTE
UNADVANTAGEOUSLY ILL
UNAFFECTED EASY REAL PLAIN HOMELY NATIVE RUSTIC SIMPLE ARTLESS BUCOLIC SINCERE SEMPLICE
UNAFRAID BOLD BRAVE DEFIANT
UNAGGRESSIVE AMIABLE
UNALERT SUPINE
UNALLOYED DEEP SOLID VIRGIN GENUINE
UNALTERABLE IMMUTABLE
UNAMBIGUOUS EXPLICIT
UNANIMATED FLAT VAPID INSIPID
UNANIMITY ATTACK CONSENT
UNANIMOUS SOLID WHOLE UNANIME UNIVOCAL
UNAPPROACHABLE STATELY
UNARMED BARE INERM UNBARBED
(PREF.) ANOPL(O)
UNASPIRATED LENE
UNASSAILABLE SECURE
UNASSUMED NATURAL
UNASSUMING SHY HUMBLE MODEST SIMPLE NATURAL RETIRING
UNATTACHED FREE LOOSE SINGLE
UNATTENDED SINGLE
UNATTRACTIVE BLAH UGLY PLAIN WORSE HOMELY FRUMPISH UNLIKELY
UNAVAILING VAIN FUTILE BOOTLESS GAINLESS NUGATORY
UNAVOIDABLE SHUNLESS NECESSARY
UNAVOWED SECRET
UNAWARE UNWARE WITLESS HEEDLESS INNOCENT UNBEWARE WARELESS OBLIVIOUS
UNAWARES ABACK SHORT
UNBALANCED ALOP HITE DOTTY NUTTY FRUITY UNEVEN FANATIC DERANGED LOPSIDED PIXILATED MOONSTRUCK
UNBAR UNSLOT
UNBARRED UNSTOKEN
UNBEARDED CALLOW
UNBECOMING RUDE INEPT PLAIN INDIGN UNMEET BENEATH IMPROPER INDECENT UNSEEMLY UNWORTHY
UNBEFITTING BENEATH
UNBELIEF UNFAITH
UNBELIEVABLE HOT THIN
UNBELIEVER PAGAN GIAOUR ATHEIST DOUBTER INFIDEL SCOFFER SKEPTIC
UNBELIEVING MISCREANT
UNBEND REST THAW FRESE RELAX UNTIE EXTEND DISBEND UNCROOK
UNBENDING RIGID STARK STERN STIFF THARF CATONIAN OBDURATE RAMRODDY RESOLUTE
UNBIASED FAIR JUST DETACHED
UNBIND FREE UNDO UNTIE UNGIRD UNDRESS
UNBLAMABLE INNOCENT
UNBLEACHED BLAE BLAY ECRU BEIGE BROWN
UNBLEMISHED FAIR PURE SOUND WHITE ENTIRE SPOTLESS

UNBLOCK REDD
UNBLOODY INCRUENT
UNBOLT OPEN UNBAR UNPIN
UNBOSOM OPEN
UNBOUGHT UNCOFT
UNBOUND FREE LOOSE
UNBOUNDED HUGE
UNBRANDED SLICK NATIVE
UNBROKEN DEAD FLAT FERAL FLUSH SHEER SOLID SOUND SINGLE CERRERO REGULAR UNRACED STRAIGHT UNBACKED WAKELESS
UNBUILD DESTROY
UNBUILT UNBIGGED
UNBURDEN EMPTY UNLOAD UNSHIP
UNBURNISHED WHITE MATTED
UNCALLED (— FOR) GRATUITOUS
UNCANNY EERY UNCO EERIE SCARY UNCOW UNKID WEIRD WISHT CREEPY SPOOKY UNCOUTH ELDRITCH POKERISH
UNCASTRATED INTACT
UNCAUGHT UNHENT
UNCEASING ENDLESS ETERNAL EASELESS MINUTELY
UNCEREMONIOUS CURT BLUFF BLUNT SHORT ABRUPT CASUAL FAMILIAR INFORMAL
UNCERTAIN WAW DARK HAZY WILD FLUKY SHADY SHAKY WAUGH CASUAL CLOUDY CRANKY FITFUL FLUKEY GLEAMY QUEASY CASALTY CHANCEY COMICAL DUBIOUS TRICKSY VAGRANT VARIOUS WILSOME CATCHING DELICATE FLICKERY FUGITIVE HOVERING INSECURE SLIPPERY TECHNOUS TICKLISH
UNCERTAINTY MIST WERE DEMUR DOUBT MAYBE BAFFLE BALANCE DUBIETY CASUALTY MISTRUST SUSPENSE UNSURETY SKEPTICISM
UNCHALLENGED ACCEPTED
UNCHANGEABLE FAST STABLE DURABLE ETERNAL
UNCHANGING STATIC ETERNAL UNIFORM CONSTANT STATICAL
UNCHASTE LEWD BAWDY FRAIL LIGHT LOOSE IMPURE WANTON FORLAIN HAGGARD SCARLET IMMODEST
UNCHASTITY BAWDRY STUPRUM ADULTERY
UNCHECKED LIBERAL RAMPANT REINLESS
UNCIFORM HAMATUM
UNCINARIA NECATOR
UNCIVIL RUDE BLUFF ROUGH RUSTY SURLY COARSE CRUSTY RUGGED UNFEEL IMPOLITE
UNCIVILIZED RUDE WILD MYALL INCULT SAVAGE UNCIVIL BARBARIC IGNORANT SYLVATIC
UNCLAD LOOSE UNDRESSED
UNCLE EME OOM TIO YEME BUNKS NUNKY NUNCLE
UNCLEAN FOUL TREF VILE BLACK TARRY TERFA TREFA COMMON FILTHY IMMUND IMPURE DEFILED
UNCLEANLINESS
(PREF.) MYS(O)
UNCLEANNESS DIRT FOULNESS
UNCLEAR DIM HAZY SHAGGY
UNCLEARLY DIMLY
UNCLENCH UNDOUBLE
UNCLE TOM'S CABIN (AUTHOR OF —) STOWE
(CHARACTER IN —) EVA TOM BIRD CASSY CHLOE ELIZA HALEY HARRY LOKER MARKS SIMON TOPSY GEORGE HARRIS LEGREE RACHEL SHELBY SIMEON OPHELIA STCLAIR EMMELINE HALLIDAY
UNCLOSE OPE OPEN UNHASP DISCLOSE
UNCLOTHE TIRL SPOIL UNRIG DEVEST DESPOIL
UNCLOTHED STARKERS
UNCLOUDED CLEAR SERENE
UNCOIL UNLINK
UNCOLORED FAIR
UNCOMBED TOUSLED UNKAMED UNTEWED
UNCOMBINED FREE FRANK LOOSE
UNCOMELY INDECENT
UNCOMFORTABLE HOT EVIL POOR HARSH UNKET UNKID QUEASY STICKY UNFELE
UNCOMMON MUCH NICE RARE SELD UNCO BYOUS FORBY UNCOW VAUDY DAINTY FORBYE SCARCE SPECIAL STRANGE UNUSUAL SINGULAR UNWONTED
UNCOMMONLY UNCO BYOUS EXTRA JOLLY UNCOW UNCOLY
UNCOMMONNESS SCARCITY
UNCOMMUNICATIVE DUMB SILENT PRIVATE RESERVED
UNCOMPLICATED RURAL HONEST SIMPLE
UNCOMPOUNDED SIMPLEX
UNCOMPROMISING ACID FIRM GRIM RIGID STERN STOUT ULTRA SEVERE STRICT STRONG EXTREME HARDSHELL BRASSBOUND
UNCONCEALED BARE OPEN OVERT OUVERT APPARENT
UNCONCERN APATHY EASINESS
UNCONCERNED COOL EASY BLAND BLASE CASUAL CARELESS
UNCONCERNEDLY LIGHTLY
UNCONDITIONAL FREE FRANK UTTER SIMPLE ABSOLUTE EXPLICIT TERMLESS
UNCONDITIONED POSITIVE
UNCONFINED LAX FREE LOOSE
UNCONGENIAL HATEFUL INGRATE KINDLESS
UNCONNECTED GAPPY REMOTE DETACHED
UNCONQUERED INVICT INVICTED
UNCONSCIOUS OUT COLD BRUTE ASLEEP BLOTTO CUCKOO TORPID UNAWARE WITLESS COMATOSE IGNORANT SENSELESS INSENSIBLE
UNCONSIDERED WILD
UNCONSTRAINED EASY FREE UNNET SIMPLE FAMILIAR
UNCONTROLLABLE WILD
UNCONTROLLED FREE MADCAP LIBERAL ABSOLUTE UNBITTED
UNCONVENTIONAL FLAKY GYPSY LOOSE CASUAL FLAKEY DEVIOUS ODDBALL OFFBEAT BOHEMIAN INFORMAL
(— IN STYLE) MOD
UNCONVINCING LAME THIN FALSE FISHY FEEBLE
UNCOOKED RAW
UNCOOL UNHIP
UNCOOPERATIVE (TO BE —) STONEWALL
UNCOUNTABLE SUMLESS
UNCOUPLE CUT UNDOCK DISLINK
UNCOUTH RUDE CRUDE DORIC GURLY ROUGH UNKED UNKID GOTHIC JUNGLY QUAINT RENISH AWKWARD BOORISH CUBBISH HIRSUTE LOUTISH AGRESTIC UNGAINLY YOKELISH
(— PERSON) TUG
UNCOVER BARE DOFF HUNT ROOT ROUT TIRL TIRR BREAK STRIP TIRVE UNLAP UNLID UNWRY DETECT EXHUME RAKEUP SEARCH UNBARE UNCASE UNHALE UNVEIL UNDRAPE UNEARTH DISCLOSE DISCOVER UNMANTLE UNMUFFLE
UNCOVERED BARE OVERT
(PREF.) GYMN(O)
UNCTION CHRISM OINTMENT
UNCTIOUS SMUG
UNCTUOUS FAT OILY SALVY SLEEK SOAPY SUAVE GREASY SMARMY COURTLY PINGUID OLEAGINOUS
UNCULTIVATED RAW BRUT FERAL DESERT FALLOW INCULT SAVAGE SLOVEN WILDERN
UNCULTURED RUDE INCULT ARTLESS
UNCUT RASPED
UNDAMAGED WHOLE
UNDARKENED CLEAR
UNDAUNTED BOLD BRAVE MANLY SPARTAN FEARLESS INTREPID
UNDE WAVY UNDEE
UNDECAYED GREEN
UNDECEIVE DISABUSE
UNDECIDED MOOT DUBIOUS PENDING DOUBTFUL WAVERING
UNDECIDEDLY HUMDRUM
UNDECLARED SECRET
UNDEFENDED UNKEPT
UNDEFILED PURE CHASTE INTACT VIRGIN
UNDEFINED OBSCURE
UNDELIVERABLE DEAD
UNDEMONSTRATIVE COLD ASEPTIC LACONIC RESERVED
UNDENIABLE BRUTAL
UNDENIABLY INDEED
UNDEPENDABLE CASUAL FLUFFY
UNDER SUB BAJO BELOW INFRA NEATH SOTTO ANEATH ANUNDER BENEATH
(— ORDERS) SUPPOSED
(— THE WORD) IV
(— THE YEAR) SA
(— THIS TITLE) HT
(— THIS WORD) SV SHV
(— WAY) AFOOT
(PREF.) HYPO SUB
UNDERBODICE JUMP BASQUINE CAMISOLE
UNDERBRUSH FILTH COVERT GARSIL MAQUIS RAMMEL ABATURE
UNDERBURNED SOFT SAMEL
UNDERBUTLER WASHPOT
UNDERCARRIAGE BOGY BOGEY BOGIE
UNDERCLAY THILL WARRANT
UNDERCLOTHES LININGS
UNDERCLOTHING LINEN SHORTS UNDIES LININGS LINGERIE BALBRIGGAN
UNDERCOAT PILE ALPACA SURFACER
(WOOL OF — OF MUSK-OX) QIVIUT
UNDERCOVER SECRET
UNDERCRUST ABAISSE
UNDERCURRENT UNDERLAY UNDERRUN UNDERSET
UNDERCUT JAD HOLE LAME POOL SUMP KIRVE NOTCH
UNDERDOG DAVID
UNDERDONE RARE REAR
UNDERDRAWERS FLANNELS
UNDERDRESS SLIP
UNDERESTIMATE DISPRIZE MINIMIZE
UNDERFLEECE PASHM
UNDERFRAME SOLE
UNDERGARMENT BAND SLIP CYMAR SIMAR SKIRT SMOCK TUNIC WAIST BANIAN BANYAN BODICE CAMISE CILICE CORSET GIRDLE STAMIN CHEMISE DOUBLET DRAWERS STAMMEL TALLITH BLOOMERS KNICKERS
(WOMAN'S —) PANTIHOSE
(WOMEN'S —) LINGERIE
(PL.) SMALLS FLANNELS FLIMSIES SNUGGIES
UNDERGO PASS SERVE ENDURE SUFFER SUSTAIN
(— GLADLY) WELCOME
UNDERGOER
(SUFF.) EE
UNDERGRADUATE MAN TASSEL SERVITOR
(CAMBRIDGE —) SUBSIZAR
(TITLED —) TUFT
UNDERGROWTH RUSH COVER RAMMEL SPRING BUSHWOOD
UNDERHAND SLY DERN SHADY BYHAND SECRET CROOKED OBLIQUE INVOLVED SINISTER SNEAKING
UNDERHANDED DERN DIRTY FUNNY FILTHY SECRET SINISTER
UNDERHANDEDLY DIRTY
UNDERIVED ORIGINAL
UNDER JAW
(PREF.) GENYO
UNDERLAYER SLASHING
UNDERLIE SUBTEND
UNDERLING MENIAL SEQUEL UNDERER HENCHMAN INFERIOR
UNDERLYING COVERT IMPLICIT
UNDERMINE SAP CAVE HOLE POOL ERODE KNIFE WEAKEN FOSSICK FOUNDER SUBVERT ENFEEBLE SUPPLANT
UNDERMINED ROTTEN
UNDERNEATH BELOW BENEATH UNNEATH
(PREF.) INTRA

UNDERNSONG TIERCE
UNDERPANTS BRIEFS BLOOMERS KNICKERS
UNDERPART BELLY
UNDERPASS DIVE SUBWAY
UNDERPINNING GAM
UNDERRATE DECRY DISCOUNT EXTENUATE
UNDERRUN BOTTOM
UNDERSACRISTAN CUSTOS
UNDERSHIRT VEST SHIFT SHIRT CAMISA JERSEY LINDER SEMMIT SINGLET WRAPPER
UNDERSHRUB HEATH PINKEYE SEEPWEED SUBSHRUB SAGEBRUSH SANTOLINA
UNDERSIDE BOTTOM BREAST
(— OF CLOUD) BASE
(— OF FINGER) BALL
(— OF FLOOR) CEILING
(— OF STAIRCASE) SOFFIT
(PREF.) **(ON THE —)** INFERO
UNDERSIZED DEENY SCRUB STUNT
UNDERSKIRT QUILT CRINOLINE PETTICOAT
UNDERSONG FABURDEN
UNDERSTAND CAN CON DIG GET KEN SEE GAUM HAVE MAKE READ TAKE TWIG BRAIN ENTER GRASP REACH SAVVY SEIZE SENSE SKILL SPELL ACCEPT COTTON FIGURE FOLLOW INTAKE INTEND SUBAUD UPTAKE CONCEIT DISCERN COMPRISE CONCEIVE CONSTRUE CONTRIVE FORSTAND PERCEIVE PERSTAND UNDERNIM
(— PROFOUNDLY) GROK
UNDERSTANDABLE PLAIN
UNDERSTANDING KEN WIT GAUM HEAD BRAIN CLASP HEART INWIT SENSE SKILL ACCORD INTENT NOTION REASON TREATY UPTAKE COMPACT CONCEIT CONCEPT ENTENTE INSIGHT MEANING WITNESS DAYLIGHT PREHENSION
(— WORDS) ISEE
(HARMONIOUS —) SYMPATHY
(IMPERFECT —) DARKNESS
(INSTINCTIVE —) FREEMASONRY
(WORDS OF —) ISEE
(PREF.) NOEMA
UNDERSTATEMENT LITOTES MEIOSIS
UNDERSTOOD LUCID SUPPOSED
(— ONLY BY SPECIALLY INITIATED) ESOTERIC
(EASILY —) EASY CLEAR EXTANT
(NOT —) DARKSOME
UNDERSTUDY DOUBLE
UNDERSURFACE SOLE
(— OF BRILLIANT) PAVILION
UNDERTAKE GO TRY DARE FANG FOND GRANT OFFER ASSUME INCEPT PLEDGE SETOUT ATTEMPT EMBRACE EMPRISE PRETEND UNDERFO CONTRACT PRESTATE
(— RESPONSIBILITY) ACCEPT ANSWER
UNDERTAKER UPHOLDER MORTICIAN
UNDERTAKING JOB AVAL TASK CAUTIO EFFORT SCHEME VOYAGE ATTEMPT CALLING PROJECT VENTURE COVENANT
(— IN CARDS) CONTRACT
(HAZARDOUS —) EMPRISE
(UNPROFITABLE —) FOLLY
UNDERTEACHER USHER
UNDERTONE INKLING SUBTONE
UNDERTOW SEAPOOSE
UNDER TWO FLAGS (AUTHOR OF —) OUIDA
(CHARACTER IN —) RAKE CECIL AMAGUE BERTIE CORONA BERKELEY CIGARETTE GUENEVERE ROYALLIEU CHATEAUROY ROCKINGHAM
UNDERVALUE DECRY DISABLE DISPRIZE DISVALUE MISPRISE MISPRIZE
UNDERVEST BODICE SEMMIT SINGLET
UNDERWAIST CAMISOLE
UNDERWATER (— DEVICE) OTTER PARAVANE
UNDERWEAR BRIEFS SHORTS SKIVVY UNDIES DESSOUS HEAVIES LONGIES LINGERIE PRETTIES SCANTIES
(MEN'S —) SKIVVIES
(PL.) SMALLS
UNDERWING CATOCALA
UNDERWOOD FRITH BOSCAGE COPPICE
UNDERWORLD DUAT DEWAT HADES ORCUS SHEOL MICTLAN XIBALBA GANGLAND
UNDERWRITE SIGN INSURE ENDORSE
UNDERWRITER INSURER
UNDESERVED INDIGN
UNDETERMINED UNSET DUBIOUS PENDENT AORISTIC DOUBTFUL INFINITE
UNDEVELOPED CRUDE MORON LATENT SLOVEN GERMING IMMATURE JUVENILE
(SEXUALLY —) NEUTER
UNDEVIATINGLY SMACK
UNDIFFERENCED ENTIRE
UNDIFFERENTIATED GLOBAL AMERISTIC
UNDIGESTED CRUDE
UNDIGNIFIED DOGGREL DOGGEREL
UNDILUTED MERE NEAT PURE NAKED SHEER SHORT STRONG STRAIGHT
UNDIMINISHED ENTIRE
UNDIMMED CLEAR
UNDINE NIX
(CHARACTER IN —) HUGO VEIT TOBIAS UNDINE BERTHALDA KUHLEBORN
(COMPOSER OF —) LORTZING
UNDISCIPLINED WANTON COLTISH
UNDISCLOSED HIDDEN SEALED
UNDISCRIMINATING GROSS
UNDISGUISED BALD NAKED PLAIN
UNDISMAYED ONFLEMED
UNDISPUTED LIQUID
UNDISTINGUISHED GROSS COMMON UNNOBLE FAMELESS NAMELESS NOTELESS
UNDISTORTED CLEAR
UNDISTURBED CALM SOUND SERENE VIRGIN TRANQUIL
UNDIVIDED WHOLE ENTIRE SINGLE
UNDO DUP COOK POOP SLIP FORDO SPEED UNPAY DEFEAT DIDDLE FOREDO UNBIND UNKNIT UNLOCK UNMAKE UNTUCK UNWORK DEFEISE DESTROY NULLIFY UNRAVEL UNRIVET UNTWIRL UNWEAVE UNWREST DECIPHER DISSOLVE DISTRUSS UNFASTEN
UNDOER ACHAN
UNDOGMATIC AGNOSTIC
UNDOING DEFEAT DOWNFALL
(PREF.) DE DIS
UNDOMESTICATED WILD FERAL FERINE
UNDOUBTEDLY SURELY FRANKLY
UNDRESS MOB DOFF FLAY PEEL TIRR STRIP UNRAY UNRIG DEVEST DIVEST UNBUSK UNCASE UNLACE UNRIND UNROBE UNTIRE DISCASE UNARRAY UNREADY UNSPOIL UNTRUSS NEGLIGEE UNATTIRE DESHABILLE DISHABILLE
UNDRESSED UNDIGHT
UNDUE EXTREME
UNDULATE SWAY WAVE WAVY FLOAT SWING BILLOW GYROSE KELTER RIPPLE UNDATE UNDOSE FLICKER UNDATED
UNDULATING SURGING FLEXUOUS INDENTED
UNDULATION FOLD ROLL WAVE CRIMP TEETER WAVING CRIMPING
UNDULATORY WAVY
UNDUTIFULNESS IMPIETY
UNDYED CORAH
UNDYING IMMORTAL
UNEARTH DIG MOOT DIGUP EXPOSE UNCOVER DISCOVER
UNEARTHLY EERY EERIE WEIRD AWESOME UNCANNY UNGODLY
UNEASINESS ENVY GENE FIDGET NETTLE SORROW UNEASE AILMENT ANXIETY DISEASE MISEASE TROUBLE DISQUIET DISTASTE
UNEASY ANTSY ONEDGE SICKLY FIDGETY INQUIET NERVOUS RESTIVE UNQUIET WORRIED RESTLESS
UNEDUCATED RUDE SIMPLE IGNORANT
UNEMBELLISHED DRY PROSE STARK AUSTERE
UNEMOTIONAL DRY COLD COOL STOIC STONY STOICAL
UNEMOTIONALLY EVENLY
UNEMPLOYED IDLE ORRA VOID IDLED ORROW OTIANT OTIOSE VACANT IDLESET LEISURE UNBUSIED
UNEMPLOYMENT IDLENESS
UNENCUMBERED VACANT EXPEDITE
UNENDING ABYSMAL AGELONG CHRONIC ENDLESS UNDYING TERMLESS TIMELESS
UNENJOYABLE JOYLESS
UNENLIGHTENED MISTY HEATHEN IGNORANT
UNENTHUSIASTIC COLD
UNEQUAL IMPAR DISPAR UNEGAL UNEVEN INEQUAL INFERIOR
(— TO STRAIN) FEEBLE
(PREF.) ANIS(O) IMPARI INEQUI
UNEQUALED UNIQUE NONESUCH
UNEQUIVOCAL DIRECT SQUARE PERFECT DEFINITE DISTINCT EXPLICIT RESOUNDING
UNERRING DEAD TRUE DEADLY INERRANT
UNERRINGLY CLEAN
UNEVEN RUDE EROSE GOBBY HAGGY JAGGY MEALY ROUGH HOBBLY PLATTY RAGGED RUGGED SPOTTY TWITTY UNFAIR UNLIKE BLOTCHY DIURNAL ERRATIC HOTTERY INEQUAL SCALENE STREAKY UNEQUAL HUMMOCKY SCRAGGED SCRATCHY SNAGGLED ACCIDENTED
(— IN COLOR) CLOUDY
UNEVENLY AWRY
UNEVENNESS BUMP WAVE FRAZE ANOMALY WRINKLE ACCIDENT ASPERITY
UNEVENTFUL STILL UNDATED
UNEXCITED LEVEL
UNEXCITING DEAD DULL TAME BORING PROSAIC
UNEXPECTED EERY EERIE ABRUPT SUDDEN UNWARY INOPINE UNLOOKED
UNEXPECTEDLY UNWARES UNAWARES
UNEXPIRED ALIVE
UNEXPLAINED HIDDEN
UNEXPOSED RAW
UNEXTINGUISHED LIT LEFTON
UNFADABLE FAST
UNFADED FRESH BRIGHT
UNFAILING SURE DEADLY INFALLID UNERRING
UNFAIR FOUL CROOK WRONG BIASED SHABBY UNEVEN UNJUST DEVIOUS PARTIAL SLANTER UNEQUAL UNSEEMLY WRONGFUL
UNFAIRLY HARDLY
UNFAIRNESS CROSS INEQUITY
UNFAITHFUL INFIDEL TRAITOR DISLOYAL RECREANT
UNFALTERING SURE TRUE STEADY UNERRING
UNFAMILIAR NEW FREMD HEATHER STRANGE UNKNOWN
UNFASTEN FREE OPEN UNDO LOOSE UNPIN UNBIND UNHASP UNLIME UNLINK UNLOCK UNMAKE UNTINE UNDIGHT UNHITCH UNSTECK UNTRUSS
UNFATHOMABLE ABYSMAL ABYSSAL PROFOUND
UNFATHOMED COSMIC
UNFAVORABLE BAD ILL FOUL HARD POOR CRONK SHREWD UNFAIR UNKIND ADVERSE AWKWARD FROWARD HOSTILE UNHAPPY BACKWARD CONTRARY INIMICAL SINISTER UNKINDLY
(PREF.) DYS
UNFAVORABLY BADLY CROSS
UNFEATHERED SQUAB
UNFEELING COLD DULL HARD CRASS CRUEL HARSH ROCKY

STERN STONY BRUTAL LEADEN MARBLE STOLID CALLOUS OBDURATE
UNFEELINGLY HARSHLY
UNFEELINGNESS APATHY
UNFEIGNED OPEN TRUE HEARTY CORDIAL NATURAL SINCERE
UNFERMENTED AZYMOUS
UNFERTILE BARREN
UNFETTERED FREE UNGYVED
UNFILLED BLANK EMPTY VACANT VACUOUS
UNFINISHED RAW GRAY GREY CRUDE KACHA ROUGH KUTCHA RAGGED KACHCHA STICKIT IMMATURE INCHOATE
UNFIRED GREEN
UNFIRM UNFAST
UNFIT BAD SICK UNAPT WISHT WRONG COMMON FAULTY NOUGHT UNTIDY DISABLE UNFITTY IMPROPER UNFITTEN UNLIKELY UNLIKING
UNFITTING UNMEETLY
UNFIXED AFLOAT
UNFLAPPABLE CALM SURE STOIC SECURE ASSURED
UNFLEDGED SQUAB CALLOW
UNFLINCHING LEVEL STAUNCH
UNFOLD OPEN BREAK BURST SOLVE UNLAP UNTIE DEPLOY EVOLVE EXPAND EXPLAT FLOWER SPREAD UNFURL UNPLAT UNROLL UNTUCK BLOSSOM DEVELOP DISPLAY DIVULGE EXPLAIN UNPLAIT UNRAVEL UNWEAVE UNDOUBLE UNPLIGHT
UNFOLDED OPEN EVOLUTE EXPANDED
UNFOLDING DISPLAY
(— OF EVENTS) ACTION
(— TO VIEW) BURST
UNFORCED EASY GLIB WILLING
UNFORESEEN CASUAL SUDDEN IMPREVU UNAWARE
UNFORGIVING STERN
UNFORMED CALLOW INFORM
UNFORTUNATE ILL EVIL POOR DONCY TOUGH WEARY SHREWD HAPLESS UNHAPPY UNLUCKY LUCKLESS UNTOWARD WANHAPPY WRETCHED
UNFREQUENTED LONE EMPTY UNCOUTH SOLITARY
UNFRIENDLY ILL COLD FOUL CHILL BITTER CHILLY FIERCE FROSTY UNSOME HOSTILE INGRATE STRANGE INIMICAL
UNFROCK DEFROCK DEGRADE DISFROCK UNPRIEST
UNFRUITFUL BLUNT ADDLED BARREN EFFETE WASTED STERILE USELESS INFECUND
UNFULFILLMENT BREACH
UNFURL BREAK SPREAD UNFOLD DEVELOP OUTROOL
UNFURNISHED BARE VACANT
UNGAINLY LANKY SPLAY WEEDY CLUMSY UNGAIN AWKWARD BOORISH NUNTING UNHEPPEN UNLICKED UNWIELDY
UNGENEROUS MEAN SHABBY STINGY GRUDGING
UNGENIAL CHILLY
UNGIRDED DISCINCT
UNGLUED UPSET
UNGODLINESS ATHEISM IMPIETY
UNGODLY SINFUL WICKED GODLESS IMPIOUS PROFANE
UNGOVERNABLE WILD UNRULY FROWARD IMPOTENT
UNGRACEFUL HARD CLUMSY ANGULAR AWKWARD HALTING UNTOWARD
UNGRACEFULLY HARSHLY
UNGRACIOUS GRUFF UNFEEL UNFELE CHURLISH SNAPPISH
UNGRATEFUL UNKIND INGRATE
UNGROOMED UNDRESSED
UNGUARDED OPEN STIFF
UNGUENT SALVE CEROMA CHRISM PIMENT POMADE SMEGMA POMATUM UNCTION OINTMENT (PREF.) MYRO
UNGULATE HOG PIG DEER HORSE TAKIN TAPIR HOOFED AMBLYPOD ELEPHANT RHINOCEROS
UNGUMMED BRIGHT
UNHALLOWED IMPURE UNHOLY PROFANE
UNHAMPERED FREE DIRECT EXPEDITE
UNHAPPINESS MISERY SORROW ILLFARE SADNESS UNBLISS
UNHAPPY SAD POOR TEARY DISMAL UNLUCKY UNLUSTY WANSOME DEJECTED DOWNBEAT DOWNGONE WOBEGONE WRETCHED
UNHARMED SAFE UNSHENT
UNHARNESS UNGEAR OUTSHUT OUTSPAN UNHORSE UNTACKLE
UNHEALED GREEN
UNHEALTHY BAD MORBID QUEASY SICKLY UNHALE NAUGHTY PECCANT EPINOSIC MALADIVE
UNHEATED COLD
UNHEEDED IGNORED UNTENTED
UNHEEDING DEAF CARELESS
UNHESITATING READY UNPOISED
UNHIDDEN OVERT
UNHITCH OUTSPAN
UNHOLY IMPURE WICKED IMPIOUS PROFANE
UNHORSE PURL THROW UNCOLT DISMOUNT UNSADDLE
UNHURRIED EASY SLOW SOFT SOBER
UNHURT SAFE HARMLESS HURTLESS UNHARMED
UNIAT MALKITE MELCHITE
UNICORN LIN REEM KILIN LICORN LICORNE NARWHAL HOWITZER
UNICORN FISH LIJA UNIE
UNICORN PLANT MARTINOE
UNICUM UNION
UNIDENTIFIED FACELESS INCOGNITO
UNIFICATION SYSTEM ENSEMBLE
UNIFIED GLOBAL
UNIFIER UMBRELLA
UNIFORM KIT DEAD EVEN FLAT JUST LIKE SAME SELF SUIT ALIKE BLUES CLOTH KHAKI SOLID SUITY GLOBAL GREENS LIVERY SINGLE STEADY EQUABLE REGULAR SIMILAR SUNTANS CONSTANT EQUIFORM EQUIPAGE MEASURED STANDARD UNIVOCAL
(— IN COLOR) SELF
(— IN HUE) FLAT
(LEATHER —) BUFF
(NOT —) MOTLEY RAGTAG SQUALLY UNKEMPT
(PRISONER'S —) STRIPES
(PREF.) IS ISO
UNIFORMITY ONENESS EQUALITY EVENNESS MONOTONY SAMENESS
(— OF MOTION) INSISTURE
UNIFORMLY EVENLY EQUALLY
UNIFY MERGE UNITE CEMENT COMPACT UNITIZE COALESCE
UNILATERAL SECUND
UNIMAGINATIVE DULL SODDEN STUPID LIMITED LITERAL PROSAIC UNIDEAL PEDANTIC PEDESTRIAN
UNIMPAIRED FRESH SOUND ENTIRE INTACT
(— BY) DEVOID
UNIMPASSIONED SOBER WHOLE STEADY
UNIMPEDED FREE EXPEDITE
UNIMPORTANT VAIN LIGHT PETTY SMALL CASUAL SIMPLE TRIVIAL IMMOMENT PEDDLING PIDDLING TRINKETY JERKWATER MINISCULE SMALLTIME INSIGNIFICANT
UNINFLECTED APTOTIC
UNINFORMED GREEN UNTOLD IGNORANT
UNINHABITED WILD EMPTY DESERT VACANT DESOLATE WASTEFUL
UNINHIBITED LARGE
UNINJURED WHOLE INTACT SINCERE
UNINSPIRED HACK STODGY POMPIER DRYASDUST
UNINSPIRING TAME
UNINSTRUCTED NAIVE IGNORANT
UNINTELLIGENT DUMB OBTUSE OPAQUE STUPID ASININE FOOLISH VACUOUS WITLESS
UNINTELLIGIBLE BLIND MISTY OPAQUE MYSTICAL
UNINTENTIONAL UNMEANT
UNINTERESTING DRY ARID COLD DRAB DREE DULL FADE FLAT TAME DREAR SANDY STALE BORING DREICH JEJUNE INSIPID BROMIDIC FRUMPISH
UNINTERMITTENT ITHAND
UNINTERRUPTED SMOOTH STEADY ENDLESS ETERNAL STRAIGHT
UNINTERRUPTEDLY AWAY
UNINVITED (ENTER —) CRASH
UNIO MUSSEL
UNION SUM ZYG BLOC DUAD JOIN ALLOY GROUP JOINT NONOP UNITY ENOSIS FUSION GREMIO TAWHID VEREIN COMPACT CONCERT CONTACT MEETING ONENESS SOCIETY ADHESION ALLIANCE COHESION ESPOUSAL JOINTURE JUNCTION JUNCTURE SODALITY SYSTASIS TRIALISM VINCULUM ZOLLVEREIN
(— OF TWO SETS) CUP
(— OF TWO VOWELS) CRASIS
(MARITAL —) BED
(POLITICAL —) ANSCHLUSS
(SEXUAL —) COPULA COUPLING
(TURKISH —) JETTRU
(PREF.) ZYG(O)(OTO)
(SEXUAL —) GAMO
(SUFF.) APSIS GAM(AE)(IST)(OUS)(Y) GAMETE
UNIONIST REFUGEE
UNIONIZE ALLY
UNION OF SOVIET SOCIALIST REPUBLICS (SEE RUSSIA)
UNIQUE ODD RARE SOLE UNIC ALONE UNION SINGLE SULLEN UNICUM ALONELY SOLEYNE SPECIAL STRANGE ISOLATED SINGULAR
UNIQUENESS SOLITUDE
UNISON FIRST CONCORD HOMOPHONY
UNIT (ALSO SEE MEASURE AND WEIGHT) (ALSO SEE MEASURE) ACE ONE ATOM BARN KLAN FLOOR HUMIT MONAD NEPER ADDRESS DIOPTER ELEMENT ENERGID KLAVERN
(— IN COUNTING FISH) MEASE
(— IN EARTHWORK) FLOAT FLOOR
(— OF ABSORPTION) SABIN
(— OF ACCELERATION) GAL MILLIGAL
(— OF ACOUSTICAL ABSORPTION) SABIN
(— OF ACTION) EPISODE
(— OF ANGULAR MEASURE) CENTRAD
(— OF ARCHEOLOGICAL CLASSIFICATION) ASPECT
(— OF AREA) DEKAR DECARE DEKARE
(— OF BINARY DIGITS) BYTE GIGABYTE
(— OF BRIGHTNESS) NIT STILB LAMBERT
(— OF CAPACITANCE) JAR FARAD
(— OF CAPACITY) COR LAST PIPE ARDAB ARDEB TIERCE AMPHORA
(— OF CARDS) TRICK
(— OF COMIC STRIP) BOX
(— OF CONDUCTANCE) SIEMENS
(— OF COUNTING) POINT
(— OF CURRENT) AMPERE
(— OF DATA TRANSMISSION SPEED) BAUD
(— OF DESIGN) LARME
(— OF DISTANCE) DAY VERST MORGAN PARSEC MEGAPARSEC
(— OF ELASTANCE) DARAF
(— OF ELECTRICAL RESISTANCE) ABOHM
(— OF ELECTRIC CAPACITY) FARAD
(— OF ELECTRIC CONDUCTANCE) MHO
(— OF ELECTRIC FORCE) VOLT KILOVOLT STATVOLT
(— OF ELECTRIC INDUCTANCE) HENRY
(— OF ELECTRIC INTENSITY) AMPERE OERSTED
(— OF ELECTRICITY) ES COULOMB
(— OF ELECTRIC RELUCTANCE) REL STATOHM

(— OF ELECTRIC RESISTANCE) BEGOHM
(— OF ENERGY) ERG RAD QUAD JOULE ATOMERG QUANTUM
(— OF FINENESS) CARAT KARAT
(— OF FLOORING) SQUARE
(— OF FLOW) CUSEC
(— OF FLUIDITY) RHE
(— OF FLUX DENSITY) GAUSS
(— OF FORCE) G DYNE STAPP NEWTON STHENE POUNDAL
(— OF FREQUENCY) HERTZ FRESNEL GIGAHERTZ MEGAHERTZ
(— OF GEOLOGIC TIME) AEON
(— OF GOVERNMENT) DEME LAND KREIS GEMEINDE
(— OF HEAT) BTU THERM CALORIE
(— OF ILLUMINANCE) LUX NIT PHOT MICROLUX
(— OF ILLUMINATION) PHOT
(— OF INFORMATION) NIT GIGABIT
(— OF INSTRUCTION) FRAME
(— OF INSULATION) TOG
(— OF INTERSTELLAR SPACE) PARSEC
(— OF JET PROPULSION) JATO
(— OF LAND AREA) ARE SULUNG
(— OF LANGUAGE) SYLLABLE
(— OF LENGTH) FERMI STADE MICRON MICROMETER
(— OF LIGHT) LUMEN
(— OF LIGHT INTENSITY) PYR PHOTON
(— OF LOUDNESS) PHON SONE DECIBEL
(— OF LUMINOUS INTENSITY) CANDELA
(— OF MACHINERY) STAND
(— OF MAGNETIC FLUX) GAUSS WEBER
(— OF MAGNETIC FLUX DENSITY) TESLA
(— OF MAGNETIC FORCE) KAPP GILBERT
(— OF MAGNETIC INTENSITY) GAMMA OERSTED MAGNETON
(— OF MAGNIFICATION) DIAMETER
(— OF MASS) AMU SLUG CRITH DALTON AVOGRAM
(— OF MEANING) SEMANTEME
(— OF MEASURE) KILOBASE
(— OF MEMORY) BIT MNEMON
(— OF METRICAL QUANTITY) MATRA
(— OF MOMENT) DEBYE
(— OF MOMENTUM) BOLE
(— OF NARCOTIC) JOLT
(— OF NYLON FINENESS) DENIER
(— OF ONE INCH) BUTTON
(— OF PAIN INTENSITY) DOL
(— OF PERMEABILITY) DARCY
(— OF PIPE) FOURBLE
(— OF POWER) WATT DYNAM GIGAWATT KILOWATT PONCELET TERAWATT
(— OF PRESSURE) BAR TORR BARAD BARIE BARYE GWELY OSMOL OSMOLE PASCAL KILOBAR MEGABAR CENTIBAR MICROBAR MILLIBAR
(— OF PRESSWORK) TOKEN
(— OF RADIATION) RAD REM REP GRAY LANGLEY
(— OF RADIOACTIVITY) CURIE
(— OF RESISTANCE) OHM
(— OF ROCKET) STAGE
(— OF SATURATION) SATRON
(— OF SOCIETY) CLAN HORDE CHAPTER
(— OF SOUND) SONE
(— OF SPACE AND CIRCULATION) MILLINE
(— OF SPEECH) WORD
(— OF SPEED) BAUD KNOT
(— OF STOCK) SHARE
(— OF STRUCTURE) MICELLE
(— OF TEMPERATURE) KELVIN
(— OF THICKNESS) POINT
(— OF TIME) AEON BEAT SVEDBERG
(— OF TRADING) CONTRACT
(— OF TRANSMISSION SPEED) BAUD
(— OF USEFULNESS) UTIL
(— OF VELOCITY) VELO
(— OF VERSE METER) FOOT
(— OF VISCOSITY) POISE STOKE SECONDS
(— OF WAVELENGTH) ANGSTROM
(— OF WEIGHT) SSU TON GERA GRAM CARAT CATTY GERAH GRAIN LIANG OUNCE POUND RATTI STEIN ARROBA GRAMME RUTTEE
(— OF WIRE MEASUREMENT) MIL
(— OF WORK) ERG CROP HOUR ERGON JOULE KILERG DINAMODE
(— OF YARN) LEA
(— OF YARN SIZE) CUT
(— OF 100 MEN) CENTURY
(— OF 20) CORGE
(ADMINISTRATIVE —) BLOCK HSIEN AGENCY BUREAU CIRCLE DISTRICT
(ARBITRARY —) OLFACTY
(ARCHERY —) END
(ARMY —) LEGION BRIGADE COMPANY MAHALLA
(ARTILLERY —) BATTERY
(ATOMIC MASS —) DALTON
(AVAILABLE AS —) MARRIED
(BOWLING —) ALLEY
(BOY SCOUT —) SHIP
(BUILDER'S —) SQUARE
(CIGAR-MANUFACTURING —) BUCKEYE
(COLLECTIVE —) COMMUNE
(COMBAT —) ARMAMENT
(DISCRETE —) FRACTION
(EDUCATIONAL —) COURSE
(ELECTROMAGNETIC —) ABFARAD ABHENRY MAXWELL ABAMPERE
(FUNDAMENTAL —) BASE
(GRAMMATICAL —) JUNCTION
(HARMONIC —) CELL
(HOUSING —) HUTMENT
(HYPOTHETICAL —) ID IDANT MICELLE
(INDIVIDUALLY OWNED LIVING —) CONDO
(LIFE —) BIOPHORE
(LIVING —) BIONT BIOGEN
(LOGARITHMIC —) BEL
(LOGGING —) CHANCE
(METRIC —) DEKAR DECARE DEKARE
(MILITARY —) ARMY GOUM CORPS GROUP LANCE SQUAD BRIGADE PLATOON SECTION COMMANDO DIVISION REGIMENT SQUADRON
(NAZI —) FEHME
(ORGANIZATIONAL —) CELL ACTIVITY
(PHOTOMETRIC —) VIOLLE
(POLITICAL —) POLITY SOVIET MUNICIPALITY
(RADIOACTIVE DISINTEGRATION —) RUTHERFORD
(RHYTHMIC —) BASIS COLON
(SELF-PERPETUATING —) BIOSOME
(SHIPPING —) CARLOAD
(SOCIAL —) SEPT GROUP KRAAL SOCIUS
(STORAGE —) BUFFER
(TELEGRAPHIC —) BAUD
(TEMPERATURE —) KELVIN
(TERRITORIAL —) STAKE STATE COMMOT CANTRED CANTREF KINGDOM
(THERMAL —) THERM CALORY CALORIE
(TRIBAL —) TOWNSHIP
(VOTING —) CENTURY
(SUFF.) MONAS ON

UNITARIAN ARIAN SOCINIAN

UNITE ADD MIX ONE OOP PAN SAM SEW UNE UNY ALLY BAND BIND CLUB COAK FUSE HASP JOIN KNIT KNOT LINK SAMM SEAM SOUD UNIT WELD BANDY CLOSE GRADE GRAFT INONE JACOB JOINT MARRY MERGE NITCH UNIFY WHOLE ATTACH CEMENT CONCUR COUPLE EMBODY ENTIRE GATHER LAUREL LEAGUE SOLDER SPLICE STRIKE SUTURE ACCRETE AMALGAM CLUSTER COALITE COMBINE CONJOIN CONNECT CONSORT JACOBUS SIAMESE ALLIGATE ANCYLOSE ANKYLOSE ASSEMBLE COALESCE COMPOUND CONCRETE CONSPIRE COPULATE FEDERATE LAMINATE COLLIGATE
(— ACCURATELY) LAP
(— BY INTERWEAVING) PLEACH SPLICE
(— BY THREADS) SEW STITCH
(— CLOSELY) FAY YOT WELD CEMENT COTTON
(— FOR INTRIGUE) CABAL
(— HOSE) COLLECT
(— IN MARRIAGE) WED SACRE SACRI SPLICE SPOUSE
(— METALS) WELD SWEAT
(— TIMBERS) SCARF
(PREF.) GAMETO GAMO

UNITED ONE TIED ADDED ASONE ATONE FUSED JOINT ALLIED CONNATE ENDLESS UNIONED COMBINED CONCRETE CONJOINT CONJUNCT FEDERATE COADUNATE
(PREF.) GAM(ETO)(O)

UNITED ARAB EMIRATES
(CAPITAL OF —) ABUDHABI
(FORMER NAME OF —) TRUCIALOMAN TRUCIALCOAST TRUCIALSTATES
(MONEY OF —) DIRHAM
(MOUNTAINS OF —) HAJAR
(STATE OF —) AJMAN DUBAI SHARJAH FUJAIRAH
(TOWN OF —) DUBAI JEBEL BURAIMI SHARJAH

UNITED KINGDOM (SEE ENGLAND)

UNITED STATES (ALSO SEE SPECIFIC STATES)

UNITED STATES

LAKE: ERIE MEAD SALT HURON TAHOE CRATER ONTARIO MICHIGAN SUPERIOR CHAMPLAIN OKEECHOBEE
MOUNTAIN: BEAR BONA SILL GREEN OZARK ROCKY UINTA WHITE ANTERO ELBERT SHASTA SIERRA BELFORD FORAKER HARVARD MASSIVE RAINIER SANFORD WASATCH WHITNEY CATSKILL MCKINLEY WRANGELL BLACKBURN ADIRONDACK BITTERROOT APPALACHIAN
PRESIDENT: ABE CAL DDE FDR IKE JFK LBJ BUSH FORD POLK TAFT ADAMS GRANT HARRY HAYES JIMMY NIXON TEDDY TYLER ARTHUR CARTER HOOVER MONROE PIERCE REAGAN TAYLOR TRUMAN WILSON CLINTON HARDING JACKSON JOHNSON KENNEDY LINCOLN MADISON BUCHANAN COOLIDGE FILLMORE GARFIELD HARRISON MCKINLEY VANBUREN JEFFERSON ROOSEVELT EISENHOWER WASHINGTON
VICE PRESIDENT: BURR BUSH FORD KING ADAMS AGNEW DAWES GERRY NIXON TYLER ARTHUR COLFAX CURTIS DALLAS GARNER HAMLIN HOBART MORTON TRUMAN WILSON BARKLEY CALHOUN CLINTON JOHNSON MONDALE SHERMAN WALLACE WHEELER COOLIDGE FILLMORE HUMPHREY MARSHALL TOMPKINS VANBUREN FAIRBANKS HENDRICKS JEFFERSON ROOSEVELT STEVENSON ROCKEFELLER BRECKINRIDGE
WATERFALL: TWIN AKAKA SEVEN NARADA RIBBON FEATHER PALOUSE PASSAIC SLUISKIN YOSEMITE BRIDALVEIL YELLOWSTONE

UNITING SUTURE

UNITS (SUFF.)
(HAVING TIME —) SEMIC

UNITY UNION SYSTEM ONENESS UNITUDE IDENTITY SODALITY SYMPATHY TOTALITY
(— OF SPIRIT AND NATURE) ABSOLUTE

UNIVALENT MONATOMIC

UNIVERSAL ALL LOCAL QUALE TOTAL WHOLE WORLD COMMON GLOBAL PUBLIC VERSAL GENERAL GENERIC CATHOLIC ECUMENIC PANDEMIC
(TRANSCENDENT —) IDEA

UNIVERSALITY ALLNESS OMNITUDE

UNIVERSE ALL LOKA MASS OLAM WORLD COSMOS SYSTEM CREATURE EXEMPLAR
(SIDEREAL —) SPACE
(PREF.) COSM(O) COSMETO COSMICO
UNIVERSITY STUDY CAMPUS SCHOOL ACADEMY COLLEGE MADRASA STUDIUM VARSITY MADRASAH REDBRICK
(OF BRITISH —S) REDBRICK
(RELATING TO BRITISH —) OXBRIDGE REDBRICK PLATEGLASS
UNJUST HARD UNFAIR WANTON WICKED UNEQUAL UNRICHT UNRIGHT WRONGFUL
UNJUSTIFIED INVALID
UNJUSTLY UNDULY FALSELY
UNKEELED RATITE
UNKEMPT ROUGH SEEDY FROWZY MOTLEY RAGTAG RUGGED SHAGGY INCOMPT RAFFISH RUFFLED SCRUFFY SHAGRAG TOUSLED DRAGGLED SCRAGGLY SLIPSHOD STRUBBLY UNCOMBED SHAMBOLIC
UNKIND BAD ILL MEAN VILE CRUEL HARSH STERN SEVERE UNMEEK
UNKINDNESS DISFAVOR
UNKNOWABLE SEALED
UNKNOWN IGN UNCO UNKET UNKID IGNOTE MUNKAR SEALED SECRET UNWARE UNWIST FARAWAY OBSCURE UNCOUTH UNHEARD IGNORANT UNAWARES UNKENNED UNWITTING
UNLADEN LEAR LEER
UNLATCH UNSNECK
UNLAWFUL ILLEGAL ILLICIT NONLICET UNLEEFUL UNLEISUM
UNLEARNED LEWD GROSS PLAIN BOOKLESS IGNORANT UNLEARED
UNLEAVENED AZYMOUS
UNLESS BUT NIF LESS LEST NISI SAVE BINNA NOBUT LESSEN ONLESS WITHOUT
(— BEFORE) NIPR NIPRI
(— OTHERWISE NOTED) NAN
UNLETTERED LEWD BORREL IGNORANT
UNLIGHTED BLIND LAMPLESS
UNLIKE DIFFORM DISLIKE DIVERSE DIFFERENT DISSIMILAR
(MOST —) OTHEREST
UNLIKELY REMOTE DUBIOUS
(MOST —) LAST
UNLIMITED VAST SOVRAN ABSOLUTE UNTERMED
(— IN POWER) ALMIGHTY
UNLINED SINGLE
UNLOAD TIP DROP DUMP HOVEL DECANT STRIKE UNLADE UNSHIP UNSTOW DELIVER DEPLETE DETRUCK DISLOAD UNTRUSS DISCHARGE
UNLOCK UNMAKE RESERATE UNLOUKEN
UNLOOSE OUTWIND UNRIVET
UNLUCKY BAD FAY ILL EVIL FOUL DONSY DISMAL DONSIE HOODOO WICKED HAPLESS INFAUST UNHAPPY SINISTER UNCHANCY UNTOWARD MISCHANCY WANCHANCY
(— THING) AMBSACE
UNMAN UNDO CRUSH UNNERVE
UNMANAGEABLE ROID DONSY RANDY WANTON RESTIVE CHURLISH STAFFISH CAMSTAIRY REFRACTORY
UNMANLY SOFT EPICENE MANLESS UNLUSTY
UNMANNERLY RUDE BOORISH UNCIVIL IMPOLITE UNGENTLE MISLEARED
UNMARKED MAVERICK NOTELESS
UNMARRIED ONE LONE SOLE OLEPI YOUNG ONLEPY SINGLE
UNMASK EXPOSE UNFACE DISMASK UNCLOAK
UNMASKING EXPOSURE
UNMEASURED UNMEET MODELESS
UNMELODIOUS SCRANNEL
UNMERCHANTABLE SALABLE SALEABLE
UNMERCIFUL CRUEL PITILESS RUTHLESS
UNMETHODICAL CURSORY
UNMINDFUL SLOWFUL CARELESS HEEDLESS MINDLESS
UNMISTAKABLE FLAT OPEN BROAD CLEAR FRANK PLAIN PATENT DECIDED EXPRESS APPARENT DECISIVE MANIFEST UNIVOCAL
UNMISTAKABLY SIGNALLY
UNMITIGATED PURE GROSS RUDDY ARRANT DAMNED SOVRAN PERFECT PUREDEE REGULAR ABSOLUTE OUTRIGHT
UNMIX EXSOLVE
UNMIXED NET DEEP MERE NEAT PURE SELF SOLE BLANK SHEER UTTER IMMIXT SIMPLE STRAIGHT
UNMODIFIED BRUTE STRAIGHT
UNMOLESTED SACKLESS
UNMOVED CALM COOL FIRM STONY TIGHT IMMOTE SERENE ADAMANT IMMOVED
UNMOVING INERT IMMOBILE IMMOTIVE
UNMUSICAL NOTELESS SCABROUS
UNNATURAL EERY EERIE STIFF CLAMMY CREEPY FORCED UNKIND STRANGE UNCANNY VIOLENT ABNORMAL ABSONANT FARCICAL KINDLESS STRAINED UNKINDLY MONSTROUS
UNNECESSARY USELESS NEEDLESS SUPERFLUOUS
UNNEEDED WASTE
UNNERVE UNMAN RATTLE UNMAKE WEAKEN ENERVATE PARALYZE
UNNERVED SHOOK
UNNILPENTIUM HAHNIUM
UNNILQUADIUM RUTHERFORDIUM
UNNOTICED SILENT
UNOBJECTIONABLE VENIAL
UNOBSERVANT HEEDLESS
UNOBSTRUCTED FAIR FREE OPEN PATENT THROUGH APPARENT
UNOBTRUSIVE SHY QUIET MODEST SEDATE DISCREET RETIRING
UNOCCUPIED IDLE VOID BLANK EMPTY WASTE OTIOSE VACANT LEISURE UNSEATED WASTEFUL
UNORGANIZED ACOSMIC INCHOATE
UNORTHODOX HERETIC
UNOSTENTATIOUS SHY QUIET LENTEN MODEST
UNPACK UNFARDLE
UNPAID DUE UNQUIT UNWAGED HONORARY WAGELESS OUTSTANDING
UNPAIRED IMPAR AZYGOUS
UNPALATABLE SOD HARD BITTER BRACKISH
UNPARALLELED ALONE UNIQUE EPOCHAL PEERLESS SINGULAR UNPEERED
UNPERTURBED BLAND STILL
UNPLEASANT BAD ACID EVIL HARD NICE SOUR UGLY VILE AWFUL CRUDE GRIMY GUMMY HAIRY HARSH MUCKY NASTY ROUGH TOUGH YUCKY YUKKY BRUTAL CRIMPY RANCID STICKY THRAWN UNFELE UNGAIN UNLIEF BEASTLY BILIOUS GHASTLY INGRATE SPINOUS UNLUSTY UNQUEME UNSONCY CHISELLY DREADFUL HORRIBLE INDECENT SCABROUS UNLOVELY TRAUMATIC ABOMINABLE
(ANNOYINGLY —) CREEPY
(PREF.) CAC(O) CACH
UNPLEASANTLY QUEER HARDLY UNWINLY
UNPLEASANTNESS ILLNESS
UNPLOWED LEA
UNPOETICAL MUSELESS
UNPOLISHED ILL RUDE BLIND CRUDE ROUGH COARSE INCULT RUGGED RUSTIC SAVAGE SHAGGY UPLAND INCOMPT UNKEMPT AGRESTIC
UNPOPULARITY ENVY
UNPRACTICED RAW FRESH UNTRADED
UNPREDICTABILITY CHAOS
UNPREDICTABLE DICEY CHANCY CRANKY ERRATIC
UNPREJUDICED FAIR
UNPREMEDITATED CASUAL
UNPREPARED TARDY
UNPREPOSSESSING SEEDY
UNPRETENDING LOWLY HOMELY HUMBLE
UNPRETENTIOUS HOMY HOMEY PLAIN SOBER COMMON HOMELY HUMBLE MODEST SIMPLE DISCREET HOMESPUN
UNPRINCIPLED LEWD LIMMER
UNPRODUCTIVE DRY SHY ARID DEAD DEAF LEAN POOR VAIN YELD YELL ADDLE DUSTY WASTE BARREN GEASON SAPLESS STERILE WOODSERE
UNPRODUCTIVENESS BORASCO BORASQUE BORRASCA
UNPROFESSIONAL LAY BUSH LAICAL JACKLEG
UNPROFITABLE BAD DRY DEAD LEAN SECK VAIN BARREN BOOTLESS GAINLESS UNGAINLY
UNPROGRESSIVE SLOW DORMANT BACKWARD
UNPROMISING BLUE DUBIOUS
UNPRONOUNCED MUTE
UNPROPITIOUS ILL EVIL FOUL THRAW MALIGN SULLEN ADVERSE AVERTED INFAUST OMINOUS THRAWART
UNPROTECTED NAKED EXPOSED HELPLESS
UNPROVOKED WANTON
UNPUBLISHED INED INEDITED
UNQUALIFIED NET BARE FULL MERE PURE VERY BLACK PLUMP SHEER UNFIT DIRECT ENTIRE UNABLE CLOTTED PLENARY IMPLICIT INHABILE POSITIVE
UNQUESTIONABLE ASSURED CERTAIN DECIDED ABSOLUTE DECISIVE DISTINCT
UNQUESTIONED CLEAR
UNQUESTIONING IMPLICIT
UNRAVEL REDD UNDO BREAK ENODE FEAZE RAVEL RETEX SOLVE EVOLVE TIFFLE UNFOLD UNKNIT UNLACE ENODATE RESOLVE
UNRAVELLING DISCOVERY DENOUEMENT
UNREAL VAIN AERIAL GOTHIC CHEMICK FANCIED SHADOWY AERIFORM CHIMERIC FARCICAL ILLUSORY NOTIONAL SCENICAL VISIONAL
(PREF.) PSEUD(O)
UNREALISTIC CHIMERIC
UNREALIZED BEHIND
UNREASONABLE ABSURD FANATIC ABSONANT
UNREASONABLENESS ALOGY INSANITY
UNREASONABLY SINFULLY
UNREASONING BRUTE RABID
UNRECOGNIZED UNSUNG CRYPTIC UNWITTED
UNRECOVERABLE DEAD
UNRECTIFIED IMPURE
UNREDEEMED CHEAP
UNREFINED RAW DARK LOUD BRUTE CRUDE DORIC GROSS COARSE COMMON EARTHY JUNGLY VULGAR BOORISH UNCOUTH UNKEMPT DREADFUL SWAINISH
UNREFLECTING GLIB VACANT
UNREGENERACY ADAM
UNREGENERATE NATURAL
UNREGENERATELY MANLY
UNREHEARSED IMPROMPTU
UNRELATED FREMD STRAY UNAKIN UNTOLD EXTREME FRAMMIT POSITIVE
UNRELAXED UNSLAKED
UNRELAXING TONIC
UNRELENTING GRIM HARD IRON CRUEL STERN BRASSY SEVERE RIGOROUS
UNRELIABLE FISHY SHADY FICKLE GREASY UNSAFE CASALTY STREAKY WILDCAT FECKLESS GLIBBERY SLIPPERY TICKLISH
UNRELIEVED DEAD BRUTE ABJECT EXQUISITE

UNREMITTING BUSY FAST HARD DOGGED
UNREMUNERATIVE HONORARY
UNRESERVED FREE CLEAN FRANK ROUND COMMON UNCLOSE EXPLICIT
UNRESERVEDNESS FREEDOM
UNRESISTING BUXOM
UNRESPONSIVE DEAD DUMB BARREN SILENT STUBBORN
UNREST ANOMY ANOMIE MOTION AILMENT DISREST WANREST DISQUIET CHEMISTRY PSYCHOSIS
UNRESTRAINED LAX MAD FREE WILD BROAD FANTI FRANK LARGE LOOSE FACILE FANTEE LAVISH UNTIED WANTON FLYAWAY RAMPANT RIOTOUS BARBARIC FAMILIAR FREEHAND LAXATIVE PINDARIC ABANDONED LIBERTINE
UNRESTRAINT LICENSE IMMUNITY
UNRESTRICTED FREE GLOBAL SOVRAN UNZONED ABSOLUTE
UNRETURNED UNYOLDEN
UNREVEALED UNTOLD
UNRHYMED BLANK
UNRIG STRIP
UNRIGHTEOUSNESS ADHARMA
UNRIPE RAW CRUDE GREEN CALLOW UNCURED IMMATURE
UNROBE DISROBE UNDRESS DISARRAY
UNROLL EVOLVE UNCURL DEVELOP OUTROLL TRINDLE UNTREND
UNROOF TIRL TIRR TIRVE DISROOF
UNRUFFLE SMOOTH SOOTHE MOLLIFY
UNRUFFLED CALM COOL EASY EVEN QUIET SOBER STILL ASLEEP PLACID SEDATE SERENE SMOOTH DECOROUS
UNRULY HIGH RAMP ROYT TOUGH HAUNTY WANTON LAWLESS RAMMAGE ROPABLE UNRULED VICIOUS WANRULY WAYWARD INDOCILE MUTINOUS CAMSTAIRY TURBULENT REFRACTORY OBSTREPEROUS RAMBUNCTIOUS
UNSADDLE OUTSPAN UNPANEL
UNSADDLED BAREBACKED
UNSAFE HOT OUT FISHY EXPOSED INSECURE PERILOUS
UNSANCTIFIED PROFANE
UNSATISFACTORY BAD ILL EVIL POOR CROOK LOUSY SHREWD WRETCHED
(— PRODUCT) LEMON
UNSATISFYING DUSTY HOLLOW
UNSATURATED
(PREF.) EN
UNSAVORY WERSH INSIPID WEARISH
UNSAY WITHDRAW
UNSCHOLARLY BOOKLESS
UNSCRUPULOUS SKIN CROOK BRAZEN DEVIOUS JACKLEG DEXTROUS RASCALLY
UNSEASONABLE LAT UNRIPE UNTIDY UNCHANCY UNTIMELY
UNSEASONED RAW GREEN
UNSEAT ADDRESS DISSEAT
UNSEEING BLIND GAZELESS
UNSEEMLY HOIDEN UNFAIR IMPROPER INDECENT SEEMLESS UNMEETLY UNWORTHY
UNSEEN SECRET UNEYED CRYPTIC VIEWLESS INVISIBLE
UNSELFISH (ABSURDLY —) QUIXOTIC
UNSERRIED LOOSE
UNSETTLE JAR TURN UNFIX UNSET UPSET COMMOVE DERANGE DISTURB STAGGER UNHINGE UNQUEME DISORDER DISQUIET DISTRACT
UNSETTLED MOOT LIGHT SHAKY UNSAD VAGUE BROKEN FICKLE QUEASY VAGOUS DUBIOUS NOMADIC SHUTTLE UNSTAID RESTLESS UNSTABLE VAGABOND
UNSETTLING NASTY
UNSHAKABLE DOGGED ADAMANT IRONCLAD
UNSHAKEN FIRM STEADY UNMOVED UNSHOOK CONSTANT RESOLUTE
UNSHAPELY DEFORMED UNMACKLY
UNSHARED SOLE
UNSHEATHE DISCASE
UNSHEATHED BARE
UNSHELTERED BLEAK
UNSHOD BAREFOOT SHOELESS DISCALCED
UNSHORN UNPOLLED
UNSIGHTLY UGLY AWFUL MESSY HOMELY INDECENT
UNSKILLED JAY PUNY GREEN PUISNE UNGAIN UNSEEN STRANGE FECKLESS
UNSKILLFUL ILL EVIL RUDE ARTLESS AWKWARD UNFEATY BUNGLING TINKERLY UNHEPPEN
UNSMILING GLUM AUSTERE
UNSOCIABLE SULLEN FAROUCHE INSOCIAL
UNSOILED CLEAN
UNSOPHISTICATE SQUARE
UNSOPHISTICATED JAY DEWY NAIF PURE FRANK GREEN NAIVE SILLY CALLOW SIMPLE BUCOLIC NATURAL VERDANT HOMEBRED HOMESPUN INNOCENT PROVINCIAL
UNSOUND BAD ILL EVIL SICK ADDLE BARMY CRAZY CRONK DICKY DOTTY DOZED SANDY SHAKY WONKY ABSURD FAULTY FLAWED HOLLOW INFIRM INSANE ROTTEN UNHALE INVALID RICKETY UNWHOLE
UNSOUNDNESS CRACK INSANITY
UNSPARING ROUND SEVERE DRASTIC RIGOROUS RUTHLESS SCATHING SLASHING
UNSPIRITUAL CARNAL
UNSPOILED RACY UNSHENT PRISTINE
UNSPOKEN TACIT SILENT
UNSPORTSMANLIKE DIRTY
UNSPOTTED CLEAR SPOTLESS
UNSPUN RAW
UNSTABLE FLUX BATTY LOOSE SANDY SHAKY BROTEL CHOPPY FICKLE FITFUL FLITTY LABILE LUBRIC ROTTEN SHIFTY TICKLE UNFIRM WANKLE WANKLY ASTATIC DWAIBLE DWAIBLY DWEEBLE RICKETY SLIDDER SLIDDRY VOLUBLE FEVERISH FIRMLESS FUGITIVE INSECURE LUBRICAL REMUABLE SKITTISH SLIPPERY TICKLISH TOTTLISH VARIABLE
(MENTALLY —) BRAINISH
UNSTEADILY GROGGILY
UNSTEADINESS FALTER
UNSTEADY WALT CRANK CRONK DOTTY FLUKY LIGHT NERVY SLACK TIPPY TIPSY TOTTY UNSAD WALTY WONKY COGGLY FICKLE FLICKY FLUFFY GROGGY JIGGLY JOGGLY SWIMMY TOTTIE WAFFLY WAGGLY WAMBLY WANKLE WEEWAW WEEWOW DODDERY GLAIKIT JIGGETY QUAVERY QUEACHY TITTUPY TOTTERY WAYWARD SKITTISH STAGGERY TICKLISH TITUBANT UNSTABLE VARIABLE VERSATILE
UNSTINTED LAVISH ENDLESS
UNSTOPPABLE SUREFIRE
UNSTRESS SLACK
UNSTRESSED SHORT
UNSTRING DISSOLVE
UNSTUDIED GLIB CASUAL CARELESS GLANCING
UNSUBDUED VIRGIN UNBOWED
UNSUBSTANTIAL TOY AIRY LIMP THIN WINDY AERIAL BUBBLE CHAFFY FLIMSY SLEAZY SLEEZY SLIGHT UNREAL FOLIOUS FRAGILE INSOLID SHADOWY TENUOUS FILIGREE FINESPUN FOOTLESS GIMCRACK VAPOROUS PASTEBOARD
UNSUCCESSFUL BAD MANQUE UNSPED STICKIT UNHAPPY ABORTIVE
UNSUITABLE INEPT UNAPT UNDUE UNFIT UNKIND UNMETE UNCOMELY UNGAINLY UNLIKELY INELIGIBLE MALAPROPOS INCONVENIENT
UNSUITABLENESS IMPOLICY
UNSUITED BAD
UNSULLIED FAIR PURE CLEAR VIRGIN INNOCENT SPOTLESS VIRGINAL
UNSUPPLIED HELPLESS
UNSUPPORTED BLIND NAKED BACKWARD STAYLESS
UNSURE TIMID INFIRM DOUBTFUL INSECURE UNSICKER
UNSURPASSED CHAMPION
UNSUSPECTING INNOCENT
UNSWEET UNSOOT
UNSWEETENED BRUT
UNSWERVING FIXED FLUSH LOYAL DIRECT STEADY STRICT STURDY STAUNCH
UNSWERVINGLY HEADLONG
UNSYMMETRICAL LOPSIDED
UNSYMPATHETIC DRY HARD STONY FROZEN GLASSY HOSTILE KINDLESS
UNTAINTED FREE GOOD PURE INNOCENT
UNTAMED WILD FERAL RAMAGE SAVAGE HAGGARD RAMMISH WARRAGAL
UNTANGLE FREE SLEAVE UNLACE
UNTARNISHED PURE
UNTAUGHT WASTE UNLERED IGNORANT
UNTHINKABLE PUERILE
UNTHINKING GLIB BRUTE CASUAL FECKLESS HEEDLESS VISCERAL
UNTHINKINGLY STUPID
UNTIDINESS JAKES LITTER
UNTIDY DOWDY GAUMY MESSY ROOKY BUNTING DRAGGLY LITTERY RUMMAGY SCRUFFY UNSIDED DRAGGLED SLOVENLY STRUBBLY UNHEPPEN SHAMBOLIC
UNTIE UNDO UNBIND UNLASH UNLATCH UNTRUSS UNTWINE UNFASTEN
UNTIL AD OR TO GIN HENT INTO UNTO FORTO TWELL WHILE WHILES WHILST PENDING
(— THEN) BEFORE
UNTILLED INCULT UNEARED
UNTIMELY UNTIDY IMMATURE PREVIOUS TIMELESS
(— ARRIVAL) LATECOMER
UNTIRING BUSY SEDULOUS TIRELESS
UNTITLED (— MEN) AUMAGA
UNTO TILL
UNTOLD VAST UNQUOD
UNTOUCHABLE DOM HARIJAN CHANDALA
(PL.) PANCHAMA
UNTOUCHED FREE INTACT PRISTINE
(PREF.) INTEGRI
UNTOWARD ILL UNRULY FROWARD WAYWARD
UNTRAINED RAW RUDE GREEN HAGGARD
UNTRAMMELED FREE
UNTRIED MAIDEN UNSOUGHT
UNTRIMMED UNTEWED
UNTRODDEN PATHLESS UNFOOTED
UNTROUBLED CHEERY
UNTRUE FLAM FALSE LEASE WRONG UNFAST DISLOYAL MENDACIOUS
(PREF.) PSEUD(O)
UNTRUSTWORTHINESS FALSITY
UNTRUSTWORTHY PUNIC SHAKY LIMBER TRICKY UNSURE SLIDDERY SLIPPERY
UNTRUTH LIE FABLE LEASE SKLENT FALSITY UNTROTH MENDACITY
UNTRUTHFUL SLANTER
UNTUNABLE ABSONANT
UNTUTORED NATURAL IGNORANT PRIMITIVE
UNTWILLED PLAIN
UNTWINE FRESE UNTWIST
UNTWIST FAG FEAZE UNLAY UNSPIN UNTWIRL
UNTWISTED SLEIDED
UNUSABLE WASTE INUTILE
UNUSED IDLE FRESH RUSTY WASTE INURED MAIDEN VACANT DERELICT INITIATE UNWONTED
UNUSUAL ODD EERY RARE SELD TALL CRAZY EERIE FORBY NOVEL

UTTER WEIRD EXEMPT FORBYE SCREWY SINGLE UNIQUE STRANGE ABNORMAL DISTINCT ESPECIAL INSOLENT KNOCKOUT SELCOUTH SINGULAR SPANKING UNCOMMON UNTRADED UNWONTED PRODIGIOUS
(PREF.) ANOM(O)
UNUSUALLY EXTRA
UNVARIED SAMELY
UNVARNISHED EVERYDAY
UNVARYING FLAT SAME FRANK LEVEL STABLE UNIFORM
UNVEIL REVEAL UNCOVER UNCROWN UNDRAPE UNSCREEN UNWIMPLE
UNVENTILATED CLOSE
UNVERSED STRANGE
UNWANTED STRAY TRAMP FAULTY
UNWARRANTED UNDUE
UNWARY RASH UNAWARE CARELESS HEEDLESS WARELESS
UNWASHED SOAPLESS
UNWASTEFUL FRUGAL
UNWAVERING FIRM CLEAN LEVEL SOLID GLASSY STABLE EXPRESS STAUNCH
UNWAVERINGLY FAST
UNWEAKENED CLEAR
UNWELL BAD ILL EVIL PUNK SICK BADLY CROOK SEEDY AILING CHIPPY WICKED COMICAL
UNWHOLESOME ILL EVIL SICK CAGMAG IMPURE MORBID SICKLY CORRUPT NOISOME NOXIOUS UNCLEAN DISEASED EPINOSIC
UNWIELDY BULKY CLUMSY UNRIDE AWKWARD HULKING CUMBROUS UNGAINLY
UNWILLING CHARY LOATH SWEER WERSE AVERSE ESCHEW BACKWARD GRUDGING
(— TO GO FORWARD) RESTIVE
UNWILLINGLY MAUGER MAUGRE
UNWILLINGNESS GRUDGE NOLITION
UNWIND UNCLEW UNREEL UNREAVE UNTWINE
UNWISE FALSE INANE SILLY SIMPLE FOOLISH WITLESS
UNWITTING UNWIST WEETLESS
UNWOMANLY MANKIND
UNWORLDLY WEIRD ASTRAL SPIRITUAL
UNWORRIED DOWNBEAT
UNWORTHY BASE INDIGN BENEATH UNDIGNE WANWORDY
UNWOUNDED COLD
UNWREATHE UNPLAT
UNWRINKLED BRANT BRENT
UNWROUGHT RAW LIVE RUDE
UNYIELDING PAT SET ACID DEAF DOUR FAST FIRM GRIM HARD RIGID STARK STEEL STIFF STITH STONY TOUGH FLINTY FROZEN GLASSY KNOBBY MARBLE STEELY STURDY ADAMANT AUSTERE COSTIVE FROWARD CHURLISH OBDURATE OBEDIENT STUBBORN ROCKRIBBED PERTINACIOUS
UNYOKE LOWSE UNTEAM OUTSHUT OUTSPAN
UNYOKED
(PREF.) AZYGO
UP ON ONE OOP ABOUT ASTIR DORMY NORTH DORMIE
(— AND ABOUT) AFOOT
(— TO) TIL INTO UNTIL
(— TO THE TIME) UNTIL
(— YONDER) UPBY UPBYE
(FARTHER —) ABOVE
(HIGH —) ALOFT
(PREF.) ANA ANO SUR
UPANISHAD ISHA KATHA
UPAS DITA ANTIAR CHETTIK
UPBEAT ARSIS AUFTAKT ANACRUSIS
UP-BOW POUSSE
UPBRAID CHEW RAIL SNUB TUCK TWIT ABUSE ROUSE SCOLD TAUNT UPBRAY EMBRAID REPROVE DISGRACE OUTBRAID
UPCARD STARTER
UPCOMING NEXT FUTURE
UPFOLD SADDLE ANTICLINE
UPHEAVAL BOIL STORM UPLIFT RUMMAGE UPTHROW
UPHILL UPBANK UPWITH
UPHOLD AID TOM ABET BACK FAVOR AFFIRM ASSERT DEFEND SOOTHE BOLSTER SUPPORT SUSTAIN CHAMPION MAINTAIN PRESERVE
UPHOLDER DEFENDER ERASTIAN FEUDALIST
UPHOLDING BEHIND
UPHOLSTER SQUAB
UPHOLSTERER TAPISER UPHOLDER
UPKEEP MAINTENANCE
UPLAND DOWN DOWNS MAUKA COTEAU FASTLAND
(PL.) BRAES DOWNS
UPLAND PLOVER QUAILY HILLBIRD PAPABOTE
UPLIFT TOSS BOOST ERECT TOWER UPTHRUST
UPLIFTED ERECT EXALTEE
UPON ON PON SUR INTO OVER ABOVE AGAINST
(— THAT) THEREAT
(PREF.) EP EPH EPI OB
UPPER OVER VAMP SKIVE VAMPEY SUPERIOR
(PL.) FINISH
(PREF.) ANO HYPER SUPERO
(SITUATED ON — SIDE) SUPRA
UPPER CRUST GRATIN
UPPERCUT BOLO
UPPER HURONIAN LAWSON
UPPERMOST UMEST UPMOST OVEREST BUNEMOST OVERMOST
UPPER VOLTA FASO BURKINA
UPRAISED SUBLIME
UPRIGHT FAIR GOOD HARR JUST PROP STUD TIDY TRUE ANEND CHEEK ERECT GUIDE JELLY MORAL ONEND RIGHT ROMAN SETUP STALE STALK STILE ARRECT DIRECT ENTIRE HONEST SQUARE FRIZZEN HOUSING JANNOCK PITPROP SINCERE GOALPOST INNOCENT RIGHTFUL STANDARD STANDING STRAIGHT VERTICAL VIRTUOUS
(NOT —) ATILT BEVEL
(PL.) STUDDING
(PREF.) ORTH(O)
UPRIGHTNESS HONOR TRUTH APLOMB EQUITY HONESTY PROBITY JUSTNESS SINCERITY
UPRISING RIOT EMEUTE MUTINY PUTSCH REVOLT TUMULT UPRISE UPRISAL REBELLION
UPROAR DIN RUT CAIN FLAW GILD HELL MOIL RIOT ROUT BABEL BURLE CHANG FUROR HOOHA HURLY RUMOR STOUN STOUR CLAMOR DIRDUM EMEUTE FRACAS HABBLE HUBBLE HUBBUB RACKET RANDAN RATTLE RIPPET RUCKUS RUMBLE RUMPUS SHINDY STEVEN STOUND TUMULT CATOUSE FERMENT GARBOIL GAUSTER ORATION OUTROAR RUCTION STASHIE TURMOIL BALLYHOO BROUHAHA SCOUTHER STIRRING STRAMASH TINTAMAR CHARIVARI SHEMOZZLE HULLABALOO PANDEMONIUM
UPROARIOUS FURIOUS ROUTOUS ROWDYDOWDY
UPROOT GRUB HACK LOUK MORE UNROUT UNPLANT DISPLANT ROOTWALT SUPPLANT
UPROOTED LUMPEN
UPSET ILL TIP TOP TUP CAVE COUP COWP FUSS JUMP PURL ROCK TILT TURN WELT EVERT FREAK KNOCK ROUSE SHAKE SKAIL SKELL SPILL WHELM BOTHER DISMAY QUELME TICKED TIPPLE TOPPLE UPCAST WALTER CAPSIZE DERANGE DISTURB FRAZZLE HAYWIRE INASTEW OVERSET PERVERT REVERSE SLATTER SUBVERT TEMPEST TURMOIL UNGLUED CAPSIZAL DISTRAIT OVERTILT OVERTURN STREAKED SUPPLANT TURNOVER OVERTHROW
(EASILY —) FUSSY FLAPPABLE
UPSHOT ISSUE SHORT UPSET EFFECT SEQUEL UPPING OUTCOME UPSHOOT UPSTROKE
UPSIDE-DOWN CRAZY REVERSE OVERHAND UPSEDOUN
UPSILON
(PREF.) YPSILI
UPSTAIRS ABOVE
UPSTANDING GRADELY
UPSTART KIP QUAT SNIP SNOB SQUIRT UPSKIP DALTEEN PARVENU ARRIVIST MUSHROOM SKIPJACK UPSPRING
UPTICK RISE INCREASE
UPTIGHT TENSE
UP-TO-DATE AGOGO WITHIT MOD MODERN TRENDY ABREAST TODAYISH
UPWARD ALOFT UPLONG UPWAYS UPWITH SKYWARD UPALONG UPWARDS
(PREF.) ANO
UPWARD-MOVING ANABATIC
URAEUS ASP
URAMIL MUREXAN
URANUS OURANOS HERSCHEL
(WIFE OF —) GAEA
URAO TRONA
URARTAEAN KHALDIAN
URARTU VAN
URATE LITHATE
URBAN TOWN URBIC URBANE BURGHAL OPPIDAN
URBANE CIVIL SUAVE POLITE SVELTE AMIABLE GRACIOUS
URBANITY COMITY SUAVITY COURTESY ELEGANCE
URCHIN IMP TYKE WAIF ELFIN GAMIN SCAMP KEELIE NIPPER HURCHEON
(PREF.) **(SEA —)** ECHIN(O)
URD MUNGO
URDEE MATELEY
URDU REKHTA REKHTI MOORISH
URDUR (SISTER OF —) SKULD VERTHANDI
URGE ART DUN EGG HIE PLY PUT SIC SUE TAR YEN BROD COAX CRAM EDGE FIRK GOAD ITCH MOVE PING POKE PROD PUSH SICK SPUR WHIP CROWD DRIVE EGGON FILIP FORCE HOOSH IMPEL LABOR PRESS PRICK SPANK TREAT COMPEL DEHORT DESIRE ENGAGE EXCITE FILLIP HARDEN HOICKS HUSTLE INCITE INDUCE INVITE MOTION PROMPT PROPEL STRAIN THREAP THREAT ANIMATE COMMOVE ENFORCE INSTANT OPPRESS PERSIST SOLICIT SUGGEST URGENCY ADMONISH INSTANCE PERSUADE
(— IMPORTUNATELY) DUN PRESS
(— ON) EGG ERT HAG SOOL WHIG ALARM CHIRK CROWD DRIVE FILIP HASTE HURRY IMPEL ROWEL YOICK ALARUM FILLIP HARDEN HASTEN INCITE
(— ON A HORSE) HUP CRAM CHUCK
(— OUT) EXTRUDE
(— STRONGLY) EXHORT SOLICIT
(— WITH VEHEMENCE) DING
(VITAL —) LIBIDO
URGENCY NEED PRESS STRESS COGENCE COGENCY URGENCE EXIGENCY INSTANCE INSTANCY PRESSURE
URGENT HOT DIRE LOUD RASH ACUTE HASTY STRONG BURNING CLAMANT EXIGENT INSTANT URGEFUL CRITICAL PRESSING PRESSIVE NECESSITOUS
URGING QUEST
URI (SON OF —) GEBER BEZALEEL
URIAH (WIFE OF —) BATHSHEBA
URIAL SHA OORIAL
URIEL (DAUGHTER OF —) MAACHAH
(FATHER OF —) TAHATH
URIJAH (FATHER OF —) SHEMAIAH
URINAL DUCK PISSOIR SANITARY
URINATE WET LEAK EMPTY STALE PIDDLE EVACUATE MICTURATE
URINATION MICTION NOCTURIA
URINE MIG SIG LAGE LANT WASH STALE WATER NETTING EMICTION
(— USED AS COSMETIC) LOTIUM
(PREF.) UR(O) URIC(O) URIN(I)(O)
(SUFF.) URIA URIC
URN JAR EWER KIST URNA VASE CAPANNA

(— FOR MAKING TEA) KITCHEN SAMOVAR
(— IN KENO) GOOSE
(BURIAL —) OSSUARY
(CINERARY —) DINOS DEINOS
(STONE —) STEEN
URN-SHAPED URCEOLAR
UROCHORDA ASCIDIA TUNICATA
UROPYGIUM RUMP
UROSTYLE COCCYX
URSA MAJOR OKNARI CHARIOT WAGONER WAGGONER
URSA MINOR CYNOSURE
URSINE ARCTOID
URTICARIA HIVES UREDO CNIDOSIS
URTICASTRUM LAPORTEA
URUBU ZOPILOTE

URUGUAY
CAPITAL: MONTEVIDEO
DEPARTMENT: ROCHA SALTO FLORES RIVERA ARTIGAS COLONIA DURAZNO FLORIDA SORIANO
ESTUARY: PLATA
LAKE: MERIN MIRIM DIFUNTOS
MEASURE: VARA LEGUA CUADRA SUERTE
RIVER: MALO MIRIM NEGRO ULIMAR CUAREIM QUEGUAY YAGUARON CEBOLLATI
TOWN: MELO AIGUA MINAS PANDO ROCHA SALTO VERAS RIVERA DURAZNO FLORIDA MERCEDES PAYSANDU
WEIGHT: QUINTAL

URUGUAYAN ORIENTAL
URUS TUR URE AUROCHS
US HIS HIZ HUZ
U.S.A. (AUTHOR OF —) DOSPASSOS
(CHARACTER IN —) ANN BEN JOE MAC MARY WARD DELLA FAINY JANEY MARGO TRENT FRENCH MAISIE SAVAGE STAPLE STRANG CHARLEY COMPTON DOWLING ELEANOR EVELINE RICHARD SPENCER ANDERSON GERTRUDE HUTCHINS MCCREARY STODDARD WILLIAMS ANNABELLE MOOREHOUSE
USABLE FIT UTIBLE SERVABLE
USAGE USE ASAL FORM WONE HABIT HAUNT SUNNA USURE CUSTOM MANNER FASHION HALACHA HALAKAH USATION PRACTICE
(BAD —) ABUSAGE
(EVIL-) MISUSE
(HARD —) GRIEF
(ILL —) ABUSE
(LEGAL —) PRACTIC
(RELIGIOUS —) RITUS
(PL.) CEREMONY
(PREF.) NOM(O)
(SUFF.) NOMY
USE URE BOOT CALL DUTY HAVE NAIT NOTE USUS WISE APPLY AVAIL GUIDE HABIT SPEND STEAD TREAT USAGE WASTE BEHOOF EMPLOY FINISH HANDLE OCCUPY USANCE ACCOUNT ADHIBIT ENTREAT IMPROVE PURPOSE SERVICE UTILITY ACCUSTOM EXERCISE FUNCTION PRACTICE
(— AS WONTED) ADOPT
(— DILIGENTLY) PLY
(— EXPERIMENTALLY) TRY
(— FIGURE OF SPEECH) TROPE
(— FOR FIRST TIME) FLESH
(— IMPROPERLY) ABUSE
(— INDISCRIMINATELY) HACK
(— OF MORE WORDS THAN NECESSARY) PLEONASM
(— OF NEW WORD) NEOLOGY
(— OF SUBTERFUGE) CHICANE
(— OSTENTATIOUSLY) SPORT
(— SELFISHLY) HOG
(— SPARINGLY) TAPE SPARE MANAGE
(— UP) EAT TIRE WEAR SHOOT SPEND ABSORB DEVOUR EXPEND GUZZLE PERUSE CONSUME EXHAUST OVERWEAR
(— WASTEFULLY) SPILL
(— WITH FULL COMMAND) WIELD
(EFFICIENT —) ECONOMY
(EXCESSIVE — OF FACE AND HANDS) ABHINAYA
(FIRST —) HANSEL HANDSEL
(FOR TEMPORARY —) JURY
(FRUGAL —) SPARE
(GENERAL —) CURRENCY
(GET EXCLUSIVE — OF) SEWUP
(LITURGICAL —) RITE
(MUCH IN —) GREAT
(UNRESTRICTED —) FREEDOM
(WRONG —) ABUSE
(PREF.) USU
USED WONT
(— CONTINUOUSLY) HOT
(— IN FLIGHT) VOLAR
(— UP) ALL BEAT SHOT SPENT FOREWORN
(CONVENTIONALLY —) STOCK
(MUCH —) GREAT HACKNEY
USEFUL GAIN GOOD UTILE UTIBLE HELPFUL THRIFTY BEHOVELY UTENSILE BEHOVEFUL
(— FOR LONG TIME) HARD
(SUFF.) CHRESIS CHRESTIC CHRESTO
USEFULNESS USE AVAIL VALUE WORTH PROFIT MILEAGE UTILITY
USELESS IDLE LEWD VAIN VOID WIDE EMPTY WASTE DOLESS GROTTY NOUGHT OTIOSE SCREWY TRASHY INUTILE STERILE VAINFUL BOOTLESS FOOTLESS FOOTLING WASTEFUL WORTHLESS INEFFECTIVE
USELESSNESS FUTILITY IDLENESS
USER USUS
(SUFF.) STER STRESS
USH SEAT
USHABTI SHAWABTI
USHER BOW USH SEAT SHOW CRIER ESCORT HERALD ISCHAR SEATER VERGER CHOBDAR HUISHER JANITOR MARSHAL STEWARD
USSR (SEE RUSSIA)
USUAL RIFE NOMIC COMMON FAMOUS NORMAL SOLEMN VULGAR WONTED AVERAGE GENERAL NATURAL REGULAR TYPICAL USITATE EVERYDAY FREQUENT HABITUAL ORDINARY ORTHODOX ACCUSTOMED
(NOT —) EXTRAORDINARY
USURER SHARK GAVELER HARPAGON
USURP ASSUME INVADE PRESUME ACCROACH ARROGATE
USURY GAVEL OCKER USURE USANCE GOMBEEN

UTAH
CAPITAL: SALTLAKECITY
COLLEGE: WEBER
COUNTY: IRON JUAB CACHE PIUTE CARBON SEVIER TOOELE UINTAH SANPETE
EARLY NAME: DESERET
INDIAN: UTE
LAKE: SALT SWAN SEVIER
MOTTO: INDUSTRY
MOUNTAIN: LENA LION WAAS KINGS PEALE TRAIL FRISCO NAVAJO SWASEY GRANITE GRIFFIN HAWKINS PENNELL LINNAEUS
MOUNTAIN RANGE: CEDAR HENRY HOGUP UINTA WAHWAH TERRACE WASATCH CONFUSION
NATIONAL PARK: ZION
NICKNAME: MORMON BEEHIVE
RIVER: UINTA WEBER JORDAN SEVIER
STATE BIRD: SEAGULL
STATE FLOWER: SEGOLILY
STATE TREE: SPRUCE
TOWN: LOA MOAB OREM DELTA HEBER KANAB LOGAN MAGNA MANTI NEPHI OGDEN PRICE PROVO KEARNS TOOELE VERNAL BRIGHAM BOUNTIFUL COALVILLE

UTENSIL (ALSO SEE IMPLEMENT AND TOOL) HOD BOAT IRON MOLD PECK STEW BAKER FRIER FRYER GRILL KNIFE MOULD RICER SCOOP SHEET SHELL SIEVE SLICE ULLER BEATER BEETLE BREWER COOKER DABBER FUNNEL GRATER GRILLE KETTLE LINGEL MASKER POPPER PUSHER SHAKER SIFTER BRAZIER BROILER DUSTPAN FLIPPER GLUEPOT MUDDLER SCUMMER SKIMMER STEAMER STIRRER TOASTER CALABASH GRIDIRON SAUCEPAN SAUCEPOT SHREDDER SPOUCHER STRAINER
(— FOR COVERING FIRE) CURFEW
(COOKING —) WOK
(LITURGICAL —) ASTERISK
(SHIP-SHAPED —) NEF
(PL.) BATTERY COOKWARE IRONWARE
UTERUS WOMB BELLY METRA MATRIX BEARING
(EXAMINATION OF —) FETOSCOPY
(PREF.) METR(O)
UTHAI (FATHER OF —) BIGVAI AMMIHUD
UTHER (WIFE OF —) IGRAINE
UTILITARIAN USEFUL ECONOMIC
UTILITY USE AVAIL USAGE PROFIT BENEFIT SERVICE
UTILIZE USE EMPLOY ENLIST CONSUME EXPLOIT HARNESS HUSBAND
UTILIZING
(SUFF.) IC(AL)
UTMOST END NTH BEST LAST MOST FINAL EXTREME OUTMOST SUPREME DAMNDEST POSSIBLE UTTEREST
UTOPIA ZION
UTOPIAN IDEAL
UTOPIANISM FUTURISM
UTRAQUIST CALIXTIN
UTRICULUS ALVEUS
UTTER ASK OUT SAY BARK BLOW BOOM DEAD DRIB EMIT FAIR GASP GIVE HURL MAIN MOOT MOVE PASS PURE RANK SEND TELL VENT VERY BLACK COUGH CRUDE FETCH FRAME FRANK GROSS ISSUE MOUTH PLAIN RAISE SHEER SLING SOUND SPEAK SPELL STARK THICK TOTAL VOICE ACCENT ARRANT BROACH DAMNED DIRECT ENTIRE INTONE PARLEY PROFER PROPER TONGUE BLUSTER BREATHE DELIVER ENOUNCE EXCLAIM EXPRESS OUTMOST OUTTELL PERFECT PHONATE PROLATE UPBRAID ABSOLUTE BLINKING COMPLETE CRASHING INTONATE PRONOUNCE BLITHERING PEREMPTORY
(— ABRUPTLY) BLURT
(— AFFECTEDLY) KNAP MINCE
(— ARGUMENTS) BLAZE
(— CASUALLY) DROP
(— EXPLOSIVELY) BOLT
(— FALSEHOODS) FABLE
(— FOOLISHLY) BLABBER
(— GLIBLY) SCREED
(— HALTINGLY) BLUBBER
(— HURRIEDLY) CHOP
(— INADVERTENTLY) SLIP
(— INDISTINCTLY) CHEW
(— IN HARSH VOICE) GRIT GRATE
(— LOUD CRY) BRAY BLARE
(— LOUDLY) CRY BLAT CALL HALLO HALLOO HULLOO PRABBLE
(— LOW SOUNDS) MURMUR WHISPER
(— MEANINGLESS SOUNDS) BABBLE
(— RAPIDLY) FIRE CHATTER
(— RAUCOUSLY) BLAT
(— REPETITIVELY) CHIME
(— RHETORICALLY) DECLAIM
(— RUTTING CALL OF THE ELK) BUGLE
(— SOLEMNLY) SWEAR
(— STUPIDLY) BLUNDER
(— SUDDENLY) CRACK
(— UNCTUOUSLY) DROOL
(— VIGOROUSLY) FLING
(— WITH EFFORT) HEAVE
UTTERANCE CRY GAB CALL OSSE BLURT DITTY PAROL VOICE ACCENT ACTION BREATH CHORUS DRIVEL GIBBER ORACLE PAROLE TONGUE EXPRESS INKLING LALLING STATUTE DELIVERY FOOTNOTE HOMESPUN JUDGMENT LOCUTION SYLLABIC

(— **FROM A DIVINITY)** ORACLE
(— **OF JESUS)** AGRAPHON
(— **OF LOVE)** ENDEARMENT
(— **OF PRAISE)** MAGNIFICAT
(— **OF VOCAL SOUNDS)** PHONESIS
(CONDEMNATORY —) INFAMY
(DEFECTIVE —) STAMMER
(ECSTATIC —) RHAPSODY
(EMPTY —) NOTHING
(FACETIOUS —) PLEASANTRY
(FAINT —) INKLING
(FLUENT —) OUTPOURING
(FOOLISH —) DRIVEL
(FOOLISH —S) GUFF
(GUSHING —) EFFUSION
(HABITUAL —) SONG
(IMPULSIVE —) BLURT
(INDISTINCT —) BUMBLE BUMMLE MUTTER
(INSIPID —) INANITY
(INSPIRED —) PROPHECY
(MALICIOUS —) SLANDER
(MOMENTOUS —) MOUTHFUL
(OFFENSIVE —) AFFRONT
(PROPHETIC —) OSSE
(PUBLIC —) AIR OUTGIVING
(SHORT —) DITTY
(SOLEMN —) EFFATE EFFATUM
(TRADITIONAL —) AGRAPHON
(UNVARIED —) MONOTONE
(VAPID —) CUCKOO
(VIOLENT —) INVECTIVE
(WISE —) ORACLE
(PL.) BYRONICS

UTTERED ORAL SPOKEN
(BOLDLY —) OUTSPOKEN
(INDISTINCTLY —) INARTICULATE

UTTERLY DOG BONE DEAD BLACK OUTLY PLUMB PROOF HOLLOW MERELY BLANKLY OUTERLY SHEERLY PROPERLY

UTU (FATHER OF —) NANNA

UVULA CION UVULE PLECTRUM STAPHYLE
(PREF.) CION(O) STAPHYL(O)

UVULARIA OAKESIA

UZ (FATHER OF —) ARAM NAHOR DISHAN
(GRANDFATHER OF —) SEIR SHEM

UZAI (SON OF —) PALAL

UZAL (FATHER OF —) JOKTAN

UZBEK JAGATAI

UZBEKISTAN (ALSO SEE RUSSIA)
AUTONOMOUS REPUBLIC: KARAKALPAK KARAKALPAKSTAN
CAPITAL: TASHKENT TOSHKENT
COIN: RUBLE
DESERT: KYZYLKUM QIZILQUM MIRZACHOL
MOUNTAIN: BESHTOR
MOUNTAIN RANGE: ALAY UGAM PSKEM GISSAR HISSAR KURAMA CHATKAL NURATAU MALGUZAR TIENSHAN TURKESTAN KARZHANTAU
NAME: UZBEK
PLAIN: TURAN
RIVER: OXUS NARYN AMUDARYA KARADARYA ZERAVSHAN KASHKADARYA SURKHANDARYA SHERABADDARYA
SEA: ARAL
TOWN: KHIVA NAVOI NUKUS QOQAN ANGREN KOKAND BEKABAD BUKHARA ANDIZHAN CHIRCHIK GULISTAN NAMANGAN YANGIYER YANGIYUL SAMARKAND
VALLEY: FERGANA ZERAVSHAN

UZZAH (BROTHER OF —) AHIO
(FATHER OF —) ABINADAB

UZZI (FATHER OF —) BANI BELA TOLA BUKKI
(SON OF —) ZERAHIAH

UZZIAH (FATHER OF —) AMAZIAH
(SON OF —) ATHAIAH JEHONATHAN

UZZIEL (FATHER OF —) ISHI KOHATH HARHAIAH
(SON OF —) ZITHRI MISHAEL ELIZAPHAN

V

V VEE FIVE VICTOR
(INVERTED —) CARET
VACANCY HOLE WANT VACUIT VACUITY VACATION
(— IN ENERGY BAND) HOLE
VACANT IDLE OPEN VOID BLANK EMPTY FISHY INANE WASTE DEVOID HOLLOW DORMANT UNFILLED
(BECOME —) FALL
(PREF.) VACUO
VACATE QUIT TOLL VOID AVOID EMPTY WAIVE VACANT ABANDON RESCIND ABROGATE EVACUATE
VACATION OUT HOLS REST LEAVE OUTING RECESS HOLIDAY NONTERM VACANCY
(SUMMER —) LONG
VACCFINE (KIND OF —) SALK
VACCINE LYMPH BACTERIN BIOLOGIC
(KIND OF —) ORAL
VACCINIA COWPOX
VACILLATE HALT SWAG WAVE WAVER DACKER DITHER HALPER SEESAW TEETER WABBLE WAFFLE WOBBLE SHAFFLE STICKLE SWITHER WHIFFLE HESITATE
VACILLATING INFIRM MOBILE HALTING
VACILLATION SEESAW WAVERING
VACUITY BLOW VACANCY FONTANEL NOTHINGNESS
(MENTAL —) INANITY
VACUOLE GUTTA
VACUOUS DULL BLANK EMPTY SILLY VACANT
VACUUM GAPE VOID HOOVER VACANCY VACUITY VACATION
VACUUM TUBE
(SUFF.) TRON
VAGABOND BUM VAG HOBO KERN JAVEL ROGUE SHACK STIFF BRIBER CANTER HARLOT JOCKEY PICARA PICARO RODNEY RUNNER TAGRAG TRUANT WAFFIE COASTER ERRATIC FAITOUR GADLING GANGREL OUTCAST SCOURER SKELDER SWAGMAN SWINGER TINKLER TRUCKER VAGRANT VAURIEN WASTREL BOHEMIAN BRODYAGA CURSITOR CUSTROUN FUGITIVE GLASSMAN PALLIARD RAPPAREE RUNABOUT RUNAGATE WHIPJACK
VAGARY WHIM FANCY FREAK VAGUE CAPRICE CONCEIT CRANKUM FLAGARIE VAGRANCY
(PL.) HUMORS
VAGINA
(PREF.) COLP(O) ELYTR(O)
VAGINATE SHEATHED
VAGRANCY MOPERY ROGUING NOMADISM
VAGRANT BUM HOBO WAFF WAIF CAIRD PIKER PIKEY ROGUE SKELB STRAG TRAMP VAGUE ARRANT CASUAL SHAKER SHULER TINKER TRUANT VAGROM VAGUER WAFFIE DEVIOUS DRIFTER ERRATIC FLOATER GANGREL ROGUISH SKILDER SWAGMAN TINKLER TRAMPER TROGGER BRODYAGA PLANETIC STROLLER VAGABOND SHACKLING
(PL.) FLOTSAM
VAGUE LAX DARK HAZY FOGGY FUZZY GROSS LOOSE MISTY MUDDY WOOZY CLOUDY DREAMY MYSTIC SHAGGY BLURRED EVASIVE OBSCURE SHADOWY UNFIXED CONFUSED INFINITE NEBULOUS NUBILOUS
VAGUELY DIMLY DARKLY DUMBLY DREAMILY
VAIN MAD IDLE NULL PUFF VOID WANE COCKY EMPTY FLORY PROUD SAUCY VOGIE WASTE FLIMSY FUTILE HOLLOW OTIOSE VAUNTY BIGGITY CARRIED TRIVIAL USELESS VAINFUL BOOTLESS CONCEITY NUGATORY PEACOCKY VAPOROUS WASTEFUL
(NOT —) SOLID
VAINGLORY POMP RUFF GLORY VANITY ELATION
VAINLY IDLY TOOMLY
VAIR POTENT
VAISRAVANA BISHAMON
VAISYA BAIS BICE
VAJEZATHA (FATHER OF —) HAMAN
VAJRA DORJE
VAKULA THE SMITH (CHARACTER IN —) CHUB DEVIL OXANA PANAS VAKULA SOLOKHA
(COMPOSER OF —) TCHAIKOVSKY
VAL LACE
VALANCE PAND PELMET FRONTLET PALMETTE
VALE DALE DEAN DELL BACHE BATCH ENNIS DINGLE
VALEDICTORY FAREWELL
VALENCE ADICITY ATOMISM
VALENTINE (SISTER OF —) GRETCHEN
(SLAYER OF —) FAUST
VALERIAN HELIO BENNET SUMBUL ALLHEAL CUTHEAL SETWALL CETEWALE
VALERIC PENTOIC
VALET MAN ANDREW JEEVES SIRDAR TARTAR WALLIE CRISPIN TIREMAN
VALIANT SAD BOLD BRAG PREU PROW WILD BRAVE LUSTY ORPED PROUD STOUT WIGHT FIERCE HEROIC DOUGHTY GAILLARD GALLIARD INTREPID STALWART VIRTUOUS
(SON OF PRINCE —) ARN
(WIFE OF PRINCE —) ALETA
VALID FAIR GOOD JUST LEGAL SOUND COGENT LAWFUL BINDING ETERNAL WEIGHTY FORCIBLE VAILABLE VALIDOUS VALUABLE
(PREF.) RATI
VALIDATE FIRM SEAL VALID AFFIRM CONFIRM
VALIDATION PROOF
VALIDITY FORCE VIGOR STRENGTH
VALISE BAG GRIP MAIL DORLACH SATCHEL VALLIES SUITCASE
VALKYRIE BRYNHILD SHIELDMAY
VALLECULA VALLEY
VALLEY DIB GUT COMB COOM COVE DALE DELL DENE GILL HOLE HOPE HOWE HOYA PARK VALE WADI WADY ATRIO BACHE BREAK CHASM COMBE COOMB DHOON GHYLL GLACK GOYAL GOYLE HEUGH SLACK SLADE SWALE TEMPE YUNGA BOLSON BOTTOM CANADA CLOUGH COULEE DINGLE HOLLOW LAAGTE LEEGTE RINCON STRATH AIJALON BLOWOUT GEHENNA VAALITE
(— BETWEEN CONES OF VOLCANO) ATRIO
(— IN OCEAN) DEEP
(— IN THESSALY) TEMPE
(— ON MOON'S SURFACE) RILL CLEFT RILLE
(— ON MT BLANC) NANT
(BROAD —) STRATH
(CIRCULAR —) RINCON
(DEEP —) CANON GRIKE CANYON
(DROWNED —) RIA VIA
(FLAT-FLOORED DESERT —) BOLSON
(GRASSY MOUNTAIN —) HOLE
(LOWEST PART OF —) SOLE
(MINIATURE —) GULLY GULLEY
(NARROW —) DEAN DENE GLEN GLACK GOYLE GRIFF KLOOF CLOUGH
(RIFT —) GRABEN
(RIVER —) WATER
(SECLUDED —) GLEN DINGLE
(TRENCHLIKE —) COULEE
VALOR ARETE MERIT VALUE BOUNTY VALOUR BRAVERY COURAGE HEROISM PROWESS STOMACH CHIVALRY VALIANCY
VALOROUS BOLD BRAVE VIRTUOUS
VALUABLE DEAR COSTLY PRIZED WORTHY EMINENT WEALTHY PRECIOUS PRIZABLE SINGULAR
VALUATION PRIZE VALOR VALUE ESTEEM EXTENT ESTIMATE TAXATION
VALUE SET COST FECK FOOT HOLD RATE TELL AVAIL CARAT CHEAP COUNT FORCE PRICE PRIZE STAMP STENT STOCK VALOR WORTH ASSESS ASSIZE EQUITY ESTEEM EXTENT FIGURE HIDAGE MATTER MOMENT PRAISE REGARD VALURE VALUTA VIRTUE ACCOUNT ADVANCE APPRIZE CAPITAL CHERISH COMPUTE PRETIUM RESPECT VALENCY WERGILD ESTIMATE EVALUATE GOODWILL SPLENDOR TREASURE VALIDITY VALLIDOM
(— HIGHLY) PRIZE ENDEAR
(— OF ANGLE) EPOCH
(— OF COW) SET
(— OF STOCKS) OMNIUM
(— OF TIMBER) STUMPAGE
(— WRONGLY) MISRATE
(ABSOLUTE —) MODULUS
(AESTHETIC —) AMENITY
(ANNUAL —) RENTAL
(ESTABLISHED —) PAR
(GOOD —) SNIP
(HIGH —) ESTEEM
(LOWEST —) MINIMUM
(MATHEMATICAL —) EXTREMUM
(MIDDLE —) MEDIAN
(NEGATIVE —) DISVALUE
(OF NO —) IMMOMENT
(SOUND —) POWER
(STUDY OF —) AXIOLOGY
(TESTED —) ASSAY
(PREF.) AXIO TIMO
VALUED DEAR
VALUELESS BAFF STRAWY NAUGHTY
VALVE TAP COCK DISC DISK GATE ORAL STOP CHOKE CLACK MIXER VALVA WAFER BINODE BOTTLE CUTOUT DAMPER KICKER PALLET POPPET POTLID SCUTUM SLUICE SUCKER VENTIL WASHER CLICKET DRAWOFF PETCOCK REDUCER SCALLOP SCOLLOP SHUTOFF VALVULA VALVULE DRAWGATE EPITHECA EPIVALVE STOPCOCK THROTTLE
(— OF BARNACLE) SCUTUM
(— OF MUSICAL INSTRUMENT) PISTON VENTIL
(— OF PUMP BOX) FANG
(ANATOMICAL —) TRICUSPID
(ELECTRODE —) TRIODE
(THERMIONIC —) TUBE
(THIN —) WAFER
(TRIPLE —) KICKER
(PREF.) THYRE(O) THYRO
(SUFF.) THYRIS
VAMBRACE BRACELET

VAMOOSE SCAT SCRAM CHEESE DECAMP SKIDDOO
VAMPIRE LAMIA ALUKAH
VAN WAN FORE LEAD SAIL FRONT TRUCK VAUNT WAGON VAWARD CARAVAN FOURGON FOREWARD KHALDIAN
(LUGGAGE —) FREIGHTCAR
(TAKE THE —) LEAD
VANADATE UVANITE TURANITE
VANDAL HUN HUNLIKE SARACEN HOOLIGAN
VANDALIZE MAR TRASH DAMAGE DEFACE RAVAGE
VANE FAN TEE WEB COCK TAIL WING FAINE BUCKET TARGET DOGVANE FLIGHTER VEXILLUM
(— OF ARROW) FEATHER
(— OF CONVEYOR BELT) FLIGHT
(— OF FEATHER) WEB FLUE VEXILLUM
(— OF SURVEYING STAFF) TRANSOM
(— OF WINDMILL) FAN FANE TAIL FAINE
(COOLING — IN BREWING) FLIGHTER
VANESSA PYRAMEIS
VANGUARD LEAD FORLORN
VANIAH (FATHER OF —) BANI
VANILLA PLAIN ORDINARY
VANISH DIE FLY DROP FADE FLEE MELT PASS SANT WEDE WEND CLEAR FLEET SAUNT SLIDE EXHALE EVANISH SCATTER CONQUEST DISSOLVE EVANESCE
(— BY DEGREES) DRILL
VANISHED LAPSED EXTINCT
VANITY ABEL POMP VAIN FOLLY PRIDE EGOISM CONCEIT FEATHER FOPPERY INANITY SANDUST IDLENESS IDLESHIP PRETENSION
VANITY FAIR (AUTHOR OF —) THACKERAY
(CHARACTER IN —) JOS PITT BECKY SHARP AMELIA DOBBIN GEORGE JOSEPH RAWDON SEDLEY STEYNE CRAWLEY OSBORNE WILLIAM
VANNER SLIMER
VANNIC KHALDIAN
VANQUISH GET WIN BEAT LICK MILL CREAM PASTE UTTER EXPUGN MASTER OUTRAY SUBDUE THRASH CONQUER OVERWIN SHELLAC SMOTHER CONQUEST OVERCOME SURMOUNT VENKISEN
VANQUISHED CRAVEN
VANUATU (CAPITAL OF —) VILA
(FORMER NAME OF —) NEWHEBRIDES
(ISLAND OF —) EPI EFATE MALEKULA PENTECOST ESPIRITUSANTO
(MONEY OF —) VATU
(VOLCANO OF —) TANNA AMBRYN LOPEVI
VAPID DRY DULL FADE FLAT STALE TRITE JEJUNE INSIPID WATERISH
VAPOR FOG FUME REEK ROKE STEW BOAST BRUME EWDER HUMOR SMOKE STEAM STIFE BREATH VAPOUR EXHAUST HALITUS
(FROZEN —) SNOW
(HOT —) LUNT
(NOXIOUS —) DAMP
(PETROL —) JUICE
(PL.) BRUME
(PREF.) ATM(O) ATMID(O) MANO PNEUMAT(O) TYPH(O)
VAPORIZATION BURNUP BOILOFF
VAPORIZE DRIVE FLASH STEAM AERATE AERIFY VAPORATE
VAPOROUS FUMY FUMID HUMID FUMISH FUMOSE STEAMY VOLATILE
VARANGIAN VARIAG WARING
(PL.) ROS
VARGUENO DESK
VARIABILITY HETERISM
VARIABLE FLUX FREE CHOPPY FICKLE FITFUL KITTLE WRAIST CEPHEID FACIENT FLUXILE MUTABLE ROLLING STREAKY UNEQUAL VARIANT VARIOUS ARGUMENT FLOATING FLUXIBLE SHIFTING SKITTISH UNSTABLE VEERABLE
(EXCEEDINGLY —) PROTEAN
(MATHEMATICAL —) FUNCTION
(RANDOM —) STATISTIC
VARIANCE ODDS DISCORD DISPUTE DISCREPANCY
(ANALYSIS OF —) ANOVA
VARIANT STATE VERSION
(— IN WHEAT) SPELTOID
(POSITIONAL —) ALLOPHONE
(SOUND —) ALTERNANT
(PL.) DIAPHONE
VARIATION REX TURN ERROR ROGUE SHADE CHANGE DOUBLE JITTER SWITCH CYCLING DESCANT EXTREME SHADING VARIETY WINDING DIVISION DYNAMICS HETERISM MUTATION
(— IN AIR PRESSURE) ROBBING
(— IN CURRENT) SURGE
(— IN FREQUENCY) SWINGING
(— IN SPEED) HUNTING
(— OF COLOR) ABRASH
(— OF PUPIL OF EYE) HIPPUS
(— OF SHOE) SPRING
(— OF VOWELS) ABLAUT
(ALLOWABLE —) LEEWAY
(BALLET —) ATTITUDE
(TOPOGRAPHICAL —) BREAK
(PL.) PIBROCH
VARICOCELE RAMEX
VARIED SORTY DAEDAL SEVERAL VARIANT VARIOUS MANIFOLD
VARIED BUNTING PRUSIANO
VARIEGATE DROP FRET FLECK FREAK SHOOT AUMAIL DAPPLE STRIPE VARIFY CHECKER
VARIEGATED FAW PIED SHOT JASPE LYART PANED SHELD DAEDAL MARLED MENALD MOSAIC MOTLEY SKEWED VEINED BROCKED BROCKIT CHECKED CLOUDED DAPPLED FREAKED FRETTED PECKLED SPARKED VARIOUS DISCOLOR FRECKLED OVERSHOT PANACHED SKEWBALD
(— AS GLASS BEADS) AGGRI AGGRY
(NOT —) UNBROKEN
(PREF.) POECIL(O)
VARIEGATION COLOR
VARIETY BREW FORM KIND MODE SORT BRAND BREED CLASS COLOR SPICE CHANGE FLAVOR NATURE STIRPS STRAIN STRIPE SPECIES VARIENS
(— OF COLOR) SHADE
(PERMANENT —) STIRPS
VARIOLA HORSEPOX SMALLPOX
VARIOUS MANY SERE DIVERS SUNDER SUNDRY VARIED DIVERSE SEVERAL VARIANT MANIFOLD MULTIPLE
(PREF.) PARTI POECIL(O) POEKIL(O)
VARISCITE UTAHITE
VARIX
(PREF.) CIRS(O)
VARLET BOY CAD LAD GIPPO JIPPO PAVISER COISTREL VARLETTO
VARNISH DOPE JAPAN LACKER MEDIUM PUNDUM FIXATIF LACQUER VEHICLE VERMEIL FIXATIVE OVERGILD THEETSEE
(— INGREDIENT) ALOE COPAL ROSIN MASTIC
VARY HUNT ALTER BREAK DRIFT SHIFT SPORT CHANGE DIFFER RECEDE VARIFY CHECKER DEVIATE DISSENT DIVERGE VARIATE DISAGREE OSCILLATE
(— PITCH) MODULATE
VARYING CURRENT
VASE PYX URN OLLA VASA VASO ASKOS CYLIX DINOS DIOTA KYLIX PYXIS BASKET BOWPOT COTULA COTYLA CRATER DEINOS DOLIUM FILLER HYDRIA KALPIS KOTYLE KRATER LEKANE SITULA AMPHORA AMPULLA CANOPUS PATELLA POTICHE PSYKTER SCYPHUS SKYPHOS STAMNOS URCEOLE BOUGHPOT LECYTHUS LEKYTHOS MURRHINE PROCHOOS
(— FOR PERFUME) CONCH
(— ON PEDESTAL) TAZZA
(—S UNDER THEATER SEATS) SCHEA
(PREF.) POTICHO VAS(I)(O) VASCUL(I)(O)
VASHNI (FATHER OF —) SAMUEL
VASHTI (HUSBAND OF —) AHASUERUS
VASODILATOR KELLIN KHELLIN MINOXIDIL
VASSAL MAN WER BOND LEUD SERF CEILE LIEGE SLAVE CLIENT GENEAT SACOPE BONDMAN FEEDMAN FEODARY HOMAGER RUDIGER SAMURAI SERVANT SUBJECT VAVASOR PALATINE
(PL.) MANRED
VASSALAGE MANRENT
VAST HUGE BROAD ENORM GREAT LARGE STOUR VASTY COSMIC IMMANE MIGHTY UNTOLD ABYSMAL IMMENSE OCEANIC VASTITY ENORMOUS INFINITE MOUNTAIN SPACIOUS
VASTNESS IMMANE GRANDEUR WIDENESS
VAT ARK BAC DIP FAT PIT TAP TUN BACK BECK COOM FATE GAAL GAIL GYLE KEEL KIER TINE APRON COOMB FETTE FLOAT KEEVE KIEVE ROUND STAND STEEP KIMNEL MOTHER BLUNGER DRAINER GRAINER KEELVAT STEEPER PRESSFAT
(— USED IN MEASURING SLIPS) ARK
(BLEACHING —) KEIR KIER
(BREWER'S —) BACK FLOAT KEEVE UNION CUMMING
(CHEESE —) CHESSEL CHESSET CHESSART
(COOLING —) KELDER
(DYER'S —) JIG LEAD DYEBECK
(EVAPORATING —) APRON GRAINER
(FERMENTING —) TUN COMB COOM GYLE KEEL COOMB FLOAT
(TANNER'S —) TAP HANGER SPENDER
(TEXTILE —) KIER
(WINE —) LAKE CUVEE
(PREF.) PYEL(O)
VATICAN CITY (BASILICA OF —) STPETERS
(WALL OF —) LEONINE
VAU DIGAMMA
VAUDEVILLE ZARZUELA
VAULT BOUT COPE JUMP LEAP PEND SKIP TOMB VOLT WOWT AZURE CROFT CRYPT EMBOW VOLTO CELLAR CUPOLA FORNIX SHROUD CONCAVE DUNGEON TESTUDO VALTAGE CATACOMB LEAPFROG MONUMENT
(— IN CEILING) LACUNAR
(— OF HEAVEN) WELKIN
(— OF SKY) CONVEX ZENITH CONCAVE
(PART OF —) PENDENTIVE
VAULTED CONCAVE CRYPTED EMBOWED
VAULTER VOLTIGEUR
VAULTING POMADA POMMADO
VAUNT GAB BRAG BOAST ROOSE VOUST AVAUNT INSULT BLUSTER GLORIFY FLOURISH
(— ONESELF) WIND
VAUNTMURE MANURE
VCR (— BUTTON) RESET
VEAL VEAU SLINK FRICANDO
(— SCALLOPS) SALTIMBOCCA
(LIKE —) VITULINE
(PIECE OF —) PAILLARD
(SCALLOPS OF —) SALTIMBOCCA
(SLICES OF —) SCALLOPINI
VECTOR I K PHASOR GRADIENT
VEDA SHASTER
VEDDOID PANYAN
VEDIC (— PRINCIPLE) RTA RITA
VEER CUT DIP FLY YAW CAST CHOP SLEW SLUE SWAY TACK WYRE FETCH SHIFT SWOOP BROACH CHANGE SLOUGH SWERVE TUMBLE BOXHAUL DEVIATE WHIFFLE
VEERING DRIFT CHOPPY
VEGA (CONSTELLATION OF —) LYRA
VEGETABLE PEA YAM BEAN BEET CORN KALE LEEK OKRA CHARD GRASS ONION SABZI SALAD VEGIE CARROT CELERY LEGUME LENTIL

POTATO RADISH SQUASH TOMATO TOPEPO TURNIP VEGGIE BLOATER CABBAGE CELTUCE LETTUCE PARSNIP PEASCOD RHUBARB SPINACH VEGETAL BROCCOLI EGGPLANT RUTABAGA
(— MATTER) SUDD
(—S FOR MARKET) TRUCK
(EARLY —) PRIMEUR
(EARLY —S) HASTINGS
(GARDEN —S) SASS SAUCE
(HYBRID —) GARLION
(RAW —S) CRUDITES
(PL.) CRUDITES
(PREF.) PHYT(I)(O)
VEGETARIAN VEGAN VEGIE VEGGIE
VEGETATION HERB COVER GREEN SCRUB GROWTH HERBAGE COVERAGE PLANTAGE PLEUSTON SMELLAGE
(DECOMPOSED —) STAPLE
(SCRUB —) BRUSH
(UNWANTED —) FILTH
(PREF.) PHYT(I)(O)
VEGETATIVE ASEXUAL PLANTAL
VEHEMENCE FURY GLOW HEAT RAGE WARMTH STRENGTH VIOLENCE
VEHEMENT HOT HIGH KEEN LOUD ANGRY EAGER FIERY HEFTY YEDER ARDENT BITTER FERVID FIERCE FLASHY HEARTY HEATED RAGING STRONG ANIMOSE ANIMOUS FURIOSO INTENSE JEALOUS VIOLENT
VEHEMENTLY AMAIN PELLMELL
VEHICLE BUS CAB CAR FLY VAN ARBA AUTO CART DUKE FLAT GOER JEEP LIMO SLED TAXI TEAM WAIN ARABA BRAKE BREAK BUGGY CARRY DILLY FLAIL GUIDE HANSA NODDY ROVER STAGE WAGON BLADER CAMPER CHARET CISIUM DIESEL HEARSE JITNEY MEDIUM RANDEM SLEDGE SLEIGH SURREY TRISHA TROIKA CARRIER CHARIOT CRUISER HOTSHOT ICEBOAT KIBITKA MACHINE MINIBUS OMNIBUS PEDICAB PEDRAIL SHEBANG SHUTTLE SPEEDER SPRAYER STEAMER STEERER TARTANA TAXICAB TRAVOIS TRISHAW TURNOUT UTILITY AUTORAIL AUTOSLED CARRIAGE CHARETTE CYCLECAR DEADHEAD DELIVERY ELECTRIC FILMOGEN SHOWCASE SOCIABLE UNICYCLE AEROTRAIN SPACESHIP LOCOMOBILE MOTORCYCLE SNOWMOBILE SPACECRAFT
(— DRAWN BY BULLOCK) EKKA
(— FOR COLORS) MEGILP
(— FOR HAULING) TRACTOR
(— FOR SAND USE) DUNEBUGGY
(— IN FINE CONDITION) CREAMPUFF
(— ON RUNNERS) SLED CARRO SLEDGE SLEIGH ICEBOAT AUTOSLED
(— ON SINGLE RAIL) AEROTRAIN
(— PULLED BY MAN) BROUETTE RICKSHAW
(— RUNNING ON RAILS) LORRY TRAIN
(— WITH RUNNERS) SKIBOB
(— WITH 3 HORSES ABREAST) TROIKA
(— WITH 3 HORSES BEHIND EACH OTHER) RANDEM
(AIR-CUSHION —) HOVERCRAFT
(AIRPORT —) SKYLOUNGE
(AMMUNITION —) CAISSON
(AMPHIBIOUS —) BUFFALO
(ARCTIC —) SNOCAT
(AWKWARD —) ARK
(CHILD'S —) PRAM WALKER SCOOTER STROLLER
(COVERED —) SEDAN LANDAU CARAVAN KIBITKA
(DRAG-RACING —) RAIL
(EARTH-MOVING —) SCOOP
(KIND OF —) LAUNCH
(LITTLE —) HINAYANA
(LUMBERING —) TUG TODE
(MILITARY —) WEASEL AMTRACK
(MOON —) LEM
(MOTOR —) WHEELS
(OBSOLETE —) CRATE
(ONE-WHEELED —) BARROW
(OPERATE MOTOR —) VROOM
(POOR-QUALITY —) DOG SHANDRYPAN
(RIVER —) HOVERCRAFT
(RUDE —) KIBITKA
(RUSSIAN —) TARANTAS TARANTASS
(SATELLITE —) SLV
(SLEDGE-LIKE —) GAMBO
(SNOW —) SKIBOB
(SPACE —) LEM LANDER
(THREE-WHEELED —) PEDICAB
(WHEELLESS —) DRAY
(2-WHEELED —) GIG CART SULKY TONGA CISIUM JINGLE LIMBER BICYCLE CALECHE CROYDON RICKSHAW
(PL.) PARK
(SUFF.) MOBILE
VEIL WRY FALL FILM HIDE MASK WRAP COVER GLOSS RUMAL SCARF SCENE SHADE VELUM VIMPA VOLET WREIL BUMBLE CHRISM FAILLE SHADOW SHROUD VEILER WEEPER WIMPLE CORTINA CURTAIN ENDOTYS PARANJA VEILING CALYPTRA ENDOTHYS HEADRAIL KALYPTRA MAHARMAH MANTILLA TELEBLEM
(— IN CHURCH) AER ENDOTYS ENDOTHYS
(— OF MUSLIM WOMEN) YASHMAK
(— ON FUNGI) CORTINA
(— OVER HELMET) LAMBREQUIN
(BIRTH —) CAUL
(DOUBLE —) YASHMAK
(HUMERAL —) SUDARY
(WIDOW'S —) WEEPER
VEILED COVERT LATENT VELATED SHROUDED
VEILING PURDAH GOSSAMER
VEIN BAR LOB RIB CAVA LODE MOOD RAKE REEF VENA AMPER CLOUD COMES COSTA LEDGE MEDIA NERVE RIDER SCRIN VARIX LEADER MEDIAL STRAIN STREAK VENULA VENULE AXILLAR AZYGOUS CUBITAL DROPPER JUGULAR NERVURE PRECAVA PRESTER SAPHENA VEINLET AXILLARY EMULGENT PREMEDIA PROFUNDA SUBCOSTA
(— IN MARBLE) CLOUD
(— OF LEAF) RIB COSTA MIDRIB
(— OF MINERAL) STREAK STRINGER
(— OF ORE) LODE ROKE BUNCH LEDGE RIDER SCRIN LEADER STRING DROPPER UNDERSET
(— OF WING) CUBIT RADIUS CUBITAL CUBITUS SUBCOSTA SUBCOSTAL
(—S OF LEAF) SKELETON
(GRANITIC —) ELVAN
(QUARTZ —) SADDLE
(VARICOSE —) AMPER
(PREF.) CIRS(O) PHLEB(O) PYL(E)(O) VENI VENO
(SWOLLEN —) CIRS(O)
VEINED MARBLED NERVOSE
VELA SAILS
VELAR PALATAL GUTTURAL
VELD BUSHVELD SOURVELD
VELELLA SALLYMAN
VELLEITY DESIRE WOULDING
VELLINCH FLINCHER
VELLUM ORIHON
VELOCIPEDE HOBBY STEED TRICAR BICYCLE DICYCLE RANTOON SPEEDER DRAISINE TRICYCLE
VELOCITY DRIFT CELERITY RAPIDITY STRENGTH
(— OF FLOW) CURRENT
(— OF 1 FOOT PER SECOND) VELO
VELOUR SOLEIL
VELOUTE POULETTE
VELUM VEIL VELAMEN VELARIUM
VELVET PILE PANNE YUZEN BIRODO VELURE FRAYING VELLUTE
VELVETEEN TRIPE
VELVET GRASS FOG
VELVETLEAF DAGGA PAREIRA
VENAL CORRUPT SALABLE BRIBABLE HIRELING SALEABLE VENDIBLE
VEND HAWK SELL UTTER MARKET PEDDLE
VENDA (CAPITAL OF —) THOHOYANDOU
(TOWN OF —) SIBASA MAKWARELA
VENDIBLE VENAL SALABLE SALEABLE
VENDITION SALE
VENDOR FAKER SELLER VENDER ALIENOR BUTCHER HUSTLER PITCHER PURLMAN VIANDER PITCHMAN SAUCEMAN VENDITOR
VENEER BURL BURR JAPAN SHOOK OVERLAY SKILLET
VENEERER DUSTER
VENERABLE OLD AGED HOAR SAGE AWFUL HOARY AUGUST SACRED VETUST ANCIENT VENERAL VINTAGE
(PREF.) SEBASTO
VENERATE FEAR DREAD HALLOW REVERE VENERE RESPECT WORSHIP
VENERATED HOLY SACRED HALLOWED
VENERATION AWE CULT DULIA CULTISM RESPECT DEVOTION
VENESECTION PHLEBOTOMY
VENETIAN RED SIENA SIERRA
VENETIAN SUMAC SCOTINO

VENEZUELA
CAPITAL: CARACAS
COIN: REAL MEDIO FUERTE BOLIVAR CENTIMO MOROCOTA
GULF: PARIA
MEASURE: GALON MILLA FANEGA ESTADEL
MOUNTAIN: PAVA YAVI DUIDA ICUTU CONCHA CUNEVA PARIMA IMUTACA MASAITI RORAIMA
NATIVE: CARIB TIMOTE GUARAUNO
RIVER: META APURE CAURA ARAUCA CARONI CUYUNI GUANARE ORINOCO ORITUCO PARAGUA SUAPURE VICHADA GUAVIARE VENTUARI
STATE: LARA APURE SUCRE ZULIA ARAGUA FALCON MERIDA BOLIVAR COJEDES GUARICO MONAGAS TACHIRA YARACUY CARABOBO TRUJILLO
TOWN: AROA CORO ATURES CUMANA MERIDA BARINAS CABELLO GUAWARE MARACAY MATURIN CARUPANO TACUPITA VALENCIA
WATERFALL: ANGEL CUQUENAN
WEIGHT: BAG LIBRA

VENGEANCE WRACK WREAK WRECK AVENGE ULTION WANION ALASTOR REVENGE VINDICT REQUITAL VINDICTA
VENICE (ISLAND NEAR —) LIDO
VENILIA (HUSBAND OF —) DAUNUS
(SISTER OF —) AMATA
(SON OF —) TURNUS
VENISON BILTONG
VENOM GALL ATTER VIRUS POISON SWELTER CROTALIN CROTALUS
VENOMOUS TOXIC ATTERN DEADLY SNAKEY VENOMY BANEFUL NOXIOUS SMITTLE SNAKISH POISONED VIPERINE VIPEROUS VIRULENT POISONOUS
VENT EMIT HOLE REEK BELCH DRAIN FROTH ISSUE TEWEL OUTAGE OUTLET CHIMNEY EXPRESS OPENING ORIFICE OUTCAST OUTFALL OUTTAKE RELEASE VENTAGE APERTURE BREATHER DIATREME FONTANEL MOFFETTE SESPERAL SPIRACLE SUSPIRAL VENTHOLE VOMITORY
(— IN EARTH'S CRUST) VOLCANO
(VOLCANIC —) BOCCA DIATREME SOLFATARA
VENTILATE AIR WIND AERATE EXPRESS
VENTILATED (BADLY —) STUFFY
VENTILATION AERAGE AIRING
VENTILATOR BADGIR LOUVER FEMERELL
VENTING GUST
VENTRAL BELLY HEMAL STERNAL ANTERIOR INFERIOR

(PREF.) **(— AREA)** GASTER(O) GASTR(I)(O)
VENTRICLE HEART TRICORN DIACOELE
(SUFF.) CELE COELE COELUS
VENTURE HAB RUN SET CAST DARE JUMP KITE LUCK MINT REST RISK WAGE ETTLE FLIER FLYER FROST RISCO SALLY STAKE TEMPT WAGER CHANCE DANGER HAZARD SASHAY FLUTTER IMPERIL JEOPARD PRESUME PRETEND ENDANGER GETPENNY
(— AT DICE) THROW
(— TO SAY) DARESAY
(RISKY —) CRAPSHOOT
VENTURESOME BOLD RASH RISKY DARING PARLOUS TEMEROUS
VENTURESOMELY CHANCILY
VENUS LOVE VESPER LUCIFER HESPERUS PHOSPHOR
(FATHER OF —) JUPITER
(HUSBAND OF —) VULCAN
(MOTHER OF —) DIONE
(SON OF —) AMOR CUPID AENEAS
VENUSIAN VENEREAN
VERACIOUS TRUE VERY TRUTHY SINCERE VERIDIC FAITHFUL TRUTHFUL
VERACITY HSIN TROTH TRUTH VERITY FIDELITY
VERANDA PYAL LANAI PORCH STOEP STOOP PIAZZA BALCONY GALERIE GALLERY
VERB RHEMA ACTIVE NOMINAL PASSIVE DEPONENT VOLITIVE INCEPTIVE INCHOATIVE INDICATIVE INFINITIVE
(AUXILIARY —) BE DO CAN MAY HAVE MUST WILL SHALL
(KIND OF —) ACTIVE PASSIVE PRETERIT TRANSITIVE
(LINKING —) COPULA
VERBAL ORAL WORDY
VERBATIM DIRECT VERBAL LITERAL DIRECTLY
VERBENA ALOYSIA VERVAIN
VERBENALIN CORNIN
VERBIAGE TALK JABBER
VERBOSE WINDY WORDY PROLIX VERBAL DIFFUSE WORDISH
(NOT —) LEAN
VERBOSITY MACROLOGY
VERDANT BOSKY GREEN VIRID
VERDICT WORD VARDI ASSIZE FINDING OPINION DECISION JUDGMENT VEREDICT
VERDIGRIS AERUGO CANKER VERDET
VERDIN GOLDTIT
VERDURE GREENTH GREENERY VIRIDITY
(PREF.) CHLO
VERGE RIM TOP EDGE WAND YARD BRINK POINT TOUCH BORDER TRENCH TRIGGER THRESHOLD
VERGER WANDSMAN
VERGILIAN MARONIAN MARONIST
VERIFICATION AUDIT AVERRAL CHECKUP AVERMENT
VERIFY AVER TRUE AUDIT CHECK PROVE ATTEST RATIFY COLLATE CONFIRM CONTROL JUSTIFY SUPPORT CONSTATE
VERILY YEA AMEN FAITH PARDY CERTES INDEED PARDIE FAITHLY
VERITABLE REAL TRUE VERY ACTUAL HONEST PROPER GENUINE VERIMENT
VERITY TROTH TRUTH REALISM VERIDITY
VERJUICE VARGE
VERMICELLI FEDELINI
VERMICULE VAALITE
VERMICULITE KERRITE MACONITE
VERMIFUGE KOSIN HARMAL HARMEL KAMALA KAMELA KOOSIN COWHAGE HELONIAS PINKROOT WORMWOOD
VERMILION RED GOYA MINIUM MINIATE PAPRIKA PIMENTO VERMEIL ZINOBER CARMETTA CINNABAR TOREADOR
VERMIN FILTH CARRION VARMINT
VERMIS WORM

VERMONT
CAPITAL: MONTPELIER
COLLEGE: BENNINGTON MIDDLEBURY
COUNTY: ESSEX ORANGE ADDISON ORLEANS WINDSOR LAMOILLE
LAKE: CASPIAN DUNMORE SEYMOUR CHAMPLAIN
MOUNTAIN: BROMLEY HOGBACK ASCUTNEY PROSPECT MANSFIELD
MOUNTAIN RANGE: GREEN TACONIC
NICKNAME: GREENMOUNTAIN
PRESIDENT: ARTHUR COOLIDGE
RIVER: SAXTONS LAMOILLE NULHEGAN POULTNEY WINOOSKI
STATE BIRD: THRUSH
STATE FLOWER: CLOVER
STATE TREE: MAPLE
TOWN: BARRE STOWE CHELSEA GRAFTON NEWFANE RUTLAND BENNINGTON BURLINGTON
UNIVERSITY: NORWICH

VERMOUTH CINZANO CHAMBERY
VERNACULAR LINGO COMMON JARGON PATOIS ROMAIC TONGUE VULGAR CHALDEE DIALECT TRIVIAL SCOTTISH
VERNALIZE IAROVIZE JAROVIZE YAROVIZE
VERNE (— CAPTAIN) NEMO
VERNIER NONIUS
VERONICA HEBE SUDARIUM VERNICLE BROOKLIME
VERRUCOSE WARTY WARTED
VERSANT SLOPE
VERSATILE HANDY FICKLE MOBILE FLEXILE
VERSE FIT EPIC LINE POSE RANN RICH RIME SONG BLANK IONIC METER METRE RHYME STAVE STICH TANKA ADONIC ALCAIC BURDEN CHIAVE CYWYDD DIPODY HEROIC JINGLE PANTUN SCAZON STANZA VERSET ANAPEST DICOLON DOGGREL ELEGIAC PAEONIC PANTOUM PENNILL SAPPHIC SAVITRI SOTADIC STICHOS TRIPODY TROILUS CHOLIAMB DACTYLIC DINGDONG DOGGEREL GLYCONIC LEONINES PRIAPEAN RESPONSE SENTENCE SINGSONG TERETISM TRIMETER VERSICLE MACARONIC
(— FORM) VIRELAY KYRIELLE
(— OF FOUR MEASURES) TETRAMETER
(— OF 14 LINES) SONNET
(— OF 2 FEET) DIPODY DIMETER
(— OF 6 FEET) CHOLIAMB SENARIAN SENARIUS
(— WITH LIMPING MOVEMENT) SCAZON
(DEVOTIONAL —) ANTIPHON OFFERTORY
(HINDU —) SLOKA
(JAPANESE —) HAIKU TANKA HAIKAI
(KOREAN — FORM) SIJO
(LINKED —) RENGA
(MEDIEVAL —) SIRVENTE
(NONSENSE —) AMPHIGORY
(NONSENSE —S) AMPHIGORY
(UNMELODIOUS —) TERETISM
(PL.) TRIPOS PINDARICS GALLIAMBICS HUDIBRASTICS
VERSED SEEN WITTY BESEEN TRADED STUDIED FREQUENT OVERSEEN SCIENCED
(WELL —) SKILLFUL
VERSICLE VERSE VERSET STICHOS SUFFRAGE
VERSIFIER BARD POET RHYMER VERSER METERER
VERSIFY METER
VERSION DRAM MODEL DRAUGHT EDITION READING TURNING REDACTION
(SHORT —) BRIEF
(SIMPLIFIED —) KEY
(TRANSLATED —) CONSTRUE
VERSO REVERSE
VERT VERD POMME VENUS PRASINE SINOPLE GREENHEW
VERTEBRA AXIS RACK ATLAS DORSAL LUMBAR SACRAL ACANTHA CENTRUM CERVICAL METAMERE PROATLAS RACKBONE SPONDYLE
(PREF.) ASTRAGAL(O) SPONDYL(O)
(SUFF.) SPONDYLI SPONDYLUS
VERTEBRATA CRANIATA CRANIOTA
VERTEBRATE CRANIATE SAUROPSID
VERTEX APEX COPE NODE POLE CROWN PITCH SUMMIT VERTICAL
VERTICAL APEAK ERECT PLUMB SHEER WHIRL ORTHAL UPRIGHT COLUMNAR SHEERING STRAIGHT
(PREF.) ORTH(O)
VERTICALLY PLUMP ENDLONG SHEERLY DIRECTLY PALEWISE
VERTICIL WHORL
VERTIGINOUS DIZZY
VERTIGO DINUS TIEGO MEGRIM MIRLIGO SWIMMING WHIRLING
VERUMONTANUM COLLICLE
VERVAIN GERVAO FROGFOOT IRONWEED
VERVE PEP BRIO DARE DASH ELAN GUSTO BOUNCE ENERGY PANACHE VITALITY VIVACITY
VERY SO ALL BIG DOG GAY GEY MUY TOO BRAW DEAD FELL FULL JUST MAIN MUCH PURE RARE REAL SAME SEHR SELF SUCH TRES UNCO WELL ASSAI AWFUL BLAME BULLY CRAZY DOOMS JOLLY MOLTO PESKY RIGHT SOWAN SUPER SWITH UNCOW VERRA BITTER BLAMED DAMNED DEUCED FREELY GAINLY LIVING MAINLY MASTER MIGHTY NATION POISON PROPER SORELY STRONG TARNAL THRICE VERRAY WONDER AWFULLY BOILING GALLOWS GREATLY PARLOUS PASSING PRECISE SOPPING STRANGE DEUCEDLY DREADFUL ENORMOUS FAMOUSLY POWERFUL PRECIOUS SPANKING SWINGING WHACKING ABSOLUTELY
(PREF.) ERI MALLO
VESICANT LEWISITE MESEREUM
VESICA PISCIS MANDORLA
VESICATORY BLISTER
VESICLE BLEB CYST APTHA BULLA BURSE FLOAT APHTHA AMPULLA BLADDER BLISTER HYDATID OTOCYST POMPHUS UTRICLE VACUOLE AEROCYST CISTERNA MIDBRAIN VESICULA PHAGOSOME
(SUFF.) YDATIS
VESICULAR BULLOSE BULLOUS
VESPERAL TOWEL
VESPERS LYCHNIC PLACEBO EVENSONG
VESSEL (ALSO SEE BOAT AND SHIP) GO CAN CAT COG CUP FAT GUM HOY KEG NEF PIG POT TUB VAS VAT VIA BARK BOAT BODY BOMB BOOT BOSS BOWL BRIG BUSH BUSS CASK CELL COWL DISH DRIP DUCT GAWN GRAB HORN HULK JACK JUNK KOFF LOTA PINK PINT POST PROW SAIL SHIP SNOW TING YAWL AMULA BAKIE BARGE BASIN BIDET BIKIE BOCAL BOYER CADUS CANNE CHURN COGUE CRACK CRAER CRAFT CRARE CRUET CRUSE DANDY DIOTA DUBBA FLASK GLOBE GUIDE JUBBE KETCH LADLE LAKER LAVER LINER PIECE PYKAR SCOOP SMACK STEAM STILL XEBEC YANKY ZABRA BANKER BARQUE BARREL BILALO BOILER BOTTLE BOUTRE BUCKET BURNER CAIQUE CANNER CAPPIE CHARGE CODMAN COFFIN CONCHA COOLER COPPER CRATER CRAYER CRUISE CUTTER DECKER DEINOS DOGGER DUBBAH ELUTOR FESSEL FIRKIN FLAGON HOLCAD HOOKER JAGGER KERNOS KETTLE KRATER LANCHA LATEEN LEKANE LORCHA MASLIN MONKEY MULLER PACKET PANKIN PATERA PICARD PITHOS POURIE ROLLER SALTER SATTIE SEALER SERVER SETTEE SHIBAR SITULA SMOKER TARTAN TENDER TOPMAN VESICA WHALER BAGGALA BALLOEN BALLOON BLICKEY BLICKIE CARAVEL CARRIER CISTERN CLIPPER CORSAIR COUGNAR

CRAGGAN CRESSET CRISSET CRUISER CUVETTE DRIFTER DRINKER DROGHER FELUCCA FLYBOAT FRIGATE GABBARD GABBART GAIASSA GALASSA GUNBOAT ORANGER PATAMAR PINNACE POACHER POLACRE PSYKTER REDUCER SALTFAT SCALDER SEEDLIP SETTLER SPARGER SPOUTER STEAMER STEEPER TRACHEA TRENDLE UTENSIL BELANDER BENITIER BILANDER BILLYBOY BIRDBATH BLEACHER BUGGALOW CORVETTE CRUCIBLE CRUISKEN CUCURBIT DECANTER DIGESTER DUTCHMAN EFFERENT EMISSARY FIREBOAT FLESHPOT GALLIPOT GALLIVAT GAROOKUH GAYDIANG HELLSHIP HONEYPOT INKSTAND INRIGGER IRONCLAD IRONSIDE KEELBOAT LATEENER LAVATORY MONOHULL NITRATOR PICAROON SCHOONER SMUGGLER SPITTOON WATERPOT BARKENTINE STIRRUPCUP
(— CUT FROM BLOCK OF WOOD) BAMBOOS
(— FOR COAL) GEORDIE
(— FOR DYE) TOBY
(— FOR FEEDING ANIMALS) TROUGH
(— FOR HEATING LIQUIDS) ETNA
(— FOR HOLY WATER) FAT FONT STOCK STOOP STOUP AMPULLA BENITIER CHRISMATORY
(— FOR HYPODERMIC USE) AMPUL AMPULE AMPOULE
(— FOR LIQUID WASTE) DRIP
(— FOR MEASURING ORE) HOPPET
(— FOR MOLTEN METAL) LADLE
(— FOR ORE WASHINGS) LOOL
(— FOR PERFUMES) CENSER
(— FOR PORRIDGE) BICKER
(— FOR SOLDIER'S FOOD) MESSTIN
(— FOR SUGAR) SUCRIER
(— FOR WINE SAMPLING) TASTER
(— HOLDING CONDIMENTS) CRUET CASTER
(— IN MINE) CORB
(— MADE OF HOLLOW LOG) GUM
(— OF BARK) COOLAMAN COOLAMON COOLIMAN
(— OF HORN) BUGLE
(— ON TRIPOD) HOLMOS
(— ROWED BY OARS) CATUR GALLEY
(— STATIONED IN ENGLISH CHANNEL) GROPER
(— USED IN MAKING GLAZE) HILLER
(ABANDONED —) DERELICT
(ARMORED —) CRUISER IRONCLAD IRONSIDE
(BAILING —) SCOOP
(BAPTISMAL —) FONT
(BARGELIKE —) PANGARA
(BLOOD —) AORTA ARTERY BLEEDER EFFERENT
(BREWER'S —) ROUND
(CANDLEMAKING —) JACK
(CHEMIST'S —) BATH FLASK STILL BEAKER RETORT
(CHINESE —) JUNK SAMPAN
(CIRCULAR —) KIT
(CLUMSY —) CRAY CRARE HAGBOAT
(COASTING —) DHOW DONI GRAB PONTIN SHEBAR SHIBAR TRADER COASTER GRIBANE MISTICO BILLYBOY HOVELLER
(CODFISHING —) BANKER CODMAN
(COOKING —) MARMITE
(DECORATIVE —) AIGUIERE
(DISTILLING —) BODY STILL RETORT MATRASS CUCURBIT
(DRINKING —) CAP CUP TIN BOOT PECE FOUNT GLASS GOURD JORUM KOVAH POKAL SCALE BICKER CAPPIE CHOPIN COOPER COOTIE DIPPER DUBBER FIRLOT GOBLET KITTIE KOVSHI QUAICH QUAIGH RABBIT RUMKIN BIBERON CANAKIN CANIKIN GALLIOT SCYPHUS SKINKER SKYPHOS TANKARD CANNIKIN CYLINDER
(DUTCH —) KOFF YANKY HOOKER SCHUIT SCHUYT
(EARTHEN —) PIG OLLA BAYAN PANKIN TINAGE CRAGGAN
(ELECTROPLATING —) TROUGH
(EUCHARISTIC —) AMA PYX AMULA PYXIS FLAGON COLUMBA CHRISMAL CIBORIUM MONSTRANCE
(GLASS —) VERRE UNDINE BALLOON
(HERRING-FISHING —) BUSS
(HOLLOW METALLIC —) BELL
(INVERTED —) BELL
(LADLING —) GAUN
(LARGE-NECKED —) JORDAN
(LATEEN-RIGGED —) DHOW LATEEN LATEENER
(LEATHER —) BOOT JACK OLPE GIRBA DUBBER
(LEVANTINE —) JERM SAIC
(LONG-NECKED —) GOGLET GUGLET
(LYMPHATIC —) LACTEAL
(MALAYAN —) PROA COUGNAR
(MELTING —) GRISSET
(OPEN —) LOOM
(PERFORATED —) LEACH
(PINECONE-SHAPED —) THYRSE
(PORTUGUESE —) MULET
(RARE —) SNOW
(SEED —) POD BUTTON BIVALVE
(SERVING —) ARGYLE ARGYLL SERVER
(SHALLOW —) KIVER SKEEL BEDPAN PANCHION
(SMALL —) CAG HOY VIAL PHIAL VEDET JIGGER LIEPOT PICARD TINLET YETLIN FLIVVER VEDETTE YETLING GALLIPOT
(TOP-HEAVY —) CRANK
(TURKISH —) MAHONE
(WHALING —) WHALER SPOUTER
(WICKER —) POT
(WINE —) AMA AMULA TINAGE
(WOODEN —) COG KIT BOSS BAKIE KIVER BICKER CAPPIE COOTIE DUDDIE FIRKIN STOUND
(PL.) CRAFT WAFTAGE
(PREF.) ANGI(O) ARTERI VAS(I)(O) VASCUL(I)(O)
(HOLLOW —) CYT(O)
(SUFF.) ANGE ANGIUM

VEST GARB GOWN ROBE GILET ACCRUE ATTACH FECKET INVEST JACKET JELICK JERKIN LINDER WESKIT ENFEOFF CLOTHING
(— IN) STATE

VESTA WAX
(FATHER OF —) SATURN
(MOTHER OF —) RHEA
(SISTER OF —) JUNO CERES

VESTED BESTEAD DONATIVE

VESTIBULE HALL ENTRY FOYER PORCH ATRIUM EXEDRA EPINAOS NARTHEX PASSAGE PRONAOS TAMNOUR ANTEROOM VESTIARY

VESTIGE TAG DREG MARK RACK SIGN PRINT RELIC SPARK TRACE TRACK TRACT UMBRA SHADOW MENTION LEFTOVER RUDIMENT TINCTURE

VESTIGIAL REDUCED OBSOLETE

VESTING ADITIO

VESTITURE TIRE RAIMENT TUNICLE

VESTMENT ALB CAP ALBE COPE PALL VEST AMICE COTTA EPHOD FANON RABAT RASON STOLE RHASON ROCHET SACCOS SAKKOS VAKASS MANIPLE ORARION PALLIUM PILLION PLUVIAL TUNICLE VESTURE CHASUBLE DALMATIC PHRYGIUM RATIONAL SCAPULAR SURPLICE VESTIARY
(PL.) GARB GEAR DRESS CLOTHING

VESTRY SACRISTY VESTIARY

VESTURE COAT

VESUVIANITE EGERAN CYPRINE IDOCRASE VESUVIAN XANTHITE

VETCH DAL ERS AKRA LUCK TARE TINE ERVIL FITCH AXSEED FECCHE THETCH ARVEJON TINETARE TINEWEED

VETERAN VET CHAUVIN EMERITUS HARDENED SEASONED WARHORSE

VETERINARIAN VET LEECH FARRIER

VETERINARY VET FARRIERY

VETIVER BEN KHUS CUSCUS KUSKUS KHASGHAS KHUSKHUS

VETO NIX KILL DISALLOW NEGATIVE

VEUGLAIRE FOWLER

VEX FRY IRE NOY TEW CARK CHAW FASH FAZE FRET FYKE GALL HALE HUMP ITCH RILE ROIL RUCK TEEN TOUT YOKE ANGER ANNOY CHAFE FRUMP GRAME GRILL GRIND GRIPE HARRY SCALD SPITE STURT TARRY TEASE WORRY WRACK WRATH YEARN BOTHER BURDEN CORSIE COTTER CUMBER GRIEVE GRUDGE HARASS HARROW INFEST NETTLE OFFEND PLAGUE POTHER RUFFLE THREAT WORRIT AFFLICT BEDEVIL CHAGRIN DESPITE PERPLEX PROVOKE TORMENT TROUBLE ACERBATE BEPESTER BULLYRAG EXERCISE IRRITATE MACERATE

VEXATION VEX CHAW FASH MOIL TEEN TRAY CHAFE CROSS ERROR GRIEF HARRY PIQUE SPITE STEAM THORN WORRY BOTHER REPINE CHAGRIN DISGUST NOISANCE SORENESS

VEXATIOUS MEAN SORE TEEN NASTY PESKY ACHING FIERCE SHREWD THORNY VEXFUL IRKSOME PEEVISH PRICKLY TARSOME ANNOYING CUMBROUS FRAMPOLD PHRAMPEL UNTOWARD VEXATORY WEARIFUL PESTILENT

VEXATIOUSLY PLAGUY

VEXED DIK MAD RILY SORE TEEN WAXY WILD WRAW ANGRY NARKY RAGGY ROILY MIFFED MUFFED SHIRTY SNUFFY FRABOUS GRIEVED IRKSOME OUTDONE
(EASILY —) CROSS

VEXILLUM WEB VEXIL BANNER STANDARD

VEXING CHRONIC TECHING WAYWARD ANNOYING NETTLING TEACHING

V-GOUGE VEINER

VIABLE VITAL HEALTHY

VIAL AMPUL CRUET PHIAL AMPULE CASTER CASTOR AMPOULE
(— OF AMYL NITRITE) POPPER

VIANDS CATE DIET FOOD CHEER VIANDRY VICTUALS

VIBRANT RINGY BRAWLING RESONANT SONOROUS VIGOROUS

VIBRATE JAR WAG BEAT CAST DIRL PLAY ROCK TIRL WHIR PULSE QUAKE SWING THIRL THROB TRILL WAVER DINDLE HOTTER JUDDER QUAVER QUIVER SHIMMY SHIVER THRILL TINGLE WARBLE CHATTER FLUTTER LIBRATE STAGGER TREMBLE TWIDDLE EVIBRATE FLICHTER RESONATE UNDULATE
(— ABNORMALLY) SHIMMY

VIBRATING PLANGENT
(— OF AIRPLANE) BUFFET

VIBRATION BUZZ DIRL FLIP TIRL VIBE KARMA SWING TRILL DINDLE JUDDER QUAVER QUIVER THRILL TREMOR DANCING FLUTTER TEMBLOR DIADROME FREMITUS VIBRANCY OSCILLATION
(— OF SAW) CUPPING
(RATTLING —) JAR

VIBRATIONS KARMA

VIBRATO TRILL WHINE TREMOLO

VIBRATOR TREMBLER

VIBRISSA HAIR FEELER SMELLER

VIBURNUM MAE MAY SNOWBALL ARROWWOOD SHEEPBERRY

VICAR PROXY DEPUTY STALLAR ALTARIST STALLARY

VICAR OF CHRIST POPE

VICAR OF WAKEFIELD (AUTHOR OF —) GOLDSMITH
(CHARACTER IN —) MOSES GEORGE OLIVIA SOPHIA WILMOT DEBORAH ARABELLA BURCHELL PRIMROSE THORNHILL

VICE SIN EVIL CRIME FAULT TAINT ULCER DEFECT DEPUTY BUGGERY OFFENSE INIQUITY

VICE-GERENT EPHOR

VICE-PRESIDENT CROUPIER

VICE PRESIDENT VEEP
VICE-PRESIDENT CROUPIER
(— OF SANHEDRIN) ABBETDIN
VICEREGENT VICAR SUBPRIOR
VICEROY EARL VALI NABOB NAWAB NAZIM SUBAH EXARCH KEHAYA PROREX PROVES SATRAP WARDEN PROVOST TSUNGTU SUBAHDAR
VICIA FABA
VICINAGE AREA
VICINITY HERE SHADOW ENVIRONS
(— OF MINE SHAFT) COLLAR
(NEAR —) SUBURBS
VICIOUS BAD ILL EVIL LAZY LEWD MEAN UGLY VILE ROWDY TOUGH SINFUL STRONG VITIAL WICKED CORRUPT IMMORAL NAUGHTY SKAITHY DEPRAVED DEVILISH FRATCHED INFAMOUS THEWLESS MONSTROUS NEFARIOUS
VICIOUSNESS VICE
VICISSITUDE CHANGE MUTATION
(— OF FORTUNE) WEATHER
VICTIM BUTT DUPE GOAT GULL PREY PATHIC QUARRY CASUALTY
(— FOR SHARPERS) JAY
(INTENDED —) CHUMP
(PERPETUAL —) NEBBISH
(SACRIFICIAL —) HOST MERIAH
(SCAM —) PATSY
(SUITABLE —) MARK
(UNFORTUNATE —) BASTARD
VICTIMIZATION RIDE
VICTIMIZE HOAX BUNCO BUNKO COZEN
VICTOR COCK CAPTOR MASTER WINNER BANGSTER
VICTORFISH AKU
VICTORIA (FATHER OF —) PALLAS
(MOTHER OF —) STYX
VICTORIA LAKE PUCE
VICTORIAN GENTEEL
VICTORIOUS FIRST VICTOR WINNING
VICTORY WIN PALM SIEG PRICE BETTER SUBDUE VICTOR MASTERY SACKING TRIUMPH WINNING CONQUEST DECISION WALKOVER
(AUTHOR OF —) CONRAD
(CHARACTER IN —) AXEL LENA WANG HEYST JONES PEDRO MARTIN RICARDO DAVIDSON MORRISON SCHOMBERG
(EASY —) BREEZE
(ONE-SIDED —) BLOWOUT
(OVERWHELMING —) SWEEP
VICTUAL BIT VITE VITTLE
(BROKEN —S) SCRAN
(PL.) KAI BITE CHOW FOOD GRUB PROG SAND VIVERS PROVENDER PROVISIONS
VICTUALER PURVEYOR
VIDELICET NAMELY SCILICET
VIDEO RECORDING
(— GAME) ATARI
(COMPUTER — DEVICE) MONITOR
VIDEODISC RECORDING
VIDEOTAPE (— RECORDER) VCR
VIDEOTEX VIEWDATA
(— SYSTEM) VIEWDATA
VIE ENVY JOSTLE STRIVE COMPARE COMPETE CONTEND CONTEST EMULATE
VIETNAM (SEE NORTH VIETNAM AND SOUTH VIETNAM)

VIETNAM
CAPITAL: HANOI
COIN: XU XU DONG DONG
COMMUNIST PARTY: VIETCONG
GULF: TONKIN TONKING
MEASURE: GANG PHAN THON
MOUNTAIN: LINH YANGSIN FANSIPAN
PEOPLE: HOA MAN MEO TAY CHAM KINH NUNG THAI MALAY MUONG
PORT: DANANG HONGAI SAIGON BENTHUY HONGGAI QUINHON HAIPHONG NHATRANG HOCHIMINHCITY
REGION: ANNAM COCHIN TONKIN
RIVER: BO CA DA LO MA CHU GAM KOK XAM CHAY BLACK CLEAR NHIHA MEKONG XONGCA DONGHAI PANLONG
TOWN: HUE VINH HOIAN DANANG BACNINH BIENHOA CAOBANG DONGHOI NAMDINH QUINHON SONGCAU TAYNINH THANHOA VIETTRI HAIPHONG PHANRANG QUANGTRI
WEIGHT: CAN YET UYEN

VIETNAMESE ANNAMESE
VIEW EYE KEN FACE GLOM MAKE VISE ADVEW AVIEW BLUSH CATCH MOUTH SCAPE SCENE SIGHT VISTA VIZZY ADVICE ADVISE ASPECT DEVICE GLANCE REGARD SURVEY ALOGISM CONCEIT FEELING GLIMPSE KENNING LOOKOUT OFFLOOK OPINION RESPECT SCENERY SURVIEW THOUGHT AIRSCAPE CONSPECT EYESIGHT OFFSCAPE PROSPECT SEASCAPE SENTENCE SENTIMENT
(— ATTENTIVELY) GAZE
(— CLOSELY) INSPECT
(— FROM AFAR) DESCRY
(— FROM ANGLE) SLANT
(— OF MAN) DUALISM
(— WITH SURPRISE) ADMIRE
(BACKWARD —) RETROSPECT RETROSPECTION
(BRIEF —) SNAPSHOT
(CATCH MOMENTARY —) GLANCE
(COMPREHENSIVE —) PANORAMA
(DEPRESSING —) PESSIMISM
(EXPRESS A —) OPINE
(GENERAL —) LANDSKIP
(OPEN —) LIGHT
(PHYSICAL —) INSIGHT
(PUBLIC —) OPEN
(SATISFYING —) EYEFUL
(SECOND —) DEUTEROSCOPY
(SECTIONAL — OF BODY) CATSCAN
(SUFF.) ORAMA SCOPE SCOPIC SCOPUS SCOPY
VIEWDATA VIDEOTEX
VIEWER (TELEVISION —) GOGGLER
VIEWING
(SUFF.) SCOPE SCOPIC SCOPUS SCOPY
VIEWPOINT SIGHT LAXISM STANDPOINT
VIGIL WAKE WATCH WAKING AGRYPNIA
VIGILANCE WATCH JEALOUSY
VIGILANT AGOG WARE WARY ALERT AWAKE AWARE CHARY SHARP JEALOUS LIDLESS WAKEFUL CAUTIOUS WATCHFUL
VIGODA ABE
VIGOR GO PEP SAP VIM VIR VIS BIRR DASH EDGE ELAN LUST PITH SEVE SNAP SOUL TUCK ARDOR DRIVE FLUSH FORCE GREEN JUICE NERVE OOMPH POWER PUNCH VERVE ENERGY ESPRIT FOISON GINGER SPRAWL SPRING STARCH STINGO VIGOUR VIRTUS FREEDOM SMEDDUM STAMINA STHENIA FLOURISH STRENGTH TONICITY VITALITY
(— OF THOUGHT) FLAME
(FULL OF —) LIFESOME
(MENTAL —) DOCITY SPIRIT
(RENEWED —) REST
VIGOROUS YEP ABLE CANT FRIM HALE LIVE RUDE SPRY YEPE ALIVE CRANK EAGER FRACK FRANK HEFTY JUICY LUSTY NIPPY PEPPY PITHY PROUD SASSY SOLID STARK STIFF STOUT TOUGH VIVID FLORID GOLDEN HEARTY LIVELY MANFUL POTENT PRETTY RAUCLE ROBUST RUGGED SINEWY SQUARE STRONG STURDY BUCKISH CHIPPER CORDIAL DRASTIC FECKFUL FURIOUS HEALTHY LUSTFUL NERVOSE NERVOUS VALIANT VIBRANT ZEALOUS ATHLETIC BOUNCING CHOPPING FORCEFUL MUSCULAR SLAMBANG SLASHING STUBBORN VEHEMENT VIGOROSO YOUTHFUL TRENCHANT
(NOT —) GENTEEL
VIGOROUSLY DOWN FELL HARD VERN AMAIN CRANK SNELL TIGHT VERNE HARDLY SNELLY FRESHLY SMARTLY STOUTLY WIGHTLY HEARTILY
VIGOROUSNESS ENERGY FREEDOM
VIKING DANE WIKING NORSEMAN
VIKRAMADITYA BIKRAM
VILE BAD BASE CLAM FOUL RANK CHEAP MUCKY POCKY RUSTY SLIMY WILLE ABJECT CRUSTY DRAFTY DRASTY FILTHY LECHER NOUGHT ODIOUS PALTRY SORDID TURPID UNKIND BEASTLY BENEATH CAITIFF CORRUPT DEBASED HATEFUL IGNOBLE SCABBED SLAVISH VICIOUS BASEBORN DEPRAVED UNKINDLY
(OPENLY —) SCANDALOUS
VILENESS FEDITY VILITY TURPITUDE
VILIFICATION SLANDER REPROACH
VILIFY ILL VILE ABUSE LIBEL SMEAR STAIN SULLY DEFAME DEFILE MALIGN REVILE SLIGHT ASPERSE BLACKEN DEBAUCH DETRACT SLANDER TRADUCE REPROACH STRUMPET
VILIPEND SLUR BELITTLE
VILL HAM TOWN TOWNSHIP
VILLA ALDEA DACHA LODGE CHALET DATCHA QUINTA TRIANON
VILLAGE BY AUL BYE GAV HAM KOM PAH REW BOMA BURG DORP HOME MURA TOWN VILL WICK ALDEA BOURG CASAL PLACE THORP VICUS ALDEIA BARRIO BUSTEE CASTLE GOTHAM HAMLET HAMMON MOUZAH PETTAH PUEBLO AMBALAM BOROUGH CAMPODY CASERIO CLACHAN ENDSHIP MAABARA MISSION OUTPORT BEREWICK BOURGADE CAMPOODY CRANFORD TOLDERIA VILLACHE VILLAGET VILLAKIN
(— IN WHICH BARLEY IS GROWN) BEREWICK
(— OUTSIDE OF FORT) PETTAH
(AFRICAN —) STAD KRAAL
(ARABIAN —) DOUAR
(ARGENTINE —) TOLDERIA
(FRENCH —) BASTIDE
(IMAGINARY —) CRANFORD
(INDIAN —) CASTLE PUEBLO CAMPODY CAMPOODY
(JAPANESE —) MURA BUSTI BUSTEE
(JAVANESE —) DESSA
(JEWISH —) SHTETL SHTETEL
(MALAY —) CAMPONG KAMPONG
(MAORI —) KAIK KAIKA KAINGA
(MEXICAN —) EJIDO
(NEWFOUNDLAND —) OUTPORT
(NEW ZEALAND FORTIFIED —) PA PAH
(RUSSIAN —) MIR STANITSA STANITZA
(TENT —) DUAR DOUAR DOWAR
VILLAIN IAGO LOUT SERF BADDY BRAVO CHURL DEMON DEVIL FAGIN FELON HEAVY KNAVE ROGUE SCAMP SHREW VIPER BADDIE VILIACO SCELERAT SCOUNDREL
VILLAINOUS BAD EVIL GALLUS GALLOWS KNAVISH RAFFISH VILEYNS FLAGRANT RASCALLY MISCREANT
VILLAINY CRIME KNAVERY
VILLEIN SERF CHURL BORDAR COTTER VILLAR BONDMAN TOWNMAN VILLAIN COTARIUS
VILLI (HAVING —) ZONARY
VILLOUS SHAGGY
VIM ZIP GIMP ZING FORCE OOMPH VIGOR ENERGY GINGER SPIRIT STARCH VINEGAR RAZZMATAZZ
VINA BEN BIN BINA
VINCENTIAN LAZARIST
VINDICATE FREE CLEAR RIGHT SALVE WREAK ACQUIT ASSERT AVENGE EXCUSE UPHOLD ABSOLVE DERAIGN JUSTIFY PROPUGN REVENGE SUSTAIN DARRAIGN MAINTAIN
VINDICATION BEHALF APOLOGY DEFENSE THEODICY COMPURGATION SATISFACTION JUSTIFICATION
VINDICATOR VINDEX ASSERTER DEFENDER
VINDICTIVE HOSTILE PUNITIVE SPITEFUL VENGEFUL

VINE AKA FIG HOP IVY IYO BINE CARO GOGO ODAL SOMA TINE AKEBI BUAZE BWAZI CAAPI CACUR GUACO KAIWI KUDZU LIANA LIANE MAILE PALAY PRIVY TACSO TIMBO TRAIL TWINE WITHE WONGA BEJUCO CISSUS COBAEA COWAGE DERRIS DODDER ECANDA GERKIN IPOMEA JICAMA LABLAB PIKAKE RUNNER TURURI TWINER ULLUCO WINDER APRICOT BIGROOT BONESET BRAMBLE CALAMUS CATVINE CERIMAN CLIMBER COWHAGE COWITCH CUPSEED EPACRID GHERKIN IPOMOEA LAVANGA PAREIRA PUMPKIN TRAILER VINELET YANGTAO ATRAGENE BINDWEED BOXTHORN CLEMATIS COMEBACK CUCUMBER CUCURBIT DECUMARY DOLICHOS EARDROPS EARTHPEA EVONYMUS GULANCHA HEARTPEA HEMPWEED MUSCATEL REDWITHE TINETARE TINEWEED TRAILERY TRAILING TREEBINE VINIFERA WINETREE WISTARIA WISTERIA OLOLIUQUI
(PREF.) AMPEL(O) VITI

VINEGAR VIM EISEL ESILL ACETUM ALEGAR ASCILL SOURING BEERGAR VINAIGRE
(— AND HONEY) OXYMEL
(PREF.) ACET(O)

VINEGAR EEL EELWORM
VINEGARY ACETOSE ACETOUS
VINEGROWER VINITOR
VINEYARD CRU CLOS COTE VINER VINERY WINEYARD
VINGT-ET-UN MACAO MACCO
VINOUS WINY
VINTAGE OLD VINT WINE CUVEE ARCHAIC CLASSIC VENDAGE OUTMODED
VIOL GUE GIGA LIRA TURR GIGUE GUDOK TARAU VOYAL VOYOL CHELYS FIDDLE VIELLE VIOLET MINIKIN QUINTON SARINDA SULTANA VIHUELA VIOLONE BARBITON BASSETTE SERINGHI VIOLETTE
VIOLA ALTO QUINT TENOR TENORE VIOLET
(BROTHER OF —) SEBASTIAN
(HUSBAND OF —) ORSINO
VIOLA BASTARDA BARITONE BARYTONE
VIOLA DA BRACCIO QUINT
VIOLA DA GAMBA GAMBA
VIOLA D'AMORE VIOLET
VIOLATE ERR SIN FLAW ABUSE BREAK CRACK FORCE FRACT HARRY LOOSE VIOLE WRONG BREACH BROACH DEFILE INVADE OFFEND RAVISH DEBAUCH DISOBEY FALSIFY INFRACT OUTRAGE POLLUTE PROFANE VITIATE DEFLOWER DISHONOR FORSWEAR FRACTURE INFRINGE MISTREAT STUPRATE SURPRISE TEMERATE TRESPASS VIOLENCE
VIOLATED FRACTED INFRACT
VIOLATION SIN DEBT ABUSE CRIME ERROR FAULT SALLY BREACH INJURY MISCONDUCT
(HOCKEY —) STICKS
(TRIVIAL —) MOPERY
VIOLATOR WRONGER
VIOLENCE FURY NEED RAGE RUFF BRUNT FORCE RIGOR STORM BENSIL ESTURE HUBRIS RANDOM RAPINE STOUSH STRESS BENSAIL BENSALL OUTRAGE FEROCITY SEVERITY SORENESS ROUGHHOUSE
(DEPICTING —) SNUFF
(LETHAL —) DEATH
(OF DEPICTION OF —) SNUFF
VIOLENT BIG HOT TEZ DERF HARD HIGH MAIN RANK RUDE WILD WOOD ACUTE FIERY HEADY HEAVY HEFTY RABID SHARP SMART STARK STERN STIFF STOOR STOUR STOUT WROTH BROTHE FIERCE HEARTY MANIAC MIGHTY SAVAGE SEVERE STORMY STRONG STURDY SUDDEN CRIMSON DRASTIC FURIOUS HOTSPUR RAMMISH RAMPANT RAPEFUL RUFFIAN TEARING VIOLOUS WILSOME CHURLISH DIABOLIC FLAGRANT FORCEFUL IMPOTENT MANIACAL PERACUTE RIGOROUS SEETHING SLAMBANG STALWART VEHEMENT
VIOLENTLY HARD AMAIN HOTLY HARDLY SORELY HOPPING SOUNDLY
VIOLET CANON GRAPE MAUVE VIOLA BLAVER CANYON DAHLIA DAMSON EVEQUE JOHNNY HOOKERS LOBELIA OPHELIA PRELATE PRIMULA PUREAYN CLEMATIS DAMEWORT FINELEAF IANTHINE ROOSTERS WISTERIA
(KIND OF,—) AFRICAN
(PREF.) IO
VIOLIN GUE KIT ALTO GIGA AMATI CROWD CRWTH GEIGE GIGUE REBAB REBEC STRAD TARAU VIOLA CATGUT CHORUS CROUTH FIDDLE FITHEL REBECK TAILLE VIOLON CATLING CHROTTA CREMONA THEYAOU VIOLAND VIOLINO GUARNERI KEMANCHA VIOLOTTA
(PART OF —) NUT PEG TOP FROG HEAD HEEL HOLE NECK BELLY TABLE BRIDGE BUTTON PEGBOX SCROLL STRING PURFLING SOUNDBOARD FINGERBOARD
VIPER ASP HABU ADDER ASPIC ATHER URUTU WYVER ASPIDE DABOIA DABOYA JESSUR KATUKA KUPPER HAGWORM HOGNOSE MAMUSHI VIPERID AMMODYTE CERASTES JARARACA VIPERINE BUSHMASTER
(KIND OF —) PIT
VIPER'S BUGLOSS BLUEWEED
VIRAGO NAG RANDY SHREW AMAZON BELDAM CALLET BELDAME TRIMMER VIRAGIN RIXATRIX
VIREO REDEYE GRASSET TEACHER GREENLET PREACHER
VIRGATE YOKE VERGE YARDLAND
(HALF —) MANTAL
VIRGILIAN MARONIAN
VIRGIN NEW LIVE MAID PURE FRESH CHASTE MAIDEN VESTAL INITIAL PUCELLE DOROTHEA PARAMOUR
(— OF PARADISE) HURI HOURI
(PREF.) PARTHEN(O)
VIRGINAL CHERRY INTACT SYMPHONY TRIANGLE

VIRGINIA
CAPITAL: RICHMOND
COLLEGE: AVERETT HOLLINS MADISON RADFORD LONGWOOD
COUNTY: LEE BATH PAGE WISE BLAND CRAIG FLOYD SMYTH SURRY WYTHE AMELIA LOUISA ACCOMAC HENRICO PATRICK PULASKI ROANOKE CULPEPER FLUVANNA TAZEWELL
INDIAN: SAPONI TUTELO MONACAN MANAHOAC MEHERRIN NOTTAWAY POWHATAN
LAKE: KERR SMITH
MOUNTAIN: CEDAR ELLIOT ROGERS BALDKNOB
MOUNTAIN RANGE: CLINCH ALLEGHENY BLUERIDGE
NICKNAME: OLDDOMINION MOTHEROFSTATES MOTHEROFPRESIDENTS
PRESIDENT: TYLER MONROE TAYLOR WILSON MADISON HARRISON JEFFERSON WASHINGTON
RIVER: DAN JAMES POTOMAC RAPIDAN
STATE BIRD: CARDINAL
STATE FLOWER: DOGWOOD
STATE TREE: DOGWOOD
TOWN: GALAX LURAY SALEM MARION BEDFORD BRISTOL EMPORIA NORFOLK PULASKI ROANOKE CULPEPER DANVILLE HOPEWELL MANASSAS STAUNTON TAZEWELL

VIRGINIA COWSLIP LUNGWORT
VIRGINIA CREEPER CREEPER WOODBIND WOODBINE
VIRGINIA KNOTWEED JUMPSEED
VIRGINIAN BEAGLE COOHEE CAVALIER TUCKAHOE
(AUTHOR OF —) WISTER
(CHARACTER IN —) WOOD HENRY MOLLY STEVE SHORTY TRAMPAS
VIRGINIANS (AUTHOR OF —) THACKERAY
(CHARACTER IN —) THEO WILL FANNY HARRY HETTY MARIA MILES ESMOND GEORGE RACHEL LAMBERT MOUNTAIN BERNSTEIN CASTLEWOOD WARRINGTON WASHINGTON
VIRGINIA SNAKEROOT SANGREL SNAGREL
VIRGINIA STICKSEED SOLDIERS
VIRGINIA WATERLEAF SHAWNY
VIRGINIA WILLOW ITEA
VIRGINITY HONOR CHERRY CHASTITY PUCELAGE
VIRGIN MARY DESPOINA THEOTOCOS
VIRGIN'S-BOWER LOVE HONESTY CLEMATIS MOONWORT
VIRGIN SOIL (AUTHOR OF —) TURGENEV
(CHARACTER IN —) KOLYA PAHKLIN SOLOMIN MARIANNA MASHURIN SIPYAGIN MARKELOFF VALENTINA NEZHDANOFF OSTRODUMOFF
VIRGO (STAR IN —) SPICA
VIRGULE SLANT VIRGULA DIAGONAL
VIRIDIAN EMERAUDE
VIRILE MALE MACHO MANLY
(AGGRESSIVELY —) MACHO
VIRILITY LUST GREEN MANHEAD MANHOOD
VIROLOGIST (FAMOUS —) SABIN
VIRTUAL IMPLICIT PRACTICAL
VIRTUALLY BUT NEARLY MORALLY
VIRTUE JEN HSIN THEW ARETE FAITH GRACE POWER VALOR VERTU WORTH BOUNTY DHARMA FOISON CHARISM CHARITY JUSTICE PROBITY QUALITY CHARISMA CHASTITY EFFICACY GOODNESS MORALITY PARAMITA PROPERTY
(CONFUCIAN —) LI
(PL.) CIVISM
(PREF.) ARETO
VIRTUOSO ACE EXPERT SAVANT ESTHETE LAPIDARY
VIRTUOUS GOOD PURE BRAVE CIVIL MORAL PIOUS CHASTE HONEST MODEST GODDARD SAINTED SINCERE UPRIGHT VIRTUAL STRAIGHT
VIRULENCE VIRUS RANCOR RANCOUR
VIRULENT RANK ACRID RABID DEADLY MALIGN VIROSE NOXIOUS VIRIFIC WASPISH VENOMOUS
(LESS THAN —) MITIS
VIRUS PARVO VENOM POISON PATHOGEN SPECIFIC
(AIDS —) HIV
(PRESENCE OF —) VIREMIA
VIS PEIKTHA
VISAGE FACE PHIZ CHEER IMAGE VISOR ASPECT FASHION
VISCERA GUTS HASLET INSIDE UMBLES GARBAGE GIBLETS HASSLET INMEATS INNARDS INSIDES NUMBLES ENTRAILS HARIGALS
(PREF.) SPLANCHNO
VISCERAL GUT
VISCID SLAB WAXY GOOEY GLAIRY STICKY LENTOUS STRINGY VISCOUS MOTHERED
VISCIDITY LENTOR
VISCOSITY BODY ROPINESS
(— UNIT) POISE
VISCOUS LIMY ROPY SIZY SLAB GOBBY GUMMY MUCIC ROPEY SLIMY STIFF TARRY SIRUPY SLABBY SMEARY SNOTTY STICKY THONGY VISCID LENTOUS SQUISHY VISCOSE MUCULENT
VISE GEE CHAP JACK SHOP VICE CHEEK CLAMP CRAMP WINCH
(PART OF —) JAW BASE BOLT ANVIL SCREW SLIDE HANDLE SWIVEL

VISHNU RAMA VASU KALKI KRISHNA BALARAMA BHAGAVAT
(AVATAR OF —) KALKI KURMA BUDDHA MATSYA VAMANA VARAHA KRISHNA NARASINHA PARASHURAMA RAMACHANDRA
(BREAST JEWEL OF —) KAUSTUBHA
(BREASTMARK OF —) SHRIVATSA
(VEHICLE OF —) GARUDA
(WIFE OF —) SHRI LAKSHMI
(WRIST JEWEL OF —) SYAMANTAKA
VISIBLE OUT FAIR SEEN CLEAR GROSS EXTANT SIGHTY EVIDENT GLARING OBVIOUS OPTICAL SIGHTLY APPARENT DIOPTRIC EXPLICIT EXTERNAL MANIFEST PROSPECT
(BARELY —) DARK
(SCARCELY —) DIM
(PREF.) DELO PHANER(O) PHANTA PHANTASMO PHANTO
VISION EYE RAY DREAM FANCY SIGHT FANTAD SEEING SWEVEN AISLING SHOWING SPECTER SPECTRE EYESIGHT PHOTOPIA PROSPECT SPECULATION
(— IN BRIGHT LIGHT) PHOTOPIA
(— IN DIM LIGHT) SCOTOPIA
(— PROBLEM) REDOUT
(BLURRED —) SWIMMING
(DEFECTIVE —) ANOPIA
(DOUBLE —) DIPLOPIA
(FALSE —) PARABLEPSY PARABLEPSIS
(FANCIED —) PHANTASM
(IMAGINARY —) SHADOW
(IMPERFECT —) CALIGO DARKNESS
(MENTAL —) VISTA
(MULTIPLE —) POLYOPIA
(PREF.) OPTI(CO) OPTO VISUO
(RANGE OF —) METROPIA
(SUFF.) OPSIA OPSIS OPSY OPTIC OPTICON
(— DEVIATION) TROPIA
VISIONARY FEY AERY AIRY WILD BIGOT IDEAL VIEWY ASTRAL INSANE SHANDY UNREAL DREAMER FANTAST LAPUTAN UTOPIAN ACADEMIC DELUSIVE FANCIFUL FINESPUN IDEALIST NOTIONAL PHANTAST QUIXOTIC ROMANTIC UTOPIAST VISIONER
VISIT DO GAM SEE VIS CALL CHAT STAY APPLY HAUNT TRYST VIZZY COSHER RESORT RETURN CEILIDH CEILIDHE FREQUENT INVASION
(— BETWEEN WHALERS) GAM
(— PERSISTENTLY) INFEST
(— PROFESSIONALLY) ATTEND
(— RELATIVES) COUSIN
(— UNEXPECTEDLY) POPIN DROPIN
(— WRETCHED NEIGHBORHOODS) SLUM
(CEREMONIAL —) SELAMLIK
VISITATION SENE VISIT SENDING
VISITING ACTIVE SOCIAL
VISITOR GUEST LAKER CALLER VISITANT
(MEALTIME —) SCAMBLER
(PL.) COMPANY
VISOR BILL SIGHT UMBER UMBRE VIZOR BEAVER MESAIL UMBRIL VIZARD EYESHADE UMBRIERE
VISTA VIEW SCENE OUTLOOK PERSPECTIVE
VISUAL OPTIC OCULAR SCOPIC VISORY VISIBLE
VISUALIZE SEE FANCY IDEATE SYMBOL IMAGINE PICTURE CONCEIVE ENVISAGE
VITAL KEY LIVE BASIC CHIEF FRESH SAPPY LIVELY MOVING VIABLE ZOETIC ANIMATE CAPITAL CORDIAL EXIGENT NEEDFUL ESSENTIAL
VITALITY SAP VIM LIFE COLOR GUSTO JUICE OOMPH PULSE PUNCH BIOSIS BREATH ENERGY FOISON HEALTH MARROW PAZAZZ PIZAZZ STARCH PIZZAZZ VIVENCY STRENGTH
(DEFICIENT —) ASTHENIA
(LACKING —) STUFFY TURNIPY
VITALIZE ACTIVATE ENERGIZE
VITAMIN BIOTIN CITRIN NIACIN ADERMIN ANEURIN CHOLINE RETINOL THIAMIN TORULIN ADVITANT INOSITOL NUTRAMIN ORYZANIN VITAMINE
VITAMIN A RETINOL
VITELLINE YOLKY
VITIATE BEAT BLEND SPOIL TAINT CANCEL DEBASE POISON CORRUPT DEBAUCH DEPRAVE
VITIATED PICAL CORRUPT
(PREF.) CAC(O) CACH
(SUFF.) CACE
VITICULTURIST VIGNERON
VITREOUS GLASSY GLAIZIE VITREAN VITROUS
VITRIFY GLAZE
VITRIOL BLUEJACK COPPERAS
(PL.) SORY
VITRIOLIC SHARP BITING BITTER CAUSTIC MORDANT SCATHING
VITRIOS GLASSWARE
VITTLES CHOW
VITUPERATE RAIL ABUSE CURSE SCOLD SLANG BERATE REVILE
VITUPERATION ABUSE VITUPER
VITUPERATIVE ABUSIVE REVILING SHAMEFUL
VIVACE VIVO LEBHAFT
VIVACIOUS GAY AIRY PERT BRISK CRISP MERRY SUNNY ACTIVE BRIGHT LIVELY LIVING SPARKY VIVACE ANIMATE JOCULAR ANIMATED SPIRITED SPORTIVE FLAMBOYANT
VIVACITY BRIO FIRE LIFE ZEAL ARDOR VERVE VIGOR ESPRIT GAIETY GAYETY SPIRIT SPRAWL SPARKLE
VIVARIUM STEW VIVARY STEWPOND
VIVAT HOCH
VIVERRINE CIVET GENET FOUSSA MUSANG LINSANG FALANAKA MONGOOSE SURICATE
VIVIANO (BROTHER OF —) MALAGIGI ALDIGIERI
(SISTER OF —) BRADAMANTE
VIVID DEEP HARD KEEN LIVE RICH VIVE BRISK FRESH GREEN LURID QUICK RUDDY SHARP GARISH LIVELY LIVING STRONG VISUAL EIDETIC FLAMING FREAKED GLARING GLOWING GRAPHIC INTENSE PEPPERY VIOLENT COLORFUL DISTINCT DRAMATIC SLASHING STRIKING VIGOROUS PICTURESQUE
(NOT —) PALE
VIVIDNESS COLOR EMPHASIS
VIVIFY LIFE FOMENT ANIMATE QUICKEN SPARKLE
VIVIPARUS PALUDINA
VIXEN BARD FURY RANDY SCOLD SHREW VIRAGO TAGSTER TRIMMER
VIZIER WAZIR ATABEG ATABEK VISIER
VLACH WALLACH
V-MAIL AIRGRAPH
VOCABULARY CANT LEXIS SLANG JARGON DICTION LEXICON POCHISMO WORDBOOK
(FAULTY —) CACOLOGY
(UNDERWORLD —) ARGOT
(PREF.) LEXICO
VOCAL GLIB ORAL VOWEL FLUENT TONGUED VOCULAR ELOQUENT
VOCALIST BOPPER SINGER BOPPIST BOPSTER SONGSTER VOCALLER
VOCALIZE MOUTH ORATE INTONE PHONATE
VOCATION CALL HOBBY METIER CALLING SCIENCE
VOCATIONAL BANAUSIC
VOCIFERATION CLAMOR OUTCRY
VOCIFEROUS LOUD NOISY BAWLING BLATANT BRAWLING STRIDENT
VODKA SAMOGON SAMOGONKA
VOGUE CUT FAD TON CHIC MODE RAGE TURN STYLE CUSTOM FASHION RECLAME PRACTICE
VOGUL MANSI
VOICE SAY VOX EMIT GIVE HARP PIPE TONE TURN WISH FROTH LEDEN RAISE RUMOR SOUND UTTER ACTIVE ASSERT CHOICE STEVEN TAISCH THROAT TONGUE EXPRESS OPINION SONORIZE DIATHESIS
(— PRAISE) SLAVER
(ARTIFICIAL —) FALSETTO
(BELLOWING —) FOGHORN
(FIFTH —) QUINTUS
(HOARSE —) FOGHORN
(LOWEST —) BASS BASSO
(MIDDLE —) MOTETUS
(OF LYRIC AND DRAMATIC —) SPINTO
(PRINCIPAL —) CANTUS
(PUBLIC —) CRY
(SINGING —) ALTO BASS TENOR BREAST SPINTO SOPRANO BARITONE FALSETTO
(SUBDUED —) UNDERBREATH
(TENOR —) TAILLE
(UPPER —) DESCANT DISCANT
(PREF.) PHON(O) PHTHONGO VOCI
(LOUD —) STENTORO
(SUFF.) PHON(E)(IA)(Y)
VOICED SOFT WEAK TONIC MEDIAL SONANT VIBRANT PHTHONGAL
VOICELESS MUM DUMB HARD MUTE SURD SHARP ATONIC FLATED SILENT ANAUDIA APHONIC SPIRATE APHONOUS BREATHED NOTELESS
VOID NO BAD FREE KORE LEAR LEER MUTE NULL PASS TOOM ABYSS AVOID BLANK EGEST EJECT EMPTY INEPT LAPSE PURGE SLICE SPACE WASTE DEVOID HOLLOW VACANT VACUUM CONCAVE INVALID VACANCY VACUITY EVACUATE INDIGENT NONBEING
(— OF FEELING) BLATE
(— OF SENSE) INANE
(— OF SUBSTANCE) JEJUNE
VOIDED FALSE CLECHE CLECHY CLECHEE
VOILE NINON ETAMINE
VOLATILE LIGHT FIGENT LIVELY VOLAGE BUOYANT DARTING ELASTIC FLIGHTY FLYAWAY GASEOUS FUGITIVE SKITTISH VAPOROSE VAPOROUS FUGACIOUS
(PREF.) PTENO
VOLATILITY LEVITY
VOLCANIC ROCK TRASS
VOLCANO APO DOME ETNA ASKJA PELEE SHASTA VULCAN FURNACE RUMBLER VULCANO FUMAROLE KRAKATOA SPITFIRE VESUVIUS
(MUD —) SALSE SALINELLE
VOLE CRABER CRICETID CAMPAGNOL
VOLITATION FLIGHT VOLATION
VOLITION WILL CHOICE INTENT VOLENCY VELLEITY
VOLLEY TIRE CROWD DRIFT VOLEE FLIGHT BARRAGE PLATOON BLIZZARD
VOLPLANE GLIDE
VOLPONE (AUTHOR OF —) JONSON
(CHARACTER IN —) CELIA MOSCA BONARIO CORVINO VOLPONE VOLTORE POLITICK CORBACCIO PEREGRINE
VOLSUNG WAELS
VOLT VOLTA REPOLON
(— AMPERE UNIT) VAR
VOLTAGE KICKBACK
VOLTAIC GUR GALVANIC
VOLTE-FACE BACKFLIP
VOLUBILITY FLUENCY
VOLUBLE GLIB WORDY FLUENT
VOLUME MO PEN BAND BOOK BULK CODE SIZE TOME CODEX SPACE CUBAGE CONTENT DIURNAL MENAION VOLUMEN CAPACITY CUBATURE SOLIDITY STRENGTH
(— OF SOUND) STRESS
(— OF WORT) LENGTH
(PATTERN —) DUMMY
VOLUMINOUS FULL AMPLE BULKY LARGE BOUFFANT
VOLUMNIA (SON OF —) CORIOLANUS
VOLUNTARILY WILLES WILLICHE
VOLUNTARY FREE WILLY SORTIE WILFUL PRELUDE SORTITA WILLFUL WILLING ELECTIVE

FREEWILL HONORARY OPTIONAL POSTLUDE UNFORCED
VOLUNTEER OFFER ENLIST PROFFER FENCIBLE STRANGER
(— SERVING AS OFFICER) REFORMADO
(— STATE) TENNESSEE
VOLUPTUARY SYBARITE
VOLUPTUOUS ADIN BUXOM LUXIVE LYDIAN SULTRY WANTON SENSUAL DELICATE LUSCIOUS SENSUOUS
VOLUPTUOUSNESS DELICE LUXURY
VOLUTE TURN HELIX SCROLL VOLUTA CILLERY VOLUTION
VOLUTION COIL TWIST WHORL VERTICIL
VOLVA CUP WRAPPER
VOMIT CAT PUT BALK BARF BOCK BOKE CACK CAST PICK PUKE SICK SPEW SPUE VOME WOOM BRAKE EVOME HEAVE RALPH REACH RETCH SHOOT POSSET REJECT VOMITO CASCADE CASTING REGORGE DISGORGE PARBREAK SICKNESS VOMITING
VOMITING BOKE EMESIS PYEMESIS (PREF.) EMET(O)
VOMITUS SPEW SPUE
VOODOO HEX OBI CHARM OBEAH HOODOO SORCERER
(— DESIGN) VERVER
(— PRIEST) BOCOR BOKOR
(— SPELL) MOJO
VOODOOISM VODUN WANGA VODOUN
VOPHSI (SON OF —) NAHBI
VORACIOUS GORB GREEDY BULIMIC ESURINE GLUTTON THROATY EDACIOUS ESURIENT RAVENING RAVENOUS
VORACITY BULIMIA EDACITY
VORTEX APEX EDDY GYRE SWIRL WHIRL
VOTARESS NUN
VOTARY PALMER ZEALOT DEVOTEE SECTARY ADHERENT DEVOTARY FOLLOWER
VOTE AYE CON NAY PRO ELECT FAGOT GRACE VOICE BALLOT DIVIDE FAGGOT TONGUE APPROVE PLUMPER SUFFRAGE
(— AGAINST) NAY KNIFE NEGATIVE
(— APPROVAL) CONFIRM
(— FOR) AY AYE PRO SUPPORT
(— ILLEGALLY) REPEAT
(— OF ASSENT) PLACET
(AFFIRMATIVE —) YEA YES
(INFORMAL —) STRAW
(KIND OF —) WRITEIN
VOTER BOLTER POLLER CHOOSER ELECTOR FLOATER ASSENTOR
(KIND OF —) CROSSOVER
VOTING POLL
(— FIRST) PREROGATIVE
VOTIVE VOWED
VOTYAK UDMURT
VOUCH ABLE ASSURE ATTEST AVOUCH ENDORSE ACCREDIT
VOUCHER CHIT CHALAN COUPON POLICY TICKET WARRANT
VOUCHSAFE GIVE SEND DEIGN GRANT VOUCH BETEEM PLEASE WITSAFE
VOUSSOIR QUOIN WEDGE KEYSTONE SPRINGER
VOW LAY VUM AVOW OATH SNUM VOTE SWEAR VOUCH BEHEST PLEDGE BEHIGHT PROMISE PROTEST
(MARRIAGE —) IDO
(PREF.) EUCHO
VOWEL SHWA WIDE GLIDE SCHWA VOCOID AUGMENT PALATAL GEMINATE ORINASAL
(— POINT) SERE
(— SOUND) LONGA
(BACK —) VELAR
(CHANGE OF —) UMLAUT
(GLIDE —) MURMUR
(GROUP OF 2 —S) BROAD DIGRAM DIGRAPH
(PREFIXED —) AUGMENT
(SHORT —) MATRA
VOYAGE SAIL TRIP VIAGE COURSE CRUISE FLIGHT TRAVEL CARAVAN JOURNEY PASSAGE SAILING STEAMER PERIPLUS SHIPPING
VOYAGING SEA NAVIGANT
VOYEUR PEEPER
VULCAN MULCIBER
(WORKSHOP OF —) AETNA
VULCANITE EBONITE
VULCANIZATION BURNING
VULCANIZE BURN CURE METALIZE
VULCANIZER CEMENTER
VULGAR LOW LEWD LOUD RUDE BANAL CHEAP FLASH GROSS SLANG SLIMY TOUGH COARSE COMMON PORTER RABBLE VULGUS WOOLEN XRATED BLATANT BOORISH GENERAL KNAVISH LOWBRED MOBBISH OBSCENE POPULAR PROFANE RAFFISH SECULAR TABLOID VILLAIN WOOLLEN BANAUSIC CHURLISH MECHANIC PANDEMIC PLEBEIAN PORTERLY POTHOUSE SOUTERLY
VULGARIAN CAD SLOB TIGER KEELIE RAFFISH
VULGARITY RAUNCH SHODDY FOULNESS HARLOTRY
VULGARIZE PLEBIFY PROFANE
VULGARIZED DEGRADED
VULGARLY CHEAPLY
VULNERABILITY GAP EXPOSURE
VULNERABLE NAKED LIABLE EXPOSED PREGNABLE
VULPINE SLY FOXY CRAFTY ALOPECOID
VULTURE AURA GEIR PAPA AREND GRAAP GRAPE GRIPE SWIPE URUBU CONDOR CORBIE FALCON GRIPHE RAPTOR SNATCH TORGOS GRIFFIN GRIFFON GRYPHON NEKHEBT AASVOGEL DIRTBIRD GEREAGLE NEKHEBET ZOPILOTE GALLINAZO
VULVA DOCK PUDENDUM (PREF.) EPISIO
VUM SNUM

W WAW WHISKEY WILLIAM

WA VU KAWA LAWA

WABBLE COCKLE COGGLE HOBBLE WAGGLE WARBLE WAUBLE WOBBLE

WABBLY COGGLE WAGGLY WOBBLY

WABBY LOON WHABBY

WABRON WAYBERRY

WACKY CRAZY FLAKY WACKO WIGGY FLAKEY INSANE MENTAL ERRATIC OFFBEAT

WAD BAT BET BOB PAD COLF LINE POKE SWAB SWOB WISP WAGER PLEDGE SCOURER GRAPHITE

WADDING BOMBAST

WADDLE WAG DAIDLE HODDLE PODDLE TODDLE WALLOP WIDDLE WAUCHLE

WADDY PEG STICK COWBOY RUSTLER WHADDIE

WADE FORD WYDE SLOSH PLODGE PLOUTER PLUTTER
(— IN MUD) LAIR

WADI OUED WASH GULLY RAVINE

WADSET PAWN PLEDGE MORTGAGE

WAFER HOST ABRET OBLEY CACHET GAUFRE LAVASH MATZOH OFLETE POPADAM FLATBROD PARTICLE

WAFF WAG FLAP GUST ODOR PUFF WAVE WHIFF PALTRY FLUTTER GLIMPSE LOWBORN

WAFFENSCHMEID, DER
(CHARACTER IN —) GEORG MARIE CONRAD LIEBENAU STADINGER
(COMPOSER OF —) LORTZING

WAFFIE VAGRANT VAGABOND

WAFFLE GOFER WAFER WAVER GAUFRE BLATHER

WAFT PUFF WING WHEFT WHIFF BECKON WINNOW

WAG LUG NOD WIG WIT WOG CARD CHAP FLAG WAFF WALK DROLL JOKER ROGUE SHAKE TROLL FARCER JESTER NICKUM WADDLE WAGGLE WAGWIT WIGWAG FARCEUR HUMORIST SLYBOOTS

WAGE FEE PAY WAR HIRE LEVY FIGHT WADGE WEDGE EMPLOY ENGAGE PACKET STIPEND OVERTIME
(— BATTLE) STRIKE

WAGER GO BET LAY PUT SET VIE WED GAGE HOLD PAWN TOSS WOID BOUND PRIZE RAISE REVIE SPORT STAKE STOOP WADGE DEPONE GAMBLE IMPONE LEVANT WEDFEE STOATER QUINELLA

WAGES FEE PAY UTU GAGE HIRE MEED STIP GAGES TUNCA REWARD SALARY PENSION SERVICE STIPEND GRATUITY LABORAGE PAYCHECK REQUITAL

WAGGERY JEST ROGUERY DROLLERY

WAGGISH ARCH DROLL JOKEY JOCOSE JESTING JOCULAR PARLOUS ROGUISH WAGSOME HUMOROUS SPORTIVE

WAGGLE WAG WIGGLE WOBBLE WOGGLE

WAGON CAR FLY VAN CART CHAR DRAG DRAY PLOW RACK TEAM TRAM WAIN WANE BUGGY DILLY JERKY RULLY TRUCK CAMION ROLLEY SPIDER TELEGA CAISSON CHARIOT COASTER FOURGON SHELVER TUMBREL TUMBRIL DEMOCRAT LANDSHIP RUNABOUT WHITETOP
(— WITHOUT SPRINGS) JERKY TELEGA
(BAGGAGE —) FOURGON
(COVERED —) VAN CARAVAN TARTANA LANDSHIP CONESTOGA
(KIND OF —) PADDY
(LUMBER —) GILLY
(MINING —) TRAM HUTCH RULLY ROLLEY
(ROUNDUP —) HOODLUM
(RUSSIAN —) TELEGA KIBITKA
(SCREENED —) ARABA
(STATION —) MICROBUS SUBURBAN
(TEA —) SERVER

WAGONER AURIGA TREKKER WAINMAN

WAGONETTE BREAK

WAGONLOAD FODDER FOTHER

WAGONMAN FOOTMAN

WAGTAIL MOLLY OATEAR WAGGIE WASHER MOTACIL WATERIE SEEDBIRD WASHDISH WASHTAIL

WAHINE WIFE WOMAN FEMALE VAHINE FEMININE MISTRESS

WAHOO ONO PETO BASSWOOD EUONYMUS GUARAPUCU

WAIF WEFT STRAY FEEBLE PALTRY STRAFE CURRENT IGNOBLE WASTREL

WAIL CRY WOW BAWL GURL HOWL KEEN MOAN RAME YARM CROON MOURN ULULU LAMENT PLAINT YAMMER EJULATE PLANGOR ULULATE ULLAGONE

WAILING WO WOE LAMENT ULULANT

WAIN CART WAGON WEYNE CHARIOT

WAINSCOT CEIL CARDIGAN

WAINSCOTING CEILING PANELING

WAIST JOSIE BASQUE BLOUSE BODICE HALTER MIDDLE TAILLE CORSAGE PIERROT

WAISTCOAT VEST BENJY GILET FECKET JERKIN VESKIT WESKIT SINGLET CAMISOLE

WAISTER TROUNCER

WAIT BIDE HOLD KEEP LITE PARK STAY TEND WHET ABIDE ABODE DEFER HOVER LURCH TARRY WATCH ATTEND DEPEND EXPECT HARKEN LAYOUT LINGER
(— A WHILE) TAIHOA
(— FOR) KEEP ABIDE AWAIT ATTEND EXPECT
(— ON) HOP SEE SERVE INTEND LACKEY
(— TABLE) HASH SERVE

WAITER MOZO CARHOP COMMIS DRAWER FLUNKY GARCON HASHER KIDNEY SALVER TENDER THOMAS DAPIFER FLUNKEY KELLNER PANNIER PICCOLO SERVITOR KITMUDGAR
(APPRENTICE —) COMMIS
(WING —) SOMMELIER

WAITING DORMANT

WAITING ROOM LOBBY ANTEROOM

WAITRESS NIPPY HASHER MOUSMEE PHYLLIS

WAIVE ABEY DEFER EVADE FORGO ABANDON DECLINE FORSAKE POSTPONE RENOUNCE RELINQUISH

WAKA CANOE

WAKE WAK CROW NECK PLAY STIR ALERT REVEL ROUSE TANGI TRAIL VIGIL WATCH AROUSE AWAKEN EXCITE FEATHER

WAKEFUL ALERT WACKER RESTLESS VIGILANT WALKRIFE WATCHFUL

WAKEFULNESS VIGIL WATCH INSOMNIA

WAKE-ROBIN ARUM SARA SARAH TRILLIUM

WAKF WAQF VAKUF VACOUF

WALACHIAN RUMAN VLACH ROMANESE

WALAHEE ALAHEE

WALAPAI HUALPAI

WALDENSIAN LEONIST PATARIN VAUDOIS SABOTIER

WALE RIB BEND PICK WEAL WELT RIDGE WHELP CHOICE HARPIN STROKE
(PL.) BEND HARPINS

WALES CYMRU CAMBRIA
(PREF.) CAMBRO

WALES

BAY: SWANSEA CARDIGAN TREMADOC
CAPITAL: CARDIFF
COUNTY: FLINT RADNOR DENBIGH ANGLESEY CARDIGAN MONMOUTH PEMBROKE
ISLAND: MONA ANGLESEY HOLYHEAD
LAKE: BALA VYRNWY
LANGUAGE: CYMRAEG
MEASURE: COVER CANTRED CANTREF LESTRAD LISTRED CRANNOCK
MOUNTAIN: SNOWDON
MOUNTAIN RANGE: BERWYN CAMBRIAN
PEOPLE: CYMRY KYMRY WELSH
PORT: CARDIFF
RIVER: DEE USK WYE TAFF TEME TOWY TEIFI SEVERN VYRNWY
TOWN: MOLD RHYL ROSS FLINT TOWYN AMLWCH BANGOR BRECON RUTHIN CARDIFF NEWPORT RHONDDA SWANSEA HEREFORD HOLYHEAD PEMBROKE BRECKNOCK
WATERFALL: CAIN RHAIADR

WALK GO JET MOG FOOT GAIT GANG HIKE HOOF LAMP PACE PAUT REEL STEP TROD ALLEE ALLEY ARBOR LEAVE MARCH PORCH SHANK SLOPE SPACE STALK TRACE TRACK TRADE TRAMP TREAD TROOP ATTEND AVENUE BEHAVE BOUNCE BRIDGE BROGUE DANDER PASEAR SASHAY STROKE TODDLE TRAVEL TRUDGE BALTEUS BERCEAU CRAMBLE FOOTING GALLERY SHUFFLE STRETCH TRACHLE TRAIPSE TURNOUT AMBULATE ARBORWAY FLAGGING FRESCADE NAVICATE TRAVERSE PROMENADE PEREGRINATE
(— ABOUT) SLOSH
(— AFFECTEDLY) PRINK
(— AIMLESSLY) PAUP POAP
(— ARROGANTLY) STRUT STRIDE
(— ARROGANTLY —) WALTZ
(— AWKWARDLY) STAUP SHAMBLE
(— BEFORE) PREAMBLE
(— BEHIND BATTLEMENTS) ALURE
(— BRISKLY) LEG SKELP
(— CARELESSLY) JAYWALK
(— CAUTIOUSLY) STALK
(— CLUMSILY) JOLL STUMP LOPPET
(— FOR CATTLE) GANG
(— FOR EXAMINING ENGINE) GALLERY
(— FOR EXERCISE) HIKE GRIND
(— HEAVILY) PLOD CLOMP CLUMP STUMP TRAMP LAMPER PLODGE
(— IDLY) DANDER POTTER SAUNTER
(— IN AFFECTED MANNER) MINCE
(— IN SUPERIOR MANNER) SWAGGER

(— LAME) LIMP HIRPLE HOBBLE CRIPPLE
(— LEISURELY) AMBLE DANDER STROLL
(— ON) BEAT TREAD
(— OUT) FLOUNCE
(— PRIMLY) MINCE
(— RAPIDLY) LAMP LINK STAVE
(— SHAKILY) DOTTER
(— SLOWLY) JET LAG
(— SMARTLY) LINK
(— STEADILY) SNOVE SNOOVE
(— THROUGH WATER) WADE
(— UNSTEADILY) REEL DADDLE FALTER STAVER STAGGER STUMBLE
(— WAVERINGLY) SHEVEL WARPLE
(— WITH DIFFICULTY) CRAMBLE CRAMMEL LOUTHER
(— WITH JERK) HIRCH
(— WITH LOFTY GAIT) JET
(— WITH LOOSE GAIT) GANGLE
(— WITH OSTENTATION) PRANCE
(— WITHOUT LIFTING FEET) SCUFF
(— WITH SHUFFLE) COONJINE
(— WITH STRIDES) STAG
(— WITH TREES) XYST XYSTUS ALAMEDA
(BACKSTAGE —) BRIDGE
(COOL —) FRESCADE
(COVERED —) PAWN PORCH CLOISTER
(FOLIAGE-COVERED —) BERCEAU
(HARD —) STRAM SWINGE
(LIMPING —) GIMP
(LONG —) STRAM
(POMPOUS —) STRUT
(PUBLIC —) XYST XYSTUS ALAMEDA
(RAISED —) GALLERY
(SHADED —) MALL ARBOR XYSTUS
(SHORT —) TURN
(TEDIOUS —) TRAIL
(TREE-PLANTED —) XYST XYSTUS
(PL.) BALTEI
(PREF.) AMBULO GRADIO GRADO

WALKER GOER FOOTER FULLER GANGER FOOTMAN TODDLER PEDESTRIAN
(PL.) FEET

WALKING HOTFOOT PASSANT AMBULANT GRADIENT TRIPPING
(— IN SLEEP) SOMNABULISM
(PREF.) BASI BASO
(SUFF.) BAT(ES)(IC) GRADE

WALKING STICK BAT CANE GIBBY KEBBY STICK WADDY KEBBIE PHASMID SPECTER ASHPLANT GIBSTAFF WOODHORSE

WALKOUT STRIKE

WALKURE, DIE (CHARACTER IN —) MIME WOTAN FRICKA HUNDING SIEGMUND SIEGLINDE BRUNNHILDE
(COMPOSER OF —) WAGNER

WALKWAY CATWALK SKYWALK SIDEWALK

WALL WA DAM FIN MUR WAW BAIL BELT CELL CORE CRIB CURB DICK DIKE DRUM DYKE FACE HEAD MURE PACK SKIN SPUR WING WOGE ATTIC BOARD CHEEK CRUST DIGUE EMURE FENCE HEDGE MEURE MURAL PIRCA SHOJI WOGHE WOUGH BAFFLE BAILEY BATTER CUTOFF DOKHMA IMMURE LEADER PARIES PARPEN PRETIL REBOTE RIPRAP SCREEN SEPTUM SHIELD VALLUM CHEMISE CURTAIN ENCLOSE MIZRACH PARAPET PERPEND PLUTEUS REREDOS TAMBOUR FIREBACK SPANDREL TRAVERSE
(— ABOVE FACADE) ATTIC
(— AROUND) IMMURE
(— BEHIND ALTAR) REREDOS
(— BETWEEN TWO OPENINGS) PIER
(— CARRYING CUPOLA) DRUM
(— CARRYING ROOF) BAHUT
(— CROSSING RAMPART) SPUR
(— HANGING) DRAPERY
(— IN) MURE ENTOMB IMMURE IMPRISON
(— IN HOCKEY RINK) BOARD
(— IN ROMAN ARENA) SPINA
(— IN TRUCK) HEADER
(— OF BLAST FURNACE) DAM INWALL FIREBACK
(— OF CASTLE) BARMKIN
(— OF CLAY) COTTLE
(— OF HOOF) CRUST
(— OF MINE) FACE
(— OF MOUTH) CHEEK
(— OF TENT) KANAT CANAUT
(BODY —) MANTLE
(CIRCULAR —) CASHEL
(CORE —) HEARTING
(CURVED —) SWEEP
(DIVIDING —) SEPTUM
(END — OF BUILDING) GABLE
(FISH —) LEADER
(HIGHEST PART OF —) CRAPWA
(INNER SLOPE OF —) BATTER
(KIND OF —) TROMBE
(LOG —) CRIB
(LOW —) BAHUT PODIUM PLUTEUS
(LOWER PART OF —) DADO
(OUTER — OF CASTLE) BAIL BAILEY
(PEAT —) COP
(PUDDLE —) HEARTING
(RETAINING —) CRIB PILING BULKHEAD
(SCARPED —) GHAT
(SEA —) GROIN
(SECONDARY —) CHEMISE
(SOMETHING ATTACHED TO —) PINUP
(SUSTAINING —) RIPRAP
(THINNED PART OF —) ALLEGE
(VENTRAL —) STERNUM
(WING —) AILERON
(PL.) PERICARP
(PREF.) MURI PARIETO TICHO
(SUFF.) **(COAT OF SPORE —)** SPORIUM

WALLABA APA

WALLABY WURRUP BRUSHER TOOLACH WURRUNG BOONGARY KANGAROO PADMELON WHIPTAIL

WALLACHIAN RUMAN

WALLAROO EURO

WALLBOARD GOBO

WALLET JAG JAGG MAIL POKE BOGET BOUGE BULCH BULGE SCRIP BUDGET READER SACKET ALFARGA ALFORJA LEATHER BILLFOLD NOTECASE POCHETTE
(PREF.) PERO

WALLEYE WHALL SAUGER LEUCOMA WATCHEYE EXOTROPIA

WALLEYED PIKE DORE DORY JACK PERCID SALMON WALLEYE PICKEREL

WALLFLOWER CUBA CHEIR GILLY JACKS KEIRI GELOFER WARRIOR GILLIVER

WALL HAWKWEED LUNGWORT

WALLOP TAN BEAT BEER FLOP SLUG SOCK PASTE POUND VALOP GALLOP IMPACT WALLOW FLUTTER TROUNCE FLOUNDER LAMBASTE

WALLOW FADE LAIR ROLL SOIL SLOSH WALWE GROVEL MUDDLE WALTER WELTER WITHER SLUDDER SWELTER FLOUNDER KOMMETJE VOLUTATE

WALLOWISH FLAT WELSH INSIPID

WALLPAPER GROUND SCENIC HANGING TENTURE TAPESTRY

WALL PEPPER SEDUM STONECROP

WALL PLATE PAN RASEN

WALL RUE TENTWORT

WALL STREET (— ORDER) BUY HOLD SELL

WALL-TO-WALL UBIQUITOUS

WALLY TOY FINE SPOIL PAMPER ROBUST STRONG STURDY SPLENDID VIGOROUS

WALLY, LA (CHARACTER IN —) WALLY GELLNER HAGENBACH
(COMPOSER OF —) CATALANI

WALNUT ACAPU NOGAL TRYMA AKHROT BANNUT HEARTNUT
(BRAZILIAN —) EMBOYA IMBUIA
(PL.) JUGLANS

WALNUT BROWN TAFFY

WALNUT SHELL BOLSTER

WALPI HUALPI

WALRUS MORSE WALTRON PELAGIAN PINNIPED ROSMARINE

WALT CRANK UNSTEADY

WALTZ LUG CARRY MARCH VALSE BOSTON BREEZE FLOUNCE

WAMARA CLUBWOOD IRONWOOD PANOCOCO

WAMBLE ROLL SPIN WAMEL NAUSEA REVOLVE

WAMBLY FAINT SHAKY

WAME WEM WAMB WYME BELLY

WAMPUM PEAG BEADS DOUGH FADME HAWOK MONEY PAAGE SEWAN FATHOM SEAWAN ROANOKE

WAMUS JACKET WAMPUS WARMUS

WAN DIM HAW ASHY FADE PALE PALY SICK ASHEN BLAKE FAINT WHITE FEEBLE PALLID SALLOW GHASTLY LANGUID

WANAPUM SOKULK

WAND ROD VARE YARD BATON STAFF STICK VERGE VIRGA FERULA THYRSE WATTLE RHABDOS THYRSUS CADUCEUS
(JESTER'S —) BAUBLE
(PREF.) RHABD(O)

WANDER BAT BUM ERR GAD WAG HAAK HAIK HAKE MAZE MUCK RAKE RAVE ROAM ROIL ROLL ROVE WALK WILL WORE DAVER DRIFT GLAIK KNOCK RANGE ROGUE SHACK SLOSH STRAY TAVER TRAIK VAGUE WAIVE WAVER CANDER CRUISE DANDER DAUNER FORAGE LOITER MITHER MOIDER MUCKER PALMER PERUSE RAMBLE RANGLE STRAKE STROLL SWERVE WILDER MEANDER TRAFFIC TRAIPSE VAGRATE VANDYKE ABERRATE CUTICULA SQUANDER STRAGGLE STRAVAGE STRAVAIG
(— ABOUT) DIVAGATE
(— ABSTRACTEDLY) MOON
(— AIMLESSLY) SWAN SLOSH TRACE MEANDER
(— AS A VAGABOND) SHACK
(— AS A VAGRANT) LOITER
(— AT RANDOM) SQUANDER
(— ERRATICALLY) SWASH
(— FROM DIRECT COURSE) STRAGGLE
(— FROM PLACE TO PLACE) WAG
(— IDLY) HAKE LOUT MAUNDER SHACKLE
(— IN DELIRIUM) DWALE DWALL
(— IN MIND) DAVER DANDER DELIRE
(— LEISURELY) BUMMEL
(— RESTLESSLY) FEEK

WANDERER HOBO WAIF ROVER TRAMP VAGUE RANGER DRIFTER PILGRIM RAMBLER VAGRANT FUGITIVE RUNAGATE TRAVELER VAGABOND
(AUTHOR OF —) FOURNIER
(CHARACTER IN —) FRANTZ GALAIS MILLIE SEUREL YVONNE AUGUSTIN BLONDEAU FRANCOIS MEAULNES VALENTINE CHARPENTIER

WANDERING GAD ROAM WAFF ERROR STRAY VAGUE ARRANT ASTRAY ERRANT MOBILE ROVING VAGANT VAGOUS DEVIOUS NOMADIC ODYSSEY VAGANCY VAGRANT WINDING ABERRANT FLOATING FUGITIVE PELASGIC PLANETAL PLANETIC RAMBLING RESTLESS TRAILING VAGABOND WINDRING ITINERANT MIGRATORY PEREGRINE
(PREF.) PLAN(O) VAGO
(SUFF.) PLANIA

WANDERING JEW (AUTHOR OF —) SUE
(CHARACTER IN —) ROSE HARDY RODIN SIMON DJALMA SAMUEL BAUDOIN GABRIEL JACQUES ADRIENNE AGRICOLA AIGRIGNY DAGOBERT FRANCOIS HERODIAS RENNEPONT CARDOVILLE

WANDFLOWER GALAX SPARAXIS

WANDOROBO WAASI

WAND-SHAPED VIRGATE

WANE GO EBB SET WELK WILK ABATE DECAY UNWAX WANZE REPINE DECLINE DWINDLE DECREASE
(— OF MOON) WADDLE

WANGA CHARM SPELL OUANGA WONGAH SORCERY

WANGLE FAKE SHAKE WIGGLE FINAGLE

WANIGAN ARK CHEST COFFER WANGUN
WANT HURT LACK LIKE MISS NEED OONT PINE VOID WANE WONT CRAVE FAULT FORGO BESOIN CHOOSE DEARTH DEFECT DESIRE MISTER PENURY PLIGHT ABSENCE BEGGARY BLEMISH BORASCA DEFAULT MISEASE NEEDHAM POVERTY REQUIRE VACANCY MISCHIEF WANTROKE
(— EXCEEDINGLY) DIE ACHE
(— OF APPETITE) ANOREXY ANOREXIA
(— OF CONTROL) ACRASY
(— OF ENERGY) ATONY
(— OF FEELING) APATHY
(— OF GOOD SENSE) FOLLY
(— OF LIBERTY) RESTRAINT
(— OF PROPER CARE) NEGLIGENCE
(— OF REST) UNRO
(— OF SPIRIT) FOZINESS POLTROONERY
(— OF SUCCESS) FAILURE
(— OF VARIETY) MONOPOLY
(— OF VIGOR) DELICACY
WANTAGE ULLAGE
WANTING LACK VOID WANE ALACK MINUS ABSENT LACKING MISSING INDIGENT
(— ORIGINALITY) BANAL
WANTON JAY NAG RIG DAFT GOLE IDLE LEWD NICE RAGE SKIT CADGY DALLY LIGHT SAUCY GIGLET GIGLOT HARLOT HAUNTY LACHES LUBRIC RAKISH RIGSBY TICKLE TOYING TOYISH UNRULY COLTISH FULSOME GIGGISH HAGGARD IMMORAL KITTOCK LUSTFUL PAPHIAN RIGGISH RIOTOUS SMICKER WAYWARD FLAGRANT LUSCIOUS MISTRESS PETULANT PLAYSOME RUMBELOW SKITTISH SLIPPERY SPITEFUL SPORTIVE UNCHASTE
WANTONNESS FOLLY PRIDE SPORT RAGERY SUCCUDRY SURQUIDY
WAP BIND BLOW WHOP WRAP BLAST FIGHT KNOCK STORM TRUSS BUNDLE STRIKE
WAPITI ELK ALCE DEER LOSH LUSH STAG MARAL MOOSE CERVID WAMPOOSE
WAR WIN CAMP FEUD MART FIGHT SWORD WORSE WORST BATTLE CONTEND CRUSADE CONFLICT GUERILLA OVERCOME
(OPPONENT OF —) DOVE PEACENIK
(RELIGIOUS —) JEHAD JIHAD
(PREF.) BELLI MACHO POLEMO
WAR AND PEACE (AUTHOR OF —) TOLSTOY
(CHARACTER IN —) LISE ELLEN MARYA ANDREY PIERRE ROSTOV ANATOLE BEZUHOV KURAGIN KUTUZOV NATASHA NIKOLAY VASSILY NAPOLEON BOLKONSKY NIKOLUSHKA
WARBLE SING CAROL CHANT CHIRL CHIRM SHAKE TRILL YODEL JARGON RALISH RELISH WARNEL WORMIL DESCANT VIBRATE WOURNIL
WARBLE FLY OXFLY BOTFLY GADFLY OESTRID OESTRIAN
WARBLER CUT KIT CHAT SMEU WREN FITTE PEGGY CANARY EYSOGE REELER SMEUTH SYLVIA TITIEN CREEPER CROMBEC FANTAIL HAYBIRD HAYSUCK PITBIRD REDPOLL SYLVIID TROCHIL BEAMBIRD BLACKCAP FAUVETTE MALURINE MOCKBIRD OVENBIRD PINCPINC REDSTART REEDBIRD RIRORIRO TROCHILUS CHIFFCHAFF
WAR CLUB MAR MER MERE MERAI MARREE
WAR CRY ALALA BANZAI SLOGAN
WARD CARE GUARD MAHAL VICUS WAIRD WATCH ALUMNA BARRIO CALPUL DEFEND ROWENA KEEPING NATUARY PROTEGE CALPOLLI CONTRADA
(— OFF) FEND WEAR WERE AVERT AWARD FENCE PARRY REPEL STAVE SHIELD BUCKLER EXPIATE FORFEND
(— OF WORKHOUSE) SPIKE
(HOSPITAL —) ICU
WARDAGE WARTH
WARDEN ALCADE DIZDAR PORTER RANGER REGENT ROLAND WARNER ALCAIDE HOGMACE LEATMAN ROWLAND BEARWARD CLAVIGER
(AUTHOR OF —) TROLLOPE
(CHARACTER IN —) TOM BOLD JOHN SUSAN FINNEY TOWERS ABRAHAM ELEANOR GRANTLY HARDING SEPTIMUS HAPHAZARD QUIVERFUL THEOPHILUS
WARDER PORTER GUARDER HEIMDAL TURNKEY WATCHMAN BEEFEATER
WARDROBE KAS CLOSET VESTRY ALMIRAH ARMOIRE VESTUARY
WARE CLOTH GOODS SPEND FABRICS SEAWEED SQUANDER
(CERAMIC —) SPODE BENNINGTON
(CLOISONNE —) SHIPPO
(ENAMELED —) BILSTON COALPORT
(GILT —) ORMOLU
(INFERIOR —S) SLUM
(JAPANESE —) IMARI YAYOI
(JAPANESE CERAMIC —) SETO BIZEN KARATSU
(KIND OF —) RAKU SETO TING BIZEN CHIEN SANDA YAYOI KUTANI MINTON KARATSU WHIELDON
(KIND OF JAPANESE POTTERY —) SANDA
(MAJOLICA —) DERUTA
(PORCELAIN —) CHINA IMARI BERLIN
(UNGLAZED —) BISQUE
(PL.) TROKE CHAFFER TROGGIN
WAREHOUSE GOLA HONG ETAPE GOLAH STORE BODEGA FONDUK GODOWN STAITH ALMACEN FUNDUCK SPICERY STOWAGE ENTREPOT MAGAZINE SERAGLIO
WARFARE WAR ARMS IRON ARMOR BATTLE PSYWAR MILITIA CONFLICT
(CHEMICAL — AGENT) SARIN
(NONAGGRESSIVE —) SITZKRIEG
(PETTY —) GUERILLA GUERRILLA
(PSYCHOLOGICAL —) PSYWAR
(SUFF.) MACHIA MACHY
WARHEAD MIRV
WAR-HORSE CHARGER COURSER DESTRER TROOPER DESTRIER
WARILY TIPTOE GINGERLY
WARINESS CAUTEL CAUTION DISTRUST WARESHIP WARIMENT
WARKLOOM TOOL WARKLUME
WARLIKE WARLY MARTIAL CAVALIER FIGHTING MILITARY BELLICOSE
(NOT —) IMBELLIC
WARLOCK IMP WITCH SPRITE WARLOW WIZARD CONJUROR SORCERER
WARLORD TUCHUN
WARM HOT LEW LOO RUG BASK BEEK KEEN LEWD MILD CALID CHAFE EAGER FRESH MALMY MUNGY SLACK TEPID TOAST ACHAFE ARDENT BIRSLE DEVOUT DIGEST FOSTER GENIAL HEARTY HEATED RIZZLE TENDER TOASTY CHERISH CLEMENT CORDIAL GLOWING THERMAL ZEALOUS FRIENDLY PRESSING SANGUINE
(— UP) SCORE
(MODERATELY —) LEW SLACK TEPID
(PREF.) CAL(E)(I)(ORI)
WARMHEARTED KIND TENDER FRIENDLY GENEROUS
WARMING FOVENT
WARMOUTH BIGMOUTH FLATFISH SACALAIT
WARMTH GLOW HEAT LIFE ZEAL ARDOR LEWTH ENERGY FERVOR ARDENCY PASSION CALIDITY FERVENCY
(— OF ADDRESS) UNCTION
(— OF MANNER) EMPRESSEMENT
(INNER —) JUICE
WARN REDE WARD WERN ALERT AREAD DETER WEIRD ADVERT ADVISE EXHORT INFORM CAUTION COMMAND COUNSEL GARNISH PREVISE ADMONISH THREATEN
(— OFF) FORBID
WARNING AHEM ITEM ALARM CHECK KNELL BEACON CAVEAT LESSON NOTICE OFFICE SAMPLE SIGNAL TIPOFF AVISION CALLING CAUTION EXAMPLE GRIFFIN JIGGERS MEMENTO MONITOR PRESAGE SUMMONS DOCUMENT GARDYLOO MONITION PREMONITION
(— OF DISASTER) DIRE
(— ON CHART) VIGIA
(— SIGNAL) RED REDFLAG REDLIGHT
(AIR-RAID —) ALERT
(ARCHERY —) FAST
(DANGER —) VIGIA
WARP CUP WEB BIAS CANE CAST LIFT WARF WERP WIND ANGLE CHAIN CHOKE CRAWL CROOK GEYZE KEDGE PORRY THRAW TWINE WEAVE BUCKLE CHEESE DEFORM WASHIN DEFLECT DISTORT SKELLER
(— IN WEAVING) CRAM
(PREF.) HIST(O)
WARPED WRY BUCKLED GNARLED HOUSING
WARPER BALLER
WARPING BOW PANDATION
WARRAGAL WILD DINGO HORSE OUTLAW
WARRANT ABLE EARN WARN AMRIT BERAT FIANT PRESS SANAD VOUCH AMRITA ASSERT BRANCH BREVET CAPIAS COUPON DOCKET ENSURE INSURE PARDON PERMIT PLEVIN POLICY POTENT SUNNUD TICKET UPHOLD WARDOG BEHIGHT CAPTION DESERVE JUSTIFY PRECEPT PROMISE GUARANTY MITTIMUS
(CUSTOMS —) TRANSIRE
WARRANTED VALID
WARRANT OFFICER BOSN BOSUN BOATSWAIN
WARRAU GUARANO
WARREN SLUM CONYGER WARRANT
WARRIOR TOA WER EARL HERO KEMP RINK WEER BERNE FREIK FREKE HAGEN LLUDD SEPAD SINGH THANE THEGN OSSIAN WARMAN WEAPON FIGHTER SOLDIER STARKAD WARWOLF ZERBINO CHAMPION RODOMONT SHARDANA STARKATH SWORDMAN WARFARER
(— CLASS) MAGANI
(— OF NOBLE RANK) EARL
(AMERICAN INDIAN —) BRAVE SANNUP
(BOASTFUL —) RODOMONT
(BRYTHONIC —) LLUDD
(BURGUNDIAN —) HAGEN
(FEMALE —) AMAZON SHIELDMAY
(GREEK —) AJAX
(IRISH —) FENIAN
(KAFFIR —S) IMPI
(MUSLIM —) GAZI GHAZI
(NOTED —) THANE THEGN
(SCANDINAVIAN —) BERSERK
(SCOTTISH —) ZERBINO
(TROJAN —) AGENOR
(VALIANT —) TOA
(VIRGIN —) CAMILLA
(PL.) IMPI CHIVALRY GAMMADIM
WARSHIP GUIDE RAZEE WAFTER CRUISER MONITOR SULTANA SULTANE CORVETTE
(— OF OLD) RAM
WART RAT WRAT AMBURY ANBURY SYCOMA PUSTULE VERRUCA VERRUGA EPIDERMA PAPILLOMA
(POTATO —) CANKER
(PREF.) VERRUCI
WART HOG EMGALLA
WARTLIKE PYRENOID
WART SNAKE XENODERM
WARTY MURICATE MURICATED PAPILLOSE
WARY SHY CAGY WISE AWARE CAGEY CANNY DOWNY HOOLY LEERY TENDER CAREFUL

GUARDED PRUDENT WAREFUL CAUTIOUS SKITTISH VIGILANT WATCHFUL
WAS VAS WIS WUZ WYS PAST WISSHE
(— ABLE) COULD
(— NOT) NAS
(I —) CHWAS
WASH DO BOG FEN LAG LAP NET TUB BEER BUCK EDDY HOSE HUSH LAVE SILT SUDS WADI BATHE CLEAN CLEAR DOLLY DRAFF ERODE MARSH RINSE SCRUB SLOSH SOUSE SWILL BUDDLE CRADLE DOLLIE LOTION PURIFY SLOOSH SLUICE SOZZLE STREAM ALLUVIO CLEANSE LAUNDER SHAMPOO ALLUVIUM EYEWATER LAVAMENT LAVATORY
(— A GAS) SCRUB
(— AWAY) GULL
(— BY TREADING IN WATER) TRAMP
(— DOWN) SIND SOOGEE
(— EDGE) LIP
(— FOR GOLD) PAN
(— GIVEN TO SWINE) DRAFF
(— GRAVEL) ROCK
(— HAIR) SHAMPOO
(— IN LYE) BUCK
(— LIGHTLY) RINSE
(— OFF) DETERGE
(— ORE) TYE HUTCH BUDDLE CRADLE STRAKE
(— OUT) SIND ELUTE FLUSH LAVAGE
(— ROUGHLY) SLUSH
(— THOROUGHLY) SCOUR
(— THROAT) GARGLE
(— VIGOROUSLY) SLOSH
(— WITH BROOM) TYE
(— WITH COSMETIC) SURFLE SURPHUL
(DRY —) ARROYA ARROYO
WASHBASIN LAVER LAVABO LAVATORY ALJOFAINA
WASHCLOTH FLANNEL
WASHED ABLUTED
(— UP) SHOT THROUGH
WASHED-OUT ANEMIC ANAEMIC
WASHER BUR BURR DRUM ROVE CLOUT BUTTON RONDEL SOURER GROMMET LEATHER RACCOON COTTEREL LAVENDER RONDELLE SCRUBBER
WASHERMAN DHOBI DHOBIE LAVANDERO
WASHERWOMAN LAUNDER
WASHING LAG BATH LAVAGE SLOOSH LAUNDRY ABLUTION LAVAMENT LAVATION
(PL.) ELUATE
WASHING MACHINE DASHWHEEL

WASHINGTON

CAPITAL: OLYMPIA
COLLEGE: GONZAGA WHITMAN EVERGREEN WHITWORTH
COUNTY: ASOTIN KITSAP SKAGIT YAKIMA CLALLAM KITTITAS
DAM: COULEE
INDIAN: HOH LUMMI MAKAH TWANA SAMISH SKAGIT YAKIMA CHINOOK CLALLAM COWLITZ SANPOIL CHIMAKUM OKANAGON
LAKE: SOAP MOSES CHELAN OZETTE CUSHMAN QUINAULT
MOUNTAIN: JACK TUNK ADAMS LEMEI LOGAN MOSES SLOAN QUARTZ SIMCOE STUART OLYMPUS RAINIER SHUKSAN
MOUNTAIN RANGE: KETTLE CASCADE OLYMPIC
NICKNAME: CHINOOK EVERGREEN
RIVER: SNAKE YAKIMA COLUMBIA
SOUND: PUGET
STATE BIRD: GOLDFINCH
STATE TREE: HEMLOCK
TOWN: OMAK PASCO TACOMA YAKIMA EPHRATA EVERETT OTHELLO SEATTLE SPOKANE LONGVIEW

WASHOUT FLOP STUMOR FAILURE
WASHROOM BASEMENT LAVATORY
WASHSTAND COMMODE
WASHTUB FLASKET
WASHY SOFT WEAK LOOSE MOIST FEEBLE PALLID WATERY DILUTED SHILPIT
WASP MASON SPHEX WHAMP WOPSE BEMBEX DAUBER DIGGER HORNET TIPHIA TREMEX VESPID CYNIPID DRYINID EUMENID MASARID SCOLIID SERPHID SIRICID SPHECID STINGER ACULEATE MUTILLID POMPILID
(KIND OF —) MASON
WASPISH TART TESTY FRETFUL PEEVISH CHOLERIC SNAPPISH
WASSAIL DRINK TOAST PLEDGE CAROUSE REVELRY CAROUSAL
WASTE EAT FUD GOB TED BURN GNAW JUNK LOSS PASS PEAK ROSS SACK TEAR TINE WEAR WILD DROSS EXILE HAVOC SCRAP SLOOM SLOTH SLOUM SPILL TABID THRUM BANGLE BEZZLE COMMON DEBRIS DESERT DEVOUR DIDDLE DRAFFY DRIVEL ELAPSE EXPEND FOREST GARBLE GOUSTY LAVISH MOLDER MUDDLE PADDLE PERISH RAVAGE REFUSE SCATHE SPILTH WESTEN CONNACH CONSUME EXHAUST FRITTER GARBAGE MULLOCK RUBBISH SLATTER CONFOUND DEMOLISH SLATTERN SQUANDER
(— AWAY) BATE MELT DECAY DWINE SWAIN SWEAL TRAIK WANZE TABEFY WINDLE DWINDLE FORPINE MISLIKE DISSOLVE EMACIATE FORSPEND MACERATE
(— GRADUALLY) WEAR ABSUME
(— IN DRUNKENNESS) SOT
(— IN RIOT) BEZZLE
(— OF INK) INKSHED
(— OF SILK COCOONS) KNUB
(— TIME) FOOL FRIG IDLE DALLY DEFER DRILL DAWDLE DIDDLE FOOTER FOOTLE LOITER DRINGLE FOOSTER GAUSTER
(COAL —) SLUDGE
(COTTON —) FLUKE SLASHER SPOOLER
(FOOD —) SLOP
(LIQUID —) DRIPPING EFFLUENT
(MINING —) GOB GOAF
(RADIOACTIVE —) RADWASTE
(WOOL —) FUD MUNGO GARNETT
(YARN —) THRUM EYEBROW
WASTEBASKET HELL HELLBOX
WASTED IDLE FORWORN RAVAGED DECREPIT
WASTEFUL LAVISH PROFUSE DESOLATE PRODIGAL SPENDFUL
WASTEFULNESS WAIT UNTHRIFT
WASTELAND MOOR HEATH CURAGH DESERT CURRACH
WASTER THIEF LEISTER WASTREL PRODIGAL
WASTING FRET DECAY LIGHT AWASTE ATROPHY CACHEXY EXEDENT MISLIKE PREYING TABIFIC CACHEXIA PHTHISIS SYNTEXIS TABESCENCE CONSUMPTION
(— AWAY) TABES MARASMUS SYNTECTIC TABEFACTION
(PREF.) PHTHISIO TABE TABI TABO
(PROGRESSIVE —) TABO
WASTREL WAIF LOSEL REFUSE WASTER ROUNDER VAGABOND STROYGOOD
WATCH EYE FOB NIT SEE SPY TAB DIAL ESPY GLIM GLOM HACK HEED KEEP LOOK MARK MIND PIPE TOUT TWIG VACH WAIK WAKE WARD YARD CLOCK GUARD SCOUT SPIAL SUPER TIMER VERGE VIGIL VIRGE WAKEN WHEEL BEHOLD DEFEND DIACLE FOLLOW HUNTER PERDUE SENTRY SHADOW TICKER TICTIC TURNIP WAKING YEMING OBSERVE OVERSEE ROSKOPF STRIKER THIMBLE TOMPION HOROLOGE MEDITATE SENTINEL SPECTATE TICKTICK STEMWINDER
(— FOR) TENT ABIDE AWAIT
(— OF ARMY) BIVOUAC
(— ON THE SLY) FOX
(— OVER) HOLD KEEP TEND TENT GUARD ATTEND OVERLOOK
(— OVER DEAD) LIKEWAKE LYKEWALK
(— PEOPLE EATING) GROAK
(— QUIETLY) HINT
(— THAT STRIKES) STRIKER REPEATER
(— UNIT) LIGNE
(— WITH HINGED COVER) HUNTER
(ALARM —) TATLER TATTLER
(CLOSE —) SCRUTINY
(NAUTICAL —) HACK DOGWATCH
(NIGHT —) LICHWAKE LYKEWAKE
(PART OF —) BOW FOB CASE DIAL FACE HAND STEM BEZEL COVER CROWN FRAME CHAPTER CRYSTAL DISPLAY NUMERAL SHOULDER
(SUFF.) SCOPE SCOPIC SCOPUS SCOPY
WATCHBAND WRISTER WRISTLET
WATCH CHAIN GUARD SLANG
WATCH CRYSTAL LUNET LUNETTE
WATCHDOG CUR GARM GARMR MATIN BANDOG KRATIM CERBERUS
WATCHER VEIL ARGUS WAKER VIEWER WAITER MUSAHAR SPOTTER WATCHMAN
WATCHFUL IRA ALERT AWARE CANNY CHARY ERECT TENTY WAKER TENTIE WACKER ANXIOUS GUARDED JEALOUS LIDLESS WAKEFUL VIGILANT WAKERIFE WAUKRIFE OBSERVANT
WATCHFULNESS OUTLOOK JEALOUSY
WATCH GLASS CRYSTAL LUNETTE
WATCHING VIGIL CUSTODY CONSERVATION
WATCHMAN FLAG MINA WAIT GUARD SCOUT VIGIL WATCH ASKARI BANTAY GHAFIR SENTRY SERENO SHOMER TOOTER WAITER WARDEN WARDER BELLMAN CHARLEY GUARDER TALLIAR WAKEMAN CHOKIDAR SENTINEL
(NIGHT —) SERENO CHARLIE
WATCHTOWER WARD BEACON GARRET MIZPAH SENTRY ATALAYA LOOKOUT MIRADOR BARBICAN SENTINEL SPECCHIE
WATCHWORD CRY MAXIM ALERTA ENSIGN PAROLE SIGNAL NAYWORD PASSWORD
WATCH WORKS MOVEABLE
WATER EAU TJI AGUA AQUA BATH BRIM BROO BURN LAGE LAKE POND POOL TIDE WAVE ABYSS BILGE FLUME LOUGH LYMPH RIVER TABBY TEARS TUBIG BALLOW BAREGE CAMLET CONGEE CONJEE PAWNEE PHLEGM SALIVA STREAM VADOSE WATHER AQUATIC CRYSTAL JAVELLE IRRIGATE SNOWMELT
(— AFTER BOILING RICE) CONGEE CONJEE
(— AS REFUGE FOR GAME) SOIL
(— AT THE MOUTH) DROOL
(— BY CALENDERING) TABBY
(— FOR BREWING) BURN
(— IN SOIL) HOLARD
(— IN WEIR) LASHER
(— REDDISH WITH IRON) RIDDAM
(— RUNNING AGAINST MAIN CURRENT) EDDY
(— SPIRIT) KELPIE
(— SURROUNDED BY ICE) WAKE
(— TRAIL) WAKE
(— UNDER PRESSURE) HUSH
(ARCH OF —) CURL
(BAPTISMAL —) LAVER
(BARLEY —) PTISAN
(BOTTOM — OF SEA) ABYSS
(BOUNDARY —) SHARD
(BUBBLING —) SPRUDEL
(DEEP —) BALLOW
(DIRTY —) SAUR PUDDLE
(FAST-MOVING —) SOUP
(FEN —) SUDS
(FROZEN —) ICE FROST
(FROZEN FLAVORED — ON A STICK) POPSICLE
(HARD —) ICE
(HOLY —) HYSSOP
(HOT —) SOUP
(LIVING —) RASA
(MINERAL —) VICHY SELTER SELTZER APOLLINARIS

(OPEN —) POLYNYA
(QUININE —) TONIC
(RED —) RESP RIDDAM
(ROUGH —) SEA
(RUNNING —) SEA
(SALT —) BRACK BRINE SEAWATER
(SOAPY —) SUDS GRAITH
(SPLASH OF —) FLASH
(STILL —) KELD LOGIN
(SULPHUR —) BAREGE
(SURFACE OF —) RYME
(SWEETENED —) AMRIT AMRITA
(WASHING —) LAVATION
(WHITE — AFTER WAVE) SOUP
(PL.) APSU
(PREF.) AQUA AQUEO AQUI AQUO HIDRO HYDAT(O) HYDR(O)
(GO THROUGH —) SILLO
(STAGNANT —) TELMAT(O)
(SUFF.) LIMNION YDATIS
WATER ARUM DRAGON
WATER BAG CHAGUL MATARA MUSSUK
WATER BATH BAINMARIE
WATERBIRD ALCATRAS
WATER BOA ANACONDA
WATER BOTTLE CARAFE
WATERBRAIN GID
WATERBUCK COB CHUZWI DEFASSA WATERDOE
WATER BUFFALO KERBAU CARABAO
(WILD —) ARNA
WATER CARRIER BHISTI AGUADOR BHEESTY
WATER CART DILLY
WATER CASK WINGER
WATER CHESTNUT LING CALTROP SALIGOT SINGHARA
WATER CHINQUAPIN BONNET NELUMBO WANKAPIN YONCOPIN RATTLENUT
WATER CLOCK GHURRY CLEPSYDRA
WATER CLOSET PETTY PRIVY STOOL SANITARY NECESSARY
WATER COCK KORA
WATERCOLOR GRAPHIC
WATERCOURSE (ALSO SEE STREAM AND RIVER) RUN URN AGOS DIKE DYKE GOTE HAHR KHOR LADE LEAT REAN WADI WADY YORA AUWAI BAYOU BROOK CANAL CANEL COWAL DITCH DRAIN RHINE ARROYO CANNEL COURSE FURROW GUTTER KENNEL NULLAH CHANNEL TRINKET
WATERCRAFT SAILER
WATERCRESS EKER KERS CARSE KERSE BILDERS NOSESMART
WATER DIVINER DOWSER
WATER DOG OTTER WATERRUG
WATER DRINKER HYDROPOT
WATERED MOIRE TABBY
WATERFALL LIN LYN FALL FOSS LINN SALT CHUTE FORCE SAULT SHOOT SPOUT LASHER CASCADE CATADUPE CATARACT OVERFALL
(FROZEN —) ICEFALL
WATER FENNEL EDGEWEED
WATER FERN PILLWORT
WATER FLEA CYCLOPS DAPHNID
WATERFOWL WADER SWIMMER
WATERFRONT PRAYA
WATERGALL WINDDOG WINDGALL JELLYFISH
WATER GATE SLUICE
WATER GERMANDER SCORDIUM
WATER HEMLOCK CICUTA COWBANE DEATHIN JELLICA
WATER HEN GALLINULE
WATER HOG BUSHPIG CAPYBARA
WATER HOLE DUB CHARCO TINAJA ALBERCA
WATER ICE SHERBET
WATERINESS AQUEITY AQUOSITY
WATERING EPIPHORA RIGATION
WATER JUG GAMLA GOMLAH GOOLAH
WATERLEAF SHAWNY NEMOPHILA
WATERLESS
(PREF.) ANHYDR(O)
WATER LETTUCE QUIAPO
WATER LILY DUCK LOTOS LOTUS WOCAS WOKAS BOBBIN CANDOCK NELUMBO CAMALOTE NENUPHAR
WATERLOGGED SOGGY SODDEN SWAMPY EDEMATOUS SATURATED
WATERMAN MERMAN QUENCH OARSMAN
WATERMARK CROWN TIDEMARK
WATERMARKED LAID
WATERMELON PEPO GOURD MELON TSAMA CITRUL SANDIA ANGURIA MILLION CUCURBIT PEPONIDA PEPONIUM SKIPJACK
WATER MOCCASIN CONGO
WATER NEWT ASK TRITON
WATER OPOSSUM YAPOK YAPOCK
WATER OUZEL PIET OOZEL OWZEL DIPPER DUCKER
WATER PARSNIP SKIRRET
WATER PEPPER LAKEWEED
WATER PIMPERNEL BROOKWEED
WATER PLANT LIMU AQUATIC
WATER PLANTAIN ALISMA THRUMWORT
WATERPOT FONTAL
WATERPROOF RAINCOAT
(— MATERIAL) KERATOL
WATER RAIL RUNNER BILCOCK MOORHEN OARCOCK
WATER RAT VOLE CRABER MUSKRAT WATERRUG
WATER SCORPION NEPID
WATERSHED BROW DIVIDE DIVORT SNOWSHED
WATER SHIELD FANWORT DEERFOOD FROGLEAF
WATERSKIN MASHAK MATARA MUSSUK MUSSACK MUSSICK
WATER SOLDIER PONDWORT
WATER SPIRIT ARIEL KELPY KELPIE UNDINE
WATERSPOUT RONE CANAL SPATE SPOUT VORTEX PRESTER TWISTER CATARACT GARGOYLE
WATER SPRITE KELPY KELPIE
WATER STRIDER SKATER SKIMMER SKIPPER SKETCHER
WATER THRUSH KICKUP WAGTAIL
WATER TIGER DYTISCID
WATERTIGHT THEAT THEET TIGHT STANCH THIGHT STAUNCH
WATER WALLY BATAMOTE
WATERWAY GUT CASH DOCK HOLE LODE DITCH INLET ARTERY SEAWAY CULVERT FAIRWAY HIGHWAY IGARAPE
(ARTIFICIAL —) LEAD CANAL
(DUTCH —) ZEE
(PL.) SCUPPERS
WATERWHEEL NORIA SAKIA SAGEER SAKIEH DANAIDE SAKIYEH TYMPANUM
WATERY WET LASH PALE SICK THIN WHEY BOGGY MOIST SAMMY WASHY BLASHY FLASHY LIQUID PALLID SEROSE SEROUS SWASHY AQUATIC AQUEOUS CHOROUS HYDROUS PHLEGMY SANIOUS HUMOROUS HYDATOID ICHOROUS SKINKING
WATT (ONE BILLION —S) GIGAWATT
WATTLE GILL JOWL PLAT SALY TWIG WAND BOREE COOBA FRITH MULGA SALLY SALWE STAVE STICK HURDLE JEWING JOLLOP LAPPET SALLOW BLUEBUSH CARUNCLE
WATTLEBIRD IAO MOHO MINER MANUAO MAOMAO GILLBIRD
WATTLE CROW KOKAKO
WAVE FAN FLY JAW SEA WAW BECK FLAG FLAP GUST LUMP PERM SUFF SULK SWAY WAFF WAFT WAWE YTHE BLESS CRIMP FLASH FLOAT FLOTE PULSE SHAKE SURGE SWELL SWING BILLOW COMBER FLAUNT MARCEL RIPPLE ROLLER WAFFLE WINNOW BREAKER BRIMMER CRIMPLE DECUMAN FEATHER FLICKER FLUTTER TSUNAMI WHIFFLE ARTEFACT BRANDISH FLOURISH GRAYBACK UNDULATE UNIPULSE WHISTLER WHITECAP
(— ABOUT) WAMPISH
(— OF EXCITATION) IMPULSE
(— OF FLAG) DOT DASH
(— OF SHIP) BONE
(ARCH OF —) CURL
(BRAIN —) DELTA
(ELECTRIC —) STRAY CARRIER
(ELECTROMAGNETIC —) ALFVEN
(HAIR —) MARCEL PERMANENT
(LARGE —) HEAVY
(LITTLE —) RIPPLE
(RIDE A —) BODYSURF
(SOLITARY —) SOLITON
(SPIN —) MAGNON
(TIDAL —) AEGIR EAGER EAGRE
(PL.) SURF
(PREF.) CUMA CYM(I)(O) CYMATO KYM(I)(O) KYMATO ONDA ONDO UNDI
WAVER HALT REEL SWAG SWAY VARY CHECK DAKER DOUBT FLOAT SWALE SWING WIVER DACKER DAIKER DITHER FALTER MAMMER QUIVER SWERVE TEETER TOTTER WABBLE WAFFLE WOBBLE BALANCE FLICKER FLITTER FLUTTER STAGGER SWITHER VIBRATE HESITATE VACILLATE
WAVERING WAW WAVY WEAK WAUCH WAUGH FICKLE GROGGY UNSURE WAVERY WIGGLY DUBIOUS LAMBENT SHUTTLE DOUBTFUL FLEXUOSE FLEXUOUS FLICKERY HOVERING WAVEROUS PENDULOUS
WAVERLEY (AUTHOR OF —) SCOTT
(CHARACTER IN —) EVAN LEAN ROSE VOHR ALICE COSMO DAVIE FLORA DONALD FERGUS STUART CHARLES EVERARD MACIVOR GARDINER PEMBROKE WAVERLEY GELLATLEY MACCOMBICH BRADWARDINE
WAVINESS CRIMP
WAVING UNDE WAFT AWAVE OUNDY UNDEE WAFTURE FLOURISH
(— OF WEAPON) FLOURISH
WAVY ONDE UNDE UNDY CRISP MOIRE SNAKY UNDEE CRIMPY FLECKY REPAND SNAKEY UNDATE WIGGLY BUCKLED CRINKLY CURVING ENDATED ROLLING SINUATE UNDULAR ENRIDGED FLEXUOUS ONDOYANT SQUIGGLY UNDULATE
(PEOPLE WITH — HAIR) VEDDOID
WAWL HOWL WAIL WOWL SQUALL
WAX WOX CERE CODE GROW RAGE WACE WOXE SCALE BECOME CAPPING CERESIN KLISTER CARNAUBA CERESINE CEROXYLE COCCERIN EPILATOR INCREASE
(— FAINT) APPAL
(— FROM INSECT) PELA
(— IN HONEYCOMB) CAPPING
(— STRONG) PREVAIL
(CHINESE —) PELA
(COBBLER'S —) CODE
(EAR —) CERUMEN
(KIND OF —) MONTAN PINSANG
(POLISH WITH —) SIMONIZE
(SKI —) KLISTER
(PREF.) CER(I)(O) KERO
WAXBILL ASTRILD REDBILL
WAXEN WAX PALLID CEREOUS
WAXER GLAZER WAXMAN
WAXFLOWER EPIPHYTE
WAXING CRESCIVE
WAX LIGHT TAPER CANDLE
WAX MYRTLE ARRAYAN
WAX PALM CARNAUBA
WAX PLANT HOYA
WAXWING WAXBIRD RECOLLET SILKTAIL
WAXY ANGRY VEXED CEREOUS PLIABLE YIELDING
WAY LAW PAD RUE TAO VIA WON WYE FARE FORE FORM GAIT GANG GATE KIND LANE LARK PACE PATH PAWK RAKE ROAD SORT TOBY WISE ALLEY CHANT FORTH GOING GUISE HABIT MOYEN ROUTE SHEAR STEPS STYLE TRACT TRADE ACCESS AVENUE CAREER CHEMIN COURSE MANNER METHOD PHASIS STREET TRAJET CHANNEL FASHION HIGHWAY PASSAGE SKIDWAY APPROACH CONTRADA DISTRICT FOOTPATH THOROUGH VICINITY LAUNCHING
(— OF DEPARTURE) EXIT
(— OF ESCAPE) BOLTHOLE
(— OF LIFE) LARK TRACE HEDONISM
(— OF LOOKING) SLANT

(— OF SPEAKING) AMBAGE
(— OF THINKING) DIET
(— OF WALKING) JET
(— ON OR OFF) RAMP
(— OUT) IT RAD EXIT SALVO RADICAL
(— THROUGH MINEFIELD) BREACH
(BY ANOTHER —) ALIA
(CLEVER —) KNACK
(COVERED —) CORRIDOR
(DEVIOUS —) ROUNDABOUT
(EVERY —) ROUND
(IN ANY —) SOEVER
(INDIRECT —) AMBAGES
(LONG —) FAR
(MAJOR —) STEM
(NARROW —) DRANG
(ODD —S) JIMJAMS
(PLANK —) BRIDGE
(RAISED —) BANQUETTE
(ROUNDABOUT —) DETOUR CIRCUIT
(ROUNDABOUT —S) AMBAGES
(SETTLED —) BIAS
(SIDE —) BRANCH
(SLOPING —) RAMP
(UNDEVIATING —) GROOVE
(PL.) DAPS
(PREF.) HODO ODO VIA
(SUFF.) ODE OID WISE

WAYBILL CHALAN WILLIE CHALLAN
WAYFARER SHULER VIATOR PILGRIM SHUILER TRAVELER PASSENGER
WAYFARING TREE WHITTEN COTTONER VIBURNUM
WAYLAY BELAY BESET BLOCK BRACE AMBUSH FORLAY FORSET FORELAY OBSTRUCT SURPRISE
WAYLAYER WAIT
WAYMARK AHU
WAY OF ALL FLESH (AUTHOR OF —) BUTLER
(CHARACTER IN —) JOHN ELIZA ELLEN MARIA PRYER ALLABY ALTHEA ERNEST GEORGE JOSEPH OVERTON SKINNER MAITLAND PONTIFEX THEOBALD CHARLOTTE CHRISTINA
WAY OF THE WORLD (AUTHOR OF —) CONGREVE
(CHARACTER IN —) FOIBLE FAINALL MARWOOD ROWLAND WILFULL WITWOOD MIRABELL WAITWELL WISHFORT MILLAMANT
WAYSIDE HEDGE
WAYWARD PEEVISH PERVERSE LOUPTHEDYKE
WEAK DIM LEW COOL DOWY FOND LAME NESH NICE PALE PUNY SELI SELY SOFT THIN WASH WAUF WOKE BAUCH BAUGH CRIMP DICKY FAINT FLASH FRAIL JERKY LIGHT NAISH REEDY ROCKY SEELY SHAKY SILLY SLACK STANK WASHY WAUGH WEARY WERSH YOUNG CADUKE DEBILE DILUTE DOTISH EFFETE FEEBLE FLABBY FLAGGY FLIMSY FOIBLE GROGGY INFIRM LIMBER LITTLE MARCID SEMMIT SICKLY SINGLE SWASHY TENDER UNSURE UNWISE WAIRCH WATERY BRICKLE DWAIBLY DWEEBLE FLACCID FOOLISH FRAGILE INSIPID INVALID LANGUID PIMPING PUERILE REGULAR RICKETY SAUGHEN SHALLOW SHILPIT SLENDER SPINDLY TOTTERY UNHARDY UNLUSTY WEARISH ASTHENIC CHILDISH DECREPIT DEFINITE FECKLESS FEMININE FLAGGING GRIPLESS HELPLESS IMBECILE IMPOTENT LADYLIKE LANGUENT PHTHISIC RESOLUTE RUSHLIKE SACKLESS SCRANNEL THEWLESS UNMIGHTY UNWIELDY SPINELESS
(— FROM FATIGUE) TANGLE
(— FROM HUNGER) LEER
(— IN RESOLUTION) FRAIL
(MENTALLY —) TOTTY
(PREF.) ASTHEN(O) LEPT(O)

WEAKEN GO LAG SAP DAMP FAIL HURT MELT PALL SINK THIN ABATE ALLAY BLUNT BREAK CRAZE DELAY QUAIL SHAKE SPEND WATER APPALL ATTRIT DEACON DEADEN DEFANG DEFEAT DEJECT DENUDE DILUTE FALTER IMPAIR INFIRM LABEFY LESSEN PERISH REBATE REDUCE SICKEN SOFTEN CORRODE CORRUPT CRIPPLE DECLINE DEPRESS DISABLE MOLLIFY QUALIFY RESOLVE THREADY UNBRACE UNNERVE CASTRATE DIMINISH EMBEZZLE ENERVATE ENFEEBLE ETIOLATE INFRINGE LABEFACT UNSTRENG
WEAKENED GROGGY ANODYNE INVALID SHOTTEN DECREPIT LABEFACT STRAINED
WEAKENING CHRONIC FAILURE FLAGGING
WEAKEST RECKLING
WEAKFISH DRUM TROUT ACOUPA SALMON CORBINA CORVINA DRUMMER SQUETEE TOTOABA TOTUAVA BLUEFISH CHICKWIT
WEAKLING TOY WRIG DUGON PULER SLINK SOFTIE DILLING RECKLING SOFTLING
WEAKLY FEEBLY FEMALE SIMPLY
WEAK-MINDED DAFT DOTY DOTED FOOLISH
WEAKNESS ATONY CRACK CRAZE FAULT FOLLY TOUCH ATONIA DEFECT FOIBLE ACRATIA FAILING FISSURE FRAILTY LANGUOR ASTHENIA DEBILITY DELICACY FONDNESS
(— OF DIGESTION) APEPSY APEPSIA
(— OF MIND) FOLLY
(— OF VOICE) PHONASTHENIA
(CARNAL —) FLESH
(SUFF.) **(— FOR)** ITIS

WEAL WHEAL RICHES STRIPE WEALTH WELFARE
WEALTH WAD WON DHAN GEAR GOLD GOOD MUCK WONE MEANS THING WORTH GRAITH MAMMON POCKET PURPLE RICHES TALENT CASHBOX FORTUNE RICHDOM WARISON WELFARE CATALLUM OPULENCE OPULENCY PROPERTY TREASURE WARRISON MONEYBAGS
(— OF NATION) STOCK
(PATRON OF —) YAKSHA
(PREF.) APHNO PLUT(O)

WEALTHY FAT BEIN BIEN FULL OOFY RICH WELI AMPLE PURSY TINNY LOADED OOFIER COUTHIE MONEYED PURSIVE ABUNDANT AFFLUENT
(— CLASS) PLUTOCRACY
WEAN CHILD SPAIN SPANE WAYNE INFANT ESTRANGE
WEANING ABLACTATION
WEAPON (ALSO SEE SPECIFIC TYPE OF WEAPON) ARM BOW GUN BILL BOLA BOLO CLUB COSH DART EDGE EPEE FALX FOIL IRON MACE NUKE PATU PIKE TOOL WIWI ADAGA ARROW BILLY CAKRA DEATH FLAIL KNIFE LANCE ONCIN ORGUE SHARP SPEAR SQUID STEEL SWORD VOUGE WAPIN CANNON CHAKRA DAGGER GLAIVE MACANA TOMBOC ARCHERY BAZOOKA FIREARM GISARME HALBERD HARPOON HURLBAT JAVELIN LIANGLE POUNAMU SHOTGUN SLASHER STICKER STUNGUN TICKLER WHIFFLE ARBALEST BLOWBACK BLUDGEON CROSSBOW FAUCHARD HEDGEHOG LEEANGLE NUNCHAKU PARTISAN TOMAHAWK TROMBASH
(CELTIC —) PALSTAFF
(DEADLY —) DEATH
(LINE OF —S) RIDGE
(NUCLEAR —) NUKE
(PREHISTORIC —) CELT
(PL.) WAR TACKLE ARCHERY WEAPONRY
(PREF.) ARMI HOPL(O)

WEAPONRY ARMS
WEAR KIT BEAR FRAY FRET GROW HAVE PASS CHAFE GUARD SPEND VOGUE WEARY ABRADE BATTER BECOME HAVEON BETHUMB CONSUME DEFENSE DEGRADE FASHION FATIGUE FRAZZLE PROCEED WEATHER PROGRESS
(— AND TEAR) GAFF SLITE GRUELING
(— AN OPENING) BREACH
(— AWAY) EAT FADE FRET GALL GNAW GULL PINE ERODE GULLY SCOUR SPEND ABRADE CORRADE CORRODE CONTRIVE
(— CLOTHES) DRESS
(— DOWN) BRAY GRIND ABRADE ABRASE GRAVEL
(— FURROWS) GUTTER
(— IN PUBLIC) SPORT
(— OFF) FADE FRAY ABRADE
(— OUT) DO BURN COOK FLOG FRAY JADE MUSH TIRE TUCK BREAK SLAVE SLITE SPEND TRASH BUGGER HATTER MAGGLE PERUSE EXHAUST FORWEAR FORWORK HACKNEY INVALID SHACHLE OVERFRET OVERWEAR
(— SHIP) CAST
(— SHOES OUT OF SHAPE) SHACHLE SHACKLE
(— TIGHT CORSETS) LACE
(WINTER —) EARMUFF

WEARIED AWEARY FORGONE FATIGUED WEARIFUL
WEARINESS TIRE FATIGUE BRAINFAG SICKNESS VEXATION
WEARING DECAY SCUFF BURNING CLOTHES ABRASION GARMENTS GRINDING
WEARISOME DRY DULL HARD SLOW WEARY BORING MORTAL PROLIX SODDEN IRKSOME TEDIOUS SAWDUSTY TIRESOME TOILSOME
WEARISOMENESS TEDIUM
WEARY FAG IRK SAD BEAT BOEG BORE CLOY MOIL PALL POOP PUNY SADE TIRE TIRY WEAK WORE WORN BORED BREAK CURSE SPENT ABRADE BETOIL HARASS PLAGUE POOPED SICKLY SQUEAL TUCKER EXHAUST FATIGUE IRKSOME SWINKED FATIGATE FORCHASE GRIEVOUS TIRESOME WRETCHED FORJASKIT
(— OUT) RAMFEEZLE
(BE —) SAG
(BECOME —) JADE
WEARY WILLIE TRAMP
WEASAND WISEN GULLET THROAT WIZZEN TRACHEA WINDPIPE
WEASEL CANE VAIR VARE WARE HULDA HURON SNEAK STOAT TAIRA TAYRA ERMINE FERRET HULDAH VERMIN ARCTOID VORMELA FUTTERET MUISHOND MUSTELIN WHITRACK
(— OUT OF) EVADE
(— RELATIVE) ZORIL
(PREF.) GALEO

WEASEL CAT LINSANG
WEATHER SKY DIRT RAIN TIME COLLA STORM WINDWARD
(— CONDITION) WHITEOUT
(— LINE) FRONT
(FAIR —) SHINE
(HOT AND HUMID —) SIZZARD
(INCLEMENT —) SEASON
(INTERVAL OF FAIR —) SLATCH
(OPEN —) FRESH
(OUT OF THE —) ALEE
(UNDER THE —) SEEDY
(VIOLENT —) ELEMENTS
(PREF.) EUDIO METEOR(O)

WEATHERBEATEN GNARLED SEAGOING
WEATHERCOCK COCK FANE VANE FAINE FANACLE
WEATHERGLASS BAROMETER
WEAVE CANE HABI HUCK JOIN LACE LENO LOOM REED ROCK SPIN WALE WARP WIND WOOF DOBBY DRAPE PLAIT TWINE UNITE BROCHE DAMASK DEVISE DIAPER DOBBIE FABRIC CANILLE ENTWINE FASHION INDRAPE SATINET SHUTTLE VANDYKE DIAGONAL DUCHESSE OVERSHOT
(— PATTERNS INTO) BROCADE
(BASKET —) BARLEYCORN
(CARPET —) FLOSSA
(HERRINGBONE —) SUMAK SOUMAK SHEMAKA
(LATTICE —) TEE

(OPEN —) LENO BAREGE
(RUG —) RYA
WEAVER KORI TANTI WEBBE DRAWBOY WEBSTER WOBSTER PENELOPE TAPESTER
WEAVERBIRD NUN BAYA MAYA TAHA FINCH MUNIA VIDUA WEBBE BISHOP CANARY OXBIRD WHIDAH WHYDAH BENGALI AMADAVAT AVADAVAT CARDINAL MANNIKIN
WEAVING TANIKO TEXTURE WEBBING
(— MAIDEN) ARACHNE
(— OF WORDS) CONTEXT
(— TOGETHER) PLEXURE
WEAZEN WIZEN SHRINK WIZENED
WEB PLY WOB CAUL FELT MAZE TENT TOIL VANE WARP WEFT SKEIN SNARE THROW TWIST FLEECE TISSUE ENSNARE FEATHER LAYETTE TEXTURE SNOWSHOE VEXILLUM
(— IN EYE) HAW
(CRANK —) THROW
(PREF.) HIST(O) HISTI(O) HYPHO
WEBBED RINGED PALMATE
WEBBING MAT WEB PALAMA
WEB-FOOTED PALMATE PALAMATE PALMIPED
WEB SPINNER EMBIID WEBWORM
WED GET BEWED BRIDE HITCH MARRY STAKE WAGER ENGAGE PLEDGE SPOUSE ESPOUSE WEDLOCK
WEDDING BRIDAL SPLICE NUPTIAL WEDLOCK ESPOUSAL MARRIAGE
(— WORDS) IDO
WEDGE KEY COIN FROE FROW GLUT HORN KYLE PLUG SHIM STOB TRIG TRIP WAGE CHOCK CHUCK CLEAT COIGN HACEK HORSE QUINE QUOIN SCOTE SLICE THROW COTTER CUNEUS QUINET SCOTCH EMBOLUS QUINNET SCHOCHE VOUSSOIR
(— BETWEEN TWO FEATHERS) KEY
(— IN) JAM JAMB
(— OF OATMEAL) FARL FARLE
(— TO PREVENT MOTION) CHOCK
(CURVED —) CAM
(WOODEN —) COW GLUT JACK
(PREF.) CUNEI CUNEO EMBOL(O) SPHEN(O)
WEDGER SPRINGER
WEDGE-SHAPED CUNEAL SPHENIC CUNEATED SPHENOID
(PREF.) CUNEO SPHEN(O)
WEDLOCK WIFE SPOUSAL MARRIAGE SPOUSAGE
WEDNESDAY MIDWEEK
WEE TINY EARLY SMALL TEENY YOUNG LITTLE ITSYBITSY
WEED BUR HOE BURR CHOP CULL DOCK FORB LOUK SHIM SIDA TARE WEID CIGAR DRANK DRAWK DRESS DROKE FLESH BLINKS CASUAL COCKLE DARNEL JIMSON KNAWEL RIPGUT SARCLE SPURGE SPURRY STROIL ASHWORT BUGLOSS COHITRE CUCKOLD EGILOPS GARMENT GOSMORE HOGWORT RAGWEED RAGWORT RIBWORT SANDBUR TOBACCO VERVAIN VERVINE CHADLOCK COCKSPUR COWWHEAT PIRIPIRI PLANTAIN PURSLANE TOADFLAX ALFILERIA MARIJUANA NIPPLEWORT
(— KILLER) PARAQUAT HERBICIDE
(— OUT) ROGUE
(MEXICAN —) BIRDEYE
(ROADSIDE —) PLANTAGO
(STINGING —) NETTLE
(TROUBLESOME —) KEX TITTER
(WATER —) ANACHARIS
(PL.) FILTH WRACK DISMAL SPRING WEEDAGE TRUMPERY
WEEDER SARCLER
WEEDY FOUL LANKY
WEEK OOK WOK OULK WOKE SENNET STANZA HEBDOMAD SENNIGHT
(TWO —S) FORTNIGHT
WEEKDAY FERIA WARDAY
WEEKLY AWEEK HEBDOMADAL HEBDOMADARY
WEEL LEAP POOL TRAP RIGHT WHIRLPOOL
WEEN MEAN VENE WEND FANCY GUESS EXPECT BELIEVE IMAGINE SUPPOSE CONCEIVE
WEENY TINY SMALL WEESHY
WEEP CRY ORP SOB BAWL BEND GIVE LEAK OOZE PIPE TEAR WAIL GREET BEWAIL BEWEEP BOOHOO BUBBLE LAMENT SHOWER BLUBBER LAPWING SQUINNY COMPLAIN
WEEPER GREETER MOURNER CAPUCHIN
(PL.) FLENTES
WEEPING WOP GREET MILCH RAINY BOOHOO LAMENT OOZING PIPING BLUBBER MAUDLIN TEARFUL DRIPPING LACRIMAL MADIDANS PLORATION
WEEPING SINEW GANGLION
WEEVER JUGULAR STINGBULL
WEEVIL MAX BOUD POPE WHULE PICUDO WEEBLE BILLBUG BRUCHUS VAQUITA CURCULIO WOODWORM
(PLUM —) TURK
WEFT WEB PICK WOOF BLAST FABRIC FILLING
WEIGH GO SIT HEFT PEIS TARE TELL COUNT HEAVE HOIST PEIZE POISE RAISE SCALE BURDEN PONDER ANALYZE BALANCE DEPRESS LIBRATE CONSIDER EVALUATE MEDITATE MILITATE
(— DOWN) LADE SWAY SWEE BESET HEAVY PEISE CADDLE CHARGE CUMBER PESTER DEPRESS FREIGHT INGRATE OPPRESS OVERLAY ENCUMBER
(— UPON) SIT GRIEVE
WEIGHER BOXMAN PEISER SCALER
WEIGHING METAGE
(— MACHINE) TRON SCALE TRONE
WEIGHT (ALSO SEE MEASURE AND UNIT) BOB FEN FOB KIN MAN NET OKE RAM SER SIR TOM TUP ABAS ATOM BEEF CLOG DROP GRAM HEFT IRON KITE LEAD LOAD MACE MEAL NAIL ONUS PEIS POND PORT ROTL SEAM SEER SINK WAIT ABBAS CLOVE CRITH GARCE LIVRE MAUND PEASE PEISE PICUL POISE POIZE PRESS RIDER SCALE STAMP AUNCEL BURDEN CHARGE DIRHEM HAMMER IMPORT MOMENT MONKEY PASSIR PONDER PONDUS SINKER STRESS BALLAST DOLPHIN GRAVITY MILLIER PAYLOAD PLATINE PLUMMET POSIURE CHALDRON DEMIMARK DUMBBELL ENCUMBER FARASULA LISPOUND PRESSURE PRESTIGE QUINCUNX STANDARD STRENGTH
(— AFTER TARE DEDUCTION) SUTTLE
(— CARRIED BY HORSE) IMPOST
(— CLOTH) FLOCK
(— FOR HURLING) HAMMER
(— FOR LEAD) FOTHER FOTMAL
(— FOR PRECIOUS STONE) CARAT
(— FOR WOOL) TOD SARPLER
(— FOR WOOL, CHEESE, ETC.) CLOVE
(— OF BROADSIDE) GUNPOWER
(— OF COAL) KEEL
(— OF COFFEE) MAT
(— OF EMPTY VEHICLE) TARE
(— OF HYDROGEN) CRITH
(— OF METAL) JOURNEY
(— OF ONE 10TH TAEL) MACE
(— OF ONE 100TH TAEL) FEN
(— OF PENDULUM) BOB
(— OF PILE DRIVER) TUP
(— OF RAW SILK) PARI
(— OF SILK OR RAYON) DRAMMAGE
(— OF 100 LBS.) CENTAL CENTENA CENTNER
(— OF 1000 LIVRES) MILLIER
(— OF 20 OR 21 LBS.) SCORE
(— OF 40 BUSHELS) WEY
(— OF 5 UNCIAE) QUINCUNX
(— ON MINE SWEEPER) KITE
(— ON STEELYARD) PEA
(— ON WATCH CHAIN) FOB
(— TO BEND HOT METAL) DUMPER
(— TO DETECT FALSE COINS) PASSIR
(— TO HINDER MOTION) CLOG
(— WHICH VESSEL CAN CARRY) TONNAGE
(ABYSSINIAN —) FARASULA
(BOXER'S —) FLY HEAVY LIGHT BANTAM MIDDLE WELTER FEATHER
(CARAT —) SILIQUA
(CLOCK —) PEISE
(COUNTERFEIT —) SLANG
(FALSE —) SLANG
(GREATLY VARYING —) MAN MAUND
(HEAVY —) MONKEY
(LIGHT —) SUTTLE
(METRIC —) TONNE
(MONEYER'S —) DROIT
(ORIENTAL —) TAEL CATTY
(SASHCORD —) MOUSE
(SHUFFLEBOARD —) SHIP
(SMALL —) MITE GERAH RIDER
(SPLINE —) DOLPHIN
(UNIT OF —) SER VIS WEY GERA LAST ROTL SEER LIANG LIBRA LINGO MINAL PECUL PERIT PIKOL KANTAR LINGOE MISKAL POCKET LISPUND PRICKLE QUINTAL ZOLOTNIK
(PREF.) BAR(I)(O)(Y) PONDERO
(SUFF.) BAR(IC)
WEIGHTED BIAS LOADED
WEIGHTER FULLER
WEIGHTLESSNESS MICROGRAVITY
WEIGHT-PRODUCING GRAVIFIC
WEIGHTY GRAVE GREAT HEAVY HEFTY MASSY SOLID VALID COGENT SOLEMN EARNEST MASSIVE ONEROUS PEISANT PESANTE SERIOUS TELLING GRIEVOUS MATERIAL POWERFUL PREGNANT PORTENTOUS SIGNIFICANT
WEIR DAM PEN CRIB KEEP LEAP STOP CAULD DOACH GARTH GORCE HATCH HEDGE SASSE STANK LASHER BURROCK MILLPOND
WEIRD ODD EERY UNCO UNKO EERIE SPACY UNCOW UNKID CREEPY SPACEY ELDRICH ELRITCH UNCANNY UNUSUAL WIZARDLY SPACEDOUT
(— SISTERS) FATES
WEIRDO NUT GEEK KOOK CREEP DINGBAT ECCENTRIC
WEITSPEKAN YUROK
WEKA RAIL WOODHEN RAILBIRD
WELCOME SEE FAIN GOOD HAIL ADOPT ALOHA CHEER GREET RESET TREAT ACCOIL INVITE SALUTE ACCLAIM ACCUEIL EMBRACE GRATIFY BIENVENU GREETING HAEREMAI PLEASANT ACCEPTABLE
WELCOMING HOMEY
WELD SHUT WELL SWAGE UNITE WOALD ACACIA
WELDED SHOT
WELDING FUSION SHUTTING
WELFARE SEL GOOD HALE HEAL SELE WEALTH BENISON BLESSING COMMONWEAL
(PUBLIC —) STATE
WELKIN SKY HEAVENS WALKENE
WELL AIN EYE GAY PIT WEL BENE FINE FLOW GOOD PANT PUIT PURE RITE SAFE SINK WINK AWEEL BOOLY BOWLY GREAT MUSHA OILER QUELL WALLY WISHA ATWEEL BUCKET CENOTE ENOUGH FAIRLY GASSER NICELY OFFSET PUMPER TUNNEL FALLWAY GRADELY HEALTHY WILDCAT BOREHOLE FOUNTAIN GRAITHLY POSTHOLE WATERPIT WEALSOME
(— AND STRONG) BUNKUM
(— IN GLACIER) MOULIN
(— THROUGH FLOORS OF WAREHOUSE) FALLWAY
(— UP) WALL WALM DIGHT
(AS —) TOO ALSO
(FAIRLY —) MIDDLING
(NONPRODUCTIVE —) DUSTER
(NOT —) DONNY SOBER INVALID
(OIL —) OILER GASSER GUSHER SPOUTER WILDCAT STRIPPER

(RECTANGULAR —) BOOLY BOWLY
(REMARKABLY—) RARELY
(SACRED — AT MECCA) ZEMZEM
(TOLERABLY —) GAYLIES GEYLIES
(VERY —) BRAWLY CLEVER
(PREF.) BENE EU
WELL-BALANCED SOBER
WELL-BEHAVED DECOROUS GOOD NICE MODEST MANNERED
WELL-BEING HEAL SKIN WEAL HEALTH WEALTH COMFORT EUCRASY WELFARE EUCRASIA PROSPERITY
WELLBORN GENTLE EUGENIC
WELL-BRED GENTIL POLITE GENTEEL REFINED CULTURED LADYLIKE
WELL-BUILT TIGHT
WELL CASING STEANING
WELL-CHOSEN CHOICE
WELL-CONDITIONED SONSY
WELL-CONSIDERED THRIFTY
WELL CURB PUTEAL
WELL-DEFINED STRICT
WELL-DISPOSED SIB FAIN GOOD VAIN
WELL DONE SHABASH
WELL-DRESSED BRAW GASH SMART BRAWLY
WELL-FED BLOWSY BLOWZY CHUBBY GAWCEY GAWSIE
WELL-FINISHED SOIGNE
WELL-FORMED TIGHT DECENT PROPER SEEMLY SHAPELY
WELL-FOUNDED VALID FIRM GOOD JUST SOUND WORTHY
WELL-GROOMED SMUG CRISP SOIGNE SOIGNEE
WELL-GROUNDED JUST VALID
WELL-GROWN THRODDY
WELL-HUSBANDED THRIFTY
WELL-INFORMED KNOWING PERFECT
WELL-INTENTIONED AMIABLE
WELL-KEPT SMUG POLITE
WELL-KNIT WIRY
WELL-KNOWN BREEM BREME BEATEN FAMOUS KENNED PUBLIC FAMILIAR PROMINENT
WELL-LIKED FANCIED POPULAR
WELL-MADE CLEVER FEATOUS
WELL-MANNERED GENTILE POLITE COURTEOUS
WELL-NIGH WELLY ALMOST NEARLY WELLMOST
WELL-ORDERED
(PREF.) COSM(ETO)(ICO)(O)
WELL-ORGANIZED SNOD
WELL-PLEASED FAIN VAIN
WELL-PROPORTIONED SUING TRETIS HANDSOME
WELL-READ STUDIED LITERARY
WELL-ROUNDED CHUBBY
WELL-SHAPED CLEANCUT CLEVER FEATOUS
WELL-TILLED NOT NOTT
WELL-TO-DO ABLE BEIN BIEN EASY WARM PODDED
WELL-TRODDEN TRITE
WELL-WISHER FRIEND FAVORER
WELS WALLER SHEATFISH
WELSH (ALSO SEE WALES) CYMRY FUDGE TAFFY CYMRIC KYMRIC CAMBRIAN
WELSHER SHICER QUITTER
WELSHMAN CELT KELT TAFFY BRYTHON CAMBRIAN
WELSH ONION CIBOL CIBOULE CHESBOLL
WELT WALE RIDGE STRIP WHELP WELTING BANDELET TURNOVER
(SHOE —S) WATTIS
WELTANSCHAUUNG FAITH IDEOLOGY
WELTER REEL RIOT TOSS WILT GROVEL TUMBLE WALLOW WRITHE SMOTHER STAGGER SWELTER
(— OF SOUNDS) DIN
WELWITSCHIA TUMBOA
WEM FLAW SCAR SPOT STAIN
WEN CYST WYNN CLIER CLYER TALPA TUMOR GOITER
WENCH DELL DILL DOXY DRAB GILL GIRL JADE MAID MOLL PRIM TRUG BIMBO GOUGE KITTY MADAM QUEAN TRULL WHORE AUDREY BLOUSE BLOWEN BLOWZE DRAZEL JILLET KITTIE MOTHER POPLET WOTLINK POPLOLLY
(CLUMSY —) MODER MODDER MOTHER MAUTHER
WENCHER DRABBER STRIKER
WEND BOW END SORB VEND STEER BETAKE DEPART DIRECT TRAVEL PROCEED SORBIAN LUSATIAN
(— ONE'S WAY) MARK
WENT GODE LANE ROAD YEDE ALLEY PASSAGE
(— ABOUT) WOLK
WENTLETRAP SCALA
WENZEL JACK
WERE (— IT NOT) SAVE
WEREWOLF TURNSKIN VERSIPEL
WERTHER (BELOVED OF —) LOTTE
WEST STY BEWEST PONENT OCCIDENT
WESTERN PONENT SCAEAN HESPERIC SANDWICH
(PREF.) HESPER(O)
WESTERN SAMOA (CAPITAL OF —) APIA
(ISLAND OF —) UPOLU MANONO SAVAII APOLIMA
(MONEY OF —) TALA
WEST HIGHLAND KYLOE

WEST INDIES
ISLAND: CAT CUBA LONG ABACO EXUMA HAITI NEVIS PELEE TURKS ANDROS BAHAMA CAICOS CAYMAN INAGUA TOBAGO VIRGIN ACKLINS ANTIGUA BONAIRE CROOKED CURACAO GRENADA JAMAICA LEEWARD STKITTS STLUCIA TORTOLA ANGUILLA BARBADOS DOMINICA STTHOMAS TRINIDAD WINDWARD ELEUTHERA MARGARITA MAYAGUANA STVINCENT GUADELOUPE HISPANIOLA MARTINIQUE MONTSERRAT PUERTORICO
NATION: BARBADOS

WEST VIRGINIA
CAPITAL: CHARLESTON
COLLEGE: SALEM BETHANY CONCORD MARSHALL BLUEFIELD
COUNTY: CLAY WIRT BOONE HARDY MINGO ROANE TUCKER UPSHUR BARBOUR KANAWHA
INDIAN: MONETON
LAKE: LYNN
NICKNAME: MOUNTAIN
RIVER: ELK OHIO KANAWHA POTOMAC GUYANDOT
STATE BIRD: CARDINAL
STATE FLOWER: RHODODENDRON
STATE TREE: MAPLE
TOWN: ELKINS KEYSER RIPLEY VIENNA WESTON BECKLEY GRAFTON SPENCER WEIRTON FAIRMONT WHEELING

WESTWARD WESSEL OCCASIVE WESTLINS
WESTWARD HO (AUTHOR OF —) KINGSLEY
(CHARACTER IN —) YEO JOHN LUCY ROSE AMYAS FRANK LEIGH DESOTO GUZMAN EUSTACE OXENHAM RICHARD GRENVILE SALTERNE AYACANORA
WET DEW DIP SOP WAT ASOP DAMP DANK LASH MOIL SLOW SOAK SOFT UVID BATHE DABBY DROOK DRUNK HUMID JUICE JUICY LEACH MADID MOIST MOOTH RAINY SLAKE SNAPY SOBBY SOPPY SPEWY STEEP TIGHT WEAKY CLASHY DABBLE DAGGLE DAMPEN HUMECT IMBRUE JARBLE LABBER MADEFY MARSHY MOISTY QUASHY SHOWER SLABBY SOBBED SPONGY SPOUTY SWASHY WATERY ARROUSE BLUBBER DRABBLE FLOTTER MOISTEN SLOPPED SOBBING SPEWING SPRINGY IRRIGATE SATURATE SLATTERY SLOBBERY SLOTTERY WATERISH
(— AND STORMY) FOUL
(— LIGHTLY) SPRINKLE
(— THOROUGHLY) SOUSE DRENCH
(DRIPPING —) ASOP
(SLIGHTLY —) DEWY
(SOFTLY —) SQUASHY
(VERY —) SOPPY
(PREF.) HYGR(O) UDO
WETHER PUR RAM HAMEL DINMAN DINMONT
WETNESS DANK
WETTING SOUCE SOUSE SOWSE MOILING
WHACK DAD LAM TRY BANG BELT BIFF DEAL HACK SWAK TIME CLONK DRIVE SHARE STATE SWACK WHANG CHANCE DEFEAT STROKE THWACK BARGAIN LAMBACK PORTION
WHACKING VERY WHALING WHOPPING EXTREMELY
WHALE SEI CETE HUEL HULL LASH ORCA WALL KOGIA POGGY SCRAG SPERM STUNT BALEEN BELUGA BLOWER FINNER GIBBAR KILLER THRASH BOWHEAD DOLPHIN FINBACK FINFISH GIBBERT GRAMPUS MARSOON RIPSACK RORQUAL SPOUTER ZIPHIAN BALAENID CACHALOT CETACEAN DOEGLING GREYBACK HARDHEAD HUMPBACK JUBARTES MUTILATE PHYSETER THRASHER ZIPHIOID
(— BUTCHER) LEMMER
(— REFUSE) GURRY
(FINBACK —) GRASO
(HERD OF —S) GAM
(KIND OF —) SEI MINKE KILLER
(NEWBORN —) SUCKER
(SCHOOL OF —S) GAM POD
(SMALL —) MINKE
(YOUNG —) CUB
(PREF.) BALAENI BALAENO CET(O)
WHALEBONE BALEEN
WHALER HEADER BUSHMAN SPOUTER SWAGMAN WHACKER WHOPPER CETICIDE
WHALESKIN MUKTUK
WHAMMY HEX
WHANG BEAT BLOW FLOG CHUNK THONG WHACK THRASH RAWHIDE
WHARF KEY POW DOCK GARE PIER QUAY SLIP BERTH JETTY LEVEE STADE STAITH STRAND LANDING PANTALAN STELLING
WHARVE WARVE WHIRL WHORL
WHAT FAT HOT HOW WET WHO HOOT HOTE WHEN STUFF WHICH MATTER PARTLY
WHATA FUTTAH FUTTER
WHAT EVERY WOMAN KNOWS
(AUTHOR OF —) BARRIE
(CHARACTER IN —) JOHN ALICK DAVID JAMES SHAND SYBIL WYLIE BRIERE MAGGIE CHARLES VENABLES TENTERDEN
WHATNOT OMNIUM ETAGERE
WHAT PRICE GLORY (AUTHOR OF —) ANDERSON
(CHARACTER IN —) FLAGG QUIRT CHARMAINE
WHATSIT GIZMO WHATSIS THINGAMAJIG
WHAT'S-ITS-NAME TIMENOGUY
WHATSOEVER MORTAL
WHEAL HIVE HUEL WALE WELT URTICA POMPHUS
WHEAT BLE WIT CORN CONES EMMER FULTZ GRAIN SPELT SPICA TRIGO BULGUR BURGUL CEREAL KANRED STAPLE TURKEY EINKORN FORMITY FRUMETY KUBANKA MARQUIS POLLARD FRUMENTY SPELTOID
(— BOILED IN MILK) FURMITY FRUMENTY
(— MEASURE) TRUG
(BEARDED —) RIVETS
(CRACKED —) GROATS
(GRANULATED —) SUJI SUJEE
(HARD —) DURUM
(PARCHED —) BULGUR
(PREF.) TRITICO
WHEATCAKE PURI
WHEATEAR CHACK ARLING WITTOL CHACKER ORTOLAN SNORTER WITTALL CHICKELL SAXICOLA
WHEATGRASS BLUESTEM

WHEATLIKE VULGARE
WHEEDLE COG CANT CLAW COAX CARNY FLUFF GLOSE GLOZE INGLE JOLLY BANTER CAJOLE CUITER FLEECH GLAVER RADDLE SMOOGE WHILLY BLARNEY CUITTLE PALAVER SMOODGE TWEEDLE BLANDISH COLLOGUE SCROUNGE
WHEEDLING BUTTERY COMETHER
WHEEL BOB BUR COG FAN NUT ORB BEAD BUFF GEAR HELM HURL PURL ROLL ROTA RULL STAR TIRL WYLE ATHEY FLIER FLUFF FLYER IDLER NORIA REWET RHOMB ROWEL SWING TRUCK BILOBE CASTER CASTOR CIRCLE DRIVEN DRIVER FANNER HORRAL JAGGER KURUMA LEADER PINION ROLLER ROTATE RUNDLE RUNNER TRACER BALANCE BICYCLE CHUKKER GUDGEON LANTERN PEDRAIL PRICKER REVOLVE STEPNEY TRAILER TRILOBE TRINDLE TROCHUS TRUCKLE TRUNDLE UNILOBE WILDCAT CARACOLE FOLLOWER ODOMETER SPROCKET
(— A SKIN) FLUFF
(— CHARGED WITH DIAMOND DUST) SLITTER
(— CONTROLLING RUDDER) HELM
(— FOR EXECUTIONS) RAT
(— IN KNITTING MACHINE) BUR BURR
(— IN TIMEPIECE) BALANCE
(— OF DAY AND NIGHT) RHOMB
(— OF LIFE) ZOETROPE
(BUCKET —) LIFTER
(DIAMOND —) SKIVE
(GEAR —) DRIVEN HELICAL
(GRINDING —) SHELL
(GROOVED —) PULLEY SHEAVE SHIVER
(INTERRUPTER —) TICKER TIKKER
(LOCOMOTIVE —) DRIVER
(METAL —) FILET FILLET
(MILL —) PIRN
(PAIR OF LOGGING —S) CATYDID KATYDID
(POINTED —) TRACER
(POLISHING —) BOB BUFF SKAIF SKEIF BUFFER SCAIFE
(POTTER'S —) LATHE THROW
(PULLEY —) TRUCKLE
(ROAD-MEASURING —) AMBULATOR
(SPARE —) STEPNEY
(SPINNING —) TURN CHARKA CHARKHA
(SPUR —) ROWEL
(TANK —) BOGY BOGEY BOGIE
(TOOTHED —) GEAR PINION ROULETTE
(TURBINE —) ROTOR
(TWO PAIRS OF —S) CUTS CUTTS
(VANED —) FLIER FLYER
(WATER —) NORIA SAKIA SAKIEH SAKIYEH TYMPANUM
(PL.) KATYDID
(PREF.) CYCL(O) ROTA ROTATO ROTI ROTO TROCH(I)(LEI)(O)
(SUFF.) TROCH(A)(AL)(OUS)(US)
WHEELBARROW GURRY BARROW CARRIAGE
(PART OF —) BED LEG GRIP TIRE TRAY BRACE FRAME WHEEL HANDLE BRACKET SUPPORT
WHEELER POLER PUSHER
WHEEL-SHAPED ROTATE TROCHAL ROTIFORM
WHEELWORK MOTION
(— IN A CLOCK) MOVEMENT
WHEELWRIGHT WHEELER WOODMAN WHEELMAN
WHEEZE JOKE HOOSE HOOZE TRICK COGHLE
WHELK FILK GRUB WELT BUCKIE MAGGOT PAPULE PIMPLE WINKLE PUSTULE
WHELP CUB PUP SON CHIT FAWN PUPPY YELPER KITLING SPROCKET
WHEMMEL UPSET FUMMEL FUMMLE WHAMBLE OVERTURN
WHEN AS BUT FAN FRO GIN THO WON THAN THEN THOA TILL SINCE UNTIL ENOUGH ALTHOUGH
WHENEVER ONCE
WHERE AS FAR FUR FAUR FEAR FERRE PLACE QUAIR THERE WHITHER LOCATION
(— ABOVE MENTIONED) US
WHEREFORE WHY CAUSE FORWHY REASON
WHERENESS UBIETY
WHEREVER THERE
WHEREWITHAL MEANS MONEY RESOURCES
WHERRET BOX CUFF SLAP HURRY TEASE WORRY TROUBLE WHIRRICK
WHERRY BARGE ROWBOAT WHIRREY
WHET WET GOAD HONE TIME TURN GRIND POINT RIFLE ROUSE SLITE WHILE AROUSE EXCITE INCITE STROKE QUICKEN SHARPEN APERITIF EXACUATE
WHETHER IF GIF GIN WHAR WHERE EITHER
WHETSTONE BUR RIP RUB BUHR BURR SLIP STONE RUBBER STRAIK SHARPER WASHITA WHITTLE OILSTONE RUBSTONE STRICKLE
WHEY PALE QUAY WHIG SERUM THRUST WATERY
(PREF.) ORO
WHIBA UEBA
WHICH AS THE WHO THAT QUILK WHILK
(— SEE) QV QQV
WHICKER NEIGH WHINNY WIGHER
WHIDAH BIRD VEUVE WEAVER WHYDAH REDBILL
WHIFF FAN GUF BLOW GUFF GUST HINT PUFF TIFT WAFT WIFT FLUFF QUIFF SMOKE EXHALE MAGRIM MEGRIM WHIFFET
WHIFFLE BLOW FIFE SWAY FLICKER FLUTTER
WHIFFLETREE HEELTREE SWINGLEBAR
WHIG JOG QUIG WHEY
WHIGMALEERIE FANCY
WHILE AS BIT GAM THO YET FILE FYLE TIDE TILL WHEN WHET WOLE FILIE PIECE SPACE STEAD STOUN THROW UNTIL STOUND WHENAS WHILOM BEGUILE TROUBLE EXERTION OCCASION SOLONGAS
(— AWAY) AMUSE FLEET DIVERT BEGUILE DECEIVE
(LITTLE —) AWEE DRASS WHILEY WHILEEN WHILOCK
WHILES UNTIL SOMETIMES
WHILLY GULL CAJOLE WHEEDLE
WHILOM ERST
WHILST TILL UNTIL
WHIM BEE FAD GIG GIN TOY FIKE FLAM KINK CRANK FANCY FLISK FOLLY FREAK HUMOR MEINY QUIRK THRUM FEGARY FITTEN MAGGOT MEGRIM SPLEEN VAGARY WHIMSY BOUTADE CAPRICE CONCEIT WRINKLE CROTCHET
WHIMBREL JACK SPOW SPOWE CURLEW MAYBIRD MAYFOWL TITTEREL
WHIMPER GIRN MEWL PULE WAIL WEAK BLEAT WHINE SIMPER WHINGE YAMMER GRIZZLE SNIFFLE SNUFFLE WHINDLE WHINNEL WHITTER WHINNOCK
WHIMSICAL FAIRY FANCY BAROCK COCKLE FLISKY NOTION QUAINT BAROQUE BIZARRE GIGGISH PUCKISH TOYSOME BIZZARRO FANCIFUL FREAKISH HUMOROUS NOTIONAL SINGULAR VAPOROUS CROTCHETY FANTASTIC PIXILATED FANTASTICAL
WHIMSY WHIM FREAK VAGARY CAPRICE WHIMWHAM
WHIN FUN ULEX FURZE WHINCOW WOODWAX
WHINCHAT TICK UTICK WHEATEAR
WHINE WOW GIRN GOWL MEWL PULE TIRM TOOT YARM YIRN BLEAT CROON MEECH QUINE TWINE WHAUP WHEWT PEENGE SNIVEL TREBLE WHINGE WINNEL YAMMER WHIMPER WHINDLE
WHINING QUERULOUS
WHINNY HINNY NEIGH PLAIN SNICKER WHICKER
WHINSTONE TRAP WHIN SCURDY
WHINYARD SWORD HANGER POCHARD WHINGER SHOVELER
WHIP CAT EEL FAN GAD ROD TAW BEAT CAST COIL DICK DUST FIRK FLOG FOAM GOAD HIDE JEHU JERK LASH LICK LOUK PLET TAWS URGE WHUP ABUSE AZOTE BASTE BIRCH CRACK FLAIL FLICK FLISK IMPEL KNOUT LEASH PLETE QUILT ROMAL SLASH STRAP SWEPE SWING SWISH TAWSE THONG THUMP AROUSE BREECH CHABUK DEFEAT FEAGUE INCITE LAINER LARRUP LICKER MAIDEN NETTLE PIZZLE QUIPPE SCUTCH SNATCH SWINGE SWITCH THRASH TICKLE CHABOUK CHICOTE COWHIDE COWSKIN CURBASH KURBASH LAMBAST LAYOVER NAGAIKA RAWHIDE SCOURGE SHINGLE SJAMBOK SLASHER TICKLER CHAWBUCK COACHMAN CONFOUND FLAGELLA KOURBASH PEPPERER BLACKSNAKE
(— EGGS) CAST
(— HANDLE) CROP
(— IN PIANO ACTION) WIPPEN
(— WITH 3 LASHES) PLET PLETE
(FURIOUS —) JEHU
(HORSE —) WAND CHABOUK
(JOCKEY'S —) BAT
(RIDING —) CROP DICK QUIRT
(RUSSIAN —) KNOUT
(PREF.) FLAGELLI MASTIG(O)
(SUFF.) MASTIX
WHIPLASH THONG COSAQUE CRACKER
WHIPPED BEATEN BROKEN DEFEATED FOUETTEE CHANTILLY
WHIPPER TICKLER THONGMAN THRASHER THREAPER
WHIPPER-IN PRICKER
WHIPPERSNAPPER SQUIRT WHIFFET WHIPSTER JACKANAPES
WHIPPING LICK TOCO TOKO HIDING CLANKER FANNING SERVING BIRCHING BROWSING SKELPING
WHIPPING POST FORK PILLAR
WHIP SCORPION GRAMPUS PHRYNID PEDIPALP WHIPTAIL
WHIPSOCKET SNEAD
WHIPSTITCH HEM SEC SEAM MINUTE INSTANT OVERCAST
WHIR BIRR ZIZZ WHIRRY
WHIRL BIRL EDDY FURL GYRE HURL PURL REEL RUSH SPIN TIRL DRILL GIDDY SKIRL SQUIR SWIRL THIRL THROW TWIRL TWIST WALTZ WHORL BUSTLE CIRCLE GYRATE HURTLE SWINGE VORTEX WHORLE WINDLE WIRBLE MIZMAZE REVOLVE TRUNDLE TURMOIL VERTICIL
(— ABOUT) DOZE GURGE
(— IN THE AIR) WARP
(— OF ACTIVITY) MERRYGOROUND
WHIRLIGIG GIG TOY SPIN TURN WHEEL FIZGIG FISHGIG
WHIRLING GIDDY WHEELY STROBIC GYRATION GYRATORY VORTICAL PIROUETTE
(PREF.) STROBO
WHIRLPOOL EDDY GULF SUCK WEEL WELL WIEL GORCE GOURD GURGE BULLER GORGES SWELTH VORTEX GURGLET SWALLOW SWILKIE SUCKHOLE MAELSTROM
(PREF.) DINO
WHIRLWIND OE DEVIL VORTEX PRESTER TORNADO TOURBILLON TOURBILLION
WHIRLYBIRD CHOPPER
WHISHT HUSH SILENCE
WHISK ZIP FISK TUFT WHID WHIP WISP CAURI FLICK FLISK HURRY SPEED SWISH CHAURI CHOWRY SWITCH COWTAIL WHISKER
(— OFF) TROUNCE
WHISKER HAIRLINE VIBRISSA
(PL.) BEARD ZIFFS WEEPER GALWAYS VIBRISSA MOUSTACHE SIDEBURNS
WHISKY RYE BOND CORN CIDER IRISH USQUE POTEEN REDEYE SCOTCH BOURBON BLOCKADE BUSTHEAD CREATURE POPSKULL USQUABAE MOONSHINE

TANGLEFOOT USQUEBAUGH MOUNTAINDEW
(GLASS OF —) RUBDOWN
(RAW —) DRUDGE
WHISPER BUZZ HARK HINT ROUN RUNE ROUND RUMOR TRACE TUTEL BREATH BREEZE HARKEN MURMUR SUSURR TITTLE WHISHT HEARKEN SUSURRUS
WHIST MORT VINT QUIET BOSTON SILENT WHEESHT
WHISTLE BLOW CALL PIPE WHEW FLUTE QUILL WHAUP WHEEP WHUTE BUMMER BUZZER CUCKOO FUSSLE HOOTER SIFFLE SISTLE SQUEAL WARBLE YELPER CATCALL TWEEDLE BIRDCALL
(— FEEBLY) WHEEDLE WHEEPLE
WHISTLE FLUTE SIFFLOT
WHISTLER PIPER MARMOT ROARER FLUTIST LAPWING SIFFLEUR
WHISTLING PIPY PIPEY ROARING SIFFLET RHONCHUS SUSSURANT
WHIT BIT JOT RAP ATOM DOIT HATE HOOT IOTA QUAT QUIT AUGHT BODLE GROAT POINT QUITE SPECK CIVITE PARTICLE TWOPENNY
WHITE CUT WAN BAWN FITE HOAR LILY PALE QUAT QUIT ASHEN BLOND HAOLE HOARY LABAN LINEN SNOWY ALBINO ARGENT BLANCH BRIGHT BUCKRA CANDID CIVITE ERMINE SILVER WINTRY CANDENT LEUCOUS NIVEOUS WHITTLE FAVORITE INNOCENT LACTEOUS
(— AND SMOOTH) IVORINE
(— OF EGG) GLAIR ALBUMEN
(— PERSON) OFAY
(POOR —) YAHOO CRACKER
(SHADE OF —) IVORY
(PREF.) ALB(I)(O) CALI CALLI LEUC(O) LEUK(O)
WHITE ALDER CLETHRA
WHITE ANT ANAY NASUTE TERMITE
WHITEBAIT SMELT ICEFISH SALANGID SALMONID
WHITEBEAM ARIA SERVICE MULBERRY
WHITEBOY PET LEVELER
WHITE BRYONY COWBIND MANDRAKE
WHITE CEDAR JUNIPER
WHITE CLOVER LADINO SHAMROCK
WHITE COMPANY (AUTHOR OF —) DOYLE
(CHARACTER IN —) JOHN MAUDE NIGEL HORDLE LORING SAMKIN ALLEYNE AYLWARD EDRICSON
WHITEFACE HEREFORD
WHITEFISH BLOAT CISCO PILOT POWAN BELUGA CHIVEY POLLAN TULIPI VENDIS BLOATER BOWBACK GWYNIAD LAVARET VENDACE BLACKFIN GREYBACK HUMPBACK MENOMINI SALMONID SCHNABEL TULLIBEE
WHITEFLY HOMOPTER MEALYWING
WHITE FRIAR CARMELITE
WHITE GUM TUART
WHITEHEAD MILIUM
WHITE-HEADED GOLDEN FAVORED FORTUNATE
WHITE HEATH BRIAR BRIER
WHITE HELLEBORE ITCHREED ITCHWEED
WHITE IPECAC ITOUBOU
WHITE LEAD CERUSE
WHITE MAPAN PIRIPIRI
WHITE MUSTARD KEDLOCK SINAPIS CRUCIFER
WHITEN CAM CAUM SCURF ALBIFY BLANCH BLANCO BLEACH BLENCH DEALBATE EMBLANCH ETIOLATE PIPECLAY
WHITENED DEALBATE
WHITENESS IVORY ALBEDO ARGENT CANDOR PURITY CANITIES PALENESS
WHITE OAK ROBLE
WHITE POPLAR ABELE ABELTREE
WHITE SNAKEROOT STEVIA POOLWORT RICHWEED WHITETOP
WHITE STURGEON BELUGA
WHITETHROAT JACK MUFF MUFTY MUGGY PEGGY EYSOGE MILLER MUFFET WHISKY WINNEL HAYSUCK WHEYBIRD
WHITEWALL TIRE
WHITEWASH LIME GLASS BLANCH PARGET STIFLE CHICAGO LIMEWASH PALLIATE
WHITEWEED DAISY
WHITE WHALE BELUGA
WHITHER GUST HURL RUSH WHIZ HURRY SHAKE WHERE FLURRY BLUSTER WHERETO
WHITING BARB HAKE CORBINA CORVINA MERLING KINGFISH MOONFISH
WHITING-POUT BIB KLEG BLENS
WHITISH BAWN PALE DILUTE SUBALBID
WHITLOW FELON AGNAIL ANCOME FETLOW BREEDER PANARIS BREDSORE RUNROUND PANARITIUM PARONYCHIA
WHITLOW GRASS DRABA NAILWORT SHADBLOW
WHITRACK WEASEL FUTTERET WHITTRET
WHITSUNDAY TERM
WHITSUNTIDE PINXTER PINGSTER PINKSTER
WHITTLE CUT PARE CARVE KNIFE STEEL TWITE EXCITE MANTLE THWITE BLANKET
WHIZ ACE BUZZ DEAL GIRL PIRR QUIZ SING WHIR ZIZZ BRAIN SOUGH WHISH WHIZZ WIZARD BARGAIN SWITHER WHIDDER WHINNER
(— KID) BRAIN GENIUS EINSTEIN
(COMPUTER —) HACKER
WHIZ-BANG EXPERT NOTABLE
WHO AS HOW THE WHA WHAT WHICH
WHOA WO WAY WHO STOP
WHOEVER WHATSO EVERWHO
WHOLE ALL HOW SUM BODY COOL EVEN HALE HALF HOLY HULL BLOCK GREAT GROSS HAILL SOLID SOUND TOTAL TOTUM TUTTA UNCUT CORPSE ENTIRE HEALED INTACT VERSAL GENERAL INFRACT INTEGER PERFECT SINCERE SOLIDUM UNITARY COMPLETE ENSEMBLE ENTIRETY GLOBULAR INTEGRAL LIVELONG OUTRIGHT UNBROKEN
(— OF ANY ORGANISM) SOMA
(— OF REALITY) ABSOLUTE
(ORGANIC —) SYSTEM
(ORGANIZED —) GESTALT CONFIGURATION
(PREF.) ALL HOL(O) INTEGRI PAN TOTI TOTO
WHOLEHEARTED HEARTY SINCERE ZESTFUL COMPLETE IMPLICIT
WHOLESALE MASSIVE SWEEPING
WHOLESALER JOBBER EXPORTER
WHOLESOME GOOD CLEAN SOUND SWEET BENIGN SAVORY HEALTHY PRUDENT CURATIVE HALESOME HEALSOME HOMELIKE REMEDIAL SALUTARY HEALTHFUL
WHOLE-SOULED SINCERE
WHOLLY ALL FAIR FLAT HALE ONLY BLACK CLEAR FULLY QUITE STARK ALGATE BODILY FLATLY HOLLOW PURELY SOLELY ALGATES ROUNDLY SOLIDLY TOTALLY DIRECTLY ENTIRELY
(PREF.) TOTI
WHOMP CREAM
WHOOP BOOM HOOP HOOT BOOST RAISE SHOUT EXCITE HALLOO HOOPOE
WHOOPING COUGH KINKHOST CHINCOUGH PERTUSSIS
WHOP TAN WAP BEAT THUD THUMP STRIKE THRASH
WHOPPER LIE TALE SIZER BOUNCER CRUMPER SLAPPER SNAPPER SWAPPER SWINGER SCROUGER STRAPPER WALLOPER
WHOPPING VERY LARGE BANGING RAPPING WAPPING WHALING SWINGING THUMPING WHACKING WALLOPING
WHORE DRAB JILT FILTH QUAIL WENCH HARLOT PUTAIN DEBAUCH PINNACE STRUMPET SUCCUBUS PROSTITUTE
WHOREMONGER HOLOUR
WHORL TURN CYCLE SPIRE SWIRL WHIRL THWORL VOLUTE WHARVE WREATH ANNULUS CALYCLE CALYCULE GYRATION VERTICIL VOLUTION
(PREF.) SPONDYL(O) VERTICILL(I)
WHORLED (NOT —) ACYCLIC
WHORTLEBERRY HOT HURT FRAWN HOOTE FRAGHAN BILBERRY COWBERRY
WHY HOW QUI ENIGMA FORWHY HOWCOME
WICK BAD EVIL FARM TOWN ANGLE CREEK DAIRY MATCH QUICK SEAVE SNAST CORNER LIVING WICKED VILLAGE FARMSTEAD
(— CLOGGED WITH TALLOW) ROUGHIE
(LONG WAXED —) TAPER
WICKED BAD SAD DARK EVIL FAST FOUL IRON LAZY LEWD MEAN PIKY VILE BLACK CURST FELON SHREW SORRY WRONG WROTH CURSED GUILTY LITHER LUTHER NEFAST PERDIT PITCHY SEVERE SHREWD SINFUL UNHOLY UNJUST UNLEAD UNLEDE UNWELL CAITIFF DARKSUM GODLESS HEINOUS HELLISH IMMORAL NAUGHTY NINETED NOXIOUS PRAVOUS PROFANE ROGUISH UNGODLY UNSEELY UNSOUND UNWREST VICIOUS VILLAIN ACCURSED CRIMINAL DARKSOME DEPRAVED DEVILISH DIABOLIC ENORMOUS FELONOUS FIENDISH FLAGRANT MESCHANT OBDURATE PERVERSE TERRIBLE UNKINDLY ABANDONED NEFARIOUS PERNICIOUS
(— ITEM) CANDLE
(PREF.) PONERO
WICKEDNESS ILL SIN EVIL HARM VICE CRIME FOLLY GUILT BELIAL FELONY NOUGHT UNGOOD ATHEISM DEVILRY ILLNESS PRAVITY DARKNESS DEVILTRY INIQUITY MISCHIEF SATANISM WANGRACE
WICKER SALE
WICKERWORK WEB WEEL TWIGGEN BASKETRY
WICKET GATE HOOP HATCH PITCH STUMP GUICHET
(FALLING OF —S) ROT
WICKETKEEPER STUMP STUMPER
WICKFORD POINT (AUTHOR OF —) MARQUAND
(CHARACTER IN —) JIM JOE BERG MARY ALLEN AVERY BELLA BRILL HARRY STOWE ARCHIE CALDER HOWARD WRIGHT GIFFORD SOUTHBY LEIGHTON PATRICIA CLOTHILDE
WICKIUP HUT WAKIUP SHELTER
WIDDRIM FIT FURY
WIDDY NOOSE WIDOW WITHY HALTER
WIDE FAR LAX DEEP ROOM SIDE AMPLE BROAD LARGE ROOMY SHARP SLACK WRONG ASTRAY ROOMWARD SPACEFUL SPACIOUS
(— OF) BESIDE
(— OF THE MARK) AWRY WILD ABROAD
(LONG AND —) SIDE
(PREF.) EURY LATI
WIDE-AWAKE FLY FOXY KEEN LIVE ALERT FLASH LEERY CADDIE SLIPPY KNOWING WAKEFUL WATCHFUL
WIDELY FAR BROAD ABROAD GREATLY LARGELY
WIDEN FLAN REAM DILATE EXPAND EXTEND FLANCH FLANGE FUNNEL BROADEN
WIDENESS WIDTH BREADTH
WIDESPREAD RIFE DIFFUSE GENERAL POPULAR PROLATE REGNANT CATHOLIC EXTENDED PANDEMIC SWEEPING EXTENSIVE
WIDGEON SMEE WHIM GOOSE WHEWER ZUISIN POACHER POTCHER BALDPATE BLUEBILL WHISTLER
WIDGET PART

WIDOW VID BALO DAME SKAT BLIND KITTY VEUVE WEEDA WIDDY MATRON RELICT TERCER DOWAGER EMPRESS BARONESS DOWERESS
(PL.) VIDUAGE
WIDOWED VIDUOUS
WIDOWHOOD VIDUAGE VIDUITY
WIDTH GAPE SIDE RANGE SCOPE BREADTH OPENING FRONTAGE FULLNESS LARGEOUR LATITUDE WIDENESS
(— OF CUT) KERF
(— OF HORSESHOE) COVER
(— OF PALM) HAND
(— OF PAPER) FILL
(— OF PULLEY) FACE
(— OF SHIP) BEAM
(— OF SHIP'S BAND) STRAKE
(— OF TYPE) SET
(— OF WEB) DECKLE
WIELD PLY RUN BEAR WALT WIND APPLY EXERT SWING VELDE EMPLOY GOVERN HANDLE MANAGE STRAIN CONTROL
WIELDER (— OF AUTHORITY) GAULEITER
(— OF POWER) POTENCY
WIENER FRANK HOTDOG FRANKFURTER
WIFE UX FEM HEN MRS RIB WYF BABY BIBI DAME DORA ENID FEME FERE FRAU FROW JAEL LADY MAKE MAMA MATE RANI UXOR DIRCE DONNA DUTCH FEMME LUCKY MAMMA MATCH MUJER SQUAW WOMAN ELMIRE EMILIA ESPOSA GAMMER KEEPER MATRON MISSIS MISSUS MULIER SPOUSE VENDER WAHINE BEDMATE DIONYZA EMPRESS PARTNER WEDLOCK DEIANIRA DEIDAMIA ERIPHYLE HELPMATE HELPMEET MISTRESS PECULIAR
(— OF COTTER) COTQUEAN
(— OF KNIGHT OR BARONET) DAME
(— OF MOHAMMEDAN) KHADIJA
(AFFIANCED —) FUTURE
(INDIAN'S —) WEBB
(OLD —) GAMMER
(SPEND TIME WITHOUT —) BACHIT
(PL.) PUNALUA
(PREF.) UXOR(I)
WIFTY DITSY DIZZY GIDDY INANE SILLY
WIG BOB JIZ RUG TIE FRIZ GIZZ JANE JIZZ LOCK TETE TOUR BUSBY CAXON FLASH JASEY MAJOR SCALP SCOLD ADONIS BRUTUS FROWZE MERKIN PERUKE REBUKE TOUPEE TOUPET COMBING RAMILIE SCRATCH SHEITEL SPENCER BOBJEROM CHEDREUX CHEWELER DALMAHOY NIGHTCAP PERUKERY POSTICHE ROGERIAN VALLANCY
(— WITH ROUGHLY CROPPED HAIR) BRUTUS
(BUSHY —) BUSBY
(GRAY —) GRIZZLE
(WORSTED —) JASEY
(18TH CENTURY —) ADONIS GEORGE
WIGGLE JET HOTCH JIGGLE WABBLE WANGLE
WIGGLER PUPA LARVA WRYER
WIGGY WACKO WACKY
WIGHT MAN SWIFT STRONG VALIANT CREATURE STALWART
WIGLET TOUPEE
WIGMAKER WIGGER PERUKER PERUKIER
WIGWAG SIGNAL
WIGWAM TIPI LODGE TEPEE WEEKWAM WICKIUP
WIKENO NIKENO HEILTSUK
WILD APE MAD REE SHY FAST RUDE SCAR WOWF CRAZY FANTI FELON FERAL GIDDY MYALL RANDY RANTY ROUGH ROYET SKEER WASTE DESERT FANTEE FERINE FIERCE LAVISH MADCAP NATIVE RAMAGE RANDOM RENISH SAVAGE SHANDY STORMY UNRULY BERSERK BREACHY ERRATIC FRANTIC GALLOUS GALLOWS HAGGARD HOWLING MADDING NATURAL OUTWARD RIOTOUS SKADDLE SKEERED WILDING ABERRANT AGRESTAL BARBARIC CHIMERIC DESOLATE FAROUCHE FRENETIC HALUCKET HELLICAT RECKLESS UNTILLED WARRAGAL WILLYARD BOISTEROUS
(— CARD) FREAK
(PREF.) AGRIO
WILD ASS GOUR KIANG KULAN COTULA KOULAN ONAGER QUAGGA CHIGETAI
WILD BALSAM APPLE CREEPER
WILD BEE KARBI
WILD BOAR APER SUID TUSKER SOUNDER SUIDIAN WILRONE SANGLIER
WILD BUFFALO ARNA ARNEE
WILD BUSH BEAN PHASEMY
WILD CABBAGE YELLOWS
WILD CARDAMOM RUEWORT KNOBWOOD
WILD CARROT DILL ELTROT FIDDLE BIRDNEST HILLTROT
WILDCAT CAT BALU EYRA CHATI CHAUS MANUL TIGER MARGAY SERVAL WAGATI COLOCOLA JAGUARONDI JAGUARUNDI
WILD CELERY ACHE ECHE EELGRASS SMALLAGE
WILD CHERRY GEAN MERRY MAZZARD
WILD CHERVIL KECK COWWEED HONEWORT MILKWEED
WILD CYCLAMEN SOWBREAD
WILD DOG ADJAG DHOLE DINGO GUARA AGUARA AGOUARA CIMARRON WARRAGAL
WILD DUCK (AUTHOR OF —) IBSEN
(CHARACTER IN —) GINA EKDAL SORBY WERLE HANSEN HEDVIG GREGERS HJALMAR RELLING
WILDEBEEST GNU
WILDERNESS BUSH WILD WASTE DESERT FOREST WESTERN SOLITUDE
WILD-EYED HAGGARD RADICAL
WILDFOWL VOLATILE
WILD GARLIC MOLY
WILD GERANIUM ALUMROOT DOVEFOOT FLUXWEED
WILD GOAT TUR IBEX TAHR EVECK PASAN MAZAME MARKHOR AEGAGRUS MARKHOOR
WILD HORSE BRUMBY KUMRAH TARPAN BRUMBIE WARRAGAL WARRIGAL
WILD HYACINTH CUCKOO CROWTOE GREGGLE BRODIAEA CROWFOOT
WILD INDIGO SHOOFLY BAPTISIA TUMBLEWEED
WILD LETTUCE FIREWEED
WILD MAN SAVAGE WOODMAN WOODSMAN
WILD MANGOSTEEN SANTOL
WILD MARJORAM ORGAN ORGAMY ORGANY ORIGAN OREGANO ORGAMENT
WILD MULBERRY YAWWEED
WILD MUSTARD RUNCH CHARLOCK
WILDNESS FERITY HEYDAY HEYDEY FEROCITY SAVAGERY SAVAGISM
WILD OAT DRANK DRAWK DROKE HAVER HEVER EGILOPS
WILD ONION UMBEL UMBELLA
WILD OX BUF YAK ANOA BUFF REEM UNICORN
WILD PARSLEY ELTROT HILLTROT
WILD PEAR DOGBERRY
WILD PLUM SLOE ISLAY
WILD POTATO MANROOT WAPATOO
WILD RADISH RUNCH
WILD RICE MANOMIN
WILD SAGE EYESEED
WILD SARSAPARILLA SHOTBUSH
WILDSCHUTZ, DER (CHARACTER IN —) BACULUS NANETTE EBERBACH FREIMANN GRETCHEN KRONTHAL
(COMPOSER OF —) LORTZING
WILD SERVICE TREE SORB SORBUS
WILD SHEEP SHA AUDAD URIAL AOUDAD ARGALI BHARAL NAYAUR BIGHORN MOUFLON
WILD SWAN ELK
WILD THYME HILLWORT SERPOLET
WILD TOBACCO GAGROOT SOURBUSH MARIJUANA SALVADORA
WILD TURNIP NAVEW
WILD VANILLA LIATRIS
WILE ART PAUK PAWK RUSE FRAUD GUILE TRICK ALLURE BLENCH DECEIT ENGINE ENTICE BEGUILE ARTIFICE TRICKERY
WILGA WILLOW
WILL EGO MAY ULL WAY FATE LIST TEST WISH LEAVE OUGHT SHALL WORST ANIMUS CHOICE CHOOSE DESIRE DEVICE DEVISE LEGATE LIKING QUETHE SCRIPT CODICIL PASSION WITWORD AMBITION APPETITE BEQUEATH PLEASING PLEASURE VOLITION
(— NOT) WONT WINNA WONNA WUNNA WONNOT
(— NOT TO DO) NOLITION
(— OF DEITY) DECREE
(— OF GOD) LAW
(— OF LEGISLATURE) ACT
(— TO LIVE) TANGHA
(FREE —) ACCORD
(GOOD —) GREE
(I —) CHILL
(ILL —) ARR ENVY HEST VENOM ANIMUS ENMITY HATRED UNTHANK AMBITION
(KIND OF —) LIVING
(SUFF.) **(CONDITION OF —)** THYMIA
(STATE OF —) BOULIA BULIA BULIC
WILLET TATLER TATTLER
WILLFUL HEADY WILLY FEISTY UNRULY HAGGARD WAYWARD WILSOME CAMSTRARY
WILLFULLY WOLDES SCIENTER
WILLIAM TELL (AUTHOR OF —) SCHILLER
(CHARACTER IN —) JOHN TELL FURST HENRY ARNOLD BERTHA ULRICH WALTER WERNER GESSLER WILLIAM MATHILDE BAUMGARTEN
(COMPOSER OF —) ROSSINI
WILLIES JUMPS CREEPS
WILLING BAIN FAIN FREE GAME GLAD LIEF RATH PRONE READY MINDED TOWARD CONTENT OBLIGING UNFORCED
(— TO FORGIVE) PACABLE PLACABLE
WILLINGLY LIEF SOON FREELY GLADLY LIEFLY FRANKLY READILY
(MORE —) RATHER
WILLINGNESS HEART FREEDOM FAINNESS
(— TO FIGHT) DEFIANCE
WILLIWAW STORM WOOLLY TEMPEST
WILLOW DULY ITEA SALE WYLW OSIER SALEW SALIX SAUGH WIDDY WITHY WOODY DUSTER SALLOW TEASER TWILLY WITHEN WUDDIE
(— FOR THATCHING) SPRAYS
(— IN TEXTILES) WOLF
(NATIVE —) COOBA COOBAH
(SIMPLE —) WHIPPER
(PREF.) **(— TWIG)** LYGO
WILLOWER DULER DUSTER TEASER WILLIER
WILLOW HERB WICOPY EPILOBE FIRETOP PIGWEED ROSEBAY BURNWEED FIREWEED
WILLOW WARBLER SMEU SMEUTH MUDDLER TROCHIL OVENBIRD
WILLOW WREN PEGGY
WILLOWY SUPPLE SLIPPER DELICATE
WILLY-NILLY PERFORCE
WILSON'S PLOVER COLLIER
WILSON'S SNIPE JACK SHADBIRD
WILSON'S TERN MEDRICK
WILSON'S THRUSH VEERY
WILT EBB SAG DROP FADE FLAG WELK DROOP SUCCUMB COLLAPSE
WILTED EMARCID
WILY SLY FOXY CANNY SLICK ARTFUL ASTUTE CLEVER CRAFTY QUAINT SHREWD STALKY SUBTLE TRICKY CUNNING POLITIC VERSUTE WINDING SERPENTINE
WIMBLE BORE AUGER BRISK ACTIVE

GIMLET LIVELY NIMBLE WIBBLE WUMMEL
WIMP NERD
WIMPLE BEND WIND CURVE TWIST GORGET RIPPLE MEANDER WIMLUNGE
WIN BAG COP HIT DRAW GAIN HAVE LAND LICK FORCE SCORE ATTACH CLINCH OBTAIN ACHIEVE ACQUIRE CONQUER DESERVE HARVEST POSSESS TRIUMPH DECISION OVERCOME STRAIGHT
(— AGAINST) BREAK SCOOP
(— AT CHESS) MATE CHECKMATE
(— AWAY) STEAL DEBAUCH
(— BACK) RECOVER
(— BY GUILE) GET POT BEAR CARRY RAISE TRAIN GATHER CAPTURE INVEIGLE PROMERIT
(— EASILY) ROMP
(— EVERY MATCH) SWEEP
(— NARROWLY) SQUEEZE
(— OVER) DEFEAT DISARM NOBBLE
(— OVERWHELMINGLY) SWEEP
(— SKILLFULLY) SNARE
(WRESTLING —) PIN
WINCE KICK CHECK QUECH CRINGE FLINCH QUATCH QUINCH QUITCH RECOIL SHRINK
WINCH CRAB JACK REEL WINK GIPSY WINZE ROLLER WHIMSY WINDLE CATHEAD TRAVELER VARIABLE WINDLASS
WIND AIR COP LAP BALL BIRR BISE BIZE COIL CONE CURL EAST FIST FLAW FOHN GALE GUST KINK PUFF PUNO ROLL WEST WRAP BATCH BLAST BLORE CRANK CREEK CROOK FOEHN QUILL SPOOL STORM TRADE TREND TWINE TWIST WEAVE WITHE BOTTOM BOUGHT BREEZE BUSTER CAURUS COLLAR KECKLE SHAMAL SPIRAL SPIRIT SQUALL WAMPLE WESTER ZEPHYR BREATHE CRANKLE CRINKLE CYCLONE ENTWINE EQUINOX ETESIAN GREGALE INVOLVE MEANDER MISTRAL SERPENT SINUATE TEMPEST TWINGLE TWISTER WEATHER WHIRLER WINDILL ARGESTES DOWNWARD EASTERLY FAVONIUS
(— ABEAM) LASK
(— ABOUT) WIRE SNAKE
(— AFTER DYEING) BATCH
(— DOWN) RELAX UNWIND
(— FROM THE ANDES) ZONDA PAMPERO
(— IN AND OUT) INDENT WINGLE
(— MAGNETS) COMPOUND
(— OF ARGENTINA) ZONDA PAMPERO
(— OF CUBA) BAYAMO
(— OF HAWAII) KONA
(— OF OREGON AND WASHINGTON) CHINOOK
(— OF TUNISIA) CHILE CHILI CHILLI
(— ROPE) WORM WOOLD
(—S OF CHILE AND PERU) SURES
(— THREAD OR YARN) QUILL CHEESE
(— TO PREVENT CHAFING) KECKLE
(— WOOL) TREND
(— YARN) BEAM SERVE WINDLE
(ADRIATIC —) BORA
(BREAKING —) FIST
(BROKEN —) HEAVES
(COLD —) BISE BIZE BORA SARSAR BLIZZARD
(COOLING —) IMBAT
(DEAD —) NOSER
(DESERT —) SAMUM GIBLEH SAMIEL SIMOOM SIMOON KHAMSIN SIROCCO SCIROCCO
(DRYING —) TRADE
(EASTERLY —) LEVANT LEVANTER
(FIERCE —) BUSTER
(GUST OF —) FLAN FLAW
(HAWAIIAN WINTER —) KONA
(HEAD —) NOSER MUZZLE
(HIGH —) RIG
(HOT —) CHILI GIBLEH SAMIEL SOLANO CHAMSIN KHAMSIN SIROCCO SCIROCCO
(LIGHT GENTLE —) BREEZE
(MOUNTAIN —) PUNA
(NORTH —) BISE AQUILO BOREAS AQUILON MISTRAL
(NORTHEAST —) BURAN GREGALE
(NORTHWEST —) CAURUS MAESTRO ARGESTES
(OF —) EOLIAN VENTAL AEOLIAN
(PERIODICAL —) ETESIAN MONSOON
(PERSIAN GULF —) SHAMAL SHARKI SHIMAL
(PERUVIAN —) PUNA PUNO
(ROARING —) BLORE
(SEVERE —) SNIFTER
(SOUTH —) NOTUS AUSTER
(SOUTHEAST —) EURUS SOLANO
(SOUTHEASTERLY —) SHARKI SHURGEE
(SOUTHWEST —) CHINOOK LIBECCIO
(STRONG —) BIRR
(VIOLENT —) BUSTER SQUALL SNORTER
(WARM —) FOHN FOEHN CHINOOK SANTANA
(WEST —) ZEPHYR FAVONIUS ZEPHYRUS
(WHISTLING —) SARSAR
(PREF.) ANEM(O) AURO VENTI VENTO
(SOUTH —) AUSTRO
WINDAGE DRIFT
WIND-BORNE EOLIC EOLIAN AEOLIAN
WINDER REEL WINCH DRUMMER PLUGGER SKEINER SPOOLER TENDRIL
WINDFALL VAIL GRAVY MANNA CADUAC FALLING BLOWDOWN BUCKSHEE
WINDGALL PUFF WINDDOG
WINDING LINK MAZY CRANK LACET SPIRE CREEKY DETOUR GYRATE SCREWY SPIRAL TWISTY WANLAS CRANKLE CRINKLE DEVIOUS MEANDER SINUATE SINUOSE SINUOUS SNAKING WRIGGLY WRINKLE SINUATED TORTUOUS MEANDERING
(PL.) AMBAGES RADDLINGS
WINDING-SHEET SHROUD SUDARY CEREMENT
WINDING STAIR COCKLE COCLEA WINDER COCHLEA
WIND INSTRUMENT
(PREF.) AEOLO
WINDLASS CRAB REEL WINK FEARN WINCH STOWCE STOWSE TACKLE TURNEL WINDAS WINDLE TWISTER WILDCAT ARTIFICE DRAWBEAM MANEUVER
WINDMILL JUMBO MOTOR COPTER PINWHEEL
(— ARM) VANE
(— BAR) UPLONG
(— SAIL) AWE EIE EIGHE FLIER FLYER SWEEP SWIFT
(PART OF —) BAR CAP FAN AXLE CORD HEEL LINE SAIL WHIP BLADE ROTOR STOCK SWEEP TOWER FANTAIL HELMATH CANNISTER WINDSHAFT
WINDOW BAY EYE LOOP ROSE SASH SLIT SLOT CHAFF GLAZE GRILL INLET LIGHT OGIVE SIGHT THURL AWNING DORMER GRILLE LANCET PEEPER ROSACE SPLITE THURLE WICKET BALCONE COUPLET DORMANT FENSTER GUICHET LUTHERN MIRADOR ORIFICE TRANSOM VENTANA WINDOCK WINNOCK CASEMENT FANLIGHT FENESTER FENESTRA JALOUSIE VENETIAN
(— IN ROOF) SKYLIGHT
(— OF TWO LIGHTS) COUPLET
(BAY —) ORIEL MIRADOR
(BLANK —) ORB
(BLIND —) ORB
(CHURCH —) LYCHNOSCOPE
(CRESCENT-SHAPED —) LUNETTE
(DORMER —) OXEYE DORMANT LUCARNE LUTHERN
(HIGH NARROW —) LANCET
(OVAL —) OXEYE
(PART OF —) BEAD JAMB LOCK PANE RAIL SASH STOP YOKE APRON FRAME SKIRT STILE STOOL STRIP CASING MUNTIN BRICKMOLD WINDOWPANE COUNTERWEIGHT
(POINTED —) OGIVE
(ROUND —) OXEYE OCULUS ROUNDEL
(SEMICIRCULAR —) FANLIGHT
(SMALL LOW —) MEZZANINE
(TICKET —) GRILLE GUICHET
(TWIN —) AJIMEZ
(PL.) STORMS
WINDOW DRESSING TRIM FRONT FACADE
WINDOW FRAME SASH REVEAL
WINDOW OYSTER COPIS
WINDOWPANE LIGHT LOZEN QUIRK LOZENGE TATTERSALL
WINDOWSILL SOLE
WINDPIPE HALS ARBER ARBOR ERBER HALSE WIZEN ARTERY GUGGLE STROUP WEEZLE KEACORN TRACHEA WEASAND THRAPPLE THROPPLE THROTTLE
(PREF.) BRONCH(I)(IO)(O) TRACHE(O) TRACHO TRACHY
WINDROW BANK HEAP RIDGE SWATH SWATHE
WINDSOR CHAIR FANBACK
WINDSTORM BLOW BURA THUD BURAN BOURRAN
(HAWAIIAN —) KONA
WINDWARD ALOOF WEATHER AWEATHER
(— SIDE) KOOLAU
WINDY BLOWY EMPTY GASSY GUSTY HUFFY PROUD STARK SWALE FLIMSY STORMY WONDIE BREATHY FEARFUL GUSTFUL NERVOUS VENTOSE VIOLENT BOISTEROUS
(— CITY) CHICAGO
WINE CUP VIN BOIS BUAL CUIT CUTE DEAL PALM PORT RAPE ROSE ROSY TENT TYRE VINO CAPRI GRAPE KRAMA LUNEL MEDOC PETER PLONK PORTO RIOJA SCIAN SHRAB SOAVE TINTO TOKAY VINUM WHITE BAROLO BARSAC CORTON COUTET GRAVES KIJAFA LISBON MASDEU PIMENT ROCHET SAUMUR SHIRAZ SOLERA TIVOLI ALICANT AMBONNA BACCHUS BANYULS BARBERA BASTARD CATAWBA CHACOLI CHATEAU DEZALEY FALERNO MARSALA MISSION MOSELLE ORVIETO PALERMO PIGMENT RHENISH ROSOLIO SERCIAL SILLERY VERNAGE VIDONIA VINTAGE APERITIF BORDEAUX BURGUNDY CHARNECO DELAWARE LACHRYMA LIBATION MALVASIA MARSALLA MOUNTAIN RIESLING ROCHELLE RULANDER RUMBOOZE SPARKLER BARDOLINO LAMBRUSCO ZINFANDEL
(— AND PUNCH) GLOGG
(— BOILED WITH HONEY) MULSE
(— CHEST) TANTALUS
(— FROM VINEGAR) ESILL
(— MIXED WITH WATER) KRASIS
(— OF EXCELLENT QUALITY) VINTAGE
(— OF SACRAMENT) BLOOD
(— SELLER) ABKAR BISTRO WINARE
(— SERVING) VOIDEE
(AROMATIZED —) DUBONNET
(BANANA —) MARAMBA
(BULK —) CUVEE
(CONSECRATED —) CUP
(DRY WHITE —) SANCERRE
(FIRST-GROWTH —) LAFITE LAFITTE
(FRANCONIAN —) STEIN LEISTEN
(GREEK —) RUMNEY RETSINA RESINATA
(HEATED —) WHITEPOT
(INFERIOR —) PLONK
(JAPANESE —) SAKI
(KIND OF —) JUG POP BLUSH
(LIGHT —) BUAL CAPRI BAROLO CANARY
(MULLED —) NEGUS WASSAIL GLUHWEIN
(NEW —) MUST
(NEW — BOILED DOWN) CUIT CUTE
(PALM —) SAGWIRE
(RED —) ZIN GAMAY MACON TINTA BAROLO BEAUNE CLARET MERLOT

CHIANTI HOLLOCK POMMARD ALICANTE BURGUNDY CABERNET FLORENCE BARDOLINO ZINFANDEL
(REVIVED —) STUM
(RHINE —) HOCK SYLVANER
(SPANISH —) SACK TENT DULCE RIOJA OPORTO SHERRY ALICANT ALIKANT BASTARD TARRAGONA
(STILL —) PONTAC PONTACQ
(SWEET —) TYRE DULCE MULSE CANARY BASTARD MALMSEY CHARNECO MUSCATEL
(TENT —) TINTO
(TOKAY —) ESSENCE
(TUSCAN —) VERDEA CHIANTI FLORENCE
(WHITE —) HOCK SACK CAPRI CASEL FORST BARSAC MALAGA BROMIAN CATAWBA CHABLIS CONTHEY LANGOON ANGELICA BUCELLAS MUSCADET RIESLING SANCERRE SAUTERNE VERMOUTH MEURSAULT VERDICCHIO
(WHITE — APERITIF) KIR
(PL.) PALUS
(PREF.) ENO OEN(O) OINO VINI VINO

WINEBERRY MAKO MAKOMAKO
WINEGLASS FLUTE
WINEGROWER WINER VIGNERON
WINESBURG OHIO (AUTHOR OF —) ANDERSON
(CHARACTER IN —) JOHN KATE WING DAVID HARDY HELEN JESSE REEFY SWIFT WHITE CURTIS GEORGE LOUISE BENTLEY HARTMAN WILLARD TRUNNION ELIZABETH BIDDLEBAUM
WINESHOP BISTRO BODEGA
WINE-VAULT SHADE
WING ALA ARM ELL FAN FLY OAR RIB VAN AILE FORE JAMB SAIL TAIL ALULA ANNEX BLOCK FLANK JAMBE PINNA POINT SHEAR VOLET BRANCH FLETCH FLIGHT HALTER PENNON PINION POISER DEMIVOL ELYTRON ELYTRUM AEROFOIL BALANCER DISPATCH TORMENTOR
(— OF ARMY) HORN
(— OF BUILDING) ELL JAMB JAMBE ALETTE ALLETTE FLANKER
(— OF SHELL) AURICLE
(— OF THEATER) COULISSE TORMENTOR
(— OF TRIPTYCH) VOLET
(—S DISPLAYED) VOL
(BASTARD —) ALULA
(BIRD'S —) FLAG
(FLY'S —S) HALTERES
(KIND OF —) DELTA SINGLE
(PL.) PENS FEATHERS
(PREF.) ALI PTER(O) PTERIDO PTERYG(O) PTERYLO PTIL(O)
(SUFF.) PTERA PTERIS PTEROUS PTERUS PTERYX
WING CASE SHEATH ELYTRON
(BEETLE'S —) SHARD
WINGDING GALA
WINGED AILE ALATE LOFTY RAPID SWIFT ALATED PENNED PENNATE ELEVATED
(PREF.) PTENO
(SUFF.) PTENE
WINGED DISK FEROHER
WINGED ELM WAHOO
WING-FOOTED FLEET SWIFT ALIPED
WINGLESS APTERAL
WING-LIKE ALARY ALIFORM PTEROID PTERTGOID
WING SHELL STROMB ELYTRON STROMBUS
WINGS OF THE DOVE (AUTHOR OF —) JAMES
(CHARACTER IN —) CROY KATE MARK MILLY MERTON THEALE DENSHER
WINGTIP SHOE
WINK BAT NAP PINK BLINK DEATH FLASH PRINK SLEEP TWINK CONNIVE FLICKER INSTANT NICTATE SPARKLE TWINKLE NICTITATE
WINKER EYE BLINKER EYELASH
WINKING BLINK
WINKLE PERIWIG TWINKLE
WINNER PLACER VICTOR FACEMAN BANGSTER
(EASY —) SHOOIN
(NOT A —) ALSORAN
(SURE —) SNIP
WINNIE-THE-POOH (AUTHOR OF —) MILNE
(CHARACTER IN —) ROO KANGA ROBIN EEYORE PIGLET RABBIT HEFFALUMP CHRISTOPHER
WINNING GAIN SWEET PROFIT GAINING VICTORY WINSOME CHARMING
(— OF ALL TRICKS) CAPOT SCHWARZ
(PL.) WIN VELVET
WINNOW FAN WIM CHAR SIFT WIND DIGHT SIEVE DELETE REMOVE SELECT WINDER SEPARATE
WINNOWER VAN WINDER DIGHTER
WINSOME GAY BUXOM SWEET CHARMING CHEERFUL PLEASANT
WINTER BISE SNOW YEAR HIEMS HIVER DECEMBER HIBERNATE
(— AILMENT) STREP
(— OVER) HOG
WINTERBERRY PRINOS HOOPWOOD
WINTERBLOOM AZALEA
WINTERGREEN JINKS CHINKS PYROLA DRUNKER BOXBERRY DRUNKARD EYEBERRY GAYWINGS IVYBERRY LIMONIUM RATSBANE SHINLEAF TEABERRY PINEDROPS PIPSISSEWA
WINTERLIKE BRUMAL
WINTERSET (AUTHOR OF —) ANDERSON
(CHARACTER IN —) MIO CARR GARTH GAUNT TROCK ESDRAS SHADOW ROMAGNA MIRIAMNE BARTOLOMEO
WINTER'S TALE (AUTHOR OF —) SHAKESPEARE
(CHARACTER IN —) DION MOPSA DORCAS EMILIA CAMILLO LEONTES PAULINA PERDITA FLORIZEL HERMIONE ANTIGONUS AUTOLYCUS CLEOMENES MAMILLIUS POLIXENES ARCHIDAMUS
WINTRY AGED COLD WHITE BOREAL HIEMAL STORMY BRUMOUS CHILLING HIBERNAL
WINTUN COPEHAN
WINY VINOUS DRUNKEN
WINZE CURSE RAISE OPENING PASSAGEWAY
WIPE BEAT BLOW DRUB DUST GIBE DICHT DIGHT SWIPE CANCEL SPONGE SPUNGE STRIKE ABOLISH CLEANSE ABSTERGE SQUEEGEE
(— BEAK OF HAWK) FEAK
(— NOSE) SNITE
(— OFF) SCUFF
(— OUT) ERASE SCRUB SWEEP EFFACE DESTROY
(— UP) SWAB SWOB
WIPEOUT MASSACRE
WIPER DUSTER TRIPPET
WIPING TERSION
(— OF INK ON PLATE) RETROUSSAGE
(— OUT) EXTINCTION
WIRE GUY TAP BINE CORE DENT DRAG FILE FUSE PURL BRACE CABLE OUTER RISER SNAKE SWEEP TAPER BRIDGE FESCUE FINGER HEATER JUMPER NEEDLE STAPLE STOLON STRAND DROPPER HAYWIRE LAMETTA LASHING PRICKER SHIFTER SNUFFER FILAMENT LIGATURE PALISADE PULLDOWN STRINGER TELEGRAM
(— BETWEEN TWO VESSELS) SWEEP
(— FASTENED TO TEETH) BRACES
(— FOR CUTTING CLAY) SLING
(— FOR SUSTAINING HAIR) PALISADE
(— HOLDING SPOOL) SPIT
(— IN BLASTING CAP) BRIDGE
(— IN CATHETER) STYLET
(— IN WEAVING LOOM) DENT
(— OF GOLD,SILVER OR BRASS) LAMETTA
(—S BOUND TOGETHER) SELVAGE
(— TO ADJUST WICK) SNUFFER
(— TO CLOSE A BREAK) JUMPER
(— TO REMOVE TUMORS) LIGATURE
(— USED AS POINTER) FESCUE
(— USED IN SPLICING CABLES) TAPER
(ENAMELED —) LITZ
(FENCE —) DROPPER
(FRAYED —) JAGGER
(GOLD —) KINSEN
(LOOPED —) OESE
(PALLET —) PULLDOWN
(PRIMING —) PICKER EPINGLETTE
(SURGICAL —) STYLET
(TWISTED —) HEALD HEADLE HEDDLE
(VENT —) PRICKER
(4 —S TWISTED TOGETHER) QUAD
WIRE CUTTER SECATEUR
WIREDRAW WREST OUTWIT DEFRAUD DISTORT ELONGATE
WIREGLASS FLUTE
WIRE GRASS POA
WIRELESS RADIO
WIRE ROPE JACKSTAY
WIRETAP BUG
(REMOVE —) DEBUG
(REMOVE — DEVICE) DEBUG
WIREWORM ELATER ELATERID MILLIPEDE
WIRY THIN HARDY STIFF WITHY FEEBLE KNOTTY SINEWY STRINGY THREADY
WIS KNOW THINK SURELY SUPPOSE

WISCONSIN
CAPITAL: MADISON
COLLEGE: RIPON BELOIT ALVERNO CARROLL VITERBO CARTHAGE
COUNTY: DOOR VILAS JUNEAU CALUMET SHAWANO WAUSHARA
INDIAN: FOX SAUK KICKAPOO WINNEBAGO
LAKE: POYGAN MENDOTA WISSOTA WINNEBAGO
MOUNTAIN: TIMSHILL SUGARBUSH
NATIVE: BADGER
NICKNAME: BADGER
RIVER: FOX BLACK STCROIX CHIPPEWA MENOMINEE
STATE BIRD: ROBIN
STATE FLOWER: VIOLET
STATE TREE: MAPLE
TOWN: ANTIGO BELOIT RACINE WAUSAU ASHLAND BARABOO KENOSHA MADISON OSHKOSH PORTAGE SHAWANO LACROSSE SUPERIOR WAUKESHA

WISDOM WIT LORE SABE SABBY SAVEY SENSE SOPHY ADVICE GNOSIS HOKMAH POLICY SATTVA SOPHIA WISURE CUNNING MINERVA SAGESSE SLEIGHT AFTERWIT JUDGMENT PRUDENCE SAPIENCE
(DIVINE —) WORD THEOMAGY
(ESOTERIC —) GNOSIS
(SUPREME —) PRAJNA
(UNIVERSAL —) PANSOPHY
(PREF.) SOPH(O) SOPHI(O)
(SUFF.) SOPH(ER)(IC)(IST)(Y)
WISE HEP SLY DEEP GASH GOOD KIND SAGE SANE SEND TURN CANNY FRESH GUIDE SMART SOUND WITTY ADVISE CRAFTY DIRECT QUAINT WITFUL WITTER ANCIENT ERUDITE GNOSTIC KNOWING LEARNED POLITIC PRUDENT SAPIENT THRIVEN PERSUADE PROFOUND SENSIBLE SPACIOUS
(— GUY) SAGE SOLON
(— MAN) MAGI SAGE MAGUS AMAUTA ORACLE
(— ONE) OWL
(PREF.) SOPH(O) SOPHI(O)
(SUFF.) SOPH(ER)(IC)(IST)(Y)
WISEACRE SAGE DUNCE GOTHAM SOLONIST WISEHEAD WISELING
WISECRACK JOKE QUIP
WISE CRACK GASSER
WISENT BISON AUROCH UROCHS BONASUS
WISH CARE GIVE GOAL HOPE LIST LUST MIND VOTE WANT WILL

BOSOM COVET CRAVE DREAM HEART TASTE VOICE DESIRE UTINAM FAREWELL GODSPEED PLEASURE
(— OTHERWISE) REGRET
(DEATH —) DESTRUDO
(EARNEST —) VOW
(SLIGHT —) VELLEITY
WISHBONE FURCULA FOURCHET FURCULUM MERRYTHOUGHT
WISHFUL EAGER HOPEFUL LONGING ALLURING
WISHING ANXIOUS DESIROUS
WISHY-WASHY PALE THIN WEAK BLAND VAPID FEEBLE DILUTED INSIPID SLIPSLOP
WISKET BASKET WHISKET
WISP TATE WUSP SCRAP SHRED SKIFF SKIFT TWIST RUMPLE CRUMPLE MASSAGE
(— OF HAY) RISP
(— OF STRAW) WAP WASE DOSSIL
(— OF THATCH) TIPPET
WISPY FRAIL NEBULOUS
WISTERIA FUJI KRAUNHIA
WISTFUL INTENT PENSIVE WISHFUL MOURNFUL YEARNING
WISTITI WISTIT MARMOSET
WIT VAT VYT WAG KNOW NOUS SALT BRAIN HUMOR IRONY SENSE THINK WHITE WOTTE ACUMEN ESPRIT POLICY SANITY SATIRE WISDOM CONCEIT CUNNING PICADOR SARCASM SUPPOSE THINKER WITWORM BADINAGE REPARTEE
(BITING —) DICACITY
(TO —) NAMELY SCILICET
(PL.) SCONCE BUTTONS
WITCH ALP ANI HAG HEG HEX MARE SAGA TRAT WYCH BRUJA BUTCH GREBE HEXER LAMIA SIBYL WEIRD WIGHT ASUANG CARLEY CARLIN CUMMER DOWSER DUESSA HECATE KIMMER PILWIZ WIZARD AGANICE CANIDIA CARLINE HAGGARD HELLCAT SYCORAX BABAJAGA CAROLINE ERICHTHO SORCERER SPAEWIFE VERSIERA WALKYRIE
(HOME OF —) ENDOR
(MEETING OF —S) ESBAT
(PL.) COVEN
WITCHCRAFT CHARM GOETY OBEAH WICCA CUNNING HEXEREI MYALISM SORCERY BRUJERIA DEVILTRY PISHOGUE WIZARDRY
WITCH DOCTOR BOCOR BOKOR GOOFER GUFFER
WITCHERY CHARM SPELL SORCERY SORTIARY
WITCHES'-BROOM STAGHEAD
WITCHGRASS COUCH PANIC PANICLE
WITCH HAZEL FOTHERGILLA
WITE WAT BLAME FAULT WAYTE CENSURE REPROACH HAMESOKEN
WITH BY CUM MID MIT WUD AVEC CHEZ DOWN AMONG ANENT WIGHT AGAINST
(— HAND ON HIP) AKIMBO
(— REGARD TO) ABOUT
(— SPEED) TIVY
(PREF.) CO COL COM CON COR META SYM SYN
WITHDRAW GO COY DROP TAKE AVOID DEMIT FREAK LOOSE REVEL SHIFT START UNSAY CHANGE DECEDE DESERT DETACH DETRAY DEVOID EFFACE FLINCH MINISH RECALL RECANT RECEDE RETIRE REVOKE ROGATE SECEDE SHRINK SINGLE SYPHON ABSCOND CONCEAL DESCEND DETRACT FORSAKE INVEIGH RETRACT RETREAT SCRATCH SCUTTLE SECLUDE SUBDUCE SUBDUCT TURNOFF UNSCREW SEPARATE SUBTRACT SEGREGATE SEQUESTER
(— ATTENTION) PRESCIND
(— FROM) VAIK ABANDON
(— FROM COMPETITION) SCRATCH
(— FROM POKER POT) DROP
(— FROM REALITY) FREAK
(— FROM USE) MOTHBALL
(— SUPPORT) ABANDON
(— TEMPORARILY) STOPOUT
(— WITHIN) INVAGINATE
WITHDRAWAL DRAIN FLIGHT HIDING OFFLAP RETIRE SHRINK ABSENCE DUNKIRK PULLOUT REGRESS RETIRAL RETREAT SCUTTLE RECESSION REVULSION RETRACTION
(— FROM WORLDLY THINGS) ABSTRACTION
(— OF BUILDING FACE) SETBACK
(— OF PROMISE) BACKWORD
(— OF SUIT) RETRAXIT
WITHDRAWN SHY ASOCIAL INGROWN SECLUSE DISTRAIT ISOLATED SECLUDED RECESSIVE ABSTRACTED
WITHE HANK ROPE TIER TWIG WITHY WATTLE WICKER CRINGLE
WITHER BURN DAZE FADE MIFF PINE RUST SEAR STUN WARP WELK WELT BLAST CLING DAVER DECAY QUAIL WIZEN COTTER GIZZEN SHRINK WALLOW WELTER WILTER WINDER AREFACT DECLINE FORWELK SENESCE SHRIVEL LANGUISH PARALYZE
WITHERED DRY ARID SEAR SERE CORKY SCRAM MARCID BLASTED UNGREEN WEARISH WIZENED AUTUMNAL
WITHERING SCATHING
WITHHELD DEFERRED SUSPENSE
WITHHOLD CURB DENY HIDE KEEP STOP CHECK SCANT ABSENT DEPORT DETAIN REFUSE RETAIN ABSTAIN BOYCOTT DEFORCE FORBEAR OUTHOLD REPRESS RESERVE SUSPEND RESTRAIN SUBTRACT
(— CONSENT) DECLINE
WITHHOLDING DETAINER
(— OF DUES) CHECKOFF
(CONDITIONAL —) SUSPENSION
WITHIN IN ON BEN BIN INBY INLY INTRA ABOARD HEREIN INSIDE INWITH INDOORS ENCLOSED INCLUDED INWARDLY
(PREF.) END(O) ENT(O) ESO IL IM IN INFRA INTER INTRA INTRO
(ARISING —) IDIO
WITHOUT EX BUT OUT SEN BOUT FREE OHNE SANS SINE MINUS SENZA FAILING OUTSIDE WANTING INNOCENT OUTDOORS
(— ACCENT) ENCLITIC
(— ACTION) DEEDLESS
(— A FLANGE) BALD
(— A MATE) ODD
(— BEGINNING OR END) ETERNAL
(— BLEMISH) CHOICE
(— BRIGHTNESS) LACKLUSTER
(— CONTENTS) INANE
(— DELAY) AWAY FOOTHOT SUMMARY
(— DELIBERATION) HEADLONG
(— EFFECT) EMPTY INSIGNIFICANT
(— EMOTION) DRYLY DULLY
(— END) ENTERNAL
(— EXCEPTION) ALWAYS
(— FEET) APOD
(— FUNDS) CLEAN
(— HORNS) ACEROUS
(— INTEREST) BARREN
(— LIFE) DULL AZOIC INANIMATE
(— LIGHT) APHOTIC
(— LIMITS OF DURATION) AGELESS
(— MONEY) IMPECUNIOUS
(— ORDER) ANYHOW
(— PAYMENT) FREE
(— POWER) ADRIFT
(— PROFIT) FRUITLESS
(— QUALIFICATION) FLAT
(— QUESTION) EASILY SECURELY
(— REALITY) AIRY
(— REASON) BLINDLY
(— REMEDY) BOOTLESS
(— ROADS) INVIOUS
(— RULE OR LAW) ANARCHIC
(— SADDLES) ASELLATE
(— SALT) FRESH
(— SHAME) BROWLESS
(— SIN) IMPECCANT
(— STRENGTH) MEAGER MEAGRE
(— TEETH, TONGUE OR CLAWS) MORNE
(— THORNS) INERM
(— WINGS) APTEROUS
(PREF.) A ECT(O) LIPO
(— GOVERNMENT) ANARCH(O)
(SUFF.) LESS
WITHSTAND BIDE DEFY TAKE ABIDE OPPOSE OPPUGN RESIST CONTAIN CONTEST FORBEAR SUSTAIN CONFRONT WITHSTAY
WITHY WIRY AGILE OSIER WOODY WILLOW WOODIE WINDING
WITLESS MAD GROSS INANE SILLY INSANE STUPID FATUOUS FOOLISH UNWITTY HEEDLESS SLAPHAPPY
WITLOOF ENDIVE CHICORY
WITNESS SEE TAKE TEST PROOF ATTEST BEHOLD MARTYR RECORD TESTIS TESTOR CURATOR TESTATE TESTIFY EVIDENCE RECORDER SUFFRAGE
(FALSE —) JUROR
(PL.) SECTA
(PREF.) TESTI
WITNESS-BOX STAND
WITOTO HUITOTE
WITTICISM WIT JEER JEST JOKE QUIP SALLY SLENT WHEEZE
WITTING NEWS TIDINGS
WITTINGLY SCIENTER
WITTOL FOOL CUCKOLD WITTALL
WITTY GASH WILY WISE DROLL LEPID PAWKY SHARP SMART CLEVER FACETE JOCOSE JOCULAR KNOWING CONCEITY HUMOROUS
(NOT —) INFICETE
WIVERN DRAGON WYVERN
WIZARD MAGE SEER SHIZ FIEND WITCH DOCTOR EXPERT PELLAR WARLOW CHARMED MAGICAL SPAEMAN WARLOCK WISEMAN CONJUROR MAGICIAN SORCERER TROLLMAN WITCHMAN ARCHIMAGE
(PL.) GOETAE
WIZARDRY SORCERY
WIZEN DRY WITHER SHRIVEL
WIZENED SERE GIZZEN WEAZEN
WOAD DYE NIL ODE ANIL KERS NILL OADE CRESS ANILLA INDICO INDIGO PASTEL
(PREF.) ISAT(O)
WOADWAXEN ALLELUIA ALLELUJA
WOBBLE COCKLE COGGLE HOBBLE QUAVER SHIMMY TEETER TITTER TOTTER WABBLE WIGGLE TREMBLE NUTATION
(KIND OF —) CHANDLER
WOBBLY LOOSE SHAKY COGGLY DRUNKEN DOUBTFUL
WODEN ODIN ALLFATHER
WOE WA WEI BALE BANE DULE PAIN PINE WAWE GRIEF MISERY SORROW TROUBLE WILLAWA CALAMITY DISTRESS WELLADAY WELLAWAY
WOEBEGONE WAFF UNHAPPY DEJECTED DESOLATE DOWNCAST
WOEFUL MEAN DISMAL PALTRY RUEFUL DIREFUL DOLEFUL RUTHFUL DOLOROUS PITIABLE WRETCHED
WOLF GLUT LOBO CANID FREKI YABBI CHANCO COYOTE FAMINE FENRIR ISGRIN KABERU LOAFER MASHER SIGRIM THOOID POVERTY ISENGRIM
(FOX —) ZORRO
(KIND OF —) LONE
(PREF.) LUPI LYC(O) VULPI
WOLFBERRY BUCKBUSH
WOLFHOUND ALAN BORZOI PSOVIE
WOLFISH LUPINE RAVENOUS
WOLFLIKE THOOID
WOLFRAMITE CAL TUNGSTEN
WOLFSBANE ACONITE DOGBANE FOXBANE
WOLF SPIDER HUNT JAGER HUNTER JAEGER JAYHAWK LYCOSID TARANTULA
WOLVERINE PIG GLUT GORB MIKER GLOTUM HELLUO GLUTTON GUTLING LURCHER MOOCHER RAVENER SWILLER CARCAJOU DRAFFMAN GOURMAND GULLYGUT
(— STATE) MICHIGAN
WOMAN BIM BIT DAM EVE HEN HER

JUG MEG SHE TEG TIT BABE BABY BINT BOSS CONY DAME FAIR FEME FLAG FROW JADE JANE LADY MAMA MARY MORT PERI SLUT WIFE BIDDY BIMBO BLADE BROAD CHINA DONAH FEMME FRAIL JATNI LUBRA LUCKY MAMMA MUJER QUEAN SKIRT SMOCK SQUAW TAGGE TOOTS TWIST UMMAN VROUW BURDIE CALICO CARLIN CUMMER FEMALE GIMMER HEIFER KIMMER LUCKIE MANESS MULIER SISTER TOMATO VIRAGO WAHINE CARLING CHANGAR DISTAFF PARTLET PINNACE PLACKET QUAEDAM MISTRESS PETTICOAT
(— DESERTED BY HUSBAND) AGUNAH
(— OF CONSEQUENCE) HERSELF
(— OF LOW CASTE) DASI
(— OF MEXICAN DESCENT) CHICANA
(— OF RANK) DOMINA
(— OF UNSTEADY CHARACTER) FLAP CALLET
(— OF WEALTH) FORTUNE
(— WHO ACTS AS ADVISER) EGERIA
(— WITH ONE CHILD) UNIPARA
(— WITH 3 CHILDREN) TRIPARA
(ABORIGINAL —) GIN LUBRA
(ABUSIVE —) FISHWIFE
(ALLURING —) DISH
(ATHENIAN — OF HIGH RANK) GERARA GERAERA
(ATTRACTIVE —) FOX DOLLY SHEBA DOLLIE LOOKER CHARMER
(AUSTRALIAN —) BINT
(AWKWARD —) ROIL
(BEAUTIFUL —) HURI PERI BELLE HOURI SIREN SPARK CHERUB EYEFUL MUSIDORA
(BIG COURAGEOUS —) VIRAGO
(BLESSED —) BEATA
(BOISTEROUS —) HOYDEN
(BOLD —) RAMP
(CLEANING —) CHAR
(COARSE —) BEAST RUDAS BLOWZE RULLION
(COOLIE —) CHANGAR
(COY —) HAGGARD
(CREMATED —) SATI SUTTEE
(DEAR —) PEAT
(DIRTY —) SLUT SLATTERN
(DISSOLUTE —) SLAG
(DUTCH OR GERMAN —) FRAU FROW FROKIN FRAULEIN
(ENGAGED —) BONDAGER
(ENTICING —) SIREN
(EVIL OLD —) HAG HELLHAG
(EXCITED —) MAENAD
(FASCINATING —) SIREN
(FASHIONABLE —) MILADY GALLANT ELEGANTE
(FAT —) BOSS FUSTILUGS
(FINE —) SCREAMER
(FIRST —) EMBLA PANDORA
(FLIGHTY —) GILLET JILLET FLIPFLOP
(FLIRTING —) CHIPPY FIZGIG
(FOOLISH —) TAWPIE
(FORWARD —) STRAP
(FOUL-MOUTHED —) RUDAS
(FRENCH HOLY —) STE SAINTE
(FRENZIED —) MAENAD
(GAUDY —) JAY
(GENTLE —) DOVE
(GOSSIPY —) HAIK HAKE BIDDY TABBY
(GOSSIPY, TALKATIVE —) YENTA
(GROSS —) SOW
(GYPSY —) ROMI ROMNI GITANA
(ILL-TEMPERED —) VIXEN CATAMARAN
(IMMODEST —) TOMBOY
(IMMORAL —) RIG GITCH FLAPPER HARLOTRY
(IMPUDENT —) YANKIE
(INDIAN —) SQUAW WENCH KLOOCH BUCKEEN
(INSPIRED —) PHOEBAD
(ITALIAN —) DONNA
(LASCIVIOUS —) GIGLET
(LEARNED —) PUNDITA CLERGESS
(LEWD —) REP SLUT BITCH HUSSY HUZZY MALKIN BROTHEL CYPRIAN
(LOOSE —) BAG BIM KIT MOB TIB DRAB FLAP BIMBO TROLL GILLOT HARLOT LIMMER BAGGAGE COCOTTE FRANION TROLLOP
(LOUD-SPOKEN —) RANDY
(LOW OR WORTHLESS —) JADE JURR BUNTER SLINGDUST
(MARRIED — OF LOWLY STATION) GOODY
(MASCULINE —) AMAZON RULLION COTQUEAN
(MEEK —) GRIZEL
(MUSLIM —) BEGUM
(MYTHOLOGICAL —) HEROINE
(NON-JEWISH —) SHIKSA
(ODD-LOOKING —) JUDY
(OLD —) GIB HEN BABA TROT CRONE FAGOT FRUMP LUCKY TROUT BELDAM CARLIN GAMMER GEEZER GRANNY LUCKIE CARLINE GRANDAM HARRIDAN CAILLEACH
(OLD SHRIVELED —) FAGOT FAGGOT
(OVERGROWN —) FUSTILUGS
(PAINTED —) PICT
(PEDANTIC —) BLUE
(PERT —) CHIT
(PERVERSE —) JADE
(PORTUGUESE —) SENHORA
(PREGNANT —) GRAVIDA
(PRIGGISH —) PRUDE
(RAPACIOUS —) HARPY
(RAW-BONED —) RANDLETREE
(RICH OLD —) DOWAGER
(RUDE —) SCOLD
(RUSTIC —) JOAN
(SCOLDING —) RANDY SHREW COTQUEAN RIXATRIX
(SHAMELESS —) JEZEBEL
(SHORT OR STUMPY —) CUTTY
(SHOWY —) ANONYMA
(SHREWISH —) JADE HARPY SKELLAT
(SLATTERNLY —) DRAB FLEABAG SLAMKIN
(SLENDER GRACEFUL —) SYLPH
(SLIPSHOD —) MAUX CLATCH TROLLIMOG
(SLOVENLY —) BAG DAW SOW SLUT BESOM TAWPY TROLL TROLLOP SLATTERN
(SPANISH —) DONA GITANA
(SPANISH-INDIAN —) CHOLA
(SPITEFUL —) CAT FURY BITCH
(SQUAT —) TRUB
(SQUEAMISH —) COCKNEY
(STAID —) MATRON
(STATELY —) JUNO
(STORMY VIOLENT —) FURY
(TRACTABLE —) SHEEP
(UGLY —) HAG GORGON
(UNATTRACTIVE —) SCRUBBER
(UNCHASTE —) JILT
(UNMARRIED —) DAME GIRL SPINSTER MADEMOISELLE
(VIOLENT —) FURY
(VIXENISH —) HARRIDAN
(WANTON —) MINX TRUB QUEAN PARNEL
(WICKED —) JEZEBEL
(WISE —) VOLVA ALRUNA ALRUNE
(WITHERED —) CRONE
(YOUNG —) BIT BIRD BURD CHIT DAME DELL DOLL GIRL LASS PUSS BEAST CHICK FILLY FLUFF TOAST DAMSEL HEIFER PIGEON SHEILA SUBDEB BAGGAGE CHICKEN DAMOZEL FLAPPER WINKLOT DAUGHTER GRISETTE
(PREF.) FEMINO GYN(AE)(AECO) (AEO)(ANDRO)(E)(EO)(O)
(SUFF.) GYN(E)(IST)(OUS)

WOMAN HATER MISOGYNIST
WOMANHOOD MULIEBRITY
WOMAN IN WHITE (AUTHOR OF —) COLLINS
(CHARACTER IN —) ANNE FOSCO GLYDE LAURA PESCA MARIAN WALTER FAIRLIE HALCOMBE PERCIVAL CATHERICK HARTRIGHT
WOMANISH FEMALE FEMININE LADYLIKE PETTICOAT
WOMANIZER ROUE
WOMANKIND WOMEN CALICO MUSLIN FEMINIE
WOMAN'S TONGUE LEBBEK
WOMB BELLY CRADLE UTERUS VENTER
(PREF.) COLP(O) HYSTER(O) METRO UTER(O) VULVI VULVO
(SUFF.) COLPOS METRA METRIUM
WOMBAT KOALA BADGER DIDELPH VOMBATID
WOMEN DISTAFF
(— OF EARLY CHURCH) SETTERS AGAPETAE
WON CITY LIVE ROOM ABIDE DWELL REGION
WONDER AWE MUSE SELI SIGN TROW UNCO UNKO VERY FARLY FERLY SELLE SELLY UNCOW ADMIRE MARVEL MIRATE MAGNALE MIRABLE MIRACLE PORTENT PRODIGY STRANGE UNCOUTH AMERVEIL SELCOUTH SURPRISE
(SMALL —) GEM
(PL.) MIRABILIA
(PREF.) TERAT(O) THAUMA(TO) THAUMO
WONDERFUL KEEN NEAT SELI FERLY GRAND GREAT SELLE SWELL WAKON GEASON MIGHTY AMAZING EPATANT GALLANT MIRABLE MIRIFIC STRANGE FRABJOUS GLORIOUS MIRABILE TERRIFIC WONDROUS
WONDERFULLY AMAZING
WONDER-WORKER THEURGIC THEURGIST
WONDER-WORKING MIRIFIC
WONG FIELD GROVE PLAIN MEADOW
WONKY AWRY SHAKY WRONG UNSTEADY
WONT APT USE FAIN USED VAIN HABIT USAGE CUSTOM INCLINED
WONTED TAME USUAL HAUNTED
WOO SUE LOVE SEEK SUIT WALE COURT SPARK SPOON ASSAIL SPLUNT SUITOR ADDRESS
WOOD (ALSO SEE TREE AND TIMBER) HAG KIP BOIS BOSK BOWL EKKI HOLT HYLE KIRI MASS MOCK PALO SHAW SUPA TREE WOLE ALDER CAHUY CHARK CROWD EDDER FLOUR GROVE HURST HYRST KOKRA RESAK SHOLA STICK STUFF WEALD ALMOND ANGILI AUSUBO BRAZIL EKHIMI FOREST ITAUBA JARANA LUMBER PALING SPINNY TIMBER APITONG AVODIRE BOSCAGE BOSKAGE COPPICE DADDOCK DUDGEON HAYBOTE SATINAY VENESIA BAGTIKAN CRANTARA FIREBOOT CALAMANDER
(— BURNT AS PERFUME) AGALLOCH
(— FOR CARPENTRY) STUFF
(— FOR OARS) ASH
(— FOR REPAIRING HEDGE) TINING HAYBOTE
(— OF SMALL EXTENT) GROVE
(— OF THE VERA) VENESIA
(— ON RAFTER) FUR
(— ROTATED ON STRING) ROMBOS RHOMBOS
(— USEFUL FOR TINDER) PUNK SPONK TOUCHWOOD
(— YIELDING PERFUME) LINALOA
(BABUL —) SUNT
(BLACK —) EBONY
(CONE-SHAPED PIECE OF —) ACORN
(DARK RED —) RATA
(DEAD —) RAMMEL
(DENSIFIED —) STAYPAK
(ELASTIC —) SYCAMORE
(FIR —) DEAL
(FLAT ROUND PIECE OF —) TRENCHER
(FLEXIBLE —) EDDER
(FOSSIL —) PINITE PEUCITES
(FRAGRANT —) CEDAR SANDALWOOD
(FUEL —) ESTOVERS
(HARD —) ASH DAO ELM SAL BAKU IPIL KARI LANA POON ANJAN EBONY GIDYA KARRI KOKRA MAPLE MAZER ZANTE BANUYO CAMARA FREIJO GIDGEE KEMPAS SABICU SAPELE WALNUT CURUPAY DATTOCK HICKORY GUAIACUM IRONBARK MAHOGANY
(HEAVY —) DAO EBON EBONY CHENGAL GUAYABI SUCUPIRA

(LIGHT —) POON BALSA HEMLOCK
(LIMBA —) KORINA
(LOGGED —) CHIP
(LOST —) CHIPPAGE
(LUSTROUS —) LEZA BOARWOOD
(MATCHBOX —) SKILLET
(MOTTLED —) AMBOINA CALAMBOUR
(NARROW BAR OF —) SLAT
(NUMBER 1 —) DRIVER
(NUMBER 2 —) BRASSIE
(NUMBER 3 —) SPOON
(NUMBER 4 —) CLEEK
(OILY —) BATETE
(OLIVE —) COLLIE
(PETRIFIED —) LITHOXYL ROCKWOOD
(PINE —) DEAL
(PINKISH —) BOSSE
(POINTED PIECE OF —) TRIPPET
(REDDISH —) KOA KARI KARRI ARANGA BANABA CHERRY DUNGON SATINE KAMBALA
(REDDISH-YELLOW —) GUYO
(ROTTEN —) DADDOCK
(SANDARAC —) ALERCE
(SMALL —) SHAW
(SOFT —) KIRI GABUN GABOON ELKWOOD AGALLOCH ALBURNUM GUATAMBU
(SPONGY —) PUNK
(SQUARE LOG OF —) NOG
(STICK OF —) BILLET
(STRIP OF —) LATH STAVE BATTEN REEPER REGLET SPLINE SPLINT SPLINTER
(WATER-RESISTING —) AMUGIS
(YELLOWISH —) HALDU FUSTIC IDIGBO KADAMBA KAMASSI GUATAMBU
(PREF.) HYL(O) LIGN(I)(O) XYL(O)
(SUFF.) XYLON XYLUM

WOOD ALCOHOL METHANOL
WOOD ANEMONE CYME EMONY BOWBELLA SNOWDROP
WOODBARK SABLE BLONDINE
WOODBINE BIND WIDBIN EGLATERE
WOODCARVER BODGER
WOODCHUCK CHUG CHUCK MONAX MARMOT SUSLIK WEJACK MOONACK GROUNDHOG
WOODCOCK QUIS PEWEE PEWIT SNIPE SNITE SHRUPS BECASSE SIMPLETON
WOODCUT BLOCK
WOODCUTTER AXEMAN LOGGER WOODMAN WOODSMAN
WOOD DUCK SQUEALER BRANCHIER
WOODED BOSKY TREEY HYLEAN SYLVAN FORESTED NEMOROUS
WOODEN DRY DULL STIFF TREEN CLUMSY STICKY STOLID TIMBER AWKWARD DEADPAN TIMBERN LIFELESS
WOOD GUM XYLAN
WOOD HEN WEKA
WOODHEWER PICUCULE
WOOD HOOPOE WHOOP WHOOPE IRRISOR DUNGBIRD PICARIAN
WOOD HYACINTH SCILLA CROWTOE GREGGLE HAREBELL
WOOD IBIS STORK GANNET JABIRU IRONHEAD
WOODLAND DESERT MIOMBO SPRING BOSCAGE
(WASTE —) WEALD
WOOD LOUSE SLATER SOWBUG PILLBUG MILLIPED
WOODPECKER AWL CHAB JYNX KATE PEEK ECCLE HECCO HEWEL ICKLE PICUS SPEKT HECKLE NICKER NICKLE PECKER PIANET PICULE SPRITE TAPPER YAFFLE YUCKER YUKKEL CLIMBER CREEPER FLICKER HEWHOLE HICKWAY LOGCOCK REDHEAD SAPSUCK SNAPPER SPEIGHT WHETILE WITWALL WRYNECK DIRTBIRD HICKWALL PICARIAN PICUCULE POPINJAY RAINBIRD RAINFOWL WALLHICK SAPSUCKER
(LIKE A —) PICIFORM
(PREF.) PICI
WOOD-PIGEON CULVER CUSHAT ZOOZOO RINGDOVE
WOOD PIGEON CUSHAT ZOOZOO
WOODPILE STRAN STRAND WOODRICK
WOOD ROBIN MIRO TOMTIT
WOODRUFF HAIROF MUGGET MUGWET WOODROW HAIRHOOF
WOODS BOSK BUSH BOSQUE
(PREF.) NEMO SILVI SYLVI
WOODSMAN BUSHY SILVAN SYLVAN BUSHMAN BUSHWACK
WOOD SORREL OCA COCKOO HEARTS LUJULA OXALIS TREFOIL ALLELUIA ALLELUJA SHAMROCK STABWORT
WOOD SPIRIT METHANOL
WOOD SUGAR XYLOSE
WOOD THRUSH MAYBIRD
WOODTURNER BODGER
WOODWIND OBOE FLUTE BASSOON PIBGORN PICCOLO CLARINET
WOODWORK CEILING
WOODWORKER JOINER TURNER MILLMAN
WOODWORM GRIBBLE
(PREF.) TERMITO
WOODY BOSKY WITHY FRITHY STICKY SYLVAN XYLOID LIGNOSE LIGNEOUS
WOOER BEAU LOVER WOWER SUITOR COURTER WOOSTER COURTIER PARAMOUR
WOOF WEFT WOUGH FILLING TEXTURE
WOOING SUIT WOHLAC
WOOL OO COT DAG HOG VOL WOW BEAT BLUE FRIB PILE PULU ROCK FADGE LAINE MUNGO STUFF TIPPY ALPACA ARGALI BOTANY BREECH FLEECE GREASE JACKET JERSEY KERSEY LUSTER SLIVER WETHER COMBING HASLOCK KASHMIR MORLING STUBBLE WIGGING CASHMERE CLOTHING COMEBACK MORTLING PICKLOCK TOMENTUM
(— AS IT COMES FROM SHEEP) GREASE
(— FROM DEAD SHEEP) MORLING MORTLING
(— FROM LEOMINSTER) ORE
(— FROM RAGS) EXTRACT
(— OF UNDERCOAT OF MUSK-OX) QIVIUT
(— ON SHEEP'S LEG) GARE BREECH
(— ON SHEEP'S THROAT) HASLOCK
(— WEIGHT) TOD
(COARSE —) ABB SHAG BRAID COWTAIL
(COTTON —) CADDIS CADDICE
(DUNGY BIT OF —) FRIB
(FINE —) MERINO
(FINE GRADE OF —) PICKLOCK SPINNERS
(GREASY —) TIPPY
(INFERIOR GRADE OF —) HEAD
(KNOT OF —) NOIL
(LAMB'S —) WASSAIL
(LOCK OF —) FLOCK STAPLE
(LONG —) BLUE
(LOW GRADE OF —) LIVERY
(MATTED —) DAG KET SHAG
(PULLED —) SLIPE
(RECLAIMED —) MUNGO SHODDY
(REFUSE —) COT COTT FLOCK PINION
(ROLL OF —) CARDING
(RUSSIAN —) DONSKY
(SMALL PIECE OF —) TATE
(SPUN —) YARN
(WOUND —) TREND
(PREF.) ERIO LAN(I)(O) MALLO
(SUFF.) LAN

WOOLCLOTH HODDEN
WOOLEN (ALSO SEE FABRIC) CADDIS CAMLET SUCLAT CADDICE PASHMINA
(PL.) LAINAGE
WOOL FAT LANOLIN
WOOLLY SHEEP WOOZY LANATE LANOSE COTTONY FLOCCOSE PERONATE
WOOLLY BEAR WOUBIT
WOOLLY CROTON HOGWORT
WOOLY
(PREF.) DASI DASY ULO
WOOZY SICK DRUNK TIGHT VAGUE BLURRY WOOLLY
WORD GIG MOT EZEL GULE HAIT NEWS RAFF TERM VERB WHID WHUD ADNEX CHEEP COUCH DERRY DILLY FITCH GLOSS HAPAX HOKEY HYNDE LEMMA MAXIM ORDER PAROL RHEMA RUMOR SPELL ACCENT ADVERB AVOWAL BREATH COPULA ETYMON KIBBER LATIVE ONEYER PAROLE PLEDGE QUATCH REMARK REPORT SAYING ACCOUNT ADJUNCT BICCHED COMMAND COMMENT DICTION DUCDAME GENTILE GITTITH HOMONYM INCIPIT MESSAGE PALABRA PARONYM PRAYFUL PRENZIE PROMISE PROVERB SYNONYM VOCABLE ACROSTIC CATCHCRY CHEVILLE COMPOUND ENCLITIC EQUIVOKE FRABJOUS FRINGENT IDEOGRAM ILLATIVE LATINISM SYLLABLE SYNTAGMA NEOLOGISM PALINDROME PARTICIPLE MONOSYLLABLE
(— AS CALL TO DUCK) DILLY
(— EXPRESSING COMMAND) JUSSIVE
(— FORMED FROM VOWELS) EUOUAE
(— FROM INITIAL LETTERS) ACRONYM
(— IN A PUZZLE) LIGHT
(— MISPRONOUNCED) BEARD
(— OF ADDRESS) SIR
(— OF CONCLUSION) AMEN EXPLICIT
(— OF GOD) LOGOS
(— OF HONOR) PAROLE
(— OF MOUTH) FIDELITY
(— OF OPPOSITE MEANING) ANTONYM
(— OF RESPECT) SIR
(— OF SECONDARY RANK) ADNEX
(— OF SEVERAL MEANINGS) POLYSEME
(— OF UNCERTAIN MEANING) FRINGENT
(— OF UNKNOWN MEANING) KIBBER ONEYER PRAYFUL PRENZIE
(— REPRESENTED BY SIGN) GRAMMALOGUE
(— SEGMENT) SYLLABLE
(—S IN LOW TONE) ASIDE
(—S OF GREETING) SALUTATION
(—S OF OPERA) LIBRETTO
(—S SIGNIFYING UNDERSTANDING) ISEE
(BIBLICAL — OF DOUBTFUL MEANING) EZEL FITCH GITTITH
(BIG —) MOUTHFUL
(CALL —) JINGO
(CHARACTERIZING —) EPITHET
(CODE —) DOG FOX JIG ABLE EASY ECHO GOLF ITEM KING BRAVO DELTA HOTEL INDIA SUGAR GEORGE CHARLIE EUPHEMISM
(DISCOURAGING —) TSK
(EMPTY —S) WAFFLE
(FINE —S) DICK
(GATHERING —) SLOGAN
(HARSH —) MISWORD
(HONEYED —S) MANNA
(HYPHENATED —) SOLID
(IDENTIFYING —) LABEL
(LAST — OF SPEECH) CUE
(MAGIC —) ABRACADABRA
(MEANINGLESS —) DERRY
(MEANINGLESS —S) NOISE
(METAPHORICAL —) KENNING
(MNEMONIC —) VIBGYOR
(MYSTIC —) ABRAXAS
(NEW —) NEOLOGISM
(NONSENSE —) RAFF RAFFE FRABJOUS RUNCIBLE
(ORIGINAL —) STEM
(PARTING —) ENVOI
(PUT INTO —S) LIMN
(QUOTED —) CITATION
(RECURRING —) REPETEND
(REDUNDANT —) CHEVILLE
(ROOT —) ETYMON PRIMITIVE
(SIGNAL —) NAYWORD SECURITY
(SIGNIFICANT —) ACCENT
(SINGLE —) PHRASE
(SMOOTH —S) SOAP
(SOURCE —) ETYMON
(SPREAD THE —) TELL
(TEST —) SHIBBOLETH

(THIEVES' SLANG —) TWAG WHID
(UNEXPLAINED —) DUCDAME
(UTTERED —S) SPEECH
(WAY WITH —S) TACT
(PL.) LIP TALK LYRIC SPEECH LANGUAGE DISCOURSE
(PREF.) LEXI LEXICO LOG(O) ONOMATO RHEMATO VERBI VERBO
(SUFF.) EPY LEXIA ONYM

WORD-BLINDNESS ALEXIA DYSLEXIA ALEXIA

WORDBOOK LEXICON SPELLER LIBRETTO

WORDINESS VERBIAGE

WORDING LEGEND DICTION PHRASING

WORDLESS DUMB TACIT SILENT TACITURN

WORDMAKING RHEMATIC

WORDPLAY EQUIVOKE

WORD PROCESSING (— DISPLAY) WYSIWYG

WORDS TEXT

WORDY PROLIX VERBAL DIFFUSE VERBOSE WORDISH REDUNDANT

WORK DO GO ACT FAG JOB DIKE DYKE FEND FRET NOTE OPUS TASK TEND TOIL ERGON GRAFT GRIND KARMA KNEAD LABOR PRESS YAKKA ARBEIT BEAVER BONNET EFFECT HUSTLE OEUVRE REDUIT RESULT STRIVE THRIFT CALLING EXECUTE EXPLOIT FERMENT HEXAPLA LOUSTER MISSION OPERATE OPIFICE OPUSCLE OUVRAGE OVERAGE PICHERY PURSUIT TRAVAIL ADVOCACY AGENTING BUSINESS CAPONIER DEMILUNE DRUDGERY ENDEAVOR FUNCTION INDUSTRY LABORAGE OPUSCULE PARERGON RETRENCH EXECUTION
(— ACROSS GRAIN) THURM
(— ACTIVELY) LOUSTER
(— AGAINST) KNIFE ATTACK COMBAT
(— AIMLESSLY) FIDDLE
(— AS MUSICIAN) GIG
(— AS REPORTER) HEEL
(— BEYOND ONE'S POWERS) OVERDO
(— BY THE PIECE) TUT
(— CARELESSLY) RABBLE
(— DILIGENTLY) PEG PLUG STRIKE BELABOR
(— DOGGEDLY) SLOG
(— DONE) WRIHTE
(— FOR) LABOR SERVE BESWINK
(— FREE) START
(— HARD) TEW MOIL SLOG SWOT BULLOCK LEATHER
(— HIDES) BEAM
(— IMPERFECTLY) MALFUNCTION
(— INEFFECTUALLY) PINGLE
(— INSIDUOUSLY) WORM
(— INTO A MASS) KNEAD
(— INTO SHAPE) REDACT
(— LAND) FLOAT
(— LEISURELY) DAKER DAIKER
(— OCCASIONALLY) SMOOT SMOUT
(— OF ACKNOWLEDGED EXCELLENCE) CLASSIC
(— OF ART) GEM CRAFT ANTIQUE CAPRICE CREATION EPIPHANY EXERCISE MANDORLA
(— OF FICTION) SHOCKER
(— OF HISTORY) STORY
(— OF MENIAL KIND) DRUDGE
(— ONE'S WAY) WISE
(— OUT) BLOCK FUDGE SOLVE TRAIN DESIGN EVOLVE
(— OUT A PROBLEM) PSYCH PSYCHE
(— OUT IN ADVANCE) FOREPLOT
(— OVER) DIGEST
(— PAID FOR IN ADVANCE) HORSE
(— PART-TIME) TEMP
(— PART TIME) TEMP
(— PERSISTENTLY) HAMMER
(— RESEMBLING PATCHWORK) CENTO
(— SLIPSHOD) MULLOCK
(— STEADILY) PLY
(— SYSTEM) FLEXTIME FLEXITIME
(— TO EXHAUSTION) FAG
(— TOGETHER) COACT
(— TO WINDWARD) CLAW
(— TRIFLINGLY) PIDDLE
(— UNDER ANOTHER NAME) ALLONYM
(— UNFAIRLY OR CRUELLY) HORSE
(— UP) MENG MING MENGE SPUNK SUBACT
(— UPON) TILL LABOR
(— UPWARD) HIKE
(— VIGOROUSLY) BEND
(— WITHOUT FINISHING) SCABBLE SCAPPLE
(ALLEGORICAL —) BESTIARY
(ANONYMOUS —) ADESPOTA
(BUNGLED —) BOTCH
(CANVAS —) POINT
(CARELESS —) SLAPDASH
(CESSATION OF —) SITIN SITDOWN
(CHASED —) CISELURE
(CLEANING —) CHAR
(CLUMSY —) BOTCH
(COMPLETED —) TRAVAIL
(CONTRACT —) GYPPO
(DAMASCENE —) KOFTGARI
(DAY'S —) DARG DARGUE
(DECORATIVE —) FLOCKING MARQUETRY
(DIVINE —) THEURGY
(DOING LEGAL —) PROBONO
(DULL —) DRUDGERY
(EMBOSSED —) CELATURE
(FRAUDULENT —) JERRY
(HAND —) CAMAY
(HARD —) TEW MOIL MUCK SWOT TWIG YERK SWEAT EFFORT MOIDER LEATHER SLAVERY SLOGGING
(INFERIOR —) KITSCH SLOPWORK
(INLAY —) INTARSIA
(JOINER —) FINISH
(LITERARY —) STUDY CHASER SEQUEL SERIAL CLASSIC DIPTYCH PREQUEL PRODUCTION
(LITTLE —) OPUSCLE OPUSCULE
(LURID —) BLOOD
(MANUAL —) FATIGUE
(METAL —) NIELLO
(MINOR —) OPUSCULE OPUSCULUM
(MOSAIC —) EMBLEM
(ORGANIZED ABSENCE FROM —) SICKOUT
(ORNAMENTAL —) BEADWORK FILIGREE LEAFWORK
(PIECE OF —) JOB
(REFERENCE —) BIBLE SOURCE
(SACRED —) HIERURGY
(SCHOLASTIC —) SUMMA
(SKILLED MECHANICAL —) SLOJD SLOYD
(SLOVENLY —) SLAISTER
(SOCIAL —) ALMONING
(USELESS —) BOONDOGGLE
(WOMAN'S —) DISTAFF
(PL.) CANON PLANT STODGE FACTORY BUSINESS
(PREF.) ERG(O) ERGAT(O) OPERA
(EMBOSSED —) TOREUMATO
(SUFF.) ERGATE ERGY

WORKABLE YOUNG PLIANT VIABLE FEASIBLE
(EASILY —) SWEET

WORKADAY HUMDRUM PROSAIC ORDINARY

WORKBASKET CABA CABAS CALATHUS

WORKBENCH SIEGE DONKEY TEMPLATE

WORKED INWROUGHT
(— OUT) DEAD
(— UP) ANGRY EXCITED

WORKER (ALSO SEE WORKMAN AND LABORER) AGER CARL DOER HAND HIND ICER SCAB AXMAN BOXER BUTTY DEMAS DRIER EDGER ENDER FILER FIRER FIXER FLYER FOXER GLUER GORER HOLER INKER JERRY LINER LURER MAXIM MINIM NURSE PROLE TAPER TOWER ASHMAN BACKER BAILER BALLER BANDER BEADER BENDER BINDER BINMAN BLADER BLOWER BOILER BONDER BOOKER BOSHER BRACER BUFFER BUMPER BURNER BURRER CAPPER CARMAN CASTER CASUAL CHASER COMBER COOKER DAYMAN DIPPER DOCKER DOGGER DOTTER DUMPER ETCHER FACTOR FAGGER FANMAN FASHER FEEDER FELLER FILLER FITTER FLAKER FLAMER FLUTER FLUXER FOILER FOLDER FORCER FORMER FRAMER GASSER GOFFER GRADER GUMMER GUTTER HASHER HEADER HEELER HELPER HEMMER HOLDER HOOKER HOOPER HOPPER HUNKIE INKMAN JOGGER JOINER LEAFER LEASER LEGGER NOILER PUGGER READER REEDER SCORER SEAMAN SEAMER SHAKER SKIVER SLAKER SLICER SLIDER SLOPER STAVER STAYER TOILER TOPPER BUILDER CREATOR EMPLOYE FIELDER LABORER OUVRIER
(— IN LEATHER) BEAMER CHUMAR JACKER BLACKER CHUCKLER
(— IN METALS) SMITH FLAPPER
(ADDITIONAL —) EXTRA
(AGRICULTURAL —) ARKIE KISAN
(AIRCRAFT —) BOOTMAN
(ANT —) MAXIM ERGATES REPLETE
(ASBESTOS —) COBBER
(AUTO —) DISKER
(BAKERY —) BRAKER COOLER DIVIDER BENCHMAN SPREADER
(BLUE-COLLAR —) STIFF
(BREWERY —) HOPPER STEEPER STILLMAN
(BRICK —) DAUBER CROWDER
(CANNERY —) SLIMER SCALDER SHEDMAN
(CLOCK —) STAKER
(CLUMSY —) BODGE BODGER
(COAL —) SUMPER GEORDIE SPRAGGER
(COMPULSIVE —) WORKAHOLIC
(CONSTRUCTION —) HARDHAT
(DOCK —) BUNGS HOLDMAN SHENANGO
(DOMESTIC —) HELP
(FARM —) HODGE
(FELLOW —) CONFRERE
(FOREIGN —) GASTARBEITER
(FOUNDRY —) FLOGGER SNAGGER
(GARMENT —) FACER SLEEVER ASSORTER INSEAMER
(GUN —) BLUER
(HARD —) SLOGGER
(HAT —) CURLER BRIMMER
(HIDE —) HEFTER COLORER
(HOSPITAL —) ALMONER
(HOTEL —) SCRUB
(ICEHOUSE —) AIRMAN
(JEWELRY —) ARBORER
(LIMITED-TIME —) TEMP
(LOGGING —) SNIPER SKIDDER
(MATTRESS —) BEATER
(MIGRATORY —) HOBO OKIE
(MILL —) BILLER SPOUTER
(MINE —) BYEMAN FOOTER GOPHER LANDER DROPPER FACEMAN SLEDGER SWAMPER DRIFTMAN
(NONUNION CONSTRUCTION —S) LUMP
(OIL WELL —) ROUGHNECK
(ORCHARD —) SMUDGER
(PACKINGHOUSE —) COOK
(PAPERMILL —) SIZER SIZEMAN
(PIANO —) BELLYMAN
(PLODDING —) GRUBBER
(POTTERY —) CASER BATTER BEDDER FETTLER JOLLIER JUSTLER
(PRINTING —) FLY FLYBOY
(PUERTO RICAN —) GIBARO JIBARO
(QUARRY —) BREAKER
(RAILROAD —) JERRY HERDER BRAKEMAN
(SAWMILL —) BOLTER SETTER BOATMAN DECKMAN CHAINMAN
(SHOE —) CASER FOXER ARCHER FUDGER HEELER CHALKER BOTTOMER
(SKILLED —) ARTISTE
(SLAUGHTERHOUSE —) FATTER SHOVER SINGER SLIMER CHEEKER CHOPPER KNOCKER LIMEMAN SCALPER SCRIBER STICKER SNATCHER
(SOCIAL —) ALMONER
(TANNERY —) GATER STONER CROPPER CURRIER DELIMER BEAMSMAN SEASONER

(TEXTILE —) DOFFER DOUPER DRAWER GIGGER LAPPER LEASER SINGER CREELER DOUBLER JACKMAN KETTLER SKEINER SPINNER SHUTTLER SOFTENER SPLITTER TEASELER
(THEATER —) FLYMAN STAGEMAN
(TOBACCO —) BULKER SIFTER STEMMER SCRAPMAN SPRIGGER STICKMAN STRIPPER
(UNSKILLED —) HELPER DILUTEE GREENER
(USELESS —) TOOL
(WHITE-COLLAR —) EFFENDI
(YARN —) SOURER CHAINER
(PL.) LABOR
(PREF.) ERG(O) ERGAT(O)
(SUFF.) ERGAT(E) URGE URGIC URGY

WORKHORSE AVER AIVER TRESTLE SAWHORSE
WORKHOUSE UNION FACTORY WORKSHOP
WORKING PLAY GOING OPENCUT FUNCTION LABORAGE OPENCAST OPENWORK OPERATIC OPERATIVE
(— ALONE) HATTING
(— HARD) HOPPING
(— IN THE MIND) MOTION
(— OF MINE) GWAG CROSSCUT
(— ON) PRACTICE
(— TOGETHER) SYNERGIC SYNERGETIC
(DISUSED —) WASTE
(MINE —S) SPLIT
(NOT —) DUFF

WORKMAN (ALSO SEE WORKER AND LABORER) BOSS HAND MATE ROTO CAGER CONER EXTRA FINER FLINT FLUER FROCK LAYER MAJOR MIXER POLER TONER TRIER TUBER BEAMER BLOUSE BOOMER BOWLER BUCKER BUMMER COATER DIPPER DRIVER FORKER GAGGER HANGER LASTER LATHER MASTER NIPPER OILMAN PUFFER RUNNER SAMMER SCORER SHAKER SKIVER SLICER SLIDER SOAKER SPIKER STAGER STAVER TAPPER TARRER TEEMER TILTER TIPMAN TIPPER TOPMAN WARMER WASHER WETTER WRIGHT ARTISAN DRUMMER HOTSHOT LUDDITE SHOPMAN
(CHIEF —) BOSS
(CLUMSY —) BUNGLER COBBLER
(FELLOW —) BULLY BUTTY
(ITINERANT —) HOBO
(PROFICIENT —) DEACON
(SKILLED —) PRUDHOMME
(UNSKILLFUL —) HUNKY BUTCHER
(PL.) VOLK

WORKMANLIKE DEFT ADEPT SKILLFUL
WORKMANSHIP HAND FABRIC FACTURE OVERAGE ARTIFICE ARTISANRY
WORKROOM DEN STUDY ATELIER
WORKS HACIENDA
(— OF CLOCK) WATCH
(SALT —) SALINA

WORKSHOP LAB SHED SHOP FORGE LODGE SMIDDY SMITHY ATELIER BOTTEGA HOSPITAL OFFICINA PLUMBERY SKINNERY
WORKTABLE BENCH
WORLD ORB LOKA VALE WARD EARTH MONDE WADRU WARDE CAREER PUBLIC KINGDOM MONDIAL CREATION CREATURE UNIVERSE
(— OF BOXING) FISTIANA
(— OF DARKNESS) SHEOL
(— OF DOGS) DOGDOM
(— OF FASHION) STYLEDOM SWELLDOM
(— OF GODS) DEVALOKA
(— OF THE DEAD) DEEP
(— OF WOMEN) FEMINIE
(ACADEMIC —) CAMPUS
(EXTERNAL —) NONEGO
(GREAT —) MACROCOSM
(LITTLE —) MICROCOSM
(LOWER —) ORCUS
(PRIVATE —) AUTOCOSM
(THE —) FOLD
(THIRD —) SOUTH
(TWO-DIMENSIONAL —) FLATLAND
(PREF.) COSM(O) MUNDI
(SUFF.) COSM

WORLDLINESS MAMMON
WORLDLING DIVES
WORLDLY LAY WARLY CARNAL EARTHY MUNDAL EARTHEN EARTHLY FLESHLY MUNDANE PROFANE SECULAR SENSUAL TERRENE
(NOT —) INTERIOR

WORLD'S ILLUSION **(AUTHOR OF —)** WASSERMANN
(CHARACTER IN —) EVA LAY IVAN VOSS CYRIL DENIS KAREN SOREL BECKER AMADEUS BERNARD CRAMMON CHRISTIAN ENGELSCHALL WAHNSCHAFFE

WORLD-WEARY JADED BLASE
WORLDWIDE GLOBAL ECUMENIC GLOBULAR PLANETAL PLANETARY
(PREF.) GLOBO
WORLD-WISE KNOWING PRUDENT
WORM BOB EEL ESS LOA MAD LURG NAIS NEMA ARTER CADEW FLUKE LYTTA PIPER SCREW SNAKE DRAGON NEREID NEREIS PALMER PALOLO SHAMIR SYLLID SYLLIS TEREDO VERMIS WRETCH ANNELID ASCARID CARBORA ENOPLAN SABELLA SAGITTA SERPENT SERPULA SETARID SHUFFLE SPIONID TAGTAIL TRICLAD WRIGGLE BRANDLIN CEPHALOB CERCARIA CHETOPOD GILTTAIL HELMINTH LEODICID MEASURER NEMATODE POLYCLAD STRONGYL TRICHINA VERMICLE NEMERTEAN TOOTHACHE SCHISTOSOME POGONOPHORAN
(— IN HAWKS) FILANDER
(— OF DOG'S TONGUE) LYTTA
(— USED FOR BAIT) TAGTAIL
(AQUATIC —) TUBIFEX
(BLOODSUCKING —) LEECH
(CADDIS —) CADEW PIPER CADBAIT
(FLUKE —) PLAICE
(MARINE —) RAGWORM
(MEASURING —) LOOPER
(MUD —) IPO LOA
(SHIP —) BROMA COBRA
(PL.) APODA ENTOZOA
(PREF.) HELMINTH(O) LUMBRICI SCOLEC(I)(O) VERMI
(SUFF.) SCOLEX

WORM-EATEN PITTED DECAYED VERMOULU WERMETHE
WORMER JAG
WORMHOLE PIQURE
WORMLIKE VERMIAN
WORMSEED EPAZOTE AMBROSIA
WORMWOOD MOXA ABSINTH CUDWEED MUGWORT ABSINTHE COMPOSIT MINGWORT SANTONICA
WORMY EARTHY
WORN SEAR SERE USED PASSE TRITE MAGGED MIZPAH SHABBY ATTRITE CONTRITE
(— NEXT TO SKIN) INTIMATE
(— OUT) SHOT BANAL JADED SEELY SPENT STALE STANK BEATEN BEDRID BLEARY EFFETE EPUISE SCREWY SHABBY CRIPPLE FORWORN DECREPID FOUGHTEN HARASSED OBSOLETE STRICKEN
(— SMOOTH) BEATEN

WORRICOW DEVIL BUGABOO BUGBEAR HOBGOBLIN
WORRIED TOEY UNEASY ANXIOUS FRETTED STREAKED CONCERNED
WORRIT VEX WORRY DISTRESS
WORRY DOG HOE HOW HOX LUG NAG RUX TEW VEX BAIT BITE CARE CARK FAZE FIKE FRAB FRET FUSS HARE MOIL SOOL STEW ANNOY CHEVY CHOKE DEAVE FEEZE GALLY HARRY HURRY LURRY PHASE SCALD SHAKE TEASE TOUSE TOWSE BOTHER CADDLE CHIVVY COTTER CUMBER FERRET FIDGET GALLOW HARASS HATTER HECTOR INFEST KIAUGH MOIDER PESTER PINGLE PLAGUE POTHER ANXIETY CHAGRIN HATCHEL TROUBLE TURMOIL WHERRET FASHERIE STRANGLE
WORRYING ANXIOUS
WORSE VER WAR SEAMY
WORSEN DESCEND
WORSHIP GOD CULT HERY PUJA RANK ADORE DULIA HONOR NAMAZ WURTH YAJNA CREDIT PRAISE REPUTE REVERE BAALISM ELOHISM ICONISM IDOLISM IDOLIZE IMAGERY OBSERVE BLESSING HIERURGY VENERATE IDOLATRIZE
(— OF ALL GODS) PANTHEISM
(— OF HOST OF HEAVEN) SABAISM
(— OF IMAGES) ICONOLATRY
(— OF SELF) AUTOLATRY
(— OF SHAKESPEARE) BARDOLATRY
(ANCESTOR —) SCIOTHEISM
(DEVIL —) DIABOLISM
(FALSE —) SUPERSTITION
(FORMAL —) EYESERVICE
(FORM OF —) RITUAL
(HERO —) ADULATION
(HIGHEST KIND OF —) LATRIA
(INFERIOR KIND OF —) DULIA
(INSINCERE —) LIPSERVICE
(SERPENT —) OPHISM
(STAR —) SABAISM
(PREF.) LITURGIO THRESKI
(SUFF.) LATER LATRIA LATROUS LATRY

WORSHIPER ISIAC BHAKTA PRAISER IDOLATER
(— OF STARS) AKKUM SABIAN
(FIRE —) PARSI GHEBER GUEBER PARSEE
(SERPENT —) SETHIAN SETHITE

WORSHIPFUL GOOD PROUD NOTABLE REVERENT
WORST ACE GET BEST LAST OUTDO SHEND WREST DEFEAT
(SOMETHING THAT IS THE —) PIT PITS
(PREF.) KAKISTO

WORSTED GARN JERRY SERGE CUBICA VESSES WHIPCORD
WORT GAIL GYLE SWAT PLANT LENGTH TUTSAN FILLING KRAUSEN POTHERB
(FERMENTED —) FEED WASH
(UNFERMENTED —) GROUT

WORTH FECK MEED CARAT MERIT PRICE VALOR VALUE BECOME BOUNTY DESERT ESTEEM REGARD RICHES VALENT VIRTUE WEALTH DIGNITY PRETIUM VALIANT WORSHIP SPLENDOR TREASURE VALIDITY VALLIDOM
(NET —) CAPITAL
(OF LITTLE —) SHLOCK SCHLOCK
(PREF.) AXIO TIMO

WORTHINESS DESERT WORSHIP
WORTHLESS BAD BUM LOW WAF BAFF BALD BARE BASE EVIL IDLE LEWD ORRA PUNK RACA SLIM VAIN VILE WAFF BLANK BLOWN DUSTY FLASH FOUTY LOSEL LOUSY PUTID SLINK SORRY STRAW WASHY ABJECT CHAFFY CHEESY CRUMMY DRAFFY DRASTY DROSSY HOLLOW LIMMER LITHER LUTHER MEASLY NAUGHT PALTRY RASCAL ROTTEN SCREWY TRASHY WOODEN BAGGAGE FUSTIAN MAUVAIS NAUGHTY NOTHING PIPERLY RAFFISH RUBBISH SCABBED SHILPIT USELESS FECKLESS HARLOTRY MAUVAISE NUGATORY PRECIOUS RASCALLY RUBBISHY SIXPENNY TRUMPERY VAGABOND WANWORDY WRETCHED NOACCOUNT STRAMINEOUS
(— THING) AMBSACE

WORTHLESSNESS BELIAL UNTHRIFT
WORTHWHILE TANTI
WORTHY BIG DEAR FAIR GOOD HOLY TIDY AUGHT CANNY DIGNE EXALT HONOR JELLY NOBLE PIOUS GENTLE CONDIGN GRADELY PAREGAL THRIFTY ELIGIBLE VALUABLE WAUREGAN
(— OF BELIEF) CREDIBLE
(— OF DEVOTION) HOLY
(— OF PRAISE) LAUDABLE
(VERY —) SUPERIOR
(SUFF.) ABLE IBLE

WOULD WAD WID WANT WISH COULD SHOULD
(— NOT) NOLD WADNA WADDENT
(I —) CHUD CHOLD
WOULD-BE MANQUE
WOUND ARR CUT HEW PIP WIN BITE CALK CLAW DUNT FAKE FOIN GALL GORE HARM HURT MAIM PAIN PINK RASE RAZE RIST SCAR SKAG SORE STAB TEAR VULN WING BLESS BROKE GANCH GRIEF KNIFE KNOCK SHOOT STICK STING SUGAT THIRL TOUCH BREACH BRUISE CREASE ENTAME GRIEVE HARROW INJURE LAUNCH LESION MARTYR OFFEND PIERCE PLAGUE SCOTCH TRAUMA AFFLICT ATTAINT BATTERY BLIGHTY DIACOPE GUNSHOT SCRATCH DISTRESS FLANKARD FLEABITE INCISION LACERATE SPURGALL VULNERATE
(— FROM BOAR'S TUSK) GANCH GAUNCH
(— FROM BULL'S HORN) CORNADA
(— FROM RUBBING) GALL
(— IN DEER'S SIDE) FLANKARD
(— MADE BY THRUST) FOIN
(— ON FOOT) FIKE
(— ON HORSE'S ANKLE) CREPANCE
(— ON HORSE'S FOOT) CREPANCE
(— PRIDE) PIQUE
(— WITH POINTED WEAPON) STAB SWORD
(DEEP —) DIACOPE
(MINUTE —) PRICK SCART
(TRIFLING —) FLEABITE
(PL.) NOUNS
(PREF.) HELC(O) TRAUMAT(O) VULNI
WOUNDED HURT WUND VULNED WINGED VULNOSE STRICKEN
WOUNDWORT BETONY ALLHEAL HERCULES
WOU-WOU WAWA WAWAH CAMPER GIBBON
WOVEN BROCHE BROWDEN DAMASSE
(— FULL WIDTH) SEAMLESS
(— WIDE) BROAD
(— WITH RIB) SOLEIL
WOW AWE HIT MEW BARK GOSH HOWL RAVE WAIL GOLLY WHINE SUCCESS
WOZZECK (CHARACTER IN —) MARIE ANDRES WOZZECK
(COMPOSER OF —) BERG
WRACK KELP RACK RUIN VAREC CUTWEED DESTROY DOWNFALL EELGRASS WRECKAGE
WRAITH WAFT FETCH GHOST SPOOK DOUBLE SHADOW SWARTH SPECTRE
WRANGLE RAG YED CAMP MOIL SPAR TIFT ARGLE ARGUE BRAWL CHIDE DAFER FLITE JOWER PLEAD STRUT ARGUFY BICKER CAFFLE CAMPLE CANGLE DACKER FRAPLE FRATCH HAGGLE HASSLE JANGLE RAGGLE THREAP BRABBLE BRANGLE DISPUTE PICKEER QUARREL SCRAFFLE SQUABBLE TIRRWIRR
WRANGLER CAMPER COWBOY GRATER HAFTER WRAGER DEBATER HAGGLER DEFENDER OPPONENT
WRANGLING JANGLE
WRAP HAP LAP LOT WAP BIND FURL ROLL WHIP AMICE CLASP CLOAK LAMBA MANTA NUBIA SERVE SHAWL TWINE WOOLD AFGHAN BURLAP CLOTHE COCOON COOLER DOLMAN EMBALE MOIDER MUFFLE PATTOO SACQUE SARAPE SERAPE SWATHE WIMPLE WRIXLE ENVELOP INVOLVE SWADDLE UMBELAP BARRACAN
(— CABLE) KECKLE
(— CLOSE) SNUGGLE
(— DEAD BODY) CERE
(— ONESELF) HUDDLE
(— UP) HAP MAIL CINCH ENROL IMPLY
(— UP HEAD) MOB MOP MOBLE
(— WIRE AROUND FISHING LINE) GANGE
(— WITH BANDAGE) SWATHE
(HEAD —) NUBIA SNOOD
(PL.) SECRECY RESTRAINT
WRAPPER APRON COVER MOTTO PILCH SHAWL SMOCK COUPON FARDEL JACKET ENVELOP OVERALL SARPLER COVERING MAHARMAH WOOLPACK
(— FOR BOOK) JACKET
(— FOR CUTLET) PAPILLOTE
(— WORN IN EGYPT) GALABIA GALABEAH
(COOKING —) PAPILLOTE
WRAPPING WAP PACK GELILAH LAPPING COVERING MANTLING
(— FOR DEAD) CEREMENT
(— MATERIAL) SARAN
(— OF HEBREW SCROLL) GELILAH
(— OF ROPE) SERVICE
WRASSE COOK BALLAN COMBER CONNER CUNNER LABRID HOGFISH PIGFISH SEAWIFE CORKWING DONCELLA JANIZARY LADYFISH SENORITA
WRATH IRE FURY GRIM ANGER WROTH CHOLER FELONY PASSION VIOLENCE
WRATHFUL IRY EVIL HIGH ANGRY IRATE WROTH IREFUL RAGING FURIOUS JEALOUS CHOLERIC
WREAK CAUSE AVENGE EXPEND GRATIFY INDULGE INFLICT REVENGE
(— DESTRUCTION) ESTREPE
WREATH LEI ORLE PLAY CROWN GREEN LAURE LORRE OLIVE TORSE WHORL WRASE ANADEM CRANTS CREASE LAUREL POTONG TORTIL CHAPLET CORONAL CORONET CROWNAL DOLPHIN FESTOON GARLAND WRINKLE KELYPHYTE
(SPIRAL —) VOLUTION
WREATHE BIND WIND CRISP TWINE TWIST WRING INTORT WRITHE CONTORT ENTWINE INTWIST INVOLVE
WREATHED SPIRY TORTILE TORTIVE WRITHED INTORTED TORTILLE
WRECK CRAB HULK RUIN BLAST CRACK CREAM PRANG SHOOT SMASH TRASH WRACK DEFACE DESPOIL DESTROY FOUNDER GODSEND SHATTER TORPEDO DEMOLISH SABOTAGE SHAMBLES
(— COMPLETELY) TOTAL
(HUMAN —) DERELICT
WRECKAGE WRACK FINDAL FLOTSAM GODSEND WAVESON SHAMBLES
WRECKED NOUGHT
WRECKERS, THE (CHARACTER IN —) AVIS MARK PASCOE THRIZA
(COMPOSER OF —) SMYTH
WREN GIRL STAG TOPE CUTTY JENNY KITTY PEGGY SALLY STAID TYDIE SCUTTY TIDIFE TIDLEY TINTIE TOMTIT WRANNY BLUECAP REGULUS MALURINE WRANNOCK
(BUSH —) RIFLEBIRD
WRENCH KEY PIN RUG PULL RACK RICK RUGG TEAR YERK CRICK CRINK FORCE THRAW THROW TWIST WRAMP WREST BEDKEY SPRAIN STRAIN TWEEZE DISTORT SPANNER SPANULE SQUINCH TORTURE TWISTLE
WREST REAR REND EXACT FORCE TWIST ARREST EXTORT WRENCH WRITHE ABSTORT WIREDRAW
(— AWAY) STRIP DESPOIL
WRESTLE PRAY RASSLE SQUIRM TUSSLE WRAXLE WRITHE GRAPPLE SCUFFLE THRIMBLE THRUMBLE
WRESTLER MATMAN WELTER CLICKER MATSTER GRAPPLER
(KIND OF —) SUMO
WRESTLING SUMO SAMBO PALESTRA WRAXLING
(— TECHNIQUE) GLIMA
(KIND OF —) WRIST
(STYLE OF —) SAMBO
WRETCH DOG MIX FILE WARY MISER SLAVE THING BUGGER PERSON SQUALL BRETHEL CAITIFF CAMOOCH CHINCHE CULLION GLUTTON HILDING SCROYLE BEZONIAN CREATURE MESCHANT POLTROON RECREANT SCULLION
WRETCHED EVIL FOUL LORN MEAN POOR DAWNY DEENY GAUNT SORRY WISHT WOFUL YEMER ABJECT CAITIF DISMAL MEAGER PALTRY RASCAL SHABBY SICKLY SORDID UNLEAD UNLEDE WOEFUL ABYSMAL BENEATH FORLORN OUTWORN PITIFUL SQUALID UNSEELY MESCHANT MISERABLE
(— PERSON OR ANIMAL) MISERY
WRIGGLE EEL REG RIG FRIG LASH WIND WRIG SLIDE WRELE WRING SQUIRM WAMBLE WANGLE WARPLE WIDDLE WIMPLE WINTLE WRITHE EYEBROW SNIGGLE TWIDDLE TWINGLE WRABILL WRESTLE SCRIGGLE SQUIGGLE
WRIGGLING EELY SCRIGGLE SQUIGGLY
WRIGGLY SNAKY SNAKISH SQUIRMING
WRING RACK DRAIN EXACT SCREW TWIST WREST EXTORT OPPRESS SQUEEZE TORMENT TORTURE
(— THE NECK) SCRAG
WRINGER RUNG WRUNG SQUEEZER
WRINKLE RUT DRAW FOLD FURL HINT KNIT LIRK RUCK RUGA SEAM BREAK CRIMP CRISP DELVE FAULT FRILL REEVE RIVEL SNIRL BUCKLE COCKLE CRAVAT CREASE FURROW METHOD PUCKER RIMPLE RUMPLE RUNKLE SCRIMP WREATH BLEMISH CRANKLE CRINKLE CRUMPLE CRUNKLE FROUNCE FRUMPLE CONTRACT IRRUGATE RUGOSITY
(— OF FLESH) CRAVAT
(— REMOVER) IRON IRONER
(PREF.) RUTI RUTID(O)
WRINKLED CRUMP PURFLY RUGATE RUGGED RUGOSE RUGOUS SEAMED COCKLED CREASED ROUCHED SAVOYED CRUMPLED FURROWED PUCKERED WRITHLED WRIZZLED
WRINKLING KNIT KNOT FROWN
WRIST CARPUS SHACKLE
(PREF.) CARP(O)
WRISTER MUFFETEE
WRISTLET STRAP WRISTER MUFFETEE
WRISTWATCH BAGUET BAGUETTE
WRIT AIEL CAPE MISE PONE TOLT ALIAS BREVE BRIEF ERROR RECTO UTRUM BRIEVE CAPIAS ELEGIT EXTENT PLAINT VENIRE ACCOUNT DEDIMUS DETINUE EXIGENT LATITAT PLURIES PRECEPT PROCESS SUMMONS WARRANT CESSAVIT COSINAGE DETAINER DOCUMENT FORMEDON MANDAMUS MITTIMUS NOVERINT PRAECIPE QUOMINUS REPLEVIN SISERARY SUBPOENA TESTATUM WARRANTY
(— FOR SUMMONING EXTRA JURORS) TALES
(LEGAL —) CERT
WRITE INK PEN BACK BOOK DITE DRAW READ SELL CLERK DRAFT STYLE AUTHOR ENFACE INDITE SCRIBE SCRIVE ADDRESS COMPILE COMPOSE DICTATE EMPAPER EXARATE SCREEVE BIOGRAPH INSCRIBE
(— ADDRESS) BACK
(— BENEATH) SUBSCRIBE
(— BETWEEN) INTERSCRIBE
(— BRIEFLY) JOT
(— CARELESSLY) DASH SCRAWL SCRIBBLE
(— DOWN) SIGN BREVE DENOTE RECORD AMORTIZE DESCRIBE
(— FOR ANOTHER) GHOSTWRITE
(— FURTHER) ADD
(— HASTILY) SCRATCH SCRIBBLE SQUIGGLE
(— IN A LARGE HAND) ENGROSS
(— IN LARGE CHARACTERS) TEXT
(— IN SHORTHAND) STENOGRAPH
(— LETTER) CORRESPOND EPISTOLIZE

(— MUSIC) NOTATE COMPOSE
(— ON FRONT OF BILL) ENFACE
(— PASTORAL POEMS) PHILLIS
(— POMPOUSLY) FUSTIANIZE
(— WHAT IS NOT TRUE) FABLE
(SUFF.) GRAPH(ER)(IA)(IC)(Y)
WRITER (ALSO SEE AUTHOR) PEN BARD HACK PUFF ALVAR GHOST ODIST SQUIB AUTHOR FATHER GLOZER HEROIC LAWYER LETTER MUNSHI NOTARY PENMAN PRABHU PROSER PURVOE SCRIBE TRAGIC YEOMAN ADAPTER ADSMITH ANALYST DIARIST ELOHIST ESSAYER GLOSSER GNOMIST HYMNIST IAMBIST JUVENAL LAUDIST MUNCHEE PENSTER PROPHET PROSAIC REVUIST SCRIVER STYLIST SUMMIST TEXTMAN AUGUSTAN BLURBIST COMEDIAN COMPOSER DECADENT DECADIST DIDACTIC EMBOSSER EPISTLER ESSAYIST FABLEIST FABULIST GROMATIC HUMORIST IDYLLIST MONODIST MOONSHEE NOVELIST PARODIST PENWOMAN PREFACER PRESSMAN PROSAIST PROSEMAN PSALMIST REVIEWER SATIRIST SCRIPTER VERSEMAN HISTORIAN LEGENDARY LEGENDIST PROSATEUR LIBRETTIST TRACTARIAN PAMPHLETEER
(— OF BURLESQUE) GABBER
(FAST —) STENO
(FREE-LANCE —) CREEPER
(HACK —) PENSTER
(INCOMPETENT —) BOTCHER
(JESUIT —) BOLLANDIST
(OBITUARY —) NECROGRAPHER
(OBSCENE —) RIBALD
(PROVERB —) PAROEMIOGRAPHER
(SACRED —) HAGIOLOGIST HAGIOGRAPHER
(SATIRICAL —) SILLOGRAPH
(SPEECH —) LOGOGRAPHER
WRITHE WRY WIND THROW TWIRL TWIST WRING SQUIRM TERVEE WAMBLE WRABBE WRENCH AGONIZE WRESTLE WRIGGLE WRINGLE CONVOLVE
WRITHING EELY WRING WRITHY
WRITING BOOK DITE FAIT PAGE POEM KANJI LIBEL SCROW CADJAN GOSSIP LEGEND LETTER PAGINE SCRIPT SCRITE SCRIVE UNCIAL ARTICLE AUTONYM DIPLOMA ESCRIPT SCREEVE APOCRYPH CONTRACT DOCUMENT GRAVAMEN HARANGUE KAKEMONO LETTRURE LIPOGRAM PAMPHLET SCRIBING SONNETRY SMALLHAND JOURNALISM SCRIVENING
(— FOR ANOTHER) ALLOGRAPH
(— OF LITTLE VALUE) STUFF SCRIBBLE
(— ON PAPER SCROLL) MAKIMONO
(— ON SILK) KAKEMONO
(— ON WAX) CEROGRAPH
(—S OF VIRGIL) POETICA
(— UNDER SEAL) BOND
(BAWDY —) SCULDUDDRY SCULDUDDERY SKULDUDDERY
(BIBLICAL —) MENE
(BITTER —) DIATRIBE
(CARELESS —) SCRAWL
(CRAMPED —) NIGGLE
(CURSIVE —) JOINHAND
(EASY —) GOSSIP
(FORMAL —) RECORD
(HINDU —) VEDA
(HUMOROUS —S) FACETIAE
(ILLUMINATED —) FRACTUR
(IN THIS —) HERETO
(IRREGULAR —) SCRAWL
(MUSICAL —) GIMEL GYMEL
(NORSE —) EDDA
(OBSCENE —) BALDERDASH
(PRETENTIOUS —) FUSTIAN
(SACRED —) ARANYAKA BRAHMANA SCRIPTURE
(SATIRICAL —) PASQUINADE
(SECRET —) SCYTALE
(SHORT —) SCRIP
(SHORTHAND —) PHONOGRAPHY
(SPY —) CODE
(STUPID —) PABLUM PABULUM
(STYLE OF —) ACADEMESE
(SWIFT —) SHORTHAND
(SYLLABIC —) KANA
(VAPID —) WASH
(VERBOSE —) TOOTLE
(VOLUMINOUS —) POLYGRAPHY
(WITTY —S) FACETIAE
(WORTHLESS —) TRIPE
(PL.) LEGENDA ARANYAKA POSTHUMA
(PREF.) GRAMO GRAPHI GRAPHO
(SUFF.) GRAM GRAPH(ER)(IA)(IC)(Y)
WRITING CASE STANDISH SCRUTOIRE
WRITTEN KETIB KETHIB KTHIBH GRAPHIC LITERAL
(— ABOVE) SS
(— AFTER) ADSCRIPT
(— HASTILY) STRAY
(SO —) SIC
(PREF.) GRAPTO
WROCLAW BRESLAU
WRONG BAD CAR ILL MIS OUT WET AWRY HARM HURT SORE SOUR TORT WITE AGATE AGLEE AGLEY AMISS CRIME DUTCH FALSE GLEED GRIEF MALUM UNFIT WATHE WOUGH AGUILT ASTRAY BLOOEY FAULTY INJURE INJURY NOUGHT OFFEND SARAAD SINFUL UNTRUE WICKED WONDER ABUSION ABUSIVE DAMNIFY DEFRAUD IMMORAL INJURIA MISBEDE NAUGHTY UNRIGHT VIOLATE AGGRIEVE COCKEYED MISTAKEN PERVERSE UNLEEFUL
(CIVIL —) TORT
(IMAGINARY —) WINDMILL
(SHOCKINGLY —) MONSTROUS
(PREF.) MIS
WRONGDOER ACTOR SINNER FAULTER MISDOER OFFENDER
WRONGDOING MISS CRIME FAULT DEFAULT MISCONDUCT MALFEASANCE
WRONGFUL UNFAIR UNJUST TORTIOUS TORTUOUS UNLAWFUL
WRONGHEADED WRY PERVERSE
WRONGLY AMISS BADLY FALSE NOUGHT UNRICHT UNRIGHT OVERWART
WROTH ANGRY IRATE IREFUL
WROUGHT BEATEN CARVEN FORMED SHAPED VROCHT CREATED HAMMERED
(ELABORATELY —) LABORED
WRY ASKEW AVERT TWIST WRING WRONG IRONIC WRITHE DEFLECT DISTORT TWISTED WRITHEN SATURNINE
WRYNECK IYNX JYNX SLAB WEET LOXIA PEABIRD WEETBIRD TORTICOLLIS
WUTHERING HEIGHTS (AUTHOR OF —) BRONTE
(CHARACTER IN —) DEAN EDGAR ELLEN JOSEPH LINTON ZILLAH FRANCES HARETON HINDLEY EARNSHAW ISABELLA LOCKWOOD CATHERINE HEATHCLIFF
WYCH ELM WITCH WITCHEN
WYLIECOAT WALYCOAT NIGHTGOWN PETTICOAT
WYND HAW ALLEY CLOSE

WYOMING

CAPITAL: CHEYENNE
COUNTY: TETON UINTA GOSHEN BIGHORN LARAMIE NIOBRARA
INDIAN: ARAPAHO
LAKE: JACKSON
MOUNTAIN: ELK CLOUD GANNET HOBACK FREMONT ATLANTIC SHERIDAN
MOUNTAIN RANGE: TETON ABSARO BIGHORN LARAMIE RATTLESNAKE
NICKNAME: EQUALITY
RIVER: GREEN SNAKE PLATTE POWDER BIGHORN
STATE BIRD: MEADOWLARK
STATE FLOWER: PAINTBRUSH
STATE TREE: COTTONWOOD
TOWN: CODY LUSK CASPER BUFFALO LARAMIE RAWLINS WORLAND GREYBULL KEMMERER SHERIDAN SUNDANCE

X EX XRAY ERROR MISTAKE
XANADU (SACRED RIVER OF —) ALPH
XANTHIC YELLOW
XANTHIPPE NAG SHREW
(HUSBAND OF —) SOCRATES
XANTHIPPUS (SON OF —) PERICLES
XEBEC SHIP CHEBEC CHEBECK SHABEQUE
XENIUM GIFT DAINTY DELICACY
XERES JEREZ SHERRY
XERIC DRY
XHOSA KAFIR KAFFIR
(PL.) AMAKOSA AMAXOSA
XIPHARES (FATHER OF —) MITHRIDATE
XIPHISTERNUM XIFOID
XIPHOSURUS LIMULUS
X-RAY UROGRAM
XUREL SCAD SAUREL
XUTHUS (ADOPTED SON OF —) ION
(BROTHER OF —) DORUS AEOLUS
(FATHER OF —) HELLEN
(MOTHER OF —) ORSEIS
(SON OF —) ION DURUS ACHAEUS
(WIFE OF —) CREUSA
XYLEM WOOD HADROM HADROME XYLOGEN
XYLOID WOODY LIGNEOUS
XYLOPHONE REGAL SARON BALAFO GAMBANG GAMELAN MARIMBA BALAPHON GAMELANG GIGELIRA STICCADO
XYSTUS WALK XYST PORTICO TERRACE

Y

Y WY YA WYE YOD YOKE YANKEE
(— CONNECTION) SIAMESE
(— COORDINATE) SINE
(PREF.) **(LETTER —)** YPSILI
YABBER TALK JABBER LANGUAGE
YABBY CRAWLIE
YACARE CAIMAN CAYMAN JACARE
YACHT SAIL SCOW BRUTE YATCH DINGHY SONDER YEAGHE CRUISER KEELBOAT
YAFF YAP BARK YELP
YAFFLE ARMFUL YAFFIL
YAHOO BRUTE CLOWN ROWDY BUMPKIN
YAHWEH GOD JAVE YHWH JAHVAH
YAHWIST JEHOVIST
YAK GAB GAG GAS JOKE YUCK LAUGH BULBUL SARLAK SARLYK YAMMER CHATTER
YAKALA JAGA
YAKKA WORK LABOR
YAKUT SAKHA
YAM HOI UBE UBI UVE JAMB LIMA RAIL TUGUI IGNAME INAMIA INHAME POTATO BONIATA
(TARO —) KOKO
YAMA (FATHER OF —) VIVASVANT
(SISTER OF —) YAMI
YAM BEAN KAMAS JICAMA WAYAKA SINCAMAS
YAMEN COURT YAMUN OFFICE
YAMEO LLAMEO
YAMMER CRY WAIL SCOLD WHINE YEARN YOMER GRUMBLE WHIMPER
YAMP YAMPA SQUAWROOT
YANAN NOZI
YANG HONK GURJUN
YANK FLOG JERK SLAP HOICK SNAKE BUFFET
YAP BARK YAWP YELP MOUTH SCOLD WAFFLE BUMPKIN CHATTER KYOODLE
YAPOK YAPOCK OPOSSUM OYAPOCK
YAQUI YAKI HIAQUI
YARD HAW HOF YED CREW CROW DUMP FOLD SKID SPAR TILT COURT GARTH PATIO STICK CANCHA HOPPET LOANIN CURTAIN GARSTON KNACKERY OUTGARTH
(— OF SAWMILL) DUMP
(— WHERE COWS ARE MILKED) LOANIN LOANING
(FINAL —) FELL
(GRASSY —) GARSTON
(PAVED —) CAUSEY
(POULTRY —) BARTON
(SAIL —) RAE
(1-16TH OF A —) NAIL
(1-3RD OF CUBIC —) CARTLOAD
(20 —S) SCORE
(5 AND A HALF —S) ROD
YARD GRASS ELEUSINE MANGRASS
YARDLAND VERGE VIRGATE
YARDMASTER DINGER
YARDSTICK VERGE YAIRD METRIC MEASURE METWAND METEWAND STANDARD CRITERION
YARE YAR AYRE YORE BRISK READY LIVELY NIMBLE PROMPT
YARETA LLARETA
YARM WAIL NOISE OUTCRY SHRIEK
YARN ABB END FOX CORD GARN GIMP PIRN SILK SLIP WEFT WHIP DYNEL FLOSS GRAIN INKLE LUREX PITCH SPIEL ALASKA ANGORA BERLIN BROACH CADDIS COTTON CREWEL CUFFER DACRON ESTRON FLORET FRIEZE MERINO MOTTLE PEELER RATINE SAXONY SINGLE STRAND TASLAN THREAD VINYON WOOLEN ZEPHYR ACETATE CADDICE FILLING GENAPPE INGRAIN MELANGE RACKING SCHAPPE VIGOGNE WORSTED ASBESTOS BOURETTE CHENILLE FORTISAN METALLIC ROUNDING SPINNING WHEELING ORGANZINE VIGOUREUX
(— FOR WARP) ABB
(— FROM FLOSS SILK) FLORET
(— MEASURE) LEA
(— SIZE) TYPP
(BALL OF —) CLEW CLUE
(BITS OF ROPE —) THRUMS
(BUNDLE OF —) PAD
(CONICAL MASS OF —) COP
(ELASTIC —) LASTEX
(EXAGGERATED —) STRETCHER
(FINE SOFT —) ZEPHYR KASHMIR CASHMERE
(LINEN —) SPINEL
(ROLL OF —) PRICK CHEESE
(ROPE —S) SOOGEE
(SILK —) TRAM
(SMALL PIECE OF SPUN —) RABAND ROBBIN ROPEBAND
(UNEVEN —) BOUCLE
(PL.) FOX MENDINGS
YARRAN GIDYA MYALL GIDGEA GIDGEE
YARROW ALLHEAL CAMMOCK MAUDLIN MILFOIL PELLITORY
YASHIRO SHA
YASHMAK VEIL ASMACK YAKMAK
YATAGHAN SABER ATAGHAN SIMITAR
YATTER CHATTER PRATTLE
YAUD MARE YADE
YAUPON ASSI HOLLY YUPON CASINA CASSINE
YAUTIA COCO TARO TANIA COCKER TANIER MALANGA
YAW GAPE YAWN LURCH SHEER BROACH SWERVE
YAWL HOWL DANDY MIZZEN SCREAM SCHOKKER
YAWN GAP GALP GANE GANT GAPE YANE ABYSM CHAUM CAVITY TEDIUM DULLNESS OSCITATE
YAWNING HIANT CHASMA GAPING OSCITANT
YAWP BAWL GAPE RANT YELP STARE SQUAWK YAMMER COMPLAIN
YAWS PIAN TUBBA TUBBOE
YAWWEED RHUBARB
YAYA COPA
YEA YA YES YOY YIGH TRULY ASSENT REALLY VERILY
YEAN EAN LAMB
YEANLING KID LAMB EANLING
YEAR EAR SUN AYRE HAAB TIME ANNEE ANNUS VAGUE WINTER ZODIAC TOWMOND TZOLKIN BIRTHDAY
(— OF EMANCIPATION) JUBILEE
(ACADEMIC —) SESSION
(IN THIS —) HA
(LAST —) FERNYEAR
(MANY —S) AGE
(MAYAN —) TUN HAAB
(ONE BILLION —S) AEON
(SABBATICAL —) JUBILE JUBILEE
(1000 —S) MILLENARY MILLENNIUM
(4320 MILLION —S) KALPA
(PL.) SEASONS
(SUFF.) ENNIAL ENNIUM
YEARBOOK ANNUAL SERIAL ANNUARY
YEARLING COLT HORNOTINE
(AUTHOR OF —) RAWLINGS
(CHARACTER IN —) LEM ORA JODY HUTTO PENNY TWINK BAXTER NELLIE OLIVER WILSON GINRIGHT FORRESTER WEATHERBY FODDERWING
YEARLY ANNUAL SOLEMN
YEARN HO YEN ACHE BURN EARN GAPE HONE IRNE LONG PANT PINE SIGH CRAVE GREEN GRIEN ASPIRE CURDLE GRIEVE HANKER YAMMER
YEARNING EROS DESIRE HANKER RENNET CRAVING EARNFUL HOMESICK
YEAST BEE EST BARM BEES EAST KOJI SOTS FROTH SPUME LEAVEN NEWING RISING SIZING TORULA FERMENT SIZZING EMPTINGS
(FILM —) FLOR
YEASTY LIGHT FROTHY TRIVIAL RESTLESS
YEGG ROBBER BURGLAR
YELL CRY CALL GOWL HOWL ROAR YARM YAUP YOWL YOWT GOLLY SHOUT TIGER BELLOW GOLLAR HOLLER SCREAM YAMMER YELLOCH SCRONACH SKELLOCH
YELLOW (ALSO SEE COLOR) OR GULL AMBER BLAKE BLOND FAVEL FLAVE JAUNE PALEW SHELL YELWE ALMOND BANANA FLAVID MELINE MIMOSA NUGGET OXGALL BISCUIT JASMINE JONQUIL LEGHORN LUTEOUS MEXICAN MUSTARD NANKEEN OATMEAL POPCORN SAFFRON TILLEUL WHEATEN YUCATAN AUREOLIN GENERALL ICTEROID LUMINOUS MARIGOLD ORPIMENT PRIMROSE
(— AS BUTTER) BLAKE
(— ORANGE) SAFFRON
(BROWNISH —) FULVID FULVOUS
(DINGY —) LURID
(GOLDEN —) FLAVID
(GREENISH —) ACACIA
(INDIAN —) PURI PURREE
(LEMON —) GENERALL
(PALE —) EGGSHELL
(PREF.) CHLOR(O) CHRYS(O) FLAV(I)(O) OCHRO XANTH(O) XANTIN(O)
YELLOW ALDER SAGEROSE
YELLOW BEDSTRAW CRUDWORT CURDWORT FLEAWEED
YELLOW BUGLE IVA IVE IVY
YELLOW CLINTONIA DOGBERRY
YELLOW-DOG MEAN CONTEMPTIBLE
YELLOW FEVER VOMITO
YELLOW FOXTAIL STICKERS
YELLOW GENTIAN FELWORT
YELLOW GREEN PISTACHE
YELLOWHAMMER SKYT YITE AMMER GOWDY SKITE GLADDY GOLDIE VERDIN YORLIN FLICKER GLADEYE YELDRIN YOLDRING
(— STATE) ALABAMA
YELLOW IRIS SEDGE LEVERS DAGGERS
YELLOWISH SALLOW ICTERINE SAFFRONY
(— GREEN) GLAUCOUS
(— RED) FALLOW
(PREF.) LUTEO
YELLOW JACKET VESPA VESPID
YELLOW JASMINE WOODBINE
YELLOWLEGS KILLCU TATLER WINTER YELPER TATTLER
YELLOW MACKEREL CREVALLE
YELLOWNESS FLAVEDO
YELLOW POND LILY DUCK CLOTE CLOTS NUPHAR
YELLOW POPLAR TULIPWOOD
YELLOW PRICKLE RUBIA
YELLOW RATTLE RATEL COCKSCOMB LOUSEWORT
YELLOW TOADFLAX RAMSTEAD
YELLOW WAGTAIL OATEAR
YELLOW WATER LILY KELP WOKAS
YELLOWWOOD FUSTIC FUSTOC GOPHER MANGWE VIRGILIA

YELP CRY YAP YIP BAFF BARK KIYI WAFF YAFF YAUP YAWP BOAST YAMPH AVOCET SQUEAL YAFFLE YELLOW
YELPING CRY

YEMEN
ANCIENT KINGDOM: SABA SHEBA
CAPITAL: SANA SANAA
COIN: RIAL RIYAL BUQSHA
MUSLIM SECT: SHIA SUNNI
OFFICIAL NAME: YEMENARABREPUBLIC
PEOPLE: ZAIDI SHAFAI
PORT: MOKA MOCHA
REGION: TIHAMA
RULER: IMAM
TOWN: MOKA DAMAR MOCHA TAIZZ HODEIDA

YEN EYES ITCH LONG URGE YEARN DESIRE SUCKER CRAVING LONGING
YENTA GOSSIP TALKER BUSYBODY
YEOMAN CHURL CLERK WRITER GOODMAN GUIDMAN GRAYCOAT RETAINER BEEFEATER
YERBA SANTA TARBUSH
YERK BEAT GOAD HURL JERK KICK STAB YARK THUMP EXCITE THRASH LASHING
YES AY DA IS JA OC SI YA AYE ISS YAS YAW YEA YEP YIS YUH YUS YEAH JOKOL TRULY
YESTERDAY HIER YESTER YESTREEN
(OF —) PRIDIAN
YET AND BUT YIT EVEN STILL ALGATE HOWEER THOUGH FINALLY HOWEVER HITHERTO
(AS —) SOFAR UPTONOW
YETI BIGFOOT SNOWMAN SASQUATCH
YETT GATE
YEUK EWK YUK ITCH YUCK ITCHING
YEW YO HEW UGH YOE YOW VIEW TAXUS TOPIARY CHINWOOD
YEX YOLK
YIDDISH JEWISH
YIELD GO BOW CUT ILD PAN PLY BEAR BEND CAST CEDE CESS COME CROP DRAG DUCK EMIT FOLD GIVE HEAR HELD LOUT QUIT SELL VAIL WAGE AGREE ALLOW AMAIN AVALE AWALE BRING BUDGE CARRY CAUSE DEFER GRANT HEALD HIELD LEAVE OFFER SLAKE STOOP ACCEDE AFFORD BOUNTY BUCKLE COMPLY CONFER FOLLOW IMPART OUTPUT RELENT RENDER RETURN SUBMIT SUPPLY SWERVE UNGIVE UPGIVE ABANDON ANALYZE BEARING CONCEDE DELIVER FURNISH HARVEST KNUCKLE OUTTURN PRODUCE PROVIDE REDOUND RUCKSEY SUCCUMB BEGRUDGE FRUITAGE OVERGIVE PICKINGS UNDERLIE RELINQUISH
(— FRUIT) ADDLE GRAIN
(— GRASS) GRAZE
(— OF FIELD) BURDEN
(— OF MINE) BONANZA
(— ON BOND) BASIS
(— TO) INDULGE
(— TO TEMPTATION) FALL
(— UP) LET FORLET FORLEIT
(— WELL) HIT BLEED
(MINERAL —) PROSPECT
(SUFF.) FER(ENCE)(ENT)(OUS)
YIELDED
(SUFF.) GENETIC
YIELDING ABLE MEEK NESH SOFT TALL WAXY NAISH WAXEN BONAIR CAVING FACILE FEEBLE FLABBY LIMBER LITHER OUTPUT PLIANT QUAGGY SUPPLE BEARING CESSION FINGENT FLACCID DEDITION LADYLIKE RECREANT COMPLIANT COMPLIANCE SUBMISSIVE
(— IRREGULARLY) BUNCHY
(— OF HORSE) FLEXION
(— STAGE) SEAR
(— TO IMPULSES) ABANDON
(— TO INFLUENCE) PLIABLE
(— UNDERFOOT) SINKY
YIN SHANG
YIRMILIK METALLIK
YODEL SONG JODEL WARBLE REFRAIN
YODH IOD JOD
YOGA JOG
(— POSITION) ASANA
YOGI JOGI FAKIR FAKEER
YOKE BOW YOK BAIL CROW DRAG FORK HOOP PAIR POKE SOLE TEAM BANGY FURCA SHEBA SPANG BANGHY COUPLE INSPAN DRAGBAR HARNESS OPPRESS ADJUGATE
(— BAR) SKEY
(— TO HOLD DRILL) CROW
(— TO RAISE CANNON) BAIL
(PREF.) ZYG(O)(OTO)
(SUFF.) ZYGOMATIC ZYGOSIS ZYGOTE
YOKED (NOT —) AZYGOUS
YOKEFELLOW MATE FELLOW PARTNER YOKEMATE
YOKEL YOB BOOR CLUB JAKE JOCK LOUT YAHOO YOBBO FARMER JOSKIN BUMPKIN HAYSEED HOODLUM WAYBACK ABDERITE CHAWBACON
YOKING BOUT CONTEST MUGGING
YOKO ONO
YOLANTA (CHARACTER IN —) RENE ROBERT YOLANTA VAUDEMONT
(COMPOSER OF —) TCHAIKOVSKY
YOLDRING YOWLEY
YOLK CENTER YELLOW ESSENCE LATEBRA VITELLUS PARABLAST
(HAVING A —) LECITHAL
(PREF.) LECITH(O) VITELLI VITELLO
(SUFF.) LECITHAL
YON YONDER THITHER BACKWARD
YONDER THAT THERE THOSE THITHER
YORE PAST YARE YEARS
(OF —) OLDEN
YORKER TICE
YORKSHIREMAN TIKE TYKE LEAROYD
YORUBA NAGO
YOU DU HE IT OW TA TU WE YA YO ONE OWE SHE SIE TOI YOW YUH THOU VOUS YOUSE YOURSELF
YOU CAN'T GO HOME AGAIN
(AUTHOR OF —) WOLFE
(CHARACTER IN —) ELSE JACK LLOYD ESTHER GEORGE KOHLER MCHARG WEBBER EDWARDS FOXHALL
YOU NEVER CAN TELL (AUTHOR OF —) SHAW
(CHARACTER IN —) BOON BOHUM DOLLY GLORIA PHILIP CLANDON MCCOMAS WILLIAM GRAMPTON VALENTINE
YOUNG FRY JUV BIRD CALF DROP BIRTH BROOD FETUS FRUIT GREEN SMALL UNOLD JUNIOR KINDLE JUVENAL IMMATURE YEANLING YOUTHFUL
(— OF ANY ANIMAL) FRY BABY CALF FOAL JOEY LAMB TOTO
(— OF BEAST) SLINK
(— OF BIRD) CHICK
(— OF CAMEL) COLT
(— OF DOG) WHELP
(— OF FISH) FRY
(— OF SEA TROUT) HERLING
(VERY —) SUCKING NEPHIONIC SHIRTTAIL
(PREF.) FETI FETO FOETI FOETO
(SUFF.) **(— ONE)** LING
(MODE OF HATCHING —) PAEDES
YOUNGER KID LESS PUNEE JUNIOR PUISNE OFFSPRING
YOUNGEST (— OF BROOD) WALLYDRAG
YOUNGSTER KID BIRD COLT CHILD MINOR YOUTH BUTTON SHAVER URCHIN YONKER YOUNKER SPALPEEN
YOUNKER DUPE CHILD KNIGHT NOVICE SQUIRE YUNKER
YOUR OR YO THY YAR YER OURE OWRE SEIN VOTRE YOURN
YOURSELF ITSELF HERSELF HIMSELF ONESELF
YOUTH BOY BUD IMP LAD CHAP COLT PAGE TEEN BAHUR CHABO GROOM HYLAS POULT PRIME SPRIG SWAIN WHELP BOCHUR BURSCH EPHEBE HOYDEN INFANT JUVENT KOUROS MASTER NONAGE SPRING SQUIRT YONKER CALLANT EPHEBOS GOSSOON JUVENAL PUBERTY SAPLING YOUDITH YOUNGTH ENDYMION JUVENILE SPRINGAL
(— WHO SERVES LIQUORS) GANYMEDE
(AWKWARD —) HOBBLEDEHOY
(DELINQUENT —) BODGIE
(GODDESS OF —) HEBE
(IMPUDENT —) SQUIRT
(INEXPERIENCED —) GUNSEL GREENHORN
(NON-JEWISH —) SHEGETZ
(PERT —) PRINCOX
(RUDE —) HOYDEN
(RUSSIAN — ORGANIZATION) KOMSOMOL
(SILLY —) CALF SLENDER
(WELLBORN —) CHILD
(WORLD'S —) PRIME
(PREF.) HEBE
YOUTHFUL RATH FRESH GREEN YOUNG BOYISH GOLDEN JUNIOR MAIDEN NEANIC VERNAL VIRGIN YOUTHY LADDISH PUERILE YOUNGLY IMMATURE JUVENILE SPRINGAL VIGOROUS
YOUTHFULNESS JEUNESSE
YOWL GOWL HOWL WAIL YELL YELP
YO-YO FLUCTUATE VACILLATE
YUAN DOLLAR
YUAPIN YARURA
YUCATAN (— PEOPLE) MAYA MAYAS
YUCATEC MAYA
YUCCA LILY PITA YUCA AGAVE DATIL IZOTE PALMA JOSHUA LILIAL LILIUM PALMITO SOAPWEED
YUCKY ICKY DIRTY NASTY SLIMY DISGUSTING
YUGA KALI

YUGOSLAVIA
CAPITAL: BEOGRAD BELGRADE
COIN: PARA DINAR
FORMER REPUBLIC: BOSNIA CROATIA SLOVENIA
GULF: KOTOR
LAKE: OHRID PRESPA SCUTARI
MEASURE: RIF AKOV RALO DONUM KHVAT LANAZ STOPA MOTYKA PALAZE RALICO
MOUNTAIN: DURMITOR
MOUNTAIN RANGE: DINARIC
PORT: KOTOR NOVISAD BELGRADE
REPUBLIC: SERBIA MONTENEGRO
RIVER: DRIM IBAR SAVA DRINA RASKA TISZA DANUBE MORAVA VARDAR
TOWN: NIS BUDVA USKUB BITOLJ PRILEP TETOVO CATTARO NOVISAD PRIZREN SKOPLJE MONASTIR SUBOTICA
WEIGHT: OKA OKE DRAMM TOVAR WAGON SATLIJK

YUKON TERRITORY (CAPITAL OF —) WHITEHORSE
(LAKE OF —) KLUANE
(MOUNTAIN OF —) LOGAN
(MOUNTAIN RANGE OF —) OGILVIE STIKINE MACKENZIE
(RIVER OF —) PEEL LEWES LIARD PELLY WHITE KLONDIKE PORCUPINE
(TOWN OF —) ELSA MAYO BARLOW DAWSON
YULE NOEL CHRISTMAS
YUMA CUCHAN
YUMAN PATAYAN
YUNX WRYNECK
YURT TENT

Z

Z ZAD ZED ZEE ZETA ZULU IZARD ZEBRA IZZARD
(SHAPED LIKE A —) OPENBAND
ZAAVAN (FATHER OF —) EZER
ZABAD (FATHER OF —) NEBO ZATTU NATHAN
(MOTHER OF —) SHIMEATH
ZABAGLIONE SABAYON
ZABBAI (SON OF —) BARUCH
ZABBUD (FATHER OF —) BIGVAI
ZABDI (FATHER OF —) ASAPH ZERAH
ZABDIEL (SON OF —) JASHOBEAM
ZABUD (FATHER OF —) NATHAN
ZACCUR (FATHER OF —) IMRI ASAPH JAAZIAH
(SON OF —) HANAN SHAMMUA
ZACHARIAH (DAUGHTER OF —) ABIJAH
(FATHER OF —) JEROBOAM
ZACHARIAS (FATHER OF —) BARACHIAS
(SON OF —) JOHN
(WIFE OF —) ELISABETH
ZACHER (FATHER OF —) JEHIEL
(MOTHER OF —) MAACHAH
ZADOK (DAUGHTER OF —) JERUSHAH
(FATHER OF —) BAANA IMMER AHITUB MERAIOTH
ZAFFER SMALT SAFFIOR ZAPHARA
ZAGREUS (FATHER OF —) JUPITER
(MOTHER OF —) PROSERPINE
ZAHAM (FATHER OF —) REHOBOAM
(MOTHER OF —) ABIHAIL

ZAIRE
BOMU UELE
ALTERNATE NAME: CONGO
CAPITAL: KINSHASA
COIN: SENGI LIKUTA MAKUTA
COINS: MAKUTA
LAKE: KIVU MWERU
LANGUAGE: KIKONGO LINGALA SWAHILI TSHILUBA
MONEY: ZAIRE
MOUNTAIN RANGE: MITUMBA VIRUNGA RUWENZORI
PROVINCE: KIVU KASAI SHABA EQUATOR KATANGA BANDUNDU EQUATEUR ORIENTAL
RIVER: RUKI UELE CONGO DENGU IBINA KASAI LINDI ZAIRE LIKATI LOMAMI LUKUGA UBANGI ARUWIMI LUALABA LULONGA
TOWN: BAYA BOMA LEBO AKETI BUKAVU KAMINA KIKWIT MATADI BUTEMBO KANANGA KOLWEZI BAKWANGA YANGAMBI KISANGANI

ZALAPH (SON OF —) HANUN

ZAMBIA
CAPITAL: LUSAKA
COIN: NGWEE KWACHA
FALLS: VICTORIA
LAKE: MWERU BANGWEULU TANGANYIKA
LANGUAGE: LOZI BEMBA TONGA LUVALE NYANJA AFRIKAANS
MOUNTAIN RANGE: MUCHINGA
RIVER: KAFUE LUANGWA LUAPULA ZAMBEZI
TOWN: KITWE NDOLA LUAPULA LUANSHYA MUFULIRA
WATERFALL: VICTORIA

ZAMBO CHINO SAMBO CAFUSO CURIBOCA
ZAMIA BANGA CICAD CYCAD COONTIE
ZAMINDAR MALIK
ZAMOUSE GAMOUS
ZAMPOGNA BAGPIPE PANPIPE
ZANDER ZANT PERCID SANDER SANDRA
ZANTHOXYLUM FAGARA
ZANY NUT FOOL CRAZY TOADY SAWNEY BUFFOON IDIOTIC CLOWNISH SCREWBALL
ZANZIBAR (SEE TANZANIA)
ZAP ZIP ZONK MICROWAVE
ZAPARO IQUITO
ZAPATERO LIMA BOXWOOD CERILLO
ZARA (FATHER OF —) JUDAH
ZARAH KAZOO
ZARPANIT (HUSBAND OF —) MERODACH
ZAZA (FATHER OF —) JONATHAN
ZEAL FIRE MOOD ARDOR FLAME HEART FERVOR WARMTH DEVOTION GOODWILL JEALOUSY
(MORBID —) ZELOTYPIA
(WITH —) DINGDONG
(PREF.) ZELO
ZEALOT BIGOT VOTARY VOTEEN ZELANT DEVOTEE FANATIC CANANEAN SERAPHIC SICARIUS VOTARESS VOTARIST
ZEALOUS HOT AVID HIGH ARDENT FERVID STRING CORDIAL DEVOTED EARNEST EMULOUS FERVENT FORWARD JEALOUS PUSHFUL VIGOROUS PERFERVID RELIGIOUS
(— ABOUT BEAUTY) ESTHETIC
ZEALOUSLY FAST INNERLY HEARTILY
ZEBADIAH (FATHER OF —) ASAHEL ISHMAEL JEROHAM MICHAEL MESHELEMIAH
ZEBAH (SLAYER OF —) GIDEON
ZEBEDEE (SON OF —) JOHN JAMES
(WIFE OF —) SALOME
ZEBINA (FATHER OF —) NEBO
ZEBRA DAUW EQUID HORSE QUAGGA SOLIPED
ZEBRA FISH DANIO
ZEBRAWOOD ARAROBA ZINGANA
ZEBU BRAMIN BRAGMAN BRAHMIN
(HYBRID OF — AND CATTLE) CATTABU
(HYBRID OF — AND YAK) ZOBO
ZEBUDAH (HUSBAND OF —) JOSIAH
(SON OF —) JEHOIAKIM
ZEBULUN (FATHER OF —) JACOB
(SON OF —) ELON
ZECCHINO SEQUIN
ZECHARIAH (DAUGHTER OF —) ABI ABIJAH
(FATHER OF —) IDDO BEBAI HOSAH JEHIEL PASHUR ISSHIAH PHAROSH JEHOIADA JONATHAN BERECHIAH JEBERECHIAH JEHOSHAPHAT MESHELEMIAH
(SON OF —) JAHAZIEL
ZEDEKIAH (BROTHER OF —) JEHOAHAZ
(FATHER OF —) JOSIAH HANANIAH MAASEIAH CHENAANAH
(MOTHER OF —) HAMUTAL
ZEDOARY SETWALL
ZELOPHEHAD (FATHER OF —) HEPHER
ZELUS (FATHER OF —) PALLAS
(MOTHER OF —) STYX
(SISTER OF —) NIKE
ZEMIRA (FATHER OF —) BECHER
ZEN (— PARADOX) KOAN
(— QUESTIONS) MONDO
ZENANA HAREM HARIM SERAGLIO
ZEND AVESTAN
ZENICK SURICATE
ZENITH ACME PEAK HIGHT PITCH HEIGHT SUMMIT VERTEX
ZENOBIA (HUSBAND OF —) ODENATHUS
ZEOLITE ANALCIME ANALCITE STILBITE GMELINITE NATROLITE PHACOLITE
ZEPHANIAH (FATHER OF —) MAASEIAH
(SON OF —) JOSIAH
ZEPHO (FATHER OF —) ELIPHAZ
ZEPHON (FATHER OF —) GAD
ZEPHYR FINE SOFT BERLIN BREEZE
ZEPHYRUS FAVONIUS
(FATHER OF —) AEOLUS ASTRAEUS
(MOTHER OF —) EOS
(SON OF —) CARPOS
(WIFE OF —) CHLORIS
ZEPPELIN ZEP ZEPP AIRSHIP
ZERAH (FATHER OF —) IDDO REUEL SIMEON
ZERBINETTE (FATHER OF —) ARGANTE
ZERBINO (BELOVED OF —) ISABELLA
(COMPANION OF —) ORLANDO
(SISTER OF —) GINEVRA
(SLAYER OF —) MANDRICARDO
ZERESH (HUSBAND OF —) HAMAN
ZERETH (FATHER OF —) ASHUR
(MOTHER OF —) HELAH
ZERI (FATHER OF —) JEDUTHUN
ZERO OH NIL NUL BLOB DUCK NULL AUGHT CLOSE EMPTY OUGHT TRAIN ZILCH ABSENT CIPHER NAUGHT LACKING NOTHING NULLITY SCRATCH NINETEEN
(EQUAL TO —) NILPOTENT
(HAVING — AS LIMIT) NULL
(HAVING VARIABLES EQUAL TO —) TRIVIAL
ZERUAH (FATHER OF —) NEBAT
(SON OF —) JEROBOAM
ZERUIAH (SON OF —) JOAB ASAHEL ABISHAI
ZEST EDGE ELAN JASM LIFE GUSTO SPICE FLAVOR RELISH STINGO MUSTARD PIQUANCY
ZESTFUL RACY SPICY BREEZY
(— QUALITY) ZAP
ZESTY ZINGY
ZETES (BROTHER OF —) CALAIS
(FATHER OF —) BOREAS
(MOTHER OF —) ORITHYIA
ZETHAM (FATHER OF —) LAADAN
ZETHUS (BROTHER OF —) AMPHION
(FATHER OF —) JUPITER
(MOTHER OF —) ANTIOPE
ZEUS ZAN SOTER ALASTOR CRONION KRONION POLIEUS CRONIDES
(BROTHER OF —) HADES POSEIDON
(FATHER OF —) CRONUS KRONOS
(MOTHER OF —) RHEA
(SISTER OF —) HERA HESTIA DEMETER
(SON OF —) ARES ARCAS ARGUS AEACUS AGACUS APOLLO HERMES TITYUS PERSEUS DARDANUS DIONYSUS HERCULES TANTALUS
(WIFE OF —) HERA JUNO METIS THEMIS EURYNOME
(PREF.) ZENO
ZEUXIS UNDERLAY
ZHIVAGO YURI
ZIBEON (SON OF —) ANAH
ZIBIA (FATHER OF —) SHAHARAIM
(MOTHER OF —) HODESH
ZIBIAH (SON OF —) JOASH
ZICHRI (FATHER OF —) ASAPH IZHAR
(SON OF —) JOEL AMASIAH ELIEZER ELISHAPHAT
ZIGZAG BOYAU CRANK BROKEN INDENT SLALOM CRANKLE CHEVRONY FLEXUOSE TRAVERSE
(PREF.) ZYZZO
ZILCH NIL ZAP ZIP ZERO ZING NOTHING

ZILIANTE (BROTHER OF —) ORRIGILLE
(FATHER OF —) MONODANTE
(SISTER OF —) BRANDIMARTE
ZILPAH (SON OF —) GAD ASHER
ZIMARRA CYMAR SIMAR CASSOCK
ZIMB FLY ZEBUB

ZIMBABWE
CAPITAL: HARARE SALISBURY
DIVISION: RHODESIA
LANGUAGE: ILA BANTU SHONA NDEBELE
PEOPLE: BANTU MASHOMA MATABELE BALOKWAKWA
RIVER: SABI GWAII LUNDI LIMPOPO SANYATI ZAMBEZI
TOWN: GWELO UMTALI BULAWAYO
WATERFALL: VICTORIA

ZIMMAH (FATHER OF —) SHIMEI
ZIMRAN (MOTHER OF —) KETURAH
ZIMRI (FATHER OF —) SALU ZERAH
ZINA (FATHER OF —) SHIMEI
ZINC FAR SPELT ZINCUM SPELTER TUTENAG EXCLUDER
(— SALT) ZIRAM
(KIND OF —) MOSSY
ZING PEP VIM ZAP ZIP DASH SNAP ENERGY SPIRIT RAZZMATAZZ
ZINGEL PERCID
ZINGER MOT
ZINGY ZESTY
ZINKE CORNET
ZINNIA CRASSINA
ZION SION ISRAEL UTOPIA
ZIONIST IRGUNIST
ZIP NIL VIM ZAP DASH NADA SEAL SNAP ZERO ZING FORCE OOMPH WHISK ZILCH BUTTON ENERGY STINGO NOTHING
ZIPHAH (FATHER OF —) JEHALELEEL
ZIPHION (FATHER OF —) GAD
ZIPPER FASTENER
(PART OF —) TAB FACE PULL STOP TAPE CHAIN SLIDE TOOTH
ZIPPOR (SON OF —) BALAK
ZIPPORAH (FATHER OF —) REUEL JETHRO
(HUSBAND OF —) MOSES
(SON OF —) ELIEZER GERSHOM
ZIPPY ZAPPY
ZIRCON JARGON AZORITE MALACON HYACINTH STARLITE
ZITHER KIN QIN CANON CANUN GUSLI KANOON CITHARA GITERNE GITTERN AUTOHARP GALEMPONG
(JAPANESE —) KOTO
ZITHER HARP KOTO
ZIZA (FATHER OF —) SHIPHI REHOBOAM
(MOTHER OF —) MAACHAH
ZIZITH SISITH FRINGES TASSELS TSITSITH
ZO DZO ZOH ZOBO
ZOARITE BIMMELER
ZOBEBAH (FATHER OF —) COZ
ZOBO ZO DZO ZOH ZOBU
ZODIAC GIRDLE BALDRIC BAWDRICK SIGNIFIER
(SECTION OF —) TRIGON
(SIGN OF —) LEO RAM BULL CRAB FISH GOAT LION ARIES LIBRA SCALE TWINS VIRGO ARCHER CANCER GEMINI PISCES TAURUS SCORPIO AQUARIUS CAPRICORN
ZOHAR (FATHER OF —) SIMEON
(SON OF —) EPHRON
ZOHETH (FATHER OF —) ISHI
ZOISITE THULITE
ZONA ZOSTER
ZONE BED AREA BAND BEAM BELT HALO PLAGE TRACT CIRCLE REGION ZODIAC CLIMATE HORIZON ZONULET CINCTURE CINGULUM FRONTIER HABENULA HISTOGEN STRINGER
(— OF CONFLICT) FRONT
(— OF FLAME) MANTLE
(— OF MINERALS) CORONA
(— OF VENUS) CEST CESTUS
(ABYSSAL —) BASSALIA
(PALEONTOLOGIC —S) ASSISE
(SAFETY —) ISLET ISLAND REFUGE
(STRATOGRAPHIC —) HEMERA
(WELDING —) ROOT
ZONK WASTE
ZONKED GONZO
ZOO (KIND OF —) PETTING
ZOOECIUM AUTOPORE
ZOOID PERSON SIPHON BRYOZOAN HYDRANTH POLYPIDE ZOOTHOME
ZOOLOGIST AMERICAN DEAN GILL ADAMS ALLEN BAIRD BAKER BIRGE CLARK GOULD GUYER MORSE SHULL BINNEY BROOKS BUTLER CASTLE ELLIOT FISHER GARMAN HOLMES KOFOID MORGAN NEWMAN OLIVER PARKER RIDDLE STILES WILDER WILSON AGASSIZ ANDREWS BARTSCH BIGELOW FERNALD KELLOGG MCCLUNG NUTTING VERRILL WHITMAN CRAMPTON GRINNELL HORNADAY KIRTLAND MELANDER SHELFORD COCKERELL DAVENPORT SANDERSON PETRUNKEVITCH
AUSTRIAN FRISCH
BELGIAN BENEDEN
CANADIAN ANDERSON
DANISH STEENSTRUP
ENGLISH BUSK GRAY OWEN ELTON FLOWER GROGAN LISTER MORGAN MORRIS MURRAY NEWTON PARKER BEDDARD DURRELL GUNTHER HASWELL MEDAWAR POULTON YARRELL GOODRICH MACBRIDE MITCHELL
FRENCH CUVIER DELAGE PERRIER DUJARDIN BLAINVILLE VALENCIENNES
GERMAN VOGT BREHM BRONN CARUS CLAUS DOHRN BOVERI FRISCH LEYDIG MOBIUS MULLER GRZIMEK HAECKEL HERTWIG SIEBOLD SPEMANN BUTSCHLI GUENTHER BECHSTEIN LEUCKHART SCHAUDINN BLUMENBACH GOLDSCHMIDT REICHENBACH LICHTENSTEIN
ITALIAN GRASSI
NORWEGIAN SARS NANSEN
RUSSIAN PANDER KOVALEVSKI METCHNIKOFF
SWEDISH LOVEN
ZOOM ZAP SPEED
ZOOPHYTE CORAL SPONGE HYDROID
ZOOSPORE MONAD SWARMER ZOOCARP
ZOPHAH (FATHER OF —) HELEM HOTHAM
ZOPHAI (FATHER OF —) ELKANAH
ZORIL SKUNK POWCAT CHINCHE POLECAT MUISHOND
ZOROASTRIAN GABAR PARSI GUEBRE PARSEE
ZOROASTRIANISM MAZDAISM
ZOUAVE ZUZU SCALER ZOUZOU
ZOUNDS OONS WAUNS ZOONS
ZUAR (SON OF —) NETHANEEL
ZUCCHETTO CALOTTE SOLIDEO SKULLCAP
ZUCCHINI COURGETTE
ZULU CAR TRAIN LUGGER MATABELE
ZUNI CIBOLAN SHALAKO
ZUR (FATHER OF —) JEHIEL
(SON OF —) COZBI
ZURIEL (FATHER OF —) ABIHAIL
ZWINGLIAN TIGURINE
ZYGOMATIC JUGAL
ZYGOSPORE COPULA
ZYGOTE OOCYST OOSPERM OOSPORE SPORONT OOKINETE
ZYME YEAST ZYMIN ENZYME FERMENT
ZYMOGEN PEPSINOGEN
ZYRIAN KOMI SYRYAN